Short forms and labels

Short forms

adj	adjective
adv	adverb
n	noun
phr v	phrasal verb
prep	preposition
pron	pronoun
v	verb
sb	someone
sth	something

Labels

Words which are used only or mainly in one region or country are marked:

BrE	British English
AmE	American English
AusE	Australian English

Words which are used in a particular situation, or show a particular attitude:

approving	a word that is used to praise things or people, although this may not be clear from its meaning
disapproving	a word that is used to show dislike or approval, although this may not be clear from its meaning
formal	a word or phrase that is suitable for formal speech or writing, but would not normally be used in everyday conversation
informal	a word or phrase that is used in normal conversation, but may not be suitable for use in more formal contexts, for example in writing essays or business letters
humorous	a word that is normally used in a joking way

Words which are used in a particular context or type of language:

biblical	a word or phrase that is used in the language of the Bible, and would sound old-fashioned to a modern speaker
law	a word or phrase with a technical meaning used by lawyers, in legal documents etc
literary	a word or phrase used mainly in English literature, and not in normal speech or writing
medical	a word or phrase that is more likely to be used by doctors than by ordinary people, and that often has a more common equivalent
not polite	a word or phrase that is considered rude, and that might offend some people
old-fashioned	a word or phrase that was commonly used in the past, but would sound old-fashioned today
old use	a word or phrase used in earlier centuries
spoken	a word or phrase used only, or nearly always, in conversation
taboo	a word or phrase that should not be used because it is very rude or offensive
technical	a word or phrase used by doctors, scientists, and other specialists
trademark	a word or phrase that is the official name of a particular product
written	a word or phrase that is used only, or nearly always, in written English

Grammar codes and patterns

Grammar codes

[C] countable a noun that has both a singular and a plural form: *He lent me a **book** about photography.* | *Some of the **books** were very old.*

[U] uncountable a noun that has no plural form and refers to something that cannot be counted: *the **importance** of education* | *a bucket of **water***

[I] intransitive a verb that has no object: *Jack **sneezed**.* | *House prices **are rising**.*

[T] transitive a verb that is followed by an object, which can be either a noun phrase or a clause: *I **love** chocolate.* | *She **said** she was too busy.* | *I **remember** going on holiday there.*

[singular] a noun that is used only in the singular, and has no plural form: *The room has a modern **feel**.* | *a **sprinkling** of snow*

[plural] a noun that is used only in the plural, and has no singular form: *His **clothes** were soaking wet.* | *Those are my **scissors**.*

[linking verb] a verb that is followed by a noun or adjective complement that describes the subject of the verb: *I **felt** very tired.* | *Her father **is** a doctor.* | *Your dinner's **getting** cold.*

[always + adv/prep] shows that a verb must be followed by an adverb or a preposition: *She **went** upstairs.* | *Robert **put** the letter in his briefcase.*

[not in progressive] shows that a verb is not used in the progressive form, that is, the -ing form after 'be': *I **admire** his work.* (not *I am admiring his work*) | *I don't **know** where it is.*

[no comparative] shows that an adjective is not used in the comparative or superlative form, that is, not with -er and -est, or 'more' and 'most': *He played a **key** role in the negotiations.*

[only before noun] shows that an adjective can be used only before a noun: *the **main** reason for her visit* | *You **poor** thing!*

[not before noun] shows that an adjective cannot be used before a noun: *I don't even know if he's still **alive**.* | *I'm **glad** you're here.*

[only after noun] shows that an adjective is used only immediately after a noun: *some matters to be discussed before the meeting **proper**.*

[sentence adverb] shows that an adverb modifies a whole sentence: ***Fortunately** no one was hurt.*

[+adj/adv] shows that an adverb of degree is used before adjectives and adverbs: *The room was **very** dark.* | *We've got to act **fairly** quickly.*

[also + plural verb *BrE*] shows that a group noun can take a plural verb in British English: *The **team** are feeling confident.*

Patterns

[+about] [+along] shows that a word can be followed immediately by a particular preposition or adverb: *I'm **worried** about Rachel.* | *The children **skipped** along.*

throw sth at sb/sth shows that a verb can be followed by an object and a particular preposition: *Tom **threw** a cushion at her.*

request that shows that a word can be followed by a clause beginning with 'that': *He **requested** that his name be removed from the list of candidates.*

surprised (that) or **tell sb (that)** shows that a word can be followed by a clause beginning with 'that', or the word 'that' can be left out: *I'm **surprised** you didn't know the answer.* | *Bill **told** me you were here.*

decide who/what/whether etc or **ask (sb) who/what/where etc** shows that a word can be followed by a clause beginning with a word such as 'who', 'what', 'whether', or 'where': *I can't **decide** what to do.* | *I **asked** her what she meant.* | *I'm not **sure** where James is.*

try to do sth or **order sb to do sth** shows that a word can be followed by an infinitive: ***Try** to forget about it.* | *He **ordered** them to leave.* | *He's **sure** to win.*

help do sth or **see sb/sth do sth** shows that a verb can be followed by an infinitive without 'to': *This can **help** prevent infection.* | *Did anyone **see** them leave?*

enjoy doing sth or **hear sb doing sth** shows that a verb can be followed by a present participle: *I **enjoy** meeting new people.* | *Peter could **hear** them laughing.*

bring sb sth shows that a verb can be followed by an indirect object and then a direct object: *Could you **bring** us the bill?* | *Let me **buy** you a drink.*

LONGMAN

Dictionary of Contemporary English

6TH EDITION

Pearson Education Limited
Edinburgh Gate
Harlow
Essex CM20 2JE
England, UK
and associated Companies throughout the world

Visit our website: pearsonELT.com/dictionaries

First published 1978
Second edition 1987
Third edition 1995
Fourth edition 2003
Fourth edition with Writing Assistant 2005
Fifth edition 2009
Sixth edition 2014
Sixth printing 2019

ISBN 978 1 4479 5408 8 (paperback edition + online access)

Typeset by Letterpart Limited, Caterham on the Hill, Surrey CR3 5XL

Printed in China (GCC/06)

Contents

Acknowledgements

Publishing Manager
Laurence Delacroix

Managing Editors
Chris Fox
Rosalind Combley

Editors
Karen Cleveland Marwick
Lucy Hollingworth
Elizabeth Manning
Michael Murphy
Laura Wedgeworth

Pronunciation Editor
Dinah Jackson

Proofreaders
Pat Dunn
Margaret Hill
Ruth Hillmore
Kate Mohideen
Alison Sadler
Nicky Thompson

Project Management
Alan Savill
Alice Willoughby

Website Development
Andy Roberts

Computational Linguist
Allan Ørsnes

Language Supplement
Chris Fox
Maria Karyda

Academic Word List
Averil Coxhead

Production Editors
Hilary Marsden
Michael Murphy
Paola Rocchetti
Alice Willoughby

Production
Susan Braund

Design
Eddi Edwards
Matthew Dickin
Johnson Banks

Keyboarder
Denise McKeough

Picture Research
Sandra Hilsdon
Louise Edgeworth

Illustrations
Ben Hasler (NB Illustration)
Maltings Partnership
Chris Pavely
Peter Richardson
Mark Turner (Beehive Illustration)

The Publishers and editorial team would like to thank the lexicographic team who worked on the *Longman Dictionary of Contemporary English* (fifth edition) and the many people who have contributed advice to the making of this dictionary for the last 35 years, in particular the Linglex Dictionary and Corpus Advisory Committee:

Lord Quirk (Chair), Professor David Crystal, Professor Geoffrey Leech, Professor John Wells, Della Summers

The Publishers would also like to thank Professor Norbert Schmitt for his guidance during the development of the *Longman Vocabulary Trainer*.

The Publishers and editors of the *Longman Dictionary of Contemporary English* would like to thank all of the teachers who took part in the research:

Monika Adamowicz, Julia Adkins, Niki Alford, Shanel Ali, Melinda Allen, Marcin Banasiak, Jamie Barnett, Fiona Bennet, Robert Bundala, Nick Canning, Shelley Carter, Marc Challans, Jaetloon Choi, Małgorzata Chomicz, Ewa Czwarno, Heather Daniell, Elin Davies, Kasia Downer, Magdalena Dworakowska, Krystyna Dybowska-Głąb, AliReza Z. Ekbatani, Kate Evans, Alicja Frątczak, Emma Meade Flynn, Helen Galer, John Gallagher, Moriana Gamboa, Thorkild Gantner, Olga Gaweł, Marianna Goral, Laila Grinberga, Harriett Han, Kathleen Hargreaves, Claire Harrison, Vanessa Harrison, Tess Hicks, Maria Hinc, Susan Holzman, Kim Hyon-hwa, Christian Ricardo Ingracio, Dorota Jaborska-Adaszewska, Jackie Jays, Rob Julian, Maimu Kado, Kaori Kaneko, Anna Kaźmierczak, Tah Eun Kim, Krystyna Krzemińska, Mick Lammond, Pip Langley, Jerzy Laskus, Du Le Khanh, Bernadette Lingani, Sara L Marlow, Kristina Maulina, Eve McEllinney, Tim McLeish, Vicky McWilliam, Steven Miller, Anne Morris, Antonio Mulima, Tom Neath, Jolanta Nyczke, Joanna Odgers, Cheriere Ophelie, Daniel Orina, Sarah Perkins, Stephen Perry, Michel Pierre, Frank Pinner, Davina Pobee, Martin Porter, Martin Poster, Tom Pritchard, Leena Punga, Jonathan Richardson, Sally Robinson, Monika Sadowska, Katarzyna Scibor, Jane Sherlock, Misako Shimoji, Elizabeth Singleton, Tomasz Siuta, Ewa Skoczeń, Mark Smith, Katarzyna Socha, Joanna Stansfield, Anna Stępień, Simon Thomas, Luke Thompson, Alison Tiernety, Ali Tierney, Philippa Titley, Olzhas Tolubayev, Maria Tsangaras, Emina Tuzovic, Rolf Tynan, Alison Waite, Ewa Wirth, Arkadiusz Witecki, Cathy Yarrow, Gizem Yilmazyurt, Ewa Zalewska, Yu Zhant, Ewa Zielinska

Every effort has been made to include the names of all the teachers who took part in the research. If your name has been inadvertently omitted please contact us and we will be happy to insert it in a future reprint.

Foreword

Randolph Quirk
Professor the Lord Quirk, FBA

People the world over know that English is the most important single tool they need to achieve success in their careers. This means acquiring and retaining an active knowledge of many thousands of words in an ever-expanding, ever-changing language. It also means using these words in grammatically correct sentences.

Vocabulary and grammar are key challenges, which, when mastered, offer learners the satisfaction of being fluent in English and of reaping the professional rewards of this achievement. The last edition of the ***Longman Dictionary of Contemporary English*** then added a large amount of information on collocations, showing that a word may not only have several meanings but also have vitally important (if subtle and invisible) relations with other words. For instance, *hot* is the opposite of *cold* if our topic is the weather, but of *mild* if we are talking about curry. Or again, one meaning of *remain* is 'stay', but these two verbs are not freely interchangeable: *stay* is far more common in general and especially in spoken English, but *remain* is more common when used with *seated*.

The ***Longman Dictionary of Contemporary English*** is brilliant both at capturing such relations between words and at presenting them to the learner in an attractive and instantly comprehensible way that makes them easily memorable. Collocation boxes present users with over 65,000 common collocations while the integrated Thesaurus explains the differences between some 18,000 synonyms and closely related words. And as you would expect from Longman dictionaries, all of this information is illustrated with examples taken from the Longman Corpus Network.

This sixth edition now also offers new grammar information in the printed dictionary, and a complete vocabulary and grammar package online. Grammar points include comparisons between verbs that have a similar meaning but a different grammatical behaviour, for instance showing key patterns such as *talk about something* and *discuss something.*

Living up to its reputation for innovation, this sixth edition is firmly exploiting 21st-century technology to improve learning. The brand-new accompanying website, ***Longman Dictionaries Online***, contains thousands more collocations and synonyms, as well as additional words and phrases, and one million additional corpus examples. It also gives users access to a wealth of interactive exercises, including a new grammar practice module with videos, and teaching resources.

But if a dictionary is no longer just a book, it is most certainly also a book. Maintaining a long tradition of skilled analysis and definition, lexicographers working on this sixth edition of the ***Longman Dictionary of Contemporary English*** are ever alert to the changing language and to the changing needs of learners. Let no one forget that the Longman name was on the title page of Johnson's epoch-making *Dictionary of the English Language* in 1755!

Introduction

The *Longman Dictionary of Contemporary English* – or *LDOCE* as it has become known over the past 35 years – is now in its sixth edition and still a best-selling dictionary worldwide.

Here at Longman Dictionaries, our goal is to provide students and teachers with the most comprehensive and accurate information on the English language while addressing our users' needs. It is important that our dictionaries are user-friendly – and in the digital age of computers, mobile phones and the Internet, this not only means that our dictionaries are easy to use, it also means that the information is available in a variety of formats so that users can access the information whenever and wherever they need it.

The sixth edition of *LDOCE* continues to be available in a variety of formats – online at the brand-new website www.longmandictionaries.com and on mobile phones and tablets – to ensure that it is accessible to as many learners of English as possible.

The starting point for any Longman dictionary is research. Research with both students and teachers. It is only in this way that we can keep up-to-date with the ever-changing needs of both groups and adapt our dictionaries accordingly. We would like to take this opportunity to thank all of the students and teachers, some of whom are listed in the acknowledgements, who gave generously of their time and ideas. None of what we have achieved with *LDOCE* over the years would have been possible without them.

So what is special about this sixth edition? We have obviously retained the features that are popular with existing users, expanded them and added new features such as grammar information, so that we now offer a full vocabulary and grammar package. The *Longman Communication 3000* is now the *Longman Communication 9000*, highlighting the most important 9000 words to learn in English, as a result of research into vocabulary acquisition. As in earlier editions, the 3000 most frequent words in spoken and written English are marked in the dictionary – Longman dictionaries are still the only learners' dictionaries to make this distinction. *LDOCE* continues to offer thousands of corpus-based examples, grammar and error notes, and signposts to help navigate long entries. (A full description of all features can be found in the '*How to use the Dictionary*' pages.)

But for this sixth edition, following feedback from existing users and new research, we have focused on offering a full grammar package and mobile access – in addition to the invaluable information on collocations, synonyms and register.

Grammar

Grammar notes throughout the dictionary help learners to avoid common grammar mistakes relating to prepositions, grammar patterns and word order.

A Grammar Guide provides helpful and concise information on key grammar topics such as verb tenses, verb patterns and the order of adjectives.

And because practice is essential to help develop sound grammar foundations, the new website www.longmandictionaries.com offers a Grammar Centre with video presentations of key grammar points and interactive practice, tests and scores to help measure progress

Collocation

Collocations – or words that are typically used together – are already a key feature, with an integrated collocations dictionary which now contains over 65,000 common collocations. Thousands of example sentences show these collocations in context so that learners know exactly how to use them. By focusing on collocational information, users are able to improve their comprehension when reading and listening, and increase their fluency when speaking or writing in English. Register now at www.longmandictionaries.com and log in using your PIN code to find an additional 82,000 collocations in the dictionary, all with corpus-based examples.

Synonyms

Vocabulary building is a key need for learners of English. Some of you may already be familiar with the Longman Language Activator – a dictionary that helps users to choose the right lexical item to express their ideas from a group of semantically related words and phrases. The Longman Language Activator database was used as the starting point for creating the Thesaurus notes in *LDOCE*. For the first time users have a Thesaurus integrated into *LDOCE*, making it easier and quicker for them to find the most appropriate word or phrase. The Thesaurus notes contain information on 18,000 related words and phrases, with an additional 30,000 online. The *LDOCE website* also contains the full contents of the Longman Language Activator, both as a separate database and as an integral part of the main dictionary.

Register

Being aware of the different register of closely related words and phrases is a common problem for learners of English. Spoken language can sound unnatural if the words and phrases are too formal or high level. Conversely, written assignments will usually be marked down if the language is that of spoken English. Throughout this dictionary, you will find hundreds of Register notes, focusing precisely on this problem area. You will see, for example, that accumulate is quite a high-level word and native speakers of English are more likely to use the phrasal verb build up in everyday spoken English. The two words 'mean' the same, but the contexts in which they are used are different. You will also find a middle section in the dictionary which groups words and phrases according to their 'function' in the language – for example, ways in which to disagree with someone, or to thank someone. The words and phrases are contrasted with each other to show which are more appropriate for written and formal English, and which are more suited to informal and spoken language.

We hope you find this sixth edition of *LDOCE* an invaluable resource when it comes to learning, teaching and generally improving your English.

How to use the Dictionary

FINDING A WORD OR PHRASE

Words that have more than one part of speech

Words that have the same spelling, but have different parts of speech, are listed separately and given different numbers.

beard[1] /bɪəd $ bɪrd/ ●●● S3 *n* [C]
1 hair that grows around a man's chin and cheeks → **moustache**
2 something similar to a beard, such as hair growing on an animal's chin —**bearded** *adj*

beard[2] *v* [T] **beard sb (in their den)** to go and see someone who has influence or authority, and tell them what you want, why you disagree with them etc

Words that have more than one spelling

If a word is spelt differently in British and American English, the definition and examples are shown at the British spelling, and there is a cross-reference from the American spelling.

If a word has more than one spelling, the different spellings are shown together at the beginning of the entry.

fa·vor·a·ble /ˈfeɪvərəbəl/ *adj* the American spelling of FAVOURABLE

fa·vour·a·ble *BrE*, **favorable** *AmE* /ˈfeɪvərəbəl/ ●○○ *adj*
1 a favourable report, opinion, or reaction shows that you think that someone or something is good or that you agree with them: *favourable film reviews | The response has been overwhelmingly favorable.*
2 suitable and likely to make something happen or succeed: *The disease spreads quickly under* ***favourable conditions****.* | **[+for/to]** *a financial environment that is favorable to job creation*
3 if a LOAN, agreement, rate etc is favourable, the conditions of it are reasonable and not too expensive or difficult: *a favourable interest rate | the* ***favorable terms*** *of the settlement*
4 making people like or approve of someone or something: *A smart appearance makes a* ***favourable impression*** *at an interview.* —**favourably** *adv*

Derived words

Derived words are shown at the end of the entry. These are words that can easily be understood if you know the meaning of the main word. Many of them end in '-ly' or '-ness'.

Compound words

Compound words are treated like ordinary words and listed in alphabetical order as if there were no space or hyphen in them.

ˈgene ˌtherapy *n* [U] a way of treating certain diseases by using GENETIC ENGINEERING

ge·net·ic /dʒəˈnetɪk/ ●○○ *adj* relating to GENES or GENETICS: *genetic defects | each person's genetic make-up | genetic research* —**genetically** /-kli/ *adv*: *genetically determined characteristics*

geˌnetically ˈmodified (*also* **geˌnetically enginˈeered**) *adj* (*abbreviation* **GM**) genetically modified foods or plants have had their genetic structure changed so that they are not affected by particular diseases or harmful insects

Position of idioms and phrases

Idioms and phrases are shown at the first important word of the phrase or idiom. For example *the jury is (still) out on sth* is shown at **jury**. Idioms and phrases are listed with the other senses of the word in frequency order.

ju·ry /ˈdʒʊəri $ ˈdʒʊri/ ●●○ S3 W3 *n* (*plural* **juries**) [C]
1 a group of often 12 ordinary people who listen to the details of a case in court and decide whether someone is guilty or not: *the* ***members of the jury*** *| The jury found him not guilty. | the right to* ***trial by jury*** | **sit/serve on a jury** (=be part of a jury)
2 a group of people chosen to judge a competition
3 the jury is (still) out on sth used to say that something has not been finally decided: *Is it good value? The jury is still out on that.* → **GRAND JURY**

Phrasal verbs

Phrasal verbs are listed in alphabetical order after the main verb.

If the phrasal verb has an object, this is shown as **sb** (=somebody) or **sth** (=something). The symbol ↔ means that the object can come before or after the particle. For example **key** something in or **key in** something.

key[3] ●●○ *v* [T]
1 *AmE informal* if you key a win for your team, you help it win a game because you play very well: *Abdul keyed the game with three touchdowns.*
2 *BrE* to prepare a surface so that a covering such as paint will stick to it

key sth ↔ **in** *phr v* to put information into a computer or other machine, using buttons or a keyboard: *Key in your password and press 'Return'.*

key sth **to** sth *phr v AmE*
1 to make or change a system so that it works well with something else: *The daycare hours are keyed to the needs of working parents.*
2 if the level, price, or value of something is keyed to something else, it is related to it and they rise and fall at the same time: *Pensions are keyed to the rate of inflation.*

LEARNING MORE ABOUT A WORD

Pronunciation

Pronunciation is shown using the International Phonetic Alphabet (IPA).

If the British and American pronunciations are different, the British pronunciation is shown first and the American pronunciation has a dollar sign ($) in front of it.

For compound words, the primary stress (ˈ) and the secondary stress (ˌ) are shown.

See inside front cover for a list of IPA symbols.

cloth /klɒθ $ klɒːθ/ ●●○ S3 *n*
1 [U] material used for making things such as clothes: **cotton/woollen/silk etc cloth** *a dress of the finest silk cloth*
2 [C] a piece of cloth used for a particular purpose: *She mopped her face with a wet cloth.* | *Is there a clean cloth for the table?* → **DISHCLOTH, FACECLOTH, TABLECLOTH**
3 man of the cloth *formal* a Christian priest

ˌcloth ˈcap *n* [C] *BrE* a soft flat cap with a stiff pointed piece at the front

Frequency

The meanings of each word are listed in order of frequency. The most common meaning is shown first.

The most important 9000 words to learn in English are highlighted in red. ●●● indicates the top 3000 words; ●●○ indicates the next most important 3000 words; ●○○ indicates the less frequent yet important next 3000 words. S1 and W1 indicate the 1000 most frequent words in spoken or written English. S2 and W2 mark the next 1000 (1000-2000) most frequent words, and S3 and W3 denote the words in the 2000-3000 frequency range.

See the end of the book for further information and a full list of the Longman Communication 9000.

There are also graphs that give you extra information about spoken and written frequency.

let¹ /let/ ●●● S1 W1 *v* (*past tense and past participle* **let**, *present participle* **letting**)
1 ALLOW [T not in passive] to allow someone to do something → **allow, permit**: *I can't come out tonight – my dad won't let me.* | **let sb do sth** *Let Johnny have a go on the computer now.* | *Some people seem to let their kids do whatever they like.* | *Let me have a look at that letter.* | **let sb have sth** (=give something to someone) *I can let you have another £10, but no more.* THESAURUS ALLOW

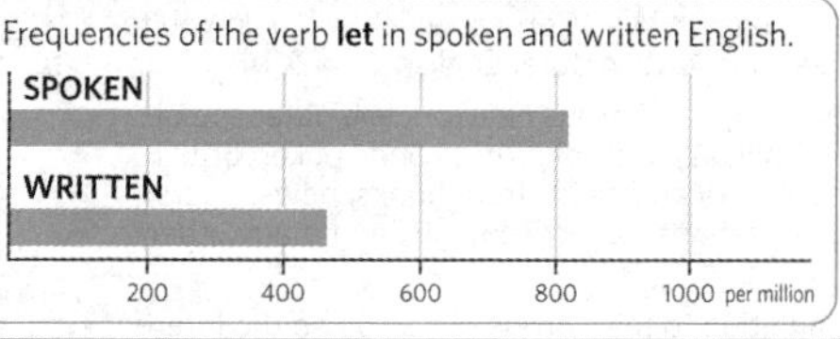

Academic words

The label AWL indicates that a word is included in the *Academic Word List*. These are important words to know if you are studying in an English-speaking environment, or if you are writing academic assignments.

For further information about the Academic Word List, go to: http://www.victoria.ac.nz/lals/resources/academicwordlist/

min·i·mize (*also* **-ise** *BrE*) /ˈmɪnəmaɪz/ ●●○ AWL *v* [T]
1 to reduce something that is difficult, dangerous, or unpleasant to the smallest possible amount or degree OPP **maximize**: *Every effort is being made to minimize civilian casualties.* | *The rail company is bringing in more trains in an effort to minimize disruption to travellers.*
2 to make something seem less serious or important than it really is SYN **play down**: *We must not minimize the problem of racial discrimination.*
3 to make a document or program on your computer very

Register

Labels before the definition show you if a word is used in informal, formal, spoken, literary, legal, technical English and so on.

ne'er /neə $ ner/ *adv literary* never
ˈne'er-do-ˌwell *n* [C] *old use* a lazy useless person
ne·far·i·ous /nɪˈfeəriəs $ -ˈfer-/ *adj formal* evil or criminal: *nefarious activities such as drug trafficking and fraud*

Register notes give additional information about the formality of a word or phrase, helping you to choose the most appropriate word for a particular context.

See page i for a list of the labels used.

See page A1 for further information about formality in spoken and written English.

pe·nul·ti·mate /peˈnʌltəmət, pə-/ *adj* [only before noun] not the last, but immediately before the last SYN **last but one** → **ultimate**: *the penultimate chapter* THESAURUS LAST

> **REGISTER**
> In everyday English, people usually say **the next to last** or, in British English, **the last but one** rather than use **penultimate**: *the* ***next to last*** *chapter* | *the* ***last but one*** *chapter*

American and British English

This dictionary has full coverage of both American and British English. If a word is only used in American English, it is marked *AmE*. If a word is only used in British English, it is marked *BrE*.

If there is another word with the same meaning in British or American English, it is shown after the definition.

If a word is only used in Australian English, it is marked *AusE*.

poˌlice ˈconstable *n* [C] *BrE formal* (*abbreviation* **PC**) a police officer of the lowest rank

poˈlice deˌpartment *n* [C] *AmE* the official police organization in a particular area or city

ˈprimary ˌschool ●●○ *n* [C] *BrE* a school for children between 5 and 11 years old in England and Wales SYN **elementary school** *AmE*

FINDING OUT ABOUT MEANING

The Longman Defining Vocabulary

Definitions explain the meaning of the word in clear simple language, using the 2000-word *Longman Defining Vocabulary*.

➲ *See the end of the book for further information about the Longman Defining Vocabulary, including a complete list of all 2000 words.*

If a word used in a definition is not part of the *Longman Defining Vocabulary*, it is shown in SMALL CAPITAL LETTERS.

at·mo·sphere /ˈætməsfɪə $ -fɪr/ ●●● S3 W2 *n*
1 [C,U] the feeling that an event or place gives you: *The hotel had a lovely* ***relaxed atmosphere****.* | *The atmosphere at home was rather tense.* | **[+of]** *An atmosphere of optimism dominated the conference.*
2 [U] if a place or event has atmosphere, it is interesting: *The castle was centuries old and full of atmosphere.* | *The match was lacking in atmosphere.*
3 the atmosphere the mixture of gases that surrounds the Earth
4 [C] the mixture of gases that surrounds a PLANET
5 [C usually singular] the air inside a room: *a smoky atmosphere*

Signposts

If a word has a lot of different meanings, signposts help to guide you quickly to the meaning you want.

Examples

There are thousands of useful examples, based on information from the Longman Corpus Network and the Longman Web Corpus, which will help you to speak and write natural English.

The Longman Corpus Network is a database of 390 million words of written and spoken British and American English from books, newspapers, conversations, advertisements, and many other sources.

In addition to the Corpus, we also use the Internet to discover new words and new meanings of existing words.

class¹ /klɑːs $ klæs/ ●●● S1 W1 *n*
1 SOCIAL GROUP **a)** [C] one of the groups in a society that different types of people are divided into according to their jobs, income, education etc: *a member of* ***the landed class*** (=people who own land) → LOWER CLASS, MIDDLE CLASS, UPPER CLASS, WORKING CLASS, → **the chattering classes** at CHATTER¹(4) **b)** [U] the system in which people are divided into these groups: *Defining the concept of class is not an easy task.* | *The old class system is slowly disappearing.*
2 STUDENTS [C] **a)** a group of students who are taught together → **classmate**: **in a class** *We're in the same class for chemistry.* | *Gary came* ***top of the class*** *in English.* | *My class are going to the science museum.* **b)** *AmE* a group of students who finished studying together in the same year → **classmate**: *a class reunion* | **the class of 1965/2001 etc** (=the group of students who finished in 1965 etc) *The class of '69 spent almost as much time protesting as learning.*
3 TEACHING PERIOD [C,U] a period of time during which

FINDING OUT ABOUT GRAMMAR

Part of speech and grammar information

The part of speech is shown first, followed by information about whether a word is countable, uncountable, transitive, intransitive etc.

Inflections

Information about irregular forms of verbs, nouns, and adjectives is shown at the beginning of the entry.

blow¹ /bləʊ $ bloʊ/ ●●● S2 W3 *v* (*past tense* **blew** /bluː/, *past participle* **blown** /bləʊn $ bloʊn/)
1 WIND MOVING [I,T] if the wind or a current of air blows, it moves: *A cold breeze was* ***blowing hard****.* | *It was blowing from an easterly direction.* | *Outside, the weather was* ***blowing a gale****.*
2 WIND MOVING STH [I,T usually + adv/prep] to move, or to move something, by the force of the wind or a current of

Grammar patterns

Common grammar patterns are shown in **bold** before the examples so that you can see clearly how the word operates in a sentence.

Common prepositions are also shown in **bold** before the examples.

➲ *See pages i and ii for lists of short forms of parts of speech and grammar codes.*

change¹ /tʃeɪndʒ/ ●●● S1 W1 *v*
1 BECOME DIFFERENT/MAKE STH DIFFERENT [I,T] to become different, or to make something become different: *Susan has changed a lot since I last saw her.* | *Changing your eating habits is the best way to lose weight.* | *The leaves on trees change colour in the autumn.* | **change (from sth) to sth** *He changed from being a nice lad to being rude and unhelpful.* | **[+into]** *The hissing sound gradually changed into a low hum.* | **change sb/sth into sth** *A witch had changed him into*

Grammar notes

Grammar notes provide detailed information about areas of grammar.

GRAMMAR: Singular or plural verb?

- You use a singular verb after **the number of**: ***The number of*** *people* ***is*** *increasing.*
- You use a plural verb after **a number of** (=several): ***A number of*** *issues* ***were*** *discussed.*

Common Error notes

Common Error notes are introduced by a warning triangle ⚠ and provide information about common mistakes that people make when using a word, based on research from the Longman Learners' Corpus (a database of over 10 million words of English written by students from around the world).

bring the number to 25, 120 etc *This will bring the number of jobs lost at the company to 85.*

COMMON ERRORS

⚠ Don't say 'a big number of people/things'. Say **a large number of people/things**.

BUILDING VOCABULARY

Synonyms, antonyms, and related words

Synonyms (=words with the same meaning), antonyms (=words with the opposite meaning), and related words are shown after the definition.

fec·und /ˈfekənd, ˈfiːkənd/ *adj formal* able to produce many children, young animals, or crops SYN **fertile** —**fecundity** /fɪˈkʌndəti/ *n* [U]

fe·male[1] /ˈfiːmeɪl/ ●●● S3 W2 *adj*
1 relating to women or girls OPP **male** → **feminine**: *female voters | Over half of the staff are female.*
2 belonging to the sex that can have babies or produce eggs OPP **male**: *a female spider*

Collocation

Collocations are words that are often used with a particular word. Collocations are shown in **bold**.

If a word has a lot of collocations, they are listed in a box at the end of the entry.

ex·tent /ɪkˈstent/ ●●● S2 W1 *n*
1 to ... extent used to say how true something is or how great an effect or change is: **to a certain extent/to some extent/to an extent** (=partly) *We all to some extent remember the good times and forget the bad. | I do agree with him to an extent.* | **to a great/large extent** *Its success will depend to a large extent on local attitudes.* | **to a lesser/greater extent** (=less or more) *It will affect farmers in Spain and to a lesser extent in France. | They examined* ***the extent to which***

COLLOCATIONS – MEANING 2

ADJECTIVES

the full extent *He refused to reveal the full extent of his debts.*
the actual/true extent *Rescue workers still do not know the true extent of the disaster.*

VERBS

know/realize the extent of sth *We do not yet know the extent of the damage.*
understand the extent of sth *Other people didn't seem to understand the extent of his disability.*
discover/find out the extent of sth *We were shocked when we discovered the extent of the fraud.*
assess/establish/determine the extent of sth *We are still trying to assess the extent of the problem.*
show/reveal the extent of sth *These pictures show the extent of the devastation caused by the earthquake.*

Thesaurus notes

Thesaurus notes explain the differences between words which are similar in meaning and give examples that show how they are used differently.

broken[2] ●●● S3 W2 *adj*
1 PIECE OF EQUIPMENT not working properly: *The CD player's broken again. | Do you know how the phone* ***got broken*** (=became broken)?
2 OBJECT in small pieces because it has been hit, dropped etc: *Mind the broken glass. | Wrap it up well so it*

THESAURUS

broken if something is broken, it does not work properly: *I think my watch is broken. | The camera got broken when we were on holiday.*
out of order [not before noun] if a machine, especially one used by the public, is out of order, it is not working for a temporary period: *Every phone I tried was out of order. | The toilets were all out of order.*
down [not before noun] if a computer system is down, it is not working: *The computer system was down all afternoon, so we went home.* | **go down** (=stop working): *The network went down at 11:00 and we lost the whole morning's work.*
there's something wrong with sth used when saying that a car, machine etc does not work properly and you do not know why: *There's something wrong with my car; I think it might be the battery.*
sth has had it *informal* used when saying that a car, machine etc is completely broken and cannot be repaired: *I'm afraid the bike's had it.*

Numbers

000 *number* the telephone number you use in Australia to call the police, the FIRE SERVICE, or an AMBULANCE in an emergency

1 used in TEXT MESSAGES instead of 'one', for example SUM1 (= someone)

2 /tuː/ *written informal* a way of writing 'to' or 'too', used especially in emails and TEXT MESSAGES: *Happy birthday 2 U* (=to you)! | *He's 2* (=too) *cool!*

2.0 /ˌtuː pɔɪnt ˈəʊ $ -ˈoʊ/ *adj* [only after noun] used to refer to a slightly improved or different form of something: *We are calling the exhibition Surrealism 2.0.*

2:1 /ˌtuː ˈwʌn/ *n* [C] the higher of the two levels of SECOND-CLASS university degree in Britain

2:2 /ˌtuː ˈtuː/ *n* [C] the lower of the two levels of SECOND-CLASS university degree in Britain

3-D (*also* **three-D**) /ˌθriː ˈdiː◂/ *adj* a 3-D film or picture is made so that it appears to have length, width, and depth, and therefore the people and things in it look much more real. 3D is short for 'three dimensional'. —**3-D** *n* [U]: *a film in 3-D*

3G /ˌθriː ˈdʒiː◂/ *adj* 3G technology makes it possible to have fast ACCESS to the Internet and watch videos when using a MOBILE PHONE. 3G is short for 'third generation': *a new 3G phone*

4 /fɔː fɔːr/ *written informal* a way of writing 'for', used especially in emails and TEXT MESSAGES: *a message 4 U* (=for you)

4x4 *n* [C] a FOUR-WHEEL DRIVE vehicle

4-D film /ˌfɔː diː ˈfɪlm $ ˌfɔːr-/ *n* [C,U] a 3-D film combined with physical effects in the cinema, such as smells

4-F /ˌfɔːr ˈef/ *n, adj* used in the US to describe someone who is not allowed to become a member of the US military forces because of physical, mental, or moral reasons

4G /ˌfɔː ˈdʒiː $ ˌfɔːr-/ *adj* 4G technology and services provide a very fast connection to the Internet from MOBILE PHONES etc. 4G is short for 'fourth generation': *When will they be launching their 4G network?*

4-H /ˌfɔːr ˈeɪtʃ/ a US organization that helps young people to be good citizens, live healthily, and develop new skills

4WD *n* [C] a FOUR-WHEEL DRIVE vehicle

➲ See page 2155 for more information on numbers.

9/11 /ˌnaɪn ɪˈlevən/ *n* [U] September 11, 2001, when TERRORISTS used planes to attack New York and Washington: *the terrifying events of 9/11* | *a 9/11 disaster relief fund*

12 /twelv/ *n* [singular, U] used in Britain to describe a film which only people aged 12 or over are allowed to see

15 /ˌfɪfˈtiːn◂/ *n* [singular, U] used in Britain to describe a film which only people aged 15 or over are allowed to see

20/20 vi·sion /ˌtwenti twenti ˈvɪʒən/ *n* [U] the ability to see perfectly without needing to wear glasses

24-7 /ˌtwenti fɔː ˈsevən $ -fɔːr-/ *adv* if something happens 24-7, it happens all the time, every day

101 /ˌwʌn əʊ ˈwʌn $ -oʊ-/ *number* **1 Psychology 101/Economics 101 etc** *AmE* a course that teaches you the most basic things about a subject **2 that's/it's Psychology 101/Marketing 101 etc** *informal* used to say that a piece of knowledge relating to something is very simple and basic: *If you're with a girl, don't stare at other girls: that's Dating 101.*

180 /wʌn ˈeɪti/ *n* **do a 180** *informal* **a)** to turn around so that you are then facing in the opposite direction, for example on a bicycle or a SKATEBOARD **b)** to completely change your attitude to something or your plans for something → **U-turn**: *They have done a 180 on the issue of immigration.*

411 /ˌfɔː wʌn ˈwʌn $ ˌfɔːr-/ **1** the telephone number you use in the US and Canada to call DIRECTORY ASSISTANCE (=a service which helps you to find someone's number) **2 the 411 on sth** *AmE* information about something: *the 411 on text messaging*

419 scam /ˌfɔː wʌn ˈnaɪn skæm $ ˌfɔːr-/ *n* [C,U] an illegal way of getting money from someone by sending them an email promising that they will make a lot of money if they INVEST in a business activity which does not really exist SYN **advance fee fraud**

911 /ˌnaɪn wʌn ˈwʌn/ *number* the telephone number you use in the US to call the police, the FIRE SERVICE, or an AMBULANCE in an emergency

999 /ˌnaɪn naɪn ˈnaɪn/ *number* the telephone number you use in Britain to call the police, the FIRE SERVICE, or an AMBULANCE in an emergency

1066 /ˌten sɪksti ˈsɪks/ the year 1066, the year of the Battle of Hastings and the Norman Conquest of Britain. This is a date known by most schoolchildren in the UK.

Symbols

@ [in email addresses] at. Also used to identify a person's name on some SOCIAL NETWORKING sites.

. [in grammar] full stop *BrE*, period *AmE*; [in email addresses] dot

" ditto

& ampersand

* asterisk

™ trademark

© copyright

hash sign *BrE*, pound sign *AmE*. Also used on some SOCIAL NETWORKING sites before a word or phrase, to identify messages on a specific topic. This is referred to as a HASHTAG.

\ back slash

/ forward slash

“ ” quotation marks, inverted commas

’ apostrophe

✗ cross - used to show that an answer is wrong.

✓ tick, check mark *AmE* - used to show that an answer is correct.

— dash

_ underscore: **john_smith@email.com** *john underscore smith at email dot com*

( ) (round) brackets

! exclamation mark

[ ] square brackets

: colon

; semicolon

{ } curly brackets, braces

= equals sign: **2+2=4** *Two plus two equals four.*

≠ does not equal

× multiplication sign: **2x3=6** *Two times three equals six.*

\+ plus sign: **4+1=5** *Four plus one equals five.*

\- minus sign: **8-2=6** *Eight minus two equals six.*

÷ division sign: **4÷2=2** *Four divided by two equals two.*

√ square root sign: **√9=3** *The square root of nine equals three.*

% percent

Aa

A[1], **a** /eɪ/ *n* (*plural* **A's, a's**) **1** [C,U] the first letter of the English alphabet **2** [C,U] the sixth note in the musical SCALE of C MAJOR or the musical KEY based on this note **3** [C] the highest mark that a student can get in an examination or for a piece of work: *I got an A in French.* | *Julia got* ***straight A's*** (=all A's) *in high school.* → **A LEVEL** **4 an A student** *AmE* someone who regularly gets the best marks possible for their work in school or college **5** [U] used to refer in a short way to one of two different things or people. You can call the second one B: *A demands £500, B offers £100.* → **plan A** at **PLAN**[1](5) **6 from A to B** from one place to another: **get/go from A to B** *Hiring a car was the best way to get from A to B.* **7 from A to Z** describing, including, or knowing everything about a subject: *the history of art from A to Z* **8 A34, A40 etc** the name of a road in Britain that is smaller than a MOTORWAY, but larger than a B-ROAD → **A-ROAD** **9** [U] a common type of blood

A[2] the written abbreviation of ***amp*** or ***amps***

a /ə; *strong* eɪ/ ●●● [S1] [W1] (*also* **an**) *indefinite article, determiner*

1 used to show that you are talking about someone or something that has not been mentioned before, or that your listener does not know about: *We have a problem.* | *There was a hole in the fence.* | *Suddenly they heard a loud bang.* → **THE**[1]

2 used to show that you are referring to a general type of person or thing and not a specific person or thing: *Would you like a sandwich?* | *I want to train to be an engineer.* | *He's a really nice man.* | *Take a look at this.* | *It needs a good clean.*

3 used before someone's family name to show that they belong to that family: *One of his daughters had married a Rothschild.*

4 one: *a thousand pounds* | *a dozen eggs* | *You'll have to wait an hour or two.*

5 used in some phrases that say how much of something there is: *There were* ***a lot*** *of people at the party.* | ***A few*** *weeks from now I'll be in Venice.* | *You have caused* ***a great deal*** *of trouble.*

6 used to mean 'each' when stating prices, rates, or speeds: *I get paid once a month.* | *The eggs cost $2 a dozen.*

7 used before singular nouns to mean all things of a particular type: *A square has four sides* (=all squares have four sides). | *A child needs love and affection.*

8 used once before two nouns that are mentioned together very often: *I'll fetch you a cup and saucer.* | *Does everyone have a knife and fork?*

9 used before the -ing forms of verbs when they are used as nouns referring to an action, event, or sound: *There was a beating of wings overhead.* | *Bernice became aware of a humming that seemed to come from all around her.*

10 used before nouns that are usually UNCOUNTABLE when other information about the quality, feeling etc is added by an adjective, phrase, or CLAUSE: *Candidates must have a good knowledge of chemistry.*

11 used before the name of a substance, food etc to refer to a particular type of it: *Use a good cheese to make the sauce.* | *plants that grow well in a moist soil*

12 used before the name of a drink to refer to a cup or glass of that drink: *Can I get you a coffee?* | *Renwick went to the bar and ordered a beer.*

13 used before the name of a famous artist to refer to a painting by that artist: *an early Rembrandt*

14 used before a name to mean someone or something that has the same qualities as that person or thing: *She was hailed as a new Marilyn Monroe.*

15 used before someone's name when you do not know who they are: *There is a Mr Tom Wilkins on the phone.*

16 used before the names of days, months, seasons, and events in the year to refer to a particular one: *We arrived in England on a cold wet Sunday in 1963.* | *I can't remember a Christmas like it.*

USAGE: A, an

- Before a word beginning with a vowel sound, use **an**: *an elephant* | *an umbrella* | *an obvious mistake*
- Use **an** before an 'h' that is not pronounced: *an hour later* | *an honest explanation*
- Use **a** before a 'u' that is pronounced like 'you': *a university* | *a unique opportunity*
- Use **an** before an abbreviation that is pronounced with a vowel sound at the start: *an SOS call* | *an MP3 file*

a-[1] /ə/ *prefix* **1** in a particular condition or way: *aloud* | *alive* (=living) | *with nerves all a-tingle* (=tingling) **2** *old use* in, to, at, or on something: *abed* (=in bed) | *afar* (=far away)

a-[2] /eɪ, æ, ə/ *prefix* not or without: *amoral* (=not moral) | *atypically* (=not typically)

A* /ˌeɪ ˈstɑː $ -ˈstɑːr/ *n* [C,U] the highest mark that a student can get in a GCSE examination

A-1 /ˌeɪ ˈwʌn/ *adj old-fashioned* very good or completely healthy: *Everything about the resort was A-1.*

A3 /ˌeɪ ˈθriː◂/ *n* [U] a standard size of paper, used in Europe and Japan. A3 paper measures 297 x 420 MILLIMETRES → **A4, A5**

A4 /ˌeɪ ˈfɔː◂ $ -ˈfɔːr◂/ *n* [U] a standard size of paper, used in Europe and Japan. A4 paper measures 210 x 297 MILLIMETRES → **A3, A5**

A5 /ˌeɪ ˈfaɪv◂/ *n* [U] a standard size of paper, used in Europe and Japan. A5 paper measures 148 x 210 MILLIMETRES → **A3, A4**

AA /eɪ ˈeɪ/ *n* **1** (***Alcoholics Anonymous***) an organization for ALCOHOLICS who want to stop drinking alcohol **2 the AA** (***Automobile Association***) a British organization which provides services for people who own cars **3** [C] (***Associate of Arts***) a two-year college degree in the US

A & E /ˌeɪ ənd ˈiː/ *n* [U] *BrE* (***accident and emergency***) the room or department in a hospital where people go if they are injured or suddenly become ill

aard·vark /ˈɑːdvɑːk $ ˈɑːrdvɑːrk/ *n* [C] a large animal from southern Africa that has a very long nose and eats small insects

aargh /ɑːx, ɑː $ ɑːrg, ər/ *interjection* used to show you are disappointed, hurt, or annoyed: *Aargh, the lid won't close!*

AB /ˌeɪ ˈbiː/ *n* [U] a common type of blood

a·back /əˈbæk/ *adv* **be taken aback (by sth)** to be very surprised or shocked by something: *For a moment, I was completely taken aback by her request.*

ab·a·cus /ˈæbəkəs/ *n* [C] a frame with small balls that can be slid along on thick wires, used for counting and calculating

ab·a·lo·ne /ˌæbəˈləʊni $ -ˈloʊ-/ *n* [C,U] a kind of SHELLFISH which is used as food and whose shell contains MOTHER-OF-PEARL

a·ban·don[1] /əˈbændən/ ●●○ [W3] [AWL] *v* [T]

1 to leave someone, especially someone you are responsible for → **abandoned**: *How could she abandon her own child?*

2 to go away from a place, vehicle etc permanently, especially because the situation makes it impossible for you to stay [SYN] **leave** → **abandoned**: *We had to abandon the car and walk the rest of the way.* | *Fearing further attacks, most of the population had abandoned the city.*

3 to stop doing something because there are too many problems and it is impossible to continue: *The game had to be abandoned due to bad weather.* | *They* ***abandoned*** *their* ***attempt*** *to recapture the castle.* | *Because of the fog they* ***abandoned*** *their* ***idea*** *of driving.*

4 to stop having a particular idea, belief, or attitude: *They*

A

were accused of abandoning their socialist principles. | *Rescuers had* ***abandoned*** *all* ***hope*** *of finding any more survivors.*
5 abandon yourself to sth *literary* to feel an emotion so strongly that you let it control you completely: *She abandoned herself to grief.*
6 abandon ship to leave a ship because it is sinking —**abandonment** *n* [U]

abandon² *n* [U] if someone does something with abandon, they behave in a careless or uncontrolled way, without thinking or caring about what they are doing: **with reckless/wild abandon** *They drank and smoked with reckless abandon.*

a·ban·doned /əˈbændənd/ AWL *adj* **1** an abandoned building, car, boat etc has been left by the people who owned or used it: *The car was found abandoned in Bristol.* | *the demolition of abandoned buildings* **2** [only before noun] an abandoned person or animal has been left completely alone by the person that was looking after them **3** *literary* behaving in a wild and uncontrolled way

a·ban·don·ware /əˈbændənˌweə $ -ˌwer/ *n* [U] old software that is no longer used by most people

a·base /əˈbeɪs/ *v* **abase yourself** to behave in a way that shows you accept that someone has complete power over you —**abasement** *n* [U]

a·bashed /əˈbæʃt/ *adj* [not before noun] *written* embarrassed or ashamed because you have done something wrong or stupid SYN **shamefaced**: *She looked rather abashed.*

a·bate /əˈbeɪt/ *v* [I] *formal* to become less strong or decrease SYN **subside**: *We waited for the storm to abate.*

ab·at·toir /ˈæbətwɑː $ -ɑːr/ *n* [C] *BrE* a place where animals are killed for their meat SYN **slaughterhouse**

a·ba·ya /əˈbeɪə/ *n* [C] a long black piece of clothing worn by Muslim women in some countries, which covers the body and is usually worn with a separate head covering → **burqa**, **chador**, **niqab**

ab·bess /ˈæbəs, ˈæbes/ *n* [C] a woman who is in charge of a CONVENT (=a place where a group of NUNS live)

ab·bey /ˈæbi/ *n* [C] a large church with buildings next to it where MONKS and NUNS live or used to live

ab·bot /ˈæbət/ *n* [C] a man who is in charge of a MONASTERY (=a place where a group of MONKS live)

abbr. (*also* **abbrev.**) the written abbreviation of ***abbreviation***

ab·bre·vi·ate /əˈbriːvieɪt/ ●○○ *v* [T] to make a word or expression shorter by not including letters or using only the first letter of each word SYN **shorten**: **be abbreviated to sth** *'Information technology' is usually abbreviated to 'IT'.*

ab·bre·vi·at·ed /əˈbriːvieɪtɪd/ *adj* made shorter: *Orders were passed to the commander at the front in an abbreviated form.*

ab·bre·vi·a·tion /əˌbriːviˈeɪʃən/ ●●○ *n*
1 [C] a short form of a word or expression: **[+of/for]** *'Dr' is the written abbreviation of 'Doctor'.*

> **REGISTER**
> In everyday English, people usually say **be short for** instead of **be the abbreviation of/for**: *W.H.O.* ***is short for*** *'World Health Organization'.*

2 [U] the act of abbreviating something

ABC /ˌeɪ biː ˈsiː/ *n* **1** [singular] *BrE*, **ABCs** [plural] *AmE* the letters of the English alphabet as taught to children **2 the ABC of sth** *BrE*, **the ABCs of sth** *AmE* the basic facts about a particular subject: *the ABCs of your computer* **3** (***the American Broadcasting Company***) one of the national television companies in the US **4** (***the Australian Broadcasting Corporation***) the national public television company of Australia

ab·di·cate /ˈæbdɪkeɪt/ *v* [I,T] **1** to give up the position of being king or queen: *King Alfonso XIII abdicated in favour of his eldest son.* | *The king was forced to* ***abdicate the throne***.
2 abdicate (your) responsibility *formal* to refuse to be responsible for something, when you should be or were before: *The government has largely abdicated its responsibility in dealing with housing needs.* —**abdication** /ˌæbdɪˈkeɪʃən/ *n* [C,U]

Ab·di·ca·tion /ˌæbdɪˈkeɪʃən/ **the Abdication** (*also* **the Abdiˈcation ˌCrisis**) the period in Britain in 1936, in which King Edward VIII abdicated so that he could marry Wallis Simpson, a woman who had been divorced (DIVORCE)

ab·do·men /ˈæbdəmən, æbˈdəʊ- $ -ˈdoʊ-/ ●○○ *n* [C]
1 the part of your body between your chest and legs which contains your stomach, BOWELS etc
2 the end part of an insect's body, joined to the THORAX → see picture at **INSECT** —**abdominal** /æbˈdɒmɪnəl $ -ˈdɑː-/ *adj*: *acute abdominal pains*

ab·duct /əbˈdʌkt, æb-/ *v* [T] to take someone away by force SYN **kidnap**: *The diplomat was abducted on his way to the airport.* —**abductor** *n* [C] —**abduction** /əbˈdʌkʃən, æb-/ *n* [C,U]: *child abduction* —**abductee** /ˌæbdʌkˈtiː/ *n* [C]

> **REGISTER**
> **Abduct** is mostly used in journalism. In everyday English, people usually say **kidnap**: *He was* ***kidnapped*** *on his way to the airport.*

a·bed /əˈbed/ *adj* [not before noun] *old use* in bed

a·ber·rant /ˈæbərənt, əˈberənt/ *adj formal* not usual or normal SYN **abnormal**: *aberrant behaviour*

ab·er·ra·tion /ˌæbəˈreɪʃən/ *n* [C] *formal* an action or event that is very different from what usually happens or what someone usually does: *a temporary aberration in US foreign policy* | *a mental aberration*

a·bet /əˈbet/ *v* (**abetted**, **abetting**) [T] to help someone do something wrong or illegal → **aid and abet** at **AID²**(3)

a·bey·ance /əˈbeɪəns/ *n* **in abeyance** something such as a custom, rule, or system that is in abeyance is not being used at the present time: **fall into abeyance** (=no longer be used)

ab·hor /əbˈhɔː $ əbˈhɔːr, æb-/ *v* (**abhorred**, **abhorring**) [T not in progressive] *formal* to hate a kind of behaviour or way of thinking, especially because you think it is morally wrong: *I abhor discrimination of any kind.* THESAURUS ▸ HATE

ab·hor·rence /əbˈhɒrəns $ -ˈhɔːr-/ *n* [U] *formal* a deep feeling of hatred towards something

ab·hor·rent /əbˈhɒrənt $ -ˈhɔːr-/ *adj* something that is abhorrent is completely unacceptable because it seems morally wrong SYN **repugnant**: **[+to]** *The practice of killing animals for food is utterly abhorrent to me.*

a·bide /əˈbaɪd/ *v* **1 sb can't abide sb/sth** used to say that someone dislikes someone or something very much: *I can't abide that man – he's so self-satisfied.* **2** (*past tense* **abode** /əˈbəʊd $ əˈboʊd/) [I always + adv/prep] *old use* to live somewhere

abide by sth *phr v* to accept and obey a decision, rule, agreement etc, even though you may not agree with it: *You have to abide by the referee's decision.*

a·bid·ing /əˈbaɪdɪŋ/ *adj* [only before noun] *written* an abiding feeling or belief continues for a long time and is not likely to change SYN **lasting**: *Phil has a deep and abiding love for his family.*

a·bil·i·ty /əˈbɪləti/ ●●● S2 W1 *n* (*plural* **abilities**)
1 [C] the state of being able to do something: **ability to do sth** *the ability to walk* | *The health center serves all patients, regardless of their ability to pay.*
2 [C,U] someone's level of skill at doing something: *The test measures your mathematical ability.* | *mixed ability classes* | **of high/low etc ability** *students of average ability* | *There are musicians of all abilities.* | **sb's abilities as sth** *He showed his abilities as a leader.*
3 to the best of your ability as well as you can: *He completed the job to the best of his ability.*

> **GRAMMAR**
> **Ability** is followed by an infinitive with 'to', not by an **-ing** form. You say: *I admire his ability to listen.*
> ✗ Don't say: *I admire his ability of listening.*
> GRAMMAR GUIDE ▸ NOUNS

COLLOCATIONS – MEANINGS 1 & 2

ADJECTIVES

high/low/average ability *a group of low ability pupils*
great/considerable ability *He was a young man of great ability.*
remarkable/outstanding/exceptional ability *a writer of remarkable ability*
mixed ability (=at different levels) *a mixed ability class*
uncanny ability (=an unusual ability that is difficult to explain) | **natural ability** (*also* **innate ability** *formal*) (=an ability that you are born with) | **physical/athletic ability** | **artistic/creative ability** | **musical ability** | **acting ability** | **mental ability** | **intellectual/academic ability** | **verbal/linguistic ability** (=language skills) | **mathematical ability** | **proven ability** (=that you have proved through your achievements)

VERBS

have the ability to do sth (*also* **possess the ability to do sth** *formal*) *She has the ability to make people feel relaxed.*
show/demonstrate the ability to do sth *a chance for candidates to demonstrate their abilities*
lack the ability to do sth

PHRASES

a level of ability/ability level *The children were of the same age and ability level.*
a range of ability/ability range *There is a wide range of ability within the class.*
a test of ability/an ability test | **an ability group** (=a group that students are taught in, based on their level of ability)

-ability /əbɪləti/ (*also* **-ibility**) *suffix* makes nouns from adjectives ending in -ABLE and -IBLE: *manageability*

ab·ject /ˈæbdʒekt/ *adj* **1 abject poverty/misery/failure etc** the state of being extremely poor, unhappy, unsuccessful etc **2** an abject action or expression shows that you feel very ashamed: *an abject apology* —**abjectly** *adv*

ab·jure /əbˈdʒʊə, æb- $ -ˈdʒʊr/ *v* [T] *formal* to state publicly that you will give up a particular belief or way of behaving SYN **renounce**

ab·la·tive /ˈæblətɪv/ *n* [C usually singular] a particular form of a noun in some languages, such as Latin or Finnish, which shows movement away or separation

a·blaze /əˈbleɪz/ *adj* [not before noun] *written* **1** burning strongly with a lot of flames → **blaze**: *Within minutes the whole house was ablaze.* | *The factory had been* ***set ablaze*** (=made to burn).

REGISTER
Ablaze is mostly used in journalism or in literature. In everyday English, people usually say **on fire**: *The whole house was* ***on fire****.*

2 very bright or colourful: *a passing pleasure-boat, with all its lights ablaze* | **[+with]** *Her yard was ablaze with summer flowers.* **3** feeling or showing strong emotion, especially anger SYN **blazing**: **[+with]** *His eyes were ablaze with fury.*

a·ble /ˈeɪbəl/ ●●● S1 W1 *adj*
1 be able to do sth a) to have the skill, strength, knowledge etc needed to do something: *I've always wanted to be able to speak Japanese.* **b)** to be in a situation in which it is possible for you to do something: *I'd like to do more gardening, but I never seem able to find the time.* | *I haven't been able to read that report yet.*
2 clever or good at doing something: *one of my more able students*

-able /əbəl/ (*also* **-ible**) *suffix* [in adjectives] **1** that you can do something to: *washable* (=it can be washed) | *unbreakable* (=it cannot be broken) | *loveable* (=easy to love) **2** having a particular quality or condition: *knowledgeable* (=knowing a lot) | *comfortable* —**-ably** /əbli/, **-ibly** *suffix* [in adverbs]: *unbelievably*

ˌable-ˈbodied *adj* **1** physically strong and healthy, especially when compared with someone who is DISABLED: *Every able-bodied man had to fight for his country.* **2 the able-bodied** [plural] people who are able-bodied

ˌable ˈseaman *n* [C] a low rank in the navy, or someone who has this rank

a·blu·tions /əˈbluːʃənz/ *n* [plural] *formal* if you perform your ablutions, you wash yourself – sometimes used humorously

a·bly /ˈeɪbli/ *adv* cleverly, skilfully, or well: *She was ably assisted by her team of researchers.*

ab·ne·ga·tion /ˌæbnəˈɡeɪʃən/ *n* [U] *formal* when you do not allow yourself to have or do something that you want → **self-denial**

ab·norm·al /æbˈnɔːməl $ -ˈnɔːr-/ ●○○ AWL *adj* very different from usual in a way that seems strange, worrying, wrong, or dangerous OPP **normal**: *abnormal behaviour* | *an abnormal level of cholesterol* | *My parents thought* ***it was abnormal*** *for a boy to be interested in ballet.* —**abnormally** *adv*: *an* ***abnormally high*** *pulse rate*

ab·nor·mal·i·ty /ˌæbnɔːˈmæləti $ -nər-/ ●○○ *n* (*plural* **abnormalities**) [C,U] an abnormal feature, especially something that is wrong with part of someone's body: *tests that can detect genetic abnormalities in the foetus*

ab·o, **Abo** /ˈæbəʊ $ -boʊ/ *n* (*plural* **abos**) [C] *taboo* a very offensive word for an Australian ABORIGINE. Do not use this word.

a·board¹ /əˈbɔːd $ əˈbɔːrd/ ●○○ *prep* on or onto a ship, plane, or train: *They finally* ***went aboard*** *the plane.*

aboard² ●○○ *adv*
1 on or onto a ship, plane, or train: *The plane crashed, killing all 200 people aboard.* | *The boat swayed as he stepped aboard.*
2 All aboard! *spoken* used to tell passengers of a ship, bus, or train that they must get on because it will leave soon

a·bode¹ /əˈbəʊd $ əˈboʊd/ *n* [C] **1** *formal* someone's home – sometimes used humorously: *Welcome to my humble abode.* | *a homeless person with* ***no fixed abode*** (=no permanent home) **2 right of abode** *law* the right to live in a country

abode² *v* the past tense of ABIDE

a·bol·ish /əˈbɒlɪʃ $ əˈbɑː-/ ●●○ *v* [T] to officially end a law, system etc, especially one that has existed for a long time: *Slavery was abolished in the US in the 19th century.*

ab·o·li·tion /ˌæbəˈlɪʃən/ *n* [U] when a law or a system is officially ended: **[+of]** *the abolition of the death penalty*

ab·o·li·tion·ist /ˌæbəˈlɪʃənɪst/ *n* [C] someone who wants to end a system or law

A-bomb /ˈeɪ bɒm $ -bɑːm/ *n* [C] *old-fashioned* an ATOMIC BOMB

a·bom·i·na·ble /əˈbɒmɪnəbəl, -mənə- $ əˈbɑː-/ *adj* extremely unpleasant or of very bad quality SYN **terrible**: *abominable cruelty* —**abominably** *adv*: *Mavis behaved abominably.*

aˌbominable ˈsnowman *n* [C] a YETI

a·bom·i·nate /əˈbɒməneɪt $ əˈbɑː-/ *v* [T] *formal* to hate something very much SYN **abhor**

a·bom·i·na·tion /əˌbɒməˈneɪʃən $ əˌbɑː-/ *n* [C] someone or something that is extremely offensive or unacceptable: *Slavery was an abomination.*

ab·o·rig·i·nal¹ /ˌæbəˈrɪdʒɪnəl◂/ *adj* **1** (*also* **Aboriginal**) relating to the Australian aborigines **2** *formal* relating to the people or animals that have existed in a place or country from the earliest times SYN **indigenous**

aboriginal², **Aboriginal** *n* [C] an aborigine

ab·o·rig·i·ne, **Aborigine** /ˌæbəˈrɪdʒɪni/ *n* [C] someone who belongs to the race of people who have lived in Australia from the earliest times

a·bort /əˈbɔːt $ -ɔːrt/ *v* **1** [T] to stop an activity because it would be difficult or dangerous to continue it: *The rescue mission had to be aborted.* **2** [T] to deliberately end a PREGNANCY when the baby is still too young to live **3** [I] if a PREGNANT woman or animal aborts, the baby is born too early and is dead when it is born SYN **miscarry**: *The disease causes pregnant animals to abort.*

a·bor·tion /əˈbɔːʃən $ əˈbɔːr-/ ●○○ *n* [C,U] a medical operation to end a PREGNANCY so that the baby is not born alive SYN **termination**: *She decided to **have** an **abortion**. | anti-abortion campaigners*

a·bor·tion·ist /əˈbɔːʃənɪst $ əˈbɔːr-/ *n* [C] someone who performs abortions, especially illegally

a·bor·tive /əˈbɔːtɪv $ əˈbɔːr-/ *adj* an abortive action is not successful: *an **abortive** military **coup*** | **abortive attempt/effort** *an abortive attempt to reform local government*

a·bound /əˈbaʊnd/ *v* [I] to exist in very large numbers: *Rumours abound as to the reasons for his resignation. | Examples of this abound in her book.*

abound with/in sth *phr v* if a place, situation etc abounds with things of a particular type, it contains a very large number of them: *The forests abound with deer, birds, and squirrels.*

a·bout¹ /əˈbaʊt/ ●●● S1 W1 *prep*

1 concerning or relating to a particular subject: *a book about politics | She said something about leaving town. | He lied about his age. | About that car of yours. How much are you selling it for? | What's he on about* (=talking about)? | ***It's about** Tommy, doctor. He's been sick again. | Naturally, my mother wanted to know **all about** it* (=all the details relating to it).

2 used to show why someone is angry, happy, upset etc: *I'm really worried about Jack. | She's upset about missing the party.*

3 in many different directions within a particular place, or in different parts of a place SYN **around, round**: *We spent the whole afternoon walking about town. | Books were scattered about the room.*

4 in the nature or character of a person or thing: ***There's something** really strange **about** Liza. | **What I like about** the job is that it's never boring.*

5 what/how about sb/sth *spoken* **a)** used to ask a question that directs attention to another person or thing: *What about Jack? We can't just leave him here. | I'm feeling hungry. How about you?* **b)** used to make a suggestion: *How about a salad for lunch?*

6 do something about sth to do something to solve a problem or stop a bad situation: *If we don't do something about it, the problem is going to get worse. | What can be done about the rising levels of pollution?*

7 if an organization, a job, an activity etc is about something, that is its basic purpose: *Leadership is **all about** getting your team to co-operate.*

8 it's all about sb/sth used to say who or what is important in a situation: *It's all about money, and who's got the most.*

9 while you're about it *spoken* used to tell someone to do something while they are doing something else because it would be easier to do both things at the same time: *Go and see what's the matter, and while you're about it you can fetch me my sweater.*

10 what was all that about? *spoken* used to ask the reason for something that has just happened, especially someone's angry behaviour

11 *literary* surrounding a person or thing: *Jo sensed fear and jealousy all about her.* → **be quick about it** at QUICK¹(5), → **go about your business** at BUSINESS(12)

THESAURUS

about used when saying what the subject of something is: *She's always talking about you. | In her novels she writes about life in South Africa. | There's something I wanted to ask you about.*

on about a particular subject: *a book on English grammar | a report on poverty in rural areas*

concerning/regarding *formal* about: *Prince Saiid answered questions concerning Kuwait's future. | The report raises a number of questions regarding food safety.*

with regard to *formal* about – used especially when you want to start talking or writing about something: *Dear Sir, I'm writing with regard to your advertisement in The Times.*

re used in business letters and in emails to introduce the subject that you are going to write about: *Re: Friday's meeting*

about² ●●● S1 W1 *adv*

1 (*also* **round about** *spoken*) a little more or less than a particular number, amount, or size SYN **roughly, approximately**: *I live about 10 miles away. | a tiny computer about as big as a postcard | We left the restaurant at round about 10.30.* **THESAURUS** ▶ APPROXIMATE

REGISTER

In written English, people usually prefer to use **approximately**, as it sounds more technical: *The cost to taxpayers is **approximately** $200 billion.*

2 *BrE* in many different directions within a place or in different parts of a place SYN **around**: *People were rushing about, trying to find the driver. | Cushions were scattered about on the chairs.*

3 near to you or in the same place as you: *Is Derek about? There's a phone call for him. | Quick! Let's go while there's no-one about.*

4 *BrE spoken* existing or available now: *I hope she hasn't caught flu. **There's a lot of it about**. | She might get temporary work, but there's not much about.*

5 *informal* almost or probably: *I was about ready to leave when somebody rang the doorbell. | 'Have you finished?' '**Just about**.' | It's **just about** the worst mistake anyone could make.*

6 that's about it/all *spoken* **a)** used to tell someone that you have told them everything you know: *He was a quiet chap, married with kids. That's about it, really.* **b)** used to say that there is nothing else available: *There's some cheese in the fridge and that's about it.*

7 so as to face in the opposite direction SYN **around**: *He quickly turned about and walked away.*

about³ ●●● S3 W2 *adj*

1 be about to do sth if someone is about to do something, or if something is about to happen, they will do it or it will happen very soon: *We were just about to leave when Jerry arrived. | Work was about to start on a new factory building.*

2 not be about to do sth *informal* used to emphasize that you have no intention of doing something: *I've never smoked in my life and I'm not about to start now.* → **out and about** at OUT¹(3), → **be up and about** at UP¹(11)

aˌbout-ˈface (*also* **aˌbout-ˈturn** *BrE*) *n* [C usually singular] a complete change in the way someone thinks or behaves SYN **U-turn**: *The administration seems to have done a complete about-face on gun-control.*

a·bove¹ /əˈbʌv/ ●●● S2 W1 *adv, prep*

1 in a higher position than something else SYN **over** OPP **below**: *Our office is above the hairdresser's. | He had a bruise just above his left eye. | I heard a strange noise coming from the room above. | The great bird hovered **high above** our heads.*

2 more than a particular number, amount, or level OPP **below**: *50 metres above sea level* | **above freezing/zero** (=higher than the temperature at which water freezes) *Tonight, temperatures should be just above freezing.* | **and/or above** *free medical care for pensioners aged 65 and above | Prize winners must have gained marks of 80% or above. | The salaries we offer are **well above*** (=much higher than) *average.*

3 to a greater degree than something else: *Many employers value personality above experience or qualifications.* | **above all (else)** (=used to say that something is more important than anything else) *Max is hard-working, cheerful, and above all honest. | medals awarded for bravery **above and beyond** the call of duty* (=greater than it is your duty to show)

4 louder or clearer than other sounds: *You can always hear her voice above everybody else's.*

5 higher in rank, power, or importance OPP **below**: *He never rose above the rank of corporal.* | **and/or above** *officers*

of the rank of Major and above | **from above** (=from people in higher authority) *We just obey orders from above.*
6 *formal* before, in the same piece of writing OPP **below**: *As mentioned above, there is a service charge. | Write to the address above for further information.*
7 not be above (doing) sth to not be too good or honest to do something: *Eileen's not above flirting with the boss when it suits her.*
8 be above suspicion/reproach/criticism etc to be so good that no one can doubt or criticize you: *Even the king's closest advisers were not above suspicion.*
9 get above yourself to think you are better or more important than you really are → **over and above** at OVER¹(14), → **be above the law** at LAW(13)

above² ●●○ W3 *adj*
1 [only before noun] used in a piece of writing to refer to something mentioned in an earlier part of the same piece of writing: *For the above reasons, the management has no choice but to close the factory.*
2 the above *formal* something mentioned before in the same piece of writing: *If none of the above applies to you, you may be able to reclaim tax.*

a,bove 'board / $.'../ *adj* [not before noun] honest and legal: *His plans for opening a coffee shop are completely above board.*

a,bove-'mentioned *adj* [only before noun] *formal* mentioned on a previous page or higher up on the same page

ab·ra·ca·dab·ra /ˌæbrəkəˈdæbrə/ *interjection* a word you say when you do a magic trick, which is supposed to make it successful

a·brade /əˈbreɪd/ *v* [I,T] *technical* to rub something so hard that the surface becomes damaged

a·bra·sion /əˈbreɪʒən/ *n* **1** [C] an area on the surface of your skin that has been injured by being rubbed against something hard: *She was treated for cuts and abrasions.* **2** [U] the process of rubbing a surface very hard so that it becomes damaged or disappears: *extra protection against abrasion*

a·bra·sive¹ /əˈbreɪsɪv/ *adj* **1** rude or unkind: *She was a tough girl with rather an abrasive manner.* **2** having a rough surface, especially one that can be used to clean something or make it smooth: *Smooth down with a fine abrasive paper.* —**abrasively** *adv*

abrasive² *n* [C] a rough powder or substance that you use for cleaning something or making it smooth

a·breast /əˈbrest/ *adv* **1 keep/stay abreast of sth** to make sure that you know all the most recent facts or information about a particular subject or situation: *It's important to keep abreast of the latest developments in computers.* **2 walk/ride etc abreast** to walk, ride etc next to each other, all facing the same way: **two/three/four etc abreast** (=with two, three, four etc people or vehicles next to each other) *The planes were flying four abreast.* **3** level with someone or something or in line with them: *As the car* ***drew abreast*** *of him, Jack suddenly recognised the driver.*

a·bridged /əˈbrɪdʒd/ *adj* [usually before noun] an abridged book, play etc has been made shorter but keeps its basic structure and meaning: *The* ***abridged edition*** *was published in 1988.* —**abridge** *v* [T] —**abridgement, abridgment** *n* [C,U]

a·broad /əˈbrɔːd $ əˈbrɒːd/ ●●● S2 W3 *adv*
1 in or to a foreign country: *I've never* ***lived abroad*** *before. | She often* ***goes abroad*** *on business. | We never* ***travelled abroad*** *when we were kids. | A lot of goods are imported* ***from abroad****. | The books about Harry Potter have been very popular, both* ***at home and abroad****.*
2 *formal* if a feeling, piece of news etc is abroad, a lot of people feel it or know about it: *There were rumours abroad that she was planning to resign.*

GRAMMAR: Comparison

abroad
• You **go abroad** or **study abroad**.
Don't use a preposition before **abroad**. ✗ Don't say: *go to abroad | study in abroad*

a foreign country
• You **go to a foreign country** or **study in a foreign country**.
GRAMMAR GUIDE ▶ ADVERBS

ab·ro·gate /ˈæbrəgeɪt/ *v* [T] *formal* to officially end a legal agreement, practice etc: *Both governments voted to abrogate the treaty.* —**abrogation** /ˌæbrəˈgeɪʃən/ *n* [C,U]

a·brupt /əˈbrʌpt/ ●○○ *adj*
1 sudden and unexpected: *an* ***abrupt change*** *of plan |* **come to an abrupt end/halt etc** *The bus came to an abrupt halt.*
2 seeming rude and unfriendly, especially because you do not waste time in friendly conversation: *Sorry, I didn't mean to be so abrupt.* —**abruptness** *n* [U]

a·brupt·ly /əˈbrʌptli/ ●○○ *adv*
1 suddenly and unexpectedly: *She stopped abruptly and looked at him.*
2 in a way that seems rude and unfriendly: *He spoke abruptly, as if he wanted to avoid the subject.*

abs /æbz/ *n* [plural] *informal* the muscles on your ABDOMEN (=stomach): *exercises that improve your legs and abs*

ABS /ˌeɪ biː ˈes/ *n* [U] (***anti-lock braking system***) a piece of equipment that makes a vehicle easier to control when you have to stop very suddenly

ab·scess /ˈæbses/ *n* [C] a painful swollen part of your skin or inside your body that has become infected and is full of a yellowish liquid

ab·scond /əbˈskɒnd, æb- $ æbˈskɑːnd/ *v* [I] *formal*
1 to escape from a place where you are being kept: **[+from]** *The boy absconded from a children's home.* THESAURUS ▶ ESCAPE **2** to secretly leave somewhere, taking with you something that does not belong to you: **[+with]** *He has to convince a judge that he wasn't going to abscond with the money.*

ab·seil /ˈæbseɪl/ *v* [I + down] *BrE* to go down a cliff or a rock by sliding down a rope and pushing against the rock with your feet SYN **rappel** *AmE*

ab·sence /ˈæbsəns/ ●●● S3 W2 *n*
1 [C,U] when you are not in the place where people expect you to be, or the time that you are away: **in/during sb's absence** *Ms Leighton will be in charge during my absence* (=while I am away). | **[+from]** *Her work involved repeated absences from home.*
2 [singular] the lack of something or the fact that it does not exist OPP **presence**: **[+of]** *a complete absence of any kind of planning |* ***In the absence of*** *any evidence, the police had to let Myers go.*
3 absence makes the heart grow fonder used to say that being away from someone makes you like them more → **leave of absence** at LEAVE²(3), → **conspicuous by your absence** at CONSPICUOUS(3)

ab·sent¹ /ˈæbsənt/ ●●● W2 *adj*
1 not at work, school, a meeting etc, because you are sick or decide not to go OPP **present**: **[+from]** *students who are regularly absent from school*

REGISTER
In everyday English, if someone is on holiday or on a business trip, people usually say that he/she **is away**: *He's* ***away*** *at the moment. He's gone to Hawaii.*
If you want to say that someone is not in a particular place, say **not there**: *I called in to see her but she* ***wasn't there****.*
If you want to say that someone is not with you, say **not here**: *I'm afraid he's* ***not here*** *at the moment. Can I take a message?*

2 if someone or something is absent, they are missing or not in the place where they are expected to be: **absent parent/father** *plans to force absent fathers to pay child maintenance |* **[+from]** *Local women were* ***conspicuously absent*** (=obviously not there) *from the meeting.*
3 [only before noun] a look etc that is absent shows you are not paying attention to or thinking about what is happening → **absently**: *The dull,* ***absent look*** *on her face implied boredom.*

A

ab·sent² /əbˈsent, æb- $ æb-/ v [T] *formal* **absent yourself (from sth)** to not go to a place or take part in an event where people expect you to be

ab·sen·tee /ˌæbsənˈtiː◂/ n [C] someone who should be in a place or at an event but is not there

ˌabsentee ˈballot n [C] *AmE* a process by which people can vote before an election because they will be away during the election

ab·sen·tee·is·m /ˌæbsənˈtiːɪzəm/ n [U] regular absence from work or school without a good reason

ˌabsentee ˈlandlord n [C] someone who lives a long way away from a house or apartment which they rent to other people, and who rarely or never visits it

ˌabsentee ˈvote n [C] *AmE* a vote which you send by post in an election because you cannot be in the place where you usually vote SYN **postal vote** *BrE*

ab·sen·ti·a /æbˈsentiə/ n *formal* **in absentia** when you are not at a court or an official meeting where a decision is made about you

ab·sent·ly /ˈæbsəntli/ adv in a way that shows that you are not paying attention to or thinking about what is happening: *Laura gazed absently out of the window.*

ˌabsent-ˈminded adj likely to forget things, especially because you are thinking about something else SYN **forgetful**: *Grandad's been getting rather absent-minded lately.* —**absent-mindedly** adv —**absent-mindedness** n [U]

ab·sinth, **absinthe** /ˈæbsɪnθ/ n [U] a bitter green very strong alcoholic drink

ab·so·lute¹ /ˈæbsəluːt/ ●●○ S3 adj

1 complete or total: *I have absolute confidence in her.* | *We don't know with absolute certainty that the project will succeed.*

2 [only before noun] *especially BrE informal* used to emphasize your opinion about something or someone: *Some of the stuff on TV is absolute rubbish.* | *How did you do that? You're an absolute genius.* | *That meal last night cost an absolute fortune.*

3 definite and not likely to change: *We need absolute proof that he took the money.*

4 not restricted or limited: *an absolute monarch* | *Parents used to have absolute power over their children.*

5 true, correct, and not changing in any situation: *You have an absolute right to refuse medical treatment.*

6 in absolute terms measured by itself, not in comparison with other things: *In absolute terms wages have risen, but not in comparison with the cost of living.*

absolute² n [C] something that is considered to be true or right in all situations: *She believed in the importance of moral absolutes.*

Frequencies of the adverb **absolutely** in spoken and written English.

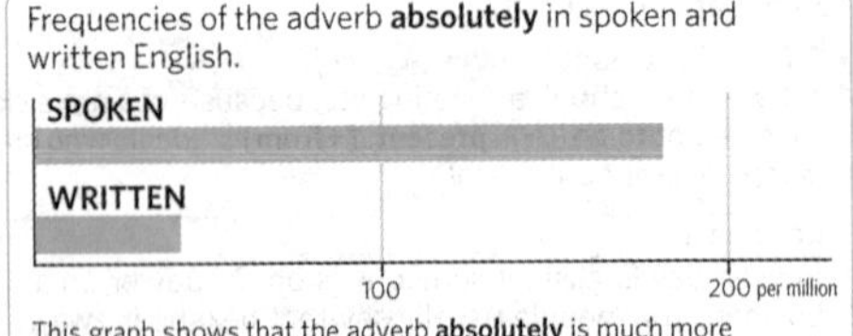

This graph shows that the adverb **absolutely** is much more common in spoken English than in written English. This is because it is used to emphasize adjectives like brilliant, stupid, fantastic etc in spoken English.

ab·so·lute·ly /ˈæbsəluːtli, ˌæbsəˈluːtli/ ●●● S1 W3 adv

1 completely and in every way: *He made his reasons for resigning absolutely clear.* | *Are you absolutely sure?* | *This cake is absolutely delicious.*

2 used to emphasize something: *The burglars took absolutely everything.* | *Jim knew **absolutely nothing** about the business when he joined the firm.* | *He has **absolutely no** experience of marketing.*

3 absolutely not! *spoken* used when you strongly disagree with someone or when you do not want someone to do something: *'Do you let your kids travel alone at night?' 'Absolutely not!'*

4 absolutely! *spoken* used to say that you completely agree with someone

ˌabsolute maˈjority n [singular] when a party or person wins more than half of the total votes in an election

ˌabsolute ˈzero n [U] the lowest temperature that is believed to be possible

ab·so·lu·tion /ˌæbsəˈluːʃən/ n [U] when someone is formally forgiven by the Christian Church or a priest for the things they have done wrong: *Pope Leo **gave** him **absolution**.*

ab·so·lut·is·m /ˈæbsəluːtɪzəm/ n [U] a political system in which a ruler has complete power and authority

ab·solve /əbˈzɒlv $ -ɑːlv/ v [T] **1** to say publicly that someone is not guilty or responsible for something: **absolve sb from/of sth** *He cannot be absolved of all responsibility for the accident.* **2** if someone is absolved by the Christian Church or a priest for something they have done wrong, they are formally forgiven → **absolution**

ab·sorb /əbˈsɔːb, əbˈzɔːb $ -ɔːrb/ ●●○ W3 v [T]

1 LIQUID/GAS to take in liquid, gas, or another substance from the surface or space around something: *Plants absorb nutrients from the soil.* | **absorb sth into sth** *Water and salts are absorbed into our bloodstream.*

2 INFORMATION to read or hear a large amount of new information and understand it: *Her capacity to absorb information is amazing.*

3 INTEREST to interest someone so much that they do not pay attention to other things: *The movement and noise of the machines absorbed him completely.* | **be absorbed in sth** *Judith lay on the settee, absorbed in her book.*

4 BECOME PART OF STH to become part of something larger: *California absorbs many of the legal immigrants to the US.* | **be absorbed into sth** *We were soon absorbed into local village life.*

5 LIGHT/HEAT/ENERGY/NOISE if something absorbs light, heat, energy, or noise, it takes it in: *Darker surfaces absorb heat.*

6 DEAL WITH CHANGE/COSTS if something absorbs changes or costs, it accepts them and deals with them successfully: *The beer industry had absorbed a doubling of federal tax in 1991.*

7 MONEY/TIME if something absorbs money, time etc, it uses a lot of it: *Defence spending absorbs almost 20% of the country's wealth.*

8 FORCE to reduce the effect of a sudden violent movement: *A well-designed sports shoe should absorb the impact on your feet.*

ab·sor·bent /əbˈsɔːbənt, -ˈzɔː- $ -ɔːr-/ adj material that is absorbent is able to take in liquids easily OPP **non-absorbent**: *absorbent kitchen paper*

ab·sorb·ing /əbˈsɔːbɪŋ, -ˈzɔː- $ -ɔːr-/ adj enjoyable and interesting, and keeping your attention for a long time: *an absorbing hobby* THESAURUS ▸ INTERESTING

ab·sorp·tion /əbˈsɔːpʃən, -ˈzɔːp- $ -ɔːr-/ n [U] **1** a process in which something takes in liquid, gas, or heat: **[+of]** *the body's absorption of iron* **2** a process in which people or things become part of something larger: **[+of]** *the absorption of Soviet immigrants into Israel* **3** when you are very interested in something: **[+with/in]** *I don't understand James' absorption with military history.*

ab·stain /əbˈsteɪn/ ●○○ v [I]

1 to choose not to vote for or against something: *Six countries voted for the change, five voted against, and two abstained.*

2 to not do or have something you enjoy, especially alcohol or sex, usually for reasons of religion or health: **[+from]** *Pilots must **abstain from alcohol** for 24 hours before flying.*

ab·ste·mi·ous /əbˈstiːmiəs/ adj *formal* careful not to have too much food, drink etc —**abstemiousness** n [U]

ab·sten·tion /əbˈstenʃən/ n **1** [C,U] an act of not voting for or against something: *The draft law was passed by 134 votes to 19, with 5 abstentions.* **2** [U] *formal* when you do not do something you enjoy doing: **[+from]** *fasting and abstention from intoxicating drinks*

ab·sti·nence /ˈæbstənəns/ *n* [U] the practice of not having something you enjoy, especially alcohol or sex, usually for reasons of religion or health —**abstinent** *adj*

ab·stract¹ /ˈæbstrækt/ ●●○ AWL *adj*
1 based on general ideas or principles rather than specific examples or real events SYN **theoretical**: **abstract idea/concept etc** *the ability to translate abstract ideas into words | By the age of seven, children are capable of thinking* ***in abstract terms****. | Human beings are the only creatures capable of* ***abstract thought*** (=thinking about ideas).
2 existing only as an idea or quality rather than as something real that you can see or touch OPP **concrete**: *the abstract nature of beauty*
3 abstract paintings, designs etc consist of shapes and patterns that do not look like real people or things → ABSTRACT NOUN

abstract² ●○○ AWL *n* [C]
1 a painting, design etc which contains shapes or images that do not look like real things or people → see picture at PAINTING
2 a short written statement containing only the most important ideas in a speech, article etc
3 in the abstract considered in a general way rather than being based on specific details and examples: *Talking about crime in the abstract just isn't enough.*

ab·stract³ /əbˈstrækt, æb-/ AWL *v* [T] **1** to write a document containing the most important ideas or points from a speech, article etc **2** *formal* to remove something from somewhere

ab·stract·ed /əbˈstræktəd, æb-/ *adj* not noticing anything around you because you are thinking carefully about something else —**abstractedly** *adv*

ab·strac·tion /əbˈstrækʃən, æb-/ AWL *n* **1** [C] a general idea about a type of situation, thing, or person rather than a specific example from real life: *He's always talking in abstractions.* **2** [U] when you do not notice what is happening around you because you are thinking carefully about something else: *She rocked the baby gently, gazing in abstraction at the flickering fire.* **3** [U] the use of shapes and patterns that do not look like real things

ˌabstract ˈnoun *n* [C] a noun that names a feeling, quality, or state rather than an object, animal, or person. For example, 'hunger' and 'beauty' are abstract nouns.

ab·struse /əbˈstruːs, æb-/ *adj formal* unnecessarily complicated and difficult to understand: *Maths is a mix of abstruse theory and detailed calculations.*

ab·surd /əbˈsɜːd, -ˈzɜːd $ -ɜːrd/ ●●○ *adj*
1 completely stupid or unreasonable SYN **ridiculous**: **quite/slightly/completely etc absurd** *It seems quite absurd to expect anyone to drive for 3 hours just for a 20-minute meeting. | It seems an absurd idea.* THESAURUS ▸ STUPID
2 the absurd something that is completely stupid and unreasonable: *Some of the stories he tells verge on the absurd.* —**absurdity** *n* [C,U]: *Duncan laughed at* ***the absurdity of*** *the situation.*

ab·surd·ly /əbˈsɜːdli, -ˈzɜːd- $ -ɜːr-/ *adv* surprisingly or unreasonably SYN **ridiculously**: **absurdly low/high** *Prices seem absurdly low to Western tourists.*

ABTA /ˈæbtə/ an organization of travel agencies and holiday companies in the UK. Members of ABTA promise to treat their customers fairly and to give them their money back if their holiday is cancelled (CANCEL). ABTA used to be known as the Association of British Travel Agents.

a·bun·dance /əˈbʌndəns/ ●○○ *n* [singular, U] a large quantity of something: **[+of]** *an abundance of wavy red hair* | **in abundance** *One quality the team possessed in abundance was fighting spirit.*

a·bun·dant /əˈbʌndənt/ ●○○ *adj* something that is abundant exists or is available in large quantities so that there is more than enough OPP **scarce**: *an abundant supply of fresh water | abundant opportunities for well-qualified staff*

a·bun·dant·ly /əˈbʌndəntli/ *adv* **1 abundantly clear** very easy to understand: *She'd* ***made*** *her feelings towards him* ***abundantly clear****.* **2** in large quantities: *Melons grow abundantly in this region.*

a·buse¹ /əˈbjuːs/ ●●○ S3 W3 *n*
1 [plural, U] cruel or violent treatment of someone: *several cases of* ***child abuse*** | **physical/sexual/racial abuse** *Many children* ***suffer*** *racial* ***abuse*** *at school. | An independent committee will look into alleged* ***human rights abuses****.*
2 [C,U] the use of something in a way that it should not be used SYN **misuse**: **[+of]** *government officials'* ***abuse of power*** *| A self-monitoring tax system is clearly* ***open to abuse*** (=able to be used wrongly). | **alcohol/drug abuse** (=the practice of drinking too much or taking illegal drugs) → SOLVENT ABUSE
3 [U] rude or offensive things that someone says when they are angry: *vandalism and* ***verbal abuse*** *directed at old people* | **a torrent/stream of abuse** (=a series of rude or angry words) | **shout/hurl/scream abuse at sb** *The other driver started hurling abuse at me.* → **a term of abuse** at TERM¹(3)

a·buse² /əˈbjuːz/ ●●○ *v* [T]
1 to treat someone in a cruel and violent way, often sexually: **sexually/physically abused** *She was sexually abused as a child.*
2 to deliberately use something for the wrong purpose or for your own advantage: *Williams* ***abused*** *his* ***position*** *as mayor to give jobs to his friends. | Morris* ***abused*** *the* ***trust*** *the firm had shown in him. | people who* ***abuse*** *the* ***system*** | **abuse alcohol/drugs** *The proportion of drinkers who abuse alcohol is actually quite small.*
3 to say rude or offensive things to someone SYN **insult**: *Many soldiers in Belfast are* ***verbally abused****. | He came to the help of another driver who was being* ***racially abused*** *by three white passengers.*
4 to treat something so badly that you start to destroy it: *James abused his body for years with heroin and cocaine.* —**abuser** *n* [C]

a·bu·sive /əˈbjuːsɪv/ *adj* using cruel words or physical violence: *Smith denies using abusive language to the referee. | He became abusive and his wife was injured in the struggle.* —**abusively** *adv* —**abusiveness** *n* [U]

a·but /əˈbʌt/ (*also* **abut on**) *v* (**abutted**, **abutting**) [T] *formal* if one piece of land or a building abuts another, it is next to it or touches one side of it → **adjoin**

ABV /ˌeɪ biː ˈviː/ (***alcohol by volume***) used on bottles of alcoholic drink to show how much alcohol the drink contains: *12% ABV*

a·bys·mal /əˈbɪzməl/ *adj* very bad or of bad quality SYN **terrible**: *The reunion was an abysmal failure.* THESAURUS ▸ BAD —**abysmally** *adv*

a·byss /əˈbɪs/ *n* [C] **1** a very dangerous or frightening situation: **[+of]** *The country might plunge into the abyss of economic ruin. | At that time Bosnia was standing on* ***the edge of an abyss****.* **2** a deep empty hole in the ground **3** a very big difference that separates two people or groups: *the gaping abyss between these grand buildings and my own miserable home*

a/c the written abbreviation of ***account*** → ACCOUNT¹(2)

AC /ˌeɪ ˈsiː/ **1** the abbreviation of ***alternating current*** → **DC** **2** the written abbreviation of ***air conditioning*** → AC/DC

a·ca·cia /əˈkeɪʃə/ *n* [C] a tree with small yellow or white flowers that grows in warm countries

ac·a·deme /ˈækədiːm, ˌækəˈdiːm/ *n* [U] the work that university teachers and students do – often used humorously

ac·a·de·mi·a /ˌækəˈdiːmiə/ *n* [U] the activities and work done at universities and colleges, or the teachers and students involved in it

ac·a·dem·ic¹ /ˌækəˈdemɪk◂/ ●●○ W2 AWL *adj*
1 [usually before noun] relating to education, especially at college or university level OPP **non-academic**: *He possessed no academic qualifications. | a program to raise academic standards*
2 [usually before noun] concerned with studying from

A

books, as opposed to practical work: *the study of art as an academic discipline*
3 good at studying OPP **unacademic**: *He's not very academic.*
4 if a discussion about something is academic, it is a waste of time because the speakers cannot change the existing situation: *The question of where we go on holiday is* ***purely academic*** *since we don't have any money.*
—**academically** /-kli/ *adv*

academic² ●○○ AWL *n* [C] a teacher in a college or university

a·cad·e·mi·cian /əˌkædəˈmɪʃən $ ˌækədə-/ *n* [C] a member of an official organization which encourages the development of literature, art, science etc

ˌacademic ˈyear *n* [C] the period of the year during which there are school or university classes

a·cad·e·my /əˈkædəmi/ *n* (*plural* **academies**) [C] **1** an official organization which encourages the development of literature, art, science etc: *the American Academy of Arts and Letters* **2** a college where students are taught a particular subject or skill: *a military academy | the Royal Academy of Music* **3** a school in Scotland for children between 11 and 16 **4** a private school in the US **5** *previously* **city academy** a type of independent SECONDARY SCHOOL in England that is run with help and money from private organizations or people. Each school SPECIALIZES in teaching a particular subject such as science, business, or technology.

a·cai ber·ry /əˈsaɪ ˌberi/ (*also* **acai**) *n* [C] a small purple fruit that grows in South America and is used especially for its juice

a cap·pel·la /ˌæ kæˈpelə $ ˌɑː kə-/ *adj, adv* sung without any musical instruments

ACAS /ˈeɪkæs/ (***Advisory Conciliation and Arbitration Service***) a British organization that tries to end disagreements about pay, conditions at work etc between the management of a business and its workers

ac·cede /əkˈsiːd, æk-/ *v*
accede to sth *phr v formal* **1** to agree to a demand, proposal etc, especially after first disagreeing with it → **accession**: *the doctor's refusal to accede to his patient's request* **2** if someone accedes to the THRONE, they become king or queen → **accession**

ac·cel·e·ran·do /ækˌseləˈrændəʊ $ -ˈrɑːndoʊ/ *adj, adv* getting gradually faster

ac·cel·er·ant /əkˈselərənt/ *n* [C] *formal* a substance such as petrol that makes a fire spread or burn more strongly: *Police suspect that an accelerant was used in the arson attack.*

ac·cel·e·rate /əkˈseləreɪt/ ●○○ *v*
1 [I,T] if a process accelerates or if something accelerates it, it happens faster than usual or sooner than you expect: *measures to accelerate the rate of economic growth*
2 [I] if a vehicle or someone who is driving it accelerates, it starts to go faster OPP **decelerate**: *The car accelerated smoothly away.*

ac·cel·e·ra·tion /əkˌseləˈreɪʃən/ ●○○ *n*
1 [singular, U] a process in which something happens more and more quickly: **[+in]** *an acceleration in the rate of inflation* | **[+of]** *the rapid acceleration of economic progress in South East Asia*
2 [U] the rate at which a car or other vehicle can go faster: *The latest model has excellent acceleration.*
3 [U] *technical* the rate at which the speed of an object increases

ac·cel·e·ra·tor /əkˈseləreɪtə $ -ər/ *n* [C] **1** the part of a car or other vehicle that you press with your foot to make it go faster SYN **gas pedal** *AmE* → see picture at CAR **2** *technical* a large machine used to make extremely small pieces of MATTER¹(3) move at extremely high speeds

ac·cel·e·rom·e·ter /əkˌseləˈrɒmɪtə $ -ˈrɑːmɪtər/ *n* [C] a piece of technology in a MOBILE PHONE or small computer that makes sure images and writing are shown in the correct way for the direction of the screen

ac·cent¹ /ˈæksənt $ ˈæksent/ ●●○ *n* [C]
1 the way someone pronounces the words of a language, showing which country or which part of a country they come from → **dialect**: *He had a strong Irish accent.*
2 the accent is on sth if the accent is on a particular quality, feeling etc, special importance is given to it: *accommodation with the accent on comfort*
3 the part of a word that you should emphasize when you say it SYN **stress**: **[+on]** *In the word 'dinner' the accent is on the first syllable.*
4 a written mark used above or below particular letters in some languages to show how to pronounce that letter

COLLOCATIONS

VERBS

have an accent *The man had a Spanish accent.*
speak with an accent *She spoke with an accent that I couldn't understand.*
pick up an accent *During his stay in England, he had picked up an English accent.*
lose your accent (=no longer speak with an accent) *After 9 years in London, Ben had lost his French accent.*
put on an accent (=deliberately speak with a different accent from your usual one) *When Mum's on the phone, she puts on a funny accent.*

ADJECTIVES/NOUN + accent

a strong/broad/thick/pronounced accent (=very noticeable) *She spoke with a strong Scottish accent.*
a slight/faint accent *He has a very slight accent.*
a French/American etc accent | **a New York/London etc accent** | **a foreign accent** | **a southern/northern accent** | **a regional accent** (=from a particular area of a country) | **an upper-class/middle-class/working-class accent** | **a posh/plummy accent** *BrE informal* (=an upper-class accent)

ac·cent² /əkˈsent $ ˈæksent/ *v* [T] **1** to make something more noticeable so that people will pay attention to it SYN **highlight**: *Use make-up to accent your cheekbones and eyes.* **2** *technical* to emphasize a part of a word in speech

ac·cen·ted /əkˈsentɪd $ ˈæksen-/ *adj* **1** spoken with a foreign accent: *He spoke* ***heavily accented*** *English.* **2** emphasized or given special importance: *accented lighting*

ac·cen·tu·ate /əkˈsentʃueɪt/ *v* [T] to make something more noticeable: *The photograph seemed to accentuate his large nose.* **THESAURUS** ▸ EMPHASIZE —**accentuation** /əkˌsentʃuˈeɪʃən/ *n* [C,U]

ac·cept /əkˈsept/ ●●● S1 W1 *v*
1 GIFT/OFFER/INVITATION [I,T] to take something that someone offers you, or to agree to do something that someone asks you to do OPP **refuse**: *Rick* ***accepted*** *her* ***offer*** *of coffee.* | *He* ***accepted*** *the* ***invitation*** *to stay with us.* | *His school reports said that he is always ready to* ***accept*** *a* ***challenge*** (=agree to do something difficult). | *Please accept this small gift.* | *They offered me a job and I accepted.* | **accept sth from sb** *He accepted a glass of water from Helen.* | *He* ***readily accepted*** *her invitation* (=accepted it quickly).

REGISTER
In everyday English, when talking about accepting a job, accepting responsibility or blame, or accepting a method of payment, people usually use **take**: *They offered me the job and I* ***accepted***. → *They offered me the job and I* ***took it***.
When talking about accepting an offer, people often say **take** someone **up on their offer**: *He decided to* ***take her up on her offer***.

2 SITUATION/PROBLEM ETC [T] to decide that there is nothing you can do to change a difficult and unpleasant situation or fact and continue with your normal life: *He's not going to change, and you just have to accept it.* | **accept that** *We have to accept that this is not an ideal world.* | *He can't* ***accept the fact that*** *his problems are his own fault.*
3 THINK SB/STH IS GOOD ENOUGH [T] to decide that someone has the necessary skill or intelligence for a particular

job, course etc or that a piece of work is good enough OPP **reject**: *Students accepted by Stanford Law School had very high scores on the LSAT.* | **accept sb/sth as sth** *They have accepted him as the representative of the company.* | **accept sb/sth for sth** *Random House accepted the book for publication.*

4 BECOME PART OF A GROUP [T] to allow someone to become part of a group, society, or organization, and to treat them in the same way as the other members OPP **reject**: **accept sb as sth** *The children gradually began to accept her as one of the family.* | **accept sb into sth** *It often takes years for immigrants to be accepted into the host community.*

5 AGREE TO TAKE/DEAL WITH STH [T] to agree to take or deal with something that someone gives you, or to say that it is suitable or good enough: *The government has* ***accepted*** *the* ***resignation*** *of a senior army commander.* | *Please* ***accept*** *my sincere* ***apologies****.* | *Sorry, we don't accept traveller's cheques.*

6 SUGGESTION/ADVICE [T] to decide to do what someone suggests or advises you should do: *Be prepared to accept the advice of members of staff.*

7 BELIEVE AN EXPLANATION/STATEMENT [T] to agree that what someone says is right or true OPP **reject**: *She has accepted your explanation as to why you didn't attend the meeting.* THESAURUS ▶ BELIEVE

GRAMMAR

In more formal English, you say **it is accepted that** when saying what people generally believe is true: *It is accepted that he was sincere in his claim.*

8 accept responsibility/blame for sth to admit that you were responsible for something bad that happened: *The University will not accept responsibility for items lost or stolen.*

GRAMMAR: Comparison

accept

- You **accept** something: *She decided to accept the offer.* | *I accepted his invitation to have dinner with him.*
✗ Don't say: *I accepted to have dinner with him.*

agree

- You **agree to** something: *Her parents would never agree to the marriage.* ✗ Don't say: *Her parents would never agree the marriage.*
- You **agree to do** something: *I agreed to have dinner with him.*

ac·cept·a·ble /əkˈseptəbəl/ ●●○ S3 W3 *adj*
1 good enough to be used for a particular purpose or to be considered satisfactory: **[+to]** *an agreement which is acceptable to all sides* | *Students who achieve an* ***acceptable standard*** *will progress to degree studies.* | *How do we reach an* ***acceptable level*** *of data security?* THESAURUS ▶ SATISFACTORY
2 acceptable behaviour is considered to be morally or socially good enough: *Alcohol is not an* ***acceptable way*** *out of your problems.* | *Here, the students set the standards for* ***acceptable behaviour****.* | **acceptable (for sb) to do sth** *It is not* ***socially acceptable*** *for parents to leave children unattended at that age.* | *It is* ***perfectly acceptable*** *to sample the food before you buy.* —**acceptably** *adv* —**acceptability** /əkˌseptəˈbɪləti/ *n* [U]

ac·cept·ance /əkˈseptəns/ ●○○ *n*
1 [U] when you officially agree to take something that you have been offered: **[+of]** *the formal acceptance of an invitation* | *He wrote a* ***letter of acceptance*** (=a letter in which you agree to accept a job, university place etc) *to the university.*
2 [singular, U] when people agree that an idea, statement, explanation etc is right or true: **[+of]** *the acceptance of Einstein's theory* | **acceptance that** *There is still not widespread acceptance that fathers can care for children as well as mothers do.* | **gain/find acceptance** *This management style gained acceptance in the 1980s.*
3 [U] the ability to accept an unpleasant situation which cannot be changed, without getting angry or upset about it: **[+of]** *By the end of the trial, Nicolas moved towards acceptance of his fate.*
4 [U] the process of allowing someone to become part of a group or a society and of treating them in the same way as the other members: *Acceptance by their peer group is important to most youngsters.*

ac·cept·ed /əkˈseptɪd/ ●○○ *adj* considered right or suitable by most people: *Having more than one wife is a normal and* ***accepted practice*** *in some countries.* | **generally/widely/universally etc accepted** *generally accepted principles of fairness and justice*

ac·cess¹ /ˈækses/ ●●● S2 W1 AWL *n* [U]
1 the right to enter a place, use something, see someone etc: **[+to]** *Access to the papers is restricted to senior management.* | *Cats should always* ***have access*** *to fresh, clean water.*
2 how easy or difficult it is for people to enter a public building, to reach a place, or talk to someone: **[+for]** *We're trying to improve access for disabled visitors.* | **[+to]** *a villa with* ***easy access*** *to the sea*
3 the way you use to enter a building or reach a place: *Access is by means of a small door on the right.* | **[+to]** *Access to the restrooms is through the foyer.*
4 have access to a car/computer etc to have a car, a computer etc that you can use
5 *BrE* the legal right to see and spend time with your children, a prisoner, an official etc: *My ex-husband has access to the children once a week.*
6 gain/get access (to sth) to succeed in entering a place or in seeing someone or something: *The police managed to gain access through an upstairs window.*

access² ●●○ AWL *v* [T] to find information, especially on a computer: *Users can access their voice mail remotely.*

ˈaccess ˌcourse *n* [C] *BrE* an educational course for adults which prepares them for study at a university or college

ac·ces·si·ble /əkˈsesəbəl/ ●○○ AWL *adj*
1 a place, building, or object that is accessible is easy to reach or get into OPP **inaccessible**: *The island is only accessible by boat.* | *There is a church which is* ***easily accessible*** *from my home.*
2 easy to obtain or use: **[+to]** *the need for a health service that is accessible to all* | **easily/readily accessible** *Computers should be made readily accessible to teachers and pupils.*
3 someone who is accessible is easy to meet and talk to, even if they are very important or powerful SYN **approachable**: *I think that you'll find she's very accessible.*
4 a book, poem, painting etc that is accessible is easy to understand and enjoy: **[+to]** *He wants his music to be accessible to everyone.* —**accessibly** *adv* —**accessibility** /əkˌsesəˈbɪləti/ *n* [U]

ac·ces·sion /əkˈseʃən/ *n* **1** [U] an official process in which someone becomes king, queen, president etc → **succession**: **[+of]** *the accession of James I* | **accession to power/to the throne** (=the act of becoming king, queen, president etc) **2** [U] *formal* the act of agreeing to a demand **3** [C] *technical* an object or work of art that is added to a collection of objects or paintings

ac·ces·so·rize (*also* **-ise** *BrE*) /əkˈsesəraɪz/ *v* [I,T] to add accessories to clothes, a room etc: *She wore a black dress, accessorized with a silver belt.*

ac·ces·so·ry /əkˈsesəri/ ●○○ *n* (*plural* **accessories**) [C]
1 [usually plural] something such as a piece of equipment or a decoration that is not necessary, but that makes a machine, car, room etc more useful or more attractive: *bathroom accessories such as mirrors and towel-rails*
2 [usually plural] something such as a bag, belt, or jewellery that you wear or carry because it is attractive: *fashion accessories* | *a set of fully matching clothes and accessories*
3 *law* someone who helps a criminal, especially by helping them hide from the police: **[+to]** *an accessory to murder* | **an accessory before/after the fact** (=someone who helps a criminal before or after the crime)

A

ˈaccess point *n* [C] *technical* (*written abbreviation* **AP**) a special piece of equipment on a computer system, which is designed to manage and control information, requests etc received from other computers that are connected to the system without wires → **wireless communication**

ˈaccess proˌvider *n* [C] a company that provides the technical services that allow people to use the Internet, usually in exchange for a monthly payment SYN **Internet Service Provider**

ˈaccess ˌroad *n* [C] a road which allows traffic to reach a particular place: *the access road to the farm*

ˈaccess ˌtime *n* [C,U] *technical* the time taken by a computer to find and use a piece of information in its memory

ac·ci·dent /ˈæksɪdənt/ ●●● S2 W2 *n*
1 by accident in a way that is not planned or intended OPP **on purpose**, **deliberately**: *I met her **quite by accident*** (=completely by accident). | *The discovery was made almost by accident.* | *The pilot, **whether by accident or design*** (=whether it was planned or not planned), *made the plane do a sharp turn.* GRAMMAR ✗ Don't say: *by an accident*
2 [C] an event in which a car, train, plane etc is damaged and often someone is hurt: *Over 70,000 people are seriously injured every year in road accidents.* | *The accident happened at the junction of Forest Road and Pine Walk.* | *a train accident*
3 [C] a situation in which someone is injured or something is damaged without anyone intending them to be: *Ken **had** an **accident** at work and had to go to hospital.* | *I'm sorry about breaking the vase – **it was an accident*** (=I did not intend to do it). | **a climbing/skiing/hunting etc accident** *He died in a climbing accident in the Himalayas.* | *She was injured in a **freak accident*** (=an unusual accident) *when a wall suddenly collapsed.* | *I had a **slight accident** with your coffee.* | *They lost their lives in a **tragic accident**.*
4 [C,U] something that happens without anyone planning or intending it: *My third baby was an accident.* | ***It is no accident that** men fill most of the top jobs in nursing, while women remain on the lower grades.* | **an accident of birth/geography/history etc** (=an event or situation caused by chance)
5 accidents (will) happen *spoken* used to tell someone who has broken something that they should not worry that it has happened
6 an accident waiting to happen used about a situation in which an accident is likely to happen because no one is trying to prevent it: *The boats are being left to drift; it's an accident waiting to happen.*

COLLOCATIONS – MEANING 2

ADJECTIVES

a bad/serious accident *There's been a bad accident on the freeway.*
a major accident *News is coming in of a major rail accident.*
a horrible/nasty/horrific accident *We narrowly avoided a nasty accident.*
a fatal accident (=in which someone is killed) *a fatal accident involving a bus and a cyclist*
a minor accident (=one that is not serious) | **a road/traffic accident** | **a car accident** (*also* **an automobile accident** *AmE formal*) | **a plane accident/an airplane accident** *AmE* (*also* **a flying accident**) | **a rail accident/a train accident** | **a hit-and-run accident** (=when someone is hit by a driver who does not stop)

VERBS

be involved in an accident *formal: Your son has been involved in a car accident.*
prevent an accident *Steps have been taken to prevent a similar accident happening again.*
an accident happens (*also* **an accident occurs** *formal*)
have an accident *Young drivers are more likely to have accidents than older drivers.*

accident + NOUN

an accident victim *One of the accident victims is still trapped in his vehicle.*
accident rates/statistics | **an accident investigation/inquiry** | **an accident investigator**

PHRASES

the scene of an accident (=the place where it happened) *Police were at the scene of the accident within minutes.*

COMMON ERRORS

⚠ Don't say 'a small accident'. Say **a minor accident**.

THESAURUS

accident an event in which a vehicle is damaged and often someone is hurt: *Her father died in a car accident.* | *Hugh had an accident on his way to work.*
crash a serious accident in which a vehicle hits something else: *Rees-Jones was the only person to survive the crash.* | *a car/plane/train crash*
collision an accident in which two or more cars, trains etc hit each other: *His car was involved in a collision with a train.* | **a head-on collision** (=between vehicles that are driving towards each other)
disaster a serious accident involving a train, plane, or boat, in which a lot of people are killed or injured: *It was Britain's worst air disaster.*
wreck *AmE* an accident in which a car or train is badly damaged: *Ben nearly died in a car wreck.*
pileup an accident that involves several cars or trucks: *The pileup happened in thick fog.*

ac·ci·den·tal /ˌæksəˈdentl◂/ ●●○ *adj* happening without being planned or intended OPP **deliberate**: *an accidental discharge of toxic waste* | *Buy an insurance policy that covers **accidental damage**.*

ˌaccidental ˈdeath *n* [U] *law especially BrE* an expression used by a court when it has decided that someone's death was caused by an accident

ac·ci·den·tal·ly /ˌæksəˈdentli/ ●○○ *adv* in a way that was not planned or intended OPP **deliberately**: *She accidentally dropped the vase on her foot.*

ˌaccident and eˈmergency *n* [U] *BrE* (*abbreviation* **A & E**) the room or department in a hospital where people go if they are injured or suddenly become ill SYN **emergency room** *AmE*

ˈaccident prone *adj* more likely to have accidents than other people

ac·claim¹ /əˈkleɪm/ *v* [T] to praise someone or something publicly: *His work was acclaimed by art critics.*

acclaim² *n* [U] praise for a person or their achievements: *The young singer is enjoying **critical acclaim*** (=praise by people who are paid to give their opinion on art, music etc). | **international/great/popular/public etc acclaim** *Their recordings have **won** great **acclaim**.*

ac·claimed /əˈkleɪmd/ *adj* publicly praised by a lot of people: **highly/widely/universally acclaimed** *The book has been widely acclaimed by teachers and pupils.* | *His work was **critically acclaimed*** (=praised by people who are paid to give their opinion on art, music etc).

ac·cla·ma·tion /ˌækləˈmeɪʃən/ *n formal* **1** [C,U] a loud expression of approval or welcome **2** [singular, U] the act of electing someone, using a spoken rather than written vote

ac·cli·ma·tize (*also* **-ise** *BrE*) /əˈklaɪmətaɪz/ (*also* **ac·cli·mate** /əˈklaɪmət $ ˈækləmeɪt, əˈklaɪmət/ *AmE*) *v* [I,T] to become used to a new place, situation, or type of weather, or to make someone become used to it: **[+to]** *Runners had to acclimatize to the humid tropical conditions.* | **acclimatize yourself (to sth)** *I found it hard to acclimatize myself to working at weekends.* —**acclimatization** /əˌklaɪmətaɪˈzeɪʃən $ -tə-/ *n* [U]

ac·co·lade /ˈækəleɪd/ *n* [C] praise for someone who is greatly admired, or a prize given to them for their work: **ultimate/highest/supreme etc accolade** *She received* *a Grammy Award, the highest accolade in the music business.*

ac·com·mo·date /əˈkɒmədeɪt $ əˈkɑː-/ ●○○ AWL *v*
1 [T] if a room, building etc can accommodate a particular number of people or things, it has enough space for them: *He bought a huge house to accommodate his library.* | *The ballroom can accommodate 400 people.*
2 [T] to provide someone with a place to stay, live, or work: *The island was used to accommodate child refugees.*
3 [T] to accept someone's opinions and try to do what they want, especially when their opinions or needs are different from yours: *We've made every effort to accommodate your point of view.*
4 [I] to get used to a new situation or to make yourself do this: **[+to]** *Her eyes took a while to accommodate to the darkness.*

ac·com·mo·dat·ing /əˈkɒmədeɪtɪŋ $ əˈkɑː-/ *adj* helpful and willing to do what someone else wants OPP **awkward**: *an accommodating child*

ac·com·mo·da·tion /əˌkɒməˈdeɪʃən $ əˌkɑː-/ ●●○ W2 AWL *n*
1 [U] *especially BrE* (*also* **accommodations** *AmE*) a place for someone to stay, live, or work: *The price for the holiday includes flights and accommodation.* | *living accommodations for the crews* | *travel and hotel accommodations* | ***rented accommodation*** | ***secure accommodation** for young offenders* | *Universities have to provide **student accommodation** for first-year students.*

> **REGISTER**
> In everyday English, people usually say **somewhere to live/stay** rather than **accommodation**: *She's trying to find **somewhere to live**.* | *Have you found **anywhere to stay** yet?*

2 [singular, U] *formal* an agreement between people or groups who have different views or opinions, that satisfies everyone: *We **reached** an **accommodation** between both parties.* | *Neither side was willing to make any kind of accommodation.*

> **GRAMMAR: Countable or uncountable?**
> • In meaning 1, **accommodation** is used as an uncountable noun, especially in British English: *Can you arrange some accommodation for me?* ✗ Don't say: *Can you arrange an accommodation?*
> • In American English, **accommodation** is often used as a plural noun in meaning 1: *The price includes meals and accommodations.*
> • In meaning 2, **accommodation** is often used as a singular noun: *They reached an accommodation.*
> GRAMMAR GUIDE ▸ NOUNS

ac·com·pa·ni·ment /əˈkʌmpənimənt/ AWL *n*
1 [C,U] music that is played in the background at the same time as another instrument or singer that plays or sings the main tune: **piano/orchestral/organ/guitar etc accompaniment** *He plays folk music with guitar accompaniment.* | **to the accompaniment of sth** *A group of children danced around to the accompaniment of drums and piano.* **2** [C] something that is provided or used with something else: *White wine makes an excellent accompaniment to fish.* **3 to the accompaniment of sth** while something else is happening or while another sound can be heard: *They were exercising to the accompaniment of cheerful music.* **4** [C] something that happens at the same time as another thing

ac·com·pa·nist /əˈkʌmpənɪst/ *n* [C] someone who plays a musical instrument while another person sings or plays the main tune

ac·com·pa·ny /əˈkʌmpəni/ ●●○ W2 AWL *v* (**accompanied, accompanying, accompanies**) [T]
1 to go somewhere with someone: *Children under 14 must be accompanied by an adult.* | *Wherever her husband went, she would accompany him.*

> **REGISTER**
> In everyday English, people usually say **go with** or **come with** someone rather than **accompany** someone: *Do you want me to **go with** you to the station?* | *She **came with** me to church.*

2 to play a musical instrument while someone sings a song or plays the main tune: *Daniel wanted Liz to accompany him on violin.*
3 to happen or exist at the same time as something else: **be accompanied by sth** *The disease is accompanied by sneezing and fever.* GRAMMAR **Accompany** is usually passive in this meaning.
4 if a book, document etc accompanies something, it comes with it: *Please see accompanying booklet for instructions.* | *Your passport application form should be accompanied by two recent photographs.*

ac·com·plice /əˈkʌmplɪs $ əˈkɑːm-, əˈkʌm-/ *n* [C] a person who helps someone such as a criminal to do something wrong

ac·com·plish /əˈkʌmplɪʃ $ əˈkɑːm-, əˈkʌm-/ ●○○ *v* [T] to succeed in doing something, especially after trying very hard SYN **achieve**: *We have accomplished all we set out to do.* | ***Mission accomplished*** (=we have done what we intended to do). THESAURUS ▸ SUCCEED

ac·com·plished /əˈkʌmplɪʃt $ əˈkɑːm-, əˈkʌm-/ *adj*
1 an accomplished writer, painter, singer etc is very skilful: **highly/very accomplished** *a highly accomplished designer* THESAURUS ▸ SKILFUL **2 an accomplished fact** *BrE* something that is known to be true and cannot be doubted

ac·com·plish·ment /əˈkʌmplɪʃmənt $ əˈkɑːm-, əˈkʌm-/ ●○○ *n*
1 [C] something successful or impressive that is achieved after a lot of effort and hard work SYN **achievement**: **impressive/significant/great etc accomplishment** *Cutting the budget was an impressive accomplishment.* | *It was a **major accomplishment** for a player who had been injured so recently.*
2 [U] the act of finishing or achieving something good: **[+of]** *the accomplishment of policy goals*
3 [C,U] an ability to do something well, or the skill involved in doing something well: *Playing the piano is one of her many accomplishments.*

ac·cord¹ /əˈkɔːd $ -ɔːrd/ ●○○ *n*
1 of sb's/sth's own accord without being asked or forced to do something: *He decided to go of his own accord.* | *The door seemed to move of its own accord.*
2 [U] *formal* a situation in which two people, ideas, or statements agree with each other: **be in accord with sth** *These results are in accord with earlier research.* | **in perfect/complete accord** *It is important to the success of any firm that its partners should be in complete accord.*
3 [C] a formal agreement between countries or groups: *the Helsinki accord on human rights*
4 with one accord *formal* if two or more people do something with one accord, they do it together or at the same time: *There was a silence as the women turned with one accord to stare at Doreen.*

accord² *v formal* **1** [T] to give someone or something special attention or a particular type of treatment: *You will not be accorded any special treatment.* | **accord sth to sth/sb** *Every school accords high priority to the quality of teaching.* **2 accord with sth** to match or agree with something: *The punishments accorded with the current code of discipline.*

ac·cord·ance /əˈkɔːdəns $ əˈkɔːr-/ ●○○ *n* **in accordance with sth** *formal* according to a rule, system etc: *Article 47 may only be used **in accordance with** international **law**.* | *Use this product only in accordance with the manufacturer's instructions.*

ac·cord·ing·ly /əˈkɔːdɪŋli $ əˈkɔːr-/ ●○○ *adv*
1 in a way that is suitable for a particular situation or that is based on what someone has done or said: *Katherine still considered him a child and treated him accordingly.*
2 [sentence adverb] as a result of something SYN **therefore**: *Some of the laws were contradictory. Accordingly, measures were taken to clarify them.*

A

ac'cording to ●●● S2 W1 *prep*
1 as shown by something or stated by someone: *According to the police, his attackers beat him with a blunt instrument.* | *There is now widespread support for these proposals, according to a recent public opinion poll.* ⚠ Don't say 'according to me' or 'according to my opinion/point of view'. Say **in my opinion**: *In my opinion his first book is much better.*
2 in a way that depends on differences in situations or amounts: *You will be paid according to the amount of work you do.*
3 in a way that agrees with a system or plan, or obeys a set of rules: *The game will be played according to rules laid down for the 1992 Cup.* | *Everything **went according to plan**, and we arrived on time.*

ac·cor·di·on /əˈkɔːdiən $ əˈkɔːr-/ (*also* **piano accordion** *BrE*) *n* [C] a musical instrument like a large box that you hold in both hands. You play it by pressing the sides together and pulling them out again, while you push buttons and KEYS. —**accordionist** *n* [C]

ACCORDION

ac·cost /əˈkɒst $ əˈkɒːst, əˈkɑːst/ *v* [T] *written* to go towards someone you do not know and speak to them in an unpleasant or threatening way: *He was accosted by four youths and forced to give them all his money.*

ac·count¹ /əˈkaʊnt/ ●●● S1 W1 *n* [C]
1 DESCRIPTION a written or spoken description that says what happens in an event or process: **[+of]** *He was too shocked to **give an account** of what had happened.* | **blow-by-blow account** (=a description of all the details of an event in the order that they happened) *a blow-by-blow account of how England lost to Portugal* | *Chomsky's account of how children learn their first language* | **eye-witness/first-hand account** (=a description of events by someone who saw them) *Eye-witness accounts told of the unprovoked shooting of civilians.* | *This gives a first-hand account of the war.*
2 AT A BANK (*written abbreviation* **a/c** *or* **acct.**) an arrangement in which a bank keeps your money safe so that you can pay more in or take money out: *My salary is paid into my bank account.* | *I've **opened an account** with Barclay's Bank.* | *My husband and I have a **joint account*** (=one that is shared between two people). → BANK ACCOUNT, CHECKING ACCOUNT, CURRENT ACCOUNT, DEPOSIT ACCOUNT, PROFIT AND LOSS ACCOUNT, SAVINGS ACCOUNT
3 take account of sth (*also* **take sth into account**) to consider or include particular facts or details when making a decision or judgment about something: *These figures do not take account of changes in the rate of inflation.*

GRAMMAR
You say: *We will take your views into account.* ✗ Don't say: *We will take your views in account.*

4 on account of sth because of something else, especially a problem or difficulty: *She was told to wear flat shoes, on account of her back problem.*
5 accounts a) [plural] an exact record of the money that a company has received and the money it has spent: *The accounts for last year showed a profit of $2 million.* **b)** [U] a department in a company that is responsible for keeping records of the amount of money spent and received: *Eileen works in accounts.*
6 on account if you buy goods on account, you take them away with you and pay for them later
7 WITH A SHOP/COMPANY an arrangement that you have with a shop or company, which allows you to buy goods or use a service now and pay for them later SYN **credit account**: *Can you charge this to my account please?* | *an unlimited-use Internet account*
8 BILL a statement that shows how much money you owe for things you have bought from a shop SYN **bill**: **pay/settle your account** (=pay what you owe) *James left the restaurant, settling his account by credit card.*
9 ARRANGEMENT TO SELL GOODS an arrangement to sell goods and services to another company over a period of time: *Our sales manager has secured several big accounts recently.*
10 by/from all accounts according to what a lot of people say: *It has, from all accounts, been a successful marriage.*
11 on sb's account if you do something on someone's account, you do it because you think they want you to: *Please don't change your plans on my account.*
12 on your own account by yourself or for yourself: *Carrie decided to do a little research on her own account.*
13 on no account/not on any account used when saying that someone must not, for any reason, do something: *On no account must you disturb me.*
14 by sb's own account according to what you have said, especially when you have admitted doing something wrong: *Bentley was, by his own account, over-sensitive to criticism.*
15 on that account/on this account concerning a particular situation: *There needn't be any more worries on that account.*
16 give a good/poor account of yourself to do something or perform very well or very badly: *Kevin gave a good account of himself in today's game.*
17 bring/call sb to account *formal* to force someone who is responsible for a mistake or a crime to explain publicly why they did it and punish them for it if necessary: *The people responsible for the accident have never been brought to account.*
18 put/turn sth to good account *formal* to use something for a good purpose: *Perhaps she could put some of her talents to good account by helping us.*
19 of no/little account *formal* not important: *As she grew up, her father was of no account to her.*

account² ●●○ S3 W3 *v*
account for sth *phr v*
1 to form a particular amount or part of something: *Afro-Americans account for 12% of the US population.*
2 to be the reason why something happens SYN **explain**: *Recent pressure at work may account for his behavior.*
3 to give a satisfactory explanation of why something has happened or why you did something SYN **explain**: *Can you account for your movements on that night?*
4 to say where all the members of a group of people or things are, especially because you are worried that some of them may be lost: *Three days after the earthquake, more than 150 people had still to be accounted for.*

ac·count·a·ble /əˈkaʊntəbəl/ ●○○ *adj* [not before noun] responsible for the effects of your actions and willing to explain or be criticized for them: **[+to]** *The government should be accountable to all the people of the country.* | **[+for]** *Managers must be accountable for their decisions.* | *The hospital should be **held accountable** for the quality of care it gives.* —**accountability** /əˌkaʊntəˈbɪləti/ *n* [U]

ac·coun·tan·cy /əˈkaʊntənsi/ *n* [U] *BrE* the profession or work of keeping or checking financial accounts, calculating taxes etc

ac·coun·tant /əˈkaʊntənt/ ●●○ *n* [C] someone whose job is to keep and check financial accounts, calculate taxes etc

ac·coun·ting /əˈkaʊntɪŋ/ ●●○ *n* [U] accountancy

ac·cou·tre·ments /əˈkuːtrəmənts/ (*also* **ac·cou·ter·ments** /əˈkuːtəmənts $ -tər-/ *AmE*) *n* [plural] *formal* the equipment needed for a particular activity or way of life: *the stylish accoutrements of an English country gentleman*

ac·cred·it·ed /əˈkredɪtɪd/ *adj* **1** having official approval to do something, especially because of having reached an acceptable standard: *an accredited counsellor* | *an accredited language school* **2** if a government official is accredited to another country, they are sent to that country to officially represent their government there: *the UK **accredited representative*** —**accredit** *v* [T] —**accreditation** /əˌkredɪˈteɪʃən/ *n* [U]

ac·cre·tion /əˈkriːʃən/ *n* [C,U] *formal* **1** a layer of a substance which slowly forms on something **2** a gradual process by which new things are added and something gradually changes or gets bigger

ac·crue /əˈkruː/ *v* **1** [I] if advantages accrue to you, you get those advantages over a period of time: **[+to]** *benefits that accrue to students* | **[+from]** *advantages accruing from the introduction of new technology* **2** [I,T] if money accrues or is accrued, it gradually increases over a period of time: *Interest will accrue until payment is made.* —**accrual** *n* [C usually singular]

acct. the written abbreviation of ***account***

ac·cu·mu·late /əˈkjuːmjəleɪt/ ●○○ AWL *v*
1 [T] to gradually get more and more money, possessions, knowledge etc over a period of time: *It is unjust that a privileged few should continue to accumulate wealth.* THESAURUS ▶ COLLECT
2 [I] to gradually increase in numbers or amount until there is a large quantity in one place: *Fat tends to accumulate around the hips and thighs.* —**accumulation** /əˌkjuːmjəˈleɪʃən/ *n* [C,U]: *the accumulation of data*

> **REGISTER**
> In everyday English, people usually say **build up** rather than **accumulate**: *These chemicals tend to **build up** in the soil.*

ac·cu·mu·la·tive /əˈkjuːmjələtɪv $ -leɪ-, -lə-/ *adj* gradually increasing in amount or degree over a period of time SYN **cumulative** —**accumulatively** *adv*

ac·cu·mu·la·tor /əˈkjuːmjəleɪtə $ -ər/ *n* [C] **1** *technical* a part of a computer that stores numbers **2** *especially BrE* a kind of BETTING on the results of a series of horse races, by which any money you win from a race is bet on the next race

ac·cu·ra·cy /ˈækjərəsi/ ●●○ AWL *n* [U]
1 the ability to do something in an exact way without making a mistake: *He passes the ball with unerring accuracy.*
2 the quality of being correct or true OPP **inaccuracy**: **[+of]** *worries about the accuracy of government statistics*

ac·cu·rate /ˈækjərət/ ●●● S2 W3 AWL *adj*
1 INFORMATION correct and true in every detail OPP **inaccurate**: *The brochure tries to give a fair and accurate description of each hotel.* | **fairly/reasonably accurate** *Police believe Derek gave a reasonably accurate account of what happened.* | **not strictly/entirely/completely accurate** *The evidence she gave to the court was not strictly accurate* (=not exactly accurate). THESAURUS ▶ RIGHT, TRUE
2 MEASUREMENT measured or calculated correctly OPP **inaccurate**: *It is difficult to get accurate figures on population numbers.*
3 MACHINE a machine that is accurate is able to do something in an exact way without making a mistake: *The cutter is accurate to within ½ a millimetre.*
4 WELL-AIMED an accurate shot, throw etc succeeds in hitting or reaching the thing that it is intended to hit: *an accurate shot* | *accurate bowling* —**accurately** *adv*: *It's impossible to predict the weather accurately.*

ac·curs·ed /əˈkɜːsəd, əˈkɜːst $ -ɜːr-/ *adj* **1** [only before noun] *formal* used to show that something makes you very angry **2** *old use* someone who is accursed has had a CURSE put on them

ac·cu·sa·tion /ˌækjəˈzeɪʃən/ ●○○ *n* [C] a statement saying that someone is guilty of a crime or of doing something wrong: **[+against]** *A number of **serious accusations** have been **made** against her.* | *The main **accusation levelled against** him was that he tried to avoid military service.* | **[+of]** *His administration now **faces accusations** of corruption.* | **[+that]** *The organizers of the march strongly **denied** government **accusations** that they intended to cause trouble.* | *Burton's enemies had made **false accusations** against him.* | *She's made all sorts of **wild accusations** against me in the past.* | *They fled the country, **amid accusations of** corruption.*

ac·cu·sa·tive /əˈkjuːzətɪv/ *n* [C] *technical* a form of a noun in languages such as Latin or German, which shows that the noun is the DIRECT OBJECT of a verb or a PREPOSITION —**accusative** *adj*

ac·cu·sa·to·ry /əˈkjuːzətəri $ -tɔːri/ *adj* an accusatory remark or look from someone shows that they think you have done something wrong

ac·cuse /əˈkjuːz/ ●●○ W3 *v* [T] to say that you believe someone is guilty of a crime or of doing something bad: **accuse sb of (doing) sth** *He was accused of murder.* | *Smith accused her of lying.* | *The professor **stands accused of*** (=has been accused of) *stealing his student's ideas and publishing them.* —**accuser** *n* [C]

> **GRAMMAR**
> You **accuse** someone **of doing** something: *They accused him of cheating.* ✗ Don't say: *accuse someone to do something*

> **THESAURUS**
> **accuse** to say that you believe that someone is guilty of a crime or of doing something bad: *Two women have been accused of kidnapping a newborn baby.* | *Are you accusing me of lying?*
> **allege** /əˈledʒ/ to accuse someone of doing something, although this has not been proved: *He alleged that the other man had attacked him first.*
> **charge** if the police charge someone, they officially tell that person that they are believed to be guilty of a crime and that they must go to court: *She was charged with murder.*
> **indict** *AmE law* to officially accuse someone of a crime so that they will be judged in court under the American legal system: *He was indicted on charges of fraud.*

ac·cused /əˈkjuːzd/ *n* **the accused** [singular or plural] the person or group of people who have been officially accused of a crime or offence in a court of law

ac·cus·ing /əˈkjuːzɪŋ/ *adj* an accusing look from someone shows that they think you have done something wrong —**accusingly** *adv*

ac·cus·tom /əˈkʌstəm/ ●○○ *v* [T] to make yourself or another person become used to a situation or place: **accustom yourself to sth** *It took a while for me to accustom myself to all the new rules and regulations.*

ac·cus·tomed /əˈkʌstəmd/ *adj* **1 be accustomed to (doing) sth** to be familiar with something and accept it as normal: *We were accustomed to working together.* | **become/grow/get accustomed to sth** *Her eyes quickly became accustomed to the dark.*

> **REGISTER**
> In everyday English, people usually say **be used to** instead of **be accustomed to,** and **get used to** instead of **get/become accustomed to**: *She's **used to** working with children.* | *It's hard at first, but you'll **get used to** it.*

2 [only before noun] *formal* usual: *The pans were in their accustomed places.*

AC/DC /ˌeɪ siː ˈdiː siː/ *adj informal* sexually attracted to both men and women

ace¹ /eɪs/ *n* [C]
1 PLAYING CARD a playing card with a single spot on it, which usually has the highest value in a game: *the ace of hearts* | *I've got a pair of aces.*
2 SKILFUL PERSON someone who is extremely skilful at doing something: *a soccer ace* | *cycling ace Chris Boardman*
3 TENNIS SHOT a first shot in tennis or VOLLEYBALL which is hit so well that your opponent cannot reach the ball and you win the point
4 hold the aces to have the advantages in a situation so that you are sure to win: *The Americans hold most of the aces in this technology.*
5 within an ace of (doing) sth very close to doing or achieving something: *The team **came within an ace of** winning the championship.*

A

6 have an ace up your sleeve to have a secret advantage which could help you to win or be successful
7 ace in the hole *AmE informal* something that you keep secretly to use when you need it: *That fifty dollars is my ace in the hole.*

ace² *adj* **1 ace pilot/player/skier etc** someone who is a very skilful pilot, player etc: *an ace marksman* **2** *BrE spoken* very good: *The party was ace.*

ace³ *v* [T] **1** *AmE informal* to do very well in an examination, a piece of written work etc: *I aced the History test.* **2** to hit your first shot in tennis or VOLLEYBALL so well that your opponent cannot reach the ball

a·cer·bic /əˈsɜːbɪk $ -ɜːr-/ *adj* criticizing someone or something in a clever but cruel way SYN **biting**: *acerbic wit* —**acerbity** *n* [U]

ac·e·tate /ˈæsɪteɪt/ *n* **1** [U] a chemical made from acetic acid **2** [U] a smooth artificial cloth used to make clothes **3** [C] a transparent sheet that you write or print something on, and that is used with an OVERHEAD PROJECTOR

a,ce·tic ˈac·id /əˌsiːtɪk ˈæsɪd/ *n* [U] the acid in VINEGAR

ac·e·tone /ˈæsətəʊn $ -toʊn/ *n* [U] a clear liquid with a strong smell, used for cleaning surfaces, making paint more liquid, or for making other chemical substances

a·cet·y·lene /əˈsetəliːn $ -tl-ən, -iːn/ *n* [U] a gas which burns with a bright flame and is used in equipment for cutting and joining pieces of metal → **oxyacetylene**

ache¹ /eɪk/ ●○○ *v* [I]
1 if part of your body aches, you feel a continuous, but not very sharp pain there SYN **hurt**: *His feet were aching from standing so long.* **THESAURUS** ▸ HURT

> **REGISTER**
> In everyday English, people usually say they **have a headache**, **have (a) backache**, **have (a) stomach ache**, or **have (a) toothache** rather than saying that their **head, back, etc aches**: *My **head aches** terribly.* → *I **have a** terrible **headache**.*

2 to want to do or have something very much: **[+for]** *I'm aching for sleep.* | **ache to do sth** *He ached to reach out and hold her close.*
3 to have a strong unhappy feeling: **[+with]** *Sarah ached with sadness that her brother was so ill.* | *Tim's **heart** was **aching** for her.*

ache² ●○○ *n* [C]
1 a continuous pain that is not sharp or very strong: *a stomach ache* | *A **dull ache** throbbed at the back of David's head.* | **aches and pains** (=slight feelings of pain that are not considered to be serious) *Apart from the usual aches and pains, she felt all right.* **THESAURUS** ▸ PAIN
2 a strong, mostly unhappy, feeling: *the ache of his loneliness* —**achy** *adj*: *I'm feeling tired and achy.*

a·chieve /əˈtʃiːv/ ●●● S2 W1 AWL *v*
1 [T] to successfully complete something or get a good result, especially by working hard: *She eventually **achieved her goal of** becoming a professor.* | *Wilson has **achieved** considerable **success** as an artist.* | *Frances achieved very good exam results.* | **THESAURUS** ▸ SUCCEED

> **REGISTER**
> In everyday English, people usually say someone **gets** a result rather than **achieves** it: *He **got** good grades in his final exams.*

2 [I] to be successful in a particular kind of job or activity: *We want all our students to achieve within their chosen profession.* —**achievable** *adj*

a·chieve·ment /əˈtʃiːvmənt/ ●●● S3 W2 AWL *n*
1 [C] something important that you succeed in doing by your own efforts: **[+of]** *We try to celebrate the achievements of our students.* | *His great achievement is to make all the players into a united team.* | **sb's achievement in (doing) sth** *The test measures children's achievements in reading, spelling, and maths.*
2 [U] when you achieve something or when people achieve something: *Roberts is researching the effect of social class on educational achievement.* | *As we climbed the final few metres, we felt a **sense of achievement**.*

a·chiev·er /əˈtʃiːvə $ -ər/ *n* [C] someone who is successful because they are determined and work hard → **underachiever, overachiever**

A·chil·les' heel /əˌkɪliːz ˈhiːl/ *n* [C] a weak part of someone's character, which could cause them to fail at something: *I think Frank's vanity is his Achilles' heel.*

A·chil·les ten·don /əˌkɪliːz ˈtendən/ *n* [C] the part of your body that connects the muscles in the back of your foot with the muscles of your lower leg

a·choo /əˈtʃuː/ *n* [C] used to represent the sound you make when you SNEEZE

ac·id¹ /ˈæsɪd/ ●●○ W3 *n*
1 [C,U] a chemical substance that has a PH of less than 7. Strong acids can burn holes in material or damage your skin: *sulphuric acid*
2 [U] *informal* the drug LSD

acid² *adj* **1** having a sharp sour taste SYN **bitter**: *a juicy apple with a slightly acid flavour* **2 acid remark/comment/tone etc** an acid remark uses humour in an unkind way to criticize someone: *I was expecting another of his acid remarks, but he remained silent.* **3 the acid test** a way of finding out whether something is as good as people say it is, whether it works, or whether it is true: *People ask if the team is good enough. This match will be the acid test.* **4** *technical* an acid soil does not contain much LIME¹(3): *Blueberry bushes need a very acid soil.* —**acidity** /əˈsɪdəti/ *n* [U]

ˈacid-free *adj* acid-free paper and paper products do not contain acid: *Store precious photographs and documents between sheets of acid-free paper.*

ˈacid house *n* [U] a kind of dance music that is played loudly using electronic instruments

a·cid·ic /əˈsɪdɪk/ *adj* **1** very sour: *Some fruit juices taste a bit acidic.* **2** containing acid

a·cid·i·fy /əˈsɪdɪfaɪ/ *v* (**acidified, acidifying, acidifies**) [I,T] *technical* to become an acid or make something become an acid

ˈacid jazz *n* [U] a type of popular music that combines features of many other kinds of music, especially JAZZ, HIP-HOP, and SOUL

ac·id·ly /ˈæsɪdli/ *adv* if you say something acidly, you say it in a cruel or unkind way: *'I'm sure you're right,' he said acidly.*

ˌacid ˈrain *n* [U] rain that contains harmful acid which can damage the environment and is caused by chemicals in the air, for example from cars or factories

ac·knowl·edge /əkˈnɒlɪdʒ $ -ˈnɑː-/ ●●○ S3 W3 AWL *v* [T]
1 ADMIT to admit or accept that something is true or that a situation exists: *The family acknowledge the need for change.* | **acknowledge that** *He acknowledges that when he's tired he gets bad-tempered.* | *Claire acknowledged that she was guilty.* | *The government must acknowledge what is happening and do something about it.* | *'Maybe you are right,' she acknowledged.* | *This is a fact that most smokers **readily acknowledge**.* **THESAURUS** ▸ ADMIT

> **GRAMMAR**
> In more formal English, you say **it is acknowledged that** when saying what people generally agree is true: *It is acknowledged that these letters are genuine.*

2 RECOGNIZE STH'S IMPORTANCE if people acknowledge something, they recognize how good or important it is: *The Brazilian coach acknowledged the talent of his players.* | **be acknowledged as sth** *The film festival is acknowledged as an event of international importance.* | **be widely/generally acknowledged to be sth** *The mill produces what is widely acknowledged to be the finest wool in the world.*
3 ACCEPT SB'S AUTHORITY to accept that someone or something has authority over people: *Both defendants refused to acknowledge the authority of the court.* | **acknowledge sb as sth** *Many of the poor acknowledged him as their spiritual leader.*

4 THANK to publicly announce that you are grateful for the help that someone has given you: *We wish to acknowledge the support of the university.*
5 SHOW YOU NOTICE SB to show someone that you have noticed them or heard what they have said: *Tom acknowledged her presence by a brief glance.*
6 SAY YOU HAVE RECEIVED STH to let someone know that you have received something from them: *I would be grateful if you would **acknowledge receipt** of this letter.*

ac·knowl·edge·ment, **acknowledgment** /əkˈnɒlɪdʒmənt $ -ˈnɑː-/ ●○○ AWL *n*
1 [C,U] the act of admitting or accepting that something is true: **[+of]** *We want an acknowledgement of the existence of the problem.* | **acknowledgement that** *The reduction in their grant is an acknowledgement that they have been paid too much.*
2 [singular, U] a movement of your body that shows that you have noticed someone or heard what they have said: *Basil nodded an acknowledgement as he entered the room.* | *He gave her a faint smile of acknowledgement.* | **in acknowledgement** *Larsen looked over and nodded in acknowledgement.*
3 [C,U] the act of publicly thanking someone for something they have done: **in acknowledgement of sth** *She received a special award in acknowledgement of all her hard work.*
4 [C,U] a letter written to tell someone that you have received their letter, message etc: *Do you want a written acknowledgement?*
5 acknowledgements [plural] a short piece of writing at the beginning or end of a book in which the writer thanks all the people who have helped him or her

ac·me /ˈækmi/ *n* **the acme of sth** *formal* the best and highest level of something SYN **pinnacle**: *the acme of perfection*

ac·ne /ˈækni/ *n* [U] a medical problem which causes a lot of red spots on your face and neck and mainly affects young people

ac·o·lyte /ˈækəlaɪt/ *n* [C] **1** *formal* someone who serves a leader or believes in their ideas **2** someone who helps a priest at a religious ceremony

a·corn /ˈeɪkɔːn $ -ɔːrn, -ərn/ *n* [C] the nut of the OAK tree → see picture at **TREE**

ACOUSTIC

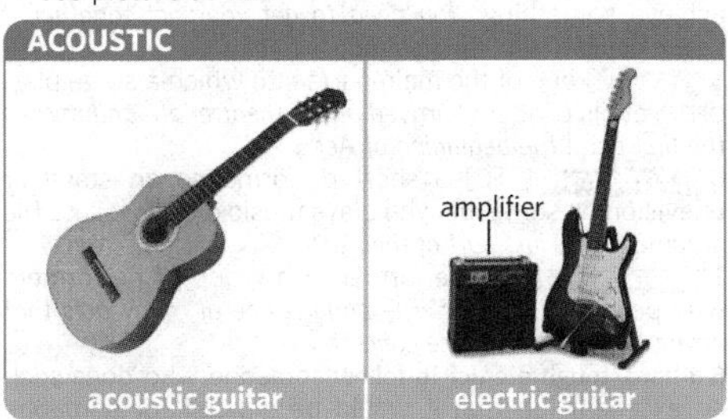

acoustic guitar | electric guitar

a·cous·tic /əˈkuːstɪk/ ●○○ *adj*
1 relating to sound and the way people hear things
2 an acoustic GUITAR or other musical instrument does not have its sound made louder electronically → **electric** —**acoustically** /-kli/ *adv*

a·cous·tics /əˈkuːstɪks/ *n* **1** [plural] the shape and size of a room, which affect the way sound is heard in it: *The hall has excellent acoustics.* **2** [U] the scientific study of sound

GRAMMAR: Singular or plural verb?
- In meaning 1, **acoustics** is followed by a plural verb: *The **acoustics** in here **are** terrible.*
- In meaning 2, **acoustics** is followed by a singular verb: ***Acoustics is** the science of sound waves.*

ac·quaint /əˈkweɪnt/ *v* [T] *formal* **1 acquaint yourself with sth** to deliberately find out about something: *I need to acquaint myself with the new regulations.* **2 acquaint sb with sth** to give someone information about something: *You need to acquaint the police with the facts.*

ac·quaint·ance /əˈkweɪntəns/ ●○○ *n*
1 SB YOU KNOW [C] someone you know, but who is not a close friend: *She was a **casual acquaintance** of my family in Vienna.* | *He heard about the job through a **mutual acquaintance*** (=someone you and another person both know). THESAURUS▸ FRIEND

REGISTER
In everyday English, people usually say **someone I know** rather than **an acquaintance**: *I got the job through **someone I know**.*

2 RELATIONSHIP [singular, U] a relationship with someone you know, but who is not a close friend: *They developed an acquaintance over the Internet.* | *You can't judge her on such short acquaintance* (=when you have not known her long). | *My uncle did not improve on further acquaintance* (=when you knew him better).
3 make sb's acquaintance *formal* to meet someone for the first time: *I should be delighted to make Mrs McGough's acquaintance.* | *At the hotel, I made the acquaintance of a young American actor.*
4 KNOWLEDGE [U] *formal* knowledge or experience of a particular subject: **[+with]** *The practice of a lawyer requires acquaintance with court procedures.* | **have a passing/nodding acquaintance with sth** (=have only slight knowledge or experience of something) *He has a passing acquaintance with a lot of different subjects.*
5 of your acquaintance *formal* a person of your acquaintance is someone that you know: *The poems were written by various women of her acquaintance.*
6 on first acquaintance *formal* when you meet someone for the first time: *Most people are nicer than you think on first acquaintance.*

acˈquaintance ˌrape *n* [C,U] a crime in which a person forces someone they know to have sex with them SYN **date rape**

ac·quaint·ance·ship /əˈkweɪntənsʃɪp/ *n* [U] **1** your experience or knowledge of a subject **2** a slight friendship with someone: *Sheridan had struck up an acquaintanceship with Giles* (=had met him and became friendly with him).

ac·quaint·ed /əˈkweɪntɪd/ ●○○ *adj* [not before noun]
1 if you are acquainted with someone, you have met them a few times but do not know them very well: **[+with]** *Were you acquainted with a friend of mine, Daniel Green?* | *We would like to get better acquainted.*
2 be acquainted with sth *formal* to know about something, because you have seen it, read it, used it etc: *She was well acquainted with classical literature.*

ac·qui·esce /ˌækwiˈes/ *v* [I] *formal* to do what someone else wants, or allow something to happen, even though you do not really agree with it: **[+in/to]** *Oil companies have been accused of acquiescing in the pollution of the ocean.*

ac·qui·es·cent /ˌækwiˈesənt◂/ *adj* too ready to agree with someone or do what they want, without complaining or saying what you want to do —**acquiescence** *n* [U]

ac·quire /əˈkwaɪə $ əˈkwaɪr/ ●●○ W2 AWL *v* [T]
1 *formal* to obtain something by buying it or being given it: *Manning hoped to acquire valuable works of art as cheaply as possible.* | *The council acquired the land using a compulsory purchase order.* THESAURUS▸ BUY
2 to get or gain something: *The college acquired a reputation for very high standards.*

REGISTER
In everyday English, people usually say **get** rather than **acquire**: *Where did you **get** that tie?* | *He soon **got** a reputation for being unfriendly.*

3 to gain knowledge or learn a skill: *He spent years acquiring his skills as a surgeon.* | *Elsie acquired a good knowledge of Chinese.* THESAURUS▸ GET
4 acquire a taste for sth to begin to like something: *She had acquired a taste for European beer.*

5 an acquired taste something that people only begin to like after they have tried it a few times

ac·qui·si·tion /ˌækwəˈzɪʃən/ [AWL] *n* **1** [U] the process by which you gain knowledge or learn a skill: *the acquisition of language* **2** [U] the act of getting land, power, money etc: **[+of]** *the acquisition of new sites for development* **3** [C] *formal* something that you have obtained by buying it or being given it: *The Art Society is holding an exhibition of recent acquisitions.*

ac·quis·i·tive /əˈkwɪzətɪv/ *adj* wanting to have and keep a lot of possessions —**acquisitiveness** *n* [U]

ac·quit /əˈkwɪt/ *v* (**acquitted**, **acquitting**) **1** [T] to give a decision in a court of law that someone is not guilty of a crime: *All the defendants were acquitted.* | **acquit sb of sth** *The judge directed the jury to acquit Phillips of the murder.* [GRAMMAR] **Acquit** is often passive in this meaning. **2 acquit yourself well/honourably** to do something well, especially something difficult that you do for the first time in front of other people

ac·quit·tal /əˈkwɪtl/ *n* [C,U] an official statement in a court of law that someone is not guilty → **conviction**

a·cre /ˈeɪkə $ -ər/ ●●○ *n* [C]

1 a unit for measuring area, equal to 4,840 square yards or 4,047 square metres: *They own 200 acres of farmland.* | *a 200-acre wood*

2 acres of space/room *BrE informal* a large amount of space

a·cre·age /ˈeɪkərɪdʒ/ *n* [U] the area of a piece of land measured in acres

ac·rid /ˈækrɪd/ *adj* **1** an acrid smell or taste is strong and unpleasant and stings your nose or throat: *a cloud of acrid smoke* **2** *formal* an acrid remark expresses anger and criticizes someone strongly

ac·ri·mo·ni·ous /ˌækrəˈməʊniəs◂ $ -ˈmoʊ-/ ●○○ *adj* an acrimonious meeting or discussion is one in which people argue a lot and get very angry [SYN] **bitter**: *The meeting ended in an acrimonious dispute.* —**acrimoniously** *adv* —**acrimoniousness** *n* [U]

ac·ri·mo·ny /ˈækrəməni $ -moʊni/ *n* [U] *formal* feelings of anger between people who disagree strongly and do not like each other

ac·ro·bat /ˈækrəbæt/ *n* [C] someone who entertains people by doing difficult physical actions such as walking on their hands or balancing on a high rope, especially at a CIRCUS

ac·ro·bat·ic /ˌækrəˈbætɪk◂/ *adj* acrobatic movements involve moving your body in a very skilful way, for example by jumping through the air or balancing on a rope: *They performed some amazing acrobatic feats.* —**acrobatically** /-kli/ *adv*

ac·ro·bat·ics /ˌækrəˈbætɪks/ *n* [plural] skilful movements of your body, for example jumping through the air or balancing on a rope

ac·ro·nym /ˈækrənɪm/ *n* [C] a word made up from the first letters of the name of something such as an organization. For example, NATO is an acronym for the North Atlantic Treaty Organization.

a·cross /əˈkrɒs $ əˈkrɔːs/ ●●● [S1] [W1] *adv, prep*

1 from one side of something to the other: *the first flight across the Atlantic* | *They ran* ***straight across*** *the road* (=without stopping). | *We'll have to swim across.* | *We'd got halfway across before Philip realized he'd left his money at home.* | *We gazed across the valley.*

2 towards someone or something on the other side of an area: *There's Brendan. Why don't you go across and say hello?* | **[+to/at]** *The referee looked across at his linesman before awarding the penalty.* | *He walked across to where I was sitting.*

3 used to say that something exists or reaches from one side of an area to the other: *a deep crack across the ceiling* | *the only bridge across the river* | *Do you think this shirt is too tight across the shoulders?* | *Someone's parked* ***right across*** *the entrance to the driveway.*

4 on the opposite side of something: *My best friend lives across the road.* | *He knew that* ***just across*** *the border lay freedom.* | **across (sth) from sb/sth** *Across the street from where we're standing, you can see the old churchyard.* | *the woman sitting across from me* (=opposite me) *on the train*

5 in every part of a country, organization etc: *a TV series that became popular across five continents* | *Teachers are expected to teach a range of subjects* ***right across*** *the curriculum.*

6 used to show how wide something is: **ten feet/five metres etc across** *The river is 2 kilometres across.*

aˌcross-the-ˈboard, **across the board** *adj, adv* affecting everyone or everything in a situation or organization: *an across-the-board pay increase* | *In July everything we sell is reduced right across the board.*

a·cros·tic /əˈkrɒstɪk $ əˈkrɒː-/ *n* [C] a poem or piece of writing in which the first or last letter of each line spells a word

a·cryl·ic /əˈkrɪlɪk/ *adj* acrylic paints or cloth are made from chemical substances, not natural substances

a·cryl·ics /əˈkrɪlɪks/ *n* [plural] acrylic paints

act¹ /ækt/ ●●● [S1] [W1] *n*

1 ACTION [C] one thing that you do: *The new president's first act should be to end the war.* | *a thoughtless act* | **act of (doing) sth** *an act of violence* | *her many acts of kindness* | *The act of writing a list can help to calm you down.* | **in the act of doing sth** (=at the moment that you are doing something) *Lindsay paused in the act of putting down the phone.*

> **REGISTER**
> In everyday English, people usually say **a thoughtless/kind/stupid etc thing to do** rather than **a thoughtless/kind/stupid etc act**.

2 LAW (*also* **Act**) [C] a law that has been officially accepted by Parliament or Congress: *the Housing and Community Development Act of 1977* | *an act of Parliament*

3 PRETENDING [singular] insincere behaviour in which you pretend to have a particular kind of feeling or to be a particular kind of person: *Mike played the loving husband in front of the children but it was all an act.* | *Be natural. Don't feel you have to* ***put on an act.***

4 get your act together *informal* to become more organized and behave in a more effective way, especially in order to achieve something: *You need to get your act together if you're going to find the right house to buy.*

5 PLAY [C] one of the main parts into which a stage play, OPERA etc is divided: *I arrived at the theatre late and missed the first act.* | *the beginning of Act 3*

6 PERFORMANCE [C] a short performance on stage or television by someone who plays music or tells jokes: *The argument was just part of their act.*

7 PERFORMER [C] a performer or a group of performers who perform together: *The band is one of many acts that have been booked for the concert.*

8 a hard/tough etc act to follow someone who does such an excellent job that it would be difficult for someone doing the same job after them to be as good: *He has been a very successful captain and will be a hard act to follow.*

9 get in on the act *informal* to take part in an activity that someone else has started, especially in order to get a share of the advantages for yourself

10 act of God an event that is caused by natural forces, such as a storm, flood, or fire, which you cannot prevent or control

11 act of worship an occasion when people pray together and show their respect for God

12 balancing/juggling act a situation in which you are trying to do several different types of work at the same time

13 do a disappearing/vanishing act to be impossible to find when you are needed → **catch sb in the act** at CATCH¹(3), → **clean up your act** at CLEAN UP

act² ●●● [S2] [W1] *v*

1 DO SOMETHING [I] to do something in a particular way or for a particular reason: *The company acted correctly in sacking him.* | *The jury decided that Walker had acted in* *self-defence.* | **act to do sth** *The UN must act now to restore democracy.* | *Politicians will only act when enough people demand that they do something.*

> **REGISTER**
> In everyday English, people often use expressions like **do the right thing** or **do a brave thing** rather than use **act** with an adverb such as **correctly** or **bravely**: *They **acted correctly** in telling her.* → *They **did the right thing** in telling her.*
> When **act** is used alone to mean 'take action', in everyday English people usually just say **do something**: *We have to **do something** now.*

2 BEHAVE [I always + adv/prep] to behave in a particular way: *They acted unreasonably when they turned down Jill's application.* | *He's been acting strangely ever since his mom died.* | **[+as if]** *Pip acted as if he was better than everyone else.* | **[+like]** *Stop acting like a baby.* | **[+with]** *She acted with dignity.* | **act your age** (=used to tell someone to behave in a more adult way, suitable for someone of their age)
3 PRETEND [I,T] to pretend to have feelings, qualities etc that are different from your true ones: *When he's angry, he acts the fool.* | *That guy is acting crazy.* | **act a part/role** *Stella felt unnatural in their company, as if she was acting a part.* | **[+as if/like]** *Why does he act as if he was stupid?* THESAURUS ▸ PRETEND
4 PLAY/FILM [I,T] to perform in a play or film: *I first started acting when I was 12 years old.* | **act a part/role** *She is acting the role of Lady Macbeth six evenings a week.* | *The movie is very well acted.*
5 HAVE AN EFFECT [I] to have an effect or use: **[+as]** *The padding acts as a cushion if the player falls or is hit by the ball.* | **[+on]** *Disinfectants act on bacteria in two main ways.*
6 act for sb/act on sb's behalf to represent someone, especially in a court of law or by doing business for them: *Makin, a solicitor, is acting for the young people in their case against the county council.* | *I am acting on behalf of the bank.* → ACTING[1]
act as sth *phr v* to do a particular job for a short time, for example while the usual person is absent: *My brother speaks French – he can act as interpreter.*
act on/upon sth *phr v* to do something because of another person's advice or order, or because you have received information or had an idea: *She is **acting on** the **advice** of her lawyers.* | *Police say they **acted on information** received.*
act sth ↔ **out** *phr v*
1 if a group of people act out an event, they show how it happened by pretending to be the people who were involved in it: *The children were acting out the story of the birth of Jesus.*
2 to express your feelings about something through your behaviour or actions, especially when you have been feeling angry or nervous: *These teenagers are likely to act out their distress by running away.*
act up *phr v*
1 if children act up, they behave badly: *He's a tough kid and he acts up a lot.*
2 if a machine or part of your body acts up, it does not work properly: *The computer is acting up again.*

act·ing[1] /ˈæktɪŋ/ *adj* **acting manager/head teacher/director etc** someone who does an important job while the usual person is not there, or until a new person is chosen for the job

acting[2] *n* [U] the job or skill of performing in plays and films → **drama**

ac·tion[1] /ˈækʃən/ ●●● S1 W1 *n*
1 DOING STH [U] the process of doing something, especially in order to achieve a particular thing: *The government must **take action*** (=do something) *now to stop the rise in violent crime.* | **[+on]** *Environmental groups want tougher action on pollution from cars.* | *She was looking forward to **putting her ideas into action*** (=doing the things she had planned). | *Ambulance crews are ready to **spring into action*** (=suddenly start doing something) *if anything goes wrong during the race.*
2 STH DONE [C] something that someone does: **quick/swift/prompt action** *Her **prompt actions** probably saved my life.* | *The child could not be **held responsible for his actions*** (=he was too young to be blamed for them). | **defend/justify your action(s)** *The chief of police tried to justify his actions.*
3 in action someone or something that is in action is doing the job or activity they are trained or designed to do: *photos of ski jumpers in action* | **see/watch sth/sb in action** *I'd like to see the new computer system in action.*
4 out of action a) broken and not working: *The photocopier is out of action again.* **b)** injured and unable to do anything: **put/keep sb out of action** *The injury will keep him out of action for a month.*
5 FIGHTING [U] fighting during a war: *There have been reports of widespread **enemy action** in the area.* | **killed/wounded in action** (=killed or wounded while fighting) *His father was killed in action in Vietnam.* | *530 servicemen were reported **missing in action*** (=they were never seen again after a battle). | *The men were **sent into action** with little or no training.* | *He had **seen action*** (=been involved in fighting) *in Korea.* THESAURUS ▸ WAR
6 LEGAL [C,U] a legal or formal process to decide whether someone has done something wrong: *They are threatening to **take legal action** against the hospital* (=start a court case against them). | *The director faces **disciplinary action*** (=official action to punish him). | *The matter is now the subject of a **court action*** (=a court case). | *The students agreed to **drop** their **action*** (=decided not to continue with a court case or an official complaint). | *The sisters **brought a libel action** against the newspaper* (=started a court case).
7 EXCITEMENT [U] **a)** *informal* exciting things that are happening: *There hasn't been much action around here for months.* | *New York **is where all the action is**.* **b)** an action film has a lot of exciting scenes in it, in which people fight, chase, and kill each other: *Gibson became famous in action movies.* | *a TV **action hero***
8 THE EVENTS IN A STORY/FILM ETC **the action** the events in a story, film, play etc: *Most of **the action takes place** in San Francisco.* | ***The action opens*** (=starts) *in a barbershop.*
9 MOVEMENT [C,U] the way something moves or works: **[+of]** *the action of the heart* | *a smooth braking action*
10 EFFECT [U] the effect that a substance, especially a chemical, has on something: **[+of]** *The drug blocks the action of the cancer gene.* | **[+on/upon]** *the action of alcohol on the liver*
11 action group/committee etc a group formed to change a social or political situation – often used in names: *the Child Poverty Action Group*
12 a piece/slice of the action *informal* an opportunity to be involved in an event or activity, especially one that will be enjoyable or will make money: *If you want a slice of the action, tickets may still be available.*
13 actions speak louder than words used to say that you are judged by what you do, and not by what you say
14 action! used by film DIRECTORS to give the instruction to begin filming: *Lights, camera, action!* → **AFFIRMATIVE ACTION**

> **COLLOCATIONS**
> **VERBS**
> **take action** (=do something to deal with a problem) *The government must take action to control inflation.*
> **demand/call for action** (=ask forcefully) *Voters are demanding tougher action on gun crime.*
> **swing/spring/leap into action** (=suddenly start doing something) | **put sth into action** (=start doing something you have planned to do)
> **ADJECTIVES**
> **immediate/prompt/swift action** *The public wants immediate action to stop the terrorists.*
> **urgent action** (=that needs to be done immediately) *The Opposition called for urgent action to reduce unemployment.*

A

firm/tough action *We need firm action to deal with the problem.*
decisive action (=that has a big effect on the way something develops) | **drastic action** (=that has a very severe effect) | **further action** | **direct action** (=that is aimed at making a government or company do something) | **political action** | **industrial/strike action** (=that workers take in order to protest about pay, working conditions etc) | **joint action** (=that two or more countries, organizations etc take together)

PHRASES

a course of action *Have you decided on a course of action?*
a plan of action *The General outlined his plan of action for the campaign.*

action² *v* [T] *formal* to do a specific thing that needs to be done, especially after discussing it: *How are we actually going to action these objectives?*

ac·tion·a·ble /ˈækʃənəbəl/ *adj law* if something you say or do is actionable, it is so bad or damaging that a claim could be made against you in a court of law: *His remarks are actionable in my view.*

ˌaction-ˈpacked *adj* an action-packed film, book etc contains a lot of exciting events

ˈaction point *n* [C] something that must be done, as a result of a meeting

ˌaction ˈreplay *n* [C] *BrE* **1** an important or exciting moment in a sports game that is shown again on television immediately after it happens, sometimes at a slower speed SYN **instant replay** *AmE* **2** [usually singular] an event in your life that is very similar to one that you have experienced before: **[+of]** *an action replay of the week we spent in Jamaica*

ˈaction ˌstations *n* [plural] *BrE* the positions that people such as soldiers or the police take when they are getting ready to fight or deal with a difficult situation – often used to tell people to go to these positions: *Crew, return to action stations!*

ac·tiv·ate /ˈæktɪveɪt/ *v* [T] *technical* to make an electrical system or chemical process start working OPP **deactivate**: *Cooking fumes may activate the alarm.* | *The yeast's growth is activated by sugar and warmth.* —**activation** /ˌæktəˈveɪʃən/ *n* [U]

REGISTER
In everyday English, people usually use **set off** rather than **activate** when talking about electrical systems: *Someone has* **set off** *the smoke alarm again.*

ac·tive¹ /ˈæktɪv/ ●●● S2 W2 *adj*
1 BUSY always busy doing things, especially physical or mental activities OPP **inactive**: *games for active youngsters* | *She's over 80, but is still very active.* | **active life/lifestyle** *My father always led a very active life.* | **active mind/imagination** *a child with a very active imagination*
2 INVOLVED involved in an organization or activity and doing lots of practical things to achieve your aims: *He became* ***politically active*** *at college.* | **be active in (doing) sth** *The Bureau is active in promoting overseas investment.* | **take/play an active part/role in sth** *Encourage students to take an active part in discussions.* | *She* ***took an active interest*** *in local charities.* | **active participation/involvement** *the importance of active participation by elderly people in the life of the community* | *We're* ***taking active steps*** (=doing practical things) *to deal with the problem.* | *We maintain* ***active links*** *with other European universities.* | **active member/supporter** *He is an active member of the Labour Party.*
3 FUNCTIONING operating in a way that is normal or expected OPP **inactive**: *The virus is active even at low temperatures.*
4 DOING STH doing something regularly: ***sexually active*** *teenagers*
5 VOLCANO an active VOLCANO is likely to ERUPT (=explode) at any time: *The* ***volcano*** *became* ***active*** *last year with a series of eruptions.*
6 GRAMMAR an active verb or sentence has the person or thing doing the action as its SUBJECT. In 'The boy kicked the ball', the verb 'kick' is active → **PASSIVE¹(2)**
7 CHEMICAL producing a chemical reaction: *nicotine, the* ***active ingredient*** *in tobacco*

active² *n* **the active** the active form of a verb, for example 'destroyed' in the sentence 'Enemy planes destroyed the village.' → **PASSIVE²**

ac·tive·ly /ˈæktɪvli/ ●●○ *adv* in a way that involves doing a lot of practical things: *Carol was* ***actively involved*** *in running the group.* | *The school actively encourages students to do their best.*

ˌactive ˈservice (*also* **ˌactive ˈduty**) *n* [U] the work that soldiers do in a war: *Powell was declared unfit for active service.* | **on active service/duty** *More than 20,000 women are on active duty.*

ac·tiv·ist /ˈæktɪvɪst/ ●○○ *n* [C] someone who works hard doing practical things to achieve social or political change: **political/gay/animal rights etc activist** —**activist** *adj* [only before noun]: *activist groups*

ac·tiv·i·ty /ækˈtɪvəti/ ●●● S2 W1 *n* (*plural* **activities**)
1 [C,U] things that people do, especially in order to achieve a particular aim: *Everyone is free to engage in peaceful political activity.* | *fund-raising activities* | *Regular physical activity helps to control your weight.*
2 [C usually plural] something that you do because you enjoy it: *leisure activities* | *outdoor activities such as hiking or climbing*
3 [U] a situation in which a lot of things are happening or a lot of things are being done: *The office was suddenly full of* ***frantic activity***. | *The farm was always* ***a hive of activity*** *at this time of year.*

COLLOCATIONS – MEANINGS 1, 2 & 3

VERBS

take part in an activity (*also* **participate in an activity** *formal*) *The children were encouraged to take part in several different activities.*
be involved in an activity *The men were involved in terrorist activities.*
do an activity *He doesn't do a lot of physical activity.*

ADJECTIVES/NOUN + activity

political activity *Political activity is closely controlled by the government.*
economic activity *The current level of economic activity will influence business confidence.*
business/commercial activity *Internet shopping is a rapidly developing area of business activity.*
human activity | **criminal/illegal activity** | **terrorist activity** | **outdoor activities** | **physical activity** | **mental activity** | **leisure activities** | **classroom activities** | **cultural activities**

PHRASES

the level of activity *The level of economic activity has increased.*

COMMON ERRORS

⚠ Don't say 'make an activity'. Say **take part in an activity** or **be involved in an activity**.
Don't say 'sport activity'. Say **sports activity**.

ac·tor /ˈæktə $ -ər/ ●●● W3 *n* [C] someone who performs in a play or film: **leading/principal actor** *She has starred with many leading actors.* | **character actor** (=an actor who takes unusual or interesting roles)

THESAURUS

actor someone who performs in a play or film: *Her son wants to be an actor.*
actress a woman who performs in a play or film. Many women prefer to be called **actors** rather than actresses: *Who was the actress who played Jane Eyre?*
star a famous actor: *Julia Roberts is a famous Hollywood star.* | *The hotel is popular with movie stars.*

the star someone who plays the most important part in a play or film: *Daniel Radcliffe is the star of the 'Harry Potter' films.*
co-star one of two or more famous actors who have important parts in a play or film: *Her co-star Jodie Foster won the Best Actress Award.*
the lead the main acting part in a play or film: *He will* ***play the lead*** *in a new version of 'Dracula'.*
extra an actor in a film who does not say anything but is part of a crowd: *She started her career as an extra in TV soap operas.*
understudy an actor who learns a part in a play so that they can act the part if the usual actor is ill: *Vanessa had flu, and her place was taken by her understudy, Miss Lisa Fennell.*

A GROUP OF ACTORS

the cast all the actors in a play or film: *Other members of the cast include Johnny Depp and Danny DeVito.* | *She will head the cast* (=she will have the most important part).
company a group of actors who perform plays together: *In 2006, he joined the Royal Shakespeare Company.* | *The play will be performed by an all-female company.*

ac·tress /ˈæktrɪs/ ●●● W3 *n* [C] a woman who performs in a play or film **THESAURUS** ACTOR

ac·tu·al /ˈæktʃuəl/ ●●● S1 W2 *adj* [only before noun] **1** used to emphasize that something is real or exact: *I'm not joking. Those were his actual words.* | *I know Germany won, but I can't tell you the actual score.* | *Interest is only charged on the actual amount borrowed.* | *In* ***actual fact*** (=really), *there is little evidence to support the allegations.* ⚠ Do not use **actual** to mean 'at the present time'. Use **current** or **present**: *the current (NOT actual) economic policy*
2 the actual sth used to introduce the most important part of an event or activity: *The programme starts at 8.00 but the actual film doesn't start until 8.30.*

ac·tu·al·i·ty /ˌæktʃuˈæləti/ *n* (*plural* **actualities**) *formal* **1** [C usually plural] facts, rather than things that people believe or imagine SYN **realities**: *the grim actualities of prison life* **2** [U] the state of being real or really existing: ***In actuality****, it's much more complex than that* (=used when talking about what a situation is really like).

ac·tu·a·lize (*also* **-ise** *BrE*) /ˈækʃuəlaɪz/ *v* [T] to make a plan or wish become true SYN **realize**: *Mistakes are a necessary part of actualizing your vision.* —**actualization** /ˌæktʃuəlaɪˈzeɪʃən $ -lə-/ *n* [U]

Frequencies of the adverb **actually** in spoken and written English.

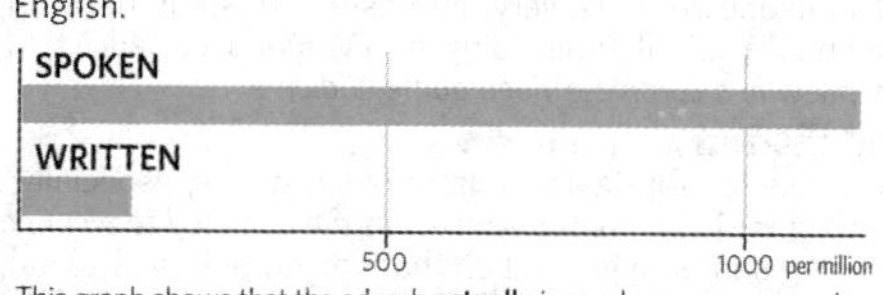

This graph shows that the adverb **actually** is much more common in spoken English than in written English.

ac·tu·al·ly /ˈæktʃuəli, -tʃəli/ ●●● S1 W1 *adv*
1 [sentence adverb] *spoken* used to add new information to what you have just said, to give your opinion, or to start a new conversation: *I've known Barbara for years. Since we were babies, actually.* | *Actually, on second thoughts, I don't think I want to go out tonight.*
2 used to emphasize the real or exact truth of a situation, rather than what people may think: *What time are you actually leaving?* | *Labor costs have actually fallen.* | *'Disappointed?' 'No, actually I'm rather glad.'*

ac·tu·als /ˈæktʃuəlz/ *n* [plural] numbers that relate to something that has actually happened, rather than what was expected to happen: *Mobile phone operators had expected monthly usage of up to 250 minutes. Actuals are very different, at 100 minutes.*

ac·tu·a·ry /ˈæktʃuəri $ -tʃueri/ *n* (*plural* **actuaries**) [C] someone whose job is to advise insurance companies on how much to charge for insurance, after calculating the risks —**actuarial** /ˌæktʃuˈeəriəl $ -ˈer-/ *adj*

ac·tu·ate /ˈæktʃueɪt/ *v* [T] *formal* **1 be actuated by sth** to behave in a particular way because of something: *He was actuated by violent jealousy.* **2** to make a piece of machinery start to operate

a·cu·i·ty /əˈkjuːəti/ *n* [U] *formal* the ability to think, see, or hear clearly: *A motorist needs good* ***visual acuity****.*

ac·u·men /ˈækjəmən, əˈkjuːmən/ *n* [U] the ability to think quickly and make good judgments: **business/political/financial etc acumen** *The firm's success is largely due to Brannon's commercial acumen.*

ac·u·pres·sure /ˈækjəˌpreʃə $ -ər/ *n* [U] a treatment for pain and disease that involves pressing your hands on particular parts of the body

ac·u·punc·ture /ˈækjəˌpʌŋktʃə $ -ər/ *n* [U] a treatment for pain and disease that involves pushing special needles into parts of the body: *the four main acupuncture points* —**acupuncturist** *n* [C]

a·cute /əˈkjuːt/ ●○○ *adj*
1 PROBLEM an acute problem is very serious: *The housing shortage is more acute than first thought.* **THESAURUS** SERIOUS
2 FEELING an acute feeling is very strong: ***acute pain*** | *acute embarrassment* | *acute anxiety*
3 ILLNESS *technical* an acute illness or disease quickly becomes very serious OPP **chronic**: *acute arthritis*
4 SENSES acute senses such as hearing, taste, touch etc are very good and sensitive: *Young children have a particularly* ***acute sense of*** *smell.*
5 INTELLIGENT quick to notice and understand things SYN **sharp**: *Simon's vague manner concealed an acute mind.* | *an acute analysis of Middle Eastern politics*
6 MATHEMATICS *technical* an acute angle is less than 90° → **obtuse**
7 PUNCTUATION an acute ACCENT (=a mark used to show pronunciation) is a small mark written above a vowel. In 'café', the letter 'e' has an acute accent. → **grave**, **circumflex** —**acuteness** *n* [U]

a·cute·ly /əˈkjuːtli/ ●○○ *adv* feeling or noticing something very strongly: **acutely aware/conscious (of/that)** *Students are becoming acutely aware that they need more than just paper qualifications.* | *acutely embarrassed*

ad /æd/ ●●● S3 W3 *n* [C] *informal* an advertisement → **classified ad** **THESAURUS** ADVERTISEMENT

AD *BrE*, **A.D.** *AmE* /ˌeɪ ˈdiː/ ●●○ (***Anno Domini***) used to show that a date is a particular number of years after the birth of Christ SYN **CE** → **BC**: *the first century AD* | *54 AD*

ad·age /ˈædɪdʒ/ *n* [C] a well-known phrase that says something wise about human experience SYN **proverb**: *the* ***old adage*** *that a picture is worth a thousand words*

a·da·gi·o /əˈdɑːdʒiəʊ $ -dʒoʊ/ *n* (*plural* **adagios**) [C] *technical* a piece of music that should be played or sung slowly —**adagio** *adj, adv*

Ad·am /ˈædəm/ **1** in the Old Testament of the Bible, the first man created by God. God put him in the Garden of Eden, and created Eve, the first woman, from one of Adam's RIBS. He was the father of Cain, Abel, and Seth. **2 not know someone from Adam** *informal* to not know someone at all

ad·a·mant /ˈædəmənt/ *adj* determined not to change your opinion or a decision that you have made: *She begged me to change my mind, but I* ***remained adamant****.* | **[+that]** *Madonna is adamant that she will not tour this year.* —**adamantly** *adv*: *Britain is* ***adamantly opposed to*** *the new directive.*

ˌAdam's ˈapple / $ ˈ.. ˌ./ *n* [C] the lump at the front of your neck that moves when you talk or swallow

a·dapt /əˈdæpt/ ●●○ W3 *v*
1 [I,T] to gradually change your behaviour and attitudes in order to be successful in a new situation: **[+to]** *The children are finding it hard to adapt to the new school.* |

A

flowers which are **well adapted** to harsh winters | The ability to adapt is a definite asset in this job. | **adapt yourself/itself etc (to sth)** How do these insects adapt themselves to new environments?
2 [T] to change something to make it suitable for a different purpose: **adapt sth to do sth** The car has been adapted to take unleaded gas. | **adapt sth for sb** These teaching materials can be adapted for older children.
3 [T] if a book or play is adapted for film, television etc, it is changed so that it can be made into a film, television programme etc → **adaptation**: **be adapted for sth** Many children buy books after they have been adapted for television. GRAMMAR **Adapt** is usually passive in this meaning. —**adapted** adj: She lives in a specially adapted flat.

a·dapt·a·ble /əˈdæptəbəl/ AWL adj [usually after noun] able to change in order to be successful in new and different situations: The American Constitution has proved adaptable in changing political conditions. | **[+to]** The catfish is adaptable to a wide range of water conditions. —**adaptability** /əˌdæptəˈbɪləti/ n [U]

ad·ap·ta·tion /ˌædæpˈteɪʃən/ AWL (also **a·dap·tion** /əˈdæpʃən/) n **1** [C] a film or television programme that is based on a book or play: **[+of]** the BBC adaptation of the best-selling book | **television/film/stage etc adaptation** He's working on a screen adaptation of his latest novel.
2 [U] formal the process of changing something to make it suitable for a new situation: **[+to]** adaptation to the environment

a·dapt·er, **adaptor** /əˈdæptə $ -ər/ n [C] an object that you use to connect two different pieces of electrical equipment, or to connect two pieces of equipment to the same power supply → see picture at PLUG[1]

add /æd/ ●●● S1 W1 v
1 PUT WITH STH ELSE [T] to put something with something else or with a group of other things: If the mixture seems dry, add water. | **add sth to sth** Do you want to add your name to the list? | Suzuki has added extra doors to its sports off-roader. | Material about recent research has been added to this new edition.
2 COUNT [I,T] if you add numbers or amounts together, you calculate their total → **subtract**: **add sth and sth (together)** Add 7 and 5 to make 12. | For tax purposes, your pension and earnings are added together. | **add sth to sth** Add £2.20 to the cost for postage.
3 INCREASE [I,T] to increase the amount or cost of something: **add (sth) to sth** Spell-checking your document adds time to the process. | Sales tax adds to the price.
4 SAY MORE [T] to say more about something that has just been said: 'And I don't care what you think,' she added defiantly. | Is there anything you'd like to add, David? | **[+that]** Everyone will be invited to vote, he said, adding that voting is likely to be via the Web. | I was refused accommodation – not, ***I hasten to add***, on account of my appearance (=used to explain more about what you have just said). | She was trying to entertain us – unsuccessfully, ***I might add*** (=used to comment on what you have just said).
THESAURUS ▸ SAY
5 GIVE A QUALITY [T] to give a particular quality to something: **add sth to sth** We've ***added value*** to the information by organizing it. | **add a touch of glamour/class (to sth)** Champagne always adds a touch of glamour to the occasion. | Coloured glass can be added for effect.
6 add(ed) to that/this used to introduce another fact that supports your opinion: Our hospitals are short of cash. Add to that the long hours doctors work, and you have a recipe for disaster.
7 add weight to sth if something adds weight to an argument, idea etc, it makes it stronger: **add weight to the suggestion/idea etc** Recent research adds weight to the theory that the climate is changing.
8 to add insult to injury to make a bad situation worse for someone who has already been treated badly: She not only deceived him but, to add insult to injury, allowed him to pay for her meal.
9 add fuel to the fire/flames to make an argument or disagreement worse: Rather than providing a solution, their statements merely added fuel to the fire.
add sth ↔ **in** phr v to include something with something else: Don't forget to add in the cost of your time.
add sth ↔ **on** (also **add sth on sth**) phr v to include or put on something extra: proposals to add a penny on income tax | **[+to]** The private chapel was added on to the church much later.
add to sth phr v to make a feeling or quality stronger and more noticeable: This show will no doubt add to his growing reputation.
add up phr v
1 to calculate the total of several numbers: I can add up in my head quite easily. | **add sth ↔ up** Specialized software adds up the statistics.
2 not add up a) if a set of facts does not add up, it does not provide a reasonable explanation for a situation: He was troubled by a feeling that things just didn't add up. **b)** if sums, numbers etc do not add up, there is a mistake in them: These figures don't add up.
3 it all adds up informal used to say that lots of small amounts gradually make a large total: There are five of us using the phone so it all adds up.
add up to sth phr v to produce a particular total or result: Rising prison population and overcrowding add up to a real crisis.

Ad·dams Fam·i·ly /ˈædəmz ˌfæməli/ trademark **the Addams Family** an imaginary family from a US CARTOON STRIP, which was later made into a humorous television programme and films. They wear black clothes and are very interested in death and frightening things. If you describe a family as being like the Addams Family, you mean that they are very strange.

ADD /ˌeɪ diː ˈdiː/ n [U] medical the abbreviation of ***attention-deficit disorder***

ad·ded /ˈædɪd/ ●○○ adj in addition to what is usual or expected SYN **extra**: cereal with added vitamins | no added sugar | **added advantage/bonus/benefit etc** The system has the added advantage of recordable DVD drives. | Include people in your picture for ***added interest***. | **added difficulty/problem etc** Our yard is only small, and has the added disadvantage of facing north. | It may not be necessary to go to the ***added expense of*** updating your anti-virus software.

ad·den·dum /əˈdendəm/ n (plural **addenda** /-də/ or **addendums**) [C] something you add to the end of a speech or book to change it or give more information: **[+to]** an addendum to section 4

ad·der /ˈædə $ -ər/ n [C] a type of poisonous snake

ad·dict /ˈædɪkt/ ●●○ n [C]
1 someone who is unable to stop taking drugs: **drug/heroin/morphine etc addict** a recovering heroin addict
2 someone who is very interested in something and spends a lot of time doing it: **TV/sports etc addict** My nephew is a complete video game addict.

ad·dic·ted /əˈdɪktɪd/ ●●○ adj
1 unable to stop taking a harmful substance, especially a drug: **[+to]** Fifty million Americans are addicted to nicotine.
2 liking something so much that you do not want to stop doing it or having it: **[+to]** kids addicted to surfing the Net

ad·dic·tion /əˈdɪkʃən/ ●●○ n [C,U]
1 the need to take a harmful drug regularly, without being able to stop: **drug/heroin/alcohol etc addiction** | **[+to]** addiction to alcohol
2 a strong desire to do or have something regularly

ad·dic·tive /əˈdɪktɪv/ ●○○ adj
1 if a substance, especially a drug, is addictive, your body starts to need it regularly and you are unable to stop taking it: Tobacco is ***highly addictive***.
2 an activity that is addictive is so enjoyable that you do not want to stop: It started as a hobby, but it got so addictive I had to keep on doing it. | addictive arcade games

ad·di·tion /əˈdɪʃən/ ●●● S3 W1 n
1 in addition used to add another piece of information to what you have just said: The company provides cheap Internet access. In addition, it makes shareware freely

available. | **in addition to sth** *In addition to his movie work, Redford is known as a champion of environmental causes.*
2 [U] the act of adding something to something else: **the addition of sth** *The addition of networking facilities will greatly enhance the system.* | **with the addition of sth** *Turn sparkling wine into Buck's Fizz with the addition of chilled orange juice.*
3 [C] something that is added to something else, often in order to improve it: **[+to]** *This excellent book will be a* ***welcome addition*** *to the library of any student.* | **latest/new/recent addition** *the latest addition to our designer range*
4 [U] the process of adding numbers or amounts to make a total → **subtraction**
5 [C] *AmE* an extra room that is added to a building: *They built a big addition onto the back of the house.*

ad·di·tion·al /əˈdɪʃənəl/ ●●○ W2 *adj* more than what was agreed or expected SYN **extra**: ***Additional information*** *can be obtained from the centre.* | **additional costs/expenditure etc** *An additional charge is made on baggage exceeding the weight allowance.* **THESAURUS** ▸ MORE

> **REGISTER**
> In everyday English, people usually say **extra** rather than **additional**: *He gets* ***extra*** *money from his parents.*

ad·di·tion·al·ly /əˈdɪʃənəli/ ●○○ *adv* [sentence adverb] in addition SYN **also**: *A new contract is in place. Additionally, staff will be offered a bonus scheme.*

ad·di·tive /ˈædətɪv/ *n* [C usually plural] a substance that is added to food to improve its taste, appearance etc: *permitted* ***food additives*** | *Our products are free from* ***artificial additives****.*

ad·dle /ˈædl/ *v* [T] *old-fashioned* to confuse someone so they cannot think properly: **addle sb's brains/wits** *All that drink has addled his brains!*

ˈadd-on *n* [C] **1** something extra that is added to an existing plan, agreement, law etc: **[+to]** *We bought legal protection as an add-on to our home insurance policy.*
2 a piece of equipment that you connect to a computer to improve its performance: *an add-on circuit board* **3** a product that is designed to be used with another product

ad·dress[1] /əˈdres $ əˈdres, ˈædres/ ●●● S2 W2 *n*
1 [C] **a)** the details of the place where someone lives or works, which you use to send them letters etc: *What's your new address?* | *I can give you the address of a good attorney.* **b)** the series of letters and other symbols that you put when sending email to a particular person, or that is the name of a website: *They have changed the address of their website.*
2 [C] a formal speech that someone makes to a group of people: **[+to]** *an address to the European Parliament* | **presidential/inaugural etc address** *The new president* ***delivered*** *his inaugural* ***address*** *in Creole.* **THESAURUS** ▸ SPEECH
3 form/mode/style of address the correct title or name that you should use when speaking or writing to someone

> **COLLOCATIONS**
> **ADJECTIVES/NOUN + address**
> **sb's home/private address** *What's your home address?*
> **sb's work/business/school address** *I sent the letter to her work address.*
> **sb's email address** *I can't find his email address.*
> **a web/website address** *Just type in the web address.*
> **the full address** *They need the full address, including the postcode.*
> **a forwarding address** (=a new address for sending mail to when you move from your old address) | **a false/fake address**
> **VERBS**
> **give sb your address** *She refused to give me her address.*
> **have/know sb's address** *Do you know Helen's address?*
> **lose sb's address** *I wanted to write to him, but I've lost his address.*
> **PHRASES**
> **sb's name and address** *We'll need your full name and address.*
> **a change of address** (=a new address when you move to a different place) | **of no fixed address** (=having no permanent home - used especially in news reports) | **an address book** (=a book or a file on your computer, where you keep people's addresses)

ad·dress[2] /əˈdres/ ●○○ *v* [T]
1 if you address an envelope, package etc, you write on it the name and address of the person you are sending it to: **address sth to sb** *That letter was addressed to me.* | *Send a* ***stamped, self-addressed envelope*** (=with your address on it so it can be sent back to you).
2 *formal* if you address a problem, you start trying to solve it: **address a problem/question/issue etc** *Our products address the needs of real users.* | **address yourself to sth** *Marlowe now addressed himself to the task of searching the room.*
3 *formal* to speak to someone directly: *She turned to address the man on her left.*
4 *formal* if you address remarks, complaints etc to someone, you say or write them directly to that person: *You will have to address your comments to our Head Office.*
5 to make a formal speech to a large group of people: **address a meeting/conference etc** *He addressed an audience of 10,000 supporters.*
6 to use a particular title or name when speaking or writing to someone: **address sb as sth** *The president should be addressed as 'Mr. President'.*

ad·dress·ee /ˌædreˈsiː, əˌdresˈiː/ *n* [C] the person a letter, package etc is addressed to

ad·duce /əˈdjuːs $ əˈduːs/ *v* [T] *formal* to give facts or reasons in order to prove that something is true

ad·e·noid·al /ˌædəˈnɔɪdl◂, ˌædənˈɔɪdl◂/ *adj* an adenoidal voice is unpleasant and sounds as if it comes mainly through someone's nose SYN **nasal**: *her adenoidal singing voice*

ad·e·noids /ˈædənɔɪdz, ˈædən-/ *n* [plural] the small soft pieces of flesh at the top of your throat, behind your nose, that sometimes become swollen

ad·ept /ˈædept, əˈdept $ əˈdept/ *adj* good at something that needs care and skill SYN **skilful**: **[+at]** *Melissa quickly became adept at predicting his moods.* | **[+in]** *Silas proved adept in the art of avoiding potholes in the road.* | *I'm afraid she's also an adept liar.* —**adept** /ˈædept/ *n* [C]: *a form of kung fu practiced by only a handful of adepts* —**adeptly** *adv*

ad·e·quate /ˈædɪkwət/ ●●○ S3 W3 AWL *adj*
1 enough in quantity or of a good enough quality for a particular purpose SYN **sufficient** OPP **inadequate**: *Farmers have been slow to make* ***adequate provision*** *for their retirement.* | *Some creams we tested failed to give adequate protection against UV light.* | *The standard of his work is* ***barely adequate****.* | *The company has yet to provide an adequate explanation for its actions.* | **[+for]** *Are the parking facilities adequate for 50 cars?* | **adequate to do sth** *The lunchtime menu is* ***more than adequate*** *to satisfy the biggest appetite.* **THESAURUS** ▸ ENOUGH
2 fairly good but not excellent → **satisfactory**: *Her performance was adequate but lacked originality.* **THESAURUS** ▸ SATISFACTORY —**adequacy** *n* [U]

ad·e·quate·ly /ˈædɪkwətli/ ●●○ AWL *adv* in a way that is enough for a particular purpose SYN **sufficiently** OPP **inadequately**: *Students need to be adequately prepared for the world of work.* | *She wasn't adequately insured.*

ADHD /ˌeɪ diː eɪtʃ ˈdiː/ *n* [U] *medical* the abbreviation of ***attention-deficit hyperactivity disorder***

ad·here /ədˈhɪə $ -ˈhɪr/ ●○○ *v* [I] *formal* to stick firmly to something: **[+to]** *The eggs of these fish adhere to plant leaves.*

A

A

adhere to sth *phr v formal* to continue to behave according to a particular rule, agreement, or belief: *We* ***adhere to*** *the* ***principles*** *of equal rights and freedom of expression for all.* | *I have* ***adhered*** *strictly* ***to*** *the* ***rules***.

ad·her·ence /ədˈhɪərəns $ -ˈhɪr-/ *n* [U] when someone behaves according to a particular rule, belief, principle etc: **[+to]** ***adherence*** *to democratic* ***principles*** | **strict/rigid/slavish adherence** *strict adherence to Judaic law*

ad·her·ent /ədˈhɪərənt $ -ˈhɪr-/ *n* [C] someone who supports a particular belief, plan, political party etc: **[+of]** *adherents of the Greek Orthodox Church* | **[+to]** *The anti-globalization movement is attracting new adherents to its principles.*

ad·he·sion /ədˈhiːʒən/ *n* **1** [U] when something sticks to something else **2** [C] *medical* a piece of TISSUE (=skin) that grows around a cut or diseased area

ad·he·sive /ədˈhiːsɪv/ *n* [C,U] a substance such as glue that you use to stick two things together: *waterproof adhesive* —**adhesive** *adj*: *adhesive tape*

ad hoc /æd ˈhɒk◂ $ -ˈhɑːk◂,-ˈhoʊk◂/ *adj, adv formal* not planned, but arranged or done only when necessary: **ad hoc committee/group etc** | *decisions made* ***on an ad hoc basis***

a·dieu /əˈdjuː/ *n* (*plural* **adieus** *or* **adieux** /əˈdjuːz/) [C] *literary* goodbye: *He* ***bid*** *her* ***adieu***. —**adieu** *interjection*

ad in·fi·ni·tum /ˌæd ɪnfəˈnaɪtəm/ *adv formal* continuing without ever ending - often used humorously: *I have to explain A, then B, and C, and so on ad infinitum.*

ad·i·os /ˌædiˈɒs $ -ˈoʊs/ *interjection* goodbye

adj. (*also* **adj** *BrE*) the written abbreviation of ***adjective***

ad·ja·cent /əˈdʒeɪsənt/ ●○○ AWL *adj* a room, building, piece of land etc that is adjacent to something is next to it: *We stayed in adjacent rooms.* | **[+to]** *the building adjacent to the library*

ad·jec·tive /ˈædʒəktɪv/ ●●● *n* [C] a word that describes a noun or PRONOUN. In the phrase 'black hat', 'black' is an adjective and in the sentence 'It makes her happy', 'happy' is an adjective. —**adjectival** /ˌædʒəkˈtaɪvəl◂/ *adj*: *an adjectival phrase*

ad·join /əˈdʒɔɪn/ *v* [T] a room, building, or piece of land that adjoins something is next to it and connected to it: *A vacant plot of land adjoins his house.* —**adjoining** *adj* [usually before noun]: *adjoining rooms*

ad·journ /əˈdʒɜːn $ -ɜːrn/ ●○○ *v*
1 [I,T] if a meeting, parliament, law court etc adjourns, or if the person in charge adjourns it, it stops for a short time: *It was almost noon when the meeting adjourned.* | **[+for/until]** *Congress has adjourned for the November elections.* | *His* ***trial*** *was* ***adjourned*** *until May.*
2 adjourn to sth to finish an activity and go somewhere - often used humorously: *The rest of us adjourned to a nearby pub for some refreshments.* —**adjournment** *n* [C,U]: *We sought an adjournment of the proceedings.*

ad·judge /əˈdʒʌdʒ/ *v* [T] *formal* to make a judgment about something or someone SYN **judge**: **be adjudged to be sth/have done sth** | *The reforms of 1979 were generally adjudged to have failed.* GRAMMAR **Adjudge** is usually passive.

ad·ju·di·cate /əˈdʒuːdɪkeɪt/ *v* **1** [I,T] to officially decide who is right in a disagreement and decide what should be done: *The Dean adjudicates any faculty disputes.* | **[+on/upon/in/between]** *The owner can appeal to the court to adjudicate on the matter.* | **adjudicate that** *The judge adjudicated that he should be released.* **2** [I] to be the judge in a competition: *He adjudicated at all the regional music competitions.* —**adjudicator** *n* [C]: *an impartial adjudicator* —**adjudication** /əˌdʒuːdɪˈkeɪʃən/ *n* [U]

ad·junct /ˈædʒʌŋkt/ *n* [C] **1** something that is added or joined to something that is bigger or more important: **[+to]** *Online instruction is a useful adjunct to the real thing.* **2** *technical* an ADVERBIAL word or phrase that adds information to another part of a sentence. In 'They arrived on Sunday', 'on Sunday' is an adjunct.

ad·jure /əˈdʒʊə $ əˈdʒʊr/ *v* [T] *formal* to order or try to persuade someone to do something: **adjure sb to do sth** *Gwen adjured him to be truthful.*

ad·just /əˈdʒʌst/ ●●○ W3 AWL *v*
1 [I,T] to gradually become familiar with a new situation SYN **adapt**: *They'll soon settle in - kids are very good at adjusting.* | **[+to]** *It took a few seconds for her eyes to adjust to the darkness.* | **adjust to doing sth** *My parents had trouble adjusting to living in an apartment.* | **adjust yourself to sth** *It took time to adjust myself to motherhood.*

> **REGISTER**
> In everyday English, people usually say **get used to** rather than **adjust (to)**: *You'll soon* ***adjust***. → *You'll soon* ***get used to it***.

2 [T] to change or move something slightly to improve it or make it more suitable for a particular purpose: *Check and adjust the brakes regularly.* | *Taste the soup and adjust the seasoning.* | *If your employment status changes, your tax code will be adjusted accordingly.*

> **REGISTER**
> In everyday English, people usually say **turn up** or **turn down** the temperature, volume etc rather than **adjust** it.

3 [T] if you adjust something you are wearing, you move it slightly so that it is neater, more comfortable etc: *He paused to adjust his spectacles.* → WELL-ADJUSTED

ad·just·a·ble /əˈdʒʌstəbəl/ *adj* something that is adjustable can be changed or moved slightly to make it suitable for different purposes: *an adjustable spanner*

ad·just·ment /əˈdʒʌstmənt/ ●●○ AWL *n* [C,U]
1 a small change made to a machine, system, or calculation: **[+for]** *Once we* ***make*** *the* ***adjustments*** *for inflation, the fall in interest rates is quite small.* | **[+to]** *a slight adjustment to the mechanism* | **minor/slight adjustment** *It just needs a few minor adjustments.*
2 a change in the way that someone behaves or thinks: *a* ***period of adjustment*** | **[+to]** *her adjustment to her new role*

ad·ju·tant /ˈædʒətənt/ *n* [C] an army officer responsible for office work

ad·land /ˈædlænd/ *n* [U] *informal* the activity or business of advertising, considered as a whole: *Anything that grabs your attention is good in adland.*

ad-lib /ˌæd ˈlɪb/ *v* (**ad-libbed**, **ad-libbing**) [I,T] to say things that you have not prepared or planned when you are performing or giving a speech SYN **improvise**: *I never use a script; I just ad lib the whole programme.* —**ad-lib** *n* [C]

ad·man /ˈædmæn/ *n* (*plural* **admen** /-men/) [C] *informal* someone who works in advertising

ad·min /ˈædmɪn/ *n* [U] *informal* ADMINISTRATION: *an admin assistant* | *She works in admin.*

ad·min·is·ter /ədˈmɪnɪstə $ -ər/ ●○○ *v*
1 [T] to manage the work or money of a company or organization: *The money will be administered by local charities.* | *Our office* ***administers the affairs*** *of the Society.*
2 [I,T] to provide or organize something officially as part of your job: **administer justice/punishment etc** *It is not the job of the police to administer justice; that falls to the courts.* | **[+to]** *Pillai had responsibility for administering to the needs of half a million people.* | **administer sth to sb** *The test was administered to all 11-year-olds.* | **administer an oath** (=be the official person who listens to it)
3 [T] *formal* to give someone a medicine or medical treatment: **administer sth to sb** *Painkillers were administered to the boy.* | *This unit teaches students how to* ***administer first aid***.

ad·min·is·tra·tion /ədˌmɪnəˈstreɪʃən/ ●●○ S3 W3 AWL *n*
1 [U] the activities that are involved in managing the work of a company or organization: *We're looking for someone with experience in administration.* | *The health service spends too much on administration.* | **the administration** (=the people who do this work) *the college administration*

2 [C] the government of a country at a particular time: *the Kennedy Administration* | *The problem has been ignored by successive administrations.* THESAURUS ▶ GOVERNMENT
3 [U] the act of administering something, especially a law, test, or medicine: **[+of]** *the administration of justice* | *the administration of sedatives*

ad·min·is·tra·tive /əd'mɪnəstrətɪv $ -streɪtɪv/ ●●○ W3 AWL *adj* relating to the work of managing a company or organization: *The job is mainly administrative.* | **administrative staff/duties/job etc** *the* ***administrative costs*** *of health care systems* | *an* ***administrative assistant*** | *staff who provide technical and* ***administrative support*** *to the college* —**administratively** *adv*

ad·min·is·tra·tor /əd'mɪnəstreɪtə $ -ər/ ●●○ *n* [C] someone whose job involves managing the work of a company or organization

ad·mi·ra·ble /'ædmərəbəl/ ●○○ *adj formal* having many good qualities that you respect and admire: *an admirable achievement* —**admirably** *adv*

ad·mi·ral /'ædmərəl/ *n* [C] a high rank in the British or US navy, or someone with this rank

Ad·mi·ral·ty /'ædmərəlti/ *n* **the Admiralty** the government department that controls the British navy

ad·mi·ra·tion /ˌædmə'reɪʃən/ ●●○ *n* [U] a feeling of great respect and liking for something or someone: *Daniel gazed at her* ***in admiration.*** | **[+for]** *I wanted to express my admiration for the way the crew handled the crisis.* | **[+of]** *Her riding soon drew the admiration of the older girls.*

COLLOCATIONS

ADJECTIVES

great/deep admiration (=that you feel strongly) *He's a man for whom I have the greatest admiration.*
genuine/real admiration *'Where did you learn to do that?' she asked with genuine admiration.*
a sneaking admiration (=that you secretly feel, but do not show) *I have always had a sneaking admiration for his music.*
open admiration (=that you do not try to hide) *Her father looked at her in open admiration.*
grudging/reluctant admiration (=unwilling admiration) | **mutual admiration** (=that two or more people feel for each other)

PHRASES

be full of admiration/be filled with admiration *I'm full of admiration for what you've done.*

VERBS

have great/deep/a lot of etc admiration *She always had great admiration for people who could speak so many languages.*
win sb's admiration (*also* **draw sb's admiration** *formal*) *His films have won the admiration of the critics.*
express your admiration (=talk or write about your admiration) *She wrote to him expressing her admiration for his work.*
show your admiration

ad·mire /əd'maɪə $ -'maɪr/ ●●● S3 *v* [T]
1 to respect and like someone because they have done something that you think is good, or to respect their qualities or skills: *I really* ***admire the way*** *she brings up those kids all on her own.* | **admire sb for (doing) sth** *Lewis was* ***much admired*** *for his work on medieval literature.*
2 to look at something and think how beautiful or impressive it is: *We stopped halfway to* ***admire the view.*** | *Sal stood back to admire her work.*
3 admire sb from afar *literary* to be attracted to someone, without letting them know

GRAMMAR: Using the progressive

• **Admire** is not used in the progressive in meaning 1. You say: *I admire him for his courage* (=I respect and like him). ✗ Don't say: *I am admiring him.*
• **Admire** is often used in the progressive in meaning 2. You say: *He was admiring himself in the mirror* (=he was looking at himself). You can also say: *He admired himself in the mirror.*
GRAMMAR GUIDE ▶ VERBS

THESAURUS

admire to like someone because they have achieved something special, or they have skills or qualities that you would like to have: *I admire your courage.* | *She admired him for the way he dealt with the situation.*
respect to have a good opinion of someone, even if you do not agree with them, for example because they have achieved a lot or have high standards: *She is respected by all her colleagues at the university.*
revere /rɪ'vɪə $ -'vɪr/ *formal* to greatly admire someone because of their achievements and personal qualities, especially someone famous: *Mandela is revered as one of the great leaders of our time.*
look up to sb to admire someone who is older or who has more experience than you: *All the young comedians look up to him.*
think highly of sb to think that someone is good at what they do: *His teachers seem to think very highly of him.*
idolize to admire someone so much that you think they are perfect – used especially about famous people or people in your family: *He idolized his brother.* | *Jane grew up idolizing Princess Diana.*

ad·mir·er /əd'maɪərə $ -'maɪrər/ ●○○ *n* [C]
1 *literary* someone who likes a person and thinks that they are attractive: *a beautiful woman with many admirers* | *a* ***secret admirer***
2 someone who respects a famous person, especially because they like their work SYN **fan**: *a crowd of fervent admirers* | **[+of]** *'I'm a great admirer of yours,' she managed to stammer.*

ad·mir·ing /əd'maɪərɪŋ $ -'maɪr-/ *adj* [usually before noun] showing that you think someone or something is very impressive or attractive: *admiring glances* —**admiringly** *adv*

ad·mis·si·ble /əd'mɪsəbəl/ *adj* admissible reasons, facts etc are acceptable or allowed, especially in a court of law OPP **inadmissible**: *admissible evidence* —**admissibility** /ədˌmɪsə'bɪləti/ *n* [U]

ad·mis·sion /əd'mɪʃən/ ●●○ W3 *n*
1 [C] a statement in which you admit that something is true or that you have done something wrong SYN **confession**: **admission that** *The Senator's admission that he had lied to Congress shocked many Americans.* | **admission of guilt/defeat/failure etc** *Silence is often interpreted as an admission of guilt.* | *Reese,* ***by his own admission,*** *lacks the necessary experience.*
2 [U] permission given to someone to enter a building or place, or to become a member of a school, club etc: *No admission after 10 pm.* | *The young men tried to enter a nightclub but were* ***refused admission.*** | *Women* ***gained admission*** *to the club only recently.* | **[+to]** *those applying for admission to university*
3 admissions [plural] the process of allowing people to enter a university, institution etc, or the number of people who can enter: **university/college/school admissions** | **admissions policy/procedures etc** *The college has a very selective admissions policy.* | *the* ***admissions officer***
4 [C,U] the process of taking someone into a hospital for treatment, tests, or care: *There are 13,000* ***hospital admissions*** *annually due to playground accidents.*
5 [U] the cost of entrance to a concert, sports event, cinema etc → **admittance**: *Admission: $10 for adults, $5 for children.* | *The cost includes* ***free admission*** *to the casinos.* | *The Museum has no* ***admission charge.***

ad·mit /əd'mɪt/ ●●● S2 W1 *v* (**admitted**, **admitting**)
1 ACCEPT TRUTH [I,T] to agree unwillingly that something is true or that someone else is right: *'Okay, so maybe I was a little bit scared,' Jenny admitted.* | **admit (that)** *You may not like her, but you* ***have to admit*** *that she's good at her job.* | **admit to sb (that)** *Paul admitted to me that he sometimes*

A

feels jealous of my friendship with Stanley. | ***I must admit**, I didn't actually do anything to help her.* | ***Admit it!** I'm right, aren't I?* | **admit (to) doing sth** *Dana admitted feeling hurt by what I had said.* | **freely/openly/frankly etc admit** (=admit without being ashamed) *Phillips openly admits to having an alcohol problem.*

2 ACCEPT BLAME [I,T] to say that you have done something wrong, especially something criminal SYN **confess** OPP **deny**: **admit doing sth** *Greene admitted causing death by reckless driving.* | **admit to (doing) sth** *A quarter of all workers admit to taking time off when they are not ill.* | *After questioning, he admitted to the murder.* | *No organization has **admitted responsibility** for the bombing.* THESAURUS ADMIT

3 ALLOW TO ENTER [T] to allow someone to enter a public place to watch a game, performance etc → **admittance**, **admission**: **admit sb to/into sth** *Only ticket-holders will be admitted into the stadium.*

> **REGISTER**
> In everyday English, people usually say **let** someone **in** rather than **admit** someone: *They won't **let you in** without a ticket.*

4 ALLOW TO JOIN [T] to allow someone to join an organization, club etc: **admit sb to/into sth** *Drake was admitted into the club in 1997.*

5 HOSPITAL [T] if people at a hospital admit someone, that person is taken in to be given treatment, tests, or care: *What time was she admitted?* | **be admitted to hospital** *BrE*, **be admitted to the hospital** *AmE*

6 admit defeat to stop trying to do something because you realize you cannot succeed: *For Haskill, selling the restaurant would be admitting defeat.*

7 admit evidence to allow a particular piece of EVIDENCE to be used in a court of law: *Courts can refuse to admit evidence obtained illegally by police.*

admit of sth *phr v formal* if a situation admits of a particular explanation, that explanation can be accepted as possible: *The facts admit of no other explanation.*

> **GRAMMAR: Comparison**
>
> **admit**
> - You **admit that** you did something: *He admitted that he had made a mistake.*
> - You **admit to** someone **that** you did something: *He admitted to me that he had made a mistake.* ✗ Don't say: *He admitted me that he had made a mistake.*
> - You **admit doing** something: *He admitted making a mistake.* ✗ Don't say: *He admitted to make a mistake.*
>
> **confess**
> - You **confess that** you did something: *He confessed that he had stolen the money.*
> - You **confess to** someone **that** you did something: *He confessed to the police that he had stolen the money.*

> **THESAURUS**
>
> **ADMIT SOMETHING IS TRUE**
>
> **admit** to agree unwillingly that something is true: *He admitted that the company was having financial difficulties.* | ***I must admit** I was disappointed by their reaction.*
>
> **concede** *formal* to admit something in a discussion or argument: *'You may be right,' Bridget conceded.* | *It was a decision which he now concedes was incorrect.*
>
> **acknowledge** /ək'nɒlɪdʒ/ *formal* to say that something is true or that a situation exists: *The report acknowledges that research on animals is not always a reliable guide when it comes to humans.*
>
> **confess** to admit something that you feel embarrassed or ashamed about: *Bradley confessed that he struggled to finish the race.* | ***I must confess** I don't like his wife at all.*
>
> **Granted/I grant you** *formal spoken* used when admitting that something is true, although you do not think it makes much difference to the main point. **Granted** is usually used at the beginning of a sentence, or on its own: *She has a lot of experience, I grant you, but she's not good at managing people.* | *Granted he did play well in the last game, but generally his form hasn't been very good recently.*
>
> **ADMIT YOU HAVE DONE SOMETHING WRONG**
>
> **admit** to say that you have done something wrong, especially something criminal: *He admitted charges of theft and false accounting.* | *Bennett admitted killing his wife.*
>
> **confess** to tell the police or someone in authority that you have done something bad, especially when they have persuaded you to do this: *He finally confessed that he had stolen the money.* | *They told him that if he confessed he would get a lighter sentence.*
>
> **own up** to admit that you have done something wrong, usually something that is not very serious. **Own up** is more informal than **admit** or **confess**: *He owned up to the mistake straight away.*
>
> **fess up** *informal* to admit that you have done something wrong that is not very serious: *Come on, fess up! Where were you last night?*
>
> **come clean** *informal* to finally admit something bad that you have been trying to hide: *They want the government to come clean on where all the money has gone.*

ad·mit·tance /əd'mɪtəns/ *n* [U] *formal* permission to enter a place → **admission**: ***Gaining admittance** to the club was no easy matter.*

ad·mit·ted·ly /əd'mɪtɪdli/ ●○○ *adv* [sentence adverb] used when you are admitting that something is true: *This has led to financial losses, though admittedly on a fairly small scale.*

ad·mix·ture /əd'mɪkstʃə, æd- $ æd'mɪkstʃər/ *n* [C] *technical* a substance that is added to another substance in a mixture

ad·mon·ish /əd'mɒnɪʃ $ -'mɑː-/ *v* [T] *formal* to tell someone severely that they have done something wrong: **admonish sb for (doing) sth** *The witness was admonished for failing to answer the question.* —**admonishment** *n* [C]

ad·mo·ni·tion /ˌædmə'nɪʃən/ *n* [C,U] *formal* a warning or expression of disapproval about someone's behaviour —**admonitory** /əd'mɒnətəri $ -'mɑːnətɔːri/ *adj*: *an admonitory glance*

ad nau·se·am /ˌæd 'nɔːziəm, -iæm $ -'nɒː-/ *adv* if you say or do something ad nauseam, you say or do it so often that it becomes annoying for other people: *Look, we've been over this ad nauseam. I think we should move on to the next item.*

a·do /ə'duː/ *n* **without more/further ado** without delaying or wasting any time: *So without further ado, I'll now ask Mr Davis to open the debate.*

a·do·be /ə'dəʊbi $ ə'doʊ-/ *n* [U] earth and STRAW that are made into bricks for building houses

ad·o·les·cence /ˌædə'lesəns/ ●○○ *n* [U] the time, usually between the ages of 12 and 18, when a young person is developing into an adult

ad·o·les·cent /ˌædə'lesənt◂/ ●○○ *n* [C] a young person, usually between the ages of 12 and 18, who is developing into an adult THESAURUS CHILD, YOUNG —**adolescent** *adj*: *adolescent girls* → CHILD

A·do·nis /ə'dəʊnɪs $ ə'dɑː-/ *n* [C usually singular] an extremely attractive young man

a·dopt /ə'dɒpt $ ə'dɑːpt/ ●●○ S3 W2 *v*

1 CHILD [I,T] to take someone else's child into your home and legally become its parent → **foster**: *Sally was adopted when she was four.* | *The couple are unable to have children of their own, but hope to adopt.*

2 adopt an approach/policy/attitude etc to start to deal with or think about something in a particular way: *The courts were asked to adopt a more flexible approach to young offenders.* | *The store recently adopted a drug testing policy for all new employees.* | *California has adopted a tough stance on the issue.*

3 STYLE/MANNER [T] to use a particular style of speaking, writing, or behaving, especially one that you do not

usually use: *Kim adopts a southern accent when speaking to family back home.*
4 LAW/RULE [T] to formally approve a proposal, AMENDMENT etc, especially by voting: *Congress finally adopted the law after a two-year debate.*
5 NAME/COUNTRY ETC [T] to choose a new name, country, custom etc, especially to replace a previous one: *Stevens became a Muslim and adopted the name Yusuf Islam.* | *Becoming a member of a society means adopting its values.*
6 ELECTION [T] *BrE* to officially choose someone to represent a political party in an election —**adopter** *n* [C] —**adoptee** /əˌdɒpˈtiː $ əˌdɑːp-/ *n* [C]

a·dopt·ed /əˈdɒptɪd $ əˈdɑːp-/ *adj* **1** an adopted child has been legally made part of a family that he or she was not born into: *his adopted son* **2** your adopted country is one that you have chosen to live in permanently

a·dop·tion /əˈdɒpʃən $ əˈdɑːp-/ *n* **1** [C,U] the act or process of adopting a child: *She decided to* ***put*** *the baby* ***up for adoption***. **2** [U] the act of starting to use a particular plan, method, way of speaking etc **3** [U] *BrE* the choice of a particular person to represent a political party in an election

a·dop·tive /əˈdɒptɪv $ əˈdɑːp-/ *adj* [only before noun] an adoptive parent is one who has adopted a child

a·dor·a·ble /əˈdɔːrəbəl/ *adj* someone or something that is adorable is so attractive that they fill you with feelings of love: *Oh what an adorable little baby!*

ad·o·ra·tion /ˌædəˈreɪʃən/ *n* [U] **1** great love and admiration: *the look of adoration in his eyes* **2** *literary* the showing of great love and respect for God

a·dore /əˈdɔː $ əˈdɔːr/ ●○○ *v* [T]
1 to love someone very much and feel very proud of them: *Betty adores her grandchildren.* **THESAURUS** LOVE
2 *informal* to like something very much: *I simply adore chocolate.* **THESAURUS** LIKE

GRAMMAR: Using the progressive

Adore is not used in the progressive. You say: *He adores his students.* | *I adore your cake.* ✗ Don't say: *he is adoring* | *I am adoring*
GRAMMAR GUIDE VERBS

a·dor·ing /əˈdɔːrɪŋ/ *adj* [only before noun] liking and admiring someone very much: *his adoring fans* —**adoringly** *adv*

a·dorn /əˈdɔːn $ -ɔːrn/ *v* [T] *formal* to decorate something: **adorn sth with sth** *church walls adorned with religious paintings*

a·dorn·ment /əˈdɔːnmənt $ -ɔːr-/ *n formal*
1 [C] something that you use to decorate something
2 [U] the act of decorating something

a·dren·a·lin, **adrenaline** /əˈdrenəl-ɪn/ *n* [U] a chemical produced by your body when you are afraid, angry, or excited, which makes your heart beat faster: *There's nothing like a good horror film to* ***get the adrenalin going*** (=make you feel nervously excited).

a·drift /əˈdrɪft/ *adj, adv* **1** a boat that is adrift is not fastened to anything or controlled by anyone: *Several of the lifeboats were still afloat a month after being* ***cast adrift***. **2** someone who is adrift is confused about what to do in their life: *a young woman adrift in London* **3 come adrift** *BrE* if something comes adrift, it is no longer fastened or attached to something: *Her hair was forever coming adrift from the pins she used to keep it in place.* **4 two points/five seconds etc adrift (of sb)** two points, five seconds etc behind someone in a competition, race etc

a·droit /əˈdrɔɪt/ *adj* clever and skilful, especially in the way you use words and arguments SYN **skilled**: *an adroit negotiator* —**adroitly** *adv* —**adroitness** *n* [U]

ADSL /ˌeɪ diː es ˈel/ *n* [U] (***asymmetric digital subscriber line***) a system that makes it possible for information such as video images to be sent to computers through telephone wires at a very high speed

ad·u·la·tion /ˌædʒəˈleɪʃən/ *n* [U] *formal* praise and admiration for someone that is more than they really deserve —**adulatory** /ˌædʒəˈleɪtəri, ˈædʒəleɪtəri $ ˈædʒələtɔːri/ *adj*

ad·ult¹ /ˈædʌlt, əˈdʌlt/ ●●● S2 W2 AWL *n* [C]
1 a fully-grown person, or one who is considered to be legally responsible for their actions → **child**: *Some children find it difficult to talk to adults.*
2 a fully-grown animal: *The adults have white bodies and grey backs.*

adult² ●●● W3 AWL *adj*
1 [only before noun] fully grown or developed: *an adult lion* | *the adult population* | *He lived most of his* ***adult life*** *in Scotland.*
2 typical of an adult's behaviour or of the things adults do: *dealing with problems in an adult way* | *That wasn't very adult of you.*
3 [only before noun] adult films, magazines etc are about sex or related to sex: *The film is rated R for language and adult themes.*

ˌadult eduˈcation *n* [U] education provided for adults outside schools and universities, usually by means of classes that are held in the evening

a·dul·ter·ant /əˈdʌltərənt/ *n* [C] *formal* a substance that is secretly added to food or drink, making it less pure

a·dul·ter·ate /əˈdʌltəreɪt/ *v* [T] to make food or drink less pure by adding another substance of lower quality to it → **unadulterated** —**adulteration** /əˌdʌltəˈreɪʃən/ *n* [U]

a·dul·ter·er /əˈdʌltərə $ -ər/ *n* [C] someone who is married and has sex with someone who is not their wife or husband

a·dul·ter·ess /əˈdʌltərɪs/ *n* [C] a married woman who has sex with a man who is not her husband

a·dul·ter·y /əˈdʌltəri/ *n* [U] sex between someone who is married and someone who is not their wife or husband: *She had* ***committed adultery*** *on several occasions.* —**adulterous** *adj*

ad·ult·hood /ˈædʌlthʊd, əˈdʌlt-/ *n* [U] the time when you are an adult OPP **childhood**

ad·um·brate /ˈædʌmbreɪt/ *v* [T] *formal* to suggest or describe something in an incomplete way

adv. (*also* **adv** *BrE*) the written abbreviation of ***adverb***

ad·vance¹ /ədˈvɑːns $ ədˈvæns/ ●●○ W3 *n*
1 in advance (of sth) before something happens or is expected to happen: *I should* ***warn*** *you* ***in advance*** *that I'm not a very good dancer.* | *Many thanks, in advance, for your help.* | **six months/a year etc in advance** *Book tickets 21 days in advance.* | *Could you distribute copies* ***well in advance*** *of the meeting?*
2 be in advance of sb/sth to be more developed or modern than someone or something else: *Their aircraft were in advance of those used by the US.*
3 DEVELOPMENT/IMPROVEMENT [C] a change, discovery, or INVENTION that brings progress: **technological/scientific/medical etc advance** *one of the great technological advances of the 20th century* | *a* ***major advance*** | **[+in]** *Recent advances in genetics have raised moral questions.* | **[+on]** *an advance on previous treatments* | *the* ***advances made*** *in the understanding of mental handicap* **THESAURUS** PROGRESS
4 FORWARD MOVEMENT [C] forward movement or progress of a group of people - used especially to talk about soldiers: **[+on]** *the enemy's advance on St. Petersburg*
5 MONEY [C usually singular] money paid to someone before the usual time, especially someone's salary: *a $500 advance* | **[+on]** *Krebs decided to ask for an advance on his salary.*
6 advances [plural] *formal* an attempt to start a sexual relationship with someone: *She accused her boss of* ***making advances to*** *her.* | *The witness said that he 'went berserk' when she rejected his* ***sexual advances***.
7 INCREASE [C] an increase in the price or value of something - used especially when talking about the STOCK EXCHANGE

advance² ●●○ W3 *v*
1 MOVE FORWARD [I] to move towards someone or something, especially in a slow and determined way - used especially to talk about soldiers: *A line of US tanks slowly advanced.* | **[+on]** *Troops advanced on the rebel stronghold*

(=moved towards it in order to attack it). | **[+across/through/towards]** *The army advanced across the plain.*
2 DEVELOP [I,T] if scientific or technical knowledge advances, or if something advances it, it develops and improves: *Our understanding of human genetics has advanced considerably.* | *The group's research has done much to advance our knowledge of the HIV virus.*
3 MONEY [T] to give someone money before they have earned it: **advance sb sth** *Will they advance you some money until you get your first paycheck?* | **advance sth to sb** *I advanced $1,500 to Kramer last Thursday.*
4 advance your career/a cause/your interests etc to do something that will help you achieve an advantage or success for yourself or someone else: *Jameson agreed to the deal in an effort to advance his political career.*
5 PRICE [I] if the price or value of something advances, it increases – used especially when talking about the STOCK EXCHANGE
6 TIME/DATE [T] *formal* to change the time or date when an event should happen to an earlier time or date: *The meeting has been advanced to ten o'clock.*
7 MACHINE [I,T] *formal* if you advance a film, clock, musical recording etc, or if it advances, it goes forward → ADVANCING

advance[3] *adj* **1 advance planning/warning/booking etc** planning etc that is done before an event: *We received no advance warning of the storm.* **2 advance party/team** a group of people who go first to a place where something will happen to prepare for it **3 advance copy** a copy of a book, record etc that has not yet been made available to the public

ad·vanced /ədˈvɑːnst $ ədˈvænst/ ●●● W3 *adj*
1 very modern: *advanced weapon systems* | *advanced technology* | *high levels of unemployment in the advanced industrial societies*
2 studying or dealing with a school subject at a difficult level: *advanced learners of English* | *advanced physics*
3 having reached a late point in time or development: *The disease was too far advanced to be treated.*
4 advanced age/years used to talk about the age of someone who is old: *Despite his advanced age, he often travelled abroad.*

THESAURUS

advanced using very modern technology and ideas: *technologically advanced nations* | *Their equipment isn't as advanced as ours.*
sophisticated very advanced, and working in a better but often more complicated way than other things: *highly sophisticated weapons* | *As machines become more sophisticated, they become more likely to break down.*
high-tech /ˌhaɪ ˈtek◂/ using very advanced technology, especially electronic equipment and computers: *high-tech industries in Silicon Valley* | *High-tech listening equipment was used to find survivors in the rubble.*
state-of-the-art using the newest and most advanced features, ideas, and materials that are available: *The football club has invested £40 million in state-of-the-art training facilities.* | *The sound system is state-of-the-art.*
cutting-edge cutting-edge technology or research is the most advanced that there is at this time: *The system uses cutting-edge technology to identify and eliminate viruses.*

Adˈvanced ˌlevel *n* [C,U] A LEVEL

adˌvance ˈfee fraud *n* [C,U] another name for 419 SCAM

ad·vance·ment /ədˈvɑːnsmənt $ ədˈvæn-/ *n* [C,U] *formal* progress or development in your job, level of knowledge etc: *career advancement* | *advancements in science*

ad·vanc·ing /ədˈvɑːnsɪŋ $ ədˈvæn-/ *adj* **advancing years/age** the fact of growing older: *Blake had grown much quieter – another sign of his advancing years.*

ad·van·tage /ədˈvɑːntɪdʒ $ ədˈvæn-/ ●●● S2 W1 *n*
1 [C,U] something that helps you to be more successful than others, or the state of having this OPP **disadvantage**: **[+over]** *Her experience meant that she had a big advantage over her opponent.* | *Younger workers tend to* **be at an advantage** (=have an advantage) *when applying for jobs.* | *It might* **be to your advantage** (=it might help you) *to take a computer course of some kind.*
2 [C,U] a good or useful feature that something has: **[+of]** *One of the many advantages of living in New York is that you can eat out at almost any time of day.* | **[+over]** *This printer has several advantages over conventional printers.*
3 take advantage of sb to treat someone unfairly in order to get what you want, especially someone who is generous or easily persuaded: *Don't lend them the car – they're taking advantage of you!*
4 take advantage of sth (to do sth) to use a particular situation to do or get what you want: *I took advantage of the good weather to paint the shed.* | *You'll want to* **take full advantage** *of the beach-front clubs.*
5 use/turn sth to your/good advantage to use something that you have or that happens in order to achieve something: *How could he turn the situation to his advantage?* | *Burns used his family connections to good advantage.*
6 show sth to (good/great) advantage to make the best features of someone or something very noticeable: *Her dress showed her tanned skin to great advantage.*
7 advantage sb used in tennis to show that the person named has won the next point after the score was 40-40

COLLOCATIONS – MEANINGS 1 & 2

VERBS

have an advantage (*also* **enjoy an advantage** *formal*) *Our parents didn't have all the advantages that we have.*
get/gain an advantage *Both teams tried to get an advantage.*
give sb an advantage *His height gives him a big advantage.*
work to your advantage (=make you have an advantage – often used when this is unexpected) *Sometimes a lack of experience can work to your advantage.*
see the advantage (=understand the advantage)

ADJECTIVES

a big/great/massive/huge advantage *It's a great advantage to be able to speak some Spanish.*
a slight advantage (=a small one) *Karpov enjoyed a slight advantage over his opponent.*
an unfair advantage *Companies that receive government subsidies have an unfair advantage.*
a definite/distinct advantage (=one that you can clearly notice) | **a real advantage** (=a definite advantage) | **an added advantage** (=an extra advantage) | **a political advantage** | **a military advantage** | **a psychological advantage**

PHRASES

the advantages and disadvantages of sth *the advantages and disadvantages of living in a big city*
the advantages outweigh the disadvantages (=the advantages are more valuable)

COMMON ERRORS

⚠ Don't say 'a good advantage'. Say **a big advantage** or **a real advantage**.

THESAURUS – MEANING 2

advantage a good feature that something has, which makes it better, more useful etc than other things: *The great advantage of digital cameras is that there is no film to process.*
benefit a feature of something that has a good effect on people's lives: *Regular exercise has many benefits, including reducing the risk of heart disease.*
merit a good feature that something has, which you

consider when you are deciding whether it is the best choice: *The committee will consider the merits of the proposals.*
virtue an advantage that makes you believe that something is a good thing: *They believed in the virtues of culture, civilization, and reason.*
the good/great/best thing about sth *especially spoken* used when mentioning a good feature of something. This phrase is rather informal and you should not use it in formal essays: *The good thing about cycling is that you don't have to worry about getting stuck in a traffic jam.*
the beauty of sth is that used when you want to emphasize that something has a very good or useful feature: *The beauty of the plan is that it is so simple.*

ad·van·taged /ədˈvɑːntɪdʒd $ ədˈvæn-/ *adj formal* having more money, a higher social position etc than someone else OPP **disadvantaged**: *Some of the boys come from* ***less advantaged*** *backgrounds.* | **socially/geographically/economically etc advantaged**

ad·van·ta·geous /ˌædvənˈteɪdʒəs, ˌædvæn-/ ●○○ *adj* helpful and likely to make you successful OPP **disadvantageous**: *He was now in a more advantageous position.* | **[+to]** *terms advantageous to foreign companies* —**advantageously** *adv*

ad·vent /ˈædvent/ ●○○ *n written* **the advent of sth** the time when something first begins to be widely used SYN **coming**: *the advent of the computer*

Advent *n* [U] the period of four weeks before Christmas in the Christian religion

ˈAdvent ˌcalendar *n* [C] a picture on thick paper which has parts like doors with smaller pictures behind them. You open one door each day in December until Christmas.

ad·ven·ti·tious /ˌædvənˈtɪʃəs◂, ˌædven-/ *adj formal* happening by chance SYN **unexpected** —**adventitiously** *adv*

ad·ven·ture /ədˈventʃə $ -ər/ ●●● W2 *n* [C,U]
1 an exciting experience in which dangerous or unusual things happen: *a great adventure* | *Ahab's adventures at sea* | *an adventure story*
2 sense/spirit of adventure willingness to try new things, take risks etc: *Come on – where's your sense of adventure?*

adˌventure ˈplayground *n* [C] *BrE* an area of ground for children to play on, with equipment and structures for climbing on

ad·ven·tur·er /ədˈventʃərə $ -ər/ *n* [C] **1** someone who enjoys adventure: *an adventurer travelling the world* **2** *old-fashioned* someone who tries to become rich or socially important by using dishonest or immoral methods – used to show disapproval

ad·ven·tur·is·m /ədˈventʃərɪzəm/ *n* [U] when someone who is in charge of a government, business, army etc takes dangerous risks

ad·ven·tur·ous /ədˈventʃərəs/ ●○○ *adj*
1 not afraid of taking risks or trying new things: *Andy isn't a very adventurous cook.* **THESAURUS** ▸ BRAVE
2 (*also* **adventuresome** *AmE*) eager to go to new places and do exciting or dangerous things

ad·verb /ˈædvɜːb $ -vɜːrb/ ●●● *n* [C] a word that adds to the meaning of a verb, an adjective, another adverb, or a whole sentence, such as 'slowly' in 'He ran slowly', 'very' in 'It's very hot', or 'naturally' in 'Naturally, we want you to come.' → ADJECTIVE

ad·ver·bi·al /ədˈvɜːbiəl $ -ɜːr-/ *adj technical* used as an adverb: *an adverbial phrase* —**adverbial** *n* [C]

ad·ver·sa·ri·al /ˌædvɜːˈseəriəl $ -vərˈser-/ *adj* an adversarial system, especially in politics and the law, is one in which two sides oppose and attack each other: *the adversarial nature of two-party politics*

ad·ver·sa·ry /ˈædvəsəri $ ˈædvərseri/ ●○○ *n* (*plural* **adversaries**) [C] *formal* a country or person you are fighting or competing against SYN **opponent**: *his* ***old adversary***

ad·verse /ˈædvɜːs $ -ɜːrs/ ●○○ *adj*
1 not good or favourable: *They fear it could have an* ***adverse effect*** *on global financial markets.* | *Miller's campaign has received a good deal of* ***adverse publicity***.
2 adverse conditions conditions that make it difficult for something to happen or exist: *The expedition was abandoned because of adverse weather conditions.* —**adversely** *adv*: *developments which had* ***adversely affected*** *their business*

ad·ver·si·ty /ədˈvɜːsəti $ -ɜːr-/ *n* [U] a situation in which you have a lot of problems that seem to be caused by bad luck: *his courage* ***in the face of adversity***

ad·vert¹ /ˈædvɜːt $ -ɜːrt/ ●●○ S3 *n* [C] *BrE* an advertisement **THESAURUS** ▸ ADVERTISEMENT

ad·vert² /ədˈvɜːt $ -ɜːrt/ *v*
advert to sth *phr v formal* to mention something

ad·ver·tise /ˈædvətaɪz $ -ər-/ ●●○ S3 W3 *v* [I,T]
1 to tell the public about a product or service in order to persuade them to buy it: *They no longer advertise alcohol or cigarettes at sporting events.* | **advertise (sth) on television/in a newspaper etc** *Many companies will only advertise in the Sunday paper.* | **be advertised as sth** *The inn is advertised as being from the early 16th century.* | *Colleges and universities have found that* ***it pays to advertise*** (=advertising brings good results).
2 to make an announcement, for example in a newspaper or on a POSTER, that a job is available, an event is going to happen etc: *a poster advertising the concert* | **[+for]** *I see they're advertising for a new Sales Director.*
3 advertise the fact (that) to let people know something about yourself: *Don't advertise the fact that you're looking for another job.*

ad·ver·tise·ment /ədˈvɜːtəsmənt $ ˌædvərˈtaɪz-/ ●●● S3 *n* [C]
1 (*also* **ad** *informal*, **advert** *BrE*) a picture, set of words, or a short film, which is intended to persuade people to buy a product or use a service, or that gives information about a job that is available, an event that is going to happen etc: **[+for]** *The Sunday papers are full of advertisements for cars.* | *She saw an advertisement for a ski vacation in Vermont.* | *They* ***put an advertisement in*** *'The Morning News', offering a high salary for the right person.* | *The organizers of the concert had* ***taken out*** *a* ***full page advertisement*** *in 'The New York Times'.* | *Only a handful of people* ***answered the advertisement***.
2 be an advertisement for sth to be a good example of something or show how effective it can be: *He's a very good advertisement for the benefits of regular exercise.*

THESAURUS

advertisement: *an* ***advertisement for*** *shampoo* | *They placed an advertisement in the newspaper.*
ad *informal* an advertisement: *She's been in several* ***TV ads***.
advert *BrE* an advertisement: *a job advert* | *He took out a front-page* ***advert for*** *his shop.*
commercial an advertisement on television or radio: *television commercials* | *He was in some* ***commercials for*** *beer.*
trailer an advertisement in the cinema, on television, or online for a film or programme which will be shown soon: *A second trailer for Richard Friedman's film has just been added to the website.*
promotion a series of advertisements for a company's products: *The company has spent more than $300 million on promotions for the brand.*
poster an advertisement on a wall: *They selected a famous artist to do the poster for the upcoming performance.*
billboard (*also* **hoarding** *BrE*) a large sign next to a road, with an advertisement on it: *billboard advertisements* | *A huge hoarding shows two contrasting images.*
flyer a piece of paper with an advertisement on it, often given to you in the street: *Someone was handing out flyers for a new nightclub.*

banner ad an advertisement across the top of a page on the Internet: *Banner ads are becoming more sophisticated.*
junk mail unwanted advertisements that you get in the post: *I never read junk mail.*
spam unwanted emails advertising things: *I'm trying to delete all the spam.*
classified ad (*also* **want ad** *AmE*, **small ad** *BrE*) a short advertisement that you put in a newspaper if you want to buy or sell something: *The bike was advertised for sale in the small ads section.*

ad·ver·tis·er /ˈædvətaɪzə $ -vərtaɪzər/ *n* [C] **1** a person or company that advertises something **2** **Advertiser** used in the names of newspapers: *the Stockport Advertiser*

ad·ver·tis·ing /ˈædvətaɪzɪŋ $ -ər-/ ●●○ W3 *n* [U] the activity or business of advertising things on television, in newspapers etc: *advertising aimed at 18–25 year olds* | *a career in advertising* | **television/radio/newspaper advertising** *Both candidates are spending millions on television advertising.* | **advertising campaign/strategy** *a major advertising campaign* | *the* **advertising slogan** *'Come alive with Pepsi'*

ˈadvertising ˌagency *n* [C] a company that designs advertisements for other companies

ad·ver·to·ri·al /ˌædvɜːˈtɔːriəl $ -vər-/ *n* [C] an advertisement in a newspaper or magazine that is made to look like a normal article

ad·vice /ədˈvaɪs/ ●●● S2 W2 *n* [U] an opinion you give someone about what they should do: *You should have followed my advice.* | **[+on/about]** *advice on saving energy* | *I need some advice about my computer.* | **on sb's advice** *On her doctor's advice* (=because her doctor advised her) *Smith decided to take early retirement.*

GRAMMAR: Comparison

advice
- You give someone **some advice**: *My father gave me some good advice.* ✗ Don't say: *some advices* **Advice** is an uncountable noun and cannot be used in the plural.
- You give someone **a piece of advice**: *My father gave me a piece of good advice.* ✗ Don't say: *an advice*

tip
- You give someone **a tip**: *My father gave me a good tip.*
- **Tip** is a countable noun and can be used in the plural: *I got some good tips.*

advise
- Don't confuse the noun **advice** /ədˈvaɪs/ with the verb **advise** /ədˈvaɪz/. You say: *Can you advise me?* ✗ Don't say: *Can you advice me?*

GRAMMAR GUIDE ▸ NOUNS

COLLOCATIONS

VERBS
give sb some advice *My father once gave me some useful advice.*
get some advice *I decided to get some advice from a specialist.*
ask sb's advice *Can I ask your advice about something?*
ask for advice *If in doubt, always ask for advice.*
take/follow sb's advice (*also* **act on sb's advice** *formal*) (=do what someone advises you to do) *He followed his doctor's advice and went on a low-fat diet.*
listen to sb's advice (*also* **heed sb's advice** *formal*) (=pay attention to someone's advice) | **ignore/disregard sb's advice** (=not do what someone tells you) | **go/turn to sb for advice** | **seek advice** (=try to get some advice) | **offer advice** | **pass on some advice** (=give someone advice that you have learned or been given)

ADJECTIVES
good/excellent/useful/helpful *The book is full of good advice.*
sound (=sensible) *I thought that this was sound advice.*
wrong *Unfortunately all the advice they gave me was wrong.*
bad advice *Financial advisors can be fined if they give bad advice to a client.*
practical advice | **detailed advice** | **professional/expert/specialist advice** | **legal/medical/financial etc advice** | **independent/impartial advice** (=from someone who is not involved and will not get an advantage) | **conflicting advice** (=very different opinions about what you should do)

PHRASES
a piece of advice (*also* **a bit of advice** *informal*) *Let me give you a piece of advice.*
a word of advice *spoken* (=used when advising someone what to do) *A word of advice: look at the small print in the contract very carefully.*

advice + NOUN
an advice centre/service/desk/bureau

adˈvice ˌcolumn *n* [C] part of a newspaper or magazine in which someone gives advice to readers who have written to them about their personal problems SYN **agony column** *BrE* —**advice columnist** *n* [C]

ad·vi·sab·le /ədˈvaɪzəbəl/ *adj* [not before noun] *formal* something that is advisable should be done in order to avoid problems or risks OPP **inadvisable**: *Regular medical check-ups are advisable.* | ***It is advisable*** *to write a career objective at the start of your resume.* —**advisability** /ədˌvaɪzəˈbɪləti/ *n* [U]

ad·vise /ədˈvaɪz/ ●●● S2 W2 *v*
1 [I,T] to tell someone what you think they should do, especially when you know more than they do about something: *She needed someone to advise her.* | **advise sb to do sth** *Evans advised him to leave London.* | *You are* ***strongly advised*** *to take out medical insurance when visiting China.* | **advise sb against (doing) sth** *I'd advise you against saying anything to the press.* | **advise that** *Experts advise that you should avoid being in strong sunlight for long periods.* | **advise caution/patience/restraint etc** (=advise people to be careful, patient etc) *The makers advise extreme caution when handling this material.* | **I/we would advise sb to do sth** (=used when advising someone what to do) *I would advise you to speak to a doctor.* | **'…,' sb advised** *'Make sure that you keep the documents in a safe place,' Otley advised him.* | **sb can advise** *If you need more information, I'm sure your lawyer can advise.*
2 [I,T] to be employed to give advice on a subject about which you have special knowledge or skill: **advise sb on/about sth** *He advises us on tax matters.* | **advise on sth** *She's been asked to advise on training the new sales team.* | **advise sb on sth** *He advises us on tax matters.* | **advise sb (on) how/where/what/when** *Matthew advises people how to invest their money.*
3 [T] *formal* to tell someone about something: **advise sb of sth** *We'll advise you of any changes in the delivery dates.* | ***Keep*** *us* ***advised of*** (=continue to tell us about) *any new developments.* | **advise sb that** *They advised him that the tour would proceed.*
4 you would be well/ill advised to do sth used to tell someone that it is wise or unwise to do something: *You would be well advised to stay in bed and rest.*

GRAMMAR: Comparison

advise
- You **advise** someone **to do** something: *His lawyer advised him to plead guilty.* ✗ Don't say: *His lawyer advised to him to plead guilty.*
- You **advise** someone **that** they **should** do something: *His lawyer advised him that he should plead guilty.*

recommend
- You **recommend** something **to** someone: *One of my friends recommended the restaurant to me.*
- You **recommend that** someone **should** do something: *One of my friends recommended that I should go to the restaurant.*

suggest
- You **suggest** something **to** someone: *Someone suggested the idea to her.*
- You **suggest that** someone **should** do something: *Someone suggested that she should write a book about her experiences.*

GRAMMAR GUIDE ▸ VERBS

THESAURUS

advise to tell someone what you think they should do, especially when you have more experience or knowledge than they do: *My lawyer advised me to plead guilty.*
give advice to advise someone about questions relating to a particular subject: *They give advice to people about loans. | Can I give you some advice?*
tell to tell someone what you think they should do, especially in order to avoid problems: *My dad told me to talk to a teacher if I was being bullied. | I told her not to worry.*
recommend to advise someone to do something, especially after careful study of that subject: *Doctors recommend eating five portions of fruit and vegetables each day.*
suggest to tell someone your ideas about what they should do: *I suggested they should visit the cathedral while they're here.*
urge to strongly advise someone to do something: *Police have urged anyone with information about the murder to contact them.*

ad·vis·ed·ly /ədˈvaɪzɪdli/ *adv formal* after careful thought SYN **deliberately**: *He behaved like a dictator, and I use the term advisedly.*

ad·vis·er, **advisor** /ədˈvaɪzə $ -ər/ ●●○ S3 W3 *n* [C] someone whose job is to give advice because they know a lot about a subject, especially in business, law, or politics: *a financial adviser*

ad·vi·so·ry[1] /ədˈvaɪzəri/ ●○○ *adj* having the purpose of giving advice: **advisory committee/body** *the Environmental Protection Advisory Committee* | **advisory role/capacity** *He was employed in a purely advisory role.*

advisory[2] *n* (*plural* **advisories**) [C] *AmE* an official warning or notice that gives information about a dangerous situation: *The State Department issues travel advisories about conditions overseas.*

ad·vo·ca·cy /ˈædvəkəsi/ AWL *n* [U] public support for a course of action or way of doing things

ad·vo·cate[1] /ˈædvəkeɪt/ ●●○ AWL *v* [I,T] to publicly support a particular way of doing something: *Extremists were openly advocating violence.* | **[+for]** *AmE: Those who advocate for doctor-assisted suicide say the terminally ill should not have to suffer.* THESAURUS ▸ RECOMMEND

ad·vo·cate[2] /ˈædvəkət, -keɪt/ ●●○ AWL *n* [C]
1 someone who publicly supports someone or something SYN **proponent**: **[+of]** *She's a passionate advocate of natural childbirth.* | **[+for]** *an advocate for the disabled*
2 a lawyer who speaks in a court of law, especially in Scotland → DEVIL'S ADVOCATE

ad·ware /ˈædweə $ -wer/ *n* [U] software that includes a program that makes advertisements appear on your computer while the software is running

adze, **adz** /ædz/ *n* [C] a sharp tool with the blade at a right angle to the handle, used to shape wood

ae·gis /ˈiːdʒɪs/ *n formal* **under the aegis of sb/sth** with the protection or support of a person or organization: *a refugee camp operating under the aegis of the UN*

ae·on, **eon** /ˈiːən/ *n* [C] an extremely long period of time

aer·ate /ˈeəreɪt $ ˈer-/ *v* [T] *technical* to put a gas or air into a liquid or into soil

aer·i·al[1] /ˈeəriəl $ ˈer-/ ●○○ *adj* [only before noun]
1 from a plane: *an aerial attack | aerial photographs | an aerial view of the Three Gorges Dam project*
2 in or moving through the air

aerial[2] *n* [C] **1** a piece of equipment for receiving or sending radio or television signals, usually consisting of a piece of metal or wire SYN **antenna** *AmE* → see picture at CAR **2 aerials** a sport in which someone goes down a mountain on SKIS and performs complicated jumps and turns in the air

aer·i·al·ist /ˈeəriəlɪst $ ˈer-/ *n* [C] someone who goes down a mountain on SKIS and performs complicated jumps and turns in the air

aero- /eərəʊ, eərə $ eroʊ, -rə/ *prefix* concerning the air or aircraft: *aerodynamics* (=the science of movement through air) | *an aeroengine*

aer·o·bat·ics /ˌeərəˈbætɪks, ˌeərəʊ- $ ˌerə-/ *n* [plural] tricks done in a plane that involve making difficult or dangerous movements in the air

ae·ro·bic /eəˈrəʊbɪk $ eˈroʊ-/ *adj* **1** *technical* using oxygen OPP **anaerobic** **2 aerobic exercise** a type of exercise intended to strengthen the heart and lungs: *running, swimming, and other forms of aerobic exercise*

aer·o·bics /eəˈrəʊbɪks $ eˈroʊ-/ *n* [U] a very active type of physical exercise done to music, usually in a class

GRAMMAR: Singular or plural verb?

Aerobics is followed by a singular verb: ***Aerobics is*** *fun when you do it to music.*

GRAMMAR GUIDE ▸ NOUNS

aer·o·drome /ˈeərədrəʊm $ ˈerədroʊm/ *n* [C] *BrE old-fashioned* a place that small planes fly from

aer·o·dy·nam·ic /ˌeərəʊdaɪˈnæmɪk◂ $ ˌeroʊ-/ *adj*
1 an aerodynamic car, design etc uses the principles of aerodynamics to achieve high speed or low use of petrol
2 *technical* related to or involving aerodynamics: *aerodynamic efficiency* —**aerodynamically** /-kli/ *adv*

aer·o·dy·nam·ics /ˌeərəʊdaɪˈnæmɪks $ ˌeroʊ-/ *n*
1 [U] the scientific study of how objects move through the air **2** [plural] the qualities needed for something to move smoothly through the air

GRAMMAR: Singular or plural verb?
- In meaning 1, **aerodynamics** is followed by a singular verb: ***Aerodynamics is*** *an important science in vehicle design.*
- In meaning 2, **aerodynamics** is followed by a plural verb: *The car's* ***aerodynamics are*** *very advanced.*

aer·o·gramme (*also* **aerogram** *AmE*) /ˈeərəgræm $ ˈerə-/ *n* [C] a very light letter you send by AIRMAIL

aer·o·nau·tics /ˌeərəˈnɔːtɪks $ ˌerəˈnɒː-/ *n* [U] the science of designing and flying planes —**aeronautical** *adj*

aer·o·plane /ˈeərəpleɪn $ ˈerə-/ *BrE*, **airplane** *AmE n* [C] a flying vehicle with wings and at least one engine SYN **plane** → AIRCRAFT

aer·o·sol /ˈeərəsɒl $ ˈerəsɑːl/ *n* [C] a small metal container with liquid inside. You press a button on the container to make the liquid come out in very small drops. → **spray**

aerospace /ˈeərəʊspeɪs $ ˈeroʊ-/ *n* [U] the industry that designs and builds aircraft and space vehicles: **aerospace company/worker etc** *employment in the aerospace industry*

aes·thete, **esthete** /ˈiːsθiːt $ ˈes-/ *n* [C] *formal* someone who loves and understands beautiful things, such as art and music

aes·thet·ic[1], **esthetic** /iːsˈθetɪk, es- $ es-/ ●○○ *adj* connected with beauty and the study of beauty: *From an esthetic point of view, it's a nice design. | a work of great aesthetic appeal* —**aesthetically** /-kli/ *adv*: *aesthetically pleasing*

aesthetic[2] *n formal* **1 aesthetics** [U] the study of beauty,

A

especially beauty in art **2** [C] a set of principles about beauty or art: *a new aesthetic*

ae·ther /ˈiːθə $ -ər/ *n* [U] an old spelling of ETHER (=the air or sky)

ae·ti·ol·o·gy, **etiology** /ˌiːtiˈɒlədʒi $ -ˈɑːl-/ *n* [U] *medical* the study of what causes disease

a·far /əˈfɑː $ əˈfɑːr/ *adv literary* **from afar** from a long distance away: *I saw him from afar.*

af·fa·ble /ˈæfəbəl/ *adj* friendly and easy to talk to SYN **pleasant**: *an affable guy* —**affably** *adv* —**affability** /ˌæfəˈbɪləti/ *n* [U]

af·fair /əˈfeə $ əˈfer/ ●●● S2 W1 *n* [C]

1 PUBLIC/POLITICAL ACTIVITIES **affairs** [plural] **a)** public or political events and activities: *Are you interested in world affairs? | the Ministry of Foreign Affairs | Women had little role in public affairs.* **b)** things connected with your personal life, your financial situation etc: *I am not prepared to discuss my financial affairs with the press.* → **state of affairs** at STATE[1](8)

2 EVENT **a)** an event or set of related events, especially one that is impressive or shocking: *the Watergate affair | The whole affair was a disaster.* **b)** used when describing an event: *The party was a very grand affair.* THESAURUS EVENT

3 RELATIONSHIP a secret sexual relationship between two people, when at least one of them is married to someone else SYN **love affair**: **[+with]** *He **had an affair** with his boss that lasted six years.*

4 OBJECT *informal old-fashioned* used when describing an object, machine etc: *The computer was one of those little portable affairs.*

5 be sb's affair if something is your affair, it only concerns you and you do not want anyone else to get involved in it: *What I do in my free time is my affair.*

COLLOCATIONS

ADJECTIVES

world/international affairs *China is now a major player in world affairs.*
current affairs (=important events that are happening now) *a 24-hour news and current affairs channel*
sb's private affairs (=things that are personal and not for other people to know about) *He never discussed his private affairs in public.*
sb's financial affairs *They offer advice on managing your financial affairs.*
sb's business affairs | **economic affairs** | **political affairs** | **military affairs** | **religious affairs** | **foreign/external affairs** (=events in other countries) | **domestic/internal affairs** (*also* **home affairs** *BrE*) (=events inside a country) | **public affairs** (=events that affect the people of a country)

PHRASES

affairs of state (=the business of the government) *The church played no role in the affairs of state.*
put your affairs in order (=organize them before you go somewhere or die)

af·fect /əˈfekt/ ●●● S2 W1 AWL *v* [T]

1 to do something that produces an effect or change in something or in someone's situation: *the areas affected by the hurricane | a disease that affects the central nervous system | decisions which **affect** our **lives** | Trading has been **adversely affected** by the downturn in consumer spending.*

2 to make someone feel strong emotions: *We were all **deeply affected** by her death.* GRAMMAR **Affect** is often passive in this meaning.

3 *formal* to pretend to have a particular feeling, way of speaking etc: *As usual, Simon affected complete boredom. | He used to affect a foreign accent.*

GRAMMAR: Comparison

affect
• You say that something **affects** another thing: *Smoking affects your health.* ✗ Don't say: *Smoking affects on your health.*

have an effect
• You say that something **has an effect on** another thing: *Smoking has a bad effect on your health.*

af·fec·ta·tion /ˌæfekˈteɪʃən/ *n* [C,U] a way of behaving, speaking etc that is not sincere or natural: *Calling everyone 'darling' is just an affectation.*

af·fect·ed /əˈfektɪd/ *adj* not sincere or natural: *an affected laugh*

af·fect·ing /əˈfektɪŋ/ *adj formal* producing strong emotions of sadness, pity etc SYN **upsetting**: *a deeply affecting story*

af·fec·tion /əˈfekʃən/ ●●○ *n* [singular, U]

1 a feeling of liking or love and caring SYN **fondness**: **[+for]** *Bart **had** a **deep affection** for the old man. | She looked back on those days **with affection**. | Their father never **showed** them much **affection**. | The church was **held in great affection** (=loved and cared about a lot) by the local residents.*

2 sb's affections the feelings of love and caring that someone has: *Africa has always had a special place in my affections.*

af·fec·tion·ate /əˈfekʃənət/ ●○○ *adj* showing in a gentle way that you love someone and care about them SYN **loving**: **[+towards]** *Jo is very affectionate towards her. | an affectionate hug* —**affectionately** *adv*

af·fec·tive /əˈfektɪv/ *adj medical or technical* relating to or having an effect on the emotions: *affective disorders*

afˌfective comˈputing *n* [U] *technical* computing in which the computer measures the user's emotional state and then uses this information in order to change the way it reacts to the user

af·fi·da·vit /ˌæfɪˈdeɪvɪt/ *n* [C] *law* a written statement that you swear is true, for use as proof in a court of law

af·fil·i·ate[1] /əˈfɪlieɪt/ *v* **1** [I,T] if a group or organization affiliates to or with another larger one, it forms a close connection with it: **[+with]** *The Society is not affiliated with any political party.* | **[+to]** *the church's right to affiliate to Rome* **2 affiliate yourself to/with sb/sth** to join or become connected with a larger group or organization: *She affiliated herself with the Impressionist school of painting.*

af·fil·i·ate[2] /əˈfɪliət/ *n* [C] a company, organization etc that is connected with or controlled by a larger one: *Volvo's Japanese affiliate, Mitsubishi*

af·fil·i·at·ed /əˈfɪlieɪtɪd/ *adj* [only before noun] **an affiliated organization/club/member etc** an organization, club etc that is a member of a larger group or organization, or is closely connected with it: *The Association provides information on affiliated clubs.*

af·fil·i·a·tion /əˌfɪliˈeɪʃən/ *n* **1** [C,U] the connection or involvement that someone or something has with a political, religious etc organization: **sb's (political/religious etc) affiliation** *the newspaper's political affiliations*
2 [U] when a smaller group or organization joins a larger one

af·fin·i·ty /əˈfɪnəti/ ●○○ *n* (*plural* **affinities**)

1 [singular] a strong feeling that you like and understand someone or something: **[+with/for/between]** *his remarkable affinity with animals*

2 [C,U] a close relationship between two things because of qualities or features that they share: **[+with/between]** *the affinity between Christian and Chinese concepts of the spirit*

afˈfinity ˌcard *n* [C] a type of CREDIT CARD, where an amount of money is given by the credit card company to a CHARITY every time the card is used

af·firm /əˈfɜːm $ -ɜːrm/ ●○○ *v* [T] *formal*

1 to state publicly that something is true SYN **confirm**: *The general affirmed rumors of an attack.* | **affirm that** *A spokesman for the company affirmed that a merger was likely.*

2 to strengthen a feeling, belief, or idea: *He claims that modern physics affirms his Christian beliefs.* —**affirmation** /ˌæfəˈmeɪʃən $ ˌæfər-/ *n* [C,U]

af·fir·ma·tive[1] /əˈfɜːmətɪv $ -ɜːr-/ *adj formal* an affirmative answer or action means 'yes' or shows agreement OPP **negative**: *an affirmative nod* —**affirmatively** *adv*

affirmative² *n* **answer/reply in the affirmative** *formal* to say 'yes' → **answer/reply in the negative** at NEGATIVE²(2)

af,firmative 'action *n* [U] *especially AmE* the practice of choosing people for a job, college etc who are usually treated unfairly because of their race, sex etc SYN **positive discrimination** *BrE*

af·fix¹ /əˈfɪks/ *v* [T] *formal* to fasten or stick something to something else: **affix sth to sth** *A label must be affixed to all parcels.* GRAMMAR **Affix** is often passive.

af·fix² /ˈæfɪks/ *n* [C] a group of letters added to the beginning or end of a word to change its meaning or use, such as 'un-', 'mis-', '-ness', or '-ly' → PREFIX¹(1), SUFFIX

af·flict /əˈflɪkt/ ●○○ *v* [T] *formal* to affect someone or something in an unpleasant way, and make them suffer: **be afflicted with/by sth** *a country afflicted by famine*

af·flic·tion /əˈflɪkʃən/ *n* [C,U] *formal* something that causes pain or suffering, especially a medical condition: *the afflictions of old age*

af·flu·ent /ˈæfluənt/ ●○○ *adj formal* having plenty of money, nice houses, expensive things etc SYN **wealthy**: *affluent families* | **an affluent society/area etc** *the affluent Côte d'Azur* THESAURUS ▸ RICH —**affluence** *n* [U]

af·ford /əˈfɔːd $ -ɔːrd/ ●●● S1 W3 *v* [T]

1 can/could afford [usually negative] **a)** to have enough money to buy or pay for something: **afford (to do) sth** *We can't afford to go on vacation this year.* | *I couldn't afford the rent on my own.* | *How can she afford to eat out every night?* **b)** to have enough time to do something: *Dad can't afford any more time off work.* **c)** if you cannot afford to do something, you must not do it because it could cause serious problems for you: **afford to do sth** *We can't afford to wait any longer or we'll miss the plane.*

> **GRAMMAR**
> **Afford** is followed by an infinitive with 'to': *I can't afford to buy a car.* ✗ Don't say: *can't afford buying* | *can't afford buy*
> GRAMMAR GUIDE ▸ VERBS

2 *formal* to provide something or allow something to happen: *The room* ***affords*** *a beautiful* ***view*** *over the city.* | **afford (sb) an opportunity/chance** *It afforded her the opportunity to improve her tennis skills.* | *The new law will* ***afford protection*** *to employees.*

af·ford·a·ble /əˈfɔːdəbəl $ -ɔːrd-/ ●○○ *adj* cheap enough for most people to afford: *affordable housing* | *This is a top-quality product at a very affordable price.*

af·for·es·ta·tion /əˌfɒrəˈsteɪʃən $ əˌfɔː-, əˌfɑː-/ *n* [U] *technical* the act of planting trees in order to make a forest OPP **deforestation**

af·fray /əˈfreɪ/ *n* [C,U] *law* a noisy fight in a public place, or when someone is involved in such a fight

af·fri·cate /ˈæfrɪkət/ *n* [C] *technical* a PLOSIVE sound such as /t/ or /d/ that is immediately followed by a FRICATIVE sound made in the same part of the mouth, such as /s/ or /ʒ/. The word 'church', for example, contains the affricate /tʃ/.

af·front¹ /əˈfrʌnt/ *v* [T] *formal* to offend or insult someone, especially by not showing respect: **be affronted by sth** *He stepped back, affronted by the question.*

affront² *n* [C usually singular] a remark or action that offends or insults someone: **[+to]** *The comments were an affront to his pride.*

Af·ghan¹ /ˈæfgæn/ *adj* relating to Afghanistan or its people

Afghan² *n* [C] **1** someone from Afghanistan **2** (*also* **Afghan hound**) a tall thin dog with a pointed nose and very long silky hair

a·fi·cio·na·do /əˌfɪʃəˈnɑːdəʊ $ -doʊ/ *n* (*plural* **aficionados**) [C] someone who is very interested in a particular activity or subject and knows a lot about it: **[+of]** *an aficionado of fine food*

a·field /əˈfiːld/ *adv* **far/further/farthest afield** far away, especially from home: *They were exporting* ***as far afield as*** *Alexandria.* | *students who come* ***from further afield***

a·fire /əˈfaɪə $ əˈfaɪr/ *adj, adv* [not before noun] *literary* burning SYN **ablaze**: *One of the boats had been* ***set afire***.

a·flame /əˈfleɪm/ *adj* [not before noun] **1** burning SYN **ablaze**: *Most of the city was aflame.* **2** very bright with colour or light SYN **ablaze**: **[+with]** *trees aflame with autumn leaves* **3** filled with strong emotions or excitement —**aflame** *adv*

AFL-CIO, the /ˌeɪ ef ˌel ˌsiː aɪ ˈəʊ $ -ˈoʊ/ (***the American Federation of Labor and Congress of Industrial Organizations***) an organization of American TRADE UNIONS

a·float /əˈfləʊt $ əˈfloʊt/ *adj* [not before noun] **1** having enough money to operate or stay out of debt: **keep (sb/sth) afloat/stay afloat** *The Treasury borrowed £40 billion, just to stay afloat.* **2** floating on water: **keep (sb/sth) afloat/stay afloat** *Somehow we kept the ship afloat.* —**afloat** *adv*

a·foot /əˈfʊt/ *adj* [not before noun] being planned or happening: **moves/plans/changes afoot** *There were plans afoot for a second attack.* —**afoot** *adv*

a·fore·men·tioned /əˈfɔːmenʃənd $ ˈæfərˌmenʃənd, əˈfɔːr-/ (*also* **a·fore·said** /əˈfɔːsed $ əˈfɔːr-/) *adj* [only before noun] *law* **the aforementioned** mentioned before in an earlier part of a document, article, book etc: *The property belongs to the aforementioned Mr Jones.* —**aforementioned** *n* [singular or plural]

a·fore·thought /əˈfɔːθɔːt $ əˈfɔːrθɒːt/ *adj* → **with malice aforethought** at MALICE(2)

a·foul /əˈfaʊl/ *adv* **run afoul of sb/sth** *formal* to do something that is not allowed or legal, or that is against people's beliefs

a·fraid /əˈfreɪd/ ●●● S1 W2 *adj* [not before noun]

1 frightened because you think that you may get hurt or that something bad may happen SYN **scared**: **be/feel afraid** *There's no need to be afraid.* | **afraid of sth** *Many children are afraid of the dark.* | **afraid of sb** *I was* ***a little afraid*** *of him when I first met him.* | **afraid of doing sth** *Some old people are afraid of going out alone.* | **afraid to do sth** *Zoe was afraid to go back into the house.* THESAURUS ▸ FRIGHTENED

> **REGISTER**
> In everyday English, people often say **scared** rather than **afraid**: *I'm* ***scared*** *of heights.*

2 worried that something bad will happen as a result of your actions: **afraid (that)** *He was afraid that the other kids would laugh at him.* | *She was* ***half afraid*** *that he would say no* (=a little afraid). | **afraid of doing sth** *I didn't tell her because I was afraid of upsetting her.* | **afraid of sth** *The government was afraid of the reaction from the public.* | **afraid to do sth** *Don't be afraid to ask for help.*

3 afraid for sb/sth worried that something bad may happen to a particular person or thing: *Her father looked ill and she was suddenly afraid for him.* | *Many of us were afraid for our jobs.*

4 I'm afraid *spoken* used to politely tell someone something that may annoy, upset, or disappoint them: *That's the most we can offer you, I'm afraid.* | **[+(that)]** *I'm afraid you've come to the wrong address.* | *'Is she very ill?'* ***'I'm afraid so*** (=yes).' | *'Did you see him?'* ***'I'm afraid not*** (=no).'

> **GRAMMAR: Comparison**
> **afraid, frightened, scared**
> • You feel **afraid of** someone or something: *A lot of people are afraid of snakes.* ✗ Don't say: *afraid about something*
> • You feel **afraid to** do something: *I was afraid to tell anyone.*
> • You can use the same patterns with **frightened** and **scared**: *I was* ***frightened of*** *my father.* | *She was too* ***scared to*** *talk.*
> **worried**
> • You feel **worried about** someone or something: *I was worried about my father.*

A

• You feel **worried by** something that has happened: *Many people were worried by the news.*

a·fresh /əˈfreʃ/ *adv* if you do something afresh, you do it again from the beginning SYN **anew**: *He moved to America to* ***start afresh***.

Af·ri·can¹ /ˈæfrɪkən/ *adj* relating to Africa or its people

African² *n* [C] someone from Africa

ˌAfrican Aˈmerican *n* [C] an American with dark skin, whose family originally came from the part of Africa south of the Sahara Desert

Af·ri·kaans /ˌæfrɪˈkɑːns/ *n* [U] a language of South Africa that is similar to Dutch

Af·ri·ka·ner /ˌæfrɪˈkɑːnə $ -ər/ *n* [C] a white South African whose first language is Afrikaans and who is usually related to the Dutch people who settled in South Africa in the 1600s → **Boer**

Af·ro /ˈæfrəʊ $ -roʊ/ *n* [C] a hairstyle popular with black people in the 1970s in which the hair is cut into a large round shape

Afro- /æfrəʊ $ -roʊ/ *prefix* [in nouns and adjectives] African and something else: *an Afro-American | Afro-Caribbean children*

Af·ro·beat /ˈæfrəʊbiːt $ -roʊ-/ *n* [U] a style of African popular music that is a mixture of American FUNK and African PERCUSSION and singing styles

aft /ɑːft $ æft/ *adj, adv technical* in or towards the back part of a boat or aircraft OPP **fore (2)**

af·ter¹ /ˈɑːftə $ ˈæftər/ ●●● S1 W1 *prep, conjunction, adv*

1 when a particular event or time has happened, or when someone has done something OPP **before**: *After the war many soldiers stayed in France. | I go swimming every day after work. | Do you believe in life after death? | The first attack started just after midnight. | David went to bed* ***straight after*** (=immediately after) *supper. | After you'd called the police, what did you do? | Zimmerman changed his name after he left Germany. | People still remember the 1958 revolution and what* ***came after*** (=happened after it). | **after doing sth** *After leaving school, Mackay worked in a restaurant for a year.* | **two days/three weeks etc after (sth)** *Ten years after he bought the painting, Carswell discovered that it was a fake.* | **the day/week/year etc after (sth)** (=the next day, week etc) *His car was outside your house the morning after Bob's engagement party. | I'll see you again tomorrow or the day after. | She retired from politics the year after she received the Nobel Prize.* | **soon/not long/shortly after (sth)** *Not long after the wedding, his wife became ill. | The family moved to Hardingham in June 1983, and Sarah's first child was born soon after.*

2 when a particular amount of time has passed OPP **before**: *After ten minutes remove the cake from the oven. | You'll get used to it after a while. | After months of negotiation, an agreement was finally reached.*

3 following someone or something else in a list or a piece of writing, or in order of importance: *Whose name is after yours on the list? | The date should be written after the address. | After football, tennis is my favourite sport. | The UK is the world's third largest arms producer, after the USA and Russia.*

4 *AmE* used when telling the time to say how many minutes have passed since a particular hour SYN **past** *BrE*: *The movie starts at a quarter* (=fifteen minutes) *after seven.*

5 day after day/year after year etc continuously for a very long time: *He's worked in that same office week after week, year after year, since he was 18.*

6 a) following someone in order to stop or speak to them: *Go after him and apologize. | I heard someone running after me, and a voice called my name.* **b)** in the direction of someone who has just left: *'Good luck,' she called after me as I left. | Harry stood in the doorway gazing after her.*

7 when someone has left a place or has finished doing something: *Remember to close the door after you. | I spend all day cleaning up after the kids.*

8 because of something that happened earlier: *I'm not surprised he walked out, after the way she treated him. | After your letter, I didn't think I'd ever see you again.*

9 in spite of something that was done in the past: *How can you treat me like this after all I've done for you?*

10 when you have passed a particular place or travelled a certain distance along a road: *Turn left after the hotel. | After a mile you will come to a crossroads.*

11 be after sb/sth a) to be looking for someone or something: *That boy's always in trouble – the police are after him again. | 'Were you after anything in particular?' 'No, we're just looking.'* **b)** *informal* to want to have something that belongs to someone else: *I think Chris is after my job.*

12 one after another/one after the other if a series of events or actions happen one after another, each one happens soon after the previous one: *Ever since we moved here it's been one problem after another.*

13 after all a) in spite of what you thought was true or expected to happen: *He wrote to say they couldn't give me a job after all. | Union leaders announced that they would, after all, take part in the national conference.* **b)** used to say that something should be remembered or considered, because it helps to explain what you have just said: *Prisoners should be treated with respect – they are human beings after all. | I don't know why you're so concerned – it isn't your problem after all.*

14 *especially BrE* used to say who or what first had the name that someone or something has been given: *His name is Alessandro, after his grandfather. | It was named Waterloo Bridge, after the famous battle.*

15 *formal* in the same style as a particular painter, musician etc: *a painting after Rembrandt*

16 a) after you *spoken* used to say politely that someone else can use or do something before you do: *'Do you need the copier?' 'After you.'* **b) after you with sth** used to ask someone if you can have or use something after they have finished: *After you with that knife, please.* → **a man/woman after my own heart** at HEART¹(22), → **take after** at TAKE¹

THESAURUS

after *prep* after something happens, or after a period of time has passed. **After** is used especially when talking about the past: *We went for a walk after lunch. | After an hour, we got tired of waiting and went home.*

in *prep* after a particular period of time. **In** is used especially when talking about the future, especially the next few minutes, hours, days etc: *The concert's due to start in a few minutes. | I'll come back in an hour. | In a few years' time, this place will look completely different.*

within *prep* after less than a month, two weeks etc has passed – used especially when the time seems surprisingly short: **within a month/two weeks etc**: *Within two days of arriving she had managed to upset everyone.*

24 hours/a year etc from now at a time 24 hours, a year etc after now: *A week from now we'll be in Paris.*

afterwards (*also* **afterward** *especially AmE*) *adv* after an event or time you have mentioned: *He moved to Belgium, and* ***soon afterwards*** *he met Angela.*

later *adv* some time after now or after the time you are talking about: *I'll tell you about it later when I'm less busy.* | **two months/three years etc later**: *James went off, and came back ten minutes later with some food.*

subsequently *adv formal* after something had happened in the past: *The book was published in 1954 and was subsequently translated into fifteen languages.*

after² *adj* [only before noun] **1 in after years** *literary* in the years after the time that has been mentioned **2** *technical* in the back part of a boat or an aircraft

af·ter·birth /ˈɑːftəbɜːθ $ ˈæftərbɜːrθ/ *n* [U] the substance that comes out of female humans or animals just after they have had a baby SYN **placenta**

af·ter·burn·er /ˈɑːftəˌbɜːnə $ ˈæftərˌbɜːrnər/ *n* [C] a piece of equipment in a JET engine that gives it more power

after- /ɑːftə $ æftər/ *prefix* coming or happening afterwards OPP **pre-**: *an after-dinner speech | after-school activities*

af·ter·care /ˈɑːftəkeə $ ˈæftərker/ *n* [U] *BrE* care or treatment given to someone after they leave hospital, prison etc: *the aftercare of ex-offenders*

ˈafter-efˌfect *BrE*, **af·ter·ef·fect** *AmE* /ˈɑːftərɪfekt $ ˈæf-/ ●○○ *n* [C usually plural] a bad effect that continues for a long time after the thing that caused it: **the after-effects (of sth)** *the after-effects of his illness*

af·ter·glow /ˈɑːftəgləʊ $ ˈæftərgloʊ/ *n* [C usually singular] **1** a pleasant feeling that remains after a good experience: **[+of]** *the afterglow of victory* **2** the light that remains in the sky after the sun goes down

af·ter·life /ˈɑːftəlaɪf $ ˈæftər-/ *n* [singular] the life that some people believe people have after death

af·ter·math /ˈɑːftəmæθ $ ˈæftər-/ ●○○ *n* [singular] the period of time after something such as a war, storm, or accident when people are still dealing with the results: **[+of]** *the danger of disease* ***in the aftermath*** *of the earthquake*

af·ter·noon¹ /ˌɑːftəˈnuːn◂ $ ˌæftər-/ ●●● S1 W2 *n* [C,U]
1 the part of the day after the morning and before the evening → **morning**, **evening**: *There's a meeting* ***on Thursday afternoon****. | It was very hot* ***in the afternoon****. | See you* ***tomorrow afternoon****. | Are you going into town* ***this afternoon****? | We met in the* ***early afternoon****. | By* ***late afternoon****, Micky had changed his mind. | He was having his* ***afternoon nap****.*
2 afternoons during the afternoon every day: *She only works afternoons.*

GRAMMAR: Patterns with afternoon

in the afternoon
• You do something **in the afternoon**: *We went shopping in the afternoon.* ✗ Don't say: *We went shopping on the afternoon.*

on Monday/Tuesday etc afternoon
• You do something **on Monday/Tuesday etc afternoon**: *I usually do the shopping on Friday afternoon.*

on the afternoon of sth
• Something happens **on the afternoon of** a particular date or event: *Diana was born on the afternoon of July 1, 1961. | He had gone there on the afternoon of the murder.*

afternoon² *interjection BrE informal* used to greet someone when you meet them in the afternoon

af·ters /ˈɑːftəz $ ˈæftərz/ *n* [plural] *BrE informal* the part of a meal that comes after the main dish SYN **dessert**

af·ter·school club /ˌɑːftəˈskuːl klʌb $ ˌæftər-/ *n* [C] a place, usually at a school, where young children in Britain can go after the normal school day has finished, and take part in organized activities until their parents can collect them after finishing work

af·ter·shave /ˈɑːftəʃeɪv $ ˈæftər-/ *n* [C,U] a liquid with a nice smell that a man puts on his face after he has shaved

af·ter·shock /ˈɑːftəʃɒk $ ˈæftərʃɑːk/ *n* [C] **1** a small EARTHQUAKE that happens after a larger one **2** the effects of a shocking event: *the war and its aftershocks*

af·ter·taste /ˈɑːftəteɪst $ ˈæftər-/ *n* [C usually singular] a taste that stays in your mouth after you have eaten or drunk something: *The wine leaves a strong aftertaste.*

af·ter·thought /ˈɑːftəθɔːt $ ˈæftərθɒːt/ *n* [C] something that you mention or add later because you did not think of it or plan it before: *He added as an afterthought, 'Bring Melanie too.'*

af·ter·wards /ˈɑːftəwədz $ ˈæftərwərdz/ ●●● S2 W3 *adv* (*also* **afterward**) after an event or time that has already been mentioned: *Charles arrived* ***shortly afterwards****.* | **days/weeks etc afterwards** *The experience haunted me* ***for years afterwards****. | She died* ***not long afterwards****. | Afterwards, I was asked to write a book.*
THESAURUS ▸ AFTER

a·gain /əˈgen, əˈgeɪn $ əˈgen/ ●●● S1 W1 *adv*
1 one more time – used when something has happened or been done before: *Can you say that again? I didn't hear. | I'll never go there again. | Mr Khan's busy. Can you try again later?* | **once again/yet again** (=used to emphasize that something has happened several or many times before) *In 1997, the family moved house yet again. | Once again, Drew was under arrest.*
2 back to the same state or situation that you were in before: *She stayed and nursed him back to health again. | It's great to have you home again.*
3 all over again if you do something all over again, you repeat it from the beginning: *I had to write the essay all over again.*
4 as much/as many/the same again the same amount or number as you have just had, said etc: *What a fantastic lunch. I could eat the same again. | Nearly as many again died from pneumonia. | The amount of crime is about* ***half as much again*** (=the same in addition to half that amount) *as it was in 1973. | 'Another drink?' 'Yes,* ***same again*** (=the same drink again), *please.'*
5 *spoken* used to give a fact or opinion that explains or adds to something you have just said: *And again, these workshops will benefit the community widely.*
6 then/there again *spoken* used to introduce an idea or fact that is different from something you have just said, or makes it seem less likely to be true: *She says she's thirty-five.* ***But then again*** *she might be lying.*
7 again and again/time and (time) again/over and over again very often – used to show disapproval: *I've told you again and again, don't do that!*
8 *spoken* used when you want someone to repeat information that they have already given you: *What did you say your name was again?* → **now and again** at NOW¹(5)

GRAMMAR: Word order

Again usually comes at the end of a sentence: *He's forgotten his keys again.* ✗ Don't say: *He's again forgotten his keys. | He's forgotten again his keys.*

a·gainst /əˈgenst, əˈgeɪnst $ əˈgenst/ ●●● S1 W1 *prep*
1 a) used to say that someone opposes or disagrees with something: *Every council member voted against the proposal. | those who are campaigning against the new road | He advised me against travelling. | Mr Howard has declared that he is against all forms of racism. | the fight against terrorism* **b)** used to say that an action is not wanted or approved of by someone: *They got married* ***against*** *her parents'* ***wishes*** (=although they knew her parents did not want them to). *| She has been kept in the house* ***against*** *her* ***will*** (=she does not want to stay in the house). *| The use of certain drugs is* ***against the law*** (=illegal). *| It's* ***against*** *my* ***principles*** *to borrow money* (=I do not believe it is right). **c)** used to say that something is not allowed by a law or rule: *There ought to be a law against it.*
2 used to say who someone is competing with or trying to defeat in a game, battle etc: *Gambotti was injured in last Saturday's game against the Lions. | We'll be competing against the best companies in Europe.*
3 used to say who is harmed, threatened, or given a disadvantage: *violence against elderly people | crimes against humanity | discrimination against women | There had been death threats against prison staff. | Your lack of experience could count against you. | The regulations tend to work against smaller companies.*
4 used to say that something touches, hits, or rubs a surface: *the sound of the rain drumming against my window | The car skidded and we could hear the crunch of metal against metal.*
5 next to and touching an upright surface, especially for support: *There was a ladder propped up against the wall. | The younger policeman was leaning against the bureau with his arms folded.*
6 in the opposite direction to the movement or flow of something OPP **with**: *sailing against the wind | She dived down and swam out strongly against the current.*

A

7 seen with something else behind or as a background: *He could see a line of figures silhouetted against the sky.* | *It is important to know what colours look good against your skin.*
8 used to show that you are considering particular events in relation to other events that are happening at the same time: *The reforms were introduced against a background of social unrest.*
9 used to say what you are comparing something with: *The pound has fallen 10% against the dollar.* | *She checked the contents of the box against the list.* | *The cost of the proposed research needs to be balanced against its benefits.*
10 used to say who or what you are trying to protect someone or something from: *insurance against accident and sickness* | *a cream to protect against sunburn* | *a vaccine which is effective against pneumonia*
11 used to say who is said or shown to have done something wrong: *He has always emphatically denied the allegations against him.* | *The evidence against you is overwhelming.*
12 be/come up against sb/sth to have to deal with a difficult opponent or problem: *You see, this is what we're up against – the suppliers just aren't reliable.*
13 have sth against sb/sth to dislike or disapprove of someone or something: *I don't have anything against babies. I just don't feel very comfortable with them.*

a·gape /əˈɡeɪp/ *adj* [not before noun] with your mouth wide open, especially because you are surprised or shocked: *Vince watched, his* ***mouth agape*** *in horror.*

ag·ate /ˈæɡət/ *n* [C,U] a hard stone with bands of different colours, used in jewellery

age[1] /eɪdʒ/ ●●● S1 W1 *n*
1 HOW OLD [C,U] the number of years someone has lived or something has existed → **old**: *Francis is the same age as me.* | *Experts disagree over the age of the drawings.* | *Dad retired* ***at the age of*** *56.* | **at age 5/18 etc** *In Britain, schooling starts at age 5.* | **4/15 etc years of age** (=4, 15 etc years old) *She was just over 16 years of age.* | **at my/your etc age** (=when you are as old as me etc) *At my age, it's quite difficult getting up the stairs.* | **over/under the age of 5/18 etc** *people over the age of 65* | **for his/her etc age** (=compared with other people of the same age) *She's tall for her age, isn't she?*

> **REGISTER**
> In everyday English, people usually use the expression **how old ...?** rather than using the noun **age**: *What age is your brother?* → ***How old*** *is your brother?* | *They asked me my age.* → *They asked me* ***how old*** *I was.*

2 LEGAL AGE [U] the age when you are legally old enough to do something: *What's the minimum age for getting a driver's license?* | *You're not allowed to buy alcohol. You're* ***under age*** (=too young by law). | *The normal retirement age is 65.*
3 PERIOD OF LIFE [C,U] one of the particular periods of someone's life: *When you get to old age, everything seems to take longer.* | *The early teens are often a difficult age.*
4 BEING OLD [U] the state of being old → **youth**: **with age** *High blood pressure increases with age.* | *Some of the furniture was* ***showing*** *signs of* ***age***.
5 PERIOD OF HISTORY [C usually singular] a particular period of history SYN **era**: *We are living in the age of technology.* | *Molecular biology is pushing medicine into a new age.* → **in this day and age** at DAY(6) THESAURUS ▸ PERIOD
6 ages [plural] (*also* **an age**) *especially BrE informal* a long time: *Simon! I haven't seen you* ***for ages***. | *That recipe* ***takes ages***. | **it's ages since/before/until etc sth** *It's ages since we've played that game.*
7 come of age a) to reach the age when you are legally considered to be a responsible adult **b)** if something comes of age, it reaches a stage of development at which people accept it as being important, valuable etc: *During this period the movies really came of age as an art form.* → NEW AGE[1], NEW AGE[2]

> **COLLOCATIONS – MEANINGS 1, 2 & 3**
>
> **ADJECTIVES/NOUN + age**
> **old age** (=the time when you are old) *the problems of old age*
> **middle age** (=between about 40 and 60) *He was in late middle age.*
> **a great/advanced age** (=a very old age) *My aunt died at a great age.*
> **a difficult/awkward age** (=used mainly about the time when people are teenagers) | **retirement age** | **school age** | **school-leaving age** *BrE* | **the legal age** | **the minimum age** | **the voting age** | **the marrying age**
>
> **PHRASES**
> **from an early/young age** *She'd been playing the piano from a very early age.*
> **at an early/young age** *Kids can start learning a second language at a young age.*
> **sb (of) your own age** *He needs to find people his own age.*
> **of childbearing age** (=at the age when a woman can have children) | **of working age** | **the age of consent** (=when you are legally allowed to marry or have sex)
>
> **age + NOUN**
> **an age group/bracket/range** *Men in the 50-65 age group are most at risk from heart disease.*
> **an age limit**
>
> **VERBS**
> **get to/reach/live to a particular age** *One in three children here die before they reach the age of 5.*
> **lower/raise the age** (=at which something can be done) *The voting age was lowered from 21 to 18.*
> **look/feel your age** (=look or feel as old as you really are) | **act your age** (=behave in the way that a person of your age should behave) | **ask/say your age** (=ask or say how old you are)

age[2] ●●○ *v* (*present participle* **aging** *or* **ageing** *BrE*)
1 [I,T] to start looking older or to make someone or something look older: *He was worried to see how much she'd aged.* | *The experience had aged him in advance of his years.*
2 [I] to become older: *The buildings are ageing, and some are unsafe.*
3 [I,T] to improve and develop in taste over a period of time, or to allow food or alcohol to do this SYN **mature**: *Cheddar cheese ages well.* | *The whisky is aged for at least ten years.*

-age /-ɪdʒ/ *suffix* [in nouns] *informal* used to form nouns referring to a quantity of something: *Here's some interesting stattage* (=stats, statistics) *about the game.*

ˈage-apˌpropriate *adj* something that is age-appropriate is suitable for people of the age who are using it or doing it: *age-appropriate toys*

ˈage ˌbracket *n* [C] the people between two particular ages, considered as a group SYN **age group**: **in the ... age bracket** *single people in the 40–50 age bracket*

aged[1] /eɪdʒd/ ●●○ W3 *adj* **aged 5/25 etc** 5 etc years old: **[+between]** *Police are looking for a man aged between 30 and 35.* | *The course is open to children aged 12 and over.*

a·ged[2] /ˈeɪdʒɪd/ *adj* **1** very old: *my aged parents* THESAURUS ▸ OLD **2 the aged** [plural] old people: *the care of children and the aged*

ˈage discrimiˌnation *n* [U] unfair treatment of people because they are old SYN **ageism** *BrE*

ˈage group *n* [C] the people between two particular ages, considered as a group: **in the ... age group** *a book for children in the 12–14 age group*

age·ing /ˈeɪdʒɪŋ/ *adj* a British spelling of AGING THESAURUS ▸ OLD

age·is·m (*also* **agism** *AmE*) /ˈeɪdʒɪzəm/ *n* [U] unfair treatment of people because they are old SYN **age discrimination** THESAURUS ▸ PREJUDICE

age·ist /ˈeɪdʒɪst/ *adj* treating older people unfairly because of a belief that they are less important than younger people: *The article seemed somewhat insensitive and ageist to me.* —**ageist** *n* [C]

age·less /ˈeɪdʒləs/ *adj* **1** never looking old or old-fashioned: *Her face seemed ageless.* **2** having existed for a very long time and continuing forever SYN **timeless**: *the ageless charm of a country kitchen* —**agelessness** *n* [U]

ˈage ˌlimit *n* [C] the oldest or youngest age at which you are allowed to do something: **[+for]** *The* ***upper age limit*** *for entrants was set at 25.*

a·gen·cy /ˈeɪdʒənsi/ ●●○ W3 *n* (*plural* **agencies**) [C]
1 a business that provides a particular service for people or organizations: **an advertising/employment/travel etc agency** *a local housing agency* → DATING AGENCY, NEWS AGENCY
2 an organization or department, especially within a government, that does a specific job: *a UN agency responsible for helping refugees | the Environmental Protection Agency*
3 by/through the agency of sb *formal* being done as the result of someone's help

a·gen·da /əˈdʒendə/ ●●○ *n* [C]
1 a list of problems or subjects that a government, organization etc is planning to deal with: **be high on the agenda/be top of the agenda** (=be one of the most important problems to deal with) *Measures to combat terrorism will be high on the agenda. | The government* ***set an agenda*** *for constitutional reform.* | **political/economic/legislative/domestic etc agenda** *Our Centre has limited its research agenda to four areas.*
2 the ideas that a political party thinks are important and the things that party aims to achieve: *The Republicans have stuck to their conservative agenda.*
3 a list of the subjects to be discussed at a meeting: *the next* ***item*** (=subject) ***on the agenda*** → **hidden agenda** at HIDDEN²(3)

a·gent /ˈeɪdʒənt/ ●●○ S3 W3 *n* [C]
1 a person or company that represents another person or company, especially in business: *Our agent in Rio deals with all our Brazilian business.* | **[+for]** *We're* ***acting as agents*** *for Mr Watson.* → ESTATE AGENT, LAND AGENT, REAL ESTATE AGENT, TRAVEL AGENT
2 someone who finds work for actors, musicians etc, or who finds someone to PUBLISH a writer's work: *My agent has a new script for me to look at. | a* ***literary agent***
3 someone who works for a government or police department, especially in order to get secret information about another country or organization: *an* ***intelligence agent*** *| an FBI agent | an* ***undercover*** (=secret) ***agent*** → SECRET AGENT, DOUBLE AGENT
4 *technical* a chemical or substance that is used for a particular purpose or that has a particular effect: *Soap is a cleansing agent.*
5 someone or something that affects or changes a situation: **agent for/of change** *Technological advances are the chief agents of change.* → FREE AGENT

a·gent pro·voc·a·teur /ˌæʒɒn prɒvɒkəˈtɜː $ ˌɑːʒɑːn proʊvɑːkəˈtɜːr/ *n* (*plural* **agents provocateurs** (*same pronunciation*)) [C] someone who is employed to encourage people who are working against a government to do something illegal so that they are caught

ˌage of conˈsent *n* **the age of consent** the age when someone can legally get married or have a sexual relationship

ˌage-ˈold *adj* having existed for a very long time: **an age-old tradition/practice/custom etc** *BrE*: *age-old customs | the* ***age-old problem*** *of sexual discrimination* THESAURUS ▸ OLD

ˈage range *n* [C] the people between two particular ages, considered as a group SYN **age group**: **in the ... age range** *young people in the 15–18 age range | This affects people across a wide age range.*

ag·fla·tion /ægˈfleɪʃən/ *n* [U] a general increase in the price of food: *A major cause of agflation is the growing use of crops for fuel.*

ag·glom·er·ate /əˈglɒmərət $ əˈglɑː-/ *n* [singular, U] *technical* a type of rock formed from pieces of material from a VOLCANO that have melted together

ag·glom·e·ra·tion /əˌglɒməˈreɪʃən $ əˌglɑː-/ *n* [C,U] a large collection of things that do not seem to belong together: **[+of]** *buildings in an agglomeration of styles*

ag·glu·ti·na·tion /əˌgluːtəˈneɪʃən $ əˌgluːtnˈeɪ-/ *n* [U] **1** the state of being stuck together **2** the process of making new words by combining two or more words, such as combining 'ship' and 'yard' to make 'shipyard'

ag·gran·dize·ment (*also* **-isement** *BrE*) /əˈgrændəzmənt/ *n* [U] when a person or country tries to increase their power or importance – used to show disapproval: *the misuse of authority for* ***personal aggrandizement***

ag·gra·vate /ˈægrəveɪt/ ●○○ *v* [T]
1 to make a bad situation, an illness, or an injury worse OPP **improve**: *Their money problems were* ***further aggravated*** *by a rise in interest rates. | Building the new road will only* ***aggravate the situation***.
2 to make someone angry or annoyed SYN **irritate**: *What really aggravates me is the way she won't listen.* —**aggravating** *adj* —**aggravatingly** *adv* —**aggravation** /ˌægrəˈveɪʃən/ *n* [C,U]

ag·gra·va·ted /ˈægrəveɪtɪd/ *adj* [only before noun] *law* an aggravated offence is one in which a criminal does something that makes their original crime more serious: *He was charged with* ***aggravated assault***.

ag·gre·gate¹ /ˈægrɪgət/ AWL *n formal* **1** [C] the total after a lot of different figures or points have been added together: **[+of]** *The smaller minorities got an aggregate of 1,327 votes.* | ***In the aggregate*** (=as a group or in total), *women outlive men by 7 or more years.* | **on aggregate** *BrE* (=when the points from two football games are added together) *Manchester United won 2-1 on aggregate.* **2** [singular, U] *technical* sand or small stones that are used in making CONCRETE

aggregate² AWL *adj* [only before noun] *technical* being the total amount of something after all the figures or points have been added together: *an increase in the aggregate production*

ag·gre·gate³ /ˈægrɪgeɪt/ AWL *v formal* **1** [linking verb] to be a particular amount when added together: *Sheila's earnings from all sources aggregated £100,000.* **2** [I,T] to put different amounts, pieces of information etc together to form a group or a total: **[+with]** *A wife's income is no longer aggregated with that of her husband.* —**aggregation** /ˌægrɪˈgeɪʃən/ *n* [U]

ag·gres·sion /əˈgreʃən/ ●○○ *n* [U]
1 angry or threatening behaviour or feelings that often result in fighting: *Television violence can encourage aggression in children.* | **[+towards]** *Our dogs have never shown aggression towards other dogs.*
2 the act of attacking a country, especially when that country has not attacked first: *an unprovoked* ***act of aggression*** | **[+against]** *Athenian aggression against Persia*

ag·gres·sive /əˈgresɪv/ ●●○ S3 W3 *adj*
1 behaving in an angry threatening way, as if you want to fight or attack someone: *Jim's voice became aggressive. | Teachers apparently expect a certain amount of aggressive behaviour from boys.*
2 very determined to succeed or get what you want: *A successful businessman has to be aggressive. | an aggressive marketing campaign*
3 an aggressive disease spreads quickly in the body: *an aggressive form of breast cancer* —**aggressively** *adv* —**aggressiveness** *n* [U]

ag·gres·sor /əˈgresə $ -ər/ *n* [C] a person or country that begins a fight or war with another person or country: *measures taken to deter potential aggressors*

ag·grieved /əˈgriːvd/ *adj* **1** angry and sad because you think you have been unfairly treated: *an aggrieved tone of voice* **2** *law* having suffered as a result of the illegal

A

actions of someone else: *the aggrieved party* (=the person who has suffered)

ag·gro /ˈæɡrəʊ $ -roʊ/ *n* [U] *BrE informal* **1** angry behaviour or fighting: *I hope he doesn't* ***cause*** *any* ***aggro***. **2** problems or difficulties that annoy you: *I can't cope with all this aggro.*

a·ghast /əˈɡɑːst $ əˈɡæst/ *adj* [not before noun] *written* feeling or looking shocked by something you have seen or just found out: **[+at]** *Everyone was aghast at the verdict.* | *Hank looked at her aghast.* **THESAURUS** SHOCKED

a·gile /ˈædʒaɪl $ ˈædʒəl/ ●○○ *adj*
1 able to move quickly and easily: *Dogs are surprisingly agile.*
2 someone who has an agile mind is able to think very quickly and intelligently: *He was physically strong and mentally agile.* —**agility** /əˈdʒɪləti/ *n* [U]: *With surprising agility, Karl darted across the road.*

ag·ing[1] (*also* **ageing** *BrE*) /ˈeɪdʒɪŋ/ *adj* [only before noun] becoming old: *aging movie stars* | *Europe's* ***ageing population*** (=with more old people than before) **THESAURUS** OLD

aging[2] (*also* **ageing** *BrE*) /ˈeɪdʒɪŋ/ *n* [U] the process of getting old: *Memory loss is often a part of ageing.*

ag·is·m /ˈeɪdʒɪzəm/ *n* an American spelling of AGEISM

a·gi·tate /ˈædʒɪteɪt/ *v* **1** [I] to argue strongly in public for something you want, especially a political or social change: **[+for/against]** *unions agitating for higher pay* | **agitate to do sth** *His family are agitating to get him freed.* **2** [T] *formal* to make someone feel anxious, upset, and nervous: *I must warn you that any mention of Clare agitates your grandmother.* **3** [T] *technical* to shake or mix a liquid quickly

a·gi·ta·ted /ˈædʒɪteɪtɪd/ *adj* so nervous or upset that you are unable to keep still or think calmly: *Amanda was getting visibly agitated.*

a·gi·ta·tion /ˌædʒɪˈteɪʃən/ *n* **1** [U] when you are so anxious, nervous, or upset that you cannot think calmly: *She was in a state of considerable agitation.* **2** [C,U] public argument or action for social or political change: **[+for/against]** *mass agitation for political reform* **3** [U] *technical* the act of shaking or mixing a liquid

a·gi·ta·tor /ˈædʒəteɪtə $ -ər/ *n* [C] someone who encourages people to work towards changing something in society - used to show disapproval: *a political agitator*

a·git·prop /ˌædʒətˈprɒp $ -ˈprɑːp/ *n* [U] music, literature, or art that tries to persuade people to follow a particular set of political ideas

a·glow /əˈɡləʊ $ əˈɡloʊ/ *adj* [not before noun] *literary* **1** having a soft light, or a strong warm colour: *The evening sky was still aglow.* **2** if someone's face is aglow, they seem happy and excited: **[+with]** *Linda's face was aglow with happiness.*

AGM /ˌeɪ dʒiː ˈem/ *n* [C] *BrE* (***annual general meeting***) a meeting held once a year by a club, business, or organization for the members to discuss the previous year's business, elect officials etc SYN **annual meeting** *AmE*

ag·nos·tic /æɡˈnɒstɪk, əɡ- $ -ˈnɑː-/ *n* [C] someone who believes that people cannot know whether God exists or not → **atheist** **THESAURUS** RELIGIOUS —**agnostic** *adj* —**agnosticism** /-tɪsɪzəm/ *n* [U]

a·go /əˈɡəʊ $ əˈɡoʊ/ ●●● S1 W1 *adv* used to show how far back in the past something happened: **5 minutes/an hour/20 years etc ago** *Her husband died 14 years ago.* | **long ago/a long time ago** *He should have finished at university long ago, but he kept taking extra courses.* | **a minute/moment ago** *The little girl you saw a moment ago was my niece.* | **a little/short while ago** *Tom got a letter from him just a little while ago.* | *They moved to a new house* ***some time ago*** (=a fairly long time ago). | *We had our bicentenary celebrations not that long ago.*

GRAMMAR: Patterns with ago

- Use the simple past, not the present perfect, with **ago**. You say: *I started a new job a few weeks ago.* ✗ Don't say: *I've started a new job a few weeks ago.*
- Don't use a preposition such as 'at', 'in', or 'on' before a phrase with **ago**. You say: *They first met fifteen years ago.* ✗ Don't say: *They first met at/in/fifteen years ago.*
- Don't use 'since' or 'before' with **ago**. You say: *I came to the US two months ago.* ✗ Don't say: *I came to the US since/before two months ago.*

a·gog /əˈɡɒɡ $ əˈɡɑːɡ/ *adj* [not before noun] very excited about something and wanting to find out more: *I've been agog all afternoon, waiting for the next part of your story.* | *Paul was agog with curiosity.*

ag·o·nize (*also* **-ise** *BrE*) /ˈæɡənaɪz/ *v* [I] to think about a difficult decision very carefully and with a lot of effort: **[+over/about]** *All the way home she agonized about what she should do.* —**agonizing** *n* [U]

ag·o·nized (*also* **-ised** *BrE*) /ˈæɡənaɪzd/ *adj* [only before noun] expressing very severe pain: *an agonized scream* | *From some place close by she heard agonized sobbing.*

ag·o·niz·ing (*also* **-ising** *BrE*) /ˈæɡənaɪzɪŋ/ *adj* **1** extremely painful: *The pain was agonizing.* **2** very unpleasant to experience, especially because of involving a difficult choice or a long wait: *an agonizing decision* —**agonizingly** *adv*: *at an agonizingly slow pace*

ag·o·ny /ˈæɡəni/ ●○○ *n* (*plural* **agonies**) [C,U]
1 very severe pain: *the agony of arthritis* | **in agony** *I was in agony.* | *He groaned in agony.* **THESAURUS** PAIN
2 a very sad, difficult, or unpleasant experience: *It was agony not knowing if she would live.* | **[+of]** *He was in agonies of remorse.* → **pile on the pressure/agony** at PILE, → **prolong the agony** at PROLONG(2)

ˈagony ˌaunt *n* [C] *BrE* someone who writes an agony column

ˈagony ˌcolumn *n* [C] *BrE* a part of a newspaper or magazine in which someone gives advice to readers about their personal problems SYN **advice column**

ag·o·ra·pho·bi·a /ˌæɡərəˈfəʊbiə $ -ˈfoʊ-/ *n* [U] fear of crowds and open spaces → **claustrophobia**

ag·o·ra·pho·bic /ˌæɡərəˈfəʊbɪk◂ $ -ˈfoʊ-/ *n* [C] someone who suffers from agoraphobia —**agoraphobic** *adj*

a·grar·i·an /əˈɡreəriən $ əˈɡrer-/ *adj* [usually before noun] relating to farming or farmers: *an agrarian economy* (=based on farming)

a·gree /əˈɡriː/ ●●● S1 W1 *v*
1 SAME OPINION [I,T] to have or express the same opinion about something as someone else OPP **disagree**: *Teenagers and their parents rarely agree.* | **[+with]** *If she felt he was right, she would agree with him.* | **agree that** *Most people nowadays would agree that a good pub is one of our best traditions.* | **[+on/about]** *We don't agree on everything, of course.* | **I quite agree/I couldn't agree more** (=I agree completely) *'We have to talk.' 'Absolutely,' Meredith replied. 'I couldn't agree more.'*
2 SAY YES [I,T] to say yes to an idea, plan, suggestion etc OPP **refuse**: *I suggested we go somewhere for the weekend and she agreed at once.* | **agree to do sth** *No one really knows why he agreed to do the film.* | **[+to]** *My sister won't agree to our mother going into a nursing home.*
3 DECIDE TOGETHER [I,T] to make a decision with someone after a discussion with them: **agree to do sth** *We agreed to meet again the following Monday.* | **[+on]** *They managed to agree on a date for the wedding.* | **agree that** *We agreed that elections would be held in May.* | **agree a price/plan/strategy etc** *We agreed a new four-year contract.*

GRAMMAR

In more formal English, you say **it was agreed that** when saying what people agreed: *It was agreed that the post would be advertised.*

4 BE THE SAME [I] if two pieces of information agree with each other, they match or are the same: **[+with]** *Your story doesn't agree with what the police have told us.*
5 agree to differ/disagree if two people agree to differ, they accept that they have different opinions about something and stop arguing about it

agree with sth *phr v*
1 to believe that a decision, action, or suggestion is correct or right: *I don't agree with hitting children.*
2 not agree with sb if a type of food does not agree with you, it makes you feel ill: *Green peppers don't agree with me.*
3 if an adjective, verb etc agrees with a word, it matches that word by being plural if the word is plural etc

GRAMMAR

Reciprocal verbs

Agree is a reciprocal verb. This type of verb is used when saying that two or more people or groups do something that involves both or all of them: *Our parties agree on this.* You can also say: *Our parties agree with each other on this.* | *My party agrees with yours on this.*

Prepositions with agree

agree with sb/sth
• You **agree with** someone: *I agree with Tanya.*
✗ Don't say: *I agree Tanya.*
• You **agree with** an opinion or statement: *He agrees with this view.* ✗ Don't say: *He agrees this view.*

agree on/about sth
• People **agree on** or **about** a subject: *My wife and I agree on most things.*

agree to sth
• You **agree to** a plan or suggestion: *They agreed to all our proposals.* ✗ Don't say: *They agreed all our proposals.*

Using the progressive

Agree is not used in the progressive. You say: *I agree completely.* ✗ Don't say: *I am agreeing completely.*

GRAMMAR GUIDE ▸ VERBS

THESAURUS

TO SAY YES

agree to say that you think that someone's plan or suggestion is a good idea and you think it should happen: *Charles suggested going for a picnic, and we all agreed.* | *The Council of Ministers would never agree to such a plan.*
say yes *especially spoken* to agree to do what someone has asked: *They asked if I would give a talk, and I stupidly said yes.*
approve to officially agree to a plan or proposal: *Congress approved the plan by a large majority.*
give your consent to say that you agree to something that will affect you, your family, or your property, when you have the legal right to say 'no': *Her parents have given their consent to the marriage.*
go along with sth to agree with someone else's plan or suggestion even though you are not sure if it is the right thing to do: *He wasn't very happy with the idea, but he decided to go along with it.*

TO HAVE THE SAME OPINION

agree to have the same opinion as someone, or to think that a statement is correct: *I totally agree with what you've just said.* | *Most experts agree that dieting needs to be accompanied by regular exercise.*
be in agreement *formal* if people are in agreement, they agree with each other, especially after discussing something: *The world's scientists are in agreement that global warming is a problem that needs to be addressed.*
share sb's view/be of the same opinion *formal* to have the same opinion as someone, especially about an important issue: *A lot of people share his view that tourism will have a negative impact on the island.* | *Professor Dawkins is of the same opinion as Dr Jones.*
concur /kənˈkɜː $ -ˈkɜːr/ *formal* to agree with someone or about something – a very formal word which is used especially in official contexts: *The committee concurred with this view.* | *She asked her colleague, and she concurred.*
see eye to eye [not in progressive] to agree with someone about something – used especially in negative sentences: *We don't always see eye to eye, but we do respect each other's opinions.*
agree up to a point to partly agree with someone: *I agree with you up to a point, but surely the situation is more complex than that?*

a·gree·a·ble /əˈgriːəbəl/ *adj* **1** *written or old-fashioned* pleasant OPP **disagreeable**: *We spent a most agreeable couple of hours.* | *an agreeable young man* **2 be agreeable to sth** *formal* to be willing to do something or willing to allow something to be done: *My parents are quite agreeable to my studying abroad.* **3** acceptable: **[+to]** *The main objective is to find a solution that is agreeable to the company in terms of cost.* —**agreeably** *adv*: *I think you'll be agreeably surprised by what I'm going to say.*

a·greed /əˈgriːd/ ●●○ *adj* [only before noun]
1 an agreed plan, price, arrangement etc is one that people have discussed and accepted: *The important thing is to have agreed objectives.*
2 be agreed if people are agreed, they have discussed something and agree about what to do: **[+on]** *All parties are now agreed on the plan.* | **be agreed that** *We're all agreed that we cannot spend what we have not earned.*
3 Agreed used to check if someone agrees, or to show that you agree: *'Let's just forget it ever happened. Agreed?' 'Agreed.'*

a·gree·ment /əˈgriːmənt/ ●●● S2 W1 *n*
1 [C] an arrangement or promise to do something, made by two or more people, companies, organizations etc: **[+that]** *They had made an agreement that they would share the profits equally.* | **[+with]** *Haydon came to an agreement with his creditors.* | **[+on]** *an agreement on arms reduction* | **under an agreement** *Under the agreement, most agricultural prices will remain at the same level.*
2 [U] when people have the same opinion as each other OPP **disagreement**: **agreement that** *There is general agreement that copyright is a good idea.* | **[+on]** *There is widespread agreement on the need for prison reform.* | **be in agreement** *A decision will not be made until everyone is in agreement.* | *It is easier for two parties to* ***reach agreement*** *than for three.*
3 [U] when someone says yes to an idea, plan, suggestion etc: **agreement to do sth** *Would their discussion result in his agreement to visit his stepmother?* | **[+of]** *Such arrangements cannot be altered without the agreement of the bank.*
4 [C] an official document that people sign to show that they have agreed to something: *Please read the agreement and sign it.* | *a hire purchase agreement*

COLLOCATIONS

VERBS

make an agreement *We made an agreement not to tell anyone.*
sign an agreement *The two countries have signed an agreement on military co-operation.*
have an agreement *They have an agreement that all workers should be union members.*
reach/come to an agreement (*also* **conclude an agreement** *formal*) *It took the two sides several weeks to reach an agreement.*
break/violate an agreement *The UN accused the country's leaders of breaking international agreements.*
keep/honour an agreement (*also* **stick to an agreement** *informal*) (=do what you have agreed) | **go back on an agreement** (*also* **renege on an agreement** *formal*) (=not do what you agreed to do) | **be bound by an agreement** (=have to obey the conditions of an official agreement) | **negotiate an agreement** (=discuss particular things in order to reach an agreement) | **draft an agreement** (=write the conditions of an agreement, which may be

changed) | **broker an agreement** (=arrange an agreement between two or more opposing groups) | **enter into an agreement** *formal* (=make an official agreement, which has legal responsibilities) | **finalize an agreement** (=agree the last part) | **an agreement breaks down** (=it stops working)

ADJECTIVES/NOUN + agreement

a written agreement *There is usually a written agreement between the borrower and the bank.*
a verbal agreement (=agreed in words, but not written down) *The doctor needs to have a verbal agreement from the patient.*
a trade agreement *The administration has signed a multi-billion dollar trade agreement with Colombia.*
a legal agreement *The golf club is also offering to enter into a legal agreement with local residents.*
a binding agreement (=an official agreement that must be obeyed) *Lawyers are in the process of drafting a legally binding agreement between both parties.*
a formal/informal agreement | **a peace agreement** (=a permanent agreement to stop fighting) | **a ceasefire agreement** (=a temporary agreement to stop fighting) | **an international agreement** | **a multilateral agreement** *formal* (=involving several countries or groups) | **a bilateral agreement** *formal* (=between two countries or groups) | **a draft agreement** (=one that is not yet in its finished form) | **a gentleman's agreement** (=an agreement that is not written down, and is based only on trust)

PHRASES

the terms of an agreement (=the conditions that people agree on) *Under the terms of the agreement, the debt would be repaid over a 20-year period.*
a breach of an agreement (=an act of breaking an agreement) | **be close to an agreement** (=have almost reached an agreement)

ag·ri·busi·ness /ˈægrɪˌbɪznəs/ *n* [C,U] the production and sale of farm products, or a company involved in this

ag·ri·cul·ture /ˈægrɪˌkʌltʃə $ -ər/ ●●○ W2 *n* [U] the practice or science of farming: *More than 75% of the land is used for agriculture.* —**agricultural** /ˌægrɪˈkʌltʃərəl◂/ *adj*: *agricultural land | agricultural labourers* —**agriculturalist** *n* [C] → HORTICULTURE

ag·ri·tour·is·m, **agrotourism** /ˈægrɪˌtʊərɪzəm $ -ˌtʊr-/ *n* [U] holidays in which visitors stay in country areas on farms or near farms

agro- /ægrəʊ $ -roʊ/ *prefix* (*also* **agri-** /ægrɪ/) relating to farming: *agrobiology*

a·gron·o·my /əˈgrɒnəmi $ əˈgrɑː-/ *n* [U] the study of the growing of crops —**agronomist** *n* [C]

a·ground /əˈgraʊnd/ *adv* **run/go aground** if a ship runs aground, it becomes stuck in a place where the water is not deep enough

a·gue /ˈeɪgjuː/ *n* [C,U] *old-fashioned* a fever that makes you shake and feel cold

ah /ɑː/ *interjection* used to show surprise, happiness, agreement etc: *Ah! There you are!*

a·ha /ɑːˈhɑː/ *interjection* used to show that you understand or realize something: *Aha! So you planned all this, did you?* → HA

a·head /əˈhed/ ●●● S1 W2 *adv*
1 IN FRONT a short distance in front of someone or something OPP **behind**: *He kept his gaze fixed on the car ahead.* | **[+of]** *A hill loomed ahead of them.* | *We could see the lights of Las Vegas* ***up ahead***. | **some/a little/a long way ahead** *The clinic was now in sight, some way ahead.* | **straight/dead ahead** (=straight in front) *The river is eight miles away dead ahead.* | *Henry hurried on ahead* (=went in front of the others).
2 FORWARD if someone or something looks or moves ahead, they look or move forward: *He stared* ***straight ahead***. | *The ship forged ahead through the thin ice.*
3 BEFORE SB ELSE before someone else: **[+of]** *There were four people ahead of me at the doctor's.*
4 FUTURE in the future: **[+of]** *You* ***have*** *a long trip* ***ahead*** *of you.* | *Problems may* ***lie ahead***. | **the years/days/months etc ahead** *We do not foresee any major changes in the years ahead.* | *Unless we* ***plan ahead*** (=plan for the future) *we are going to be in a mess.*
5 BEFORE AN EVENT before an event happens SYN **in advance**: *I cook rice two or three hours ahead.* | *Can you tell me* ***ahead of time*** *if you're coming?* | **[+of]** *He's giving a series of concerts in London ahead of his international tour.*
6 ahead of schedule earlier than planned or arranged: *I arrived at Jack's suite half an hour ahead of schedule.*
7 PROGRESS/SUCCESS making progress and being successful in your job, education etc: **get/keep/stay ahead** *Getting ahead at work is the most important thing to her at the moment.*
8 ADVANCED ideas, achievements etc that are ahead of others have made more progress or are more developed: *This design is* ***light years ahead*** (=much more advanced) *in performance and comfort.* | **ahead of your/its time** (=very advanced or new, and not understood or accepted) *Coleridge was in many ways far ahead of his time.*
9 WINNING winning in a competition or election: *Two shots from Gardner* ***put*** *the Giants 80–75* ***ahead***. | *We are 10 points ahead in the polls.* | **[+of]** *At this stage, Smith appeared to be ahead of his rivals.*
10 go ahead a) *spoken* used to tell someone they can do something: *'Can I have the sports section?' 'Yeah, go ahead, I've read it.'* **b)** to do something that was planned, especially in spite of a problem: **[+with]** *Frank'll be late but we'll go ahead with the meeting anyway.* **c)** to take place: *Tests of anti-cancer drugs are to go ahead this year.* → GO-AHEAD[1]
11 ahead of the game/curve *informal* in a position where you are more advanced or more successful than your competitors: *Belmont city leaders have never been ahead of the curve in environmental matters.*

a·hem /mˈhm; *spelling pronunciation* əˈhem/ *interjection* a sound like a cough that you make to attract someone's attention, or when you are saying something embarrassing

-aholic /əhɒlɪk $ əhɒː-, əhɑː-/ *suffix* [in nouns and adjectives] someone who cannot stop doing something or using something: **a workaholic** (=someone who never stops working) | **a chocaholic** (=someone who loves chocolate)

a·hoy /əˈhɔɪ/ *interjection old-fashioned* used by sailors to get someone's attention or greet them

AI /ˌeɪ ˈaɪ/ *n* [U] the abbreviation of ***artificial intelligence***

aid[1] /eɪd/ ●●○ W3 AWL *n*
1 [U] help, such as money or food, given by an organization or government to a country or to people who are in a difficult situation: ***Foreign aid*** *from many countries poured into the famine area.* | *convoys delivering* ***humanitarian aid*** | *a substantial* ***aid programme*** | *He has been granted* ***legal aid*** (=free legal services).
2 [U] help that you need to do a particular thing: **with/without the aid of sth** *Father Poole walked painfully, with the aid of a stick.*
3 in aid of sth in order to help a CHARITY: *We're collecting money in aid of cancer research.*
4 [U] help or advice that is given to someone who needs it: **come/go to sb's aid** (=help someone) *I didn't speak any French, but a nice man came to my aid.*
5 [C] something such as a machine or tool that helps someone do something: *A video is a useful aid in the classroom.* | *a hearing aid*
6 what's this in aid of? *BrE spoken* used to ask what something is used for or why someone is doing something: *What's this meeting tomorrow in aid of, then?*
7 an American spelling of AIDE → FIRST AID

aid[2] ●●○ AWL *v* [T]
1 to help someone do something: *an index to aid the reader* | **aid sb in/with (doing) sth** *Mrs Coxen was aided in looking after the children by her niece.* THESAURUS ▸ HELP
2 to make something happen more quickly or easily:

Welfare spending aids economic development in three ways.
3 aid and abet *law* to help someone do something illegal

aide /eɪd/ ●○○ *n* [C] someone whose job is to help someone who has an important job, especially a politician: *a presidential aide*

aide-de-camp /ˌeɪd də ˈkɑːmp/ *n* (*plural* **aides-de-camp** *(same pronunciation)*) [C] a military officer whose job is to help an officer of a higher rank

AIDS (*also* **Aids** *BrE*) /eɪdz/ *n* [U] (***Acquired Immune Deficiency Syndrome***) a very serious disease that stops your body from defending itself against infections, and usually causes death: *the AIDS virus* | *Aids sufferers* | ***full-blown AIDS*** (=AIDS at its most advanced stage)

ˈaid ˌworker *n* [C] someone who works for an organization that brings food and other supplies to people in danger from wars, floods etc: *UN aid workers*

ail /eɪl/ *v* **1 what ails sth** *formal* the thing or things that are causing difficulties for something: *This initiative is not the answer to what ails our educational system.* **2** [I,T] *old-fashioned* to be ill, or to make someone feel ill or unhappy

ail·ing /ˈeɪlɪŋ/ *adj* [usually before noun] **1** an ailing company, organization, or ECONOMY is having a lot of problems and is not successful: *the ailing car industry* **2** *formal* ill and not likely to get better

ail·ment /ˈeɪlmənt/ ●○○ *n* [C] an illness that is not very serious: ***minor ailments*** THESAURUS▸ ILLNESS

aim¹ /eɪm/ ●●● S2 W2 *n*

1 [C] something you hope to achieve by doing something: **[+of]** *The aim of the research is to find new food sources.* | *The* ***main aim*** *of the course is to improve your writing.* | **with the aim of doing sth** *a campaign with the aim of helping victims of crime* | *Teamwork is required in order to* ***achieve*** *these* ***aims****.* | *a policy which sets out the school's* ***aims and objectives*** THESAURUS▸ PURPOSE

2 take aim to point a gun or weapon at someone or something you want to shoot: **[+at]** *Alan took aim at the target.*

3 take aim at sb/sth *AmE* to criticize someone or something: *Critics took aim at the president.*

4 [U] someone's ability to hit what they are aiming at when they throw or shoot something: *Val's aim was very good.*

THESAURUS

aim something you hope to achieve by doing something: *The main aim of the plan was to provide employment for local people.*

goal something important that you hope to achieve in the future, even though it may take a long time: *The country can still achieve its goal of reducing poverty by a third.*

target a particular amount or total that you want to achieve: *The company is on track to meet its target of increasing profits by 10%.*

objective the specific thing that you are trying to achieve – used especially about things that have been officially discussed and agreed upon in business, politics etc: *Their main objective is to halt the flow of drugs.* | *We met to set the business objectives for the coming year.*

ambition something that you very much want to achieve in your future career: *Her ambition was to go to law school and become an attorney.*

aim² ●●● S2 W2 *v*

1 [I,T] to try or intend to achieve something: **aim to do sth** *We aim to finish by Friday.* | **be aimed at doing sth** *an initiative aimed at reducing road accidents* | **aim for sth** *We're aiming for a big improvement.*

2 aim sth at sb to say or do something that is intended for a particular person or group of people: *The anti-smoking campaign is aimed at teenagers.* | *The criticism wasn't aimed at you.* | *He aimed his attacks at his opponent, calling him a "political dinosaur."*

3 [I,T] to choose the place, person etc that you want to hit or reach and point a weapon or another object towards them: *Denver aimed his gun but did not shoot.* | **[+at/for]** *The pilot was aiming for the runway but came down in a nearby field.*

GRAMMAR: Patterns with aim

• You **aim to do** something: *I aim to study medicine.*
✗ Don't say: *I aim at studying medicine.*

• An action is **aimed at doing** something: *Our policies are aimed at encouraging economic growth.* ✗ Don't say: *Our policies are aimed to encourage economic growth.*

aim·less /ˈeɪmləs/ *adj* not having a clear purpose or reason: *a young man drifting through life in an aimless way* —**aimlessly** *adv* —**aimlessness** *n* [U]

ain't /eɪnt/ a short form of 'am not', 'is not', 'are not', 'has not', or 'have not', that many people think is incorrect

Ain·tree /ˈeɪntriː/ a RACECOURSE in northwest England where a famous horse race, the Grand National, takes place each year

air¹ /eə $ er/ ●●● S1 W1 *n*

1 GAS [U] the mixture of gases around the Earth, that we breathe: *Let's go outside and get some fresh air.* | *You need to put some air in the tyres.* | **in the air** *There was a strong smell of burning in the air.* → **a breath of fresh air** at BREATH(2)

2 SPACE ABOVE THE GROUND **the air** the space above the ground or around things: **into the air** *Flames leapt into the air.* | **through the air** *He fell 2,000 metres through the air without a parachute.*

3 PLANES **a) by air** travelling by, or using, a plane: *I'd prefer to travel by air.* **b)** relating to or involving planes: *the victims of Britain's worst air disaster* | ***Air travel*** *was growing rapidly.* | ***air traffic*** *congestion* | *His brother died in an* ***air crash****.*

4 be in the air a) if a feeling is in the air, a lot of people feel it at the same time: *There was a sense of excitement in the air.* **b)** to be going to happen very soon: *Change is in the air.*

5 APPEARANCE [singular] if something or someone has an air of confidence, mystery etc, they seem confident, mysterious etc: **[+of]** *She had an air of quiet confidence.* | *She looked at him with a determined air.*

6 be up in the air if something is up in the air, no decision has been made about it yet: *Our trip is still very much up in the air.*

7 be on/off (the) air to be broadcasting on the radio or television at the present moment, or to stop broadcasting: *We'll be on air in three minutes.*

8 MUSIC [C] a simple tune, often used in the title of a piece of CLASSICAL music

9 airs [plural] a way of behaving that shows someone thinks they are more important than they really are: **put on airs/give yourself airs** *Trudy is always putting on airs.* | *an actor with no* ***airs and graces***

10 be walking/floating on air to feel very happy → HOT AIR, ON-AIR, → **clear the air** at CLEAR²(15), → **disappear/vanish into thin air** at THIN¹(15), → **out of thin air** at THIN¹(16)

COLLOCATIONS

ADJECTIVES

fresh *She opened the window to let in some fresh air.*
clean *London's air is cleaner than it has been at any time since 1585.*
warm/hot *Warm air rises and is replaced by cooler and denser air.*
cool/cold *The air had turned a little cooler.*
crisp (=pleasantly cool) *the crisp autumn air*
clear | **damp/humid** | **polluted** | **stale** (=not fresh and often full of smoke) | **the air is thin** (=there is less oxygen because you are in a high place) | **the morning/evening/night air** | **the sea/mountain/country air** | **the still air** (=air in which there is no wind)

air + NOUN

air pollution *Most air pollution is caused by cars.*

A

the air quality *The air quality is very poor on hot days.*
the air pressure

PHRASES

a breath of air *I went outside for a breath of air.*
a rush/blast/stream of air | a current of air

VERBS

breathe in the air *She breathed in the cool mountain air.*
fight/gasp for air (=try to breathe with difficulty) *He clutched his throat as he fought for air.*
let in some air (=let fresh air into a room) | **put air into sth** (=fill a tyre, balloon etc with air)

air² ●○○ *v*
1 OPINION [T] to express your opinions publicly: **air your views/grievances/complaints etc** *Staff will get a chance to ask questions and air their views.* THESAURUS SAY
2 TV/RADIO [I,T] to broadcast a programme on television or radio: *KPBS airs such popular children's programs as 'Barney' and 'Sesame Street'. | The program is due to air next month.*
3 ROOM [T] *especially BrE*, **air sth out** *AmE* to let fresh air into a room, especially one that has been closed for a long time
4 CLOTHES [I,T] *especially BrE*, **air (sth) out** *AmE* to put a piece of clothing in a place that is warm or has a lot of air, so that it smells clean: *I've left my sweater outside to air.*
→ AIRING, → **air your dirty laundry** at DIRTY¹(7)

ˈair ˌambulance *n* [C] a special aircraft used for taking people to hospital

air·bag /ˈeəbæg $ ˈer-/ *n* [C] a bag in a car that fills with air to protect the driver or passenger in an accident → see picture at CAR

air·base /ˈeəbeɪs $ ˈer-/ *n* [C] a place where military aircraft begin and end their flights, and where members of an air force live

air·bed /ˈeəbed $ ˈer-/ *n* [C] something that you fill with air and use as a bed

air·borne /ˈeəbɔːn $ ˈerbɔːrn/ *adj* **1** a plane that is airborne is in the air **2** airborne soldiers are trained to fight in areas that they get to by jumping out of a plane **3** carried through the air: *airborne pollutants*

ˈair brakes *n* [plural] BRAKES that work using air pressure

air·brush¹ /ˈeəbrʌʃ $ ˈer-/ *n* [C] a piece of equipment that uses air to put paint onto a surface

airbrush² *v* [T] to use an airbrush to make a picture or photograph look better
airbrush sb/sth ↔ **out** *phr v* to remove someone or something from a picture or photograph using an airbrush

Air·bus /ˈeəbʌs $ ˈer-/ *n* [C] *trademark* a large plane that carries a lot of people for short distances

ˌair chief ˈmarshal *n* [C] a high rank in the British air force, or someone who has this rank

ˌair ˈcommodore *n* [C] a high rank in the British air force, or someone who has this rank

ˈair conˌditioner *n* [C] a machine that makes the air in a room or building cooler and drier

ˈair conˌditioning *n* [U] (*written abbreviation* **AC**) a system that makes the air in a room or building cooler and drier —**air-conditioned** *adj*

air·craft /ˈeəkrɑːft $ ˈerkræft/ ●●● S2 W2 *n* [C] (*plural* **aircraft**) a plane or other vehicle that can fly → LIGHT AIRCRAFT

ˈaircraft ˌcarrier *n* [C] a type of ship that planes can fly from and land on

air·craft·man /ˈeəkrɑːftmən $ ˈerkræft-/ *n* (*plural* **aircraftmen** /-mən/) [C] a low rank in the British air force, or someone who has this rank

air·crew /ˈeəkruː $ ˈer-/ *n* [C] the pilot and the people who are responsible for flying a plane

air·drop /ˈeədrɒp $ ˈerdrɑːp/ *n* [C] the action of delivering supplies to people by dropping them from a plane —**airdrop** *v* [T]

air·fare /ˈeəfeə $ ˈerfer/ *n* [C] the price of a journey by plane

air·field /ˈeəfiːld $ ˈer-/ *n* [C] a place where planes can fly from, especially one used by military planes

air·flow /ˈeəfləʊ $ ˈerfloʊ/ *n* [U] the movement of air through or around something

ˈair force ●●○ *n* [C] the part of a country's military organization that uses planes to fight → **army, navy**

ˌAir Force ˈOne the name of the plane that the US president uses

ˈair ˌfreshener *n* [C,U] a substance or object used to make a room smell pleasant

ˈair guiˌtar *n* [C,U] if someone plays air guitar, they pretend to play an imaginary GUITAR, usually while listening to ROCK music

air·gun /ˈeəgʌn $ ˈer-/ *n* [C] a gun that uses air pressure to fire a small round bullet

air·head /ˈeəhed $ ˈer-/ *n* [C] *informal* someone who behaves in a stupid way

ˈair ˌhostess *n* [C] *BrE old-fashioned* a woman who serves food and drink to passengers on a plane

air·i·ly /ˈeərəli $ ˈer-/ *adv* in a way that shows you are not worried about something or do not think it is serious: *'I don't really care,' he replied airily.*

air·ing /ˈeərɪŋ $ ˈer-/ *n* **1** [singular] an occasion when an opinion, idea etc is discussed: **be given/get an airing** *an issue that wasn't given an airing during the campaign* **2** [C] an occasion when a programme is broadcast on television or radio: *the program's first airing in 2000* **3** [C] an occasion when something is shown to people: *a car which had its first airing at the Paris Motor Show* **4** [singular] an occasion when you let fresh air move around something: *Put your houseplants outside to* ***give*** *them* ***an airing.***

ˈairing ˌcupboard *n* [C] *BrE* a warm cupboard in a house where you keep sheets

ˈair kiss *n* [C] a way of greeting someone with a kiss that is near the side of their face, but that does not touch them —**air-kiss** *v* [I,T]

air·less /ˈeələs $ ˈer-/ *adj* airless places or conditions are unpleasant because there is not enough fresh air → **airy**: *an airless room*

air·lift /ˈeəˌlɪft $ ˈer-/ *n* [C] an occasion when people or supplies are taken to a place by plane, especially during a war or dangerous situation —**airlift** *v* [T]

air·line /ˈeəlaɪn $ ˈer-/ ●●○ S3 W3 *n* [C] a company that takes passengers and goods to different places by plane: *an airline pilot*

air·lin·er /ˈeəˌlaɪnə $ ˈerˌlaɪnər/ *n* [C] a large plane for passengers

ˈair lock *n* [C] **1** a small room used for moving between two places that do not have the same air pressure, for example in a spacecraft **2** a small amount of air in a pipe that stops liquid flowing through it

air·mail /ˈeəmeɪl $ ˈer-/ *n* [U] letters and packages that are sent somewhere using a plane, or the system of doing this: *Send the letter by airmail.*

air·man /ˈeəmən $ ˈer-/ *n* (*plural* **airmen** /-mən/) [C] someone who is a member of their country's air force

ˈair ˌmarshal *n* [C] another name for a SKY MARSHAL

Air Miles /ˈeəmaɪlz $ ˈer-/ *trademark* a system in which people collect points when they buy things from certain companies. These points can be exchanged for free or cheaper flights. The name of the system has been changed in the UK to Avios.

air·plane /ˈeəpleɪn $ ˈer-/ *n* [C] *AmE* a vehicle that flies through the air and has one or more engines SYN **aeroplane** *BrE*, **plane**

air·play /ˈeəpleɪ $ ˈer-/ *n* [U] the number of times that a particular song is played on the radio: *The new single is already* ***getting airplay.***

ˈair ˌpocket *n* [C] **1** a current of air that makes a plane suddenly move down **2** a small area that becomes filled with air

air·port /ˈeəpɔːt $ ˈerpɔːrt/ ●●● S3 W3 *n* [C] a place where planes take off and land, with buildings for passengers to wait in → **airfield**: *The plane landed at Heathrow Airport.* | *Her family went to see her off at the airport.*

ˈairport ˌfiction *n* [U] books that are not very serious, and that people buy at airports to read when they are on a plane journey

ˈair pump *n* [C] a piece of equipment used to put air into something

ˈair quote *n* [C usually plural] a movement that someone makes in the air with their fingers to show that what they are saying should be in QUOTATION MARKS, and that it should not be taken as their real opinion or their usual way of speaking

ˈair rage *n* [U] violence and angry behaviour by a passenger on a plane towards other passengers or the people who work on it

ˈair raid *n* [C] an attack in which bombs are dropped on a place by planes

ˈair ˌrifle *n* [C] a gun that uses air pressure to fire a small bullet

air·ship /ˈeəʃɪp $ ˈer-/ *n* [C] a large aircraft with no wings, that has an engine and is filled with gas to make it float

air·show /ˈeəʃəʊ $ ˈerʃoʊ/ *n* [C] an event at which people watch planes fly and do very complicated movements in the sky

air·sick /ˈeəˌsɪk $ ˈer-/ *adj* feeling sick because of the movement of a plane —**airsickness** *n* [U]

air·space /ˈeəspeɪs $ ˈer-/ *n* [U] the sky above a particular country, that is legally controlled by that country: *Canadian airspace*

air·speed /ˈeəspiːd $ ˈer-/ *n* [singular, U] the speed at which a plane travels

ˈair strike *n* [C] an attack in which military aircraft drop bombs

air·strip /ˈeəˌstrɪp $ ˈer-/ *n* [C] a long narrow piece of land that planes can fly from or land on

ˈair ˌterminal *n* [C] a large building at an airport where passengers wait to get on planes

air·tight /ˈeətaɪt $ ˈer-/ *adj* **1** not allowing air to get in or out: *airtight containers* **2** planned or done so carefully that there is no chance of any problems or mistakes SYN **watertight**: *an airtight alibi*

air·time /ˈeətaɪm $ ˈer-/ *n* [U] **1** the amount of time that a radio or television station gives to a particular subject, advertisement etc: *Advertisers have bought airtime on all the major TV networks.* **2** the amount of time that has been paid for when using a MOBILE PHONE

ˈairtime proˌvider *n* [C] a company that provides the service that allows you to make and receive calls on a MOBILE PHONE

ˌair-to-ˈair *adj* shot from one plane to another while both planes are flying: *an air-to-air missile*

ˌair ˈtraffic conˌtrol *n* [U] **1** the process or job of giving instructions to pilots by radio **2** the people whose job is to do this

ˌair ˈtraffic conˌtroller *n* [C] someone at an airport whose job is to give instructions to pilots by radio

ˌair vice-ˈmarshal *n* [C] a high rank in the British air force, or someone who has this rank

air·waves /ˈeəweɪvz $ ˈer-/ *n* **the airwaves** *informal* radio and television broadcasts: **on/over the airwaves** *a subject that's been debated on the airwaves*

air·way /ˈeəweɪ $ ˈer-/ *n* [C] **1** the passage in your throat that you breathe through **2** an area of the sky that is regularly used by planes

air·wor·thy /ˈeəˌwɜːði $ ˈerˌwɜːrði/ *adj* a plane that is airworthy is safe to fly —**airworthiness** *n* [U]

air·y /ˈeəri $ ˈeri/ *adj* **1** an airy room or building has plenty of fresh air because it is large or has a lot of windows: *All the hotel's bedrooms are* ***light and airy***. **2** done in a happy and confident way, even when you should be serious or worried: *He dismissed her concerns with an airy wave of the hand.*

ˌairy ˈfairy *adj BrE informal* not sensible or practical: *airy fairy ideas*

aisle /aɪl/ ●○○ *n* [C]
1 a long passage between rows of seats in a church, plane, theatre etc, or between rows of shelves in a shop: *Would you like a window seat or an* ***aisle seat*** (=seat next to the aisle)?
2 go/walk down the aisle *informal* to get married → **be rolling in the aisles** at ROLL[1](20)

aitch /eɪtʃ/ *n* (*plural* **aitches**) [C,U] the letter H when written as a word not a letter: **drop your aitches** (=not pronounce the letter H at the beginning of words) *People with Cockney accents tend to drop their aitches.*

a·jar /əˈdʒɑː $ əˈdʒɑːr/ ●○○ *adj* [not before noun] a door that is ajar is slightly open

ak·a, **aka** /ˌeɪ keɪ ˈeɪ, ˈækə/ (***also known as***) used when giving someone or something's real name together with a different name they are known by: *John Phillips, aka The Mississippi Mauler*

a·kim·bo /əˈkɪmbəʊ $ -boʊ/ *adj* **1 (with) arms akimbo** with your hands on your HIPS so that your elbows point away from your body **2 (with) legs akimbo** with your legs wide apart

a·kin /əˈkɪn/ *adj formal* **akin to sth** very similar to something: *Something akin to panic overwhelmed him.*

à la /ˈæ lə, ˈɑː lɑː/ *prep* in the same style as someone or something else: *detective stories à la Agatha Christie*

al·a·bas·ter[1] /ˈæləbɑːstə $ -bæstər/ *n* [U] a white stone, used for making STATUES or other objects for decoration

alabaster[2] *adj* **1** made of alabaster **2** white and smooth

à la carte /ˌæ lə ˈkɑːt, ˌɑː lɑː- $ -ˈkɑːrt/ *adj, adv* if food in a restaurant is à la carte, each dish has a separate price

a·lac·ri·ty /əˈlækrəti/ *n* [U] *formal* quickness and eagerness: **with alacrity** | *She accepted with alacrity.*

A·lad·din's Cave /əˌlædənz ˈkeɪv/ *n* **an Aladdin's Cave** a place that contains a large variety of interesting, valuable, or exciting things. This expression comes from the story of Aladdin in *The Arabian Nights*: *Her apartment is an Aladdin's Cave of antiques, old books, and fine paintings.*

Al·a·mo /ˈæləməʊ/ **the Alamo** a famous battle that took place in 1836, when the US and Mexico were fighting each other for the control of Texas. The Americans were eventually all killed, but their brave action encouraged others, and Texas later became part of the US. The phrase 'Remember the Alamo!' is used to encourage people to continue doing something very difficult.

à la mode /ˌæ lə ˈməʊd, ˌɑː lɑː- $ -ˈmoʊd/ *adj, adv* **1** *old-fashioned* fashionable **2** *AmE* served with ICE CREAM: *apple pie à la mode*

ALARM

smoke alarm | alarm clock

a·larm[1] /əˈlɑːm $ əˈlɑːrm/ ●●● S2 *n*
1 [C] a piece of equipment that makes a loud noise to warn you of danger: *I forgot to set the burglar alarm.* | *Car alarms are always going off in the street.* | *a sophisticated alarm system*
2 [U] a feeling of fear or worry because something bad or dangerous might happen: **[+at]** *There is growing alarm at*

the increase in crime. | **in alarm** *She looked up in alarm.* | *Scientists have said* ***there is no cause for alarm.*** THESAURUS FEAR
3 [C] an alarm clock: *I've* ***set the alarm*** *for 7 o'clock.* | *I was still asleep when the* ***alarm went off.***
4 raise/sound the alarm *especially BrE* to warn people that something bad is happening: *Neighbours raised the alarm when they smelled smoke.*
5 alarm bells ring if alarm bells ring, you feel worried that something bad may be happening: *Alarm bells started to ring when he failed to return home.* → FALSE ALARM

COLLOCATIONS

ADJECTIVES/NOUN + alarm

a burglar alarm *Neighbours heard the burglar alarm and called the police.*
a fire/smoke alarm *A fire alarm went off and the building had to be evacuated.*
a car alarm (=for when someone tries to steal a car) *I was woken by a car alarm in the middle of the night.*
a baby alarm (=for when a baby wakes up and cries) *Is the baby alarm switched on?*
a personal alarm (=that you carry with you in case you are attacked)

alarm + NOUN

an alarm button *He hit the alarm button under the desk.*
an alarm system

VERBS

set off/trigger/activate the alarm (=make it start ringing) *A window blew open, setting off the alarm.*
set the alarm (=make it ready to operate) *Did you set the burglar alarm?*
an alarm goes off (*also* **an alarm sounds** *formal*) *The thieves fled when an alarm went off.*
switch/turn off the alarm

alarm² ●●○ *v* [T] to make someone feel worried or frightened: *I don't want to alarm you, but I can't find the key.*

a'larm clock *n* [C] a clock that makes a noise at a particular time to wake you up → see picture at CLOCK¹

a·larmed /ə'lɑːmd $ -ɑːr-/ ●●○ *adj*
1 worried or frightened: **[+by/at]** *Environmentalists are alarmed by the increase in pollution.* | **alarmed to see/hear etc** *He was alarmed to discover that his car was gone.* THESAURUS FRIGHTENED
2 protected by an alarm: *The whole building is alarmed.*

a·larm·ing /ə'lɑːmɪŋ $ -ɑːr-/ ●●○ *adj* making you feel worried or frightened SYN **disturbing**: *an alarming increase in violent crime* | *The rainforest is disappearing* ***at an alarming rate.*** —**alarmingly** *adv*

a·larm·ist /ə'lɑːmɪst $ -ɑːr-/ *adj* making people feel worried about dangers that do not really exist: *alarmist reports of health risks*

a·las¹ /ə'læs/ *adv* [sentence adverb] *formal* used when mentioning a fact that you wish was not true: *Donald, alas, died last year.*

alas² *interjection literary* used to express sadness, shame, or fear

al·ba·tross /'ælbətrɒs $ -trɒːs, -trɑːs/ *n* **1** [C] a very large white sea bird **2 an albatross (around your neck)** something that causes problems for you and prevents you from succeeding: *The issue has become a political albatross for the government.*

al·be·it /ɔːl'biːɪt $ ɒːl-/ ●○○ AWL *conjunction formal* used to add information that reduces the force or importance of what you have just said SYN **although**: *He accepted the job, albeit with some hesitation.* | *Chris went with her, albeit reluctantly.*

al·bi·no /æl'biːnəʊ $ æl'baɪnoʊ/ *n* (*plural* **albinos**) [C] a person or animal with a GENETIC condition that makes their skin and hair very white and their eyes pink

al·bum /'ælbəm/ ●●○ S3 W3 *n* [C]
1 a group of songs or pieces of music on a record, CD, DOWNLOAD etc: *The band plan to release their new album next week.*
2 a book that you put photographs, stamps etc in: *a photograph album*

al·bu·men /'ælbjʊmɪn $ æl'bjuː-/ *n* [U] *technical* the colourless part inside an egg SYN **white**

Al·ca·traz /'ælkətræz/ a prison on a rocky island in San Francisco Bay, in California. It was known for being almost impossible to escape from, and for having very strict rules for its prisoners. When people are describing a place that is very difficult to escape from, they often compare it to Alcatraz.

al·che·my /'ælkəmi/ *n* [U] **1** a science studied in the Middle Ages, that involved trying to change ordinary metals into gold **2** *literary* magic —**alchemist** *n* [C]

al·co·hol /'ælkəhɒl $ -hɒːl/ ●●● S2 W2 *n*
1 [U] drinks such as beer or wine that contain a substance which can make you drunk: *I don't drink alcohol anymore.* | ***alcohol abuse*** (=when someone drinks too much) | *people with* ***alcohol problems*** (=people who drink too much)
2 [C,U] the chemical substance in alcoholic drinks that can make you drunk, which is also used in other types of products: *low alcohol drinks*

al·co·hol·ic¹ /ˌælkə'hɒlɪk◂ $ -'hɒː-/ ●●○ *adj*
1 relating to alcohol or containing alcohol OPP **nonalcoholic**: *alcoholic drinks*
2 caused by drinking alcohol: *an alcoholic stupor*

alcoholic² ●○○ *n* [C] someone who regularly drinks too much alcohol and has difficulty stopping

al·co·hol·is·m /'ælkəhɒlɪzəm $ -hɒː-/ *n* [U] the medical condition of being an alcoholic

al·co·pop /'ælkəʊpɒp $ -koʊpɑːp/ *n* [C] *BrE* a sweet FIZZY drink that contains alcohol

ALCOVE

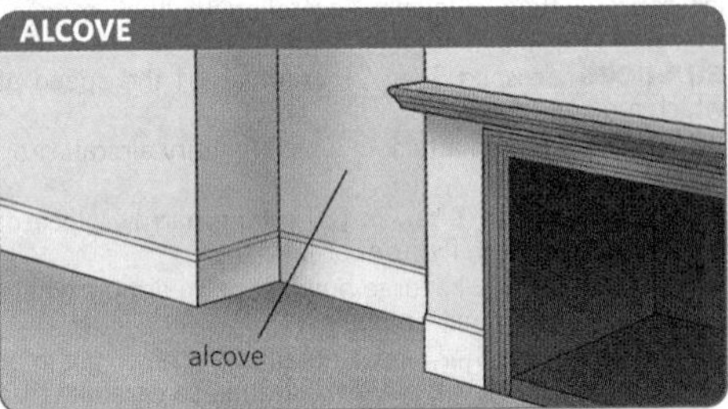

al·cove /'ælkəʊv $ -koʊv/ *n* [C] a place in the wall of a room that is built further back than the rest of the wall SYN **recess**

al den·te /æl 'denti, -teɪ/ *adj* food, especially PASTA that is al dente is still pleasantly firm after it has been cooked

al·der·man /'ɔːldəmən $ 'ɒːldər-/ *n* (*plural* **aldermen** /-mən/) [C] **1** an elected member of a town or city council in the US **2** an important member of a town council in Britain in the past

ale /eɪl/ *n* [U] **1** a type of beer made from MALT(1) **2** *old-fashioned* beer → LIGHT ALE

al·eck /'ælək/ → SMART ALEC

ale·house /'eɪlhaʊs/ *n* [C] *old-fashioned* a place where people drank beer in the past

a·lert¹ /ə'lɜːt $ -ɜːrt/ ●●○ *adj*
1 giving all your attention to what is happening, being said etc: *The animal raised its head, suddenly alert.* | *Taking notes is one of the best ways to* ***stay alert*** *in lectures.*
2 able to think quickly and clearly: *Jack was as* ***mentally alert*** *as a man half his age.*
3 be alert to sth to know about or understand something, especially a possible danger or problem: *The authorities should have been* ***alert to the possibility*** *of invasion.* —**alertness** *n* [U]

alert² ●●○ *v* [T]
1 to officially warn someone about a problem or danger so that they are ready to deal with it: *The school immediately* ***alerted the police.*** THESAURUS WARN

A

2 to make someone realize something important or dangerous: **alert sb to sth** *campaigns to alert the public to the dangers of HIV*

alert³ *n* **1** [C] a warning to be ready for possible danger: **a bomb/fire/terrorist etc alert** *a full-scale flood alert | The bomb alert was raised soon after midnight.* → RED ALERT **2 on (the) alert (for sth/sb)** ready to notice and deal with a situation or problem: *Be **on the alert** for anyone acting suspiciously. | Troops in the vicinity were **put on alert**.* | **on full alert** (*also* **on high alert**) (=completely ready to deal with a dangerous situation) *All our border points are on full alert.*

A lev·el /ˈeɪ ˌlevəl/ *n* [C,U] (*Advanced level*) an examination that students in England and Wales take, usually when they are 18 → **A/S level, GCSE, GNVQ, O level**: **do/take (your) A levels** *She decided to stay on at school and do her A levels.* | **at A level** *I took maths, physics, and chemistry at A level.*

Al·ex·an·der tech·nique /ˌælɪɡˈzɑːndə tekˌniːk $ -ˈzændər-/ *trademark* **the Alexander technique** a special way of sitting, standing, and moving, which some people believe helps to improve general health, cure back problems etc

al·fal·fa /ælˈfælfə/ *n* [U] a plant grown especially in the US to feed farm animals

al·fres·co /ælˈfreskəʊ $ -koʊ/ *adj, adv* if you eat alfresco, you eat in the open air: *We **dined alfresco**, on a balcony overlooking the sea.* | **alfresco lunch/supper etc**

al·gae /ˈældʒiː, -ɡiː/ *n* [U] a very simple plant without stems or leaves that grows in or near water

al·ge·bra /ˈældʒəbrə/ *n* [U] a type of mathematics that uses letters and other signs to represent numbers and values —**algebraic** /ˌældʒəˈbreɪ-ɪk◂/ *adj* —**algebraically** /-kli/ *adv*

al·go·rith·m /ˈælɡərɪðəm/ *n* [C] *technical* a set of instructions that are followed in a fixed order and used for solving a mathematical problem, making a computer program etc

a·li·as¹ /ˈeɪliəs/ *prep* used when giving someone's real name, especially an actor's or a criminal's name, together with another name they use: *'Friends' star Jennifer Aniston, alias Rachel Green*

alias² *n* [C] a false name, usually used by a criminal: *a spy operating **under** the **alias** Barsad*

al·i·bi /ˈæləbaɪ/ ●○○ *n* [C]
1 something that proves that someone was not where a crime happened and therefore could not have done it: **a perfect/cast-iron/unshakeable etc alibi** *He **had** a perfect **alibi** and the police let him go.*
2 an excuse for something you have failed to do or have done wrong

Al·ice in Won·der·land /ˌæləs ɪn ˈwʌndəlænd $ -dər-/ (*also* **ˌAlice's Adˌventures in ˈWonderland**) a book written in 1865 by Lewis Carroll about a girl called Alice who has many strange adventures. People sometimes describe something as being 'Alice-in-Wonderland', when they mean it is the opposite of what is normal or what you expect: *The book is a good introduction to the strange, Alice-in-Wonderland world of theoretical physics.*

a·li·en¹ /ˈeɪliən/ ●●○ *adj*
1 very different from what you are used to, especially in a way that is difficult to understand or accept SYN **strange**: *the alien environment of the city* | **be alien to sb** *a way of life that is totally alien to us*
2 belonging to another country or race SYN **foreign**: *alien cultures | an alien multiracial society*
3 [only before noun] relating to creatures from another world: ***alien beings** from another planet*

alien² ●○○ *n* [C]
1 someone who is not a legal citizen of the country they are living or working in: ***illegal aliens** entering the country*

> **REGISTER**
> **Alien** is used in official contexts. In everyday English, **foreigner** is used, but can sound disapproving or unfriendly. To avoid this, people often use the expression **people from other countries** instead: *In those days **people from other countries** rarely came to Japan.*

2 in stories, a creature from another world

a·li·en·ate /ˈeɪliəneɪt/ ●○○ *v* [T]
1 to do something that makes someone unfriendly or unwilling to support you: *The latest tax proposals will alienate many voters.*
2 to make it difficult for someone to belong to a particular group or to feel comfortable with a particular person: **alienate sb from sth** *He felt that his experiences had alienated him from society.* —**alienated** *adj*: *Gina had become alienated from her family.*

a·li·en·a·tion /ˌeɪliəˈneɪʃən/ *n* [U] **1** the feeling of not being part of society or a group: **[+from]** *Unemployment may provoke a **sense of alienation** from society.* **2** when someone becomes less friendly, understanding, or willing to give support as the result of something that happens or is done: **[+of]** *the alienation of voters*

a·light¹ /əˈlaɪt/ ●○○ *adj* [not before noun]
1 burning: *The car was **set alight** and pushed over a hill.*

> **REGISTER**
> **Alight** is mostly used in journalism or in literature. In everyday English, people usually say **on fire**: *The car had been deliberately **set on fire**.*

2 *literary* someone whose face or eyes are alight looks excited, happy, etc: **alight with excitement/pleasure/laughter etc** *Jed's face was alight with excitement.*
3 *literary* bright with light or colour

alight² *v* [I] *formal* **1** if a bird or insect alights on something, it stops flying and stands on it SYN **land** **2** to step out of a vehicle after a journey: **[+from]** *She alighted from the train at 74th Street.*
alight on/upon sth *phr v formal* to suddenly think of or notice something or someone: *His mind alighted on several possible answers.*

a·lign /əˈlaɪn/ ●○○ *v*
1 [T] to publicly support a political group, country, or person that you agree with: **align yourself with sb/sth** *Church leaders have aligned themselves with the opposition. | a country **closely aligned** with the West*
2 [I,T] to arrange things so that they form a line or are parallel to each other, or to be in a position that forms a line etc: *The desks were neatly aligned in rows. | Make sure that all the holes align.*
3 [T] to organize or change something so that it has the right relationship to something else: **be aligned with sth** *This policy is **closely aligned** with the goals of the organization.*

a·lign·ment /əˈlaɪnmənt/ ●○○ *n*
1 [U] the state of being arranged in a line with something or parallel to something: **[+of]** *the geometrical alignment of the Sun, Moon, and Earth at the eclipse* | **out of/into alignment** *The wheels were out of alignment.*
2 [C,U] support given by one country or group to another in politics, defence etc: **[+with]** *their military alignment with the US*

a·like¹ /əˈlaɪk/ ●●○ *adj* [not before noun] very similar: *My mother and I are alike in many ways.* THESAURUS SIMILAR

alike² ●●○ *adv*
1 in a similar way: *The twins were dressed alike.* → **great minds think alike** at GREAT¹(15)
2 used to emphasize that you mean both the people, groups, or things that you have just mentioned: *I learned a lot from teachers and students alike.*

al·i·men·ta·ry ca·nal /ˌæləmentəri kəˈnæl/ *n* [C] the tube in your body that takes food through your body from your mouth to your ANUS SYN **digestive tract**

al·i·mo·ny /ˈæləməni $ -moʊni/ *n* [U] money that a court orders someone to pay regularly to their former wife or husband after their marriage has ended → **maintenance**

A-list /ˈeɪ lɪst/ *n* **the A-list** all the most popular or famous film stars, musicians etc → **B-list**: *the Hollywood A-list | A-list celebrities*

A-list·er /ˈeɪ ˌlɪstə $ -ər/ *n* [C] *informal* a very famous film star, musician etc – used especially in newspapers and magazines: *Several A-listers are expected to be at the movie premiere.*

a·lit /əˈlɪt/ a past tense and past participle of ALIGHT

a·live /əˈlaɪv/ ●●● S2 W3 *adj* [not before noun]
1 NOT DEAD still living and not dead: *It was a bad accident – they're lucky to be alive. | My grandparents are **still alive**. | We **stayed alive** by eating berries. | He was **kept alive** on a life-support machine. | Apparently he's **alive and well** and living in Brazil.*
2 STILL EXISTING continuing to exist: *Ancient traditions are very much alive in rural areas. | Christianity is **alive and well** in Asia. | The sport is still very much **alive and kicking** in this country.*
3 CHEERFUL full of energy, happiness, activity etc: *It was the kind of morning when you wake up and **feel** really **alive**. |* **[+with]** *Her face was alive with excitement. | The whole house was alive with activity.*
4 come alive a) if a subject or event comes alive, it becomes interesting and seems real: *Hopefully, we can make history come alive for the children.* **b)** if someone comes alive, they suddenly become happy and interested in what is happening: *She only came alive when she sat down at the piano.* **c)** if a town, city etc comes alive, it becomes busy: *seaside resorts that come alive in the summer*
5 be alive to a fact/possibility/danger etc to know that a particular fact etc exists and that it is important: *The company is alive to the threat posed by foreign imports.*
6 be alive with sth to be full of living things that are moving: *The pond was alive with fish.*
7 bring sth alive to make something interesting and real: *The way he describes his characters really brings them alive.*
→ **skin sb alive** at SKIN²(3)

al·ka·li /ˈælkəlaɪ/ *n* [C,U] a substance that forms a chemical salt when combined with an acid → **acid**

al·ka·line /ˈælkəlaɪn/ *adj* containing an alkali

all¹ /ɔːl $ ɒːl/ ●●● S1 W1 *determiner, predeterminer, pron*
1 the whole of an amount, thing, or type of thing: *Have you done all your homework? |* **all your life/all day/all year etc** (=during the whole of your life, a day, a year etc) *He had worked all his life in the mine. | The boys played video games all day. | They were quarrelling **all the time*** (=very often or continuously). *| Hannah didn't say a single word **all the way** back home* (=during the whole of the journey). *|* **[+of]** *Almost all of the music was from Italian operas. | I've heard it all before. | She'd given up all hope of having a child.*
2 every one of a number of people or things, or every thing or person of a particular type: *Someone's taken all my books! | Will all the girls please stand over here. | All children should be taught to swim. | Sixteen per cent of all new cars sold in Western Europe these days are diesel-engined. | They all speak excellent English. |* **[+of]** *important changes that will affect all of us*
3 the only thing or things: *All you need is a hammer and some nails. | All I'm asking for is a little respect.*
4 *formal* everything: *I'm doing all I can to help her. | I hope all is well with you. | All was dark and silent down by the harbour wall.*
5 used to emphasize that you mean the greatest possible amount of the quality you are mentioning: *Can any of us say in all honesty that we did everything we could?*
6 at all used in negative statements and questions to emphasize what you are saying: *They've done nothing at all to try and put the problem right. | He's not looking at all well. | 'Do you mind if I stay a little longer?' 'No, not at all.' | Has the situation improved at all?*
7 all sorts/kinds/types of sth many different kinds of something: *Social workers have to deal with all kinds of problems.*
8 of all people/things/places etc used to emphasize that your statement is true of one particular person, thing, or place more than any other: *You shouldn't have done it. You of all people should know that. | She did not want to quarrel with Maria today, of all days.*
9 all in all used to show that you are considering every part of a situation: *All in all, it had been one of the most miserable days of Henry's life.*
10 for all sth in spite of a particular fact: *For all his faults, he's a kind-hearted old soul. | For all my love of landscape, nothing could persuade me to spend another day in the Highlands.*
11 in all including every thing or person: *In all, there were 215 candidates. | We received £1,550 in cash and promises of another £650, making £2,200 in all.*
12 and all a) including the thing or things just mentioned: *They ate the whole fish – head, bones, tail, and all.* **b)** *spoken informal* used to emphasize a remark that you have just added: *And you can take that smelly old coat out of here, and all!*
13 all of 50p/20 minutes etc *spoken* used to emphasize how large or small an amount actually is: *The game lasted all of 58 seconds. | The repairs are going to cost all of £15,000.*
14 it's all or nothing used to say that unless something is done completely, it is not acceptable: *Half-heartedness won't do – it's got to be all or nothing.*
15 give your all to make the greatest possible effort in order to achieve something: *The coach expects every player to give their all in every game.*
16 it was all I could do to do sth used to say that you only just succeeded in doing something: *It was all I could do to stop them hitting each other.*
17 when all's said and done *spoken* used to remind someone about an important point that needs to be considered: *When all's said and done, he's only a kid.*
18 all sorts/kinds of wrong/crazy etc *informal* wrong, crazy etc in many ways, or very wrong, crazy etc: *Her beach outfit is all sorts of wrong.* → **for all sb cares** at CARE²(8), → **for all sb knows** at KNOW¹(33), → **all and sundry** at SUNDRY(1), → **after all** at AFTER¹(13)

GRAMMAR: Patterns with all

- You use **all the** or **all of the** when talking about every one of a particular group of people or things: ***All the** students have gone home. | **All of the** students have gone home.*
- You use **all** directly before a plural noun to mean every person or thing of a particular type: *All men are created equal. | All children like chocolate.*

all² ●●● S1 W1 *adv*
1 [always + adj/adv/prep] completely: *You shouldn't be sitting here by yourself, all alone. | a strange woman, dressed all in black | If people want more freedom of choice, then I'm **all for** it* (=I strongly support it). *| 'It was a dreadful experience.' 'Never mind, it's **all over*** (=completely finished) *now.'*
2 all over (sth) a) everywhere on an object or surface: *There were bits of paper all over the floor. | He has cuts all over his legs. | She ached all over* (=her whole body ached). **b)** everywhere in a place: *Antique clocks from all over the world are on display. | People came from all over the country. | They're putting up new offices all over the place.*
3 all the better/easier/more etc used to emphasize how much better, easier etc something is than it would be in a different situation: *Clayton's achievement is all the more remarkable when you consider his poor performance last season. | The job was made all the easier by having the proper tools.*
4 all but almost completely: *Britain's coal industry has all but disappeared. | His left arm was all but useless.*
5 all too used to mean 'very' when talking about a bad situation: *All too often it's the mother who gets blamed for her children's behaviour. | In these conditions it was all too easy to make mistakes.*
6 all along *informal* all the time from the beginning while

something was happening: *Chapman had known all along that the plan wouldn't work.* | *We had to admit that Dad had been right all along.*
7 all round *BrE*, **all around** *AmE* **a)** used to say that you are describing the general quality or effect of something: *All round it's not a bad car.* | *It was a nasty business all round.* **b)** from everyone, for everyone, or involving everyone: *There were smiles all round.* | *He paid for drinks all round.*
8 one-all/two-all etc used when giving the score of a game in which both players or teams have scored the same number of points: *The game ended one-all.*
9 all told including everything or everyone: *a project costing £10,000, all told*
10 it's all up (with sb) *BrE informal* used to say that someone's success or happiness has ended: *If someone tells the police, then it'll be all up with me.*
11 be not all there *informal* someone who is not all there seems stupid or slightly crazy
12 be all smiles/innocence/sweetness etc to be showing a lot of a particular quality or type of behaviour: *The mayor and mayoress were all smiles and kisses during the grand ceremony.*
13 be all over sb *informal* to be trying to kiss someone and touch them, especially in a sexual way: *Before I could speak, he was all over me.*

SPOKEN PHRASES
14 very: *You're getting me all confused.*
15 that's sb all over used to say that a particular way of behaving is typical of someone: *He was late of course, but that's Tim all over!*
16 be all in *BrE* to be very tired
17 sb was all ... *AmE* used to report what someone said or did, when telling a story: *He drove me home, and he was all, 'I love this car ... it's like a rocket.'*
18 not all that not very: *It doesn't sound all that good, does it?* | *I don't think it matters all that much.*
19 sb/sth is not all that used to say that someone or something is not very attractive or desirable: *I don't know why you keep chasing her around. She's not all that.*

all- /ɔːl $ ɒːl/ *prefix* **1** consisting of or made of only one kind of thing: *an all-male club* | *an all-wool coat* **2 all-day/all-night** continuing for the whole day or night: *an all-day seminar* | *an all-night café*

Al·lah /ˈælə $ ˈælə, ˈɑː-/ the Muslim name for God

ˌall-Aˈmerican *adj* [usually before noun] **1** having qualities that are considered to be typically American and that American people admire, such as being healthy and working hard: *an all-American family* **2** belonging to a group of players who have been chosen as the best in their sport at American universities: *an all-American football player*

ˌall-aˈround *adj* [only before noun] *AmE* good at doing many different things, especially sports SYN **all-round** *BrE*: *an all-around athlete*

al·lay /əˈleɪ/ *v* [T] **allay (sb's) fear/concern/suspicion etc** to make someone feel less afraid, worried etc: *The president made a statement to allay public anxiety.*

ˌall ˈclear, **all-clear** *n* **the all clear a)** official permission to begin doing something: **give (sb)/get the all clear** *We've got the all clear for the new project.* **b)** a signal such as a loud whistle that tells you that a dangerous situation has ended

ˌall ˈcomers, **all-comers** *n* [plural] everyone who wants to take part in something, especially a competition: *The marathon is open to all comers.*

al·le·ga·tion /ˌælɪˈɡeɪʃən/ ●●○ *n* [C usually plural] a statement that someone has done something wrong or illegal, but that has not been proved: **allegations of corruption/fraud/misconduct etc** *Mr Singh has strongly* ***denied*** *the* ***allegations*** *of sexual harassment.* | **allegation that** *an allegation that senior government figures were involved* | **[+against]** *The teacher* ***made*** *serious* ***allegations*** *against a colleague.* | **[+of]** *A committee will* ***investigate allegations*** *of racial discrimination.* **THESAURUS▸** CLAIM

al·lege /əˈledʒ/ ●●○ *v* [T] *formal* to say that something is true or that someone has done something wrong, although it has not been proved: **it is alleged (that)** *It was alleged that the policeman had accepted bribes.* | **allege that** *The prosecution alleged that the man had been responsible for an act of terrorism.* | **be alleged to be/do sth** *The water is alleged to be polluted with mercury.* **THESAURUS▸** ACCUSE

al·leged /əˈledʒd/ *adj* [only before noun] *formal* an alleged crime, fact etc is one that someone says has happened or is true, although it has not been proved: **alleged offence/crime/incident etc** *their alleged involvement in international terrorism* | *The* ***alleged victim*** *made the complaint at a police station in York.*

al·leg·ed·ly /əˈledʒɪdli/ ●○○ *adv* [sentence adverb] *formal* used when reporting something that people say is true, although it has not been proved: *a sports car, allegedly stolen in Manchester*

al·le·giance /əˈliːdʒəns/ ●○○ *n* [C,U] loyalty to a leader, country, belief etc: **[+to]** *You* ***owe allegiance*** (=have a duty to give allegiance) *to your king.* | **swear/pledge allegiance** *I pledge allegiance to the flag of the United States of America.* | *an oath of allegiance* | **switch/transfer allegiance** (=start to support a different person, group etc) | *The people here have strong* ***political allegiances****.*

al·le·go·ry /ˈæləɡəri $ -ɡɔːri/ *n* (*plural* **allegories**) [C,U] a story, painting etc in which the events and characters represent ideas or teach a moral lesson —**allegorical** /ˌæləˈɡɒrɪkəl $ -ˈɡɔːr-/ *adj* —**allegorically** /-kli/ *adv*

al·leg·ro /əˈleɡrəʊ, əˈleɪ- $ -ɡroʊ/ *n* (*plural* **allegros**) [C] a piece of music played or sung quickly —**allegro** *adj, adv*

al·le·lu·ia /ˌæləˈluːjə◂/ *interjection* another spelling of HALLELUJAH

ˌall-emˈbracing *adj* including everyone or everything: *an all-embracing vision of society*

Al·len key /ˈælən kiː/ *n* [C] *BrE* a tool used to turn an Allen screw SYN **Allen wrench** *AmE*

Allen screw /ˈælən skruː/ *n* [C] a type of screw with a hole that has six sides

Allen wrench /ˈælən rentʃ/ *n* [C] *AmE* a tool used to turn an Allen screw SYN **Allen key** *BrE*

al·ler·gen /ˈælədʒən $ -lər-/ *n* [C] a substance that causes an allergy

al·ler·gic /əˈlɜːdʒɪk $ -ɜːr-/ ●○○ *adj*
1 having an allergy: **[+to]** *I'm allergic to penicillin.*
2 caused by an allergy: *an* ***allergic reaction*** *to nuts* | *an* ***allergic rash***
3 be allergic to sth *informal* if you are allergic to something, you do not like it and try to avoid it – used humorously: *Most men are allergic to housework!*

al·ler·gy /ˈælədʒi $ -ər-/ ●○○ *n* (*plural* **allergies**) [C,U] a medical condition in which you become ill or in which your skin becomes red and painful because you have eaten or touched a particular substance: **[+to]** *I* ***have an allergy*** *to cats.* | *a* ***food allergy***

al·le·vi·ate /əˈliːvieɪt/ ●○○ *v* [T] to make something less painful or difficult to deal with: **alleviate the problem/situation/suffering etc** *a new medicine to alleviate the symptoms of flu* | *measures to alleviate poverty* —**alleviation** /əˌliːviˈeɪʃən/ *n* [U]

al·ley /ˈæli/ ●●○ *n*
1 [C] (*also* **alleyway**) a narrow street between or behind buildings, not usually used by cars: *The alley led to the railway bridge.* | *She found the side alley where the stage door was located.*
2 right up/down sb's alley very suitable for someone: *The job sounds right up your alley.* → BLIND ALLEY, BOWLING ALLEY

ˈalley cat *n* [C] a cat that lives on the streets and does not belong to anyone

al·ley·way /ˈæliweɪ/ *n* [C] an ALLEY

ˌall-ˈfired *adv AmE* completely – used when describing a quality that you think is extreme: *If he weren't so all-fired sure of himself, I'd like him better.*

all ˈfours → **on all fours** at FOUR(2)

ˌall ˈgo *adj BrE* **it's all go** *spoken* used to say that a situation is very busy and full of activity: *It was all go from 8.00 until we finished at 5.00.*

al·li·ance /əˈlaɪəns/ ●○○ *n* [C]
1 an arrangement in which two or more countries, groups etc agree to work together to try to change or achieve something: **[+with]** *Britain's* ***military alliance*** *with her NATO partners* | **[+between]** *the possibility of a* ***political alliance*** *between the two parties* | **make/enter into/form/forge an alliance** (=agree to work together) *The companies have formed an alliance to market the product.*
2 a group of two or more countries, groups etc who work together to achieve something: *independent organizations and alliances*
3 in alliance (with sb/sth) if two groups, countries etc are in alliance, they work together to achieve something or protect each another: *Relief workers in alliance with local charities are trying to help the victims.*
4 *formal* a close relationship, especially a marriage, between people → **unholy alliance** at UNHOLY(1)

al·lied /ˈælaɪd, əˈlaɪd/ ●○○ *adj*
1 *usually* **Allied** [only before noun] belonging or relating to the countries that fought with Britain, the US etc in the First or Second World War: *an Allied bombing raid* | *Allied forces*
2 (be) allied to/with sth *formal* to be related to something or to be very similar: *Anthropology is closely allied to the field of psychology.*
3 allied industries/organizations/trades etc connected with each other because of being similar to or dependent on each other: *agriculture and allied industries*
4 joined by the same political, military, or economic aims: *loosely allied guerilla groups*

al·li·ga·tor /ˈæləgeɪtə $ -ər/ *n* **1** [C] a large animal with a long mouth and tail and sharp teeth that lives in the hot wet parts of the US and China → see picture at **REPTILE 2** [U] the skin of this animal used as leather: *alligator shoes*

ˌall-imˈportant *adj* extremely important: *the all-important question in everyone's minds*

ˌall ˈin, all-in *adj, adv BrE* used to describe the total cost of something, or the total amount of money charged for something SYN **inclusive**: **all-in price/package/deal etc** *all-in deals to Australia and New Zealand* | *The hourly rate is £20 all in.*

ˌall-inˈclusive *adj* including the cost of everything in the price charged SYN **all in**: **an all-inclusive price/package/holiday etc** *an all-inclusive vacation cruise*

ˌall-in-ˈone¹ *n* [C] a DESKTOP COMPUTER with the PROCESSOR, DRIVE etc combined with the screen, rather than being in a separate box

ˌall-in-ˈone² *adj* [only before noun] *BrE* combining two or more things that are usually separate into one thing: *an all-in-one TV and video*

al·lit·er·a·tion /əˌlɪtəˈreɪʃən/ *n* [U] the use of several words together that begin with the same sound or letter in order to make a special effect, especially in poetry **THESAURUS** LANGUAGE

ˌall-ˈnighter *n* [C] *AmE informal* an occasion when you spend the whole night studying or doing written work at university

al·lo·cate /ˈæləkeɪt/ ●○○ AWL *v* [T] to use something for a particular purpose, give something to a particular person etc, especially after an official decision has been made: **allocate sth to sb/sth** *the importance of* ***allocating resources*** *to local communities* | *You should allocate the same amount of time to each question.* | **allocate sth for sth** *One million dollars was allocated for disaster relief.* | **allocate sb/sth sth** *Several patients were waiting to be allocated a bed.*

al·lo·ca·tion /ˌæləˈkeɪʃən/ ●○○ AWL *n*
1 [C] the amount or share of something that has been allocated for a particular purpose: *Twelve hours a week seemed a generous allocation of your time.*
2 [U] the decision to allocate something, or the act of allocating it: **[+of]** *the allocation of funds to universities*

al·lot /əˈlɒt $ əˈlɑːt/ *v* (**allotted, allotting**) [T] to use a particular amount of time for something, or give a particular share of money, space etc to someone or something SYN **allocate**: **allot sth to sth/sb** *Try and allot two or three hours a day to revision.* | *Each school will be allotted twenty seats.* | **allot sb sth** *Everyone who works for the company has been allotted ten shares.* —**allotted** *adj* [only before noun]: *The department has already spent more than its allotted budget.*

al·lot·ment /əˈlɒtmənt $ əˈlɑːt-/ *n* **1** [C,U] an amount or share of something such as money or time that is given to someone or something, or the process of doing this: *The budget allotment for each county is below what is needed.* | **[+of]** *the allotment of shares in the company* **2** [C] *BrE* a small area of land that people can rent for growing vegetables

ˌall-ˈout *adj* [only before noun] done in a very determined way, and involving a lot of energy or anger: **all-out war/attack/offensive etc** | *an all-out effort to win* —**all out** *adv*: *Canada will have to* ***go all out*** *on the ice if they want to win.*

al·low /əˈlaʊ/ ●●● S1 W1 *v* [T]
1 CAN DO STH to let someone do or have something, or let something happen SYN **permit**: **allow sb to do sth** *My parents wouldn't allow me to go to the party.* | *Students are not allowed to eat in class.* | **sth is allowed** (=something is officially permitted) *Are dictionaries allowed in the exam?* | **allow sb sth** *Passengers are allowed one item of hand luggage each.* | *How much time are we allowed?* | **allow yourself sth** *He allowed himself the occasional glass of wine.* | **allow sth** *We don't allow diving in the pool.* | **allow sb in/out/up etc** *I don't allow the cat in the bedroom.* | *The audience is not allowed backstage.* | **sb should be allowed to do sth** *Students should be allowed to make their own decisions.* | **allow sth to do sth** *Don't allow your problems to dominate your life.*
2 MAKE STH POSSIBLE to make it possible for something to happen or for someone to do something, especially something helpful or useful SYN **permit**: **allow for sth** *Our new system will allow for more efficient use of resources.* | **allow sb to do sth** *A 24-hour ceasefire allowed the two armies to reach an agreement.* | **allow sb sth** *a seat belt that allows the driver greater freedom of movement* | **allow sth** *This adjustment of the figures allows a fairer comparison.*
3 HAVE ENOUGH OF STH to be sure that you have enough time, money, food etc available for a particular purpose: **allow sb sth** *Allow yourselves plenty of time to get to the airport.* | **allow sth for sb/sth** *I've allowed half a bottle of wine for each person.*
4 CORRECT/PERMITTED *formal* to accept that something is correct or true, or that something is acceptable according to the rules or law: *The judge allowed the evidence.* | **allow that** *I allow that there may have been a mistake.*
5 allow me *formal* used as a polite way of offering to help someone do something: *'Allow me,' the waiter said, opening the door.* → **LET¹**, **FORBID(1)**

GRAMMAR: Comparison

allow
• You **allow** someone **to do** something: *Her boss allows her to work from home.*
• Something **is allowed**: *Working from home is allowed.*
Allow is often used in the passive.

let
• You **let** someone **do** something: *Her boss lets her work from home.* ✗ Don't say: *let someone to do something*
Let is not used in the passive.

permit
• Something **is permitted**: *Working from home is permitted.*
• Someone **is permitted to do** something: *Employees are permitted to work from home.*
Permit is usually used in the passive.
GRAMMAR GUIDE VERBS

THESAURUS

allow to say that someone can do something – used about parents, teachers, or people in authority: *They*

don't allow students to chew gum in the classroom. | *I'm not allowed to stay out after ten o'clock.*
let [not in passive] to allow someone to do something. **Let** is not used in the passive, and is much more commonly used in everyday English than allow: *Will your mum let you come to the party?* | *I'll borrow John's bicycle, if he'll let me.*
permit *formal* if something is permitted, it is allowed according to the rules – used especially on written notices and announcements: *Smoking is not permitted anywhere in the building.*
give sb permission used when someone in an important official position decides to allow someone to do something: *He was given special permission to leave school early.* | *The Home Office has given him permission to stay in Britain indefinitely.*
give your consent to say that you will allow someone to do something that will affect you personally, or a member of your family, when you have a legal right to say 'no': *Her parents have given their consent to the marriage.*
give sth the go-ahead to officially allow a planned project or activity to happen: *The government finally gave the go-ahead for a new terminal at Heathrow airport.* | *A new nuclear plant has been given the go-ahead.*
authorize to officially or legally allow someone to do something – used about laws or people: *The UN resolution would authorize the use of force.* | *I never authorized them to give information about me to other banks.*
entitle to give someone the right to do or have something: *The pass entitles you to travel on any bus, at any time, in Norwich.* | *If the goods are faulty, the customer is entitled to a refund.*
sanction *formal* to give official approval and support for something: *The Truman administration refused to sanction a military attack.* | *The advertisements were sanctioned by the candidate himself.*

allow for sb/sth *phr v* to consider the possible facts, problems, costs etc involved in something when making a plan, calculation, or judgment: *Allowing for inflation, the cost of the project will be $2 million.* | *You should always allow for the possibility that it might rain.*
allow of sth *phr v formal* to make it possible for something to happen or be accepted: *The facts allow of only one interpretation.*

al·low·a·ble /əˈlaʊəbəl/ *adj* **1** acceptable according to the rules SYN **permissible**: *The maximum allowable dosage is two tablets a day.* **2** allowable costs are costs that you do not pay tax on: *allowable deductions such as alimony and business expenses*

al·low·ance /əˈlaʊəns/ ●●○ *n*
1 [C usually singular] an amount of money that you are given regularly or for a special purpose: **a monthly/annual etc allowance** *His father gives him a monthly allowance of £200.* | **[+for]** *Do you* ***get an allowance*** *for clothes?* | *Sales staff get a generous mileage allowance or a company car.* | *If you are entitled to sickness allowance, you must claim it from your employer.*
2 [C usually singular] an amount of something that is acceptable or safe: *the recommended* ***daily allowance*** *of Vitamin C* | *Passengers' baggage allowance is 75 pounds per person.*
3 [C] *BrE* an amount of money that you can earn without paying tax on it: *a new* ***tax allowance***
4 [C usually singular] *especially AmE* a small amount of money that a parent regularly gives to a child SYN **pocket money** *BrE*
5 [C,U] something that you consider when deciding what is likely to happen, what you should expect etc: **[+for]** *There is always an allowance in insurance premiums for whether someone smokes or not.* | **make (an) allowance/make allowances (for sth)** *The budget makes allowances for extra staff when needed.*
6 make allowance/allowances (for sb) to let someone behave in a way you do not normally approve of, because you know there are special reasons for their behaviour: *Dad's under pressure – you have to make allowances.*

al·loy¹ /ˈælɔɪ $ ˈælɔɪ, əˈlɔɪ/ *n* [C,U] a metal that consists of two or more metals mixed together: *Brass is an alloy of copper and zinc.*

al·loy² /əˈlɔɪ $ əˈlɔɪ, ˈælɔɪ/ *v* [T + with] *technical* to mix one metal with another

ˌall-ˈpowerful *adj* having complete power or control SYN **omnipotent**: *an all-powerful dictator*

ˌall-ˈpurpose *adj* [only before noun] able to be used in any situation: *an all-purpose cleaner*

all ˈright ●●● S1 W2 *adj* [not before noun], *adv, interjection*
1 GOOD satisfactory, but not excellent SYN **okay**: *'What's the food like?' 'It's all right, but the place on campus is better.'* | *'How's school going, Steve?' 'Oh, all right, I guess.'*
2 NO PROBLEMS not ill, hurt, or upset or not having any problems SYN **okay**: *Kate looks really unhappy – I'd better make sure she's all right.* | *Are you* ***feeling all right***? | *The kids seem to be* ***getting on all right*** *at school.* | *Tony was worried about the meeting but it* ***went all right*** (=happened with no problems). | *Don't worry, it'll* ***turn out all right***.
3 do all right (for yourself/herself etc) to be successful in your job, life etc: *She's doing all right – she's got a job with Microsoft.*
4 SUITABLE used to say whether something is suitable or convenient SYN **okay**: **[+with/by/for]** *Is Thursday morning all right with you?* | *We'll eat at eight. Does that* ***sound all right*** *to you?*
5 it's all right used to make someone feel less afraid or worried: *It's all right, Mommy's here.*
6 it's/that's all right used to reply to someone who thanks you or says they are sorry about something: *'Thanks for all your help!' 'That's* ***quite all right***.*'*
7 PERMISSION used to ask or give permission for something SYN **okay**: *Would it be all right if I left early?* | **be all right to do sth** *Is it all right to bring my dog?*
8 AGREEMENT used to agree with someone's suggestion, although you may be slightly unwilling SYN **okay**: *'Why not come along?' 'Oh, all right.'*
9 UNDERSTANDING [sentence adverb] used to check that someone understands what you have said, or to show that you understand SYN **okay**: *I'll leave a key with the neighbours, all right?* | *'The train leaves at 5.30.' 'All right, I'm coming!'*
10 THREATEN used when asking in a threatening or angry way what someone's intentions are SYN **okay**: *All right, you two. What are you doing in my room?*
11 CHANGE/END SUBJECT used to introduce a new subject or to end a conversation SYN **okay**: *All right, now I'd like to introduce our first speaker.*
12 it's all right for sb *BrE informal* used to say that someone else does not have the problems that you have, or that you are jealous because someone else is luckier than you: *'I get eight weeks' holiday a year.' 'Well,* ***it's all right for some***.*'*
13 EMPHASIZE *informal* used to emphasize that you are certain about something: *'Are you sure it was Bill?' 'Oh, yes, it was him all right.'*
14 HAPPY *AmE informal* used to say you are happy about something you have just been told: *You passed? All right!*
15 LIKE *BrE* used to describe someone you like or approve of: *'The new boss isn't too bad, is she?' 'No, she's all right.'*
16 GREETING *especially BrE informal* used as a greeting when you meet someone you know well, or reply to a greeting: *'How are you, John?' 'Oh, all right – can't complain.'*
17 I'm all right Jack *BrE informal* used to describe someone's attitude when they do not care about other people as long as they themselves are happy, comfortable etc
18 it'll be all right on the night *BrE informal* used to say that something will be successful, even though there have been lots of problems: *Workmen have yet to finish the new complex, but the organisers are confident it will be all right on the night.* → **a bit of all right** at BIT¹(12)

A

ˌall-ˈround *BrE*, **all-aˈround** *AmE adj* [only before noun] good at doing many different things: *an all-round athlete*

all-ˈrounder *n* [C] *BrE* someone with many different skills: *a good all-rounder*

ˌall-ˈseater *adj BrE* an all-seater football ground, STADIUM etc is one where everyone has a seat

all-ˌsinging, all-ˈdancing *adj* [only before noun] *BrE* an all-singing, all-dancing machine or system can do many things because it is so technically advanced - used humorously

all·spice /ˈɔːlspaɪs $ ˈɒːl-/ *n* [U] the dried fruit of a tropical American tree, crushed and used in cooking

ˈall-star *adj* [only before noun] including many famous actors, sports players etc: *an all-star cast*

ˌall-terˈrain *adj* [only before noun] all-terrain vehicles are very strong with thick tyres and are suitable for use in many different conditions: *an all-terrain bike*

ˈall-through *adj* an all-through system of education is one where students attend the same school for the whole of their education

ˈall-time *adj* used when you compare things to say that one of them is the best, worst etc that there has ever been: **an all-time high/low** *The price of wheat had reached an all-time low.* | *They reached an* ***all-time record*** *score.*

al·lude /əˈluːd/ ●○○ *v*
allude to sb/sth *phr v formal* to mention something or someone indirectly: *Rick didn't want to discuss his past, though he alluded darkly to 'some bad things that happened.'*

al·lure /əˈljʊə $ əˈlʊr/ *n* [singular, U] a mysterious, exciting, or desirable quality: **[+of]** *the allure of foreign travel* | *At 50, she had lost none of her sexual allure.* —**allure** *v* [T]: *harmonies that never fail to allure the listener* —**alluring** *adj*: *the alluring magic of Hong Kong* —**allurement** *n* [C,U]

al·lu·sion /əˈluːʒən/ *n* [C,U] something said or written that mentions a subject, person etc indirectly: **[+to]** *The committee* ***made*** *no* ***allusion*** *to the former president in its report.* | **literary/classical/cultural etc allusions** *Eliot's poetry is full of biblical allusions.* | *In his poetry we find many allusions to the human body.* —**allusive** /-sɪv/ *adj* [only before noun]

al·lu·vi·al /əˈluːviəl/ *adj* [usually before noun] *technical* made of soil left by rivers, lakes, floods etc: *alluvial flood plains*

al·lu·vi·um /əˈluːviəm/ *n* [U] *technical* soil left by rivers, lakes, floods etc

al·ly¹ /ˈælaɪ $ ˈælaɪ, əˈlaɪ/ ●○○ *n* (*plural* **allies**) [C]
1 a country that agrees to help or support another country in a war: *a meeting of the European allies*
2 the Allies the group of countries including Britain and the US that fought together in the First and Second World Wars
3 someone who helps and supports you when other people are trying to oppose you: *Ridley was one of the Queen's* ***closest allies***. | *a* ***staunch ally*** (=very close ally) *of President Soares* | *a network of* ***political allies*** | *She knew she had found an ally in Ted.*
4 something that helps you succeed in a difficult situation: *Exercise is an important ally in your campaign to lose weight.*

al·ly² /əˈlaɪ $ əˈlaɪ,ˈælaɪ/ *v* (**allied**, **allying**, **allies**) [T always +adv/prep] to help and support other people or countries, especially in a war or disagreement: **ally yourself to/with sb** *Some of the northern cities allied themselves with the emperor.* → ALLIED

al·ma ma·ter /ˌælmə ˈmɑːtə, -ˈmeɪ- $ -ˈmɑːtər/ *n* [singular] **1 sb's alma mater** the school, college etc that someone used to attend **2** *AmE* the song of a particular school, college etc

al·ma·nac, **almanack** *old-fashioned* /ˈɔːlmənæk $ ˈɒːl-, ˈæl-/ *n* [C] a book produced each year containing information about a particular subject, especially a sport, or important dates, times etc SYN **yearbook**: *a football almanac* | *a nautical almanac*

al·might·y /ɔːlˈmaɪti $ ɒːl-/ ●○○ *adj*
1 the Almighty/Almighty God/Almighty Father expressions used to talk about God that emphasize His power
2 God/Christ Almighty an expression used when you are angry or upset. Some people consider this use offensive.
3 almighty din/crash/row etc *BrE old-fashioned informal* a very loud noise, argument etc: *There was an almighty bang and the car came to a halt.*

al·mond /ˈɑːmənd $ ˈɑː-, ˈæ-, ˈæl-/ *n* [C] a flat pale nut with brown skin that tastes sweet, or the tree that produces these nuts: *Stir in the ground almonds and egg.* → see picture at NUT¹

al·most /ˈɔːlməʊst $ ˈɒːlmoʊst, ɒːlˈmoʊst/ ●●● S1 W1 *adv* nearly, but not completely or not quite: *Have you almost finished?* | *Supper's almost ready.* | *It was almost midnight.* | *Almost nothing was done to improve the situation.* | *The story is* ***almost certainly*** *true.* | *He's* ***almost as*** *old* ***as*** *I am.* | **almost all/every/everything** *Marsha visits her son almost every day.*

GRAMMAR: Word order

- **Almost** usually comes before a main verb: *I* ***almost*** *cried.*
- **Almost** usually comes after 'be' when it is the main verb: *I* ***am almost*** *ready.*
- **Almost** comes after the first auxiliary verb: *She* ***has almost*** *decided.* | *It* ***could almost*** *be described as luminous.* ✗ Don't say: *She almost has decided.*

THESAURUS

almost not completely or not quite: *I've almost finished my essay.* | *It's almost lunchtime.*
nearly almost. Nearly is more commonly used in British English than American English: *I've been a teacher for nearly 10 years now.* | *It's* ***very nearly*** *time to go home.*
not quite almost, but not yet: *'Is he 60?' 'Not quite!'* | *It's not quite time to go yet.* | *I'm not quite ready yet.*
practically/virtually very nearly: *The room was practically empty.* | **practically all/everything/everyone etc**: *The frost killed practically every plant in the garden.* | *Virtually everyone had gone home.*
more or less/just about/pretty much *especially spoken* very nearly - use this when saying that the difference is not important: *All the rooms are more or less the same size.* | *His jacket was pretty much the same colour as his trousers.*
getting on for *BrE informal*, **getting on toward** *especially AmE informal* almost a particular time, age, or period of time - used especially when you are not sure of the exact time, age etc: *It's getting on for 10 years since we last saw each other.* | *'How old's Diane?' 'She must be getting on toward 50.'*
close to almost a particular number, amount, or time - used especially when the number or amount is surprisingly large or the time is very late: *It was close to midnight by the time we arrived.* | *They've spent close to $1.3 billion on the project.*
approaching/nearing almost - used when a number or amount is still increasing or a time is getting nearer: *The unemployment rate was nearing 20%.*
be on the verge of (doing) sth to be very close to doing something: *She was on the verge of tears* (=almost crying). | *I was on the verge of giving up.*
be on the brink of sth to be very close to an extremely bad situation: *The two countries are on the brink of war.* | *The company was on the brink of bankruptcy.*

alms /ɑːmz $ ɑːmz, ɑːlmz/ *n* [plural] *literary* money, food etc given to poor people in the past

alms·house /ˈɑːmzhaʊs/ (*plural* **-houses** /-haʊzɪz/) *n* [C] in Britain in the past, a house where a poor person was allowed to live without paying rent

a·loe ve·ra /ˌæləʊ ˈvɪərə $ ˌæloʊ ˈverə/ *n* [U] a tropical plant with thick leaves that are filled with a liquid which is used to make medicine, COSMETICS etc

a·loft /əˈlɒft $ əˈlɒːft/ *adv formal* high up in the air: **hold/bear sth aloft** *He emerged, holding a baby aloft.*

Frequencies of **alone, on your own** and **by yourself** in spoken and written English.

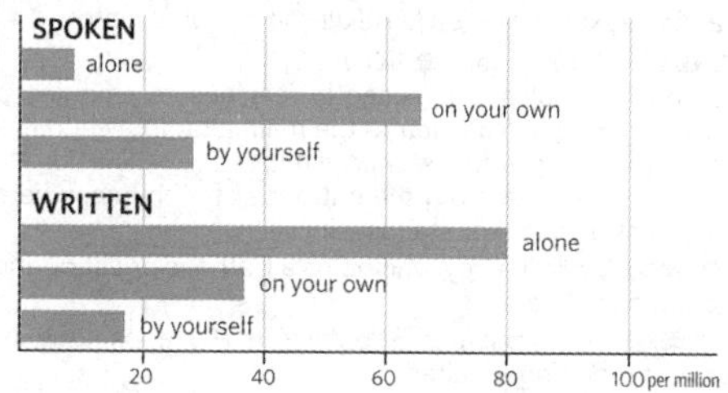

In spoken English it is more usual to say **on your own** or **by yourself** rather than **alone**. In written or more formal English **alone** is more common.

a·lone /əˈləʊn $ əˈloʊn/ ●●● S2 W1 *adj* [not before noun], *adv*
1 if you are alone in a place, there is no one with you SYN **by yourself**: *She* **lives alone**. | *You shouldn't* **leave** *a child* **alone** *in the house.* | *My wife and I like to spend time* **alone together** *away from the kids.*

REGISTER
In everyday English, people often say **by yourself** or **on your own** rather than **alone**: *She lives* **by herself/on her own**.

2 without any friends or people you know: *It was scary being* **all alone** *in a strange city.* | *She was* **all alone in the world** (=she had no family or friends to help her or look after her).
3 feeling unhappy and lonely: *I cried like a child because I* **felt so alone**.
4 without any help from other people: *He was left to raise their two children alone.*
5 without including anything else: *The case will cost thousands of pounds in legal fees alone.*
6 you/he etc alone used to emphasize that there is only one person who knows, can do something etc: *Julie alone knew the truth.*
7 go it alone to start working or living on your own, especially after working or living with other people: *After years of working for a big company I decided to go it alone.*
8 leave sb alone (*also* **let sb alone** *old-fashioned*) to stop annoying or interrupting someone: *'Leave me alone!' she screamed.*
9 leave sth alone (*also* **let sth alone** *old-fashioned*) to stop touching an object or changing something: *Leave those cakes alone. They're for the guests.* | **leave well (enough) alone** (=not change something that is satisfactory) *In economic matters, they should leave well alone.*
10 be yours/hers/his etc alone used to emphasize that something belongs to someone: *The responsibility is yours and yours alone.*
11 not be alone in (doing) sth to not be the only person to do something: *You're not alone in feeling upset, believe me.*
12 stand alone a) to be strong and independent: *the courage to stand alone* **b)** to be at a distance from other objects or buildings: *The house stood alone at the end of the road.*

a·long¹ /əˈlɒŋ $ əˈlɒːŋ/ ●●● S1 W1 *adv*
1 going forward: *I was driving along, thinking about Chris.* | *a group of children walking along in a line*
2 go/come along to go or come to a place where something is happening: *You're welcome to come along if you like.* | *I think I'll go along and watch the game.*
3 take/bring sb/sth along to take someone or something with you to a place: *Mandy brought some of her friends along.* | *Why don't you take your guitar along?*
4 be/come along to arrive: *Another bus should be along in a minute.* | *Every so often, a band comes along that changes music history.*
5 come/go/get along to improve, develop, or make progress: *After a five-hour operation, Wendy is coming along just fine.*
6 along with sb/sth together with someone or something else: *Dunne was murdered, along with three guards.*
7 all along all the time from the beginning, while something was happening: *They should have known all along that she was lying.*

along² ●●● S1 W1 *prep*
1 from one place on something such as a line, road, or edge towards the other end of it: *We were driving along Follyfoot Road.* | *She glanced anxiously along the line of faces.* | *He slid his hand along her arm.*
2 forming a line beside something long: *The palm trees along the shore swayed in the wind.* | *the toolbar along the top of your screen* | *There were cheering crowds* **all along** *Pennsylvania Avenue.*
3 a particular distance away, on or beside something long such as a line, road, edge etc: *Hugo's house was about two hundred yards away along the main street.* | *The bathroom is* **just along** (=a short distance along) *the corridor.*
4 along the way/line during a process or experience, or during someone's life: *I've been lucky, but I've had my share of heartbreak along the way.*

a·long·side /əˌlɒŋˈsaɪd $ əˌlɒːŋ-/ ●●○ W3 *adv, prep*
1 next to the side of something: *A car* **drew up alongside**. | *Children's prices are shown alongside adult prices.*
2 used to say that people or things do something or exist together at the same time: *Charles spent a week working alongside the miners.* | *Organized crime continued to flourish alongside the mainstream economy.*
3 in comparison with something: *His achievement may seem small alongside the great triumphs of 20th-century technology.* | *Athletics should* **rank alongside** (=be equal to) *soccer and cricket as a major sport.*

a·loof /əˈluːf/ *adj, adv* **1** unfriendly and deliberately not talking to other people: **remain/stay aloof (from sb)** *They worked hard, but tended to stay aloof from the local inhabitants.* | **keep/hold yourself aloof (from sb)** *She had always kept herself aloof from the boys in class.* | *Beneath that aloof exterior, Gayle is a warm, sympathetic person.* **THESAURUS** UNFRIENDLY **2** deliberately not becoming involved in something: **remain/stand aloof (from sth)** *Initially, the President remained aloof from the campaign.* | **hold/keep (yourself) aloof from sth** *The doctor held himself somewhat aloof from the rest of the ship's crew.* —**aloofness** *n* [U]

al·o·pe·cia /ˌæləˈpiːʃə/ *n* [U] *medical* a condition in which you lose some or all of your hair

a·loud /əˈlaʊd/ ●●● S3 W2 *adv* if you read, laugh, say something etc aloud, you read etc so that people can hear you SYN **out loud**: **read/say sth aloud** *Joanne, would you read the poem aloud?* | **laugh/groan/cry etc aloud** *The pain made him cry aloud.* | *She could have laughed aloud.* | **think aloud** (=say the things you are thinking) *'What did you say?' 'Sorry, I was just thinking aloud.'* ⚠ Do not use **aloud** to mean 'in a loud voice'. Use **loudly**: *You need to speak quite loudly for the people at the back.*

al·pac·a /ælˈpækə/ *n* **1** [C] an animal from South America with long hair that looks like a LLAMA **2** [U] cloth made from the wool of an alpaca

al·pha /ˈælfə/ *n* [C usually singular] **1** the first letter of the Greek alphabet **2 the alpha and omega** *formal* the start and finish of something, and therefore the whole of it: *Collective bargaining was viewed as the alpha and omega of trade unionism.*

al·pha·bet /ˈælfəbet/ ●●● W3 *n* [C] a set of letters, arranged in a particular order, and used in writing: **the Greek/Roman etc alphabet** *the international phonetic alphabet*

al·pha·bet·i·cal /ˌælfəˈbetɪkəl◂/ ●●● W3 (*also* **al·pha·bet·ic** /ˌælfəˈbetɪk◂/) *adj* relating to the alphabet:

The files are arranged ***in alphabetical order****.* —**alphabetically** /-kli/ *adv*: *Are the records* ***filed alphabetically****?*

al·pha·bet·ize (*also* **-ise** *BrE*) /ˈælfəbetaɪz/ *v* [T] to arrange things in order according to the letters of the alphabet

ˈalpha girl *n* [C usually singular] a teenage girl who is the most important and powerful member of a group of girls who regularly spend time together. Alpha girls are typically confident, attractive, and determined to be successful. Often used humorously.

ˌalpha ˈmale *n* [C usually singular] **1** the male with the highest rank in a group of animals such as CHIMPANZEES **2** the man who has the most power and influence and the highest social position in a particular group – used humorously

al·pha·nu·mer·ic /ˌælfənjuːˈmerɪk◂ $ -nuː-/ (*also* **al·pha·nu·mer·i·cal** /-ˈmerɪkəl/) *adj* using letters and numbers: *alphanumeric codes*

ˈalpha ˌparticle *n* [C] *technical* an ATOMIC PARTICLE consisting of two PROTONS and two NEUTRONS that is sent out by some RADIOACTIVE substances

ˈalpha ˌtest *n* [C] a test of software to see if it works properly, done by the company that is writing the software → **beta test**

ˈalpha ˌversion *n* [C] software that is being tested by the company that is writing it, to see if it works properly → **beta version**

al·pine /ˈælpaɪn/ *adj* [only before noun] relating to the Alps (=a mountain range in central Europe) or to mountains in general: *breathtaking alpine scenery* | *alpine flowers* | *alpine skiing*

al·read·y /ɔːlˈredi $ ɒːl-/ ●●● S1 W1 *adv*
1 before now, or before a particular time: *The design of the new house is similar to those that have already been built.* | *The performance had already started when we arrived.*
2 used to say that something has been done before and does not need doing again: *You already told me that.* | *'Fancy a coffee?' 'No thanks, I already have one.'*
3 used to say that something has happened too soon or before the expected time: *Have you eaten all that food already?* | *Is it 5 o'clock already?*
4 used to say that a situation exists and it might get worse, greater etc: *Hurry up, we're already late.*

GRAMMAR: Word order

• **Already** often comes at the end of a sentence: *I knew that already.* | *I was tired already.* | *I have booked the tickets already.*
As well as at the end of a sentence, **already** can be used in the following ways:
• **Already** can come before a main verb: *I already knew that.*
• **Already** comes after 'be' when it is the main verb: *I was already tired.* ✗ Don't say: *I already was tired.*
• **Already** comes after the first auxiliary verb: *I have already booked the tickets.* ✗ Don't say: *I already have booked the tickets.*

al·right /ˌɔːlˈraɪt $ ˌɒːl-/ *adj, adv* another spelling of ALL RIGHT that some people think is incorrect

Al·sa·tian /ælˈseɪʃən/ *n* [C] *BrE* a large dog, often used by the police or to guard places SYN **German Shepherd**

al·so /ˈɔːlsəʊ $ ˈɒːlsoʊ/ ●●● S1 W1 *adv*
1 in addition to something else that you have mentioned → **as well**, **too**: *Information is also available on women's health care.* | *She sings beautifully* ***and also*** *plays the flute and piano.* | *The system was* ***not only*** *complicated* ***but also*** *ineffective.*

REGISTER
In written English, avoid starting a sentence with **also**. Use **furthermore** or **moreover** instead, or put **also** before the main verb: ***Also****, it costs more.*
→ ***Furthermore****, it costs more.* | *It* ***also*** *costs more.*

2 used to say that the same thing is true about another person or thing: *My girlfriend was also called Helen.*

ˈalso-ran *n* [C] someone who fails to win a competition, election etc: *Ten months ago he was just an also-ran for the Democratic nomination.*

alt- /ɒlt $ ɒːlt/ *prefix* [in nouns] used to refer to something, especially music, that is ALTERNATIVE (=not of the usual or traditional kind): *She is a fan of alt-folk and alt-country.*

al·tar /ˈɔːltə $ ˈɒːltər/ ●○○ *n* [C]
1 a holy table or surface used in religious ceremonies: *a crucifix above the* ***high altar*** (=the main altar in a church) | *The victim was tied to a sacrificial altar.*
2 the area furthest from the entrance of a church, where the priest or minister stands

ˈaltar boy *n* [C] a boy who helps a Catholic priest during a church service

al·tar·piece /ˈɔːltəpiːs $ ˈɒːltər-/ *n* [C] a painting or SCULPTURE behind an altar

al·ter /ˈɔːltə $ ˈɒːltər/ ●●● S3 W3 AWL *v*
1 [I,T] to change, or to make someone or something change: *Her face hadn't altered much over the years.* | *The city centre has altered beyond recognition* (=changed very much). | *Nothing can alter the fact that the refugees are our responsibility.*
2 [T] to make a piece of clothing longer, wider etc so that it fits: **have/get sth altered** *She had the dress altered for the wedding.*

al·ter·a·tion /ˌɔːltəˈreɪʃən $ ˌɒːl-/ ●●○ AWL *n* [C,U] a small change that makes someone or something slightly different, or the process of this change: **[+to]** *If you* ***make alterations to*** *the Windows setup, save the new settings before closing.* | **[+in]** *Have you noticed any alteration in the patient's behaviour?* | **minor/major etc alterations** *The King's Arms pub is to* ***undergo*** *extensive* ***alterations****.*

al·ter·ca·tion /ˌɔːltəˈkeɪʃən $ ˌɒːltər-/ *n* [C] *formal* a short noisy argument: *They became involved in an altercation.*

al·ter e·go /ˌæltər ˈiːgəʊ, ˌɔːl- $ ˌæltər ˈiːgoʊ, ˌɒːl-/ *n* [C] **1 sb's alter ego** an invented person that you use to represent part of your character that is very different from your usual one: *Gissing used his fictional alter ego to attack Victorian morals.* **2** someone you trust and who has similar opinions, attitudes etc: *Mrs Reagan was widely regarded as the president's alter ego.*

al·ter·nate¹ /ɔːlˈtɜːnət $ ˈɒːltər-, ˈæl-/ ●○○ AWL *adj* [usually before noun]
1 if something happens on alternate days, weeks etc, it happens on one day etc and not the next, and continues in this pattern → **every other**: **alternate Mondays/weekends etc** *The service runs on alternate days.*

REGISTER
In everyday English, instead of **alternate days/Fridays/weeks** etc, people usually use the phrase **every other day/Friday/week** etc: *We meet on* ***alternate*** *Saturdays.* → *We meet* ***every other*** *Saturday.*

2 two alternate things are placed one after the other in a regular pattern: *alternate blue and red stripes* | *Arrange the leeks and noodles in* ***alternate layers****.*
3 used to replace another thing of the same type SYN **alternative**: *the appointment of an alternate director*

al·ter·nate² /ˈɔːltəneɪt $ ˈɒːltər-, ˈæl-/ ●○○ AWL *v* [I,T] if two things alternate, or if you alternate them, they happen one after the other in a repeated pattern: **[+between]** *She alternated between outrage and sympathy.* | **[+with]** *Periods of depression alternate with excited behavior.* | **alternate sth and/with sth** *Twist your body, alternating right and left stretches.* —**alternation** /ˌɔːltəˈneɪʃən $ ˌɒːltər-, ˌæl-/ *n* [C,U]

ˌalternating ˈcurrent *n* [U] (*abbreviation* **AC**) a flow of electricity that changes direction regularly and quickly → **direct current**

al·ter·na·tive¹ /ɔːlˈtɜːnətɪv $ ɒːlˈtɜːr-, æl-/ ●●○ S3 W2 AWL *adj*
1 [only before noun] an alternative idea, plan etc is different

from the one you have and can be used instead: **alternative ways/approach/methods etc** *alternative approaches to learning* | *Have you any* ***alternative suggestions****?* | *An* ***alternative route*** *is along the Via Unione.*
2 deliberately different from what is usual, expected, or traditional: **alternative music/theatre etc** *Tucson's alternative radio station* | *sources of* ***alternative energy*** (=energy produced by the sun, wind etc rather than by gas, coal etc) | *tolerance of* ***alternative lifestyles*** | **alternative medicine/therapies** (=medical treatment that is not based on the usual western methods) *Acupuncture is widely used by practitioners of alternative medicine.*

alternative² ●●○ S3 W3 AWL *n* [C] something you can choose to do or use instead of something else: **[+to]** *Is there a* ***viable alternative*** *to the present system?* | *If payment is not received, legal action will be our* ***only alternative****.* | *I* ***had no alternative*** *but to report him to the police.* | *He quickly assessed the alternatives open to him.*

COLLOCATIONS

VERBS

have an alternative *You have a few alternatives to choose from.*
offer/provide an alternative *If your first choice is not available, we always have alternatives to offer.*
suggest an alternative *Do you have an alternative you can suggest?*
seek an alternative *People are seeking alternatives to meat-based dishes.*
find an alternative *The program is directed to finding alternatives to oil and natural gas.*

PHRASES

have no/little alternative (but to do sth) *He had no alternative but to resign.*
leave sb with no alternative (but to do sth) *I was left with no alternative but to seek legal advice.*

alˌternative ˈlifestyle *n* [C] the way that someone lives their life, when this is not the usual way that other people live: *Some people say schools need to teach tolerance of alternative lifestyles.*

al·ter·na·tive·ly /ɔːlˈtɜːnətɪvli $ ɒːlˈtɜːr-, æl-/ ●○○ AWL *adv* [sentence adverb] used for suggesting something different: *You can relax on the beach* ***or alternatively*** *visit the bustling town centre.*

al·ter·na·tor /ˈɔːltəneɪtə $ ˈɒːltərneɪtər, ˈæl-/ *n* [C] an object that produces an ALTERNATING CURRENT, especially in a car

al·though /ɔːlˈðəʊ $ ɒːlˈðoʊ/ ●●● S1 W1 *conjunction*
1 used to introduce a statement that makes your main statement seem surprising or unlikely SYN **though**: *Although in poor health, she continued to carry out her duties.* | *We decided to take rooms in Longwood House, although we knew we could not really afford the rent.* | *Although I can't help admiring the man's courage, I do not approve of his methods.*
2 used to add a statement that balances or reduces the effect of what you have just said SYN **but**: *You can copy down my answers, although I'm not sure they're right.* | *No, this is my responsibility, although I appreciate your offer.*
THESAURUS ▸ BUT

al·ti·me·ter /ˈæltɪˌmiːtə $ ælˈtɪmɪtər/ *n* [C] an instrument in an aircraft that tells you how high you are

al·ti·tude /ˈæltɪtjuːd $ -tuːd/ ●○○ *n* [C] the height of an object or place above the sea: **[+of]** *We're* ***flying at an altitude*** *of 40,000 feet.* | **high/low altitudes** *At high altitudes it is difficult to get enough oxygen.*

al·to¹ /ˈæltəʊ $ -toʊ/ *adj* an alto instrument or voice produces notes at the second highest level, below a SOPRANO: *an alto sax*

alto² *n* (*plural* **altos**) **1** [C] a singing voice that is lower than a SOPRANO, or a singer with a voice like this **2** [singular] the part of a musical work that is written for an alto voice or instrument → BARITONE¹(2), BASS¹(2), SOPRANO¹(2), TENOR¹(2)

al·to·geth·er¹ /ˌɔːltəˈgeðə◂ $ ˌɒːltəˈgeðər◂/ ●●● S2 W3 *adv*
1 used to emphasize that something has been done completely or has finished completely: *an old custom that has vanished altogether* | *Congress could ban the procession altogether.*
2 [+adj/adv] used to emphasize that the way you describe something is completely true: *In Canada, the situation is altogether different.* | *This latest problem is* ***altogether more*** *serious.* | **not altogether** (=not completely) *I wasn't altogether happy about Mike staying over.* | *The results were not altogether surprising.*
3 used to show that you are referring to the total amount: *There were five people altogether.* | *How much do I owe you altogether?*
4 used to make a final statement about several things you have just mentioned SYN **all in all**: *Lots of sunshine, wonderful food, and amazing nightlife – altogether a great vacation!*

altogether² *n* **in the altogether** not wearing any clothes – used humorously: *Several of the men were parading around in the altogether.*

al·tru·is·m /ˈæltru-ɪzəm/ *n* [U] when you care about or help other people, even though this brings no advantage to yourself: *Many choose to work in developing countries out of altruism.* —**altruist** *n* [C]

al·tru·is·tic /ˌæltruˈɪstɪk◂/ *adj* altruistic behaviour shows that you care about and will help other people, even though this brings no advantage for yourself OPP **selfish**: *Were his motives entirely altruistic?* —**altruistically** /-kli/ *adv*

al·um /ˈæləm/ *n* [C] *AmE informal* a former student of a school, college etc: *a Crawford High alum*

al·u·min·i·um /ˌæləˈmɪniəm/ *BrE*, **a·lu·mi·num** /əˈluːmənəm/ *AmE* ●●○ *n* [U] a silver-white metal that is very light and is used to make cans, cooking pans, window frames etc. It is a chemical ELEMENT: symbol Al: *recycled aluminium cans*

a·lum·na /əˈlʌmnə/ *n* (*plural* **alumnae** /-niː/) [C] *formal* a woman who is a former student of a school, college etc

a·lum·ni /əˈlʌmnaɪ/ *n* [plural] the former students of a school, college etc: *the University alumni association*

a·lum·nus /əˈlʌmnəs/ *n* (*plural* **alumni** /-naɪ/) [C] *formal* a former student of a school, college etc

al·ve·o·lar /ˌælviˈəʊlə◂, ælˈviːələ $ ælˈviːələr/ *n* [C] *technical* a CONSONANT sound such as /t/ or /d/ that you make by putting the end of your tongue behind your upper front teeth

al·ways /ˈɔːlwəz, -weɪz $ ˈɒːl-/ ●●● S1 W1 *adv*
1 all the time, at all times, or every time: *Always lock your bicycle to something secure.* | *She'd always assumed that Gabriel was a girl's name.* | *He hadn't always been a butler.*
2 for a very long time: *I've always wanted to go to Paris.* | *John's always been keen on music.*
3 for ever: *I'll always remember that day.*
4 if someone or something is always doing something, they do it often, especially in an annoying way: *That woman next door's always complaining.*
5 always assuming/supposing (that) sth *BrE* used to say that one important fact has to be accepted as true for something else to happen, be true etc: *We'll leave on Tuesday – always assuming the car's repaired by then.*
6 as always as is usual or expected: *The truth, as always, is more complicated.* | *As always, Deborah was the last to arrive.*
7 can/could always do sth (*also* **there's always sth**) *spoken* used to make a polite suggestion: *You could always try ringing again.* | *If you can't get it locally, there's always the Internet.*
8 sb always was lucky/untidy etc used to say you are not surprised by what someone has done because it is typical of them: *You always were a stubborn creature.* | *He's a troublemaker! Always was and always will be!*

A

GRAMMAR: Word order

- **Always** usually comes before a verb: *I **always travel** with my girlfriend.* ✗ Don't say: *Always I travel with my girlfriend.*
- **Always** usually comes after the verb 'be': *He **was always** very intelligent.*
- You sometimes use **always** before 'be' to emphasize that two statements are connected: *Henry did well in his exams. He **always was** very intelligent.*
- **Always** usually comes after the auxiliary: *I **have always** loved Japan.*
- You sometimes use **always** before an auxiliary to emphasize that two statements are connected: *I had a great time in Tokyo. I **always have** loved Japan.*

GRAMMAR GUIDE ▸ ADVERBS

USAGE: Always or still?

You use **still** when you want to emphasize that a situation has not changed: *He still lives with his parents.* ✗ Don't say: *He always lives with his parents.*

THESAURUS

always all the time, at all times, or every time: *I will always love you.* | *He always carries his medicine wherever he goes.* | *People will always need houses.*
forever (*also* **for ever** *BrE*) if something lasts or continues forever, it remains or continues for all future time: *Nothing lasts forever.* | *He seemed to think he would live forever.*
permanently always, or for a very long time – used about changes that you expect to last forever. Permanently can be used with a verb or with an adjective: *His eyesight may be permanently damaged.* | *They decided to move to Portugal permanently.*
for life for the rest of your life: *Marriage is supposed to be for life.* | *He was sent to jail for life.*
for good *especially spoken* forever – used to talk about a permanent change: *This time, he's coming back for good.* | *Once a species dies out, it is gone for good.*
for all time forever – used when saying that something will last or be remembered forever because it is very good or special: *Their deeds will be remembered for all time.*
to/until your dying day for the rest of your life – used when something has affected you very deeply: *I'll remember what he said to my dying day.*

ˈalways-on *adj* [only before noun] permanently switched on: *an always-on Internet connection*

Alz·heim·er's dis·ease /ˈæltshaɪməz dɪˌziːz $ -ərz-/ (*also* **Alzheimer's**) *n* [U] a disease that affects the brain, especially of old people, and that gradually makes it difficult to move, talk, or remember things SYN **dementia**

am /m, əm; *strong* æm/ *v* the first person singular of the present tense of the verb BE

a.m. (*also* **am** *BrE*) /ˌeɪ ˈem/ ●●● W2 (***ante meridiem***) used to talk about times that are after MIDNIGHT but before MIDDAY → **p.m.**: *Work starts at 9 am.*

AM /ˌeɪ ˈem/ *n* [U] (***amplitude modulation***) a system used for broadcasting radio programmes → **FM**

A.M.A., the /ˌeɪ em ˈeɪ/ (***the American Medical Association***) an organization in the US for doctors and people who do medical RESEARCH. There is a similar organization in the UK called the BMA (British Medical Association).

a·mal·gam /əˈmælgəm/ *n* [C] *formal* a mixture of different things: **[+of]** *an amalgam of different styles* THESAURUS ▸ MIXTURE

a·mal·ga·mate /əˈmælgəmeɪt/ *v formal* **1** [I,T] if two organizations amalgamate, or if one amalgamates with another, they join and make one big organization SYN **merge**: **amalgamate sth with/into/under sth** *The agency is expected to amalgamate with the National Rivers Authority.* **2** [T] to combine two or more things together to make one thing: *Stir until the ingredients are amalgamated.* | **amalgamate sth with/into sth** *The editors will amalgamate all the information into one article.* —**amalgamation** /əˌmælgəˈmeɪʃən/ *n* [C,U]: *an **amalgamation between** two companies*

a·man·u·en·sis /əˌmænjuˈensɪs/ *n* (*plural* **amanuenses**) [C] *formal* someone whose job is to write down what someone else says

a·mass /əˈmæs/ *v* [T] if you amass money, knowledge, information etc, you gradually collect a large amount of it: *For 25 years, Darwin amassed evidence to support his theories.* | *He **amassed** a **fortune** after the war.* THESAURUS ▸ COLLECT

am·a·teur¹ /ˈamətə, -tʃʊə, -tʃə, ˌæməˈtɜː $ ˈæmətʃʊr, -tər/ ●○○ *n* [C]
1 someone who does an activity just for pleasure, not as their job OPP **professional**: *a gifted amateur* | *Mickelson won his first major golf tournament while still an amateur.*
2 *informal* someone who you think is not very skilled at something: *You English are a bunch of amateurs when it comes to romance.* —**amateurism** *n* [U]: *well-meaning amateurism*

amateur² ●○○ *adj*
1 doing something for pleasure, or done for pleasure, and not as a job OPP **professional**: *an amateur golfer* | ***amateur dramatics*** *BrE* (=producing or acting in plays for pleasure)
2 amateurish: *It was a very amateur performance.*

am·a·teur·ish /ˈæmətərɪʃ, -tʃʊə-, -tʃə- ˌæməˈtɜːrɪʃ $ ˌæməˈtʊr-, -ˈtɜːr-/ *adj* not skilfully done or made OPP **professional**: *His paintings are rather amateurish.* —**amateurishly** *adv* —**amateurishness** *n* [U]

am·a·to·ry /ˈæmətəri $ -tɔːri/ *adj formal* expressing sexual or romantic love

a·maze /əˈmeɪz/ ●●○ *v* [T] to surprise someone very much SYN **astonish**: *Dave amazed his friends by suddenly getting married.* | **it amazes sb how/what/that** *It still amazes me how much she has improved.* | ***It never ceased to amaze*** *him that women were attracted to Sam.*

a·mazed /əˈmeɪzd/ ●●● S2 *adj* very surprised SYN **astonished**: **amazed (that)/how** *I'm amazed you've never heard of the Rolling Stones.* | *You'd be amazed how much money you can save.* | **[+at/by]** *We were **absolutely amazed** at his rapid recovery.* | **amazed to see/find/discover sth** *Visitors are often amazed to discover how little the town has changed.* THESAURUS ▸ SURPRISED

a·maze·ment /əˈmeɪzmənt/ ●●○ *n* [U] a feeling of great surprise SYN **astonishment**: **do sth in amazement** *Ralph gasped in amazement.* | **to sb's amazement** *To everyone's amazement, the goal was disallowed.*

a·maz·ing /əˈmeɪzɪŋ/ ●●● S2 *adj*
1 very good, especially in an unexpected way: *He's an amazing player to watch.* | *an amazing bargain* THESAURUS ▸ GOOD
2 so surprising you can hardly believe it: ***It's amazing how*** *often you see drivers using mobile phones.* THESAURUS ▸ SURPRISING —**amazingly** *adv*: *These shoes were amazingly cheap.*

GRAMMAR

Amazing is not used with 'very'. You say: *It was an absolutely amazing day.* ✗ Don't say: *It was a very amazing day.*

GRAMMAR GUIDE ▸ ADJECTIVES

Am·a·zon /ˈæməzən $ -zɑːn -zən/ *n* [C] *literary* a strong tall woman —**Amazonian** /ˌæməˈzəʊniən◂ $ -ˈzoʊ-/ *adj*

am·bas·sa·dor /æmˈbæsədə $ -ər/ ●●○ *n* [C]
1 an important official who represents his or her government in a foreign country: **[+to]** *the US ambassador to Spain*
2 someone who represents a particular sport, business etc because they behave in a way that people admire: **[+for]** *He has made some good films and he is a good*

ambassador for the industry. —**ambassadorial** /æmˌbæsəˈdɔːriəl/ *adj*: *relations at ambassadorial level*

am·ber /ˈæmbə $ -ər/ *n* [U] **1** a yellowish brown colour **2** a hard yellowish brown substance used to make jewellery: *an amber necklace* —**amber** *adj*

am·bi·ance /ˈæmbiəns/ *n* [singular] another spelling of AMBIENCE

am·bi·dex·trous /ˌæmbɪˈdekstrəs◂/ *adj* able to use either hand equally well → **left-handed**, **right-handed**

am·bi·ence, **ambiance** /ˈæmbiəns/ *n* [singular] the qualities and character of a particular place and the way these make you feel SYN **atmosphere**: **pleasant/relaxing/friendly etc ambience** *The restaurant's new owners have created a welcoming ambience.*

am·bi·ent /ˈæmbiənt/ *adj* **1 ambient temperature/light etc** *technical* the temperature etc of the surrounding area **2 ambient music/sounds** a type of modern music or sound that is slow, peaceful, and does not have a formal structure

ˌambient ˈadvertising *n* [U] advertising that is present on objects that are not usually expected to have advertising, for example on a train ticket or a RECEIPT

am·bi·gu·i·ty /ˌæmbɪˈgjuːəti/ ●○○ AWL *n* (*plural* **ambiguities**) [C,U] the state of being unclear, confusing, or not certain, or things that produce this effect: **[+in]** *There was an element of ambiguity in the president's reply.* | *legal ambiguities*

am·big·u·ous /æmˈbɪgjuəs/ ●●○ AWL *adj* something that is ambiguous is unclear, confusing, or not certain, especially because it can be understood in more than one way OPP **unambiguous**: *The language in the Minister's statement is highly ambiguous.* | *His role in the affair is ambiguous.* —**ambiguously** *adv*: *The legislation had been* ***ambiguously worded****.*

REGISTER

In everyday English, people also use the phrase **you can take sth two ways** instead of saying it is **ambiguous**: *What she says is* ***ambiguous****.* → *You* ***can take*** *what she says* ***two ways****.*

am·bit /ˈæmbɪt/ *n* [singular] *formal* the range or limit of someone's authority, influence etc → **remit**: **fall within the ambit of sth** *areas falling within the ambit of our research*

am·bi·tion /æmˈbɪʃən/ ●●○ W3 *n*
1 [C] a strong desire to achieve something: **an ambition to do sth** *She had always had an ambition to be a pilot.* | **sb's ambitions of doing sth** *An injury ended his ambitions of becoming a professional footballer.* THESAURUS ▶ AIM
2 [U] determination to be successful, rich, powerful etc: *He was young and full of ambition.*
3 have no ambition to do sth used when saying that you definitely do not want to do something: *I have no ambition to go back there again.*

GRAMMAR: Patterns with ambition

- You say that someone's **ambition is to do** something: *His ambition is to become a doctor.*
- You can also say that someone **has the ambition of doing** something: *He has the ambition of becoming a doctor.*
- You can also say that someone **has an ambition to do** something. This pattern is often used when talking about the past: *He had always had an ambition to become a doctor.*

COLLOCATIONS – MEANINGS 1 & 2

VERBS

sb's ambition is to be/do sth *My ambition was to be a journalist.*
have an ambition *He had an ambition to be a top cello player.*
achieve/fulfil/realize your ambition (=do what you wanted to do) *It took her ten years to achieve her ambition.*
lack ambition/have no ambition *Many of the students lack ambition.*
nurse/harbour/cherish an ambition (=have it for a long time, especially secretly) | **frustrate/thwart sb's ambitions** *formal* (=prevent someone from achieving them)

ADJECTIVES/NOUN + ambition

sb's main ambition *What's your main ambition in life?*
sb's great ambition *He didn't achieve his greatest ambition – to be Wimbledon Champion.*
a lifelong/long-held ambition (=one that you have had all your life) | **a personal ambition** | **a secret ambition** | **a burning/driving ambition** (=a very strong ambition) | **career ambitions** | **political/presidential ambitions**

PHRASES

sb's dreams and ambitions *He told her all about his dreams and ambitions.*
sb's lack of ambition *I was frustrated by their apparent lack of ambition.*
be full of ambition

am·bi·tious /æmˈbɪʃəs/ ●●○ *adj*
1 determined to be successful, rich, powerful etc: *Alfred was intensely ambitious, obsessed with the idea of becoming rich.* | **[+for]** *mothers who are* ***highly ambitious*** *for their children* (=who want their children to be successful)
2 an ambitious plan, idea etc shows a desire to do something good but difficult: *an ambitious engineering project* | *an* ***over-ambitious*** *health reform program* —**ambitiously** *adv* —**ambitiousness** *n* [U]

am·biv·a·lent /æmˈbɪvələnt/ *adj* not sure whether you want or like something or not: **[+about]** *We are both somewhat ambivalent about having a child.* | **ambivalent attitude/feelings etc** —**ambivalence** *n* [singular, U]: *O'Neill had a genuine* ***ambivalence toward*** *US involvement in the war.* —**ambivalently** *adv*

am·ble /ˈæmbəl/ *v* [I always + adv/prep] to walk slowly in a relaxed way SYN **saunter**: *An old man came out and ambled over for a chat.* —**amble** *n* [singular]: *a pleasant amble by the river*

am·bro·si·a /æmˈbrəʊziə $ -ˈbroʊʒə/ *n* [U] *literary* food or drink that tastes very good

am·bu·lance /ˈæmbjələns/ ●●○ S3 *n* [C] a special vehicle that is used to take people who are ill or injured to hospital: *the ambulance service* | **ambulance staff/crew/worker** *The ambulance crew removed him from the wreckage.* | *the* ***ambulance driver*** | **by ambulance** *Mike had to be taken by ambulance to hospital.* | *Do you think we need to* ***call an ambulance*** (=phone to ask an ambulance to come)?

ˈambulance ˌchaser *n* [C] a lawyer who uses a lot of pressure to persuade someone who has been hurt in an accident to SUE other people or companies in court, so that the lawyer will get part of the money if they win – used to show disapproval

am·bush /ˈæmbʊʃ/ ●○○ *n* [C,U] a sudden attack on someone by people who have been hiding and waiting for them, or the place where this happens: *The soldiers were killed in an ambush.* | *In winter the danger of ambush is much reduced.* | **lie/wait in ambush** *Armed police lay in ambush behind the hedge.* THESAURUS ▶ ATTACK —**ambush** *v* [T]: *Everybody thought our train would be ambushed, but we got out safely.*

a·me·ba /əˈmiːbə/ *n* [C] an American spelling of AMOEBA

a·me·li·o·rate /əˈmiːliəreɪt/ *v* [T] *formal* to make a bad situation better or less harmful SYN **improve**: *It is not clear what can be done to ameliorate the situation.* —**amelioration** /əˌmiːliəˈreɪʃən/ *n* [U]

a·men /ɑːˈmen, eɪ-/ *interjection*, *n* [C] **1** a word used to end a prayer: *Blessed be the Lord, Amen!* | *McAllister murmured a fervent amen.* **2 amen to that** *informal* used to show that you agree with a suggestion or remark: *'I think we can close the meeting now.' 'Amen to that.'*

A

a·me·na·ble /əˈmiːnəbəl $ əˈmiːn- əˈmen-/ *adj* **1** willing to accept what someone says or does without arguing: *She was always a very amenable child.* | **[+to]** *Young people are more amenable than older citizens to the idea of immigration.* **2** suitable for a particular type of treatment: **[+for/to]** *Such conditions may be amenable to medical intervention.*

a·mend /əˈmend/ ●○○ AWL *v* [T] *formal* to correct or make small changes to something that is written or spoken: *The law was amended to include women.* | *The defendant later amended his evidence.* | *'Steve stole it – or rather borrowed it,' he amended.* —**amended** *adj*: *an amended version*

a·mend·ment /əˈmendmənt/ ●○○ AWL *n* [C,U] a small change, improvement, or addition that is made to a law or document, or the process of doing this: *constitutional amendments* | **[+to]** *an amendment to the resolution*

a·mends /əˈmendz/ *n* **make amends (to sb/for sth)** to do something to show you are sorry for hurting or upsetting someone, especially something that makes it better for them: *He seized the chance to make amends for his behavior.*

a·me·ni·ty /əˈmiːnəti $ əˈme-/ ●○○ *n* (*plural* **amenities**) [C usually plural] something that makes a place comfortable or easy to live in: *The hotel is in the city centre, close to shops and local amenities.* | *houses that lack* ***basic amenities*** (=basic things that people need, such as heat and running water)

Am·er·a·sian /ˌæməˈreɪʒən◂, -ʃən◂/ *n* [C] someone from Asia who has one American parent and one Asian parent → **Asian-American**

A·mer·i·can¹ /əˈmerɪkən/ *adj* **1** relating to the US or its people: *Her mother is American.* | *a famous American writer* **2 sth is as American as apple pie** used to say that something is very typically American → **LATIN AMERICAN**

American² *n* [C] someone from the US

A·mer·i·ca·na /əˌmerəˈkɑːnə $ -ˈkɑːnə, -ˈkænə/ *n* [U] objects that are considered to be typical of the US, especially when they are in a COLLECTION: *1940s Americana*

Aˌmerican ˈDream, the the idea that the US is a place where everyone has the chance of becoming rich and successful. Many IMMIGRANTS to the US in the early 20th century believed in the American Dream.

Aˌmerican ˈfootball *n* [U] *BrE* a game played in the US by two teams of eleven players, who carry, throw, or kick an OVAL ball SYN **football** *AmE*

Aˌmerican ˈIndian *n* [C] another name for a NATIVE AMERICAN (=someone who belongs to one of the races that lived in North America before Europeans arrived)

A·mer·i·can·is·m /əˈmerəkənɪzəm/ *n* [C] a word or phrase that is typically used in American English

A·mer·i·can·ize (*also* **-ise** *BrE*) /əˈmerəkənaɪz/ *v* [T] to change a society, language, system etc so that it becomes more American in character —**Americanization** /əˌmerəkənaɪˈzeɪʃən $ -nə-/ *n* [U]: *the Americanization of youth culture*

Aˌmerican ˈLeague, the one of two groups of professional baseball teams that make up the highest level of baseball in the US and Canada. Every year, the team that wins in this LEAGUE plays against the winning team of the National League in the World Series. Its full name is the American League of Professional Baseball Clubs.

a·mer·i·ca·no /əˌmerəˈkɑːnəʊ $ -noʊ/ *n* (*plural* **americanos**) [C] a cup of coffee made with ESPRESSO (=strong black Italian coffee) and hot water

Aˌmerican ˈWay, the a set of beliefs or values that many Americans hold but which are not laws or written down in any form

Aˌmerica's ˈCup, the a sailing competition held every three or four years, in which teams from the US, Australia, and other nations compete. It is the most important yacht race in the world.

Aˌmerica the ˈBeautiful a PATRIOTIC song which most people in the US learn when they are children

am·e·thyst /ˈæmɪθɪst/ *n* **1** [C] a valuable purple stone used in jewellery **2** [U] a light purple colour —**amethyst** *adj*

a·mi·a·ble /ˈeɪmiəbəl/ *adj* friendly and easy to like: *The driver was an amiable young man.* | *She was in an amiable mood.* **THESAURUS** ▸ **FRIENDLY** —**amiably** *adv* —**amiability** /ˌeɪmiəˈbɪləti/ *n* [U]

am·i·ca·ble /ˈæmɪkəbəl/ ●○○ *adj* an amicable agreement, relationship etc is one in which people feel friendly towards each other and do not want to quarrel: *Their relationship hasn't always been amicable.* | **amicable settlement/agreement** *The two parties have reached an amicable settlement.* —**amicably** *adv*: *In the end, the matter was resolved amicably.*

a·mid /əˈmɪd/ ●○○ *prep* **1** while noisy, busy, or confused events are happening – used in writing or news reports: *The dollar has fallen in value amid rumors of weakness in the US economy.* | *Demonstrators ripped up the national flag amid shouts of 'Death to the tyrants!'* **2** *literary* among or surrounded by things: *He sat amid the trees.*

a·mid·ships /əˈmɪdʃɪps/ *adv technical* in the middle part of a ship

a·midst /əˈmɪdst/ *prep literary* amid: *a light that shines amidst the darkness*

AMERICAN FOOTBALL

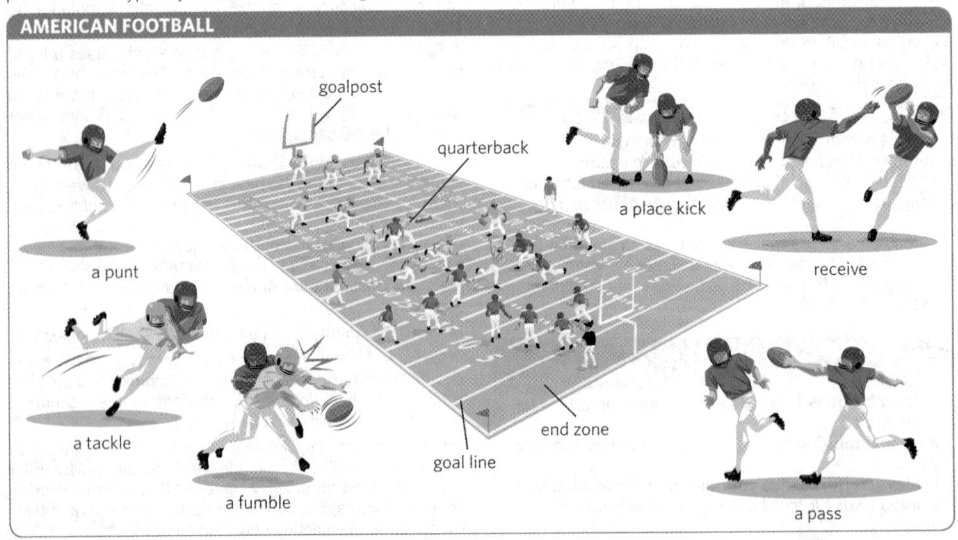

a·mi·no ac·id /əˌmiːnəʊ 'æsəd, əˌmaɪ- $ -noʊ-/ *n* [C] one of the substances that combine to form PROTEINS

a·miss¹ /ə'mɪs/ *adj* [not before noun] if something is amiss, there is a problem SYN **wrong**: *Elsa continued as if nothing was amiss.* | **[+with/in]** *There's something amiss in their relationship.*

amiss² *adv BrE* **1 sth would not come/go amiss** *informal* used to say that something would be suitable or useful in a situation: *A cup of tea wouldn't go amiss.* **2 take sth amiss** to feel upset or offended about something that someone has said or done: *Don't take it amiss – I was just teasing.*

am·i·ty /'æməti/ *n* [U] *formal* friendship, especially between countries OPP **hostility**: *a spirit of perfect amity*

am·me·ter /'æmɪtə, 'æmˌmiːtə $ -ər/ *n* [C] a piece of equipment used to measure the strength of an electric current

am·mo /'æməʊ $ -moʊ/ *n* [U] *informal* ammunition

am·mo·ni·a /ə'məʊniə $ -'moʊ-/ *n* [U] **1** a clear liquid with a strong bad smell that is used for cleaning or in cleaning products **2** a poisonous gas with a strong bad smell that is used in making many chemicals, FERTILIZERS etc

am·mo·nite /'æmənaɪt/ *n* [C] *technical* an EXTINCT sea creature with a SPIRAL shell that can be found as a FOSSIL

am·mu·ni·tion /ˌæmjə'nɪʃən/ ●○○ *n* [U]
1 bullets, shells (SHELL) etc that are fired from guns
2 information that you can use to criticize someone or win an argument against them: **give sb ammunition/provide sb with ammunition** *His mistakes provided political opponents with even more ammunition.*

am·ne·si·a /æm'niːziə $ -ʒə/ *n* [U] the medical condition of not being able to remember anything —**amnesiac** /-ziæk $ -ʒiæk, -ziæk/ *n* [C]

am·nes·ty /'æmnəsti/ ●○○ *n* (*plural* **amnesties**) [C]
1 an official order by a government that allows a particular group of prisoners to go free: **[+for]** *The government* ***granted an amnesty*** *for all former terrorists.*
2 a period of time when you can admit to doing something illegal without being punished: **[+on]** *an amnesty on illegal handguns* —**amnesty** *v* [T]

am·ni·o·cen·te·sis /ˌæmniəʊsen'tiːsɪs $ -nioʊ-/ *n* [U] a test to see if an unborn baby has a disease or other problem, done by taking liquid from the mother's WOMB

ˌamniotic 'fluid *n* [U] *medical* the liquid that surrounds and protects a baby when it is growing inside its mother's body

a·moe·ba (*also* **ameba** *AmE*) /ə'miːbə/ *n* [C] a very small creature that has only one cell —**amoebic** *adj*

a·mok /ə'mɒk $ ə'mɑːk/ (*also* **amuck**) *adv* **run amok**
a) to suddenly behave in a very violent and uncontrolled way: *Drunken troops ran amok in the town.* **b)** to get out of control and cause a lot of problems: *an age in which global capitalism has run amok*

a·mong /ə'mʌŋ/ ●●● S2 W1 (*also* **a·mongst** /ə'mʌŋst/) *prep*
1 in or through the middle of a group of people or things: *The girl quickly disappeared among the crowd.* | *I could hear voices coming from somewhere among the bushes.* | *We walked among the chestnut woods on the mountain slopes.* | *She began rummaging among the books on her desk.* → BETWEEN
2 with a particular group of people: *Jim relaxed, knowing he was* ***among friends***.
3 used to say that many people in a group have the same feeling or opinion, or that something affects many people in a group: *The problem is causing widespread concern among scientists.* | *The general opinion among police officers was that the law should be tightened.* | *The changes will mean 7,000 job losses among railway workers.*
4 used to talk about a particular person, thing, or group as belonging to a larger group: *She was the eldest among them.* | *Innocent civilians were among the casualties.* | *My grandfather had among his possessions a portrait by Matisse.* | *Representatives were chosen by the students from among themselves.*
5 among other things/places/factors etc used to say that you are only mentioning one or two people or things out of a much larger group: *At the meeting they discussed, among other things, recent events in Japan.*
6 if something is divided or shared among a group of people, each person is given a part of it: *A father's property was divided among his heirs.*
7 among yourselves/ourselves/themselves with each other: *The allies found it hard to agree among themselves.*

USAGE: Among, between

• To talk about position, use **among** if there are more than two people or things around someone or something, and **between** if there is just one person or thing on each side: *They hid among the reeds.* | *I put my bag down between my feet.*
• After words such as 'relationship' or 'difference', use **between**, even when there are more than two people or things: *the relationship between the three friends* ✗ Don't say: *the relationship among the three friends*

a·mor·al /eɪ'mɒrəl, æ- $ eɪ'mɔː-, -'mɑː-/ *adj* having no moral standards at all OPP **moral** → **immoral**: *a completely amoral person* —**amorality** /ˌeɪmɒ'ræləti, ˌæ- $ ˌeɪmə-/ *n* [U]

am·o·rous /'æmərəs/ *adj formal* showing or concerning sexual love: *She resisted his* ***amorous advances***. | *He was always boasting about his* ***amorous adventures***. —**amorously** *adv*

a·mor·phous /ə'mɔːfəs $ -ɔːr-/ *adj formal* having no definite shape or features: *an* ***amorphous mass*** *of twisted metal*

a·mor·tize (*also* **-ise** *BrE*) /ə'mɔːtaɪz $ 'æmərtaɪz/ *v* [T] *technical* to pay a debt by making regular payments —**amortization** /əˌmɔːtaɪ'zeɪʃən $ ˌæmərtə-/ *n* [C,U]

a·mount¹ /ə'maʊnt/ ●●● S1 W1 *n* [C,U]
1 a quantity of something such as time, money, or a substance: **[+of]** *They spend equal amounts of time in California and New York.* | **a considerable/large/enormous etc amount** *a considerable amount of money* | **a small/tiny etc amount** *a tiny amount of dirt* | *Please pay* ***the full amount*** *(=of money) by the end of the month.*
2 used to talk about how much there is of a feeling or quality: **a large/considerable etc amount of sth** *Her case has attracted an enormous amount of public sympathy.* | **a certain/fair amount of sth** *Dina encountered a fair amount of envy among her colleagues.*
3 no amount of sth can/will etc do sth used to say that something has no effect: *No amount of persuasion could make her change her mind.*
4 any amount of sth used to say that there is plenty of something, and no more is needed: *The school has any amount of resources and equipment.*

THESAURUS

amount how much of something there is: *Try to reduce the amount of fat in your diet.* | *a tiny amount of poison*
quantity a particular amount of food, liquid, or another substance that can be measured - used especially in written descriptions and instructions: *Make sure that you add the right quantity of milk.* | *They buy the wood in large quantities.*
volume the amount of something such as business activity or traffic, especially when this is large or increasing: *The volume of traffic on our roads has risen sharply.* | *the huge volume of trade with China*
level the exact amount of something at one time, which can go up or down at other times: *They measured the level of alcohol in his blood.* | *There is a high level of unemployment.*
proportion the amount of something, compared with the whole amount that exists: *the proportion of road accidents caused by drunk drivers* | *A high proportion of the students were from poor families.*
quota a maximum amount of something that can be

produced, sold, brought into a country etc: *import quotas on Japanese cars*
yield /jiːld/ the amount of something that is produced, especially crops: *this year's cotton yield*

amount² ●○○ *v*
amount to sth *phr v*
1 if figures, sums etc amount to a particular total, they equal that total when they are added together: *Time lost through illness amounted to 1,357 working days.*
2 if an attitude, remark, situation etc amounts to something, it has the same effect: *The court's decision amounts to a not guilty verdict.* | *Ultimately, their ideas* ***amount to the same thing.***
3 not amount to much/anything/a great deal etc to not be important, valuable, or successful: *Her academic achievements don't amount to much.* | *Jim's never going to amount to much.*

a·mour /əˈmʊə $ əˈmʊr/ *n* [C] *literary* a sexual relationship, especially a secret one

amp /æmp/ *n* [C] **1** (*also* **am·pere** /ˈæmpeə $ -pɪr/) a unit for measuring electric current: *a 3-amp fuse* **2** *informal* an AMPLIFIER

am·per·sand /ˈæmpəsænd $ -ər-/ *n* [C] the sign '&' that means 'and': *Mills & Boon*

am·phet·a·mine /æmˈfetəmiːn, -mɪn/ *n* [C,U] a drug that gives you a feeling of excitement and a lot of energy

am·phib·i·an /æmˈfɪbiən/ *n* [C] an animal such as a FROG that can live both on land and in water

am·phib·i·ous /æmˈfɪbiəs/ *adj* **1** able to live both on land and in water: *amphibious creatures* **2 amphibious vehicle** a vehicle that is able to move both on land and in water **3 amphibious operation/force/assault** an amphibious operation etc involves both sea and land vehicles

am·phi·thea·tre *BrE*, **amphitheater** *AmE* /ˈæmfəˌθɪətə $ -ər/ *n* [C] a large circular building without a roof and with many rows of seats

am·pho·ra /ˈæmfərə/ *n* [C] a tall clay container for oil or wine, used in ancient times

am·ple /ˈæmpəl/ ●○○ *adj*
1 more than enough SYN **sufficient** OPP **insufficient**: **ample time/evidence/opportunity** *You'll have ample time for questions later.* | *There is ample evidence that climate patterns are changing.* | **ample room/space etc** *She found ample room for her things in the wardrobe.* THESAURUS ENOUGH
2 *literary* large in a way that is attractive or pleasant: *an ample bosom* —**amply** *adv*: *Recent US history has amply demonstrated the risks of foreign intervention.*

am·pli·fi·er /ˈæmpləfaɪə $ -faɪər/ *n* [C] a piece of electrical equipment that makes sound louder SYN **amp** → see picture at ACOUSTIC

am·pli·fy /ˈæmplɪfaɪ/ *v* (**amplified**, **amplifying**, **amplifies**) [T] **1** to make sound louder, especially musical sound: *an amplified guitar* **2** *formal* to increase the effects or strength of something: *These stories only amplified her fears.* **3** *formal* to explain something that you have said by giving more information about it: *Would you care to amplify that remark?* —**amplification** /ˌæmplɪfɪˈkeɪʃən/ *n* [U]

am·pli·tude /ˈæmplɪtjuːd $ -tuːd/ *n* [U] *technical* the distance between the middle and the top or bottom of a WAVE such as a SOUND WAVE

am·poule, **ampule** /ˈæmpuːl $ -pjuːl/ *n* [C] a small container for medicine that will be put into someone with a special needle

am·pu·tate /ˈæmpjəteɪt/ *v* [I,T] to cut off someone's arm, leg, finger etc during a medical operation: *Two of her toes were amputated because of frostbite.* —**amputation** /ˌæmpjəˈteɪʃən/ *n* [C,U]

am·pu·tee /ˌæmpjəˈtiː/ *n* [C] someone who has had an arm or a leg amputated

a·muck /əˈmʌk/ *adv* AMOK

am·u·let /ˈæmjələt, -let $ -lət/ *n* [C] a small piece of jewellery worn to protect against bad luck, disease etc

a·muse /əˈmjuːz/ ●●○ *v* [T]
1 to make someone laugh or smile: *He made funny faces to amuse the children.* | *The question seemed to amuse him in some way.* | **it amuses sb that/how/to do** *It amused me to think back to my life in London.*

> **REGISTER**
> In everyday English, people usually say they **think** something **is funny** rather than say that it **amuses** them: *The joke really* ***amused*** *them.* → *They* ***thought*** *the joke was really* ***funny.***

2 to make time pass in an enjoyable way for someone, so that they do not get bored SYN **entertain**: *Doing jigsaws would amuse Amy for hours on end.* | *The kids* ***amused themselves*** *playing hide-and-seek.*

a·mused /əˈmjuːzd/ ●●○ *adj*
1 if you are amused by something, you think it is funny and you smile or laugh: **[+at/by]** *Ellen seemed amused by the whole situation.* | *I could see she was* ***highly amused*** (=very amused). | *The man looked a little amused.* | *He* ***won't*** *be very* ***amused*** (=he will be annoyed) *when he finds out what's happened to his garden.* | **an amused smile/look/expression etc**
2 keep sb amused to entertain or interest someone for a long time so that they do not get bored: *There were puzzles and games to keep the children amused.*

a·muse·ment /əˈmjuːzmənt/ ●●○ *n*
1 [U] the feeling you have when you think something is funny: **with/in amusement** *Her eyes sparkled with amusement.* | *She looked at him in amusement.* | *Steve couldn't hide his amusement.* | **to sb's amusement** (=in a way that makes someone laugh or smile) *They were dancing and singing in the car,* ***much to the amusement*** *of passers-by.* | *The cats are a constant* ***source of amusement*** *to us.*
2 amusements [plural] **a)** things that entertain you and make time pass in an enjoyable way: *childhood amusements* **b)** *BrE* special machines or games that are intended to entertain people, for example at a FAIR: *The kids can ride on the amusements.*
3 [U] the process of getting or providing pleasure and enjoyment: *What do you do for amusement in this town?*

aˈmusement arˌcade *n* [C] *BrE* a place where you play games on machines by putting coins into them SYN **video arcade** *AmE*

AMUSEMENT PARK

aˈmusement ˌpark *n* [C] a large park with many special machines that you can ride on, such as ROLLER COASTERS and MERRY-GO-ROUNDS

a·mus·ing /əˈmjuːzɪŋ/ ●●○ *adj* funny and entertaining: *I don't* ***find*** *his jokes at all* ***amusing.*** | *a* ***highly amusing*** (=very amusing) *film* | **an amusing story/anecdote/incident etc** *The book is full of amusing stories about his childhood.* | **mildly/vaguely amusing** (=a little amusing, but not very) *a mildly amusing spectacle* THESAURUS FUNNY —**amusingly** *adv*

> **REGISTER**
> In everyday English, people usually say **funny** rather than **amusing**: *Someone told me a really* ***funny*** *joke.*

an /ən; *strong* æn/ ●●● S1 W1 *indefinite article, determiner* used when the following word begins with a vowel sound → **a**: *an orange* | *an X-ray*

an- /ən, æn/ *prefix* **1** the form used for A before a vowel sound **2** not SYN **without**: *anarchy* (=without government) | *anoxia* (=a condition caused by lack of oxygen)

-an /ən/ (*also* **-ean**, **-ian**) *suffix* **1** [in adjectives and nouns] someone or something of, from, or connected with a particular thing, place, or person: *suburban* | *Jamesian* **2** [in nouns] someone skilled in or studying a particular subject: *a historian* (=someone who studies history)

-ana /ɑːnə $ ɑːnə, ænə/ *suffix* [in nouns] another form of the suffix -IANA: *Americana*

an·a·bol·ic ste·roid /ˌænəbɒlɪk ˈstɪərɔɪd, -ˈster- $ -bɑːlɪk ˈstɪrɔɪd, -ˈster-/ *n* [C] a drug that makes muscles grow quickly, sometimes used illegally by people in sport

a·nach·ro·nis·m /əˈnækrənɪzəm/ *n* [C] **1** someone or something that seems to belong to the past, not the present: *The monarchy is something of an anachronism these days.* **2** something in a play, film etc that seems wrong because it did not exist in the period of history in which the play etc is set: *The film is full of anachronisms.* —**anachronistic** /əˌnækrəˈnɪstɪk◂/ *adj*: *His painting style was seen as outdated and anachronistic.*

an·a·con·da /ˌænəˈkɒndə $ -ˈkɑːn-/ *n* [C] a very large South American snake

a·nae·mi·a (*also* **anemia** *AmE*) /əˈniːmiə/ *n* [U] a medical condition in which there are too few red cells in your blood

a·nae·mic (*also* **anemic** *AmE*) /əˈniːmɪk/ *adj* **1** suffering from anaemia: *his anaemic-looking face* **2** *written* seeming weak and uninteresting: *an anaemic first novel*

an·ae·ro·bic /ˌænəˈrəʊbɪk◂ $ -ˈroʊ-/ *adj* **1** not needing oxygen in order to live OPP **aerobic**: *anaerobic bacteria* **2** without oxygen, or happening without oxygen OPP **aerobic**: *anaerobic fermentation*

an·aes·the·si·a (*also* **anesthesia** *AmE*) /ˌænəsˈθiːziə $ -ʒə/ *n* [U] **1** the use of anaesthetics in medicine **2** the state of being unable to feel pain

an·aes·thet·ic (*also* **anesthetic** *AmE*) /ˌænəsˈθetɪk◂/ ●○○ *n* [C,U] a drug that stops you feeling pain: **under anaesthetic** *The operation will have to be done under anaesthetic* (=using anaesthetic). | *Eye surgery is often performed using a* ***local anaesthetic*** (=one that only affects a particular area of your body). | *You will need to have a* ***general anaesthetic*** (=one that makes you completely unconscious). —**anaesthetic** *adj* [only before noun]: *anaesthetic drugs*

a·naes·the·tist (*also* **anesthetist** *AmE*) /əˈniːsθətɪst $ əˈnes-/ *n* [C] a doctor or nurse who has been specially trained to give people anaesthetics

a·naes·the·tize (*also* **-ise** *BrE*, **anesthetize** *AmE*) /əˈniːsθətaɪz $ əˈnes-/ *v* [T] to give someone an anaesthetic so that they do not feel pain

an·a·gram /ˈænəgræm/ ●○○ *n* [C] a word or phrase that is made by changing the order of the letters in another word or phrase: *'Silent' is an anagram of 'listen'.*

a·nal /ˈeɪnl/ *adj* **1** connected with the ANUS **2** (*also* **anal retentive**) showing too much concern with small details, especially in a way that annoys other people – used to show disapproval: *Don't be so anal.*

an·al·ge·si·a /ˌænəlˈdʒiːziə $ -ʒə/ *n* [U] *technical* the condition of being unable to feel pain while conscious

an·al·ge·sic /ˌænəlˈdʒiːzɪk◂/ *n* [C] *technical* a drug that reduces pain SYN **painkiller**: *Aspirin is a popular analgesic.* —**analgesic** *adj* [only before noun]: *drugs that have an analgesic effect on ulcers*

a·nal·o·gous /əˈnæləgəs/ ●○○ AWL *adj formal* similar to another situation or thing so that a comparison can be made: **[+to/with]** *The report's findings are analogous with our own.*

an·a·logue (*also* **analog** *AmE*) /ˈænəlɒg $ -lɒːg, -lɑːg/ *adj* **1 analogue clock/watch** a clock or watch that uses POINTERS, not changing numbers → **digital** **2** *technical* analogue technology uses changing physical quantities such as VOLTAGE to store data → **digital**: **analogue computer/circuit/technology**

a·nal·o·gy /əˈnælədʒi/ ●○○ AWL *n* (*plural* **analogies**) [C,U] something that seems similar between two situations, processes etc: **[+with/to/between]** *analogies between human and animal behaviour* | **draw/make an analogy** (=make a comparison) *She drew an analogy between childbirth and the creative process.* | **by analogy with** *Dr Wood explained the movement of light by analogy with* (=using the analogy of) *the movement of water.*

an·a·lyse *BrE*, **analyze** *AmE* /ˈænəl-aɪz/ ●●○ W3 AWL *v* [T]
1 to examine or think about something carefully, in order to understand it: *She still needs to analyse the data.* | *You need to sit down and analyse why you feel so upset.* | *Joe had never tried to analyze their relationship.* **THESAURUS** EXAMINE
2 to examine a substance to see what it is made of: *The cell samples are analyzed by a lab.*
3 to examine someone's mental or emotional problems by using PSYCHOANALYSIS

a·nal·y·sis /əˈnælɪsɪs/ ●●○ S3 W3 AWL *n* (*plural* **analyses** /-siːz/)
1 [C,U] **a)** a careful examination of something in order to understand it better: **[+of]** *a* ***detailed analysis*** *of the week's news* | *Further analysis of the data is needed.* | **do/carry out/conduct an analysis** *They were doing some type of* ***statistical analysis***. **b)** the way in which someone describes a situation or problem, and says what causes it to happen: **[+of]** *Do you agree with Marx's analysis of the failure of free-market capitalism?*
2 [C,U] a careful examination of a substance to see what it is made of: **[+of]** *analysis of genetic material* | **for analysis** *Blood samples were sent for analysis.* | *You'll get the results when the analysis is complete.*
3 [U] a process in which a doctor makes someone talk about their past experiences, relationships etc in order to help them with mental or emotional problems SYN **psychoanalysis** → **therapy**: *She's been in analysis for three years.*
4 in the final/last analysis used when giving the most basic or important facts about a situation: *In the final analysis, profit is the motive.*

an·a·lyst /ˈænəl-ɪst/ ●●○ W3 AWL *n* [C]
1 someone whose job is to think about something carefully in order to understand it, and often to advise other people about it: ***Political analysts*** *expect the Conservatives to win.* | **investment/financial/business analyst** *Cleary has been working as a* ***computer analyst*** *in Winchester.*
2 a doctor who helps people who have mental or emotional problems by making them talk about their experiences and relationships SYN **psychoanalyst** → SYSTEMS ANALYST

an·a·lyt·ical /ˌænəlˈɪtɪkəl/ ●○○ AWL (*also* **an·a·lyt·ic** /ˌænəlˈɪtɪk◂/) *adj*
1 thinking about things in a detailed and intelligent way, so that you can examine and understand things: *She's got an analytical mind.* | **analytical method/techniques/approach/skills** *During the course, students will develop their analytical skills.*
2 using scientific analysis to examine something: *analytical chemistry* —**analytically** /-kli/ *adv*

an·a·lyze /ˈænəl-aɪz/ *v* [T] the American spelling of ANALYSE **THESAURUS** EXAMINE

an·a·phy·lac·tic shock /ˌænəfəlæktɪk ˈʃɒk $ -ˈʃɑːk/ *n* [U] *medical* a very sudden serious physical reaction that is caused by an ALLERGY to something such as nuts, eggs, or the STING of some insects. The reaction causes shock, breathing difficulties, and sometimes death.

an·ar·chic /æˈnɑːkɪk $ -ɑːr-/ *adj* lacking any rules or order, or not following the moral rules of society: *a lawless, anarchic city* | *an anarchic sense of humour*

an·ar·chis·m /ˈænəkɪzəm $ -ər-/ *n* [U] the political belief that there should be no government and ordinary people should work together to improve society

A

an·ar·chist /'ænəkɪst $ -ər-/ *n* [C] someone who believes that governments, laws etc are not necessary —**anarchistic** /ˌænə'kɪstɪk◂ $ -ər-/ *adj*

an·ar·chy /'ænəki $ -ər-/ ●○○ *n* [U] a situation in which there is no effective government in a country or no order in an organization or situation: *The prison is close to anarchy.* | *The classroom was* ***in a constant state of anarchy***. | **slide/fall/descend into anarchy** *The nation is in danger of falling into anarchy.*

a·nath·e·ma /ə'næθəmə/ *n* [singular, U] *formal* something that is completely the opposite of what you believe in: **[+to]** *His political views were anathema to me.*

an·a·tom·i·cal /ˌænə'tɒmɪkəl◂ $ -'tɑː-/ *adj* relating to the structure of human or animal bodies: *an anatomical examination* —**anatomically** /-kli/ *adv*

a·nat·o·mist /ə'nætəmɪst/ *n* [C] a scientist who studies anatomy

a·nat·o·my /ə'nætəmi/ ●○○ *n* (*plural* **anatomies**)
1 [U] the scientific study of the structure of human or animal bodies: *a professor of anatomy* | **human/animal anatomy** *Knowledge of human anatomy is essential to figure drawing.*
2 [C usually singular] the structure of a body, or of a part of a body: **[+of]** *the anatomy of the nervous system*
3 [C] your body – often used in a humorous way: *You could see a part of his anatomy that I'd rather not mention.*
4 the/an anatomy of sth a) a study or examination of an organization, process etc in order to understand and explain how it works: *Elkind's book is an anatomy of one man's discussion with his son about life.* **b)** the structure of an organization, process etc or the way it works: *For the first time, we have the chance to examine the anatomy of a secret government operation.*

-ance /əns/, **-ence** *suffix* [in nouns] the action, state, or quality of doing something or of being something: *his sudden appearance* (=he appeared suddenly) | *her brilliance* (=she is BRILLIANT)

an·ces·tor /'ænsəstə, -ses- $ -sestər/ ●●○ *n* [C]
1 a member of your family who lived a long time ago → **descendant**: *My ancestors were French.* **THESAURUS** ▸ RELATIVE
2 an animal that lived in the past, that modern animals have developed from: *Lions and house cats evolved from* ***a common ancestor*** (=the same ancestor).
3 the form in which a modern machine, vehicle etc first existed SYN **forerunner**: **[+of]** *Babbage's invention was the ancestor of the modern computer.* —**ancestral** /æn'sestrəl/ *adj*: *the family's ancestral home*

an·ces·try /'ænsəstri, -ses- $ -ses-/ *n* (*plural* **ancestries**) [C usually singular, U] *formal* the members of your family who lived a long time ago: **of ... ancestry** *Her mother is of German ancestry* (=has German ancestors). | *Helen's family can trace their ancestry back to the 1700s.*

an·chor¹ /'æŋkə $ -ər/ *n* [C] **1** a piece of heavy metal that is lowered to the bottom of the sea, a lake etc to prevent a ship or boat moving: **at anchor** *The ship was at anchor.* | *We* ***dropped anchor*** *a few yards offshore.* | *The next morning, they* ***weighed anchor*** (=lifted the anchor) *and began to move south again.* **2** *especially AmE* someone who reads the news on TV and introduces news reports SYN **newsreader** *BrE*: *Dan Rather, anchor of the CBC Evening News* **3** someone or something that provides a feeling of support and safety: *Dad was the anchor of the family.*

anchor² *v* **1** [I,T] to lower the anchor on a ship or boat to hold it in one place SYN **moor**: *Three tankers were anchored in the harbor.* **2** [T] to fasten something firmly so that it cannot move: *The shelves should be securely anchored to the wall.* GRAMMAR **Anchor** is usually passive in this meaning. **3 be anchored in sth** to be strongly connected with a particular system, way of life etc: *John's outlook has always been anchored in the political mainstream.* **4** [T] to provide a feeling of support, safety, or help for someone or an organization: *Steve anchors the team's defense.* | *Her life was anchored by her religion.* **5** [T] *AmE* to be the person who reads the news and introduces reports on television SYN **present**: *Collins anchors the 6 o'clock news.*

an·chor·age /'æŋkərɪdʒ/ *n* **1** [C] a place where ships can anchor **2** [C,U] a place where something can be firmly fastened

'anchor ˌbaby *n* [C] *AmE informal* a child who has the right to be a US citizen because they were born there, but their parents are not US citizens – used to show disapproval

an·chor·per·son /'æŋkəˌpɜːsən $ -kərˌpɜːr-/, **an·chor·man** /-mæn/, **an·chor·wom·an** /-ˌwʊmən/ *n* [C] someone who reads the news on TV and introduces reports SYN **anchor**

'anchor store *n* [C] *AmE* a large, well-known, and popular store in a SHOPPING MALL (=place containing a lot of shops), that attracts a lot of customers to the mall and to the other shops. An anchor store is usually part of a successful chain that has stores in many cities.

an·cho·vy /'æntʃəvi $ 'æntʃoʊvi/ *n* (*plural* **anchovies**) [C,U] a very small fish that tastes strongly of salt

an·cient¹ /'eɪnʃənt/ ●●● W2 *adj*
1 belonging to a time long ago in history, especially thousands of years ago OPP **modern**: *the ancient civilizations of Asia* | **ancient Greece/Egypt/Rome** *the religion of ancient Egypt*
2 having existed for a very long time OPP **new**: *an ancient walled city* | *an ancient forest* | *the ancient art of calligraphy*
3 very old – used humorously: *That photo makes me look ancient!* **THESAURUS** ▸ OLD
4 ancient history a) the history of ancient societies, such as Greece or Rome: *a professor of ancient history* **b)** *informal* if you say that something is ancient history, you mean that it happened a long time ago and is not important now: *It's all ancient history and I'm not upset anymore.*

ancient² *n* **the ancients** [plural] people who lived long ago, especially the Greeks and Romans: *The ancients believed that the Sun and Moon were planets.*

an·cil·la·ry /æn'sɪləri $ 'ænsəleri/ *adj* **1 ancillary workers/staff etc** workers who provide additional help and services for the people who do the main work in hospitals, schools etc **2** *formal* connected with or supporting something else, but less important than it: *Agreement was reached on several ancillary matters.*

-ancy /ənsi/, **-ency** *suffix* [in nouns] the state or quality of doing something or of being something: *expectancy* (=state of expecting) | *hesitancy* | *complacency* (=being complacent)

and /ənd, ən; *strong* ænd/ ●●● S1 W1 *conjunction*
1 used to join two words, phrases etc referring to things that are related in some way: *He's gone to get some fish and chips.* | *The film starred Jack Lemmon and Shirley Maclaine.* | *We've dealt with items one, two, and eleven.* | *He was tall, dark, and handsome.* | *He plays the guitar and sings folk songs.* | *She didn't speak to anyone and nobody spoke to her.*
2 used to say that one action or event follows another: *Sit down and tell me all about it.* | *She picked up the kitten and put it in the box.* | *He knocked on the door and went in.* | *You'll have to wait and see what happens.*
3 used to say that something is caused by something else: *I missed supper and I'm starving!* | *She fell downstairs and broke her leg.*
4 used when adding numbers: *Six and four is ten.*
5 *especially BrE* used after verbs such as 'go', 'come', and 'try' to show what your intention is: *Shall we go and have a cup of coffee?* | *I'll see if I can try and persuade her to come.*
6 *spoken* used to introduce a statement, remark, question etc: *And now I'd like to introduce our next speaker, Mrs Thompson.* | *'She's getting married in June.' 'And who's the lucky man?'*

REGISTER
In written English, avoid starting a sentence with **and**: ***And now we*** *come onto the issue of homelessness.*
→ ***We now*** *come onto the issue of homelessness.*

7 used between repeated words to emphasize what you are saying: *More and more people are losing their jobs.* | *We waited for hours and hours!* | *That was years and years ago.* | *We ran and ran.*
8 a) used before saying the part of a large number which is less than 100: *a hundred and four* | *five hundred and seventy-six* | *by the year two thousand and ten* **b)** used when saying a number which consists of a whole number followed by a FRACTION: *three and three-quarters* | *in about two and a half hours' time* | *five and a quarter per cent*
9 used between repeated plural nouns to say that some things of a particular kind are much better than others: *'They said this guy was an expert.' 'Yes, but there are experts and experts.'*
10 and? *spoken* used when you want someone to add something to what they have just said: *'I'm sorry.' 'And?' 'And I promise it won't happen again.'*

andante /æn'dænti, -teɪ $ ɑːn'dɑːn-/ *n* [C] a piece of music played or sung at a speed that is neither very fast nor very slow —**andante** *adj, adv*

an·drog·y·nous /æn'drɒdʒɪnəs $ -'drɑː-/ *adj* **1** having both male and female parts **2** someone who is androgynous looks both female and male: *Bowie had a kind of androgynous sex appeal.*

an·droid /'ændrɔɪd/ *n* [C] a ROBOT that looks completely human

an·dro·pause /'ændrəʊpɔːz $ -droʊpɒːz/ *n* [U] the period in a man's life when the amount of TESTOSTERONE in his body begins to reduce, after about age 50 SYN **male menopause** —**andropausal** /ˌændrəʊ'pɔːzəl $ -droʊ'pɒː-/ *adj*

an·ec·da·ta /'ænəkdeɪtə, -dɑːtə/ *n* [U] information which is presented as if it is the result of serious research, but which is actually based on what someone thinks but cannot prove: *All this is just anecdata, when what we need now is some hard evidence of what UK firms are doing.*

an·ec·dot·al /ˌænɪk'dəʊtl◂ $ -'doʊ-/ *adj* consisting of short stories based on someone's personal experience: *His findings are based on* ***anecdotal evidence*** *rather than serious research.*

an·ec·dote /'ænɪkdəʊt $ -doʊt/ ●○○ *n* [C] a short story based on your personal experience: *The book is full of amusing anecdotes about his life in Japan.*

a·ne·mi·a /ə'niːmiə/ *n* [U] the usual American spelling of ANAEMIA

a·ne·mic /ə'niːmɪk/ *adj* the usual American spelling of ANAEMIC

a·nem·o·ne /ə'neməni/ *n* [C] a plant with red, white, or blue flowers → SEA ANEMONE

an·es·the·si·a /ˌænəs'θiːziə $ -ʒə/ *n* [U] the usual American spelling of ANAESTHESIA

an·es·the·si·ol·o·gist /ˌænɪsθiːzi'ɒlədʒɪst $ -'ɑːl-/ *n* [C] *AmE* a doctor who gives ANAESTHETICS to a patient

an·es·thet·ic /ˌænəs'θetɪk◂/ *n* [C,U] the usual American spelling of ANAESTHETIC

a·nes·the·tist /ə'niːsθɪtɪst $ ə'nes-/ *n* [C] the usual American spelling of ANAESTHETIST

a·nes·the·tize /ə'niːsθətaɪz $ ə'nes-/ *v* [T] the usual American spelling of ANAESTHETIZE

an·eu·rysm, **aneurism** /'ænjəˌrɪzəm/ *n* [C] a small place on the surface of a BLOOD VESSEL that is swollen and full of blood, and that can kill you if it breaks open

a·new /ə'njuː $ ə'nuː/ *adv written* **1 start/begin anew** to begin a different job, start to live in a different place etc, especially after a difficult period in your life: *I was ready to leave everything behind and start anew in California.* **2** if you do something anew, you start doing it again: *The committee is going to examine the whole situation anew.*

an·gel /'eɪndʒəl/ ●●○ *n* [C]
1 a SPIRIT who is God's servant in heaven, and who is often shown as a person dressed in white with wings: *the angel Gabriel*
2 someone who is very kind, very good, or very beautiful: *That little girl of theirs is an angel.* | *Sam* ***is no angel*** (=often behaves badly).
3 *old-fashioned spoken* used when asking someone to help you or when thanking someone for helping you: *Thanks for mailing those letters,* ***you're an angel***. | ***Be an angel*** *and get me my glasses, will you?*
4 (*also* **business angel**, **angel investor**) someone who gives new businesses money, often in exchange for a share of the company → GUARDIAN ANGEL

an·gel·ic /æn'dʒelɪk/ *adj* **1** looking good, kind, and gentle or behaving in this way: *She had an angelic smile, but a dreadful temper.* **2** connected with angels: *the angelic hosts* —**angelically** /-kli/ *adv*

an·gel·i·ca /æn'dʒelɪkə/ *n* [U] a plant that smells sweet and is used in cooking

an·ger¹ /'æŋgə $ -ər/ ●●○ W3 *n* [U]
1 a strong feeling of wanting to hurt or criticize someone because they have done something bad to you or been unkind to you: *There is growing anger among the people against the government.* | **[+at]** *She struggled to control her anger at her son's disobedience.* | **in anger** *'That's a lie!' he shouted in anger.*
2 do/use sth in anger to do or use something for the first time, or in a real situation: *He joined the club last month, but has yet to kick a ball in anger.*

COLLOCATIONS

VERBS

be filled with anger/be full of anger *His face was suddenly filled with anger.*
be shaking with anger *My aunt was shaking with anger as she left the room.*
be seething with anger (=be extremely angry) *Seething with anger and frustration, Polly pushed back her chair and stood up.*
express your anger (*also* **vent your anger** *formal*) (=show your anger) *Demonstrators expressed their anger by burning American flags.*
hide your anger | **control/contain your anger** | **arouse/provoke anger** (*also* **stir up anger** *informal*) (=make people angry) | **fuel anger** (=make people even more angry) | **sb's anger goes away/subsides/fades** (=it stops)

ADJECTIVES

deep/great/fierce anger *There is deep anger against the occupying forces.*
growing/rising/mounting anger *There is growing anger among drivers over the rise in fuel prices.*
widespread anger (=among many people) *The decision to build the airport has provoked widespread anger.*
public/popular anger | **suppressed/pent-up anger** (=that you have tried not to show) | **real anger** | **righteous anger** *often disapproving* (=anger felt when you think something should not be allowed to happen)

PHRASES

a fit/outburst of anger (=an occasion when someone suddenly becomes angry) *His occasional outbursts of anger shocked those around him.*
a feeling of anger

anger² ●●○ *v* [T] to make someone angry SYN **annoy**: *What angered me most was his total lack of remorse.* | **be angered by/at sth** *Environmental groups were disappointed and angered by the president's decision.*

REGISTER

In everyday English, people usually say something **makes them angry** rather than say that it **angers** them: *I didn't want to* ***anger*** *him.* → *I didn't want to* ***make*** *him* ***angry***.

'anger ˌmanagement *n* [U] good ways of dealing with your angry feelings

an·gi·na /æn'dʒaɪnə/ *n* [U] a medical condition in which you have bad pains in your chest because your heart is weak

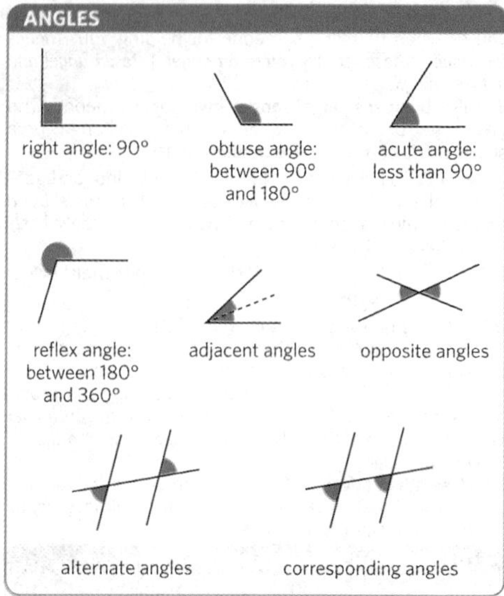

an·gle¹ /ˈæŋɡəl/ ●●● S3 W3 *n* [C]
1 the space between two straight lines or surfaces that join each other, measured in degrees: **an angle of sth** *an angle of 45°* | **[+of]** *the angles of a triangle* | *You didn't measure the angle accurately.* | **[+between]** *the angle between walls and ceiling* → RIGHT ANGLE
2 a way of considering a problem or situation: *We're approaching the issue* ***from*** *many* ***different angles****.* | *Look at* ***every angle*** *of the situation.* | **[+to]** *There's another angle to this question.*
3 a position from which you look at something or photograph it: **from a ... angle** *This drawing of the monastery was done from an unusual angle.* | *Some of the pictures have strange camera angles.*
4 at an angle leaning to one side and not straight or upright: *The portrait was hanging at an angle.* | **at a slight/steep angle** *The sign leaned over at a slight angle.*
5 the shape formed when two lines or surfaces join: **[+of]** *My head struck the angle of the shelf.*

angle² *v* [T] **1** to move or place something so that it is not straight or upright: *a mirror angled to reflect light from a window* | *Philip angled his chair towards the door.* **2** to present information from a particular point of view or for a specific group of people: *The book is angled towards a business audience.*

angle for sth *phr v* to try to get something you want without asking directly for it: *She was obviously angling for an invitation.* | *I didn't want him to think I was just angling for sympathy.*

ˈ**angle** ˌ**brackets** *n* [plural] *BrE* a pair of BRACKETS < > used for enclosing information

an·gler /ˈæŋɡlə $ -ər/ *n* [C] someone who catches fish as a sport → **fisherman**

An·gli·can /ˈæŋɡlɪkən/ *n* [C] a Christian who is a member of the Church of England or related churches —**Anglican** *adj*: *members of the Anglican Church* —**Anglicanism** *n* [U]

an·gli·cize (*also* **-ise** *BrE*) /ˈæŋɡlɪsaɪz/ *v* [T] to make something or someone more English: *Leszek anglicized his name to 'Lester'.*

an·gling /ˈæŋɡlɪŋ/ *n* [U] the sport of catching fish with a fishing rod SYN **fishing**

Anglo- /æŋɡləʊ $ -ɡloʊ/ *prefix* [in nouns and adjectives] **1** relating to England or Britain: *an anglophile* (=someone who loves Britain) **2** English or British and something else: *an Anglo-Scottish family* | *an improvement in Anglo-American relations*

ˌ**Anglo-ˈCatholic** *n* [C] a Christian who is a member of the part of the Church of England that is similar to the Roman Catholic Church —**Anglo-Catholic** *adj* —ˌ**Anglo-Caˈtholicism** *n* [U]

ˌ**Anglo-ˈIndian** *n* [C] someone whose family is partly British and partly Indian —**Anglo-Indian** *adj*

an·glo·phile /ˈæŋɡləʊfaɪl, -ɡlə- $ -ɡloʊ-, -ɡlə-/ *n* [C] someone who is not English but likes England and anything English

an·glo·phobe /ˈæŋɡləʊfəʊb, -ɡlə- $ -ɡloʊfoʊb, -ɡlə-/ *n* [C] someone who dislikes anything English —**anglophobia** /ˌæŋɡləʊˈfəʊbiə, -ɡlə- $ -ɡloʊˈfoʊ-, -ɡlə-/ *n* [U]

an·glo·phone /ˈæŋɡləʊfəʊn, -ɡlə- $ -ɡloʊfoʊn, -ɡlə-/ *n* [C] someone who speaks English as their first language —**anglophone** *adj*: *the US and other anglophone countries*

ˌ**Anglo-ˈSaxon** *n* **1** [C] someone who belonged to the race of people who lived in England from about 600 AD **2** [U] the language used by the Anglo-Saxons **3** [C] a white person, especially someone whose family originally came from England —**Anglo-Saxon** *adj*

an·go·ra /æŋˈɡɔːrə/ *n* **1** [C] a type of goat, rabbit, or cat with very long soft hair or fur **2** [U] wool or thread made

THESAURUS: angry

angry feeling strong emotions because you think someone has behaved badly, or because a situation seems bad or unfair: *He gets really angry if people keep him waiting.* | *a crowd of angry protesters*
mad [not before noun] *informal* angry: *Dad was mad at me for damaging the car.*
cross [not before noun] *spoken* rather angry - used when speaking to people you know well: *She was cross with me for being late.*
annoyed [not before noun] a little angry: *I was annoyed no one had told me the class was cancelled.*
irritated annoyed and impatient, especially by something that keeps happening or something someone keeps saying: *I was irritated by their stupid questions.* | *an irritated voice*
bad-tempered becoming annoyed or angry easily: *a bad-tempered old man* | *He's always bad-tempered when he doesn't get what he wants.*
in a bad/foul mood feeling a little angry for a period of time, often for no particular reason: *I woke up in a bad mood.*
in a huff /hʌf/ in an angry mood for a short time, especially because someone has just said something to offend or annoy you: *He walked off in a huff when they refused to let him join in their game.*
sb has got up on the wrong side of the bed *informal* used when you think someone has been in an angry mood all day, for no particular reason - often used humorously: *I don't know what's wrong - she must have got up on the wrong side of the bed today.*

EXTREMELY ANGRY

furious/livid extremely angry: *She was furious when she found out he'd been lying to her.* | *He looked absolutely livid.*
outraged very angry and shocked by something you think is unfair or wrong: *Most people were outraged by the 9/11 attacks.* | *complaints from outraged viewers*
incandescent with rage *BrE formal* extremely angry - used mainly in writing, for example in newspaper reports: *Gordon Brown was reported to be incandescent with rage over the article.*
lose your temper to suddenly become very angry and start shouting at someone: *It was the first time I'd seen her lose her temper.*

from the fur of an angora goat or rabbit: *soft pink angora sweaters*

This graph shows how common different grammar patterns of the adjective **angry** are.

be/get angry
angry person/look etc
angry with sb
angry about sth
angry (that)
angry at sth
other

10% 20% 30% 40% 50%

an·gry /ˈæŋgri/ ●●● S2 W2 *adj* (*comparative* **angrier**, *superlative* **angriest**)
1 feeling strong emotions which make you want to shout at someone or hurt them because they have behaved in an unfair, cruel, offensive etc way, or because you think that a situation is unfair, unacceptable etc → **annoyed**: *I was angry because he hadn't told me his plans.* | *He was beginning to* ***get angry***. | *His comments brought an angry response from opposition politicians.* | *'Calm down,' she said, looking at his angry face.* | *Jesse laughed, which* ***made*** *me even* ***angrier***. | **[+with]** *'Please don't be angry with me,' she said.* | **[+at]** *They are angry at the way they have been treated.* | **[+about/over]** *Kate's still so angry about the whole thing.* | **angry (that)** *The workers are angry that they haven't been paid for the week.*
2 angry with/at yourself feeling strongly that you wish you had done something or had not done something: *David was angry with himself for letting the others see his true feelings.*
3 *literary* an angry sky or cloud looks dark and stormy
4 *literary* an angry wound etc is painful and red and looks infected SYN **inflamed** —**angrily** *adv*: *Joey reacted angrily.*

GRAMMAR: Patterns with angry

angry with
• You say that someone is **angry with** another person: *My parents were very angry with me.* ✗ Don't say: *My parents were angry to me.*

angry about
• You say that someone is **angry about** something: *I was really angry about what had happened.*

angry at
• You can say that someone is **angry at** someone, or **angry at** something: *Please don't get angry at me.* | *I was really angry at what had happened.*

ˌAngry Young ˈMan *n* [C] *BrE* a young man who strongly criticizes society and the government. The phrase was first used to describe John Osborne and other British writers in the 1950s.

angst /æŋst/ *n* [U] strong feelings of anxiety and unhappiness because you are worried about your life, your future, or what you should do in a particular situation: *love letters full of angst*

angst·y /ˈæŋsti/ *adj informal* full of anxiety and unhappiness because you are worried about your life, your future, or what you should do in a particular situation: *angsty teenagers*

an·guish /ˈæŋgwɪʃ/ ●○○ *n* [U] *written* mental or physical suffering caused by extreme pain or worry: *the anguish of not knowing what had happened to her* —**anguished** *adj*: *an anguished cry for help*

an·gu·lar /ˈæŋgjələ $ -ər/ *adj* **1** thin and not having much flesh on your bones: *a tall, angular young man* **2** having sharp and definite corners: *a cubist painting with angular shapes*

an·i·mal¹ /ˈænəməl/ ●●● S1 W1 *n* [C]
1 a living creature such as a dog or cat, that is not an insect, plant, bird, fish, or person: *furry little animals* | **wild/domestic/farm animals** *cattle, sheep, and other domestic animals* | *The cosmetics have not been tested on animals.* | *Beth is an* ***animal lover*** (=someone who likes animals).
2 any living creature that is not a plant or a person: *He can't stand* ***cruelty to animals*** *of any sort.* | *the animal welfare movement in Britain* | *the enormous diversity of* ***the animal kingdom***
3 any living creature, including people: *Man is a highly intelligent animal.*
4 *informal* someone who behaves in a cruel, violent, or very rude way: *Football hooligans are just animals.*
5 a (very/completely/entirely) different animal *informal* something that is very different from the thing you have mentioned: *Writing email is a very different animal from all other forms of writing.*
6 a political/social etc animal *informal* someone who is interested in politics, in meeting other people etc: *He is simply not a social animal.*

THESAURUS

animal a living thing such as a dog, cow, or tiger, but not an insect, fish, or bird: *farm animals such as cows, sheep, and pigs* | *People are becoming more concerned about animal welfare.*
creature /ˈkriːtʃə $ -ər/ an animal - used especially when describing a particular animal's characteristics or when referring to animals generally: *The cheetah is a magnificent creature.* | *all the living creatures in the sea*
beast an animal, especially a large or dangerous one: *To most people, lions are savage beasts.* | *a wild beast*
living thing an animal considered as one of a group of things that grow and then die, including humans and plants: *The only living things we saw were dogs and cats.*
species /ˈspiːʃiːz/ a group of animals whose members are similar and can breed together to produce young animals: *Seven species of birds of prey have been observed.*
mammal an animal that drinks milk from its mother's body when it is young: *Humans, dogs, and whales are all mammals.*
vertebrate a living creature that has a backbone: *viruses that affect chickens, monkeys, and most other vertebrates*
invertebrate a living creature that does not have a backbone: *earthworms and other small invertebrates*

animal² *adj* **1 animal urges/instincts etc** human feelings, desires etc that are connected with sex, food, and other basic needs **2 animal products/fats/protein etc** things that are made or come from animals: *a diet rich in red meat and animal fats*

ˌanimal ˈhusbandry *n* [U] farming that involves keeping animals and producing milk, meat etc

ˌanimal ˈrights *n* [U or plural] the idea that people should treat animals well, and especially not use them in tests to develop medicines or other products: **animal rights activists/campaigners/groups etc** *Bill has been involved in the animal rights movement for years.*

an·i·mate¹ /ˈænəmət/ *adj formal* living OPP **inanimate**: *animate beings*

an·i·mate² /ˈænɪmeɪt/ *v* [T] to give life or energy to something: *Laughter animated his face for a moment.*

an·i·ma·ted /ˈænɪmeɪtɪd/ *adj* **1** showing a lot of interest and energy: **animated discussion/conversation** *The performance was followed by an animated discussion.* **2 animated cartoon/film/feature etc** a film or programme that shows pictures, clay models etc that seem to be really moving: *an animated Disney film* —**animatedly** *adv*

an·i·ma·tion /ˌænəˈmeɪʃən/ *n* **1** [U] the process of making animated films, television programmes, computer games etc: *They used computer animation in the film.* **2** [C] a film, television programme, computer game etc that has pictures, clay models etc that seem to be really moving: *3-D animations* **3** [U] liveliness and excitement: **with animation** *They were talking with animation.*

A

A

an·i·ma·tor /ˈænəmeɪtə $ -ər/ *n* [C] someone who makes animated films

an·i·ma·tron·ics /ˌænəməˈtrɒnɪks $ -ˈtrɑː-/ *n* [U] the method or process of making or using moving models that look like real animals or people in films —**animatronic** *adj*

an·i·me /ˈænɪmeɪ, -mə/ *n* [U] Japanese CARTOONS and computer ANIMATION (=pictures, films etc produced using a computer) **THESAURUS** MOVIE → MANGA

an·i·mis·m /ˈænəmɪzəm/ *n* [U] a religion in which animals and plants are believed to have spirits

an·i·mos·i·ty /ˌænəˈmɒsəti $ -ˈmɑː-/ ●○○ *n* (*plural* **animosities**) [C,U] strong dislike or hatred SYN **hostility**: **[+between]** *There is no personal animosity between the party leaders.* | **[+towards/against]** *She felt a certain amount of animosity towards him.*

an·i·mus /ˈænɪməs/ *n* [singular, U] *formal* a feeling of strong dislike or hatred SYN **animosity**, **hostility**: **[+against/towards]** *I have no animus towards Robert.*

an·ise /ˈænɪs/ *n* [U] a plant with seeds that have a strong taste

an·i·seed /ˈænəsiːd/ *n* [U] the seeds of an anise plant, which are used in alcoholic drinks and in sweets

an·kle /ˈæŋkəl/ ●●○ *n* [C]
1 the joint between your foot and your leg: **break/twist/sprain your ankle** *Janet slipped on the stairs and twisted her ankle.* | *slender ankles*
2 ankle socks/boots socks or boots that only come up to your ankle

an·klet /ˈæŋklɪt/ *n* [C] a ring or BRACELET worn around your ankle

an·nals /ˈænlz/ *n* [plural] **1 in the annals of sth** in the whole history of something: *one of the most unusual cases in the annals of crime* **2** used in the titles of official records of events or activities: *the Annals of the Zoological Society*

an·neal /əˈniːl/ *v* [T] *technical* to make metal or glass hard by heating it and then slowly letting it get cold

an·nex /əˈneks $ əˈneks, ˈæneks/ *v* [T] to take control of a country or area next to your own, especially by using force: *The Baltic republics were annexed by the Soviet Union in 1940.* —**annexation** /ˌænekˈseɪʃən/ *n* [C,U]

an·nexe, **annex** /ˈæneks/ *n* [C] **1** a separate building that has been added to a larger one: *Some of us will be sleeping in the annexe.* **2** *formal* a part that has been added to the end of a document, report etc

an·ni·hi·late /əˈnaɪəleɪt/ *v* [T] **1** to destroy something or someone completely: *Just one of these bombs could annihilate a city the size of New York.* **2** to defeat someone easily and completely in a game or competition: *Tyson annihilated his opponent in the first round.* —**annihilation** /əˌnaɪəˈleɪʃən/ *n* [U]

an·ni·ver·sa·ry /ˌænəˈvɜːsəri $ -ɜːr-/ ●●○ *n* (*plural* **anniversaries**) [C] a date on which something special or important happened in a previous year: *Jack and Kim celebrated their twentieth* ***wedding anniversary*** *in January.* | **[+of]** *A huge parade was held on the anniversary of the 1959 revolution.*

An·no Dom·i·ni /ˌænəʊ ˈdɒmənaɪ $ ˌænoʊ ˈdɑː-/ AD

an·no·tate /ˈænəteɪt/ *v* [T] to add short notes to a book or piece of writing to explain parts of it: *an annotated edition of 'Othello'* GRAMMAR **Annotate** is usually passive. —**annotation** /ˌænəˈteɪʃən/ *n* [C,U]

an·nounce /əˈnaʊns/ ●●● S2 W1 *v* [T]
1 to officially tell people about something, especially about a plan or a decision: *They announced their engagement in 'The Times'.* | **announce a decision/intention/plan** *The government has announced plans to create 10,000 new jobs.* | **announce that** *A government spokesman announced that the hostages had been released.* | *At the end of their meeting,* ***it was announced that*** *an agreement had been reached.* | **announce sth to sb** *Cordon announced his resignation to staff members on Wednesday.* **THESAURUS** TELL
2 to say something, especially something that other people will not like, in a loud and confident way SYN **state**: *'I'm not going to their party,' Maggie announced.* | **announce (that)** *He stood up and announced that he was ready to go.* **THESAURUS** SAY
3 to give information to people using a LOUDSPEAKER or MICROPHONE, especially at an airport or railway station: *We arrived just as they were announcing the arrival of Flight 207 from Minneapolis.*
4 announce sb/yourself to officially tell people that someone has arrived at a particular place: *All visitors to the apartment building must be announced.* | *After announcing himself at the reception desk, James was led upstairs.*
5 to introduce a programme on television or radio

an·nounce·ment /əˈnaʊnsmənt/ ●●● S3 W3 *n*
1 [C] an important or official statement: *The minister made the announcement at a news conference.* | **[+about]** *an important announcement about tax increases* | **[+ that]** *They heard the announcement that the mayor was resigning.*
2 [U] the act of telling people that something important is going to happen: **[+of]** *the announcement of the company's annual results*
3 [C] a small advertisement or statement in a newspaper: *a wedding announcement in the local paper*

COLLOCATIONS

VERBS

make/issue an announcement *The next day an announcement was issued to staff, saying the company would be closing.*
hear an announcement *Everyone was shocked when they heard the announcement.*
welcome an announcement (=say that you are pleased about it) *Environmental groups welcomed the announcement.*
an announcement comes (=it happens) *His announcement came after two days of peace talks.*

ADJECTIVES

a formal announcement *A formal announcement will be made in Parliament.*
an official announcement *No official announcement is expected until next year.*
a surprise announcement/an unexpected announcement | **a dramatic announcement** (=sudden and important) | **a further announcement**

an·nounc·er /əˈnaʊnsə $ -ər/ *n* [C] **1** someone who reads news or information on the television or radio **2** someone who gives information to people using a LOUDSPEAKER or MICROPHONE, especially at an airport or railway station

an·noy /əˈnɔɪ/ ●●○ S3 *v* [T] to make someone feel slightly angry and unhappy about something SYN **irritate**: *What annoyed him most was that he had received no apology.* | *She annoyed him with her stupid questions.* | **it annoys sb when/how/that** *It really annoys me when I see people dropping litter.*

REGISTER
In everyday English, people also often use the phrase **get on** someone's **nerves**: *She* ***got on his nerves*** *with her stupid questions.*

an·noy·ance /əˈnɔɪəns/ *n* **1** [U] a feeling of slight anger SYN **irritation**: *A look of annoyance crossed her face.* | **to sb's annoyance** *To his annoyance, he discovered they hadn't waited.* | **in annoyance** *Kelly shook her head in annoyance.* **2** [C] something that makes you slightly angry: *Alan found the constant noise of the traffic an annoyance.*

an·noyed /əˈnɔɪd/ ●●● S2 *adj* slightly angry SYN **irritated** → **angry**: *I'll be annoyed if we don't finish by eight.* | **be annoyed at/with sb** *She was annoyed with Duncan for forgetting to phone.* | **be annoyed about/by sth** *He was annoyed by her apparent indifference.* | **annoyed that** *Mr Davies was annoyed that the books were missing.* **THESAURUS** ANGRY

an·noy·ing /əˈnɔɪ-ɪŋ/ ●●● S2 *adj* making you feel slightly angry SYN **irritating**: *an annoying habit of interrupting* | *The annoying thing is he's usually right.* | ***It's annoying that** we didn't know about this before.* —**annoyingly** *adv*

an·nu·al[1] /ˈænjuəl/ ●●○ W2 AWL *adj*
1 happening once a year SYN **yearly**: *The school trip has become an annual event.* | **annual report/meeting/conference**
2 based on or calculated over a period of one year SYN **yearly**: **annual budget/income/cost etc** *a household with an annual income of $60,000*

annual[2] *n* [C] **1** a plant that lives for one year or season → **biennial**, **perennial** **2** a book, especially for children, that is produced once a year with the same title but different stories, pictures etc

an·nu·a·lized (*also* **-ised** *BrE*) /ˈænjuəlaɪzd/ *adj* [only before noun] *technical* if money or an amount is annualized, it is calculated for one year, based on amounts for shorter periods of time: *an annualized **inflation rate** of 15%*

an·nu·al·ly /ˈænjuəli/ ●●○ *adv* once every year: *The jazz festival is held annually in July.*

an·nu·i·ty /əˈnjuːəti $ əˈnuː-/ *n* (*plural* **annuities**) [C] a fixed amount of money that is paid each year to someone, usually until they die

an·nul /əˈnʌl/ *v* (**annulled**, **annulling**) [T] to officially state that a marriage or legal agreement no longer exists: *Their marriage was annulled last year.* **THESAURUS** ▸ CANCEL —**annulment** *n* [C,U]

an·ode /ˈænəʊd $ ˈænoʊd/ *n* [C] *technical* the part of a BATTERY that collects ELECTRONS, often a wire or piece of metal with the sign (+) → **cathode**

an·o·dyne[1] /ˈænədaɪn/ *adj formal* expressed in a way that is unlikely to offend anyone SYN **bland**: *anodyne topics of conversation*

anodyne[2] *n* [C] **1** *technical* a medicine that reduces pain SYN **painkiller** **2** *formal* an activity or thing that comforts people

a·noint /əˈnɔɪnt/ *v* [T] to put oil or water on someone's head or body, usually as part of a religious ceremony: *the anointed king* | **anoint sb with sth** *He was anointed with sacred oil.* —**anointment** *n* [C,U]

a·nom·a·lous /əˈnɒmələs $ əˈnɑː-/ *adj formal* different from what you expected to find: *a highly anomalous situation* | *anomalous results* —**anomalously** *adv*

a·nom·a·ly /əˈnɒməli $ əˈnɑː-/ ●○○ *n* (*plural* **anomalies**) [C,U] *formal* something that is noticeable because it is different from what is usual: *In those days, a woman professor was still an anomaly.* | **[+in]** *various anomalies in the tax system*

a·non /əˈnɒn $ əˈnɑːn/ *adv literary* soon: *See you anon.*

anon. (*also* **anon** *BrE*) the written abbreviation of ***anonymous***

an·o·nym·i·ty /ˌænəˈnɪməti/ *n* [U] when other people do not know who you are or what your name is: *Every step will be taken to preserve your anonymity.* | *One official, who spoke on condition of anonymity* (=he would only speak if his name was not told), *said the White House took the threat very seriously.* | *the anonymity of city streets* (=you do not know anyone, and no one knows you)

a·non·y·mize (*also* **-ise** *BrE*) /əˈnɒnɪmaɪz $ əˈnɑː-/ *v* [T] to remove the name or names from something such as information, so that people cannot know exactly who it belongs or relates to: *All the data we gather will be anonymized to protect the participants' privacy.*

a·non·y·mous /əˈnɒnɪməs $ əˈnɑː-/ ●○○ *adj*
1 unknown by name: *the anonymous author of a collection of poems* | **anonymous donor/benefactor** *the anonymous donor of a large sum of money* | *According to one employee, who wishes to **remain anonymous**, the company engaged in illegal activities.*
2 done, sent, or given by someone who does not want their name to be known: *an anonymous donation of $5,000* | **anonymous phone call/letter etc** (=one that is often unpleasant or contains threats)
3 *written* uninteresting in features or qualities – used to show disapproval: *grey, anonymous housing estates* —**anonymously** *adv*

an·o·rak /ˈænəræk/ *n* [C] **1** *especially BrE* a short coat with a HOOD that keeps out the wind and rain **2** *BrE informal* a boring person who is interested in the unimportant details of a particular subject and does not know how to behave properly in social situations SYN **nerd**

an·o·rex·i·a /ˌænəˈreksiə/ (*also* **anorexia ner·vo·sa** /-nɜːˈvəʊsə $ -nɜːrˈvoʊ-/) *n* [U] a mental illness that makes someone stop eating

an·o·rex·ic /ˌænəˈreksɪk◂/ *adj* suffering from or relating to anorexia **THESAURUS** ▸ THIN —**anorexic** *n* [C]

an·oth·er /əˈnʌðə $ -ər/ ●●● S1 W1 *determiner, pron*
1 ADDITIONAL one more person or thing of the same type: *I'm going to have another cup of coffee.* | *There'll be another bus along in a few minutes.* | *Buy two CDs and get another completely free.* | **[+of]** *Is this another of your schemes to make money?* | ***Not another** word was spoken.* | *Oh look, there's **another one** of those birds.* | *This misunderstanding is **yet another** example of bad communication* (=there have already been several). | **another 2/10/100 etc** (=an additional amount or number) *We'll have to wait another three weeks for the results.* | *There's still another £100 to pay.*
2 A DIFFERENT ONE not the same thing, person etc, but a different one: *They must have returned by another route.* | *We finally moved to another apartment.* | *I'm busy right now. Could you come back another time?* | *Helen resigned from her last job and has yet to find another.* | **[+of]** *The gold watch was a present from another of his girlfriends.* | **from one ... to another** *She spends the day rushing from one meeting to another.*
3 one another used to say that two or more people or things do the same thing to each other or share a relationship: *They seem to love one another very much.* | *The streets are all at right angles to one another.*
4 one ... or another used to say that there are many different types of something, or many possibilities, rather than being specific: *All the kids in this class have learning difficulties of one sort or another.* | *people who, for one reason or another, can't have children*
5 one after another used to talk about a series of similar things or events: *Small businesses have been collapsing one after another.*
6 not another ... ! *spoken* used when a series of bad or annoying things have happened and something of the same type seems to have just happened again: *Oh no! Not another accident!*
7 be another thing/matter used to suggest that something may not be true, possible, easy etc, after mentioning something that is: *It is true that his programme is original, though whether it is funny is quite another matter.* | *It is one thing to talk about 'involving the students'; it is quite another thing to actually do this.*
8 and another thing *spoken* used to introduce something additional that you want to say to someone about a different subject: *And another thing. You were late for work again this morning.*
9 SIMILAR PERSON/THING used with the name of a well-known person, thing, event etc to mean someone or something else that is similar because they have the same good or bad qualities: *warnings that not enough has been done to prevent another Chernobyl* | *There'll never be another Elvis Presley.*

> **GRAMMAR: Spelling**
> **Another** is written as one word: *There must be another way of doing it.* ✗ Don't write: *an other*

an·swer[1] /ˈɑːnsə $ ˈænsər/ ●●● S1 W1 *n*
1 REPLY [C,U] something you say when you reply to a question that someone has asked you SYN **response**: *You don't have to **give** them **an answer** now.* | *Every time I ask him about it, I **get a** different **answer**.* | **[+to]** *These are important*

A

questions, and we want answers to them. | *She's still* ***waiting for an answer*** *from the school.* | *The* ***honest answer*** *was that I didn't know.* | *He was never able to get a* ***straight answer*** *about why it happened.* | *It's impossible for me to give you a* ***definite answer*** *at this time.* | ***The short answer*** *is that it can't be done.* | ***In answer to your question****, yes, you can go.* | *If it's money you want,* ***the answer is no****!*

2 TEST/COMPETITION ETC [C] something that you write or say in reply to a question in a test or competition: **[+to]** *What was the answer to question 4?* | **the right/wrong/correct/incorrect answer** *Score two points for each correct answer.*

3 INVITATION/LETTER ETC [C] a written reply to a letter, invitation, advertisement etc: **[+to]** *Did you ever get an answer to your letter?*

4 PROBLEM [C] a way of dealing with a problem SYN **solution**: **simple/easy/obvious answer** *There is no simple answer.* | **[+to]** *The police do not have an answer to rising crime.* | *Some people think cars should be banned from the city, but I don't think that's the answer.* | **be the answer to sb's problems/worries etc** *If he could get a job, it'd be the answer to all his worries.*

5 ON THE PHONE [singular, U usually in negative] if you get an answer when you call someone on the phone, they pick up the phone and talk to you: *I tried calling him all day but couldn't get an answer.*

6 AT THE DOOR [singular, U usually in negative] if you get an answer when you knock on a door, someone opens it and talks to you: *I tried knocking on her door, but there was* ***no answer****.*

7 have/know all the answers *informal* to be very sure that you know everything about a situation, especially when you do not: *He acts like he has all the answers.*

8 sb's answer to sth *written* someone or something that is considered to be just as good as a more famous person or thing: *The Space Needle is Seattle's answer to the Eiffel Tower.*

answer[2] ●●● S1 W2 *v*

1 REPLY [I,T] to say something to someone as a reply when they have asked you a question, made a suggestion etc: *She thought for a moment before answering.* | *He still hadn't* ***answered*** *my* ***question****.* | *'Why don't you just leave?' 'I'd like to,' she answered, 'but I have nowhere else to go.'* | **answer (that)** *When questioned, Hughes answered that he knew nothing about the robbery.* | *How much was it? Come on, answer me.*

2 TEST [I,T] to write or say the answer to a question in a test or competition: *Answer as many questions as possible in the time provided.*

3 answer the phone/a call/the door to pick up the telephone and speak when it rings or open the door when someone knocks or rings the bell

4 LETTER [T] if you answer a letter or advertisement, you write a letter to the person who has written it: *Simon got the job by answering an advert in the paper.*

5 answer criticism/charges/accusations etc to explain why you did something when people are criticizing you – used in news reports: *How do you answer the criticism that your government has done nothing to help the homeless?*

6 REACT TO STH [I,T] to do something as a reaction to criticism or an attack SYN **respond**: *The army answered by firing into the crowd.*

7 DEAL WITH A PROBLEM [T] to be a way of dealing with or solving a problem: *'You can borrow my car if you like.' 'Well, that answers one problem.'*

8 answer a need to provide something that is needed: *Our transportation system is designed to answer the needs of the city's commuters.*

9 answer a description if someone answers a description, they match that description: *A man answering the police's description was seen entering the building.*

THESAURUS

answer to say something to someone when they have asked you a question or spoken to you: *You don't have to answer the question if you don't want to.* | *I said hello to her, but she didn't answer.*

reply to answer someone – used especially in written English to report what someone said: *'I'm so sorry,' he replied.* | *We asked Jane to help, but she replied that she was too busy.*

respond *formal* to answer someone: *How do you respond to the allegation that you deliberately deceived your employers?*

give sb an answer to answer someone by telling them what you have decided or giving them a piece of information they asked for: *He asked me to marry him, but I didn't give him an answer straight away.*

get back to sb to answer someone at a later time especially by telephoning them, usually because you need to think about their question or find out more information: *She's promised to get back to me as soon as she hears any more news from the hospital.*

retort *written* to answer someone angrily, especially because they have annoyed you or criticized you: *'You're not afraid?' Brenda asked. 'Of course not,' he retorted angrily.*

GRAMMAR: Comparison

answer

- You **answer** someone: *Why won't you answer me?*

✗ Don't say *answer to someone* in this meaning.

- You **answer** someone's question: *You still have not answered my question.*
- You can use **answer** with speech marks ('...') when quoting someone's exact words: *'I'm fine, thank you,' she answered.*
- You can use **answer that** to report what someone says. After **answered**, the verb in the other clause is usually also in the past tense: *She answered that she* ***was*** *fine.*

reply

- You **reply to** someone's question: *You still have not replied to my question.*
- You can use **reply** with speech marks ('...') when quoting someone's exact words: *'I'm fine, thank you,' she replied.*
- You can use **reply that** to report what someone says. After **replied**, the verb in the other clause is usually also in the past tense: *She replied that she* ***was*** *fine.*

GRAMMAR GUIDE ▸ VERBS

answer back *phr v* to reply in a rude way to someone that you are supposed to obey: **answer sb back** *Don't answer me back young man!*

answer for sb/sth *phr v*

1 to explain to people in authority why you did something wrong or why something happened, and be punished if necessary: *Their coach must answer for the team's poor performance.*

2 have a lot to answer for *informal* to be responsible for causing a lot of trouble

3 can't answer for sb *spoken* used to say that you cannot make a decision for someone who is not there, or give their opinion: *I'm sure John will help us – I can't really answer for the others.*

answer to sb/sth *phr v*

1 to give an explanation to someone, especially about something that you have done wrong: *Phipps answers to me and me alone.*

2 answer to the name of sth to be called a particular name – used humorously: *a well-dressed young woman answering to the name of Suzanne*

an·swer·a·ble /ˈɑːnsərəbəl $ ˈæn-/ *adj* **1 be answerable to sb (for sth)** to have to explain your actions to someone in authority: *The agency is answerable to the governor.* **2** a question that is answerable can be answered

ˈanswering maˌchine (*also* **an·swer·phone** *BrE* /ˈɑːnsəfəʊn $ ˈænsərfoʊn/) *n* [C] a machine that records your telephone calls when you cannot answer them

ant /ænt/ ●●○ *n* [C]

1 a small insect that lives in large groups

2 have ants in your pants *spoken* to be so excited or full of energy that you are unable to sit or stand still – used humorously

-ant /ənt/, **-ent** *suffix* [in nouns and adjectives] someone or something that does something: *a servant* (=someone who serves others) | *disinfectant* (=substance for killing germs) | *expectant* (=expecting) | *pleasant* (=pleasing)

ant·a·cid /ænt'æsɪd/ *n* [C] a substance that gets rid of the burning feeling in your stomach when you have eaten too much, drunk too much alcohol etc

an·tag·o·nis·m /æn'tægənɪzəm/ *n* [U] **1** hatred between people or groups of people SYN **hostility**: **[+between]** *the antagonism between the army and other military groups* **2** opposition to an idea, plan etc: **[+to/towards]** *his antagonism towards the press*

an·tag·o·nist /æn'tægənɪst/ *n* [C] your opponent in a competition, battle, quarrel etc → PROTAGONIST

an·tag·o·nis·tic /æn,tægə'nɪstɪk◂/ *adj* **1** unfriendly; wanting to argue or disagree SYN **hostile**: *an antagonistic attitude* THESAURUS UNFRIENDLY **2** opposed to an idea or group: **[+to/towards]** *antagonistic to new ideas* —**antagonistically** /-kli/ *adv*

an·tag·o·nize (*also* **-ise** *BrE*) /æn'tægənaɪz/ *v* [T] to annoy someone very much by doing something that they do not like: *Do not antagonize your customers.*

An·tarc·tic /æn'tɑ:ktɪk $ -ɑ:r-/ *n* **the Antarctic** the very cold most southern part of the world → see picture at EARTH[1]

An,tarctic 'Circle *n* **the Antarctic Circle** an imaginary line drawn around the world at a certain distance from the most southern point (the South Pole) → see picture at EARTH[1]

an·te[1] /'ænti/ *n* **up/raise the ante** to increase your demands or try to get more things from a situation, even though this involves more risks: *They've upped the ante by making a $120 million bid to buy the company.* → PENNY ANTE

ante[2] *v* (*past tense and past participle* **anted** *or* **anteed**, *present participle* **anteing**)

ante up (sth) *phr v* to pay an amount of money in order to be able to do or be involved in something: *Small firms that want to expand must ante up large legal fees.*

ante- /æntɪ/ *prefix* before → **anti-**, **post-**, **pre-**: *antedate* (=earlier than something) | *antenatal* (=before birth)

ant·eat·er /'ænt,i:tə $ -ər/ *n* [C] an animal that has a very long nose and eats small insects

an·te·bel·lum /,ænti'beləm/ *adj* [only before noun] existing before a war, especially the American Civil War: *an antebellum plantation*

an·te·ced·ent /,æntə'si:dənt/ *n* [C] **1** *formal* an event, organization, or thing that is similar to the one you have mentioned but existed earlier: *historical antecedents* **2 antecedents** [plural] *formal* the people in your family who lived a long time ago SYN **ancestors** **3** *technical* a word, phrase, or sentence that is represented by another word, for example a PRONOUN —**antecedent** *adj*

an·te·cham·ber /'æntɪ,tʃeɪmbə $ -ər/ *n* [C] ANTEROOM

an·te·date /'æntɪdeɪt, ,æntɪ'deɪt/ *v* [T] *formal* to come from an earlier time in history than something else SYN **predate** OPP **postdate**: *The economic troubles antedate the current administration.*

an·te·di·lu·vi·an /,æntɪdə'lu:viən◂/ *adj formal* very old-fashioned SYN **outdated**: *antediluvian ideas about women*

an·te·lope /'æntələʊp $ 'æntəl-oʊp/ *n* [C] an animal with long horns that can run very fast and is very graceful

an·te·na·tal /,æntɪ'neɪtl◂/ *adj* [only before noun] *BrE* relating to the medical care given to women who are going to have a baby SYN **prenatal** → **postnatal**: *an **antenatal clinic** | regular **antenatal care** | Many young mothers do not attend **antenatal classes**.*

an·ten·na /æn'tenə/ *n* [C] **1** (*plural* **antennae** /-ni:/) one of two long thin parts on an insect's head, that it uses to feel things → see picture at INSECT **2** (*plural* **antennas** *or* **antennae**) a wire ROD etc used for receiving radio and television signals SYN **aerial**: *television antennas* → see picture at CAR

an·ter·i·or /æn'tɪəriə $ -'tɪriər/ *adj* [no comparative] **1** *technical* at or towards the front → **posterior**: *anterior vertebrae* **2** *formal* happening or existing before something else

an·te·room /'æntɪrʊm, -ru:m/ *n* [C] a small room that is connected to a larger room, especially where people wait to go into the larger room SYN **antechamber**

an·them /'ænθəm/ ●○○ *n* [C]
1 a formal or religious song → NATIONAL ANTHEM
2 a song that a particular group of people consider to be very important: *The Rolling Stones' 'Satisfaction' was an anthem for a generation.*

an·the·mic /æn'θemɪk, -'θi:-/ *adj* having the qualities of an anthem: *anthemic rock music*

an·ther /'ænθə $ -ər/ *n* [C] *technical* the part of a male flower which contains POLLEN

ant·hill /'ænt,hɪl/ *n* [C] a place where ANTs live

an·thol·o·gy /æn'θɒlədʒi $ æn'θɑ:-/ ●○○ *n* (*plural* **anthologies**) [C] a set of stories, poems, songs etc by different people collected together in one book SYN **collection**: *an anthology of American literature* —**anthologist** *n* [C]

an·thra·cite /'ænθrəsaɪt/ *n* [U] a very hard type of coal that burns slowly and produces a lot of heat

an·thrax /'ænθræks/ *n* [U] a serious disease affecting cattle and sheep, which can affect humans

anthropo- /ænθrəpə, -pəʊ $ -pə, -poʊ/ *prefix* like or concerning HUMAN BEINGS: *anthropomorphic* (=having human form or qualities)

an·thro·poid /'ænθrəpɔɪd/ *adj* an anthropoid animal, such as an APE, looks like a human —**anthropoid** *n* [C]

an·thro·pol·o·gy /,ænθrə'pɒlədʒi $ -'pɑ:-/ *n* [U] the scientific study of people, their societies, CULTUREs etc → **ethnology**, **sociology** —**anthropologist** *n* [C] —**anthropological** /,ænθrəpə'lɒdʒɪkəl◂ $ -'lɑ:-/ *adj*

an·thro·po·mor·phis·m /,ænθrəpə'mɔ:fɪzəm $ -ɔ:r-/ *n* [U] **1** the belief that animals or objects have the same feelings and qualities as humans **2** *technical* the belief that God can appear in a human or animal form —**anthropomorphic** *adj*

anti- /æntɪ $ æntɪ, æntaɪ/ *prefix* **1** opposed to OPP **pro-**: *antinuclear* (=opposing the use of NUCLEAR weapons and power) | *anti-American* **2** the opposite of something: *anticlimax* (=an unexciting ending instead of the expected exciting ending) | *antimatter* (=material completely opposite in kind to the ordinary material in the universe) **3** acting to prevent something: *antifreeze* (=a liquid added to a car's engine to prevent freezing) | *antiseptic* (=a liquid that kills harmful bacteria)

,anti-'aircraft *adj* [only before noun] anti-aircraft weapons are used against enemy aircraft: *anti-aircraft missiles*

an·ti·bi·ot·ic /,æntɪbaɪ'ɒtɪk◂ $ -'ɑ:-/ ●○○ *n* [C usually plural] a drug that is used to kill BACTERIA and cure infections

an·ti·bod·y /'æntɪ,bɒdi $ -,bɑ:-/ *n* (*plural* **antibodies**) [C] a substance produced by your body to fight disease

,anti-'choice *adj* against women having the right to have an ABORTION OPP **pro-choice**

an·tic·i·pate /æn'tɪsəpeɪt/ ●●○ S3 W3 AWL *v* [T]
1 to expect that something will happen and be ready for it: *Sales are better than anticipated.* | **anticipate changes/developments** *The schedule isn't final, but we don't anticipate many changes.* | **anticipate problems/difficulties** *We don't anticipate any problems.* | *A good speaker is able to anticipate an audience's needs and concerns.* | **anticipate (that)** *This year, we anticipate that our expenses will be 15% greater.* | ***It is anticipated that** the research will have many different practical applications.* | **anticipate doing sth** *I didn't anticipate having to do the cooking myself!*

A

2 to think about something that is going to happen, especially something pleasant SYN **look forward to**: *Daniel was eagerly anticipating her arrival.*
3 to do something before someone else: *Copernicus anticipated in part the discoveries of the 17th and 18th centuries.*
—**anticipatory** /æn,tɪsəˈpeɪtəri $ ænˈtɪsəpətɔːri/ *adj formal*: *the anticipatory atmosphere of a big college football game*

GRAMMAR: Comparison

anticipate
- You **anticipate** something: *We don't anticipate any problems.*
- You **anticipate that** something will happen: *No one could have anticipated that this would happen.*

expect
- You **expect** something: *We don't expect any problems.*
- You **expect that** something will happen, or someone will do something: *Everyone expected that the team would win.*
- You **expect** something **to** happen, or **expect** someone **to do** something: *Everyone expected them to win.*

predict
- You **predict** something: *No one could have predicted the result.*
- You **predict that** something will happen, or someone will do something: *He predicted that the team would win.*

an·tic·i·pa·tion /æn,tɪsəˈpeɪʃən/ ●○○ AWL *n* [U]
1 when you are expecting something to happen: *She waited in eager anticipation for Robert to arrive.* | *Taylor was excited and full of anticipation at the prospect of the trip.*
2 **do sth in anticipation of sth** to do something because you expect something to happen: *The workers have called off their strike in anticipation of a pay offer.*

an·ti·cler·i·cal /,æntiˈklerɪkəl◂/ *adj* being opposed to priests having any political power or influence —**anticlericalism** *n* [U]

an·ti·cli·max /,æntɪˈklaɪmæks/ *n* [C,U] a situation or event that does not seem exciting because it happens after something that was much better: *Going back to work after a month travelling in China was bound to be an anticlimax.*

an·ti·clock·wise /,æntɪˈklɒkwaɪz◂ $ -ˈklɑːk-/ *adv, adj BrE* moving in the opposite direction to the hands of a clock SYN **counterclockwise** *AmE* OPP **clockwise**: *Turn the lid anticlockwise.*

an·tics /ˈæntɪks/ *n* [plural] behaviour that seems strange, funny, silly, or annoying: *We're all growing tired of his childish antics.* THESAURUS ▸ BEHAVIOUR

an·ti·cy·clone /,æntɪˈsaɪkləʊn $ -kloʊn/ *n* [C] an area of high air pressure that causes calm weather in the place it is moving over → **cyclone**

an·ti·de·pres·sant /,æntidɪˈpresənt/ *n* [C,U] a drug used to treat DEPRESSION (=a mental illness that makes people very unhappy)

an·ti·dote /ˈæntɪdəʊt $ -doʊt/ ●○○ *n* [C]
1 a substance that stops the effects of a poison: **[+to]** *There is no known antidote to a bite from this snake.*
2 something that makes an unpleasant situation better: *laughter, the antidote to stress*

an·ti·freeze /ˈæntɪfriːz/ *n* [U] a liquid that is put in the water in car engines to stop it from freezing

,anti-ˈfungal *adj* anti-fungal medicines are used to cure FUNGAL infections such as ATHLETE'S FOOT, RINGWORM, and THRUSH

an·ti·gen /ˈæntɪdʒən/ *n* [C] *technical* a substance that makes the body produce ANTIBODIES

,anti-globaliˈzation (*also* **-isation** *BrE*) *n* [U] a belief shared by various political groups that people must oppose GLOBALIZATION (=the process of making something such as a business operate in different countries around the world) because of bad effects it has on people, especially in developing countries, and because of the damage it does to the environment: *anti-globalization protests*

an·ti·her·o /ˈæntɪ,hɪərəʊ $ -,hɪroʊ/ *n* (*plural* **antiheroes**) [C] a main character in a book, play, or film who is an ordinary or unpleasant person and lacks the qualities that you expect a hero to have

an·ti·his·ta·mine /,æntɪˈhɪstəmiːn, -mɪn/ *n* [C,U] a drug that is used to treat an ALLERGY (=an unpleasant reaction to particular foods, substances etc)

,anti-inˈflammatory *adj* [only before noun] *medical* anti-inflammatory drugs reduce INFLAMMATION (=painful swelling) in part of your body: *anti-inflammatory painkillers for treating arthritis* —**anti-inflammatory** *n* [C]

,anti-lock ˈbraking ,system *n* [U] (*abbreviation* **ABS**) a piece of equipment that makes a vehicle easier to control when you have to stop very suddenly

an·ti·mat·ter /ˈænti,mætə $ -ər/ *n* [U] a form of MATTER(30) (=substance which the things in the universe are made of) consisting of antiparticles

an·tim·o·ny /ænˈtɪməni $ ˈæntəmoʊni/ *n* [U] a silver-white metal that breaks easily and is often combined with other metals. It is a chemical ELEMENT: symbol Sb

an·ti·ox·i·dant /,æntiˈɒksɪdənt $ -ˈɑːk-/ *n* [C] a substance in some foods that cleans the body and protects it from CANCER

an·ti·par·ti·cle /ˈænti,pɑːtɪkəl $ -,pɑːr-/ *n* [C] a very small part of an atom that has the opposite electrical charge to the one usually found in atoms

an·ti·pas·to /ˈæntipæstəʊ $,æntiˈpɑːstoʊ/ *n* (*plural* **antipasti** /-ti/) [U] an Italian dish consisting of cold meat or vegetables that you eat before the main part of a meal

an·ti·pa·thet·ic /,æntɪpəˈθetɪk◂/ *adj formal* having a very strong feeling of disliking or opposing someone or something SYN **hostile**: **[+to]** *It's human nature to be antipathetic to change.*

an·tip·a·thy /ænˈtɪpəθi/ *n* [U] *formal* a feeling of strong dislike towards someone or something SYN **hostility**: **[+to/towards]** *a growing antipathy towards the government* | **[+between]** *There's always been a certain amount of antipathy between the two doctors.*

,anti-personˈnel *adj* [only before noun] an anti-personnel weapon is designed to hurt people rather than to damage buildings, vehicles etc

,anti-ˈperspirant *n* [U] a substance that prevents you SWEATing → **deodorant**

an·ti·quar·i·an /,æntəˈkweəriən◂ $ -ˈkwer-/ *adj* [only before noun] an antiquarian bookshop sells old books

an·ti·quat·ed /ˈæntɪkweɪtɪd/ *adj* old-fashioned and not suitable for modern needs or conditions – used to show disapproval SYN **outdated**: *antiquated laws* THESAURUS ▸ OLD-FASHIONED

an·tique[1] /,ænˈtiːk◂/ ●○○ *adj* [usually before noun] antique furniture, jewellery etc is old and often valuable: *an antique rosewood desk* THESAURUS ▸ OLD

antique[2] ●○○ *n* [C] a piece of furniture, jewellery etc that was made a very long time ago and is therefore valuable: *The palace is full of priceless antiques.* | *They bought the clock at an **antique shop** in Bath.* | *an **antique dealer*** (=someone who buys and sells antiques)

an·tiq·ui·ty /ænˈtɪkwəti/ *n* (*plural* **antiquities**)
1 [U] ancient times: **in antiquity** *The common household fork was nearly unknown in antiquity.* 2 [U] the state of being very old: *a building of great antiquity* 3 [C usually plural] a building or object made in ancient times: *a collection of Roman antiquities*

an·ti·ret·ro·vi·ral drug /,æntiretrəʊˈvaɪərəl ,drʌg $ -troʊˈvaɪrəl-/ *n* [C] a type of drug that is used against HIV infection

anti-Se·mite /,ænti ˈsiːmaɪt $ -ˈsem-/ *n* [C] someone who hates Jewish people —**anti-Semitic** /,æntisəˈmɪtɪk◂/ *adj*: *He made a few anti-Semitic remarks.*

anti-Sem·i·tis·m /,æntɪ ˈsemətɪzəm/ *n* [U] hatred of Jewish people: *the struggle against fascism and anti-Semitism* THESAURUS ▸ PREJUDICE

an·ti·sep·tic¹ /ˌæntəˈseptɪk◂/ *n* [C,U] a medicine that you put onto a wound to stop it from becoming infected: *He dabbed the cut with antiseptic.* | *Mint is a mild antiseptic.*

antiseptic² *adj* helping to prevent infection: *an antiseptic cream* | *Some herbs have antiseptic qualities.* → see picture at FIRST AID KIT

an·ti·so·cial /ˌæntɪˈsəʊʃəl $ -ˈsoʊ-/ *adj* **1** antisocial behaviour is violent or harmful to other people, or shows that you do not care about other people: *She was finding it hard to cope with her son's increasingly* ***antisocial behaviour***. | *Smoking is an antisocial habit.* THESAURUS UNFRIENDLY **2** someone who is antisocial does not enjoy meeting or being with other people OPP **sociable**: *If I don't go tonight, everyone will accuse me of being antisocial.* THESAURUS SHY **3** an activity or job that is antisocial does not give you the chance to meet other people SYN **unsocial**: *I got fed up with the low pay and* ***antisocial hours***.

ˌanti-ˈtank *adj* an anti-tank weapon is designed to destroy enemy TANKS

an·tith·e·sis /ænˈtɪθɪsɪs/ *n* (*plural* **antitheses** /-siːz/) [C] *formal* the complete opposite of something: **[+of]** *This is not democratic. It is the antithesis of democracy.*

an·ti·thet·i·cal /ˌæntɪˈθetɪkəl/ (*also* **an·ti·thet·ic** /-ˈθetɪk◂/) *adj formal* exactly opposite to something: **[+to]** *This violence is completely antithetical to the teaching of the church.*

an·ti·tox·in /ˌæntiˈtɒksɪn $ -ˈtɑːk-/ *n* [C] a medicine or substance produced by your body which stops the effects of a poison

an·ti·trust /ˌæntiˈtrʌst/ *adj* [only before noun] intended to prevent companies from unfairly controlling prices: *new tougher* ***antitrust laws*** | *an antitrust investigation*

ˌanti-ˈvirus ˌsoftware (*also* **ˌanti-ˈvirus ˌprogram**) *n* [U] a type of SOFTWARE that looks for and removes VIRUSES in programs and documents on your computer: *You need to update your anti-virus software regularly.*

ant·ler /ˈæntlə $ -ər/ *n* [C] one of the two horns of a male DEER

an·to·nym /ˈæntənɪm/ ●○○ *n* [C] a word that means the opposite of another word → **synonym**: *a dictionary of synonyms and antonyms*

ant·sy /ˈæntsi/ *adj informal* nervous and unable to keep still because you are waiting for something to happen

a·nus /ˈeɪnəs/ *n* [C] the hole in your bottom through which solid waste leaves your body → **anal**

an·vil /ˈænvəl/ *n* [C] a heavy iron block on which pieces of hot metal are shaped using a hammer

anx·i·e·ty /æŋˈzaɪəti/ ●●○ S3 W3 *n* (*plural* **anxieties**)
1 [C,U] the feeling of being very worried about something SYN **concern**: **[+about/over]** *There is* ***considerable anxiety*** *among staff about job losses.* | *There is growing public anxiety over levels of air pollution in our cities.* | **deep/acute/great anxiety** *The fear of unemployment can be a source of deep anxiety to people.* | *his feelings of anxiety* | *A high level of anxiety was created by the introduction of cameras into the factory.* | *It can help if you discuss your anxieties with someone.*
2 [U] a feeling of wanting to do something very much: **anxiety to do sth** *I nearly fell in my anxiety to get downstairs quickly.*

anx·ious /ˈæŋkʃəs/ ●●○ S3 W3 *adj*
1 worried about something: **[+about]** *He was a bit anxious about the safety of the machinery.* | **[+for]** *We were anxious for you.* | **anxious (that)** *She was anxious that it might be cancer.* | **an anxious look/expression** *She gave me an anxious look.* THESAURUS WORRIED

GRAMMAR: Prepositions with anxious

- You are **anxious about** something: *She is anxious about the interview.* ✗ Don't say: *She is anxious for the interview.*
- You are **anxious for** another person (=worried that something bad might have happened to them): *They are anxious for their son.*

2 an anxious time or situation is one in which you feel nervous or worried SYN **worrying**: *We had an anxious couple of weeks waiting for the test results.* | *There was an anxious moment when the plane suddenly dropped.*
3 feeling strongly that you want to do something or want something to happen SYN **keen**: **anxious to do sth** *The company is anxious to improve its image.* | *He seemed* ***most anxious*** *to speak to me alone.* | *The president is anxious not to have another crisis.* | **anxious for sb to do sth** *Why was she so anxious for me to stay?* | **[+for]** *We were all anxious for news.* | **anxious (that)** *Both sides were anxious that the agreement should be signed as quickly as possible.*
—**anxiously** *adv*: *She waited anxiously by the phone.*

an·y¹ /ˈeni/ ●●● S1 W1 *determiner, pron*
1 [usually in questions and negatives] some or even the smallest amount or number: *Have you got any money?* | *Do you need any further information?* | **[+of]** *Are any of the paintings for sale?* | *They didn't invite any of us.* | *Are there* ***any other*** *questions?* | *They haven't shown* ***any*** *interest* ***at all*** *in my research.* | *The universities have shown* ***few if any*** *signs of a willingness to change.*
2 used to refer to a person or thing of a particular type when what you are saying is true of all people or things of that type: *Any child who breaks the rules will be punished.* | *Always check the details carefully before you sign any written agreement.* | *I can see you any time on Monday.* | *If I can help in any way, let me know.* | **[+of]** *You can choose any of the books on the list.* | *This excuse was as good as* ***any other***.
3 as much as possible: *They're going to need any help they can get.*
4 not just any (old) man/woman/job etc used to say that someone or something is special: *She's not just any actress, she's one of the best.* → **any old thing** at OLD(10), → **any old how** at OLD(11), → **not in any way** at WAY¹(40)

any² ●●● S2 *adv* [usually in questions and negatives]
1 used before the comparative form of an adjective to mean 'even a small amount': *I can't run any faster.* | *Are you feeling any better?*
2 not anymore/any longer if something does not happen anymore or any longer, it used to happen but does not happen now: *It used to be quite cheap to fly there, but not anymore.* | *He was told he wasn't wanted any longer.*
3 *AmE spoken* used with a verb to mean 'at all': *We tried talking to him but that didn't help any.*

an·y·bod·y /ˈeniˌbɒdi, ˈenibədi $ -ˌbɑːdi/ ●●● S1 W3 *pron* ANYONE

an·y·how /ˈenihaʊ/ ●●○ S3 *adv*
1 [sentence adverb] *informal* ANYWAY: *The scandal could damage her reputation but the press reported it anyhow.* | *I've never been to a circus, not recently anyhow.*
2 in a careless or untidy way: *The cupboard would hardly close, with all the shoes thrown in anyhow.*

an·y·more /ˌeniˈmɔː $ -ˈmɔːr/ ●●● S1 W3 *adv* **not anymore** used when something used to happen or be true in the past but does not happen or is not true now SYN **no longer**: *Nick doesn't live here anymore.* | *I don't really like her anymore.* | *You're describing a world that just doesn't exist anymore.*

an·y·one /ˈeniwʌn/ ●●● S1 W1 *pron*
1 used to refer to any person, when it is not important to say exactly who: *Anyone could win tonight.* | *They offer help and advice to anyone interested in becoming a teacher.* | *If anyone sees Lisa, ask her to call me.* | ***Anyone else*** *who is interested in going on the trip should see me at the end of this lesson.*
2 used in questions to mean 'someone': *Does anyone want a drink?* | *Is there anyone new coming to tonight's meeting?* | *Do you know* ***anyone else*** *who wants a ticket?*
3 used in negative sentences to mean no person: *I went to the bar but there wasn't anyone there.* | *I haven't spoken to anyone all day.*
4 anyone? used after mentioning something to show that you think it is not a good thing: *I think people are dressing way too casually. I mean, shorts in the office, anyone?*

A

USAGE: Anyone or any one?

- **Anyone** is written as one word in this meaning: *I didn't see anyone.* ✗ Don't write: *I didn't see any one.*
- **Any one of** is usually written as separate words. You usually write: *The same is true for any one of us.*
- You don't usually use **of** after **anyone**.

an·y·place /ˈenipleɪs/ *adv AmE* ANYWHERE: *I can't imagine living anyplace else now.*

an·y·thing /ˈeniθɪŋ/ ●●● S1 W1 *pron*
1 any thing, event, situation etc, when it is not important to say exactly which: *You can buy anything you want.* | *He was prepared to do anything to make a bit of money.* | *Anything would be better than staying at home!* | *You can write about swimming, skiing, or **anything else** you enjoy doing.*
2 used in questions to mean 'something': *Is there anything I can do to help?* | *Do you want anything from the shops?* | *Would you like **anything else** to eat?*
3 used in negative sentences to mean no thing, event etc: *We didn't have anything to eat for three days.* | *Don't do anything until we get there.*
4 anything but used to emphasize that someone or something does not have a particular quality: *Maria is anything but stupid!*
5 anything like sb/sth similar in any way to someone or something else: *You don't look anything like your mother.* | *If you're anything like me, you'll want to be where the action is.*
6 not anything like/near *spoken* used to emphasize a negative sentence: *We don't have anything like enough money to buy a new car.*
7 as important/clear/big etc as anything *informal* extremely important, clear etc: *He was as nice as anything to me.*
8 or anything *spoken* or something that is similar: *Would you like a drink or anything?*
9 anything goes *informal* used to say that anything someone says or does is acceptable: *From what other people were wearing, it looked like anything goes.*
10 for anything *informal* if you will not do something for anything, you will definitely not do it: *I wouldn't go back there for anything.*
11 like anything *informal* if you do something like anything, you do it a lot: *We all encouraged him like anything.*
12 if anything *spoken* used when you are adding something to emphasize what you have just said: *Sam didn't seem too disappointed at losing. If anything, he seemed relieved that it was all over.*
13 anything you say *spoken* used to tell someone you agree with what they suggest: *Yes, of course, anything you say.*

an·y·time /ˈenitaɪm/ ●●● S3 *adv* at any time: *Call me anytime. I'm always home.* | *They should arrive anytime between noon and 3 p.m.*

an·y·way /ˈeniweɪ/ ●●● S1 W2 (*also* **anyhow**) *adv* [sentence adverb]
1 in spite of the fact that you have just mentioned: *Catherine wasn't sure the book was the right one, but she bought it anyway.* | *This idea probably won't work, but let's try it anyway.*
2 used when adding a remark which shows that the fact just mentioned is not important: *They didn't have any trainers in my size, and anyway I'd already decided I'd rather save the money.* | *'I hope you haven't told anyone.' 'No. Who would believe me anyway?'*
3 used when adding something that corrects or slightly changes what you have just said: *Let's think about it for a while, for a few days anyway.* | *There seems to have been a technical problem – anyway, that's what they told me.*
4 *spoken* used when you are ignoring details so that you can talk immediately about the most important thing: *He got lost and spent hours looking for the station, and anyway it was past midnight by the time he got home.* | *Anyway, why didn't you call the police?*
5 *spoken* used when you are changing the subject of a conversation or returning to a previous subject: *Anyway, let's leave that for the moment and look at this month's profit figures.* | *Anyway, how are you?*
6 *spoken* used when you want to end a conversation or leave a place: *Anyway, I must be going now.*

an·y·ways /ˈeniweɪz/ *adv* [sentence adverb] ANYWAY. Many teachers think this is not correct English.

an·y·where /ˈeniweə $ -wer/ ●●● S1 W3 (*also* **anyplace** *AmE*) *adv*
1 in or to any place: *Sit anywhere you like.* | *You can buy clothes like these anywhere.* | *I don't want to live in London, but I'd be happy living **anywhere else**.*
2 used in questions to mean 'somewhere': *Do you need anywhere to stay for the night?* | *Did you go anywhere exotic on vacation this year?* | *Have you been **anywhere else** in Spain?*
3 used in negative sentences to mean no place: *I can't find my passport anywhere.*
4 not anywhere near a) not at all near: *I wasn't anywhere near him when he fell.* **b)** not at all: *I don't think these figures are anywhere near accurate.*
5 anywhere between one and ten/anywhere from one to ten etc used to mean any age, number, amount etc between the ones that you say: *She could have been anywhere between 45 and 60 years of age.* | *We can accommodate anywhere between 60 and 300 people.*
6 not get anywhere *informal* to not be successful at all: *You won't get anywhere without qualifications.*
7 not get sb anywhere *informal* if something does not get you anywhere, it does not change a situation or help you to achieve something: *You can try writing to complain, but I don't think it will get you anywhere.*
8 not be going anywhere *informal* to not be achieving success in your life: *He's a nice enough lad, but he's not going anywhere.*

An·zac /ˈænzæk/ *n* [C] a soldier from Australia or New Zealand, especially in World War I

AOB /ˌeɪ əʊ ˈbiː $ -oʊ-/ *BrE* (***any other business***) things which are not written on the list of subjects to discuss at a meeting, but which people want to talk about after all the other subjects have been discussed

A-OK /ˌeɪ əʊˈkeɪ $ -oʊ-/ *adj AmE spoken informal* in good condition SYN **satisfactory**: *We took the car in for a check, and it was A-OK.* —**A-OK** *adv*: *Everything's been going A-OK since Jack got home.*

a·or·ta /eɪˈɔːtə $ -ˈɔːr-/ *n* [C] the largest ARTERY that takes blood away from your heart

AP /ˌeɪ ˈpiː/ *n* [C] the abbreviation of ***access point***

a·pace /əˈpeɪs/ *adv* happening quickly: *Expansion of the company has **continued apace**.*

a·part /əˈpɑːt $ -ɑːrt/ ●●● S2 W1 *adv, adj*
1 NOT CLOSE/TOUCHING if things are apart, they are not close to each other or touching each other: **two miles/six feet etc apart** *Place the two posts 6 metres apart.* | *They have offices in countries as **far apart** as India and Peru.* | *The police try to **keep** rival supporters **apart** at all matches.* | *A couple of men started fighting and we had to **pull** them **apart**.* | *Joel stood apart from the group, frowning.*
2 IN DIFFERENT PIECES if something comes apart, or you take it apart, it is separated into different pieces: *The whole thing **comes apart** so that you can clean it.* | *They **took** the engine **apart** to see what was wrong.*
3 SEPARATE if you keep things apart, you keep them separate from each other: *I try to keep my work and private life as far apart as possible.*
4 NOT AT SAME TIME if things are a particular time apart, they do not happen at the same time but have that much time between them: **two days/three weeks/five years etc apart** *Our birthdays are exactly a month apart.*
5 PEOPLE if people are apart, they are not together in the same place, or not having a relationship with each other: *The children have never been apart before.* | *My wife and I are living apart at the moment.* | **[+from]** *He's never been apart from his mother.*
6 fall apart a) if something falls apart, it breaks into different pieces: *It just fell apart in my hands!* **b)** if something is falling apart, it is in very bad condition: *He drives around in an old car that's falling apart.* **c)** if something falls apart, it

fails completely: *He lost his job and his marriage fell apart.* | *The country's economy is in danger of falling apart.*
7 be torn apart if a marriage, family etc is torn apart, it can no longer continue because of serious difficulties: *The play portrays a good marriage torn apart by external forces.*
8 be worlds/poles apart if people, beliefs, or ideas are worlds or poles apart, they are completely different from each other: *I realized we were still worlds apart.*
9 grow/drift apart if people drift or grow apart, their relationship slowly becomes less close: *Lewis and his father drifted apart after he moved to New York.*
10 joking apart used to say that you want to say something seriously: *Joking apart, they did do quite a good job for us.*
11 sb/sth apart except for someone or something: *The car industry apart, most industries are now seeing an improvement in their economic performance.*
12 set sb/sth apart to make someone or something different from other people or things: *Her unusual lifestyle set her apart as a child.*

a'part from (*also* **a'side from** *AmE*) *prep* **1** except for: *We didn't see anyone all day, apart from a couple of kids on the beach.* | *Apart from the ending, it's a really good film.* **2** as well as: *Apart from his earnings as a football coach, he also owns and runs a chain of sports shops.* | ***Quite apart from** the cost, we need to think about how much time the job will take.*

a·part·heid /ə'pɑːtaɪt, -teɪt, -taɪd $ -ɑːr-/ *n* [U] the former political and social system in South Africa, in which only white people had full political rights and people of other races, especially black people, were forced to go to separate schools, live in separate areas etc

a·part·ment /ə'pɑːtmənt $ -ɑːr-/ ●●● S2 W3 *n* [C]
1 *especially AmE* a set of rooms on one floor of a large building, where someone lives SYN **flat** *BrE*: *She lives in a small apartment.*
2 [usually plural] a room or set of rooms used by an important person such as a president: *I had never been in the prince's private apartments before.* | *the presidential apartments*

COLLOCATIONS

ADJECTIVES/NOUN + apartment

a one-bedroom/two-bedroom etc apartment (*also* **one-bedroomed/two-bedroomed apartment** *BrE*) *A tiny one-bedroom apartment was all she could afford.*
a studio apartment (=with just one main room, which you use for sleeping, cooking, and eating) | **a first-floor/second-floor etc apartment** | **a basement apartment** (=below the level of the ground) | **a penthouse apartment** (=on the top floor of a building) | **a luxury apartment** | **a furnished/unfurnished apartment** (=with or without furniture) | **a holiday apartment** *BrE*, **a vacation apartment** *AmE*

VERBS

live in an apartment *He lived in a small apartment on the third floor.*
buy/rent an apartment *Tom rented an apartment at the top of the building.*
share an apartment | **own an apartment**

NOUN + apartment

an apartment building (*also* **an apartment block** *BrE*, **apartment house** *AmE*) *a five-storey apartment block*
an apartment complex (=a group of buildings containing apartments)

a'partment ˌblock *BrE*, **a'partment ˌhouse** *AmE*, **a'partment ˌbuilding** *n* [C] a large building containing many apartments → see picture at HOUSE[1]

ap·a·thet·ic /ˌæpə'θetɪk◂/ ●○○ *adj* not interested in something, and not willing to make any effort to change or improve things: *She felt too apathetic even to move.* | [+about] *How can you be so apathetic about the world and its problems?* —**apathetically** /-kli/ *adv*

ap·a·thy /'æpəθi/ ●○○ *n* [U] the feeling of not being interested in something, and not willing to make any effort to change or improve things: *The campaign failed because of public apathy.*

ape[1] /eɪp/ ●○○ *n* [C]
1 an animal that is similar to a monkey but has no tail or only a very short tail
2 go ape *informal* to suddenly become very angry

ape[2] *v* [T] **1** to copy the way someone speaks or behaves in order to make fun of them SYN **mimic**: *He could ape his teachers perfectly.* **2** to copy someone's way of doing something, so that what you do or produce is not good or original SYN **mimic**: *cheap clothes which ape the high fashions of the day*

a·per·i·tif /əˌperə'tiːf/ *n* [C] an alcoholic drink that people drink before a meal

ap·er·ture /'æpətʃə $ 'æpərtʃʊr/ *n* [C] **1** *formal* a small hole or space in something **2** the small hole at the front of a camera, which can be made larger or smaller to let more or less light in when you take a photograph

ape·shit /'eɪpʃɪt/ *adj* **go apeshit** *informal* to suddenly become very angry

a·pex /'eɪpeks/ *n* [C] **1** *technical* the top or highest part of something pointed or curved: *the apex of the roof* | *the apex of a pyramid* **2** *formal* the most important position in an organization or society: *The king was at the apex of society.* **3** *formal* the most successful part of something SYN **peak**: *He was at the apex of his career.*

a·pha·si·a /ə'feɪziə, eɪ- $ ə'feɪʒə/ *n* [U] *medical* a medical condition in which it is difficult to speak, write, or understand words, caused by a brain disease or injury

a·phid /'eɪfɪd, 'æfɪd/ *n* [C] a type of small insect that feeds on the juices of plants

aph·o·ris·m /'æfərɪzəm/ *n* [C] *formal* a short phrase that contains a wise idea SYN **saying** —**aphoristic** /ˌæfə'rɪstɪk◂/ *adj*

aph·ro·dis·i·ac /ˌæfrə'dɪziæk◂/ *n* [C] a food, drink, or drug that makes you want to have sex —**aphrodisiac** *adj*: *a fruit that is believed to have aphrodisiac properties*

a·piece /ə'piːs/ *adv* [only after number or noun] costing or having a particular amount each SYN **each**: *The pictures are worth about £10,000 apiece.* | *The two top teams have ten points apiece.*

a·plen·ty /ə'plenti/ *adj* [only after noun] *literary* in large amounts, especially more than you need: *There was food aplenty.*

a·plomb /ə'plɒm $ ə'plɑːm/ *n* [U] *formal* **with aplomb** in a confident and skilful way, especially when you have to deal with difficult problems or a difficult situation: *Ms Sharpe handled their questions with great aplomb.*

a·poc·a·lypse /ə'pɒkəlɪps $ ə'pɑː-/ *n* [C]
1 the apocalypse the destruction and end of the world: *anti-nuclear protesters who fear the apocalypse* **2** a situation in which a lot of people die or suffer, and a lot of damage is done: *A lot of investors now fear a stock market apocalypse.*

a·poc·a·lyp·tic /əˌpɒkə'lɪptɪk◂ $ əˌpɑː-/ *adj* **1** warning people about terrible events that will happen in the future: *The novel presents us with an apocalyptic vision of the future.* **2** connected with the final destruction and end of the world, or with any great destruction: *Before them was an apocalyptic landscape of burnt villages and bomb craters.*

a·poc·ry·phal /ə'pɒkrəfəl $ ə'pɑː-/ *adj* an apocryphal story is well-known but probably not true

ap·o·gee /'æpədʒiː/ *n* [C] *formal* the most successful part of something SYN **apex**: *His political career reached its apogee in the 1960s.*

a·po·lit·i·cal /ˌeɪpə'lɪtɪkəl◂/ *adj* not interested in politics, or not connected with any political party: *a group of apolitical young professional people* | *an apolitical organization*

A

a·pol·o·get·ic /əˌpɒləˈdʒetɪk◂ $ əˌpɑː-/ ●○○ *adj* showing or saying that you are sorry that something has happened, especially because you feel guilty or embarrassed about it: **[+about]** *The manager was very apologetic about everything.* | *She gave me an* ***apologetic smile.*** | **look/sound apologetic** *Dan came in looking very apologetic.* —**apologetically** /-kli/ *adv*: *'I know,' she said apologetically.*

ap·o·lo·gi·a /ˌæpəˈləʊdʒiə, -dʒə $ -ˈloʊ-/ *n* [C] *formal* a statement in which you defend an idea or organization that you believe in: **[+for]** *an apologia for the Christian church*

a·pol·o·gist /əˈpɒlədʒɪst $ əˈpɑː-/ *n* [C] someone who tries to explain and defend an idea, person, or political system: **[+for]** *an apologist for socialism*

a·pol·o·gize (*also* **-ise** *BrE*) /əˈpɒlədʒaɪz $ əˈpɑː-/ ●●● S2 *v* [I] to tell someone that you are sorry that you have done something wrong → **apologetic**: *I'm so sorry, I do apologize.* | **[+to]** *I think you should apologize to your brother.* | **apologize for (doing) sth** *He later apologized for his behaviour.* | *I apologize for losing my temper.*

REGISTER
In everyday English, people often use the phrases **say (you are) sorry** or **tell** someone **you are sorry**, rather than **apologize (to sb)**: *I've already apologized to him.* → *I've already* ***told him I'm sorry.***

GRAMMAR: Patterns with apologize
- You **apologize for** something: *We would like to apologize for the delay.*
- You **apologize for doing** something: *He apologized for being late.*
- You **apologize to** someone: *We apologize to passengers for the delay.* ✗ Don't say: *We apologize passengers for the delay.*

a·pol·o·gy /əˈpɒlədʒi $ əˈpɑː-/ ●●● S3 *n* (*plural* **apologies**)
1 [C,U] something that you say or write to show that you are sorry for doing something wrong: **[+for]** *The minister had to issue a formal public apology for his remarks.* | **[+from]** *She finally received an apology from the company.* | **[+to]** *an apology to passengers for any inconvenience caused*
2 apologies [plural] a message that you send to a meeting to say that you will not be able to come to the meeting: *Edward can't be here today, but he* ***sends*** *his* ***apologies.***
3 make your apologies to say that you are sorry but you have to leave: *I quickly made my apologies and left.*
4 make no apology for sth to not say that you are sorry for something, because you do not regret it and you think it is the right thing to do: *We make no apology for defending our members' interests – that is our job.*
5 [C] *literary* a statement in which you defend something you believe in after it has been criticized by other people: **[+for]** *an apology for Christianity*
6 an apology for sth a very bad example of something: *They served us up an apology for a meal.*

COLLOCATIONS

VERBS
make an apology *I hope you are going to make an apology.*
issue an apology (=make an official public apology) *North Korea issued an official apology for the incident.*
get/receive an apology *He received a formal apology from the company.*
offer an apology *We would like to offer our sincere apologies for the delay.*
accept sb's apology *Please accept my apologies for having to cancel our meeting.*
demand an apology | **owe sb an apology** | **publish an apology** (=print it in a newspaper) | **mumble/mutter an apology** (=say it quietly, especially because you are embarrassed)

ADJECTIVES
my sincere/profound apologies (=used when you feel very sorry) *Firstly, my sincere apologies for not having contacted you earlier.*
a public apology *The authorities published a public apology in the newspaper.*
a formal apology *Russia is demanding a formal apology.*
an official apology | **a written apology** | **a full apology** | **an abject apology** *formal* (=one that shows that you are very sorry)

PHRASES
a letter of apology

ap·o·plec·tic /ˌæpəˈplektɪk◂/ *adj* **1** *informal* so angry that your face becomes red: *The colonel was apoplectic with rage.* **2** *old-fashioned* relating to apoplexy

ap·o·plex·y /ˈæpəpleksi/ *n* [U] *old-fashioned* an illness in your brain which causes you to suddenly lose your ability to move or think SYN **stroke**

a·pos·ta·sy /əˈpɒstəsi $ əˈpɑː-/ *n* [U] *formal* when someone suddenly stops believing in a religion or supporting a political party

a·pos·tate /əˈpɒsteɪt, -stət $ əˈpɑː-/ *n* [C] *formal* someone who has stopped believing in a religion or supporting a political party

a pos·ter·i·o·ri /ˌeɪ pɒsteriˈɔːraɪ, ˌɑː pɒsteriˈɔːri $ ˌɑː poʊstɪriˈɔːri, ˌeɪ pɑː-/ *adj, adv formal* using facts that you know now to form a judgment about what must have happened before → A PRIORI

a·pos·tle /əˈpɒsəl $ əˈpɑː-/ *n* [C] **1** one of the 12 people chosen by Jesus Christ to teach and spread the Christian religion **2** *formal* someone who believes strongly in an idea and tries to persuade other people about it SYN **proponent**: **[+of]** *a great apostle of non-violence*

ap·o·stol·ic /ˌæpəˈstɒlɪk◂ $ -ˈstɑː-/ *adj technical* **1** connected with the Pope (=leader of the Catholic church) **2** connected with one of Christ's 12 apostles

a·pos·tro·phe /əˈpɒstrəfi $ əˈpɑː-/ *n* [C] **a)** the sign (') that is used in writing to show that numbers or letters have been left out, as in 'don't' (=do not) and '86 (=1986) **b)** the same sign used before 's' to show that something belongs to someone or something, or is connected with them, as in 'John's book', or 'Charles' mother', or 'Henry's first year as a teacher' **c)** the same sign used before 's' to show the plural of letters and numbers as in "Your r's look like v's."

a·poth·e·ca·ry /əˈpɒθəkəri $ əˈpɑːθəkeri/ *n* (*plural* **apothecaries**) [C] someone who mixed and sold medicines in the past

a·poth·e·o·sis /əˌpɒθiˈəʊsɪs $ əˌpɑːθiˈoʊsɪs, ˌæpəˈθiːəsɪs/ *n* [singular] *formal* **1** the best and most perfect example of something: **[+of]** *the apotheosis of romantic art* **2** the best or highest point in someone's life or job SYN **apex**: **[+of]** *the apotheosis of his career*

app /æp/ *n* [C] a piece of computer software that does a particular job SYN **application**: *You can download an app that reminds you of things you have to do.*

ap·pal *BrE*, **appall** *AmE* /əˈpɔːl $ əˈpɒːl/ ●○○ *v* [T] to make someone feel very shocked and upset SYN **horrify**: *The way we kill animals appals a lot of people.* | *The decision to execute the two men has appalled many politicians.*

ap·palled /əˈpɔːld $ əˈpɒːld/ ●○○ *adj* very shocked and upset by something very bad or unpleasant: **[+by]** *I was appalled by what I saw.* | **[+at]** *He was appalled at how dirty the place was.* | *When I heard what had happened I was* ***absolutely appalled.*** THESAURUS ▸ SHOCKED

ap·pal·ling /əˈpɔːlɪŋ $ əˈpɒː-/ ●○○ *adj*
1 very unpleasant and shocking SYN **terrible**: *She suffered appalling injuries.* | *He was kept in appalling conditions in prison.* | *an appalling famine*
2 very bad SYN **atrocious**: *The weather was* ***absolutely appalling.*** THESAURUS ▸ BAD —**appallingly** *adv*: *He behaved appallingly.* | *an appallingly difficult job*

ap·pa·loo·sa /ˌæpəˈluːsə/ *n* [C] *AmE* a type of horse that is pale in colour, with dark spots

ap·par·at·chik /ˌɑːpəˈrɑːtʃɪk/ *n* [C] an official who works for a government or other organization and who obeys orders without thinking: *a Communist party apparatchik*

ap·pa·ra·tus /ˌæpəˈreɪtəs $ -ˈræ-/ ●○○ *n*
1 [U] the set of tools and machines that you use for a particular scientific, medical, or technical purpose SYN **equipment**: *Astronauts have special breathing apparatus.*
2 [C] the way in which a lot of people are organized to work together to do a job or control a company or country SYN **machinery**: *The tax will require a massive administrative apparatus.* | *The state apparatus has become corrupt.* | *the apparatus of government*

ap·par·el /əˈpærəl/ *n* [U] *formal* clothes: *She looked lovely, despite her strange apparel.* | *men wearing protective apparel* | *We sell a full range of sports apparel.*

ap·par·ent /əˈpærənt/ ●●○ W2 AWL *adj*
1 easy to notice SYN **obvious**: **it is apparent (that)** *It soon became apparent that we had a major problem.* | **it is apparent from sth that** *It is apparent from scientific studies that the drug has some fairly nasty side effects.* | **it is apparent to sb that** *It was apparent to everyone that he was seriously ill.* | *The difference in quality was* ***immediately apparent***. | *He left suddenly,* ***for no apparent reason***.
2 seeming to have a particular feeling or attitude, although this may not be true: *He did well in his exams, despite his apparent lack of interest in his work.*

ap·par·ent·ly /əˈpærəntli/ ●●● S1 W2 *adv*
1 [sentence adverb] used to say that you have heard that something is true, although you are not completely sure about it: *Apparently the company is losing a lot of money.* | *I wasn't there, but apparently it went well.*
2 according to the way someone looks or a situation appears, although you cannot be sure: *She turned to face him, her anger apparently gone.*

ap·pa·ri·tion /ˌæpəˈrɪʃən/ *n* [C] something that you imagine you can see, especially the spirit of a dead person: *He stared at the strange apparition before him.* | *a ghostly apparition of a man*

ap·peal[1] /əˈpiːl/ ●●● S2 W1 *n*
1 REQUEST [C] an urgent request for something important: **[+for]** *The police have issued a new appeal for information.* | **[+to]** *All the organizations involved have sent urgent appeals to the government, asking for extra funding.* | *The girl's family have made a public appeal for help to try and catch her killer.* | **appeal to sb to do sth** *an appeal to the army to not use too much force*
2 REQUEST FOR MONEY [C] an attempt to persuade people to give money in order to help people who need something: *The appeal has nearly reached its target of £100,000.*
3 REQUEST TO CHANGE DECISION [C,U] a formal request to a court or to someone in authority asking for a decision to be changed: **[+to]** *an appeal to the European Court of Human Rights* | **on appeal** *The sentence was reduced to three years on appeal.*
4 BEING ATTRACTIVE [U] a quality that makes people like something or someone: *What is the particular appeal of this island?* | *The programme has a very* ***wide appeal***. | **[+for]** *The film has great appeal for young audiences.* | *She's definitely got* ***sex appeal*** (=she is sexually attractive). → COURT OF APPEAL

COLLOCATIONS – MEANINGS 1 & 2

VERBS

make/issue/launch an appeal *Detectives are making an urgent appeal for information.*
renew an appeal (=make an appeal again) *Detectives renewed their appeal for help from the public.*

ADJECTIVES

an urgent appeal *The fire service has made an urgent appeal for more part-time firefighters.*
a desperate appeal *The family made a desperate appeal to their daughter to come home.* | *The London-based relief agency issued a desperate appeal for aid.*
a direct appeal *The police have issued a direct appeal to the witness to come forward with information.*
a personal appeal *Muslim leaders made a personal appeal for the hostage's freedom.*
a public appeal | **a fresh appeal** (=one that you make again) | **a nationwide appeal** | **an international appeal** | **a television appeal**

COLLOCATIONS – MEANING 3

VERBS

make an appeal *My client is planning to make an appeal.*
lodge/file/bring an appeal (=make an appeal) *Mr Sarhadi, who has lived here for three years, has lodged an appeal against extradition.*
consider an appeal *The US Supreme Court could refuse to consider the appeal.*
hear an appeal (=listen to all the facts) *The FA will hear Chelsea's appeal against the fine next week.*
win/lose an appeal | **uphold/allow an appeal** (=give permission for a decision to be changed) | **dismiss/throw out/turn down an appeal** (=not give permission for a decision to be changed) | **an appeal fails/succeeds**

ADJECTIVES

a formal appeal *She decided to make a formal appeal through her lawyer.*

PHRASES

grounds for an appeal (=reasons for making an appeal) *You need to have reasonable grounds for your appeal.*
a right of appeal | **pending appeal** (=until an appeal can take place)

appeal[2] ●●● S3 W3 *v*
1 ASK [I] to make a serious public request for help, money, information etc: **[+for]** *Church and community leaders have appealed for calm.* | **[+to]** *Farmers have appealed to the government for help.* | **appeal to sb to do sth** *The police have appealed to anyone with information to come forward and talk to them.*
2 ASK TO CHANGE DECISION [I,T] to make a formal request to a court or someone in authority asking for a decision to be changed: *She is not happy with the decision and plans to appeal.* | **[+against]** *Both men intend to appeal against their convictions.* | **[+to]** *Appealing to the referee does not often result in a decision being changed.*
3 BE ATTRACTIVE [I] if someone or something appeals to you, they seem attractive and interesting: **[+to]** *The programme appeals to young children.* | *The idea of working abroad* ***really appeals*** *to me.*
4 appeal to sb's better nature/sense of justice etc to try to persuade someone to do something by reminding them that it is a good or fair thing to do: *You could always try appealing to his better nature.*

Apˈpeal ˌCourt *n* [singular] the COURT OF APPEAL

ap·peal·ing /əˈpiːlɪŋ/ *adj* **1** attractive or interesting OPP **unappealing**: *The city offers an appealing combination of sporting and cultural events.* | *It creates an atmosphere which visitors* ***find*** *so* ***appealing***. **2 appealing look/expression/voice etc** a look etc that shows that someone wants help or sympathy: *'Are you sure it's okay?' she said with an appealing smile.* —**appealingly** *adv*: *She looked appealingly at Ben.*

apˈpeals ˌcourt *n* [C] a court of law in some countries which deals with cases when people are not satisfied with the judgment given by a lower court SYN **Court of Appeals**: *a ruling by a US federal appeals court*

ap·pear /əˈpɪə $ əˈpɪr/ ●●● S2 W1 *v*
1 SEEM [linking verb] used when saying how someone or something seems. **Appear** is more formal than **seem**: **appear to be sth** *The diamonds appeared to be genuine.* |

appear to do sth *The research appears to show that the drug is effective in most cases.* | **appear to sb** *He didn't appear to me to be a violent man.* | **it appears (that)** (=used when saying what you think has happened or is true) *It appears that all the files have been deleted.* | **there appear(s) to be sth** (=used when saying what you think has happened or is true) *There appears to be some kind of problem.* | *Police have found* ***what appear to be*** *human remains.* | *He tried to* ***make it appear that*** *she had committed suicide.* | *It may be less useful* ***than it first appears.*** | **appear + adj** *During the interview she appeared calm and relaxed.* | *I don't want to appear rude.* | **so it would appear** (=used when saying that something seems to be true, although you are not completely sure) *'Have they gone?' 'So it would appear.'*

GRAMMAR

Linking verbs

Appear is a linking verb. This type of verb links the subject of the sentence with an adjective or noun: *His explanation appears unlikely.* | *This appears a good solution.*

Using the progressive

Appear is not used in the progressive in this meaning. You say: *He appears to be unhappy.*
✗ Don't say: *He is appearing to be unhappy.*
GRAMMAR GUIDE ▸ VERBS

2 START TO BE SEEN [I always + adv/prep] to start to be seen, to arrive, or to exist in a place, especially suddenly: *Two faces appeared at our window.* | *A man suddenly appeared from behind a tree.* | *Small cracks appeared in the wall.* | *It was nearly an hour before Sweeney appeared in the pub.* | **appear from nowhere/out of nowhere** (=appear suddenly and unexpectedly) *The car seemed to appear from nowhere.*

3 FILM/TV PROGRAMME ETC [I always + adv/prep] to take part in a film, play, concert, television programme etc: **appear in a film/play** *She has already appeared in a number of films.* | **appear on television/stage** *He appeared on national television to deny the claims.* | **appear at a theatre etc**

4 BOOK/NEWSPAPER ETC [I always + adv/prep] to be written or shown on a list, in a book or newspaper, in a document etc: *The story appeared in all the national newspapers.* | *Some of the material used has* ***appeared in print*** *before* (=has been published).

5 AVAILABLE/KNOWN [I always + adv/prep] to become widely available or known about: *The new range will be appearing in shops in the autumn.* | *New courses are appearing every year.*

6 LAW COURT/MEETING [I always + adv/prep] to go to a law court or other official meeting to give information, answer questions etc: *The three men are due to* ***appear in court*** *tomorrow.* | **appear before a court/judge/committee etc** *She appeared before Colchester magistrates charged with attempted murder.* | **appear for sb/on behalf of sb** (=to be the legal representative for someone) *Sir Nicholas Gammon QC appeared on behalf of the defendant.*

THESAURUS

appear to start to be seen, especially suddenly: *A few small white clouds appeared on the horizon.*
pop up to appear very suddenly: *A woman's face popped up from the other side of the fence.*
become visible to gradually start to be able to be seen: *The shape of the baby's head gradually became visible on the screen.*
come into view if something comes into view, you start to see it as you move closer to it, or it gets closer to you: *The white cliffs of Dover came into view.*
come out if the sun, moon, or the stars come out, they suddenly appear: *The sun came out from behind a cloud.*
loom/loom up if a large frightening object or person looms, they appear suddenly: *The dark shape of the castle loomed up out of the mist.* | *The man's face suddenly loomed over him.*
resurface to appear again after being lost or missing: *The girl's father has resurfaced after six years of no contact.*

ap·pear·ance /əˈpɪərəns $ əˈpɪr-/ ●●● W2 *n*
1 WAY SB/STH LOOKS [C,U] the way someone or something looks to other people: *He was always criticising his wife's appearance.* | **[+of]** *They've changed the appearance of the whole building.* | *We are often attracted to somebody first by their* ***physical appearance.*** | *Women, in general, tend to be more concerned than men about their* ***personal appearance.*** | *She had an* ***outward appearance*** *of calm, but deep down she was really worried.* | *The metal posts* ***spoiled the appearance*** *of the garden.* | *A garnish helps to* ***enhance the appearance of*** *any dish.* | *She's the kind of woman who* ***takes pride in her appearance.*** | *You shouldn't* ***judge by appearances.*** | *They work hard at school without* ***giving the appearance of*** *being particularly hard-working.* | *The case* ***had all the appearances of*** *a straightforward murder.* | *The pupils looked angelic – but* ***appearances can be deceptive.*** | *He was,* ***to all appearances,*** *a respectable, successful businessman.*
2 SB TAKES PART IN A PUBLIC EVENT [C] when a famous person takes part in a film, concert, or other public event: *It was his first* ***public appearance*** *since the election.* | *He* ***made*** *his last* ***appearance*** *for the club in the Cup Final.* | **appearance money/fee** (=money paid to a famous person to attend an event)
3 STH NEW STARTS TO EXIST [singular] when something new begins to exist or starts being used: **[+of]** *The industry has changed greatly with the appearance of new technologies.* | *the appearance of buds on the trees*
4 ARRIVAL [C usually singular] the unexpected or sudden arrival of someone or something: **[+of]** *Eileen was deep in concentration, and the sudden appearance of her daughter startled her.*
5 keep up appearances to dress and behave in the way in which people expect you to, especially to hide your true situation: *She just wanted to keep up appearances for the kids.*
6 for appearances' sake/for the sake of appearances if you do something for appearances' sake, you are trying to behave how people expect you to, especially to hide your true situation or feelings
7 put in an appearance/make an appearance to go to an event for a short time, because you think you should rather than because you want to: *At least Marc managed to put in an appearance at the party.*
8 AT A LAW COURT/MEETING [C] an occasion when someone goes to a court of law or official meeting to give information, answer questions etc: *He is due to make another court appearance on Monday.*

ap·pease /əˈpiːz/ *v* [T] *formal* to make someone less angry or stop them from attacking you by giving them what they want: *They attempted to appease international opposition by promising to hold talks.* —**appeasement** *n* [C,U]: *Chamberlain's policy of appeasement towards Hitler in the 30s*

ap·pel·lant /əˈpelənt/ *n* [C] *law* a person who APPEALS against the decision in a court of law

ap·pel·late court /əˌpelət ˈkɔːt $ -ˈkɔːrt/ *n* [C] a court in which people APPEAL against decisions made in other courts of law

ap·pel·la·tion /ˌæpəˈleɪʃən/ *n* [C] *literary* a name or title

ap·pend /əˈpend/ AWL *v* [T] *formal* to add something to a piece of writing → **appendix**: **[+to]** *The results of the client survey are appended to this document.*

ap·pend·age /əˈpendɪdʒ/ *n* [C] **1** something that is connected to a larger or more important thing **2** *formal* an arm, leg, or other body part

ap·pen·dec·to·my /ˌæpənˈdektəmi/ *n* (*plural* **appendectomies**) [C,U] a medical operation in which your APPENDIX is removed

ap·pen·di·ci·tis /əˌpendɪˈsaɪtɪs/ *n* [U] an illness in which your APPENDIX swells and causes pain

ap·pen·dix /əˈpendɪks/ ●○○ AWL *n* [C]
1 (*plural* **appendixes**) a small organ near your BOWEL, which has little or no use: *Christine had to go into hospital to have her appendix out* (=have it removed).
2 (*plural* **appendices** /-dəsiːz/) a part at the end of a book containing additional information: *See Appendix 2.6.*

ap·per·tain /ˌæpəˈteɪn $ -ər-/ *v*
appertain to sth *phr v formal* to belong to or concern something: *A forum was set up to deal with all issues appertaining to Everton Park.*

ap·pe·tite /ˈæpətaɪt/ ●●○ *n*
1 [C usually singular, U] a desire for food: *Her husband always had a huge appetite.* | *Symptoms include tiredness and loss of appetite.*
2 [C] a desire or liking for a particular activity: **[+for]** *She has an amazing appetite for knowledge.* | *People seem to have an* ***insatiable appetite*** (=always wanting more of something) *for news of any kind.* | *a loss of* ***sexual appetite***
→ **whet sb's appetite** at WHET(1)

COLLOCATIONS

ADJECTIVES

a good/healthy appetite *Growing children should have a healthy appetite.*
a big/huge/enormous appetite *By the time Ron was 16 he had an enormous appetite.*
a poor appetite *A poor appetite may be a sign of illness.*
a small appetite

VERBS

have an appetite *There's lots of food – I hope you have a good appetite.*
lose your appetite *She was so miserable that she completely lost her appetite.*
give sb an appetite (*also* **stimulate your appetite** *formal*) *The exercise and fresh air had given us an appetite.*
spoil/ruin your appetite (=make you not feel like eating a meal) *Don't give the children any more sweets – it will spoil their appetite.*

PHRASES

loss/lack of appetite *Symptoms include fever and loss of appetite.*

ap·pe·tiz·er (*also* **-iser** *BrE*) /ˈæpətaɪzə $ -ər/ *n* [C] a small dish that you eat at the beginning of a meal

ap·pe·tiz·ing (*also* **-ising** *BrE*) /ˈæpətaɪzɪŋ/ ●○○ *adj* food that is appetizing smells or looks very good, making you want to eat it OPP **unappetizing**: *an appetizing aroma* | *The food wasn't particularly appetizing.*

ap·plaud /əˈplɔːd $ əˈplɒːd/ ●○○ *v*
1 [I,T] to hit your open hands together, to show that you have enjoyed a play, concert, speaker etc SYN **clap**: *The* ***audience applauded*** *loudly.* | *A crowd of 300 supporters* ***warmly applauded*** *her speech.*

REGISTER
In everyday English, people usually say **clap** rather than **applaud**: *Everyone was* ***clapping*** *and cheering.*

2 [T] *formal* to express strong approval of an idea, plan etc: *I* ***applaud*** *the* ***decision*** *to install more security cameras.* | **applaud sb for sth** *She should be applauded for her honesty.*
THESAURUS ▶ PRAISE

ap·plause /əˈplɔːz $ əˈplɒːz/ ●○○ *n* [U] the sound of many people hitting their hands together and shouting, to show that they have enjoyed something: *She got a* ***round of applause*** (=a short period of applause) *when she finished.* | **rapturous/enthusiastic applause** *He left the stage to rapturous applause.* | **loud/thunderous applause**

ap·ple /ˈæpəl/ ●●● S2 W3 *n*
1 [C,U] a hard round fruit that has red, light green, or yellow skin and is white inside: *apple pie* | *an apple tree* | *roast pork and apple sauce* (=a thick sauce made from cooked apples) → COOKING APPLE, EATING APPLE, see picture at FRUIT[1]
2 be the apple of sb's eye to be loved very much by someone: *Ben was always the apple of his father's eye.*
3 bob/dunk/dip for apples to play a game in which you must use your teeth to pick up apples floating in water
4 be as American as apple pie used to describe something that is typically American
5 the apple doesn't fall far from the tree *AmE* used to say that children are usually similar to their parents, especially in a bad way → **upset the apple cart** at UPSET[1], → **a rotten apple** at ROTTEN[1](7), → ADAM'S APPLE

ˈapple ˌpolisher *n* [C] *AmE spoken* someone who tries to gain something, become popular etc by praising or helping someone else without being sincere

ap·plet /ˈæplɪt/ *n* [C] *technical* a computer program that is part of a larger program, and which performs a particular job, such as finding documents on the Internet

ap·pli·ance /əˈplaɪəns/ *n* [C] a piece of equipment, especially electrical equipment, such as a COOKER or WASHING MACHINE, used in people's homes: **domestic/household etc appliance** *There's plenty of space for all the usual kitchen appliances.* | **electrical/gas appliance**

ap·plic·a·ble /əˈplɪkəbəl, ˈæplɪkəbəl/ *adj* if something is applicable to a particular person, group, or situation, it affects them or is related to them → **apply**: **[+to]** *The offer is only applicable to bookings for double rooms.* | **where/if/as applicable** *Ms/Miss/Mrs/Mr Please delete as applicable.* —**applicability** /əˌplɪkəˈbɪləti/ *n* [U]

ap·pli·cant /ˈæplɪkənt/ ●○○ *n* [C] someone who has formally asked, usually in writing, for a job, university place etc → **apply**: **[+for]** *He was one of 30 applicants for the manager's job.* | **successful/unsuccessful applicant** (=someone who is accepted or not accepted for a job etc) *Successful applicants will be expected to travel extensively.*

ap·pli·ca·tion /ˌæplɪˈkeɪʃən/ ●●● S1 W1 *n*
1 WRITTEN REQUEST [C,U] a formal, usually written, request for something such as a job, place at university, or permission to do something: **[+for]** *an application for a grant* | **[+from]** *The university welcomes applications from overseas students.* | *We receive hundreds of* ***job applications*** *each year.* | *I* ***filled in*** *the* ***application form*** *and sent it off.* | *You have to* ***submit*** *your* ***application*** *before the end of the month.* | *I've* ***put in an application*** *for a transfer.* | *He received a letter saying that his* ***application*** *had been* ***rejected***. | *It can take a long time for your visa* ***application*** *to be* ***processed***. | *The Council is currently reviewing the way it deals with* ***planning applications***. | *Thank you for your* ***letter of application***, *which we received yesterday.*
2 PRACTICAL USE [C,U] the practical purpose for which a machine, idea etc can be used, or a situation when this is used: **[+of/to/in]** *the applications of genetic engineering in agriculture* | *The research has many* ***practical applications***.
3 COMPUTERS [C] a piece of computer software which does a particular job: *We received training on a number of spreadsheet and database applications.*
4 PAINT/LIQUID [C,U] when you put something such as paint, liquid, medicine etc onto a surface: **[+of]** *The application of fertilizer increased the size of the plants.*
5 EFFORT [U] attention or effort over a long period of time: *Making your new business successful requires luck, patience, and application.*

ˌapplication ˈservice proˌvider *n* [C] an ASP

ˌapplication ˈsoftware *n* [U] *technical* computer software that is designed for a particular use or user: *We need to ensure that the application software on both the PC and the Macintosh produces compatible files.*

ap·pli·ca·tor /ˈæplɪkeɪtə $ -ər/ *n* [C] a special brush or tool used to spread a cream, liquid, medicine etc onto a surface

ap·plied /əˈplaɪd/ ●○○ *adj* **applied science/physics/linguistics etc** science etc that has a practical use → PURE(10), → THEORETICAL(1)

ap·pli·qué /əˈpliːkeɪ $ ˌæpləˈkeɪ/ *n* [C,U] the process of

A

sewing pieces of material onto a piece of clothing for decoration, or the pieces themselves —**appliqué** *v* [T]

ap·ply /əˈplaɪ/ ●●● S1 W1 *v* (**applied**, **applying**, **applies**)

1 REQUEST [I] to make a formal request, usually written, for something such as a job, a place at a university, or permission to do something: **[+for]** *She applied for a job with the local newspaper.* | *We need to* ***apply for*** *planning* ***permission*** *to build a garage.* | **[+to]** *I applied to four universities and was accepted by all of them.*

2 AFFECT [I,T not in progressive] to have an effect on or to concern a particular person, group, or situation: **[+to]** *Do the same rules apply to part-time workers?* | *The offer only applies to flights from London and Manchester.*

3 USE [T] to use something such as a method, idea, or law in a particular situation, activity, or process: **apply sth to sth** *New technology is being applied to almost every industrial process.* | *These ideas are often difficult to apply in practice.* THESAURUS ▶ USE

4 apply yourself to work hard at something, especially with a lot of attention for a long time: *Stephen would do well if only he applied himself.* | **[+to]** *Over the next months, he applied himself to improving the technique.*

5 MAKE STH WORK [T] to make something such as a piece of equipment operate, usually by pushing or pressing something: *apply the brakes*

6 SPREAD PAINT/LIQUID ETC [T] to put or spread something such as paint, liquid, or medicine onto a surface: *Apply the cream evenly over the skin.* | **apply make-up/lipstick etc**

7 apply force/pressure to push on something

8 USE A WORD [T] to use a particular word or name to describe something or someone: *The term 'mat' can be applied to any small rug.*

ap·point /əˈpɔɪnt/ ●●○ W3 *v* [T]

1 to choose someone for a position or a job: *officials appointed by the government* | **appoint sb to sth** *He's been appointed to the State Supreme Court.* | **appoint sb to do sth** *A committee was appointed to consider the plans.* | **appoint (sb) as sth** *O'Connell was appointed as chairman.*

2 *formal* to arrange or decide a time or place for something to happen: *The committee appointed a day in June for celebrations.* | *Everyone assembled in the hall* ***at the appointed time*** (=at the time that had been arranged). —**appointee** /əˌpɔɪnˈtiː, ˌæpɔɪn-/ *n* [C]: *a presidential appointee* → SELF-APPOINTED, WELL-APPOINTED

GRAMMAR: Patterns with appoint

- You **appoint** someone **to** a post or position: *He promised to appoint more women to senior positions.*
- You **appoint** someone **as** chairman, manager, ambassador etc: *The board appointed him as chairman.*
- You **appoint** someone **to do** something: *Schwarzkopf was appointed to command US forces.*

ap·point·ment /əˈpɔɪntmənt/ ●●● S2 W2 *n*

1 [C] an arrangement for a meeting at an agreed time and place, for a particular purpose: **an appointment to do sth** *I'd like to make an appointment to see the doctor.* | **[+with]** *He has an appointment with a client at 10.30.* | *All consultations are* ***by appointment only***.

2 [C,U] when someone is chosen for a position or job: **[+of]** *Other changes included the appointment of a new Foreign Minister.* | **[+as]** *They congratulated him on his appointment as chairman.*

3 [C] a job or position, usually involving some responsibility: **[+as]** *He has taken up an appointment as Professor of Chemistry.* THESAURUS ▶ JOB

4 by appointment to the Queen *BrE* a phrase that can be used by a business that sells goods or services to the Queen

COLLOCATIONS

VERBS

have an appointment *She has an appointment with the dentist at 5 o'clock.*

make/arrange an appointment *Can you phone the hairdresser and make an appointment?*

book an appointment *BrE*, **schedule an appointment** *AmE* (=make an appointment) *I've scheduled your appointment for 9.30.*

cancel an appointment | **get an appointment** (=succeed in arranging one) | **miss an appointment** (=not go to an appointment you have arranged) | **keep an appointment** (=go to an appointment that you have arranged)

ADJECTIVES/NOUN + appointment

a hospital appointment *BrE My hospital appointment lasted half an hour.*

a doctor's appointment (*also* **an appointment at the doctor's**) *What time is your doctor's appointment?*

an urgent appointment *I can't talk now – I have an urgent appointment to get to.*

a dentist's/dental appointment | **a medical appointment** | **a business appointment** | **a morning/afternoon appointment**

apˈpointment ˌbook *n* [C] **1** *AmE* a DIARY **2** a large book divided into days and times containing the names of people you have appointments with, for example a doctor or a HAIRDRESSER etc

ap·por·tion /əˈpɔːʃən $ -ɔːr-/ *v* [T] *formal* to decide how something should be shared among various people: *It's not easy to* ***apportion blame*** (=say who deserves to be blamed) *when a marriage breaks up.* | **[+among/between]** *Court costs were equally apportioned between them.* —**apportionment** *n* [C,U]

ap·po·site /ˈæpəzət/ *adj formal* suitable to what is happening or being discussed SYN **appropriate** OPP **inappropriate**: **[+to]** *His observations are, indeed, apposite to the present discussion.* —**appositely** *adv* —**appositeness** *n* [U]

ap·po·si·tion /ˌæpəˈzɪʃən/ *n* [U] *technical* in grammar, an occasion when a simple sentence contains two or more noun phrases that describe the same thing or person, appearing one after the other without a word such as 'and' or 'or' between them. For example, in the sentence 'The defendant, a woman of thirty, denies kicking the policeman' the two phrases 'the defendant' and 'a woman of thirty' are in apposition.

ap·prais·al /əˈpreɪzəl/ ●○○ *n*

1 [C,U] a statement or opinion judging the worth, value, or condition of something: **[+of]** *It needed a calmer appraisal of her situation.* | *a critical appraisal of the existing facilities*

2 [C] a meeting between a manager and a worker to discuss the quality of someone's work and how well they do their job

ap·praise /əˈpreɪz/ *v* [T] **1** *formal* to officially judge how successful, effective, or valuable something is SYN **evaluate**: *Greenpeace has been invited to appraise the environmental costs of such an operation.* **2** *literary* to look carefully at someone or something to make an opinion about them: *His eyes appraised her face.*

ap·pre·cia·ble /əˈpriːʃəbəl/ AWL *adj* large enough to be noticed or considered important SYN **significant**: *There's no appreciable change in the patient's condition.* —**appreciably** *adv*: *The two plans are not appreciably different.*

ap·pre·ci·ate /əˈpriːʃieɪt/ ●●○ S3 W3 AWL *v*

1 [T] to understand how serious or important a situation or problem is or what someone's feelings are SYN **realize**: **appreciate the significance/importance/value of sth** *He did not fully appreciate the significance of signing the contract.* | **appreciate that** *We appreciate that caring for children is an important job.* | **appreciate what/how/why** *It is difficult to appreciate how bad the situation had become.*

2 [T] used to thank someone in a polite way or to say that you are grateful for something they have done: *Thanks ever so much for your help, I really appreciate it.* | ***I appreciate*** *your* ***concern****, but honestly, I'm fine.* | ***I'd appreciate it if*** *you let me get on with my job.*

3 [T] to understand how good or useful someone or something is: *Her abilities are not fully appreciated by her employer.* | *I'm not an expert, but I appreciate fine works of art.*
4 [I] *technical* to gradually become more valuable over a period of time OPP **depreciate**: *Most investments are expected to appreciate at a steady rate.*

GRAMMAR
Patterns with appreciate
• You say: *I appreciate your advice* | *I appreciate having your advice.* ✗ Don't say: *I appreciate to have your advice.*
Using the progressive
• **Appreciate** is not used in the progressive in meanings 1, 2, and 3. You say: *I appreciate what you are saying.* ✗ Don't say: *I am appreciating what you are saying.*
• **Appreciate** is used in the progressive in meaning 4: *The value of his work is still appreciating.*
GRAMMAR GUIDE ▸ VERBS

ap·pre·ci·a·tion /əˌpriːʃiˈeɪʃən/ ●●○ AWL *n*
1 [U] pleasure you feel when you realize something is good, useful, or well done: **[+of]** *It helps children to develop an appreciation of poetry and literature.*
2 [U] a feeling of being grateful for something someone has done: **show/express your appreciation** *The chairman asked me to express our appreciation of all your hard work.* | *He was presented with a watch* ***in appreciation of*** *his long service.*
3 [C,U] an understanding of the importance or meaning of something: **[+of]** *a realistic appreciation of the situation*
4 [singular, U] a rise in value, especially of land or possessions OPP **depreciation**: *an appreciation of 50% in property values*

ap·pre·cia·tive /əˈpriːʃətɪv/ *adj* **1** feeling or showing that you enjoy something or are pleased about it: **appreciative audience/crowd** | **appreciative laughter/applause** **2** [not before noun] grateful for something: **[+of]** *She was appreciative of Greg's concern for her health.* —**appreciatively** *adv*

ap·pre·hend /ˌæprɪˈhend/ *v* [T] **1** *formal* if the police apprehend a criminal, they catch him or her SYN **arrest**: *The police have failed to apprehend the culprits.* THESAURUS ▸ CATCH **2** *old-fashioned* to understand something: *They were slow to apprehend the danger.*

ap·pre·hen·sion /ˌæprɪˈhenʃən/ ●○○ *n*
1 [C,U] anxiety about the future, especially about dealing with something unpleasant or difficult SYN **anxiety**: *a feeling of apprehension* | *I woke before the alarm, filled with apprehension.*
2 [U] *formal* the act of apprehending a criminal SYN **arrest**
3 [U] *old-fashioned* understanding

ap·pre·hen·sive /ˌæprɪˈhensɪv◂/ ●○○ *adj* worried or nervous about something that you are going to do, or about the future: **[+about/of]** *We'd been a little apprehensive about their visit.* | **apprehensive that** *I was apprehensive that something would go wrong.* | *Some had apprehensive looks on their faces.* THESAURUS ▸ WORRIED —**apprehensively** *adv*: *'What's wrong?' I asked apprehensively.*

ap·pren·tice /əˈprentɪs/ ●○○ *n* [C] someone who works for an employer for a fixed period of time in order to learn a particular skill or job: *She works in the hairdresser's as an apprentice.* | *an apprentice electrician* —**apprentice** *v* [T]: *He was* ***apprenticed to*** *a local architect.*

ap·pren·tice·ship /əˈprentəsʃɪp/ *n* [C,U] the job of being an apprentice, or the period of time in which you are an apprentice: *He's* ***serving*** *an* ***apprenticeship*** *as a printer.* | *a five-year apprenticeship*

ap·prise /əˈpraɪz/ *v* [T] *formal* to tell or give someone information about something SYN **inform**: **apprise sb of sth** *The district chairman was fully apprised of all the details.*

ap·proach¹ /əˈprəʊtʃ $ əˈproʊtʃ/ ●●● S2 W1 AWL *n*
1 METHOD [C] a method of doing something or dealing with a problem: **[+to]** *a new approach to teaching languages* | *He decided to* ***adopt a*** *different* ***approach*** *and teach the Bible through story-telling.* | *This book* ***takes an*** *unorthodox* ***approach*** *to art criticism.* | *organizations which take a* ***positive approach*** *to creative thinking* THESAURUS ▸ METHOD, WAY
2 ASK [C] a request from someone, asking you to do something for them: *They* ***made*** *a direct* ***approach to*** *the minister of education.*
3 the approach of sth the approach of a particular time or event is the fact that it is getting closer: *the approach of autumn* | *It's a sign of the approach of middle age.*
4 MOVEMENT TOWARDS [U] movement towards or near to something: *Our approach frightened the birds.*
5 PATH/ROAD [C] a road, path etc that leads to a place, and is the main way of reaching it: *Soldiers were guarding the approaches to the city.* | *an* ***approach road***
6 AIRCRAFT [C] the final part of a plane's flight, before it lands at an airport: *It was clear to land so we* ***made*** *our* ***approach****.*

ap·proach² ●●● S3 W2 AWL *v*
1 MOVE TOWARDS [I,T] to move towards or nearer to someone or something: *As I approached the house, I noticed a light on upstairs.* | *She heard footsteps approaching.*
2 ASK [T] to ask someone for something, or ask them to do something, especially when you are asking them for the first time or when you are not sure if they will do it: **approach sb for sth** *Students should be able to approach teachers for advice.* | **approach sb/sth about (doing) sth** *The charity approached several stores about giving food aid.* | *I have already been approached by several other companies* (=offered a job, work etc). → APPROACHABLE
3 FUTURE EVENT [I,T] if an event or a particular time approaches, or you approach it, it is coming nearer and will happen soon: *She was then approaching the end of her career.* | *The time is* ***fast approaching*** *when we will have to make a decision.* | *With winter approaching, many animals are storing food.*
4 DEAL WITH [T] to begin to deal with a situation or problem in a particular way or with a particular attitude: **approach a problem/task/matter etc** *It might be possible to approach the problem in a different way.*
5 ALMOST [I,T] to be almost equal to something: *temperatures approaching 35°C* | *He's never had anything approaching a normal life.*

ap·proach·a·ble /əˈprəʊtʃəbəl $ əˈproʊtʃ-/ *adj* friendly and easy to talk to OPP **unapproachable**: *The head teacher is very approachable.* THESAURUS ▸ FRIENDLY

ap·pro·ba·tion /ˌæprəˈbeɪʃən/ *n* [U] *formal* official praise or approval

ap·pro·pri·ate¹ /əˈprəʊpri-ət $ əˈproʊ-/ ●●● S2 W1 AWL *adj* correct or suitable for a particular time, situation, or purpose OPP **inappropriate**: **[+for]** *clothes appropriate for a job interview* | **[+to]** *an education system which is more appropriate to the needs of the students* | **it is appropriate (for sb) to do sth** *It would not be appropriate for me to discuss that now.* | **it is appropriate (that)** *It seemed somehow appropriate that we should begin our journey here.* | **appropriate time/place etc** *I didn't feel that this was an appropriate time to mention the subject of money.* | **highly/entirely/wholly appropriate** *I thought his remark was highly appropriate, given the circumstances.* | *The timing of the announcement was* ***particularly appropriate****.* | ***Where appropriate****, I delegate as much work as possible.* | *Mark box 1 or 2,* ***as appropriate****.* | *I can assure you that* ***appropriate action*** *will be taken.* THESAURUS ▸ SUITABLE —**appropriateness** *n* [U]

ap·pro·pri·ate² /əˈprəʊprieɪt $ əˈproʊ-/ *v* [T] *formal* **1** to take something for yourself when you do not have the right to do this SYN **steal**: *He is suspected of appropriating government funds.* **2** to take something, especially money, to use for a particular purpose: **appropriate sth for sth** *Congress appropriated $5 million for International Women's Year.* → **misappropriate**

A

ap·pro·pri·ate·ly /əˈprəʊpri-ətli $ əˈproʊ-/ ●●○ AWL *adv* correctly or suitably for a particular time, situation, or purpose SYN **suitably** OPP **inappropriately**: *The painters met,* ***appropriately enough****, in an art gallery* (=used to emphasize that something is very appropriate). | *appropriately dressed*

ap·pro·pri·a·tion /əˌprəʊpriˈeɪʃən $ əˌproʊ-/ *n* [C,U] *formal* **1** the process of saving money for a special purpose, or the money that is saved, especially by a business or government: **[+of]** *the appropriation of $2 million for the new hospital* **2** the act of taking control of something without asking permission → **misappropriation**: **[+of]** *the appropriation of company property*

ap·prov·al /əˈpruːvəl/ ●●○ W3 *n*
1 [C,U] when a plan, decision, or person is officially accepted: *The president has already* ***given his approval*** *to the plan.* | *It is just three months since we* ***received official approval*** *to go ahead with the project.* | *A company cannot be sold* ***without the approval*** *of the shareholders.* | *The bill will be* ***submitted for approval*** *by Congress.* | *The president would appoint the Council of Ministers,* ***subject to the approval of*** *the National Assembly.* | *The IMF has given its* ***seal of approval*** *to the government's economic strategy.* | *appointments requiring* ***parliamentary approval***
2 [U] *formal* when someone likes something or someone and thinks that they are good OPP **disapproval**: *A murmur of approval passed through the crowd.* | **nod/smile/clap etc in approval** *They clapped their hands in approval.* | *His ideas have* ***won*** *widespread public* ***approval*** (=many people agree with them and think they are good). | *Does the design* ***meet with your approval*** (=do you like it?)? | *Children are always* ***seeking approval*** *from their parents.* | *She* ***looked to*** *Greg* ***for approval****.*
3 on approval if you buy something on approval, you have the right to return it to the shop if you decide you do not want it

ap·prove /əˈpruːv/ ●●● S3 W2 *v*
1 [T] to officially accept a plan, proposal etc: *The conference approved a proposal for a referendum.* **THESAURUS** AGREE
2 [I] to think that someone or something is good, right, or suitable OPP **disapprove**: **[+of]** *Catherine's parents now approve of her marriage.* | *I don't approve of cosmetic surgery.*

GRAMMAR: Comparison

approve of
• You use **approve of** when saying that someone thinks that someone or something is good or right: *Her parents didn't* ***approve of*** *her boyfriend.* ✗ Don't say: *Her parents didn't approve her boyfriend.*

approve
• You use **approve** when saying that a person or group of people officially agrees to allow something to happen: *Congress approved the budget.*

THESAURUS

approve to officially accept a plan, proposal etc: *The Medical Research Council has approved the use of a new drug for breast cancer.*
pass to approve a law or proposal, especially by voting: *Many anti-smoking laws have been passed.*
ratify to make a written agreement official by signing it: *The treaty was ratified by the Senate in 1988.*
rubber-stamp to approve something without really thinking about it - used to show disapproval: *Parliament merely rubber-stamped the president's decisions.*

ap·proved /əˈpruːvd/ *adj* [only before noun] officially recognized as being of a particular level or standard: *Funding is available for approved courses.*

apˈproved ˌschool *n* [C] *BrE* a special school in Britain in the past, where children who had done something illegal were sent if they were under 18

ap·prov·ing /əˈpruːvɪŋ/ *adj* showing support or agreement for something OPP **disapproving**: **an approving nod/glance/smile etc** —**approvingly** *adv*: *She smiled approvingly at the child.*

approx. (*also* **approx** *BrE*) /əˈprɒks $ əˈprɑːks/ the written abbreviation of ***approximately***

ap·prox·i·mate¹ /əˈprɒksəmət $ əˈprɑːk-/ ●●○ W3 AWL *adj* an approximate number, amount, or time is close to the exact number, amount etc, but could be a little bit more or less than it SYN **rough** OPP **exact**: *What is the approximate number of students in each class?* | *These percentages are only approximate.*

REGISTER
In everyday English, people usually say **rough** rather than **approximate**: *Can you give me a* ***rough*** *idea of how much it would cost?*

ap·prox·i·mate² /əˈprɒksɪmeɪt $ əˈprɑːk-/ AWL *v* [I, linking verb] *formal* **1** to be close to a particular number: **[+to]** *This figure approximates to a quarter of the UK's annual consumption.* **2** to be similar to but not exactly the same as something: **[+to]** *Your story only approximates to the real facts.*

ap·prox·i·mate·ly /əˈprɒksəmətli $ əˈprɑːk-/ ●●○ W3 AWL *adv* more or less than a number or amount SYN **roughly**: *The plane will be landing in approximately 20 minutes.* | *How much do you think it will cost, approximately?*

THESAURUS

approximately more or less than a number or amount - used especially in technical or scientific contexts: *The company had total revenues of approximately $2 million.* | *The disease affects approximately 10% of the adult population.*
about more or less than a number or amount. 'About' is the usual word to use in everyday English: *It costs about $30 to get a visa.* | *There were about 50 people at the meeting.*
roughly /ˈrʌfli/ about - used when you are trying to give someone a general idea of the size, amount, or number of something: *The two countries are roughly the same size.* | *Roughly how many miles do you travel a year?*
around about a number or time - used when you are guessing: *I'll be there around 5 o'clock.* | *The BBC broadcasts around 2,000 radio dramas every year.*
somewhere/something in the region of *formal* about - used with very large numbers or amounts: *Last year he earned something in the region of $60 million.*
or so *informal* about - used after a period of time, a number, or an amount: *The journey takes an hour or so.*
circa /ˈsɜːkə $ ˈsɜːr-/ *formal* about - used with dates a long time ago in the past: *The house was built circa 1530.*
or more used after a number or amount, when the total may be a lot more: *A thirty-second commercial can cost £60,000 or more.*
upwards of more than a number or amount: *The aircraft can carry upwards of 400 passengers.*

ap·prox·i·ma·tion /əˌprɒksəˈmeɪʃən $ əˌprɑːk-/ ●○○ AWL *n* [C,U]
1 a number, amount etc that is not exact, but is almost correct SYN **estimate**: **[+of]** *an approximation of the total* | **a rough/crude approximation** (=one that is not very exact) *Could you give us a rough approximation of the cost?* | **a good/close/reasonable approximation**
2 something that is similar to another thing, but not exactly the same: **[+of/to]** *It was the* ***nearest approximation*** *to a crisis she'd ever experienced.*

ap·pur·te·nance /əˈpɜːtɪnəns, -tən- $ əˈpɜːrtənəns/ *n* [C usually plural] *formal* a part of something more important

Apr. (*also* **Apr** *BrE*) the written abbreviation of ***April***

APR /ˌeɪ piː ˈɑː $ -ˈɑːr/ *n* [C usually singular] (***annual percentage rate***) the rate of INTEREST that you must pay when you borrow money

ap·rès-ski /ˌæpreɪ ˈskiː◂ $ ˌɑː-/ *n* [U] activities such as eating and drinking that you do after SKIing —**après-ski** *adj*

a·pri·cot /ˈeɪprəkɒt $ ˈæprəkɑːt/ *n* **1** [C] a small round fruit that is orange or yellow and has a single large seed **2** [U] the orange-yellow colour of an apricot → see picture at **FRUIT**[1] —**apricot** *adj*

A·pril /ˈeɪprəl/ ●●● S2 W2 *n* [C,U] (*written abbreviation* **Apr.**) the fourth month of the year, between March and May: **next/last April** *I'm going to Cuba next April.* | **in April** *Our new office opened in April 2001.* | **on April 6th** *The meeting will be on April 6th.* | **on 6th April** *BrE: I arrived on 6th April.* | **April 6** *AmE: Jim's birthday's April 6.*

ˌApril ˈfool *n* [C] someone who is tricked on April Fools' Day, or the trick that is played on them

ˌApril ˈFools' Day (*also* **All ˈFools' Day**) *n* April 1st, a day when people play tricks on each other

a pri·o·ri /ˌeɪ praɪˈɔːraɪ, ˌɑː priˈɔːriː/ *adj, adv formal* using previous experiences or facts to decide what the likely result or effect of something will be → **a posteriori**: *a ruling made on a priori grounds*

a·pron /ˈeɪprən/ ●●○ *n* [C]
1 a piece of clothing that covers the front part of your clothes and is tied around your waist, worn to keep your clothes clean, especially while cooking
2 apron strings *informal* the relationship between a child and its mother, especially if the mother controls an adult son or daughter too much: *You're 25 years old, and you still haven't* ***cut the apron strings****.* | *Jeff is still* ***tied to*** *his mother's* ***apron strings****.*
3 *technical* the hard surface in an airport on which planes are turned around, loaded, unloaded etc
4 *technical* (*also* **apron stage**) the part of the stage in a theatre that is in front of the curtain

ap·ro·pos /ˌæprəˈpəʊ, ˈæprəpoʊ $ -poʊ/ *adv formal* **apropos of sth** used to introduce a new subject that is related to something just mentioned: *He had nothing to say apropos of the latest developments.* | **apropos of nothing** (=not relating to anything previously mentioned) *Apropos of nothing, he suddenly asked me if I liked cats!*

apse /æps/ *n* [C] *technical* the curved inside end of a building, especially the east end of a church

apt /æpt/ ●○○ *adj*
1 be apt to do sth to have a natural tendency to do something SYN **tend to**: *Some of the staff are apt to arrive late on Mondays.*
2 exactly right for a particular situation or purpose SYN **appropriate**: *'Love at first sight' is a very* ***apt description*** *of how he felt when he saw her.* | **[+for]** *The punishment should be apt for the crime.*
3 an apt pupil/student *formal* a student who is quick to learn and understand SYN **able** —**aptness** *n* [U]

ap·ti·tude /ˈæptɪtjuːd $ -tuːd/ *n* [C,U] **1** natural ability or skill, especially in learning: **[+for]** *He has a* ***natural aptitude*** *for teaching.* **2 aptitude test** a test that measures your natural skills or abilities

apt·ly /ˈæptli/ *adv* **aptly named/described/called etc** named, described etc in a way that seems very suitable SYN **appropriately**: *The aptly named Skyline Restaurant provides spectacular views of the city below.*

aq·ua·lung /ˈækwəlʌŋ/ *n* [C] *trademark BrE* a piece of equipment that provides a DIVER (=someone who swims underwater) with air, and which they wear on their backs

aq·ua·ma·rine /ˌækwəməˈriːn◂ $ ˌæ-, ˌɑː-/ *n* **1** [C,U] a greenish blue jewel, or the type of stone it comes from **2** [U] a greenish blue colour —**aquamarine** *adj*

aq·ua·plane[1] /ˈækwəpleɪn/ *v* [I] *BrE* **1** if a car aquaplanes, it slides over a wet road in an uncontrolled way SYN **hydroplane** *AmE* **2** to be pulled over the water on an aquaplane

aquaplane[2] *n* [C] *BrE* a thin board that you stand on while you are pulled over the water by a fast boat

a·quar·i·um /əˈkweəriəm $ əˈkwer-/ ●○○ *n* (*plural* **aquariums** *or* **aquaria** /-riə/) [C]
1 a clear glass or plastic container for fish and other water animals
2 a building where people go to look at fish and other water animals

A·quar·i·us /əˈkweəriəs $ əˈkwer-/ *n* **1** [U] the 11th sign of the ZODIAC, represented by a person pouring water, which some people believe affects the character and life of people born between January 21 and February 19 **2** (*also* **Aquarian**) [C] someone who was born between January 21 and February 19 —**Aquarian** *adj*

aq·ua·ro·bics /ˌækwəˈrəʊbɪks $ -ˈroʊ-/ *n* [U] AEROBICS (=very active physical exercise done to music, usually in a class) that you do in a swimming pool

a·quat·ic /əˈkwætɪk, əˈkwɒ- $ əˈkwæ-, əˈkwɑː-/ *adj* **1** living or growing in water: *an aquatic plant* **2** involving or happening in water: *aquatic sports*

a·quat·ics /əˈkwætɪks, əˈkwɒ- $ əˈkwæ-, əˈkwɑː-/ *n* [U] the five Olympic sports that involve swimming or diving (DIVE)

aq·ua·tint /ˈækwətɪnt/ *n* [C,U] a method of producing a picture using acid on a sheet of metal, or a picture printed using this method

aq·ue·duct /ˈækwədʌkt/ *n* [C] a structure like a bridge, that carries water across a river or valley

a·que·ous /ˈeɪkwiəs, ˈækwiəs/ *adj technical* containing water or similar to water

aq·ui·line /ˈækwəlaɪn $ -laɪn, -lən/ *adj* **aquiline nose** a nose with a curved shape like the beak of an EAGLE

-ar /ə, ɑː $ ər, ɑːr/ *suffix* **1** [in adjectives] relating to something: *stellar* (=relating to stars) | *polar* (=relating to the North or South Pole) **2** [in nouns] someone who does something: *a liar* (=someone who lies)

AR /ˌeɪ, ˈɑː $ -ˈɑːr/ *n* [U] the abbreviation of ***augmented reality***

Ar·ab /ˈærəb/ *n* [C] someone whose language is Arabic and whose family comes from, or originally came from, the Middle East or North Africa

ar·a·besque /ˌærəˈbesk/ *n* [C] **1** a position in BALLET, in which you stand on one foot with the other leg stretched out straight behind you **2** a decorative pattern of flowing lines

A·ra·bi·an /əˈreɪbiən/ *adj* relating to Arabia or its people

Ar·a·bic /ˈærəbɪk/ *n* [U] the language or writing of the Arabs, which is the main language of North Africa and the Middle East —**Arabic** *adj*

ˌArabic ˈnumeral *n* [C] the sign 1,2,3,4,5,6,7,8,9, or 0, or a combination of these signs, used as a number → **Roman numeral**

ar·a·ble /ˈærəbəl/ *adj* relating to growing crops: *arable farming* | *arable land* (=land that is suitable for growing crops)

a·rach·nid /əˈræknɪd/ *n* [C] a small creature such as a SPIDER, that has eight legs and a body with two parts

ar·bi·ter /ˈɑːbɪtə $ ˈɑːrbɪtər/ *n* [C] **1** someone who influences society's opinions about what is STYLISH, socially acceptable etc: *The designer has received rave reviews from such* ***arbiters of taste*** *as 'Elle' magazine.* **2** someone or something that settles an argument between two opposing sides SYN **judge**: *The European Court of Justice will be* ***the final arbiter*** (=make the final decision) *in the dispute.*

ar·bi·trage /ˈɑːbətrɑːʒ $ ˈɑːr-/ *n* [U] *technical* the process of buying something such as raw materials or CURRENCY in one place and selling them immediately in another place in order to make a profit from the difference in prices —**arbitrageur** /ˌɑːbətrɑːˈʒɜː $ ˌɑːrbətrɑːˈʒɜːr/ (*also* **arbitrager** *BrE* /ˈɑːbətrɑːʒə $ ˈɑːrbətrɑːʒər/) *n* [C]

ar·bi·tra·ry /ˈɑːbətrəri, -tri $ ˈɑːrbətreri/ ●○○ AWL *adj* decided or arranged without any reason or plan, often unfairly: *an* ***arbitrary decision*** | *the* ***arbitrary arrests*** *of political opponents* —**arbitrariness** *n* [U] —**arbitrarily**

/ˈɑːbətrərəli $ ˌɑːrbəˈtrerəli/ *adv*: *an* ***arbitrarily chosen*** *number*

ar·bi·trate /ˈɑːbətreɪt $ ˈɑːr-/ *v* [I,T] to officially judge how an argument between two opposing sides should be settled: **[+between]** *A committee will arbitrate between management and unions.* | **[+in]** *The tribunal arbitrates in disputes.* —**arbitrator** *n* [C]

ar·bi·tra·tion /ˌɑːbəˈtreɪʃən $ ˌɑːr-/ *n* [U] the process of judging officially how an argument should be settled: *The dispute is* ***going to arbitration*** (=someone is being asked to arbitrate). | *Both sides in the dispute have agreed to* ***binding arbitration***.

ar·bo·re·al /ɑːˈbɔːriəl $ ɑːr-/ *adj technical or literary* relating to trees, or living in trees

ar·bo·re·tum /ˌɑːbəˈriːtəm $ ˌɑːr-/ *n* (*plural* **arboretums** *or* **arboreta** /-tə/) [C] a place where trees are grown for scientific study

ar·bour *BrE*, **arbor** *AmE* /ˈɑːbə $ ˈɑːrbər/ *n* [C] a shelter in a garden made by making plants grow together on a frame shaped like an ARCH

arc /ɑːk $ ɑːrk/ ●○○ *n* [C]
1 a curved shape or line: *the arc of a rainbow*
2 part of a curved line or a circle: *The Sun moves across the sky in an arc.*
3 a flash of light formed by the flow of electricity between two points —**arc** *v* [I]

ar·cade /ɑːˈkeɪd $ ɑːr-/ *n* [C] **1** a covered passage at the side of a row of buildings with PILLARS and ARCHes supporting it on one side **2** a covered passage between two streets with shops on each side of it **3** *BrE* (*also* **shopping arcade**) a large building or part of a building where there are many shops **4** an AMUSEMENT ARCADE: *arcade games*

arˈcade ˌgame *n* [C] a type of electronic game that was first popular in AMUSEMENT ARCADES (=a place where you play games by putting coins in machines) in the early 1980s, but is now usually played on a computer → **video game**

Ar·ca·di·a /ɑːˈkeɪdiə $ ɑːr-/ *literary* an area in the country where people have a pleasant simple life. Arcadia was first used in ancient Greek and Latin poetry as the name of a beautiful area of countryside in ancient Greece.

ar·cane /ɑːˈkeɪn $ ɑːr-/ *adj* secret and known or understood by only a few people: *the arcane language of the law*

arch¹ /ɑːtʃ $ ɑːrtʃ/ ●●○ *n* [C]
1 a structure with a curved top and straight sides that supports the weight of a bridge or building
2 a curved structure above a door, window etc
3 a curved structure of bones in the middle of your foot
4 something with a curved top and straight sides

ARCH

arch² *v* [I,T] to form or make something form a curved shape: *Two rows of trees arched over the driveway.* | *The dog* ***arched*** *its* ***back***.

arch³ *adj* amused because you think you understand something better than other people: *'I think he's in for a surprise,' Ian said, in a somewhat arch tone.* —**archly** *adv*

arch- /ɑːtʃ, ɑːk $ ɑːrtʃ, ɑːrk/ *prefix* belonging to the highest class or rank: *an archbishop* (=an important BISHOP) | *our archenemy* (=our worst enemy) | *the company's arch-rivals* (=main competitors)

ar·chae·ol·o·gy (*also* **archeology** *AmE*) /ˌɑːkiˈɒlədʒi $ ˌɑːrkiˈɑː-/ ●○○ *n* [U] the study of ancient societies by examining what remains of their buildings, GRAVES, tools etc —**archaeologist** *n* —**archaeological** /ˌɑːkiəˈlɒdʒɪkəl◂ $ ˌɑːrkiəˈlɑː-/ *adj*: *an* ***archaeological site*** —**archaeologically** /-kli/ *adv*

ar·cha·ic /ɑːˈkeɪ-ɪk $ ɑːr-/ *adj* **1** old and no longer used SYN **outdated** OPP **modern**: *archaic words* **2** old-fashioned and needing to be replaced: *Many smaller radio stations broadcast on archaic equipment.* **3** from or relating to ancient times SYN **ancient**: *archaic civilizations*

ar·cha·is·m /ˈɑːkeɪ-ɪzəm, ɑːˈkeɪ- $ ˈɑːrki-/ *n* [C] an old word or phrase that is no longer used

arch·an·gel /ˈɑːkeɪndʒəl $ ˈɑːrk-/ *n* [C] one of the most important ANGELs in the Jewish, Christian, and Muslim religions

arch·bish·op /ˌɑːtʃˈbɪʃəp◂ $ ˌɑːrtʃ-/ *n* [C] a priest of the highest rank, who is in charge of all the churches in a particular area

arch·bish·op·ric /ˌɑːtʃˈbɪʃəprɪk $ ˌɑːrtʃ-/ *n* [C] **1** the area governed by an archbishop **2** the rank of archbishop

arch·dea·con /ˌɑːtʃˈdiːkən◂ $ ˌɑːrtʃ-/ *n* [C] a priest of a high rank in the Anglican Church who works under a BISHOP

arch·di·o·cese /ˌɑːtʃˈdaɪəsəs, -siːs $ ˌɑːrtʃ-/ *n* [C] the area that is governed by an archbishop

arch·duke /ˌɑːtʃˈdjuːk◂ $ ˌɑːrtʃˈduːk◂/ *n* [C] a prince who belonged to the royal family of Austria

arch·en·e·my /ˌɑːtʃˈenəmi $ ˌɑːrtʃ-/ *n* (*plural* **archenemies**) [C] the main enemy

ar·che·ol·o·gy /ˌɑːkiˈɒlədʒi $ ˌɑːrkiˈɑː-/ *n* [U] an American spelling of ARCHAEOLOGY

ar·cher /ˈɑːtʃə $ ˈɑːrtʃər/ *n* [C] someone who shoots ARROWS from a BOW

ar·cher·y /ˈɑːtʃəri $ ˈɑːr-/ *n* [U] the sport of shooting ARROWS from a BOW

ar·che·type /ˈɑːkɪtaɪp $ ˈɑːr-/ *n* [C usually singular] a perfect example of something, because it has all the most important qualities of things that belong to that type: **[+of]** *France is the archetype of the centralized nation-state.* —**archetypal** /ˌɑːkɪˈtaɪpəl◂ $ ˌɑːr-/ *adj*: *Byron was the archetypal Romantic hero.*

ar·chi·pel·a·go /ˌɑːkəˈpeləgəʊ $ ˌɑːrkəˈpeləgoʊ/ *n* (*plural* **archipelagos**) [C] a group of small islands → see picture at **ISLAND**

ar·chi·tect /ˈɑːkətekt $ ˈɑːr-/ ●●○ W3 *n* [C]
1 someone whose job is to design buildings
2 the architect of sth the person who originally thought of an important and successful idea: *Tinoco was one of the architects of the government's economic reforms.*

ar·chi·tec·ture /ˈɑːkətektʃə $ ˈɑːrkətektʃər/ ●●○ S3 W3 *n*
1 [U] the style and design of a building or buildings: **[+of]** *the architecture of Venice* | **modern/classical/medieval etc architecture**
2 [U] the art and practice of planning and designing buildings: *He studied architecture at university.*
3 [U] the structure of something: *the architecture of DNA*
4 [C,U] *technical* the structure of a computer system and the way it works —**architectural** /ˌɑːkəˈtektʃərəl◂ $ ˌɑːr-/ *adj*: *architectural features* —**architecturally** *adv*: *Architecturally, Chengdu is quite different from most of China.*

ar·chive¹ /ˈɑːkaɪv $ ˈɑːr-/ ●○○ *n* [C]
1 a place where a large number of historical records are stored, or the records that are stored: *an archive of the writer's unpublished work*
2 *technical* copies of a computer's FILEs that are stored on a DISK or in the computer's memory in a way that uses less space than usual, so that the computer can keep them for a long time —**archive** *adj*: *interesting archive material* —**archival** /ɑːˈkaɪvəl $ ɑːr-/ *adj*: *archival footage of the president's visit in 1969*

archive² *v* [T] **1** to put documents, books, information etc in an archive **2** to save a computer FILE in a way that uses less space than usual, because you do not use that file often but may need it in the future —**archiving** *n* [U]: *electronic archiving systems*

ar·chi·vist /ˈɑːkɪvɪst $ ˈɑːr-/ *n* [C] someone who works in an archive

arch·way /ˈɑːtʃweɪ $ ˈɑːrtʃ-/ *n* [C] a passage or entrance under an ARCH or arches: *He was standing in the archway outside the club.*

-archy /əki, ɑːki $ ərki, ɑːrki/ *suffix* [in nouns] used to talk about a particular type of government: *anarchy* (=no government) | *monarchy* (=having a king or queen)

Arc·tic, arctic /ˈɑːktɪk $ ˈɑːrk-/ *adj* [only before noun] **1** relating to the most northern part of the world → **Antarctic**: *the Arctic island of Novaya Zemlya* → see picture at EARTH[1] **2** extremely cold: *arctic conditions* THESAURUS COLD

ˌarc ˈwelding *n* [U] a method of joining two pieces of metal together by heating them with a special tool

-ard /əd $ ərd/ *suffix* [in nouns] someone who is usually or always in a particular state: *a drunkard*

ar·dent /ˈɑːdənt $ ˈɑːr-/ *adj* [usually before noun] **1** showing strong positive feelings about an activity and determination to succeed at it: *an* ***ardent supporter*** *of free trade* **2** *literary* showing strong feelings of love: *an ardent lover* —**ardently** *adv*

ar·dour *BrE*, **ardor** *AmE* /ˈɑːdə $ ˈɑːrdər/ *n* [U] **1** very strong admiration or excitement SYN **passion**: **with ardour** *They sang with real ardour.* **2** *literary* strong feelings of love SYN **passion**

ar·du·ous /ˈɑːdjuəs $ ˈɑːrdʒuəs/ *adj* involving a lot of strength and effort: **arduous task/work** *the arduous task of loading all the boxes into the van* | **arduous journey/voyage** *an arduous journey through the mountains* —**arduously** *adv*

are /ə; *strong* ɑː $ ər ; *strong* ɑːr/ the present tense and plural of 'be'

ar·e·a /ˈeəriə $ ˈeriə/ ●●● S1 W1 AWL *n* [C]
1 a particular part of a country, town etc: *Only cheeses made in this area may be labelled 'Roquefort'.* | *Crime rates are much higher in urban areas.* | **[+of]** *Many areas of Africa have suffered severe drought this year.*
2 a part of a house, office, garden etc that is used for a particular purpose: *a* ***no-smoking area*** | *Their apartment has a large* ***kitchen area***. | *Come through into the* ***dining area***. | *the* ***reception area*** *of the hotel* | *a* ***storage area*** *on the ground floor*
3 a particular subject, range of activities, or group of related subjects: *The course covers three main* ***subject areas***. | *This study has clearly identified a major* ***problem area*** *for the National Health Service.* | *We're funding research into new areas such as law enforcement technology.* | **[+of]** *reforms in the* ***key areas*** *of health and education*
4 the amount of space that a flat surface or shape covers: **[+of]** *an area of 2,000 square miles* | *a formula to calculate the area of a circle* THESAURUS SIZE → **grey area** at GREY[1](7)

COLLOCATIONS

ADJECTIVES/NOUN + area

a rural area (=in the countryside) *Schools in rural areas are often very small.*
an urban area (=in a town or city) *90% of the English population live in urban areas.*
a remote/isolated area (=a long way from towns and cities) *a remote area of northeast Afghanistan*
the local area *He quickly made friends in the local area.*
the surrounding area (=the area around a place) | **outlying areas** (=far from the centre of a town, village etc) | **a wooded area** | **a mountainous area** | **a coastal area** | **a desert area** | **a residential area** (=a part of a town where people live) | **an industrial area** | **a built-up area** (=with a lot of buildings close together) | **a deprived area** (=where many poor people live) | **an inner-city area** (=the central part of a city, where many poor people live) | **a middle-class/working-class etc area** (=where a particular class of people live) | **a metropolitan area** (=a very large city) | **a conservation area** (=for preserving nature or old buildings) | **a geographical area** (=one that is shown on a map)

VERBS

move into/out of an area *She had just moved into the area and knew very few people.*
keep/stay away from an area *The police ordered people to stay away from the area.*
be spread out over a wide area *The town is spread out over a wide area.*

THESAURUS

area a part of a town or country, or of the world: *They live in a very wealthy area.* | *coastal areas*
region a large area of a country or the world: *the northwest region of Russia* | *desert regions*
zone an area that is different from other areas around it in some way: *a war zone* | *a no-parking zone*
district one of the areas a city or town is officially divided into, or an area of a city where a particular group live or an activity happens: *the Chelsea district of Manhattan* | **the business/financial/theatre etc district**: *the financial district of London*
neighbourhood *BrE*, **neighborhood** *AmE* /ˈneɪbəhʊd $ -ər-/ an area of a town where people live: *a friendly neighbourhood* | *There are lots of trees in our neighborhood.*
suburb an area outside the centre of a city, where people live: *a suburb of Boston*
quarter an area of a town or city where people of a particular nationality live: *the French quarter of New Orleans*
slum an area of a city that is in very bad condition, where many poor people live: *He grew up in the slums of East London.*
ghetto an area of a city where poor people of a particular race or class live: *a black baby born in the ghetto*

ˈarea ˌcode *n* [C] numbers you use before a phone number when you phone someone in a different area of the country

a·re·na /əˈriːnə/ ●○○ *n* [C]
1 a building with a large flat central area surrounded by seats, where sports or entertainments take place: *a* ***sports arena*** | *an* ***indoor arena***
2 the political/international/public etc arena all the activities and people connected with politics, public life etc: *Women are entering the political arena in larger numbers.* | *American economic activity in the international arena*

aren't /ɑːnt $ ˈɑːrənt/ **1** the short form of 'are not': *They aren't here.* **2** the short form of 'am not', used in questions: *I'm in big trouble, aren't I?*

ar·gan oil /ˈɑːgæn ˌɔɪl $ ˈɑːr-/ *n* [U] an oil obtained from the nuts of a north African tree, which is used in cooking and COSMETICS

Ar·gen·tin·i·an[1] /ˌɑːdʒənˈtɪniən◂ $ ˌɑːr-/ (*also* **Ar·gen·tine** /ˈɑːdʒəntaɪn, -tiːn $ ˈɑːr-/) *adj* relating to Argentina or its people

Argentinian[2] (*also* **Argentine**) *n* [C] someone from Argentina

ar·gon /ˈɑːgɒn $ ˈɑːrgɑːn/ *n* [U] a colourless gas that is found in very small quantities in the air and is sometimes used in electric light BULBS. It is a chemical ELEMENT: symbol Ar

ar·got /ˈɑːgəʊ $ ˈɑːrgət/ *n* [C,U] *written* expressions used by a particular group of people SYN **jargon**: *teenage argot*

ar·gu·a·ble /ˈɑːgjuəbəl $ ˈɑːr-/ ●○○ *adj*
1 not certain, or not definitely true or correct, and therefore easy to doubt SYN **debatable**: *Whether or not Webb is the best person for the job is arguable.*
2 it is arguable that used in order to give good reasons why something might be true: *It's arguable that the legislation has had little effect on young people's behaviour.*

ar·gu·a·bly /ˈɑːgjuəbli $ ˈɑːr-/ ●○○ *adv* [sentence adverb] used when giving your opinion to say that there are good reasons why something might be true: *Senna was arguably the greatest racing driver of all time.*

ar·gue /ˈɑːgjuː $ ˈɑːr-/ ●●● S2 W1 *v*
1 [I] to disagree with someone in words, often in an angry way: *We could hear the neighbours arguing.* | **[+with]** *Gallacher continued to argue with the referee throughout the game.* | **[+about]** *They were arguing about how to spend the*

A

money. | **[+over]** *The children were arguing over which TV programme to watch.*

GRAMMAR

Reciprocal verbs

Argue is a reciprocal verb. This type of verb is used when saying that two or more people do something that involves both or all of them: *He and the waiter started arguing.* You can also say: *He and the waiter started arguing with each other.* | *He started arguing with the waiter.*

Patterns with argue

- You **argue with** someone: *I wish you two would stop arguing with each other!*
- You **argue about** something or **over** something: *Let's not argue about/over small details.*

2 [I,T] to state, giving clear reasons, that something is true, should be done etc: **argue that** *Croft argued that a date should be set for the withdrawal of troops.* | ***It could be argued that*** *a dam might actually increase the risk of flooding.* | **argue for/against (doing) sth** *Baker argued against cutting the military budget.* | *She* ***argued the case*** *for changing the law.* | *The researchers put forward a* ***well-argued case*** *for banning the drug.* | *They* ***argued the point*** (=discussed it) *for hours without reaching a conclusion.*
3 argue sb into/out of doing sth *BrE* to persuade someone to do or not do something: *Joyce argued me into buying a new jacket.*
4 [T] *formal* to show that something clearly exists or is true: *The statement argues a change of attitude by the management.*
5 argue the toss *BrE informal* to continue to argue about a decision that has been made and cannot be changed: *There was no point arguing the toss after the goal had been disallowed.*

THESAURUS

argue to speak angrily to someone because you disagree with them about something: *Those two are always arguing.* | *We rarely argue with each other.*
have an argument to argue with someone for a period of time about a particular thing: *She had a long argument with the man who was selling the tickets.*
have a row /raʊ/ *BrE*, **have a fight** *especially AmE* to have an argument with someone, especially with your boyfriend, girlfriend, or a member of your family: *She was upset because she'd had a fight with her boyfriend.*
quarrel *especially BrE* to argue with someone, especially for a long time and about many different things: *The children quarrel all the time.*
squabble /ˈskwɒbəl $ ˈskwɑː-/ to argue about unimportant things: *The kids were squabbling over what to watch on TV.*
fall out with sb *BrE* to have a big argument with someone that results in you stopping having a friendly relationship with them: *I've fallen out with my best friend.*
be at each other's throats if two people are at each other's throats, they are always arguing in a very angry way: *His parents are constantly at each other's throats.*

ar·gu·ment /ˈɑːgjəmənt $ ˈɑːr-/ ●●● S1 W1 *n*
1 [C] a situation in which two or more people disagree, often angrily: **[+with]** *She had a big argument with her husband.* | **[+about/over]** *There have been a lot of arguments about who was responsible for the accident.*
2 [C] a set of reasons that show that something is true or untrue, right or wrong etc: *We need to provide a* ***convincing argument*** *as to why the system should be changed.* | **[+for/against]** *a* ***powerful argument*** *against smoking* | *A* ***good argument*** *can be made for comparing the IT revolution with the invention of writing itself.* | **[+in favour of]** *the arguments in favour of banning tobacco advertising* | **[+that]** *the familiar argument that the costs outweigh the benefits*
3 [U] when you disagree with something or question whether it is right: **do sth without (further) argument** *Ian accepted the suggestion without argument.* | **for the sake of argument** (=in order to discuss all the possibilities) *If, for the sake of argument, you aren't offered the job, what will you do?*

COLLOCATIONS

VERBS

have an argument *I could hear my parents having an argument downstairs.*
get into an argument/become involved in an argument *She didn't want to get into another argument about money.*
start/cause an argument *He was deliberately trying to start an argument.*
avoid an argument *I was anxious to avoid an argument.*
win/lose an argument | **an argument breaks out** (=it starts) | **an argument erupts** (=a big argument suddenly starts)

ADJECTIVES

a big/huge/massive argument *There was a big argument about whether we should move to a new house.*
a heated argument (=involving very strong feelings) | **a bitter argument** | **a furious/fierce argument** | **a violent argument**

THESAURUS

argument a situation in which people speak angrily to each other because they disagree about something: *an argument between two drivers over who had right of way*
row /raʊ/ *BrE*, **fight** *especially AmE* a loud angry argument with someone, especially your boyfriend, girlfriend, or someone in your family. **Row** is also used about a serious disagreement between politicians about important public issues: *There were always fights between my parents.* | *the continuing row over tax increases*
disagreement a situation in which people disagree with each other, but without shouting or getting angry: *There were the occasional disagreements about money, but mostly we got on well.*
quarrel *especially BrE* an argument, especially one in which people get angry and that lasts a long time. **Quarrel** sounds more formal and more serious than **argument** or **row**: *a bitter family quarrel*
feud /fjuːd/ a very bitter argument between two groups, especially families, which lasts for many years and causes people to hate each other: *The feud between the Hatfields and the McCoys raged for 20 years.*
dispute a public or legal argument about something, especially one which continues for a long time: *Morris has been involved in a long legal dispute with his publisher.*

AN ARGUMENT THAT IS NOT VERY SERIOUS

squabble /ˈskwɒbəl $ ˈskwɑː-/ an argument about something that is not important: *There were the usual squabbles between brothers and sisters.*
tiff *informal* an argument that is not very serious, between people who are in love: *Gary had a bit of a tiff with his girlfriend.*
misunderstanding a slight argument – a rather formal word which is often used humorously: *There was a slight misunderstanding over the bill, but everything's been sorted out now.*

ar·gu·men·ta·tive /ˌɑːgjəˈmentətɪv◂ $ ˌɑːr-/ ●○○ *adj* someone who is argumentative often argues or likes arguing: *He quickly becomes argumentative after a few drinks.*

ar·gy-bar·gy /ˌɑːdʒi ˈbɑːdʒi $ ˌɑːrdʒi ˈbɑːr-/ *n* [U] *BrE* *informal* noisy arguments or quarrelling: *Jones was sent off after a bit of argy-bargy with other players.*

a·ri·a /ˈɑːriə/ *n* [C] a song that is sung by only one person in an OPERA or ORATORIO

-arian /eəriən $ eriən/ *suffix* **1** [in nouns] someone who believes in or does a particular thing: *a vegetarian* (=someone who does not eat meat) | *a librarian* (=someone who works in a library) **2** [in adjectives] for people of this type, or relating to them: *a vegetarian restaurant*

ar·id /ˈærɪd/ *adj* **1** arid land or an arid CLIMATE is very dry because it has very little rain: *Water from the Great Lakes is pumped to* ***arid regions****.* **2** not having any new, interesting, or exciting features or qualities: *My mind was arid, all inspiration gone.* —**aridity** /əˈrɪdəti/ *n* [U]

Ar·ies /ˈeəriːz, ˈeəri-iːz $ ˈeriːz/ *n* **1** [U] the first sign of the ZODIAC, represented by a RAM (=male sheep), which some people believe affects the character and life of people born between March 21 and April 20 **2** [C] someone who was born between March 21 and April 20

a·right /əˈraɪt/ *adv BrE old use* **1** correctly: *I was not certain I had heard aright.* **2 set things aright** to deal with problems or difficulties

a·rise /əˈraɪz/ ●●○ W2 *v* (*past tense* **arose** /əˈrəʊz $ əˈroʊz/, *past participle* **arisen** /əˈrɪzən/) [I]

1 if a problem or difficult situation arises, it begins to happen: *A crisis has arisen in the Foreign Office.* | *More problems like those at the nuclear power plant are certain to arise.* THESAURUS ▸ HAPPEN

> **REGISTER**
> In everyday English, people usually say that a problem or difficult situation **comes up** rather than **arises**: *The same problems* ***come up*** *every time.*

2 if something arises from or out of a situation, event etc, it is caused or started by that situation etc: *Several important legal questions arose in the contract negotiations.* | **[+from/out of]** *Can we begin by discussing matters arising from the last meeting?*

3 when/if the need arises (*also* **should the need arise** *formal*) when or if it is necessary: *Should the need arise for extra staff, we will contact you.*

4 *literary* to get out of bed, or stand up

5 *literary* if a group of people arise, they fight for or demand something they want

6 *literary* if something arises when you are moving towards it, you are gradually able to see it as you move closer

ar·is·toc·ra·cy /ˌærəˈstɒkrəsi $ -ˈstɑː-/ *n* (*plural* **aristocracies**) [C usually singular] the people in the highest social class, who traditionally have a lot of land, money, and power: *dukes, earls, and other* ***members of the aristocracy*** | *the* ***landed aristocracy*** (=who own a lot of land) → UPPER CLASS

ar·is·to·crat /ˈærəstəkræt, əˈrɪs- $ əˈrɪs-/ *n* [C] someone who belongs to the highest social class

ar·is·to·crat·ic /ˌærəstəˈkrætɪk◂, əˌrɪs- $ əˌrɪs-/ *adj* belonging to or typical of the aristocracy SYN **noble**: *an* ***aristocratic family***

a·rith·me·tic¹ /əˈrɪθmətɪk/ ●○○ *n* [U] the science of numbers involving adding, multiplying etc → **mathematics**

ar·ith·met·ic² /ˌærɪθˈmetɪk◂/ (*also* **ar·ith·met·i·cal** /-tɪkəl/) *adj technical* involving or relating to arithmetic: *the* ***arithmetic mean*** (=average) —**arithmetically** /-kli/ *adv*

ˌarithmetic proˈgression *n* [C] a set of numbers in order of value in which a particular number is added to each to produce the next (as in 2, 4, 6, 8, ...) → **geometric progression**

ark /ɑːk $ ɑːrk/ *n* [C] **1** a large ship **2 the Ark** in the Bible, the large boat built by Noah to save his family and the animals from a flood that covered the earth → **sth went out with the ark** at GO OUT(8)

arm¹ /ɑːm $ ɑːrm/ ●●● S1 W1 *n* [C]

1 BODY one of the two long parts of your body between your shoulders and your hands: *Dave has a* ***broken arm****.* | **left/right arm** *He had a tattoo on his left arm.* | *Tim's mother* ***put*** *her* ***arms around*** *him.* | *Pat was carrying a box* ***under*** *his* ***arm****.* | *He had a pile of books* ***in his arms****.* | *They walked along the beach* ***arm in arm*** (=with their arms bent around each other's). | **take sb by the arm** (=lead someone somewhere by holding their arm) *She took him by the arm and pushed him out of the door.* | **take sb in your arms** (=gently hold someone with your arms) *Gerry took Fiona in his arms and kissed her.* | **cross/fold your arms** (=bend your arms so that they are resting on top of each other against your body) *He folded his arms and leaned back in his chair.* | *The old lady rushed to greet him,* ***arms outstretched****.*

2 WEAPONS **arms** [plural] weapons used for fighting wars: *Sales of arms to the Middle East have dramatically increased.* | **nuclear arms** | *the* ***arms trade*** | *an* ***arms dealer*** | *The government is cutting arms expenditure.* | *The United Nations will lift its* ***arms embargo*** *against the country.* | **take up arms (against sb)** (=get weapons and fight) *Boys as young as 13 are taking up arms to defend the city.* | *He appealed for the rebels to* ***lay down*** *their* ***arms*** (=stop fighting). | **under arms** (=with weapons and ready to fight) *All available forces are under arms.* → **small arms** at SMALL¹(15)

3 FURNITURE the part of a chair, SOFA etc that you rest your arms on

4 CLOTHING the part of a piece of clothing that covers your arm SYN **sleeve**

5 be up in arms to be very angry and ready to argue or fight: *Residents are up in arms about plans for a new road along the beach.*

6 with open arms if you do something with open arms, you show that you are happy to see someone or eager to accept an idea, plan etc: *We* ***welcomed*** *Henry's offer* ***with open arms****.* | *My new in-laws* ***accepted*** *me* ***with open arms****.*

7 sb would give their right arm to do sth used to say that someone would be willing to do anything to get or do something because they want it very much: *I'd give my right arm to be 21 again.*

8 hold sth at arm's length to hold something away from your body

9 keep/hold sb at arm's length to avoid developing a relationship with someone: *Petra keeps all men at arm's length to avoid getting hurt.*

10 as long as your arm *informal* a list or written document that is as long as your arm is very long: *I've got a list of things to do as long as your arm.*

11 PART OF GROUP a part of a large group that is responsible for a particular type of activity: *the* ***political arm*** *of a terrorist organization* | *Epson America is the US marketing arm of a Japanese company.*

12 OBJECT/MACHINE a long part of an object or piece of equipment: *the arm of a record player* | *There is a 15-foot arm supporting the antenna.* → see picture at **MICROSCOPE**

13 on sb's arm *old-fashioned* if a man has a woman on his arm, she is walking beside him holding his arm

14 DESIGN **arms** [plural] a set of pictures or patterns, usually painted on a SHIELD, that is used as the special sign of a family, town, university etc SYN **coat of arms**

→ **arms akimbo** at AKIMBO(1), → **babe in arms** at BABE(1), → **brothers in arms** at BROTHER¹(6), → **cost an arm and a leg** at COST²(1), → **fold sb in your arms** at FOLD¹(7), → **twist sb's arm** at TWIST¹(9)

arm² *v* [T] **1** to provide weapons for yourself, an army, a country etc in order to prepare for a fight or a war: **arm sb with sth** *The local farmers have armed themselves with rifles and pistols.* | *The rebels armed a group of 2,000 men to attack the city.* → ARMED, UNARMED **2** to provide all the information, skills, or equipment you need to do something SYN **equip**: **arm sb with sth** *Arm yourself with all the facts you need to argue your case.* | *The guidebook arms the reader with a mass of useful information.*

ar·ma·da /ɑːˈmɑːdə $ ɑːr-/ *n* [C] a large group of things, especially ships or boats: *an armada of US naval vessels*

ar·ma·dil·lo /ˌɑːməˈdɪləʊ $ ˌɑːrməˈdɪloʊ/ *n* (*plural* **armadillos**) [C] a small animal that has a shell made of hard material, and lives in parts of North and South America

A

Ar·ma·ged·don /ˌɑːməˈgedn $ ˌɑːr-/ *n* [singular, U] a terrible battle that will destroy the world: *a nuclear Armageddon*

ar·ma·ment /ˈɑːməmənt $ ˈɑːr-/ *n* **1** [C usually plural] the weapons and military equipment used by an army: *nuclear armaments* **2** [U] the process of preparing an army or country for war by giving it weapons → **disarmament**

ar·ma·ture /ˈɑːmətʃə $ ˈɑːrmətʃər/ *n* [C] *technical* **1** the part of a GENERATOR, motor etc that turns around to produce electricity, movement etc **2** a frame that you cover with clay or other soft material to make a model

arm·band /ˈɑːmbænd $ ˈɑːrm-/ *n* [C] **1** a band of material that you wear around your arm to show that you have an official position, or as a sign of MOURNING **2** [usually plural] *BrE* one of two bands of plastic filled with air that you wear around your arms when you are learning to swim SYN **waterwings**

ˈarm ˌcandy *n* [U] *informal* an attractive woman or man that someone takes with them to a public event so that people will admire them → **eye candy**: *He had just invited me along as arm candy.*

arm·chair[1] /ˈɑːmtʃeə, ˌɑːmˈtʃeə $ ˈɑːrmtʃer, ˌɑːrmˈtʃer/ ●●○ *n* [C] a comfortable chair with sides that you can rest your arms on

arm·chair[2] /ˈɑːmtʃeə $ ˈɑːrmtʃer/ *adj* **armchair traveller/fan etc** someone who talks or reads about being a traveller, or watches sport on television but does not have any real experience of doing it: *Her books about her adventures give enjoyment and inspiration to armchair travellers.* | *Armchair fans will have to pay extra to watch the best games live.*

armed /ɑːmd $ ɑːrmd/ ●●○ S3 W3 *adj*
1 carrying weapons, especially a gun OPP **unarmed**: ***Armed police** raided the building.* | *The Minister was kidnapped by **armed men** on his way to the airport.* | *The prisoners were kept under **armed guard**.* | **[+with]** *The suspect is armed with a shotgun.* | *She got ten years in prison for **armed robbery*** (=stealing using a gun). | *The president fears that **armed conflict*** (=a war) *is possible.* | *There is very little support for an **armed struggle*** (=fighting with weapons) *against the government.* | *a **heavily armed** battleship* | *Many of the gangs are **armed to the teeth*** (=carrying a lot of weapons).
2 having the knowledge, skills, or equipment you need to do something: **[+with]** *She came to the meeting armed with all the facts and figures to prove us wrong.* | *I went out, armed with my binoculars, to see what I could find in the fields.*

ˌarmed ˈforces *n* **the armed forces** [plural] a country's military organizations, including the army, navy, and air force → **military**

arm·ful /ˈɑːmfʊl $ ˈɑːrm-/ *n* [C] the amount of something that you can hold in one or both arms: **[+of]** *an armful of books*

arm·hole /ˈɑːmhəʊl $ ˈɑːrmhoʊl/ *n* [C] a hole in a shirt, dress, jacket etc that you put your arm through

ar·mi·stice /ˈɑːmɪstɪs $ ˈɑːrm-/ *n* [C] an agreement to stop fighting → **ceasefire**, **truce**

arm·let /ˈɑːmlət $ ˈɑːrm-/ *n* [C] a piece of jewellery that you wear around the top of your arm

arm·lock /ˈɑːmlɒk $ ˈɑːrmlɑːk/ *n* [C] a way in which a WRESTLER holds an opponent's arm so that he or she cannot move

ar·moire /ɑːmˈwɑː $ ɑːrmˈwɑːr/ *n* [C] *AmE* a large piece of furniture with doors, and sometimes shelves, that you hang clothes in SYN **wardrobe** *BrE*

ar·mour *BrE*, **armor** *AmE* /ˈɑːmə $ ˈɑːrmər/ ●○○ *n* [U]
1 metal or leather clothing that protects your body, worn by soldiers in battles in past times: *a knight wearing a **suit of armour***
2 a strong metal layer that protects military vehicles: *armour-clad warships*
3 a strong layer or shell that protects some plants and animals → **a chink in sb's armour** at CHINK[1](3), → **a knight in shining armour** at KNIGHT[1](4)

ar·moured *BrE*, **armored** *AmE* /ˈɑːməd $ ˈɑːrmərd/ *adj* **1** armoured vehicles have an outside layer made of metal to protect them from attack: *armored personnel carriers* **2** an armoured army uses armoured vehicles: *an armoured division*

ˌarmoured ˈcar *n* [C] **1** a military vehicle with a strong metal cover and usually a powerful gun **2** a car that has special protection from bullets etc, used especially by important people

ar·mour·er *BrE*, **armorer** *AmE* /ˈɑːmərə $ ˈɑːrmərər/ *n* [C] someone who makes or repairs weapons and ARMOUR

ˌarmour-ˈplated *BrE*, **armor-plated** *AmE adj* something, especially a vehicle, that is armour-plated has an outer metal layer to protect it —**armour plating** *n* [U] —**armour plate** *n* [U]

ar·mour·y *BrE*, **armory** *AmE* /ˈɑːməri $ ˈɑːr-/ *n* (*plural* **armouries**) [C] **1** a place where weapons are stored **2** all the skills, information etc someone has available to achieve something: *Interest rates have become powerful weapons in the government's armoury.*

arm·pit /ˈɑːmˌpɪt $ ˈɑːrm-/ *n* [C] **1** the hollow place under your arm where it joins your body **2 the armpit of sth** *AmE informal* the ugliest or worst place in a particular city or area: *Dale says Butte is the armpit of Montana.*

ˈarms conˌtrol *n* [U] the attempts by powerful countries to limit the number and types of war weapons that exist

ˈarms race *n* [C usually singular] the competition between different countries to have a larger number of powerful weapons: *the **nuclear arms race***

ˈarm-ˌtwisting *n* [U] *informal* an attempt to persuade someone to do something that they do not want to do: *No amount of arm-twisting will get me to reveal who told me.*

ˈarm-ˌwrestling *n* [U] a competition in which two people sit facing each other with one elbow on a table, and try to force the other person's hand down onto the table

ar·my /ˈɑːmi $ ˈɑːr-/ ●●● S1 W1 *n* (*plural* **armies**)
1 the army the part of a country's military force that is trained to fight on land in a war: *The army are helping to clear up after the floods.* | *an **army officer*** | ***Army units** launched attacks on bases near Jounieh port.* | *He **joined the army** when he was 17.* | **in the army** *My son is in the army.*
2 [C] a large organized group of people trained to fight on land in a war: *Rebel armies have taken control of the radio station.* | **raise an army** (=collect together and organize an army to fight a battle) *The Slovenians say they can raise an army of 20,000 men.*
3 [C] a large number of people involved in the same activity: **[+of]** *The village hall is maintained by an **army of volunteers**.*

GRAMMAR: Singular or plural verb?
- **Army** is usually followed by a singular verb: *The army **has** taken control of the country.*
- In British English, you can also use a plural verb: *The army **have** taken control of the country.*

GRAMMAR GUIDE ▸ NOUNS

A-road /ˈeɪ rəʊd $ -roʊd/ *n* [C] a type of road in Britain that is smaller than a MOTORWAY, but larger than a B-ROAD

a·ro·ma /əˈrəʊmə $ əˈroʊ-/ ●○○ *n* [C] a strong pleasant smell: *the aroma of fresh coffee* THESAURUS ▸ SMELL

a·ro·ma·ther·a·py /əˌrəʊməˈθerəpi $ əˌroʊ-/ *n* [U] a treatment that uses MASSAGE (=rubbing the body) with pleasant smelling natural oils to reduce pain and make you feel well —**aromatherapist** *n* [C]

ar·o·mat·ic /ˌærəˈmætɪk◂/ *adj* having a strong pleasant smell SYN **fragrant**: *aromatic oils* | *aromatic herbs*

a·rose /əˈrəʊz $ əˈroʊz/ *v* the past tense of ARISE

a·round /əˈraʊnd/ ●●● S1 W1 *adv, prep*
1 surrounding or on all sides of something or someone SYN **round** *BrE*: *The whole family was sitting around the*

dinner table. | *The Romans built a defensive wall around the city.* | *She wore a beautiful silk shawl around her shoulders.* | *People crowded around to see what was happening.* | *We would hear the birds singing* ***all around*** *us.*
2 moving in a circle SYN **round** *BrE*: *A helicopter was circling around, looking for somewhere to land.* | *They danced around the bonfire.*
3 in or to many places or parts of an area SYN **about** *BrE*: *He wandered around the streets, looking in shop windows.* | *There are over 40 radio stations dotted around the country.* | *When I finished college, I travelled around for a while.* | *Since it's your first day here, would you like me to show you around?* | *We started looking around for somewhere to live.*
4 a) *BrE* in an area near a place or person SYN **round**: *Is there a bank around here?* | *When you've been around a person long enough, you start to know how they'll react.* | *the new housing areas* ***in and around*** *Dublin* | *Catherine was the most beautiful girl* ***for miles around.*** **b)** if someone or something is around, they are somewhere in the place where you are: *Why is there never a policeman around when you need one?* | *Jake went down to the bar, but there was no one around that he knew.* | *Is your dad around?* | *The list is* ***somewhere around.***
5 *BrE* on the other side of something, or to the other side of it without going through it or over it SYN **round**: *If the gate's locked, you'll have to go around the side of the house.* | *There's a door around the back.* | *She ran* ***around the corner*** *and straight into the arms of John Delaney.*
6 used to say that someone or something turns so that they face in the opposite direction SYN **round** *BrE*: *Rex spun around and kicked the gun from her hand.* | *Slowly he turned the boat around towards the open sea.*
7 (*also* **around about**) used when guessing a number, amount, time etc, without being exact: *There must have been around 40,000 people in the stadium.* | *The whole project will probably cost around $3 million.* | *Most guests started to make their way home around about ten o'clock.*
THESAURUS APPROXIMATE
8 existing SYN **about** *BrE*: *That joke's been around for years.* | *Manson has a reputation as one of the most stylish designers around.*
9 if something is organized around a particular person or thing, it is organized according to their needs, wishes, ideas etc: *Why does everything have to be arranged around what Callum wants to do?* | *Their whole society was built around their religious beliefs.*
10 used to show that someone spends time in a place without doing anything useful SYN **about** *BrE*: *I've been waiting around all morning.* | *They could be seen hanging around street corners, watching the girls go by.*
11 a way around a difficult situation or problem is a way to solve it or avoid it SYN **round** *BrE*: *We must find a way around these difficulties.* | *The company is expected to get around this problem by borrowing from the banks.*
12 to other people or positions SYN **round** *BrE*: *Write your name on this list and pass it around.* | *Someone's been moving the furniture around.*
13 have been around (*also* **have been around the block a few times**) *informal* **a)** to have had experience of many different situations so that you can deal with new situations confidently: *You could tell this guy had been around a bit by the knowing way he talked.* **b)** to have had many sexual experiences – used humorously
14 *AmE* used to show the length of a line surrounding something: *Redwood trees can measure 30 or 40 feet around.* → ROUND[1], → **get around (sth)** at GET AROUND, → **go around in circles** at CIRCLE[1](5)

ˌaround-the-ˈclock *adj* [only before noun] ROUND-THE-CLOCK

a·rous·al /əˈraʊzəl/ *n* [U] excitement, especially sexual excitement

a·rouse /əˈraʊz/ ●○○ *v* [T]
1 arouse interest/expectations etc to make you become interested, expect something etc: *Matt's behavior was arousing the interest of the neighbors.*
2 arouse hostility/suspicion/resentment/anger etc to make someone feel very unfriendly and angry, or SUSPICIOUS: *A great deal of anger was aroused by Campbell's decision.*
3 to make someone feel sexually excited SYN **excite**: *She felt aroused by the pressure of his body so close to hers.*
4 *literary* to wake someone: **[+from]** *Anne had to be aroused from a deep sleep.*

ar·peg·gi·o /ɑːˈpedʒiəʊ $ ɑːrˈpedʒioʊ/ *n* (*plural* **arpeggios**) [C] the notes of a musical CHORD played separately but quickly one after the other

arr. (*also* **arr** *BrE*) **1** the written abbreviation of ***arranged by***: *music by Mozart, arr. Britten* **2** the written abbreviation of ***arrives*** or ***arrival***

ar·raign /əˈreɪn/ *v* [T] *law* to make someone come to court to hear what their crime is: **arraign sb on sth** *Thompson was arraigned on a charge of murder.* —**arraignment** *n* [C,U]

ar·range /əˈreɪndʒ/ ●●● S2 W2 *v*
1 [I,T] to organize or make plans for something such as a meeting, party, or trip: *Contact your local branch to arrange an appointment.* | *I'd like to arrange a business loan.* | **arrange to do sth** *Have you arranged to meet Mark this weekend?* | **arrange sth with sb** *Beth arranged a meeting with the marketing director.* | **arrange when/where/how etc** *We still have to arrange how to get home.* | **arrange that** *We had arranged that I would go for the weekend.* | *Matthew arrived at 2 o'clock* ***as arranged.***
2 [I,T] to make it possible for someone to have or do something: **arrange for sth** *The company will arrange for a taxi to meet you at the airport.* | **arrange for sb to do sth** *Dave arranged for someone to drive him home.*
3 [T] to put a group of things or people in a particular order or position: *Ben arranged the flowers in a vase.* | *The list is arranged alphabetically.* | **arrange sth in pairs/groups etc** *The children were arranged in lines according to height.*
4 [T] to write or change a piece of music so that it is suitable for a particular instrument: **arrange sth for sth** *a symphony arranged for the piano*

arˌranged ˈmarriage *n* [C,U] a marriage in which your parents choose a husband or wife for you

ar·range·ment /əˈreɪndʒmənt/ ●●● S2 W2 *n*
1 PLAN [C usually plural] plans and preparations that you must make so that something can happen: *Have you made all your travel arrangements?* | **[+for]** *I've agreed to help with arrangements for the party.* | *The family made arrangements for his body to be flown back.*
2 AGREEMENT [C,U] something that has been organized or agreed on SYN **agreement**: **[+between]** *An arrangement between the two couples ensured there was always someone to look after the children.* | **[+with]** *The school has an arrangement with local businesses.* | **an arrangement to do sth** *Maxine cancelled our arrangement to meet.* | **come to an/some arrangement (with sb)** (=make an agreement that is acceptable to everyone) *It would usually cost $500, but I'm sure we can come to some kind of arrangement.* | *Pets are permitted at the resort* ***by prior arrangement.***
3 WAY STH IS ORGANIZED [C usually plural] the way in which something is organized: *The airport is currently reviewing its* ***security arrangements.*** | *domestic arrangements*
4 POSITION [C,U] a group of things that are put in a particular position, or the process of doing this: **[+of]** *the traditional arrangement of desks in rows* | *a beautiful flower arrangement*
5 MUSIC [C] a piece of music that has been written or changed for a particular instrument: *a piano arrangement of an old folk song*

COLLOCATIONS
VERBS
make arrangements *You are advised to make travel arrangements well in advance.*
discuss the arrangements *We need to discuss the wedding arrangements.*
finalize the arrangements *I'm meeting him tomorrow to finalize the arrangements.*

A

ADJECTIVES/NOUN + arrangement

alternative arrangements *If the flight is cancelled you'll have to make alternative arrangements.*
special arrangements (=particular preparations other than those usually made) *Please inform us if any guests have disabilities or need any special arrangements.*
security arrangements *He was in charge of security arrangements for the president's visit.*
financial arrangements | **travel arrangements** | **holiday arrangements** *BrE* | **seating/sleeping arrangements** (=plans for where people will sit/sleep)

ar·rang·er /əˈreɪndʒə $ -ər/ *n* [C] **1** someone who changes music that has been written by someone else so that it is suitable for a particular instrument or performance **2** someone who arranges things for other people

ar·rant /ˈærənt/ *adj formal* used to emphasize how bad something is: *What **arrant nonsense**!*

ar·ray[1] /əˈreɪ/ ●○○ *n* [C]
1 [usually singular] a group of people or things, especially one that is large or impressive: **[+of]** *a dazzling array of flowers* | *a **bewildering array** of options* | **a vast/impressive/wide array** *There was a vast array of colours to choose from.*
2 *technical* a set of numbers or signs, or of computer memory units, arranged in lines across or down

array[2] *v* [T] **1** *literary* to wear particular clothes, especially clothes of good quality: **arrayed in sth** *She came in arrayed in all her finery.* **2** *literary* to arrange something in an attractive way: **arrayed on sth** *make-up arrayed on the bathroom counter* **3** *formal* to put soldiers in position ready to fight GRAMMAR **Array** is usually passive.

ar·rears /əˈrɪəz $ əˈrɪrz/ *n* [plural] **1 be in arrears** if someone is in arrears, or if their payments are in arrears, they are late in paying something that they should pay regularly, such as rent: *Many people are in arrears with their rent.* | **be four weeks/three months etc in arrears** *The rent money is two months in arrears.* | **fall/get into arrears** (=become late with payments) **2** money that you owe someone because you have not made regular payments at the correct time: *We've got 3 months' arrears to pay.* | **rent/mortgage/tax arrears** *He was ordered to pay rent arrears of £550.* **3 paid in arrears** *BrE* if your salary is paid in arrears, it is paid at the end of the period you have worked: *a salary paid monthly in arrears*

ar·rest[1] /əˈrest/ ●●● S3 W2 *v* [T]
1 if the police arrest someone, the person is taken to a POLICE STATION because the police think they have done something illegal: *He was arrested and charged with murder.* | **arrest sb for sth** *Her father was arrested for fraud.* | *I **got arrested** for careless driving.* | **arrest sb in connection with sth** *Five youths were arrested in connection with the attack.* | **arrest sb on charges/suspicion of (doing) sth** *He was arrested on suspicion of supplying drugs.* THESAURUS ▸ CATCH
2 *formal* to stop something happening or to make it happen more slowly: *The drug is used to arrest the spread of the disease.*
3 *literary* if something arrests you or arrests your attention, you notice it because it is interesting or unusual: *The mountains are the most arresting feature of the glen.*

GRAMMAR: Comparison

arrest
• The police **arrest** someone: *The police arrested a man as he fled the scene.*
• The police **arrest** someone **for** a crime: *He was arrested for robbery.*
• The police **arrest** someone **for doing** something: *They arrested him for possessing an illegal weapon.*

catch
• The police **catch** someone: *The police believe they have caught the killer.*
• You **catch** someone **doing** something: *I caught him stealing money from my purse.*

arrest[2] ●●● S3 W2 *n* [C,U] when the police take someone away and guard them because they may have done something illegal: *The police **made** several **arrests**.* | *A man is **under arrest** (=the police are guarding him) following the suspicious death of his wife.* | **place/put sb under arrest** (=arrest someone) | *He sued the police for **wrongful arrest*** (=when someone who is not guilty is arrested). → HOUSE ARREST, → **cardiac arrest** at CARDIAC

ar·riv·al /əˈraɪvəl/ ●●● W3 *n*
1 [C,U] when someone or something arrives somewhere OPP **departure**: *Only the timely arrival of the police prevented the situation from becoming worse.* | *Traffic problems account for one third of late arrivals.* | **[+at/in]** *Shortly after our arrival in London, Lisa was attacked.* | **on arrival** *A deposit is payable on arrival* (=when you arrive).
2 the arrival of sth a) the time when a new idea, product etc is first used or discovered: *The demand for phone numbers has increased since the arrival of mobile phones.* **b)** the time when an event or period of time starts to happen: *The arrival of winter can make many people feel depressed.*
3 [C] someone who has just arrived in a place: ***New arrivals** were greeted with suspicion.* | ***Late arrivals** will not be admitted to the theatre.*
4 arrivals the place at an airport where people arrive when they get off a plane: *the arrivals lounge*
5 new arrival a baby who has just been born

ar·rive /əˈraɪv/ ●●● S2 W1 *v* [I]
1 GET SOMEWHERE to get to the place you are going to: *Give me a call to let me know you've arrived safely.* | **[+in/at]** *What time does the plane arrive in New York?* | **arrive late/early** *He arrived late as usual.* | *By the time the police **arrived on the scene**, the burglars had fled.*
2 BE DELIVERED if something arrives, it is brought or delivered to you SYN **come**: *The card arrived on my birthday.*
3 HAPPEN if an event or particular period of time arrives, it happens SYN **come**: *When her wedding day arrived, she was really nervous.*
4 STH NEW if a new idea, method, product etc arrives, it begins to exist or starts being used: *Since computers arrived, my job has become much easier.*
5 BE BORN to be born: *Sharon's baby arrived just after midnight.*
6 arrive at a decision/solution/compromise etc to reach a decision, solution etc after a lot of effort: *After much consideration, we have arrived at a decision.*
7 SUCCESS **sb has arrived** used to say that someone has become successful or famous: *When he saw his name painted on the door he knew he'd arrived!*

GRAMMAR: Comparison

arrive
• You **arrive in** a city or country: *We arrived in London at 2 a.m.*
• You **arrive at** a place such as a house, hotel, or airport: *They arrived at the airport at 10.30.*
• You **arrive home**: *He arrived home at midnight.*
• You **arrive here/there/back**: *Call me when you arrive there.* ✗ Don't say: *arrive to a place* | *arrive to home* | *arrive to here/there*

get
• You **get to** a city, country, or other place: *We got to London at 2 a.m.* | *We got to the airport at 10.30.*
• You **get home**: *He got home at midnight.*
• You **get here/there/back**: *Call me when you get there.*

reach
• You **reach** a city, country, or other place: *The climbers reached the summit of the mountain.*
• You **reach home** or **reach here/there**: *You should reach there around 9.45 a.m.* ✗ Don't say: *reach to a place* | *reach to home/here/there*

THESAURUS

arrive to get to the place you are going to: *I arrived at the party at around 7 o'clock.* | *They were due to arrive home from Spain yesterday.*

get to arrive somewhere. Get is much more common in everyday English than **arrive**: *What time do you usually get to work? | I'll call you when I get home.*
reach to arrive somewhere, especially after a long journey: *When we finally reached the port, we were all very tired.*
come if someone comes, they arrive at the place where you are: *She came home yesterday. | What time did the plumber say he'd come?*
turn up (*also* **show up**) *informal* to arrive somewhere, especially when someone is waiting for you: *I'd arranged to meet Tom, but he never turned up.*
roll in *informal* to arrive somewhere later than you should and not seem worried about it: *Rebecca usually rolls in around noon.*
get in to arrive somewhere - used especially about people arriving home, or a plane, train etc arriving at an airport, station etc: *I usually get in at around 6 o'clock. | What time did your plane get in?*
come in if a plane, train, or ship comes in, it arrives in the place where you are: *We liked to watch the cruise ships come in.*
land if a plane or the passengers on it land, they arrive on the ground: *We finally landed at 2 a.m. | They watched the planes taking off and landing.*

ar·ro·gance /ˈærəgəns/ ●○○ *n* [U] when someone behaves in a rude way because they think they are very important: *I couldn't believe the arrogance of the man!*

ar·ro·gant /ˈærəgənt/ ●○○ *adj* behaving in an unpleasant or rude way because you think you are more important than other people: *He was unbearably arrogant. | an arrogant attitude* THESAURUS PROUD
—**arrogantly** *adv*

ar·ro·gate /ˈærəgeɪt/ *v* **arrogate (to yourself) sth** *formal* to claim that you have a particular right, position etc, without having the legal right to it

ar·row /ˈærəʊ $ ˈæroʊ/ ●●○ *n* [C]
1 a weapon usually made from a thin straight piece of wood with a sharp point at one end, that you shoot with a BOW
2 a sign in the shape of an arrow, used to show direction: *Follow the arrows to the X-ray department.* → STRAIGHT ARROW

ar·row·head /ˈærəʊhed $ ˈæroʊ-/ *n* [C] the sharp pointed end of an arrow

ar·row·root /ˈærəʊruːt, ˈærəruːt $ ˈæroʊ-, ˈærə-/ *n* [U] a type of flour made from the root of a tropical American plant, used in cooking to make sauces thicker

arse[1] /ɑːs $ ɑːrs/ *n* [C] *BrE spoken* **1** *not polite* the part of your body that you sit on SYN **ass** *AmE* **2** *taboo* a stupid and annoying person. Do not use this word. **3 my arse!** *not polite* used to say that you do not believe something **4 get off your arse** *not polite* used to tell someone to stop being lazy and start doing something **5 shift/move your arse** (*also* **get your arse into gear**) *not polite* used to tell someone to hurry up **6 not know your arse from your elbow** used to tell someone to hurry up to be stupid and confused about simple things → ASS, → **be a pain in the arse** at PAIN[1](3), → SMART ARSE, → **work your arse off** at WORK[1](30)

arse[2] *v BrE spoken not polite* **can't/couldn't be arsed (to do sth)** to not do something because you are feeling too lazy
arse about/around *phr v* to waste time behaving in a silly way instead of doing the things you should do

arse·hole /ˈɑːshəʊl $ ˈɑːrshoʊl/ *n* [C] *BrE spoken* **1** *taboo* a stupid and annoying person. Do not use this word. **2** *not polite* someone's ANUS

ˈarse-ˌlicker *n* [C] *BrE spoken not polite* someone who is always very nice to people in authority because he or she wants to be liked by them - used to show disapproval
—**arse-licking** *n* [U]

ar·se·nal /ˈɑːsənəl $ ˈɑːr-/ *n* [C] **1** a large group of weapons that someone has: *Britain's nuclear arsenal |* **[+of]** *an arsenal of guns* **2** a building where weapons are stored **3** the equipment, methods etc that someone can use to help them achieve something: *a software package that's now part of our arsenal |* **[+of]** *He has a whole arsenal of cameras.*

ar·se·nic /ˈɑːsənɪk $ ˈɑːr-/ *n* [U] a strong poison. It is a chemical ELEMENT: symbol As

ar·son /ˈɑːsən $ ˈɑːr-/ *n* [U] the crime of deliberately making something burn, especially a building: *The school was destroyed in an* ***arson attack***. THESAURUS CRIME

ar·son·ist /ˈɑːsənɪst $ ˈɑːr-/ *n* [C] someone who commits the crime of arson

art[1] /ɑːt $ ɑːrt/ ●●● S1 W1 *n*
1 [U] the use of painting, drawing, SCULPTURE etc to represent things or express ideas: *the Museum of Modern Art in New York | an example of early Indian art*
2 [plural, U] objects that are produced by art, such as paintings, drawings etc: *an art exhibition | an art critic | an arts and crafts fair | The exhibition features* ***works of art*** *by Picasso and Matisse.*
3 [U] the skill of drawing or painting: *He's very good at art. | an art teacher | art college*
4 the arts [plural] art, music, theatre, film, literature etc all considered together: *Government funding for the arts has been reduced.*
5 arts (*also* **the arts**) [plural] subjects you can study that are not scientific, for example history, languages etc → **humanities**
6 [C,U] the ability or skill involved in doing or making something: *Television is ruining the art of conversation. | Writing advertisements* ***is quite an art*** (=it is difficult to do). | **have/get sth down to a fine art** (=do something very well) *I've got the early morning routine down to a fine art.*

GRAMMAR
• You use **art** when talking in general about paintings, drawings etc: *She believes that art should be beautiful.* ✗ Don't say: *She believes that the art should be beautiful.*
• You use **art** when talking about a particular type of art: *He is fond of modern art.* ✗ Don't say: *He is fond of the modern art.*
• You use **the art of** when talking about the paintings, drawings etc that were produced in a particular place, or at a particular time: *There is an exhibition of the art of nineteenth-century Italy.*
• You also often use **the art of** when talking about the skill of doing something: *He is an expert in the art of lying.*
GRAMMAR GUIDE NOUNS

art[2] *v old-fashioned or biblical* **thou art** a phrase meaning 'you are'

Art Dec·o /ˌɑːt ˈdekəʊ $ ˌɑːrt ˈdekoʊ/ *n* [U] a style of art and decoration that uses simple shapes and was popular in Europe and America in the 1920s and 1930s

ˈart diˌrector *n* [C] someone whose job is to decide on how pictures, photographs etc will look in a magazine, film, advertisement etc

ar·te·fact *especially BrE* (*also* **artifact** *especially AmE*) /ˈɑːtəfækt $ ˈɑːr-/ ●○○ *n* [C] an object such as a tool, weapon etc that was made in the past and is historically important: *ancient Egyptian artefacts* THESAURUS THING

ar·ter·i·al /ɑːˈtɪəriəl $ ɑːrˈtɪr-/ *adj* **1** involving the arteries: *arterial blood* **2** [only before noun] an arterial road is one of the main roads in a city, country etc

ar·ter·i·o·scle·ro·sis /ɑːˌtɪəriəʊskləˈrəʊsəs, $ ɑːrˌtɪrioʊskləˈroʊ-/ *n* [U] a disease in which your arteries become hard, which makes it difficult for the blood to flow through

ar·te·ry /ˈɑːtəri $ ˈɑːr-/ *n* (*plural* **arteries**) [C] **1** one of the tubes that carries blood from your heart to the rest of your body → **vein** → see picture at HUMAN[1] **2** a main road, railway line, river etc

ar·te·si·an well /ɑːˌtiːziən ˈwel $ ɑːrˌtiːʒən-/ *n* [C] a WELL from which the water is forced up out of the ground by natural pressure

ˈart form *n* [C] **1** a way of expressing ideas, for example in a painting, dance, piece of writing etc: *Music is quite*

unlike any other art form. **2 make/turn sth into an art form** to do something so often that you become very good at it: *a company that's in danger of turning mismanagement into an art form*

art·ful /ˈɑːtfəl $ ˈɑːrt-/ *adj* **1** clever at deceiving people SYN **cunning**: *artful tricks* **2** designed or done in a clever and attractive way: *artful photographs* —**artfully** *adv*: *artfully concealed pockets* —**artfulness** *n* [U]

ˈ**art ˌgallery** *n* [C] a building where paintings are shown to the public

ˈ**art house** *n* [C] a cinema that shows mainly foreign films, or films made by small film companies: *art house films*

ar·thri·tis /ɑːˈθraɪtɪs $ ɑːr-/ *n* [U] a disease that causes the joints of your body to become swollen and very painful —**arthritic** /-ˈθrɪtɪk/ *adj*: *arthritic fingers*

ar·ti·choke /ˈɑːtətʃəʊk $ ˈɑːrtətʃoʊk/ *n* [C] **1** (*also* **globe artichoke**) a type of round green vegetable, which has BUDs with leaves that you eat, which are like the PETALS of a flower **2** (*also* **Jerusalem artichoke**) a plant that has a root like a potato that you can eat

ARTICHOKE
leaf
heart

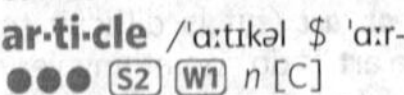

ar·ti·cle /ˈɑːtɪkəl $ ˈɑːr-/ ●●● S2 W1 *n* [C]

1 NEWSPAPER/MAGAZINE a piece of writing about a particular subject in a newspaper or magazine: **[+on/about]** *an article on environmental issues* | *The paper's* ***leading article*** (=the main article) *described the government as weak.* | *newspaper articles*

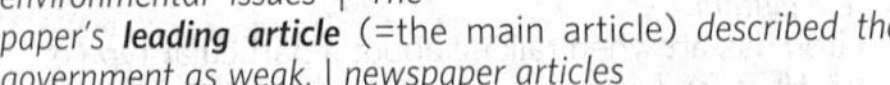

2 OBJECT *formal* a thing, especially one of a group of things SYN **item**: *household articles* | *She only took a few* ***articles of clothing*** *with her.* THESAURUS ▸ THING

3 LAW a part of a law or legal agreement that deals with a particular point: *Article 1 of the constitution guarantees freedom of religion.*

4 GRAMMAR *technical* a word used before a noun to show whether the noun refers to a particular example of something or to a general example of something. In English, 'the' is called the definite article and 'a' and 'an' are called the indefinite article.

5 articles *BrE* an agreement by which someone finishes their training, especially as a lawyer, by working for a company

6 an article of faith something that you feel very strongly about so that it affects how you think or behave

ar·ti·cled /ˈɑːtɪkəld $ ˈɑːr-/ *adj BrE* someone who is articled to a company of lawyers, ACCOUNTANTS etc, is employed by that company while they are training to become a lawyer etc: *an articled clerk* | **[+to]** *He was articled to a firm of architects.*

ar·tic·u·late[1] /ɑːˈtɪkjəleɪt $ ɑːr-/ ●○○ *v*

1 [T] *formal* to express your ideas or feelings in words: *Many people are unable to articulate the unhappiness they feel.*

2 [I,T] to pronounce what you are saying in a clear and careful way: *He was so drunk that he could barely articulate his words.*

3 [I,T] *technical* if something such as a bone in your body is articulated to another thing, it is joined to it in a way that allows movement

4 articulate sth with sth *formal* if one idea, system etc articulates with another idea, system etc, the two things are related and exist together: *a new course that is designed to articulate with the current degree course*

ar·tic·u·late[2] /ɑːˈtɪkjələt $ ɑːr-/ ●○○ *adj*

1 able to talk easily and effectively about things, especially difficult subjects OPP **inarticulate**: *bright, articulate 17-year-olds* | *a* ***highly articulate*** *speaker*

2 writing or speech that is articulate is very clear and easy to understand even if the subject is difficult —**articulately** *adv*

ar·tic·u·la·ted /ɑːˈtɪkjəleɪtɪd $ ɑːr-/ *adj* an articulated vehicle has two parts joined together to make it easier to turn

ar·tic·u·la·tion /ɑːˌtɪkjəˈleɪʃən $ ɑːr-/ *n* **1** [U] the act of making a sound or of speaking words **2** [U] the expression of thoughts or feelings in words: **[+of]** *the articulation of ideas* **3** [C,U] *technical* a joint that allows movement

ar·ti·fact /ˈɑːtəfækt $ ˈɑːr-/ *n* [C] *especially AmE* another spelling of ARTEFACT THESAURUS ▸ THING

ar·ti·fice /ˈɑːtɪfɪs $ ˈɑːr-/ *n formal* **1** [U] the use of clever tricks to deceive someone SYN **cunning** **2** [C] a trick used to deceive someone

ar·ti·fi·cial /ˌɑːtɪˈfɪʃəl◂ $ ˌɑːr-/ ●●● S3 *adj* [usually before noun]

1 not real or not made of natural things but made to be like something that is real or natural SYN **false** OPP **natural**: *artificial flowers* | *artificial light* | *artificial fertilizers*

2 an artificial situation or quality exists because someone has made it exist, and not because it is really necessary: *artificial distinctions* | *artificial barriers of gender and race*

3 artificial behaviour is not sincere – used to show disapproval OPP **genuine**: *an artificial smile* —**artificially** *adv*: *Food prices are being kept artificially low.* —**artificiality** /ˌɑːtəfɪʃiˈæləti $ ˌɑːr-/ *n* [U]

THESAURUS

artificial not real or natural, but made to look or work like something real or natural: *artificial flowers* | *He was given an artificial heart.*

synthetic made using chemical processes rather than by natural processes: *synthetic fabrics* | *a synthetic version of the drug*

man-made made by people – used especially about geographical features and materials: *a man-made lake* | *man-made fibres*

fake made to look or seem like something else, especially in order to deceive people: *a fake passport* | *fake fur*

imitation made to look like something, but not real – used especially about guns, jewellery, and leather: *imitation firearms* | *imitation pearls*

false artificial – used especially about teeth, EYELASHes, and BEARDS: *a set of false teeth*

simulated not real, but made to look, sound, or feel real, especially by means of special computers or machines: *a simulated space flight*

virtual made, done, seen etc on a computer, rather than in the real world: *a virtual tour of the garden*

ˌartificial insemiˈnation *n* [U] the medical process of making a woman or female animal PREGNANT by using a piece of equipment, rather than by having sex

ˌartificial inˈtelligence *n* [U] (*abbreviation* **AI**) the study of how to make computers do intelligent things that people can do, such as think and make decisions

ˌartificial respiˈration *n* [U] a way of making someone breathe again when they have stopped, by blowing air into their mouth

ar·til·le·ry /ɑːˈtɪləri $ ɑːr-/ *n* **1** [U] large guns, either on wheels or fixed in one place **2 the artillery** the part of the army that uses these weapons

ar·ti·san[1] /ˌɑːtɪˈzæn $ ˈɑːrtɪzən/ *n* [C] someone who does skilled work, making things with their hands SYN **craftsman**

artisan[2], **ar·tis·a·nal** /ɑːˈtɪsənəl $ ɑːr-/ *adj* **artisan bread/cheese/cider etc** food or drink that is not made in a large factory but is made in small quantities by skilled people using good quality, natural INGREDIENTS

art·ist /ˈɑːtɪst $ ˈɑːr-/ ●●● S3 W2 *n* [C]

1 someone who produces art, especially paintings or drawings: *an exhibition of paintings by local artists* → **make-up artist** at MAKE-UP(1)

2 a professional performer, especially a singer, dancer, or actor: *Many of the artists in the show donated their fee to charity.*
3 *informal* someone who is extremely good at something: *He's an artist in the kitchen.* → CON ARTIST

ar·tiste /ɑːˈtiːst $ ɑːr-/ *n* [C] a professional singer, dancer, actor etc who performs in a show

ar·tis·tic /ɑːˈtɪstɪk $ ɑːr-/ ●●○ *adj*
1 relating to art or culture: *artistic work | Opinion about the artistic merit of his paintings has been mixed.*
2 good at painting, drawing, or producing beautiful things: *John is very artistic.*
3 an artistic arrangement, design etc looks attractive and has been done with skill and imagination: *food presented in an artistic way* —**artistically** /-kli/ *adv*

art·ist·ry /ˈɑːtəstri $ ˈɑːr-/ *n* [U] skill in a particular artistic activity: *the artistry of dance*

art·less /ˈɑːtləs $ ˈɑːrt-/ *adj* **1** *literary* natural, honest, and sincere: *artless sincerity* **2** *formal* made or done without any skill: *an artless copy of European art* —**artlessly** *adv* —**artlessness** *n* [U]

Art Nou·veau /ˌɑːt nuːˈvəʊ $ ˌɑːrt nuːˈvoʊ/ *n* [U] a style of art that used plants and flowers in paintings and in the design of objects and buildings, popular in Europe and America at the end of the 19th century

ˈarts ˌcinema *n* [C] *BrE* a cinema that shows mainly foreign films or films made by small film companies

art·work /ˈɑːtwɜːk $ ˈɑːrtwɜːrk/ ●○○ *n*
1 [U] drawings and photographs that are specially prepared to be in a book, magazine, or advertisement
2 [C,U] paintings and other objects produced by artists

art·y /ˈɑːti $ ˈɑːrti/ *BrE*, **art·sy** /ˈɑːtsi $ ˈɑːrt-/ *AmE adj*
1 someone who is arty knows a lot about art, film, theatre etc – often used to show disapproval: *He was one of those arty types.* **2** intended for, or used by people who are interested in art, film, theatre etc: *an arty film | Paris's arty Marais district*

art·y-fart·y /ˌɑːti ˈfɑːti◂ $ ˌɑːrti ˈfɑːr-/ *BrE*, **art·sy-fart·sy** /ˌɑːtsi ˈfɑːtsi $ ˌɑːrtsi ˈfɑːr-/ *AmE adj informal* trying too hard to show that you are interested in art – used to show disapproval

Ar·y·an /ˈeəriən $ ˈer-/ *n* [C] someone from Northern Europe, especially someone with BLOND hair and blue eyes —**Aryan** *adj*

a·ru·gu·la /əˈruːgjələ $ -gələ/ *n* [U] ROCKET[1](4)

ar·vo /ˈɑːvəʊ $ ˈɑːrvoʊ/ *n* [C] *AusE informal* afternoon: *I'm going fishing this arvo.*

as[1] /əz; *strong* æz/ ●●● S1 W1 *prep, adv*
1 used when you are comparing two people, things, situations etc: **as ... as** *Tom's not as old as you, is he? | an old woman with hair as white as snow | Some of the doctors are paid almost twice as much as the nurses. | We work as hard as any other team in England. | Please let me know your decision* **as soon as possible** (=as soon as you can). *| His last album sold half a million copies and we hope this one will be* **just as** (=equally) *popular.*
2 used to say what job, duty, use, or appearance someone or something has: *As a parent, I feel that more should be done to protect our children. | A flat stone was used as a table. | Dad dressed up as Santa Claus.*
3 used to say what someone thinks or says a person or thing is: *The problem is regarded as serious. | The result of last week's election will be seen as a victory for the right-wing government. | He's described as being in his late teens, tall, and of slim build.*
4 when someone was in a particular age group: *As a young man, Eliot had studied art in Paris. | I'll take you to all the places I loved as a girl.* → **such as** at SUCH(2), → **as one** at ONE[2](15)

USAGE: As, like, as if/though

- Use **as** in comparisons in the expression **as ... as**, with an adjective or adverb in between: *Basketball is as popular as football here. | He can't sing as well as his brother.*
- **As** is also used after **be the same (age/size etc)**: *He is the same age as me.*
- Do not use **as** on its own before a noun or pronoun in comparisons. Use **like**: *A movie is not like a book. | Like other people, he values his privacy.*
✗ Don't say: *A movie is not as a book. | As other people, he values his privacy.*
- Use **as if/as though** before a clause describing an imaginary situation: *He talked to them as if they were children.*
- Some people also use **like** in this way, although this is often considered to be incorrect: *They act like they own the place.*
- Do not use **as if/as though** directly before a noun. You say: *You treat him as if he were your servant.*
✗ Don't say: *You treat him as if your servant.*

as[2] ●●● S1 W1 *conjunction*
1 used in comparisons: **as ... as** *They want peace as much as we do. | Helen comes to visit me as often as she can. | I can't run as fast as I used to.*
2 in the way that someone says or that something happens, or in the condition something is in: *Do as I say! | We'd better leave things as they are until the police arrive. | The money was repaid, as promised. | He did not need to keep moving house, as his father had. | Roberta was late* **as usual** (=in the way that she usually was).
3 used to say that what you are saying is already known or has been stated before: *David, as you know, has not been well lately. | As I explained on the phone, your request will be considered at the next meeting. | As Napoleon once said, attack is the best method of defence.*
4 while or when: *I saw Peter as I was getting off the bus. | As time passed, things seemed to get worse. | Just as the two men were leaving, a message arrived.*
5 used to state why a particular situation exists or why someone does something: *As it was getting late, I turned around to start for home. | We asked Philip to come with us, as he knew the road.* **THESAURUS** ▸ BECAUSE
6 though: *Unlikely as it might seem, I'm tired too. | Try as she might, Sue couldn't get the door open. | As popular as he is, the president hasn't always managed to have his own way.*
7 as for sb/sth used when you are starting to talk about someone or something new that is connected with what you were talking about before: *Kitty's got so thin. And as for Carl, he always seems to be ill. | You can ask the others, but as for myself, I'll be busy in the office.*
8 as yet [used in negatives] until and including the present time – used to say that something has not happened although it may happen in the future: *We've had no word from Colin as yet.*
9 as if .../as though ... a) in a way that makes it seem that something is true or that something is happening: *It sounds as though she's been really ill. | Gary was behaving as though nothing had happened. | Mrs Crump looked as if she was going to explode. | Beckworth shook his head as if to say 'Don't trust her'.* **b)** used to emphasize that something is not true or will not happen: *She said she'd never speak to me again. As if I cared* (=I do not care at all). *| 'Don't try any funny business, now.' 'As if I would.'* | **As if!** *spoken informal: He asked if I'd go out with him. As if* (=it is extremely unlikely that I would go out with him)*!*
10 it's not as if used to say that something cannot be the explanation for a situation or someone's behaviour because it is not true: *Why do they never go on holiday? I mean it's not as if they're poor is it? | I don't know why you're so frightened of her, it's not as if she's got any power over you.*
11 as it is a) because of the situation that actually exists – used when that situation is different from what you expected or needed: *They hoped to finish the kitchen by Friday, but as it is they'll probably have to come back next week.* **b)** already: *Just keep quiet – you're in enough trouble as it is.*
12 as from/of sth starting from a particular time or date and continuing: *As from today, you are in charge of the office. | As of now, there will be no more paid overtime.*

A

13 as against sth in comparison with something: *Profits this year are $2.5 million as against $4 million last year.*
14 as to sth a) concerning something: *Frank was very uncertain as to whether it was the right job for him.* | *advice as to which suppliers to approach* | *He kept his rivals guessing as to his real intentions.* **b)** *formal* used when you are starting to talk about something new that is connected with what you were talking about before: *As to our future plans, I think I need only say that the company intends to expand at a steady rate.*
15 as it were used when describing someone or something in a way that is not quite exact: *Jim Radcliffe became our idol, as it were, the man we all wanted to be.*
16 as is/was/does etc *formal* used to add that what you have said is also true of someone or something else: *Eve's very tall, as was her mother.* | *I voted Labour, as did my wife.*
17 as you do *BrE spoken* in the way that people usually do something or how they normally behave - often used humorously by people after they have mentioned doing something strange or unusual: *We talked, exchanged email addresses and phone numbers, as you do on planes.* | *I was driving a Ferrari through town yesterday - as you do - when I saw an old school friend outside the cinema.* → **not as such** at SUCH(8), → **as well** at WELL[1](5), → **as well as** at WELL[1](6), → **might (just) as well** at MIGHT[1](9), → **so as to do sth** at SO[2](3)

ASA /ˌeɪ es ˈeɪ/ **the ASA** (***the Advertising Standards Authority***); a British organization that controls the advertising industry in the UK. If people think that an advertisement is offensive or untrue, they can complain to this organization, which can stop the advertisement being used.

asap, **ASAP** /ˌeɪ es eɪ ˈpiː, ˈeɪsæp/ the abbreviation of ***as soon as possible***

as·bes·tos /æsˈbestəs/ *n* [U] a grey mineral that does not burn easily, that was used in the past as a building material or in protective clothing

ASBO /ˈæzbəʊ $ -boʊ/ *n* [C] (***anti-social behaviour order***) an official order in Britain which tells someone not to go to particular places or not to see particular people. The order is given by a court to someone who has been found guilty of ANTI-SOCIAL behaviour such as VANDALISM (=deliberately damaging things, especially public property) or violence towards other people. If they do not obey the order, they are given a stronger punishment, such as being sent to prison.

as·cend /əˈsend/ ●○○ *v*
1 [I] *formal* to move up through the air OPP **descend**: *The plane ascended rapidly.*
2 [T] *written* to climb something or move to a higher position OPP **descend**: *Without a word, he began to ascend the stairs.*

> **REGISTER**
> **Ascend** is used mostly in literary or technical contexts. In everyday English, people usually say **climb** or **go up**: *We started to **climb** the mountain.* | *She slowly **went up** the stairs.*

3 [I] *written* to lead up to a higher position OPP **descend**: *The road ascends steeply from the harbour.*
4 [I,T] *formal* to move to a more important or powerful job: *The number of women decreases as you ascend the professional hierarchy.*
5 ascend the throne to become king or queen
6 in ascending order if a group of things are arranged in ascending order, each thing is higher, or greater in amount, than the one before it

as·cen·dan·cy, **ascendency** /əˈsendənsi/ *n* [U] *formal* a position of power, influence, or control → **ascendant**: *moral ascendancy* | **[+of]** *the ascendancy of nationalist forces* | **[+over]** *Butler established ascendancy over his critics.* | *He slowly **gained ascendancy** in the group.* | **in the ascendancy** *a teaching method that is currently in the ascendancy*

as·cen·dant[1], **ascendent** /əˈsendənt/ *n* **be in the ascendant** *formal* to be or become powerful or popular: *a political party that's in the ascendant*

ascendant[2], **ascendent** *adj formal* becoming more powerful or popular: *a politically ascendant country*

as·cen·sion /əˈsenʃən/ *n* **1 the Ascension** in the Christian religion, when Jesus Christ left the earth and went to heaven **2** [U] *formal* when someone moves to a more important or higher position or job: *his ascension to the ranks of senior management*

as·cent /əˈsent/ *n* **1** [C usually singular] the act of climbing something or moving upwards OPP **descent**: *the first ascent of Everest* **2** [C usually singular] a path or way up to the top of something, for example a mountain OPP **descent**: *a rugged and steep ascent* **3** [U] the process of becoming more important, powerful, or successful than before SYN **rise** OPP **fall**: **[+to]** *the president's ascent to power*

as·cer·tain /ˌæsəˈteɪn $ ˌæsər-/ ●○○ *v* [I,T] *formal* to find out something SYN **establish**: *A postmortem was ordered to try to ascertain the cause of death.* | **ascertain whether/what/how etc** *Tests were conducted to ascertain whether pollution levels have dropped.* | **ascertain that** *Police had ascertained that the dead man knew his killer.* | **ascertain sth from sb/sth** *You should ascertain the level of insurance cover from the car rental company.* —**ascertainable** *adj*

> **REGISTER**
> **Ascertain** is used mainly in formal or technical contexts. In everyday English, people usually say **find out**: *We need to **find out** exactly what happened before we jump to any conclusions.*

as·cet·ic /əˈsetɪk/ *adj* living without any physical pleasures or comforts, especially for religious reasons: *an ascetic life* —**ascetic** *n* [C] —**asceticism** /-tɪsɪzəm/ *n* [U]

ASCII /ˈæski/ *n* [U] *technical* (***American Standard Code for Information Interchange***) a system used for exchanging information between computers by allowing them to recognize letters, numbers etc in the same way

as·cot /ˈæskɒt $ -kɑt/ *n* [C] *AmE* a wide piece of material that a man wears loosely folded around his neck and inside his collar SYN **cravat**

as·cribe /əˈskraɪb/ *v*
ascribe sth **to** sb/sth *phr v written* **1** to claim that something is caused by a particular person, situation etc: *The report ascribes the rise in childhood asthma to the increase in pollution.* **2** to claim that something has been written, said, made etc by a particular person: *a quotation that's often been ascribed to Marilyn Monroe* **3** to believe that something or someone has a particular quality: *Local people ascribe healing properties to this fruit.* —**ascribable** *adj*: *Most of the accidents were ascribable to the bad weather.*

ASD /ˌeɪ es ˈdiː/ *n* [C,U] the abbreviation of ***autistic spectrum disorder***

a·sep·tic /eɪˈseptɪk, ə-/ *adj technical* a wound that is aseptic is completely clean without any harmful BACTERIA OPP **infected**

a·sex·u·al /eɪˈsekʃuəl/ *adj* **1** *technical* not having sexual organs or not involving sex: *asexual reproduction* **2 a)** not having any sexual qualities **b)** not interested in sex —**asexually** *adv*

ash /æʃ/ ●○○ *n*
1 [C,U] the soft grey powder that remains after something has been burned: *cigarette ash* | *The house burnt to ashes.* → see picture at VOLCANO
2 ashes [plural] **a)** the ash that remains when a dead person's body is burned: *His **ashes were scattered** at sea.* **b)** a situation in which something is completely destroyed: *The organization has **risen from the ashes** to become very successful.* | *All her hopes and dreams had **turned to ashes**.*
3 [C,U] a tree that is common in Britain and North America, or the wood from this tree

ˌAsh ˈWednesday *n* [C,U] the first day of LENT

a·shamed /əˈʃeɪmd/ ●●○ S3 *adj* [not before noun]
1 feeling very sorry and embarrassed because of something you have done: **[+of/at]** *I felt ashamed of the things I'd said to him.* | **be ashamed to do sth** *I'm ashamed to admit that I've never read any of his books.* | **ashamed that** *She felt ashamed that she had missed her sister's wedding.* | **deeply/bitterly/thoroughly ashamed** *Alan was deeply ashamed when he remembered what he'd said.* | *Everyone cries sometimes – it's* ***nothing to be ashamed of.*** | **be/feel ashamed of yourself** *You should be ashamed of yourself.*
2 feeling uncomfortable because someone does something that embarrasses you: **[+of]** *Many children feel ashamed of their parents.* | **ashamed to be/do sth** *Their behaviour makes me ashamed to be British.*

GRAMMAR: Comparison

ashamed
• You feel **ashamed of** something or someone: *She was ashamed of her behaviour.| You should be ashamed of yourself!*

embarrassed
• You feel **embarrassed by** something or someone: *I was embarrassed by the fact that I knew nothing about cars.* | *Minna felt embarrassed by her parents.*
• You feel **embarrassed about** something: *He was clearly embarrassed about what had happened.*

THESAURUS

ashamed [not before noun] feeling very sorry and embarrassed because of something you have done, or someone connected with you has done: *You should be ashamed of yourself.* | *She felt deeply ashamed of her son's behaviour.*
humiliated [not before noun] very ashamed and upset, because someone has made you look weak or stupid, especially in front of other people: *I came out of the class feeling humiliated.*
mortified /ˈmɔːtɪfaɪd $ ˈmɔːr-/ extremely ashamed and embarrassed, especially about something you have done accidentally: *She'll be mortified when she realizes her mistake.* | *a mortified expression*
shamefaced showing by the expression on your face that you are ashamed about something: *Paul came into my office looking shamefaced and apologized for what he had done.*
feel guilty (*also* **feel bad** *especially spoken*) to feel worried and unhappy because you know that you have done something wrong. **Feel bad** is more informal than **feel guilty**: *He felt guilty about lying to his parents.* | *I felt bad about letting the team down.*
lose face to lose people's respect for you, especially by doing something that makes you look weak or stupid in front of other people: *He feels he'll lose face if he admits to his staff that he was wrong.*

ash·can /ˈæʃkæn/ *n* [C] *AmE old-fashioned* a GARBAGE CAN
ash·en /ˈæʃən/ *adj* **1** looking very pale because you are ill, shocked, or frightened SYN **white**: *His face was ashen.* **2** *literary* pale grey in colour: *ashen hills*
Ash·es, the /ˈæʃɪz/ the name given to the competition between the English and Australian cricket teams: *Australia have retained the Ashes for the third year running.*
a·shore /əˈʃɔː $ əˈʃɔːr/ *adv* on or towards the shore of a lake, river, sea etc SYN **onshore**: **come/go ashore** *Seals come ashore to breed.* | *Several dead birds had been* ***washed ashore.***
ash·ram /ˈæʃrəm/ *n* [C] a place where Hindus live together, away from other people
ash·tray /ˈæʃtreɪ/ *n* [C] a small dish where you put used cigarettes → see picture at TRAY
A·sian¹ /ˈeɪʃən, ˈeɪʒən $ ˈeɪʒən, ˈeɪʃən/ *n* [C] **1** *BrE* someone from Asia, or whose family originally came from Asia, especially India or Pakistan **2** *AmE* someone from Asia, or whose family originally came from Asia, especially from Japan, China, Korea etc
Asian² *adj* **1** *BrE* from or relating to Asia, especially India or Pakistan **2** *AmE* from or relating to Asia, especially Japan, China, Korea etc
ˌAsian-Aˈmerican *n* [C] an American citizen whose family originally came from Asia
ASIC /ˈeɪsɪk/ *n* [C] *technical* (***application specific integrated circuit***) a computer CHIP that is specially designed to do one particular job, rather than perform several jobs as part of a computer's CIRCUIT BOARD
a·side¹ /əˈsaɪd/ ●●○ S3 W3 *adv*
1 kept to be used later: *I've been* ***setting aside*** *a few pounds each week.* | *One of the rooms was* ***set aside*** *for a yoga class.* | *Try to* ***set aside*** *a few hours a week for exercise.* | *Could you* ***put*** *this cake* ***aside*** *for me?*
2 moved to one side or away from you: *He* ***pushed*** *his half-eaten salad* ***aside*** *and left.* | *He* ***stepped aside*** *to let Katherine go in first.* | *Mark* ***drew*** *me* ***aside*** *and explained the problem.* | *She swept her thick hair aside.*
3 left to be considered or dealt with later, or not considered and dealt with at all: *He* ***brushed aside*** *criticisms of his performance.* | ***Leaving aside*** *the heat, we really enjoyed our holiday.* | *You must* ***put aside*** *your pride and call her.*
4 [only after noun] used to show that something you have just said is not as important as what you are going to say next: *These problems aside, we think the plan should go ahead.*
5 aside from sb/sth *especially AmE* **a)** except for SYN **apart from**: *Aside from Durang's performance, the actors are ordinary.* **b)** in addition to: *In the poetry competition, aside from Hass, are four other entrants.*
aside² *n* [C] **1** words spoken by an actor to the people watching a play, that the other characters in the play do not hear **2** a remark made in a low voice that you only intend particular people to hear THESAURUS COMMENT **3** a remark or story that is not part of the main subject of a speech: *I should add, as an aside, that the younger the child, the faster they learn.*
as·i·nine /ˈæsənaɪn/ *adj* extremely stupid or silly SYN **ridiculous**: *What an asinine remark!*
ask¹ /ɑːsk $ æsk/ ●●● S1 W1 *v*
1 QUESTION [I,T] to speak or write to someone in order to get an answer, information, or a solution: *'What's your name?' she asked.* | *Don't ask him – he won't know.* | *That kid's always* ***asking*** *awkward* ***questions.*** | **ask who/what/where etc** *I asked him where he lived.* | **ask sb sth** *We'll have to ask someone the way to the station.* | **ask sb if/whether** *Go and ask Tom whether he's coming tonight.* | **ask (sb) about sth** *Visitors usually ask about the history of the castle.* | **ask around** (=ask in a lot of places or ask a lot of people) *I'll ask around, see if I can find you a place to stay.*
2 FOR HELP/ADVICE ETC [I,T] to make a request for help, advice, information etc: *If you need anything, you only have to ask.* | **ask sb to do sth** *Ask John to mail those letters tomorrow.* | **ask to do sth** *Karen asked to see the doctor.* | **[+for]** *Some people find it difficult to ask for help.* | **ask sb for sth** *He repeatedly asked Bailey for the report.* | **ask (sb) if/whether you can do sth** *Ask your mom if you can come with us.* | **ask that** *Was it too much to ask that he be allowed some privacy?*
3 PRICE [T] to want a particular amount of money for something you are selling: *How much is he asking?* | **ask $50/$1,000 etc for sth** *He's asking £2,000 for his car.* | *They're asking a fortune for that house.*
4 INVITE [T usually + adv/prep] to invite someone to your home, to go out with you etc: **ask sb to do sth** *Let's ask them to have dinner with us some time.* | **ask sb out** (=ask someone, especially someone of the opposite sex, to go to a film, a restaurant etc with you) *Jerry's too scared to ask her out.* | **ask sb in** (=invite someone into your house, office etc) *Don't leave them standing on the doorstep – ask them in!* | **ask sb over/round** (=invite someone to come to your home) *We must ask our new neighbours over for a drink.*
5 DEMAND [T] if you ask something of someone, you want them to do it for you: *It would be better if he cooperated, but perhaps I'm asking too much.* | **ask sth of sb** *You have no right to ask anything of me.* | *Expecting the*

A

children to do an hour's homework after school is asking a lot of them.
6 I/you can't/couldn't ask for a better sth (*also* **I/you can't/couldn't ask for more**) used to say that you are very happy with what you have or with a situation: *I couldn't ask for a better boss.*
7 be asking for trouble to do something that is very likely to have a bad effect or result: *Saying that to a feminist is just asking for trouble.*
8 ask yourself sth to think carefully and honestly about something: *You have to ask yourself where your responsibilities really lie.*

SPOKEN PHRASES
9 if you ask me used to emphasize your own opinion: *He's just plain crazy, if you ask me.*
10 don't ask me used to say you do not know the answer to something: *'Where's she gone then?' 'Don't ask me!'*
11 don't ask used to say that something is too embarrassing or strange to explain: *'What was that woman selling?' 'Don't ask.'*
12 be asking for it used to say that someone deserves something bad that happens to them: *It's his own fault he got hit – he was asking for it.*

13 be sb's for the asking *informal* if something is yours for the asking, you can have it if you want it: *The job was hers for the asking.*
ask after sb *phr v BrE* if you ask after someone, you want to know whether they are well, what they are doing etc: *I spoke to James today. He was asking after you.*
ask for sb *phr v* if you ask for someone, you want to speak to them: *There's someone at the door asking for Dad.*

GRAMMAR: Patterns with ask

- You **ask** someone something: *They asked me some difficult questions at the interview.* ✗ Don't say: *ask to someone*
- You **ask** someone **to do** something: *I asked him to open the window.*
- You **ask** someone **if** or **whether** something is true: *Ask them if they want anything to drink.*
- When you report what someone **asked**, use a verb in the past tense: *She asked if I* ***wanted*** *to go.* ✗ Don't say: *She asked if I want to go.*

GRAMMAR GUIDE ▸ **VERBS**

THESAURUS

ASK A QUESTION

ask to speak or write to someone to get an answer: *Did you ask about the price? | They asked me a lot of questions.*
inquire/enquire /ɪnˈkwaɪə $ -ˈkwaɪr/ *formal* to ask someone for information about something: *I'm writing to inquire about the job that was advertised in yesterday's 'Times'.*
demand *especially written* to ask a question in a firm or angry way: *'Why didn't you call me?', she demanded.*
interview to ask someone questions, to find out if they are suitable for a job, or as part of a television or radio interview: *When they interviewed me for the job, they didn't mention the salary.*
poll to officially ask a lot of people in order to find out their opinion on something: *Over 1,000 people were polled for the report.*

TO ASK SOMEONE ABOUT A CRIME

question/interview to ask someone a lot of questions in order to get information about a crime: *He was arrested and questioned by the police. | Detectives are interviewing the father of the missing girl.*
interrogate to ask someone a lot of detailed questions, often in an aggressive way: *The men were interrogated by the US authorities for over six hours.*
cross-examine to ask someone questions in court about the statements they made: *A second lawyer began to cross-examine the witness.*
sb is helping the police with their inquiries *formal* used in news reports when saying that the police are asking someone questions about a crime – especially when they think this person is guilty, but have not yet charged them: *He is helping the police with their inquiries in connection with the murder of Diane Jones.*

TO ASK FOR SOMETHING

ask for to tell someone you want them to give you something: *I'm going to ask for a pay rise.*
order to ask for food or drink in a restaurant: *We ordered some more coffee.*
demand to ask for something in a firm way, insisting that someone gives you what you ask for: *They're demanding immediate payment.*
request *formal* to ask for something: *The pilot requested permission to land.*
beg/plead to ask for something in an urgent way, because you want it very much and will be very unhappy if you do not get it: *He begged me for some money. | I'm not going to plead for forgiveness.*
nag/pester to keep asking someone for something, in an annoying way: *She keeps nagging me for a new phone. | People were pestering him for his autograph.*

ask² *n* **a big ask** a situation in a sports competition when someone needs to get a lot of points or do something very difficult in order to win: *We need to win the next three games. It's a big ask, but I'm confident we can do it.*
a·skance /əˈskæns, əˈskɑːns $ əˈskæns/ *adv* **look askance (at sb/sth)** if you look askance at someone or something, you do not approve of them or think they are good: *A waiter looked askance at Ellis's jeans.*
a·skew /əˈskjuː/ *adv* [not before noun] not quite straight or in the right position: *Matilda ran towards us with her hat askew.*
ˈasking ˌprice *n* [usually singular] the price that someone wants to sell something for → **selling price**
a·slant /əˈslɑːnt $ əˈslænt/ *adj, adv* [not before noun] *formal* not straight up or down, but across at an angle
a·sleep /əˈsliːp/ ●●● S2 *adj* [not before noun]
1 sleeping OPP **awake**: *Quiet! The baby's asleep.* | **fast/sound asleep** (=sleeping deeply)
2 fall asleep a) to begin to sleep: *Grandad fell asleep watching TV. | One in seven road accidents is caused by drivers* ***falling asleep at the wheel*** (=falling asleep while driving). **b)** *literary* used to mean that someone dies, when you want to avoid saying this directly
3 half asleep very tired or not completely awake: *Still half asleep, Jenny began to make the kids' breakfast.*
4 an arm or leg that is asleep has been in one position for too long, so you cannot feel it properly
5 asleep at the wheel/switch not paying attention to a situation, so that something bad happens: *Several publishers were asleep at the switch, and missed the book's potential.* → **go to sleep** at SLEEP²(3)
ASLEF /ˈæzlef/ (***Associated Society for Locomotive Engineers and Firemen***) a TRADE UNION in the UK for workers who drive or operate trains
A/S level /ˌeɪ ˈes ˌlevəl/ *n* [C,U] (***Advanced Supplementary level***) an examination that is taken by students in schools in England and Wales the year after they finish their GCSES. Students usually continue with three or four of the same subjects after A/S level, in order to complete their A LEVELS: **do/take A/S levels** | **[+in]** *I'm taking A/S levels in French, Spanish, English, and Maths.*
asp /æsp/ *n* [C] a small poisonous snake from North Africa
ASP /ˌeɪ es ˈpiː/ *n* [C] *technical* (***application service provider***) a company that supplies organized sets of computer software to other companies so that they can do business on the Internet
as·par·a·gus /əˈspærəgəs/ *n* [U] a long thin green vegetable with a point at one end → see picture at **VEGETABLE**
ASP bat·on /ˌeɪ es ˈpiː ˌbætɒn, -tn $ -bəˌtɑːn/ *n* [C] a

type of metal stick that can be made longer, used especially by police

ASPCA, the /ˌeɪ es ˌpi siː ˈeɪ/ *trademark* (**the American Society for the Prevention of Cruelty to Animals**) a CHARITY organization that takes care of animals, especially pets who have been badly treated or are not wanted, and tries to find new homes for them

as·pect /ˈæspekt/ ●●● S2 W1 AWL *n*
1 [C] one part of a situation, idea, plan etc that has many parts: **[+of]** *Dealing with people is the most important aspect of my work.* | *Alcoholism affects all aspects of family life.*
2 [C] the direction in which a window, room, front of a building etc faces: *a south-facing aspect*
3 [singular, U] *literary* the appearance of someone or something: *The storm outside gave the room a sinister aspect.*
4 [C,U] *technical* the form of a verb in grammar that shows whether an action is continuing, or happens always, again and again, or once: *'He sings' differs from 'He is singing' in aspect.*

COLLOCATIONS

ADJECTIVES

an important/significant aspect *A person's nationality is an important aspect of their identity.*
a key aspect (=a very important aspect) *There have been changes in five key aspects of education.*
a positive aspect *Describe some of the positive aspects of technological development.*
negative aspect *We have to consider tourism's negative aspects.*
a worrying/disturbing aspect | **the technical/practical/financial etc aspects**

VERBS

deal with an aspect *International banks have departments to deal with this aspect of trade.*
look at/consider/examine an aspect *Managers were asked to look at every aspect of their work.*
discuss an aspect *Police are reluctant to discuss any aspect of the investigation.*
concentrate/focus on an aspect | **cover all aspects of sth**

NOUN + aspect

the safety/security aspect *the safety aspect of nuclear power generation*
the health/business/money etc aspect

as·pen /ˈæspən/ *n* [C] a type of tree from western North America with leaves that shake a lot in the wind

As·per·ger's syn·drome /ˈæspɜːgəz ˌsɪndrəʊm $ -pɜːrgərz ˌsɪndroʊm/ (*also* **Asperger's**) *n* [U] a mental condition that makes it difficult for a person to form relationships, and can make them very interested in one particular thing

as·per·i·ty /æˈsperəti, ə-/ *n* [U] *formal* if you speak with asperity, you say something in a way that is rough or severe, showing that you are feeling impatient

as·per·sion /əˈspɜːʃən, -ʒən $ əˈspɜːrʒən/ *n* [C] *formal* an unkind remark or an unfair judgment: *No one is* ***casting aspersions on*** *you or your men, Major.*

as·phalt /ˈæsfælt $ ˈæsfɒːlt/ *n* [U] a black sticky substance that becomes hard when it dries, used for making the surface of roads —**asphalt** *v* [T]

as·phyx·i·a /æsˈfɪksiə, əs-/ *n* [U] *formal* death caused by not being able to breathe SYN **suffocation**

as·phyx·i·ate /æsˈfɪksieɪt, əs-/ *v* [I,T] *formal* to prevent someone from breathing normally, usually so that they die, or stop breathing SYN **suffocate** —**asphyxiation** /æsˌfɪksiˈeɪʃən, əs-/ *n* [U]

as·pic /ˈæspɪk/ *n* [U] **1** a clear brownish JELLY in which cold meat is sometimes served **2 preserve sth in aspic** *BrE* if something has been preserved in aspic, it has not changed for a very long time: *a part of town preserved in aspic for tourists*

as·pi·dis·tra /ˌæspəˈdɪstrə/ *n* [C] an indoor plant with broad green pointed leaves

As·pie /ˈæspi/ *n* [C] *informal* a person who has ASPERGER'S SYNDROME – used especially by people who have the condition

as·pi·rant /əˈspaɪərənt, ˈæspərənt $ əˈspaɪr-, ˈæsp-/ *n* [C] *formal* someone who hopes to get a position of importance or honour

as·pi·rate[1] /ˈæspəreɪt/ *v* [T] *technical* to make the sound of an 'h' when speaking, or to blow out air when pronouncing some CONSONANTS

as·pi·rate[2] /ˈæspərət/ *n* [C] *technical* the sound of the letter 'h', or the letter itself

as·pi·ra·tion /ˌæspəˈreɪʃən/ ●○○ *n*
1 [C usually plural, U] a strong desire to have or achieve something SYN **ambition**: *a high level of political aspiration* | **[+of]** *the aspirations of the working classes* | **[+for]** *their* ***hopes and aspirations*** *for the future*
2 [U] *technical* the sound of air blowing out that happens when some CONSONANTS are pronounced, such as the /p/ in 'pin'

as·pi·ra·tion·al /ˌæspəˈreɪʃənəl/ *adj* **1** having a strong desire to have or achieve something: *aspirational young women* **2** something that is aspirational is wanted by people because they connect it with wealth or success: *The advertisements had an aspirational look, using silk and pearls.*

as·pire /əˈspaɪə $ əˈspaɪr/ ●○○ *v* [I] to desire and work towards achieving something important: **[+to]** *college graduates aspiring to careers in finance* | **aspire to do sth** *At that time, all serious artists aspired to go to Rome.*

as·pirin /ˈæsprɪn/ ●●○ *n* (*plural* **aspirin** *or* **aspirins**) [C,U] a medicine that reduces pain, INFLAMMATION, and fever

as·pir·ing /əˈspaɪərɪŋ $ əˈspaɪr-/ *adj* [only before noun] hoping to be successful in a particular job, activity, or way of life: *aspiring young writers* | *the aspiring middle classes*

ass /æs/ *n* [C] **1** *not polite* a stupid annoying person SYN **fool**: *He's a pompous ass.* | **make an ass of yourself** (=do something stupid or embarrassing) **2** *AmE not polite* the part of your body that you sit on **3** *old use* a DONKEY → **ARSE**[1], → **get your butt/ass in gear** at **GEAR**[1](8), → **haul ass** at **HAUL**[1](5), → **kick ass** at **KICK**[1](8), → **kick sb's ass** at **KICK**[1](7), → **kiss sb's ass** at **KISS**[1](6), → **be a pain in the ass** at **PAIN**[1](3), → **piece of ass** at **PIECE**[1](24), → **SMART ARSE**, → **work your ass off** at **WORK**[1](30)

as·sail /əˈseɪl/ *v* [T] *formal* **1** if you are assailed by unpleasant thoughts or feelings, they worry or upset you: *Carla was suddenly assailed by doubts.* **2** if a strong smell or loud sound assails you, you suddenly experience it: *The smell of rotten meat assailed her nostrils.* **3** to attack someone or something violently **4** to criticize someone or something severely: *The press assailed the proposals.*

as·sai·lant /əˈseɪlənt/ *n* [C] *formal* someone who attacks another person SYN **attacker**

as·sas·sin /əˈsæsɪn/ ●○○ *n* [C] someone who murders an important person: *Kennedy's assassin is assumed to have been Lee Harvey Oswald.*

as·sas·sin·ate /əˈsæsəneɪt $ -səneɪt/ ●○○ *v* [T] to murder an important person: *a plot to assassinate the president* THESAURUS ▸ KILL

as·sas·sin·a·tion /əˌsæsəˈneɪʃən $ əˌsæsənˈeɪ-/ ●○○ *n* [C,U] the act of murdering an important person: **[+of]** *the assassination of Anwar Sadat* | *He narrowly escaped an* ***assassination attempt*** (=when someone tries but fails to kill someone else). → **character assassination** at **CHARACTER**(6)

as·sault[1] /əˈsɔːlt $ əˈsɒːlt/ ●●○ *n*
1 [C,U] the crime of physically attacking someone: *a case of robbery and assault* | **for assault** *He was jailed for assault.* | **sexual/indecent assault** *victims of indecent assault* | **[+on/against]** *sexual assaults on women* | *Several soldiers have been* ***charged with assault.*** THESAURUS ▸ CRIME

A

2 [C,U] a military attack to take control of a place controlled by the enemy: **[+on]** *an unsuccessful assault on the enemy lines* | *The refugee camp* ***came under assault*** *again last night.* | *a powerful assault rifle*
3 [C,U] a strong spoken or written criticism of someone else's ideas, plans etc SYN **attack**: **[+on]** *an assault on the capitalist system* | **under assault** *Traditional family values are increasingly under assault.*
4 [C] an attempt to achieve something difficult, especially using physical force: **[+on]** *an assault on Mt Everest* (=an attempt to climb it)

assault² ●●○ *v* [T]
1 to attack someone in a violent way: *Two men assaulted him after he left the bar.* | **sexually/indecently assault** *He was found guilty of indecently assaulting a student.* THESAURUS ATTACK
2 *literary* if a feeling, sound, smell etc assaults you, it affects you in a way that makes you uncomfortable or upset: *The noises and smells of the market assaulted her senses.*
3 to strongly criticize someone's ideas, plans etc
4 to try to do something very difficult: *a task force to assault the problems*

as,sault and 'battery *n* [U] *law* the crime of threatening to attack someone physically and then attacking them

as'sault ,course *n* [C] *BrE* an area of land with special equipment to climb, jump over, run through etc that is used for developing physical strength, especially by soldiers SYN **obstacle course** *AmE*

as·say /ə'seɪ/ *v* [T] to test a substance, especially a metal, to see how pure it is or what it is made of —**assay** /ə'seɪ, 'æseɪ $ 'æseɪ, æ'seɪ/ *n* [C]

as·sem·blage /ə'semblɪdʒ/ *n formal* **1** [C] a group of things collected together: **[+of]** *a unique assemblage of wildlife* **2** [U +of] when parts are put together in order to make something

ASSEMBLE

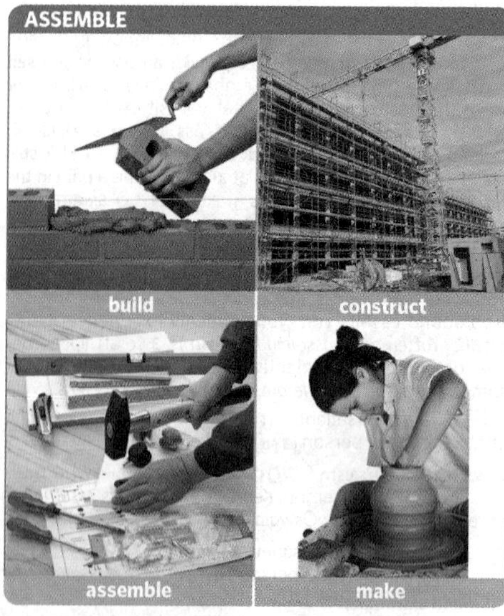

as·sem·ble /ə'sembəl/ ●○○ AWL *v*
1 [I,T] if you assemble a large number of people or things, or if they assemble, they are gathered together in one place, often for a particular purpose: *A large crowd had assembled outside the American embassy.* | *He looked around at the* ***assembled company*** (=all the people who had come there). | *She had assembled a collection of her favourite songs.* THESAURUS COLLECT, MEET
2 [T] to put all the parts of something together: *The aircraft will continue to be assembled in France.*

as·sem·bly /ə'sembli/ ●○○ AWL *n* (*plural* **assemblies**)
1 [C] a group of people who are elected to make decisions or laws for a particular country, area, or organization: *the General Assembly of the Church of Scotland* | *the speaker of the California state assembly*
2 [C,U] the meeting together of a group of people for a particular purpose: **[+of]** *an assembly of reporters* | *Police have imposed conditions on* ***public assemblies****.* | *Restrictions on* ***freedom of assembly*** *have gradually been relaxed.* | *an* ***assembly point*** (=a place where people go in a particular situation)
3 [C,U] a regular meeting of all the teachers and students of a school
4 [U] the process of putting the parts of something together: *instructions for assembly*

as'sembly ,language *n* [C,U] *technical* a computer language used in programs that are written to work with a specific kind of PROCESSOR

as'sembly ,line *n* [C] a system for making things in a factory in which the products move past a line of workers who each make or check one part

as·sem·bly·man /ə'semblimən/ *n* (*plural* **assemblymen** /-mən/) [C] *AmE* a male member of an assembly

as·sem·bly·wom·an /ə'sembli,wʊmən/ *n* (*plural* **assemblywomen** /-,wɪmɪn/) [C] *AmE* a female member of an assembly

as·sent¹ /ə'sent/ *n* [U] *formal* approval or agreement from someone who has authority: *a nod of assent* | **[+of]** *the assent of the Board of Governors* | **[+to]** *Parliament* ***gave*** *its* ***assent*** *to war.*

assent² *v* [I] *formal* to agree to a suggestion, idea etc after considering it carefully: **[+to]** *They assented to his request to work from home.*

as·sert /ə'sɜːt $ -ɜːrt/ ●○○ *v* [T]
1 to state firmly that something is true: *French cooking, she asserted, is the best in the world.* | **assert that** *He asserted that nuclear power was a safe and non-polluting energy source.*
2 assert your rights/independence/superiority etc to state very strongly your right to something: *Native Americans asserting their rights to ancestral land*
3 assert yourself to behave in a determined way and say clearly what you think: *Women began to assert themselves politically.*
4 assert itself if an idea or belief asserts itself, it begins to influence something: *National pride began to assert itself.*

as·ser·tion /ə'sɜːʃən $ -ɜːr-/ ●○○ *n* [C] something that you say or write that you strongly believe: **assertion that** *the assertion that house prices are falling* | **[+of]** *her assertion of independence* | **[+about]** *her assertions about the murder of her father* | *She* ***makes*** *very general* ***assertions*** *about marriage in the poem.* THESAURUS CLAIM

as·ser·tive /ə'sɜːtɪv $ -ɜːr-/ ●○○ *adj* behaving in a confident way, so that people notice you THESAURUS CONFIDENT —**assertively** *adv* —**assertiveness** *n* [U]: *assertiveness training*

as·sess /ə'ses/ ●●○ AWL *v* [T]
1 to make a judgment about a person or situation after thinking carefully about it SYN **judge**: **assess the impact/extent/effectiveness etc of sth** *a report to assess the impact of advertising on children* | **assess what/how etc** *The technique is being tried in classrooms to assess what effects it may have.* | **be assessed as sth** *Many of the adults were assessed as having learning difficulties.*
2 to calculate the value or cost of something: **be assessed at sth** *The value of the business was assessed at £1.25 million.*

as·sess·ment /ə'sesmənt/ ●●○ AWL *n* [C,U]
1 a process in which you make a judgment about a person or situation, or the judgment you make: **[+of]** *What's Michael's assessment of the situation?* | *a reading assessment test*
2 a calculation about the cost or value of something: *a tax assessment* → **continuous assessment** at CONTINUOUS(3)

as·ses·sor /ə'sesə $ -ər/ *n* [C] **1** someone whose job is to calculate the value of something or the amount of tax someone should pay **2** *BrE* someone who decides how well someone has done in an examination SYN **examiner**

3 someone who knows a lot about a subject or activity and who advises a judge or an official committee

as·set /'æset/ ●○○ *n* [C]
1 [usually plural] the things that a company owns, that can be sold to pay debts: **in assets** *a corporation with $9 billion in assets* | *the value of a company's assets*
2 [usually singular] something or someone that is useful because they help you succeed or deal with problems OPP **liability**: *A sense of humor is a great asset in this business.* | **be an asset to sb/sth** *I think Rachel would be an asset to the department.* → FIXED ASSETS, LIQUID ASSETS

'asset ,stripping *n* [U] the practice of buying a company cheaply and then selling all the things it owns to make a quick profit – used to show disapproval

ass·hole /'æshəʊl $ -hoʊl/ *n* [C] *AmE spoken* **1** *taboo* someone who you think is stupid and annoying. Do not use this word. **2** *not polite* the ANUS

as·sid·u·ous /ə'sɪdjuəs $ -dʒuəs/ *adj formal* very careful to make sure that something is done properly or completely SYN **meticulous**: **[+in]** *He was assiduous in his attendance at church.* —**assiduously** *adv*: *Even young children worked assiduously for a reward.* —**assiduity** /,æsə'djuːəti $ -'duː-/ *n* [U]

as·sign /ə'saɪn/ ●○○ AWL *v* [T]
1 to give someone a particular job or make them responsible for a particular person or thing: **assign sb a task/role** *I've been assigned the task of looking after the new students.* | **assign sb to sth** *Jan's been assigned to the Asian Affairs Bureau.* | **assign sb to do sth** *Madison was assigned to investigate a balloon accident.* | **assign sb sth** *Assign each student a partner.*
2 to give a particular time, value, place etc to something: *How much time have you assigned for the meeting?* | **assign sth to sth** *A code was assigned to each batch of work.*
3 to give money, equipment etc to someone to use: **assign sth to sb** *A personal bodyguard had been assigned to her.* | **assign sb sth** *They assigned me a small room.*

as·sig·na·tion /,æsɪg'neɪʃən/ *n* [C] *formal* a secret meeting, especially with someone you are having a romantic relationship with – often used humorously

as·sign·ment /ə'saɪnmənt/ ●●● S2 AWL *n*
1 [C,U] a piece of work that is given to someone as part of their job: **on an assignment** *She's gone to Italy on a special assignment.* | **on assignment** *He was killed while on assignment abroad.*
2 [C] a piece of work that a student is asked to do: *a history assignment*
3 [U] when people are given particular jobs to do
4 [C] something such as a place to sit, piece of equipment etc that you are given to use for a particular purpose: *an aeroplane seat assignment*

as·sim·i·late /ə'sɪməleɪt/ *v* **1** [T] to completely understand and begin to use new ideas, information etc SYN **absorb**: *It will take time to assimilate all these facts.* **2** [I,T] if people assimilate, or are assimilated into a country or group, they become part of that group and are accepted by the people in that group: **[+into]** *Refugees find it difficult to become assimilated into the community.*

as·sim·i·la·tion /ə,sɪmə'leɪʃən/ *n* **1** [U + of] the process of understanding and using new ideas **2** [U + into] the process of becoming an accepted part of a country or group

as·sist¹ /ə'sɪst/ ●●○ W3 AWL *v formal*
1 [I,T] to help someone to do something: **assist (sb) with/in sth** *You will be employed to assist in the development of new equipment.* | **assist sb to do sth** *We want to assist people to stay in their own homes.* **THESAURUS** ▸ HELP
2 [T] to make it easier for someone to do something: *They had no maps to assist them.*

> **REGISTER**
> In everyday English, people usually say **help** rather than **assist**: *We'll **help** in any way we can.* | *They have special software to **help** them process invoices.*

assist² *n* [C] an action that helps another player on your sports team to make a point

as·sist·ance /ə'sɪstəns/ ●●○ W2 AWL *n* [U] help or support: *We offer financial assistance to students.* | *Can I* **be of** *any* **assistance** (=can I help you)? | **with the assistance of sb/sth** *We've rebuilt the theatre with the assistance of the National Lottery.*

> **COLLOCATIONS**
>
> **VERBS**
> **need assistance** *Phone this number if you need any assistance.*
> **get/receive assistance** *She got no assistance from her family.*
> **seek assistance** *If side-effects are severe, seek medical assistance.*
> **give (sb) assistance** *Our staff can give assistance with any problems that may arise.*
> **offer assistance** *I would be grateful for any assistance you can offer.*
> **provide assistance** | **pledge/promise assistance** | **ask for/request assistance**
>
> **ADJECTIVES**
> **financial assistance** *The company may also provide financial assistance.*
> **economic assistance** *humanitarian aid and other forms of economic assistance*
> **technical assistance** *Most of our time is spent providing technical assistance to companies.*
> **legal/medical assistance** | **military assistance**
>
> **PHRASES**
> **be of assistance** (=help) *'How can I be of assistance to you?' she asked.*
> **come to sb's assistance** (=help someone) *One of her fellow passengers came to her assistance.*
> **turn to sb for assistance** (=ask them to help)

as·sis·tant¹ /ə'sɪstənt/ ●●○ W3 *adj* **assistant manager/director/cook etc** someone whose job is just below the level of manager etc

assistant² ●●○ W3 *n* [C]
1 someone who helps someone else in their work, especially by doing the less important jobs: *a clerical assistant*
2 *BrE* a SHOP ASSISTANT → **PERSONAL ASSISTANT**

as,sistant pro'fessor *n* [C] the lowest rank of PROFESSOR at an American university

as,sisted 'death *n* [C,U] ASSISTED SUICIDE

as,sisted repro'duction *n* [U] medical methods that are used to help a woman have a baby

as,sisted 'suicide *n* [C,U] when a doctor or someone else helps a person who is very ill to kill themselves in order to end their suffering → **euthanasia**

as,sistive tech'nology *n* [U] technology which helps people who have a DISABILITY

as·siz·es /ə'saɪzɪz/ *n* [plural] *old use* a meeting of a court in which a judge who travelled to different towns in Britain dealt with cases

assn. (*also* **assn** *BrE*) a written abbreviation of ***association***

assoc. (*also* **assoc** *BrE*) a written abbreviation of ***association***

as·so·ci·ate¹ /ə'səʊʃieɪt, ə'səʊsi- $ ə'soʊ-/ ●●○ S3 W2 *v*
1 [T] to make a connection in your mind between one thing or person and another: **associate sb/sth with sth** *I don't associate him with energetic sports.*
2 be associated (with sb/sth) a) to be related to a particular subject, activity etc: *problems associated with cancer treatment* **b)** (*also* **associate yourself with sb/sth**) to show that you support someone or something: *He did not associate himself with the pro-democracy movement.*

> **REGISTER**
> In everyday English, people usually say something **comes with** or **goes with** something rather than **is associated with** it: *There are some problems that **go with** this way of doing things.*

A

3 associate with sb to spend time with someone, especially someone that other people disapprove of: *I don't like these layabouts you're associating with.*

as·so·ci·ate² /əˈsəʊʃiət, əˈsəʊsi- $ əˈsoʊ-/ ●●○ *n* [C] someone who you work or do business with SYN **colleague**: *one of his business associates*

associate³ *adj* **associate member/director/head etc** someone who is a member etc of something, but who is at a lower level and has fewer rights

asˌsociated ˈcompany *n* [C] a company of which 20 to 50 per cent of the SHARES are owned by another company

Asˌsociate of ˈArts (*also* **asˈsociate deˌgree**) *n* [C] *AmE* a degree given after two years of study at a COMMUNITY COLLEGE in the US

asˌsociate proˈfessor *n* [C] a PROFESSOR at an American university whose job is above the level of ASSISTANT PROFESSOR and below the level of PROFESSOR

as·so·ci·a·tion /əˌsəʊsiˈeɪʃən, əˌsəʊʃi- $ əˌsoʊ-/ ●●○ W3 *n*

1 [C] an organization that consists of a group of people who have the same aims, do the same kind of work etc: *the Association of Master Builders* → HOUSING ASSOCIATION

THESAURUS ORGANIZATION

2 [C,U] a relationship with a particular person, organization, group etc: **[+with]** *his **close association** with the Green Party*

3 in association with sb/sth made or done with another person, organization etc: *concerts sponsored by the Arts Council in association with local businesses*

4 [C] a connection or relationship between two events, ideas, situations etc: **[+between]** *the **strong association** between the disease and middle-aged women*

5 [C] a feeling or memory that is related to a particular place, event, word etc: *Scotland has all kinds of happy associations for me.*

asˌsociation ˈfootball *n* [U] *BrE* FOOTBALL

as·so·cia·tive /əˈsəʊʃətɪv, əˈsəʊsiə- $ əˈsoʊ-/ *adj technical* reminding you of something else: *the brain's ability to form associative links between different things*

as·so·nance /ˈæsənəns/ *n* [U] *technical* similarity in the vowel sounds of words that are close together in a poem, for example between 'born' and 'warm'

as·sort·ed /əˈsɔːtɪd $ -ɔːr-/ *adj* of various different types: *paintbrushes in assorted sizes | assorted vegetables* → ILL-ASSORTED

as·sort·ment /əˈsɔːtmənt $ -ɔːr-/ *n* [C] a mixture of different things or of various kinds of the same thing: **[+of]** *a **wide assortment** of friends | an **odd assortment** of knives and forks*

asst. (*also* **asst** *BrE*) the written abbreviation of ***assistant***

as·suage /əˈsweɪdʒ/ *v* [T] *literary* to make an unpleasant feeling less painful or severe SYN **relieve**: *Nothing could **assuage** his **guilt**.*

as·sume /əˈsjuːm $ əˈsuːm/ ●●● S2 W1 AWL *v* [T]

1 to think that something is true, although you do not have definite proof SYN **presume**: **assume (that)** *I didn't see your car, so I assumed you'd gone out.* | **it seems/is reasonable to assume (that)** *It seems reasonable to assume that the book was written around 70 AD.* | **sb can safely assume that** (=it is almost certain) *I think we can safely assume that interest rates will go up again soon.* | **let us/let's assume (that)** (=used when thinking about a possible event or situation and its possible results) *Let us assume for a moment that we could indeed fire her. Should we?* | **sb/sth is assumed to be (doing) sth** *The rest of the system is assumed to be functioning well.* | **assume the worst** (=think that the worst possible thing has happened) *When it got to midnight and Paul was still not back, I began to assume the worst.*

GRAMMAR

In more formal English, you say **it is assumed that** something is true: *It is assumed that the person is innocent.*

2 assume control/responsibility etc *formal* to start to have control, responsibility etc or to start in a particular position or job: *Whoever they appoint will **assume responsibility for** all financial matters. | He **assumed power** in a bloody coup in 1990. | Jim Paton will **assume the role of** managing director.*

3 assume a manner/air/expression etc *formal* to behave in a way that does not show how you really feel, especially in order to seem more confident, happy etc than you are SYN **put on**: *Andy assumed an air of indifference whenever her name was mentioned.*

4 to start to have a particular quality or appearance SYN **take on**: *These relationships **assume** great **importance** in times of crisis. | The problem is beginning to **assume** massive **proportions**.*

5 to be based on the idea that something else is correct SYN **presuppose**: **assume (that)** *The theory assumes that both labour and capital are mobile. | Coen's economic forecast assumes a 3.5% growth rate.* → ASSUMING

asˌsumed ˈname *n* [C] if you do something under an assumed name, you do it using a name that is not your real name SYN **pseudonym**: *He's been living in Peru under an assumed name.*

as·sum·ing /əˈsjuːmɪŋ $ əˈsuː-/ AWL (*also* **asˈsuming that**) *conjunction* used when talking about an event or situation that might happen, and what you will do if it happens: *Assuming that you get a place at university, how are you going to finance your studies?*

as·sump·tion /əˈsʌmpʃən/ ●●○ W2 AWL *n*

1 [C] something that you think is true although you have no definite proof → **assume**: **[+that]** *A lot of people make the assumption that poverty only exists in the Third World. | My calculations were based on the assumption that house prices would remain steady.* | **[+about]** *People make a lot of assumptions about me.*

2 [U] *formal* when someone starts to have control or power: **[+of]** *the assumption of responsibility*

COLLOCATIONS

VERBS

make an assumption *You're making a lot of assumptions for which you have no proof.*

be based on/rest on an assumption *Our plans were based on the assumption that everyone would be willing to help.*

work on an assumption (=act according to something that may not be true) *The police seemed to be working on the assumption that he was guilty.*

ADJECTIVES

a reasonable/valid assumption *This seemed like a reasonable assumption.*

a common/general/widespread assumption *There's a common assumption that science is more difficult than other subjects.*

a basic/fundamental/underlying assumption *There is a basic assumption in international law that a state will protect its citizens.*

a correct assumption *Many people acted on the correct assumption that interest rates would rise.*

a wrong/false/mistaken assumption | **an underlying assumption** (=a belief that is used as the basis for an idea, but which may not be correct) | **a tacit/unspoken assumption** (=one that no one says aloud) | **a questionable assumption** (=one that is likely to be wrong)

as·sur·ance /əˈʃʊərəns $ əˈʃʊr-/ ●●○ AWL *n*

1 [C] a promise that something will definitely happen or is definitely true, made especially to make someone less worried: *Despite my repeated assurances, Rob still looked very nervous.* | **give/seek/receive an assurance (that)** *He gave an assurance that the work would be completed by Wednesday.*

2 [U] a feeling of calm confidence about your own abilities, or that you are right about something: *the calm*

assurance with which she handled the horse | *'Jack will never agree to that,' he said with assurance.*
3 [U] *BrE technical* insurance, especially to provide money when someone dies SYN **insurance** *AmE* → LIFE ASSURANCE

as·sure /əˈʃʊə $ əˈʃʊr/ ●●○ W3 AWL *v* [T]
1 to tell someone that something will definitely happen or is definitely true so that they are less worried SYN **reassure**: **assure sb that** *Her doctor has assured us that she'll be fine.* | *The document is genuine, **I can assure you**.* | **assure sb of sth** *The dealer had assured me of its quality.* → **rest assured** at REST[2](5) THESAURUS PROMISE
2 to make something certain to happen or to be achieved SYN **ensure**: *Excellent reviews have assured the film's success.* | **assure sb (of) sth** *A win on Saturday will assure them of promotion to Division One.*
3 assure yourself *formal* to check that something is correct or true: **assure yourself that** *Tim waited a moment to assure himself that he was not being followed.* | **[+of]** *I took steps to assure myself of her guilt.*
4 the sum assured *formal* the amount of insurance money to be paid out when someone dies

GRAMMAR: Comparison

assure
- You **assure** someone **that** something is true or will happen: *He assured them that they would be safe.*
- You **assure** someone **of** something: *He assured them of their safety.*

guarantee
- You **guarantee that** something is true or will happen: *We guarantee that you will get your money back.*
- You **guarantee to do** something: *We guarantee to give you your money back.*
- You **guarantee** someone something: *We guarantee you a full refund.*

as·sured /əˈʃʊəd $ əˈʃʊrd/ ●○○ *adj*
1 confident about your own abilities SYN **self-assured**: *an assured manner*
2 be assured of sth if you are assured of something, you will definitely get it or achieve it: *His victory means that he is now assured of a place in the final.*
3 certain to happen or to be achieved: *Her political future looks assured.*
4 the assured *BrE technical* someone whose life has been insured

as·sur·ed·ly /əˈʃʊərɪdli $ əˈʃʊr-/ *adv formal* definitely or certainly: *I am most assuredly in favour.*

as·te·risk /ˈæstərɪsk/ *n* [C] a mark like a star (*), used especially to show something interesting or important —**asterisk** *v* [T]

a·stern /əˈstɜːn $ -ɜːrn/ *adv* in or at the back of a ship

as·te·roid /ˈæstərɔɪd/ *n* [C] one of the many small PLANETS that move around the Sun, especially between Mars and Jupiter

asth·ma /ˈæsmə $ ˈæzmə/ ●○○ *n* [U] a medical condition that causes difficulties in breathing

asth·mat·ic /æsˈmætɪk $ æz-/ *n* [C] someone who suffers from asthma —**asthmatic** *adj*: *My son's asthmatic.* | *an **asthmatic attack***

as·tig·ma·tis·m /əˈstɪgmətɪzəm/ *n* [U] difficulty in seeing clearly that is caused by a change in the inner shape of the eye

as·ton·ish /əˈstɒnɪʃ $ əˈstɑː-/ ●○○ *v* [T] to surprise someone very much SYN **amaze**: *Her reply astonished me.* | ***It astonished** him **that** she had changed so little.* | ***What astonishes** me most **is** his complete lack of fear.*

as·ton·ished /əˈstɒnɪʃt $ əˈstɑː-/ ●○○ *adj* very surprised about something SYN **amazed**: **astonished to see/find/hear/learn etc** *We were astonished to find the temple still in its original condition.* | **[+by/at]** *I was astonished by the result.* | **astonished (that)** *I'm astonished that you should even think such a thing!* THESAURUS SURPRISED

as·ton·ish·ing /əˈstɒnɪʃɪŋ $ əˈstɑː-/ ●○○ *adj* so surprising that it is difficult to believe SYN **amazing**: *an astonishing decision* | *their astonishing success* THESAURUS SURPRISING —**astonishingly** *adv*: *an astonishingly good voice*

as·ton·ish·ment /əˈstɒnɪʃmənt $ əˈstɑː-/ ●○○ *n* [U] complete surprise SYN **amazement**: **in astonishment** *She stared at him in astonishment.* | **to sb's astonishment** *To my astonishment, the car was gone.*

as·tound /əˈstaʊnd/ *v* [T] to make someone very surprised or shocked SYN **astonish**: *The judge's decision astounded everyone.* | ***It astounded** me **that** she succeeded.*

as·tound·ed /əˈstaʊndɪd/ *adj* very surprised or shocked SYN **astonished**: **[+by/at]** *She was astounded by his arrogance.* THESAURUS SURPRISED

as·tound·ing /əˈstaʊndɪŋ/ *adj* so surprising that it is almost impossible to believe SYN **astonishing**: *The concert was an astounding success.* THESAURUS SURPRISING —**astoundingly** *adv*: *astoundingly beautiful scenery*

as·tra·khan /ˌæstrəˈkæn◂ $ ˈæstrəkən/ *n* [U] curly black or grey fur used for making coats and hats

as·tral /ˈæstrəl/ *adj* **1** relating to ideas and experiences connected with the mind and SPIRIT rather than the body: *out-of-body experiences and astral travel* **2** relating to the stars

a·stray /əˈstreɪ/ *adv* **1 go astray a)** to be lost or stolen: *The letter had gone astray in the post.* **b)** if a plan or action goes astray, it goes wrong: *The best-laid plans can go astray.* **2 lead sb astray a)** to encourage someone to do bad or illegal things that they would not normally do: *The older boys led him astray.* **b)** to make someone believe something that is not true: *It's easy to be led astray by the reports in the papers.*

a·stride /əˈstraɪd/ *adv, prep* **1** with one leg on each side of something: *a photograph of my mother **sitting astride** a horse* **2** on both sides of a river, road etc: *The ancient town of Bridgwater, astride the River Parrett, is an ideal touring centre.*

as·trin·gent[1] /əˈstrɪndʒənt/ *adj* **1** an astringent liquid is able to make your skin less oily or stop a wound from bleeding **2** criticizing someone very severely: *astringent remarks* **3** having a sharp acid taste —**astringency** *n* [U]

astringent[2] *n* [C,U] *technical* a liquid used to make your skin less oily or to stop a wound from bleeding

astro- /æstrəʊ, -trə $ -troʊ, -trə/ *prefix* relating to the stars, the PLANETS, or space: *an astronaut* (=someone who travels in space) | *astronomy* (=scientific study of the stars)

as·trol·o·ger /əˈstrɒlədʒə $ əˈstrɑːlədʒər/ *n* [C] someone who uses astrology to tell people about their character, life, or future

as·trol·o·gy /əˈstrɒlədʒi $ əˈstrɑː-/ *n* [U] the study of the positions and movements of the stars and how they might influence people and events → **astronomy** —**astrological** /ˌæstrəˈlɒdʒɪkəl◂ $ -ˈlɑː-/ *adj*

as·tro·naut /ˈæstrənɔːt $ -nɒːt, -nɑːt/ ●○○ *n* [C] someone who travels and works in a spacecraft

as·tron·o·mer /əˈstrɒnəmə $ əˈstrɑːnəmər/ *n* [C] a scientist who studies the stars and PLANETS

as·tro·nom·i·cal /ˌæstrəˈnɒmɪkəl◂ $ -ˈnɑː-/ *adj* **1** *informal* astronomical prices, costs etc are extremely high THESAURUS EXPENSIVE **2** [only before noun] relating to the scientific study of the stars —**astronomically** /-kli/ *adv*: *astronomically high rents*

as·tron·o·my /əˈstrɒnəmi $ əˈstrɑː-/ ●○○ *n* [U] the scientific study of the stars and PLANETS → **astrology**

as·tro·phys·ics /ˌæstrəʊˈfɪzɪks $ ˌæstrə-, -troʊ-/ *n* [U] the scientific study of the chemical structure of the stars and the forces that influence them —**astrophysicist** /-ˈfɪzɪsɪst/ *n* [C]

As·tro·Turf /ˈæstrəʊtɜːf $ -troʊtɜːrf/ *n* [U] *trademark* an artificial surface like grass that sports are played on

as·tute /əˈstjuːt $ əˈstuːt/ ●○○ *adj* able to understand situations or behaviour very well and very quickly, especially so that you can get an advantage for yourself SYN **clever**: *an astute politician | astute investments* —**astutely** *adv* —**astuteness** *n* [U]

a·sun·der /əˈsʌndə $ -ər/ *adv literary* **be torn/split/rent etc asunder** to be torn violently apart or destroyed: *a nation torn asunder by internal conflicts*

a·sy·lum /əˈsaɪləm/ ●○○ *n*
1 [U] protection given to someone by a government because they have escaped from fighting or political trouble in their own country: **apply for/seek/be granted asylum** *He has been granted asylum in France.* → POLITICAL ASYLUM
2 [C] *old use* a MENTAL HOSPITAL

aˈsylum ˌseeker *n* [C] someone who leaves their own country because they are in danger, especially for political reasons, and who asks the government of another country to allow them to live there → **refugee**: *The government halted its policy of returning Zimbabwean asylum seekers to their homeland.*

a·sym·met·ri·cal /ˌeɪsəˈmetrɪkəl/ (*also* **a·sym·met·ric** /-ˈmetrɪk◂/) *adj* **1** having two sides that are different in shape OPP **symmetrical**: *asymmetrical patterns* **2** *formal* not equal OPP **symmetrical** —**asymmetrically** /-kli/ *adv* —**asymmetry** /eɪˈsɪmətri/ *n* [U]

a·symp·to·mat·ic /æˌsɪmptəˈmætɪk, eɪ- $ eɪ-/ *adj medical* if someone or the illness that they have is asymptomatic, the illness has no physical signs

a·syn·chro·nous /eɪˈsɪŋkrənəs/ *adj technical* asynchronous computer processes happen at different times or rates

at /ət; *strong* æt/ ●●● S1 W1 *prep*
1 used to say exactly where something or someone is, or where something happens: *They live at 18 Victoria Street. | Does this train stop at Preston? | I was waiting at the bus stop. | Liz and her friend sat down at a corner table. | Turn left at the church. | We'll meet at Harry's* (=at Harry's house). *| I spent an unpleasant hour at the dentist's. | Dad's at work* (=in the place where he works). | **at the top/bottom/end etc (of sth)** *At the top of the stairs, she paused.*
2 used to say what event or activity someone is taking part in: *I met my wife at a disco. | The matter was discussed at a meeting of the finance committee. | I'm sorry, Pam's at lunch just now.*
3 used to say that someone is studying somewhere regularly: *Is Jessica still at school? | Hulme was a student at Oxford in the 1960s.*
4 used to say exactly when something happens: *The film starts at 8 o'clock.*
5 during a particular period of time: *My husband often works at night. | We go to Midnight Mass at Christmas.*
6 used to say which thing or person an action is directed towards or intended for: *He gazed up at the sky. | You don't have to shout at me. | The older girls used to throw stones at me. | The course is aimed at those aged 16 or over.*
7 used to say what or who causes an action or feeling: *The children all laughed at his jokes. | I'm surprised at you! | Dad got really mad at me for scratching the car. | her distress at having to leave*
8 used to say which subject or activity you are talking about when you say whether someone is skilful, successful etc or not: *Barbara's getting on really well at her new job.* | **good/bad etc at (doing) sth** *I've always been good at maths. | Matt's bad at handling people. | He's an expert at making things out of junk.*
9 used to say that someone or something is in a particular state: *two nations at war | Many children are still at risk from neglect or abuse.*
10 used to show a price, rate, level, age, speed etc: *old books selling at 10 cents each | You should have more sense at your age. | The Renault was travelling at about 50 mph. | Amanda rode off at a gallop.*
11 at your best/worst/most effective etc used to say that, at a particular time, someone or something is as good, bad etc as they can be: *The garden is at its best in June. | This was Federer at his most powerful.*
12 used to say what someone tries to touch, or keeps touching: *I clutched at the rope. | George was just picking at his food. | Sarah took another sip at her wine.*
13 used to say what someone tries to do: *the student's first attempt at a piece of research | They were so beautiful that I decided to have a go at growing them.*
14 because of what someone has said: *Chapman visited Austria at the invitation of his friend, Hugo Meisl. | At my suggestion, Bernard went to see his former teacher.*
15 while I'm/you're etc at it *spoken* used to suggest that someone should do something while they are doing something else: *I'm just going for a cup of coffee. Shall I bring you one while I'm at it?*
16 be at it again *informal* if you say that someone is at it again, you mean that they are doing something you disapprove of, which they have done before: *She's at it again, interfering in other people's business.*
17 at that a) also or besides: *It's a new idea, and a good one, at that.* **b)** after something is said: *Tess called him a liar and at that he stormed out of the room.*
18 be where it's at *old-fashioned informal* used to say that a place or activity is very popular, exciting, and fashionable → **at all** at ALL[1](6)

USAGE: At, in, on

Talking about time
Use **at**
- with clock times: *at one o'clock | at 6.30*
- with points of time in the day: *at midnight | at noon | at dawn | at sunset*
- with holiday periods, meaning the few days around the holiday: *at Easter | at Diwali*
- with **weekend**, in British English: *See you at the weekend! | At weekends we go out.*
Use **in**
- with parts of the day: *in the morning | in the evening | I never watch TV in the daytime.*
- with months, seasons, years, and centuries: *in May | in the summer | in 2004 | in the 21st century*
Use **on**
- with dates and specific days: *on 29th July | on Tuesday afternoons | on the last day of term*
- with **weekend**, in American English: *We sometimes go there on weekends.*

Talking about position and place
Use **at**
- with particular positions or places: *at the end of the corridor | at the back of the room | at the corner of the street*
- to mean 'next to' or 'beside': *She sat at her desk. | He stopped me at the door.*
- with words for buildings, for example **airport**, **university**, **restaurant**, **art gallery**: *at the airport | at the Lyceum theatre*
- with city or place names, when you are talking about stopping during a journey: *Does this train stop at Watford?*
Use **in**
- with a position or place, when something or someone is inside a larger thing such as a room: *in the bath | in the kitchen | in the garden | in the doorway*
- with cities, counties, states, and countries: *When will you arrive in Tokyo? | He lives in Germany. | She's working in California.*
- with the names of squares, plazas etc: *in Times Square*
Use **on**
- with a position or place, when one thing is attached to or touching another: *a spot on the end of her nose | He hung his jacket on the back of a chair.*
You can use either **in** or **on** with street names in British English. In American English, use **on**: *in Oxford Street | on the High Street | on 42nd Street | on Broadway*

at·a·vis·tic /ˌætəˈvɪstɪk◂/ *adj formal* atavistic feelings are very basic human feelings that people have felt since humans have existed

ate /et,eɪt $ eɪt/ *v* the past tense of EAT

-ate /ət, eɪt/ *suffix* **1** [in adjectives] full of or showing a particular quality: *affectionate* (=showing love) **2** [in verbs] to make something have a particular quality: *activate* (=make something start working) | *regulate* (=control something or make it regular) **3** [in nouns] a group of people with particular duties: *the electorate* (=voters) **4** [in nouns] the job, rank, or degree of a particular type of person: *She was awarded her doctorate* (=PHD). **5** [in nouns] a chemical salt formed from a particular acid: *phosphate* **—-ately** /ətli/ [in adverbs]: *fortunately*

a·tel·i·er /əˈtelieɪ $ ˌætəlˈjeɪ/ *n* [C] a room or building where an artist works SYN **studio**

a·the·is·m /ˈeɪθi-ɪzəm/ *n* [U] the belief that God does not exist → **agnosticism (agnostic)** —**atheist** *n* [C] —**atheistic** /ˌeɪθiˈɪstɪk◂/ *adj*

ath·lete /ˈæθliːt/ ●●○ *n* [C]
1 someone who competes in sports competitions, especially running, jumping, and throwing: *a professional athlete*
2 someone who is good at sports and who often does sports: *I was a natural athlete as a kid.*

ˌathlete's ˈfoot *n* [U] a medical condition in which the skin between your toes cracks

ath·let·ic /æθˈletɪk, əθ-/ ●●○ *adj*
1 physically strong and good at sport: *a tall athletic man*
2 [only before noun] relating to athletics: *athletic ability*

ath·let·i·cis·m /æθˈletəsɪzəm, əθ-/ *n* [U] the ability to play sports or do physical activities well

ath·let·ics /æθˈletɪks, əθ-/ ●○○ *n* [U]
1 *BrE* sports such as running and jumping SYN **track and field** *AmE*
2 *AmE* physical activities such as sports and exercise

GRAMMAR: Singular or plural verb?

Athletics is followed by a singular verb: ***Athletics is** largely an individual sport.*
GRAMMAR GUIDE ▸ NOUNS

-athon /əθən $ əθɑːn/ *suffix* [in nouns] an event in which a particular thing is done for a very long time, especially to collect money: *a swimathon*

-ation /eɪʃən/ *suffix* [in nouns] the act, state, or result of doing something: *an examination of the contents* (=examining them) | *the combination of several factors*

a·tish·oo /əˈtɪʃuː/ (*also* **achoo**) *BrE* a word used to represent the sound you make when you SNEEZE

-ative /ətɪv $ ətɪv, eɪtɪv/ *suffix* [in adjectives] liking something or tending to do something or show a particular quality: *talkative* (=liking to talk a lot) | *argumentative* (=enjoying arguments) | *imaginative* (=showing imagination)

at·las /ˈætləs/ ●○○ *n* [C] a book containing maps, especially of the whole world → **ROAD ATLAS**

ATM /ˌeɪ tiː ˈem/ *n* [C] (***automated teller machine***) a machine outside a bank that you use to get money from your account SYN **cashpoint**

at·mo·sphere /ˈætməsfɪə $ -fɪr/ ●●● S3 W2 *n*
1 [C,U] the feeling that an event or place gives you: *The hotel had a lovely* ***relaxed atmosphere****.* | *The atmosphere at home was rather tense.* | **[+of]** *An atmosphere of optimism dominated the conference.*
2 [U] if a place or event has atmosphere, it is interesting: *The castle was centuries old and full of atmosphere.* | *The match was lacking in atmosphere.*
3 the atmosphere the mixture of gases that surrounds the Earth
4 [C] the mixture of gases that surrounds a PLANET
5 [C usually singular] the air inside a room: *a smoky atmosphere*

at·mo·spher·ic /ˌætməsˈferɪk◂/ *adj* **1** [only before noun] relating to the Earth's atmosphere: *atmospheric pressure* **2** if a place, event, sound etc is atmospheric, it gives you a particular feeling, especially a pleasant or mysterious one: *the atmospheric decor in the restaurant* | *atmospheric music*

at·mo·spher·ics /ˌætməsˈferɪks/ *n* [plural] **1** features or qualities in something, especially a piece of music or a book, that give you a particular feeling **2** continuous crackling noises that sometimes interrupt radio broadcasts

at·oll /ˈætɒl $ ˈætɒːl, ˈætɑːl/ *n* [C] a CORAL island in the shape of a ring

at·om /ˈætəm/ ●●○ *n* [C]
1 the smallest part of an ELEMENT that can exist alone or can combine with other substances to form a MOLECULE: *carbon atoms* | **[+of]** *two atoms of hydrogen*
2 a very small amount of something - used for emphasis: **[+of]** *There isn't an atom of truth in it.*

ATOM

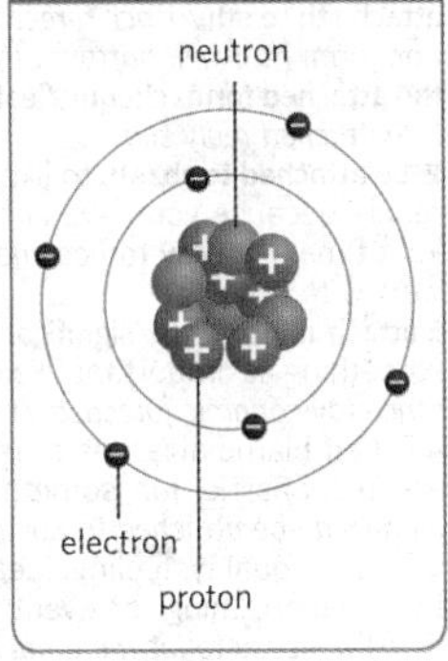

a·tom·ic /əˈtɒmɪk $ əˈtɑː-/ ●●○ *adj*
1 relating to the energy produced by splitting atoms or the weapons that use this energy: *atomic power* | *an atomic submarine*
2 relating to the atoms in a substance: *atomic weight*

aˌtomic ˈbomb (*also* **ˈatom ˌbomb**) *n* [C] a NUCLEAR bomb that splits atoms to cause an extremely large explosion

aˌtomic ˈenergy *n* [U] NUCLEAR energy

aˌtomic ˈnumber *n* [U] *technical* the number of PROTONS in the NUCLEUS (=central part) of an atom

at·om·ize (*also* **-ise** *BrE*) /ˈætəmaɪz/ *v* [T] **1** to make a substance change into ATOMS **2** *especially AmE* to divide something so that it is no longer whole or united: *a society that has become atomized*

at·om·izer (*also* **-iser** *BrE*) /ˈætəmaɪzə $ -ər/ *n* [C] a container from which you can make a liquid such as PERFUME come out in very small drops like mist

a·ton·al /eɪˈtəʊnəl, æ- $ -ˈtoʊ-/ *adj* a piece of music that is atonal is not based on a particular KEY²(4) —**atonality** /ˌeɪtəʊˈnæləti, ˌæ- $ -toʊ-/ *n* [U]

a·tone /əˈtəʊn $ əˈtoʊn/ *v* [I] *formal* to do something to show that you are sorry for having done something wrong: **[+for]** *Richard was anxious to atone for his thoughtlessness.*

a·tone·ment /əˈtəʊnmənt $ əˈtoʊn-/ *n* [singular, U] *formal* something you do to show that you are sorry for having done something wrong: **[+for]** *The priest is a representative of his people, making atonement for their sin.*

a·top /əˈtɒp $ əˈtɑːp/ *prep literary* on top of something

-ator /eɪtə $ -ər/ *suffix* [in nouns] someone or something that does something: *a narrator* (=someone who tells a story) | *a generator* (=a machine that produces electricity)

A to Z, **A-Z** /ˌeɪ tə ˈzed $ -ˈziː/ *n* [C] *trademark* a book with maps that show every street in a British city

ˌat-ˈrisk *adj* **at-risk children/patients/groups etc** people who need special care because they are likely to be in danger from violent parents, to become ill etc: **at-risk register** (=an official list of people in this situation)

at·ri·um /ˈeɪtriəm/ *n* [C] **1** a large high open space in a tall building **2** one of the two spaces in the top of your heart that push blood into the VENTRICLES

a·tro·cious /əˈtrəʊʃəs $ əˈtroʊ-/ *adj* extremely bad SYN **awful**: *atrocious weather* | *Her singing was atrocious.* THESAURUS ▸ BAD —**atrociously** *adv*

a·troc·i·ty /əˈtrɒsəti $ əˈtrɑː-/ *n* (*plural* **atrocities**) [C usually plural, U] an extremely cruel and violent action, especially during a war

A

at·ro·phy /ˈætrəfi/ *v* (**atrophied**, **atrophying**, **atrophies**) [I,T] if a part of the body atrophies or is atrophied, it becomes weak because of lack of use or lack of blood: *therapy to prevent the leg muscles from atrophying* —**atrophy** *n* [U]

at·ta·boy /ˈætəbɔɪ/ *interjection* used to tell a male person or dog that he has done something well, or to encourage him

at·tach /əˈtætʃ/ ●●● S2 W2 AWL *v*
1 [T] to fasten or connect one object to another SYN **fix**: **attach sth to sth** *Attach a recent photograph to your application form.* | *a small battery attached to a little loudspeaker* | **the attached form/cheque/leaflet etc** *Please fill in and return the attached reply slip.*
2 be attached to sb/sth to like someone or something very much, because you have known them or had them for a long time: *It's easy to become attached to the children you work with.*
3 attach importance/significance etc to sth to believe that something is important: *People attach too much importance to economic forecasts.*
4 [I,T] if blame attaches or is attached to someone, they are responsible for something bad that happens: *No blame can be attached to Roy for the incident.*
5 [I,T] if a quality, feeling, idea etc attaches or is attached to a person, thing, or event, it is connected with them: **[+to]** *It's easy to let the emotions attached to one situation spill over into others.*
6 be attached to sth a) to work for part of a particular organization, especially for a short period of time: *He was attached to the foreign affairs department of a Japanese newspaper.* **b)** to be part of a bigger organization: *The Food Ministry is attached to the Ministry of Agriculture.*
7 [T] to connect a document or FILE to an email so that you can send them together → **attachment**
8 attach yourself to sb to join someone and spend a lot of time with them, often without being invited or welcome: *A young man from Canada had attached himself to Sam.*
9 attach a condition (to sth) to allow something to happen, but only if someone agrees to do a particular thing or accept a particular idea: *When approving a merger, the commission can attach conditions.*
10 attach a label to sb/sth to think of or describe someone or something as being a particular thing, especially in a very general way: *You can't really attach a label to this type of art.*

at·taché /əˈtæʃeɪ $ ˌætəˈʃeɪ/ *n* [C] someone who works in an EMBASSY and deals with a particular subject: *a cultural attaché*

atˈtaché ˌcase / $ ˌ..ˈ. ˌ./ *n* [C] a thin case used for carrying business documents

at·tach·ment /əˈtætʃmənt/ ●●○ AWL *n*
1 [C,U] a feeling that you like or love someone or something and that you would be unhappy without them: **[+to/for]** *a child's attachment to its mother*
2 [C] a part that you can put onto a machine to make it do a particular job: *The vacuum cleaner has various attachments.*
3 [U] belief in and loyalty towards a particular idea, organization etc: **[+to/for]** *old people's attachment to traditional customs*
4 [C] a document or FILE that is sent with an email message: *I'll send the spreadsheet as an attachment.*
5 [C,U] when you fasten or connect one thing to another, or the thing that you use to do this: *Hooks were fixed to the wall for the attachment of the ropes.* | *the attachments that secure your boots firmly to the skis*
6 on attachment working for a particular organization, especially for a short period of time: *He was sent on attachment to their offices in Hong Kong.*
7 [C,U] *law* a situation in which part of the money someone earns or money that is owed to them is taken by a court of law and used to pay their debts
8 [C] *technical* a piece of paper fastened to a document such as an insurance agreement, which shows a special condition of the agreement

at·tack¹ /əˈtæk/ ●●● S2 W2 *n*
1 VIOLENCE AGAINST SB/STH [C] an act of violence that is intended to hurt a person or damage a place: **[+on]** *There have been several attacks on foreigners recently.* | *a* **bomb attack** | *a* **knife attack** | *an* **arson attack** (=an attempt to destroy a building using fire) | *victims of* **racial attacks**
2 IN A WAR [C,U] the act of using weapons against an enemy in a war: *The attack began at dawn.* | **[+on]** *the attack on Pearl Harbor* | **be/come under attack** *Once again we came under attack from enemy fighter planes.* | *Rebel forces* **launched** (=started) *an* **attack** *late Sunday night.* | **air/missile/nuclear etc attack** *the threat of nuclear attack*
3 CRITICISM [C,U] a strong and direct criticism of someone or something: **[+on]** *The magazine recently published a vicious* **personal attack** *on the novelist.* | **be/come under attack** (=be strongly criticized) *The company has come under fierce attack for its decision to close the factory.* | **go on the attack** (=start to criticize someone severely)
4 ILLNESS [C] a sudden short period of suffering from an illness, especially an illness that you have often: **[+of]** *I had a bad attack of flu at Christmas.* | *He died after* **suffering** *a severe asthma* **attack**. → HEART ATTACK
5 EMOTION [C] a short period of time when you suddenly feel extremely frightened or worried and cannot think normally or deal with the situation: **panic/anxiety attack** *Her heart began to pound frantically, as if she were having a panic attack.* | **[+of]** *a sudden attack of nerves*
6 ATTEMPT TO STOP STH [C,U] actions that are intended to get rid of or stop something such as a system, a set of laws etc: **[+on]** *The new measures were seen by many as an attack on the Scottish way of life.*
7 SPORT **a)** [C,U] an attempt by a player or group of players to score GOALS or win points **b)** [singular] *BrE* the players in a team that are responsible for trying to score GOALS or win points SYN **offense** *AmE* → **defence**: **in attack** *Heath will play alongside Smith in attack.*
8 DAMAGE [C,U] when something such as a disease, insect, or chemical damages something: *Unfortunately, the carved ceilings have suffered woodworm attack over the years.*

attack² ●●● S3 W2 *v*
1 USE VIOLENCE [I,T] to deliberately use violence to hurt a person or damage a place: *She was attacked while walking home late at night.* | *His shop was attacked by a gang of youths.* | *Snakes will only attack if you disturb them.* | **attack sb/sth with sth** *He needed 200 stitches after being attacked with a broken bottle.*
2 IN A WAR [I,T] to start using guns, bombs etc against an enemy in a war: *Army tanks attacked a village near the capital on Sunday.*
3 CRITICIZE [T] to criticize someone or something very strongly: *Last year Dr Travis publicly attacked the idea that abortion should be available on demand.* | **attack sb for (doing) sth** *Newspapers attacked the government for failing to cut taxes.* | **strongly/bitterly/savagely etc attack sb/sth**
THESAURUS ▸ CRITICIZE
4 DAMAGE [T] if something such as a disease, insect, or chemical attacks something, it damages it: *a cruel disease that attacks the brain and nervous system*
5 BEGIN DOING [T] to begin to do something in a determined and eager way: *She immediately set about attacking the problem.* | *Martin attacked his meal* (=started eating) *with vigour.*
6 SPORT [I,T] to move forward and try to score GOALS or win points → **defend**: *Brazil began to attack more in the second half of the match.*

THESAURUS

TO ATTACK A PERSON

attack to use violence against someone and try to hurt them: *She was attacked by a man with a baseball bat.* | *Police dogs are trained to attack.*

ambush /ˈæmbʊʃ/ if a group of people ambush someone, they hide and wait for them and then attack them: *The judge was ambushed by gunmen as he drove to work at the courthouse.*

mug to attack someone and take money from them in a public place such as a street: *He was mugged on his way home from school.*
stab to attack someone with a knife: *The victim had been stabbed in the neck.*
assault to attack and hurt someone - used especially when talking about this as a criminal OFFENCE: *He assaulted a flight attendant who refused to serve him more drinks.*
be set upon by sb/sth *written* to be attacked by a group of people: *He died outside his home after being set upon by a gang of youths.*
turn on to suddenly change your behaviour and attack the person you are with, when they do not expect this: *The dog suddenly turned on him, sinking its teeth into his arm.*

TO ATTACK A PLACE

attack to use weapons to try to damage or take control of a place: *The village was attacked by enemy warplanes.*
invade to enter a country and try to get control of it using force: *The Romans invaded Britain 2,000 years ago.*
storm to suddenly attack a city or building that is well defended by getting inside it and taking control: *Elite troops stormed the building and rescued the hostages.*
besiege /bɪˈsiːdʒ/ to surround a city or building with soldiers in order to stop the people inside from getting out or from receiving supplies: *In April 655, Osman's palace was besieged by rebels.*

atˈtack ad *n* [C] an advertisement which criticizes another company very strongly

at·tack·er /əˈtækə $ -ər/ ●○○ *n* [C]
1 a person who deliberately uses violence to hurt someone: *Her attacker then dragged her into the bushes.* | *a* **sex** *attacker*
2 a member of a sports team whose job is to move forward and try to score GOALS or win points → **defender**

at·ta·girl /ˈætəgɜːl $ -gɜːrl/ *interjection* used to tell a female person or dog that she has done something well, or to encourage her

at·tain /əˈteɪn/ ●○○ AWL *v* [T] *formal*
1 to succeed in achieving something after trying for a long time: *More women are attaining positions of power.*
2 to reach a particular level, age, size etc: *Share prices attained a high of $3.27.* | *After a year she had attained her ideal weight.* —**attainable** *adj*: *This target should be attainable.*

at·tain·ment /əˈteɪnmənt/ ●○○ AWL *n formal*
1 [U] success in achieving something or reaching a particular level SYN **achievement**: *a low level of educational attainment*
2 [C] something that you have succeeded in achieving or learning, such as a skill SYN **achievement**: *a society remarkable for its cultural attainments*

at·tempt¹ /əˈtempt/ ●●● S2 W1 *n* [C]
1 an act of trying to do something, especially something difficult: **attempt to do sth** *All attempts to control inflation have failed.* | **attempt at (doing) sth** *her feeble attempts at humour* | **at the first/second etc attempt** *She passed her driving test at the first attempt.*
2 make no attempt to do sth to not try to do something at all: *He made no attempt to hide his anger.*
3 an attempt on sb's life an occasion when someone tries to kill a famous or important person: *She has already survived two attempts on her life.*

COLLOCATIONS

VERBS

make an attempt *She made several attempts to escape.*
abandon/give up an attempt *They had to abandon their attempt to climb the mountain.*
fail/succeed in your attempt *He failed in his attempt to set a new Olympic record.*
an attempt fails/succeeds *All attempts to find a cure have failed.*

ADJECTIVES

on the first/second etc attempt (*also* **at the first/second etc attempt** *BrE*) *The car started at the second attempt.*
a vain attempt (=one that does not succeed) *They worked through the night in a vain attempt to finish on schedule.*
a desperate attempt (=that involves a lot of effort) *Doctors made a desperate attempt to save his life.*
a deliberate/conscious attempt | **a serious/genuine attempt** | **an unsuccessful/successful attempt** | **an abortive attempt** *formal* (=unsuccessful) | **a futile attempt** (= certain to fail and not worth doing) | **a doomed attempt** (=certain to fail, and causing something very bad to happen) | **a brave/bold/gallant/valiant attempt** *approving* (=one that you admire, but that is unsuccessful) | **a blatant attempt** *disapproving* (=when someone openly tries to do something bad) | **a final/last attempt** | **a last-ditch attempt** (=a final attempt to achieve something before it is too late)

NOUN + attempt

a rescue attempt *Two firefighters were hurt in the rescue attempt.*
an assassination attempt (=an attempt to kill a leader) *De Gaulle survived an assassination attempt in 1961.*
a suicide attempt (=an attempt to kill yourself) | **a coup attempt** (=an attempt to change the government, usually by force)

attempt² ●●● S2 W2 *v* [T]
1 to try to do something, especially something difficult: **attempt to do sth** *In this chapter I will attempt to explain what led up to the revolution.* | **attempt sth** *Weather conditions prevented them from attempting the jump.* **THESAURUS** TRY
2 attempted murder/suicide/rape etc an act of trying to kill or harm someone, kill yourself etc: *He pleaded guilty to attempted murder.*

GRAMMAR: Comparison

attempt
• You **attempt to do** something: *They were attempting to climb the mountain.*
• You **attempt** something: *The prisoners attempted an escape.*

try
• You **try to do** something: *I tried to call him at home.*
• In everyday spoken English, you say that you will **try and do** something (=try to do something): *I will try and call him at home.*
• If you **try** something, you taste or experience something for the first time: *I've never tried sushi before.*

Frequencies of **attend** and **go to** in spoken and written English.

Attend is more formal than **go to**.

at·tend /əˈtend/ ●●● S2 W2 *v formal*
1 [I,T] to go to an event such as a meeting or a class: *Only*

12 people attended the meeting. | Please let us know if you are unable to attend.

> **REGISTER**
> In everyday English, people usually say **go (to)** or **come (to)** instead of **attend**: *I didn't **go to** the parents' meeting. | Please let us know if you can't **come**.*

2 [I,T] to go regularly to a school, church etc: *I am the first child in my family to attend college.*
3 [T] *formal* to happen or exist at the same time as something: *the peculiar atmosphere which attends such an event*
4 [T] to look after someone, especially because they are ill: *On his deathbed the General was attended by several doctors.*
attend to sb/sth *phr v*
1 to deal with business or personal matters: *I may be late – I have got one or two things to attend to.*
2 to help a customer in a shop or a restaurant SYN **serve**

at·tend·ance /əˈtendəns/ ●○○ *n*
1 [C,U] the number of people who attend a game, concert, meeting etc: *We have an average attendance of 4,000 fans per game. | Last year's fair saw **attendance figures** of 32,000.*
2 [C,U] when someone goes to a meeting, class etc, or an occasion when they go: **[+at]** *Most courses involve an average of eight hours' attendance at college each week. | The doctor will have a record of her attendances.*
3 be in attendance (at sth) *formal* to be at a special or important event: *Over 2,000 people were in attendance at yesterday's demonstration.*
4 be in attendance on sb *formal* to look after someone or serve them → **dance attendance on sb** at DANCE²(5)

at·tend·ant¹ /əˈtendənt/ *n* [C] **1** someone whose job is to look after or help customers in a public place: *a car park attendant* **2** someone who looks after a very important person, for example a king or queen

attendant² *adj formal* relating to or caused by something: **attendant problems/difficulties/dangers etc** *nuclear power, with all its attendant risks* | **[+on]** *Drugs are one of the issues attendant on running a school.*

at·ten·dee /əˌtenˈdiː, ˌæten-/ *n* [C] someone who is at an event such as a meeting or a course

at·tend·er /əˈtendə $ -ər/ *n* [C] someone who regularly goes to an event such as a meeting or a class: *Daniel was a **regular attender** at the Baptist church.*

at·ten·tion /əˈtenʃən/ ●●● S2 W1 *n*
1 LISTEN/LOOK/THINK CAREFULLY [U] when you carefully listen to, look at, or think about someone or something: *My **attention wasn't** really **on** the game. | She tried to **pay attention to** what he was saying. | If you **paid** more **attention** in class, you might actually learn something! | Scott sat down at his desk and **turned** his **attention to** the file he had in front of him. | As a society we need to **give** more **attention to** the needs of older people. | Now he's gone, I can **give you my undivided attention**. | This game is fun and is sure to **keep the attention of** any young student. | They listened to the speech with **close attention**. | **Attention to detail** is essential in this job. | During the lecture Sarah's **attention** began to **wander**.*
2 INTEREST [plural, U] the interest that people show in someone or something: *She was flattered by all the **attention** he was **giving** her.* | **attract/receive/enjoy attention** *a player who quickly attracted the attention of several clubs | The exhibition received little attention in the press.* | **public/media/press attention** *Her case attracted a great deal of media attention.* | **hold/keep sb's attention** (=make someone stay interested and keep reading, listening, watching etc) *The book holds the reader's attention right to the very end. | Rob loves being **the centre of attention*** (=the person who everyone is interested in, listens to etc). | *She spent a lot of time trying to avoid the attentions* (=romantic interest) *of her boss. | The man then **turned his attentions to*** (=became romantically interested in) *her sister.*
3 NOTICE **a) attract/catch/get sb's attention** to make someone notice you, especially because you want to speak to them or you need their help: *She waved to attract the attention of the waitress.* **b) get attention** to make someone notice you and be interested in what you are doing: *Children often misbehave in order to get attention.* **c) draw/call attention to sth** (*also* **focus attention on sth**) to make people notice and be concerned or think about something: *The purpose of the article was to draw attention to the problems faced by single parents. | We wanted to focus public attention on this matter. | He left quietly to avoid drawing attention to himself.* **d) divert/distract/draw attention from sth** to make people stop being concerned about something such as a social problem: *All this talk of war is just an attempt to draw attention away from the serious economic problems that face our country.* **e) bring sth to sb's attention** to tell someone, especially someone in authority, about something such as a problem: *The matter was first brought to my attention earlier this year.* **f) come to sb's attention** if something such as a problem comes to the attention of someone in authority, they find out about it: *It came to my attention that Jenny was claiming overtime pay for hours she had not worked.* **g) escape your attention** if something escaped your attention, you did not notice it: *This fact had not escaped the attention of the authorities.*
4 REPAIR/CLEANING [U] something you do to repair or clean something: *The bike's in fairly good condition, but the gears **need** a bit of **attention**.*
5 CARE [U] things that you do to help or to take care of someone or something: *Pets need a lot of **care and attention**. | Anyone who comes into contact with these chemicals should seek urgent **medical attention**. | Your plants look like they **could do with a bit of attention**.*
6 stand to/at attention if soldiers stand to attention, they stand up straight in neat lines
7 attention! a) used to ask people to listen to important information that is being announced, especially on a LOUDSPEAKER (=piece of equipment used to make sounds louder): *Attention, please! Could passenger Marie Thomas please proceed to Gate 25 immediately.* **b)** used when ordering a group of soldiers to stand up straight in neat lines
8 for the attention of sb used on the front of an official letter when you want a particular person to read it or deal with it: *Letters should be marked 'for the attention of Joe Benson'.*

atˈtention-ˌdeficit disˌorder *n* [U] *medical* (*abbreviation* **ADD**) the former name of ATTENTION-DEFICIT HYPERACTIVITY DISORDER

atˌtention-ˌdeficit hyperacˈtivity disˌorder (*also* **attention-deficit syndrome**) *n* [U] *medical* (*abbreviation* **ADHD**) a medical condition that especially affects children. It causes them to be too active and to be unable to pay attention or be quiet for very long.

atˈtention ˌspan *n* [C usually singular] the period of time during which you continue to be interested in something: *Children often have a **short attention span**.*

at·ten·tive /əˈtentɪv/ *adj* **1** listening to or watching someone carefully because you are interested OPP **inattentive**: *an attentive audience* **2** making sure someone has everything they need: **[+to]** *Customers want companies that are attentive to their needs.* —**attentively** *adv* —**attentiveness** *n* [U]

at·ten·u·ate /əˈtenjueɪt/ *v* [T] *formal* to make something weaker or less: *an attenuated form of the polio virus*

at·test /əˈtest/ *v formal* **1** [I,T] to show or prove that something is true SYN **testify**: **[+to]** *Luxurious furnishings attested to the wealth of the owner.* **2** [T] to officially state that you believe something is true, especially in a court of law SYN **testify**

at·tes·ta·tion /ˌæteˈsteɪʃən/ *n* [C,U] *formal* a legal statement made by someone in which they say that something is definitely true → **testimony**

at·tic /ˈætɪk/ ●○○ *n* [C] a space or room just below the roof of a house, often used for storing things: *a small attic room*

at·tire /əˈtaɪə $ əˈtaɪr/ *n* [U] *formal* clothes: *business attire*

at·tired /əˈtaɪəd $ əˈtaɪrd/ *adj* [not before noun] *formal* dressed in a particular way: *He arrived* **suitably attired** *in a dark dinner suit.*

at·ti·tude /ˈætɪtjuːd $ -tuːd/ ●●● S2 W1 AWL *n*
1 [C,U] the opinions and feelings that you usually have about something, especially when this is shown in your behaviour: *As soon as they found out I was a doctor, their whole attitude changed.* | **[+to/towards]** *The people have a very positive attitude to life.*
2 [U] *informal* a style of dressing, behaving etc that shows you have the confidence to do unusual and exciting things without caring what other people think: **with attitude** *a coat with attitude* —**attitudinal** /ˌætəˈtjuːdənəl $ -ˈtuː-/ *adj*

COLLOCATIONS

ADJECTIVES

good/bad *a lazy student with a bad attitude*
positive/negative *A positive attitude is essential if you want to be successful.*
relaxed *On Bali, there is a healthier, more relaxed attitude to life.*
favourable (=having a good opinion of something or someone) *Older people tend to have a favourable attitude to the police.*
critical (=showing you disagree with or disapprove of someone or something) *People's attitude towards US foreign policy has become increasingly critical.*
ambivalent (=not sure if you approve of something) | **cavalier** (=very careless, especially about something serious or important) | **patronizing/condescending** (=showing that you think you are more important or intelligent than someone) | **aggressive/hostile** (=showing anger) | **public attitudes/people's attitudes** | **political attitudes** | **mental attitude** | **sb's whole attitude** | **the general attitude**

VERBS

have/take/adopt an attitude *Not everyone takes a positive attitude towards modern art.*
sb's attitude changes *As you get older, your attitude changes.*
an attitude exists *This attitude no longer exists in the church.*
sb's attitude hardens (=they feel less sympathy and they want to be stricter or firmer)

PHRASES

an attitude of mind *BrE* (=a way of thinking) *Being young is simply an attitude of mind.*
sb has an attitude problem (=someone is not helpful or pleasant to be with) *Some of the male students have a real attitude problem.*

attn. (***attention***) used to say that a letter or package is for a particular person

at·tor·ney /əˈtɜːni $ -ɜːr-/ ●●● S2 W3 *n* [C] *AmE* a lawyer

atˌtorney ˈgeneral *n* [C] the lawyer with the highest rank in some countries or in the US government

at·to·sec·ond /ˈætəʊˌsekənd $ -toʊ-/ *n* [C] *technical* a unit of time that is equal to 10 to the power of MINUS 18

at·tract /əˈtrækt/ ●●● S2 W2 *v* [T]
1 to make someone interested in something, or make them want to take part in something: **attract sb to sth** *What attracted me most to the job was the chance to travel.* | **attract attention/interest etc** *The story has attracted a lot of interest from the media.*
2 be attracted to sb to feel that you like someone and want to have a sexual relationship with them: *I'm not usually attracted to blondes.*
3 to make someone like or admire something or feel romantically interested in someone: *I guess it was his eyes that attracted me first.*
4 to make someone or something move towards another thing: *Leftover food attracts flies.* | *low rents designed to attract new businesses to the area*

at·trac·tion /əˈtrækʃən/ ●●○ W3 *n*
1 [C,U] a feeling of liking someone, especially in a sexual way: *The attraction between them was almost immediate.*
2 [C] something interesting or enjoyable to see or do: *The beautiful beaches are the island's* ***main attraction*** (=most popular place, activity etc). | **tourist attraction** (=a place that many tourists visit)
3 [C,U] a feature or quality that makes something seem interesting or enjoyable: **[+of]** *Being your own boss is one of the attractions of owning your own business.*
4 [C,U] *technical* a force which makes things move together or stay together: *the* ***gravitational attraction*** *between the Earth and the Moon*

at·trac·tive /əˈtræktɪv/ ●●● S2 W2 *adj*
1 someone who is attractive is good looking, especially in a way that makes you sexually interested in them: *an attractive young woman* | *Women seem to* ***find*** *him* ***attractive.*** **THESAURUS** ▶ BEAUTIFUL
2 pleasant to look at: *Kitchen utensils should be attractive as well as functional.*
3 having qualities that make you want to accept something or be involved in it: **[+to]** *a political movement that is attractive to young people* | **attractive offer/proposition/package etc** *I must say, it's a very attractive offer.* **THESAURUS** ▶ GOOD —**attractively** *adv* —**attractiveness** *n* [U]

at·trib·u·ta·ble /əˈtrɪbjətəbəl/ AWL *adj* [not before noun] likely to have been caused by something: **[+to]** *Death was attributable to gunshot wounds.*

at·tri·bute¹ /əˈtrɪbjuːt $ -bjət/ ●○○ AWL *v*
attribute sth **to** sb/sth *phr v*
1 to believe or say that a situation or event is caused by something: *The fall in the number of deaths from heart disease is generally attributed to improvements in diet.*
2 if people in general attribute a particular statement, painting, piece of music etc to someone, they believe that person said it, painted it etc: *a saying usually attributed to Confucius*
3 to believe or say that someone or something has a particular quality: *One should not attribute human motives to animals.* —**attribution** /ˌætrəˈbjuːʃən/ *n* [U]

at·tri·bute² /ˈætrəbjuːt/ ●○○ AWL *n* [C] a quality or feature, especially one that is considered to be good or useful: *What attributes should a good manager possess?*

at·trib·u·tive /əˈtrɪbjətɪv/ *adj* describing and coming before a noun. For example, in the phrase 'big city', 'big' is an attributive adjective, and in the phrase 'school bus', 'school' is a noun in an attributive position. → **predicative** —**attributively** *adv*

at·tri·tion /əˈtrɪʃən/ *n* [U] *formal* **1** the process of gradually destroying your enemy or making them weak by attacking them continuously: *a* ***war of attrition***
2 *especially AmE* when people leave a company or course of study and are not replaced: *Staff reductions could be achieved through attrition and early retirements.*

at·tuned /əˈtjuːnd $ əˈtuːnd/ *adj* **be/become attuned to sth** to be or become familiar with the way someone thinks or behaves so that you can react to them in a suitable way: *British companies still aren't really attuned to the needs of the Japanese market.*

atty. *n AmE* the written abbreviation of ***attorney***

ATV /ˌeɪ tiː ˈviː/ *n* [C] (***all terrain vehicle***) a vehicle which is designed to be ridden on rough ground where there are no roads. ATVs have one seat, no roof, and three or four large wheels.

a·typ·i·cal /eɪˈtɪpɪkəl/ ●○○ *adj* not typical or usual

au·ber·gine /ˈəʊbəʒiːn $ ˈoʊbər-/ *n* [C,U] *BrE* a large dark purple vegetable SYN **eggplant** *AmE* → see picture at VEGETABLE

au·burn /ˈɔːbən $ ˈɒːbərn/ *adj* auburn hair is a reddish brown colour —**auburn** *n* [U]

auc·tion¹ /ˈɔːkʃən $ ˈɒːk-/ ●○○ *n* [C,U] a public meeting where land, buildings, paintings etc are sold to the person who offers the most money for them: **at auction** *The house was sold at auction.* | **put sth up for auction** (=try

A

to sell something at an auction) *This week 14 of his paintings were put up for auction.* | **auction house** (=a company that arranges auctions)

auction² (*also* **auction off**) *v* [T] to sell something at an auction

auc·tio·neer /ˌɔːkʃəˈnɪə $ ˌɒːkʃəˈnɪr/ *n* [C] someone who is in charge of selling the things at an auction and who calls out how much money has already been offered for something

au·da·cious /ɔːˈdeɪʃəs $ ɒː-/ *adj* showing great courage or confidence in a way that is impressive or slightly shocking: *the risks involved in such an audacious operation* —**audaciously** *adv*

au·dac·i·ty /ɔːˈdæsəti $ ɒː-/ *n* [U] the quality of having enough courage to take risks or say impolite things: **have the audacity to do sth** | *I can't believe he had the audacity to ask me for more money!*

au·di·ble /ˈɔːdəbəl $ ˈɒː-/ *adj* a sound that is audible is loud enough for you to hear it OPP **inaudible**: *His voice was* ***barely audible*** (=could only just be heard) *above the roar of the crowd.* —**audibly** *adv* —**audibility** /ˌɔːdəˈbɪləti $ ˌɒː-/ *n* [U]

au·di·ence /ˈɔːdiəns $ ˈɒː-, ˈɑː-/ ●●● S2 W2 *n*

1 [C] a group of people who come to watch and listen to someone speaking or performing in public: *The audience began clapping and cheering.* | **[+of]** *an audience of 250 business people* | *One* ***member of the audience*** *described the opera as 'boring'.*

2 [C also + plural verb] *BrE* the people who watch or listen to a particular programme, or who see or hear a particular artist's, writer's etc work: *The show attracts a regular audience of about 20 million.* | **target audience** (=the type of people that a programme, advertisement etc is supposed to attract) | *Goya was one of the first painters to look for* ***a wider audience*** *for his work.* | *The book is not intended for a purely academic audience.*

3 [C] a formal meeting with a very important person: **[+with]** *He was* ***granted*** *an* ***audience*** *with the Pope.*

GRAMMAR: Singular or plural verb?

- **Audience** is usually followed by a singular verb: *The audience* ***was*** *cheering and shouting.*
- In British English, you can also use a plural verb: *The audience* ***were*** *cheering and shouting.*

GRAMMAR GUIDE ▶ NOUNS

au·di·o¹ /ˈɔːdiəʊ $ ˈɒːdioʊ/ *adj* [only before noun] relating to sound that is recorded or broadcast: *audio and video equipment*

audio² *n* [U] the part of a recording that contains sounds and music but not pictures: *You can save the audio for editing later.*

audio- /ɔːdiəʊ $ ɒːdioʊ/ *prefix* [in nouns and adjectives] relating to hearing or sound: *an audio-cassette*

au·di·o·book /ˈɔːdiəʊbʊk $ ˈɒːdioʊ-/ *n* [C] a recording of a book being read

au·di·o·guide /ˈɔːdiəʊgaɪd $ ˈɒːdioʊ-/ *n* [C] a piece of electronic equipment that visitors to a MUSEUM or ART GALLERY can use. They carry the audioguide with them and it gives them spoken information about objects or paintings in the museum or gallery.

au·di·o·tape /ˈɔːdiəʊteɪp $ ˈɒːdioʊ-/ *n* [C,U] *technical* a long thin band of MAGNETIC material used to record sound

au·di·o·ty·pist /ˈɔːdiəʊˌtaɪpɪst $ ˈɒːdioʊ-/ *n* [C] *BrE* someone whose job is to type letters that have been recorded

au·di·o·vis·u·al /ˌɔːdiəʊˈvɪʒuəl◂ $ ˌɒːdioʊ-/ *adj* [only before noun] involving the use of recorded pictures and sound: *the use of audiovisual materials in the classroom*

au·dit¹ /ˈɔːdɪt $ ˈɒː-/ *n* [C,U] **1** an official examination of a company's financial records in order to check that they are correct: *the annual audit* | **internal audit** (=an audit carried out by a company's own staff) **2** *formal* a detailed examination of something in order to check if it is good enough: *Start with an audit of existing services within the community.*

audit² *v* [T] **1** to officially examine a company's financial records in order to check that they are correct **2** *AmE* to attend a course at university without intending to take examinations in it or get a CREDIT for it

au·di·tion¹ /ɔːˈdɪʃən $ ɒː-/ *n* [C] a short performance by an actor, singer etc that someone watches to judge if they are good enough to act in a play, sing in a concert etc: **[+for]** *I've got an audition for the Bournemouth Symphony Orchestra on Friday.*

audition² *v* **1** [I] to take part in an audition: **[+for]** *She's auditioning for Ophelia in 'Hamlet'.* **2** [T] to watch and judge someone's performance in an audition: *We auditioned more than 200 dancers before deciding on Carole Ann.*

au·di·tor /ˈɔːdɪtə $ ˈɒːdɪtər/ *n* [C] someone whose job is to officially examine a company's financial records

au·di·to·ri·um /ˌɔːdəˈtɔːriəm $ ˌɒː-/ ●○○ *n* (*plural* **auditoriums** *or* **auditoria** /-riə/) [C]

1 the part of a theatre where people sit when watching a play, concert etc

2 *AmE* a large building used for concerts or public meetings

au·di·to·ry /ˈɔːdətəri $ ˈɒːdətɔːri/ *adj* [only before noun] *technical* relating to the ability to hear

ˈaudit trail *n* [C] *technical* **1** ACCOUNTING records which show a series of steps leading to the present financial situation: *The lack of a physical audit trail in electronic commerce increases the possibilities for tax avoidance.* **2** an electronic or paper record of how a computer is used

au fait /əʊ ˈfeɪ $ oʊ-/ *adj* **be au fait with sth** to be familiar with a system or way of doing something: *I'm not really au fait with the computer system yet.*

Aug. (*also* **Aug** *BrE*) the written abbreviation of ***August***

Au·ge·an sta·bles, the /ɔːˌdʒiːən ˈsteɪbəlz/ in ancient Greek stories, the very dirty buildings where King Augeas kept thousands of cattle, which Hercules was ordered to clean. The expression 'to clean the Augean stables' is sometimes used in literature to describe a very difficult and unpleasant job.

au·ger /ˈɔːgə $ ˈɒːgər/ *n* [C] a tool used for making a hole in wood or in the ground

aught /ɔːt $ ɒːt, ɑːt/ *pron old use* anything

aug·ment /ɔːgˈment $ ɒːg-/ ●○○ *v* [T] *formal* to increase the value, amount, effectiveness etc of something: *Any surplus was sold to augment their income.* —**augmentation** /ˌɔːgmenˈteɪʃən, -mən- $ ˌɒːg-/ *n* [C,U]

augˌmented reˈality *n* [U] (*abbreviation* **AR**) a situation in which COMPUTER-GENERATED information, images etc are combined with things in the real world or images of real things

au·gur /ˈɔːgə $ ˈɒːgər/ *v* **augur well/badly/ill** *formal* to be a sign that something will be successful or unsuccessful SYN **bode**: *Today's announcement of 300 redundancies does not augur well for the local economy.*

au·gu·ry /ˈɔːgjəri $ ˈɒː/ *n* (*plural* **auguries**) [C] *literary* a sign of what will happen in the future

au·gust /ɔːˈgʌst $ ɒː-/ *adj* impressive and respected: *an august institution*

Au·gust /ˈɔːgəst $ ˈɒː-/ ●●● S2 W2 *n* [C,U] (*written abbreviation* **Aug.**) the eighth month of the year, between July and September: **next/last August** *I was there last August.* | **in August** *My birthday's in August.* | **on August 6th** *The new store opened on August 6th.* | **on 6th August** *BrE*: *He arrived at Berwick on 6th August 1823.* | **August 6** *AmE*: *We'll expect you to call August 6.*

auk /ɔːk $ ɒːk/ *n* [C] a black and white seabird with short wings

Auld Lang Syne /ˌɔːld læŋ ˈzaɪn, ˌəʊld-, -ˈsaɪn $ ˌoʊld-/ a Scottish song that people sing when they celebrate the beginning of the new year at 12 o'clock MIDNIGHT on December 31st

au nat·u·rel /əʊ ˌnætjʊˈrel $ oʊ ˌnætʃəˈrel/ *adv* not wearing any clothes, or not wearing MAKE-UP, hair products etc that change the way you would naturally look

aunt /ɑːnt $ ænt/ ●●● S3 W3 *n* [C] the sister of your father or mother, or the wife of your father's or mother's brother: *Aunt Mary* → AGONY AUNT

aunt·ie, aunty /ˈɑːnti $ ˈæn-/ *n* [C] *informal* **1** an aunt: *Auntie Lou* **2** used by children to address a woman who is a friend of their parents

au pair /əʊ ˈpeə $ oʊ ˈper/ *n* [C] a young person, usually a woman, who stays with a family in a foreign country to learn the language, and looks after their children for a small wage

au·ra /ˈɔːrə/ ●○○ *n* [C] a quality or feeling that seems to surround or come from a person or a place: **[+of]** *The building retains an* ***aura of mystery****.*

au·ral /ˈɔːrəl/ *adj* relating to the sense of hearing, or someone's ability to understand sounds: *an aural stimulus* —**aurally** *adv*

au·re·ole /ˈɔːriəʊl $ -oʊl/ *n* [C] *literary* a bright circle of light SYN **halo**

au re·voir /ˌəʊ rəˈvwɑː, ˌɒ- $ ˌoʊ rəˈvwɑːr/ *interjection* goodbye

au·ro·ra bo·re·a·lis /əˌrɔːrə bɔːriˈeɪləs, ɔː- $ -ˈæl-/ *n* [singular] the NORTHERN LIGHTS

aus·pic·es /ˈɔːspɪsɪz $ ˈɒː-/ *n* [plural] **under the auspices of sb/sth** *formal* with the help and support of a particular organization or person: *negotiations held under the auspices of the United Nations*

aus·pi·cious /ɔːˈspɪʃəs $ ɒː-/ *adj formal* showing that something is likely to be successful OPP **inauspicious**: **auspicious start/beginning** *Saccani's excellent recording is an auspicious start to what promises to be a distinguished musical career.* —**auspiciously** *adv*

Aus·sie /ˈɒzi $ ˈɒːzi, ˈɑːzi/ *n* [C] *informal* someone from Australia —**Aussie** *adj*

aus·tere /ɔːˈstɪə, ɒ- $ ɒːˈstɪr/ ●○○ *adj*
1 plain and simple and without any decoration: *the church's austere simplicity*
2 someone who is austere is very strict and serious – used to show disapproval: *Her father is a very austere man.*
3 an austere way of life is very simple and has few things to make it comfortable or enjoyable: *Cuthbert led an austere life of prayer and solitude.* —**austerely** *adv*

aus·ter·i·ty /ɔːˈsterəti, ɒ- $ ɒː-/ *n* (*plural* **austerities**) **1** [C usually plural, U] bad economic conditions in which people do not have much money to spend: *a time of great austerity after the war* | *the austerities of post-communist Eastern Europe* **2** [U] when a government has a deliberate policy of trying to reduce the amount of money it spends: **austerity programme/plan/package** *a tough new austerity programme* | *IMF-backed* ***austerity measures*** (=reductions in government spending) **3** [U] the quality of being austere: *a life of austerity*

Aus·tra·la·sian /ˌɒstrəˈleɪʒən◂, -ʃən $ ˌɒː-, ˌɑː-/ *adj* relating to Australasia (=Australia and the islands that are near to it) or its people

Aus·tra·li·an¹ /ɒˈstreɪliən $ ɒː-, ɑː-/ *adj* relating to Australia or its people

Australian² *n* [C] someone from Australia

Ausˌtralian ˌRules ˈfootball *n* [U] a game played between two teams of 18 players on an oval field with an oval ball which is passed by kicking or striking with the hand, the aim being to get points by putting the ball between a set of four posts at either end of the field. The informal name for the game is Aussie Rules.

Aus·tri·an¹ /ˈɒstriən $ ˈɒː-,ˈɑː-/ *adj* relating to Austria or its people

Austrian² *n* [C] someone from Austria

Austro- /ɒstrəʊ $ ɒːstroʊ, -trə, ɑːs-/ *prefix* [in nouns and adjectives] Austrian and something else: *Austro-Hungarian*

au·tar·chy *especially BrE*, **autarky** *AmE* /ˈɔːtɑːki $ ˈɒːtɑːr-/ *n* (*plural* **autarchies**) [C,U] *formal* a policy in which a country or area does not want or need goods, food etc from any other country or area, or a country which has this policy

au·teur /əʊˈtɜː $ oʊˈtɜːr/ *n* [C] a film DIRECTOR who has a strong influence on the style of the films that he or she makes

au·then·tic /ɔːˈθentɪk $ ɒː-/ ●●○ *adj*
1 done or made in the traditional or original way SYN **genuine**: *authentic French food* THESAURUS ▸ GENUINE
2 a painting, document, book etc that is authentic has been proved to be by a particular person SYN **genuine**: *an authentic work by Picasso*

> **REGISTER**
> In everyday English, people usually say that something is **real** or **the real thing** rather than **authentic**: *This is* ***real*** *Indian cooking.* | *How do you know if the picture is* ***the real thing****?*

3 based on facts: *an authentic account*
4 used to describe a copy that is the same as, or as good as, the original: *Actors dressed in authentic costumes re-enact the battle.* —**authentically** /-kli/ *adv*

au·then·tic·ate /ɔːˈθentɪkeɪt $ ɒː-/ *v* [T] to prove that something is true or real: *The painting has been authenticated by experts.* | *passwords which can authenticate electronic documents* —**authentication** /ɔːˌθentɪˈkeɪʃən $ ɒː-/ *n* [U]

au·then·tic·i·ty /ˌɔːθenˈtɪsəti, -θən- $ ˌɒː-/ *n* [U] the quality of being real or true: **[+of]** *Archaeological evidence may help to establish the authenticity of the statue.*

au·thor¹ /ˈɔːθə $ ˈɒːθər/ ●●● W2 AWL *n* [C]
1 someone who has written a book SYN **writer**: *Nothomb is a Belgian author.* | **[+of]** *He was the author of two books on China.* | *It's clear that the author is a woman.*
2 *formal* the person who starts a plan or idea SYN **initiator**: **[+of]** *the author of the state reforms* —**authorial** /ɔːˈθɔːriəl $ ɒː-/ *adj* [only before noun]

author² AWL *v* [T] to be the writer of a book, report etc

au·thor·ess /ˈɔːθərɪs $ ˈɒː-/ *n* [C] *old-fashioned* a woman who writes books SYN **writer**

au·thor·ing /ˈɔːθərɪŋ $ ˈɒː-/ *n* [U] the activity of writing and designing WEBSITES: *Here are a few tips on authoring and site design.*

au·thor·i·tar·i·an /ɔːˌθɒrəˈteəriən◂ $ ɒːˌθɑːrəˈter-, əˌθɔː-/ ●○○ *adj* strictly forcing people to obey a set of rules or laws, especially ones that are wrong or unfair: *an authoritarian government* | *Critics claim his management has become too authoritarian.* THESAURUS ▸ STRICT —**authoritarian** *n* [C] —**authoritarianism** *n* [U]

au·thor·i·ta·tive /ɔːˈθɒrətətɪv, ə- $ ɒːˈθɑːrəteɪtɪv, əˈθɔː-/ ●○○ AWL *adj*
1 an authoritative book, account etc is respected because the person who wrote it knows a lot about the subject: *the most authoritative work on English surnames*
2 behaving or speaking in a confident determined way that makes people respect and obey you: *He has a commanding presence and an authoritative voice.* —**authoritatively** *adv*

au·thor·i·ty /ɔːˈθɒrəti, ə- $ ɒːˈθɑː-, əˈθɔː-/ ●●● W1 AWL *n* (*plural* **authorities**)
1 POWER [U] the power you have because of your official position: **the authority to do sth** *Only the president has the authority to declare war.* | **[+over]** *Several countries claim authority over the islands.* | **in authority** *I need to speak to someone in authority* (=who has a position of power).
2 the authorities [plural] the people or organizations that are in charge of a particular country or area: *an agreement between the US and Colombian authorities*
3 ORGANIZATION [C] an official organization or a government department that has the power to make decisions, and has particular responsibilities: *the* ***local authority*** | *East Sussex Education Authority* | *the San Diego Water Authority* | *Welsh* ***health authorities*** *face a £13m deficit this year.*
4 EXPERT [C] someone who knows a lot about a subject

A

and whose knowledge and opinions are greatly respected: **[+on]** *Mr Li is a **leading authority** on Chinese food.* THESAURUS EXPERT

5 PERMISSION [C,U] official permission to do something: **under the authority of sb** *The attack took place under the authority of the UN Security Council.* | **without sb's authority** *No one may enter without my authority.*

6 authority figure someone who has a position of power, especially because of their job: *teenage rebellion against authority figures*

7 PERSONAL QUALITY [U] a quality in the way you speak or behave which makes people obey you: *Jack's air of quiet authority*

8 I have it on good authority used to say that you are sure that something is true because you trust the person who told you about it

9 speak with authority to be sure of what you are saying, because of your knowledge or experience

COLLOCATIONS

VERBS

have authority *Teachers should have the authority to discipline their students.*

exercise/exert your authority (*also* **wield authority** *formal*) (=use your authority) *In practice it's very difficult for the president to exercise his authority.*

abuse/misuse your authority (=use your authority in a bad way) *The mayor was accused of abusing his authority and taking bribes.*

establish/assert/impose/stamp your authority (=show people that you have authority) *The new manager was anxious to establish her authority.*

lose your authority | **undermine/weaken sb's authority** (=make someone's authority weaker) | **exceed/overstep your authority** (=do more than you have the power or right to do) | **challenge sb's authority** (=try to take the power away from someone)

ADJECTIVES

full/complete/total authority *The manager has full authority to make decisions.*

absolute authority (=complete authority over everyone - used especially about the leader of a country) *In those days, the emperor had absolute authority.*

parental authority | **governmental authority** | **presidential authority** | **legal authority**

PHRASES

be in a position of authority *I've never been in a position of authority before.*

have an air of authority *approving* (=look like you have authority, in a way that makes people obey you) *The commander had an unmistakeable air of authority.*

a challenge to sb's authority | **an authority figure** (=someone, such as a parent or teacher, who has the power to tell young people what they can do)

au·thor·i·za·tion (*also* **-isation** *BrE*) /ˌɔːθəraɪˈzeɪʃən $ ˌɒːθərə-/ ●○○ *n* [C,U] official permission to do something, or the document giving this permission SYN **authority**: *You need special authorization to park here.* | *Children may not leave the building without the authorization of the principal.*

au·thor·ize (*also* **-ise** *BrE*) /ˈɔːθəraɪz $ ˈɒː-/ ●○○ *v* [T] to give official permission for something: *an authorized biography* | **authorize sb to do sth** *Napoleon III authorized Haussmann to rebuild Paris.* THESAURUS ALLOW

au·thor·ship /ˈɔːθəʃɪp $ ˈɒːθər-/ AWL *n* [U] **1** the fact that you have written a particular book, document etc: *There's no evidence to dispute his claim to authorship.* | **[+of]** *an investigation into the authorship of the Bible* **2** *formal* the profession of writing books

au·tis·m /ˈɔːtɪzəm $ ˈɒː-/ *n* [U] a mental DISORDER (=problem) that makes people unable to communicate properly, or to form relationships —**autistic** /ɔːˈtɪstɪk $ ɒː-/ *adj*: *an autistic child*

auˌtistic ˈspectrum *n* [singular] the range of autistic DISORDERS

auˌtistic ˈspectrum disˌorder *n* [C,U] one of a group of related DISORDERS from ASPERGER'S SYNDROME to severe autism

au·to /ˈɔːtəʊ $ ˈɒːtoʊ/ *n* (*plural* **autos**) [C] a car: *imported autos* | *the auto industry* | *auto insurance*

auto- /ɔːtəʊ, -tə $ ɒːtoʊ, -tə/ *prefix* **1** of or by yourself: *an autobiography* **2** working by itself: *a camera with an auto-focus lens*

au·to·bi·og·ra·phy /ˌɔːtəbaɪˈɒɡrəfi $ ˌɒːtəbaɪˈɑː-/ ●●○ *n* (*plural* **autobiographies**) [C,U] a book in which someone writes about their own life, or books of this type → **biography** THESAURUS BOOK —**autobiographical** /ˌɔːtəbaɪəˈɡræfɪkəl $ ˌɒː-/ *adj*: *an autobiographical novel* (=one based on the author's own experiences)

au·toc·ra·cy /ɔːˈtɒkrəsi $ ɒːˈtɑː-/ *n* (*plural* **autocracies**) **1** [U] a system of government in which one person or group has unlimited power SYN **dictatorship** **2** [C] a country or organization that is completely controlled by one powerful person or group SYN **dictatorship**

au·to·crat /ˈɔːtəkræt $ ˈɒː-/ *n* [C] **1** someone who makes decisions and gives orders to people without asking them for their opinion **2** a ruler who has complete power over a country —**autocratic** /ˌɔːtəˈkrætɪk◂ $ ˌɒː-/ *adj*: *an autocratic leadership style* —**autocratically** /-kli/ *adv*

Au·to·cue /ˈɔːtəʊkjuː $ ˈɒːtoʊ-/ *n* [C] *trademark* a machine that shows the words that someone must say while they are speaking in public, especially on television

au·to·dial·ler *BrE*, **autodialer** *AmE* /ˈɔːtəʊdaɪələ $ ˈɒːtoʊˌdaɪələr/ *n* [C] a machine that DIALs people's telephone numbers and plays a recorded advertisement SYN **robodialer** *AmE*

au·to·gas /ˈɔːtəʊɡæs $ ˈɒːtoʊ-/ *n* [U] *BrE* a type of liquid FUEL used in vehicles SYN **LPG**

au·to·graph¹ /ˈɔːtəɡrɑːf $ ˈɒːtəɡræf/ *n* [C] a famous person's signature that they give to someone who admires them: *Can I have your autograph?* | *a player who would always **sign autographs** and chat with fans*

autograph² *v* [T] if a famous person autographs a book, photograph etc, they sign it: *a shirt autographed by the whole team*

ˈautograph ˌdriving *n* [U] *informal* the activity of driving OFF-ROAD (=on rough ground rather than on the road) without a DRIVING LICENCE

ˌauto-immune disˈease *n* [U] a condition in which substances that normally prevent illness in the body attack and harm parts of it instead

au·to·ma·gi·cally /ˌɔːtəʊˈmædʒɪkli $ ˌɒːtoʊ-/ *adv technical* by the action of a machine, without a person making it work - used especially when you want to describe what a piece of software can do without giving a technical explanation SYN **automatically**

au·to·mak·er /ˈɔːtəʊˌmeɪkə $ ˈɒːtoʊˌmeɪkər/ *n* [C] *AmE* a company that makes cars - used especially in newspapers: *US automakers*

au·to·mate /ˈɔːtəmeɪt $ ˈɒː-/ AWL *v* [T] to start using computers and machines to do a job, rather than people: *Cash machines automate two basic functions of a bank - deposits and withdrawals.*

au·to·ma·ted /ˈɔːtəmeɪtɪd $ ˈɒː-/ AWL *adj* using computers and machines to do a job, rather than people → **automation**: *a **highly automated** factory* | *The production process is now **fully automated**.*

au·to·mat·ic¹ /ˌɔːtəˈmætɪk◂ $ ˌɒː-/ ●●○ S3 AWL *adj* **1** an automatic machine is designed to work without needing someone to operate it for each part of a process → **manual**: *an automatic weapon* | *an automatic gearbox* | *My camera is **fully automatic**.*

2 something that is automatic always happens as a result of something you have done, especially because of a rule or law: *Littering results in an automatic fine.*

3 done without thinking, especially because you have done the same thing many times before: *Practise the breathing techniques until they become automatic.*

automatic² *n* [C] **1** a weapon that can fire bullets continuously **2** a car with a system of GEARS that operate themselves without the driver needing to change them

au·to·mat·i·cally /ˌɔːtəˈmætɪkli $ ˌɒː-/ ●●○ S3 W3 AWL *adv*
1 as the result of a situation or action, and without you having to do anything more: *Join now and you will automatically receive 50% off your first purchase.*
2 without thinking about what you are doing: *Of course I automatically said yes.*
3 by the action of a machine, without a person making it work: *The doors opened automatically as we approached.*

ˌautomatic ˈpilot *n* [C,U] **1** a machine that flies a plane by itself without the need for a pilot **2 on automatic pilot** doing something without thinking about it, especially because you have done it many times before: *Moving on automatic pilot, she tidied the room.*

ˌautomatic transˈmission *n* [C,U] a system that operates the GEARS of a car without the driver needing to change them

au·to·mation /ˌɔːtəˈmeɪʃən $ ˌɒː-/ AWL *n* [U] the use of computers and machines instead of people to do a job → **automated**

au·tom·a·ton /ɔːˈtɒmətən $ ɒːˈtɑː-/ *n* (*plural* **automata** /-tə/ *or* **automatons**) [C] **1** a machine, especially one in the shape of a human, that moves without anyone controlling it SYN **robot 2** someone who seems unable to feel emotions or to think about what they are doing

au·to·mo·bile /ˈɔːtəməbiːl $ ˈɒːtəmoʊ-/ ●○○ *n* [C] *AmE* a car: *the automobile industry*

au·to·mo·tive /ˌɔːtəˈməʊtɪv◂ $ ˌɒːtəˈmoʊ-/ *adj* [only before noun] relating to cars: *automotive technology*

au·ton·o·mous /ɔːˈtɒnəməs $ ɒːˈtɑː-/ ●○○ *adj*
1 an autonomous place or organization is free to govern or control itself SYN **independent**: **an autonomous region/state/republic etc** *Galicia is an autonomous region of Spain.*
2 *formal* having the ability to work and make decisions by yourself without any help from anyone else SYN **independent** —**autonomously** *adv*

au·ton·o·my /ɔːˈtɒnəmi $ ɒːˈtɑː-/ ●○○ *n* [U]
1 freedom that a place or an organization has to govern or control itself SYN **independence**: *campaigners who want greater autonomy for Corsica*
2 the ability or opportunity to make your own decisions without being controlled by anyone else SYN **independence**: *Teachers are given considerable individual autonomy.*

au·to·pi·lot /ˈɔːtəʊˌpaɪlət $ ˈɒːtoʊ-/ *n* [C,U] AUTOMATIC PILOT

au·top·sy /ˈɔːtɒpsi $ ˈɒːtɑːp-/ *n* (*plural* **autopsies**) [C] *especially AmE* an examination of a dead body to discover the cause of death SYN **post mortem** *BrE*: *an autopsy report*

au·tumn /ˈɔːtəm $ ˈɒː-/ ●●● W3 (*also* **fall** *AmE*) *n* [C,U] the season between summer and winter, when leaves change colour and the weather becomes cooler: *autumn mists*

GRAMMAR: Patterns with autumn

in autumn/in the autumn
• You use **in autumn** or **in the autumn** when saying that something happens at that time: *In autumn the leaves turn red.* | *She is planning to go back to college in the autumn.*

last autumn/this autumn etc
Don't use **in** with these words:
• You say **last autumn**: *They got married last autumn.*
✗ Don't say: *They got married in last autumn.*
• You say **this autumn**: *The frost is early this autumn.*
✗ Don't say: *The frost is early in this autumn.*
• You say **next autumn**: *The novel will be published next autumn.* ✗ Don't say: *The novel will be published in next autumn.*
• You say **that autumn**: *It was very stormy that autumn.*
✗ Don't say: *It was very stormy in that autumn.*

au·tum·nal /ɔːˈtʌmnəl $ ɒː-/ *adj* relating to or typical of autumn: *autumnal colours*

aux. (*also* **aux** *BrE*) /ɔːks $ ɒːks/ the written abbreviation of ***auxiliary*** or ***auxiliary verb***

aux·il·ia·ry¹ /ɔːɡˈzɪljəri, ɔːk- $ ɒːɡˈzɪljəri, -ˈzɪləri/ *adj*
1 auxiliary workers provide additional help for another group of workers: *an auxiliary nurse* | *auxiliary staff*
2 an auxiliary motor, piece of equipment etc is kept ready to be used if the main one stops working properly: *an auxiliary power supply* | *auxiliary equipment*

auxiliary² *n* (*plural* **auxiliaries**) [C] **1** a worker who provides additional help for another group of workers: *a nursing auxiliary* **2** an auxiliary verb: *a modal auxiliary*

auxˌiliary ˈverb *n* [C] a verb that is used with another verb to show its tense, PERSON, MOOD etc. In English the auxiliary verbs are 'be', 'do', and 'have' (as in 'I am running', 'I didn't go', 'they have gone'), and all the MODALS.

AV, **A.V.** /ˌeɪ ˈviː/ **1** the abbreviation of ***audiovisual*** **2** the abbreviation of ***Alternative Vote***

a·vail¹ /əˈveɪl/ *n* **to/of no avail** if something you do is to no avail or of no avail, you do not succeed in getting what you want: *We searched the whole area but all to no avail. Robbie had disappeared.*

avail² *v* **avail yourself of sth** *formal* to accept an offer or use an opportunity to do something: *How many schools avail themselves of this opportunity each year?*

a·vail·a·bil·i·ty /əˌveɪləˈbɪləti/ ●●○ AWL *n* [U]
1 the state of being able to be used, bought, or found: **[+of]** *the availability of affordable housing* | *Rooms are offered* ***subject to availability*** (=only if they are available).
2 the state of being able to do something because you have enough time: *He has been asked about his availability to take part in the competition.*

a·vail·a·ble /əˈveɪləbəl/ ●●● S1 W1 AWL *adj*
1 something that is available is able to be used or can easily be bought or found: *Tickets are available from the box office.* | **[+to]** *Not enough data is available to scientists.* | **available to do sth** *Funds are available to assist teachers who want to attend the conference.* | **[+for]** *No figures are available for the number of goods sold.* | **[+in]** *There are plenty of jobs available in the area.* | **readily/widely available** (=very easy to obtain) *Parking is readily available near the station entrance.* | *Meetings were held to update employees as soon as new information* ***became available.*** | *Further building can continue when money is* ***made available.*** | ***Every available*** *space on the wall was covered in pictures.*

REGISTER
In everyday English, people usually say that a book, record etc is **out** rather than **available**: *His new album is* ***out*** *now.*

2 [not before noun] someone who is available is not busy and has enough time to talk to you: *Collins was not available for comment on Thursday night.*
3 someone who is available does not have a wife, BOYFRIEND etc, and therefore may want to start a new romantic relationship with someone else

av·a·lanche /ˈævəlɑːntʃ $ -læntʃ/ ●○○ *n* [C]
1 a large mass of snow, ice, and rocks that falls down the side of a mountain: *Two skiers were killed in the avalanche.*
2 an avalanche of sth a very large number of things such as letters, messages etc that arrive suddenly at the same time: *The school received an avalanche of applications.*

av·ant-garde /ˌævɒŋ ˈɡɑːd◂ $ ˌævɑːŋ ˈɡɑːrd◂/ *adj* **1** avant-garde music, literature etc is extremely modern and often seems strange or slightly shocking: *an avant-garde play* **2 the avant-garde** the group of artists, writers etc who produce avant-garde books, paintings etc: *a member of the avant-garde*

av·a·rice /ˈævərɪs/ *n* [U] *formal* a desire to have a lot of money that is considered to be too strong SYN **greed** —**avaricious** /ˌævəˈrɪʃəs/ *adj* —**avariciously** *adv*

av·a·tar /ˈævətɑː $ -tɑːr/ *n* [C] **1** *literary* a person or animal who is really a god in human or animal form **2** *formal* a person who represents an idea or quality **3** a picture of a person or animal that represents you on a computer screen, for example in some CHAT ROOMS or when you are playing games over the Internet

Ave. (*also* **Ave** *BrE*) the written abbreviation of ***Avenue***, used in addresses: *36, Rokesly Ave*

a·venge /əˈvendʒ/ *v* [T] *literary* to do something to hurt or punish someone because they have harmed or offended you → **revenge**: *He wanted to avenge his brother's death.* —**avenger** *n* [C]

av·e·nue /ˈævənjuː $ -nuː/ ●●○ *n* [C]
1 **Avenue** used in the names of streets in a town or city: *Fifth Avenue | Shaftesbury Avenue*
2 a possible way of achieving something: *The president wants to* ***explore every avenue*** *towards peace in the region. | There are many avenues open to researchers.*
3 *BrE* a road or broad path between two rows of trees, especially one leading to a big house: *a tree-lined avenue*

a·ver /əˈvɜː $ əˈvɜːr/ *v* (**averred**, **averring**) [T] *formal* to say something firmly and strongly because you are sure that it is true SYN **declare**

av·e·rage¹ /ˈævərɪdʒ/ ●●● S2 W2 *adj*
1 the average amount is the amount you get when you add together several quantities and divide this by the total number of quantities: *The age of the candidates ranged from 29 to 49 with an* ***average age*** *of 37. | The* ***average cost*** *of making a movie has risen by 15%. | Last winter was colder than average. | The cars were being sold at an* ***average price*** *of $11,000.*
2 an average amount or quantity is not unusually big or small: *They have an average-size front garden and a large rear garden.* | **of average height/build/intelligence etc** *He was in his late twenties and of average height.*
3 having qualities that are typical of most people or things: *The average American has not even thought about next year's election. | In an average week I drive about 250 miles.* THESAURUS ▸ NORMAL
4 neither very good nor very bad

average² ●●● S2 W2 *n*
1 [C] the amount calculated by adding together several quantities, and then dividing this amount by the total number of quantities: **[+of]** *The average of 3, 8, and 10 is 7. | Each person raised an average of £60 to plant an acre of trees. | The December figures brought the annual average for 2001 up to 10.6 per cent.*
2 **on average** based on a calculation about how many times something usually happens, how much money someone usually gets, how often people usually do something etc: *On average, men still earn more than women. | Nearly 80% of Swiss citizens on average turn out to vote.*
3 [C,U] the usual level or amount for most people or things: *Streets in the town centre are wider than the average.* | **above/below average** *The school's eighth-graders are above average in science. | The murder rate in the city has risen to four times* ***the national average***. → **law of averages** at LAW(9)

average³ ●●○ *v*
1 [linking verb] to usually do something or usually happen a particular number of times, or to usually be a particular size or amount: *The water in the lake is not particularly deep, averaging about 12 metres. | The airport averages about a thousand flights a month. | Inflation averaged just under 2.8% per year.*
2 [T] to calculate the average of figures: *The rate of growth was averaged over a period of three years.*

average out *phr v*
1 if something averages out at a particular figure, it has that figure as an average over a period of time: **[+at]** *Training costs for last year averaged out at £5,100 per trainee. | The government's share of the cost was intended to average out at 25%.*
2 **average sth ↔ out** to calculate the average of something: *I averaged out the total increase at about 10%.*

a·verse /əˈvɜːs $ -ɜːrs/ *adj* **1** **not be averse to sth** to quite enjoy something, especially something that is slightly wrong or bad for you: *I was not averse to fighting with any boy who challenged me.* **2** *formal* unwilling to do something or not liking something: **be averse to (doing) sth** *Jim is averse to using chemicals in the garden. | Some banks are* ***risk averse*** (=do not like taking a risk).

a·ver·sion /əˈvɜːʃən $ əˈvɜːrʒən/ *n* [singular, U] a strong dislike of something or someone SYN **hatred**: **[+to]** *Despite his aversion to publicity, Arnold was persuaded to talk to the press.* | **have an aversion to sth** *I have an aversion to housework.*

a·vert /əˈvɜːt $ -ɜːrt/ ●○○ *v* [T]
1 to prevent something unpleasant from happening: *The tragedy could have been averted if the crew had followed safety procedures.*
2 **avert your eyes/gaze etc** to look away from something so that you do not see it: *Henry averted his eyes as she undressed.*

a·vi·an flu /ˌeɪviən ˈfluː/ (*also* **ˌavian influˈenza**) *n* [U] an infectious disease that spreads very quickly among birds and can sometimes kill them. People can also catch the disease.

a·vi·a·ry /ˈeɪviəri $ ˈeɪvieri/ *n* (*plural* **aviaries**) [C] a large CAGE where birds are kept

a·vi·a·tion /ˌeɪviˈeɪʃən $ ˌeɪ-, ˌæ-/ *n* [U] **1** the science or practice of flying in aircraft **2** the industry that makes aircraft

a·vi·a·tor /ˈeɪvieɪtə $ ˈeɪvieɪtər, ˈæ-/ *n* [C] *old-fashioned* a pilot

ˈaviator ˌsunglasses (*also* **aviators**) *n* [plural] SUNGLASSES with large OVAL metal frames and a bar across the top, between the parts that cover your eyes. Aviator sunglasses were originally worn by pilots.

av·id /ˈævɪd/ *adj* [only before noun] doing something as much as possible SYN **keen**: *an avid collector of old jazz records | an avid reader*

a·vi·on·ics /ˌeɪviˈɒnɪks $ -ˈɑːn-/ *n* [U] *technical* the electronic equipment used in aircraft and the science of developing it

av·o·ca·do /ˌævəˈkɑːdəʊ◂ $ -doʊ◂/ (*also* **ˌavocado ˈpear**) *n* (*plural* **avocados**) [C] a fruit with a thick green or dark purple skin that is green inside and has a large seed in the middle → see picture at FRUIT¹

a·void /əˈvɔɪd/ ●●● S2 W1 *v* [T]
1 to prevent something bad from happening: *Road safety is taught to young children to avoid road accidents. | It is important to take measures to avoid the risk of fire.* | **avoid doing sth** *The refugees left to avoid getting bombed. | Alan* ***narrowly avoided*** *an accident.*
2 to stay away from someone or something, or not use something: *Everyone seemed to be avoiding Nick. | She carefully avoided his eyes* (=did not look directly at his face). *| Pregnant women should avoid certain foods such as raw eggs. | Why did you speak to him? You usually* ***avoid*** *him* ***like the plague*** (=try hard to avoid him).
3 to deliberately not do something, especially something wrong, dangerous, or harmful: *There are ways of legally avoiding taxes.* | **avoid doing sth** *You should avoid overspending in the first half of the year.*

GRAMMAR

Avoid is followed by an **-ing** form, not an infinitive. You say: *They are able to avoid paying taxes.* ✗ Don't say: *They are able to avoid to pay taxes.*
GRAMMAR GUIDE ▸ VERBS

THESAURUS

TO AVOID A PERSON OR PLACE

avoid to deliberately not go near a person or place: *Why have you been avoiding me? | We avoided Park Street because of the traffic.*
stay away/keep away to avoid a person or place, especially a dangerous one: *She walked along the path, keeping well away from the edge of the cliff. | That man is trouble – I'd stay away from him.*
steer clear of sb/sth *informal* to avoid a person or place, because there could be problems if you do not: *I usually steer clear of the kitchen when Alan's cooking.*
make a detour to avoid a place by travelling around it instead of through the centre: *We had to make a long detour because of the floods.*

TO AVOID DOING SOMETHING

avoid to find a way of not doing something that you should do: *Some people will do anything to avoid work.*
get out of sth to avoid doing something you should do or something you promised to do. **Get out of** is more common than **avoid** in everyday spoken English: *We promised we'd go – we can't get out of it now.*
wriggle out of sth (*also* **wiggle out of sth** *AmE*) to avoid doing something you should do by making up excuses – used to show disapproval: *He always seems to wriggle out of helping with the kids.*
evade *formal* to avoid doing something that legally or morally you should do – used especially about taxes or responsibilities: *It is an offence to evade taxes. | The US cannot evade its responsibility for the war.*

a·void·a·ble /əˈvɔɪdəbəl/ *adj* something bad that is avoidable can be avoided or prevented: *an almost entirely avoidable cause of death | Nearly 1,000 children die each year from accidents in the home which are avoidable.*

a·void·ance /əˈvɔɪdəns/ *n* [U] the act of avoiding someone or something: **[+of]** *the avoidance of issues such as domestic violence | a **tax avoidance** scheme* (=legal way of not paying tax)

av·oir·du·pois /ˌævwɑːdjuːˈpwɑː, ˌævədəˈpɔɪz $ ˌævərdəˈpɔɪz/ *n* [U] the system of weighing things that uses the standard measures of the OUNCE, POUND, and TON → METRIC SYSTEM

a·vow /əˈvaʊ/ *v* [T] *formal* to make a public statement about something you believe in SYN **swear**: *He avowed his commitment to Marxist ideals.* —**avowal** *n* [C,U]

a·vowed /əˈvaʊd/ *adj* [only before noun] admitted or said publicly SYN **sworn**: *an avowed atheist*

a·vun·cu·lar /əˈvʌŋkjələ $ -ər/ *adj* behaving in a kind and nice way to someone who is younger, rather like an uncle: *an avuncular pat on the shoulder*

a·wait /əˈweɪt/ ●○○ *v* [T]
1 to wait for something: *Several men are awaiting trial for robbery.* THESAURUS ▸ WAIT
2 if a situation, event etc awaits you, it is going to happen in the future: *A terrible surprise awaited them at Mr Tumnus' house.*

a·wake[1] /əˈweɪk/ ●●● S2 *adj* [not before noun]
1 not sleeping: *I hope he's awake now. | She was still only half awake when I brought her a cup of coffee. | How do you **stay awake** during boring lectures? | Emma **lay awake** half the night, worrying. | The noise brought him **wide awake*** (=completely awake). *| To **keep** themselves **awake*** (=stop themselves from going to sleep) *they sat on the floor and told each other stories.*
2 be awake to sth to understand a situation and its possible effects SYN **be aware of sth**: *Too few people are awake to the dangers of noise pollution.*

awake[2] *v* (*past tense* **awoke** /əˈwəʊk $ əˈwoʊk/, *past participle* **awoken** /əˈwəʊkən $ əˈwoʊ-/) [I,T] **1** *formal* to wake up, or to make someone wake up: *It was midday when she awoke. | We awoke to a day of brilliant sunshine.*

REGISTER
In everyday English, people usually use **wake up** rather than **awake**: *I **woke up** at 4 o'clock this morning.*

2 *literary* if something awakes an emotion, or if an emotion awakes, you suddenly begin to feel that emotion: *The gesture awoke an unexpected flood of tenderness towards her.*
awake to sth *phr v* to begin to realize the possible effects of a situation SYN **wake up to**: *Artists finally awoke to the aesthetic possibilities of photography.*

a·wak·en /əˈweɪkən/ ●○○ *v formal*
1 [I,T] to wake up or to make someone wake up: *She was awakened by a noise at two in the morning. | Bill slept a little until he was awakened to take his turn on guard.*

REGISTER
In everyday English, people usually use **wake up** rather than **awaken**: *She was **woken up** by the phone ringing.*

2 [T] if something awakens an emotion, interest, memory etc it makes you suddenly begin to feel that emotion etc: *Early involvement in music can awaken an interest that will last a lifetime.*
awaken sb **to** sth *phr v* to make someone understand a situation and its possible effects: *We must awaken people to the dangers for the environment.*

a·wak·en·ing /əˈweɪkənɪŋ/ *n* [C] **1** an occasion when you suddenly realize that you understand something or feel something: *It was during the period of 1943–1945 that his political awakening took place. | Confident that he would win, he had a **rude awakening*** (=very unpleasant surprise) *on election day.* **2** the act of waking from sleep

a·ward[1] /əˈwɔːd $ -ɔːrd/ ●●● S3 W2 *n* [C]
1 something such as a prize or money given to someone to reward them for something they have done: *The movie has won a number of awards. | an award-winning restaurant |* **[+for]** *the award for best student*
2 something, especially money, that is officially given to someone as a payment or after a legal decision: *the teachers' pay award | an award for unfair dismissal*

COLLOCATIONS

VERBS

win an award *Caprio won the award for best actor. | an award-winning novel*
get/receive an award *He is the youngest person ever to receive the award.*
give sb an award *The award is given each year to the best new artist.*
present sb with an award (=give someone an award at a formal ceremony) *She cried when she was presented with her award.*
be nominated for an award (*also* **be up for an award** *informal*) (=to be chosen as one of the people, films etc that could receive an award) | **pick up/scoop up an award** (=to get an award – used especially in news reports) | **the award goes to sb/sth** (=that person, film etc is chosen to receive it)

ADJECTIVES/NOUN + award

the highest award *The Victoria Cross is Britain's highest military award.*
a top award/a major award *The restaurant has won several top awards.*
a special award *He received a special award for his work as a movie director.*
a prestigious award (=very well-respected) | **a film/music/poetry etc award** | **a literary award**

award + NOUN

an awards ceremony *My parents wanted to be at the awards ceremony.*
an award winner | **an award scheme** *BrE*

A

award² ●●○ W3 *v* [T]
1 to officially give someone something such as a prize or money to reward them for something they have done: *Moodie has been awarded a golf scholarship at the University of Hawaii.* | **award sb sth** *The judge awarded me first prize.* | **award sth to sb** *A Nobel Prize was awarded to Waksman in 1952.* THESAURUS ▸ GIVE
2 to officially decide that someone should receive a payment or a formal agreement: **award sb sth** *The government awarded a German company the contract.* | **award sth to sb** *£45,000 was awarded to a typist with an injured hand.*

a·ware /əˈweə $ əˈwer/ ●●● S1 W1 AWL *adj* [not before noun]
1 if you are aware that a situation exists, you realize or know that it exists: **[+of]** *The children are aware of the danger of taking drugs.* | *Mr Braley has been* ***made aware*** *of the need for absolute secrecy.* | **aware that** *Were you aware that Joe had this problem with his knee?* | **well/fully/acutely aware** *They were well aware that the company was losing money.* | *As you are aware, a fee will be charged annually.*
2 if you are aware of something, you notice it, especially because you can see, hear, feel, or smell it: **[+of]** *She was aware of a tall dark figure watching her.* | *He was aware of the wind in his face.* | **aware that** *Bill* ***became aware*** *that he was still holding his glass.*
3 understanding a lot about what is happening around you and paying attention to it, especially because you realize possible dangers and problems: **politically/socially/environmentally etc aware** *the socially aware novels of Dickens* | *We should promote environmentally aware and responsible science.*
4 so/as far as I am aware *spoken* used when you are saying something that you think is true, although you might be wrong because you do not know all the facts: *As far as I am aware, they are a happily married couple.*

a·ware·ness /əˈweənəs $ əˈwer-/ ●●○ W3 AWL *n* [U]
1 knowledge or understanding of a particular subject or situation: **environmental/political/social awareness** | *Health officials have tried to* ***raise awareness*** (=improve people's knowledge) *about AIDS.*
2 the ability to notice something using your senses: **[+of]** *an artist's awareness of light and color*

a·wash /əˈwɒʃ $ əˈwɒːʃ, əˈwɑːʃ/ *adj* [not before noun]
1 covered with water or another liquid **2** containing too many things or people of a particular kind: **[+with]** *All the pavements were awash with rubbish.*

a·way¹ /əˈweɪ/ ●●● S1 W1 *adv*
1 used to say that someone leaves a place or person, or stays some distance from a place or person: *Go away!* | *Dinah was crying as she drove slowly away.* | **[+from]** *Stay away from the fire.*
2 towards a different direction: *She turned away and stared out of the window.* | *Charley blushed and looked away, embarrassed.*
3 if someone is away from school, work, or home, they are not there SYN **absent**: *Simon is away with flu.* | *Kate is away on holiday.* | **[+from]** *You must bring a note from your parents if you've been away from school.*
4 used to say how far it is to a place or thing: **five miles/ten feet etc away** *Geneva is about 20 miles away.* | *There's another hotel not far away.* | **[+from]** *She was sitting ten feet away from the microphone.* | **five minutes/two hours etc away** *The beach is only five minutes away* (=it only takes five minutes to get there).
5 if an event is two days, three weeks etc away, it will happen after that period of time has passed: *Christmas is only a month away.*
6 used to say how close someone is to achieving something or experiencing something: **[+from]** *At one stage, they were just two points away from victory.*
7 into or in a safe or enclosed place: *Put your money away, I'm paying.* | *Thousands of archaeological treasures are being kept hidden away.*
8 used to show that something disappears or is removed: *The music died away.* | *Ruben gave all his money away to charity.* | *Support for the Democrats has dropped away.* | *Cut away all the dead wood.*
9 used to emphasize that an action continues: *Sue was singing away to herself in the bath.* | *They've been hammering away all day.*
10 used to say that someone spends the whole of a period of time doing something: *You can dance the night away in one of Benidorm's many discos.*
11 if a team is playing away, it is playing a game at its opponent's field or sports hall OPP **at home**: *Liverpool are playing away at Everton on Saturday.* → **far and away** at FAR¹(12), → **right away** at RIGHT²(2), → **straight away** at STRAIGHT¹(7)

away² *adj* [only before noun] an away game or match is played at your opponent's field or sports hall OPP **home**

awe¹ /ɔː $ ɒː/ ●○○ *n* [U]
1 a feeling of great respect and liking for someone or something: *He felt great awe for the landscape.* | **with/in awe** *Kate gazed at the statue with awe.*
2 be/stand in awe of sb (*also* **hold sb in awe**) to admire someone and have great respect for them and sometimes a slight fear of them: *All of the neighbours were a little in awe of my mother.* | *The villagers hold them in awe and think of them as gods.*

awe² *v* [T] *formal* if you are awed by someone or something, you feel great respect and liking for them, and are often slightly afraid of them: *The girls were awed by the splendour of the cathedral.* —**awed** *adj*: *an awed silence*

ˈawe-inˌspiring *adj* extremely impressive in a way that makes you feel great respect: *a truly awe-inspiring achievement*

awe·some /ˈɔːsəm $ ˈɒː-/ ●●○ *adj*
1 extremely impressive, serious, or difficult so that you feel great respect, worry, or fear: *an awesome responsibility* | *the awesome sweep of the scenery*
2 *especially AmE informal* very good: *Their last concert was really awesome.* —**awesomely** *adv*

ˈawe-ˌstricken *adj* AWESTRUCK

awe·struck /ˈɔːstrʌk $ ˈɒː-/ *adj* feeling great respect for the importance, difficulty, or seriousness of someone or something: *She gazed awestruck at the jewels.*

aw·ful¹ /ˈɔːfəl $ ˈɒː-/ ●●● S1 *adj*
1 very bad or unpleasant SYN **terrible**: *The weather was awful.* | *He is a pretty awful driver.* | *That fridge smells awful.* | *The last six months have been awful for her.* | *I've stopped believing most of what he says. Isn't that awful?* | *I'm sure Suzy is dead but the* ***awful thing*** *is not knowing how it happened.* THESAURUS ▸ BAD, HORRIBLE
2 [only before noun] *spoken* used to emphasize how much or how good, bad etc something is: ***An awful lot of*** *people* (=a large number of people) *died in the war.* | *He made me feel an awful fool.*
3 look/feel awful to look or feel ill: *She's lost a lot of weight and she looks awful.*
4 *literary* making you feel great respect or fear —**awfulness** *n* [U]

> **GRAMMAR**
> **Awful** is not used with 'very'. You say: *It was a really awful experience.* ✗ Don't say: *It was a very awful experience.*
> GRAMMAR GUIDE ▸ ADJECTIVES

awful² *adv* [+adj/adv] *AmE spoken* very: *That kid's awful cute, with her red curls.*

aw·ful·ly /ˈɔːfəli $ ˈɒː-/ *adv* very: *It's awfully cold in here. Is the heater on?*

a·while /əˈwaɪl/ *adv* for a short time

awk·ward /ˈɔːkwəd $ ˈɒːkwərd/ ●●○ S3 *adj*
1 making you feel embarrassed so that you are not sure what to do or say SYN **difficult**: *I hoped he would stop asking* ***awkward questions****.* | *There was an awkward moment when she didn't know whether to shake his hand or kiss his cheek.* | *an* ***awkward silence*** | *A laugh can help people over an awkward situation.* | *Philip's remarks* **put** *her* ***in an awkward***

position (=made it difficult for her to know what to do). **THESAURUS** ▶ **EMBARRASSED**
2 not relaxed or comfortable: *She liked to dance but felt awkward if someone was watching her. | Geoff looked uneasy and awkward. | Make sure that the baby is not sleeping in an awkward position.*
3 difficult to do, use, or deal with: *It'll be awkward getting cars in and out. | The new financial arrangements were awkward to manage. | A good carpenter can make a cupboard to fit the most awkward space. | She was afraid he was going to ask an awkward question.* **THESAURUS** ▶ **DIFFICULT**
4 not convenient: *I'm sorry to call at such an awkward time but I won't keep you a minute.*
5 an awkward person is deliberately unhelpful SYN **difficult**: **[+about]** *The staff wanted to go home and they were getting awkward about a meeting starting so late. | an* ***awkward customer*** (=person who is difficult and unhelpful) —**awkwardly** *adv*: *'I'm very sorry about your sister,' he said awkwardly. | Vera smiled awkwardly.* —**awkwardness** *n* [U]: *He tried to smooth over the awkwardness of the situation.*

awl /ɔːl $ ɒːl/ *n* [C] a pointed tool for making holes in leather

AWNING

aw·ning /ˈɔːnɪŋ $ ˈɒː-/ *n* [C] a sheet of material outside a shop, tent etc to keep off the sun or the rain

a·woke /əˈwəʊk $ əˈwoʊk/ *v* the past tense of AWAKE

a·wok·en /əˈwəʊkən $ əˈwoʊ-/ *v* the past participle of AWAKE

AWOL /ˌeɪ ˌdʌbəljuː əʊ ˈel, ˈeɪwɒl $ -oʊ-, ˈeɪwɒːl/ *adj* (***absent without leave***) absent from somewhere without permission, especially from the army: *Two soldiers had* ***gone AWOL*** *the night before.*

a·wry /əˈraɪ/ *adj* **1 go awry** if something goes awry, it does not happen in the way that was planned: *My carefully laid plans had already gone awry.* **2** not in the correct position: *He rushed out, hat awry.*

aw shucks /ˌɔː ˈʃʌks $ ˌɒː-/ *interjection AmE* used in a joking way to show that you feel embarrassed or sad

axe[1] (*also* **ax** *AmE*) /æks/ ●●○ *n* [C]
1 a tool with a heavy metal blade on the end of a long handle, used to cut down trees or split pieces of wood → PICKAXE
2 the axe *informal* if someone gets the axe, they are dismissed from their job: *A hundred workers are facing the axe in a cost-cutting exercise.*
3 the axe *informal* if a plan, system, or service gets the axe, someone gets rid of it: *MPs know there will be cuts in public spending but do not know on which department the axe will fall.*
4 have an axe to grind to have a strong personal opinion about something which is the reason why you do something: *I need objective advice from someone with no axe to grind.*

axe[2] (*also* **ax** *AmE*) *v* [T] **1** to suddenly dismiss someone from their job: *There are plans to axe 2,600 staff.* **2** to get rid of a plan, system, or service, especially in order to save money: *TV's longest running show is to be axed.*

ax·i·om /ˈæksiəm/ *n* [C] *formal* a rule or principle that is generally considered to be true

ax·i·o·mat·ic /ˌæksiəˈmætɪk◂/ *adj* something that is axiomatic does not need to be proved because you can easily see that it is true SYN **self-evident** —**axiomatically** /-kli/ *adv*

ax·is /ˈæksɪs/ ●○○ *n* (*plural* **axes** /-siːz/) [C]
1 the imaginary line around which a large round object, such as the Earth, turns: *The Earth rotates on an axis between the north and south poles.* → see picture at EARTH[1]
2 a line drawn across the middle of a regular shape that divides it into two equal parts
3 either of the two lines of a GRAPH, by which the positions of points are measured: **the vertical/horizontal axis**

ˌAxis of ˈEvil, the a phrase used by US President George W. Bush in a speech in April 2002 to describe countries that he claimed supported TERRORISM (=use of violence to obtain political demands) and wanted to obtain chemical, BIOLOGICAL, or NUCLEAR weapons

ax·le /ˈæksəl/ *n* [C] the bar connecting two wheels on a car or other vehicle

Ax·min·ster /ˈæksmɪnstə $ -ər/ *n* [U] *trademark* a type of high-quality CARPET

a·ya·tol·lah /ˌaɪəˈtɒlə $ -ˈtoʊ-/ *n* [C] a religious leader of the Shiite Muslims, especially a very powerful one

aye /aɪ/ *adv* **1** used to say yes when voting OPP **nay**: **the ayes have it** (=used to say that most people in a meeting have voted in favour of something) **2** a word meaning yes, used especially in Scotland

Ay·ur·ve·dic med·i·cine /ˌaɪjəveɪdɪk ˈmedsən $ -jərveɪdɪk ˈmedəsən/ *n* [U] a traditional Indian medical treatment that involves using herbs, eating certain types of food, and doing YOGA (=exercises that help you relax by controlling your mind and body) in order to stay healthy

a·za·le·a /əˈzeɪliə $ -jə/ *n* [C] a small bush that has large flowers → see picture at FLOWER[1]

AZT /ˌeɪ zed ˈtiː $ -ziː-/ *trademark* azidothymidine - a drug used to treat AIDS

az·ure /ˈæʒə, ˈæʒjʊə, ˈæzjʊə $ ˈæʒər/ *adj* having a bright blue colour like the sky —**azure** *n* [U]

Bb

B

B, **b** /biː/ *n* (*plural* **B's**, **b's**) **1** [C,U] the second letter of the English alphabet **2** [C,U] the seventh note in the musical SCALE of C MAJOR or the musical KEY based on this note **3** [C] a mark given to a student's work to show that it is good but not excellent: *I got a B in history.* **4** [U] used to refer in a short way to one of two different things or people. You can call the first one A: *the advantages and disadvantages of choosing product A or B* → **plan B** at PLAN¹(6) **5 B4509/B1049 etc** the name of a road in Britain that is smaller than an A-ROAD **6** [U] a common type of blood → **from A to B** at A¹(6), → **B-MOVIE**, **B-SIDE**, **B-ROAD**

b. (*also* **b** *BrE*) the written abbreviation of ***born***: *Andrew Lanham, b. 1885*

BA *BrE*, **B.A.** *AmE* /ˌbiː ˈeɪ/ *n* [C] (***Bachelor of Arts***) a first university DEGREE in a subject such as history, languages, or English literature → **BS**, **BSc**, **MA**: **[+in]** *He has a BA in French.* | *Susan Potter, BA*

baa /bɑː/ *v* [I] to make a sound like a sheep —**baa** *n* [C]

bab·ble¹ /ˈbæbəl/ *v* **1** [I,T] to speak quickly in a way that is difficult to understand or sounds silly: *I have no idea what he was babbling on about.* **2** [I] to make a sound like water moving over stones —**babbler** *n* [C]

babble² *n* [singular] **1** the confused sound of many people talking at the same time: *the babble of a crowded party* **2** a sound like water moving over stones

babe /beɪb/ *n* [C] **1** *literary* a baby: **babe in arms** (=one that has to be carried) **2** *spoken informal* a word for an attractive young woman **3** *spoken informal not polite* a way of speaking to a young woman, often considered offensive **4** *spoken* a way of speaking to someone you love, especially your wife or husband **5 babe in the woods** *AmE* someone who can be easily deceived: *He was like a babe in the woods when he first came to New York.*

ba·bel /ˈbeɪbəl $ ˈbeɪ-, ˈbæ-/ *n* [singular, U] the confusing sound of many voices talking together: *a babel of French and Italian*

ba·boon /bəˈbuːn $ bæ-/ *n* [C] a large monkey that lives in Africa and South Asia

ba·by¹ /ˈbeɪbi/ ●●● S1 W1 *n* (*plural* **babies**) [C]

1 YOUNG CHILD a very young child who has not yet learned to speak or walk: *The baby is crying.* | *She gave birth to a baby on Thursday.* | *What do you think of your new baby sister?* → **TEST-TUBE BABY**

2 YOUNG ANIMAL a very young animal: *baby birds*

3 VEGETABLE a type of vegetable which is grown to be much smaller than usual or is eaten before it has grown to its normal size: *baby carrots* | *baby sweetcorn*

4 YOUNGEST a younger child in a family, often the youngest: *Clare is the baby of the family.*

5 WOMAN *spoken* **a)** used to address someone that you love: *Relax, baby – we're on holiday.* **b)** *not polite* used to address a young woman that you do not know

6 SILLY PERSON someone, especially an older child, who is not behaving in a brave way: *Don't be a baby!*

7 RESPONSIBILITY something special that someone has developed or is responsible for: *Don't ask me about the building contract – that's Robert's baby.*

8 THING *informal* something, especially a piece of equipment or a machine, that you care about a lot: *This baby can reach speeds of 130 miles per hour.* → **throw the baby out with the bathwater** at THROW¹(37)

COLLOCATIONS

VERBS

a baby is born *Let me know as soon as the baby is born.*
have a baby/give birth to a baby *She had the baby at home.*
be expecting a baby (=be pregnant) *My wife's expecting a baby.*
a baby is due (=is expected to be born) *When is your baby due?*
lose a baby (=have a baby that dies when it is born too soon) *She was three months pregnant when she lost the baby.*
deliver a baby (=help a woman to give birth to a baby) | **abandon a baby** (=leave your baby somewhere because you do not want it)

ADJECTIVES

a newborn baby *There's plenty of help and advice for people with newborn babies.*
an unborn baby (=not yet born) *Drinking alcohol is bad for your unborn baby.*
a premature baby (=born before the normal time) *Lesley's baby was three weeks premature.*
an illegitimate baby (=born to an unmarried mother) | **an unwanted baby**

baby + NOUN

a baby boy/girl *She's just had a lovely healthy baby girl.*
a baby son/daughter/brother/sister | **baby clothes/food**

COMMON ERRORS

⚠ Don't say 'she is waiting a baby'. Say **she is expecting a baby**.

THESAURUS

baby a very young child who has not yet learned to speak or walk: *I sat next to a woman holding a baby.*
toddler a baby who has learned how to walk: *The playground has a special area for toddlers.*
infant *formal* a baby or a very young child: *The disease is mainly found in infants.*
little one *spoken informal* a baby, or a small child up to the age of about three: *How old is your little one?*
young the babies of an animal or bird: *Kangaroos carry their young in a pouch.*
litter a group of baby animals that are born at the same time to the same mother: *Our cat has just had a litter of six kittens.*

baby² *v* (**babied**, **babying**, **babies**) [T] to be too kind to someone and look after them as if they were a baby

ˈbaby blues *n* [plural] *informal* an illness in which a woman feels unhappy and tired after her baby is born

ˈbaby boom *n* [C] an increase in the number of babies born during a particular period, compared to other times – used especially about people born between 1946 and 1964: *the baby boom generation*

ˈbaby ˌboomer *n* [C] someone born during a period when a lot of babies were born, especially between 1946 and 1964

ˈbaby ˌbuggy *n* [C] **1** *BrE* BUGGY **2** *AmE* PRAM

ˈbaby ˌcarriage *n* [C] *AmE* a thing like a small bed with four wheels, used for taking a baby from one place to another SYN **pram** *BrE* → **pushchair**

ˈbaby ˌdaddy (*also* **ˈbaby ˌfather**) *n* [C] *informal* the man who is the father of a woman's child but is not married to her

ˈbaby-faced *adj* a baby-faced adult has a face like a child

Ba·by·gro /ˈbeɪbigrəʊ $ -groʊ/ *n* (*plural* **Babygros**) [C] *trademark BrE* a piece of clothing for a baby, that covers their whole body

ba·by·hood /ˈbeɪbihʊd/ *n* [U] the period of time when you are a baby

ba·by·ish /ˈbeɪbi-ɪʃ/ *adj* like a baby, or suitable for a baby: *The games were a little babyish for nine-year-olds.*

ˈbaby milk *n* [U] *BrE* dried milk that is mixed with water and fed to babies instead of breast milk SYN **formula** *AmE*

ba·by·moon /ˈbeɪbimuːn/ *n* [C] **1** a holiday taken by a PREGNANT woman and her husband or partner, usually before their first baby is born **2** a period just after a baby is born when the parents spend time alone with their baby

ba·by·sit /ˈbeɪbisɪt/ *v* (*past tense and past participle* **babysat** /-sæt/, *present participle* **babysitting**) [I,T] to take care of children while their parents are away for a short time —**babysitting** *n* [U]: *a babysitting service* —**babysitter** *n* [C]

ˈbaby talk *n* [U] sounds or words that babies use when they are learning to talk

ˈbaby tooth *n* (*plural* **baby teeth**) [C] a tooth from the first set of teeth that young children have SYN **milk tooth** *BrE*

ˈbaby ˌwalker *n* [C] a small frame on wheels that a baby uses to support itself while it is learning to walk

bac·ca·lau·re·ate /ˌbækəˈlɔːriət/ *n* [C] **1** an examination in a range of subjects that students do in their final school year in France and some other countries, and in some international schools **2** *AmE formal* a BACHELOR'S DEGREE

bac·ca·rat /ˈbækərɑː $ ˌbækəˈrɑː/ *n* [U] a card game

bac·cha·na·li·an, **Bacchanalian** /ˌbækəˈneɪliən◂/ *adj literary* a bacchanalian party involves a lot of alcohol, sex, and uncontrolled behaviour: *a bacchanalian orgy*

bac·cy /ˈbæki/ *n* [U] *BrE informal* tobacco

bach·e·lor /ˈbætʃələ $ -ər/ ●○○ *n* [C]

1 a man who has never been married: *Gerald was 38, and a **confirmed bachelor*** (=a man who has decided that he will never marry). | *The Crown Prince was Japan's most **eligible bachelor*** (=a rich young man who has not yet married).

THESAURUS MARRIED

2 **Bachelor of Arts/Science/Education etc** a first university DEGREE in an ARTS subject, a science subject etc → **BA, BSc, BEd**

ˈbachelor ˌflat *n* [C] *BrE* an apartment where an unmarried man or woman lives

ˈbachelor ˌparty *n* [C] *AmE* a party for a man and his male friends before he gets married, especially on the night before his wedding SYN **stag night** *BrE*

ˈbachelor's deˌgree *n* [C] a first university DEGREE, such as a BA, B.S., or BSC → **master's degree**

ba·cil·lus /bəˈsɪləs/ *n* (*plural* **bacilli** /-laɪ/) [C] *technical* a type of BACTERIA. Some types of bacillus cause diseases.

back¹ /bæk/ ●●● S1 W1 *adv*

1 RETURN TO PLACE in, into, or to the place or position where someone or something was before: *I'll be back in a minute.* | *Put that book back where you found it!* | **[+in/to/into etc]** *Rory plugged the cable back into the socket.* | *I feel like going back to bed.* | **go/get/head etc back** *We ought to try and get back before it gets dark.* | *He was **back home** by half past eleven.* | *It's possible to travel **there and back** in a day.*

GRAMMAR

- You go **back to** a place: *We decided to go back to Athens.* | *I'm going back to school tomorrow.*
- You go **back home**: *It's time to go back home.* ✗ Don't say: *go back to home*

2 AS BEFORE in or into the condition or situation you were in before: *Gary woke at 4 am and couldn't get back to sleep.* | *It took me a long time to get my confidence back.* | *If you decide to marry him, there will be **no going back*** (=you will not be able to get back to your previous situation). | **go/get back to (doing) sth** *There's no way I'm going back to being poor.* | *It'll take a while for things to get back to normal.*

3 PREVIOUS PLACE in or to a place where you lived or worked before: **[+in/at]** *She was the one who had fired him from his first job back in South Africa.* | **back home** (=in the place that you come from and think of as your home) *It reminded me of evenings back home.*

4 BACKWARDS in the opposite direction from the way you are facing OPP **forwards**: *He glanced back at the house.* | *Kirov stepped back a pace.* | *She tilted her head back to look at him.*

5 REPLY/REACTION if you do something back, you do it as a reply or reaction to what someone has said or done: *Can I call you back later?* | *I'll pay you back on Friday.* | *'No, thanks!' he shouted back.* | *If he hits you, you just hit him back.*

6 RETURN STH TO SB if you give something, get something etc back, you return it to the person who first had it, or you have it returned to you: *Can we have our ball back, please?* | *I want all my books back as soon as you've finished with them.* | *Give me back that letter! It's none of your business!*

7 IN THE PAST in or towards a time in the past: *a pile of newspapers dating back to the 1970s* | *A lot of emotional problems can be traced back to childhood.* | *Looking back on it, I should have known he was unhappy.* | *At times, I think back to my life in Moscow.* | **[+in]** *The house was built back in 1235.* | **three years/two months etc back** (=three years etc ago) *His wife died a couple of years back.* | *He called me **a while back**.*

8 AGAIN once again: *Go back over your work to check for any mistakes.* | *Liverpool were back level again two minutes later with a superb goal.*

9 **sit/lie/lean back** to sit or lie in a comfortable relaxed way: *Sit back, relax, and enjoy the show!*

10 AWAY away from a surface, person, or thing: *She pulled the bandage back very carefully.* | *Her hair was brushed back from her face.* | *The woman nodded and stood back, allowing Patrick to enter.*

11 **back and forth** going in one direction and then in the opposite direction, and repeating this several times: *We travel back and forth all the time between Canada and England.* | *He was pacing back and forth.*

12 TOWARDS BEGINNING towards the beginning of a book, film, or computer document etc: *Turn back to the summaries at the end of section 1.5.* | *Clicking on the icon will take you back to the previous web page.* | *Wind the tape back to the beginning.*

back² ●●● S1 W1 *n* [C]

1 PART OF YOUR BODY **a)** the part of the body between the neck and legs, on the opposite side to the stomach and chest: *The cat arched its back and hissed.* | *My feet were sore and my back was aching.* | *Keep your head up and your back straight.* | *To avoid back problems, always bend your knees when you lift heavy objects.* | *He lay **on his back** and gazed at the ceiling.* | *Johnny was lying **flat on** his **back** in the middle of the floor.* | *Anna stood **with** her **back to** the window.* | **on sb's back** (=carried on someone's back) *The girl appeared again, now with a little baby on her back.* **b)** the bones between your neck and the top of your legs SYN **spine**: *He broke his back in a motorbike accident.*

2 NOT AT FRONT [usually singular] the part of something that is furthest from the front OPP **front**: *a T-shirt with a picture of a snake **on the back*** | **[+of]** *He kissed her on the back of her head.* | *Her window faced the backs of the houses.* | **in the back (of sth)** (=used especially about the back of a vehicle) *Two men were sitting in the back of the car.* | **at the back (of sth)** *a small shop with an office at the back* | **in back (of sth)** *AmE* (=in or at the back of something) *Kids should always wear seat belts, even in back.* | **out back** *AmE* (=behind a house or other building) *Tom's working on the car out back.* | **round/out the back** *BrE* (=behind a house or building) *Have you looked round the back?*

3 LESS IMPORTANT SIDE [usually singular] the less important side or surface of something such as a piece of paper or card OPP **front**: *Paul scribbled his address on the back of an envelope.* | *The credits are listed on the back of the album.*

4 PART OF SEAT the part of a seat that you lean against

when you are sitting: **[+of]** *He rested his arm on the back of the sofa.*
5 BOOK/NEWSPAPER [usually singular] the last pages of a book or newspaper OPP **front**: **at the back (of)** *The sports pages are usually at the back.* | **in the back (of)** *The answers are in the back of the book.*
6 at/in the back of your mind a thought that is at the back of your mind is one you try to ignore because you do not want it to be true: *At the back of her mind was the thought that he might be with someone else.* | **put/push sth to the back of your mind** *He tried to push these uncomfortable thoughts to the back of his mind.*
7 back to back a) with the backs towards each other: *Stand back to back and we'll see who's tallest.* **b)** happening immediately one after the other: *He performed up to three times a day, often back to back.* → BACK-TO-BACK[1]
8 back to front *BrE* **a)** in an incorrect position so that what should be at the back is at the front: *You've got your sweater on back to front.* **b)** doing something the wrong way round and starting with the part that should be at the end: *He got the commands back to front and the program didn't work.*
9 behind sb's back if you do something behind someone's back, you do it without them knowing: *I don't like the idea of the two of them talking about me behind my back.* | *I should have realized that he'd* ***go behind*** *my* ***back*** (=do something without telling me).
10 when/while sb's back is turned if something happens when your back is turned, it happens when you are not able to see or know what someone is doing: *What are your kids up to when your back is turned?*
11 get/put sb's back up *BrE informal* to annoy someone: *Simone was the kind of person who was always putting people's backs up.*
12 get (sb) off sb's back *spoken* to stop annoying someone with a lot of questions, criticisms etc, or to make someone stop annoying you in this way: *Maybe the only way to get him off my back is to tell him the truth.* | *Do me a favour and* ***get off my back****!*
13 be on sb's back *spoken* to be trying to make someone do something they do not want to do: *Why are you and Dad always on my back?*
14 on the back of sth as a result of something that already exists or something you have already done: *The company should be able to generate business on the back of existing contracts.*
15 on the backs of sb using the work of a particular group to achieve something that they will not get any advantage from: *Economic prosperity was won on the backs of the urban poor.*
16 SPORTS a defending player in a sports team SYN **defender**
17 the back of beyond *informal* a place that is a long way from other places and is difficult to get to: *It's a nice little cottage but it really is in the back of beyond.*
18 be (flat) on your back a) to be lying on your back – used to emphasize that someone seems unlikely to get up soon: *He was drunk and flat on his back on the street.* **b)** to be so ill that you cannot get out of bed: *Their best player was flat on his back in hospital.* **c)** if a business, country, ECONOMY etc is on its back, it is not successful: *The UK market was flat on its back.*
19 put your back into it *informal* to work extremely hard at something: *If we really put our backs into it, we could finish today.*
20 be glad/delighted/pleased etc to see the back of sb/sth to be happy that someone is leaving or because you no longer have to deal with something: *No, I'm not too upset that he left – in fact, I was glad to see the back of him.* | *I* ***can't wait to see the back of*** *this project, I can tell you* (=I will be happy when it ends).
21 have your back to/against the wall *informal* to be in a difficult situation with no choice about what to do
22 at your back a) behind you: *They had the wind at their backs as they set off.* **b)** supporting you: *Caesar marched into Rome with an army at his back.*
23 on your back *informal not polite* if someone achieves something on their back, they achieve it by having sex with someone
24 high-backed/straight-backed/low-backed etc with a high, straight, low etc back: *a high-backed chair* → **know sth like the back of your hand** at KNOW[1](3), → **turn your back on sb/sth** at TURN[1](7)

back[3] ●●● S2 W3 *v*

1 SUPPORT [T] **a)** to support someone or something, especially by giving them money or using your influence: *The scheme has been backed by several major companies in the region.* | *Some suspected that the rebellion was backed and financed by the US.* | *government-backed loans* **b)** (*also* **back up**) to support an idea by providing facts, proof etc: *His claims are not backed by any scientific evidence.* THESAURUS SUPPORT GRAMMAR **Back** is usually passive in this meaning.
2 MOVE BACKWARDS [I always + adv/prep, T] to move backwards, or make someone or something move backwards: **[+into/out of/away from etc]** *She backed into a doorway to let the crowds pass by.* | **back sb into/towards/out of etc sth** *He began to back her towards the open door.* | **back sth into/towards/out of etc sth** *I backed the car into the garage.*
3 PUT STH ON THE BACK [T] to put a material or substance onto the back of something, in order to protect it or make it stronger: *The photograph is backed with cardboard.* | *a plastic-backed shower curtain* GRAMMAR **Back** is usually passive in this meaning.
4 BE BEHIND STH [T] to be at the back of something or behind it: *The Jandia Peninsula is a stretch of white sands backed by a mountain range.* GRAMMAR **Back** is usually passive in this meaning.
5 MUSIC [T] to play or sing the music that supports the main singer or musician: *They performed all their hits, backed by a 40-piece orchestra.* GRAMMAR **Back** is usually passive in this meaning.
6 RISK MONEY [T] to risk money on whether a particular horse, dog, team etc wins something
7 back the wrong horse to support someone or something that is not successful

back away *phr v*
1 to move backwards and away from someone or something, especially because you are frightened: **[+from]** *She backed away from the menacing look on his face.*
2 to stop supporting a plan or idea, or stop being involved in something: **[+from]** *The government has backed away from its nuclear weapons strategy.*

back down *phr v* to admit that you are wrong or that you have lost an argument: *Both sides have refused to back down.*

back off *phr v*
1 to move backwards, away from someone or something: *She backed off and then turned and ran.*
2 to stop telling someone what to do, or stop criticizing them, especially so that they can deal with something themselves: *I think you should back off for a while.* | *Back off, Marc! Let me run my own life!*
3 to stop supporting something, or decide not to do something you were planning to do: *Jerry backed off when he realized how much work was involved.* | **[+from]** *The company has backed off from investing new money.*

back onto sth *phr v* if a building backs onto something, its back faces it: *The hotel backs onto St Mark's Square.*

back out *phr v* to decide not to do something that you had promised to do: *It's too late to back out now.* | *After you've signed the contract, it will be impossible to back out.* | **[+of]** *The government is trying to back out of its commitment to reduce pollution.*

back up *phr v*
1 back sb/sth ↔ up to say or show that what someone is saying is true: *Jane would back me up if she were here.* | *There's no evidence to back up his accusations.* | *These theories have not been backed up by research.*
2 back sb/sth ↔ up to provide support or help for someone or something: *The plan's success depends on how vigorously the UN will back it up with action.* | *The police officers are backed up by extra teams of people at the weekend.* → BACKUP

3 to make a copy of information stored on a computer: *Make sure you back up.* | **back sth ↔ up** *These devices can back up the whole system.* | **back sth ↔ up onto sth** *Back all your files up onto a storage device or Cloud.* → BACKUP
4 *especially AmE* to make a vehicle move backwards: *The truck stopped and then backed up.* | **back sth ↔ up** *I backed the car up a little.*
5 to move backwards: *Back up a bit so that everyone can see.* → BACKUP
6 if traffic backs up, it forms a long line of vehicles that cannot move: *The traffic was starting to back up in both directions.*
7 if a toilet, sink etc backs up, it becomes blocked so that water cannot flow out of it

back⁴ ●●● S2 W3 *adj* [only before noun]
1 at or in the back of something OPP **front**: *You'll be sleeping in the back bedroom.* | *Turn to the back page.* | *I keep my keys in my back pocket.* | *There was the sound of giggling from the back row.* | *The rabbit had one of its back legs caught in a trap.* → BACK DOOR
2 behind something, especially a building OPP **front**: *the back garden* | *We left by the back gate.*
3 from the back: *The back view of the hotel was even less appealing than the front.*
4 **back street/lane/road etc** a street etc that is away from the main streets: *a short cut down a back lane*
5 **back rent/taxes/pay etc** money that someone owes from an earlier date
6 **back issue/copy/number** a copy of a magazine or newspaper from an earlier date
7 *technical* a back vowel sound is made by lifting your tongue at the back of your mouth

back·ache /ˈbækeɪk/ *n* [C,U] a pain in your back

back·bench /ˌbækˈbentʃ◂/ *adj* [only before noun] *BrE* a backbench Member of Parliament is an ordinary British Member of Parliament who does not have an important official position: *He has the support of a lot of backbench MPs.* | *a backbench revolt*

back·bench·er /ˌbækˈbentʃə◂ $ -ər◂/ *n* [C] *BrE* an ordinary British Member of Parliament who does not have an important official position

back·benches /ˌbækˈbentʃɪz/ *n* **the backbenches** [plural] *BrE* the seats in the British parliament where ordinary Members of Parliament sit

back·bit·ing /ˈbækbaɪtɪŋ/ *n* [U] unpleasant or cruel talk about someone who is not present: *All this backbiting is destroying company morale.*

back·board /ˈbækbɔːd $ -bɔːrd/ *n* [C] the board behind the basket in the game of BASKETBALL → see picture at BASKETBALL

back·bone /ˈbækbəʊn $ -boʊn/ ●○○ *n*
1 [C] the row of connected bones that go down the middle of your back SYN **spine**
2 **the backbone of sth** the most important part of an organization or group of people: *Farmers are the backbone of this community.*
3 [U] courage and determination: *Stuart doesn't have the backbone to be a good manager.*

back·break·ing /ˈbækbreɪkɪŋ/ *adj* backbreaking work is physically difficult and makes you very tired THESAURUS TIRING

ˈback-ˌburner, **back·bur·ner** /ˈbækˌbɜːnə $ -ˌbɜːrnər/ *v* [T] *informal* to delay doing something, because it does not need your attention immediately or because it is not as important as other things that you need to do immediately: *Allison back-burnered her prestigious law career when she had a baby.* | *The project has been backburnered.* → **leave/put sth on the back burner** at BURNER(3)

ˈback ˌcatalogue *n* [C] music that a performer has recorded in the past

back·chat /ˈbæktʃæt/ *n* [U] *BrE informal* a rude reply to someone who is telling you what to do SYN **backtalk** *AmE*: *None of your backchat – do your homework!*

back·cloth /ˈbæk-klɒθ $ -klɒːθ/ *n* [C] *especially BrE* **1** a BACKDROP(3) **2** a BACKDROP(2)

back·comb /ˈbæk-kəʊm $ -koʊm/ *v* [T] *BrE* to comb your hair against the way it grows in order to make it look thicker and shape it into a style SYN **tease** *AmE*

ˈback ˌcountry *n* [U] **1** *especially AusE* a country area where few people live **2** *AmE* an area, especially in the mountains, away from roads and towns

back·date /ˌbækˈdeɪt $ ˈbækdeɪt/ *v* [T] **1** to make something have its effect from an earlier date: **backdate sth from/to sth** *The pay increase will be backdated to January.* **2** *AmE* to write an earlier date on a document or cheque than when it was actually written

ˌback ˈdoor *n* [C] **1** a door at the back or side of a building **2** **get in through the back door** to achieve something by having an unfair secret advantage: *His father works there, so he got in through the back door.*

back·door /ˈbækdɔː $ -dɔːr/ *adj* [only before noun] secret, or not publicly stated as your intention: *a backdoor tax rise*

back·drop /ˈbækdrɒp $ -drɑːp/ *n* [C] **1** *literary* the SCENERY behind something that you are looking at: **[+to]** *The sea made a splendid backdrop to the garden.* **2** the conditions or situation in which something happens: **against a backdrop of sth** *a love story set against a backdrop of war and despair* **3** a painted cloth hung across the back of a stage

ˈback-end *adj* used by a computer or program, not directly by the user: *back-end software*

back·er /ˈbækə $ -ər/ *n* [C] someone who supports a plan, especially by providing money: *We're still trying to find backers for the housing development scheme.*

back·fire /ˌbækˈfaɪə $ ˈbækfaɪr/ ●○○ *v* [I]
1 if a plan or action backfires, it has the opposite effect to the one you intended: *The company's new policy backfired when a number of employees threatened to quit.* THESAURUS FAIL
2 if a car backfires, it makes a sudden loud noise because the engine is not working correctly

ˈback forˌmation *n* [C] *technical* a new word formed from an older word, for example 'televise', which is formed from 'television'

back·gam·mon /ˈbækgæmən/ *n* [U] a game for two players, using flat round pieces and DICE on a special board → see picture at BOARD GAME

BACKGROUND

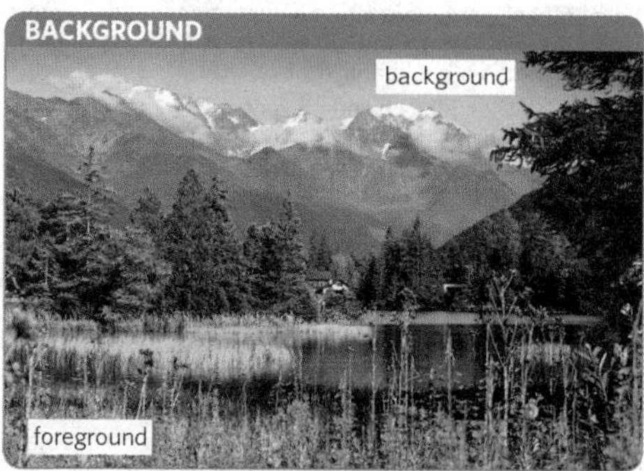

back·ground /ˈbækgraʊnd/ ●●● S2 W2 *n*
1 [C] someone's family, education, previous work etc: *Students with a background in chemistry will probably find the course easier.* | *It's important to understand other people, people* ***from different backgrounds****.* | *Do you know anything about his background?*
2 [C,U] the situation or past events that explain why something happens in the way that it does: **[+to]** *Without knowing the background to the case, I couldn't possibly comment.* | **against a background of sth** *The peace talks are being held against a background of increasing violence.* | **background information/details/data etc** *The author included a new chapter of background material for the second edition of the book.*
3 [C usually singular] the area that is behind the main thing

that you are looking at, especially in a picture: *The background looks out of focus.* | **in the background** *In the background, you can see my college friends.*
4 [C] the pattern or colour on top of which something has been drawn, printed etc: *red lettering on a white background*
5 in the background someone who keeps or stays in the background tries not to be noticed: *The president's advisors are content to remain in the background.*
6 [C,U] the sounds that you can hear apart from the main thing that you are listening to: **in the background** *In the background, I could hear the sound of traffic.* | *All of the* ***background noise*** *made it difficult to have a phone conversation.*

B

COLLOCATIONS

ADJECTIVES

family background *Many kids lack a stable family background.*
social background *Universities aim to attract students from varied social backgrounds.*
cultural background *Some of his attitudes were due to his cultural background.*
ethnic background *We do not discriminate against people because of their ethnic background or gender.*
socio-economic background *Smokers often come from poorer socio-economic backgrounds.*
educational/academic background *The interviewer will ask you about your educational background and work experience.*
a working-class/middle-class background | a deprived/disadvantaged background | a privileged/wealthy background

VERBS

have a background (in sth) *We are looking for someone who has a background in science.*
come from a background *Mark and I came from very similar backgrounds.*

back·hand /ˈbækhænd/ *n* [C usually singular] a way of hitting the ball in tennis and some other games, in which the back of your hand is turned in the direction of the ball when you hit it → **forehand** → see picture at TENNIS —**backhand** *adj*

back·hand·ed /ˌbækˈhændɪd◂ $ ˈbækhændɪd/ *adj* **1** a backhanded remark or COMPLIMENT seems to express praise or admiration but in fact is insulting **2** a backhanded shot is a backhand shot

back·hand·er /ˈbækhændə $ -ər/ *n* [C] **1** a hit or shot that you do using the back of your hand **2** *BrE informal* money that you pay illegally and secretly to get something done SYN **bribe**: *Investigators estimate that £35m had been spent on bribes and backhanders.*

back·hoe /ˈbækhəʊ $ -hoʊ/ *n* [C] *AmE* a large digging machine used for making roads etc

back·ing /ˈbækɪŋ/ ●○○ *n*
1 [U] support or help, especially with money: *She flew to New York to try to raise some* ***financial backing*** *for the project.*
2 [C] material that is used to make the back of an object
3 [C] the music that is played at the same time as a singer's voice —**backing** *adj*: *backing singers*

back·lash /ˈbæklæʃ/ *n* [C] a strong negative reaction by a number of people against recent events, especially against political or social developments: **[+against]** *The 1970s saw the first backlash against the women's movement.* | **[+from]** *The management fear a backlash from fans over the team's poor performances.*

back·less /ˈbækləs/ *adj* a backless dress, SWIMSUIT etc does not cover much or any of a woman's back

back·link /ˈbæklɪŋk/ *n* [C] *technical* a LINK that comes to a website from another website

back·log /ˈbæklɒg $ -lɒːg, -lɑːg/ *n* [C usually singular] a large amount of work that you need to complete, especially work that should already have been completed: **[+of]** *a backlog of requests* | *It's going to take us months to* ***clear*** *the* ***backlog****.*

ˈback ˌoffice *n* [C] the department of a bank or other financial institution that manages or organizes the work of the institution, but that does not deal with customers —**back-office** *adj* [only before noun]: *back-office operations*

back·pack /ˈbækpæk/ ●●○ *n* [C] a RUCKSACK → see picture at BAG[1]

back·pack·er /ˈbækpækə $ -ər/ *n* [C] someone who is travelling for pleasure, usually with not very much money, and who walks or uses public transport and carries a backpack **THESAURUS** TOURIST, TRAVEL

back·pack·ing /ˈbækˌpækɪŋ/ *n* [U] the activity of travelling for pleasure, usually without very much money, and carrying a backpack

back·ped·al /ˌbækˈpedl $ ˈbækˌpedl/ *v* (**backpedalled**, **backpedalling** *BrE*, **backpedaled**, **backpedaling** *AmE*) [I] **1** to change your opinion or not do something that you had promised to do → **backtrack**: *They are backpedalling on the commitment to cut taxes.* **2** to PEDAL backwards on a bicycle **3** to run or walk backwards

back·rest /ˈbækrest/ *n* [C] the part of a chair or seat that supports your back

back·room boy /ˈbækrʊm ˌbɔɪ, -ruːm-/ *n* [C usually plural] *BrE informal* someone such as an engineer or scientist whose work is important but who does not get much attention or fame

ˈback-ˌscratching *n* [U] the act of doing nice things for someone in order to get something in return

ˌback ˈseat *n* **1** [C] a seat at the back of a car, behind where the driver sits **2 back seat driver** *informal* **a)** a passenger in the back of a car who gives unwanted advice to the driver about how to drive **b)** someone in business or politics who tries to control things that they are not really responsible for **3 take a back seat** to accept a less important position than someone or something else: *Finally, Bryant decided to take a back seat and let his son run the company.*

back·side /ˈbæksaɪd/ *n* [C] *informal* **1** the part of your body that you sit on SYN **bottom 2 get off your backside** to start doing something or taking action, instead of not doing anything → **be a pain in the backside** at PAIN[1](3)

back·slap·ping /ˈbækˌslæpɪŋ/ *n* [U] behaviour in which people praise each other's achievements more than they deserve

back·slash /ˈbækslæʃ/ ●○○ *n* [C] a line (\) used in writing to separate words, numbers, or letters

back·slide /ˌbækˈslaɪd $ ˈbækslaɪd/ *v* (*past tense and past participle* **backslid** /-slɪd/) [I] to start doing the bad things that you used to do, after having improved your behaviour —**backslider** *n* [C]

back·space /ˈbækspeɪs/ *n* [C usually singular] a button on a computer KEYBOARD or TYPEWRITER that you press to move backwards towards the beginning of the line

back·spin /ˈbækspɪn/ *n* [U] a turning movement in a ball that has been hit so that the top of the ball turns backwards as the ball travels forwards → **topspin**

back·stab·bing /ˈbækstæbɪŋ/ *n* [U] the act of secretly doing bad things to someone else, especially saying bad things about them, in order to gain an advantage for yourself —**backstabber** *n* [C]

back·stage /ˌbækˈsteɪdʒ◂/ *adj, adv* **1** behind the stage in a theatre, especially in the actors' dressing rooms **2** in private, especially within the secret parts of an organization: *intensive backstage negotiations*

ˈback ˌstory *n* [C] the things that happened to a character in a book or film before the beginning of the story being told in the book or film: *The back story of why she hates her father is a bit too contrived.*

back·street[1] /ˈbækstriːt/ *adj* [only before noun] backstreet activities are done in a secret or illegal way, and are often done badly: *a backstreet abortion*

backstreet[2], **ˈback street** *n* [C] a small quiet street that is away from the main part of a town

back·stroke /ˈbækstrəʊk $ -stroʊk/ *n* [singular, U] a way of swimming on your back by moving first one arm then the other backwards while kicking your feet → see picture at SWIM

back·talk /ˈbæktɔːk $ -tɒːk/ *n* [U] *AmE informal* a rude reply to someone who is telling you what to do (SYN) **backchat** *BrE*

ˌback-to-ˈback¹ *adj* [only before noun] happening one after another: *They have had five back-to-back wins.*

back-to-back² *n* [C] *BrE* a house in a row or TERRACE built with its back touching the back of the next row of houses

back·track /ˈbæktræk/ *v* [I] **1** to change an opinion or promise that you gave so that it is not as strong as it was earlier → **backpedal**: **[+on]** *The president is backtracking on his promise to increase health care spending.* **2** to return by the same way that you came: *We had to backtrack about a mile.*

back·up /ˈbækʌp/ ●○○ *n*
1 [C] something that you can use to replace something that does not work or is lost: *Always have a backup plan.* | *a backup generator*
2 [C] a copy of a computer document, program etc, which is made in case the original becomes lost or damaged: *Make a backup of any work you do on the computer.*
3 [U] people or things that can be used to provide support and help if they are needed: *Army units can only operate if they have sufficient backup.* | *a backup team*
4 [C] *AmE* someone who will play in a sports team if one of the other players is injured or ill (SYN) **reserve**: *a backup goalie*

back·ward /ˈbækwəd $ -wərd/ ●●○ *adj*
1 [only before noun] looking or facing in the direction that is behind you (OPP) **forward**: *She went without a backward glance.*
2 developing slowly and less successfully than most others: *a backward country* | *a backward child* —**backwardness** *n* [U]

ˌbackward-ˈlooking *adj* using the methods and ideas of the past rather than modern ones – used to show disapproval (OPP) **forward-looking**: *Darwin transformed a backward-looking organisation into a respected art school.*

back·wards /ˈbækwədz $ -wərdz/ ●●● (S3) (*also* **backward** /-wəd $ -wərd/ *AmE*) *adv*
1 in the direction that is behind you (OPP) **forwards**: *Hannah took a step backward.* | *She pushed me and I fell backwards into the chair.*
2 towards the beginning or the past (OPP) **forwards**: *Count backwards from 100.*
3 with the back part in front: *Your T-shirt is on backwards.*
4 towards a worse state (OPP) **forwards**: *The new measures are seen by some as a major step backwards.*
5 backwards and forwards first in one direction and then in the opposite direction, usually many times: *Kip stumbled backwards and forwards before falling down.*
6 bend/lean over backwards (to do sth) to try as hard as possible to help or please someone: *City officials bent over backwards to help downtown businesses.*
7 know sth backwards *BrE*, **know sth backwards and forwards** *AmE* to know something very well or perfectly: *She practiced her part until she knew it backwards and forwards.*

ˌbackwards comˈpatible *adj* able to be used with earlier forms of software

back·wash /ˈbækwɒʃ $ -wɒːʃ, -wɑːʃ/ *n* [U] **1** a backward flow of water, caused by an OAR, wave etc **2** the bad situation that remains after something bad has happened: *the backwash of the company's failure*

back·wa·ter /ˈbækwɔːtə $ -wɒːtər, -wɑː-/ *n* [C] **1** a very quiet place not influenced by outside events or new ideas – used to show disapproval: *a rural backwater* **2** a part of a river away from the main part, where the water does not move

back·woods /ˈbækwʊdz/ *n* [plural] a distant and undeveloped area away from any towns

back·woods·man /ˈbækwʊdzmən/ *n* (*plural* **backwoodsmen** /-mən/) [C] **1** someone who lives in the backwoods **2** *BrE* a member of a political party or parliament, especially the House of Lords, who is not very active politically and only sometimes votes, attends meetings etc

back·yard, **ˌback ˈyard** /ˌbækˈjɑːd◂ $ -ˈjɑːrd◂/ *n* [C] **1** *BrE* a small area behind a house, covered with a hard surface **2** *AmE* an area of land behind a house, often covered with grass: *The old man grew vegetables in his backyard.* **3 in sb's own backyard** *informal* very near where someone lives, works etc: *Americans would probably react differently to the war if it was in their own back yard.* **4 not in my backyard** used to say that you do not want something to happen near where you live —**backyard** *adj* [only before noun]: *a backyard pool*

bacn /ˈbeɪkən/ *n* [U] *especially AmE* email that you have chosen to receive from an organization or service but which you may not want to read immediately or at all

ba·con /ˈbeɪkən/ ●●○ (S3) *n* [U]
1 salted or smoked meat from the back or sides of a pig, often served in narrow thin pieces: *bacon and eggs* | **rasher of bacon** *BrE* (=piece of bacon)
2 bring home the bacon *informal* to provide enough money to support your family → **save sb's bacon** at SAVE¹(11)

bac·te·ri·a /bækˈtɪəriə $ -ˈtɪr-/ ●○○ *n* [plural] (*singular* **bacterium** /-riəm/) very small living things, some of which cause illness or disease → **virus** —**bacterial** *adj*: *a bacterial infection*

bac·te·ri·ol·o·gy /bækˌtɪəriˈɒlədʒi $ -ˌtɪriˈɑːl-/ *n* [U] the scientific study of bacteria —**bacteriologist** *n* [C] —**bacteriological** /bækˌtɪəriəˈlɒdʒɪkəl $ -ˌtɪriəˈlɑː-/ *adj*

bad¹ /bæd/ ●●● (S1) (W1) *adj* (*comparative* **worse** /wɜːs $ wɜːrs/, *superlative* **worst** /wɜːst $ wɜːrst/)
1 NOT GOOD unpleasant or likely to cause problems (OPP) **good**: *I have some bad news for you.* | *I thought things couldn't possibly get any worse.* | *The plane was delayed for several hours by bad weather.* | *It's difficult to break bad habits.* | *a bad smell*
2 LOW QUALITY low in quality or below an acceptable standard (OPP) **good**: *The failure of the company was due to bad management.* | *Your handwriting is so bad I can hardly read it.* | *That was the worst movie I've ever seen.*
3 NOT SENSIBLE [usually before noun] not sensible, or not suitable in a particular situation (OPP) **good**: *Cutting spending at this time is a bad idea.* | *Making big changes in your diet all at once is a* **bad thing to do**.
4 MORALLY WRONG morally wrong or evil (OPP) **good**: *He's a bad man – keep away from him.* → BAD GUY
5 WRONG BEHAVIOUR spoken doing something you should not do, or behaving in a wrong way – used especially about children or pets (SYN) **naughty**: *Katie was very bad today!* | **bad girl/dog etc** *Bad cat! Get off the table!*
6 SERIOUS serious or severe: *He was in a bad accident.* | *The pain in my side is worse than it was yesterday.*
7 a bad time/moment etc a time that is not suitable or causes problems: *It's a bad time to have to borrow money, with interest rates so high.* | *You've come at the worst possible moment. I have a meeting in five minutes.*
8 HARMFUL damaging or harmful: *Pollution is having a bad effect on fish stocks.* | **[+for]** *Smoking is bad for your health.* | *Too much salt can be* **bad for you**. | **It is bad** *for kids to be on their own so much.*
9 FOOD food that is bad is not safe to eat because it has decayed: *bad fish* | *This milk has* **gone bad**.
10 NO SKILL having no skill or ability in a particular activity: **bad at (doing) sth** *I'm really bad at chess.* | *They have got to be the worst band on the planet.*
11 bad heart/leg/back etc a heart, leg etc that is injured or does not work correctly: *I haven't been able to do much because of my bad back.*
12 LANGUAGE bad language is rude or offensive: *We were shocked to hear the little boy using bad language in front of his mother.* | *Jacky said a bad word!*
13 be in a bad mood (*also* **be in a bad temper** *BrE*) to feel annoyed or angry: *The boss is in a bad mood.*

B

14 feel bad a) to feel ashamed or sorry about something: **feel bad about (doing) sth** *I felt bad about not being able to come last night.* | **[+for]** *I feel bad for Ann – she studied so hard for that test and she still didn't pass.* **b)** to feel ill
15 not bad *spoken* used to say that something is good, or better than you expected: *'How are you?' 'Oh, not bad.'* | *That's not a bad idea.*
16 not too/so bad *spoken* used to say that something is not as bad as expected: *The exams weren't so bad.*
17 too bad *spoken* **a)** used to say that you do not care that something bad happens to someone: *'I'm going to be late now!' 'Too bad – you should have gotten up earlier.'* **b)** used to say that you are sorry that something bad has happened to someone: *It's too bad that you couldn't come to the party last night.*
18 go from bad to worse to become even more unpleasant or difficult: *The schools have gone from bad to worse in this area.*
19 be in a bad way *informal* to be very ill, unhappy, or injured, or not in a good condition: *She was in a bad way after the funeral.*
20 a bad name if something has a bad name, people do not respect or trust it: **have/get a bad name** *The bar had a bad name and was avoided by all the locals.* | **give sb/sth a bad name** *These annoying tourists give all Americans a bad name.*
21 bad lot/sort/type *BrE old-fashioned* someone who is morally bad or cannot be trusted
22 bad penny *BrE* someone or something that causes trouble and is difficult to avoid: *Sure enough, Steve* ***turned up like*** *the proverbial* ***bad penny*** (=suddenly appeared).
23 be taken bad *BrE informal* to become ill: *He was taken bad in the middle of the night.*
24 in bad faith if someone does something in bad faith, they are behaving dishonestly and have no intention of keeping a promise: *In order to sue, you have to prove that the company was* ***acting in bad faith***.
25 bad news *spoken informal* someone or something that always causes trouble: *I'd avoid her if I were you. She's bad news.*
26 bad form *BrE old-fashioned* socially unacceptable behaviour: *It's bad form to argue with the umpire.*
27 bad blood angry or bitter feelings between people: **[+between]** *There's too much bad blood between them.*
28 not have a bad word to say about/against sb if no one has a bad word to say about a particular person, everyone likes and respects that person
29 it's bad enough ... *spoken* used to say that you already have one problem, so that you do not want to worry about or deal with another one: *It's bad enough having to bring up three kids on your own, without having to worry about money as well!*
30 sth can't be bad *spoken* used to persuade someone that something is good or worth doing: *You only pay £10 deposit and no interest – that can't be bad, can it?*
31 (*comparative* **badder**, *superlative* **baddest**) *spoken informal especially AmE* **a)** used when you think something is very good: *Now that's a bad car!* **b)** someone who is bad is very determined and does not always obey rules – used to show approval —**badness** *n* [U]

THESAURUS

bad not good: *a bad idea* | *His behaviour is getting worse.*
poor not as good as it could be or should be: *A poor diet can lead to ill health.* | *his poor performance at school*
not very good not good – often used instead of saying directly that something was 'bad', especially when you were disappointed by it: *The film wasn't very good.*
disappointing not as good as you hoped or expected: *Her exam results were disappointing.* | *a disappointing start to the campaign*
negative bad – used when talking about the bad result or effect of something: *All the publicity had a negative impact on sales.*
undesirable *formal* bad and not wanted: *The policy had some undesirable consequences.*
unfavourable *formal* unfavourable conditions are not good for doing something: *The boat race was cancelled because of unfavourable weather.*

VERY BAD

awful/terrible/dreadful *especially BrE* very bad: *The movie was awful.* | *Her house is in a terrible state.*
horrible very bad, especially in a way that shocks or upsets you: *He describes prison as 'a horrible place'.*
disgusting smelling or tasting very bad: *The food was disgusting.* | *The fish smelled disgusting.*
lousy /ˈlaʊzi/ *informal* very bad or disappointing: *The weather has been lousy all week.* | *I'm fed up with this lousy job.*
ghastly /ˈɡɑːstli $ ˈɡæstli/ *BrE informal* very bad: *I've had a ghastly day.* | *a ghastly mistake*
severe severe problems, injuries, illnesses etc are very bad and serious: *The country faces severe economic problems.* | *severe delays*
atrocious/appalling/horrendous extremely bad in a way that is shocking: *Her behaviour has been absolutely atrocious.* | *The country has an appalling human rights record.*
abysmal /əˈbɪzməl/ very bad and of a very low standard: *The team's performance was abysmal.*

bad² *n* **1 to the bad** *BrE informal* if you are a particular amount to the bad, you are that much poorer or you owe that much: *Thanks to your mistake, I'm £500 to the bad!* **2 my bad!** *AmE spoken informal* used to say that you have made a mistake or that something is your fault **3 go to the bad** *BrE old-fashioned* to begin living in a wrong or immoral way

bad³ *adv spoken* a word used to mean 'badly' that many people think is incorrect: *I need that money bad.*

ˈbad-ass *adj* [only before noun] *AmE informal* **1** very good or impressive: *bad-ass biker gear* **2** a bad-ass person is very determined and does not always obey rules – used to show approval: *Johnson plays this bad-ass cop named O'Riley.* —**bad-ass, badass** *n* [C]

ˈbad bank *n* [C] a bank that is set up so that it will take on LOANS from another bank that are unlikely to be repaid

ˈbad choˌlesterol (*also* **LDL**) *n* [U] a type of CHOLESTEROL (=chemical substance found in your blood) that can gradually turn into a hard substance that can stop your blood flowing properly and can eventually cause heart disease → **GOOD CHOLESTEROL**

ˌbad ˈdebt *n* [C] a debt that is unlikely to be paid

bad·die, **baddy** /ˈbædi/ *n* (*plural* **baddies**) [C] *BrE informal* someone who is bad, especially in a book or film SYN **bad guy** *AmE*

bade /bæd,beɪd/ *v* the past tense of BID

badge /bædʒ/ ●●○ *n* [C]
1 *BrE* a small piece of metal, cloth, or plastic with a picture or words on it, worn to show rank, membership of a group, support for a political idea etc SYN **button**, **pin** *AmE*: *We were each handed a badge with our name on it.* → see picture at PATCH¹
2 a small piece of metal or plastic that you carry to show people that you work for a particular organization, for example that you are a police officer
3 a badge of honour/courage etc something that shows that you have a particular quality: *He now sees his wartime injuries as a badge of honor.*
4 (*also* **merit badge** *AmE*) a small piece of cloth with a picture on it, given to SCOUTS, GUIDEs etc to show what skills they have learned: *Steve won a photography badge in the Boy Scouts.*
5 badge of office *BrE* an object which shows that you have an official position: *Mayors wear chains around their necks as badges of office.*
6 an ICON that provides a link to another web page, for example to your page on a SOCIAL NETWORKING SITE: *How do I add a badge to my blog?*

bad·ger¹ /ˈbædʒə $ -ər/ *n* [C] an animal that has black and white fur, lives in holes in the ground, and is active at night

badger² *v* [T] to try to persuade someone by asking them something several times SYN **pester**: *She badgered me for weeks until I finally gave in.* | **badger sb to do sth** *My friends keep badgering me to get a cell phone.* | **badger sb into doing sth** *I had to badger the kids into doing their homework.*

ˈbad guy *n* [C] *AmE informal* a man in a film, book etc who is evil or dangerous SYN **baddie** *BrE*

ˌbad ˈhair day *n* [C] *informal* a day when you are unhappy and easily upset, especially because your hair does not look the way you want it to look

bad·i·nage /ˈbædɪnɑːʒ $ ˌbædənˈɑːʒ/ *n* [U] *literary* conversation that involves a lot of jokes or humour

bad·ly /ˈbædli/ ●●● S3 W3 *adv* (*comparative* **worse** /wɜːs $ wɜːrs/, *superlative* **worst** /wɜːst $ wɜːrst/)
1 in an unsatisfactory or unsuccessful way OPP **well**: *The company has been very badly managed.* | *The novel was translated badly into English.* | *badly made furniture* | *Rob* ***did very badly*** *in the History exam.*
2 to a great or serious degree: *He's been limping badly ever since the skiing accident.* | *We badly wanted to help, but there was nothing we could do.* | *He was beaten so badly that his brother didn't recognize him.* | *The school* ***is badly in need of*** (=very much needs) *some new computers.* | *Things started to* ***go badly wrong*** (=go wrong in a serious way) *for Eric after he lost his job.*
3 think badly of sb/sth to have a bad opinion of someone or something: *I'm sure they won't think badly of you if you tell them you need some help.*

ˌbadly ˈoff *adj* (*comparative* **worse-off**, *superlative* **worst-off**) [not before noun] *especially BrE* **1** (*also* **bad-off** *AmE*) not having much money SYN **poor** OPP **well-off**
2 badly off for sth *BrE* not having enough of something that you need OPP **well-off**: *The school is rather badly off for equipment.*

bad·min·ton /ˈbædmɪntən/ *n* [U] a game that is similar to tennis but played with a SHUTTLECOCK (=small feathered object) instead of a ball → see picture at **SPORT¹**

ˈbad-mouth *v* [T] *especially AmE informal* to criticize someone or something: *Her former colleagues accused her of bad-mouthing them in public.*

ˌbad-ˈtempered ●●○ *adj BrE* someone who is bad-tempered becomes easily annoyed and talks in an angry way to people SYN **irritable** **THESAURUS** ANGRY

bad·ware /ˈbædweə $ -wer/ *n* [U] another word for MALWARE

baf·fle¹ /ˈbæfəl/ ●○○ *v* [T] if something baffles you, you cannot understand or explain it at all: *The question baffled me completely.* —**baffled** *adj*: *We were all utterly baffled.* —**baffling** *adj*: *a baffling mystery* —**bafflement** *n* [U]

baffle² *n* [C] *technical* a board, sheet of metal etc that controls the flow of air, water, or sound into or out of something

BAFTA /ˈbæftə/ *n* [C] a prize given each year by the British Academy of Film and Television Arts for the best films, television programmes, actors etc: *Her film won two BAFTAs.* | *the BAFTA award ceremony*

bag¹ /bæg/ ●●● S1 W2 *n* [C]
1 CONTAINER **a)** a container made of paper, cloth, or thin plastic, that usually opens at the top: *a paper bag* | *a plastic bag* | *a garbage bag* **b)** a HANDBAG: *Don't leave your bag in the car.* **c)** a large bag that you use to carry your clothes etc when you are travelling: *Just throw your bags in the back of the car.* | *a garment bag*
2 AMOUNT the amount that a bag will hold: **[+of]** *a bag of popcorn*
3 old/stupid bag *spoken* an insulting word for an old woman: *You silly old bag!*
4 A LOT OF STH **bags of sth** *BrE spoken* a lot of something SYN **plenty**: *She's got bags of money.* | *No need to rush – we've got bags of time.*

BAGS

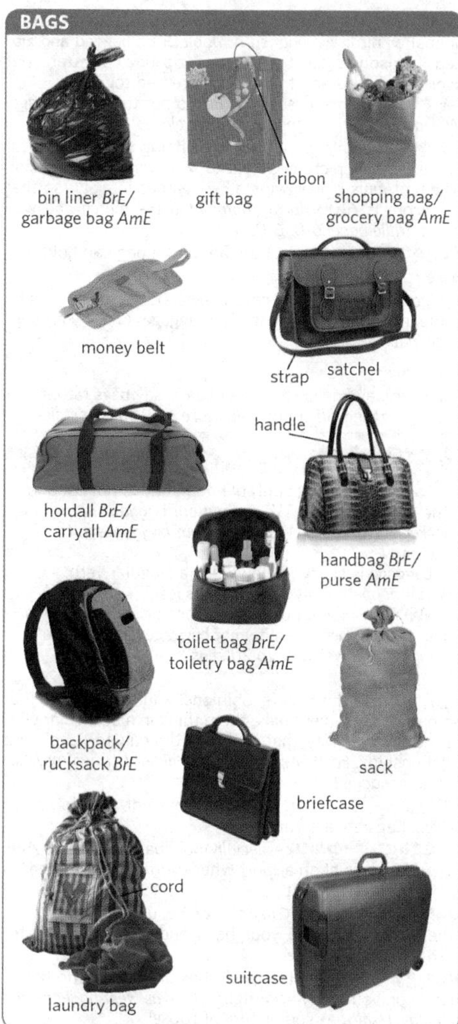

5 pack your bags *informal* to leave a place where you have been living, usually after an argument: *We told her to pack her bags at once.*
6 EYES **bags** [plural] dark circles or loose skin under your eyes, usually because of old age or being tired
7 a bag of bones *informal* a person or animal who is too thin
8 in the bag *informal* certain to be won or achieved: *The governor's advisors believe the election is in the bag.*
9 TROUSERS **bags** [plural] *BrE old-fashioned* loose-fitting trousers: *Oxford bags*
10 not sb's bag *old-fashioned informal* something that someone is not very interested in or not very good at: *Thanks, but dancing is not really my bag.*
11 bag and baggage *BrE* with all your possessions: *They threw her out of the house, bag and baggage.*
12 HUNTING [usually singular] *BrE* the number of birds or animals that someone kills when they go hunting: *We had a good bag that day.* → **SLEEPING BAG, AIRBAG, DUFFEL BAG, TOTE BAG, BEANBAG, PUNCHBAG, SANDBAG¹, TEABAG,** → **let the cat out of the bag** at **CAT(2)**, → **be left holding the bag** at **HOLD¹(26)**, → **a mixed bag** at **MIXED(6)**

bag² *v* (**bagged, bagging**) [T] **1** to put things into bags: *He got a job bagging groceries.* **2** *informal* to manage to get something that a lot of people want: *Try to bag a couple of seats at the front.* **3** *BrE informal* to score a GOAL or a point in sport: *Larsson bagged his thirtieth goal of the season in*

Celtic's win. **4** *especially BrE informal* to kill or catch an animal or bird: *We bagged a rabbit.* **5 be bagged and zip-tied** if prisoners are bagged and zip-tied, bags are put over their heads and their hands are tied together

bag sth ↔ **up** *phr v especially BrE* to put things into bags: *We bagged up the money before we closed the shop.*

ba·gel /ˈbeɪɡəl/ *n* [C] **1** a small ring-shaped type of bread → see picture at BREAD **2** *informal* an occasion when a tennis player wins all six games in a SET, so that the score is 6-0: *Murray dominated the match and won with a triple bagel 6-0, 6-0, 6-0.*

bag·ful /ˈbæɡfʊl/ *n* [C] the amount a bag can hold

bag·gage /ˈbæɡɪdʒ/ ●●○ *n*

1 [U] *especially AmE* the cases, bags, boxes etc carried by someone who is travelling SYN **luggage**: *Check your baggage in at the desk.*

REGISTER
In everyday English, people usually say **bags** rather than **baggage**: *Shall I help you take your **bags** upstairs?*

GRAMMAR: Countable or uncountable?

- **Baggage** is an uncountable noun and is not used in the plural. You say: *We can put our baggage in the locker.* ✗ Don't say: *We can put our baggages in the locker.*
- **Baggage** is always followed by a singular verb: *What happens if my baggage **gets** lost?*
- When talking about one suitcase or bag, you say a **piece of baggage** or an **item of baggage**: *Each piece of baggage can weigh up to 20 kilos.*

2 [U] *informal* the beliefs, opinions, and experiences that someone has, which make them think in a particular way, especially in a way that makes it difficult to have good relationships: *Each employee brings his or her own psychological baggage to the workplace.*

ˈbaggage ˌcar *n* [C] *AmE* the part of a train where boxes, bags etc are carried

ˈbaggage ˌreclaim *especially BrE*, **ˈbaggage ˌclaim** *AmE* *n* [U] the place at an airport where you collect your cases and bags after a flight

ˈbaggage room *n* [C] *AmE* a place, usually in a station, where you can leave your bags and collect them later SYN **left luggage office**

bag·gy /ˈbæɡi/ *adj* baggy clothes are big and do not fit tightly on your body OPP **tight**: *She was wearing jeans and a baggy T-shirt.* → see picture at LOOSE[1]

ˈbag ˌlady *n* [C] *informal* an impolite word for a homeless woman who lives on the streets and carries all her possessions with her

bag·pipes /ˈbæɡpaɪps/ *n* [plural] a musical instrument played especially in Scotland, in which air blown into a bag is forced out through pipes to produce a sound → see picture at KILT —**bagpipe** *adj*

ba·guette /bæˈɡet/ *n* [C] a long thin LOAF of bread, made especially in France → see picture at BREAD

bah /bɑː/ *interjection old-fashioned* used to show disapproval of something: *Bah! That's stupid.*

bahahaha used on SOCIAL NETWORKING SITES to express laughter, especially evil laughter

bail[1] /beɪl/ ●○○ *n*

1 [U] money left with a court of law to make sure that a prisoner will return when their TRIAL starts: *Carpenter is free **on bail** while he appeals his conviction.* | *She was murdered by a man who was **out on bail** for rape.* | *The three men were **released on bail** pending an appeal.* | *He is not likely to be **granted bail**.* | *Carter has been **refused bail** and will remain in custody.* | *The judge ordered that Jones be **held without bail**.* | *Why can't you ask your father to **put up bail** for you?* | *Two of the defendants **jumped bail** and fled to New York.* | ***Bail** was **set** at $30,000.*

2 [C usually plural] one of the two small pieces of wood laid on top of the STUMPS in a game of CRICKET

bail[2] *v* **1** (*also* **bail out** *AmE*, **bale out** *BrE*) [I] *informal* to escape from a situation that you do not want to be in anymore: *After ten years in the business, McArthur is baling out.* **2** [T] *BrE* if someone is bailed, they are let out of prison to wait for their TRIAL after they have left a sum of money with the court: *Dakers was **bailed to appear** at Durham Crown Court.*

bail out *phr v* **1 bail sb/sth ↔ out** (*also* **bale sb/sth ↔ out** *BrE*) to do something to help someone out of trouble, especially financial problems: *Some local businesses have offered to bail out the museum.* | *Sutton bailed his team out with a goal in the last minute.* **2 bail sb ↔ out** to leave a large sum of money with a court so that someone can be let out of prison while waiting for their TRIAL: *Clarke's family paid £500 to bail him out.* **3** *AmE* to escape from a plane, using a PARACHUTE SYN **bale out** *BrE* **4 bail sth ↔ out** (*also* **bale sth ↔ out** *BrE*) to remove water that has come into a boat

bai·ley /ˈbeɪli/ *n* [C] an open area inside the outer wall of a castle

bai·liff /ˈbeɪlɪf/ *n* [C] **1** *BrE* someone who looks after a farm or land that belongs to someone else **2** *AmE* an official of the legal system who watches prisoners and keeps order in a court of law **3** *BrE* an official of the legal system who can take people's goods or property when they owe money

ˈbail-in *n* [C] a way of helping a bank or other institution in financial difficulty, in which people who are owed money by it accept that part of the money they are owed will not be paid back

ˈbail-out *n* [C] *informal* financial help given to a person or a company that is in difficulty

bain ma·rie /ˌbæn məˈriː/ *n* [C] a pan that floats in a larger pan full of water, used for cooking things gently

bairn /beən $ bern/ *n* [C] a baby or child - used in Scotland

bait[1] /beɪt/ ●○○ *n* [singular, U]

1 food used to attract fish, animals, or birds so that you can catch them: *We used worms as bait.* | *The fish wouldn't **take the bait**.* → see picture at FISHING

2 something attractive that is offered to someone to make them do something or buy something, especially when this is done in a dishonest way that tricks people: *Plenty of people **took the bait*** (=accepted what was on offer) *and lost their life savings.*

3 rise to the bait to become angry when someone is deliberately trying to make you angry: *Senator O'Brien just smiled, refusing to rise to the bait.*

bait[2] *v* [T] **1** to put bait on a hook to catch fish or in a trap to catch animals **2** to deliberately try to make someone angry by criticizing them, using rude names etc **3 bear-baiting/badger-baiting etc** the activity of attacking a wild animal with dogs

baize /beɪz/ *n* [U] thick cloth that is usually green, and is used to cover tables on which games such as POOL are played → see picture at POOL[1]

ba·jil·lion /bəˈdʒɪljən/ *n* [C] *informal humorous* a very large number of things: *I gave him a bajillion reasons why it was a bad idea.*

bake /beɪk/ ●●● S3 *v* [I,T]

1 to cook something using dry heat, in an OVEN: *I'm baking some bread.* | *baked potatoes* | *Bake at 250 degrees for 20 minutes.* THESAURUS ▸ COOK

2 to make something become hard by heating it: *The bricks were baked in the sun.* → BAKING[1], HALF-BAKED

GRAMMAR

Bake belongs to a group of verbs where the same noun can be the subject of the verb or its object.

- You can say: *Bake the cake for 40 minutes.* In this sentence, 'the cake' is the object of **bake**.
- You can also say: *The cake should bake for 40 minutes.* In this sentence, 'the cake' is the subject of **bake**.

GRAMMAR GUIDE ▸ VERBS

ˌbaked ˈbeans *n* [plural] small white beans cooked in a sauce made from tomatoes, usually sold in cans

Ba·ke·lite /ˈbeɪkəlaɪt/ *n* [U] *trademark* a hard plastic used especially in the 1930s and 1940s to make things such as telephones and radios

bak·er /ˈbeɪkə $ -ər/ ●●○ *n* [C]
1 someone who bakes bread and cakes, especially in order to sell them in a shop
2 baker's *BrE* a shop that makes and sells bread and cakes SYN **bakery**

ˌbaker's ˈdozen *n* [singular] thirteen of something

bak·er·y /ˈbeɪkəri/ ●●○ (*also* **baker's** /ˈbeɪkəz $ -ərz/ *BrE*) *n* (*plural* **bakeries**) [C] a place where bread and cakes are baked, or a shop where they are sold

bak·ing¹ /ˈbeɪkɪŋ/ *n* [U] the activity of making cakes, bread etc

baking² *adj spoken* used to say that a person or place is very hot: *I'm baking! | a baking hot day*

ˈbaking ˌpowder *n* [U] a powder used when baking cakes to make them lighter

ˈbaking sheet *n* [C] a baking tray

ˈbaking ˌsoda *n* [U] a powder used when baking cakes to make them lighter SYN **bicarbonate of soda**

ˈbaking tray *n* [C] *BrE* a flat piece of metal that you bake food on → see picture at TRAY

bak·sheesh /ˌbækˈʃiːʃ/ *n* [U] money that people in the Middle East give to poor people, to someone who has helped them, or as a BRIBE

bal·a·cla·va /ˌbæləˈklɑːvə◂/ (*also* **ˌbalaclava ˈhelmet**) *n* [C] a warm hat made of wool, that covers your head and most of your face

bal·a·lai·ka /ˌbæləˈlaɪkə/ *n* [C] a musical instrument like a GUITAR, with a body shaped like a TRIANGLE and three strings, played especially in Russia → see picture at STRINGED INSTRUMENT

bal·ance¹ /ˈbæləns/ ●●● S2 W2 *n*
1 STEADY [U] a state in which all your weight is evenly spread so that you do not fall: *I lost my balance and fell on my face.*
2 EQUAL AMOUNTS [singular, U] a state in which opposite forces or influences exist in equal or the correct amounts, in a way that is good OPP **imbalance**: **[+between]** *Try to keep a balance between work and play.* | **[+of]** *Pesticides seriously upset the balance of nature.*
3 on balance if you think something on balance, you think it after considering all the facts: *I think on balance I prefer the old system.*
4 SURPRISE SB **catch/throw sb off balance** to surprise someone and make them confused and no longer calm: *The question caught him off balance.*
5 BANK [C] the amount of money that you have in your bank account: *My **bank balance** isn't good.*
6 MONEY OWED [C] the balance of a debt is the amount of money that you still owe after you have paid some of it: *The balance is due at the end of the month.*
7 REMAINING **the balance** the amount of something that remains after some has been used, spent, mentioned etc SYN **the rest**: *The firm owns about 96% of the portfolio, with the balance belonging to our family.*
8 be/hang in the balance if the future or success of something hangs in the balance, you cannot yet know whether the result will be bad or good: *Meanwhile, the fate of the refugees continues to hang in the balance.*
9 tip/swing the balance to influence the result of an event: *The dignity and courage shown by the president may **tip the balance in** his party's **favour**.*
10 FOR WEIGHING [C] an instrument for weighing things, with two dishes that hang from a bar SYN **scales**
11 MENTAL/EMOTIONAL HEALTH [singular] when someone's mind is healthy and their emotional state is normal: *The death of her friend had disturbed the **balance of** her **mind**.*
12 the balance of evidence/probability etc the most likely answer or result produced by opposing information, reasons etc → **checks and balances** at CHECK²(4)

COLLOCATIONS – MEANING 1

VERBS

keep your balance (=stay steady) *The sea was so rough that it was hard to keep your balance.*
lose your balance (=become unsteady) *She nearly lost her balance as the bus suddenly moved forward.*
regain/recover your balance (=become steady again) *He held onto Carrie until he regained his balance.*
knock/throw sb off balance *The blow was hard enough to knock him off balance.*

PHRASES

a sense of balance *A good sense of balance is always useful when you are sailing.*

COLLOCATIONS – MEANING 2

VERBS

strike/achieve/find a balance (=succeed in getting the right balance) *It is necessary to strike a balance between the needs of employers and employees.*
keep/maintain a balance *Try to keep a balance between your spending and your earnings.*
upset the balance (=make it less equal or correct) *The move could upset the delicate balance of power in the Middle East.*
change/alter/shift the balance *Will this alter the balance of power in the EU?*
redress the balance (*also* **restore the balance** *BrE*) (=make it equal or correct again) *What can be done to redress the balance in favour of women?*

ADJECTIVES

a good/healthy balance *You should eat a good balance of carbohydrates and protein.*
a delicate balance (=easily damaged) *Too much carbon dioxide in the atmosphere upsets the delicate balance of gases.*
the right/proper/correct balance *With sport, you have to find the right balance between competition and fun.*
the natural balance *Chemicals will upset the natural balance of the pond.*

PHRASES

the balance of power *the European balance of power*
the balance of nature *Nothing can justify permanent damage to the balance of nature.*

balance² ●●● S3 *v*
1 [I,T] to be in or get into a steady position, without falling to one side or the other, or to put something into this position: **balance sth on sth** *She was balancing a plate of food on her knees.* | **[+on]** *He turned around, balancing awkwardly on one foot.*
2 [I,T] to be equal in importance, amount, value, or effect to something that has the opposite effect: *Job losses in manufacturing were balanced by job increases in the service sector. | just enough sugar to balance the acidity of the fruit*
3 [T] to consider the importance of one thing in relation to something else when you are making a decision: **balance sth against sth** *The courts must balance our liberty against the security of the nation.*
4 balance the budget if a government balances the budget, they make the amount of money that they spend equal to the amount of money available
5 balance the books to show that the amount of money a business has received is equal to the amount spent

balance out *phr v* if two or more things balance out, the final result is that they are equal in amount, importance, or effect: *Sometimes I look after the kids and sometimes John does – it all balances out.* → BALANCING ACT

ˈbalance ˌbeam *n* [C] a long narrow wooden board on which a GYMNAST performs

bal·anced /ˈbælənst/ ●●○ *adj*
1 giving equal attention to all sides or opinions SYN **fair**: **a balanced view/account** *a balanced account of what*

happened | ***balanced reporting*** *of the election campaign* THESAURUS ▸ FAIR
2 arranged to include things or people of different kinds in the right amounts: *a balanced programme of events* | *the importance of* ***a balanced diet*** (=one that is healthy because it contains the right foods in the right amounts) | *Nature is* ***perfectly balanced***. | **finely/delicately balanced** (=very carefully balanced) *soup with a delicately balanced flavor*
3 someone who is balanced is calm and sensible, and has good mental health OPP **unbalanced**
4 balanced budget when a government is not spending more money than it has available

ˌbalance of ˈpayments *n* [singular] the difference between what a country spends in order to buy goods and services abroad, and the money it earns selling goods and services abroad

ˌbalance of ˈpower *n* [singular] a situation in which political or military strength is shared evenly: *The election of so many Republicans to Congress has changed the balance of power in Washington.* | *A small centre party* ***holds the balance of power*** (=is able to make either side more powerful than the other by supporting them) *in the Assembly.*

ˌbalance of ˈtrade *n* [singular] the difference in value between the goods a country buys from abroad and the goods it sells abroad

ˈbalance sheet *n* [C] a document showing a company's financial position and wealth at a particular time, often the last day of the financial year: *a healthy balance sheet*

ˈbalancing ˌact *n* [C usually singular] when you are trying to please two or more people or groups who all want different things, or who have ideas that are completely different from each other: *Gilmore had to perform the difficult balancing act of attracting moderate voters without losing his Conservative base.*

bal·co·ny /ˈbælkəni/ ●●○ *n* (*plural* **balconies**) [C]
1 a structure that you can stand on, that is attached to the outside wall of a building, above ground level: *Has your flat got a balcony?*
2 the seats upstairs at a theatre → **stalls** → see picture at THEATRE

bald /bɔːld $ bɒːld/ ●●○ *adj*
1 having little or no hair on your head: *a bald man* | *his shiny bald head* | *Dad started* ***going bald*** *when he was in his thirties.* | *He combed his hair and tried to hide his* ***bald patch*** (=part of someone's head where there is no hair). → see picture at HAIRSTYLE
2 not having enough of what usually covers something: *The car's tires are completely bald.*
3 bald statement/facts/truth a statement etc that is correct but gives no additional information to help you understand or accept what is said: *The bald truth was that Lori didn't love her husband anymore.* —**baldness** *n* [U]

ˈbald ˌeagle *n* [C] a large North American bird with a white head and neck that is the national bird of the US

bal·der·dash /ˈbɔːldədæʃ $ ˈbɒːldər-/ *n* [U] talk or writing that is silly nonsense

ˌbald-ˈfaced *adj* making no attempt to hide the fact that you know you are saying or doing something wrong SYN **barefaced**: *a bald-faced lie*

bald·ing /ˈbɔːldɪŋ $ ˈbɒːl-/ *adj* a balding man is losing the hair on his head: *a balding man in his mid-thirties*

bald·ly /ˈbɔːldli $ ˈbɒːld-/ *adv* in a way that is true but makes no attempt to be polite SYN **bluntly**: *'I'm not coming,' Rosa said baldly next morning at breakfast.*

bald·y /ˈbɔːldi $ ˈbɒːl-/ *n* (*plural* **baldies**) [C] *informal* someone who is BALD – used humorously

bale[1] /beɪl/ *n* [C] a large quantity of something such as paper or HAY that is tightly tied together especially into a block: *a bale of straw*

bale[2] *v* [T] to tie something such as paper or HAY into a large block

bale out *phr v* → BAIL[2], BAIL-OUT

bale·ful /ˈbeɪlfəl/ *adj literary* expressing anger, hatred, or a wish to harm someone: *a baleful look* —**balefully** *adv*

balk (*also* **baulk** *BrE*) /bɔːk, bɔːlk $ bɒːk, bɒːlk/ *v* **1** [I] to not want to do or try something, because it seems difficult, unpleasant, or frightening: **[+at]** *Many people would balk at setting up a new business during a recession.* | *Westerners balk at the prospect of snake on the menu.*
2 [I] if a horse balks at a fence, it stops in front of it and refuses to jump over it **3** [I] *AmE* in baseball, to stop in the middle of the action of throwing the ball to the player who is trying to hit it **4** [T] *formal* to stop someone or something from getting or achieving what they want

bal·kan·i·za·tion (*also* **-isation** *BrE*) /ˌbɔːlkənaɪˈzeɪʃən $ ˌbɒːlkənə-/ *n* [U] the practice of dividing a country into separate independent states – used to show disapproval

bal·ky /ˈbɔːki $ ˈbɒː-/ *adj especially AmE informal* someone or something that is balky does not do what they are expected to do: *a balky air-conditioning system*

ball[1] /bɔːl $ bɒːl/ ●●● S1 W2 *n*
1 ROUND OBJECT [C] a round object that is thrown, kicked, or hit in a game or sport: **throw/hit/kick/catch etc a ball** *Weiskopf hit the ball 330 yards and a cheer went up.* | **a tennis/golf/cricket etc ball** → see pictures at CROQUET, SPORT[1]
2 ROUND SHAPE [C] something formed or rolled into a round shape: *a ball of string* | *Shape the dough into balls.*
3 GAME/SPORT [U] any game or sport played with a ball, especially baseball or BASKETBALL: *D'you want to go out and* ***play ball****?* | *Dad likes college ball.*
4 FOOT/HAND **the ball of the foot/hand** the rounded part of the foot at the base of the toes, or the rounded part of the hand at the base of the thumb
5 on the ball *informal* able to think or act quickly and intelligently: *an assistant who's really on the ball*
6 set/start/keep the ball rolling to start something happening: *To start the ball rolling, the government was asked to contribute £1 million.*
7 the ball is in sb's court it is their turn to take action or to reply: *I've emailed him – now the ball's in his court.*
8 FORMAL OCCASION [C] a large formal occasion at which people dance THESAURUS ▸ PARTY
9 have a ball *informal* to have a very good time
10 balls [plural] *informal not polite* **a)** TESTICLES **b)** courage: *I didn't have the balls to ask.* **c)** *BrE spoken* something that is stupid or wrong SYN **nonsense**: *That's a load of balls!* → BALLS[1]
11 a fast/good/long etc ball a ball that is thrown, hit, or kicked fast etc in a game or sport: *He hit a long ball to right field.*
12 CRICKET **no ball** a ball that is thrown too high, low etc towards someone trying to hit it, in the game of CRICKET or ROUNDERS
13 BASEBALL **no ball** [C] a ball that the hitter does not try to hit, because it is not within the correct area
14 the whole ball of wax *AmE informal* the whole thing SYN **everything**
15 a ball of fire *informal* someone who has a lot of energy and enthusiasm
16 keep several/too many etc balls in the air to struggle to deal with more than one problem or job at the same time: *The company just won't be able to keep that many balls in the air.*
17 drop the ball (*also* **take your eye off the ball**) to make a mistake when dealing with something because you stop thinking carefully or paying attention
18 ball-buster/ball-breaker *informal* **a)** a problem that is very difficult to deal with **b)** an offensive word for a woman who uses her authority over men → **CANNONBALL, CRYSTAL BALL, WRECKING BALL,** → **play ball** at PLAY[1](7)

ball[2] *v* [T] **1** (*also* **ball up**) to make something form a small round shape: *Ray balled up his fists.* **2** *AmE informal not polite* to have sex with a woman

bal·lad /ˈbæləd/ ●○○ *n* [C]
1 a slow love song
2 a short story in the form of a poem or song

ˌball and ˈchain *n* [singular] **1** something that limits your freedom and stops you from doing what you want to do: *The lower-tech side of the business was seen as a ball and chain.* **2** a heavy metal ball on a chain, tied to a prisoner's legs, to stop the prisoner from escaping

bal·last /ˈbæləst/ *n* [U] **1** heavy material that is carried by a ship to make it more steady in the water **2** material such as sand that is carried in a BALLOON so that it can be thrown out to make it rise **3** a layer of broken stones that a road or railway line is built on

ˌball ˈbearing *n* [C] **1** an arrangement of small metal balls that move in a ring, to make a part inside a machine turn more easily **2** one of these metal balls

ˈball boy *n* [C] a boy who picks up the balls for people playing in important tennis matches → see picture at TENNIS

ball·cock /ˈbɔːlkɒk $ ˈbɒːlkɑːk/ *n* [C] a hollow floating ball on a stick that opens and closes a hole to allow water to flow into a container, for example in a toilet

ball·er /ˈbɔːlə $ ˈbɒːlər/ *n* [C] a BASKETBALL player, especially a good player in informal games

bal·le·ri·na /ˌbæləˈriːnə/ ●○○ *n* [C] a woman who dances in ballets

bal·let /ˈbæleɪ $ bæˈleɪ, ˈbæleɪ/ ●●○ *n*
1 [C] a performance in which dancing and music tell a story without any speaking: *We're going to the ballet tomorrow evening.*
2 [U] this type of dancing
3 [C] a group of BALLET dancers who work together: *the Bolshoi ballet*

ˈballet ˌdancer / $.ˈ. ˌ../ *n* [C] someone who dances in ballets

bal·let·ic /bəˈletɪk/ *adj* movements that are balletic are graceful like the movements in ballet: *a balletic leap*

ˈball game *n* [C] **1** *AmE* a game of baseball, football, or BASKETBALL **2** *BrE* any game played with a ball **3 a whole new ball game** a situation that is very different from the one you are used to: *I used to be a teacher, so working in an office is a whole new ball game.*

ˈball girl *n* [C] a girl who picks up the balls for people playing in important tennis matches → see picture at TENNIS

ball·gown /ˈbɔːlgaʊn $ ˈbɒːl-/ *n* [C] a long dress made of expensive material, that a woman wears to formal parties SYN **evening dress**

bal·lis·tic /bəˈlɪstɪk/ *adj* **go ballistic** *spoken* to suddenly become very angry: *I couldn't believe it! She went ballistic just because there were peas in her pasta.*

balˌlistic ˈmissile *n* [C] a powerful weapon that can travel extremely long distances, and that flies very high up into the sky and then back down to earth, where it explodes

bal·lis·tics /bəˈlɪstɪks/ *n* [U] the scientific study of the movement of objects that are thrown or fired through the air, such as bullets shot from a gun

BALLOON

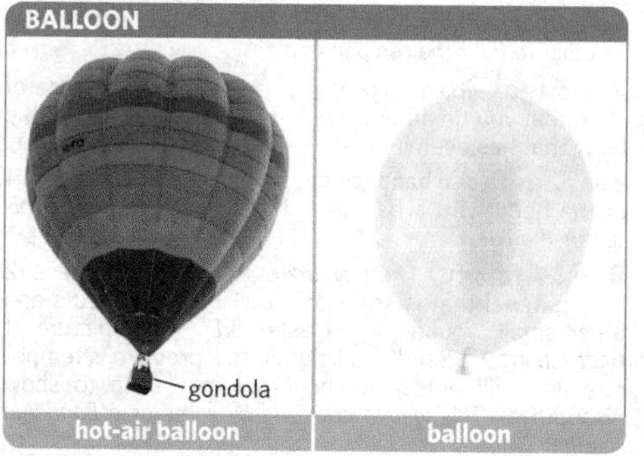

hot-air balloon | balloon

bal·loon¹ /bəˈluːn/ ●●○ *n* [C]
1 an object made of brightly coloured thin rubber, that is filled with air and used as a toy or decoration for parties: *Can you help me* **blow up** *these balloons?* | *He* **burst** *the* **balloon** *in my face.*
2 (*also* **hot-air balloon**) a large bag of strong light cloth filled with gas or heated air so that it can float in the air. It has a basket hanging below it for people to stand in: *a* **balloon flight** *over the Yorkshire Moors*
3 the circle drawn around the words spoken by the characters in a CARTOON SYN **bubble**
4 a balloon payment *AmE* money borrowed that must be paid back in one large sum after several smaller payments have been made: *a $10,000 balloon payment due in two years*
5 the balloon goes up *BrE informal* used to refer to the moment when a situation starts to become really bad: *We'll have to get out of there before the balloon goes up.*
→ **go down like a lead balloon** at LEAD³(3)

balloon² (*also* **balloon out**) *v* [I] **1** to suddenly become larger in amount SYN **explode**: *The company's debt has ballooned in the past year.* **2** if someone balloons, they suddenly become fat: *Paul ballooned after he got married.* **3** to get bigger and rounder: *The sheet flapped and ballooned in the wind.*

bal·loon·ing /bəˈluːnɪŋ/ *n* [U] the sport of flying in a balloon

bal·loon·ist /bəˈluːnɪst/ *n* [C] someone who flies a balloon

bal·lot¹ /ˈbælət/ ●○○ *n*
1 [C,U] a system of voting, usually in secret, or an occasion when you vote in this way: *The party leader is elected by* **secret ballot**. | *Workers at the plant* **held a ballot** *and rejected strike action.* **THESAURUS** ▸ ELECTION
2 [C] a piece of paper on which you make a secret vote SYN **ballot paper**: *Only 22% of voters* **cast** *their* **ballots**.
3 the ballot the total number of votes in an election SYN **the vote**: *He won 54% of the ballot.*

ballot² *v* [I,T] **1** to ask someone to vote for something: **[+on/over]** *Train drivers are being balloted on industrial action.* **2** to vote for something: **[+for]** *Staff balloted for strike action yesterday.* **THESAURUS** ▸ VOTE

ˈballot box *n* **1** [C] a box that ballot papers are put in after voting **2 the ballot box** the system or process of voting in an election: **through the ballot box** *The people have expressed their views through the ballot box.*

ˈballot ˌpaper *n* [C] a piece of paper on which you record your vote: **spoiled ballot papers** (=ones that have been marked incorrectly and so cannot be counted)

ˈballot ˌrigging *n* [U] the practice of cheating in an election by not counting the ballot papers correctly

ˈball park *n* **1** [C] *AmE* a field for playing baseball with seats for watching the game **2 in the (right) ball park** *informal* close to the amount, price etc that you want or are thinking about: *Their estimate is in the right ball park.* **3 a ball-park figure/estimate/amount** a number or amount that is almost but not exactly correct: *He said $25,000, but it's just a ball-park figure.*

ball·play·er /ˈbɔːlˌpleɪə $ ˈbɒːlˌpleɪər/ *n* [C] *AmE* someone who plays baseball

ball·point /bɔːlpɔɪnt/ (*also* **ˌballpoint ˈpen**) *n* [C] a pen with a ball at the end that rolls ink onto the paper

ball·room /ˈbɔːlrʊm, -ruːm $ ˈbɒːl-/ *n* [C] a very large room used for dancing on formal occasions

ˌballroom ˈdancing *n* [U] a type of dancing that is done with a partner and has different steps for particular types of music, such as the WALTZ

balls¹ /bɔːlz $ bɒːlz/ *interjection BrE not polite* used to show strong disapproval or disappointment: *Balls to that!*
→ **balls** at BALL¹(10)

balls² *v*
balls *sth* ↔ **up** *phr v BrE informal not polite* to do something very badly or unsuccessfully SYN **mess up**

ˈballs-up *n* [singular] *BrE informal* something that has been done very badly or not successfully: *Nigel made a complete balls-up of the arrangements.*

B

B

ball·sy /ˈbɔːlzi $ ˈbɒːl-/ *adj informal* brave and determined, and not afraid of other people's disapproval: *a very ballsy lady*

bal·ly /ˈbæli/ *adj, adv BrE old-fashioned* an expression meaning BLOODY[1] – used to avoid offending people

bal·ly·hoo /ˌbæliˈhuː $ ˈbælihuː/ *n* [U] *informal* when there is a lot of excitement or anger about something – used to show disapproval SYN **fuss**: *After all the ballyhoo, the film was a flop.* —**ballyhoo** *v* [T]: *a much ballyhooed program to recruit more police officers*

balm /bɑːm $ bɑːm, bɑːlm/ *n* [C,U] **1** an oily liquid with a strong pleasant smell that you rub into your skin, often to reduce pain: *lip balm* **2** *literary* something that gives you comfort: **[+for/to]** *A drive through the countryside is balm for a weary soul.*

balm·y /ˈbɑːmi $ ˈbɑːmi, ˈbɑːlmi/ *adj* balmy air, weather etc is warm and pleasant SYN **mild**: *a balmy summer night*

ba·lo·ney /bəˈləʊni $ -ˈloʊ-/ *n* [U] *informal* something that is silly or not true SYN **nonsense**: *Don't give me that baloney.*

bal·sa /ˈbɔːlsə $ ˈbɒːl-/ *n* [C,U] a tropical American tree or the wood from this tree, which is very light

bal·sam /ˈbɔːlsəm $ ˈbɒːl-/ *n* [C,U] BALM, or the tree that produces it

bal·sam·ic vin·e·gar /bɔːlˌsæmɪk ˈvɪnəgə $ bɒːl-, -gər/ *n* [U] a type of dark-coloured VINEGAR that has a strong taste

bal·us·trade /ˌbæləˈstreɪd $ ˈbæləstreɪd/ *n* [C] a row of wooden, stone, or metal posts that stop someone falling from a bridge or BALCONY

bam /bæm/ *interjection* **1** used to show that something happens quickly: *He made a run for it and, bam, they shot him in the leg.* **2** used to show that something has hit something else **3** used to make the sound of a gun

bam·boo /ˌbæmˈbuː◂/ *n* [C,U] a tall tropical plant with hollow stems that is used for making furniture

bam·boo·zle /bæmˈbuːzəl/ *v* [T] *informal* to deceive, trick, or confuse someone

BAME /beɪm/ *BrE* the abbreviation of 'black, Asian, and minority ethnic': *a survey of BAME women*

ban[1] /bæn/ ●●○ W3 *n* [C] an official order that prevents something from being used or done: **[+on]** *a total ban on cigarette advertising* | *a call to lift the ban on homosexuals in the military* → TEST BAN

COLLOCATIONS

ADJECTIVES/NOUN + ban

a complete/total ban *They are seeking a complete ban on nuclear testing.*
an outright ban (=a complete ban) *an outright ban on gun ownership*
an international/worldwide/global ban *an international ban on trade in endangered species*
a blanket ban (=including all possible cases) *They imposed a blanket ban on beef products from Europe.*
a lifetime ban *He faces a lifetime ban from athletics.*
an export/import ban *The export ban on live cattle was brought in some years ago.*
an advertising ban | **a driving ban** *BrE*

VERBS

put/place/impose a ban *The government has imposed an outright ban on fox hunting.*
lift a ban *They promised to lift the immigration ban.*
call for a ban *French farmers have called for a ban on imports.*
enforce a ban (=make sure that it is obeyed)

ban[2] ●●○ *v* (**banned**, **banning**) [T] to say that something must not be done, seen, used etc SYN **prohibit** OPP **allow**: *Smoking is banned in the building.* | **ban sb from doing sth** *Charlie's been banned from driving for a year.* | **a banned substance/drug** (=a drug that people competing in a sport are not allowed to take because it improves their performance) THESAURUS FORBID —**banning** *n* [U]: *the banning of trade unions*

ba·nal /bəˈnɑːl, bəˈnæl/ ●○○ *adj* ordinary and not interesting, because of a lack of new or different ideas SYN **trivial**: *conversations about the most banal subjects* —**banality** /bəˈnæləti/ *n* [C,U]

ba·na·na /bəˈnɑːnə $ -ˈnæ-/ ●●● S2 *n* [C] a long curved tropical fruit with a yellow skin → see picture at FRUIT[1]

baˈnana ˌpeel *n* [C] *AmE* an embarrassing mistake made by someone in a public position, especially a politician or someone in a government SYN **banana skin** *BrE*

baˈnana reˌpublic *n* [C] an insulting word for a small poor country with weak government that depends on financial help from abroad

ba·na·nas /bəˈnɑːnəz $ -ˈnæ-/ *adj informal* **1 go bananas** to become very angry or excited: *Mum went bananas when I said I was going to leave nursing.* **2** crazy or silly

baˈnana ˌskin *n* [C] *BrE* an embarrassing mistake made by someone in a public position, especially a politician or someone in a government SYN **banana peel** *AmE*: *This government has an unhappy knack of* ***slipping on banana skins***.

baˌnana ˈsplit *n* [C] a dish with bananas and ICE CREAM

band[1] /bænd/ ●●● S2 W2 *n* [C]
1 a group of musicians, especially a group that plays popular music: *The band was playing old Beatles songs.* | *I grew up* ***playing in*** *rock bands.* | *Smith* ***joined the band*** *in 1989.* | *They* ***formed a band*** *when they were still at school.* | *The entertainment includes a disco and* ***live band***. | *interviews with* ***band members*** → BIG BAND, BRASS BAND, MARCHING BAND, ONE-MAN BAND

GRAMMAR: Singular or plural verb?

- In this meaning, **band** is usually followed by a singular verb: *The band* ***has*** *made a video.*
- In British English, you can also use a plural verb: *The band* ***have*** *made a video.*

GRAMMAR GUIDE NOUNS

2 a group of people formed because of a common belief or purpose: **[+of]** *a small band of volunteers* | *bands of soldiers*
3 a range of numbers within a system: *Interest rates stayed within a relatively narrow band.* | **age/tax/income etc band** *people within the $20,000–$30,000 income band*
4 a flat narrow piece of something with one end joined to the other to form a circle: *papers held together with a rubber band* | *a slim gold band on her finger*
5 a narrow area of light, colour, land etc that is different from the areas around it: *The birds have a distinctive blue band round their eyes.* | **[+of]** *a thin band of cloud*
6 *technical* a range of radio signals SYN **waveband**

band[2] *v* [T] *BrE* to put people or things into different groups, usually according to income, value, or price: *After valuation, properties will be banded in groups of £20,000 or more.* GRAMMAR **Band** is usually passive.

band together *phr v* if people band together, they unite in order to achieve something: *Local people have banded together to fight the company's plans.*

ban·dage[1] /ˈbændɪdʒ/ ●●○ *n* [C] a narrow piece of cloth that you tie around a wound or around a part of the body that has been injured → see picture at FIRST AID KIT

bandage[2] (*also* **bandage up**) *v* [T] to tie or cover a part of the body with a bandage: *The nurse bandaged up his sprained ankle.*

ˈBand-Aid *n* [C] **1** *trademark especially AmE* a piece of thin material that is stuck to the skin to cover cuts and other small wounds SYN **plaster** *BrE* → see picture at FIRST AID KIT **2** a Band-Aid solution to a problem is temporary and will not solve the problem – used to show disapproval: *This idea is criticized by some as a Band-Aid solution.*

ban·dan·na, **bandana** /bænˈdænə/ *n* [C] a large brightly coloured piece of cloth that you wear around your head or neck

B and B, **B & B** /ˌbiː ənd ˈbiː/ the abbreviation of ***bed and breakfast***: *a small B and B in the Cotswolds*

band·ed /ˈbændɪd/ *adj* if an object or animal is banded, it has bands of colour or bands of a material around it: *banded snakes* | **[+with/in]** *a heavy door banded with steel*

ban·dit /ˈbændɪt/ *n* [C] someone who robs people, especially one of a group of people who attack travellers: *They travelled 30 miles through bandit country.* **THESAURUS** THIEF —**banditry** *n* [U] → ONE-ARMED BANDIT

band·lead·er /ˈbændˌliːdə $ -ər/ *n* [C] someone who CONDUCTS a band, especially a dance or JAZZ band

band·mas·ter /ˈbændˌmɑːstə $ -ˌmæstər/ *n* [C] someone who CONDUCTS a military band, BRASS band etc

ban·do·lier /ˌbændəˈlɪə $ -ˈlɪr/ *n* [C] a belt that goes over someone's shoulder and is used to carry bullets

bands·man /ˈbændzmən/ *n* (*plural* **bandsmen** /-mən/) [C] a musician who plays in a military band, BRASS band etc

band·stand /ˈbændstænd/ *n* [C] a structure in a park that has a roof but no walls and is used by a band playing music

band·wag·on /ˈbændˌwægən/ *n* [C] **1** an activity that a lot of people are doing: *The keep-fit bandwagon started rolling in the mid-80s.* **2 climb/jump/get on the bandwagon** to start doing or saying something that a lot of people are already doing or saying – used to show disapproval: *I don't want to look as if I'm jumping on a green bandwagon.*

band·width /ˈbændwɪdθ/ *n* [U] *technical* the amount of information that can be carried through a telephone wire, computer connection etc at one time

ban·dy[1] /ˈbændi/ *adj* bandy legs curve out at the knees —**bandy-legged** /ˌbændi ˈlegd◂, -ˈlegɪd◂/ *adj*

bandy[2] (**bandied**, **bandying**, **bandies**) *v* **bandy words (with sb)** *old-fashioned* to argue

bandy sth ↔ **about/around** *phr v* to mention an idea, name, remark etc several times, especially in order to seem impressive: *Many names have been bandied about in the press as the manager's replacement.*

bane /beɪn/ *n* [singular] something that causes trouble or makes people unhappy: **be the bane of sth** *Drugs are the bane of the inner cities.* | *Her brother is* ***the bane of*** *her* ***life****.*

bane·ful /ˈbeɪnfəl/ *adj literary* evil or bad

bang[1] /bæŋ/ ●●○ S3 *n*

1 [C] a sudden loud noise caused by something such as a gun or an object hitting a hard surface: *There was a loud bang outside the kitchen door.* **THESAURUS** SOUND

2 [C] a painful blow to the body when you hit against something or something hits you SYN **bump**: *a bang on the head*

3 bangs [plural] *AmE* hair cut straight across your forehead SYN **fringe** *BrE*

4 with a bang in a very successful way: *Stock markets started the year with a bang.*

5 (get) a bigger/better etc bang for your buck *informal* something that gives you a good effect or a lot of value for the effort or money you spend on it: *Are taxpayers getting enough bang for their buck?*

6 get a bang out of sth *AmE spoken* to enjoy something very much → BIG BANG THEORY

bang[2] ●●○ S3 *v*

1 [I,T] to hit something hard, making a loud noise: **[+on]** *Stop banging on the door!* | **bang your fist/hand on sth** *She banged her fist on the table.* | *The baby kept banging the table with his spoon.* **THESAURUS** HIT

2 [T] to put something down or against something with a lot of force, making a loud noise: **bang sth down** *She banged the phone down.* | **bang sth on/against sth** *He banged a teapot on the table.*

3 [I always + adv/prep, T] to close something violently, making a loud noise, or to be closed in this way SYN **slam**: *I ran out, banging the door behind me.* | *The window* ***banged shut****.*

4 [T] to hit a part of your body, or something you are carrying, against something by accident SYN **bump**: **bang sth on sth** *I fell and banged my head on the pavement.*

5 [I] to make a loud noise or loud noises: *The gate keeps banging in the wind.*

6 [T] *not polite* to have sex with someone → **bang the drum for sb/sth** at DRUM[1](4), → **bang sb's heads together** at HEAD[1](32), → **be (like) banging your head against a brick wall** at HEAD[1](31)

bang about/around *phr v* to move around a place, making a lot of noise: *We could hear them banging about upstairs.*

bang on *phr v BrE informal* to talk continuously about something in a boring way SYN **go on**: **[+about]** *I wish he wouldn't keep banging on about politics.*

bang sth ↔ **out** *phr v informal*

1 to play a tune or song loudly and badly on a piano

2 to write something in a hurry, especially using a KEYBOARD

bang sb/sth ↔ **up** *phr v informal*

1 *BrE* to put someone in prison

2 *AmE* to seriously damage something: *a banged-up old Buick*

bang[3] *adv* **1** *informal* directly or exactly: *The train arrived* ***bang on time****.* | *The technology is* ***bang up to date****.* **THESAURUS** EXACTLY **2 bang on** *BrE spoken* exactly correct: *'Is that right?' 'Bang on!'* **3 bang goes sth** *BrE spoken* used to show that you are unhappy because something you had hoped for will not happen: *Bang goes my brilliant plan.* **4** *spoken* in a sudden violent way: *I skidded and went bang into the wall.* **5 go bang** *informal* to explode or burst with a loud noise

bang[4] *interjection* used to make a sound like a gun or bomb: *Bang bang, you're dead!*

bang·er /ˈbæŋə $ -ər/ *n* [C] *BrE informal* **1** a SAUSAGE: *bangers and mash* (=sausages and mashed potato) **2** an old car in bad condition: *an* ***old banger*** **3** a type of noisy FIREWORK

bang·ing /ˈbæŋɪŋ/ *adj BrE informal* very good: *That party was banging.*

ban·gle /ˈbæŋgəl/ *n* [C] a solid band of gold, silver etc that you wear loosely around your wrist as jewellery SYN **bracelet** → see picture at JEWELLERY

ˈbang-up *adj AmE informal* very good: *He* ***did a bang-up job*** *fixing the plumbing.*

ban·ish /ˈbænɪʃ/ ●○○ *v* [T]

1 to not allow someone or something to stay in a particular place: **banish sb/sth from/to sth** *I was banished to a distant corridor.*

2 to send someone away permanently from their country or the area where they live, especially as an official punishment SYN **exile**: **banish sb from/to** *Thousands were banished to Siberia.*

3 *literary* to try to stop thinking about something or someone: **banish the memory/thought/image etc (of sb/sth)** *They tried to banish the memory from their minds.* —**banishment** *n* [U]

ban·is·ter /ˈbænɪstə $ -ər/ *n* [C] a row of wooden posts with a bar along the top, that stops you from falling over the edge of stairs → see picture at STAIRCASE

ban·jo /ˈbændʒəʊ $ -dʒoʊ/ *n* (*plural* **banjos**) [C] a musical instrument like a guitar, with a round body and four or more strings, played especially in COUNTRY AND WESTERN music → see picture at STRINGED INSTRUMENT

bank[1] /bæŋk/ ●●● S1 W1 *n* [C]

1 PLACE FOR MONEY **a)** a business that keeps and lends money and provides other financial services: **in the bank** *We have very little money in the bank.* | *Barclays Bank* | *a* ***bank loan*** **b)** a local office of a bank: *I have to* ***go to the bank*** *at lunch time.* → CLEARING BANK, MERCHANT BANK

2 RIVER/LAKE land along the side of a river or lake: **[+of]** *the banks of the River Dee* | *the river bank*

3 blood/sperm/organ bank a place where human blood etc is stored until someone needs it

4 CLOUDS/MIST a large mass of clouds, mist etc: *a* ***fog bank*** | **[+of]** *banks of mist*

5 RAISED AREA a large sloping mass of earth, sand, snow etc: *She was sitting on a grassy bank.* | **[+of]** *steep banks of snow* | *banks of flowers*

B

6 MACHINES a large number of machines, television screens etc arranged close together in a row: **[+of]** *banks of TV monitors*
7 GAME a supply of money used to GAMBLE, that people can win → **break the bank** at BREAK[1](24)
8 be makin' bank *AmE spoken informal* to earn a lot of money for the work that you do: *Check out Omar's new car. The brother must be makin' bank.*
9 the bank of Mum and Dad *BrE informal* used when saying that your parents will provide you with the money that you need for something: *Some young people turn to the bank of Mum and Dad when they want to buy a house.*
10 ROAD a slope made at a bend in a road or RACETRACK to make it safer for cars to go around → **BOTTLE BANK, FOOD BANK, MEMORY BANK**

bank² *v*
1 MONEY **a)** [T] to put or keep money in a bank: *Did you bank that check?* **b)** [I always + adv/prep] to keep your money in a particular bank: **[+with]** *Who do you bank with?* | **[+at]** *I've always banked at First Interstate.*
2 PLANE [I] if a plane banks, it slopes to one side when turning: *The plane banked, and circled back toward us.*
3 PILE/ROWS (*also* **bank up**) [T] *BrE* to arrange something into a pile or into rows: *Snow was banked up on either side of the road.*
4 CLOUD/MIST (*also* **bank up**) [T] to form a mass of cloud, mist etc: *Banked clouds promised rain.*
5 FIRE (*also* **bank up**) [T] to cover a fire with wood or coal to keep it going for a long time: *Josie banked up the fire to last till morning.*

bank on sb/sth *phr v* to depend on something happening or someone doing something SYN **count on**: **bank on (sb) doing sth** *I was banking on being able to get some coffee on the train.*

bank·a·ble /ˈbæŋkəbəl/ *adj* likely to be profitable or make a lot of money: *Hollywood's most bankable stars*

ˈbank acˌcount *n* [C] an arrangement between a bank and a customer that allows the customer to pay in and take out money: *I'd like to* ***open a bank account****.*

ˈbank ˌbalance *n* [singular] the amount of money someone has in their bank account

ˈbank·book /ˈbæŋkbʊk/ *n* [C] *AmE* a book in which a record is kept of the money you put into and take out of your bank account SYN **passbook**

ˈbank card *n* [C] **1** *AmE* a CREDIT CARD provided by your bank **2** *BrE* CHEQUE CARD

ˈbank draft (*also* **banker's draft**) *n* [C] a cheque from one bank to another, especially a foreign bank, to pay a certain amount of money to a person or organization

bank·er /ˈbæŋkə $ -ər/ ●●○ *n* [C]
1 someone who works in a bank in an important position
2 the player who is in charge of the money in some GAMBLING games

ˈbanker's ˌcard *n* [C] *BrE* CHEQUE CARD

ˈbanker's ˌdraft *n* [C] BANK DRAFT

ˈbanker's ˌorder *n* [C] *BrE* STANDING ORDER

ˌbank ˈholiday *n* [C] *BrE* an official holiday when banks and most businesses are closed SYN **public holiday** *AmE*: *Next Monday is a bank holiday.* | **bank holiday weekend** (=a weekend on which there is a bank holiday on Friday or Monday)

bank·ing /ˈbæŋkɪŋ/ ●●○ *n* [U] the business of a bank: *the international banking system*

ˈbank ˌmanager *n* [C] *BrE* someone who is in charge of a local bank

bank·note, **ˈbank note** /ˈbæŋknəʊt $ -noʊt/ *n* [C] a piece of paper money SYN **note** *BrE*, **bill** *AmE*

ˈbank rate *n* [C] the rate of INTEREST charged by banks lending money, decided by a country's main bank SYN **interest rate**

bank·roll¹ /ˈbæŋkrəʊl $ -roʊl/ *v* [T] *informal* to provide the money that someone needs for a business, a plan etc SYN **finance**: *a software company bankrolled by the Samsung Group*

bankroll² *n* [C] a supply of money

bank·rupt¹ /ˈbæŋkrʌpt/ ●●○ *adj*
1 without enough money to pay what you owe SYN **insolvent**: *The firm* ***went bankrupt*** *before the building work was completed.* | *In 1977 he was* ***declared bankrupt*** (=by a court). | *Mr Trent lost his house when he was* ***made bankrupt****.* | *Seventeen years of war left the country bankrupt.* | *a bankrupt electrical company*
2 completely lacking a particular good quality: *The opposition attacked the government as* ***morally bankrupt****.*

bankrupt² *v* [T] to make a person, business, or country bankrupt or very poor SYN **ruin**: *Johns had been nearly bankrupted through a failed business venture.*

bankrupt³ *n* [C] someone who has officially said that they cannot pay their debts: **certified/uncertified bankrupt** *BrE* (=one a court does or does not allow to start a business again)

bank·rupt·cy /ˈbæŋkrʌptsi/ ●●○ *n* (*plural* **bankruptcies**)
1 [C,U] the state of being unable to pay your debts SYN **insolvency**: *In 1999 it was revealed that he was close to bankruptcy.* | *When inflation rises, so do bankruptcies.*
2 [U] a total lack of a particular good quality: *the moral bankruptcy of terrorism*

ˈbank ˌstatement *n* [C] a document sent regularly by a bank to a customer that lists the amounts of money taken out of and paid into their BANK ACCOUNT

banned /bænd/ *adj* [only before noun] not officially allowed to meet, exist, or be used: *Leaders of the banned party were arrested last night.* | *He was suspended for using a* ***banned substance*** (=a drug that people competing in sport are not allowed to take).

ban·ner /ˈbænə $ -ər/ ●●○ *n* [C]
1 a long piece of cloth on which something is written, often carried between two poles: *The onlookers were shouting, cheering, and waving banners.*
2 a belief or principle: **carry/raise/wave etc the banner of sth** (=publicly support a particular belief etc) *She'd never felt the need to carry the banner of feminism.* | **under the banner of sth** *They marched under the banner of equal educational opportunity.*
3 under the banner of sth as part of a particular group or organization: *The oil-producing countries joined together under the banner of OPEC.*
4 a flag

ˈbanner ad *n* [C] an advertisement that appears across the top of a page on the Internet —**ˈbanner ˌadvertising** *n* [U]

ˌbanner ˈheadline *n* [C] words printed in very large letters across the top of the first page of a newspaper: *The front-page banner headline read 'Disgraced police chief to stand trial'.*

ˈbanner ˌyear *n* [C] *AmE* a year that is good because something is successful

ban·nis·ter /ˈbænɪstə $ -ər/ *n* [C] BANISTER

banns /bænz/ *n* [plural] a public statement that two people intend to get married, made in a church in Britain

ba·nof·fi pie, **banoffee pie** /bəˌnɒfi ˈpaɪ $ -ˌnɑː-/ *n* [C,U] a sweet food which has a BISCUIT layer on the bottom, a TOFFEE layer in the middle, and thin flat pieces of BANANA and cream on the top

ban·quet /ˈbæŋkwɪt/ ●○○ *n* [C]
1 a formal dinner for many people on an important occasion: *a state banquet* (=one attended by heads of government and other important people)
2 a large and impressive meal

ˈbanqueting ˌhall, **ˈbanquet room** *n* [C] a large room in which banquets take place

ban·shee /ˈbænʃiː/ *n* [C] a female SPIRIT whose loud cry is believed to be heard when someone is going to die: *She was* ***screaming like a banshee****.*

ban·tam /ˈbæntəm/ *n* [C] a type of small chicken

ban·tam·weight /ˈbæntəmweɪt/ *n* [C] a BOXER who

weighs less than 53.52 kilograms, and who is heavier than a FLYWEIGHT but lighter than a FEATHERWEIGHT

ban·ter /ˈbæntə $ -ər/ *n* [U] friendly conversation in which people make a lot of jokes with, and amusing remarks about, each other: **friendly/good-natured/light-hearted banter [+with/between]** *easy banter between her cousins* —**banter** *v* [I]: *I watched the guys as they bantered with the waitresses.* —**bantering** *adj*

bap /bæp/ *n* [C] *BrE* a round soft bread ROLL

bap·tis·m /ˈbæptɪzəm/ ●○○ *n* [C,U]
1 a Christian religious ceremony in which someone is touched or covered with water to welcome them into the Christian faith, and sometimes to officially name them → **christening**
2 baptism of/by fire a difficult or painful first experience of something: *The campaign has been a baptism of fire.* —**baptismal** /bæpˈtɪzməl/ *adj* [only before noun]: *a baptismal font* (=container for holding the water used at baptism)

Bap·tist /ˈbæptɪst/ *n* [C] a member of a Christian group that believes baptism should only be for people old enough to understand its meaning

bap·tize (*also* **-ise** *BrE*) /bæpˈtaɪz $ ˈbæptaɪz/ ●○○ *v* [T]
1 to perform the ceremony of baptism on someone → **christen**
2 to accept someone as a member of a particular Christian church by a ceremony of baptism: *He was baptized a Roman Catholic.*
3 to give a child a name in a baptism ceremony: *She was baptized Jane.*

BARS

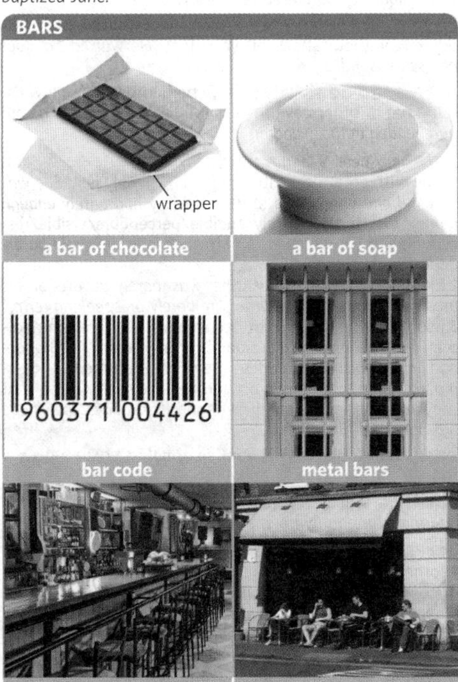

a bar of chocolate | a bar of soap | bar code | metal bars | the bar | coffee bar *BrE*

bar¹ /bɑː $ bɑːr/ ●●● S1 W1 *n* [C]
1 PLACE TO DRINK IN **a)** a place where alcoholic drinks are served → **pub**: *The hotel has a* ***licensed bar****.* | *a* ***cocktail bar*** **b)** *BrE* one of the rooms inside a pub: *The* ***public bar*** *was crowded.*
2 PLACE TO BUY DRINK a COUNTER where alcoholic drinks are served: *They stood at the bar.*
3 a wine/coffee/snack etc bar a place where a particular kind of food or drink is served
4 a breakfast bar *BrE* a place in your kitchen at home where you eat breakfast or a quick meal
5 BLOCK SHAPE a small block of solid material that is longer than it is wide: *a* ***chocolate bar*** | *a* ***candy bar*** | **[+of]** *a* ***bar of soap*** → see picture at PIECE¹
6 PIECE OF METAL/WOOD a length of metal or wood put across a door, window etc to keep it shut or to prevent people going in or out: *houses with bars across the windows* **THESAURUS** ▸ PIECE
7 behind bars *informal* in prison: *Her killer was finally* ***put behind bars****.*
8 MUSIC a group of notes and RESTS, separated from other groups by vertical lines, into which a line of written music is divided: *a few bars of the song*
9 bar to (doing) sth *written* something that prevents you from achieving something that you want: *I could see no bar to our happiness.*
10 the bar a) *BrE* the group of people who are BARRISTERS **b)** *AmE* an organization consisting of lawyers
11 be called to the bar a) *BrE* to become a BARRISTER **b)** *AmE* to become a lawyer
12 ON COMPUTER SCREEN a long narrow shape along the sides or at the top of a computer screen, usually containing signs that you can CLICK on: *the main menu bar at the top of the screen* | *the toolbar* → **SCROLL BAR**
13 IN SPORTS the long piece of wood or metal across the top of the goal in sports such as football: *The ball hit the bar.*
14 PILE OF SAND/STONES a long pile of sand or stones under the water at the entrance to a HARBOUR
15 COLOUR/LIGHT a narrow band of colour or light
16 UNIFORMS a narrow band of metal or cloth worn on a military uniform to show rank
17 HEATER *BrE* the part of an electric heater that provides heat and has a red light

bar² ●○○ *v* (**barred**, **barring**) [T]
1 to officially prevent someone from entering a place or from doing something: **bar sb from (doing) sth** *They seized his passport and barred him from leaving the country.* **THESAURUS** ▸ FORBID
2 to prevent people from going somewhere by placing something in their way: *She ran back, but Francis* ***barred*** *her* ***way****.* | *A locked gate barred my entrance to the wood.*
3 (*also* **bar up**) to shut a door or window using a bar or piece of wood so that people cannot get in or out

bar³ *prep* **1** except: *We had recorded the whole album, bar one track.* **2 bar none** used to emphasize that someone is the best of a particular group: *He's the most talented actor in the country, bar none.* → **BARRING**

barb /bɑːb $ bɑːrb/ *n* [C] **1** the sharp curved point of a hook, ARROW etc that prevents it from being easily pulled out **2** a remark that is clever and amusing, but also cruel → **BARBED**

bar·bar·i·an /bɑːˈbeəriən $ bɑːrˈber-/ *n* [C] **1** someone from a different tribe or land, who people believe to be wild and not CIVILIZED: *The Roman Empire came under severe pressure from the barbarians across the Rhine.* **2** someone who does not behave properly, and does not show proper respect for education, art etc: *The youths were described as uncivilised barbarians who savagely attacked innocent victims.* **3** someone who behaves in a way that is cruel and UNCIVILIZED

bar·bar·ic /bɑːˈbærɪk $ bɑːr-/ ●○○ *adj* very cruel and violent SYN **barbarous**: *The way the whales are killed is nothing short of barbaric.* **THESAURUS** ▸ **CRUEL**

bar·bar·is·m /ˈbɑːbərɪzəm $ ˈbɑːr-/ *n* [U] **1** extremely violent and cruel behaviour **2** a situation in which people have no respect for CIVILIZED things such as art and culture: *cultural barbarism*

bar·bar·i·ty /bɑːˈbærəti $ bɑːr-/ *n* (*plural* **barbarities**) [C,U] a very cruel act: *the medieval barbarity of putting people in prison for debt*

bar·bar·ous /ˈbɑːbərəs $ ˈbɑːr-/ *adj* **1** extremely cruel in a way that is shocking SYN **barbaric**: *The trade in exotic birds is barbarous.* **2** wild and not CIVILIZED: *a savage barbarous people* —**barbarously** *adv*

bar·be·cue[1] (*also* **bar·beque** *AmE*) /ˈbɑːbɪkjuː $ ˈbɑːr-/ ●●● S3 *n* [C]
1 (*written abbreviation* **BBQ**) a meal or party during which food is cooked on a metal frame over a fire and eaten outdoors: *We **had a barbecue** on the beach.*
2 a metal frame for cooking food on outdoors

BARBECUE

barbecue[2] (*also* **bar·beque** *AmE*) *v* [T] to cook food on a metal frame over a fire outdoors: *barbecued chicken* THESAURUS COOK

barbed /bɑːbd $ bɑːrbd/ *adj* **1** a barbed hook or ARROW has one or more sharp curved points on it **2** a barbed remark is unkind: *a barbed comment on his appearance*

ˌbarbed ˈwire *n* [U] wire with short sharp points on it: *a high barbed wire fence* → see picture at FENCE[1]

bar·bell /ˈbɑːbel $ ˈbɑːr-/ *n* [C] *AmE* a metal bar with weights at each end, that you lift to make you stronger SYN **dumbbell** *BrE* → see picture at GYM

bar·ber /ˈbɑːbə $ ˈbɑːrbər/ *n* [C] **1** a man whose job is to cut men's hair and sometimes to SHAVE them **2 barber's** *BrE* a shop where men's hair is cut SYN **barbershop** *AmE*

bar·ber·shop /ˈbɑːbəʃɒp $ ˈbɑːrbərʃɑːp/ *n* **1** [U] a style of singing popular songs with parts for four men, usually without music: *a barbershop quartet* **2** [C] *AmE* a shop where men's hair is cut SYN **barber's** *BrE*

bar·bie /ˈbɑːbi $ ˈbɑːr-/ *n* [C] *BrE, AusE informal* a BARBECUE

ˈBarbie doll *n* [C] *trademark* a popular type of DOLL in the shape of an attractive young woman, that can be dressed in a large variety of fashionable clothes. A woman is sometimes compared to a Barbie doll if she is attractive and always has new clothes, but is not very intelligent.

ˈbar ˌbilliards *n* [U] a type of BILLIARDS played in PUBs in Britain

bar·bi·tu·rate /bɑːˈbɪtʃərət $ bɑːrˈbɪtʃərət, -reɪt/ *n* [C,U] a powerful drug that makes people calm and helps them to sleep

Bar·bour /ˈbɑːbəʳ $ ˈbɑːr-/ (*also* **Barbour jacket**) *n* [C] *trademark* a type of good-quality expensive coat made in the UK, traditionally worn by farmers and country people to protect them from wind and rain. It has also become fashionable with some people in cities.

ˈbar chart (*also* **bar graph**) *n* [C] a picture of boxes of different heights, in which each box represents a different amount or quantity → see picture at CHART[1]

ˈbar code ●○○ *n* [C] a group of thin and thick lines printed on products you buy in a shop, that a computer can read. It contains information such as the price. → see picture at BAR[1]

bard /bɑːd $ bɑːrd/ *n* **1** [C] *literary* a poet **2 the Bard** William Shakespeare

bare[1] /beə $ ber/ ●●○ *adj*
1 WITHOUT CLOTHES not covered by clothes SYN **naked**: *a ragged child with bare feet | She felt the warm sun on her bare arms.* | **bare-headed/bare-chested/bare-legged etc**
2 LAND/TREES not covered by trees or grass, or not having any leaves: *The trees soon gave way to bare rock.*
3 NOT COVERED/EMPTY empty, not covered by anything, or not having any decorations: *She looked round her tiny bare room. | a bare wood staircase* THESAURUS EMPTY
4 the bare facts a statement that tells someone only what they need to know, with no additional details: *The newspaper had simply published the bare facts.*
5 SMALLEST AMOUNT NECESSARY [only before noun] the very least amount of something that you need to do something: *He got 40% – a bare pass. | The room had the **bare minimum** (=the smallest amount possible) of furniture.* | **the bare essentials/necessities** *Her bag was light, packed with only the bare essentials. | If you ask her about herself, she gives only **the barest** (=the smallest amount possible) of details.*
6 the bare bones the most important parts or facts of something without any detail: *We have outlined only the bare bones of the method.*
7 lay sth bare a) to uncover something that was previously hidden: *When the river is low, vast stretches of sand are laid bare.* **b)** to make known something that was secret: *historical writing which seeks to lay bare the true nature of an event*
8 with your bare hands without using a weapon or a tool: *He had **killed** a man **with his bare hands**.*
9 bare infinitive *technical* the basic form of a verb, for example 'go' or 'eat' —**bareness** *n* [U]

bare[2] *v* [T] **1** to remove something that was covering or hiding something: *The dog **bared** its **teeth**. | He bared his back to the hot sun.* **2 bare your soul** to reveal your most secret feelings

bare[3] /beə $ ber/ *adv BrE spoken informal* very, or a lot of – used by young people: *Check out this new game – it's bare hard. | His dad's got bare money.*

bare-assed /ˌbeər ˈæst◂ $ ˈber æst/ *AmE*, **bare-arsed** /-ˈɑːst◂ $ -ɑːrst/ *BrE adj informal* having no clothes on

bare·back /ˈbeəbæk $ ˈber-/ *adj, adv* on a horse without a SADDLE: *He'd been **riding bareback** all his life.*

bare·faced, **bare-faced** /ˌbeəˈfeɪst◂ $ ˈberfeɪst/ *adj* [only before noun] used to describe a remark or action that is clearly untrue or unpleasant, and that shows that you do not care about offending someone SYN **blatant**: *Why are you telling such **barefaced lies**?*

bare·foot /ˈbeəfʊt $ ˈber-/ (*also* **ˌbare-ˈfooted** / $ ˈ. ˌ../) *adj, adv* without shoes on your feet: *He walked barefoot across the sand.*

bare·head·ed /ˌbeəˈhedɪd◂ $ ˈberhedɪd/ *adj, adv* without a hat or other covering on your head: *You can't go out bareheaded in this weather.*

bare·ly /ˈbeəli $ ˈberli/ ●●○ *adv*
1 only with great difficulty or effort SYN **only just**: *She was very old and **barely able** to walk. | Mary had **barely enough** money to live on.* | **barely audible/perceptible/visible/discernible etc** *His voice was barely audible. | She **could barely** understand English.*
2 almost not SYN **hardly**: *She was barely aware of his presence. | Joe and his brother are barely on speaking terms.*
3 used to emphasize that something happens immediately after a previous action SYN **only just** *BrE*: *Graham had barely finished his coffee when Henry returned.*
4 used before amounts or numbers to emphasize that they are surprisingly small SYN **only**: *Nowadays, the village has barely 100 inhabitants.*

barf /bɑːf $ bɑːrf/ *v* [I] *AmE informal* to VOMIT —**barf** *n* [U]

bar·fly /ˈbɑːflaɪ $ ˈbɑːr-/ *n* (*plural* **barflies**) [C] *AmE informal* someone who spends a lot of time in bars

bar·gain[1] /ˈbɑːgɪn $ ˈbɑːr-/ ●●○ *n* [C]
1 something you buy cheaply or for less than its usual price: *There are no bargains in the clothes shops at the moment. | It's an attractive little home, and I think **it's a bargain**. | That second-hand table was a **real bargain**. | Good watches don't come **at bargain prices**. | **Bargain hunters** (=people looking for things to buy at low prices) queued outside the store for hours.*
2 an agreement, made between two people or groups, to do something in return for something else: **make/strike a bargain** *Management and unions have struck a bargain over wage increases. | I've **kept** my **side of the bargain** and I expect you to keep yours.* → **drive a hard bargain** at HARD[1](18)
3 into the bargain (*also* **in the bargain** *AmE*) in addition to everything else: *I am now tired, cold, and hungry, with a headache into the bargain.*

bargain[2] ●○○ *v* [I] to discuss the conditions of a sale, agreement etc, for example to try and get a lower price: **[+for]** *workers bargaining for better pay* | **[+over]** *They* bargained over the level of wages. | **[+with]** women bargaining with traders —**bargainer** n [C]: He's the hardest bargainer in the business.

bargain for sth (also **bargain on sth**) phr v [usually in negatives] to expect that something will happen and make it part of your plans: *They hadn't bargained for such a dramatic change in the weather.* | **bargain on doing sth** *I hadn't bargained on being stuck in traffic on the way home.* | *The thief **got more than** he **bargained for**, as Mr Cox tripped him up with his walking stick.*

ˌbargain ˈbasement n [C] a part of a large shop, usually below ground level, where goods are sold at reduced prices

bar·gain·ing /ˈbɑːɡənɪŋ $ ˈbɑːr-/ n [U] **1** discussion in order to reach an agreement about a sale, contract etc SYN **negotiation**: **wage/pay bargaining** *The government would not intervene in private-sector wage bargaining.* | *The 4% pay raise was the result of some **hard bargaining**.* **2 bargaining position/power** the amount of influence someone has and their ability to achieve what they want when starting a discussion or making an agreement: *Most new artists and bands aren't in **a strong bargaining position**.* | *This will increase the bargaining power of management in wage negotiations.* → COLLECTIVE BARGAINING

ˈbargaining ˌchip especially AmE, **ˈbargaining ˌcounter** BrE n [C] something that one person or group in a business deal or political agreement has, that can be used to gain an advantage in the deal

barge¹ /bɑːdʒ $ bɑːrdʒ/ n [C] a large low boat with a flat bottom, used for carrying goods on a CANAL or river

barge² v [I always + adv/prep, T] to move somewhere in a rough careless way, often hitting against things SYN **push**: *She ran outside, barging past bushes and shrubs.* | **barge your way through/to etc sth** *She barged her way through the shopping crowds.*

barge in (also **barge into sth**) phr v to enter somewhere rudely, or to rudely interrupt someone: *George barged into my office without knocking.* | **[+on]** *'Sorry to barge in on your evening,' James said.*

barg·ee /bɑːˈdʒiː $ bɑːr-/ BrE (also **barge·man** /ˈbɑːdʒmən $ ˈbɑːrdʒ-/) n [C] someone who drives or works on a barge

barge·pole /ˈbɑːdʒpəʊl $ bɑːrdʒpoʊl/ n [C] a long pole used to guide a barge → **not touch sb/sth with a bargepole** at TOUCH¹(12)

ˈbar graph n [C] a BAR CHART

bar·hop /ˈbɑːhɒp $ ˈbɑːrhɑːp/ v (**barhopped**, **barhopping**) [I] AmE informal to visit and drink at several bars, one after another

bar·i·at·rics /ˌbæriˈætrɪks/ n [U] technical the area of medicine that deals with OBESITY (=the condition of being very fat) —**bariatric** adj

bar·is·ta /bɑːˈriːstə/ n [C] someone whose job is to prepare coffee in a COFFEE BAR

bar·i·tone¹ /ˈbærətəʊn $ -toʊn/ n **1** [C] a male singing voice that is lower than a TENOR but higher than a BASS, or a man with a voice like this: *a famous baritone* **2** [singular] the part of a musical work that is written for a baritone voice or instrument: *Can you sing the baritone?* → ALTO²(2), BASS¹(2), SOPRANO¹(2), TENOR¹(2)

baritone² adj [only before noun] a baritone voice or instrument is lower than a TENOR but higher than a BASS

ba·ri·um /ˈbeəriəm $ ˈber-/ n [U] **1** a soft silver-white metal that is used to make PIGMENTS (=dry coloured powders used to make paints). It is a chemical ELEMENT: symbol Ba **2 a barium meal/enema/swallow** a substance containing barium that you swallow or that is put in your BOWELS before you have an X-RAY, because it makes the organs in your body easier to see

bark¹ /bɑːk $ bɑːrk/ ●●○ v
1 [I] when a dog barks, it makes a short loud sound or series of sounds → **growl**: **[+at]** *The dog always barks at strangers.*
2 (also **bark out**) [T] to say something quickly in a loud voice: **[+at]** *'Don't just stand there, give me a hand,' she barked at the shop assistant.*
3 bark up the wrong tree informal to have a wrong idea, or do something in a way that will not give you the information or result you want: *The police spent three months barking up the wrong tree on the murder investigation.*
4 [T] to rub the skin off your knee, elbow etc by falling or knocking against something SYN **graze**: *I barked my shin against the step.*

bark² ●●○ n
1 [C] the sharp loud sound made by a dog
2 [U] the outer covering of a tree → see picture at TREE
3 [C] a loud sound or voice: *Amy's voice was a hoarse bark.*
4 sb's bark is worse than their bite used to say that someone who seems unpleasant or difficult to deal with is not really too bad

bar·keep·er /ˈbɑːkiːpə $ ˈbɑːrkiːpər/ (also **bar·keep** /ˈbɑːkiːp $ ˈbɑːr-/) n [C] AmE someone who serves drinks in a bar SYN **bartender**

bark·er /ˈbɑːkə $ ˈbɑːrkər/ n [C] in the past, someone who stood outside a place where there was a CIRCUS or FAIR, shouting to people to come in

ˌbarking ˈmad (also **bark·ing** /ˈbɑːkɪŋ $ ˈbɑːr-/) adj [not before noun] BrE completely crazy or acting very strangely - used humorously

bar·ley /ˈbɑːli $ ˈbɑːrli/ n [U] a plant that produces a grain used for making food or alcohol

ˈbarley ˌsugar n [C,U] BrE a hard sweet made of boiled sugar

ˈbarley ˌwater n [U] BrE a drink made from barley boiled with water, with the flavour of lemon or orange

ˌbarley ˈwine n [U] BrE a type of very strong beer

bar·maid /ˈbɑːmeɪd $ ˈbɑːr-/ n [C] BrE a woman who serves drinks in a bar SYN **bartender**

bar·man /ˈbɑːmən $ ˈbɑːr-/ n (plural **barmen** /-mən/) [C] especially BrE a man who serves drinks in a bar SYN **bartender**

bar mitz·vah /ˌbɑː ˈmɪtsvə $ ˌbɑːr-/ n [C] **1** the religious ceremony held when a Jewish boy reaches the age of 13 and is considered an adult → **bat mitzvah** **2** a boy for whom this ceremony is held

barm·y /ˈbɑːmi $ ˈbɑːrmi/ adj BrE informal slightly crazy: *That's a barmy idea.*

barn /bɑːn $ bɑːrn/ n [C] **1** a large farm building for storing crops, or for keeping animals in → see picture at HOME¹ **2** informal a large plain building: *a huge barn of a house*

bar·na·cle /ˈbɑːnəkəl $ ˈbɑːr-/ n [C] a small sea animal with a hard shell that sticks firmly to rocks and the bottom of boats

ˈbarn dance n [C] BrE a social event at which there is COUNTRY DANCING → **square dance**

bar·net /ˈbɑːnɪt $ ˈbɑːr-/ n [C] BrE informal old-fashioned hair, or a way of wearing your hair

bar·ney /ˈbɑːni $ ˈbɑːrni/ n [C usually singular] BrE informal a noisy argument

barn·storm /ˈbɑːnstɔːm $ ˈbɑːrnstɔːrm/ v [I] AmE to travel from place to place making short stops to give political speeches, theatre performances, or aircraft flying shows —**barnstormer** n [C]

barn·storm·ing /ˈbɑːnˌstɔːmɪŋ $ ˈbɑːrnˌstɔːr-/ adj [only before noun] done with a lot of energy and very exciting to watch: *a barnstorming speech*

barn·yard /ˈbɑːnjɑːd $ ˈbɑːrnjɑːrd/ n [C] an area on a farm, surrounded by farm buildings SYN **farmyard**

ba·rom·e·ter /bəˈrɒmɪtə $ -ˈrɑːmɪtər/ n [C] **1** an instrument that measures changes in the air pressure and the weather, or that calculates height above sea level **2** something that shows any changes that are happening in a particular situation: *The skin is an accurate barometer of emotional and physical health.* —**barometric** /ˌbærəˈmetrɪk◂/ adj [only before noun] —**barometrically** /-kli/ adv

bar·on /ˈbærən/ n [C] **1** a man who is a member of a low rank of the British NOBILITY or of a rank of European NOBILITY **2** a businessman with a lot of power or influence: ***drug barons*** | *conservative* ***press barons*** *like Beaverbrook* → ROBBER BARON

bar·on·ess /ˈbærənəs/ *n* [C] **1** a woman who is a member of a low rank of the British NOBILITY **2** the wife of a baron

bar·on·et /ˈbærənət, -net/ *n* [C] a member of the British NOBILITY, lower in rank than a baron, whose title passes to his son when he dies

B

bar·on·et·cy /ˈbærənətsi/ *n* (*plural* **baronetcies**) [C] the rank of a baronet

ba·ro·ni·al /bəˈrəʊniəl $ -ˈroʊ-/ *adj* **1** very large and richly decorated: *a splendid baronial house* **2** belonging to or involving BARONS

bar·on·y /ˈbærəni/ *n* (*plural* **baronies**) [C] the rank of BARON

ba·roque¹ /bəˈrɒk, bəˈrəʊk $ bəˈroʊk, -ˈrɑːk/ *adj* relating to the very decorated style of art, music, buildings etc, that was common in Europe in the 17th and early 18th centuries: *furnished in a* ***baroque style*** | **baroque music/architecture/paintings etc**

baroque² *n* **the baroque** used to describe baroque art, music, buildings etc

barque /bɑːk $ bɑːrk/ *n* [C] a sailing ship with three, four, or five MASTS (=poles that the sails are fixed to)

bar·rack /ˈbærək/ *v* [I,T] **1** *BrE* to interrupt someone, especially a performer or a player, by shouting criticism at them: *At the 1965 Newport Folk Festival Bob Dylan was barracked for using electric instruments.* **2** *AusE* to shout to show that you support someone or something

bar·racks /ˈbærəks/ *n* [plural] a building or group of buildings in which soldiers live

bar·ra·cu·da /ˌbærəˈkjuːdə $ -ˈkuːdə/ *n* [C] a large tropical fish that eats flesh

bar·rage¹ /ˈbærɑːʒ $ bəˈrɑːʒ/ ●○○ *n*

1 [C usually singular] the continuous firing of guns, dropping of bombs etc, especially to protect soldiers as they move towards an enemy: **[+of]** *a barrage of anti-aircraft fire*

2 [singular] a lot of criticism, questions, complaints etc that are said at the same time, or very quickly one after another: **[+of]** *a barrage of questions*

bar·rage² /ˈbærɑːʒ $ ˈbɑːrɪdʒ/ *n* [C] a wall of earth, stones etc built across a river to provide water for farming or to prevent flooding → **dam**

ˈbarrage balˌloon / $ ˈ..ˌ./ *n* [C] a large bag that floats in the air to prevent enemy planes from flying near the ground

barred /bɑːd $ bɑːrd/ *adj* **1** a barred window, gate etc has bars across it → **bar 2** *formal* having bands of different colour → **bar**: *red barred tail feathers*

bar·rel¹ /ˈbærəl/ ●●○ *n* [C]

1 a large curved container with a flat top and bottom, made of wood or metal, and used for storing beer, wine etc: *The wine is aged in oak barrels.* | **[+of]** *barrels of beer* → see picture at CONTAINER

2 a unit of measurement for oil, equal to 159 litres: **[+of]** *two million barrels of oil*

3 the part of a gun that the bullets are fired through

4 have sb over a barrel to put someone in a situation in which they are forced to accept or do what you want: *The manager has us over a barrel – either we work on a Saturday or we lose our jobs.*

5 be a barrel of laughs [often in negatives] to be very enjoyable: ***Life is not*** *exactly* ***a barrel of laughs*** *at the moment.* → PORK BARREL, → **scrape (the bottom of) the barrel** at SCRAPE¹(5), → **lock, stock, and barrel** at LOCK²(3)

barrel² *v* [I] *AmE informal* to move very fast, especially in an uncontrolled way: *A vehicle barreled out of a shopping center and crashed into the side of my car.*

ˌbarrel-ˈchested *adj* a man who is barrel-chested has a round chest that sticks out

ˈbarrel ˌorgan *n* [C] a musical instrument that you play by turning a handle, often used on the streets in order to get money, especially in the past

bar·ren /ˈbærən/ ●○○ *adj*

1 land or soil that is barren has no plants growing on it: *Thousands of years ago the surface was barren desert.*

2 *old-fashioned* unable to produce children or baby animals – used of a woman or of female animals SYN **infertile** OPP **fertile**

3 a tree or plant that is barren does not produce fruit or seeds

4 used to describe something that does not look interesting or attractive: *The sports hall was a rather barren concrete building.*

5 used to describe a period of time during which you do not achieve anything or get any useful results: *I scored five in the first seven games, but I've had a bit of a barren patch since then.*

bar·rette /bæˈret/ *n* [C] *AmE* a small metal or plastic object used to keep a woman's hair in place SYN **hair-slide** *BrE*

bar·ri·cade¹ /ˈbærəkeɪd, ˌbærəˈkeɪd/ ●○○ *n* [C] a temporary wall or fence across a road, door etc that prevents people from going through: *The fans were kept back behind barricades.*

barricade² *v* [T] to build a barricade to prevent someone or something from getting in: *During the riots, some of the prisoners barricaded their cells.* | **barricade sb/yourself in/into sth** *Shopkeepers had to barricade themselves in.*

bar·ri·er /ˈbæriə $ -ər/ ●●○ W3 *n* [C]

1 a rule, problem etc that prevents people from doing something, or limits what they can do: *He advocated the removal of trade barriers.* | **[+to]** *Problems with childcare remain the biggest barrier to women succeeding at work.* | **[+between]** *barriers between doctors and patients*

2 a type of fence or gate that prevents people from moving in a particular direction: *Crowds burst through the barriers and ran onto the pitch.*

3 a physical object that keeps two areas, people etc apart: **[+between]** *The mountains form a* ***natural barrier*** *between the two countries.*

4 the 10-second/40% etc barrier a level or amount of 10 seconds, 40% etc that is seen as a limit which it is difficult to get beyond: *I'm hoping to crash the 20-second barrier in the final and get a bronze.* → SOUND BARRIER, CRASH BARRIER

COLLOCATIONS

ADJECTIVES/NOUN + barrier

trade barriers (=things such as taxes that make trade between countries difficult) *The aim was to remove trade barriers and open up free markets.*

the language barrier (=the problem of understanding people who do not speak the same language) *Living in China was hard for me at first because of the language barrier.*

cultural/racial/class barriers | **technical/legal/political barriers**

VERBS

break/tear down barriers *Most companies have broken down the old barriers of status among the workers.*

cross/transcend barriers (=avoid barriers that usually exist) *Music has the great advantage of crossing cultural barriers.*

remove/eliminate/lift barriers *Will this remove the barriers to change?*

overcome barriers *There are still many more barriers that need to be overcome.*

ˈbarrier ˌmethod *n* [C] barrier methods of CONTRACEPTION involve the use of CONDOMS etc, which physically prevent the SPERM from reaching the egg

ˌbarrier ˈreef *n* [C] a line of CORAL (=pink stone-like substance) separated from the shore by water

bar·ring /ˈbɑːrɪŋ/ *prep* unless something happens: *Barring a miracle, he won't walk again.*

bar·ri·o /ˈbæriəʊ $ ˈbɑːrioʊ/ *n* (*plural* **barrios**) [C] *AmE* a part of an American town or city where many poor Spanish-speaking people live

bar·ris·ter /ˈbærɪstə $ -ər/ *n* [C] a lawyer in Britain who can argue cases in the higher law courts → **solicitor**

ˈ**bar·room**, ˈ**bar room** *n* [C] a bar

bar·row /ˈbærəʊ $ -roʊ/ *n* [C] **1** a small vehicle like a box on wheels, from which fruits, vegetables etc used to be sold **2** a large pile of earth like a small hill that was put over a GRAVE in ancient times **3** a WHEELBARROW

bar·row·boy /ˈbærəʊbɔɪ $ -roʊ-/ *n* [C] *BrE* a man or boy who sells fruit, vegetables etc from a barrow

bar·tend·er /ˈbɑːˌtendə $ ˈbɑːrˌtendər/ *n* [C] *AmE* someone who makes, pours, and serves drinks in a bar or restaurant SYN **barman, barmaid** *BrE*

bar·ter¹ /ˈbɑːtə $ ˈbɑːrtər/ *v* [I,T] to exchange goods, work, or services for other goods or services rather than for money: **barter (with sb) for sth** *I had to barter with the locals for food.* | **barter sth for sth** *They bartered their grain for salt.*

barter² *n* [U] **1** a system of exchanging goods and services for other goods and services rather than using money: *Trading was carried out under a barter system.* **2** goods or services that are exchanged by bartering: *We used cigarettes for barter.*

bas·alt /ˈbæsɔːlt, bəˈsɔːlt $ ˈbæsɒːlt, ˈbeɪ-/ *n* [U] a type of dark green-black rock

base¹ /beɪs/ ●●● S1 W1 *v* [T] to have your main place of work, business etc in a particular place: *The paper had intended to base itself in London.* | **be based in sth** *The new organization will be based in Dallas.* → BASED

base sth **on/upon** sth *phr v* to use something as the thing from which something else is developed → **basis**: *Their relationship was based upon mutual respect.* | *an economy based on farming*

base² ●●● S2 W2 *n*

1 LOWEST PART [C usually singular] **a)** the lowest part or surface of something SYN **bottom**: **[+of]** *There is a door at the base of the tower.* | *the base of a triangle* | *a frozen dessert with a biscuit base* | *a wine glass with a heavy base* | *The leather of his left trainer was coming away from its rubber base.* **b)** the lowest point on a plant or part of your body, where it joins another part SYN **bottom**: **[+of]** *a hole in the base of the tree* | *He was killed by an axe blow to the base of his skull.* **THESAURUS** ▶ BOTTOM

2 KNOWLEDGE/IDEAS [C] the most important part of something, from which new ideas develop SYN **foundation**: *India has a good scientific research base.* | **[+for]** *They were laying the base for a new economic recovery.*

3 MILITARY [C] a place where people in a military organization live and work: **military/naval/air base**

4 COMPANY/ORGANIZATION [C,U] the main place from which a person, company, or organization controls their activities: **[+for]** *He used the house as a base for his printing business.*

5 PEOPLE/GROUPS [C usually singular] the people, money, groups etc that form the main part of something: *The company has built up a loyal* ***customer base***. | *By broadening the* ***tax base*** (=all the people who pay taxes), *he could raise more revenues.* | *an attempt to strengthen the city's* ***economic base*** (=things that produce jobs and money) | *The country's* ***manufacturing base*** (=all the factories, companies etc that produce goods in a country) *has shrunk by 20%.* → POWER BASE

6 SUBSTANCE/MIXTURE [singular, U] the main part of a substance, meal etc to which other things are added: *paint with an oil base* | **[+for]** *Vodka is the base for many cocktails.*

7 SPORT [C] one of the four places that a player must touch in order to get a point in games such as BASEBALL → see picture at **BASEBALL**

8 be off base *AmE informal* to be completely wrong: *His estimate for painting the kitchen seems way off base.*

9 CHEMICAL [C] *technical* a chemical substance that combines with an acid to form a SALT

10 NUMBERS [C usually singular] *technical* the number in relation to which a number system or mathematical table is built up, for example 10 in the DECIMAL system

11 touch base (with sb) to talk to someone to find out what is happening about something —**basal** *adj* → **cover (all) the bases** at **COVER¹**(12)

base³ *adj* not having good moral principles: *base attitudes and desires* → **BASE METAL**

base·ball /ˈbeɪsbɔːl $ -bɒːl/ ●●● S3 W2 *n*

1 [U] an outdoor game between two teams of nine players, in which players try to get points by hitting a ball and running around four BASES

2 [C] the ball used in baseball

ˈ**baseball ˌcap** *n* [C] a hat that fits closely around your head with a round part that sticks out at the front → see picture at **HAT**

base·board /ˈbeɪsbɔːd $ -bɔːrd/ *n* [C] *AmE* a narrow board fixed to the bottom of indoor walls where they meet the floor SYN **skirting board** *BrE*

based /beɪst/ *adj* **1** [not before noun] if you are based somewhere, that is the place where you work or where your main business is: *It is a professional service based at*

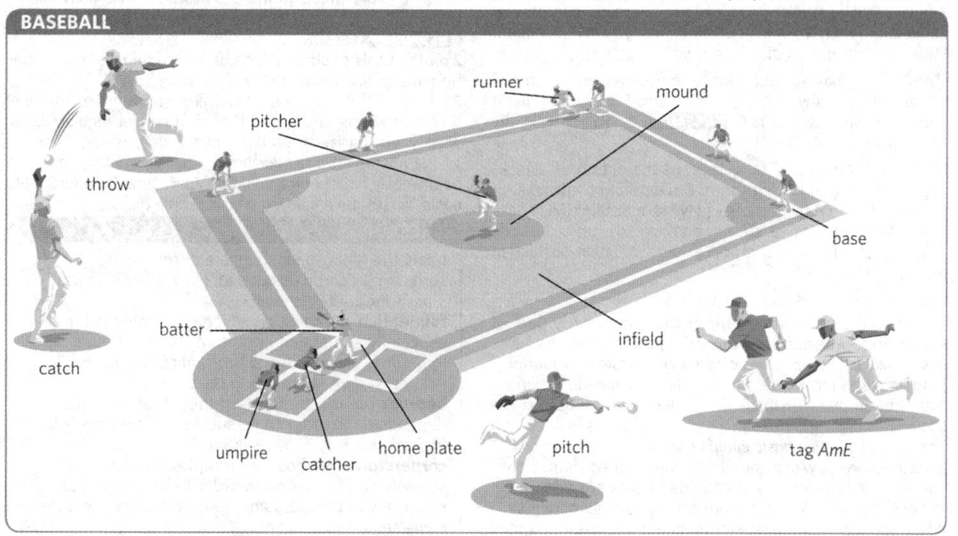

our offices in Oxford. | **London-based/New York-based etc** *a London-based firm of accountants* **2 oil-based/carbon-based/computer-based etc** used to describe the basic feature or part of something: *computer-based teaching* | *community-based services* | *carbon-based fuels* **3 broadly-based** based on many kinds of things or people: *a broadly-based government of national reconciliation*

BASE jumping, **base jumping** /ˈbeɪs ˌdʒʌmpɪŋ/ *n* [U] (***Building, Antenna, Span, Earth***) a sport in which people jump off tall objects such as buildings, bridges, or cliffs, using a PARACHUTE

B

base·less /ˈbeɪsləs/ *adj* not based on facts or good reasons – used to show disapproval SYN **unfounded**: **baseless rumours/charges/accusations**

base·line /ˈbeɪslaɪn/ *n* [C usually singular] **1** *technical* a standard measurement or fact against which other measurements or facts are compared, especially in medicine or science: *The company's waste emissions were 14% lower than in 1998, the baseline year.* **2** the line at the back of the court in games such as tennis or VOLLEYBALL → see picture at **TENNIS** **3** the area that a player must run within, on a BASEBALL field

base·ment /ˈbeɪsmənt/ ●●● S2 *n* [C] a room or area in a building that is under the level of the ground → **cellar**

ˌbase ˈmetal *n* [C,U] a metal that is not very valuable, such as iron or lead

ˈbase rate *n* [C] *BrE* in Britain, the standard rate of INTEREST[1](4), set by the Bank of England, on which all British banks base their charges → **prime rate**

bas·es /ˈbeɪsiːz/ the plural of BASIS

bash[1] /bæʃ/ *v* **1** [I always + adv/prep, T] to hit someone or something hard, in a way that causes pain or damage: *Someone bashed him on the back of his head.* | *Police bashed down the door to get in.* | **bash sth on/against sth** *He bashed his head on the back of the seat.* | **[+into]** *I accidentally bashed into a woman pushing a pram.* THESAURUS HIT

2 [T] to criticize someone or something very strongly: *He was always bashing the trade unions.* —**-basher** [in nouns]: *union-bashers*

bash on *phr v BrE informal* to continue working in order to finish something: *Well, I'd better bash on.*

bash sth ↔ **out** *phr v informal* to produce something quickly or in great quantities but without much care or thought: *I bashed out replies as fast as I could.*

bash sb ↔ **up** *phr v* to seriously hurt someone by attacking them violently

bash[2] *n* [C] **1** *informal* a hard strong hit SYN **bang**: **[+on]** *a bash on the head* **2** *informal* a party or an event to celebrate something: *a birthday bash* THESAURUS PARTY **3 have a bash (at sth)** *BrE spoken* to try to do something, especially when you are not sure that you will succeed: *Why not have a bash at windsurfing?*

bash·ful /ˈbæʃfəl/ *adj* easily embarrassed in social situations SYN **shy**: *a bashful grin* | *Don't be bashful about telling people how you feel.* THESAURUS SHY —**bashfully** *adv* —**bashfulness** *n* [U]

bash·ing /ˈbæʃɪŋ/ *n* [singular, U] **1** the action of attacking someone and hitting them: *Gay-bashing* (=attacks on gay people) *is on the increase.* | **give sb a bashing** *They gave him a real bashing.* **2** strong and usually unfair public criticism of a particular group or person: *union-bashing in the right-wing press*

ba·sic /ˈbeɪsɪk/ ●●● S2 W1 *adj*

1 forming the most important or most necessary part of something → **basics**: *the* ***basic principles*** *of chemistry* | *The* ***basic idea*** *is simple.* | ***basic research*** | ***basic information*** | **[+to]** *medical techniques basic to the control of infection*

2 at the simplest or least developed level → **basics**: *the* ***basic skills*** *of programming* | *Their knowledge is very basic.* | *The farm lacks even* ***basic equipment***.

3 basic salary/pay/pension etc the amount of money that you are paid before any special payments are added: *On top of the basic salary, there are numerous other benefits.*

4 [only before noun] basic rights, needs etc are ones that everyone needs or should have: *basic human rights* | *poor families unable to meet their basic needs*

ba·sic·ally /ˈbeɪsɪkli/ ●●● S1 *adv*

1 [sentence adverb] *spoken* used to emphasize the most important reason or fact about something, or a simple explanation of something: *Basically, I'm just lazy.* | *Well, basically, it's a matter of filling in a few forms.* | *I used to see him every night, basically.*

2 in the main or most important ways, without considering additional details or differences SYN **fundamentally**: *All cheeses are made in basically the same way.* | *I believe that human beings are basically good.* | *Basically, he hadn't changed at all.*

ba·sics /ˈbeɪsɪks/ ●○○ *n* [plural]

1 the most important and necessary facts about something, from which other possibilities and ideas may develop: **[+of]** *the basics of French grammar* | *Here are some of the basics you will need to know.*

2 things that everyone needs in order to live or to deal with a particular situation: *basics like food and education*

3 back to basics used to describe a return to teaching or doing the most important or simplest things: *A lot of parents want schools to get back to basics.*

ˌbasic ˈtraining *n* [U] the period when a new soldier learns military rules and does a lot of exercise

bas·il /ˈbæzəl $ ˈbeɪ-/ *n* [U] a strong-smelling and strong-tasting HERB used in cooking

ba·sil·i·ca /bəˈsɪlɪkə, -ˈzɪl-/ *n* [C] a church in the shape of a long room with a round end: *the basilica of St Peter's in Rome*

bas·i·lisk /ˈbæsəlɪsk, ˈbæz-/ *n* [C] an imaginary animal like a snake in ancient stories, supposed to be able to kill people by looking at them

ba·sin /ˈbeɪsən/ ●●○ *n* [C]

1 *BrE* a round container attached to the wall in a bathroom, where you wash your hands and face SYN **sink**: *a wash basin*

2 a large bowl-shaped container for liquids or food: *Fill the basin with the cake mixture.*

3 (*also* **basinful** /ˈbeɪsənfʊl/) the amount of liquid that a basin can contain: *a basin of hot water*

4 an area of land that is lower at the centre than at the edges, especially one from which water runs down into a river: *the Amazon basin*

5 a place where the Earth's surface is lower than in other areas: *the Pacific Basin* → **PUDDING BASIN**

ba·sis /ˈbeɪsɪs/ ●●● S2 W1 *n* (*plural* **bases** /-siːz/)

1 [C] the facts, ideas, or things from which something can be developed: *Their claim had no basis in fact* (=it was not true). | **[+of]** *Bread* ***forms*** *the* ***basis*** *of their daily diet.* | **[+for]** *The video will* ***provide a basis*** *for class discussion.* THESAURUS REASON

2 on the basis of sth because of a particular fact or situation: *discrimination on the basis of sex*

3 [singular] the way that something happens, or the way that something is organized or done: **on a regular/daily/weekly etc basis** (=regularly, every day, week, etc) *I'm saving money on a regular basis.* | *Board meetings are held on a weekly basis.* | **on a voluntary/part-time/temporary etc basis** *Nurses are employed on a full-time basis.*

THESAURUS

basis the facts, ideas, things etc from which something can be developed: *His work will be used as a basis for future research.*

foundation the thing on which something is based, especially something important that continues for a long time: *Their ideas were the foundation for the political system that exists in the UK today.*

bedrock the most important thing that something depends on in order to be successful: *Honesty is the bedrock of any healthy relationship.*

cornerstone the most important thing that something depends on in order to be successful, especially in business and politics: *Confidence is the cornerstone of our business.*

bask /bɑːsk $ bæsk/ *v* [I] **1** to enjoy sitting or lying in the heat of the sun or a fire: **[+in]** *Lizards were basking in the morning sun.* **2** if a place basks in the sun, it is sunny and warm: **[+in]** *Tenerife was basking in afternoon sunshine as they arrived.* **3** to enjoy the approval or attention that you are getting from other people: **[+in]** *She **basked in the admiration** of the media.* → **bask/bathe in sb's reflected glory** at GLORY[1](4)

bas·ket /ˈbɑːskɪt $ ˈbæ-/ ●●● S3 *n* [C]
1 a container made of thin pieces of plastic, wire, or wood woven together, used to carry things or put things in: *a shopping basket | a basket full of vegetables |* **clothes/laundry basket** (=for dirty clothes)
2 a net with a hole at the bottom, attached to a metal ring, through which the ball is thrown in BASKETBALL: **make/shoot a basket** (=to throw the ball through the basket) → see picture at **BASKETBALL**
3 *technical* the average or total value of a number of different goods or CURRENCIES
4 the part of a website, often represented by a picture of a basket, where you collect things to buy → **put all your eggs in one basket** at EGG[1](6), → **WASTEPAPER BASKET**

bas·ket·ball /ˈbɑːskətbɔːl $ ˈbæskətbɒːl/ ●●● S3 *n*
1 [U] a game played indoors between two teams of five players, in which each team tries to win points by throwing a ball through a net
2 [C] the ball used in this game

ˈbasket case *n* [C] **1** *informal* someone who you think is crazy SYN **nut case** **2** a country with many severe economic and social problems that are likely to continue for a long time

bas·ket·ry /ˈbɑːskətri $ ˈbæs-/ (*also* **bas·ket·work** /ˈbɑːskətwɜːk $ ˈbæskətwɜːrk/) *n* [U] **1** baskets or other objects made by weaving together thin dried branches **2** the skill of making baskets

basque /bæsk/ *n* [C] a piece of underwear for a woman that covers her body from under her arms to the top of her legs

bas-re·lief /ˌbɑː rɪˈliːf, ˌbæs-/ *n* [C,U] *technical* a style of art in which stone or wood is cut so that shapes are raised above the surrounding surface → **high relief**

bass[1] /beɪs/ *n* **1** [C] a very low male singing voice, or a man with a voice like this **2** [singular] the part of a musical work that is written for a singer with a bass voice → **ALTO[2](2), BARITONE[1](2), SOPRANO[1](2), TENOR[1](2)** **3** [U] the lower half of the whole range of musical notes → **treble** **4** [C] a BASS GUITAR: *The band features Johnson **on bass*** (=playing the bass guitar). **5** [C] a DOUBLE BASS

bass[2] *adj* [only before noun] a bass instrument or voice produces low notes: *a bass drum*

bass[3] /bæs/ *n* (*plural* **bass**) [C] a fish that can be eaten and lives in both rivers and the sea

bass clef /ˌbeɪs ˈklef/ *n* [C] a sign (𝄢) at the beginning of a line of written music that shows that the top line of the STAVE is the A below MIDDLE C

bas·set /ˈbæsɪt/ (*also* **ˈbasset ˌhound**) *n* [C] a dog with short legs and long ears, used for hunting

bass gui·tar /ˌbeɪs gɪˈtɑː $ -ˈtɑːr/ (*also* **bass**) *n* [C] an electric GUITAR with four strings, that plays low notes → **BASSIST**

bas·sist /ˈbeɪsɪst/ *n* [C] someone who plays a BASS GUITAR or a DOUBLE BASS

bas·soon /bəˈsuːn/ *n* [C] a musical instrument like a very long wooden tube, that produces a low sound. You hold it upright and play it by blowing into a thin curved metal pipe. → see picture at **WOODWIND** —**bassoonist** *n* [C]

bas·tard /ˈbɑːstəd, ˈbæ- $ ˈbæstərd/ *n* [C]
1 *taboo* someone, especially a man, who you think is unpleasant. Do not use this word: *You lying bastard!*
2 *spoken informal not polite* a man who you think is very lucky or very unlucky – often used humorously: *He's gone straight to the top, the lucky bastard. | The poor bastard fell off his horse.* **3** *BrE spoken informal* something that causes difficulties or problems: *Life's a bastard sometimes.*
4 *old-fashioned* someone who was born to parents who were not married

bas·tard·ize (*also* **-ise** *BrE*) /ˈbɑːstədaɪz, ˈbæ- $ ˈbæstər-/ *v* [T] to spoil something by changing its good parts: *a bastardized version of the play*

baste /beɪst/ *v* [I,T] **1** to pour liquid or melted fat over food that is cooking: *Baste the potatoes occasionally.* **2** to fasten cloth with long loose stitches, in order to hold it together so that you can SEW it later SYN **tack**

bas·ti·on /ˈbæstiən $ -tʃən/ *n* [C] **1** something that protects a way of life, principle etc that seems likely to change or end completely: **[+of]** *These clubs are the **last bastions** of male privilege.* **2** a place where a country or army has strong military defences: *Pearl Harbor was the principal American bastion in the Pacific.* **3** *technical* a part of a castle wall that sticks out from the rest

bat[1] /bæt/ ●●● S3 *n* [C]
1 a small animal like a mouse with wings that flies around at night → **FRUIT BAT**
2 a) a long wooden stick with a special shape that is used in some sports and games: *a baseball bat | a cricket bat* **b)** *BrE* a round flat piece of wood with a handle, used to hit a ball in TABLE TENNIS SYN **paddle** *AmE* → see picture at **SPORT[1]**

BASKETBALL

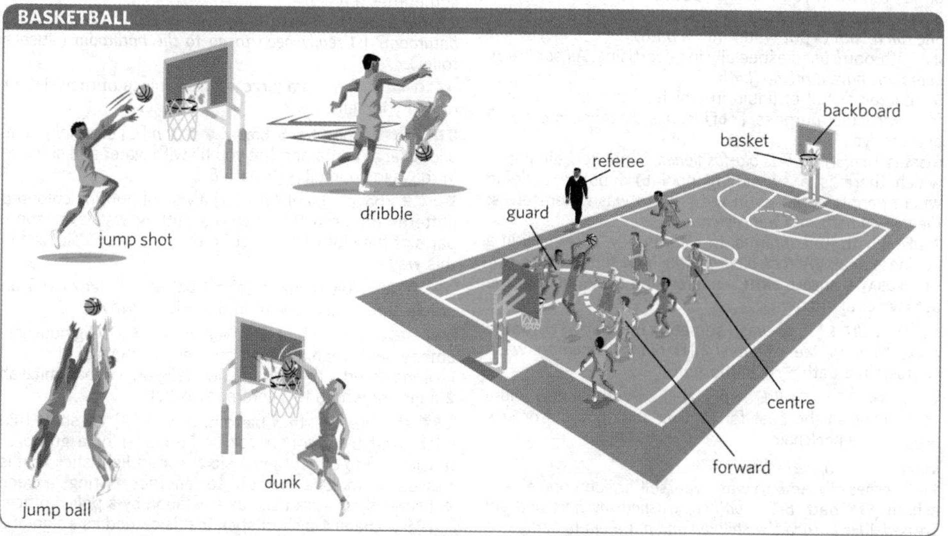

3 be at bat to be the person who is trying to hit the ball in a game of BASEBALL
4 do sth off your own bat *BrE informal* to do something without being told to do it: *She went to see a solicitor off her own bat.*
5 do sth right off the bat *AmE informal* to do something immediately: *He said yes right off the bat.*
6 like a bat out of hell *informal* very fast: *I drove like a bat out of hell to the hospital.*
7 old bat *spoken* an unpleasant old woman → **as blind as a bat** at BLIND[1]

B

bat² *v* (**batted**, **batting**) **1** [I,T] to hit the ball with a bat in CRICKET or BASEBALL **2 not bat an eye/eyelid** *informal* to not seem to be shocked, surprised, or embarrassed: *They started talking about sex, but she didn't bat an eyelid.* **3 bat your eyes/eyelashes** if a woman bats her eyes, she opens and closes them several times quickly, in order to look attractive to men **4 go to bat for sb** *AmE informal* to help and support someone **5 be batting a thousand** *AmE informal* to be very successful: *She's been batting a thousand since she got that job.*

bat sth ↔ **around** *phr v informal* to discuss various ideas or suggestions

bat·boy /ˈbætbɔɪ/ *n* [C] a boy whose job is to look after the equipment of a BASEBALL team

batch /bætʃ/ ●●○ *n* [C]
1 a group of people or things that arrive or are dealt with together: **[+of]** *Every day another batch of papers reaches the manager, demanding his attention.*
2 a quantity of food, medicine etc that is produced or prepared at the same time: **[+of]** *She was in the kitchen taking a batch of bread out of the oven.*
3 a set of jobs that are dealt with together on a computer: *an overnight* ***batch file*** | *a* ***batch job***

ˌbatch ˈprocessing *n* [U] *technical* a type of computer system in which the computer does several jobs one after the other, without needing instructions between each job

bat·ed /ˈbeɪtɪd/ *adj* **with bated breath** feeling very anxious or excited: *He* ***waited*** *for a reply to his offer* ***with bated breath.***

bath¹ /bɑːθ $ bæθ/ ●●● S2 W3 *n* (*plural* **baths** /bɑːðz, bɑːθs $ bæðz, bæθs/) [C]
1 if you take a bath, you wash your body in a bath: *After a week of camping, I really needed a bath.* | **have a bath** *BrE* **take a bath** *AmE*: *I'll have a bath and go to bed.* | *How often do you take a bath?* | *I'll* ***give*** *the children their* ***bath*** (=wash them in a bath).
2 *BrE* a large long container that you fill with water and sit or lie in to wash yourself SYN **bathtub** *AmE*
3 water that you sit or lie in to wash yourself: *a hot bath* | *She* ***ran a bath*** (=put water into a bath).
4 a bathroom, used especially in advertising: *All our luxury bedrooms have a private bath.*
5 a container full of liquid in which something is placed for a particular purpose: **[+of]** *Plunge the fabric into a bath of black dye.*
6 baths [plural] **a)** *BrE old-fashioned* a public building in which there is a swimming pool **b)** a public building where people could go in the past to wash themselves: *the Roman baths at Cirencester*
7 take a bath *AmE informal* to lose money, especially in a business deal: *We took a bath in the market over that stock.*
→ **BIRDBATH, BUBBLE BATH,** → **throw the baby out with the bath water** at THROW[1](37)

bath² *v BrE* **1** [T] to wash someone in a bath SYN **bathe** *AmE*: *I'll bath the children.* **2** [I] *old-fashioned* to wash yourself in a bath SYN **bathe** *AmE*

ˈbath chair *n* [C] *BrE* a special chair with wheels and a cover, used in the past for moving someone old or sick around → **wheelchair**

bathe¹ /beɪð/ ●○○ *v*
1 [I,T] *especially AmE* to wash yourself or someone else in a bath SYN **bath** *BrE*: *I bathed, washed my hair, and got dressed.* | *He bathed the children and put them to bed.*
2 [I] *BrE old-fashioned* to swim in the sea, a river, or a lake: *They bathed in the lake in the moonlight.*

> **REGISTER**
> In everyday English, people usually say **go for/have a swim** rather than **bathe**: *They* ***went for a swim*** *in the lake.*

3 [T] to wash or cover part of your body with a liquid, especially as a medical treatment: *She brought a bowl of water and began to bathe the injured arm.* **THESAURUS** CLEAN
4 be bathed in light/sunshine etc *written* an area or building that is bathed in light has light shining onto it in a way that makes it look pleasant or attractive: *The top of Pea Hill was bathed in brilliant sunshine.*
5 be bathed in sweat *written* to be covered in SWEAT: *I was tired and bathed in sweat.*

bathe² *n* **a bathe** *BrE old-fashioned* when you swim in the sea, a river, or a lake SYN **swim**: *They went for a bathe.*

bath·er /ˈbeɪðə $ -ər/ *n* **1** [C] *BrE* someone who is swimming in the sea, a river, or a lake **2 bathers** [plural] *AusE* a SWIMSUIT

bath·ing /ˈbeɪðɪŋ/ *n* [U] *BrE* the activity of swimming in the sea, a river, or a lake SYN **swimming**: *Is the beach safe for bathing?*

bathing cap /ˈbeɪðɪŋ kæp/ *n* [C] *old-fashioned* a special hat that you wear for swimming SYN **swimming cap**

bathing cos·tume /ˈbeɪðɪŋ ˌkɒstjuːm $ -ˌkɑːstuːm/ *n* [C] *BrE old-fashioned* a SWIMSUIT

bathing suit /ˈbeɪðɪŋ suːt, -sjuːt $ -suːt/ *n* [C] *old-fashioned* a SWIMSUIT

bathing trunks /ˈbeɪðɪŋ trʌŋks/ *n* [plural] *BrE old-fashioned* a piece of clothing worn by men for swimming SYN **swimming trunks**

ˈbath mat *n* [C] **1** a piece of thick cloth that you put on the floor next to the bath **2** a piece of rubber that you put in the bath to prevent yourself from slipping

ba·thos /ˈbeɪθɒs $ -θɑːs/ *n* [U] *formal* in writing, a play etc, a sudden change from a subject that is beautiful, moral, or serious to something that is ordinary, silly, or not important **THESAURUS** LANGUAGE

bath·robe /ˈbɑːθrəʊb $ ˈbæθroʊb/ *n* [C] a long loose piece of clothing shaped like a coat, that you wear especially before or after having a bath or SHOWER → **dressing gown**

bath·room /ˈbɑːθrʊm, -ruːm $ ˈbæθ-/ ●●● S2 W3 *n* [C]
1 a room where there is a bath or SHOWER, a BASIN, and sometimes a toilet
2 *AmE* a room where there is a toilet: *Where's the bathroom?* | *I really need to* ***go to the bathroom*** (=use a toilet).

ˈbath towel *n* [C] a large TOWEL (=piece of material for drying yourself)

bath·tub /ˈbɑːθtʌb $ ˈbæθ-/ ●●○ *n* [C] *especially AmE* a long large container that you fill with water and sit or lie in to wash yourself SYN **bath** *BrE*

ba·tik /bəˈtiːk, ˈbætɪk/ *n* **1** [U] a way of printing coloured patterns on cloth that involves putting WAX over some parts of the cloth **2** [C,U] cloth that has been coloured in this way

bat·man /ˈbætmən/ *n* (*plural* **batmen** /-mən/) [C] an officer's personal servant in the British army

bat mitzvah /ˌbɑːt ˈmɪtsvə/ *n* [C] **1** a religious ceremony held when a Jewish girl reaches the age of 13 and is considered an adult in her religion → **bar mitzvah** **2** a girl for whom this ceremony is held

bat·on /ˈbætɒn, -tn $ bæˈtɑːn, bə-/ *n* [C] **1** a short thin stick used by a CONDUCTOR (=the leader of a group of musicians) to direct the music **2** a short light stick that is passed from one person to another during a race **3** a short thick stick used as a weapon by a police officer SYN **truncheon** **4** a short stick that is carried as a sign of a special office or rank **5** a light metal stick that is spun and thrown into the air by a MAJORETTE

bats·man /ˈbætsmən/ *n* (*plural* **batsmen** /-mən/) [C] the person who is trying to hit the ball in CRICKET → **bowler**

bat·tal·ion /bəˈtæljən/ *n* [C] **1** a large group of soldiers consisting of several companies (COMPANY) **2** a large group of people who are doing something with a particular purpose: **[+of]** *a battalion of supporters*

bat·ten¹ /ˈbætn/ *v* **1 batten down the hatches a)** to prepare yourself for a period of difficulty or trouble **b)** to firmly fasten the entrances to the lower part of a ship **2 batten on sb** *BrE formal* to live well by using someone else's money, possessions etc - used to show disapproval

batten² *n* [C] a long narrow piece of wood that is attached to other pieces of wood or another building material to strengthen them and keep them in place

bat·ter¹ /ˈbætə $ -ər/ *v* [I always + adv/prep, T] to hit someone or something many times, in a way that hurts or damages them: *He was **battered to death**.* | *As a child, she was battered by her father.* | **[+at/on/against etc]** *People were battering at the door.* | **batter sb with sth** *He was battered on the head with a cricket bat.* | **[+away]** *She battered away at his chest with her fists.* | **batter sth down** *Armed police battered his door down.*

batter² *n* **1** [C,U] a mixture of flour, eggs, milk etc, used in cooking and for making bread, cakes etc: *Fry the fish in batter.* | *pancake batter* **2** [C] the person who is trying to hit the ball in BASEBALL → see picture at **BASEBALL**

bat·tered /ˈbætəd $ -ərd/ *adj* **1** old and in bad condition: *a battered old suitcase* **2 battered woman/wife/husband/baby etc** someone who has been violently attacked by their husband, wife, father etc

bat·tering /ˈbætərɪŋ/ *n* [C,U] **1** when someone or something is severely damaged, defeated, criticized etc: *Her self-confidence had **taken a battering**.* **2** *BrE* when someone or something is hit many times

ˈbattering ˌram *n* [C] a long heavy piece of wood, used in wars in the past to break through walls or doors

bat·ter·y /ˈbætəri/ ●●● S2 *n* (*plural* **batteries**)

1 ELECTRICITY [C] an object that provides a supply of electricity for something such as a radio, car, or toy: *You have to take the top off to **change the batteries**.* | *When the red light comes on, you should **recharge the battery**.* | *The car's got a **flat battery**.* | *a **battery-operated** hairdryer*

2 a battery of sth a group of many things of the same type: *a battery of medical tests*

3 FARM [C] *BrE* a row of small CAGES in which chickens are kept, so that the farm can produce large numbers of eggs: *battery hens* → **FREE-RANGE**

4 GUNS [C] several large guns used together: *an anti-aircraft battery*

5 CRIME [U] *law* the crime of hitting someone: *He was charged with **assault and battery**.* → **ASSAULT AND BATTERY**

6 recharge your batteries *informal* to rest or relax in order to get back your energy: *A week in the mountains should recharge my batteries.*

bat·tle¹ /ˈbætl/ ●●● W2 *n* [C]

1 FIGHT a fight between opposing armies, groups of ships, groups of people etc, especially one that is part of a larger war: *the Battle of Trafalgar* | **in battle** *Her son was killed in battle.* | **into battle** *a knight riding into battle* | **[+between]** *battles between government forces and the rebels* | *a **pitched battle*** (=a long and serious battle) *between police and drug gangs* THESAURUS ▸ **WAR**

2 COMPETITION/ARGUMENT a situation in which opposing groups or people compete or argue with each other when trying to achieve success or control: *a long-running **legal battle*** | **[+for]** *a battle for custody of their children* | **[+between]** *a fierce ratings battle between rival TV stations* | **[+with]** *an ongoing battle with my mother about eating properly*

3 CHANGE BAD SITUATION an attempt to solve a difficult problem or change an unpleasant situation: **[+against]** *a battle against the racism of the school system* | **[+with]** *a long battle with lung cancer* | **[+for]** *Scientology has fought long battles for acceptance as a religion.*

4 be half the battle to be a difficult or important part of what you have to do: *Just getting an interview is half the battle.*

5 a battle of wits a situation in which opposing sides try to win by using their intelligence: *A good mystery story is a battle of wits between author and reader.*

6 battle of wills a situation in which opposing sides refuse to change what they want, in the hope that the other side will decide to change first: *a battle of wills between teacher and student*

7 do battle (with sb) to argue with someone or fight against someone: *She walked into the room with her eyes blazing, ready to do battle.*

8 fight your own battles to argue with someone, or compete in a difficult situation, without having help from other people - used to show approval: *It's all right, Mum. I can fight my own battles.*

9 the battle of the sexes the relationship between men and women when it is considered as a fight for power

10 the battle of the bulge the act of trying to lose weight - used humorously

COLLOCATIONS - MEANING 3

VERBS

fight a battle (*also* **wage a battle** *formal*) *The police are fighting a tough battle against crime.*
win a battle *It's essential to win the battle against inflation.*
lose a battle *a brave little girl who lost her battle against cancer*

ADJECTIVES

a long/lengthy battle *his long battle with alcoholism*
an uphill battle (=one that is very difficult) *For most people losing weight is an uphill battle.*
a tough/hard battle *He faces a tough battle to prove his innocence.*
a constant battle *As a student, life was a constant battle against debt.*
a losing battle (=one that is going to fail) *She was fighting a losing battle to stop herself from crying.*

battle² ●○○ *v*

1 [I,T] to try very hard to achieve something that is difficult or dangerous: *Firefighters battled the flames.* | **[+against/with]** *She had battled against cancer.* | **[+for]** *a pressure group battling for better schools* | **battle to do sth** *Doctors battled to save his life.*

2 battle it out to keep fighting or opposing each other until one person or team wins: *Sixteen teams will battle it out.*

3 [I] *literary* to take part in a fight or war

bat·tle·axe (*also* **battleax** *AmE*) /ˈbætl-æks/ *n* [C] **1** *informal* a very unpleasant woman who tries to control other people **2** a large AXE used as a weapon in the past

ˈbattle ˌcruiser *n* [C] a large fast ship used in war

ˈbattle cry *n* [C usually singular] **1** a phrase used to encourage people, especially members of a political organization: *'Socialism Now!' was their battle cry.* **2** a loud shout used in war to encourage your side and frighten the enemy

bat·tle·dress /ˈbætldres/ *n* [U] (*also* **ˈbattle ˌfatigues** [plural] *BrE*) clothes worn by soldiers when they are fighting

ˈbattle faˌtigue *n* [U] *old-fashioned* a type of mental illness caused by the frightening experiences of war, in which someone feels very anxious and upset

bat·tle·field /ˈbætlfiːld/ ●○○ (*also* **bat·tle·ground** /ˈbætlgraʊnd/) *n* [C]

1 a place where a battle is being fought or has been fought

2 a subject that people disagree or argue a lot about: *Education has become a political battleground.*

3 a place where an argument or disagreement happens, or where people are competing against each other: *a battleground state during the election*

bat·tle·ments /ˈbætlmənts/ *n* [plural] a low wall around the top of a castle, that has spaces to shoot guns or ARROWS through

bat·tle·ship /ˈbætlʃɪp/ *n* [C] the largest type of ship used in war, with very big guns and heavy ARMOUR

ˌbattleship ˈgrey *BrE*, **battleship gray** *AmE n* [U] a medium grey colour —**battleship grey** *adj*

bat·ty /ˈbæti/ *adj* slightly crazy, but not in an unpleasant or frightening way SYN **nutty**

bau·ble /ˈbɔːbəl $ ˈbɒː-/ *n* [C] **1** a cheap piece of jewellery **2** *BrE* a brightly coloured decoration that looks like a ball and is used to decorate a CHRISTMAS TREE

baud rate /ˈbɔːd reɪt $ ˈbɒːd-/ *n* [C] *technical* a measurement of how fast information is sent to or from a computer, for example through a telephone line

baulk /bɔːk, bɔːlk $ bɒːk, bɒːlk/ *v* [I,T] a British spelling of BALK

baux·ite /ˈbɔːksaɪt $ ˈbɒːk-/ *n* [U] a soft substance that ALUMINIUM is obtained from

bawd·y /ˈbɔːdi $ ˈbɒːdi/ *adj* bawdy songs, jokes, stories etc are about sex and are funny, enjoyable, and often noisy: *a bawdy new play* —**bawdiness** *n* [U]

ˈbawdy house *n* [C] *old use* a place where women have sex with men for money

bawl /bɔːl $ bɒːl/ *v* **1** [I,T] (*also* **bawl out**) to shout in a loud voice SYN **yell**: *'Tickets, please!' bawled the conductor.* THESAURUS ▸ SHOUT **2** [I] to cry loudly SYN **scream**: *They could hear a baby bawling somewhere.*

bawl sb ↔ **out** *phr v* to speak angrily to someone because they have done something wrong: *He was afraid Vic would bawl him out for being late.*

bay[1] /beɪ/ ●●○ *n* [C]

1 SEA a part of the sea that is partly enclosed by a curve in the land: *a house with a view across the bay | Montego Bay*

2 keep/hold sth at bay to prevent something dangerous or unpleasant from happening or from coming too close: *A thick wall keeps the noise at bay.*

3 AREA an area within a large room or just outside a building that is used for a particular purpose: *a storage bay | loading bay*

4 FOR CARGO the part of a ship or plane where things are stored: *the cargo bay*

5 TREE (*also* **bay tree**) a tree that has leaves that smell sweet and are often used in cooking

6 HORSE a horse that is a reddish brown colour

bay[2] *v* [I] **1** if a dog bays, it makes a long high noise, especially when it is chasing something SYN **howl**: *dogs baying at the moon* **2** to make strong demands to get answers to questions or force someone to give you something: **[+for]** *Reporters began* ***baying for*** *the president's* ***blood*** (=demanding that he be punished).

bay[3] *adj* a bay horse is reddish brown in colour

ˈbay leaf *n* [C] a sweet-smelling leaf from the bay tree, used in cooking

ˌBay of ˈPigs, the an area on the south coast of Cuba which is famous for a military attack that took place in 1961. A group of Cubans living in the US tried to enter Cuba with the aim of ending the government of Fidel Castro. They were trained and supported by the US, but the attack failed and they were all put into prison or killed. → CUBAN MISSILE CRISIS, THE

bay·o·net[1] /ˈbeɪənət, -net/ *n* [C] a long knife that is fixed to the end of a RIFLE (=long gun)

bayonet[2] *v* [T] to push the point of a bayonet into someone

bay·ou /ˈbaɪuː $ ˈbaɪuː, -oʊ/ *n* [C] a large area of water in the southeast US that moves very slowly and has many water plants

ˌbay ˈwindow *n* [C] a window that sticks out from the wall of a house, usually with glass on three sides → see picture at WINDOW

ba·zaar /bəˈzɑː $ -ˈzɑːr/ ●○○ *n* [C]

1 a market or area where there are a lot of small shops, especially in India or the Middle East

2 an occasion when a lot of people sell different things to collect money for a good purpose: *a church bazaar*

ba·zil·lion /bəˈzɪljən/ *n* [C] *informal humorous* a very large number of things: *Bazillions of people have already seen the video.*

ba·zoo·ka /bəˈzuːkə/ *n* [C] a long light gun that rests on your shoulder and is used for shooting at TANKS

BBC, the /ˌbiː biː ˈsiː◂/ (***the British Broadcasting Corporation***) the British radio and television company that is paid for by the public

ˌBBC ˈEnglish *n* [U] a standard form of British English pronunciation that was traditionally taught to people learning English in many parts of the world. For many years, almost everyone speaking on BBC programmes used this form of pronunciation, but many different types of British pronunciation can now be heard on the BBC.

BB gun /ˈbiː biː gʌn/ *n* [C] *AmE* a gun that uses air pressure to shoot small round metal balls SYN **airgun**

BBQ *n* [C] the abbreviation of ***barbecue***

BC *BrE*, **B.C.** *AmE* /ˌbiː ˈsiː/ (***before Christ***) used after a date to show that it was before the birth of Christ → **AD**: *The Great Pyramid dates from around 2600 BC.*

bcc (***blind carbon copy***) used in an EMAIL when you are sending a copy of a message to various people, when you do not give a complete list of all the people you are sending the message to

BCE *BrE*, **B.C.E.** *AmE* /ˌbiː siː ˈiː/ (***before common era***) used after a date to show that it is before the birth of Christ

BCG /ˌbiː siː ˈdʒiː/ *n* [U] *medical* a VACCINE used to protect people from getting the disease TUBERCULOSIS: *a BCG vaccination*

BDD /ˌbiː diː ˈdiː/ *n* [U] the abbreviation of ***body dysmorphic disorder***

be[1] /bi; *strong* biː/ ●●● S1 W1 *auxiliary verb* (*past tense* **was**, **were**, *past participle* **been**, *present participle* **being**, *first person singular* **am**, *second person singular and plural* **are**, *third person singular* **is**)

1 used with a present participle to form the CONTINUOUS(4) tenses of verbs: *Don't disturb me while I'm working. | Gemma was reading. | They've been asking a lot of questions. | That guy's always causing trouble. | We'll be starting in about an hour. | He isn't leaving, is he?*

2 used with past participles to form the PASSIVE: *Smoking is not permitted. | I was told about it yesterday. | The house is being painted. | She's been invited to a party. | The flames could be seen several miles away. | The police should have been informed about this.*

3 be to do sth *formal* **a)** used to talk about arrangements for the future: *Audrey and Jimmy are to be married in June. | Two men are to appear in court on charges of armed robbery.* **b)** used to give an order or to tell someone about a rule: *You are to wait here in this room until I return. | All staff are to wear uniforms.* **c)** used to say or ask what someone should do or what should happen: *What am I to tell her? | He is not to be blamed.* **d)** used to ask how something can be done: *How are we to get out of the present mess?*

4 be to be seen/found/heard etc used to say that something can be seen, found, or heard somewhere: *A large range of species are to be seen in the aquarium. | We searched everywhere but the ring* ***was nowhere to be found*** (=could not be found). *| The only sound to be heard was the twittering of the birds above us.*

5 was/were to do sth used when talking about a time in the past to say what happened later: *This discovery was to have a major effect on the treatment of heart disease.*

6 a) used in CONDITIONAL[1](2) sentences about an imagined situation: **were sb to do sth/if sb were to do sth** *Even if England were to win the next two matches, Germany would still be three points ahead. | Were we to offer you the job, would you take it?* **b)** used in CONDITIONAL sentences to introduce an aim when you are saying what must be done in order to achieve it: **if sb/sth is to do sth** *If we are to succeed in this enterprise, we shall need to plan everything very carefully.*

7 *old use* used instead of 'have' to form the PERFECT[3] tense of some verbs: *The hour is come.*

be² ●●● S1 W1 *v*
1 [linking verb] used to say that someone or something is the same as the subject of the sentence: *My name is Susan. | These are my favourite pictures. | He's my brother. | The problem is finding the time to get things done. | Our aim was to reduce the number of accidents.*
2 [I always + adv/prep] used to say where something or someone is: *Jane's upstairs. | Are my keys in the drawer? | The principal's in his office. | How long has she been here?*
3 [I always + adv/prep] used to say when something happens: *The concert was last night. | The party is on Saturday.*
4 [linking verb] used to describe someone or something, or say what group or type they belong to: *The sky was grey. | Spiders are not really insects. | Mr Cardew was a tall thin man. | She wants to be a doctor when she leaves school. | Her dress was pure silk. | I'm not ready yet.*
5 there is/are used to say that something exists or happens: *There's a hole in your trousers. | There was a loud explosion. | 'I thought there was going to be a party.' 'No, there isn't.' | Is there a problem?*
6 [linking verb] to behave in a particular way: *He was just being rude. | Don't be silly. | You'd better be careful.*
7 [linking verb] used to say how old someone is: *His mother died when he was 20. | Rachel will be three in November.*
8 [linking verb] used to say who something belongs to: *Whose is this bag? It isn't mine and it isn't Sarah's.*
9 [linking verb] used to talk about the price of something: *'How much are the melons?' 'The big ones are £2 each.'*
THESAURUS ▸ COST
10 [linking verb] to be equal to a particular number or amount: *32 divided by 8 is 4.*
11 be that as it may *formal* used to say that even though you accept that something is true, it does not change a situation: *'He was only joking.' 'Be that as it may, silly remarks like that can do a lot of harm.'*
12 [I] *formal* to exist: *What was once a great and powerful empire has effectively ceased to be.*
13 be yourself to behave in a natural way, rather than trying to pretend to be different: *Don't try too hard – just be yourself.*
14 not be yourself to be behaving in a way that is unusual for you, especially because you are ill or upset: *Sorry – I'm not myself this morning.*
15 the be-all and end-all the most important part of a situation or of someone's life: **[+of]** *For Jim, making money was the be-all and end-all of his job.*

GRAMMAR: Linking verbs

Be is a linking verb. This type of verb links the subject of the sentence with an adjective or noun: *The water was cold.| Leeds is a city in the north of England.*

be- /bɪ/ *prefix* **1** [in verbs] used to mean that someone or something is treated in a particular way: *Don't belittle him* (=say he is unimportant). | *He befriended me* (=became my friend). **2** [in adjectives] *literary* wearing or covered by a particular thing: *a bespectacled boy* (=wearing glasses)

beach¹ /biːtʃ/ ●●● S2 W2 *n* [C] an area of sand or small stones at the edge of the sea or a lake: *There is a beautiful sandy beach. | It's a nice day for going to the beach. | We walked along the beach. | Our hotel was right next to the beach.*

GRAMMAR: Patterns with beach

on the beach
• You use **on the beach** when thinking of the beach as a surface: *I just wanted to lie on the beach and read a book. | We played volleyball on the beach.* ✗ Don't say: *in the beach*

at the beach
• You use **at the beach** when thinking of the beach as a place: *The kids are at the beach. | We spent the day at the beach. | You can go swimming at the beach. | There is a café at the beach.* ✗ Don't say: *in the beach*

beach² *v* [T] **1** to pull a boat onto the shore away from the water **2** if a WHALE beaches itself or is beached, it swims onto the shore and cannot get back in the water

ˈbeach ball *n* [C] a large coloured plastic ball that you blow air into and use for playing games on the beach

ˈbeach chair *n* [C] *AmE* a folding chair with a seat and back made of cloth or plastic that is used outdoors, especially at the beach SYN **deckchair** *BrE*

beach·comb·er /ˈbiːtʃˌkəʊmə $ -ˌkoʊmər/ *n* [C] someone who searches beaches for interesting or useful things

beach·head /ˈbiːtʃhed/ *n* [C] an area of shore that has been taken from an enemy by force, and from which the army can prepare to attack a country

beach·wear /ˈbiːtʃweə $ -wer/ *n* [U] clothes that you wear for swimming, lying on the beach etc

bea·con /ˈbiːkən/ ●○○ *n* [C]
1 a light that is put somewhere to warn or guide people, ships, vehicles, or aircraft
2 a radio or RADAR signal used by aircraft or boats to help them find their position and direction
3 *especially literary* a person, idea etc that guides or encourages you: **[+of]** *The education program offers a* ***beacon of hope*** *to these children.*
4 a fire on top of a hill used in the past as a signal → BELISHA BEACON

bead /biːd/ ●○○ *n* [C]
1 one of a set of small, usually round, pieces of glass, wood, plastic etc, that you can put on a string and wear as jewellery: *She wore a string of green glass beads around her neck.* → see picture at JEWELLERY
2 a small drop of liquid such as water or blood: *Beads of sweat trickled down his face.*
3 draw a bead on sb/sth to aim carefully before shooting a weapon → WORRY BEADS

bead·ed /ˈbiːdɪd/ *adj* **1** decorated with beads: *a beaded dress* **2 beaded with sweat/perspiration** having drops of SWEAT (=liquid produced by your body when you are hot) on your skin

bead·ing /ˈbiːdɪŋ/ *n* [U] **1** long thin pieces of wood or stone that are used as a decoration on the edges of walls, furniture etc **2** a lot of beads sewn close together on clothes, leather etc as decoration

bea·dle /ˈbiːdl/ *n* [C] an officer in British churches in the past, who helped the priest in various ways, especially by keeping order

bead·y /ˈbiːdi/ *adj* **1** beady eyes are small, round, and shiny – used especially about someone who you think looks dishonest or strange **2 have/keep your beady eye(s) on sb/sth** *especially BrE* to watch someone or something very carefully – used humorously

bea·gle /ˈbiːɡəl/ *n* [C] a dog with short legs and smooth fur, sometimes used in hunting

beak /biːk/ ●●○ *n* [C]
1 the hard pointed mouth of a bird SYN **bill** → see picture at BIRD OF PREY
2 a large pointed nose – used humorously
3 the beak *BrE old-fashioned informal* a judge or a male teacher

bea·ker /ˈbiːkə $ -ər/ *n* [C] **1** *BrE* a drinking cup with straight sides and no handle, usually made of plastic **2** a glass cup with straight sides that is used in chemistry for measuring and heating liquids

beam¹ /biːm/ ●●○ *n* [C]
1 a) a line of light shining from the sun, a lamp etc: *the beam of a powerful flashlight* **b)** a line of light, energy etc that you cannot see: *a laser beam*
2 a long heavy piece of wood or metal used in building houses, bridges etc → see picture at ROOF[1]
3 a wide happy smile: *a beam of delight*
4 off beam *BrE informal* incorrect or mistaken: *Our guesses were way off beam.*
5 a BALANCE BEAM
6 *technical* the widest part of a ship from side to side → **broad in the beam** at BROAD¹(1)

B

beam² ●○○ *v*
1 [I] to smile very happily: *Sherman looked at his sons and beamed proudly.* | **[+with]** *Connie beamed with pleasure.* | **[+at]** *McLeish beamed at her.*
2 [T always + adv/prep] to send a radio or television signal through the air, especially to somewhere very distant: *the first sports broadcast to be beamed across the Atlantic*
3 [I,T] to send out a line of light, heat, energy etc: *The sun beamed through the clouds.*

Bea·mer, **Beemer** /ˈbiːmə/ *n* [C] *especially AmE informal* a name for any car made by BMW: *That's his white Beamer convertible over there.*

bean¹ /biːn/ ●●● S2 *n* [C]
1 a seed or a POD (=case containing seeds), that comes from a climbing plant and is cooked as food. There are very many types of beans: *baked beans* | *Soak the beans overnight.* | *kidney beans* | *green beans* → see picture at VEGETABLE¹
2 a plant that produces beans
3 a seed used in making some types of food or drinks: *coffee beans* | *cocoa beans*
4 be full of beans *informal* to be very eager and full of energy: *She's full of beans this morning.*
5 not have a bean *BrE informal* to have no money at all
6 not know/care beans (about sb/sth) *AmE informal* to not know anything or care at all about someone or something
→ **spill the beans** at SPILL¹(3), → **not amount to a hill of beans** at HILL(5), → JELLY BEAN

bean² *v* [T] *informal* to hit someone on the head with an object

bean·bag /ˈbiːnbæg/ *n* [C] **1** (*also* ˈ**beanbag** ˌ**chair**) a very large cloth bag that is filled with small balls of soft plastic and used for sitting on **2** a small cloth bag filled with beans, used for throwing and catching in children's games

ˈ**bean** ˌ**counter** *n* [C] *informal* someone whose job is to examine the cost of doing something, and who is concerned only with making a profit – used to show disapproval: *Since the bean counters took over the radio station, it's become a boring place to work.*

ˈ**bean curd** *n* [U] a soft white food made from SOYA BEANS SYN **tofu**

ˈ**bean feast** *n* [C] *BrE informal* a party or celebration

bea·nie /ˈbiːni/ *n* [C] *AmE* a small round hat that fits close to your head

bean·pole /ˈbiːnpəʊl $ -poʊl/ *n* [C] a very tall thin person – used humorously

bean·sprout /ˈbiːnspraʊt/ *n* [C] the small white stem from a bean seed that is eaten as a vegetable

Frequencies of the verbs **bear**, **stand**, and **endure** in spoken and written English, with the meaning 'accept or deal with an unpleasant situation'.

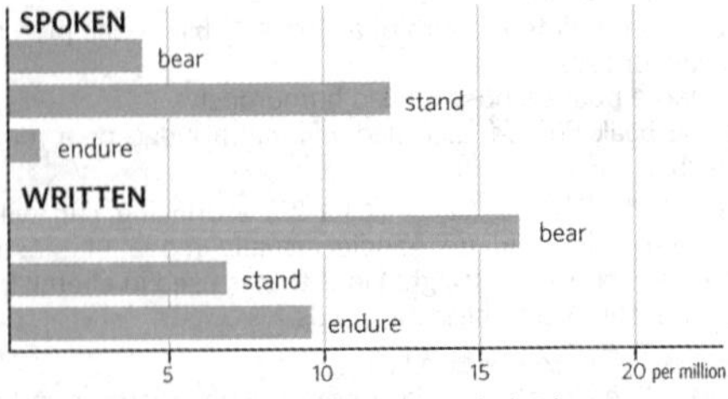

All three verbs are used to mean 'accept or deal with an unpleasant situation'. The graph shows that in this meaning **stand** and **bear** are much more common than **endure** in spoken English. In written English, **bear** is the most common and **endure**, a formal word, is fairly common.

bear¹ /beə $ ber/ ●●● S2 W2 *v* (*past tense* **bore** /bɔː $ bɔːr/, *past participle* **borne** /bɔːn $ bɔːrn/) [T]
1 DEAL WITH STH to bravely accept or deal with a painful, difficult, or upsetting situation SYN **stand**: *She was afraid she wouldn't be able to bear the pain.* | *Overcrowding makes prison life even harder to bear.* | *Make the water as hot as you* ***can bear***. | *The humiliation was* ***more than*** *he* ***could bear***. | *Black people continue to* ***bear the brunt of*** *most racial violence* (=have to deal with the most difficult or damaging part). | *Passengers could be insulting, and stewardesses just had to* ***grin and bear it*** (=accept it without complaining). | *Experts were worried the financial system would not be able to* ***bear the strain***.

> **REGISTER**
> In everyday English, people usually say that they **can't stand** something, rather than that they **can't bear** it: *I* ***couldn't stand*** *the noise any longer.*

2 can't bear sth *spoken* **a)** to be so upset about something that you feel unable to accept it or let it happen SYN **can't stand**: *Please don't leave me. I couldn't bear it.* | **can't bear the thought of (doing) sth** *I just can't bear the thought of having to start all over.* | **can't bear to do sth** *I can't bear to see her cry.* | **can't bear doing sth** *I couldn't bear not seeing him again.* **b)** to dislike something or someone very much, often so that they make you feel annoyed or impatient SYN **can't stand**: *Oh, I really can't bear him.* | **can't bear sb doing sth** *He can't bear people smoking while he's eating.* | **can't bear doing sth** *I can't bear being cold.*
3 bear (sth) in mind to remember a fact or piece of information that is important or could be useful in the future SYN **keep (sth) in mind**: **bear in mind (that)** *Bear in mind that some children will need help.*
4 ACCEPT/BE RESPONSIBLE FOR *formal* to be responsible for or accept something: **bear the costs/burden** *Each company will bear half the costs of development.* | *Fares have gone up, perhaps to more than the market will bear.* | **bear the responsibility/blame etc** *Developed countries bear much of the responsibility for environmental problems.*
5 SUPPORT to be under something and support it SYN **hold**: *My leg was painful, and I wasn't sure it would* ***bear*** *my* ***weight***. | *a tray bearing a bottle and several glasses* | *a load-bearing wall*
6 SIGN/MARK *formal* to have or show a sign, mark, or particular appearance, especially when this shows that something has happened or is true SYN **have**: *The letter bore no signature.* | *a car bearing diplomatic license plates* | *The labels bear a yellow and black symbol.* | *The town still* ***bears the scars*** *of the bombings during the war.* | *The store* ***bears the hallmarks*** (=it has the qualities) *of a family-owned business.*
7 bear a resemblance/relation to sb/sth to be similar to someone or something else: *The child* ***bore a striking resemblance*** *to his father.* | *The things she says bear little relation to what she actually does.*
8 BABY *formal* to give birth to a baby: *She might never be able to bear children.* | **bear sb a child/son/daughter** *She bore him three sons.*
9 bear fruit a) if a plan, decision etc bears fruit, it is successful, especially after a long period of time: *Charles's diplomacy eventually bore fruit.* **b)** if a tree bears fruit, it produces fruit
10 ABLE TO BE EXAMINED/COMPARED ETC [often in negatives] to be suitable or good enough to be examined, compared, repeated etc without failing or being wrong: *The production figures did not* ***bear scrutiny***. | *We believe our pupils' results will* ***bear comparison*** *with any in Scotland.* | *The story is well known, but it certainly* ***bears repeating***.
11 sth doesn't bear thinking about used to say that something is so upsetting or shocking that you prefer not to think about it: *The long-term consequences of a nuclear leak don't bear thinking about.*
12 bear interest if a bank account, INVESTMENT etc bears interest, the bank pays you a particular amount of money for keeping your money in the account
13 CARRY *literary* to carry someone or something, especially something important: *The wedding guests arrived, bearing gifts.* | *The US Constitution states that the people have a right to* ***bear arms***.
14 bring pressure/influence to bear (on sb/sth) to use your

influence or power to get what you want: *Unions can bring pressure to bear on governments.*
15 bear witness/testimony to sth *formal* to show that something is true or exists: *The empty workshops bear witness to the industrial past.*
16 HAVE FEELINGS *formal* to have a particular feeling, especially a bad feeling: **bear (sb) a grudge** (=continue to feel annoyed after a long time) *It was an accident. I don't bear any grudges.* | **bear sb no malice/ill will etc** (=not feel angry) *He was just doing his job, and I bore him no malice.*
17 bear right/left to turn towards the right or left: *When you reach the fork in the trail, bear left.*
18 bear yourself *formal* to walk, stand etc in a particular way, especially when this shows your character: *She bore herself with great dignity.*
19 WIND/WATER *literary* if wind, water, or air bears something, it carries it somewhere: *The sound of music was borne along on the wind.*
20 NAME/TITLE *formal* to have a particular name or title: *He bore the name 'Magnus'.*
bear down *phr v*
1 bear down on sb/sth a) to move quickly towards a person or place in a threatening way: *a storm bearing down on the island* **b)** to behave in a threatening or controlling way towards a person or group: *Federal regulators have been bearing down on campaign contributors.*
2 to use all your strength and effort to push or press down on something
bear on/upon sth *phr v formal* to relate to and possibly influence something: *the national policies which bear on these problems*
bear sb/sth↔ **out** *phr v* if facts or information bear out a claim, story, opinion etc, they help to prove that it is true SYN **support**: *Evidence bears out the idea that students learn best in small groups.*
bear up *phr v* to show courage or determination during a difficult or unpleasant time: *How is he bearing up since the accident?*
bear with sb/sth *phr v*
1 bear with me *spoken* used to ask someone politely to wait while you find out information, finish what you are doing etc: *Bear with me a minute, and I'll check if Mr Garrard's in.*
2 to be patient or continue to do something difficult or unpleasant: *It's boring, but please bear with it.*

BEARS

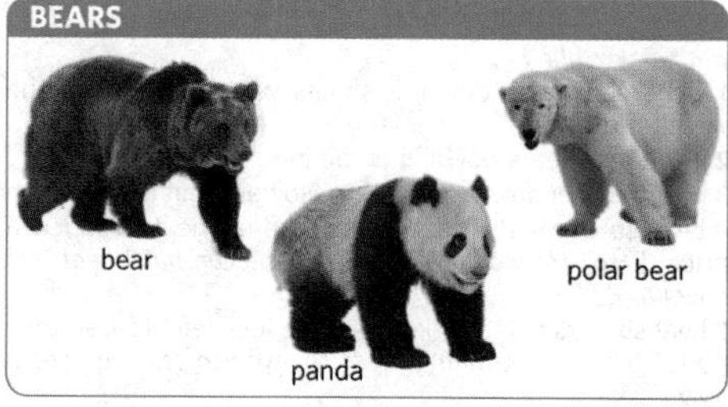

bear² ●●○ *n* [C]
1 a large strong animal with thick fur, that eats flesh, fruit, and insects: *a mother bear and her cubs* → GRIZZLY BEAR, POLAR BEAR, TEDDY BEAR
2 *AmE informal* something that is very difficult to do or to deal with: *The chemistry test was a bear.*
3 be like a bear with a sore head *BrE informal* to be rude to people because you are feeling bad-tempered
4 *technical* someone who sells SHARES or goods when they expect the price to fall → **bull**
bear·a·ble /ˈbeərəbəl $ ˈber-/ *adj* something that is bearable is difficult or unpleasant, but you can deal with it OPP **unbearable**: *His friendship was the one thing that made life bearable.* —**bearably** *adv*
ˈbear claw *n* [C] *AmE* a PASTRY filled with fruit, that has a row of long cuts across the top
beard¹ /bɪəd $ bɪrd/ ●●● S3 *n* [C]
1 hair that grows around a man's chin and cheeks → **moustache**
2 something similar to a beard, such as hair growing on an animal's chin —**bearded** *adj*
beard² *v* [T] **beard sb (in their den)** to go and see someone who has influence or authority, and tell them what you want, why you disagree with them etc
bear·er /ˈbeərə $ ˈberər/ *n* [C] **1** *formal* someone who carries something such as a flag or a STRETCHER (=light bed for a sick person) **2** someone who brings you information, a letter etc: *I hate to be* ***the bearer of bad news****, but ...* **3** *formal* the bearer of a legal document, for example a PASSPORT, is the person that it officially belongs to **4** someone who knows about traditions and customs, and makes sure that younger people learn about them: *They see themselves as the bearers of Jewish tradition.*
ˈbear hug *n* [C] an action in which you put your arms around someone and hold them very tightly because you like them or are pleased to see them
bear·ing /ˈbeərɪŋ $ ˈber-/ *n* **1 have a/some/no etc bearing on sth** to have an effect or influence on something, or not have any effect or influence: *Exercise has a direct bearing on how healthy you are.* **2 lose your bearings a)** to become confused about where you are: *I completely lost my bearings in the dark.* **b)** to become confused about what you should do next: *young men who have lost their bearings in a changing society* **3 get/find your bearings a)** to find out exactly where you are: *He paused to get his bearings.* **b)** to feel confident that you know what you should do next: *An introduction session helps new students get their bearings.* **4** [singular, U] the way in which you move, stand, or behave, especially when this shows your character **5** [C] *technical* a direction or angle that is shown by a COMPASS: *learning to* ***take*** *a compass* ***bearing*** **6** [C] *technical* a part of a machine that turns on another part, or in which a turning part is held → BALL BEARING
bear·ish /ˈbeərɪʃ $ ˈber-/ *adj* **1** a bearish market is one where the prices of SHARES are decreasing → **bullish** **2** someone who is bearish expects the price of business shares to go down → **bullish** —**bearishly** *adv* —**bearishness** *n* [U]
ˈbear ˌmarket *n* [C] a situation in which the value of STOCKS is decreasing → **bull market**
bear·skin /ˈbeəˌskɪn $ ˈber-/ *n* **1** [C,U] the skin of a bear **2** [C] a tall hat made of black fur, worn by some British soldiers for special ceremonies
beast /biːst/ ●○○ *n* [C]
1 *written* an animal, especially a large or dangerous one THESAURUS ANIMAL
2 *old-fashioned* someone who is cruel or unpleasant: *You beast! Let go!*
3 something of a particular type or that has a particular quality – usually used humorously SYN **animal**: *A city at night is a very* ***different beast****.*
4 the beast in sb the part of someone's character that makes them experience hatred, strong sexual feelings, violence etc
beast·ly /ˈbiːstli/ *adj BrE* very unpleasant SYN **nasty**: *beastly weather* —**beastly** *adv* —**beastliness** *n* [U]
ˌbeast of ˈburden *n* [C] *old use* an animal that does heavy work
beat¹ /biːt/ ●●● S2 W2 *v* (*past tense* **beat**, *past participle* **beaten** /ˈbiːtn/)
1 COMPETITION/ELECTION [T] to get the most points, votes etc in a game, race, or competition SYN **defeat**: *Brazil were beaten 2–1.* | *Labour easily beat the Conservatives in the last election.* | **beat sb at/in sth** *I beat him more often at pool than he beats me.* | **beat sb hollow** *BrE*, **beat the pants off sb** *AmE* (=defeat them easily)
2 HIT [T] to hit someone or something many times with your hand, a stick etc: *photographs of rioters beating a policeman* | *He was questioned and beaten.* | *The woman had been* ***beaten to death*** *by her husband.* | *Two prisoners were* ***beaten unconscious****.* | **beat sb black and blue** (=hit someone until it makes marks on their body) | **beat the living**

daylights out of sb (=beat someone very hard) THESAURUS ▸ HIT

3 HIT AGAINST [I always + adv/prep] to hit against something many times or continuously: **[+on/against/at etc]** *Waves beat against the cliffs.* | *rain beating on the windows* | *Sid beat on the door with his hand.*

4 DO BETTER [T] to do something better, faster etc than what was best before: **beat a record/score etc** *The record set by Kierson in '84 has yet to be beaten.* | *The company's profits are unlikely to beat last year's £10 million.*

5 BE BETTER [T not in progressive] *especially spoken* to be much better and more enjoyable than something else: *Fresh milk beats powdered milk any time.* | **beat doing sth** *'Well,' said Culley, 'it beats going to the office.'* | ***You can't beat*** *swimming as a good all-body exercise.* | ***Nothing beats*** *homemade cake.* | **you can't beat sth (for sth)** *For excitement, you just can't beat college basketball.*

6 FOOD [I,T] to mix things together quickly with a fork or special kitchen machine: *Beat the eggs, then add the milk.* | **beat sth in** *Gradually beat in the sugar.* | **beat sth together** *Beat the butter and sugar together until fluffy.* THESAURUS ▸ MIX

7 CONTROL/DEAL WITH [T] to successfully deal with a problem that you have been struggling with SYN **conquer**: *advice on how to beat depression* | *the government's long fight to beat inflation*

8 HEART [I] when your heart beats, it moves in a regular RHYTHM as it pumps your blood: *The average person's heart beats 70 times a minute.* | *Jennifer's heart was beating fast.*

9 DRUMS [I,T] if you beat drums, or if drums beat, they make a regular continuous sound

10 WINGS [I,T] if a bird beats its wings, or if its wings beat, they move up and down quickly and regularly SYN **flap**

11 take some beating if something or someone will take some beating, it will be difficult for anyone or anything to be or do better: *Raikkonen has 42 points, which will take some beating.* | *Florida takes some beating as a vacation destination.*

12 AVOID [T] to avoid situations in which a lot of people are trying to do something, usually by doing something early: *We left at four a.m. to beat the traffic.* | *Shopping by mail order lets you beat the queues.* | *Shop now and* ***beat the*** *Christmas* ***rush****!*

13 DO BEFORE SB ELSE [T] *informal* to get or do something before someone else, especially if you are both trying to do it first: **beat sb to sth** *John had beaten me to the breakfast table.* | *I wanted the last piece of pie, but somebody* ***beat*** *me* ***to it****.* | *They wanted to make it into a film, but another studio* ***beat*** *them* ***to the punch****.*

14 beat about/around the bush to avoid or delay talking about something embarrassing or unpleasant: *Don't beat around the bush. Ask for your account to be paid, and paid quickly.*

15 beat the system to find ways of avoiding or breaking the rules of an organization, system etc, in order to achieve what you want: *Accountants know a few ways to beat the system.*

16 beat a path to sb's door (*also* **beat down sb's door**) if people beat a path to your door, they are interested in something you are selling, a service you are providing etc: *The new design was supposed to have consumers beating a path to their door.*

17 beat a (hasty) retreat to leave somewhere or stop doing something very quickly, in order to avoid a bad situation: *He beat a hasty retreat when he spotted me.*

18 beat the clock to finish something very quickly, especially before a particular time: *The company managed to beat the clock on delivering its new system.*

SPOKEN PHRASES

19 (it) beats me used to say that you do not know something, or cannot understand or explain it: *Beats me why he wants such a big car.* | *'What's he saying?' 'Beats me.'*

20 beat it! used to tell someone to leave at once, because they are annoying you or should not be there

21 can you beat that/it? used to show that you are surprised or annoyed by something: *They've got eight children! Can you beat that?*

22 beat your brains out to think about something very hard and for a long time: *I've been beating my brains out all week trying to finish this essay.*

23 if you can't beat 'em, join 'em used when you decide to take part in something even though you disapprove of it, because everyone else is doing it and you cannot stop them

---

24 beat the rap *AmE informal* to avoid being punished for something you have done

25 beat time to make regular movements or sounds to show the speed at which music should be played: *a conductor beating time with his baton*

26 beat a path/track to make a path by walking over an area of land

27 to beat the band *AmE informal* in large amounts or with great force: *It's raining to beat the band.*

28 beat the heat *AmE informal* to make yourself cooler: *Fresh lemonade is a great way to beat the heat.*

29 METAL (*also* **beat out**) [T] to hit metal with a hammer in order to shape it or make it thinner

30 HUNTING [I,T] to force wild birds and animals out of bushes, long grass etc so that they can be shot for sport

31 beat your breast *literary* to show clearly that you are very upset or sorry about something → BEATEN, BEATING

THESAURUS

beat to get more points, votes etc than someone. Beat is used especially in spoken English: *We should have beaten them easily.* | *I always beat my brother at tennis.*

defeat to beat someone. **Defeat** is more formal than beat and is used especially in writing: *England were defeated by 2 goals to 1.* | *Bush defeated Kerry in the election.*

trounce /traʊns/ to defeat someone completely in a game: *They were trounced 20–0 by Kuwait.*

thrash *BrE informal*, **cream** *AmE informal* to beat someone very easily in a game: *Of course, they totally creamed the other team.*

wipe the floor with sb *informal* to beat someone completely in a game or argument: *She wiped the floor with her opponent in the debate.*

beat down *phr v*

1 if the sun beats down, it shines very brightly and the weather is hot

2 if the rain beats down, it is raining very hard

3 beat the door down to hit a door so hard that it falls down

4 beat sb down *BrE* to persuade someone to reduce a price: **[+to]** *He wanted £4,500 for the car, but I beat him down to £3,850.*

5 beat sb ↔ down to make someone feel defeated, so they no longer respect themselves: *The women seemed beaten down.*

beat off *phr v*

1 beat sb/sth ↔ off to succeed in defeating someone who is attacking, opposing, or competing with you: *McConnell beat off a challenge for his Senate seat.*

2 *AmE informal not polite* if a man beats off, he MASTURBATES

beat sb/sth **↔ out** *phr v*

1 if a drum or something else beats out a RHYTHM, or if you beat out a rhythm on a drum, it makes a continuous regular sound

2 *especially AmE* to defeat someone in a competition: *Lockheed beat out a rival company to win the contract.* | **[+for]** *Roberts beat out Tony Gwynn for the Most Valuable Player Award.*

3 to put out a fire by hitting it many times with something such as a cloth

beat up *phr v*

1 beat sb ↔ up to hurt someone badly by hitting them: *Her boyfriend got drunk and beat her up.*

2 beat up on sb *AmE* to hit someone and harm them, especially someone younger or weaker than yourself
3 beat yourself up (*also* **beat up on yourself** *AmE*) *informal* to blame yourself too much for something: *If you do your best and you lose, you can't beat yourself up about it.*

beat² ●●○ S3 *n*
1 [C] one of a series of regular movements or hitting actions: *a heart rate of 80 beats a minute* | *the steady beat of the drum*
2 [singular] a regular repeated noise SYN **rhythm**: **[+of]** *the beat of marching feet*
3 [C] the main RHYTHM that a piece of music or a poem has: *a song with a beat you can dance to*
4 [singular] a subject or area of a city that someone is responsible for as their job: *journalists covering the Washington beat* | **on the beat** *People like to see police officers on the beat.*
5 [C] one of the notes in a piece of music that sounds stronger than the other notes

beat³ *adj* [not before noun] *informal* very tired SYN **exhausted**: *I'm beat.* | *Come and sit down – you must be* ***dead beat***. THESAURUS ▸ TIRED

beat·box /ˈbiːtbɒks $ -bɑːks/ *n* **1** (*also* **beat·box·er** /-bɒksə $ -bɑːksər/) [C] someone who provides the words or other spoken sounds that go with HIP HOP **2** [U] a computer program that is used to mix the sounds of popular electronic music with a strong beat, or the type of music produced by this —**beatboxing** *n* [U]

beat·en /ˈbiːtn/ *adj* [only before noun] **1 off the beaten track/path** a place that is off the beaten track is not well known and is far away from the places that people usually visit **2** a beaten path, track etc has been made by many people walking the same way: *a well-beaten path through the forest* **3** a beaten person feels defeated and not respected: *a beaten man who had lost his job* **4** beaten metal has been shaped with a hammer to make it thinner

beat·er /ˈbiːtə $ -ər/ *n* [C] **1** an object that is designed to beat something: *an egg beater* | *a carpet beater* **2 wife/child beater** someone who hits his wife or child, especially someone who does this often **3** someone who forces wild birds or animals out of bushes, long grass etc so that they can be shot for sport **4** *AmE informal* an old car in bad condition → WORLD-BEATER

bea·tif·ic /ˌbiːəˈtɪfɪk◂/ *adj* a beatific look, smile etc shows great peace and happiness —**beatifically** /-kli/ *adv*

be·at·i·fy /biˈætɪfaɪ/ *v* (**beatified**, **beatifying**, **beatifies**) [T] if the Pope beatifies someone, he says officially that they are a holy or special person —**beatification** /biˌætɪfɪˈkeɪʃən/ *n* [U]

beat·ing /ˈbiːtɪŋ/ *n* **1** [C] an act of hitting someone many times as a punishment or in a fight: *a brutal beating* **2 take a beating** to lose very badly in a game or competition: *The Dodgers took a real beating on Saturday.* → **take some beating** at BEAT¹(11)

beat·nik /ˈbiːtnɪk/ *n* [C] one of a group of young people in the late 1950s and early 1960s, who did not accept the values of society and showed this by their clothes and the way they lived

ˈbeat-up *adj* a beat-up car, bicycle etc is old and in bad condition SYN **battered**: *a beat-up old Ford Escort*

beau /bəʊ $ boʊ/ *n* (*plural* **beaux** /bəʊz $ boʊz/ *or* **beaus**) [C] *old-fashioned* **1** a woman's close friend or lover **2** a fashionable well-dressed man

beaut /bjuːt/ *n* [singular] *AmE, AusE spoken* used to say that something is either very good, attractive, or impressive: *That last catch was a beaut.*

beau·te·ous /ˈbjuːtiəs/ *adj literary* beautiful: *the beauteous Helen of Troy* —**beauteously** *adv*

beau·ti·cian /bjuːˈtɪʃən/ *n* [C] someone whose job is to give beauty treatments to your skin, hair etc

beau·ti·ful /ˈbjuːtəfəl/ ●●● S1 W2 *adj*
1 someone or something that is beautiful is extremely attractive to look at: *She was even more beautiful than I had remembered.* | *a beautiful bunch of flowers*
2 very good or giving you great pleasure SYN **lovely**: *beautiful music* | *What a beautiful shot!* | *The weather was beautiful.* THESAURUS ▸ GOOD —**beautifully** *adv*

THESAURUS: beautiful

PERSON

beautiful a beautiful woman or child has perfect good looks: *Grace Kelly was a very beautiful woman.* | *a beautiful baby*
good-looking a good-looking person looks nice. **Good-looking** is very common in spoken English: *He's a good-looking guy, but he's a bit boring.*
attractive an attractive person looks nice, especially in a way that makes you feel sexually interested in them: *She's a very attractive woman.* | *A lot of women find him attractive.*
pretty a pretty girl or woman looks nice - used especially about a woman who has a nice face: *You look pretty with your hair down.*
handsome a handsome man or boy looks nice - used especially about a man who has a nice face. **Handsome** is also sometimes used, especially in literature, to describe a woman who is good-looking and has a strong face: *He was tall, dark, and handsome.*
gorgeous/stunning *spoken* extremely attractive. **Gorgeous** is used especially by women: *She thinks Brad Pitt is gorgeous.* | *You look absolutely stunning in that dress!*
cute *spoken* nice to look at - used about animals, babies, children, and young adults: *a cute little puppy* | *She thinks you're cute!*
lovely *spoken* used when saying that someone looks very nice: *You look lovely tonight.*

PLACE/THING ETC

beautiful used to describe something that looks, feels, sounds etc so good that it gives you a lot of pleasure: *a beautiful tropical beach* | *a beautiful song* | *The weather was beautiful.*
lovely *spoken* used when saying that something looks, feels, or sounds very nice: *What a lovely day!* | *a lovely voice*
pretty pleasant to look at - often used about things that are not big or impressive: *a pretty little pink dress* | *a pretty village*
attractive pleasant to look at. **Attractive** sounds more formal than **pretty**: *an attractive white-painted cottage with green shutters*
magnificent very big, beautiful, and impressive - used about buildings, objects, and views: *The Taj Mahal always looks magnificent.* | *a magnificent Persian carpet*
picturesque *written* pleasant to look at - used in written descriptions of towns, buildings, and places: *the picturesque harbour town of Castleton*
stunning/breathtaking extremely beautiful and impressive - used especially about views: *All around is a stunning view of Cape Town.* | *The landscape is breathtaking.*
exquisite /ɪkˈskwɪzət, ˈekskwɪ-/ used to describe things that have very beautiful small details, especially things that have been made with a lot of skill: *an exquisite piece of jewellery* | *an exquisite flower*

GRAMMAR: Order of adjectives

If there is more than one adjective, the adjectives are usually used in a fixed order.
You say: *It's a beautiful old village.* ✗ Don't say: *It's an old beautiful village.*
You say: *He has beautiful brown eyes.* ✗ Don't say: *He has brown beautiful eyes.*
GRAMMAR GUIDE ▸ ADJECTIVES

beau·ti·fy /ˈbjuːtɪfaɪ/ *v* (**beautified**, **beautifying**, **beautifies**) [T] *formal* to make someone or something beautiful: *plants to beautify the garden*

beau·ty /ˈbjuːti/ ●●● S3 W2 *n* (*plural* **beauties**)
1 APPEARANCE [U] a quality that people, places, or things have that makes them very attractive to look at: *her beauty and grace | an area of outstanding* ***natural beauty*** *| Millions of dollars are spent each year on* ***beauty products****.*
2 WOMAN [C] a woman who is very beautiful: *She was considered a great beauty in her youth.*
3 POEM/MUSIC/EMOTION ETC [U] a quality that something such as a poem, song, emotion etc has that gives you pleasure or joy: **[+of]** *the beauty of Shakespeare's verse*
4 ADVANTAGE **the beauty of sth** a particularly good quality that makes something especially suitable or useful: *The beauty of e-mail is its speed and ease of use.*
5 [C] *spoken* a very good, large etc example of something: *You should have seen the boat – a real beauty.*
6 beauty is in the eye of the beholder used to say that different people have different opinions about what is beautiful
7 beauty is only skin-deep used to say that how someone looks is not as important as a good character

ˈbeauty ˌcontest *n* [C] a competition in which women are judged on how attractive they look

ˈbeauty mark *n* [C] *AmE* a small dark mark on a woman's face – used when you think it is attractive SYN **beauty spot** *BrE*

ˈbeauty ˌparlor *n* [C] *AmE* a beauty salon

ˈbeauty queen *n* [C] the winner of a beauty contest

ˈbeauty ˌsalon / $ ˈ.. ˌ./ (*also* **ˈbeauty ˌshop** *AmE*) *n* [C] a place where you can receive treatments for your skin, hair, nails etc to make you look more attractive

ˈbeauty sleep *n* [U] enough sleep to keep you healthy and looking good – used humorously

ˈbeauty spot *n* [C] *BrE* **1** a place in the countryside that is famous because it is very pretty: *Guests will be able to visit some of the local beauty spots.* **2** a small dark mark on a woman's face – used when you think it is attractive SYN **beauty mark** *AmE*

bea·ver[1] /ˈbiːvə $ -ər/ *n* [C] a North American animal that has thick fur and a wide flat tail, and cuts down trees with its teeth → **eager beaver** at EAGER(2)

beaver[2] *v*
beaver away *phr v informal* to work very hard, especially at writing or calculating something: **[+at]** *He's been beavering away at his homework for hours.*

be·bop /ˈbiːbɒp $ -bɑːp/ *n* [U] a type of JAZZ music

be·calmed /bɪˈkɑːmd $ -ˈkɑːmd, -ˈkɑːlmd/ *adj formal*
1 a sailing boat that is becalmed cannot move because there is no wind **2** if something such as a company, the economy, or a discussion about something is becalmed, no progress is being made: *The Stock Market was becalmed yesterday as dealers waited for company results.*

be·came /bɪˈkeɪm/ *v* the past tense of BECOME

be·cause[1] /bɪˈkɒz, bɪˈkəz $ bɪˈkɒːz, bɪˈkəz/ ●●● S1 W1 *conjunction*
1 used when you are giving the reason for something: *We didn't enjoy the day because the weather was so awful. | 'Why can't I go?' 'Because you're not old enough.' | Hubert never experienced any fear, and this was* ***partly because*** *he was not particularly intelligent. | Many exam candidates lose marks* ***simply because*** *they do not read the questions properly. | I decided to go with them,* ***mainly because*** *I had nothing better to do.*
**2 just because … ** *spoken* used to say that, although one thing is true, it does not mean that something else is true: *Just because you're my brother doesn't mean I have to like you!*

GRAMMAR: Comparison

because
• You use **because** at the beginning of a clause, when giving the reason for something: *I was late because the traffic was bad.*
• In formal written English, don't use **because** at the beginning of a sentence.

because of
• You use **because of** before a noun, when giving the reason for something: *I was late because of the traffic.*
✗ Don't say: *because the traffic*

THESAURUS

because *conjunction* used when giving the reason for something: *I went home because I was tired. | The streets were flooded because of all the rain.*
due to/owing to *prep* used to give the reason why something has happened. **Due to** and **owing to** are more formal than **because**: *The delay was due to a problem with the ship's engines. | The parade had to be cancelled owing to bad weather.*
through *prep* because of something. **Through** is used especially when saying why someone succeeded or failed to do something: *They won the game, more through luck than skill. | You failed that test through carelessness.*
thanks to *prep* used when explaining that something good has happened because of someone's efforts, or because something exists: *Thanks to modern medicine, the disease can now be cured.*
since/as *conjunction* used when giving the reason why someone decides to do something or decides that something is true: *We decided to go to the beach since it was a nice day. | I thought Kevin was out as his car wasn't there.*
out of *prep* because of a particular feeling or quality: *He started reading the book out of curiosity. | I only asked out of politeness.*

because[2] ●●● S1 W1 *prep* **because of sb/sth** used to say who or what causes something to happen or is the reason for something: *He had to retire because of ill health. | We spent three hours waiting in the rain because of you!*

REGISTER

In written English, people often prefer to use the expressions **due to** something, **owing to** something, or **as a result of** something, which sound more formal than **because of** something: *Many businesses fail* ***due to*** *cash-flow problems.*

beck /bek/ *n* [C] **1 be at sb's beck and call** to always be ready to do what someone wants: *I was tired of being at her beck and call all day long.* **2** *BrE* a small stream

beck·on /ˈbekən/ ●○○ *v*
1 [I,T] to make a signal to someone with your hand, to show that you want them to come towards you or to follow you: *I could see my husband beckoning me.* | **beckon (to) sb to do sth** *She beckoned to the waitress to bring more wine.* | **beckon sb forward/over etc** *He beckoned us over and introduced us to his wife.*
2 [I,T] if something such as a place or opportunity beckons, it appears so attractive that you want to have it: *A career in the film industry beckoned.*
3 [I] if something beckons for someone, it will probably happen to them: **[+for]** *Early retirement beckoned for George.*

be·come /bɪˈkʌm/ ●●● S1 W1 *v* (*past tense* **became** /-ˈkeɪm/, *past participle* **become**)
1 [linking verb] to start to have a feeling or quality, or to

start to develop into something: *The weather became warmer.* | *Slowly my eyes became accustomed to the darkness.* | *Helen became increasingly anxious about her husband's strange behaviour.* | *Pollution from cars has become a major problem.*
2 [linking verb] to start to have a job or position: *George became king at the age of 54.* | *When did you first want to become a teacher?*
3 [T not in progressive] *formal* to be suitable for someone, or to look attractive on them SYN **suit**: *Blue really becomes her.* | *Don't try to be clever – it doesn't become you.*
4 what became of ... ? whatever will become of ... ? used to ask what has happened to someone or something, especially when you have not seen them for a long time, or what will happen to someone that you are worried about: *What became of those Chinese vases that Mum used to have?* | *Whatever will become of Sam when his wife dies?*

GRAMMAR: Linking verbs

Become is a linking verb. This type of verb links the subject of the sentence with an adjective or noun: *It became more difficult.* | *She hoped to become a lawyer.*

THESAURUS

become to start to have a feeling or quality, or to start to develop into something: *His parents became worried when he was late home from school.* | *Violent crime is becoming a major problem.*
get to start to have a feeling or quality. **Get** is less formal than **become** and is much more commonly used in everyday English: *I was getting very tired.* | *Make sure you're home before it gets dark.*
go to become something – used about things becoming a different colour, or things or people becoming worse in some way: *Her hair was going grey.* | *He went blind.* | *I think I'm going mad.*
turn to become something – used about things becoming a different colour, or the weather or people's behaviour changing: *The water had turned bright green.* | *The weather is expected to turn cold again.* | *He suddenly turned nasty.*
grow *especially written* to gradually become something: *People were growing impatient.* | *The rich grew richer.*
come undone/loose/apart to become undone, loose, or separated into pieces: *The screws had come loose.*
change into sth to become something completely different: *The caterpillar changed into a beautiful butterfly.*

be·com·ing /bɪˈkʌmɪŋ/ *adj formal* **1** a piece of clothing, a hairstyle etc that is becoming makes you look attractive: *Her short hairstyle is very becoming.* **2** words or actions that are becoming are suitable for you or for the situation you are in: *She received the praise with becoming modesty.* —**becomingly** *adv*

bec·que·rel /ˌbekəˈrel/ *n* [C] a unit for measuring RADIOACTIVITY

bed¹ /bed/ ●●● S1 W1 *n*
1 SLEEP [C,U] a piece of furniture that you sleep on: **in bed** *Simon lay in bed thinking.* | *You should go to bed early.* | *She got into bed and turned out the light.* | **before bed** (=before going to bed) *Dad has a whisky before bed.* → CAMP BED, FOUR-POSTER BED, SOFA BED
2 SEX [U] *informal* used to refer to having sex: *I came home and found him* ***in bed with*** (=having sex with) *my best friend.* | *He wanted me to* ***go to bed with*** *him.* | *He's been trying to* ***get*** *his secretary* ***into bed.*** | *She told me he was* ***good in bed*** (=a skilful lover).
3 RIVER/LAKE/SEA [C] the flat ground at the bottom of a river, lake, or sea: *the sea bed* THESAURUS BOTTOM
4 GARDEN [C] an area of a garden, park etc that has been prepared for plants to grow in: *rose beds*
5 ROCK [C] a layer of rock → BEDROCK(2)
6 LOWEST LAYER [singular] a layer of something that forms

BEDS

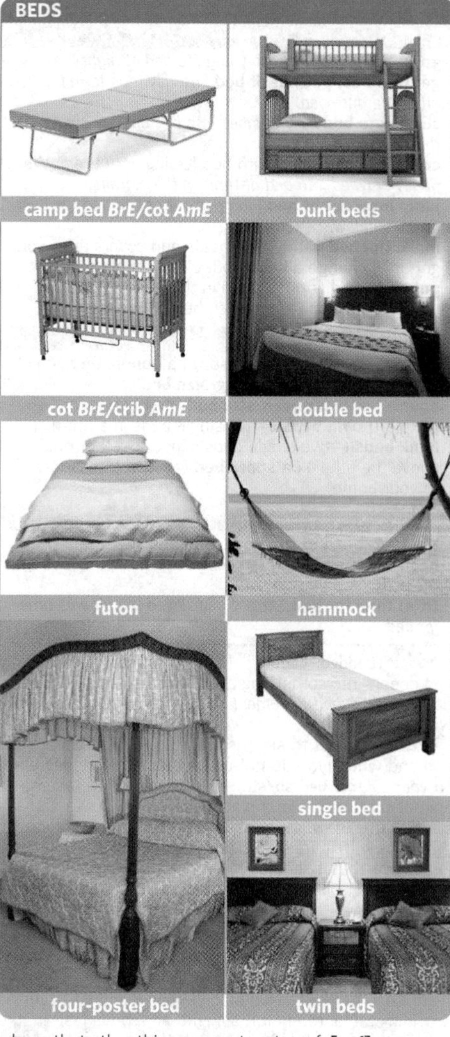

camp bed *BrE*/cot *AmE* | bunk beds | cot *BrE*/crib *AmE* | double bed | futon | hammock | four-poster bed | single bed | twin beds

a base that other things are put on top of: **[+of]** *prawns on a bed of lettuce*
7 IN RIVER/WATER [C] an area at the edge of a river or in deeper water where things grow: *an oyster bed* | *The birds build their nests in reed beds along the river bank.*
8 get out of bed on the wrong side *BrE*, **get up on the wrong side of the bed** *AmE* to feel slightly angry or annoyed for no particular reason
9 not a bed of roses not a happy, comfortable, or easy situation: *Life isn't always a bed of roses, you know.*
10 you've made your bed and you must lie on it *spoken* used to say that you must accept the results of your actions, even if they are bad
11 put sth to bed *technical* to complete a newspaper, magazine, or book, so that it is ready to be printed

GRAMMAR: Patterns with bed

on the bed
• You use **on the bed** when someone is not covered by sheets or blankets: *He sat on the bed and took off his shoes.* | *I lay on the bed and looked at the ceiling.*

in bed
• You use **in bed** when someone is covered with sheets or blankets: *I spent the morning in bed.*

in the bed
• You use **in the bed** to refer to a particular bed: *There was no one in the bed.*

COLLOCATIONS

VERBS

go to bed *What time do you go to bed at night?*
get into bed/get out of bed *I usually read for a bit after I get into bed.*
climb into bed *Lucy climbed into bed and lay awake thinking.*
crawl into bed (=get into bed feeling very tired) *We finally crawled into bed at three in the morning.*
jump into/out of bed *I jumped out of bed and ran over to the window.*
make the bed (=tidy the sheets and covers after you get up) | **change a bed** (=put clean sheets on it) | **put sb to bed** (=put a child in their bed) | **take to your bed** *written* (=go to bed because you feel ill)

ADJECTIVES

a single bed (=for one person) | **a double bed** (=a bed for two people) | **a king-size bed** (=a very big double bed) | **a queen-size bed** (=a big bed for two people) | **twin beds** (=two single beds in a room) | **bunk beds** (=two single beds joined together one above the other) | **a spare bed** (=a bed for visitors to your home)

PHRASES

the foot/head of the bed (=the bottom/top of the bed) *I woke up to find someone standing at the foot of the bed.*
(it's) time for bed *She sat and sewed until it was time for bed.*

bed² *v* (**bedded**, **bedding**) [T] **1** to fix something firmly and deeply into something else: **bed sth in sth** *The foundations were bedded in cement.* **2** *old-fashioned* to have sex with someone

bed down *phr v* **1** to sleep somewhere which is not your bed and where you do not usually sleep: *Can I bed down on your sofa?* **2 bed sb/sth ↔ down** to make a person or animal comfortable in a place where they do not usually sleep **3** if a new system or arrangement beds down, problems with it are solved and it gradually starts to work in the way that it should

bed sth ↔ **out** *phr v* to put plants into the ground so that they can grow

BEd *BrE*, **B.Ed.** *AmE* /biː ˈed/ *n* [C] (***Bachelor of Education***) a first university DEGREE in education

ˌbed and ˈboard *n* [U] *BrE* food and a place to sleep

ˌbed and ˈbreakfast *n* (*abbreviation* **B and B**) **1** [U] the providing of a room for a night and breakfast in the morning, for example in a hotel: *Is there anyone who does bed and breakfast round here?* | *bed and breakfast accommodation* **2** [C] a private house or small hotel where you can sleep and have breakfast: *There's a bed and breakfast in the next village.*

be·daz·zled /bɪˈdæzəld/ *adj literary* if you are bedazzled by something, you find it so impressive that it surprises and confuses you SYN **dazzled**

ˈbed bath *n* [C] a thorough body wash given to someone who cannot leave their bed

ˈbed-ˌblocking *n* [U] *BrE* a situation in which someone stays in hospital because there is no other suitable place where they can go to be looked after. This means that other people cannot go into hospital when they need to, because there is no bed for them.

bed·bug /ˈbedbʌg/ *n* [C] an insect that sucks blood and lives in dirty houses, especially in beds

bed·cham·ber /ˈbedˌtʃeɪmbə $ -ər/ *n* [C] *old use* a bedroom

bed·clothes /ˈbedkləʊðz, -kləʊz $ -kloʊðz, -kloʊz/ *n* [plural] the sheets, covers etc that you put on a bed

bed·ding /ˈbedɪŋ/ *n* [U] **1** sheets, covers etc that you put on a bed **2** something soft for animals to sleep on, such as dried grass or STRAW **3** garden plants that will look good for one season and then be removed

be·deck /bɪˈdek/ *v* [T] *literary* to decorate something such as a building or street by hanging things all over it SYN **deck out**: **be bedecked with sth** *a balcony bedecked with hanging baskets*

be·dev·il /bɪˈdevəl/ *v* (**bedevilled**, **bedevilling** *BrE*, **bedeviled**, **bedeviling** *AmE*) [T] to cause a lot of problems and difficulties for someone or something over a period of time SYN **plague**: *a society bedevilled by racial tensions*

bed·fel·low /ˈbedˌfeləʊ $ -loʊ/ *n* **strange bedfellows** two or more people, ideas etc that are related or working together in an unexpected way: *Rugby and art seem strange bedfellows.*

bed·head /ˈbedhed/ *n* [C] *BrE* the part of a bed that is behind your head when you are sleeping SYN **headboard**

bed·lam /ˈbedləm/ *n* [U] a situation where there is a lot of noise and confusion SYN **chaos**: *When the bomb exploded, there was bedlam.*

ˈbed ˌlinen *n* [U] the sheets and PILLOWCASES for a bed

Bed·ou·in /ˈbeduɪn/ (*also* **Bedu**) *n* (*plural* **Bedouin** *or* **Bedouins**) [C] **1** someone who belongs to an Arab tribe that traditionally lives in tents in the desert **2 the Bedouin** the people who belong to this tribe —**Bedouin** *adj*

bed·pan /ˈbedpæn/ *n* [C] a low wide container used as a toilet by someone who is too ill to get out of bed

bed·post /ˈbedpəʊst $ -poʊst/ *n* [C] one of the four main supports at the corners of an old-fashioned bed

be·drag·gled /bɪˈdrægəld/ *adj* looking untidy, wet, and dirty, especially because you have been out in the rain: *Bedraggled soldiers crawled into camp.*

bed·rid·den /ˈbedˌrɪdn/ *adj* unable to leave your bed, especially because you are old or ill

bed·rock /ˈbedrɒk $ -rɑːk/ *n* **1** [singular] the basic ideas, features, or facts on which something is based: *Marriage and children are the bedrock of family life.* THESAURUS▸ **BASIS** **2** [U] solid rock in the ground below soil or sand

bed·roll /ˈbedrəʊl $ -roʊl/ *n* [C] *AmE* a number of BLANKETS rolled together and used for sleeping outdoors

bed·room /ˈbedrʊm, -ruːm/ ●●● S1 W2 *n* [C]
1 a room for sleeping in: *a hotel with 50 bedrooms* | **three-bedroomed/five-bedroomed etc** *They've just bought a new four-bedroomed house in Edinburgh.*
2 bedroom eyes a look in your eyes that shows that you are sexually attracted to someone

ˈbedroom comˌmunity (*also* **ˈbedroom ˌsuburb**) *n* [C] *AmE* a place where people live but that does not have many businesses, so that people have to go to another town or city to work SYN **dormitory town** *BrE*

bed·side /ˈbedsaɪd/ *n* [C usually singular] the area beside your bed – used especially when talking about someone who is ill in bed: **at sb's bedside** *Relatives have been at his bedside all week.* | **bedside lamp/table/cabinet etc** *The clock on her bedside table said half past four.* → see picture at TABLE¹

ˌbedside ˈmanner *n* [singular] the way that a doctor talks to the people that he or she is treating

bed·sit /ˌbedˈsɪt/ (*also* **bed·sit·ter** /-ˈsɪtə $ -ər/), **bedsitting room** /bedˈsɪtɪŋ rʊm,- ruːm/ *n* [C] *BrE* a rented room used for both living and sleeping in

bed·sore /ˈbedsɔː $ -sɔːr/ *n* [C] a sore place on your skin caused by lying in bed for a long time

bed·spread /ˈbedspred/ *n* [C] an attractive cover for a bed that goes on top of all the other covers

bed·stead /ˈbedsted/ *n* [C] the wooden or metal frame of a bed

bed·time /ˈbedtaɪm/ *n* [C,U] the time when you usually go to bed: *It's way past your bedtime!* | *a bedtime story*

Bed·u /ˈbeduː/ *n* (*plural* **Bedu**) [C] another word for a BEDOUIN

ˈbed-ˌwetting *n* [U] the problem that some children have of passing URINE (=liquid from the body) while they are asleep

bee /biː/ ●●○ *n* [C]
1 a black and yellow flying insect that makes HONEY and can sting you: *a swarm of bees* | *a bee sting* → **BUMBLEBEE**, see picture at **INSECT**

2 have a bee in your bonnet (about sth) *informal* to think something is so important, so necessary etc that you keep mentioning it or thinking about it: *Dad's got a bee in his bonnet about saving electricity.*
3 sewing/quilting etc bee *AmE informal* an occasion when people, usually women, meet in order to do a particular type of work
4 a busy bee *spoken* someone who enjoys being busy or active
5 be the bee's knees *spoken old-fashioned* to be very good: *She thought the party was just the bee's knees.* → SPELLING BEE, → **the birds and the bees** at BIRD(3)

Beeb, the /biːb/ *informal* the BBC

beech /biːtʃ/ *n* [C,U] a large tree with smooth grey BARK (=outer covering), or the wood from this tree

beef[1] /biːf/ ●●● S3 *n*
1 [U] the meat from a cow: *roast beef | We have both dairy and beef cattle on the farm.*
2 [C] *informal* a complaint: *OK, so what's the beef this time?*
3 where's the beef? *AmE spoken* used when you think someone's promises sound good, but you want to know what they actually plan to do → CORNED BEEF

beef[2] *v* [I] *informal* to complain a lot: **[+about]** *They're always beefing about something.*

beef sth ↔ **up** *phr v informal* to improve something or make it more interesting, more important etc: *a beefed-up news story | We need to beef the campaign up.*

beef·bur·ger /ˈbiːfbɜːɡə $ -bɜːrɡər/ *n* [C] *BrE* a HAMBURGER

beef·cake /ˈbiːfkeɪk/ *n* [U] *informal* strong attractive men with large muscles

Beef·eat·er /ˈbiːfˌiːtə $ -ər/ *n* [C] *BrE* a traditional guard at the Tower of London

beef·steak /ˈbiːfsteɪk/ *n* [C,U] STEAK

ˌbeef ˈtea *n* [U] a hot drink made from BEEF that used to be given to people when they were ill

beef·y /ˈbiːfi/ *adj* (*comparative* **beefier**, *superlative* **beefiest**) someone who is beefy is big, strong, and often quite fat

bee·hive /ˈbiːhaɪv/ *n* [C] **1** a structure where BEES are kept for producing HONEY **2** a way of arranging a woman's hair in a high pile on the top of her head, that was popular in the 1960s

bee·keep·er /ˈbiːkiːpə $ -ər/ *n* [C] someone who owns or takes care of BEES —**beekeeping** *n* [U]

bee·line /ˈbiːlaɪn/ *n* **make a beeline for sb/sth** *informal* to go quickly and directly towards someone or something: *Rob always makes a beeline for beautiful women.*

been /biːn, bɪn $ bɪn/ *v* **1** the past participle of BE **2 a)** used to say that someone has gone to a place and come back: **[+to]** *I've never been to Japan.* | **have been to do sth** *Have you been to see the Van Gogh exhibition yet?* **b)** *BrE* used to say that someone has come to a place and left again: *The postman hasn't been yet.* **3 been there, seen that, done that** *spoken* used to say that you are no longer interested in doing something, because you already have a lot of experience of it

GRAMMAR: Comparison

have been
• You use **have been to** when someone has visited a place and come back again: *She's been to the hospital for a check-up.*
• You use **have been in** when someone has lived or stayed in the same place: *How long have you been in London?*

have gone
• You use **have gone to** when someone has travelled to a place and not come back: *Mark's not here. He's gone to the shops.*

went
• You use **went to** to talk about a trip that someone made in the past: *Last May I went to a conference in Montreal.*

beep /biːp/ ●●○ *v*
1 [I] if a machine beeps, it makes a short high sound SYN **bleep**: *Why does the computer keep beeping?* THESAURUS SOUND
2 [I,T] if a car horn beeps, or if you beep your car horn, it makes a loud noise —**beep** *n* [C]: *Leave your message after the beep.*

beep·er /ˈbiːpə $ -ər/ *n* [C] a small machine that you carry with you that makes short high electronic sounds to tell you that you must telephone someone SYN **bleeper, pager**

beer /bɪə $ bɪr/ ●●● S2 W3 *n*
1 [U] an alcoholic drink made from MALT and HOPS: *a pint of beer | We sell* ***draught beer*** (=beer served from a large container, not a bottle).
2 [C] a glass, bottle, or can of beer: *Do you fancy a beer?* → see picture at GLASS[1] —**beery** *adj*: *his beery breath* → GINGER BEER, ROOT BEER, → **small beer** at SMALL[1](16)

ˈbeer ˌbelly (*also* **ˈbeer gut**) *n* [C] an unattractive fat stomach caused by drinking too much beer

beered up /ˌbɪəd ˈʌp $ ˌbɪrd-/ *adj BrE informal* if someone is beered up, they have drunk a lot of beer

ˈbeer mat *n* [C] *BrE* a small piece of CARDBOARD that you put under a glass, especially in a bar

ˈbeer ˌmoney *n* [U] *BrE informal* a little extra money to buy a drink or have fun with: *The job was never going to make me rich, but it kept me in beer money for a while.*

bees·wax /ˈbiːzwæks/ *n* [U] **1** a substance produced by BEES, used especially for making furniture POLISH and CANDLES **2 none of your beeswax** *AmE spoken* used to tell someone that what they have asked you is private or personal

beet /biːt/ *n* [C,U] **1** (*also* **sugar beet**) a vegetable that sugar is made from **2** *AmE* a plant with a round dark red root that you cook and eat as a vegetable SYN **beetroot** *BrE* → see picture at VEGETABLE[1] **3 red as a beet** *AmE informal* having a red face, especially because you are embarrassed

bee·tle[1] /ˈbiːtl/ *n* [C] an insect with a round hard back that is usually black → see picture at INSECT

beetle[2] *v* [I always + adv/prep] *BrE informal* to go somewhere quickly and leaning forward SYN **scurry**: *He went beetling off down the corridor.*

beet·root /ˈbiːtruːt/ *n* [C,U] **1** *BrE* a plant with a round dark red root that you cook and eat as a vegetable SYN **beet** *AmE* → see picture at VEGETABLE[1] **2 go beetroot** *BrE informal* to become red in the face, especially because you are embarrassed

be·fall /bɪˈfɔːl $ -ˈfɒːl/ *v* (*past tense* **befell** /-ˈfel/, *past participle* **befallen** /-ˈfɔːlən $ -ˈfɒː-/) [T] *literary* if something unpleasant or dangerous befalls you, it happens to you: *We prayed that no harm should befall them.*

be·fit /bɪˈfɪt/ *v* (**befitted**, **befitting**) [T] *formal* to be proper or suitable for someone or something: ***As befits*** *a castle of such national importance, there are many stories connected with its history.*

be·fore[1] /bɪˈfɔː $ -ˈfɔːr/ ●●● S1 W1 *conjunction*
1 earlier than a particular event or action OPP **after**: *Say goodbye before you go. | I saw her a few days before she died.*
2 so that something does not or cannot happen: *Put that money somewhere safe before it gets stolen. | That dog ought to be destroyed before it attacks any more children. | Before I could say anything more, Holmes had rushed off towards the station.*
3 used to say that something happens after a period of time: *It was several minutes before we realised what was happening. | It will be a while before we know the results.*
4 used to say that something must happen in order for something else to be possible: *You have to pass a test before you can get a licence.*
5 *spoken* used to warn someone that something bad will happen to them if they do not do something: *Get out before I call the police!*
6 used to emphasize that someone does not want to do

B

something: *She would die before she would admit she was wrong.*

GRAMMAR: Choosing the right tense

You use the present simple with **before** to talk about a future event. Don't use 'will'. You say: *I want to get home before it rains.* ✗ Don't say: *before it will rain*

GRAMMAR GUIDE ▸ VERBS

before² ●●● S1 W1 *prep*
1 earlier than something or someone OPP **after**: *The new road should be completed before the end of the year.* | *Let's meet at our house before the show.* | *Larry arrived home before me.* | **five minutes/two hours etc before sth** *Hugh arrived just five minutes before the ceremony.* | **before doing sth** *I usually take a shower before having my breakfast.* | *We only got back from Scotland* ***the day before yesterday*** (=two days ago). | *Other students joined in the protest, and* ***before long*** (=soon) *there was a crowd of 200 or so.*
2 ahead of someone or something else in a list or order OPP **after**: *You were before me in the queue.* | *The files are in alphabetical order, so B1 comes before C1.*
3 used to say that something happens where it can be watched by people SYN **in front of**: *Italy will face Brazil this afternoon before a crowd of 100,000 spectators.* | *an actor who had performed before the Queen*
4 used to say that someone or something comes to be judged or considered by a person or group of people: *The proposal was put before the planning committee.*
5 used to say that one thing or person is considered more important than another: *I put my wife and kids before anyone else.* | *In the air transport business, safety must always come before profit.*
6 *formal* in front of something or someone: *The priest stood before the altar.* | *The sea stretched out before them.*
7 if one place is before another place on a road or journey, the first place is nearer to you than the second, so you will reach it first OPP **after**: *The pub is 100 metres before the church on the right.* | *the last station before the Simplon Tunnel*
8 *formal* if there is a job or situation before you, you will have to do the job or face the situation SYN **ahead of**: *The task of emptying the house lay before us.*
9 *formal* if a period of time is before you, it is about to start and you can do what you want during it SYN **in front of**: *We had a glorious summer afternoon before us to do as we pleased.* | *You have your whole life before you.*

THESAURUS

before earlier than something or someone: *She could read before she started school.* | *Do you want to have a shower before me?*
prior to *formal* before something happens: *Please arrive at the airport two hours prior to departure.*
by no later than a particular time or date: *The children are usually in bed by 9 o'clock.*
earlier before now, or before the time you are talking about: *I saw her earlier.* | *I had sent the letter earlier in the week.*
previously before now, or before a time in the past: *He previously worked as an electrician.*
in advance before something happens – used especially when talking about the arrangements for something: *Let me know in advance if you are going to be late.* | *The landlord wants three months' rent in advance.*
beforehand (*also* **ahead of time**) before something happens, especially so that you are ready: *I wish we had known about all this beforehand.*

before³ ●●● S1 W1 *adv*
1 at an earlier time: *Haven't I met you before somewhere?* | *Never before had he seen so many people starving.* | *She looked just the same as before.*
2 the day/week/month etc before the previous day, week, month etc OPP **after**: *She was in Paris last week and in Rome the week before.*
3 *old use* ahead of someone or something else: *The king's herald walked before.*

be·fore·hand /bɪˈfɔːhænd $ -ˈfɔːr-/ ●○○ *adv* before something else happens or is done: *The police need to be briefed beforehand on how to deal with this sort of situation.* | *When you give a speech, it's natural to feel nervous beforehand.* THESAURUS ▸ BEFORE

be·friend /bɪˈfrend/ *v* [T] to behave in a friendly way towards someone, especially someone who is younger or needs help: *They befriended me when I first arrived in London as a student.*

be·fud·dled /bɪˈfʌdəld/ *adj* completely confused: *Even in my befuddled state, I could find my key.*

beg /beg/ ●●○ *v* (**begged**, **begging**)
1 ASK [I,T] to ask for something in an anxious or urgent way, because you want it very much: *She begged and pleaded with them until they finally agreed.* | *She fought back the sudden urge to run to him and* ***beg*** *his* ***forgiveness***. | **beg to do sth** *The children begged to come with us.* | **beg sb to do sth** *I begged Helen to stay, but she wouldn't listen.* | **beg (sb) for sth** *She ran to the nearest house and* ***begged for help***. | *We could hear the prisoners* ***begging for mercy***. | **I beg of you** *formal* (=please) *Listen, I beg of you.* | **beg leave to do sth** *formal* (=ask permission to do something) THESAURUS ▸ ASK
2 MONEY/FOOD [I,T] to ask people to give you food, money etc, usually because you are very poor: **beg (sth) from sb** *a ragged child begging from passing shoppers* | **[+for]** *The old man went from door to door begging for food.* | *a* ***begging letter*** (=a letter asking for money)
3 ANIMAL [I] if a dog begs, it sits up with its front legs off the ground
4 I beg your pardon *spoken* **a)** used to ask someone to repeat what they have just said: *'The meeting's on Wednesday.' 'I beg your pardon?' 'I said the meeting's on Wednesday.'* **b)** used to say sorry when you have made a mistake, or said something wrong or embarrassing: *Oh, I beg your pardon. I thought you said 15 pence, not 50.* **c)** used to show that you strongly disagree with something that someone has said, or think it is unacceptable: *'Chicago's an awful place.' 'I beg your pardon, that's where I'm from!'*
5 I beg to differ *spoken formal* used to say firmly that you do not agree with something that has been said: *I must beg to differ on this point.*
6 beg the question a) to make you want to ask a question that has not yet been answered: **[+of]** *This proposal begs the question of who is going to pay for the new building.* **b)** to treat an idea as though it were true or had been proved, when this may not be the case
7 be going begging *BrE spoken* if something is going begging, it is available for anyone who wants it: *There's a beer going begging, if anyone's interested.*
8 beg, borrow, or steal to do whatever you must in order to get what you want – often used humorously: *She'd beg, borrow, or steal the money for those shoes.*

be·gan /bɪˈgæn/ *v* the past tense of BEGIN

be·get /bɪˈget/ *v* (*past tense* **begot** /-ˈgɒt $ -ˈgɑːt/, *past participle* **begotten** /-ˈgɒtn $ -ˈgɑːtn/, *present participle* **begetting**) [T] **1** *old use* to become the father of a child **2** to cause something or make it happen: *Hunger begets crime.* —**begetter** *n* [C]

beg·gar¹ /ˈbegə $ -ər/ ●○○ *n* [C]
1 someone who lives by asking people for food and money: *the beggars on the streets*
2 lucky/lazy/cheeky etc beggar *BrE spoken* used when speaking to or about someone you like: *'How's Dave?' 'The lucky beggar's in the South of France!'*
3 beggars can't be choosers used to say that, when you have no money or no power to choose, you have to accept whatever you are given

beggar² *v* [T] **1 beggar description/belief** if something beggars description or belief, it is impossible to describe or believe it: *They showed a lack of common sense that beggars belief.* **2** *literary* to make someone very poor: *Why should he beggar himself for you?*

beg·gar·ly /ˈbegəli $ -ərli/ *adj literary* poor

beg·gar·y /ˈbegəri/ *n* [U] *formal* the state of being very poor

ˈbegging ˌbowl *n* [C] **1** used to talk about a request for money made by an organization or country: *Arts and theatre groups are constantly thrusting the begging bowl at the government.* **2** a container that a beggar holds out to people for money

This graph shows how common different grammar patterns of the verb **begin** are.

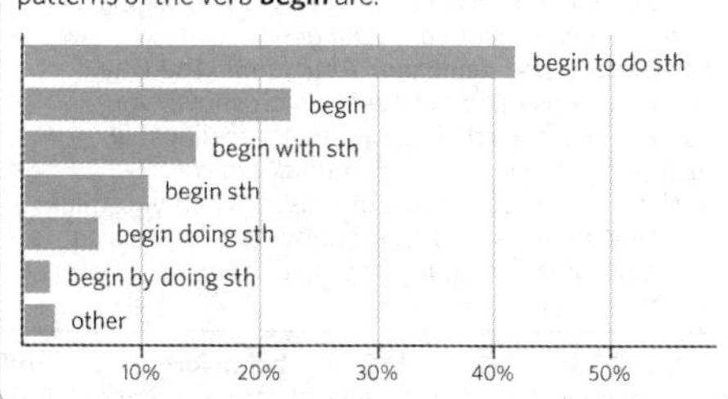

be·gin /bɪˈɡɪn/ ●●● S1 W1 *v* (*past tense* **began** /-ˈɡæn/, *past participle* **begun** /-ˈɡʌn/, *present participle* **beginning**)

1 START DOING STH [I,T] to start doing something: *As everybody's here, let's begin.* | *In the third year, students begin the study of classical Chinese.* | *The president begins talks with the prime minister tonight.* | **begin to do sth** *She began to feel a sense of panic.* | **begin doing sth** *I began teaching in 1984.* THESAURUS ▶ START

2 START HAPPENING [I,T] if something begins, or you begin something, it starts to happen or exist from a particular time: *It was the coldest winter since records began.* | **[+at]** *The meeting begins at 10.30 am.*

3 DO FIRST [I] if you begin with something or begin by doing something, this is the first thing you do: **[+with]** *Shall we begin with a prayer?* | **begin by doing sth** *I'll begin by thanking you all for being here tonight.*

4 BOOK/WORD ETC [I] if a book, film, or word begins with something, it starts with a particular event or letter: **[+with]** *'Psychosis' begins with a P.*

REGISTER

In everyday English, people usually say **start** rather than **begin**: *The movie **starts** at 7.45.* | *Let's **start** by introducing ourselves.* | *Not many English names **start** with X.*

5 SPEECH [I,T] to start speaking: *'Ladies and gentlemen,' he began. 'I am delighted to be here.'*

6 to begin with a) *spoken* used to introduce the first and most important point you want to make: *Well, to begin with, he shouldn't even have been driving my car.* **b)** used to say that something was already in a particular condition before something else happened: *I didn't break it! It was like that to begin with.* **c)** during the first part of a process or activity: *The kids helped me to begin with, but they soon got bored.*

7 can't begin to understand/imagine etc *spoken* used to emphasize how difficult something is to understand etc: *I can't begin to imagine how awful it was.*

GRAMMAR

Begin belongs to a group of verbs where the same noun can be the subject of the verb or its object.
- You can say: *They began the meeting at 9.* In this sentence, 'the meeting' is the object of **begin**.
- You can also say: *The meeting began at 9.* In this sentence, 'the meeting' is the subject of **begin**.

GRAMMAR GUIDE ▶ VERBS

begin (sth) **as** sth *phr v* to be a particular thing at the start of your existence, working life etc: *Roger began his career as an office boy.*

be·gin·ner /bɪˈɡɪnə $ -ər/ ●●● W3 *n* [C]
1 someone who has just started to do or learn something: *an **absolute beginner***
2 beginner's luck unusual success that you have when you start something new

be·gin·ning /bɪˈɡɪnɪŋ/ ●●● S1 W2 *n* [C usually singular]
1 the start or first part of an event, story, period of time etc: **[+of]** *She's been here **since the beginning** of the year.* | *There's a short poem **at the beginning** of every chapter.* | ***From the beginning** of my career as a journalist, I've been writing about gender issues.* | *I thought he loved me; perhaps he did **in the beginning**.* | *That chance meeting **marked the beginning** of a long and happy relationship.* | *This is **just the beginning** of a new and different life for you.* | *I said he would cause trouble, **right from the beginning**.* | *I opposed it from **the very beginning**.* | *The whole trip was a disaster **from beginning to end**.* | *I feel like I've been offered **a new beginning**.* | *Could we **start at the beginning**? Tell me where you first met him.*
2 beginnings [plural] the early signs or stages of something that later develops into something bigger or more important: **[+of]** *I think I **have the beginnings** of a cold.* | **from humble/small beginnings** *He rose from humble beginnings to great wealth.*
3 the beginning of the end the time when something good starts to end

GRAMMAR: Prepositions with beginning
- You say **in the beginning**: *In the beginning, she didn't like him.*
- You say **at the beginning of** a period of time: *I started my new job at the beginning of the year.*

✗ Don't say: *in the beginning of the year*

THESAURUS

beginning the first part of something such as a story, event, or period of time: *The beginning of the movie is very violent.* | *Let's go back to the beginning.*
start the beginning of something, or the way something begins: *Tomorrow marks the start of the presidential election campaign.* | *It was not a good start to the day.*
commencement *formal* the beginning of something – used especially in official contexts: *the commencement of the academic year*
origin the point from which something starts to exist: *He wrote a book about the origins of the universe.* | *The tradition has its origins in medieval times.*
the onset of sth the time when something bad begins, such as illness, old age, or cold weather: *the onset of winter* | *An active lifestyle can delay the onset of many diseases common to aging.*
dawn *literary* the beginning of an important period of time in history: *People have worshipped gods since the dawn of civilization.*
birth the beginning of something important that will change many people's lives: *the birth of democracy in South Africa* | *the birth of the environmental movement*

be·gone /bɪˈɡɒn $ bɪˈɡɒːn/ *interjection old use* used to tell someone to go away

be·go·ni·a /bɪˈɡəʊniə $ -ˈɡoʊ-/ *n* [C] a plant with yellow, pink, red, or white flowers

be·got /bɪˈɡɒt $ bɪˈɡɑːt/ *v* the past tense of BEGET

be·got·ten /bɪˈɡɒtn $ bɪˈɡɑːtn/ *v* the past participle of BEGET

be·grudge /bɪˈɡrʌdʒ/ *v* [T usually in negatives] **1** to feel angry or upset with someone because they have something that you think they do not deserve: **begrudge sb sth** *We shouldn't begrudge her this success.* **2** to feel annoyed or unhappy that you have to pay something, give someone something etc: **begrudge sb sth** *The farmer's wife never begrudged him a meal at the end of the day.* | **begrudge doing sth** *I begrudge spending so much money on train fares.*

be·guile /bɪˈɡaɪl/ *v* [T] **1** to interest and attract someone: *She was beguiled by his smooth talk.* **2** to persuade or trick someone into doing something: **beguile sb into doing sth** *He was beguiled into buying another copy of her book.*

3 *literary* to do something that makes the time pass in an enjoyable way

be·guil·ing /bɪˈɡaɪlɪŋ/ *adj* attractive and interesting: *a beguiling smile* —**beguilingly** *adv*

be·gum /ˈbeɪɡəm, ˈbiː-/ *n* [C] a title of respect, used for married Muslim women, especially of high rank

be·gun /bɪˈɡʌn/ *v* the past participle of BEGIN

B

be·half /bɪˈhɑːf $ bɪˈhæf/ ●●○ S3 W3 AWL *n* **on behalf of sb** (*also* **in behalf of sb** *AmE*) **a)** instead of someone, or as their representative: *She asked the doctor to speak to her parents on her behalf.* | *On behalf of everyone here, may I wish you a very happy retirement.* **b)** because of or for someone: *Oh, don't go to any trouble on my behalf.*

be·have /bɪˈheɪv/ ●●● S3 W3 *v* [I]

1 [always + adv/prep] to do things that are good, bad, sensible etc SYN **act**: *She* ***behaved in a*** *very responsible* ***way***. | **[+towards]** *I think he behaved disgracefully towards you.* | **[+like]** *grown men behaving like schoolboys* | **behave as if/though** *He was a little boy, but he behaved as if he was an adult.*

2 (*also* **behave yourself**) to not do things that annoy or offend people OPP **misbehave**: *Will you children please behave!* | *I hope Nicholas behaved himself at the party.* | **well-behaved/badly-behaved** *a badly-behaved class*

3 [always + adv/prep] if something behaves in a particular way, it does those things: *Quantum mechanics is the study of the way atoms behave.*

be·hav·iour *BrE*, **behavior** *AmE* /bɪˈheɪvjə $ -ər/ ●●● S2 W1 *n* [U]

1 the things that a person or animal does: *It is important to reward good behaviour.* | **[+towards]** *She complained of her boss's inappropriate behavior towards her.* | *the effects of alcohol on human behaviour*

2 be on your best behaviour to behave as well and politely as you can in order to please someone: *I want you both to be on your best behaviour at Grandad's.*

3 the things that something in science normally does: **[+of]** *the behaviour of human chromosomes* —**behavioural** *adj*: *behavioural science* —**behaviourally** *adv*

COLLOCATIONS

ADJECTIVES

good/bad *The boys were suspended from school for bad behaviour.*
normal/abnormal *They thought that their son's behaviour was perfectly normal.*
aggressive/violent/threatening *His behavior became increasingly violent.*
antisocial *antisocial behaviour such as spitting and swearing in public*
acceptable/unacceptable *This sort of behavior is completely unacceptable.*
appropriate/inappropriate *formal* (=suitable/not suitable for that situation) | **human/animal behaviour** | **criminal behaviour**

behaviour + NOUN

behaviour problems *She teaches children with behaviour problems.*

PHRASES

standards of behaviour *declining standards of behaviour among young people*
a pattern of behaviour

VERBS

change your behaviour (*also* **modify your behaviour** *formal*) *He has no reason to change his behaviour.*
influence sb's behaviour *The genes we inherit influence our behaviour.*

THESAURUS

behaviour *BrE*, **behavior** *AmE* the way someone behaves: *Chemicals added to food may be responsible for children's bad behaviour.* | *Tatsuya apologized for his behaviour towards me.*
conduct *formal* the way someone behaves in public or in their job – used mainly in official or legal contexts: *Bates was arrested and charged with* ***disorderly conduct*** (=noisy and violent). | *The committee found him guilty of unsatisfactory* ***professional conduct***.
manner the way someone behaves when they are talking to or dealing with other people, which is shown in their expression, their voice etc: *She had a pleasant friendly manner.* | *Suddenly his whole manner changed, and he started shouting.*
demeanour *BrE*, **demeanor** *AmE formal* the way someone looks and behaves, which shows you something about their character or feelings: *She maintained a calm demeanour at all times.*
antics someone's behaviour – used when you think it is silly, funny, strange, or annoying: *The drunken antics of some English football fans has brought shame on the country.*

be·hav·iour·is·m *BrE*, **behaviorism** *AmE* /bɪˈheɪvjərɪzəm/ *n* [U] the belief that the scientific study of the mind should be based only on people's behaviour, not on what they say about their thoughts and feelings —**behaviourist** *n* [C]

be·head /bɪˈhed/ *v* [T] to cut off someone's head as a punishment: *Charles I was beheaded in 1649.*

be·held /bɪˈheld/ the past tense and past participle of BEHOLD

be·he·moth /bəˈhiːmɒθ $ -mɑːθ/ *n* [C] *formal* something that is very large: *a trade behemoth that shipped abroad $800 billion worth of goods*

be·hest /bɪˈhest/ *n* **at the behest of sb** *formal* because someone has asked for something or ordered something to happen: *The committee was set up at the behest of the president.*

be·hind¹ /bɪˈhaɪnd/ ●●● S1 W1 *prep, adv*

1 at or towards the back of a thing or person: *I turned to speak to the person standing behind me.* | *Someone could easily creep up behind us.* | *The car behind was hooting impatiently.* | *Jane shut the door behind her.* | *The manager was sitting behind a large desk.* | **close behind/not far behind** *He set off down the road with the rest of us following close behind.* ⚠ Don't say 'behind of': *He hid behind a chair* (*NOT behind of a chair*).

2 not as successful or not having made as much progress as someone or something else: *Mark's always behind the rest of his class in mathematics.* | *This victory lifts Ferguson's team into fifth place, nine points behind leaders Norwich.* | *Europe was falling behind in the important field of computer technology.*

3 used to say that someone is late in doing what they have to do: *This work should have been finished yesterday. I'm getting terribly behind.* | *Victor had fallen behind with his mortgage payments after losing his job.* | *an important research project that is already two years* ***behind schedule*** (=not ready at the time planned)

4 used for talking about the hidden reason for something: *I wonder what's behind this change of plan.* | *Perhaps a bitter experience lay behind her anger.*

5 supporting a person, idea etc: *The workers are very much behind these proposals.* | *I suppose I'm lucky because my parents were behind me all the way.*

6 responsible for a plan, idea etc or for organizing something: *It was alleged that foreign agents were behind the recent violence.* | *The Rotary Club is behind the fund-raising for the new hospital.*

7 if an unpleasant experience or situation is behind you, it no longer upsets you or affects your life: *Now you can put all these worries behind you.* | *a chance to start a new life and leave all your troubles behind*

8 if you have experience behind you, you have gained valuable skills or important qualities that can be used: *Marjorie is one of the top designers in the business, with years of experience behind her.*

9 used when the real facts about a situation or someone's character are hidden by the way things seem or by the

way a person behaves: *We were determined to find the truth behind this mystery.* | *You could see the burning hatred behind Graham's calm manner.*
10 if a student stays behind after school or after a lesson, they stay after it has finished → **behind sb's back** at BACK[2](9), → **behind bars** at BAR[1](7), → **behind the times** at TIME[1](38)

behind² *n* [C] *informal* the part of your body that you sit on SYN **bottom**

be·hold /bɪˈhəʊld $ -ˈhoʊld/ *v* (*past tense and past participle* **beheld**) [T] *literary* to see or to look at something – sometimes used humorously: **be a sight/joy/pleasure etc to behold** *The beauty of the garden was a pleasure to behold.* —**beholder** *n* [C] → **lo and behold** at LO(2)

be·hold·en /bɪˈhəʊldn $ -ˈhoʊl-/ *adj* **feel/be beholden to sb** to feel that you have a duty to someone because they have done something for you

be·hove /bɪˈhəʊv $ bɪˈhoʊv/ *BrE*, **be·hoove** /bɪˈhuːv/ *AmE v* **it behoves sb to do sth** *formal* used to say that someone should do something because it is right or necessary, or it will help them

beige /beɪʒ/ *n* [U] a pale brown colour —**beige** *adj*

being¹ ●●○ W3 *n*
1 come into being/be brought into being to start to exist: *a law that first came into being in 1912*
2 [C] a living thing, especially a person: *a* ***human being*** | **intelligent/conscious/rational etc being** *a story about alien beings who invade Earth*
3 [U] *literary* the most important quality or nature of something, especially of a person: **the core/roots/whole of sb's being** *The whole of her being had been taken over by a desire to return to her homeland.*

be·ing² /ˈbiːɪŋ/ *v* [linking verb] **1** the present participle of BE **2** used to give the reason for something: *Being a quiet sort of person, I didn't want to get involved.* | *You can't expect them to sit still for that long, children being what they are.* **3 being as** *BrE spoken* because SYN **as**: *You might as well drink it, being as you've paid for it.*

be·jew·elled *BrE*, **bejeweled** *AmE* /bɪˈdʒuːəld/ *adj literary* wearing jewels, or decorated with jewels: *bejewelled hands*

be·la·bour *BrE*, **belabor** *AmE* /bɪˈleɪbə $ -ər/ *v* [T] **1 belabour the point** *formal* to keep emphasizing a fact or idea in a way that is annoying **2** *old-fashioned* to hit someone or something hard

be·lat·ed /bɪˈleɪtɪd/ *adj* happening or arriving late: ***a belated attempt*** *to increase support* | **belated recognition/realization/acknowledgement** *The statement was a belated acknowledgement that the project had not been a success.* | *a belated birthday present* THESAURUS LATE —**belatedly** *adv*

be·lay /bɪˈleɪ/ *v* [I,T] *technical* to make someone who is climbing a mountain etc safe by attaching a rope to them and to a rock

belch /beltʃ/ *v* **1** [I] to let air from your stomach come out loudly through your mouth SYN **burp 2** (*also* **belch out**) [I,T] to send out a large amount of smoke, flames etc, or to come out of something in large amounts: *a line of chimneys belching out smoke* | *Flames belched from the wreckage.* —**belch** *n* [C]

be·lea·guered /bɪˈliːgəd $ -ərd/ *adj* [usually before noun] *formal* **1** experiencing a lot of problems or criticism: *the country's beleaguered steel industry* **2** surrounded by an army: *Supplies are being brought into the beleaguered city.*

bel·fry /ˈbelfri/ *n* (*plural* **belfries**) [C] a tower for a bell, especially on a church

Bel·gian¹ /ˈbeldʒən/ *adj* from or relating to Belgium or its people

Belgian² *n* [C] someone from Belgium

be·lie /bɪˈlaɪ/ *v* (**belied**, **belying**, **belies**) [T] **1** to give someone a false idea about something: *Her pleasant manner belied her true character.* **2** to show that something cannot be true or real: *His cheerful smile belied his words.*

be·lief /bəˈliːf/ ●●● S3 W2 *n*
1 [singular, U] the feeling that something is definitely true or definitely exists: **[+in]** *a strong belief in God* | **[+that]** *her sincere belief that her brother was not the murderer* | **in the belief that** *Thieves broke into the building in the mistaken belief that there was expensive computer equipment inside.*
2 [singular] the feeling that something is good and can be trusted: **[+in]** *If you're selling, you have to have genuine belief in the product.* | *When you get something wrong, it can shake your belief in yourself.*
3 [C] an idea that you believe to be true, especially one that forms part of a system of ideas: *religious beliefs* | *Several members* ***hold*** *very right-wing* ***beliefs***.
4 beyond belief used to emphasize that something is so extreme that it is difficult to believe: *What she did was stupid beyond belief.* → **it beggars belief** at BEGGAR[2](1), → **to the best of your belief** at BEST[3](4), → DISBELIEF, UNBELIEF

COLLOCATIONS

ADJECTIVES

a firm/strong belief *It is still my firm belief that we did the right thing.*
a strongly-held/deeply-held belief (=that you believe very much) *her strongly-held belief that things were much better in the past*
a common/popular/widespread belief (=that a lot of people believe) *There is a common belief that educational standards are declining.*
a mistaken/false belief *the mistaken belief that cannabis is not an addictive drug*
a sincere belief (=based on what you really feel is true) | **a passionate belief**

VERBS

have a belief *You must always have the belief that you can succeed.*
hold a belief *He held this belief until the day he died.*

PHRASES

it is my belief that *It is my belief that most teachers are doing a good job.*
contrary to popular belief (=opposite to what most people think) *Contrary to popular belief, boys are not usually better at maths than girls.*

be·liev·a·ble /bəˈliːvəbəl/ *adj* something that is believable can be believed because it seems possible, likely, or real: *a story with believable characters in it* | *That scenario is entirely believable.*

be·lieve /bəˈliːv/ ●●● S1 W1 *v*
1 [T] to be sure that something is true or that someone is telling the truth: *You shouldn't believe everything you read.* | *I believed him, even though his story sounded unlikely.* | **believe (that)** *I don't believe he's only 25.* | *I* ***don't believe a word of it*** (=I think it is completely untrue).
2 [T] to think that something is true or possible, although you are not completely sure: **believe (that)** *Detectives believe that the victim knew his killer.* | **it is believed (that)** *It is believed that the house was built in 1735.* | **believe so** (=think that something is true) *'Have they arrived yet?' 'Yes, I believe so.'* | **be believed to be sth** *At 115, Mrs Jackson is believed to be the oldest person in the country.* | *The four men are* ***widely believed*** (=believed by a lot of people) *to have been killed by their captors.* | *Did you* ***honestly believe*** *that I'd be stupid enough to do that?* | *I* ***firmly believe*** *that the business will be a success.* THESAURUS THINK
3 it's difficult/hard to believe (that) used when you are surprised that something is true: *Sometimes, it's hard to believe we've been married for 50 years.*

SPOKEN PHRASES

4 can't/don't believe sth used when you are very surprised or shocked by something: *I can't believe he's expecting us to work on Sunday!* | *I couldn't believe it when he told me what had happened.* | **can hardly/scarcely believe sth** *I could scarcely believe my luck.*
5 believe it or not used when you are saying something that is true but surprising: *He enjoys school, believe it or not.*
6 would you believe it! (*also* **I don't believe it!**) used when

you are surprised or angry about something: *And then he just walked out. Would you believe it!*
7 believe (you) me used to emphasize that something is definitely true: *There'll be trouble when they find out about this, believe you me!*
8 you'd better believe it! used to emphasize that something is true
9 don't you believe it! used to emphasize that something is definitely not true
10 can't believe your eyes/ears used to say that someone is very surprised by something they see or hear
11 if you believe that, you'll believe anything used to say that something is definitely not true, and that anyone who believes it must be stupid
12 seeing is believing (*also* **I'll believe it when I see it**) used to say that you will only believe that something happens or exists when you actually see it

13 [I] to have a religious faith: *She says those who believe will go to heaven.* → **make believe** at MAKE¹(19)

GRAMMAR
Patterns with believe
- You **believe that** something is true: *We believe that all men are equal.*
- You **believe that** something **should** happen: *We believe all men should be treated equally.*
- You **believe that** someone **can** do something: *I still believe that we can win.*
- You **believe that** something **might** or **could** happen: *Do you believe that things might change?*
- In more formal English, you can say **it is believed that**: *It was believed that the King's touch could cure diseases.*
- In all the above patterns with **that**, 'that' can be omitted: *We believe all men are equal.*
- You can use the phrases **I believe so** or **I don't believe so**, usually to give a short answer: *'Are they married?' 'I believe so.' | 'Were there any problems?' 'I don't believe so.'* ✗ Don't say: *I believe it.*

Using the progressive
Believe is not used in the progressive. You say: *I believe you.* ✗ Don't say: *I am believing you.*
GRAMMAR GUIDE ▸ VERBS

THESAURUS
TO BELIEVE SOMETHING
believe to be sure that something is true or that someone is telling the truth: *I believed her when she said that she loved me. | Don't believe anything he tells you.*
accept to believe that something is true, especially because someone has persuaded you to believe it: *His wife accepted his explanation for why he was late.*
take sb's word for it *especially spoken* to believe what someone says is true, even though you have no proof or experience of it: *I don't know anything about him, so I'll just have to take your word for it.*
give sb the benefit of the doubt to believe what someone says, even though you think it might not be true: *Unless you have proof, you should give him the benefit of the doubt.*
TO BELIEVE SOMETHING THAT IS UNTRUE
be taken in (*also* **fall for sth** *informal*) to be tricked into believing something that is not true: *A lot of people were taken in by these claims. | I can't believe she fell for that old excuse!*
swallow *informal* to believe a story or explanation that is not true, especially when this makes you seem silly: *His aunt had swallowed his story unquestioningly.*

believe in sb/sth *phr v*
1 to be sure that someone or something exists: *Do you believe in God?*
2 to think that something is effective or right: *I don't believe in these diets.* | **believe in doing sth** *The school believes in letting children learn at their own pace.*
3 to trust someone and be confident that they will be successful: *The people want a president they can believe in. | Believe in yourself, or you'll never succeed.*

be·liev·er /bəˈliːvə $ -ər/ ●○○ *n* [C]
1 be a (great/firm) believer in sth to believe strongly that something is good and effective: *I'm a great believer in regular exercise.*
2 someone who believes in a particular god, religion, or system of beliefs OPP **unbeliever**

Be·li·sha bea·con /bəˌliːʃə ˈbiːkən/ *n* [C] in Britain, one of two posts with a round flashing orange light on the top, marking a place that cars must stop at to allow people to cross a road

be·lit·tle /bɪˈlɪtl/ *v* [T] *formal* to make someone or something seem small or unimportant: *He tends to belittle her efforts.*

BELLS
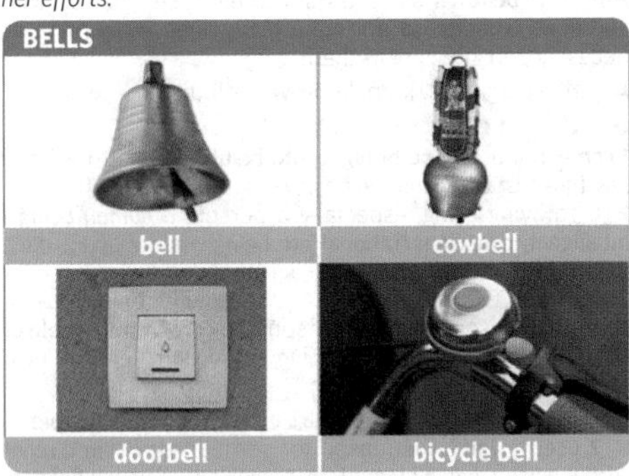
bell | cowbell | doorbell | bicycle bell

bell /bel/ ●●● S2 W3 *n* [C]
1 a piece of electrical equipment that makes a ringing sound, used as a signal or to get someone's attention: **ring/press the bell** *He rang the bell and waited for someone to answer the door. | She pressed the bell for the nurse.* | **a bell rings/goes** *The bell went and everyone rushed out of the classroom.*
2 a hollow metal object like a cup with a piece of metal hanging inside it, that makes a ringing noise when it moves or you shake it: *church bells*
3 give sb a bell *BrE spoken* to telephone someone: *I must give Vicky a bell later.*
4 something that is shaped like a bell: *the bell of a flower*
→ **alarm bells ring** at ALARM¹(5), → **as clear as a bell** at CLEAR¹(10), → **ring a bell** at RING²(4), → DIVING BELL, DOORBELL

bel·la·don·na /ˌbeləˈdɒnə $ -ˈdɑːnə/ *n* [U] **1** a poisonous plant SYN **deadly nightshade** **2** a substance from this plant, used as a drug

ˈbell-ˌbottoms *n* [plural] trousers with legs that get wider from the knee to the bottom SYN **flares**

bell·boy /ˈbelbɔɪ/ *n* [C] *especially BrE* a young man who carries bags, takes messages etc in a hotel

belle /bel/ *n* [C] *old-fashioned* a beautiful girl or woman: **the belle of the ball** (=the most beautiful girl at a dance or party)

bell·hop /ˈbelhɒp $ -hɑːp/ *n* [C] *especially AmE* a young man who carries bags, takes messages etc in a hotel

bel·li·cose /ˈbelɪkəʊs $ -koʊs/ *adj formal* behaving in a way that is likely to start an argument or fight SYN **aggressive**: *bellicose criticism* —**bellicosity** /ˌbelɪˈkɒsəti $ -ˈkɑː-/ *n* [U]

bel·lig·er·ent /bəˈlɪdʒərənt/ *adj* **1** very unfriendly and wanting to argue or fight SYN **aggressive**: *a belligerent attitude* **2** [only before noun] *formal* a belligerent country is fighting a war against another country —**belligerence, belligerency** *n* [U]

bel·low¹ /ˈbeləʊ $ -loʊ/ *v* **1** [I,T] to shout loudly in a deep voice SYN **yell**: *'That's your problem!' bellowed Hurley. | Tony was bellowing orders.* THESAURUS ▸ SHOUT
2 [I] to make the deep sound that a BULL makes

bellow² *n* [C] **1** a loud deep shout: *His voice rose to a bellow.* | **a bellow of rage/laughter etc** *Alex gave another bellow of laughter.* **2** the deep sound that a BULL makes **3 bellows** [plural] **a)** an object used for blowing air into a fire to make it burn better **b)** part of a musical instrument that pushes air through pipes to produce a sound, for example in an ORGAN

ˈbell ˌpepper *n* [C] *AmE* a hollow red, green, or yellow vegetable SYN **pepper** *BrE* → see picture at **VEGETABLE¹**

ˈbell-ˌringer *n* [C] someone who rings church bells → **campanology** —**bell-ringing** *n* [U]

bel·ly¹ /ˈbeli/ ●●○ *n* (*plural* **bellies**) [C]
1 a) your stomach: *a full belly* **b)** *BrE* the front part of your body between your chest and your legs SYN **abdomen**: *She was lying on her belly.*
2 the middle part of an animal's body, near its stomach → see picture at **HORSE¹**
3 *literary* a curved or rounded part of an object: *the belly of a plane*
4 black-bellied/fat-bellied/big-bellied etc having a black, fat, big etc stomach
5 go belly up *informal* if a business or company goes belly up, it stops operating because it cannot pay its debts → **BEER BELLY, POTBELLY**

belly² (*also* **belly out**) *v* (**bellied, bellying, bellies**) [I] *literary* to fill with air and become rounder in shape

bel·ly·ache¹ /ˈbeli-eɪk/ *n* [C,U] *informal* a pain in your stomach SYN **stomachache**

bellyache² *v* [I] *informal* to complain a lot, especially about something unimportant SYN **whinge**: **[+about]** *She never stops bellyaching about money.*

ˈbelly ˌbutton *n* [C] *informal* the small round mark in the middle of your stomach SYN **navel**

ˈbelly dance *n* [C] a dance from the Middle East in which a woman moves her stomach and HIPS around —**belly dancer** *n* [C] —**belly dancing** *n* [U]

ˈbelly flop *n* [C] a way of jumping into water, in which the front of your body falls flat against the surface of the water —**bellyflop** *v* [I]

bel·ly·ful /ˈbelifʊl/ *n* **have had a bellyful of sb/sth** *informal* to be annoyed by someone or something because you have had to deal with them for too long: *I'd had a bellyful of his family by the end of the weekend.*

ˈbelly laugh *n* [C] *informal* a deep loud laugh

be·long /bɪˈlɒŋ $ bɪˈlɒːŋ/ ●●● S2 W2 *v* [I]
1 [always + adv/prep] if something belongs somewhere, that is the right place or situation for it: *Put the chair back where it belongs.* | **[+in]** *an attitude that doesn't belong in modern society*
2 if you feel you belong in a place or situation, you feel happy and comfortable in it, because you have the same interests and ideas as other people: *I worked there for five years but never really felt I belonged.* —**belonging** *n* [U]: *It's important to have a* ***sense of belonging*** (=a feeling that you are happy and comfortable somewhere).

belong to sb/sth *phr v*
1 if something belongs to someone, they own it: *The book belongs to Dan.* | *Who does this scarf belong to?*
2 to be a member of a group or organization: *He belongs to the golf club.*
3 to be related to something or form part of it: *cars that belong to a different era*
4 to be related to or produced by a particular person: *She recognized the voice as belonging to the man who had attacked her.*
5 if a competition or period of time belongs to someone, they are the most important or successful person in it: *All the acts were good, but the evening belonged to a dance group from Moscow.*

GRAMMAR: Using the progressive

Belong is not used in the progressive. You say: *My friend belongs to the choir.* ✗ Don't say: *My friend is belonging to the choir.*
GRAMMAR GUIDE ▸ VERBS

be·long·ings /bɪˈlɒŋɪŋz $ bɪˈlɒːŋ-/ ●●○ *n* [plural] the things you own, especially things that you can carry with you SYN **possessions**: *an insurance policy that covers your* ***personal belongings***

be·lov·ed¹ /bɪˈlʌvɪd/ *adj literary or humorous* loved very much by someone: *He never recovered from the death of his beloved daughter.* | *He's always talking about his beloved computer!* | **[+of/by]** *a book beloved of children everywhere*

beloved² *n* **my/her etc beloved** *literary* someone who is loved very much → **dearly beloved** at **DEARLY(3)**

be·low /bɪˈləʊ $ -ˈloʊ/ ●●● S2 W2 *adv, prep*
1 in a lower place or position, or on a lower level OPP **above**: *an animal that lives* ***below ground*** | *Water was dripping onto the floor below.* | *I could hear voices in the courtyard below my window.* | *They camped a few hundred feet below the summit.* | ***Down below,*** *people were talking and laughing.* | *Somewhere* ***far below,*** *a door slammed.* | *The kitchen is* ***directly below*** *her bedroom.* | *Captain Parker* ***went below*** (=to the lower level of the ship), *leaving Clooney in charge.* THESAURUS ▸ UNDER
2 of a lower rank or having a less important job than someone else OPP **above**: *No one below the level of senior manager was present at the meeting.* | **and/or below** *officers of the rank of captain and below*
3 less than a particular number, amount, level etc OPP **above**: *Test scores below 50 were classed as 'unsatisfactory'.* | *In June the rate of inflation fell below 3%.* | *Tom's spelling is* ***well below*** *average* (=much worse than the normal standard). | **below freezing/zero** (=lower than the temperature at which water freezes) *In winter, temperatures dip to 40 degrees below freezing.* | **and/or below** *free travel for children four years old and below*
4 lower on the same page, or on a later page OPP **above**: *Details of courses are listed below.* | *For more information, see below.* → **below par** at **PAR(2)**, → **below the belt** at **BELT¹(4)**

belt¹ /belt/ ●●● S2 W3 *n* [C]
1 a band of leather, cloth etc that you wear around your waist to hold up your clothes or for decoration: *He unbuckled his leather belt.*
2 a large area of land that has particular features or where particular people live: *America's farming belt* | *the green* (=countryside) *belt BrE* → **GREEN BELT**
3 a circular band of something such as rubber that connects or moves parts of a machine → **CONVEYOR BELT, FAN BELT**
4 below the belt *informal* unfair or cruel: *That was a bit below the belt, Paul.* | *The comments* ***hit below the belt*** (=they were unfair or cruel).
5 have sth under your belt to have achieved something useful or important: *a secretary with several years' experience under her belt*
6 belt and braces *BrE informal* a belt and braces way of doing something is one in which you do more than necessary in order to make sure that it succeeds → **BLACK BELT, GARTER BELT, SAFETY BELT, SEAT BELT, SUSPENDER BELT,** → **tighten your belt** at **TIGHTEN(6)**

belt² *v*
1 HIT [T] *informal* to hit someone or something hard: *Dan belted the ball towards the goal.*
2 GO QUICKLY [I always + adv/prep] *BrE spoken* to go somewhere very fast SYN **charge**: **[+down/along etc]** *We were belting down the motorway at 95 miles per hour.*
3 FASTEN [T] to fasten something with a belt: *Maria belted her raincoat firmly.* | *a dress belted loosely at the waist*

belt sth ↔ **out** *phr v* to sing a song or play an instrument loudly: *She was belting out old Broadway favourites.*

belt up *phr v BrE*
1 *spoken* used to tell someone rudely to be quiet
2 *informal* to fasten your SEAT BELT in a vehicle

belt·ed /ˈbeltɪd/ *adj* fastened with a belt: *a belted jacket*

belt·way /ˈbeltweɪ/ *n* [C] *AmE* a fast main road that goes around a city, not through the centre SYN **ring road** *BrE*

be·moan /bɪˈməʊn $ -ˈmoʊn/ *v* [T] *formal* to complain or say that you are disappointed about something: *He*

B

was ***bemoaning the fact that*** *lawyers charge so much.* | **bemoan the lack/absence/loss of sth** *an article bemoaning the lack of sports facilities in the area*

be·mused /bɪˈmjuːzd/ *adj* looking as if you are confused SYN **bewildered**: *a bemused expression* | **[+by]** *He looked slightly bemused by all the questions.* THESAURUS CONFUSED —**bemusedly** /bɪˈmjuːzɪdli/ *adv* —**bemusement** *n* [U]: *a look of bemusement* —**bemuse** *v* [T]

B

bench¹ /bentʃ/ ●●● S2 W3 *n*

1 OUTDOOR SEAT [C] a long seat for two or more people, especially outdoors: *We sat on a park bench.*

2 IN A LAW COURT **the bench a)** the seat where a judge or MAGISTRATE sits in a court of law: *Would the prisoner please approach the bench?* **b)** the position of being a judge or MAGISTRATE in a court of law: *He was appointed to the bench last year.* | **sit/serve on the bench** (=work as a judge or MAGISTRATE)

3 SPORTS **the bench** the seat where members of a sports team sit when they are not playing in the game: *Batts and Dorigo are* ***on the bench*** *tonight.* | *Simpson* ***came off the bench*** *to play in midfield.*

4 PARLIAMENT **benches** [plural] *BrE* the seats in the British parliament where members of a particular party sit: *There was cheering from the Conservative benches.* → BACKBENCH, BACKBENCHES, FRONT BENCH

5 TABLE [C] a long heavy table used for working on with tools or equipment: *a carpenter's bench*

bench² *v* [T] *AmE* to not allow a sports player to play in a game, or to remove them from a game: *Anderson has been benched until his injury has healed.*

bench·mark¹ /ˈbentʃmɑːk $ -mɑːrk/ ●○○ *n* [C] something that is used as a standard by which other things can be judged or measured: *benchmark data* | *The valuation becomes a benchmark against which to judge other prices.* | **[+for]** *figures that are a useful benchmark for measuring the company's performance* | **[+of]** *results that are used as a benchmark of success*

benchmark² *v* [T] to use a company's good performance as a standard by which to judge the performance of other companies of the same type: **benchmark sb/sth against sth** *British Steel is benchmarked against the best operations anywhere in the world.* —**benchmarking** *n* [U]

bench·warm·er /ˈbentʃˌwɔːmə $ ˌ-wɔːrmər/ *n* [C] *informal* a player in a sports team who does not play in many matches, but is usually a SUBSTITUTE

bend¹ /bend/ ●●● S3 W3 *v* (*past tense and past participle* **bent** /bent/)

1 [I,T] to move part of your body so that it is not straight or so that you are not upright: *Lee bent and kissed her.* | *She bent her head.* | *Bend your knees, but keep your back straight.* | **[+over]** *Emma bent over to pick up the coins.* | **[+down]** *I bent down to lift the box off the floor.* | **[+towards/across etc]** *He bent towards me and whispered in my ear.*

2 [T] to push or press something so that it is no longer flat or straight: *You need a special tool to bend the steel.*

3 [I] to become curved and no longer flat or straight: *Several branches started bending towards the ground.*

4 [I] when a road bends, it changes direction to form a curve: *The road bends sharply to the left.*

5 bend the truth to say something that is not completely true

6 bend over backwards (to do sth) to try very hard to be helpful: *We bent over backwards to finish it on time.*

7 bend sb's ear *spoken* to talk to someone, especially for a long time, about something that is worrying you

8 on bended knee a) trying very hard to persuade someone to do something: *He begged on bended knee for another chance.* **b)** in a kneeling position: *He went down on bended knee and asked her to marry him.*

9 bend your mind/efforts to sth *formal* to give all your energy or attention to one activity, plan etc

10 bend to sb's will *formal* to do what someone else wants, especially when you do not want to → **bend the rules** at RULE¹(1)

bend² *n* [C] **1** a curved part of something, especially a road or river: *The car came round the bend at a terrifying speed.* | **[+in]** *a sharp bend in the road* **2** an action in which you bend a part of your body: *We started the session with a few knee bends to warm up.* **3 drive sb round the bend** *BrE spoken* to annoy someone: *His attitude drives me round the bend.* **4 be/go round the bend** *BrE spoken* to be or become crazy: *I sometimes feel I'm going round the bend looking after young children all day.* **5 the bends** a painful and serious condition that DIVERS get if they come up from deep water too quickly

ben·der /ˈbendə $ -ər/ *n* [C] *informal* **1** a time when people drink a lot of alcohol or take a lot of drugs: *The whole team* ***went on a bender*** *and were arrested.* **2** *BrE taboo* a very offensive word for a man who is attracted to other men. Do not use this word. SYN **homosexual**

bend·y /ˈbendi/ *adj* **1** easy to bend SYN **flexible**: *a bendy rubber doll* **2** with many curves or angles OPP **straight**: *a bendy road*

ˈbendy ˌbus *n* [C] *BrE* a long bus that can bend in the middle

be·neath /bɪˈniːθ/ ●●● W2 *adv, prep formal*

1 in or to a lower position than something, or directly under something SYN **underneath**: *The dolphins disappeared beneath the waves.* | *Jo enjoyed feeling the warm sand beneath her feet.* | *He was standing on the bridge looking at the river beneath.* | *Some roofs collapsed* ***beneath the weight of*** (=unable to support the weight of) *so much snow.* THESAURUS UNDER

> **REGISTER**
> In everyday English, people usually use **underneath** (as an adverb or preposition) or **under** (as a preposition) when talking about position: *They hid* ***under*** *the table.* | *a picture with a caption* ***underneath***

2 covered by something: *Shiona shivered beneath the bedclothes.*

3 used to say that someone's real character or feelings are not shown because their appearance or behaviour is different SYN **underneath**: *Dave sensed that something more sinister lay beneath the woman's cheerful exterior.* | ***Beneath the surface*** *she was angry.*

4 not good enough or suitable for someone: *She acts as if even speaking to us is beneath her.* | *He felt it would be* ***beneath*** *his* ***dignity*** *to comment.* | *His mother felt he was* ***marrying beneath*** *him* (=marrying someone who was not good enough). | *I consider such behaviour to be* ***beneath contempt*** (=so bad that you have no respect for the person involved).

5 in a lower, less important rank or job than someone else SYN **below**

ben·e·dic·tine /ˌbenəˈdɪktiːn/ *n* [C,U] a strong alcoholic drink that is a type of LIQUEUR

Ben·e·dic·tine /ˌbenəˈdɪktɪn◂/ *n* [C] a member of a Christian religious order of MONKS —**Benedictine** *adj*

ben·e·dic·tion /ˌbenəˈdɪkʃən/ *n* [C,U] a Christian prayer that asks God to protect and help someone

ben·e·fac·tion /ˌbenəˈfækʃən/ *n* [C,U] *formal* something, especially money, that someone gives a person or organization in order to help them do something good, or when someone gives money in this way SYN **donation**

ben·e·fac·tor /ˈbenəˌfæktə $ -ər/ *n* [C] someone who gives money for a good purpose: *An anonymous benefactor donated $2 million.* | **[+of/to]** *a generous benefactor of the university*

ben·e·fice /ˈbenɪfɪs/ *n* [C] the pay and position of a Christian priest who is in charge of a PARISH

be·nef·i·cent /bɪˈnefəsənt/ *adj formal* helping people, or resulting in something good: *the beneficent properties of natural remedies* —**beneficence** *n* [U] —**beneficently** *adv*

ben·e·fi·cial /ˌbenɪˈfɪʃəl◂/ ●●○ AWL *adj* having a good effect OPP **detrimental**: *a drug that has a* ***beneficial effect*** *on the immune system* | **[+to/for]** *Cycling is* ***highly beneficial*** *to health and the environment.* | *an arrangement* *that is* ***mutually beneficial*** (=it has advantages for everyone who is involved) —**beneficially** *adv*

ben·e·fi·cia·ry /ˌbenəˈfɪʃəri $ -ˈfɪʃieri/ ●○○ AWL *n* (*plural* **beneficiaries**) [C]
1 someone who gets advantages from an action or change: **[+of]** *The rich were the main beneficiaries of the tax cuts.*
2 someone who receives money or property from someone else who has died: **[+of]** *He was the chief beneficiary of his father's will.*

ben·e·fit¹ /ˈbenəfɪt/ ●●● S2 W1 AWL *n*
1 ADVANTAGE [C,U] an advantage, improvement, or help that you get from something → **beneficial**: **[+of]** *the benefits of contact lenses | I never had the benefit of a university education. | The new credit cards will* ***be of*** *great* ***benefit*** *to our customers. | I hope that the decision taken today will* ***be to the benefit of*** *the whole nation.* | **for sb's benefit** *Could you just explain again for Mark's benefit?* | **without the benefit of sth** *Most motorists manage without the benefit of four-wheel drive.* THESAURUS ADVANTAGE
2 MONEY FROM GOVERNMENT [C,U] *BrE* money provided by the government to people who are sick, unemployed, or have little money SYN **welfare** *AmE*: **unemployment/housing/child etc benefit** *You might be entitled to housing benefit.* | **on benefit** *families on benefit | those people eligible to* ***claim benefit***
3 EXTRA THINGS [C usually plural] extra money or other advantages that you get as part of your job or from insurance that you have → **perk**: *We offer an excellent* ***benefits package****. | medical benefits* → FRINGE BENEFIT
4 give sb the benefit of the doubt to accept what someone tells you, even though you think they may be wrong or lying but you cannot be sure: *The referee gave him the benefit of the doubt.*
5 with the benefit of hindsight/experience used to say it is easier to know the right thing to do after something has happened or if you have a lot of experience: *He admitted that, with the benefit of hindsight, the original launch had not been large enough.*
6 benefit concert/performance/match a concert, performance etc arranged to make money for CHARITY: *a benefit concert for famine relief*

COLLOCATIONS

VERBS

have the benefit of sth *All the hotel rooms have the benefit of a balcony.*
get a benefit (*also* **gain/derive a benefit** *formal*) *In this way, students will gain maximum benefit from their classes.*
enjoy the benefits *You'll enjoy all the benefits of being a member.*
reap the benefits (=enjoy the advantages of something you have worked hard to get) *He was looking forward to reaping the benefits of all his hard work.*
bring/provide benefits *The new bridge has brought considerable benefits.*
sth outweighs the benefits (=something is more important than the benefits) *Make sure that the risks don't outweigh the benefits.*

ADJECTIVES/NOUN + benefit

a great/major/substantial benefit *The new system will be a great benefit to the company.*
a real benefit *To get some real benefit from the exercise, you should continue for at least half an hour.*
the full benefit of sth *They will have the full benefit of our facilities.*
economic/social/environmental etc benefits *Tourism has brought considerable economic benefits to the island.*
health benefits | **mutual benefit** (=something good for both people, companies etc involved)

benefit² ●●○ W3 AWL *v* (**benefited, benefiting**) [I,T] if you benefit from something, or it benefits you, it gives you an advantage, improves your life, or helps you in some way: *They are working together to benefit the whole community.* | **[+from/by]** *Many thousands have benefited from the new treatment. | They would benefit by reducing their labour costs.* | **benefit greatly/enormously/considerably etc** *I'm sure you'll benefit greatly from the visit.*

Ben·e·lux /ˈbenəlʌks/ *n* [singular] the countries of Belgium, the Netherlands, and Luxembourg considered as a group

be·nev·o·lent /bəˈnevələnt/ *adj* kind and generous: *A benevolent uncle paid for her to have music lessons. | a benevolent smile* THESAURUS KIND —**benevolence** *n* [U] —**benevolently** *adv*

BEng *BrE*, **B.Eng.** *AmE* /ˌbiː ˈeŋ/ *n* [C] (***Bachelor of Engineering***) a first university DEGREE in ENGINEERING

Ben·ga·li /benˈɡɔːli $ -ˈɡɒːli/ *n* **1** [U] the language used in Bangladesh and West Bengal **2** [C] someone from Bengal —**Bengali** *adj*

be·night·ed /bɪˈnaɪtɪd/ *adj literary* having no knowledge or understanding —**benightedly** *adv*

be·nign /bɪˈnaɪn/ ●○○ *adj*
1 kind and gentle: *He shook his head in benign amusement.*
2 a benign TUMOUR (=unnatural growth in the body) is not caused by CANCER OPP **malignant**

bent¹ /bent/ the past tense and past participle of BEND

bent² *adj* **1** no longer straight: *a bent nail | Stand with your knees slightly bent. | He breathed in deeply,* ***bent double*** *in pain* (=with the top part of your body leaning forward towards your legs). | *a bent old man* (=not standing straight) → see picture at CURVED **2 bent on sth** completely determined to do something, especially something bad: *a crowd of hooligans bent on violence* | **be bent on doing sth** *They seemed bent on destroying his career.* → HELL-BENT **3** *BrE informal* financially dishonest and willing to use your official position unfairly OPP **honest**: *a bent policeman* **4** *BrE informal not polite* an insulting word meaning HOMOSEXUAL **5 bent out of shape** *AmE spoken* very angry or upset

bent³ *n* [singular] *formal* special natural skill or interest in a particular area: **musical/artistic/literary etc bent** *readers of a more literary bent*

ben·zene /ˈbenziːn, benˈziːn/ *n* [U] a liquid obtained from coal, used for making plastics

ben·zine /ˈbenziːn, benˈziːn/ *n* [U] a liquid obtained from PETROLEUM, used to clean clothes

be·queath /bɪˈkwiːð, bɪˈkwiːθ/ *v* [T] **1** to officially arrange for someone to have something that you own after your death SYN **leave**: **bequeath sth to sb** *She bequeathed her collection of paintings to the National Gallery.* | **bequeath sb sth** *His father bequeathed him a fortune.* **2** to pass knowledge, customs etc to people who come after you or live after you

be·quest /bɪˈkwest/ *n* [C] *formal* money or property that you arrange to give to someone after your death: *a bequest of $5,000*

be·rate /bɪˈreɪt/ *v* [T + for] *formal* to speak angrily to someone because they have done something wrong

be·reaved /bəˈriːvd/ *adj* **1** having lost a close friend or relative because they have recently died: *a bereaved mother* **2 the bereaved** the person or people whose close friend or relative has just died: *Our sympathies go to the bereaved.*

be·reave·ment /bəˈriːvmənt/ *n* [C,U] *formal* when someone loses a close friend or relative because they have died: *depression caused by bereavement or divorce*

be·reft /bəˈreft/ *adj* **1 bereft of hope/meaning/life etc** completely without any hope etc: *The team now seems bereft of inspiration.* **2** feeling very sad and lonely: *His death in 1990 left her completely bereft.*

be·ret /ˈbereɪ $ bəˈreɪ/ *n* [C] a round cap with a tight band around the head and a soft loose top part → see picture at HAT

ber·i·ber·i /ˌberiˈberi/ *n* [U] a disease of the nerves caused by lack of VITAMIN B

berk /bɜːk $ bɜːrk/ *n* [C] *BrE informal* a stupid person

Ber·mu·da shorts /bəˌmjuːdə ˈʃɔːts $ bərˌmjuːdə ˈʃɔːrts/ (*also* **Bermudas**) *n* [plural] short trousers that end at the knee

ber·ry /ˈberi/ ●●○ *n* (*plural* **berries**) [C] a small soft fruit with small seeds

ber·serk /bɜːˈsɜːk, bə- $ bɜːrˈsɜːrk, ˈbɜːrsɜːrk/ *adj* **go berserk** *informal* to become very angry and violent: *Dad went berserk when he found out.*

B

berth¹ /bɜːθ $ bɜːrθ/ *n* [C] **1** a place where a ship can stop and be tied up **2** a place for someone to sleep on a ship or on a train SYN **bunk** → **give sb/sth a wide berth** at WIDE¹(7)

berth² *v* [I,T] to bring a ship into a berth, or arrive at a berth

ber·yl /ˈberəl/ *n* [C] a valuable stone that is usually green or yellow

be·seech /bɪˈsiːtʃ/ *v* (*past tense and past participle* **besought** /-ˈsɔːt $ -ˈsɒːt/ *or* **beseeched**) [T] *literary* to eagerly and anxiously ask someone for something SYN **beg**

be·set /bɪˈset/ *v* (*past tense and past participle* **beset**, *present participle* **besetting**) [T] *formal* **1** to make someone experience serious problems or dangers: **be beset with/by sth** *The business has been beset with financial problems.* GRAMMAR **Beset** is usually passive in this meaning. **2 besetting sin** a particular bad feature or habit – often used humorously

be·side /bɪˈsaɪd/ ●●● S3 W2 *prep*
1 next to or very close to the side of someone or something: *Wendy came up and sat beside me.* | *the table beside the bed* | *I was standing* **right beside** *her at the time.* ⚠ Do not confuse **beside** (=next to) and **besides** (=in addition to): *He sat down beside Mary.* | *Who was there besides you?*
2 in comparison with something or someone: *This year's sales figures don't look very good beside last year's results.* | *The children seemed tiny beside him.*
3 be beside yourself to be feeling so angry, excited etc that you find it difficult to control yourself: *The poor girl was almost beside herself.* | **be beside yourself with anger/excitement/rage etc** *Mom and Dad will be beside themselves with worry.*
4 be beside the point to not be directly connected with the main subject or problem that you are talking about: *He's very charming, but that's beside the point.*

be·sides /bɪˈsaɪdz/ ●●○ *adv, prep informal*
1 *spoken* used when adding another reason: *I need the money. And besides, when I agree to do something, I do it.*

> REGISTER
> In written English, people do not usually use **besides** as a sentence adverb. They start a sentence with the more formal **moreover** instead: ***Moreover**, smoking is linked with heart disease and strokes.*

2 in addition to someone or something else that you are mentioning: *The area has stunning scenery, beautiful beaches, and much more besides.* | *People choose jobs for other reasons besides money.* | *Besides myself, the only English people there were Keith and Doreen.* | **besides doing sth** *Besides being heartbroken, she felt foolish.*

be·siege /bɪˈsiːdʒ/ *v* [T] **1** to surround a city or castle with military force until the people inside let you take control → **siege**: *In April 655, Osman's palace was besieged by rebels.* THESAURUS ATTACK **2** if you are besieged by people, you have a lot of them around you: *Miller was besieged by press photographers.* **3 be besieged with letters/demands/requests etc** to receive a very large number of letters, requests etc SYN **be inundated**

be·smirch /bɪˈsmɜːtʃ $ -ɜːrtʃ/ *v* [T] *literary* **besmirch sb's honour/reputation** to spoil the good opinion that people have of someone

be·sot·ted /bɪˈsɒtɪd $ bɪˈsɑː-/ *adj* **be besotted (with sb/sth)** to love or want someone or something so much that you cannot think or behave sensibly: *He's completely besotted with her.*

be·sought /bɪˈsɔːt $ -ˈsɒːt/ the past tense and past participle of BESEECH

be·speak /bɪˈspiːk/ *v* (*past tense* **bespoke** /-ˈspəʊk $ -ˈspoʊk/, *past participle* **bespoken** /-ˈspəʊkən $ -ˈspoʊ-/) [T] *literary* to be a sign of something

be·spec·ta·cled /bɪˈspektəkəld/ *adj formal* wearing glasses

be·spoke /bɪˈspəʊk $ -ˈspoʊk/ *adj BrE* a bespoke product, especially computer software or a piece of clothing, has been specially made for a particular customer: *the cost of development of a bespoke system*

best¹ /best/ ●●● S1 W1 *adj* [superlative of good]
1 better than anything else or anyone else in quality, skill, how effective it is etc: *He won the best actor award.* | *What's the* **best way** *to cook this fish?* | *The* **best thing** *to do is to stop worrying.* | **it's best to do sth** *It's best to go later in the season.* | **easily the best/by far the best** (=much better than anything else) *John's idea is by far the best option.* | *Our pilots are given* **the best possible** *training.* | *We use only* **the very best** *ingredients.*
2 best friend the friend that you know and like better than anyone else: *She was my best friend in college.*
3 best dress/shoes/clothes etc clothing that you keep for special occasions: *I put on my best suit for the wedding.*
4 the next best thing something that is not exactly what you want but is as similar to it as possible: *If sterile equipment isn't available, the next best thing is to clean equipment with disinfectant.*
5 best of all used to introduce the fact about a situation that is even better than the other good things: *It's clean and well-located, but best of all, it's affordable.*
6 best before *BrE* written on food packets with the date that the food should be eaten before: *Best before 13 July.* | *a best-before date* → **be on your best behaviour** at BEHAVIOUR(2), → **your best bet** at BET²(2), → **the best/better part of** at PART¹(6)

best² ●●● S1 W2 *adv* [superlative of well]
1 in a way that is better than any other: *It works best if you let it warm up first.* | *This can best be described as a series of steps.* | *the best-dressed man in Paris*
2 to the greatest degree SYN **most**: *You know him best – you should ask him.* | *The part I like best is the meal afterwards.* | *He's perhaps* **best known** *for his role in 'Midnight Cowboy'.*
3 as best you can *spoken* as well as you can, even if this is not very good: *I'll try and fix it as best I can.*
4 had best *spoken* ought to: *We'd best be getting back.* → **had better** at BETTER²(3)

best³ ●●● S2 W2 *n*
1 the best a) the most helpful, most successful etc situation or results that you can achieve: *We all want the best for our children.* | *It's the best we can do in the circumstances.* **b)** the person or thing that is better than any other: *She's the best of the new young writers.*
2 do your best to try as hard as you can to do something: *As long as you do your best, we'll be happy.* | **do your best to do sth** *She did her best to make him comfortable.*
3 at best used to emphasize that something is not very good, pleasant, honest etc even if you consider it in the best possible way: *The campaign was at best only partially successful.* | *The technique is at best ineffective and at worst dangerous.*
4 to the best of your knowledge/belief/ability etc used to say that something is as much as you know, believe, or are able to do: *I'm sure he'll do the work to the best of his ability.*
5 the best of sth used to refer to something very good: *We wish him* **the best of luck** *with this venture.* | *He hasn't been* **in the best of health** *lately.* | *They didn't part* **on the best of terms**. | *They became* **the best of friends** (=very close friends).
6 with the best of intentions/for the best of reasons used to

mean that someone does something with good intentions or for good reasons, even if the result is not always good: *I'm sure he went there with the best of intentions.*
7 the best of both worlds a situation in which you have the advantages of two different things without any of the disadvantages: *They live in a village but it's only an hour from London, so they have the best of both worlds.*
8 at your best performing as well or effectively as you are able to: *At her best, she's a really stylish player.* | *He was never at his best early in the morning.*
9 make the best of sth (*also* **make the best of a bad job/situation etc** *BrE*) to accept a situation that is not very good, and do whatever you can to make it better: *We are stuck here, so we might as well make the best of it.*
10 all the best used to express good wishes to someone for the future: *We'd just like to* ***wish*** *him* ***all the best*** *in his new job.* | **[+for]** *All the best for the New Year!*
11 at the best of times if something is not very good, pleasant etc at the best of times, it is usually even worse than this: *It's crowded at the best of times, but today it was unbearable.*
12 the best of a bad lot/bunch *BrE* the least bad person or thing in a group of not very good people or things
13 be for the best *especially spoken* used to say that a particular event may seem bad now, but might have a good result later: *I still don't want him to go, but maybe it's for the best.*
14 your Sunday best *old-fashioned* your best clothes, that you only wear on special occasions

best[4] *v* [T] *old-fashioned* to defeat someone

bes·ti·al /ˈbestiəl $ ˈbestʃəl/ *adj literary* behaving like an animal, especially in a cruel way: *bestial and barbaric acts* —**bestially** *adv*

bes·ti·al·i·ty /ˌbestiˈæləti $ ˌbestʃi-/ *n* [U] **1** sexual relations between a person and an animal **2** *formal* very cruel behaviour

bes·ti·ar·y /ˈbestiəri $ ˈbestʃieri/ *n* (*plural* **bestiaries**) [C] an old book about strange animals, written in the Middle Ages

ˌbest ˈman *n* [singular] the man who helps the BRIDEGROOM at a wedding ceremony

be·stow /bɪˈstəʊ $ -ˈstoʊ/ *v* [T] *formal* to give someone something of great value or importance: **bestow sth on/upon sb** *honours bestowed on him by the Queen*

ˌbest ˈpractice *n* [C,U] a description of the best way of performing a particular activity, especially in business, that can be used by other people or companies as a set of rules to follow

ˌbest-ˈsel·ler, **best·sell·er** /ˌbestˈselə $ -ər/ *n* [C] a popular product, especially a book, that many people buy: *His new book went straight to number one on the* ***best-seller list***. | *The game is already a bestseller in Japan.* —**best-selling** *adj* [only before noun]: *a best-selling author* | *the UK's best-selling album*

best·y /ˈbesti/ *n* [C] *informal* a best friend

Frequencies of the verb **bet** in spoken and written English.

SPOKEN

WRITTEN

50 100 per million

This graph shows that the verb **bet** is much more common in spoken English than in written English. This is because it is used in some common spoken phrases.

bet[1] /bet/ ●●● S1 *v* (*past tense and past participle* **bet**, *present participle* **betting**)
1 [I,T] to risk money on the result of a race, game, competition, or other future event → **gamble**: *How much do you want to bet?* | **bet (sb) that** *He bet me £10 that I wouldn't do it.* | **bet (sth) on sth** *She bet all her money on a horse that came last.* | **[+against]** *I wouldn't bet against him winning the championship this year.*
2 I bet/I'll bet *spoken* **a)** used to say that you are fairly sure that something is true, something is happening etc, although you cannot prove this: *Bet you wish you'd arrived earlier.* | *I bet you she won't come.* **b)** used to show that you understand or can imagine the situation that someone has just told you about: *'God, I was so angry.' 'I bet you were.'* | *'It makes things much easier.' 'Yeah, I'll bet it does.'* **c)** used to show that you do not believe what someone has just told you: *'I'm definitely going to give up smoking this time.' 'Yeah, I bet!'*
3 you bet! *spoken* used to emphasize that you agree with someone or are keen to do what they suggest: *'Going to the party on Saturday?' 'You bet!'*
4 (do you) want to bet?/wanna bet? *spoken* used to say that you think something that someone has just said is not true or not likely to happen: *'I'm sure Tom'll be here soon.' 'Wanna bet?'*
5 don't bet on it/I wouldn't bet on it *spoken* used to say that you do not think something is likely to happen: *He said he'd finish by tomorrow, but I wouldn't bet on it.*
6 you (can) bet your life/your bottom dollar *spoken* used when you are sure that you know what someone will do or what will happen: *You can bet your bottom dollar he won't be back.*
7 bet the farm/ranch *AmE informal* to risk everything that you own: *Do we really want to bet the ranch on this deal?*

bet[2] ●●● S3 *n* [C]
1 an agreement to risk money on the result of a race, game etc or on something happening, or the money that you risk: *a £50 bet* | **[+on]** *A few of us* ***had*** *a* ***bet*** *on who'd get married first.* | **place/put/lay a bet** *We placed bets on three horses.* | *Bookmakers are already* ***taking bets*** *on the outcome.* | **win/lose a bet** *If he scores now, I'll win my bet.*
2 your best bet *spoken* used when advising someone what to do: *Your best bet is to put an advert in the local newspaper.* | *The train might be a better bet.*
3 a good/safe bet an action or situation that is likely to be successful or does not involve much risk: *If you're looking for long-term growth, the government's own saving certificates are a pretty good bet.* → **hedge your bets** at HEDGE[2](2)
4 it's a safe/sure/fair bet (that) *spoken* used to say that something seems almost certain: *I think it's a pretty safe bet that he'll get the job.*
5 my bet *spoken* used when saying what you expect to happen in the future: *My bet is he'll be back this time next week.*
6 do sth for a bet to do something stupid, dangerous etc to win money from someone or to prove that you can do it: *He climbed the tree for a bet.*

be·ta /ˈbiːtə $ ˈbeɪtə/ *n* [singular] the second letter of the Greek alphabet, β or B

ˈbeta-ˌblock·er *n* [C] a drug used to help prevent HEART ATTACKS

ˈbeta ˌparticle *n* [C] *technical* an ELECTRON or POSITRON that is sent out by some RADIOACTIVE substances

ˈbeta ˌtest *n* [C] *technical* a test of software in which it is given to customers to use, so that any problems will be found → **alpha test**

ˈbeta ˌversion *n* [C] *technical* software that is being tested by people who will use it, to see if it works properly → **alpha version**

be·tel /ˈbiːtl/ *n* [U] a plant whose leaves have a fresh taste, and that some people chew, especially in Asia

ˈbetel nut *n* [C,U] small pieces of red nut with a bitter taste, that are wrapped in a betel leaf and chewed

bête noire /ˌbet ˈnwɑː $ -ˈnwɑːr/ *n* [singular] **sb's bête noire** the person or thing that someone dislikes most

be·tide /bɪˈtaɪd/ *v* **woe betide sb** used to say that someone will be in trouble if they do something – often humorous: *Woe betide anyone who wakes the baby!*

be·to·ken /bɪˈtəʊkən $ -ˈtoʊ-/ *v* [T] *literary* to be a sign of something

be·tray /bɪˈtreɪ/ ●●○ *v* [T]
1 FRIENDS to be disloyal to someone who trusts you, so that they are harmed or upset: *He felt that she had betrayed him.* | **betray sb to sb** *What kind of man would*

betray his own sister to the police? | *She had* ***betrayed*** *her parents'* ***trust***. | *I would never* ***betray*** *a* ***confidence*** (=tell a secret that someone has trusted me with).
2 COUNTRY to be disloyal to your country, company etc, for example by giving secret information to its enemies: *people who betray their country for money*
3 EMOTIONS to show feelings that you are trying to hide SYN **give away**: *His voice betrayed his nervousness.* | *His face* ***betrayed nothing*** (=showed no emotion).
4 TRUTH to show that something is true or exists, especially when it is not easily noticed SYN **give away**: *The slightest sound might* ***betray his presence***. | *The crumpled sheets* ***betrayed the fact that*** *someone had been sleeping there.*
5 betray your beliefs/principles/ideals etc to stop supporting your old beliefs and principles, especially in order to get power or avoid trouble —**betrayer** *n* [C]

be·tray·al /bɪˈtreɪəl/ ●○○ *n* [C,U] when you betray your country, friends, or someone who trusts you: **[+of]** *a ruthless betrayal of their election pledges* | *She felt a great* ***sense of betrayal***.

be·troth·al /bɪˈtrəʊðəl $ -ˈtroʊ-/ *n* [C] *old-fashioned* an agreement that two people will be married SYN **engagement**

be·trothed¹ /bɪˈtrəʊðd $ -ˈtroʊðd/ *adj old-fashioned* **be betrothed to sb** to have promised to marry someone —**betroth** *v* [T]

betrothed² *n* **sb's betrothed** the person that someone has agreed to marry

bet·ter¹ /ˈbetə $ -ər/ ●●● S1 W1 *adj*
1 [comparative of good] more useful, interesting, satisfactory, effective, suitable etc OPP **worse**: *Your stereo is better than mine.* | *There must be a better way to do this.* | *a better-quality car* | **much/a lot/far better** *We now have a much better understanding of the disease.* | **better still/even better** *It was even better than last year.* ⚠ **Better** is a comparative form. Don't say 'more better'.
2 [comparative of well] **a)** more healthy or less ill or painful than before OPP **worse**: *She is a little better today, the doctor says.* | *I'm* ***feeling*** *much* ***better****, thank you.* **b)** completely well again after an illness: *When you're better we can see about planning a trip.* | *I hope he* ***gets better*** (=recovers from an illness) *soon.* THESAURUS ▸ HEALTHY
3 it is better/it would be better used to give your opinion or make a suggestion about what you think should be done or happen: **it is better to do sth** *It's much better to get a proper written agreement.* | **[+if]** *It might be better if you stayed here.*
4 get better to improve: *Her English isn't really getting any better.* | *Things can only get better.*
5 no better a) not better than something else or something before: *The following day the weather was no better.* **b)** used to say that something is the best: **there is no better way/example/place etc** *There's no better way of exploring the region.*
6 nothing better a) used to say that you really like something or think that something is very good: **like/love/enjoy nothing better (than)** *She likes nothing better than a nice long walk along the beach.* | *There's nothing better than beating someone who's playing well.* **b)** used to say that a thing or situation is not very good, but is the only thing possible or available: **have nothing better to do** *Have you got nothing better to do than sit there playing that silly game?* | *I only picked it up because there was nothing better to read.*
7 that's better *spoken* used to say that something has improved, that you are happier or more comfortable, or to encourage someone: *Ah, that's better. I needed to sit down.* | *'Can you turn it down?' 'Is that better?'*
8 better late than never *spoken* used to say that it is better for someone or something to be late than never to arrive or happen at all → **your better half/other half** at HALF²(8), → **the best/better part of sth** at PART¹(9), → **against your better judgment** at JUDGMENT(1), → **sb's better nature** at NATURE(2), → **better luck next time** at LUCK¹(14), → **better the devil you know** at DEVIL(11), → **have seen better days** at SEE¹(29)

THESAURUS

better the COMPARATIVE of good: *She wants a better job.* | *The sales figures were far better than expected.*
superior better, especially in quality: *German cars are far superior.* | *a superior product* | *He thinks men are superior to women.*
preferable *formal* more suitable or useful – used when saying which one you prefer: *Cash would be preferable.*
be an improvement on sth to be better than something that existed before: *The engine is a huge improvement on previous diesel engines.*
have the edge to be slightly better than another person or thing – used especially when saying which one will win in a game or competition: *Federer is likely to have the edge in Sunday's game.* | *For me, this film has the edge over the others.*
be miles ahead (of sb/sth) (*also* **be streets ahead (of sb/sth)** *BrE*) *informal* to be very much better than someone or something that you are competing against: *The company is streets ahead of its rivals.*
there's no comparison *spoken* used to emphasize that one person or thing is clearly much better than someone or something else: *There's no comparison between the two teams.*

better² ●●● S1 W1 *adv* [comparative of well]
1 to a higher standard or quality OPP **worse**: *He can speak French a lot better than I can.* | *Your bike will run better if you oil it.* → **fare better** at FARE²
2 to a higher degree SYN **more**: *She knows this town better than you do.* | *I think I like the red one better.* | *Potter is* ***better known*** *for his TV work.*
3 had better a) used to give advice about what someone should do, or to say what you should do or need to do: *I'd better go and get ready.* | *I think you'd better ask Jo first.* | *You* ***had better not*** *tell Oliver* (=it is not a good idea). **b)** used to threaten someone: *You'd better keep your mouth shut about this.* ⚠ In speech, people usually shorten **had** to **'d**, and may not pronounce it at all. But do not leave out **had** or **'d** in writing: *You'd better (NOT You better) come here!*
4 do better to perform better or reach a higher standard: *We did better than all the other schools.*
5 the sooner the better/the bigger the better etc used to emphasize that you would prefer something to happen as soon as possible, want something to be as big as possible etc: *School finishes at the end of the week, and the sooner the better as far as I'm concerned.* | *The younger you start learning a language, the better you'll speak it.*
6 go one better (than sb) *informal* to do something more successfully than someone else: *The following year Lewis went one better by winning the gold medal.* | *Of course, they had to go one better and have the whole garden redesigned.* → BETTER OFF

better³ ●●○ *n*
1 the better the one that is higher in quality, more suitable etc when you are comparing two similar people or things: *It's hard to decide which one's the better.*
2 get the better of sb a) if your feelings or wishes get the better of you, they make you behave in a way you would not normally behave: *My curiosity finally got the better of me and I opened the letter.* | *I think her nerves got the better of her.* **b)** to defeat someone or deal successfully with a problem
3 for the better in a way that improves the situation: *a definite* ***change for the better*** | *The president's fortunes seem, at last, to have* ***taken a turn for the better*** (=started to improve).
4 so much the better used to say that something would be even better or bring even more advantages: *If they can do them both at the same time, then so much the better.*
5 be all the better for sth to be improved by a particular

action, change etc: *I think it's all the better for that extra ten minutes' cooking.*
6 for better or (for) worse used to say that something must be accepted, whether it is good or bad, because it cannot be changed: *Work is, for better or worse, becoming more flexible nowadays.*
7 your betters *old-fashioned* people who are more important than you or deserve more respect → WORSE³, → **elders and betters** at ELDER²(2)

better⁴ *v* [T] **1** to be higher in quality, amount etc than someone or something else: *His total of five gold medals is unlikely to be bettered.* **2 better yourself** to improve your position in society by getting a better education or earning more money **3** *formal* to improve something: *bettering the lot of the working classes*

bet·ter·ment /ˈbetəmənt $ -tər-/ *n* [singular] *formal* improvement, especially in someone's social and economic position: **for the betterment of sb/sth** *social change for the betterment of society as a whole*

ˌbetter ˈoff *adj* [no comparative] **1** having more money than someone else or than you had before OPP **worse off**: *She'll be about £50 a week better off.* → WELL-OFF(1) **2** happier, improved, more successful etc OPP **worse off**: **[+with/without]** *I think she's better off without him.* | **be better off doing sth** (=used to give advice or an opinion) *He'd be better off starting with something simpler.*

bet·ting /ˈbetɪŋ/ *n* **1** [U] when people risk money on the results of games, competitions etc or other future events → **gambling 2 what's the betting** (*also* **the betting is** *BrE*) used to say that something seems very likely to happen or to be true: *What's the betting Dan's involved in this somewhere?*

ˈbetting ˌshop *n* [C] a place in Britain where people go to place BETs on the results of races, competitions etc SYN **bookmaker's**

ˌBetty ˌFord ˈClinic, the an expensive hospital in the US where rich or famous people go for treatment to help them stop drinking too much alcohol or taking illegal drugs. Its official name is the Betty Ford Center.

be·tween /bɪˈtwiːn/ ●●● S1 W1 *adv, prep*
1 (*also* **in between**) in or through the space that separates two things, people, or places: *I sat down between Sue and Jane.* | *a house and stables, with a yard in between* | *The ball rolled between his feet.*
2 (*also* **in between**) in the time that separates two times or events: *Are there any public holidays between Christmas and Easter?* | *You shouldn't eat between meals.* | *The team have a lot of work to do between now and Sunday.* | *A lot of students spend a year abroad in between school and university.* | *I've had a few jobs, with long periods of unemployment in between.*
3 within a range of amounts, numbers, distances etc: *The project will cost between eight and ten million dollars.* | *Most of the victims were young men between the ages of 16 and 21.*
4 used to say which two places are joined or connected by something: *They're building a new road between Manchester and Sheffield.*
5 used to say which people or things are involved in something together or are connected: *the long-standing friendship between Bob and Bryan* | *co-operation between the two countries* | *She had overheard a private conversation between two MPs.* | *the link between serious sunburn and deadly skin cancer*
6 used to say which people or things get, have, or are involved in something that is shared: *Tom divided his money between his children.* | *Between the four of them they managed to lift her into the ambulance.* | *We collected £17 between us.*
7 used to say which two things or people you are comparing: *the contrast between town and country life* | *In her book she makes a comparison between Russian and British ballet.* | *the difference between good music and really great music*
8 between you and me (*also* **between ourselves**) *spoken* used before telling someone something that you do not want them to tell anyone else: *Between you and me, I think Schmidt's about to resign.*
9 come between sb if something comes between two people, it causes an argument or problems between them: *I let my stupid pride come between us.*
10 used when it is difficult to give an exact description of something and you therefore have to compare it to two things that are similar to it: *He uttered a sound that was something between a sigh and a groan.*

be·twixt /bɪˈtwɪkst/ *prep* **1** *literary* between **2 betwixt and between** *old-fashioned* not quite belonging to one group or to another

bev·el /ˈbevəl/ *n* [C] **1** a sloping edge or surface, usually along the edge of a piece of wood or glass **2** a tool for making this kind of edge or surface —**bevelled** *adj*: *bevelled glass*

bev·er·age /ˈbevərɪdʒ/ ●○○ *n* [C] *formal* a hot or cold drink: *alcoholic beverages* | *the Food and Beverage Manager* THESAURUS DRINK

bev·vied up /ˌbevid ˈʌp/ *adj* [not before noun] *BrE informal* drunk: *We're all going out to* ***get bevvied up****.*

bev·vy /ˈbevi/ *n* (*plural* **bevvies**) [C] *BrE informal* a drink, especially an alcoholic drink

bev·y /ˈbevi/ *n* [singular] a large group of people of the same kind, especially girls or young women: **[+of]** *a bevy of beauties*

be·wail /bɪˈweɪl/ *v* [T] *literary* to express deep sadness or disappointment about something

be·ware /bɪˈweə $ -ˈwer/ ●○○ *v* [I,T only in imperative and infinitive] used to warn someone to be careful because something is dangerous: **[+of]** *Beware of the dog!* | **beware of doing sth** *They should beware of making hasty decisions.* | *Police warned drivers to beware.*

be·wil·der /bɪˈwɪldə $ -ər/ *v* [T] to confuse someone: *He was bewildered by his daughter's reaction.* GRAMMAR **Bewilder** is usually passive.

be·wil·dered /bɪˈwɪldəd $ -ərd/ ●○○ *adj* totally confused: *a bewildered expression on his face* THESAURUS CONFUSED

be·wil·der·ing /bɪˈwɪldərɪŋ/ ●○○ *adj* confusing, especially because there are too many choices or things happening at the same time: **a bewildering variety/array/range** *a bewildering variety of choices* —**bewilderingly** *adv*: *The details are bewilderingly complex.*

be·wil·der·ment /bɪˈwɪldəmənt $ -dər-/ *n* [U] a feeling of being very confused SYN **confusion**: **in bewilderment** *She looked at him in bewilderment.*

be·witch /bɪˈwɪtʃ/ *v* [T] **1** to make someone feel so interested or attracted that they cannot think clearly: *Tim is utterly bewitched by her.* **2** to get control over someone by putting a magic SPELL on them —**bewitching** *adj*: *a bewitching smile*

be·yond¹ /bɪˈjɒnd $ -ˈjɑːnd/ ●●● S2 W1 *prep, adv*
1 on or to the further side of something: *They crossed the mountains and headed for the valleys beyond.* | *Beyond the river, cattle were grazing.* | *She drove through Westport, and stopped a few miles beyond at a wayside inn.*
2 later than a particular time, date etc SYN **after**: *What changes await us in the coming year and beyond?* | *The ban has been extended beyond 2003.* | *The disco went on until beyond midnight.*
3 more or greater than a particular amount, level, or limit: *More people are choosing to work beyond retirement age.* | *Inflation has risen beyond the 5% level.*
4 outside the range or limits of something or someone: *Such tasks are* ***far beyond*** *the scope of the average schoolkid.* | *expensive luxuries that are beyond the reach of ordinary people*
5 used to say that something is impossible to do: **beyond repair/control/belief etc** (=impossible to repair, control, believe etc) *Scott's equipment was damaged beyond repair.* | *The town centre had changed beyond all recognition.* | *Due to circumstances beyond our control, the performance has had to be cancelled.*
6 be beyond sb to be too difficult for someone to understand: *The whole problem was quite beyond him.* | *Why Joan ever married such an idiot in the first place is beyond me.*

B

7 used to mean 'except' in negative sentences: *Fred owns nothing beyond the clothes on his back.*

beyond² *n* **the beyond** *literary* whatever comes after this life

bez·zie /ˈbezi/ *n* [C] *BrE informal* a best friend: *I didn't like her then but now we're bezzies.* —**bezzie** *adj* [only before noun]: *Me and my bezzie mate are going on holiday next week.*

B

BF /biː ˈef/ *n* [C] **1** the abbreviation of ***best friend*** – used by young people and in magazines **2** the abbreviation of ***boyfriend*** – used by young people and in magazines

BFF /ˌbiː ef ˈef/ *n* [C] *informal* (***best friend forever***) someone's best friend – used especially by young people, in magazines, and in emails: *It's my BFF's birthday tomorrow.*

bha·ji, **bhajee** /ˈbɑːdʒiː/ *n* [C] a hot-tasting Indian vegetable cake cooked in BATTER (=a liquid mixture of flour, egg, and milk or water): *onion bhajis*

bhan·gra /ˈbʌŋgrə/ *n* [U] a type of music that is a mixture of Punjabi traditional music and Western popular music

bi- /baɪ/ *prefix* two, twice, or double → **semi-**, **di-**, **tri-**: *bilingual* (=speaking two languages) | *to bisect* (=cut in two)

bi·an·nu·al /baɪˈænjuəl/ *adj* happening twice each year: *a biannual report* → **annual**, **biennial**

bi·as¹ /ˈbaɪəs/ ●○○ AWL *n*

1 [singular, U] an opinion about whether a person, group, or idea is good or bad that influences how you deal with it → **discrimination**: **political/gender/racial etc bias** *political bias in the press* | *Students were evaluated without bias.* | **[+against/towards/in favour of]** *It's clear that the company has a bias against women and minorities.*

2 [singular] a natural skill or interest in one type of thing: *Lydia has a strong artistic bias.*

3 on the bias in a DIAGONAL direction

bias² AWL *v* [T] to unfairly influence attitudes, choices, or decisions: *Several factors could have biased the results of the study.*

bi·ased, **biassed** /ˈbaɪəst/ ●○○ AWL *adj*

1 unfairly preferring one person or group over another: *Of course I'm biased, but I thought my daughter's paintings were the best.* | *racially biased attitudes* | **[+against/towards/in favour of]** *news reporting that was* ***heavily biased*** *towards the government*

2 more interested in a particular thing than in another: **[+towards]** *The majority of infants are biased towards being social rather than being antisocial.*

bi·ath·lon /baɪˈæθlən $ -lɑːn, -lən/ *n* [C] a sports competition in which competitors SKI across fields and then shoot a RIFLE → **decathlon**, **pentathlon**

bib /bɪb/ *n* [C] **1** a piece of cloth or plastic tied under a baby's chin to protect its clothes when it is eating **2** the part of an APRON, DUNGAREES, or OVERALLS that covers your chest **3 your best bib and tucker** your best clothes – used humorously

bi·ble, **Bible** /ˈbaɪbəl/ *n* **1 the Bible** the holy book of the Christian religion, consisting of the OLD TESTAMENT and the NEW TESTAMENT **2** [C] a copy of the bible **3** [singular] *informal* the most useful and important book on a particular subject: *It's the anatomy student's bible!*

ˈbible-ˌbasher *n* [C] *BrE informal* a Christian who believes very strongly in what the Bible says and tries to get other people to accept the Bible too – used to show disapproval —**bible-bashing** *adj*

ˈBible Belt, the an area in the south of the US known for its very religious Christian people who follow the teachings of the Bible very strictly

bib·li·cal /ˈbɪblɪkəl/ *adj* [usually before noun] **1** relating to or written in the Bible: *The disease dates back to* ***biblical times.*** | **biblical story/text/reference** *the biblical story of Noah* **2 of biblical proportions** a bad situation or event that is of biblical proportions is very great or severe: *This could result in an environmental disaster of biblical proportions.*

bib·li·og·ra·phy /ˌbɪbliˈɒgrəfi $ -ˈɑːg-/ ●○○ *n* (*plural* **bibliographies**) [C]

1 a list of all the books and articles used in preparing a piece of writing

2 a list of books and articles that are all about a particular subject —**bibliographer** *n* [C]

bib·li·o·phile /ˈbɪbliəfaɪl/ *n* [C] *formal* someone who likes books

bib·u·lous /ˈbɪbjələs/ *adj formal* liking to drink too much alcohol – sometimes used humorously

bi·cam·er·al /baɪˈkæmərəl/ *adj* [only before noun] *technical* a bicameral LEGISLATURE (=part of the government that makes laws) consists of two parts, such as the Senate and the House of Representatives in the US Congress → **unicameral**

bi·car·bon·ate of so·da /baɪˌkɑːbənət əv ˈsəʊdə, -bəneɪt- $ -ˌkɑːr-, -ˈsoʊdə/ (*also* **bicarbonate**, **bi·carb** *informal* /ˈbaɪkɑːb $ -kɑːrb/) *n* [U] *informal* a chemical substance used especially in baking, and sometimes taken with water as a medicine SYN **baking soda**

bi·cen·te·na·ry /ˌbaɪsenˈtiːnəri $ -ˈtenəri, -ˈsentəneri/ *n* (*plural* **bicentenaries**) [C] *especially BrE* the day or year exactly 200 years after an important event → **centenary**: **[+of]** *the bicentenary of Mozart's death* —**bicentenary** *adj* [only before noun]

bi·cen·ten·ni·al /ˌbaɪsenˈteniəl/ *n* [C] *AmE* the day or year exactly 200 years after an important event: *the bicentennial of the Declaration of Independence* —**bicentennial** *adj*: *bicentennial celebrations*

bi·cep /ˈbaɪsep/ *n* [C usually plural] the large muscle on the front of your upper arm: *He had an eagle tattoo on one of his biceps.*

bick·er /ˈbɪkə $ -ər/ *v* [I] to argue, especially about something very unimportant: *I wish you two would stop bickering.* | **[+about/over]** *They kept bickering over who should answer the phone.* —**bickering** *n* [U]

bi·cy·cle¹ /ˈbaɪsɪkəl/ ●●● W3 *n* [C] a vehicle with two wheels that you ride by pushing its PEDALS with your feet SYN **bike**: *Can James* ***ride a bicycle*** *yet?* → **EXERCISE BIKE**

GRAMMAR: Patterns with bicycle

- You say **get on your bicycle**: *She got on her bicycle and rode away.*
- You say **get off your bicycle**: *I stopped and got off my bicycle.*
- You say that someone is **on a bicycle**: *I saw her out on her bicycle.*
- You go somewhere **by bicycle**: *Can you get to work by bicycle?* ✗ Don't say: *Can you get to work with bicycle?*

bicycle² *v* [I always + adv/prep] *formal* to go somewhere by bicycle SYN **bike**, **cycle** —**bicyclist** *n* [C]

ˈbicycle ˌshorts *n* [plural] *especially AmE* CYCLING SHORTS

bid¹ /bɪd/ ●●○ W3 *n* [C]

1 an offer to pay a particular price for something, especially at an AUCTION: **[+for]** *They put in a bid for the house.* | *the person who places* ***the highest bid*** | *We've* ***made a bid*** *of nearly £400 million for the company.* | *A* ***takeover bid*** *for the airline was launched today.*

2 an offer to do work or provide services for a specific price: **[+for]** *rival bids for the cleaning contract*

3 an attempt to achieve or obtain something: **[+for]** *a bid for power* | **a bid to do sth** *a desperate bid to free herself from a loveless marriage*

4 a statement of how many points you hope to win in a card game

bid² ●●○ *v* (*past tense and past participle* **bid**, *present participle* **bidding**)

1 [I,T] to offer to pay a particular price for goods, especially in an AUCTION: **bid (sb) sth for sth** *She bid £100 for a Victorian chair.* | *What am I bid for lot 227? Shall we start at $500?* | **[+against]** *The two men ended up bidding against each other at the auction.*

2 [I] to offer to do work or provide services for a specific

price, in competition with others offers: **[+for]** *Three firms bid for the contract on the new buildings.*
3 [I,T] to say how many points you think you will win in a game of cards

bid³ *v* (*past tense* **bade** /bæd, beɪd/ *or* **bid**, *past participle* **bid** *or* **bidden** /ˈbɪdn/, *present participle* **bidding**) *literary* **1 bid sb good afternoon/good morning etc** to greet someone **2** [T] to order or tell someone what to do: **bid sb (to) do sth** *The queen bade us enter.*

bid·da·ble /ˈbɪdəbəl/ *adj* willing to do what you are told without arguing

bid·der /ˈbɪdə $ -ər/ ●○○ *n* [C]
1 someone who offers to pay a particular amount of money for something that is being sold: *The antiques will be sold to the* ***highest bidder*** (=the person who offers to pay the most).
2 someone who offers to do work or provide services for a particular amount of money, in competition with others: *one of 13 bidders for the contract*

bid·ding /ˈbɪdɪŋ/ *n* [U] **1** when you BID for goods, especially in an AUCTION: *The bidding was brisk and sales went well.* **2 at sb's bidding** *formal* because someone has told you to **3 do sb's bidding** *formal* to obey someone's requests or orders

bid·dy /ˈbɪdi/ *n* (*plural* **biddies**) **old biddy** *informal* an old woman, especially one who is unpleasant or annoying

bide /baɪd/ *v* **1 bide your time** to wait until the right moment to do something: *They are stronger than us and can afford to bide their time.* **2** [I] *old use* to wait or stay somewhere, often for a long time SYN **abide**

bi·det /ˈbiːdeɪ $ bɪˈdeɪ/ *n* [C] a small low bath that you sit on to wash your bottom

bi·en·ni·al /baɪˈeniəl/ *adj* **1** a biennial event happens once every two years → **annual 2** a biennial plant stays alive for two years → **annual**, **perennial** —**biennially** *adv*

bier /bɪə $ bɪr/ *n* [C] a frame like a table, on which a dead body or COFFIN is placed

biff¹ /bɪf/ *v* **1** [T] *old-fashioned informal* to hit someone hard with your FIST SYN **thump**: *He biffed me on the nose.* **2** [I] *informal* to fall or hit something when riding a bicycle, SNOWBOARD etc

biff² *n* [C] *informal* an embarrassing mistake

bi·fo·cals /baɪˈfəʊkəlz $ ˈbaɪfoʊ-/ *n* [plural] special glasses with an upper part made for seeing things that are far away, and a lower part made for reading —**bifocal** *adj*

bi·fur·cate /ˈbaɪfəkeɪt $ -ər-/ *v* [I] *formal* if a road, river etc bifurcates, it divides into two separate parts SYN **fork** —**bifurcation** /ˌbaɪfəˈkeɪʃən $ -fər-/ *n* [C,U]

big¹ /bɪg/ ●●● S1 W1 *adj* (*comparative* **bigger**, *superlative* **biggest**)
1 SIZE of more than average size or amount: *a big house* | *I need a bigger desk.* | *She had a big grin on her face.* | *a big increase in crime* | *Los Angeles is the biggest city in California.* | *The garage isn't big enough for two cars.* | *When they lose, they lose* ***in a big way*** (=to a large degree). | *There was this* ***great big*** (=extremely big) *spider in the sink.* THESAURUS FAT
2 IMPORTANT important and serious: *a big decision* | *Buying your own house is a big commitment.* | *The big game is on Friday.* | *There's a* ***big difference*** *between understanding something and being able to explain it to others.* | *Everyone was getting ready for the* ***big day*** (=a day when an important event will happen). THESAURUS IMPORTANT
3 POPULAR/SUCCESSFUL successful or popular, especially in business or entertainment: *Julia Roberts became a big star.* | *She's very big in Australia.* | *After years as a small-time actor, he suddenly* ***made it big*** (=became very successful) *in Hollywood.* | **the big boys** (=the most powerful people or companies) → **BIG CHEESE**, **BIG NOISE**, → **big shot** at **SHOT¹**(14), → **BIG TIME¹**

BICYCLE

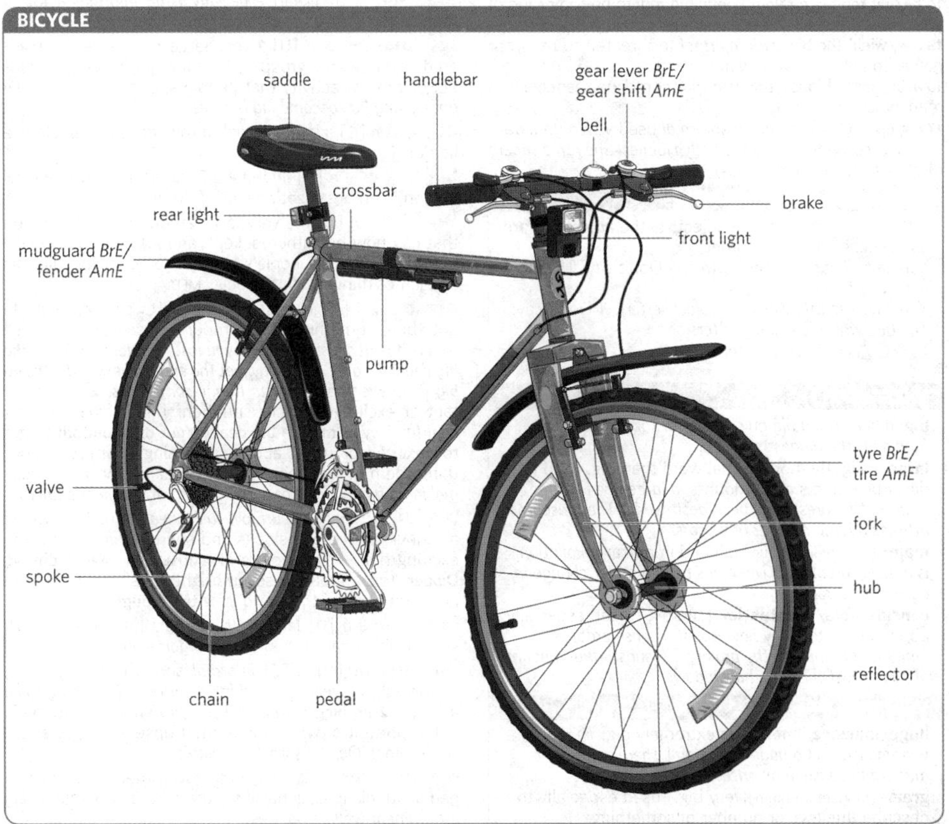

4 OLDER **a) big sister/brother** your older sister or brother **b)** older or more like an adult – used especially by children or when you are talking to children: *Come on, don't cry. You're a big girl now.*
5 LARGE DEGREE [only before noun] *informal* **a)** doing something to a large degree: **a big eater/drinker/spender etc** *Des is a big gambler, you know.* | **be a big fan/admirer of sb/sth** **b)** done to a large degree or with great energy: **give sb a big hug/kiss** *Mama gave me a big hug.* | **give sb a big hand** (=hit your hands together with enthusiasm, to show you have enjoyed a performance)
6 BAD [only before noun] *informal* used to emphasize how bad something is: *AIDS remains a* **big problem** *in many parts of the world.* | *Buying that house was a* **big mistake**. | *I never said that, you big liar!*
7 have big ideas/plans to have impressive plans for the future: *I've got big plans for this place.*
8 be big on sth *spoken* **a)** to like something very much: *I'm not big on kids.* **b)** to have a lot of a quality or feature: *The new BMW is big on safety features.*
9 what's the big idea? *spoken* used when someone has done something annoying, especially when you want them to explain why they did it: *Hey, what's the big idea? Who said you could use my computer?*
10 GENEROUS **it is big of sb to do sth** *spoken* **a)** used to say that someone is very kind or generous to do something **b)** used when you really think that someone is not kind or helpful at all: *£5! That was big of her!*
11 big mouth *spoken* someone who has a big mouth cannot be trusted to keep things secret: *I'm sorry. I shouldn't have opened my big mouth.* | **me and my big mouth** (=said when you wish you had not told someone a secret) → BIGMOUTH
12 LETTERS *informal* big letters are CAPITALS, for example G, R, A etc
13 WORDS *informal* big words are long or unusual and are difficult to read or understand
14 be/get too big for your boots *informal* to be too proud of yourself
15 use/wield the big stick *informal* to threaten to use your power to get what you want
16 a big girl's blouse *BrE informal* someone, especially a man, who is not brave
17 big up (to/for) sb *spoken informal* used when you want to praise someone: *Big up to Kelly Holmes! She ran a superb race.* → **think big** at THINK[1](39)

GRAMMAR: Order of adjectives

If there is more than one adjective, the adjectives are usually used in a fixed order.
You say: *That's a lovely big tree.* ✗ Don't say: *That's a big lovely tree.*
You say: *The title was in big black letters.* ✗ Don't say: *The title was in black big letters.*
GRAMMAR GUIDE ADJECTIVES

THESAURUS

big: *a big city | a big guy | a big mistake | Lack of funding is the biggest problem.*
large a slightly more formal word than **big**, used to describe objects and amounts: *a large bowl | Large areas of the forest have been destroyed. | The museum attracts a large number of visitors.*
major [only before noun] big and important: *Pollution is a major problem. | There has been a major change in government policy.*
considerable/substantial quite big – used especially about amounts: *They have spent a considerable amount of money on the project. | A substantial amount of heat is lost through the windows.*

VERY BIG

huge/massive/enormous extremely big: *The table was enormous. | a huge explosion | There has been a massive increase in oil prices.*
great [only before noun] very big – used especially to describe the level or number of something: *He achieved great success in America. | The college offers a great number of courses. | a great advantage*
vast extremely big – used about areas, distances, numbers, or amounts: *vast areas of rainforest | A vast number of tourists visit the island every year.*
gigantic extremely big and much bigger than other things of the same type: *Gigantic waves crashed onto the beach.*
colossal extremely big – used about amounts or objects: *James ran up a colossal phone bill. | a colossal statue of Napoleon*
tremendous having an extremely big effect: *There have been some tremendous changes. | My new job will be a tremendous challenge.*

big² *v* (**bigged, bigging**)
big sb/sth ↔ **up** *phr v BrE spoken informal* **1** to say that someone or something is very good, especially in public: *He's always on TV bigging up his new band.* **2 big it up** to spend a lot of money and enjoy yourself in a social situation, in a way that other people will notice

big·a·my /ˈbɪɡəmi/ *n* [U] the crime of being married to two people at the same time → **monogamy**, **polygamy** —**bigamist** *n* [C] —**bigamous** *adj*

ˈbig band *n* [C] a large musical band, especially popular in the 1940s and 1950s, that plays JAZZ or dance music and has a leader who plays SOLOS: *Tommy Dorsey's big band* —**big-band** *adj*

ˌbig ˈbang ˌtheory *n* **the big bang theory** the idea that the universe began with a single large explosion (the 'big bang'), and that the pieces are still flying apart → **steady state theory**

ˌbig-ˈboned *adj* a big-boned person is large without being fat

ˈbig-box *adj* [only before noun] *AmE* a big-box store is a very large store, usually on the edge of a town

ˌbig ˈbucks *n* [plural] *especially AmE informal* a lot of money: *Her parents spent big bucks on her wedding.*

ˌbig ˈbusiness *n* [U] **1** very large companies, considered as a powerful group with a lot of influence **2** a product or type of activity that people spend a lot of money on: *Dieting has become big business.*

ˌbig ˈcat *n* [C] a large animal of the cat family, such as a lion or tiger

ˌbig ˈcheese *n* [C] *informal* an important and powerful person in an organization – used humorously

ˌBig ˈData *n* [U] the very large amounts of information that can now be gathered, kept, and ANALYSEd, especially information about people's interests or what they like, as a result of things such as SOCIAL MEDIA use

ˌbig ˈdeal *n* [singular] *spoken* **1** used to say that you do not think something is as important as someone else thinks it is: *It's just a game. If you lose, big deal.* | ***What's the big deal?*** *It's only a birthday, not the end of the world.* | ***It's no big deal.*** *Everybody forgets things sometimes.* **2** an important or exciting event or situation: *This audition is a big deal for Joey.* **3 make a big deal of/out of/about sth** to get too excited or upset about something, or make something seem more important than it is: *I know I'm probably making a big deal out of nothing, but I'm worried about you.*

ˌbig ˈdipper *n* [C] **1** *BrE old-fashioned* a small railway in a FUNFAIR, with steep slopes and sharp curves to give an exciting ride → see picture at **AMUSEMENT PARK** **2 the Big Dipper** *AmE* a group of seven bright stars seen only from northern parts of the world SYN **the Plough** *BrE*

ˌbig ˈgame *n* [U] large wild animals hunted for sport, such as lions and ELEPHANTS: *a big game hunter*

big·gie /ˈbɪɡi/ *n* **1** [C] *informal* something very large, important, or successful: *I think their new CD is going to be a biggie.* **2 no biggie** *AmE spoken* said when something is not important or when you are not upset or angry about something: *'Oh, I'm sorry.' 'No biggie.'*

ˈbig ˌgovernment *n* [U] *AmE* government – used when people think it is controlling their lives too much: *big government welfare policies*

BIG CATS

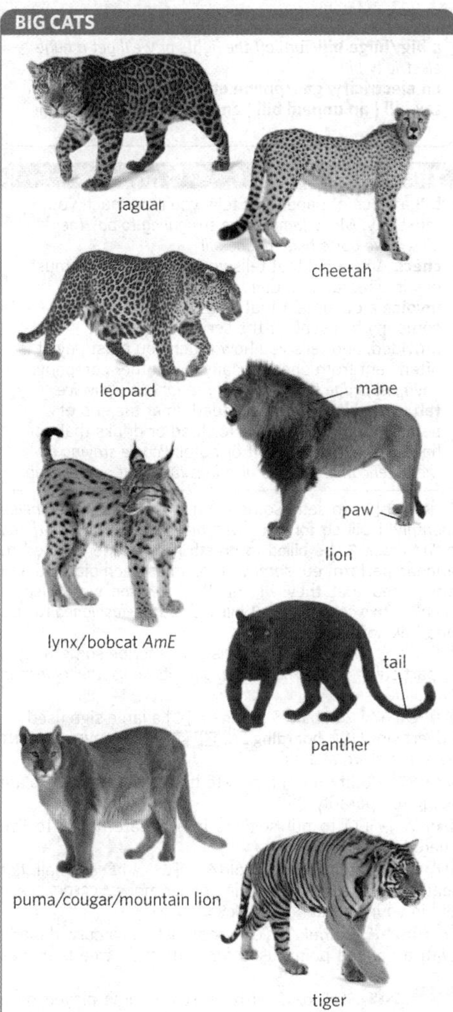

ˌbig ˈgun *n* [C] *informal* a person or company that has a lot of power and influence: *one of the party's big guns*

big·head·ed /ˌbɪɡˈhedɪd◂/ ●○○ *adj informal* someone who is big-headed thinks they are very important, clever etc – used to show disapproval OPP **modest** THESAURUS ▸ PROUD —**ˈbig-head** *n* [C]

big-heart·ed /ˌbɪɡ ˈhɑːtɪd◂ $ -ɑːr-/ *adj* very kind and generous

ˌbig ˈhitter *n* [C] someone who is very important and successful and who has a lot of influence: *one of the big hitters of the Conservative Party*

big·horn sheep /ˌbɪɡhɔːn ˈʃiːp $ -hɔːrn-/ *n* [C] a wild sheep with long curved horns that lives in the mountains of western North America

bight /baɪt/ *n* [C] a slight bend or curve in a coast

ˌBig Man on ˈCampus *n* [C] *AmE informal* an important and popular male student at a college or university, especially someone who is good at sports

ˌbig ˈmoney *n* [U] *informal* a large amount of money: *Carter won big money in Vegas last year.*

big·mouth /ˈbɪɡmaʊθ/ *n* [C] *informal* someone who cannot be trusted to keep secrets SYN **gossip**

ˌbig ˈname *n* [C] a famous person or group, especially a musician, actor etc: *Poor attendance at the concert was put down to the lack of big names.*

ˌbig ˈnoise *n* [C] *informal* an important and powerful person in an organization

big·ot /ˈbɪɡət/ *n* [C] someone who is bigoted: *racist bigots*

big·ot·ed /ˈbɪɡətɪd/ *adj* having such strong opinions about a group of people that you are unwilling to listen to anyone else's opinions SYN **prejudiced**: *a bigoted old man*

big·ot·ry /ˈbɪɡətri/ *n* [U] bigoted behaviour or beliefs SYN **prejudice**: *sensational news stories that just encourage bigotry* THESAURUS ▸ PREJUDICE

ˌbig ˈpharma *n* [U] the big PHARMACEUTICAL companies – used especially in newspapers and in business

ˌbig ˈscreen *n* **the big screen** the cinema, rather than television or the theatre: **on the big screen** *She was last seen on the big screen in the comedy 'Jawbreaker'.*

ˈbig-screen *adj* [only before noun] **1** relating to the cinema, rather than to television or the theatre: *his big-screen career* **2** a big-screen television is very big

ˈbig shot *n* [C] *informal* someone who has a lot of power or influence in a company or an area of business: *His father's a big shot and he thinks he is, too.*

ˌbig ˈsociety *n* **the big society** *BrE* the idea that members of the public should provide or organize services, rather than the government doing this

ˈbig ticket *adj* [only before noun] *AmE informal* expensive: *big ticket items such as cars or jewelry*

ˈbig time¹ *n* **the big time** *informal* the position of being very famous or important, for example in the entertainment business or in politics: *The 46-year-old author has finally* ***hit the big time***. —**big-time** *adj* [only before noun]: *big-time cocaine dealers*

big time² *adv spoken* to a very large degree: *Morris messed up big time.*

ˌbig ˈtoe *n* [C] the largest toe on your foot

ˌbig ˈtop *n* [C] the very large tent in which a CIRCUS performance takes place

ˌbig ˈwheel *n* [C] *BrE* a machine used in AMUSEMENT PARKS, consisting of a very large upright wheel with seats hanging from it, that turns round slowly SYN **ferris wheel** → see picture at **AMUSEMENT PARK**

big·wig /ˈbɪɡwɪɡ/ *n* [C] *informal* an important person: *A few of the company bigwigs have their own jets.*

bi·jou /ˈbiːʒuː/ *adj* [only before noun] *BrE* a bijou house or apartment is small and fashionable – often used humorously: *a bijou residence in Mayfair*

bike¹ /baɪk/ ●●● S2 *n* [C]

1 a bicycle: *Let's* ***go for a bike ride***. | **by bike** *They'll be coming by bike.*

2 *informal* a MOTORCYCLE

3 on your bike! *BrE spoken* used to tell someone rudely to go away

GRAMMAR: Patterns with bike

- You say **get on your bike**: *We got on our bikes and went for a picnic.*
- You say **get off your bike**: *You have to get off your bike here.*
- You say that someone is **on a bike**: *You should always wear a helmet when you're on a bike.*
- You go somewhere **by bike**: *We get to school by bike.*

✗ Don't say: *We get to school with a bike.*

bike² *v* **1** [I always + adv/prep] *informal* to ride a bicycle: *She bikes to work every day.* **2** [T] to take something to someone by MOTORCYCLE in order to get it there quickly: **bike sth over/round** *We're late for our deadline. Can you bike the photos over to us?*

bik·er /ˈbaɪkə $ -ər/ *n* [C] **1** someone who rides a MOTORCYCLE, especially as part of a group: *Most of the bikers rode Harley-Davidsons.* **2** someone who rides a bicycle: *trails for bikers and hikers*

bi·ki·ni /bəˈkiːni/ ●●○ *n* [C] a set of clothes worn by women for swimming, which consists of a top part covering the breasts, and a bottom part

biˈkini line *n* [C] the place on a woman's legs where the hair around her sexual organs stops growing

bi·la·bi·al /baɪˈleɪbiəl/ *n* [C] *technical* a CONSONANT sound such as /p/ or /b/ that is made using both lips —**bilabial** *adj* → LABIAL

bi·lat·er·al /baɪˈlætərəl/ ●○○ *adj* involving two groups or nations: **bilateral relations/trade/agreements/negotiations etc** *bilateral negotiations between Israel and Syria* —**bilaterally** *adv* → MULTILATERAL, UNILATERAL

B

bil·ber·ry /ˈbɪlbəri $ -beri/ *n* (*plural* **bilberries**) [C] a blue-black fruit that grows in Northern Europe, or the bush it grows on

bile /baɪl/ *n* [U] **1** a bitter green-brown liquid formed in the LIVER, which helps you to DIGEST fats **2** *literary* anger and hatred

bilge /bɪldʒ/ *n* **1** [C usually plural] the broad bottom part of a ship **2** [U] *old-fashioned informal* nonsense

bi·lin·gual /baɪˈlɪŋɡwəl/ ●●○ *adj*
1 written or spoken in two languages: *a bilingual dictionary* | *The report proposed* ***bilingual education*** *in schools.*
2 able to speak two languages equally well: *Their kids are bilingual.* | **[+in]** *Louis is virtually bilingual in Dutch and German.* —**bilingual** *n* [C] → **monolingual**

bil·i·ous /ˈbɪliəs/ *adj* **1** feeling as if you might VOMIT: *She felt a bilious attack coming on.* **2** very unpleasant: *bilious green walls* **3** *literary* bad-tempered —**biliousness** *n* [U]

bilk /bɪlk/ *v* [T] *informal* to cheat someone, especially by taking their money SYN **swindle**: **bilk sb out of sth** *Consumers were bilked out of more than $15,000.*

bill¹ /bɪl/ ●●● S1 W1 *n* [C]
1 REQUEST FOR PAYMENT a written list showing how much you have to pay for services you have received, work that has been done etc: **[+for]** *The bill for the repairs came to $650.* | *Have you paid the phone bill?*
2 RESTAURANT *especially BrE* a list showing how much you have to pay for food you have eaten in a restaurant SYN **check** *AmE*: *Could we have the bill, please?*
3 LAW a written proposal for a new law, that is brought to a parliament so that it can be discussed: **approve/pass/veto a bill** *The House of Representatives passed a new gun-control bill.* | *The senator* ***introduced*** *a* ***bill*** *that would increase the minimum wage.*
4 MONEY *AmE* a piece of paper money SYN **note** *BrE* → **coin**: *a five-dollar bill*
5 fit/fill the bill to be exactly what you need: *This car fits the bill perfectly. It's cheap and gets good mileage.*
6 CONCERT/SHOW ETC a programme of entertainment at a theatre, concert, cinema etc, with details of who is performing, what is being shown etc: *Tricia* ***topped the bill*** (=was the most important performer) *at the Children's Variety Show.*
7 give sb/sth a clean bill of health to officially state that someone is in good health or that something is working correctly: *Maddox was given a clean bill of health.*
8 BIRD a bird's beak
9 ADVERTISEMENT a printed notice advertising an event
10 PART OF A HAT *AmE* the front part that sticks out on a hat such as a BASEBALL CAP
11 the (old) bill *BrE spoken* the police

COLLOCATIONS

VERBS

pay a bill *Most people pay their bills on time.*
settle a bill (=pay it) *She went down to the lobby to settle the bill for their rooms.*
foot the bill/pick up the bill (=pay for something, especially when you do not want to) *Taxpayers will probably have to foot the bill.*
run up a bill (=use a lot of something so that you have a big bill to pay) *It's easy to run up a big bill on your mobile phone.*
a bill comes to sth (=is for that amount) *The bill came to $60.*

ADJECTIVES/NOUN + bill

a big/huge bill *Turn off the lights or we'll get a huge electricity bill.*
an electricity/gas/phone etc bill | **a hotel bill** | **a tax bill** | **an unpaid bill** | **an outstanding bill** (=still unpaid)

THESAURUS

bill a piece of paper that tells you how much you must pay: *Many families are struggling to pay their bills.* | *We got a huge phone bill.*
check *AmE* a bill that tells you how much you must pay in a restaurant: *Can I have the check, please?*
invoice a document that lists the goods that a company has sent, or the services they have provided, and tells you how much you must pay. It is often sent from one company to another company: *Payment is due ten days after receipt of the invoice.*
tab *informal* a bill that is added up at the end of a period of time, especially for food or drinks that you have had in a restaurant or hotel: *People staying in the hotel can order food or drinks to be put on their tab.*

bill² *v* **1** [T] to send someone a bill: *Clients will be billed monthly.* | **bill sb for sth** *I was billed for equipment that I didn't order.* **2 be billed to do sth** if someone is billed to appear, perform etc somewhere, it has been planned and advertised that they will do this: *Johnson was billed to speak at two conferences.* **3 bill and coo** *old-fashioned* to kiss and talk softly

bill sth **as** sth *phr v* to advertise or describe something in a particular way: *The castle bills itself as the oldest in England.*

bill·board /ˈbɪlbɔːd $ -bɔːrd/ *n* [C] a large sign used for advertising SYN **hoarding** *BrE* THESAURUS ADVERTISEMENT → see picture at SIGN¹

bil·let¹ /ˈbɪlɪt/ *n* [C] a private house where soldiers are living temporarily

billet² *v* [T] to put soldiers in a private house to live there temporarily

bill·fold /ˈbɪlfəʊld $ -foʊld/ *n* [C] *AmE* a small flat leather case, used for carrying paper money, CREDIT CARDS etc in your pocket SYN **wallet**

bill·hook /ˈbɪlhʊk/ *n* [C] a tool that has a curved blade with a hooked point, used for cutting off tree branches etc

bil·liards /ˈbɪljədz $ -ərdz/ *n* [U] a game played on a cloth-covered table in which balls are hit with a CUE (=a long stick) against each other and into pockets at the edge of the table → **pool**, **snooker** —**billiard** *adj* [only before noun]: *a billiard table*

bill·ing /ˈbɪlɪŋ/ *n* **give sb top/star billing** to name a particular performer, actor etc as being the most important person in a show, play etc

bil·lion /ˈbɪljən/ ●●● W2 *number* (*plural* **billion** *or* **billions**)
1 the number 1,000,000,000: *The final cost could be as much as one billion dollars.* | **two/three/four etc billion** *3.5 billion years ago* | *Overseas debt is a staggering £16 billion.* | **billions of pounds/dollars etc** *Airlines have lost billions of dollars.*
2 an extremely large number of things or people: **a billion** *A billion stars shone in the night sky.* | **billions of sth** *There are billions of things I want to say.*
3 *BrE old use* the number 1,000,000,000,000 —**billionth** *adj* —**billionth** *n* [C]

bil·lion·aire /ˌbɪljəˈneə◂ $ -ˈner◂/ *n* [C] someone who has more than a billion dollars or pounds

ˌbill of exˈchange *n* (*plural* **bills of exchange**) [C] *technical* a signed document ordering someone to pay someone else a particular amount of money

ˌbill of ˈfare *n* (*plural* **bills of fare**) [C] *old-fashioned* a list of the food that is served in a restaurant SYN **menu**

ˌbill of ˈlading *n* (*plural* **bills of lading**) [C] *technical* a list of the goods being carried, especially on a ship

ˌbill of ˈrights *n* (*plural* **bills of rights**) [C] a written statement of the most important rights of the citizens of a country

ˌbill of ˈsale *n* (*plural* **bills of sale**) [C] *technical* a written document showing that someone has bought something

bil·low¹ /ˈbɪləʊ $ -loʊ/ *v* [I] **1** (*also* **billow out**) if something made of cloth billows, it moves in the wind: *Her long skirt billowed in the breeze.* **2** if a cloud or smoke billows, it rises in a round mass: **[+out of/up etc]** *There was smoke billowing out of the windows.*

billow² *n* [C usually plural] **1** a moving cloud or mass of something such as smoke or cloth **2** *literary* a wave, especially a very large one

bil·ly /ˈbɪli/ (*also* **bil·ly·can** /ˈbɪlikæn/) *n* (*plural* **billies**) [C] *BrE* a pot for cooking or boiling water when you are camping

ˈbilly goat *n* [C] a male goat – used especially by or to children → **nanny goat** → see picture at GOAT

ˌBilly ˈno-mates *n* [singular, U] *BrE informal* someone who has no friends: *I was left sitting on my own, looking like Billy no-mates.*

bim·bo /ˈbɪmbəʊ $ -boʊ/ *n* (*plural* **bimbos**) [C] *informal* an insulting word for an attractive but unintelligent young woman: *He picked up some bimbo at the club.*

bi·month·ly /baɪˈmʌnθli/ *adj* appearing or happening every two months or twice each month → **monthly**, **quarterly**: *a bimonthly magazine* —**bimonthly** *adv*

BINS

pedal bin *BrE*; recycling bin; wastepaper basket *BrE*/ wastebasket *AmE*; dustbin *BrE*/ garbage can *AmE*; wheelie bin *BrE*; litter bin *BrE*/ trash can *AmE*

bin¹ /bɪn/ ●●● S2 *n* [C]
1 *BrE* a container for putting waste in → **trash can**, **waste paper basket**: *Throw it in the bin.* → DUSTBIN, LITTER BIN
2 a large container for storing things, such as goods in a shop or substances in a factory

bin² *v* (**binned**, **binning**) [T] *BrE informal* to throw something away: *Just bin that letter.*

bi·na·ry /ˈbaɪnəri/ *adj* **1 the binary system** a system of counting, used in computers, in which only the numbers 0 and 1 are used **2** consisting of two parts SYN **double**: *a binary star system*

bind¹ /baɪnd/ ●●○ *v* (*past tense and past participle* **bound** /baʊnd/)
1 TIE/FASTEN [T] *written* **a)** to tie someone so that they cannot move or escape: *They bound my arms and legs with rope.* | **bound and gagged** (=tied up, and with cloth tied around your mouth so you cannot speak) **b)** (*also* **bind up**) to tie things firmly together with cloth or string: *The pile of newspapers was bound with string.*
2 FORM A CONNECTION [T] to form a strong emotional or economic connection between two people, countries etc SYN **unite**: **bind sb/sth together** *Their shared experiences in war helped to bind the two communities together.*
3 MAKE SB DO STH [T] if you are bound by an agreement, promise etc, you must do what you have agreed to do or promised to do: **be bound by sth** *The monks are bound by vows of silence.* | **be bound to do sth** *Employees are not bound to give their reasons for leaving.* GRAMMAR **Bind** is usually passive in this meaning.
4 STICK TOGETHER [I,T] *technical* to stick together in a mass, or to make small pieces of something stick together: *The flour mixture isn't wet enough to bind properly.* | **[+with]** *The hydrogen molecule binds with the oxygen molecule.*
5 BOOK [T] to fasten the pages of a book together and put them in a cover → BOUND²(9)
6 STITCH [T] to sew cloth over the edge of a piece of material, or stitch over it, to strengthen it: *The edges of the blanket were bound with ribbon.*

bind sb **over** *phr v* [usually passive] *law* **a)** *BrE* if someone is bound over by a court of law, they are warned that, if they cause more trouble, they will be legally punished: *The demonstrators were bound over to keep the peace.* **b)** *AmE* if someone is bound over for TRIAL, they are forced by law to appear in a court

bind² *n* [singular] *informal* an annoying or difficult situation: *It's a real bind having to look after the children.* | **in a bind** *Caroline was really in a bind.*

bind·er /ˈbaɪndə $ -ər/ *n* **1** [C] a removable cover for holding loose sheets of paper, magazines etc → RING BINDER **2** [C] a person or machine that fastens the parts of a book together **3** [C,U] a substance that makes things stick together **4** [C] *AmE* an agreement in which you pay money to show that you intend to buy a property

bind·ing¹ /ˈbaɪndɪŋ/ *adj* **a binding contract/promise/agreement etc** a promise, agreement etc that must be obeyed

binding² *n* **1** [C] a book cover **2** [U] material sewn or stuck along the edge of a piece of cloth for strength or decoration

bind·weed /ˈbaɪndwiːd/ *n* [U] a wild plant that winds itself around other plants

binge¹ /bɪndʒ/ *n* [C] *informal* a short period when you do too much of something, such as eating or drinking: *a drinking binge* | *a week-long binge of shopping* | **on a binge** *Ken's* **gone on a binge** *with his mates.*

binge² *v* [I] *informal* to do too much of something, such as eating or drinking, in a short period of time: **[+on]** *Whenever she's depressed, she binges on chocolates.*

ˈbinge ˌdrinking *n* [U] the activity of drinking a large amount of alcohol in a short period of time, usually in order to become DRUNK: *Binge drinking is an increasing problem among young people.* —**binge drinker** *n* [C]

bin·go¹ /ˈbɪŋgəʊ $ -goʊ/ *n* [U] a game played for money or prizes, in which numbers are chosen by chance and called out, and if you have the right numbers on your card, you win: *Vera won £20 at bingo.*

bingo² *interjection* used when you have just done something successfully and are pleased: *Bingo! That's the one I've been looking for.*

ˈbin ˌliner *n* [C] *BrE* a plastic bag used inside a BIN for holding waste → see picture at BAG

bin·man /ˈbɪnmæn/ *n* (*plural* **binmen** /-men/) [C] *BrE* someone who comes to people's houses to collect their waste SYN **garbage collector** *AmE*

bi·noc·u·lars /bɪˈnɒkjələz, baɪ- $ -ˈnɑːkjələrz/ ●○○ *n* [plural] a pair of special glasses, that you hold up to your eyes to look at objects that are a long distance away SYN **field glasses** → see picture at OPTICAL

B

bi,nocular 'vision *n* [U] *technical* the ability to FOCUS both eyes on one object, which humans, monkeys, and some birds and other animals have

bi·no·mi·al /baɪˈnəʊmiəl $ -ˈnoʊ-/ *n* [C] *technical* a mathematical expression that has two parts connected by the sign + or the sign -, for example 3x + 4y or x - 7 —**binomial** *adj*

bio- /baɪəʊ, baɪə $ baɪoʊ, baɪə/ *prefix* relating to or using living things: *bio-genetics* | *biophysics*

bi·o·char /ˈbaɪəʊˌtʃɑː $ -oʊˌtʃɑːr/ *n* [U] CHARCOAL made from BIOLOGICAL waste. It can be used to improve soil, or used as a way of storing CARBON rather than letting it into the atmosphere.

bi·o·chem·ist /ˌbaɪəʊˈkemɪst $ ˌbaɪoʊ-/ *n* [C] someone who studies or works in biochemistry

bi·o·chem·is·try /ˌbaɪəʊˈkeməstri $ ˌbaɪoʊ-/ *n* [U] the scientific study of the chemistry of living things —**biochemical** *adj*

bi·o·de·gra·da·ble /ˌbaɪəʊdɪˈgreɪdəbəl◂ $ ˌbaɪoʊ-/ *adj* materials, chemicals etc that are biodegradable are changed naturally by BACTERIA into substances that do not harm the environment OPP **non biodegradable**, **non-biodegradable**: *This carton is made of biodegradable plastic.*

bi·o·die·sel /ˈbaɪəʊˌdiːzəl $ ˈbaɪoʊ-/ *n* [U] a liquid made from vegetable oil or animal fat, which can be used instead of DIESEL in engines

bi·o·di·gest·er /ˌbaɪəʊdaɪˈdʒestə, -də- $ -oʊdaɪˈdʒestər, -də-/ *n* [C] a large container in which plant material or animal waste is changed by bacteria, producing METHANE and CARBON DIOXIDE

bi·o·di·ver·si·ty /ˌbaɪəʊdaɪˈvɜːsəti, -də- $ ˌbaɪoʊdaɪˈvɜːr-, -də-/ *n* [U] *technical* the variety of plants and animals in a particular place: *the biodiversity of the rainforest*

bi·ody·nam·ic /ˌbaɪəʊdaɪˈnæmɪk $ ˌbaɪoʊ-/ *adj* biodynamic farming and gardening is a type of ORGANIC farming and gardening based on a SPIRITUAL view of nature in which plants, animals, and soil are considered to be a system working together —**biodynamics** *n* [U]

bi·o·en·er·gy /ˈbaɪəʊˌenədʒi $ -oʊˌenər-/ *n* [U] energy that is obtained from plants or animal waste

bi·o·eth·a·nol /ˌbaɪəʊˈeθənɒl, -ˈiːθ- $ ˌbaɪoʊˈeθəˌnoʊl, -ˈiːθ-/ *n* [U] FUEL that is made from plants and can be mixed with petrol for use in cars

bi·o·feed·back /ˌbaɪəʊˈfiːdbæk $ ˌbaɪoʊ-/ *n* [U] a method of helping people to relax by teaching them to control their heart rate, breathing etc, using an instrument attached to the body

bi·o·fu·el /ˈbaɪəʊˌfjuːəl $ ˈbaɪoʊ-/ *n* [C,U] a substance made from plants or animal waste that can be used to produce heat or power

bi·o·gas /ˈbaɪəʊgæs $ ˈbaɪoʊ-/ *n* [U] gas produced from decaying plant material that can be used as FUEL

bi·og·ra·pher /baɪˈɒgrəfə $ -ˈɑːgrəfər/ *n* [C] someone who writes a biography of someone else

bi·og·ra·phy /baɪˈɒgrəfi $ -ˈɑːg-/ ●●○ *n* (*plural* **biographies**)
1 [C] a book that tells what has happened in someone's life, written by someone else: **[+of]** *Boswell's biography of Samuel Johnson* THESAURUS ▸ BOOK
2 [U] literature that consists of biographies → **autobiography** —**biographical** /ˌbaɪəˈgræfɪkəl◂/ *adj*: *biographical information*

bi·o·haz·ard /ˈbaɪəʊˌhæzəd $ ˈbaɪoʊˌhæzəd/ *n* [C] *medical* something biological, such as a type of BACTERIA or a VIRUS, that is dangerous to people's health

bi·o·in·di·ca·tor /ˌbaɪəʊˈɪndəkeɪtə $ ˌbaɪoʊˈɪndəkeɪtər/ *n* [C] *technical* a small number of animals, plants, insects etc that are typical of all the animals, plants etc normally found in a particular area, which scientists study in order to get information about the whole area: *This insect-bacteria bioindicator is a reliable tool for assessing environmental damage to the country's wetlands.*

bi·o·in·for·mat·ics /ˌbaɪəʊɪnfəˈmætɪks $ ˌbaɪoʊɪnfər-/ *n* [U] *technical* the use of mathematics and computer science to solve biological problems, for example when studying the human GENOME

bi·o·lo·gi·cal /ˌbaɪəˈlɒdʒɪkəl◂ $ -ˈlɑː-/ ●●○ *adj*
1 relating to the natural processes performed by living things: *the biological functions of the body* | *Depression is both biological and psychological.*
2 biological weapons/warfare/attack etc weapons, attacks etc that involve the use of living things, including BACTERIA, to harm other living things: *a ban on chemical and biological weapons*
3 [only before noun] relating to biology: *the biological sciences*
4 biological parent/father/mother etc a child's parent through birth, rather than through ADOPTION —**biologically** /-kli/ *adv*

ˌbiological ˈclock *n* [singular] **1** *technical* the system in plants and animals that controls when they sleep, eat, produce babies etc SYN **body clock** **2** the idea that when a woman reaches a certain age, she will soon be too old to have a baby: *career women who hear the* ***biological clock ticking***

bi·ol·o·gist /baɪˈɒlədʒɪst $ -ˈɑːl-/ ●○○ *n* [C] someone who studies or works in biology

bi·ol·o·gy /baɪˈɒlədʒi $ -ˈɑːl-/ ●●● W3 *n* [U]
1 the scientific study of living things: *a degree in biology*
2 the scientific laws that control the life of a particular type of animal, plant etc: *the biology of bacteria*

biomarker /ˈbæɪəʊˌmɑːk $ -oʊˌmɑrkər/ *n* [C] *medical* a chemical substance in your body, which can show doctors whether you have a particular medical condition, are likely to have it, or whether a treatment is successful: *The diagnosis of these patients is based on a biomarker.*

bi·o·mass /ˈbaɪəʊmæs $ ˈbaɪoʊ-/ *n* [U] *technical* plant and animal matter used to provide power or energy

bi·ome /ˈbaɪəʊm $ -oʊm/ *n* [C] *technical* a type of environment that is described according to the typical weather conditions and plants that exist there

bi·o·met·ric /ˌbaɪəʊˈmetrɪk◂ $ ˌbaɪoʊ-/ *adj* [usually before noun] relating to technology that can be used to measure things such as people's eyes or fingerprints. These measurements can be kept on computer and then used to check someone's IDENTITY, for example when they show a passport at an airport: ***biometric data*** | *biometric identifiers such as fingerprints or iris patterns*

bi·on·ic /baɪˈɒnɪk $ -ˈɑːn-/ *adj* bionic arms, legs etc are electronic and therefore stronger or faster than normal arms etc - often used humorously: *I swear Mom has bionic ears.*

bi·o·phys·ics /ˌbaɪəʊˈfɪzɪks $ ˌbaɪoʊ-/ *n* [U] the scientific study of how PHYSICS relates to biological processes

bi·o·pic /ˈbaɪəʊˌpɪk $ ˈbaɪoʊ-/ *n* [C] *informal* a film that tells the story of someone's life

bi·o·pi·ra·cy /ˌbaɪəʊˈpaɪərəsi $ ˌbaɪoʊˈpaɪr-/ *n* [U] the process in which large companies try to get PATENTs on (=legal rights to) products that make use of plants, animals, GENEs etc that were developed over many years by nature or by farmers, especially farmers in poorer countries

bi·o·pro·spec·ting /ˌbaɪəʊprəˈspektɪŋ $ ˌbaɪoʊˈprɑːspek-/ (*also* **ˌbiodiversity proˈspecting** / $ ˌ...... ˈ.../) *n* [U] the scientific study of plants and other living things found in nature, such as BACTERIA, in order to discover new drugs that can be used as medicines —**bioprospect** *v* [I] —**bioprospector** *n* [C]

bi·op·sy /ˈbaɪɒpsi $ -ɑːp-/ *n* (*plural* **biopsies**) [C] the removal of cells, TISSUE etc from someone's body in order to find out more about a disease they may have: *a breast biopsy*

bi·o·rhyth·ms /ˈbaɪəʊˌrɪðəmz $ ˈbaɪoʊ-/ *n* [plural] regular changes in the speed at which physical processes happen in your body, which some people believe can affect the way you feel

bi·o·sci·ence /ˈbaɪəʊˌsaɪəns $ ˈbaɪoʊ-/ *n* [C,U] the science subjects that relate to living things, or one of these subjects

bi·o·se·cu·ri·ty /ˌbaɪəʊsɪˈkjʊərəti $ ˌbaɪoʊsɪˈkjʊr-/ *n* [U] things that are done to prevent diseases from spreading between people, animals, or crops: *Poultry producers have started to adopt strict **biosecurity measures**.*

bi·o·sphere /ˈbaɪəsfɪə $ -sfɪr/ *n* [singular] *technical* the part of the world in which animals, plants etc can live

bi·o·tech·nol·o·gy /ˌbaɪəʊtekˈnɒlədʒi $ ˌbaɪoʊtekˈnɑː-/ ●○○ (*also* **bi·o·tech** /ˈbaɪəʊtek $ ˈbaɪoʊ-/ *informal*) *n* [U] the use of living things such as cells, BACTERIA etc to make drugs, destroy waste matter etc: *the biotech industries* —**biotechnological** /ˌbaɪəʊteknəˈlɒdʒɪkəl $ ˌbaɪoʊteknəˈlɑː-/ *adj*

bi·o·ter·ror·ism /ˈbaɪəʊˌterərɪzəm $ ˈbaɪoʊ-/ *n* [U] the use of BACTERIA or VIRUSes by a person or group to attack people and achieve a political aim —**bioterrorist** *n* [C]

bi·o·weap·on /ˈbaɪəʊwepən $ ˈbaɪoʊ-/ *n* [C] BACTERIA or VIRUSes (=very small living things that cause illness or disease) used as a weapon to kill a lot of people SYN **biological weapon**: *He warned that influenza could be used as a bioweapon.*

bi·par·ti·san /ˌbaɪpɑːtɪˈzæn $ baɪˈpɑːrtɪzən/ *adj* involving two political parties, especially parties with opposing views: *a bipartisan committee*

bi·par·tite /baɪˈpɑːtaɪt $ -ˈpɑːr-/ *adj formal* involving two different parts or groups: *a bipartite treaty*

bi·ped /ˈbaɪped/ *n* [C] *technical* an animal with two legs, such as a human

bi·plane /ˈbaɪpleɪn/ *n* [C] a type of aircraft with two sets of wings, especially one built in the early 20th century

bi·po·lar /baɪˈpəʊlə $ -ˈpoʊlər/ *adj* **1** [usually before noun] involving two opposing countries, groups etc: *the bipolar view of the world during the Cold War* **2** **bipolar disorder** *technical* MANIC DEPRESSION **3** someone who is bipolar has bipolar disorder

bi·ra·cial /ˌbaɪˈreɪʃəl◂/ *adj AmE* representing or including people from two different races SYN **mixed race** *BrE*: *biracial families*

birch /bɜːtʃ $ bɜːrtʃ/ *n* **1** [C,U] a tree with smooth BARK (=outer covering) and thin branches, or the wood from this tree **2** **the birch** *BrE* the practice of hitting people with birch sticks as an official punishment → **SILVER BIRCH**

bird /bɜːd $ bɜːrd/ ●●● S2 W2 *n* [C]

1 a creature with wings and feathers that can usually fly. Many birds sing and build nests, and female birds lay eggs: *wild birds | The dawn was filled with the sound of birds. | a **flock of birds*** (=a group of birds flying together) | *a wooden bird cage*

2 *BrE informal not polite* a word meaning a young woman, which some people think is offensive

3 **the birds and the bees** the facts about sex – used humorously or to children

4 **a little bird told me (sth)** *informal* used to say that you know something, but you will not say how you found out: *A little bird told me that you've got engaged.*

5 **birds of a feather (flock together)** *informal* used to say that two or more people have similar attitudes, beliefs etc

6 **give sb the bird a)** *AmE informal* to make a very rude sign at someone by holding your middle finger up **b)** *BrE* to show strong disapproval of someone who is performing or speaking in public, by shouting, making rude noises etc

7 **a bird in the hand (is worth two in the bush)** used to say that it is better to keep what you have than to risk losing it by trying to get more

8 **the bird has flown** *informal* used to say that the person you are looking for has already left or escaped

9 **be (strictly) for the birds** *old-fashioned informal* to be silly, useless, or not practical

10 **wise/wily/funny/weird etc old bird** *old-fashioned informal* a person who seems wise, funny etc

11 **do bird** *BrE old-fashioned informal* to serve a prison sentence SYN **do time** → **early bird** at EARLY[1](9), → **kill two birds with one stone** at KILL[1](13)

bird·bath /ˈbɜːdbɑːθ $ ˈbɜːrdbæθ/ *n* [C] a bowl in a garden that is filled with water for birds to wash in

ˈbird-brain *n* [C] *AmE informal* someone who is silly or stupid —**bird-brain** (*also* **birdbrained**) *adj*

ˈbird dog *n* [C] *AmE* a dog that is trained to find and return with birds that have been shot for sport SYN **gun dog** *BrE*

ˈbird flu *n* [U] *informal* another name for AVIAN FLU

bird·ie¹ /ˈbɜːdi $ ˈbɜːrdi/ *n* [C] **1** *spoken* a word meaning a little bird, used especially by or to children **2** in golf, a score that is one less than PAR **3** *AmE* a small object with feathers that you hit across the net in a game of BADMINTON SYN **shuttlecock** *BrE* → see picture at **SPORT¹**

birdie² *v* [T] in golf, to get the ball into the hole in one hit less than PAR: *Woods birdied the last two holes.*

ˌbird of ˈparadise *n* (*plural* **birds of paradise**) [C] **1** a brightly coloured bird from New Guinea **2** a tall orange flower

ˌbird of ˈpassage *n* (*plural* **birds of passage**) [C] **1** *technical* a bird that flies from one area or country to another, according to the seasons **2** *literary* someone who never stays in the same place for long

BIRDS OF PREY

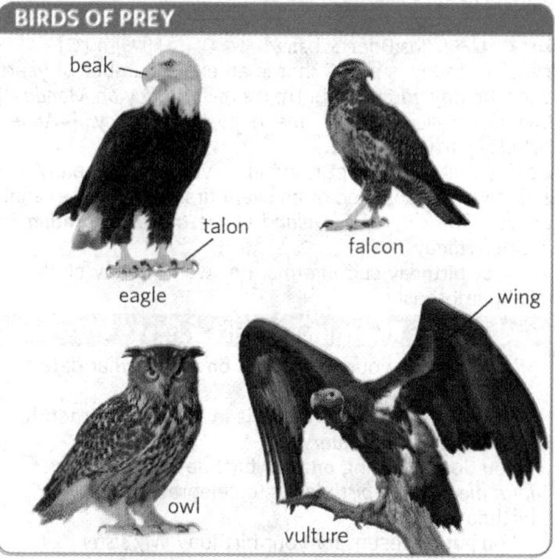

ˌbird of ˈprey *n* (*plural* **birds of prey**) [C] a bird that kills other birds or small animals for food

bird·seed /ˈbɜːdsiːd $ ˈbɜːrd-/ *n* [U] a mixture of seeds for feeding birds

ˌbird's-eye ˈview *n* [singular] **1** a view of something from high above it: *Visitors can enjoy a bird's-eye view of the area from the castle turrets.* **2** a general report or account of something, without many details: *a bird's-eye view of recent research*

bird·shot /ˈbɜːdʃɒt $ ˈbɜːrdʃɑːt/ *n* [U] a type of very small bullet that is fired in large numbers: *The crowd was dispersed by police using tear gas and birdshot.*

bird·song /ˈbɜːdsɒŋ $ ˈbɜːrdsɒːŋ/ *n* [U] the musical noises made by birds

ˈbird ˌtable *n* [C] *BrE* a high wooden structure in a garden that you put food on for birds

ˈbird-ˌwatcher *n* [C] someone who watches wild birds and tries to recognize different types —**bird-watching** *n* [U]

bi·ret·ta /bəˈretə/ *n* [C] a square cap worn by Roman Catholic priests

Bir·ken·stocks /ˈbɜːkənstɒks $ ˈbɜːrkənstɑːks/ *n* [plural] *trademark* a type of leather SANDAL (=a shoe that is open at the toes and heel) with a wide flat bottom

bi·ro /ˈbaɪərəʊ $ ˈbaɪroʊ/ *n* (*plural* **biros**) [C] *trademark BrE* a pen with a small ball at the end that puts ink onto paper SYN **ball point** → **PEN¹**

birth /bɜːθ $ bɜːrθ/ ●●● S2 W2 *n*

1 **give birth (to sb)** if a woman gives birth, she produces a

baby from her body: *Patsy was celebrating last night after giving birth to twins.*
2 [C,U] the time when a baby comes out of its mother's body: *Congratulations on the birth of your daughter!* | *He only weighed 2 kilos* ***at birth***. | *Henry has been blind* ***from birth***. | *What's your* ***date of birth***? | *The exact* ***place of birth*** *is not recorded.* | *They believe that the position of the planets at the* ***time of birth*** *determines the fate of the individual.* | *More and more women are choosing to have* ***home births***. | *Smoking in pregnancy has been linked to* ***premature birth***. | *the association between* ***birth weight*** *and blood pressure* | *The drug was found to cause serious* ***birth defects***.
3 [singular] the time when something new starts to exist: **[+of]** *the birth of a nation* | *The film* ***gave birth to*** *a TV show of the same name.* **THESAURUS** BEGINNING
4 [U] the character, language, social position etc that you have because of the family or country you come from: *a woman of noble birth* | **French/German etc by birth**

ˈbirth cerˌtificate *n* [C] an official document showing when and where you were born, and your parents' names

ˈbirth conˌtrol *n* [U] the practice of controlling the number of children you have SYN **contraception**: *a safe method of birth control*

birth·day /ˈbɜːθdeɪ $ ˈbɜːr-/ ●●● S1 W3 *n* [C]
1 your birthday is a day that is an exact number of years after the day you were born: *It's my birthday on Monday.* | *My aunt called to wish me a happy birthday.* | *Anne's birthday party*
2 a day that is an exact number of years since an organization was established or an event first happened → **anniversary**: *The City of Cleveland Orchestra is* ***celebrating*** *its 200th* ***birthday***.
3 in your birthday suit *informal* not wearing any clothes – used humorously

GRAMMAR: Prepositions with birthday

- You say that your birthday is **on** a particular date: *My birthday is on July 22nd.*
- You say that your birthday is **in** a particular month: *His birthday is in January.*
- You do something **on** your birthday: *We went out for a meal on my birthday* (=to celebrate your birthday).
- You get a present **for** your birthday: *My sister bought me a sweater for my birthday.*

COLLOCATIONS

ADJECTIVES

sb's first/18th/40th etc birthday *It's Mum's 50th birthday tomorrow.*
Happy Birthday! (=said to someone on their birthday)

VERBS

have a good/nice etc birthday *Did you have a nice birthday?*
get sth for your birthday *What did you get for your birthday?*
celebrate sb's birthday *He will celebrate his 90th birthday on 25th August.*
remember sb's birthday (=remember to send a card or present) | **forget sb's birthday** (=forget to send a card or present)

birthday + NOUN

a birthday card | **a birthday present** | **a birthday party** | **a birthday cake** | **birthday celebrations** | **the birthday girl/boy** *informal* (=the person whose birthday it is)

ˈbirth ˌfather *n* [C] a child's natural father, rather than a man who has become the child's legal father through ADOPTION

birth·ing /ˈbɜːθɪŋ $ ˈbɜːrθ-/ *n* [U] the process of giving birth to a baby: *a birthing class*

birth·mark /ˈbɜːθmɑːk $ ˈbɜːrθmɑːrk/ *n* [C] a permanent mark on your skin that you have had since you were born: *Paul had a birthmark on his left cheek.*

ˈbirth ˌmother *n* [C] a child's natural mother, rather than a woman who has become the child's legal mother through ADOPTION

ˈbirth ˌparent *n* [C] a child's natural mother or father, rather than someone who has become the child's legal mother or father through ADOPTION

ˈbirth ˌpartner *n* [C] a person that a woman chooses to be present when she gives birth

birth·place /ˈbɜːθpleɪs $ ˈbɜːrθ-/ *n* [C usually singular] **1** the place where someone was born, used especially when talking about someone famous: *Stratford-upon-Avon was Shakespeare's birthplace.* **2** the place where something first started to happen or exist: *New Orleans is the birthplace of jazz.*

ˈbirth plan *n* [C] a plan that a PREGNANT woman writes to tell doctors and nurses how she would like to give birth, for example what positions she would like to be in and what drugs, if any, she would like to take

birth·rate /ˈbɜːθreɪt $ ˈbɜːrθ-/ *n* [C] the number of births for every 100 or every 1,000 people in a particular year in a particular place: *the rising birthrate*

birth·right /ˈbɜːθraɪt $ ˈbɜːrθ-/ *n* [C usually singular] something such as a right, property, money etc that you believe you should have because of the family or country you belong to: *Freedom of speech is every American's birthright.*

bis·cuit /ˈbɪskɪt/ ●●● S2 *n*
1 [C] *BrE* a small thin dry cake that is usually sweet and made for one person to eat SYN **cookie** *AmE*: *a packet of chocolate biscuits* | *cheese and biscuits*
2 [C] *AmE* a type of soft bread baked in small round pieces
3 [U] a light brown colour
4 take the biscuit *BrE informal* to be the most surprising, annoying etc thing you have ever heard SYN **take the cake** *especially AmE*: *I've heard some excuses, but this really takes the biscuit!*

bi·sect /baɪˈsekt $ ˈbaɪsekt/ *v* [T] *formal* to divide something into two equal parts: *A long cobbled street bisects the town from east to west.*

bi·sex·u·al /baɪˈsekʃuəl/ *adj* **1** sexually attracted to both men and women **2** *technical* having features of both males and females: *a bisexual plant* —**bisexual** *n* [C] —**bisexuality** /ˌbaɪsekʃuˈæləti/ *n* [U]

bish·op /ˈbɪʃəp/ *n* [C] **1** a priest with a high rank in some Christian religions, who is the head of all the churches and priests in a large area: *the Bishop of Durham* **2** a piece in the game of CHESS that can be moved sideways over any number of squares of the same colour → see picture at **CHESS**

bish·op·ric /ˈbɪʃəprɪk/ *n* [C] **1** the area that a bishop is in charge of SYN **diocese** **2** the position of being a bishop

bis·muth /ˈbɪzməθ/ *n* [U] a grey-white metal that is often used in medicines. It is a chemical ELEMENT: symbol Bi

bi·son /ˈbaɪsən/ *n* (*plural* **bison** *or* **bisons**) [C] an animal like a large cow, with hair on its head and shoulders → **buffalo**

bisque /bɪsk/ *n* [U] a thick creamy soup made from SHELLFISH: *lobster bisque*

bis·tro /ˈbiːstrəʊ $ -troʊ/ *n* (*plural* **bistros**) [C] a small restaurant or bar: *a French bistro*

bit¹ /bɪt/ ●●● S1 *adv, pron*
1 ONLY SLIGHTLY **a bit** *especially BrE* **a)** slightly or to a small degree SYN **a little**: *Could you turn the TV up a bit?* | *That's a bit odd.* | *'Are you sorry to be leaving?' 'Yes, I am a bit.'* | *Aren't you being* ***a little bit*** *unfair?* | *I think you're* ***a bit too*** *young to be watching this.* | *She looks* ***a bit like*** *my sister.* | **a bit better/older/easier etc** *I feel a bit*

better now. **b)** sometimes, but not very often: *I used to act a bit when I was younger.*

REGISTER
In written English, people usually avoid **a (little) bit** and use **slightly**, **rather**, or **somewhat** instead: *This system is **slightly** more efficient.* | *The final cost was **somewhat** higher than expected.*

2 AMOUNT **a bit** *especially BrE informal* a small amount of a substance or of something that is not a physical object SYN **a little**: **[+of]** *I may need a bit of help.* | *He still likes to do a bit of gardening.* | *I want to spend a bit of time with him before he goes.* | *With a bit of luck, we should have finished by five o'clock.* | *Everyone needs **a little bit** of encouragement.* | *'Would you like cream in your coffee?' 'Yes please, just a bit.'* | **a bit more/less** *Can we have a bit less noise, please?*
3 QUITE A LOT **quite a bit** (*also* **a good bit** *BrE*) a fairly large amount or to a fairly large degree: *She's quite a bit older than you, isn't she?* | *He knows quite a bit about painting.* | **[+of]** *I expect you do quite a bit of travelling?* | **quite a bit more/less** *They're worth quite a bit more than I thought.*
4 TIME/DISTANCE **a bit** *especially BrE* a short period of time or a short distance SYN **a while**: *You'll have to wait a bit.* | *I walked on a bit.* | **in a bit** *I'll see you in a bit.* | **for a bit** *We sat around for a bit, chatting.*
5 a bit of a sth *especially BrE* used to show that the way you describe something is only true to a limited degree: *The news came as a bit of a shock.* | *I felt a bit of a fool.* | *It looks like they left in a bit of a hurry.*
6 not a bit/not one bit *especially BrE* not at all: *You're **not a bit like** your brother.* | *Am I cross? No, **not a bit of it**.* | *I'm **not in the least bit** interested in whose fault it is.* | *Well, you haven't surprised me, not one bit.*
7 every bit as important/bad/good etc *especially BrE* used to emphasize that something is equally important, bad etc as something else: *Jodi plays every bit as well as the men.*
8 bit by bit *especially BrE* gradually: *Bit by bit, I was starting to change my mind.*
9 a/one bit at a time *especially BrE* in several small parts or stages: *Memorize it a bit at a time.*
10 take a bit of doing/explaining etc *BrE* to be difficult to do, explain etc: *The new system took a bit of getting used to.*
11 be a bit much *BrE* to be unacceptable, impolite, or unfair: *It's a bit much when he criticizes us for doing something that he does himself.*
12 be a bit of all right *BrE informal* used to say that someone is sexually attractive
13 bit on the side *BrE informal* someone's bit on the side is a person they are having a sexual relationship with, even though they already have a wife, husband, or partner – used humorously or to show disapproval: *She stayed, in the hope that he'd tire of his bit on the side.*
14 a bit of stuff/fluff/skirt *BrE informal not polite* offensive expressions meaning a young woman, especially one who is sexually attractive
15 a bit of rough *BrE informal* someone of a lower social class that someone has a sexual relationship with – used humorously

GRAMMAR: Comparison
a bit
• You use **a bit** before an adjective: *He's a bit shy.* | *I'm feeling a bit tired.*
a bit of
• You use **a bit of** before an uncountable noun: *We had a bit of trouble with the engine.*
a bit of a
• You use **a bit of a** before a countable noun, or before an adjective and a countable noun: *She has a bit of a cold.* | *It was a bit of a strange decision.*

bit² ●●● S1 W1 *n* [C]
1 PIECE a small piece of something: **[+of]** *bits of broken glass* | *He wedged the door open with a bit of wood.* | **break/rip/shake etc sth to bits** *The aircraft was blown to bits.* | *He's **taken** the engine **to bits**.* | **fall/come to bits** *The old house was falling to bits.* THESAURUS ▸ PIECE

Frequencies of the noun **bit** in spoken and written English.

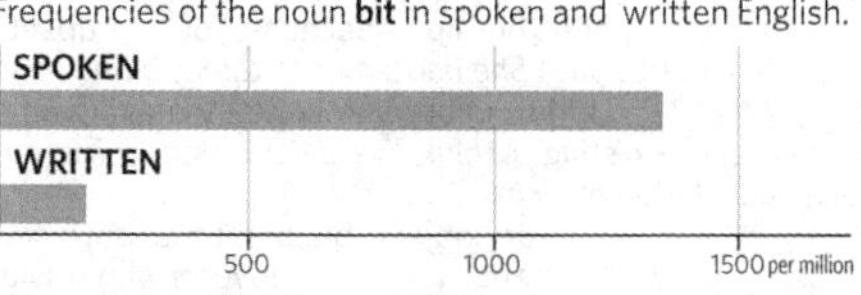

This graph shows that the noun **bit** is much more common in spoken English than in written English. This is because **a bit** is more common than **a little** in spoken English, and **bit** is used in a lot of common spoken phrases.

2 PART *BrE informal* a part of something larger: *This is the boring bit.* | **[+of]** *We did **the last bit** of the journey on foot.* | **[+about]** *Did you like the bit about the monkey?* THESAURUS ▸ PART
3 to bits *BrE informal* very much or extremely: *Mark's a darling – I **love** him **to bits**.* | **thrilled/chuffed/pleased to bits** *I've always wanted a car, so I'm thrilled to bits.*
4 COMPUTER the smallest unit of information that a computer uses: *a 32-bit processor*
5 TOOL the sharp part of a tool for cutting or making holes: *a drill bit*
6 HORSE the metal bar attached to a horse's BRIDLE that is put into its mouth and used to control it → **be champing at the bit** at CHAMP¹(2)
7 bits and pieces (*also* **bits and bobs** *BrE*) *informal* any small things of various kinds: *Let me get all my bits and pieces together.*
8 do your bit *informal* to do a fair share of the work, effort etc that is needed to achieve something good or important: *Everyone should do their bit for the environment.*
9 get the bit between your teeth *BrE*, **take the bit between your teeth** *AmE* to do something or deal with something in a very determined way, so that you are not likely to stop until it is done
10 MONEY **a) two bits/four bits** *AmE informal* 25 cents or 50 cents **b)** *BrE old-fashioned* a small coin
11 pull sth to bits *BrE informal* to criticize something strongly: *The critics pulled his new play to bits.*
12 TYPICAL BEHAVIOUR/EXPERIENCE *informal* used to mean a kind of behaviour or experience that is typical of someone or something: **the (whole) student/movie star/travelling etc bit** *Then she gave us the concerned mother bit.*
13 be in bits *BrE spoken informal* to be extremely upset because something unpleasant or disappointing has happened: *She was in bits after the race, and looked totally gutted.*

bit³ *v* the past tense of BITE

bitch¹ /bɪtʃ/ *n* [C] **1** *especially BrE* a female dog **2** *informal* an insulting word for a woman that you dislike or think is unpleasant – also used humorously between friends: *The silly bitch went and told the police.* | *Ooh, you're such a bitch!* **3** *informal* something that causes problems or difficulties: *I love that silk dress, but it's a bitch to wash.* → SON OF A BITCH, → **life's a bitch** at LIFE(20)

bitch² *v* [I] *informal* **1** to make unpleasant remarks about someone: **[+about]** *He never bitches about other members of the team.* **2** *AmE* to complain continuously: *Stop bitching!* | **[+at]** *He's always bitching at me.*

bitch·in, **bitching** /ˈbɪtʃən/ *adj AmE spoken informal* very good: *That guy has one bitchin truck.*

bitch·y /ˈbɪtʃi/ *adj* unkind and unpleasant about other people SYN **catty**: *a bitchy remark* | *She can be really bitchy sometimes.* —**bitchily** *adv* —**bitchiness** *n* [U]

Bit·coin /ˈbɪtkɔɪn/ *n* [C,U] a form of money that is used on the Internet

bite¹ /baɪt/ ●●● S2 *v* (*past tense* **bit** /bɪt/, *past participle* **bitten** /ˈbɪtn/, *present participle* **biting**)
1 TEETH [I,T] to use your teeth to cut, crush, or chew something: *The dog bit him and made his hand bleed.* | **[+into/through/at/down]** *She bit into a croissant and took a sip of coffee.* | *An adult conger eel can easily bite through a man's leg.* | *Nina pushed her fist into her mouth and **bit** down **hard**.* | **bite sth off** *a man whose arm was bitten off by an alligator* | **bite your nails** (=bite the nails on your fingers,

especially because you are nervous) *I wish I could stop biting my nails.* | **bite your lip** (=because you are upset or not sure what to say) *She paused uncertainly, biting her lip.*
2 INSECT/SNAKE [I,T] to injure someone by making a hole in their skin → **sting**: *I think I've been bitten.* | *The dog's been badly bitten by fleas.*
3 PRESS HARD [I] if an object bites into a surface, it presses firmly into it and does not move or slip: **[+into]** *The hooves of the galloping horses had bitten deep into the soft earth.* | *He wore boots that bit into the ice.*
4 EFFECT [I] to start to have an unpleasant effect: *The new tobacco taxes have begun to bite.* | **[+into]** *The recession is biting into the music industry.*
5 ACCEPT [I] to believe what someone tells you, or to buy something they are selling, especially when they have persuaded you to do this: *The new camcorders were withdrawn after consumers failed to bite.*
6 FISH [I] if a fish bites, it takes food from a hook and so gets caught: *The fish just aren't biting today.*
7 bite your tongue to stop yourself from saying what you really think, even though this is difficult: *She should have bitten her tongue.*
8 bite the dust *informal* to die, fail, or be defeated: *Italy's championship hopes eventually bit the dust.*
9 bite the bullet *informal* to start dealing with an unpleasant or dangerous situation because you cannot avoid it any longer: *I finally bit the bullet and left.*
10 bite off more than you can chew to try to do more than you are able to do
11 he/she won't bite *spoken* used to say that there is no need to be afraid of someone, especially someone in authority: *Well, go and ask him – he won't bite!*
12 what's biting you/her etc? *spoken* used to ask why someone is annoyed or upset
13 sb/sth bites *spoken not polite* used to say that you dislike someone or something very much or think that something is very bad
14 once bitten, twice shy used to say that if you have failed or been hurt once, you will be more careful next time
15 bite the hand that feeds you to harm someone who has helped or supported you
16 be bitten by the showbiz/travel/flying etc bug to develop a very strong interest in something
17 Bite me! *AmE spoken informal* used to show that you are offended by something someone has just said about you
→ **bite sb's head off** at HEAD[1](33), → NAIL-BITING

THESAURUS

bite to use your teeth to cut, crush, or chew something: *The dog bit me!* | *I sometimes bite my fingernails when I'm nervous.* | *He bit into the apple.*
chew to keep biting something that is in your mouth: *Helen was chewing a piece of gum.* | *He was chewing on a cigar.*
gnaw if an animal gnaws something, it bites it repeatedly: *The dog was in the yard gnawing on a bone.*
nip sb/give sb a nip to give someone or something a small sharp bite: *When I took the hamster out of his cage, he nipped me.*
nibble to take a lot of small bites from something: *A fish nibbled at the bait.* | *She sat at her desk, nibbling her sandwich.*
sink your teeth into sb/sth to bite someone or something with a lot of force, so that your teeth go right into them: *The dog sank its teeth into my leg.*
chomp on sth *informal* to bite something and chew it in a noisy way: *The donkey was chomping on a carrot.*
sting if an insect stings you, it makes a very small hole in your skin. You use **sting** about bees, wasps, and scorpions, and **bite** about mosquitoes, ants, spiders, and snakes: *She stepped on a wasps' nest and must have been stung at least 20 times.*

bite back *phr v*
1 bite sth ↔ back to stop yourself from saying or showing what you really think: *Tamar bit back the retort that sprang to her lips.*
2 to react strongly and angrily to something: **[+at]** *Determined to bite back at car thieves, he wired his car to an electric fence.*

bite² ●●● S3 *n*
1 USING TEETH [C] the act of cutting or crushing something with your teeth: *Antonio devoured half his burger in one bite.* | **take/have a bite (of sth/out of sth)** *She picked up the sandwich and took a bite.* | *Can I have a bite of your apple?* | **give sb a bite** *Some fish can give you a nasty bite.* | *Her body was covered in* ***bite marks****.*
2 WOUND [C] a small hole made where an animal or insect has bitten you: **snake/ant etc bite** | **[+of]** *The infection is passed by the bite of a mosquito.*
3 a bite (to eat) *informal* a small meal: *We had a bite to eat and a couple of drinks before the flight.*
4 TASTE [U] a pleasantly sharp taste: *Goat's cheese adds extra bite to any pasta dish.*
5 COLD [singular] a feeling of coldness: *There was no mistaking the approach of winter; he could feel its bite.*
6 STRONG EFFECT [U] a special quality in a performance, piece of writing etc that makes its arguments very effective and likely to persuade people: *The film gains incisive bite from Sellers' performance as the union chief.*
7 FISH [C] when a fish takes the food from a hook: *Sometimes I sit for hours and never* ***get a bite****.*
8 another/a second bite at the cherry *BrE* a second chance to do something
9 JAW [C usually singular] *technical* the way that a person or animal's top and bottom teeth touch when their mouth is closed: *Our dentist said that Emmy should wear a brace to improve her bite.* → LOVE BITE, SOUND BITE, → **sb's bark is worse than their bite** at BARK²(4)

ˈbite-sized (*also* **ˈbite-size**) *adj* [only before noun] small enough to put into your mouth to eat: *sushi served in convenient* ***bite-size pieces***

bit·ing /ˈbaɪtɪŋ/ *adj* **1** a biting wind is unpleasantly cold SYN **icy**: *A biting wind blew down from the hills.* **2** a biting criticism, remark etc is cruel or unkind: *a biting satire on corruption* —**bitingly** *adv*

bit·map /ˈbɪtmæp/ *n* [C] *technical* (*abbreviation* **BMP**) a computer image that is stored or printed as an arrangement of BITS: *bitmap fonts* —**bitmapped** *adj*: *bitmapped graphics*

ˈbit part *n* [C] a small and unimportant acting job in a play or film: *He's had bit parts in a couple of soaps.*

ˈbit ˌplayer *n* [C] someone who is not important and who has little influence in a particular situation: *Although he was NRC chairman, Hervey was strictly a bit player in government.*

bit·ten /ˈbɪtn/ *v* the past participle of BITE

bit·ter¹ /ˈbɪtə $ -ər/ ●●○ S3 W3 *adj*
1 feeling angry, jealous, and upset because you think you have been treated unfairly → **bitterly**: **[+about]** *I* ***feel*** *very* ***bitter*** *about it.* | *a bitter old man*
2 [only before noun] making you feel very unhappy and upset → **bitterly**: **a bitter disappointment/blow** *If he failed, it would be a bitter disappointment to his parents.* | *His photo stirred up bitter memories.* | **from bitter experience** (=because of your own very unpleasant experiences) *She* ***knew from bitter experience*** *that it would be impossible to talk it over with Julian.*
3 a bitter argument, battle etc is one in which people oppose or criticize each other with strong feelings of hate and anger: **bitter dispute/battle/struggle etc** *The couple are locked in a bitter battle for custody of the children.* | *The government faces* ***bitter opposition*** *to these policies.* | *The countries are still* ***bitter enemies****.*
4 having a strong sharp taste, like black coffee without sugar → **sour, sweet**: *Enjoy the beer's* ***bitter taste*** *as you slowly drink it.* | *bitter chocolate* THESAURUS TASTE
5 unpleasantly cold → **bitterly**: *a bitter wind* | *the* ***bitter cold*** *of the Midwestern winters*
6 to the bitter end continuing until the end, even though this is difficult: *Employees have vowed to* ***fight*** *the closure* ***to the bitter end****.*
7 a bitter pill (to swallow) something very unpleasant that

you must accept: *The knowledge that his friends no longer trusted him was a bitter pill to swallow.* —**bitterness** *n* [U]

bitter² *n* **1** [C,U] *BrE* a type of dark beer that is popular in Britain, or a glass of this: *A pint of bitter, please.* THESAURUS TASTE **2 bitters** [U] a strong bitter liquid made from plants that is added to alcoholic drinks

bit·ter·ly /ˈbɪtəli $ -ər-/ ●●○ *adv*
1 in a way that produces or shows feelings of great sadness or anger: *He **complained bitterly** about his exam grades.* | *I was **bitterly disappointed**.* | *The march was **bitterly opposed** by local residents.*
2 bitterly cold very cold

bit·ter·sweet /ˌbɪtəˈswiːt◂ $ -tər-/ *adj* **1** feelings, memories, or experiences that are bittersweet are happy and sad at the same time: *bittersweet memories of childhood* **2** a taste or smell that is bittersweet is both sweet and bitter at the same time

bit·ty /ˈbɪti/ *adj BrE* having too many small parts that do not seem to be related or connected to each other: *I thought the film was rather bitty.* —**bittiness** *n* [U]

bi·tu·men /ˈbɪtʃʊmɪn $ bɪˈtuː-/ *n* [U] a dark sticky substance that is used for making the surface of roads —**bituminous** /bɪˈtjuːmɪnəs $ -ˈtuː-/ *adj*

bi·valve /ˈbaɪvælv/ *n* [C] *technical* any sea animal that has two shells joined together: *bivalve molluscs*

biv·ou·ac¹ /ˈbɪvu-æk/ *n* [C] a temporary camp built outside without any tents

bivouac² *v* (**bivouacked**, **bivouacking**) [I] to spend the night outside without tents in a temporary camp: *The climbers bivouacked halfway up the mountain.*

bi·week·ly /ˌbaɪˈwiːkli◂/ *adj, adv* **1** appearing or happening every two weeks SYN **fortnightly**: *a biweekly magazine* **2** appearing or happening twice a week: *a biweekly television drama*

biz /bɪz/ *n* [singular] *informal* a particular type of business, especially one relating to entertainment: *the **music biz*** → SHOWBIZ

bi·zarre /bəˈzɑː $ -ˈzɑːr/ ●●○ *adj* very unusual or strange: *a bizarre coincidence* | *dancers in rather bizarre costumes* THESAURUS STRANGE —**bizarrely** *adv*

blab /blæb/ *v* (**blabbed**, **blabbing**) [I] *informal* to tell someone something that should be kept secret SYN **gossip**: **[+to]** *Don't go blabbing to your friends about this.*

blab·ber /ˈblæbə $ -ər/ *v* [I] *informal* to talk in a silly or annoying way for a long time: **[+on]** *I wish she'd stop blabbering on about her boyfriends.*

blab·ber·mouth /ˈblæbəmaʊθ $ -ər-/ *n* [C] *informal* someone who tells secrets because they always talk too much

black¹ /blæk/ ●●● S1 W1 *adj* (*comparative* **blacker**, *superlative* **blackest**)
1 COLOUR having the darkest colour, like coal or night: *a black evening dress* | **jet/inky black** (=very dark) *jet black hair*
2 NO LIGHT very dark because there is no light: *It was still **pitch black*** (=very dark) *out.*
3 PEOPLE (*also* **Black**) **a)** belonging to the race of people who originally came from Africa and who have dark brown skin → **white**: *Over half the students are black.* **b)** [only before noun] relating to black people: *politics from a black perspective* | *Black and Asian music*
4 DRINK [only before noun] black coffee or tea does not have milk in it OPP **white**: *Black coffee, no sugar, please.*
5 DIRTY *informal* very dirty: **be black with soot/dirt/age etc**
6 WITHOUT HOPE sad and without hope for the future: *the blackest period of European history* | *a mood of black despair* | *It's been another **black day** for the car industry, with more job losses announced.*
7 HUMOUR making jokes about serious subjects, especially death: *a very **black joke***
8 ANGRY [only before noun] full of feelings of anger or hate → **blackly**: *Denise gave me a **black look**.*
9 a black mark (against sb) if there is a black mark against you, someone has a bad opinion of you because of something you have done
10 not be as black as you are painted not to be as bad as people say you are
11 BAD *literary* very bad: *black deeds* —**blackness** *n*

black² ●●● S2 W2 *n*
1 [U] the dark colour of coal or night: *You look good wearing black.* → COAL-BLACK
2 (*also* **Black**) [C] someone who belongs to the race of people who originally came from Africa and who have dark brown skin → **white**: *laws that discriminated against blacks*
3 be in the black to have money in your bank account OPP **be in the red**

black³ *v* [T] **1** *BrE* if a TRADE UNION blacks goods or a company, it refuses to work with them: *The union has blacked all non-urgent work.* **2** *old-fashioned* to make something black

black out *phr v* **1** to become UNCONSCIOUS SYN **faint, pass out**: *For a few seconds, he thought he was going to black out.* **2 black sth ↔ out** to put a dark mark over something so that it cannot be seen: *The censors had blacked out several words.* **3 black sth ↔ out** to hide or turn off all the lights in a town or city, especially during war → **blackout**

ˌblack and ˈblue *adj* skin that is black and blue has BRUISES (=dark marks) on it as a result of being hit: *If you do that again, I'll beat you black and blue.*

ˌblack and ˈwhite *adj* **1** showing pictures or images only in black, white, and grey → **colour**: *black and white photos* | *an old black and white TV* **2 black and white** considering things in a way that is too simple and as if things are either completely good or completely bad: *There's still a tendency to see the issues in black and white.* **3 in black and white** in written form, and therefore definite: *Once it's down in black and white, you can't forget it.*

ˌblack ˈart *n* [U] (*also* **the black arts** [plural]) BLACK MAGIC

black·ball /ˈblækbɔːl $ -bɒːl/ *v* [T] to vote against someone, especially so that they cannot join a club or social group

ˈblack belt *n* [C] **1** a high rank in sports such as JUDO and KARATE **2** someone who has this rank: **[+in]** *Sandy's a black belt in judo.*

black·ber·ry /ˈblækbəri $ -beri/ *n* (*plural* **blackberries**) [C] a small black or purple BERRY from a bush that has THORNS (=sharp points) → see picture at **FRUIT¹**

Black·Ber·ry /ˈblækberi/ *n* [C] *trademark* a piece of WIRELESS (=using electronic signals not wires) electronic equipment that you can hold in your hand. You can use it as a PDA (=small computer that you use to store information such as telephone numbers, addresses, and appointments), as a MOBILE PHONE, to send and receive emails and TEXT MESSAGES, and to look at the Internet.

black·bird /ˈblækbɜːd $ -bɜːrd/ *n* [C] a common European and American bird, the male of which is completely black

black·board /ˈblækbɔːd $ -bɔːrd/ ●●● S3 *n* [C] a board with a dark smooth surface, used in schools for writing on with CHALK → **whiteboard**

ˌblack ˈbox *n* [C] *informal* a piece of equipment on an aircraft that records what happens on a flight and can be used to discover the cause of accidents SYN **flight recorder**

ˌblack ˈcomedy *n* [C,U] a play, story etc that is funny, but also shows the unpleasant side of human life

ˈBlack ˌCountry, the an industrial area in the West Midlands of England

black·cur·rant /ˌblækˈkʌrənt◂ $ -ˈkɜːr-/ *n* [C] a small blue-black BERRY that grows in bunches on a bush → see picture at **FRUIT¹**

ˌBlack ˈDeath, the the illness that killed large numbers of people in Europe and Asia in the 14th century → **BUBONIC PLAGUE, PLAGUE¹**(2)

ˌblack eˈconomy *n* [singular] business activity that takes place secretly, especially in order to avoid tax → **black market**

black·en /ˈblækən/ *v* **1** [I,T] to become black, or to make something black: *The thunder became louder and the sky blackened.* **2 blacken sb's name/character/reputation** to say unpleasant things about someone in order to make other people have a bad opinion of them

ˌblack ˈeye *n* [C] if you have a black eye, you have a dark area around your eye because you have been hit: *Jack looked like someone had* ***given*** *him a* ***black eye***.

ˌblack-eyed ˈbean (*also* **ˌblack-eyed ˈpea**) *n* [C] a small white bean with a black spot on it

ˌblack ˈgold *n* [U] *informal* oil

black·guard /ˈblægɑːd, -əd $ -ərd, -ɑːrd/ *n* [C] *old use* a man who treats other people very badly

black·head /ˈblækhed/ *n* [C] a small dark spot on the skin, with a black centre

ˌblack ˈhole *n* [C] **1** an area in outer space into which everything near it, including light, is pulled **2** *informal* something that uses up a lot of money: *I'm worried that the project could become a financial black hole.*

Black ˌHole of Calˈcutta, the a small, very crowded room or dark place is sometimes described as being 'like the Black Hole of Calcutta'. This phrase comes from a small room used as a prison in Calcutta, India where many British prisoners died during one night in 1756.

ˌblack ˈhumour *n* [U] jokes or funny stories that deal with the unpleasant parts of human life

ˌblack ˈice *n* [U] an area of ice that is very difficult to see: *Driving conditions are dangerous, with black ice in many areas.*

black·jack /ˈblækdʒæk/ *n* **1** [U] a card game, usually played for money, in which you try to get as close to 21 points as possible **2** [C] a weapon like a stick covered with leather, used to hit people

black·leg /ˈblækleg/ *n* [C] *BrE* someone who continues to work when other workers are on STRIKE – used to show disapproval

black·list¹ /ˈblæklɪst/ *v* [T] to put a person, country, product etc on a blacklist: *Many people in the industry were blacklisted for their communist sympathies.*

blacklist² *n* [C] a list of people, countries, products etc that are disapproved of, and should therefore be avoided or punished: *Friends of the Earth have produced a blacklist of environmentally damaging products.*

ˌblack ˈmagic *n* [U] magic that is believed to use the power of the Devil for evil purposes → **white magic**

black·mail¹ /ˈblækmeɪl/ ●○○ *n* [U]
1 when someone tries to get money from you or make you do what they want by threatening to tell other people your secrets
2 when someone tries to make you do what they want by making threats or by making you feel guilty if you do not do it: *She had already tried* ***emotional blackmail*** (=tried to make him feel guilty) *to stop him leaving.*

blackmail² ●○○ *v* [T] to use blackmail against someone: *He was jailed for four years for blackmailing gay businessmen.* | **blackmail sb into (doing) sth** *I refuse to be blackmailed into making a quick decision.* **THESAURUS** FORCE —**blackmailer** *n* [C]

ˌblack ˈmarket *n* [C] the system by which people illegally buy and sell foreign money, goods that are difficult to obtain etc: **[+in]** *There was a thriving black market in foreign currency.* | *Many foods were only available* ***on the black market***. | *black market cigarettes* → **black economy**

ˌblack marketˈeer *n* [C] someone who sells things on the black market

ˌBlack ˈMuslim *n* [C] a member of a group of black people who believe in the religion of Islam and want a separate black society

black·out /ˈblækaʊt/ *n* [C] **1** a period of darkness caused by a failure of the electricity supply SYN **power cut** **2** a situation in which particular pieces of news or information are not allowed to be reported: *As the crisis worsened, the authorities imposed a* ***news blackout***. **3** a period during a war when all the lights in a town or city must be turned off **4** if someone has a blackout, they suddenly become unconscious

ˌblack ˈpepper *n* [U] pepper made from crushed seeds from which the dark outer covering has not been removed → **white pepper**

ˌblack ˈpudding *n* [C,U] *BrE* a kind of thick dark SAUSAGE made from animal blood and fat

ˌblack ˈsheep *n* [C usually singular] someone who is regarded by other members of their family or group as a failure or embarrassment: *Amy's always been* ***the black sheep of the family***.

black·smith /ˈblækˌsmɪθ/ *n* [C] someone who makes and repairs things made of iron, especially HORSESHOES SYN **smith**

black·spot /ˈblækspɒt $ -spɑːt/ *n* [C] *BrE* a place or area where there are more problems than usual: *Arbroath is now the* ***unemployment blackspot*** *of northeast Scotland.* | *an* ***accident blackspot*** (=where there are a lot of road accidents)

black·thorn /ˈblækθɔːn $ -θɔːrn/ *n* [C] a European bush that has small white flowers

ˌblack-ˈtie *adj* a black-tie event is one at which people wear special formal clothes, such as TUXEDOs for men → **white-tie**

black·top /ˈblæktɒp $ -tɑːp/ *n AmE* **1** [U] a thick black sticky substance that becomes hard as it dries, used to cover roads SYN **tarmac** *BrE* **2 the blacktop** the surface of a road covered by this substance

ˌblack-water ˈrafting *n* [U] the activity of riding in an INNER TUBE (=large rubber tube filled with air, like those inside a tyre) along a fast-flowing river that runs under the ground through CAVES

ˌblack ˈwidow *n* [C] a very poisonous type of SPIDER that is black with red marks

blad·der /ˈblædə $ -ər/ *n* [C] **1** the organ in your body that holds URINE (=waste liquid) until it is passed out of your body **2** a bag of skin, leather, or rubber, for example inside a football, that can be filled with air or liquid → **GALL BLADDER**

blad·dered /ˈblædəd $ -ərd/ *adj* [not before noun] *BrE informal* very drunk

blade /bleɪd/ ●●○ S3 *n* [C]
1 the flat cutting part of a tool or weapon → **edge**: **[+of]** *The blade of the knife flashed in the moonlight.* | *a* ***razor blade***
2 the flat wide part of an object that pushes against air or water: *the blade of an oar*
3 blade of grass a single thin flat piece of grass
4 the metal part on the bottom of an ICE-SKATE
5 a thin curved piece of a strong material that someone with the lower part of their leg missing attaches to their leg in order to run → **SHOULDER BLADE**

blad·er /ˈbleɪdə $ -ər/ *n* [C] *informal* someone who SKATES or ROLLERBLADES

ˈblade ˌrunner *n* [C] *informal* a runner who runs with blades attached to their legs because the lower part of their legs are missing

blag /blæg/ *v* (**blagged**, **blagging**) [I,T] *BrE informal* to obtain something you want by talking in a clever way: *He blagged his way in by saying he was a friend of the owner.*

blag·ger /ˈblægə $ -ər/ *n* [C] *BrE informal* someone who gets something they want by lying to people in a clever way

blah¹ /blɑː/ *n* **1 blah, blah, blah** *spoken* used when you do not need to complete what you are saying because it is boring or because the person you are talking to already knows it: *You know how Michelle talks: 'Tommy did this, and Jesse did that, blah, blah, blah.'* **2** [U] *BrE spoken* remarks or statements that are boring and do not mean much: *the usual blah about everyone working harder* **3 the blahs** [plural] *AmE informal* a feeling of being sad and bored: *a case of the winter blahs*

blah² *adj AmE spoken informal* **1** not having an interesting taste, appearance, character etc: *The chili was kind of blah.* **2** slightly ill or unhappy: *I feel really blah today.*

blame¹ /bleɪm/ ●●● S2 W3 *v* [T]
1 to say or think that someone or something is responsible for something bad: *Don't blame me – it's not my fault.* | *I blame his mother. She does everything for him.* | **blame sb/sth for sth** *Marie still blames herself for Patrick's death.* | *The report blames poor safety standards for the accident.* | *The decision to increase interest rates was* ***widely blamed*** (=blamed by many people) *for the crisis.* | **blame sth on sb/sth** *One of the computers is broken and she's blaming it on me.* | *The crash was blamed on pilot error.*
2 sb/sth is to blame (for sth) used to say that someone or something is responsible for something bad: *Officials believe that more than one person may be to blame for the fire.* | **partly/largely/entirely etc to blame** *Television is partly to blame.*

REGISTER
In everyday English, people usually say something **is** someone's **fault**, rather than saying they **are to blame**: ***He was to blame for*** *the accident.* → *The accident* ***was his fault.***

3 I don't blame you/you can hardly blame him etc *spoken* used to say that you think it was right or reasonable for someone to do what they did: *'She's left her husband.' 'I don't blame her, after the way he treated her.'* | *You can hardly blame him for not waiting.*
4 don't blame me *spoken* used when you are advising someone not to do something but you think that they will do it in spite of your advice: *Buy it then, but don't blame me when it breaks down.*
5 sb only has himself/herself to blame *spoken* used to say that someone's problems are their own fault: *If he fails his exams, he'll only have himself to blame.*

THESAURUS
blame *v* [T] to say or think that someone or something is responsible for something bad that has happened: *Democrats have blamed Republicans for the failure to reach an agreement.* | *For many years I blamed myself for her death.*
put/place/lay the blame on sb/sth to say who or what you think is responsible for something bad that has happened, often unfairly or wrongly: *Don't try to put the blame on me!* | *Farmers have laid the blame for their problems entirely on EU policies.*
say it's sb's fault *especially spoken* to say that someone is responsible for something bad that has happened: *Are you saying it's my fault that we lost the game?*
hold sb responsible to say that someone is responsible for something bad that has happened, because it was their duty to prevent it from happening: *He was held personally responsible for the failure of the project.*

blame² ●●● S3 W2 *n* [U] responsibility for a mistake or for something bad: **[+for]** *Do you accept any blame for what happened?* | *I always* ***get the blame*** (=am blamed) *for his mistakes!* | *She stole the money but she's trying to* ***put the blame on*** (=blame) *me.*

COLLOCATIONS
VERBS
get the blame (=be blamed) *Sam knew that if something went wrong, he'd get the blame.*
take/accept/shoulder the blame (=say that something is your fault) *No one was prepared to take the blame for the disaster.*
put/pin the blame on sb (*also* **lay/place the blame on sb** *written*) (=blame someone, especially when it is not their fault) *Don't try to put the blame on me.*
shift the blame (onto sb) (=blame someone else for something you did) *She always tried to shift the blame onto her brother.*
apportion/assign blame *formal* (=find someone to blame for something) *He seemed to want to apportion blame for her death.*
the blame lies with sb (=used to say that someone is responsible for something bad) *In this case, the blame lay with the police.*
PHRASES
point the finger of blame at sb (=say that someone is responsible for something bad) *I couldn't believe it when they started pointing the finger of blame at me.*

blame·less /ˈbleɪmləs/ *adj* not guilty of anything bad SYN **innocent**: *The police are* ***not*** *always* ***entirely blameless*** (=are guilty of doing something bad) *in these matters.* | *She had led a* ***blameless life.*** —**blamelessly** *adv*

blame·wor·thy /ˈbleɪmˌwɜːði $ -ɜːr-/ *adj* deserving blame or disapproval: *blameworthy conduct*

blanch /blɑːntʃ $ blæntʃ/ *v* **1** [T] to put vegetables, fruit, or nuts into boiling water for a short time: *Blanch the peaches and remove the skins.* **2** [I] *literary* to become pale because you are frightened or shocked: *Patrick visibly blanched.*

blanc·mange /bləˈmɒnʒ, -ˈmɒndʒ $ -ˈmɑː-/ *n* [C,U] *BrE* a cold sweet food made from CORNFLOUR, milk, and sugar SYN **pudding** *AmE*

bland /blænd/ ●○○ *adj*
1 without any excitement, strong opinions, or special character SYN **dull**: *a few bland comments*
2 food that is bland has very little taste SYN **tasteless**: *a bland diet* THESAURUS ▸ TASTE —**blandly** *adv* —**blandness** *n* [U]

blan·dish·ments /ˈblændɪʃmənts/ *n* [plural] *formal* pleasant things that you say in order to persuade or influence someone: *How sensible she had been to resist his blandishments.*

blank¹ /blæŋk/ ●●○ S3 *adj*
1 without any writing, print, or recorded sound: ***Leave*** *the last page* ***blank.*** | *a blank cassette* THESAURUS ▸ EMPTY
2 a blank face or look shows no emotion, understanding, or interest → **blankly**: **blank face/look/expression/eyes** *Zoe looked at me with a blank expression.* | *She gazed at him in blank astonishment.*
3 go blank a) if your mind goes blank, or if you go blank, you are suddenly unable to remember something: *My heart began to race and my mind went blank.* **b)** to stop showing any images, writing etc: *Suddenly the screen went blank.* —**blankness** *n* [U] → BLANK VERSE

blank² *n* [C] **1** an empty space on a piece of paper, where you are supposed to write a word or letter: *When you've* ***filled in*** *the* ***blanks,*** *hand the form back to me.* **2 my mind's a blank** *spoken* used to say that you cannot remember something: *I'm trying to think of his name, but my mind's a complete blank.* **3** a CARTRIDGE (=container for a bullet in a gun) that contains an explosive but no bullet: *Soldiers* ***fired blanks*** *into the crowd.* **4 be shooting/firing blanks** *informal* if a man is shooting blanks or firing blanks, his SPERM is not able to make a woman PREGNANT → **draw a blank** at DRAW¹(32)

blank³ *v* **1** (*also* **blank out**) [I] *informal* if you blank, or if your mind blanks, you are suddenly unable to remember something: *I just blanked in the oral exam.* **2** [T] *BrE informal* to ignore someone who you would usually greet or speak to: *Last time I saw Mike Adams he completely blanked me.*

blank sth ↔ **out** *phr v* **1** to cover something so that it cannot be seen: *The actual names had been blanked out.* **2** to completely forget something, especially deliberately: *I tried to blank out everything he had said.*

ˌblank ˈcheque *BrE*, **ˌblank ˈcheck** *AmE n* [C] **1** a cheque that has been signed, but has not had the amount written on it **2 give sb a blank cheque** *BrE*, **give sb a blank check** *AmE* to give someone permission to do whatever they think is necessary in a particular situation

blan·ket¹ /ˈblæŋkɪt/ ●●○ *n*
1 [C] a cover for a bed, usually made of wool → **duvet**
2 [singular] a thick covering or area of something: **[+of]** *The hills were covered with a* ***blanket of snow.*** | **blanket of fog/cloud**

B

3 [singular] something that makes it hard for you to find information or the truth about something SYN **cloak**: **[+of]** *The trial was held under* ***a blanket of secrecy***. → **electric blanket** at ELECTRIC(1), **WET BLANKET**, **SECURITY BLANKET**

blanket² *v* [T] to cover something with a thick layer: **be blanketed in/with sth** *The rooftops were blanketed in snow.*

blanket³ *adj* [only before noun] **blanket statement/rule/ban etc** a statement, rule etc that affects everyone or includes all possible cases: *the proposed blanket ban on tobacco advertising* | *a blanket strategy*

blank·e·ty-blank /ˌblæŋkəti ˈblæŋk/ *adj* [only before noun] *AmE spoken* used to show annoyance when you want to avoid swearing: *The blankety-blank key is stuck!*

blank·ly /ˈblæŋkli/ *adv* in a way that shows no emotion, understanding, or interest: *Anna stared blankly at the wall.*

ˌblank ˈverse *n* [U] poetry that has a fixed RHYTHM but does not RHYME → **FREE VERSE**

blare /bleə $ bler/ ●○○ (*also* **blare out**) *v* [I,T] to make a very loud unpleasant noise: *Horns blared in the street outside.* —**blare** *n* [singular]

blar·ney /ˈblɑːni $ -ɑːr-/ *n* [U] *informal* pleasant but untrue things that you say to someone in order to trick or persuade them

ˈBlarney ˌStone, the a stone in the wall of Blarney Castle in the Republic of Ireland. People believe that, if you kiss it, it will bring you good luck and the ability to persuade people to do what you want.

bla·sé /ˈblɑːzeɪ $ blɑːˈzeɪ/ *adj* not worried or excited about things that most people think are important, impressive etc: **[+about]** *He's very blasé about money now that he's got that job.*

blas·pheme /blæsˈfiːm/ *v* [I] to speak in a way that insults God or people's religious beliefs, or to use the names of God and holy things when swearing —**blasphemer** *n* [C]

blas·phe·my /ˈblæsfəmi/ *n* (*plural* **blasphemies**) [C,U] something you say or do that is insulting to God or people's religious beliefs —**blasphemous** *adj*: *The book has been widely condemned as blasphemous.* —**blasphemously** *adv*

blast¹ /blɑːst $ blæst/ ●○○ *n* [C]

1 AIR/WIND a sudden strong movement of wind or air: **[+of]** *A* ***blast of*** *cold* ***air*** *swept through the hut.*

2 EXPLOSION an explosion, or the very strong movement of air that it causes: **in the blast** *Thirty-six people died in the blast.* | **bomb/shotgun/nuclear etc blast** *A bomb blast completely destroyed the building.*

3 LOUD NOISE a sudden very loud noise, especially one made by a whistle or horn: **[+on]** *The station master* ***gave*** *a* ***blast*** *on his whistle and we were off.* | **long/short blast** *a long trumpet blast*

4 (at) full blast as powerfully or loudly as possible: *I had the gas fire* ***going full blast***. | *The radio was* ***on at full blast***.

5 FUN **a blast** *informal* an enjoyable and exciting experience: *The concert* ***was a blast***. | *We* ***had a blast*** *at the fair.*

6 EMOTION a sudden strong expression of a powerful emotion: **[+of]** *She was totally unprepared for the blast of criticism she received.*

7 a blast from the past *informal* something from the past that you remember, see, or hear again, and that reminds you of that time in your life: *That's a blast from the past. No one has called me that for years.*

blast² ●○○ *v*

1 GUN/BOMB [T] to damage or destroy something, or to injure or kill someone, using a gun or a bomb: **blast sb with sth** *She blasted her husband with a shotgun because he was having an affair.* | *The first shot missed and* ***blasted*** *a* ***hole*** *in the far wall.* | *The plane was blasted out of the sky by a terrorist bomb.*

2 BREAK STH INTO PIECES [I,T] to break something into pieces using explosives, especially in order to build something such as a road: **blast sth through sth** *A 1.5 km tunnel was blasted through the mountain.* | **blast sth out of sth** *The road will have to be blasted out of solid rock.* | **[+through]** *Railway workers had blasted through the mountains 90 years before.*

3 LOUD NOISE (*also* **blast out**) [I,T] to produce a lot of loud noise, especially music: *He was woken by the radio alarm clock blasting out rock music.* | **[+from]** *Dance music blasted from the stereo.*

4 CRITICIZE [T] to criticize someone or something very strongly – used especially in news reports: **blast sb for (doing) sth** *Union leaders blasted the government for failing to tackle the jobs crisis.*

5 KICK/HIT A BALL [T] to hit or kick a ball very hard: *With six minutes remaining, he* ***blasted*** *the* ***ball*** *through the Coleraine defences for his 19th goal of the season.*

6 AIR/WATER [I,T] if air or water is blasted somewhere, or if it blasts somewhere, it moves there with great force: *The wind ripped through the trees and blasted a curtain of rain up the meadow.* | *Icy winds and driving snow blasted through the pine trees.*

7 SPORTS [T] *AmE informal* to beat another team very easily: *The Seahawks were blasted 35-14 by the Broncos.*

blast off *phr v* if a spacecraft blasts off, it leaves the ground → **BLAST-OFF**

blast³ (*also* ˌ**blast her/it etc**) *interjection* used when you are very annoyed about something: *Oh blast! I've forgotten my key.*

blas·ted /ˈblɑːstɪd $ ˈblæs-/ *adj* [only before noun] *spoken informal* used to express annoyance: *I wish that blasted baby would stop crying!*

ˈblast ˌfurnace *n* [C] a large industrial structure in which iron is separated from the rock that surrounds it

ˈblast-off *n* [U] the moment when a SPACECRAFT leaves the ground: *Ten seconds to blast-off.* → **blast off** at **BLAST²**

bla·tant /ˈbleɪtənt/ ●○○ *adj* something bad that is blatant is very clear and easy to see, but the person responsible for it does not seem embarrassed or ashamed: *blatant discrimination* THESAURUS **OBVIOUS** —**blatantly** *adv*

blath·er /ˈblæðə $ -ər/ *v* [I] to talk for a long time about unimportant things —**blather** *n* [C,U]

blax·ploi·ta·tion /ˌblæksplɔɪˈteɪʃən/ *n* [U] a type of American film made in the 1970s, in which the main characters are black: *blaxploitation films such as 'Shaft'*

blaze¹ /bleɪz/ ●○○ *n*

1 FIRE **a)** [C usually singular] a big dangerous fire – used especially in news reports → **ablaze**: *It took almost 100 firemen to bring the blaze under control.* | **fight/tackle/control a blaze** *Helicopters were used to help fight the blaze.* | **house/factory/barn etc blaze** *a huge chemical factory blaze* **b)** [singular] a fire burning with strong bright flames: *I lit the fire and soon had a* ***cheerful blaze*** *going.* THESAURUS **FIRE**

2 LIGHT/COLOUR [singular] very bright light or colour → **ablaze**: **[+of]** *the blaze of light from the security lamps* | *The garden is a* ***blaze of colour*** *at this time of year.*

3 blaze of publicity/glory a lot of public attention or success and praise: *As soon as the trial was over, the blaze of publicity surrounding him vanished.* | *She played the Canada tournament, then retired,* ***going out in a blaze of glory*** (=ending her career with a lot of success and praise).

4 [singular] a sudden show of very strong emotion: *A* ***blaze of anger*** *flashed across his face.*

5 what the blazes/who the blazes etc *old-fashioned spoken* used to emphasize a question when you are annoyed: *What the blazes is going on here?*

6 like blazes *old-fashioned spoken* as fast, as much, or as strongly as possible: *We had to run like blazes.*

7 [C usually singular] a white mark, especially one down the front of a horse's face

blaze² ●○○ *v* [I]

1 FIRE to burn very brightly and strongly → **blazing**: *The room was warm, with a* ***fire blazing*** *in the hearth.* THESAURUS **BURN**

2 LIGHT to shine with a very bright light: *A huge truck was advancing towards us, its headlights blazing.* | *The* ***sun blazed down*** *as we walked along the valley.* THESAURUS **SHINE**

3 EYES [usually in progressive] *literary* if someone's eyes are

blazing, their eyes are shining brightly because they are feeling a very strong emotion, usually anger: **[+with]** *Linda leapt to her feet, her dark eyes blazing with anger.*
4 GUN (*also* **blaze away**) if guns blaze, they fire bullets quickly and continuously: *An enemy plane roared overhead, its guns blazing.*
5 blaze a trail to develop or do something new and important, or to do something important that no one has done before: *an innovative young company that has blazed a trail for others to follow*
6 be blazed across/all over sth if something is blazed across a newspaper etc, it is written in a way that everyone will notice: *News of their divorce was blazed across all the tabloids.*

blaz·er /ˈbleɪzə $ -ər/ *n* [C] a jacket, sometimes with the special sign of a school, club etc on it

blaz·ing /ˈbleɪzɪŋ/ *adj* [only before noun] **1** extremely hot: *a blazing August afternoon* **2** full of strong emotions, especially anger: *He jumped to his feet in a blazing fury.* | **blazing row** (=very angry argument)

bla·zon /ˈbleɪzən/ *v* [T] **be blazoned across/on/over sth** to be written or shown on something in a very noticeable way

bleach¹ /bliːtʃ/ ●○○ *n* [U] a chemical used to make things pale or white, or to kill GERMS

bleach² *v* [T] to make something pale or white, especially by using chemicals or the sun: *She* ***bleached*** *her* ***hair*** *blonde.* | *The wood had been* ***bleached by the sun****.*

bleach·ers /ˈbliːtʃəz $ -ərz/ *n* [plural] *especially AmE* long wooden BENCHes arranged in rows, where you sit to watch sport

bleak /bliːk/ ●○○ *adj*
1 without anything to make you feel happy or hopeful: **a bleak future/prospect** *The company still hopes to find a buyer, but the future* ***looks bleak****.*
2 cold and without any pleasant or comfortable features: *a bleak January afternoon* | *The landscape was bleak.* —**bleakly** *adv* —**bleakness** *n* [U]

blear·y /ˈblɪəri $ ˈblɪri/ (*also* ˌ**bleary-ˈeyed**) *adj* unable to see very clearly, because you are tired or have been crying: *Steve emerged from his room, unshaven and bleary-eyed.* —**blearily** *adv* —**bleariness** *n* [U]

bleat /bliːt/ *v* **1** [I] to make the sound that a sheep or goat makes **2** [I,T] *informal* to complain in a silly or annoying way: *'But I've only just got here,' bleated Simon.* —**bleat** *n* [C]

bleed /bliːd/ ●●○ *v* (*past tense and past participle* **bled** /bled/)
1 BLOOD **a)** [I] to lose blood, especially because of an injury: *Your nose is bleeding.* | *Tragically, she* ***bled to death****.* | **bleed profusely/heavily** (=bleed a lot) *Mrs Burke was found unconscious and bleeding profusely.* **b)** [T] to take some blood from someone's body, done in the past in order to treat a disease: *When he fell sick several days later, he had a doctor bleed him.*
2 MONEY [T] to force someone to pay an unreasonable amount of money over a period of time: *His ex-wife clearly intends to bleed him for every last penny.* | **bleed sb dry/white** (=take all their money, possessions etc) *The ten-year war has bled the country dry.*
3 AIR/LIQUID [T] to remove air or liquid from a system in order to make it work properly, for example from a heating system: *We need to bleed the radiators.*
4 COLOUR [I] to spread from one area of cloth or paper to another SYN **run**: *Wash it in cold water so the colours don't bleed.*
5 bleed red ink *informal* if a company or business bleeds red ink, it loses a lot of money, rather than making money: *Analysts predict the retailer will continue to bleed red ink, with losses topping $180 million.* → **my heart bleeds (for sb)** at HEART¹(38)

bleed·er /ˈbliːdə $ -ər/ *n* [C] *BrE spoken not polite* a very offensive word for a person, especially a man that you dislike

bleed·ing¹ /ˈbliːdɪŋ/ *n* [U] the condition of losing blood from your body → **haemorrhage**: *Use pressure to* ***control*** *the* ***bleeding****.* | *The* ***bleeding*** *had almost* ***stopped****.* | *He died of* ***internal bleeding****.* | **severe/heavy bleeding** (=when someone is losing a lot of blood)

bleeding² *adj* [only before noun] *BrE spoken not polite* an offensive way of emphasizing something when you are angry: *Get your bleeding hands off my car!*

ˌ**bleeding ˈheart** (*also* ˌ**bleeding heart ˈliberal**) *n* [C] *informal* someone who feels sympathy for poor people or criminals, in a way that you think is not practical or helpful

bleep¹ /bliːp/ *n* [C] a short high sound made by a piece of electronic equipment

bleep² *v* **1** [I] to make a high electronic sound: *The timer on the cooker started to bleep.* **2** [T] *BrE* to let someone know, through their bleeper, that you want them to telephone you SYN **beep** *AmE* **3** [T] (*also* **bleep out**) to prevent an offensive word being heard on television or the radio by making a high electronic sound: *All the swear words had been bleeped out.*

bleep·er /ˈbliːpə $ -ər/ *n* [C] *BrE* a small machine that you carry with you, that makes short high electronic sounds to tell you that you must telephone someone SYN **pager, beeper** *AmE*

blem·ish¹ /ˈblemɪʃ/ *n* [C] a small mark, especially a mark on someone's skin or on the surface of an object, that spoils its appearance

blemish² *v* [T] to spoil something so that it is no longer beautiful or perfect → **unblemished**: *His record will be blemished by this failure.* —**blemished** *adj*

blend¹ /blend/ ●●○ *v*
1 [I,T] to combine different things in a way that produces an effective or pleasant result, or to become combined in this way: *a story that blends fact and legend* | **[+with/together]** *Leave the sauce to allow the flavours to blend together.*
2 [T] to thoroughly mix together soft or liquid substances to form a single smooth substance: *Blend the sugar, eggs, and flour.* THESAURUS ▸ MIX
3 [T] to produce tea, tobacco, WHISKY etc by mixing several different types together: *blended whisky*
GRAMMAR **Blend** is usually passive in this meaning.

blend in *phr v* if someone or something blends in with people or objects, they match them or are similar, and you do not notice them: **[+with]** *The old house blends in perfectly with the countryside.*

blend² *n* [C] **1** a product such as tea, tobacco, or WHISKY that is a mixture of several different types **2** a mixture of different things that combine together well: *an excellent team, with a nice blend of experience and youthful enthusiasm* THESAURUS ▸ MIXTURE

ˌ**blended ˈfamily** *n* [C] a family in which one or both parents have children from previous marriages living with the family

blend·er /ˈblendə $ -ər/ *n* [C] an electric machine that you use to mix liquids and soft foods together SYN **liquidizer** *BrE*

bless /bles/ ●●○ S3 *v* [T]
1 bless you! *spoken* **a)** what you say when someone SNEEZES **b)** used to thank someone for doing something for you
2 bless (him/her etc) *spoken* used to show that you are fond of someone, amused by them, or pleased by something they have done: *He's always willing to help. Bless him!* | *'Jess made this card for me.' 'Bless!'*
3 be blessed with sth to have a special ability, good quality etc: *We're both blessed with good health.*
4 if God blesses someone or something, he helps and protects them: *May God bless you.*
5 to ask God to protect someone or something: *The couple later* ***had*** *their* ***marriage blessed*** *in their local parish church.*
6 to make something holy: *Then the priest blesses the bread and wine.*

B

7 bless my soul/I'll be blessed! *old-fashioned spoken* used to express surprise

bless·ed /ˈblesɪd/ *adj* **1** [only before noun] *spoken* used to express annoyance: *Now where have I put that blessed book?* **2** [only before noun] very enjoyable or desirable: *a few moments of blessed silence* **3** holy: *the Blessed Virgin* —**blessedly** *adv* —**blessedness** *n* [U]

bless·ing /ˈblesɪŋ/ ●○○ *n*
1 [C] something that you have or something that happens which is good because it improves your life, helps you in some way, or makes you happy: *The dishwasher has been a real blessing!* | **it is a blessing (that)** *It's a blessing no one was badly hurt.*
2 [U] someone's approval or encouragement for a plan, activity, idea etc: **with sb's blessing** *They were determined to marry, with or without their parents' blessing.* | *The Defense Department* **has given** *its* **blessing to** *the scheme.*
3 a mixed blessing a situation that has both good and bad parts: *Having children so early in their marriage was a mixed blessing.*
4 a blessing in disguise something that seems to be bad or unlucky at first, but which you later realize is good or lucky
5 count your blessings used to tell someone to remember how lucky they are, especially when they are complaining about something
6 [C,U] protection and help from God, or words spoken to ask for this: *The priest gave the blessing.*

bleth·er /ˈbleðə $ -ər/ *v* [I] to talk about things that are not important - used especially in Scotland —**blether** *n* [C,U]

blew /bluː/ *v* the past tense of BLOW

blight¹ /blaɪt/ *n* **1** [singular, U] an unhealthy condition of plants in which parts of them dry up and die **2** [singular] something that makes people unhappy or that spoils their lives or the environment they live in: **[+on]** *Her guilty secret was a blight on her happiness.* | *the blight of poverty*

blight² *v* [T] to spoil or damage something, especially by preventing people from doing what they want to do: *a disease which, though not fatal, can blight the lives of its victims* | *a country blighted by poverty* —**blight·ed** *adj*: *blighted hopes*

blight·er /ˈblaɪtə $ -ər/ *n* [C] *BrE old-fashioned informal* **1** used to talk about someone that you feel sorry for or JEALOUS of: *Poor old blighter.* | *You lucky blighter!* **2** a bad or unpleasant person

Bligh·ty /ˈblaɪti/ *BrE old use* a name for Britain which was used especially by British soldiers and other British people working abroad for the British Empire during the 19th and early 20th centuries. It is now sometimes used humorously.

bli·mey /ˈblaɪmi/ *interjection BrE spoken informal* used to express surprise: *Blimey, look at that!*

blimp /blɪmp/ *n* [C] **1** a small AIRSHIP (=type of aircraft without wings) **2** *AmE spoken not polite* an offensive word for a very fat person

Blimp (*also* ˌ**Colonel** ˈ**Blimp**) *n* [C] *BrE* someone, especially an old man, with old-fashioned political ideas - used to show disapproval —**Blimpish** *adj*

blind¹ /blaɪnd/ ●●● S2 W3 *adj*
1 UNABLE TO SEE **a)** unable to see → **colour-blind**, **visually impaired**, **handicapped**: *a school for blind children* | *the needs of blind people* | **totally/completely/almost/partially blind** *She's almost blind in her right eye.* | *He was slowly* **going blind** (=becoming blind). | *Beverley was* **born blind**. **b) the blind** [plural] people who are unable to see: *talking books for the blind* **c) as blind as a bat** unable to see well - used humorously: *I'm as blind as a bat without my glasses.* **d) blind with tears/rage/pain etc** unable to see because of tears, pain, or a strong emotion → **blindly**: *She screamed at him, her eyes blind with tears.*
2 be blind to sth to completely fail to notice or realize something → **blindly**: *International companies are all too often blind to local needs.* | *He was totally blind to the faults of his children.*
3 turn a blind eye (to sth) to deliberately ignore something that you know should not be happening: *Teachers were turning a blind eye to smoking in school.*
4 not take/pay a blind bit of notice *BrE informal* to completely ignore what someone does or says, especially in a way that is annoying: *He never pays a blind bit of notice to what his staff tell him.*
5 not make a blind bit of difference *BrE informal* used to emphasize that whatever someone says or does will not change the situation at all: *Try and talk to her if you want, but I don't think it'll make a blind bit of difference.*
6 FEELINGS **a) blind faith/prejudice/obedience etc** strong feelings that someone has without thinking about why they have them - used to show disapproval: *Blind faith sent thousands of people to a pointless war.* | *a story about blind loyalty* **b) blind panic/rage** strong feelings of fear or anger that you cannot control: *In a moment of blind panic, she had pulled the trigger and shot the man dead.* | *Blind rage took hold of him.*
7 ROAD **blind bend/corner** a corner in a road that you cannot see beyond when you are driving
8 the blind leading the blind used to say that people who do not know much about what they are doing are guiding or advising others who know nothing at all
9 AIRCRAFT blind flying is when you use only instruments to fly an aircraft because you cannot see through cloud, mist etc —**blindness** *n*

blind² ●●○ *v* [T]
1 to make it difficult for someone to see for a short time: *For a moment, I was blinded by the glare of headlights coming towards me.* | *The dust choked and blinded him.* | *Blinded by tears, I walked towards the door.*
2 to make someone lose their good sense or judgment and be unable to see the truth about something: *He should have known better, but he was blinded by his own wants.* | **blind sb to sth** *Children's bad behaviour should not blind us to their need for love.* | *His single-minded determination to win the war is blinding him to other dangers.*
3 to permanently destroy someone's ability to see: *He had been blinded in an explosion.*
4 blind sb with science to confuse or trick someone by using complicated language → **effing and blinding** at EFF(1)

blind³ ●●○ *n*
1 (*also* **(window) shade** *AmE*) [C] a covering, especially one made of cloth, that can be rolled up and down to cover a window inside a building: *The* **blinds** *were* **drawn** (=pulled down) *to protect the new furniture from the sun.* |

open/pull down/draw the blinds → ROLLER BLIND, VENETIAN BLIND
2 [C] *AmE* a small shelter where you can watch birds or animals without being seen by them SYN **hide** *BrE*
3 [singular] a trick or excuse to stop someone from discovering the truth
blind⁴ *adv* **blind drunk** *BrE informal* extremely drunk → **rob sb blind** at ROB(3), → **swear blind** at SWEAR(3)
ˌblind ˈalley *n* [C] **1** a small narrow street with no way out at one end **2** a way of doing something that seems as if it will have a successful result, but which in fact does not: *False information has led the police up a series of blind alleys.*
ˌblind ˈdate *n* [C] an arranged meeting between two people who have not met each other before: *Would you ever go on a blind date?*
blind·er /ˈblaɪndə $ -ər/ *n* **1** [singular] *BrE informal* an excellent performance, especially in sport: *He played an absolute blinder!* **2 blinders** [plural] *AmE* pieces of leather that are put beside a horse's eyes to stop it from seeing objects on either side SYN **blinkers** *BrE*
blind·fold¹ /ˈblaɪndfəʊld $ -foʊld/ *n* [C] a piece of cloth that covers someone's eyes to prevent them from seeing anything
blindfold² *v* [T] to cover someone's eyes with a piece of cloth: *Blindfold the prisoner!*
blindfold³ *BrE* (*also* **blind·fold·ed** /ˈblaɪndfəʊldɪd $ -foʊld-/) *adv* **1** with your eyes covered by a piece of cloth **2 can do sth blindfold** *informal* used to say that it is very easy for you to do something because you have done it so often
blind·ing /ˈblaɪndɪŋ/ *adj* **1** [usually before noun] so bright or strong that you cannot see properly: **blinding flash/light/glare etc** *the desert with its strange twisted plants and its blinding light* | **blinding rain/snow/heat etc** *I struggled back to the hut through blinding rain.* THESAURUS ▸ BRIGHT **2 blinding headache** a very bad HEADACHE **3 blinding realization/clarity/revelation etc** a sudden realization, clear understanding, or new idea about something: *It was then that she realised, with blinding clarity, that she loved him.* | *Suddenly, I had a* ***blinding flash*** *of inspiration.* **4** *BrE spoken informal* very good and enjoyable: *It's a blinding album.*
blind·ing·ly /ˈblaɪndɪŋli/ *adv* very or extremely: *It was* ***blindingly obvious*** *that Max wasn't interested.*
blind·ly /ˈblaɪndli/ *adv* **1** not thinking about something or trying to understand it: *Don't just blindly accept what you are told.* **2** not seeing or noticing what is around you, especially because you are upset: *'I don't know,' she repeated as she* ***stared blindly*** *down into her glass.* | *I ran blindly upstairs.*
ˌblind man's ˈbuff *n* [U] a children's game in which one player whose eyes are covered tries to catch the others
blind·side /ˈblaɪndsaɪd/ *v* [T] *AmE informal* **1** to hit the side of a vehicle with your vehicle in an accident: *Their car was blindsided by a bus at the intersection.* **2** to give someone an unpleasant surprise: *I was blindsided by his suggestion.*
ˈblind spot *n* [C] **1** something that you are unable or unwilling to understand: *I have a blind spot where computers are concerned.* **2** the part of the road that you cannot see when you are driving a car **3** the point in your eye where the nerve enters, which is not sensitive to light
bling /blɪŋ/ (*also* **bling bling** /blɪŋ ˈblɪŋ/) *n* [U] *informal* expensive objects such as JEWELLERY that are worn in a way that is very easy to notice
blink¹ /blɪŋk/ ●●○ *v*
1 [I,T] to shut and open your eyes quickly: *I blinked as I came out into the sunlight.*
2 [I] if lights blink, they shine unsteadily or go on and off quickly: *The light on your answering machine is blinking.*
3 not (even) blink to not seem at all surprised: *When I told her how much it would cost, she didn't even blink.*
4 before you could blink *spoken* extremely quickly
5 blink back/away tears to shut and open your eyes in order to get rid of tears: *Lynn laughed, blinking back unexpected tears.*
blink² *n* **1 on the blink** *spoken* not working properly: *My computer's on the blink again.* **2 in the blink of an eye** very quickly **3** [C] the action of quickly shutting and opening your eyes
blink·ered /ˈblɪŋkəd $ -ərd/ *adj* **1** having a limited view of a subject, or refusing to accept or consider different ideas SYN **narrow-minded**: **a blinkered attitude/approach** *a blinkered attitude to other cultures* **2** a horse that is blinkered is wearing blinkers
blink·ers /ˈblɪŋkəz $ -ərz/ *n* [plural] **1** *BrE* pieces of leather that are put beside a horse's eyes to stop it from seeing objects on either side SYN **blinders** *AmE* **2** *AmE informal* the small lights on a car that you flash on and off to show which way you are turning SYN **indicators**
blink·ing /ˈblɪŋkɪŋ/ *adj* [only before noun] *BrE informal* used to show that you are annoyed: *Turn that blinking music down!*
blip /blɪp/ *n* [C] **1** a short high electronic sound, or a flashing light on the screen of a piece of electronic equipment: *blips on a radar screen* **2** a short pause or change in a process or activity, especially when the situation gets worse for a while before it improves again: *A government spokesman described the rise in inflation as a* ***temporary blip***.
bliss /blɪs/ ●○○ *n* [U] perfect happiness or enjoyment: **domestic/wedded/marital bliss** *six months of wedded bliss* | *I didn't have to get up till 11 – it was sheer bliss.*
blissed-out /ˌblɪst ˈaʊt/ *adj BrE informal* extremely happy and relaxed, especially as a result of using illegal drugs: *blissed-out partygoers* —**bliss out** *v* [I]
bliss·ful /ˈblɪsfəl/ *adj* **1** extremely happy or enjoyable: *blissful sunny days* THESAURUS ▸ HAPPY **2 blissful ignorance** a situation in which you do not yet know about something unpleasant —**blissfully** *adv*: *Jean seems blissfully happy.* | *blissfully unaware of the impending danger*
B-list /ˈbiː lɪst/ *adj* [only before noun] among the group of film stars, musicians etc who are fairly famous or popular, but are not the most popular or famous → **A-list**: *B-list celebrities*
blis·ter¹ /ˈblɪstə $ -ər/ ●○○ *n* [C]
1 a swelling on your skin containing clear liquid, caused, for example, by a burn or continuous rubbing: *New shoes always give me blisters.*
2 a swelling on the surface of metal, rubber, painted wood etc
blister² *v* [I,T] to develop blisters, or make blisters form: *The paint will blister in the heat.* —**blistered** *adj*: *My hands were blistered from all the digging.*
blis·ter·ing /ˈblɪstərɪŋ/ *adj* **1** extremely hot SYN **blazing**: *the blistering heat of the desert* **2 blistering attack/criticism etc** very critical remarks expressing anger and disapproval: *a blistering attack on her boss* **3** used to describe actions in sport that are very fast or forceful: *Hamilton set a blistering pace.* —**blisteringly** *adv*: *a blisteringly hot day*
ˈblister pack *n* [C] a package that is made from hard clear plastic. It fits closely round the object inside it, and can hang on a hook. Blister packs are used so that customers in shops can see the things that are for sale without being able to touch them.
blithe /blaɪð $ blaɪð, blaɪθ/ *adj* **1** seeming not to care or worry about the effects of what you do: *a blithe disregard for the facts* **2** *literary* happy and having no worries —**blithely** *adv*: *He seems blithely unaware of how much anger he's caused.*
blith·er·ing /ˈblɪðərɪŋ/ *adj* **blithering idiot** *spoken* someone who has done something very stupid
blitz /blɪts/ *n* [C usually singular] **1** a sudden military attack, especially from the air: **the Blitz** (=the bombing of British cities by German aircraft in 1940 and 1941) **2** *informal* a period of great effort in order to deal with something quickly and completely: **[+on]** *We'll have to have a blitz on the house before your parents arrive.* **3** a big

B

effort to make people notice something or buy something: **a media/marketing/advertising etc blitz** *The campaign was launched with a nationwide publicity blitz.* —**blitz** *v* [T]: *News came that Rotterdam had been blitzed.*

bliz·zard /ˈblɪzəd $ -ərd/ ●○○ *n* [C]
1 a severe snowstorm: *We got stuck in a blizzard.* THESAURUS ▸ STORM
2 a sudden large amount of something unpleasant or annoying that you must deal with → **flood**: **[+of]** *a blizzard of emails*

bloat·ed /ˈbləʊtɪd $ ˈbloʊ-/ *adj* **1** full of liquid, gas, food etc, so that you look or feel much larger than normal: *a red bloated face | I feel really bloated after that meal.* **2** if you describe an organization as bloated, you mean that it is too big and does not work effectively: *the bloated state bureaucracy*

bloa·ter /ˈbləʊtə $ ˈbloʊtər/ *n* [C] a smoked fish

blob /blɒb $ blɑːb/ *n* [C] **1** a very small round mass of a liquid or sticky substance: **[+of]** *a blob of honey* **2** something that cannot be clearly seen, especially because it is far away: *Without a telescope, the comet will look like a fuzzy blob.*

bloc /blɒk $ blɑːk/ *n* [C usually singular] a large group of people or countries with the same political aims, working together: *the former Soviet bloc* → EN BLOC

BLOCK

breeze-block *BrE*/ cinder block *AmE*

block of flats *BrE*/ apartment block *AmE*

wooden blocks

block[1] /blɒk $ blɑːk/ ●●● S2 W2 *n* [C]
1 SOLID MATERIAL a piece of hard material such as wood or stone with straight sides → BREEZE-BLOCK, BUILDING BLOCK, CINDER BLOCK: **[+of]** *a block of ice | a wall made of concrete blocks* THESAURUS ▸ PIECE → see picture at PIECE[1]
2 STREETS/AREA **a)** *AmE* the distance along a city street from where one street crosses it to the next: *Head for 44th Street, a few blocks east of Sixth Avenue. | The church is down the block.* **b)** the four city streets that form a square around an area of buildings: *Let's walk round the block. | She grew up playing with the other kids on the block.* **c)** *AusE* a large piece of land: *a ten-acre block near the city*
3 LARGE BUILDING a large building divided into separate parts: **[+of]** ***a block of flats** | an **office block** | an **apartment block** | the school science block*
4 QUANTITY OF THINGS a quantity of things of the same kind, considered as a single unit: **[+of]** *New employees receive a block of shares in the firm. | Set aside blocks of time for doing your homework.*
5 block booking/voting an arrangement that is made for a whole group to buy something or to vote together
6 INABILITY TO THINK [usually singular] the temporary loss of your normal ability to think, learn, write etc: *I have a **mental block** whenever I try to remember my password. | After his second novel, Garland had **writer's block*** (=he could not write anything).
7 STOPPING MOVEMENT [usually singular] something that prevents movement or progress: **[+to]** *a major block to progress* → ROADBLOCK, STUMBLING BLOCK
8 PUNISHMENT **the block** in the past, a solid block of wood on which someone's head was cut off as a punishment
9 put your head/neck on the block to risk destroying other people's opinion of you or losing your job by doing or saying something: *I'm not prepared to put my head on the block for him.*
10 SPORT a movement in sport that stops an opponent going forward or playing the ball forward
11 SELL **go on the block** to be sold, especially at an AUCTION: *$500 million worth of art will go on the block.* → BLOCK CAPITALS, TOWER BLOCK, → **be a chip off the old block** at CHIP[1](7), → **I'll knock your block off** at KNOCK[1](24)

block[2] ●●● S3 *v* [T]
1 (*also* **block up**) to prevent anything moving through a space by being or placing something across it or in it: *A fallen tree is blocking the road. | The sink's blocked up.*
2 block sb's way/path/exit/escape etc to stand in front of someone, so that they cannot go past: *I tried to get through, but there were people blocking my way.*
3 to stop something happening, developing, or succeeding: *The Senate blocked publication of the report. | laws designed to block imports of cheap tobacco*
4 block sb's view to be in front of someone, so that they cannot see something: *The huge building across the street blocked our view of the sea.*
5 (*also* **block out**) to stop light reaching a place: *Can you move? You're blocking my light.*
6 to stop a ball, a blow etc from getting to where your opponent wants it to: *a shot blocked by the goalkeeper*

block sb/sth ↔ **in** *phr v*
1 to park your car too close to another car, so that the other one cannot drive away
2 to paint or draw simple shapes or areas of colour: *I'll just block in the main buildings.*

block sth ↔ **off** *phr v* to completely close something such as a road or an opening: *Police blocked off the city centre streets. | The fireplace had been blocked off.*

block sth ↔ **out**
1 to stop light reaching a place: *There was a heavy curtain blocking out the light.*
2 to stop yourself thinking about something or remembering it: *a memory so terrible that she tried to block it out*

block·ade[1] /blɒˈkeɪd $ blɑː-/ *n* [C] **1** [usually singular] the surrounding of an area by soldiers or ships to stop people or supplies entering or leaving: *a naval blockade | They've **imposed** an economic **blockade** on the country. | an agreement to **lift** the **blockade*** (=end it) **2** something that is used to stop vehicles or people entering or leaving a place: *Angry farmers used tractors as blockades on the streets.*

blockade[2] *v* [T] to put a place under a blockade: *The ships blockaded the port.*

block·age /ˈblɒkɪdʒ $ ˈblɑː-/ *n* **1** [C] something that is stopping movement in a narrow place: *a blockage in the pipe* **2** [U] the state of being blocked or prevented

ˌblock and ˈtackle *n* [C usually singular] a piece of equipment with wheels and ropes, used for lifting heavy things

block·bust·er /ˈblɒkˌbʌstə $ ˈblɑːkˌbʌstər/ *n* [C] *informal* a book or film that is very good or successful: *the latest Hollywood blockbuster* THESAURUS ▸ MOVIE —**blockbusting** *adj*

ˌblock ˈcapitals *n* [plural] letters in their large form, such as A, B, C, rather than a, b, c SYN **capital letters**: *Complete the form in block capitals.*

block·head /ˈblɒkhed $ ˈblɑːk-/ *n* [C] *old-fashioned informal* a very stupid person

block·house /ˈblɒkhaʊs $ ˈblɑːk-/ *n* [C] a small strong building used as a shelter from enemy guns

ˌblock ˈletters *n* [plural] block capitals

ˈblock ˌparty *n* [C] *AmE* a party held in the street for all the people living in the area

blog /blɒg $ blɑːg/ ●●○ *n* [C] a web page containing information or opinions from a particular person or about a particular subject, to which new information is added regularly SYN **web log** —**blog** *v* [I] —**blogger** *n* [C]

blog·o·sphere /ˈblɒgəsfɪə $ -ˈblɑːgəsfɪr/ *n* [C] *informal* personal websites and WEBLOGS, considered as a group

blog·post /ˈblɒgpəʊst $ ˈblɑːgpoʊst/ *n* [C] something that has been written as part of a blog

blog·zine /ˈblɒgziːn $ ˈblɑːg-/ *n* [C] a magazine on the Internet that is like a BLOG

bloke /bləʊk $ bloʊk/ ●●○ S3 *n* [C] *BrE informal* a man: *He's a nice bloke.*

blok·ish, **blokeish** /ˈbləʊkɪʃ $ ˈbloʊ-/ *adj BrE informal* if you do blokish things, you behave in a traditionally male way: *playing football, fixing the car, and other blokish activities*

blond /blɒnd $ blɑːnd/ ●●● S3 *adj*
1 another spelling of BLONDE
2 a man who is blond has pale or yellow hair

blonde[1] /blɒnd $ blɑːnd/ ●●● S3 *adj*
1 blonde hair is pale or yellow in colour
2 a woman who is blonde has pale or yellow hair

blonde[2] *n* [C] *informal* a woman with pale or yellow-coloured hair → **brunette**: *a beautiful blonde*

blood[1] /blʌd/ ●●● S2 W1 *n* [U]
1 the red liquid that your heart pumps around your body: *Her body was found in a pool of blood.* | *Blood oozed from a cut on his forehead.* | *Blood tests proved he was not the father.*
2 (have) sb's blood on your hands to have caused someone's death: *dictators with blood on their hands*
3 in cold blood in a cruel and deliberate way: *Evans had been* ***murdered in cold blood****.*
4 make sb's blood boil to make someone extremely angry: *The way they treat people makes my blood boil.*
5 make sb's blood run cold to make someone feel extremely frightened
6 like getting blood out of a stone almost impossible: *Getting the truth out of her is like getting blood out of a stone.*
7 blood is thicker than water used to say that family relationships are more important than any other kind
8 be after sb's blood to be angry enough to want to hurt someone
9 sb's blood is up *BrE* someone is extremely angry about something and determined to do something about it: *They tried to stop me, but my blood was up.*
10 the family to which you belong from the time that you are born: *There's Irish blood on his mother's side.*
11 be/run in sb's blood if an ability or tendency is in, or runs in, someone's blood, it is natural to them and others in their family
12 sweat blood to work extremely hard to achieve something: *Beth sweated blood over that article.*
13 blood, sweat, and tears extremely hard work
14 new/fresh blood new members in a group or organization who bring new ideas and energy: *We need to bring in some new blood and fresh ideas.*
15 blood on the carpet a situation where people have a very strong disagreement, with the result that something serious happens, such as someone losing his or her job
16 young blood *old-fashioned* a fashionable young man
17 *spoken informal* a way of greeting a friend, used by young men → **bad blood** at BAD[1](27), → **BLUE-BLOODED, RED BLOOD CELL, WHITE BLOOD CELL,** → **your own flesh and blood** at FLESH[1](6), → **shed blood** at SHED[2](5)

COLLOCATIONS

VERBS

lose blood (=from a cut or wound) *He had lost a lot of blood and was very weak.*
give/donate blood (=provide blood from your body for the medical treatment of other people) *The Health Service is asking for more people to donate blood.*
draw blood (=make someone bleed) *He touched me with the knife and it drew blood.*
blood flows *A quick walk will get the blood in your legs flowing again.*
blood trickles (=moves slowly) *The blood was beginning to trickle down his leg.*
blood oozes (=comes out slowly) *Blood was oozing from her forehead.*
be covered in blood *His face was covered in blood.*
blood gushes/streams (=moves fast) | **be caked with blood** (=covered with dry blood) | **be spattered/splattered with blood** (=covered with small spots of blood)

blood + NOUN

blood pressure (=the force with which blood moves through your body) *High blood pressure increases the risk of a heart attack.*
sb's blood type/group (=one of the different types of human blood) *What blood type are you?*
a blood cell *The red blood cells carry oxygen.*
a blood vessel (=a tube in your body through which blood flows) | **a blood clot** (=a mass formed when blood dries or sticks together) | **the blood supply** (=the blood that flows to a part of the body) | **a blood test** (=a test done on your blood to see if you have a disease or another condition) | **a blood sample** (=a small amount of blood taken from your body to test) | **a blood transfusion** (=putting more blood in someone's body for medical reasons)

PHRASES

a drop of blood *Police found tiny drops of blood in the apartment.*
loss of blood *She suffered a massive loss of blood.*
a pool of blood | **a trickle of blood**

blood[2] *v* [T] *BrE* to give someone their first experience of an activity, especially a difficult or unpleasant one

ˌblood-and-ˈguts *adj* [only before noun] full of action or violence: *a blood-and-guts struggle between the two teams*

ˌblood-and-ˈthunder *adj* [only before noun] *BrE* full of exciting and violent action or emotion

ˈblood bank *n* [C] a store of human blood to be used in hospital treatment

blood·bath /ˈblʌdbɑːθ $ -bæθ/ *n* [singular] the violent killing of many people at one time SYN **massacre**

ˌblood ˈbrother *n* [C] a man who promises loyalty to another, often in a ceremony in which the men's blood is mixed together

ˈblood count *n* [C] **1** a medical examination of someone's blood to see if it contains the right substances in the right amounts **2** the number of cells in someone's blood: *Her blood count is very low.*

blood·cur·dling /ˈblʌdˌkɜːdlɪŋ $ -ɜːr-/ *adj* extremely frightening: *a bloodcurdling scream*

ˈblood ˌdiamond (*also* **ˈconflict ˌdiamond**) *n* [C] a diamond that comes from a place where there is a war and is sold illegally, in order to provide money so that the war can continue – used to show disapproval

ˈblood ˌdonor *n* [C] someone who gives their blood to be used in the medical treatment of other people

blood·fest /ˈblʌdfest/ *n* [C] *informal* something such as a film or computer game that involves a lot of killing with weapons

ˈblood feud *n* [C] a quarrel between people or families that lasts for many years, in which each side murders or injures members of the other side

ˈblood group *n* [C] *especially BrE* one of the classes into which human blood can be separated, including A, B, AB, and O SYN **blood type** *AmE*

ˈblood heat *n* [U] the normal temperature of the human body

blood·hound /ˈblʌdhaʊnd/ *n* [C] a large dog with a very good sense of smell, often used for hunting

blood·less /ˈblʌdləs/ *adj* **1** without killing or violence: *a bloodless coup* **2** a bloodless part of your body is very pale: *His lips were thin and bloodless.* **3** lacking in human feeling —**bloodlessly** *adv*

blood·let·ting /ˈblʌdˌletɪŋ/ *n* [U] **1** killing people SYN **bloodshed**: *The movie contains scenes of violence and bloodletting.* **2** a medical treatment used in the past that involved removing some of a person's blood **3** a reduction in the number of people working for an organization, industry etc: *Many jobs have been lost, and the bloodletting isn't over yet.*

blood·line /ˈblʌdlaɪn/ *n* [C] all the members of a family of people or animals over a period of time → **pedigree**: *a royal bloodline*

ˈblood lust *n* [U] a strong desire to be violent

ˈblood ˌmoney *n* [U] **1** money paid for murdering someone **2** money paid to the family of someone who has been murdered

B

ˈblood ˌorange *n* [C] an orange with red juice

ˈblood ˌpoisoning *n* [U] a serious illness in which an infection spreads through your blood

ˈblood ˌpressure *n* [U] the force with which blood travels through your body: *high blood pressure* | **check/take sb's blood pressure** (=measure it) *The nurse will take your blood pressure.*

ˈblood-red *adj* dark red, like blood —**blood-red** *n* [U]

ˈblood reˌlation (*also* **ˈblood ˌrelative**) *n* [C] someone related to you by birth rather than by marriage

blood·shed /ˈblʌdʃed/ *n* [U] the killing of people, usually in fighting or war: *diplomacy aimed at stopping further bloodshed*

blood·shot /ˈblʌdʃɒt $ -ʃɑːt/ *adj* if your eyes are bloodshot, the parts that are normally white are red or pink

ˈblood sport *n* [C] a sport that involves the killing of animals: *a demonstration against blood sports*

blood·stain /ˈblʌdsteɪn/ *n* [C] a mark or spot of blood —**bloodstained** *adj*: *a bloodstained handkerchief*

blood·stock /ˈblʌdstɒk $ -stɑːk/ *n* [U] horses that have been bred for racing: *a bloodstock auction*

blood·stream /ˈblʌdstriːm/ *n* [C usually singular] the blood flowing in your body: *The drug is injected directly into the bloodstream.*

blood·suck·er /ˈblʌdˌsʌkə $ -ər/ *n* [C] **1** a creature that sucks blood from the bodies of other animals **2** *informal* someone who always uses other people's money or help - used to show disapproval

blood·thirst·y /ˈblʌdˌθɜːsti $ -ɜːr-/ *adj* **1** eager to kill and wound, or enjoying killing and violence: *a bloodthirsty crowd* **THESAURUS** VIOLENT **2** describing or showing violence SYN **violent**: *The film was too bloodthirsty for me.*

ˈblood transˌfusion *n* [C,U] the process of putting blood into someone's body as a medical treatment

ˈblood type *n* [C] *especially AmE* one of the classes into which human blood can be separated, including A, B, AB, and O SYN **blood group** *BrE*

ˈblood ˌvessel *n* [C] one of the tubes through which blood flows in your body → **artery**, **vein**

blood·y¹ /ˈblʌdi/ *adj, adv spoken* **1** *especially BrE* used to emphasize what you are saying, in a slightly rude way: *It's bloody cold out there!* | *That's a bloody good idea.* | *Bloody hell!* **2** **bloody well** *BrE* used to emphasize an angry statement or order: *It serves you bloody well right.*

bloody² *adj* **1** covered in blood, or bleeding **2** with a lot of killing and injuries: *a bloody battle* **THESAURUS** VIOLENT **3** **scream/yell bloody murder** *AmE informal* to protest in a loud very angry way: *She was furious, screaming bloody murder at the manager!* **4** **bloody/bloodied but unbowed** harmed by events but not defeated by them: *He emerged from the discussions bloody but unbowed.*

bloody³ *v* (**bloodied**, **bloodying**, **bloodies**) [T] to injure someone so that blood comes, or to cover something with blood

ˌBloody ˈMary /ˌblʌdi ˈmeəri $ -ˈmeri/ *n* [C] an alcoholic drink made from VODKA, tomato juice, and spices

ˌbloody-ˈminded *adj* deliberately making things difficult for other people → **awkward**: *Stop being so bloody-minded!* —**bloody-mindedness** *n* [U]

bloom¹ /bluːm/ *n* **1** [C,U] a flower or flowers: *beautiful red blooms* | *a mass of bloom on the apple trees* **2** **in (full) bloom** with the flowers fully open **3** [singular, U] the healthy happy appearance that someone has, especially when they are young: *The rosy bloom of her cheeks had faded.*

bloom² *v* [I] **1** if a plant or a flower blooms, its flowers appear or open **2** to become happier, healthier, or more successful in a way that is very noticeable SYN **blossom**: *She was blooming the last time I saw her.*

bloom·er /ˈbluːmə $ -ər/ *n* **1** **bloomers** [plural] underwear that women wore in the past, like loose trousers that end at the knees **2** [C] *BrE old-fashioned* an embarrassing mistake that you make in front of other people - used humorously SYN **blooper** *AmE*

bloom·ing /ˈbluːmɪŋ, ˈblʊmɪn/ *adj* [only before noun], *adv BrE spoken old-fashioned* used for emphasizing a remark, especially when you are angry or surprised: *It's blooming ridiculous!*

ˈBloomsbury ˌGroup, the a group of artists and writers who lived and met regularly in Bloomsbury, an area of Central London, in the early 20th century. The most famous member of the group was Virginia Woolf.

bloop·er /ˈbluːpə $ -ər/ *n* [C] *AmE* **1** an embarrassing mistake that you make in front of other people SYN **bloomer** *BrE* **2** a ball in baseball that is high and slow, and easy to catch or hit

blos·som¹ /ˈblɒsəm $ ˈblɑː-/ ●○○ *n*
1 [C,U] a flower or the flowers on a tree or bush: *pale pink blossoms* | *The cherry tree was covered in blossom.* → see picture at TREE
2 **in (full) blossom** with the flowers fully open

blossom² ●○○ *v* [I]
1 if trees blossom, they produce flowers: *The apple trees are just beginning to blossom.*
2 (*also* **blossom out**) to become happier, more beautiful, more successful etc: *Pete's blossomed out in his new school.* | **[+into]** *The idea blossomed into a successful mail order business.*

blot¹ /blɒt $ blɑːt/ ●○○ *v* (**blotted**, **blotting**) [T]
1 to make a wet surface become dry by pressing soft paper or cloth on it
2 **blot your copybook** *BrE informal* to do something that spoils the idea that people have of you

blot sth ↔ **out** *phr v*
1 to cover or hide something completely: *Thick white smoke blotted out the sun.*
2 if you blot out an unpleasant memory, a thought etc, you deliberately try to forget it: *She said she took drugs to blot out her problems.*

blot sth ↔ **up** *phr v* to remove liquid from a surface by pressing soft paper or cloth onto it

blot² *n* [C] **1** a mark or dirty spot on something, especially made by ink: ***ink blots*** **2** a building, structure etc that is ugly and spoils the appearance of a place: *The new power station is a* ***blot on the landscape***. **3** something that spoils the good opinion that people have of someone or something: **[+on]** *The increase in juvenile crime is a blot on our time.*

blotch /blɒtʃ $ blɑːtʃ/ *n* [C] a pink or red mark on the skin, or a coloured mark on something —**blotchy** *adj* —**blotched** *adj*

blot·ter /ˈblɒtə $ ˈblɑːtər/ *n* **1** [C] a large piece of blotting paper kept on top of a desk **2** [C] *AmE* a book in which an official daily record is kept: *the police blotter* **3** [U] *AmE informal* the drug LSD

ˈblotting ˌpaper *n* [U] soft thick paper used for drying wet ink on a page after writing

blot·to /ˈblɒtəʊ $ ˈblɑːtoʊ/ *adj BrE informal* drunk

blouse /blaʊz $ blaʊs/ ●●● S3 *n* [C] a shirt for women: *a silk blouse*

blou·son /ˈbluːzɒn $ ˈblaʊsɑːn, ˈbluːzɑːn/ *n* [C] a short loose jacket that fits tightly around your waist

blov·i·ate /ˈbləʊvieɪt $ ˈbloʊ-/ *v* [I] *informal* to speak or write for too long and to use words that are too long and formal, especially on a BLOG

blow[1] /bləʊ $ bloʊ/ ●●● S2 W3 *v* (*past tense* **blew** /bluː/, *past participle* **blown** /bləʊn $ bloʊn/)

1 WIND MOVING [I,T] if the wind or a current of air blows, it moves: *A cold breeze was* ***blowing hard****.* | *It was blowing from an easterly direction.* | *Outside, the weather was* ***blowing a gale****.*

2 WIND MOVING STH [I,T usually + adv/prep] to move, or to move something, by the force of the wind or a current of air: *Her hair was blowing in the breeze.* | *The wind blew the rain into our faces.* | *My ticket blew away.* | **blow (sth) open/shut** *A sudden draught* ***blew*** *the* ***door shut****.*

3 AIR FROM YOUR MOUTH [I,T always + adv/prep] to send air out from your mouth: **blow (sth) into/onto/out etc** *She blew onto her coffee to cool it down.* | *He blew the smoke right in my face.*

4 MAKE A NOISE [I,T] to make a sound by passing air through a whistle, horn etc: *The whistle blew for half time.* | *A truck went by and blew its horn at her.*

5 VIOLENCE [T always + adv/prep] to damage or destroy something violently with an explosion or by shooting: **blow sth away/out/off sth** *Part of his leg had been blown off.* | **blow sb/sth to pieces/bits/smithereens** *A bomb like that could blow you to bits.*

6 LOSE AN OPPORTUNITY [T] *informal* to lose a good opportunity by making a mistake or by being careless: *We've* ***blown*** *our* ***chances*** *of getting that contract.* | *You've got a great future ahead of you. Don't* ***blow it****.*

7 WASTE MONEY [T] *informal* to spend a lot of money in a careless way, especially on one thing: *I blew all the money I won on a trip to Hawaii.* **THESAURUS** ▸ SPEND

8 blow your nose to clean your nose by forcing air through it into a cloth or a piece of soft paper

9 blow sb a kiss to kiss your hand and then pretend to blow the kiss towards someone: *She leant out of the window and blew him a kiss.*

10 ELECTRICITY STOPS [I,T] if an electrical FUSE blows, or a piece of electrical equipment blows a fuse, the electricity suddenly stops working because a thin wire has melted: *The floodlights blew a fuse.*

11 TYRE [I,T] if a tyre blows, or if a car blows a tyre, it bursts

12 MAKE A SHAPE [T] to make or shape something by sending air out from your mouth: *The kids were* ***blowing bubbles*** *in the backyard.* | **blow glass** (=shape glass by blowing into it when it is very hot and soft)

13 SURPRISE/ANNOYANCE **blow/blow me/blow it etc** *BrE spoken* said to show annoyance or surprise: *Blow it! I forgot to phone Jane.* | ***Blow me down*** *if she didn't just run off!* | *Well,* ***I'm blowed****!*

14 TELL A SECRET [T] to make known something that was meant to be a secret: *Your coming here has blown the whole operation.* | **blow sb's cover** (=make known what someone's real job or name is) *It would only take one phone call to blow his cover.*

15 blow sb's mind *spoken* to make you feel very surprised and excited by something: *Seeing her again really blew my mind.* → MIND-BLOWING

16 blow your top/stack/cool (*also* **blow a fuse/gasket**) *informal* to become extremely angry quickly or suddenly: *One day, I just blew my top and hit him.*

17 blow the whistle on sb *informal* to tell someone in authority about something wrong that someone is doing: *He blew the whistle on his colleagues.* → WHISTLE-BLOWER

18 blow sth (up) out of (all) proportion to make something seem much more serious or important than it is

19 blow your own trumpet *especially BrE*, **blow your own horn** *AmE informal* to talk a lot about your own achievements – used to show disapproval: *Dave spent the whole evening blowing his own trumpet.*

20 blow sb/sth out of the water to defeat someone or something that you are competing with, or to achieve much more than they do: *Motown had blown all the other record companies out of the water.*

21 blow hot and cold *BrE informal* to keep changing your attitude towards someone or something

22 blow sth sky-high *BrE* to destroy an idea, plan etc by showing that it cannot be true or effective: *This new information blows his theory sky-high.*

GRAMMAR

Blow belongs to a group of verbs where the same noun can be the subject of the verb or its object.

- You can say: *Someone blew a whistle.* In this sentence, 'a whistle' is the object of **blow**.
- You can also say: *A whistle blew.* In this sentence, 'a whistle' is the subject of **blow**.

GRAMMAR GUIDE ▸ VERBS

blow sb ↔ **away** *phr v especially AmE informal*
1 to make someone feel very surprised, especially about something they like or admire: *It just blows me away, the way everyone's so friendly round here.*
2 to kill someone by shooting them with a gun
3 to defeat someone completely, especially in a game: *Nancy blew away the rest of the skaters.*

blow down *phr v* if the wind blows something down, or if something blows down, the wind makes it fall: *The garden gate has blown down.* | **blow sth ↔ down** *Several trees were blown down in the night.*

blow in *phr v*
1 (*also* **blow into sth**) *informal* to arrive in a place, especially suddenly: *Jim blew in about an hour ago.* | *Guess who's just* ***blown into town****?*
2 if a storm or bad weather blows in, it arrives and begins to affect a particular area: *The first snowstorm blew in from the north.*

blow sb/sth ↔ **off** *phr v AmE informal*
1 to treat someone or something as unimportant, for example by not meeting someone or not going to an event: *Bud got into trouble for blowing off the meeting.*
2 blow the lid off sth to make known something that was secret, especially something involving important or famous people: *Her book blew the lid off the Reagan years.*
3 blow sb's head off to kill someone by shooting them in the head
4 blow off steam *AmE* to get rid of anger or energy by doing something SYN **let off steam** *BrE*: *I went jogging to blow off some steam.*

blow out *phr v*
1 if you blow a flame or a fire out, or if it blows out, it stops burning: *The match blew out in the wind.* | **blow sth ↔ out** *Blow out all the candles.*
2 if a tyre blows out, it bursts
3 blow itself out if a storm blows itself out, it ends
4 blow your/sb's brains out to kill yourself, or someone else, with a shot to the head
5 blow sb ↔ out *AmE spoken* to easily defeat someone: *We blew them out 28–0.*
6 *AmE* if you blow out your knee or another joint in your body, or if it blows out, you injure it badly
7 if an oil or gas WELL blows out, oil or gas suddenly escapes from it
8 blow sb ↔ out to stop having a friendship or relationship with someone

blow over *phr v*
1 if the wind blows something over, or if something blows over, the wind makes it fall: *Our fence blew over in the storm.* | **blow sth ↔ over** *The hurricane blew many trees over.*
2 if an argument or unpleasant situation blows over, it ends or is forgotten: *They weren't speaking to each other, but I think it's blown over now.*
3 if a storm blows over, it goes away

blow up *phr v*
1 to destroy something, or to be destroyed, by an explosion: *The plane blew up in midair.* | **blow sth ↔ up** *Rebels attempted to blow up the bridge.*
2 blow sth ↔ up to fill something with air or gas: *Can you* ***blow up*** *this* ***balloon****?* | *We'll* ***blow*** *the* ***tyres up****.*
3 if a situation, argument etc blows up, it suddenly becomes important or dangerous: *A crisis had blown up over the peace talks.*
4 blow sth ↔ up if you blow up a photograph, you make it larger SYN **enlarge**
5 *informal* to become very angry with someone: *Jenny's*

father blew up when she didn't come home last night. | **[+at]** *I was surprised at the way he blew up at Hardy.*
6 if bad weather blows up, it suddenly arrives: *It looks as if there's a storm blowing up.*
7 blow up in sb's face if something you have done or planned to do blows up in your face, it suddenly goes wrong: *One of his deals had just blown up in his face.*

B

blow² ●●○ S3 W3 *n* [C]
1 BAD EFFECT an action or event that causes difficulty or sadness for someone: *Joe resigned, which was a* ***severe blow*** *because we needed him desperately.* | *His mother's death was a* ***shattering blow****.* | *The election result* ***dealt a*** *further* ***blow to*** *the party.* | *The factory closures* ***came as a blow*** *to the local economy.* | *The* ***final blow*** *for many firms was the government's abolition of import duties.*
2 HARD HIT a hard hit with someone's hand, a tool, or a weapon: *She died from a* ***heavy blow*** *to the head.* | *He* ***struck a blow*** *which threw her to the floor.* | *Martin* ***received a blow*** *on the nose.* | *He had been struck a* ***glancing blow*** (=a blow that did not hit him directly) *by the car.* | **[+to]** *He gave her a violent blow to the head.*

> **REGISTER**
> In everyday English, people usually say that someone **gets hit** or that something **hits** them, rather than using the noun **blow**: *He* ***received a blow to*** *the head.* → *He* ***got hit on*** *the head.*

3 BLOWING an action of blowing: *One big blow and the candles were out.*
4 come to blows (with sb) if two people come to blows, they start arguing or hitting each other because they disagree about something: **[+over]** *They almost came to blows over the money.*
5 soften/cushion the blow to make something unpleasant easier for someone to accept: *A reduction in interest rates would soften the blow of tax increases.*
6 low blow *AmE informal* something unkind you say to deliberately embarrass or upset someone → **strike a blow for sb/sth** at STRIKE¹(13)

blow·back /ˈbləʊbæk $ ˈbloʊ-/ *n* [U] **1** bad results of an action which were not intended: *We are now suffering the blowback of the terrible foreign policy choices made by the previous president.* **2** the powder that is sent out when a gun is fired: *Other inconsistencies included the absence of fingerprints on the gun and of blowback material from the gun blast.*

ˌblow-by-ˈblow *adj* **a blow-by-blow account/description etc** an account that includes all the details of an event exactly as they happened

ˈblow-dry *v* (**blow-dried, blow-drying, blow-dries**) [T] to dry hair and give it shape by using an electric HAIRDRYER —**blow-dry** *n* [C]: *a cut and blow-dry*

ˈblow-ˌdryer *n* [C] a small electric machine that blows hot air onto your hair in order to dry it SYN **hair dryer**

blow·er /ˈbləʊə $ ˈbloʊər/ *n* [C] **1** a machine that blows out air, for example inside a car **2 on the blower** *BrE old-fashioned* on the telephone in order to talk to someone

ˈblow-fly *n* [C] a fly that lays its eggs on meat or wounds

blow·hard /ˈbləʊhɑːd $ ˈbloʊhɑːrd/ *n* [C] *AmE informal* someone who talks too much and has very strong opinions

ˈblow-hole *n* [C] **1** a hole in the surface of ice where water animals such as SEALS come to breathe **2** a hole in the top of the head of a WHALE, DOLPHIN etc through which they breathe

ˈblow job *n* [C] *informal* the practice of touching a man's sexual organs with your lips and tongue to give him sexual pleasure

blow·lamp /ˈbləʊlæmp $ ˈbloʊ-/ *n* [C] *BrE* a piece of equipment that produces a very hot flame, used especially for removing paint SYN **blowtorch**

blown /bləʊn $ bloʊn/ *v* the past participle of BLOW

blow·out, **blow-out** /ˈbləʊaʊt $ ˈbloʊ-/ *n* [C] **1** a sudden bursting of a tyre → **puncture**: *I had a blow-out on the driver's side.* **2** [usually singular] *informal* a big expensive meal or large social occasion: *We went for a real blow-out to celebrate.* **3** *AmE informal* an easy victory over someone in a game **4** a sudden uncontrolled escape of oil or gas from a WELL

blow·pipe /ˈbləʊpaɪp $ ˈbloʊ-/ *n* [C] a tube through which you can blow a small stone, ARROW etc, used as a weapon

blow·sy, **blowzy** /ˈblaʊzi/ *adj* a blowsy woman is fat and looks untidy

blow·torch /ˈbləʊtɔːtʃ $ ˈbloʊtɔːrtʃ/ *n* [C] a piece of equipment that produces a small very hot flame, used especially for removing paint SYN **blowlamp** *BrE*

ˈblow-up *n* **1** [C] a photograph, or part of a photograph, that has been made larger **2** [C usually singular] *AmE* a sudden big argument or disagreement → **blow up** at BLOW¹

blow·y /ˈbləʊi $ ˈbloʊi/ *adj* windy

blow·zy /ˈblaʊzi/ *adj* another spelling of blowsy

BLT /ˌbiː el ˈtiː/ *n* [C] (***bacon, lettuce, and tomato***) the name of a sandwich that contains these foods

blub·ber¹ /ˈblʌbə $ -ər/ (*also* **blub** /blʌb/) *v* [I] to cry noisily, especially in a way that annoys people

blubber² *n* [U] the fat of sea animals, especially WHALES

blud·geon¹ /ˈblʌdʒən/ *v* [T] **1** to hit someone several times with something heavy: *He was* ***bludgeoned to death*** *with a hammer.* **2** to force someone to do something by making threats or arguing with them: **[+into]** *I won't let myself be bludgeoned into marriage.* **3 bludgeon your way through/to/past etc sb/sth** to get somewhere, or achieve something, by pushing past other people or not caring about them

bludgeon² *n* [C] a heavy stick with a thick end, used as a weapon

blue¹ /bluː/ ●●● S1 W2 *adj*
1 having the colour of the sky or the sea on a fine day → **navy, navy blue**: *the blue waters of the lake* | **dark/light/pale/bright blue** *a dark blue raincoat*
2 [not before noun] *informal* sad and without hope SYN **depressed**: *I've been* ***feeling*** *kind of* ***blue****.*
3 *informal* blue jokes, stories etc are about sex, in a way that might offend some people → BLUE MOVIE
4 argue/talk etc till you're blue in the face *informal* to argue, talk etc about something a lot, but without achieving what you want: *You can tell them till you're blue in the face, but they'll still do what they want.*
5 blue with cold *especially BrE* someone who is blue with cold looks extremely cold
6 go blue *BrE* if someone goes blue, their skin becomes blue because they are cold or cannot breathe properly
7 talk a blue streak *AmE informal* to talk very quickly without stopping —**blueness** *n* [U] → BLACK AND BLUE, → **once in a blue moon** at ONCE¹(15), → **scream blue murder** at SCREAM¹(1)

blue² ●●● S3 W3 *n*
1 [C,U] the colour of the sky or the sea on a fine day: *She nearly always dresses in blue.* | *the rich greens and blues of the tapestry*
2 blues (*also* **the blues**) [U] a slow sad style of music that came from the southern US: *a blues singer* → RHYTHM AND BLUES
3 the blues [plural] *informal* feelings of sadness: *A lot of women* ***get the blues*** *after the baby is born.*
4 out of the blue *informal* if something happens out of the blue, it is very unexpected → **a bolt from/out of the blue** at BOLT¹(3)
5 Blue [C] *BrE* someone who has represented Oxford or Cambridge University at a sport, or the title given to such a person
6 the blue *literary* the sea or the sky → **boys in blue** at BOY¹(9)

ˈblue ˌbaby *n* [C] a baby whose skin is slightly blue when it is born because it has a heart problem

blue·bell /ˈbluːbel/ *n* [C] a small plant with blue flowers that grows in woods

blue·ber·ry /ˈbluːbəri $ -beri/ *n* (*plural* **blueberries**) [C,U] a small blue fruit, or the plant it grows on → see picture at FRUIT[1]

blue·bird /ˈbluːbɜːd $ -bɜːrd/ *n* [C] a small blue bird that lives in North America

ˌblue-ˈblooded *adj* a blue-blooded person belongs to a royal or NOBLE family —ˌ**blue-ˈblood** *n* [U]

ˈblue book *n* [C] *AmE* **1** a book with a list of prices that you can expect to pay for any used car **2** a book with a blue cover that is used in American colleges for writing answers to examination questions

blue·bot·tle /ˈbluːˌbɒtl $ -ˌbɑːtl/ *n* [C] *BrE* a large blue fly

ˌblue ˈcheese *n* [C,U] a type of cheese with blue lines in it and a strong taste

ˈblue-chip *adj* **blue-chip companies/shares etc** companies or SHARES that make a profit and are considered safe —**blue chip** *n* [C]

ˌblue-ˈcollar *adj* [only before noun] blue-collar workers do physical work, rather than working in offices → **white-collar**, **pink-collar**

ˌblue-eyed ˈboy *n* [C usually singular] *BrE informal* the man or boy in a group who is most liked and approved of by someone in authority

blue·grass /ˈbluːgrɑːs $ -græs/ *n* [U] a type of music from the southern and western US, played on instruments such as the GUITAR and VIOLIN

blue·jack·ing /ˈbluːdʒækɪŋ/ *n* [U] the practice of using a MOBILE PHONE with BLUETOOTH technology to send a TEXT MESSAGE to another person near you, without letting them know who has sent the message. This is usually done as a joke to surprise the person who receives the message. —**bluejack** *v* [I,T] —**bluejacker** *n* [C]

blue·jay /ˈbluːˌdʒeɪ/ *n* [C] a common large North American bird with blue feathers

ˈblue jeans *n* [plural] *AmE* blue trousers made in a heavy material SYN **jeans**

ˈblue law *n* [C] *AmE* a law used in the past in the US to control activities that were considered immoral, such as drinking alcohol and working on Sundays

ˌblue ˈmovie *n* [C] a film that shows a lot of sexual activity

ˌblue on ˈblue *adj* used to describe an occasion during a battle or a war when a soldier, sailor, or pilot is accidentally killed by their own army: *a 'Blue on Blue' incident which saw an RAF jet brought down by a Patriot missile*

blue·print /ˈbluːˌprɪnt/ *n* [C] **1** a plan for achieving something: **[+for]** *a blueprint for health-care reform* **2** a photographic print of a plan for a building, machine etc on special blue paper: **[+for]** *a blueprint for the new shopping mall* **3** *technical* a pattern that all living cells contain, which decides how a person, animal, or plant develops and what it looks like: *By changing the tomato's* ***genetic blueprint****, scientists can alter the rate at which it ripens.*

ˌblue ˈribbon (*also* **blue rib·and** /ˌbluː ˈrɪbənd/ *BrE*) *n* [C] the first prize in a competition, sometimes consisting of a small piece of blue material —**blue ribbon** (*also* **blue riband** *BrE*) *adj* [only before noun]: *the club's prized blue riband award*

ˈblue-sky *adj* concerned with thinking of new and interesting ideas, without worrying about whether they are practical or not: *blue-sky thinking*

blue·stock·ing /ˈbluːˌstɒkɪŋ $ -ˌstɑː-/ *n* [C] *BrE* a woman who is more interested in ideas and studying than in parties, men etc – sometimes used to show disapproval

blue·sy /ˈbluːzi/ *adj* bluesy music is slow and sad, like BLUES

Blue·tooth /ˈbluːtuːθ/ *n* [U] *trademark* a system that allows you to connect computer equipment, such as a KEYBOARD or PRINTER, to a computer that is near it by using radio waves instead of wires. You can also use the system to connect a MOBILE PHONE to a computer without using wires.

bluff[1] /blʌf/ *v* [I,T] to pretend something, especially in order to achieve what you want in a difficult or dangerous situation: *You wouldn't really tell her. You're bluffing!* | **bluff your way out of/through/past etc sb/sth** (=go somewhere or succeed in doing something by deceiving someone) *I hope we'll be able to bluff our way past the guard.* | *'I was with Don,' she said, deciding to* ***bluff it out*** (=continue to pretend something). | **bluff sb into (doing) sth** (=make someone do something by deceiving them)

bluff[2] *n* **1** [C,U] an attempt to deceive someone by making them think you will do something, when you do not intend to do it: *The threat was only a bluff.* | *Whatever you say, you must do it. This isn't a* ***game of bluff****.* → DOUBLE BLUFF **2 call sb's bluff** to tell someone to do what they have threatened because you do not believe that they will really do it **3** [C] a very steep cliff or slope

bluff[3] *adj* a bluff person, usually a man, is pleasant but very direct and does not always consider other people: *He was a bluff no-nonsense administrator.*

blu·ish /ˈbluːɪʃ/ *adj* slightly blue: *Her skin had* ***a bluish tinge****.*

blun·der[1] /ˈblʌndə $ -ər/ *n* [C] a careless or stupid mistake: *A last-minute blunder cost them the match.* **THESAURUS** ▸ MISTAKE

blunder[2] *v* **1** [I always + adv/prep] to move in an unsteady way, as if you cannot see properly: **[+about/around]** *Someone was blundering about in the kitchen.* | **blunder into/past/through etc sth** *Phil came blundering down the stairs.* **2** [I] to make a big mistake, especially because you have been careless or stupid: *They blundered badly when they gave him the job.* **3** [I always + adv/prep] to enter a place or become involved in a difficult situation by mistake: **[+into]** *Somehow we blundered into the war.* | **[+in]** *He would have agreed if you hadn't blundered in.*

blun·der·buss /ˈblʌndəbʌs $ -ər-/ *n* [C] a type of gun used in the past

blun·der·ing /ˈblʌndərɪŋ/ *adj* [only before noun] careless or stupid: *You blundering idiot!*

blunt[1] /blʌnt/ ●○○ *adj*

1 not sharp or pointed OPP **sharp**: *Sharpen all your blunt knives.* | *a blunt pencil*

2 speaking in an honest way even if this upsets people → **bluntly**: *To be blunt, many of the candidates cannot read or write.* | *Julian's blunt words hurt her.* **THESAURUS** ▸ HONEST

3 blunt instrument a) a heavy object that is used to hit someone: *The victim suffered a blow to the head from a blunt instrument.* **b)** a method of doing something that does not work very well because it has a lot of other effects that you do not want: *The exams are a blunt instrument that will reveal little about children's abilities.* —**bluntness** *n* [U]

blunt[2] *v* [T] **1** to make a feeling less strong OPP **sharpen**: *The bad weather blunted their enthusiasm for camping.* **2** to make the point of a pencil or the edge of a knife less sharp OPP **sharpen**

blunt·ly /ˈblʌntli/ ●○○ *adv* speaking in a direct honest way that sometimes upsets people: *'You're drunk,' she said bluntly.* | ***To put it bluntly****, she's not up to the job.*

blur[1] /blɜː $ blɜːr/ ●○○ *n* [C usually singular]

1 a shape that you cannot see clearly: **[+of]** *I saw the blur of the car as it passed in front of me.* | *The island was a blur through misty rain.*

2 something that you cannot remember clearly: *The days before the accident were a blur.*

blur[2] ●○○ *v* (**blurred**, **blurring**) [I,T]

1 to become difficult to see, or to make something difficult to see, because the edges are not clear: *The street lights were blurred by the fog.* | *Many of the details in the picture are blurred.*

2 to be unable to see clearly: *Tears* ***blurred*** *her* ***eyes****.* | *His* ***vision*** *was* ***blurred****.*

3 to make the difference between two ideas, subjects etc less clear: *His films blur the boundaries between fact and* fiction. | *The design of the conservatory is meant to blur the distinction between the house and the garden.* —**blurry** *adj*: *a few blurry photos of their holiday* → BLURRED

Blu-ray /ˈbluː reɪ/ *n* [U] *trademark* a way of storing HIGH-DEFINITION (=very clear) video images on a DISC

blurb /blɜːb $ blɜːrb/ *n* [C] a short description giving information about a book, new product etc

blurred /blɜːd $ blɜːrd/ ●○○ *adj*
1 unclear in shape, or making it difficult to see shapes: *a blurred photo*
2 difficult to remember or understand clearly: *blurred memories*

blurt /blɜːt $ blɜːrt/ *v*
blurt sth ↔ **out** *phr v* to say something suddenly and without thinking, usually because you are nervous or excited: *Peter blurted the news out before we could stop him.*

blush¹ /blʌʃ/ ●○○ *v* [I]
1 to become red in the face, usually because you are embarrassed: *Wilson saw she was watching him and blushed.* | *Joan blushed at the unexpected compliment.* | *Kate blushed scarlet.*

> **REGISTER**
> In everyday British English, people often say **go red** rather than **blush**: *She **went red** when he looked at her.*

2 to feel ashamed or embarrassed about something: **blush to do sth** *I blush to admit that I haven't read it.*
3 sth that would make sb blush something so shocking that it would shock someone who is not normally easily shocked: *language that would make a sailor blush*
4 the blushing bride a young woman on her wedding day – used humorously —**blushingly** *adv*

blush² *n* **1** [C] the red colour on your face that appears when you are embarrassed: *Donald felt a blush warm his cheeks.* | *She bent her head to hide her blushes.* **2 at first blush** *literary* when first thought of or considered: *At first blush, this sounds like good news.* → **spare sb's blushes** at SPARE²(10)

blush·er /ˈblʌʃə $ -ər/ (*also* **blush** *AmE*) *n* [U] cream or powder used for making your cheeks look red or pink → see picture at MAKE-UP

blus·ter /ˈblʌstə $ -ər/ *v* **1** [I,T] to speak in a loud angry way that is not really very impressive: *'That's hardly the point,' he blustered.* **2** [I] if the wind blusters, it blows violently —**bluster** *n* [U] —**blustering** *adj*: *blustering wintry weather*

blus·ter·y /ˈblʌstəri/ *adj* blustery weather is very windy: *a cold and blustery day*

Blvd. (*also* **Blvd** *BrE*) the written abbreviation of ***boulevard***

BMA, the /ˌbiː em ˈeɪ/ (***the British Medical Association***) an organization that represents medical doctors in the UK. There is a similar organization in the US called the A.M.A. (American Medical Association). The BMA produces a well-known medical magazine, *The British Medical Journal.*

BMI /ˌbiː em ˈaɪ/ *medical* the abbreviation of BODY MASS INDEX

B-mov·ie /ˈbiː ˌmuːvi/ *n* [C] a film that is made cheaply and is of low quality

BMP /ˌbiː em ˈpiː/ *n* [C,U] *technical* (***bitmap***) a type of computer FILE that contains images

BMX /ˌbiː em ˈeks/ *n* [C] a strong bicycle with a frame that is very low to the ground, used to do special movements such as jumping high into the air —**BMXing** *n* [U]

BO /ˌbiː ˈəʊ $ -ˈoʊ/ *n* [U] (***body odour***) an unpleasant smell from someone's body caused by SWEAT

bo·a /ˈbəʊə $ ˈboʊə/ *n* [C] **1** (*also* **ˈboa conˌstrictor**) a large snake that is not poisonous, but kills animals by crushing them **2** a FEATHER BOA

boar /bɔː $ bɔːr/ *n* [C] **1** a wild pig **2** a male pig

board¹ /bɔːd $ bɔːrd/ ●●● S1 W1 *n*
1 INFORMATION [C] a flat wide piece of wood, plastic etc that you can use to show information: **on a board** *The plan of the new building is displayed on a board at the back of the room.* | *I've put a list of names up on the board.* | *I'll check the departure board for train times.* → BILLBOARD, BLACKBOARD, NOTICEBOARD, SCOREBOARD
2 FOR PUTTING THINGS ON [C] a flat piece of wood, plastic, card etc that you use for a particular purpose such as cutting things on, or for playing indoor games: *Martha was chopping vegetables on a wooden board.* | *a chess board* → BREADBOARD, CHEESEBOARD, CHOPPING BOARD
3 GROUP OF PEOPLE (*also* **Board**) [C] a group of people in a company or other organization who make the rules and important decisions: **[+of]** *The Board of Directors met yesterday.* | *There was disagreement among the agency's board of governors.* | **sit on a board/have a seat on a board** (=be a member of a board) *He gave up his seat on the board after 40 years.* | *a* ***board meeting*** | *a* ***board member***

> **GRAMMAR: Singular or plural verb?**
> • **Board** is usually followed by a singular verb in this meaning: *The board **meets** once a month.*
> • In British English, you can also use a plural verb: *The board **meet** once a month.*
> **GRAMMAR GUIDE** NOUNS

4 IN NAMES **Board** used in the name of some organizations: *the New York State Board of Elections* | *the British Boxing Board of Control*
5 IN BUILDING [C] a long thin flat piece of wood used for making floors, walls, fences etc: *We'll have to take the boards up to check the wiring.* → FLOORBOARD
6 on board a) on a ship, plane, or spacecraft SYN **aboard**: *There are 12 children on board the ship.* **b)** involved with something or working for an organization: *Supporters of the treaty say that it will be necessary to have the United States on board.* | *He* ***came on board*** *in the late sixties and spent two decades with the agency.*
7 MEALS [U] the meals that are provided for you when you pay to stay somewhere: *In the nursing home she will have to pay for* ***room and board***. | *The landlord provides* ***board and lodging*** (=meals and a place to stay). → FULL BOARD, HALF BOARD
8 go by the board if an idea, way of behaving, or plan goes by the board, it fails to happen, ends, or is no longer possible: *Loyalty has gone by the board.*
9 IN WATER SPORTS [C] a SURFBOARD or SAILBOARD
10 across the board if something happens or is done across the board, it affects everyone in a particular group, place etc: *The changes will affect local authorities across the board.* | *We find jobs for people* ***right across the board****, from chief executives to cleaners.*
11 take sth on board to listen to and accept a suggestion, idea etc: *The school refused to take any of the parents' criticisms on board.*
12 ELECTRICITY [C] a CIRCUIT BOARD
13 THEATRE **the boards** [plural] the stage in a theatre → **tread the boards** at TREAD¹(7)
14 SPORTS AREA **boards** [plural] *AmE* the low wooden wall around the area in which you play ICE HOCKEY
15 college/medical boards *AmE* examinations that you take in the US when you formally ask to be accepted as a student at a college or medical school → ABOVE BOARD, DIVING BOARD, DRAWING BOARD, IRONING BOARD, SOUNDING BOARD, → **sweep the board** at SWEEP¹(11)

board² ●●○ *v*
1 [I,T] *formal* to get on a bus, plane, train etc in order to travel somewhere: *The couple boarded the train for New York.* | *Passengers were standing on the dock, waiting to board.*

> **REGISTER**
> In everyday English, people usually say **get on** a bus, plane etc rather than **board**: *When she heard the news, she **got on** the next plane for Chicago.*

2 be boarding if a plane or ship is boarding, passengers are getting onto it: *Olympic Airways Flight 172 to Istanbul is now boarding at Gate No. 37.*

3 [I always + adv/prep] to stay in a room in someone's house that you pay for: *Several students boarded with Mrs. Smith.*
4 [I] to stay at a school at night as well as during the day: *Dickie was sent away to school as soon as he was old enough to board.*
board sth ↔ **out** *phr v* to pay money and arrange for an animal to stay somewhere
board sth ↔ **up** *phr v* to cover a window or door, or all the windows and doors of a building, with wooden boards: *The shop was boarded up.*
board·er /ˈbɔːdə $ ˈbɔːrdər/ *n* [C] **1** a student who stays at a school during the night, as well as during the day → **day pupil 2** someone who pays to live in another person's house, with some or all of their meals provided SYN **lodger**

BOARD GAMES

ˈ**board game** *n* [C] an indoor game played on a specially designed board made of thick card or wood
board·ing /ˈbɔːdɪŋ $ ˈbɔːr-/ *n* [U] **1** the act of getting on a ship, plane etc in order to travel somewhere: *Boarding is now taking place at Gate 38.* **2** narrow pieces of wood that are fixed side by side, usually to cover a broken door or window
ˈ**boarding card** *n* [C] a British word for BOARDING PASS
ˈ**boarding house** *n* [C] a private house where you pay to sleep and eat SYN **guesthouse**
ˈ**boarding pass** (*also* **boarding card** *BrE*) *n* [C] an official card that you have to show before you get onto a plane
ˈ**boarding school** *n* [C] a school where students live as well as study → **DAY SCHOOL**
board·room /ˈbɔːdruːm, -rʊm $ ˈbɔːrd-/ *n* [C] a room where the DIRECTORS of a company have meetings
ˈ**board shorts** *n* [plural] trousers that reach the knees, worn by men when swimming or SURFING
board·walk /ˈbɔːdwɔːk $ ˈbɔːrdwɒːk/ *n* [C] *AmE* a raised path made of wood, usually built next to the sea
boast¹ /bəʊst $ boʊst/ ●●○ *v*
1 [I,T] to talk too proudly about your abilities, achievements, or possessions: *'I wouldn't be afraid,' she boasted.* | **boast that** *Amy boasted that her son was a genius.* | **[+about]** *He's boasting about how much money he has made.* | **[+of]** *The company is inclined to boast of its success.*
2 [T not in progressive] if a place, object, or organization boasts something, it has something that is very good: *The city boasts two excellent museums.* | *The Society boasts 3,000 members worldwide.* —**boaster** *n* [C]
boast² ●○○ *n* [C] something that you like telling people because you are proud of it: *It is the company's **proud boast** that it can deal with all a customer's needs in one phone call.* | *Philip's boast is that he started out without any outside financial backing.* | **an empty/idle/vain boast** (=a false statement that something is good or possible) *'Making knowledge work' is the university's phrase, and it is no idle boast* (=not a boast, but true).
boast·ful /ˈbəʊstfəl $ ˈboʊst-/ ●○○ *adj* talking too proudly about yourself OPP **modest** —**boastfully** *adv* —**boastfulness** *n* [U]
boat /bəʊt $ boʊt/ ●●● S1 W2 *n* [C]
1 a vehicle that travels across water: *a fishing boat* | *The boat **capsized** (=turned over) in heavy seas.* | *a boat trip around the islands* | **by boat** *Some of the beaches can only be reached by boat.* | **on/in a boat** *MacKay said he would sleep on his boat.* → **LIFEBOAT, MOTORBOAT, POWERBOAT, SPEEDBOAT, STEAMBOAT**
2 *informal* a ship, especially one that carries passengers: *We're taking the night boat to St. Malo.*
3 be in the same boat (as sb) to be in the same unpleasant situation as someone else: *Everyone has lost their job. We're all in the same boat.* → **GRAVY BOAT, SAUCE BOAT**, → **burn your bridges/boats** at BURN¹(18), → **miss the boat** at MISS¹(14), → **push the boat out** at PUSH¹(15), → **rock the boat** at ROCK²(3)
boat·er /ˈbəʊtə $ ˈboʊtər/ *n* [C] a hard STRAW hat with a flat top
ˈ**boat hook** *n* [C] a long pole with an iron hook at the end, used to pull or push a small boat
boat·house /ˈbəʊthaʊs $ ˈboʊt-/ *n* [C] a building beside a lake or river where boats are kept
boat·ing /ˈbəʊtɪŋ $ ˈboʊt-/ *n* [U] the activity of travelling in a small boat for pleasure: *Let's **go boating** on the lake.*
boat·man /ˈbəʊtmən $ ˈboʊt-/ *n* (*plural* **boatmen** /-mən/) [C] a man who you pay to take you out in a boat or for the use of a boat
ˈ**boat ˌpeople** *n* [plural] people who escape from bad conditions in their country in small boats → **refugees**
ˈ**Boat Race, the** a rowing race on the River Thames, held every year between teams from Oxford University and Cambridge University. The Boat Race is a popular national event and is shown on television.
boat·swain /ˈbəʊsən $ ˈboʊ-/ *n* [C] another spelling of BOSUN
ˈ**boat train** *n* [C] a train that takes people to or from ships in a port
boat·yard /ˈbəʊtjɑːd $ ˈboʊtjɑːrd/ *n* [C] an area where boats are built and repaired
bob¹ /bɒb $ bɑːb/ *v* (**bobbed, bobbing**)
1 MOVE ON WATER [I] to move up and down when floating on the surface of water: *The boat **bobbed** gently **up and down** on the water.*
2 MOVE SOMEWHERE [I always + adv/prep] to move quickly in a particular direction: *Mrs Foster bobbed about, gathering up her things.*
3 bob your head to move your head down quickly as a way of showing respect, greeting someone, or agreeing with them: *He spoke to the girl, who bobbed her head.*
4 CUT HAIR [T] to cut someone's, especially a woman's, hair in a bob: *her neatly bobbed hair*
bob² *n* [C] **1** a way of cutting hair so that it hangs to the level of your chin and is the same length all the way round your head → see picture at **HAIRSTYLE 2** a quick up and down movement of your head or body, to show respect, agreement, greeting etc: *The maid gave a little bob and left the room.* **3** (*plural* **bob**) *informal* a SHILLING (=coin used in the past in Britain): *At last I'm making a few bob* (=a reasonable amount of money). → **bits and bobs** at BIT²(7)
Bob /bɒb $ bɑːb/ *n* **Bob's your uncle!** *BrE spoken* used to say that something will be easy to do: *Just copy the disk, and Bob's your uncle!*
bob·bin /ˈbɒbɪn $ ˈbɑː-/ *n* [C] a small round object that

you wind thread onto, especially for a SEWING MACHINE → **spool**, **reel**

bob·ble¹ /ˈbɒbəl $ ˈbɑː-/ *n* [C] *BrE* a small soft ball, usually made of wool, that is used especially for decorating clothes: *Her pullover had bobbles on the front.* —**bobbly** *adj*

bobble² *v* **1** [T] *AmE* to drop or hold a ball in an uncontrolled way SYN **fumble 2** [I] *BrE* if a piece of clothing bobbles, especially a sweater, it forms little balls on the surface of the cloth after it has been worn or washed SYN **pill** *AmE*

B

ˈ**bobble hat** *n* [C] a WOOLLEN hat with a bobble on the top → see picture at **HAT**

bob·by /ˈbɒbi $ ˈbɑːbi/ *n* (*plural* **bobbies**) [C] *BrE informal old-fashioned* a policeman

ˈ**bobby pin** *n* [C] *AmE* a thin piece of metal bent into a narrow U shape that you use to hold your hair in place SYN **hairgrip** *BrE*

ˈ**bobby socks**, ˈ**bobby sox** *n* [plural] *AmE* girls' short socks that have the tops turned over

bob·cat /ˈbɒbkæt $ ˈbɑːb-/ *n* [C] a large North American wild cat that has no tail SYN **lynx** → see picture at **BIG CAT**

bobs /bɒbz $ bɑːbz/ *n* [plural] → **bits and bobs** at **BIT²**(7)

bob·sleigh /ˈbɒbsleɪ $ ˈbɑːb-/ (*also* **bob·sled** /ˈbɒbsled $ ˈbɑːb-/) *n* **1** [C] a small vehicle with two long thin metal blades instead of wheels, that is used for racing down a special ice track **2** [U] a sports event in which people race against each other in bobsleighs: *Sixteen teams took part in the 400 m bobsleigh.* —**bobsleigh** *v* [I]

bob·tail /ˈbɒbteɪl $ ˈbɑːb-/ *n* [C] → **ragtag and bobtail** at **RAGTAG**

bob·white /ˈbɒbwaɪt $ ˈbɑːb-/ *n* [C] a bird from North America, often shot for sport SYN **quail**

bod /bɒd $ bɑːd/ *n* [C] **1** *BrE spoken* a person: *He's a clever bod.* **2** *informal* someone's body: *She's got a lovely bod.* **3 odd bod** *informal* a strange person: *He's a bit of an odd bod but very pleasant.*

bo·da·cious /bəʊˈdeɪʃəs $ boʊ-/ *adj AmE informal* **1** excellent: *a bodacious video* **2** surprising or extreme: *Smith's bodacious promise*

bode /bəʊd $ boʊd/ *v* **1** the past tense of BIDE **2 bode well/ill (for sb/sth)** to be a good or bad sign for the future SYN **augur**: *The opinion polls do not bode well for the Democrats.*

bodge /bɒdʒ $ bɑːdʒ/ (*also* **bodge up**) *n* [singular] *spoken* a mistake, or something that is not as good as it should be → **botch**: *The builders have made a complete bodge of the kitchen.* —**bodge** *v* [T]

bod·ice /ˈbɒdɪs $ ˈbɑː-/ *n* [C] **1** the part of a woman's dress above her waist **2** a tight-fitting woman's WAISTCOAT, worn over a BLOUSE in former times **3** *old use* a piece of a woman's underwear that covers the upper part of her body SYN **corset**

-bodied /ˈbɒdiːd/ *suffix* **long-bodied/short-bodied etc** having a long, short etc body: *a wide-bodied aircraft* → **ABLE-BODIED**, **FULL-BODIED**

bod·i·ly¹ /ˈbɒdəli $ ˈbɑː-/ *adj* [only before noun] related to the human body: *bodily sensations*

bodily² *adv* **1** by moving the whole of your or someone else's body: *He lifted the child bodily aboard.* **2** by moving a large object in one piece: *The column was transferred bodily to a new site by the bank of the river.*

bod·kin /ˈbɒdkɪn $ ˈbɑːd-/ *n* [C] a long thick needle without a point

bod·y /ˈbɒdi $ ˈbɑːdi/ ●●● S1 W1 *n* (*plural* **bodies**)

1 PEOPLE/ANIMALS [C] the physical structure of a person or animal: *the human body* | *My fingers were numb and my whole body ached.* | **body weight/temperature/size** *Your body temperature is higher in the daytime than at night.* | *For their body size, these birds lay very small eggs.* | *He needs to overcome a negative* ***body image*** (=what you think about your own body).

2 DEAD PERSON [C] the dead body of a person: *A dog found the body of a girl in the woods.*

3 GROUP [C] a group of people who work together to do a particular job or who are together for a particular purpose: *The British Medical Association is the doctors' professional body.* | **[+of]** *There were reports of a large body of armed men near the border.* | *Kaplan served on the* ***governing body*** *of the museum* (=the group who control the museum). | *The* ***student body*** (=all the students in a school or college) *numbers 5,000.* | *The research will be used by government departments and other* ***public bodies*** (=groups whose work is connected to the government). | **in a body** (=as a group, together) *The women moved towards the building in a body.* THESAURUS ▸ ORGANIZATION

4 body of sth a) a large amount or mass of something, especially something that has been collected: **body of knowledge/evidence/opinion etc** *There is now a considerable body of knowledge of the different stages of childhood.* | *There is a growing body of evidence that charges are too high.* **b)** the main, central, or most important part of something: *The arguments are explained in the body of the text.* | *Leave three blank lines between the date and the body of the letter.*

5 body of water a large area of water such as a lake: *The city was built near a large body of water.*

6 MIDDLE PART [C] the central part of a person or animal's body, not including the head, arms, legs, or wings: *Nick had bruises on his face and body.* | *The bird has a small body and long wings.*

7 VEHICLE [C] the main structure of a vehicle not including the engine, wheels etc: *Workers at the factory are making steel bodies for cars.*

8 OBJECT [C] *technical* an object that is separate from other objects: *Keep the caps on the bottles to prevent* ***foreign bodies*** *entering them* (=objects that should not be there). → **heavenly body** at **HEAVENLY**(3)

9 HAIR [U] if your hair has body, it is thick and healthy: *This shampoo will give more body to your hair.*

10 TASTE [U] if food or an alcoholic drink has body, it has a strong FLAVOUR (=taste): *A small amount of tomato paste will give extra colour and body to the sauce.*

11 keep body and soul together to continue to exist with only just enough food, money etc: *He's working at the shop to keep body and soul together.*

12 body and soul a) completely: *She threw herself body and soul into her work.* **b)** the whole of a person: *They think they own the employees, body and soul.*

13 INSTRUMENT [C] the wide part of a musical instrument such as a VIOLIN or GUITAR, or of a sports RACKET (=bat): *The guitar is 16 inches wide across the body.*

14 CLOTHING [C] *BrE* a type of tight-fitting shirt worn by women that fastens between their legs SYN **body suit** *AmE* → see picture at **UNDERWEAR** → **over my dead body** at **DEAD¹**(11)

ˈ**body ˌarmour** *n* [U] clothing worn by the police that protects them against bullets

ˈ**body bag** *n* [C] a large bag in which a dead body is removed

ˈ**body blow** *n* [C] **1** a serious loss, disappointment, or defeat → **blow**: *Hopes of economic recovery were dealt a body blow by this latest announcement.* **2** a hard hit between your neck and waist during a fight

bod·y·board /ˈbɒdiˌbɔːd $ ˈbɑːdiˌbɔːrd/ *n* [C] a short SURFBOARD which you use lying on your front SYN **boogie board** —**bodyboarding** *n* [U]

ˈ**body ˌbuilding** *n* [U] an activity in which you do hard physical exercise in order to develop big muscles —**body builder** *n* [C]

ˈ**body clock** *n* [C] the system in your body that controls types of behaviour that happen at regular times, such as sleeping or eating SYN **biological clock**

ˈ**body con** *adj* [only before noun] *BrE* a body con piece of clothing fits closely to your body, showing its shape: *The actress was wearing a stunning body con dress.*

ˈ**body ˌcount** *n* [C] the number of dead soldiers after a period of fighting, or the process of counting their bodies

ˈ**body ˌdouble** *n* [C] someone whose body appears instead of an actor's or actress's in a film, especially in scenes where they are not wearing any clothes → **double**

body dys·morph·ic dis·or·der /ˌbɒdi dɪsˈmɔːfɪk dɪsˌɔːdə $ ˌbɑːdi dɪsˈmɔːrfɪk dɪsˌɔːrdər/ (*also* **body dys·mor·phi·a** /-ˈmɔːfiə $ -ˈmɔːr-/) *n* [U] (*abbreviation* **BDD**) a mental condition in which someone wrongly believes that part of their body is very ugly or not normal

bod·y·guard /ˈbɒdigɑːd $ ˈbɑːdigɑːrd/ ●○○ *n* [C] **1** someone whose job is to protect an important person: *The senator arrived, surrounded by personal bodyguards.* **2** a group of people who work together to protect an important person

ˈ**body** ˌ**language** ●○○ *n* [U] changes in your body position and movements that show what you are feeling or thinking: *It was obvious from Luke's body language that he was nervous.*

ˈ**body mass** ˌ**index** *n* [U] (*abbreviation* **BMI**) the relationship between your height and your weight, used as a measure of whether you have too much flesh on your body: *Your body mass index is your weight in kilograms divided by the square of your height in meters.* | *Individuals with a BMI of 25 to 29.9 are considered overweight.*

ˈ**body** ˌ**odour** *n* [U] the natural smell of someone's body, especially when this is unpleasant SYN **BO**

ˈ**body** ˌ**piercing** *n* [U] making a hole in a part of the body in order to fix a ring or other piece of jewellery to the body

ˌ**body** ˈ**politic** *n* [singular] *formal* all the people in a nation forming a state under the control of a single government

ˈ**body** ˌ**popping** *n* [U] a type of dancing to popular music, with movements that make you look like a ROBOT

ˈ**body search** *n* [C] a thorough search for drugs, weapons etc that might be hidden on someone's body: *Everyone entering the building had a body search.* —**body-search** *v* [T]

ˈ**body shape** *n* [C,U] the shape of someone's body, used especially when talking about exercise and DIETS: *If you're not happy with your body shape, you should do more exercise.*

ˈ**body shop** *n* [C] a building where the main structure of a car is repaired

ˈ**body spray** *n* [U] a chemical substance that you put onto your body to make it smell nice → **deodorant**

ˈ**body** ˌ**stocking** *n* [C] a close-fitting piece of clothing that covers the whole of your body

ˈ**body suit** *n* [C] *AmE* a type of tight-fitting shirt worn by women that fastens between their legs SYN **body** *BrE* → see picture at **UNDERWEAR**

ˈ**body** ˌ**warmer** *n* [C] *BrE* a piece of warm clothing without arms that you wear over a SWEATER or a shirt, especially when you are outside: *a fleece body warmer*

bod·y·work /ˈbɒdiwɜːk $ ˈbɑːdiwɜːrk/ *n* [U] the metal frame of a vehicle, not including the engine, wheels etc: *The bodywork's beginning to rust.*

Boer /bɔː, bʊə $ bɔːr, bʊr/ *n* [C] a white South African whose family is related to the Dutch people who settled in South Africa in the 1600s → **Afrikaner**

bof·fin /ˈbɒfɪn $ ˈbɑː-/ *n* [C] *BrE informal* **1** a scientist **2** someone who is very clever: *He was always a bit of a boffin, even at school.* | ***computer boffins***

bog¹ /bɒg $ bɑːg, bɔːg/ *n* **1** [C,U] an area of low wet muddy ground, sometimes containing bushes or grasses → **marsh**, **swamp** **2** [C] *BrE informal* a toilet

bog² *v* (**bogged**, **bogging**)

bog sb/sth ↔ **down** *phr v* **1** if a process or plan becomes bogged down, it is delayed so that no progress is made: *Talks to settle the pay dispute have become bogged down.* | **be/get bogged down in sth** *Don't let yourself get bogged down in minor details.* **2** if something gets bogged down, it becomes stuck in soft ground and is unable to move: **be/get bogged down in sth** *The car got bogged down in the mud.*

bog off *phr v BrE spoken informal* used to tell someone rudely to go away: *Just bog off!*

bo·gey, **bogie** /ˈbəʊgi $ ˈboʊgi/ *n* [C] **1** *technical* when you take one more shot than PAR (=the usual number of shots) to get the ball into the hole in GOLF → **birdie**, **eagle** **2** a problem or difficult situation that makes you feel anxious: **[+of]** *the bogey of recession* **3** *BrE informal* a piece of MUCUS from inside your nose **4** a bogeyman

bo·gey·man /ˈbəʊgimæn $ ˈboʊ-/ *n* (*plural* **bogeymen** /-men/) [C] **1** an evil spirit, especially in children's imagination or stories **2** someone who people think is evil or unpleasant: *Manson was and remains America's number one bogeyman.*

bog·gle /ˈbɒgəl $ ˈbɑː-/ *v* **the/your mind boggles,** (*also* **sth makes the/your mind boggle**, **sth boggles the/your mind**) *informal* if your mind boggles when you think of something, it is difficult for you to imagine or accept it: *The sheer amount of data makes the mind boggle.* | **[+at]** *My mind boggles at the amount of work still to do.*

bog·gy /ˈbɒgi $ ˈbɑː-/ *adj* boggy ground is wet and muddy → **bog**: *a boggy patch at the edge of the field*

bo·gie¹ /ˈbəʊgi $ ˈboʊ-/ *n* [C] a BOGEY

bogie² *v* [T] to use one more than PAR (=the usual number of strokes) to get the ball into the hole in GOLF

BOGOF, **bog·of** /ˈbɒgɒf $ ˈbɑːgɔːf, ˈbɔːg-/ *n* [C,U] (***buy one get one free***) an offer from a shop to sell you two things of the same type for the price of one: *Take advantage of special offers and BOGOFs in supermarkets.*

ˈ**bog roll** *n* [C,U] *BrE informal* TOILET PAPER

ˌ**bog-**ˈ**standard** *adj* [only before noun] *BrE informal* not special or interesting in any way SYN **average**

bo·gus /ˈbəʊgəs $ ˈboʊ-/ *adj* not true or real, although someone is trying to make you think it is SYN **false**: *bogus insurance claims* | *bogus applications for asylum*

bo·he·mi·an /bəʊˈhiːmiən, bə- $ boʊ-, bə-/ *adj* living in a very informal or relaxed way and not accepting society's rules of behaviour: *bohemian cafés frequented by artists, musicians, and actors* —**bohemian** *n* [C]

bo·ho /ˈbəʊhəʊ $ boʊhoʊ/ *adj informal* bohemian: *a boho lifestyle*

boil¹ /bɔɪl/ ●●● S3 *v*

1 [I,T] when a liquid boils, or when you boil it, it becomes hot enough to turn into gas: **[+at]** *The solution boiled at 57.4°C.* | *Put the spaghetti into plenty of boiling salted water.* | *We were advised to boil the water before drinking it.*

2 [I,T] to cook something in boiling water: *a boiled egg* | *Boil the rice for 15 minutes.* | *She fried the chicken and* ***put*** *the vegetables* ***on to boil.*** **THESAURUS** COOK → see picture at **EGG**¹

3 [I,T] if something containing liquid boils, the liquid inside it is boiling: *The kettle's boiling – shall I turn it off?* | *The saucepan* ***boiled dry*** *on the stove.*

4 [T] to wash something, using boiling water: *I always boil the cotton sheets.*

5 [I] if you are boiling with anger, you are extremely angry: **[+with]** *Lewis was boiling with rage and misery.* → **BOILING POINT**(2), → **make sb's blood boil** at **BLOOD**¹(4)

GRAMMAR

Boil belongs to a group of verbs where the same noun can be the subject of the verb or its object.

• You can say: *I'm boiling the potatoes.* In this sentence, 'the potatoes' is the object of **boil**.

• You can also say: *The potatoes are boiling.* In this sentence, 'the potatoes' is the subject of **boil**.

GRAMMAR GUIDE VERBS

boil away *phr v* if a liquid boils away, it disappears because it has been heated too much: *The soup's almost boiled away.*

boil down *phr v*

1 boil down to sth *informal* if a long statement, argument etc boils down to a single statement, that statement is the main point or cause: *It boils down to a question of priorities.*

2 boil sth ↔ down to make a list or piece of writing shorter by not including anything that is not necessary: *You can boil this down so that there are just two main categories.*

3 if a food or liquid boils down, or if you boil it down, it becomes less after it is cooked: *Spinach tends to boil down a lot.* | **boil sth ↔ down** *glue made from boiling down old sheepskins*

boil over *phr v*
1 if a liquid boils over when it is heated, it rises and flows over the side of the container: *The milk was boiling over on the stove behind her.*
2 if a situation or an emotion boils over, the people involved stop being calm: *All the bitterness of the last two years seemed to boil over.* | **[+into]** *Anger eventually boils over into words that are later regretted.*

B

boil up *phr v*
1 if a situation or emotion boils up, bad feelings grow until they reach a dangerous level: *She could sense that trouble was boiling up at work.* | *He could feel the anger boiling up inside him.*
2 boil sth ↔ up to heat food or a liquid until it begins to boil: *Boil the fruit up with sugar.*

boil² *n* **1 the boil** *BrE*, **a boil** *AmE* the act or state of boiling: *Add the seasoning and **bring** the sauce **to the boil**.* | *She waited for the water to **come to the boil*** (=begin to boil). **2** [C] a painful infected swelling under someone's skin: *The boy's body is covered in boils.* **3 go off the boil** *BrE* to become less good at something that you are usually very good at: *He's gone off the boil after a tournament win in Dubai.*

ˈboiled sweet *n* [C] *BrE* a hard SWEET that often tastes of fruit SYN **hard candy** *AmE*

boil·er /ˈbɔɪlə $ -ər/ ●○○ *n* [C] a container for boiling water that is part of a steam engine, or is used to provide heating in a house

boil·er·plate /ˈbɔɪləpleɪt $ -ər-/ *n* [C,U] *AmE* a standard piece of writing or a design for something that can be easily used each time you need it, for example in business or legal documents → **template**: *a boilerplate for a fax message* | *lawyers selling boilerplate wills*

ˈboiler room *n* [C] **1** a room in a large building where the building's boiler is **2** *AmE informal* a room or office where people sell SHARES or services on the telephone, using unfair and sometimes dishonest methods

ˈboiler suit *n* [C] *BrE* a piece of loose clothing like trousers and a shirt joined together, that you wear over your clothes to protect them → **overalls**

boil·ing /ˈbɔɪlɪŋ/ ●○○ *adj, adv spoken* very hot OPP **freezing**: *Can I open a window? It's boiling in here.* | *It was a **boiling hot** morning.*

ˈboiling point *n* [C usually singular] **1** the temperature at which a liquid boils **2** a point where people can no longer deal calmly with a problem → **flashpoint**: *Relations between the two countries have almost **reached boiling point**.*

bois·ter·ous /ˈbɔɪstərəs/ *adj* someone, especially a child, who is boisterous makes a lot of noise and has a lot of energy: *a class of boisterous five-year-olds*

bok choy /ˌbɒk ˈtʃɔɪ $ ˌbɑːk-/ *n* [U] another spelling of PAK CHOI

bold /bəʊld $ boʊld/ ●●○ *adj*
1 PERSON/ACTION not afraid of taking risks and making difficult decisions: *In a surprisingly **bold move**, he is threatening court action against the company.* | *My aunt Flo was a bold determined woman.* | *He had the ability to take bold imaginative decisions.* THESAURUS▸ BRAVE
2 MANNER/APPEARANCE so confident or determined that you sometimes offend people: *You should be feeling confident and bold when you meet your bank manager.* | *She marched into his office **as bold as brass*** (=very confident and not showing enough respect).
3 COLOURS/SHAPES very strong or bright so that you notice them: *bold geometric shapes* | *Stripes are bold, bright, and fun to wear.* | *bold colours*
4 LINES/WRITING written or drawn in a very clear way: *an envelope addressed to her in a bold black hand* | *The graphics are bold and colourful.* | *The print should be bold and easy to read.*
5 PRINTED LETTERS printed in letters that are darker and thicker than ordinary printed letters: *All the headings are in bold type.* → see picture at FONT
6 make/be so bold (as to do sth) *formal* to do something that other people feel is rude or not acceptable: *I see you have been so bold as to ask for food at this hour.*
7 if I may be so bold *BrE spoken formal* used when asking someone a question, to show that you are slightly annoyed with them: *Tell me, if I may be so bold as to ask, precisely what you are talking about.* —**boldly** *adv* —**boldness** *n* [U]

bold·face /ˈbəʊldfeɪs $ ˈboʊld-/ *n* [U] *technical* a way of printing letters that makes them thicker and darker than normal —**boldfaced** *adj* —**boldface** *adj*

bole /bəʊl $ boʊl/ *n* [C] *literary* the main part of a tree SYN **trunk**

bo·le·ro¹ /bəˈleərəʊ $ -ˈleroʊ/ *n* (*plural* **boleros**) [C] a type of Spanish dance, or the music for this dance

bol·e·ro² /ˈbɒlərəʊ $ bəˈleroʊ/ *n* (*plural* **boleros**) [C] a short jacket for a woman

boll /bəʊl $ boʊl/ *n* [C] the part of a cotton plant that contains the seeds

bol·lard /ˈbɒləd, -lɑːd $ ˈbɑːlərd/ *n* [C] **1** *BrE* a short thick post in the street that is used to stop traffic entering an area or to show a JUNCTION more clearly **2** a thick stone or metal post used for tying ships to when they are in port

bol·lock /ˈbɒlək $ ˈbɑː-/ *v* [T] *BrE spoken informal* to tell someone angrily that you do not like what they have done: *I'll bollock him for sticking his rubbish in my cupboard.*

bol·lock·ing /ˈbɒləkɪŋ $ ˈbɑː-/ *n* [C] *BrE spoken informal* when someone tells you that they are very angry with you: *I expect I'll **get** a right **bollocking** from my boss when she finds out.*

bol·locks /ˈbɒləks $ ˈbɑː-/ *n* [plural] *BrE spoken informal*
1 used to say rudely that you think something is wrong or stupid SYN **rubbish**: *Your lyrics are complete bollocks; they don't actually mean anything, do they?* | *She's just talking **a load of old bollocks**.* **2** a word used to emphasize that you are annoyed or angry: *Oh, bollocks! We've missed it.* **3 bollocks to you/that/it etc** used when you refuse to accept or obey something: *Yeah? Well, bollocks to you too, mate!* **4** the two round male organs that produce SPERM SYN **testicle**

ˌboll ˈweevil *n* [C] an insect that eats and destroys cotton plants

Bol·ly·wood /ˈbɒliwʊd $ ˈbɑː-/ *informal* the Indian film industry

bo·lo·gna /bəˈləʊni, -njə $ -ˈloʊ-/ *n* [U] a type of cooked meat often eaten in sandwiches

bo·lo·ney /bəˈləʊni $ -ˈloʊ-/ *n* [U] another spelling of BALONEY

bo·lo tie /ˈbəʊləʊ taɪ $ ˈboʊloʊ-/ *n* [C] *AmE* a string worn around your neck that you fasten with a decoration

Bol·she·vik /ˈbɒlʃəvɪk $ ˈboʊl-/ *n* [C] **1** someone who supported the COMMUNIST party at the time of the Russian Revolution in 1917 **2** *old-fashioned* an insulting way of talking about a Communist or someone who has strong LEFT-WING opinions —**bolshevik** *adj*

bol·shie, **bolshy** /ˈbəʊlʃi $ ˈboʊl-/ *adj BrE informal* tending to be angry or annoyed and not to obey people: *There's no need to be so bolshie.* —**bolshiness** *n* [U]

bol·ster¹ /ˈbəʊlstə $ ˈboʊlstər/ ●○○ (*also* **bolster up**) *v* [T]
1 to help someone to feel better and more positive SYN **boost**: *He is making a bold attempt to bolster the territory's confidence.*
2 to improve something SYN **boost**: *his efforts to bolster his career*

bolster² *n* [C] a long firm PILLOW, usually shaped like a tube

bolt¹ /bəʊlt $ boʊlt/ ●●○ *n* [C]
1 LOCK a metal bar that you slide across a door or window to fasten it → see picture at LOCK²
2 SCREW a screw with a flat head and no point, for fastening things together → see picture at SCREW¹

3 a bolt from/out of the blue news that is sudden and unexpected: *Was this money a bolt from the blue or did you know you were going to get it?*
4 bolt of lightning lightning that appears as a white line in the sky: *There's not much left of his house after it was* ***struck by a bolt of lightning****.* → THUNDERBOLT
5 make a bolt for it *BrE* to suddenly try to escape from somewhere: *They attacked the driver and he straightaway made a bolt for it.*
6 WEAPON a short heavy ARROW that is fired from a CROSSBOW
7 CLOTH a large long roll of cloth → **have shot your bolt** at SHOOT[1](24), → **the nuts and bolts of sth** at NUT[1](6)

bolt² ●○○ *v*
1 [I] to suddenly run somewhere very quickly, especially in order to escape or because you are frightened: *The horse reared up and bolted.* | *Kevin had bolted through the open window.* THESAURUS RUN
2 [T] (*also* **bolt down**) to eat very quickly SYN **gobble**: *He bolted down his breakfast.*
3 [T] to fasten two things together using a bolt: **bolt sth to sth** *The cell contained an iron bedframe bolted to the floor.* | **bolt sth together** *The boxes were made of heavy panels of metal bolted together.*
4 [T] to lock a door or window by sliding a bolt across

bolt³ *adv* **sit/stand bolt upright** to sit or stand with your back very straight, often because something has frightened you: *She sat bolt upright in the back seat.*

bolt·hole /ˈbəʊlthəʊl $ ˈboʊlthoʊl/ *n* [C] *BrE* a place where you can escape to and hide: *a bolthole in the country*

ˈbolt-on *adj especially BrE* **bolt-on part/component/extra** something that is connected to the outside of a machine after it has been made, and is then part of the machine

bomb¹ /bɒm $ bɑːm/ ●●● S3 W3 *n* [C]
1 WEAPON a weapon made of material that will explode: *The bomb went off at 9.30 in the morning.* | *Enemy planes dropped over 200 bombs during the raid.* | *He was killed in a bomb explosion.* → SMOKE BOMB, STINK BOMB
2 BAD PERFORMANCE/EVENT *AmE informal* a play, film, event etc that is not successful: *This is just another one of Hollywood's bland and boring bombs.*
3 be the bomb *informal* to be very good or exciting: *That new P Diddy CD is the bomb.*
4 the bomb used to describe NUCLEAR weapons, and especially the HYDROGEN BOMB: *Voices of dissent began to rise against the bomb.*
5 cost a bomb *BrE informal* to cost a lot of money
6 make a bomb *BrE informal* to get a lot of money by doing something
7 drop the c-bomb/f-bomb *informal* to say a very rude word beginning with C or F

COLLOCATIONS

VERBS

a bomb explodes/goes off *Forty people were injured when the bomb exploded.*
set off a bomb (*also* **detonate a bomb** *formal*) (=make a bomb explode) *The area was cleared and the police safely detonated the bomb.*
drop a bomb (=from a plane) *Government forces began dropping bombs on rebel positions.*
a bomb falls on sth *A bomb fell on the cathedral during the war.*
plant a bomb (=put a bomb somewhere)

ADJECTIVES/NOUN + bomb

a nuclear/hydrogen bomb *The North Koreans were developing a nuclear bomb.*
an atom/atomic bomb *Oppenheimer was the father of the atomic bomb.*
a neutron bomb (=that kills people but does not damage buildings much) | **a car bomb** (=that makes a car explode) | **a letter bomb** (*also* **a parcel bomb** *BrE*) (=sent in a letter or parcel) | **a time bomb** (=that is set to explode at a particular time) | **a petrol bomb** *BrE* (=containing petrol) | **a nail bomb** (=containing nails) | **a cluster bomb** (=that sends out smaller bombs when it explodes) | **a dirty bomb** (=that spreads radioactive material) | **a smart bomb** (=that is guided to the right place) | **a terrorist bomb** | **a suicide bomb** (=the person carrying the bomb dies when it explodes) | **a homemade bomb** | **an unexploded bomb**

bomb + NOUN

a bomb blast/explosion *The restaurant was destroyed in a massive bomb blast.*
a bomb attack *No one has yet claimed responsibility for the bomb attack.*
a bomb threat (=when someone leaves a message saying there is a bomb somewhere) | **a bomb scare** (=when people think there might be a bomb somewhere)

bomb² ●●● W3 *v*
1 [T] to attack a place by leaving a bomb there, or by dropping bombs on it from a plane: *The town was heavily bombed in World War II.* | *Government aircraft have been bombing civilian areas.* → CARPET-BOMB, DIVE-BOMB
2 [I always + adv/prep] *BrE informal* to move or drive very quickly: *Suddenly a police car came bombing down the high street.*
3 [I,T] *AmE informal* to fail a test very badly: *I bombed my midterm.*
4 [I] *AmE* if a play, film, event etc bombs, it is not successful: *His latest play bombed on Broadway.*

be bombed out *phr v* if a building or the people in it are bombed out, the building is completely destroyed: *My family were bombed out in 1941.*

bom·bard /bɒmˈbɑːd $ bɑːmˈbɑːrd/ ●○○ *v* [T]
1 to attack a place for a long time using large weapons, bombs etc: *I had been in action, bombarding the Normandy coast.* THESAURUS SHOOT
2 to do something too often or too much, for example criticizing or questioning someone, or giving too much information: *The office was bombarded by telephone calls.* | **bombard sb with sth** *They bombarded him with questions.* | *Today we are bombarded with advice on what to eat and what to avoid.*

bom·bar·dier /ˌbɒmbəˈdɪə◂ $ ˌbɑːmbərˈdɪr/ *n* [C] **1** the person on a military aircraft who is responsible for dropping bombs **2** a low rank in the British army

bom·bard·ment /bɒmˈbɑːdmənt $ bɑːmˈbɑːrd-/ *n* [C,U] a continuous attack on a place by big guns and bombs: *The bombardment continued for a terrible nine hours.* | **aerial/artillery/naval bombardment** (=attack from the air, land, or sea)

bom·bas·tic /bɒmˈbæstɪk $ bɑːm-/ *adj* bombastic language contains long words that sound important but have no real meaning: *He is best known for three rather bombastic poems.* —**bombast** /ˈbɒmbæst $ ˈbɑːm-/ *n* [U]

ˈbomb disˌposal *n* [U] the job of dealing with bombs that have not exploded, and making them safe: **bomb disposal experts/team/squad/unit** *The device, which contained 400lbs of explosive, was made safe by army bomb disposal experts.*

bombed /bɒmd $ bɑːmd/ *adj* [not before noun] *informal* very drunk or affected by illegal drugs SYN **stoned**: *I feel like going out and getting completely bombed.*

bomb·er /ˈbɒmə $ ˈbɑːmər/ ●●○ *n* [C]
1 a plane that carries and drops bombs
2 someone who hides a bomb somewhere in order to destroy something

ˈbomber ˌjacket *n* [C] a short jacket that fits tightly around your waist

bomb·ing /ˈbɒmɪŋ $ ˈbɑːm-/ ●●○ *n* [C,U] the use of bombs to attack a place: *The southwest of the country suffered an intensive* ***bombing campaign****.* | *They were planning* ***bombing raids*** *in some of America's major cities.* | *a terrorist network responsible for a* ***wave of bombings*** *in Paris* | **[+of]** *the bombing of Hiroshima*

ˈbomb scare *n* [C] when people have to be moved out

of a building because there may be a bomb there: *a bomb scare in Central London*

bomb·shell /ˈbɒmʃel $ ˈbɑːm-/ *n* [C] **1** an unexpected and very shocking piece of news: *Then came the bombshell: the factory was to close down.* | *Finally, she* ***dropped the bombshell****. She was pregnant, she said.* **2 blonde bombshell** *humorous* a sexually attractive woman with light-coloured hair

ˈbomb ˌshelter *n* [C] a room or building that is built to protect people from bomb attacks

B

ˈbomb site *n* [C] a place where a bomb has destroyed several buildings in a town: *They've pulled down so many buildings around here it looks like a bomb site.*

bo·na fi·de /ˌbəʊnə ˈfaɪdi $ ˈbəʊnə faɪd/ *adj* real, true, and not intended to deceive anyone: *Only bona fide members are allowed to use the club pool.*

bona fi·des /ˌbəʊnə ˈfaɪdiːz $ ˌboʊnə-, ˈboʊnə faɪdz/ *n* [plural] *BrE* if you check someone's bona fides, you check that they are who they say they are, and that their intentions are good and honest

bo·nan·za /bəˈnænzə, bəʊ- $ bə-, boʊ-/ *n* [C] a lucky or successful situation where people can make a lot of money: *2008 was a bonanza year for the oil industry.* | *an amazing cash bonanza*

bon ap·pe·tit /ˌbɒn æpəˈtiː $ ˌboʊn æpeɪ-/ *interjection* said to someone before they start eating a meal, to tell them you hope they enjoy their food

bonce /bɒns $ bɑːns/ *n* [C] *BrE informal* your head

bond¹ /bɒnd $ bɑːnd/ ●●○ AWL *n* [C]

1 MONEY an official document promising that a government or company will pay back money that it has borrowed, often with INTEREST: *My father put all his money into stock market bonds.* | *furious trading on the bond market* → see also **JUNK BOND, PREMIUM BOND, SAVINGS BOND**

2 RELATIONSHIP something that unites two or more people or groups, such as love, or a shared interest or idea → **tie**: **[+between]** *the emotional bond between mother and child* | **[+with]** *the United States' special bond with Britain* | **[+of]** *lifelong bonds of friendship*

3 bonds [plural] *literary* something that limits your freedom and prevents you from doing what you want: **[+of]** *the bonds of fear and guilt*

4 WITH GLUE the way in which two surfaces become attached to each other using glue: *Use a glue gun to form a strong bond on wood or china.*

5 CHEMISTRY *technical* the chemical force that holds atoms together in a MOLECULE: *In each methane molecule there are four CH bonds.*

6 WRITTEN AGREEMENT a written agreement to do something, that makes you legally responsible for doing it → **contract**

7 my word is my bond *formal* used to say that you will definitely do what you have promised

8 in/out of bond *technical* in or out of a BONDED WAREHOUSE

bond² AWL *v* **1** [I] if two things bond with each other, they become firmly fixed together, especially after they have been joined with glue: *It takes less than ten minutes for the two surfaces to bond.* **2** [I] to develop a special relationship with someone → **bonding**: **[+with]** *Time must be given for the mother to bond with her baby.* **3** [T] *technical* to keep goods in a bonded warehouse

bond·age /ˈbɒndɪdʒ $ ˈbɑːn-/ *n* [U] **1** the state of having your freedom limited, or being prevented from doing what you want: *the bondage of early motherhood* **2** *literary* the state of being a slave: **in bondage** *Since the age of 13, he had been in bondage.* **3** the practice of being tied up for sexual pleasure

ˌbonded ˈwarehouse *n* [C] *technical* an official place for storing goods that have been brought into a country before tax has been paid on them

bond·hold·er /ˈbɒndˌhəʊldə $ ˈbɑːndˌhoʊldər/ *n* [C] *technical* someone who owns government or industrial BONDS

bond·ing /ˈbɒndɪŋ $ ˈbɑːn-/ *n* [U] **1** a process in which a special relationship develops between two or more people: **[+between]** *the bonding between mare and foal* **2 male/female bonding** *informal* the activity of doing things with other people of the same sex, so that you feel good about being a man or a woman: *They're in the bar again, doing some male bonding!* **3** *technical* the connection of atoms or of two surfaces that are glued together: *chemical bonding*

bone¹ /bəʊn $ boʊn/ ●●● S2 W2 *n*

1 [C] one of the hard parts that together form the frame of a human, animal, or fish body: *The X-ray showed that the bone was broken in two places.* | **hip/leg/cheek etc bone** (=the bone in your hip etc) *He broke his collar bone.* | **big-boned/fine-boned/small-boned etc** (=with big etc bones) *She was tall and big-boned.* | *Amelia had inherited her mother's good* ***bone structure****.*

2 [U] a substance made of bones: *the bone handle of his dagger*

3 the bare bones the simplest and most important details of something: *I can't tell you more than the bare bones of what happened.*

4 make no bones about (doing) sth to not feel nervous or ashamed about doing or saying something: *Mary made no bones about enjoying a drink.*

5 bone of contention something that causes arguments between people: *The examination system has long been a serious bone of contention in this country.*

6 be chilled/frozen to the bone to be extremely cold

7 skin and bone very thin: *She was all skin and bone.*

8 a bag of bones someone who is much too thin

9 feel/know sth in your bones to be certain that something is true, even though you have no proof and cannot explain why you are certain: *She knew that something good was sure to happen; she could feel it in her bones.*

10 have a bone to pick with sb *spoken* used to tell someone that you are annoyed with them and want to talk about it

11 close to the bone a remark, statement etc that is close to the bone is close to the truth in a way that may offend someone: *His jokes were a bit close to the bone.*

12 cut sth to the bone to reduce costs, services etc as much as possible: *Shops cut prices to the bone in the January sales.*

13 on the bone meat that is served on the bone is still joined to the bone: *a boiled ham on the bone*

14 off the bone meat that is served off the bone has been cut away from the bone: *roasted duck, off the bone* → **dry as a bone** at DRY¹(1), → **work your fingers to the bone** at WORK¹(29)

bone² *v* [T] to remove the bones from fish or meat: *boned breast and thigh meat*

bone up on sth *phr v* to learn as much as you can about a subject, because you need the knowledge, for example for an examination: *I have to bone up on criminal law for a test next week.*

ˌbone ˈchina *n* [U] delicate and expensive cups, plates etc that are made partly with crushed bone

ˌbone ˈdry *adj* completely dry: *There had been no rain for months and the land was bone dry.*

bone·head /ˈbəʊnhed $ ˈboʊn-/ *n* [C] *informal* a stupid person

ˌbone ˈidle *adj BrE* extremely lazy: *He's just bone idle.*

bone·less /ˈbəʊnləs $ ˈboʊn-/ *adj* boneless meat or fish has had the bones taken out

ˈbone ˌmarrow *n* [U] the soft substance in the hollow centre of bones SYN **marrow**: *a bone marrow transplant*

bone·meal, bone meal /ˈbəʊnmiːl $ ˈboʊn-/ *n* [U] a substance used to feed plants that is made of crushed bones

bon·er /ˈbəʊnə $ ˈboʊnər/ *n* [C] *informal not polite* an ERECTION

bon·fire /ˈbɒnfaɪə $ ˈbɑːnfaɪr/ *n* [C] a large outdoor fire, either for burning waste or for a party

ˈbonfire ˌnight, Bonfire Night *n* [U] November 5th, when people in Britain light FIREWORKS and burn a GUY (=model of a man) on a large outdoor fire SYN **Guy Fawkes' Night**

bong /bɒŋ $ bɑːŋ/ *n* [C] **1** a deep sound made by a large bell **2** *informal* an object used for smoking CANNABIS, in which the smoke goes through water to make it cool

bon·gos /ˈbɒŋɡəʊz $ ˈbɑːŋɡoʊz/ (*also* ˈ**bongo drums**) *n* [plural] a pair of small drums that you play with your hands

bon·ho·mie /ˈbɒnəmi $ ˌbɑːnəˈmiː/ *n* [U] *formal* a friendly feeling among a group of people: *They were relaxed and full of bonhomie.*

bonk¹ /bɒŋk $ bɑːŋk/ *v* [I,T] *informal* **1** *BrE* to have sex with someone – used humorously **2** to hit someone lightly on the head or to hit your head on something: *He fell, bonking his head against a tree.*

bonk² *n informal* **1** [singular] *BrE* the action of having sex – used humorously: *a quick bonk* **2** [C] the action of hitting someone lightly on the head, or hitting your head against something **3** [C] a sudden short deep sound, for example when something hits the ground

bon·kers /ˈbɒŋkəz $ ˈbɑːŋkərz/ *adj* [not before noun] *informal* **1** slightly crazy **2 drive sb bonkers** to make someone feel crazy or very annoyed: *Thinking about the whole problem has driven me nearly bonkers.*

bon mot /ˌbɒn ˈməʊ $ ˌbɔːn ˈmoʊ/ *n* [C] *written* a clever remark

bon·net /ˈbɒnɪt $ ˈbɑː-/ *n* [C] **1** *BrE* the metal lid over the front of a car SYN **hood** *AmE*: *I'll need to check under the bonnet.* → see picture at CAR **2 a)** a warm hat that a baby wears which ties under its chin **b)** a type of hat that women wore in the past which tied under their chin and often had a wide BRIM → see picture at HAT → **have a bee in your bonnet** at BEE(2)

Bon·nie and Clyde /ˌbɒni ən ˈklaɪd $ ˌbɑː-/ when a man and woman work together as criminals, newspapers sometimes refer to them as being like 'Bonnie and Clyde'. These names come from two young criminals, Bonnie Parker (a woman) and Clyde Barrow (a man), who stole from US banks and businesses in the 1930s. A popular film was made about them in 1967.

bon·ny /ˈbɒni $ ˈbɑːni/ *adj BrE* pretty and healthy: *a bonny baby*

bon·sai /ˈbɒnsaɪ, ˈbəʊn- $ bɔːnˈsaɪ, ˈbɑːnsaɪ/ *n* [C,U] a tree that is grown so that it always stays very small, or the art of growing trees in this way —**bonsai** *adj*

bo·nus /ˈbəʊnəs $ ˈboʊ-/ ●●○ *n* [C]
1 money added to someone's wages, especially as a reward for good work: *Long-term savers qualify for a cash bonus.* | *Further additions to your pay may take the form of bonus payments.* | *a Christmas bonus* | *Each worker receives an annual bonus.* | *a £20,000 bonus*
2 something good that you did not expect in a situation: **[+for]** *Britain's possession of North Sea oil has proved a bonus for British technology.* | *He promised to take me to the match, with the* ***added bonus*** *of an afternoon off school.*
3 no-claims bonus *BrE* a reduction in the cost of your car insurance when you do not make a CLAIM in a particular year

bon vi·vant /ˌbɒn viːˈvɒnt $ ˌbɔːn viːˈvɑːnt/ (*also* **bon viveur** /-viːˈvɜː $ -viːˈvɜːr/) *n* [C] *formal* someone who enjoys good food and wine, and being with people

bon voy·age /ˌbɒn vɔɪˈɑːʒ $ ˌbɔːn-/ *interjection* used to wish someone a good journey

bon·y /ˈbəʊni $ ˈboʊ-/ *adj* **1** someone or part of their body that is bony is very thin: *She had a bony intelligent face.* | *He was tall and bony.* **2** bony meat or fish contains a lot of small bones **3** a part of an animal that is bony consists mostly of bone

boo¹ /buː/ *v* [I,T] to shout 'boo' to show that you do not like a person, performance, idea etc: *Some of the audience started booing.* | *She was* ***booed off stage*** (=they shouted 'boo' until she left the stage).

boo² *interjection* **1** a noise made by people who do not like a person, performance, idea etc **2** a word you shout suddenly to someone as a joke in order to frighten them **3 wouldn't say boo to a goose** an expression used to describe a shy quiet person

boob¹ /buːb/ *n* [C] **1** [usually plural] *informal* a woman's breast **2** *BrE informal* a silly mistake **3** *AmE old-fashioned* a stupid or silly person

boob² *v* [I] *BrE informal* to make a stupid mistake SYN **goof** *AmE*: *I think Jean's boobed again.*

ˈ**boo-boo** *n* [C] *informal* a silly mistake: *I* ***made*** *a bit of a* ***boo-boo*** *asking her about David!*

ˈ**boob tube** *n* [C] **1** *BrE* a piece of women's clothing made of material that stretches, that covers her chest SYN **tube top** *AmE* **2 the boob tube** *AmE informal* the television

boo·by /ˈbuːbi/ *n* (*plural* **boobies**) [C] *informal* a silly or stupid person

ˈ**booby hatch** *n* [singular] *AmE old-fashioned informal* a mental hospital

ˈ**booby prize** *n* [C] *informal* a prize given as a joke to the person who is last in a competition

ˈ**booby trap**, **booby-trap** *n* [C] **1** a hidden bomb that explodes when you touch something else that is connected to it: *He lost both legs in a booby trap bomb blast.* **2** a HARMLESS trap that you arrange for someone as a joke —**booby-trapped** *adj* —**booby trap** *v* [T]

boo·ga·loo /ˈbuːɡəˌluː/ *n* **1** [U] a type of music that was popular especially in the US during the 1960s and 70s, which is a combination of Latin American dance music and RHYTHM AND BLUES **2 the boogaloo** a dance that young people did to this music, which involves moving your feet in a regular pattern of usually 12 steps

boog·er /ˈbʊɡə, ˈbuː- $ -ər/ *n* [C] *AmE informal* a thick piece of MUCUS from your nose

boo·gey·man /ˈbuːɡimæn/ *n* [C] a BOGEYMAN

boo·gie¹ /ˈbuːɡi $ ˈbʊɡi/ *v* [I] *informal* to dance, especially to fast popular music

boogie² (*also* **boogie woo·gie** /ˌbuːɡi ˈwuːɡi $ ˌbʊɡi ˈwʊɡi/) *n* [U] **1** a type of music played on the piano with a strong fast RHYTHM: *boogie rock at its finest* **2 a boogie** *informal* a dance, or an occasion when you dance, especially to fast popular music

ˈ**boogie board** *n* [C] a BODYBOARD

boo·hoo /ˌbuː ˈhuː/ *interjection written* used in stories to show that someone is crying

book¹ /bʊk/ ●●● S1 W1 *n*
1 PRINTED PAGES [C] a set of printed pages that are held together in a cover so that you can read them: *I've just started reading a book by Graham Greene.* | *a cookery book* | **[+about/on]** *a book about cats*
2 TO WRITE IN [C] a set of sheets of paper held together in a cover so that you can write on them: *a black address book* | *a notebook*
3 SET OF THINGS [C] a set of things such as stamps, matches, or tickets, held together inside a paper cover: *a cheque book*
4 books [plural] **a)** ACCOUNTS written records of the financial accounts of a business: *An accountant will examine the company's books.* | *a small firm that is having problems* ***balancing*** *the* ***books*** (=keeping its profits and spending equal) | **on the books** *They have £50 billion worth of orders on the books.* → **cook the books** at COOK¹(3) **b)** JOBS the names of people who use a company's services, or who are sent by a company to work for other people: **on sb's books** *an agent with a lot of popular actors on his books*
5 by the book exactly according to rules or instructions: *She feels she has to* ***go by the book*** *and can't use her creativity.* | **do/play sth by the book** *The police were careful to do everything by the book.*
6 a closed book a subject that you do not understand or know anything about: *Chemistry is a closed book to me.*
7 be in sb's good/bad books *informal* used to say that someone is pleased or annoyed with you
8 LAW **be on the books** if a law is on the books, it is part of the set of laws in a country, town, area etc
9 PART OF A BOOK [C] one of the parts that a very large book such as the Bible is divided into: **[+of]** *the Book of Isaiah*

10 in my book *spoken* said when giving your opinion: *In my book, nothing is more important than football.*
11 bring sb to book to punish someone for breaking laws or rules, especially when you have been trying to punish them for a long time: *War criminals must be brought to book.* → STATUTE BOOK, → **take a leaf out of sb's book** at LEAF[1](2), → **read sb like a book** at READ[1](16), → **suit sb's book** at SUIT[2](5), → **a turn-up for the book** at TURN-UP(2), → **throw the book at sb** at THROW[1](26)

GRAMMAR: Patterns with book

• You read something **in a book**: *I read about him in a book at school.*
• You say **a book about** a subject or **a book on** a subject: *I like books about sport.* ✗ Don't say: *I like books of sport.*
• **A book of** essays, poems etc is one that contains several essays, poems etc: *It's a book of interviews with artists.*
• You say **a book by** someone: *I'm reading a book by John Gray.* ✗ Don't say: *I'm reading a book of John Gray.*

COLLOCATIONS

VERBS

read a book *What book are you reading at the moment?*
look through a book (=look at the pages quickly) *I looked through the book until I found the right section.*
write a book *He's written several interesting travel books.*
publish a book *The book is published by Penguin.*
a book comes out (=it is published for the first time) *Everyone was waiting for the new Harry Potter book to come out.*
borrow a book (*also* **take out a book** *BrE*) (=from a library) | **return a book** (=to a library) | **renew a book** (=arrange to continue borrowing it from a library)

book + NOUN

a book shop (*also* **book store** *AmE*) *I got it from that little book shop in the village.*
a book seller (=a person, shop, or company selling books) *High street book sellers are experiencing a drop in sales.*
a book token *BrE* (=a ticket that you can use to pay for a book) *She always bought me book tokens for my birthday.*
a book review (=an article giving critical opinions of a book) | **a book fair**

PHRASES

the cover of a book *His picture is on the cover of the book.*
a chapter of a book *The first chapter of the book is about his childhood.*

THESAURUS

TYPES OF BOOK

novel *n* [C] a book about imaginary people and events: *The film is based on Nick Hornby's best-selling novel.* | *a historical novel*
fiction *n* [U] books that describe imaginary people and events: *She reads a lot of romantic fiction.*
literature *n* [U] novels and plays that are considered to be important works of art: *I'm studying American literature at university.*
non-fiction *n* [U] books that describe real people and events: *Men tend to prefer non-fiction.*
science fiction *n* [U] books about imaginary events in the future or space travel
reference book *n* [C] a book such as a dictionary or encyclopedia, which you look at to find information
textbook *n* [C] a book about a particular subject that you use in a classroom
set book *BrE*, **course book** *BrE n* [C] a book that you have to study as part of your course
guidebook *n* [C] a book telling visitors about a city or country
hardcover/hardback *n* [C] a book that has a hard stiff cover
paperback *n* [C] a book that has a paper cover
biography *n* [C] a book about a real person's life, written by another person
autobiography *n* [C] a book that someone has written about their own life
recipe book/cookery book *BrE* (*also* **cookbook** *AmE*) *n* [C] a book that tells you how to cook different meals

book² ●●○ S3 *v*
1 [I,T] to make arrangements to stay in a place, eat in a restaurant, go to a theatre etc at a particular time in the future → **reserve**: *Have you booked a holiday this year?* | *The flight was already* ***fully booked*** (=no more seats were available). | *To get tickets, you have to* **book in advance**. | *The show's* **booked solid** (=all the tickets have been sold) *until February.*
2 [T] to arrange for someone such as a singer to perform on a particular date: *The band was booked for a benefit show in Los Angeles.*
3 be booked up a) if a hotel, restaurant etc is booked up, there are no more rooms, places, seats etc still available: *The courses quickly get booked up.* **b)** if someone is booked up, they are extremely busy and have arranged a lot of things they must do: *I'm all booked up this week – can we get together next Friday?*
4 [T] to arrange for someone to go to a hotel, fly on a plane etc: *I've booked you a flight on Saturday.* | **book sb on/in etc** *I'll book you in at the Hilton.*
5 [T] to put someone's name officially in police records, along with the charge made against them: *Smith was booked on suspicion of attempted murder.*
6 [T] *BrE* when a REFEREE in a sports game books a player who has broken the rules, he or she officially writes down the player's name in a book as a punishment
book in (*also* **book into sth**) *phr v BrE* to arrive at a hotel and say who you are etc SYN **check in**: *Several tourists were booking in.*

book·a·ble /ˈbʊkəbəl/ *adj BrE* **1** tickets for a concert, performance etc that are bookable can be ordered before it happens **2 bookable offence** an offence for which a sports player can be punished by having his or her name written into the REFEREE's book

book·bind·ing /ˈbʊkˌbaɪndɪŋ/ *n* [U] the process of fastening the pages of books inside a cover —**bookbinder** *n* [C]

book·case /ˈbʊk-keɪs/ ●○○ *n* [C] a piece of furniture with shelves to hold books

ˈbook club *n* [C] **1** a club that offers books cheaply to its members **2** a group of people who meet regularly to discuss a particular book they have all read

book·cross·ing /ˈbʊkˌkrɒsɪŋ $ -ˌkrɒːs-/ *n* [U] the practice of leaving books in public places or on buses, trains etc, so that other people will read them and then leave them for others to read. There is a website where people can record details of the books and the places where they found or left them. —**bookcrosser** *n* [C]

book·end /ˈbʊkend/ *n* [C usually plural] one of a pair of objects that you put at the end of a row of books to prevent them from falling over

Book·er Prize, the /ˈbʊkə ˌpraɪz $ -kər-/ → MAN BOOKER PRIZE, THE

ˈbook group *n* [C] a group of people who meet regularly to discuss books that they have all agreed to read

book·ie /ˈbʊki/ *n* [C] *informal* a BOOKMAKER

book·ing /ˈbʊkɪŋ/ ●○○ *n* [C]
1 an arrangement to travel by train, use a hotel room etc at a particular time in the future → **reservation**: *bookings on cruise ships* | *I* **made** *a* **booking** *for two double rooms.* | *I'm calling to* **confirm** *my* **booking** (=say definitely that I want to travel etc). | *If you* **cancel** *your* **booking**, *there will be a small charge.* | *Places on the course are limited and* **advance**

booking is essential. | **block booking** (=a booking for a large number of dates, seats, rooms etc)
2 an arrangement made by a performer to perform at a particular time in the future
3 *BrE* the act of writing a football player's name in a book as a punishment for breaking the rules

ˈbooking ˌoffice *n* [C] *BrE* a place where you can buy train or bus tickets SYN **ticket office** → BOX OFFICE

book·ish /ˈbʊkɪʃ/ *adj* someone who is bookish is more interested in reading and studying than in sports or other activities: *a shy bookish man*

book·keep·ing /ˈbʊkˌkiːpɪŋ/ *n* [U] the job or activity of recording the financial accounts of an organization → **accountancy**

book·let /ˈbʊklɪt/ ●○○ *n* [C] a very short book that usually contains information on one particular subject → **leaflet**: *a free booklet on drug abuse*

book·mak·er /ˈbʊkˌmeɪkə $ -ər/ (*also* **bookie** *informal*) *n* [C] someone whose job is to collect money that people want to risk on the result of a race, competition etc, and who pays them if they guess correctly

book·mark¹ /ˈbʊkmɑːk $ -mɑːrk/ *n* [C] **1** a piece of paper, leather etc that you put in a book to show you the last page you have read **2** a way of saving the address of a page on the Internet so that you can find it again

bookmark² *v* [T] to save the address of a page on the Internet so that you can find it again easily

book·mo·bile /ˈbʊkməbiːl/ *n* [C] *AmE* a vehicle that contains a library and travels to different places so that people can use it SYN **mobile library** *BrE*

book·plate /ˈbʊkpleɪt/ *n* [C] a decorated piece of paper with your name on it, that you stick in the front of your books

book·rest /ˈbʊk-rest/ *n* [C] a metal or wooden frame that holds a book upright so that you can read it without holding it in your hands

book·sell·er /ˈbʊkˌselə $ -ər/ *n* [C] a person or company that sells books

book·shelf /ˈbʊkʃelf/ ●●● S3 *n* (*plural* **bookshelves** /-ʃelvz/) [C] a shelf that you keep books on, or a piece of furniture used for holding books → **bookcase**

book·shop /ˈbʊkʃɒp $ -ʃɑːp/ ●●● W3 *n* [C] *especially BrE* a shop that sells books SYN **bookstore** *AmE*

book·stall /ˈbʊkstɔːl $ -stɒːl/ *n* [C] *BrE* a small shop that has an open front and sells books and magazines, often at a railway station SYN **newsstand** *AmE*

book·store /ˈbʊkstɔː $ -stɔːr/ *n* [C] *AmE* a shop that sells books SYN **bookshop**

ˈbook ˌtoken *n* [C] *BrE* a card that you can exchange for books: *She gave me a book token for Christmas.*

ˈbook ˌvalue *n* [C] **1** how much a car of a particular age, style etc should be worth if you sold it **2** *technical* **a)** the value of a business after you sell all of its ASSETS and pay all of its debts **b)** the value of something that a company owns, which it lists in its accounts

book·worm /ˈbʊkwɜːm $ -wɜːrm/ *n* [C] **1** someone who likes reading very much **2** an insect that eats books

Boo·le·an /ˈbuːliən/ *adj* [only before noun] *technical* a Boolean system is based on things that can be either true or false, but not both. It links statements with words called OPERATORS, such as AND, OR, and NOT. Boolean systems are used to write computer programs, especially Internet search programs: *The program searches for information using **Boolean logic**.*

boom¹ /buːm/ ●○○ *n*
1 INCREASE IN BUSINESS [singular] a quick increase of business activity OPP **slump**: *The boom has created job opportunities.* | **[+in]** *a sudden boom in the housing market* | **consumer/investment/property etc boom** *the post-war property boom* | **boom years/times** *In boom times, airlines do well.* | *the **economic boom** of the 1950s* | *The economy went from **boom to bust*** (=from increasing to decreasing) *very quickly.* → BOOM TOWN
2 WHEN STH IS POPULAR [singular] an increase in how popular or successful something is, or in how often it happens: *the disco boom of the 1970s* | **[+in]** *the boom in youth soccer in the U.S.* → BABY BOOM
3 SOUND [C] a deep loud sound that you can hear for several seconds after it begins, especially the sound of an explosion or a large gun → SONIC BOOM THESAURUS SOUND
4 BOAT [C] a long pole on a boat that is attached to the bottom of a sail, and that you move to change the position of the sail
5 LONG POLE [C] **a)** a long pole used as part of a piece of equipment that loads and unloads things **b)** a long pole that has a camera or MICROPHONE on the end
6 ON A RIVER/HARBOUR [C] something that is stretched across a river or a BAY to prevent things floating down or across it

boom² ●○○ *v*
1 [I usually in progressive] if business, trade, or a particular area is booming, it is increasing and being very successful: ***Business** was **booming**, and money wasn't a problem.* | *Tourism on the island has boomed.*
2 (*also* **boom out**) [T] to say something in a loud deep voice: *'Ladies and gentlemen,' his voice boomed out.*
3 (*also* **boom out**) [I] to make a loud deep sound: *Guns boomed in the distance.* —**booming** *adj*: *a booming economy*

ˈboom box *n* [C] *AmE informal* a GHETTO BLASTER

boo·me·rang¹ /ˈbuːməræŋ/ *n* [C] a curved stick that flies in a circle and comes back to you when you throw it, first used in Australia

boomerang² *v* [I] if a plan or action boomerangs on someone, it affects them badly instead of affecting the person who it was intended to affect SYN **backfire**

ˈboomerang ˌchild *n* [C] someone who returns to live in their parents' home in their twenties or thirties after a period of being at university or living away from home

ˈboomerang geneˌration *n* [singular] young people who come back to live with their parents after finishing university: *The boomerang generation are saving thousands in rent by living at home.*

ˈboom town *n* [C] a town or city that suddenly becomes very successful because there is a lot of new industry

boon /buːn/ *n* [C usually singular] something that is very useful and makes your life a lot easier or better: *The bus service is a real boon to people in the village.*

ˌboon comˈpanion *n* [C] *literary* a very close friend

boon·docks /ˈbuːndɒks $ -dɑːks/ *n* [plural] *AmE informal* **the boondocks** a place that is a long way from the nearest town

boon·dog·gle /ˈbuːn ˌdɒgl $ -ˌdɑːgl/ *n* [singular] *AmE informal* an officially organized plan or activity that is very complicated and wastes a lot of time, money, and effort: *a bureaucratic boondoggle*

boo·nies /ˈbuːniz/ *n* [plural] *AmE informal* the boondocks

boor /bʊə $ bʊr/ *n* [C] a man who behaves in a very rude way —**boorish** *adj* —**boorishly** *adv*

boost¹ /buːst/ ●●○ *v* [T]
1 to increase or improve something and make it more successful: *The new resort area has boosted tourism.* | **boost sb's confidence/morale/ego** *The win boosted the team's confidence.* THESAURUS INCREASE
2 (*also* **boost up**) to help someone reach a higher place by lifting or pushing them: *He boosted her up.*
3 if a ROCKET or motor boosts a SPACECRAFT, it makes it go up into space or go in a particular direction
4 *AmE informal* to steal something

boost² ●●○ *n*
1 [singular] something that gives someone more confidence, or that helps something increase, improve, or become successful: **[+to]** *a major boost to the economy* | **[+for]** *a multimillion-pound boost for the British film industry* | *Add a little more vanilla, to **give** the flavor **a boost**.* | **get/receive a boost** *The community will get a boost from a new library and recreation center.* | **morale/ego boost** *The poll provided a morale boost for the Conservatives.*

2 give sb a boost (up) to lift someone so that they can reach a higher place: *If I give you a boost, could you reach the window?*
3 [U] an increase in the amount of power available to a ROCKET, piece of electrical equipment etc

boost·er /ˈbuːstə $ -ər/ *n* [C] **1** a small quantity of a drug that increases the effect of one that was given before, so that someone continues to be protected against a disease: *a booster shot* **2** something that helps someone or something to increase or improve, or to be more successful or confident: *a booster pump* | *a profit booster for the company* | **morale/confidence booster** *Mail from home is a big morale booster for faraway troops.* **3** a rocket that is used to provide extra power for a SPACECRAFT to leave the Earth: *a giant booster rocket* **4** *AmE* someone who gives a lot of support to a person, organization, or idea: *a dance organized by the school's booster club*

ˈbooster ˌseat (*also* **ˈbooster ˌchair**, **ˈbooster ˌcushion** *BrE*) *n* [C] a special seat for a small child that lets them sit in a higher position in a car or at a table

boot¹ /buːt/ ●●● S2 W3 *n* [C]
1 a type of shoe that covers your whole foot and the lower part of your leg → **Wellington**: *hiking boots* | *a pair of boots* → RUBBER BOOT, see picture at **SHOE¹**
2 *BrE* an enclosed space at the back of a car, used for carrying bags etc SYN **trunk** *AmE*: *The new model has a bigger boot.*
3 the boot *informal* when someone is forced to leave their job SYN **the sack** *BrE* → **dismiss**: *The chairman denied that he had been* ***given the boot***. | *He should have* ***got the boot*** *years ago.*
4 to boot in addition to everything else you have mentioned: *She was a great sportswoman, and beautiful to boot.*
5 put the boot in *BrE informal* **a)** to criticize or be cruel to someone who is already in a bad situation **b)** to attack someone by kicking them repeatedly, especially when they are on the ground
6 the boot is on the other foot *BrE* used to say someone who has caused problems for other people in the past is now in a situation in which people are causing problems for them
7 *AmE* a metal object that the police attach to one of the wheels of an illegally parked car so that it cannot be moved SYN **wheel clamp** *BrE*
8 boots on the ground soldiers present somewhere taking military action, or prepared to take military action → **be/get too big for your boots** at BIG¹(14), → **lick sb's boots** at LICK¹(7), → **tough as old boots** at TOUGH¹(2)

boot² *v* **1** (*also* **boot up**) [I,T] to start the program that makes a computer ready to be used → **load 2** [T] *informal* to kick someone or something hard: **boot sth in/round/down etc** *The goalkeeper booted the ball upfield.* **3** [T] *AmE* to stop someone from moving their illegally parked vehicle by fixing a piece of equipment to one of the wheels SYN **clamp** *BrE*

boot sb ↔ **out** *phr v informal* to force someone to leave a place, job, or organization, especially because they have done something wrong SYN **throw out**: *His fellow students booted him out of the class.*

ˈboot camp *n* [C] a training camp for people who have just joined the US army, navy, or Marine Corps

boot·cut /ˈbuːtkʌt/ *adj* [only before noun] *BrE* bootcut JEANS and trousers become slightly wider at the end of each leg SYN **bootleg** *AmE*

boot·ee, **bootie** /ˈbuːtiː, buːˈtiː/ *n* [C] a short thick sock that a baby wears instead of a shoe

booth /buːð $ buːθ/ ●○○ *n* [C]
1 a small partly enclosed place where one person can do something privately, such as use the telephone or vote: *a voting booth*
2 a small partly enclosed structure where you can buy things, play games, or get information, usually at a market or a FAIR: *a crafts booth*
3 a partly enclosed place in a restaurant, with a table between two long seats

ˈbooth bunny *n* [C] *AmE informal* an attractive woman who works in a company's booth at a TRADE FAIR (=an event when many companies show their goods or services in one place) in order to encourage people to visit the booth

boot·lace /ˈbuːtleɪs/ *n* [C usually plural] a long piece of string that you use to fasten a boot

boot·leg¹ /ˈbuːtleg/ *adj* [only before noun] **1** bootleg alcohol, software, or RECORDINGS are made and sold illegally: *bootleg tapes* **2** *AmE* bootleg JEANS, trousers etc become wider at the end of each leg SYN **bootcut** *BrE*

bootleg² *n* [C] an illegal recording of a music performance

bootleg³ *v* (**bootlegged**, **bootlegging**) [I,T] to illegally make or sell alcohol, or to illegally make or sell copies of software or RECORDINGS —**bootlegger** *n* [C] —**bootlegging** *n* [U]

ˈboot sale *n* [C] *BrE* a CAR BOOT SALE

boot·straps /ˈbuːtstræps/ *n* [plural] **pull/haul yourself up by your bootstraps** to improve your position and get out of a difficult situation by your own efforts, without help from other people

boot·y /ˈbuːti/ *n* **1** [U] *especially literary* valuable things that a group of people, especially an army that has just won a victory, take away from somewhere SYN **loot** **2** [C] *AmE informal* the part of your body that you sit on SYN **backside, bottom**

boo·ty·li·cious /ˌbuːtəˈlɪʃəs/ *adj informal* extremely nice, enjoyable, or attractive: *bootylicious babes*

booze¹ /buːz/ *n* [singular, U] *informal* alcoholic drink: *a bottle of booze* | **on the booze** *He's been on the booze* (=drinking too much alcohol) *for five days.* | **off the booze** *My husband is now off the booze* (=no longer drinking too much alcohol) *and he is a different person.*

booze² *v* [I] *informal* to drink alcohol, especially a lot of it: *He went out boozing with his mates after work.*

ˈbooze cruise *n* [C] *BrE informal* an occasion when a group of people travel together on a FERRY from England to France in order to buy a lot of wine, beer, or SPIRITS cheaply

booz·er /ˈbuːzə $ -ər/ *n* [C] **1** *BrE* a PUB **2** someone who often drinks a lot of alcohol

ˈbooze-up *n* [C] *BrE old-fashioned informal* a party where people drink a lot of alcohol

booz·y /ˈbuːzi/ *adj* showing that someone has drunk too much alcohol: *boozy laughter*

bop¹ /bɒp $ bɑːp/ *v* (**bopped**, **bopping**) *informal* **1** [T] to hit someone, especially gently: *Tom bopped him on the nose.* **2** [I] to dance to popular music: *kids happily bopping on the dance floor* **3** [I always + adv/prep] *informal* to go somewhere or to several different places, especially to enjoy yourself: *We spent the afternoon just bopping around town.*

bop² *n* **1** [U] another word for BEBOP **2** [C] a gentle hit: *a bop on the head* **3** [singular] *BrE informal* a dance

bop·per /ˈbɒpə $ ˈbɑːpər/ *n* [C] *old-fashioned* another word for TEENYBOPPER

bo·rax /ˈbɔːræks/ *n* [U] a mineral used for cleaning

bor·del·lo /bɔːˈdeləʊ $ bɔːrˈdeloʊ/ *n* (*plural* **bordellos**) [C] *especially literary* a house where men can pay to have sex SYN **brothel**

bor·der¹ /ˈbɔːdə $ ˈbɔːrdər/ ●●● S3 W2 *n* [C]
1 the official line that separates two countries, states, or areas, or the area close to this line: *To cross the border, you will need a valid passport.* | **[+between]** *the border between the US and Mexico* | **[+with]** *regular patrols along the border with France* | **on the border** *a market town on the border of England and Wales* | **across the border** *He helped them to get across the border.* | **south/north etc of the border** *The coach took us south of the border to Tijuana.*
2 a band along or around the edge of something such as a picture or piece of material: *writing paper with a black border* → see picture at **EDGE¹**
3 an area of soil where you plant flowers or bushes, along the edge of an area of grass: *a flower and shrub border*

4 something that separates one situation, state etc from another: *new scientific discoveries that are stretching the borders of knowledge*

COLLOCATIONS

VERBS

cross the border *The army crossed the border and advanced on Warsaw.*
flee/escape across the border *Over 100,000 civilians fled across the border.*
form the border *The river forms the border between the two countries.*
close the border (=prevent people from crossing) | **open the border** (=start allowing people to cross)

ADJECTIVES

the Welsh/Mexican etc border *I had reached the Swiss border.*
the southern/eastern etc border *They renewed their attacks on Ethiopia's northern border.*
a common border (=that countries share)

border + NOUN

a border dispute (=a disagreement about where the border should be) *a long-running border dispute between Iraq and Iran*
a border town | **a border area/region** | **a border crossing** (=a place where you cross a border) | **a border guard** | **border controls** (=controls on who crosses a border)

PHRASES

this/the other side of the border *Her friend lives on the other side of the border.*

THESAURUS

border the official line that separates two countries, or the area close to this line: *The town lies on the border between Chile and Argentina.* | *Strasbourg is very close to the German border.*
frontier *especially BrE* the border: *They crossed the Libyan frontier into Egypt.*
line the official line that separates states and counties in the US: *His family lived across the state line in West Virginia.*
boundary the line that marks the edge of an area of land that someone owns, or one of the parts of a country: *The fence marks the boundary between the two properties.* | *The Mississippi River forms the boundary between Tennessee and Arkansas.*

border² *v* **1** [I,T] if one country, state, or area borders another, it is next to it and shares a border with it: *countries that border the Mediterranean* | **[+on]** *The area borders on the Yorkshire Dales.* **2** [T] to form a border along the edge of something: *a path bordered by a high brick wall*
border on sth *phr v* to be very close to being something extreme: *His confidence bordered on arrogance.*

bor·der·land /ˈbɔːdəlænd $ ˈbɔːrdər-/ *n* [C] **1** the land near the border between two countries **2** the borderland between two qualities is an unclear area that contains features of both of them

bor·der·line¹ /ˈbɔːdəlaɪn $ ˈbɔːrdər-/ ●○○ *adj*
1 very close to not being acceptable: *In **borderline cases**, the student's coursework is considered, as well as exam grades.* | *The referee's decision was borderline.*
2 [usually before noun] having qualities of both one situation, state etc and another more extreme situation or state: *a borderline schizophrenic* (=someone who has some signs of being mentally ill)

borderline² *n* **1** [singular] the point at which one quality, situation, emotion etc ends and another begins: *She slipped over the borderline into sleep.* | **on the borderline** *I was on the borderline between a first- and a second-class degree.* **2** [C] a border between two countries

bore¹ /bɔː $ bɔːr/ *v* the past tense of BEAR

bore² ●●○ *v*
1 [T] to make someone feel bored, especially by talking too much about something they are not interested in: *He's the sort of person who bores you at parties.* | *a film that will bore its young audience* | **bore sb with sth** *I won't bore you with all the technical details.* | **bore sb to death/tears** (=make them very bored)
2 [I,T] to make a deep round hole in a hard surface: **bore sth through/into/in sth** *The machine bores a hole through the cards.* | **[+through/into]** *To build the tunnel they had to bore through solid rock.* THESAURUS ▸ DIG
3 [I + into] if someone's eyes bore into you, they look at you in a way that makes you feel uncomfortable

bore³ ●●○ *n*
1 [singular] something that is not interesting to you or that annoys you: *Waiting is a bore.* | *You'll find it's a terrible bore.*
2 [C] someone who is boring, especially because they talk too much about themselves or about things that do not interest you: *He turned out to be a crashing bore* (=used to emphasize that someone is very boring).
3 [singular] the measurement of the width of the inside of a long hollow object such as a pipe or the BARREL of a gun: *Take a length of piping with a bore of about 15 mm.* | **12-/16-/20- etc bore** *a **12-bore** shotgun* | **wide-/narrow-/fine-bore** *a fine-bore tube*
4 [singular] a wave of water that moves quickly along a river from the sea at particular times of the year: *the Severn bore*
5 [C] a BOREHOLE

bored /bɔːd $ bɔːrd/ ●●● S3 *adj* tired and impatient because you do not think something is interesting, or because you have nothing to do: *He was easily bored.* | *After a while, I **got bored** and left.* | **[+with]** *Are you bored with your present job?* | **bored stiff/to tears/to death/out of your mind** (=extremely bored)

USAGE: Bored or boring?

• You use **bored** about a person who is not interested in something: *I'm bored!*
• You use **boring** about something that makes you feel bored: *a boring film*

bore·dom /ˈbɔːdəm $ ˈbɔːr-/ ●○○ *n* [U] the feeling you have when you are bored, or the quality of being boring: *a game to **relieve the boredom** of a long journey* | *the **sheer boredom** of being in jail* | **[+with]** *his boredom with life in a small town*

bore·fest /ˈbɔːfest $ ˈbɔːr-/ *n* [C] *informal* something that is very boring SYN **snoozefest**: *The game was turning out to be a borefest.*

bore·hole /ˈbɔːhəʊl $ ˈbɔːrhoʊl/ *n* [C] a deep hole made using special equipment, especially in order to get water or oil out of the ground

bor·ing /ˈbɔːrɪŋ/ ●●● S2 *adj* not interesting in any way: *Her husband is about the most boring person I've ever met.* | *The job was dull and boring.* | **dead/incredibly/terribly etc boring** (=very boring)

THESAURUS

boring not interesting in any way: *a boring speech* | *He found school incredibly boring.*
not very interesting [not before noun] very ordinary and therefore rather boring. People often use this phrase in everyday English, instead of saying directly that something is **boring**: *The story wasn't very interesting.*
dull *especially written* boring: *The conference was usually a dull affair.* | *Life was never dull.*
tedious /ˈtiːdiəs/ very boring and continuing for a long time: *The process was tedious and slow.* | *Jake began the tedious task of sorting through his papers.*
monotonous /məˈnɒtənəs $ məˈnɑː-/ boring and always the same: *The work was monotonous and unchallenging.* | *He was only half listening to the monotonous voice of the teacher.*
mundane /mʌnˈdeɪn/ rather boring, because it is connected with things you do regularly as part of

your daily life: *He busied himself with the mundane task of cleaning the house.* | *Most arguments are over mundane issues like spending or saving money.*
humdrum /ˈhʌmdrʌm/ [usually before noun] boring because nothing new or interesting ever happens: *He wanted to escape his humdrum life.* | *a humdrum existence*
dry a subject, piece of writing etc that is dry is boring because it is very serious and does not contain any humour: *The students complained that the lecture was dry and uninspiring.* | *a dry academic volume*

B

born[1] ●●● S1 W1 *v*
1 be born when a person or animal is born, they come out of their mother's body or out of an egg: *Forty lambs were born this spring.* | **[+in]** *Swift was born in 1667.* | **[+at]** *Then, most babies were born at home.* | **[+on]** *I was born on December 15th, 1973.* | **be born into/to/of sth** (=be born in a particular situation, type of family etc) *One third of all children are born into single-parent families.* | **be born with sth** (=have a particular disease, type of character etc since birth) *Jenny was born with a small hole in her heart.* | *I was* ***born and raised*** (=was born and grew up) *in Alabama.* | **be born blind/deaf etc** (=be blind, deaf etc when born) | *a* ***newly-born baby*** | *the queen's* ***firstborn*** *son* | **be born lucky/unlucky etc** (=always be lucky, unlucky etc) | **Australian/French etc born** (=born in or as a citizen of Australia etc) ⚠ Don't say 'I born', 'I have been born', or 'I am born'. Say **I was born**: *I was born in Pakistan.*
2 START EXISTING **be born** something that is born starts to exist: *the country where the sport of cricket was born* | **[+(out) of]** (=as a result of a particular situation) *The alliance was born of necessity in 1941.* | *Bill spoke with a cynicism born of bitter experience.*
3 born and bred born and having grown up in a particular place and having the typical qualities of someone from that place: *I was born and bred in Liverpool.*
4 be born to do/be sth to be very suitable for a particular job, activity etc: *He was born to be a politician.*
5 I wasn't born yesterday *spoken* used to tell someone you think is lying to you that you are not stupid enough to believe them
6 there's one born every minute *spoken* used to say that someone has been very stupid or easily deceived
7 be born under a lucky/unlucky star to always have good or bad luck in your life
8 be born with a silver spoon in your mouth to be born into a rich family → NATURAL-BORN

born[2] *adj* [only before noun] **1 born leader/musician/teacher etc** someone who has a strong natural ability to lead, play music etc: *the skill of a born actor* **2 born loser** someone who always seems to have bad things happen to them **3 in all your born days** *old-fashioned* used to express surprise or annoyance at something that you have never heard about before

ˈborn-again *adj* **1 born-again Christian** someone who has become an EVANGELICAL Christian **2 born-again non-smoker/vegetarian etc** *informal* someone who has recently stopped smoking, eating meat etc, and who is always talking about it and suggesting that other people do the same

borne[1] /bɔːn $ bɔːrn/ *v* the past participle of BEAR

borne[2] *adj* **1 water-borne/sea-borne/air-borne etc** carried by water, the sea, air etc: *water-borne diseases* **2 be borne in on/upon sb** if a fact is borne in on someone, they realize that it is true

bo·rough /ˈbʌrə $ -roʊ/ *n* [C] a town, or part of a large city, that is responsible for managing its own schools, hospitals, roads etc: *the borough of Queens in New York City* | *Lambeth Borough Council*

ˌborough ˈcouncil *n* [C] *especially BrE* the organization that controls a borough

bor·row /ˈbɒrəʊ $ ˈbɑːroʊ, ˈbɔː-/ ●●● S2 W3 *v* [I,T]
1 to use something that belongs to someone else and that you must give back to them later → **lend**, **loan**: *Can I borrow your pen for a minute?* | **borrow sth from sb** *You are allowed to borrow six books from the library at a time.* | *They* ***borrowed heavily*** (=borrowed a lot of money) *from the bank to start their new business.* ⚠ Do not confuse **borrow** and **lend** (=give someone permission to use something of yours): *I borrowed his bike.* | *Can you lend me your pen?*
2 to take or copy someone's ideas, words etc and use them in your own work, language etc: **borrow sth from sb/sth** *I borrowed my ideas from Eliot's famous poem 'The Waste Land'.* | *To* ***borrow a phrase*** (=use what someone else has said), *if you can't stand the heat, get out of the kitchen.* | **[+from]** *English has borrowed words from many languages.*
3 borrow trouble *AmE informal* to worry about something when it is not necessary → **be living on borrowed time** at LIVE[1](17), → **beg, borrow, or steal** at BEG(8)

bor·row·er /ˈbɒrəʊə $ ˈbɑːroʊər, ˈbɔː-/ *n* [C] someone who has borrowed money and has not yet paid it all back → **lender**: *Most borrowers pay 7% interest.*

bor·row·ing /ˈbɒrəʊɪŋ $ ˈbɑːroʊ-, ˈbɔː-/ *n* **1** [C,U] when a person, government, company etc borrows money, or the money that they borrow: *Public borrowing has increased.* **2** [C] something such as a word, phrase, or idea that has been copied from another language, book etc: *words that are French borrowings* | **[+from]** *his musical borrowings from other composers* **3 borrowings** [plural] the total amount of money that a company or organization owes

ˈborrowing ˌpowers *n* [plural] the amount of money that a company is allowed to borrow, according to its own rules

bor·stal /ˈbɔːstl $ ˈbɔːr-/ *n* [C,U] *BrE old-fashioned* a special prison for criminals who are not old enough to be in an ordinary prison

bosh /bɒʃ $ bɑːʃ/ *n* [U] *especially BrE old-fashioned* something that you think is silly, not good, or not true: *He thinks modern art is bosh.* —**bosh** *interjection*

bos·om /ˈbʊzəm/ *n* **1** [C usually singular] *written* the front part of a woman's chest: *She cradled the child to her bosom.* **2** [C usually plural] a woman's breast **3 the bosom of the family/the Church etc** the situation where you feel safe because you are with people who love and protect you **4** [singular] *literary* a word meaning someone's feelings and emotions, used especially when these are bad or unpleasant: *Drury harboured bitterness in his bosom.* **5 bosom friend/buddy/pal** *literary* a very close friend

bos·om·y /ˈbʊzəmi/ *adj* having large breasts

boss[1] /bɒs $ bɒːs/ ●●● S2 W3 *n* [C]
1 the person who employs you or who is in charge of you at work → **employer**, **manager**, **supervisor**: *I'll have to ask my boss for a day off.* | *Since I'm* ***my own boss*** (=I work for myself, rather than for an employer), *my hours are flexible.*
2 *informal* someone with an important position in a company or other organization: *the new boss at Paramount Pictures* | *union bosses*
3 the person who is the strongest in a relationship, who controls a situation etc: *When you first start training a dog, it's important to let him see that you're the boss.* | *You've got to* ***show*** *the kids* ***who's boss***.
4 a round decoration on the surface of something, for example on the ceiling of an old building

boss[2] *v* [T] to tell people to do things, give them orders etc, especially when you have no authority to do it: **boss sb about** *BrE*, **boss sb around** *AmE*: *Five-year-old girls love to boss people around.*

boss[3] *adj informal* very good, attractive, or fashionable: *a boss car*

bos·sa no·va /ˌbɒsəˈnəʊvə $ ˌbɑːsəˈnoʊ-/ *n* [C] a dance that comes from Brazil, or the music for this dance

boss·y /ˈbɒsi $ ˈbɒːsi/ ●●○ *adj* (*comparative* **bossier**, *superlative* **bossiest**)
1 always telling other people what to do, in a way that is annoying: *her loud bossy sister*
2 bossy-boots *BrE informal* someone who you think tells other people what to do too often —**bossily** *adv* —**bossiness** *n* [U]

ˌBoston ˈTea ˌParty, the a protest in Boston in

1773 against the British tax on tea, when tea was thrown from British ships into the water. This is often considered to be the event that started the American Revolution.

bo·sun /ˈbəʊsən $ ˈboʊ-/ *n* [C] an officer on a ship whose job is to organize the work and look after the equipment SYN **boatswain**

bot /bɒt $ bɑːt/ *n* [C] *technical* a computer PROGRAM that performs the same operation many times in a row, for example one that searches for information on the Internet as part of a SEARCH ENGINE

bo·tan·i·cal /bəˈtænɪkəl/ *adj* [only before noun] relating to plants or the scientific study of plants —**botanically** /-kli/ *adv*

boˌtanical ˈgarden *n* [C] a large public garden where many different types of flowers and plants are grown for scientific study

bot·a·nist /ˈbɒtənɪst $ ˈbɑː-/ *n* [C] someone whose job is to make scientific studies of wild plants

bot·a·ny /ˈbɒtəni $ ˈbɑː-/ *n* [U] the scientific study of plants

botch¹ /bɒtʃ $ bɑːtʃ/ (*also* **botch up**) *v* [T] *informal* to do something badly, because you have been careless or because you do not have the skill to do it properly: *The builders really botched up our patio.* | *a botched investigation*

botch² (*also* **ˈbotch-up** *BrE*) *n* [C] *especially BrE informal* a piece of work, a job etc that has been badly or carelessly done: *I've just* ***made*** *an awful* ***botch of*** *my translation.* | *The whole thing was a* ***botch job****.*

both¹ /bəʊθ $ boʊθ/ ●●● S1 W1 *determiner, predeterminer, pron*

1 used to talk about two people, things etc together, and emphasize that each is included → **either**: *Both Helen's parents are doctors.* | *Hold it in both hands.* | *You can both swim, can't you?* | *They both started speaking together.* | *Oxford is not far from Stratford, so you can easily visit both in a day.* | **[+of]** *Both of my grandfathers are farmers.*

2 sb can't have it both ways used to say that someone cannot have the advantages that come from two separate situations because they cannot exist together: *It's either me or her. You can't have it both ways.*

> **GRAMMAR**
>
> **Word order**
>
> • You use **both** before a plural noun: *Both women were tall.*
>
> • You use **both** or **both of** before a determiner such as 'the', 'these', or 'my': *Both (of) the women were tall.* | *Both (of) her parents are dead.* ✗ Don't say: *the both women* | *her both parents*
>
> • You use **both** after a pronoun: ***We both*** *come from Scotland.*
>
> • You use **both** after the first auxiliary verb: *We* ***have both*** *worked there.* | *They* ***could both be*** *described as robots.*
>
> **Negatives**
>
> **Both** is not usually used in negative clauses. You say: *Neither of these methods is perfect.* ✗ Don't say: *Both of these methods are not perfect.*

both² *conjunction* **both ... and ...** used to emphasize that something is true not just of one person, thing, or situation but also of another: *He's lived in both Britain and America.* | *She can both speak and write Japanese.* | *Both he and his wife enjoy tennis.*

both·er¹ /ˈbɒðə $ ˈbɑːðər/ ●●● S1 W3 *v*

1 MAKE AN EFFORT [I,T usually in questions and negatives] to make the effort to do something: **(not) bother to do sth** *He didn't bother to answer the question.* | **not bother about/with** *He didn't bother with a reply.* | **(not) bother doing sth** *Many young people didn't bother voting.* | **don't/didn't/won't etc bother** *'Do you want me to wait for you?' 'No, don't bother.'* | ***Why bother*** *to go abroad, when there are so many nice places here?*

2 WORRY [I,T] to make someone feel slightly worried, upset, or concerned: *Being in a crowd really bothers me.* | *It was very noisy, but that didn't bother me.* | **[+about]** *especially BrE*: *I try not to bother about what other people think.* | **it bothers sb that/how/when** *It really bothered me that he'd forgotten my birthday.*

3 ANNOY [I,T] to annoy someone, especially by interrupting them when they are trying to do something: *Danny, don't bother Ellen while she's reading.* | *Would it bother you if I put on some music?* | **bother sb about/with sth** ***It didn't seem worth bothering*** *the doctor about.*

4 sb can't/couldn't be bothered (to do sth) *especially BrE* used to say that you do not want to make the effort to do something, or that you are not interested in doing something: *It was so hot I couldn't be bothered to cook.* | *I should be revising, but I just can't be bothered.*

5 CAUSE PAIN [T] if a part of your body bothers you, it is slightly painful or uncomfortable: *My back's been bothering me.*

6 sorry to bother you *spoken* used as a very polite way of interrupting someone when you want their attention: *Sorry to bother you, but Mr. Grey is on the line.*

7 FRIGHTEN [T] to upset or frighten someone by talking to them when they do not want to talk to you, trying to hurt them, touch them sexually etc: *Don't worry – my dog won't bother you.* | *If he starts bothering you, let me know.*

8 not bother yourself/not bother your head to not spend time or effort on something, either because it is not important or because it is too difficult: **[+with/about]** *Cliff didn't want to bother himself with details.*

9 bother it/them etc *BrE spoken old-fashioned* used to express a sudden feeling of annoyance about something: *Oh bother it! The thread's broken again!*

bother² *n* **1** [U] *especially BrE* trouble or difficulty that has been caused by small problems and that usually only continues for a short time SYN **trouble**: *It's an old car, but it's never caused me any bother.* | **[+with]** *Joe's been having a bit of bother with his back again.* | *'Thanks for your help.'* ***'It was no bother*** (=used to emphasize that you were happy to help someone) *at all.'* | *My mother hardly ever went to* ***the bother of*** (=the effort of) *making cakes.* | *Are you sure the station is on your way? I don't want to* ***give*** *you any extra* ***bother****.* | *I should have phoned the shop first and* ***saved*** *myself* ***the bother of*** *going there.* | **sth is more bother than it's worth** (=it is too difficult to be worth doing) **2 a bother** *especially BrE* a person or job that slightly annoys you by causing trouble or problems: *I hate to be a bother, but could you show me how the copier works?*

bother³ *interjection BrE informal* used when you are slightly annoyed: *Oh bother! I forgot to phone Jean.*

both·er·a·tion /ˌbɒðəˈreɪʃən $ ˌbɑː-/ *interjection old-fashioned* used when you are slightly annoyed: *Botheration. I forgot my glasses.*

both·ered /ˈbɒðəd $ ˈbɑːðərd/ *adj* [not before noun] **1** worried or upset: **[+about]** *He doesn't seem too bothered about the things that are written about him in the papers.* | **bothered that** *No one else seemed bothered that Grandfather wasn't there.* THESAURUS▸ WORRIED **2 not bothered** *especially BrE* if you are not bothered about something, it is not important to you: *'What film do you want to see?' 'I'm not bothered.'* | **[+about]** *He's not bothered about getting the facts right.* → **hot and bothered** at HOT¹(12)

both·er·some /ˈbɒðəsəm $ ˈbɑːðər-/ *adj* slightly annoying

bot·net /ˈbɒtnet $ ˈbɑːt-/ *n* [C] a large number of computers that someone has secretly gained control of and uses to do things such as send SPAM (=unwanted emails)

bot·tle¹ /ˈbɒtl $ ˈbɑːtl/ ●●● S1 W2 *n*

1 [C] a container with a narrow top for keeping liquids in, usually made of plastic or glass: *an empty bottle* | **a wine/milk/beer etc bottle** | **[+of]** *a bottle of champagne*

2 [C] (*also* **bottleful**) the amount of liquid that a bottle contains: *Between us, we drank three bottles of wine.*

3 [C] a container for babies to drink from, with a rubber part on top that they suck, or the milk contained in this bottle: *My first baby just wouldn't* ***take a bottle*** *at all.*

4 the bottle alcoholic drink – used when talking about the problems drinking can cause: *Peter let the bottle ruin his*

life. | **hit the bottle** (=regularly drink too much) *She was under a lot of stress, and started hitting the bottle.* | **be on the bottle** *BrE* (=be drinking a lot of alcohol regularly)
5 [U] *BrE informal* courage to do something that is dangerous or unpleasant SYN **nerve**: *I never thought she'd have the bottle to do it!*
6 bring a bottle *BrE*, **bring your own bottle** *AmE* used when you invite someone to an informal party, to tell them that they should bring their own bottle of alcoholic drink
→ HOT-WATER BOTTLE

bottle² *v* [T] **1** to put a liquid, especially wine or beer, into a bottle after you have made it: *The whisky is bottled here before being sent abroad.* **2** *BrE* to put vegetables or fruit into special glass containers in order to preserve them SYN **can** *AmE*

bottle out (*also* **bottle it**) *phr v BrE informal* to suddenly decide not to do something because you are frightened SYN **cop out**: *'Did you tell him?' 'No, I bottled out at the last minute.'*

bottle sth ↔ **up** *phr v* **1** to deliberately not allow yourself to show a strong feeling or emotion: *It is far better to cry than to bottle up your feelings.* **2** to cause problems by delaying something: *The bill has been bottled up in Congress.*

ˈbottle bank *n* [C] *BrE* a container in the street that you put empty bottles into, so that the glass can be used again

bot·tled /ˈbɒtld $ ˈbɑː-/ *adj* **bottled water/beer etc** water, beer etc that is sold in a bottle

ˈbottle-feed *v* (*past tense and past participle* **bottle-fed**) [T] to feed a baby or young animal with milk from a bottle rather than from their mother's breast —**bottle-feeding** *n* [U] —**bottle-fed** *adj*

ˌbottle ˈgreen *n* [U] a very dark green colour —**bottle green** *adj*

bot·tle·neck /ˈbɒtlnek $ ˈbɑː-/ *n* [C] **1** a place in a road where the traffic cannot pass easily, so that there are a lot of delays **2** a delay in one stage of a process that makes the whole process take longer: *Understaffing has caused a real bottleneck.*

ˈbottle ˌopener *n* [C] a small tool used for removing the metal lids from bottles

bot·tom¹ /ˈbɒtəm $ ˈbɑː-/ ●●● S1 W3 *n*
1 LOWEST PART **the bottom** the lowest part of something OPP **the top**: **[+of]** *Can you hold the bottom of the ladder for me?* | **at the bottom (of sth)** *Grandma was standing at the bottom of the stairs.* | *at the bottom of the page* | *Go downstairs and wait for me at the bottom.* | **the bottom of the page/screen** *There should be a menu bar at the bottom of your screen.*
2 LOWEST SIDE [C usually singular] the flat surface on the lowest side of an object: **the bottom of sth** *What's that on the bottom of your shoe?*
3 LOWEST INNER PART [C usually singular] the lowest inner surface of something such as a container: **at/in the bottom of sth** *I found the keys – they were at the bottom of my handbag.* | *The drugs had been hidden in a suitcase with a false bottom.*
4 LOWEST SOCIAL POSITION/RANK **the bottom** the lowest position in an organization or company OPP **the top**: **[+of]** *The Giants are at the bottom of the league.* | **the bottom of the ladder/pile/heap** (=the lowest position in society, an organization etc) *Immigrants were at the bottom of the pile.* | *Higgins had* **started at the bottom** (=in a low position in a company) *and worked his way up to become managing director.* | **second/third etc from bottom** *United currently lie second from bottom of the Premier League.*
5 OCEAN/RIVER **the bottom** the ground under a sea, river etc, or the flat land in a valley: **[+of]** *The bottom of the pool is very slippery.* | **at/on the bottom (of sth)** *A body was found at the bottom of the canal.* | **the sea/river bottom** *fish living on the sea bottom*
6 BODY [C] the part of your body that you sit on SYN **backside**: *I just sat on my bottom and slid down.*
7 CLOTHES [C usually plural] the part of a set of clothes that you wear on the lower part of your body: *pyjama bottoms* | *a blue bikini bottom*
8 FURTHEST PART **the bottom of a road/garden etc** *especially BrE* the part of a road, area of land etc that is furthest from where you are: *There's a shop at the bottom of the street.*
9 get to the bottom of sth to find out the cause of a problem or situation: *I never got to the bottom of this!*
10 be/lie at the bottom of sth to be the basic cause of a problem or situation: *Lack of money is at the bottom of many family problems.*
11 be at/hit/reach rock bottom a) to be in a very bad situation that could not be any worse: *I was at rock bottom, and knew I had to try and stop drinking.* **b)** to be at a very low level: *We bought the house when prices were at rock bottom.*
12 from the bottom of your heart in a very sincere way: *Thank you from the bottom of my heart.*
13 the bottom drops/falls out of the market when people stop buying a particular product, so that the people who sell it can no longer make any money
14 bottoms up! *spoken* used to tell someone to enjoy or finish their alcoholic drink
15 big-bottomed/round-bottomed etc having a bottom or base that is big, round etc

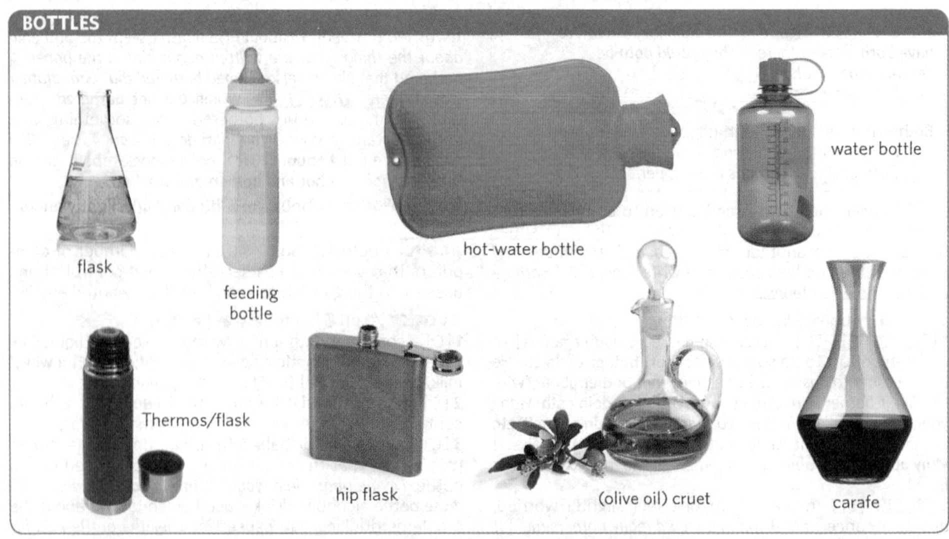

16 at bottom *formal* the way a person or situation really is, although they may seem different: *She's a good kind person at bottom.* → **top,** → **you can bet your bottom dollar** at BET[1](6), → **knock the bottom out of** at KNOCK[1](25), → **from top to bottom** at TOP[1](22), → **the bottom of the list** at LIST[1](2), → **scrape the bottom of the barrel** at SCRAPE[1](5)

THESAURUS

the bottom the lowest part of something: *The house is at the bottom of that hill.* | *She scrolled down to the bottom of the screen.*
the underneath/the underside the bottom surface on the outside of something: *You will find the serial number on the underneath of the vacuum cleaner.*
base the lowest part or the wide bottom part on which something stands: *The lamp has a square base.* | *He had broken a bone at the base of his spine.*
the foot *literary* the bottom of a tree, a hill, or some stairs: *There was a small village at the foot of the mountain.*
bed the ground at the bottom of a river, a lake, or the sea: *the sea bed* | *They found some interesting stones on the river bed.*
the foundations the layer of cement and stones that forms the bottom of a building: *The builders have begun laying the foundations for the house.*

bottom² ●●● S1 W3 *adj*
1 [only before noun] in the lowest place or position OPP **top**: *It's on the **bottom shelf**.* | *The towels are in the **bottom drawer**.* | *You've got some butter on your **bottom lip**.* | *the **bottom** right-hand **corner** of the page*
2 [not before noun] the least important, successful etc OPP **top**: *I was **bottom of the class** (=the least successful student) in Spanish.* | *Britain **came bottom** on efforts to tackle pollution and global warming.*
3 [only before noun] *especially BrE* in the place furthest away from where you are: *the bottom field*
4 bottom gear the lowest GEAR of a vehicle

bottom³ *v*
bottom out *phr v* if a situation, price etc bottoms out, it stops getting worse or lower, usually before improving again → **level off/out**: *There are signs that the recession has bottomed out.*

ˌbottom ˈdrawer *n* [C] *BrE* all the things, especially things that you use in a house, that a woman collects to use when she is married SYN **hope chest** *AmE*

ˈbottom-ˌfeeder *n* [C] *informal* someone who uses and profits from opportunities that are provided when bad things happen to other people – used to show disapproval

bot·tom·less /ˈbɒtəmləs $ ˈbɑː-/ *adj* **1** a bottomless hole, sea etc is one that is extremely deep: *There was a rope dangling down into a dark bottomless hole.* **2** seeming to have no end or limit: *the bottomless well of information available through the Internet* | *The government does not have **a bottomless pit** (=a supply with no limits) of money to spend on public services.*

ˌbottom ˈline *n* [singular] **1 the bottom line** used to tell someone what the most important part of a situation is, or what the most important thing to consider is: *In radio, you have to keep the listener listening. That's the bottom line.* **2** the profit or the amount of money that a business makes or loses **3** the least amount of money that you are willing to accept in a business deal —**bottom-line** *adj*

bot·tom·most /ˈbɒtəmˌməʊst $ ˈbɑːtəmˌmoʊst/ *adj* [only before noun] in the lowest, furthest, or deepest position or place OPP **topmost**

ˌbottom-ˈup *adj* a bottom-up plan is one in which you decide on practical details before thinking about general principles OPP **top-down**

bot·u·lis·m /ˈbɒtʃəlɪzəm $ ˈbɑː-/ *n* [U] serious food poisoning caused by BACTERIA in preserved meat and vegetables

bou·doir /ˈbuːdwɑː $ -wɑːr/ *n* [C] *old use* a woman's bedroom or private sitting room

bouf·fant /ˈbuːfɒŋ, -fɒnt $ buːˈfɑːnt/ *adj* a bouffant hairstyle is one in which your hair is raised away from your head at the top

bou·gain·vil·le·a /ˌbuːgənˈvɪliə/ *n* [C,U] a tropical plant that has red or purple flowers and grows up walls

bough /baʊ/ *n* [C] *literary* a main branch on a tree

bought /bɔːt $ bɒːt/ the past tense and past participle of BUY

bouil·lon /ˈbuːjɒn $ -jɑːn/ *n* [C,U] a clear soup made by boiling meat and vegetables in water

ˈbouillon cube *n* [C] *AmE* a small square made of dried meat or vegetables, used to give a stronger taste to soups SYN **stock cube** *BrE*

boul·der /ˈbəʊldə $ ˈboʊldər/ *n* [C] a large round piece of rock

boule·vard /ˈbuːlvɑːd $ ˈbuːləvɑːrd, ˈbʊ-/ *n* [C] **1** a wide road in a town or city, often with trees along the sides **2** (*written abbreviation* **Blvd.**) used as part of the name of a particular road: *Sunset Boulevard*

bounce¹ /baʊns/ ●●● S3 *v*
1 BALL/OBJECT [I,T] if a ball or other object bounces, or you bounce it, it immediately moves up or away from a surface after hitting it: **[+off]** *The ball bounced off the post and into the goal.* | **bounce sth on/against etc sth** *The kids were bouncing a ball against the wall.*
2 JUMP UP AND DOWN [I] to move up and down, especially because you are hitting a surface that is made of rubber, has springs etc: **[+on]** *Lyn was bouncing on the trampoline.* | *Stop **bouncing up and down** on the sofa.*
THESAURUS JUMP → see picture at JUMP¹
3 CHEQUE [I,T] if a cheque bounces, or if a bank bounces a cheque, the bank will not pay any money because there is not enough money in the account of the person who wrote it
4 WALK [I always + adv/prep] to walk quickly and with a lot of energy: *Olivia came bouncing into the room.*
5 STH MOVES UP AND DOWN [I] if something bounces, it moves quickly up and down as you move: *Her hair bounced when she walked.*
6 LIGHT/SOUND [I,T] if light or sound bounces, it hits a surface and then moves quickly away from it: **bounce (sth) off sth** *The radio signals are bounced off a satellite.*
7 EMAIL (*also* **bounce back**) [I,T] if an email that you send bounces or is bounced, it is returned to you and the other person does not receive it because of a technical problem
8 bounce ideas off sb to talk about your ideas with someone in order to get their opinion: *When you work in a team you can bounce your ideas off each other.*
9 FORCE SB TO LEAVE [T] *informal* to force someone to leave a place, job, or organization, especially because they have done something wrong: **bounce sb from sth** *Taylor was bounced from the team for assaulting another player.*

bounce sth ↔ **around** *phr v informal* to discuss ideas with other people: *I wanted to have a meeting so that we could bounce a few ideas around.*

bounce back *phr v*
1 to feel better quickly after being ill, or to become successful again after failing or having been defeated SYN **recover**: *The company's had a lot of problems in the past, but it's always managed to bounce back.*
2 if an email that you send bounces back or is bounced back, it is returned to you and the other person does not receive it because of a technical problem

bounce sb **into** sth *phr v BrE* to force someone to decide to do something, especially without giving them time to consider it carefully: **bounce sb into doing sth** *Party members feel that they were bounced into accepting the policy.*

bounce² *n* **1** [C] the action of moving up and down on a surface: *Try to catch the ball on the second bounce.* **2** [U] the ability to move up and down on a surface, or that surface's ability to make something move up and down: *The ball had completely lost its bounce.* | *a basketball court with good bounce* **3** [singular, U] a lot of energy that someone has: *Exercise is great. I feel like there's a new bounce in my step.* **4** [U] hair that has bounce is in very good condition and goes back to its shape if you press it: *a brand-new styling spray that gives your hair body and bounce* **5** [C] a sudden increase in something such as how popular a leader is: **[+in]** *the bounce in the property market*

bounc·er /ˈbaʊnsə $ -ər/ *n* [C] **1** someone whose job is to stand at the door of a club, bar etc and stop unwanted people coming in, or make people leave if they are behaving badly **2** a fast ball in CRICKET that passes or hits the BATSMAN above the chest after it bounces

ˈbounce rate *n* [singular] the PERCENTAGE of people who only look at one page of a website, rather than looking at several pages

B

bounc·ing /ˈbaʊnsɪŋ/ *adj* healthy and full of energy: *a bouncing baby girl*

bounc·y /ˈbaʊnsi/ *adj* **1** a bouncy ball etc quickly moves away from a surface after it has hit it **2** a bouncy surface is made of a substance that makes people move up and down when they are on it: *The new bed is nice and bouncy.* **3** someone who is bouncy is always very happy, confident, and full of energy **4** hair or material that is bouncy goes back to its shape when you press it —**bouncily** *adv* —**bounciness** *n* [U]

ˌbouncy ˈcastle *n* [C] *BrE* a large object filled with air, often shaped like a castle, that children jump on for fun

bound[1] /baʊnd/ the past tense and past participle of BIND

bound[2] ●●○ S3 *adj* [no comparative]

1 LIKELY **be bound to** to be very likely to do or feel a particular thing: *Don't lie to her. She's bound to find out.* | **it is bound to be** (=used to say that something should have been expected) *'It's hot!' 'Well, it was bound to be – I just took it out of the oven.'* | *When you are dealing with so many patients, mistakes are* ***bound to happen****.*

> REGISTER
> **Bound to** is used mainly in spoken English. In written English, people usually use **certain to, it is inevitable that** instead: *Mistakes are* ***bound to*** *happen.* → ***It is inevitable that*** *mistakes will happen.*

2 LAW/AGREEMENT **be bound (by sth)** to be forced to do what a law or agreement says you must do → **binding**: **bound (by sth) to do sth** *The Foundation is bound by the treaty to help any nation that requests aid.* | *You are* ***legally bound*** *to report the accident.*

3 DUTY **be/feel bound to do sth** to feel that you ought to do something, because it is morally right or your duty to do it: *Ian felt bound to tell Joanna the truth.* | *Well, I'm* ***bound to say*** (=I feel I ought to say), *I think you're taking a huge risk.* | **be duty bound/honour bound to do sth** *A son is duty bound to look after his mother.*

4 TRAVELLING TOWARDS **bound for London/Mexico etc** (*also* **London-bound/Mexico-bound etc**) travelling towards a particular place or in a particular direction: *a plane bound for Somalia* | *We tried to get seats on a Rome-bound flight.* | ***homeward-bound*** (=travelling towards home) *commuters* | **northbound/southbound/eastbound/westbound** *All eastbound trains have been cancelled due to faulty signals.*

5 RELATIONSHIP **be bound (together) by sth** if two people or groups are bound together by something, they share a particular experience or situation that causes them to have a relationship → **unite**: *The two nations were bound together by a common history.*

6 be bound up in sth to be very involved in something, so that you cannot think about anything else: *He was too bound up in his own problems to listen to mine.*

7 be bound up with sth to be very closely connected with a particular problem or situation: *Mark's problems are all bound up with his mother's death when he was ten.* | *The people of Transkei began to realize that their future was inseparably bound up with that of South Africa.*

8 snow-bound/strike-bound/tradition-bound etc controlled or limited by something, so that you cannot do what you want or what other people want you to: *a* ***fog-bound*** *airport* | *people who are* ***wheelchair-bound*** | *a* ***desk-bound sergeant*** (=having to work in an office, instead of doing a more active job)

9 a bound book is covered on the outside with paper, leather etc → **bind**: **[+in]** *a Bible bound in leather* | *a* ***leather-bound*** *volume of Shakespeare's plays*

10 I'll be bound *old-fashioned* used when you are very sure that what you have just said is true: *He had good reasons for doing that, I'll be bound.*

11 bound and determined *AmE* very determined to do or achieve something, especially something difficult: *Klein is bound and determined to win at least five races this year.*

bound[3] *v* **1** [I always + adv/prep] to run with a lot of energy, because you are happy, excited, or frightened: **[+up/towards/across etc]** *Suddenly a huge dog came bounding towards me.* **2 be bounded by sth** if a country or area of land is bounded by something such as a wall, river etc, it has the wall etc at its edge → **boundary**: *a yard bounded by a wooden fence* | *The US is bounded in the north by Canada and in the south by Mexico.*

bound[4] *n* **1 bounds** [plural] **a)** the limits of what is possible or acceptable: **within the bounds of sth** *We are here to make sure that the police operate within the bounds of the law.* | **be/go beyond the bounds of credibility/reason/decency etc** *The humor in the movie sometimes goes beyond the bounds of good taste.* | **be within/beyond the bounds of possibility** (=be possible/not possible) *It was not beyond the bounds of possibility that they could meet again.* **b)** *old-fashioned* the edges of a town, city etc **2 out of bounds** if a place is out of bounds, you are not allowed to go there SYN **off-limits** *AmE*: **[+to/for]** *The path by the railway line is officially out of bounds to both cyclists and walkers.* **3 by leaps and bounds/in leaps and bounds** *BrE* if someone or something increases, develops etc by leaps and bounds, they increase etc very quickly: *Julie's reading is improving in leaps and bounds.* **4 know no bounds** *formal* if someone's honesty, kindness etc knows no bounds, they are extremely honest etc **5 in bounds/out of bounds** inside or outside the legal playing area in a sport such as American football or BASKETBALL **6** [C] a long or high jump made with a lot of energy

bound·a·ry /ˈbaʊndəri/ ●●○ *n* (*plural* **boundaries**)

1 [C] the real or imaginary line that marks the edge of a state, country etc, or the edge of an area of land that belongs to someone: **[+between]** *The Mississippi River forms a* ***natural boundary*** *between Iowa and Illinois.* | ***National boundaries*** *are becoming increasingly meaningless in the global economy.* | *We would need their agreement to build outside the* ***city boundary****.* | *The stream curves round to* ***mark the boundary*** *of his property.* | *Anything that* ***crosses the boundary*** *of a black hole cannot get back.* | *We walked through the churchyard towards the* ***boundary wall****.* | *The property's* ***boundary line*** *is 25 feet from the back of the house.* | ***boundary disputes*** *between neighbouring countries*

THESAURUS ▸ BORDER

2 [C usually plural] the limit of what is acceptable or thought to be possible: **[+of]** *the boundaries of human knowledge* | **within/beyond the boundaries of sth** *within the boundaries of the law* | **push back the boundaries (of sth)** (=to make a new discovery, work of art etc that is very different from what people have known before, and that changes the way they think) *art that pushes back the boundaries*

3 [C] the point at which one feeling, idea, quality etc stops and another starts: **[+of/between]** *the boundaries between work and play* | *the blurring of the boundaries between high and popular culture*

4 [C] the outer limit of the playing area in CRICKET, or a shot that sends the ball across this limit for extra points

bound·en /ˈbaʊndən/ *adj* **your bounden duty** *old use* something that you should do because it is morally correct

bound·er /ˈbaʊndə $ -ər/ *n* [C] *old-fashioned* a man who has behaved in a way that is morally wrong

bound·less /ˈbaʊndləs/ *adj* having no limit or end: *boundless energy and enthusiasm* —**boundlessly** *adv* —**boundlessness** *n* [U]

boun·te·ous /ˈbaʊntiəs/ *adj* very generous

boun·ti·ful /ˈbaʊntɪfəl/ *adj* **1** if something is bountiful, there is more than enough of it: *bountiful harvests* **2** generous: *bountiful God*

boun·ty /ˈbaʊnti/ *n* (*plural* **bounties**) **1** [C] an amount of money that is given to someone by the government as a reward for doing something, especially catching or killing a criminal: **[+on]** *a notorious cattle rustler with* ***a bounty on his head*** **2** [U] *literary* food or wealth that is provided in large amounts: *People came from all over the world to enjoy America's bounty.* **3** [U] *literary* the quality of being generous

ˈbounty ˌhunter *n* [C] someone who catches criminals and brings them to the police for a reward

BOUQUET

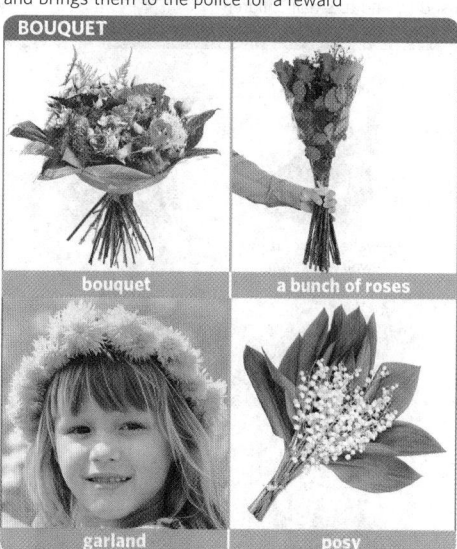

bouquet — a bunch of roses — garland — posy

bou·quet /bəʊˈkeɪ, buː- $ boʊ-, buː-/ ●○○ *n*
1 [C] an arrangement of flowers, especially one that you give to someone
2 [C,U] the smell of a wine

bouquet gar·ni /ˌbuːkeɪ ˈɡɑːni $ -ɡɑːrˈniː/ *n* (*plural* **bouquets garnis**) [C] a small bag full of herbs that you put into food that you are cooking to give it a special taste

bour·bon /ˈbʊəbən $ ˈbɜːr-/ *n* [U] a type of American WHISKY

bour·geois /ˈbʊəʒwɑː $ bʊrˈʒwɑː/ *adj* **1** belonging to the MIDDLE CLASS: *She came from a bourgeois family.* | *bourgeois morality* **2** too interested in having a lot of possessions and a high position in society: *the backlash against bourgeois materialism* **3** belonging to or typical of the part of society that is rich, educated, owns land etc, according to Marxism → **proletarian** —**bourgeois** *n* [C] → PETTY BOURGEOIS

bour·geoi·sie /ˌbʊəʒwɑːˈziː $ ˌbʊr-/ *n* **the bourgeoisie** the people in a society who are rich, educated, own land etc, according to Marxism → **the proletariat**

bout /baʊt/ ●○○ *n* [C]
1 **a bout of depression/flu/sickness etc** a short period of time during which you suffer from an illness
2 a short period of time during which you do something a lot, especially something that is bad for you: *a drinking bout* | **[+of]** *a bout of unemployment*
3 a BOXING or WRESTLING match

ˈbout /baʊt/ *adv, prep spoken informal* about: *What are you talking ˈbout?*

bou·tique¹ /buːˈtiːk/ ●●○ *n* [C] a small shop that sells fashionable clothes or other objects

boutique² *adj AmE* special, good in quality, and expensive, or producing things that are special, good in quality, and expensive: *a boutique winery*

bouˈtique hoˌtel *n* [C] a small expensive hotel, decorated in a fashionable way

bou·ton·ni·ere /buːˌtɒniˈeə $ ˌbuːtnˈɪr/ *n* [C] *AmE* a flower that a man wears fastened to his jacket at a wedding SYN **buttonhole** *BrE*

bou·zou·ki /bʊˈzuːki/ *n* [C] a Greek musical instrument similar to a GUITAR

bo·vine /ˈbəʊvaɪn $ ˈboʊ-/ *adj* **1** *technical* relating to cows: *bovine diseases* **2** *written* slow and slightly stupid, like a cow – used to show disapproval: *a bovine expression of contentment*

bov·ver /ˈbɒvə $ ˈbɑːvər/ *n* [U] *BrE old-fashioned informal* violent behaviour, especially by a group of young men: **bovver boy** (=someone who behaves in a violent way)

bow¹ /baʊ/ ●●○ *v*
1 [I] to bend the top part of your body forward in order to show respect for someone important, or as a way of thanking an AUDIENCE: *She bowed and left the stage.* | *Corbett entered the room, bowing respectfully.* | *The servant* ***bowed low*** *and handed his master the sealed note.* | **[+before/to]** *He bowed before the king.*
2 **bow your head** to bend your neck so that you are looking at the ground, especially because you want to show respect for God, or because you are embarrassed or upset: *She bowed her head and prayed.* | *Phil stood, his head bowed in shame.*
3 [I,T] to bend your body over something, especially in order to see it more closely: **[+over]** *Teague sat at his desk, bowed over a book.*
4 [I,T] to bend, or to make something bend: *The trees bowed in the wind.* | *His back was bowed under the weight of the heavy bag.*
5 **bow and scrape** to show too much respect to someone in authority – used to show disapproval

bow down *phr v*
1 to bend your body forward, especially when you are already kneeling, in order to show respect: **[+before/to etc]** *Maria bowed down before the statue.* | *Come, let us* ***bow down in worship***.
2 **bow down to sb** *literary* to let someone give you orders or tell you what to do – used to show disapproval

bow out *phr v*
1 to stop taking part in an activity, job etc, especially one that you have been doing for a long time: **[+of]** *Reeves thinks it is time for him to bow out of politics.*
2 to not do something that you have promised or agreed to do: **[+of]** *You're not trying to bow out of this, are you?*

bow to sb/sth *phr v* to finally agree to do something, even though you do not want to do it: *Congress may* ***bow to public pressure*** *and lift the arms embargo.* | *Myers finally* ***bowed to the inevitable*** (=accepted something he could not change) *and withdrew from the campaign.*

bow² /baʊ/ ●●○ *n*
1 [C] the act of bending the top part of your body forward to show respect for someone when you meet them, or as a way of thanking an AUDIENCE: **take/give a bow** (=bow to the audience at the end of a performance) *The music ended and the girl took a bow.* | *He gave a final bow just as the curtains came down.* | *This is done with a* ***formal bow*** *to the king or queen.*
2 (*also* **bows** [plural]) [C] the front part of a ship → **stern**, **yacht**

bow³ /bəʊ/ *n* [C] **1** a weapon used for shooting ARROWS, made of a long thin piece of wood held in a curve by a tight string: *a* ***bow and arrow*** **2** a knot of cloth or string, with a curved part on either side and two loose ends, worn in the hair as decoration or for tying SHOELACES: *Ella wore a bow in her hair.* | **in a bow** *long chestnut hair tied back in a bow* **3** a long thin piece of wood with a tight string fastened along it, used to play musical instruments such as the VIOLIN or CELLO → **have more than one string to your bow** at STRING¹(8)

bow⁴ /bəʊ/ *v* [I,T] to play a piece of music on a musical instrument with a BOW³

B

Bow Bells /ˌbəʊ ˈbelz $ ˌboʊ-/ the bells of St Mary-le-Bow Church in London. It is said that a person born in a place where you can hear Bow Bells is a true cockney.

bowd·ler·ize (*also* **-ise** *BrE*) /ˈbaʊdləraɪz/ *v* [T] to remove all the parts of a book, play etc that you think might offend someone – used to show disapproval: *a bowdlerized version of 'Antony and Cleopatra'*

bow·el /ˈbaʊəl/ ●○○ *n*
1 **bowels** [plural] the system of tubes inside your body where food is made into solid waste material and through which it passes out of your body → **intestine**: **move/empty/open your bowels** (=get rid of solid waste from your body)
2 [singular] one part of this system of tubes: *cancer of the bowel*
3 **a bowel movement** *formal* the act of getting rid of solid waste from your body
4 **the bowels of sth** *literary* the lowest or deepest part of something: **the bowels of the earth** (=deep under the ground)

bow·er /ˈbaʊə $ -ər/ *n* [C] *literary* a pleasant place in the shade under a tree: *a rose-scented bower*

bowl¹ /bəʊl $ boʊl/ ●●● S2 W3 *n*
1 CONTAINER [C] a wide round container that is open at the top, used to hold liquids, food, flowers etc → **dish**: *Mix all the ingredients thoroughly in a large bowl.* | *Fill the bowl with water.* | **a mixing/serving bowl** (=a bowl used for mixing foods or serving them) *Beat the butter in a mixing bowl until creamy and soft.* | **a soup/salad/cereal etc bowl** (=a bowl to eat or serve soup, salad etc from)
2 AMOUNT [C] (*also* **bowlful**) the amount of something contained in a bowl: **[+of]** *a bowl of rice* | *a bowl of fruit*
3 GAME **a)** **bowls** *BrE* [plural] an outdoor game played on grass, in which you try to roll big balls as near as possible to a small ball SYN **lawn bowling** *AmE* **b)** [C usually singular] a special game in American football played by the best teams after the normal playing season: *the Rose Bowl*
4 BALL [C] *BrE* a ball that you use in the game of bowls
5 SHAPE [C] the part of an object such as a spoon, pipe, toilet etc that is shaped like a bowl: *the bowl of a pipe* | **a toilet/lavatory bowl**
6 STADIUM [C usually singular] *AmE* a large STADIUM shaped like a bowl, where people go to watch special events such as sports games or music CONCERTS: *the Hollywood Bowl*

bowl² *v* **1** [I,T] to roll a ball along a surface when you are playing the game of bowls **2** **a)** [I,T] to throw a ball at the BATSMAN (=the person who hits the ball) in CRICKET → **bat b)** [T] to make a batsman have to leave the field by throwing a ball so that it hits the WICKET behind him THESAURUS THROW **3** [I always + adv/prep] to travel along very quickly and smoothly: **[+along/down]** *We were bowling along at about 90 miles per hour.*

bowl sb ↔ **out** *phr v* in CRICKET, when a team is bowled out, each member of the team has had to leave the field and there is no one left to BAT

bowl sb ↔ **over** *phr v* **1** to accidentally hit someone and knock them down because you are running in a place that is full of people or things SYN **knock over** **2** to surprise, please, or excite someone very much SYN **knock out**: *He was bowled over by her beauty.*

bow legs /ˌbəʊ ˈlegz $ ˌboʊ-/ *n* [plural] legs that curve outwards at the knees —**bow-legged** /-ˈlegd◂, -ˈlegɪd◂/ *adj*

bowl·er /ˈbəʊlə $ ˈboʊlər/ *n* [C] **1** a player in CRICKET who throws the ball at a BATSMAN **2** (*also* **bowler hat** *BrE*) a hard round black hat that businessmen sometimes wear SYN **derby** *AmE* → see picture at **HAT**

bowl·ing /ˈbəʊlɪŋ $ ˈboʊ-/ ●●● S3 *n* [U]
1 an indoor game in which you roll a large heavy ball along a wooden track in order to knock down a group of PINS (=wooden objects shaped like bottles): *Do you want to* **go bowling** *with us Friday?*
2 the act of throwing a ball at the BATSMAN in CRICKET

ˈbowling ˌalley *n* [C] a building where you go bowling

ˈbowling ball *n* [C] the heavy ball you use in bowling

ˈbowling green *n* [C] an area of short grass where you play the game of BOWLS

bow·man /ˈbəʊmən $ ˈboʊ-/ *n* (*plural* **bowmen** /-mən/) [C] a soldier in the past whose weapon was a BOW

bow tie /ˌbəʊ ˈtaɪ $ ˈboʊ taɪ/ *n* [C] a short piece of cloth tied in the shape of a bow that men sometimes wear around their neck

bow win·dow /ˌbəʊ ˈwɪndəʊ $ ˌboʊ ˈwɪndoʊ/ *n* [C] a window that curves out from a wall → see picture at **WINDOW**

bow·wow /ˌbaʊˈwaʊ/ *interjection* a word used to make the sound a dog makes, used by and to small children

bow-wow /ˈbaʊ waʊ/ *n* [C] a word meaning a dog, used by and to small children

BOXES

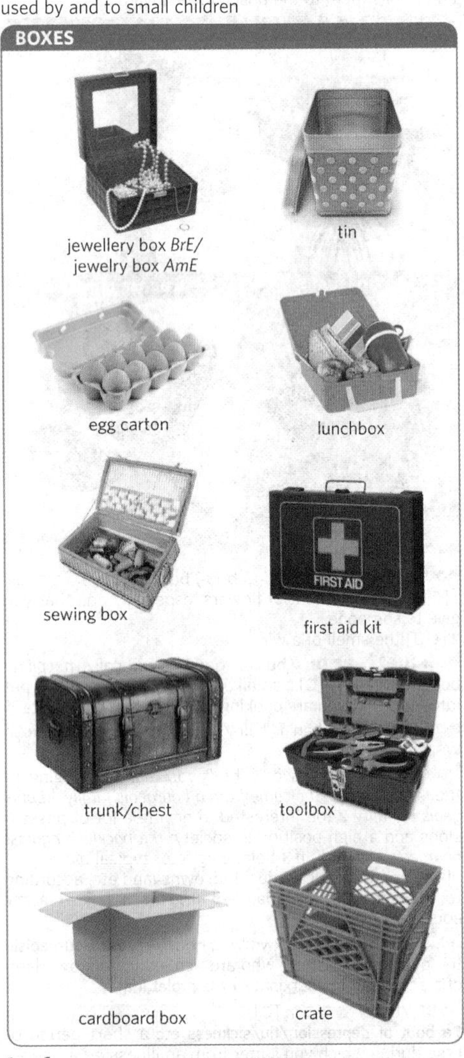

jewellery box *BrE*/ jewelry box *AmE*; tin; egg carton; lunchbox; sewing box; first aid kit; trunk/chest; toolbox; cardboard box; crate

box¹ /bɒks $ bɑːks/ ●●● S1 W1 *n*
1 CONTAINER [C] a container for putting things in, especially one with four stiff straight sides: **cardboard/wooden/plastic etc box** *a strong cardboard box* | **toolbox/shoebox/matchbox etc** (=a box used for keeping tools etc in)
2 AMOUNT (*also* **boxful**) [C] the amount of something contained in a box: **[+of]** *a box of chocolates*
3 SHAPE [C] **a)** a small square on a page for people to write information in: *Put an 'X' in the box if you would like to join our mailing list.* **b)** a SQUARE or RECTANGLE on a page where information is given or where an answer can be

written: *The box on the left gives a short history of the battle.*
4 IN A COURT/THEATRE ETC [C] a small area of a theatre or court that is separate from where other people are sitting: *the jury box* → see picture at THEATRE
5 SMALL BUILDING [C] a small building or structure used for a particular purpose SYN **booth**: *a sentry box* | **telephone box** *BrE*
6 AT A POST OFFICE **box 25/450 etc** a box with a number in a POST OFFICE, where you can have letters etc sent instead of to your own address SYN **PO Box**
7 SPORTS FIELD [C usually singular] a special area of a sports field that is marked by lines and used for a particular purpose: *the **penalty box***
8 PROTECTION [C] *BrE* a piece of plastic that a man wears over his sex organs to protect them when he is playing a sport, especially CRICKET
9 TREE [C,U] a small tree that keeps its leaves in winter and is often planted around the edge of a garden or field: *a **box hedge***
10 TELEVISION **the box** *informal* the television: *What's on the box tonight?*
11 be out of your box *BrE informal* to be very drunk or have taken an illegal drug → BLACK BOX

box² ●○○ *v*
1 [I,T] to fight someone as a sport by hitting them with your closed hands inside big leather GLOVES
2 (*also* **box up**) [T] to put things in boxes: *Help me box up the Christmas tree lights.* → BOXED
3 [T] to draw a box around something on a page
4 box sb's ears *old-fashioned* to hit someone on the side of their head

box sb/sth ↔ **in** *phr v*
1 to surround someone or something so that they are unable to move freely: *Someone had parked right behind them, boxing them in.*
2 feel boxed in a) to feel that you cannot do what you want to do because a person or situation is limiting you: *Married for only a year, Connie already felt boxed in.* **b)** to feel that you cannot move freely, because you are in a small space

box sth ↔ **off** *phr v* to separate a particular area from a larger one by putting walls around it: *We're going to box off that corner to get extra storage space.*

ˈbox ˌcanyon *n* [C] *AmE* a deep narrow valley with very straight sides and no way out SYN **gorge**

box·car /ˈbɒkskɑː $ ˈbɑːkskɑːr/ *n* [C] *AmE* a railway carriage with high sides and a roof, used for carrying goods

boxed /bɒkst $ bɑːkst/ *adj* [usually before noun] sold in a box or boxes: *a **boxed set** of CDs*

ˌbox end ˈwrench *n* [C] *AmE* a type of WRENCH with a hollow end that fits over a NUT that is being screwed or unscrewed SYN **ring spanner** *BrE*

box·er /ˈbɒksə $ ˈbɑːksər/ ●●○ *n* [C]
1 someone who BOXES, especially as a job
2 a large dog with short light brown hair and a flat nose

box·er·cise /ˈbɒksəsaɪz $ ˈbɑːksər-/ *n* [U] a type of exercise based on AEROBICS (=very active physical exercise done to music, usually in a class) that includes some BOXING movements

ˈboxer ˌshorts ●●○ *n* [plural] loose cotton underwear for men → see picture at UNDERWEAR

box·ing /ˈbɒksɪŋ $ ˈbɑːk-/ ●●○ *n* [U] the sport of fighting while wearing big leather GLOVES → see picture at SPORT¹

ˈBoxing Day *n* [C,U] *BrE* a national holiday in England and Wales, on the day after Christmas Day

ˈbox ˌjunction *n* [C] *BrE* a place marked with yellow painted lines where two roads cross each other

ˈbox lunch *n* [C] *AmE* a LUNCH (=a meal eaten in the middle of the day) that you take to school or work with you in a LUNCHBOX SYN **packed lunch** *BrE*

ˈbox ˌnumber *n* [C] an address at the POST OFFICE that people can have their letters etc sent to instead of their own address → **PO Box**

ˈbox ˌoffice *n* **1** [C] the place in a theatre, cinema etc where tickets are sold → **ticket office**: **at the box office** *Collect your tickets at the box office.* **2** [singular] used to describe how successful a film, play, or actor is, by the number of people who pay to see them: **a (huge) box office hit/success** | **a (big) box office draw** (=a successful actor who many people will pay to see) | **box office receipts/takings etc** (=the number of tickets sold or the money received)

ˈbox room *n* [C] *BrE* a small room in a house where you can store things

boy¹ /bɔɪ/ ●●● S1 W1 *n* [C]
1 a male child, or a male person in general → **girl**: *The boys wanted to play football.* | *boys and girls aged 11-18* | **a teenage/adolescent boy** *A group of teenage boys stood talking in a group outside.* | **bad/naughty boy** *'You naughty boy!' she said in a harsh voice.* | *What a polite **little boy** (=young male child) you are.* | *Come on, Timmy, act like a **big boy** (=an older boy) now.* THESAURUS MAN
2 a son: *I love my boys, but I'd like to have a girl, too.* | *How old is your **little boy** (=young son)?*
3 office/paper/delivery etc boy a young man who does a particular job
4 city/local/country boy *informal* a man of any age who is typical of people from a particular place, or who feels a strong connection with the place he grew up in: *The classic story of a local boy who's made good (=who has succeeded).* | *I'm just a country boy.*
5 the boys [plural] *informal* a group of men who are friends and often go out together: *Friday is his **night out with the boys**.* | *He considers himself just **one of the boys** (=not anyone special, but liked by other men).*
6 a way of talking to a male horse or dog: *Good boy!*
7 boys [plural] *informal* **a)** a group of men who do the same job: *Oh no! Wait until the press boys get hold of this story.* **b)** men in the army, navy etc, especially those who are fighting in a war: *our boys on the front lines*
8 boys will be boys used to say that you should not be surprised when boys or men behave badly, are noisy etc
9 the boys in blue *informal* the police
10 old boy/my dear boy *BrE old-fashioned* a friendly way for one man to speak to another man
11 *AmE not polite* an offensive way of talking to a black man → BLUE-EYED BOY, → **jobs for the boys** at JOB(16), → MAMA'S BOY, MUMMY'S BOY, OLD BOY, WIDE BOY

boy² *interjection AmE informal* **1** used when you are excited or pleased about something: *Boy, that was a great meal!* **2 oh boy!** used when you are slightly annoyed or disappointed about something: *Oh boy! Bethany's sick again.*

ˈboy band *n* [C] a group of attractive young men who perform by singing and dancing, and who are especially popular with teenage girls

boy·cott¹ /ˈbɔɪkɒt $ -kɑːt/ ●○○ *v* [T] to refuse to buy something, use something, or take part in something as a way of protesting: *We boycott all products tested on animals.*

boycott² ●○○ *n* [C] an act of boycotting something, or the period of time when it is boycotted: *They are now trying to **organize** a **boycott**.* | **[+of/on/against]** *a boycott on GM crops* | *He **called for** a **boycott** of the elections.*

boy·friend /ˈbɔɪfrend/ ●●● S3 *n* [C]
1 a man that you are having a romantic relationship with → **girlfriend**
2 boyfriend jeans/cardigan/jacket etc used to refer to a piece of clothing for women that is quite big and loose

boy·hood /ˈbɔɪhʊd/ *n* [U] the time of a man's life when he is a boy → **girlhood**: *boyhood memories*

boy·ish /ˈbɔɪ-ɪʃ/ *adj* someone who is boyish looks or behaves like a boy in a way that is attractive → **girlish**: *boyish good looks* | *At 45, she still had a trim **boyish figure**.* —**boyishly** *adv*: *boyishly handsome* —**boyishness** *n* [U]

ˌboy ˈracer *n* [C] *BrE informal* a young man who likes driving cars very fast - used to show disapproval

ˌBoy ˈScout / $ ˈ../ *n* [C] a member of the SCOUTS → **Girl Scout, guide**

ˌBoys' ˈOwn *adj* used to describe men doing brave exciting things, like a HERO in an adventure story: *His life story is like a nonstop Boys' Own adventure.*

ˈboy toy *n* [C] an attractive young man who an older, usually rich or successful woman has a sexual relationship with

ˌboy ˈwonder *n* [C] a young man who is very successful: *Robson, the boy wonder of the department*

bo·zo /ˈbəʊzəʊ $ ˈboʊzoʊ/ *n* (*plural* **bozos**) [C] *informal* someone who you think is silly or stupid: *Who's the bozo in the pyjamas?*

B

BPO /ˌbiː piː ˈəʊ $ -ˈoʊ/ *n* [U] (***business process outsourcing***) the practice of asking people from outside a company to take charge of running a part of its activities

bps, **BPS** /ˌbiː piː ˈes/ *technical* (***bits per second***) a measurement of how fast a computer or MODEM can send or receive information: *a 28,800 bps modem*

Br. (*also* **Br** *BrE*) **1** the written abbreviation of ***brother*** **2** the written abbreviation of ***British***

bra /brɑː/ ●●○ *n* [C] a piece of underwear that a woman wears to support her breasts → see picture at UNDERWEAR

brace¹ /breɪs/ *v* **1** [T] to mentally or physically prepare yourself or someone else for something unpleasant that is going to happen: **brace yourself (for sth)** *Nancy braced herself for the inevitable arguments.* | *The military needs to brace itself for further spending cuts, says McCoy.* | **brace yourself to do sth** *Cathy braced herself to see Matthew, who she expected to arrive at any minute.* | **be braced for sth** *The base was braced for an attack.* **2** [T] to push part of your body against something solid in order to make yourself more steady: **brace sth against sth** *Gina braced her back against the wall and pushed as hard as she could.* | **brace yourself (for sth)** *The pilot told passengers and crew to brace themselves for a rough landing.* **3** [T] to make something stronger by supporting it: *Wait until we've braced the ladder.* | *Workers used steel beams to brace the roof.* **4** [I,T] to make your body or part of your body stiff in order to prepare to do something difficult

brace² *n* **1** [C] something that is used to strengthen or support something, or to make it stiff: *The miners used special braces to keep the walls from collapsing.* | **neck/back/knee brace** (=a brace that supports the neck etc) *He was being fitted for a back brace.* | *She had to* ***wear*** *a* ***brace*** *after the accident.* **2** [C] (*also* **braces** [plural]) a system of metal wires that people, usually children, wear on their teeth to make them grow straight **3** [C usually plural] *AmE* a metal support that someone with weak legs wears to help them walk SYN **callipers** *BrE* **4 braces** [plural] *BrE* two long pieces of material that stretch over someone's shoulders and fasten to their trousers at the front and the back to stop them falling down SYN **suspenders** *AmE* **5** [C] one of a pair of signs { } used to show that information written between them should be considered together → **bracket 6 a brace of sth** *especially BrE* two things of the same type, especially two birds or animals that have been killed for food or sport: *a brace of partridge*

brace·let /ˈbreɪslɪt/ ●●○ *n* [C] a band or chain that you wear around your wrist or arm as a decoration → **bangle**: *a gold bracelet* → see picture at JEWELLERY

brac·ing /ˈbreɪsɪŋ/ *adj* bracing air or weather is cold and makes you feel very awake and healthy: *a bracing sea breeze*

brack·en /ˈbrækən/ *n* [U] a plant that often grows in forests and becomes reddish brown in the autumn

brack·et¹ /ˈbrækɪt/ ●●○ *n* [C]

1 (*also* **round bracket**) [usually plural] *BrE* one of the pair of signs ( ) put around words to show extra information SYN **parenthesis** *AmE*: **in brackets** *Last year's sales figures are given in brackets.* → ANGLE BRACKETS, SQUARE BRACKET, PUNCTUATION MARK

2 income/tax/age etc bracket a particular income, tax etc range: *the highest tax bracket* | *families in lower income brackets*

3 a piece of metal, wood, or plastic, often in the shape of the letter L, fixed to a wall to support something such as a shelf

bracket² *v* [T] **1** to consider two or more people or things as being similar or the same: **be bracketed together** *Women and minors were bracketed together for the legislation.* | **be bracketed with sb/sth** *Arizona has been bracketed with Iowa in the tournament.* **2** to put brackets around a written word, piece of information etc: *Debit amounts are bracketed.*

brack·ish /ˈbrækɪʃ/ *adj* brackish water is not pure because it is slightly salty

brad /bræd/ *n* [C] *AmE* **1** a small metal object like a button with two metal sticks that are put through several pieces of paper and folded down to hold the papers together **2** a small thin wire nail with either a small head or a part that sticks out to the side instead of a head

brad·awl /ˈbrædɔːl $ -ɒːl/ *n* [C] *especially BrE* a small tool with a sharp point for making holes SYN **awl**

brag /bræg/ ●○○ *v* (**bragged**, **bragging**) [I,T] to talk too proudly about what you have done, what you own etc – used to show disapproval SYN **boast**: *'I came out top in the test,' he bragged.* | **[+about]** *Ben's always bragging about his success with women.* | **brag that** *Julia used to brag that her family had a villa in Spain.*

brag·ga·do·ci·o /ˌbrægəˈdəʊʃiəʊ $ -ˈdoʊʃioʊ/ *n* [U] *especially literary* proud talk about something that you claim to own, to have done etc

brag·gart /ˈbrægət $ -ərt/ *n* [C] *old-fashioned* someone who is always talking too proudly about what they own or have done

Brah·man /ˈbrɑːmən/ (*also* **Brah·min** /ˈbrɑːmɪn/) *n* [C] someone of the highest rank in the Hindu faith

braid¹ /breɪd/ *n* **1** [U] a narrow band of material formed by twisting threads together, used to decorate the edges of clothes: *a jacket* ***trimmed with*** *red* ***braid*** **2** [C] a length of hair that has been separated into three parts and then woven together SYN **plait** *BrE*: **in braids** *Suzy always wears her hair in braids.* → see picture at HAIRSTYLE —**braided** *adj*

braid² *v* [T] to weave or twist together three pieces of hair or cloth to form one length SYN **plait** *BrE*

braille /breɪl/ *n* [U] a form of printing for blind people, with raised parts that they can read by touching the paper with their fingers

brain¹ /breɪn/ ●●● S2 W2 *n*

1 ORGAN [C] the organ inside your head that controls how you think, feel, and move: *Messages from the brain are carried by the central nervous system.* | *the chemistry of the brain* | *the human brain* | **the right/left hemisphere of the brain** (=the right or left side of the brain) *Emotional responses are a function of the right hemisphere of the brain.* | *She died of a* ***brain tumour***. | **brain tissue/cell** → see picture at HUMAN¹

2 INTELLIGENCE [C usually plural, U] the ability to think clearly and learn quickly: *If you had any brains, you'd know what I meant.* | *The job requires brains.* | *Something's* ***addled*** *your* ***brains*** (=made you confused). | *Come on,* ***use*** *your* ***brain****, John.*

3 PERSON [C usually plural] *informal* someone who is intelligent, with good ideas and useful skills: *Some of our best brains are leaving the country to work in the US.* → BRAIN DRAIN

4 FOOD [U] (*also* **brains** [plural]) the brain of an animal, used as food

5 have sth on the brain *informal* to be always thinking about something: *I've got that song on the brain today.*

6 be the brains behind/of sth to be the person who thought of and developed a particular plan, system, or organization, especially a successful one: *Danny's definitely the brains of the project.*

7 brain dead a) in a state where your brain has stopped working properly, even though your heart may still be beating **b)** *informal* in a state in which you seem stupid or uninteresting, especially because you live a boring life or are very tired

8 sth is not brain surgery *informal* used to say that something is not difficult to do → BIRD-BRAIN, HARE-BRAINED, → **beat your brains out** at BEAT¹(22), → **pick sb's brains** at PICK¹(7), → **rack your brain(s)** at RACK²(2)

brain² *v* [T] *informal* to hit someone very hard on the head - used humorously: *I wanted to brain him.*

brain·box /ˈbreɪnbɒks $ -bɑːks/ *n* [C] *BrE informal* someone who is very intelligent

brain·child /ˈbreɪntʃaɪld/ *n* [singular] an idea, plan, organization etc that someone has thought of without any help from anyone else: **[+of]** *The festival was the brainchild of Reeves.*

ˈbrain ˌdamage *n* [U] damage to someone's brain caused by an accident or illness: *Potts* ***suffered*** *severe* ***brain damage*** *in the crash.* —**brain-damaged** *adj*

ˈbrain drain *n* **the brain drain** a movement of highly skilled or professional people from their own country to a country where they can earn more money

ˈbrain dump *n* [C] *informal* the process of writing everything you know about something on paper or storing it electronically on a computer

brain·fart /ˈbreɪnfɑːt $ -fɑːrt/ *n* [C] *informal* an occasion when you suddenly cannot think of what you should say when you are in the middle of saying something

ˈbrain ˌfingerprinting *n* [U] the process of measuring the electrical activity in someone's brain to see if they react to a particular object or picture. This process could be used to check if someone is telling the truth, for example if they are answering questions from the police.

brain·freeze /ˈbreɪnfriːz/ *n* [U] *informal* an unpleasant feeling in the head that you get, for example, when eating very cold food such as ice cream

brain·i·ac /ˈbreɪniæk/ *n* [C] *AmE informal* someone who is very intelligent

brain·less /ˈbreɪnləs/ *adj* completely stupid: *What a brainless thing to do!* —**brainlessly** *adv*

brain·melt /ˈbreɪnmelt/ *n* [U] *informal* a state of complete confusion, because you are very tired or are dealing with something very complicated

brain·pow·er, **ˈbrain power** /ˈbreɪnpaʊə $ -paʊr/ *n* [U] **1** intelligence, or the ability to think: *A lot of brainpower went into solving the problem.* **2** educated intelligent people who have special skills, especially in science, considered as a group: *the country's shortage of scientific brainpower*

ˈbrain scan *n* [C] a process in which detailed photographs of the inside of your brain are taken and examined by a doctor

brain·storm¹ /ˈbreɪnstɔːm $ -stɔːrm/ ●○○ *n*
1 [C usually singular] *AmE* a sudden clever idea SYN **brainwave** *BrE*: *Kirby* ***had a sudden brainstorm***.
2 [C] *BrE informal* if you have a brainstorm, you are suddenly unable to think clearly or sensibly: *I must have* ***had a brainstorm*** *that afternoon.*

brainstorm² *v* [I,T] to have a discussion or meeting with other people at work, to suggest a lot of ideas for an activity or for solving a problem: *Employees get together and* ***brainstorm ideas*** *some of which get developed and some don't.*

brain·storm·ing /ˈbreɪnstɔːmɪŋ $ -ɔːr-/ *n* [U] when a group of people meet in order to try to develop ideas and think of ways of solving problems: *a* ***brainstorming session*** *to come up with slogans for new products*

ˈbrain ˌteaser *n* [C] a difficult problem that is fun trying to solve

brain·wash /ˈbreɪnwɒʃ $ -wɒːʃ, -wɑːʃ/ *v* [T] to make someone believe something that is not true, by using force, confusing them, or continuously repeating it over a long period of time: *Young people are being brainwashed by this religious group.* | **brainwash sb into doing sth** *Commercials brainwash consumers into buying things they don't need.* —**brainwashing** *n* [U]

brain·wave /ˈbreɪnweɪv/ ●○○ *n* [C]
1 *BrE* a sudden clever idea SYN **brainstorm** *AmE*: *I've had a brainwave! Let's go this weekend instead.* **THESAURUS** IDEA
2 an electrical force that is produced by the brain and that can be measured

brain·y /ˈbreɪni/ ●○○ *adj* (*comparative* **brainier**, *superlative* **brainiest**) able to learn easily and think quickly SYN **clever**, **smart** *AmE*: *He always was the brainy one.* **THESAURUS** INTELLIGENT

braise /breɪz/ *v* [T] to cook meat or vegetables slowly in a small amount of liquid in a closed container → **stew** —**braised** *adj*

brake¹ /breɪk/ ●●● S3 *n* [C]
1 [often plural] a piece of equipment that makes a vehicle go more slowly or stop: *Test your brakes after driving through water.* | *I managed to* ***put the brakes on*** *just in time.* | *Moira* ***slammed on the brakes*** (=used them suddenly and with a lot of force). | **apply the brakes** *formal*: *He applied the brakes but failed to stop in time.* | **the rear/front brakes** | *the* ***screech of brakes*** (=the loud unpleasant noise they can make) → ANTI-LOCK BRAKING SYSTEM, EMERGENCY BRAKE, HANDBRAKE, PARKING BRAKE, see picture at CAR
2 act as a brake on sth to make something develop more slowly, be more difficult to do, or happen less: *Rises in interest rates act as a brake on expenditure.*
3 put the brakes on sth to stop something that is happening

brake² ●●○ *v* [I] to make a vehicle or bicycle go more slowly or stop by using its brake: **brake sharply/hard** (=brake quickly) *He braked sharply to avoid the dog.*

ˈbrake ˌfluid *n* [U] liquid used in certain kinds of brakes so that the different parts move smoothly

ˈbrake light *n* [C] a light on the back of a vehicle that comes on when you use the brake → see picture at CAR

ˈbrake ˌshoe *n* [C] one of the two curved parts that press against the wheel of a vehicle in order to make it go more slowly or stop

bram·ble /ˈbræmbəl/ *n* [C] a wild BLACKBERRY bush

bran /bræn/ *n* [U] the crushed outer skin of wheat or a similar grain that is separated from the rest of the grain when making white flour

branch¹ /brɑːntʃ $ bræntʃ/ ●●● S2 W2 *n* [C]
1 OF A TREE a part of a tree that grows out from the TRUNK (=main stem) and that has leaves, fruit, or smaller branches growing from it → **limb**: *After the storm, the ground was littered with twigs and branches.* | *The* ***topmost branches*** *were full of birds.* → see picture at TREE
2 OF A BUSINESS/SHOP/COMPANY ETC a local business, shop etc that is part of a larger business etc: *The bank has branches all over the country.* | *a* ***branch office*** *in Boston* | *She now works in our Denver branch.* | *Where's their nearest branch?* | *They're planning to* ***open*** *a* ***branch*** *in St. Louis next year.* | *Have you met our* ***branch manager***, *Mr. Carlson?*
3 OF GOVERNMENT a part of a government or other organization that deals with one particular part of its work → **department**: *All branches of government are having to cut costs.* | **the executive/judicial/legislative branch** (=the three main parts of the US government)
4 OF A SUBJECT one part of a large subject of study or knowledge → **field**: **a branch of mathematics/physics/biology etc**
5 OF A FAMILY a group of members of a family who all have the same ANCESTORS → **side**: *the wealthy South American branch of the family*
6 OF A RIVER/ROAD ETC a smaller less important part of a river, road, or railway that leads away from the larger more important part of it: *The rail company may have to close the* ***branch line*** *to Uckfield.*

branch² *v* [I] to divide into two or more smaller, narrower, or less important parts → **fork**: *When you reach the village green, the street* ***branches into two***.

branch off *phr v* **1** if a road, passage, railway etc branches off from another road etc, it separates from it and goes in a different direction SYN **fork off**: **[+from]** *a passage* *branching off from the main tunnel* **2** *BrE* to leave a main road SYN **fork off**: **[+from/into]** *We branched off from the main road and turned down a country lane.* **3** to start talking about something different from what you were talking about before: **[+into]** *Then the conversation branched off into a discussion about movies.*

branch out *phr v* to start doing something different from the work or activities that you normally do: *Don't be afraid to branch out and try something new.* | **branch out into (doing) sth** *Profits were falling until the bookstore branched out into selling CDs.*

brand[1] /brænd/ ●●○ *n* [C]
1 a type of product made by a particular company, that has a particular name or design → **make**: **[+of]** *What brand of detergent do you use?* | **brand leader/leading brand** (=the brand that sells the most) | *products which lack a strong* ***brand image*** | **brand loyalty** (=the tendency to always buy a particular brand) | **own brand** *BrE*, **store brand** *AmE* (=a product made and sold by a particular store)
2 brand of humour/politics/religion etc a particular type of humour, politics, religion etc: *a strange macabre brand of humour*
3 a mark made or burned on a farm animal's skin that shows who it belongs to

brand[2] ●○○ *v* [T]
1 to describe someone or something as a very bad type of person or thing, often unfairly: **brand sb (as) sth** *You can't brand all football supporters as hooligans.* | *Stealing that money has* ***branded*** *Jim* ***for life*** *– no one will trust him again.*
2 to burn a mark onto something, especially a farm animal, in order to show who it belongs to: **brand sth with sth** *Each cow was branded with the ranch's logo.*
3 *technical* to give a name to a product or group of products so that they can be easily recognized by their name or design

brand·ed /ˈbrændɪd/ *adj* [only before noun] a branded product is made by a well-known company and has the company's name on it

brand·ing /ˈbrændɪŋ/ *n* [U] a practice that involves a company giving a group of their products the same brand name, helping this name to become well-known

ˈbranding ˌiron *n* [C] a piece of metal that is heated and used for burning marks on cattle or sheep, to show who they belong to

bran·dish /ˈbrændɪʃ/ *v* [T] *written* to wave something around in a dangerous or threatening way, especially a weapon: *A man leapt out, brandishing a kitchen knife.*

ˈbrand ˌname *n* [C] the name given to a product by the company that makes it SYN **trade name**

ˌbrand-ˈnew ●●○ *adj* new and not yet used: *a brand-new car* | *His clothes looked brand-new.*

bran·dy /ˈbrændi/ *n* (*plural* **brandies**) [C,U] a strong alcoholic drink made from wine, or a glass of this drink → see picture at GLASS[1]

ˈbrandy ˌbutter *n* [U] a mixture of butter, sugar, and brandy, usually eaten with CHRISTMAS PUDDING

brash /bræʃ/ *adj* **1** behaving too confidently and speaking too loudly – used to show disapproval: *brash journalists* **2** a brash building, place, or object attracts attention by being very colourful, large, exciting etc: *The painting was bold, brash, and modern.* —**brashly** *adv* —**brashness** *n* [U]

brass /brɑːs $ bræs/ ●●○ *n*
1 METAL [U] a very hard bright yellow metal that is a mixture of COPPER and ZINC: *an old brass bedstead*
2 MUSIC **a)** [U] musical instruments that are made of metal, such as the TRUMPET and the TROMBONE: *brass instruments* → PERCUSSION, STRINGED INSTRUMENT, WIND INSTRUMENT, WOODWIND **b) the brass (section)** the people in an ORCHESTRA or band who play musical instruments that are made of metal
3 DECORATIONS [C usually plural] an object made of brass, usually with a design cut into it, or several brass objects
4 get down to brass tacks *informal* to start talking about the most important facts or details of something

BRASS INSTRUMENTS

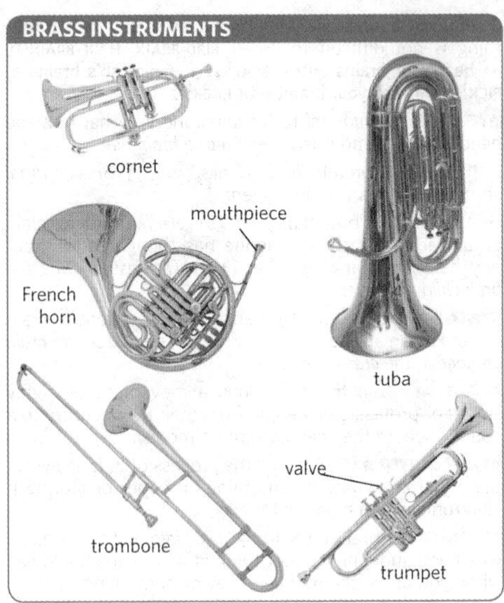

5 PEOPLE WITH TOP JOBS **the brass** *AmE informal* people who hold the most important positions SYN **top brass** *BrE*
6 it's brass monkeys/brass monkey weather *BrE spoken informal* used to say that it is very cold
7 MONEY [U] *BrE old-fashioned informal* money → **as bold as brass** at BOLD(2)

ˌbrass ˈband *n* [C] a band consisting mostly of brass musical instruments such as TRUMPETS, horns etc

brassed off /ˌbrɑːst ˈɒf $ ˌbræst ˈɒːf/ *adj BrE informal* annoyed SYN **fed up**

bras·se·rie /ˈbræsəri $ ˌbræsəˈriː/ *n* [C] a cheap informal restaurant, usually serving French food

bras·si·ere /ˈbræziə $ brəˈzɪr/ *n* [C] *formal* a BRA

ˌbrass ˈknuckles *n* [plural] *AmE* a set of connected metal rings worn over a person's fingers, used as a weapon SYN **knuckle-duster** *BrE*

brass·y /ˈbrɑːsi $ ˈbræsi/ *adj* **1** a woman who is brassy is too loud, confident, or brightly dressed: *a drunken brassy nightclub singer* **2** sounding hard and loud like the sound made by a BRASS musical instrument **3** having a bright gold-yellow colour like BRASS

brat /bræt/ *n* [C] *informal* **1** a badly behaved child: *a* ***spoiled brat*** **2 army/navy/military etc brat** *AmE* a child whose family moves often, because one or both parents work for the army, navy etc —**bratty** *adj*

brat·wurst /ˈbrætwɜːst $ -wɜːrst/ *n* [C,U] a type of German sausage

bra·va·do /brəˈvɑːdəʊ $ -doʊ/ *n* [U] behaviour that is deliberately intended to make other people believe you are brave and confident: *youthful bravado*

brave[1] /breɪv/ ●●● S3 *adj* (*comparative* **braver**, *superlative* **bravest**)
1 a) dealing with danger, pain, or difficult situations with courage and confidence SYN **courageous**: *brave soldiers* | *her brave fight against cancer* | **it is brave of sb (to do sth)** *It was brave of you to speak in front of all those people.* **b) the brave** [plural] brave people: *Today we remember the brave who died in the last war.*
2 very good: *Despite their captain's brave performance, Arsenal lost 2–1.* | **brave effort/attempt** *the brave efforts of the medical staff to save his life*
3 put on a brave face/front to pretend that you are happy when you are really very upset
4 brave new world a situation or a way of doing something that is new and exciting and meant to improve people's lives: *the brave new world of digital television* —**bravely** *adv*: *She smiled bravely.*

THESAURUS

brave showing that you are not afraid to do things that other people find dangerous or difficult: *I think he was incredibly brave to do a parachute jump.* | *a brave attempt to change the system*
courageous /kəˈreɪdʒəs/ *especially written* very brave – used especially about someone fighting for what they believe in, or fighting against a disease: *a courageous speech* | *her courageous fight against cancer*
daring brave and willing to take a lot of risks: *a daring escape from a prison camp* | *a daring fighter pilot*
bold willing to make difficult decisions or say what you think, even though it may involve risks: *It was a bold move to set up his own company.* | *She was very bold in criticizing the leadership.*
intrepid *written* willing to do dangerous things or go to dangerous places: *an intrepid traveller* | *We sent our intrepid reporter to find out what is happening.*
adventurous used about someone who enjoys going to new places and doing new, possibly dangerous, things: *More adventurous visitors can go skiing or snowboarding.*
fearless not afraid of anything or anyone: *a fearless campaigner for human rights*
heroic very brave and admired by many people: *heroic rescuers* | *Despite heroic efforts to save him, he died.*

brave² *v* [T] **1** to deal with a difficult, dangerous, or unpleasant situation: *I decided to take the train to work rather than brave the traffic.* | **brave the elements/weather etc** (=go out in bad weather) *More than 100 people braved the elements and attended the rally.* **2 brave it out** to deal bravely with something that is frightening or difficult

brave³ *n* [C] a young fighting man from a Native American tribe

ˌBrave New ˈWorld an advanced society of the future, in which many people seem to have easy and pleasant lives but in fact nobody has any freedom. This type of society is described in the novel *Brave New World* by Aldous Huxley. The phrase was first used in Shakespeare's play *The Tempest*.

brav·e·ry /ˈbreɪvəri/ ●●○ *n* [U] actions, behaviour, or an attitude that shows courage and confidence SYN **courage** OPP **cowardice**: *an act of great bravery*

bra·vo /ˈbrɑːvəʊ, brɑːˈvəʊ $ -voʊ/ *interjection* used to show your approval when someone, especially a performer, has done something very well: *Bravo! Encore!*

bra·vu·ra /brəˈvjʊərə $ -ˈvjʊrə/ *n* [U] great skill shown in the way you perform, write, paint etc, especially when you do something very difficult: *a bravura performance*

brawl¹ /brɔːl $ brɒːl/ *n* [C] a noisy quarrel or fight among a group of people, especially in a public place: *a drunken brawl in the street*

brawl² *v* [I] to quarrel or fight in a noisy way, especially in a public place: *Fans brawled outside the stadium.* —**brawler** *n* [C]

brawn /brɔːn $ brɒːn/ *n* [U] **1** physical strength, especially when compared with intelligence: *Mina has the brains, I have the brawn.* **2** *BrE* meat from a pig's head that has been boiled and pressed in a container and is often served in thin flat pieces SYN **headcheese** *AmE*

brawn·y /ˈbrɔːni $ ˈbrɒː-/ *adj* very large and strong: *His brawny arms glistened with sweat.*

bray /breɪ/ *v* [I] **1** if a DONKEY brays, it makes a loud sound **2** if someone brays, they laugh or talk in a loud, slightly annoying way —**bray** *n* [C]

bra·zen¹ /ˈbreɪzən/ *adj* **1** used to describe a person, or the actions of a person, who is not embarrassed about behaving in a wrong or immoral way: *her brazen admission that she was cheating on him* **2** *literary* having a shiny yellow colour

brazen² *v*
brazen sth ↔ **out** *phr v* to deal with a situation that is difficult or embarrassing for you by appearing to be confident rather than ashamed: *She knew she could either admit the truth or brazen it out.*

bra·zen·ly /ˈbreɪzənli/ *adv* doing something openly, without showing or feeling any shame: *She smiled at him brazenly.*

bra·zi·er /ˈbreɪziə $ -ʒər/ *n* [C] a metal container that holds a fire and is used to keep people warm outside

bra·zil /brəˈzɪl/ (*also* **braˈzil nut**) *n* [C] a type of curved nut that has a hard shell

Bra·zil·i·an¹ /brəˈzɪliən/ *adj* relating to Brazil or its people

Brazilian² *n* [C] **1** someone from Brazil **2** (*also* **Brazilian wax**) a beauty treatment in which most of a woman's PUBIC HAIR is removed, leaving just a small strip

breach¹ /briːtʃ/ ●○○ *n*
1 [C,U] an action that breaks a law, rule, or agreement: **[+of]** *This was a clear breach of the 1994 Trade Agreement.* | *They sued the company for* **breach of contract**. | *a breach of professional duty* | **be in breach of sth** *He was clearly in breach of the law.*
2 [C] a serious disagreement between people, groups, or countries: **[+with]** *Britain did not want to risk a breach with the US over sanctions.* | **[+between]** *What had caused the sudden breach between Henry and his son?* | *She wanted to help* **heal** *the* **breach** *between them.*
3 breach of confidence/trust an action in which someone does something that people have trusted them not to do: *We regard the publication of this information as a serious breach of trust.*
4 breach of security an action in which someone manages to learn secret information or manages to get into a place that is guarded: *There had been a major breach of security at the airbase.*
5 breach of the peace *BrE* the crime of making too much noise or fighting in a public place: *He was arrested and charged with breach of the peace.*
6 [C] a hole made in a wall that is intended to protect a place: **[+in]** *a breach in the castle wall*
7 step into the breach to help by doing someone else's job or work when they are unable to do it SYN **step in**: *Thanks for stepping into the breach last week.*

breach² ●○○ *v* [T]
1 to break a law, rule, or agreement SYN **break**: *The company accused him of breaching his contract.*
2 to break a hole in a wall that is intended to protect a place: *The storm had breached the sea wall in two places.*

BREAD

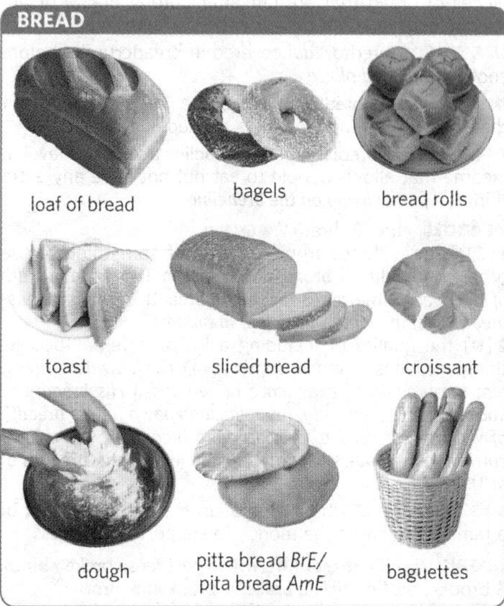

bread /bred/ ●●● S2 W3 *n* [U]
1 a type of food made from flour and water that is mixed

together and then baked: *Would you like some bread with your soup? | a loaf of brown bread | a piece of bread and butter*
2 your/sb's bread and butter *informal* the work that provides you with most of the money that you need in order to live: *Writing is my bread and butter.*
3 know which side your bread is buttered on *informal* to know which people to be nice to in order to get advantages for yourself
4 *old-fashioned informal* money

COLLOCATIONS

ADJECTIVES

fresh *Eat the bread while it's nice and fresh.*
stale (=hard and no longer fresh) *This bread's stale - shall I throw it away?*
crusty (=having a hard crust that is nice to eat) *Serve the soup with crusty bread.*
white/brown bread | **wholewheat bread** (*also* **wholemeal bread** *BrE*) (=bread made with flour that contains all of the grain) | **home-made/home-baked bread**

PHRASES

a slice/piece of bread *Can I have another slice of bread?*
a loaf of bread *He's gone to buy a loaf of bread.*

VERBS

make/bake bread *We usually make our own bread.*
cut/slice bread *Could you cut some bread?*

ˌbread-and-ˈbutter *adj* [only before noun] **1** *BrE* bread-and-butter questions are very important basic ones: *bread-and-butter political issues such as jobs and housing* **2** bread-and-butter work is work that is not very exciting but provides you with most of the money that you need in order to live

bread·bas·ket /ˈbredˌbɑːskɪt $ -ˌbæ-/ *n* **1** [C] a basket in which you keep or serve bread **2** [singular] the part of a country or area that provides most of its food: *Zambia could be the breadbasket of Africa.*

ˈbread bin *n* [C] *BrE* a container that you keep bread in so that it stays fresh (SYN) **breadbox**

bread·board /ˈbredbɔːd $ -bɔːrd/ *n* [C] a wooden board on which you cut bread

bread·box /ˈbredbɒks $ -bɑːks/ *n* [C] a BREAD BIN

bread·crumbs /ˈbredkrʌmz/ *n* [plural] very small pieces of bread that are left after cutting bread, or are used in cooking: *Coat the fish in breadcrumbs and fry.*

bread·ed /ˈbredɪd/ *adj* covered in breadcrumbs before cooking: *breaded plaice*

bread·fruit /ˈbredfruːt/ *n* [C,U] a large tropical fruit that looks like bread when it is cooked

bread·line /ˈbredlaɪn/ *n* **the breadline** a very low level of income that allows people to eat but not have any extra things: *a family* ***living on the breadline***

breadth /bredθ, bretθ/ ●○○ *n*
1 [C,U] the distance from one side of something to the other (SYN) **width** → **broad, depth, length**: **[+of]** *the breadth of the river* | **5 metres/3 feet etc in breadth** *The boat measured 15 feet in length and 4 feet in breadth.*
2 [U] the quality of including a lot of different people, things, or ideas → **broad, depth**: **[+of]** *The job wasn't giving him the breadth of experience he wanted. | His* ***breadth of knowledge*** *was amazing. | a politician known for his* ***breadth of vision*** *| We need to provide more breadth in the college curriculum.* → HAIR'S BREADTH, → **the length and breadth of** at LENGTH(8)

bread·win·ner /ˈbredˌwɪnə $ -ər/ *n* [C] the member of a family who earns the money to support the others

break¹ /breɪk/ ●●● (S1) (W1) *v* (*past tense* **broke** /brəʊk $ broʊk/, *past participle* **broken** /ˈbrəʊkən $ ˈbroʊ-/)
1 SEPARATE INTO PIECES **a)** [T] if you break something, you make it separate into two or more pieces, for example by hitting it, dropping it, or bending it: *I had to break a window*

BREAK

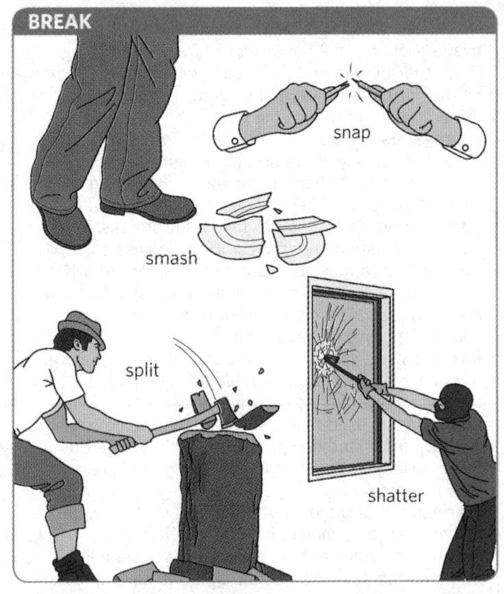

to get into the house. | Don't lean on the fence like that - you'll break it! | **break sth in half/two** *He broke the biscuit in half and handed one piece to me. |* ***Break*** *the chocolate* ***into*** *small* ***pieces*** *and melt it over a gentle heat.* **b)** [I] if something breaks, it separates into two or more pieces: *He kept pulling at the rope until it broke. | The frames are made of plastic and they tend to break quite easily.*
2 BONES [T] to damage a bone in your body by making it crack or split: *She fell downstairs and broke her hip.* THESAURUS ▸ HURT
3 MACHINES **a)** [T] to damage a machine so that it does not work properly: *Don't mess about with my camera - you'll break it. | Someone's broken the TV.* **b)** [I] if a machine breaks, it stops working properly: *The washing machine's broken again.*
4 RULES/LAWS [T] to disobey a rule or law: *They're* ***breaking the law*** *by employing such young children. | If you* ***break*** *the* ***rules****, you will be punished. | The cameras catch motorists who break the speed limit.*
5 PROMISE/AGREEMENT [T] to not do something that you have promised to do or signed an agreement to do: *I never* ***break*** *my* ***promises****. | You betrayed me. You* ***broke*** *your* ***word****.* | **break an agreement/contract** *He was worried that he might be breaking his contract.*
6 STOP/REST [I] to stop for a short time in order to have a rest or eat something: **[+for]** *Shall we break for lunch now?*
7 END STH [T] to stop something from continuing: *We need to break the cycle of poverty and crime in the inner cities. | We took turns driving, in order to try and break the monotony. | New talks will begin on Monday in an effort to* ***break*** *the* ***deadlock****.*
8 DEFEAT SB [T] to make someone feel that they have been completely defeated and they cannot continue working or living: *Losing his business nearly broke him. | I won't give in. I won't be broken by him.*
9 DESTROY AN ORGANIZATION [T] to damage an organization so badly that it no longer has any power: *The government succeeded in breaking the unions.*
10 DAY/DAWN [I] when the day or the DAWN breaks, the sky gets light: *Dawn was breaking by the time we arrived home.*
11 STORM [I] if a storm breaks, it begins: *We were keen to get back to the hotel before the storm broke.*
12 WEATHER [I] if the weather breaks, it suddenly changes and becomes cold or wet: *The following day the weather broke and we had ten days of solid rain.*
13 WAVES [I] when waves break, they fall onto the land at the edge of the water: *We sat and watched the waves breaking on the shore.*

14 SB'S VOICE [I] **a)** when a boy's voice breaks, it becomes lower and starts to sound like a man's voice: *He was fifteen, and his voice was just beginning to break.* **b)** if your voice breaks, it does not sound smooth because you are feeling strong emotions: *Her voice broke as she told us what had happened.*

15 NEWS **a)** [I] if news about an important event breaks, it becomes known: *News of his resignation broke yesterday.* | *The minister has refused to give any interviews since the scandal broke.* **b)** [T] if you break unpleasant news to someone, you tell it to them: *I didn't know how I was going to **break** the **news** to my mother.* | *The doctor finally broke it to me that there was no cure.*

16 break a habit to stop doing something that you do regularly, especially something that you should not do: *a new drug which helps smokers to break their habit*

17 break a record to do something even faster or even better than the previous best time, amount etc: *an attempt to break the 10,000-metres world record*

18 break a journey *BrE* to stop somewhere for a short time during a long journey: *We decided to break our journey in Oxford.*

19 break sb's heart to make someone very unhappy by ending a relationship with them or doing something that upsets them a lot: *He broke my heart when he left me.* | *It'll break your father's heart if you tell him you're giving up college.*

20 break a strike to force workers to end a STRIKE: *The government has threatened to bring in the army to break the 10-month-old strike.*

21 break a link/tie/connection to end a relationship with a person or organization: *The US has now broken all diplomatic links with the regime.* | *Sometimes it is necessary to break family ties in order to protect the child.*

22 break the skin to cut the skin on your body: *Their teeth are sharp enough to break the skin.*

23 break the back of sth to finish the main or worst part of something: *I think we've broken the back of the job now.*

24 break the bank to cost a lot of money, or more money than you have: *A new hard drive doesn't have to break the bank.*

25 break sb's concentration to interrupt someone and stop them from being able to continue thinking or talking about something: *The slightest sound would break his concentration.*

26 break the silence to end a period of silence by talking or making a noise: *The silence was broken by a loud scream.*

27 break sb's spirit to destroy someone's feeling of determination: *They could not break her spirit.* | *The spirit of our soldiers will never be broken.*

28 break sb's power to take away someone's position of power or control: *At last the power of the Church had been broken.*

29 break the ice *informal* to make people feel more friendly and willing to talk to each other: *Sam's arrival broke the ice and people began to talk and laugh.*

30 break a code to succeed in understanding something that is written in a secret way: *Scientists worked day and night to break the code.*

31 break wind to allow gas to escape from your bottom, making a noise and an unpleasant smell

32 break (sb's) serve to win a game in tennis when your opponent is starting the game by hitting the ball first: *Hewitt broke serve twice in the second set.*

33 break a leg *spoken* used to wish someone luck, especially just before they perform on stage

GRAMMAR

Break belongs to a group of verbs where the same noun can be the subject of the verb or its object.

- You can say: *I broke a glass.* In this sentence, 'a glass' is the object of **break**.
- You can also say: *A glass broke.* In this sentence, 'a glass' is the subject of **break**.

GRAMMAR GUIDE ▶ VERBS

THESAURUS

TO BREAK SOMETHING

break *v* [T] to damage something and make it separate into pieces, for example by dropping it or hitting it: *Careful you don't break the chair.* | *He broke his leg.*

smash *v* [T] to break something with a lot of force: *A policeman smashed his camera.*

snap *v* [T] to break something into two pieces, making a loud noise – used especially about long thin objects: *He snapped the sticks in two.*

split *v* [T] to separate something into two pieces along a straight line: *Using a sharp knife, split the melon in half.*

fracture *v* [T] to damage a bone, especially so that a line appears on the surface: *I fell over and fractured my wrist.*

tear /teə $ ter/ *v* [T] to damage paper or cloth by pulling it so that it separates into pieces: *She tore up the letter and put it in the bin.* | *I tore my jacket.*

TO BECOME BROKEN

break *v* [I] to become damaged and separate into pieces: *Plastic breaks quite easily.*

smash *v* [I] to break after being hit with a lot of force: *The bowl smashed as it hit the floor.*

shatter *v* [I] to break into a lot of small pieces: *The glass shattered all over the pavement.*

crack *v* [I] if something cracks, a line appears on the surface, which means that it could later break into separate pieces: *The ice was starting to crack.*

burst *v* [I] if a tyre, balloon, pipe etc bursts, it gets a hole and air or liquid suddenly comes out of it: *She blew up the balloon until it burst.*

split *v* [I] to break in a straight line: *The damp had caused the wood to split.*

crumble *v* [I] to break into a powder or a lot of small pieces: *The cork just crumbled in my hand.*

break away *phr v*

1 to leave a group or political party and form another group, usually because of a disagreement: *More than 30 Labour MPs broke away to form a new left-wing party.* | **[+from]** *They broke away from the national union and set up their own local organization.* → BREAKAWAY[2]

2 to leave your home, family, or job and become independent: **[+from]** *I felt the need to break away from home.*

3 to move away from someone who is holding you: *She started crying and tried to break away.* | **[+from]** *She broke away from him and ran to the door.*

4 to move away from other people in a race or game: *Radcliffe broke away 200 metres before the finish.*

5 to become loose and no longer attached to something: *Part of the plane's wing had broken away.*

break down *phr v*

1 if a car or machine breaks down, it stops working: *The car broke down just north of Paris.* | *The printing machines are always breaking down.* → BREAKDOWN

2 to fail or stop working in a successful way: *Negotiations broke down after only two days.* | *I left London when my marriage broke down.* → BREAKDOWN

3 break sth ↔ down if you break down a door, you hit it so hard that it breaks and falls to the ground: *Police had to break down the door to get into the flat.*

4 break sth ↔ down to change or remove something that prevents people from working together and having a successful relationship with each other: *Getting young people together will help to **break down** the **barriers** between them.* | *It takes a long time to break down prejudices.*

5 if a substance breaks down, or something breaks it down, it changes as a result of a chemical process: **break sth ↔ down** *Food is broken down in the stomach.* | *Bacteria are added to help break down the sewage.*

6 to be unable to stop yourself crying, especially in public: *He broke down and cried.* | *She **broke down in tears** when she heard the news.*

7 break sth ↔ down to separate something into smaller

parts so that it is easier to do or understand: *He showed us the whole dance, then broke it down so that we could learn it more easily.* | *The question can be broken down into two parts.* → BREAKDOWN

break for sth *phr v* to suddenly run towards something, especially in order to escape from someone: *He broke for the door, but the guards got there before he did.*

break in *phr v*

1 to enter a building by using force, in order to steal something: *Thieves broke in and stole £10,000 worth of computer equipment.* → BREAK-IN

2 to interrupt someone when they are speaking: **[+on]** *I didn't want to break in on his telephone conversation.* | **[+with]** *Dad would occasionally break in with an amusing comment.*

3 break sth ↔ in to make new shoes or boots less stiff and more comfortable by wearing them: *I went for a walk to break in my new boots.*

4 break sb in to help a person get used to a certain way of behaving or working: *She's quite new to the job, so we're still breaking her in.*

5 break sth ↔ in to teach a young horse to carry people on its back: *We break the horses in when they're about two years old.*

break into sth *phr v*

1 to enter a building or car by using force, in order to steal something: *Someone broke into my car and stole the radio.* | *Her house was broken into last week.*

2 to become involved in a new job or business activity: *She made an attempt to break into journalism.* | *It's a profession that is very hard to break into.* | *Many British firms have failed in their attempts to break into the American market.*

3 to start to spend money that you did not want to spend: *I don't want to break into my savings unless I have to.*

4 break into a run/trot etc to suddenly start running: *He broke into a run as he came round the corner.*

5 break into a smile/a song/applause etc to suddenly start smiling, singing etc: *Her face broke into a smile.* | *The audience broke into loud applause.*

break sb **of** sth *phr v* to make someone stop having a bad habit: *Try to* ***break*** *yourself* ***of*** *the* ***habit*** *of eating between meals.*

break off *phr v*

1 to suddenly stop talking: *She started to speak, then broke off while a waitress served us coffee.* | *He broke off in mid-sentence to shake hands with the new arrivals.* | **break sth ↔ off** *I broke off the conversation and answered the phone.*

2 break sth ↔ off to end a relationship: *She* ***broke off*** *their* ***engagement*** *only a few weeks before they were due to be married.* | *The US has* ***broken off*** *diplomatic* ***relations*** *with the regime.*

3 if something breaks off, or if you break it off, it comes loose and is no longer attached to something else: *One of the car's wing mirrors had broken off.* | **break sth ↔ off** *He broke off a piece of bread.*

break out *phr v*

1 if something unpleasant such as a fire, fight, or war breaks out, it starts to happen: *I was still living in London when the war broke out.* | *Does everyone know what to do if a fire breaks out?* | *Fighting broke out between demonstrators and the police.* → OUTBREAK

2 to escape from a prison: **[+of]** *Three men have broken out of a top-security jail.* → BREAKOUT

3 to change the way you live because you feel bored: **[+of]** *She felt the need to break out of her daily routine.*

4 break out in spots/a rash/a sweat etc if you break out in spots etc, they appear on your skin: *I broke out in a painful rash.* | *My whole body broke out in a sweat.*

break through *phr v*

1 break through (sth) to manage to get past or through something that is in your way: *Several demonstrators broke through the barriers despite warnings from the police.* | *After hours of fierce fighting, rebels broke through and captured the capital.*

2 break through (sth) if the sun breaks through, you can see it when you could not see it before because there were clouds: *The sun broke through at around lunch time.* | *The sun soon broke through the mist.*

3 to manage to do something successfully when there is a difficulty that is preventing you: *He's a very talented young actor who's just ready to break through.* | **[+into]** *It is possible that at this election some of the minority parties might succeed in breaking through into parliament.* → BREAKTHROUGH

break up *phr v*

1 if something breaks up, or if you break it up, it breaks into a lot of small pieces: *It seems that the plane just broke up in the air.* | **break sth ↔ up** *Use a fork to break up the soil.*

2 break sth ↔ up to separate something into several smaller parts: *There are plans to break the company up into several smaller independent companies.* | *You need a few trees and bushes to break up the lawn.*

3 break sth ↔ up to stop a fight: *Three policemen were needed to break up the fight.*

4 break sth ↔ up to make people leave a place where they have been meeting or protesting: *Government soldiers* ***broke up*** *the* ***demonstration***. | *Police moved in to* ***break up*** *the* ***meeting***.

5 if a marriage, group of people, or relationship breaks up, the people in it separate and do not live or work together anymore: *He lost his job and his* ***marriage broke up***. | *The couple broke up last year.* | *Many bands break up because of personality clashes between the musicians.* | **[+with]** *Has Sam really broken up with Lucy?* → BREAKUP

6 if a meeting or party breaks up, people start to leave: *The party didn't break up until after midnight.* | *The meeting broke up without any agreement.*

7 *BrE* when a school breaks up, it closes for a holiday: *School breaks up next week.* | **[+for]** *When do you break up for Easter?*

8 break sb up *AmE informal* to make someone laugh by saying or doing something funny: *He breaks me up!*

break with sb/sth *phr v*

1 to leave a group of people or an organization, especially because you have had a disagreement with them: *She had broken with her family years ago.* | *They broke with the Communist Party and set up a new party.*

2 break with tradition/the past to stop following old customs and do something in a completely different way: *Now is the time to break with the past.* | *His work broke with tradition in many ways.*

break² ●●● (S2) (W2) *n*

1 STOP WORKING [C] a period of time when you stop working in order to rest, eat etc: *We'll* ***have a*** *short* ***break*** *for lunch, then start again at two o'clock.* | *Let's* ***take a*** *ten-minute* ***break***. | *We'd worked for ten hours* ***without a break***. | *I'll go shopping during my* ***lunch break***.

2 STOP DOING STH [C] a period of time when you stop doing something before you start again: **[+from]** *I wanted a break from university life.* | *She decided to take a* ***career break*** *when she had children.* | **[+in]** *a welcome break in my normal routine*

3 HOLIDAY [C] a short holiday: *I was beginning to feel that I needed a break.* | *We flew off for a week's break in Spain.* | *They're offering* ***weekend breaks*** *in Paris for only £100.* | **the Easter/Christmas etc break** *Are you looking forward to the summer break?*

4 AT SCHOOL [U] the time during the school day when classes stop and teachers and students can rest, eat, play etc: **at break** *I'll speak to you at break.* | *They get together with their friends at* ***break time***.

5 ON TV [C] a pause for advertisements during a television or radio programme: *Join us again after the break.* | *We'll be back with more after a short break.*

6 STH STOPS HAPPENING [C] a period of time when something stops happening before it starts again: **[+in]** *We'll go for a walk if there's a break in the rain.* | *Latecomers will be admitted at a suitable break in the performance.* | *She waited for a break in the conversation.* | *There was no sign of a* ***break in the weather*** (=an improvement in bad weather).

7 END A RELATIONSHIP [singular] a time when you leave a person or group, or end a relationship with someone:

*I wanted a **clean break** so that I could restart my life.* | *It was years before I plucked up enough courage to **make** the **break** and leave him.* | **[+with]** *He was beginning to regret his break with the Labour Party.*
8 SPACE/HOLE [C] a space or hole in something: **[+in]** *We crawled through a break in the hedge.* | *The sun shone through a break in the clouds.*
9 CHANCE [C] *informal* a sudden or unexpected chance to do something that allows you to become successful in your job: *There are hundreds of young musicians out there looking for their first break.* | *He got his first **big break** in 1998.* | *a **lucky break***
10 BONES [C] the place where a bone in your body has broken: *It's quite a bad break, which will take several months to heal.*
11 TENNIS [C] a situation in a game of tennis in which you win a game when your opponent is starting the game by hitting the ball first: *She really needs a **break of serve** now if she wants to win this match.*
12 SNOOKER [C] the number of points that a player wins when it is their turn to hit the ball in a game such as SNOOKER
13 break with tradition/the past a time when people stop following old customs and do something in a completely different way: *It is time for a complete break with the past.*
14 make a break for sth to suddenly start running towards something in order to escape from a place: *As soon as the guard's back was turned, they made a break for the door.* | *Two of the prisoners **made a break for it** but were soon recaptured.*
15 give me/it a break! *spoken* used when you want someone to stop doing or saying something that is annoying you
16 give sb a break *spoken* to stop being strict with someone so that a situation becomes easier for them: *Give the kid a break. It's only his second day on the job.*
17 the break of day *literary* the time early in the morning when it starts getting light

break·a·ble /ˈbreɪkəbəl/ *adj* made of a material such as glass or clay that breaks easily → **fragile**: *Make sure you pack breakable ornaments carefully.*

break·age /ˈbreɪkɪdʒ/ *n* [C,U] something that someone breaks, especially when they must pay for it: *All breakages must be paid for.*

break·a·way[1] /ˈbreɪkəweɪ/ *adj* **breakaway group/party/movement** a breakaway group etc is formed by people who have left another group because of a disagreement: *a breakaway group of journalists* | *Hundreds of miners joined the breakaway union.* → **break away** at BREAK[1]

breakaway[2] *n* [singular] **1** a situation in which some people leave a group or organization after a disagreement and start a new group or organization: **[+from]** *He led a breakaway from the Communist Party.* **2** a change from the usual or accepted way of doing something: **[+from]** *His work marks a breakaway from traditional building styles.*

break·beat /ˈbreɪkbiːt/ *n* [U] a type of dance music that uses different patterns of sound based on one, two, or three beats in every BAR (=group of notes into which music can be divided), rather than the regular four beats in every bar

break·danc·ing /ˈbreɪkˌdɑːnsɪŋ $ -ˌdæn-/ *n* [U] a type of dancing to popular music that involves a lot of jumping and rolling on the floor

break·down /ˈbreɪkdaʊn/ ●○○ *n*
1 [C,U] the failure of a relationship or system: **[+of]** *He moved away after the breakdown of his marriage.* | *A sudden rise in oil prices could lead to a breakdown of the economy.* | **[+in]** *There has been a serious breakdown in relations between the two countries.* | **marriage/marital/family breakdown** *Family breakdown can lead to behavioural problems in children.*
2 [C] a serious medical condition in which someone becomes mentally ill and is unable to work or deal with ordinary situations in life: *I was worried he might **have a breakdown** if he carried on working so hard.* | *Two years ago he **suffered** a mental **breakdown**.* | *She had already had one **nervous breakdown**.*
3 [C] an occasion when a car or a piece of machinery breaks and stops working: *Always carry a phone with you in case you **have a breakdown** on the motorway.* | **[+in]** *a breakdown in the cooling system*
4 [C] a list of all the separate parts of something: **[+of]** *Can you give us a breakdown of the figures?*
5 [singular] the changing of a substance into other substances: *the breakdown of glucose in the body to release energy* → **break down** at BREAK[1]

ˈbreakdown ˌtruck (*also* **ˈbreakdown ˌlorry**) *n* [C] *BrE* a vehicle with special equipment that is used to pull a car that is broken and does not work to a place where it can be repaired SYN **tow truck** *AmE* → see picture at TRUCK[1]

break·er /ˈbreɪkə $ -ər/ *n* [C] a large wave with a white top that rolls onto the shore → CIRCUIT BREAKER

break·e·ven, **break-even** /ˌbreɪkˈiːvən◂/ *n* [U] the level of business activity at which a company is making neither a profit nor a loss: **(the) breakeven point/level** *The firm should reach breakeven point after one year.* → **break even** at EVEN[2](11)

break·fast /ˈbrekfəst/ ●●● S2 W2 *n* [C,U] the meal you have in the morning: *We **had** bacon and eggs **for breakfast**.* | *I never **eat breakfast**.* | *After a **hearty breakfast*** (=large breakfast), *we set out for a hike.* | *a **light breakfast*** (=small breakfast) | *a **working breakfast*** (=a breakfast at which you talk about business) —**breakfast** *v* [I] → BED AND BREAKFAST, CONTINENTAL BREAKFAST, ENGLISH BREAKFAST, → **wedding breakfast** at WEDDING(1), → **make a dog's breakfast of sth** at DOG[1](8)

> **GRAMMAR: Patterns with breakfast**
>
> **for breakfast**
> • You eat something **for breakfast**: *I had toast and coffee for breakfast.* ✗ Don't say: *At breakfast I had toast and coffee.*
>
> **at breakfast**
> • You use **at breakfast** to talk about something that happens while you are eating breakfast: *I saw her this morning at breakfast.*

ˌbreakfast ˈtelevision *n* [U] *BrE* television programmes that are broadcast in the early part of the morning

ˈbreak-in *n* [C] an act of entering a building illegally and by force, especially in order to steal things: *Since the break-in we've had all our locks changed.* → **break in** at BREAK[1]

ˌbreaking and ˈentering *n* [U] *law* the crime of entering a building illegally and by force

break·neck /ˈbreɪknek/ *adj* **at breakneck speed/pace** extremely and often dangerously fast: *He drove away at breakneck speed.*

break·out /ˈbreɪkaʊt/ *n* [C] an escape from a prison, especially one involving a lot of prisoners → **break out** at BREAK[1]

break·through /ˈbreɪkθruː/ ●●○ *n* [C] an important new discovery in something you are studying, especially one made after trying for a long time: **[+in]** *Scientists have **made** a major **breakthrough** in the treatment of cancer.* → **break through** at BREAK[1] THESAURUS PROGRESS

break·up /ˈbreɪkʌp/ *n* [C,U] **1** the act of ending a marriage or relationship: *the breakup of her marriage* **2** the separation of a group, organization, or country into smaller parts: **[+of]** *the breakup of the Soviet Union* → **break up** at BREAK[1]

break·wa·ter /ˈbreɪkˌwɔːtə $ -ˌwɔːtər, -ˌwɑː-/ *n* [C] a wall built out into the sea to protect the shore from the force of the waves

breast[1] /brest/ ●●● S3 *n*
1 WOMAN'S BODY [C] one of the two round raised parts on a woman's chest that produce milk when she has a baby: *These bras are specially designed for women with large*

breasts. | **breast** milk | **breast** cancer | **bare-breasted/small-breasted etc**
2 CHEST [C] *written* the part of your body between your neck and your stomach: *Dick cradled her photograph against his breast.*
3 BIRD [C] the front part of a bird's body, below its neck: *a robin with a red breast* | **red-breasted/white-breasted etc** *red-breasted geese*
4 MEAT [U] meat that comes from the front part of the body of a bird such as a chicken: *turkey breast*
5 CLOTHES [C usually singular] the part of a jacket, shirt etc that covers the top part of your chest → DOUBLE-BREASTED, SINGLE-BREASTED
6 make a clean breast of it/things to admit that you have done something wrong
7 EMOTIONS [C] *literary* where your feelings of sadness, love, anger, fear etc come from: *a troubled breast* → **beat your breast** at BEAT[1](31), → CHIMNEY BREAST

breast² *v* [T] *formal* **1** to reach the top of a hill or slope **2** to push against something with your chest

breast·bone /ˈbrestbəʊn $ -boʊn/ *n* [C] a long flat bone in the front of your chest that is connected to the top seven pairs of RIBS SYN **sternum**

ˈ**breast-feed** *v* (*past tense and past participle* **breast-fed**) [I,T] if a woman breast-feeds, she feeds her baby with milk from her breast rather than from a bottle SYN **nurse** → **suckle**, **bottle-feed**

breast·plate /ˈbrestpleɪt/ *n* [C] a leather or metal protective covering worn over the chest by soldiers during battles in the past

ˌ**breast-ˈpocket** *n* [C] a pocket on the outside of a shirt or JACKET, above the breast

breast·stroke /ˈbrest-strəʊk $ -stroʊk/ *n* [U] a way of swimming in which you push your arms out and then bring them back in a circle towards you while bending your knees towards your body and then kicking out → see picture at SWIM

breath /breθ/ ●●● S3 W2 *n*
1 a) [U] the air that you send out of your lungs when you breathe: *Leo could smell the wine on her breath.* | *Let your breath out slowly.* **b)** [U] air that you take into your lungs: *When he reached the top of the stairs, his heart was pounding and he was gasping for breath.* **c)** [C] an amount of air that you take into your lungs: *Shaun took a deep breath and dived in.* ⚠ Do not confuse the noun **breath** /breθ/ with the verb **breathe** /briːð/: *She took a deep breath and continued.* | *I can't breathe in here!*
2 a breath of fresh air a) something that is new and different in a way you think is exciting and good: *Osborne's play brought a breath of fresh air to the British theatre.* **b)** clean air outside, that you feel you need after being inside for a long time: *I'm going outside for a breath of fresh air.*
3 don't hold your breath *informal* used to say that something is not going to happen soon: *The system's due for an update, but don't hold your breath.*
4 catch your breath (*also* **get your breath back**) to start breathing normally again after running or making a lot of effort: *Slow down, I need to catch my breath.*
5 don't waste your breath (*also* **save your breath**) *spoken* used to say that someone will not be able to persuade someone else, so there is no point in trying: *Save your breath. She's already made up her mind.* | *Will he listen to me or will I just be wasting my breath?*
6 take sb's breath away to be extremely beautiful or exciting: *The view from the top will take your breath away.*
7 under your breath in a quiet voice so that no one can hear you: *'Son of a bitch,' he muttered under his breath.*
8 in the same breath a) (*also* **in the next breath**) used to say that someone has said two things at once that are so different from each other they cannot both be true: *He criticized the film, then predicted in the same breath that it would be a great success.* **b)** if you mention two people or things in the same breath, you show that you think they are alike or are related: *I became nervous when the doctor mentioned my mother's name and 'cancer' in the same breath.* | **[+as/with]** *a young poet mentioned in the same breath as T.S. Eliot*
9 with your last/dying breath at the moment when you are dying: *With his last breath, he cursed his captors.*
10 [singular] *written* a very small amount or a sign of something: **[+of]** *They did everything they could to avoid the slightest breath of scandal.*
11 a breath of air/wind *literary* a slight movement of air: *Scarcely a breath of air disturbed the stillness of the day.*
→ **with bated breath** at BATED

COLLOCATIONS

VERBS

take a breath (=breathe in) *Alex took a deep breath, then jumped into the pool.*
let your breath out (=breathe out) *Let your breath out slowly and relax.*
hold your breath (=not breathe out for a few seconds or minutes) *How long can you hold your breath underwater?*
be out of breath (=have difficulty breathing after running, hurrying etc) *Andrew hurried in, slightly out of breath.*
be short of breath (=be unable to breathe easily because you are ill, old etc) | **gasp/fight for breath** (=have difficulty breathing) | **pause for breath** | **draw breath** *written* (=breathe)

ADJECTIVES

bad breath (=that smells unpleasant) *Smoking gives you bad breath.*
a deep/long breath (=in which you breathe a lot of air in slowly) *She took a deep breath and knocked on the door.*
a shallow breath (=in which you breathe a small amount of air in)

PHRASES

shortness of breath (=when you are unable to breathe easily) *Symptoms include dizziness and shortness of breath.*
an intake of breath (=when you breathe in very quickly and suddenly, especially because you are surprised) *He gave a sharp intake of breath.*

breath·a·ble /ˈbriːðəbəl/ *adj* clothing that is breathable allows air to pass through it easily

breath·a·lyze (*also* **-lyse** *BrE*) /ˈbreθəl-aɪz/ *v* [T] to make someone breathe into a special piece of equipment in order to see if they have drunk too much alcohol to be allowed to drive

Breath·a·lyz·er (*also* **Breathalyser** *BrE*) /ˈbreθəl-aɪzə $ -ər/ *n* [C] *trademark* a piece of equipment used by the police to see if a driver of a car has drunk too much alcohol

breathe /briːð/ ●●● S3 W3 *v*
1 AIR [I,T] to take air into your lungs and send it out again: *The room filled with smoke, and it was becoming difficult to breathe.* | *People are concerned about the quality of the air they breathe.* | *Relax and* **breathe deeply** (=take in a lot of air).
2 BLOW [I,T] to blow air or smoke out of your mouth: **[+on]** *Roy breathed on his hands and rubbed them together vigorously.* | **breathe sth over sb** *The fat man opposite was breathing garlic all over me.*
3 sb can breathe easy/easily used when saying that someone can relax because a worrying or dangerous situation has ended: *With stocks going up, investors can breathe easily.*
4 breathe a sigh of relief to stop being worried or frightened about something: *Once the deadline passed, everyone breathed a sigh of relief.*
5 be breathing down sb's neck *informal* to pay very close attention to what someone is doing, in a way that makes them feel nervous or annoyed: *How can I concentrate with you breathing down my neck all the time?*
6 not breathe a word to not tell anyone anything at all

about something, because it is a secret: *Don't breathe a word; it's supposed to be a surprise.*
7 breathe life into sth to change a situation so that people feel more excited or interested: *Critics are hoping the young director can breathe new life into the French film industry.*
8 SKIN [I] if your skin can breathe, air can reach it
9 CLOTHES/FABRIC [I] if cloth or clothing breathes, air can pass through it so that your body feels pleasantly cool and dry
10 WINE [I] if you let wine breathe, you open the bottle to let the air get to it before you drink it
11 SAY STH QUIETLY [T] *written* to say something very quietly, almost in a whisper: *'Wait,' he breathed.*
12 breathe your last (breath) *literary* to die
13 breathe fire to talk and behave in a very angry way
→ **live and breathe sth** at LIVE[1](19)

THESAURUS

breathe [I,T] to take air into your lungs and send it out again: *Mary knew he was asleep because he was breathing deeply.* | *He breathed the clear spring air.*
sigh to breathe out slowly and make a noise that shows you are disappointed, tired, RELIEVED etc: *She just sighed and shook her head.*
pant to breathe quickly and noisily through your mouth, because you have been using a lot of effort: *They were panting by the time they got to the finish line.*
gasp to breathe very quickly and deeply and with difficulty: *Her eyes were wide, and she was gasping for breath.*
snore to breathe noisily while you are sleeping: *I couldn't sleep because my husband was snoring.*
wheeze to breathe with difficulty, making a noise in your throat and chest, because you are ill: *His asthma was making him wheeze.*

breathe in *phr v* to take air into your lungs → **inhale**: *The doctor made me breathe in while he listened to my chest.* | **breathe sth ↔ in** *Wyatt breathed in the cool ocean air.*

breathe out *phr v* to send air out from your lungs → **exhale**: *Jim breathed out deeply.* | **breathe sth ↔ out** *Lauren lit up a cigarette, then breathed out a puff of smoke.*

breath·er /ˈbriːðə $ -ər/ *n* **have/take a breather** *informal* to stop what you are doing for a short time in order to rest, especially when you are exercising → HEAVY BREATHER

breath·ing /ˈbriːðɪŋ/ ●○○ *n* [U] the process of breathing air in and out: *His breathing was deep and regular.* | *When I picked up the phone, all I heard was* ***heavy breathing*** (=loud breathing).

ˈbreathing ˌspace (*also* **ˈbreathing ˌroom**) *n* [U] **1** a short time when you have a rest from doing something before starting again: *This deal should* ***give*** *the company some extra* ***breathing room*** *before its loans are due.* **2** enough room to move or breathe easily and comfortably in

breath·less /ˈbreθləs/ *adj* **1** having difficulty breathing, especially because you are very tired, excited, or frightened: *The long climb left Jan feeling breathless.* | **[+with]** *They waited, breathless with anticipation.* **2** *written* excited: *His first novel drew breathless superlatives from critics.* **3 at (a) breathless pace/speed** extremely fast **4** *literary* unpleasantly hot, with no fresh air or wind: *the breathless heat of a midsummer night in Rome* —**breathlessly** *adv* —**breathlessness** *n* [U]

breath·tak·ing /ˈbreθˌteɪkɪŋ/ *adj* very impressive, exciting, or surprising: *The view from my bedroom window was absolutely breathtaking.* | *an act of breathtaking arrogance* THESAURUS▸ BEAUTIFUL —**breathtakingly** *adv*

ˈbreath ˌtest *n* [C] *BrE* a test in which the police make a car driver breathe into a special bag to see if he or she has drunk too much alcohol → **breathalyze**

breath·y /ˈbreθi/ *adj* if someone's voice is breathy, you can hear their breath when they speak

bred /bred/ the past tense and past participle of BREED

breech /briːtʃ/ *n* [C] the part of a gun into which you put the bullets

ˈbreech birth (*also* **ˈbreech deˌlivery**) *n* [C] a birth in which the lower part of a baby's body comes out of its mother first

breech·es /ˈbrɪtʃɪz/ *n* [plural] short trousers that fasten just below the knees: *riding breeches*

breed[1] /briːd/ ●●○ *v* (*past tense and past participle* **bred** /bred/)
1 [I] if animals breed, they MATE in order to have babies: *Eagles breed during the cooler months of the year.*
2 [T] to keep animals or plants in order to produce babies or new plants, especially ones with particular qualities: *These dogs were originally bred in Scotland to round up sheep.* → CROSSBREED[1], PUREBRED, THOROUGHBRED
3 [T] to cause a particular feeling or condition: *Poor living conditions breed violence and despair.*
4 [T] if a place, situation, or thing breeds a particular type of person, it produces that type: *Society's obsession with sex has bred a generation of unhappy children.* → WELL-BRED,
→ **born and bred** at BORN[1](3)

breed[2] ●●○ *n* [C]
1 a type of animal that is kept as a pet or on a farm: **[+of]** *Spaniels are my favourite breed of dog.*
2 a particular kind of person or type of thing: *Real cowboys are* ***a dying breed*** (=not many exist anymore). | *Dodd was one of that* ***rare breed*** (=there are not many of them) *who could make the game of football look simple.* | **[+of]** ***a new breed of*** *international criminal*

breed·er /ˈbriːdə $ -ər/ *n* [C] someone who breeds animals or plants as a job: *a dog breeder*

breed·ing /ˈbriːdɪŋ/ *n* [U] **1** when animals produce babies: *Open-sea fish lay several million eggs each* ***breeding season***. **2** the activity of keeping animals or plants in order to produce animals or plants that have particular qualities: *the breeding of pedigree dogs* | *Benson took great care in selecting* ***breeding stock*** (=animals you keep to breed from). **3** the fact of coming from a family of high rank and having polite social behaviour: *The young lieutenant had an air of wealth and* ***good breeding***.

ˈbreeding ˌground *n* [C] **1** a place or situation where something bad or harmful develops: **[+for]** *Overcrowded slums are breeding grounds for crime.* **2** a place where animals go in order to breed

breeze[1] /briːz/ ●●○ *n* [C]
1 a gentle wind → **breezy**: *flowers waving in the breeze* THESAURUS▸ WIND
2 be a breeze *informal* to be very easy: *Don't think that learning Dutch will be a breeze.* → **shoot the breeze** at SHOOT[1](13)

breeze[2] *v* **1** [I always + adv/prep] to walk somewhere in a calm confident way: **[+in/into/out etc]** *She just breezed into my office and said she wanted a job.* **2** [T] to do very well in a test, a piece of written work etc, with very little effort: *Don't bother studying for the English exam – you'll breeze it.*

breeze through sth *phr v* to achieve something very easily SYN **sail through**: *He breezed through the exam.*

ˈbreeze-block *n* [C] *BrE* a light brick used in building, made of CEMENT and CINDERS SYN **cinder block** *AmE* → see picture at BLOCK[1]

breez·y /ˈbriːzi/ *adj* **1** a breezy person is happy, confident, and relaxed: *a breezy and relaxed air of confidence* **2** if the weather is breezy, the wind blows quite strongly —**breezily** *adv*

breth·ren /ˈbreðrən/ *n* [plural] *old use* used to address or talk about the members of an organization or group, especially a religious group

breve /briːv/ *n* [C] *BrE* a musical note that continues for twice as long as a SEMIBREVE

brev·i·ty /ˈbrevəti/ AWL *n* [U] *formal* **1** the quality of expressing something in very few words → **brief**: *Letters published in the newspaper are edited for brevity and clarity.* **2** the quality of continuing for only a short time → **brief**: *the brevity of her visit*

B

brew¹ /bruː/ ●○○ *v*
1 [T] to make beer: *Every beer on the menu was brewed locally.*
2 [I] if a drink of tea or coffee is brewing, the taste is getting into the hot water: *He read the paper while the tea brewed.*
3 [T] to make a drink of tea or coffee: *freshly brewed coffee*
4 be brewing a) if something unpleasant is brewing, it will happen soon: *There's* ***trouble brewing*** *in the office.* **b)** if a storm is brewing, it will happen soon
brew up *phr v BrE informal* to make a drink of tea

brew² *n* **1** [C] *especially BrE* a drink that is brewed, especially tea **2** [C,U] *AmE* beer, or a can or glass of beer: *a cold brew in a frosty glass* **3** [C usually singular] a combination of different things: **[+of]** *The band played a strange brew of rock, jazz, and country music.* → HOME BREW

brew·er /ˈbruːə $ -ər/ *n* [C] a person or company that makes beer

brew·er·y /ˈbruːəri/ ●○○ *n* (*plural* **breweries**) [C] a place where beer is made, or a company that makes beer

bri·ar, **brier** /ˈbraɪə $ -ər/ *n* **1** [C,U] a wild bush with branches that have small sharp points **2** [C] a tobacco pipe made from briar

bribe¹ /braɪb/ ●○○ *v* [T]
1 to illegally give someone, especially a public official, money or a gift in order to persuade them to do something for you: *The only way we could get into the country was by bribing the border officials.* | **bribe sb to do sth** *He bribed one of the guards to smuggle out a note.*
2 to offer someone, especially a child, something special in order to persuade them to do something: **bribe sb with sth** *Sam wouldn't do her homework until I bribed her with ice cream.*

bribe² ●○○ *n* [C]
1 money or a gift that you illegally give someone to persuade them to do something for you: *The officials said that they had been* ***offered bribes*** *before an important game.* | **accept/take a bribe** *A Supreme Court judge was charged with taking bribes.*
2 something special offered to someone, especially a child, in order to persuade them to do something

brib·er·y /ˈbraɪbəri/ ●○○ *n* [U] the act of giving bribes: *We tried everything – persuasion, bribery, threats.* | *He was found guilty of* ***bribery and corruption*** (=bribery and dishonest behaviour).

bric-a-brac /ˈbrɪk ə ˌbræk/ *n* [U] *BrE* small objects that are not worth very much money but are interesting or attractive

BRIC coun·tries /ˈbrɪk ˌkʌntriz/ *n* [plural] Brazil, Russia, India, and China, considered to be countries whose economies are developing quickly

brick¹ /brɪk/ ●●● S2 W3 *n*
1 [C,U] a hard block of baked clay used for building walls, houses etc: *a brick wall* | *a house made of brick* | *Protesters attacked the police with stones and bricks.*
2 bricks and mortar houses – used especially when talking about them as an INVESTMENT
3 [C] *BrE* a small square block of wood, plastic etc used as a toy
4 [C] *old-fashioned* a good person who you can depend on when you are in trouble
5 bricks to clicks used to talk about changing from selling things in shops to selling things on the Internet → **be (like) banging/bashing etc your head against a brick wall** at HEAD¹(31), → **drop a brick** at DROP¹(27)

brick² *v* **be bricking it** *BrE informal* to feel very nervous or frightened
brick sth ↔ **off** *phr v* to separate an area from a larger area by building a wall of bricks: *Some of the rooms had been bricked off.*
brick sth ↔ **up/in** *phr v* to fill or close a space by building a wall of bricks in it: *The windows were bricked up.*

brick·bat /ˈbrɪkbæt/ *n* [C] *written* a criticism of something: *The plan has drawn both brickbats and praise.*

brick·lay·er /ˈbrɪkˌleɪə $ -ər/ (*also* **brick·ie** /ˈbrɪki/ *BrE informal*) *n* [C] someone whose job is to build walls, buildings etc with bricks —**bricklaying** *n* [U]

ˌbrick ˈred *n* [U] a brownish red colour —**brick red** *adj*

brick·work /ˈbrɪkwɜːk $ -wɜːrk/ *n* [U] **1** the bricks that have been used to build something: *The brickwork was cracked and in need of repair.* **2** the work of building something with bricks

brid·al /ˈbraɪdl/ *adj* [only before noun] relating to a wedding or a woman who is getting married → **bride**: *a bridal gown*

ˈbridal ˌparty *n* [C] the group of people who arrive at the church with the bride

ˈbridal ˌsuite *n* [C] a special set of rooms in a hotel for two people who have just got married

bride /braɪd/ ●●○ *n* [C] a woman at the time she gets married or just after she is married → **groom**

bride·groom /ˈbraɪdgruːm, -grʊm/ ●●○ (*also* **groom**) *n* [C] a man at the time he gets married, or just after he is married

brides·maid /ˈbraɪdzmeɪd/ ●●○ *n* [C] a girl or woman, usually unmarried, who helps a bride on her wedding day and is with her at the wedding → BEST MAN

ˌbride-to-ˈbe *n* (*plural* **brides-to-be**) [C] a woman who is going to be married soon: *Jonathan's bride-to-be*

BRIDGES

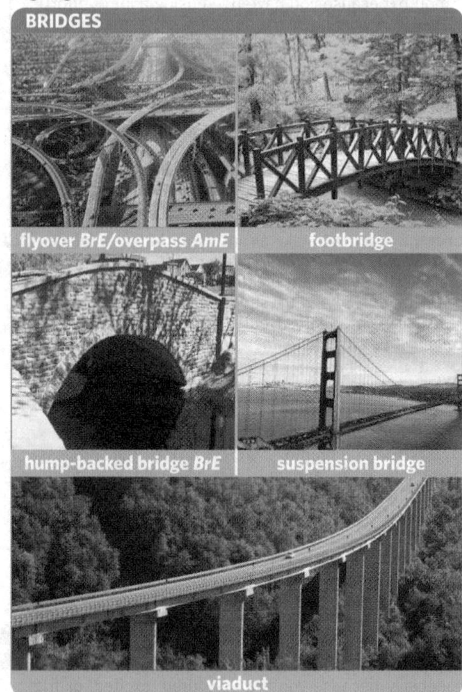

flyover *BrE*/overpass *AmE* — footbridge — hump-backed bridge *BrE* — suspension bridge — viaduct

bridge¹ /brɪdʒ/ ●●● S2 W2 *n*
1 OVER A RIVER/ROAD ETC [C] a structure built over a river, road etc that allows people or vehicles to cross from one side to the other → SUSPENSION BRIDGE, SWING BRIDGE
2 CONNECTION [C] something that provides a connection between two things SYN **link**: **[+between/to]** *The training programme is seen as a bridge between school and work.* | *a scheme to* ***build bridges*** (=make a better relationship) *between the police and the community*
3 SHIP [C usually singular] the raised part of a ship from which the officers control it
4 CARD GAME [U] a card game for four players, who play in pairs
5 the bridge of your nose the upper part of your nose between your eyes
6 PAIR OF GLASSES [C usually singular] the part of a pair of glasses that rests on your nose

7 MUSICAL INSTRUMENT [C usually singular] a small piece of wood under the strings of a VIOLIN or GUITAR, used to keep them in position
8 FOR TEETH [C] a small piece of metal that keeps false teeth in place by attaching them to your real teeth → **burn your bridges** at BURN[1](18), → **cross that bridge when you come to it** at CROSS[1](10), → **be (all) water under the bridge** at WATER[1](6)

bridge² ●○○ *v* [T]
1 to reduce or get rid of the difference between two things: *The differences between our two cultures can be bridged if we continue to communicate.* | *Alvin managed to* ***bridge the gap between*** *ballet and modern dance.*
2 *written* to build or form a bridge over something: *a fallen tree bridging the stream*

bridge·head /ˈbrɪdʒhed/ *n* [C] a strong position far forward in enemy land from which an army can go forward or attack

ˈbridging ˌloan *BrE*, **ˈbridge loan** *AmE n* [C] an amount of money that a bank lends you for a short period of time until you receive money from somewhere else

bri·dle¹ /ˈbraɪdl/ *n* [C] a set of leather bands put around a horse's head and used to control its movements

bridle² *v* **1** [I] *written* to become angry and offended about something: **[+at]** *The senator bridled at the reporter's question.* **2** [T] to put a bridle on a horse

ˈbridle path (*also* **bri·dle·way** /ˈbraɪdlweɪ/) *n* [C] a path that you ride a horse on

Brie /briː/ *n* [U] a soft French cheese

brief¹ /briːf/ ●●● S2 W2 AWL *adj*
1 continuing for a short time → **brevity**: *We stopped by Alice's house for a brief visit.* | *Let's keep this conversation brief; I have a plane to catch.* | **a brief period/moment/spell etc** *Greene spent a brief time at Cambridge.* THESAURUS SHORT
2 using very few words or including few details → **brevity**: *The president read a brief statement to reporters before boarding his plane.* | *a brief description of the film*
3 be brief to say or write something using only a few words, especially because there is little time: *I'll be brief; a lot of changes are going to happen.*
4 clothes that are brief are short and cover only a small area of your body: *a very brief bikini*

brief² ●○○ AWL *n* [C]
1 [usually singular] official instructions that explain what someone's job is, what their duties are etc: *The architect's brief is to design an extension that is modern but blends with the rest of the building.*
2 *law* a short spoken or written statement giving facts about a law case: *The ACLU filed a brief* (=gave one to the court) *opposing the decision.*
3 *BrE law* a law case that a lawyer will argue in a court
4 a short report about something
5 in brief a) in as few words as possible: *We should, in brief, invest heavily in digital systems.* **b)** without any details: *Here again are today's headlines in brief.*
6 briefs [plural] men's or women's underwear worn on the lower part of the body

brief³ ●○○ AWL *v* [T] to give someone all the information about a situation that they will need → **briefing**: **brief sb on sth** *The president has been fully briefed on the current situation in Haiti.* THESAURUS TELL → DEBRIEF

brief·case /ˈbriːfkeɪs/ ●●○ *n* [C] a flat case used especially by business people for carrying papers or documents → see picture at CASE¹

brief·ing /ˈbriːfɪŋ/ ●○○ AWL *n* [C,U] information or instructions that you get before you have to do something

brief·ly /ˈbriːfli/ ●●○ W3 AWL *adv*
1 for a short time: *We stopped off briefly in London.*
2 in as few words as possible SYN **in brief**: *Sonia explained briefly what we had to do.* | *Briefly, I think we should accept their offer.*

bri·er /ˈbraɪə $ -ər/ *n* [U] a BRIAR

brig /brɪɡ/ *n* [C] **1** a ship with two MASTS (=poles) and large square sails **2** *AmE* a military prison, especially on a ship

bri·gade /brɪˈɡeɪd/ *n* [C] **1** a large group of soldiers forming part of an army **2** an insulting word for a group of people who have the same beliefs: *the anti-nuclear brigade* **3** a group of people who are organized to do something: *Snowmobile brigades delivered food and medicine.* → FIRE BRIGADE

brig·a·dier /ˌbrɪɡəˈdɪə◂ $ -ˈdɪr◂/ *n* [C] a high military rank in the British army, or the person who has this rank

ˌbrigadier-ˈgeneral *n* [C] a high army rank, or someone holding this rank

brig·and /ˈbrɪɡənd/ *n* [C] *literary* a thief, especially one of a group that attacks people in mountains or forests

bright /braɪt/ ●●● S2 W2 *adj* (*comparative* **brighter**, *superlative* **brightest**)
1 LIGHT shining strongly, or with plenty of light: *Her eyes were hurting from the bright lights.* | *bright sunshine* | *a large bright room*
2 SUNNY if the weather is bright, the sun is shining and there is a lot of light OPP **dull**: *The weather was bright and sunny.* | *a bright autumn day*
3 INTELLIGENT intelligent and able to learn things quickly: *He was an exceptionally bright child.* | *a bright ambitious young man* THESAURUS INTELLIGENT
4 a bright idea a very good idea – sometimes used ironically (IRONIC): *Whose bright idea was this?* | *He is constantly coming up with* ***bright ideas*** *for making money.*
5 COLOURS bright colours are strong and easy to see: *a bright red jumper* | *I never wear bright colours.* THESAURUS COLOUR
6 CHEERFUL happy and full of energy: *Her voice was bright and cheerful.* | *She gave him a bright smile.* | *He looked up at me with bright eyes.*
7 SUCCESSFUL if the future looks bright, you think that something will be successful SYN **promising**: *The school's future now looks very bright.* | *I'm sure the company* ***has a bright future*** *now.*
8 as bright as a button very intelligent and full of energy
9 look on the bright side to see the good points in a situation that seems to be bad: *Come on, try to look on the bright side.*
10 bright and early very early in the morning: *He was up bright and early, keen to get started.*
11 bright spark *informal* someone who says or does something that they think is intelligent but is really wrong or stupid: *Some bright spark thought the building was on fire and called the fire brigade.*
12 bright and breezy happy and confident
13 bright-eyed and bushy-tailed happy and full of energy
14 the bright lights the interesting exciting life in a big city: *She missed the bright lights of London.*
15 bright spot an event or a period of time that is more pleasant when everything else is unpleasant: *The only bright spot of the weekend was our trip to the theatre.*
—**brightly** *adv*: *The sun shone brightly.* | *brightly coloured clothes* | *She smiled brightly.* —**brightness** *n* [U]

THESAURUS

A BRIGHT LIGHT

bright shining strongly: *The sunshine was very bright.* | *the bright light of the torch*
strong very bright: *Photographs fade if they are exposed to strong sunlight.*
brilliant extremely bright, especially in a way that seems good: *The garden was full of brilliant autumn sunshine.*
dazzling a dazzling light is so bright that it hurts your eyes and you cannot look at it: *dazzling headlights*
blinding a blinding light is very bright and makes you unable to see for a short time after you have looked at it: *There was a sudden blinding light, followed by the sound of a huge explosion.*

harsh a harsh light is bright and unpleasant: *In the harsh light of the kitchen, she looked older than she was.*
good if the light is good in a place where you are working, it is bright enough for you to see what you are doing: *The light wasn't good enough to read.*

A BRIGHT PLACE

bright full of light: *I wish the room was a bit brighter.*
light bright because there are big windows: *The dining room was light and airy.*
well-lit bright because there are plenty of electric lights: *Try to park in a well-lit place.*

B

bright·en /ˈbraɪtn/ *v*
1 MAKE LIGHTER [T] (*also* **brighten sth ↔ up**) to make something lighter or brighter: *Use blonde highlights to brighten your hair.* | *The morning sunshine brightened up the room.*
2 MAKE MORE ATTRACTIVE [T] (*also* **brighten sth ↔ up**) to make something more colourful or attractive: *She bought some flowers to brighten the room.* | *I want to brighten the place up a bit.*
3 MAKE MORE ENJOYABLE [T] (*also* **brighten sth ↔ up**) to make something more enjoyable, exciting, or interesting: *His letter brightened my day.* | *I felt I needed something to brighten up my life.*
4 BECOME LIGHTER/BRIGHTER [I] to shine more strongly, or become brighter in colour: *The stage lights brightened to reveal a street scene.*
5 BECOME SUNNY [I] (*also* **brighten up**) if the weather brightens, the sun begins to shine and it becomes lighter: *The sky brightened after lunch.* | *Let's hope the weather brightens up later.* | *It brightened up a bit in the afternoon.*
6 BECOME HAPPY [I] (*also* **brighten up**) to become happier or more excited: *His eyes brightened when we started talking about money.* | *She brightened up a bit when she saw us.*

brights /braɪts/ *n* [plural] *AmE* car HEADLIGHTS when they are shining as brightly as possible: *driving with your brights on*

brill /brɪl/ *adj BrE informal* very good: *It sounds really brill!*

bril·liance /ˈbrɪljəns/ *n* [U] **1** a very high level of intelligence or skill: *He is also respected for his brilliance as an artist.* **2** very great brightness: *The stars glittered with the brilliance of jewels.*

bril·liant /ˈbrɪljənt/ ●●● S2 W3 *adj*
1 BRIGHT brilliant light or colour is very bright and strong: *She closed her eyes against the **brilliant light**.* | *We sat outside in the **brilliant sunshine**.* | *She was dressed in brilliant white.* THESAURUS BRIGHT, COLOUR
2 CLEVER extremely clever or skilful: *I think that's a **brilliant idea**.* | *a brilliant performance* | *a brilliant young musician* THESAURUS INTELLIGENT
3 EXCELLENT *BrE* excellent: *The film was **absolutely brilliant**.* THESAURUS GOOD

GRAMMAR

In this meaning, **brilliant** is not used with 'very'. You say: *We had an absolutely brilliant time.* ✗ Don't say: *We had a very brilliant time.*
GRAMMAR GUIDE ADJECTIVES

4 SUCCESSFUL very successful: *He had a long and **brilliant career**.* | *The project was a **brilliant success**.* —**brilliantly** *adv*: *The sun was shining brilliantly.* | *The goalkeeper played brilliantly.*

bril·lian·tine /ˈbrɪljəntiːn/ *n* [U] an oily substance that was used in the past on men's hair

Bril·lo pad /ˈbrɪləʊ pæd $ -loʊ-/ *n* [C] *trademark* a ball of wire filled with soap, which is used for cleaning pans

brim[1] /brɪm/ *n* [C] **1** the bottom part of a hat that sticks out to protect you from sun and rain: *an old straw hat with a broad brim* → see picture at HAT **2** the top edge of a container: *She filled each glass to the brim.* | **filled/full to the brim** (=completely full) *The cup was filled to the brim with coffee.*

brim[2] *v* (**brimmed, brimming**) [I] **1** if your eyes brim with tears, or if tears brim from your eyes, you start to cry: **[+with]** *Her eyes brimmed with tears.* | *Her tears brimmed over again as she started to speak.* **2 be brimming (over) with sth** to have a lot of a particular thing, quality, or emotion: *The flowerbeds were brimming over with flowers.* | *He seemed to be **brimming with confidence**.* | *Rob was just brimming with enthusiasm.*

brim·ful /ˈbrɪmfʊl/ *adj* [not before noun] very full of something: **[+of]** *The team is brimful of confidence after their win last week.* | *a glass brimful of red wine*

brin·dled /ˈbrɪndld/ (*also* **brin·dle** /ˈbrɪndl/) *adj* a brindled animal is brown and has marks or bands of another colour —**brindle** *n* [C,U]

brine /braɪn/ *n* [U] **1** water that contains a lot of salt and is used for preserving food: *fish pickled in brine* **2** sea water

bring /brɪŋ/ ●●● S1 W1 *v* (*past tense and past participle* **brought** /brɔːt $ brɒːt/) [T]
1 a) to take something or someone with you to the place where you are now, or to the place you are talking about → **take**: *Did you bring an umbrella?* | *It was the first time Joey had ever **brought** a girl **home**.* | *They **brought news** of further fighting along the border.* | **bring sb/sth to sb/sth** *Is it OK if I bring some friends to the party?* | **bring sb/sth with you** *For some reason, Jesse had brought a tape recorder with him.* **b)** to get something for someone and take it to them: **bring sb sth** *Can you bring me another beer?* | *Robert asked the waiter to bring him the check.* | *While she was in prison, friends used to bring her books.* | **bring sb/sth to sb/sth** *He expects me to bring everything to him.* THESAURUS TAKE
2 a) to make a particular situation exist, or cause a particular feeling: *efforts to **bring peace** to the region* | *The strikes are expected to bring chaos.* | *The senator's speech brought an angry response from civil rights groups.* **b)** to cause someone or something to reach a particular state or condition: **bring sth to an end/close/halt/conclusion** (=make something stop) *The trial was swiftly brought to an end.* | *It was the war that first **brought** him **to power*** (=made him have power over a country). | *So far the US has been unable to **bring** him **to justice*** (=make him be punished for his actions). | ***Bring** the sauce **to the boil*** (=heat it until it boils). | *The country had been **brought to its knees*** (=caused to be in such a bad condition that it is almost impossible to continue).
3 [always + adv/prep] to make something move in a particular direction: **bring sth up/down/round etc** *Bring your arm up slowly until it's level with your shoulder.* | *The storm brought the old oak tree crashing down.*
4 [always + adv/prep] if something brings people to a place, it makes them go there: *The discovery of gold brought thousands of people to the Transvaal.* | **what brings you here?** (=used to ask why someone is in a particular place) *What brings you here on a night like this?*
5 to make something available for people to use, have, enjoy etc: *The expansion of state education brought new and wider opportunities for working class children.* | **bring sth to sb/sth** *The government is launching a new initiative to bring jobs to deprived areas.* | **bring sb sth** *It's a good sign – let's hope it will bring us some luck.*
6 if a period of time brings a particular event or situation, the event or situation happens during that time: *The 1930s brought unemployment and economic recession.* | *Who knows what the future will bring?*
7 bring charges/a lawsuit/a court case/a prosecution/a claim (against sb) to begin a court case in order to try to prove that someone has done something wrong or is legally responsible for something wrong: *Survivors of the fire later brought a billion-dollar lawsuit against the company.* | *The police say they are planning to bring charges against him.*
8 bring a smile to sb's lips/face to make someone smile: *Her words brought a sudden smile to his lips.*
9 bring tears to sb's eyes to make someone start to cry: *The pain brought tears to his eyes.*
10 bring the total/number/score etc to sth used when saying what the new total etc is: *This brings the total to 46.*

11 cannot/could not bring yourself to do sth to feel unable to do something because it would upset you or someone else too much: *She still can't bring herself to talk about it.*
12 *spoken* used when saying that something is the next thing that you want to talk about: **that/this/which brings me to ...** *This brings me to the main point of today's meeting.*
13 if a programme is brought to you by a particular television or radio company, they broadcast it or make it: **sth is brought to you by sb** *This programme is brought to you by the BBC.*
14 bring sth to bear (on/upon sth) *formal* to use something, for example your power, authority, or your knowledge, in a way that will have a big effect on something or someone: *The full force of the law was brought to bear on anyone who criticized the government.*
15 bring home the bacon *informal* to earn the money that your family needs to live

THESAURUS

bring to take something or someone to the place where you are now, or the place where you are going: *Have you brought your ticket with you? | He asked his father if he could bring a friend to stay.*
take to move something to another place, or help someone go to another place: *I took a book with me to read on the train. | He was taken to hospital by ambulance.*
get (*also* **fetch** *especially BrE*) to go to another place and come back with something or someone: *I went upstairs to get my jacket. | Joseph told me to fetch the doctor, so I ran to the village.*

bring sth ↔ **about** *phr v* to make something happen SYN **cause**: *How can we bring about a change in attitudes? | A huge amount of environmental damage has been brought about by the destruction of the rainforests.*
bring sb/sth ↔ **along** *phr v* to take someone or something with you when you go somewhere: *You're welcome to bring along a friend. | I've brought some pictures along to show you.*
bring sb/sth **around/round** *phr v*
1 bring the conversation around/round to sth to deliberately and gradually introduce a new subject into a conversation: *I'll try to bring the conversation around to the subject of money.*
2 to make someone become conscious again: *I slapped his face a couple of times to try to bring him round.*
3 to manage to persuade someone to do something or to agree with you: *She won't listen to me. Let's see if Sue can bring her round.* | **[+to]** *I'm sure I can bring him around to our point of view.*
4 to bring someone or something to someone's house: *I'll bring the books around tomorrow.*
bring back *phr v*
1 bring sth ↔ back to start to use something again that was used in the past SYN **reintroduce**: *The city council has decided to bring back the old electric trams. | Bringing back the death penalty has done absolutely nothing to reduce crime.*
2 bring sth ↔ back to make you remember something: *The trip* ***brought back*** *a lot of happy* ***memories****. | Seeing those pictures on TV* ***brought it all back*** *to me.*
3 bring sth ↔ back to take something or someone with you when you come back from somewhere: **bring sth back for sb** *Don't forget to bring something back for the kids.* | **bring sb back sth** *If you're going to the store, could you bring me back a six-pack?*
4 bring sb ↔ back to return someone to their previous job or position of authority SYN **reinstate**: *Following their latest defeat, soccer fans are urging the club to bring back the former manager.*
5 bring sb back to sth if something that is said brings you back to a particular subject, it is connected with that subject, so you will start talking about it again: *This brings us back to the question of funding.*
bring sb/sth ↔ **down** *phr v*
1 to reduce something to a lower level: *The government hopes these measures will help to bring down inflation.*
2 to fly a plane down to the ground SYN **land**: *The pilot managed to bring the plane down safely.*
3 to make a plane, bird, or animal fall to the ground by shooting at it: *A bomber had been brought down by anti-aircraft fire.*
4 to force a government or ruler to stop ruling a country: *a crisis that could bring down the government*
5 to make someone fall over: *He was brought down by the goalkeeper and awarded a penalty.*
bring sth ↔ **down on/upon** sb *phr v* to make something bad happen to someone, especially to yourself or to people connected with you: *His recklessness brought down disaster on the whole family.*
bring sth ↔ **forth** *phr v literary* to produce something or make it appear: *a tragic love affair that brought forth only pain*
bring sth ↔ **forward** *phr v*
1 to change an arrangement so that something happens sooner: **[+to]** *The meeting's been brought forward to Thursday.*
2 bring forward legislation/plans/policies etc to officially introduce plans etc for people to discuss: *The government has brought forward new proposals to tackle the problem of increasing crime.*
3 to record the result of a calculation so that it can be used in a further calculation: *The balance brought forward is £21,765.*
bring sb/sth ↔ **in** *phr v*
1 to introduce a new law: *Harsh anti-trade union laws were brought in in the early 1980s.*
2 to ask someone to become involved in a discussion or situation: *I'd like to bring in Doctor Hall here and ask him his views.* | **bring sb in to do sth** *The police were brought in to investigate the matter.*
3 to earn a particular amount or produce a particular amount of profit: *The sale of the house only brought in about £45,000.*
4 to attract customers to a shop or business: *We've got to bring in more business if we want the restaurant to survive.*
5 bring in a verdict to say officially in a law court whether someone is guilty or not guilty of a crime SYN **return a verdict**: *The jury brought in a verdict of not guilty.*
bring sb/sth **into** sth *phr v*
1 to cause someone or something to be in a particular situation: *Most of the land has now been brought into cultivation. | The work brought me into contact with a lot of very interesting people.*
2 to make someone become involved in a discussion or situation: *The government is trying to bring teachers into the debate on education. | There is a danger that this could bring other countries into the war.*
bring sth ↔ **off** *phr v* to succeed in doing something difficult SYN **pull off**: *They managed to bring off the most daring jewellery robbery in history.*
bring sth ↔ **on** *phr v*
1 to make something bad or unpleasant happen SYN **cause**: *Stress can bring on an asthma attack. | What's brought this on? Have I upset you somehow?*
2 to help someone to improve or make progress: *Teachers have to bring on the bright children and at the same time give extra help to those who need it.*
3 to make plants or crops grow faster: *Keeping the young plants in a greenhouse will help bring them on.*
4 bring it on *informal* used to say that you are prepared and willing to deal with something bad that is likely to happen
bring sth **on/upon** sb *phr v* to make something unpleasant happen to someone: *You have brought disaster on the whole village!* | **bring sth on/upon yourself** *I've got no sympathy for him – he's brought this all on himself!*
bring sb **onto** sth *phr v* if something brings you onto a particular subject, it is a good time for you to start talking about it: *This brings me onto the question of pay rises.*
bring sth ↔ **out** *phr v*
1 to make something easier to see, taste, notice etc: *The*

B

spices really bring out the flavour of the meat. | *Fatherhood seems to have brought out the caring side of him.*
2 to produce something that will be sold to the public: *He's bringing out a new album next month.*
3 to take something out of a place: *Jenny opened the cupboard and brought out a couple of bottles.*
4 bring out the best/worst in sb to make someone behave in the best or worst way that they can: *Alcohol just brings out the worst in her.*
5 bring sb out of himself/herself to make someone feel more confident and able to talk to people: *Changing schools has really brought her out of herself.*
bring sb **out in** sth *phr v* if something brings you out in spots, it makes them appear on your skin: *Any foods containing wheat bring him out in a rash.*
bring sb/sth **round** → **bring sb/sth around/round**
bring sb **through** (sth) *phr v* to help someone to successfully deal with a very difficult event or period of time: *Both my children have brought me through extremely difficult times since my husband died.*
bring sb ↔ **together** *phr v*
1 to arrange for people to meet and do something together: *We brought together researchers from three different universities to work on the project.*
2 to make people have a better relationship or feel closer to each other: *Any attack by a foreign power will inevitably bring the people of a country together.*
bring sb/sth ↔ **up** *phr v*
1 to mention a subject or start to talk about it SYN **raise**: *Why did you have to bring up the subject of money?*
2 to look after and influence a child until he or she is grown up SYN **raise**: *He was brought up by his grandparents.* | **bring sb up to do sth** *In my day, children were brought up to respect the law.* | **be brought up (as) a Catholic/Muslim etc** *I was brought up a Catholic.* → UPBRINGING
3 to make something appear on a computer screen: *Can you bring up the list of candidates again?*
4 *BrE* if you bring food up, it comes back up from your stomach and out of your mouth: *I had a sandwich for lunch and promptly brought it up again.*
5 to charge someone with a particular crime and make them go to a court to be judged: **[+before]** *He was brought up before a magistrate, charged with dangerous driving.*
6 bring sb up short/with a start to surprise someone and make them suddenly stop talking or doing something: *Her question brought me up short.*

brink /brɪŋk/ ●○○ *n*
1 the brink (of sth) a situation when you are almost in a new situation, usually a bad one: **on the brink of death/disaster/war etc** *In October 1962 the world seemed on the brink of nuclear war.* | *The company had huge debts and was on the brink of collapse.* | **to the brink (of sth)** *managers who have taken their companies to the brink of disaster* | **back from the brink (of sth)** *He will go down in history as the leader who pulled us back from the brink* (=saved us from disaster).
2 push/tip sb over the brink to make someone start doing crazy or extreme things
3 the brink of sth *literary* the edge of a very high place such as a cliff

brink·man·ship /ˈbrɪŋkmənʃɪp/ (*also* **brinks·man·ship** /ˈbrɪŋksmən-/ *AmE*) *n* [U] a method of gaining political advantage by pretending that you are willing to do something very dangerous

brin·y[1] /ˈbraɪni/ *adj* briny water is water that contains a lot of salt

briny[2] *n* **the briny** *old-fashioned* the sea

bri·o /ˈbriːəʊ $ -oʊ/ *n* [U] *literary* energy and confidence

bri·oche /ˈbriːɒʃ, briːˈəʊʃ $ briːˈoʊʃ, -ˈɔːʃ/ *n* [C,U] a type of sweet bread made with flour, eggs, and butter

bri·quette /brɪˈket/ *n* [C] a block of pressed coal dust, to burn in a fire or BARBECUE

brisk /brɪsk/ ●○○ *adj*
1 quick and full of energy: *a* ***brisk walk*** | *They set off at a* ***brisk pace.*** THESAURUS ▸ FAST
2 quick, practical, and showing that you want to get things done quickly: *Her tone of voice is brisk.*
3 trade or business that is brisk is very busy, with a lot of products being sold: *The public bar was already doing a* ***brisk trade.***
4 weather that is brisk is cold and clear —**briskly** *adv*: *They walked briskly.* —**briskness** *n* [U]

bris·ket /ˈbrɪskɪt/ *n* [U] meat from the chest of an animal, especially a cow

bris·tle[1] /ˈbrɪsəl/ *n* **1** [C,U] a short stiff hair that feels rough: *His chin was covered with bristles.* **2** [C] a short stiff hair, wire etc that forms part of a brush

bristle[2] *v* [I] **1** to behave in a way that shows you are very angry or annoyed: **bristle with rage/indignation etc** *John pushed back his chair, bristling with rage.* | **[+at]** *He bristled at her rudeness.* **2** if an animal's hair bristles, it stands up stiffly because the animal is afraid or angry
bristle with sth *phr v* to have a lot of something, or be full of something: *a battleship bristling with guns*

bris·tly /ˈbrɪsli/ *adj* **1** bristly hair is short and stiff **2** a bristly part of your body has short stiff hairs on it: *a bristly chin*

Brit /brɪt/ *n* [C] *informal* someone from Britain

ˈ**Brit A**ˌ**wards, the** (*also* **the Brits** *informal*) a set of prizes given every year at a public ceremony to the best British pop and rock musicians

britch·es /ˈbrɪtʃɪz/ *n* [plural] *old-fashioned* trousers

Brit·ish[1] /ˈbrɪtɪʃ/ *adj* relating to Britain or its people: *the British government* | *a British-born scientist* —**Britishness** *n* [U]

British[2] *n* **the British** [plural] people from Britain

Brit·ish·er /ˈbrɪtɪʃə $ -ər/ *n* [C] *AmE old-fashioned* someone from Britain

ˌ**British ˈSummer Time** *n* [U] (*written abbreviation* **BST**) the time one hour ahead of Greenwich Mean Time that is used in Britain from late March to late October → **daylight saving time**

Brit·on /ˈbrɪtn/ *n* [C] *formal* someone from Britain: *the ancient Britons* | *the first Briton to win a medal*

brit·tle /ˈbrɪtl/ *adj* **1** hard but easily broken: *The branches were dry and brittle.* | *Joanna was diagnosed as having brittle bones.* **2** a situation, relationship, or feeling that is brittle is easily damaged or destroyed: *He spoke with the brittle confidence of someone who, underneath, was very worried.* **3** showing no warm feelings: *a brittle laugh*

bro /brəʊ $ broʊ/ *n* (*plural* **bros**) [C] *spoken* **1** your brother **2** *AmE* a way of greeting a friend

broach /brəʊtʃ $ broʊtʃ/ *v* [T] **1 broach the subject/question/matter etc** to mention a subject that may be embarrassing or unpleasant or cause an argument: *I broached the subject of his past.* THESAURUS ▸ MENTION
2 to open a bottle or BARREL containing wine, beer etc

broad[1] /brɔːd $ brɒːd/ ●●● S2 W2 *adj*
1 WIDE a road, river, or part of someone's body etc that is broad is wide OPP **narrow** → **breadth**: *We went along a broad passage.* | *He was six feet tall, with broad shoulders.* | **six feet/three metres etc broad** *The room is three metres long and two metres broad.*

> **REGISTER**
> In everyday English, **wide** is more common than **broad**: *a* ***wide*** *river/street/corridor* | *They sell a* ***wide*** *range of bikes.*
> **Broad** is often used when describing someone's shoulders.

2 INCLUDING A LOT including many different kinds of things or people OPP **narrow** → **breadth**: *The show aims to reach the broadest possible audience.* | **broad range/spectrum** *Students here study a broad range of subjects.* | **broad category/field/area etc** *Private pension schemes fall into two broad categories.* | *a party which lacks a* ***broad base*** *of political support* | *The play is a comedy,* ***in the broadest sense of the word.***
3 GENERAL concerning the main ideas or parts of

something rather than all the details: *The client should understand, **in broad terms**, the likely cost of the case.* | **broad consensus/agreement etc** *The members were in broad agreement.* | **broad outline/framework** *I'll give you a broad outline of the plan.*
4 LARGE AREA covering a large area: *a broad expanse of water*
5 WAY OF SPEAKING a broad ACCENT clearly shows where you come from SYN **strong**: *a broad Scottish accent*
6 broad smile/grin a big smile: *Abby came in with a broad smile on her face.*
7 in broad daylight if something, especially a crime, happens in broad daylight, it happens in the daytime and in public: *The attack happened in broad daylight, in one of the busiest parts of town.*
8 broad hint a HINT (=suggestion) that is very clear and easy to understand: *In June he gave a broad hint that he might retire.*
9 a broad church *BrE* an organization that contains a wide range of opinions: *The Labour Party has to be a broad church.*
10 HUMOUR broad humour is rather rude or concerned with sex
11 broad in the beam *informal* having large or fat HIPS

broad[2] *n* [C] *AmE spoken not polite* an offensive word for a woman

B-road /'bi: rəʊd $ -roʊd/ *n* [C] a type of road in Britain that is smaller than an A-ROAD

broad·band /'brɔːdbænd $ 'brɒːd-/ ●●○ *n* [U]
1 *technical* a system of sending radio signals, that allows several messages to be sent at the same time
2 a system of connecting computers to the Internet and moving information, such as messages or pictures, at a very high speed —**broadband** *adj* [only before noun]: *broadband communications*

,broad 'bean / $ '../ *n* [C] *BrE* a round pale green bean

broad·brush /'brɔːdbrʌʃ $ 'brɒːd-/ *adj* [only before noun] dealing only with the main parts of something, and not with the details SYN **general**: *a broadbrush strategy*

broad·cast[1] /'brɔːdkɑːst $ 'brɒːdkæst/ ●●○ *n* [C] a programme on the radio or on television: *a news broadcast* | *CNN's **live broadcast** of the trial* (=sent out at the same time as the events are happening)

broadcast[2] ●●○ *v* (*past tense and past participle* **broadcast**)
1 [I,T] to send out radio or television programmes: *The interview was **broadcast live** across Europe.*
2 [T] to tell something to a lot of people: *Don't broadcast the fact that he lost his job.*

broad·cast·er /'brɔːdkɑːstə $ 'brɒːdkæstər/ *n* [C] **1** someone who speaks on radio or television programmes: *a well-known broadcaster* **2** a company that sends out television or radio programmes: *the British broadcaster Channel 4*

broad·cast·ing /'brɔːdkɑːstɪŋ $ 'brɒːdkæstɪŋ/ *n* [U] the business of making television and radio programmes: *a career in broadcasting*

broad·en /'brɔːdn $ 'brɒːdn/ ●○○ *v*
1 [T] to increase something such as your knowledge, experience, or range of activities: *The course helps school-leavers broaden their knowledge of the world of work.* | *I'd like to work abroad to **broaden** my **horizons*** (=learn, experience, or attempt new things). | *Travel **broadens** the **mind*** (=helps you to understand and accept other people's beliefs, customs etc).
2 [I,T] to affect or include more people or things, or to make something affect or include more people or things SYN **widen, expand**: *Mr Mates said the party must broaden its appeal to younger voters.* | *Flynn's appeal broadened as the campaign continued into the summer months.* | *I want to broaden the discussion to other aspects of the problem.*
3 [I,T] to make something wider, or to become wider SYN **widen**: *Mark's smile broadened.* | *The council decided to broaden the pavement.*

broaden out *phr v* if something, especially a river or road, broadens out, it becomes wider SYN **widen out**: *The river broadens out at this point.*

'broad jump *n AmE* **the broad jump** the LONG JUMP

broad·leaved /'brɔːdliːvd $ 'brɒːd-/ *adj technical* a broadleaved tree or plant has wide leaves rather than leaves shaped like needles

broad·loom /'brɔːdluːm $ 'brɒːd-/ *n* [U] CARPET that is woven in a single wide piece

broad·ly /'brɔːdli $ 'brɒːd-/ ●○○ *adv*
1 in a general way, relating to the main facts rather than details: *She knows broadly what to expect.* | **broadly similar/comparable/equivalent etc** *We reached broadly similar conclusions.* | ***Broadly speaking**, there are four types of champagne.* | *Independent films are, **broadly defined**, movies that appeal to sophisticated audiences.*
2 smile/grin broadly to have a big smile on your face that clearly shows that you are happy or amused
3 including a range of different things or subjects: *a **broadly based** school curriculum* | *We invest broadly to lessen the risk.*

broad·mind·ed, broad-minded /ˌbrɔːd'maɪndɪd◂ $ ˌbrɒːd-/ *adj* willing to respect opinions or behaviour that are very different from your own OPP **narrow-minded**: *Her parents were broadminded, tolerant, and liberal.* —**broad-mindedness** *n* [U] → SMALL-MINDED

broad·sheet /'brɔːdʃiːt $ 'brɒːd-/ *n* [C] a newspaper printed on large sheets of paper, especially a serious newspaper → **tabloid** THESAURUS NEWSPAPER

broad·side[1] /'brɔːdsaɪd $ 'brɒːd-/ *n* [C] **1** a strong criticism of someone or something: *Can the government survive this latest broadside from its own supporters?* **2** an attack in which all the guns on one side of a ship are fired at the same time

broadside[2] *adv* with the longest side facing something SYN **sideways**: **[+to]** *I brought the boat in broadside to the beach.*

broadside[3] *v* [T] *especially AmE* to crash into the side of another vehicle

ˌbroad-'spectrum *adj* [only before noun] broad-spectrum chemicals or medicines are effective against a wide range of PESTS, diseases etc

broad·sword /'brɔːdsɔːd $ 'brɒːdsɔːrd/ *n* [C] a heavy sword with a broad flat blade

bro·cade /brə'keɪd $ broʊ-/ *n* [C,U] thick heavy decorative cloth that has a pattern of gold and silver threads: *brocade curtains* | *deluxe brocades and satins* —**brocaded** *adj*

broc·co·li /'brɒkəli $ 'brɑː-/ *n* [U] a green vegetable that has short branch-like stems → see picture at VEGETABLE[1]

bro·chure /'brəʊʃə, -ʃʊə $ broʊ'ʃʊr/ ●●○ *n* [C] a thin book giving information or advertising something: *a holiday brochure*

brogue /brəʊg $ broʊg/ *n* [C] **1** [usually plural] a thick strong leather shoe with a pattern in the leather: *a new pair of brogues* **2** [usually singular] an ACCENT, especially an Irish or Scottish accent

broil /brɔɪl/ *v AmE* **1** [T] to cook something under direct heat, or over a flame on a BARBECUE SYN **grill**: *broiled chicken* **2** [I] to become very hot: *We lay broiling in the sun.*

broil·er /'brɔɪlə $ -ər/ *n* [C] **1** *AmE* a special area of a STOVE, used for cooking food under direct heat SYN **grill** *BrE* **2** a broiler chicken

'broiler ˌchicken *n* [C] a chicken that is suitable to be cooked by broiling

broil·ing /'brɔɪlɪŋ/ *adj AmE* broiling weather, sun etc makes you feel extremely hot SYN **boiling**: *a broiling day*

broke[1] /brəʊk $ broʊk/ *v* the past tense of BREAK

broke[2] *adj* [not before noun] **1** having no money: *I'm fed up with being broke all the time.* | **flat/stony broke** (=completely broke) **2 go broke** if a company or business goes broke, it can no longer operate because it has no money: *A lot of small businesses went broke in the recession.* **3 go for broke** *informal* to take big risks when you try to achieve something: *At 2-0 down with ten minutes left, you have to go for broke.* **4 if it ain't broke, don't fix it** *informal* used to say that you should not try to improve a system, situation etc that is satisfactory

bro·ken¹ /ˈbrəʊkən $ ˈbroʊ/ *v* the past participle of BREAK

BROKEN

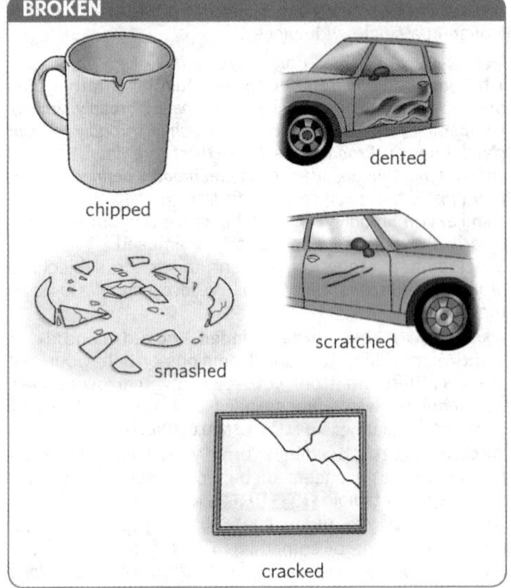

broken² ●●● S3 W2 *adj*
1 PIECE OF EQUIPMENT not working properly: *The CD player's broken again. | Do you know how the phone* **got broken** (=became broken)?
2 OBJECT in small pieces because it has been hit, dropped etc: *Mind the broken glass. | Wrap it up well so it doesn't* **get broken** (=become broken) *in the mail.*
3 BONE cracked because you have had an accident: *a badly broken leg | Gibbs had an X-ray, which revealed no broken bones.*
4 NOT CONTINUOUS interrupted and not continuous: *a broken white line | a long noisy night of broken sleep*
5 PERSON extremely weak mentally or physically because you have suffered a lot: *He returned from the war a broken man.*
6 broken English/French etc if you speak in broken English, French etc, you speak slowly and make a lot of mistakes because you know only a little of the language
7 broken home a family that no longer lives together because the parents have DIVORCEd: *The majority of offenders do not come from broken homes.*
8 broken marriage a marriage that has ended because the husband and wife do not live together anymore
9 a broken heart a feeling of extreme sadness, especially because someone you love has died or left you: *I reckon she died of a broken heart.*
10 a broken society a society which has many social and financial problems: *This report paints a depressing picture of Britain's broken society.*

THESAURUS

broken if something is broken, it does not work properly: *I think my watch is broken. | The camera got broken when we were on holiday.*
out of order [not before noun] if a machine, especially one used by the public, is out of order, it is not working for a temporary period: *Every phone I tried was out of order. | The toilets were all out of order.*
down [not before noun] if a computer system is down, it is not working: *The computer system was down all afternoon, so we went home.* | **go down** (=stop working): *The network went down at 11:00 and we lost the whole morning's work.*
there's something wrong with sth used when saying that a car, machine etc does not work properly and you do not know why: *There's something wrong with my car; I think it might be the battery.*
sth has had it *informal* used when saying that a car, machine etc is completely broken and cannot be repaired: *I'm afraid the bike's had it.*

ˌbroken-ˈdown *adj* not working, or in very bad condition: *a broken-down truck*

ˌbroken-ˈhearted *adj* extremely sad, especially because someone you love has died or left you SYN **heartbroken**: *He was broken-hearted when she left.*

bro·ken·ly /ˈbrəʊkənli $ ˈbroʊ-/ *adv written* if you say something brokenly, you speak in short phrases with a lot of pauses, because you are feeling a strong emotion

bro·ker¹ /ˈbrəʊkə $ ˈbroʊkər/ ●○○ *n* [C]
1 someone who buys and sells things such as SHARES in companies or foreign money for other people → STOCKBROKER
2 someone who arranges sales or business agreements for other people: *a real estate broker*

broker² *v* [T] **broker a deal/settlement/treaty etc** to arrange the details of a deal etc so that everyone can agree to it: *a ceasefire agreement brokered by the UN*

bro·ker·age /ˈbrəʊkərɪdʒ $ ˈbroʊ-/ *n* [U] **1** the business of being a broker **2** the amount of money a broker charges **3 brokerage house/firm** a company of brokers, or the place where they work

brol·ly /ˈbrɒli $ ˈbrɑːli/ *n* (*plural* **brollies**) [C] *BrE informal* an UMBRELLA

bro·mance /ˈbrəʊmæns $ ˈbroʊ-/ *n* [C] a very close friendship between two men, or a film about this – used especially in newspapers and magazines

bro·mide /ˈbrəʊmaɪd $ ˈbroʊ-/ *n* **1** [C,U] a chemical that is sometimes used in medicine to make people feel calm **2** [C] *formal* a statement that is intended to make someone less angry but which is not effective

bronc /brɒŋk $ brɑːŋk/ *n* [C] *AmE informal* a BRONCO

bron·chi·al /ˈbrɒŋkiəl $ ˈbrɑːŋ-/ *adj medical* affecting the bronchial tubes: *a bronchial infection*

ˈbronchial ˌtube *n* [C] *medical* one of the tubes that take air into your lungs

bron·chi·tis /brɒŋˈkaɪtɪs $ brɑːŋ-/ *n* [U] an illness that affects your bronchial tubes and makes you cough —**bronchitic** /-ˈkɪtɪk/ *adj*

bron·co /ˈbrɒŋkəʊ $ ˈbrɑːŋkoʊ/ *n* (*plural* **broncos**) [C] a wild horse from the western US: *a bucking bronco*

bron·to·sau·rus /ˌbrɒntəˈsɔːrəs $ ˌbrɑːn-/ *n* [C] a large DINOSAUR with a small head and a long neck

Bronx cheer /ˌbrɒŋks ˈtʃɪə $ ˌbrɑːŋks ˈtʃɪr/ *n* [C] *AmE* a sound that you make by sticking out your tongue and blowing, often considered rude SYN **raspberry** *BrE*

bronze¹ /brɒnz $ brɑːnz/ ●●○ *n*
1 [U] a hard metal that is a mixture of COPPER and TIN: *a bell cast in bronze*
2 [U] the dark reddish brown colour of bronze
3 [C] a work of art such as a STATUE (=model of a person), made of bronze: *three bronzes by Giacometti*
4 [C,U] a BRONZE MEDAL: *King won a bronze in the 100-metres.*

bronze² ●●○ *adj*
1 made of bronze: *a bronze statuette*
2 having the dark reddish brown colour of bronze

ˈBronze Age *n* **the Bronze Age** the time, between about 6,000 and 4,000 years ago, when bronze was used for making tools, weapons etc → IRON AGE, STONE AGE

bronzed /brɒnzd $ brɑːnzd/ *adj* having skin that is attractively brown because you have been in the sun SYN **tanned**

ˌbronze ˈmedal *n* [C] a MEDAL made of bronze given to the person who comes third in a race or competition: *The bronze medal went to Nool of Estonia.* —**bronze medallist** *BrE*, **bronze medalist** *AmE n* [C]: *an Olympic bronze medallist* → GOLD MEDAL, SILVER MEDAL

brooch /brəʊtʃ $ broʊtʃ/ *n* [C] a piece of jewellery that you fasten to your clothes, usually worn by women SYN **pin** *AmE*

brood¹ /bru:d/ *v* [I] **1** to keep thinking about something that you are worried or upset about: *Don't sit at home brooding all day.* | **[+over/about/on]** *There's no point brooding over it – she's gone.* THESAURUS THINK **2** if a bird broods, it sits on its eggs to make the young birds break out

brood² *n* [C] **1** a family of young birds all born at the same time **2** a family with a lot of children – used humorously: **[+of]** *Mary has a whole brood of grandchildren.*

brood·ing /ˈbru:dɪŋ/ *adj literary* **1** mysterious and threatening: *the brooding silence of the forest* **2** looking thoughtful and sad: *brooding eyes* —**broodingly** *adv*

ˈ**brood mare** *n* [C] a MARE (=female horse) that is kept for breeding

brood·y /ˈbru:di/ *adj* **1** *BrE informal* wishing that you had a baby: *I get broody when I see baby clothes.* **2** silent because you are thinking or worrying about something: *Damian's been broody lately.* **3** if a female bird is broody, it wants to lay eggs or to sit on them to make the young birds break out —**broodiness** *n* [U]

brook¹ /brʊk/ *n* [C] a small stream: *a babbling brook*

brook² *v* **not brook sth/brook no sth** *formal* to not allow or accept something: *He would brook no criticism, even from his beloved daughter.*

ˌ**Brooklyn ˈBridge, the** a bridge in New York that connects Brooklyn with Manhattan. It is a famous LANDMARK on the New York SKYLINE (=shape made by buildings against the sky). If something is difficult to believe, people sometimes talk about 'selling the Brooklyn Bridge', because this is something that is very unlikely to happen.

broom /bru:m, brʊm/ ●●○ *n*
1 [C] a large brush with a long handle, used for sweeping floors → see picture at BRUSH¹
2 [U] a large bush with small yellow flowers

broom·stick /ˈbru:mˌstɪk, ˈbrʊm-/ *n* [C] a broom with a long handle and thin sticks tied at one end that a WITCH is supposed to fly on in stories

Bros. (*also* **Bros** *BrE*) /brɒs $ brɒ:s/ the written abbreviation of ***Brothers***, used in the names of companies: *Warner Bros.*

broth /brɒθ $ brɒ:θ/ *n* [C,U] soup with meat, rice, or vegetables: *chicken broth* → SCOTCH BROTH

broth·el /ˈbrɒθəl $ ˈbrɑ:-, ˈbrɒ:-/ *n* [C] a house where men pay to have sex with PROSTITUTES

broth·er¹ /ˈbrʌðə $ -ər/ ●●● S1 W1 *n* [C]
1 a male who has the same parents as you → **sister**: *I have two brothers, William and Mark.* | **elder/older/younger etc brother** *My younger brother is a doctor.* | **little/kid brother** (=younger brother) *I have to take my little brother to school.* | *My* ***big brother*** (=older brother) *has always looked after me.* | *my twin brother*
2 *spoken informal* a word meaning a black man, used especially by other black men
3 a male member of a group with the same interests, religion, profession etc as you
4 (*plural* **brothers** *or* **brethren**) a male member of a religious group, especially a MONK: *Brother Justin*
5 *AmE* a member of a FRATERNITY (=a club of male university students)
6 brothers in arms *literary* soldiers who have fought together in a war → BLOOD BROTHER, HALF-BROTHER, STEPBROTHER

brother² *interjection especially AmE* used to show you are annoyed or surprised: *Oh, brother – I really don't want to deal with this now.*

broth·er·hood /ˈbrʌðəhʊd $ -ər-/ *n* **1** [U] a feeling of friendship between people: *the spirit of brotherhood* **2** [C] an organization formed for a particular purpose, especially a religious one: *the Franciscan brotherhood* **3** [C] *old-fashioned* a union of workers in a particular trade **4** [U] the relationship between brothers

ˈ**brother-in-law** ●●○ *n* (*plural* **brothers-in-law**) [C]
1 the brother of your husband or wife
2 the husband of your sister
3 the husband of your husband or wife's sister → **sister-in-law**

broth·er·ly /ˈbrʌðəli $ -ər-/ *adj* showing feelings of kindness, loyalty etc that you would expect a brother to show → **sisterly**: *brotherly love* | *brotherly advice*

brough·am /ˈbru:əm/ *n* [C] a carriage used in the past, that had four wheels and a roof and was pulled by a horse

brought /brɔ:t $ brɒ:t/ the past tense and past participle of BRING

brou·ha·ha /ˈbru:hɑ:hɑ: $ bru:ˈhɑ:hɑ:/ *n* [singular, U] unnecessary excitement, criticism, or activity – used especially in news reports to show disapproval: *the pre-election brouhaha*

brow /braʊ/ ●○○ *n* [C]
1 *literary* the part of your face above your eyes and below your hair SYN **forehead**: **mop/wipe your brow** (=dry your brow with your hand or a cloth because you are hot or nervous) | **your brow furrows/creases/wrinkles** (=lines appear on your brow because you are thinking or are worried) *His brow furrowed. 'I don't understand,' he said.*
2 an EYEBROW
3 the brow of a hill the top part of a slope or hill

brow·beat /ˈbraʊbi:t/ *v* (*past tense* **browbeat**, *past participle* **browbeaten** /-bi:tn/) [T] to try to make someone do something, especially in a threatening way: **browbeat sb into doing sth** *She was determined to browbeat everyone into believing her.*

brown¹ /braʊn/ ●●● S2 W2 *adj*
1 having the colour of earth, wood, or coffee: *dark brown hair*
2 having skin that has been turned brown by the sun: *He'd been on vacation and looked very brown.* | *He was as* ***brown as a berry*** *after two weeks in the sun.*

brown² ●●● S2 W2 *n* [C,U] the colour of earth, wood, or coffee: *This particular model is available in brown, white, or grey.* | *the browns and greens of the landscape*

brown³ *v* [I,T] **1** to heat food so that it turns brown, or to become brown by being heated: *First, brown the meat in a pan.* **2** to become brown because of the sun's heat, or to make something brown in this way: *The children's faces were browned by the sun.* **3 browned off** *BrE informal* annoyed or bored SYN **fed up**: *They are* ***getting browned off*** *by the situation.*

ˈ**brown-bag** *v* [I] *AmE* **1** to bring your LUNCH to work, usually in a brown paper bag **2** to bring your own alcohol to a restaurant that does not serve alcohol —**brown-bagging** *n* [U]

brown·field site /ˈbraʊnfi:ld ˌsaɪt/ *n* [C] *BrE* a place, especially in a city, that is used for building homes, offices etc, where in the past there have already been buildings, industries etc → **greenfield site**

ˈ**brown goods** *n* [plural] *BrE* electrical goods that provide entertainment at home, such as televisions and computers → WHITE GOODS

brown·ie /ˈbraʊni/ *n* [C] a thick flat chocolate cake

ˈ**brownie ˌpoints** *n* [plural] **get/win/score brownie points** *informal* if you do something in order to get brownie points from your teacher, boss etc, you do it in order to make them have a good opinion of you: *I'm not doing it just to get brownie points.*

ˈ**brown-nose** *v* [I,T] *informal* to try to make someone in authority like you by being very nice to them – used to show disapproval —**brown-noser** *n* [C] —**brown-nosing** *n* [U]

brown·out /ˈbraʊnaʊt/ *n* [C] *AmE* a time when the amount of electrical power supplied to an area is reduced

ˌ**brown ˈrice** *n* [U] rice that still has its outer layer

brown·stone /ˈbraʊnstəʊn $ -stoʊn/ *n* [C] a house in the US with a front made of reddish-brown stone, common in New York City

B

ˌbrown ˈsugar *n* [U] a type of sugar that is brown in colour and contains MOLASSES

browse /braʊz/ ●●○ *v*
1 [I] to look through the pages of a book, magazine etc without a particular purpose, just looking at the most interesting parts: **[+through]** *Jon was browsing through the photographs.*
2 [I,T] to look at the goods in a shop without wanting to buy any particular thing: **[+around]** *The trip allows you plenty of time for browsing around the shops.* | *tourists browsing the boutiques and souvenir stalls*
3 [I,T] to search for information on a computer or on the Internet: *a feature that allows you to browse your hard drive and choose the graphic you want to display*
4 [I] if a goat, DEER etc browses, it eats plants —**browse** *n* [singular]: *We had a quick browse around the shops.*

brows·er /ˈbraʊzə $ -ər/ ●●○ *n* [C] a computer program that finds information on the Internet and shows it on your computer screen: *a Web browser*

Bruce, Rob·ert (the) /ˈrɒbət $ ˈrɑːbərt/ (1274-1329) the King of Scotland from 1306 till his death. Scotland was recognized as independent under him in 1328. The story that most people know about Robert the Bruce is that he watched a SPIDER trying to make a WEB. Each time the spider failed, it started again. This showed determination, which encouraged Bruce to do the same.

bruise¹ /bruːz/ ●●○ *n* [C]
1 a purple or brown mark on your skin that you get because you have fallen, been hit etc: *minor cuts and bruises* THESAURUS ➤ INJURY
2 a mark on a piece of fruit that spoils its appearance

bruise² ●○○ *v*
1 [I,T] if part of your body bruises, or if you bruise part of your body, it gets hit or hurt and a bruise appears: *She fell off her bike and bruised her knee.* THESAURUS ➤ HURT
2 [T] to affect someone badly and make them feel less confident: **bruise sb's pride/ego** *The incident had bruised his pride.*
3 [I,T] if a piece of fruit bruises, or is bruised, it gets a bruise by being hit, dropped etc —**bruised** *adj*: *a badly bruised knee* | *a bruised ego*

bruis·er /ˈbruːzə $ -ər/ *n* [C] *informal* a big strong man who likes fighting or arguing

bruis·ing¹ /ˈbruːzɪŋ/ *n* [U] purple or brown marks that you get on your skin where you have fallen, been hit etc: **[+to/on]** *She **suffered** severe **bruising** to her arms and legs.*

bruising² *adj* difficult and unpleasant, and leaving you feeling tired or emotionally harmed: *a bruising contest*

Brum·mie /ˈbrʌmi/ *n* [C] *BrE informal* someone from the city of Birmingham in England —**Brummie** *adj*

brunch /brʌntʃ/ ●●○ *n* [C,U] a meal eaten in the late morning, as a combination of breakfast and LUNCH

bru·nette /bruːˈnet/ *n* [C] a woman with dark brown hair → **blonde**

brunt /brʌnt/ *n* **bear/take/suffer etc the brunt of sth** to receive the worst part of an attack, criticism, bad situation etc: *an industry that bore the brunt of the recession* | *The car took **the full brunt** of the explosion.*

brush¹ /brʌʃ/ ●●● S3 *n*
1 OBJECT FOR CLEANING/PAINTING [C] an object that you use for cleaning, painting, making your hair tidy etc, made with a lot of hairs, BRISTLES, or thin pieces of plastic, fastened to a handle → **broom**: *a scrubbing brush* → HAIRBRUSH, NAILBRUSH, PAINTBRUSH, TOOTHBRUSH, see picture at MAKE-UP
2 TREES [U] **a)** small bushes and trees that cover an area of land **b)** branches that have broken off bushes and trees
3 MOVEMENT [singular] a movement in which you brush something to remove dirt, make something smooth, tidy etc: *I'll just **give** my hair a quick **brush**.*
4 TOUCH [singular] a quick light touch, made by chance when two things or people pass each other: *the brush of her silk dress as she walked past*
5 [C] a time when you only just avoid an unpleasant situation or argument: **[+with]** *His first **brush with the law** came when he was 16.* | *A **brush with death** can make you appreciate life more.*
6 TAIL [C] the tail of a FOX

BRUSHES

brush² ●●● S3 *v*
1 CLEAN/MAKE TIDY [T] to clean something or make something smooth and tidy using a brush → **sweep**: *Don't forget to brush your teeth.*
2 REMOVE [T always + adv/prep] to remove something with a brush or with your hand: **brush sth off/from etc sth** *Ella brushed the crumbs off her jacket.* | *He brushed the tears from his eyes.* → see picture at CLEAN²
3 TOUCH LIGHTLY [I always + adv/prep, T] to touch someone or something lightly when passing them: *Something brushed her shoulders.* | **[+against]** *I felt her hair brush against my arm.* | **[+past]** *Nell brushed past him in the doorway.*
4 PUT STH ON STH [T always + adv/prep] to put a liquid onto something using a brush: **brush sth with sth** *Brush the pastry with milk.* | **brush sth over/onto sth** *Brush a little oil over the top of the pizza.* → **brush sth under the carpet** at SWEEP¹(15)

brush sb/sth ↔ **aside** *phr v* to refuse to listen to someone, or refuse to consider something SYN **dismiss**: *He simply brushed all my objections aside.*

brush sb/sth ↔ **down** *phr v*
1 to clean something using a brush: *He was brushing the pony down.*
2 brush yourself down to use your hands to remove dirt from your clothes, especially after you have fallen

brush sb/sth ↔ **off** *phr v* to refuse to listen to someone or their ideas, especially by ignoring them or saying something rude: *Corman brushed off the accusations.* → BRUSH-OFF

brush up (on) sth *phr v* to practise and improve your skills or your knowledge of something that you learned in the past: *I must brush up on my French before I go to Paris.*

brushed /brʌʃt/ *adj* [only before noun] brushed cloth has been made so it is soft: *brushed cotton*

ˈbrush-off *n* [singular] rude or unfriendly behaviour that shows you are not interested in someone: *She **gave** him **the brush-off**.* | *I tried to be friendly but I just **got the brush-off**.* → **brush off** at BRUSH²

brush·wood /ˈbrʌʃwʊd/ *n* [U] small dead branches broken from trees or bushes

brush·work /ˈbrʌʃwɜːk $ -wɜːrk/ *n* [U] the way in which an artist puts paint on a picture using a brush

brusque /bruːsk, brʊsk $ brʌsk/ *adj* using very few words, in a way that seems rude SYN **abrupt**: *a brusque manner* —**brusquely** *adv* —**brusqueness** *n* [U]

Brus·sels sprout /ˌbrʌsəlz ˈspraʊt/ *n* [C] a small round green vegetable that looks like a very small CABBAGE → see picture at **VEGETABLE**[1]

bru·tal /ˈbruːtl/ ●○○ *adj*

1 very cruel and violent: **brutal murder/attack/assault** *a brutal attack on a defenceless old man* | *a brutal man*
THESAURUS ▸ **CRUEL, VIOLENT**

2 not pleasant and not sensitive to people's feelings: *He replied with* ***brutal honesty***. —**brutally** *adv*: *He was brutally murdered.* | *If I'm brutally honest, I don't like her dress.*

bru·tal·ist, **Brutalist** /ˈbruːtlɪst/ *adj* brutalist buildings are large buildings made of CONCRETE, with no decoration —**brutalism** *n* [U]

bru·tal·i·ty /bruːˈtæləti/ *n* (*plural* **brutalities**) [C,U] cruel and violent behaviour, or an event involving cruel and violent treatment: *allegations of police brutality* | **[+of]** *the brutalities of war*

bru·tal·ize (*also* **-ise** *BrE*) /ˈbruːtəl-aɪz/ *v* [T] **1** to affect someone so badly that they lose their normal human feelings: *He was brutalized by his experiences in jail.* **2** to treat someone in a cruel or violent way: *Demonstrators claimed they had been brutalized by police officers.* —**brutalization** /ˌbruːtl-aɪˈzeɪʃən $ -tl-ə-/ *n* [U]

brute[1] /bruːt/ *n* [C] a man who is cruel, violent, and not sensitive

brute[2] *adj* **1 brute force/strength** physical strength, rather than intelligence and careful thinking: *Discussion can be more effective than the use of brute force.* **2** [only before noun] simple and not involving any other facts or qualities: *The brute fact is that the situation will not improve.* | *brute stupidity*

brut·ish /ˈbruːtɪʃ/ *adj* cruel and not sensitive to people's feelings —**brutishness** *n* [U]

Bryl·creem /ˈbrɪlkriːm/ *n* [U] *trademark* a type of oil used on men's hair to make it shiny and smooth

B.S. /ˌbiː ˈes/ *n AmE* **1** [C] (***Bachelor of Science***) a first university DEGREE in a science subject SYN **BSc** *BrE* → **B.A.**: **[+in]** *a B.S. in Biology* **2** [U] *not polite* the abbreviation of ***bullshit***

BSc, **B.Sc.** /ˌbiː es ˈsiː/ *n* [C] *BrE* (***Bachelor of Science***) a first university DEGREE in a science subject SYN **B.S.** *AmE*: **[+in]** *He's going to Birmingham to* ***do*** *a* ***BSc*** *in Biochemistry.* | *Catherine McBride, BSc*

BSE /ˌbiː es ˈiː/ *n* [U] (***bovine spongiform encephalopathy***) a serious brain disease that affects cows SYN **mad cow disease**

B-side /ˈbiː saɪd/ *n* [C] **1** the side of a record that has the less well-known song on it **2** the song on this side of the record

BST /ˌbiː es ˈtiː/ *n* [U] the abbreviation of ***British Summer Time***

B2B /ˌbiː tə ˈbiː/ *adj* (***business to business***) used to refer to business activities between companies, especially using the Internet

BTEC /ˈbiːtek/ *n* [C,U] (***Business and Technical Education Council***) a range of examinations that are done by students in England and Wales at different levels in a variety of subjects relating to work. BTEC courses are usually done after the age of 17. → **GNVQ**: *a BTEC Diploma in Art and Design*

BTW, **btw** the written abbreviation of ***by the way***, often used in email or TEXT MESSAGES on MOBILE PHONES

bub /bʌb/ *n* [C] *AmE old-fashioned* used to speak to a man, especially when you are angry: *Hey, what do you think you're doing, bub?*

bub·ble[1] /ˈbʌbəl/ ●●○ *n* [C]

1 a ball of air or gas in liquid: *When water boils, bubbles rise to the surface.* | *soap bubbles* | *She was* ***blowing bubbles*** *in her milk with a straw.*

2 a small amount of air trapped in a solid substance: *Examine the glass carefully for bubbles.*

3 a bubble of sth *literary* a small amount of a feeling: *A bubble of anger rose in Pol's throat.*

4 (*also* **speech bubble**) a circle around the words said by someone in a CARTOON

5 a situation in which the prices of something such as company SHARES or houses increase a lot very quickly, so they are too high and will quickly come down again: *Eager investors created a stock market bubble.*

6 the bubble bursts used for saying that a very successful or happy period of time suddenly ends: *The bubble has finally burst in the mobile phone industry.*

7 burst/prick sb's bubble to make someone suddenly realize that something is not as good as they thought it was

bubble[2] *v* [I] **1** to produce bubbles: *Heat the cheese until it bubbles.* | **[+up]** *The cola bubbled up when I unscrewed the lid.* **2** to make the sound that water makes when it boils: **[+away]** *The water was bubbling away on the stove.* **3** (*also* **bubble over**) to be excited: **[+with]** *Mary was bubbling over with excitement.* **4** (*also* **bubble away/up**) if a feeling or activity bubbles, it continues to exist: *Resentment was still bubbling inside her.* | *Speculation that he plans to resign has been bubbling away for months.*

ˌbubble and ˈsqueak *n* [U] a British dish of potatoes and CABBAGE mixed together and cooked in fat

ˈbubble bath *n* **1** [U] a liquid soap that smells pleasant and makes bubbles in your bath water **2** [C] a bath with this in the water

ˈbubble gum *n* [U] a type of CHEWING GUM that you can blow into a bubble

ˈbubble jet ˌprinter *n* [C] a type of machine for printing from a computer, that SPRAYS ink onto the paper

ˈbubble wrap (*also* **ˈbubble pack**) *n* [U] a sheet of plastic covered with bubbles of air, used for wrapping and protecting things

bub·bly[1] /ˈbʌbli/ *adj* **1** always happy, friendly, and eager to do things: *She has a very bubbly personality.* **2** full of bubbles

bubbly[2] *n* [U] *informal* CHAMPAGNE: *a glass of bubbly*

bu·bon·ic plague /bjuːˌbɒnɪk ˈpleɪg $ buːˌbɑː-/ *n* [U] a very serious disease spread by rats, that killed a lot of people in the Middle Ages → **Black Death**

buc·ca·neer /ˌbʌkəˈnɪə $ -ˈnɪr/ *n* [C] **1** someone who attacks ships at sea and steals from them SYN **pirate** **2** someone who is very successful, especially in business, but may not be honest

buck[1] /bʌk/ *n* [C]

1 DOLLAR *informal* a US, Canadian, or Australian dollar: *He owes me ten bucks.* | *The movie is about a group of men trying to* ***make a buck*** (=earn some money) *as male strippers.* | **big/mega bucks** (=a lot of money) *Using celebrities in advertising is guaranteed to pull in big bucks.* | **make a fast/quick buck** (=make some money quickly, often dishonestly)

2 the buck stops here (*also* **the buck stops with sb**) used to say that a particular person is responsible for something: *The buck stops firmly with the boss.*

3 pass the buck to make someone else responsible for something that you should deal with

4 feel/look like a million bucks *especially AmE informal* to feel or look very healthy, happy, and beautiful

5 ANIMAL (*plural* **buck** *or* **bucks**) a male rabbit, DEER, and some other male animals → **doe**

6 MAN *old-fashioned* a young man → **(get) a bigger/better etc bang for your buck** at BANG[1](5)

buck[2] *v*

1 HORSE [I] if a horse bucks, it kicks its back feet into the air, or jumps with all four feet off the ground

2 MOVE SUDDENLY [I] to suddenly move up and down, or backwards and forwards, in an uncontrolled way: *The plane bucked sharply.*

3 OPPOSE [I,T] to oppose something in a direct way: *He was a rebel who* ***bucked*** *the* ***system*** (=opposed rules or

authority). | *Unemployment in the area has* **bucked** *the* **trend** *by falling over the last month.* | **[+against]** *Initially, he had bucked against her restraints.*
4 MAKE SB HAPPIER [T] to make someone feel more happy, confident, or healthy: *He was bucked by the success he'd had.* | *She gave me a tonic which bucked me a little.*
buck for sth *phr v* to try very hard to get something, especially a good position at work: *He's bucking for promotion.*
buck up *phr v*
1 to become happier, or to make someone happier: *Come on, buck up, things aren't that bad!* | **buck sb ↔ up** *You need something to buck you up.*
2 buck up! *BrE old-fashioned* used to tell someone to hurry up: *Buck up, John! We'll be late.*
3 *informal* to improve, or to make something improve: *It'll be a long time before the situation starts to buck up.* | **buck sth ↔ up** *a company that is looking to buck up its networking capabilities*
4 buck your ideas up *BrE informal* used to tell someone to improve their behaviour or attitude
buck³ *adv AmE* **buck naked** not wearing any clothes
buck·a·roo /ˌbʌkəˈruː/ *n* [C] *AmE informal* a COWBOY – used especially when talking to children
buck·board /ˈbʌkbɔːd $ -bɔːrd/ *n* [C] a light vehicle with four wheels that is pulled by a horse, and was used in the US in the 19th century
buck·et¹ /ˈbʌkɪt/ ●●● S2 *n* [C]
1 an open container with a handle, used for carrying and holding things, especially liquids SYN **pail**
2 (*also* **bucketful**) the quantity of liquid that a bucket can hold: **[+of]** *a bucket of water*
3 a part of a machine shaped like a large bucket and used for moving earth, water etc
4 *informal* a large amount of something: *They were drinking beer by the bucket.* | **[+of]** *They made buckets of cash on the deal.*
5 weep buckets *informal* to cry a lot
6 in buckets *informal* if rain comes down in buckets, it is raining very hard → **kick the bucket** at KICK¹(20), → **a drop in the bucket** at DROP²(8)
bucket² *v*
bucket down *phr v BrE informal* to rain very hard SYN **pour**: *It's been bucketing down all day.*
ˈ**bucket list** *n* [C] a list of things that you want to do before you die: *Swimming with dolphins is one of the things on my bucket list.*
ˈ**bucket seat** *n* [C] a car seat with a high curved back, for one person
ˈ**bucket shop** *n* [C] *BrE informal* a place that sells cheap plane tickets
Buck·ing·ham Pa·lace /ˌbʌkɪŋəm ˈpælɪs/ (*also* **the Palace**) the official home of the British royal family in London. Since 1995, some parts of the building have been open to tourists. The name of the Palace is sometimes used to mean the officials who are in charge of organizing the Queen's public life: *Buckingham Palace announced today that Her Majesty will be visiting Japan next year.*
buck·le¹ /ˈbʌkəl/ *v*
1 BEND [I,T] to become bent or curved because of heat or pressure, or to make something bend or curve in this way: *The steel pillars began to buckle.* | **[+under]** *The rails buckled under the intense heat of the fire.*
2 KNEES/LEGS [I] if your knees or legs buckle, they become weak and bend SYN **give way**: *John felt his knees start to buckle.*
3 DO STH YOU DO NOT WANT [I] to do something that you do not want to do because a difficult situation forces you to do it SYN **give in**: *He refused to buckle.* | **buckle under the pressure/strain/weight** *A weaker person would have buckled under the weight of criticism.*
4 FASTEN [I,T] to fasten a buckle, or be fastened with a buckle: *Amy buckled the belt around her waist.* | **buckle sth on/up/together** *Lou was buckling on his revolver.*
buckle down *phr v* to start working very hard: **[+to]** *You'd better buckle down to some revision now.*
buckle up *phr v* to fasten your SEAT BELT in a car, aircraft etc
buckle² *n* [C] a piece of metal used for fastening the two ends of a belt, for fastening a shoe, bag etc, or for decoration
buck·ram /ˈbʌkrəm/ *n* [U] stiff cloth, used in the past for covering books and making the stiff parts of clothes
Buck's Fizz /ˌbʌks ˈfɪz/ *n* [C,U] *BrE* a mixture of CHAMPAGNE and orange juice, or a glass of this
buck·shot /ˈbʌkʃɒt $ -ʃɑːt/ *n* [U] a lot of small metal balls that are fired together from a gun
buck·skin /ˈbʌkˌskɪn/ *n* [U] strong soft leather made from the skin of a DEER or goat
ˌ**buck ˈteeth** *n* [plural] teeth that stick forward out of your mouth —**buck-toothed** /ˌbʌk ˈtuːθt◂/ *adj*
buck·wheat /ˈbʌkwiːt/ *n* [U] a type of small grain used as food for chickens, and for making flour
bu·col·ic /bjuːˈkɒlɪk $ -ˈkɑː-/ *adj literary* relating to the countryside → **pastoral**
bud¹ /bʌd/ ●○○ *n* [C]
1 a young tightly rolled-up flower or leaf before it opens: *rose buds* | **in bud** (=having buds but no flowers yet) | **come into bud** (=start to produce buds) → see picture at TREE
2 *AmE spoken* BUDDY: *Hey, bud, how's it going?* → **COTTON BUD, TASTE BUD,** → **nip sth in the bud** at NIP¹(3)
bud² *v* (**budded, budding**) [I] to produce buds
Bud·dhis·m /ˈbʊdɪzəm $ ˈbuː-, ˈbʊ-/ *n* [U] a religion of east and central Asia, based on the teaching of Gautama Buddha —**Buddhist** *n* [C] —**Buddhist** *adj*
bud·ding /ˈbʌdɪŋ/ *adj* **1 budding artist/actor/writer etc** someone who is just starting to paint, act etc and will probably be successful at it **2** [only before noun] beginning to develop: *a budding romance*
bud·dy /ˈbʌdi/ *n* (*plural* **buddies**) [C] **1** *informal* a friend: *We're good buddies.* THESAURUS▸ FRIEND **2** *AmE spoken* used to talk to a man or boy, especially one you do not know: *Hey, buddy! This your car?*
ˈ**buddy-buddy** *adj informal especially AmE* **be buddy-buddy (with sb)** to be very friendly with someone
ˈ**buddy list** *n* [C] a place on a computer where you keep a list of the names of people that you regularly send INSTANT MESSAGES to
ˈ**buddy ˌsystem** *n* [C] *AmE* a system in which two people in a group are put together to help each other or keep each other safe
budge /bʌdʒ/ *v* [I,T usually in negatives] **1** to move, or to make someone or something move: *She leaned on the door, but it wouldn't budge.* | **[+from]** *Will hasn't budged from his room all day.* | *The horse refused to* **budge an inch**. THESAURUS▸ MOVE **2** to change your opinion, or to make someone change their opinion: *The government has refused to budge.* | **[+on]** *He won't budge on the issue.* | **[+from]** *Treacy refuses to budge from his principles.*
bud·ge·ri·gar /ˈbʌdʒərɪɡɑː $ -ɡɑːr/ *n* [C] *BrE formal* a BUDGIE
bud·get¹ /ˈbʌdʒɪt/ ●●○ S3 W3 *n* [C]
1 the money that is available to an organization or person, or a plan of how it will be spent: **[+of]** *a welfare program with a budget of $2 million* | **[+for]** *The budget for photography has been cut.* | *We had a really* **tight budget**. | **on/within budget** (=not using more money than planned) *The project was completed within budget.* | **under budget** (=using less money than planned) *If you come in under budget, everyone will be very impressed.* | **over budget** (=using more money than planned) *Feature movies always run over budget.*
2 on a budget if you are on a budget, you do not have much money to spend: *Travellers on a budget might prefer to camp.* | *a book which offers great ideas for decorating on a budget* | *families* **on a tight budget**
3 (*also* **Budget**) *BrE* an official statement that a government makes about how much it intends to spend and what taxes will be necessary

COLLOCATIONS

ADJECTIVES/NOUN + budget

an annual/monthly/weekly budget *The organization has an annual budget of $24 million.*
the national/federal/state budget *He has a plan to balance the federal budget.*
the defence/education etc budget *We had to make cuts in the defence budget.*
the family/household budget *Often the husband and wife contribute equally to the family budget.*
a big/large budget *The club does not have a large budget for new players.*
a small/low/limited budget *It was a project with a low budget.*
a tight budget (=small and limited) | **a fixed budget**

VERBS

have a budget *Hospital caterers have a budget of about £20 per person per week.*
overspend your budget *The Metropolitan Police has overspent its budget by £70 million.*
keep within a budget (=spend only the money that is available) | **balance the budget** (=spend only the money that is available)

budget + NOUN

a budget deficit (=when a government has spent more money than it has) *The country has a budget deficit of over $4 billion.*
a budget surplus (=when a government has more money than it spends) *A huge budget surplus of over £16 billion was recorded.*
budget cuts (=reductions in the amount of money that is available)

budget² *v* [I,T] **1** to carefully plan and control how much money you spend and what you will buy with it: *We'll have to budget more carefully.* | *This scheme enables you to budget the cost through fixed monthly payments.* | **[+for]** *We've budgeted for a new car next year.* **2** if you budget something such as time, you decide how much of it you will need —**budgeting** *n* [U]

budget³ *adj* [only before noun] **1** very low in price – often used in advertisements SYN **cheap**: *budget flights* THESAURUS CHEAP **2 low-budget/big-budget** used for saying how much money has been spent on doing something, especially making a film: *low-budget movies*

bud·get·a·ry /ˈbʌdʒətəri $ -teri/ *adj* relating to the way money is spent in a budget THESAURUS FINANCIAL

bud·gie /ˈbʌdʒi/ *n* [C] *BrE* a small brightly coloured bird that people keep as a pet

buff¹ /bʌf/ *n* **1 wine/film/opera etc buff** someone who is interested in wine, films etc and knows a lot about them THESAURUS EXPERT **2** [U] a pale yellow-brown colour SYN **beige 3 in the buff** *old-fashioned* not wearing any clothes SYN **naked**

buff² (*also* **buff up**) *v* [T] to polish something with a cloth: *Sandra was buffing her nails.*

buff up *phr v informal* to exercise in order to make your muscles bigger: *Smith buffed up for his role as Muhammad Ali.*

buff³ *adj* **1** having a pale yellow-brown colour: *buff envelopes* **2** *informal* attractive and looking as if you do a lot of exercise – used especially by young people: *He's so buff!*

buf·fa·lo /ˈbʌfələʊ $ -loʊ/ *n* (*plural* **buffaloes** *or* **buffalo**) [C] **1** an African animal similar to a large cow with long curved horns → WATER BUFFALO **2** a BISON

buff·er¹ /ˈbʌfə $ -ər/ *n* [C]
1 PROTECTION someone or something that protects one thing or person from being harmed by another: **[+against]** *Eastern Europe was important to Russia as a buffer against the West.* | **[+between]** *She often had to act as a buffer between father and son.*
2 RAILWAY one of the two special metal springs on the front or back of a train or at the end of a railway track, to take the shock if the train hits something
3 buffer zone an area between two armies, that is intended to separate them so that they do not fight
4 buffer state a smaller country between two larger countries, that makes war between them less likely
5 COMPUTER a place in a computer's memory for storing information temporarily
6 PERSON *BrE old-fashioned* an old man who is not good at managing things: *He's a nice old buffer.*
7 FOR POLISHING something used to polish a surface
8 run into/hit the buffers *informal* an activity or plan that hits the buffers is stopped and does not succeed

buffer² *v* [T] **1** to reduce the bad effects of something: *Consumer spending is buffering the effects of the recession.* **2** if a computer buffers information, it holds it for a short while before using it

buf·fet¹ /ˈbʊfeɪ $ bəˈfeɪ/ ●○○ *n* [C]
1 a meal at a party or other occasion, in which people serve themselves at a table and then move away to eat: *a cold buffet* | **buffet breakfast/lunch/supper** *The price includes morning coffee, buffet lunch, and afternoon tea.*
2 a place in a railway station, bus station etc where you can buy and eat food or drink
3 *AmE* a piece of furniture in which you keep the things you use to serve and eat a meal SYN **sideboard** *BrE*

buf·fet² /ˈbʌfɪt/ *v* [T] **1** if something, especially wind, rain, or the sea, buffets something, it hits it with a lot of force: *London was buffeted by storms last night.* | *High winds buffeted the region.* **2** *literary* to treat someone unkindly: *I was weary of being buffeted by life.* —**buffeting** *n* [C,U]

buffet sth **about** *phr v* to move something in one direction and then another, again and again, with force: *The body was buffeted about in the waves.*

buffet car /ˈbʊfeɪ kɑː $ bəˈfeɪ kɑːr/ (*also* **buffet**) *n* [C] *BrE* a part of a train where you can buy food and drink

buf·foon /bəˈfuːn/ *n* [C] *old-fashioned* someone who does silly amusing things —**buffoonery** *n* [U]

bug¹ /bʌg/ ●●○ S3 *n* [C]
1 *informal* an illness that people catch very easily from each other but is not very serious: **catch/pick up/get a bug** *I picked up a bug last weekend.* | *There's* ***a*** *nasty* ***bug going round*** (=that a lot of people have caught). | **tummy/stomach bug** (=illness affecting your stomach) *He's off work with a stomach bug.* | *a 24-hour* ***flu bug*** THESAURUS ILLNESS
2 *especially AmE* a small insect
3 a fault in the system of instructions that operates a computer: *a bug in the software* → DEBUG THESAURUS FAULT
4 a small piece of electronic equipment for listening secretly to other people's conversations
5 *informal* a sudden strong interest in doing something: **the travel/sailing etc bug** *She's got the travel bug.* | *I had one flying lesson and immediately* ***caught the bug*** (=became very interested in flying).

bug² *v* (**bugged**, **bugging**) [T] **1** *informal* to annoy someone: *It just bugs me that I have to work so many extra hours for no extra money.* | *The baby's crying is really bugging him.* **2** to put a BUG (=small piece of electronic equipment) somewhere secretly in order to listen to conversations: *Do you think the room is bugged?*

bug·a·boo /ˈbʌgəbuː/ *n* [C] *AmE* something that makes people anxious or afraid

bug·bear /ˈbʌgbeə $ -ber/ *n* [C] something that makes people feel annoyed or worried: *Paperwork is our worst bugbear.*

bug·eyed /ˌbʌgˈaɪd◂/ *adj* having eyes that stick out

bug·ger¹ /ˈbʌgə $ -ər/ *n* [C] *not polite* **1** *BrE* an offensive word for someone who is very annoying or unpleasant **2** someone that you pretend to be annoyed with, although you actually like or love them: *The poor little bugger got an awful shock.* **3** *BrE* a job or activity that is very difficult: *The exam was a bit of a bugger.* **4 bugger all** *BrE* nothing: *There's bugger all wrong with this machine.*

bugger² *v* [T] *BrE* **1** *spoken not polite* said when you are annoyed or angry: *Bugger it! I don't see why I should pay for everything.* **2 I'm buggered/bugger me!** *spoken not polite* said when you are surprised about something: *Well I'm buggered! I never thought you'd do that.* **3 I'm buggered if ...** *spoken not polite* used to say that you do not know something, will not do something, or are not able to do something: *I'm buggered if I can remember.* **4 bugger the ...** *spoken not polite* used to say that you do not care about the person or thing you are talking about: *Bugger the expense – I'm going to buy it!* **5** *taboo or law* to have ANAL sex with someone

bugger about/around *phr v spoken not polite* **1** to behave in a stupid way or waste time SYN **mess about/around**: *Let's stop buggering about and go.* **2 bugger sb about** to cause unnecessary problems for someone SYN **mess sb about/around**: *Don't let Peter bugger you about.*

bugger off *phr v spoken not polite* to go away or leave a place: *Tim buggered off to Australia years ago.* | *'Bugger off!' she screamed.*

bugger sth ↔ **up** *phr v spoken not polite* to ruin something or do something very badly SYN **cock up, mess up**: *It really buggered up our plans when the train was cancelled.*

bug·gered /ˈbʌɡəd $ -ərd/ *adj* [not before noun] *BrE spoken not polite* **1** extremely tired **2** completely ruined or broken: *The washing machine's buggered.*

bug·ger·y /ˈbʌɡəri/ *n* [U] *BrE law* ANAL sex

bug·gy /ˈbʌɡi/ *n* (*plural* **buggies**) [C] **1** *BrE* a light folding chair on wheels that you push small children in SYN **pushchair, stroller** *AmE* **2** a light carriage pulled by a horse **3** *AmE* a small bed on wheels, that a baby lies in SYN **baby carriage, pram** *BrE*

bu·gle /ˈbjuːɡəl/ *n* [C] a musical instrument like a TRUMPET, that is used in the army to call soldiers —**bugler** *n* [C]

build¹ /bɪld/ ●●● S1 W1 *v* (*past tense and past participle* **built** /bɪlt/)

1 MAKE STH [I,T] to make something, especially a building or something large: *The purpose is to build new houses for local people.* | *The road took many years to build.* | *They needed $3 million to build the bridge.* | *It is the female birds that build the nests.* | *Developers want to build on the site of the old gasworks.* | *a row of recently built houses* | **build sb sth** *He's going to build the children a doll's house.* → see picture at ASSEMBLE

2 MAKE STH DEVELOP (*also* **build up**) [T] to make something develop or form: *She had built a reputation as a criminal lawyer.* | *She's been busy building her career.* | *Ross took 20 years to build up his business.* | **build (up) a picture of sb/sth** (=form a clear idea about someone or something) *We're trying to build up a picture of what happened.*

3 be built of sth to be made using particular materials: *The church was built of brick.*

4 FEELING (*also* **build up**) [I,T] if a feeling builds, or if you build it, it increases gradually over a period of time: *Tension began to build as they argued more frequently.* | *In order to build your self-esteem, set yourself targets you can reach.*

5 build bridges to try to establish a better relationship between people who do not like each other: *Peter needs to try and build bridges with Lizzie.*

build sth **around** sth *phr v* to base something on an idea or thing and develop it from there: *Successful businesses are built around good personal relationships.*

build sth ↔ **in** *phr v* to make something so that it is a permanent part of a wall, room etc: *You could build in a wardrobe with mirrored doors.* → BUILT-IN

build sth **into** sth *phr v*

1 to make something so that it is a permanent part of a wall, room etc: *There are three cash machines* ***built into the wall.***

2 to make something a permanent part of a system, agreement etc: *Opportunities for reviewing the timings should be built into the plan.*

build on *phr v*

1 build sth on sth to base something on an idea or thing: *Our relationship is built on trust.*

2 build on sth to use your achievements as a base for further development: *The new plan will build on the success of the previous programme.*

3 to add another room to a building in order to have more space: **build sth ↔ on** *We're planning to build on a conservatory.*

build up *phr v*

1 INCREASE GRADUALLY if something builds up somewhere, or if you build it up, it gradually becomes bigger or greater: *the rate at which the pension builds up* | **build sth ↔ up** *The museum has built up a fine art collection.* → BUILD-UP

2 DEVELOP **build sth ↔ up** to make something develop or form: **[+into]** *He's built up the family firm into a multinational company.*

3 FEELING if a feeling builds up, or if you build it up, it increases gradually over a period of time: *If you don't express your feelings, frustration and anger can build up.* | **build up sth** *You have to build up trust.*

4 MAKE HEALTHY **build sb/sth ↔ up** to make someone well and strong again, especially after an illness: *Taking exercise will build up your strength.*

5 PRAISE **build sb/sth ↔ up** to praise someone or something so that other people think they are really good, or so that they have more confidence: *The coach has been building his men up before the match.*

6 build up sb's hopes (*also* **build sb's hopes up**) to unfairly encourage someone to think that they will get what they hope for: *Don't build your hopes up too much.*

build up to sth *phr v* to prepare for a particular moment or event: *I could tell she was building up to some kind of announcement.*

build² ●○○ *n* [singular, U] the shape and size of someone's body → **built**: *a woman of* ***slim build*** | *You're a surprisingly strong swimmer for one of such a* ***slight build.*** | *I wanted a more* ***athletic*** *and* ***muscular build.***

build·er /ˈbɪldə $ -ər/ ●●○ S3 *n* [C] *especially BrE* a person or a company that builds or repairs buildings

build·ing /ˈbɪldɪŋ/ ●●● S1 W1 *n*

1 [C] a structure such as a house, church, or factory, that has a roof and walls: *The offices are on the top two floors of the building.* | *a farmhouse and other farm buildings*

2 [U] the process or business of building things → **construction**: *There is a limited supply of land for building.* | *stone, timber, and other building materials* | **[+of]** *The enquiry recommended the building of a tunnel.*

COLLOCATIONS

VERBS

put up a building (*also* **erect a building** *formal*) *They keep pulling down the old buildings and putting up new ones.*

pull down/knock down/tear down a building *All the medieval buildings were torn down.*

demolish/destroy a building (=pull it down) *Permission is needed to demolish listed buildings.*

ADJECTIVES/NOUN + building

a tall building *The park was surrounded by tall buildings.*

a high-rise building (=very tall with many floors)

a low building *That low building is a stable block.*

an office/school/hospital etc building *Our office building is just ten minutes' walk from where I live.*

a public building *The town has a number of interesting public buildings, including the old town hall.*

a beautiful building (*also* **a fine/handsome building** *BrE*) | **an impressive/imposing building** | **a brick/stone/wooden building** | **a two-storey/three-storey etc building** (=with two, three etc floors) | **a single-storey/one-storey building** (=with only one floor) | **a historic building** (=an old building of historical interest)

a listed building *BrE* (=a historic building that is protected by a government order) *The school is actually a listed building.*

a derelict building (=empty and in very bad condition) | **a dilapidated building** (=in bad condition)
a ramshackle building (*also* **a tumbledown building** *BrE*) (=old and almost falling down) *The farm was surrounded by tumbledown buildings.*

ˈbuilding ˌblock *n* [C] **1** a block of wood or plastic for young children to build things with → see picture at BLOCK[1] **2 building blocks** [plural] the pieces or parts that together make it possible for something big or important to exist: *Amino acids are the building blocks of protein.*

ˈbuilding conˌtractor / $ ˈ.. ˌ.../ *n* [C] someone whose job is to organize the building of a house, office, factory etc

ˈbuilding ˌsite *n* [C] a place where a house, factory etc is being built

ˈbuilding soˌciety *n* [C] *BrE* a type of bank that you pay money into in order to save it and earn interest, and that will lend you money to buy a house or apartment SYN **savings and loan association** *AmE*

ˈbuild-up *n* [C usually singular] **1** an increase over a period of time: **[+of]** *a heavy build-up of traffic on the motorway* **2** a description of someone or something before an event, in which you say they are very special or important: *The presenter* ***gave*** *her* ***a big build-up***. **3** the length of time spent preparing an event: *I was running 20 miles a week in my build-up for the race.* → **build up** at BUILD[1]

built[1] /bɪlt/ the past tense and past participle of BUILD

built[2] *adj* used to describe someone's size or shape → **build**: *She is built like a dancer.* | *a heavily built man*

ˌbuilt enˈvironment *n* [singular] *especially BrE* places where there are buildings and roads, and not the countryside

ˌbuilt-ˈin ●○○ *adj* forming a part of something that cannot be separated from it → **inbuilt**: *a built-in microphone*

ˌbuilt-ˈup *adj* a built-up area has a lot of buildings and not many open spaces: *He was fined for speeding in a built-up area.*

bulb /bʌlb/ ●●○ *n* [C]
1 the glass part of an electric light, that the light shines from SYN **light bulb**: *a 100-watt bulb*
2 a root shaped like a ball that grows into a flower or plant: *tulip bulbs* → see picture at TREE

bul·bous /ˈbʌlbəs/ *adj* fat, round, and unattractive: *a bulbous nose*

bulge[1] /bʌldʒ/ *n* [C] **1** a curved mass on the surface of something, usually caused by something under or inside it: *The gun made a bulge under his jacket.* **2** a sudden temporary increase in the amount or level of something: *a bulge in the birthrate* —**bulgy** *adj*

bulge[2] (*also* **bulge out**) *v* [I] to stick out in a rounded shape, especially because something is very full or too tight: **[+with]** *His pockets were bulging with candy.* | *He fell heavily to the floor, his* ***eyes bulging*** *wide with fear.*

bu·lim·i·a /bjuːˈlɪmiə, bʊ-, -ˈliː-/ *n* [U] an illness in which a person cannot stop themselves from eating too much, and then VOMITs in order to control their weight —**bulimic** *adj*

bulk[1] /bʌlk/ ●○○ AWL *n*
1 the bulk (of sth) the main or largest part of something: *The bulk of consumers are based in towns.*
2 [C usually singular] a big mass or shape of something: *the great bulk of a building* THESAURUS SIZE
3 [U] the size of something or someone: *The dough will rise until it is double in bulk.*
4 in bulk if you buy goods in bulk, you buy large amounts each time you buy them

bulk[2] *adj* **1 bulk buying/orders etc** the buying etc of goods in large quantities at one time **2** [only before noun] bulk goods are sold or moved in large quantities: *bulk flour for commercial bakeries* **3 bulk mail** if you send something bulk mail, you send large amounts of it for a smaller cost than normal

bulk[3] *v* **bulk large** to be the main or most important part of something

bulk sth ↔ **out** *phr v* to make something bigger or thicker by adding something else: *We can bulk out the report with lots of diagrams.*

bulk up *phr v* to increase the amount of muscle you have

bulk·head /ˈbʌlkhed/ *n* [C] a wall that divides the structure of a ship or aircraft into separate parts

bulk·y /ˈbʌlki/ AWL *adj* **1** something that is bulky is bigger than other things of its type, and is difficult to carry or store: *a bulky parcel* **2** someone who is bulky is big and heavy: *Andrew is a bulky man.* —**bulkiness** *n* [U]

bull[1] /bʊl/ ●●○ *n*
1 MALE COW [C] an adult male animal of the cattle family: *a herd of cows with one bull*
2 MALE ANIMAL [C] the male of some other large animals such as the ELEPHANT or WHALE
3 take the bull by the horns to bravely or confidently deal with a difficult, dangerous, or unpleasant problem: *Nora decided to take the bull by the horns and organize things for herself.*
4 NONSENSE [U] *informal* nonsense or something that is completely untrue SYN **rubbish**: *What a load of bull!*
5 like a bull in a china shop if you are like a bull in a china shop, you keep knocking things over, dropping things, breaking things etc
6 like a bull at a gate if you move somewhere like a bull at a gate, you move there very fast, ignoring everything in your way
7 RELIGION [C] an official statement from the Pope
8 CENTRE [C] (*also* **bullseye**) the centre of a TARGET that you are shooting at
9 BUSINESS [C] *technical* someone who buys SHARES because they expect prices to rise → **bear** → **BULL MARKET** → **cock and bull story** at COCK[1](4), → **like a red rag to a bull** at RED[1](5), → **shoot the bull** at SHOOT[1](13)

bull[2] *interjection* used to say that you do not believe or agree with what someone has said: *Bull! Where did you get that idea?*

ˈbull bars *n* [plural] *BrE* a set of metal bars fixed to the front of a large vehicle such as a Jeep or Land Rover, in order to protect it from damage —**bullbarred** /ˈbʊlbɑːd $ -bɑːrd/ *adj*: *bullbarred vehicles*

bull·dog /ˈbʊldɒg $ -dɒːg/ *n* [C] a powerful dog with a large head, a short neck, and short thick legs

ˈBulldog ˌclip *n* [C] *trademark BrE* a small metal object that shuts tightly to hold papers together → see picture at STATIONERY

bull·doze /ˈbʊldəʊz $ -doʊz/ *v* [T] **1** to destroy buildings etc with a bulldozer **2** to push objects such as earth and rocks out of the way with a bulldozer **3 bulldoze sb into (doing) sth** to force someone to do something that they do not really want to do

bull·doz·er /ˈbʊldəʊzə $ -doʊzər/ *n* [C] a powerful vehicle with a broad metal blade, used for moving earth and rocks, destroying buildings etc

bul·let /ˈbʊlɪt/ ●●○ *n* [C] a small piece of metal that you fire from a gun → **shell**, **shot**: *He was killed by a single bullet.* | *a* ***bullet wound*** *in the shoulder* | *Several* ***bullet holes*** *could be seen beside a window.* → **PLASTIC BULLET**, → **bite the bullet** at BITE[1](9)

bul·le·tin /ˈbʊlətɪn/ ●●○ *n* [C]
1 a news report on radio or television
2 an official statement that tells people about something important
3 a letter or printed statement that a group or organization produces to tell people its news

ˈbulletin ˌboard *n* [C] **1** *AmE* a board on the wall that you put information or pictures on SYN **noticeboard** *BrE* **2** a place in a computer information system where you can read or leave messages

ˈbullet point *n* [C] a thing in a list that consists of a word or short phrase, with a small printed symbol in front of it

ˈbullet-ˌproof *adj* something that is bullet-proof is

designed to stop bullets from going through it: *an inch-thick wall of bullet-proof glass*

ˈbullet train *n* [C] a very fast passenger train, especially in Japan

bull·fight /ˈbʊlfaɪt/ *n* [C] a type of entertainment popular in Spain, in which a person fights and kills a BULL —**bullfighter** *n* [C] —**bullfighting** *n* [U]

bull·finch /ˈbʊlˌfɪntʃ/ *n* [C] a small grey and red European bird

bull·frog /ˈbʊlfrɒg $ -frɑːg, -frɒːg/ *n* [C] a kind of large FROG that makes a loud noise

ˌbull-ˈheaded *adj* determined to get what you want without really thinking enough about it —**bullheadedly** *adv*

bull·horn /ˈbʊlhɔːn $ -hɔːrn/ *n* [C] *AmE old-fashioned* a piece of equipment that you hold up to your mouth to make your voice louder SYN **megaphone** *BrE*

bul·lion /ˈbʊljən/ *n* [U] bars of gold or silver: *gold bullion*

bul·lish /ˈbʊlɪʃ/ *adj* **1** [not before noun] feeling confident about the future: *He's very bullish about the company's prospects.* **2** *technical* in a business market that is bullish, the prices of SHARES are rising or seem likely to rise → **bearish** —**bullishly** *adv* —**bullishness** *n* [U]

ˈbull ˌmarket *n* [C] *technical* a STOCK MARKET in which the price of SHARES is going up and people are buying them → **bear market**

bull·necked /ˌbʊlˈnekt◂/ *adj* having a short and very thick neck

bul·lock /ˈbʊlək/ *n* [C] a young male cow that cannot breed

ˈbull pen *n* [C] **1** the area in a baseball field in which PITCHERS practise throwing **2** the PITCHERS of a baseball team

bull·ring /ˈbʊlˌrɪŋ/ *n* [C] the place where a BULLFIGHT is held

ˈbull ˌsession *n* [C] *AmE informal* an occasion when a group of people meet to talk in a relaxed and friendly way: *an all-night bull session*

bulls·eye, **bull's-eye** /ˈbʊlzaɪ/ *n* [C] **1** the centre of a TARGET that you try to hit when shooting or in games like DARTS SYN **bull** **2** *BrE* a large hard round sweet

bull·shit¹ /ˈbʊlˌʃɪt/ *n* [U] *spoken not polite* something that is stupid and completely untrue SYN **rubbish**: *Forget all that bullshit and listen to me!* | *What he told me was a **load of bullshit**.*

bullshit² *v* (**bullshitted**, **bullshitting**) [I,T] to say something stupid or completely untrue, especially in order to deceive someone or make them think you are important —**bullshitter** *n* [C]

ˌbull ˈterrier *n* [C] a strong short-haired dog → **PIT BULL TERRIER**

bul·ly¹ /ˈbʊli/ ●●○ *n* (*plural* **bullies**) [C] someone who uses their strength or power to frighten or hurt someone who is weaker: *Bullies are often cowards.*

bully² ●●○ *v* (**bullied**, **bullying**, **bullies**) [T]
1 to threaten to hurt someone or frighten them, especially someone smaller or weaker
2 to put pressure on someone in order to make them do what you want: **bully sb into (doing) sth** *Don't let them bully you into working on Saturdays.* —**bullying** *n* [U]: *an attempt to tackle the problem of bullying in schools*

bully off *phr v BrE* to start a game of HOCKEY —**bully-off** *n* [C]

bully³ *adj* **bully for you/him etc** *spoken* used when you do not think that someone has done anything special but they want you to praise them: *Yes, I know you've done all the dishes. Bully for you!*

ˈbully boy *n* [C] *BrE informal* someone who behaves in a violent and threatening way

bul·rush /ˈbʊlrʌʃ/ *n* [C] a tall plant that looks like grass and grows by water

bul·wark /ˈbʊlwək $ -wərk/ *n* [C] **1** something that protects you from an unpleasant situation: **[+against]** *a bulwark against dictatorship* **2** **bulwarks** [plural] the sides of a boat or ship above the DECK **3** a strong structure like a wall, built for defence

bum¹ /bʌm/ ●○○ *n* [C] *informal*
1 *BrE* the part of your body that you sit on SYN **bottom**
2 *AmE* someone, especially a man, who has no home or job, and who asks people for money
3 beach/ski etc bum someone who spends all their time on the beach, SKIing etc without having a job
4 someone who is very lazy
5 get/put bums on seats *BrE informal* to make a large number of people go to see a film, play, sports match etc: *She's the kind of star who will put bums on seats.*
6 give sb the bum's rush *informal* to make someone leave a place, especially a public place, quickly

bum² *v* (**bummed**, **bumming**) [T] *BrE informal* to ask someone for something such as money, food, or cigarettes SYN **cadge**: *She bummed a little cash off me.*

bum around *phr v informal* **1** (*also* **bum about**) to spend time lazily doing nothing **2 bum around sth** to travel around, living very cheaply, without having any plans: *He spent a year bumming around Australia.*

bum³ *adj* [only before noun] *informal* **1** bad and useless: *The orchestra was excellent. No one played a bum note.* | *Jim got **a bum deal** (=unfair treatment).* **2 a bum ankle/leg etc** *AmE* an injured ANKLE, leg etc

ˈbum bag *n* [C] *BrE* a small bag that you wear around your waist to hold money, keys etc

bum·ble /ˈbʌmbəl/ *v* [I] **1** (*also* **bumble on**) to speak in a confused way, so that no one can understand you: *What was Karl bumbling on about?* **2** (*also* **bumble around**) to move in an unsteady way

bum·ble·bee /ˈbʌmbəlˌbiː/ *n* [C] a large hairy BEE

bum·bling /ˈbʌmblɪŋ/ *adj* [only before noun] behaving in a careless way and making a lot of mistakes: *a kind bumbling man with a gentle smile*

bumf, **bumph** /bʌmf/ *n* [U] *BrE informal* boring written information that you have to read: *I got loads of bumf about the introduction of the euro.*

bum·mer /ˈbʌmə $ -ər/ *n* **a bummer** *informal* a situation that is disappointing or annoying: *It was a real bummer being ill on holiday.*

bump¹ /bʌmp/ ●●● S3 *v*
1 [I always + adv/prep, T] to hit or knock against something: **[+against]** *I ran after him, bumping against people in my hurry.* | **[+into]** *Tim was a clumsy boy, always bumping into the furniture.* | **bump sth on sth** *She bumped her arm on the table.* | *The roof was so low he **bumped** his **head** (=his head hit the roof).* THESAURUS ▸ HIT
2 [I always + adv/prep] to move up and down as you move forward, especially in a vehicle: *A police car bumped down the track.* | **[+along]** *The plane was bumping along the runway.*
3 [T always + adv/prep] to push or pull something somewhere in an irregular or unsteady way: *Flora was bumping her bags down the steps.*
4 [T] *informal* to move someone or something into a different class or group, or to remove them from a class or group altogether: *The flight was overbooked, and Dad was the first one to be bumped.* | **bump sb up to/out of/from etc sth** *The reforms bumped many families off the state-provided health care list.*
5 [T] to move a radio or television programme to a different time: *'Married with Children' will be bumped from Sundays to Saturdays.*

bump into sb *phr v* to meet someone who you know, when you were not expecting to SYN **run into**: *I bumped into Jean in town.*

bump sb ↔ **off** *phr v informal* to kill someone

bump sth ↔ **up** *phr v* to suddenly increase something by a large amount: *Prices were bumped up by 10 percent last week.*

bump² ●●○ *n* [C]
1 an area of skin that is raised because you have hit it on something → **lump**: *She has a bump on the back of her*

head. | *He had a few injuries, mostly bumps and bruises.* **THESAURUS** INJURY
2 a small raised area on a surface: *The car hit a bump on the road.* → SPEED BUMP
3 the sound or sudden movement of something hitting a hard surface: *We heard a bump in the next room.* | **fall/sit down etc with a bump** *Rose fell, landing with a bump.*
4 *informal* a small accident in which your car hits something but you are not hurt

bump·er¹ /ˈbʌmpə $ -ər/ *n* [C] **1** *BrE* a bar fixed on the front and back of a car to protect it if it hits anything SYN **fender** *AmE* → see picture at CAR **2 bumper-to-bumper** bumper-to-bumper traffic is very close together and moving slowly

bumper² *adj* [only before noun] unusually large: **bumper crop/harvest** | *We hope readers will enjoy this bumper issue of 'Homes and Gardens'.*

ˈbumper car *n* [C] a small electric car that you drive in a special area at a FUNFAIR and deliberately try to hit other cars → **dodgems**

ˈbumper ˌsticker *n* [C] a small sign on the bumper of a car, with a humorous, political, or religious message

bumph /bʌmf/ *n* [U] *BrE* another spelling of BUMF

bump·kin /ˈbʌmpkɪn/ *n* [C] *informal* someone from the countryside who is considered to be stupid

bump 'n' grind /ˌbʌmp ən ˈgraɪnd/ *n* [U] a dance in which people move parts of their body, especially their HIPS, together in a sexually exciting way

bump·tious /ˈbʌmpʃəs/ *adj* too proud of your abilities in a way that annoys other people SYN **arrogant** —**bumptiously** *adv* —**bumptiousness** *n* [U]

bump·y /ˈbʌmpi/ ●●○ *adj* (*comparative* **bumpier**, *superlative* **bumpiest**)
1 a bumpy surface is flat but has a lot of raised parts, so it is difficult to walk or drive on it SYN **uneven** OPP **smooth**: *a bumpy road* | *The ground is bumpy in places.* **THESAURUS** ROUGH
2 a bumpy journey by car or plane is uncomfortable, with movements up and down because of bad road or weather conditions OPP **smooth**: *The plane made a bumpy landing.*
3 a bumpy ride/time having a lot of problems for a long time: *Shareholders have had a bumpy ride.*

bun /bʌn/ *n* [C] **1** *BrE* a small round sweet cake: *a sticky bun* **2** a small round type of bread: *a hamburger bun* **3** if a woman has her hair in a bun, she fastens it in a small round shape at the back of her head → see picture at HAIRSTYLE **4 buns** [plural] *AmE informal* the two round parts of a person's bottom SYN **buttocks** **5 have a bun in the oven** *BrE informal* to be PREGNANT - used humorously

bunch¹ /bʌntʃ/ ●●● S2 *n*
1 GROUP OF THINGS [C] a group of things that are fastened, held, or growing together: **[+of]** *I'll send her a* **bunch** *of flowers.* | *He had a* **bunch of keys** *on his belt.* | *a* **bunch of grapes** **THESAURUS** GROUP → see picture at BOUQUET
2 GROUP OF PEOPLE [singular] *informal* a group of people: *The ancient Egyptians were a clever bunch.* | **[+of]** *a friendly bunch of people*
3 the best/pick of the bunch the best among a group of people or things
4 LARGE AMOUNT [singular] *AmE informal* a large number of people or things, or a large amount of something: **[+of]** *There's a* **whole bunch** *of places I want to visit.*
5 bunches [plural] *BrE* if a girl wears her hair in bunches, she ties it together at each side of her head → see picture at HAIRSTYLE → **thanks a bunch** at THANKS¹

bunch² (*also* **bunch together**, **bunch up**) *v* **1** [I,T] to stay close together in a group, or to make people do this: *The children bunched together in small groups.* | *John stopped, forcing the rest of the group to bunch up behind him.* **2** [I,T] to make part of your body tight, or to become tight like this: *Sean bunched his fists.* **3** [I,T] to pull material together tightly in folds: *She bunched the cloth up and threw it away.* **4** [T] to hold or tie things together in a bunch

bun·dle¹ /ˈbʌndl/ ●○○ *n* [C]
1 a group of things such as papers, clothes, or sticks that are fastened or tied together: **[+of]** *bundles of newspapers* | *a small bundle containing mostly clothing* **THESAURUS** GROUP
2 a number of things that belong or are dealt with together: **[+of]** *bundles of data*
3 computer software, and sometimes other equipment or services that are included with a new computer at no extra cost
4 a bundle *informal* a lot of money: *College evening classes cost a bundle.* | *A company can* **make a bundle** *by selling unwanted property.*
5 be a bundle of nerves *informal* to be very nervous
6 be a bundle of laughs/fun *BrE informal* an expression meaning a person or situation that is fun or makes you laugh, often used jokingly when they are not fun at all: *Being a teenager isn't a bundle of laughs.*
7 not go a bundle on sth/sb *BrE informal* to not like something or someone very much: *Jim never drank, and certainly didn't go a bundle on gambling.*

bundle² *v* **1** [T always + adv/prep] to quickly push someone or something somewhere because you are in a hurry or you want to hide them: **bundle sb into/through etc sth** *They bundled Perez into the car and drove off.* **2** [I always + adv/prep] *BrE* to move somewhere quickly in a group: **[+into/through etc]** *Six of us bundled into a taxi.* **3** [T] to include computer software or other services with a new computer at no extra cost: **bundle sth with/into sth** *Microsoft can bundle Windows Vista at discounted prices with its popular desktop application programs.* | **bundle sth together** *The company offered customers a single computer solution, bundling together hardware and software.*

bundle sb ↔ **off** *phr v* to send someone somewhere quickly without asking them if they want to go

bundle sb/sth ↔ **up** *phr v* **1** (*also* **bundle sth ↔ together**) to make a bundle by tying things together: *Bundle up the newspapers and take them to the skip.* **2** (*also* **bundle sth ↔ together**) to put different things together so that they are dealt with at the same time: *The lawsuit bundles together the claims of many individuals into one big case.* **3** to put warm clothes on someone or yourself because it is cold SYN **wrap up**: *People sat bundled up in scarves, coats, and boots.* | **[+against]** *spectators bundled up against the cold*

bund·ler /ˈbʌndlə $ -ər/ *n* [C] *AmE* someone who collects money from different people and gives it to a political party to help with its CAMPAIGN

bun·fight /ˈbʌnfaɪt/ *n* [C] *BrE informal* **1** an argument: *There was a bunfight over who should pay for the damage.* **2** a party with food, arranged by an organization: *The Rugby Club is planning a bunfight.*

bung¹ /bʌŋ/ *n* [C] **1** a round piece of rubber, wood etc used to close the top of a container **2** *BrE informal* money given to someone secretly, and usually illegally, to make them do something SYN **bribe**

bung² *v* [T always + adv/prep] *BrE informal* to put something somewhere quickly and carelessly: **bung sth in/into etc sth** *Can you bung these clothes in the washing machine?* **THESAURUS** PUT

bung sth ↔ **up** *phr v BrE* **1** to block something, especially a hole **2 be bunged up** to find it difficult to breathe because you have a cold

bun·ga·low /ˈbʌŋgələʊ $ -loʊ/ ●○○ *n* [C]
1 *BrE* a house that is all on ground level → see picture at HOUSE¹
2 *AmE* a small house that is often on one level

bun·gee jump·ing /ˈbʌndʒi ˌdʒʌmpɪŋ/ *n* [U] a sport in which you jump off something very high with a long length of special rope that stretches tied to your legs, so that you go up again without touching the ground —**bungee jump** *n* [C] —**bungee jumper** *n* [C]

bun·gle /ˈbʌŋgəl/ *v* [T] to fail to do something properly, because you have made stupid mistakes - used especially in news reports: *The whole police operation was bungled.* —**bungled** *adj*: *a bungled rescue attempt* —**bungle** *n* [C] —**bungler** *n* [C]

B

B

bun·ion /ˈbʌnjən/ *n* [C] a painful lump on the first joint of your big toe

bunk¹ /bʌŋk/ *n* **1** [C] a narrow bed that is attached to the wall, for example on a train or ship **2** (*also* **bunk bed**) [often plural] one of two beds that are attached together, one on top of the other **3 do a bunk** *BrE informal* to suddenly leave a place without telling anyone **4** [U] *informal* nonsense SYN **bunkum**: *What a load of bunk!*

bunk² (*also* **bunk down**) *v* [I] *informal* to sleep somewhere, especially in someone else's house: *You can bunk down on the sofa for tonight.*

bunk off (sth) *phr v BrE informal* to stay away from somewhere such as school or to leave somewhere early without permission SYN **skive**: *John and I used to bunk off school.*

bun·ker¹ /ˈbʌŋkə $ -ər/ *n* [C] **1** a strongly built shelter for soldiers, usually underground **2** *BrE* a large hole on a golf course filled with sand SYN **sand trap** *AmE* → see picture at GOLF **3** a place where you store coal, especially on a ship or outside a house

bunker² *v* [T] *BrE* to hit a golf ball into a bunker

ˈbunker ˌbuster *n* [C] a bomb that goes deep into the ground before exploding, and that is used to destroy BUNKERS

bunk·house /ˈbʌŋkhaʊs/ *n* [C] a building where workers sleep

bun·kum /ˈbʌŋkəm/ *n* [U] BUNK

bun·ny /ˈbʌni/ (*also* **ˈbunny ˌrabbit**) *n* (*plural* **bunnies**) [C] a word for a rabbit, used especially by or to children

ˈbunny ˌboiler *n* [C] *informal* a woman who is always thinking and worrying about whether her husband or boyfriend loves her, and is willing to deceive or threaten him so that he will do what she wants him to

ˈbunny ˌslope *n* [C] *AmE* the area of a mountain where people learn to SKI SYN **nursery slope** *BrE*

bun·ra·ku /bʊnˈrɑːku/ *n* [U] the Japanese art of puppet theatre, which is performed using very large PUPPETS (=models of a person or animal that you move by pulling wires)

Bun·sen bur·ner /ˌbʌnsən ˈbɜːnə $ -ˈbɜːrnər/ *n* [C] a piece of equipment that produces a hot gas flame, for scientific EXPERIMENTS

bunt /bʌnt/ *v* [I] *AmE* to deliberately hit the ball a short distance in a game of baseball —**bunt** *n* [C]

bun·ting /ˈbʌntɪŋ/ *n* [U] small flags on strings, used to decorate buildings and streets on special occasions

buoy¹ /bɔɪ $ ˈbuːi, bɔɪ/ *n* [C] an object that floats on the sea, a lake etc to mark a safe or dangerous area

buoy² (*also* **buoy up**) *v* [T] **1** to make someone feel happier or more confident: *The party is buoyed up by the latest opinion poll results.* **2** to keep profits, prices etc at a high level: *Increased demand for computers buoyed their profits.* **3** to keep something floating

buoy·an·cy /ˈbɔɪənsi $ ˈbɔɪənsi, ˈbuːjənsi/ *n* [U] **1** the ability of an object to float **2** the power of a liquid to make an object float: *Salt water has more buoyancy than fresh water.* **3** a feeling of happiness and a belief that you can deal with problems easily **4** the ability of prices, a business etc to quickly get back to a high level after a difficult period

buoy·ant /ˈbɔɪənt $ ˈbɔɪənt, ˈbuːjənt/ *adj* **1** happy and confident: *Phil was in a buoyant mood.* **2** buoyant prices etc tend to rise: *a buoyant economy* **3** able to float or keep things floating: *Cork is very buoyant.* —**buoyantly** *adv*

bur /bɜː $ bɜːr/ *n* [C] another spelling of BURR(1)

bur·ble /ˈbɜːbəl $ ˈbɜːr-/ *v* **1** [I,T] to talk about something in a confused way that is difficult to understand: **[+on/away]** *I had to listen for an hour while she burbled away.* **2** [I] to make a sound like a stream flowing over stones —**burble** *n* [singular]

burbs /bɜːbz $ bɜːrbz/ *n* **the burbs** [plural] *AmE informal* the SUBURBS (=areas around a city, where people live)

bur·den¹ /ˈbɜːdn $ ˈbɜːrdn/ ●○○ *n*
1 [C] something difficult or worrying that you are responsible for: *His family responsibilities had started to become a burden.* | **[+of]** *The burden of taxation has risen considerably.* | **[+on]** *I don't like being a burden on other people.* | **bear/carry the burden** *If things go wrong he will bear the burden of guilt.* | **the tax/financial/debt burden**
2 the burden of proof *law* the duty to prove that something is true
3 [C] something that is carried SYN **load** → BEAST OF BURDEN

burden² *v* **1 be burdened with/by sth** to have a lot of problems because of a particular thing: *a company burdened with debt* → UNBURDEN **2 be burdened with sth** to be carrying something heavy

bur·den·some /ˈbɜːdnsəm $ ˈbɜːr-/ *adj formal* causing problems or additional work: *These charges are particularly burdensome for poor parents.*

bu·reau /ˈbjʊərəʊ $ ˈbjʊroʊ/ ●○○ *n* (*plural* **bureaus** *or* **bureaux** /-rəʊz $ -roʊz/) [C]
1 an office or organization that collects or provides information: *an employment bureau | the Citizens Advice Bureau*
2 a government department or a part of a government department in the US: *the Federal Bureau of Investigation*
3 an office of a company or organization that has its main office somewhere else: *the London bureau of the Washington Post*
4 *BrE* a large desk or writing table
5 *AmE* a piece of furniture with several drawers, used to keep clothes in SYN **chest of drawers** *BrE*

bu·reauc·ra·cy /bjʊəˈrɒkrəsi $ bjʊˈrɑː-/ ●○○ *n* (*plural* **bureaucracies**)
1 [U] a complicated official system that is annoying or confusing because it has a lot of rules, processes etc → **red tape**: *the reduction of unnecessary bureaucracy*
2 [C,U] the officials who are employed rather than elected to do the work of a government, business etc

bu·reau·crat /ˈbjʊərəkræt $ ˈbjʊr-/ ●○○ *n* [C] someone who works in a bureaucracy and uses official rules very strictly

bu·reau·crat·ic /ˌbjʊərəˈkrætɪk◂ $ ˌbjʊr-/ ●○○ *adj* involving a lot of complicated official rules and processes —**bureaucratically** /-kli/ *adv*

bureau de change /ˌbjʊərəʊ də ˈʃɒndʒ $ ˌbjʊroʊ də ˈʃɑːndʒ/ *n* (*plural* **bureaux de change** /-rəʊ- $ -roʊ-/) [C] *BrE* a shop where you can change foreign money → **exchange**

bu·rette (*also* **buret** *AmE*) /bjʊˈret/ *n* [C] a glass tube with measurements on it, used in scientific EXPERIMENTS

bur·geon /ˈbɜːdʒən $ ˈbɜːr-/ *v* [I] *formal* to grow or develop quickly: *the burgeoning market for digital cameras*

burg·er /ˈbɜːgə $ ˈbɜːrgər/ ●●● S3 *n* [C] a flat round piece of finely cut BEEF, which is cooked and eaten, or one of these served in a bread BUN SYN **hamburger** → CHEESEBURGER, VEGEBURGER

burgh /ˈbʌrə $ bɜːrg, ˈbʌroʊ/ *n* [C] a BOROUGH – used in Scotland

bur·gher /ˈbɜːgə $ ˈbɜːrgər/ *n* [C] *old use* someone who lives in a particular town

bur·glar /ˈbɜːglə $ ˈbɜːrglər/ ●●○ *n* [C] someone who goes into houses, shops etc to steal things → **robber**, **thief**, **cat burglar** THESAURUS THIEF

ˈburglar aˌlarm ●●○ *n* [C] a piece of equipment that makes a loud noise when someone tries to get into a building illegally

bur·gla·rize /ˈbɜːgləraɪz $ ˈbɜːr-/ *v* [T] *AmE* to go into a building and steal things SYN **burgle** *BrE*

bur·glar·y /ˈbɜːgləri $ ˈbɜːr-/ ●●○ *n* (*plural* **burglaries**) [C,U] the crime of getting into a building to steal things: *Burglaries have risen by 5%.* | *He was* ***charged with burglary****.* | *Most burglaries happen at night.* THESAURUS CRIME

bur·gle /ˈbɜːgəl $ ˈbɜːr-/ *v* [T] *BrE* to go into a building and steal things SYN **burglarize** *AmE*: *We've been burgled three times.* THESAURUS STEAL

bur·gun·dy /ˈbɜːɡəndi $ ˈbɜːr-/ *n* (*plural* **burgundies**) **1** [C,U] red or white wine from the Burgundy area of France **2** [U] a dark red colour —**burgundy** *adj*: *a burgundy skirt*

bur·i·al /ˈberiəl/ ●●○ *n* [C,U]
1 the act or ceremony of putting a dead body into a GRAVE
2 the act of burying something in the ground: **[+of]** *the burial of solid waste*

bur·ka /ˈbɜːkə $ ˈbɜːr-/ *n* [C] another spelling of BURQA

bur·lap /ˈbɜːlæp $ ˈbɜːr-/ *n* [U] *AmE* a type of thick rough cloth SYN **hessian** *BrE*

bur·lesque /bɜːˈlesk $ bɜːr-/ *n* [C,U] **1** speech, acting, or writing in which a serious subject is made to seem silly or an unimportant subject is treated in a serious way **2** *AmE* a performance involving a mixture of COMEDY and STRIPTEASE, popular in America in the past

bur·ly /ˈbɜːli $ ˈbɜːrli/ *adj* a burly man is big and strong: *a burly policeman*

burn¹ /bɜːn $ bɜːrn/ ●●● S2 W3 *v* (*past tense and past participle* **burnt** /bɜːnt $ bɜːrnt/ *or* **burned**)

1 PRODUCE FLAMES AND HEAT [I] **a)** if a fire burns, it produces heat and flames: *There was a fire burning in the fireplace.* | *An average household candle will burn for about six hours.* **b)** if something is burning, it is producing flames and being damaged or destroyed by fire: *Parts of the building are still burning.*

2 DESTROY STH WITH FIRE [T] to destroy or damage something with fire: *I burnt all his old letters.* | *Cars were burned and shops were looted during the rioting.* | *The Grand Hotel had* ***burnt to the ground.*** | *Make sure the iron isn't too hot or you'll burn the cloth.* | *He dropped his cigarette and* ***burnt a hole in*** *the carpet.*

3 INJURE/KILL SB WITH FIRE [T] to hurt yourself or someone else with fire or something hot: *I* ***burned my hand*** *on the oven door.* | *She was* ***badly burned*** *in a road accident.* | *Sixteen passengers were* ***burned to death*** (=died in a fire). | *A family of five were* ***burned alive*** *in their home last night* (=died in a fire). | *Heretics were* ***burnt at the stake*** (=burnt in a fire as a punishment).

4 SUN [I,T] if the sun burns your skin, or if your skin burns, it becomes red and painful from the heat of the sun → **sunburn**: *I burn quite easily.* | *Don't forget you can still* ***get burnt*** *when you're swimming or when it's cloudy.* | *Her face and neck were quite* ***badly burned.***

5 FOOD [I,T] to spoil food by cooking it for too long, or to become spoiled in this way: *I'm afraid I've burnt the pizza.* | **burn sth to a crisp/cinder** *The meat was burned to a crisp.*

6 CHEMICALS [T] to damage or destroy something by a chemical action: *Quite a lot of household chemicals can burn your skin.*

7 FUEL [I,T] if you burn a FUEL, or if it burns, it is used to produce power, heat, light etc: *The boiler burns oil to produce heat.* | *greenhouse gases caused by the burning of fossil fuels*

8 FAT/ENERGY [T] if you burn fat or CALORIES, you use up energy stored in your body by being physically active: *Taking a brisk walk every morning is a great way to burn calories.* | *a fat-burning exercise*

9 LIGHT [I] if a light or lamp burns, it shines or produces light: *A lamp was burning in the kitchen window.* | *The hall light was still burning.*

10 FEEL HOT AND PAINFUL [I,T] if a part of your body burns, or if something burns it, it feels unpleasantly hot: *The whisky burned my throat as it went down.* | *My eyes were burning from the smoke.*

11 FACE/CHEEKS [I] if your face or cheeks are burning, they feel hot because you are embarrassed or upset: *I could feel my cheeks burning as I spoke.*

12 CD [T] if you burn a CD or DVD, you record music, images, or other information onto it using special computer equipment

13 be burning with rage/desire etc to feel a particular emotion very strongly: *She was burning with curiosity.*

14 be burning to do sth to want to do or find out something very much: *I was burning to know how he had got on in New York.*

15 be/get burned *informal* **a)** to be emotionally hurt by someone or something: *Take things slowly – don't get burned again.* **b)** to lose a lot of money: *The company got badly burned in the dot.com collapse.*

16 burn your fingers/get your fingers burned *informal* to suffer the unpleasant results of something that you have done: *I tried a dating agency once, but got my fingers badly burnt – I'll never do it again.*

17 burn a hole in your pocket if money burns a hole in your pocket, you want to spend it as soon as you can

18 burn your bridges/boats *informal* to do something with the result that you will not be able to return to a previous situation again, even if you want to: *I'm really tempted to take up that job offer in Washington, but I don't want to burn my boats with this company.*

19 burn the candle at both ends *informal* to get very tired by doing things until very late at night and getting up early in the mornings

20 burn the midnight oil *informal* to work or study until late at night

21 it burns sb that/how etc *AmE* used to say that something makes someone feel angry or jealous: *It really burns me the way they treat us.*

22 GO FAST [I always + adv/prep] *informal* to travel very fast: **[+along/up etc]** *a sports car burning up the motorway*

GRAMMAR

Burn belongs to a group of verbs where the same noun can be the subject of the verb or its object.
• You can say: *You're burning the toast!* In this sentence, 'the toast' is the object of **burn**.
• You can also say: *The toast is burning!* In this sentence, 'the toast' is the subject of **burn**.

GRAMMAR GUIDE VERBS

THESAURUS

TO BE BURNING

burn to produce heat and flames: *The fire was still burning.* | *A pile of branches was burning in the yard.*

be on fire if a building, car, piece of clothing etc is on fire, it is burning and being damaged: *Before long, the neighbouring houses were on fire too.*

be alight *especially written* if something is alight, it is burning: *By the time the fire engines got there, the whole building was already alight.*

be ablaze *especially written* if something is ablaze, it is burning with a lot of flames, so that it is seriously damaged: *Twelve hours after the bombing raid, many parts of the city were still ablaze.*

blaze to burn very brightly with a lot of flames and heat: *A big log fire was blazing in the fireplace.*

smoulder *BrE*, **smolder** *AmE* /ˈsməʊldə $ ˈsmoʊldər/ to burn slowly and continuously, producing smoke but no flames: *A cigarette smouldered in the ashtray.*

TO START BURNING

catch fire to start burning accidentally: *We were worried the house would catch fire.*

burst into flames to suddenly start burning and produce a lot of flames that cause serious damage: *The plane crashed into the side of the mountain and burst into flames.*

ignite /ɪɡˈnaɪt/ *technical* if a chemical or gas ignites, it starts burning: *The compound ignites at 450 degrees Celsius.*

TO BURN SOMETHING

burn to damage or destroy something with fire or heat: *She lit a fire and burned his letters one by one.*

set fire to sth (*also* **set sth on fire**) to make something start burning so that it gets damaged: *Vandals set fire to an empty warehouse.*

scorch to damage the surface of something by burning it so that a dark mark is left on it: *Having the iron on a very high heat can scorch the fabric.*

singe /sɪndʒ/ to damage hair, wool, paper etc by burning it slightly so that the ends or edges are burnt: *The flames were hot enough to singe your eyebrows.*
scald to burn your skin with very hot liquid or steam: *The coffee was so hot it nearly scalded his tongue.*

TO MAKE SOMETHING STOP BURNING

put out to make something such as a fire, cigarette, or candle stop burning: *It took firefighters four hours to put out the blaze.* | *I put out my cigarette and went back into the house.*
extinguish /ɪkˈstɪŋgwɪʃ/ *formal* to make something such as a fire, cigarette, or candle stop burning: *He managed to extinguish the flames with his coat.* | *Customers who smoke will be asked to extinguish their cigarettes or leave the premises.*
blow out to make a flame or fire stop burning by blowing on it: *He blew out the candle and went to sleep.* | *The wind blew out the fire.*

burn away *phr v* if something burns away or is burned away, it is destroyed by fire: **burn sth ↔ away** *All her hair had been burnt away.*

burn down *phr v*
1 if a building burns down or is burned down, it is destroyed by fire: *She was worried that the house might burn down while they were away.* | **burn sth ↔ down** *The old town hall was burnt down in the 1970s.*
2 if a fire burns down, the flames become weaker and it produces less heat

burn sth ↔ **off** *phr v*
1 to remove something by burning it: *You can use a blow-lamp to burn off the old paint.*
2 to use energy that is stored in your body by doing physical exercise: *I decided to go for a run to try and burn off a few calories.*

burn out *phr v*
1 if a fire burns out or burns itself out, it stops burning because there is no coal, wood etc left: *He left the fire to **burn itself out**.*
2 be burnt out if a building or vehicle is burnt out, the inside of it is destroyed by fire: *The hotel was completely burnt out. Only the walls remained.* | *We passed several burnt out cars.*
3 burn sth ↔ out to remove something by burning it: *The cancer cells are burnt out using a laser beam.*
4 to work so hard over a period of time that you become unable to continue working because you are tired, ill, or unable to think of any new ideas: *It's a high-pressure job and you could burn out young.* | **be/get burnt out** *He was almost burnt out by the time he was 21.* | **burn yourself out** *She's in danger of burning herself out.* → BURNOUT(1)
5 if an engine or electric wire burns out or is burnt out, it stops working because it has been damaged by getting too hot: *The plugs are wired so that if one burns out, the others will still start the engine.* | **burn sth ↔ out** *I think you've burnt out one of the gaskets.*
6 if a ROCKET or JET burns out, it stops working because all its FUEL has been used → BURNOUT(2)

burn up *phr v*
1 if something burns up or is burnt up, it is completely destroyed by fire or heat: *The satellite will burn up as it re-enters the Earth's atmosphere.* | **burn sth ↔ up** *Most of the woodland has now been burnt up.*
2 burn sth ↔ up *informal* to use a lot of something in a careless way: *Most household appliances burn up loads of electricity.* | *He just burns up money!*
3 be burning up *spoken* if someone is burning up, they are very hot, usually because they are ill: *Feel his forehead – he's burning up.*
4 burn sb up *AmE informal* to make someone very angry: *The way he treats her really burns me up.*
5 burn sth ↔ up to use energy that is stored in your body, by being physically active: *As we get older, our body becomes less efficient at burning up calories.*

burn² ●●○ S3 *n* [C]
1 an injury caused by fire, heat, the light of the sun, or acid: *His body was covered in cigarette burns.* | **severe/serious burns** *She was taken to the hospital with serious burns.* | *Several of the survivors **suffered** severe **burns**.* | *She is being treated for **minor burns**.*
2 a mark on something caused by fire or heat: *The desk was covered with graffiti and **burn marks**.*
3 a painful mark on the skin caused by it rubbing hard against something rough
4 the burn *informal* a painful hot feeling in your muscles when you exercise a lot: *Go for the burn.*
5 *BrE* a small stream

burn·er /ˈbɜːnə $ ˈbɜːrnər/ *n* [C] **1** *BrE* the part of an OVEN or heater that produces heat or a flame: *a gas burner* **2** *AmE* one of the round parts on the top of a COOKER that produce heat **3 put/leave sth on the back burner** *informal* to delay doing something until a later time: *The government quietly put the scheme on the back burner.* → BUNSEN BURNER

burn·ing¹ /ˈbɜːnɪŋ $ ˈbɜːr-/ ●●○ *adj* [only before noun]
1 on fire: *She was rescued from a burning building.*
2 feeling very hot: *Claudia put her hands to her burning face.*
3 burning ambition/desire/need etc a burning AMBITION, desire, need etc is very strong: *My burning ambition is to be world champion.*
4 burning issue/question a burning ISSUE or question is very important and urgent: *Education has become a burning issue in this election.*
5 *written* burning eyes look at you very hard or show very strong feeling

burning² *adv* **burning hot** very hot

bur·nish /ˈbɜːnɪʃ $ ˈbɜːr-/ *v* [T] *formal* **1** to polish metal or another substance until it shines **2** to work hard in order to improve something: *He missed no opportunity to burnish his image.* —**burnished** *adj*

burn·out /ˈbɜːnaʊt $ ˈbɜːrn-/ *n* **1** [U] the feeling of always being tired because you have been working too hard: *Many of the teachers are suffering from burnout.* **2** [C,U] the time when a ROCKET or JET has finished all of its FUEL and stops operating

burnt¹ /bɜːnt $ bɜːrnt/ *especially BrE* the past tense and past participle of BURN

burnt² ●●○ *adj*
1 damaged or hurt by burning: *burnt toast*
2 burnt offering a) something that is offered as a gift to a god by being burnt on an ALTAR **b)** *BrE humorous* food that you accidentally burnt while you were cooking it

burp /bɜːp $ bɜːrp/ *v* **1** [I] to pass gas loudly from your stomach out through your mouth SYN **belch** **2** [T] to help a baby to do this, especially by rubbing or gently hitting its back —**burp** *n* [C]

bur·qa, **burka** /ˈbɜːkə $ ˈbɜːr-/ *n* [C] a long piece of clothing worn by Muslim women in some countries, which covers the head, face, and body, with only a small square to see through → **abaya**, **chador**

Bur·qi·ni /bɜːˈkiːni $ bɜːr-/ *n* [C] *trademark* (*also* **burkini**) a piece of clothing designed to be worn for swimming by Muslim women who want their whole bodies to be covered

burr /bɜː $ bɜːr/ *n* [C] **1** (*also* **bur**) the seed container of some plants, covered with sharp points that make it stick to things **2** *BrE* a way of pronouncing English with a strong 'r' sound **3** a fairly quiet regular sound like something turning quickly SYN **whirr**: *the burr of a motor* **4** a rough spot on a piece of metal

bur·ri·to /bəˈriːtəʊ $ -toʊ/ *n* (*plural* **burritos**) [C] a Mexican dish made with a TORTILLA (=flat thin bread) folded around meat or beans with cheese

bur·ro /ˈbʊrəʊ $ ˈbɜːroʊ/ *n* (*plural* **burros**) [C] *AmE* a small DONKEY

bur·row¹ /ˈbʌrəʊ $ ˈbɜːroʊ/ *v* **1** [I always + adv/prep, T] to make a hole or passage in the ground SYN **dig down**: **[+into/under/through etc]** *Mother turtles burrow into the sand to lay their eggs.* THESAURUS DIG **2** [I,T always + adv/prep] to press your body close to someone or under something because you want to get warm or feel safe SYN nestle: **[+into/under/down etc]** *The child stirred and burrowed deeper into the bed.* | **burrow sth into/against etc sth** *She burrowed her head into his shoulder.* **3** [I always + adv/prep] to search for something that is hidden in a container or under other things SYN **rummage**: **[+in/into/through etc]** *Helen burrowed in her bag for a handkerchief.*

burrow² *n* [C] a passage in the ground made by an animal such as a rabbit or FOX as a place to live

bur·sar /ˈbɜːsə $ ˈbɜːrsər/ *n* [C] someone at a school or college who deals with the accounts and office work

bur·sa·ry /ˈbɜːsəri $ ˈbɜːr-/ *n* (*plural* **bursaries**) [C] *BrE* an amount of money given to someone so that they can study at a university or college SYN **grant**

burst¹ /bɜːst $ bɜːrst/ ●●○ W3 *v* (*past tense and past participle* **burst**)

1 BREAK OPEN [I,T] if something bursts, or if you burst it, it breaks open or apart suddenly and violently so that its contents come out: *The* ***pipes*** *had* ***burst*** *and the house was under two feet of water.* THESAURUS ▸ BREAK, EXPLODE

2 be bursting with sth to have a lot of something or be filled with something: *John was bursting with ideas and good humour.* | *The shops are bursting with food.* | **be bursting with pride/energy/excitement etc** *Your mum's bursting with pride for you.*

3 MOVE SUDDENLY [I always + adv/prep] to move somewhere suddenly or quickly, especially into or out of a place: **[+into/through/in etc]** *Jo burst into the room.*

4 burst open to open suddenly: *The door burst open and Tom ran into the room.*

5 be bursting to do sth *informal* to want to do something very much: *Zach was bursting to tell them something.*

6 be bursting a) *BrE informal* to need to go to the toilet very soon **b)** (*also* **be bursting at the seams**) to be so full that nothing else can fit inside

7 burst sb's bubble to make someone suddenly realize that something is not as good as they thought it was: *Steve was so happy I couldn't bear to burst his bubble.*

8 burst its banks if a river bursts its banks, water from it goes onto the land → **full (up) to bursting** at FULL¹(1), → **burst/prick sb's bubble** at BUBBLE¹(7), → **the bubble bursts** at BUBBLE¹(6)

burst in on/upon sb/sth *phr v* to interrupt someone or something by entering a room, in a way that embarrasses you or other people: *I'm sorry to burst in on you like this.*

burst into sth *phr v*

1 to suddenly begin to make a sound, especially to start singing, crying, or laughing: *Claire looked as if she were about to* ***burst into tears****.* | *Suddenly, the group* ***burst into laughter****.* | *Lydia* ***burst into song****.*

2 burst into flames/flame to suddenly start to burn very strongly: *Their car crashed and burst into flames.*

burst onto/upon/on sth *phr v* to suddenly appear and become very successful: *The band* ***burst onto the*** *music* ***scene*** *in 1997.*

burst out *phr v*

1 burst out laughing/crying/singing etc to suddenly start to laugh, cry etc: *Everyone burst out laughing.*

2 to suddenly say something in a forceful way: *'I don't believe it!' she burst out angrily.* → OUTBURST(1)

burst² ●○○ *n* [C]

1 the act of something bursting or the place where it has burst: *a burst in the water pipe*

2 a) a short sudden effort or increase in activity: **[+of]** *The van gave a sudden burst of speed.* **b)** a short sudden and usually loud sound: **[+of]** *sharp bursts of machine gun fire* **c)** a sudden strong feeling or emotion: **burst of anger/enthusiasm/temper etc**

bur·then /ˈbɜːðən $ ˈbɜːr-/ *n* [C] *literary* a BURDEN

bur·ton /ˈbɜːtn $ ˈbɜːrtn/ *n* **gone for a burton** *BrE old-fashioned informal* lost, broken, or dead

bur·y /ˈberi/ ●●● W3 *v* (**buried**, **burying**, **buries**) [T]

1 DEAD PERSON to put someone who has died in a GRAVE: **bury sb in/at etc sth** *He was buried in the churchyard of St Mary's.*

2 OBJECT to put something under the ground, often in order to hide it: *Electric cables are buried beneath the streets.*

3 FALL ON STH [usually passive] to fall on top of someone or something, usually harming or destroying them: **be buried under/beneath etc sth** *The skiers were buried under the snow.* | *Fifty-seven miners were* ***buried alive****.*

4 HIDDEN to cover something so that it cannot be found: **be buried under/in sth** *His glasses were buried under a pile of papers.* GRAMMAR **Bury** is usually passive in this meaning.

5 FEELING/MEMORY to ignore a feeling or memory and pretend that it does not exist: *a deeply buried memory*

6 bury your face/head etc (in sth) to press your face etc into something soft: *Noel buried his face in the pillow.*

7 bury your face/head in your hands to cover your face with your hands because you are very upset

8 bury your head in the sand to ignore an unpleasant situation and hope it will stop if you do not think about it

9 bury the hatchet/bury your differences to agree to stop arguing about something and become friends

10 IN A SURFACE to push something, especially something sharp, into something else with a lot of force: **bury sth in sth** *The dog buried its teeth in my leg.* | *The bullet buried itself in the wall.*

11 bury yourself in your work/studies etc to give all your attention to something: *After the divorce, she buried herself in her work.*

12 INFORMATION to put information in a document in a place where it is unlikely to be noticed, or to not make it available to people: *The story was buried at the back of the paper.*

13 LOVED ONE *literary* to have someone you love die: *She had buried her husband, two sons, and a daughter.* → **be dead and buried** at DEAD¹(14)

bus¹ /bʌs/ ●●● S1 W2 *n* (*plural* **buses** *or* **busses** *especially AmE*) [C]

1 a large vehicle that people pay to travel on: **on a bus** *There were a lot of people on the bus.* | **by bus** *The best way to get there is by bus.* | *I took a bus to San Francisco.* | *Buses run at 15 and 30 minutes past the hour.*

2 a CIRCUIT that connects the main parts of a computer so that signals can be sent from one part of the computer to another

GRAMMAR: Patterns with bus

- You usually say **get on a bus**: *I got on the bus at the station.* 'Get in' is much less common.
- You usually say **get off a bus**: *She got off the bus at her usual stop.* 'Get out of' is much less common.
- You usually say that someone is **on a bus**: *All the people on the bus stared at me.* 'In a bus' is much less common.
- You go somewhere **by bus**: *The children travel to school by bus.*
- You often talk about **the bus**: *It's quicker if you take the bus.* | *I was waiting for the bus for the airport.*

COLLOCATIONS

VERBS

go/travel by bus *I usually go to work by bus.*
go on the bus/use the bus (=travel by bus) *It's easier to go on the bus than to drive.*
get/take/catch a bus *Can we get a bus from here to Reading?*
ride a bus *AmE It was the first time Craig had ridden a bus downtown by himself.*
get on/off a bus *Several more passengers got on the bus.*
wait for a bus | **miss the bus** (=be too late to get on a bus) | **buses run** (=go at regular times)

bus + NOUN

a bus ride/journey/trip *It's a 20-minute bus ride into town.*
a bus stop (=a place where a bus stops for passengers) *She got off at the next bus stop.*

B

a bus shelter (=a small covered area where you wait for a bus) | **a bus service** (=a service that provides regular buses) | **a bus route** | **a bus fare** (=the money you pay for a bus journey) | **a bus ticket** | **a bus pass** (=a ticket giving cheap or free bus travel) | **a bus station** (=a place where buses start and finish their journeys) | **a bus lane** (=a part of the road where only buses are allowed to drive) | **a bus driver**

ADJECTIVES/NOUN + bus

a school bus | **a shuttle bus** (=one that makes regular short journeys between two places) | **a double-decker bus** (=one with two levels for passengers) | **an open-topped bus** (=one without a roof, used for showing tourists a town etc)

B

bus² *v* (**bused** *or* **bussed**, **busing** *or* **bussing**) [T] **1** to take a person or a group of people somewhere in a bus: **bus sb to/in/into sth** *Casey was bussed to the school.* **2** *AmE* to take away dirty dishes from the tables in a restaurant: *Shelley had a job* ***bussing tables***.

bus·boy /ˈbʌsbɔɪ/ *n* [C] *AmE* a young man whose job is to take away dirty dishes from the tables in a restaurant

bus·by /ˈbʌzbi/ *n* [C] a tall fur hat worn by some British soldiers

bush /bʊʃ/ ●●● S3 *n* [C]

1 a plant with many thin branches growing up from the ground → **tree**, **shrub**: *a rose bush* | *The child was hiding in the bushes.*

2 the bush wild country that has not been cleared, especially in Australia or Africa

3 a bush of hair is a lot of thick untidy hair → **beat about the bush** at BEAT¹(14)

bushed /bʊʃt/ *adj* [not before noun] *informal* very tired **THESAURUS** TIRED

bush·el /ˈbʊʃəl/ *n* **hide your light under a bushel** to not tell anyone that you are good at something

ˈ**bush league** *adj AmE informal* badly done or of such bad quality that it is not acceptable: *bush league reporting*

Bush·man /ˈbʊʃmən/ *n* (*plural* **Bushmen** /-mən/) [C] someone who belongs to a southern African tribe who live in the BUSH (=wild country)

bush·whack /ˈbʊʃwæk/ *v* [I,T] to push or cut your way through thick trees or bushes

bush·y /ˈbʊʃi/ *adj* (*comparative* **bushier**, *superlative* **bushiest**) **1** bushy hair or fur grows thickly: *a bushy tail* **2** bushy plants grow thickly, with a lot of branches and leaves —**bushiness** *n* [U]

bus·i·ly /ˈbɪzəli/ *adv* in a busy way: *Students were busily writing notes.*

busi·ness /ˈbɪznəs/ ●●● S1 W1 *n*

1 BUYING OR SELLING GOODS OR SERVICES [U] the activity of making money by producing or buying and selling goods, or providing services: *Students on the course learn about all aspects of business.* | *Carl began in the music business by running a recording studio.* | *We do business with a number of Italian companies.* | *He has a wide range of business interests.*

GRAMMAR

Don't use 'the business' when talking in general about the activity of making money. You say: *Tourism is good for business.* ✗ Don't say: *Tourism is good for the business.*

GRAMMAR GUIDE NOUNS

2 COMPANY [C] an organization such as a company, shop, or factory that produces or sells goods or provides a service: *She now has her own $25 million home-shopping business.* | *They don't know how to run a business.* | *The company began as a small family business.* **THESAURUS** COMPANY

3 HOW MUCH WORK A COMPANY HAS [U] the amount of work a company does or the amount of money it makes: *We're now* ***doing*** *twice as much* ***business*** *as we did last year.* | *Exports account for 72% of overall business.* | **business is good/bad/slow etc** *Business is slow during the summer.* | **drum up business** (=try to get more work for you or your company) *Perot was in Europe, drumming up business for his new investment company.*

4 FOR YOUR JOB [U] work that you do as part of your job: *She's in New York this week* ***on business*** (=for her work). | *Hi Maggie! Is this phone call* ***business or pleasure****?* | **business trip/meeting etc** *We discussed the idea over a business lunch.* | *useful* ***business contacts***

5 WHAT SOMEONE SHOULD BE INVOLVED IN [U] **a)** if something is not your business or none of your business, you should not be involved in it or ask about it: *It was not her business, she decided, to ask where the money came from.* | *It's* ***none of your business*** *how much I weigh.* | *'Who's that girl you were with?' '****Mind your own business*** (=Don't ask questions about something that does not concern you)*!'* | *'Are you going out with Kate tonight?' '****That's my business*** (=it doesn't concern you, so don't ask me questions about it)*'.* **b)** if it is someone's business to do something, it is their duty or responsibility to do it: **it is the business of sb to do sth** *It is the business of government to listen to the various groups within society.*

6 THINGS TO BE DEALT WITH [U] things that need to be done or discussed: *Okay, let's* ***get down to business*** (=start doing or discussing something). | *'Is there* ***any other business****?' the chairman asked.*

7 MATTER [singular] a situation or activity, especially one that you have a particular opinion about or attitude towards: **a serious/strange/funny etc business** *Leon regards keeping fit as a serious business.* | *Tanya found* ***the whole business*** *ridiculous.*

8 be in business a) to be involved in business activities: *The company has been in business for over 30 years.* **b)** *spoken* to have all that you need to start doing something: *I've just got to buy the paint and then we're in business.*

9 (go) out of business if a company goes out of business, or something puts it out of business, it stops operating, especially because of financial problems: *Higher interest rates will drive small firms out of business.*

10 be back in business to be working or operating in a normal way again: *The band are back in business after a long break.*

11 sb was (just) minding their own business *spoken* used to say that someone was not doing anything unusual or wrong at the time when something unfair or bad happened to them: *I was driving along, minding my own business, when the police stopped my car.*

12 go about your business to do the things that you normally do: *The street was full of ordinary people going about their business.*

13 make it your business to do sth to make a special effort to do something: *Ruth made it her business to get to know the customers.*

14 mean business *informal* to be serious about doing something even if it involves harming someone: *The border is guarded by troops who mean business.*

15 unfinished business something you need to discuss further with someone or a situation that has not yet reached a satisfactory solution: *The sudden death of a loved one can often leave the bereaved with an agonising sense of unfinished business.*

16 business is business *spoken* used to say that profit is the most important thing to consider: *We can't afford to employ someone who isn't good at the job – business is business.*

17 business as usual when someone or something is still working or operating normally when you think they might not be: *Despite last night's scare, it was business as usual in the White House today.*

18 have no business doing sth/have no business to do sth to do something you should not be doing: *He was drunk and had no business driving.*

19 not be in the business of doing sth to not be intending to do something because you think it is a bad idea: *I'm not in the business of selling my best players.*

20 and all that business *spoken informal* and other things of the same general kind: *She handles the publicity and all that business.*

21 (it's) the business *BrE informal* used to say that something is very good or works well: *Have you seen David's new car? It's the business!*
22 do the business *BrE informal* **a)** to do what you are expected to do or what people want you to do: *Come on, then, and do the business.* **b)** to have sex → BIG BUSINESS, → **funny business** at FUNNY(3), → **like nobody's business** at NOBODY[1](2), → **monkey business** at MONKEY[1](3), → SHOW BUSINESS

COLLOCATIONS – MEANING 1

VERBS

do business *A lot of firms are keen to do business in Japan.*
conduct business *formal* (=do business) *It is not a sensible way to conduct business.*
go into business (=start working in business) *A lot of university graduates want to go into business.*
set up/start up in business *The bank gave me a loan to help me set up in business.*
stay in business (=continue operating and not become bankrupt) *Even if they manage to stay in business for another year, their long-term survival remains under threat.*
go out of business (=stop doing business because of financial problems) *In a recession smaller firms often go out of business.*

NOUN + business

the music/entertainment/computer etc business *He started out working in the computer business.*

business + NOUN

a business deal (=an occasion when you buy or sell something) *Negotiation is the most important part of a business deal.*
business activities *His wife refused to get involved in his business activities.*
business interests (=business activities, or shares in companies) *Both companies have substantial business interests in Indonesia.*
the business community (=people who work in business) *There was pressure on the government from the business community.*
the business world *You need to be flexible in today's highly competitive business world.*

COMMON ERRORS

⚠ Don't say 'make business'. Say **do business.**

COLLOCATIONS – MEANING 2

VERBS

have/own a business *Nick owned a software business in Boston.*
run a business (=manage it) *There's plenty of advice available on how to run your own business.*
start/set up a business *When you're starting a business, you have to work longer hours.*
take over a business (=buy it or start running it) *When my father retired, I took over the business.*
build (up)/develop a business *He spent years trying to build a business in Antigua.*
a business succeeds | a business collapses/fails (=stops operating)

ADJECTIVES/NOUN + business

a small business (=that employs only a few people) *Many small businesses have been badly hit by the recession.*
a software/catering/construction etc business *His girlfriend runs a catering business.*
a family business (=owned and controlled by one family) *For many years the hotel was a family business.*
an import/export business | a successful/profitable/thriving business | a viable business (=one that is likely to be successful)

business + NOUN

a business partner (=someone who shares a business with you) *Margie was his wife and also his business partner.*
a business manager | a business customer/client

ˈbusiness ˌcard *n* [C] a card that shows a business person's name, position, company, address etc
ˈbusiness ˌclass *n* [U] travelling conditions on an aircraft that are more expensive than TOURIST CLASS, but not as expensive as FIRST CLASS → **ECONOMY CLASS**
ˈbusiness end *n* **the business end (of sth)** *informal* the end of a tool or weapon that does the work or causes the damage: *the business end of a gun*
ˈbusiness ˌhours *n* [plural] the normal hours that shops and offices are open
busi·ness·like /ˈbɪznəs-laɪk/ *adj* effective and practical in the way that you do things: *a businesslike manner*
busi·ness·man /ˈbɪznəsmən/ ●●● W3 *n* (*plural* **businessmen** /-mən/) [C] a man who works in business
ˈbusiness ˌpark *n* [C] an area where many companies and businesses have buildings and offices
ˈbusiness ˌperson *n* (*plural* **business people**) [C] a person who works in business
ˈbusiness ˌplan *n* [C] a document that explains what a company wants to do in the future, and how it plans to do it
ˈbusiness ˌschool *n* [C,U] a college or part of a college where students can study economic and financial subjects and learn about managing a business
ˈbusiness ˌstudies *n* [U] a course of study on economic and financial subjects and managing a business

GRAMMAR: Singular or plural verb?

Business studies is followed by a singular verb:
***Business studies** is now a popular subject.*

ˈbusiness ˌsuit *n* [C] *AmE* a suit that someone wears during the day at work
busi·ness·wom·an /ˈbɪznəsˌwʊmən/ *n* (*plural* **businesswomen** /-ˌwɪmɪn/) [C] a woman who works in business
bus·ing /ˈbʌsɪŋ/ *n* [U] a system in the US in which students ride buses to schools that are far from where they live, so that a school has students of different races
busk /bʌsk/ *v* [I] *BrE* to play music in a public place in order to earn money —**busker** *n* [C]
ˈbus lane *n* [C] a part of a wide road that only buses are allowed to use
bus·load /ˈbʌsləʊd $ -loʊd/ *n* [C] *AmE* an amount of people on a bus that is full
bus·man's hol·i·day /ˌbʌsmənz ˈhɒlədi $ -ˈhɑːlədeɪ/ *n* [singular] *BrE* a holiday spent doing the same work as you do in your job – often used humorously
ˈbus pass *n* [C] a special ticket giving cheap or free bus travel
buss /bʌs/ *v* [T] *AmE old-fashioned* to kiss someone in a friendly rather than sexual way: *politicians bussing babies*
bus·ses /ˈbʌsɪz/ *n* a plural of bus
ˈbus ˌshelter *n* [C] a small structure with a roof that keeps people dry while they are waiting for a bus
ˈbus ˌstation (*also* **ˈbus ˌterminal**) *n* [C] a place where buses start and finish their journeys
ˈbus stop ●●○ *n* [C] a place at the side of a road, marked with a sign, where buses stop for passengers
bust[1] /bʌst/ ●●○ *v* (*past tense and past participle* **bust** *BrE*, **busted** *especially AmE*) [T]
1 BREAK *informal* to break something: *I bust my watch this morning.* | *Tony busted the door down.*
2 POLICE **a)** if the police bust someone, they charge them with a crime: *He was busted by US inspectors at the border.* | **bust sb for sth** *Davis **got busted for drugs**.* **b)** *informal* if the police bust a place, they go into it to look for something

illegal: *Federal agents busted several money-exchange businesses.*
3 TRY HARD **bust a gut** (*also* **bust your butt/ass** *AmE spoken*) *informal* to try extremely hard to do something: *I bust a gut trying to finish that work on time.*
4 MONEY *AmE informal* to use too much money, so that a business etc must stop operating: *The trip to Spain will probably bust our budget.*
5 crime-busting/union-busting/budget-busting etc *informal* used with nouns to show that a situation is being ended or an activity is being stopped: *crime-busting laws*
6 ... or bust! *informal* used to say that you will try very hard to go somewhere or do something: *Idaho or bust!*
7 MILITARY *especially AmE* to give someone a lower military rank as a punishment SYN **demote**
bust out *phr v informal* to escape from a place, especially prison
bust up *phr v informal*
1 *BrE* if people bust up, they end their relationship or friendship SYN **break up**: *They bust up after six years of marriage.* → BUST-UP(1)
2 bust sth ↔ up to prevent an illegal activity or bad situation from continuing SYN **break up**: *A couple of teachers stepped in to bust up the fight.*
3 bust sth ↔ up *AmE* to damage or break something: *A bunch of bikers busted up the bar.*
4 *AmE* to start laughing a lot SYN **crack up**: *Elaine busted up laughing at the sight of him.*

bust² ●○○ *n* [C]
1 a model of someone's head, shoulders, and upper chest, usually made of stone or metal: **[+of]** *a bust of Beethoven*
2 a woman's breasts, or the part of her clothes that covers her breasts
3 a measurement around a woman's breast and back: *a 36-inch bust*
4 *informal* a situation in which the police go into a place in order to catch people doing something illegal: *a* ***drug bust***
→ **boom to bust** at BOOM¹(1)

bust³ *adj* [not before noun] **1 go bust** *informal* a business that goes bust cannot continue operating **2** *BrE informal* broken: *The television's bust again.*

bust·ed /ˈbʌstɪd/ *adj AmE spoken informal* **1** broken: *a busted arm* **2** [not before noun] caught doing something wrong and likely to be punished: *You guys are so busted!*

bus·ter /ˈbʌstə $ -ər/ *n* **1** *AmE spoken* used to speak to a man who is annoying you or who you do not respect: *You're under arrest, buster!* **2 crime-buster/budget-buster/sanctions-buster etc** *informal* used with nouns to mean someone or something that ends a situation or stops an activity

bus·ti·er /ˈbʌstieɪ, ˈbʊs- $ buːsˈtjeɪ, bʌs-/ *n* [C] a tight piece of clothing that women wear on the top half of the body, which does not cover their shoulders or arms

bus·tle¹ /ˈbʌsəl/ *v* [I always + adv/prep] to move around quickly, looking very busy: **[+about/round etc]** *Madge bustled round the room, putting things away.*

bustle² *n* **1** [singular] busy and usually noisy activity: **[+of]** *a continual bustle of people coming and going* → **hustle and bustle** at HUSTLE²(1) **2** [C] a frame worn by women in the past to hold out the back of their skirts

bus·tling /ˈbʌsəlɪŋ/ *adj* a bustling place is very busy: **bustling with sb/sth** *The flower market was bustling with shoppers.*

ˈbust-up *n* [C] *informal* **1** the end of a relationship: **[+of]** *the bust-up of their marriage* → **bust up** at BUST¹ **2** *BrE* a very bad quarrel or fight: *Cathy and I had a real bust-up yesterday.*

bust·y /ˈbʌsti/ *adj informal* a woman who is busty has large breasts

bus·y¹ /ˈbɪzi/ ●●● S1 W2 *adj* (*comparative* **busier**, *superlative* **busiest**)
1 PERSON if you are busy, you are working hard and have a lot of things to do: *She's busy now – can you phone later?* | *a busy mother of four* | **[+with]** *Mr Haynes is busy with a customer at the moment.* | **busy doing sth** *Rachel's busy studying for her exams.* | *There were lots of activities to* ***keep*** *the kids* ***busy***.

GRAMMAR
You are **busy with** something: *I'm very busy with work at the moment.* ✗ Don't say: *busy for something* | *busy on something*
GRAMMAR GUIDE ▸ ADJECTIVES

2 TIME a busy period of time is full of work or other activities: *December is the busiest time of year for shops.* | *a* ***busy day*** | *He took time out of his* ***busy schedule*** *to visit us.*
3 PLACE a busy place is very full of people or vehicles and movement: *We live on a very* ***busy road***.
4 TELEPHONE *especially AmE* if a telephone you are calling is busy, it makes a repeated sound to tell you that the person you are calling is talking on their telephone SYN **engaged** *BrE*: *I called Sonya, but her line was busy.* | *I keep getting a* ***busy signal***.
5 PATTERN a pattern or design that is busy is too full of small details – used to show disapproval

THESAURUS

PERSON

busy if you are busy, you have a lot of things you need to do: *Sorry I haven't called you, but I've been really busy.* | *a busy housewife*
rushed/run off your feet [not before noun] *BrE spoken* very busy and in a hurry, because you have too many things to do: *We've been absolutely rushed off our feet getting ready for our son's birthday party.*
snowed under [not before noun] so busy that you can hardly deal with all the work you have to do: *I can't stop for lunch today – I'm completely snowed under.*
up to your ears/neck in sth [not before noun] *informal* extremely busy because you have a lot of work to deal with: *Teachers say they are up to their ears in paperwork and don't have enough time for teaching.*
tied up [not before noun] busy in your job, so that you cannot do anything else: *I'm sorry, but he's tied up at the moment. Could you call back later?*
have a lot to do *especially spoken* to have to do a lot of things, so that you need to hurry or work hard: *Let's get started – we have a lot to do.*
have a lot on *BrE*, **have a lot going on** *AmE spoken* to be busy, especially because you have arranged to do a lot of things during a particular period: *I've got a lot on this weekend.*

TIME

busy use this about times when you have a lot of things you need to do: *We have a busy day ahead of us tomorrow.*
hectic a hectic time or situation is extremely busy, so that you are always in a hurry and often feel excited or worried: *It was really hectic at work today.*
the rush hour the time in the morning and evening when a lot of people are travelling to or from work: *The buses are so crowded during the rush hour you never get a seat.*

busy² *v* (**busied**, **busying**, **busies**) [T] **busy yourself with sth** to use your time dealing with something: *He busied himself with answering letters.*

bus·y·bod·y /ˈbɪziˌbɒdi $ -ˌbɑːdi/ *n* (*plural* **busybodies**) [C] someone who is too interested in other people's private activities – used to show disapproval

busy Liz·zie /ˌbɪzi ˈlɪzi/ *n* [C] a small plant with bright flowers

bus·y·work /ˈbɪziwɜːk $ -wɜːrk/ *n* [U] *AmE* work that gives someone something to do, but that is not really necessary

but¹ /bət; *strong* bʌt/ ●●● S1 W1 *conjunction*
1 used to connect two statements or phrases when the second one adds something different or seems surprising after the first one: *It's an old car, but it's very reliable.* | *They rushed to the hospital, but they were too late.* | *We've invited the boss, but she may decide not to come.* | *an expensive but*

extremely useful book | *'Has he got any experience?' 'No, but he's keen to learn.'*

2 used to introduce a statement that explains why the thing you have mentioned did not happen or is not possible: *I'd like to go but I'm too busy.* | *They would have married sooner, but they had to wait for her divorce.*

3 used after a negative to emphasize that it is the second part of the sentence that is true: *He lied to the court not just once, but on several occasions.* | *The purpose of the scheme is not to help the employers but to provide work for young people.*

4 except: *What can we do but sit and wait?* | *I had no choice but to accept the challenge.* | *Not a day goes by but I think of dear old Larry* (=I think of him every day). **THESAURUS** EXCEPT

5 but for a) used when you are saying that something would have happened if something or someone else had not prevented it: *But for these interruptions, the meeting would have finished earlier.* | *The score could have been higher but for some excellent goalkeeping by Simon.* | *I might never have got to university but for you.* **b)** except for something or someone: *All was silent but for the sound of the wind in the trees.*

6 but then (again) *spoken* **a)** used when you are adding a statement that says almost the opposite of what you have just said: *John might be ready to help us, but then again, he might not.* | *You feel really sorry for him. But then again, it's hard to like him.* **b)** used when you are adding a statement that makes what you have just said seem less surprising: *Dinah missed the last rehearsal, but then she always was unreliable, wasn't she?*

7 *spoken* used when you are replying to someone and expressing strong feelings such as anger, surprise etc: *But that's marvellous news!* | *'They won't even discuss the problem.' 'But how stupid!'*

8 sb cannot but do sth *formal* used to say that someone has to do something or cannot stop themselves from doing it: *I could not but admire her.*

9 *spoken* used when disagreeing with someone: *'It was a good idea.' 'But it didn't work.'*

10 *spoken* used to emphasize a word or statement: *It'll be a great party – everyone, but everyone, is coming.* | *They're rich, but I mean rich.*

11 *spoken* used to change the subject of a conversation: *But now to the main question.* | *But tell me, are you really planning to retire?*

12 *spoken* used after expressions such as 'Excuse me' and 'I'm sorry': *Excuse me, but I'm afraid this is a no-smoking area.*

THESAURUS

but *conjunction* used when linking two words or phrases that seem opposite or very different in meaning. Don't use **but** at the beginning of a sentence in written English: *The plant's leaves are big, but its flowers are quite small.* | *Her books are fascinating but often rather disturbing.*

although *conjunction* used when contrasting one clause with another in the same sentence: *Although you are in the middle of the city, you feel as if you are in the countryside.* | *I enjoyed German although I wasn't very good at it.*

however *conjunction* used when saying something that seems different or surprising after your previous statement. It is usually used in the middle of a sentence, separated from the rest of the sentence by commas. It can also come at the beginning: *Jack and his family managed to escape before the soldiers arrived. Other families in the village, however, were less lucky.* | *The town is a long way from the nearest big city. However, there is a good bus service.*

nevertheless/nonetheless *conjunction* used when saying something that seems different or surprising after your previous statement. It is used at the beginning or end of a sentence: *It was certainly a terrible accident. Nevertheless, air travel is still the safest form of transport.* | *The weather turned bad early in the day, but the festival was a great success nonetheless.*

while/whereas /weər'æz/ *conjunction* used when making comparisons and saying that something is true of one person, thing, or situation, but it is different for another. They are used when contrasting one clause with another in the same sentence: *Some people visit their doctor once every few weeks, while others may not visit a doctor for several years.* | *Whereas in most of the world they drive on the right, in the UK and Japan they drive on the left.*

by contrast *formal* used when making comparisons and saying that a person, thing, or situation is very different from the one you have just mentioned. It is used when referring back to the previous sentence: *The surface temperature on Venus is higher than the boiling point of water. Mars, by contrast, is very cold.*

but² ●●● S2 W3 *prep*

1 apart from SYN **except**: *I could come any day but Thursday.* | *There's no one here but me.* | *I could still see nothing but the spirals of desert dust.* | *He was unable to swallow anything but liquids.*

2 the last but one/the next but two etc *especially BrE* the last or next thing or person except for one, two etc: *Pauline and Derek live in the next house but one* (=they live two houses away from us).

but³ *adv* only: *This is but one example of what can happen when things go badly wrong.* | *It's going to be difficult. Anyway, we can but try.* | *We have relationships of many different sorts – with our children, our parents, our boss and our friends, to name but a few.*

but⁴ /bʌt/ *n* **buts** [plural] *spoken* reasons that someone gives for not doing something or agreeing with something: *'I don't want to hear any buts,' Jo snapped.* | *He is the best player –* ***no ifs, ands, or buts*** *about that.*

bu·tane /'bjuːteɪn/ *n* [U] a gas stored in liquid form, used for cooking and heating

butch /bʊtʃ/ *adj informal* **1** a woman who is butch looks, behaves, or dresses like a man **2** a man who is butch seems big and strong, and typically male

butch·er¹ /'bʊtʃə $ -ər/ ●●○ S3 *n*

1 [C] someone who owns or works in a shop that sells meat

2 the butcher's a shop where you can buy meat

3 [C] someone who has killed someone else cruelly and unnecessarily, especially someone who has killed a lot of people

4 have/take a butcher's *BrE spoken informal* to have a look at something

butcher² *v* [T] **1** to kill animals and prepare them to be used as meat **2** to kill someone cruelly or unnecessarily, especially to kill a lot of people **3** *informal* to spoil something by working carelessly: *That hairdresser really butchered my hair!*

butch·er·y /'bʊtʃəri/ *n* [U] **1** cruel and unnecessary killing: *the butchery of battle* **2** the preparation of meat for sale

but·ler /'bʌtlə $ -ər/ *n* [C] the main male servant of a house

But·lins /'bʌtlənz/ *trademark* a group of HOLIDAY CAMPS in various seaside towns in the UK. They were started by Sir Billy Butlin (1899-1980) with the aim of providing inexpensive holidays for ordinary working people, and they were especially popular in the 1950s and 1960s.

butt¹ /bʌt/ *n* [C]

1 PART OF YOUR BODY *AmE informal* the part of your body that you sit on SYN **buttocks**: *a baby's soft little butt* → **be a pain in the butt** at PAIN¹(3)

2 CIGARETTE the end of a cigarette after most of it has been smoked

3 be the butt of sth to be the person or thing that other people often make jokes about: *Paul quickly became the butt of everyone's jokes.*

4 GUN the thick end of the handle of a gun: *a rifle butt*

5 get your butt in/out/over etc *AmE spoken* used to rudely

tell someone to go somewhere or do something: *Kevin, get your butt over here!*
6 work/play etc your butt off *AmE spoken* to work, play etc very hard: *I worked my butt off in college.*
7 CONTAINER *BrE* a large round container for collecting or storing liquids: *a rainwater butt*
8 HITTING WITH YOUR HEAD the act of hitting someone with your head
butt[2] *v* [I,T] **1** to hit or push against something or someone with your head **2** if an animal butts someone, it hits them with its horns
butt in *phr v* **1** to interrupt a conversation rudely: *Stop butting in!* **2** to become involved in a private situation that does not concern you: **[+on]** *They don't want outsiders butting in on their decision-making.*
butt out *phr v especially AmE spoken* used to tell someone rudely that you do not want them to be involved in a conversation or situation: *This has nothing to do with you, so just butt out!*
butte /bjuːt/ *n* [C] a hill with steep sides and a flat top in the western US
but·ter[1] /ˈbʌtə $ -ər/ ●●● S2 *n* [U]
1 a solid yellow food made from milk or cream that you spread on bread or use in cooking → BREAD-AND-BUTTER
2 butter wouldn't melt in sb's mouth used to say that someone seems to be very kind and sincere but is not really
—**buttery** *adj*
butter[2] *v* [T] to spread butter on something: *buttered toast*
butter sb ↔ **up** *phr v informal* to say nice things to someone so that they will do what you want: *Don't think you can butter me up that easily.*
ˈ**butter bean** *n* [C] a large pale yellow bean
but·ter·cream /ˈbʌtəkriːm $ -ər-/ *n* [U] a soft mixture of butter and sugar used inside or on top of cakes
but·ter·cup /ˈbʌtəkʌp $ -ər-/ *n* [C] a small shiny yellow wild flower
but·ter·fat /ˈbʌtəfæt $ -ər-/ *n* [U] the natural fat in milk
but·ter·fin·gers /ˈbʌtəˌfɪŋgəz $ ˈbʌtərˌfɪŋgərz/ *n* [singular] *informal* someone who often drops things they are carrying or trying to catch
but·ter·fly /ˈbʌtəflaɪ $ -ər-/ ●●○ *n* (*plural* **butterflies**) [C]
1 a type of insect that has large wings, often with beautiful colours → see picture at INSECT
2 have/get butterflies (in your stomach) *informal* to feel very nervous before doing something: *I always get butterflies before an exam.*
3 the butterfly a way of swimming by lying on your front and moving your arms together over your head while your legs move up and down → see picture at SWIM
4 someone who usually moves on quickly from one activity or person to the next: *Gwen's a real* ***social butterfly****.*
but·ter·milk /ˈbʌtəˌmɪlk $ -ər-/ *n* [U] the liquid that remains after butter has been made
but·ter·scotch /ˈbʌtəskɒtʃ $ -ərskɑːtʃ/ *n* [U] a type of sweet or sauce made from butter and sugar boiled together, or the taste this has: *butterscotch pudding*
butt·hole /ˈbʌthəʊl $ -hoʊl/ *n* [C] *AmE spoken not polite* **1** someone's ANUS **2** used to insult someone: *You butthole!*
but·tock /ˈbʌtək/ ●○○ *n* [C usually plural] one of the fleshy parts of your body that you sit on
but·ton[1] /ˈbʌtn/ ●●● S2 *n* [C]
1 a small round flat object on your shirt, coat etc that you pass through a hole to fasten it: *small pearl buttons* | *A button was missing from his shirt.* | *She* ***undid*** (=unfastened) *the* ***buttons*** *of her blouse.* | **do up a button** *BrE* (=fasten a button)
2 a small part or area of a machine that you press to make it do something: ***Press*** *the pause* ***button****.* | *Click on the icon with the right* ***mouse button****.* → PUSH-BUTTON
3 a small area on a computer screen, especially on a website, that you CLICK on in order to perform an action
4 *AmE* a small metal or plastic pin with a message or picture on it SYN **badge** *BrE*: *presidential campaign buttons*
5 button nose/eyes a nose or eyes that are small and round
6 on the button *especially AmE informal* exactly right, or at exactly the right time: *She got to our house at two, on the button.*
7 press/push (all) the right buttons to get what you want by behaving in a clever way: *She seemed to push all the right buttons.*
8 press/push sb's buttons to make someone angry by doing or saying something that annoys them: *He really knows how to push Dad's buttons.*
9 at/with the push/touch of a button used to emphasize how easy a machine is to use because it is controlled by pushing a button: *The instrument can gauge a distance with the push of a button.* → **as bright as a button** at BRIGHT(8)
button[2] *v* [I,T] **1** (*also* **button up**) to fasten clothes with buttons, or to be fastened with buttons: *Sam, make sure Nina buttons up her jacket.* **2 button it!** *BrE*, **button your lip/mouth!** *AmE spoken* used to tell someone in a rude way to stop talking
ˈ**button-down** *adj* [only before noun] **1** a button-down shirt or collar has the ends of the collar fastened to the shirt with buttons **2** a button-down company or style is formal and traditional: *He didn't fit in with the button-down culture of his new boss.*
ˌ**buttoned-ˈup** *adj informal* someone who is buttoned-up is not able to express their feelings, especially sexual feelings
but·ton·hole /ˈbʌtnhəʊl $ -hoʊl/ *n* [C] **1** a hole for a button to be put through to fasten a shirt, coat etc **2** *BrE* a flower you fasten to your clothes SYN **boutonniere** *AmE*
but·tress[1] /ˈbʌtrəs/ *n* [C] a brick or stone structure built to support a wall
buttress[2] *v* [T] *formal* to support a system, idea, argument etc, especially by providing money: *The evidence seemed to buttress their argument.*
but·ty /ˈbʌti/ *n* (*plural* **butties**) [C] *BrE informal* a SANDWICH
bux·om /ˈbʌksəm/ *adj* a woman who is buxom is attractively large and healthy and has big breasts

Frequencies of the verbs **buy**, **get** and **purchase** in spoken and written English.

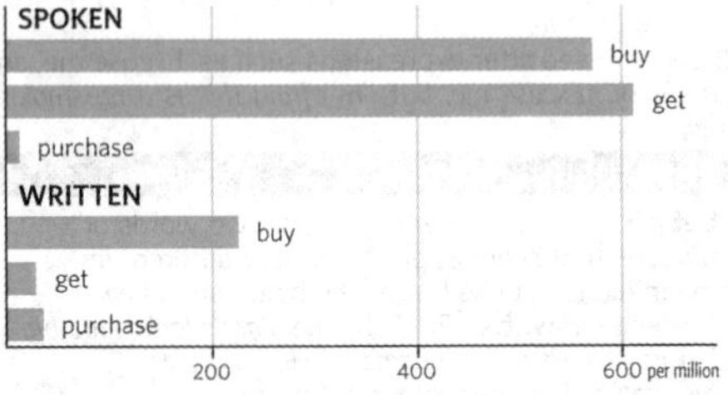

SPOKEN
buy
get
purchase
WRITTEN
buy
get
purchase
200 400 600 per million

All three verbs are used to mean 'get something by paying for it'. The graph shows that in this meaning **get** is extremely common in spoken English. However, **get** is informal and is not at all common in written English. **Purchase** is used in formal or business contexts. It is not very common and is used more in written English than in spoken English.

buy[1] /baɪ/ ●●● S1 W1 *v* (*past tense and past participle* **bought** /bɔːt $ bɒːt/)
1 a) [I,T] to get something by paying money for it OPP **sell**: *Where did you buy that dress?* | *Ricky showed her the painting he'd bought that morning.* | **buy sb sth** *Let me buy you a drink.* | **buy sth for sb/sth** *The money will be used to buy equipment for the school.* | **buy (sth) from sb** *It's cheaper to buy direct from the manufacturer.* | **buy sth for $10/£200 etc** *Dan bought the car for $2,000.* | *It's much cheaper to* ***buy in bulk*** (=buy large quantities of something). **b)** [T] if a sum of money buys something, it is enough to pay for it: *$50 doesn't buy much these days.* | **buy sb sth** *$15 should buy us a pizza and a drink.*
2 buy (sb) time to deliberately make more time for yourself to do something, for example by delaying a decision:

'Can we talk about it later?' he said, trying to buy a little more time.
3 [T] *informal* to believe something that someone tells you, especially when it is not likely to be true: *'Let's just say it was an accident.' **'He'll never buy that.'***
4 [T] *informal* to pay money to someone, especially someone in a position of authority, in order to persuade them to do something dishonest SYN **bribe**: *People say the judge had been bought by the Mafia.*
5 buy sth at the cost/expense/price of sth to get something that you want, but only by losing something else: *The town has been careful not to buy prosperity at the expense of its character.*
6 sb bought it *old-fashioned informal* someone was killed
7 buy off-plan if you buy property off-plan, you buy a house, flat etc that is just starting to be built, with an arrangement to pay part of the cost of the property at that time and the balance when the property is finished

THESAURUS

buy to pay money for something so that you can own it: *I've just bought a new car.* | *The painting was bought by a museum in New York.*
purchase *formal* to buy something, especially something large or expensive, in a business deal or by a legal contract: *They purchased 5,000 acres of land.*
acquire *formal* to become the owner of something large or expensive such as property, a company, or a valuable object: *In 2007 the business was acquired by a Dutch company.*
get *especially spoken* to buy something, especially ordinary things such as food, clothes, or things for your house: *Did you remember to get some bread?* | *I never know what to get Dad for his birthday.*
snap sth up *informal* to buy something immediately, especially because it is very cheap, or because you want it very much and you are worried that someone else might buy it first: *Real estate in the area is being snapped up by developers.*
pick sth up *informal* to buy something, especially something ordinary such as food or a newspaper, or something that you have found by chance and are pleased about owning: *Could you pick up some milk on your way home?* | *It's just a little thing I picked up when I was in Kathmandu.*
stock up to buy a lot of something you use regularly, because you may not be able to buy it later, or because you are planning to use more of it than usual: *The supermarkets are full of people stocking up for the New Year's holiday.*

buy sth ↔ **in** *phr v* to buy something in large quantities: *Companies are buying in supplies of paper, in case the price goes up.*
buy into sth *phr v*
1 *informal* to accept that an idea is right and allow it to influence you: *I never bought into this idea that you have to be thin to be attractive.*
2 to buy part of a business or organization, especially because you want to control it: *Investors were invited to buy into state-owned enterprises.*
buy sb ↔ **off** *phr v* to pay someone money to stop them causing trouble or threatening you SYN **bribe**
buy out *phr v*
1 buy sb/sth ↔ out to buy someone's share of a business or property that you previously owned together, so that you have complete control → BUYOUT
2 buy sb out of sth to pay money so that someone can leave an organization such as the army before their contract has ended
buy sth ↔ **up** *phr v* to quickly buy as much of something as possible, for example land, tickets, or goods: *Much of the land was bought up by property developers.*

buy² *n* [C, usually singular] **1** something that is worth buying, because it is cheap, good quality, or likely to gain in value: **a good/excellent etc buy** *The wine is a good buy at $6.50.* | *It's worth shopping around for* ***the best buy*** (=what you want at the lowest price). **2** *informal* an act of buying something, especially something illegal SYN **deal**

buy·er /ˈbaɪə $ -ər/ ●●○ S3 W3 *n* [C]
1 someone who buys something expensive such as a house or car OPP **seller**, **vendor**: *There were several potential buyers.* | *discounts for **first-time buyers***
2 someone whose job is to choose and buy the goods for a shop or company: *a buyer for a chain store*

ˌbuyer's ˈmarket *n* [singular] a situation in which there is plenty of something available, so that buyers have a lot of choice and prices tend to be low OPP **seller's market**

buy·out /ˈbaɪaʊt/ *n* [C] a situation in which someone gains control of a company by buying all or most of its SHARES: *a management buyout* → **buy out** at BUY¹

buzz¹ /bʌz/ ●○○ *v*
1 MAKE A SOUND [I] to make a continuous sound, like the sound of a BEE: *a loud buzzing noise*
2 MOVING AROUND [I always + adv/prep] **a)** to move around in the air making a continuous sound like a BEE: *Bees were buzzing around the picnic tables.* **b)** to move quickly around a place: *Pamela buzzed around checking that everything was ready.* | *There were all sorts of rumours buzzing through the office.*
3 EXCITEMENT [I] if a group of people or a place is buzzing, there is a lot of activity or excitement: **[+with]** *a classroom **buzzing with activity***
4 CALL [I,T] **a)** to call someone by pressing a BUZZER: *Kramer buzzed at the security door, and I let him in.* | **[+for]** *Tina buzzed for her secretary.* **b)** to make something happen, for example make a door or gate open or close, by pressing a buzzer: **buzz sb in/out** *She buzzed them in and greeted them warmly.* | **buzz sb through sth** *The guard buzzed me through the gate.*
5 THOUGHTS [I] if your head or mind is buzzing with thoughts, ideas etc, you cannot stop thinking about them: **[+with]** *My mind was buzzing with new ideas.* | *Questions started buzzing round in my head.*
6 EARS [I] if your ears or head are buzzing, you can hear a continuous low unpleasant sound
7 AIRCRAFT [T] *informal* to fly an aircraft low and fast over buildings, people etc: *Military jets buzzed the city.*
buzz off *phr v spoken*
1 buzz off! used to tell someone in a rude way to go away
2 *BrE* to go away: *I've finished everything, so I'll buzz off now.*

buzz² *n* **1** [C] a continuous noise like the sound of a BEE: **[+of]** *the buzz of mosquitoes* **2** [singular] a lot of activity, noise, and excitement: **[+of]** *the buzz of conversation and laughter* **3** [singular] *informal* a strong feeling of excitement, pleasure, or success, or a similar feeling from drinking alcohol or taking drugs: *Playing well **gives** me **a buzz**.* | *Neil **gets a buzz** from drinking one beer.* **4 give sb a buzz** *informal* to telephone someone: *I'll give you a buzz on Monday.* **5 the buzz** *informal* unofficial news or information that is spread by people telling each other → **gossip**, **rumour**

buz·zard /ˈbʌzəd $ -ərd/ *n* [C] **1** *BrE* a type of large HAWK (=hunting bird) **2** *AmE* a type of large bird that eats dead animals

buzz·cut /ˈbʌzkʌt/ *n* [C] *AmE* a hair style that is very short, usually worn by men

buzz·er /ˈbʌzə $ -ər/ *n* [C] a small thing, usually shaped like a button, that BUZZes when you press it: *Press the buzzer if you know the answer.*

ˈbuzz saw *n* [C] *AmE* a SAW with a round blade that is spun around by a motor SYN **circular saw**

buzz·word /ˈbʌzwɜːd $ -wɜːrd/ *n* [C] a word or phrase from one special area of knowledge that people suddenly think is very important: *'Multimedia' has been a buzzword in the computer industry for years.* THESAURUS ▸ WORD

buzz·y /ˈbʌzi/ *adj informal* exciting, especially because a lot of things are going on: *The restaurant has quite a buzzy atmosphere.*

B

by¹ /baɪ/ ●●● S1 W1 *prep*
1 WHO/WHAT DOES STH used especially with a PASSIVE verb to say who or what does something or makes something happen: *I was attacked by a dog.* | *a church designed by the famous architect, Sir Christopher Wren* | *We are all alarmed by the rise in violent crime.* | *interference by the state in the affairs of the Church* | *his appointment by the BBC as a producer*
2 MEANS/METHOD used to say what means or method someone uses to do something: *You can reserve the tickets by phone.* | *Send it by airmail.* | *Some customers prefer to pay by cheque.* | **by car/train/bus/taxi etc** *They travelled to Chicago by train.* | **by air/sea/land/road/rail etc** *All supplies are transported by air.* | **by doing sth** *She earns her living by selling insurance.* | *He was taken from his home by force.*
3 ROAD/DOOR used to say which road, entrance, door etc someone uses to get to a place: *They came in by the back door.* | *It's quicker to go by the country route.*
4 TAKING HOLD used to say which part of an object or of a person's body someone takes hold of: *He took Elaine by the arm and led her across the road.* | *She grabbed the hammer by the handle.*
5 WRITER/COMPOSER ETC used to give the name of someone who wrote a book, produced a film, wrote a piece of music etc: *the 'New World symphony' by Dvorak* | *a short story by Charles Dickens* | *Who's it by?*
6 BESIDE beside or near something: *She stood by the window.* | *Jane went and sat by Patrick.*
7 PAST past someone or something without stopping: *He walked right by me without even saying hello.* | *I pass by the farm every day on my way to work.*
8 BEFORE before or not later than a particular time: *The documents need to be ready by next Friday.* | *I reckon the film should be over by 9.30.* | *By the end of the day we had sold over 2,000 tickets.* | *By the time we got home we were tired and hungry.* THESAURUS ▸ BEFORE
9 ACCORDING TO according to a particular rule, method, or way of doing things: *You've got to play by the rules.* | *Profits were £6 million, but by our standards this is low.*
10 CHANGE/DIFFERENCE used to say how great a change or difference is: *The price of oil fell by a further $2 a barrel.* | *I was overcharged by £3.* | *Godard's first film was better* ***by far*** (=by a large amount or degree).
11 MEASUREMENTS used to give the measurements of a room, container etc: *a room 15 metres by 23 metres*
12 QUANTITY used to show what unit of measurement or quantity is involved in selling, paying for, producing etc something: *Eggs are sold by the dozen.* | *We're paid by the hour.* | *She wanted to tear his hair out by the handful.*
13 GRADUAL CHANGE used to say that something happens gradually: *Day by day, he grew weaker.* | *Little by little, I was beginning to discover the truth about Garfield.* | *One by one, the men stepped forward.*
14 QUICK CHANGE used to say that something or someone is quickly becoming worse, better etc: *The financial crisis was growing more serious by the hour.*
15 LIGHT used to say that something happens in a particular kind of light: *We walked through the palace gardens by moonlight.*
16 by day/night during the day or the night: *a tour of Paris by night*
17 JOB/NATURE ETC used when you are giving information about someone's character, job, origin etc: *George I and George II were Germans by birth.* | *Cautious by nature, Simpkin was reluctant to interfere.* | *Robert Key was a teacher by profession.*
18 VISITING in order to visit a person or place for a short time: *On the way, I stopped by the post office.*
19 (all) by yourself a) completely alone: *Dave spent Christmas all by himself.* **b)** without help from anyone: *You can't move the furniture all by yourself.*
20 MULTIPLYING/DIVIDING used between two numbers when talking about multiplying or dividing: *What's 48 divided by 4?*
21 EMPHASIS used when expressing strong feelings or making serious promises: *By God, I'll kill that boy when I see him!*
22 FATHER if a woman has children by a particular man, that man is the children's father: *She's got two children by her previous husband.*
23 by the by *spoken* used when mentioning something that may be interesting but is not particularly important: *By the by, Ian said he might call round tonight.* → **by the way** at WAY¹

USAGE: By, with
- **By** is used, especially after passive verbs, to say who or what does something: *The article was written by a university professor.* | *She was hit by a truck.*
- **With** is used after verbs that describe a state rather than an action: *The books were covered with dust.* | *Her house is always filled with music.* ✗ Don't say: *covered by dust* | *filled by music*
- **By** is used to say what means or method someone uses to do something: *He replied by email.*
- **With** is used to say what tool is used to do something: *Clean the surface thoroughly with a wire brush.* ✗ Don't say: *by a wire brush*

by² ●●● S1 W1 *adv*
1 past someone or something: *As I was standing on the platform, the Liverpool train went whizzing by.* | *James walked by without even looking in my direction.*
2 used to say that time passes: *As the summer days slipped by, it was easy to forget about the war.* | *Ten years had gone by since I had last seen Marilyn.*
3 beside or near someone or something: *A crowd of people were standing by, waiting for an announcement.*
4 in order to visit a person or place for a short time: *Why don't you stop by for a drink after work?*
5 by and large used when making a general statement: *By and large, the new arrangements have worked well.*
6 by and by *old use* soon: *She will be better by and by.*

by-, **bye-** /baɪ/ *prefix* less important: *a by-product* (=something made in addition to the main product) | *a by-election* (=one held between regular elections)

bye¹ /baɪ/ ●●● S1 *interjection informal* goodbye: *Bye, Dave.* | **bye for now** (=used to say that you will see or speak to someone again soon)

bye² *n* [C] a situation in a sports competition in which a player or a team does not have an opponent to play against and continues to the next part of the competition

bye- /baɪ/ *prefix* another spelling of BY-

bye-'bye *interjection informal* goodbye – used especially when speaking to children, friends, or members of your family: *Say bye-bye to Daddy, Tommy.*

'bye-byes *n* **go (to) bye-byes** *BrE* an expression meaning go to sleep, used by or to children

'by-eˌlection, **'bye-eˌlection** *n* [C] *especially BrE* a special election to replace a politician who has left parliament or died → **general election**

by·gone /ˈbaɪɡɒn $ -ɡɔːn/ *adj* **bygone age/era/days etc** a period of time in the past: *The buildings reflect the elegance of a bygone era.*

by·gones /ˈbaɪɡɒnz $ -ɡɔːnz/ *n* **let bygones be bygones** to forget something bad that someone has done to you and forgive them

by·law /ˈbaɪlɔː $ -lɒː/ *n* [C] **1** a law made by a local government that people in that area must obey **2** *AmE* a rule made by an organization to control the people who belong to it

'by-line *n* [C] a line at the beginning of an article in a newspaper or magazine that gives the writer's name

BYOD /ˌbiː waɪ əʊ ˈdiː $ -oʊ-/ *n* [U] (***bring your own device***) the practice of allowing or asking an EMPLOYEE or student to bring their own equipment, for example a LAPTOP, to work on: *BYOD has implications for a company's security.*

by·pass¹ /ˈbaɪpɑːs $ -pæs/ *n* [C] **1 (heart) bypass operation/surgery** an operation to direct blood through new VEINS (=blood tubes) outside the heart because the veins in the heart are blocked or diseased: *a triple heart bypass operation* **2** a road that goes around a town or other busy area rather than through it → **ring road** **3** *technical* a tube that allows gas or liquid to flow around something rather than through it

bypass² *v* [T] **1** to go around a town or other busy place rather than through it: *Interstate 8 bypasses the town to the north.* **2** to avoid obeying a rule, system, or someone in an official position: *Francis bypassed his manager and wrote straight to the director.*

ˈby-ˌproduct, **by·prod·uct** /ˈbaɪˌprɒdʌkt $ -ˌprɑː-/ *n* [C] **1** something additional that is produced during a natural or industrial process: **[+of]** *a by-product of oil refining* **2** an unplanned additional result of something that you do: **[+of]** *Job losses are an unfortunate byproduct of the recession.* → END PRODUCT

byre /baɪə $ baɪr/ *n* [C] *BrE old-fashioned* a farm building in which cattle are kept SYN **cowshed**

by·stand·er /ˈbaɪˌstændə $ -ər/ *n* [C] someone who watches what is happening without taking part SYN **onlooker**: *Several* ***innocent bystanders*** *were killed by the blast.*

byte /baɪt/ *n* [C] a unit for measuring computer information, equal to eight BITS (=the smallest unit on which information is stored on a computer): *Each character requires one byte of storage space.* → GIGABYTE, KILOBYTE, MEGABYTE, TERABYTE

by·way /ˈbaɪweɪ/ *n* [C] **1** a small road or path that is not used very much **2 byways** [plural] the less important parts of an activity or subject: *a scholar exploring the* ***highways and byways*** *of Russian music* (=the important and less important parts)

by·word /ˈbaɪwɜːd $ -wɜːrd/ *n* **1 be a byword for sth** to be so well known for a particular quality that your name is used to represent that quality: *His name has become a byword for honesty in the community.* **2** [singular] a word, phrase, or saying that is very well known: *Caution should be a byword for investors.*

By·zan·tine /baɪˈzæntaɪn, -tiːn, bɪ- $ ˈbɪzəntiːn, -taɪn/ *adj* **1** (*also* **byzantine**) complicated and difficult to understand: *the byzantine complexity of our tax laws* **2** relating to the Byzantines or the Byzantine Empire: *a 5th-century Byzantine church*

B

Cc

C[1], **c** /siː/ *n* (*plural* **C's**, **c's**) [C,U] **1** the third letter of the English alphabet **2** the first note in the musical SCALE of C MAJOR, or the musical KEY based on this note **3** a mark given to a student's work to show that it is of average quality **4** the number 100 in the system of ROMAN NUMERALS

C[2] **1** the written abbreviation of ***Celsius*** or ***Centigrade***: *Water boils at 100°C.* **2** *written informal* a way of writing 'see', used especially in emails and TEXT MESSAGES: *CU* (=see you) *in class!*

c (*also* **c.**) **1** (*also* **C**) the written abbreviation of ***century***: *the economic changes of the C20th* **2** a written abbreviation of ***circa*** (=about), used especially before dates: *c. 1830* **3** © the written abbreviation of ***copyright*** **4** *AmE* the written abbreviation of ***cup***, used in cooking

ca. (*also* **ca** *BrE*) a written abbreviation of ***circa*** (=about): *dating from ca. 1900*

CAA, the /ˌsiː eɪ ˈeɪ/ (***the Civil Aviation Authority***) a British organization that controls the operation of the air travel industry, especially by making safety rules and directing the traffic of planes in the UK

cab /kæb/ ●●● S3 *n* [C]
1 a taxi: *New York's yellow cabs* | **take/get a cab** *I took a cab to the airport.* | **call (sb) a cab** (=telephone for a taxi) | *Ralph tried to* ***hail a cab*** (=wave to get a cab to stop for you).
2 the part of a bus, train, or truck in which the driver sits
3 a carriage pulled by horses that was used like a taxi in the past

CAB, the /ˌsiː eɪ ˈbiː/ (***the Citizens Advice Bureau***) a British organization supported by the government which gives free advice to ordinary people about legal, financial, and other problems. Most towns and cities in the UK have a Citizens Advice Bureau, and most of the people who work for it are VOLUNTEERS (=they are not paid for their work).

ca·bal /kəˈbæl/ *n* [C] *formal* a small group of people who make secret plans, especially in order to have political power

ca·ba·na /kəˈbɑːnə $ -ˈbæ-/ *n* [C] a tent or small wooden structure used for changing clothes at a beach or pool

cab·a·ret /ˈkæbəreɪ $ ˌkæbəˈreɪ/ *n* **1** [C,U] entertainment, usually with music, songs, and dancing, performed in a restaurant or club while the customers eat and drink: *a cabaret singer* **2** [C] a restaurant or club where this is performed: *the most famous Parisian cabaret, the Moulin Rouge*

cab·bage /ˈkæbɪdʒ/ ●●○ *n*
1 [C,U] a large round vegetable with thick green or purple leaves → see picture at **VEGETABLE**[1]
2 [C] *BrE informal* someone who cannot think, move, speak etc as a result of brain injury SYN **vegetable**

cab·bie, **cabby** /ˈkæbi/ *n* [C] *informal* a taxi driver

ca·ber /ˈkeɪbə $ -ər/ *n* [C] a long heavy wooden pole that is thrown into the air as a test of strength in sports competitions in Scotland

cab·in /ˈkæbɪn/ ●●○ *n* [C]
1 a small house, especially one built of wood in an area of forest or mountains: *a* ***log cabin***
2 a small room on a ship in which you live or sleep
3 an area inside a plane where the passengers sit or where the pilot works: *the First Class cabin*

ˈcabin boy *n* [C] a young man who works as a servant on a ship

ˈcabin class *n* [U] travelling conditions on a ship that are better than TOURIST CLASS but not as good as FIRST CLASS

ˈcabin crew *n* [U] the group of people whose job is to take care of the passengers on a plane → **flight attendant**, **stewardess**

ˈcabin ˌcruiser *n* [C] a large motorboat with one or more cabins for people to sleep in

cab·i·net /ˈkæbɪnɪt/ ●●○ *n* [C]
1 (*also* **Cabinet**) *BrE* the politicians with important positions in a government who meet to make decisions or advise the leader of the government: *a cabinet meeting* | *a member of the Cabinet* → **Shadow Cabinet** at **SHADOW**[3](2)

> **GRAMMAR: Singular or plural verb?**
> **Cabinet** can be followed by a singular or a plural verb: *The cabinet* ***has*** *been discussing the plans.* | *The cabinet* ***have*** *been discussing the plans.*
> GRAMMAR GUIDE ▸ **NOUNS**

2 a piece of furniture with doors and shelves or drawers, used for storing or showing things SYN **cupboard**: *the medicine cabinet* → **FILING CABINET**

ˈcabinet-ˌmaker *n* [C] someone whose job is to make good-quality wooden furniture

ˈcabin ˌfever *n* [U] *informal* when you feel upset and impatient because you have not been outside for a long time

ca·ble[1] /ˈkeɪbəl/ ●●● W3 *n*
1 [C] a plastic or rubber tube containing wires that carry telephone messages, electronic signals, television pictures etc: *cables and switches for computers* | **overhead/underground/undersea cable** *overhead power cables*
2 [C,U] a thick strong metal rope used on ships, to support bridges etc
3 [U] a system of broadcasting television by using cables, paid for by the person watching it: **on cable** *I'll wait for the movie to come out on cable.* | **cable network/channel/programme**
4 [C] a TELEGRAM

cable[2] *v* [I,T] to send someone a TELEGRAM: **cable sb sth** *I cabled Mary the good news.*

ˈcable car *n* [C] **1** a vehicle that hangs from a moving cable, and is used to take people up and down mountains **2** a vehicle similar to a train that is pulled along by a moving cable

ca·ble·cast /ˈkeɪbəlkɑːst $ -kæst/ *n* [C] *AmE* a show, sports event etc that is broadcast on a CABLE TELEVISION station → **broadcast**: *the MTV Video Awards cablecast* —**cablecast** *v* [T]

ˈcable-knit *adj* a cable-knit SWEATER has a raised pattern of crossing lines on it

ˈcable ˌmodem *n* [C] a MODEM (=piece of computer equipment that allows information from one computer to be sent to another) that uses CABLE connections instead of telephone wires, and allows you to search the Internet very quickly

ˈcable ˌrailway *n* [C] a railway on which vehicles are pulled up steep slopes by a moving CABLE

ˈcable-ˌready *adj* a television that is cable-ready is able to receive cable television signals directly without needing any special equipment

ˌcable ˈtelevision (*also* **ˌcable TˈV**) *n* [U] a system of broadcasting television programmes by CABLE → **SATELLITE TELEVISION**

ca·bling /ˈkeɪblɪŋ/ *n* [U] all the wires that are used for electrical equipment or an electrical system

ca·boo·dle /kəˈbuːdl/ *n* **the whole (kit and) caboodle** *informal* everything: *I think it's time to replace the whole caboodle: computer, printer, and monitor.*

ca·boose /kəˈbuːs/ *n* [C] *AmE* a small railway carriage at the back of a train, usually where the person in charge of it travels SYN **guard's van** *BrE*

ˈcab rank *n* [C] *BrE* a place where taxis wait for customers SYN **cabstand** *AmE*

cab·ri·o·let /ˈkæbriəleɪ $ ˌkæbriəˈleɪ/ *n* [C] *BrE* a car with a roof that can be folded back SYN **convertible**

cab·stand /ˈkæbstænd/ *n* [C] *AmE* a place where taxis wait for customers SYN **taxi rank**, **cab rank** *BrE*

ca·cao /kəˈkaʊ/ *n* [U] the seed from which chocolate and COCOA are made

cache¹ /kæʃ/ *n* [C] **1** a number of things that have been hidden, especially weapons, or the place where they have been hidden: **[+of]** *a cache of explosives* | *a large* ***arms cache*** **2** *technical* a special part of a computer's memory that helps it work faster by storing information for a short time: *cache memory*

cache² *v* [T] **1** to hide something in a secret place, especially weapons **2** *technical* to store information in a computer's memory for a short time

cach·et /ˈkæʃeɪ $ kæˈʃeɪ/ *n* [singular, U] *formal* if something has cachet, people think it is very good or special SYN **kudos**: *It's a good college, but lacks the cachet of Harvard.*

cack-hand·ed /ˌkæk ˈhændɪd◂/ *adj BrE informal* careless and tending to drop things, or badly done SYN **clumsy**

cack·le¹ /ˈkækəl/ *v* [I] **1** to laugh in a loud unpleasant way, making short high sounds THESAURUS LAUGH **2** when a chicken cackles, it makes a loud high sound

cackle² *n* [C] **1** a loud high sound that a chicken makes → **cluck 2** a short high unpleasant laugh

ca·coph·o·ny /kəˈkɒfəni $ kəˈkɑː-/ *n* [singular] a loud unpleasant mixture of sounds: **[+of]** *a cacophony of car horns* —**cacophonous** *adj*

cac·tus /ˈkæktəs/ *n* (*plural* **cacti** /-taɪ/ *or* **cactuses**) [C] a desert plant with sharp points instead of leaves

cad /kæd/ *n* [C] *old-fashioned* a man who cannot be trusted, especially one who treats women badly

CAD /kæd, ˌsiː eɪ ˈdiː/ *n* [U] (***computer-aided design***) the use of computers to design industrial products

ca·dav·er /kəˈdævə, kəˈdeɪ- $ kəˈdævər/ *n* [C] *technical* a dead human body, especially one used for study SYN **corpse**

ca·dav·er·ous /kəˈdævərəs/ *adj literary* looking extremely thin, pale, and unhealthy: *cadaverous cheeks*

cad·dy¹ /ˈkædi/ *n* (*plural* **caddies**) [C] **1** (*also* **caddie**) someone who carries the GOLF CLUBS for someone who is playing golf → see picture at GOLF **2** a small box for storing tea

caddy², **caddie** *v* (**caddied**, **caddying**, **caddies**) [I + for] to carry GOLF CLUBS for someone who is playing golf

ca·dence /ˈkeɪdəns/ *n* [C] **1** the way someone's voice rises and falls, especially when reading out loud: *the cadence of my mother's voice* **2** a regular repeated pattern of sounds or movements: *the Brazilian cadences of the music* **3** *technical* a set of CHORDS

ca·den·za /kəˈdenzə/ *n* [C] *technical* a difficult part of a long piece of music, which a performer plays alone in order to show his or her skill

ca·det /kəˈdet/ *n* [C] someone who is training to be an officer in the army, navy, air force, or police

cadge /kædʒ/ *v* [I,T] *BrE informal* to ask someone you know for something such as food, money, or cigarettes, because you do not have any or do not want to pay: **cadge sth from/off sb** *I cadged a lift from Joanna.*

Cad·il·lac /ˈkædɪlæk, -dəl-/ *n* [C] *trademark* **1** a very expensive and comfortable car **2** *AmE informal* something that is regarded as an example of the highest quality of a particular type of product: **[+of]** *the Cadillac of stereo systems*

cad·mi·um /ˈkædmiəm/ *n* [U] a soft poisonous metal that is used in BATTERIES and in the protective SHIELDS in NUCLEAR REACTORS. It is a chemical ELEMENT: symbol Cd

ca·dre /ˈkɑːdə, -drə, ˈkeɪdə $ ˈkædri, ˈkɑːdrə/ *n* [C] a small group of specially trained people in a profession, political party, or military force: **[+of]** *a cadre of highly trained scientists*

GRAMMAR: Singular or plural verb?

- **Cadre** is usually followed by a singular verb: *A new cadre of leaders* ***has*** *emerged.*
- In British English, you can also use a plural verb: *A new cadre of leaders* ***have*** *emerged.*

GRAMMAR GUIDE NOUNS

cae·sar·e·an /səˈzeəriən $ -ˈzer-/ (*also* **caeˌsarean ˈsection**) *n* [C] an operation in which a woman's body is cut open to take a baby out: **born/delivered etc by caesarean** *Both her children were born by caesarean section.* | *She had to* ***have*** *a* ***caesarean***.

cae·si·um *BrE*, **cesium** *AmE* /ˈsiːziəm/ *n* [U] a soft silver-white metal that is used in PHOTOELECTRIC CELLS. It is a chemical ELEMENT: symbol Cs

cae·su·ra /sɪˈzjʊərə $ sɪˈʒʊrə, sɪˈzʊrə/ *n* [C] *technical* a pause in the middle of a line of poetry

ca·fé /ˈkæfeɪ $ kæˈfeɪ, kə-/ ●●● S2 *n* [C]
1 a small restaurant where you can buy drinks and simple meals
2 Internet café/cybercafé a public place where you can pay to use the Internet and buy drinks etc

caf·e·te·ri·a /ˌkæfəˈtɪəriə $ -ˈtɪr-/ ●●● S3 *n* [C] a restaurant, often in a factory, college etc, where you choose from foods that have already been cooked and carry your own food to a table SYN **canteen** *BrE*: *the school cafeteria* THESAURUS RESTAURANT

caf·e·tière /ˌkæfəˈtjeə $ -ˈtjer/ *n* [C] *BrE* a pot for making coffee, with a metal FILTER that you push down

caff /kæf/ *n* [C] *BrE informal* a café

caf·feine /ˈkæfiːn $ kæˈfiːn/ *n* [U] a substance in tea, coffee, and some other drinks that makes you feel more active → **decaffeinated**: *Avoid caffeine* (=drinks with caffeine) *before bedtime.* | *a caffeine-free cola* —**caffeinated** /ˈkæfɪneɪtɪd/ *adj*

caf·fè lat·te /ˌkæfeɪ ˈlæteɪ $ ˌkɑːfeɪ ˈlɑːteɪ, ˌkæf-/ *n* [C,U] a drink made with coffee and hot milk

caf·tan, **kaftan** /ˈkæftæn $ kæfˈtæn/ *n* [C] a long loose piece of clothing, usually made of silk or cotton, and worn in the Middle East

cage¹ /keɪdʒ/ ●●○ *n* [C] a structure made of wires or bars in which birds or animals can be kept

cage² *v* [T] to put or keep an animal or bird in a cage: *caged birds*

ˈcage ˌfighting *n* [U] a sport in which two people fight in an area surrounded by NETTING, using punches, kicks, and movements from different types of fighting —**cage fighter** *n* [C]

ˈcage-free *adj* cage-free egg production is production that does not involve keeping chickens in small cages: *We only offer cage-free eggs for sale.*

cag·ey /ˈkeɪdʒi/ *adj* unwilling to tell people about your plans, intentions, or opinions OPP **open**: **[+about]** *He was very cagey about the deal.* —**cagily** *adv* —**caginess** *n*

ca·goule /kəˈguːl/ *n* [C] *BrE* a thin coat with a HOOD that stops you from getting wet

ca·hoots /kəˈhuːts/ *n* **be in cahoots (with sb)** to be working secretly with another person or group, especially in order to do something dishonest: *The Forest Service and the timber industry were in cahoots.*

cairn /keən $ kern/ *n* [C] a pile of stones that marks a particular place, especially at the top of a mountain

cais·son /ˈkeɪsən, kəˈsuːn $ ˈkeɪsɑːn, -sən/ *n* [C] **1** a large box filled with air, that people go into to work under water, for example when building bridges **2** a large box for carrying AMMUNITION

ca·jole /kəˈdʒəʊl $ -ˈdʒoʊl/ *v* [I,T] to gradually persuade someone to do something by being nice to them, or making promises to them: **cajole sb into doing sth** *We do our best to cajole rich countries into helping.* THESAURUS PERSUADE

Ca·jun /ˈkeɪdʒən/ *n* **1** [C] someone from Louisiana in the US who has French-Canadian ANCESTORS **2** [U] a type of music played by Cajun people —**Cajun** *adj*: *Cajun cooking*

cake¹ /keɪk/ ●●● S2 W3 *n*
1 [C,U] a soft sweet food made by baking a mixture of

flour, butter, sugar, and eggs: *We had cake and ice cream.* | *a chocolate cake*
2 fish/rice/potato etc cake fish, rice etc that has been formed into a flat round shape and then cooked
3 [C] a small block of something: **[+of]** *a cake of soap*
4 be a piece of cake *spoken* to be very easy: *'How do you do that?' 'It's a piece of cake! Watch!'*
5 take the cake (*also* **take the biscuit** *BrE*) *informal* to be worse than anything else you can imagine: *I've heard some pretty dumb ideas, but that takes the cake!*
6 have your cake and eat it *BrE*, **have your cake and eat it too** *AmE spoken* to have all the advantages of something without its disadvantages
7 a slice of the cake *BrE* a share of the profit, help etc that is available: *Both companies expect to get a big slice of the cake.* → **sell like hot cakes** at HOT CAKE(1)

C

COLLOCATIONS

VERBS

make/bake a cake *Let's make a cake for his birthday.*
decorate a cake *We decorated the cake with strawberries and cream.*
ice a cake *BrE*, **frost a cake** *AmE* (=cover a cake with fine sugar mixed with a liquid)

PHRASES

a piece/slice of cake *Would you like a slice of cake?*
a cake recipe | **a cake tin** *BrE*, **a cake pan** *AmE* (=that you bake a cake in) | **a cake shop** | **cake mix** (=a mixture that you buy in a packet and use for making a cake)

TYPES OF CAKE

a birthday/Christmas/wedding cake (=a special cake for a birthday etc) *Lucy had twelve candles on her birthday cake.*
a home-made cake *Home-made cakes are much nicer than bought ones.*
a fruit cake (=one with dried fruit in it) | **a sponge cake** (=one made from flour, butter, sugar, and eggs) | **a chocolate/lemon etc cake** (=a sponge cake with a chocolate etc flavour) | **a cream cake** (=one with thick cream inside it)

COMMON ERRORS

⚠ Don't say 'cook a cake'. Say **make a cake** or **bake a cake**.

cake² *v* **1 be caked with/in sth** to be covered with a layer of something soft or wet that becomes thick and hard when it dries: *Our boots were caked with mud.* **2** [I] if a substance cakes, it forms a thick hard layer when it dries

cake·hole /ˈkeɪkhəʊl $ -hoʊl/ *n* [C] *BrE spoken* someone's mouth

ˈcake pan *n* [C] *AmE* a cake TIN¹(4) → see picture at **PAN¹**

ˈcake slice *n* [C] a piece of kitchen equipment with a handle and a wide flat end that you use for cutting and serving cakes, TARTS etc

ˈcake tin *n* [C] **1** *BrE* a metal container in which you bake a cake SYN **cake pan** *AmE* → see picture at **PAN¹** **2** a metal container with a lid, that you keep a cake in

cake·walk /ˈkeɪkwɔːk $ -wɒːk/ *n* [singular] *AmE informal* a very easy thing to do, or a very easy victory SYN **piece of cake**: *The game was a cakewalk.*

cal·a·mine lo·tion /ˈkæləmaɪn ˌləʊʃən $ -ˌloʊ-/ *n* [U] a pink liquid that you put on sore, ITCHY, or SUNBURNed skin to make it less painful

ca·lam·i·ty /kəˈlæməti/ *n* (*plural* **calamities**) [C] a terrible and unexpected event that causes a lot of damage or suffering SYN **disaster**: *It will be a calamity for farmers if the crops fail again.* —**calamitous** *adj*

cal·ci·fy /ˈkælsɪfaɪ/ *v* (**calcified**, **calcifying**, **calcifies**) [I,T] *technical* to become hard, or make something hard, by adding LIME

cal·ci·um /ˈkælsiəm/ ●●○ *n* [U] a silver-white metal that helps to form teeth, bones, and CHALK. It is a chemical ELEMENT: symbol Ca

cal·cu·la·ble /ˈkælkjələbəl/ *adj* [no comparative] something that is calculable can be measured by using numbers, or by studying the facts available OPP **incalculable**: *clear and calculable benefits*

cal·cu·late /ˈkælkjəleɪt/ ●●● S2 W3 *v* [T]
1 to find out how much something will cost, how long something will take etc, by using numbers: *These instruments calculate distances precisely.* | **calculate how much/how many etc** *I'm trying to calculate how much paint we need.* | **calculate (that)** *Sally calculated that she'd have about £100 left.* | **calculate sth on sth** *Rates are calculated on an hourly basis.*

REGISTER

In everyday English, people usually say that they **work** something **out** or, in American English, **figure** something **out**, rather than **calculate** it: *We still haven't* ***worked out*** *how much it's all going to cost.*

GRAMMAR

In more formal English, you say **it is calculated that**: *It is calculated that over $16 billion has been spent on the project.*

2 to guess something using as many facts as you can find: **calculate (that)** *Researchers calculated that this group was at a higher risk of heart disease.* | **calculate how/what/whether etc** *It's difficult to calculate what effect all these changes will have on the company.*
3 be calculated to do sth to be intended to have a particular effect: *a question calculated to embarrass him*
calculate on sth *phr v* if you calculate on something, you are depending on it for your plans to succeed: *We're calculating on an early start.* | **calculate on sb/sth doing sth** *Ken hadn't calculated on Polson refusing his offer.*

cal·cu·lat·ed /ˈkælkjəleɪtɪd/ *adj* **1** a calculated crime or dishonest action is deliberately and carefully planned – used to show disapproval: *a* ***calculated attempt*** *to deceive the American public* **2 a calculated risk/gamble** something risky that you do after thinking carefully about what might happen: *The police* ***took a calculated risk*** *in releasing him.* —**calculatedly** *adv*

cal·cu·lat·ing /ˈkælkjəleɪtɪŋ/ *adj* thinking carefully about how to get exactly what you want, often without caring about anyone else – used to show disapproval: *He gave her a calculating look.*

cal·cu·la·tion /ˌkælkjəˈleɪʃən/ ●●○ *n*
1 [C usually plural, U] when you use numbers in order to find out an amount, price, or value: *Dee looked at the bill and made some rapid calculations.* | **by sb's/some/many calculations** *By some calculations, the population will reach eight million soon.*
2 [C,U] careful planning in order to get what you want, especially without caring about the effects on other people → **miscalculation**: *political calculation*
3 [U] when you think carefully about what the probable results will be if you do something → **miscalculation**

COLLOCATIONS

VERBS

do/make a calculation *The children should be able to do that calculation in their heads.*
perform a calculation *formal* (=do one) *Computers can perform calculations very quickly.*

ADJECTIVES

a simple calculation *A simple calculation will show that these figures are incorrect.*
a rough calculation (=not very detailed or exact) *I made a few rough calculations of how much it would cost.*
a quick/rapid calculation | **a detailed calculation** | **complex calculations** | **mathematical calculations** | **sb's calculations are right/correct/accurate** | **sb's calculations are wrong/inaccurate**

cal·cu·la·tor /ˈkælkjəleɪtə $ -ər/ ●●● S3 *n* [C] a small electronic machine that can add, multiply etc → see picture at MATHEMATICS

cal·cu·lus /ˈkælkjələs/ *n* [U] the part of mathematics that deals with changing quantities, such as the speed of a falling stone or the slope of a curved line

cal·dron /ˈkɔːldrən $ ˈkɒːl-/ *n* [C] the American spelling of CAULDRON

cal·en·dar /ˈkæləndə $ -ər/ ●●● S3 *n* [C]
1 a set of pages that show the days, weeks, and months of a particular year, that you usually hang on a wall
2 *AmE* **a)** a book with separate spaces or pages for each day of the year, on which you write down the things you have to do SYN **diary** *BrE*: *a desk calendar* **b)** all the things you plan to do in the next days, months etc: *an event that deserves a place on your calendar*
3 a system that divides and measures time in a particular way, usually starting from a particular event: **the Roman/Islamic/Gregorian etc calendar**
4 all the events in a year that are important for a particular organization or activity: **golfing/sporting/racing etc calendar** *The Derby is a major event in the racing calendar.*

ˌcalendar ˈmonth *n* [C] **1** one of the 12 months of the year: *Salaries will be paid at the end of the calendar month.* **2** a period of time from a specific date in one month to the same date in the next month

ˌcalendar ˈyear *n* [C] the period of time from January 1st to December 31st of the same year

calf /kɑːf $ kæf/ ●●○ *n* (*plural* **calves** /kɑːvz $ kævz/) [C]
1 the part of the back of your leg between your knee and your ANKLE
2 the baby of a cow, or of some other large animals, such as an ELEPHANT
3 be in/with calf if a cow is in or with calf, it is going to have a baby → **kill the fatted calf** at KILL[1](15)

calf·skin /ˈkɑːfskɪn $ ˈkæf-/ *n* [U] the skin of a calf, used for making shoes, bags etc

cal·i·ber /ˈkæləbə $ -ər/ *n* [C,U] the American spelling of CALIBRE

cal·i·brate /ˈkæləbreɪt/ *v* [T] *technical* **1** to check or slightly change an instrument or tool, so that it does something correctly **2** to mark an instrument or tool so that you can use it for measuring

cal·i·bra·tion /ˌkæləˈbreɪʃən/ *n* [U] *technical* **1** the process of checking or slightly changing an instrument or tool so that it does something correctly: *the calibration of flight instruments* **2** a set of marks on an instrument or tool used for measuring, or the act of making these marks correct

cal·i·bre *BrE*, **caliber** *AmE* /ˈkæləbə $ -ər/ *n* **1** [U] the level of quality or ability that someone or something has achieved: **of sb's calibre** *Where will we find another man of his calibre?* | *The school attracts a* ***high calibre*** *of student.* | **of high/the right etc calibre** *The paintings were of the highest caliber.* | **of this/that calibre** *The city needs a hotel of this calibre* (=of this high standard). **2** [C] **a)** the width of the inside of a gun or tube: *a .22 caliber rifle* **b)** the width of a bullet

cal·i·co /ˈkælɪkəʊ $ -koʊ/ *n* [U] **1** *BrE* heavy cotton cloth that is usually white **2** *AmE* light cotton cloth with a small printed pattern **3 calico cat** *AmE* a cat that has black, white, and brown fur

cal·i·pers /ˈkæləpəz $ -ərz/ *n* [plural] the American spelling of CALLIPERS

ca·liph /ˈkeɪlɪf/ *n* [C] a Muslim ruler, especially in the past

ca·li·phate /ˈkeɪləfeɪt/ *n* [C] the country a caliph rules, or the period of time when they rule it

cal·is·then·ics /ˌkæləsˈθenɪks/ *n* [U] the American spelling of CALLISTHENICS

calk /kɔːk $ kɒːk/ *v* [T] an American spelling of CAULK

call[1] /kɔːl $ kɒːl/ ●●● S1 W1 *v*
1 TELEPHONE [I,T] to telephone someone: *She calls her father every couple of days.* | *I'll call you soon.* | *What time did Tony call?* | **call a doctor/the police/a cab etc** (=telephone someone and ask them to come to you) *I think we should call a doctor.* | *I'm gonna call the cops!* THESAURUS PHONE

> **GRAMMAR**
> • You **call** someone on the phone: *Call me tomorrow.*
> ✗ Don't say: *Call to me tomorrow.*
> • If you **call to** someone, you shout at them to get their attention: *He called to the driver to stop.*

2 DESCRIBE [T] to use a word or name to describe someone or something in a particular way: **call sb sth** *Are you calling me a liar?* | *You may call it harmless fun, but I call it pornography.* | **call sb names** (=use insulting names for someone) *The other kids used to call me names, but I tried to ignore them.*
3 HAVE A NAME [T] to have a particular name or title, or use a particular name or title for someone or something: **be called sth** *Our son is called Matthew.* | *The arrow that appears on the screen is called a cursor.* | **call sb sth** *My name's Virginia, but my friends call me Ginny.* | *Do you want to be called Miss or Ms?* | **call sb by sth** *I prefer to be called by my middle name.*
4 GIVE SB/STH A NAME [T] *especially BrE* to give someone or something the name they will be known by in the future SYN **name** *AmE*: *What are you going to call the new puppy?* | **call sb sth** *They've decided to call the baby Louise.*
5 ASK/ORDER BY SPEAKING [T] to ask or order someone to come to you: **call sb into/over/across etc** *Peter called the waitress over and ordered a large brandy.* | *Marcie was called up to the principal's office.*
6 ARRANGE [T] to arrange for something to happen at a particular time: **call a meeting/strike/election etc** *The Security Council has called an emergency session to discuss the crisis.* | *According to the law, the election must be called within the next two months.*
7 SAY/SHOUT [I,T] to say or shout something loudly so that someone can hear you: *I heard someone calling in the distance.* | *'I'm coming!' she called down the stairs.* | *Sheila was just sneaking out when her mother called her.* | *She heard him* ***call*** *her* ***name***. | **[+to]** *The foreman called to the workmen.*
8 call yourself sth to say that you are a particular type of person, although you do nothing to show this is true: *How could Julian call himself a friend and then let me down so badly?*
9 call the shots/tune *informal* to be in a position of authority so that you can give orders and make decisions: *It was a job in which she was able to call the shots.*
10 call it a day *informal* to decide to stop working, especially because you have done enough or you are tired: *Come on, let's call it a day and go home.*
11 call collect *AmE* to make a telephone call that is paid for by the person who receives it SYN **reverse the charges** *BrE*
12 READ NAMES [T] (*also* **call out**) to read names or numbers in a loud voice in order to get someone's attention: *When I call your name, go and stand in line.*
13 COURT [T] to tell someone that they must answer questions in a law court or in front of an official committee: *The prosecution called its next witness.* | **call sb to do sth** *They were called to give evidence at the trial.* GRAMMAR **Call** is often passive in this meaning.
14 call (sth) into question to make people uncertain about whether something is right, good, or true: *I feel that my competence is being called into question here.*
15 be/feel called to do sth to feel strongly that you should do something: *He felt called to write to all his fellow investors, warning them of the impending crisis.*
16 call sb/sth to order *formal* to tell people to obey the rules of a formal meeting
17 VISIT [I] (*also* **call round** *BrE*) to stop at a house or other place for a short time to see someone or do something: *She called round for a chat.* | **call on sb** *Let's call on James on the way home.* | **call (in) at sth** *I regularly called in at his office for news.* | **call into sth** *People often call into the library while they're out shopping.*

C

18 call it £10/two hours etc *spoken* used to suggest a general figure rather than a more specific one, especially in order to make things simpler: *'I owe you £10.20.' 'Oh, call it £10!'*

19 call it a draw if two opponents in a game call it a draw, they agree that neither of them has won → **call it quits** at QUITS(2)

20 call it/things even *spoken* use this to say that someone who owes you something does not have to give you anything more than they have already given you

21 call (sb's) attention to a) to ask people to pay attention to a particular subject or problem: *May I call your attention to item seven on the agenda?* **b)** to make someone notice someone or something: *I wanted to shout out to Ken, but I didn't want to call attention to myself.*

22 call sth to mind a) to remind you of something: *Don't those two call to mind the days when we were courting?* **b)** to remember something: *I couldn't call to mind where I'd seen him before.*

23 call a huddle *AmE informal* to make people come together to talk about something

24 call time (on sb/sth) to say that it is time for something to finish or stop

25 TRAINS/SHIPS [I] if a train, ship, bus etc calls at a place, it stops there for a short time SYN **stop**: *This train calls at all stations to Broxbourne.*

26 COIN [I,T] to guess which side of a coin will land upwards when it is thrown in the air, in order to decide who will play first in a game: *It's your turn to call.*

27 CARD GAME [I,T] to risk the same amount of money as the player who plays before you in a POKER game → SO-CALLED, → **call sb's bluff** at BLUFF²(2), → **too close to call** at CLOSE²(8)

call back *phr v*

1 call (sb) back to telephone someone again, for example because they were not at home when you telephoned last time: *I'll call back later.* | *Can you ask John to call me back when he gets in?*

2 *BrE* to return to a place you went to earlier: *You could call back to collect her at noon.*

call by *phr v* to stop and visit someone when you are near the place where they live or work: *I thought I'd call by and see how you were.*

call down sth *phr v formal* to ask for someone, especially a god, to make something unpleasant happen to someone or something: **[+on/upon]** *He called down vengeance on them.*

call for sb/sth *phr v*

1 if a group of people call for something, they ask publicly for something to be done: *Human Rights groups are calling for the release of political prisoners.*

2 to need or deserve a particular type of behaviour or treatment: *Dealing with children who are so damaged calls for immense tact and sensitivity.* | *That kind of abuse is really* ***not called for*** (=it is unnecessary and unwelcome). → UNCALLED FOR

3 *BrE* to meet someone at their home in order to take them somewhere: *I'll call for you at eight o'clock.*

4 *AmE* to say that a particular kind of weather is likely to happen SYN **predict**: *The forecast calls for more rain.*

call sth ↔ **forth** *phr v formal* to produce a particular reaction: *Great works of classical music can often call forth a mixture of responses from the listener.*

call in *phr v*

1 call sb/sth ↔ in to ask someone to come and help you with a difficult situation: *The government then called in troops to deal with the disturbances.*

2 to telephone somewhere, especially the place where you work, to tell them where you are, what you are doing etc: *Rachael* ***called in sick*** (=telephoned to say she was too ill to come to work).

3 to telephone a radio or television show to give your opinion or to ask a question: *Over 2,000 viewers called in with complaints about the bad language used in the programme.*

4 call in a loan/debt to officially tell someone to pay back money you lent them: *The bank can call in the loan at any time.*

5 *BrE* to visit a person or place while you are on your way to somewhere else: **[+on/at]** *Could you call in on Mum on your way home?*

call sb/sth ↔ **off** *phr v*

1 to decide that a planned event will not take place SYN **cancel**: *The trip to Italy might be called off.*

2 to officially decide that something should be stopped after it has already started: *Rescuers had to call off the search because of worsening weather conditions.*

3 to order an animal or person to stop attacking or threatening someone: *Call your dog off.*

call on/upon sb/sth *phr v*

1 to formally ask someone to do something: **call on sb to do sth** *The UN has called on both sides to observe the ceasefire.*

2 to visit someone for a short time: *Why don't you call on my sister when you're in Brighton?*

call out *phr v*

1 to say something loudly: **call sth ↔ out** *'Hi there!' I called out.* | **[+to]** *The firemen called out to him.*

2 call sb ↔ out to ask or order a person or an organization to help, especially in a difficult or dangerous situation: *The army was called out to help fight fires.*

3 call sb/sth ↔ out *BrE* to order workers to go on STRIKE: *The transport workers were called out.*

call up *phr v*

1 *especially AmE informal* to telephone someone: **call sb ↔ up** *He called me up to tell me about it.* | *I'm going to call up and cancel my subscription.*

2 call sth ↔ up if you call up information on a computer, you make the computer show it to you: *I called up their website, but it didn't have the information I was looking for.*

3 call sb ↔ up *BrE* to officially order someone to join the army, navy, or air force SYN **draft** *AmE*: *I was called up three months after war broke out.*

4 call sb ↔ up to choose someone for a national sports team → **call-up**: *Hurst was called up for the game against Mexico.*

5 call sth ↔ up to produce something or make it appear: *She can call up the spirits of the dead.*

call² ●●● S1 W1 *n*

1 TELEPHONE [C] when you speak to someone on the telephone: **[+for]** *Were there any phone calls for me while I was out?* | **[+from]** *I received a call from an old friend last week.* | *It's cheaper to make calls after 6 pm.* | *I'll give you a call at the weekend.*

2 be on call if someone such as a doctor or engineer is on call, they are ready to go and help whenever they are needed as part of their job: *Don't worry, there's a doctor on call 24 hours a day.*

3 SHOUT/CRY [C] **a)** a loud sound that a bird or animal makes SYN **cry**: **[+of]** *the call of an owl* **b)** a shout that you make to get someone's attention

4 VISIT [C] a visit, especially for a particular reason: *Sorry, Doctor Pugh is out on a call at the moment.* | **pay/make a call (on sb)** (=visit someone)

5 REQUEST/ORDER [C] a request or order for something or for someone to do something: *Members obediently answered the calls for funds.* | **call for sb to do sth** *There have been calls for the secretary to resign.* | **a call to arms** (=an order for people to fight against an enemy)

6 DECISION **a)** [C] the decision made by a REFEREE in a sports game: **make a good/bad call** *There may have been a few bad calls, but they're making them for a reason.* **b)** [singular] *informal* a decision: *Don't just say what you think I would like.* ***It's your call.*** | **make a call** (=decide something) | **an easy/hard call** (=an easy or difficult decision) | **judgment call** (=a decision based on your personal judgment of a situation)

7 there isn't much call for sth used for saying that not many people want a particular thing: *There isn't much call for black and white televisions these days.*

8 there is no call for sth *spoken* used to tell someone that

their behaviour is wrong and unnecessary: *There's no call for that kind of language!*
9 AT AN AIRPORT [C] a message announced at an airport that a particular plane will soon leave: *This is the last call for flight BA872 to Moscow.*
10 have first call on sth a) to have the right to be the first person to use something **b)** to be the first person that you will help because they are important to you: *Her children had first call on her time.*
11 the call of sth *literary* the power that a place or way of life has to attract someone: *the call of the sea*
12 the call of nature a need to URINATE (=pass liquid from your body) – used especially humorously → **be at sb's beck and call** at BECK(1), → **PORT OF CALL, ROLL-CALL, WAKE-UP CALL**

COLLOCATIONS

VERBS

make a call *He made a few calls and then went out.*
give sb a call (=phone someone) *I'll give him a call later today.*
get/have a call (*also* **receive a call** *formal*) *At 11 in the evening we got a call from the police.*
there is/was a call *There was a phone call for you.*
answer a call *We're sorry that we cannot answer your call right now.*
take a call (=answer one) *Monica took the call upstairs.*
return sb's call (=call someone after they have tried to call you) | **transfer a call** (=connect one to another person's phone) | **put through a call** (=transfer or make one)

ADJECTIVES/NOUN + call

a phone/telephone call *I had a phone call from Barbara in Australia.*
a quick call *This is just a quick call to make sure you're OK.*
a local call *Local calls are free at weekends.*
a long-distance call | **an international call** | **a collect call** *AmE* (=one paid for by the person who receives it) | **incoming/outgoing calls** (=coming into or going out of a place) | **an emergency call** (=to the police, fire service, or ambulance service) | **a hoax call** (=one intended to trick someone) | **an anonymous call** (=in which the caller does not give their name)

CALL /kɔːl $ kɒːl/ *n* [U] (***computer-assisted language learning***) the use of computers to help people learn foreign languages

ˈcall box *n* [C] **1** *BrE* a PHONE BOX **2** *AmE* a public telephone beside a road or FREEWAY used to telephone for help

ˈcall ˌcentre *BrE*, **call center** *AmE* ●○○ *n* [C] an office where people answer customers' questions, make sales etc by using the telephone rather than by meeting people

call·er /ˈkɔːlə $ ˈkɒːlər/ *n* [C] **1** someone making a telephone call: *'Could you hold for one moment?' he asked the caller.* **2** *old-fashioned* someone who visits your house

ˌcaller diˈsplay *BrE*, **ˌcaller I'D** *AmE* *n* [C,U] a special service on your telephone that lets you know who is calling before you answer the telephone

ˈcall girl *n* [C] a PROSTITUTE who arranges by telephone to meet men

cal·lig·ra·phy /kəˈlɪgrəfi/ *n* [U] the art of producing beautiful writing using special pens or brushes, or the writing produced this way —**calligrapher** *n* [C]

ˈcall-in *n* [C] *AmE* a radio or television programme in which people telephone to give their opinions SYN **phone-in** *BrE*: *a **call-in** talk **show***

call·ing /ˈkɔːlɪŋ $ ˈkɒː-/ *n* [C] **1** a strong desire or feeling of duty to do a particular kind of work, especially religious work SYN **vocation**: *It wasn't until Durant was in her 30s that she **found** her **calling**.* **2** *formal* someone's profession or trade

ˈcalling card *n* [C] *AmE* a small card with a name and often an address printed on it, that people in the past gave to people they visited SYN **visiting card** *BrE*

cal·li·pers *BrE*, **calipers** *AmE* /ˈkæləpəz $ -ərz/ *n* [plural] **1** a tool used for measuring thickness, or the distance between two surfaces, or the DIAMETER (=inside width) of something **2** *BrE* metal bars that someone wears on their legs to help them walk SYN **brace** *AmE*

cal·lis·then·ics *BrE*, **calisthenics** *AmE* /ˌkæləsˈθenɪks/ *n* [U] a set of physical exercises that are intended to make you strong and healthy

ˈcall ˌletters *n* [plural] *especially AmE* a CALL SIGN

ˈcall ˌoption *n* [C] *technical* the right to buy a particular number of SHARES at a special price within a particular period of time

cal·lous /ˈkæləs/ *adj* not caring that other people are suffering: *We were shocked at the callous disregard for human life.* | *a callous attitude* | *the callous slaughter of seals* —**callously** *adv* —**callousness** *n* [U]

cal·loused /ˈkæləst/ *adj* calloused skin is rough and covered in CALLUSes: *rough **calloused hands***

ˈcall-out *n* [C] *BrE* a situation in which someone is called to another person's house or place of business to do repairs, help them etc: *The lifeboat has had ten call-outs in the past year.* | *call-out charges*

cal·low /ˈkæləʊ $ -loʊ/ *adj* young and without experience – used to show disapproval SYN **immature**: *a **callow youth***

ˈcall ˌscreening *n* [U] **1** a special service that you can buy from your telephone company which prevents particular people from calling you **2** when you let an answering machine answer your telephone calls, and you then only talk to callers that you want to speak to

ˈcall sign *n* [C usually singular] (*also* **call letters** *especially AmE*) a name made up of letters and numbers, used by people operating communication radios to prove who they are

call·time /ˈkɔːltaɪm $ ˈkɒːl-/ *n* [U] the amount of time that is available for the user of a MOBILE PHONE to make calls

ˈcall-up *n* [C] *BrE* **1** an order to join the army, navy etc SYN **draft** *AmE*: *He got his **call-up papers** in July.* **2** an opportunity or invitation to play for a professional sports team, especially a national one: **[+to]** *Stewart's recent call-up to the Wales squad*

cal·lus /ˈkæləs/ *n* [C] an area of thick hard skin: *the calluses on his hands*

ˌcall ˈwaiting *n* [U] a telephone service that allows you to receive another call when you are already talking on the telephone, without ending the first call

calm¹ /kɑːm $ kɑːm, kɑːlm/ ●●● S3 W3 *adj* (*comparative* **calmer**, *superlative* **calmest**)
1 relaxed and quiet, not angry, nervous, or upset: *Glen was calm and composed at the funeral.* | **remain/stay/keep calm** *I tried to stay calm and just ignore him.*
2 if a place, period of time, or situation is calm, there is less activity, trouble etc than there sometimes is, or than there has been recently: *The financial markets are calm at the moment.* | *The streets are calm again after last night's disturbances.*
3 a sea, lake etc that is calm is smooth or has only gentle waves: *The seas were **dead calm**.* —**calmly** *adv* —**calmness** *n* [U]

THESAURUS

calm not getting angry, nervous, or upset, even in a difficult situation: *We'll talk about this later when you're feeling calmer.*
relaxed not worried about anything, especially so that people feel comfortable: *Looking relaxed and confident, the president answered questions from the press.* | *There was a relaxed atmosphere.*

chilled-out (*also* **chilled**) *informal* very relaxed and not worried – used especially by young people: *I'm much more chilled-out about the whole thing this year.*
laid-back *informal* someone who is laid-back is always relaxed and never seems to get worried or annoyed about anything: *I like his laid-back attitude to life.* | *My parents are pretty laid-back and don't mind me staying out late.*
mellow *informal* relaxed, friendly, and happy, especially after drinking alcohol: *After a few drinks, everyone was pretty mellow.*
cool *informal* staying calm and not showing your emotions, especially when other people are getting excited or angry: *He is the kind of player who always manages to stay cool, even under pressure.* | *She was as cool as a cucumber* (=very cool).
keep your head to manage to stay calm and behave in a sensible way in a difficult or frightening situation: *In this job you need to be good at keeping your head in a crisis.*

C

calm² ●●○ *n* [singular, U]
1 a situation or time that is quiet and peaceful: **[+of]** *They remained on the terrace after dinner, enjoying the calm of the evening.* | **morning/afternoon/evening calm** *A scream shattered the late afternoon calm.* | *Hindu leaders* ***appealed for calm*** (=asked that the public stay calm) *after a temple was burnt to the ground.* | *The presence of soldiers helped* ***restore calm***. | *The last five years have seen a period of* ***relative calm***.
2 the calm before the storm a calm peaceful situation that will not continue because a big argument, problem etc is coming

calm³ ●●○ (*also* **calm down**) *v* [I,T]
1 to become quiet and relaxed after you have been angry, excited, nervous, or upset, or to make someone become quiet and relaxed: *He tried to calm the frightened children.* | *Calm down and tell me what happened.* | *We tried to* ***calm*** *people's* ***fears***. | **calm yourself (down)** *She lit a cigarette to calm herself down.*
2 if a situation calms down, it becomes easier to deal with because there are fewer problems and it is not as busy as it was before: *It took months for* ***things*** *to* ***calm down*** *after we had the baby.*

Cal·or gas /ˈkælə gæs $ -lər-/ *n* [U] *trademark BrE* a type of gas that is sold in metal containers and used for heating and cooking where there is no gas supply

cal·o·rie /ˈkæləri/ ●●○ *n* [C]
1 a unit for measuring the amount of ENERGY that food will produce: *A potato has about 90 calories.* | *a calorie-controlled diet* | **low-calorie/high-calorie** *a low-calorie snack* | *I need to* ***burn off*** *a few* ***calories*** (=lose some weight by exercising). | *My wife convinced me to finally start* ***counting calories*** (=control my weight by being careful about what I eat).
2 *technical* the amount of heat that is needed to raise the temperature of one gram of water by one degree Celsius. It is used as a unit for measuring energy. —**caloric** /kəˈlɒrɪk, ˈkælərɪk $ kəˈlɔːrɪk/ *adj*

cal·o·rif·ic /ˌkæləˈrɪfɪk◂/ *adj* **1** food that is calorific tends to make you fat **2** *technical* producing heat

cal·um·ny /ˈkæləmni/ *n* (*plural* **calumnies**) **1** [C] an untrue and unfair statement about someone that is intended to give people a bad opinion of them **2** [U] when someone says things like this

calve /kɑːv $ kæv/ *v* [I] to give birth to a CALF

calves /kɑːvz $ kævz/ the plural of CALF

Cal·vin·is·m /ˈkælvənɪzəm/ *n* [U] the Christian religious teachings of John Calvin, based on the idea that events on Earth are controlled by God and cannot be changed by humans

Cal·vin·ist /ˈkælvɪnɪst/ *adj* **1** following the teachings of Calvinism **2** (*also* **Calvinistic** /ˌkælvəˈnɪstɪk◂/) having strict moral standards and tending to disapprove of pleasure SYN **puritanical** —**Calvinist** *n* [C]

ca·lyp·so /kəˈlɪpsəʊ $ -soʊ/ *n* (*plural* **calypsos**) [C] a type of Caribbean song based on subjects of interest in the news

ca·lyx /ˈkeɪlɪks, ˈkæ- $ ˈkeɪ-/ *n* (*plural* **calyxes** *or* **calyces** /-ləsiːz/) [C] the green outer part of a flower that protects it before it opens

cam /kæm/ *n* [C] a wheel or part of a wheel that is shaped to change circular movement into backwards and forwards movement

CAM /kæm/ *n* [U] (***computer-aided manufacturing***) the use of computers to make industrial products

cam·a·ra·de·rie /ˌkæməˈrɑːdəri $ -ˈræ-, -ˈrɑː-/ *n* [U] a feeling of friendship that a group of people have, especially when they work together: *the camaraderie of the women's basketball team*

cam·ber /ˈkæmbə $ -ər/ *n* [C,U] *technical* a slight curve from the centre of a road or other surface to the side, which makes water flow to the side

cam·bric /ˈkeɪmbrɪk/ *n* [U] thin white cloth made of LINEN or cotton

cam·cor·der /ˈkæmˌkɔːdə $ -ˌkɔːrdər/ *n* [C] a type of camera that records pictures and sound on VIDEOTAPE

came /keɪm/ *v* the past tense of COME

cam·el /ˈkæməl/ ●○○ *n* [C] a large desert animal with a long neck and either one or two HUMPS (=large raised parts) on its back

cam·el·hair /ˈkæməlheə $ -her/ *n* [U] a thick yellowish brown cloth, usually used for making coats

ca·mel·li·a /kəˈmiːliə/ *n* [C] a plant with dark green leaves and red, pink, or white flowers, or the flowers of this plant

Cam·em·bert /ˈkæməmbeə $ -ber/ *n* [C,U] a soft French cheese that is white outside and yellow inside

cam·e·o /ˈkæmi-əʊ $ -oʊ/ *n* (*plural* **cameos**) [C] **1** a short appearance in a film or play by a well-known actor: **cameo role/appearance** **2** a short appearance in a game of sport by a player **3** a small piece of jewellery with a raised shape, usually a person's face, on a flat background of a different colour: *a cameo brooch* → see picture at **JEWELLERY** **4** a short piece of writing that gives a clear idea of a person, place, or event

cam·e·ra /ˈkæmərə/ ●●● S2 W3 *n* [C]
1 a piece of equipment used to take photographs or make films or television programmes → **camcorder**, **video camera**: **on/off camera** (=while a camera is recording or not recording) *The crime was* ***caught on camera*** *by police.*
2 in camera *law* a law case that is held in camera takes place secretly or privately

cam·e·ra·man /ˈkæmərəmən/ *n* (*plural* **cameramen** /-mən/) [C] someone who operates a camera for films or television ⚠ Do not confuse with **photographer** (=a person who takes still photographs).

cam·e·ra·phone /ˈkæmərəˌfəʊn $ -ˌfoʊn/ *n* [C] a MOBILE PHONE that you can use to take photographs

ˈcamera-ˌshy *adj* not liking to have your photograph taken

cam·i·knick·ers /ˈkæmiˌnɪkəz $ -ərz/ *n* [plural] *BrE* a piece of women's underwear that combines a CAMISOLE and KNICKERS

cam·i·sole /ˈkæməsəʊl $ -soʊl/ *n* [C] a light piece of women's underwear that covers the chest down to the waist and has narrow bands over the shoulders → see picture at **UNDERWEAR**

cam·o·mile, **chamomile** /ˈkæməmaɪl/ *n* [C,U] a plant with small white and yellow flowers that are sometimes used to make tea

cam·ou·flage¹ /ˈkæməflɑːʒ/ *n* **1** [U] a way of hiding something, especially soldiers and military equipment, by using paint, leaves etc to make it look like the things around it: *soldiers learning camouflage technique* | *the camouflage netting over the tanks* **2** [U] the type of green and brown clothes, paint etc that soldiers wear to make themselves more difficult to see: *The men were dressed* ***in camouflage*** *and carrying automatic weapons.* | *camouflage trousers* **3** [singular, U] the way that the colour or shape of an animal protects it by making it difficult to see in the area in which it lives: *The whiteness of the arctic fox* ***acts as camouflage****, hiding it from its enemies.* **4** [singular, U] behaviour that is designed to hide something: **[+for]** *Aggression is often a camouflage for insecurity.*

camouflage² *v* [T] to hide something, especially by making it look the same as the things around it, or by making it seem like something else: **camouflage sth with sth** *I saw a truck, heavily camouflaged with netting and branches.* | *The strain she was under was* ***well camouflaged*** *by skilful make-up.* **THESAURUS** ▸ **HIDE**

camp¹ /kæmp/ ●●● S3 W3 *n*

1 IN THE MOUNTAINS/FOREST ETC [C,U] a place where people stay in tents, shelters etc for a short time, usually in the mountains, a forest etc: *Let's go back to camp – it's getting dark.* | *a camp near Lake Ellen Wilson* | *The soldiers* ***broke camp*** (=took down their tents etc) *and left before dawn.* | **pitch/make camp** (=set up a tent or shelter) *It was dark by the time we pitched camp.* | *We* ***set up camp*** (=made the camping place ready) *at nearby Icicle Lake.* | *The expedition's* ***base camp*** (=main camp) *was 6,000 feet below the summit.* | **mining/logging etc camp** (=a camp where people stay when they are doing these kinds of jobs)

2 prison/labour/detention etc camp a place where people are kept for a particular reason, when they do not want to be there: *a* ***refugee camp*** *just across the border* → **CONCENTRATION CAMP**

3 FOR CHILDREN [C,U] a place where young people go to take part in activities, and where they usually stay for several days or weeks: *The camp offers hiking, fishing, canoeing, and boating.* | *scout camp* | *Two years ago, she started a* ***summer camp*** *for girls aged eight and older.* | **tennis/football etc camp** (=a camp where you can do one particular activity) → **DAY CAMP, HOLIDAY CAMP**

4 GROUP OF PEOPLE [C] a group of people or organizations who have the same ideas or principles, especially in politics: *the extreme right-wing camp of the party* | *At least Lynne is definitely* ***in your camp*** (=supports you rather than someone else, and agrees with your ideas). → **have a foot in both camps** at **FOOT¹**(21)

5 MILITARY [C] a permanent place where soldiers live or train: *Donny is stationed at Camp Pendleton.*

camp² ●●○ *v* [I]

1 to set up a tent or shelter and stay there for a short time: *We'll camp by the river for the night, and move on tomorrow.* | **camping gear/equipment** *camping gear such as a sleeping bag, tent, and backpack*

2 go camping to visit an area, especially the mountains or a forest, and stay in a tent: *We went camping in the San Bernardino Mountains.*

camp out *phr v*

1 to sleep outdoors, usually in a tent: *What he liked best about scouting was camping out.*

2 to stay somewhere where you do not have all the usual things that a house has: *We'll just have to camp out until our furniture arrives.*

camp sth **up** *phr v* **camp it up** *informal* to deliberately use unnatural body or face movements, in a way that some people think is typical of a HOMOSEXUAL man

camp³ *adj* **1** a man who is camp moves or speaks in the way that people used to think was typical of HOMOSEXUALS **2** (*also* **campy** *AmE*) clothes, decorations etc that are camp are very strange, bright, or unusual

cam·paign¹ /kæmˈpeɪn/ ●●○ S3 W3 *n* [C]

1 a series of actions intended to achieve a particular result relating to politics or business, or a social improvement: *an advertising campaign* | **[+for/against]** *a campaign for equal rights* | *Jones ran a good campaign.* | *Police have launched a campaign to crack down on drug dealers.*

2 a series of battles, attacks etc intended to achieve a particular result in a war

COLLOCATIONS

VERBS

launch/mount a campaign (=begin a campaign) *They have launched a campaign to end world poverty.*

run/wage/conduct a campaign (=carry out a campaign) *He ran an aggressive campaign.*

lead a campaign *The government is leading a 'walk to school' campaign.*

spearhead a campaign (=lead it - used especially in news reports)

ADJECTIVES/NOUN + campaign

a national/nationwide campaign *The walk was part of a national campaign to raise £900,000.*

a worldwide/global/international campaign *a worldwide campaign for peace*

an advertising/marketing/sales campaign *The store ran a television advertising campaign just before Christmas.*

a publicity campaign (=to tell the public about something) *The interview was the start of a publicity campaign for his new book.*

an election/electoral campaign *He was a candidate in the 2008 election campaign.*

a presidential campaign | **a political campaign** | **a media/press campaign** | **a fundraising campaign** (=to get money for something) | **an anti-smoking/anti-bullying etc campaign** | **a smear campaign** (=in which unpleasant or untrue stories are spread about an important person) | **a long campaign** | **an effective/successful campaign** | **a strong campaign** (=forceful and effective) | **a deliberate/concerted campaign** (=done by people in a determined way) | **an orchestrated campaign** *disapproving* (=organized secretly to make political events happen in the way you want)

campaign + NOUN

campaign funds/money *He was found guilty of using campaign funds illegally.*

a campaign manager (=for a political campaign) *She's a campaign manager for Amnesty International.*

the campaign trail (=the places someone visits as part of their election campaign)

COMMON ERRORS

⚠ Don't say 'make a campaign'. Say **launch a campaign**.

campaign² ●●○ *v* [I] to lead or take part in a series of actions intended to achieve a particular social or political result: **[+for/against]** *a group campaigning against the destruction of the rain forests*

cam·paign·er /kæmˈpeɪnə $ -ər/ ●○○ *n* [C] someone who leads or takes part in actions which are intended to achieve a particular social or political result: **[+for]** *a campaigner for greater democracy* | **peace/human rights/environmental campaigners**

cam·pa·ni·le /ˌkæmpəˈniːli/ *n* [C] a high bell tower that is usually separate from any other building

cam·pa·nol·o·gy /ˌkæmpəˈnɒlədʒi $ -ˈnɑː-/ *n* [U] *formal* the skill of ringing bells, and the study of bells

ˌcamp ˈbed / $ ˈ. ˌ./ *n* [C] *BrE* a light narrow bed that folds flat and is easy to carry SYN **cot** *AmE*

camp·er /ˈkæmpə $ -ər/ *n* [C] **1** someone who is staying in a tent or shelter **2** (*also* **camper van** *BrE*) a vehicle that has cooking equipment and beds in it **3** *AmE* a special type of tent on wheels that has cooking equipment and beds in it **4** *AmE* a child who is taking part in a camp **5 happy camper** *spoken* someone who seems to be happy with their situation

camp·fire /ˈkæmpfaɪə $ -faɪr/ *n* [C] a fire made outdoors by people who are camping

ˈcamp ˌfollower *n* [C] *especially BrE* someone who supports an organization or a political party, but who is not actually a member of it

camp·ground /ˈkæmpgraʊnd/ *n* [C] *AmE* an area where people can camp, often with a water supply and toilets SYN **campsite** *BrE*

cam·phor /ˈkæmfə $ -ər/ *n* [U] a white substance with a strong smell, used especially to keep insects away

camp·ing /ˈkæmpɪŋ/ ●●● S3 *n* [U] the holiday activity of living in a tent: **camping gear/equipment**: *The shop sells camping equipment such as sleeping bags and backpacks.*

camp·site /ˈkæmpsaɪt/ ●●○ *n* [C]
1 *BrE* an area where people can camp, often with a water supply and toilets SYN **campground** *AmE*
2 *AmE* a place, usually within a campground, where one person or group can camp SYN **pitch** *BrE*

camp·stool /ˈkæmpstuːl/ *n* [C] *BrE* a small folding seat with no back

C

cam·pus /ˈkæmpəs/ ●●● S2 W3 *n* [C,U]
1 the land and buildings of a university or college, including the buildings where students live: *a beautiful campus in New England* | **on/off campus** *Most first-year students live on campus.*
2 the land and buildings belonging to a large company: *the Microsoft campus outside Seattle*

camp·y /ˈkæmpi/ *adj AmE* clothes, decorations etc that are campy are very strange, bright, or unusual SYN **camp**

CAMRA /ˈkæmrə/ *n* (***Campaign For Real Ale***) a British organization that encourages people to drink beer made using traditional methods, and supports PUBs that sell this type of beer

cam·shaft /ˈkæmʃɑːft $ -ʃæft/ *n* [C] a metal bar that a CAM is fastened to in an engine

can¹ /kən; *strong* kæn/ ●●● S1 W1 *modal verb* (*negative short form* **can't**)
1 ABILITY to be able to do something or to know how to do something: *You can swim, can't you?* | *Even a small personal computer can store vast amounts of information.* | *Gabriella can speak French fluently.* | *I'm afraid Mr Harding can't see you now – he's busy.* | *The police are doing all they can to find her.*
2 REQUESTING *spoken* used to ask someone to do something or give you something: *Can I have a drink, please?* | *Can you help me lift this box?*
3 ALLOWED to be allowed to do something or to have the right or power to do something: *You can't park here – it's a no parking zone.* | *'Can we go home now?' 'No we can't.'* | *A police officer can insist on seeing a driver's license.*
4 POSSIBILITY used to say that something is possible: *I am confident a solution can be found.* | *There can be no doubt that he is guilty.* | *The boxes can be stored flat.* | *Can he still be alive after all this time?*
5 SEEING/HEARING ETC used with the verbs 'see', 'hear', 'feel', 'taste', and 'smell', and with verbs connected with thinking, to mean that someone sees something, hears something etc: *Here they are – I can see their car.* | *Can you smell something burning?* | *I can't understand why you're so upset.* | *He can't remember where he put the tickets.*
6 NOT TRUE [in negatives] used to say that you do not believe that something is true: *This can't be the right road.* | *It can't be easy caring for someone else's children.*
7 SHOULD NOT [in questions and negatives] used to say that someone should not or must not do something: *You can't expect the world to change overnight.* | *We can't go on like this.* | *Jill's left her husband, but can you blame her after the way he treated her?*
8 SURPRISE/ANGER [usually in questions and negatives] *spoken* used when you are surprised or angry: *You can't be serious!* | *They can't have arrived already, surely!* | *How can you be so stupid!*
9 SOMETIMES used to say what sometimes happens or how someone sometimes behaves: *It can be quite cold here at night.* | *Peter can be really annoying.*
10 GIVING ORDERS *spoken* used to tell someone in an angry way to do something: *And you can stop that quarrelling, the pair of you.* | *If you won't keep quiet, you can get out.*
11 **no can do** *spoken* used to say that it is impossible for you to do what someone has asked you to do: *Sorry, John, no can do.*

THESAURUS: can

TO BE ABLE TO DO STH

can do sth to have the ability, opportunity, time, or equipment that you need in order to do something. **Could** is used as the past form, and is also used to say what is or may be possible: *'I don't think Mike can drive.' 'Yes, he can.'* | *Can you see the TV, or should I move?* | *Adrian could read when he was four.* | *Why didn't they ask me? I could have done it for them for half the price.* | *She could win.*
be able to do sth used when talking about ability or success in the past or ability in the future, or when you need to use an INFINITIVE. It is also used instead of **can** in more formal English: *I was able to get a good job* (=I got one). | *Will you be able to carry those bags on your own?* | *If you want to join the expedition, you must be able to speak Spanish.* | *The young birds are now able to fly.*
be capable of sth to have the ability, energy, or qualities needed to do something, especially something very difficult or unusual – use this about people or machines: *She's perfectly capable* (=completely capable) *of dealing with the situation.* | *The car is capable of a top speed of 200 mph.*
have the ability to do sth to be able to do something, especially something that is unusual or that most people cannot do: *She seemed to have the ability to make people do anything she wanted.*
be in a position to do sth to be able to do something because you have enough knowledge, power, money, or equipment to do it: *We will have to run more tests before we are in a position to say whether the document is authentic or not.*
manage to do sth to succeed in doing something difficult, especially after trying very hard: *He finally managed to find an apartment near his office.*

TO BE UNABLE TO DO STH

can't/cannot do sth to be unable to do something because you do not have the ability, opportunity, time, or equipment that you need. **Couldn't/could not** is used as the past form: *Louise can't see anything without her glasses.* | *He couldn't remember where he had left the car.* | *I couldn't have done it without your help.*
not be able to do sth used when talking about inability in the past or the future, when you need to use an INFINITIVE, and in more formal English: *Unfortunately, I wasn't able to help them.* | *I don't think I'll be able to come to the meeting after all.* | *The doctor told Tina she wouldn't be able to have children.*
be unable to do sth *especially written* to not be able to do something, especially something important that you want to do or need to do: *He was unable to sleep and lay awake all night.* | *Many passengers were unable to reach the lifeboats in time.*
not be in a position to do sth (*also* **be in no position to do sth**) *formal* to not be able to do something because you do not have enough knowledge, power, money, or equipment to do it: *I'm afraid I'm not in a position to answer your questions.*
not be capable of sth (*also* **be incapable of sth**) to not have the physical strength or mental ability to do something – often used when criticizing someone: *My son seems to be incapable of keeping a job.* | *She's not capable of looking after herself anymore.*

GRAMMAR: Patterns with can

- Like other modal verbs, you use **can** before the base form of the main verb (=the infinitive without 'to'): *We can hear the birds singing.| You can go home now.* | *Sharks can be dangerous.* ✗ Don't say: *We can to go home.* | *We can going home.*
- The past tense of **can** is **could**: *We could hear the birds singing.* | *The teacher said we could go home.*
- You also use **was/were able to** when talking about the ability to do something in the past, especially something that was difficult: *He was able to walk a few steps.*
- In questions you say **Can I/he/she etc**: *Can we go home?*
- In negatives you say **can't** (spoken) or **cannot** (written): *I can't hear you!| He cannot leave prison.*
- You also use **is/are unable to** when saying that someone does not have the ability to do something: *He is unable to walk.*

GRAMMAR GUIDE ▸ **VERBS**

CANS

can² /kæn/ ●●● S2 *n* [C]
1 a metal container in which food or drink is preserved without air: *a Coke can* | **[+of]** *All we've got is a couple of cans of soup.* → see picture at CONTAINER
2 a special metal container that keeps the liquid inside it under pressure. The liquid is released as a SPRAY when you press the button: **[+of]** *a can of hairspray*
3 *especially AmE* a metal container with a lid that can be removed, used for holding liquid: *Two large cans of paint ought to be enough.*
4 can of worms a very complicated situation that causes a lot of problems when you start to deal with it: *I just don't know what to do – every solution I can think of would just* ***open*** *up a whole new* ***can of worms***.
5 in the can *informal* a film that is in the can is complete and ready to be shown
6 the can *informal* **a)** a prison **b)** *AmE* a toilet
7 cans [plural] *informal* HEADPHONES → **carry the can** at CARRY¹(26)

can³ *v* (**canned, canning**) [T] *AmE* **1** to preserve food by putting it into a metal container from which all the air is removed SYN **tin** *BrE* → **canned 2** *informal* to dismiss someone from a job SYN **sack 3 can it!** *spoken* used to tell someone to stop talking or making a noise

Ca·na·di·an¹ /kəˈneɪdiən/ *adj* relating to Canada or its people

Canadian² *n* [C] someone from Canada

Caˌnadian ˈbacon *n* [U] *AmE* meat from the back or sides of a pig, served in thin narrow pieces

ca·nal /kəˈnæl/ ●●○ *n* [C] a long passage dug into the ground and filled with water, either for boats to travel along, or to take water to a place: *We walked along by the side of the canal.* | *the Panama Canal* | **by canal** *The goods were transported by canal to London.*

caˈnal boat *n* [C] a long narrow boat that is used for travelling on a canal

can·a·lize (*also* **-ise** *BrE*) /ˈkænəl-aɪz/ *v* [T] **1** *technical* to make a river deeper or straighter, especially in order to prevent flooding **2** *formal* to direct people's energy or feelings towards one particular thing

can·a·pé /ˈkænəpeɪ $ -pi, -peɪ/ *n* [C] a small piece of bread with cheese, meat etc on top, which is served with drinks at a party

ca·nard /kæˈnɑːd $ kəˈnɑːrd/ *n* [C] *written* a piece of news that is false and is told to people deliberately in order to harm someone

ca·nar·y /kəˈneəri $ -ˈneri/ *n* (*plural* **canaries**) [C] a small yellow bird that people often keep as a pet

ca·nas·ta /kəˈnæstə/ *n* [U] a card game

can·can /ˈkænkæn/ *n* [C] a fast dance in which a line of women kick their legs high into the air

can·cel /ˈkænsəl/ ●●● S2 *v* (**cancelled, cancelling** *BrE*, **canceled, canceling** *AmE*)
1 [I,T] to decide that something that was officially planned will not happen: *Our flight was cancelled.* | *I'm afraid I'll have to cancel our meeting tomorrow.* | *You'll just have to ring John and cancel.*
2 [I,T] to end an agreement or arrangement that you have with someone: *I phoned the hotel to cancel my reservation.* | *The bank agreed to cancel all the company's debts.*
3 [T] to say officially that a document can no longer be used or no longer has any legal effect: *I phoned the bank to cancel the cheque.*

THESAURUS

cancel to decide that something that was officially planned will not happen: *The teacher was ill so classes were cancelled for the day.* | *I was feeling better so I cancelled my doctor's appointment.* | *They were forced to cancel the concert when the conductor became ill.*
call off to cancel a meeting, game, or event that you have organized. **Call off** is less formal than **cancel** and is very commonly used in everyday English: *Linda decided to call the wedding off.* | *The game was called off due to heavy rain.*
be off if an event or activity is off, it has been cancelled because of a sudden problem or change in someone's plans: *I'm afraid the party's off. Nick won't let us use his apartment.* | *Myers called me yesterday to tell me that the deal was off.*
postpone to decide to do something at a later time, instead of the time that was officially planned: *The show has been postponed until next Saturday.*
shelve (*also* **put sth on ice**) to decide not to continue with a plan, project etc although it may be considered again at some time in the future: *Plans for a new stadium have been shelved for now.* | *The project had to be put on ice due to lack of funding.*
annul *formal* to officially decide that a marriage, result, or agreement has no legal authority and is therefore cancelled: *The election results were annulled by the courts.* | *A marriage can be annulled if there has been lack of consent.*

cancel sth ↔ **out** *phr v* if two things cancel each other out, they are equally important and have an opposite effect to each other, so that neither one has any effect → **negate**: *The losses in our overseas division have cancelled out the profits made in the home market.*

can·cel·la·tion /ˌkænsəˈleɪʃən/ ●●○ *n* [C,U]
1 a decision that an event that was planned will not happen: *Rail passengers are fed up with cancellations and delays.* | *Bad weather led to the cancellation of the game.*
2 a decision to end an agreement or arrangement that you have with someone: *There is a cancellation fee of £20.* | *The hotel is fully booked, but we will let you know if there are any cancellations.*

can·cer /ˈkænsə $ -ər/ ●●● S2 W2 *n*
1 [C,U] a very serious disease in which cells in one part of the body start to grow in a way that is not normal → **tumour**: *A lot of cancers can now be treated successfully.* | **lung/breast/stomach etc cancer** *Smoking causes lung cancer.* | *She was told last year that she* ***had cancer***. | *He* ***died of cancer*** *last month.* | **[+of]** *cancer of the womb* | *a new treatment which effectively kills* ***cancer cells***
2 [C] an evil influence that affects a lot of people and is difficult to stop: *Drug abuse is the cancer of our society.* —**cancerous** *adj*: *a cancerous growth* | *cancerous cells*

Cancer *n* **1** [U] the fourth sign of the ZODIAC, represented by a CRAB, which some people believe affects the character and life of people born between June 22 and July 23 **2** (*also* **Can·cer·i·an** /kænˈsɪəriən $ -ˈsɪr-/) [C] someone who was born between June 22 and July 23 —**Cancerian** *adj*

can·de·la·bra /ˌkændəˈlɑːbrə/ (*also* **can·de·la·brum** /-ˈlɑːbrəm/) *n* (*plural* **candelabra**) [C] a decorative object which holds several CANDLES or lamps

can·did /ˈkændɪd/ ●○○ *adj* telling the truth, even when the truth may be unpleasant or embarrassing SYN **frank**: **[+about]** *She was quite candid about the difficulties the government is having.* | **[+with]** *He was remarkably candid with me.* | *It struck me as an unusually candid confession for a politician.* **THESAURUS** HONEST —**candidly** *adv* → CANDOUR

can·di·da /ˈkændədə/ *n* [U] an infection in the mouth and throat of children or in a woman's VAGINA

can·di·da·cy /ˈkændədəsi/ *n* (*plural* **candidacies**) (*also* **can·di·da·ture** /ˈkændədətʃə $ -ər/) [C,U] the position of being one of the people who are competing in an election → **candidate**: **[+for]** *The local party supported her candidacy for the post of chairman.* | **announce/declare your candidacy** *He has not yet officially announced his candidacy for the presidential election.* | *She later* ***withdrew*** *her* ***candidacy***.

can·di·date /ˈkændədət $ -deɪt, -dət/ ●●● W2 *n* [C]
1 someone who is being considered for a job or is competing in an election: *a presidential candidate* | **[+for]** *There are only three candidates for the job.*
2 *BrE* someone who is taking an examination: *Candidates are not allowed to use a calculator in this exam.*
3 someone or something that is likely to experience or get something: **[+for]** *The school is an obvious candidate for extra funding.* | *The novel must be a* ***prime candidate*** *for the award.*

can·died /ˈkændid/ *adj* [only before noun] candied fruit has been cooked in sugar as a way of preserving it

can·dle /ˈkændl/ ●●○ S3 *n* [C]
1 a stick of WAX with a string through the middle, which you burn to give light
2 can't hold a candle to sb/sth *informal* if something or someone cannot hold a candle to something or someone else, they are not as good as the other thing or person: *No other singer can hold a candle to her.* → **burn the candle at both ends** at BURN[1](19)

can·dle·light /ˈkændl-laɪt/ *n* [U] the gentle light produced when a candle burns: *The jewels sparkled in the candlelight.* | **by candlelight** *We ate by candlelight.*

ˈcandle-lit *adj* lit by the gentle light of candles: *a candle-lit dinner for two*

can·dle·stick /ˈkændlˌstɪk/ *n* [C] a specially shaped metal or wooden stick that you put a candle into

can·dle·wick /ˈkændlˌwɪk/ *n* [U] cloth decorated with patterns of raised threads

ˌcan-ˈdo *adj* [only before noun] *informal* willing to try anything and expect that it will work: *He has a wonderful can-do attitude towards work.*

can·dour *BrE*, **candor** *AmE* /ˈkændə $ -ər/ *n* [U] the quality of being honest and telling the truth, even when the truth may be unpleasant or embarrassing → **candid**: *She spoke with candour about her life.*

C & W the written abbreviation of ***country and western***

can·dy /ˈkændi/ ●●● S3 *n* (*plural* **candies**) [C,U]
1 *AmE* a sweet food made from sugar or chocolate: *a box of candies* | *a candy bar* | *Do you want a piece of candy?*
2 mind/brain candy *informal* something that is entertaining or pleasant to look at, but which you do not approve of because you think it is not serious: *Most video games are just brain candy.*

ˈcandy ˌapple *n* [C] *AmE* an apple covered with a sweet sticky mixture

ˈcandy cane *n* [C] *AmE* a stick of hard red and white sugar with a curved end

can·dy·floss /ˈkændiflɒs $ -flɑːs, -flɔːs/ *n* [U] *BrE* a type of sweet food made from sticky threads of pink sugar wound around a stick

ˈcandy-ˌstriped *adj* candy-striped cloth has narrow coloured lines on a white background

cane[1] /keɪn/ ●○○ *n*
1 [U] thin pieces of the stems of plants, used for making furniture and baskets: *a cane chair* | *cane furniture*
2 [C] a long thin stick made from the stem of a plant, used for supporting other plants in a garden
3 [C] a long thin stick with a curved handle that you can use to help you walk
4 [C] a stick that was used in the past by teachers to hit children with as a punishment: *Children knew that if they misbehaved they would* ***get the cane***.

cane[2] *v* [T] **1** to punish someone, especially a child, by hitting them with a stick **2 cane it** *BrE spoken informal* **a)** to drive along very fast **b)** to drink a lot of alcohol

can·er /ˈkeɪnə $ -ər/ *n* [C] *BrE informal* someone who drinks a lot of alcohol

ca·nine[1] /ˈkeɪnaɪn, ˈkæ- $ ˈkeɪ-/ *adj* relating to dogs: *canine diseases* | *her loyal canine friend*

canine[2] *n* [C] **1** (*also* **canine tooth**) one of the four sharp pointed teeth in the front of your mouth **2** *formal* a dog

can·is·ter /ˈkænɪstə $ -ər/ *n* [C] **1** a round metal case that contains gas and bursts when it is thrown or fired from a gun: *Police fired tear gas canisters into the crowd.* **2** a metal container for keeping something in: *a tea canister* | *a petrol canister*

can·ker /ˈkæŋkə $ -ər/ *n* [C,U] **1** an evil influence that spreads quickly among people and is difficult to destroy: *the canker of violence in modern society* **2** a disease that affects trees or plants

can·na·bis /ˈkænəbɪs/ *n* [U] *especially BrE* an illegal drug that is usually smoked SYN **marijuana** *AmE*

canned /kænd/ *adj* **1** canned food is preserved in a round metal container SYN **tinned** *BrE*: *canned tomatoes* | *canned fruit* **2 canned music/laughter** music or laughter that has been recorded and is used on television or in radio programmes

can·nel·lo·ni /ˌkænəˈləʊni $ -ˈloʊ-/ *n* [U] small tubes of PASTA filled with meat and sometimes cheese, and covered in a sauce

can·ne·ry /ˈkænəri/ *n* (*plural* **canneries**) [C] a factory where food is put into cans

can·ni·bal /ˈkænəbəl/ *n* [C] **1** a person who eats human flesh **2** an animal that eats the flesh of other animals of the same kind —**cannibalism** *n* [U] —**cannibalistic** /ˌkænəbəˈlɪstɪk◂/ *adj*

can·ni·bal·ize (*also* **-ise** *BrE*) /ˈkænəbəlaɪz/ *v* [T]
1 to take parts of one machine to use in another, for example to repair it: *The truck was cannibalized for parts.*
2 *technical* if one of a company's products cannibalizes another, it takes sales away from it

can·non[1] /ˈkænən/ *n* [C] a large heavy powerful gun that was used in the past to fire heavy metal balls

cannon[2] *v* [I always + adv/prep] to hit someone or something while moving fast: **[+into]** *She came hurtling round the corner and cannoned straight into me.* | **[+off]** *The ball cannoned off the far post.*

can·non·ade /ˌkænəˈneɪd/ *n* [C] a continuous heavy attack by large guns

can·non·ball /ˈkænənbɔːl $ -bɒːl/ *n* [C] a heavy iron ball fired from a cannon

ˈcannon ˌfodder *n* [U] ordinary soldiers whose lives are not considered to be very important, and who are sent to fight where they are likely to get killed

can·not /ˈkænət, -nɒt $ -nɑːt/ ●●● W1 *modal verb*
1 a negative form of 'can': *Mrs Armstrong regrets that she cannot accept your kind invitation.*
2 cannot but *formal* used to say that you feel you have to do something: *One cannot but admire her determination.*

can·ny /ˈkæni/ *adj* **1** clever, careful, and not easily deceived, especially in business or politics: *a canny political advisor* **2** nice, good - used in Scotland: *a canny lass* —**cannily** *adv*

ca·noe¹ /kəˈnuː/ ●●○ *n* [C] a long light boat that is pointed at both ends and which you move along using a PADDLE → **paddle your own canoe** at **PADDLE²**(5)

canoe² *v* [I] to travel by canoe —**canoeist** *n* [C]

can·oe·ing /kəˈnuːɪŋ/ *n* [U] the sport of travelling in a canoe

can·on /ˈkænən/ *n* [C] **1** a Christian priest who has special duties in a CATHEDRAL **2** *formal* a standard, rule, or principle, or set of these, that are believed by a group of people to be right and good: **[+of]** *Mapplethorpe's pictures offended the canons of American good taste.* **3** *formal* **a)** a list of books or pieces of music that are officially recognized as being the work of a certain writer: *the Shakespearean canon* **b)** all the books that are recognized as being the most important pieces of literature: *the literary canon* **4** a piece of music in which a tune is started by one singer or instrument and is copied by each of the others **5** an established law of the Christian Church

ca·non·i·cal /kəˈnɒnɪkəl $ kəˈnɑː-/ *adj* **1** according to CANON LAW **2** *technical* in the simplest mathematical form

can·on·ize (*also* **-ise** *BrE*) /ˈkænənaɪz/ *v* [T] to officially state that a dead person is a SAINT —**canonization** /ˌkænənaɪˈzeɪʃən $ -nənə-/ *n* [C,U]

ˌcanon ˈlaw *n* [U] the laws of the Christian Church

ca·noo·dle /kəˈnuːdl/ *v* [I] *BrE old-fashioned* if two people canoodle, they kiss and hold each other in a sexual way

ˈcan ˌopener ●●○ *n* [C] a tool for opening a can of food

can·o·py /ˈkænəpi/ *n* (*plural* **canopies**) [C] **1** a cover made of cloth that is fixed above a bed, seat etc as a decoration or as a shelter **2** the leaves and branches of trees, that make a kind of roof in a forest: *the forest canopy* **3** *literary* something that spreads above you like a roof: *a canopy of twinkling stars* —**canopied** *adj*

canst /kənst; *strong* kænst/ *v* **thou canst** *old use* used to mean 'you can' when talking to one person

cant¹ /kænt/ *n* [U] **1** insincere talk about moral or religious principles by someone who is pretending to be better than they really are **2** *formal* special words used by a particular group of people, especially in order to keep things secret SYN **slang**: *thieves' cant*

cant² *v* [I,T] to lean, or make something lean

can't /kɑːnt $ kænt/ ●●● S1
1 the short form of 'cannot': *Sorry, I can't help you.* | *You can swim, can't you?*
2 used to say that something is impossible or unlikely: *You can't miss it – it's a huge building.*

Can·tab /ˈkæntæb/ used after the title of a degree from Cambridge University: *Jane Smith MA (Cantab)*

can·ta·loup, **cantaloupe** /ˈkæntəluːp $ -loʊp/ *n* [C,U] a type of MELON with a hard green skin and sweet orange flesh

can·tan·ker·ous /kænˈtæŋkərəs/ *adj* bad-tempered and complaining a lot: *a cantankerous old man*

can·ta·ta /kænˈtɑːtə, kən- $ kən-/ *n* [C] a piece of religious music for singers and instruments

can·teen /kænˈtiːn/ *n* [C] **1** *BrE* a place in a factory, school etc where meals are provided, usually quite cheaply **2** a small container in which water or other drink is carried by soldiers, travellers etc **3 a canteen of cutlery** *BrE* a set of knives, forks, and spoons in a box

can·ter /ˈkæntə $ -ər/ *v* [I,T] to ride or make a horse run quite fast, but not as fast as possible → **gallop** —**canter** *n* [C]: *She rode off at a canter.*

can·ti·cle /ˈkæntɪkəl/ *n* [C] a short religious song usually using words from the Bible

can·ti·le·ver /ˈkæntəliːvə $ -tl-iːvər/ *n* [C] a long piece of metal or wood that sticks out from an upright post or wall and supports a shelf, the end of a bridge etc —**cantilevered** *adj*: *a cantilevered staircase*

can·to /ˈkæntəʊ $ -toʊ/ *n* (*plural* **cantos**) [C] one of the parts into which a very long poem is divided → **stanza**

can·ton /ˈkæntɒn, kænˈtɒn $ ˈkæntən, -tɑːn/ *n* [C] one of the areas that a country such as Switzerland is divided up into, that has limited political powers

Can·to·nese /ˌkæntəˈniːz◂/ *n* [U] a Chinese language spoken in Southern China and Hong Kong

can·ton·ment /kænˈtuːnmənt $ -ˈtɑːn-/ *n* [C] *technical* a camp where soldiers live

can·tor /ˈkæntə, -tɔː $ -ər, -ɔːr/ *n* [C] **1** a man who leads the prayers and songs in a Jewish religious service **2** the leader of a group of singers in a church

Ca·nuck /kəˈnʌk/ *n* [C] *AmE informal* a Canadian

can·vas /ˈkænvəs/ ●●○ *n*
1 [U] strong cloth used to make bags, tents, shoes etc: *a canvas bag*
2 [C] a painting done with oil paints, or the piece of cloth it is painted on: *The gallery has a canvas by Paul Cézanne.* | *'Four Women on a Bench', oil on canvas, 1991*
3 a broader/wider/larger canvas the whole of a situation, and not just a part of it: *These questions must be considered on a broader canvas.*
4 under canvas *BrE* in a tent

can·vass /ˈkænvəs/ *v* **1** [I,T] to try to persuade people to support a political party, politician, plan etc by going to see them and talking to them, especially when you want them to vote for you in an election: *Candidates from all three parties were out canvassing in Darlington today.* | **[+for]** *Chapman spent the rest of May canvassing for votes.* | *The US has been* ***canvassing support*** *from other Asian states.* **2** [I,T] to ask people about something in order to get their opinion or to get information: *Police canvassed the neighborhood, but didn't find any witnesses.* **3** [T] to talk about a problem, suggestion etc in detail: *A committee was set up to* ***canvass*** *the city's educational* ***options***. —**canvasser** *n* [C] —**canvass** *n* [C]

can·yon /ˈkænjən/ ●●○ *n* [C] a deep valley with very steep sides of rock that usually has a river running through it

can·yon·ing /ˈkænjənɪŋ/ (*also* **can·yon·eer·ing** /ˌkænjəˈnɪərɪŋ $ -ˈnɪr-/ *AmE*) *n* [U] a sport in which you walk and swim along a fast-moving river at the bottom of a canyon

cap¹ /kæp/ ●●● S3 *n* [C]
1 HAT **a)** a type of flat hat that has a curved part sticking out at the front, and is often worn as part of a uniform: *a baseball cap* | *old men in flat caps* | *a chauffeur's peaked cap* **b)** a covering that fits very closely to your head: *a swimming cap* | *a shower cap* **c)** a type of simple hat that fits very closely to your head, worn especially by women in the past: *a white lace cap*
2 COVERING a protective covering that you put on the end or top of an object SYN **top**: *Make sure you put the cap back on the pen.* | *a bottle cap*
3 LIMIT an upper limit that is put on the amount of money that someone can earn, spend, or borrow: *a cap on local council spending*
4 SPORT *BrE* **a)** if a sportsperson wins a cap or is given a cap, he or she is chosen to play for their country: *He won his first England cap against Wales in 1994.* **b)** a sportsperson who has played for his or her country: *Mason is one of two new caps in the team.*
5 SMALL EXPLOSIVE a small paper container with explosive inside it, used especially in toy guns

6 SEX a CONTRACEPTIVE made of a round piece of rubber that a woman puts inside her VAGINA SYN **diaphragm**
7 go cap in hand (to sb) *BrE*, **go hat in hand** *AmE* to ask for money or help in a very respectful way, from someone who has a lot more power than you: *Elderly people should receive a heating allowance every winter, instead of having to go cap in hand to the government.* → **FLAT CAP, ICE CAP, KNEECAP, MOB CAP, SKULL CAP, TOECAP,** → **a feather in your cap** at FEATHER¹(2), → **if the cap fits (, wear it)** at FIT¹(8), → **put your thinking cap on** at THINKING¹(3)

cap² *v* (**capped, capping**) [T]
1 COVER **be capped with sth** to have a particular substance on top: *a graceful tower capped with a golden dome | magnificent cliffs capped by lovely wild flowers*
2 LIMIT to limit the amount of something, especially money, that can be used, allowed, or spent: *the only county to have its spending capped by the government* GRAMMAR **Cap** is often passive in this meaning.
3 GOOD/BAD to say, do, or be something that is better, worse, or more extreme than something that has just happened or been said: *Well, we went three nights with no sleep at all. I bet you can't cap that!*
4 be capped by sth to have something very good or very bad at the end of an event: *a fabulous weekend, capped by dinner in the Times Square Hotel*
5 SPORT *BrE* to choose someone for a national sports team: *He's been capped three times for England.* GRAMMAR **Cap** is usually passive in this meaning.
6 to cap it all (off) *BrE spoken* used before a statement to say that something is the last in a series of annoying, unpleasant, or funny events: *To cap it all, the phones didn't work, and there was no hot water.*
7 snow-capped, white-capped etc with snow on top, with white on top etc: *snow-capped mountains*
8 TOOTH to cover a tooth with a special hard white substance: *He's had his teeth capped.*

ca·pa·bil·i·ty /ˌkeɪpəˈbɪləti/ ●●○ AWL *n* (*plural* **capabilities**) [C]
1 the natural ability, skill, or power that makes a machine, person, or organization able to do something, especially something difficult: *the country's manufacturing capability* | **capability to do sth** *Does the company have the capability to change to meet market needs?* | *I can speak French, but simultaneous translation is* ***beyond*** *my* ***capabilities*** (=too difficult).
2 the ability that a country has to take a particular kind of military action: **military/nuclear etc capability** *America's nuclear capability*

ca·pa·ble /ˈkeɪpəbəl/ ●●○ S3 W2 AWL *adj*
1 capable of (doing) sth having the qualities or ability needed to do something: *I don't think he's capable of murder.* | *The company isn't capable of handling an order that large.* | *I'm perfectly capable of looking after myself, thank you!*

> **GRAMMAR**
> You say that someone is **capable of doing** something: *He is capable of doing it by himself.* ✗ Don't say: *He is capable to do it by himself.*
> GRAMMAR GUIDE **ADJECTIVES**

2 able to do things well: *a strong capable woman*
3 capable hands someone who is able to do something well: *Helen was put in the capable hands of hair stylist Daniel Herson.* —**capably** *adv*

ca·pa·cious /kəˈpeɪʃəs/ *adj formal* able to contain a lot: *a capacious suitcase* —**capaciousness** *n* [U]

ca·pac·i·tor /kəˈpæsɪtə $ -ər/ *n* [C] a piece of equipment that collects and stores electricity

ca·pac·i·ty /kəˈpæsəti/ ●●○ W3 AWL *n* (*plural* **capacities**)
1 [singular] the amount of space a container, room etc has to hold things or people: **[+of]** *The fuel tank has a capacity of 40 litres.* | *The room had seating capacity for about 80.* | *The orchestra played to a* ***capacity crowd*** (=the largest number of people who can fit into a hall, theatre etc). | *All the hotels were* ***filled to capacity***. THESAURUS **SIZE**
2 [C,U] someone's ability to do something OPP **incapacity**: **[+for]** *a child's capacity for learning | an infinite capacity for love* | **capacity to do sth** *a capacity to think in an original way*
3 [singular] *formal* someone's job, position, or duty SYN **role**: **in a professional/official etc capacity** *Rollins will be working in an advisory capacity on this project.* | **(do sth) in your capacity as sth** *I attended the meeting in my capacity as chairman of the safety committee.*
4 [singular, U] the amount of something that a factory, company, machine etc can produce or deal with: *The company has the capacity to build 1,500 trucks a year.* | *The factory has been working* ***at full capacity*** (=making the most amount of things that it can).
5 [singular, U] the size or power of something such as an engine: *The tax on cars is still based on engine capacity.*

ˌcap-and-ˈtrade *n* [U] a system in which companies are only allowed to produce a limited amount of substances that harm the environment. If they produce more than the amount allowed, they have to buy permission from other companies that produce less.

cape /keɪp/ ●○○ *n* [C]
1 a long loose piece of clothing without SLEEVES that fastens around your neck and hangs from your shoulders
2 a large piece of land surrounded on three sides by water: *Cape Cod*

ca·per¹ /ˈkeɪpə $ -ər/ *v* [I always + adv/prep] to jump around and play in a happy excited way

caper² *n* [C] **1** a small dark green part of a flower used in cooking to give a sour taste to food **2** *informal* a planned activity, especially an illegal or dangerous one: *I'm too old for this sort of caper.* **3** behaviour or an activity that is amusing or silly and not serious: *the comic capers of a cartoon cat and mouse* **4** a short jumping or dancing movement

ca·pil·la·ry /kəˈpɪləri $ ˈkæpəleri/ *n* (*plural* **capillaries**) [C] the smallest type of BLOOD VESSEL (=tube carrying blood) in the body

caˌpillary ˈaction / $ ˌ.... ˈ../ *n* [U] *technical* the force that makes a liquid rise up a narrow tube

cap·i·tal¹ /ˈkæpətl/ ●●● S3 W1 *n*
1 CITY [C] an important city where the main government of a country, state etc is: *Washington D.C., the capital of the United States* THESAURUS **CITY**
2 MONEY [singular, U] money or property, especially when it is used to start a business or to produce more wealth: *The government is eager to attract foreign capital.* → **VENTURE CAPITAL, WORKING CAPITAL**
3 LETTER [C] a letter of the alphabet written in its large form, used for example at the beginning of someone's name → **lower case, upper case**
4 CENTRE OF ACTIVITY [C] a place that is a centre for an industry, business, or other activity: *Hollywood is the capital of the movie industry.*
5 make capital from/out of sth to use a situation or event to help you get an advantage
6 BUILDING [C] *technical* the top part of a COLUMN (=a long stone post used in some buildings)

capital² ●●○ *adj*
1 a capital letter is one that is written or printed in its large form → **lower case, upper case**: *capital 'B'*
2 relating to money that you use to start a business or to make more money: *capital investments*
3 capital offence/crime an offence that is punished by death
4 trouble with a capital T, fast with a capital F etc *informal* used with any word in order to emphasize that you are talking about an extreme type of something
5 *old-fashioned* excellent

ˌcapital ˈassets *n* [plural] *technical* machines, buildings, and other property belonging to a company

ˌcapital ˈgains *n* [plural] profits you make by selling your possessions

ˌcapital ˈgains tax *n* [U] a tax that you pay on profits that you make when you sell your possessions

ˌcapital ˈgoods *n* [plural] goods such as machines or buildings that are made for the purpose of producing other goods → **consumer goods**

ˌcapital-inˈtensive *adj* a capital-intensive business, industry etc needs a lot of money in order to operate properly → **labour-intensive**

cap·i·tal·is·m /ˈkæpətl-ɪzəm/ ●○○ *n* [U] an economic and political system in which businesses belong mostly to private owners, not to the government → **communism, socialism**

cap·i·tal·ist¹ /ˈkæpɪtl-ɪst/ ●○○ *n* [C]
1 someone who supports capitalism → **communist, socialist**
2 someone who owns or controls a lot of money and lends it to businesses, banks etc to produce more wealth → **venture capitalist** at VENTURE CAPITAL

capitalist² ●○○ (*also* **cap·i·ta·lis·tic** /ˌkæpətlˈɪstɪk◂/) *adj* using or supporting capitalism → **communist, socialist**: *the capitalist system*

cap·i·tal·ize (*also* **-ise** *BrE*) /ˈkæpətl-aɪz/ *v* [T] **1** to write a letter of the alphabet using a CAPITAL letter **2** to supply a business with money so that it can operate **3** *technical* to calculate the value of a business based on the value of its SHARES or on the amount of money it makes —**capitalization** /ˌkæpɪtl-aɪˈzeɪʃən $ -tl-ə-/ *n* [U]

capitalize on sth *phr v* to use a situation or something good that you have, in order to get an advantage for yourself: *Ecuador has capitalized on its natural beauty to attract tourism.*

ˌcapital ˈlevy *n* [C] *technical* a tax on private or industrial wealth that is paid to the government

ˌcapital ˈpunishment ●○○ *n* [U] punishment which involves killing someone who has committed a crime → **death penalty**

cap·i·ta·tion /ˌkæpɪˈteɪʃən/ *n* [C] a tax or payment of the same amount from each person

Cap·i·tol Hill /ˌkæpətl ˈhɪl/ *n* **1** the US Congress **2** the hill in Washington D.C. where the Capitol building stands

ca·pit·u·late /kəˈpɪtʃəleɪt/ *v* [I] **1** *formal* to accept or agree to something that you have been opposing for a long time SYN **give in**: *Helen finally capitulated and let her son have a car.* **2** *formal* to accept defeat by your enemies in a war SYN **surrender** —**capitulation** /kəˌpɪtʃəˈleɪʃən/ *n* [C,U]

cap·let /kæplɪt/ *n* [C] a small smooth PILL (=solid piece of medicine) with a shape that is slightly longer and narrower than a TABLET (=a small round pill)

cap·o·ei·ra /ˌkæpəʊˈeərə $ ˌkɑːpoʊˈerə/ *n* [U] an Afro-Brazilian mixture of dance, song, and fighting that is similar to the MARTIAL ARTS

ca·pon /ˈkeɪpən $ -pɑːn, -pən/ *n* [C] a male chicken that has had its sex organs removed to make it grow big and fat

capped /kæpt/ *adj* [only before noun] if you borrow an amount of money at a capped rate of interest, the rate is not allowed to rise, but it is allowed to come down → **fixed-rate**: *capped rate mortgage deals*

cap·puc·ci·no /ˌkæpəˈtʃiːnəʊ $ -noʊ/ *n* (*plural* **cappuccinos**) [C,U] Italian coffee made with hot milk and with chocolate powder on top

ca·price /kəˈpriːs/ *n* **1** [C,U] a sudden and unreasonable change of mind or behaviour: *the caprices of a spoilt child* **2** [U] the tendency to change your mind suddenly or behave in an unexpected way

ca·pri·cious /kəˈprɪʃəs/ *adj* **1** likely to change your mind suddenly or behave in an unexpected way: *She was as capricious as her mother had been.* **2** *literary* changing quickly and suddenly: *a capricious wind* —**capriciously** *adv*

Cap·ri·corn /ˈkæprɪkɔːn $ -kɔːrn/ *n* **1** [U] the tenth sign of the ZODIAC, represented by a goat, which some people believe affects the character and life of people born between December 22 and January 20 **2** [C] someone born between December 22 and January 20

caps the written abbreviation of ***capital letters***

cap·si·cum /ˈkæpsɪkəm/ *n* [C,U] *technical* a kind of PEPPER (=a green, red, or yellow vegetable)

cap·size /kæpˈsaɪz $ ˈkæpsaɪz/ *v* [I,T] if a boat capsizes, or if you capsize it, it turns over in the water

ˈcaps lock *n* [singular, U] the button that you press on a computer when you want to use capital letters

cap·stan /ˈkæpstən/ *n* [C] a round machine shaped like a drum, used to wind up a rope that pulls or lifts heavy objects

cap·sule /ˈkæpsjuːl $ -səl/ *n* [C] **1** a plastic container shaped like a very small tube with medicine inside that you swallow whole → **tablet** **2** a small plastic container with a substance or liquid inside **3** the part of a spacecraft in which people live and work: *a space capsule orbiting the Earth* → TIME CAPSULE

ˈcapsule ˌwardrobe *n* [C usually singular] a small set of clothes which all look good with each other and will not go out of fashion: *Your capsule wardrobe will probably include a classic white shirt and a good pair of jeans.*

cap·tain¹ /ˈkæptɪn/ ●●● W3 *n* [C]
1 the sailor in charge of a ship, or the pilot in charge of an aircraft: *The captain and crew welcome you aboard.*
2 a military officer with a fairly high rank → GROUP CAPTAIN
3 someone who leads a team or other group of people: **[+of]** *Julie's captain of the quiz team.* | *The Blackhawks'* ***team captain*** *was the first to score.*
4 captain of industry someone who owns or has an important job in a big company

captain² *v* [T] **1** to lead a group or team of people and be their captain: *The U.S. team, captained by Arthur Ashe, won the Davis Cup in 1981 and 1982.* **2** to be in charge of a ship, aircraft etc

cap·tain·cy /ˈkæptənsi/ *n* (*plural* **captaincies**) [C,U] the position of being captain of a team, or the period during which someone is captain

CAPTCHA /ˈkæptʃə/ *n* [C,U] *trademark* a system or test for checking that a computer user is human, often a test that asks the user to recognize a word written with letters that are a strange shape and hard to recognize

cap·tion /ˈkæpʃən/ *n* [C] words printed above or below a picture in a book or newspaper or on a television screen to explain what the picture is showing → **subtitle** —**caption** *v* [T]: *a photograph of the couple captioned 'rebuilding their romance'*

cap·ti·vate /ˈkæptɪveɪt/ *v* [T] to attract someone very much, and hold their attention: **be captivated by sb/sth** *He was captivated by her beauty.*

cap·ti·vat·ing /ˈkæptəveɪtɪŋ/ *adj* very attractive and interesting, in a way that holds your attention: *a captivating smile*

cap·tive¹ /ˈkæptɪv/ *adj* **1** kept in prison or in a place that you are not allowed to leave: *captive soldiers* | *captive animals* | *His son had been* ***taken captive*** (=became a prisoner) *during the raid.* | *a pilot who was* ***held captive*** (=kept as a prisoner) *for six years* **2 captive audience** people who listen or watch someone or something because they have to, not because they are interested **3 captive market** the people who must buy a particular product or service, because they need it and there is only one company selling it **4 be captive to sth** to be unable to think or speak freely, because of being influenced too much by something: *Our communities should not be captive to the mistakes of the past.*

captive² *n* [C] someone who is kept as a prisoner, especially in a war

cap·tiv·i·ty /kæpˈtɪvəti/ *n* [U] when a person or animal is kept in a prison, CAGE etc and not allowed to go where they want OPP **freedom**: *The hostages were released from captivity.* | **in captivity** *animals bred in captivity*

cap·tor /ˈkæptə $ -ər/ *n* [C] someone who is keeping another person prisoner → **captive**: *He managed to escape from his captors.*

C

cap·ture¹ /ˈkæptʃə $ -ər/ ●●○ W3 *v* [T]
1 PERSON to catch a person and keep them as a prisoner: *Government troops have succeeded in capturing the rebel leader.* | *40 captured French soldiers* THESAURUS ➤ CATCH
2 PLACE/THING to get control of a place or object that previously belonged to an enemy, during a war: *The town was captured after a siege lasting ten days.* | *The Dutch fleet captured two English ships.*
3 ANIMAL to catch an animal after chasing or following it: *The tiger was finally captured two miles outside the village.*
4 FILM/RECORD/ART to succeed in recording, showing, or describing a situation or feeling, using words or pictures: *These photographs capture the essence of working-class life at the turn of the century.* | *The robbery was captured on police video cameras.*
5 capture sb's imagination/attention etc to make someone feel very interested in something: *His stories of foreign adventure captured my imagination.*
6 capture sb's heart to make someone love you
7 BUSINESS/POLITICS to get something that previously belonged to one of your competitors: *We aim to capture eight percent of the UK wine market.* | *Republicans captured three Senate seats from the Democrats.*
8 capture the headlines to be talked or written about a lot in the newspapers or on television: *Irvine Welsh first captured the headlines with his novel 'Trainspotting'.*
9 COMPUTER *technical* to put something in a form that a computer can use: *The data is captured by an optical scanner.*
10 CHESS to remove one of your opponent's pieces from the board in CHESS

capture² *n* [U] **1** when you catch someone in order to make them a prisoner: *The two soldiers somehow managed to avoid capture.* **2** when soldiers get control of a place that previously belonged to an enemy: **[+of]** *the capture of Jerusalem in 1099* **3** when you get control of something that previously belonged to one of your competitors **4** when you put information into a form a computer can use

car /kɑː $ kɑːr/ ●●● S1 W1 *n* [C]
1 a vehicle with four wheels and an engine, that can carry a small number of passengers: *Dan got out of the car and locked the door.* | *He isn't old enough to drive a car.* | **by car** *I always go to work by car.* | *Coughlan was killed in a car accident.*
2 sleeping/dining/buffet car a train carriage used for sleeping, eating etc
3 *AmE* a train carriage
4 the part of a lift, BALLOON, or AIRSHIP in which people or goods are carried

GRAMMAR: Patterns with car

• You say **get in a car** or **get into a car**: *He got into the car and drove away.* ✗ Don't say: *get on a car*
• You say **get out of a car**: *We got out of the car to see what had happened.* ✗ Don't say: *get off the car*
• You say that someone is **in a car**: *I like to listen to the radio when I'm in the car.* ✗ Don't say: *on a car*
• You go somewhere **by car**: *It's quicker to get there by car.* ✗ Don't say: *by a car*

COLLOCATIONS

VERBS

go/travel by car *I try to use public transport instead of going by car.*
get in/into a car *The man stopped and she got into the car.*
get out of a car *He got out of the car and went into the newsagent's.*
drive a car *In England you can learn to drive a car when you are 17.*
take the car (=use a car to go somewhere) *Is it all right if I take the car this evening?*
park a car *She parked the car by the side of the road.*
back/reverse a car (=make it move backwards) *Suzy backed the car into the driveway.*
a car passes/overtakes sb *A small black car overtook me on my left.*
a car drives off/away *The police car drove off at top speed.*
a car pulls out (=moves away from the side of the road) | **a car slows down** | **a car pulls up** (=stops) | **a car pulls over** (=stops on the side of a road) | **a car breaks down** (=stops working because something is wrong with it) | **a car hits sth/crashes into sth**

car + NOUN

a car crash/accident (*also* **a car wreck** *AmE*) *He was involved in a car crash.*
a car park *She couldn't find a space in the car park.*
a car door/engine/key etc | **a car dealer** (=someone who buys and sells used cars) | **a car chase** | **car crime** *BrE*

ADJECTIVES/NOUNS + car

a used/second-hand car (=one that is not new) | **a sports car** (=a low fast car) | **an estate car** *BrE* (=one with a door at the back and folding seats) | **a racing car** (*also* **a race car** *AmE*) | **a police car** | **a company car** (=one that your company gives you to use) | **a hire car** *BrE*, **a rental car** *AmE*

ca·rafe /kəˈræf, kəˈrɑːf/ *n* [C] a glass container with a wide neck, used for serving wine or water at meals

ˈcar aˌlarm *n* [C] equipment in a car that makes a loud noise if anyone tries to steal or damage the car

car·a·mel /ˈkærəməl, -mel/ *n* **1** [C,U] a sticky brown sweet made of boiled sugar, butter, and milk **2** [U] burnt sugar used for giving food a special taste and colour **3** [U] a light yellow-brown colour → CRÈME CARAMEL

car·a·mel·ize (*also* **-ise** *BrE*) /ˈkærəməlaɪz/ *v* **1** [I] if sugar caramelizes, it becomes brown and hard when it is heated **2** [T] to cook food such as fruit or vegetables with sugar —**caramelized** *adj*: *caramelized onions*

car·a·pace /ˈkærəpeɪs/ *n* [C] *technical* a hard shell on the outside of some animals such as a CRAB or TORTOISE SYN **shell**

car·at /ˈkærət/ *n* [C] *BrE* **1** (*also* **karat** *AmE*) a unit for measuring how pure gold is: **9/18/22/24 carat gold** *a 22 carat gold chain* | *Pure gold is 24 carats.* **2** a unit for measuring the weight of jewels, equal to 200 MILLIGRAMS: *the Orloff diamond, a stone of 194.5 carats*

car·a·van /ˈkærəvæn/ ●●○ *n* [C]
1 *BrE* a vehicle that a car can pull and in which people can live and sleep when they are on holiday SYN **trailer** *AmE*: **caravan site/park** (=area of land where people can park their caravans)
2 *BrE* a covered vehicle that is pulled by a horse, and in which people can live SYN **wagon** *AmE*: *a gipsy caravan*
3 a group of people with animals or vehicles who travel together for safety, especially through a desert

car·a·van·ning /ˈkærəvænɪŋ/ *n* [U] *BrE* the activity of taking holidays in a caravan: *a caravanning holiday*

car·a·van·se·rai /ˌkærəˈvænsəraɪ/ *n* [C] a hotel with a large open central area, used in the past in Eastern countries by groups of people and animals travelling together

car·a·way /ˈkærəweɪ/ *n* [C,U] a plant whose seeds are used in cooking

carb /kɑːb $ kɑːrb/ *n* [C] *informal* **1** *BrE* a CARBURETTOR **2** [usually plural] *especially AmE* a food such as rice, potatoes, or bread that contains CARBOHYDRATE: *Before a race I eat plenty of carbs.*

car·bine /ˈkɑːbaɪn $ ˈkɑːr-/ *n* [C] a short light RIFLE

car·bo·hy·drate /ˌkɑːbəʊˈhaɪdreɪt, -drət $ ˌkɑːrboʊ-/ ●○○ *n*
1 [C,U] a substance that is in foods such as sugar, bread, and potatoes, which provides your body with heat and energy and which consists of oxygen, HYDROGEN, and CARBON

Car

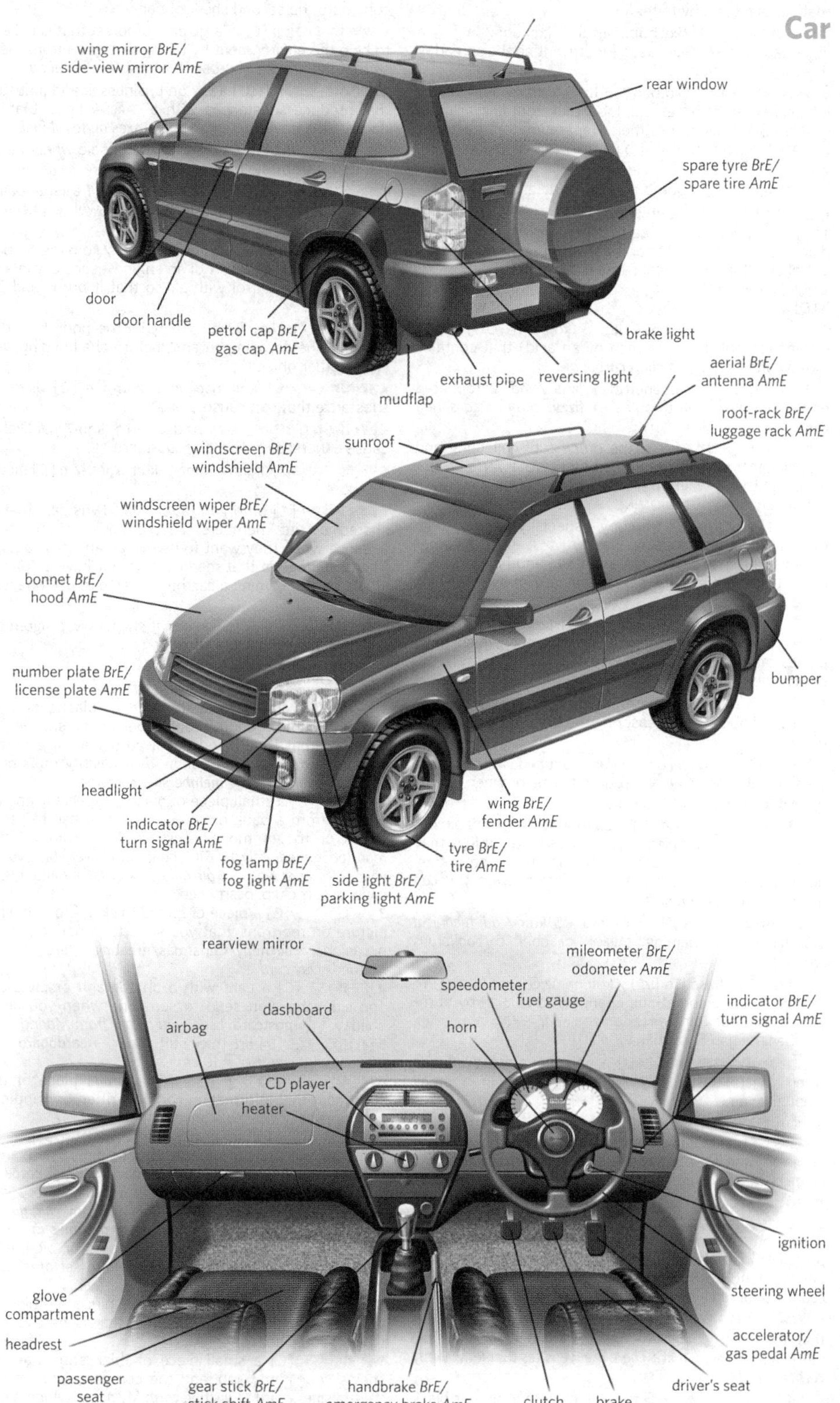
wing mirror BrE/
side-view mirror AmE
rear window
spare tyre BrE/
spare tire AmE
door
door handle
petrol cap BrE/
gas cap AmE
brake light
exhaust pipe
reversing light
mudflap
aerial BrE/
antenna AmE
roof-rack BrE/
luggage rack AmE
sunroof
windscreen BrE/
windshield AmE
windscreen wiper BrE/
windshield wiper AmE
bonnet BrE/
hood AmE
number plate BrE/
license plate AmE
bumper
headlight
indicator BrE/
turn signal AmE
wing BrE/
fender AmE
tyre BrE/
tire AmE
fog lamp BrE/
fog light AmE
side light BrE/
parking light AmE
rearview mirror
mileometer BrE/
odometer AmE
speedometer
fuel gauge
dashboard
indicator BrE/
turn signal AmE
airbag
horn
CD player
heater
ignition
steering wheel
glove
compartment
headrest
accelerator/
gas pedal AmE
passenger
seat
gear stick BrE/
stick shift AmE
handbrake BrE/
emergency brake AmE
clutch
brake
driver's seat

2 [C usually plural] foods such as rice, bread, and potatoes that contain carbohydrates

car·bol·ic a·cid /ˌkɑːbɒlɪk ˈæsɪd $ kɑːrˌbɑː-/ *n* [U] a liquid that kills BACTERIA, used for preventing the spread of disease or infection

car·bo load·ing /ˈkɑːbəʊ ˌləʊdɪŋ $ ˈkɑːrboʊ ˌloʊ-/ *n* [U] *informal* when ATHLETES eat food that contains a lot of CARBOHYDRATES as part of their preparation for a race etc, so that their muscles will have extra energy during the event —**carbo load** *v* [I]

ˈcar bomb *n* [C] a bomb hidden inside a car

car·bon /ˈkɑːbən $ ˈkɑːr-/ ●●○ *n*
1 [U] a chemical substance that exists in a pure form as diamonds, GRAPHITE etc, or in an impure form as coal, petrol etc. It is a chemical ELEMENT: symbol C
2 [C,U] CARBON PAPER
3 [C] a CARBON COPY(1)

C

car·bon·ate /ˈkɑːbənət, -neɪt $ ˈkɑːr-/ *n* [C,U] a salt (=chemical substance formed by an acid) that contains CARBON and oxygen: *calcium carbonate*

car·bon·at·ed /ˈkɑːbəneɪtɪd $ ˈkɑːr-/ *adj* carbonated drinks contain small bubbles → **fizzy**: *carbonated spring water*

ˌcarbon ˈcapture *n* [U] the process of collecting and storing CARBON DIOXIDE produced by POWER PLANTS or factories, so that it will not escape into the air and increase the effects of GLOBAL WARMING

ˌcarbon ˈcopy *n* [C] **1** a copy, especially of something that has been TYPEd using CARBON PAPER → **cc** **2** someone or something that is very similar to another person or thing: **[+of]** *The robbery is a carbon copy of one that took place last year.*

ˌcarbon ˈcredit *n* [C usually plural] permission to produce a particular amount of CARBON DIOXIDE, which companies can buy and sell as a way of reducing harm to the environment

ˌcarbon ˈdating *n* [U] a method of finding out the age of very old objects by measuring the amount of CARBON in them

ˌcarbon diˈoxide *n* [U] the gas produced when animals breathe out, when CARBON is burned in air, or when animal or vegetable substances decay

ˌcarbon ˈfootprint *n* [C] the amount of CARBON DIOXIDE that a person or organization produces by the things they do, used as a way of measuring the amount of harm they do to the environment: *There are lots of ways you can* ***reduce*** *your* ***carbon footprint****.*

car·bon·if·er·ous /ˌkɑːbəˈnɪfərəs◂ $ ˌkɑːr-/ *adj technical* producing or containing CARBON or coal: *carboniferous rocks*

car·bon·ize (*also* **ise** *BrE*) /ˈkɑːbənaɪz $ ˈkɑːr-/ *v* [I,T] to change or make something change into CARBON by burning it without air —**carbonized** *adj* —**carbonization** /ˌkɑːbənaɪˈzeɪʃən $ ˌkɑːrbənə-/ *n* [U]

ˌcarbon moˈnoxide *n* [U] a poisonous gas produced when CARBON, especially in petrol, burns in a small amount of air

ˌcarbon ˈnegative *adj* if an organization, activity, or thing is carbon negative, it takes more CARBON DIOXIDE out of the air than it produces: *We eventually hope to develop a range of carbon negative construction products.*

ˌcarbon ˈneutral *adj* if an organization or activity is carbon neutral, it takes the same amount of CARBON DIOXIDE out of the air, for example by planting trees, as it produces. This is done in order to avoid harming the environment: *Costa Rica wants to be the first developing country to become carbon neutral.*

ˌcarbon ˈoffsetting *n* [U] the practice of doing things that will make your activities carbon neutral —**carbon offset** *n* [C usually plural]: *There are websites that let you buy carbon offsets.*

ˈcarbon ˌpaper *n* [C,U] thin paper with a blue or black substance on one side, that you put between sheets of paper when TYPING on a typewriter in order to make a copy onto the second sheet of paper

ˈcarbon sink *n* [C] a large area of forest that is believed to help the environment by taking in CARBON from the air so that the effects of GLOBAL WARMING are reduced

ˈcarbon ˌtax *n* [C,U] a tax on businesses and industries that produce substances with a CARBON base, that can damage the environment: *carbon taxes on fossil fuels*

ˌcar ˈboot ˌsale *n* [C] *BrE* an outdoor sale where people sell things from the back of their cars

car·bun·cle /ˈkɑːbʌŋkəl $ ˈkɑːr-/ *n* [C] **1** a large painful lump under someone's skin **2** a red jewel, especially a GARNET

car·bu·ret·tor *BrE*, **carburetor** *AmE* /ˌkɑːbjəˈretə, -bə- $ ˈkɑːrbəreɪtər/ *n* [C] a part of an engine, especially in a car, that mixes the petrol with air so that it burns and provides power

car·cass /ˈkɑːkəs $ ˈkɑːr-/ *n* [C] **1** the body of a dead animal **2** the decaying outer structure of a building, vehicle, or other object

car·cin·o·gen /kɑːˈsɪnədʒən $ kɑːr-/ *n* [C] *medical* a substance that can cause CANCER

car·cin·o·gen·ic /ˌkɑːsənəˈdʒenɪk◂ $ ˌkɑːr-/ *adj* likely to cause CANCER: *a carcinogenic substance*

car·ci·no·ma /ˌkɑːsəˈnəʊmə $ ˌkɑːrsəˈnoʊ-/ *n* [C] *medical* a CANCER

ˈcar club *n* [C] an organization that owns cars that are shared by its members. People have to arrange in advance when they want to use a car, and pay to use it. The advantage is that members do not have to pay the whole cost of owning a car, but are able to use one when they need to.

ˌcar-crash TˈV *n* [U] *informal* REALITY TV programmes which people think are of poor quality, but which they cannot stop themselves watching

card¹ /kɑːd $ kɑːrd/ ●●● S1 W2 *n*
1 INFORMATION [C] a small piece of plastic or paper containing information about a person or showing, for example, that they belong to a particular organization, club etc: *Employees must show their* ***identity cards*** *at the gate.* | *I haven't got my* ***membership card*** *yet.*
2 MONEY [C] a small piece of plastic, especially one that you get from a bank or shop, which you use to pay for goods or to get money: *Lost or stolen cards must be reported immediately.* | *a £10 phone card* | *Every time you use your store card, you get air miles.* → **CHARGE CARD, CHEQUE CARD, CREDIT CARD, DEBIT CARD**
3 GREETINGS [C] a piece of folded thick stiff paper with a picture on the front, that you send to people on special occasions: **birthday/Christmas/greetings etc card** *a Mother's Day card*
4 HOLIDAY [C] a card with a photograph or picture on one side, that you send to someone when you are on holiday SYN **postcard**: *I sent you a card from Madrid.*
5 STIFF PAPER [U] *BrE* thick stiff paper → **cardboard**: *Cut a piece of white card 12 × 10 cm.*
6 FOR WRITING INFORMATION [C] a small piece of thick stiff paper that information can be written or printed on: *a set of recipe cards* | *a score card*
7 GAMES [C] **a)** a small piece of thick stiff paper with numbers and signs or pictures on one side. There are 52 cards in a set. SYN **playing card**: **pack/deck of cards** (=a complete set of cards) **b)** a game in which these cards are used: *I'm no good at cards.* | *We were having* ***a game of cards****.* | *Let's* ***play cards****.* | *a book of* ***card games*** **c)** a small piece of thick stiff paper with numbers or pictures on them, used to play a particular game: *a set of cards for playing Snap*
8 football/baseball etc card a small piece of thick stiff paper with a picture on one side, that is part of a set which people collect
9 BUSINESS [C] a small piece of thick stiff paper that shows your name, job, and the company you work for SYN **business card** → **visiting card**: *My name's Adam Carver. Here's my card.*

10 COMPUTER [C] a piece of equipment inside a computer that the CHIPS are attached to, that allows the computer to do specific things: *a graphics card*
11 be on the cards *BrE*, **be in the cards** *AmE* to seem likely to happen: *At 3-1 down, another defeat seemed to be on the cards.*
12 play your cards right to deal with a situation in the right way, so that you are successful in getting what you want: *If he plays his cards right, Tony might get a promotion.*
13 put/lay your cards on the table to tell people what your plans and intentions are in a clear honest way: *What I'd like us to do is put our cards on the table and discuss the situation in a rational manner.*
14 play/keep your cards close to your chest to keep your plans, thoughts, or feelings secret
15 get/be given your cards *BrE informal* to have your job taken away from you
16 have another card up your sleeve to have another advantage that you can use to be successful in a particular situation
17 trump/best/strongest card something that gives you a big advantage in a particular situation: *The promise of tax cuts proved, as always, to be the Republican Party's trump card.*
18 sb's card is marked *BrE* if someone's card is marked, they have done something that makes people in authority disapprove of them
19 PERSON [C] *old-fashioned informal* an amusing or unusual person: *Fred's a real card, isn't he!*
20 SPORT [C] a small piece of stiff red or yellow paper, shown to a player who has done something wrong in a game such as football
21 LIST AT SPORTS EVENT [C] a list of races or matches at a sports event, especially a horse race: *a full card of 120 riders for the Veterans race*
22 TAROT [C] a small piece of thick stiff paper with a special picture on one side, that is put down in a pattern in order to tell someone what will happen in their future
23 TOOL [C] *technical* a tool that is similar to a comb and is used for combing, cleaning, and preparing wool or cotton for spinning (SPIN) → **hold all the cards** at HOLD[1](30), → **play the race/nationalist/environmentalist etc card** at PLAY[1](14), → **stack the cards** at STACK[2](4)

card[2] *v* [T] **1** *especially AmE* to ask someone to show a card proving that they are old enough to do something, especially to buy alcohol **2** to show a red or yellow card to someone playing a sport such as football, to show that they have done something wrong **3** to comb, clean, and prepare wool or cotton, before making cloth

car·da·mom /ˈkɑːdəməm $ ˈkɑːr-/ *n* [C,U] the seeds of an Asian fruit, used to give a special taste to Indian and Middle Eastern food

card·board[1] /ˈkɑːdbɔːd $ ˈkɑːrdbɔːrd/ *n* [U] stiff thick brown paper, used especially for making boxes: *a sheet of cardboard* → see picture at BOX[1]

cardboard[2] *adj* **1** made from cardboard: *a cardboard box* **2** [only before noun] seeming silly and not real: *a romantic novel full of cardboard characters*

ˌcardboard ˈcity *n* [C] an area in a large town or city where people who have no home sleep outside using cardboard boxes to try to keep warm

ˌcardboard ˈcut-out *n* [C] **1** a picture drawn on cardboard so that it can stand up on a surface **2** a person or character in a book, film etc who does not seem natural or real: *the sort of movie in which the characters are just cardboard cut-outs*

ˈcard-ˌcarrying *adj* [only before noun] **1 card-carrying member** someone who has paid money to a political organization and is an official and active member of it: *a card-carrying member of the Labour Party* **2** believing very strongly in something – used to show disapproval: *One of them is a card-carrying ecology freak.*

ˈcard ˌcatalog *n* [C] *AmE* a box of cards that contain information about something and are arranged in order, especially the cards with book information on them in a library SYN **card index** *BrE*

card·hold·er /ˈkɑːdˌhəʊldə $ ˈkɑːrdˌhoʊldər/ *n* [C] someone who has a CREDIT CARD

car·di·ac /ˈkɑːdi-æk $ ˈkɑːr-/ *adj* [only before noun] *medical* relating to the heart: *cardiac surgery* | **cardiac arrest/failure** (=when the heart stops working)

car·die /ˈkɑːdi $ ˈkɑːr-/ *n* [C] *BrE informal* a cardigan

car·di·gan /ˈkɑːdɪgən $ ˈkɑːr-/ ●●● S3 (*also* **ˈcardigan ˌsweater** *AmE*) *n* [C] a SWEATER similar to a short coat, fastened at the front with buttons or a zip

car·di·nal[1] /ˈkɑːdənəl $ ˈkɑːr-/ *n* [C] **1** a priest of high rank in the Roman Catholic Church **2** a North American bird. The male is a bright red colour. **3** a CARDINAL NUMBER

cardinal[2] *adj* [only before noun] very important or basic SYN **fundamental**: *Having clean hands is one of the* ***cardinal rules*** *when preparing food.* | *an issue of cardinal importance*

ˌcardinal ˈnumber (*also* **cardinal**) *n* [C] a number such as 1, 2, or 3, that shows how many of something there are, but not what order they are in → **ORDINAL NUMBER**

ˌcardinal ˈpoint *n* [C] *BrE technical* one of the four main points (north, south, east, or west) on a COMPASS

ˌcardinal ˈsin *n* [C] **1** *informal* something bad or stupid that you must avoid doing: *politicians who commit the cardinal sin of ignoring public opinion* **2** a serious SIN in the Christian religion

ˈcard ˌindex *n* [C] *BrE* a box of cards that contain information about something and are arranged in order, especially the cards with book information on them in a library SYN **card catalog** *AmE*

car·di·o /ˈkɑːdiəʊ $ ˈkɑːrdioʊ/ *n* [U] *informal* any type of exercise that makes the heart stronger and healthier, for example running: *a combination of cardio, weight training, and kung fu*

cardio- /kɑːdiəʊ, -diə $ kɑːrdioʊ, -diə/ *prefix medical* relating to the heart: *a cardiograph* (=machine that measures movements of the heart)

car·di·ol·o·gist /ˌkɑːdiˈɒlədʒɪst $ ˌkɑːrdiˈɑː-/ *n* [C] *medical* a doctor who studies or treats heart diseases

car·di·ol·o·gy /ˌkɑːdiˈɒlədʒi $ ˌkɑːrdiˈɑː-/ *n* [U] the medical study of the heart

car·di·o·vas·cu·lar /ˌkɑːdiəʊˈvæskjələ $ ˌkɑːrdioʊˈvæskjələr/ *adj* [usually before noun] *medical* relating to the heart and BLOOD VESSELS (=tubes through which blood flows around your body): *cardiovascular disease*

card·shark /ˈkɑːdʃɑːk $ ˈkɑːrdʃɑːrk/ (*also* **card·sharp** /ˈkɑːdʃɑːp $ ˈkɑːrdʃɑːrp/ *BrE*) *n* [C] someone who cheats when playing cards in order to make money

ˈcard ˌtable *n* [C] a small light table, usually with folding legs, used for playing card games on

ˈcard vote *n* [C] *BrE* a way of voting at a TRADE UNION meeting in which your vote represents the votes of all the members of your organization

care[1] /keə $ ker/ ●●● S1 W1 *n*
1 LOOKING AFTER SB [U] the process of looking after someone, especially because they are ill, old, or very young: *high standards of medical care* | *They shared the care of the children.* | *Care facilities for the elderly are inadequate.* | **in sb's care** (=being looked after by someone) *The children had been left in the care of a babysitter.* | **be under sb's care** (=be officially looked after or treated by someone) *Mentally ill patients will be under the care of a psychiatrist.* → **DAY CARE, HEALTH CARE, INTENSIVE CARE,** → **tender loving care** at TENDER[1](5)
2 take care of sb/sth a) to look after someone or something: *Who's taking care of the dog while you're away?* | **take care of yourself** *The children are old enough to take care of themselves.* **b)** to deal with all the necessary work, arrangements etc: *Her secretary always took care of the details.* | *Don't worry about your accommodation – it's all taken care of.* **c)** to pay for something – used when you want to avoid saying this directly: *We'll take care of the fees.*
3 take care a) *spoken* used when saying goodbye to family and friends: *Take care! See you next week!* **b)** to be careful: *Take care when driving in icy conditions.* | **take care to do sth**

Take care to ensure that the ladder is steady before you climb it. | **take care (that)** *Take care that the meat is cooked properly.*
4 KEEPING STH IN GOOD CONDITION [U] the process of doing things to keep something in good condition and working correctly: *With proper care, the washing machine should last for years.* | *advice on skin care*
5 CAREFULNESS [U] when you are careful to avoid damage, mistakes etc: *The note on the box said 'Fragile – **handle with care**'.* | *The picture had been drawn with **great care**.*
6 take care over/with sth to spend a lot of time and effort making sure that something is perfect: *Paul always takes great care over his appearance.*
7 in care *BrE* a child who is in care is being looked after by the government, not by their parents: *When he was sent to prison, the children were **taken into care**.*
8 PROBLEM/WORRY [C,U] *literary* something that causes problems and makes you anxious or sad: *At last I felt free from my cares.* | *Alex looked as though he **didn't have a care in the world*** (=had no problems or worries). | *a man **with the cares of the world on his shoulders*** (=with a lot of problems or worries)
9 care of sb *BrE*, **in care of sb** *AmE* used when sending letters to someone at someone else's address SYN **c/o**: *Send me the letter care of my uncle.*
10 have a care! *BrE spoken old-fashioned* used to tell someone to be more careful

care² ●●● S1 W2 *v* [I,T]
1 to think that something is important, so that you are interested in it, worried about it etc: **[+about]** *The only thing he seems to care about is money.* | **care what/how/whether etc** *She didn't care what her father thought.* | *'He looked angry.' '**I don't care**!'*
2 to be concerned about what happens to someone, because you like or love them → **caring**: **[+about]** *I care about him and hate to see him hurt like this.* | *She felt that nobody cared.*
3 who cares? *spoken* used to say that something does not worry or upset you because it is not important: *It's rather old and scruffy, but who cares?*
4 see if I care! *spoken* used when you are angry or upset, to say that you do not care about what someone will do: *Go with William, then – see if I care!*
5 sb couldn't care less *spoken* used to say that someone does not care at all about something: *I really couldn't care less what you think!*
6 what does sb care? *spoken* used to say that someone does not care at all about something: *What do I care? It's your responsibility now!*
7 as if I cared! *spoken* used to say that something is not important to you at all: *As if I cared whether he comes with us or not!*
8 for all sb cares *spoken* used when you are angry that someone does not seem concerned about someone or something: *We could be starving for all they care!*
9 not care to do sth *old-fashioned* to not like doing something: *She doesn't care to spend much time with her relatives.* | *I wouldn't care to meet him in a dark alley!* | *I've experienced **more** reorganizations **than I care to remember*** (=a lot of them).
10 any ... you care to name/mention any thing of a particular kind: *Virtually any piece of equipment you care to name can be hired these days.*
11 would you care to do sth? *spoken formal* used to ask someone politely whether they want to do something: *Would you care to join us for dinner?*

care for sb/sth *phr v*
1 to look after someone who is not able to look after themselves SYN **take care of**: *He thanked the nurses who had cared for him.* | *The children are well cared for.*
2 to do things that keep something in good condition: *Instructions on caring for your new sofa are included.*
3 would you care for sth? *spoken formal* used to ask someone politely if they would like something: *Would you care for another drink?*
4 not care for sb/sth *formal* to not like someone or something: *I don't much care for his parents.*

ca·reen /kəˈriːn/ *v* [I always + adv/prep] *AmE* to move forwards quickly without control, making sudden sideways movements SYN **career** *BrE*: **[+down/over/along etc]** *The car careened around the corner.*

ca·reer¹ /kəˈrɪə $ -ˈrɪr/ ●●● S2 W2 *n* [C]
1 a job or profession that you have been trained for, and which you do for a long period of your life: **[+in]** *a career in journalism* | *a teaching career* | *He realized that his acting career was over.* | **career development/advancement/progression etc** *Career prospects within the company are excellent.* | *a physiotherapist who wanted to make a dramatic **career change** by becoming an author* | *Nurses want an improved **career structure*** (=better opportunities to move upwards in their jobs). THESAURUS ▸ JOB
2 career soldier/teacher etc someone who intends to be a soldier, teacher etc for most of their life, not just for a particular period of time: *a career diplomat*
3 the period of time in your life that you spend doing a particular activity: *She had not had a very impressive school career up till then.* | *My career as an English teacher didn't last long.* | *Beating the defending champion has to be the highlight of my career.*

career² *v* [I always + adv/prep] *BrE* to move forwards quickly without control, making sudden sideways movements SYN **careen** *AmE*: **[+down/along/towards etc]** *The truck careered down the hill and into a tree.*

caˈreer ˌbreak *n* [C] a short period of time when you do not work in your usual job or profession, for example because you want to look after your children

caˈreer coach *n* [C] someone whose job is to help people to plan their careers —**career coaching** *n* [U]

caˈreer ˌcounselor *n* [C] *AmE* a CAREERS OFFICER

ca·reer·ist /kəˈrɪərɪst $ -ˈrɪr-/ *adj* someone who is careerist considers their career to be more important to them than anything else – often used to show disapproval —**careerism** *n* [U] —**careerist** *n* [C]

caˈreers ˌofficer (*also* **caˈreers adˌviser**) *n* [C] *BrE* someone whose job is to give people advice about what jobs and professional training might be suitable for them SYN **career counselor** *AmE*

caˈreer ˌwoman *n* [C] a woman whose career is very important to her, so that she may not want to get married or have children: *independent career women*

care·free /ˈkeəfriː $ ˈker-/ ●○○ *adj* having no worries or problems: *He thought back to the carefree days of his childhood.* | *a carefree attitude*

This graph shows how common different grammar patterns of the adjective **careful** are.

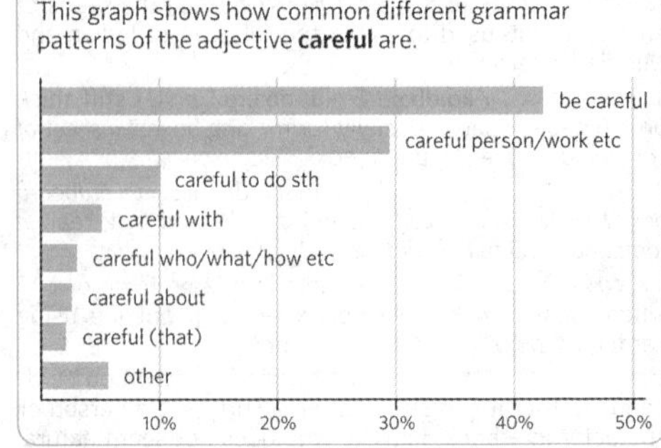

care·ful /ˈkeəfəl $ ˈker-/ ●●● S1 W2 *adj*
1 (be) careful! *spoken* used to tell someone to think about what they are doing so that something bad does not happen: *Be careful – the floor's slippery.*
2 trying very hard to avoid doing anything wrong or to avoid damaging or losing something OPP **careless**: *a careful driver* | **careful to do sth** *Be careful to dispose of your litter properly.* | **[+with]** *He was being very careful with the coffee so as not to spill it.* | **careful who/what/how etc** *I'll be more careful what I say in the future.* | **[+about]** *Mara was careful about what she ate.* | **careful (that)** *We were very careful that he didn't find out.*

GRAMMAR: Prepositions with careful

- You are **careful with** something: *You must be careful with the knife.*
- You are **careful about** what you do: *I was careful about how I spoke to him.*

GRAMMAR GUIDE ADJECTIVES

3 paying a lot of attention to details, so that something is done correctly and thoroughly: *Any school trip requires careful planning.* | **careful consideration/attention/thought** *Careful consideration has been given to all applications.* | **careful analysis/examination/study etc** *careful analysis of the data*

4 careful with money not spending more money than you need to

5 you can't be too careful *spoken* used to say that you should do everything you can to avoid problems or danger —**carefulness** *n* [U]

THESAURUS

careful trying to avoid mistakes and do everything correctly by paying a lot of attention to details: *Try to be more careful with your punctuation.* | *A careful inspection showed cracks in the foundation of the building.*

methodical always doing things in a careful and well-organized way: *He is very methodical in his work and likes to plan everything in advance.* | *This time the researchers used a more methodical approach to the problem.*

thorough /ˈθʌrə $ ˈθʌroʊ, ˈθʌrə/ careful to examine or deal with every part of something, so that you do not miss anything important: *There will be a thorough investigation into the circumstances of her death.* | *Our mechanics will check everything – they're very thorough.*

meticulous very careful about every small detail in order to make sure everything is done correctly: *She keeps meticulous records of the students' progress.* | *He was meticulous about keeping the place clean and tidy.*

systematic using a fixed plan in a careful and well-organized way in order to do everything that you should: *a systematic review of the scientific evidence* | *We need a systematic way to evaluate employees.*

painstaking using a lot of time and effort to do something in a very careful and thorough way: *The book is the result of ten years of painstaking research.* | *They began the long and painstaking task of translating his work into English.*

care·ful·ly /ˈkeəfəli $ ˈker-/ ●●● S2 W2 *adv* in a careful way OPP **carelessly**: *He folded the sheets up carefully.* | **look/listen/think etc carefully** *You need to think very carefully about which course you want to do.* | **carefully planned/chosen/controlled etc** *carefully chosen words*

care·giv·er /ˈkeəˌɡɪvə $ ˈkerˌɡɪvər/ *n* [C] *AmE* someone who takes care of a child or sick person

ˈcare ˌhome *n* [C] *BrE* a building where people who are old or ill live and are looked after

ˌCare in the Comˈmunity *n* [U] when people with mental illnesses are allowed to live among ordinary people in the COMMUNITY, instead of staying in special hospitals

ˈcare ˌlabel *n* [C] a small piece of cloth in a piece of clothing that tells you how to wash it

care·less /ˈkeələs $ ˈker-/ ●●○ *adj*

1 not paying enough attention to what you are doing, so that you make mistakes, damage things etc OPP **careful**: *It was careless of him to leave the door unlocked.* | *a careless mistake* | *careless driving* | **[+with]** *He's careless with his glasses and has lost three pairs.* | ***Careless talk** can be disastrous for a business.*

2 [usually before noun] natural and not done with any deliberate effort or attention: *He ran a hand through his hair with a careless gesture.*

3 not concerned about something: **[+of]** *a man careless of his own safety* | *She gave a careless shrug.* ⚠ Do not use 'careless' to mean that someone has no worries. Use **carefree**: *They all felt happy and carefree.* —**carelessly** *adv* —**carelessness** *n* [U]

THESAURUS

careless not paying enough attention to what you are doing, so that you make mistakes, damage things etc: *I made a few careless mistakes.* | *It was careless of you to leave your purse lying about.*

clumsy often dropping or breaking things because you move around in a careless way: *I'm so clumsy, I spilt milk all over the floor.* | *a clumsy child*

sloppy careless and lazy in the way you do your work or in your behaviour generally: *As a student, he was brilliant but sloppy.* | *I will not tolerate sloppy work.*

reckless *especially written* doing dangerous or stupid things without thinking about your own or other people's safety: *The driver of the car was arrested for reckless driving.* | *His actions showed a reckless disregard for human life.*

irresponsible careless in a way that might affect other people, especially when you should be taking care of them: *It's irresponsible for parents to let their children smoke.* | *his irresponsible attitude to keeping animals*

tactless carelessly saying something that upsets or embarrasses someone, without intending to do this: *He kept making tactless remarks about her appearance.* | *a tactless question*

casual not being careful enough about something and treating it as though it is not important: *He seems to have a very casual attitude towards his work.* | *She disliked the casual way in which he made decisions affecting other people's lives.*

negligent careless about something that you are responsible for, so that serious mistakes are made – used especially when someone will be officially punished for this: *The doctor was negligent in using the wrong type of needle.* | *They found him guilty of negligent conduct.*

ˈcare ˌpackage *n* [C] *AmE* a package of food, sweets etc that is sent to someone living away from home, especially a student at college

car·er /ˈkeərə $ ˈkerər/ ●●○ *n* [C] *BrE* someone who looks after an old or ill person at home SYN **caretaker** *AmE*

ca·ress¹ /kəˈres/ *v* [T] **1** *especially literary* to touch someone gently in a way that shows you love them SYN **stroke**: *His hands gently caressed her body.* THESAURUS TOUCH **2** *literary* to touch something gently, in a way that seems pleasant or romantic: *Waves caressed the shore.*

caress² *n* [C] *especially literary* a gentle touch or kiss that shows you love someone

care·tak·er /ˈkeəˌteɪkə $ ˈkerˌteɪkər/ ●○○ *n* [C]

1 *BrE* someone whose job is to look after a building, especially a school SYN **janitor** *AmE*

2 someone who looks after a house or land while the person who owns it is not there

3 caretaker manager/government/boss etc a manager, government etc that is in charge for a short period of time until another manager or government is chosen

4 *AmE* someone who looks after other people, especially a teacher, parent, nurse etc SYN **carer** *BrE*

ˈcare ˌworker *n* [C] *BrE* someone whose job is to look after people who need care

care·worn /ˈkeəwɔːn $ ˈkerwɔːrn/ *adj* looking sad, worried, and tired: *a careworn expression*

car·go /ˈkɑːɡəʊ $ ˈkɑːrɡoʊ/ ●●○ *n* (*plural* **cargos** *or* **cargoes**) [C,U] the goods that are being carried in a ship or plane SYN **freight**: **[+of]** *A ship carrying a cargo of oil has run aground.* | *a cargo plane*

ˈcargo bike *n* [C] a bicycle with a large container at the front, used for carrying children or goods

Car·ib·be·an /ˌkærəˈbiːən◂/ *adj* from or relating to the islands in the Caribbean Sea —**Caribbean** *n* [C]

car·i·bou /ˈkærəbuː/ *n* (*plural* **caribou**) [C] a North American REINDEER

car·i·ca·ture[1] /ˈkærɪkətʃʊə $ -tʃʊr/ *n* **1** [C] a funny drawing of someone that makes them look silly: **[+of]** *caricatures of politicians* **2** [C] a description of someone or something that is only partly true and makes them seem silly: **[+of]** *The report presents a caricature of the true situation.* **3** [U] the activity of drawing or writing caricatures

caricature[2] *v* [T] to draw or describe someone or something in a way that makes them seem silly: **caricature sb/sth as sth** *Scientists are often caricatured as absent-minded professors.*

car·i·ca·tur·ist /ˈkærɪkətʃʊərɪst $ -tʃʊr-/ *n* [C] someone who draws or writes caricatures

C

car·ies /ˈkeəriz $ ˈker-/ *n* [U] *technical* decay in someone's teeth

car·ill·on /kəˈrɪljən, ˈkærəljən, $ ˈkærəljɑːn, -lən/ *n* [C] a set of bells in a tower that are controlled from a piano KEYBOARD, or a tune played on these bells

car·ing /ˈkeərɪŋ $ ˈker-/ ●○○ *adj*
1 thinking about what other people need or want and trying to help them → **care**: *a warm and caring man | a caring attitude | The school aims to provide a caring environment.* **THESAURUS** KIND, SYMPATHETIC
2 [only before noun] involving the job of looking after other people: *Many of* ***the caring professions*** *are badly paid. | More men are taking on a* ***caring role****.*

car·jack·ing /ˈkɑːˌdʒækɪŋ $ ˈkɑːr-/ *n* [C,U] the crime of using a weapon to force the driver of a car to drive you somewhere or give you their car → **hijacking** —**carjacker** *n* [C] —**carjack** *v* [T]

car·load /ˈkɑːləʊd $ ˈkɑːrloʊd/ *n* [C] the amount of people or things a car can hold: **[+of]** *A carload of tourists pulled up and asked for directions.*

car·mine /ˈkɑːmən, -maɪn $ ˈkɑːr-/ *n* [U] *literary* a dark red colour SYN **crimson** —**carmine** *adj*

car·nage /ˈkɑːnɪdʒ $ ˈkɑːr-/ *n* [U] when a lot of people are killed and injured, especially in a war: *a scene of terrible carnage*

car·nal /ˈkɑːnl $ ˈkɑːrnl/ *adj formal* **1** relating to sex or someone's body: *carnal desires* **2 carnal knowledge/relations** sexual activity —**carnally** *adv*

car·na·tion /kɑːˈneɪʃən $ kɑːr-/ *n* [C] a flower that smells sweet. Men often wear a carnation on their jacket on formal occasions. → see picture at **FLOWER[1]**

car·net /ˈkɑːneɪ $ ˈkɑːr-/ *n* [C] **1** *BrE* a small book of tickets that you can use on trains, buses etc **2** an official document that allows you to go somewhere, especially to drive across the border into another country for a limited period → **pass**

car·ni·val /ˈkɑːnəvəl $ ˈkɑːr-/ ●●○ *n*
1 [C,U] a public event at which people play music, wear special clothes, and dance in the streets: *preparations for this year's carnival | when it's Carnival in Rio | a* ***carnival atmosphere*** *in the town*
2 [C] *AmE* a noisy outdoor event at which you can ride on special machines and play games for prizes SYN **funfair** *BrE*
3 [C] *AmE* a school event at which students play games for prizes
4 carnival of sth *literary* an exciting mixture of things: *Shakespeare's carnival of images*

car·ni·vore /ˈkɑːnəvɔː $ ˈkɑːrnəvɔːr/ *n* [C] **1** an animal that eats flesh → **herbivore**, **omnivore** **2** *humorous* someone who eats meat → **vegetarian** —**carnivorous** /kɑːˈnɪvərəs $ kɑːr-/ *adj*

car·ob /ˈkærəb/ *n* [U] the fruit of a Mediterranean tree, which tastes similar to chocolate

car·ol[1] /ˈkærəl/ (*also* **Christmas carol**) *n* [C] a traditional Christmas song

carol[2] *v* (**carolled**, **carolling** *BrE*, **caroled**, **caroling** *AmE*) [I,T] *literary* to sing or say something in a happy way: *'Goodbye,' carolled Boris happily.*

ca·rot·id ar·te·ry /kəˈrɒtəd ˌɑːtəri $ -ˈrɑːtəd ˌɑːr-/ *n* [C] *medical* one of the two ARTERIES in your neck that supply blood to your head

ca·rouse /kəˈraʊz/ *v* [I] *literary* to drink a lot, be noisy, and have fun —**carousal** *n* [C,U]

car·ou·sel (*also* **carrousel** *AmE*) /ˌkærəˈsel/ *n* [C] **1** *especially AmE* a machine with wooden horses on it that turns around and around, which people can ride on for fun **2** the moving belt that you collect your bags from at an airport

carp[1] /kɑːp $ kɑːrp/ *v* [I] to keep complaining about something in a way that is annoying: **[+about]** *He always finds something to carp about.*

carp[2] *n* (*plural* **carp**) [C] a large fish that lives in lakes and rivers and can be eaten

car·pac·cio /kɑːˈpætʃəʊ $ kɑːrˈpɑːtʃoʊ/ *n* [U] raw BEEF or SALMON that has been cut into very small thin pieces, served as part of a meal: *carpaccio of beef*

car·pal tun·nel syn·drome /ˌkɑːpəl ˈtʌnl ˌsɪndrəʊm $ ˌkɑːr-, -droʊm/ *n* [U] a medical condition which causes pain and weakness in your wrist

ˈcar park ●●● S3 *n* [C] *BrE*
1 an area where people can park their cars SYN **parking lot** *AmE*
2 an enclosed building in a public place where people can park their cars SYN **parking garage** *AmE*

car·pen·ter /ˈkɑːpəntə $ ˈkɑːrpəntər/ ●●○ *n* [C] someone whose job is making and repairing wooden objects

car·pen·try /ˈkɑːpəntri $ ˈkɑːr-/ *n* [U] the skill or work of a carpenter

car·pet[1] /ˈkɑːpɪt $ ˈkɑːr-/ ●●● S2 W3 *n*
1 [C,U] heavy woven material for covering floors or stairs, or a piece of this material → **carpeting**, **rug**: *My bedroom carpet is green. | All the rooms had* ***fitted carpets*** (=carpets cut to fit the shape of the rooms).
2 a carpet of sth *literary* a thick layer of something on the ground: *a carpet of flowers*
3 be/get called on the carpet *AmE informal* to be criticized by someone in authority because you have done something wrong: *He was called on the carpet by his boss to explain his excessive spending.* → MAGIC CARPET, → **sweep/brush sth under the carpet** at SWEEP[1](15)

carpet[2] *v* [T] **1** to cover a floor with carpet: *The building has been carpeted throughout.* **2** *especially BrE informal* to talk in an angry way to someone because they have done something wrong: **be carpeted for sth** *Top officers were carpeted for bullying younger officers.* **3** *literary* if leaves, flowers etc carpet the ground, they cover it in a thick layer: **be carpeted with sth** *The whole garden was carpeted with daffodils.* GRAMMAR **Carpet** is usually passive.

car·pet·bag·ger /ˈkɑːpətˌbægə $ ˈkɑːrpɪtˌbægər/ *n* [C] **1** someone from the northern US who went to the southern US after the Civil War in order to make money, especially in a dishonest way **2** someone who moves to a different place to try to be politically successful – used to show disapproval **3** *BrE* someone who opens an account at a BUILDING SOCIETY because they think that the building society will soon become a bank, and then they will receive money or SHARES in the bank

ˈcarpet-bomb *v* [T] to drop a lot of bombs over a small area to destroy everything in it —**carpet bombing** *n* [U]

car·pet·ing /ˈkɑːpətɪŋ $ ˈkɑːr-/ *n* **1** [U] carpets in general, or the material used for making them: *a spacious room with* ***wall-to-wall carpeting*** (=covering the whole floor) **2** [C] *BrE informal* an occasion when you talk to someone in an angry way because they have done something wrong: *He was called to the manager's office for a carpeting.*

ˈcarpet ˌslipper *n* [C] *BrE old-fashioned* a type of soft shoe that you wear in your house SYN **slipper**

ˈcarpet ˌsweeper *n* [C] a simple machine for sweeping carpets, which does not use electricity

ˈcar pool, **carpool** *n* [C] **1** a group of people who agree to travel together to work, school etc in one car and share the cost **2** a group of cars that a company or organization owns for its workers or members to use

car·pool, **car-pool** /ˈkɑːpuːl $ ˈkɑːr-/ *v* [I] *especially AmE* if a group of people carpool, they travel together to work, school etc in one car and share the cost —**carpooling** *n* [U]

car·port /ˈkɑːpɔːt $ ˈkɑːrpɔːrt/ *n* [C] a shelter for a car which consists of a roof supported by posts or walls

car·rel /ˈkærəl/ *n* [C] a small enclosed desk for one person to use in a library

car·riage /ˈkærɪdʒ/ ●●○ *n*

1 VEHICLE PULLED BY HORSE [C] a vehicle with wheels that is pulled by a horse, used in the past

2 TRAIN [C] *BrE* one of the parts of a train where passengers sit SYN **car** *AmE*

3 MOVEMENT OF GOODS [U] *BrE formal* the act of moving goods from one place to another or the cost of moving them: *Canals were originally built for the carriage of coal.* | *It costs £45.50 including carriage.*

4 MACHINE PART [C] a moving part of a machine that supports or moves another part: *the carriage of a typewriter*

5 POSITION OF BODY [U] *formal* used when describing the position of someone's body as they walk, stand, or sit: *her graceful carriage*

6 FOR MOVING HEAVY OBJECTS [C] something with wheels that is used to move a heavy object, especially a gun → BABY CARRIAGE

ˈcarriage clock *n* [C] a clock inside a glass case with a handle on top

car·riage·way /ˈkærɪdʒweɪ/ *n* [C] *BrE* one of the two sides of a MOTORWAY or main road, for vehicles travelling in the same direction: *the northbound carriageway of the M1* → DUAL CARRIAGEWAY

car·ri·er /ˈkæriə $ -ər/ *n* [C] **1** a company that moves goods or passengers from one place to another → **carry**: *an international carrier* **2** a military vehicle or ship used to move soldiers, weapons etc → AIRCRAFT CARRIER, PEOPLE CARRIER **3** *medical* someone who passes a disease or GENE to other people, especially without being affected by it themselves → **carry**: *carriers of the lung disease, TB* **4** something used for carrying something → **carry**: *a baby carrier* **5** *BrE* a carrier bag **6** *AmE* a company that provides a service such as insurance or telephones

ˈcarrier ˌbag ●●○ *n* [C] *BrE* a bag that you are given in a shop, to carry the things you have bought

ˈcarrier ˌpigeon *n* [C] a PIGEON (=type of bird) that has been trained to carry messages

car·ri·on /ˈkæriən/ *n* [U] the decaying flesh of dead animals, which is eaten by some animals and birds

car·rot /ˈkærət/ ●●● S3 *n*

1 [C,U] a long pointed orange vegetable that grows under the ground: *grated carrots* | *carrot juice* → see picture at VEGETABLE[1]

2 [C] *informal* something that is offered to someone in order to try and persuade them to do something: *They have refused to sign the agreement despite a carrot of £140 million.*

3 carrot and stick *informal* a way of trying to persuade someone to do something by offering them something good if they do it, and a punishment if they do not: *the government's* ***carrot and stick approach*** *in getting young people to find jobs*

car·rot·y /ˈkærəti/ *adj BrE* carroty hair is orange

car·rou·sel /ˌkærəˈsel/ *n* [C] an American spelling of CAROUSEL

car·ry[1] /ˈkæri/ ●●● S1 W1 *v* (**carried**, **carrying**, **carries**)

1 LIFT AND TAKE [T] to hold something in your hand or arms, or support it as you take it somewhere: *Gina was carrying a small bunch of flowers.* | *Angela carried the child in her arms.* | *Let me carry that for you.* | *Jack carried his grandson up the stairs.* | **carry sth to sth/sb** *The waiter carried our drinks to the table.* THESAURUS ▶ TAKE

2 VEHICLE/SHIP/PLANE [T] to take people or things from one place to another in a vehicle, ship, or plane: *The ship was carrying drugs.* | *There are more airplanes carrying more people than ever before.*

3 PIPE/WIRE ETC [T] if a pipe, wire etc carries something such as liquid or electricity, the liquid, electricity etc flows or travels along it: *A drain carries surplus water to the river.* | *The aim is for one wire to carry both television and telephone calls.*

4 MOVE STH [T] to cause something to move along or support something as it moves along: *This stretch of water carries a lot of shipping.* | *The bridge carries the main road over the railway.* | *Pollution was carried inland by the wind.*

5 HAVE WITH YOU [T] to have something with you in your pocket, on your belt, in your bag etc everywhere you go: *I don't carry a handbag. I just carry money in my pocket.* | *All the soldiers carried rifles.* | *He says he's got to carry a knife to protect himself.*

6 HAVE A QUALITY [T] to have something as a particular quality: *Degree qualifications carry international recognition.* | *Few medical procedures* ***carry*** *no* ***risk*** *of any kind.* | *Older managers* ***carry*** *more* ***authority*** *in a crisis.* | *The plan is not likely to* ***carry*** *much* ***weight*** *with* (=have much influence over) *the authorities.* | *If the child believes in what she is saying, she will* ***carry conviction*** (=make others believe what she says is true).

7 NEWS/PROGRAMMES [T] if a newspaper, a television or radio broadcast, or a website carries a piece of news, an advertisement etc, it prints it or broadcasts it: *The morning paper* ***carried*** *a* ***story*** *about demonstrations in New York and Washington D.C.* | *The national TV network carries religious programmes.*

8 INFORMATION [T] if something carries information, the information is written on it: *All tobacco products must carry a health warning.* | *goods carrying the label 'Made in the USA'*

9 BE RESPONSIBLE [T] to be responsible for doing something: *Each team member is expected to carry a fair share of the workload.* | *Which minister* ***carries responsibility*** *for the police?* | *Parents* ***carry the burden of*** *ensuring that children go to school.*

10 SHOP [T] if a shop carries goods, it has a supply of them for sale: *The sports shop* ***carries*** *a full* ***range of*** *equipment.*

11 BUILDING [T] if a wall etc carries something, it supports the weight of that thing: *These two columns carry the whole roof.*

12 TAKE SB/STH [T] to take something or someone to a new place, point, or position: **carry sb/sth to sth** *The president wanted to carry the war to the northern states.* | *Blair carried his party to victory in 1997.* | **carry sb/sth into sth** *Clinton carried his campaign into Republican areas.*

13 DISEASE [T] if a person, animal, or insect carries a disease, they can pass it to other people or animals even if they are not ill themselves → **carrier**: *The disease is carried by a black fly which lives in the rivers.* | *Birds and monkeys can carry disease.*

14 carry insurance/a guarantee etc to have insurance etc: *All our products carry a 12-month guarantee.*

15 be/get carried away to be so excited, angry, interested etc that you are no longer really in control of what you do or say, or you forget everything else: *It's easy to get carried away when you can do so much with the graphics software.*

16 be carried along (by sth) to become excited about something or determined to do something: *The crowd were carried along on a tide of enthusiasm.* | *You can be carried along by the atmosphere of an auction and spend more than you planned.*

17 CRIME [T] if a crime carries a particular punishment, that is the usual punishment for the crime: *Drink-driving should* ***carry*** *an automatic prison* ***sentence.*** | *Murder still* ***carries*** *the death* ***penalty.***

18 SOUND [I] if a sound carries, it goes a long way: *In the winter air, sounds carry clearly.* | *The songs of the whales carry through the water over long distances.*

19 BALL [I] if a ball carries a particular distance when it is thrown, hit, or kicked, it travels that distance

C

20 carry sth in your head/mind to remember information that you need, without writing it down: *Alice carried a map of the London Underground in her head.*
21 TUNE [T] to sing a tune using the correct notes: *I sang solos when I was six because I could carry a tune.* | *The highest voice carries the melody.*
22 PERSUADE [T] to persuade a group of people to support you: *He had to carry a large majority of his colleagues to get the leadership.* | *Her appeal to common sense was what finally* ***carried the day*** (=persuaded people to support her).
23 VOTE **be carried** if a suggestion, proposal etc is carried, most of the people at an official meeting vote for it and it is accepted: *The amendment was carried by 292 votes to 246.* | *The resolution was* ***carried unanimously*** (=everyone agreed). | *Those in favour of the motion raise your arm. Those against? The* ***motion is carried*** (=proposal is accepted).
24 ELECTION [T] *AmE* if someone carries a state or local area in a US election, they win in that state or area: *Cuban Americans play an important role in whether he carries Florida in the fall campaign.*
25 YOUR BODY [T always + adv/prep] to stand and move in a particular way, or to hold part of your body in a particular way: *He had a way of carrying his head on one side.* | **carry yourself** *She carried herself straight and with confidence.*
26 carry the can (for sb/sth) *BrE informal* to be the person who has to take the blame for something even if it was not their fault, or not their fault alone: *He has been left to carry the can for a decision he didn't make.*
27 NOT ENOUGH EFFORT [T] if a group carries someone who is not doing enough work, they have to manage without the work that person should be doing: *The team can't afford to carry any weak players.*
28 CHILD [I,T] *old-fashioned* if a woman is carrying a child, she is PREGNANT
29 carry all/everything before you *literary* to be completely successful in a struggle against other people
30 carry sth too far/to extremes/to excess to do or say too much about something: *I don't mind a joke, but this is carrying it too far.*
31 WEIGHT [T] to weigh a particular amount more than you should or than you did: *Joe carries only nine pounds more than when he was 20.*
32 carry a torch for sb to love someone romantically who does not love you: *He's been carrying a torch for your sister for years.*
33 carry the torch of sth to support an important belief or tradition when other people do not: *Leaders in the mountains carried the torch of Greek independence.*
34 as fast as his/her legs could carry him/her as fast as possible: *She ran as fast as her legs could carry her.*
35 ADDING NUMBERS [T] to put a number into the next row to the left when you are adding numbers together → CARD-CARRYING, CASH AND CARRY, → **fetch and carry** at FETCH[1](3)

carry sth ↔ **forward** *phr v*
1 to succeed in making progress with something: *The new team have to carry the work forward.*
2 to include an amount of money in a later set of figures or calculations

carry sth ↔ **off** *phr v*
1 to do something difficult successfully: *I was flattered to be offered the job but wasn't sure if I could carry it off.*
2 to win a prize: *a film that carried off three Oscars*

carry on *phr v*
1 *especially BrE* to continue doing something: *Sorry, I interrupted you. Please carry on.* | **carry on doing sth** *You'll have an accident if you carry on driving like that.* | **[+with]** *I want to carry on with my course.* | **carry on as usual/as you are/regardless etc**
2 to continue moving: *He stopped and looked back, then carried on down the stairs.* | *Carry straight on until you get to the traffic lights.*
3 carry on sth if you carry on a particular kind of work or activity, you do it or take part in it: *Mr Dean carried on his baking business until he retired.* | *It was so noisy it was hard to* ***carry on*** *a* ***conversation***.
4 *spoken* to talk in an annoying way: **[+about]** *I wish everyone would stop carrying on about it.*
5 *old-fashioned* to have a sexual relationship with someone, when you should not: *Lucy confessed to carrying on behind her husband's back.* | **[+with]** *She was carrying on with a neighbour.*

carry sth ↔ **out** *phr v*
1 to do something that needs to be organized and planned: *We need to carry out more research.* | *A survey is now being carried out nationwide.* | *Turn off the water supply before carrying out repairs.*

> **REGISTER**
> In written English, people often use **conduct** when writing about research, experiments etc, because this sounds more formal than **carry out**: *They* ***conducted*** *experiments to test this theory.*

2 to do something that you have said you will do or that someone has asked you to do: *Nicholson didn't* ***carry out*** *his* ***threat*** *to take legal action.* | *We* ***carried out*** *her* ***instructions*** *precisely.* | *Will the government* ***carry out*** *its* ***promise*** *to reform the law?*

carry sth ↔ **over** *phr v*
1 if something is carried over into a new situation, it continues to exist in the new situation: *The pain and violence of his childhood were carried over into his marriage.*
2 to make an official arrangement to do something or use something at a later time: *Up to five days' holiday can be carried over from one year to the next.*

carry sb/sth **through** *phr v*
1 to complete or finish something successfully, in spite of difficulties: *I'm determined to carry this through.*
2 carry sb through (sth) to help someone to manage during an illness or a difficult period: *Her confidence carried her through.*

carry[2] *n* [U] *technical* the distance a ball or bullet travels after it has been thrown, hit, or fired

car·ry·all /ˈkæri-ɔːl $ -ɒːl/ *n* [C] *AmE* a large soft bag SYN **holdall** *BrE* → see picture at BAG[1]

car·ry·cot /ˈkærikɒt $ -kɑːt/ *n* [C] *BrE* a small bed used for carrying a baby

ˈcarry-on[1] *n* [C] **1** *BrE spoken* a situation in which someone behaves in a silly or annoying way: *What a carry-on!* **2** *AmE* a bag that you are allowed to take onto a plane with you → **carry on** at CARRY[1]

carry-on[2] *adj* [only before noun] carry-on bags are ones that you are allowed to take onto a plane with you

ˈcarry-out *n* [C] *especially AmE* food that you can take away from a restaurant to eat somewhere else, or a restaurant that sells food like this SYN **takeaway** *BrE*

ˈcarry-ˌover *n* [singular] **1** something you do, or something that happens now, that is the result of a situation that existed in the past: **[+from]** *Some of the problems schools are facing are a carry-over from the previous government's policies.* **2** an amount of money that has not been used and is available to use later: **[+from]** *The budget includes a £7 million carry-over from last year.* → **carry over** at CARRY[1]

ˈcar seat *n* [C] **1** a special seat for a baby or young child that can be used in a car **2** a seat in a car

car·sick /ˈkɑːˌsɪk $ ˈkɑːr-/ *adj* feeling sick because you are travelling in a car —**carsickness** *n* [U]

cart[1] /kɑːt $ kɑːrt/ ●●○ *n* [C]
1 a vehicle with no roof that is pulled by a horse and used for carrying heavy things → HANDCART
2 *AmE* a large wire basket on wheels that you use in a SUPERMARKET SYN **trolley** *BrE*
3 the place on an Internet shopping website where you put things that you wish to buy
4 *AmE* a small table with wheels, used for moving and serving food and drinks SYN **trolley** *BrE*
5 put the cart before the horse to do two things in the wrong order → **upset the apple cart** at UPSET[2](5)

cart² *v* [T always + adv/prep] **1** to take something somewhere in a cart, truck etc: **cart sth away** *Household waste is carted away by the city's Sanitation Department.* **2** *informal* to carry something somewhere, especially something that is heavy or difficult to carry: *We carted all the furniture upstairs.*

cart sb **off/away** *phr v informal* to take someone somewhere, especially to prison or hospital: *He collapsed and had to be carted off to hospital.*

ˈcar tax *n* [U] money that people in Britain must pay if they want to drive a car on the roads SYN **road tax**

carte blanche /ˌkɑːt ˈblɑːnʃ $ ˌkɑːrt-/ *n* [U] permission or freedom to do whatever you want: *The new manager will be* ***given carte blanche*** *as long as she can increase the company's profits.* | *She* ***had carte blanche*** *to produce a film suitable for children.*

car·tel /kɑːˈtel $ kɑːr-/ *n* [C] a group of people or companies who agree to sell something at a particular price in order to prevent competition and increase profits → **monopoly**: *an illegal drug cartel*

cart·er /ˈkɑːtə $ ˈkɑːrtər/ *n* [C] someone whose job was to drive a CART in the past

cart·horse /ˈkɑːthɔːs $ ˈkɑːrthɔːrs/ *n* [C] a large strong horse, often used for pulling heavy loads

car·ti·lage /ˈkɑːtəlɪdʒ $ ˈkɑːrtəlɪdʒ/ *n* [C,U] a strong substance that can bend, which is around the joints in your body and in your outer ear

cart·load /ˈkɑːtləʊd $ ˈkɑːrtloʊd/ *n* [C] the amount that a CART can hold: **[+of]** *cartloads of hay*

car·tog·ra·phy /kɑːˈtɒɡrəfi $ kɑːrˈtɑː-/ *n* [U] the activity of making maps —**cartographer** *n* [C]

car·ton /ˈkɑːtn $ ˈkɑːrtn/ ●○○ *n* [C]
1 a small box made of CARDBOARD or plastic that contains food or a drink: **[+of]** *a carton of fruit juice* | *a milk carton* → see pictures at **BOX¹**, **CONTAINER**
2 *especially AmE* a large container with smaller containers of goods inside it: **[+of]** *a carton of cigarettes*

car·toon /kɑːˈtuːn $ kɑːr-/ ●●○ S3 *n* [C]
1 a short film that is made by photographing a series of drawings: *cartoon characters such as Donald Duck*
2 a funny drawing in a newspaper or magazine, especially about politicians or events in the news
3 (*also* **cartoon strip**) a set of drawings that tell a funny story, especially in a newspaper or magazine SYN **comic strip**
4 *technical* a drawing that an artist does before starting to do a painting

car·toon·ist /kɑːˈtuːnɪst $ kɑːr-/ *n* [C] someone who draws cartoons

carˈtoon ˌstrip *n* [C] a CARTOON(3)

car·tridge /ˈkɑːtrɪdʒ $ ˈkɑːr-/ *n* [C] **1** a small container or piece of equipment that you put inside something to make it work: *computer game cartridges* | *an ink cartridge for a printer* **2** a tube containing explosive powder and a bullet that you put in a gun SYN **shell**

ˈcartridge ˌpaper *n* [U] *BrE* thick strong paper used for drawing on

ˈcart track *n* [C] a narrow road with a rough surface, usually on a farm

cart·wheel /ˈkɑːt-wiːl $ ˈkɑːrt-/ *n* [C] **1** a movement in which you turn completely over by throwing your body sideways onto your hands while bringing your legs over your head: **do/turn cartwheels** *The children were doing cartwheels in the park.* **2** the wheel of a CART —**cartwheel** *v* [I]

carve /kɑːv $ kɑːrv/ ●●○ *v*
1 MAKE OBJECT OR PATTERN [T] to make an object or pattern by cutting a piece of wood or stone → **carving**: **carve sth out of/from sth** *a statue carved from a single block of marble* | *carved wooden chairs*
2 CUT STH INTO A SURFACE [T] to cut a pattern or letter on the surface of something: **carve sth on/in/into sth** *Someone had carved their initials on the tree.*
3 CUT MEAT [I,T] to cut a large piece of cooked meat into smaller pieces using a knife: *Carve the meat into slices.* | *Who's going to carve?* THESAURUS ▸ CUT
4 JOB/POSITION/LIFE [T] (*also* **carve out**) to succeed in getting the job, position, life etc that you want: *He* ***carved a niche*** *for himself as a writer.* | *She* ***carved out*** *a successful* ***career*** *in the film industry.* | *He moved to Boston to carve out a new life for himself.*
5 WATER/WIND [T] if a river, the wind etc carves land or rock, it removes some of it: *The river had carved channels in the limestone rock.* → **not be carved in stone** at **STONE¹**(9)
6 REDUCE STH [T always + adv/prep] to reduce the size of something by removing some of it: **carve sth from sth** *The company carved $1 million from its budget.*

carve sb/sth ↔ **up** *phr v*
1 to divide land, a company etc into smaller parts and share it between people – used especially to show disapproval: *The Ottoman Empire was carved up by Britain and France after World War I.* | *The two companies are attempting to carve up a large slice of America's publishing industry between them.*
2 *BrE informal* to drive past a car and then suddenly move in front of it so that you are too close

carv·er /ˈkɑːvə $ ˈkɑːrvər/ *n* [C] someone who carves wood or stone

car·ver·y /ˈkɑːvəri $ ˈkɑːr-/ *n* (*plural* **carveries**) [C] *BrE* a restaurant that serves ROAST meat

ˈcarve-up *n* [singular] *informal* an arrangement between two or more people, governments etc by which they divide something among themselves even though this is wrong

carv·ing /ˈkɑːvɪŋ $ ˈkɑːr-/ *n* **1** [C] an object or pattern made by cutting a shape in wood or stone for decoration → **carve 2** [U] the activity or skill of carving something

ˈcarving fork *n* [C] a large fork used to hold cooked meat firmly while you are cutting it

ˈcarving knife *n* [C] a large knife used for cutting large pieces of meat → see picture at **KNIFE¹**

ˈcar wash *n* [C] a place where there is special equipment for washing cars

car·y·at·id /ˌkæriˈætɪd/ *n* [C] *technical* a PILLAR in the shape of a female figure

Cas·a·no·va /ˌkæsəˈnəʊvə $ -ˈnoʊ-/ *n* [C] a man who has had sexual relationships with many women

cas·bah /ˈkæzbɑː/ *n* [C] an ancient Arab city or the market in it

cas·cade¹ /kæˈskeɪd/ *n* [C] **1** a small steep WATERFALL that is one of several together **2** something that hangs down in large quantities: **[+of]** *Her hair fell over her shoulders in a cascade of curls.*

cascade² *v* **1** [I always + adv/prep] to flow, fall, or hang down in large quantities: *Her thick black hair cascaded down below her waist.* | *Gallons of water cascaded over the side of the bath.* **2** [I,T always + adv/prep] to pass information or skills to people at a lower level in your organization, or to be passed down in this way: *This information will be cascaded down to employees through their line managers.*

case¹ /keɪs/ ●●● S1 W1 *n*
1 EXAMPLE [C] an example of a particular situation or of something happening: **[+of]** *There were 16 cases of damage to cars in the area.* | **in the case of sth** *The amount of fruit in fruit juices must be 6% in the case of berries and 10% in the case of other fruits.* | **in some/many/most etc cases** *In many cases standards have improved.* | *Tom's career is* ***a case in point*** (=a clear example of something that you are discussing or explaining). | *a* ***classic case*** (=typical example) *of poor design* THESAURUS ▸ EXAMPLE
2 SITUATION [C usually singular] a situation that exists, especially as it affects a particular person or group: **in sb's case** *Like the others, he produced a written explanation, but in Scott's case this was a 30-page printed booklet.* | *Changing men's and women's traditional roles is not easy, but in our case it has been helpful.* | **it is the case (that)** *It may be the case that the scheme will need more money.* | *We tend to think of these people as untrustworthy, but that is not the*

C

CASES

case. | **in this case** *In this case, several solutions could be tried.* | **in which case** *He won't want to eat it unless he's really hungry, in which case he'll eat almost anything.*

3 (just) in case a) as a way of being safe from something that might happen or might be true: *Take an umbrella, in case it rains.* | *He had his camera ready, just in case he saw something that would make a good picture.* **b)** *AmE* if: *In case I'm late, start without me.*

GRAMMAR: Choosing the right tense

- Use the simple present tense with **in case** to talk about a possible future event. Don't use 'will'. You say: *Write it down* ***in case*** *you* ***forget***. ✗ Don't say: *in case you will forget*
- Use the simple past tense with **in case** when talking about the past. Don't use 'would'. You say: *I took my umbrella* ***in case*** *it* ***rained***. ✗ Don't say: *in case it would rain*
- In more formal English, you can say **in case** something **should** happen: *Here's a contact number, in case there should be a problem.*

GRAMMAR GUIDE ▸ VERBS

4 in any case whatever happens or happened: *I don't see why I couldn't do it. In any case, I'm going to try.* | *He's too young to come and in any case I want him to spend the time with Mom.*

5 in that case if that is the situation: *'He didn't want to talk to Sally.' 'In that case why did he agree to meet her?'*

6 REASON/ARGUMENT [C usually singular] a set of reasons why something should happen or be done: *Let me research the facts before I* ***put forward*** *a* ***case***. | **[+for]** *A group of us met to* ***make*** *our* ***case*** *for more women in the cabinet.* | *There is a* ***strong case*** (=very good set of reasons) *for getting parents more involved in the school's activities.*

7 LAW/CRIME [C] **a)** a question or problem that will be dealt with by a law court: *She is keen to avoid a court case.* | *The lawyers will only be paid if they win the case.* | **[+against]** *Marshall has dropped the case against us.* **b)** all the reasons that one side in a legal argument can give against the other side: *The evidence does not support the prosecution's case.* | *The court ruled that we* ***had*** *a* ***case*** (=had enough evidence or good arguments). **c)** an event or set of events that need to be dealt with by the police in order to find out if a crime has been committed and who committed it: **[+of]** *a case of armed robbery* | **on the case** *Around 50 police officers are on the case.*

8 BOX/CONTAINER [C] **a)** a large box or container in which things can be stored or moved: *a packing case* | *a case of wine* **b)** a special box used as a container for holding or protecting something: *a jewellery case* | *Jim put his violin back in its case.* **c)** *BrE* a SUITCASE: *Polly carried her cases upstairs to the bedroom.* → **BOOKCASE, BRIEFCASE, PILLOWCASE**

9 it's a case of sth *spoken* used before describing a situation: *Everyone can learn, it's just a case of practising.* | *It's a case of too many people and not enough jobs.*

10 DISEASE [C] an example of a disease or a person who has a disease: **[+of]** *There are thousands of new cases of AIDS in Africa every year.*

11 in case of sth used to describe what you should do in a particular situation, especially on official notices: *In case of fire, break the glass.*

12 GRAMMAR [C,U] *technical* the way in which the form of a word changes, showing its relationship to other words in a sentence: *case endings*

13 be on sb's case *informal* to be criticizing someone constantly: *Dad's always on my case about something or other.*

14 be on the case *spoken* if someone says they are on the case, they know about a problem and are going to try to solve it

15 get off my case *spoken* used to tell someone to stop criticizing you or complaining about you: *OK, OK, just get off my case!*

16 PERSON [C] someone who is being dealt with by a doctor, a SOCIAL WORKER, the police etc → **BASKET CASE, LOWER CASE, NUTCASE,** → **I rest my case** at REST²(9), → **UPPER CASE**

COLLOCATIONS – MEANING 7a

ADJECTIVES/NOUN + case

a court case *There was a lot of publicity surrounding the court case.*
a murder case *He had been a witness in a murder case.*
a libel case (=against someone who has written a bad statement about someone else) *damages awarded by juries in libel cases*
a criminal case *It was the longest and most expensive criminal case in US history.*
a civil case (=not a criminal case) | **a test case** (=one that will establish a principle for the first time) | **a landmark case** (=one that established a principle for the first time) | **a high-profile case** (=one that gets a lot of attention)

VERBS

bring a case (against sb) *There was not enough evidence to bring a case against him.*
hear/try a case (=listen to the evidence before making a judgment) *The case will be heard by a federal judge.*
win/lose a case (=be successful or unsuccessful in proving someone guilty or not guilty) *Lomax was a brilliant lawyer who had never lost a case.*
settle a case (=end it finally) *He paid a $15,000 fine to settle the case.*
adjourn a case (=stop it for a short time) *The case was adjourned until next month for further reports.*
dismiss/throw out a case (=officially stop it from continuing) | **drop a case** (=not continue with it) | **a case comes/goes to court** | **a case comes/goes to trial** | **a case comes before a judge/court**

case² *v* [T] **1 be cased in sth** to be completely surrounded by a material or substance: *The reactor will be cased in metal.* → **CASING 2 case the joint** *informal* to look around a place that you intend to steal from in order to find out information

case·book /ˈkeɪsbʊk/ *n* [C] a detailed written record kept by a doctor, SOCIAL WORKER, or police officer of the cases they have dealt with

ˈcase ˌhistory *n* [C] a detailed record of someone's past illnesses, problems etc that a doctor or SOCIAL WORKER studies

ˈcase law *n* [U] *law* a type of law that is based on decisions judges have made in the past

case·load /ˈkeɪsləʊd $ -loʊd/ *n* [C] the number of people a doctor, SOCIAL WORKER etc has to deal with

case·ment /ˈkeɪsmənt/ (*also* **ˈcasement ˌwindow**) *n* [C] a window that opens like a door with HINGES at one side

ˌcase-ˈsensitive *adj* a case-sensitive computer program recognizes whether a letter is a capital or LOWER CASE

ˈcase ˌstudy *n* [C] a detailed account of the development of a particular person, group, or situation that has been studied over a period of time

casework /ˈkeɪswɜːk/ *n* [U] work that a SOCIAL WORKER does which is concerned with the problems of a particular person or family who needs help —**caseworker** *n* [C]

cash¹ /kæʃ/ ●●● S2 W2 *n* [U]
1 money in the form of coins or notes rather than cheques, CREDIT CARDS etc: *Cash was taken during a burglary of the apartment.* | **in cash** *The traffic police will accept fines in cash immediately.* | *The shop charges less if the customer* ***pays in cash.*** → HARD CASH, PETTY CASH
THESAURUS MONEY
2 money: *Health and education need cash from the government.* | *A phone line to help children in trouble has been closed due to lack of cash.* | *Charity workers must constantly* ***raise*** *more* ***cash*** (=collect more money) *for the needy.* | *The company found itself* ***strapped for cash*** (=without enough money) *to pay taxes.*
3 cash down *BrE*, **cash up front** *AmE* if you pay for something cash down, you pay before you receive it
4 cash on delivery (*abbreviation* **COD**) a payment system in which the customer pays the person who delivers the goods to them

cash² *v* [T] **cash a cheque/postal order/draft etc** to exchange a cheque etc for the amount of money it is worth: *Traveller's cheques can be cashed at most hotels for a small charge.* | *Where can I get this cashed?* —**cashable** *adj*
cash in *phr v* **1** to make a profit from a situation in a way that other people think is wrong or unfair: **[+on]** *The record company was trying to cash in on her fame by releasing early teenage recordings.* **2 cash sth ↔ in** to exchange something such as an insurance POLICY for its value in money **3 cash in your chips** to die – used humorously
cash up *BrE*, **cash out** *AmE phr v* to add up the amount of money received in a shop in a day so that it can be checked

ˈcash adˌvance *n* [C] money that you get from a bank, using a CREDIT CARD: *It seems so easy to get a $100 cash advance every few days at a local ATM machine.*

ˌcash and ˈcarry *n* [C] *BrE* a shop where customers representing a business or organization can buy large amounts of goods at cheap prices

cash·back /ˈkæʃbæk/ *n* [U] **1** a way of getting money at a shop when you use a DEBIT CARD to pay for the things you are buying, in which the shop gives you money which it takes from your bank account: *I got £40 cashback.* **2** a way of reducing the price of a car, piece of furniture etc where the seller says what the price is and offers to give a certain amount of money back to the person who buys it: *Price on the road – £8,750. But on top of that, we'll give you £500 cashback.*

ˈcash bar *n* [C] a place at a big party, wedding etc where guests have to pay for their own drinks

ˈcash box *n* [C] a small metal box with a lock that you keep money in

ˈcash card *n* [C] a special plastic card used for getting money from a machine outside a bank, SUPERMARKET, or other public building → **debit card**

ˈcash cow *n* [C] something that a company sells very successfully and that brings in a lot of money

ˈcash crop *n* [C] a crop grown in order to be sold rather than to be used by the people growing it → **subsistence crop** at SUBSISTENCE(2)

ˈcash desk *n* [C] *BrE* the desk in a shop where you pay

ˌcash ˈdiscount *n* [C] an amount by which a seller reduces a price if the buyer pays immediately or before a particular date

ˈcash disˌpenser *n* [C] *BrE* a CASH MACHINE

ca·shew /ˈkæʃuː, kəˈʃuː/ *n* [C] **1** a small curved nut → see picture at NUT¹ **2** the tropical American tree that produces the cashew nut

ˈcash flow *n* [singular, U] the movement of money coming into a business as income and going out as wages, materials etc: *We expect a rise in both our production and our cash flow.* | *The builder is unable to pay due to* ***cash flow problems.***

cash·ier¹ /kæˈʃɪə $ -ˈʃɪr/ *n* [C] someone whose job is to receive or pay out money in a shop

cashier² *v* [T] to force an officer to leave the army, navy etc because they have done something wrong

ˌcash-in-ˈhand *adj* a cash-in-hand payment is made in the form of notes and coins so that there is no record of the payment

cash·less /ˈkæʃləs/ *adj* done or working without using money in the form of coins and notes: *a cashless pay system* | *the cashless society*

ˈcash maˌchine ●●○ *n* [C] a machine in or outside a bank, SUPERMARKET, or other public building, from which you can obtain money with a special plastic card SYN **ATM**

cash·mere /ˈkæʃmɪə $ ˈkæʒmɪr, ˈkæʃ-/ *n* [U] a type of fine soft wool: *I wish I could afford a cashmere sweater.*

Cash·point /ˈkæʃpɔɪnt/ *n* [C] *trademark BrE* a CASH MACHINE

ˈcash ˌregister *n* [C] a machine used in shops to keep the money in and record the amount of money received from each sale SYN **till** *BrE*

ˈcash-starved *adj* not having as much money as is needed: *cash-starved public services*

ˈcash-strapped *adj* not having enough money: *cash-strapped governments* | *cash-strapped shoppers*

cas·ing /ˈkeɪsɪŋ/ *n* [C] an outer layer of metal, rubber etc that covers and protects something such as a wire

ca·si·no /kəˈsiːnəʊ $ -noʊ/ ●●○ *n* (*plural* **casinos**) [C] a place where people try to win money by playing card games or ROULETTE: *Doesn't that club have a casino upstairs?*

caˈsino bank *n* [C] *BrE informal* an INVESTMENT BANK – used to show disapproval

cask /kɑːsk $ kæsk/ *n* [C] a round wooden container used for storing wine or other liquids, or the amount of liquid that it contains SYN **barrel**: *a cask of rum*

cas·ket /ˈkɑːskɪt $ ˈkæs-/ *n* [C] **1** a small decorated box in which you keep jewellery and other valuable objects **2** *AmE* a COFFIN

Cas·san·dra /kəˈsændrə/ people are sometimes called a 'Cassandra' if they warn that something bad will happen, but nobody believes them. In ancient Greek stories, Cassandra was the daughter of Priam, King of Troy. She had the power to see the future, and warned that the Greeks could use the Trojan Horse to take control of Troy, but no one believed her.

cas·sa·va /kəˈsɑːvə/ *n* [C,U] a tropical plant with thick roots that you can eat, or the flour made from these roots

cas·se·role¹ /ˈkæsərəʊl $ -roʊl/ *n* [C] **1** food that is cooked slowly in liquid in a covered dish in the OVEN: *chicken casserole* **2** a deep covered dish used for cooking food in an oven

casserole² *v* [T] to cook food in a casserole

cas·sette /kəˈset/ *n* [C] **1** a small flat plastic case containing MAGNETIC TAPE, that can be used for playing or recording sound **2** a closed container with photographic film in it, that can be fitted into a camera

casˈsette ˌplayer *n* [C] a piece of electrical equipment used for playing cassettes

casˈsette reˌcorder *n* [C] a piece of electrical equipment used for recording sound or for playing cassettes on SYN **tape recorder**

cas·sock /ˈkæsək/ *n* [C] a long, usually black, piece of clothing worn by priests

C

cast¹ /kɑːst $ kæst/ ●●○ W3 *v* (*past tense and past participle* **cast**)
1 cast light on/onto sth to provide new information about something, making it easier to understand: *research findings that cast new light on the origin of our universe | The numerous biographies of Baldwin cast little light on the subject.*
2 cast doubt(s) on sth to make people feel less certain about something: *Her documentary casts serious doubt on Gilligan's conviction.*
3 LIGHT AND SHADE [T] *literary* to make light or a shadow appear somewhere: **cast sth over/on/across sth** *The flames cast dancing shadows on the walls. | the shade cast by low-hanging branches*
4 cast a shadow/cloud over sth *literary* to make people feel less happy or hopeful about something: *The allegations cast a cloud over the mayor's visit. | Her father's illness cast a shadow over the wedding celebrations.*
5 LOOK [T] *literary* to look quickly in a particular direction: **cast a look/glance at sb/sth** *She cast an anguished look at Guy.* | **cast sb a glance/look** *The young tramp cast him a wary glance. | She blushed,* ***casting her eyes down****.*
6 cast an eye on/over sth to examine or read something quickly in order to judge whether it is correct, good etc: *Mellor cast an eye over the draft for inaccuracies.* | **cast a critical/expert etc eye** *Tonight, Tim Goodman casts a cynical eye on TV ads.*
7 cast a vote/ballot to vote in an election: *Barely one in three will bother to cast a ballot on February 26th. | To qualify, candidates must get at least 10% of the votes cast.*
→ CASTING VOTE
8 cast a spell on/over sb a) to attract someone very strongly and to keep their attention completely: *Hong Kong casts a spell over the visitor almost as soon as the aircraft touches down.* **b)** to use magic words or acts to change someone or something: *She's a witch, and she'll cast a spell on you if she catches you.*
9 cast your mind back *literary* to try to remember something that happened in the past: **[+to]** *Cast your mind back to your first day at school.* | **[+over]** *He frowned, casting his mind back over the conversation.*
10 cast aspersions on sth/sb *formal* to suggest that someone is not as truthful, honest etc as they seem: *remarks that cast aspersions on the integrity of the jury*
11 METAL [T] to make an object by pouring liquid metal, plastic etc into a MOULD (=hollow container): **cast sth in/from sth** *a statue of a horse cast in bronze*
12 ACTING [T] to choose which people will act particular parts in a play, film etc: **cast sb alongside/opposite sb** (=choose people for the two main roles) *Pfeiffer was expected to be cast alongside Douglas in 'Basic Instinct'.* | **cast sb as sth** *Coppola cast him as Sodapop in 'The Outsiders'.* | **cast sb in a role/a part/the lead** *The producer finally cast Finch in the male lead.*
13 DESCRIBE [T] to regard or describe someone as a particular type of person: **cast sb as sth** *Clinton had cast himself as the candidate of new economic opportunity. | Clarke's trying to* ***cast*** *me* ***in the role of*** *villain here.*
14 THROW [T always + adv/prep] *literary* to throw something somewhere SYN **toss**: *Sparks leapt as he cast more wood on the fire.*
15 FISHING [I,T] to throw a fishing line or net into the water: *There's a trick to casting properly.*
16 SEND AWAY [T always + adv/prep] *literary* to force someone to go somewhere unpleasant: **cast sb into prison/Hell etc** *Memet should, in her opinion, be cast into prison.*
17 cast your net (far and) wide to consider or try as many things as possible in order to find what you want: *We cast our net wide to get the right person for the job.*
18 SKIN [T] when a snake casts its skin, the top layer of skin falls off slowly SYN **shed**
19 cast a shoe if a horse casts a shoe, the shoe falls off by accident
20 cast a horoscope to prepare and write a HOROSCOPE for someone → **the die is cast** at DIE²(3), → **throw in/cast your lot with sb/sth** at LOT²(8), → **cast pearls before swine** at PEARL(4)

cast about/around for sth *phr v* to try hard to think of the right thing to do or say: *She cast about frantically for an excuse. | Telecoms companies are casting around for ways of recouping huge losses.*
cast sb/sth ↔ **aside** *phr v literary* to remove or get rid of someone or something because you no longer want or need them: *When Henry became king, he cast aside all his former friends.* | **cast aside your inhibitions/doubts etc** *Cast aside your fears.*
cast away *phr v* if you are cast away on an island, you are left alone there, because your ship has sunk: *If you were cast away on a desert island, what would you miss most?*
cast off *phr v*
1 to untie the rope that fastens your boat to the shore so that you can sail away
2 cast sb/sth ↔ off *literary* to remove or get rid of something or someone that you no longer want or need: *His family had cast him off without a penny.*
3 to finish a piece of KNITTING by removing the stitches from the needle to make an edge that will not come undone: **cast sth ↔ off** *Cast off four stitches.*
cast on *phr v* to start a piece of KNITTING by making the first stitches on the needle: **cast sth ↔ on** *Cast on 132 stitches.*
cast sb/sth ↔ **out** *phr v literary* to force someone or something to leave a place: *God has cast out the demons from your soul.*
cast sth ↔ **up** *phr v literary* if the sea casts something up, it carries it onto the shore: *A body had been cast up on the rocks.*

cast² ●●○ *n* [C]
1 ACTORS all the people who perform in a play, film etc: **[+of]** *Films like 'Ben Hur' have a cast of thousands. | the entire cast of 'Les Misérables' | an* ***all-star cast*** *| a strong* ***supporting cast*** (=everyone except the main actors) | *a* ***member*** *of the* ***cast***
2 ON ARM/LEG (*also* **plaster cast**) a hard protective case that is put over your arm, leg etc because the bone is broken: *Murray* ***has*** *his leg* ***in a cast****.*
3 FOR MAKING A SHAPE a MOULD (=hollow container) into which you pour liquid metal, plastic etc in order to make an object of a particular shape, or the object made in this way: **[+of]** ***Make*** *a* ***cast*** *of the statue.*
4 sb's cast of mind *formal* the way that a person thinks and the type of opinions or mental abilities they have: *Mary was of a far less intellectual cast of mind.*
5 FISHING the act of throwing a fishing line into the water
6 COLOUR *literary* a small amount of a particular colour: *Sage leaves have a silvery cast.*
7 EYE *old-fashioned* a problem with your eye which causes it to look sideways
8 EARTH a small pile of earth that a WORM produces on the surface of the ground

-cast /kɑːst $ kæst/ *suffix* [in nouns] a program that is put on the Internet for people to DOWNLOAD: *a podcast* —**-casting** *suffix* [in nouns]: *Lifecasting involves showing every event in your life on the Internet.*

cas·ta·nets /ˌkæstəˈnets/ *n* [plural] a musical instrument made of two small round pieces of wood or plastic that you hold in one hand and knock together, used especially by Spanish dancers

cast·a·way /ˈkɑːstəweɪ $ ˈkæst-/ *n* [C] someone who is left alone on an island after their ship has sunk

ˌcast ˈdown *adj* [not before noun] *literary* sad and disappointed: *She could not bear to see him so miserable and cast down.*

caste /kɑːst $ kæst/ *n* [C,U] **1** one of the fixed social classes, which cannot be changed, into which people are born in India: *the caste system* **2** a group of people who have the same position in society

cas·tel·lat·ed /ˈkæstɪleɪtɪd/ *adj technical* built to look like a castle

cast·er, castor /ˈkɑːstə $ ˈkæstər/ *n* [C] **1** a small wheel fixed to the bottom of a piece of furniture so that it can move in any direction **2** *BrE* a small container with holes in the top, used to spread sugar, salt etc on food SYN **shaker** *AmE*

ˈcaster ˌsugar, **castor sugar** *n* [U] *BrE* sugar with very small grains used for cooking

cas·ti·gate /ˈkæstɪgeɪt/ *v* [T] *formal* to criticize or punish someone severely —**castigation** /ˌkæstəˈgeɪʃən/ *n* [U]

cast·ing /ˈkɑːstɪŋ $ ˈkæstɪŋ/ *n* **1** [U] the process of choosing the actors for a film or play → **cast**: *a casting director* **2** [C] an object made by pouring liquid metal, plastic etc into a MOULD (=specially shaped container) **3 the casting couch** a situation in which an actress is persuaded to have sex in return for a part in a film, play etc – used humorously

ˈcasting ˌvote *n* [C usually singular] *BrE* the vote of the person in charge of a meeting, which can be used to make a decision when there is an equal number of votes supporting and opposing a proposal

ˌcast ˈiron *n* [U] a type of iron that is hard, breaks easily, and is shaped in a MOULD

ˌcast-ˈiron *adj* **1 a cast-iron excuse/alibi/guarantee etc** an excuse etc that is very certain and cannot fail **2** made of cast iron: *a cast-iron frying pan*

cas·tle /ˈkɑːsəl $ ˈkæ-/ ●●● W3 *n* [C]
1 (*also* **Castle**) a very large strong building, built in the past as a safe place that could be easily defended against attack: *Edinburgh Castle* | *a ruined castle* → see picture at HOUSE[1]
2 one of the pieces used in a game of CHESS. Each player has two castles, which start the game in the corner squares, and can move only forwards or sideways. SYN **rook** → see picture at CHESS
3 castles in the air plans or hopes that you have that are unlikely ever to become real

ˈcast-off *adj* [only before noun] cast-off clothes or other goods are not wanted or have been thrown away

ˈcast-offs *n* [plural] clothes that you do not wear anymore and give to someone else: *As the youngest of five kids, I was always dressed in other people's cast-offs.*

cast·or /ˈkɑːstə $ ˈkæstər/ *n* [C] another spelling of CASTER

ˌcastor ˈoil *n* [U] a thick oil made from the seeds of a plant and used in the past as a medicine to make the BOWELS empty

ˈcastor ˌsugar *n* [U] another spelling of CASTER SUGAR

cas·trate /kæˈstreɪt $ ˈkæstreɪt/ *v* [T] to remove the TESTICLES of a male animal or a man —**castration** /kæˈstreɪʃən/ *n* [U]

cas·u·al /ˈkæʒuəl/ ●●○ *adj*
1 RELAXED relaxed and not worried, or seeming not to care about something: *a casual manner* | *His eyes were angry, though he sounded casual.* | *Marsha was quite casual about appearing on TV.* | *She had a casual attitude to life.*
2 NOT FORMAL not formal or not for a formal situation OPP **formal**: *Jean felt more comfortable in* ***casual clothes***. | *a casual jacket*
3 WORK employed as a temporary worker or working for only a short period of time: *casual labour* | *staff employed* ***on a casual basis*** | *Chris has occasional* ***casual work*** *but mostly he is unemployed.*
4 RELATIONSHIP knowing someone or having sex with someone without wanting a close relationship with them OPP **serious**: *She will never be more than a casual acquaintance.* | *They had been conducting a casual affair for years.* | *John just wanted* ***casual sex***.
5 WITHOUT ATTENTION without any serious interest or attention: *He gave us a casual glance as he walked by, but didn't stop.* | ***To the casual observer*** (=to someone who is not looking carefully) *Mary seemed quite calm.* THESAURUS CARELESS
6 NOT PLANNED [only before noun] happening by chance without being planned: *a casual conversation* | *He made some* ***casual remark*** (=one without thinking much about it) *about her holiday.*
7 NOT REGULAR [only before noun] doing something or using something sometimes but not regularly or often SYN **occasional**: *a casual drug user* | *The museum is of great interest, both to experts and to casual visitors.* —**casually** *adv*: *a* ***casually dressed*** *young man* | *'Where do you work?' she asked casually.* | *He walked down the road, casually swinging his bag.* —**casualness** *n* [U]

ˌcasual ˈFriday *n* [C,U] *AmE* DRESS-DOWN FRIDAY

ˈcasual game *n* [C] a very simple video or computer game that can be played by anyone

ˈcasual gamer *n* [C] someone who plays casual games

cas·u·al·i·za·tion (*also* **-isation** *BrE*) /ˌkæʒuəlaɪˈzeɪʃən $ -lə-/ *n* [U] **1** a tendency to make things less formal in places where people work, for example by allowing office workers to wear informal clothes **2** a tendency for companies to use temporary workers instead of permanent ones

cas·u·al·ty /ˈkæʒuəlti/ ●●○ *n* (*plural* **casualties**)
1 [C] someone who is hurt or killed in an accident or war: *Our aim is to reduce* ***road casualties***. | ***civilian casualties*** (=people who are not soldiers who are injured or killed) | **cause/inflict casualties** *The rebels have inflicted* ***heavy casualties***.
2 [singular] someone or something that suffers as a result of a particular event or situation: **[+of]** *The Safer City Project is the latest casualty of financial cutbacks.*
3 [U] (*also* **Casualty**) *BrE* the part of a hospital that people are taken to when they are hurt in an accident or suddenly become ill SYN **Emergency Room** *AmE*: **in casualty** *Jean ended up in casualty last night.*

cas·u·is·try /ˈkæʒuəstri/ *n* [U] *formal* the use of clever but often false arguments to answer moral or legal questions

cat /kæt/ ●●● S1 W3 *n* [C]
1 a) a small animal with four legs that people often keep as a pet → **feline**: **tabby/ginger/tortoiseshell etc cat** (=colours of cats) | ***a tom cat*** (=a male cat) **b)** (*also* **big cat**) a large animal such as a lion or TIGER
2 let the cat out of the bag to tell someone a secret, especially without intending to
3 put/set the cat among the pigeons to do or say something that causes arguments, trouble etc
4 play (a game of) cat and mouse (with sb) to pretend to allow someone to do or have what they want, and then to stop them from doing or having it: *The police played an elaborate game of cat and mouse to trap him.*
5 the cat's whiskers/pyjamas *informal* something or someone that is better than everything else: *I really thought I looked the cat's whiskers in that dress.*
6 like a cat on hot bricks *BrE*, **like a cat on a hot tin roof** *AmE* so nervous or anxious that you cannot keep still or keep your attention on one thing
7 not stand/have a cat in hell's chance (of doing sth) *informal* to not have any chance of succeeding: *They don't have a cat in hell's chance of being elected.*
8 when the cat's away (the mice will play) used to say that people will not behave well when the person who has authority over them is not there
9 like the cat that got the cream *BrE*, **like the cat that ate the canary** *AmE informal* very proud or pleased because of something you have achieved or got
10 look like sth the cat dragged/brought in *BrE informal* to look very dirty or untidy → **raining cats and dogs** at RAIN[2](1), → **there's not enough room to swing a cat** at ROOM[1](5)

cat·a·clys·m /ˈkætəklɪzəm/ *n* [C] *literary* a violent or sudden event or change, such as a serious flood or EARTHQUAKE —**cataclysmic** /ˌkætəˈklɪzmɪk◂/ *adj*

cat·a·comb /ˈkætəkuːm $ -koʊm/ *n* [C usually plural] an area underground where dead people are buried SYN **tomb**

cat·a·falque /ˈkætəfælk/ *n* [C] *formal* a decorated raised structure on which the dead body of an important person is placed before their funeral

Cat·a·lan /ˈkætəlæn $ -tl-æn, -ən/ *n* [U] a language spoken in part of Spain around Barcelona

cat·a·logue[1] (*also* **catalog** *AmE*) /ˈkætəlɒg $ -lɒːg, -lɑːg/ ●●○ W3 *n* [C]
1 a complete list of things that you can look at, buy, or

C

use, for example in a library or at an art show: *a mail order catalog | an online catalogue*
2 catalogue of mistakes/crimes/cruelty etc a series of mistakes, crimes etc that happen one after the other and never seem to stop: *a catalogue of terrorist crimes | an appalling* ***catalogue of errors***

catalogue² (*also* **catalog** *AmE*) *v* [T] **1** to make a complete list of all the things in a group: *The manuscripts have never been systematically catalogued.* **2** to list all the things that are connected with a particular person, event, plan etc: *The report catalogued numerous dangerous work practices.*

ca·tal·y·sis /kəˈtæləsɪs/ *n* [U] *technical* the process of making a chemical reaction quicker by adding a catalyst

cat·a·lyst /ˈkætl-ɪst/ ●○○ *n* [C]
1 *technical* a substance that makes a chemical reaction happen more quickly without being changed itself
2 something or someone that causes an important change or event to happen: **[+for]** *They hope his election will* ***act as a catalyst*** *for reform.* —**catalytic** /ˌkætlˈɪtɪk◂/ *adj*

ˌcatalytic conˈverter *n* [C] a piece of equipment fitted to a car's EXHAUST system that reduces the amount of poisonous gases the engine sends out

cat·a·ma·ran /ˌkætəməˈræn/ *n* [C] a sailing boat with two separate HULLS (=the part that goes in the water)

cat·a·pult¹ /ˈkætəpʌlt/ *n* [C] **1** a large weapon used in former times to throw heavy stones, iron balls etc **2** *BrE* a small stick in the shape of a Y with a thin rubber band fastened over the two ends, used by children to throw stones SYN **slingshot** *AmE* **3** a piece of equipment used to send an aircraft into the air from a ship

catapult² *v* **1** [T always + adv/prep] to push or throw something very hard so that it moves through the air very quickly: *Sam was catapulted into the air by the force of the blast.* **2 catapult sb to fame/stardom etc** to suddenly make someone very famous: *A remarkable series of events catapulted her into the limelight.*

cat·a·ract /ˈkætərækt/ *n* [C] **1** a medical condition that causes the LENS of your eye to become white, so that you slowly lose your sight **2** *literary* a large WATERFALL

ca·tarrh /kəˈtɑː $ -ˈtɑːr/ *n* [U] *BrE* an uncomfortable condition in which your body produces a thick liquid that blocks your nose and throat: *After a cold, many patients complain of persistent catarrh.*

ca·tas·tro·phe /kəˈtæstrəfi/ ●○○ *n*
1 [C,U] a terrible event in which there is a lot of destruction, suffering, or death SYN **disaster**: **environmental/nuclear/economic etc catastrophe** *The Black Sea is facing ecological catastrophe as a result of pollution.* | **prevent/avert a catastrophe** *Sudan requires food immediately to avert a humanitarian catastrophe.*
2 [C] an event which is very bad for the people involved SYN **disaster**: **[+for]** *If the contract is cancelled, it'll be a catastrophe for everyone concerned.*

ca·tas·tro·phic /ˌkætəˈstrɒfɪk◂ $ -ˈstrɑː-/ ●○○ *adj*
1 causing a lot of destruction, suffering, or death: *catastrophic floods*
2 extremely bad: *The failure of the talks could have* ***catastrophic consequences.*** —**catastrophically** /-li/ *adv*

ca·tas·tro·phize (*also* **-ise** *BrE*) /kəˈtæstrəfaɪz/ *v* [I] to think that something terrible may happen, although this is unlikely, or think that something that has happened is much worse than it actually is: *I have a tendency to catastrophize, so I imagined that I would die on the operating table.*

cat·a·ton·ic /ˌkætəˈtɒnɪk◂ $ -ˈtɑː-/ *adj* not able to move or talk because of an illness, shock etc: **catatonic stupor/trance**

cat·bird seat /ˈkætbɜːd ˌsiːt $ -bɜːrd-/ *n* **be (sitting) in the catbird seat** *AmE informal* to be in a position where you have an advantage

ˈcat ˌburglar *n* [C] a thief who enters a building by climbing up walls, pipes etc

cat·call /ˈkætkɔːl $ -kɒːl/ *n* [C] a loud whistle or shout expressing disapproval of a speech or performance: *jeers and catcalls from the audience* —**catcall** *v* [I]

catch¹ /kætʃ/ ●●● S1 W1 *v* (*past tense and past participle* **caught** /kɔːt $ kɒːt/)
1 TAKE AND HOLD **a)** [I,T] to get hold of and stop an object such as a ball that is moving through the air → **throw**: *Stephen leapt up and caught the ball in one hand. | 'Pass me that pen, would you?' 'Here you are. Catch!' | The kids were throwing and catching a Frisbee down on the beach.* **b)** [T] to suddenly take hold of someone or something with your hand: *He caught her elbow to steady her. | Miss Perry* ***caught hold of*** *my sleeve and pulled me back.* → see picture at BASEBALL
2 FIND/STOP SB [T] **a)** to stop someone after you have been chasing them and not let them get away: *'You can't catch me!' she yelled, running away.* **b)** to find a criminal or enemy and stop them from escaping SYN **capture**: *State police have launched a massive operation to catch the murderer. | If you go back to the city, you're bound to* ***get caught.***
3 SEE SB DOING STH [T] to see someone doing something that they did not want you to know they were doing: **catch sb doing sth** *I caught him reading my private letters. | Gemma turned around and caught the stranger looking at her intently.* | **catch sb in the act (of doing sth)** (=catch someone while they are doing something illegal) *The gang was caught in the act of unloading the cigarettes. | He was* ***caught red-handed*** (=as he was doing something wrong) *taking money from the cash register.* | **catch sb at it** *We knew he'd been cheating, but we'd never caught him at it before.*
4 ILLNESS [T] to get an infectious disease: *Anton caught malaria in Mali, and nearly died. | Many young people are still ignorant about how HIV is caught.* | **catch sth from/off sb/sth** *Typhoid and cholera are often caught from contaminated water supplies. | I caught chicken pox off my friend at school.* | **catch your death (of cold)** *BrE spoken* (=get a very bad cold) *Don't stand out in the rain. You'll catch your death.*
5 catch sb by surprise, catch sb off guard, catch sb napping/unawares (*also* **catch sb on the hop** *BrE*) to do something or to happen when someone is not expecting it or prepared for it: *Her question caught him off guard.*
6 catch sb with their pants/trousers down to discover that someone is doing something that they should not be doing or has not done something that they should have done: *He's not the first politician to be caught with his pants down, and he won't be the last.*
7 ANIMAL/FISH [T] to trap an animal or fish by using a trap, net, or hook, or by hunting it: *Did you catch any fish? | Early settlers caught rabbits and squirrels and even rats in order to survive.*
8 catch a train/plane/bus to get on a train, plane etc in order to travel on it, or to be in time to get on a train, plane etc before it leaves: *I caught the 7.15 train to London. | There's a train in now. If you run, you'll just catch it. | I have to hurry – I* ***have a*** *bus* ***to catch.***
9 NOT MISS SB/STH [T] to not be too late to do something, see something, talk to someone etc OPP **miss**: *I managed to catch her just as she was leaving. | I just caught the last few minutes of the documentary. | Tumours like these can be treated quite easily if they're caught early enough.* | **catch the post** *BrE* (=post letters in time for them to be collected that day)
10 GET STUCK [I,T] if your hand, finger, clothing etc catches or is caught in something, it gets stuck in it accidentally: *His overalls caught in the engine. | Her microphone was forever* ***getting caught*** *on her clothes.*
11 catch sb's attention/interest/imagination etc to make you notice something and feel interested in it: *Lucie whistled sharply to catch the other girl's attention. | This is a story that will catch the imagination of every child.*
12 not catch sth *spoken* to not hear or understand what someone says: *I'm afraid I didn't catch your name.*
13 HEAR [T] to manage to hear a sound: *I caught the muffled thud of a car door slamming in the street.*
THESAURUS▸ HEAR
14 catch you later *spoken* used to say goodbye: *'I'll give you a call in a couple of days.' 'Okay. Catch you later.'*

15 DO/SEE STH [T] *spoken especially AmE* to go somewhere in order to do or see something: *We could **catch a movie*** (=go to a movie). | *M Records caught his act and signed him immediately.*

16 catch a ride *AmE spoken* to go somewhere in someone else's car: *I caught a ride as far as Columbus.*

17 you won't catch me doing sth (*also* **you won't catch me somewhere**) *spoken* used to say that you would never do something: *I love dancing but you won't catch me being the first on the dance floor!*

18 catch it *informal* to be punished by someone such as a parent or teacher because you have done something wrong: *You'll catch it if Dad finds out.*

19 catch a glimpse of sb/sth to see someone or something for a very short time: *Fans waited for hours at the airport to catch a glimpse of their idol.*

20 catch sight of sb/sth to suddenly see someone or something that you have been looking for or have been hoping to see: *I caught sight of her in the crowd.*

21 DESCRIBE WELL [T] to show or describe the character or quality of something well in a picture, piece of writing etc SYN **capture**: *a novel that catches the mood of post-war Britain*

22 BURN **a) catch fire** if something catches fire, it starts to burn accidentally: *Two farm workers died when a barn caught fire.* **b)** [I] if a fire catches, it starts to burn: *For some reason the charcoal wasn't catching.*

23 catch sb's eye a) to attract someone's attention and make them look at something: *Out on the freeway, a billboard caught his eye.* **b)** to look at someone at the same moment that they are looking at you: *Every time she caught his eye, she would glance away embarrassed.*

24 catch yourself doing sth to suddenly realize you are doing something: *Standing there listening to the song, he caught himself smiling from ear to ear.*

25 HIT [T] to hit someone in or on a particular part of their body: *The punch caught him right in the face.*

26 be/get caught in/without etc sth to be in a situation that you cannot easily get out of or in which you do not have something you need: *We got caught in a rainstorm on the way here.* | *Here's a useful tip if you're caught without a mirror.*

27 catch your breath a) to pause for a moment after a lot of physical effort in order to breathe normally again: *Hang on a minute – let me catch my breath!* **b)** to stop breathing for a moment because something has surprised, frightened, or shocked you **c)** to take some time to stop and think about what you will do next after having been very busy or active: *It was an enforced absence from work, but at least it gave me a little time to catch my breath before the final push.*

28 CONTAINER [T] if a container catches liquid, it is in a position where the liquid falls into it: *Place the baking sheet under the muffin pan to catch the drips.*

29 SHINE [T] if the light catches something or if something catches the light, the light shines on it: *The sunlight caught her hair and turned it to gold.*

30 catch the sun *informal* if you catch the sun, your skin becomes red and sometimes sore because of the effects of sunlight: *You've caught the sun on the back of your neck.*

31 WIND [T] if something catches the wind or the wind catches something, it blows on it: *Gary swung the sail round to catch the light wind.*

32 SPORT **a)** [T] to end a player's INNINGS in CRICKET by catching the ball that is hit off their BAT before it touches the ground **b)** [I] to be the CATCHER in a game of baseball

THESAURUS – MEANING 2

catch to stop someone who is trying to escape, especially by running after them and then holding them: *He raced after her, but he couldn't catch her.* | *The police caught the bank robbers after a car chase through the city.*

arrest if the police arrest someone, they take him or her to a police station because they think that person has done something illegal: *Wayne was arrested for dangerous driving.* | *The police arrested him and charged him with murder.*

apprehend *formal* if the police apprehend someone they think has done something illegal, they catch him or her: *The two men were later apprehended after they robbed another store.* | *The killers were never apprehended.*

capture to catch an enemy or a criminal in order to keep them as a prisoner: *The French king was captured by the English at the Battle of Poitiers in 1356.* | *The gunmen were finally captured after a shoot-out with the police.*

take sb prisoner to catch someone, especially in a war, in order to keep them as a prisoner: *350 soldiers were killed and another 300 taken prisoner.*

trap to make someone go to a place from which they cannot escape, especially by using your skill and intelligence: *Police trapped the man inside a bar on the city's southside.*

corner to force someone into a place from which they cannot escape: *He was cornered outside the school by three gang members.*

catch at sth *phr v* to try to take hold of something: *She caught at his arm, 'Hang on. I'm coming with you.'*

catch on *phr v*

1 to become popular and fashionable: *The idea of glasses being a fashion item has been slow to catch on.*

2 to begin to understand or realize something: **[+to]** *It was a long time before the police caught on to what he was really doing.*

catch sb **out** *phr v*

1 to make someone make a mistake, especially deliberately and in order to prove that they are lying: *The interviewer may try to catch you out.*

2 if something unexpected catches you out, it puts you in a difficult situation because you were not expecting it or not fully prepared for it: *Even the best whitewater rafters get caught out by the fierce rapids here.*

catch up *phr v*

1 to improve and reach the same standard as other people in your class, group etc: *If you miss a lot of classes, it's very difficult to catch up.* | **[+with]** *At the moment our technology is more advanced, but other countries are catching up with us.*

2 to come from behind and reach someone in front of you by going faster: **[+with]** *Drive faster – they're catching up with us.* | **catch sb up** *BrE*: *You go on ahead. I'll catch you up in a minute.*

3 to do what needs to be done because you have not been able to do it until now: **[+on]** *I have some work to catch up on.* | *I need to **catch up on some sleep*** (=after a period without enough sleep).

4 to spend time finding out what has been happening while you have been away or during the time you have not seen someone: **[+on]** *When I got home I phoned Jo to catch up on all the gossip.* | *I'll leave you two alone – I'm sure you've got a lot of **catching up** to do.*

5 be/get caught up in sth to be or get involved in something, especially something bad: *I didn't want to get caught up in endless petty arguments.*

catch up with sb *phr v*

1 to finally find someone who has been doing something illegal and punish them: *It took six years for the law to catch up with them.*

2 if something bad from the past catches up with you, you cannot avoid dealing with it any longer: *At the end of the movie his murky **past catches up with** him.*

catch² ●●○ *n*

1 [C] an act of catching a ball that has been thrown or hit: *Hey! Nice catch!*

2 [C usually singular] *informal* a hidden problem or difficulty: *This deal looks too good to be true – there must be a catch somewhere.* | **the catch is (that)** *The catch is that you can't enter the competition unless you've spent $100 in the store.*

3 [C] a hook or something similar for fastening a door or lid and keeping it shut
4 [C] a quantity of fish that has been caught at one time
5 [U] a simple game in which two or more people throw a ball to each other: *Let's go outside and play catch.*
6 a catch in your voice/throat a short pause that you make when you are speaking, because you feel upset or are beginning to cry: *There was a catch in Anne's voice and she seemed close to tears.*
7 a (good) catch someone who is a good person to have a relationship with or to marry because they are rich, attractive etc - often used humorously

catch·all /ˈkætʃɔːl $ -ɒːl/ *n* [C] *AmE* a drawer, cupboard etc where you put any small objects

ˈcatch-all *adj* intended to include all possibilities: *a vague catch-all clause in the contract | a catch-all term*

C

catch·er /ˈkætʃə $ -ər/ *n* [C] in baseball, the player behind the BATTER, who catches missed balls → **pitcher** → see pictures at **BASEBALL**, **SPORT**[1]

catch·ing /ˈkætʃɪŋ/ *adj* [not before noun] **1** an illness that is catching is easily passed to other people SYN **infectious** **2** an emotion or feeling that is catching spreads quickly among people: *Julia's enthusiasm was catching.*

catch·ment ar·e·a /ˈkætʃmənt ˌeəriə $ -ˌeriə/ *n* [C] **1** *BrE* the catchment area of a school, hospital etc is the area that its students, patients etc come from **2** *technical* the area that a river or lake gets water from

catch·phrase /ˈkætʃfreɪz/ *n* [C] a short well-known phrase made popular by an entertainer or politician, so that people think of that person when they hear it

Catch-22 /ˌkætʃ twentiˈtuː/ *n* [U] an impossible situation that you cannot solve because you need to do one thing in order to do a second thing, but you cannot do the first thing until you have done the second: *It's a* ***Catch-22 situation*** *- without experience you can't get a job and without a job you can't get experience.*

ˌcatch-up TˈV *n* [U] a system in which you use the Internet to watch television programmes after they have been broadcast

catch·word /ˈkætʃwɜːd $ -wɜːrd/ *n* [C] a word or phrase that refers to a feature of a situation, product etc that is considered important: *Variety is the catchword at our latest venue, the Beehive Club.*

catch·y /ˈkætʃi/ *adj* a catchy tune or phrase is easy to remember: *a* ***catchy song*** | ***catchy*** *advertising* ***slogans***

cat·e·chis·m /ˈkætəˌkɪzəm/ *n* [singular] a set of questions and answers about the Christian religion that people learn in order to become full members of a church: *We were taught to recite the catechism.*

cat·e·gor·i·cal /ˌkætəˈɡɒrɪkəl◂ $ -ˈɡɔː-, -ˈɡɑː-/ *adj* [usually before noun] a categorical statement is a clear statement that something is definitely true or false: **categorical denial/assurance etc** *Can you give us a categorical assurance that no jobs will be lost?*

cat·e·gor·i·cally /ˌkætəˈɡɒrɪkli $ -ˈɡɔː-, -ˈɡɑː-/ *adv* in such a sure and certain way that there is no doubt: **categorically deny/refuse etc sth** *He has categorically denied his guilt all along. | Can you* ***state categorically*** *that her death was caused by lack of food?*

cat·e·go·rize (*also* **-ise** *BrE*) /ˈkætəɡəraɪz/ ●●○ *v* [T] to put people or things into groups according to the type of person or thing they are SYN **classify**: *The population is categorized according to age, sex, and social group.* | **categorize sth/sb as sth** *Keene doesn't like to be categorized as a socialist.* —**categorization** /ˌkætəɡəraɪˈzeɪʃən $ -rə-/ *n* [C,U]

cat·e·go·ry /ˈkætəɡəri $ -ɡɔːri/ ●●● S2 W2 AWL *n* (*plural* **categories**) [C] a group of people or things that are all of the same type: **[+of]** *There are five categories of workers. | people in the over-45* ***age category*** *| Seats are available in eight of the ten* ***price categories****.* | **fall into/belong in/fit into a category** *Voters fall into three* ***main categories****. | Williams' style does not fit easily into the category of jazz.*

ca·ter /ˈkeɪtə $ -ər/ ●○○ *v* [I,T] to provide and serve food and drinks at a party, meeting etc, usually as a business: **[+for]** *This is the biggest event we've ever catered for. | Joan has catered functions for up to 200 people.*
cater for sb/sth (*also* **cater to sb/sth**) *phr v* to provide a particular group of people with the things they need or want: *an LA bank catering to Asian businesses | Vegetarians are well catered for. | Most perfume ads cater to male fantasies.*

ca·ter·er /ˈkeɪtərə $ -ər/ *n* [C] a person or company that provides and serves food and drinks at a party, meeting etc

ca·ter·ing /ˈkeɪtərɪŋ/ *n* [U] the activity of providing and serving food and drinks at parties, meetings etc for money → **self-catering**: *Who did the catering?* | **catering business/service etc**

cat·er·pil·lar /ˈkætəˌpɪlə $ -tərˌpɪlər/ *n* [C] a small creature like a WORM with many legs that eats leaves and that develops into a BUTTERFLY or other flying insect

Caterpillar (*also* **ˈCaterpillar ˌtrack**) *n* [C] *trademark* a metal belt made of short connected pieces that is fastened over the wheels of a heavy vehicle to help it to move over soft ground: *a Caterpillar tractor* (=a vehicle fitted with this belt)

cat·er·waul /ˈkætəwɔːl $ -tərwɒːl/ *v* [I] to make a loud high unpleasant noise like the sound a cat makes —**caterwauling** *n* [U]: *the sound of drunken caterwauling coming from next door*

cat·fight /ˈkætfaɪt/ *n* [C] *informal* a word for a fight between women, that some people consider offensive

cat·fish /ˈkætˌfɪʃ/ *n* (*plural* **catfish**) **1** [C,U] a type of fish that has WHISKERS (=strong hairs) around its mouth and lives in rivers or lakes **2** [C] *informal* someone who lies about themselves on the Internet in order to impress people, especially so that someone will start a relationship with them

cat·fish·ing /ˈkætˌfɪʃɪŋ/ *n* [U] *informal* the practice of lying about yourself on the Internet in order to make people admire you, especially so that someone will start a relationship with you

ˈcat flap *BrE*, **pet door** *AmE n* [C] a small hole cut into a door and covered with wood or plastic that moves to allow a pet cat to enter or leave a house

cat·gut /ˈkætɡʌt/ *n* [U] strong thread made from the INTESTINES of animals and used for the strings of musical instruments

ca·thar·sis /kəˈθɑːsɪs $ -ɑːr-/ *n* [U] *formal* the act or process of removing strong or violent emotions by expressing them through writing, talking, acting etc: *Music is a means of catharsis for me.*

ca·thar·tic /kəˈθɑːtɪk $ -ɑːr-/ *adj formal* helping you to remove strong or violent emotions: *a* ***cathartic experience***

ca·the·dral /kəˈθiːdrəl/ ●●○ *n* [C] the main church of a particular area under the control of a BISHOP: *St Paul's Cathedral* | **cathedral city** *BrE* (=one with a cathedral)

Cath·er·ine wheel /ˈkæθərən wiːl/ *BrE*, **pinwheel** *AmE n* [C] a round flat FIREWORK that spins around as it burns

cath·e·ter /ˈkæθɪtə $ -ər/ *n* [C] *medical* a thin tube that is put into your body to remove liquids —**catheterize** (*also* **-ise** *BrE*) *v* [T]

cath·ode /ˈkæθəʊd $ -θoʊd/ *n* [C] *technical* the negative ELECTRODE, marked (−), from which an electric current leaves a piece of equipment such as a BATTERY OPP **anode**

ˌcathode ˈray tube *n* [C] a piece of equipment used in televisions and computer MONITORS, in which ELECTRONS from the cathode produce an image on a screen

cath·o·lic /ˈkæθəlɪk/ *adj* including a very wide variety of things: *She has* ***catholic tastes*** *(=likes a lot of different things). | a catholic collection of records*

Catholic *adj* connected with the Roman Catholic Church —**Catholic** *n* [C] —**Catholicism** /kəˈθɒlɪsɪzəm $ kəˈθɑː-/ *n* [U]

cat·house /ˈkæthaʊs/ *n* [C] *AmE informal* a place where men can pay women to have sex with them SYN **brothel**

cat·kin /ˈkætkɪn/ *n* [C] *BrE* a long soft flower that hangs in groups from the branches of trees such as the WILLOW

ˈcat ˌlitter (*also* **kitty litter** *AmE*) *n* [U] a substance like small grey stones that people put in boxes for cats that live indoors, and which the cats use as a toilet

cat·nap /ˈkætnæp/ *n* [C] *informal* a very short sleep: **have/take a catnap** *Nomes slept badly, and had to take catnaps during the day.* —**catnap** *v* [I]

cat-o'-nine-tails /ˌkæt ə ˈnaɪn teɪlz/ *n* [singular] a whip made of nine knotted strings, used in the past for punishing people

CAT scan /ˈkæt ˌskæn/ (*also* **CT scan**) *n* [C] a medical examination in which an image of the inside of someone's body is produced on a computer using X-RAYS —**CAT scanner** *n* [C]

ˌcat's ˈcradle *n* **1** [U] a game you play by winding string around your fingers to make different patterns **2** [singular] a set of lines, threads etc that form a complicated pattern: *The searchlights wove a cat's cradle of light.*

Cats·eye /ˈkætsaɪ/ *n* [C] *trademark BrE* one of a line of small flat objects fixed in the middle of the road that shine when lit by car lights and guide traffic in the dark

ˈcat's paw, **cats·paw** /ˈkætspɔː $ -pɒː/ *n* [C] *old-fashioned* someone who is used by someone else to achieve something bad

ˈcat suit *n* [C] a tight piece of women's clothing that covers the body and legs in one piece

cat·sup /ˈkætsəp/ *n* [U] an American spelling of KETCHUP

cat·te·ry /ˈkætəri/ *n* (*plural* **catteries**) [C] *BrE* a place where people can pay to leave their pet cats to be cared for while they are away from home

cat·tle /ˈkætl/ ●●● W3 *n* [plural] cows and BULLs kept on a farm for their meat or milk: *herds of cattle* | **dairy/beef cattle** | **20/100 etc head of cattle** (=20, 100 etc cattle) | *a cattle rancher*

ˈcattle grid *BrE*, **ˈcattle guard** *AmE n* [C] a set of bars placed over a hole in the road, so that animals cannot go across but cars can

cat·tle·man /ˈkætlmən/ *n* (*plural* **cattlemen** /-mən/) [C] someone who looks after or owns cattle

ˈcattle ˌmarket (*also* **ˈcattle ˌauction** *AmE*) *n* [C] **1** a place where cattle are bought and sold **2** *informal* a beauty competition or a social event where women are judged only by their appearance - used to show disapproval

ˈcattle prod *n* [C] a type of stick that gives cattle an electric shock when it touches them, used to make them move

ˈcattle truck *n* [C] a vehicle or part of a train that is used for carrying cattle

cat·ty /ˈkæti/ *adj* someone who is catty says unkind things about people —**cattily** *adv* —**cattiness** *n* [U]

ˈcatty-ˌcorner *adv* KITTY-CORNER

cat·walk /ˈkætwɔːk $ -wɒːk/ *n* [C] **1** a long raised structure that MODELs walk along in a fashion show SYN **runway** *AmE* **2 the catwalk** the business of designing clothes for fashion shows **3** a narrow structure for people to walk on that is high up inside or outside a building

Cau·ca·sian /kɔːˈkeɪziən $ kɒːˈkeɪʒən/ *n* [C] a member of the race of people with white or pale skin —**Caucasian** *adj*

cau·cus /ˈkɔːkəs $ ˈkɒː-/ *n* [C] **1** a meeting of the members of a political party to choose people to represent them in a larger meeting, election etc **2** *AmE* an organized group of people who have similar aims or interests, especially political ones: *the chairman of the Congressional Black Caucus*

cau·dal /ˈkɔːdl $ ˈkɒːdl/ *adj* [only before noun] *technical* relating to an animal's tail

caught /kɔːt $ kɒːt/ the past tense and past participle of CATCH

caul·dron, **caldron** /ˈkɔːldrən $ ˈkɒːl-/ *n* [C] a large round metal pot for boiling liquids over a fire: *a witch's cauldron*

cau·li·flow·er /ˈkɒlɪˌflaʊə $ ˈkɒːliˌflaʊər, ˈkɑː-/ *n* [C,U] a vegetable with green leaves around a firm white centre → see picture at **VEGETABLE**[1]

ˌcauliflower ˈear *n* [C] an ear permanently swollen into a strange shape, as a result of an injury

caulk (*also* **calk** *AmE*) /kɔːk $ kɒːk/ *v* [T] to fill the holes or cracks in a ship with an oily or sticky substance in order to keep water out

caus·al /ˈkɔːzəl $ ˈkɒː-/ *adj* **1** relating to the connection between two things, where one causes the other to happen or exist → **cause**: **causal relationship/link/factor etc** *a causal relationship between unemployment and crime* **2** *technical* a causal CONJUNCTION, such as 'because', introduces a statement about the cause of something —**causally** *adv*

cau·sal·i·ty /kɔːˈzæləti $ kɒː-/ *n* [U] *formal* the relationship between a cause and the effect that it has

cau·sa·tion /kɔːˈzeɪʃən $ kɒː-/ *n* [U] *formal* **1** the action of causing something to happen or exist **2** causality

caus·a·tive /ˈkɔːzətɪv $ ˈkɒː-/ *adj formal* acting as the cause of something: *Smoking is a causative factor in several major diseases.*

cause[1] /kɔːz $ kɒːz/ ●●● S1 W1 *v* [T] to make something happen, especially something bad: *Heavy traffic is causing delays on the freeway.* | *The fire caused £15,000 worth of damage.* | **cause sth for sb** *The oil spill is causing problems for coastal fisheries.* | **cause concern/uncertainty/embarrassment etc** *The policy changes have caused great uncertainty for the workforce.* | *I'm sorry if I* ***caused*** *any* ***confusion***. | **cause sb trouble/problems etc** *You've caused us all a lot of unnecessary worry.* | *Sorry, I didn't mean to* ***cause offence*** (=offend you). | **cause sb/sth to do sth** *What caused you to change your mind?*

GRAMMAR: Comparison

cause
- Someone or something **causes** something: *Investigators are trying to find out what caused the accident.*
- Something **causes** a person or thing **to do** something: *The warmer temperatures caused the ice caps to melt.* | *The injury caused him to lose the game.*

✗ Don't say: *cause that someone does something*

make
- Someone or something **makes** another person or thing **do** something: *The warmer temperatures made the ice caps melt.* | *The injury made him lose the game.*

✗ Don't say: *make someone/something to do something*

THESAURUS

cause to make something happen, especially something bad: *Bad weather has caused a lot of problems on the roads.* | *The fault caused the whole computer system to shut down.*

make sb/sth do sth to cause someone to do something, or cause something to happen. **Make** is less formal than **cause**, and is the usual word to use in everyday English: *What made you decide to become a teacher?* | *I'm sorry, I didn't mean to make you cry.* | *Gravity is the force which makes the planets move round the Sun.*

be responsible for sth if someone or something is responsible for something bad, they caused it to happen: *The excessive heat was responsible for their deaths.* | *A small militant group was responsible for the bombing.*

bring about sth to make something happen - used especially about changes or improvements: *The Internet has brought about enormous changes in society.* | *It's important that we do everything we can to bring about peace.*

result in sth if an action or event results in something, it makes that thing happen: *The fire resulted in the deaths of two children.* | *The decision is likely to result in a large number of job losses.*

lead to sth to cause something to happen eventually after a period of time: *The information led to several arrests.* | *A poor diet in childhood can lead to health problems later in life.*

trigger if one event triggers another, it suddenly makes the second event happen: *The incident triggered a wave of violence.* | *An earthquake off Java's southern coast triggered a tsunami.*
precipitate *formal* to make a very serious event happen very suddenly, which will affect a lot of people: *The withdrawal of foreign investment would precipitate an economic crisis.* | *The assassination of Archduke Franz Ferdinand precipitated World War I.*

cause² ●●● S2 W1 *n*
1 [C] a person, event, or thing that makes something happen → **effect**: **[+of]** *Breast cancer is the leading cause of death for American women in their 40s.* | *It's our job to establish the cause of the fire.*
2 [U] a fact that makes it right or reasonable for you to feel or behave in a particular way SYN **reason**: **[+for]** *There is* ***no cause for alarm****.* | *The patient's condition is* ***giving cause for concern****.* | *The present political climate* ***gives*** *little* ***cause for optimism****.* | **have (good) cause to do sth** *His father has good cause to be proud of him.* | **with/without good cause** *Many people are worried about the economy, and with good cause.*
3 [C] an aim, belief, or organization that a group of people support or fight for: *My father fought for the Nationalist cause.* | **[+of]** *her lifelong devotion to the cause of women's rights* | *He has* ***championed the cause*** *of independence* (=he has supported it publicly). | *You can get fit, and at the same time raise money for* ***a worthy cause****.* | *Please give generously - it's all* ***in a good cause*** (=done in order to help people).
4 have/make common cause (with/against sb) *formal* to join with other people or groups in order to oppose an enemy: *U.S. officials expect other Western governments to make common cause with them over the arrests.*
5 [C] *law* a case that is brought to a court of law → **lost cause** at LOST²(12)

GRAMMAR: Comparison
cause
• You say the **cause of** something: *What was the cause of the problem?* ✗ Don't say: *the cause for the problem*
• You say there is **cause for concern/alarm/complaint etc**: *The doctor said there was cause for concern.* ✗ Don't say: *There was a cause for concern.*
reason
• You say the **reason for** something: *What do you think was the reason for their success?* ✗ Don't say: *the reason of their success*
• You talk about the **reason why** something happens: *Can you tell me the reason why you did this?*

COLLOCATIONS
ADJECTIVES
a common cause of sth *Alcohol is the most common cause of road accidents.*
the main/primary cause of sth *Smoking is the main cause of lung disease.*
a major/leading cause of sth *In this country, debt is a major cause of homelessness.*
a direct/indirect cause *Government policies are the direct cause of the problems facing the economy.*
the root cause (=the most basic cause) *People often deal with the symptoms rather than the root cause of a problem.*
the fundamental/underlying cause (=the root cause) | **the probable/likely cause**
VERBS
discover/find the cause *An investigation has failed to discover the cause of the epidemic.*
determine/establish/identify the cause (=discover definitely what it is) | **investigate the cause**
PHRASES
the cause of death *A snake bite was the cause of death.*
die of/from natural causes (=die of illness, old age etc, not because of an accident or crime) | **cause and effect** (=the idea that one thing directly causes another)

cause cé·lè·bre /ˌkəʊz seˈlebrə, ˌkɔːz- $ ˌkɒːz-, ˌkoʊz-/ *n* (*plural* **causes célèbres** (*same pronunciation*)) [C] an event or legal case that a lot of people become interested in, because it is an exciting subject to discuss or argue about: *The case became a cause célèbre among feminists.*
cause·way /ˈkɔːzweɪ $ ˈkɒːz-/ *n* [C] a raised road or path across wet ground or through water
caus·tic /ˈkɔːstɪk $ ˈkɒːs-/ *adj* **1** a caustic substance can burn through things by chemical action: *caustic soda* (=a chemical used for cleaning things) **2** a caustic remark criticizes someone in a way that is unkind but often cleverly humorous SYN **acerbic**: **caustic wit/comments/remark etc** *Eliot appreciated Pound's caustic wit.* —**caustically** /-kli/ *adv*: *'I can hardly wait,' Sir Trevor replied caustically.*
cau·ter·ize (*also* **-ise** *BrE*) /ˈkɔːtəraɪz $ ˈkɒː-/ *v* [T] *medical* to treat a wound or a growth on your body by burning it with hot metal, a LASER, or a chemical
cau·tion¹ /ˈkɔːʃən $ ˈkɒː-/ ●●○ *n*
1 [U] the quality of being very careful to avoid danger or risks → **cautious**: **with caution** *We must* ***proceed with*** *extreme* ***caution****.* | *The physician must* ***exercise caution*** *when prescribing antidepressants.* | **counsel/urge caution** *Many parents are tempted to intervene, but most experts counsel caution.* | **treat/view sth with caution** (=think carefully about something because it might not be true) *Evidence given by convicted criminals should always be treated with* ***the utmost caution****.* → **err on the side of caution** at ERR(1)
2 [C] a warning or piece of advice telling you to be careful: *Although pleased, Henson added a caution that the team still has a long way to go.* | **word/note of caution** *A final word of caution - never try any of this without backing up your system.*
3 throw/cast caution to the winds *literary* to stop worrying about danger and to take a big risk: *Throwing caution to the winds, she swung around to face him.*
4 [C,U] *BrE* a spoken official warning given to someone who has been ARRESTed or who has done something wrong that is not a serious crime: *He was let off with a caution.* | **under caution** *The defendant may make a statement under caution.*
caution² ●○○ *v*
1 [I,T] to warn someone that something might be dangerous, difficult etc: **caution (sb) against sth** *Business leaders are cautioning against hasty action that would hamper flexibility.* | **caution (sb) that** *Officials were quick to caution that these remarks did not mean an end to the peace process.* | **caution sb to do sth** *He cautioned them to avoid the forest at night.* THESAURUS ▸ WARN
2 [T] *BrE* **a)** to warn someone officially that the next time they do something illegal they will be punished: **caution sb for (doing) sth** *She was cautioned for speeding.* **b)** to warn someone officially that what they say to a police officer may be used as EVIDENCE in a court of law
cau·tion·ar·y /ˈkɔːʃənəri $ ˈkɒːʃəneri/ *adj* [usually before noun] giving a warning about what not to do: **cautionary note/comment/words etc** *Most observers were optimistic, yet some* ***sounded*** *a* ***cautionary note****.* | **cautionary tale** (=the story of an event that is used to warn people) *a cautionary tale about how not to buy a computer*
cau·tious /ˈkɔːʃəs $ ˈkɒː-/ ●●○ *adj* careful to avoid danger or risks → **caution**: *a cautious driver* | *a cautious approach to the crisis* | *The air-pollution board has reacted with* ***cautious optimism*** *to the announcement.* | **cautious about (doing) sth** *Keller is cautious about making predictions for the success of the program.* —**cautiousness** *n* [U]
cau·tious·ly /ˈkɔːʃəsli $ ˈkɒː-/ ●●○ *adv* in a cautious way: *The government* ***reacted cautiously*** *to the move.* | *We're* ***cautiously optimistic*** (=fairly hopeful) *that some form of agreement will be reached.*
cav·al·cade /ˌkævəlˈkeɪd, ˈkævəlkeɪd/ *n* [C] a line of

people on horses or in cars or carriages moving along as part of a ceremony

cav·a·lier /ˌkævəˈlɪə◂ $ -ˈlɪr◂/ *adj* [usually before noun] not caring enough about rules, principles, or people's feelings: *a* ***cavalier attitude*** *to the laws*

cav·al·ry /ˈkævəlri/ *n* [plural, U] **1** the part of an army that fights on horses, especially in the past: *The Black Prince led a cavalry charge against them.* **2** the part of a modern army that uses TANKS

cav·al·ry·man /ˈkævəlrimən/ *n* (*plural* **cavalrymen** /-mən/) [C] a soldier who fights on a horse

cave¹ /keɪv/ ●●○ *n* [C] a large natural hole in the side of a cliff or hill, or under the ground → **caving**: *the entrance to a cave*

cave² *v*

cave in *phr v* **1** if the top or sides of something cave in, they fall down or inwards: **[+on]** *The roof of the tunnel caved in on them.* **2** to finally stop opposing something, especially because someone has persuaded or threatened you: **[+to]** *The chairman is expected to cave in to pressure from shareholders.*

ca·ve·at /ˈkæviæt, ˈkeɪv-/ *n* [C] *formal* a warning that something may not be completely true, effective etc: **caveat that** *She will be offered treatment, with the caveat that it may not work.*

caveat emp·tor /ˌkæviæt ˈemptɔː, ˌkeɪv- $ -tɔːr/ *n* [U] *law* the principle that the person who buys something is responsible for checking that it is not broken, damaged etc

ˈcave-in *n* [C] **1** when the roof of something such as a mine falls in **2** when someone stops opposing something

cave·man /ˈkeɪvmæn/ *n* (*plural* **cavemen** /-men/) [C] **1** someone who lived in a CAVE many thousands of years ago **2** *informal* an insulting word for a man who you think is rude, violent etc: *Are you going to give me the macho caveman act?*

cav·er /ˈkeɪvə $ -ər/ *n* [C] *BrE* someone who goes into CAVES deep under the ground as a sport SYN **spelunker** *AmE*

cav·ern /ˈkævən $ -ərn/ *n* [C] a large CAVE

cav·ern·ous /ˈkævənəs $ -ərnəs/ *adj literary* a cavernous room, space, or hole is very large and deep: *a cavernous dining hall*

cav·i·ar, **caviare** /ˈkæviɑː $ -ɑːr/ *n* [U] the preserved eggs of various large fish, eaten as a special very expensive food: *caviare and champagne*

cav·il /ˈkævəl/ *v* (**cavilled**, **cavilling** *BrE*, **caviled**, **caviling** *AmE*) [I] *formal* to make unnecessary complaints about someone or something: **[+at]** *They cavilled at our calculations.* —**cavil** *n* [C,U]

cav·ing /ˈkeɪvɪŋ/ *n* [U] *BrE* the sport of going into CAVES deep under the ground SYN **spelunking** *AmE*

cav·i·ty /ˈkævəti/ *n* (*plural* **cavities**) [C] *formal* a hole or space inside something: *Put herbs inside the body cavity of the fish.* | *I have no cavities* (=no holes in my teeth).

ˈcavity ˌwall *n* [C] a wall consisting of two walls with a space between them to keep out cold and noise: *cavity wall insulation*

ca·vort /kəˈvɔːt $ -ɔːrt/ *v* [I] to jump or dance around in a playful or sexual way: **[+about/around]** *She cavorted about in the water.* | **[+with]** *The photograph shows him cavorting with two young women.*

caw /kɔː $ kɒː/ *n* [C] the loud sound made by some types of bird, especially CROWS —**caw** *v* [I]

cay /kiː, keɪ/ *n* [C] *AmE* a very small low island formed of CORAL or sand

cay·enne pep·per /ˌkeɪen ˈpepə $ -ər/ *n* [U] the red powder made from a PEPPER that has a very hot taste

cay·man /ˈkeɪmən/ *n* (*plural* **caymans**) [C] a South American animal like an ALLIGATOR

CB /ˌsiː ˈbiː◂/ *n* [U] (***Citizens' Band***) a type of radio communication which people use to speak to each other over short distances, especially when driving

CBE /ˌsiː biː ˈiː/ *n* [C] (***Commander of the British Empire***) an honour given to some British people for things they have done for their country

CBI, the /ˌsiː biː ˈaɪ/ (***the Confederation of British Industry***) a British organization that represents employers and managers in British businesses. It provides information about the economic situation, and tries to influence the government to make decisions that will help its members.

CBT /ˌsiː biː ˈtiː/ *n* [U] **1** (***computer-based testing***) a way of taking standard tests such as the GRE on a computer **2** (***computer-based training***) the use of computers to teach people to do something: *CBT software*

cc /ˌsiː ˈsiː/ **1** (***carbon copy to***) used in a business letter or email to show that you are sending a copy to someone else: *To Neil Fry, cc: Anthea Baker, Matt Fox* **2** the abbreviation of ***cubic centimetre*** or ***cubic centimetres***: *a 200 cc engine*

CCTV /ˌsiː siː tiː ˈviː/ *n* [U] the written abbreviation of ***closed circuit television***

CD /ˌsiː ˈdiː◂/ ●●○ S3 W3 *n* [C] (***compact disc***) a small circular piece of hard plastic on which high-quality recorded sound or large quantities of information can be stored

C. dif·fi·cile /ˌsiː dɪfɪˈsiːl/ *n* [U] (***Clostridium difficile***) a type of BACTERIA that causes serious illness, especially in people who have been taking ANTIBIOTIC drugs in hospital

CˈD ˌplayer *n* [C] a piece of equipment used to play COMPACT DISCS

CD-R /ˌsiː diː ˈɑː $ -ˈɑːr/ *n* [C,U] (***compact disc - recordable***) a type of CD that you can record music, images, or other information onto, using special equipment on your computer, and that can be recorded onto only once

CD-ROM /ˌsiː diː ˈrɒm $ -ˈrɑːm/ *n* [C,U] (***compact disc read-only memory***) a CD on which large quantities of information can be stored to be used by a computer

CD-RW /ˌsiː diː ɑː ˈdʌbəljuː $ -ɑːr-/ *n* [C,U] (***compact disc - rewritable***) a type of CD that you can record music, images, or other information onto, using special equipment on your computer, and that can be recorded onto several times

CDT /ˌsiː diː ˈtiː/ *n* [U] (***Craft, Design, and Technology***) a practical subject studied in British schools

CE *BrE*, **C.E.** *AmE* /ˌsiː ˈiː/ (***Common Era***) used after a date to show it was after the birth of Christ SYN **AD** → **BC**

cease¹ /siːs/ ●●○ W3 AWL *v* [I,T]

1 *formal* to stop doing something or stop happening: **cease to do sth** *He ceased to be a member of the association.* | *The things people will do for charity* ***never cease to amaze me*** (=I am always surprised by them). | **cease doing sth** *the decision to cease using CFCs in packaging* | *The rain ceased and the sky cleared.* | **cease trading/production/operations etc** (=stop operating a business) *The company ceased production at their Norwich plant last year.* | **cease fire!** (=used to order soldiers to stop shooting) **THESAURUS** STOP

> **REGISTER**
> In everyday English, people usually use **stop** rather than **cease**: *They have* ***stopped*** *using CFCs in packaging.* | *The rain* ***stopped*** *just as the fireworks began.*

2 cease and desist *law* to stop doing something → CEASEFIRE, → **wonders will never cease** at WONDER²(5)

cease² *n* **without cease** *formal* without stopping

cease·fire /ˈsiːsfaɪə $ -faɪr/ ●○○ *n* [C] an agreement to stop fighting for a period of time, especially so that a more permanent agreement can be made: *a ceasefire agreement* | *They have* ***called*** *a temporary* ***ceasefire*** *in the region.* → ARMISTICE, TRUCE

cease·less /ˈsiːsləs/ *adj* happening for a long time without stopping: *the ceaseless fight against crime* —**ceaselessly** *adv*: *The men worked ceaselessly through the night.*

ce·dar /ˈsiːdə $ -ər/ *n* **1** [C] a large EVERGREEN tree with leaves shaped like needles **2** (*also* **cedarwood**) [U] the hard red wood of the cedar tree, which smells pleasant

cede /siːd/ *v* [T] *formal* to give something such as an area of land or a right to a country or person, especially when you are forced to: **cede sth to sb** *Hong Kong was ceded to Britain in 1842.* → CESSION

ce·dil·la /sɪˈdɪlə/ *n* [C] a mark under the letter 'c' in French and some other languages, to show that it is an 's' sound instead of a 'k' sound. The letter is written 'ç'.

cei·lidh /ˈkeɪli/ *n* [C] an evening entertainment with Scottish or Irish singing and dancing

ceil·ing /ˈsiːlɪŋ/ ●●● S3 W3 *n* [C]
1 the inner surface of the top part of a room → **roof**: *rooms with high ceilings* | *a light hanging from the ceiling*
2 the largest number or amount of something that is officially allowed: **[+of]** *a public spending ceiling of £240 billion* | **impose/set/put a ceiling (on sth)** *The government imposed a ceiling on imports of foreign cars.* | **raise/lower the ceiling (on sth)**
3 *technical* the greatest height an aircraft can fly at or the level of the clouds → GLASS CEILING

ce·leb /səˈleb/ *n* [C] *informal* a CELEBRITY: *TV celebs*

cel·e·brant /ˈseləbrənt/ *n* [C] *formal* someone who performs or takes part in a religious ceremony

cel·e·brate /ˈseləbreɪt/ ●●● W3 *v*
1 [I,T] to show that an event or occasion is important by doing something special or enjoyable → **celebration**: *It's Dad's birthday and we're going out for a meal to celebrate.* | *My folks are celebrating their 50th anniversary.* | *We hope to give fans something to celebrate this season.* | **celebrate Christmas/Thanksgiving etc** *How do you usually celebrate New Year?*
2 [T] *formal* to praise someone or something: *poems that celebrate the joys of love*
3 [T] to perform a religious ceremony, especially the Christian Mass

cel·e·brat·ed /ˈselɪbreɪtɪd/ *adj* famous: *a celebrated actress* | *a celebrated legal case* THESAURUS FAMOUS

cel·e·bra·tion /ˌseləˈbreɪʃən/ ●●○ S3 *n*
1 [C] an occasion or party when you celebrate something: *the lively New Year celebrations in the city centre* THESAURUS PARTY
2 [singular, U] the act of celebrating: **in celebration of sth** *a reception in celebration of the Fund's 70th Anniversary* | *The show is a celebration of new young talent.* | *I think this is a* ***cause for celebration*** (=reason to celebrate).

COLLOCATIONS

ADJECTIVES/NOUN + celebration

a big/small celebration *We're having a small celebration for Dad's birthday.*
a family celebration (=for family members) *Everyone's coming here for a family celebration.*
a double celebration (=for two good things) *It's a double celebration for our first wedding anniversary and my birthday.*
a birthday/anniversary celebration *He is planning a very special 40th birthday celebration.*
a victory celebration *Some football fans were arrested during the victory celebrations.*
Christmas/New Year celebrations | **wedding celebrations**

VERBS

have a celebration *The villagers were having a celebration of some kind.*
hold/host a celebration *formal: The company is holding a celebration for its 75th anniversary.*
join in the celebrations *You're welcome to come and join in the celebrations!*

cel·e·bra·to·ry /ˌseləˈbreɪtəri◂ $ ˈseləbrətɔːri/ *adj* [only before noun] done in order to celebrate a particular event or occasion: *Join us for a celebratory drink in the bar.*

ce·leb·ri·ty /səˈlebrəti/ ●●○ *n* (*plural* **celebrities**)
1 [C] a famous living person SYN **star**: *a sporting celebrity* | *He's a national celebrity.* | *We invited a number of* ***minor celebrities*** (=people who are not very famous). | **celebrity chef/gardener etc** THESAURUS STAR
2 [U] *formal* the state of being famous SYN **fame**

ce·ler·i·ac /səˈleriæk/ *n* [U] a large white root vegetable which is a type of CELERY

cel·e·ry /ˈseləri/ *n* [U] a vegetable with long pale green stems that you can eat cooked or uncooked: *a* ***stick of celery*** → see picture at VEGETABLE[1]

ce·les·ti·al /səˈlestiəl $ -tʃəl/ *adj* [usually before noun]
1 relating to the sky or heaven: **celestial bodies** (=the Sun, Moon, stars etc) **2** *literary* very beautiful

cel·i·bate /ˈseləbət/ *adj* not married and not having sex, especially because of your religious beliefs → **virgin**: *Catholic priests are required to be celibate.* —**celibate** *n* [C] —**celibacy** /-bəsi/ *n* [U]: *a vow of celibacy*

cell /sel/ ●●● S3 W2 *n* [C]
1 BODY the smallest part of a living thing that can exist independently: **blood/brain/nerve cell** *red blood cells* | *cancer cells* | *Embryos grow by* ***cell division*** (=the splitting of cells).
2 PRISON a small room in a prison or police station where prisoners are kept: *He spent a night in the cells at the local police station.* | *the walls of his* ***prison cell*** THESAURUS PRISON
3 PHONE *AmE* a CELLULAR PHONE; a telephone that you can carry around with you, that works by using a network of radio stations to pass on signals SYN **mobile** *BrE*: *Call me on my cell if you're running late.*
4 ELECTRIC a piece of equipment for producing electricity from chemicals, heat, or light: *a car powered by electric fuel cells*
5 SECRET GROUP a small group of people who are working secretly as part of a larger political organization: *a terrorist cell*
6 RELIGIOUS a small room in a MONASTERY or CONVENT where someone sleeps
7 INSECT/SMALL ANIMAL a small space that an insect or other small creature has made to live in or use: *the cells of a honeycomb*

cel·lar /ˈselə $ -ər/ ●○○ *n* [C]
1 a room under a house or other building, often used for storing things SYN **basement**: *a coal cellar*
2 a store of wine belonging to a person, restaurant etc → SALT CELLAR

cel·list /ˈtʃelɪst/ *n* [C] someone who plays the cello

cell·mate /ˈselmeɪt/ *n* [C] someone who shares a prison cell with someone else

cel·lo /ˈtʃeləʊ $ -loʊ/ *n* (*plural* **cellos**) [C] a musical instrument like a large VIOLIN that you hold between your knees and play by pulling a BOW (=special stick) across the strings → see picture at STRINGED INSTRUMENT

Cel·lo·phane /ˈseləfeɪn/ *n* [U] *trademark* a thin transparent material used for wrapping things

cell·phone, **ˈcell phone** /ˈselfəʊn $ -foʊn/ ●●● S2 W3 *n* [C] *especially AmE* a CELLULAR PHONE SYN **mobile phone** *BrE*

ˈcell ˌtower *n* [C] a place where communication equipment for MOBILE PHONES is placed

cel·lu·lar /ˈseljələ $ -ər/ *adj* **1** consisting of or relating to the cells of plants or animals **2** a cellular telephone system works by using a network of radio stations to pass on signals: *a cellular network*

ˌcellular ˈphone *n* [C] *especially AmE* a telephone that you can carry with you and use in any place SYN **mobile phone** *BrE*

cel·lu·lite /ˈseljəlaɪt/ *n* [U] fat just below someone's skin, that makes it look uneven and unattractive

cel·lu·loid /ˈseljəlɔɪd/ *n* [U] **1** **on celluloid** on cinema film: *Chaplin's comic genius is preserved on celluloid.* **2** a plastic substance made mainly from CELLULOSE that was used in the past to make photographic film and other objects

cel·lu·lose /ˈseljələʊs $ -loʊs/ *n* [U] **1** the material that the cell walls of plants are made of and that is used to make plastics, paper etc **2** (*also* **cellulose acetate**) *technical* a plastic that is used for many industrial purposes, especially making photographic film and explosives

Cel·si·us /ˈselsiəs/ *n* [U] (*written abbreviation* **C**) a scale of temperature in which water freezes at 0° and boils at 100° SYN **Centigrade** → **Fahrenheit**: *12° Celsius* (=12 degrees on the Celsius scale) —**Celsius** *adj*

Celt /kelt, selt/ *n* [C] a member of a race of people who lived in ancient Britain and Western Europe before the Romans came, or a person living now whose ANCESTORS were members of this race

Cel·tic /ˈkeltɪk, ˈseltɪk/ *adj* relating to the Celts or their languages

ce·ment[1] /sɪˈment/ ●○○ *n* [U]
1 a grey powder made from LIME and clay that becomes hard when it is mixed with water and allowed to dry, and that is used in building → **concrete**: *a bag of cement*
2 a thick sticky substance that becomes very hard when it dries and is used for filling holes or sticking things together

cement[2] *v* [T] **1** (*also* **cement over**) to cover something with cement **2** to make a relationship between people, countries, or organizations firm and strong: **cement a relationship/alliance** *They want to cement a good working relationship between the government and trade unions.*

ceˈment ˌmixer *n* [C] a machine with a round drum that turns around, into which you put cement, sand, and water to make CONCRETE

cem·e·tery /ˈsemətri $ -teri/ ●●○ *n* (*plural* **cemeteries**) [C] a piece of land, usually not belonging to a church, in which dead people are buried → **graveyard**

cen·o·taph /ˈsenətɑːf $ -tæf/ *n* [C] a MONUMENT built to remind people of soldiers, sailors etc who were killed in a war and are buried somewhere else

censor[1] ●○○ *v* [T] to examine books, films, letters etc to remove anything that is considered offensive, morally harmful, or politically dangerous etc → **censorship**, **ban**: *The information given to the press was carefully censored by the Ministry of Defence.*

cen·sor[2] /ˈsensə $ -ər/ *n* [C] someone whose job is to examine books, films, letters etc and remove anything considered to be offensive, morally harmful, or politically dangerous → **censorship**

cen·so·ri·ous /senˈsɔːriəs/ *adj formal* criticizing and expressing disapproval: *His tone was censorious.* —**censoriously** *adv* —**censoriousness** *n* [U]

cen·sor·ship /ˈsensəʃɪp $ -ər-/ ●○○ *n* [U] the practice or system of censoring something: *censorship of books*

cen·sure[1] /ˈsenʃə $ -ər/ *n* [U] *formal* the act of expressing strong disapproval and criticism: *a vote of censure*

censure[2] *v* [T] *formal* to officially criticize someone for something they have done wrong: *He was officially censured for his handling of the situation.*

cen·sus /ˈsensəs/ ●○○ *n* (*plural* **censuses**) [C]
1 an official process of counting a country's population and finding out about the people
2 an official process of counting something for government planning: *a traffic census*

cent /sent/ ●●● S1 W1 *n* [C]
1 1/100th of the standard unit of money in some countries. For example, there are 100 cents in one dollar or in one EURO: symbol ¢
2 put in your two cents' worth *AmE* to give your opinion about something, when other people do not want to hear it → **not one red cent** at **RED[1]**(7)

cen·taur /ˈsentɔː $ -tɔːr/ *n* [C] a creature in ancient Greek stories with the head, chest, and arms of a man and the body and legs of a horse

cen·te·nar·i·an /ˌsentəˈneəriən $ -ˈner-/ *n* [C] someone who is 100 years old or older

cen·te·na·ry /senˈtiːnəri $ -ˈten-, ˈsentəneri/ *n* (*plural* **centenaries**) *especially BrE* (*also* **cen·ten·ni·al** /senˈteniəl/ *especially AmE*) [C] the day or year exactly 100 years after a particular event: **[+of]** *a concert to mark the centenary of the composer's birth*

cen·ter /ˈsentə $ -ər/ *n* the American spelling of CENTRE

centi- /sentə/ (*also* **cent-** /sent/) *prefix* [in nouns] **1** a hundred: *a centipede* (=creature with 100 legs) **2** a 100th part of a unit: *a centimetre* (=0.01 metres)

Cen·ti·grade /ˈsentəgreɪd/ *n* [U] (*written abbreviation* **C**) CELSIUS —**Centigrade** *adj*

cen·ti·li·tre *BrE*, **centiliter** *AmE* /ˈsentəliːtə $ -ər/ *n* [C] (*written abbreviation* **cl**) a unit for measuring an amount of liquid. There are 100 centilitres in one litre.

cen·time /ˈsɒntiːm $ ˈsɑːn-/ *n* [C] 1/100th of a FRANC or some other units of money

cen·ti·me·tre *BrE*, **centimeter** *AmE* /ˈsentəˌmiːtə $ -ər/ ●●● S3 W3 *n* [C] (*written abbreviation* **cm**) a unit for measuring length. There are 100 centimetres in one metre.

cen·ti·pede /ˈsentəpiːd/ *n* [C] a small creature like a WORM with a lot of very small legs

cen·tral /ˈsentrəl/ ●●● S1 W1 *adj*
1 MIDDLE [only before noun, no comparative] in the middle of an area or an object: *He lives in central London.* | *The roof is supported by a central column.* | **Central America/Asia/Europe etc**
2 FROM ONE PLACE [only before noun, no comparative] used about the part of an organization, system etc which controls the rest of it, or its work: *the party's central office* | *the system's central control unit* | *central planning*
3 IMPORTANT more important and having more influence than anything else: **[+to]** *values which are central to our society* | *Owen* ***played a central role*** *in the negotiations.* | *His ideas were* ***of central importance*** *in the development of the theory.* | **central idea/theme/concern etc** *Education has become a central issue in public debate.* THESAURUS IMPORTANT, MAIN
4 EASY ACCESS a place that is central is easy to reach because it is near the middle of a town or area: *It's very central, just five minutes' walk from the main square.* —**centrally** *adv*: *Our office is centrally situated.* | *All data is held centrally.* —**centrality** /senˈtræləti/ *n* [U]

-central /sentrəl/ *suffix* [in nouns] *informal* full of a particular type of thing or person: *It was mosquito-central down by the river.* | *In the 1990s, London's docklands became yuppie-central* (=full of rich young people).

ˌcentral ˈbank *n* [C] a national bank that does business with the government, and controls the amount of money available and the general system of banks

ˌcentral ˈcasting *n* [U] **1** an organization that supplies actors for small roles in films, plays etc **2** if you say that someone has come from central casting, you mean that they look like the perfect example of a particular type of person, as if an actor is playing the part: *Wearing black shoes and a pinstripe suit, he looked like central casting's idea of the perfect civil servant.*

ˌcentral ˈgovernment *n* [C,U] *especially BrE* the level of government which deals with national rather than local things → **local government**

ˌcentral ˈheating ●●○ *n* [U] a system of heating buildings in which water or air is heated in one place and then sent around the rest of the building through pipes etc: *the central heating boiler* —**centrally heated** *adj*

cen·tral·is·m /ˈsentrəlɪzəm/ *n* [U] a way of governing a country or controlling an organization in which one group has power and tells people in other places what to do

cen·tral·ize (*also* **-ise** *BrE*) /ˈsentrəlaɪz/ *v* [T] to organize the control of a country, organization, or system so that everything is done or decided in one place OPP **decentralize**: *plans to centralize the company's U.S. activities* —**centralized** *adj*: *a centralized database* —**centralization** /ˌsentrəlaɪˈzeɪʃən $ -lə-/ *n* [U]

ˌcentral ˈlocking *n* [U] *BrE* a system for locking all the doors of a car at the same time when you turn the key in one lock or use a key with a REMOTE CONTROL

ˌcentral ˈnervous ˌsystem *n* [C] the main part of

your NERVOUS SYSTEM, consisting of your brain and your SPINAL CORD

ˌcentral ˈprocessing ˌunit *n* [C] a CPU

ˌcentral reserˈvation *n* [C] *BrE* a narrow piece of ground that divides the two parts of a MOTORWAY or other main road

cen·tre¹ *BrE*, **center** *AmE* /ˈsentə $ -ər/ ●●● S1 W1 *n*
1 MIDDLE [C usually singular] the middle of a space, area, or object, especially the exact middle: **in the centre (of sth)** *There was an enormous oak table in the center of the room.* | *The hotel is* ***right in the centre*** *of the village.* | **[+of]** *Draw a line through the centre of the circle.* | *lines radiating out from the centre* | *chocolates with soft centres*
2 BUILDING [C] a building which is used for a particular purpose or activity: **[+for]** *the European Centre for Nuclear Research* | *an exhibition at the Community Arts Centre* | *a* ***conference centre***
3 PLACE OF ACTIVITY [C] a place where there is a lot of a particular type of business, activity etc: **business/commercial/financial etc centre** *a major banking centre* | *It's not exactly a cultural center like Paris.* | **[+of/for]** *The city became a centre for the paper industry.* | *a* ***center of*** *academic* ***excellence*** (=a very good place for education)
4 OF A TOWN [C] *BrE* the part of a town or city where most of the shops, restaurants, cinemas, theatres etc are SYN **downtown** *AmE*: **town/city centre** *shops in the town centre* | *the main route into Leeds city centre*
5 INVOLVEMENT **be at the centre of sth** if a person or thing is at the centre of something that is happening, they are involved in it more than other people or things: *He always seems to be at the centre of things.* | **be at the centre of a row/dispute/controversy etc** *the businessman at the centre of the row over political donations*
6 be the centre of attention to be the person that everyone is giving attention to: *Betty just loves being the centre of attention.*
7 be/take centre stage if something or someone is centre stage, they have an important position and get a lot of attention: *After his father's death, he was able to rise to power and take centre stage.*
8 POLITICS **the centre** a MODERATE (=middle) position in politics in which you do not support extreme ideas: *The party's new policies show a swing towards the centre.* | **left/right of centre** *Her political views are slightly left of centre.* | **centre-right/centre-left** *a centre-left government*
9 SPORT [C] a player in sports such as American football and BASKETBALL who plays in or near the middle of the field or playing area: *the Sonics' six-foot-four-inch center* | **centre forward/half/back etc** (=players in different parts of the middle section of the playing area) → see picture at BASKETBALL
10 centre of population/urban centre an area where a large number of people live: *Nuclear installations are built well away from the main centres of population.*

centre² *BrE*, **center** *AmE* ●●○ *v* [T] to move something to a position at the centre of something else: *The title isn't quite centred on the page, is it?*

centre around/round sth (*also* **be centred around/round sth** *BrE*) *phr v* if your thoughts, activities etc centre around something or are centred around it, it is the main thing that you are concerned with or interested in: *In the 16th century, village life centred around religion.*

centre on/upon sth (*also* **be centred on/upon sth**) *phr v* if your attention centres on something or someone, or is centred on them, you pay more attention to them than anything else: *The debate centred on funding for health services.* | *Much of their work is centred on local development projects.*

cen·tred *BrE*, **centered** *AmE* /ˈsentəd $ -ərd/ *adj* **1** (*also* **-centred**) [only after noun] having a particular person or group as the most important part or FOCUS of something: *a student-centred approach* | *family-centered care* **2** feeling calm and in control of your life and feelings: *Julia seems very centred nowadays.*

cen·tre·fold *BrE*, **centerfold** *AmE* /ˈsentəfəʊld $ -tərfoʊld/ *n* [C] **1** the two pages that face each other in the middle of a magazine or newspaper **2** a picture of a woman with no clothes on that covers the two pages in the middle of a magazine

ˌcentre ˈforward *BrE*, **center forward** *AmE n* [C] an attacking player who plays in the centre of the field in soccer

ˌcentre of ˈgravity *BrE*, **center of gravity** *AmE n* [singular] the point in any object on which it can balance

cen·tre·piece *BrE*, **centerpiece** *AmE* /ˈsentəpiːs $ -ər-/ *n*
1 [singular] the most important, noticeable, or attractive part of something: **[+of]** *The centrepiece of Bevan's policy was the National Health Service.* **2** [C] a decoration, especially an arrangement of flowers, in the middle of a table

-centric /sentrɪk/ *suffix* [in adjectives] giving most attention to a particular thing, person, or group: *malecentric* (=giving males most attention)

cen·tri·fu·gal force /ˌsentrɪfjuːgəl ˈfɔːs senˌtrɪfjəgəl- $ senˌtrɪfjəgəl ˈfɔːrs/ *n* [U] a force which makes things move away from the centre of something when they are moving around it

cen·tri·fuge /ˈsentrəfjuːdʒ/ *n* [C] a machine that spins a container around very quickly so that the heavier liquids and any solids are forced to the outer edge or bottom

cen·trip·e·tal force /senˌtrɪpətl ˈfɔːs $ -ˈfɔːrs/ *n* [U] *technical* a force which makes things move towards the centre of something when they are moving around it

cen·trist /ˈsentrɪst/ *adj* having political beliefs that are not extreme SYN **moderate** OPP **extremist** —**centrist** *n* [C]

cen·tu·ri·on /senˈtjʊəriən $ -ˈtʊr-/ *n* [C] an army officer of ancient Rome, who was in charge of about 100 soldiers

cen·tu·ry /ˈsentʃəri/ ●●● S2 W1 *n* (*plural* **centuries**) [C]
1 one of the 100-year periods measured from before or after the year of Christ's birth: **the 11th/18th/21st etc century** *The church was built in the 13th century.* | **the next/last century** *by the beginning of the next century* | *the story of life on a small farm at* ***the turn of the century*** (=the beginning of the century)
2 a period of 100 years: *many centuries ago*
3 100 RUNS scored by one CRICKET player in an INNINGS

CEO /ˌsiː iː ˈəʊ $ -ˈoʊ/ *n* [C] (***Chief Executive Officer***) the person with the most authority in a large company

ceph·a·lo·pod /ˈsefələpɒd $ -pɑːd/ *n* [C] a sea creature that has TENTACLES, such as an OCTOPUS or SQUID

ce·ram·ics /səˈræmɪks/ ●○○ *n*
1 [U] the art of making pots, bowls, TILES etc, by shaping pieces of clay and baking them until they are hard
2 [plural] things that are made this way: *an exhibition of ceramics* —**ceramic** *adj*: *ceramic tiles*

GRAMMAR: Singular or plural verb?

- In meaning 1, **ceramics** is followed by a singular verb: ***Ceramics is*** *an ancient art.*
- In meaning 2, **ceramics** is followed by a plural verb: *These Portuguese* ***ceramics are*** *beautiful.*

ce·re·al /ˈsɪəriəl $ ˈsɪr-/ ●●● S3 *n*
1 [C,U] a breakfast food made from grain and usually eaten with milk: *a bowl of* ***breakfast cereal***
2 [C] a plant grown to produce grain, for example wheat, rice etc: *cereal crops*

cer·e·bel·lum /ˌserəˈbeləm/ *n* (*plural* **cerebellums** *or* **cerebella** /-lə/) [C] *technical* the bottom part of your brain that controls your muscles

cer·e·bral /ˈserəbrəl $ səˈriː-, ˈserə-/ *adj* **1** [only before noun] *medical* relating to or affecting your brain: *a* ***cerebral haemorrhage*** (=bleeding in the brain) **2** having or involving complicated ideas rather than strong emotions: *a cerebral film*

ˌcerebral ˈpalsy / $ ˌ.,.. ˈ../ *n* [U] a disease caused by damage to the brain before or during birth which results in difficulties of movement and speech

cer·e·mo·ni·al¹ /ˌserəˈməʊniəl◂ $ -ˈmoʊ-/ *adj*
1 [usually before noun] used in a ceremony or done as part of a ceremony: *the mayor's ceremonial duties* | *Native*

American ceremonial robes **2** if a position in a country or organization is ceremonial, it gives no real power: *the largely ceremonial post of president*

ceremonial² *n* [C,U] a special ceremony, or special formal actions: *an occasion for public ceremonial*

cer·e·mo·ni·ous /ˌserəˈməʊniəs◂ $ -ˈmoʊ-/ *adj* done in a formal serious way, as if you were in a ceremony —**ceremoniously** *adv*: *He ceremoniously burnt the offending documents.*

cer·e·mo·ny /ˈserəməni $ -moʊni/ ●●● S3 W2 *n* (*plural* **ceremonies**)

1 [C] an important social or religious event, when a traditional set of actions is performed in a formal way → **ceremonial**: *a wedding ceremony | the opening ceremony of the Olympic Games*

2 [U] the special actions and formal words traditionally used on particular occasions: *The queen was crowned with due ceremony.*

3 without ceremony in a very informal way, without politeness: *He wished me good luck in the future and left without further ceremony.* → **not stand on ceremony** at STAND¹(42)

COLLOCATIONS

VERBS

hold a ceremony *A ceremony was held in Berlin to mark the occasion.*
attend a ceremony *I attended the ceremony at the cathedral.*
be present at a ceremony *The French ambassador was present at the ceremony.*
perform/conduct a ceremony *The Bishop of Louisiana performed the ceremony.*
a ceremony takes place *The ceremony took place on 13th June at 2.30.*
a ceremony marks sth *a ceremony marking the beginning of adulthood*

ADJECTIVES/NOUN + ceremony

a religious ceremony *Did you have a religious ceremony when you got married?*
a wedding/marriage ceremony *It was a beautiful wedding ceremony.*
a civil ceremony (=a wedding ceremony that is not a religious one) *They married in a registrar's office, in a civil ceremony.*
a special ceremony *The winners will receive their awards at a special ceremony in London.*
a simple ceremony | **a grand/elaborate ceremony** | **a solemn ceremony** (=a very serious one) | **a traditional ceremony** | **an opening/closing ceremony** (=at the beginning or end of a special event) | **an awards ceremony** (=to give people prizes for good achievements) | **a graduation ceremony** (=when you get your university degree) | **an inauguration ceremony** (=when someone becomes president, chancellor etc) | **an initiation ceremony** (=in which someone officially becomes an adult, a member of a group etc)

ce·rise /səˈriːs, -ˈriːz/ *n* [U] a bright pinkish-red colour —**cerise** *adj*

cert /sɜːt $ sɜːrt/ *n* **be a (dead) cert** *BrE informal* to be certain to happen or to succeed: *Put your money on Thorpe to win, he's a dead cert.*

cert. **1** the written abbreviation of ***certificate*** **2** the written abbreviation of ***certified***

cer·tain¹ /ˈsɜːtn $ ˈsɜːr-/ ●●● S1 W1 *adj*

1 [not before noun] confident and sure, without any doubts SYN **sure**: **certain (that)** *I'm **absolutely certain** that I left the keys in the kitchen. | I **felt certain** that I'd passed the test.* | **certain who/what/how etc** *I'm not certain when it will be ready.* | **[+about/of]** *Now, are you certain about that? | They were watching him. He was certain of it.* THESAURUS ▸ SURE

REGISTER
In everyday English, people usually say **sure** rather than **certain**: *I'm **sure** I gave him the money.*

2 if something is certain, it will definitely happen or is definitely true: ***It** now **seems certain that** there will be an election in May. | Many people **look certain to** lose their jobs. | It is wise to apply early to **be certain of** obtaining a place. | **It's not certain where** he lived. | His re-election was considered **virtually certain**. | It is **by no means certain** that the deal will be accepted. | If they stayed in the war zone they would face **certain death**.*

3 make certain a) to check that something is correct or true SYN **make sure**: **make certain (that)** *We need to make certain that it's going to fit first.* **b)** to do something in order to be sure that something will happen SYN **make sure**: **make certain (that)** *Secure the edges firmly to make certain that no moisture can get in.*

4 for certain without doubt SYN **for sure**: **know/say (sth) for certain** *I know for certain it's in here somewhere.* | **that's/one thing's for certain** *One thing's for certain, he won't be back.*

5 [only before noun] used to talk about a particular person, thing, group of things etc without naming them or describing them exactly: *The library's only open at certain times of day. | I promised to be in a certain place by lunchtime. | There are certain things I just can't discuss with my mother.* | **certain kind/type/sort** *the expectation of a certain kind of behaviour* | **in certain circumstances/cases etc** *Extra funding may be available in certain circumstances.*

6 a certain a) used to say that an amount is not great: *You may need to do **a certain amount of** work in the evenings.* | **to a certain extent/degree** (=partly, but not completely) *I do agree with his ideas to a certain extent.* **b)** enough of a particular quality to be noticed: *There's a certain prestige about going to a private school.* **c)** *formal* used to talk about someone you do not know but whose name you have been told: *a certain Mr Franks*

THESAURUS - MEANING 2

certain if something is certain, you are completely sure that it will happen or is true: *Success seems certain. | It is almost certain that there will be a change of government.*
definite if something is definite, it is certain because someone has officially stated that it will happen, is true etc: *I hope you can give me a definite answer soon. | The wedding will be next summer but a definite date has not been arranged yet.*
inevitable if something, especially something bad, is inevitable, it is certain to happen and you cannot do anything to prevent it: *War now seems inevitable. | It was inevitable that he would find out her secret sooner or later.*
be bound to if something is bound to happen, it is very likely to happen, especially because that is what usually happens in that kind of situation. **Be bound to** is less formal than **certain** and is very common in everyday spoken English: *The kids are bound to be hungry when they get home – they always are. | My car broke down today. It was bound to happen sooner or later.*
be assured of sth *formal* to be certain to get something good, or to be successful: *After the success of its recent single, the band is now assured of a contract with a major record company.*
sth is a foregone conclusion if something is a foregone conclusion, its result is certain even though it has not happened yet: *They were winning by such a large margin that victory seemed to be a foregone conclusion. | Party members believe it is a foregone conclusion that he will resign.*

certain² *pron* **certain of sb/sth** *formal* particular people or things in a group: *Certain of the payments were made on Mr Maxwell's authority.*

cer·tain·ly /ˈsɜːtnli $ ˈsɜːr-/ ●●● S1 W1 *adv* [sentence adverb]

1 without any doubt SYN **definitely**: *I certainly never expected to become a writer. | They're certainly not mine.* | **it is certainly true/possible etc** *It is certainly true that there are*

Frequencies of the adverb **certainly** in spoken and written English.

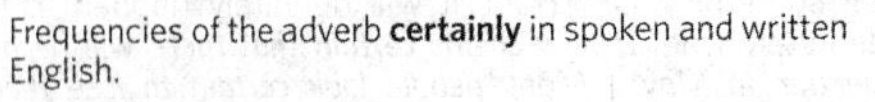

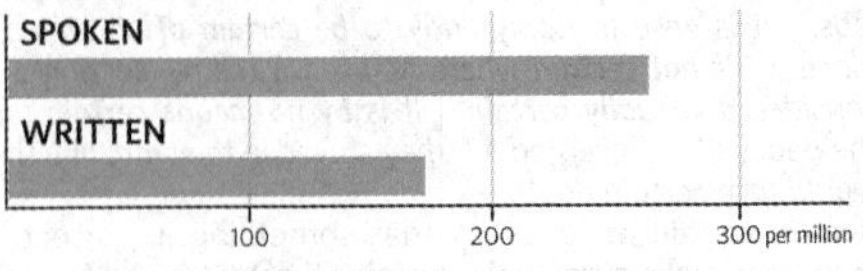

This graph shows that the adverb **certainly** is more common in spoken English than in written English. This is because it has some special uses in spoken English.

more courses on offer. | *The girl was* ***almost certainly*** *murdered.* | *'Not smoking has made a real difference.' 'It* ***most certainly*** *has.'*
2 *spoken* used to agree or give your permission: *'I'd like a beer, please.' 'Certainly, sir.'* | *'Can I come along?' 'Certainly.'*
3 certainly not *spoken* used to disagree completely or to refuse to give permission: *'May I go?' 'Certainly not!'*

REGISTER
In everyday English, people usually say **of course** or **sure** rather than **certainly** when agreeing or giving permission: *'Can I sit down?'* ***'Of course.'***

cer·tain·ty /ˈsɜːtnti $ ˈsɜːr-/ ●●○ *n* (*plural* **certainties**)
1 [U] the state of being completely certain: **with certainty** *She knew with absolute certainty that he'd say no.* | *The result is impossible to predict with any* ***degree of certainty****.*
2 [U] the fact that something is certain to happen: **certainty of (doing) sth** *the certainty of being caught* | **certainty that** *There's no certainty that he'll remember.*
3 [C] something that is definitely true or that will definitely happen: *He usually does quite well, but it's not a certainty.* | *The only certainty is that there will need to be major changes.*

cer·ti·fi·ab·le /ˈsɜːtəfaɪəbəl $ ˌsɜːrtəˈfaɪ-/ *adj* **1** *informal* crazy, especially in a way that is dangerous: *If you ask me, that man is certifiable.* **2** *especially AmE* definitely a particular thing: *The guy's a certifiable megastar.* **3** *especially AmE* good enough to be officially approved: *grade A certifiable beef*

cer·tif·i·cate /səˈtɪfɪkət $ sər-/ ●●○ S3 W3 *n* [C]
1 an official document that states that a fact or facts are true: **birth/death/marriage certificate** (=giving details of someone's birth, death, or marriage)
2 an official paper stating that you have completed a course of study or passed an examination: *a degree certificate*

cer·tif·i·cat·ed /səˈtɪfɪkeɪtɪd $ sər-/ *adj BrE* having successfully completed a course of training for a profession: *a certificated nurse*

cer·tif·i·ca·tion /ˌsəˌtɪfɪˈkeɪʃən $ sər-/ *n* **1** [C,U] an official document that says that someone is allowed to do a certain job, that something is of good quality etc: *We successfully completed the certification for open water diving.* **2** [U] the process of giving someone or something an official document that says they are allowed to do a certain job, that something is of good quality etc: **[+of]** *certification of competence*

ˌcertified ˈmail *n* [U] *AmE* a way of sending post in which someone records that you have sent it, and the person it is sent to must sign their name to prove they have received it

ˌcertified ˌpublic acˈcountant *n* [C] a CPA

cer·ti·fy /ˈsɜːtɪfaɪ $ ˈsɜːr-/ *v* (**certified, certifying, certifies**) [T] **1** to state that something is correct or true, especially after some kind of test: *The accounts were certified by an auditor.* | **certify (that)** *We need to certify that the repairs have been satisfactorily carried out.* | **certify sb dead** *BrE* (=when a doctor says officially that a person is dead) *The driver was certified dead at the scene.* **2** to give an official paper to someone which states that they have completed a course of training for a profession → **certificate**: **certify sb as sth** *She was certified as a teacher in 1990.* **3** to officially state that someone is mentally ill

cer·ti·tude /ˈsɜːtɪtjuːd $ ˈsɜːrtɪtuːd/ *n* [U] *formal* the state of being or feeling certain about something SYN **certainty**

ce·ru·le·an /səˈruːliən/ (*also* **ceˌrulean ˈblue**) *n* [U] *literary* a deep blue colour like a clear sky —**cerulean** *adj*

cer·vi·cal /ˈsɜːvɪkəl, səˈvaɪkəl $ ˈsɜːrvɪkəl/ *adj* **1** related to the neck: *cervical vertebrae* (=the bones in the back of your neck) **2** related to the cervix: *cervical cancer*

ˌcervical ˈsmear *n* [C] *BrE technical* a test for CANCER of a woman's CERVIX SYN **pap smear** *AmE*

cer·vix /ˈsɜːvɪks $ ˈsɜːr-/ *n* [C] the narrow passage into a woman's UTERUS

ce·sar·e·an /səˈzeəriən $ -ˈzer-/ *n* [C] another spelling of CAESAREAN

ce·si·um /ˈsiːziəm/ *n* [U] the American spelling of CAESIUM

ces·sa·tion /seˈseɪʃən/ *n* [C,U] *formal* a pause or stop → **cease**: **[+of]** *a cessation of hostilities* (=when the fighting stops in a war)

ces·sion /ˈseʃən/ *n* [C,U] the act of giving up land, property, or rights, especially to another country after a war, or something that is given up in this way → **cede**: *Spanish cession of the territory in 1818*

cess·pit /ˈsesˌpɪt/ *n* [C] **1** (*also* **cess·pool** /ˈsesˌpuːl/) a large hole or container under the ground in which waste from a building, especially from the toilets, is collected **2** a place or situation in which people behave in a bad or immoral way: *For weeks the affair threatened to be a cesspit of scandal.*

ce·tac·ean /sɪˈteɪʃən/ *n* [C] *technical* a MAMMAL that lives in the sea, such as a WHALE —**cetacean** *adj*

ce·vi·che, **seviche** /səˈviːtʃeɪ/ *n* [U] a dish originally from Latin America, made from pieces of raw fish in LEMON or LIME juice, oil, and spices

cf ●○○ used in writing to introduce something else that should be compared or considered

CFC /ˌsiː ef ˈsiː/ *n* [C] (***chlorofluorocarbon***) a gas used in FRIDGES and AEROSOL cans, believed to be responsible for damaging the OZONE LAYER

CGI /ˌsiː dʒiː ˈaɪ/ *n* [U] (***computer-generated imagery***) images in films, television programmes etc that are produced using computers: *The movie is an epic fantasy full of CGI.* **THESAURUS** ▸ **MOVIE**

cha-cha /ˈtʃɑː ʃɑː/ (*also* **ˌcha-cha-ˈcha**) *n* [C] a dance from South America with small fast steps

cha·dor /ˈtʃɑːdɔː, -də $ -dɔːr, -dər/ *n* [C] a long, usually black, piece of clothing worn by Muslim women in some countries, which covers the head and body → **abaya**, **burqa**

chafe /tʃeɪf/ *v* **1** [I,T] if a part of your body chafes or if something chafes it, it becomes sore because of something rubbing against it: *Wear a T-shirt under your wet suit to stop it chafing.* **2** [I] to feel impatient or annoyed: **[+at/against/under]** *Some hunters are chafing under the new restrictions.* **3** [T] *BrE* to rub part of your body to make it warm

chaff /tʃɑːf $ tʃæf/ *n* [U] **1** the outer seed covers that are separated from grain before it is used as food **2** dried grasses and plant stems that are used for food for farm animals → **separate the wheat from the chaff** at **WHEAT(2)**

chaf·finch /ˈtʃæfɪntʃ/ *n* [C] a common small European bird

chag·rin[1] /ˈʃægrɪn $ ʃəˈgrɪn/ *n* [U] annoyance and disappointment because something has not happened the way you hoped: **to sb's chagrin** *Much to her chagrin, I got the job.*

chagrin[2] *v* **be chagrined** *formal* to feel annoyed and disappointed: *Dale was chagrined that she wasn't impressed.*

chai /tʃaɪ/ *n* [U] sweet Indian tea with spices

chain[1] /tʃeɪn/ ●●● S3 W2 *n*
1 JOINED RINGS [C,U] a series of metal rings which are joined together in a line and used for fastening things,

supporting weights, decoration etc → **link**: *She had a gold chain around her neck.* | *a length of heavy chain* | *the mayor's* ***chain of office*** (=a decoration worn by some British officials at ceremonies) | **pull the chain** *BrE* (=flush the toilet) | **a bicycle chain** (=that makes the wheels turn) → see pictures at BICYCLE, JEWELLERY

2 CONNECTED EVENTS [C] a connected series of events or actions, especially which lead to a final result: *the* ***chain of events*** *that led to World War I* | *The salesmen are just one* ***link in the chain*** (=part of a process) *of distribution.* | *a rather complicated chain of reasoning* → CHAIN OF COMMAND, FOOD CHAIN

3 SHOPS/HOTELS [C] a number of shops, hotels, cinemas etc owned or managed by the same company or person: **[+of]** *a chain of restaurants* | **hotel/restaurant/retail etc chain** *several major UK supermarket chains* → CHAIN STORE

4 CONNECTED LINE [C] people or things which are connected or next to each other forming a line: **mountain/island chain** *the Andean mountain chain* | **chain of atoms/molecules etc** *technical*: *a chain of amino acids* | *They formed a* ***human chain*** (=a line of people who pass things from one person to the next) *to move the equipment.* | *daisy chains* (=flowers tied together)

5 PRISONERS [C usually plural] metal chains fastened to the legs and arms of a prisoner, to prevent them from escaping: **in chains** *He was led away in chains.* | **ball and chain** (=a chain attached to someone's ankle at one end with a heavy metal ball at the other)

6 BUYING A HOUSE [C usually singular] *BrE* a number of people buying houses, where each person must complete the sale of their own house before they can buy the next person's house

chain² *v* **1** [T] to fasten someone or something to something else using a chain, especially in order to prevent them from escaping or being stolen: **chain sb/sth to sth** *a bicycle chained to the fence* | *Four activists chained themselves to the gates.* | **chain sb/sth up** *The elephants were chained up by their legs.* | **chain sb/sth together** *Their hands and feet were chained together.* **2 be chained to sth** to have your freedom restricted because of something you must do: *She felt chained to the kitchen sink.* | *I don't want a job where I'm chained to a desk all day.*

ˈchain gang *n* [C] a group of prisoners chained together to work outside their prison

ˈchain ˌletter *n* [C] a letter sent to several people asking them to send a copy of the letter to several more people

ˌchain-link ˈfence *n* [C] a type of fence made of wire twisted together into a diamond pattern

ˈchain mail *n* [U] protective clothing made by joining many small metal rings together, worn by soldiers in the past

ˌchain of comˈmand *n* [C] a system in an organization by which decisions are made and passed from people at the top of the organization to people lower down: *Symonds is third in the chain of command.*

ˌchain reˈaction *n* [C] **1** *technical* a chemical or NUCLEAR reaction which produces energy and causes more reactions of the same kind **2** a series of related events, each of which causes the next: *A sudden drop on Wall Street can set off a chain reaction in other financial markets.*

chain·saw /ˈtʃeɪnsɔː $ -sɒː/ *n* [C] a tool used for cutting wood, consisting of a circular chain with teeth which is driven by a motor → CIRCULAR SAW → see picture at TOOL¹

ˈchain-smoke *v* [I,T] to smoke cigarettes one immediately after another —**chain-smoker** *n* [C]

ˈchain stitch *n* [C,U] a way of sewing in which each new stitch is pulled through the last one

ˈchain store, **chain·store** /ˈtʃeɪnstɔː $ -stɔːr/ *n* [C] one of a group of shops, all of which are owned by one organization SYN **chain**

chair¹ /tʃeə $ tʃer/ ●●● S1 W2 *n*

1 [C] a piece of furniture for one person to sit on, which has a back, a seat, and four legs: *a kitchen chair* | *They bought a new table and chairs.* | *One of the* ***chair legs*** *was broken.* | **on/in a chair** *She was sitting on a wooden chair.* | *He sat back in his chair.*

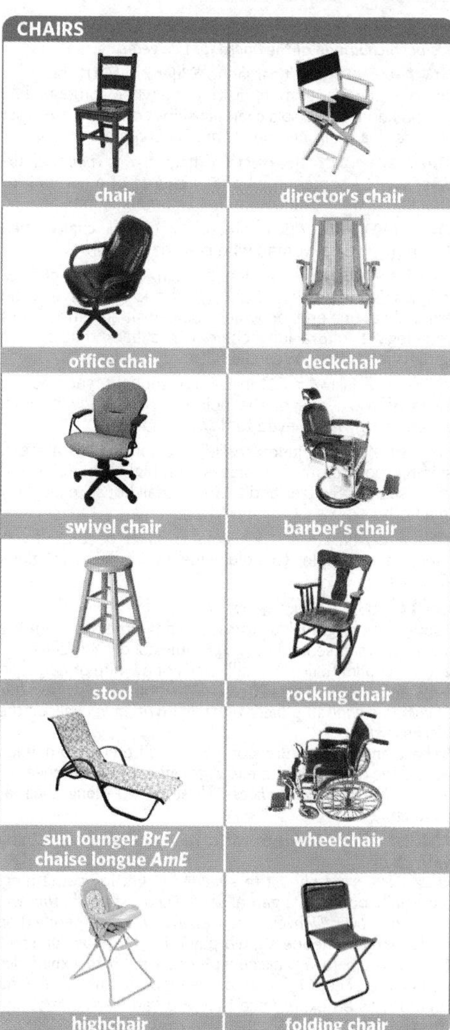

2 [singular] the position of being in charge of a meeting or committee, or the person who is in charge of it: *Address your questions to the chair, please.* | **be in the chair** *Who will be in the chair at tomorrow's meeting?* | **[+of]** *He was nominated as chair of the board of governors.*

3 [C] the position of being a university PROFESSOR: **[+of]** *a new Chair of Medicine*

4 the chair *AmE informal* the ELECTRIC CHAIR

chair² ●○○ *v* [T] to be the CHAIRPERSON of a meeting or committee: *The inquiry was chaired by a judge.*

chair·lift, **ˈchair lift** /ˈtʃeəlɪft $ ˈtʃer-/ *n* [C] a line of chairs hanging from a moving wire, used for carrying people up and down mountains, especially to SKI

chair·man /ˈtʃeəmən $ ˈtʃer-/ ●●○ W3 *n* (*plural* **chairmen** /-mən/) [C]

1 someone, especially a man, who is in charge of a meeting or directs the work of a committee or an organization → **chairwoman**: **[+of]** *Potts was appointed chairman of the education committee.* | **deputy/vice chairman** *Barrett serves as vice chairman.* ⚠ Many people use **chairperson** or **chair** instead, to avoid suggesting that this person must be a man.

2 *BrE* someone who is in charge of a large company or

C

organization: *the chairman of British Aerospace* | *Williams has been* ***chairman of the board*** *for five years.*

chair·man·ship /ˈtʃeəmənʃɪp $ ˈtʃer-/ *n* [C,U] the position of being a chairman, or the time when someone has this position: **under sb's chairmanship** *A committee was set up under the chairmanship of Edmund Compton.*

chair·per·son /ˈtʃeəˌpɜːsən $ ˈtʃerˌpɜːr-/ *n* (*plural* **chairpersons**) [C] someone who is in charge of a meeting or directs the work of a committee or organization

chair·wom·an /ˈtʃeəˌwʊmən/ *n* (*plural* **chairwomen** /-ˌwɪmɪn/) [C] a woman who is a chairperson

chaise longue /ʃeɪz ˈlɒŋ $ -ˈlɔːŋ/ *n* (*plural* **chaises longues** (*same pronunciation*)) [C] **1** a long chair with an arm only at one end, on which you can sit and stretch out your legs **2** *AmE* a long chair with a back that can be upright for sitting, or can lie flat for lying down

C

chak·ra /ˈtʃʌkrə/ *n* [C] in Eastern thought, such as the ideas of YOGA, one of the points on the body through which energy is believed to flow in and out

chal·et /ˈʃæleɪ $ ʃæˈleɪ/ *n* [C] **1** a house with a steep sloping roof, common in places with high mountains and snow such as Switzerland **2** *BrE* a small house, especially in a HOLIDAY CAMP

chal·ice /ˈtʃælɪs/ *n* [C] a gold or silver decorated cup used, for example, to hold wine in Christian religious services

chalk¹ /tʃɔːk $ tʃɒːk/ ●○○ *n* [U]
1 soft white or grey rock formed a long time ago from the shells of small sea animals SYN **limestone**: *chalk cliffs*
2 (*also* **chalks** [plural]) small sticks of a white or coloured substance like soft rock, used for writing or drawing: *a box of coloured chalks* | *a piece of chalk* | *writing in chalk on the blackboard*
3 chalk and cheese *BrE* completely different from each other: *The two brothers are* ***as different as chalk and cheese.*** | *They're* ***like chalk and cheese****, those two.* → **long chalk** at LONG¹(21)

chalk² *v* [T + up/on] to write, mark, or draw something with chalk

chalk sth ↔ **up** *phr v* **1** to succeed in getting something, especially points in a game: *Seattle chalked up another win last night over Denver.* **2** to record what someone has done, what someone should pay etc: **[+to]** *You can chalk the drinks up to my account.* **3 chalk it up to experience** *informal* to accept a failure or disappointment calmly and regard it as an experience that you can learn something from

chalk·board /ˈtʃɔːkbɔːd $ ˈtʃɒːkbɔːrd/ *n* [C] *AmE* a BLACKBOARD: *She wrote the day's menu up on a chalkboard.*

chalk·y /ˈtʃɔːki $ ˈtʃɒː-/ *adj* similar to chalk or containing chalk: *white chalky soil* | *There were chalky bits in the bottom of the drink.* —**chalkiness** *n* [U]

chal·lenge¹ /ˈtʃæləndʒ/ ●●● S2 W2 AWL *n*
1 STH DIFFICULT [C,U] something that tests strength, skill, or ability, especially in a way that is interesting: **[+of]** *The company is ready to meet the challenges of the next few years.* | **the challenge of doing sth** *I relish the challenge of rebuilding the club.* | **face/take on/accept etc a challenge** (=be ready to deal with one) *Martins now faces the biggest challenge of his career.* | **meet a challenge/rise to a challenge** (=successfully deal with one) *a new and vibrant initiative to meet the challenge of the 21st century* | **intellectual/physical challenge** *the intellectual challenge of postgraduate research*
2 QUESTION STH [C] when someone refuses to accept that someone or something is right and legal: **[+to]** *a direct challenge to the Governor's authority* | **[+from]** *The president faces a strong challenge from nationalists.* | **pose/represent/present a challenge (to sb)** *The strike represented a serious challenge to the government.* | **mount/launch a challenge** *They decided to mount a* ***legal challenge*** *to the decision.*
3 COMPETITION [C] when someone tries to win something or invites someone to try to beat them in a fight, competition etc: **[+for]** *They are ready to mount a challenge for the championship.* | *They* ***threw down*** *the* ***challenge*** *that he couldn't wash 40 cars in one hour* (=invited him to try to do it). | *The prime minister narrowly avoided a* ***leadership challenge*** *last year.*
4 STOP [C] a demand from someone such as a guard to stop and give proof of who you are, and an explanation of what you are doing
5 IN LAW [C] *law* a statement made before the start of a court case that a JUROR is not acceptable

challenge² ●●● S3 W3 AWL *v* [T]
1 QUESTION STH to refuse to accept that something is right, fair, or legal: *a boy with a reputation for* ***challenging*** *the* ***authority*** *of his teachers* | **challenge a view/an idea/an assumption etc** *Viewpoints such as these are strongly challenged by environmentalists.* | *They went to the High Court to* ***challenge*** *the* ***decision***. | **challenge sb to do sth** *I challenge Dr. Carver to deny his involvement!*
2 COMPETITION to invite someone to compete or fight against you, or to try to win something → **challenger, dare**: **challenge sb to sth** *After lunch, Carey challenged me to a game of tennis.* | **[+for]** *Liverpool are challenging for the title* (=in a position where they could win).
3 STH DIFFICULT to test the skills or abilities of someone or something SYN **stimulate**: *I'm really at my best when I'm challenged.* | **challenge sb to do sth** *Every teacher ought to be challenging kids to think about current issues.*
4 STOP SB to stop someone and demand proof of who they are, and an explanation of what they are doing: *We were challenged by the security guard at the gate.*
5 IN LAW *law* to state before the start of a court case that a JUROR is not acceptable —**challenger** *n* [C]: *Lewis is his main challenger for the world title.*

chal·lenged /ˈtʃæləndʒd/ *adj* **visually/physically/mentally etc challenged** *AmE* used as a polite expression for describing someone who has difficulty doing things because they are blind etc

chal·leng·ing /ˈtʃæləndʒɪŋ/ ●○○ AWL *adj* difficult in an interesting or enjoyable way: *Teaching young children is a challenging and rewarding job.* | *a challenging problem*
THESAURUS ▸ DIFFICULT —**challengingly** *adv*

cham·ber /ˈtʃeɪmbə $ -ər/ ●○○ *n*
1 ENCLOSED SPACE [C] an enclosed space, especially in your body or inside a machine: *a combustion chamber* | *The heart has four chambers.*
2 ROOM [C] a room used for a special purpose, especially an unpleasant one: **gas/torture chamber** (=used for killing people by gas or for hurting them)
3 MEETING ROOM [C] a large room in a public building used for important meetings: *the council chamber*
4 PARLIAMENT [C] one of the two parts of a parliament or of the US Congress. For example, in Britain the upper chamber is the House of Lords and the lower chamber is the House of Commons.
5 PRIVATE ROOM [C] a word used in the past to mean a bedroom or private room: *the Queen's private chambers*
6 chambers [plural] *especially BrE* an office or offices used by BARRISTERS or judges
7 GUN [C] the part of a gun where you put the bullets

cham·ber·lain /ˈtʃeɪmbəlɪn $ -bər-/ *n* [C] an important official who managed the house of a king or queen in the past

cham·ber·maid /ˈtʃeɪmbəmeɪd $ -ər-/ *n* [C] a female worker whose job is to clean and tidy bedrooms, especially in a hotel

ˈchamber ˌmusic *n* [U] CLASSICAL music written for a small group of instruments

ˌchamber of ˈcommerce *n* (*plural* **chambers of commerce**) [C] a group of business people in a particular town or area, working together to improve trade

ˈchamber ˌorchestra *n* [C] a small group of musicians who play CLASSICAL music together

ˈchamber pot *n* [C] a round container for URINE, used in a bedroom and kept under the bed in the past

cha·me·le·on /kəˈmiːliən/ *n* [C] **1** a LIZARD that can change its colour to match the colours around it **2** someone who changes their ideas, behaviour etc to fit different situations

cham·ois /ˈʃæmwɑː $ ˈʃæmi/ *n* (*plural* **chamois**) **1** [C] a wild animal like a small goat that lives in the mountains of Europe and southwest Asia **2** (*also* **ˈchamois ˌleather** /ˈʃæmi leðər $ -ər/) [C,U] soft leather prepared from the skin of chamois, sheep, or goats and used for cleaning or polishing, or a piece of this leather → **shammy**

cham·o·mile /ˈkæməmaɪl/ *n* [C,U] another spelling of CAMOMILE

champ¹ /tʃæmp/ *v* [I,T] *BrE* **1** to bite food in a noisy way SYN **chomp 2 be champing at the bit** to be unable to wait for something patiently

champ² *n* [C] *informal* a CHAMPION: *the world champ*

cham·pagne /ʃæmˈpeɪn/ ●●○ *n* [U] a French white wine with a lot of BUBBLES, drunk on special occasions

cham·pers /ˈʃæmpəz $ -pərz/ *n* [U] *BrE informal* champagne

cham·pi·on¹ /ˈtʃæmpiən/ ●●● W3 *n* [C]
1 someone or something that has won a competition, especially in sport: *the* ***world*** *heavyweight boxing* ***champion*** | *the Olympic champion* | **reigning/defending champion** (=the champion at the present time)
2 champion of sth/sb someone who publicly fights for and defends an aim or principle, such as the rights of a group of people: *a champion of women's rights*

champion² ●○○ *v* [T] *written* to publicly fight for and defend an aim or principle, such as the rights of a group of people: *She championed the cause of religious freedom.*

cham·pi·on·ship /ˈtʃæmpiənʃɪp/ ●●● W3 *n*
1 [C] (*also* **championships** [plural]) a competition to find which player, team etc is the best in a particular sport: *the women's figure skating championships* | *Greece won the European Championship.*
2 [C] the position or period of being a champion SYN **title**: *Warwickshire are the current holders of the cricket championship.*
3 [U + of] *written* the act of championing something or someone

chance¹ /tʃɑːns $ tʃæns/ ●●● S1 W1 *n*
1 POSSIBILITY [C,U] the possibility that something will happen, especially something you want: *There's always the chance that something will go wrong.* | **[+of]** *What are the team's chances of success?* | *If we did move to London, I'd* ***stand a*** *much better* ***chance*** (=have a much better chance) *of getting a job.* | *There is little chance of her being found alive.* | ***Chances are*** (=it is likely that) *you'll be fine.*
2 OPPORTUNITY [C] a time or situation which you can use to do something that you want to do SYN **opportunity**: **chance to do sth** *Ralph was waiting for a chance to introduce himself.* | **[+of]** *our only chance of escape* | *I'm sorry, I haven't had a chance to look at it yet.* | *If someone invited me over to Florida, I'd* ***jump at the chance*** (=use the opportunity eagerly).
3 RISK **take a chance** to do something that involves risks: *The rope might break, but that's a chance we'll have to take.* | *After losing $20,000 on my last business venture, I'm* ***not taking any chances*** *this time.* | **[+on]** *He was taking a chance on a relatively new young actor.* | *He decided to take his chances in the boat.*
4 LIKELY TO SUCCEED **sb's chances** how likely it is that someone will succeed: *Ryan will be a candidate in next month's elections, but his chances are not good.* | **sb's chances of doing sth** *England's chances of winning the series have all but disappeared.* | **not fancy/not rate sb's chances** *BrE* (=think someone is unlikely to succeed) *I don't fancy their chances against Brazil.* ⚠ Don't say 'someone's chances to do something'. Say **someone's chances of doing something**.
5 LUCK [U] the way some things happen without being planned or caused by people → **fate**: **by chance** *I bumped into her quite by chance in Oxford Street.* | **leave sth to chance** (=to not plan something but just hope that everything will happen as intended) *Dave had thought of every possibility, he was leaving nothing to chance.* | **pure/sheer/blind chance** (=not at all planned) *It was pure chance that they ended up working in the same office in the same town.* | ***As chance would have it****, the one time I wanted to see her, she wasn't in.*
6 by any chance *spoken* used to ask politely whether something is true: *Are you Mrs Grant, by any chance?*
7 any chance of ...? *spoken* used to ask whether you can have something or whether something is possible: *Any chance of a cup of coffee?* | *Any chance of you coming to the party on Saturday?*
8 be in with a chance if a competitor is in with a chance, it is possible that they will win: *I think we're in with a good chance of beating them.*
9 no chance!/fat chance! *spoken* used to emphasize that you are sure something could never happen: *'Maybe your brother would lend you the money?' 'Huh, fat chance!'*
10 on the off chance if you do something on the off chance, you do it hoping for a particular result, although you know it is not likely: *I didn't really expect her to be at home. I just called on the off chance.* → **OFF-CHANCE**
11 chance would be a fine thing! *BrE spoken* used to mean that the thing you want to happen is very unlikely: *'Do you think you'll get married?' 'Chance would be a fine thing!'*
→ **game of chance** at GAME¹(15)

COLLOCATIONS - MEANING 1

VERBS

have/stand a chance (of sth) (=it is possible you will do it) *I think you have a good chance of getting the job.*
give sb a chance of doing sth (=say how likely it is that they will do it) *He has been given a fifty-fifty chance of being fit for Sunday's match.*
increase the chance of sth *Certain foods increase the chance of heart disease.*
improve the chance of sth *The book shows you how to improve your chance of success.*
reduce/lessen the chance of sth | **ruin any chance of sth** (=make it impossible for something to happen)

ADJECTIVES

a good chance (=when something is likely) *I think there is a good chance that he will say yes.*
every chance (=a good chance) *There's every chance that the baby will survive.*
some chance *There's some chance of snow later this week.*
a small/slight/slim chance *He only has a very small chance of being elected.*
no/little/not much chance *The prisoners knew there was little chance of escape.*
a one in three/four/ten etc chance (=used to say how likely something is) *People in their 30s have a one in 3,000 chance of getting the disease.*
a fair chance (=a fairly good chance) | **a sporting chance** (=a fairly good chance) | **a fighting chance** (=a small but real chance) | **a fifty-fifty chance** (=an equal chance that something will or will not happen) | **an outside/a remote chance** (=a very small chance) | **a million-to-one chance/a one in a million chance** (=when something is extremely unlikely)

COLLOCATIONS - MEANING 2

VERBS

get/have a chance to do sth *I'd like a job in which I get the chance to travel.*
give sb/offer/provide a chance *I was given the chance to play the main part in the play.*
take a chance (=accept an opportunity) *If I was offered the chance to be in the team, I'd take it.*
jump at a chance (=use an opportunity eagerly) *Ed jumped at the chance to earn some extra money.*

grab/seize a chance (=quickly use an opportunity) *As soon as she stopped speaking, I grabbed the chance to leave.*
miss/lose a chance (=not use an opportunity) *He missed a chance to score just before half time.*
throw away/pass up/turn down a chance (=not accept or use an opportunity) | **welcome the chance to do sth** | **deserve a chance** | **blow a chance** *informal* (=have a special opportunity and fail to use it)

ADJECTIVES

a second chance/another chance *The interview went badly, so I didn't think they would give me a second chance.*
sb's last chance *This is my last chance to try and pass the exam.*

PHRASES

the chance of a lifetime (=one that you are very unlikely to have again) *If you don't decide soon, you'll have missed the chance of a lifetime.*
now's your chance *spoken* (=you have the opportunity to do something now) *You're not working so now's your chance to write a book.*
given the chance/given half a chance (=if there is an opportunity to do something) *Goats will eat anything, given half a chance.*

chance² *v* **1** [T] to do something that you know involves a risk: *I wasn't sure if I'd got quite enough petrol to get me home, but I decided to **chance it**.* | *We decided not to **chance** our **luck** in the storm.* | *She'd never played before, but she was ready to **chance** her **arm*** (=take a risk by doing something which may fail). | **chance doing sth** *I decided to stay where I was. I couldn't chance being seen.* **2** [I] *literary* to happen in a way which is not expected and not planned: **chance to do sth** *She chanced to be passing when I came out of the house.* | ***It chanced that** we both went to Paris that year.*

chance on/upon/across sb/sth *phr v formal* to find something or meet someone when you are not expecting to: *Henry chanced upon some valuable coins in the attic.*

chance³ *adj* [only before noun] not planned or expected SYN **accidental**: **chance meeting/encounter/event etc** *A chance meeting with a journalist changed everything.* | *A **chance remark** by one of his colleagues got him thinking.*

chan·cel /ˈtʃɑːnsəl $ ˈtʃæn-/ *n* [C] the part of a church where the priests and the CHOIR (=singers) sit

chan·cel·ler·y /ˈtʃɑːnsələri $ ˈtʃæn-/ *n* (*plural* **chancelleries**) [C] **1** the building in which a chancellor has his or her office **2** the officials who work in a chancellor's office **3** the offices of an official representative of a foreign country SYN **chancery**

chan·cel·lor /ˈtʃɑːnsələ $ ˈtʃænsələr/ *n* [C] **1** the Chancellor of the Exchequer **2 a)** the person who officially represents a British university on special occasions **b)** the person in charge of some American universities **3** the leader of the government or the main government minister of some countries: *Helmut Kohl, the former German Chancellor*

ˌChancellor of the Exˈchequer *n* (*plural* **Chancellors of the Exchequer**) [C] the British government minister in charge of taxes and government spending

chan·ce·ry /ˈtʃɑːnsəri $ ˈtʃæn-/ *n* [singular] **1** *especially BrE* a government office that collects and stores official papers **2** the part of the British system of law courts which deals with EQUITY **3** the offices of an official representative of a foreign country SYN **chancellery**

chanc·y /ˈtʃɑːnsi $ ˈtʃænsi/ *adj* not certain, or involving a lot of risk SYN **risky**: *Acting professionally is a chancy business.* —**chanciness** *n* [U]

chan·de·lier /ˌʃændəˈlɪə $ -ˈlɪr/ *n* [C] a large round frame for holding CANDLES or lights that hangs from the ceiling and is decorated with small pieces of glass → see picture at **LAMP**

chand·ler /ˈtʃɑːndlə $ ˈtʃændlər/ *n* [C] someone who made or sold CANDLES in the past → **SHIP'S CHANDLER**

change¹ /tʃeɪndʒ/ ●●● S1 W1 *v*

1 BECOME DIFFERENT/MAKE STH DIFFERENT [I,T] to become different, or to make something become different: *Susan has changed a lot since I last saw her.* | *Changing your eating habits is the best way to lose weight.* | *The leaves on trees change colour in the autumn.* | **change (from sth) to sth** *He changed from being a nice lad to being rude and unhelpful.* | **[+into]** *The hissing sound gradually changed into a low hum.* | **change sb/sth into sth** *A witch had changed him into a mouse.* | **change sth to sth** *Mueller changed his name to Miller when he became a U.S. citizen.*

2 START DOING/USING STH DIFFERENT [I,T] to stop doing or using one thing, and start doing or using something else instead SYN **switch**: *She changed jobs in May.* | **change (from sth) to sth** *The company has recently changed to a more powerful computer system.* | *The ship changed course and headed south.* | *The company has had to change direction because of developments in technology.* | *Piper awkwardly tried to **change the subject*** (=talk about something else).

3 REPLACE STH [T] to put or use something new or different in place of something else, especially because it is old, damaged, or broken: *Three boys were changing a tyre by the side of the road.* | *When I lost my keys, we had to change all the locks.* | **change sth (from sth) to sth** *The time of the meeting has been changed from 11:00 to 10:30.* | *How often do you change cars* (=buy a new car and sell the old one)?

4 change your mind to change your decision, plan, or opinion about something: *Her father tried to get her to change her mind.* | **[+about]** *If you change your mind about the job, just give me a call.*

5 change sides to leave one party, group etc and join an opposing party, group etc: *It's quite rare for politicians to change sides.*

6 CLOTHES a) [I,T] to take off your clothes and put on different ones: *Francis came in while Jay was changing.* | *Change your dress – that one looks dirty.* | **[+into/out of]** *Sara changed into her swimsuit and ran out for a quick swim.* | *You'd better go and **get changed**.* **b)** [T] to put a clean NAPPY on a baby, or to put clean clothes on a baby or small child: *I bathed him and changed his diaper.* | *Can you change the baby?*

7 BED [T] to take the dirty SHEETS off a bed and put on clean ones

8 EXCHANGE GOODS [T] *BrE* **a)** to take back to a shop something that you have bought and get something different instead, especially because there is something wrong with it SYN **exchange** *AmE*: **change sth for sth** *I bought these gloves for my daughter, but they're too large. Can I change them for a smaller size?* **b)** to give a customer something different instead of what they have bought, especially because there is something wrong with it SYN **exchange** *AmE*: *I'm sure the shop will change them for you.*

9 EXCHANGE MONEY [T] **a)** to get smaller units of money that add up to the same value as a larger unit: *Can you change a £20 note?* **b)** to get money from one country for the same value of money from another country: **change sth into/for sth** *I want to change my dollars into pesos, please.*

10 TRAINS/BUSES/AIRCRAFT [I,T] to get off one train, bus, or aircraft and onto another in order to continue your journey: **[+at]** *Passengers for Liverpool should change at Crewe.* | **change trains/buses/planes etc** *I had to change planes in Denver.* | **all change!** (=used to tell passengers to get off a train because it does not go any further)

11 change hands if property changes hands, it starts to belong to someone else: *The house has changed hands three times in the last two years.*

12 change places (with sb) a) to give someone your place and take their place: *Would you mind changing places with me so I can sit next to my friend?* **b)** to take someone else's social position or situation in life instead of yours: *She may be rich, but I wouldn't want to change places with her.*

13 GEAR [I,T] to put the engine of a vehicle into a higher or lower GEAR in order to go faster or slower: **change (into/**

out of) gear *Change into second gear as you approach the corner.* | **[+up/down]** *BrE*: *Change down before you get to the hill.*
14 change your tune *informal* to start expressing a different attitude and reacting in a different way, after something has happened: *The question is, will the president change his tune on taxes?*
15 WIND [I] if the wind changes, it starts to blow in a different direction
16 change your spots to change your character completely: *US business has changed its spots in recent years.* → **chop and change** at CHOP[1](3)

GRAMMAR

Change belongs to a group of verbs where the same noun can be the subject of the verb or its object.
• You can say: *They've changed the password.* In this sentence, 'the password' is the object of **change**.
• You can say: *The password has changed.* In this sentence, 'the password' is the subject of **change**.
GRAMMAR GUIDE ▸ VERBS

THESAURUS

TO CHANGE SOMETHING

change to make someone or something different: *Unfortunately, there's nothing we can do to change the situation.* | *Being at college has changed her – she's much more confident now.*
alter *especially written* to change something so that it is better or more suitable: *You can alter the colour and size of the image using a remote control.* | *Can we alter the date of the meeting?*
adapt to change something slightly in order to improve it or make it more suitable: *How much would it cost to adapt the existing equipment?* | *You can adapt the recipe to suit your own requirements.*
adjust to make small changes in the position or level of something in order to improve it or make it more suitable: *How do you adjust the volume on the television?* | *He adjusted his tie in the mirror.*
modify *especially written* to make small changes to something such as a piece of equipment, a set of ideas, or a way of behaving in order to improve it or use it in a different way: *He's modified his opinions since then.* | *a modified version of the original program*
reform to change a law, system, organization etc so that it is fairer or more effective: *plans to reform the tax system* | *Health care needs to be completely reformed.*
revise to change a plan, idea, law etc because of new information and ideas: *In July, China revised the rules for foreign investment.* | *The findings could force the scientists to revise their ideas about climate change.*
reorganize to change the way that a system or organization works: *We've had to reorganize our database.* | *During the 1980s, the government reorganized the civil service.*
restructure to make big changes to the way something is organized, especially a large political or economic system or a big company, in order to make it more effective: *The company has been restructured from top to bottom.*

TO CHANGE SOMETHING COMPLETELY

transform to change something completely, especially so that it is much better: *Well, you've certainly transformed this place – it looks great!* | *Putin transformed the Russian economy.*
revolutionize to completely and permanently change the way people do something or think about something, especially because of a new idea or invention: *Computers have revolutionized the way we work.* | *This important discovery revolutionized our understanding of the universe.*

change sth ↔ **around** *phr v* to move things into different positions: *When we'd changed the furniture around, the room looked bigger.*

change over *phr v* to stop doing or using one thing and start doing or using another → **changeover**: *Complete all the exercises on one leg, then change over.* | **[+to]** *We hope to change over to the new software by next month.*

change² ●●● S1 W1 *n*

1 THINGS BECOMING DIFFERENT [C,U] the process or result of something or someone becoming different: *I find it hard to cope with change.* | *scientists worried about climatic change* | **[+in]** *changes in the immigration laws* | *A change in personality may mean your teenager has a drug problem.* | **[+of]** *a change of temperature* | *No* ***major changes*** *were made to the book.* | **change for the better/worse** (=a change that makes a situation better or worse) *There was a change for the better in the patient's condition.* | **social/political/economic etc change** *the sweeping political changes after the fall of communism* | *She had a* ***change of heart*** (=change in attitude) *and decided to stay.* | *Family life has* ***undergone*** *dramatic* ***change*** *in recent years.*
2 FROM ONE THING TO ANOTHER [C] the fact of one thing or person being replaced by another: *The car needs an oil change.* | **[+of]** *a change of government* | *a change of address* | **change from sth to sth** *the gradual change from grasslands to true desert* | *The government has* ***made*** *some major policy* ***changes****.*
3 PLEASANT NEW SITUATION [singular] a situation or experience that is different from what happened before, and is usually interesting or enjoyable: **[+from]** *The morning was cool; a* ***welcome change*** *from the heat of the day before.* | **for a change** *How about dinner out for a change?* | **it/that makes a change** (=used to say that something is better than and different from usual) *'Ron's buying the drinks.' 'That makes a change.'* | **change of scene/air/pace etc** (=when you go to a different place or do something different) *The patients benefit greatly from a change of scenery.* | **a change is as good as a rest** (=used to say that starting to do something different is as good as having a rest)
4 MONEY [U] **a)** the money that you get back when you have paid for something with more money than it costs: *Here's your change, sir.* **b)** money in the form of coins, not paper money: **in change** *I have about a dollar in change.* | *Matt emptied the* ***loose change*** *from his pockets.* | *A beggar asked for some* ***spare change*** (=coins that you do not need). **c)** coins or paper money that you give in exchange for the same amount of money in a larger unit: **change for £1/$10** *Excuse me, have you got change for a pound?* | **make change** *AmE* (=give someone change) *Can you make change for $20?* THESAURUS ▸ MONEY
5 small change a) coins you have that do not have a high value: *I only had about a pound in small change.* **b)** used to emphasize that something is a small amount of money when it is compared to a larger amount: *The program costs $20 million a year, small change by Washington standards.*
6 change of clothes/underwear etc an additional set of clothes that you have with you, for example when you are travelling
7 TRAIN/BUS/AIRCRAFT [C] a situation in which you get off one train, bus, or aircraft and get on another in order to continue your journey: *Even with a change of trains, the subway is quicker than a cab at rush hour.*
8 get no change out of sb *BrE spoken* to get no useful information or help from someone: *I wouldn't bother asking Richard – you'll get no change out of him.* → **ring the changes** at RING²(6)

COLLOCATIONS

ADJECTIVES

big/major *Going to a new school is a big change for children.*
slight/small/minor *The proposed changes were relatively minor.*
gradual *There has been a gradual change in the weather.*
dramatic/drastic/radical (=very big, especially in way that is surprising) *The Industrial Revolution was a period of dramatic change.*
significant *The change in blood pressure was not significant.*

C

marked (=very noticeable) *There was a marked change in his behaviour.*
fundamental *Reducing waste requires a fundamental change in attitude.*
social/political/economic etc change *Demands for political and social change are growing.*
sweeping changes (=affecting many things or people, especially because of an official decision) *There are likely to be sweeping changes in the company.*
far-reaching changes (=important and having a great effect that will last a long time) *The Internet has brought about far-reaching changes in the way we work.*

VERBS

make a change *We've had to make some changes to the design.*
introduce a change *A number of changes were introduced to the curriculum.*
bring (about) change (*also* **effect a change** *formal*) (=cause change) *The war brought about radical social change.*
see/notice/observe a change *I saw a big change in her when I met her again.*
undergo a change (=be affected by a change) *The body undergoes a number of changes during this time.*
signal a change (=be a sign of a change)

PHRASES

the pace/rate of change *People sometimes feel alarmed by the pace of technological change.*

change·a·ble /ˈtʃeɪndʒəbəl/ *adj* likely to change, or changing often OPP **reliable**: *changeable weather*

changed /tʃeɪndʒd/ *adj* **1 a changed man/woman** someone who has become very different from what they were before, as a result of a very important experience: *Since she stopped drinking, she's a changed woman.* **2** relating to a change in someone's situation: *Businesses need to adapt to changed circumstances.*

change·less /ˈtʃeɪndʒləs/ *adj* never seeming to change: *a changeless desert landscape*

change·ling /ˈtʃeɪndʒlɪŋ/ *n* [C] *literary* a baby that is believed to have been secretly exchanged for another baby by FAIRIES

ˌchange of ˈlife *n* [singular] the MENOPAUSE

change·o·ver /ˈtʃeɪndʒəʊvə $ -ˌoʊvər/ *n* [C] a change from one activity, system, or way of working to another: **changeover (from sth) to sth** *a changeover from military to civilian government*

ˈchange purse *n* [C] *AmE* a small bag in which coins are kept SYN **purse** *BrE*

ˈchanging room *n* [C] *BrE* a room where people change their clothes when they play sports, go swimming etc SYN **locker room** *AmE*

ˈchanging ˌtable *n* [C] a special piece of furniture that you put a baby on when you change its NAPPY

chan·nel¹ /ˈtʃænl/ ●●● S3 W2 AWL *n* [C]
1 TELEVISION a television station and all the programmes that it broadcasts: *the news on Channel 4 | The kids are watching cartoons on the Disney Channel. | What channel is 'ER' on? | He* **changed channels** *to watch the basketball game.*
2 FOR GETTING INFORMATION/GOODS ETC a system or method that you use to send or obtain information, goods, permission etc: *The U.S. is working through* **diplomatic channels** *to find a solution. | The new software will be sold through existing* **distribution channels**. | **[+of]** *It is important that we open* **channels of communication** *with the police.*
3 SEA/RIVER **a)** an area of water that connects two larger areas of water: *St George's Channel* **b) the Channel** *BrE* the area of water between France and England SYN **the English Channel c)** the deepest part of a river, HARBOUR, or sea, especially where it is deep enough to allow ships to sail in
4 WATER a passage that water or other liquids flow along: *an irrigation channel*
5 RADIO a particular range of SOUND WAVES which can be used to send and receive radio messages
6 IN A SURFACE a long deep line cut into a surface or a long deep space between two edges SYN **groove**: *The sliding doors fit into these plastic channels.*
7 WAY TO EXPRESS YOURSELF a way of expressing your thoughts, feelings, or physical energy SYN **vehicle**: **[+for]** *Art provides a channel for the children's creativity.*

channel² ●○○ AWL *v* (**channelled**, **channelling** *BrE*, **channeled**, **channeling** *AmE*) [T]
1 to control and direct something such as money or energy towards a particular purpose SYN **direct**: **channel sth into sth** *Most of his energy was channeled into writing and lecturing.* | **channel sth to sb** *Profits are channelled to conservation groups.* | **channel sth through sth** *The famine relief money was channelled through the UN.*
2 to control or direct people or things to a particular place, work, situation etc: **channel sb/sth into sth** *Women were likely to be channeled into jobs as teachers or nurses. | Drugs from government pharmacies were being channeled into illegal drug markets.*
3 to cut a long deep line in something: *Water had channelled grooves in the rock.*
4 to send water through a passage: *An efficient irrigation system channels water to the crops.*
5 to allow a spirit to come into your body and speak through you, or to tell people a message that you have received in this way: *She claims to channel the spirit of a 2,000-year-old hunter.*
6 to look or sound like a famous person, especially someone who is dead: *In her latest video, Kylie is channelling Marilyn Monroe.*

chan·nel·ling *BrE*, **channeling** *AmE* /ˈtʃænl-ɪŋ/ *n* [U] a practice based on the belief that dead people can communicate with living people by making their spirit enter a living person's body and speaking through them —**channeller** *n* [C]

ˈchannel ˌsurfing (*also* **ˈchannel ˌhopping**) *n* [U] when you change from one television channel to another, only watching a few minutes of any programme

chant¹ /tʃɑːnt $ tʃænt/ ●○○ *v* [I,T]
1 to repeat a word or phrase again and again: *protesters chanting anti-government slogans*
2 to sing or say a religious song or prayer in a way that involves using only one note or TONE: *a priest chanting the liturgy*

chant² ●○○ *n* [C]
1 words or phrases that are repeated again and again by a group of people: *Others in the crowd took up the chant* (=began chanting). | **[+of]** *chants of 'oh no, we won't go'*
2 a regularly repeated tune, often with many words sung on one note, especially used for religious prayers —**chanter** *n* [C]

chan·try /ˈtʃɑːntri $ ˈtʃæn-/ (*also* **ˈchantry ˌchapel**) *n* (*plural* **chantries**) [C] a small church or part of a church paid for by someone so that priests can pray for them there after they die

Cha·nu·kah /ˈhɑːnəkə $ ˈkɑːnəkə, ˈhɑː-/ *n* [C,U] HANUKKAH

cha·os /ˈkeɪ-ɒs $ -ɑːs/ ●●○ *n* [U]
1 a situation in which everything is happening in a confused way and nothing is organized or arranged in order: *The country was plunged into economic chaos.* | **complete/utter/absolute etc chaos** *There was total chaos on the roads.* | **in chaos** *The kitchen was in chaos.*
2 the state of the universe before there was any order

cha·ot·ic /keɪˈɒtɪk $ -ˈɑːtɪk/ ●○○ *adj* a chaotic situation is one in which everything is happening in a confused way: *a chaotic mixture of images*

chap /tʃæp/ ●●○ S3 *n*
1 [C] *especially BrE* a man, especially a man you know and like: *a decent sort of chap*
2 chaps [plural] protective leather covers worn over your trousers when riding a horse → **CHAPPED**

chap·ar·ral /ʃæpəˈræl/ *n* [U] *AmE* land on which small OAK trees grow close together

chap·book /ˈtʃæpbʊk/ *n* [C] *AmE* a small printed book, usually consisting of writings about literature, poetry, or religion

chap·el /ˈtʃæpəl/ ●●○ *n*
1 [C] a small church, or a room in a hospital, prison, big church etc in which Christians pray and have religious services
2 [C] a building where Christians who are Nonconformists have religious services
3 [U] *BrE* the religious services held in a chapel: *Bethan* ***goes to chapel*** *every Sunday.*
4 [C] *BrE* the members of a UNION in the newspaper or printing industry

chap·e·rone[1], **chaperon** /ˈʃæpərəʊn $ -roʊn/ *n* [C] **1** an older woman in the past who went out with a young unmarried woman on social occasions and was responsible for her behaviour **2** *AmE* someone, usually a parent or teacher, who is responsible for young people on social occasions: *Three parents went on the school ski trip as chaperones.*

chaperone[2], **chaperon** *v* [T] to go somewhere with someone as a chaperone

chap·lain /ˈtʃæplɪn/ *n* [C] a priest or other religious minister responsible for the religious needs of a club, the army, a hospital etc: *the prison chaplain*

chap·lain·cy /ˈtʃæplənsi/ *n* (*plural* **chaplaincies**) [C] the job of being a chaplain, or the place where a chaplain works

chapped /tʃæpt/ *adj* chapped lips or hands are sore, dry, and cracked, especially as a result of cold weather or wind —**chap** *v* [T]

chap·py /ˈtʃæpi/ *n* (*plural* **chappies**) [C] *BrE* a CHAP

chap·ter /ˈtʃæptə $ -ər/ ●●● S3 W1 AWL *n* [C]
1 one of the parts into which a book is divided: *Read Chapter 11 as your homework.* | *This chapter discusses power, and how people use it.* **THESAURUS** ▸ PART
2 a particular period or event in someone's life or in history → **era**: **[+of]** *a new chapter of peace and cooperation* | **[+in]** *the noblest chapter in our history*
3 all the priests belonging to a CATHEDRAL, or a meeting of these priests
4 the local members of a large organization such as a club: *the local chapter of the American Legion*
5 give/quote sb chapter and verse to give someone exact details about where to find some information
6 a chapter of accidents *BrE* a series of unlucky events coming one after another

chap·ter·house /ˈtʃæptəhaʊs $ -ər-/ *n* [C] a building where the priests belonging to a CATHEDRAL meet

char[1] /tʃɑː $ tʃɑːr/ *v* (**charred**, **charring**) **1** [I,T] to burn something so that its outside becomes black: *Roast the peppers until the skin begins to char and blister.* → **CHARRED**
2 [I] *BrE old-fashioned* to work as a cleaner in a house, office, public building etc

char[2] *n BrE old-fashioned* **1** [C] a CHARWOMAN **2** [U] tea: *a cup of char*

char·a·banc /ˈʃærəbæŋ/ *n* [C] *BrE old-fashioned* a large comfortable bus used for pleasure trips

char·ac·ter /ˈkærəktə $ -ər/ ●●● S1 W1 *n*
1 ALL SB'S QUALITIES [C usually singular] the particular combination of qualities that makes someone a particular type of person → **characteristic**: *He has a cheerful but quiet character.* | *Children grow up with a mixture of* ***character traits*** (=character qualities) *from both sides of their family.* | *his temper and other* ***character flaws*** (=bad qualities) | **in character/out of character** (=typical or untypical of someone's character) *He swore, which was out of character for him.* | **the English/French etc character** *Openness is at the heart of the American character.* | **character sketch** (=a description of someone's character)
2 PERSON [C] **a)** a person in a book, play, film etc: *Candida is the most interesting character in the play.* | *In the story, the main character has left his girlfriend and baby.* | *Everyone recognizes Disney's cartoon characters.* **b)** a person of a particular type, especially a strange or dishonest one: *a couple of shady characters standing on the corner* | *I'm considered a* ***reformed character*** *these days* (=someone who has stopped doing bad things). **c)** an interesting and unusual person: *Linda was something of a character.*
3 QUALITIES OF STH [singular, U] the particular combination of features and qualities that makes a thing or place different from all others SYN **nature**: **[+of]** *The whole character of the school has changed.* | *the unspoilt character of the coast* | **in character** *The southern state became more nationalist in character.*
4 MORAL STRENGTH [U] a combination of qualities such as courage, loyalty, and honesty that are admired and regarded as valuable: *a woman of great character* | *Schools were created to teach reading and mathematics, not moral character.* | *It takes* ***strength of character*** *to admit you are wrong.* | *Sport can be* ***character building*** (=develop good moral qualities).
5 INTERESTING QUALITY [U] a quality that makes someone or something special and interesting: *a red wine with a meaty character* | *suburban houses that lack character*
6 REPUTATION [U] *formal* the opinion that people have about whether you are a good person and can be trusted: *a man* ***of*** *previous* ***good character*** | *The campaign was accused of* ***character assassination*** (=an unfair attack on someone's character) *because of its negative ads.* | *His defence called several people as* ***character witnesses*** (=people who think that someone has a good character). | *Mr Wetherby wrote him a* ***character reference*** (=a statement about his good qualities).
7 LETTER/SIGN [C] a letter, mark, or sign used in writing, printing, or on a computer: *the Chinese character for 'horse'*

COLLOCATIONS – MEANING 2a

ADJECTIVES/NOUN + character

the main/central/leading character *Alec is the central character in the play.*
a minor character *Two of the minor characters get killed.*
a television/movie/cartoon character *Who's your favourite television character?*
a comic/tragic character (=a funny or sad one) *Homer Simpson is a great comic character.*
fictional/fictitious (=not existing in real life) *People sometimes forget that television characters are fictional.*
convincing (=seeming like a real person) *The characters were totally convincing.*
a sympathetic character (=one you like)

VERBS

play a character *I wanted to play the character of Danny.*
portray a character (=show one in a play, book, film etc) *The main characters are brilliantly portrayed.*

ˈcharacter ˌactor *n* [C] an actor who typically plays unusual characters, rather than the most important characters

char·ac·ter·ise /ˈkærəktəraɪz/ *v* a British spelling of CHARACTERIZE

char·ac·ter·is·tic[1] /ˌkærəktəˈrɪstɪk◂/ ●●○ S3 W2 *n* [C usually plural] a quality or feature of something or someone that is typical of them and easy to recognize: **[+of]** *a baby discovering the physical characteristics of objects* | **defining/distinguishing characteristic** (=one that separates someone or something from others of the same type) *Violent images are a defining characteristic of his work.*

characteristic[2] ●●○ *adj* very typical of a particular thing or of someone's character: *the* ***highly characteristic*** (=very typical) *flint walls of the local houses* | **[+of]** *the qualities that were characteristic of the Nixon administration* **THESAURUS** ▸ TYPICAL —**characteristically** /-kli/ *adv*

REGISTER
In everyday English, people usually say **typical** rather than **characteristic**: *The building is* ***typical*** *of those in the area.*

char·ac·ter·i·za·tion (*also* **-isation** *BrE*) /ˌkærəktəraɪˈzeɪʃən $ -tərə-/ *n* [C,U] **1** the way in which a writer makes a person in a book, film, or play seem like a real person: *Pilcher's books have humour, good characterization, and lively dialogue.* **2** the way in which the character of a real person or thing is described: **characterization of sb/sth as sth** *the characterization of the enemy as 'fanatics'*

char·ac·ter·ize (*also* **-ise** *BrE*) /ˈkærəktəraɪz/ ●●○ W3 *v* [T]
1 to describe the qualities of someone or something in a particular way SYN **portray**: **characterize sb as (being) sth** *The group was characterized as being well-educated and liberal.*
2 to be typical of a person, place, or thing: *Bright colours characterize his paintings.*

char·ac·ter·less /ˈkærəktələs $ -tər-/ *adj* not having any special or interesting qualities: *a characterless modern building*

C

cha·rade /ʃəˈrɑːd $ ʃəˈreɪd/ *n* **1 charades** [U] a game in which one person uses actions and no words to show the meaning of a word or phrase, and other people have to guess what it is **2** [C] a situation in which people behave as though something is true or serious, when it is not really true: *Unless more money is given to schools, all this talk of improving education is just a charade.*

char·broil /ˈtʃɑːbrɔɪl $ ˈtʃɑːr-/ *v* [T] *AmE* to cook food over a very hot charcoal fire —**charbroiled** *adj*

char·coal /ˈtʃɑːkəʊl $ ˈtʃɑːrkoʊl/ *n* **1** [U] a black substance made of burnt wood that can be used as FUEL: *cooking over a charcoal fire* **2** [C,U] a stick of this substance used for drawing: *a sketch drawn in charcoal* **3** (*also* ˌ**charcoal ˈgrey**) [U] a dark grey colour —**charcoal** *adj*

chard /tʃɑːd $ tʃɑːrd/ *n* [U] a vegetable with large leaves

charge[1] /tʃɑːdʒ $ tʃɑːrdʒ/ ●●● S1 W1 *n*
1 PRICE [C,U] the amount of money you have to pay for goods or services: **[+of]** *an admission charge of $5* | **[+for]** *There is a charge for the use of the swimming pool.* | *Guided tours are provided* **at no charge**. | *Your order will be sent* **free of charge** (=with no cost). THESAURUS ▸ COST
2 CONTROL [U] the position of having control or responsibility for a group of people or an activity: **in charge (of sth)** *He asked to speak to the person in charge.* | *the officer in charge of the investigation* | *Stern* **put** *Travis* **in charge of** (=gave him control of) *the research team.* | *Owens came in and* **took charge of** (=took control of) *the situation.* | *A commander in each county was to* **have charge of** *the local militia.*
3 SB/STH YOU LOOK AFTER **a) be in/under sb's charge** if someone or something is in your charge, you are responsible for looking after them: *teachers that do their best for the children in their charge* | *The files were left in your charge.* **b)** [C] *formal* someone that you are responsible for looking after: *Sarah bought some chocolate for her three young charges.*
4 CRIME [C] an official statement by the police that someone may be guilty of a crime: **[+against]** *He was found guilty of all six charges against him.* | **[+of]** *Higgins is facing a charge of armed robbery.* | **on a charge (of sth)** *The following morning, he was arrested on a charge of burglary.*
5 BLAME [C] a written or spoken statement blaming someone for doing something bad or illegal SYN **allegation**: **charge that** *the charge that tobacco companies target young people with their ads* | **[+of]** *a charge of racial discrimination against the company* | **deny/counter a charge** (=say that a charge is untrue) *Wallace denied charges that he had lied to investigators.* | **lay/leave yourself open to a charge of sth** (=be likely to be blamed for something) *The speech laid him open to charges of political bias.*
6 ATTACK [C] an attack in which soldiers or animals move towards someone or something very quickly
7 EFFORT **lead the charge** to make a strong effort to do something: *It was small businesses that led the charge against health care changes.*
8 ELECTRICITY [U] electricity that is put into a piece of electrical equipment such as a BATTERY: **on charge** (=taking in a charge of electricity) *Leave the battery on charge all night.*
9 EXPLOSIVE [C] an explosive put into something such as a bomb or gun
10 STRENGTH OF FEELINGS [singular] the power of strong feelings: *Cases of child abuse have a strong emotional charge.*
11 get a charge out of sth *AmE spoken* to be excited by something and enjoy it very much: *I got a real charge out of seeing my niece take her first steps.*
12 AN ORDER TO DO STH [C] *formal* an order to do something: **charge to do sth** *The old servant fulfilled his master's charge to care for the children.* → **reverse the charges** at REVERSE[1](6)

COLLOCATIONS – MEANING 1

ADJECTIVES/NOUN + charge

a small charge *For a small charge guests can use the hotel sauna.*
an extra/additional charge *Breakfast may be served in your bedroom at no extra charge.*
free of charge (=with no cost) *Delivery is free of charge.*
sb's charges are high/low (=you have to pay a lot/a little) *His charges are too high.*
a fixed charge | **a nominal charge** (=a very small amount of money) | **a minimum charge** (=an amount that is the least you can pay) | **a service charge** (=for service in a hotel, restaurant etc) | **an admission charge** (=for being allowed to enter a place) | **a call-out charge** *BrE* (=that you must pay a workman to come to your home) | **bank charges** (=fees charged by a bank for some services)

VERBS

pay a charge *There will be a small charge to pay.*
make a charge (=ask you to pay a charge) *We make no charge for this service.*
incur a charge *formal* (=result in you paying a charge) *All cancellations incur a charge.*
introduce/impose a charge | **waive a charge** (=allow you not to pay it)

COLLOCATIONS – MEANING 4

ADJECTIVES/NOUN + charge

a murder/burglary/drugs etc charge *He appeared in court on fraud charges.*
criminal charges *The investigation resulted in criminal charges against three police officers.*
a serious charge *Drinking and driving is a very serious charge.*
a felony charge *AmE* (=for a serious crime)

VERBS

press/bring charges (=make someone be brought to court for a crime) *Sometimes the victim of an assault does not want to press charges.*
face charges (=have been charged with a crime) *A farmer is facing charges of cruelty and neglect.*
deny/admit a charge *All three men denied the charge of manslaughter.*
plead guilty to a charge (=say formally in court that you are guilty) | **drop the charges** (=decide not to go on with a court case) | **dismiss the charges** (=say that a court case should not continue) | **be released without charge** | **be convicted of/on a charge** (=be judged to be guilty) | **be acquitted of/on a charge** (=be judged to be not guilty)

charge[2] ●●● S1 W2 *v*
1 MONEY **a)** [I,T] to ask someone for a particular amount of money for something you are selling: *The hotel charges $125 a night.* | **charge sb £10/$50 etc (for sth)** *The restaurant charged us £40 for the wine.* | **charge sth at sth** *Calls will be charged at 44p per minute.* | **[+for]** *We won't charge for delivery if you pay now.* | **charge rent/a fee/interest etc** *The gallery charges an entrance fee.* **b) charge sth to sb's account/room etc** to record the cost of something on someone's account, so that they can pay for it later:

Wilson charged the drinks to his room. | *Use a courier and charge it to the department.* **c)** [T] *AmE* to pay for something with a CREDIT CARD: **charge sth on sth** *I charged the shoes on Visa.* | *'How would you like to pay?' 'I'll* ***charge it****.'*
2 CRIME [T] to state officially that someone may be guilty of a crime: **charge sb with sth** *Gibbons has been charged with murder.* THESAURUS ACCUSE
3 BLAME SB [T] *formal* to say publicly that you think someone has done something wrong: **charge that** *Demonstrators have charged that the police used excessive force against them.*
4 RUN [I always + adv/prep] to deliberately run or walk somewhere quickly: **[+around/through/out etc]** *The boys charged noisily into the water.* THESAURUS RUN
5 ATTACK [I,T] to deliberately rush quickly towards someone or something in order to attack them: *Then, with a final effort, our men charged the enemy for the last time.* | **[+at/towards/into]** *The bear charged towards her at full speed.*
6 ELECTRICITY [I,T] (*also* **charge up**) if a BATTERY charges, or if you charge it, it takes in and stores electricity: *The shaver can be charged up.*
7 ORDER SB [T] *formal* to order someone to do something or make them responsible for it: **charge sb with doing sth** *The commission is charged with investigating war crimes.*
8 GUN [T] *old use* to load a gun
9 GLASS [T] *BrE formal* to fill a glass → CHARGED

charge·a·ble /ˈtʃɑːdʒəbəl $ ˈtʃɑːr-/ *adj BrE* **1** needing to be paid for: *Advice will be given as a chargeable service.* **2** something that is chargeable must have tax paid on it: *chargeable assets*

ˈcharge acˌcount *n* [C] *AmE* an account you have at a shop that allows you to take goods away with you now and pay later

ˈcharge card *n* [C] a plastic card from a particular shop that you can use to buy goods there and pay for them later → **credit card**

charged /tʃɑːdʒd $ tʃɑːrdʒd/ *adj* a charged situation or subject makes people feel very angry, anxious, or excited, and is likely to cause arguments or violence: *the* ***charged atmosphere*** *in the room* | *a* ***highly charged*** *debate*

char·gé d'af·faires /ˌʃɑːʒeɪ dæˈfeə $ ˌʃɑːrʒeɪ dæˈfer/ *n* (*plural* **chargés d'affaires** *(same pronunciation)*) [C] an official who represents a particular government during the absence of an AMBASSADOR or in a country where there is no ambassador

ˈcharge hand *n* [C] *BrE* a worker in charge of other workers, whose position is below that of a FOREMAN

ˈcharge nurse *n* [C] a nurse who is responsible for the work done in one part of a hospital

ˌCharge of the ˈLight Briˌgade, the an unsuccessful attack made by the British CAVALRY (=soldiers riding horses) during the Crimean War. Many British soldiers were killed because they were ordered to ride into a valley full of Russian soldiers with heavy guns. Tennyson describes this battle in his poem *The Charge of the Light Brigade.*

charg·er /ˈtʃɑːdʒə $ ˈtʃɑːrdʒər/ *n* [C] **1** a piece of equipment used to put electricity into a BATTERY **2** *literary* a horse that a soldier or KNIGHT rides in battle

ˈcharge sheet *n* [C] a record kept in a police station of the names of people the police have stated may be guilty of a particular crime

char·i·ot /ˈtʃæriət/ *n* [C] a vehicle with two wheels pulled by a horse, used in ancient times in battles and races

char·i·o·teer /ˌtʃæriəˈtɪə $ -ˈtɪr/ *n* [C] the driver of a chariot

cha·ris·ma /kəˈrɪzmə/ ●○○ *n* [U] a natural ability to attract and interest other people and make them admire you: *He lacks charisma.*

char·is·mat·ic /ˌkærəzˈmætɪk◂/ ●○○ *adj*
1 having charisma: *Martin Luther King was a very charismatic speaker.*
2 **charismatic church/movement** groups of Christians who believe that God can give them special abilities, for example the ability to cure illness

char·it·a·ble /ˈtʃærətəbəl/ *adj* **1** relating to giving help to the poor → **charity**: *charitable groups* | *a charitable donation* **2** kind and sympathetic in the way you judge people OPP **uncharitable**: *a charitable view of his actions* —**charitably** *adv*

char·i·ty /ˈtʃærəti/ ●●○ S3 W3 *n* (*plural* **charities**)
1 [C] an organization that gives money, goods, or help to people who are poor, sick etc → **charitable**: *Several charities sent aid to the flood victims.* | **charity event/walk/concert etc** (=an event organized to collect money for a charity) THESAURUS ORGANIZATION
2 [U] charity organizations in general: *All the money raised by the concert will* ***go to charity****.* | **for charity** *The children raised over £200 for charity.*
3 [U] money or gifts given to help people who are poor, sick etc: *refugees living on charity* | *Her pride wouldn't allow her to* ***accept charity****.*
4 [U] *formal* kindness or sympathy that you show towards other people: *Mother Teresa's works of charity* | *Newspaper reports* ***showed*** *him little* ***charity****.*
5 **charity begins at home** a phrase meaning that you should take care of your own family, country etc before you help other people

ˈcharity shop *n* [C] *BrE* a shop that sells used goods that are given to it, in order to collect money for a charity SYN **thrift shop**

char·la·dy /ˈtʃɑːˌleɪdi $ ˈtʃɑːr-/ *n* (*plural* **charladies**) [C] *BrE old-fashioned* a CHARWOMAN

char·la·tan /ˈʃɑːlətən $ ˈʃɑːr-/ *n* [C] *literary* someone who pretends to have special skills or knowledge - used to show disapproval

Charles·ton /ˈtʃɑːlstən $ ˈtʃɑːrl-/ *n* **the Charleston** a quick dance popular in the 1920s

char·ley horse /ˌtʃɑːli ˈhɔːs $ ˌtʃɑːrli ˈhɔːrs/ *n* [C, singular] *AmE informal* a pain in a large muscle, for example in your leg, caused by the muscle becoming tight SYN **cramp**

char·lie /ˈtʃɑːli $ ˈtʃɑːr-/ *n* [C] *BrE spoken* a stupid person: **feel a right/proper charlie** (=feel very stupid)

charm¹ /tʃɑːm $ tʃɑːrm/ ●●○ *n*
1 [C,U] a special quality someone or something has that makes people like them, feel attracted to them, or be easily influenced by them - used to show approval → **charming**: *Joe's boyish charm* | **[+of]** *the charm of this small Southern city* | *She* ***turned on the charm*** (=used her charm) *to all the men.* | *The room had no windows and* ***all the charm of*** *a prison cell* (=used to say that something has no charm).
2 [C] a very small object worn on a chain or BRACELET: *a charm bracelet* | *a small gold horseshoe worn as a* ***lucky charm***
3 [C] a phrase or action believed to have special magic powers SYN **spell**
4 **work like a charm** to work exactly as you had hoped: *The new sales program has worked like a charm.*

charm² ●○○ *v* [T]
1 to attract someone and make them like you, sometimes in order to make them do something for you → **charming**: *We were charmed by the friendliness of the local people.*
2 to please and interest someone: *a story that has charmed generations of children*
3 to gain power over someone or something by using magic

charmed /tʃɑːmd $ tʃɑːrmd/ *adj* **have/lead a charmed life** to be lucky all the time, so that although you are often in dangerous situations nothing ever harms you

ˌcharmed ˈcircle *n* [singular] *written* a group of people who have special power or influence: *politicians outside the charmed circle*

charm·er /ˈtʃɑːmə $ ˈtʃɑːrmər/ *n* [C] someone who uses their charm to please or influence people: *Even at ten years old, he was a real charmer.* → SNAKE CHARMER

charm·ing /ˈtʃɑːmɪŋ $ ˈtʃɑːr-/ ●●○ *adj* very pleasing or attractive: *a charming little Italian restaurant | Harry can be very charming.* **THESAURUS** NICE —**charmingly** *adv*

Charming, Prince → PRINCE CHARMING

ˈcharm school *n* [C] *especially AmE* a school where young women were sometimes sent in the past to learn how to behave politely and gracefully

char·nel house /ˈtʃɑːnl haʊs $ ˈtʃɑːr-/ *n* [C] *literary* a place where the bodies and bones of dead people are stored

charred /tʃɑːd $ tʃɑːrd/ *adj* something that is charred has been burned until it is black: *the charred remains of a body*

C

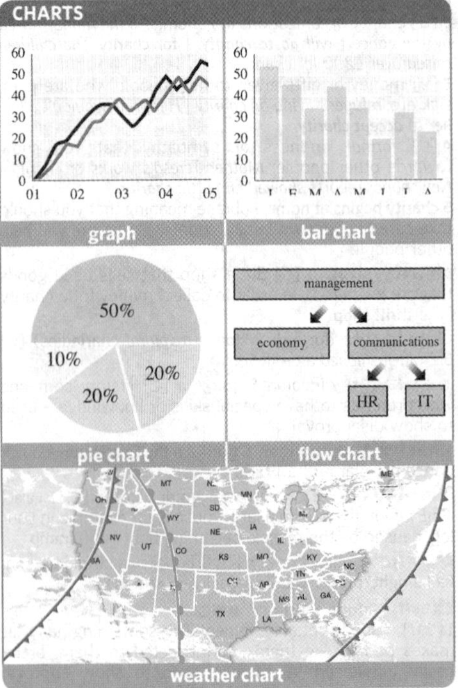

chart¹ /tʃɑːt $ tʃɑːrt/ ●●● S3 W3 AWL *n* [C]
1 information that is clearly arranged in the form of a simple picture, set of figures, GRAPH etc, or a piece of paper with this information on it SYN **diagram**: *a chart showing last year's sales | a weather chart | the theatre's seating chart* → BAR CHART, FLOW CHART, PIE CHART
2 the charts the lists, which come out weekly, of the most popular records: *Her new single went straight to number one in the* ***pop charts***. *| Brooks again* ***topped the charts*** (=was the most popular). | **chart hit/success/star etc** *the Beatles' first chart hit*
3 a detailed map, especially of an area of the sea or the stars

chart² ●○○ AWL *v*
1 [T] to record information about a situation or set of events over a period of time, in order to see how it changes or develops: *Scientists have been charting temperature changes in the oceans.*
2 [T] to make a plan of what should be done to achieve a particular result: *Each team was responsible for making its own decisions and charting its own course.*
3 [T] to make a map of an area of land, sea, or stars, or to draw lines on a map to show where you have travelled → **uncharted**
4 [I] if a record charts, it enters the weekly list of the most popular records: *Their next single didn't chart.*

char·ter¹ /ˈtʃɑːtə $ ˈtʃɑːrtər/ ●●○ *n*
1 [C] a statement of the principles, duties, and purposes of an organization: *the freedoms embodied in the UN charter*
2 [U] the practice of paying money to a company to use their boats, aircraft etc, or the boat, aircraft etc used in this way: *boats available for charter | a charter service*
3 [C] a signed statement from a government or ruler which allows a town, organization, or university to officially exist and have special rights: *The town's charter was granted in 1838.*
4 [singular] *BrE informal* a law or official decision that seems to give someone the right to do something most people consider morally wrong: *Reducing the number of police is just a thieves' charter.*

charter² *v* [T] **1** to pay a company for the use of their aircraft, boat etc: *We chartered a boat to take us to some of the smaller islands.* **2** to say officially that a town, organization, or university officially exists and has special rights

char·tered /ˈtʃɑːtəd $ ˈtʃɑːrtərd/ *adj* [only before noun] *BrE* **chartered accountant/surveyor/engineer etc** an ACCOUNTANT, SURVEYOR etc who has successfully completed special examinations

ˈcharter flight *n* [C] an aircraft journey that is arranged for a particular group or for a particular purpose, and that usually costs less than an ordinary aircraft journey → **scheduled flight**

ˌcharter ˈmember *n* [C] *AmE* an original member of a club or organization SYN **founder member** *BrE*

ˈcharter ˌschool *n* [C] a school in the US that is run by parents, companies etc rather than by the public school system, but which the state government supports

char·treuse /ʃɑːˈtrɜːz $ ʃɑːrˈtruːz/ *n* [U] **1** a green or yellow alcoholic drink **2** a bright yellow-green colour

ˈchart-ˌtopping *adj* **chart-topping record/group/hit etc** a record, group etc that has sold the most records in a particular week

char·wom·an /ˈtʃɑːˌwʊmən $ ˈtʃɑːr-/ *n* (*plural* **charwomen** /-ˌwɪmɪn/) [C] *BrE old-fashioned* a woman who works as a cleaner, especially in someone's house

char·y /ˈtʃeəri $ ˈtʃeri/ *adj especially BrE* unwilling to risk doing something SYN **wary**: **chary about/of doing sth** *Banks were chary of lending the company more money.*

chase¹ /tʃeɪs/ ●●● S3 *v*
1 FOLLOW [I,T] to quickly follow someone or something in order to catch them: *The dogs saw him running and chased him. | kids chasing around the house |* **chase sb along/down/up sth etc** *The police chased the suspect along Severn Avenue. |* **[+after]** *A gang of boys chased after her, calling her names.* **THESAURUS** FOLLOW → see picture at FOLLOW
2 MAKE SB/STH LEAVE [T always + adv/prep] to make someone or something leave, especially by following them for a short distance and threatening them: **chase sb away/off** *The men were chased off by troops, who fired warning shots. |* **chase sb out of sth** *Anne went to chase the dog out of the garden.*
3 TRY TO GET STH [I,T] to use a lot of time and effort trying to get something such as work or money: *Top graduates from the university are chased by major companies. |* **[+after]** *reporters chasing after a story*
4 HURRY [I always + adv/prep] *BrE* to rush or hurry somewhere: **[+around/up/down etc]** *I was chasing around getting everything organized.*
5 ROMANCE [T] to try hard to make someone notice you and pay attention to you, because you want to have a romantic relationship with them: *'Sometimes a girl wants to be chased,' Amelia said.*
6 METAL [T] *technical* to decorate metal with a special tool: *chased silver*
7 chase the dragon *informal* to smoke the drug HEROIN

chase sb/sth ↔ **down** *phr v* to find something or someone that you have been looking for: *We had to chase down everyone we'd sold a bike to.*

chase sb/sth ↔ **up** *phr v BrE*
1 to remind someone to do something they promised to do for you: *David hasn't paid yet – you'd better chase him up.*
2 to try to make something happen or arrive more quickly, because it has been taking too long: *Can you chase up those photos for me tomorrow?*

chase² ●●○ *n*
1 [C] the act of following someone or something quickly in order to catch them: *a high-speed* ***car chase*** | *Police spotted the car and* ***gave chase*** (=chased it).
2 [singular] when you use a lot of time and effort trying to get something: **[+after]** *the chase after higher-paying jobs*
→ PAPER CHASE, WILD GOOSE CHASE

chas·er /ˈtʃeɪsə $ -ər/ *n* [C] a weaker alcoholic drink which is drunk after a strong one, or a stronger alcoholic drink which is drunk after a weak one: *a pint of bitter and a whisky chaser*

chas·m /ˈkæzəm/ *n* **1** [C] a very deep space between two areas of rock or ice, especially one that is dangerous: *a rope bridge across the chasm* **2** [singular] a big difference between two people, groups, or things SYN **gulf**: **[+between]** *the chasm between rich and poor*

chas·sis /ˈʃæsiː/ *n* (*plural* **chassis** /-siːz/) [C] **1** the frame on which the body, engine, wheels etc of a vehicle are built **2** the landing equipment of a plane

chaste /tʃeɪst/ *adj* **1** *old-fashioned* not having sex with anyone, or not with anyone except your husband or wife → **celibate**, **chastity**: *She led a chaste decent life.*
2 not showing sexual feelings: *a* ***chaste kiss*** *on the cheek*
3 simple and plain in style: *a chaste nightgown* —**chastely** *adv*

chas·ten /ˈtʃeɪsən/ *v* [T] *formal* to make someone realize that their behaviour was wrong or mistaken: *Party workers have returned to their home towns, chastened by their overwhelming defeat.* GRAMMAR **Chasten** is usually passive. —**chastening** *adj*: *a chastening experience*

chas·tise /tʃæˈstaɪz/ *v* [T] **1** *formal* to criticize someone severely: *'You're a fool,' she chastised herself.*
2 *old-fashioned* to physically punish someone —**chastisement** *n* [C,U]

chas·ti·ty /ˈtʃæstəti/ *n* [U] the principle or state of not having sex with anyone, or not with anyone except your husband or wife → **celibacy**

chat¹ /tʃæt/ ●●○ *v* (**chatted**, **chatting**) [I]
1 (*also* **chat away**) *especially BrE* to talk in a friendly informal way, especially about things that are not important: *John and I sat up until the early hours chatting.* | **[+with/to]** *Mary was there, chatting to her mother.* | **[+about]** *Susie chatted away about her social life.*
2 to communicate with several people in a chat room on the Internet

GRAMMAR: Reciprocal verbs

Chat is a reciprocal verb. This type of verb is used when saying that two or more people or things do something that involves both or all of them: *The boys were chatting.* You can also say: *The boys were chatting with each other.* | *He was chatting with the boys.*

GRAMMAR GUIDE ▸ VERBS

chat sb ↔ **up** *phr v BrE informal* to talk to someone in a way that shows you are sexually attracted to them: *I spent the evening chatting up Liz.*

chat² ●●○ *n* [C,U] *especially BrE* an informal friendly conversation: **[+with]** *I've* ***had*** *a long* ***chat*** *with Vinnie.* | **[+about]** *a chat about the weather* | *She was enjoying their friendly* ***little chat***. | *She used to drop in for a chat quite often.*
→ BACKCHAT

chat·bot /ˈtʃætbɒt $ -bɑːt/ *n* [C] a computer program designed to send messages back to a human user, as if it is having a conversation

chat·eau /ˈʃætəʊ $ ʃæˈtoʊ/ *n* (*plural* **chateaux** /-təʊz $ -ˈtoʊz/) [C] a castle or large country house in France → see picture at HOUSE¹

chat·e·laine /ˈʃætl-eɪn/ *n* [C] *formal* the female owner, or wife of the owner, of a castle or large country house in France

ˈchat line *n* [C] a telephone service that people call to talk to other people who have called the same service

ˈchat room *n* [C] a place on the Internet where you can write messages to other people and receive messages back from them immediately, so that you can have a conversation while you are ONLINE

ˈchat show *n* [C] *BrE* a television or radio show on which people talk about themselves in reply to questions SYN **talk show** *AmE*: *a TV* ***chat show host*** (=person who asks the questions on the show)

chat·tel /ˈtʃætl/ *n* [C] *law old-fashioned* a piece of personal property that you can move from one place to another: *a society in which women are considered to be chattels* → GOODS AND CHATTELS

chat·ter¹ /ˈtʃætə $ -ər/ *v* [I] **1** (*also* **chatter away/on**) to talk quickly in a friendly way without stopping, especially about things that are not serious or important: *She chattered away happily until she noticed I wasn't listening.* | *She chattered excitedly like a child.* | **[+about]** *We were chattering about the events of last night.* **2** if birds or monkeys chatter, they make short high sounds **3** if your teeth are chattering, you are so cold or frightened that your teeth are knocking together **4 the chattering classes** *BrE* educated MIDDLE-CLASS people who like to discuss and have opinions about recent events and situations in society —**chatterer** *n* [C]

chatter² *n* [U] **1** informal talk, especially about things that are not serious or important: **[+of]** *the excited chatter of the audience* | *Jane's* ***constant chatter*** *was annoying him.* | *gossip and* ***idle chatter*** | *She was full of chatter about her new friends.* **2** a series of short high sounds made by some birds or monkeys: **[+of]** *the chatter of birds* **3** a hard quick repeated sound made by your teeth knocking together or by machines: **[+of]** *the chatter of the printer*

chat·ter·box /ˈtʃætəbɒks $ -tərbɑːks/ *n* [C] *informal* someone, especially a child, who talks too much

chat·ty /ˈtʃæti/ *adj* **1** liking to talk a lot in a friendly way: *He was in an unusually chatty mood.* **2** a piece of writing that is chatty has a friendly informal style: *a chatty letter*

ˈchat-up line *n* [C] *BrE* something that someone says in order to start a conversation with someone they think is sexually attractive

chauf·feur¹ /ˈʃəʊfə, ʃəʊˈfɜː $ ˈʃoʊfər, ʃoʊˈfɜːr/ *n* [C] someone whose job is to drive a car for someone else

chauffeur² *v* [T] **1** to drive a car for someone as your job **2** (*also* **chauffeur sb ↔ around**) to drive someone in your car, especially when you do not want to: *I spent most of the day chauffeuring the kids around.*

chau·vin·is·m /ˈʃəʊvənɪzəm $ ˈʃoʊ-/ *n* [U] **1** a belief that your own sex is better or more important than the other sex, especially if you are a man: ***male chauvinism***
2 a strong belief that your country or race is better or more important than any other: *national chauvinism*

chau·vin·ist /ˈʃəʊvɪnɪst $ ˈʃoʊ-/ *n* [C] **1** someone, especially a man, who believes that their own sex is better or more important than the other sex: *He's a bit of a* ***male chauvinist***. | *a* ***male chauvinist pig*** (=an insulting name for a male chauvinist) **2** someone who believes that their own country or race is better or more important than any other —**chauvinist** *adj*

chau·vi·nis·tic /ˌʃəʊvəˈnɪstɪk◂ $ ʃoʊ-/ *adj* **1** having the belief that your own country or race is better or more important than any other: *a chauvinistic dislike of foreigners*
2 having the belief that your own sex is better or more important than the other sex, especially if you are a man

chav /tʃæv/ *n* [C] *BrE* an offensive word used especially by newspapers to talk about a young WORKING-CLASS person who is rude and AGGRESSIVE, has a low level of education, and who wears a certain style of fashionable clothing such as TRAINERS, SPORTSWEAR, and BASEBALL CAPS

chav·vy /ˈtʃævi/ *adj BrE informal* typical of or like a chav - used to show disapproval: *She was wearing horrible chavvy earrings.*

cheap¹ /tʃiːp/ ●●● S1 W2 *adj* (*comparative* **cheaper**, *superlative* **cheapest**)
1 LOW PRICE not at all expensive, or lower in price than you expected OPP **expensive**: *cheap rail fares* | *the cheapest TV on the market* | *Property is cheaper in Spain than here.* | *a cheap shop* (=one that sells goods cheaply) | *The*

*equipment is **relatively cheap** and simple to use.* | *This coat was **dirt cheap*** (= very cheap - an informal expression) | **cheap and cheerful** *BrE* (=simple and not expensive, but of reasonable quality) *a cheap and cheerful Italian restaurant*
2 BAD QUALITY low in price and quality: *Cheap wine gives me a headache.* | *cheap jewellery* | *The furniture looked **cheap and nasty**.* | *a **cheap imitation** of the real thing*
3 NOT EXPENSIVE TO USE not costing much to use or to employ SYN **inexpensive**: **cheap to run/use/maintain etc** *Gas appliances are usually cheaper to run than electric ones.* | *For the employer, a part-time workforce means a **cheap labour** supply.*
4 NOT DESERVING RESPECT showing a lack of honesty, moral principles, or sincere feelings, so that you do not deserve respect: *She felt cheap and stupid, like a naughty child caught stealing.* | *You're lying, aren't you? You're so cheap.* | *His remark was a **cheap shot** at short people.* | *another **cheap** political **stunt*** | *It was nothing but a **cheap trick*** (=unkind trick).
5 NOT GENEROUS *AmE* not liking to spend money SYN **mean** *BrE*: *She's too cheap to take a cab.*
6 cheap thrill excitement that does not take much effort to get: *Bella will sleep with anyone for a cheap thrill.*
7 life is cheap used to say that it is not important if people die
8 cheap at the price/at any price *BrE*, **cheap at twice the price** so good, useful, or desirable that the cost is not important —**cheaply** *adv*: *a cheaply furnished room* | *They lived as cheaply as possible.* —**cheapness** *n* [U]: *the relative cheapness of housing*

THESAURUS

cheap costing very little money, or less than you expected: *My shoes were really cheap - they only cost £25.* | *The cheapest way to get to Chicago is to take the bus.* | *cheap flights*
low low prices, rents, and fees do not cost a lot of money. Do not use **cheap** with these words: *Why is the share price so low?* | *You could get equally good accommodation elsewhere at a lower rent.*
inexpensive *especially written* not expensive - use this especially about things that are of good quality, even though they do not cost a lot: *The furniture is inexpensive, but well made.* | *a simple inexpensive meal*
reasonable a reasonable price seems fair because it is not too high: *The restaurant serves good food at reasonable prices.*
economical cheap because you do not need to use a lot of money or fuel: *an economical car* | *It is usually more economical to buy in large quantities.*
affordable cheap enough for most people to be able to buy or pay for: *affordable housing* | *Single mothers often have trouble finding affordable childcare.*
competitive competitive prices and rates are as low as those charged by other shops or companies: *I think you'll find our prices are extremely competitive.* | *The hotel offers a high standard of service at very competitive rates.*
budget [only before noun] budget flights, airlines, hotels etc have especially low prices: *You can get a budget flight to Amsterdam for only £19.* | *a list of budget hotels for under $50 a night*
be good/great value to be worth at least the price you pay for it, so that you feel pleased and think you have spent your money well: *The meals at Charlie's Pizza are really good value.* | *The holiday is great value for money.*
be a bargain *informal* to be extremely cheap: *I got this shirt when I was in Indonesia. It was a real bargain.*

COLLOCATIONS CHECK

low price/cost/rent/fee/charge
reasonable price/cost
economical car/way/method
affordable accommodation/housing/price
competitive price/rate
budget flight/airline/hotel/accommodation

cheap² *adv* at a low price: *Air fares to Africa **don't come cheap*** (=are expensive). | *I bought this house because it was **going cheap*** (=selling for a lower price than usual). | *She used to **get** meat **cheap** at the butcher's.* | *They're selling linen off cheap in Lewis's.*

cheap³ *n* **on the cheap** spending less money than is needed to do something properly: *A clean environment cannot be had on the cheap.* | *holidaying on the cheap*

cheap·en /ˈtʃiːpən/ *v* **1** [I,T] to become or make something become lower in price or value: *The good harvest that year cheapened the costs of some raw materials.* **2** [T] to make something or someone seem less deserving of respect: *She never compromised or cheapened herself.*

cheap·o /ˈtʃiːpəʊ $ -oʊ/ *adj* [only before noun] *informal* not of good quality and not costing very much: *a cheapo camera*

cheap·skate /ˈtʃiːpskeɪt/ *n* [C] *informal* someone who spends as little money as possible - used to show disapproval: *The cheapskate didn't even pay for the cab.*

cheat¹ /tʃiːt/ ●●○ S3 *v*
1 [I,T] to behave in a dishonest way in order to win or to get an advantage, especially in a competition, game, or examination: *He had cheated in the test by using a calculator.* | *Don't look at my cards - **that's cheating**.* | **[+at]** *She claimed that I cheated at chess.*
2 [T] to trick or deceive someone so that they do not get or keep something they have a right to have: *Illegal workers are often cheated by employers.* | **cheat sb (out) of sth** *She cheated her aged aunt out of her fortune.*
3 feel cheated to feel that you have been treated wrongly or unfairly and have not got what you deserve: *She felt cheated and used.*
4 cheat death/fate etc to manage to avoid death or a very bad situation even though it seemed that you would not be able to: *The Italian ace cheated death in a spectacular 100 mph crash.*
5 be cheated of victory/success etc if you are cheated of victory, success etc, you do not achieve it because of something unfortunate that happens
cheat on sb *phr v* to be unfaithful to your husband, wife, or sexual partner by secretly having sex with someone else: *The magazine claims that almost half of Britain's women cheat on their partners.*

cheat² ●●○ *n* [C]
1 someone who is dishonest and cheats: *His addiction has turned him into a cheat and a liar.*
2 a cheat something that is dishonest or unfair
3 a set of instructions given to a computer that make it easier for someone who is playing a computer game to win

check¹ /tʃek/ ●●● S1 W2 *v*
1 FIND OUT [I,T] to do something in order to find out whether something really is correct, true, or in good condition: *Check the tiles carefully before you buy them.* | *A first rule in solving any mystery is to check the facts.* | *Fill in the cash book carefully and always check your calculations.* | **check (that)** *Check that all the doors are locked securely.* | **check whether/how/who etc** *Let me just check whether the potatoes are cooked.* | *They paused to check how the other climbers were getting on.* | **check (sth) for sth** *I checked the typing for errors.* | *Turn the tap on and check for leaks.* | **check sth against/with sth** (=compare something with something else to see whether they are the same) *You must check the evidence against other sources and decide if it is reliable.* | *Positive test results are **double-checked*** (=looked at twice) *to make absolutely sure.*
2 ASK SB [I,T] to ask someone whether something is correct, true, or allowed: *I'm not authorized to give you a refund - I'll have to check first.* | **check (that)** *Make a phone call to check that you're writing to the right person.* | **check whether/how/who etc** *Call the factory to check whether the beds can be delivered today.* | **[+with]** *Check with your doctor before going on a diet.*
3 NOT DO STH [T] to suddenly stop yourself from saying or doing something because you realize it would be

better not to: *I had to check the urge to laugh out loud.* | **check yourself** *He grinned, and then checked himself, not wanting to upset Jack.*

4 STOP STH [T] to stop something bad from getting worse or continuing to happen: *The police are failing to take adequate measures to check the growth in crime.*

5 BAGS/CASES ETC [T] *AmE*, **check in** *BrE* to leave your bags at an official place so they can be put on a plane or a train, or to take someone's bags in order to do this: *Any luggage over five kilos must be checked.*

6 MAKE A MARK [T] *AmE* to make a mark (✓) next to an answer, something on a list etc to show you have chosen it, that it is correct, or that you have dealt with it SYN **tick** *BrE*

7 Check *AmE spoken* say this when someone mentions each thing on a list, to tell them that you have it or have done it: *'Passport?' 'Check.' 'Ticket?' 'Check'.*

THESAURUS

check to look at something carefully and thoroughly in order to make sure that it is correct, safe, or working properly: *I'll just check the water level in the battery.* | *The immigration officer checked their passports.*

examine to look at something carefully and thoroughly because you want to find out something about it: *Experts who examined the painting believe it is genuine.* | *The police will examine the weapon for fingerprints.*

inspect to look at something carefully and thoroughly in order to make sure that it is correct, safe, or working properly, especially when it is your job to do this: *The building is regularly inspected by a fire-safety officer.*

go through sth to examine something such as a document or plan from beginning to end, especially in order to check that it is correct: *You should go through the contract before you sign.*

double-check to check something again so that you are completely sure it is correct, safe, or working properly: *I double-checked all my calculations and they seemed fine.*

test to examine or use something in order to find out whether it works or what its qualities are, or in order to check that it is satisfactory: *Test your brakes to check they are working correctly.* | *These products have not been tested on animals.*

monitor to carefully watch or keep checking someone or something in order to see what happens over a period of time: *Doctors monitored her progress during the night.* | *Observers have been monitoring the situation in Burma closely.*

check in *phr v*

1 if you check in or are checked in at a hotel or airport, you go to the desk and report that you have arrived: *Check in two hours before the flight.* | **[+at]** *He checked in at the Europa Hotel.* | **check sb ↔ in** *Airline employees were checking in passengers.* → CHECK-IN

2 check sth ↔ in to leave your bags at an official place so they can be put on a plane or a train, or to take someone's bags in order to do this: *I said goodbye and went to check in my suitcases.*

3 *AmE* to call someone to tell them that you are safe or where you are: *He just called to check in and tell them how he was doing.*

4 if a user of a SOCIAL NETWORKING system checks in to a place, they show on the system that they are there

check sth ↔ **off** *phr v* to write a mark next to something on a list to show that you have chosen it, dealt with it, or made sure that it is correct: *One by one he checked them off on his register.*

check on sb/sth *phr v*

1 to make sure that someone or something is safe, is in a satisfactory state, or is doing what they should be doing: *Honey, can you go upstairs and check on the kids?* | *My neighbour comes in once a week to check on things and feed the fish.*

2 to try to find out if something is true or correct: *He wanted to check on the girl's story.*

check out *phr v*

1 MAKE SURE **a) check sth ↔ out** to make sure that something is actually true, correct, or acceptable SYN **investigate**: *I made a phone call to check out his address.* | **[+with]** *Check it out with your boss before you do anything.* **b)** if information checks out, it is proved to be true, correct, or acceptable: *His credit record checks out.*

2 LOOK AT SB/STH **check sb/sth ↔ out** to look at someone or something because they are interesting or attractive: *If I hear about a website that sounds interesting, I check it out.* | *Hey, check out that car!*

3 GET INFORMATION **check sb ↔ out** *informal* to get information about someone, especially to find out if they are suitable for something: *I'll check them out as potential employers.*

4 HOTEL to leave a hotel after paying the bill: *We checked out at noon.* → CHECKOUT

5 BOOKS **check sth ↔ out** *AmE* to borrow a book from a library: *The library allows you to check out six books at a time.*

check sth/sb ↔ **over** *phr v*

1 to look closely at something to make sure it is correct or acceptable: *They spent the rest of the morning checking over their equipment.*

2 to examine someone to make sure they are healthy: *I'd like the doctor to check you over and do a few tests.*

check up on sb/sth *phr v*

1 to try to find out if someone is doing what they said they would do or what you want them to do: *Don't worry; no one is going to check up on you.*

2 to make sure that something is true or correct: *Dustin called me to check up on some facts.*

check² ●●● S1 W3 *n*

1 FINDING OUT [C] the process of finding out if something is safe, correct, true, or in the condition it should be: **[+on]** *the need for tighter checks on arms sales* | *Conduct* ***regular checks*** *on your water quality.* | **run/carry out/make a check** *I decided to run a check on all personnel.* | *I* ***keep a*** *careful* ***check on*** *my blood pressure.* | **have a check** *BrE*: *Have a check in your bag first and see if it's there.* | *the airport's routine* ***security checks*** | ***random*** *drug* ***checks*** | **health/medical/dental etc check** (=a test done to make sure you are healthy) | **spot check** (=a quick check of one thing among a group of things, that you do without warning) *a spot check on the accounts*

2 keep/hold sb/sth in check keep someone or something under control: *You must learn to keep your emotions in check.* | *attempts to keep global warming in check* | *He made an effort to hold himself in check.*

3 A CONTROL ON STH [C usually singular] something that controls something else and stops it from getting worse, continuing to happen etc: **[+on]** *Higher interest rates will act as a check on public spending.*

4 checks and balances a system that makes it possible for some people or parts of an organization to control the others, so that no particular person or part has too much power or influence

5 PATTERN [C,U] a pattern of squares, especially on cloth: *a shirt with brown and black checks* | **check suit/jacket etc** (=made with cloth patterned with checks) *a blue cotton check dress* → CHECKED

6 FROM YOUR BANK [C] the American spelling of CHEQUE: **[+for]** *a check for $30* | **by check** *Can I pay by check?*

7 IN A RESTAURANT [C] *AmE* a list that you are given in a restaurant showing what you have eaten and how much you must pay SYN **bill** *BrE* THESAURUS ➤ BILL

8 coat/hat check [C] *AmE* **a)** a place in a restaurant, theatre etc where you can leave your coat, bag etc to be guarded **b)** a ticket that you are given so you can claim your things from this place

9 MARK [C] *AmE* a mark (✓) that you put next to an answer to show that it is correct or next to something on a list to show that you have dealt with it SYN **tick** *BrE*

10 CHESS [U] the position of the KING (=most important piece) in CHESS where it can be directly attacked by the opponent's pieces

check·book /ˈtʃekbʊk/ *n* [C] the American spelling of CHEQUEBOOK

check·box /ˈtʃekbɒks $ -bɑːks/ *n* [C] *especially AmE* a small square space on a document or computer screen where you can put a mark to choose something SYN **tickbox**

ˈ**check card** *n* [C] *AmE* a special plastic card, similar to a CREDIT CARD, that you can use to pay for things directly from your CHECKING ACCOUNT SYN **debit card**

ˈ**check ˌdigit** *n* [C] *technical* the number on the far right of a BAR CODE. It is used to check that the information on the bar code is correct.

C

checked /tʃekt/ ●●○ *adj* checked cloth has a regular pattern of differently coloured squares: *a checked blouse* → see picture at **PATTERN**[1]

check·er /ˈtʃekə $ -ər/ *n* [C] **1** *AmE* someone who works at the CHECKOUT in a SUPERMARKET **2 spell/grammar checker** a computer program that checks whether the spelling of words or the grammar of a sentence is correct **3** someone who makes sure that something is written or done correctly **4 checkers** [U] *AmE* a game for two players using 12 flat round pieces each and a board with 64 squares, in which the purpose is to take the other player's pieces by jumping over them with your pieces SYN **draughts** *BrE* → see picture at **BOARD GAME** → **CHINESE CHEQUERS**

check·er·board /ˈtʃekəbɔːd $ -kərbɔːrd/ *n* [C] *AmE* a board that you play checkers on, with 32 white squares and 32 black squares SYN **draughtboard** *BrE*

check·ered (*also* **chequered** *BrE*) /ˈtʃekəd $ -ərd/ *adj* **1** having a pattern made up of squares of two different colours: *a red and white checkered tablecloth* | *a checkered marble floor* **2 have a checkered history/career/past etc** to have had periods of failure as well as successful times in your past: *This is an unusual building with a checkered history.*

ˌ**checkered ˈflag** (*also* **chequered flag** *BrE*) *n* [C] a flag covered with black and white squares that is waved at the end of a motor race

ˈ**check-in** *n* **1** [singular] a place where you report your arrival at an airport, hotel, hospital etc: *the* ***check-in desk*** | *Make sure you're at the check-in by 5.30.* **2** [U] the process of reporting your arrival at an airport, hotel, hospital etc: *Ask your travel agent about check-in times.* **3** [C] the act of showing on a SOCIAL NETWORKING system that you are at a particular place → **check in** at **CHECK**[1]

ˈ**checking acˌcount** *n* [C] *AmE* a bank account that you can take money out of at any time, and for which you are given checks to use to pay for things SYN **current account** *BrE* → **DEPOSIT ACCOUNT**

check·list /ˈtʃekˌlɪst/ ●●○ *n* [C] a list that helps you by reminding you of the things you need to do or get for a particular job or activity: *The guide contains a useful checklist of points to look for when buying a car.*

check·mate /ˈtʃekmeɪt/ *n* [C,U] **1** the position of the KING (=most important piece) in CHESS at the end of the game, when it is being directly attacked and cannot escape **2** a situation in which someone has been completely defeated —**checkmate** *v* [T]: *The king is checkmated and the game is over.*

check·out /ˈtʃek-aʊt/ ●●○ *n*
1 [C] the place in a SUPERMARKET where you pay for the goods you have collected: *Why can't they have more checkouts open?* | *the checkout assistant*
2 [C,U] the time by which you must leave a hotel room: *Checkout is at noon.* → **check out** at **CHECK**[1]

check·point /ˈtʃekpɔɪnt/ ●○○ *n* [C] a place, especially on a border, where an official person examines vehicles or people: *They had to cross five military checkpoints.*

check·room /ˈtʃek-rʊm, -ruːm/ *n* [C] *AmE* a place in a restaurant, theatre etc where you can leave your coat, bags etc to be guarded SYN **cloakroom** *BrE*

check·sum char·ac·ter /ˈtʃeksʌm ˌkærəktə $ -tər/ *n* [C] *technical* a CHECK DIGIT

check-up, **check-up** /ˈtʃek-ʌp/ *n* [C] a general medical examination that a doctor or DENTIST gives you to make sure you are healthy: *It's important to* ***have*** *regular* ***check-ups***.

ched·dar /ˈtʃedə $ -ər/ *n* [U] a firm smooth yellow cheese

cheek[1] /tʃiːk/ ●●● W3 *n*
1 [C] the soft round part of your face below each of your eyes: *Lucy stretched up to kiss his cheek.* | *Billy had rosy cheeks and blue eyes.* | *her tear-stained cheeks* | *Julie's cheeks flushed with pleasure at the compliment.* | **red-cheeked/hollow-cheeked/rosy-cheeked etc** *a red-cheeked plump old fellow*
2 [singular, U] *BrE* disrespectful or rude behaviour, especially towards someone in a position of authority: *I've had enough of your cheek.* | **have the cheek to do sth** *He had the cheek to make personal remarks and expect no reaction.* | *She's* ***got a cheek****; she just goes on till she gets what she wants.* | *It's* ***a bit of a cheek****, asking me for money.* | ***What a cheek****! Of course I read the instructions!*
3 cheek by jowl (with sb/sth) very close to someone or something else: *an expensive French restaurant cheek by jowl with a cheap clothes shop*
4 turn the other cheek to deliberately avoid reacting in an angry or violent way when someone has hurt or upset you
5 cheek to cheek if two people dance cheek to cheek, they dance very close to each other in a romantic way
6 [C] *informal* one of the two soft fleshy parts of your bottom SYN **buttock** → **tongue in cheek** at **TONGUE**[1](6), → **TONGUE-IN-CHEEK**

cheek[2] *v* [T] *BrE* to speak rudely or with disrespect to someone, especially to someone older such as your teacher or parents SYN **sass** *AmE*: *You can cheek some teachers and they just don't do anything.*

cheek·bone /ˈtʃiːkbəʊn $ -boʊn/ *n* [C usually plural] one of the two bones above your cheeks, just below your eyes: *She had* ***high cheekbones*** *and green eyes.*

cheek·y /ˈtʃiːki/ *adj BrE* rude or disrespectful, sometimes in a way that is amusing: **cheeky devil/monkey etc** *You did that on purpose, you cheeky little devil!* | *Now don't be cheeky to your elders, young woman.* | *a chubby five-year-old with a* ***cheeky grin*** THESAURUS ▸ RUDE —**cheekily** *adv*: *He grinned cheekily.* —**cheekiness** *n* [U]

cheep /tʃiːp/ *v* [I] if a young bird cheeps, it makes a weak high noise: *chicks cheeping for food* —**cheep** *n* [C]

cheer[1] /tʃɪə $ tʃɪr/ ●●○ *n*
1 [C] a shout of happiness, praise, approval, or encouragement OPP **boo**: *A great* ***cheer went up*** *from the crowd.* | *So let's* ***give a cheer*** *to the kids who passed their exams.* | *The final whistle was greeted with triumphant cheers from players and spectators.*
2 three cheers for sb! *spoken* used to tell a group of people to shout three times as a way of showing support, happiness, thanks etc: *Three cheers for the birthday girl!*
3 [U] *formal* a feeling of happiness and confidence: *'Hello,' said Auguste cheerily. His* ***good cheer*** *was not returned.* | *Christmas cheer*
4 [C] a special CHANT (=phrase that is repeated) that the crowds at a US sports game shout in order to encourage their team to win → **CHEERS**

cheer[2] ●●○ *v*
1 [I,T] to shout as a way of showing happiness, praise, approval, or support of someone or something: *Everybody cheered when the firemen arrived.* | *The audience was shouting and cheering.* | *The spectators cheered him wildly.* THESAURUS ▸ SHOUT
2 [T] to make someone feel more hopeful when they are worried: *By late afternoon there came news that cheered them all.* | *Government policy towards higher education*

contains little to cheer university students. —**cheering** *adj*: *cheering news*

cheer sb ↔ **on** *phr v* to shout encouragement at a person or team to help them do well in a race or competition: *They gathered round the swimming pool and cheered her on.*

cheer up *phr v*
1 to become less sad, or to make someone feel less sad: *Cheer up! The worst is over.* | *They cheered up when they saw us coming along.* | **cheer sb ↔ up** *Here's a bit of news that will cheer you up.* | *You both need cheering up, I think.*
2 cheer sth ↔ up to make a place look more attractive: *I bought some posters to cheer the place up a bit.*

cheer·ful /ˈtʃɪəfəl $ ˈtʃɪr-/ ●●○ *adj*
1 happy, or behaving in a way that shows you are happy: *She's feeling more cheerful today.* | *I'm making a real effort to be cheerful despite everything.* | **cheerful voice/smile/manner etc** *'I'm Robyn,' she said with a cheerful smile.* | *It does me good to see a cheerful face.* **THESAURUS** HAPPY
2 something that is cheerful makes you feel happy because it is so bright or pleasant: *a bright cheerful Italian restaurant* | *There was a cheerful picture on the wall.* | *The house has a cheerful atmosphere.*
3 tending to be happy most of the time: *She was a cheerful and agreeable companion.* | *Before the accident he had been cheerful and confident.*
4 [only before noun] a cheerful attitude shows that you are willing to do whatever is necessary in a happy way: *a cheerful approach to the job* —**cheerfully** *adv*: *He smiled cheerfully.* | *'Morning!' she called cheerfully.* —**cheerfulness** *n* [U] → **cheap and cheerful** at CHEAP[1](1)

cheer·i·o /ˌtʃɪəriˈəʊ $ ˌtʃɪriˈoʊ/ *interjection BrE informal* goodbye

cheer·lead·er /ˈtʃɪəˌliːdə $ ˈtʃɪrˌliːdər/ *n* [C] **1** a member of a team of young women who encourage a crowd to cheer at a US sports game by shouting special words and dancing: *She was a popular cheerleader at the University of Texas.* **2** someone who encourages other people to do something: *She was our cheerleader, teacher, and friend.*

cheer·lead·ing /ˈtʃɪəˌliːdɪŋ $ ˈtʃɪr-/ *n* [U] **1** the activity of being a cheerleader: *a cheerleading camp for girls* **2** *AmE* the act of loudly supporting an organization, idea etc and not being willing to listen to criticism of it: *The conventions have become nothing but cheerleading rallies for the presidential campaign.*

cheer·less /ˈtʃɪələs $ ˈtʃɪr-/ *adj* cheerless weather, places, or times make you feel sad, bored, or uncomfortable SYN **gloomy**: *This is a cold cheerless place.* | *The day was grey and cheerless.* —**cheerlessness** *n* [U]

cheers /tʃɪəz $ tʃɪrz/ *interjection* **1** used when you lift a glass of alcohol before you drink it, in order to say that you hope the people you are drinking with will be happy and have good health **2** *BrE informal* thank you **3** *BrE informal* goodbye

cheer·y /ˈtʃɪəri $ ˈtʃɪri/ *adj* happy or making you feel happy: *She gave me a* ***cheery smile***. | *He left them with a* ***cheery wave***. —**cheerily** *adv*

cheese /tʃiːz/ ●●● S2 W3 *n* [C,U]
1 a solid food made from milk, which is usually yellow or white in colour, and can be soft or hard: *half a kilo of cheese* | *a cheese sandwich* | *Sprinkle with the grated cheese.* | *a selection of English cheeses* | **piece/bit/slice/lump etc of cheese** | **cow's/goat's/sheep's cheese** (=from the milk of a cow etc)
2 (say) cheese! *spoken* used to tell people to smile when you are going to take their photograph → BIG CHEESE, → **chalk and cheese** at CHALK[1](3)

cheese·board /ˈtʃiːzbɔːd $ -bɔːrd/ *n* [C] **1** a board used to cut cheese on **2** a variety of cheeses that are served at the end of a meal: *The meal was finished with the cheeseboard and a dish of fruit.*

cheese·bur·ger /ˈtʃiːzbɜːgə $ -bɜːrgər/ *n* [C] a HAMBURGER cooked with a piece of cheese on top of the meat

cheese·cake /ˈtʃiːzkeɪk/ *n* **1** [C,U] a cake made from a mixture containing soft cheese: *a slice of cheesecake* **2** [U] *old-fashioned* photographs of pretty women with few clothes on → **beefcake**

cheese·cloth /ˈtʃiːzklɒθ $ -klɒːθ/ *n* [U] thin cotton cloth used for putting around some kinds of cheeses, and sometimes for making clothes

cheesed off /ˌtʃiːzd ˈɒf $ -ˈɒːf/ *adj BrE* bored and annoyed with something: *You sound really cheesed off.*

ˈcheese-ˌparing *n* [U] *BrE* behaviour that shows you are unwilling to give or spend money —**cheese-paring** *adj*

chees·y /ˈtʃizi/ *adj* **1** tasting like cheese or containing cheese: *cheesy sauces* **2** *informal* cheap and not of good quality: *a cheesy soap opera* **3** *informal* not sincere: *a cheesy grin*

chee·tah /ˈtʃiːtə/ *n* [C] a member of the cat family that has long legs and black spots on its fur, and can run extremely fast → see picture at BIG CAT

chef /ʃef/ ●●○ *n* [C] a skilled cook, especially the main cook in a hotel or restaurant: *a master chef* | *a pastry chef*

Chel·sea bun /ˌtʃelsi ˈbʌn/ *n* [C] *BrE* a small round sweet cake with dried fruit in it

chem·i·cal[1] /ˈkemɪkəl/ ●●● S3 W3 AWL *n* [C] a substance used in chemistry or produced by a chemical process: **toxic/hazardous/dangerous chemicals** *the organic chemicals industry* | *synthetic chemicals*

chemical[2] ●●● W3 AWL *adj* [only before noun] relating to substances, the study of substances, or processes involving changes in substances: *the chemical composition of bleach* | *a chemical analysis of the soil* —**chemically** /-kli/ *adv*: *Chemically, the substances are similar.*

ˌchemical engiˈneering *n* [U] the study of machines used in industrial chemical processes —**chemical engineer** *n* [C]

ˌchemical reˈaction *n* [C,U] a natural process in which the atoms of chemicals mix and arrange themselves differently to form new substances: *the chemical reaction between ozone and chlorine*

ˌchemical ˈwarfare *n* [U] methods of fighting a war using chemical weapons

ˌchemical ˈweapon *n* [C] a poisonous substance, especially a gas, used as a weapon in war

che·mise /ʃəˈmiːz/ *n* [C] **1** a piece of women's underwear for the top half of the body **2** a simple dress that hangs straight from a woman's shoulders

chem·ist /ˈkemɪst/ ●●○ S3 *n* [C]
1 a scientist who has special knowledge and training in chemistry
2 *BrE* someone trained to prepare drugs and medicines, who works in a shop SYN **pharmacist** *AmE*
3 *BrE* a shop where you can buy medicines, beauty products etc SYN **pharmacy**, **drugstore** *AmE*

chem·is·try /ˈkeməstri/ ●●● W3 *n* [U]
1 the science that is concerned with studying the structure of substances and the way that they change or combine with each other → **biochemistry**, **biology**, **physics**
2 if there is chemistry between two people, they like each other and find each other attractive: **[+between]** *It's obvious that there's a very real chemistry between them.*
3 the way substances combine in a particular process, thing, person etc: *a person's body chemistry*

ˈchemistry ˌset *n* [C] a box containing equipment for children to do simple chemistry at home

chem·ist's /ˈkeməsts/ *n* [C] *BrE* a shop where medicines and TOILETRIES are sold SYN **drugstore** *AmE* → **pharmacy**

che·mo·ther·a·py /ˌkiːməʊˈθerəpi, ˌke- $ -moʊ-/ *n* [U] the use of drugs to control and try to cure CANCER → **radiotherapy**

che·nille /ʃəˈniːl/ *n* [U] twisted thread with a surface like a soft brush, or cloth made from this and used for decorations, curtains etc

cheque *BrE*, **check** *AmE* /tʃek/ ●●● S2 *n* [C] a printed piece of paper that you write an amount of money on, sign, and use instead of money to pay for things: **[+for]** *They sent me a cheque for £100.* | **by cheque** *Can I pay* ***by cheque***? | *You could* ***write*** *her a* ***cheque***. | **cash a**

cheque (=get cash in exchange for a cheque) → BLANK CHEQUE, TRAVELLER'S CHEQUE

cheque·book *BrE*, **checkbook** *AmE* /ˈtʃekbʊk/ *n* [C] a small book of cheques that your bank gives you

ˌchequebook ˈjournalism *n* [U] *BrE* when newspapers get material for articles by paying people a lot of money for information about crimes or the private lives of famous people – used to show disapproval

ˈcheque card (*also* **ˌcheque guaranˈtee card**) *n* [C] *BrE* a card given to you by your bank that you must show when you write a cheque, which promises that the bank will pay out the amount written on the cheque → **cash card**, **check card**

chequ·ered /ˈtʃekəd $ -ərd/ *adj* a British spelling of CHECKERED

ˌchequered ˈflag *n* [C] a British spelling of CHECKERED FLAG

cheq·uers /ˈtʃekəz $ -ərz/ *n* → CHINESE CHEQUERS

cher·ish /ˈtʃerɪʃ/ ●○○ *v* [T]
1 if you cherish something, it is very important to you: *He cherished his privacy.* | *I* **cherish** *the* **memory** *of that day.* | **cherish a hope/an idea/a dream etc** *willingness to re-examine cherished beliefs*
2 to love someone or something very much and take care of them well: *In marriage, a man promises to cherish his wife.* | *his most* **cherished possession**

Cher·no·byl /tʃɜːˈnəʊbəl $ tʃərˈnoʊ-/ a town in Ukraine (formerly part of the Soviet Union) where in 1986 an explosion destroyed large parts of a NUCLEAR power station. At least 30 people were killed at the time, but it is believed that there may have been many more deaths as a result of the RADIOACTIVE dust which spread over many countries. When people are discussing the safety of nuclear power, they sometimes say that they 'do not want another Chernobyl'.

che·root /ʃəˈruːt/ *n* [C] a small CIGAR with both ends cut straight

cher·ry /ˈtʃeri/ ●●○ S3 *n* (*plural* **cherries**)
1 [C] a small round red or black fruit with a long thin stem and a stone in the middle: *a bunch of cherries* | *cherry pie* → see picture at FRUIT[1]
2 a) (*also* **ˈcherry tree**) [C] the tree on which this fruit grows **b)** (*also* **cherrywood**) [U] the wood of this tree, used for making furniture
3 [U] (*also* **ˌcherry ˈred**) a bright red colour —**cherry** *adj*
→ **another bite/a second bite at the cherry** at BITE[2](8)

ˈcherry bomb *n* [C] *AmE* a large round red FIRECRACKER (=small loud explosive)

cher·ry·pick /ˈtʃeripɪk/ *v* [I,T] to choose the best things or people you want from a group before anyone else has the chance to take them

ˈcherry toˌmato *n* [C] a type of very small TOMATO

cher·ub /ˈtʃerəb/ *n* [C] **1** an ANGEL shown in works of art as a fat pretty child with small wings **2** *informal* a young pretty child who behaves very well **3** (*plural* **cherubim** /ˈtʃerəbɪm/) one of the ANGELS who guard the seat where God sits —**cherubic** /tʃəˈruːbɪk/ *adj*: *a smile of cherubic innocence*

cher·vil /ˈtʃɜːvəl $ ˈtʃɜːr-/ *n* [U] a strong-smelling garden plant used as a herb

Chesh·ire cat, the /ˌtʃeʃə ˈkæt $ -ʃər-/ people sometimes say someone is 'grinning like a Cheshire cat' to mean that they have a big and rather silly smile on their face. This phrase comes from a character in *Alice's Adventures in Wonderland* by Lewis Carroll, which disappears until only its big smile can be seen.

chess /tʃes/ ●●○ *n* [U] a game for two players, who move their playing pieces according to particular rules across a special board to try to trap their opponent's KING (=most important piece): *They meet fairly often to* **play chess**.

chess·board /ˈtʃesbɔːd $ -bɔːrd/ *n* [C] a square board with 64 black and white squares, on which you play chess

CHESS

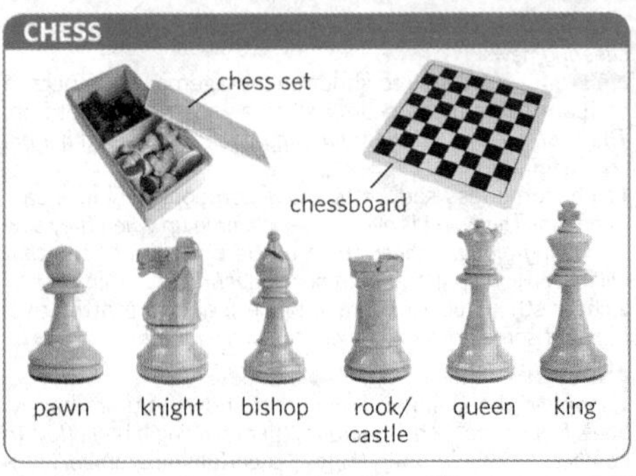

chess·man /ˈtʃesmæn/ *n* (*plural* **chessmen** /-men/) (*also* **chess·piece** /ˈtʃespiːs/) [C] any of the 16 black or 16 white playing pieces used in the game of chess

chest /tʃest/ ●●● S2 W3 *n* [C]
1 the front part of your body between your neck and your stomach → **breast**: *Her heart was pounding in her chest.* | *a hairy chest* | **chest pain/infection/injury** *He collapsed with severe chest pains.* → FLAT-CHESTED
2 a large strong box that you use to store things in or to move your personal possessions from one place to another: *a large wooden chest* → CHEST OF DRAWERS, TEA CHEST, WAR CHEST, see picture at BOX[1]
3 get something off your chest to tell someone about something that has been worrying or annoying you for a long time, so that you feel better afterwards

ches·ter·field /ˈtʃestəfiːld $ -ər-/ *n* [C] *BrE* a soft comfortable SOFA, usually covered with leather

chest·nut¹ /ˈtʃesnʌt/ *n* **1** [C] a smooth red-brown nut that you can eat: *roast chestnuts* → see picture at NUT[1] **2** (*also* **chestnut tree**) [C] the tree on which this nut grows **3** [U] a red-brown colour **4** [C] a horse that is red-brown in colour **5 an old chestnut** a joke or story that has been repeated many times **6** [C] a HORSE CHESTNUT → WATER CHESTNUT

chestnut² *adj* red-brown in colour: *her chestnut hair*

ˌchest of ˈdrawers *n* (*plural* **chests of drawers**) [C] *especially BrE* a piece of furniture with drawers, used for storing clothes SYN **dresser** *AmE*

chest·y /ˈtʃesti/ *adj* **1** *BrE* if you have a chesty cough, or if you are a bit chesty, you have a lot of MUCUS (=thick liquid) in your lungs **2** *informal* used to describe a woman with large breasts, when you want to avoid saying this directly

chev·ron /ˈʃevrən/ *n* [C] **1** a pattern in a V shape **2** a piece of cloth in the shape of a V which soldiers have on their sleeve to show their rank

chew¹ /tʃuː/ ●●● S2 *v*
1 [I,T] to bite food several times before swallowing it: *This meat's so tough I can hardly chew it!* | **[+at/on]** *a dog chewing on a bone* THESAURUS BITE
2 [I,T] to bite something continuously in order to taste it or because you are nervous: **[+on]** *We gave the dog an old shoe to chew on.* | **chew your lip/nails** | **chew gum/tobacco**
3 chew the cud if a cow or sheep chews the cud, it keeps biting on food it has brought up from its stomach
4 chew the fat *informal* to have a long friendly conversation → **bite off more than you can chew** at BITE[1](10)

chew on sth *phr v informal* to think carefully about something for a period of time

chew sb ↔ **out** *phr v AmE informal* to talk angrily to someone in order to show them that you disapprove of what they have done: *John couldn't get the guy to cooperate and so I had to call and chew him out.*

chew sth ↔ **over** *phr v* to think carefully about something for a period of time: *Let me chew it over for a few days.*

chew sth ↔ **up** *phr v*
1 to damage or destroy something by tearing it into small pieces: *Be careful if you use that video recorder. It tends to chew tapes up.*

2 to bite something many times with your teeth so that you can make it smaller or softer and swallow it: *The dog's chewed up my slippers again.*

chew² *n* [C] **1** the act of biting something many times with your teeth **2** a sweet that you chew **3** a piece of tobacco that you chew but do not swallow

ˈchewing gum ●●○ *n* [U] a type of sweet that you chew for a long time but do not swallow

chew·y /ˈtʃuːi/ *adj* food that is chewy has to be chewed a lot before it is soft enough to swallow: *chewy toffees*

chic /ʃiːk/ *adj* very fashionable and expensive, and showing good judgment of what is attractive and good style: *Margaret was looking very chic in blue.* | *a chic restaurant* —**chic** *n* [U]: *the art of comfortable chic*

chi·cane /ʃɪˈkeɪn/ *n* [C] *BrE* an S-shaped bend in a straight road, especially on a track for racing cars

chi·ca·ne·ry /ʃɪˈkeɪnəri/ *n* [U] *formal* the use of clever plans or actions to deceive people: *Clearly there is some chicanery going on.*

Chi·ca·no /tʃɪˈkɑːnəʊ $ -noʊ/ *n* (*plural* **Chicanos**) [C] a US citizen who was born in Mexico or whose family came from Mexico → **Hispanic** —**Chicano** *adj*

chi·chi /ˈʃiːʃiː/ *adj* very fashionable and expensive, or very concerned with fashionable things: *a chichi restaurant*

chick /tʃɪk/ ●●○ *n* [C]
1 a baby bird: *a mother hen with her chicks*
2 *informal not polite* a word meaning a young woman, that some people think is offensive

chick·a·dee /ˈtʃɪkədiː/ *n* [C] a North American bird with a black head

chick·en¹ /ˈtʃɪkɪn/ ●●● S2 *n*
1 [C] a common farm bird that is kept for its meat and eggs → **hen**, **cock**, **rooster**, **chick**
2 [U] the meat from this bird eaten as food: *roast chicken* | *fried chicken* | *chicken soup*
3 [C] *informal* someone who is not at all brave SYN **coward**: *Don't be such a chicken!*
4 [U] a game in which children do something dangerous, for example stand on a railway line when a train is coming, and try to be the one who continues doing it for the longest time
5 which came first, the chicken or the egg? used to say that it is difficult or impossible to decide which of two things happened first, or which action is the cause and which is the effect
6 a chicken and egg situation/problem etc a situation in which it is impossible to decide which of two things happened first, or which action is the cause and which is the effect
7 sb's chickens have come home to roost used to say that someone's bad or dishonest actions in the past have caused the problems that they have now → **don't count your chickens before they've hatched** at COUNT¹(8), → SPRING CHICKEN

chicken² *v*
chicken out *phr v informal* to decide at the last moment not to do something you said you would do, because you are afraid: *You're not chickening out, are you?*

chicken³ *adj* [not before noun] *informal* not brave enough to do something SYN **cowardly**: *Dave's too chicken to ask her out.*

ˈchicken ˌfeed *n* [U] an amount of money that is so small that it is almost not worth having: *The bank offered to lend us £1,000 but that's chicken feed compared to what we need.*

ˈchicken flu *n* [U] *informal* another name for AVIAN FLU

ˌchicken-fried ˈsteak *n* [C,U] *AmE* a thin piece of BEEF covered in BREADCRUMBS and cooked in hot fat

ˈchicken ˌpox, **chick·en·pox** /ˈtʃɪkənpɒks $ -pɑːks/ *n* [U] an infectious illness which causes a slight fever and spots on your skin

ˈchicken run *n* [C] an area surrounded by a fence where chickens are kept

chick·en·shit /ˈtʃɪkənʃɪt/ *n* [C] *AmE informal not polite* an offensive word for someone who is not at all brave SYN **coward** —**chickenshit** *adj*

ˈchicken wire *n* [U] a type of thin wire net used to make fences for chickens

ˈchick flick *n* [C] *informal* a film that women, but not men, are likely to enjoy – used humorously

ˈchick lit *n* [U] *informal* books about young women and the typical problems they have with men, sex, losing weight etc, especially books written by women for women to read – used humorously

chick·pea /ˈtʃɪkpiː/ *n* [C] a large brown PEA which is cooked and eaten SYN **garbanzo** *AmE*

chick·weed /ˈtʃɪkwiːd/ *n* [U] a garden WEED with small white flowers

chic·o·ry /ˈtʃɪkəri/ *n* [U] **1** a European plant whose bitter leaves are eaten in SALADS **2** the roots of this plant, used in coffee or instead of coffee

chide /tʃaɪd/ *v* [I,T] *written* to tell someone that you do not approve of something that they have done or said SYN **scold**: *'Edward, you are naughty,' Dorothy chided.* | **chide sb for (doing) sth** *She chided him for not responding to her Christmas cards.* | *He swiftly chided himself for such thoughts.*

chief¹ /tʃiːf/ ●●● S2 W2 *adj*
1 [only before noun] highest in rank: *He was recently appointed chief economist at the Bank of Scotland.* | *the government's chief medical officer*
2 most important SYN **main** → **chiefly**: *One of the* ***chief causes*** *of crime today is drugs.* | *Safety is our* ***chief concern.*** | *The* ***chief reason*** *for this is that people are living longer.* | *his* ***chief rival*** *for the job* | *the prosecution's chief witness* | *She had many reasons for taking the money, but* ***chief among*** *them was revenge.* THESAURUS IMPORTANT, MAIN
3 chief cook and bottle washer someone who does a lot of small jobs to make sure that an event is successful – used humorously

chief² ●●● W3 *n* [C]
1 SB IN CHARGE OF AN ORGANIZATION the most important person, or one of the most important people, in a company or organization – used especially in job titles and in news reports: **police/army/fire etc chief** *Los Angeles Police Chief Willie L. Williams* | **[+of]** *the British Chief of Defence Staff* | *Most health chiefs believe the reforms have gone too far.* | *industry chiefs* | **commander-in-chief/editor-in-chief etc** (=used in job titles for people with the highest rank) *They offered him the position of editor-in-chief.*
2 RULER OF TRIBE the ruler of a tribe: *the Zulu leader, Chief Mangosuthu Buthelezi* | *Native American* ***tribal chiefs***
3 too many chiefs and not enough Indians *BrE* used to say there are too many people saying how something should be done and not enough people doing it
4 great white chief *BrE old-fashioned* the person in charge of a group of people, company, organization etc – used humorously

ˌchief ˈconstable *n* [C] a police officer in charge of the police in a large area of Britain

ˌChief Exˈecutive *n* **the Chief Executive** the president of the US

ˌchief exˈecutive ˌofficer *n* [C] (*abbreviation* **CEO**) the person with the most authority in a large company

ˌchief inˈspector *n* [C] a British police officer of middle rank

ˌchief ˈjustice *n* [C] the most important judge in a court of law, especially the US Supreme Court

chief·ly /ˈtʃiːfli/ ●○○ *adv* mostly but not completely SYN **mainly**: *The work consists chiefly of interviewing the public.* | *I lived abroad for years, chiefly in Italy.*

ˌchief of ˈstaff *n* (*plural* **chiefs of staff**) [C] **1** an officer of high rank in the army, navy etc who advises the officer in charge of a particular military group or operation **2** an official of high rank who advises the person in charge of an organization or government: *the White House chief of staff*

ˌChief ˈRabbi *n* **the Chief Rabbi** the main leader of the JEWISH religion in a country

ˌchief superinˈtendent *n* [C] a British police officer of high rank

chief·tain /ˈtʃiːftɪn/ *n* [C] the leader of a tribe or a Scottish CLAN

chif·fon /ˈʃɪfɒn $ ʃɪˈfɑːn/ *n* [U] a soft thin silk or NYLON material that you can see through: *a pink chiffon ballgown*

chi·gnon /ˈʃiːnjɒn $ -jɑːn/ *n* [C] hair that is tied in a smooth knot at the back of a woman's head SYN **bun**

chi·hua·hua /tʃəˈwɑːwə/ *n* [C] a very small dog with smooth hair, originally from Mexico

chil·blains /ˈtʃɪlbleɪnz/ *n* [plural] painful red areas on your fingers or toes that are caused by cold weather

child /tʃaɪld/ ●●● S1 W1 *n* (*plural* **children** /ˈtʃɪldrən/) [C]

1 YOUNG PERSON someone who is not yet an adult SYN **kid**: *The hotel is ideal for families with young children.* | *The film is not suitable for children under 12.* | *I was very happy* ***as a child*** (=when I was a child). | **a child of five/eight etc** *For a child of five this was a terrifying experience.* | *a famous writer of children's books* | *child victims of war*

2 SON/DAUGHTER a son or daughter of any age: *I have five children, all happily married.* | *She lives with her husband, Paul, and three* ***grown-up children****.* | *Annie had always wanted to get married and have children.* | *Alex is* ***an only child*** (=he has no brothers or sisters). | *Our* ***youngest child****, Sam, has just started university.* | **eldest child** *especially BrE*, **oldest child** *especially AmE* | *the decision to* ***bring a child into the world*** (=have a baby)

3 SB INFLUENCED BY AN IDEA someone who is very strongly influenced by the ideas and attitudes of a particular period of history: **[+of]** *a real child of the sixties*

4 SB WHO IS LIKE A CHILD someone who behaves like a child and is not sensible or responsible – used to show disapproval: *She's* ***such a child****!*

5 sth is child's play used to say that something is very easy to do: *I've cooked for 200 people before now. So, tonight is child's play by comparison.*

6 children should be seen and not heard an expression meaning that children should be quiet and not talk – used when you disapprove of the way a child is behaving

7 be with child *old use* to be PREGNANT

8 be heavy/great with child *old use* to be nearly ready to give birth

COLLOCATIONS

ADJECTIVES/NOUN + child

a four-year-old/ten-year-old etc child *A four-year-old child should not be left on their own.*
a young child *Young children are naturally curious about the world.*
a small child (=a young one) *My family lived in France when I was a small child.*
an unborn child (=a baby that is still inside its mother) *Smoking can damage your unborn child.*
a spoilt/spoiled child (=allowed to do or have whatever he or she wants, and behaving badly) *He's behaving like a spoilt child.*
a gifted child (=extremely intelligent) *a special school for gifted children*
a good/bad child | **a naughty child** (=doing things that are not allowed) | **a problem child** (=very difficult to deal with) | **street children** (=living on the streets because they have no homes)

VERBS

bring up a child *especially BrE*, **raise a child** *especially AmE The cost of bringing up a child has risen rapidly.*
a child is born | **a child grows up**

child + NOUN

child abuse (=treating children in a very bad way, especially sexually) *He was arrested on suspicion of child abuse.*
child development *She's an expert in child development.*
child labour *BrE*, **child labor** *AmE* (=the use of children as workers) *The garments were made using child labour.*

THESAURUS

child someone who is not yet an adult. You don't usually use child to talk about babies or teenagers: *Many children are scared of the dark.* | *He's just a child.*
kid *informal* a child. Kid is the usual word to use in everyday spoken English: *We left the kids in the car.*
little boy/little girl a young male or female child: *I lived there when I was a little girl.* | *Little boys love dinosaurs.*
teenager someone between the ages of 13 and 19: *There's not much for teenagers to do around here.*
adolescent a young person who is developing into an adult – used especially when talking about the problems these people have: *He changed from a cheerful child to a confused adolescent.*
youth *especially disapproving* a teenage boy – especially one who is violent and commits crimes: *He was attacked by a gang of youths.* | *a youth court*
minor *law* someone who is not yet legally an adult: *It is illegal to sell alcohol to a minor.*

ˈchild aˌbuse *n* [U] the crime of harming a child physically, sexually, or emotionally

child·bear·ing /ˈtʃaɪldˌbeərɪŋ $ -ˌber-/ *n* [U] **1** the process of being PREGNANT and giving birth to children: *the trend towards later marriage and childbearing* **2 childbearing age/years** if a woman is of childbearing age or in her childbearing years, she is of an age when it is physically possible for her to have babies

ˌchild ˈbenefit *n* [U] an amount of money that the British government gives to families with children

child·birth /ˈtʃaɪldbɜːθ $ -bɜːrθ/ *n* [U] the act of having a baby → **labour**: **in/during/after childbirth** *His wife died in childbirth.*

child·care /ˈtʃaɪldkeə $ -ker/ ●○○ *n* [U] an arrangement in which someone who is trained to look after children cares for them while the parents are at work: *People earning low wages will find it difficult to pay for childcare.* | *I think more women would work if there were better* ***childcare facilities****.*

child·hood /ˈtʃaɪldhʊd/ ●●○ W3 *n* [C,U] the period of time when you are a child: *I had a very happy childhood.* | **in/during/since (sb's) childhood** *Most infections occur in childhood.* | *She had been writing poems since her childhood.* | **childhood home/friend/experience etc** (=a home etc that you had when you were a child) | **childhood memories** (=the memories you have of your childhood) → SECOND CHILDHOOD

REGISTER

In everyday English, people usually say **when I was a child** when talking about their **childhood**: *During my* ***childhood*** *we lived by the ocean.* → ***When I was a child*** *we lived by the ocean.* | *She's known him* ***since childhood****.* → *She's known him* ***since she was a child****.*

child·ish /ˈtʃaɪldɪʃ/ *adj* **1** [usually before noun] relating to or typical of a child OPP **adult**: *a high childish laugh* | *her childish excitement* **2** behaving in a silly way that makes you seem much younger than you really are – used to show disapproval SYN **immature** OPP **mature**: *Don't be so childish!* | *I wish politicians would stop this childish name-calling.* ⚠ To describe someone who is as innocent, eager etc as a child, use **childlike**. —**childishly** *adv* —**childishness** *n* [U]

child·less /ˈtʃaɪldləs/ *adj* having no children: **childless couple/woman/marriage** *It was a happy but childless marriage.* | *couples who deliberately remain childless* —**childlessness** *n* [U]

child·like /ˈtʃaɪldlaɪk/ *adj* having qualities that are typical of a child, especially positive qualities such as INNOCENCE and eagerness: **childlike innocence/simplicity/**

directness *'You know I love you,' she said with childlike simplicity.* | **childlike delight/wonder/excitement** *The sight filled her with childlike excitement.* | *Standing, she looked less childlike.*

child·min·der /ˈtʃaɪldˌmaɪndə $ -ər/ *n* [C] *BrE* someone who is paid to look after young children while their parents are at work —**childminding** *n* [U]

ˈchild moˌlester *n* [C] someone who harms children by touching them in a sexual way, or trying to have sex with them —**child molesting** *n* [U]

ˌchild ˈprodigy *n* [C] a child who is unusually skilful at doing something such as playing a musical instrument

child·proof /ˈtʃaɪldpruːf/ *adj* something that is childproof is designed to prevent a child from opening, damaging, or breaking it: *a childproof lock*

chil·dren /ˈtʃɪldrən/ the plural of CHILD

ˈchildren's home *n* [C] *BrE* a place where children live if their own parents have died or cannot look after them

ˈchild seat *n* [C] a special seat for a young child that is put in a car SYN **car seat**

ˈchild supˌport (*also* **maintenance** *BrE*) *n* [U] money that someone pays regularly to their former wife or husband in order to support their children

chil·i /ˈtʃɪli/ *n* [C] the American spelling of CHILLI

chill¹ /tʃɪl/ ●○○ *n*

1 [singular] a feeling of coldness: *There was a slight* ***chill in the air***. | **morning/autumnal/January etc chill** *Suddenly aware of the morning chill, she closed the window.* | **[+of]** *He sat in the chill of the evening, staring out over the city below.* | *I turned on the heater in the hall* ***to take the chill off*** *the house* (=to heat it slightly).

2 [C] a sudden feeling of fear or worry, especially because of something cruel or violent: *The sound of his dark laugh* ***sent a chill through*** *her.* | **chill of fear/apprehension/disquiet etc** *Fay felt a chill of fear as she watched Max go off with her daughter.* | *There was something in his tone that* ***sent a chill down*** *Melissa's* ***spine*** (=made her very frightened).

3 a) [C] an illness which causes a slight fever, headache, and SHIVERing (=slight shaking of the body): *Let's get these wet clothes off you before you* ***catch a chill***. **b)** [C usually plural] a feeling of being cold, caused by being ill

chill² ●○○ *v*

1 [I,T] if you chill something such as food or drink, or if it chills, it becomes very cold but does not freeze: *Spoon the mixture into a bowl and chill for two hours.* | *The longer this salad chills, the better the flavour.*

2 [I] (*also* **chill out**) *informal* to relax completely instead of feeling angry, tired, or nervous: *'Hold it! Just chill for a second, won't you!'* | *I spent the afternoon chilling out in front of the TV.*

3 [T] to make someone very cold: *The wind blew across her body, chilling her wet skin.* | **chilled to the bone/marrow** (=extremely cold) *Come and sit by the fire – you look chilled to the bone.*

4 [T] *literary* to suddenly frighten someone, especially by seeming very cruel or violent: *The anger in his face chilled her.* | **chill sb to the bone/chill sb to the marrow/chill sb's blood** (=frighten someone a lot) *He jerked his head round and saw something that chilled his blood.*

chill³ *adj* [usually before noun] unpleasantly cold: *the chill night air* | *a chill wind*

chil·lax /tʃɪˈlæks/ *v* [I] *informal* to relax and be calm – used especially by young people: *Dude, just chillax.* —**chillaxed** *adj*

chilled /tʃɪld/ *adj* **1** chilled food or drink has been kept in a REFRIGERATOR to make it cold: *a bottle of chilled white wine* **2** *informal* relaxed: *He's usually quite chilled.* | *The restaurant offers great food and a chilled atmosphere.*

chil·ler /ˈtʃɪlə $ -ər/ *n* [C] *informal* a film or book that is intended to frighten you

chil·li *BrE*, **chili** *AmE* /ˈtʃɪli/ ●●○ *n* (*plural* **chillies** *BrE*, **chilies** *AmE*)

1 [C] (*also* **ˈchilli pepper** *BrE*, **chili pepper** *AmE*) a small thin red or green PEPPER with a very strong hot taste

2 [U] (*also* **chilli con carne** *BrE*, **chili con carne** *AmE* /-kɒn ˈkɑːni $ -kɑːn ˈkɑːrni/) a spicy dish made with beans, meat, and chillies

chil·ling /ˈtʃɪlɪŋ/ *adj* something that is chilling makes you feel frightened, especially because it is cruel, violent, or dangerous: *the chilling sound of wolves howling* **THESAURUS** FRIGHTENING —**chillingly** *adv*: *It was chillingly clear that he wanted revenge.*

ˈchilli ˌpowder *BrE*, **chili powder** *AmE* *n* [U] a hot-tasting red powder made from dried chillies

chill-out mu·sic /ˈtʃɪlaʊt ˌmjuːzɪk/ (*also* **chillout**) *n* [U] music that you listen to when you want to relax

ˈchill room (*also* **chillout room**) *n* [C] **1** a room in a bar, office etc where people go to play games, listen to music, watch television etc so that they can relax **2** a website that contains games, pictures, music etc and is designed for people who want to relax or have fun

chill·y /ˈtʃɪli/ ●●○ *adj*

1 chilly weather or places are cold enough to make you feel uncomfortable: **chilly day/night/evening etc** *a chilly November morning* | **chilly wind/breeze/air etc** | *Getting chilly, isn't it?* | *The bathroom's a bit chilly.* **THESAURUS** COLD

2 if you feel chilly, you feel uncomfortably cold

3 unfriendly SYN **frosty**: *The speech met with a* ***chilly reception***. —**chilliness** *n* [singular, U]

chi·mae·ra /kaɪˈmɪərə, kə- $ -ˈmɪrə/ *n* [C] another spelling of CHIMERA

chime¹ /tʃaɪm/ *v* **1** [I,T] if a bell or clock chimes, it makes a ringing sound, especially to tell you what time it is: *The clock in the hall chimed six.* **2** [I] to be the same as something else or to have the same effect: **[+with]** *Her views on life didn't quite chime with mine.*

chime in *phr v* to say something in a conversation, especially to agree with what someone has just said: *'We'll miss you too,' the children chimed in.*

chime² *n* **1** [C] a ringing sound made by a bell or clock **2 chimes** [plural] a set of bells or other objects that produce musical sounds, used as a musical instrument or, for example, as a type of doorbell → **WIND CHIMES**

chim·e·ne·a, **chiminea** /ˌtʃɪməˈneɪə/ *n* [C] a round clay or metal container with a chimney, in which you make a fire. Chimeneas are used in gardens for heating.

chi·me·ra, **chimaera** /kaɪˈmɪərə, kə- $ -ˈmɪrə/ *n* [C] **1** *formal* something, especially an idea or hope, that is not really possible and can never exist: *trying to present that chimera, 'a balanced view'* **2** an imaginary creature that breathes fire and has a lion's head, a goat's body, and a snake's tail **3** *technical* a living thing that contains cells from another living thing

chi·me·ri·cal /kaɪˈmerɪkəl, kə-/ *adj formal* imaginary or not really possible

chim·i·chur·ri /ˌtʃɪmiˈtʃʊri/ *n* [U] a sauce, originally from Argentina, that is put on BEEF, lamb, or chicken as it is being cooked to improve the taste

chim·ney /ˈtʃɪmni/ ●●○ *n* [C]

1 a vertical pipe that allows smoke from a fire to pass out of a building up into the air, or the part of this pipe that is above the roof: *We can't light a fire because the chimney hasn't been swept.* → see picture at ROOF¹

2 a tall vertical structure containing a chimney → **smokestack**: *a factory chimney*

3 *technical* a narrow opening in tall rocks or cliffs that you can climb up

4 smoke like a chimney if someone smokes like a chimney, they smoke a lot of cigarettes or tobacco – used humorously

ˈchimney breast *n* [C] *BrE* the part of a wall in a room that encloses a chimney

ˈchimney-piece *n* [C] *BrE* a decoration, usually made of brick or stone, built above a FIREPLACE

ˈchimney pot *n* [C] *BrE* a short wide pipe made of baked clay or metal, that is attached to the top of a chimney

C

ˈchimney stack *n* [C] *BrE* **1** the tall chimney of a building such as a factory SYN **smokestack** *AmE* **2** a group of small chimneys on a roof

ˈchimney sweep *n* [C] someone whose job is to clean chimneys using special long brushes

chim·pan·zee /ˌtʃɪmpænˈziː, -pən-/ ●○○ (*also* **chimp** /tʃɪmp/) *n* [C] an intelligent African animal that is like a large monkey without a tail

chin /tʃɪn/ ●●● W3 *n* [C]
1 the front part of your face below your mouth: *He rubbed his chin thoughtfully.*
2 (keep your) chin up! *spoken* used to tell someone to make an effort to stay brave and confident when they are in a difficult situation: *Chin up! It'll be over soon.*
3 take sth on the chin to accept a difficult or unpleasant situation without complaining – used to show approval: *One of our great strengths is our ability to **take it on the chin** and come out fighting.*

C

chi·na /ˈtʃaɪnə/ *n* [U] **1** a hard white substance produced by baking a type of clay at a high temperature: *china teacups* **2** (*also* **chi·na·ware** /ˈtʃaɪnəweə $ -wer/) plates, cups etc made of china: *I'll get my best china out.*

Chi·na·town /ˈtʃaɪnətaʊn/ *n* [singular, U] an area in a city where there are Chinese restaurants and shops, and where a lot of Chinese people live

chin·chil·la /tʃɪnˈtʃɪlə/ *n* [C] a small South American animal bred for its fur

Chi·nese[1] /ˌtʃaɪˈniːz◂/ *n* **1** [U] the language used in China **2 the Chinese** [plural] people from China **3** [singular] *BrE informal* a meal of Chinese food, or a restaurant that sells Chinese food: *Do you fancy going out for a Chinese?*

Chinese[2] *adj* relating to China, its people, or its language

ˌChinese ˈchequers *BrE*, **Chinese checkers** *AmE n* [U] a game in which you move small balls from hole to hole on a board in the shape of a star → see picture at **BOARD GAME**

ˌChinese ˈlantern *n* [C] a small box made of thin paper that you put a light inside as a decoration

ˌChinese ˈleaves *n* [plural] *BrE* a type of CABBAGE eaten especially in East Asia

ˌChinese ˈmedicine *n* [U] a kind of medicine that uses herbs and ACUPUNCTURE

ˌChinese ˈwhispers *n* [U] *BrE* the passing of information from one person to another, and then to others, when the information gets slightly changed each time

chink[1] /tʃɪŋk/ *n* **1** [C] a small hole in a wall, or between two things that join together, that lets light or air through SYN **crack**: **[+in]** *The sun came through a chink in the curtains.* **2** [C] *BrE* a high ringing sound made by metal or glass objects hitting each other SYN **clink**: *the chink of coins* **3 a chink in sb's armour** a weakness in someone's character or in something they have said, that you can use to attack them

chink[2] *v* [I,T] *BrE* if glass or metal objects chink, or if you chink them, they make a high ringing sound when they knock together SYN **clink**: *They chinked their glasses and drank a toast to the couple.*

Chink *n* [C] *taboo* a very offensive word for someone from China. Do not use this word.

chin·less /ˈtʃɪnləs/ *adj BrE* lacking courage or determination

chi·nos /ˈtʃiːnəʊz $ -noʊz/ *n* [plural] loose trousers made from strong woven cotton

chin·strap /ˈtʃɪnstræp/ *n* [C] a band of cloth under your chin to keep a hat or HELMET in place

chintz /tʃɪnts/ *n* [U] smooth cotton cloth that is printed with a flowery pattern and is used for making curtains, furniture covers etc: *pink chintz curtains*

chintz·y /ˈtʃɪntsi/ *adj* **1** *BrE* covered with chintz: *a chintzy sofa* **2** *AmE informal* cheap and badly made SYN **cheap**: *a chintzy lamp* **3** *AmE informal* unwilling to give people things or spend money SYN **stingy**

ˈchin-up, **chin·up** /ˈtʃɪnʌp/ *n* [C] *AmE* an exercise in which you hang on a bar and pull yourself up until your chin is above the bar SYN **pull-up** *BrE*

chin·wag /ˈtʃɪnwæg/ *n* [singular] *BrE informal* an informal conversation SYN **chat** —**chinwag** *v* [I]

chip[1] /tʃɪp/ ●●● S2 W3 *n* [C]
1 FOOD [usually plural] **a)** *BrE* a long thin piece of potato cooked in oil SYN **French fry** *AmE*: ***fish and chips** | a **bag of chips*** **b)** *AmE* a thin flat round piece of food such as potato cooked in very hot oil and eaten cold SYN **crisp** *BrE*: *a bag of **potato chips***
2 COMPUTER a small piece of SILICON that has a set of complicated electrical connections on it and is used to store and PROCESS information in computers: *the age of the **silicon chip** | chip technology*
3 PIECE a small piece of wood, stone, metal etc that has been broken off something: *Wood chips covered the floor of the workshop. | a chocolate chip cookie* (=one that contains small pieces of chocolate)
4 MARK a small hole or mark on a plate, cup etc where a piece has broken off: **[+in]** *There's a chip in this bowl.*
5 have a chip on your shoulder to easily become offended or angry because you think you have been treated unfairly in the past
6 when the chips are down *spoken* in a serious or difficult situation, especially one in which you realize what is really true or important: *When the chips are down, you've only got yourself to depend on.*
7 be a chip off the old block *informal* to be very similar to your mother or father in appearance or character
8 GAME [usually plural] a small flat coloured piece of plastic used in games such as POKER or BLACKJACK to represent a particular amount of money
9 SPORT (*also* **chip shot, chip kick**) a hit in golf, or a kick in football or RUGBY, that makes the ball go high into the air for a short distance
10 have had your chips *BrE informal* to be in a situation in which you no longer have any hope of improvement
→ **BLUE-CHIP**, → **cash in your chips** at **CASH IN**

chip[2] ●○○ *v* (**chipped, chipping**)
1 ACCIDENTALLY BREAK (STH) [I,T] if you chip something, or if it chips, a small piece of it breaks off accidentally: *Gary fell and chipped one of his front teeth. | He chipped a bone in his knee and was carried off the pitch. | These plates chip really easily.* | **[+off]** *The paint had chipped off the gate.*
2 REMOVE STH [I,T always + adv/prep] to remove something, especially something hard that is covering a surface, by hitting it with a tool so that small pieces break off: *Archaeologists were carefully chipping away at the rock. | Chip out the plaster with a steel chisel.*
3 SPORT [T] to hit a golf ball or kick a football or a RUGBY ball so that it goes high into the air for a short distance: *United scored just before half-time when Adcock cleverly **chipped** the **ball** over the keeper.*
4 POTATOES [T] *BrE* to cut potatoes into thin pieces ready to be cooked in hot oil
5 MICROCHIP [T] *BrE* to put a MICROCHIP in an animal, person, or thing to identify or give information about them

chip away at sth *phr v* to gradually make something less effective or destroy it: *Writers such as Voltaire and Diderot were chipping away at the foundations of society. | Fears about the future chipped away at her sense of well-being.*

chip in *phr v*
1 to interrupt a conversation by saying something that adds more detail: **[+with]** *Other committee members chipped in with suggestions. | 'It won't be easy,' Jeff chipped in. | I'd just like to chip in, Bill, if I might.*
2 if each person in a group chips in, they each give a small amount of money so that they can buy something together: *We all chipped in to buy Amy a graduation present.* | **chip in (with) sth** *Fifty-two people in the music industry each chipped in $250 apiece.*

ˌchip and ˈpin *n* [U] a system for CREDIT CARDS and DEBIT CARDS, in which the card has a CHIP containing a secret number that only the owner of the card knows. The owner has to use this number every time the card is used.

The secret number makes it more difficult for people to use the card if it has been stolen: *Most shoppers prefer chip and pin to the old system.*

chip·board /ˈtʃɪpbɔːd $ -bɔːrd/ *n* [U] a type of board made from small pieces of wood pressed together with glue

chip·munk /ˈtʃɪpmʌŋk/ *n* [C] a small American animal similar to a SQUIRREL with black lines on its fur

chip·o·la·ta /ˌtʃɪpəˈlɑːtə◂/ *n* [C] *BrE* a small thin SAUSAGE

ˈchip pan *n* [C] *BrE* a deep pan with a wire basket inside used for cooking food in hot oil, especially CHIPS

chipped /tʃɪpt/ *adj* something that is chipped has a small piece broken off the edge of it: *The paint was chipped.* | *a chipped saucer* | *a chipped tooth*

chip·per /ˈtʃɪpə $ -ər/ *adj old-fashioned informal* happy and active: *You're looking very chipper this morning.*

chip·pings /ˈtʃɪpɪŋz/ *n* [plural] *BrE* small pieces of stone used when putting new surfaces on roads or railway tracks

ˈchip shop (*also* **chippie**, **chip·py** /ˈtʃɪpi/ *informal*) *n* [C] *BrE* a shop that cooks and sells FISH AND CHIPS and other FRIED food

chi·rop·o·dist /kəˈrɒpədɪst, ʃə- $ -ˈrɑː-/ *n* [C] *BrE* someone who is trained to examine and treat foot injuries and diseases SYN **podiatrist** —**chiropody** *n* [U]

chi·ro·prac·tic /ˈkaɪrəʊpræktɪk $ -rə-/ *n* [U] the treatment of physical problems by pressing on and moving the bones in someone's back and joints → **osteopathy**

chi·ro·prac·tor /ˈkaɪrəʊˌpræktə $ -rəˌpræktər/ *n* [C] someone who treats physical problems using chiropractic → **osteopath**

chirp /tʃɜːp $ tʃɜːrp/ (*also* **chirrup** *BrE*) *v* **1** [I] if a bird or insect chirps, it makes short high sounds **2** [I,T] to speak in a happy high voice: *'Yes, all finished,' he chirped.* —**chirp** *n* [C]

chirp·y /ˈtʃɜːpi $ ˈtʃɜːrpi/ *adj* happy and active: *You're very chirpy this morning – have you had some good news?* —**chirpily** *adv* —**chirpiness** *n* [U]

chir·rup /ˈtʃɪrəp $ ˈtʃɪ-, ˈtʃɜː-/ *v* [I,T] CHIRP

chis·el[1] /ˈtʃɪzəl/ *n* [C] a metal tool with a sharp edge, used to cut wood or stone → see picture at **TOOL**[1]

chisel[2] *v* (**chiselled**, **chiselling** *BrE*, **chiseled**, **chiseling** *AmE*) [T] to use a chisel to cut wood or stone into a particular shape: **chisel sth into/from/in etc sth** *Martin chiselled a hole in the door for the new lock.*

chis·elled *BrE*, **chiseled** *AmE* /ˈtʃɪzəld/ *adj* [usually before noun] if a man has chiselled features, his chin, mouth, nose etc have a strong clear shape: **chiselled features/chin/mouth/nose etc** *his chiselled good looks*

chit /tʃɪt/ *n* [C] *BrE* **1** an official note that shows that you are allowed to have something: *Take the chit to the counter and collect your books.* **2** *old-fashioned* a young woman who behaves badly and does not respect older people

ˈchit-chat *n* [U] *informal* conversation about things that are not very important: *boring social chit-chat*

chit·ter·lings /ˈtʃɪtəlɪŋz $ -ər-/ (*also* **chit·lings** /ˈtʃɪtlɪŋz/, **chit·lins** /-lənz/) *n* [plural] the INTESTINE of a pig eaten as food, especially in the southern US

chiv·al·rous /ˈʃɪvəlrəs/ *adj* a man who is chivalrous behaves in a polite, kind, generous, and honourable way, especially towards women —**chivalrously** *adv*

chiv·al·ry /ˈʃɪvəlri/ *n* [U] **1** behaviour that is honourable, kind, generous, and brave, especially men's behaviour towards women **2** a system of religious beliefs and honourable behaviour that KNIGHTs in the Middle Ages were expected to follow

chives /tʃaɪvz/ *n* [plural] the long thin green leaves of a plant with purple flowers. Chives taste like onion and are used in cooking.

chiv·vy, **chivy** /ˈtʃɪvi/ *v* (**chivvied**, **chivvying**, **chivvies**) [T] *BrE informal* to try to make someone do something more quickly, especially in an annoying way: **chivvy sb along/up** *Go and see if you can chivvy the kids up a bit.*

chla·myd·i·a /kləˈmɪdiə/ *n* [U] a disease that is passed on during sex

chlo·ride /ˈklɔːraɪd/ *n* [C,U] a chemical COMPOUND that is a mixture of chlorine and another substance: *sodium chloride*

chlo·ri·nate /ˈklɔːrəneɪt/ *v* [T] to add chlorine to water to kill BACTERIA

chlo·rine /ˈklɔːriːn/ *n* [U] a greenish-yellow gas with a strong smell that is used to keep the water in swimming pools clean. It is a chemical ELEMENT: symbol Cl

chlo·ro·fluo·ro·car·bon /ˌklɔːrəʊfluərəʊˈkɑːbən $ -roʊflʊroʊˈkɑːr-/ *n* [C] a CFC

chlor·o·form /ˈklɒrəfɔːm, ˈklɔː- $ ˈklɔːrəfɔːrm/ *n* [U] a liquid that makes you become unconscious if you breathe it —**chloroform** *v* [T]

chlo·ro·phyll /ˈklɒrəfɪl, ˈklɔː- $ ˈklɔː-/ *n* [U] the green-coloured substance in plants

choc /tʃɒk $ tʃɑːk, tʃɒːk/ *n* [C,U] *BrE informal* CHOCOLATE

choc·a·hol·ic /ˌtʃɒkəˈhɒlɪk $ ˌtʃɑːkəˈhɒː-, ˌtʃɒːk-/ *n* [C] another spelling of CHOCOHOLIC

choc·cy /ˈtʃɒki $ ˈtʃɑːki, ˈtʃɒːki/ *n* (*plural* **choccies**) [C] *BrE spoken* a CHOCOLATE(2)

ˈchoc-ice *n* [C] *BrE* a small block of ICE CREAM covered with chocolate

chock /tʃɒk $ tʃɑːk/ *n* [C] a block of wood or metal that you put in front of the wheel of a vehicle to prevent it from moving

chock-a-block /ˌtʃɒk ə ˈblɒk◂ $ ˈtʃɑːk ə ˌblɑːk/ *adj* [not before noun] *BrE* completely full of people or things: **[+with]** *Paris was chock-a-block with tourists.*

ˌchock-ˈfull *adj* [not before noun] *informal* completely full of people or things: **[+of]** *a pond chock-full of weeds*

choc·o·hol·ic, **chocaholic** /ˌtʃɒkəˈhɒlɪk $ ˌtʃɑːkəˈhɒː-, ˌtʃɒːk-/ *n* [C] *informal* someone who likes chocolate very much and eats a lot of it

choco·late /ˈtʃɒklət $ ˈtʃɑːkələt, ˈtʃɒːk-/ ●●● S2 *n*

1 [U] a sweet brown food that you can eat as a sweet or use in cooking to give foods such as cakes a special sweet taste: *a chocolate bar* | *a chocolate cake* | *a packet of chocolate biscuits* | *I prefer* ***milk chocolate*** *to* ***dark chocolate***. → see picture at **BAR**[1]

2 [C] a small sweet that is covered with chocolate: *Would you like a chocolate?* | *a box of chocolates*

3 [C,U] a hot sweet drink made with milk and chocolate, or a cup of this drink: *a mug of* ***hot chocolate*** | *Two coffees and one chocolate, please.*

4 [U] a dark brown colour

ˈchocolate box *adj* [only before noun] *BrE informal* a chocolate box place looks pretty, but in a way that is false because it seems too perfect: *He had grown tired of the chocolate box views.*

ˌchocolate chip ˈcookie *n* [C] a kind of small BISCUIT with small pieces of chocolate in it

choco·lat·ey /ˈtʃɒkləti $ ˈtʃɑːkələti, ˈtʃɒːk-/ *adj* tasting or smelling of chocolate: *a chocolatey taste*

choc·o·lat·i·er /ˌtʃɒkəˈlætiə $ ˌtʃɑːkəˈlætiər/ *n* [C] someone whose job is making chocolate or making things out of chocolate

choice[1] /tʃɔɪs/ ●●● S1 W1 *n*

1 [C,U] if you have a choice, you can choose between several things → **choose**: **[+between]** *Voters have a choice between three main political parties.* | **[+of]** *You have a choice of hotel or self-catering accommodation.* | *He has to make some important choices.* | *They gave us no choice in the matter.*

2 [singular, U] the range of people or things that you can choose from: *It was a small shop and there wasn't much choice.* | **[+of]** *There is a choice of four different colours.* | *We offer a* ***wide choice*** *of wines and beers.* | **spoilt for choice** *BrE*: *Consumers these days are spoilt for choice* (=have a lot of things to choose from).

3 [C] the person or thing that someone chooses: **[+of]** *I don't really like her choice of jewellery.* | *I think London was a*

C

***good choice** as a venue.* | **sb's first/second choice** *My first choice of college was Stanford.*
4 by choice if you do something by choice, you do it because you want to do it and not because you are forced to do it: *She lives alone by choice.*
5 the sth of your choice the person or thing of your choice is the one that you would most like to choose: *My children cannot go to the school of their choice.*
6 the sth of choice the thing of choice is the one that people prefer to use: *It is the drug of choice for this type of illness.* → HOBSON'S CHOICE

COLLOCATIONS

VERBS

have a choice *Students have a choice between German and Spanish.*
make a choice (=choose something) *One of our course advisors can help you to make your choice.*
give sb a choice *Her doctor gave her a choice: take medicine or lose weight.*
be faced with a choice *He was faced with a difficult choice.*
have no choice (but to do sth) *The men had no choice but to obey.*
leave sb with no choice *I was left with no choice but to resign.*
exercise your choice *formal* (=make a choice – used especially when talking about someone using their right to choose)

ADJECTIVES/NOUN + choice

the right/wrong choice *I think you've made the right choice.*
a difficult choice *It was a very difficult choice for me.*
a stark choice (=a choice between two unpleasant things that you must make) *We faced a stark choice: steal or starve.*
(a) free choice *Students have an entirely free choice of what to study at university.*
an informed choice (=a choice based on knowledge of the facts about something) *The patient should have enough information to make an informed choice.*
consumer choice (=the opportunity for people to choose between different products) | **parental choice**

PHRASES

freedom of choice *Patients should have more freedom of choice.*
given the choice (=if you had a choice) *Given the choice, I probably wouldn't work.*

choice² *adj* **1** [only before noun] *formal* choice food is of very good quality: *choice steak* | *We select only the choicest apples for our pies.* **2 a few choice words/phrases** if you use a few choice words, you say exactly what you mean in an angry way: *He told us what he thought of the idea in a few choice words.*

choir /kwaɪə $ kwaɪr/ ●●○ *n* [C]
1 a group of people who sing together for other people to listen to → **choral**: *He joined a church choir at the age of eight.*
2 [usually singular] the part of a church in which a choir sits during religious ceremonies

choir·boy /ˈkwaɪəbɔɪ $ ˈkwaɪr-/ *n* [C] a young boy who sings in a church choir

choir·mas·ter /ˈkwaɪəˌmɑːstə $ ˈkwaɪrˌmæstər/ *n* [C] someone who teaches a choir to sing together

choke¹ /tʃəʊk $ tʃoʊk/ ●●○ *v*
1 [I] to be unable to breathe properly because something is in your throat or there is not enough air: **[+on]** *He choked on a piece of bread.* | *Six people **choked to death** on the fumes.*
2 [T] if something chokes you, it makes you unable to breathe properly: *I felt as if there was a weight on my chest, choking me.* | *The smoke was choking me.*
3 [T] to prevent someone from breathing by putting your hands around their throat and pressing on it: *His hands were round her throat, choking her.*
4 [I,T] to be unable to talk clearly because you are feeling a strong emotion: **[+with]** *He was choking with rage.* | *I was too choked with emotion to speak.* | *Her voice was choked with rage.*
5 [T] (*also* **choke sth ↔ out**) to say something with difficulty because you are very upset or angry: *'Get out,' she choked.*
6 [T] (*also* **choke sth ↔ up**) to fill a place so that things cannot move through it: *Weeds were choking the stream.* | **be choked (up) with sth** *The gutters were choked up with leaves.*
7 [I] *informal* to fail at doing something, especially a sport, because there is a lot of pressure on you: *People said I choked, but I just had a bad day on the golf course.*
8 [T] if one plant chokes another, it kills it by growing all around it and taking away its light and room to grow: *Weeds can quickly choke delicate garden plants.*
9 choke a horse *AmE spoken* if you say that something is big enough to choke a horse, you are emphasizing that it is very big: *a wad of bills big enough to choke a horse*
choke sth ↔ **back** *phr v* to control your anger, sadness etc so that you do not show it: *He **choked back tears** as he described what had happened.* | *She choked back a sob.* | *I choked back my anger.*
choke off sth *phr v* to prevent something from happening: *It is feared that higher interest rates might choke off economic recovery.*
choke sth ↔ **out** *phr v* to say something with difficulty because you are very upset or angry: *His heart hammered as he choked out the words.* | *'No!' she choked out.*
choke up *phr v*
1 choke sth ↔ up to fill a place so that things cannot move through it: **be choked up with sth** *The stream was choked up with weeds.*
2 choke sb up to make someone feel very upset and unable to talk: *This song really chokes me up.* | *I was really choked up when I saw her again.*

choke² *n* [C] **1** a piece of equipment in a vehicle that controls the amount of air going into the engine, and that is used to help the engine start **2** the sound that someone makes when they cannot breathe properly because something is in their throat or there is not enough air: *She gave a little choke of laughter.*

ˈchoke chain *BrE*, **ˈchoke collar** *AmE n* [C] a chain that is fastened around the neck of a dog to control it

choke·cher·ry /ˈtʃəʊktʃeri $ ˈtʃoʊk-/ *n* (*plural* **chokecherries**) [C] a North American tree that produces small sour fruit

choked /tʃəʊkt $ tʃoʊkt/ *adj* [not before noun] *BrE* very upset: *I was really choked when I heard he'd died.*

chok·er /ˈtʃəʊkə $ ˈtʃoʊkər/ *n* [C] a piece of jewellery that fits very tightly around a woman's neck: *a diamond choker* → see picture at JEWELLERY

chol·er /ˈkɒlə $ ˈkɑːlər/ *n* [U] *literary* great anger: *What had brought on this fit of choler?*

chol·e·ra /ˈkɒlərə $ ˈkɑː-/ *n* [U] a serious disease that causes sickness and sometimes death. It is caused by eating infected food or drinking infected water.

chol·e·ric /ˈkɒlərɪk $ ˈkɑː-/ *adj literary* bad-tempered or angry: *He was a choleric, ill-tempered man.*

cho·les·te·rol /kəˈlestərɒl $ -roʊl/ ●○○ *n* [U] a chemical substance found in your blood. Too much cholesterol in your body may cause heart disease.

chomp /tʃɒmp $ tʃɑːmp, tʃɒːmp/ *v* [I] *informal* to eat something: **[+on]** *She was chomping on a bread roll.* | **[+away]** *a boy chomping away on a banana* | *British people **chomp their way through** more than a billion bars of chocolate every year.*

choo-choo /ˈtʃuː tʃuː/ *n* [C] *spoken* a train – used by children or when speaking to children

This graph shows how common different grammar patterns of the verb **choose** are.

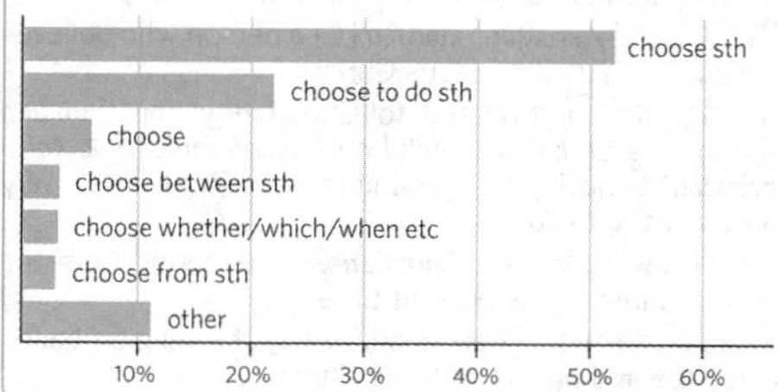

choose /tʃuːz/ ●●● S1 W1 *v (past tense* **chose** /tʃəʊz $ tʃoʊz/, *past participle* **chosen** /ˈtʃəʊzən $ ˈtʃoʊ-/) [I,T]
1 to decide which one of a number of things or people you want → **choice**: *It took us ages to choose a new carpet.* | *A panel of judges will choose the winner.* | *He* **chose** *his* **words** *carefully as he spoke.* | *I don't mind which one we have – you choose.* | **[+between]** *For pudding we could choose between ice cream and apple tart.* | **[+from]** *You can choose from a wide range of vehicles.* | **choose to do sth** *I chose to learn German rather than French.* | **choose sb/sth to do sth** *They chose Donald to be their leader.* | **choose sb/sth as sth** *The company chose London as its base.* | **choose sb/sth for sth** *Why did you choose me for the job?* | **choose which/whether/what etc** *You can choose what you want to do first.*
2 to decide to do something because that is what you prefer to do: **choose to do sth** *I chose to ignore his advice.* | *You can, if you choose, invest in the stock market.*
3 there is little/nothing to choose between sth used when you think that two or more things are equally good and you cannot decide which is better: *There was little to choose between the two candidates.*

THESAURUS

choose to decide which one of several things you want: *I chose a black dress.* | *Which dessert should I choose?*
pick to choose something, especially without thinking carefully. **Pick** is more informal than **choose**: *Pick any number from one to ten.*
select *formal* to choose something, especially after thinking carefully: *The committee will meet to select a new chairman.*
opt for/go for to choose one thing instead of another: *Many car buyers opt for used vehicles.* | *I think I'll go for the chocolate cake.*
decide on to choose something from many possible things, especially when the decision has been difficult or taken a long time: *Thomas had decided on a career as a writer.*
single out to choose one person or thing from a group because they are better, worse, more important etc than the others: *Why should he be singled out for special treatment?*
take your pick *especially spoken* to choose anything you want, especially when there are many different things available: *You can take your pick from Bodrum's many bars and restaurants.*

choos·y, **choosey** /ˈtʃuːzi/ *adj informal* someone who is choosy will only accept things that they like a lot or they consider to be very good: **[+about]** *She's very choosy about clothes.*

chop¹ /tʃɒp $ tʃɑːp/ ●●● S3 *v* (**chopped**, **chopping**) [T]
1 (*also* **chop up**) to cut something into smaller pieces: *He went outside to chop some more wood for the fire.* | *Can you chop up some carrots for me?* | *Add two* **finely chopped** *onions and a clove of garlic.* | **chop sth into pieces/chunks etc** *Chop the meat into small cubes.* **THESAURUS** ▶ **CUT**
2 *informal* to reduce an amount of money by a large amount: *He suddenly found that his income had been chopped in half.*
3 chop and change *BrE informal* to keep changing your mind: *You can't keep chopping and changing like this!*

chop at sth *phr v* to hit something with a sharp tool in order to cut it: *They chopped at the bushes with their knives.*
chop sth ↔ **down** *phr v* to make a tree fall down by cutting it with a sharp tool: *A couple of the older trees will have to be chopped down.* | *Large areas of rainforest are being chopped down every day.*
chop sth ↔ **off** *phr v* to remove something by cutting it with a sharp tool: *The branch had been chopped off.*

chop² *n* [C] **1** a small piece of meat on a bone, usually cut from a sheep or pig → **steak**: *a grilled* **pork/lamb chop** **2 the chop** *BrE* **a)** if you get or are given the chop, you lose your job: *Six more staff got the chop last week.* | *I might be* **for the chop** (=lose my job). **b)** if something gets or is given the chop, it is closed or stopped because people do not want to pay for it anymore: *The project might get the chop.* | *This factory might now be* **for the chop** (=likely to be closed). **3** a hard downward movement that you make with your hand: *a karate chop* **4** the act of hitting something with a sharp tool in order to cut it: *With one last chop he split the log in two.* **5 chops** [plural] *informal* the lower part of the face of a person or animal – used humorously: *Jack was grinning all over his chops.* **6 the chops** *informal* technical skill, especially at music, COMEDY, acting etc: *Has she got the chops to carry off such a big role?*

ˌchop-ˈchop *interjection* an expression used when you want someone to hurry: *Come on! Chop-chop!*

chop·per /ˈtʃɒpə $ ˈtʃɑːpər/ *n* [C] **1** *BrE* a large knife that you use for cutting large pieces of meat **2** *informal* a HELICOPTER: *There was a police chopper waiting for us.* **3** a type of MOTORCYCLE on which the front wheel is further forward than the place where your hands rest **4 choppers** [plural] *informal* teeth: *a row of huge white choppers*

ˈchopping board *BrE*, **ˈchopping block** *AmE* *n* [C] a large piece of wood or plastic that you cut meat or vegetables on when you are cooking

chop·py /ˈtʃɒpi $ ˈtʃɑːpi/ *adj* choppy water has a lot of waves and is not smooth to sail on: *The small boat bobbed about on the choppy water.*

chop·stick /ˈtʃɒp-stɪk $ ˈtʃɑːp-/ *n* [C usually plural] one of the two thin sticks that you use to eat food in many countries in Asia

CHOPSTICK

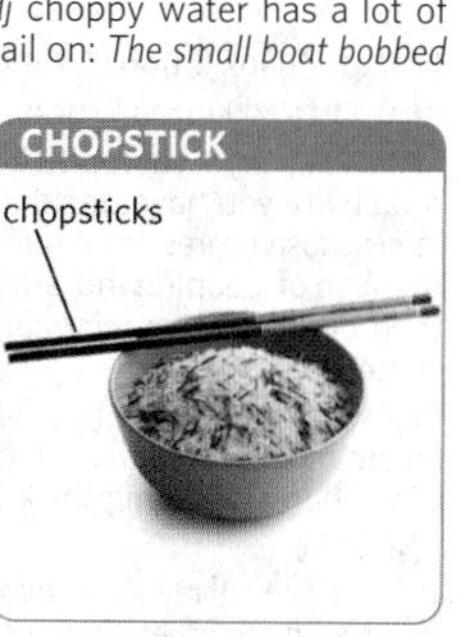

chop su·ey /ˌtʃɒp ˈsuːi $ ˌtʃɑːp-/ *n* [U] a Chinese dish of meat and vegetables, served with rice

cho·ral /ˈkɔːrəl/ *adj* [only before noun] related to music that is sung by a large group of people together → **choir**: *an evening of choral music*

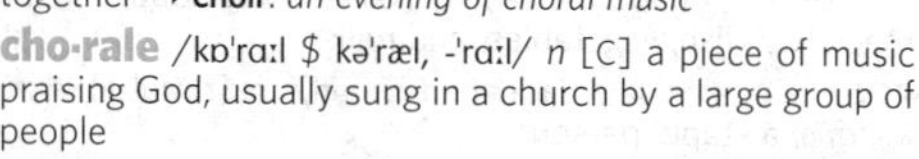

cho·rale /kɒˈrɑːl $ kəˈræl, -ˈrɑːl/ *n* [C] a piece of music praising God, usually sung in a church by a large group of people

chord /kɔːd $ kɔːrd/ ●●○ *n* [C]
1 a combination of several musical notes that are played at the same time and sound pleasant together
2 strike/touch a chord (with sb) to do or say something that people feel is familiar or true: *Many of the things she says will strike a chord with other young women.* | *He knew that what he was saying had touched a chord.*
3 *technical* a straight line joining two points on a curve → see picture at CIRCLE¹ ⚠ Do not confuse with **cord** (=thick string), which has the same pronunciation.

chore /tʃɔː $ tʃɔːr/ ●○○ *n* [C]
1 a small job that you have to do regularly, especially work that you do to keep a house clean: *everyday chores like shopping and housework* | *We share the domestic chores.*
2 something you have to do that is very boring and unpleasant: *I find driving a real chore.*

chor·e·og·raph /ˈkɒriəgrɑːf, ˈkɔː- $ ˈkɔːriəgræf/ *v* [T] to arrange how dancers should move during a performance: *The show is very cleverly choreographed.*

chor·e·og·ra·phy /ˌkɒriˈɒɡrəfi, ˌkɔː- $ ˌkɔːriˈɑːɡ-/ *n* [U] the art of arranging how dancers should move during a performance —**choreographer** *n* [C]

chor·is·ter /ˈkɒrɪstə $ ˈkɔːrɪstər, ˈkɑː-/ *n* [C] a singer in a church CHOIR

cho·ri·zo /tʃəˈriːzəʊ $ -zoʊ/ *n* [U] a spicy SAUSAGE made in Spain

chor·tle /ˈtʃɔːtl $ ˈtʃɔːrtl/ *v* [I] *formal* to laugh because you are amused or pleased about something: *Harry chortled with delight.* —**chortle** *n* [C]

cho·rus¹ /ˈkɔːrəs/ ●●○ *n* [C]

1 the part of a song that is repeated after each VERSE: *Everyone joined in the chorus.*

2 a large group of people who sing together SYN **choir**: *I sing with the university chorus.*

3 a piece of music written to be sung by a large group of people: *a recording of the 'Hallelujah Chorus'*

4 a group of singers, dancers, or actors who act together in a show but do not have the main parts: *New voices are needed to join the chorus for the annual festival in October.*

5 a chorus of thanks/disapproval/protest etc something that a lot of people all say at the same time: *The minister was greeted with a chorus of boos.* | *There was a chorus of agreement from the committee.* | *More politicians have now joined in the chorus of complaints.*

6 in chorus if people say something in chorus, they say the same thing at the same time: *'Thank you,' they said in chorus.*

chorus² *v* [T] if people chorus something, they say it at the same time: *'Hurry up!' chorused the girls.*

ˈchorus girl *n* [C] a woman who sings and dances with a group of other performers in a show or film

ˈchorus line *n* [C] a group of people who stand in a straight line and sing and dance together in a show or film

chose /tʃəʊz $ tʃoʊz/ *v* the past tense of CHOOSE

cho·sen¹ /ˈtʃəʊzən $ ˈtʃoʊ-/ the past participle of CHOOSE

chosen² *adj* **1 chosen field/career/profession etc** the job or activity you have decided to do: *He was very successful in his chosen career as a barrister.* **2 the chosen few** a small number of people who are treated as special and better than other people: *information made available only to the chosen few*

chow¹ /tʃaʊ/ *n* **1** [U] *old-fashioned informal* food: *I ordered some chow and sat down.* **2** [C] (*also* **ˈchow chow**) a type of dog with long thick fur that first came from China

chow² *v*

chow down *phr v AmE informal* to eat: *She had to chow down with the others in the cafeteria.*

chow·der /ˈtʃaʊdə $ -ər/ *n* [U] a thick soup usually made with fish, vegetables, and milk

chow·der·head /ˈtʃaʊdəhed $ -ər-/ *n* [singular] *AmE informal* a stupid person

chow mein /ˌtʃaʊ ˈmeɪn/ *n* [U] a Chinese dish made with meat, vegetables, and NOODLES

Christ¹ /kraɪst/ (*also* **Jesus Christ**) the man who is worshipped by Christians as the son of God → **Christian**: *a follower of Christ*

Christ² *interjection* used to express annoyance or surprise. Some Christian people think this use is offensive: *Christ! That's hot!*

chris·ten /ˈkrɪsən/ *v* [T] **1** to officially give a child its name at a Christian religious ceremony → **baptize**: *She was christened Sarah.* **2** to give something or someone a name: *His fans christened him the king of rock.* | *The new plane has been christened the Hawk.* **3** *informal* to use something for the first time: *We haven't christened the new garden chairs yet.*

Chris·ten·dom /ˈkrɪsəndəm/ *n* [U] *formal* all the Christian people or countries in the world

chris·ten·ing /ˈkrɪsənɪŋ/ *n* [C] a Christian religious ceremony at which a child is officially given a name and becomes a member of a Christian church → **baptism**

Chris·tian¹ /ˈkrɪstʃən, -tiən/ *n* [C] a person who believes in the ideas taught by Jesus Christ

Christian² *adj* **1** related to Christianity: *the Christian religion* | *the Christian church* | *a Christian minister* **2** (*also* **christian**) behaving in a good kind way: *That wasn't a very christian thing to do!*

ˌChristian ˈera *n* **the Christian era** the period from the birth of Christ to the present time

Chris·ti·an·i·ty /ˌkrɪstiˈænəti/ *n* [U] the religion based on the life and beliefs of Jesus Christ

ˈChristian name *n* [C] a person's first name, especially when they are given this name in a Christian religious ceremony → **surname**: *She didn't like children to call her by her Christian name.*

ˌChristian ˈScience *n* [U] a religion started in America in 1866, which includes the belief that illnesses can be cured by faith —**Christian Scientist** *n* [C]

Chris·tie's /ˈkrɪstiz/ *trademark* a famous AUCTION company with its main offices in London and New York City, where valuable paintings, old furniture, rare books etc are sold

Christ·mas /ˈkrɪsməs/ ●●● S2 W2 *n* [C,U] the period of time around December 25th, the day when Christians celebrate the birth of Christ: **at Christmas** *We'll see you at Christmas.* | **over Christmas** *I'll be in Scotland over Christmas.* | *Are you going home for Christmas?* | *a Christmas present* | *the Christmas holidays* | *Merry Christmas and a happy New Year everyone!*

GRAMMAR: Patterns with Christmas

at Christmas

- You use **at Christmas** when saying that something happens during the Christmas holiday period: *I'll see you at Christmas.* ✗ Don't say: *I'll see you on Christmas.*
- You can also say **at Christmas time**: *At Christmas time, the whole family gets together.*

on Christmas Day

- You say **on Christmas Day** when saying that something happens on December 25th: *I have to work on Christmas Day.* ✗ Don't say: *I have to work at Christmas Day.*

for Christmas

- You get a present **for Christmas**: *He gave me a new watch for Christmas.* ✗ Don't say: *He gave me a new watch on Christmas.*

ˈChristmas cake *n* [C,U] a special cake that people eat in Britain at Christmas

ˈChristmas card *n* [C] a special card that people send to friends and relatives at Christmas

ˌChristmas ˈcarol *n* [C] a Christian song that people sing at Christmas

ˌChristmas ˈcookie *n* [C] a special COOKIE that people eat in the US at Christmas

ˌChristmas ˈcracker *n* [C] a tube of coloured paper that two people pull apart at Christmas in Britain for fun. It makes a loud sound as it is pulled apart, and usually contains a small toy.

ˌChristmas ˈDay *n* [U] December 25th, the day when most Christians celebrate the birth of Christ: *I always spend Christmas Day with my family.*

ˌChristmas ˈdinner *n* [C] a special meal that people eat on Christmas Day

ˌChristmas ˈEve *n* [U] December 24th, the day before Christmas Day: *We spent Christmas Eve cooking and getting ready for Christmas Day.* | *Unfortunately, I've got to work on Christmas Eve.*

ˌChristmas ˈpudding *n* [C] a special sweet food that contains a lot of dried fruit and is eaten in Britain at the end of the main meal on Christmas Day

ˌChristmas ˈstocking *n* [C] a long sock which children

leave in their house on Christmas Eve to be filled with presents

Christ·mas·sy /ˈkrɪsməsi/ *adj* typical of Christmas: *It looked very Christmassy with lights on the trees.*

Christ·mas·time /ˈkrɪsməstaɪm/ *n* [U] the period around Christmas

ˈChristmas tree *n* [C] a FIR tree that people put in their houses and decorate for Christmas

chro·mat·ic /krəʊˈmætɪk, krə- $ kroʊ-, krə-/ *adj* **1** *technical* related to a musical scale which consists of SEMITONES: *a chromatic scale | chromatic harmonies* **2** *formal* related to bright colours

chrome /krəʊm $ kroʊm/ *n* [U] a type of hard shiny metal: *a chrome candleholder*

ˌchrome ˈyellow *n* [U] a very bright yellow colour —**chrome yellow** *adj*

chro·mi·um /ˈkrəʊmiəm $ ˈkroʊ-/ *n* [U] a hard blue-white metal that is used to cover metal objects with a shiny silver protective surface. It is a chemical ELEMENT: symbol Cr: *a* ***chromium-plated*** *handrail*

chro·mo·pho·bi·a /ˌkrəʊməˈfəʊbiə $ ˌkroʊməˈfoʊ-/ *n* [U] *technical* a strong fear of colours, often combined with the unreasonable belief that something will be bad if it is a particular colour —**chromophobic** *adj*

chro·mo·some /ˈkrəʊməsəʊm $ ˈkroʊməsoʊm/ *n* [C] a part of every living cell that is shaped like a thread and contains the GENEs that control the size, shape etc that a plant or animal has → **y chromosome**

chron·ic /ˈkrɒnɪk $ ˈkrɑː-/ ●●○ *adj*
1 a chronic disease or illness is one that continues for a long time and cannot be cured → **acute**: *chronic arthritis | chronic asthma | chronic heart disease*
2 a chronic problem is one that continues for a long time and cannot easily be solved: *chronic unemployment | There is a chronic shortage of teachers.*
3 chronic alcoholic/gambler etc someone who has behaved in a particular way for a long time and cannot stop: *He was a chronic alcoholic and unable to hold down a job. | a chronic smoker*
4 *BrE informal* extremely bad: *The food was absolutely chronic!* —**chronically** /-kli/ *adv*: *patients who are chronically ill | The service is chronically underfunded.*

ˌchronic faˈtigue ˌsyndrome *n* [U] an illness that makes you feel very tired and weak and can last for a long time

chron·i·cle¹ /ˈkrɒnɪkəl $ ˈkrɑː-/ ●○○ *n* [C] a written record of a series of events, especially historical events, written in the order in which they happened: **[+of]** *a chronicle of his life during the war years*

chronicle² *v* [T] to describe events in the order in which they happened: *His life is chronicled in a new biography published last week. | The book chronicles the events leading up to the war.*

chron·o·graph /ˈkrɒnəgrɑːf $ ˈkrɑːnəgræf/ *n* [C] a scientific instrument for measuring periods of time

chron·o·log·i·cal /ˌkrɒnəˈlɒdʒɪkəl◂ $ ˌkrɑːnəˈlɑː-/ *adj* **1** arranged according to when things happened or were made: *We arranged the documents* ***in chronological order***. **2 chronological age** a person's chronological age is how old they actually are, rather than how old their mind or body seems —**chronologically** /-kli/ *adv*: *The paintings are displayed chronologically.*

chro·nol·o·gy /krəˈnɒlədʒi $ -ˈnɑː-/ *n* (*plural* **chronologies**) **1** [U] the order in which events happened in the past: **[+of]** *It is important to establish the chronology of the events.* **2** [C] an account of events in the order in which they happened: *The book includes a chronology of his life and works.*

chro·nom·e·ter /krəˈnɒmɪtə $ -ˈnɑːmɪtər/ *n* [C] a very exact clock, used for scientific purposes

chrys·a·lis /ˈkrɪsəlɪs/ *n* [C] a MOTH or BUTTERFLY at the stage of development when it has a hard outer shell and is changing into its adult form

chry·san·the·mum /krɪˈsænθəməm/ *n* [C] a garden plant with large brightly coloured flowers → see picture at **FLOWER¹**

chub /tʃʌb/ *n* [C] a fish that lives in lakes and rivers

chub·by /ˈtʃʌbi/ *adj* slightly fat in a way that looks healthy and attractive: *a chubby six-year-old | a baby with round chubby cheeks* **THESAURUS** ▸ **FAT** —**chubbiness** *n* [U]

chuck¹ /tʃʌk/ *v* [T] *especially BrE informal* **1** to throw something in a careless or relaxed way: **chuck sth on/out of/into etc sth** *Tania chucked her bag down on the sofa. | I chucked a few things into a suitcase and left.* | **chuck sb sth** *Chuck me that pen, would you?* **2** to throw something away because you do not want it anymore: *I think I might have chucked it by mistake.* **3** (*also* **chuck sth ↔ in**) to leave your job: *You haven't chucked your job, have you?* **4** *BrE* to end a romantic relationship with someone: *Why did Judy chuck him?* **5 chuck it down** to rain very heavily: *It chucked it down all afternoon.* **6 chuck sb under the chin** to gently touch someone under their chin in a friendly way

chuck sth ↔ **away** *phr v informal* to throw something away because you do not want it anymore: *I chucked all my old clothes away when we moved house.*

chuck sth ↔ **in** *phr v* to leave your job: *He had a job but he chucked it in. | I decided to* ***chuck it all in*** *and go to Australia.*

chuck sb **off** sth *phr v informal* **1** to make someone leave a place or stop using something: *He'll chuck you off his land if he finds you.* **2 chuck yourself off sth** to jump from somewhere that is very high: *She tried to chuck herself off the bridge twice last week.*

chuck sb/sth ↔ **out** *phr v informal* **1** to throw something away because you do not want it anymore: *It was broken so I chucked it out.* **2** to make someone leave a place or a job: *Their landlord chucked them out when they couldn't pay the rent.* | **[+of]** *They got chucked out of the pub for fighting.*

chuck² *n* **1** [C] part of a machine that holds something firmly so that it does not move **2** [singular] *spoken* a friendly word used to address someone in some parts of northern England

chuck·le /ˈtʃʌkəl/ ●○○ *v* [I] to laugh quietly: *What are you chuckling about?* **THESAURUS** ▸ **LAUGH** —**chuckle** *n* [C]: *Rosie gave a little chuckle.*

ˌchuck ˈsteak *n* [U] meat that comes from just above the shoulder of a cow

ˈchuck ˌwagon *n* [C] *AmE old-fashioned* a vehicle that carries food for a group of people

chuffed /tʃʌft/ *adj* [not before noun] *BrE informal* very pleased or happy: *He's really chuffed about passing the exam.*

chug /tʃʌg/ *v* (**chugged**, **chugging**) **1** [I always + adv/prep] if a car, train etc chugs somewhere, it moves there slowly, with the engine making a repeated low sound: **[+along/up/around etc]** *The boat chugged out of the harbour.* **2** [T] (*also* **chug-a-lug**) *AmE informal* to drink all of something in a glass or bottle without stopping **3** [I always + adv/prep] to make slow but steady progress: *The economy just keeps chugging along.* —**chug** *n* [C usually singular]

chug·ger /ˈtʃʌgə $ -ər/ *n* [C] *BrE informal* someone who is paid to stop people in the street and persuade them to give money regularly to a CHARITY. The word comes from combining the words CHARITY and MUGGER.

chum /tʃʌm/ *n* **1** [C] *informal old-fashioned* a good friend: *Freddie's an old* ***school chum*** *of mine.* **2** [U] small pieces of oily fish, used to catch other fish

chum·my /ˈtʃʌmi/ *adj informal* friendly: *You and Eric have become quite chummy, haven't you?*

chump /tʃʌmp/ *n* [C] **1** *informal* someone who is silly or stupid, and who is easily deceived **2 chump chop/steak** *BrE* a thick piece of meat with a bone in it

chun·der /ˈtʃʌndə $ -ər/ *v* [I] *informal* to VOMIT

chunk /tʃʌŋk/ ●●○ *n* [C]
1 a large thick piece of something that does not have an even shape: *ice chunks* | **[+of]** *a chunk of bread* **THESAURUS** ▸ **PIECE** → see picture at **PIECE¹**
2 a large part or amount of something: *The rent takes a large chunk out of my monthly salary.* | **[+of]** *A huge chunk of the audience got up and left before the end of the show.*

C

3 a chunk of change *AmE informal* a large amount of money: *Lurie risked a pretty big chunk of change on the race.*

chunk·y /ˈtʃʌŋki/ ●○○ *adj*
1 thick, solid, and heavy: *chunky jewellery* → see picture at THICK[1]
2 chunky food has large pieces in it: *chunky peanut butter*
3 someone who is chunky has a broad heavy body

chun·ter /ˈtʃʌntə $ -ər/ *v* [I] *BrE informal* to talk for a long time, usually about something that is not interesting: *He was chuntering on about the problems he was having with his car.*

church /tʃɜːtʃ $ tʃɜːrtʃ/ ●●● S1 W1 *n*
1 [C] a building where Christians go to worship → **cathedral**: *a short church service | church bells*
2 [U] the religious ceremonies in a church: *Mrs Dobson invited us to dinner after church. | My parents* **go to church** *every Sunday.* | **at church** *We didn't see you at church this morning.*
3 [C] (*also* **Church**) one of the separate groups within the Christian religion: *the Catholic Church*
4 [singular, U] the institution of the Christian religion, and all the priests and other ministers who are part of it: *the church's attitude towards marriage | separation of church and state*

church·go·er /ˈtʃɜːtʃˌɡəʊə $ ˈtʃɜːrtʃˌɡoʊər/ *n* [C] someone who goes to church regularly

church·man /ˈtʃɜːtʃmən $ ˈtʃɜːrtʃ-/ *n* (*plural* **churchmen** /-mən/) [C] a priest SYN **clergyman**

ˌChurch of ˈEngland *n* **the Church of England** the state church in England, the official leader of which is the king or queen

ˌChurch of ˈScotland *n* **the Church of Scotland** the state church in Scotland

ˈchurch ˌschool *n* [C] a school in Britain that is partly controlled by a church

church·war·den /ˌtʃɜːtʃˈwɔːdn $ ˈtʃɜːrtʃwɔːrdn/ *n* [C] someone who looks after church property and money

church·wom·an /ˈtʃɜːtʃˌwʊmən $ ˈtʃɜːrtʃ-/ *n* (*plural* **churchwomen** /-ˌwɪmɪn/) [C] a female priest SYN **clergywoman**

church·yard /ˈtʃɜːtʃjɑːd $ ˈtʃɜːrtʃjɑːrd/ *n* [C] a piece of land around a church where people are buried → **graveyard**

churl·ish /ˈtʃɜːlɪʃ $ ˈtʃɜːr-/ *adj formal* not polite or friendly: *It seemed churlish to refuse his invitation.*

churn[1] /tʃɜːn $ tʃɜːrn/ ●○○ *v*
1 [I] if your stomach churns, you feel sick because you are nervous or frightened: *My stomach was churning on the day of the exam.*
2 [I,T] (*also* **churn up**) if water, mud etc churns, or if something churns it, it moves about violently: *We watched the ocean churn.*
3 [I] if a machine, engine, wheel etc churns, it or its parts begin to move: *I pressed the gas pedal, and slowly the wheels began to churn.*
4 [T] to make milk by using a churn

churn sth ↔ **out** *phr v* to produce large quantities of something, especially without caring about quality: *She's been churning out novels for 20 years.*

churn sb/sth ↔ **up** *phr v*
1 churn sth ↔ up to damage the surface of the ground, especially by walking on it or driving a vehicle over it: *The lawn had been churned up by the tractor.*
2 churn sth ↔ up to move water, mud etc around violently: *The oars had churned up the mud, clouding the water.*
3 *BrE* to make someone upset or angry: *Though she looked calm, in reality she was churned up inside.*

churn[2] *n* **1** [C] a container used for shaking milk in order to make it into butter **2** (*also* **milk churn**) [C] *BrE* a large metal container used to carry milk in **3** [U] the number of people who stop buying or using a company's products or services during a particular period

chute /ʃuːt/ *n* [C] **1** a long narrow structure that slopes down, so that things or people can slide down it from one place to another: *a rubbish chute | a laundry chute | The pool had several water chutes.* **2** *informal* a PARACHUTE

chut·ney /ˈtʃʌtni/ *n* [U] a mixture of fruits, hot-tasting SPICES, and sugar, that is eaten especially with meat or cheese: *mango chutney*

chutz·pah /ˈhʊtspə/ *n* [U] *informal* a lot of confidence and courage to do something, especially something that might involve being impolite to someone in authority – used to show approval SYN **nerve**: *It took a lot of chutzpah to talk to your boss like that.*

CIA, the /ˌsiː aɪ ˈeɪ/ (***the Central Intelligence Agency***) the department of the US government that collects information about other countries, especially secretly → **FBI**

cia·bat·ta /tʃəˈbætə/ *n* [U] a type of flat Italian bread made with olive oil

ciao /tʃaʊ/ *interjection informal* used to say goodbye

ci·ca·da /səˈkɑːdə $ səˈkeɪdə, -ˈkɑː-/ *n* [C] an insect that lives in hot countries, has large transparent wings, and makes a high singing noise

CID, the /ˌsiː aɪ ˈdiː/ (***the Criminal Investigation Department***) the department of the British police that deals with very serious crimes

-cide /saɪd/ *suffix* [in nouns] another form of the suffix -ICIDE: *genocide* (=killing a whole race of people) —**-cidal** [in adjectives] —**-cidally** [in adverbs]

ci·der /ˈsaɪdə $ -ər/ *n* **1** [C,U] *BrE* an alcoholic drink made from apples, or a glass of this drink SYN **hard cider** *AmE* **2** [U] (*also* **apple cider**) *AmE* a non-alcoholic drink made from apples

ci·gar /sɪˈɡɑː $ -ˈɡɑːr/ ●●○ *n* [C] a thick tube-shaped thing that people smoke, and which is made from tobacco leaves that have been rolled up → **cigarette**

cig·a·rette /ˌsɪɡəˈret $ ˈsɪɡəˌret, ˌsɪɡəˈret/ ●●● S2 W3 *n* [C] a thin tube of paper filled with finely cut tobacco that people smoke → **cigar**: *a packet of cigarettes*

cigaˈrette ˌbutt / $ ˈ... ˌ./ (*also* **cigaˈrette end** *BrE*) *n* [C] the part of a cigarette that remains when someone has finished smoking it

cigaˈrette ˌholder / $ ˈ... ˌ../ *n* [C] a narrow tube for holding a cigarette

cigaˈrette ˌlighter / $ ˈ... ˌ../ *n* [C] a small object that produces a flame for lighting cigarettes, CIGARS etc SYN **lighter**

cigaˈrette ˌpaper / $ ˈ... ˌ../ *n* [C,U] thin paper that people put tobacco in to make their own cigarettes

cig·gy /ˈsɪɡi/ *n* (*plural* **ciggies**) [C] *BrE spoken informal* a cigarette

ci·lan·tro /səˈlæntrəʊ $ səˈlɑːntroʊ, -ˈlæn-/ *n* [U] *AmE* a herb, used especially in Asian and Mexican cooking SYN **coriander** *BrE*

C in C /ˌsiː ɪn ˈsiː/ *n* [C] a COMMANDER IN CHIEF

cinch[1] /sɪntʃ/ *n* [singular] *informal* **1** something that is very easy: *'How was the exam?' 'Oh, it was a cinch!'* | **be a cinch to do sth** *The program is a cinch to install.* **2** *AmE* something that will definitely happen, or someone who will definitely do something: **be a cinch to do sth** *Most observers say the president is a cinch to win re-election.*

cinch[2] *v* [T] **1** to pull a belt, STRAP etc tightly around something: *a blue dress cinched at the waist by a wide belt* **2** *AmE* to make something certain to happen: *They cinched a place in the play-off.*

cin·der /ˈsɪndə $ -ər/ *n* [C usually plural] a very small piece of burnt wood, coal etc: *a cold hearth full of cinders | The cake was* ***burnt to a cinder*** (=completely burnt).

ˈcinder block *n* [C] *AmE* a large grey brick used to build houses and other buildings, made from CEMENT and cinders SYN **breeze-block** *BrE* → see picture at BLOCK[1]

Cin·der·el·la /ˌsɪndəˈrelə/ *n* [C] a person or thing that has been ignored or treated as less important than other people or things: **[+of]** *Their economy was the Cinderella of the industrialized world.* —**Cinderella** *adj* [only before noun]: *Mental health care has been the Cinderella service for too long.*

cine- /sɪnɪ/ *adj BrE* relating to films or to the film industry: *a cine-projector*

cine·cam·e·ra /ˈsɪni ˌkæmərə/ *n* [C] *BrE* a camera for making moving films, rather than photographs

cin·e·film /ˈsɪni ˌfɪlm/ *n* [U] *BrE* film used in a cine-camera

cin·e·ma /ˈsɪnəmə/ ●●● S3 *n*
1 [C] *especially BrE* a building in which films are shown SYN **movie theater** *AmE*: *It's on at the local cinema.*
2 the cinema *BrE* if you go to the cinema, you go to a cinema to see a film: *We decided to **go to the cinema**.*
3 [singular, U] the skill or industry of making films → **cinematic**: *a leading figure in Italian cinema*

cin·e·ma·go·er /ˈsɪnəməˌɡəʊə $ -ˌɡoʊər/ *n* [C usually plural] *BrE* someone who goes to the cinema to see a film SYN **moviegoer** *AmE*

cin·e·mat·ic /ˌsɪnəˈmætɪk◂/ *adj* relating to films: *a cinematic masterpiece*

cin·e·ma·tog·ra·phy /ˌsɪnəməˈtɒɡrəfi $ -ˈtɑː-/ *n* [U] the skill or study of making films —**cinematographer** *n* [C]

cin·e·phile /ˈsɪnɪfaɪl/ *n* [C] someone who likes films very much and considers them to be a form of art, not just entertainment: *He is a complete cinephile.*

cin·na·mon /ˈsɪnəmən/ *n* [U] a sweet-smelling brown substance used for giving a special taste to cakes and other sweet foods: *a cinnamon roll*

ci·pher, **cypher** /ˈsaɪfə $ -ər/ *n* **1** [C,U] *formal* a system of secret writing SYN **code**: *an expert in ciphers | messages written in cipher* **2** [C] someone who is not important and has no power or influence: *At work, she was a cipher, a functionary, nothing more.* **3** [C] *literary* the number 0 SYN **zero**

cir·ca /ˈsɜːkə $ ˈsɜːr-/ *prep formal* used before a date to show that something happened close to but not exactly on that date SYN **around**: *manuscripts dating from circa 1100* THESAURUS ▸ APPROXIMATE

cir·ca·di·an /sɜːˈkeɪdiən $ sɜːr-/ *adj* [only before noun] *technical* relating to a period of 24 hours, used especially when talking about changes in people's bodies: *the body's circadian rhythm*

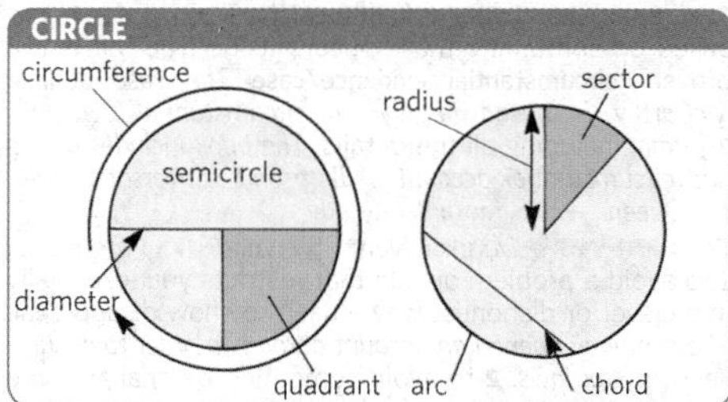

cir·cle¹ /ˈsɜːkəl $ ˈsɜːr-/ ●●● S2 W2 *n* [C]
1 SHAPE a completely round shape, like the letter O: *Draw a circle 10 cm in diameter. | Cut the pastry into circles.*
2 ARRANGED IN A CIRCLE a group of people or things arranged in the shape of a circle: *The children stood round **in a circle**. |* **[+of]** *a circle of chairs*
3 GROUP OF PEOPLE a group of people who know each other and meet regularly, or who have similar interests or jobs: **[+of]** *a circle of friends |* **political/legal/literary etc circles** *He's well-known **in** fashionable **circles**. | Johnson was part of the president's **inner circle*** (=the people who have the most influence).
4 THEATRE *BrE* the upper floor of a theatre, that has seats arranged in curved rows SYN **balcony** *AmE* → see picture at THEATRE
5 go/run around in circles to think or argue about something without deciding anything or making progress
6 come/go full circle (*also* **turn full circle** *BrE*) to end in the same situation in which you began, even though there have been changes in the time in between: *Sooner or later, fashion comes full circle.*
7 (dark) circles under your eyes dark areas under your eyes that you have when you are very tired → **square the circle** at SQUARE³(5), → **VICIOUS CIRCLE**

circle² ●●○ *v*
1 [T] to draw a circle around something: *Circle the correct answer.*
2 [I,T] to move in the shape of a circle around something, especially in the air: *The plane circled the airport before landing.* | **[+round/above/over etc]** *The pigeons circled above the terrace.*

cir·clet /ˈsɜːklɪt $ ˈsɜːr-/ *n* [C] a narrow band of gold, silver, or jewels worn around someone's head or arms

cir·cuit /ˈsɜːkɪt $ ˈsɜːr-/ ●●○ W3 *n* [C]
1 a path that forms a circle around an area, or a journey along this path: *We did a circuit of the old city.*
2 *BrE* a track that cars, MOTORBIKES etc race around
3 the tennis/lecture/cabaret etc circuit all the places that are usually visited by someone who plays tennis etc: *a well-known entertainer on the club circuit*
4 the complete circle that an electric current travels: *an electrical circuit*
5 a regular trip around an area made by a judge or a religious leader, so that a court of law or church can meet in several different places: *a circuit judge | a circuit preacher*
6 do circuits *BrE informal* to do CIRCUIT TRAINING → **CLOSED CIRCUIT TELEVISION, PRINTED CIRCUIT, SHORT CIRCUIT**

ˈcircuit board *n* [C] a board in a piece of electrical equipment that uses thin lines of metal to CONDUCT (=carry) electricity between different points

ˈcircuit ˌbreaker *n* [C] a piece of equipment that stops an electric current reaching a machine if the machine becomes dangerous

ˈcircuit ˌcourt *n* [C] a court of law that meets in small towns within a particular area whenever a judge visits from a larger town

cir·cu·i·tous /sɜːˈkjuːɪtəs $ sɜːr-/ *adj* going from one place to another in a way that is longer than the most direct way: *a hard circuitous hike* —**circuitously** *adv*

cir·cuit·ry /ˈsɜːkətri $ ˈsɜːr-/ *n* [U] a system of electric circuits

ˈcircuit ˌtraining *n* [U] *BrE* a series of many different exercises done quickly after each other, in order to increase your fitness

cir·cu·lar¹ /ˈsɜːkjələ $ ˈsɜːrkjələr/ ●●○ *adj*
1 shaped like a circle: *a circular table*
2 moving around in a circle: *a circular bus route*
3 circular argument/logic/reasoning an argument or way of thinking that is not right because the statement it uses to prove that the argument is true can only be true if the original argument is already true —**circularity** /ˌsɜːkjəˈlærəti $ ˌsɜːr-/ *n* [U]

circular² *n* [C] a printed advertisement, notice etc that is sent to lots of people at the same time

ˌcircular ˈfile *n* [C] a WASTEPAPER BASKET - used humorously

ˌcircular ˈsaw *n* [C] an electric tool with a round metal blade that has small sharp parts around the edge, used for cutting wood

cir·cu·late /ˈsɜːkjəleɪt $ ˈsɜːr-/ ●○○ *v*
1 [I,T] to move around within a system, or to make something do this: *Swimming helps to get the blood circulating through the muscles. | Ceiling fans circulated warm air around the room.*
2 [I] if information, facts, ideas etc circulate, they become known by many people: ***Rumours** began **circulating** that the prime minister was seriously ill.*
3 [T] to send goods, information etc to people: *The group circulated petitions calling for a federal law to ban handguns.*
4 [I] to talk to a lot of different people in a group, especially at a party

cir·cu·la·tion /ˌsɜːkjəˈleɪʃən $ ˌsɜːr-/ ●○○ *n*
1 [singular, U] the movement of blood around your body: *Exercise improves the circulation.* | **good/bad circulation** *Doctors had to remove her leg because of bad circulation.*
2 [U] the exchange of information, money etc from one person to another in a group or society: **in/out of circulation** *Police believe there are thousands of illegal guns in*

circulation. | *The book was taken out of circulation.* | **remove/withdraw sth from circulation** *The Treasury Department plans to remove older coins from circulation and replace them with new ones.*
3 [C usually singular] the average number of copies of a newspaper or magazine that are usually sold each day, week, month etc: **[+of]** *The newspaper has a daily circulation of 55,000.*
4 [C,U] the movement of liquid, air etc in a system: *Let's open the windows and get some circulation in here.*
5 in circulation/out of circulation *informal* when someone takes part or does not take part in social activities at a particular time: *Sandy's out of circulation until after her exams.*

C

cir·cu·la·to·ry /ˌsɜːkjəˈleɪtəri, ˈsɜːkjələtəri $ ˈsɜːrkjələtɔːri/ *adj* [only before noun] relating to the movement of blood around your body: *the heart and circulatory system*

cir·cum·cise /ˈsɜːkəmsaɪz $ ˈsɜːr-/ *v* [T] **1** to cut off the skin at the end of the PENIS (=male sex organ) **2** to cut off a woman's CLITORIS (=part of her sex organs)

cir·cum·ci·sion /ˌsɜːkəmˈsɪʒən $ ˌsɜːr-/ *n* [C,U] the act of circumcising someone, or an occasion when a baby is circumcised as part of a religious ceremony

cir·cum·fer·ence /səˈkʌmfərəns $ sər-/ *n* [C usually singular, U] the distance or measurement around the outside of a circle or any round shape → **diameter**, **perimeter**, **radius**: **[+of]** *the circumference of the Earth* | **in circumference** *The island is only nine miles in circumference.* → see picture at CIRCLE[1]

cir·cum·flex /ˈsɜːkəmfleks $ ˈsɜːr-/ *n* [C] a mark placed above a letter in various languages such as French, for example ô

cir·cum·lo·cu·tion /ˌsɜːkəmləˈkjuːʃən $ ˌsɜːr-/ *n* [C,U] *formal* the practice of using too many words to express an idea, instead of saying it directly —**circumlocutory** /ˌsɜːkəmˈlɒkjʊtəri/ *adj*: *a circumlocutory reply*

cir·cum·nav·i·gate /ˌsɜːkəmˈnævɪgeɪt $ ˌsɜːr-/ *v* [T] to sail, fly, or travel completely around the Earth, an island etc —**circumnavigation** /ˌsɜːkəmnævəˈgeɪʃən $ ˌsɜːr-/ *n* [C,U]: *circumnavigation of the world*

cir·cum·scribe /ˈsɜːkəmskraɪb $ ˈsɜːr-/ *v* [T] **1** *formal* to limit power, rights, or abilities SYN **restrict**: *The president's power is circumscribed by Congress and the Supreme Court.* **2** *technical* to draw a line around something: *a circle circumscribed by a square* GRAMMAR **Circumscribe** is usually passive.

cir·cum·spect /ˈsɜːkəmspekt $ ˈsɜːr-/ *adj formal* thinking carefully about something before doing it, in order to avoid risk SYN **cautious**: *The governor was usually circumspect when dealing with the media.* —**circumspectly** *adv* —**circumspection** /ˌsɜːkəmˈspekʃən $ ˌsɜːr-/ *n* [U]

cir·cum·stance /ˈsɜːkəmstæns, -stəns $ ˈsɜːr-/ ●●● S2 W1 AWL *n*
1 [C usually plural] the conditions that affect a situation, action, event etc: *The Soviet Union had been forced by circumstances to sign a pact with Nazi Germany.* | *I can't imagine a circumstance in which I would be willing to steal.* | **in ... circumstances** *The rules can only be waived in exceptional circumstances.* | **under ... circumstances** *Prisoners can only leave their cells under certain circumstances.*
2 under no circumstances (*also* **in no circumstances** *BrE*) used to emphasize that something must definitely not happen: *Under no circumstances are you to go out.*
3 under/given the circumstances (*also* **in the circumstances** *BrE*) used to say that a particular situation makes an action, decision etc necessary, acceptable, or true when it would not normally be: *It's the best result that could be expected under the circumstances.*
4 [U] *formal* the combination of facts, events etc that influence your life, and that you cannot control: *He was a **victim of circumstance**.*
5 circumstances [plural] *formal* the conditions in which you live, especially how much money you have: **economic/financial/personal etc circumstances** *Whether or not you qualify for a loan will depend on your financial circumstances.* | *people living in difficult social circumstances* | **in reduced circumstances** *old-fashioned* (=with much less money than you used to have) → **pomp and circumstance** at POMP

COLLOCATIONS

ADJECTIVES

in/under certain circumstances (=if particular conditions exist) *In certain circumstances you may be refused a visa.*
exceptional/special circumstances *The court may allow this evidence in exceptional circumstances.*
normal circumstances *In normal circumstances, a child's language will develop naturally.*
particular circumstances (=special or specific) *There may be particular circumstances in which this rule will not apply.*
difficult circumstances *Many teachers are doing a very good job under difficult circumstances.*
suspicious circumstances (=making you think something illegal has happened) *Officers said there were no suspicious circumstances surrounding his death.*
mysterious circumstances (=strange or suspicious) *One of their colleagues had vanished in mysterious circumstances.*
unusual circumstances | **unforeseen circumstances** (=that you did not realize would happen) | **tragic circumstances** (=extremely sad and unfortunate) | **extenuating/mitigating circumstances** (=conditions that make it reasonable for someone to break the rules or law)

PHRASES

a set/combination of circumstances *This was a very unusual set of circumstances.*
the circumstances surrounding sth *Police are investigating the circumstances surrounding the accident.*
due to circumstances beyond sb's control *Occasionally flights are cancelled due to circumstances beyond our control.*

cir·cum·stan·tial /ˌsɜːkəmˈstænʃəl◂ $ ˌsɜːr-/ *adj* **1** *law* based on something that appears to be true but is not proven: **circumstantial evidence/case** *The case against McCarthy is based largely on circumstantial evidence.* **2** *formal* including all the details: *The book includes a long and circumstantial account of Empson's conversation with the Queen.* —**circumstantially** *adv*

cir·cum·vent /ˌsɜːkəmˈvent $ ˌsɜːr-/ *v* [T] *formal* **1** to avoid a problem or rule that restricts you, especially in a clever or dishonest way - used to show disapproval: *The company opened an account abroad, in order to circumvent the tax laws.* **2** to avoid something by changing the direction in which you are travelling: *We went north in order to circumvent the mountains.* —**circumvention** /-ˈvenʃən/ *n* [U]

cir·cus /ˈsɜːkəs $ ˈsɜːr-/ ●●○ *n*
1 [C] a group of people and animals who travel to different places performing skilful tricks as entertainment: **circus act** (=a trick performed in a circus) | **circus ring** (=a large circular area where tricks are performed)
2 [singular] *informal* a situation in which there is too much excitement or noise: *The first day of school is always such a circus.* | *The trial has turned into a **media circus**.*
3 [C usually singular] *BrE* a round open area where several streets join together, often used in place names: *Piccadilly Circus*
4 [C] a place in ancient Rome where fights, races etc took place, with seats built in a circle

cir·rho·sis /sɪˈrəʊsɪs $ -ˈroʊ-/ *n* [U] a serious disease of the LIVER, often caused by drinking too much alcohol

cir·rus /ˈsɪrəs/ *n* [U] a form of cloud that is light and shaped like feathers, high in the sky

CIS /ˌsiː aɪ ˈes/ *n* (***Commonwealth of Independent States***) an association formed by countries that were formerly part of the Soviet Union

cis·sy /ˈsɪsi/ *n* (*plural* **cissies**) [C] *BrE informal* SISSY

cis·tern /ˈsɪstən $ -ərn/ *n* [C] a container in which the supply of water for a building is stored inside the building SYN **tank**

cit·a·del /ˈsɪtədəl, -del/ *n* [C] **1** a strong FORT (=small castle) built in the past as a place where people could go for safety if their city was attacked SYN **fortress**
2 the citadel of sth *literary* a place or situation in which an idea, principle, system etc that you think is important is kept safe SYN **stronghold**: *the last citadel of freedom*

ci·ta·tion /saɪˈteɪʃən/ ●○○ AWL *n* [C]
1 *AmE* a formal statement or piece of writing publicly praising someone's actions or achievements: **[+for]** *a citation for bravery*
2 an official order for someone to appear in court or pay a FINE for doing something illegal: **[+for]** *Turner was issued a traffic citation for reckless driving.*
3 a line taken from a book, speech etc SYN **quotation**: *The essay begins with a citation from 'Hamlet'.*

cite /saɪt/ ●●○ AWL *v* [T] *formal*
1 to mention something as an example, especially one that supports, proves, or explains an idea or situation: *The judge cited a 1956 Supreme Court ruling in her decision.* | **cite sth as sth** *Several factors have been cited as the cause of the unrest.* THESAURUS ➤ MENTION
2 to give the exact words of something that has been written, especially in order to support an opinion or prove an idea SYN **quote**: *The passage cited above is from a Robert Frost poem.*
3 to order someone to appear before a court of law SYN **summon**: **cite sb for sth** *Two managers had been cited for similar infractions.*
4 *BrE* to mention someone by name in a court case: *Sue was cited in the divorce proceedings.*
5 to mention someone because they deserve praise: **cite sb (for sth)** *Garcia was cited for her work with disabled children.*

cit·i·zen /ˈsɪtɪzən/ ●●● S2 W2 *n* [C]
1 someone who lives in a particular town, country, or state: *We need our schools to teach students to be good citizens.* | *The mayor urged citizens to begin preparing for a major storm.* → SENIOR CITIZEN
2 someone who legally belongs to a particular country and has rights and responsibilities there, whether they are living there or not → **national**: *At the time, there were over 2,000 British citizens living in Iraq.*
3 second-class citizen someone who is made to feel unimportant because of the way people treat them

ˌcitizen ˈjournalism *n* [U] a way of making information available about news events, in which members of the public put out reports, opinions, or pictures, usually on the Internet

cit·i·zen·ry /ˈsɪtəzənri/ *n* [U] *formal* all the citizens in a particular town, country, or state

ˌcitizen's arˈrest *n* [C] when a person who is not a police officer catches someone and presents them to the police because they have done something illegal: *Brown* ***made a citizen's arrest*** *when a youth attempted to rob an elderly woman.*

ˌCitizens' ˈBand *n* [U] CB

cit·i·zen·ship /ˈsɪtəzənʃɪp/ ●○○ *n* [U]
1 the legal right of belonging to a particular country → **nationality**: **French/US/Brazilian etc citizenship** *I have applied for French citizenship.* | *McGuirk holds* ***dual citizenship*** (=the legal right of being a citizen in two countries) *in Ireland and the US.*
2 the ways in which a good citizen behaves, for example being responsible and helping their COMMUNITY: *The schools should be responsible for teaching our children* ***good citizenship****.*

cit·ric ac·id /ˌsɪtrɪk ˈæsɪd/ *n* [U] a weak acid found in some fruits such as LEMONS

cit·ron /ˈsɪtrən/ *n* [C] a fruit like a LEMON but bigger

cit·ron·el·la /ˌsɪtrəˈnelə/ *n* [U] an oil used for keeping insects away

cit·rus /ˈsɪtrəs/ *n* [C] **1** (*also* **ˈcitrus tree**) a type of tree that produces citrus fruits **2** (*also* **ˈcitrus fruit**) a fruit with thick skin, such as an orange or LEMON —**citrus** *adj*

cit·y /ˈsɪti/ ●●● S1 W1 *n* (*plural* **cities**) [C]
1 a large important town: *The nearest big city was St. Louis.* → INNER CITY
2 a) *BrE* a large town that has been given an official title by a king or queen: *the city of Oxford* **b)** *AmE* a town of any size that has definite borders and powers that were officially given by the state government: *The city of Cleveland celebrated its 200th birthday with fireworks and an outdoor concert.*
3 [usually singular] the people who live in a city: *The city has been living in fear since last week's earthquake.*
4 the city *AmE* the government of a city: *The city is working to improve public transportation.* → CITY, THE

COLLOCATIONS

ADJECTIVES

a big/large/major city *They have stores in Houston, Dallas, and other big cities.*
a great city (=very important and interesting) *Cairo is one of the world's great cities.*
a capital city (=where the government of a country or state is) *Cuba's capital city is Havana.*
sb's home/native city (=where they were born or grew up) *He said that he never wanted to leave his home city.*
a cosmopolitan city (=full of people from different parts of the world) *San Francisco is a very cosmopolitan city.*
an industrial city | **an ancient city** | **a historic city** (=very old and with an interesting history)

city + NOUN

the city centre *BrE*, **the city center** *AmE* *The hotel is in the city centre.*
the city limits *AmE* (=the furthest parts of the city) *rural areas south of the city limits*
city life | **a city dweller** (=someone who lives in a city)

THESAURUS

PLACE WITH HOUSES, SHOPS, AND OFFICES

city a large area with houses, shops, offices etc that is often the centre of government for an area. A city is bigger than a **town**: *The nearest big city is San Francisco.*
town a large area with houses, shops, offices etc. A town is smaller than a **city**: *La Coruña is a pretty seaside town.*
capital (*also* **capital city**) the city where the government of a country or state is: *We travelled to Budapest, the capital of Hungary.*
metropolis a big busy city that is full of people and activity: *After 1850 Paris grew quickly into a busy metropolis.*
urban *adj* [only before noun] relating to towns and cities: *Air pollution is particularly bad in urban areas.* | *urban development*

OUTSIDE PART OF CITY

the outskirts the area around the edge of a city or just outside it: *Disneyland is on the outskirts of Paris.*
suburb an area around the edges of a city, where many people live: *He lives in a suburb of London.* | **the suburbs**: *More and more people are moving to the suburbs.*

City, the (*also* **the ˌCity of ˈLondon**) *BrE* an area in central London where there are many large banks and financial organizations, including the Bank of England and the STOCK EXCHANGE. The City has an area of about one square mile (about 2.5 square kilometres), and it is sometimes called 'the Square Mile', especially in newspapers. Its name is sometimes used to mean people who work there and make financial decisions. There is a similar area in

New York City called Wall Street: *The City is optimistic about the outlook for inflation.* | *a firm of City stockbrokers*

ˌcity ˈcentre *n* [C] *BrE* the main shopping or business area in a city → **downtown**

ˌcity ˈcouncil *n* [C] the group of elected officials who are responsible for governing a city

ˈcity desk *n* [C] **1** *BrE* a department of a newspaper that deals with financial news **2** *AmE* a department of a newspaper that deals with local news

ˈcity ˌeditor *n* [C] **1** (*also* **financial editor**) *BrE* a JOURNALIST responsible for the financial news in a newspaper **2** *AmE* a newspaper EDITOR who is responsible for local news

ˌcity ˈfathers *n* [plural] the group of people who govern a city

ˌcity ˈhall *n* **1** [U] *AmE* the government of a city: *The recycling program simply hasn't been a high priority at City Hall.* **2** [C usually singular] the building a city government uses as its offices

ˌcity ˈplanning *n* [U] *AmE* the study of the way cities work, so that roads, houses, services etc can be provided effectively SYN **town planning** *BrE*

cit·y·scape /ˈsɪtiskeɪp/ *n* [C,U] the way a city looks, or the way it looks from a particular place: *the gray New York cityscape*

ˌcity ˈslicker *n* [C] someone who lives and works in a city and has no experience of anything outside it – often used to show disapproval

ˌcity-ˈstate / $ ˈ.. ˌ.ˌ ˌ.. ˈ./ *n* [C] an independent state that consists of a city and the surrounding country area, especially in the past: *the city-state of Athens*

cit·y·wide /ˈsɪtiwaɪd/ *adj* involving all the areas of a city: *a citywide campaign to fight racism*

CIVETS coun·tries /ˈsɪvəts ˌkʌntriz/ *n* [plural] Colombia, Indonesia, Vietnam, Egypt, Turkey, and South Africa, considered to be countries whose economies are developing

civ·ic /ˈsɪvɪk/ ●○○ *adj* [only before noun]
1 relating to a town or city: *Jackson spent the day meeting with local religious and civic leaders.*
2 relating to the people who live in a town or city: *It is your* ***civic duty*** *to vote in the local elections.* | ***civic pride*** (=people's pride in their own city)

ˌcivic ˈcentre *BrE*, **civic center** *AmE n* [C] **1** *BrE* an area in a city where all the public buildings are **2** *AmE* a large public building where events such as sports games and concerts are held

civ·ics /ˈsɪvɪks/ *n* [U] *especially AmE* a school subject dealing with the rights and duties of citizens and the way government works

GRAMMAR: Singular or plural verb?

Civics is followed by a singular verb: ***Civics is*** *her favourite subject.*

civ·il /ˈsɪvəl/ ●●○ S3 W2 AWL *adj*
1 [only before noun] relating to the people who live in a country: **civil war/disturbance/unrest etc** (=fighting etc between different groups of people living in the same country) → CIVIL LIBERTY, CIVIL RIGHTS
2 [only before noun] relating to the ordinary people or things in a country that are not part of military, government, or religious organizations: *They were married in a civil ceremony in May.*
3 [only before noun] relating to the laws about the private affairs of citizens, such as laws about business or property, rather than laws about crime → **civil law**, **criminal**: *Many* ***civil cases*** *can be settled out of court.*
4 polite in a formal but not very friendly way → **civility**: *Try at least to be civil.* THESAURUS POLITE

ˌcivil deˈfence *BrE*, **civil defense** *AmE n* [U] the organization of ordinary rather than military people to help defend their country from military attack

ˌcivil disoˈbedience *n* [U] when people, especially a large group of people, refuse to obey a law in order to protest in a peaceful way against the government

ˌcivil engiˈneering *n* [U] the planning, building, and repair of roads, bridges, large buildings etc —**civil engineer** *n* [C]

ci·vil·ian /səˈvɪljən/ ●●○ *n* [C] anyone who is not a member of the military forces or the police: *Many innocent civilians were killed during the war.* —**civilian** *adj* [only before noun]: *It was difficult to return to civilian life after ten years in the military.*

ci·vil·i·ty /səˈvɪləti/ *n formal* **1** [U] polite behaviour which most people consider normal → **civil**: *Please have the civility to knock before you enter next time.* **2 civilities** [plural] something that you say or do in order to be polite: *We exchanged civilities when we were neighbours, but nothing more.*

civ·i·li·za·tion (*also* **-isation** *BrE*) /ˌsɪvəl-aɪˈzeɪʃən $ -vələ-/ ●●○ *n*
1 [C,U] a society that is well organized and developed, used especially about a particular society in a particular place or at a particular time → **civilized**: *modern American civilization* | **[+of]** *the ancient civilizations of Greece and Rome*
2 [U] all the societies in the world considered as a whole: *The book explores the relationship between religion and civilization.* | ***the dawn of civilization*** (=the beginning of civilization)
3 [U] a place such as a city where you feel comfortable, especially because it is modern → **civilized**: *After a week in the mountains, all I wanted to do was get back to civilization.*

civ·i·lize (*also* **-ise** *BrE*) /ˈsɪvəl-aɪz/ *v* [T] **1** to influence someone's behaviour, making or teaching them to act in a more sensible or gentle way: *The missionaries went out to civilize other places.* **2** to improve a society so that it is more organized and developed, and often more fair or comfortable: *Ellis was credited with civilizing the Texas prison system.*

civ·i·lized (*also* **-ised** *BrE*) /ˈsɪvəl-aɪzd/ *adj* **1** a civilized society is well organized and developed, and has fair laws and customs → **civilization**: *Such things should not happen in a civilized society.* **2** pleasant and comfortable → **civilized**: *'This is very civilized,' she said, lying back with a gin and tonic.* **3** behaving in a polite sensible way instead of getting angry: *Let's try and be civilized about this, shall we?* **4 a civilized hour** a time that is not too early in the morning: *Can't we have the meeting at a more civilized hour?*

ˌcivil ˈlaw *n* [U] the area of law relating to the affairs of private citizens rather than crime → **criminal law**

ˌcivil ˈliberty *n* [U] (*also* **civil liberties** [plural]) the right of all citizens to be free to do whatever they want while respecting the rights of other people

ˈCivil List *n* **the Civil List** the sum of money given every year by Parliament to the king or queen of Britain and members of their family

ˌcivil ˈpartner *n* [C] someone who has an official relationship with another person of the same sex, so that he or she has the same rights in law as a husband or wife in a marriage

ˌcivil ˈpartnership *n* [C] an official relationship between two people of the same sex, which gives them the same legal rights as two people who are married

ˌcivil ˈrights *n* [plural] the rights that every person should have, such as the right to vote or to be treated fairly by the law, whatever their sex, race, or religion: **civil rights demonstration/movement etc** *a civil rights leader* → BILL OF RIGHTS

ˌcivil ˈservant *n* [C] someone employed in the civil service

ˌcivil ˈservice *n* **the civil service** the government departments that manage the affairs of the country

ˌcivil ˈwar *n* [C,U] a war in which opposing groups of people from the same country fight each other in order to gain political control: *the Spanish Civil War*

civ·vies, **civies** /ˈsɪviz/ *n* [plural] *informal* ordinary clothes, rather than military uniform: *Sam! I didn't recognise you in civvies.*

civ·vy street /ˈsɪvi striːt/ *n* [U] *BrE old-fashioned informal* ordinary life as it is lived outside the army, navy, or air force: *I bet your family will be glad to see you when you get back to civvy street.*

CJD /ˌsiː dʒeɪ ˈdiː/ *n* [U] the abbreviation of ***Creutzfeldt-Jakob disease***

cl (*plural* **cl** *or* **cls**) the written abbreviation of ***centilitre*** or ***centilitres***

clack /klæk/ *v* [I] to make a continuous short hard sound: *the sound of high heels clacking across the courtyard* —**clack** *n* [singular]: *the clack of typewriters*

clad /klæd/ *adj literary* **1** wearing a particular kind of clothing: **[+in]** *She felt hot, despite being clad only in a thin cotton dress.* | **warmly/suitably/scantily clad** (=dressed warmly etc) **2 snow-clad/ivy-clad etc** covered in a particular thing: *an armour-clad ship*

clad·ding /ˈklædɪŋ/ *n* [U] *especially BrE* a cover of hard material that protects the outside of a building, piece of equipment etc: *decorative timber cladding*

claim¹ /kleɪm/ ●●● S1 W1 *v*

1 TRUTH [T] to state that something is true, even though it has not been proved: **claim (that)** *The product claims that it can make you thin without dieting.* | **claim to do/be sth** *No responsible therapist will claim to cure your insomnia.* | *I* ***don't claim to be*** *a feminist, but I'd like to see more women in top jobs.* | **claim to have done sth** *The girls claim to have seen the fairies.* | **claim responsibility/credit (for sth)** (=say officially that you are responsible for something that has happened) *The group claimed responsibility for the bombings.* | *Opposition leaders will* ***claim victory*** *if the turnout is lower than 50%.* | **claim sb/sth as sth** *A letter appeared in 'The Times' claiming Fleming as the discoverer of penicillin.*

GRAMMAR

In more formal English, you say **it is claimed that** something is true: *It has been claimed that he was difficult to work with.*

2 MONEY [I,T] to officially demand or receive money from an organization because you have a right to it: **claim sth back** *He should be able to claim the price of the ticket back.* | **[+on]** *BrE: You can claim on the insurance if you have an accident while on holiday.* | **claim benefit/an allowance/damages etc** *If you're still not satisfied, you may be able to* ***claim compensation***.

3 LEGAL RIGHT [T] to state that you have a right to take or have something that is legally yours: *The majority of those who* ***claim asylum*** *are genuine refugees.* | *Lost property can be claimed between 10 a.m. and 4 p.m.*

4 DEATH [T] if a war, accident etc claims lives, people die because of it – used especially in news reports: *The earthquake has so far claimed over 3,000 lives.*

5 ATTENTION [T] if something claims your attention, you notice and consider it carefully: *The military conflict continues to claim our undivided attention.*

claim² ●●● S2 W1 *n* [C]

1 TRUTH a statement that something is true, even though it has not been proved: **claim that** *Gould rejected claims that he had acted irresponsibly.* | **false/extravagant/dubious etc claims** *firms that make false claims about their products* | *They* ***made claims*** *they couldn't live up to.* | *the* ***competing claims*** *of scientists* | **dispute/deny/reject a claim** *The police denied claims that the men were tortured.* | *Evidence to* ***support*** *these* ***claims*** *is still lacking.* | **claim to do/be sth** *his claim to be the rightful owner of the painting* | *I* ***make no claim*** *to understand the complexities of the situation.*

2 MONEY **a)** an official request for money that you think you have a right to: **[+for]** *claims for compensation* | **reject/uphold/lose etc a claim** *He lost his claim for unfair dismissal.* | **make/put in/file a claim** *All claims should be made in writing.* | **pay/wage claim** (=a request from workers for more money) | *Fill in and return the* ***claim form*** *as soon as it arrives.* **b)** the sum of money you request when you make a claim: *The insurance company cannot* ***meet*** (=pay) *such enormous* ***claims***.

3 RIGHTS a right to do something or to have something, especially because it belongs to you or because you deserve it: **[+to/on]** *Surely they* ***have a rightful claim*** *on their father's land?* | *The Maldives* ***pressed*** *its* ***claim*** *to hold the summit.* | *Philip feared Edward would* ***lay claim to*** *the Scottish crown.* | *the* ***competing claims*** *of parents and teachers* | **have a claim on sb's time/attention etc** *A woman who has given a man children will always have a claim on his love.*

4 stake your claim (for sth) to say that you have a right to own or do something, especially when other people also say they have a right to it: *Tickets are on a 'first come, first served' basis, so stake your claim now.*

5 sb's/sth's claim to fame a place or person's claim to fame is the reason why they are famous – often used humorously to mention something that is not very important: *My main claim to fame is that I once shook Madonna's hand.*

6 LAND something such as a piece of land that contains valuable minerals

THESAURUS

claim a statement that something is true, even though it has not been proved: *It is difficult to believe some of the manufacturer's claims for its products.*
allegation a statement that someone has done something wrong or illegal, but that has not been proved: *He has strongly denied the allegations of sexual harassment.*
assertion *formal* something that you say or write that you strongly believe: *the assertion that house prices are falling*
contention *formal* a strong opinion that someone expresses: *Her main contention is that doctors should do more to encourage healthy eating.*

clai·mant /ˈkleɪmənt/ *n* [C] someone who claims something, especially money, from the government, a court etc because they think they have a right to it: *benefit claimants*

clair·voy·ant /kleəˈvɔɪənt $ kler-/ *n* [C] someone who says they can see what will happen in the future —**clairvoyance** *n* [U]: *the gifts of telepathy and clairvoyance* —**clairvoyant** *adj*

clam¹ /klæm/ *n* [C] **1** a SHELLFISH you can eat that has a shell in two parts that open up: *clam chowder* (=a type of soup) → see picture at **SHELLFISH** **2 as happy as a clam** *AmE informal* very happy **3** *AmE informal* someone who does not say what they are thinking or feeling

clam² *v* (**clammed, clamming**)
clam up *phr v informal* to suddenly stop talking, especially when you are nervous or shy: *A sensitive child is likely just to clam up.*

clam·bake /ˈklæmbeɪk/ *n* [C] *AmE* an informal outdoor party near the sea, where clams are cooked and eaten

clam·ber /ˈklæmbə $ -ər/ *v* [I always + adv/prep] to climb or move slowly somewhere, using your hands and feet because it is difficult or steep: **[+over/across etc]** *They clambered over the slippery rocks.* | *We all clambered aboard and the boat pulled out.*

clam·my /ˈklæmi/ *adj* feeling unpleasantly wet, cold, and sticky: *Get your clammy hands off me!* THESAURUS DAMP, WET —**clammily** *adv* —**clamminess** *n* [U]

clam·our¹ *BrE*, **clamor** *AmE* /ˈklæmə $ -ər/ *n* [singular, U] **1** a very loud noise made by a large group of people or animals: *He shouted over the rising clamour of voices.* **2** the expression of feelings of anger and shock by a large number of people – used especially in news reports: **[+for]** *Trouillot disregarded the growing* ***public clamour*** *for her resignation.* —**clamorous** *adj*

clamour² *BrE*, **clamor** *AmE* *v* [I] **1** [always + adv/prep] to demand something loudly: **[+for]** *The audience cheered, clamoring for more.* | **clamour to do sth** *All his friends were clamouring to know where he'd been.* **2** to talk or shout loudly: *Children clamored excitedly.*

C

clamp[1] /klæmp/ *v* [T] **1** [always + adv/prep] to put or hold something in a position so that it cannot move: *She clamped her hands over her ears.* | *Creed opened his mouth to speak, then* ***clamped*** *it* ***shut***. **2 clamp sanctions/restrictions etc on sb** to put limits on what someone is allowed to do: *The president clamped sanctions on the island after the bomb attack.* **3** [always + adv/prep] to hold two things together using a clamp: *Clamp the two parts together until the glue dries.* **4** (*also* **wheel-clamp**) *BrE* to put a clamp on the wheel of a car so that the car cannot be driven away. This is usually done because the car is illegally parked SYN **boot** *AmE*: *He returned, only to discover his car had been clamped.* GRAMMAR **Clamp** is usually passive in this meaning.

clamp down *phr v* to take firm action to stop a particular type of crime → **clampdown**: **[+on]** *The police are clamping down on drink-driving offenders.*

C

clamp[2] *n* [C] **1** a piece of equipment for holding things together **2** (*also* **wheel clamp**) *BrE* a metal object that is fastened to the wheel of a car so that the car cannot be driven away. This is usually done because the car is illegally parked SYN **boot** *AmE*

clamp·down /ˈklæmpdaʊn/ *n* [C usually singular] sudden firm action that is taken to reduce crime: **[+on]** *a clamp-down on drug dealers*

clam·shell phone /ˈklæmʃel ˌfəʊn $ -ˌfoʊn/ *n* [C] a MOBILE PHONE that has a top part which folds over the bottom part

clan /klæn/ ●○○ *n* [C]
1 a large group of families who often share the same name: *the Campbell clan* | *warring clans*
2 *informal* a very large family: *The whole clan will be here over Christmas.*

clan·des·tine /klænˈdestɪn/ *adj* done or kept secret: *a clandestine affair* | *clandestine meetings* THESAURUS▸ SECRET

clang /klæŋ/ *v* [I,T] if a metal object clangs, or if you clang it, it makes a loud ringing sound: *The gates clanged shut behind her.* —**clang** *n* [singular]

clang·er /ˈklæŋə $ -ər/ *n* [C usually singular] *BrE informal* a silly or embarrassing mistake: *I can't help noticing the occasional clanger in war films.* | *He's being blamed for* ***dropping a*** *massive political* ***clanger*** (=making a silly or embarrassing remark).

clang·our *BrE*, **clangor** *AmE* /ˈklæŋə $ -ər/ *n* [U] *literary* a loud sound that continues for a long time

clank /klæŋk/ *v* [I] if a metal object clanks, it makes a loud heavy sound: *A tram clanked past.* —**clank** *n* [C] —**clanking** *n* [U]: *the clanking of machinery*

clan·nish /ˈklænɪʃ/ *adj written* a group of people who are clannish are very close to each other, and seem unfriendly towards strangers: *a clannish community*

clans·man /ˈklænzmən/ *n* (*plural* **clansmen** /-mən/) [C] a male member of a CLAN

clans·wom·an /ˈklænzˌwʊmən/ *n* (*plural* **clanswomen** /-ˌwɪmɪn/) [C] a female member of a CLAN

clap[1] /klæp/ ●●○ *v* (**clapped**, **clapping**)
1 [I,T] to hit your hands against each other many times to make a sound that shows your approval, agreement, or enjoyment → **applause**: *One man began to clap, and others joined in.* | *The couple were cheered and clapped on their arrival.* | *The audience clapped politely but without much enthusiasm.*
2 [T] if you clap your hands, you hit your hands together a few times to attract someone's attention or to show that you are pleased: *Narouz clapped his hands and a servant entered.* | *Mandy laughed and clapped her hands in delight.*
3 [T] to put your hand on something quickly and firmly: *'Mick!' She* ***clapped*** *her* ***hand over*** *her mouth. 'I'd forgotten!'* | *Ben grinned and* ***clapped*** *me amiably* ***on the shoulder***.
4 clap eyes on sb/sth *BrE informal* to see someone or something, especially when you did not expect to: *Mark had loved the house from the moment he clapped eyes on it.*
5 clap sb in prison/jail/irons *literary* to suddenly put someone in prison or chains —**clapping** *n* [U]: *Each song was greeted with enthusiastic clapping.*

clap[2] *n* **1** [singular] the loud sound that you make when you hit your hands together many times to show that you enjoyed something: **give sb a clap** *BrE*: *Come on everyone, let's give Tommy a clap.* **2** [singular] a sudden loud noise: *an ear-splitting* ***clap of thunder*** **3 the clap** *informal* GONORRHEA

clap·board /ˈklæpbɔːd $ ˈklæbərd, ˈklæpbɔːrd/ *n* [C,U] *especially BrE* a set of boards used to cover the outside of a building, or one of these boards: *clapboard houses*

Clap·ham Junc·tion /ˌklæpəm ˈdʒʌŋkʃən/ a railway station in southwest London where a lot of people catch a train to work or change trains. A busy place with a lot of people coming and going is sometimes described as being 'like Clapham Junction'.

ˌclapped-ˈout *adj BrE* a clapped-out car, machine etc is old and in very bad condition

clap·per /ˈklæpə $ -ər/ *n* [C] **1** the metal part inside a bell that hits it to make it ring **2 run/go/drive etc like the clappers** *BrE informal* to run, drive etc very fast

clap·trap /ˈklæptræp/ *n* [U] *informal* talk that is stupid or shows a lack of knowledge: *romantic claptrap*

claque /klæk/ *n* [C] a group of people who show approval of everything that a politician, performer etc says: *There was applause from the claque of supporters around him.*

clar·et /ˈklærət/ *n* **1** [C,U] red wine from the Bordeaux area of France: *a bottle of claret* **2** [U] a dark red colour —**claret** *adj*

clar·i·fi·ca·tion /ˌklærɪfɪˈkeɪʃən/ AWL *n* [C,U] *formal* the act of making something clearer or easier to understand, or an explanation that makes something clearer: *There have been a number of official changes and clarifications.* | **[+on/of]** *Email us if you require further clarification on how to order.* | **seek/ask for clarification** *I asked for clarification on the legal position.*

clar·i·fy /ˈklærɪfaɪ/ ●●○ AWL *v* (**clarified**, **clarifying**, **clarifies**) [T]
1 *formal* to make something clearer or easier to understand → **clarification**: **clarify issues/a statement/matters etc** *Could you* ***clarify*** *one or two* ***points*** *for me?* | *Reporters asked him to* ***clarify*** *his* ***position*** (=say exactly what his beliefs are) *on welfare reform.* | **clarify how/what etc** *The report aims to clarify how these conclusions were reached.*
2 to make something cleaner or purer by heating it: *clarified butter*

clar·i·net /ˌklærəˈnet/ *n* [C] a musical instrument like a long black tube, that you play by blowing into it and pressing KEYS to change the notes → see picture at WOODWIND —**clarinettist** *n* [C]

clar·i·on call /ˈklæriən ˌkɔːl $ -ˌkɒːl/ *n* [C] *formal* a strong and direct request for people to do something: *This election is a clarion call for our country to face the challenges ahead.*

clar·i·ty /ˈklærəti/ ●●○ AWL *n* [U]
1 the clarity of a piece of writing, law, argument etc is its quality of being expressed clearly → **clear**: *Letters may be edited for length and clarity.* | *a lack of clarity in the law on property rights*
2 the ability to think, understand, or remember something clearly → **clear**: *He had only visited the village once, but remembered it with surprising clarity.* | **clarity of vision/purpose/thought etc** *Churchill's clarity of vision impressed all who knew him.*
3 the quality of being clear and easy to see or hear → **clear**: *The picture was of such clarity that it could have been a photograph.*

clash[1] /klæʃ/ ●●○ *v*
1 [I] if two armies, groups etc clash, they start fighting – used in news reports: *Troops clashed near the border.* | **[+with]** *Police have clashed with demonstrators again today.*
2 [I] if two people or groups clash, they argue because they have very different beliefs and opinions – used in news reports: **[+with]** *Democrats clashed with Republicans in a heated debate.* | **[+over/on]** *The two men have clashed over the report's conclusions.*
3 [I] if two colours or designs clash, they look very bad

together: **[+with]** *I can't wear red – it clashes with my hair.*
4 [I] *especially BrE* if two events clash, they happen at the same time in a way that is inconvenient SYN **conflict** *AmE*: **[+with]** *The announcement has been delayed to avoid clashing with the prime minister's speech.*
5 [I,T] if two pieces of metal clash, or if you clash them, they make a loud ringing sound: *The cymbals clashed.*

clash² ●●○ *n* [C]
1 a short fight between two armies or groups – used in news reports: ***armed clashes*** *along the border* | **[+between/with]** ***violent clashes*** *between police and demonstrators*
2 an argument between two people or groups because they have very different beliefs or opinions – used in news reports: **[+between/with]** *The plans put oil companies in a* ***head-on clash*** *with environmentalists.* | **personality/culture clash** (=a situation in which two people or groups do not like each other)
3 a sports match between two teams, players etc that is expected to be very exciting – used in sports reports: *The heavyweight clash goes ahead in Las Vegas on 8 May.*
4 a situation in which two events happen at the same time in a way that is inconvenient: *a scheduling clash on TV*
5 a loud sound made by two metal objects hitting each other: *the clash of swords*
6 a combination of two colours, designs etc that look bad together: *a colour clash*

clasp¹ ●○○ *v* [T] *written*
1 to hold someone or something tightly, closing your fingers or arms around them SYN **grip**: *A baby monkey clasps its mother's fur tightly.* | **clasp your hands/arms around/behind sth** *Fenella leaned forward, clasping her hands around her knees.* | *She stood with her* ***hands clasped*** *tightly* ***together****.* | **clasp sb/sth in your hands/arms** *She clasped the photograph in her hands.* | **clasp sb to your chest/bosom** (=hold someone tightly with your arms) THESAURUS ▸ HOLD
2 to fasten something with a clasp

clasp² /klɑːsp $ klæsp/ *n* **1** [C] a small metal object for fastening a bag, belt, piece of jewellery etc **2** [singular] a tight hold SYN **grip**: *the firm clasp of her hand*

class¹ /klɑːs $ klæs/ ●●● S1 W1 *n*
1 SOCIAL GROUP **a)** [C] one of the groups in a society that different types of people are divided into according to their jobs, income, education etc: *a member of* ***the landed class*** (=people who own land) → LOWER CLASS, MIDDLE CLASS, UPPER CLASS, WORKING CLASS, → **the chattering classes** at CHATTER¹(4) **b)** [U] the system in which people are divided into these groups: *Defining the concept of class is not an easy task.* | *The class system is slowly disappearing.*
2 STUDENTS [C] **a)** a group of students who are taught together → **classmate**: **in a class** *We're in the same class for chemistry.* | *Gary came* ***top of the class*** *in English.* | *My class are going to the science museum.* **b)** *AmE* a group of students who finished studying together in the same year → **classmate**: *a class reunion* | **the class of 1965/2001 etc** (=the group of students who finished in 1965 etc) *The class of '69 spent almost as much time protesting as learning.*

> **GRAMMAR: Singular or plural verb?**
> • **Class** is usually followed by a singular verb: *The class* ***was*** *working on some maths problems.*
> • In British English, you can also use a plural verb: *The class* ***were*** *working on some maths problems.*
> GRAMMAR GUIDE ▸ NOUNS

3 TEACHING PERIOD [C,U] a period of time during which someone teaches a group of people, especially in a school SYN **lesson** *BrE*: *I missed Bible class last week.* | **in class** (=during the class) *No talking in class!* | *He was injured in a science class.*
4 STUDYING [C] a series of classes in a particular subject SYN **course** *BrE*: **[+in]** *a class in photography at night school* | *a dance class*
5 SAME TYPE OF STH [C] a group of people, animals, or things that are considered together because they are similar in some way: **[+of]** *Have you passed a test for this class of vehicle?*
6 TRAIN/AIRCRAFT ETC [C usually singular] one of the different standards of seats, food etc available on a train, aircraft etc: **first/business/tourist etc class** *We always travel first class.*
7 QUALITY [C] a group into which people or things are divided according to their quality or abilities: **nicer/better etc class of sth** *The port now attracts a wealthier class of visitor.* | **in a class of its own/in a different class** (=better than everything else) *Its sheer versatility puts this computer in a different class.* | *He's* ***not in the same class*** (=not as good) *as her at tennis.*
8 STYLE/SKILL [U] *informal* a high level of style or skill in something → **classy**: **have/show class** *The team showed real class in this afternoon's match.* | *A fountain will* ***give*** *your garden* ***a touch of class****.* | **class player/actress etc** | **a class act** *informal* (=someone who is skilful, attractive etc) *Laughton is a class act who's proved his worth in the game.*
→ HIGH-CLASS, LOW-CLASS
9 UNIVERSITY DEGREE [C] *BrE* one of the three levels of a university degree: *a second class degree*

> **COLLOCATIONS – MEANING 1**
> **ADJECTIVES**
> **social class** *Is there a link between crime and social class?*
> **the working/lower class** *At this time most of the working class was very poor.*
> **the middle class** *A new middle class emerged after the war.*
> **the upper class** *Members of the upper class didn't have to work.*
> **the ruling class** (=the people in power) | **the professional class** (=the people with professional jobs) | **the landowning/landed class** (=the people who own land) | **the educated class** | **the privileged class** (=people with advantages because of their wealth, social position etc)
> **VERBS**
> **belong to a class** *Like you, I belong to the working class.*
> **be a member of a class** *I suppose I'm a member of the middle class.*
> **class + NOUN**
> **a class system/structure** (=a social system that has classes) *He felt he was a victim of the class system.*
> **a class division** *Nowadays, class divisions are related to economic status.*
> **class differences** (=differences that exist because of your class) *There are noticeable class differences in family size.*
> **the class struggle/war** (=disagreement or fighting between different classes) | **class conflict**

> **COLLOCATIONS – MEANINGS 3 & 4**
> **ADJECTIVES/NOUN + class**
> **a French/geography/history etc class** *I have a history class at nine o'clock today.*
> **an evening class** *Mum goes to an evening class on Tuesdays.*
> **a beginners'/elementary/intermediate/advanced class** (=teaching different levels of a subject)
> **VERBS**
> **go to/attend a class** *I've got to go to a science class now.*
> **attend class** (=go to classes regularly) *You can't pass your exams if you don't attend class.*
> **take a class** (=go to classes as a student) *I'm taking some art classes at the moment.*
> **teach a class** *One of the other teachers was ill so I taught her class.*
> **miss a class** (=not go to one) | **be late for class** | **have a class** *especially AmE* (=as a student or teacher) | **hold a class** (=provide a class)

class² ●●○ *v* [T] to consider people, things etc as belonging to a particular group, using an official system SYN **classify**: **class sb/sth as sth** *Heroin and cocaine are classed as hard drugs.* GRAMMAR **Class** is often passive.

ˌclass ˈaction *n* [C] *AmE* a LAWSUIT arranged by a group of people for themselves and other people with the same problem —**class-action** *adj* [only before noun]: *class-action lawsuits*

ˌclass ˈconsciousness *n* [U] *technical* knowledge and understanding of the class system, and of your own and other people's social class

clas·sic¹ /ˈklæsɪk/ ●●○ W3 AWL *adj* [usually before noun]

1 TYPICAL having all the features that are typical or expected of a particular thing or situation: **classic example/mistake/case etc** *Too many job hunters make the classic mistake of thinking only about what's in it for them.* THESAURUS ▸ TYPICAL

2 ADMIRED admired by many people, and having a value that has continued for a long time: *The Coca-Cola bottle is one of the* ***classic designs*** *of the last century.* | *a collection of* ***classic cars***

3 VERY GOOD of excellent quality: *Roy scored a classic goal in the 90th minute.*

4 TRADITIONAL a classic style of art or clothing is attractive in a simple traditional way → **classical**: *She chose a classic navy suit for the ceremony.*

classic² ●●○ AWL *n* [C]

1 a book, play, or film that is important and has been admired for a long time: *'La Grande Illusion' is one of the classics of French cinema.* | **all-time/modern/design etc classic** *The play has become an American classic.*

2 something that is very good and one of the best examples of its kind: *What makes a car a classic?*

3 classics [plural] the language, literature, and history of ancient Rome and Greece → **classicist**: *Judith studied classics at Oxford.*

clas·si·cal /ˈklæsɪkəl/ ●●○ W3 AWL *adj*

1 belonging to a traditional style or set of ideas: **classical ballet/dance etc** | *the classical theory of relativity*

2 relating to music that is considered to be important and serious and that has a value that continues for a long time: **classical music/musician/composer etc** *a leading classical violinist* | *a classical repertoire*

3 relating to the language, literature etc of ancient Greece and Rome: *classical literature* | *a classical scholar* | *classical mythology*

4 (*also* **classic**) typical of a particular thing or situation: *the classical argument against democracy* —**classically** /-kli/ *adv*: *a classically trained singer* | *Classically, infection appears in the lower jaw.*

clas·si·cis·m /ˈklæsɪsɪzəm/ *n* [U] a style of art, literature etc that is simple, regular, and does not show strong emotions → **realism**, **romanticism**

clas·si·cist /ˈklæsɪsɪst/ *n* [C] someone who studies CLASSICS

clas·si·fi·ca·tion /ˌklæsɪfɪˈkeɪʃən/ ●○○ *n* [C,U] a process in which you put something into the group or class it belongs to → **classify**: *the classification of wines according to quality* | *There are five job classifications.*

clas·si·fied /ˈklæsɪfaɪd/ ●○○ *adj* classified information, documents etc are ones which the government has ordered to be kept secret THESAURUS ▸ SECRET

ˌclassified ˈad *n* [C] a small advertisement you put in a newspaper to buy or sell something SYN **small ad** *BrE*, **want ad** *AmE*

clas·si·fy /ˈklæsɪfaɪ/ ●○○ *v* (**classified**, **classifying**, **classifies**) [T]

1 to decide what group something belongs to → **classification**: **classify sth as/under sth** *In law, beer is classified as a food product.* | *We'd classify Drabble's novels under 'Romance'.* | *Families are* ***classified according to*** *the father's occupation.*

2 to regard people or things as belonging to a particular group because they have similar qualities → **classification**: *As a musician, Cage is hard to classify.* —**classifiable** *adj*

class·less /ˈklɑːsləs $ ˈklæs-/ *adj* [usually before noun] a classless society is one in which people are not divided into different social classes: *Is Australia really a classless society?* —**classlessness** *n* [U]

class·mate /ˈklɑːsmeɪt $ ˈklæs-/ ●●○ *n* [C] a member of the same class in a school, college, or – in the US – a university

class·room /ˈklɑːs-rʊm, -ruːm $ ˈklæs-/ ●●● S3 W3 *n* [C] a room that you have lessons in at a school or college

ˌclass ˈstruggle (*also* **ˌclass ˈwar**) *n* [singular, U] in MARXIST THEORY, political opposition and the fight for economic power between CAPITALISTS (=the owners of property, factories etc) and the PROLETARIAT (=the workers)

class·work /ˈklɑːswɜːk $ ˈklæswɜːrk/ *n* [U] school work done by students while they are in a class rather than at home OPP **homework**

class·y /ˈklɑːsi $ ˈklæsi/ *adj informal* **1** fashionable and expensive: *classy restaurants* **2** very good: *a classy player*

clat·ter /ˈklætə $ -ər/ *v* **1** [I] if heavy hard objects clatter, or if you clatter them, they make a loud unpleasant noise: *The tray slipped and clattered to the floor.* **2** [I always + adv/prep] to move quickly and noisily: *children clattering up and down the stairs* —**clatter** *n* [singular, U]: *the clatter of dishes*

clause /klɔːz $ klɒːz/ ●●○ AWL *n* [C]

1 a part of a written law or legal document covering a particular subject of the whole law or document: *A confidentiality clause was added to the contract.*

2 *technical* a group of words that contains a subject and a verb, but which is usually only part of a sentence

claus·tro·pho·bi·a /ˌklɔːstrəˈfəʊbiə $ ˌklɒːstrəˈfoʊ-/ *n* [U] a strong fear of being in a small enclosed space or in a situation that limits what you can do → **agoraphobia** —**claustrophobic** *adj*: *I get claustrophobic in elevators.* | *a claustrophobic atmosphere*

clav·i·chord /ˈklævəkɔːd $ -kɔːrd/ *n* [C] a musical instrument like a piano, that was played especially in the past

clav·i·cle /ˈklævɪkəl/ *n* [C] *medical* a COLLARBONE

claw¹ /klɔː $ klɒː/ ●●○ *n* [C]

1 a sharp curved nail on an animal, bird, or some insects: *The cat dug his claws into my leg.* | *lobster claws* → see picture at BIG CAT

2 get your claws into sb a) if someone gets their claws into another person, they influence them in a harmful way: *The thought of Eloise getting her claws into the child made his blood run cold.* **b)** to say unpleasant things about someone in order to upset them: *Wait till the papers get their claws into him.*

3 the curved end of a tool or machine, used for lifting things: *a claw hammer*

claw² *v* [I,T] **1** to tear or pull at something, using claws or your fingers: **[+at]** *The cat keeps clawing at the rug.* **2 claw your way** to try very hard to reach a place or position, using a lot of effort and determination: **claw your way up/along/back etc** *He clawed his way forward inch by inch.* | *Benson clawed his way back into the lead.*

claw sth ↔ **back** *phr v* **1** to get back something that you had lost, by trying very hard: *The company has managed to claw back its share of the market.* **2** *BrE* if a government or organization claws back money it has given to people, it takes it back

clay /kleɪ/ ●●○ *n* [U] a type of heavy sticky earth that can be used for making pots, bricks etc → **feet of clay** at FOOT¹(27)

ˌclay ˈpigeon ˌshooting *n* [U] *BrE* a sport in which you shoot at circles of hard clay that are thrown up into the air SYN **skeet shooting** *AmE*

clean¹ /kliːn/ ●●● S2 W2 *adj* (*comparative* **cleaner**, *superlative* **cleanest**)

1 NOT DIRTY without any dirt, marks etc OPP **dirty**: *Are your hands clean?* | *clean towels* | *Make sure you* ***keep*** *the wound* ***clean***. | ***Wipe*** *that sink* ***clean*** *when you're done.* | *As*

*usual, she left her room **clean and tidy** before going to school.* | *a **spotlessly clean** kitchen* | *I want you to get those plates **as clean as a whistle**.*
2 PEOPLE/ANIMALS having a clean appearance and habits: *Cats are naturally clean.*
3 ENVIRONMENT containing or producing nothing that is dirty or harmful → **cleanly**: **clean air/water/energy etc** *the Clean Air Act* | ***cleaner fuels*** THESAURUS ENVIRONMENTALLY FRIENDLY
4 FAIR OR LEGAL **a)** done in a fair or legal way OPP **dirty**: *a clean fight* **b)** showing that you have followed the rules: *a clean driving licence* | *He's got a **clean record**.* **c)** [not before noun] *informal* not hiding any weapons or illegal drugs: *They searched him, but he was clean.* **d)** [not before noun] no longer taking illegal drugs: *Dave's been clean for two years now.*
5 NOT OFFENSIVE talk, jokes, behaviour etc that are clean are not offensive or about sex OPP **dirty**: *Oh, don't get mad – it's just **good clean fun**!* | ***Keep it clean*** (=do not offend people with what you say). | **clean living** (=a way of life which is healthy and moral)
6 come clean *informal* to finally tell the truth about something you have been hiding: **[+about]** *The government should come clean about its plans.*
7 make a clean breast of it to admit that you have done something wrong so that you no longer feel guilty
8 a clean break a complete and sudden separation from a person, organization, or situation: *Den left the next day, needing to **make a clean break**.*
9 clean sheet/slate a record of someone's work, behaviour, performance etc that shows they have not done anything wrong or made any mistakes: *Jed looked forward to starting life again with a clean sheet.* | *Lewis has **kept a clean sheet** in every game* (=not let the other team score).
10 clean hands if a person, government, organization etc has clean hands, they have done something in a fair or legal way: *Neither side is coming to the negotiating table with completely clean hands.*
11 PAPER a piece of paper that is clean has not yet been used SYN **fresh**
12 SMOOTH having a smooth or regular edge or surface → **cleanly**: *a clean cut* | *Use a clean simple typeface for signs.*
13 a clean bill of health a report that says you are healthy or that a machine or building is safe: *Inspectors **gave** the factory **a clean bill of health**.*
14 a clean sweep a) a very impressive victory in a competition, election etc: **[+for]** *All the polls had pointed to a clean sweep for the Democrats.* | *Hopes that the French would **make a clean sweep** at the Games were dashed.* **b)** a complete change in a company or organization, often by removing people
15 TASTE having a fresh pleasant taste: *Add a little lemon juice to give the pasta a cool clean taste.*
16 clean copy a piece of writing without mistakes or other marks written on it
17 MOVEMENT a clean movement in sport is skilful and exact: *He steadied his arm, hoping for a clean shot.*
—**cleanness** *n* [U] → CLEAN-CUT, → **keep your nose clean** at NOSE[1](9)

THESAURUS

clean without any dirt or marks: *They need clean water to drink.* | *I don't have any clean clothes.*
pure water or air that is pure does not contain any dirt, pollution, or bacteria: *I breathed in the pure mountain air.*
sterile /ˈsteraɪl $ -rəl/ completely clean, with no bacteria, and therefore safe for medical or scientific use: *Place a sterile bandage on the wound.*
spotless completely clean – used mainly about rooms and clothes: *Her kitchen is always spotless.*
pristine /ˈprɪstiːn/ completely clean and new-looking: *He wore a pristine white shirt.*
immaculate as clean and tidy as it is possible to be: *The soldiers' uniforms have to be immaculate.*
spick and span [not before noun] *informal* clean and tidy, especially after having just been cleaned: *By the end of the day, the whole place was spick and span.*

clean[2] ●●● S1 W3 *v*
1 [I,T] to remove dirt from something by rubbing or washing → **cleanse**: *Your shoes **need cleaning**.* | *Is it **easy to clean**?* | **clean sth down/off** *We clean the machines down at the end of each day.* | **clean sth off/from sth** *He used a tissue to clean his fingerprints off the gun.* → DRY-CLEAN, → **spring-clean** at SPRING-CLEANING → see picture on *p. 312*
2 [I,T] to clean a building or other people's houses as your job: *Anne comes in to clean twice a week.*
3 clean your teeth *BrE* to make your teeth clean using a TOOTHBRUSH and TOOTHPASTE SYN **brush your teeth** *AmE*
4 [T] to remove the inside parts of an animal or bird before cooking it: *Harry caught the fish and cleaned them himself.*
5 clean your plate to eat all your food

THESAURUS

clean to remove dirt from something: *I need to clean the car.* | *Clean the mud off your shoes.*
wash to clean something with water and usually soap: *She's washing her hair.* | *There's nowhere to wash your clothes.*
wipe to clean a surface with a cloth, often a wet cloth: *Wipe the worktop when you've finished cooking.*
scrub to wash something by rubbing it hard, especially with a brush: *They made her scrub the floor.*
rinse to remove dirt from something using water, especially after washing it with soap: *Rinse your hair thoroughly after shampooing it.*
cleanse *formal* to clean your skin, using water or a special cream: *There are many products available for cleansing your skin.*
bathe /beɪð/ to clean a wound or a part of your body with water: *Bathe the cut and put a plaster on it.*
do the dishes (*also* **do the washing-up** *BrE*) to wash plates and pans after a meal: *Who's going to help me do the dishes?*
do the laundry (*also* **do the washing** *BrE*) to wash clothes: *On Tuesdays, he does the washing.*

clean sb/sth **out** *phr v*
1 clean sth ↔ out to make the inside of a room, house etc clean or tidy: *We'd better clean out the attic this week.*
2 clean sb out *informal* if something expensive cleans you out, you spend so much money on it that you now have very little left: *Our trip to Paris cleaned me out.*
3 clean sb/sth out *informal* to steal everything from a place, or all of someone's possessions
clean up *phr v*
1 to make a place completely clean and tidy: *We spent all Saturday morning cleaning up.* | **clean sth ↔ up** *plans to clean up the beaches* | **[+after]** *John always expects other people to clean up after him* (=to make a place clean after he has used it).
2 to wash yourself after you have got very dirty: **clean yourself up** *Let me just go clean myself up.* | *Dad's upstairs **getting cleaned up**.*
3 clean up your act *informal* to start behaving sensibly and responsibly: *Some companies could face heavy fines if they fail to clean up their act.*
4 *informal* to win a lot of money or make a lot of money in a business deal: *He cleaned up at the races yesterday.*
5 clean sth ↔ up to improve moral standards in a place or organization: *It's high time British soccer **cleaned up** its **image**.* → CLEAN-UP

clean[3] *adv* used to emphasize the fact that an action or movement is complete and thorough: **clean away/through/out** *The thieves got clean away with $300,000 worth of equipment.* | *The car hit her with such force that she was lifted clean off the ground.* | *Sorry, I **clean forgot** (=completely forgot) your birthday.*

clean[4] *n* [singular] *BrE* a process in which you clean something: *The car needs a good clean.*

ˌclean-ˈcut *adj* someone who is clean-cut looks neat and clean, and appears to have a good moral character: *clean-cut college boys*

C

Clean

wipe
wipe up
dust
brush
mop
sweep
scrub
wash up *BrE*/do the dishes *AmE*
hoover *BrE*/vacuum
wash the car

clean·er /ˈkliːnə $ -ər/ ●●○ S3 *n*
1 [C] *especially BrE* someone whose job is to clean other people's houses, offices etc
2 [C,U] a machine or substance used for cleaning: *a vacuum cleaner | toilet bowl cleaner*
3 the cleaner's a DRY CLEANER'S
4 take sb to the cleaner's *informal* **a)** to cheat someone and take all their money or possessions **b)** to defeat someone completely: *The Lakers took the Bulls to the cleaner's, winning 96–72.*

clean·ing /ˈkliːnɪŋ/ *n* [U] the process or job of making a house, office etc clean: *Liz comes on Thursdays to* ***do the cleaning***. | **cleaning lady/woman** (=a woman who cleans houses, offices etc as her job)

clean·li·ness /ˈklenlinəs/ *n* [U] the practice of keeping yourself or the things around you clean: *a high standard of cleanliness*

clean·ly /ˈkliːnli/ *adv* **1** quickly and smoothly with a single movement: *The branch snapped cleanly in two.* **2** without producing dirt, pollution etc: *a fuel that burns cleanly without loss of power*

cleanse /klenz/ *v* [T] **1** to make something completely clean: *Use a piece of gauze to cleanse the cut. | The water is cleansed and reused.* **THESAURUS** ▸ **CLEAN 2** to remove everything that is bad or immoral from a person's character, an organization, or a place – used especially in news reports: **cleanse sb/sth of sth** *The mayor was elected on a promise to cleanse the city government of corruption.* → **ETHNIC CLEANSING**

cleans·er /ˈklenzə $ -ər/ *n* [C,U] **1** a substance used for removing dirt or MAKE-UP from your face **2** a substance containing chemicals that is used for cleaning surfaces inside a house, office etc: *cream cleanser for the bathroom*

ˌclean-ˈshaven *adj* a man who is clean-shaven does not have a BEARD or MOUSTACHE

clean·tech /ˈkliːntek/ *adj* [only before noun] involving products, actions, or processes that are better for the environment, for example ones which reduce waste or POLLUTION: *cleantech companies involved in renewable energy*

ˈclean-up, **clean·up** /ˈkliːnʌp/ *n* [C usually singular] a process by which you get rid of dirt or waste from a place: *The cleanup of the oil spill took months. | millions of dollars in clean-up costs*

clear¹ /klɪə $ klɪr/ ●●● S1 W1 *adj* (*comparative* **clearer**, *superlative* **clearest**)
1 EASY TO UNDERSTAND expressed in a simple and direct way so that people understand → **clarity**, **clearly**: *clear instructions | The question wasn't very clear. | It's the clearest guide I've used.* | **[+about]** *The school is clear about its policy on bullying.* | **clear about what/when/how etc** *Be very clear about what jobs should be completed, and by when.* | **[+on]** *The rules are quite clear on the point.* | **[+to]** *It was clear to him that Tolkien was a literary genius.* | **make sth clear** *The bishop made his views clear in a letter to the publisher. | How can you make the meaning clearer?* | **make it clear that** *Make it clear that you will not take sides.* | **absolutely/abundantly clear** *Can I make it absolutely clear that we did not intend this to happen? | Perhaps I tried to cover too much and didn't* ***make myself clear*** (=express myself well). | *If you don't understand, it's best to say so and* ***get*** *things* ***clear***. | *If I catch you smoking again, you're grounded.* ***Do I make myself clear?*** (=used when you are angry) | **clear picture/idea** (=a good understanding) *The report gave a clear picture of the property's condition.* | *He writes* ***crystal clear*** (=very easy to understand) *prose.*
2 IMPOSSIBLE TO DOUBT impossible to doubt, question, or make a mistake about → **clearly**: *clear evidence of guilt | They won by a clear majority.* | **it is clear whether/why/how etc** *It's not clear whether he shares her views.* | **it is clear (that)** *It's clear that the drug does benefit some patients. | When it became clear that I was pregnant, he left me.* | **clear case/example of sth** *a clear case of sexual discrimination* **THESAURUS** ▸ **OBVIOUS**
3 SURE ABOUT STH feeling certain that you know or understand something → **clearly**: **[+about/on]** *Are you all clear now about what you have to do?* | **clear whether/what/how etc** *I'm still not really clear how this machine works. | Let me* ***get*** *this* ***clear*** *– you hadn't seen her in three days? | a clearer understanding of the issues*
4 THINKING able to think sensibly and quickly → **clarity**, **clearly**: *She felt that her thinking was clearer now. | In the morning, with a* ***clear head***, *she'd tackle the problem.*
5 SUBSTANCE/LIQUID easy to see through, rather than coloured or dirty SYN **transparent** OPP **cloudy**, **opaque**: *clear glass bottles | a* ***crystal clear*** *mountain lake*
6 WEATHER clean and fresh, without clouds or mist: *a clear June morning | The skies were clear and blue.*
7 EYES healthy, very pure in colour, and without any redness: *clear blue eyes*
8 SKIN smooth and without any red spots: *a clear complexion*
9 EASY TO SEE having details, edges, lines etc that are easy to see, or shapes that are easy to recognize → **clarity**: *a TV with a clear picture and high-quality sound*
10 EASY TO HEAR easy to hear, and therefore easy to understand → **clarity**, **clearly**: *a clear speaking voice | The radio reception isn't very clear. | It's a good recording; the sound is* ***as clear as a bell*** (=very clear).
11 AFTER TAX a clear amount of profit, wages etc is what is left after taxes have been paid on it SYN **net**: *I get £200 a week clear. | Sam makes a clear $90,000 per year.*
12 a clear conscience the knowledge that you have done the right thing and should not feel guilty: *I don't think I could vote for him with a clear conscience. | She had done what she could and her conscience was clear.*
13 PERIOD OF TIME without any planned activities or events: *Next Monday is clear; how about ten o'clock?*
14 NOT BUSY complete or whole: *Allow three clear days for delivery.*
15 NOT BLOCKED/COVERED not covered or blocked by anything that stops you from doing or seeing what you want: *The roads were fairly clear this morning.* | **clear view/look** *From the top floor you get a clear view of the bay.* | **[+of]** *To prevent fires, the sides of the roads are kept clear of underbrush.*
16 see your way clear (to doing sth) *informal* to have the necessary time or willingness to be able to do something: *We expect good results soon, if the board can see its way clear to continuing funding the project.*
17 be clear of sth to not be touching something, or to be past someone or something: *Wait to cross until the street is clear of cars. | The curtains should be a couple of inches clear of the floor.*
18 as clear as mud *spoken* used humorously to say that something is very difficult to understand —**clearness** *n* [U] → **ALL CLEAR**, → **the coast is clear** at COAST¹(2)

clear² ●●● S1 W2 *v*
1 SURFACE/PLACE [T] to make somewhere emptier or tidier by removing things from it: *Snowplows have been out clearing the roads.* | **clear sth of sth** *Large areas of land had been cleared of forest.* | **clear sth from sth** *Workers began clearing wreckage from the tracks. | Dad* ***cleared a space*** (=moved things so there was room) *in the garage for Jim's tools. | It's Kelly's turn to* ***clear the table*** (=remove the dirty plates, forks etc).
2 REMOVE PEOPLE [T] to make people, cars etc leave a place: *Within minutes, police had cleared the area.* | **clear sb/sth from sth** *Crowds of demonstrators were cleared from the streets.*
3 CRIME/BLAME ETC [T] to prove that someone is not guilty of something: *Rawlings was cleared after new evidence was produced.* | **clear sb of (doing) sth** *Maya was cleared of manslaughter. | a long-running legal battle to* ***clear*** *his* ***name*** GRAMMAR **Clear** is often passive in this meaning.
4 PERMISSION [T] **a)** to give or get official permission for something to be done: *He was cleared by doctors to resume skating in August.* | **clear sth with sb** *Defence policies must often be cleared with NATO allies first.* **b)** to give official

C

permission for a person, ship, or aircraft to enter or leave a country: *The plane took off as soon as it was cleared.*
5 clear your throat to cough in order to be able to speak with a clear voice
6 WEATHER [I] (*also* **clear up**) if the weather, sky, mist etc clears, it becomes better and there is more sun: *The haze usually clears by lunchtime.*
7 LIQUID [I] if a liquid clears, it becomes more transparent and you can see through it: *Wait for the water to clear before adding any fish.*
8 CHEQUE [I,T] if a cheque clears, or if a bank clears it, the bank allows the money to be paid into the account of the person whose name is on the cheque
9 GO OVER/PAST [T] to go over a fence, wall etc without touching it, or to go past or through something and no longer be in it: *The plane barely cleared the fence at the end of the runway.* | *Edwards cleared 18 feet in the pole vault.* | *The plane cleared Chinese airspace.*
10 clear a debt/loan to get rid of a debt by paying what you owe
11 clear your head/mind to stop worrying or thinking about something, or get rid of the effects of drinking too much alcohol: *A good walk might clear my head.*
12 FACE/EXPRESSION [I] *literary* if your face or expression clears, you stop looking worried or angry: *She looked embarrassed, but then her face cleared.*
13 clear the way for sth *written* to make it possible for a process to happen: *This agreement will clear the way for further talks.*
14 SKIN [I] (*also* **clear up**) if your skin clears, red marks on it disappear: *The rash has finally cleared.*
15 clear the air to do something to end an argument or bad situation, for example discuss a problem calmly
16 clear (sth through) customs to be allowed to take things through CUSTOMS
17 clear the decks to do all the work that needs to be done before you can do other things: *I'm trying to clear the decks before Christmas.*
18 EARN [T] *informal* to earn a particular amount of money after taxes have been paid on it: *Diane clears £20,000 a year.*

clear sth ↔ **away** *phr v* to make a place look tidier by removing things or putting things back where they belong: *When dinner was done and cleared away, Auntie Lou made some tea.* | *Homeowners are clearing away brush near their houses to prevent fires.*

clear off *phr v BrE informal* to leave a place quickly: *They cleared off when they saw the police coming.* | **clear off!** (=used to tell someone angrily to go away)

clear out *phr v*
1 clear sth ↔ out to make a place tidy by removing things from it and getting rid of them: *I need to clear out my closet.*
2 to leave a place or building quickly: *Wait to get on the train until the people getting off have cleared out.* | **clear out!** *BrE* (=used to tell someone angrily to go away) → CLEAR-OUT

clear up *phr v*
1 to make a place look tidier by putting things back where they belong: *I don't mind you using the kitchen as long as you clear up afterwards.* | **clear sth ↔ up** *Adam, clear up this mess before your father sees it.* | **[+after]** *I get really tired of clearing up after you* (=tidying places that you have made untidy).
2 clear sth ↔ up to explain or solve something, or make it easier to understand: *The White House hopes these problems can be cleared up soon.* | *There are a couple of points we need to clear up before the meeting begins.*
3 if the weather clears up, it gets better
4 if an illness or infection clears up, it disappears

clear³ ●●○ *adv*
1 away from something, or out of the way: *Firefighters pulled her clear of the wreckage.* | *Please stand clear of the doors.*
2 keep/stay/steer clear (of sb/sth) to avoid someone or something because of possible danger or trouble: *If you're a beginner, steer clear of resorts with reputations for difficult skiing.*
3 *especially AmE informal* used to emphasize a long distance: *You can see clear to the hills.* → **loud and clear** at LOUD²(2)

clear⁴ *n* **in the clear** not guilty of something

clear·ance /ˈklɪərəns $ ˈklɪr-/ ●○○ *n*
1 [C,U] the process of getting official permission or approval for something: *She'll race if she* **gets** *medical* **clearance** *from her doctor.* | *Morris did not have a* **security clearance**.
2 [C,U] official permission for a plane to take off or land: **[+for]** *The pilot requested clearance for an emergency landing.*
3 [C,U] the removal of unwanted things from a place: *the clearance of minefields* | **snow/land/slum etc clearance** *flooding caused by forest clearance*
4 [C,U] the amount of space around one object that is needed for it to avoid touching another object: *There was less than a foot's clearance between the ship's sides and the wharf.*
5 [C,U] a process by which a cheque goes from one bank to another
6 [C] an occasion when a player in a game such as football kicks the ball away from his or her GOAL

ˈclearance sale *n* [C] an occasion when goods in a shop are sold cheaply in order to get rid of them

ˌclear-ˈcut¹ *adj* easy to understand or be certain about SYN **definite**: *There is not always a clear-cut distinction between right and wrong.*

ˈclear-cut² *n* [C] *AmE* an area of forest that has been completely cut down —**clear-cut** *v* [T]

ˌclear-ˈheaded *adj* able to think in a clear and sensible way

clear·ing /ˈklɪərɪŋ $ ˈklɪr-/ ●○○ *n* [C] a small area in a forest where there are no trees

ˈclearing ˌbank *n* [C] one of the banks in Britain that uses a clearing house when dealing with other banks

ˈclearing house *n* [C] **1** a central office where banks exchange cheques and other financial documents **2** an office that receives and gives out or sells information or goods for several other organizations

clear·ly /ˈklɪəli $ ˈklɪrli/ ●●● S1 W1 *adv*
1 [sentence adverb] without any doubt SYN **obviously**: *Clearly, ignoring him had been a mistake.*
2 in a way that is easy to see, hear, or understand: *Please speak clearly.* | *The economy was clearly failing.*
3 in a way that is sensible: *I wasn't thinking clearly.*

ˈclear-out *n* [C usually singular] *BrE informal* a process in which you get rid of unwanted objects or possessions: *I* **had a clear-out** *and got rid of a lot of old toys.*

ˌclear-ˈsighted *adj* able to understand a problem or situation well: *a clear-sighted analysis* —**clear-sightedness** *n* [U]

clear·way /ˈklɪəweɪ $ ˈklɪr-/ *n* [C] a road in Britain on which vehicles must not stop

cleat /kliːt/ *n* [C] **1** a small bar with two short arms around which ropes can be tied, especially on a ship **2** [usually plural] a short piece of rubber, metal etc attached to the bottom of a sports shoe in order to prevent someone from slipping SYN **stud 3 cleats** [plural] *AmE* a pair of sports shoes with these pieces attached to them → **spikes** → see picture at SHOE¹

cleav·age /ˈkliːvɪdʒ/ *n* [C,U] **1** the space between a woman's breasts **2** *formal* a difference between two people or things that often causes problems or arguments

cleave /kliːv/ *v* (*past tense* **cleaved**, **clove** /kləʊv $ kloʊv/ *or* **cleft** /kleft/, *past participle* **cleaved**, **cloven** /ˈkləʊvən $ ˈkloʊ-/ *or* **cleft**) **1** [I,T always + adv/prep] *literary* to cut something into separate parts using a heavy tool, or to be able to be cut in this way: *The wooden door had been cleft in two.* **2** [T] *formal* to divide something into two completely separate parts: *the racial problems that still cleave*

American society **3 cleave the air/darkness etc** *literary* to move quickly through the air etc: *His fist cleft the air.*

cleave to sb/sth *phr v* **1** *formal* to continue to think that a method, belief, person etc is true or valuable, even when this seems unlikely: *John still cleaves to his romantic ideals.* **2** *literary* to stick to someone or something, or seem to surround them

cleav·er /ˈkliːvə $ -ər/ *n* [C] a heavy knife for cutting up large pieces of meat

clef /klef/ *n* [C] a sign at the beginning of a line of written music to show the PITCH of the notes: **treble/bass clef**

cleft[1] /kleft/ *n* [C] **1** a natural crack in something, especially the surface of rocks or the Earth **2** an area on the chin or lip that goes slightly inwards

cleft[2] *adj* **be (caught) in a cleft stick** *BrE* to be in a very difficult situation in which any action or decision you make will cause problems

cleft[3] a past tense and past participle of CLEAVE

ˌcleft ˈlip *n* [C] a split in someone's upper lip, that they are born with

ˌcleft ˈpalate *n* [C] a split in the top of the inside of someone's mouth, that they are born with and that makes it difficult for them to speak clearly

clem·a·tis /ˈklemətɪs, klɪˈmeɪtɪs/ *n* [C,U] a plant that attaches itself to trees, buildings, fences etc as it grows, and that has white or coloured flowers → see picture at **FLOWER**[1]

clem·en·cy /ˈklemənsi/ *n* [U] *formal* forgiveness and less severe punishment for a crime: **grant/give sb clemency** *She was granted clemency after killing her violent husband.*

clem·ent /ˈklemənt/ *adj formal* clement weather is neither too hot nor too cold SYN **mild** OPP **inclement**

clem·en·tine /ˈklementiːn, -taɪn/ *n* [C] *BrE* a kind of small sweet orange → see picture at **FRUIT**[1]

clench /klentʃ/ ●○○ *v* [T]

1 clench your fists/teeth/jaw etc to hold your hands, teeth etc together tightly, usually because you feel angry or determined: *Jody was pacing the sidelines, her fists clenched.*

2 to hold something tightly in your hand or between your teeth: *a cigar clenched between his teeth*

cler·gy /ˈklɜːdʒi $ ˈklɜːr-/ *n* **the clergy** [plural] the official leaders of religious activities in organized religions, such as priests, RABBIS, and MULLAHS → **clerical**

cler·gy·man /ˈklɜːdʒimən $ ˈklɜːr-/ *n* (*plural* **clergymen** /-mən/) [C] a male member of the clergy

cler·gy·wom·an /ˈklɜːdʒiˌwʊmən $ ˈklɜːr-/ *n* (*plural* **clergywomen** /-ˌwɪmɪn/) [C] a female member of the clergy

cler·ic /ˈklerɪk/ ●○○ *n* [C] a member of the clergy

cler·i·cal /ˈklerɪkəl/ *adj* **1** relating to office work, especially work such as keeping records or accounts: *a clerical error* | *clerical workers* **2** relating to the clergy: *a clerical collar*

clerk[1] /klɑːk $ klɜːrk/ ●●○ S3 *n* [C]

1 someone who keeps records or accounts in an office: *a clerk in a commercial firm*

2 *AmE* someone whose job is to help people in a shop: *the clerk in the shoe store*

3 *AmE* someone whose job is to help people when they arrive at and leave a hotel: *Leave the keys with the* ***desk clerk.***

4 an official in charge of the records of a court, town council etc

5 *old use* a priest in the Church of England

clerk[2] *v* [I] *especially AmE informal* to work as a clerk

ˌclerk of ˈworks *n* (*plural* **clerks of works**) [C] *BrE* someone who is in charge of repairs to the buildings in a particular place

clev·er /ˈklevə $ -ər/ ●●● S2 *adj*

1 *especially BrE* able to learn and understand things quickly SYN **intelligent**, **smart** *AmE*: *a clever man* | **very/extremely/quite/pretty etc clever** *Lucy is quite clever and does well at school.* THESAURUS INTELLIGENT

2 able to use your intelligence to get what you want, especially in a slightly dishonest way: *a clever lawyer's tricks*

3 *especially BrE* skilful at doing a particular thing: *Bill's very clever with his hands.* | *his clever ball control* | **clever at doing sth** *He was clever at finding bargains.*

4 done or made in an unusual or interesting way that is very effective: *What a clever little gadget!* | *a clever marketing strategy*

5 *BrE spoken* used jokingly when someone has done something silly or stupid: *'When I got to the library I found I'd left the books at home.' 'That was clever!'*

6 clever clogs/dick *BrE spoken* used to describe someone who is annoying because they are always right or always think they are right

7 be too clever by half *BrE spoken* to be clever, and to show that you are clever in a way that annoys other people —**cleverly** *adv* —**cleverness** *n* [U]

cli·ché /ˈkliːʃeɪ $ kliːˈʃeɪ/ ●○○ *n* [C] an idea or phrase that has been used so much that it is not effective or does not have any meaning any longer: *There is plenty of truth in the cliché that a trouble shared is a trouble halved.* THESAURUS PHRASE, WORD —**clichéd** *adj*

click[1] /klɪk/ ●●● S3 *v*

1 [I,T] to make a short hard sound, or make something produce this sound: *The door* ***clicked shut*** *behind me.* | *Mother* ***clicked*** *her* ***tongue*** (=made a short sound to show disapproval) *and sighed.* | *Edmund* ***clicked his fingers*** (=made a short sound to get someone's attention) *for John to follow him.* | *Vogel* ***clicked*** *his* ***heels*** (=hit the heels of his shoes together) *and bowed.* | *Twist the lever and the gears* ***click into place.***

2 [I,T] to press a button on a computer MOUSE to choose something from the screen that you want the computer to do, or to press a button on a REMOTE CONTROL: *Choose the image you want by clicking twice.* | **[+on]** *Children can click on a sentence to hear it read aloud.*

3 [I] *informal* to suddenly understand or realize something: *It's hard work, but one day* ***it*** *will just* ***click.*** | *I thought, 'What is he doing?' and then suddenly it all* ***clicked into place*** (=I understood how all the events related to each other).

4 [I] *informal* if two people click, they like, understand, and agree with each other: *They clicked straight away.*

5 [I] *informal* to happen in a good or successful way, especially because people are working together well: *If everything clicks, we should have a good season.*

click[2] ●●○ *n* [C]

1 a short hard sound: *The door closed with a click.*

2 the click of a mouse used to show how quickly something can be done on a computer: *Your photos can be viewed with the click of a mouse.*

click·a·ble /ˈklɪkəbəl/ *adj* if a word or picture that you can see on a computer screen is clickable, it will connect you to more information when you click on it by pressing a button on the computer MOUSE

ˌclick and colˈlect *n* [U] *BrE* the practice of ordering or buying goods on the Internet and then picking them up from a store

ˈclick-fit *adj* [only before noun] having a metal or plastic connector that allows you to join two pieces of equipment together without using tools: *a click-fit coupling*

click·stream /ˈklɪkstriːm/ *n* [C] *informal* a record of the particular websites someone visits when they use the Internet, how long they spend visiting each website, the pages they looked at etc. This information is collected and stored by ISPs and some WEBSITES.

ˈclick-through *n* [C,U] when someone clicks on an advertisement or link on the Internet: *Click-throughs are one of the standard ways to measure the effectiveness of online ads.* | *click-through rates*

click·tiv·ism /ˈklɪktɪvɪzəm/ *n* [U] the use of the Internet to show that you want to protest against something or support something, for example by signing an Internet PETITION —**clicktivist** *n* [C]

C

cli·ent /ˈklaɪənt/ ●●● S2 W1 *n* [C]
1 someone who gets services or advice from a professional person, company, or organization SYN **customer**: *a meeting with an important client* THESAURUS ► CUSTOMER
2 *technical* a computer on a NETWORK that receives information from a SERVER (=large powerful computer)

cli·en·tele /ˌkliːənˈtel $ ˌklaɪənˈtel, ˌkliː-/ *n* [singular] all the people who regularly use a shop, restaurant etc: *The restaurant attracts a young clientele.* THESAURUS ► CUSTOMER

ˈclient-side *adj* relating to software that runs on the user's own machine rather than a SERVER

ˌclient ˈstate *n* [C] a country that is dependent on the support and protection of a more powerful country – used in news reports

cliff /klɪf/ ●●○ *n* [C] a large area of rock or a mountain with a very steep side, often at the edge of the sea or a river

cliff·hang·er /ˈklɪfˌhæŋə $ -ər/ *n* [C] a situation in a story, film, or competition that makes you feel very excited or nervous because you do not know what will happen or have to wait a long time to see how it will end: *Tonight's vote may be a cliffhanger.* | *the episode's cliffhanger ending* —**cliffhanging** *adj*

cli·mac·tic /klaɪˈmæktɪk/ *adj* forming a very exciting or important part of an event or story, especially near the end of it → **climax**: *a climactic moment*

cli·mate /ˈklaɪmət/ ●●○ W3 *n*
1 [C,U] the typical weather conditions in a particular area: *Los Angeles' warm dry climate*
2 [C] an area with particular weather conditions: *These flowers will not grow in cold climates.*
3 [C usually singular] the general feeling or situation in a place at a particular time: **political/economic/social etc climate** *Small businesses are finding it hard to survive in the present economic climate.* | **[+of]** *a climate of growing racial intolerance in large cities*

ˈclimate ˌchange ●●○ *n* [U] a permanent change in the Earth's weather conditions

cli·mat·ic /klaɪˈmætɪk/ *adj* [only before noun] relating to the weather in a particular area: *climatic conditions*

cli·ma·tol·o·gy /ˌklaɪməˈtɒlədʒi $ -ˈtɑː-/ *n* [U] the scientific study of climate —**climatologist** *n* [C]

cli·max¹ /ˈklaɪmæks/ ●○○ *n* [C usually singular]
1 the most exciting or important part of a story or experience, which usually comes near the end → **climactic**: **[+of]** *the climax of his naval career* | **[+to]** *a thrilling climax to the game* | *The festival* ***reaches*** *its* ***climax*** *with the traditional boat-burning ceremony.*
2 an ORGASM

climax² *v* **1** [I,T] if a situation, process, or story climaxes, it reaches its most important or exciting part: **[+in/with]** *a series of special events climaxing with a spectacular fireworks show* **2** [I] to have an ORGASM

climb¹ /klaɪm/ ●●● W2 *v*
1 MOVE UP/DOWN [I always + adv/prep, T] to move up, down, or across something using your feet and hands, especially when this is difficult to do: *Harry climbed the stairs.* | *Boys were climbing trees along the river bank.* | **[+up/down/along etc]** *The wall is too high to climb over.* | *They climbed up into the loft of the old barn.*
2 TEMPERATURE/PRICES ETC [I] to increase in number, amount, or level SYN **go up**: *The temperature has climbed steadily since this morning.* | *Inflation climbed 2% last month.* | **[+to]** *The divorce rate had climbed to almost 30% of all marriages.*
3 WITH DIFFICULTY [I always + adv/prep] to move into, out of, or through something slowly and awkwardly: *The bus pulled in, and we climbed aboard.* | **[+through/over/into etc]** *John climbed through the window into the kitchen.* | *I turned the TV on and climbed into bed.*
4 PATH/SUN/PLANE [I] to move gradually to a higher position: *The roller coaster climbs 91 feet and reaches speeds of 45 miles an hour.* | **[+into/up etc]** *The path climbs high into the hills.* | *The plane climbed to 11,600 feet to try to get above the clouds.*
5 SPORT [I,T] to climb mountains or rocks as a sport: *Hillary and Tenzing were the first men to climb Mount Everest.* | *She loves to hike and climb.* → CLIMBING
6 PLANT [I] to grow up a wall or other structure: **climbing rose/plant**
7 IN A LIST [I,T] to move higher in a list of teams, records etc as you become more popular or successful SYN **rise**: **[+to]** *The song climbed to number two in the US charts.*
8 IN YOUR LIFE/JOB [I,T] to move to a better position in your social or professional life: *Steve climbed rapidly in the sales division.* | *men who* ***climbed the*** *career* ***ladder*** *in the 1980s*
9 be climbing the walls *spoken* to become extremely anxious, annoyed, or impatient: *If I don't get a drink soon, I'll be climbing the walls.*

climb down *phr v BrE* to admit that you were wrong, especially after being certain that you were right → **climb-down**

climb² ●●○ *n*
1 MOVEMENT UPWARDS [C usually singular] a process in which you move up towards a place, especially while using a lot of effort: *a long steady climb to the top*
2 INCREASE [C usually singular] an increase in value or amount: *The dollar continued its climb against the yen.* | **[+in]** *a steady climb in house prices*
3 IMPROVEMENT [C usually singular] the process of improving something, especially your professional or social position: *a slow climb out of the recession* | **[+to]** *the Labour Party's climb to power*
4 LIST/COMPETITION [singular] a process in which someone or something reaches a higher position in a list or in a competition because of being popular or successful: *the Giants' climb from twelfth to fifth in the league* | *the song's steady climb up the charts*
5 ROCK/MOUNTAIN [C] a steep rock, cliff, or mountain that you climb up: *one of the hardest rock climbs in the world*

ˈclimb-down *n* [C usually singular] *BrE* an occasion when you admit that you were wrong: *a humiliating climb-down by the government*

climb·er /ˈklaɪmə $ -ər/ ●●○ *n* [C]
1 someone who climbs as a sport: *a mountain climber*
2 a person or animal that can climb easily: *Monkeys are good climbers.*
3 a plant that grows up a wall or other structure → SOCIAL CLIMBER

climb·ing /ˈklaɪmɪŋ/ ●●○ *n* [U] the sport of climbing mountains or rocks → **mountaineering**: *a climbing rope* | **rock/mountain climbing** | *He* ***goes climbing*** *nearly every weekend.*

ˈclimbing ˌframe *n* [C] *BrE* a structure for children to climb on, made from metal bars, wood, or rope SYN **jungle gym** *AmE*

clime /klaɪm/ *n* [C usually plural] *literary* a place that has a particular type of CLIMATE: *sunnier climes*

clinch¹ /klɪntʃ/ ●○○ *v*
1 [T] to finally agree on something or get something after trying very hard: *a young salesman eager to* ***clinch*** *the* ***deal*** | **clinch a match/championship/victory etc** *A last-minute touchdown clinched the game.*
2 clinch it *informal* if an event, situation, process etc clinches it, it makes someone finally decide to do something that they were already thinking of doing: *We'd talked about moving, and the burglary clinched it for us.*
3 [I] if two people clinch, they hold each other's arms tightly, especially when fighting

clinch² *n* [C] **1** a situation in which two people hold each other's arms tightly, especially when they are fighting **2** a situation in which two people who love each other hold each other tightly SYN **embrace**

clinch·er /ˈklɪntʃə $ -ər/ *n* [C] *informal* a fact, action, or remark that finally persuades someone to do something, or that ends an argument, discussion, or competition: *Sixsmith scored the clincher after 81 minutes.*

cline /klaɪn/ *n* [C] *technical* a series of very small differences in a group of things of the same kind SYN **continuum**

cling /klɪŋ/ ●●○ *v* (*past tense and past participle* **clung** /klʌŋ/) [I]

1 [always + adv/prep] to hold someone or something tightly, especially because you do not feel safe: **[+to/on/at etc]** *He wailed and clung to his mother.* | *Passengers clung desperately on to the lifeboats.*

2 [always + adv/prep] to stick to someone or something, or seem to surround them: **[+to/around etc]** *His wet shirt clung to his body.* | *The smell of cigarette smoke clung to her clothes.*

3 to stay close to someone all the time because you are too dependent on them or do not feel safe – used to show disapproval: *Some children tend to cling on their first day at school.*

cling on *phr v* to continue trying to stay in power, in business etc: *Other businesses cling on and hope.*

cling to sth (*also* **cling on to sth**) *phr v*

1 to continue to believe or do something, even though it may not be true or useful any longer: **cling to the hope/belief/idea etc (that)** *He clung to the hope that she would be cured.*

2 to stay in a position of power or stay ahead, when this is difficult, or to try to do this: *an attempt to cling to power*

cling·film /ˈklɪŋfɪlm/ *n* [U] *BrE* very thin transparent plastic, used to cover food and keep it fresh SYN **plastic wrap** *AmE*

cling·y /ˈklɪŋi/ (*also* **cling·ing** /ˈklɪŋɪŋ/) *adj* **1** someone who is clingy is too dependent on another person, and will often hold on to them – used to show disapproval: *a shy clingy child* **2** clingy clothing or material sticks tightly to your body and shows its shape – use this to show approval: *She wore a clingy red dress.*

clin·ic /ˈklɪnɪk/ ●●○ *n* [C]

1 a place, often in a hospital, where medical treatment is given to people who do not need to stay in the hospital: **dental/family planning/antenatal etc clinic** *women attending an antenatal clinic* | *an appointment at an* ***outpatient clinic*** (=clinic for someone who does not need to stay in a hospital)

2 *especially BrE* a period of time during which doctors give treatment or advice to people with particular health problems: *The baby* ***clinic*** *is* ***held*** *on Monday afternoons.*

3 a meeting during which a professional person gives advice or help to people: *an MP's clinic* | *a free clinic on caring for roses*

4 *AmE* a place where medical treatment is given at a low cost: *the doctors who volunteer at the inner-city clinic*

5 *AmE* a group of doctors who work together and share the same offices SYN **practice**

6 an occasion when medical students are taught how to decide what illness a patient has and how to treat it

clin·i·cal /ˈklɪnɪkəl/ ●○○ *adj*

1 [only before noun] relating to treating or testing people who are sick: *The drug has undergone extensive* ***clinical trials*** (=tests to see if it is effective in treating people). | **clinical medicine/experience/training etc** (=medicine etc that deals directly with people, rather than with research or ideas) | *The therapy has helped people with clinical depression* (=a strong feeling of sadness, for which you need medical help).

2 relating to a hospital or clinic: *The program gives the students experience in a clinical setting.*

3 considering only the facts and not influenced by personal feelings: *A formal marriage agreement sounds clinical, but it can be a good idea.*

4 a clinical building or room is very plain and clean, but not attractive or comfortable: *The walls were painted a clinical white.* —**clinically** /-kli/ *adv*: *clinically tested drugs*

ˌclinical therˈmometer *n* [C] a THERMOMETER for measuring the temperature of your body

cli·ni·cian /klɪˈnɪʃən/ *n* [C] a doctor who treats and examines people, rather than one who does RESEARCH

clink¹ /klɪŋk/ *v* [I,T] if two glass or metal objects clink, or if you clink them, they make a short ringing sound when they are hit together: *Spoons clinked against the crockery.*

clink² *n* [singular] **1** the short ringing sound made by metal or glass objects hitting each other: *the clink of glasses* **THESAURUS** ▶ **SOUND** **2** *old-fashioned informal* prison

clink·er /ˈklɪŋkə $ -ər/ *n* **1** [C,U] the hard material like rocks, which is left after coal has been burnt **2** [C] *AmE* a bad note in a musical performance: *The singer hit a real clinker.* **3** [C] *AmE informal* something or someone that is a total failure: *Most of the songs are good, but there are a few clinkers.*

clip¹ /klɪp/ ●●○ *n*

1 FOR FASTENING [C] a small metal or plastic object that holds or fastens things together: *The wire is held on with a metal clip.* | *a wad of money in a gold clip* → **BULLDOG CLIP**, **PAPERCLIP**, see picture at **STATIONERY**

2 FILM [C] a short part of a film or television programme that is shown by itself, especially as an advertisement: *clips from the new James Bond film*

3 GUN [C] a container for bullets which passes them quickly into the gun so that they can be fired

4 at a good/rapid/fast etc clip quickly: *Traffic was moving at a good clip.*

5 CUT [singular] *BrE* the act of cutting something to make it shorter or tidier: *I gave the hedge a clip.*

6 a clip round the ear/earhole *BrE informal* a short hit on the side of someone's head

7 NEWSPAPER [C] an article that is cut from a newspaper or magazine for a particular reason

8 $100/50 cents etc a clip *AmE informal* if things cost $100, 50 cents etc a clip, they cost that amount of money each

clip² ●●○ *v* (**clipped**, **clipping**)

1 FASTEN [I always + adv/prep, T] to fasten something together or to be fastened together using a clip: **clip sth into/onto etc sth** *A microphone was clipped to his tie.* | *a stack of bills* ***clipped together***

2 CUT [T] to cut small amounts of something in order to make it tidier: *The hedges had just been clipped.*

3 CUT FROM NEWSPAPER [T always + adv/prep] to cut an article or picture from a newspaper, magazine etc: **clip sth out of/from sth** *a cartoon clipped from a Minneapolis newspaper*

4 HIT [T] to hit something quickly at an angle, often by accident: *A truck swerved and clipped a parked car.*

5 REDUCE [T] to slightly reduce an amount, quantity etc – used in news reports: **clip sth off/from sth** *Gunnell clipped a second off the world record.*

6 clip sb's wings to restrict someone's freedom, activities, or power

7 clip sb round the ear/earhole *BrE informal* to hit someone quickly on the side of the head

8 TICKET [T] *BrE* to make a hole in a bus or train ticket to show that it has been used SYN **punch** *AmE*

9 clip your words to say words in a quick, short, and not very friendly way

ˈclip art *n* [U] images, photographs, or pictures that are on particular websites and CD-ROMS, and that you can copy and use in your own computer documents

clip·board /ˈklɪpbɔːd $ -bɔːrd/ *n* [C] **1** a small flat board with a CLIP on top that holds paper so that you can write on it **2** a part of a computer's MEMORY that stores information when you are moving it from one document to another

ˌclip-ˈclop *n* [singular] the sound made by a horse as it walks on a hard surface —**clip-clop** *v* [I]

ˈclip joint *n* [C] *informal* a NIGHTCLUB that charges an unfairly high price for drinks

ˈclip-on *adj* [only before noun] attached to something with a CLIP: *clip-on earrings* —**clip-on** *n* [C]

clipped /klɪpt/ *adj* **1** cut so that it is short and neat: *a neatly clipped hedge* **2** a clipped voice is quick and clear but not very friendly

clip·per /ˈklɪpə $ -ər/ *n* **1 clippers** [plural] a special tool with two blades, used for cutting small pieces from

C

something: *nail clippers* **2** [C] a fast sailing ship used in the past

clip·ping /ˈklɪpɪŋ/ *n* [C] **1** an article or picture that has been cut out of a newspaper or magazine SYN **cutting**: **newspaper/press clippings** *old press clippings about movie stars* **2** [usually plural] a small piece cut from something bigger: *hedge clippings*

clique /kliːk/ *n* [C] a small group of people who think they are special and do not want other people to join them – used to show disapproval: **[+of]** *a ruling clique of officials | the cliques formed by high school students*

cliqu·ey /ˈkliːki/ (*also* **cliqu·ish** /ˈkliːkɪʃ/) *adj* a cliquey organization, club etc has a lot of cliques or is controlled by them – used to show disapproval

clit·o·ris /ˈklɪtərɪs/ *n* [C] a small part of a woman's outer sexual organs, where she can feel sexual pleasure

Cllr *BrE* the written abbreviation of ***councillor***

cloak[1] /kləʊk $ kloʊk/ ●○○ *n*

1 [C] a warm piece of clothing like a coat without sleeves that hangs loosely from your shoulders

2 [singular] an organization, activity, or way of behaving that deliberately protects someone or keeps something secret: **[+of]** *the cloak of secrecy around the affair* | **[+for]** *The political party is used as a cloak for terrorist activities.* | **under the cloak of sth** *prejudice hiding under the cloak of religion*

cloak[2] *v* [T] **1** to deliberately hide facts, feelings etc so that people do not see or understand them – used especially in news reports: **be cloaked in secrecy/mystery** *The talks have been cloaked in secrecy.* **2** *literary* to cover something, for example with darkness or snow: **be cloaked in sth** *hills cloaked in mist* GRAMMAR **Cloak** is usually passive. —**cloaked** *adj*: *The riders were cloaked* (=they wore cloaks).

ˌcloak-and-ˈdagger *adj* [usually before noun] very secret and mysterious, and usually involving the work of SPIES: *a cloak-and-dagger operation*

cloak·ing /ˈkləʊkɪŋ $ ˈkloʊ-/ *n* [U] the practice of giving false information about what is on a website to a SEARCH ENGINE (=the computer program that finds the information people ask for on the Internet). This is usually done to attract a lot of people to the website because the false information contains words that people often type into a search engine when using the Internet.

cloak·room /ˈkləʊkrʊm, -ruːm $ ˈkloʊk-/ *n* [C] **1** a small room where you can leave your coat SYN **coatroom** *AmE* **2** *BrE* a room in a public building where there are toilets – used when you want to be polite SYN **rest room** *AmE*: *Where's the ladies' cloakroom?*

clob·ber[1] /ˈklɒbə $ ˈklɑːbər/ *v* [T] *informal* **1** to hit someone very hard **2** to affect or punish someone or something badly, especially by making them lose money: *The paper got clobbered for libel. | The company has been clobbered by falling property prices.* **3** to defeat someone very easily in a way that is embarrassing for the team that loses: *The Dallas Cowboys clobbered the Buffalo Bills last night.*

clobber[2] *n* [U] *BrE informal* someone's possessions, especially their clothes: *Liam's football clobber*

cloche /klɒʃ $ kloʊʃ/ *n* [C] **1** a hat shaped like a bell, worn by women in the 1920s **2** *BrE* a glass or transparent plastic cover put over young plants to protect them during cold weather

clock[1] /klɒk $ klɑːk/ ●●● S2 W3 *n* [C]

1 an instrument that shows what time it is, in a room or outside on a building: *I heard* ***the clock strike six*** (=make six loud sounds). | *The station clock* ***was*** *ten minutes* ***slow*** (=showed a time ten minutes earlier than the real time). | **by the hall/kitchen/church etc clock** (=according to a particular clock) *What time is it by the kitchen clock?* → **watch the clock** at WATCH[1](8)

2 around the clock (*also* **round the clock** *BrE*) all day and all night without stopping: *Kim has been* ***working round the clock*** *to finish it in time.*

3 put/turn the clock back a) (*also* **set the clock back** *AmE*) to go back to the way things were done in the past instead of doing things in a modern way – used to show disapproval: *The new employment bill will put the clock back 50 years.* **b)** to return to a good situation that you experienced in the past or to make someone remember such a situation: *The kids are all grown up now and you* ***can't put the clock back***.

4 put the clock(s) back/forward *BrE* to change the time shown on the clock to one hour earlier or later, when the time officially changes

5 the clocks go back/forward *BrE* the time changes officially to one hour earlier or later: *The clocks go back in October.*

6 against the clock a) if you work against the clock, you work as quickly as you can because you do not have much time: *Everyone is* ***racing against the clock*** *to get things ready in time.* **b)** if you run, swim etc against the clock, you run or swim a particular distance while your speed is measured

7 twenty-four hour clock a system for measuring time in which the hours of the day and night have numbers from 0 to 23

8 start/stop the clock to start or stop measuring how much time is left in a game or sport that has a time limit

9 the clock is ticking used to say that there is not much time left to do something: *The clock is ticking for those who have not yet filled in their tax form.*

10 the clock a) an instrument in a vehicle that measures how far it has travelled: **on the clock** *a car with 43,000 miles on the clock* **b)** an instrument in a vehicle that measures the speed at which it is travelling

11 run out the clock/kill the clock *AmE* if a team runs out the clock at the end of a game, it tries to keep the ball for the rest of the game so that its opponents cannot get any points → **BIOLOGICAL CLOCK, BODY CLOCK, DANDELION CLOCK, TIME CLOCK**

CLOCKS

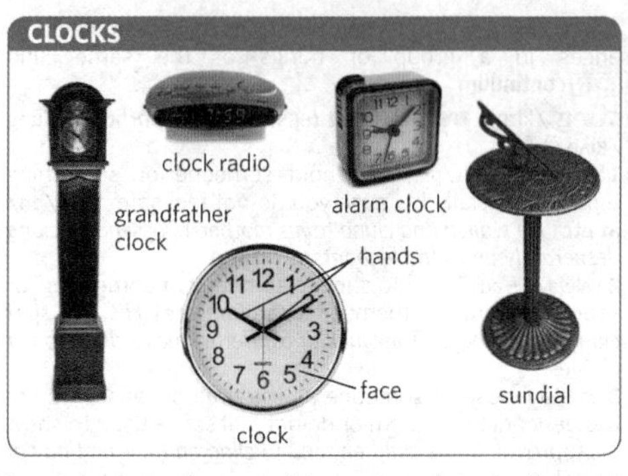

COLLOCATIONS

VERBS

look/glance at the clock *She looked at the clock. It was eight thirty.*

the clock says eight/nine etc (=shows a particular time) *The clock said five so I went back to sleep.*

a clock strikes eight/nine etc (=makes eight/nine etc sounds according to the hour) *In the distance I heard a church clock strike eleven.*

a clock ticks (=makes regular quiet sounds that show it is working) *There was no sound in the room apart from a clock ticking.*

a clock is fast/slow (=shows a later or earlier time than the real time) *There's no need to hurry – that clock's fast.*

a clock stops (=stops working) | **an alarm clock goes off** (=rings at a particular time) | **set a clock** (=make it say the right time) | **wind (up) a clock** (=turn a key to keep it working)

PHRASES

the hands of/on a clock (=the long thin pieces that point at the numbers) *The hands on the clock said ten past two.*

the face of a clock/the clock face (=the front part that you look at)

ADJECTIVES/NOUN + clock

the kitchen/sitting-room etc clock *Harry glanced at the kitchen clock and saw that he was late.*
an alarm clock (=that makes a noise to wake you up) | **a wall clock** (=that hangs on a wall) | **a grandfather clock** (=an old-style tall clock that stands on the floor) | **a digital clock** (=that shows the time as numbers that keep changing) | **a travel/travelling clock** (=a small one for taking on journeys) | **a cuckoo clock** (=a clock with a wooden bird inside that comes out every hour and makes a sound) | **a carriage clock** *BrE* (=a clock inside a glass case with a handle on top)

COMMON ERRORS

⚠ Don't say 'the clock shows five o'clock'. Say **the clock says five o'clock.**

clock² *v* [T] **1** to cover a distance in a particular time, or to reach a particular speed in a race: *Karen won in the 300 metres, clocking 42.9 seconds.* | *the first steam engine to clock 100 miles an hour* **2** to measure or record the time or speed that someone or something is travelling at: **clock sb at/doing sth** *The police clocked him doing between 100 and 110 miles per hour.* **3** *BrE informal* to notice someone or something, or to look at them carefully: *Did you clock the bloke by the door?* **4** *BrE* to reduce the number of miles or kilometres shown on the instrument in a car that says how far it has gone, in order to sell the car for more money: *He knew the car had been clocked, but he couldn't prove it.*

clock in/on *phr v especially BrE* to record on a special card the time you arrive at or begin work SYN **punch in** *AmE*: *I clock on at 8:30.*

clock off *phr v BrE* **1** *informal* to leave work at the end of the day: *What time do you clock off?* **2** to record on a special card the time you stop or leave work: *By 6 p.m. most workers have clocked off.*

clock out *phr v especially BrE* to record on a special card the time you stop or leave work SYN **punch out** *AmE*

clock up sth *phr v* to reach or achieve a particular number or amount: *The Dodgers have clocked up six wins in a row.* | *I clocked up 90,000 miles in my Ford.* | *Councillor Scott has clocked up more than 25 years on the borough council.*

'clock ˌcycle *n* [C] *technical* the basic unit of time used to measure how fast a computer can perform an instruction

ˌclock-'radio *n* [C] a machine that is a clock and a radio. You can set the clock to turn the radio on and wake you up.

'clock speed *n* [C usually singular] *technical* a measurement of how quickly a computer's CPU (=main controlling part) can deal with instructions: *a clock speed of 1 gigahertz*

clock·watch·ing /ˈklɒkˌwɒtʃɪŋ $ ˈklɑːkˌwɑːtʃɪŋ, -ˌwɒːtʃ-/ *n* [U] *BrE* when you often look at a clock to see what time it is because you are bored or want to stop working —**clockwatcher** *n* [C]

clock·wise /ˈklɒk-waɪz $ ˈklɑːk-/ *adv* in the same direction as the HANDS of a clock move OPP **anticlockwise, counterclockwise**: *Screw the lid on clockwise.* —**clockwise** *adj* → ANTICLOCKWISE, COUNTERCLOCKWISE

clock·work /ˈklɒk-wɜːk $ ˈklɑːk-wɜːrk/ *n* [U] **1** *BrE* clockwork toys, trains, soldiers etc have machinery inside them that makes them move when you turn a key: *mechanical toys powered by clockwork* | *The tape was driven by a clockwork motor.* **2 go/run like clockwork** to happen in exactly the way you had planned: *The concert went like clockwork.* **3 like clockwork** (*also* **(as) regular as clockwork**) happening at the same time and in the same way every time: *Matt came round each Friday, regular as clockwork.* **4 with clockwork precision/accuracy** in an extremely exact way

clod /klɒd $ klɑːd/ *n* [C] **1** a lump of mud or earth **2** *informal* a stupid person

clod·hop·per /ˈklɒdˌhɒpə $ ˈklɑːdˌhɑːpər/ *n* [C] **1 clodhoppers** [plural] a pair of heavy strong shoes – used humorously **2** *BrE informal* someone who is awkward and rough

clog¹ /klɒg $ klɑːg/ (*also* **clog up**) *v* (**clogged, clogging**) [I,T] to block something or become blocked: *tourists whose cars clog the roads each summer* | **[+with]** *Over many years, the pipes had* **got clogged up** *with grease.* —**clogged** *adj*: *clogged highways*

clog² *n* [C usually plural] a shoe made of wood with a leather top that covers the front of your foot but not your heel → see picture at SHOE¹ → **clever clogs** at CLEVER(6), → **pop your clogs** at POP¹(13)

clois·ter /ˈklɔɪstə $ -ər/ *n* [C] **1** [usually plural] a covered passage that surrounds one side of a square garden in a church, MONASTERY etc **2** a building where MONKS or NUNS live

clois·tered /ˈklɔɪstəd $ -ərd/ *adj* **1** protected from the difficulties and demands of ordinary life: *Academics lead a cloistered life.* **2** a cloistered building contains cloisters

clone¹ /kləʊn $ kloʊn/ ●○○ *n* [C]
1 *technical* an animal or plant produced by scientists from one cell of another animal or plant, so that they are exactly the same
2 *technical* a computer that is built as an exact copy of a more famous computer: *an IBM clone*
3 *informal* someone or something that looks and behaves exactly the same as someone or something else: **[+of]** *She's an exact clone of her sister!*

clone² ●○○ *v* [T]
1 to make an exact copy of a plant or animal by taking a cell from it and developing it artificially
2 to copy the number of someone else's MOBILE PHONE onto a new CHIP and then use that number on a different telephone, so that the mobile phone's owner receives the telephone bill

clonk /klɒŋk $ klɑːŋk/ *n* [singular] the sound made when a heavy object falls to the ground or hits another heavy object —**clonk** *v* [I,T]

clop /klɒp $ klɑːp/ *v* (**clopped, clopping**) [I] if a horse clops, its HOOVES make a loud sound as they touch the ground —**clop** *n* [singular]

close¹ /kləʊz $ kloʊz/ ●●● S1 W1 *v*
1 SHUT [I,T] to shut something in order to cover an opening, or to become shut in this way SYN **shut** OPP **open** → **closed**: *Would you mind if I closed the window?* | *She closed the curtains.* | *Let me do the car door – it won't close properly.* | *Beth* **closed** *her* **eyes** *and tried to sleep.* | *She heard the door close behind her.*
2 MOVE PARTS TOGETHER [I,T] to move the parts of something together so that there is no longer a space between them: *Anne closed her book and stood up.*
3 SHUT FOR PERIOD OF TIME [I,T] (*also* **close up**) if a shop or building closes, or you close it, it stops being open to the public for a period of time OPP **open** SYN **shut** *BrE* → **closed**: *The shops close at six.* | *Harry usually closes the store completely when he goes on vacation.*
4 STOP OPERATING [I,T] (*also* **close down**) if a company, shop etc closes, or you close it, it stops operating permanently SYN **shut down** → **closed**: *We have reluctantly decided to close the factory.* | *The shop closed down some time last year.*
5 END [I,T] to end or to make something end, especially in a particular way: **close sth with/by etc** *I will now close the meeting by asking you to join me in a final toast.* | **[+with]** *The movie closes with an emotional reunion in Prague.* | **closing remarks** (=something you say at the end of a speech) *In her closing remarks, the judge urged the jury to consider the facts only.*
6 close an account to stop having and using a bank account or other financial account: *My husband closed all my credit card accounts without even asking me.*
7 IN MONEY MARKETS [I always + adv/prep] to be worth a

particular amount of money at the end of a day's TRADING (=the buying and selling of shares) on the STOCK EXCHANGE: **[+at]** *The dollar closed at 64p against the pound.* **[+up/down]** *Their shares closed 27p up* (=worth 27p more).

8 close a deal/sale/contract etc to successfully agree a business deal, sale etc

9 OFFER FINISHES [I] to finish on a particular date SYN **end**: *Our special offer closes on June 3.*

10 MAKE DISTANCE/DIFFERENCE SMALLER [I,T] to make the distance or difference between two things smaller: *an attempt to* ***close the gap*** *between the rich and poor* | **[+on]** *The other car was closing on us fast.*

11 MAKE STH UNAVAILABLE [I,T] to make taking part in an activity or using an opportunity no longer possible → **closed**: *Bidding for the painting will close on Friday.* | *The country has now* ***closed*** *its* ***borders*** *to all foreign nationals* (=will not let foreigners in). | *The legislation aims to close a lot of legal loopholes.*

12 be closed if a subject is closed, you are no longer willing to discuss it: *It was a regrettable incident but I now consider the matter closed.*

13 close your doors (to sb) to stop operating permanently: *In 1977 the Skyfame Aircraft Museum closed its doors to the public for the last time.*

14 close your mind to/against sth to refuse to think about something: *She wanted to close her mind to the outside world.*

15 HOLD STH [I always + adv/prep, T] if someone's hands, arms etc close around something, or are closed around something, they hold it firmly: **close (sth) around/round/over etc sth** *Her left hand closed over his arm.* | *She closed her hand tightly around her bag.*

16 WOUND [I,T] (*also* **close up**) if a wound closes, or if someone closes it, the edges grow together again or are sewn together: *The surgeon closed the incision neatly.*

17 close ranks a) if people close ranks, they join together to protect each other, especially because their group, organization etc is being criticized **b)** if soldiers close ranks, they stand closer together

18 close the book on sth to stop working on something, especially a police operation, because it is not making any progress: *Detectives had closed the book on the Hornsey Murders case three years previously.* → CLOSING DATE, CLOSING TIME, → **close/shut the door on sth** at DOOR[1](9), → **close your eyes to sth** at EYE[1](16)

GRAMMAR

Close belongs to a group of verbs where the same noun can be the subject of the verb or its object.
• You can say: *She closed the door.* In this sentence, 'the door' is the object of **close**.
• You can say: *The door closed.* In this sentence, 'the door' is the subject of **close**.
GRAMMAR GUIDE ▸ VERBS

THESAURUS

close to stop being open, or to make something stop being open. You use **close** and **shut** especially about your eyes, your mouth, a door, a window, or a container: *Can I close the window?* | *Her eyes slowly closed.* | *He closed the door gently, so as not to wake the children.*
shut to close something. **Shut** sometimes has a feeling of doing something quickly and firmly, whereas **close** sounds more careful: *He shut the door with a loud bang.* | *Shut your eyes and go to sleep.*
slam to close a door or lid quickly and noisily, especially because you are angry: *She left the room, slamming the door behind her.*
draw the curtains to close curtains by pulling them across a window: *The curtains were still drawn at ten o'clock in the morning.*
put the lid on sth to close a container by putting a lid onto it: *Did you put the lid on the cookie jar?*
seal to close something so that no air or water can get in or out: *In this experiment, the chamber must be completely sealed.*

close down *phr v*
1 close sth ↔ down if a company, shop etc closes down or is closed down, it stops operating permanently: *Paramount closed down its London office in 1968.*
2 *BrE* to stop broadcasting radio or television programmes at the end of the day: *BBC 2 closes down at 12.45 tonight.*

close in *phr v*
1 to move closer to someone or something, especially in order to attack them: *The snake closed in for the kill.* | **[+on/around/upon etc]** *enemy soldiers closing in on them from all sides*
2 if the night, bad weather etc closes in, it becomes darker or gets worse: *The sun had set and dusk was closing in.*
3 if the days close in, they become shorter because it is autumn

close sth ↔ **off** *phr v* to separate a road, room etc from the area around it so that people cannot go there or use it: *The roads into the docks were closed off by iron gates.*

close on sb/sth *phr v*
1 to get nearer to someone or something that is moving in front or ahead of you: *The patrol car was rapidly closing on us.*
2 *AmE* to successfully arrange a LOAN, especially in order to buy a house

close sth ↔ **out** *phr v AmE*
1 to finish in a particular way: *The bond market closed out the week on a strong note.*
2 if a store closes out a type of goods, they sell all of them cheaply: *We're closing out this line of swimwear.*

close up *phr v*
1 close sth ↔ up if a shop or building closes up or is closed up, it stops being open to the public for a period of time: *The resorts are all closed up for the season.*
2 close up shop to stop doing something for a period of time or permanently: *When it rains, there is no alternative but to close up shop.*
3 if a group of people close up, they move closer together
4 close sth ↔ up if a wound closes up or if someone closes it up, the edges grow together again or are sewn together: *The scar is closing up nicely – it'll soon be time to take the stitches out.*
5 to become narrower or to shut: *The flowers close up at night.* | *Occasionally the channel widened then closed up tight again.*
6 to refuse to talk to someone about something: *The moment I said I was a police officer, everyone would close up like a clam.*

close with sb/sth *phr v*
1 to agree a business deal with someone: *It was such a good offer that I closed with him on the spot.*
2 *literary* to move towards someone in order to fight with them

close² /kləʊs $ kloʊs/ ●●● S1 W1 *adj* (*comparative* **closer**, *superlative* **closest**)
1 NEAR not far from someone or something SYN **near**: *If you need to buy bread or milk, the closest shop is about a mile away.* | **[+to]** *Susan sat on a chair close to the window.* | *I don't mind where we go on vacation as long as it's close to a beach.* | *His eyes were small and* ***close together****.* | *There are several accounts of dolphins living* ***in close proximity*** *to humans* (=close to humans). | *The victim had been shot* ***at close range*** (=from very close).
2 NEAR IN TIME near to something in time: **[+to]** *It was close to 1:15 a.m.* | **[+together]** *Our birthdays are quite close together.*
3 LIKELY TO HAPPEN seeming very likely to happen or very likely to do something soon: **close to doing sth** *The two countries are close to signing a peace agreement.* | *We're close to clinching the deal.* | **close to death/tears/despair etc** *The old dog could barely whimper and seemed close to*

death. | *The prosecution's main witness was close to tears as she described the assault.*
4 LIKE/LOVE if two people are close, they like or love each other very much: *My brother and I are very close.* | **[+to]** *I felt closer to Rob that evening than ever before.* | *Fiona and I have always been* ***close friends****.*
5 SIMILAR very similar to each other: **[+to]** *When I saw Henry with another woman I felt something close to jealousy.* | *Fitt was* ***the closest thing to*** *a socialist in the party.* | *Their newest model* ***bears a close resemblance to*** (=is very similar to) *that of their rival competitor.* THESAURUS SIMILAR
6 CAREFUL [usually before noun] looking at, thinking about, or watching something very carefully → **closely**: **take/have/get a close look (at sth)** | *She lifted up Jenny's silver medallion to take a closer look.* | **keep a close watch/eye on** (=watch someone or something very carefully) *Don't worry, I'll keep a close eye on the kids.* | *You could have improved your answers by* ***closer attention*** *to detail.*
7 NUMBER/AMOUNT if a number or amount is close to another number or amount, it is not much higher or lower than it: *We don't know the exact figures, but about 10,000 might be a close approximation* (=close to the actual figure). | **[+to]** *Inflation is close to 7 percent.*
8 COMPETITION/ELECTION ETC finishing or being played, fought etc with both sides almost equal: *It was a close game that could have gone either way.* | **a close second/third etc** (=very nearly first, second etc) | *The result is* ***too close to call*** (=so close that it is impossible to know who will win).
9 close relation/relative a member of your family such as your brother, sister, parent etc OPP **distant**: *The wedding was attended by close family only.*
10 VERY NEARLY BAD used when you have only just managed to avoid something bad, dangerous, or embarrassing happening: *'Phew,* ***that was close****,' Frank said as he swerved to avoid the cyclist.* | **a close call/thing/shave** (=a situation in which something dangerous, embarrassing etc almost happens) *United had a close shave when Liverpool almost scored.*
11 ALMOST very nearly getting, finding, or achieving something: **[+to]** *At this point, the investigators were closer to the truth than they realized.*
12 keep in close contact/touch if two people keep in close contact, they see, talk to, or write to each other often: *Text messaging enables people to keep in close contact at all times.*
13 WORK/TALK TOGETHER relating to a situation in which people work well with each other or talk to each other often: *He retained very* ***close links*** *with France throughout his life.* | *What we need now is* ***closer cooperation*** *between the club and supporters.*
14 WITH LITTLE SPACE with little or no space around something or between things: *The horses are always eager for exercise after the close confinement of the stables.* | *The shoe is a close fit* (=there is no space around the foot). | *I find it difficult to read such close print* (=with letters printed so close together).
15 close/you're close/that's close *spoken* used to tell someone that they have almost guessed or answered something correctly: *'I reckon he must be about 38.' 'Close – he was 40 last week.'*
16 close to the bone if something someone says is close to the bone, it makes you feel uncomfortable or offends you, especially because it is about something you do not want to admit is true
17 close, but no cigar *spoken* used when something someone does or says is almost correct or successful: *It was close, but no cigar for the Dodgers as they lost to the Reds 4–3.*
18 too close for comfort if something that happens is too close for comfort, it is near enough to make you feel nervous or afraid: *From somewhere too close for comfort came the sound of machine-gun fire.*
19 close to home a) if a remark or criticism is close to home, it makes you feel uncomfortable because it is likely to be true: *His comments struck unpleasantly close to home.* **b)** if something unpleasant happens close to home, you are directly affected by it: *It's one thing seeing riots on TV, but when they happen so close to home it's a different matter.*
20 at close quarters if something happens or is done at close quarters, it happens inside a small space or is done from a short distance away: *The troops had been fighting at close quarters.*
21 WEATHER *BrE* uncomfortably warm because there seems to be no air: *The weather that night was hot and close, with a hint of thunder in the distance.*
22 UNWILLING TO TALK ABOUT STH [not before noun] unwilling to tell people about something SYN **secretive**: **[+about]** *You're very close about your work, aren't you?*
23 UNWILLING TO SPEND MONEY [not before noun] not generous: **[+with]** *You won't get a penny out of Jack – he's very close with his money.*
24 a close shave when the hair on someone's face is cut very close to the skin
25 close work work that involves looking at or handling things in a very skilful, detailed, and careful way: *After years of close work, she could hardly see a thing if it was over a yard away.*
26 close vowel *technical* a close vowel is pronounced with only a small space between the tongue and the top of the mouth —**closeness** *n* [U]: *She had never had the physical or emotional closeness that she needed.* → **play your cards close to your chest** at CARD[1](14)

close[3] /kləʊs $ kloʊs/ ●●● S2 W2 *adv*
1 not far away SYN **near**: *Come a little closer, so you can see better.* | *Her father lives quite* ***close by****.* | *They were sitting* ***close together*** *on the couch.* | *A variety of good restaurants are* ***close at hand*** (=very near). | *James heard footsteps* ***close behind*** *him.* | *Ronnie sped off, with his brother's car following* ***close behind****.* | **stay/keep close** *We must all stay close.* | **hold/draw sb close** (=hold someone against your body) *He drew her close to him.* THESAURUS NEAR
2 close up/up close/close to from only a short distance away: *Now that I could see him close up, I saw that he was very attractive.*
3 close on sth/close to sth *spoken* used to talk about a number, amount etc that is almost exact, but not completely: *a voyage of close on 2,000 miles*
4 come close (to doing sth) a) to almost do something: *I tell you, I was so mad I came close to hitting her.* | *She came so close to the finals she must have been bitterly disappointed to go out now.* **b)** to be almost as good as someone or something else: *It's not as good as his last movie, but it comes pretty close.*
5 a close run thing *BrE* a situation in which the people competing with each other are almost equal, so neither of them is more likely to win than the other: *The upcoming election looks likely to be a close run thing.*
6 close on the heels of sth very soon after something else: **come/follow close on the heels of sth** *Yet another scandal followed close on the heels of the senator's resignation.*
7 near to the surface of something: *An electric razor doesn't really shave as close as a blade.*
8 run sb close *BrE* to be almost as successful, skilful etc as someone else: *Last season United ran them close both at home and away.* → **sail close to the wind** at SAIL[1](6)

close[4] /kləʊz $ kloʊz/ ●○○ *n* [singular] *formal* the end of an activity or of a period of time: ***At the close of*** *trade, the Dow Jones index was 1.92 points down.* | *The monsoon season was* ***drawing to a close*** (=ending). | *The event* ***came to a close*** (=finished) *with a disco.* | *Finally the meeting was* ***brought to a close*** (=ended).

close[5] /kləʊs $ kloʊs/ *n BrE* **1** [singular] used in street names for a road that has only one way in or out: *Take a left turn into Brown's Close.* **2** [C usually singular] the area and buildings surrounding a CATHEDRAL

close-cropped /ˌkləʊs ˈkrɒpt◂ $ ˌkloʊs ˈkrɑːpt◂/ *adj* close-cropped grass or hair is cut very short

closed /kləʊzd $ kloʊzd/ ●●● S3 *adj*
1 not open SYN **shut** OPP **open**: *Make sure all the windows are closed.* | *She kept her eyes* ***tightly closed****.*

C

2 [not before noun] if a shop, public building etc is closed, it is not open and people cannot enter or use it SYN **shut** OPP **open**: *The shops here are closed on Sundays.* | **closed to the public/visitors etc** *The castle is closed to visitors in winter.*
3 restricted to a particular group of people OPP **open**: *The golf club has* ***closed membership****.* | *a* ***closed meeting*** | *The police have a* ***closed circle*** *of suspects.*
4 not willing to accept new ideas or influences OPP **open**: *You're facing this situation with a* ***closed mind****.* | **closed society/world/way of life** *Venetian art in this period was a closed world.*
5 behind closed doors if something happens behind closed doors, it happens in private and the public are not allowed in: *It seems that the deal was made behind closed doors.* | *Football authorities ordered the club to play its next two games behind closed doors after the riots in February.*
6 a closed book (to sb) a subject or problem that someone does not know about or understand: *Mathematics has always been a closed book to me.*
7 a closed set (of sth) a restricted group, or a group that cannot change or grow: *The law is not a closed set of rules and principles.* → **in closed session** at SESSION(2)

ˌclosed ˈcaptioned *adj AmE* if a television programme is closed captioned, you can read the words that are said at the bottom of your screen, if you have the necessary equipment attached to your television

ˌclosed circuit ˈtelevision *n* [U] (*abbreviation* **CCTV**) a system of cameras placed in public buildings or in the street, used to help prevent crime

ˌclosed-ˈdoor *adj* [only before noun] closed-door meetings or talks take place secretly

ˌclosed eˈconomy *n* [C usually singular] a country that does not trade with any other countries

close-down /ˈkləʊzdaʊn $ ˈkloʊz-/ *n* **1** [C] a situation in which work in a company, factory etc stops, especially permanently SYN **shutdown** **2** [C,U] *BrE* the end of radio or television broadcasts each day

ˌclosed ˈseason *n* [C] *especially AmE* another form of CLOSE SEASON(1)

ˌclosed ˈshop *n* [C] a company, factory etc where all the workers must belong to a particular TRADE UNION

close-fit·ting /ˌkləʊs ˈfɪtɪŋ◂ $ ˌkloʊs-/ *adj* close-fitting clothes are tight and show the shape of your body

close-knit /ˌkləʊs ˈnɪt◂ $ ˌkloʊs-/ (*also* **ˌclosely-ˈknit**) *adj* a close-knit group of people is one in which everyone knows each other well and gives each other support when they need it: *a* ***close-knit community***

close·ly /ˈkləʊsli $ ˈkloʊs-/ ●●● S3 W2 *adv*
1 very carefully: *The detective* ***watched*** *him* ***closely****, waiting for a reply.* | **closely controlled/guarded/monitored etc** *Political activity is closely controlled.* | *Details of the program are* ***a closely-guarded secret****.*
2 to a very great degree: *I have been* ***closely involved*** *in the work of both committees.* | *The successful applicant will be* ***working closely*** *with our international staff.* | *a creature that* ***closely resembles*** *a red monkey*
3 closely related/connected/associated etc if two or more things are closely related etc, there is a strong connection between them: *closely related subjects such as physics, chemistry, and maths* | *Her development as a writer is closely connected with her religion.*
4 in a way that is close to other things in time or space: *lightning,* ***followed closely*** *by thunder* | *We were so closely packed in the elevator I could hardly move.*

close-mouthed /ˌkləʊs ˈmaʊðd◂, -ˈmaʊθt◂ $ ˌkloʊs-/ (*also* **closed mouthed** /ˌkləʊzd- $ ˌkloʊzd-/ *AmE*) *adj* not willing to say much because you are trying to keep a secret SYN **tight-lipped**

close-out /ˈkləʊz aʊt $ ˈkloʊz-/ *adj* **closeout sale/price** *AmE* a sale or price that is intended to get rid of goods cheaply —**closeout** *n* [C]

close-run /ˌkləʊs ˈrʌn◂ $ ˌkloʊs-/ *adj* [only before noun] *BrE* in a close-run competition, the winner succeeds by a very small distance or number of points, votes etc: *The Labour Party won the seat, but it was* ***a close-run thing****.*

close sea·son /ˈkləʊs ˌsiːzən $ ˈkloʊs-/ *n* [C] *BrE* **1** the period each year when particular animals, birds, or fish cannot legally be killed for sport OPP **open season** SYN **closed season** *AmE* **2** the period of a year when particular sports are not normally played

close-set /ˌkləʊs ˈset◂ $ ˌkloʊs-/ *adj* close-set eyes are near to each other

clos·et¹ /ˈklɒzɪt $ ˈklɑː-, ˈklɒː-/ ●●● S3 *n* [C]
1 *especially AmE* a cupboard built into the wall of a room from the floor to the ceiling → **wardrobe**: *a closet full of beautiful clothes*
2 come out of the closet a) to tell people that you are HOMOSEXUAL after hiding the fact SYN **come out b)** to admit something or to start to discuss something that was kept secret before
3 be in the closet *AmE informal* to not tell people that you are HOMOSEXUAL → **WATER CLOSET**, → **a skeleton in the closet** at **SKELETON(5)**

closet² *adj* **closet homosexual/alcoholic etc** someone who is a HOMOSEXUAL etc but who does not want to admit it: *a closet communist*

closet³ *v* [T] to shut someone in a room away from other people in order to discuss something private, to be alone etc: **be closeted with sb** *All morning he'd been closeted with various officials.* | **closet yourself** *Don't let her closet herself away in her room.*

close-up /ˈkləʊs ʌp $ ˈkloʊs-/ *n* [C,U] a photograph or part of a film in which the camera seems to have been very close to the picture it took: **[+of]** *a close-up of her face* | **in close-up** *Much of the movie is shot in close-up.*

clos·ing¹ /ˈkləʊzɪŋ $ ˈkloʊ-/ ●●○ *adj* [only before noun] happening or done at the end of an event or a period of time OPP **opening**: **closing remarks/words/ceremony etc** *The judge gave his closing speech to the jury.* | **closing stages/seconds/minutes etc** *in the closing years of his life*
THESAURUS ▸ LAST

closing² *n* [U] the shutting of a factory, school, hospital etc permanently OPP **opening**: **[+of]** *the closing of an old railway station*

ˈclosing ˌdate *n* [C] the last date on which it is possible to do something: **[+for]** *The closing date for applications is 6 August.*

ˈclosing time *n* [C,U] the time when a PUB must stop serving drinks and close

clo·sure /ˈkləʊʒə $ ˈkloʊʒər/ ●●○ *n*
1 [C,U] when a factory, school, hospital etc has to close permanently: *Several military bases are* ***threatened with closure****.* | **factory/hospital/school etc closure** *the problem of school closures* | **[+of]** *the closure of St Bartholomew's Hospital*
2 [C,U] when a road, bridge etc is closed for a short time so that people cannot use it: *On the M40, there are* ***lane closures*** *near Oxford.*
3 [U] when an event or a period of time is brought to an end, or the feeling that something has been completely dealt with: *Funerals help give people a sense of closure.*

clot¹ /klɒt $ klɑːt/ *v* (**clotted**, **clotting**) [I,T] if a liquid such as blood or milk clots, or if something clots it, it becomes thicker and more solid → **CLOTTED CREAM**

clot² *n* [C] **1** a thick almost solid mass formed when blood or milk dries: *He developed a* ***blood clot*** *on his brain and died.* **2** *BrE informal* a stupid person

cloth /klɒθ $ klɒːθ/ ●●○ S3 *n*
1 [U] material used for making things such as clothes: **cotton/woollen/silk etc cloth** *a dress of the finest silk cloth*
2 [C] a piece of cloth used for a particular purpose: *She mopped her face with a wet cloth.* | *Is there a clean cloth for the table?* → **DISHCLOTH, FACECLOTH, TABLECLOTH**
3 man of the cloth *formal* a Christian priest

ˌcloth ˈcap *n* [C] *BrE* a soft flat cap with a stiff pointed piece at the front

clothe /kləʊð $ kloʊð/ ●●○ *v* [T]
1 *formal* to put clothes on your body SYN **dress**: **be clothed in sth** *The King was clothed in a purple gown.* | **fully/partially/scantily etc clothed** *The children lay on the bed, fully clothed and fast asleep.*
2 to provide clothes for yourself or other people: *They could barely keep the family fed and clothed.* GRAMMAR **Clothe** is usually passive.

clothes /kləʊðz, kləʊz $ kloʊðz, kloʊz/ ●●● S2 W2 *n* [plural] the things that people wear to cover their body or keep warm: *What sort of clothes was he wearing?* | *I showered and put on clean clothes.* | *He was still in his work clothes.* | *a clothes shop* → **a change of clothes** at CHANGE²(6), → PLAIN-CLOTHES

GRAMMAR: Singular or plural verb?

- **Clothes** is a plural noun. If you want to talk about one shirt, one sock etc, you say a **piece of clothing** or an **item of clothing**.
- **Clothes** is always followed by a plural verb: *All my clothes **are** packed and I'm ready for my trip.*

COLLOCATIONS

VERBS

wear clothes *She always wears beautiful clothes.*
be dressed in … clothes *The man was dressed in ordinary clothes.*
put your clothes on *I told him to get up and put some clothes on.*
take off/remove your clothes *She took off her clothes and slipped into bed.*
change your clothes *I usually change my clothes as soon as I get home from work.*

ADJECTIVES/NOUN + clothes

warm clothes *If you're walking in the mountains, take plenty of warm clothes.*
casual clothes *Most people feel more comfortable in casual clothes.*
designer clothes (=made by a well-known designer) *She spends hundreds of pounds on designer clothes.*
sb's best clothes *They wore their best clothes for the photograph.*
formal clothes | **school/work clothes** | **ordinary/everyday clothes** | **civilian clothes** (=ordinary clothes rather than a military uniform) | **baby clothes** | **maternity clothes** (=for women who are having a baby) | **winter/summer clothes** | **clean clothes** | **fashionable/trendy clothes** | **second-hand clothes** (=not new)

THESAURUS

clothes *n* [plural] things you wear to cover your body or keep you warm. **Clothes** is always plural: *I like your clothes!* | *Don't throw your dirty clothes on the floor!* | *a clothes shop*
clothing *n* [U] used when talking in general about a type of clothes, or about making or selling clothes. Also used in the phrase **a piece/item/article of clothing** (=one of the things that someone wears): *You'll need to take some **warm clothing**.* | *It is important to wear **protective clothing** at all times.* | *a clothing manufacturer* | *a clothing retailer* | *Police found **a piece of clothing** in the bushes.*
garment *n* [C] *formal* one thing that you wear. Also used when talking about buying and selling clothes: *a long velvet garment* | *the garment industry* | *garment workers* | *garment factories*
dress *n* [U] a particular style of clothes. Don't use **dress** on its own: *Casual dress is not appropriate for an interview.* | *men in evening dress*
wear *n* [U] used about types of clothes sold in a shop, in the following phrases. Don't use **wear** on its own: *children's wear* | *sports wear* | *casual wear*
gear /gɪə $ gɪr/ *n* [U] *informal* clothes for a particular sport or activity: *She was wearing her running gear.*
wardrobe *n* [singular] all the clothes that you own, or all the clothes that you wear at a particular time of year: *Her wardrobe consisted mainly of smart clothes for work.* | *I will need a new summer wardrobe.*

ˈclothes ˌbasket *n* [C] a large basket for clothes that need to be washed, dried, or IRONed

ˈclothes brush *n* [C] *BrE* a brush used to remove dirt, dust etc from clothes

ˈclothes ˌhanger *n* [C] *BrE* a curved piece of metal, plastic, or wood with a hook on it that you use for hanging clothes SYN **hanger** *AmE*

ˈclothes horse *n* [C] **1** *BrE* a frame that you hang clothes on to dry indoors **2** *AmE informal* a woman who is very interested in clothes and who likes to have many different clothes – used to show disapproval

clothes·line /ˈkləʊðzlaɪn, ˈkləʊz- $ ˈkloʊðz-, ˈkloʊz-/ *n* [C] a long thin rope on which you hang clothes to dry outdoors SYN **washing line** *BrE*

ˈclothes peg *n* [C] *BrE* a wooden or plastic object that you use to fasten wet clothes to a clothesline SYN **clothespin** *AmE*

cloth·i·er /ˈkləʊðiə $ ˈkloʊðiər/ *n* [C] *old-fashioned* someone who makes or sells men's clothes or material for clothes

cloth·ing /ˈkləʊðɪŋ $ ˈkloʊ-/ ●●● S3 W3 *n* [U] the clothes that people wear: *basic necessities such as food and clothing* | *She took only a few items of clothing.* THESAURUS CLOTHES → **a change of clothing** at CHANGE²(6)

COLLOCATIONS

ADJECTIVES/NOUN + clothing

warm clothing *The flood victims need shelter and warm clothing.*
light clothing (=made from thin materials) *You'll only need light clothing during the day.*
outdoor clothing *The shop sells ski-wear and other outdoor clothing.*
protective clothing *Laboratory technicians have to wear special protective clothing.*
waterproof clothing | **outer clothing** (=that you wear over other clothes) | **designer clothing** (=made by a well-known designer) | **sports clothing**

PHRASES

a piece of clothing *There were pieces of clothing scattered around the room.*
an item/article of clothing *formal* (=a piece of clothing) *All items of clothing should be clearly labelled.*
a layer of clothing *In very cold weather it's good to wear several layers of clothing.*

clothing + NOUN

the clothing industry | **a clothing manufacturer**

ˌclotted ˈcream *n* [U] *BrE* very thick cream made by slowly heating milk and taking the cream from the top

clo·ture /ˈkləʊtʃə $ ˈkloʊtʃər/ *n* [C] *AmE technical* a way of ending an argument over a BILL in the US government and forcing a vote on it

cloud¹ /klaʊd/ ●●● S3 W3 *n*
1 IN THE SKY [C,U] a white or grey mass in the sky that forms from very small drops of water: **heavy/thick/dense etc clouds** *Dark clouds floated across the moon.* | *Heavy **clouds** had **gathered** over the summit of Mont Blanc.* | **low/high cloud** *Visibility was bad due to low cloud.* → STORM CLOUD, THUNDERCLOUD
2 IN THE AIR [C] a mass of dust, smoke etc in the air, or a large number of insects flying together: **cloud of dust/smoke/gas etc** *A cloud of steam rose into the air.* | *clouds of mosquitoes buzzing around us*
3 PROBLEM [C] something that makes you feel afraid, worried, unhappy etc: **[+of]** *the cloud of economic recession* | **cloud on the horizon** (=something that might spoil a happy situation) *The only cloud on the horizon was her mother's illness.* | *Fears of renewed terrorist attacks **cast a***

cloud over the event (=spoilt the happy situation). | *He returned to New York* **under a cloud of** *gloom and despair.*
4 under a cloud (of suspicion) *informal* if someone is under a cloud, people have a bad opinion of them because they think they have done something wrong: *He left the company under a cloud of suspicion.*
5 be on cloud nine *informal* to be very happy about something
6 every cloud has a silver lining used to say that there is something good even in a situation that seems very sad or difficult
7 be/live in cloud-cuckoo-land *BrE* to think that a situation is much better than it really is, in a way that is slightly stupid
8 the cloud *technical* the Internet used as something that provides software or space for storing information, rather than having it on your own computer: *They offer a variety of services* **in the cloud**. → **have your head in the clouds** at HEAD[1](24)

C

cloud² *v* **1** [T] to make someone less able to think clearly or make sensible decisions: **cloud sb's judgment/mind/vision etc** *Don't let your personal feelings cloud your judgement.* | *Fear had clouded his vision.* **2** [I,T] (*also* **cloud over**) if someone's face or eyes cloud, or if something clouds them, they start to look angry, sad, or worried: *Ann's eyes clouded with the pain.* | *Then suspicion clouded his face.* **3** [T] to make something less pleasant or more difficult than it should have been: *Her happiness was clouded by having to leave her son behind.* GRAMMAR **Cloud** is usually passive in this meaning. **4 cloud the issue/picture etc** to make a subject or problem more difficult to understand or deal with, especially by introducing unnecessary ideas: *Uninformed judgments only cloud the issue.* **5** [I,T] (*also* **cloud up**) if glass or a liquid clouds, or if something clouds it, it becomes less clear and more difficult to see through: *windows clouded up with steam* | *The water clouded and I could no longer see the river bed.* **6** [T] to cover something with clouds: *Thick mist clouded the mountain tops.*

cloud over *phr v* **1** (*also* **cloud up** *AmE*) if the sky clouds over, it becomes dark and full of black clouds **2** if someone's face or eyes cloud over, they start to look angry or sad: *His face clouded over in disappointment.*

cloud³ *adj* [only before noun] using or related to cloud computing: *cloud storage of data*

cloud·bank /ˈklaʊdbæŋk/ *n* [C] *BrE* a thick mass of low cloud

ˈcloud-based *adj* using software or space for storage that is on the Internet rather than on your own computer: *Cloud-based services can be used by large numbers of people.*

cloud·burst /ˈklaʊdbɜːst $ -bɜːrst/ *n* [C] a sudden short rainstorm

ˈcloud comˌputing *n* [U] a way of using computers in which you use software or space for storing that is on the Internet rather than on your own computer

ˈcloud ˌgaming *n* [U] the activity of playing computer games on the Internet, rather than on a GAMES CONSOLE

cloud·less /ˈklaʊdləs/ *adj* a cloudless sky is clear and has no clouds in it

cloud·y /ˈklaʊdi/ ●●● S2 W3 *adj*
1 a cloudy sky, day etc is dark because there are a lot of clouds OPP **clear**: *a cloudy night with some light rain* | *Tomorrow, it will be cloudy and cool.*
2 cloudy liquids are not clear: *a rather cloudy wine*
3 cloudy thoughts, memories etc are not very clear or exact

clout¹ /klaʊt/ *n* **1** [U] *informal* power or the authority to influence other people's decisions: **political/economic etc clout** *people with financial clout* | **the clout to do sth** *Few companies* **have the clout** *to handle such large deals.* | *An official protest could* **carry** *considerable* **clout**. **2** [C] *BrE informal* a hard blow given with the hand: *He* **gave** *him a* **clout** *round the ear.*

clout² *v* [T] *informal* to hit someone or something hard: *She clouted the boy across the face.*

clove¹ /kləʊv $ kloʊv/ *n* [C] **1** one of the separate parts that form a GARLIC plant: *a* **clove of garlic** **2** a black SPICE (=something used to give a special taste to food) with a strong sweet smell

clove² a past tense of CLEAVE

clo·ven /ˈkləʊvən $ ˈkloʊ-/ a past participle of CLEAVE

ˌcloven ˈhoof *n* [C] the type of foot that sheep, cows, and goats have, that is divided into two parts

clo·ver /ˈkləʊvə $ ˈkloʊvər/ *n* [U] **1** a small plant, usually with three leaves on each stem. If you find one with four leaves, it is thought to bring you luck: *a four-leaf clover* **2 in clover** *informal* living comfortably because you have plenty of money: *The money* **kept** *him* **in clover** *for years.*

clover·leaf /ˈkləʊvəliːf $ ˈkloʊvər-/ *n* [C] **1** the leaf of a clover plant **2** a network of curved roads which connect two main roads where they cross

clown¹ /klaʊn/ ●○○ *n* [C]
1 someone who wears funny clothes, a red nose, bright MAKE-UP on their face etc, and does silly things to make people laugh, especially at a CIRCUS
2 someone who often makes jokes or behaves in a funny way: *Frankie's a bit of a clown.* | **class clown** (=someone in a school class who behaves in a funny or silly way)
3 a stupid or annoying person: *I can't understand what she sees in that clown.*

clown² (*also* **clown around/about**) *v* [I] to behave in a silly or funny way: *Stop clowning around!*

clown·ish /ˈklaʊnɪʃ/ *adj* silly or stupid

cloy /klɔɪ/ *v* [I] if something sweet or pleasant cloys, it begins to annoy you because there is too much of it: *Her sweet submissive smile began to cloy after a while.*

cloy·ing /ˈklɔɪ-ɪŋ/ *adj* **1** a cloying attitude or quality annoys you because it is too sweet or nice: *cloying sentimentality* **2** cloying food or smells are sweet and make you feel sick: *the thick cloying smell of cheap perfume* THESAURUS ▶ SWEET —**cloyingly** *adv*

cloze test /ˈkləʊz test $ ˈkloʊz-/ *n* [C] a test in which words have been removed from a short piece of writing, and students have to write what they think are the correct words in the empty spaces

club¹ /klʌb/ ●●● S1 W1 *n* [C]
1 FOR AN ACTIVITY OR SPORT **a)** [also + plural verb *BrE*] an organization for people who share a particular interest or enjoy similar activities, or a group of people who meet together to do something they are interested in: **rugby/golf/squash etc club** *Our chess club really needs new members.* | **[+for]** *a club for unemployed young people* | *It costs £15 to* **join the club**. | *She* **belongs to** *a local health* **club**. **b)** the building or place where the members of a particular club meet or play sport: *We could have dinner at the golf club.* THESAURUS ▶ ORGANIZATION → COUNTRY CLUB, FAN CLUB, YOUTH CLUB
2 PROFESSIONAL SPORT [also + plural verb *BrE*] *especially BrE* a professional organization including the players, managers, and owners of a sports team: *Manchester United Football Club*

GRAMMAR: Singular or plural verb?
- In meanings 1 and 2, **club** is usually followed by a singular verb: *The club* **meets** *on Mondays after school.*
- In British English, you can also use a plural verb: *The club* **meet** *on Mondays after school.*

GRAMMAR GUIDE ▶ NOUNS

3 FOR DANCING/MUSIC a place where people go to dance, listen to music, and meet socially: *a jazz club* | *Shall we go to a club?* | *I'm not into the* **club scene** *at all.*
4 TRADITIONAL MEN'S CLUB *especially BrE* **a)** an organization, traditionally for men only, which provides a comfortable place for its members to relax, eat, or stay the night: *I always stay at my London club.* **b)** the building where this organization is based
5 book/record/wine etc club an organization which people join to buy books, records, wine etc cheaply
6 GOLF (*also* **golf club**) a long thin metal stick used in golf to hit the ball

7 WEAPON a thick heavy stick used to hit people
8 IN CARD GAMES **a) clubs** one of the four SUITS (=types of cards) in a set of playing cards, which has the design of three round black leaves in a group together: **ten/king etc of clubs** *the ace of clubs* **b)** a card from this suit: *You have to play a club.*
9 in the club *BrE old-fashioned* if a woman is in the club, she is going to have a baby – used humorously SYN **pregnant**
10 join the club (*also* **welcome to the club** *AmE*) *spoken* used after someone has described a bad situation that they are in, to tell them that you are in the same situation: *'He never listens to me.' 'Join the club.'*

club² *v* (**clubbed**, **clubbing**) [T] to hit someone hard with a heavy object: *baby seals being* ***clubbed to death***

club together *phr v* if people club together, they share the cost of something: *We clubbed together to buy her a present.*

club·ba·ble /ˈklʌbəbəl/ *adj BrE* friendly and good at talking to other people in a relaxed way

club·bing /ˈklʌbɪŋ/ *n* [U] *informal* the activity of going to NIGHTCLUBS: *She always* ***goes clubbing*** *when she's in New York.* —**clubber** *n* [C]

club·by /ˈklʌbi/ *adj informal* a clubby place is where everyone is very friendly to each other, but people who are outside their group are not very welcome: *the clubby atmosphere of the media*

ˈclub class *n* [U] a part of some planes where each seat has more space and more comfort than the usual seat, but is more expensive SYN **business class**

ˌclub ˈfoot *n* [C,U] a foot that has been badly twisted since birth and that prevents someone from walking properly —**club-footed** *adj*

club·house /ˈklʌbhaʊs/ *n* [C] a building used by a club, especially a sports club

club·land /ˈklʌbˌlænd/ *n* [U] **1** the part of a town which contains a lot of NIGHTCLUBS: *New York's clubland* **2** the most popular NIGHTCLUBS and the people who go to them: *She's become a clubland favourite.*

ˌclub ˈsandwich *n* [C] a sandwich consisting of three pieces of bread

ˌclub ˈsoda *n* [C,U] water filled with BUBBLES that is often mixed with other drinks SYN **soda water**

cluck¹ /klʌk/ *v* **1** [I] if a chicken clucks, it makes a short low sound **2** [I,T] to express sympathy or disapproval by saying something, or by making a short low noise with your tongue: *Edith clucked her tongue impatiently.* | **[+over/around etc]** *She stood clucking over the baby.* —**clucking** *adj*: *clucking noises*

cluck² *n* [C usually singular] **1** a low short noise made by chickens **2** a sound made with your tongue, used to show disapproval or sympathy: *a disapproving cluck* **3 dumb/stupid cluck** *AmE* a stupid person

clue¹ /kluː/ ●●● S2 *n* [C]
1 an object or piece of information that helps someone solve a crime or mystery: *Police have found a* ***vital clue***. | **[+to/about/as to]** *We now have an important clue as to the time of the murder.* | *Archaeological evidence will* ***provide clues*** *about what the building was used for.* | **[+in]** *This information is a valuable clue in our hunt for the bombers.* | *a desperate* ***search for clues***
2 information that helps you understand the reasons why something happens: **[+to/about/as to]** *Childhood experiences may provide a clue as to why some adults develop eating disorders.*
3 a piece of information that helps you solve a CROSSWORD PUZZLE, answer a question etc: *I'll* ***give*** *you* ***a clue***, *Kevin, it's a kind of bird.*
4 not have a clue (where/why/how etc) *informal* **a)** to not have any idea about the answer to a question, how to do something, what a situation is etc: *'Do you know how to switch this thing off?' 'I haven't a clue.'* | *Until I arrived here, I hadn't got a clue what I was going to say to her.* **b)** to be very stupid, or very bad at a particular activity: *Don't let Mike cook you dinner; he hasn't got a clue.* | *I haven't a clue how to talk to girls.* | **[+about]** *No point asking Jill – she hasn't got a clue about maths.*

clue² *v*

clue sb ↔ **in** *phr v informal* to give someone information about something: **[+on/about]** *Somebody must have clued him in on our sales strategy.*

ˌclued-ˈup *BrE*, **ˌclued-ˈin** *AmE adj informal* knowing a lot about something: **[+on/about]** *Ask Margaret. She's pretty clued-up about that sort of thing.*

clue·less /ˈkluːləs/ *adj informal* having no understanding or knowledge of something – used to show disapproval: **[+about]** *Many teachers are clueless about the needs of immigrant students.*

clump¹ /klʌmp/ *n* **1** [C] a group of trees, bushes, or other plants growing very close together: **[+of]** *a thick clump of grass* | **in a clump** *The roses were planted in clumps across the park.* **2** [C + of] a small mass of something such as earth or mud **3** [U] the sound of someone walking with heavy steps: *I heard the clump of Ralph's boots going up the stairs.*

clump² *v* **1** [I always + adv/prep] to walk with slow noisy steps: **[+up/down/along etc]** *The kids clumped up the stairs in their boots.* **2** [I,T] (*also* **clump together**) if separate objects clump together, or are clumped together, they form a group or solid mass: *Hair and soap had clumped together in the drain.*

clum·sy /ˈklʌmzi/ ●●○ *adj* (*comparative* **clumsier**, *superlative* **clumsiest**)
1 moving or doing things in a careless way, especially so that you drop things, knock into things etc: *A clumsy waiter spilled wine all over her new skirt.* | *a* ***clumsy attempt*** *to catch the ball* THESAURUS ▸ CARELESS
2 a clumsy object is not easy to use and is often large and heavy
3 a clumsy action or statement is said or done carelessly or badly, and likely to upset someone: *David made a* ***clumsy attempt*** *to comfort us.* —**clumsily** *adv* —**clumsiness** *n* [U]

clung /klʌŋ/ the past tense and past participle of CLING

clunk /klʌŋk/ *n* [C] a loud sound made when two solid objects hit each other: *the clunk of the car door being shut* —**clunk** *v* [I,T]

clunk·er /ˈklʌŋkə $ -ər/ *n* [C] *AmE informal* **1** an old car or other machine that does not work well **2** something that is completely unsuccessful because people think it is stupid or wrong

clunk·y /ˈklʌŋki/ *adj* **1** heavy and awkward to wear or use: *clunky old shoes* **2** clunky software is slow or does not work well

clus·ter¹ /ˈklʌstə $ -ər/ ●○○ *n* [C]
1 a group of things of the same kind that are very close together: **[+of]** *a cluster of low farm buildings* | *a cluster of red berries* | *a diamond cluster ring* THESAURUS ▸ GROUP
2 a group of people all in the same place: **[+of]** *A cluster of children stood around the ice cream van.*
3 *technical* a group of SECTORS on one or more computer DISKS

cluster² *v* [I,T always + adv/prep] if a group of people or things cluster somewhere, or are clustered somewhere, they form a small group in that place: **[+around/together etc]** *Reporters clustered around the palace gates for news.* | *Industries in Britain tend to be clustered together.*

ˈcluster ˌbomb *n* [C] a bomb that sends out smaller bombs when it explodes —**cluster-bomb** *v* [T]

clutch¹ /klʌtʃ/ ●●○ *v*
1 [T] to hold something tightly because you do not want to lose it SYN **grip**, **grasp**: *She was clutching a bottle of champagne.* THESAURUS ▸ HOLD
2 [I,T] (*also* **clutch at sb/sth**) **a)** to suddenly take hold of someone or something because you are frightened, in pain, or in danger SYN **grab**: *He clutched at a pillar for support.* | *Tom fell to the ground clutching his stomach.* **b) clutch at sb's heart** if something clutches at your heart, you suddenly feel fear or nervousness

C

3 be clutching at straws *especially BrE* to be trying everything possible to find a solution or hope in a difficult situation, even though it will probably be unsuccessful: *I knew that trying the alternative medicine was just clutching at straws.*

clutch² ●○○ *n*
1 [C] the PEDAL that you press with your foot when driving a vehicle in order to change GEAR, or the part of the vehicle that this controls → see picture at **CAR**
2 sb's clutches [plural] the power, influence, or control that someone has: *a small boy trying to escape from his mother's clutches* | **in sb's clutches** *She'll have him in her clutches soon enough.*
3 clutch of sth a small group of similar things: *a clutch of eggs* (=the number of eggs laid by a bird at one time) | *a clutch of young mothers*
4 [singular] a tight hold that someone has on something SYN **grip, grasp**: *I shook myself free of her clutch.*

ˈclutch bag *n* [C] a small bag that women carry in their hand, used especially on formal social occasions

clut·ter¹ /ˈklʌtə $ -ər/ (*also* **clutter up**) *v* [T] **1** to cover or fill a space or room with too many things, so that it looks very untidy: *Piles of books and papers cluttered his desk.* | **be cluttered (up) with sth** *The walls were cluttered with paintings and prints.* **2** to fill your mind with a lot of different things: *the everyday tasks that clutter our lives* —**cluttered** *adj*

clutter² *n* [singular, U] a large number of things that are scattered somewhere in an untidy way SYN **junk**: **[+of]** *the clutter of soaps, shampoos, and towels in the bathroom* | *Could you get rid of some of that clutter in your bedroom?*

cm (*plural* **cm** *or* **cms**) the written abbreviation of ***centimetre*** or ***centimetres***

C-note /ˈsiː nəʊt $ -noʊt/ *n* [C] *AmE informal* a 100 dollar note

co- /kəʊ $ koʊ/ *prefix* **1** together with: *to coexist* (=exist together or at the same time) | *coeducation* (=with boys and girls together) **2** doing something with someone else as an equal or with less responsibility: *my co-author* (=someone who wrote the book with me) | *the co-pilot* (=someone who helps a pilot)

c/o ●○○ the written abbreviation of ***care of***, used especially in addresses when you are sending a letter or package to someone who is living in someone else's house: *John Hammond, c/o Mrs Pearce, The Old Rectory, Reepham*

Co. /kəʊ $ koʊ/ **1** the abbreviation of ***company***: *James Smith & Co.* **2 and co** *BrE spoken* the other members of a particular group of people: *I can't say I'm looking forward to seeing Angela and co again.* **3** the written abbreviation of ***county***: *Co. Durham*

C.O. /ˌsiː ˈəʊ◂ $ -ˈoʊ◂/ *n* [C] (***Commanding Officer***) an officer who is in charge of a military unit

coach¹ /kəʊtʃ $ koʊtʃ/ ●●● S3 W2 *n*
1 SPORT [C] someone who trains a person or team in a sport: *a tennis coach* | *the Norwegian national coach* THESAURUS ▸ TEACHER
2 HELP FOR EXAM [C] *especially BrE* someone who gives private lessons to someone in a particular subject, especially so that they can pass an examination
3 BUS [C] *BrE* a bus with comfortable seats used for long journeys SYN **bus** *AmE*: **by coach** *We went to Paris by coach.* | **on a coach** *She's going to Grimsby on a coach.* | *a **coach trip** to Scotland* | *The restaurant was full of **coach parties*** (=groups of people travelling together on a coach).
4 TRAIN [C] *BrE* one of the parts of the train in which the passengers sit SYN **car** *AmE*
5 HORSES [C] a large carriage pulled by horses and used in the past for carrying passengers
6 IN PLANE/TRAIN [U] *AmE* the cheapest type of seats on a plane or train: *We **flew coach** out to Atlanta.*

coach² ●●○ *v* [T]
1 to teach a person or team the skills they need for a sport SYN **train** → **coaching**: *Nigel coaches a cricket team in his spare time.* THESAURUS ▸ TEACH
2 *especially BrE* to give someone private lessons in a particular subject, especially so that they can pass an important test → **coaching**: **coach sb in/for sth** *The child was coached for stardom by her mother.*
3 to help someone prepare what they should say or do in a particular situation – used to show disapproval → **coaching**: **coach sb in/on sth** *The girl must have been carefully coached in what to say in court.*

coach·buil·der /ˈkəʊtʃˌbɪldə $ ˈkoʊtʃˌbɪldər/ *n* [C] *BrE* someone who builds the main outer structure of a car

ˈcoach house *n* [C] *BrE* a building, similar to a GARAGE, used in the past in Britain for storing a carriage which was pulled by horses

coach·ing /ˈkəʊtʃɪŋ $ ˈkoʊ-/ *n* [U] **1** a process in which you teach a person or team the skills they need for a sport → **coach**: **tennis/football/rugby etc coaching** | *a **coaching session** with one of England's leading boxers* **2** the process of helping someone prepare for an important test or prepare what they should say or do in a particular situation → **coach**

ˈcoaching ˌinn *n* [C] *BrE* a small hotel in Britain used in the past by people travelling in carriages pulled by horses

coach·load /ˈkəʊtʃləʊd $ ˈkoʊtʃloʊd/ *n* [C] *BrE* a group of people travelling in a COACH, especially when it is full: **[+of]** *coachloads of Japanese tourists*

coach·man /ˈkəʊtʃmən $ ˈkoʊtʃ-/ *n* (*plural* **coachmen** /-mən/) [C] someone who drove a COACH pulled by horses in the past

ˈcoach ˌstation *n* [C] *BrE* the place where people begin or end their journeys on buses that travel a long distance SYN **bus station** *AmE*

coach·work /ˈkəʊtʃwɜːk $ ˈkoʊtʃwɜːrk/ *n* [U] *BrE* the main outer structure of a car

co·ag·u·late /kəʊˈægjəleɪt $ koʊ-/ *v* [I,T] if a liquid coagulates, or something coagulates it, it becomes thick and almost solid: *The blood had not coagulated.* —**coagulation** /kəʊˌægjəˈleɪʃən $ koʊ-/ *n* [U]

coal /kəʊl $ koʊl/ ●●● S2 W2 *n*
1 [U] a hard black mineral which is dug out of the ground and burnt to produce heat: *Put some coal on the fire.* | *the coal mining industry* | *a lump of coal* → see picture at **PIECE¹**
2 [C usually plural] a piece of coal, especially one that is burning: *Red hot coals glowed in the grate.*
3 [C usually plural] *AmE* a piece of wood or coal that is burning → **charcoal**: *Grill over hot coals for two minutes.*
4 carry/take coals to Newcastle *BrE* to take something to a place where there is already plenty of it available
5 haul/rake/drag sb over the coals to speak angrily to someone because they have done something wrong

ˌcoal-ˈblack *adj* very dark black: *coal-black eyes*

ˈcoal ˌbunker *n* [C] *BrE* a small building or large container where coal is stored

ˈcoal ˌcellar *n* [C] a small underground room where coal is stored

co·a·lesce /ˌkəʊəˈles $ ˌkoʊ-/ *v* [I] *formal* if objects or ideas coalesce, they combine to form one single group SYN **fuse**: **[+into/with]** *Gradually the different groups of people coalesced into one dominant racial group.* —**coalescence** *n* [U]

coal·face /ˈkəʊlfeɪs $ ˈkoʊl-/ *n BrE* **1** [C] the part of a coal mine where the coal is cut from the ground **2 at the coalface** where the real work is done, not just talked about: *Academics will be working at the coalface alongside the doctors.*

coal·field /ˈkəʊlfiːld $ ˈkoʊl-/ *n* [C] an area where there is coal under the ground

ˌcoal-ˈfired *adj BrE* using coal to make something work: *a coal-fired electricity generating station*

ˈcoal gas *n* [U] gas produced by burning coal, used especially for electricity and heating → **NATURAL GAS**

ˈcoal hole *n* [C] *BrE* a COAL CELLAR

coal·house /ˈkəʊlhaʊs $ ˈkoʊl-/ *n* [C] *BrE* a small building where coal is stored

co·a·li·tion /ˌkəʊəˈlɪʃən $ ˌkoʊə-/ ●○○ *n*
1 [C] a union of two or more political parties that allows them to form a government or fight an election together: **[+of]** *a coalition of democratic forces* | *the centre-right* ***coalition government*** | *an emergency meeting of the three* ***coalition parties***
2 [C] a group of people who join together to achieve a particular purpose, usually a political one: **[+of]** *a coalition of environmental groups*
3 [U] a process in which two or more political parties or groups join together: *He hoped to convert his party members to a belief in coalition.* | **in coalition with sb** *He was working in coalition with other Unionist leaders.*

coal·man /ˈkəʊlmən $ ˈkoʊl-/ *n* (*plural* **coalmen** /-mən/) [C] a man who delivers coal to people's houses

ˈcoal mine (*also* **ˈcoal pit** *BrE*) *n* [C] a place from which coal is dug out of the ground —**coal miner** *n* [C]

ˈcoal ˌscuttle *n* [C] *BrE* a specially shaped container with a handle for carrying coal

ˈcoal tar *n* [U] a thick black sticky liquid made by heating coal without air, from which many drugs and chemical products are made: *coal tar soap*

coarse /kɔːs $ kɔːrs/ ●○○ *adj*
1 having a rough surface that feels slightly hard SYN **rough** OPP **smooth**: *a jacket of coarse wool* THESAURUS ROUGH
2 consisting of threads or parts that are thick or large OPP **fine**: *The coarse sand was hot and rough under her feet.* | *tufts of coarse grass*
3 talking in a rude and offensive way, especially about sex SYN **crude**: *coarse jokes* —**coarsely** *adv*: *coarsely ground black pepper* —**coarseness** *n* [U]

ˌcoarse ˈfishing *n* [U] *BrE* the sport of catching fish, except for TROUT or SALMON, in rivers and lakes

coars·en /ˈkɔːsən $ ˈkɔːr-/ *v* [I,T] **1** to become thicker or rougher, or to make something thicker or rougher: *Hard work had coarsened his hands.* **2** to become or to make someone become less polite in the way they talk or behave: *He's been coarsened by his experience of war.*

coast¹ /kəʊst $ koʊst/ ●●● S3 W2 *n*
1 [C] the area where the land meets the sea → **coastal**: **[+of]** *the west coast of Africa* | *We drove along the Pacific coast to Seattle.* | **on the coast** *I used to live in a small village on the coast* (=on the land near the sea). | **off the coast** *a small island off the coast* (=in the sea near the land) *of Scotland* | *the first European to cross Africa* ***coast to coast*** | *a deserted* ***stretch of coast***
2 the coast is clear *informal* if the coast is clear, it is safe for you to do something without being seen or caught

coast² *v* [I] **1** [usually + adv/prep] if a car or bicycle coasts, it moves without any effort from you or any power from the engine: **[+down/around/along etc]** *Bev coasted downhill on her bicycle.* **2** to not try very hard to do something well - used to show disapproval: *Janey's teacher says she's just coasting at school.* **3** to be successful at something without much effort: *They scored three goals in the first half and from then on United were coasting.* | **[+to/through]** *The Ugandan relay team are* ***coasting to victory***. **4** to sail along the coast while staying close to land

coast·al /ˈkəʊstl $ ˈkoʊstl/ *adj* [only before noun] in the sea or on the land near the coast: *the* ***coastal waters*** *of Britain* | *the* ***coastal path***

coast·er /ˈkəʊstə $ ˈkoʊstər/ *n* [C] **1** a small thin object on which you put a glass, or cup, to protect a table from heat or liquids **2** a ship that sails from port to port along a coast, but does not go further out to sea → **ROLLER COASTER**

ˈcoaster brake *n* [C] a BRAKE on some types of bicycle that works by moving the PEDALS backwards

coast·guard /ˈkəʊstgɑːd $ ˈkoʊstgɑːrd/ *n*
1 the Coastguard the organization that helps swimmers and ships that are in danger and helps to prevent illegal activities around the coast: *the* ***Coastguard station*** *at Stornoway* | *Contact the Coastguard immediately if you see a boat in trouble.* **2** [C] *BrE* a member of this organization

> **GRAMMAR: Singular or plural verb?**
> • **The coastguard** is usually followed by a singular verb: *The coastguard* ***was*** *alerted and a lifeboat sent out.*
> • In British English, you can also use a plural verb: *The coastguard* ***were*** *alerted and a lifeboat sent out.*
> GRAMMAR GUIDE NOUNS

coast·line /ˈkəʊstlaɪn $ ˈkoʊst-/ ●○○ *n* [C] the land on the edge of the coast, especially the shape of this land as seen from the air: *California's* ***rugged coastline*** | *a beautiful* ***stretch of coastline*** | **along/around the coastline** *the sandy hills along the coastline of New England*

coat¹ /kəʊt $ koʊt/ ●●● S2 W3 *n* [C]
1 a piece of clothing with long sleeves that is worn over your clothes to protect them or to keep you warm: *Billy!* ***Put*** *your* ***coat on***, *it's cold outside!* | *The kids* ***took off*** *their* ***coats*** *and threw them on the floor.* | *I need a new* ***winter coat***. | *The lab assistants wear long white coats.* → **MORNING COAT**
2 *AmE* a jacket that you wear as part of a suit SYN **jacket**
3 the fur, wool, or hair that covers an animal's body: *a dog with a glossy coat*
4 a thin layer of a paint or other substance that you spread thinly over the surface of something: **[+of]** *He applied a light coat of varnish.* → **cut your coat according to your cloth** at CUT¹(43)

coat² *v* [T] to cover something with a thin layer of something else: *A layer of snow coated the trees.* | **coat sth with/in sth** *Next, coat the fish with breadcrumbs.*

ˈcoat check *n* [C] *AmE* a place in a public building where you can leave your coat while you are in the building SYN **cloakroom** *BrE*

-coated /kəʊtɪd $ koʊ-/ *suffix* **1 metal-coated/plastic-coated etc** covered with a thin layer of metal, plastic etc → **SUGAR-COATED 2 white-coated/fur-coated etc** wearing a white coat, fur coat etc

ˈcoat ˌhanger *n* [C] an object that you use to hang clothes on SYN **hanger**

coat·ing /ˈkəʊtɪŋ $ ˈkoʊ-/ *n* [C] a thin layer of something that covers a surface: **[+of]** *a fine coating of dust* | *The tent has a waterproof coating on both sides.*

ˌcoat of ˈarms *n* (*plural* **coats of arms**) [C] a set of pictures or patterns painted on a SHIELD and used as the special sign of a family, town, university etc

ˈcoat rack *n* [C] a board or pole with hooks on it that you hang coats on

coat·room /ˈkəʊtrʊm, -ruːm $ ˈkoʊt-/ *n* [C] *AmE* a COAT CHECK

coat·stand /ˈkəʊtstænd $ ˈkoʊt-/ *n* [C] a tall pole with hooks at the top that you hang coats on → see picture at **STAND²**

coat·tails /ˈkəʊt-teɪlz $ ˈkoʊt-/ *n* [plural] **1** if you achieve something on someone's coattails, you achieve it because of the other person's power or success: **on sb's coattails** *A number of Republican congressmen were elected on Bush's coattails.* **2** the cloth at the back of a TAILCOAT that is divided into two pieces

coax /kəʊks $ koʊks/ *v* [T] **1** to persuade someone to do something that they do not want to do by talking to them in a kind, gentle, and patient way: *'Please, Vic, come with us,' Nancy coaxed.* | **coax sb into/out of (doing) sth** *We had to coax Alan into going to school.* | **coax sb to do sth** *We watched the bear coax its cubs to enter the water.* | **coax sb down/out/back etc** *Firefighters managed to coax the man down from the roof.* THESAURUS PERSUADE **2** to make something such as a machine do something by dealing with it in a slow, patient, and careful way: **coax sth out of/from/into etc sth** *He coaxed a fire out of some dry grass and twigs.* | *The driver coaxed his bus through the snow.*

—**coaxing** *n* [U]: *She needs a bit of gentle coaxing.* —**coaxingly** *adv*

coax sth **out of/from** sb *phr v* to persuade someone to tell you something or give you something: *I managed to coax some money out of Dad.*

cob /kɒb $ kɑːb/ *n* [C] **1** a CORNCOB → **CORN ON THE COB** **2** *BrE* a round LOAF of bread **3** a type of horse that is strong and has short legs **4** a male SWAN

co·balt /ˈkəʊbɔːlt $ ˈkoʊbɒːlt/ *n* [U] **1** a shiny silver-white metal that is often combined with other metals or used to give a blue colour to substances such as glass. It is a chemical ELEMENT: symbol Co **2** (*also* **cobalt blue**) a bright blue-green colour —**cobalt** *adj*

cob·ble[1] /ˈkɒbəl $ ˈkɑː-/ *v* [T] *old-fashioned* **1** to repair or make shoes **2** to put cobblestones on a street

cobble sth ↔ **together** *phr v* to quickly produce or make something that is useful but not perfect: *The diplomats cobbled an agreement together.* | *She cobbled together a tent from a few pieces of string and a sheet.*

cobble[2] *n* [C] a cobblestone

cob·bled /ˈkɒbəld $ ˈkɑː-/ *adj* a cobbled street is covered with cobblestones

cob·bler /ˈkɒblə $ ˈkɑːblər/ *n* **1** [C,U] cooked fruit covered with a sweet bread-like mixture: *peach cobbler* **2** [C] *old-fashioned* someone who makes and repairs shoes **3 cobblers** [plural] *BrE spoken informal* nonsense: *I've never heard such **a load of** old **cobblers**!*

cob·ble·stone /ˈkɒbəlstəʊn $ ˈkɑːbəlstoʊn/ *n* [C] a small round stone set in the ground, especially in the past, to make a hard surface for a road

co·bra /ˈkəʊbrə $ ˈkoʊ-/ *n* [C] a poisonous African or Asian snake that can spread the skin of its neck to make itself look bigger

cob·web /ˈkɒbweb $ ˈkɑːb-/ *n* [C] **1** a net of sticky threads made by a SPIDER to catch insects, that is inside a building and has not been removed **2 blow/clear the cobwebs away** to do something, especially go outside, in order to help yourself to think more clearly and feel better → **web**: *A brisk walk will soon blow the cobwebs away.* —**cobwebbed** *adj*

ˈcobweb site *n* [C] *informal humorous* a website that has not had new information added for a long time

co·ca /ˈkəʊkə $ ˈkoʊ-/ *n* [U] a South American bush whose leaves are used to make the drug COCAINE

co·caine /kəʊˈkeɪn, kə- $ koʊ-/ *n* [U] a drug, usually in the form of a white powder, that is taken illegally for pleasure or used in some medical situations to prevent pain → **CRACK**[2](7)

coc·cyx /ˈkɒksɪks $ ˈkɑːk-/ *n* (*plural* **coccyxes** *or* **coccyges** /kɒkˈsaɪdʒiːz $ ˈkɑːksə-/) [C] *technical* the small bone at the bottom of your SPINE SYN **tailbone**

coch·i·neal /ˌkɒtʃəˈniːl◂ $ ˌkɑː-/ *n* [U] a substance used to give food a red colour

coch·le·a /ˈkɒkliə $ ˈkɑː-/ *n* (*plural* **cochleas** *or* **cochleae** /-li-aɪ/) [C] *technical* a part of the inner ear

cock[1] /kɒk $ kɑːk/ ●○○ *n* [C]

1 CHICKEN an adult male chicken SYN **rooster** *BrE* → **hen**: *A **cock crowed** in the distance.*

2 MALE BIRD *especially BrE* an adult male bird of any kind: *A cock pheasant rose from the hill in front of me.*

3 SEX ORGAN *informal not polite* a PENIS

4 cock and bull story *BrE* a story or excuse that is silly and unlikely but is told as if it were true: *a cock and bull story about the dog eating her homework*

5 OBJECT THAT CONTROLS FLOW something that controls the flow of liquid or gas out of a pipe or container SYN **tap** → **BALLCOCK, STOPCOCK**

6 MAN *BrE old-fashioned* used by some people when talking to a man they know well → **HALF COCKED**

cock[2] *v* [T] **1** to lift a part of your body, or hold a part of your body at an angle: *She **cocked** her **head** and considered the offer.* | *He cocked a quizzical eyebrow at her.* **2** to pull back the HAMMER of a gun so that it is ready to be fired **3** to move your hat so that it is at an angle **4 cock an ear/eye** to listen or look very carefully: *The little dog looked up and cocked its ears.* **5 cock a snook at sb/sth** *BrE informal* to show clearly that you do not respect someone or something: *He has always tried to cock a snook at authority.*

cock sth ↔ **up** *phr v BrE informal not polite* to spoil something by making a stupid mistake or doing it badly: *His secretary cocked up his travelling schedule and he's furious about it.* → **COCK-UP**

cock·ade /kɒˈkeɪd $ kɑː-/ *n* [C] a small piece of cloth used as a decoration on a hat to show rank, membership of a club etc

cock-a-doo·dle-doo /ˌkɒk ə ˌduːdl ˈduː $ ˌkɑːk-/ *n* [C] the loud sound made by an adult male chicken

cock-a-hoop /ˌkɒk ə ˈhuːp $ ˌkɑːk-/ *adj* [not before noun] *BrE* pleased and excited about something, especially something you have done: **[+at/about/over]** *Robert's cock-a-hoop about his new job.*

cock-a-leek·ie /ˌkɒk ə ˈliːki $ ˌkɑːk-/ *n* [U] a type of Scottish soup made with chicken, vegetables, and LEEKS

cock·a·ma·mie /ˌkɒkəˈmeɪmi◂ $ ˌkɑːk-/ *adj AmE informal* a cockamamie story or excuse is not believable or does not make sense: *That's a cockamamie idea.*

cock·a·too /ˌkɒkəˈtuː $ ˈkɑːkətuː/ *n* [C] an Australian PARROT with a lot of feathers on the top of its head

cock·chaf·er /ˈkɒkˌtʃeɪfə $ ˈkɑːkˌtʃeɪfər/ *n* [C] a European BEETLE (=a kind of insect) that damages trees and plants

cock·crow /ˈkɒk-krəʊ $ ˈkɑːk-kroʊ/ *n* [U] *literary* the time in the early morning when the sun rises SYN **dawn**

ˌcocked ˈhat *n* [C] *BrE* **1 knock/beat sb/sth into a cocked hat** to be a lot better than someone or something else: *My mother is such a good cook she knocks everybody else into a cocked hat.* **2** a hat with the edges turned up on three sides, worn in the past

cock·e·rel /ˈkɒkərəl $ ˈkɑː-/ *n* [C] a young male chicken

cock·er span·iel /ˌkɒkə ˈspænjəl $ ˌkɑːkər-/ *n* [C] a dog with long ears and long silky fur

ˌcock-ˈeyed *adj* **1** unlikely to succeed: *The whole idea is completely cock-eyed.* **2** not straight but set at an angle: *I think you put that shelf up cock-eyed.*

ˈcock fight *n* [C] an occasion when two male chickens are made to fight as a sport —**cockfighting** *n* [U]

cock·le /ˈkɒkəl $ ˈkɑː-/ *n* [C] **1** a common European SHELLFISH that is used for food **2 warm the cockles of sb's heart** *especially BrE* to make someone feel happy and full of good feelings towards other people: *Seeing her new baby just warms the cockles of your heart.*

cock·ney, **Cockney** /ˈkɒkni $ ˈkɑːk-/ *n* **1** [C] someone who comes from the east part of London, and who has a particular way of speaking which is typical of working-class people who live there **2** [U] a way of speaking English that is typical of working-class people in the east part of London —**cockney** *adj*: *She has a broad cockney accent.*

cock·pit /ˈkɒkˌpɪt $ ˈkɑːk-/ *n* [C] **1** the area in a plane, small boat, or racing car where the pilot or driver sits → see picture at **PLANE**[1] **2** a small enclosed area where COCK FIGHTS took place in the past

cock·roach /ˈkɒk-rəʊtʃ $ ˈkɑːk-roʊtʃ/ (*also* **roach** *AmE*) *n* [C] a large black or brown insect that lives in dirty houses, especially if they are warm and there is food to eat

cocks·comb /ˈkɒks-kəʊm $ ˈkɑːks-koʊm/ *n* [C] the red flesh that grows from the top of a male chicken's head

cock·suck·er /ˈkɒkˌsʌkə $ ˈkɑːkˌsʌkər/ *n* [C] *taboo informal* a very insulting word for a man. Do not use this word.

cock·sure /ˌkɒkˈʃʊə $ ˌkɑːkˈʃʊr/ *adj old-fashioned* too confident of your abilities or knowledge, in a way that is annoying to other people: *He seemed rather too cocksure for my liking.*

cock·tail /ˈkɒkteɪl $ ˈkɑːk-/ ●●○ *n* [C]

1 an alcoholic drink made from a mixture of different drinks

2 seafood/prawn/lobster cocktail small pieces of fish, PRAWNS, or LOBSTER served cold with a sauce and eaten as the first part of a meal

3 fruit cocktail a mixture of small pieces of fruit

4 a mixture of several things which is dangerous, unpleasant, confusing, or exciting: **[+of]** *a **lethal cocktail** of painkillers and whisky* | *The book contains a powerful cocktail of romance, family crises, and big business.* → MOLOTOV COCKTAIL

ˈcocktail ˌbar *n* [C] an area in a hotel or other place where you can buy cocktails as well as beer and wine

ˈcocktail ˌdress *n* [C] a formal dress for wearing to parties or other evening social events

ˈcocktail ˌlounge *n* [C] a public room in a hotel, restaurant etc, where you can buy alcoholic drinks

ˈcocktail ˌparty *n* [C] a party, usually in the early evening, at which alcoholic drinks are served and for which people usually dress formally

ˈcocktail ˌshaker *n* [C] a container in which cocktails are mixed

ˈcocktail stick *n* [C] a short pointed piece of wood on which small pieces of food are served

ˈcocktail ˌwaitress *n* [C] *AmE* a woman who serves drinks to people sitting at tables in a bar

ˈcock-up *n* [C] *BrE spoken informal* something that has been spoiled by someone's stupid mistake or by being done badly: *He's **made a** monumental **cock-up of** his first assignment.* | **[+over]** *There's been a cock-up over the tickets for the football on Saturday.*

cock·y /ˈkɒki $ ˈkɑːki/ *adj informal* too confident about yourself and your abilities, especially in a way that annoys other people: *He's a cocky little man and I don't like him.* —**cockily** *adv* —**cockiness** *n* [U]

co·coa /ˈkəʊkəʊ $ ˈkoʊkoʊ/ ●○○ *n* [U]
1 (*also* **cocoa powder**) a brown powder made from cocoa beans, used to make chocolate and to give a chocolate taste to foods
2 a sweet hot drink made with cocoa powder, sugar, and milk or water: *a cup of cocoa*

ˈcocoa bean *n* [C] the small seed of a tropical tree which is used to make cocoa

ˈcocoa ˌbutter *n* [U] a fat obtained from the seeds of a tropical tree, used in making some COSMETICS

co·co·nut /ˈkəʊkənʌt $ ˈkoʊ-/ *n* **1** [C] the large brown seed of a tropical tree, which has a hard shell containing white flesh that you can eat and a milky liquid that you can drink: *large tropical gardens of coconut palms* → see picture at FRUIT[1] **2** [U] the white flesh of a coconut, often used in cooking: *desiccated coconut* (=dried coconut)

ˌcoconut ˈmatting *n* [U] *BrE* a rough material used to cover floors that is made from the FIBRES covering a coconut shell

ˈcoconut ˌmilk *n* [U] the liquid inside a coconut

ˈcoconut ˌshy *n* (*plural* **coconut shies**) [C] *BrE* an outdoor game in which you try to knock coconuts off posts by throwing balls at them

co·coon[1] /kəˈkuːn/ *n* [C] **1** a silk cover that young MOTHS and other insects make to protect themselves while they are growing **2** something that wraps around you completely, especially to protect you: **[+of]** *The baby peered out of its cocoon of blankets.* **3** a place or situation in which you feel comfortable and safe, and are protected from anything unpleasant: **[+of]** *She was surrounded by the cocoon of a loving family.*

cocoon[2] *v* [T] to protect or surround someone or something completely, especially so that they feel safe: **be cocooned in sth** *She was cocooned in a reassuring network of friends and relatives.* | *Usually she lay for ages cocooned in her warm bed.* —**cocooned** *adj*: *a rich cocooned existence*

cocooning /kəˈkuːnɪŋ/ *n* [U] the practice of spending a lot of time at home, where you are relaxed and comfortable, rather than going out and doing things: *As our lives get busier, cocooning becomes more and more appealing.*

cod[1] /kɒd $ kɑːd/ *n* (*plural* **cod**) **1** [C] a large sea fish that lives in the North Atlantic **2** [U] the white flesh of a cod, eaten as food: *Two cod fillets, please.*

cod[2] *adj* [only before noun] *BrE* not real, but intended to look or sound real - often used humorously: *a cod English accent*

COD *BrE*, **C.O.D.** *AmE* /ˌsiː əʊ ˈdiː $ -oʊ-/ *n* [U] (***cash on delivery***) a payment system in which the customer pays the person who delivers the goods to them

co·da /ˈkəʊdə $ ˈkoʊ-/ *n* [C] **1** an additional separate part at the end of a piece of music **2** a separate piece of writing at the end of a work of literature or a speech

cod·dle /ˈkɒdl $ ˈkɑːdl/ *v* [T] to treat someone in a way that is too kind and gentle and that protects them from pain or difficulty SYN **mollycoddle**: *Don't coddle the child - he's fine!*

code[1] /kəʊd $ koʊd/ ●●● S2 W2 *n*
1 LAWS/BEHAVIOUR [C] a set of rules, laws, or principles that tell people how to behave: *The Torah is the basis for all the Jewish laws and their **moral code**.* | *Each state in the US has a different criminal and civil code.* | *The judge ruled that there had been no **breach** of the **code**.* | *There were plans to introduce a **dress code*** (=rules about what to wear) *for civil servants.* | **code of conduct/behaviour/ethics** *the **strict code of conduct** that is so much a part of karate* | **code of practice** (=a set of rules that people in a particular business or profession agree to obey) *The Textile Services Association has **drawn up a code of practice** endorsed by the Office of Fair Trading.* THESAURUS RULE → HIGHWAY CODE, PENAL CODE
2 SECRET MESSAGE [C,U] a system of words, letters, or symbols that you use instead of ordinary writing, so that the information can only be understood by someone else who knows the system: **in code** *All reports must be sent in code.* | **break/crack a code** (=manage to understand a code) *They didn't realise that we'd broken their secret code.*
3 SYMBOLS GIVING INFORMATION [C] a set of numbers, letters, or symbols that shows what something is or gives information about it: *Goods that you order must have a product code.* | *Every item found on the archaeological dig is given a **code number**.* → BAR CODE, GENETIC CODE, POSTCODE, ZIP CODE
4 TELEPHONES [C] (*also* **dialling code**, **STD code** *BrE*) the group of numbers that comes before a telephone number when you are calling from a different area SYN **area code** *AmE*: *What's the code for Aberdeen?*
5 COMPUTERS [C,U] a set of instructions that tell a computer what to do → MACHINE CODE, SOURCE CODE
6 SOUNDS/SIGNALS [C] a system of sounds or signals that represent words or letters when they are sent by machine → MORSE CODE

code[2] ●●○ AWL *v*
1 [T] to put a set of numbers, letters, or symbols on something to show what it is or give information about it: *Each path is coded to show the level of difficulty.* | *The researcher codes them X or Y.*
2 [T] to put a message into code so that it is secret OPP **decode**: *a coded message* GRAMMAR **Code** is usually passive in this meaning.
3 [I,T] to write computer programs: *I think kids should be taught how to code.*

cod·ed /ˈkəʊdɪd $ ˈkoʊ-/ AWL *adj* **1** coded information uses a system of words, letters, or symbols instead of ordinary writing so that it can only be understood by someone else who knows the system: *He sent a **coded message** to CIA headquarters.* **2** having a set of numbers, letters, or symbols to show what something is or give information about it: *The wires are **colour coded** for easy identification.* **3** coded language expresses your opinion in an indirect way because it will probably offend someone: *They voiced their criticism in coded statements.* **4** *technical* coded sounds or signals can only be understood by special machines: *coded signals broadcast by the BBC radio transmitters*

co·deine /ˈkəʊdiːn $ ˈkoʊ-/ *n* [U] a drug used to stop pain

ˈcode name *n* [C] a name that is used to keep someone's or something's real name a secret —**code-name** *v* [T]: *a crime busting operation code-named Jeeves*

ˌco-deˈpendent[1], **codependent** *adj* someone who is co-dependent thinks that they cannot be happy or successful without another person, especially someone with a problem, and so tries to keep that person happy without taking care of their own needs, in a way that seems unhealthy —**co-dependence**, **codependency** *n* [U]

co-dependent², **codependent** *n* [C] someone who is co-dependent

cod·er /ˈkəʊdə $ ˈkoʊdər/ *n* [C] *informal* a computer PROGRAMMER: *a coders' convention*

ˈcode-ˌsharing *n* [U] when two AIRLINE companies sell tickets together and use the same numbers for their flights

ˈcode word *n* [C] **1** a word or phrase that is given a different meaning to its usual meaning, so that it can be used to communicate something secretly **2** a word or expression that you use instead of a more direct one when you want to avoid shocking someone SYN **euphemism**: **[+for]** *'Lively discussion' is a code word for 'argument'.*

C

co·dex /ˈkəʊdeks $ ˈkoʊ-/ *n* (*plural* **codices** /-dəsiːz/) [C] *technical* an ancient book written by hand: *a sixth-century codex*

cod·ger /ˈkɒdʒə $ ˈkɑːdʒər/ *n* **old codger** *informal not polite* an offensive word for an old man

co·di·cil /ˈkəʊdəsɪl $ ˈkɑː-/ *n* [C] *law* a document making a change or addition to a WILL (=a legal document saying who you want your money and property to go to when you die)

co·di·fy /ˈkəʊdɪfaɪ $ ˈkɑː-/ *v* (**codified**, **codifying**, **codifies**) [T] to arrange laws, principles, facts etc in a system —**codification** /ˌkəʊdɪfɪˈkeɪʃən $ ˌkɑː-/ *n* [C,U]

cod·ing /ˈkəʊdɪŋ $ ˈkoʊ-/ AWL *n* [U] **1** a system of marking something with letters, symbols etc so that facts about it can be understood by someone who knows the system: *Most petrol stations use* ***colour coding*** *for different types of petrol.* | *A* ***coding system*** *is used to record what is found and when.* **2** the activity of writing computer programs

ˌcod-liver ˈoil *n* [U] a yellow oil from a fish, that contains a lot of substances that are important for good health

cod·piece /ˈkɒdpiːs $ ˈkɑːd-/ *n* [C] a piece of coloured cloth worn by men in the 15th and 16th centuries to cover the opening in the front of their trousers

cods·wal·lop /ˈkɒdzˌwɒləp $ ˈkɑːdzˌwɑː-/ *n* [U] *BrE informal* nonsense: *What* ***a load of codswallop***!

co·ed¹ /ˌkəʊˈed◂ $ ˈkoʊed/ *adj* **1** using a system in which students of both sexes are educated together: *a coed college* **2** *AmE* a coed place, team etc is used by or includes people of both sexes SYN **mixed** *BrE*

coed² *n* [C] *AmE old-fashioned* a woman student at a university

co·ed·u·ca·tion /ˌkəʊedjəˈkeɪʃən $ ˌkoʊedʒə-/ *n* [U] a system in which students of both sexes are educated together —**coeducational** *adj*

co·ef·fi·cient /ˌkəʊəˈfɪʃənt $ ˌkoʊ-/ *n* [C] *technical* the number by which an unknown quantity is multiplied: *In 8pq, the coefficient of pq is 8.*

coe·la·canth /ˈsiːləkænθ/ *n* [C] a large fish that was thought to have become EXTINCT millions of years ago, but still exists in the Indian Ocean

coe·li·ac dis·ease *BrE*, **celiac disease** *AmE* /ˈsiːliæk dɪˌziːz/ *n* [U] a medical condition in which someone cannot DIGEST food properly that contains GLUTEN (=a substance found in wheat)

co·e·qual /ˌkəʊˈiːkwəl◂ $ ˌkoʊ-/ *adj formal* if people are coequal, they have the same rank, ability, importance etc

co·erce /kəʊˈɜːs $ koʊˈɜːrs/ *v* [T] to force someone to do something they do not want to do by threatening them: **coerce sb into (doing) sth** *The rebels coerced the villagers into hiding them from the army.* THESAURUS ▸ FORCE

co·er·cion /kəʊˈɜːʃən $ koʊˈɜːrʒən/ *n* [U] the use of threats or orders to make someone do something they do not want to do: *The defendant explained that he had been acting under coercion.*

co·er·cive /kəʊˈɜːsɪv $ koʊˈɜːr-/ *adj formal* using threats or orders to make someone do something they do not want to do: *coercive measures to reduce absenteeism* —**coercively** *adv*

co·ex·ist /ˌkəʊɪgˈzɪst $ ˌkoʊ-/ *v* [I] if two different things coexist, they exist at the same time or in the same place: **[+with]** *wealth coexisting with poverty*

co·ex·ist·ence /ˌkəʊɪgˈzɪstəns $ ˌkoʊ-/ *n* [U] when two different things or groups of people exist together at the same time or in the same place: **[+of]** *the coexistence of two systems of measurement* | *over 50 years of* ***peaceful coexistence***

C of E /ˌsiː əv ˈiː/ *n* **the C of E** (***the Church of England***) the state church in England, which has the Queen or the King as its official leader —**C of E** *adj*

cof·fee /ˈkɒfi $ ˈkɒːfi, ˈkɑːfi/ ●●● S1 W2 *n*
1 [U] a hot dark brown drink that has a slightly bitter taste: *Do you want a cup of coffee?* | *Do you like your* ***coffee white*** (=with milk) *or* ***black***? (=without milk)
2 [C,U] a cup of coffee: *Who wants a coffee?* | **over coffee** *dinner guests chatting over coffee* (=while drinking coffee) → DECAFFEINATED
3 [U] whole coffee beans, crushed coffee beans, or a powder to which you add water to make coffee: *a jar of coffee* | ***instant coffee*** (=powdered coffee) | *I haven't got any* ***real coffee*** (=coffee beans) *at the moment.*
4 [U] a light brown colour → **wake up and smell the coffee** at WAKE UP

ˈcoffee bar *n* [C] a small restaurant that serves coffee and other non-alcoholic drinks, sandwiches, cakes etc → COFFEE SHOP

ˈcoffee bean *n* [C] the seed of a tropical bush that is used to make coffee

ˈcoffee break *n* [C] a short time when you stop working to have a cup of coffee SYN **tea break** *BrE*

ˈcoffee ˌgrinder *n* [C] a small machine that crushes coffee beans

ˈcoffee house *n* [C] a restaurant that serves coffee, cakes etc

ˈcoffee maˌchine *n* [C] a machine that gives you a cup of coffee, tea etc when you put money in it

cof·fee·mak·er /ˈkɒfiˌmeɪkə $ ˈkɒːfiˌmeɪkər, ˈkɑː-/ *n* [C] an electric machine that makes coffee

ˈcoffee mill *n* [C] a COFFEE GRINDER

ˈcoffee ˌmorning *n* [C] *BrE* a social occasion when a group of people meet in the morning to talk and drink coffee, and usually give money to help a church or another organization

ˈcoffee pot *n* [C] a container from which coffee is served → see picture at POT¹

ˈcoffee shop *n* [C] **1** *AmE* a restaurant that serves cheap meals **2** *BrE* a place in a large shop or a hotel that serves meals and non-alcoholic drinks

ˈcoffee ˌtable *n* [C] a low table on which you put cups, newspapers etc → see picture at TABLE¹

ˈcoffee table ˌbook *n* [C] a large expensive book that has a lot of pictures in it and is meant to be looked at rather than read

cof·fer /ˈkɒfə $ ˈkɒːfər, ˈkɑː-/ *n* [C] **1 sb's coffers** the money that an organization, government etc has available to spend: *The money from the exhibition should* ***swell*** *the hospital's* ***coffers*** *a little.* **2** a large strong box used to hold valuable or religious objects

cof·fin /ˈkɒfɪn $ ˈkɒː-, ˈkɑː-/ ●●○ *n* [C] a long box in which a dead person is buried or burnt SYN **casket** *AmE* → **a nail in sb's/sth's coffin** at NAIL¹(3)

cog /kɒg $ kɑːg/ *n* [C] **1** a wheel with small bits sticking out around the edge that fit together with the bits of another wheel as they turn in a machine **2** one of the small bits that stick out on a cog **3 a cog in the machine/wheel** someone who only has a small unimportant job in a large organization

co·gent /ˈkəʊdʒənt $ ˈkoʊ-/ *adj formal* if a statement is cogent, it seems reasonable and correct: **cogent**

argument/reason/case etc *a cogent argument for banning the drug* —**cogently** *adv* —**cogency** *n* [U]

cog·i·tate /ˈkɒdʒɪteɪt $ ˈkɑː-/ *v* [I + about/on] *formal* to think carefully and seriously about something —**cogitation** /ˌkɒdʒɪˈteɪʃən $ ˌkɑː-/ *n* [U]

co·gnac /ˈkɒnjæk $ ˈkoʊ-, ˈkɑː-/ *n* [C,U] a kind of BRANDY (=strong alcoholic drink) made in France, or a glass of this drink

cog·nate¹ /ˈkɒgneɪt $ ˈkɑːg-/ *adj technical* cognate words or languages have the same origin

cognate² *n* [C] *technical* a word in one language that has the same origin as a word in another language: *The German 'Hund' is a cognate of the English 'hound'.*

cog·ni·tion /kɒgˈnɪʃən $ kɑːg-/ *n* [U] *formal* the process of knowing, understanding, and learning something SYN **thought**: *the regions of the brain that are responsible for memory and cognition*

cog·ni·tive /ˈkɒgnətɪv $ ˈkɑːg-/ ●○○ *adj formal* related to the process of knowing, understanding, and learning something: *cognitive psychology* —**cognitively** *adv*

cog·ni·zance, **cognisance** /ˈkɒgnəzəns $ ˈkɑːg-/ *n* [U] *formal* **1** knowledge or understanding of something **2 take cognizance of sth** to understand something and consider it when you take action or make a decision

cog·ni·zant, **cognisant** /ˈkɒgnəzənt $ ˈkɑːg-/ *adj* [not before noun] *formal* if someone is cognizant of something, they know about it and understand it: **[+of]** *He was cognizant of the peculiarities of the case.*

co·gno·scen·ti /ˌkɒnjəʊˈʃenti $ ˌkɑːnjə-/ *n* **the cognoscenti** *formal* people who have special knowledge about a subject, especially art, literature, or food

cog·wheel /ˈkɒg-wiːl $ ˈkɑːg-/ *n* [C] a COG

co·hab·it /kəʊˈhæbɪt $ koʊ-/ *v* [I] to live with another person and have a sexual relationship with them without being married SYN **live together** —**cohabitation** /kəʊˌhæbɪˈteɪʃən $ koʊ-/ *n* [U]

co·here /kəʊˈhɪə $ koʊˈhɪr/ *v* [I] **1** if ideas, arguments, beliefs, statements etc cohere, they are connected in a clear and reasonable way → **coherent**: *All the details are there and are correct but they don't cohere.* **2** if two objects cohere, they stick together

co·her·ence /kəʊˈhɪərəns $ koʊˈhɪr-/ AWL (*also* **co·her·en·cy** /-rənsi/) *n* [U] **1** when something such as a piece of writing is easy to understand because its parts are connected in a clear and reasonable way: *An overall theme will help to give your essay coherence.* | *He had a coherence of outlook and thought.* **2** if a group has coherence, its members are connected or united because they share common aims, qualities, or beliefs: *A common religion ensures the coherence of the tribe.*

co·her·ent /kəʊˈhɪərənt $ koʊˈhɪr-/ ●○○ AWL *adj*
1 if a piece of writing, set of ideas etc is coherent, it is easy to understand because it is clear and reasonable: *The three years of the course are planned as a coherent whole.* | *a coherent account of the incident*
2 if someone is coherent, they are talking in a way that is clear and easy to understand: *He sounded coherent, but he was too ill to have any idea what he was saying.*
3 if a group is coherent, its members are connected or united because they share common aims, qualities, or beliefs: *They were never a coherent group.* —**coherently** *adv*: *She could not think coherently.*

co·he·sion /kəʊˈhiːʒən $ koʊ-/ ●○○ *n* [U]
1 if there is cohesion among a group of people, a set of ideas etc, all the parts or members of it are connected or related in a reasonable way to form a whole: *a sense of community and social cohesion*
2 *technical* a close relationship, based on grammar or meaning, between two parts of a sentence or a larger piece of writing

co·he·sive /kəʊˈhiːsɪv $ koʊ-/ *adj* **1** connected or related in a reasonable way to form a whole: *a cohesive community* **2** uniting people or things: *Historically, sport has been a cohesive force in international relations.* —**cohesively** *adv* —**cohesiveness** *n* [U]

co·hort /ˈkəʊhɔːt $ ˈkoʊhɔːrt/ *n* [C] **1** someone's cohorts are their friends who support them and stay loyal to them - used to show disapproval: *Mark and his cohorts eventually emerged from the studio.* **2** *technical* a group of people of the same age, social class etc, especially when they are being studied: *a cohort of 386 patients aged 65 plus*

coif·fure /kwɑːˈfjʊə $ -ˈfjʊr/ *n* [C] *formal* the way someone's hair is arranged SYN **hairstyle** —**coiffured, coiffed** /kwɑːft/ *adj*

coil¹ /kɔɪl/ ●○○ (*also* **coil up**) *v* [I,T] to wind or twist into a series of rings, or to make something do this: *The snake coiled around the branches of the tree.* | *Her long hair was coiled up in a plait at the top of her head.* | *He coiled the rope.* —**coiled** *adj* [only before noun]

coil² *n* [C] **1** a continuous series of circular rings into which something such as wire or rope has been wound or twisted: **[+of]** *a coil of rope* **2** one ring of wire, rope etc in a continuous series **3** a wire or a metal tube in a continuous circular shape that produces light or heat when electricity is passed through it: *the coil in a light bulb* **4** the part of a car engine that sends electricity to the SPARK PLUGS **5** a CONTRACEPTIVE that is a flat curved piece of metal or plastic that is fitted inside a woman's UTERUS SYN **IUD**

coin¹ /kɔɪn/ ●●● S3 *n*
1 [C] a piece of metal, usually flat and round, that is used as money → **bill**, **note** THESAURUS MONEY
2 toss/flip a coin to choose or decide something by throwing a coin into the air and guessing which side of it will show when it falls: *Toss a coin to see who goes first.*
3 the other/opposite side of the coin a different or opposite way of thinking about something: *Making the rules is only part of it. How the rules are carried out is the other side of the coin.*
4 two sides of the same coin two problems or situations that are so closely connected that they are really just two parts of the same thing: *Great opportunity and great danger are two sides of the same coin.*
5 [U] money in the form of metal coins

coin² *v* [T] **1** to invent a new word or expression, especially one that many people start to use: *The word 'aromatherapy' was coined in the 1920s.* **2 to coin a phrase** *spoken* said in a joking way when you use a very common expression, to show that you know it is used a lot: *He'd thought the flight would never - to coin a phrase - get off the ground.* **3 coin money/coin it (in)** *BrE informal* to earn a lot of money very quickly: *BT at its profitable peak was coining it at the rate of £90 a second.* **4** to make pieces of money from metal

coin·age /ˈkɔɪnɪdʒ/ *n* **1** [U] the system or type of money used in a country: *the gold coinage of the Roman empire* **2** [C] a word or phrase that has been recently invented: *The phrase 'glass ceiling' is a fairly recent coinage.* **3** [U] the invention of new words or phrases **4** [U] the making of coins

co·in·cide /ˌkəʊənˈsaɪd $ ˌkoʊ-/ ●●○ AWL *v* [I]
1 to happen at the same time as something else, especially by chance → **coincidence**: **[+with]** *His entry to the party coincided with his marriage.* | *When our vacations coincided, we often holidayed together.* | **planned/timed/arranged to coincide** *The show is timed to coincide with the launch of a new book.*
2 [not in progressive] if two people's ideas, opinions etc coincide, they are the same → **coincidence**: *The interests of the US and those of the islanders may not coincide.* | **[+with]** *The cloth had a natural look which coincided perfectly with the image Laura sought.*
3 to meet or be in the same place: *The journey coincides in part with the Pennine Way.*

co·in·ci·dence /kəʊˈɪnsɪdəns $ koʊ-/ ●●○ *n*
1 [C,U] when two things happen at the same time, in the same place, or to the same people in a way that seems surprising or unusual → **coincide**, **coincidental**: *'I'm going to Appleby tomorrow.' '**What a coincidence**! I'm going there too.'* | **by coincidence** *By coincidence, John and I both ended up at Yale.* | **sheer/pure coincidence** (=completely by

C

chance) *It was sheer coincidence that we were staying in the same hotel.* | **not a coincidence/more than coincidence** (=not chance, but deliberate) *I think it is more than coincidence that all the complaints have come from the same group of people.*
2 [singular] *formal* when two ideas, opinions etc are the same: **[+of]** *a coincidence of interest between the mining companies and certain politicians*

co·in·ci·dent /kəʊˈɪnsɪdənt $ koʊ-/ AWL *adj formal* existing or happening at the same place or time: **[+with]** *The rise of the novel was coincident with the decline of storytelling.*

co·in·ci·den·tal /kəʊˌɪnsəˈdentl $ koʊ-/ AWL *adj* happening completely by chance without being planned → **coincidence**: **purely/completely/entirely coincidental** *Any similarity between this film and real events is purely coincidental.* —**coincidentally** *adv* [sentence adverb]: *We have become profitable. Not coincidentally, we have only half as many employees as we did in 1988.*

C

co·in·sur·ance /ˌkəʊɪnˈʃʊərəns $ ˌkoʊɪnˈʃʊr-/ *n* [U] *AmE* **1** a type of insurance in which the payment is split between two people, especially between an employer and a worker: *health coinsurance* **2** insurance that will only pay for part of the value or cost of something

co·in·sure /ˌkəʊɪnˈʃʊə $ ˌkoʊɪnˈʃʊr/ *v* [T] *AmE* to buy or provide insurance in which the payment is split between two people, or insurance that will only pay for part of the value or cost of something

coir /kɔɪə $ kɔɪr/ *n* [U] the rough material that covers the shell of a COCONUT, used for making MATS, ropes etc

co·i·tus /ˈkəʊətəs, ˈkɔɪtəs $ ˈkoʊ-, ˈkɔɪ-/ *n* [U] *technical* the act of having sex SYN **sexual intercourse** —**coital** *adj*

coke /kəʊk $ koʊk/ *n* **1 Coke** [C,U] *trademark* the drink Coca-Cola, or a bottle, can, or glass of this drink **2** [U] *informal* COCAINE **3** [U] a solid black substance produced from coal and burned to provide heat

coke·head /ˈkəʊkhed $ ˈkoʊk-/ *n* [C] *informal* someone who uses the drug COCAINE

col[1] /kɒl $ kɑːl/ *n* [C] *technical* a low point between two high places in a mountain range

col[2] the written abbreviation of ***column***

Col. the written abbreviation of ***colonel***

co·la /ˈkəʊlə $ ˈkoʊ-/ ●●○ *n* [C,U] a brown sweet SOFT DRINK, or a bottle, can, or glass of this drink: *a can of cola*

col·an·der /ˈkʌləndə, ˈkɒ- $ ˈkʌləndər, ˈkɑː-/ *n* [C] a metal or plastic bowl with a lot of small holes in the bottom and sides, used to separate liquid from food

cold[1] /kəʊld $ koʊld/ ●●● S1 W1 *adj* (*comparative* **colder**, *superlative* **coldest**)
1 OBJECTS/SURFACES/LIQUIDS/ROOMS something that is cold has a low temperature OPP **hot** → **coldness**: *She splashed her face with cold water.* | *a blast of cold air* | *We slept on the cold ground.* | *The house **felt cold** and empty.* | **ice/stone/freezing cold** (=very cold) *The radiator is stone cold; isn't the heating working?* | **go/get cold** (=become cold) *My tea's gone cold.* | *Come and eat or your dinner will get cold!*
2 WEATHER when there is cold weather, the temperature of the air is very low OPP **hot** → **coldness**: *It was so cold this morning I had to scrape the ice off my windshield.* | *The day was **bitterly cold**.* | *The hut sheltered her from the cold wind.* | **cold winter/evening/January etc** *the coldest winter on record* | **cold out/outside** *It was raining and freezing cold outside.* | *The weather **gets colder** around the middle of October.* | **turn/grow cold** (=become cold or colder, especially suddenly) *The nights grew colder.*
3 be/feel/look/get cold if you are cold, your body is at a low temperature: *Could you turn up the heater, I'm cold.* | *I feel so cold!* | *My feet are **as cold as ice*** (=very cold).
4 FOOD cold food is cooked but not eaten hot: *a plate of cold meats* | *a cold buffet* | *Serve the potatoes cold.*
5 LACKING FEELING unfriendly or lacking normal human feelings such as sympathy, pity, humour etc OPP **warm** → **coldly**, **coldness**: *Martin was really cold towards me at the party.* | *His voice was as cold as ice.* | *She gave him a cold stare.* | *a cold calculated murder* THESAURUS ▸ UNFRIENDLY
6 get/have cold feet *informal* to suddenly feel that you are not brave enough to do something you planned to do: *The plan failed after sponsors got cold feet.*
7 give sb the cold shoulder *informal* to deliberately ignore someone or be unfriendly to them, especially because they have upset or offended you
8 LIGHT/COLOUR a cold colour or light reminds you of things that are cold OPP **warm** → **coldness**: *the cold light of a fluorescent tube*
9 in the cold light of day in the morning, when you can think clearly or see something clearly: *The house seemed less threatening in the cold light of day.*
10 cold (hard) cash *AmE* money in the form of paper money and coins rather than cheques or CREDIT CARDS
11 leave sb cold to not feel interested in or affected by something in any way: *Opera left him cold.*
12 take/need a cold shower used humorously to say that someone is sexually excited and the cold water will stop them feeling that way
13 sb's trail/scent is cold used to say that you cannot find someone because it has been too long since they passed or lived in a particular place: *I tracked the boy as far as the factory, but there his trail went cold.*
14 IN GAMES [not before noun] used in children's games, to say that someone is far away from the hidden object or answer they are trying to find: *You're getting colder!*
15 cold facts facts without anything added to make them more pleasant or interesting: *Statistics can be merely cold facts.*
16 cold steel *literary* a weapon such as a knife or sword
→ **in cold blood** at BLOOD[1](3), → **cold fish** at FISH[1](8), → **blow hot and cold** at BLOW[1](21), → **cold comfort** at COMFORT[1](7), → **pour cold water over/on** at POUR(6), → **a cold sweat** at SWEAT[2](3)

THESAURUS

PERSON

cold used especially when you feel uncomfortable: *I'm cold – can I borrow a sweater?*
cool a little cold, especially in a way that feels comfortable: *The air-conditioning keeps everyone cool.*
freezing (cold) *spoken* very cold and very uncomfortable: *You look absolutely freezing!*
shivery cold and unable to stop shivering, especially because you are ill: *I felt shivery and had a headache.*

WEATHER

cold used especially when you feel uncomfortable: *It gets very cold here in the winter.*
cool a little cold, often in a way that feels comfortable: *It's very hot in the day, but cooler at night.* | *a nice cool breeze*
chilly a little cold, but not very cold, in a way that feels rather uncomfortable: *a chilly autumn day* | *It's a bit chilly.*
freezing (cold) *spoken* very cold and very uncomfortable: *It's freezing outside.*
bitterly cold very cold and very uncomfortable: *It can be bitterly cold in the mountains.*
icy (cold) very cold, especially when the temperature is below zero: *The wind was icy cold.*
crisp cold, dry, and clear, in a way that seems pleasant: *I love these crisp autumn mornings.*
frosty in frosty weather, the ground is covered in a frozen white powder: *It was a bright frosty morning.*
arctic extremely cold and unpleasant, with snow and ice: *He would not survive for long in the arctic conditions.* | *arctic weather*

ROOM

cold used especially when you feel uncomfortable: *It's cold in here.*
cool a little cold, especially in a way that feels comfortable: *Let's go inside where it's cool.*
freezing (cold) *spoken* very cold: *I had to sleep in a freezing cold room.*

draughty *BrE*, **drafty** *AmE* /ˈdrɑːfti $ ˈdræfti/ with cold air blowing in from outside, in a way that feels uncomfortable: *Old houses can be very draughty.*

FOOD, LIQUID, OR SOMETHING YOU TOUCH

cold: *The water's too cold for swimming.* | *a cold stone floor*
cool a little cold, especially in a way that seems pleasant: *a nice cool drink* | *cool white sheets*
freezing (cold) very cold: *His friends pulled him from the freezing water.*
chilled food and drinks that are chilled have been deliberately made cold: *a bottle of chilled champagne*
frozen kept at a temperature which is below zero: *frozen peas*

cold² ●●● S2 W3 *n*
1 [C] a common illness that makes it difficult to breathe through your nose and often makes your throat hurt: *I've got a bad cold.* | *Keep your feet dry so you don't catch a cold.* → COMMON COLD
2 [U] (*also* **the cold**) a low temperature or cold weather: *I was shivering with cold.* | *Don't go out in the cold without your coat!* | **you'll catch your death of cold** *BrE* (=used to warn someone that they may become very ill if they do not keep themselves warm in cold weather)
3 come in from the cold to become accepted or recognized, especially by a powerful group of people
4 leave sb out in the cold *informal* to not include someone in an activity: *He chose to favour us one at a time and the others were left out in the cold.*

COLLOCATIONS
VERBS

have (got) a cold *She's staying at home today because she's got a cold.*
be getting a cold (=be starting to have a cold) *I think I might be getting a cold.*
catch a cold (=start to have one) *I caught a cold and had to miss the match.*
come down with a cold (*also* **go down with a cold** *BrE*) *informal* (=catch one) | **be suffering from a cold** *formal* (=have one)

ADJECTIVES/NOUN + cold

a bad cold *If you have a bad cold, just stay in bed.*
a nasty cold (*also* **a heavy cold** *BrE*) (=a bad one) *He sounded as if he had a heavy cold.*
a streaming cold *BrE* (=in which a lot of liquid comes from your nose) | **a slight cold** | **a chest cold** (=affecting your chest) | **a head cold** (=affecting your nose and head)

cold³ *adv* **1** *AmE* suddenly and completely: *Paul stopped cold. 'What was that noise?'* **2 out cold** *informal* unconscious: *He drank until he was out cold.* | *You were* ***knocked out cold*** (=hit on the head so that you became unconscious). **3** without preparation: *I can't just get up there and make a speech cold!*

ˌcold-ˈblooded *adj* **1** not showing or involving any emotions or pity for other people's suffering: *a* ***cold-blooded*** *killer* | *cold-blooded murder* THESAURUS CRUEL **2** a cold-blooded animal, such as a snake, has a body temperature that changes with the temperature of the air or ground around it → **warm-blooded** —**cold-bloodedly** *adv* —**cold-bloodedness** *n* [U]

ˌcold ˈcall *v* [T] to telephone or visit someone you have never met before and try to sell them something —**cold call** *n* [C] —**cold-calling** *n* [U]

ˌcold ˈcomfort *n* [U] if something that is slightly positive is cold comfort to someone who is feeling very bad about a situation, it does not make them feel any better: *The drop in the unemployment figures is cold comfort to those still looking for work.*

ˈcold cream *n* [U] a thick white oily cream used for cleaning your face and making it softer

ˈcold cuts *n* [plural] thinly cut pieces of cooked meat eaten cold

ˈcold frame *n* [C] *BrE* a box-like structure with sides and a top made of glass or clear plastic, used for keeping young plants warm as they start to grow

ˈcold front *n* [C] the front edge of a mass of cold air heading towards a place → WARM FRONT

ˌcold ˈfusion *n* [U] a type of NUCLEAR FUSION (=the joining together of the centre of two atoms, which releases energy) which some scientists believe can happen at extremely low temperatures, but which other scientists believe is impossible

cold-heart·ed /ˌkəʊld ˈhɑːtɪd◂ $ ˌkoʊld ˈhɑːr-/ *adj* behaving in a way that shows no pity or sympathy → **warm-hearted**: *I had no idea you could be so cold-hearted.* —**cold-heartedly** *adv* —**cold-heartedness** *n* [U]

Col·ditz /ˈkəʊldɪts/ a castle in Germany in which prisoners of war were kept during World War II. People sometimes compare a place to Colditz if it is almost impossible to escape from.

cold·ly /ˈkəʊldli $ ˈkoʊld-/ *adv* if you do something coldly, you do it without any emotion or warm feeling, making you seem unfriendly → **cold**, **coldness**: **say/speak/reply etc coldly** *'Well, what can I do for you?' he asked coldly.* | *Janine looked at her coldly.*

cold·ness /ˈkəʊldnəs $ ˈkoʊld-/ *n* [U] **1** when someone is unfriendly and does not show any warm feelings OPP **warmth**: *There was a certain coldness about him.* **2** the state of being cold → **warmth**: **[+of]** *the icy coldness of the water*

ˌcold ˈshoulder *n* **(give sb/get) the cold shoulder** to behave in an unfriendly way towards someone that you know —**cold shoulder** *v* [T]

ˈcold snap *n* [C] a sudden short period of very cold weather

ˈcold sore *n* [C] a painful spot on your lip or inside your mouth that is caused by a VIRUS

ˈcold spell *n* [C] a period of several days or weeks when the weather is much colder than usual OPP **heat wave**

ˌcold ˈstorage *n* [U] **1** if you keep something such as food in cold storage, you keep it in a cold place so that it will stay fresh and in good condition **2 put sth in cold storage** to not do or use something such as a plan or idea until later in the future: *He aims to please even if it means putting his principles in cold storage.*

ˈcold store *n* [C] *BrE* a room that is kept very cold and used to store food etc to keep it fresh

ˌcold ˈturkey *n* [U] an unpleasant physical condition suffered by people who stop taking a drug that they are ADDICTED to: *addicts who are made to* ***go cold turkey***

ˌcold ˈwar *n* [singular, U] **1** an unfriendly political relationship between two countries who do not actually fight each other **2 the Cold War** the unfriendly relationship between the US and the Soviet Union after the Second World War

cole·slaw (*also* **cole slaw** *AmE*) /ˈkəʊlslɔː $ ˈkoʊlslɒː/ *n* [U] a SALAD made with thinly cut raw CABBAGE

col·ic /ˈkɒlɪk $ ˈkɑː-/ *n* [U] if a baby has colic, it has severe pain in its stomach and BOWELS —**colicky** *adj*

co·li·tis /kəˈlaɪtɪs/ *n* [U] an illness in which part of your COLON swells, causing pain

col·lab·o·rate /kəˈlæbəreɪt/ ●○○ *v* [I]
1 to work together with a person or group in order to achieve something, especially in science or art → **collaborator**: **[+on]** *The two nations are collaborating on several satellite projects.* | **[+with]** *During the late seventies, he collaborated with the legendary Muddy Waters.* | **collaborate to do sth** *Researchers are collaborating to develop the vaccine.* | **collaborate in (doing) sth** *Elephants collaborate in looking after their young.*

REGISTER
In everyday English, people usually say they **work together on** something rather than **collaborate on** something: *They are* ***working together on*** *some new songs.*

C

2 to help a country that your country is fighting a war with, especially one that has taken control of your country → **collaborator**: **[+with]** *Vigilantes began combing the city for anyone known to have collaborated with the enemy.*

col·lab·o·ra·tion /kəˌlæbəˈreɪʃən/ ●○○ *n*
1 [C,U] when you work together with another person or group to achieve something, especially in science or art: *The company is building the centre in collaboration with the Institute of Offshore Engineering.* | **[+between]** *a collaboration between the two theatres* | **[+with]** *The project has involved collaboration with the geography department.*
2 [U] when someone gives help to a country that their country is fighting a war with, especially one that has taken control of their country

col·lab·o·ra·tive /kəˈlæbərətɪv $ -reɪ-/ ●○○ *adj* **collaborative effort/work/project etc** a job or piece of work that involves two or more people working together to achieve something

col·lab·o·ra·tor /kəˈlæbəreɪtə $ -ər/ *n* [C] **1** someone who helps their country's enemies, for example by giving them information, when the enemy has taken control of their country → **collaborate**, **collaboration**: *Their job was to identify enemy collaborators.* **2** someone who works with other people or groups in order to achieve something, especially in science or art → **collaborate**, **collaboration**: *collaborators on a biography of Dickens*

col·lage /ˈkɒlɑːʒ $ kəˈlɑːʒ/ *n* **1** [C] a picture made by sticking other pictures, photographs, cloth etc onto a surface **2** [U] the art of making pictures in this way

col·la·gen /ˈkɒlədʒən $ ˈkɑː-/ *n* [U] a PROTEIN found in people and animals. It is often used in beauty products and treatments to make people look younger and more attractive.

col·lapse¹ /kəˈlæps/ ●●○ S3 AWL *v*
1 STRUCTURE [I] if a building, wall etc collapses, it falls down suddenly, usually because it is weak or damaged: *Uncle Ted's chair collapsed under his weight.* | *The roof had collapsed long ago.* **THESAURUS** ► **FALL**
2 ILLNESS/INJURY [I] to suddenly fall down or become unconscious because you are ill or weak: *He collapsed with a heart attack while he was dancing.* | *Marion's legs collapsed under her.*
3 FAIL [I] if a system, idea, or organization collapses, it suddenly fails or becomes too weak to continue: *The luxury car market has collapsed.* | *I thought that without me the whole project would collapse.*
4 PRICES [I] if prices, levels etc collapse, they suddenly become much lower: *There were fears that property prices would collapse.*
5 SIT/LIE [I] to suddenly sit down, especially because you are very tired or want to relax: *I was so exhausted when I got home, I just collapsed on the sofa.*
6 FOLD STH SMALLER [I,T] if a piece of furniture or equipment collapses, or if you collapse it, you can fold it so that it becomes smaller → **collapsible**: *The legs on our card table collapse so we can store it in the closet.*
7 MEDICAL [I] if a lung or a BLOOD VESSEL collapses, it suddenly becomes flat, so that it no longer has any air or blood in it

collapse² ●●○ AWL *n*
1 BUSINESS/SYSTEM/IDEA ETC [singular, U] a sudden failure in the way something works, so that it cannot continue: **[+of]** *the collapse of the Soviet Union* | *the threat of* ***economic collapse*** | *His business was* ***in danger of collapse***.
2 BUILDING/STRUCTURE/FURNITURE ETC [U] when something suddenly falls down: *the collapse of an apartment building during the earthquake* | *The ancient abbey was in imminent danger of collapse.*
3 ILLNESS/INJURY [singular, U] when someone suddenly falls down or becomes unconscious because of an illness or injury: *The president said he was fine after his collapse yesterday.* | *She suffered a collapse under anaesthetic.*
4 MONEY/PRICES ETC [singular] a sudden decrease in the value of something: *the collapse of the stock market* | **[+in]** *a collapse in the value of pensions*

col·lap·si·ble /kəˈlæpsəbəl/ *adj* something collapsible can be folded so that it uses less space: *a collapsible chair*

col·lar¹ /ˈkɒlə $ ˈkɑːlər/ ●●● S3 *n* [C]
1 CLOTHING the part of a shirt, coat etc that fits around your neck, and is usually folded over: *He grabbed me by the collar.* | *He loosened his* ***collar and tie***.
2 CAT/DOG a narrow band of leather or plastic that is fastened around an animal's neck
3 INJURED NECK an object that someone wears around their neck to support it when it has been injured
4 BUSINESS a way of making sure that STOCKS you own do not lose money, even if their price goes down
5 MACHINE a circular ring that goes round a pipe to make it stronger, especially where two pipes join together
6 COLOURED FUR/FEATHERS a band of fur, feathers, or skin around an animal's neck that is a different colour from the rest of the animal → **BLUE-COLLAR**, **DOG COLLAR**, **WHITE-COLLAR**

collar² *v* [T] **1** to catch someone and hold them so that they cannot escape: *The police collared him less than 20 minutes after the robbery.* **2** to find someone so that you can talk to them, especially when they would prefer to avoid you: *He collared her in the staff room at lunchtime and started telling her about his holiday plans.* **3 high-collared/open-collared/fur-collared etc** used about clothes that have a particular type of collar: *a high-collared blouse*

col·lar·bone /ˈkɒləbəʊn $ ˈkɑːlərboʊn/ *n* [C] one of the pair of bones that go from the bottom part of your neck to your shoulders → see picture at **SKELETON**

col·lard greens /ˌkɒləd ˈgriːnz $ ˈkɑːlərd ˌgriːnz/ *n* [plural] *AmE* a vegetable with large green leaves, eaten cooked

col·lar·less /ˈkɒləlǝs $ ˈkɑːlər-/ *adj* a collarless jacket, shirt etc is one that does not have a collar

ˈcollar stud *n* [C] an object like a button, used to fasten old-fashioned collars to shirts

col·late /kəˈleɪt/ *v* [T] **1** *formal* to gather information together, examine it carefully, and compare it with other information to find any differences: **collate information/results/data/figures** *A computer system is used to collate information from across Britain.* **2** to arrange sheets of paper in the correct order SYN **sort** —**collation** /kəˈleɪʃən/ *n* [U]

col·lat·e·ral¹ /kəˈlætərəl/ *n* [U] property or other goods that you promise to give someone if you cannot pay back the money they lend you SYN **security**: *We* ***put up*** *our home* ***as collateral*** *in order to raise the money to invest in the scheme.* —**collateralize** *AmE v* [T]

collateral² *adj* [only before noun] **1 collateral damage** **a)** when non-military people are hurt or killed, or non-military property is damaged, as a result of actions in a war - used especially by the army, navy etc: *Hitting any non-military targets would risk 'collateral damage'.* **b)** unintended harm that happens to people as a result of something that is done **2** relating to something or happening as a result of it, but not as important: *There may be collateral benefits to the scheme.* **3** collateral relatives are members of your family who are not closely related to you

col·league /ˈkɒliːg $ ˈkɑː-/ ●●● S2 W2 AWL *n* [C] someone you work with - used especially by professional people SYN **co-worker**: *a colleague of mine from the bank* | *She discussed the idea with some of her colleagues.*

col·lect¹ /kəˈlekt/ ●●● S1 W2 *v*
1 BRING TOGETHER [T] to get things of the same type from different places and bring them together → **collection**, **collector**: *After 25 years of collecting recipes, she has compiled them into a cookbook.* | *The company collects information about consumer trends.* | *We've been out collecting signatures for our petition.*
2 KEEP OBJECTS [T] to get and keep objects of the same type, because you think they are attractive or interesting → **collection**, **collector**: *Arlene collects teddy bears.*
3 RENT/DEBTS/TAXES [T] to get money that you are owed → **collector**: **collect tax/rent/a debt** *The landlady came around once a month to collect the rent.*

4 MONEY TO HELP PEOPLE [I,T] to ask people to give you money or goods for an organization that helps people: **[+for]** *I'm collecting for Children in Need.*
5 INCREASE IN AMOUNT [I,T] if something collects in a place, or you collect it there, it gradually increases in amount: *Rain collected in pools on the road.* | *solar panels for collecting energy from the sun* | *I didn't know what to do with it, so it just sat there* ***collecting dust.***
6 WIN STH [T] to receive something because you have won a race, game etc: *Redgrave collected his fifth Olympic gold medal in Sydney.*
7 collect yourself/collect your thoughts to make an effort to remain calm and think clearly and carefully about something: *I got there early so I had a few minutes to collect my thoughts before the meeting began.*
8 TAKE SB/STH FROM A PLACE [T] *especially BrE* to come to a particular place in order to take someone or something away SYN **pick up** *AmE*: *Martin's gone to collect the children from school.* | *I've got to go and collect the book I ordered from the library.*
9 CROWD [I] *formal* to come together gradually to form a group of people SYN **gather**: *A crowd was beginning to collect around the scene of the accident.*

THESAURUS

collect to get things of the same type from different places and bring them together: *She collects stamps* (=as a hobby). | *They have collected 650 signatures for their petition.*
gather to collect information from different places, or to collect crops, flowers, wood etc, especially from the ground: *Computers make it easier to gather information.* | *The men gathered firewood.*
assemble *formal* to collect something such as information in an organized way: *When all the evidence is assembled, we will write our report.*
build up to gradually collect more things of the same type over time: *He has built up one of the country's finest collections of art.*
accumulate to gradually get more and more of something such as money, possessions, or knowledge, over time. **Accumulate** is more formal than **build up**: *He is driven by the desire to accumulate wealth.*
amass to collect a large amount of something such as money, information, or knowledge, over time: *Carnegie amassed a fortune in the steel industry.*
run up a bill/debt/loss *informal* to allow a debt to increase quickly, especially by spending too much: *He ran up huge gambling debts.*

collect sth ↔ **up** *phr v BrE* to pick up several things, and put them together SYN **gather up**: *Can you collect up all the dirty plates and cups?*

collect² *adv* **call/phone sb collect** *AmE* if you telephone someone collect, the person who receives the call pays for it → **collect call** SYN **reverse the charges** *BrE*

col·lect³ /ˈkɒlɪkt, -lekt $ ˈkɑː-/ *n* [C] a short prayer in some Christian services

col·lect·a·ble /kəˈlektəbəl/ (*also* **col·lect·i·ble** /-əbəl/) *adj* something that is collectable is likely to be bought and kept as part of a group of similar things, especially because it might increase in value —**collectable** *n* [C]: *shops selling antiques and collectables*

colˈlect ˌcall *n* [C] *AmE* a telephone call paid for by the person who receives it

col·lect·ed /kəˈlektɪd/ *adj* **1** in control of yourself and your thoughts, feelings etc: *She wanted to arrive feeling* ***cool, calm, and collected.*** **2 collected works/poems/essays/edition** all of someone's books, poems etc printed in one book or set of books: *the Collected Works of Shakespeare*

col·lec·tion /kəˈlekʃən/ ●●● S2 W1 *n*
1 SET/GROUP [C] **a)** a set of similar things that are kept or brought together because they are attractive or interesting → **collect**, **collector**: *a stamp collection* | *my record collection* | **[+of]** *a collection of Japanese vases* **b)** a group of objects together in the same place: *a collection of empty wine bottles on the back porch*
2 MONEY [C] the act of asking people to give you money for an organization that helps people, or during a church service, or the money collected in this way → **collect**: **[+for]** *Every Christmas we* ***have a collection*** *for a local charity.* | *We'll be* ***taking up a collection*** *at the end of tonight's service.*
3 RENT/DEBTS/TAXES [U] the act of obtaining money that is owed to you → **collect**, **collector**: *a debt collection agency*
4 BRINGING TOGETHER [U] the act of bringing together things of the same type from different places to form a group → **collect**: *a computerized* ***data collection*** *system*
5 TAKING STH AWAY [C,U] the act of taking something from a place → **collect**: *Garbage collections are made every Tuesday morning.* | *Please collect your purchases from the customer* ***collection point.***
6 FASHION [C] the clothes designed by a fashion company for a particular season: *Donna Karen's new spring collection*
7 BOOKS/MUSIC [C] several stories, poems, pieces of music etc that are in one book or on one record: **[+of]** *a new collection of Frost's poetry*
8 PEOPLE [C usually singular] a group of people, especially people you think are strange or unusual in some way: **[+of]** *There was an interesting collection of people at the wedding.*

colˈlection ˌbox *n* [C] a container with a small hole in the top, that people put money for CHARITY into

colˈlection ˌplate *n* [C] a large almost flat dish that you put money into during some religious services

col·lec·tive¹ /kəˈlektɪv/ ●○○ *adj* [only before noun] shared or made by every member of a group or society: *a* ***collective decision*** *made by all board members* | *our* ***collective responsibility*** *for the environment*

collective² *n* [C] **1** a group of people who work together to run something such as a business or farm, and who share the profits equally **2** the business or farm that is run by this type of group

colˌlective ˈbargaining *n* [U] the discussions held between employers and a union in order to reach agreement on wages, working conditions etc

colˌlective ˈfarm *n* [C] a large farm that is owned by the government and controlled by the farm workers

col·lec·tive·ly /kəˈlektɪvli/ ●○○ *adv* as a group: *All members of the cabinet are collectively responsible for decisions taken.* | *Rain, snow, and hail are* ***collectively known as*** *precipitation.*

colˌlective ˈnoun *n* [C] *technical* a noun, such as 'family' or 'flock', that is the name of people or things considered as a unit

col·lec·tiv·is·m /kəˈlektɪvɪzəm/ *n* [U] a political system in which all businesses, farms etc are owned by the government —**collectivist** *adj*

col·lec·tiv·ize (*also* **-ise** *BrE*) /kəˈlektɪvaɪz/ *v* [T] to join privately owned farms or businesses together, so that they can be owned by the government in a Communist political system —**collectivization** /kəˌlektɪvaɪˈzeɪʃən $ -və-/ *n* [U]

col·lec·tor /kəˈlektə $ -ər/ ●●○ *n* [C]
1 someone who collects things that are interesting or attractive → **collect**, **collection**: *a stamp collector* | *The painting was bought by a private collector.*
2 someone whose job is to collect taxes, tickets, debts etc → **collect**, **collection**: **tax/ticket/debt/refuse collector**

colˈlector's ˌitem *n* [C] an object that people want to have because it is interesting or rare, and might become valuable: *The dolls are real collector's items.*

col·leen /kɒˈliːn $ kɑː-/ *n* [C] *old-fashioned* a girl or young woman - used in Ireland

col·lege /ˈkɒlɪdʒ $ ˈkɑː-/ ●●● S1 W2 *n*
1 SPECIALIZED EDUCATION [C,U] a school for advanced education, especially in a particular profession or skill: *a teacher training college* | *Donna left school and went to art*

college. | **[+of]** *the London College of Fashion* | **at college** *We were great friends when we were at college.*

2 US UNIVERSITY [C,U] *AmE* a large school where you can study after HIGH SCHOOL and get a degree SYN **university** *BrE*: *Some people who want to* ***go to college*** *still can't get there.* | **in college** *Fran just finished her freshman year in college.* | *a decline in the number of* ***college students*** *studying history* | ***college graduates*** | *a* ***college education*** | ***college campuses*** → COMMUNITY COLLEGE, JUNIOR COLLEGE

3 PART OF A UNIVERSITY [C] one of the groups of teachers and students that form a separate part of some universities, especially in Britain: *Trinity College, Cambridge*

4 STUDENTS AND TEACHERS [C] the students and teachers of one of these organizations

GRAMMAR: Singular or plural verb?

- In this meaning, **college** is usually followed by a singular verb: *The college* ***is*** *putting on a production of 'Twelfth Night'.*
- In British English, you can also use a plural verb: *The college* ***are*** *putting on a production of 'Twelfth Night'.*

GRAMMAR GUIDE ▸ NOUNS

5 PROFESSIONAL ORGANIZATION [C] a group of people who have special rights, duties, or powers within a profession or organization: *the American College of Surgeons*

6 NAME OF A SCHOOL [C] *BrE* a word used in the name of some large schools, especially PUBLIC SCHOOLS → ELECTORAL COLLEGE

ˌCollege ˈBoards *n* [plural] *trademark* tests taken by students in order to attend some US universities

col·le·gi·an /kəˈliːdʒiən/ *n* [C] a member of a college —**collegian** *adj*

col·le·gi·ate /kəˈliːdʒiət/ *adj* **1** relating to college or a college: *collegiate sports* **2** a collegiate university is one that is organized into separate colleges

col·lide /kəˈlaɪd/ ●○○ *v* [I]

1 to hit something or someone that is moving in a different direction from you → **collision**: *A car and a van collided on the motorway.* | **[+with]** *I ran around the corner, and almost collided with Mrs Laurence.* | *Two trains* ***collided head-on*** (=when they were moving directly towards each other).

REGISTER

In everyday English, people usually say **run into** rather than **collide with**: *Her car* ***ran into*** *the back of a truck.*

2 to disagree strongly with a person or group, especially on a particular subject: **[+with]** *The president has again collided with Congress over his budget plans.*

3 if two very different ideas, ways of thinking etc collide, they come together and produce an interesting result: *Istanbul, where East and West collide.*

col·lid·er /kəˈlaɪdə $ -ər/ *n* [C] a machine used in scientific studies in which parts of atoms are made to move very fast and crash into each other → **particle accelerator**

col·lie /ˈkɒli $ ˈkɑːli/ *n* [C] a middle-sized dog with long hair, kept as a pet or trained to control sheep

col·li·er /ˈkɒliə $ ˈkɑːliər/ *n* [C] *BrE old-fashioned* someone who works in a coal mine

col·lie·ry /ˈkɒljəri $ ˈkɑːl-/ *n* (*plural* **collieries**) [C] *BrE* a coal mine and the buildings around it

col·li·sion /kəˈlɪʒən/ ●●○ *n* [C,U]

1 an accident in which two or more people or vehicles hit each other while moving in different directions → **collide**: **[+with]** *The school bus was involved in a collision with a truck.* | *Two people were killed in a* ***head-on collision*** (=between two vehicles that are moving directly towards each other) *on highway 218.* THESAURUS ▸ ACCIDENT

2 a strong disagreement between two people or groups: **[+between]** *a collision between the two countries over fishing rights*

3 be on a collision course a) to be likely to have serious trouble because your aims are very different from someone else's: *The two nations are on a collision course that could lead to war.* **b)** to be moving in a direction in which you will hit something: *an asteroid on a collision course with Earth*

col·lo·cate /ˈkɒləkeɪt $ ˈkɑː-/ *v* [I] *technical* when words collocate, they are often used together and sound natural together: **[+with]** *'Enigmatic' collocates with 'smile'.* —**collocate** /-kət/ *n* [C]

col·lo·ca·tion /ˌkɒləˈkeɪʃən $ ˌkɑː-/ *n* [C,U] *technical* the way in which some words are often used together, or a particular combination of words used in this way: *'Commit a crime' is a typical collocation in English.*

col·lo·qui·al /kəˈləʊkwiəl $ -ˈloʊ-/ ●○○ *adj* language or words that are colloquial are used mainly in informal conversations rather than in writing or formal speech —**colloquially** *adv*

col·lo·qui·al·is·m /kəˈləʊkwiəlɪzəm $ -ˈloʊ-/ *n* [C] an expression or word used in informal conversation

col·lo·qui·um /kəˈləʊkwiəm $ -ˈloʊ-/ *n* [C] *formal* a CONFERENCE

col·lo·quy /ˈkɒləkwi $ ˈkɑː-/ *n* [C] *formal* a conversation → SOLILOQUY

col·lude /kəˈluːd/ *v* [I] to work with someone secretly, especially in order to do something dishonest or illegal: **[+with]** *Several customs officials have been accused of colluding with drug traffickers.* | **[+in]** *She knew about the plan, and colluded in it.*

col·lu·sion /kəˈluːʒən/ *n* [U] a secret agreement that two or more people make in order to do something dishonest

col·ly·wob·bles /ˈkɒliˌwɒbəlz $ ˈkɑːliˌwɑː-/ *n* **the collywobbles** *BrE informal* an uncomfortable feeling that you get when you are very nervous

co·logne /kəˈləʊn $ -ˈloʊn/ (*also* **eau de cologne**) *n* [U] a liquid that smells slightly of flowers or plants, that you put on your neck or wrists → **perfume**

co·lon /ˈkəʊlən $ ˈkoʊ-/ ●○○ *n* [C]

1 *technical* the lower part of the BOWELS, in which food is changed into waste matter

2 the sign (:) that is used in writing and printing to introduce an explanation, example, QUOTATION(1) etc → **semicolon**

colo·nel /ˈkɜːnl $ ˈkɜːr-/ ●●○ *n* [C] a high rank in the army, Marines, or the US air force, or someone who has this rank

co·lo·ni·al¹ /kəˈləʊniəl $ -ˈloʊ-/ ●○○ *adj*

1 relating to a country that controls and rules other countries, usually ones that are far away → **colony**: *the struggle against* ***colonial rule*** | *Britain was the largest* ***colonial power***.

2 made in a style that was common in the US in the 18th century: *a large colonial house*

3 relating to the US when it was under British rule: *The town was first established in colonial times.*

colonial² *n* [C] someone who lives in a COLONY but who is a citizen of the country that rules the colony

co·lo·ni·al·is·m /kəˈləʊniəlɪzəm $ -ˈloʊ-/ *n* [U] when a powerful country rules a weaker one, and establishes its own trade and society there → **colony, imperialism**: *a legacy of European colonialism*

co·lo·ni·al·ist /kəˈləʊniəlɪst $ -ˈloʊ-/ *n* [C] a supporter of colonialism —**colonialist** *adj*: *colonialist attitudes*

co·lon·ic /kəˈlɒnɪk $ -ˈlɑː-/ *adj* relating to the COLON

coˌlonic irriˈgation *n* [C,U] a medical treatment which involves cleaning the COLON by passing water through it. Some doctors believe that the treatment can help prevent various diseases by washing out poisonous substances, but other doctors think that it does not have any good effects.

col·o·nist /ˈkɒlənɪst $ ˈkɑː-/ *n* [C] someone who settles in a new colony: *The colonists struggled through their first winter.*

col·o·nize (*also* **-ise** *BrE*) /ˈkɒlənaɪz $ ˈkɑː-/ *v* [T] **1** to establish political control over an area or over another country, and send your citizens there to settle → **colony 2** if animals or plants colonize an area, large numbers of them start to live there: *a dead tree that has been colonized by ants* —**colonizer** *n* [C] —**colonization** /ˌkɒlənaɪˈzeɪʃən $ ˌkɑːlənə-/ *n* [U]

col·on·nade /ˌkɒləˈneɪd $ ˌkɑː-/ *n* [C] a row of upright stone posts that usually support a roof or row of ARCHES —**colonnaded** *adj*

co·lo·nos·copy /ˌkəʊləˈnɒskəpi $ ˌkoʊləˈnɑːs-/ *n* [C,U] *medical* a medical examination of the COLON

col·o·ny /ˈkɒləni $ ˈkɑː-/ ●●○ *n* (*plural* **colonies**) [C]
1 a country or area that is under the political control of a more powerful country, usually one that is far away → **colonial**, **colonize**: *Algeria was formerly a French colony.* → CROWN COLONY
2 one of the 13 areas of land on the east coast of North America that later became the United States
3 a group of people who are similar in some way and who live together, or the place where they live: *an artists' colony | a leper colony*
4 a group of animals or plants of the same type that are living or growing together: *a seal colony | breeding colonies of rare birds*

col·or[1] /ˈkʌlə $ -ər/ *n,v* the American spelling of COLOUR

color[2] *v* **color me surprised/confused/embarrassed etc** *AmE spoken informal* used to say that you are very surprised, confused etc by something: *'Color me amazed!' says prize-winner Angela Harris.*

col·o·ra·tion (*also* **colouration** *BrE*) /ˌkʌləˈreɪʃən/ *n* [U] the colours or pattern of colours on a plant or animal

col·o·ra·tu·ra /ˌkɒlərəˈtʊərə, -ˈtjʊə- $ ˌkʌlərəˈtʊrə/ *n* **1** [U] a difficult piece of music that is meant to be sung fast **2** [C] a woman, especially a SOPRANO, who sings this type of music

ˈcolor ˌguard *n* [C] *AmE* a group of people who carry flags in an official ceremony

col·or·ize (*also* **colourise** *BrE*) /ˈkʌləraɪz/ *v* [T] to add colour to a film that was first made in black and white —**colorization** /ˌkʌləraɪˈzeɪʃən $ -rə-/ *n* [U]

ˈcolor line *n* [singular] *AmE* the set of laws or social customs that prevents people of different races from going to the same places or taking part in the same activities SYN **colour bar** *BrE*

co·los·sal /kəˈlɒsəl $ kəˈlɑː-/ *adj* used to emphasize that something is extremely large: *a colossal statue of the King | The whole holiday was a colossal waste of money.* THESAURUS▸ BIG —**colossally** *adv*

co·los·sus /kəˈlɒsəs $ kəˈlɑː-/ *n* [C] someone or something that is extremely big or extremely important: *an intellectual colossus like Leonardo*

col·our[1] *BrE*, **color** *AmE* /ˈkʌlə $ -ər/ ●●● S1 W1 *n*
1 RED/BLUE/GREEN ETC [C] red, blue, yellow, green, brown, purple etc: *What colour dress did you buy? | What colour are his eyes? | The pens come in a wide range of colours.* | **light/bright/pastel etc colour** *I love wearing bright colours.* | **reddish-brown/yellowy-green/deep blue etc colour** *The walls were a lovely reddish-brown color.* → see Thesaurus box on *p.338*
2 COLOUR IN GENERAL [U] (*also* **colours**) the appearance of something as a result of the way it REFLECTS (=throws back) light, especially when its appearance is very bright or is made up of a lot of different colours: *Bright bold accessories are the quickest way to* **add colour** *to a room.* | **in colour** *The wine was almost pink in colour* (=was almost pink). | **blaze/riot/mass of colour** (=lots of different bright colours) *In summer the gardens are a blaze of colour.* | *a* **splash of colour** (=a small area of a bright colour) | *The sky began to slowly* **change colour**. | *the fall colors* (=the colours of the trees in autumn)
3 SB'S RACE [C,U] how dark or light someone's skin is, which shows which race they belong to: *Everyone has a right to a job, regardless of their race, sex, or colour. | people of all colors | the continuing battle against* **colour prejudice** → COLOURED[2]
4 people/women/students etc of color *especially AmE* people, women etc who are not white: *I'm the only person of color in my class.*
5 SUBSTANCE [C,U] a substance such as paint or DYE that makes something red, blue, yellow etc: *Wash the garment separately, as the* **colour** *may* **run** (=come out when washed). | *jams that contain no* **artificial colours** *or preservatives* | **lip/nail/eye colour** *our new range of eyeshadows and lip colours*
6 in (full) colour a television programme, film, or photograph that is in colour contains colours such as red, green, and blue rather than just black and white OPP **in black and white**: *All the recipes in the book are* **illustrated in full colour**.
7 SB'S FACE [U] if you have some colour in your face, your face is pink or red, usually because you are healthy or embarrassed: *You look a lot better today. At least you've* **got** *a bit of* **colour** *now.* | *One of the girls giggled nervously as* **colour flooded** *her* **cheeks** (=her cheeks suddenly went very pink or red). | *He stared at her, the* **colour draining from** *his face.*
8 STH INTERESTING [U] interesting and exciting details or qualities that someone or something has: *The old market is lively,* **full of colour** *and activity.* | *a travel writer in search of* **local colour** | **add/give colour to sth** (=make something more interesting) *Intelligent use of metaphors can add colour to your writing.*
9 lend/give colour to sth to make something, especially something unusual, appear likely or true: *We have new evidence that lends colour to the accusation of fraud.*
10 off colour a) [not before noun] *BrE* someone who is off colour is feeling slightly ill **b)** [usually before noun] *especially AmE* off-colour jokes, stories etc are rude and often about sex
11 colours [plural] **a)** the colours that are used to represent a team, school, club, country etc: **club/team/school colours** *a cap in the team colours | Australia's* **national colours** *are gold and green.* **b)** *BrE* a flag, shirt etc that shows that someone or something belongs to or supports a particular team, school, club, or country
12 see the colour of sb's money *spoken* to have definite proof that someone has enough money to pay for something: *'A whiskey, please.' 'Let's see the color of your money first.'* → **with flying colours** at FLYING[1](2), → **nail your colours to the mast** at NAIL[2](6), → **your true colours** at TRUE[1](13)

colour[2] *BrE*, **color** *AmE* ●●○ *v*
1 [T] to change the colour of something, especially by using DYE: *If I didn't* **colour** *my* **hair** *I'd be totally grey. | Colour the icing with a little green food colouring.* | **colour sth red/blue etc** *Sunset came and coloured the sky a brilliant red.*
2 [I,T] (*also* **colour in**) to use coloured pencils to put colours inside the lines of a picture: *On the back page is a picture for your child to colour in. | She has no idea how to colour a picture – she just scribbles all over it.*
3 [I] *literary* when someone colours, their face becomes redder because they are embarrassed SYN **blush**: *Her eyes suddenly met his and she coloured slightly.*
4 colour sb's judgment/opinions/attitudes etc to influence the way someone thinks about something, especially so that they become less fair or reasonable: *In my position, I can't afford to let my judgment be coloured by personal feelings.*

colour[3] *BrE*, **color** *AmE adj* **colour television/photograph/printer etc** a colour television, photograph etc produces or shows pictures in colour rather than in black, white, and grey → **black and white**: *a large color TV | Please ask for our free colour brochure.*

col·our·ant *BrE*, **colorant** *AmE* /ˈkʌlərənt/ *n* [C] a substance used to change the colour of something, especially someone's hair SYN **dye**

col·our·ation /ˌkʌləˈreɪʃən/ *n* a British spelling of COLORATION

ˈcolour bar *n* [C usually singular] *BrE* a set of laws or social customs that prevents people of different races from going to the same places or taking part in the same activities SYN **color line** *AmE*

ˈcolour-blind *BrE*, **color-blind** *AmE adj* **1** unable to see the difference between all or some colours **2** treating people from different races equally and fairly: *The law should be colour-blind.* —**colour-blindness** *n* [U]

ˈcolour ˌblocking *BrE*, **color blocking** *AmE n* [U] the practice of wearing clothes of different plain strong colours together

ˈcolour ˌcoded *BrE*, **color coded** *AmE adj* things that are colour coded are marked with different colours so that it is easy to see what they are to be used for

ˈcolour-coˌordinated *BrE*, **color-coordinated** *AmE adj* clothes, decorations etc that are colour-coordinated have colours which look good together —**ˌcolour-coordiˈnation** *n* [U]

col·oured¹ *BrE*, **colored** *AmE* /ˈkʌləd $ -ərd/ ●●○ *adj*
1 brightly/highly/richly etc coloured having a bright colour such as red, blue, or yellow etc, or a deep shade of a particular colour, but not black, white, or plain
2 having a colour other than black or white: *coloured glass | a cream-coloured sweater*
3 *taboo old-fashioned* a very offensive word used to describe someone who is a member of a race of people with dark or black skin. Do not use this word.
4 used in South Africa to describe someone whose parents or grandparents were not of the same race as each other

coloured² *BrE*, **colored** *AmE n* [C] **1** *taboo old-fashioned* a very offensive word for someone who is a member of a race of people with dark or black skin. Do not use this word. **2** a person whose parents or grandparents were not of the same race as each other - used in South Africa

col·our·fast *BrE*, **colorfast** *AmE* /ˈkʌləfɑːst $ ˈkʌlərfæst/ *adj* cloth that is colourfast will not lose its colour when it is washed

col·our·ful *BrE*, **colorful** *AmE* /ˈkʌləfəl $ -lər-/ ●●○ *adj*
1 having bright colours or a lot of different colours: *a colourful display of flowers | colorful costumes* **THESAURUS** COLOUR
2 interesting, exciting, and full of variety: **colourful history/past/career/life** *Charlie Chaplin had a long and colorful career.* | **colourful character/figure** (=someone who is interesting and unusual)
3 colourful language, speech etc uses a lot of swearing —**colourfully** *adv*

col·our·ing *BrE*, **coloring** *AmE* /ˈkʌlərɪŋ/ ●○○ *n*
1 [C,U] a substance used to give a particular colour to food: *green* ***food colouring***
2 [U] the activity of putting colours into drawings, or of drawing using CRAYONS, coloured pencils etc: *a children's colouring competition*
3 [U] the colour of someone's skin, hair, and eyes: *Mandy has her mother's fair coloring.*
4 [U] the colours of an animal, bird, or plant

ˈcolouring ˌbook *BrE*, **coloring book** *AmE n* [C] a book full of pictures that are drawn without colour so that a child can colour them in

col·our·ist *BrE*, **colorist** *AmE* /ˈkʌlərɪst/ *n* [C]
1 *technical* a painter who uses colour itself as a subject of a painting **2** someone whose job is to DYE people's hair (=change the colour)

col·our·less *BrE*, **colorless** *AmE* /ˈkʌlələs $ ˈkʌlər-/ *adj*
1 having no colour: *a colourless odourless gas* **2** if your face, hair, eyes, skin, or lips are colourless, they are very pale, usually because you are ill or frightened **3** not interesting or exciting SYN **dull**: *his colourless personality* —**colourlessly** *adv*

ˈcolour scheme *BrE*, **color scheme** *AmE n* [C] the combination of colours that someone chooses for a room, painting etc

ˈcolour ˌsupplement *n* [C] *BrE* a magazine printed in colour and given free with a newspaper, especially on Saturdays or Sundays

colt /kəʊlt $ koʊlt/ *n* [C] **1** a young male horse → **filly**
2 [usually plural] *BrE* a member of a sports team for young people: *our colts team*

col·umn /ˈkɒləm $ ˈkɑː-/ ●●○ W2 *n* [C]
1 a tall solid upright stone post used to support a building or as a decoration
2 a line of numbers or words written under each other that goes down a page → **row**: **in a column** *Add up the numbers in each column.* | **[+of]** *a* ***column of figures***
3 an article on a particular subject or by a particular writer that appears regularly in a newspaper or magazine: *He* ***writes*** *a weekly* ***column*** *for 'The Times'.* | **music/science/gardening etc column**
4 one of two or more areas of print that go down the page of a newspaper or book and that are separated from each other by a narrow space: *Turn to page 5, column 2.* | *'The*

THESAURUS: colour

colour red, blue, yellow etc: *Blue is my favourite colour. | Matisse was famous for his use of colour.*
shade a particular type of a colour: *The dress is a light shade of pink. | He uses different shades of green.*
hue /hjuː/ *literary or technical* a particular colour or shade of a colour: *Her face had lost its golden hue.*
tint a small amount of a colour in something that is mostly another colour: *He wears sunglasses that have a pinky-orange tint.*
tone one of the many different shades of a colour, each slightly darker, lighter, brighter etc than the next: *Carpets in neutral tones give a feeling of space.*

DARK COLOURS

dark used about a colour that is strong and fairly close to black: *a dark blue suit | His eyes are dark brown.*
deep fairly dark - often used when you think this colour looks attractive: *His eyes were a beautiful deep blue. | deep red lips*
rich used about a colour that is fairly dark in a way that gives a pleasant feeling of warmth: *The walls were painted a rich red colour.*

LIGHT COLOURS

light used about a colour that is not dark: *a light blue sweater | His T-shirt was light green.*
pale used about a colour that is very light: *He has very pale blue eyes.*
soft used about a colour that is light in a way that is attractive because it is not too obvious: *She wears soft colours such as cream, which match her complexion.*
pastel used about a colour that has a lot of white in it: *The girls wore pastel pink sundresses.*

BRIGHT COLOURS

bright used about a colour that is strong and easy to see: *The front door was painted bright red.*
brilliant/vivid used about a colour that is very bright: *I looked out at the brilliant blue sky. | vivid red flowers*
colourful *BrE*, **colorful** *AmE* used about things that have many different bright colours: *There were window boxes full of colourful flowers.*
multicoloured *BrE*, **multicolored** *AmE* used about things that have a pattern of many different bright colours: *A multicoloured flag waved in the midday sun.*
gaudy/garish too brightly coloured, in a way that is unattractive: *The wallpaper was much too gaudy for me. | a garish orange tie*

*Sun' devoted ten **column inches** to the event* (=their article filled a column ten inches long).
5 something that has a tall thin shape: **[+of]** *a **column** of **smoke***
6 a long moving line of people or things: **[+of]** *a column of marching men* → **FIFTH COLUMN, GOSSIP COLUMN, PERSONAL COLUMN, SPINAL COLUMN**

col·umn·ist /ˈkɒləmɪst, -ləmnɪst $ ˈkɑː-/ ●○○ *n* [C] someone who writes articles, especially about a particular subject, that appear regularly in a newspaper or magazine

com /kɒm $ kɑːm/ the abbreviation of ***commercial organization***, used in Internet addresses

co·ma /ˈkəʊmə $ ˈkoʊ-/ *n* [C,U] someone who is in a coma has been unconscious for a long time, usually because of a serious illness or injury: **be in/go into/come out of a coma** *He went into a coma and died soon afterwards.*

co·ma·tose /ˈkəʊmətəʊs $ ˈkoʊmətoʊs/ *adj* **1** *technical* in a coma **2** not moving because of being drunk or very tired

comb¹ /kəʊm $ koʊm/ ●●● S3 *n*
1 [C] a flat piece of plastic, metal etc with a row of thin teeth on one side, used for making your hair tidy → **brush**
2 [C] a small flat piece of plastic, metal etc with a row of thin teeth on one side, used for keeping your hair back or for decoration
3 [singular] if you give your hair a comb, you make it tidy using a comb: *Your hair needs a good comb.*
4 [C] the red piece of flesh that grows on top of a male chicken's head
5 [C] a HONEYCOMB → **FINE-TOOTH COMB**

comb² ●●● S3 *v* [T]
1 to make hair look tidy using a comb: *Melanie ran upstairs to **comb** her **hair**.*
2 to search a place thoroughly: **comb sth for sb/sth** *Police are still combing the woods for the missing boy.*

comb sth ↔ **out** *phr v* to use a comb to make untidy hair look smooth and tidy: *She sat combing out her hair in front of the kitchen mirror.*

comb through sth *phr v* to search through a lot of objects or information in order to find a specific thing or piece of information: *We spent weeks combing through huge piles of old documents.*

com·bat¹ /ˈkɒmbæt $ ˈkɑːm-/ ●●○ *n*
1 [U] fighting, especially during a war: **in combat** *Corporal Gierson was killed in combat.* | *We flew over 200 **combat missions**.* | *training in **unarmed combat*** (=fighting without weapons) | **mortal combat** (=fighting until one person kills another) | **hand-to-hand combat** (=fighting in which you are close enough to touch your opponent) | **combat aircraft/jacket/boots etc** **THESAURUS** WAR
2 [C] a fight or battle
3 combats [plural] loose trousers, with many pockets: *She always wore combats, which were more fashionable than jeans.*

com·bat² /ˈkɒmbæt, kəmˈbæt $ kəmˈbæt, ˈkɑːmbæt/ ●●○ *v* (**combated**, **combating** *or* **combatted**, **combatting**) [T] to try to stop something bad from happening or getting worse – used especially in news reports: **combat inflation/crime/racism etc** *To combat inflation, the government raised interest rates.* | *new strategies for combatting terrorism*

com·ba·tant /ˈkɒmbətənt $ kəmˈbætnt/ *n* [C] someone who fights in a war

ˈcombat faˌtigue *n* [U] a type of mental illness caused by the terrible experiences of fighting in a war or battle → **post-traumatic stress disorder**: *These treatment methods enabled 80 percent of combat-fatigue-affected troops to return to duty.*

com·ba·tive /ˈkɒmbətɪv $ kəmˈbætɪv/ *adj* ready and willing to fight or argue: *Congress is in a combative mood.* —**combativeness** *n* [U]

com·bi /ˈkɒmbi $ ˈkɑːm-/ *n* [C] a machine or vehicle that can be used in two or more different ways – used especially in product names: *The new Combi can be used either as a passenger plane or for transporting freight.*

com·bi·na·tion /ˌkɒmbəˈneɪʃən $ ˌkɑːm-/ ●●● S3 W2 *n*
1 [C,U] two or more different things that exist together or are used or put together → **combine**: **[+of]** *A **combination of factors** may be responsible for the increase in cancer.* | *A combination of tact and authority was needed to deal with the situation.* | *Certain combinations of sounds are not possible in English.* | **in combination (with sth)** *Some drugs which are safe when taken separately are lethal in combination.* **THESAURUS** MIXTURE
2 [C] the series of numbers or letters you need to open a combination lock
3 winning combination a mixture of different people or things that work successfully together
4 [U] *especially AmE* used before a noun to mean that something has more than one purpose or uses more than one method: *a combination nightclub and café* | *new **combination drug therapies***

ˌcombiˈnation lock *n* [C] a lock which can only be opened by using a series of numbers or letters in a particular order → see picture at **LOCK²**

ˌcombination ˈoven *n* [C] an OVEN that uses gas or electricity and MICROWAVES

com·bine¹ /kəmˈbaɪn/ ●●● S3 W2 *v*
1 [I,T] if you combine two or more different things, or if they combine, they begin to exist or work together → **combination**: **combine sth with sth** *Augustine was later to combine elements of this philosophy with the teachings of Christianity.* | *Diets are most effective when combined with exercise.* | **combine to do sth** *A number of **factors** have **combined** to create this difficult situation.* | *Ruth hesitated, uncertain of how to combine honesty and diplomacy in her answer.* | **combined effect/effects** (=the result of two or more different things used or mixed together) *The combined effects of the war and the drought resulted in famine.* **THESAURUS** MIX
2 [T] to have two or more different features or qualities at the same time → **combination**: **combine sth with/and sth** *Good carpet wool needs to combine softness with strength.*
3 [I,T] if two or more different substances combine, or if you combine them, they mix or join together to produce a new single substance → **combination**: **combine to do sth** *Different amino acids combine to form proteins.* | *Combine all the ingredients in a large bowl.* | **combine sth with sth** *Steel is produced by combining iron with carbon.* **THESAURUS** MIX
4 [T] to do two different activities at the same time: **combine sth with sth** *Many people enjoy combining a holiday with learning a new skill.* | **combine sth and sth** *the problems facing women who wish to combine a career and family* | **combine business with pleasure** (=work and enjoy yourself at the same time)
5 [I,T] if two or more groups, organizations etc combine, or if you combine them, they join or work together in order to do something: **combine to do sth** *Ten British and French companies combined to form the Channel Tunnel Group.* | *University zoologists and government vets are **combining forces*** (=working together) *to investigate the disease.*

com·bine² /ˈkɒmbaɪn $ ˈkɑːm-/ *n* [C] **1** (*also* **combine harvester**) a machine used by farmers to cut grain, separate the seeds from it, and clean it **2** a group of people, businesses etc who work together: *The factory was sold to a British combine after the war.*

com·bined /kəmˈbaɪnd/ ●●○ *adj* [only before noun]
1 done, made, or achieved by several people or groups working together SYN **joint**: **combined effort/action/operation** *Dinner was a combined effort.*
2 a combined total is the sum of two or more quantities or figures added together: *Her records have sold a **combined total** of 14 million copies.* | *We could only afford a small flat, even on our combined salaries.*

comˈbining ˌform *n* [C] *technical* a word that is combined with another word or another combining form to make a new word, for example 'Anglo', meaning 'English', in the word 'Anglo-American'

com·bo /ˈkɒmbəʊ $ ˈkɑːmboʊ/ *n* (*plural* **combos**) [C]
1 a small band that plays JAZZ or dance music: *He played*

C

trumpet professionally in a jazz combo. **2** a COMBINATION of different things, especially of different types of foods – used especially in product names: *I chose the vegetarian combo.*

comb·o·ver /ˈkəʊməʊvə $ ˈkoʊmoʊvər/ *n* [C] *BrE informal* a way of arranging a man's hair, in which a long piece of hair from one side is COMBed over the top of the head in an attempt to hide the fact that the man is going BALD (=losing his hair) – used humorously SYN **scrapeover** *AmE*

com·bus·ti·ble /kəmˈbʌstəbəl/ *adj* able to burn easily: **combustible material/gas etc**

com·bus·tion /kəmˈbʌstʃən/ *n* [U] **1** the process of burning **2** *technical* chemical activity which uses oxygen to produce light and heat → **INTERNAL COMBUSTION ENGINE**

comˈbustion ˌchamber *n* [C] the enclosed space, for example in an engine, in which combustion happens

come[1] /kʌm/ ●●● S1 W1 *v* (*past tense* **came** /keɪm/, *past participle* **come**) [I]

1 MOVE TOWARDS SB/STH to move towards you or arrive at the place where you are OPP **go**: *Let me know when they come.* | *Can you* **come here** *for a minute?* | **Come** *a bit* **closer** *and you'll be able to see better.* | *What time will you be* **coming home**? | **[+in/into/out of etc]** *There was a knock on the door and a young woman came into the room.* | **[+to/towards]** *I could see a figure coming towards me.* | **[+across/down/up etc]** *As they came down the track, the car skidded.* | **come to do sth** *I've come to see Philip.* | **come and do sth** *I'll come and help you move the rest of the boxes.* | *Come and look at this!* | **come running/flying/speeding etc** *Jess came flying round the corner and banged straight into me.* | **come to dinner/lunch** *What day are your folks coming to dinner?* | **here comes sb/sth** *spoken* (=used to say that someone or something is coming towards you) *Ah, here comes the bus at last!* THESAURUS ▸ **ARRIVE**

2 GO WITH SB if someone comes with you, they go to a place with you: *We're going for a drink this evening. Would you like to come?* | **[+with]** *I asked Rosie if she'd like to come with us.* | **[+along]** *It should be good fun. Why don't you come along?*

3 TRAVEL TO A PLACE to travel to or reach a place: *Which way did you come?* | **[+through/across/by way of etc]** *They came over the mountains in the north.* | **[+from]** *Legend has it that the tribe came from across the Pacific Ocean.* | **come by car/train/bus etc** *Will you be coming by train?* | *Have you* **come far** (=travelled a long way) *today?* | *I've* **come a long way** *to see you.* | **come 50/100 etc miles/kilometres** *Some of the birds have come thousands of miles to winter here.*

4 POST if a letter etc comes, it is delivered to you by post SYN **arrive**: *A letter came for you this morning.* | *The phone bill hasn't come yet.*

5 HAPPEN if a time or an event comes, it arrives or happens: *At last the day came for us to set off.* | *The moment had come for me to break the news to her.* | *The time will come when you'll thank me for this.* | *Christmas seems to come earlier every year.* | **be/have yet to come** (=used when something has not happened yet but will happen) *The most exciting part is yet to come.* | *I knew he'd be able to take care of himself,* **come what may** (=whatever happens).

6 REACH A LEVEL/PLACE [always + adv/prep] to reach a particular level or place: **[+up/down]** *She had blonde hair which came down to her waist.* | *The water came up as far as my chest.*

7 BE PRODUCED/SOLD [always + adv/prep] to be produced or sold with particular features: **[+in]** *This particular sofa comes in four different colours.* | *Cats come in many shapes and sizes.* | **[+with]** *The computer* **comes complete with** *software and games.*

8 ORDER [always + adv/prep] to be in a particular position in an order, a series, or a list: **[+before/after]** *P comes before Q in the alphabet.* | **come first/second etc** *She came first in the 200 metres.*

9 come open/undone/loose etc to become open etc: *His shoelace had come undone.* | *The rope came loose.*

10 come to do sth a) to begin to have a feeling or opinion: *He came to think of Italy as his home.* | *I came to believe that he was innocent after all.* **b)** to do something by chance, without planning or intending to do it: *Can you tell me how the body came to be discovered?* | **come to be doing sth** *I often wondered how I came to be living in such a place.*

11 come and go a) to be allowed to go into and leave a place whenever you want: *The students can come and go as they please.* **b)** to keep starting and stopping: *The pain comes and goes.*

12 take sth as it comes to accept something as it happens, without trying to plan for it or change it: *We just take each year as it comes.* | *He takes life as it comes.*

13 have sth coming (to you) *informal* to deserve to be punished or to have something bad happen to you: *I do feel sorry for him, but I'm afraid he had it coming.*

14 as nice/as stupid etc as they come *informal* extremely nice, stupid etc: *My uncle Walter is as obstinate as they come.*

15 for years/weeks/days etc to come used to emphasize that something will continue for a long time into the future: *This is a moment that will be remembered and celebrated for years to come.*

16 in years/days to come in the future: *In years to come, some of the practices we take for granted now will seem quite barbaric.*

17 have come a long way to have made a lot of progress: *Computer technology has come a long way since the 1970s.*

18 come as a surprise/relief/blow etc (to sb) to make someone feel surprised, RELIEVEd, disappointed etc: *The decision came as a great relief to us all.* | *The news will* **come as no surprise** *to his colleagues.*

19 come easily/naturally (to sb) to be easy for someone to do: *Public speaking does not come easily to most people.* | *Writing came naturally to her, even as a child.*

20 come of age a) to reach the age when you are legally considered to be an adult: *He'll inherit the money when he comes of age.* **b)** to develop into an advanced or successful form: *Space technology didn't really come of age until the 1950s.*

21 come right out with sth/come right out and say sth *informal* to say something in a very direct way, often when other people think this is surprising: *You came right out and told him? I don't know how you dared!*

22 come clean *informal* to tell the truth about something you have done: **[+about]** *I think you should come clean about where you were last night.*

23 not know whether you are coming or going *informal* to feel very confused because a lot of different things are happening: *I don't know whether I'm coming or going this week.*

24 come good/right *BrE informal* to end well, after there have been a lot of problems: *Don't worry, it'll all come right in the end.*

25 come to pass *literary* to happen after a period of time: *It came to pass that they had a son.*

26 SEX *informal* to have an ORGASM

SPOKEN PHRASES

27 come in! used to tell someone who has knocked on your door to enter your room, house etc: *She tapped timidly on the door. 'Come in!' boomed a deep voice from inside.*

28 how come? used to ask someone why or how something happened: *How come you've ended up here?* | *'Last I heard, she was teaching in Mexico.' 'How come?'*

29 come to think of it/come to that used to add something that you have just realized or remembered: *Come to think of it, George did seem a bit depressed yesterday.* | *He had never expected to have a wife, or even a girlfriend come to that.*

30 come July/next year/the next day etc used to talk about a particular time in the future: *Come spring, you'll have plenty of colour in the garden.*

31 come again? used to ask someone to repeat what they have just said

32 don't come the innocent/victim/helpless male etc with me *BrE* used to tell someone not to pretend that they are something they are not in order to get sympathy or help

from you: *Don't come the poor struggling artist with me. You're just lazy!*
33 come (now) *old-fashioned* used to comfort or gently encourage someone
34 come, come/come now *old-fashioned* used to tell someone that you do not accept what they are saying or doing

come about *phr v*
1 to happen, especially in a way that is not planned: *The opportunity to get into computing came about quite by accident. | How did this situation come about?*
2 if a ship comes about, it changes direction
come across *phr v*
1 come across sb/sth to meet, find, or discover someone or something by chance: *I came across an old diary in her desk. | I've never come across anyone quite like her before. | We've come across a few problems that need resolving.*

REGISTER
In written English, people often use **encounter** when writing about problems or difficulties because this sounds more formal than **come across**: *The team of researchers had* ***encountered*** *similar problems before.*

2 if an idea comes across well, it is easy for people to understand: *Your point really came across at the meeting.*
3 if someone comes across in a particular way, they seem to have particular qualities SYN **come over**: **[+as]** *He comes across as a very intelligent sensitive man. | She sometimes comes across as being rather arrogant. | I don't think I* ***came across*** *very* ***well*** (=seemed to have good qualities) *in the interview.*
come across with sth *phr v* to provide money or information when it is needed: *I hoped he might come across with a few facts.*
come after sb *phr v* to look for someone in order to hurt them, punish them, or get something from them: *She was terrified that Trevor would come after her.*
come along *phr v*
1 be coming along *informal* to be developing or making progress SYN **progress**: *He opened the oven door to see how the food was coming along. | Your English is coming along really well.*
2 to appear or arrive: *A bus should come along any minute now. | Take any job opportunity that comes along.*
3 a) to go to a place with someone: *We're going into town – do you want to come along?* **b)** to go somewhere after someone: *You go on ahead – I'll come along later.*
4 come along! a) used to tell someone to hurry up SYN **come on**: *Come along! We're all waiting for you!* **b)** used to encourage someone to try harder SYN **come on**: *Come along! Don't give up yet!*
come apart *phr v*
1 to split or fall into pieces: *I picked the magazine up and it came apart in my hands.*
2 to begin to fail: *The whole basis of the agreement was coming apart. | She felt as if her life was* ***coming apart at the seams*** (=failing completely).
come around *phr v*
1 (*also* **come round** *BrE*) to come to someone's home or the place where they work in order to visit them SYN **come over**: *I'll come around later and see how you are. | Why don't you come round for lunch?*
2 (*also* **come round** *BrE*) to change your opinion so that you now agree with someone or are no longer angry with them: **[+to]** *It took him a while to come around to the idea. | Don't worry – she'll come round eventually.*
3 (*also* **come round** *BrE*) if a regular event comes around, it happens as usual: *By the time the summer came around, Kelly was feeling much better.*
4 *AmE* to become conscious again after you have been unconscious SYN **come round** *BrE*: *When she came around her mother was sitting by her bed.* | **[+from]** *You might feel a little sick when you come around from the anesthetic.*
come at sb/sth *phr v*
1 to move towards someone in a threatening way: *Suddenly, he came at me with a knife.*
2 if images, questions, facts etc come at you, you feel confused because there are too many of them at the same time: *Questions were coming at me from all directions.*
3 *informal* to consider or deal with a problem in a particular way SYN **approach**: *We need to come at the problem from a different angle.*
come away *phr v*
1 to become separated from the main part of something SYN **come off**: *One of the wires in the plug had come away. | I turned some of the pages and they came away in my hand.*
2 to leave a place with a particular feeling or idea: *We came away thinking that we had done quite well.* | **[+with]** *I came away with the impression that the school was very well run.*
come back *phr v*
1 to return to a particular place or person SYN **return**: *My mother was scared that if I left home I'd never come back. | Ginny's left me, and there's nothing I can do to persuade her to come back.*
2 to become fashionable or popular again → **comeback**: *Who'd have thought hippy gear would ever come back! | High heels are* ***coming back into fashion****.*
3 to appear or start to affect someone or something again SYN **return**: *The pain in her arm came back again. | It took a while for my confidence to come back.*
4 if something comes back to you, you remember it or remember how to do it: *As I walked the city streets, the memories came flooding back.* | **[+to]** *I can't think of her name at the moment, but it'll come back to me.*
5 to reply to someone quickly, often in an angry or unkind way → **comeback**: **[+at]** *He came back at me immediately, accusing me of being a liar.*
come before sb/sth *phr v formal* to be brought to someone in authority, especially a judge in a law court, to be judged or discussed by them: *When you come before the judge, it's best to tell the truth. | The case will come before the courts next month.*
come between sb *phr v*
1 to make people argue and feel angry with each other, when they had been friends before: *Nothing will ever come between us now. | I didn't want to come between a husband and wife.*
2 to prevent someone from giving enough attention to something: *She never let anything come between her and her work.*
come by *phr v*
1 come by sth to manage to get something that is rare or difficult to get: *How did you come by these pictures? | Jobs were* ***hard to come by****.*
2 come by (sth) to make a short visit to a place on your way to somewhere else: *He said he'd come by later. | I'll come by the house and get my stuff later, OK?*
come down *phr v*
1 a) if a price, level etc comes down, it gets lower: *It looks as if interest rates will come down again this month.* **b)** to accept a lower price: **[+to]** *He's asking £5,000, but he may be willing to come down to £4,800.*
2 if someone comes down to a place, they travel south to the place where you are: *Why don't you come down for the weekend sometime?* | **[+to]** *Are you coming down to Knoxville for Christmas?*
3 to fall to the ground: *A lot of trees came down in the storm. | We were still out in the fields when the rain started coming down.*
4 come down on the side of sb/sth (*also* **come down in favour of sb/sth**) to decide to support someone or something: *The committee came down in favour of making the information public.*
5 *informal* to start to feel normal again after you have been feeling very happy and excited: *He was on a real high all last week and he's only just come down.*
6 *informal* to stop feeling the effects of a strong drug: *When I came down, I remembered with horror some of the things I'd said.*
7 *BrE old-fashioned* to leave a university after completing a period of study
come down on sb *phr v* to punish someone or criticize them severely: *We need to* ***come down hard on*** *young*

C

offenders. | *I made the mistake of answering back, and she* ***came down on*** *me* ***like a ton of bricks*** (=very severely).

come down to sb/sth *phr v*

1 if a complicated situation or problem comes down to something, that is the single most important thing: ***It all comes down to*** *money in the end.*

2 if something old has come down to you, it has been passed between people over a long period of time until you have it: *The text which has come down to us is only a fragment of the original.*

come down with sth *phr v* to get an illness: *I think I'm coming down with a cold.*

come for sb/sth *phr v*

1 to arrive to collect someone or something: *I'll come for you at about eight o'clock.*

2 to arrive at a place in order to take someone away by force: *Members of the secret police came for him in the middle of the night.*

come forward *phr v* to offer help to someone, or offer to do something: *So far, only one candidate has come forward.* | *The police appealed for witnesses to come forward with information.*

come from sb/sth *phr v*

1 if you come from a place, you were born there or lived there when you were young: *I come from London originally.*

2 to be obtained from a place, thing, or person, or to start or be made somewhere: *A lot of drugs come from quite common plants.* | *My information comes from a very reputable source.* | *The idea came from America.*

3 to happen as the result of doing something: **come from doing sth** *Most of her problems come from expecting too much of people.*

4 coming from him/her/you etc *spoken* used to say that someone should not criticize another person for doing something, because they have done the same thing themselves: *You think I'm too selfish? That's rich coming from you!*

5 where sb is coming from *informal* the basic attitude or opinion someone has, which influences what they think, say, or do: *I see where you're coming from now.*

come in *phr v*

1 if a train, bus, plane, or ship comes in, it arrives at a place: *What time does your train come in?* | **[+to]** *We come in to Heathrow at nine in the morning.*

2 if money or information comes in, you receive it: *Reports are coming in of a massive earthquake in Mexico.* | *We haven't got enough money coming in.*

3 to be involved in a plan, deal etc: *We need some financial advice – that's where Kate comes in.* | **[+on]** *You had the chance to come in on the deal.*

4 to join in a conversation or discussion: *Can I come in here and add something to what you're saying?*

5 to become fashionable or popular OPP **go out**: *Trainers really became popular in the 1980s, when casual sportswear came in.*

6 to finish a race: **come in first/second etc** *His horse came in second to last.*

7 if the TIDE comes in, the sea moves towards the land and covers the edge of it OPP **go out**

come in for sth *phr v* **come in for criticism/blame/scrutiny** to be criticized, blamed etc for something: *The government has come in for fierce criticism over its handling of this affair.*

come into sth *phr v*

1 to receive money, land, or property from someone after they have died: *She'll come into quite a lot of money when her father dies.*

2 to be involved in something: *Josie doesn't come into the movie until quite near the end.* | *Where do I come into all this?*

3 come into view/sight if something comes into view, you begin to see it: *The mountains were just coming into view.*

4 come into leaf/flower/blossom to start to produce leaves or flowers: *The roses are just coming into flower.*

5 not come into it *spoken* used to say that something is not important: *Money doesn't really come into it.*

6 come into your own to become very good, useful, or important in a particular situation: *On icy roads, a four-wheel drive vehicle really comes into its own.*

come of sth *phr v* to happen as a result of something: *I did ask a few questions, but nothing came of it.* | *That's what comes of not practising – you've forgotten everything!*

come off *phr v*

1 come off (sth) to become removed from something: *The label had come off, so there was no way of knowing what was on the disk.*

2 come off (sth) *BrE* to fall off something: *Dyson came off his bike as he rounded the last corner, but wasn't badly hurt.*

3 *informal* if something that has been planned comes off, it happens: *In the end the trip never came off.*

4 *informal* to be successful: *It was a good idea, but it didn't quite come off.* | *The performance on the first night* ***came off*** *pretty* ***well.***

5 come off sth to stop taking a drug that you have been taking regularly: *It wasn't until I tried to come off the pills that I realized I was addicted.*

6 come off best/better/worst etc *BrE* to be the most or least successful, or get the most or least advantages from a situation: *As far as pensions go, it's still women who come off worst.*

7 come off it! *BrE spoken* used to tell someone that you do not believe what they are saying: *Oh come off it! You can't seriously be saying you knew nothing about this.*

come on *phr v*

1 come on! *spoken* **a)** used to tell someone to hurry: *Come on, we'll be late!* **b)** used to encourage someone to do something: *Come on, you can do it!* | *Come on, cheer up!* **c)** used to tell someone that you know that what they have just said was not true or right: *Oh come on, don't lie!* **d)** used to make someone angry enough to want to fight you: *Come on, then, hit me!*

2 come on in/over/up etc *spoken* used to tell someone to come in, over, up etc, usually in a friendly way: *Come on in – I've made some coffee.*

3 if a light or machine comes on, it starts working: *A dog started barking and lights came on in the house.*

4 if an illness comes on, you start to be ill with it: *I can feel a headache coming on.*

5 if a television or radio programme comes on, it starts: *Just at that moment, the news came on.*

6 if rain or snow comes on, it starts: *The rain came on just before lunchtime.*

7 to come onto a stage or sports field: *He scored only two minutes after he'd come on.*

8 to improve or make progress: *The children are really coming on now.* | *Your English is coming on really well.*

9 come on sb/sth to find or discover someone or something by chance: *We came on a group of students having a picnic.*

10 come on strong *informal* to make it very clear to someone that you think they are sexually attractive

come on to sb/sth *phr v*

1 to start talking about a new subject: *I'll come on to this question in a few moments.*

2 *informal* if someone comes on to another person, they make it very clear that they are sexually interested in them → **come-on**: *The way she was coming on to Jack, I'm amazed he managed to get out alive!*

come out *phr v*

1 if something comes out, it is removed from a place: *These stains will never come out!*

2 if information comes out, people learn about it, especially after it has been kept secret: *No doubt the truth will come out one day.* | ***It's come out that*** *several ministers received payments from the company.*

3 if a photograph comes out, it shows a clear picture: *I took some photographs, but they didn't come out.* | *The wedding photos have come out really well.*

4 if a book, record etc comes out, it becomes publicly available: *When is the new edition coming out?*

5 if something comes out in a particular way, that is what it is like after it has been made or produced: *I've made a cake, but it hasn't come out very well.* | *The cover has come out a bit too big.*

6 if something you say comes out in a particular way, that is how it sounds or how it is understood: *His words came out as little more than a whisper.* | *That didn't come out the way I meant it to.* | *I tried to explain everything to her, but it* ***came out all wrong*** (=not in the way I intended).
7 if someone comes out in a particular way, that is the situation they are in at the end of an event or series of events: *The more experienced team came out on top.* | **[+of]** *She came out of the divorce quite well.*
8 to be easy to notice: *His right-wing opinions come out quite strongly in his later writings.*
9 to say publicly that you strongly support or oppose a plan, belief etc: **[+in favour of]** *The board of directors has come out in favour of a merger.* | **[+against]** *Teachers have come out against the proposed changes.* | *At least he's got the courage to* ***come out and say*** *what he thinks.*
10 if the sun, moon, or stars come out, they appear in the sky: *The sky cleared and the sun came out.*
11 if a flower comes out, it opens: *The snowdrops were just starting to come out.*
12 if someone comes out, they say that they are GAY when this was a secret before: **[+to]** *That summer, I decided to come out to my parents.*
13 *BrE informal* to refuse to work, as a protest: *Nurses have threatened to come out in support of their pay claim.* | *We decided to* ***come out on strike.***
14 if a young woman came out in the past, she was formally introduced into upper-class society at a large formal dance
come out at sth *phr v* if something comes out at a particular amount, that is the amount it adds up to: *The whole trip, including fares, comes out at $900.*
come out in sth *phr v* **come out in spots/a rash etc** if you come out in spots etc, spots appear on your body: *If I eat eggs, I come out in a rash.*
come out of sth *phr v*
1 to no longer be in a bad situation: *There are signs that the country is coming out of recession.*
2 to happen as a result of something: *One or two excellent ideas came out of the meeting.*
3 come out of yourself *informal* to start to behave in a more confident way: *Penny's really come out of herself since she started that course.*
come out with sth *phr v* to say something, especially something unusual or unexpected: *The things he comes out with are so funny!*
come over *phr v*
1 a) if someone comes over, they visit you at your house: *Do you want to come over on Friday evening?* **b)** if someone comes over, they come to the country where you are: **[+to/from]** *When did your family first come over to America?*
2 come over sb if a strong feeling comes over you, you suddenly experience it: *A wave of sleepiness came over me.* | *I'm sorry about that – I* ***don't know what came over*** *me* (=I do not know why I behaved in that way).
3 if an idea comes over well, people can understand it easily: *I thought that the points he was making came over quite clearly.*
4 if someone comes over in a particular way, they seem to have particular qualities SYN **come across**: *He didn't* ***come over*** *very* ***well*** (=seem to have good qualities) *in the interview.* | **[+as]** *She comes over as a very efficient businesswoman.*
5 come over (all) shy/nervous etc *informal* to suddenly become very shy, nervous etc
come round *phr v BrE* to COME AROUND
come through *phr v*
1 if a piece of information, news etc comes through, it arrives somewhere: *We're still waiting for our exam results to come through.* | *There is news just coming through of an explosion in a chemical factory.*
2 to be made official, especially by having the correct documents officially approved: *I'm still waiting for my divorce to come through.*
3 come through (sth) to continue to live, be strong, or succeed after a difficult or dangerous time SYN **survive**: *If he comes through the operation OK he should be back to normal within a month.* | *It's been a tough time, but I'm sure you'll come through and be all the wiser for it.*
come through with sth *phr v* to give someone something they need, especially when they have been worried that you would not produce it in time: *Our representative in Hong Kong finally came through with the figures.*
come to *phr v*
1 come to a decision/conclusion/agreement etc to decide something, agree on something etc after considering or discussing a situation SYN **reach**: *We came to the conclusion that there was no other way back to the camp.* | *If they don't come to a decision by midnight, the talks will be abandoned.*
2 come to a halt/stop a) to slow down and stop SYN **stop**: *The train came to a stop just yards from the barrier.* **b)** to stop operating or continuing: *After the election our funding came to an abrupt halt.*
3 come to sth to develop so that a particular situation exists, usually a bad one: *I never thought* ***it*** *would* ***come to this.*** | *We need to be prepared to fight, but hopefully* ***it won't come to that*** (=that won't be necessary). | *All those years of studying, and in the end it all* ***came to nothing.*** | ***It's come to something when*** *I'm not allowed to express an opinion in my own house!* | **what is the world/the country etc coming to?** (=used to say that the world etc is in a bad situation)
4 come to sth to add up to a total amount: *That comes to £23.50.* | *The bill came to £48.50.*
5 come to sb if a thought or idea comes to you, you realize or remember something: *The answer came to me in a flash.* | *I've forgotten her name, but maybe it'll come to me later.*
6 to become conscious again after you have been unconscious: *When he came to, he was lying on the floor with his hands tied behind his back.*
7 when it comes to sth *informal* when you are dealing with something or talking about something: *He's a bit of an expert when it comes to computers.*
come under sth *phr v*
1 come under attack/fire/scrutiny etc to be attacked, shot at etc: *The government has come under attack from opposition leaders over proposals to cut health spending.*
2 to be governed or controlled by a particular organization or person: *The organization comes under the authority of the EU.*
3 if a piece of information comes under a particular title, you can find it under that title: *The proposals come under three main headings.*
come up *phr v*
1 if someone comes up to you, they come close to you, especially in order to speak to you: *One of the teachers came up and started talking to me.* | **[+to]** *A man came up to him and asked for a light.*
2 if someone comes up to a place, they travel north to the place where you are: **[+to]** *Why don't you come up to New York for the weekend?*
3 if a subject comes up, people mention it and discuss it SYN **arise**: *His name came up in the conversation.* | *The subject of salaries didn't come up.*
4 if a problem or difficulty comes up, it appears or starts to affect you SYN **arise**: *I'm afraid I'll have to cancel our date –* ***something's come up.*** | *The same problems come up every time.*
5 if a job or an opportunity comes up, it becomes available: *A vacancy has come up in the accounts department.*
6 to be dealt with in a law court: *Your case comes up next week.*
7 be coming up to be going to happen soon: *With Christmas coming up, few people have much money to spare.*
8 if the sun or moon comes up, it moves up into the sky where you can see it SYN **rise**: *It was six o'clock, and the sun was just coming up.*
9 if a plant comes up, it begins to appear above the ground: *The first spring bulbs are just coming up.*
10 if food comes up, it goes back through your mouth from your stomach after being swallowed → **vomit**
11 coming (right) up! *spoken* used to say that food or drink

will be ready very soon: *'Two Martinis, please.' 'Coming up!'*

come up against sth/sb *phr v* to have to deal with problems or difficulties: *We may find we come up against quite a lot of opposition from local people. | You've got no idea of what you're going to come up against.*

come up for sth *phr v*
1 come up for discussion/examination/review etc to be discussed, examined etc: *This matter will come up for discussion at next month's meeting. | The regulations come up for review in April.*
2 come up for election/re-election/selection etc to reach the time when people have to vote about whether you should continue in a political position: *The governors come up for re-election next year.*

come upon sb/sth *phr v*
1 to find or discover something or someone by chance: *We came upon a cottage just on the edge of the wood.*
2 *literary* if a feeling comes upon you, you suddenly feel it: *A wave of tiredness came upon her.*

C

come up to sth/sb *phr v*
1 to reach a particular standard or to be as good as you expected: *This doesn't come up to the standard of your usual work. | The resort certainly failed to* ***come up to expectations****.*
2 be (just) coming up to sth to be nearly a particular time: *It's just coming up to 11 o'clock.*

come up with sth *phr v*
1 to think of an idea, answer etc: *Is that the best excuse you can come up with? | We've been asked to come up with some new ideas.*
2 *informal* to produce an amount of money: *We wanted to buy the house but we couldn't come up with the cash. | How am I supposed to come up with $10,000?*

come[2] *n* [U] *informal* a man's SEMEN (=the liquid he produces during sex)

come·back /ˈkʌmbæk/ ●○○ *n* [C usually singular]
1 make/stage a comeback if a person, activity, style etc makes a comeback, they become popular again after being unpopular for a long time: *The miniskirt made a comeback in the late 1980s.*
2 a quick reply that is often clever, funny, and insulting SYN **retort**: *I couldn't think of a good comeback.*
3 a way of getting payment or a reward for something wrong or unfair that has been done to you: *Check your contract carefully, or you may have no comeback if something goes wrong.* → **come back** at COME[1]

co·me·di·an /kəˈmiːdiən/ ●●○ *n* [C]
1 someone whose job is to tell jokes and make people laugh: *He started as a* ***stand-up comedian*** (=someone who tells jokes to an audience).
2 someone who is amusing: *You'll like Matt. He's a real comedian.*

co·me·di·enne /kəˌmiːdiˈen/ *n* [C] a female comedian

come·down /ˈkʌmdaʊn/ *n* [singular] a situation that is not as good, important, interesting etc as the situation you had previously: *The film marks a real comedown for the director.* → **come down** at COME[1]

com·e·dy /ˈkɒmədi $ ˈkɑː-/ ●●● W3 *n* (*plural* **comedies**)
1 [U] entertainment that is intended to make people laugh: **comedy writer/series/show/actor etc** | *a career in* ***stand-up comedy*** (=telling jokes in front of people as a job) THESAURUS ▸ FUNNY
2 [C] a play, film, or television programme that is intended to make people laugh: *a highly successful TV comedy* THESAURUS ▸ MOVIE
3 [U] the quality in something such as a book or play that makes people laugh SYN **humour** → **tragedy**: *Can't you see the comedy of the situation?* → BLACK COMEDY, SITUATION COMEDY

ˌComedy of ˈErrors, The a humorous play by William Shakespeare about two sets of IDENTICAL TWINS. There are many confusing and amusing situations because characters think that one twin is the other. The phrase 'a comedy of errors' is often used to describe a situation that is so full of mistakes and problems that it seems funny.

ˌcomedy of ˈmanners *n* (*plural* **comedies of manners**) [C] a play, film, or television programme that shows how silly people's behaviour is or can be

come·ly /ˈkʌmli/ *adj literary old-fashioned* a comely woman is attractive —**comeliness** *n* [U]

ˈcome-on *n* [C usually singular] *informal* something that someone does deliberately to make someone else sexually interested in them: *Rick's the kind of guy who thinks every smile is a come-on.* | **give sb the come-on** (=do something to show you are sexually interested in someone) → **come on to sb/sth** at COME ON

com·er /ˈkʌmə $ -ər/ *n* **all comers** *informal* anyone who wants to take part in an activity, especially a sporting competition: *The contest is open to all comers.* → LATECOMER, NEWCOMER

com·et /ˈkɒmɪt $ ˈkɑː-/ ●○○ *n* [C] an object in space like a bright ball with a long tail, that moves around the sun: *Halley's Comet*

come·up·pance /kʌmˈʌpəns/ *n* [singular] a punishment or something bad which happens to you that you really deserve: *You'll* ***get*** *your* ***comeuppance*** *one day!*

com·fort[1] /ˈkʌmfət $ -ərt/ ●●○ W3 *n*
1 PHYSICAL [U] a feeling of being physically relaxed and satisfied, so that nothing is hurting you, making you feel too hot or cold etc → **comfortable**, **discomfort**: **built/made/designed for comfort** *All our sports shoes are designed for comfort and performance.* | **too hot/high/tight etc for comfort** (=physically unpleasant for a particular reason) *The temperature was too low for comfort. | I dress for comfort, not fashion. | Alan was very reluctant to leave the warmth and comfort of the fire.* | **in comfort** *Upstairs is a more intimate bar where guests can relax in comfort. | Now you can watch your favorite movies* ***in the comfort of*** *your own home.*
2 EMOTIONAL [U] if someone or something gives you comfort, they make you feel calmer, happier, or more hopeful after you have been worried or unhappy → **comforting**: *Whenever he was upset, he would turn to her for comfort and advice.* | **give/bring/provide/offer comfort** *a book which offers comfort and help to the parents of children with cancer | The knowledge that Cara was safe gave him some comfort.* | **great/much/little comfort** *My faith has been a* ***source of*** *great* ***comfort*** *over the years.* | **take/draw/derive comfort from (doing) sth** *He drew comfort from her warm support.* | **find/take comfort in (doing) sth** *You can take some comfort in the fact that you did your best.* | **it's no/some comfort** *It was no comfort to think he might be as frightened as she was.* | **if it's any comfort** (=used to introduce a statement that you think may make someone feel slightly less worried or unhappy) *Well, if it's any comfort, I don't think he'll try again.*
3 SB/STH THAT HELPS [C] someone or something that helps you feel calmer, happier, or more hopeful after you have been worried or unhappy → **comforting**: **be a comfort (to sb)** *Louisa's been a* ***great comfort*** *to me since Mary died.* | ***It's a comfort*** *to know there's someone to keep an eye on the kids.*
4 MONEY/POSSESSIONS [U] a way of living in which you have all the money and possessions that you need or want → **comfortable**: **in comfort** *When Dad died, he left us both enough to* ***live in comfort*** *for the rest of our lives. | He was used to a life of comfort.*
5 comforts [plural] the things that make your life nicer and more comfortable, especially things that are not necessary: *Modern caravans offer* ***all the comforts of*** *home. | hotels with all the* ***modern comforts*** (=things such as a television, telephone etc) | **material comforts** (=money and possessions) → CREATURE COMFORTS
6 too close/near for comfort something that is too close for comfort makes you feel worried, unhappy, or uncomfortable, because it is dangerous in some way: *The cars were whizzing past us much too close for comfort.*
7 cold/small comfort a small piece of good news that does not make you feel better about a bad situation: **[+for/to]** *Another drop in the inflation rate was cold comfort yesterday for the 2.74 million jobless.* → COMFORT FOOD, COMFORT ZONE

comfort² ●●○ *v* [T] to make someone feel less worried, unhappy, or upset, for example by saying kind things to them or touching them → **comforting**: *Within hours of the news, Helen arrived to comfort her heartbroken friend.* | *He longed to take her in his arms and comfort her.* | *Mr Aston's father was last night being comforted by relatives.* | **comfort yourself** *She comforted herself with the thought that it would soon be spring.*

com·fort·a·ble /ˈkʌmftəbəl, ˈkʌmfət- $ ˈkʌmfərt-, ˈkʌmft-/ ●●● S2 W3 *adj*

1 FURNITURE/PLACES/CLOTHES ETC making you feel physically relaxed, without any pain or without being too hot, cold etc → **comfort**: **comfortable chair/bed/sofa etc** *The bed wasn't particularly comfortable.* | **comfortable room/lounge/hotel etc** *Joyce has a comfortable apartment in Portland.* | **comfortable clothes/shoes/boots etc** *Wear loose comfortable clothing.* | **comfortable to wear/use/sit on etc** *Linen is very comfortable to wear.*

2 PHYSICALLY RELAXED feeling physically relaxed, without any pain or without being too hot, cold etc → **comfort**: *I was so comfortable and warm in bed I didn't want to get up.* | *Sit down and* ***make yourself comfortable****.* | *With difficulty, she rolled her body into a more* ***comfortable position****.*

3 CONFIDENT [not before noun] confident, relaxed, and not worried: **[+with]** *She's never* ***felt*** *very* ***comfortable*** *with men.* | *In our business, we need people who are comfortable in an unstructured environment.*

4 MONEY having enough money to buy the things you need or want, without having to worry about how much they cost: **comfortable life/retirement/existence etc** *Jean's looking forward to a comfortable retirement.*

5 COMPETITION/VOTE [usually before noun] if you have a comfortable win or lead, you win or are leading by a large amount: **comfortable win/victory** *The pair had a comfortable win, beating the German team by nearly three seconds.* | *The bill should pass in the House by a* ***comfortable margin****.* | *Another penalty from Roberts gave the home team a* ***comfortable*** *half-time* ***lead****.*

6 ILL/INJURED [not before noun] if someone who is ill or injured is comfortable, they are not in too much pain

THESAURUS

comfortable making you feel physically relaxed, and not too hard, hot, cold etc. Also used about people feeling physically relaxed: *The hotel was very comfortable.* | *I tried to get into a more comfortable position.*

comfy *informal* comfortable – used especially about furniture and clothes: *a comfy armchair* | *These shoes are very comfy.* | *Are you comfy?*

cosy *BrE*, **cozy** *AmE* comfortable and warm – used especially about small rooms, houses etc: *There's a cosy lounge with a real fire.* | *a cozy apartment*

snug small, warm, and comfortable, especially in a way that makes you feel protected – used especially about rooms, houses etc. Also used about people feeling warm and comfortable: *It was very cold outside, but our tents were snug and warm.* | *She wished she was back in her snug little house.* | *I'm* ***snug as a bug in a rug*** *in here!* (=very snug – used in informal British English)

smooth a smooth journey is comfortable because your car or plane does not shake, or the sea is not rough: *Did you have a smooth flight?* | *a smooth crossing*

COLLOCATIONS CHECK

comfortable chair/bed/house/position/person
comfy chair/clothes/person
cosy room/house/fire
snug room/house/person
smooth journey/crossing/flight

com·fort·a·bly /ˈkʌmftəbli, ˈkʌmfət- $ ˈkʌmfərt-, ˈkʌmft-/ ●●○ *adv*

1 FURNITURE/PLACES/CLOTHES in a way that makes you feel physically relaxed, without any pain, or without being too hot, cold etc: *The hotel is modern and* ***comfortably furnished****.* | *his comfortably baggy jeans*

2 PHYSICALLY RELAXED in a way that feels physically relaxed, without any pain, or without being too hot, cold etc: *I was* ***sitting comfortably*** *in the lounge, reading a newspaper.*

3 MONEY with enough money to live on without having to worry about paying for things: *She earns enough money to* ***live comfortably****.* | *His family were* ***comfortably off*** (=fairly rich).

4 WIN/ACHIEVEMENT easily and without problems: *Davis* ***won comfortably****, 9–1, 9–3, 9–2.* | *the amount of work you can comfortably deal with*

5 CONFIDENT in a confident and relaxed way: *They were soon chatting comfortably with each other.*

ˈcomfort break *n* [C] a short pause in a meeting or journey so that people can go to the toilet: *I think it's time for a comfort break.*

com·fort·er /ˈkʌmfətə $ -fərtər/ *n* [C] **1** *AmE* a cover for a bed that is filled with a soft warm material such as feathers SYN **duvet** *BrE* **2** someone or something that comforts you

ˈcomfort ˌfood *n* [C,U] simple food that makes you feel relaxed and happy

com·fort·ing /ˈkʌmfətɪŋ $ -fər-/ *adj* making you feel less worried, unhappy, or upset SYN **reassuring**: **it is comforting to think/have/know etc** *It's comforting to know I can call my parents any time.* | *With this* ***comforting thought****, Harry fell asleep.* | *His voice was strangely comforting.* —**comfortingly** *adv*

ˈcomfort ˌzone *n* [C usually singular] your comfort zone is the range of activities or situations that you feel happy and confident in

com·fy /ˈkʌmfi/ *adj informal* comfortable: *a comfy chair* THESAURUS ▸ COMFORTABLE

com·ic¹ /ˈkɒmɪk $ ˈkɑː-/ ●●○ *adj* amusing you and making you want to laugh OPP **tragic**: *a comic novel* | **comic writer/actress/performer etc** (=someone who writes or performs things that make you laugh) | **comic relief** (=a situation in a serious story that makes you relax a little because it is funny) *The song provides some* ***comic relief*** *from the intensity of the scene.* THESAURUS ▸ FUNNY

comic² ●○○ *n* [C]

1 (*also* ˈ**comic book**) a magazine for children that tells a story using comic strips

2 someone whose job is to tell jokes and make people laugh SYN **comedian**: *a* ***stand-up comic***

com·i·cal /ˈkɒmɪkəl $ ˈkɑː-/ *adj* behaviour or situations that are comical are funny in a strange or unexpected way: *The note of pure panic in his voice was almost comical.* THESAURUS ▸ FUNNY —**comically** /-kli/ *adv*

ˈcomic strip *n* [C] a series of pictures drawn inside boxes that tell a story → **cartoon**

com·ing¹ /ˈkʌmɪŋ/ *n* **1 the coming of sth/sb** the time when something new begins, especially something that will cause a lot of changes: *With the coming of railways, new markets opened up.* **2 comings and goings** *informal* the movements of people as they arrive at and leave places: **[+of]** *Beds are arranged so that patients can watch the comings and goings of visitors and staff.*

coming² *adj* [only before noun] *formal* happening soon: *the coming winter* → UP-AND-COMING

ˌcoming of ˈage *n* [singular] the point in a young person's life, usually the age of 18 or 21, at which their society considers them to be an adult

com·ma /ˈkɒmə $ ˈkɑːmə/ ●●○ *n* [C] the mark (,) used in writing to show a short pause or to separate things in a list → INVERTED COMMA, PUNCTUATION MARK

com·mand¹ /kəˈmɑːnd $ kəˈmænd/ ●●○ W3 *n*

1 CONTROL [U] the control of a group of people or a situation: **under sb's command** *troops under the command of General Roberts* | **in command (of sth)** *Lieutenant Peters was now in command.* | *He felt fully* ***in command of the situation****.* | **take command (of sth)** (=begin controlling a group or

situation and making decisions) *The fire officer took command, ordering everyone to leave the building.* | **at sb's command** *Each congressman has a large staff at his command* (=available to be used). | *By 1944, Fletcher **had command of** a B-17 bomber and a ten-man crew.*
2 ORDER [C] an order that should be obeyed: *Shoot when I give the **command**.*
3 COMPUTER [C] an instruction to a computer to do something
4 command of sth knowledge of something, especially a language, or ability to use something: **(have a) good/excellent/poor etc command of sth** *He's studied in the US and has a good command of English.*
5 MILITARY [C] **a)** a part of an army, navy etc that is controlled separately and has a particular job: *pilots of the Southern Air Command* **b)** a group of officers or officials who give orders: *the Army High Command* **c)** the group of soldiers that an officer is in control of
6 at your command if you have a particular skill at your command, you are able to use that skill well and easily: *a pianist with the keys at his command*
7 be in command of yourself to be able to control your emotions and thoughts: *Kathleen walked in – tall, slim, confident, and in total command of herself.*

command² ●●○ *v*
1 ORDER [I,T] to tell someone officially to do something, especially if you are a military leader, a king etc: **command sb to do sth** *Captain Picard commanded the crew to report to the main deck.* | **command that** *The General commanded that the regiment attack at once.* THESAURUS ORDER
2 LEAD THE MILITARY [I,T] to be responsible for giving orders to a group of people in the army, navy etc → **commander**: *He commands the 4th Battalion.*
3 DESERVE AND GET [T] to get something such as respect or attention because you do something well or are important or popular: **command respect/attention/support etc** *Philip was a remarkable teacher, able to command instant respect.* | **command a high fee/wage/price etc** *Which graduates command the highest salaries?*
4 CONTROL [T] to control something: *The party that commands a majority of seats in Parliament forms the government.*
5 VIEW [T] if a place commands a view, you can see something clearly from it: *The Ramses Hilton commands a magnificent view of Cairo.*

com·man·dant /ˌkɒmənˈdænt $ ˈkɑːməndænt/ *n* [C] the army officer in charge of a place or group of people

com·man·deer /ˌkɒmənˈdɪə $ ˌkɑːmənˈdɪr/ *v* [T] to take someone else's property for your own use, especially during a war: *The local hotel was commandeered for the wounded.*

com·mand·er /kəˈmɑːndə $ kəˈmændər/ ●●○ *n* [C]
1 an officer of any rank who is in charge of a group of soldiers or a particular military activity: *the American Commander, General Otis* | *our platoon commander*
2 a high rank in the navy, or someone who holds this rank
3 a British police officer of high rank → WING COMMANDER

comˌmander in ˈchief *n* (*plural* **commanders in chief**) [C usually singular] someone of high rank who is in control of all the military organizations in a country or of a specific military activity: *The king or queen is commander in chief of the British armed forces.*

com·mand·ing /kəˈmɑːndɪŋ $ kəˈmæn-/ *adj*
1 [only before noun] having the authority or position that allows you to give orders: *a **commanding officer*** **2** having the confidence to make people respect and obey you – used to show approval: *Papa's **commanding presence*** **3** a commanding view or position is one from which you can clearly see a long way **4** being in a position from which you are likely to win a race or competition easily: *a **commanding lead***

com·mand·ment /kəˈmɑːndmənt $ kəˈmænd-/ *n* [C] one of the ten rules given by God in the Bible that tell people how they must behave

comˈmand ˌmodule *n* [C] the part of a space vehicle from which its activities are controlled

com·man·do /kəˈmɑːndəʊ $ kəˈmændoʊ/ *n* (*plural* **commandos** *or* **commandoes**) **1** [C] a soldier who is specially trained to make quick attacks into enemy areas: *a commando raid* **2 go commando** *AmE spoken* to not wear any underwear – used humorously

comˌmand perˈformance *n* [C usually singular] a special performance at a theatre that is given for a king, president etc

comˈmand post *n* [C] the place from which military leaders and their officers control activities

com·mem·o·rate /kəˈmeməreɪt/ ●○○ *v* [T] to do something to show that you remember and respect someone important or an important event in the past: *a parade to commemorate the town's bicentenary* —**commemorative** /kəˈmemərətɪv/ *adj*: *a commemorative plaque*

com·mem·o·ra·tion /kəˌmeməˈreɪʃən/ *n* [U] something that makes you remember and respect someone important or an important event in the past SYN **remembrance**: **in commemoration of sb/sth** *a service in commemoration of those who died in the war*

Frequencies of **commence**, **start**, and **begin** in spoken and written English.

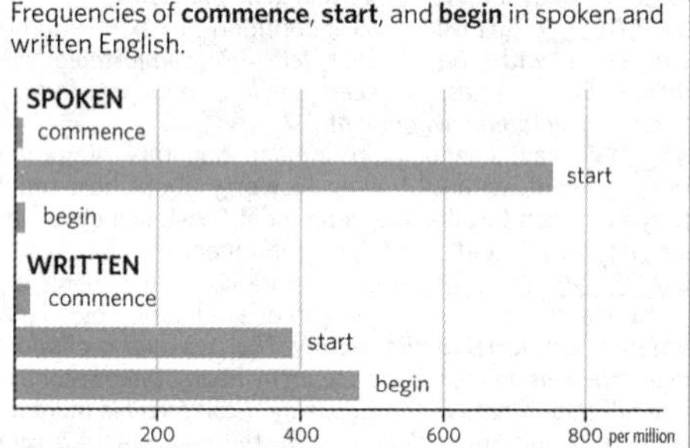

This graph shows that in spoken English **start** is the most common of the three verbs. In written English **begin** is the most common. **Commence** is much more formal than **start** and **begin**.

com·mence /kəˈmens/ ●○○ AWL *v* [I,T] *formal* to begin or to start something: *Work will commence on the new building immediately.* | *Your first evaluation will be six months after you commence employment.* | **[+with]** *The course commences with a one week introduction to Art Theory.* | **commence doing sth** *The planes commenced bombing at midnight.* THESAURUS START

REGISTER
In everyday English, people usually say **start** rather than **commence**: *The concert was just about to **start**.*

com·mence·ment /kəˈmensmənt/ AWL *n formal*
1 [U] the beginning of something: **[+of]** *the commencement of building work* THESAURUS BEGINNING **2** [C,U] *AmE* a ceremony at which university, college, or high school students receive their DIPLOMAS SYN **graduation**

com·mend /kəˈmend/ ●○○ *v* [T] *formal*
1 to praise or approve of someone or something publicly: **commend sb for sth** *Inspector Marshall was commended for his professional attitude.* | *The paper was **highly commended** in the UK Press Awards.* THESAURUS PRAISE
2 to tell someone that something is good or that it deserves attention SYN **recommend**: *Colleagues, I commend this report to you.* | *McKellen's performance **had much to commend it*** (=was very good).
3 commend itself (to sb) *formal* if something commends itself to you, you approve of it: *The plan did not commend itself to the Allies.*

com·mend·a·ble /kəˈmendəbəl/ *adj formal* deserving praise: *Your enthusiasm is **highly commendable**.* | *Baldwin answered with commendable honesty.* —**commendably** *adv*

com·men·da·tion /ˌkɒmənˈdeɪʃən $ ˌkɑː-/ *n* [C,U] *formal* an official statement praising someone, especially someone who has been brave or very successful

com·men·su·rate /kəˈmenʃərət/ *adj* matching something in size, quality, or length of time: **[+with]** *Salary will be commensurate with age and experience.*

com·ment¹ /ˈkɒment $ ˈkɑː-/ ●●● S1 W2 AWL *n*
1 [C,U] an opinion that you express about someone or something SYN **remark**: **[+on/about]** *his comments about asylum seekers | He was fined for making abusive comments to the referee.* | **no comment** (=used by people in public life when they do not want to answer questions)
2 [U] criticism or discussion of something someone has said or done: *The speech received much comment in the press.*
3 be a comment on sth to be a sign of the bad quality of something: *The number of adults who cannot read is **a sad comment on** the quality of our schools.*

COLLOCATIONS

VERBS

make a comment *Everyone was making appreciative comments about the delicious food.*
have a comment (=want to make a comment) *Do you have any comments on that, David?*
pass (a) comment *BrE* (=give an opinion) *He looked at my photos but he didn't pass comment.*
invite comment(s) (=ask people to give an opinion) *The website invites comments from people who visit it.*
welcome comments (=be glad to hear people's opinions) | **receive comments**

ADJECTIVES

a brief/quick comment *I just want to make a very brief comment.*
a helpful/constructive comment (=one that helps you make progress) *Pay close attention to your teacher's constructive comments.*
a positive/negative comment *There were some very positive comments in the report.*
a critical comment *The school has received critical comments from inspectors.*
(a) fair comment (=a criticism that is reasonable) *I accepted as fair comment 90% of what he said.*
a snide comment (=unkind and made in a secret or indirect way) | **a disparaging/derogatory comment** (=criticizing someone or something in an unpleasant way) | **an appreciative comment** (=showing that you think something is good or nice) | **a sarcastic comment** (=in which you say the opposite of what you mean, as an unkind joke) | **a passing comment** (=a quick comment made without thinking about it very carefully)

THESAURUS

comment something that you say or write in order to give your opinion: *Does anyone have any comments? | Readers are invited to send in their comments and suggestions.*
remark something that you say: *Just ignore them if they start making rude remarks. | I'm not sure what he meant by that last remark.*
point something that someone mentions about a subject in a discussion, argument, article etc: *That's an interesting point, Steve. | He raises* (=mentions) *a number of important points in his paper.*
observation a comment in which you say what you think or have noticed about something: *Karl Marx made the observation that history repeats itself first as tragedy, second as farce.*
aside a comment made in a low voice, that you intend only certain people to hear: *'Is that true?' she whispered in an aside to Don.*
quip /kwɪp/ a clever and amusing comment: *She knew she should reply with some light-hearted quip.*
dig *informal* a comment you make to annoy or criticize someone: *I'm tired of her little digs at me.*
taunt /tɔːnt $ tɒːnt/ a comment intended to make someone angry or upset: *The fans made racist taunts throughout the game.*

comment² ●●○ S3 W3 AWL *v* [I,T] to express an opinion about someone or something SYN **remark**: **[+on]** *People were always commenting on his size.* | **comment that** *Smith's lawyer commented that the decision was 'outrageous'.* THESAURUS ▸ SAY

com·men·ta·ry /ˈkɒməntəri $ ˈkɑːmənteri/ ●●○ AWL *n* (*plural* **commentaries**) [C,U]
1 a spoken description of an event, given while the event is happening, especially on the television or radio: *Commentary is by Tom Ferris.* | **[+on]** *We'll be bringing you full commentary on the game between Notts and Brescia.* | **running commentary** (=a continuous description of something)
2 something such as a book or an article that explains or discusses a book, poem, idea etc: *political commentary*
3 be a sad/tragic/devastating etc commentary on sth to be a sign of how bad a particular situation is: *The incident was a sad commentary on British football.*

com·men·tate /ˈkɒmənteɪt $ ˈkɑː-/ *v* [I + on] to describe an event such as a sports game on television or radio

com·men·ta·tor /ˈkɒmənteɪtə $ ˈkɑːmənteɪtər/ ●●○ AWL *n* [C]
1 someone who knows a lot about a particular subject, and who writes about it or discusses it on the television or radio: *political commentators*
2 someone on television or radio who describes an event as it is happening: *a **sports commentator***

com·merce /ˈkɒmɜːs $ ˈkɑːmɜːrs/ ●●○ *n* [U] the buying and selling of goods and services SYN **trade**: *measures promoting local commerce and industry* → CHAMBER OF COMMERCE, E-COMMERCE

com·mer·cial¹ /kəˈmɜːʃəl $ -ɜːr-/ ●●○ S3 W3 *adj*
1 related to business and the buying and selling of goods and services: *Our top priorities must be profit and commercial growth.*
2 related to the ability of a product or business to make a profit: *Gibbons failed to see the commercial value of his discovery.* | **commercial success/failure** *The film was a huge commercial success.*
3 [only before noun] a commercial product is one that is produced and sold in large quantities
4 more concerned with money than with quality: *Their music has become very commercial.*
5 commercial radio/TV/channel etc radio or television broadcasts that are produced by companies that earn money through advertising

commercial² ●●○ *n*
1 [C] an advertisement on television or radio: *a soap powder commercial* THESAURUS ▸ ADVERTISEMENT
2 commercial break the time when advertisements are broadcast during a television or radio programme

com·mer·cial·is·m /kəˈmɜːʃəlɪzəm $ -ɜːr-/ *n* [U] the principle or practice of being more concerned with making money from buying and selling goods than you are about their quality – used to show disapproval: *the commercialism of modern culture*

com·mer·cial·ize (*also* **-ise** *BrE*) /kəˈmɜːʃəlaɪz $ -ɜːr-/ *v* [T] **1** to be more concerned with making money from something than about its quality – used to show disapproval: *Christmas has become so commercialized.* GRAMMAR **Commercialize** is usually passive in this meaning. **2** to sell something completely new to the public for the first time: *Some space launches will be commercialized to help pay for more space research.* —**commercialization** /kəˌmɜːʃəlaɪˈzeɪʃən $ -ˌmɜːrʃələ-/ *n* [U]

com·mer·cial·ly /kəˈmɜːʃəli $ -ɜːr-/ ●○○ *adv*
1 considering whether a business or product is making a profit: *The project is no longer **commercially viable*** (=certain to make money). | [sentence adverb] *Commercially, the movie was a flop.*
2 produced or used in large quantities as a business: *commercially farmed land*
3 if a new product is commercially available, you can buy it in shops: *the world's first commercially available 3-D computer screen*

C

com,mercial 'traveller *n* [C] *BrE old-fashioned* someone who travels from place to place selling goods for a company SYN **sales representative**

com·mie /ˈkɒmi $ ˈkɑː-/ *n* [C] *informal* an insulting word for a COMMUNIST

com·min·gle /kəˈmɪŋgəl/ *v* **1** [I,T] *formal* to mix together, or to make different things do this: *Many towns allow recyclable items to be commingled for collection in a single container.* **2** [T] *AmE technical* if a financial organization commingles money, it mixes its own money with money that belongs to its customers or to another part of the business, usually in an illegal way: **commingle sth with sth** *The company faces charges that it commingled its own funds with customer funds.* —**commingling** *n* [U]

C

com·mis·e·rate /kəˈmɪzəreɪt/ *v* [I + with] *formal* to express your sympathy for someone who is unhappy about something

com·mis·e·ra·tion /kəˌmɪzəˈreɪʃən/ *n* [plural, U] *formal* a feeling of sympathy for someone when something unpleasant has happened to them: *Congratulations to the winners, commiserations to the losers.* → CONDOLENCE

com·mis·sar·i·at /ˌkɒməˈseəriət $ ˌkɑːməˈser-/ *n* [C] a military department that is responsible for supplying food

com·mis·sa·ry /ˈkɒməsəri $ ˈkɑːməseri/ *n* (*plural* **commissaries**) [C] **1** *BrE* an officer in the army who is in charge of food supplies **2** *AmE* a shop that supplies food and other goods in a military camp **3** *AmE* a place where you can eat in a large organization such as a film STUDIO, factory etc

com·mis·sion[1] /kəˈmɪʃən/ ●●○ S3 W3 *n*

1 [C] a group of people who have been given the official job of finding out about something or controlling something: *The Government **set up** a **commission** to investigate allegations of police violence.* | **[+on]** *the Royal Commission on Environmental Pollution*

2 [C,U] an extra amount of money that is paid to a person or organization according to the value of the goods they have sold or the services they have provided: *The dealer takes a 20% commission on the sales he makes.* | **on commission** *He sold cosmetics on commission.*

3 [C] a request for an artist, designer, or musician to make a piece of art or music, for which they are paid: *a commission from the Academy for a new sculpture*

4 [C] the position of an officer in the army, navy etc

5 [U] *formal* the commission of a crime is the act of doing it → **commit**

6 out of commission a) not working or not available for use: *One of the ship's anchors was out of commission.* **b)** *informal* ill or injured, and unable to work

7 in commission available to be used: *The operating theatres will be back in commission next week.*

commission[2] ●○○ AWL *v*

1 [T] to formally ask someone to write an official report, produce a work of art for you etc: *The report was commissioned by the Welsh Office.* | **commission sb to do sth** *Macmillan commissioned her to illustrate a book by Spike Milligan.*

2 be commissioned (into sth) to be given an officer's rank in the army, navy etc: *I was commissioned into the RAF.*

com·mis·sion·aire /kəˌmɪʃəˈneə $ -ˈner/ *n* [C] *BrE* someone whose job is to stand at the entrance to a hotel or theatre wearing a uniform and help people SYN **doorman**

com,missioned 'officer *n* [C] a military officer who has a commission

com·mis·sion·er /kəˈmɪʃənə $ -ər/ ●○○ *n* [C]

1 someone who is officially in charge of a government department in some countries

2 the head of the police department in some parts of the US

3 a member of a commission

com,missioner for 'oaths *n* [C] *BrE* a lawyer who may legally be a WITNESS to particular legal documents

com·mit /kəˈmɪt/ ●●● S2 W2 *v* (**committed, committing**)

1 CRIME [T] to do something wrong or illegal: *Women **commit** fewer **crimes** than men.* | **commit murder/rape/arson etc** *Brady committed a series of brutal murders.*

2 commit suicide to kill yourself deliberately

3 commit adultery if a married person commits adultery, they have sex with someone who is not their husband or wife

4 SAY YOU WILL DO STH [I,T] to say that someone will definitely do something or must do something: **commit sb to doing sth** *He has clearly committed his government to continuing down the path of economic reform.* | **commit sb to sth** *Meeting them doesn't commit us to anything.* | **commit yourself** *I'd committed myself and there was no turning back.* | **commit yourself to (doing) sth** *The banks have committed themselves to boosting profits by slashing costs.*

5 RELATIONSHIP [I,T] to give someone your love or support in a serious and permanent way: *Anna wants to get married, but Bob's not sure he wants to commit.* | **[+to]** *He has not yet committed to any of the candidates.*

6 MONEY/TIME [T] to decide to use money, time, people etc for a particular purpose: **commit sth to sth** *A lot of money has been committed to this project.*

7 FOR TRIAL [T] *BrE* to send someone to be tried in a court of law: *The two men **were committed for trial** at Bristol Crown Court.*

8 PRISON/HOSPITAL [T] to order someone to be put in a hospital or prison: **commit sb to sth** *The judge committed him to prison for six months.*

9 commit sth to memory *formal* to learn something so that you remember it SYN **memorize**

10 commit sth to paper *formal* to write something down

→ COMMITTED

com·mit·ment /kəˈmɪtmənt/ ●●○ S3 W2 *n*

1 [C] a promise to do something or to behave in a particular way: *Are you ready to **make** a long-term **commitment**?* | **[+to]** *Our company has a commitment to quality and customer service.*

2 [U] the hard work and loyalty that someone gives to an organization, activity etc: *I was impressed by the energy and commitment shown by the players.* | **[+to]** *Her commitment to work is beyond question.*

3 [C] something that you have promised you will do or that you have to do: *Will the job fit in with your **family commitments**?*

4 [C] an amount of money that you have to pay regularly: *I had a lot of financial commitments.*

5 [C,U] the use of money, time, people etc for a particular purpose: *commitments of food and medical aid of over $4 billion*

com·mit·tal /kəˈmɪtl/ *n* [C,U] **1** the process in which a court sends someone to a mental hospital or prison **2** *formal* the burying or CREMATING of a dead person

com·mit·ted /kəˈmɪtɪd/ ●○○ *adj* willing to work very hard at something SYN **dedicated**: *The party has a core of committed supporters.* | **[+to]** *We are fully committed to Equal Opportunity policies.*

com·mit·tee /kəˈmɪti/ ●●● S3 W1 *n* [C] a group of people chosen to do a particular job, make decisions etc: **[+of]** *the International Committee of the Red Cross* | **[+on]** *a ministerial committee on security affairs* | **on a committee** *He's on the finance committee.* | *a committee meeting*

GRAMMAR: Singular or plural verb?

- **Committee** is usually followed by a singular verb: *The management committee **meets** regularly.*
- In British English, you can also use a plural verb: *The management committee **meet** regularly.*

GRAMMAR GUIDE ▶ NOUNS

COLLOCATIONS

VERBS

a committee meets (=has a meeting) *The environmental health committee will meet again next Wednesday.*

be on a committee (=be a member of a committee) *I was on the parents' committee at my kids' school.*

serve/sit on a committee (=be a member of an

important committee) *Our organization is always in need of volunteers to serve on the committee.*
chair a committee (=be the person in charge of a committee) *Professor Peacock was appointed to chair the committee.*
appoint/set up/form a committee | join a committee

committee + NOUN

a committee meeting *There's a committee meeting once a month.*
a committee member *Four committee members did not attend the meeting.*
the committee chairman/chair

ADJECTIVES/NOUN + committee

a special committee *A special committee of scientists was set up to study the disease.*
an executive committee (=that manages an organization and makes decisions for it) *He sat on the firm's Executive Committee.*
an advisory committee | a standing committee (=a permanent one) | **a joint committee** (=involving two or more groups) | **a steering committee** (=one that directs a particular activity) | **a select committee** (=one of politicians and advisers who look at a particular subject) | **a management committee | a government/departmental/ministerial committee | a planning committee** *BrE* (=one that considers requests to build new buildings) | **the finance/education etc committee**

com·mode /kəˈməʊd $ -ˈmoʊd/ *n* [C] **1** a piece of furniture shaped like a chair that can be used as a toilet **2** an old-fashioned piece of furniture with drawers or shelves **3** *AmE* a word meaning 'toilet' used by people who do not like saying 'toilet'

com·mod·i·fi·ca·tion /kəˌmɒdɪfɪˈkeɪʃən $ kəˌmɑː-/ *n* [U] *formal* a process by which something starts being sold for money, or its importance starts being measured according to its value in money – usually used showing disapproval: *the commodification of art*

com·mo·di·ous /kəˈməʊdiəs $ -ˈmoʊ-/ *adj formal* a house or room that is commodious is very big

com·mod·i·ty /kəˈmɒdəti $ kəˈmɑː-/ ●○○ *n* (*plural* **commodities**) [C]
1 a product that is bought and sold: *agricultural commodities | Commodity prices fell sharply.* THESAURUS PRODUCT
2 *formal* a useful quality or thing: *Time is a precious commodity.*

com·mo·dore /ˈkɒmədɔː $ ˈkɑːmədɔːr/ *n* [C] **1** a high rank in the navy, or someone who has this rank **2** the CAPTAIN in charge of a group of ships that are carrying goods

com·mon[1] /ˈkɒmən $ ˈkɑː-/ ●●● S1 W1 *adj*
1 HAPPENING OFTEN happening often and to many people or in many places OPP **rare**: *Heart disease is one of the commonest causes of death.* | **[+among]** *Bad dreams are fairly common among children.* | **it's common for sb to do sth** *It's common for new fathers to feel jealous of the baby.*
⚠ Don't say 'It is common that ... ' Say **'It is common for ... '**: *It is common for children to be afraid (NOT It is common that children are afraid) of the dark.* THESAURUS NORMAL
2 A LOT existing in large numbers OPP **rare**: *Daisies are very common flowers.*
3 SAME/SIMILAR [usually before noun, no comparative] common aims, beliefs, ideas etc are shared by several people or groups: *people working towards a common goal | countries that share a common language* | **[+to]** *a theme that is common to all her novels*
4 common ground facts, features, or beliefs that are shared by people or things that are very different: **[+between]** *There is a great deal of common ground between management and trade unions on this issue.*
5 SHARED BY EVERYONE [no comparative] belonging to or shared by everyone in a society: **[+to]** *These problems are common to all societies. | Joe was chosen as captain* ***by common consent*** (=with everyone's agreement).
6 common knowledge something everyone knows: ***It is common knowledge that*** *travel broadens the mind.*
7 the common good the advantage of everyone: *They work together for the common good.*
8 common practice a usual or accepted way of doing things: *It was common practice for families to attend church together.*
9 ORDINARY [only before noun, no comparative] ordinary and not special in any way: *common salt | The 20th century was called the century of* ***the common man*** (=ordinary people). | *He insists that he is a revolutionary, not a common criminal.*
10 common courtesy/decency/politeness a polite way of behaving that you expect from people: *It would be common courtesy to return their hospitality.*
11 common or garden *BrE* ordinary SYN **garden-variety** *AmE*: *a common or garden dispute*
12 make/find common cause (with/against sb) *formal* to join with other people or groups in order to achieve something: *France and Russia made common cause against Britain.*
13 common touch the ability of someone in a position of power or authority to talk to and understand ordinary people – used to show approval: *He's made it to the top without losing the common touch.*
14 SOCIAL CLASS *BrE old-fashioned* an offensive word used for describing someone from a low social class

THESAURUS

common if something is common, there are a lot of them: *Jones is a very common name in Great Britain. | Foxes are common in the area.*
widespread happening in a lot of places or done by a lot of people: *Racism is much more widespread than people imagine. | the widespread availability of antibiotics*
commonplace [not before noun] *especially written* common in a particular place or time – used especially when saying that this seems surprising or unusual: *Crimes such as robbery are commonplace in big cities. | Expensive foreign cars are commonplace in this Chicago suburb.*
prevalent *formal* common in a place or among a group of people – used especially about illnesses, problems, or ideas: *Flu is most prevalent during the winter months.*
rife /raɪf/ [not before noun] very common – used about illnesses or problems: *AIDS is rife in some parts of the world.*
ubiquitous /juːˈbɪkwɪtəs/ *formal* very common and seen in many different places – often used humorously in written descriptions: *He was carrying the ubiquitous MP3 player.*
sth is everywhere *especially spoken* used when saying that you can see something a lot in many different places: *Images of the dictator were everywhere.*

common[2] ●●○ *n*
1 have sth in common (with sb) to have the same interests, attitudes etc as someone else: *I found I* ***had a lot in common with*** *these people. | four women with almost* ***nothing in common***
2 have sth in common (with sth) if objects or ideas have something in common, they share the same features: *The two games* ***have much in common.***
3 in common with sb/sth in the same way as someone or something else: *In common with a lot of other countries, we're in an economic recession.*
4 [C] a large area of open land in a town or village that people walk or play sport on: *Boston Common*

com·mo·nal·i·ty /ˌkɒməˈnæləti $ ˌkɑː-/ *n* [U] *formal* the fact of having things in common

ˌcommon ˈcold *n* [C] a slight illness in which your throat hurts and it is difficult to breathe normally SYN **cold**

C

ˌcommon ˈcurrency *n* [U] used to say that something is used by a lot of people or accepted by everyone: *Words like 'spliff' and 'blunt' have become common currency.*

ˌcommon deˈnominator *n* [C] **1** an attitude or quality that all the different members of a group have: *The common denominator of both types of novel is the vulnerable threatened heroine.* **2 the lowest common denominator** the least attractive, least intelligent people or features in a situation: *trashy TV programs that appeal to the lowest common denominator* **3** *technical* a number that can be divided exactly by all the DENOMINATORS (=bottom number) in a set of FRACTIONS

com·mon·er /ˈkɒmənə $ ˈkɑːmənər/ *n* [C] someone who is not a member of the NOBILITY

ˈcommon ˌland *n* [U] *BrE* land that belongs to or can be used by everyone living in an area

C

ˌcommon ˈlaw *n* [U] the system of laws that has developed from customs and the decisions of judges rather than from laws made by Parliament → **statute law**

ˈcommon-law *adj* [only before noun] **1 common-law marriage/husband/wife** a relationship that is considered to be a marriage because the man and woman have lived together for a long time **2** according to or related to common law: **common-law rules/courts/rights etc**

com·mon·ly /ˈkɒmənli $ ˈkɑː-/ ●●○ *adv*
1 usually or by most people SYN **widely**: *Sodium chloride is more commonly known as salt.* | *a commonly used industrial chemical*
2 often, in many places, or in large numbers SYN **widely**: *Lung cancer is the most commonly found cancer in men.* | *commonly available software packages*

ˌcommon ˈnoun *n* [C] in grammar, a common noun is any noun that is not the name of a particular person, place, or thing. For example, 'book', 'sugar', and 'stuff' are common nouns. → **proper noun, noun**

com·mon·place¹ /ˈkɒmənpleɪs $ ˈkɑː-/ ●○○ *adj* happening or existing in many places, and therefore not special or unusual: *Car thefts are commonplace in this part of town.* **THESAURUS** COMMON

commonplace² *n* [C usually singular] **1** something that happens or exists in many places, so that it is not unusual: *Women's groups have become a commonplace.* **2** something that has been said so often that it is no longer interesting or original **3 the commonplace** something that is ordinary or boring SYN **the everyday**

ˈcommon room *n* [C] *BrE* a room in a school or college that a group of teachers or students use when they are not teaching or studying

Com·mons /ˈkɒmənz $ ˈkɑː-/ *n* **the Commons** the larger and more powerful of the two parts of the British Parliament, whose members are elected by citizens → **the Lords**: *The Government has a huge majority in the Commons.*

ˌcommon ˈsense ●○○ *n* [U] the ability to behave in a sensible way and make practical decisions: *Use your common sense for once!* | *a common-sense approach to education*

com·mo·tion /kəˈməʊʃən $ -ˈmoʊ-/ *n* [singular, U] sudden noisy activity: *They heard a commotion downstairs.* | *Everyone looked to see what was* ***causing*** *the* ***commotion***.

comms /kɒmz $ kɑːmz/ *n* [plural] *BrE technical* (***communications***) used when talking about computer programs that allow communication between different computers SYN **communications software** *AmE*

com·mu·nal /ˈkɒmjənəl, kəˈmjuːnl $ ˈkɑː-/ ●○○ *adj*
1 shared by a group of people or animals, especially a group who live together: *a communal bathroom*
2 involving people from many different races, religions, or language groups: *the worst communal violence in two years*
3 relating or belonging to all the people living in a particular COMMUNITY: *crops grown on communal land*

com·mune¹ /ˈkɒmjuːn $ ˈkɑː-, kəˈmjuːn/ *n* [C] **1** a group of people who live together and who share the work and their possessions: *a hippie commune* **2** the smallest unit of local government in countries such as France and Belgium **3** a group of people in a Communist country who work as a team on a farm, and give what they produce to the state

com·mune² /kəˈmjuːn/ *v*

commune with sb/sth *phr v formal* **1** to communicate with a person, god, or animal, especially in a mysterious SPIRITUAL way **2 commune with nature** to spend time outside in a natural place, enjoying it in a quiet peaceful way: *Take time to relax and commune with nature.*

com·mu·ni·ca·ble /kəˈmjuːnɪkəbəl/ AWL *adj formal* **1** a communicable disease can be passed on to other people SYN **infectious 2** able to be communicated

com·mu·ni·cant /kəˈmjuːnəkənt/ *n* [C] someone who receives COMMUNION regularly in the Christian Church

com·mu·ni·cate /kəˈmjuːnɪkeɪt/ ●●● S3 W3 AWL *v*
1 EXCHANGE INFORMATION [I,T] to exchange information or conversation with other people, using words, signs, writing etc: *We communicated mostly by e-mail.* | **[+with]** *People use more than words when they communicate with each other.* | **communicate sth to sb** *The decision was communicated to our staff late in 1998.*
2 TELL PEOPLE STH [I,T] to express your thoughts and feelings clearly, so that other people understand them → **convey**: *A baby communicates its needs by crying.* | **communicate sth to sb** *Without meaning to, she communicated her anxiety to her child.* | *His enthusiasm* ***communicated itself*** *to the voters.* | *A teacher must be able to* ***communicate effectively*** *to students.*
3 UNDERSTAND [I] if two people communicate, they are able to talk about and understand each other's feelings or desires: *Many couples make themselves miserable by not communicating.* | **[+with]** *Parents sometimes find it difficult to communicate with their teenage children.*
4 DISEASE [T] to pass a disease from one person or animal to another → **communicable**
GRAMMAR **Communicate** is often passive in this meaning.
5 ROOMS [I] if rooms or parts of a building communicate, you can get directly to one from the other: *communicating doors*

com·mu·ni·ca·tion /kəˌmjuːnɪˈkeɪʃən/ ●●● S2 W1 *n*
1 [U] the process by which people exchange information or express their thoughts and feelings: *Good communication is vital in a large organization.* | *Radio was the pilot's only* ***means of communication***.
2 communications a) [plural] ways of sending information, especially using radio, telephone, or computers: *Modern communications are enabling more people to work from home.* **b)** [plural] roads, railways etc that are used for travelling and sending goods: **[+with]** *Paris has good communications with many European cities.* **c)** [U] the study of using radio, television, cinema etc to communicate: *a diploma in communications*
3 [U] the way people express themselves so that other people will understand: *a week's course in improving* ***communication skills*** | *There has been a* ***breakdown in communication*** (=failure to communicate).
4 be in communication with sb *formal* to talk or write to someone regularly
5 [C] *formal* a letter, message, or telephone call: *a communication from the Ministry of Defence*

comˌmuniˈcation ˌcord *n* [C] *BrE* a chain that a passenger can pull to stop a train in an EMERGENCY (=a sudden dangerous situation)

comˌmuniˈcations ˌsatellite *n* [C] a SATELLITE that is used to send radio, television, and telephone signals around the world

com·mu·ni·ca·tive /kəˈmjuːnəkətɪv $ -keɪtɪv/ AWL *adj* **1** able to talk easily to other people: *Tom wasn't very communicative, and kept himself to himself.* **2** relating to the ability to communicate, especially in a foreign language: *students' communicative skills*

com·mu·ni·ca·tor /kəˈmjuːnəkeɪtə $ -ər/ *n* [C] someone who is able to express ideas or their feelings clearly to other people: *She's a skilled communicator.*

com·mu·nion /kəˈmjuːnjən/ ●○○ *n*
1 Communion [U] (*also* **Holy Communion**) the Christian ceremony in which people eat bread and drink wine as signs of Christ's body and blood
2 [U] *formal* a special relationship with someone or something which makes you feel that you understand them very well: **[+with]** *Prayer is a form of communion with God.*
3 [C] *formal* a group of people or organizations that share the same religious beliefs SYN **denomination**: *He belongs to the Anglican communion.*

com·mu·ni·qué /kəˈmjuːnəkeɪ $ kəˌmjuːnəˈkeɪ/ *n* [C] an official report or announcement: *A* ***communiqué*** *was* ***issued*** *by NATO Defence Ministers.*

com·mu·nis·m, **Communism** /ˈkɒmjənɪzəm $ ˈkɑː-/ ●●○ *n* [U]
1 a political system in which the government controls the production of all food and goods, and there is no privately owned property → **capitalism**, **socialism**
2 the belief in this political system

com·mu·nist[1], **Communist** /ˈkɒmjənɪst $ ˈkɑː-/ ●●○ *n* [C] someone who is a member of a political party that supports communism, or who believes in communism → **capitalist**, **socialist**

communist[2], **Communist** *adj* relating to communism → **capitalist**, **socialist**: *a* ***communist country*** | *a* ***communist regime***

com·mu·ni·ty /kəˈmjuːnəti/ ●●● S1 W1 *n* (*plural* **communities**)
1 [C] the people who live in the same area, town etc: *The new arts centre will serve the whole community.* | ***community education*** *programmes* | **community relations/affairs/needs etc** *We meet once a month to discuss community problems.* | **community groups/leaders etc** *Community leaders met to discuss the proposed golf course.* | **community spirit** (=the desire to be friendly with and help other people who live in the same community)
2 [C] a group of people who have the same interests, religion, race etc: *different* ***ethnic communities*** | **the gay/black/Asian etc community** *the gay community in San Francisco* | **the business/academic/scientific etc community**
3 the community society and the people in it: *The trend is towards reintegrating mentally ill people into the community.* | **the international community** (=all the countries of the world) *The president appealed to the international community for aid for the flood victims.*
4 sense of community the feeling that you belong to a community
5 [C] a group of plants or animals that live in the same environment: *Communities of otters are slowly returning to British rivers.*

GRAMMAR: Singular or plural verb?
• **Community** is usually followed by a singular verb: *The whole community* ***gets*** *involved in planning the festival.*
• In British English, you can also use a plural verb: *The whole community* ***get*** *involved in planning the festival.*
GRAMMAR GUIDE ▸ NOUNS

comˈmunity ˌcentre *BrE*, **community center** *AmE* *n* [C] a place where people from the same area can go for social events, classes etc

comˈmunity ˌchest *n* [C] *AmE old-fashioned* money that is collected by the people and businesses in an area to help poor people

comˈmunity ˌcollege *n* [C] **1** a SECONDARY SCHOOL in the UK that students from the local area can go to, and which also has classes for adults **2** a college in the US that students can go to for two years in order to learn a skill or prepare for university SYN **junior college**

comˌmunity poˈlicing *n* [U] the practice by the police of trying to build good relationships with the people in the area where they work

comˈmunity ˌproperty *n* [U] *law* property that is considered to be owned equally by both a husband and wife in US law

comˌmunity ˈservice *n* [U] work that is not paid that someone does to help other people, sometimes as punishment for a crime

comˌmunity supˈport ˌofficer *n* [C] *BrE* a type of police officer in Britain who does some police work but does not have all the powers of an ordinary police officer

com·mu·ta·tion /ˌkɒmjəˈteɪʃən $ ˌkɑː-/ *n* [C,U] *law* a reduction in how severe a punishment is: *Activists campaigned for a commutation of Lee's sentence.*

com·mute[1] /kəˈmjuːt/ ●●○ *v*
1 [I] to regularly travel a long distance to get to work: **[+to/from/between]** *Jim commutes to Manhattan every day.* THESAURUS ▸ TRAVEL
2 commute a sentence (to sth) *technical* to change the punishment given to a criminal to one that is less severe: *Baldry's 20-year prison sentence was commuted to three years.*
3 commute sth for/into sth *technical* to exchange one thing, especially one kind of payment, for another: *He commuted his pension for a lump sum.*

commute[2] *n* [C usually singular] the journey to work every day: *My morning commute takes 45 minutes.* THESAURUS ▸ JOURNEY

com·mut·er /kəˈmjuːtə $ -ər/ ●●○ *n* [C] someone who travels a long distance to work every day THESAURUS ▸ TRAVEL

comˈmuter ˌbelt *n* [C] *BrE* an area around a large city, from which many people travel to work every day

comp[1] /kɒmp $ kɑːmp/ *n* [C] *informal* **1** *AmE* a ticket for a play, sports game etc that is given away free **2** *BrE* a COMPREHENSIVE SCHOOL

comp[2] *v* [T] *AmE spoken* to give something, such as a ticket, away free

com·pact[1] /kəmˈpækt, ˈkɒmpækt $ kəmˈpækt/ ●●○ *adj*
1 small, but arranged so that everything fits neatly into the space available – used to show approval: *The compact design of the machine allows it to be stored easily.* | *The students' rooms were compact, with a desk, bed, and closet built in.* THESAURUS ▸ SMALL
2 packed or put together firmly and closely: *The bushes grew in a compact mass.*
3 small, but solid and strong: *a short compact-looking man* —**compactly** *adv* —**compactness** *n* [U]

com·pact[2] /ˈkɒmpækt $ ˈkɑːm-/ *n* [C] **1** a small flat container with a mirror, containing powder for a woman's face **2** a COMPACT CAMERA **3** *AmE* a small car **4** *formal* an agreement between countries or people: *A compact was negotiated between the company and the union.*

com·pact[3] /kəmˈpækt/ *v* [T] to press something together so that it becomes smaller or more solid: *compacted earth*

ˌcompact ˈcamera *n* [C] a small camera with a LENS that cannot be removed

ˌcompact ˈdisc *n* [C,U] (*abbreviation* **CD**) a small circular piece of hard plastic on which high-quality recorded sound or large quantities of information can be stored: *The new album is available on vinyl, cassette, or compact disc.*

ˌcompact ˈdisc ˌplayer *n* [C] a CD PLAYER

Com·pact·Flash /ˌkɒmpæktˈflæʃ $ ˌkɑːm-/ *n* [U] *trademark* a MEMORY CARD for DIGITAL CAMERAS that allows you to take high-quality photographs of things that are moving

com·pan·ion /kəmˈpænjən/ ●●○ *n* [C]
1 someone you spend a lot of time with, especially a friend: *For ten years he had been her* ***constant companion.*** | *His dog became his* ***closest companion.*** | *a* ***travelling companion*** | **dinner/drinking companion** THESAURUS ▸ FRIEND
2 one of a pair of things that go together or can be used together: **[+to]** *This book is a companion to Professor Farrer's first work.* | **companion volume/piece etc** *The*

'Encyclopedia of Gardening' is a companion volume to the 'Encyclopedia of Plants and Flowers'.
3 used in the titles of books about a particular subject: *'A Companion to Japanese Literature'*
4 someone, especially a woman, who is paid to live or travel with an older person

com·pan·ion·a·ble /kəmˈpænjənəbəl/ *adj literary* friendly and pleasant to be with: *They sat together in* ***companionable silence***. —**companionably** *adv*

com·pan·ion·ship /kəmˈpænjənʃɪp/ *n* [U] when you are with someone you enjoy being with, and are not alone: *When Stan died, I missed his companionship.*

com·pan·ion·way /kəmˈpænjənweɪ/ *n* [C] *technical* the steps going from one DECK (=level) of a ship to another deck

C

com·pa·ny /ˈkʌmpəni/ ●●● S1 W1 *n* (*plural* **companies**)
1 BUSINESS [C] a business organization that makes or sells goods or services SYN **business**, **firm**: *Which company do you work for?* | *I called the phone company about the bill.* | *The company was set up just after the war.* | *The company directors have awarded themselves a massive pay increase.*

GRAMMAR: Singular or plural verb?

- In this meaning, **company** is usually followed by a singular verb: *The company* ***makes*** *machine parts.*
- In British English, you can also use a plural verb: *The company* ***make*** *machine parts.*

GRAMMAR GUIDE ▸ NOUNS

2 OTHER PEOPLE [U] when you are with other people and not alone: *The two men* ***enjoy*** *each other's* ***company***. | *Rita's husband is away for the week, so I thought I'd go over and* ***keep*** *her* ***company*** (=be with her so that she doesn't feel lonely). | *Come over for dinner – I* ***could use the company*** (=would like to be with other people). | *James* ***is good company*** (=is a cheerful person who is enjoyable to be with). | **as company** *Bessie was glad to have the dog as company.* | **in sb's company** (=with someone) *I felt nervous in the company of such an important man.* | **in company with sb** (=together with another person or group) *He's performing in company with saxophonist Ernie Watts.*
3 GUESTS [U] people who are visiting you in your home: *It looks like the Hammills* ***have company***. | *We're* ***expecting company*** *this evening.*
4 FRIENDS [U] your friends or the group of people you spend time with: *People judge you by* ***the company*** *you* ***keep*** (=the people you spend time with). | *Things began to go wrong when he got into* ***bad company***.
5 PERFORMERS [C] a group of actors, dancers, or singers who work together: *a* ***theatre company*** | *a* ***touring company*** | *the Kirov Ballet Company* THESAURUS ▸ ACTOR
6 be in good company used to tell someone who has made a mistake that they should not be embarrassed because some important or respected people have made the same mistake: *If you can't program the video recorder, you're in good company.*
7 GROUP [U] *formal* a group of people who are together in the same place, often for a particular purpose or for social reasons: *He glanced around at the* ***assembled company***. | *Some jokes are just not appropriate to tell* ***in mixed company*** (=in a group of both men and women). | **in company** (=when surrounded by other people, especially at a social occasion) *Parents should teach their children how to behave in company.*
8 sb and company *informal* used after a person's name to mean that person and their friends: *This has not stopped Senator Biden and company from trying to make it an issue in the election.*
9 ARMY [C] a group of about 120 soldiers who are usually part of a larger group
10 two's company, three's a crowd used to suggest that two people would rather be alone together than have other people with them → **part company** at PART²(4), → **present company excepted** at PRESENT¹(6)

COLLOCATIONS

ADJECTIVES/NOUN + company

a computer/phone/oil etc company *an international oil company*
a manufacturing/shipping/publishing etc company *I'm working for a printing company at the moment.*
a large/big company *She has a senior position in a large manufacturing company.*
a small company | **an international company** (=with offices in different countries) | **a multinational company** (=with offices in many countries) | **a private company** (=not owned by the government) | **a state-owned company** (=owned by the government) | **a public/listed company** (=offering its shares for sale on the stock exchange) | **a limited company** (=one whose owners only have to pay a limited amount if it gets into debt) | **a subsidiary company** (=owned or controlled by a larger company) | **the parent company** (=the one that owns or controls a smaller one)

VERBS

work for a company *How long have you been working for your present company?*
join a company (=become an employee) *I joined the company ten years ago.*
run/manage a company *Nick runs a property company.*
set up/start/form a company *Two years later he started his own software company.*
found/establish a company *The company was founded in 1993 by William J. Nutt.*
take over a company (=buy it and run it) | **a company grows/expands** | **a company goes bankrupt/goes out of business** (=stops doing business after losing too much money) | **a company fails** (=goes bankrupt) | **a company goes bust** *informal* (=goes bankrupt)

company + NOUN

company policy *It is not company policy to give that information.*
a company director/executive | **a company car** (=that your company gives you to use)

THESAURUS

company an organization that makes or sells something, or provides a service: *big oil companies* | *He runs a software company.*
firm a company, especially one that provides a service rather than producing goods: *a law firm* | *a firm of accountants* | *a security firm*
business a company – often used when talking about a company that employs only a small number of people: *She set up her own catering business.* | *small businesses* | *a family business*
corporation a large company that often includes several smaller companies: *IBM is one of the biggest corporations in the world.*
multinational a very large company with offices in many different countries: *American multinationals are establishing research and development facilities across the developing world.*
conglomerate /kənˈglɒmərət $ -ˈglɑː-/ a very large company that consists of several different companies which have joined together: *The company was taken over by a German media conglomerate.*
giant a word used mainly by newspapers for a very large company: *Their clients include the retail giant, Wal-Mart.*
subsidiary a company that is owned by a larger company: *The company runs its New York operations through a US subsidiary.*

ˌcompany ˈcar *n* [C] a car that your employer gives you while you work for them

ˌ**company 'law** *n* [U] *law* the laws relating to the way in which companies operate

ˌ**company 'secretary** *n* (*plural* **company secretaries**) [C] someone with a high position in a company who deals with ADMINISTRATIVE and legal matters

com·pa·ra·ble /'kɒmpərəbəl $ 'kɑːm-/ ●○○ *adj*
1 similar to something else in size, number, quality etc, so that you can make a comparison → **compare**, **comparison**: *A car of* ***comparable size*** *would cost far more abroad.* | **comparable figures/data/results** *comparable figures for the same period of time last year* | **[+with/to]** *Pluto is* ***comparable in size*** *to the Moon.*
2 being equally important, good, bad etc OPP **incomparable**: *These two artists just aren't comparable.* | **[+with/to]** *His poetry is hardly comparable with Shakespeare's.* —**comparability** /ˌkɒmpərə'bɪləti $ ˌkɑːm-/ *n* [U]

com·pa·ra·bly /'kɒmpərəbli $ 'kɑːm-/ *adv* in a similar way or to a similar degree OPP **incomparably**: *comparably priced products*

com·par·a·tive[1] /kəm'pærətɪv/ ●○○ *adj*
1 comparative comfort/freedom/wealth etc comfort, freedom, wealth etc that is quite good when compared to how comfortable, free, or rich etc something or someone else is SYN **relative**: *After a lifetime of poverty, his last few years were spent in comparative comfort.* | *She didn't want to leave the* ***comparative safety*** *of the shelter.*
2 comparative study/analysis etc a study etc that involves comparing something to something else: *a comparative study of the US and British steel industries*
3 comparative beginner/newcomer etc someone who is not really a beginner etc, but who seems to be one when compared to other people who have lived or worked somewhere for a long time: *After living here five years, we're still considered comparative newcomers.*
4 comparative figures/data comparative figures etc are similar to other figures, so that you can make a comparison: *Comparative figures for last year clearly show how sales have declined.*
5 *technical* the comparative form of an adjective or adverb shows an increase in size, quality, degree etc when it is considered in relation to something else. For example, 'bigger' is the comparative form of 'big', and 'more slowly' is the comparative form of 'slowly'. → **superlative**

comparative[2] *n* **the comparative** *technical* the form of an adjective or adverb that shows an increase in size, degree etc when something is considered in relation to something else. For example, 'bigger' is the comparative of 'big', and 'more slowly' is the comparative of 'slowly'. → **the superlative**

com·par·a·tive·ly /kəm'pærətəvli/ ●○○ *adv* as compared to something else or to a previous state SYN **relatively**: *a* ***comparatively small*** *number of people* | ***Comparatively few*** *books have been written on the subject.* | *Crime on the island is* ***comparatively rare***. | ***Comparatively speaking***, *this part of the coast is still unspoiled.*

com·pare[1] /kəm'peə $ -'per/ ●●● S1 W1 *v*
1 [T] to consider two or more things or people, in order to show how they are similar or different → **comparison**: *The report compares the different types of home computer available.* | **compare sth/sb with sth/sb** *The police compared the suspect's fingerprints with those found at the crime scene.* | **compare sth/sb to sth/sb** *Davies' style of writing has been compared to Dickens'.* | **compare and contrast** (=an expression used when telling students to write about the things that are similar or different in works of literature or art) *Compare and contrast the main characters of these two novels.*
2 compared to/with sth used when considering the size, quality, or amount of something in relation to something similar: *a 20% reduction in burglary compared with last year* | *Compared to our small flat, Bill's house seemed like a palace.*
3 [I] to be better or worse than something else: **compare (favourably/unfavourably) with sth** *The quality of English wines can now compare with wines from Germany.* | *How does life in Britain compare with life in the States?* | *The imported fabric is 30% cheaper and compares favourably* (=is as good) *in quality.*
4 sth doesn't/can't compare (with sth) if something does not compare with something else, it is not as good, large etc: *The rides at the fair just can't compare with the rides at Disneyland.*
5 compare notes (with sb) *informal* to talk to someone in order to find out if their experience of something is the same as yours: *Leading scientists got together in Paris to compare notes on current research.*

THESAURUS

compare to consider two or more things or people, in order to show how they are similar or different: *Scientists compared the results of both experiments.*
make/draw a comparison to compare two or more things or people and say how they are similar: *In her article, she makes a comparison between people's lives now and 50 years ago.* | *It is possible to draw a comparison between the two poets' work.*
draw an analogy to say that two situations are similar – a rather formal use: *Some people have attempted to draw an analogy between America's invasion of Iraq and the war in Vietnam.*
draw a parallel to say that some features of things are similar, especially things that are actually very different – a rather formal use: *He draws a parallel between football and religion.*
contrast to compare two things, situations etc, in order to show how they are different from each other: *In her novel she contrasts the lives of two families in very different circumstances.*
make/draw a distinction between to say that you think two things are very different: *The author draws a distinction between allowing death to occur, and causing it.*
measure sb/sth against sb/sth to compare two people or things, in order to judge which is better, bigger etc: *As a young actress, she was nervous of being measured against her famous father.*

compare[2] *n* **beyond/without compare** *literary* a quality that is beyond compare is the best of its kind: *a beauty and an elegance beyond compare*

com·pa·ri·son /kəm'pærəsən/ ●●○ W2 *n*
1 COMPARING [U] the process of comparing two or more people or things → **compare**, **comparative**: **[+with]** *Comparison with his previous movies shows how Lee has developed as a director.* | **in comparison (with/to sth)** *In comparison to other recent video games, this one isn't very exciting.* | *He was a loud friendly man. In comparison, his brother was rather shy.* | **by comparison (with sth)** *By comparison with other European countries, car prices in the UK are very high.* | *After months of living in a tropical climate, Spain seemed cool by comparison.* | **for comparison (with sth)** *These figures are provided for comparison with the results of previous studies.* | *He showed us the original text for comparison.* | *Her paintings* ***invite comparison*** *with those of the early Impressionists* (=they remind you of them). | **stand/bear comparison** (=is as good as someone or something else) *Irving's work bears comparison with the best of the modern novelists.* | **on comparison** *BrE* (=after you have compared two things to see if they are similar or different) *On comparison, the Renault was the more reliable of the two cars.*
2 JUDGMENT [C] a statement or examination of how similar or different two people or things are: **[+of]** *a comparison of pollution levels in Chicago and Detroit* | **[+between]** *The article* ***makes*** *a* ***comparison*** *between the two poems.*

REGISTER

In written English, people often use **draw a comparison** rather than **make a comparison**, as it sounds more formal: *The writer* ***draws a comparison*** *between the 1950s and the present day.*

C

3 BE LIKE STH [C] a statement that someone or something is like someone or something else: **(make/draw) a comparison between sb/sth** (=show the similarities between two people or things) *The writer draws comparisons between the two presidents.* | *You can't make a comparison between American and Japanese schools – they're too different.*
4 **there's no comparison** *spoken* used when you think that someone or something is much better than someone or something else: **[+between]** *There's just no comparison between canned vegetables and fresh ones.*
5 GRAMMAR [U] a word used in grammar meaning the way an adverb or adjective changes its form to show whether it is COMPARATIVE or SUPERLATIVE

C

com'parison-ˌshop *v* [I] to go to different shops in order to compare the prices of things, so that you can buy things for the cheapest possible price —**comparison shopping** *n* [U]

com·part·ment /kəmˈpɑːtmənt $ -ɑːr-/ ●○○ *n* [C]
1 a smaller enclosed space inside something larger: *The bag is divided into* ***separate compartments***. | ***engine compartment*** | *She kept the money hidden in a secret compartment in her briefcase.* → GLOVE COMPARTMENT
2 one of the separate areas into which a plane, ship, or train is divided: *a* ***first-class compartment***

com·part·men·tal·ize (*also* **-ise** *BrE*) /ˌkɒmpɑːtˈmentl-aɪz $ kəmˌpɑːrt-/ *v* [T] to divide something into separate areas or groups: *Women are better than men at compartmentalizing their lives.* —**compartmentalized** *adj* —**compartmentalization** /ˌkɒmpɑːtˌmentl-aɪˈzeɪʃən $ kəmˌpɑːrtmentl-ə-/ *n* [U]

com·pass /ˈkʌmpəs/ ●○○ *n*
1 [C] an instrument that shows directions and has a needle that always points north: *a map and compass* | **compass points/points of the compass** (=the marks on a compass that show you north, south, east, west etc)
2 [C] (*also* **compasses**) a V-shaped instrument with one sharp point and a pen or pencil at the other end, used for drawing circles or measuring distances on maps
3 [U] *formal* the area or range of subjects that someone is responsible for or that is discussed in a book: **[+of]** *Within the brief compass of a single page, the author covers most of the major points.*

COMPASS
compass
compass/ compasses

com·pas·sion /kəmˈpæʃən/ ●●○ *n* [U] a strong feeling of sympathy for someone who is suffering, and a desire to help them: **[+for]** *compassion for the sick* | **feel/show/have compassion** *Did he feel any compassion for the victim of his crime?* | **with compassion** *Lieberman explores this sensitive topic with compassion.* | *I was shocked by the doctor's* ***lack of compassion***.

com·pas·sion·ate /kəmˈpæʃənət/ ●○○ *adj* feeling sympathy for people who are suffering: *a caring compassionate man* | *I allowed him to go home* ***on compassionate grounds***. | *One measure of a civilized and compassionate society is how well it treats its prison population.* THESAURUS SYMPATHETIC —**compassionately** *adv*

comˌpassionate ˈleave *n* [U] special permission to have time away from work because one of your relatives has died or is very ill

comˈpassion faˌtigue *n* [U] if you are suffering from compassion fatigue, you have stopped feeling sympathy for people and do not want to give any more money to help them, because you have seen so many reports on television, in newspapers etc about other groups of people who are in trouble: *Some donors, battered by so many appeals for help, may find themselves battling compassion fatigue.*

ˈcompass rose *n* [singular] *technical* a symbol that consists of a circle with a pointed star in it, which is printed on maps and shows which direction is north, south, east, west etc

com·pat·i·bil·ity /kəmˌpætəˈbɪləti/ AWL *n* [U]
1 *technical* the ability of one piece of computer equipment to be used with another one, especially when they are made by different companies OPP **incompatibility**: **[+with]** *the system's compatibility with Windows software*
2 the ability to exist or be used together without causing problems OPP **incompatibility**: *compatibility of flavours*
3 the ability to have a good relationship with someone because you have similar interests, ideas etc OPP **incompatibility**: *sexual compatibility*

com·pat·i·ble[1] /kəmˈpætəbəl/ ●●○ AWL *adj*
1 if two pieces of computer equipment of SOFTWARE are compatible, they can be used together, especially when they are made by different companies → **compatibility**: *Will the software on my PC be compatible with a Mac?*
2 able to exist or be used together without causing problems → **compatibility**: **[+with]** *Stephen's political views often weren't compatible with her own.*
3 two people that are compatible are able to have a good relationship because they have similar opinions or interests → **compatibility**

> REGISTER
> In everyday English, people often say that two people are **(just) right for each other**, because **compatible** sounds rather formal: *On paper they seemed like the perfect couple, but maybe they* ***just*** *weren't* ***right for each other***.

compatible[2] *n* [C] *technical* a piece of computer equipment or SOFTWARE that can be used in or with another piece of equipment, especially one made by a different company

com·pat·ri·ot /kəmˈpætriət $ -ˈpeɪt-/ *n* [C] someone who was born in or is a citizen of the same country as someone else SYN **countryman**: **sb's compatriot** *Schmidt defeated his compatriot Hausmann in the quarter final.*

com·pel /kəmˈpel/ ●●○ *v* (**compelled, compelling**) [T]
1 to force someone to do something → **compulsion**: **compel sb to do sth** *The law will compel employers to provide health insurance.* | *She* ***felt compelled*** *to resign because of the scandal.* THESAURUS FORCE
2 *formal* to make people have a particular feeling or attitude → **compulsion**: *His performance* ***compelled*** *the audience's* ***attention***.

com·pel·ling /kəmˈpelɪŋ/ ●○○ *adj*
1 **compelling reason/argument/case etc** an argument etc that makes you feel certain that something is true or that you must do something about it: *Lucy had no compelling reason to go into town.* | *The court was presented with* ***compelling evidence*** *that she'd murdered her husband.*
2 very interesting or exciting, so that you have to pay attention: *His life makes a* ***compelling story***. THESAURUS INTERESTING
3 **compelling need/desire/urge (to do sth)** a strong need, desire etc to do something, making you feel that you must do it: *He felt a compelling need to tell someone about his idea.* —**compellingly** *adv*

com·pen·di·um /kəmˈpendiəm/ *n* (*plural* **compendiums** *or* **compendia** /-diə/) [C] **1** *formal* a book that contains a complete collection of facts, drawings etc on a particular subject: *a cricketing compendium* **2** *BrE* a set of different BOARD GAMES in a box

com·pen·sate /ˈkɒmpənseɪt $ ˈkɑːm-/ ●○○ AWL *v*
1 [I] to replace or balance the effect of something bad: *Because my left eye is so weak, my right eye has to work harder to compensate.* | **[+for]** *Her intelligence more than compensates for her lack of experience.*

> REGISTER
> In everyday English, people usually say **make up for** something rather than **compensate for** something: *What she lacks in patience she* ***makes up for*** *in determination.*

2 [T] to pay someone money because they have suffered injury, loss, or damage: *the government's promise to compensate victims of the flood* | **compensate sb for sth** *The firm will compensate workers for their loss of earnings.*

GRAMMAR: Patterns with compensate

• Something **compensates for** something: *Nothing can compensate for this loss.* ✗ Don't say: *Nothing can compensate this loss.*
• You **compensate** someone **for** something: *We will compensate you for your expenses.* ✗ Don't say: *We will compensate you your expenses.*

com·pen·sa·tion /ˌkɒmpənˈseɪʃən $ ˌkɑːm-/ ●●○ AWL *n*
1 [U] money paid to someone because they have suffered injury or loss, or because something they own has been damaged: **[+for]** *compensation for injuries at work* | **[+from]** *She received compensation from the government for the damage caused to her property.* | **in compensation** *The jury awarded Tyler $1.7 million in compensation.* | **as compensation** *The workers were given 30 days' pay as compensation.* | *People who are wrongly arrested may be* ***paid compensation***. | **demand/seek/claim compensation** *The parents are seeking compensation for birth defects caused by the drug.* | **award/grant compensation** *The court awarded Jamieson £30,000 compensation.*
2 [C,U] something that makes a bad situation better: *One of the few compensations of losing my job was seeing more of my family.* | **by way of compensation** (=in order to make a situation better) *By way of compensation he offered to take her out for a meal.*
3 [C,U] when someone behaves in a particular way in order to replace something that is missing or to balance the bad effects of something: **[+for]** *Linda's aggressiveness is just a compensation for her feelings of insecurity.* | **as compensation (for sth)** *Lip-reading can act as compensation for loss of hearing.*
4 [U] *AmE* the money someone is paid for doing their job SYN **remuneration**

com·pen·sa·to·ry /ˌkɒmpənˈseɪtəri◂ $ kəmˈpen-səˌtɔːri/ AWL *adj* [usually before noun] *formal* **1** compensatory payments are paid to someone who has been harmed or hurt in some way: *She was awarded a large sum in* ***compensatory damages***. **2** intended to reduce the bad effects of something: *Workers are given a compensatory day off when a national holiday falls on a weekend.*

com·pere /ˈkɒmpeə $ ˈkɑːmper/ *n* [C] *BrE* someone who introduces the people who are performing in a television programme, theatre show etc SYN **host** *AmE* —**compere** *v* [I,T]: *Ballentine will compere the show.*

com·pete /kəmˈpiːt/ ●●● S3 W3 *v* [I]
1 BUSINESS if one company or country competes with another, it tries to get people to buy its goods or services rather than those available from another company or country → **competition**, **competitor**, **competitive**: **[+with/against]** *They found themselves competing with foreign companies for a share of the market.* | *The Renault Clio competes against such cars as the Peugeot 206.* | **[+for]** *The stores have to compete for customers in the Christmas season.* | **[+in]** *The company must be able to compete in the international marketplace.* | **compete to do sth** *Several advertising agencies are competing to get the contract.* | **can't compete (with sth)** (=be unable to be more successful) *Small independent bookstores simply can't compete with the big national chains.*
2 PERSON to try to gain something and stop someone else from having it or having as much of it → **competition**, **competitive**: **[+for]** *She and her sister are always competing for attention.* | **[+against]** *I had to compete against 19 other people for the job.* | **[+with]** *As a stepmother, don't even try to compete with the children's mother for their love.*
3 IN A COMPETITION to take part in a competition or sports event → **competitor**: **[+in/at]** *How many runners will be competing in the marathon?* | *Professional athletes may now compete at the Olympics.* | **[+against]** *He'll be competing against the world's best.* THESAURUS ▸ PARTICIPATE
4 **sb/sth can't compete with sb/sth** to not be as interesting, attractive etc as someone or something else: *Melinda was plain and knew she couldn't compete with her sister where boys were concerned.*

GRAMMAR: Reciprocal verbs

Compete is a reciprocal verb. This type of verb is used when saying that two or more people or groups do something that involves both or all of them: *We were competing for her attention.* You can also say: *We were competing with each other for her attention.* | *I was competing with them for her attention.*
GRAMMAR GUIDE ▸ VERBS

com·pe·tence /ˈkɒmpətəns $ ˈkɑːm-/ ●●○ *n*
1 [U] (*also* **compe·ten·cy** /-tənsi/) the ability to do something well OPP **incompetence**: **[+in]** *Students will gain competence in a wide range of skills.* | **[+of]** *He questioned the competence of the government.* | **professional/linguistic/technical etc competence** *Doctors have to constantly update their knowledge in order to maintain their professional competence.*
2 [U] *law* the legal power of a court of law to hear and judge something in court, or of a government to do something: **be within the competence of sth** *Many legal issues are within the competence of individual states rather than the federal government.*
3 [C] (*also* **competency**) *formal* a skill needed to do a particular job: *Typing is considered by most employers to be a basic competence.*

com·pe·tent /ˈkɒmpɪtənt $ ˈkɑːm-/ ●●○ *adj*
1 having enough skill or knowledge to do something to a satisfactory standard OPP **incompetent**: *A competent mechanic should be able to fix the problem.* | **very/highly/extremely competent** *She's a highly competent linguist.* | **competent to do sth** *I don't feel competent to give an opinion at the moment.* | *He is the only party leader competent enough to govern this country.*
2 satisfactory but not especially good: *The workmen did a* ***competent job***.
3 *technical* having normal mental abilities: *We believe the patient was not* ***mentally competent***. | *A psychiatrist said McKibben was* ***competent to stand trial***.
4 [not before noun] *law* having the legal power to deal with something in a court of law: **competent to do sth** *This court is not competent to hear your case.* —**competently** *adv*

com·pet·ing /kəmˈpiːtɪŋ/ *adj* [only before noun] **1** competing stories, ideas etc cannot all be right or accepted: *Several people gave* ***competing accounts*** *of the accident.* | *a compromise between* ***competing interests*** *within the organization* | *competing claims* **2 competing products/brands/companies etc** products etc that are trying to be more successful than each other

com·pe·ti·tion /ˌkɒmpəˈtɪʃən $ ˌkɑːm-/ ●●● S2 W1 *n*
1 [U] a situation in which people or organizations try to be more successful than other people or organizations → **compete**, **competitor**: **[+for]** *Competition for the job was intense.* | **[+between/among]** *Sometimes there's a lot of competition between children for their mother's attention.* | *This price reduction is due to competition among suppliers.* | **[+in]** *competition in the automobile industry* | **fierce/stiff/intense etc competition** *There is fierce competition between the three leading soap manufacturers.* | **be in competition with sb/sth** *Government departments are in direct competition with each other for limited resources.* | **in the face of competition (from sb/sth)** (=in a situation where you are competing with someone or something) *Small grocery stores are going out of business in the face of stiff competition from the large supermarket chains.*
2 [singular, U] the people or groups that are competing against you, especially in business or in a sport → **compete**, **competitor**: *Going to trade fairs is an ideal opportunity to size up* ***the competition***. | **no/not much/little etc competition** (=no one who is likely to be better than you) *Jones is certain to win the race; there's just no competition.* | **a lot of/considerable/fierce etc competition** *The team overcame fierce competition for their place in the finals.* | **foreign/**

international competition (=companies from other countries that you are competing with) *Japanese PC makers now face foreign competition in their home market.*
3 [C] an organized event in which people or teams compete against each other → **competitor**: *a photography competition* | **competition to do sth** *a competition to find a designer for the new building* | *Teams from high schools all over the state have entered the competition.* | *With France out of the competition, England have a great chance to win.*

COLLOCATIONS - MEANING 3

VERBS

take part in a competition *Ten schools took part in the competition.*
enter a competition *You must be over 16 to enter the competition.*
win a competition *Lucy was thrilled to hear that she had won the short-story competition.*
come first/second/third etc in a competition *Stuart came second in the swimming competition.*
have/hold a competition *Each year the school holds a painting competition.*
run a competition (=organize it) | **judge a competition** (=decide who has won it) | **withdraw from a competition** (=not take part, when you had planned to) | **be out of a competition** (=no longer be in a competition because you have been defeated) | **put/knock sb out of a competition** (=defeat someone so that they are no longer in a competition)

ADJECTIVES/NOUN + competition

a football/music/essay etc competition *There's a music competition in the town on June 12th.*
a writing/painting/dancing etc competition | **a national/international/European etc competition** | **an annual competition** | **an open competition** (=that everyone can take part in) | **a knock-out competition** *BrE* (=in which if you lose a game, you are no longer in the competition)

PHRASES

the result of a competition *The result of the competition will be announced on April 3rd.*
the winner of a competition | **the rules of a competition**

THESAURUS

competition an organized event in which people or teams compete against each other, especially in order to win a prize: *My sister entered a dance competition.* | *The winner of the competition will be announced in June.*
contest a competition in which people do an activity, and a group of judges decide the winner: *a beauty contest* | *a contest to find America's strongest man*
championship an important sports competition to find the best player or team in the world or in a particular area: *the European Athletics Championship* | *Brazil went on to win the world championship.*
tournament a competition in a sport or game, in which many players or teams compete against each other until there is one winner: *a golf tournament*
quiz a competition in which people have to answer questions: *a TV quiz show*

PART OF A COMPETITION

round one of the parts of a competition that you have to finish or win before you can go on to the next part: *Henman lost in the second round of the competition.*
heat one of several races or competitions whose winners then compete against each other: *She came second in her heat, with a time of 23.2 seconds.*

com·pet·i·tive /kəmˈpetətɪv/ ●●○ S3 W3 *adj*
1 determined or trying very hard to be more successful than other people or businesses → **compete**, **competitor**: *Some US industries are not as competitive as they have been in the past.* | *The team seems to have lost its* ***competitive edge*** *recently* (=its ability to compete well).
2 relating to competition → **compete**, **competitor**: *Competitive sports encourage children to work together as a team.* | **highly/fiercely/intensely etc competitive** *Advertising is an intensely competitive business.*
3 products or prices that are competitive are cheaper than others but still of good quality: *The hotel offers a high standard of service at competitive rates.* THESAURUS ▸ CHEAP
—**competitively** *adv*

com·pet·i·tive·ness /kəmˈpetətɪvnəs/ *n* [U] **1** the ability of a company, country, or a product to compete with others: *New machinery has enhanced the company's productivity and competitiveness.* | *Europe's competitiveness in international markets* **2** the desire to be more successful than other people: *Her enthusiasm and competitiveness rubbed off on everyone.*

com·pet·i·tor /kəmˈpetɪtə $ -ər/ ●●○ *n* [C]
1 a person, team, company etc that is competing with another: *Last year they sold twice as many computers as their competitors.* | **major/main competitors** *The company's four major competitors have nothing to rival the new product.*
2 someone who takes part in a competition: *Two of the competitors failed to turn up for the race.*

com·pi·la·tion /ˌkɒmpəˈleɪʃən $ ˌkɑːm-/ AWL *n* **1** [C] a book, list, record etc which consists of different pieces of information, songs etc: **[+of]** *a compilation of love songs* | **compilation CD/album/tape 2** [U] the process of making a book, list, record etc from different pieces of information, songs etc: *dictionary compilation*

com·pile /kəmˈpaɪl/ ●●○ AWL *v* [T]
1 to make a book, list, record etc, using different pieces of information, music etc → **compilation**: *The document was compiled by the Department of Health* | **compile sth from/for sth** *The report was compiled from a survey of 5,000 households.*
2 *technical* to put a set of instructions into a computer in a form that it can understand and use

com·pil·er /kəmˈpaɪlə $ -ər/ *n* [C] **1** someone who collects different pieces of information to be used in a book, report, or list **2** *technical* a set of instructions in a computer that changes a computer language known to the computer user into the form needed by the computer

com·pla·cen·cy /kəmˈpleɪsənsi/ *n* [U] a feeling of satisfaction with a situation or with what you have achieved, so that you stop trying to improve or change things - used to show disapproval: *Doctors have warned against complacency in fighting common diseases.* | *Despite yesterday's win, there is clearly* ***no room for complacency*** *if the team want to stay top of the league.*

com·pla·cent /kəmˈpleɪsənt/ *adj* pleased with a situation, especially something you have achieved, so that you stop trying to improve or change things - used to show disapproval: *There's a danger of becoming complacent if you win a few games.* | *a* ***complacent attitude*** *towards the problem* | **[+about]** *We simply cannot afford to be complacent about the future of our car industry.* —**complacently** *adv*

com·plain /kəmˈpleɪn/ ●●● S2 W3 *v*
1 [I,T] to say that you are annoyed, not satisfied, or unhappy about something or someone → **complaint**: *Residents are complaining because traffic in the area has increased.* | *'You never ask my opinion about anything,' Rod complained.* | **complain (that)** *She complained that no one had been at the airport to meet her.* | **[+about]** *She often complains about not feeling appreciated at work.* | **[+of]** *Several women have complained of sexual harassment.* | **[+to]** *Neighbours complained to the police about the dogs barking.* | *Employees* ***complained bitterly*** *about working conditions.*

GRAMMAR

You **complain about** something or someone: *They complained about the service.* ✗ Don't say: *They complained against the service.* | *They complained for the service.*

2 (I/you/he etc) can't complain *spoken* used to say that a situation is satisfactory, even though there may be a few problems: *I make a good living. I can't complain.*

THESAURUS

complain to say that you are annoyed, unhappy, or not satisfied about something or someone: *Several customers complained about the service they received.*
make a complaint to formally complain about something to someone in authority: *His parents made a complaint to the head teacher.*
protest to complain about something that you think is wrong, especially publicly: *Demonstrators were protesting against the war.*
object to say that you oppose or disapprove of something: *Local residents have objected to the plan.*
grumble to keep complaining in a bad-tempered way about something: *Rail travellers have been grumbling about the increase in ticket prices.*
moan/whine *informal* (*also* **whinge** /wɪndʒ/ *BrE informal*) to keep complaining in an annoying way: *Everyone was moaning about the hotel food.* | *Stop whingeing and get on with your work!*
kick up/make a fuss to complain or become angry about something, especially something that is not very important: *The soup wasn't hot enough, but he didn't want to make a fuss.*

complain of sth *phr v formal* to say that you feel ill or have a pain in a part of your body: *Dan's been complaining of severe headaches.*

com·plain·ant /kəmˈpleɪnənt/ *n* [C] *law* someone who makes a formal complaint in a court of law SYN **plaintiff**

com·plaint /kəmˈpleɪnt/ ●●● S3 W3 *n*
1 [C,U] a statement in which someone complains about something: *If you wish to make a complaint, you should see the manager.* | *The sales assistants are trained to deal with customer complaints in a friendly manner.* | **[+about]** *Keating was dismissed after complaints about the quality of his work.* | **[+of]** *complaints of police brutality* | **[+from/to]** *complaints from local residents* | *a complaint to the Advertising Standards Authority* | **[+against]** *All complaints against police officers are carefully investigated.* | **complaint that** *We are concerned by complaints that children are being bullied.*
2 [C] something that you complain about: *Our main complaint was the poor standard of service.* | *My only complaint is that the price is rather high.*
3 [C] *formal* an illness that affects a particular part of your body: *He is having treatment for a **chest complaint**.* **THESAURUS** ILLNESS

COLLOCATIONS

VERBS

make a complaint (=complain formally to someone) *The manager of the team decided to make a complaint about the referee.*
file/lodge a complaint *formal* (=make a complaint) *She filed a complaint against several of her colleagues.*
have a complaint (=want to complain about something) *Please let us know if you have any complaints about our service.*
receive a complaint (*also* **have a complaint**) *Our department has received a number of complaints from the public.*
deal with/handle a complaint *Police officers came to the house to deal with a complaint about noise.*
investigate a complaint | **uphold a complaint** (=say it is reasonable)

ADJECTIVES/NOUN + complaint

a formal/official complaint *The man has lodged a formal complaint against the police.*
a common/widespread/frequent complaint *A common complaint of children is that parents do not listen to them.*
a serious complaint *Serious complaints of negligence have been made.*
a customer/consumer complaint *As a result of the improvements, customer complaints went down by 70%.*

PHRASES

cause/grounds for complaint (=a good reason to complain) *I do not think that he has any cause for complaint.*
a letter of complaint | **a complaints procedure** (=a system for dealing with complaints)

com·plai·sance /kəmˈpleɪzəns/ *n* [U] *formal* willingness to do what pleases other people —**complaisant** *adj* —**complaisantly** *adv*

com·plect·ed /kəmˈplektɪd/ *adj AmE* **light/fair/dark complected** having light or dark skin

com·ple·ment¹ /ˈkɒmpləment $ ˈkɑːm-/ ●○○ AWL *v* [T] to make a good combination with someone or something else: *John and Bob complemented each other well.* | *The dark red walls complement the red leather chairs.*

REGISTER
In everyday English, people usually say that something **goes well with** another thing, or they **go well together**, rather than say they **complement** each other: *White wine **goes well with** fish.*

com·ple·ment² /ˈkɒmpləmənt $ ˈkɑːm-/ AWL *n* [C]
1 someone or something that emphasizes the good qualities of another person or thing: **[+to]** *This wine would be a nice complement to grilled dishes.* **2** the number or quantity needed to make a group complete: **[+of]** *Each new cell will carry its **full complement** of chromosomes.* **3** *technical* a word or phrase that follows a verb and describes the subject of the verb. In 'John is cold' and 'John became chairman', 'cold' and 'chairman' are complements.

com·ple·men·ta·ry /ˌkɒmpləˈmentəri◂ $ ˌkɑːm-/ ●○○ AWL *adj*
1 complementary things go well together, although they are usually different: *The computer and the human mind have different but complementary abilities.*
2 *technical* complementary colours of light are very different and combine to make white
3 *technical* two angles that are complementary add up to 90 degrees —**complementarity** /ˌkɒmpləmenˈtærəti $ ˌkɑːm-/ *n* [U]

ˌcomplementary ˈmedicine *n* [U] *especially BrE* complementary medicine uses treatments that are not part of traditional Western medicine → **conventional medicine**: *acupuncture and other types of complementary medicines*

com·plete¹ /kəmˈpliːt/ ●●● S2 W1 *adj*
1 [usually before noun] used to emphasize that a quality or situation is as great as it could possibly be SYN **total**: *The police were in **complete control** of the situation.* | *Their engagement came as a **complete surprise** to me.* | *This is a **complete waste of time**.* | **a complete fool/idiot etc** *Meg realized she'd been a complete fool.* | *a **complete stranger*** | *The darkness was almost complete.*
2 including all parts, details, facts etc and with nothing missing SYN **whole** OPP **incomplete**: *a complete set of china* | *The list below is not complete.* | ***the complete works of** Shakespeare* (=a book, CD etc containing everything Shakespeare wrote)
3 [not before noun] finished OPP **incomplete**: *Work on the new building is nearly complete.*
4 complete with sth having particular equipment or features: *The house **comes complete with** swimming pool and sauna.* —**completeness** *n* [U]: *For the sake of completeness I should mention one further argument.*

complete² ●●● S2 W1 *v* [T]
1 to finish doing or making something, especially when it has taken a long time: *Students must complete the course.* | *The building took two years to complete.* **THESAURUS** FINISH
2 to make something whole or perfect by adding what is missing: *The child's task was to complete the sentences.* | *I need one more stamp to complete the set.*

3 to write the information that is needed on a form SYN **fill out**: *In all, more than 650 people completed the questionnaire.* | *Send your completed form to the following address.*

com·plete·ly /kəm'pliːtli/ ●●● S1 W2 *adv* to the greatest degree possible SYN **totally**: *I completely forgot that it's his birthday today.* | *He had never completely recovered from his illness.* | *a completely new range of low-cost computers* | *I'm not completely sure.* | *Portuguese is pronounced completely differently from Spanish.*

com·ple·tion /kəm'pliːʃən/ ●○○ *n* [U]
1 the state of being finished: *The house is* ***nearing completion*** (=almost finished). | *The project has a* ***completion date*** *of December 22nd.*
2 the act of finishing something: **[+of]** *The job is subject to your satisfactory completion of the training course.* | **on completion (of sth)** *On completion of the building, they make a final inspection.*
3 *law* the final point in the sale of a house, when all the documents have been signed and all the money paid

com·plex¹ /'kɒmpleks $ ˌkaːm'pleks◂/ ●●○ W2 AWL *adj*
1 consisting of many different parts and often difficult to understand SYN **complicated** OPP **simple**: *a* ***complex system*** *of highways* | *Photosynthesis is a* ***highly complex*** *process.* | *Peter seemed to have an instant understanding of the most complex issues.* | *It was a very complex relationship between two complex people.* THESAURUS ▸ COMPLICATED
2 *technical* a complex word or sentence contains a main part and one or more other parts → **compound**

com·plex² /'kɒmpleks $ 'kaːm-/ ●●○ AWL *n* [C]
1 a group of buildings, or a large building with many parts, used for a particular purpose: *The town has one of the best* ***leisure complexes*** *in the country.* | *a three-story apartment complex*
2 **a complex of sth** *formal* a large number of things which are closely related: *China was a complex of different societies.*
3 an emotional problem in which someone is unnecessarily anxious about something or thinks too much about something: *I used to* ***have a complex about*** *my looks.* → INFERIORITY COMPLEX, OEDIPUS COMPLEX, PERSECUTION COMPLEX

com·plex·ion /kəm'plekʃən/ *n* **1** [C] the natural colour or appearance of the skin on your face: *Drinking water is good for the complexion.* | **pale/fair/ruddy etc complexion** (=a pale, fair, red etc face) | **fair-complexioned/smooth-complexioned etc** *She was fair-complexioned with blonde hair.* **2** [singular] the general character or nature of something: *Crime has risen under governments of every political complexion.* **3 put a different/new/fresh complexion on sth** to make a situation or event seem different: *This document puts a different complexion on the matter.*

com·plex·i·ty /kəm'pleksəti/ ●○○ AWL *n* (*plural* **complexities**)
1 [U] the state of being complicated: **[+of]** *There is increasing recognition of the complexity of the causes of poverty.* | *a design of great complexity*
2 [C usually plural] one of the many details or features of something that make it hard to understand or deal with: **[+of]** *The complexities of economics are clearly explained.*

com·pli·ance /kəm'plaɪəns/ *n* [U] *formal* when someone obeys a rule, agreement, or demand → **comply**: **in compliance with sth** *He changed his name to Lee in 1815 in compliance with his uncle's will.* | **[+with]** *Patients should have a history of good compliance with treatment.* | **ensure/secure/enforce compliance** *The staff involved should be monitored to ensure compliance with the policy.*

com·pli·ant /kəm'plaɪənt/ *adj* **1** willing to obey or to agree to other people's wishes and demands → **comply**: *For years I had tried to be a compliant and dutiful wife.* **2** made or done according to particular rules or standards → **comply**: **[+with]** *Future versions will be fully compliant with the industry standard.*

com·pli·cate /'kɒmplɪkeɪt $ 'kaːm-/ ●●○ *v* [T]
1 to make a problem or situation more difficult: *The situation is complicated by the fact that I've got to work late on Friday.* | ***To complicate matters further****, differences exist as regards legal systems, trade customs, and language.*
2 to make an illness worse: *a heart condition complicated by pneumonia* GRAMMAR **Complicate** is usually passive in this meaning.

com·pli·cat·ed /'kɒmplɪkeɪtɪd $ 'kaːm-/ ●●● S2 W3 *adj*
1 difficult to understand or deal with, because many parts or details are involved SYN **complex**: *a complicated voting system* | *For young children, getting dressed is a complicated business.* | **very/extremely/immensely/highly etc complicated** *Mental illness is a very complicated subject.*

REGISTER
In written English, people often use **complex** rather than **complicated**, because it sounds more formal: *The problem is very* ***complex****.*

2 consisting of many closely connected parts SYN **complex**: *a complicated pattern* | *The human brain is an incredibly complicated organ.*

THESAURUS

complicated consisting of a lot of different parts or details and therefore difficult to understand: *The rules of the game seemed very complicated.* | *a complicated issue*
complex a complex process, relationship etc is difficult to understand because it has a lot of parts that are all connected in different ways: *The chemical processes involved are extremely complex.* | *the complex relationship between government and the media*
elaborate having a lot of parts or details and very carefully planned, but often more complicated than is necessary: *Mike had worked out an elaborate system for categorizing his collection of DVDs.*
involved very long and complicated - use this especially about something that you think should be made simpler: *The system for choosing candidates is very involved, and I won't go into it here.* | *Adopting a child can be a long involved process.*
convoluted too complicated and difficult to understand - used especially about someone's language or arguments, or about a system: *convoluted sentences* | *Procedures for government funding have become more convoluted.*
intricate having a lot of small parts or details - used especially about something that is cleverly designed or made: *Lasers are used to cut intricate designs in the metal.*

com·pli·ca·tion /ˌkɒmplɪ'keɪʃən $ ˌkaːm-/ ●●○ *n*
1 [C,U] a problem or situation that makes something more difficult to understand or deal with: *The fact that the plane was late added a further complication to our journey.*
2 [C usually plural] *medical* a medical problem or illness that happens while someone is already ill and makes treatment more difficult: *Pneumonia is one of the common complications faced by bed-ridden patients.*

com·plic·i·ty /kəm'plɪsəti/ *n* [U] *formal* **1** involvement in a crime, together with other people: **[+in]** *Jennings denied complicity in the murder.* **2** involvement in or knowledge of a situation, especially one that is morally wrong or dishonest: **[+with]** *His complicity with the former government had led to his downfall.* —**complicit** *adj*: *The careers of officers* ***complicit in*** *the cover-up were ruined.*

com·pli·ment¹ /'kɒmpləmənt $ 'kaːm-/ ●○○ *n*
1 [C] a remark that shows you admire someone or something: *All the guests paid her extravagant compliments.* | *Being compared to Abba is a great compliment.* | **[+on]** *compliments on her appearance*
2 **take sth as a compliment** to be pleased about what someone says about you, even though they may not

mean to be nice: *They all seem to think that I ask rather cheeky questions, which I'll take as a compliment.*
3 [singular] an action that shows you admire someone: *He* ***paid*** *MacLennan the finest* ***compliment*** *of all by imitating him.* | **[+to]** *It's a great compliment to the band that he came out of retirement to interview them.*
4 fish for compliments to try to make someone say something nice about you
5 compliments [plural] praise or good wishes: *This soup is delicious; my* ***compliments to*** *the chef.*
6 with the compliments of sb/with our compliments *formal* used by a person or company when they send or give something to you: *With the compliments of J. Smith & Son.* | *Please accept these tickets with our compliments.*
7 the compliments of the season *old-fashioned* used as a spoken or written greeting at Christmas and New Year
8 return the compliment to behave towards someone in the same way as they have behaved towards you: *They didn't take a lot of notice of me, and I returned the compliment.*
9 back-handed compliment *BrE*, **left-handed compliment** *AmE* something that someone says to you which is nice and not nice at the same time: *'You've got a brain. Try using it.' 'Thanks for the back-handed compliment!'*

COLLOCATIONS

VERBS

pay/give sb a compliment *He was always paying her compliments.*
mean sth as a compliment *When I said she'd lost weight, I meant it as a compliment.*
get/receive a compliment *The exhibition has received a lot of compliments from the public.*
accept a compliment (=show that you are pleased to have been given a compliment) *She accepted his compliment graciously.*

ADJECTIVES

a great compliment *He said he loved my paintings, which was a great compliment.*
the highest compliment (=the best thing you can say) *The highest compliment you can pay an actor is to say they don't look as if they are acting.*

com·pli·ment² /ˈkɒmpləmənt $ ˈkɑːm-/ ●○○ *v* [T] to say something nice to someone in order to praise them: **compliment sb on sth** *Bob complimented me on my new hairstyle.* | *The groom was so nervous he forgot to compliment the bridesmaids.* THESAURUS ▸ PRAISE

com·pli·men·ta·ry /ˌkɒmpləˈmentəri◂ $ ˌkɑːm-/ *adj* **1** given free to people: *There was a complimentary bottle of champagne in the hotel room.* | *I've got some complimentary tickets for the theatre tonight.* THESAURUS ▸ FREE **2** saying that you admire someone or something: **[+about]** *Jennie was very complimentary about Katharine's riding.* | *complimentary remarks*

ˈcompliment ˌslip (*also* **ˈcompliments slip**) *n* [C] *BrE* a small piece of paper with a company's name and address on it, which it sends with goods instead of a letter

com·pline /ˈkɒmplɪn $ ˈkɑːm-/ *n* [U] a Christian church service held late in the evening, especially in the Roman Catholic Church

com·ply /kəmˈplaɪ/ ●○○ *v* (**complied**, **complying**, **complies**) [I] *formal* to do what you have to do or are asked to do → **compliance**, **compliant**: **[+with]** *Failure to comply with the regulations will result in prosecution.* | *The newspaper was asked by federal agents for assistance and agreed to comply.*

com·po·nent¹ /kəmˈpəʊnənt $ -ˈpoʊ-/ ●●○ AWL *n* [C] one of several parts that together make up a whole machine, system etc SYN **constituent**: *companies that make electronic components for computer products* | **[+of]** *each component of their work* | **key/major/important etc component** *Exercise is one of the key components of a healthy lifestyle.* THESAURUS ▸ PART

component² AWL *adj* [only before noun] the component parts of something are the parts that it consists of SYN **constituent**: **component parts/elements etc** *We've been breaking down the budget into its component parts.*

com·port /kəmˈpɔːt $ -ˈpɔːrt/ *v* **comport yourself** *formal* to behave in a particular way: *He comported himself in a way that won him respect.* —**comportment** *n* [U]
comport with sth *phr v formal* to follow or be in agreement with an idea, belief, or rule

com·pose /kəmˈpəʊz $ -ˈpoʊz/ ●●○ *v*
1 a) be composed of sth to be formed from a number of substances, parts, or people SYN **consist of**: *Water is composed of hydrogen and oxygen.* | *The legal system is composed of people, and people make mistakes.* ⚠ Do not say that something 'is composed by' or 'is composed with' things or people. Say that it **is composed of** things or people. **b)** [T not in progressive] *formal* to combine together to form something SYN **make up**: *More than 17.6 million firms compose the business sector of our economy.*
2 [I,T] to write a piece of music → **composer**, **composition**: *Barrington has composed the music for a new production of 'A Midsummer Night's Dream'.*
3 compose a letter/poem/speech etc to write a letter, poem etc, thinking very carefully about it as you write it: *Compose a letter to your local paper stating your views on an issue of your choice.*
4 a) compose yourself to try hard to become calm after feeling very angry, upset, or excited: *Lynn took several deep breaths to compose herself.* **b) compose your face/features/thoughts** to make yourself look or feel calm → **composure**: *When asked a question, give yourself a second to compose your thoughts.*
5 [T] to arrange the parts of a painting, photograph, or scene in a way that achieves a particular result: *I like the way he composes his photographs.*

com·posed /kəmˈpəʊzd $ -ˈpoʊzd/ *adj* **1** seeming calm and not upset or angry: *He appeared very composed despite the stress he was under.* **2** a composed SALAD is arranged carefully on a plate rather than being mixed together

com·pos·er /kəmˈpəʊzə $ -ˈpoʊzər/ ●●○ *n* [C] someone who writes music → **composition**

com·po·site¹ /ˈkɒmpəzət $ kɑːmˈpɑː-/ *adj* [only before noun] **1** made up of different parts or materials: *The author builds up a useful composite picture of contemporary consumer culture.* | *composite metals* **2** *AmE* a composite drawing or photograph consists of pictures of each separate part of the face put together into one drawing, and is used especially to help catch criminals: *a composite sketch*

composite² *n* [C] **1** something made up of different parts or materials: **[+of]** *The child's character was a composite of two girls I knew.* **2** *AmE* a picture of a possible criminal, made by police from descriptions given by WITNESSES SYN **identikit** *BrE*

com·po·si·tion /ˌkɒmpəˈzɪʃən $ ˌkɑːm-/ ●○○ *n*
1 PARTS/MEMBERS [C,U] the way in which something is made up of different parts, things, or members → **compose**: **[+of]** *The composition of the group that is studied depends on the interests of the researcher.* | *Some minerals have complex chemical compositions.*
2 MUSIC/WRITING **a)** [C] a piece of music, a poem, or a piece of writing → **compose**, **composer**: *a composition by jazzman Dave Brubeck, called 'Chromatic Fantasy'* | *a mixture of traditional songs and original compositions* **b)** [U] the art or process of writing pieces of music, poems etc: *The Journals contain accounts of literary composition.* THESAURUS ▸ MUSIC
3 PICTURE [C,U] the way in which the different parts that make up a photograph or picture are arranged: *Martin starts by lightly sketching in the compositions for his paintings.*
4 WRITING AT SCHOOL [C] a short piece of writing about a particular subject, that is done at school SYN **essay**: *I had to write a composition about the Royal visit.*
5 PRINTING [U] *technical* the process of arranging words, pictures etc on a page before they are printed —**compositional** *adj*

C

com·pos·i·tor /kəm'pɒzɪtə $ -'pɑːzɪtər/ *n* [C] someone who arranges words, pictures etc on a page before they are printed

com·pos men·tis /ˌkɒmpəs 'mentɪs $ ˌkɑːm-/ *adj* [not before noun] able to think clearly and be responsible for your actions - often used humorously

com·post¹ /'kɒmpɒst $ 'kɑːmpoʊst/ *n* [U] a mixture of decayed plants, leaves etc used to improve the quality of soil

compost² *v* [T] to make plants, leaves etc into compost

com·post·a·ble /'kɒmpɒstəbəl $ 'kɑːmpoʊst-/ *adj* suitable for making into compost: *compostable garden waste*

'compost heap *BrE*, **'compost pile** *AmE* *n* [C] leaves, plants etc that you have put in a pile in your garden in order to make compost

C

com·po·sure /kəm'pəʊʒə $ -'poʊʒər/ *n* [U] the state of feeling or seeming calm: **recover/regain your composure** (=become calm after feeling angry or upset) *Carter looked stunned, but he soon regained his composure.* | **keep/maintain your composure** (=stay calm) *The widow broke down in tears, but her daughters maintained their composure.* | *He has* ***lost*** *his* ***composure*** *under the pressure of the situation.*

com·pote /'kɒmpɒt, -pəʊt $ 'kɑːmpoʊt/ *n* [C,U] fruit that has been cooked in sugar and water and is eaten cold

com·pound¹ /'kɒmpaʊnd $ 'kɑːm-/ ●●○ AWL *n* [C]
1 *technical* a substance containing atoms from two or more ELEMENTS → **element**: *man-made organic compounds* | **[+of]** *Sulphur dioxide is a compound of sulphur and oxygen.*
2 a combination of two or more parts, substances, or qualities: **[+of]** *Teaching is a compound of several different skills.* | *Brush on a damp-proofing compound.*
3 an area that contains a group of buildings and is surrounded by a fence or wall: *a prison compound*
4 *technical* a noun, adjective etc that is made up of two or more words. The noun 'flower shop' and the adjective 'self-made' are compounds.

com·pound² /kəm'paʊnd/ AWL *v* [T] **1** to make a difficult situation worse by adding more problems: **compound a problem/difficulty etc** *Helmut's problems were compounded by his lack of concentration.* **2** *BrE* to make a bad action worse by doing more bad things: **compound a crime/an offence etc** *He compounded the offence by calling his opponents liars.* **3 be compounded of sth** *formal* to be a mixture of things: *a smell compounded of dust and dead flowers* **4** *AmE* to pay INTEREST that is calculated on both the sum of money and the interest: *Interest is compounded quarterly.*

com·pound³ /'kɒmpaʊnd $ 'kɑːm-/ AWL *adj technical* **1 compound eye/leaf etc** a single eye, leaf etc that is made up of two or more parts → **simple** **2 compound noun/adjective etc** a noun, adjective etc that is made up of two or more words. For example, 'ice cream' is a compound noun. **3 compound sentence** a sentence that has two or more main parts → **complex sentence**

ˌcompound 'fracture *n* [C] a broken bone that cuts through someone's skin

ˌcompound 'interest *n* [U] INTEREST that is calculated on both the sum of money lent or borrowed and the unpaid interest already earned or charged → **simple interest**

com·pre·hend /ˌkɒmprɪ'hend $ ˌkɑːm-/ ●○○ *v* [I,T] to understand something that is complicated or difficult SYN **understand, grasp** → **comprehension**: *She cannot comprehend the extent of the disaster.* | *I did not* ***fully comprehend*** *what had happened.* | **comprehend what/how/why etc** *It may be hard to comprehend how much this gift means for my country.* | **comprehend that** *Finally, she comprehended that he wanted his pay.* THESAURUS ▸ UNDERSTAND

> **REGISTER**
> In everyday English, people usually say **understand** rather than **comprehend**: *I could* ***understand*** *most of what she was saying.*

> **GRAMMAR: Patterns with comprehend**
> • **Comprehend** is often used in the negative, especially with **can't/cannot**: *I cannot comprehend why anyone would do that.*
> • **Comprehend** is not used in the progressive. ✗ Don't say: *I am not comprehending why anyone would do that.*
> GRAMMAR GUIDE ▸ VERBS

com·pre·hen·si·ble /ˌkɒmprɪ'hensəbəl $ ˌkɑːm-/ *adj* easy to understand SYN **understandable** OPP **incomprehensible**: *Her speech was slurred and barely comprehensible.* | **[+to]** *The procedure must be clear and comprehensible to all staff.* —**comprehensibility** /ˌkɒmprɪhensə'bɪləti $ ˌkɑːm-/ *n* [U]

com·pre·hen·sion /ˌkɒmprɪ'henʃən $ ˌkɑːm-/ ●●○ *n*
1 [U] the ability to understand something SYN **understanding** → **comprehend**: **[+of]** *They don't have the least comprehension of what I'm trying to do.* | *The research project will focus on children's comprehension of pretence.* | *Why you let her talk you into doing such a foolish thing is* ***beyond*** *my* ***comprehension*** (=impossible for me to understand).
2 [C,U] an exercise given to students to test how well they understand written or spoken language: *new methods of testing reading comprehension* | *a comprehension task*

com·pre·hen·sive /ˌkɒmprɪ'hensɪv◂ $ ˌkɑːm-/ ●●○ W3 AWL *adj*
1 including all the necessary facts, details, or problems that need to be dealt with SYN **thorough**: *We offer our customers a comprehensive range of financial products.* | *a* ***comprehensive guide*** *to British hotels and restaurants* | *The following guidelines do not aim to be totally comprehensive.* | **comprehensive review/study/survey/account etc** *a thorough and comprehensive review of the case* | *a comprehensive study of alcoholism* ⚠ Do not confuse with **comprehensible** (=able to be understood) or **understanding** (=sympathetic about people's problems): *His report was barely comprehensible.* | *My parents are very understanding.*
2 comprehensive insurance/cover/policy motor insurance that pays for damage whether it is caused by you or someone else
3 comprehensive education/system a system of education in Britain in which children of different abilities go to the same school and are taught together —**comprehensively** *adv*: *No system has failed as comprehensively as the prison system.* —**comprehensiveness** *n* [U]

ˌcompre'hensive ˌschool (*also* **comprehensive**) *n* [C] a state school in Britain for children over the age of 11 of different abilities: *Kylie goes to the local comprehensive.* | *Nine out of ten secondary school children are in comprehensive schools.*

com·press¹ /kəm'pres/ *v* **1** [I,T] to press something or make it smaller so that it takes up less space, or to become smaller: *Light silk is best for parachutes, as it compresses well and then expands rapidly.* | *Isobel nodded, her lips compressed.* | **compress sth into sth** *Snow falling on the mountainsides is compressed into ice.* | *The miners used rock drills and* ***compressed air*** *to drive through hard rock.* **2** [I,T] to make a computer FILE smaller by using a special computer PROGRAM, which makes the file easier to store or send, or to become smaller in this way: *The program compresses any data saved to the disk.* **3** [T] to write or express something using fewer words SYN **condense**: **compress sth into sth** *In this chapter we compress into summary form the main issues discussed so far.* **4** [T] to reduce the amount of time that it takes for something to happen or be done: **compress sth into sth** *Many couples want to compress their childbearing into a short space of time in their married life.* —**compressible** *adj* —**compression** /-'preʃən/ *n* [U]: *data compression*

com·press² /'kɒmpres $ 'kɑːm-/ *n* [C] a small thick piece of material that you put on part of someone's body to stop blood flowing out or to make it less painful: **cold/hot compress** *Apply a cold compress to the injury.*

com·pres·sor /kəmˈpresə $ -ər/ *n* [C] a machine or part of a machine that compresses air or gas

com·prise /kəmˈpraɪz/ ●●○ W3 AWL *v formal*
1 [linking verb] to consist of particular parts, groups etc: *The house comprises two bedrooms, a kitchen, and a living room.* | **be comprised of sb/sth** *The committee is comprised of well-known mountaineers.* THESAURUS ▸ CONSIST
2 [T] to form part of a larger group of people or things SYN **constitute, make up**: *Women comprise a high proportion of part-time workers.*

GRAMMAR

• **Comprise** is not used in the progressive. You say: *The exam comprises four questions.* ✗ Don't say: *The exam is comprising four questions.*
• The participle form **comprising** is often used: *Food exports are very important, comprising 74% of the total.*
• **Comprise** is often used in the passive with **of**: *The organization is comprised of four parts.* ✗ Don't say: *The organization comprises of four parts.*
GRAMMAR GUIDE ▸ VERBS

com·pro·mise¹ /ˈkɒmprəmaɪz $ ˈkɑːm-/ ●●○ *n*
1 [C,U] an agreement that is achieved after everyone involved accepts less than what they wanted at first, or the act of making this agreement: *Compromise is an inevitable part of marriage.* | *To stop the argument they decided on a compromise.* | **[+with]** *Fresh attempts at compromise with the legislature were also on the agenda.* | **[+between]** *a compromise between government and opposition* | *If moderates fail to* ***reach*** *a* ***compromise****, the extremists will dominate the agenda.* | *Be prepared to* ***make compromises****.*
2 [C] a solution to a problem in which two things or situations are changed slightly so that they can exist together: **[+between]** *a happy compromise between the needs of family and work*

compromise² ●●○ *v*
1 [I] to reach an agreement in which everyone involved accepts less than what they wanted at first: *She admitted that she was unable to compromise.* | **[+with]** *His workmates demanded that he never compromise with the bosses.* | **[+on]** *The new regime was prepared to compromise on the oil dispute.*
2 [T] to do something which is against your principles and which therefore seems dishonest or shameful: **compromise your principles/standards/integrity etc** *As soon as you compromise your principles you are lost.* | **compromise yourself** *She had already compromised herself by accepting his invitation.*

com·pro·mis·ing /ˈkɒmprəmaɪzɪŋ $ ˈkɑːm-/ *adj* proving that you have done something morally wrong or embarrassing, or making it seem as if you have done so: **compromising position/situation** *The doctor was found in a compromising position with a nurse* (=having sex with her). | **compromising letter/photograph/picture etc**

comp·trol·ler /kənˈtrəʊlə, kæmp- $ -ˈtroʊlər/ *n* [C] *formal* an official title for a CONTROLLER

com·pul·sion /kəmˈpʌlʃən/ *n* **1** [C] a strong and unreasonable desire to do something → **compel**: *The desire to laugh became a compulsion.* | **compulsion to do sth** *Leith felt an overwhelming compulsion to tell him the truth.* | *the compulsion to smoke or eat too much* **2** [singular, U] the act of forcing or influencing someone to do something they do not want to do → **compel**: **under (no) compulsion to do sth** *Owners are under no compulsion to sell their land.* | *The use of compulsion in psychiatric care cannot be justified.*

com·pul·sive /kəmˈpʌlsɪv/ *adj* **1** compulsive behaviour is very difficult to stop or control, and is often a result of or a sign of a mental problem → **obsessive**: **compulsive gambling/overeating/spending etc** *Compulsive overspending in these days of credit cards has become more common.* **2 compulsive overeater/gambler/spender/liar etc** someone who has such a strong desire to eat too much etc that they are unable to control it: *a help group for compulsive overeaters* **3** a book, programme etc that is compulsive is so interesting that you cannot stop reading or watching it: **compulsive reading/viewing** *'Gardening World' is compulsive viewing for gardeners.* —**compulsively** *adv* —**compulsiveness** *n* [U]

com·pul·so·ry /kəmˈpʌlsəri/ ●●○ *adj* something that is compulsory must be done because it is the law or because someone in authority orders you to → **voluntary**: *the threat of* ***compulsory redundancies*** | **compulsory schooling/education** *11 years of compulsory education* | *Car insurance is compulsory.* THESAURUS ▸ NECESSARY —**compulsorily** *adv*

com·punc·tion /kəmˈpʌŋkʃən/ *n* [U usually in negatives] *formal* a feeling that you should not do something because it is bad or wrong: **have/feel no compunction about (doing) sth** *He had no compunction about interfering in her private affairs.* | *They used their tanks against the leftists* ***without compunction****.*

com·pu·ta·tion /ˌkɒmpjəˈteɪʃən $ ˌkɑːm-/ AWL *n* [C,U] *formal* the process of calculating or the result of calculating SYN **calculation**: *the computation of the monthly statistics* —**computational** *adj*: *computational linguistics*

com·pute /kəmˈpjuːt/ AWL *v* [I,T] *formal* to calculate a result, answer, sum etc: *Final results had not yet been computed.*

com·put·er /kəmˈpjuːtə $ -ər/ ●●● S1 W1 AWL *n* [C] an electronic machine that stores information and uses programs to help you find, organize, or change the information: *a huge global computer network* | *the latest computer software* | **on computer** *The information is stored on computer.* | **by computer** *Shoppers can send in their orders by computer and pick up their goods later.*

COLLOCATIONS

VERBS

use a computer *Most people do jobs in which they have to use a computer.*
log onto a computer (=start using it by typing a password) *Next time you log onto your computer, you will have to use a new password.*
switch a computer on/off | **start up/boot up a computer** (=make it start working) | **shut down a computer** (=close the programs and stop it working) | **restart/reboot a computer** (=make it start working again) | **program a computer** (=give it instructions so that it will do a particular job) | **hold/store sth on a computer** | **a computer starts up/boots up** | **a computer crashes** (=suddenly stops working) | **a computer is down** (=is not working) | **software/a program runs on a computer**

computer + NOUN

a computer system *Our office is installing a new computer system.*
a computer screen/monitor *Make sure your computer screen is at the right height.*
a computer keyboard | **a computer network** (=a set of computers connected to each other) | **a computer program** (=a set of instructions stored inside a computer) | **computer software** (=computer programs) | **computer hardware/equipment** (=machines and equipment, not programs) | **a computer game** | **computer graphics** (=images created by computers) | **computer technology** | **computer science** (=the study of computers and what they can do) | **a computer user** | **a computer programmer** (=someone who writes the instructions a computer uses to do a particular job) | **a computer virus** (=a program that secretly destroys information stored on computers) | **a computer error**

comˌputer-aided deˈsign *n* [U] CAD

comˌputer-aided manuˈfacturing *n* [U] CAM

com·put·er·ate /kəmˈpjuːtərət/ *adj* able to use a computer well: *Students need to be computerate as well as literate.*

com·put·er·ize (*also* **-ise** *BrE*) /kəmˈpjuːtəraɪz/ *v* [T] to use a computer to control the way something is done, to store information etc: *a scheme to computerize the library service* | *a* **computerized system** *for compiling the weekly charts of record sales* | **computerized information** | *a* **computerized database** —**computerization** /kəmˌpjuːtəraɪˈzeɪʃən $ -rə-/ *n* [U]: *the computerization of the printing industry*

comˌputer-ˈliterate *adj* able to use a computer: *Nowadays, all graduates are computer-literate.* —**computer literacy** *n* [U]

comˌputer ˈmodelling *n* [U] the use of computer images that are models of real things, used to help improve the way that something is designed or to solve a problem: *computer modelling of the city's traffic flow*

comˌputer ˈscience *n* [U] the study of computers and what they can do → **information technology**: *a BSc in Computer Science*

comˌputer ˈvirus *n* [C] a set of instructions secretly put into a computer, usually spread through emails, which can destroy information stored on the computer

com·put·ing /kəmˈpjuːtɪŋ/ ●●○ AWL *n* [U] the use of computers as a job, in a business etc: *Have you ever done any computing?* | *computing facilities for language research*

com·rade /ˈkɒmrəd, -reɪd $ ˈkɑːmræd/ *n* [C] **1** *formal* a friend, especially someone who shares difficult work or danger: *He misses his comrades from his days in the army.* **2** SOCIALISTS or COMMUNISTS often call each other 'comrade', especially in meetings: *Comrades, please support this motion.* —**comradely** *adj*

ˌcomrade in ˈarms *n* (*plural* **comrades in arms**) [C] someone who has fought with you or worked with you to achieve particular aims

com·rade·ship /ˈkɒmrədʃɪp, -reɪd- $ ˈkɑːmræd-/ *n* [U] *formal* friendship and loyalty among people who work together, fight together etc: *It was the spirit of comradeship that made victory possible.*

con¹ /kɒn $ kɑːn/ *v* (**conned**, **conning**) [T] *informal* **1** to get money from someone by deceiving them SYN **swindle**: **con sb out of sth** *He conned me out of £300.* **2** to persuade someone to do something by deceiving them SYN **trick**: **con sb into doing sth** *You had no right to con me into thinking I could trust you.*

con² *n* [C] *informal* **1** a trick to get someone's money or make them do something: *a con to make people pay for goods they hadn't actually received* **2** a prisoner → MOD CONS, → **the pros and cons** at PRO¹(3)

con- /kən, kɒn $ kən, kɑːn/ *prefix* together SYN **with**: *a confederation* | *to conspire* (=plan together)

Con *BrE* the written abbreviation of ***Conservative***, in British politics: *Sir Teddy Taylor (Con)*

ˈcon ˌartist *n* [C] *informal* someone who tricks or deceives people in order to get money from them

con·cat·e·na·tion /kɒnˌkætəˈneɪʃən $ kɑːn-/ *n* [C,U] *formal* a series of events or things joined together one after another: **[+of]** *a strange concatenation of events*

CONCAVE

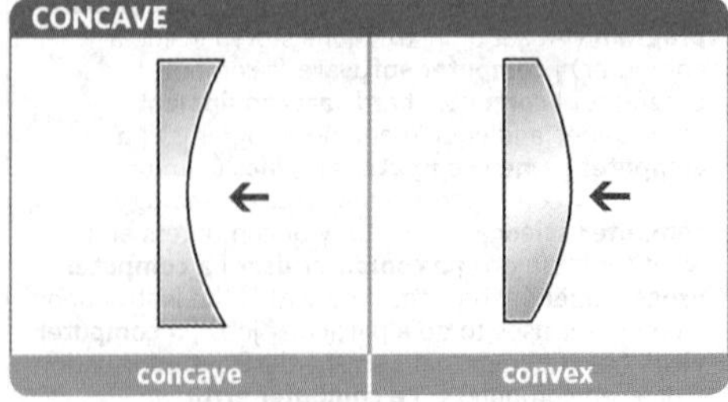

con·cave /ˌkɒnˈkeɪv◂, kən- $ ˌkɑːnˈkeɪv◂, kən-/ *adj* a concave surface is curved inwards in the middle OPP **convex**: *a concave lens*

con·cav·i·ty /kənˈkævəti/ *n* (*plural* **concavities**) *formal* **1** [U] the state of being concave **2** [C] a place or shape that is curved inwards

con·ceal /kənˈsiːl/ ●●○ *v* [T] *formal* **1** to hide something carefully: *The shadows concealed her as she crept up to the house.* | *The path was concealed by long grass.* | *a* **concealed weapon** THESAURUS ▸ HIDE **2** to hide your real feelings or the truth: *She tried to* **conceal the fact that** *she was pregnant.* | **conceal sth from sb** *She was taking drugs and trying to conceal it from me.* —**concealment** *n* [U]: *deliberate concealment of his activities*

con·cede /kənˈsiːd/ ●○○ *v*

1 ADMIT STH IS TRUE [I,T] to admit that something is true or correct, although you wish it were not true → **concession**: *'That's the only possible solution.' 'Yes, I suppose so,' Charles conceded.* | **concede (that)** *I conceded that I had made a number of errors.* THESAURUS ▸ ADMIT

2 ADMIT DEFEAT [I,T] to admit that you are not going to win a game, argument, battle etc → **concession**: *The Georgian forces defended the capital but were finally obliged to concede.* | *In May 1949, Stalin* **conceded defeat** *and reopened land access to Berlin.*

3 concede a goal/point/penalty to not be able to stop your opponent from getting a GOAL etc during a game: *The team has conceded only 19 goals in 28 games.*

4 GIVE STH AS A RIGHT [T] to give something to someone as a right or PRIVILEGE, often unwillingly → **concession**: **concede sth to sb** *The King finally agreed to concede further powers to Parliament.* | *Finally the company conceded wage increases to their workers.*

con·ceit /kənˈsiːt/ *n* **1** [U] an attitude that shows you have too high an opinion of your own abilities or importance SYN **conceitedness**: *The conceit of the woman!* **2** [C] *technical* an unusual way of showing or describing something in a play, film, work of art etc: *His sermons were full of puns and conceits.*

con·ceit·ed /kənˈsiːtɪd/ ●○○ *adj* someone who is conceited thinks they are very clever, skilful, beautiful etc - used to show disapproval SYN **vain**: *You're the most conceited selfish person I've ever known.* THESAURUS ▸ PROUD —**conceitedly** *adv* —**conceitedness** *n* [U]

con·ceiv·a·ble /kənˈsiːvəbəl/ ●○○ AWL *adj* able to be believed or imagined OPP **inconceivable**: ***It is conceivable that*** *you may get full compensation, but it's not likely.* | *We were discussing the problems from* **every conceivable** *angle.* —**conceivably** *adv*: *Conceivably, interest rates could rise very high indeed.*

con·ceive /kənˈsiːv/ ●●○ AWL *v*

1 [I,T] *formal* to imagine a particular situation or to think about something in a particular way: **(cannot) conceive of (doing) sth** *Many people can't conceive of a dinner without meat or fish.* | **conceive that** *He could not conceive that anything really serious could be worrying his friend.* | **conceive what/why/how etc** *I can hardly conceive what it must be like here in winter.* | **conceive of sth/sb as sth** *Language may be conceived of as a process which arises from social interaction.*

2 [T] to think of a new idea, plan etc and develop it in your mind → **conception**: *Scientists first conceived the idea of the atomic bomb in the 1930s.* THESAURUS ▸ INVENT

3 [I,T] to become PREGNANT → **conception**: *fertility treatment for women who have difficulty conceiving*

con·cen·trate¹ /ˈkɒnsəntreɪt $ ˈkɑːn-/ ●●● S2 W2 AWL *v*

1 [I] to think very carefully about something that you are doing → **concentration**: *Now please concentrate.* | *Adrian was finding it difficult to concentrate.* | **[+on]** *Be quiet – let me concentrate on my homework.*

GRAMMAR

You **concentrate on** something: *I'm trying to concentrate on my work.* ✗ Don't say: *I'm trying to concentrate in my work.*

2 [I,T] to be present in large numbers or amounts somewhere, or to cause people or things to be present in large numbers or amounts somewhere → **concentration**: **be concentrated in/at sth** *Italian industry is concentrated mainly in the north.* | *Construction of the aircraft is being concentrated at Prestwick.* | **[+in/at]** *Women concentrate in a small*

number of occupations. GRAMMAR **Concentrate** is usually passive in this meaning, when used as a transitive verb.
3 sth concentrates the mind if something concentrates the mind, it makes you think very clearly: *Relaxing in a Jacuzzi concentrates the mind wonderfully.*
4 [T] to make a substance or liquid stronger by removing some of the water from it → **concentrated**
concentrate (sth) **on** sth *phr v* to give most of your attention or effort to one thing SYN **focus on**: *Doctors are aiming to concentrate more on prevention than cure.* | **concentrate your efforts/attention/energy/mind etc on sth** *I'm concentrating my efforts on writing my autobiography.*

concentrate² *n* [C,U] a substance or liquid which has been made stronger by removing most of the water from it: *orange juice concentrate*

con·cen·trat·ed /ˈkɒnsəntreɪtɪd $ ˈkɑːn-/ *adj* **1** a concentrated liquid or substance has been made stronger by removing water from it: *concentrated orange juice* | *a concentrated cream detergent* **2** [only before noun] showing a lot of effort or determination: *He made a concentrated effort to improve his work.*

con·cen·tra·tion /ˌkɒnsənˈtreɪʃən $ ˌkɑːn-/ ●●● S3 W2 AWL *n*
1 [U] the ability to think about something carefully or for a long time → **concentrate**: *She needed all her* **powers of concentration** *to stop herself from slipping on the icy road.* | *Lack of concentration was a real problem.* | *I* **lost** *my* **concentration** *and fell asleep.*
2 [U] a process in which you put a lot of attention, energy etc into a particular activity → **concentrate**: **concentration on (doing) sth** *concentration on your health* | *concentration on providing value and service*
3 [C,U] a large amount of something in a particular place or among particular people → **concentrate**: **[+of]** *the concentration of greenhouse gases in the atmosphere* | *the concentration of power in the hands of a few*
4 [C] *technical* the amount of a substance contained in a liquid → **concentrate**: **high/low concentrations** *Additives are expensive but are used in very low concentrations.* | **[+of]** *allowable concentrations of pesticides in drinking water*

conceˈntration ˌcamp *n* [C] a prison where political prisoners and other people who are not soldiers are kept and treated cruelly, especially during a war

con·cen·tric /kənˈsentrɪk/ *adj* having the same centre → **eccentric**: *concentric circles*

con·cept /ˈkɒnsept $ ˈkɑːn-/ ●●○ W2 AWL *n* [C] an idea of how something is, or how something should be done: **[+of]** *the concept of total patient care* | *the concept of infinite space* | **concept that** *the concept that we are citizens of one world* | *a* **new concept** *in business travel* | *our* **basic concepts** *of decent human behaviour* | *It's very simple, once you* **grasp** *the* **concept**. THESAURUS ▸ IDEA

con·cep·tion /kənˈsepʃən/ ●○○ AWL *n*
1 [C,U] an idea about what something is like, or a general understanding of something → **concept**: **[+of]** *the conception of parliamentary democracy* | *changing conceptions of the world* | **have (no) conception of sth** *They have no conception of what women really feel and want.*
2 [U] a process in which someone forms a plan or idea → **conceive**: *the original conception of the book*
3 [C,U] the process by which a woman or female animal becomes PREGNANT, or the time when this happens → **conceive**: *the moment of conception*

con·cep·tu·al /kənˈseptʃuəl/ ●○○ AWL *adj formal* dealing with ideas, or based on them: *the conceptual framework of the play* —**conceptually** *adv*

conˌceptual ˈart *n* [U] *technical* art in which the main aim of the artist is to show an idea, rather than to represent actual things or people

con·cep·tu·al·ize (*also* **-ise** *BrE*) /kənˈseptʃuəlaɪz/ *v* [I,T] to form an idea: *How do older people conceptualize their health?* —**conceptualization** /kənˌseptʃuəlaɪˈzeɪʃən $ -lə-/ *n* [C,U]

con·cern¹ /kənˈsɜːn $ -ɜːrn/ ●●● S3 W1 *n*
1 WORRY **a)** [U] a feeling of worry about something important: *The recent rise in crime is a matter of considerable public concern.* | **[+for]** *our concern for human rights* | **[+about/over/with]** *the rise of concern about the environment* | *the growing concern over inflation* | *concern with worsening law and order* | **concern that** *increased concern that the war could continue for a long time* | **be a cause for concern/cause concern** *The activities of the far right have been a cause for concern for a while now.* | *In her last days the poet* **expressed concern** *for her father.* **b)** [C] something that worries you: *One of the concerns that people have is the side effects of treatment.* | *Education remains the electorate's main concern.* | *the* **concerns expressed** *by parents*
2 STH IMPORTANT [C,U] something that is important to you or that involves you: *His main concern is to be able to provide for his family.* | **[+for]** *The consumer has become a major concern for this government.* | **of concern to sb** *topics of concern to television viewers*
3 FEELING FOR SB [singular, U] a feeling of wanting someone to be happy and healthy: *He was moved by her obvious concern.* | **[+for]** *parents' loving concern for their children*
4 sb's concern if something is your concern, you are responsible for it: *The money side of the business is your concern.*
5 not sb's concern/none of sb's concern if something is not your concern, you are not interested in it and you do not need to worry about it or become involved in it: *His affairs were none of her concern.*
6 BUSINESS [C] a business or company: *The restaurant is a family concern.* | *We will continue to run the company as* **a going concern** (=a business that is financially successful).

concern² ●●○ W3 *v* [T]
1 [not in passive] if a story, book, report etc concerns someone or something, it is about them: *This study concerns couples' expectations of marriage.* | *The report concerns the drug traffic on the Mexican–US border.*

> **REGISTER**
> In everyday English, people usually say something **is about** something or, in British English, **is/has to do with** something, rather than say it **concerns** something: *The book* **is about** *women's experiences of war.*

2 to make someone feel worried or upset: *Issues like food additives do concern me.*
3 if an activity, situation, rule etc concerns you, it affects you or involves you: *The tax changes will concern large corporations rather than small businesses.* GRAMMAR **Concern** is never passive in this meaning.
4 concern yourself with/about sth *formal* to become involved in something because you are interested in it or because it worries you: *He told them not to concern themselves about him.* | *He loved his wife, and concerned himself with her needs and desires.*
5 to whom it may concern an expression written at the beginning of a formal letter when you do not know the name of the person you want to communicate with

con·cerned /kənˈsɜːnd $ -ɜːrnd/ ●●● S2 W2 *adj*
1 INVOLVED [not before noun] involved in something or affected by it: *Divorce is very painful, especially when children are concerned.* | *Some of the farmers concerned suffer particularly from the low prices.* | *We are trying to reach an agreement with* **all concerned** (=everyone who is involved or affected). | **[+with]** *all the people concerned with children's education* | **[+in]** *There was no evidence that he was concerned in any criminal activity.*
2 WORRIED worried about something: **[+about]** *She is concerned about how little food I eat.* | **[+for]** *He called the police because he was concerned for Gemma's safety.* | **concerned (that)** *Pamela was concerned that her schoolwork had deteriorated despite her hard work.* | *The drug came under strong attack from concerned professional observers.* THESAURUS ▸ WORRIED
3 as far as sb is concerned *spoken* used to show what someone's opinion on a subject is or how it affects them: *As far as Americans are concerned, a lot of our hotels are*

below average. | *As far as I'm concerned, you can forget about it.*
4 as far as sth is concerned (*also* **where sth is concerned**) *spoken* used to show which subject or thing you are talking about: *As far as traffic is concerned there are no delays at the moment.*
5 THINK STH IS IMPORTANT [not before noun] believing that something is important: **[+with]** *Many politicians are more concerned with power and control than with the good of the people.* | **concerned to do sth** *Mr Quinn is simply concerned to hold on to his job.*
6 LOVE/CARE caring about someone and whether they are happy and healthy: **[+for/about]** *He was genuinely concerned for the children.*
7 concerned with sb/sth if a book, story etc is concerned with a person, subject etc, it is about that subject: *This chapter is concerned with the mental health of older people.*

C

con·cern·ing /kən'sɜːnɪŋ $ -ɜːr-/ ●●○ W3 *prep* about or relating to: *calls from young children concerning lost pets* | *the facts concerning Marr's car crash* THESAURUS ABOUT

REGISTER
In everyday English, people usually say **about** rather than **concerning**: *I've already written to him* ***about*** *the problem.*

con·cert /'kɒnsət $ 'kɑːnsərt/ ●●● S3 W3 *n* [C]
1 a performance given by musicians or singers: *a rock concert* | *a concert of French choral music* | *We were going to a concert in Bath Abbey.* | *She still does about 100 concerts every year.*
2 in concert (with sb) a) *formal* people who do something in concert do it together after having agreed on it: *Britain has to pursue policies in concert with other EU members.* | *It appeared that both the accused were* ***acting in concert*** *in the attack upon the deceased.* **b)** playing or singing at a concert: *They're appearing in concert tonight at the Royal Concert Hall.*

COLLOCATIONS

VERBS

go to a concert (*also* **attend a concert** *formal*) *Do you want to go to the concert in the park this weekend?*
give/do a concert *The group gave concerts for charity throughout Europe.*
play in/perform in a concert *I'm playing in a jazz concert on Saturday night.*
put on a concert (*also* **stage a concert** *formal*) (=arrange one) *The music club puts on regular concerts throughout the year.*

ADJECTIVES/NOUN + concert

a pop/rock/jazz/classical concert *There were 150,000 people at the rock concert in Frankfurt.*
an orchestral concert/a symphony concert (=one in which an orchestra plays) *Tickets for orchestral concerts range from $15 to $35.*
a live concert (=that you watch as the performers play, rather than as a recording) *a live concert in front of 500 fans*
an open-air/outdoor concert

concert + NOUN

a concert performance *She gave a number of concert performances in Berlin.*
a concert tour (=a journey made by musicians to perform in different places) *This year we did a concert tour of the United States.*
a concert hall | **a concert ticket** | **a concert pianist** (=who performs in concerts)

con·cert·ed /kən'sɜːtɪd $ -ɜːr-/ *adj* **concerted effort/action/attack etc** a concerted effort etc is done by people working together in a carefully planned and very determined way: *Libraries have* ***made*** *a* ***concerted effort*** *to attract young people.* —**concertedly** *adv*

con·cert·go·er /'kɒnsət,gəʊə $ 'kɑːnsərt,goʊər/ *n* [C] someone who often goes to concerts, or someone who is at a particular concert

'concert hall *n* [C] a large public building where concerts are performed

con·cer·ti·na¹ /,kɒnsə'tiːnə $,kɑːnsər-/ *n* [C] a musical instrument like a small ACCORDION, that you hold in both hands and play by pressing in from each side

concertina² *v* [I] *BrE* if something concertinas, it folds together on itself

con·cert·mas·ter /'kɒnsət,mɑːstə $ 'kɑːnsərt,mæstər/ *n* [C] the most important VIOLIN player in an ORCHESTRA

con·cer·to /kən'tʃɜːtəʊ $ -'tʃertoʊ/ *n* (*plural* **concertos**) [C] a piece of CLASSICAL music, usually for one instrument and an ORCHESTRA

con·ces·sion /kən'seʃən/ ●○○ *n*
1 STH YOU ALLOW SB [C] something that you allow someone to have in order to end an argument or a disagreement → **concede**: **[+to]** *a policy of no concessions to terrorists* | *The British were not prepared to* ***make*** *any* ***concessions***. | **[+on]** *his readiness to make concessions on many of the issues raised* | **[+from]** *We will try to force further concessions from the government.* | **major/important/substantial concession** *The committee has* ***won*** *a number of major* ***concessions*** *from the prison authorities.*
2 A RIGHT [C,U] a special right that a particular person or group of people is allowed to have, for example by the government or an employer, or the act of giving or allowing something as a right: *the ending of* ***tax concessions*** *for home owners* | *the import/export* ***concessions*** *that had been* ***granted*** *to the island* | **[+of]** *the concession of autonomy to the universities*
3 PRICE REDUCTION [C] *BrE* a reduction in the price of tickets, FEES etc for certain groups of people, for example old people or children SYN **reduction**: *To qualify for travel concessions you have to be 60.* | *Open daily, adults £4, concessions £2* (=people who have the right to a concession pay £2).
4 CHANGE OF BEHAVIOUR [C] a change in your behaviour that you make because of a particular situation or idea: *He took off his jacket* ***as a concession to*** *the heat.* | *He* ***made*** *no* ***concessions to*** *fashion.*
5 BUSINESS [C] *AmE* **a)** the right to have a business in a particular place, especially in a place owned by someone else: *The company owns valuable logging and mining concessions.* **b)** a small business that sells things in a place owned by someone else: *Joe runs a hamburger concession in the mall.*
6 THINGS SOLD **concessions** [plural] *AmE* the things sold at a concession stand

con·ces·sion·aire /kən,seʃə'neə $ -'ner/ *n* [C] someone who has been given the right to have a business in a particular place, especially in a place owned by someone else

con·ces·sion·ar·y /kən'seʃənəri $ -neri/ *adj* **1** given as a concession **2** *BrE* specially reduced in price, for example for old people or children: *a* ***concessionary fares*** *scheme for pensioners*

con'cession ,stand *n* [C] *AmE* a small business that sells food, drinks, or other things at sports events, theatres etc

conch /kɒntʃ, kɒŋk $ kɑːntʃ, kɑːŋk/ *n* [C] the large twisted shell of a tropical sea animal that looks like a SNAIL

con·ci·erge /'kɒnsieəʒ $,kɑːnsi'erʒ/ *n* [C] **1** someone in a hotel whose job is to help guests by telling them about places to visit, restaurants to eat in etc **2** someone who looks after a block of apartments and who checks who is going in and coming out, especially in France

con·cil·i·ate /kən'sɪlieɪt/ *v* [I,T] *formal* to do something to make people more likely to stop arguing, especially by giving them something they want: *efforts to conciliate the unions* —**conciliator** *n* [C]

con·cil·i·a·tion /kən,sɪli'eɪʃən/ *n* [U] *formal* the process of trying to get people to stop arguing and agree → **reconciliation**: *conciliation talks between the two sides*

con·cil·i·a·tory /kənˈsɪliətəri $ -tɔːri/ *adj* doing something that is intended to make someone stop arguing with you: **conciliatory approach/tone/gesture etc** *Perhaps you should adopt a more conciliatory approach.* | *Brooks felt in no mood to be conciliatory.*

con·cise /kənˈsaɪs/ ●○○ *adj*
1 short, with no unnecessary words SYN **brief**: *Your summary should be as* ***clear and concise*** *as possible.*
2 [only before noun] shorter than the original book on which something is based: *the 'Concise Dictionary of Spoken Chinese'* —**concisely** *adv* —**conciseness** *n* [U]

con·clave /ˈkɒŋkleɪv $ ˈkɑːŋ-/ *n* [C] *formal* a private and secret meeting

con·clude /kənˈkluːd/ ●●○ W2 AWL *v*
1 [T] to decide that something is true after considering all the information you have → **conclusion**: **conclude that** *The report concluded that the school should be closed immediately.* | **conclude from sth that** *Richardson concluded from his studies that equality between the sexes is still a long way off.*

GRAMMAR
In more formal English, you can say **it is concluded that** something is true: *It was concluded that the treatment should be stopped.*

2 [T] *formal* to complete something you have been doing, especially for a long time: *When the investigation is concluded, the results will be sent to the US Attorney's office.* | *Francis, having concluded his business with James, left for Miami.* **THESAURUS** FINISH
3 [I,T] to end something such as a meeting, book, event, or speech by doing or saying one final thing: **[+with]** *Each chapter concludes with a short summary.* | **conclude by doing sth** *She concluded by saying she was proud to be from Salford.* | ***To conclude****, I'd like to express my thanks to my family.* | *'So now,' she concluded, 'I'm trying to bring some order to the garden.'*
4 conclude an agreement/treaty/contract etc to finish arranging an agreement etc successfully: *That same year, France concluded a trading agreement with Spain.*

con·clu·ding /kənˈkluːdɪŋ/ AWL *adj* **concluding remark/section/stage etc** the last remark etc in an event or piece of writing: *the concluding section of Chapter 6* **THESAURUS** LAST

con·clu·sion /kənˈkluːʒən/ ●●○ S3 W2 AWL *n*
1 [C] something you decide after considering all the information you have → **conclude**: *These are the report's main conclusions.* | **conclusion (that)** *I soon* ***came to the conclusion that*** *she was lying.* | *It is still too early to* ***reach*** *a* ***conclusion*** *on this point.* | *There are perhaps two main* ***conclusions*** *to be* ***drawn*** *from the above discussion.* | *All the evidence* ***pointed to the conclusion*** *that he was guilty.* | *It's important not to* ***jump to conclusions****.* | *The police came to the* ***inescapable conclusion*** *that the children had been murdered.*
2 [C] *formal* the end or final part of something SYN **end**: **[+of]** *At the conclusion of the meeting, little progress had been made.*
3 in conclusion used in a piece of writing or a speech to show that you are about to finish what you are saying SYN **finally**: *In conclusion, I would like to say how much I have enjoyed myself today.*

GRAMMAR
You say: *In conclusion, education reinforces democracy.*
✗ Don't say: *As a conclusion ...* | *As conclusion ...*
GRAMMAR GUIDE NOUNS

4 [U] the final arrangement of an agreement, a business deal etc: **[+of]** *the conclusion of a peace treaty*
5 be a foregone conclusion to be certain to happen, even though it has not yet officially happened: *The outcome of the battle was a foregone conclusion.*

THESAURUS
conclusion something you decide after considering all the information you have: *Doctors failed to reach a conclusion on the exact cause of death.* | *The report's main conclusion was that global warming was a serious threat.*
findings the information that someone has discovered as a result of their study, work etc: *Surveys conducted in other countries reported similar findings.*
result the answers that are provided by a scientific study or test: *Have you had the result of your blood test yet?*

con·clu·sive /kənˈkluːsɪv/ AWL *adj* showing that something is definitely true OPP **inconclusive**: **conclusive proof/evidence/findings etc** *The investigation failed to provide any conclusive evidence.* —**conclusively** *adv*

con·coct /kənˈkɒkt $ -ˈkɑːkt/ *v* [T] **1** to invent a clever story, excuse, or plan, especially in order to deceive someone: *John* ***concocted*** *an elaborate* ***excuse*** *for being late.* **2** to make something, especially food or drink, by mixing different things, especially things that are not usually combined: *Jean concocted a great meal from the leftovers.*

con·coc·tion /kənˈkɒkʃən $ -ˈkɑːk-/ *n* [C] something, especially a drink or food, made by mixing different things, especially things that are not usually combined: *He sipped the concoction cautiously.*

con·com·i·tant¹ /kənˈkɒmɪtənt $ -ˈkɑː-/ *adj formal* existing or happening together, especially as a result of something SYN **attendant**: *war with all its concomitant sufferings* —**concomitantly** *adv*

concomitant² *n* [C] *formal* something that often or naturally happens with something else: **[+of]** *Deafness is a frequent concomitant of old age.*

con·cord /ˈkɒŋkɔːd $ ˈkɑːŋkɔːrd/ *n* [U] **1** *formal* the state of having a friendly relationship, so that you agree on things and live in peace OPP **discord 2** *technical* in grammar, concord between words happens when they match correctly, for example when a plural noun has a plural verb following it

con·cor·dance /kənˈkɔːdəns $ -ɔːr-/ *n* **1** [C] an alphabetical list of all the words used in a book or set of books, with information about where they can be found and usually about how they are used: *a Shakespeare concordance* | **[+to]** *a concordance to the Bible* **2** [C] a list of all the words in a book, magazine etc, held on a computer DATABASE, showing every example of a particular word in the book etc: *concordance lines* **3** [U] *formal* the state of being similar to something else or in agreement with it: *the concordance between the proposals*

con·cor·dant /kənˈkɔːdənt $ -ɔːr-/ *adj formal* being in agreement or having the same regular pattern

con·course /ˈkɒŋkɔːs $ ˈkɑːŋkɔːrs/ *n* [C] **1** a large hall or open place in a building such as an airport or train station **2** *formal* a large crowd that has gathered together: **[+of]** *an immense concourse of spectators*

con·crete¹ /ˈkɒŋkriːt $ kɑːnˈkriːt/ ●●○ *adj*
1 made of concrete: *a concrete floor*
2 definite and specific → **abstract**: *What does that mean* ***in concrete terms****?* | *the lack of any* ***concrete evidence*** | *a dialogue about concrete issues and problems* —**concretely** *adv*

con·crete² /ˈkɒŋkriːt $ ˈkɑːŋ-/ ●●○ *n* [U] a substance used for building that is made by mixing sand, small stones, CEMENT, and water

con·crete³ /ˈkɒŋkriːt $ ˈkɑːŋ-/ *v* [T] to cover something such as a path, wall etc with concrete

ˌconcrete ˈjungle *n* [C usually singular] an unpleasant area in a city that is full of big ugly buildings and has no open spaces

ˈconcrete ˌmixer *n* [C] a CEMENT MIXER

ˌconcrete ˈnoun *n* [C] a noun that names a physical thing, animal, or person that you are able to hear, see, smell, touch, or taste. For example, 'book' and 'child' are concrete nouns. → **abstract noun**

con·cu·bine /ˈkɒŋkjəbaɪn $ ˈkɑːŋ-/ *n* [C] a woman in the past who lived with and had sex with a man who already had a wife or wives, but who was socially less important than the wives

con·cur /kən'kɜː $ -'kɜːr/ *v* (**concurred**, **concurring**) [I] *formal* **1** to agree with someone or have the same opinion as them: **[+with]** *The committee largely concurred with these views.* THESAURUS ▸ AGREE **2** to happen at the same time SYN **coincide**: **concur to do sth** *Everything concurred to produce the desired effect.*

con·cur·rence /kən'kʌrəns $ -'kɜːr-/ *n formal* **1** [C] an example of events, actions etc happening at the same time: **[+of]** *a strange concurrence of events* **2** [U] agreement: **[+with]** *Jules expressed his concurrence with the suggestion.*

con·cur·rent /kən'kʌrənt $ -'kɜːr-/ AWL *adj* **1** existing or happening at the same time: *The exhibition reflected concurrent developments abroad.* **2** *formal* in agreement: **[+with]** *My opinions are concurrent with yours.* —**concurrently** *adv*: *Because his prison sentences* ***run concurrently****, he could be free in two years.*

con·cuss /kən'kʌs/ *v* [T] if you are concussed, something hits you on the head, making you lose consciousness or feel sick for a short time: *He was concussed by the blast.*

con·cus·sion /kən'kʌʃən/ *n* **1** [U] *BrE* temporary damage to the brain that makes you lose consciousness or feel sick for a short time, usually caused by something hitting your head: **with concussion** *He was taken into hospital with concussion.* **2** [C] *AmE* an injury to the brain that makes you lose consciousness or feel sick for a short time, usually caused by something hitting your head: *I* ***had*** *a* ***concussion****, a broken leg and some minor injuries.* | *He suffered a* ***mild/serious concussion*** *as a result of the accident.* **3** [C usually singular] a violent shaking movement, caused by the very loud sound of something such as an explosion: *The ground shuddered and heaved with the concussion of the blast.*

con·demn /kən'dem/ ●○○ *v* [T]

1 DISAPPROVE to say very strongly that you do not approve of something or someone, especially because you think it is morally wrong: *Politicians were quick to condemn the bombing.* | **condemn sth/sb as sth** *The law has been condemned as an attack on personal liberty.* | **condemn sb/sth for (doing) sth** *She knew that society would condemn her for leaving her children.* THESAURUS ▸ CRITICIZE

2 PUNISH to give someone a severe punishment after deciding they are guilty of a crime: **condemn sb to sth** *He was found guilty and* ***condemned to death****.*

3 FORCE TO DO STH if a particular situation condemns someone to something, it forces them to live in an unpleasant way or to do something unpleasant: **condemn sb to (do) sth** *people condemned to a life of poverty* | *His occupation condemned him to spend long periods of time away from his family.*

4 NOT SAFE to state officially that something is not safe enough to be used: *an old house that had been condemned* | **condemn sth as sth** *The pool was closed after being condemned as a health hazard.*

con·dem·na·tion /ˌkɒndəm'neɪʃən, -dem- $ ˌkɑːn-/ ●○○ *n* [C,U] an expression of very strong disapproval of someone or something, especially something you think is morally wrong: **[+of]** *There was widespread international condemnation of the bombing.*

con·dem·na·to·ry /kən'demnətəri, ˌkɒndem'neɪtəri $ kən'demnətɔːri/ *adj* expressing strong disapproval: *my father's condemnatory attitude*

con·demned /kən'demd/ *adj* [only before noun] **1** a condemned person is going to be punished by being killed **2** a condemned building is officially not safe to live in or use

con'demned ˌcell *n* [C] *BrE* a room for a prisoner who was going to be punished by death → **death row**

con·den·sa·tion /ˌkɒnden'seɪʃən, -dən- $ ˌkɑːn-/ *n* **1** [U] small drops of water that are formed when steam or warm air touches a cold surface: *There was a lot of condensation on the windows.* **2** [U] *technical* when a gas becomes a liquid **3** [C,U] *formal* the act of making something shorter

con·dense /kən'dens/ ●○○ *v*

1 [I,T] if a gas condenses, or is condensed, it becomes a liquid: *the mist which condensed on every cold surface* | **[+into]** *The gaseous metal is cooled and condenses into liquid zinc.*

2 [T] to make something that is spoken or written shorter, by not giving as much detail or using fewer words to give the same information: **condense sth into sth** *This whole chapter could be condensed into a few paragraphs.*

3 [T] to make a liquid thicker by removing some of the water: ***condensed soup***

conˌdensed 'milk *n* [U] a type of thick sweet milk sold in cans

con·dens·er /kən'densə $ -ər/ *n* [C] **1** a piece of equipment that changes a gas into a liquid **2** a machine for storing electricity, especially in a car engine

con·de·scend /ˌkɒndɪ'send $ ˌkɑːn-/ *v* [I] **1** to behave as if you think you are better, more intelligent, or more important than other people – used to show disapproval: **[+to]** *Take care not to condescend to your readers.* **2** to do something in a way that shows you think it is below your social or professional position – used to show disapproval: **condescend to do sth** *'Yes. I know,' Clara said, condescending to look at Rose for the first time.* —**condescension** /-'senʃən/ *n* [U]

con·de·scend·ing /ˌkɒndɪ'sendɪŋ◂ $ ˌkɑːn-/ *adj* behaving as though you think you are better, more intelligent, or more important than other people – used to show disapproval SYN **patronizing**: *Professor Hutter's manner is extremely condescending.* —**condescendingly** *adv*

con·di·ment /'kɒndəmənt $ 'kɑːn-/ *n* [C] *formal* a powder or liquid, such as salt or KETCHUP, that you use to give a special taste to food

con·di·tion[1] /kən'dɪʃən/ ●●● S2 W1 *n*

1 SITUATION **conditions** [plural] the situation in which people live or work, especially the physical things that affect the quality of their lives: *Conditions in the prison were atrocious.* | **living/working conditions** *an attempt to improve living conditions for the working classes* | ***Poor working conditions*** *lead to demoralized and unproductive employees.* | **in appalling/overcrowded/dreadful etc conditions** *These children work 70 metres below ground in appalling conditions.* | *In May, staff went on strike, demanding better* ***pay and conditions****.*

2 WEATHER **conditions** [plural] the weather at a particular time, especially when you are considering how this affects people: *The conditions during the first half of the match were appalling.* | **cold/windy/icy etc conditions** *In cold conditions you'll need a sleeping bag with a hood.* | *the worsening weather conditions*

3 THINGS AFFECTING SITUATION **conditions** [plural] all the things that affect the way something happens: **under ... conditions** *Under normal conditions, people will usually do what requires least effort.* | *Under these conditions, the fire can be rapidly controlled.* | *Profits increased by £1.5m, despite the difficult economic conditions.* | *The combination of rain and greasy surfaces made driving conditions treacherous.*

4 STATE [singular, U] the state that something is in, especially how good or bad its physical state is: **in (a) good/poor/excellent/terrible etc condition** *The car has been well maintained and is in excellent condition.* | *The house was in a terrible condition.* | **[+of]** *The condition of nuclear plants is a matter of great concern.*

5 HEALTH/FITNESS [singular, U] how healthy or fit you are: *She is being treated at Walton Hospital, where her condition is described as 'satisfactory'.* | **in (a) critical/stable/satisfactory condition** *One of the victims was in a critical condition after suffering severe burns.* | **physical/mental condition** *If you are uncertain about your physical condition, check with your doctor before trying these exercises.* | *'I'm so* ***out of condition*** *(=unfit),' she panted.* | *an athlete* ***in peak condition*** | **in no condition to do sth** (=too drunk, ill, or upset to be able to do something) *I was in no condition to cope* *with a train journey.* | *Mark can't possibly drive home* ***in that condition*** (=when he is so drunk, ill, or upset).

6 AGREEMENT/CONTRACT [C] something that you must agree to in order for something to happen, especially when this is included in a contract: *She* ***laid down*** *only one* ***condition****: that her name not be revealed.* | **[+for]** *There were* ***strict conditions*** *for letting us use their information.* | *The bank agreed to extend the loan if* ***certain conditions*** *were* ***met****.* | *A statement of your* ***terms and conditions*** *of employment can be found in the Personnel Handbook.* | *He was released on bail* ***on condition that*** *he did not go within half a mile of his mother's address.* | *The application was approved,* ***subject to*** *certain* ***conditions****.*

7 FOR STH TO HAPPEN [C] something that must exist or happen first, before something else can happen: **[+for/of]** *Our goal is to create the conditions for a lasting peace.* | *Investment is a* ***necessary condition*** *of economic growth.*

8 ILLNESS [C] an illness or health problem that affects you permanently or for a very long time: *People* ***suffering from*** *this* ***condition*** *should not smoke.* | **heart/lung etc condition** *She has a serious heart condition.* | *Was he being treated for any* ***medical condition****?* **THESAURUS** ILLNESS

9 SITUATION OF GROUP [singular] *formal* the situation or state of a particular group of people, especially when they have problems and difficulties: *the condition of the poor in our cities* | *All my paintings are ultimately about the* ***human condition****.*

10 NEVER **on no condition** never: *On no condition should untrained personnel use the equipment.*

condition[2] *v* **1** [T] to make a person or an animal think or behave in a certain way by influencing or training them over a period of time → **conditioning**: *People are conditioned by society.* | **condition sb to do sth** *Many women are conditioned from birth to be accepting rather than questioning.* **2** [T] *formal* to control or decide the way in which something can happen or exist SYN **determine**: *What I buy is conditioned by the amount I earn.* **3** [I,T] to keep hair or skin healthy by putting a special liquid on it → **conditioner**: *a shampoo that washes and conditions all in one*

con·di·tion·al[1] /kən'dɪʃənəl/ ●○○ *adj*
1 if an offer, agreement etc is conditional, it will only be done if something else happens first OPP **unconditional**: *a conditional acceptance* | **[+on/upon]** *His agreement to buy our house was conditional on our leaving all the furniture in it.*
2 in grammar, a conditional sentence is one that begins with 'if' or 'unless' and expresses something that must be true or happen before something else can be true or happen —**conditionally** *adv*

conditional[2] *n* [C] a sentence or CLAUSE that is expressed in a conditional form

con,ditional 'discharge *n* [C usually singular] a judgment made by a court that allows someone who has done something illegal not to be punished if they obey rules set by the court

con·di·tion·er /kən'dɪʃənə $ -ər/ *n* [C,U] **1** a liquid that you put onto your hair after washing it to make it softer **2** *BrE* a liquid that you wash clothes in to make them softer SYN **softener** *AmE*

con·di·tion·ing /kən'dɪʃənɪŋ/ *n* [U] the process by which people or animals are trained to behave in a particular way when particular things happen: ***Social conditioning*** *makes crying more difficult for men.* → AIR CONDITIONING

con·do /'kɒndəʊ $ 'kɑːndoʊ/ *n* (*plural* **condos**) [C] *AmE informal* a CONDOMINIUM

con·do·lence /kən'dəʊləns $ -'doʊ-/ *n* [C usually plural, U] sympathy for someone who has had something bad happen to them, especially when someone has died: ***a letter of condolence*** | **send/offer your condolences** (=formally express your sympathy when someone has died)

con·dom /'kɒndəm $ 'kɑːn-, 'kʌn-/ ●○○ *n* [C] a thin rubber bag that a man wears over his PENIS (=sex organ) during sex, to prevent a woman having a baby or to protect against disease

con·do·min·i·um /,kɒndə'mɪniəm $,kɑːn-/ ●●○ *n* [C] *especially AmE*
1 one apartment in a building with several apartments, each of which is owned by the people living in it
2 a building containing several of these apartments → **apartment block**

con·done /kən'dəʊn $ -'doʊn/ *v* [T] to accept or forgive behaviour that most people think is morally wrong: *I cannot condone the use of violence under any circumstances.*

con·dor /'kɒndɔː $ 'kɑːndər, -dɔːr/ *n* [C] a very large South American VULTURE (=a bird that eats dead animals)

con·du·cive /kən'djuːsɪv $ -'duː-/ *adj* **be conducive to sth** *formal* if a situation is conducive to something such as work, rest etc, it provides conditions that make it easy for you to work etc: *an environment conducive to learning*

con·duct[1] /kən'dʌkt/ ●●○ W2 AWL *v*
1 CARRY OUT [T] to carry out a particular activity or process, especially in order to get information or prove facts: **conduct a survey/investigation/review etc** *We are conducting a survey of consumer attitudes towards organic food.* | **conduct an experiment/a test** *Is it really necessary to conduct experiments on animals?* | **conduct a campaign** *They conducted a campaign of bombings and assassinations.* | **conduct an interview** *The interview was conducted in English.* | *The memorial service was conducted by the Rev. David Prior.* | *It was the first time that I had conducted business in Brazil.*

> **REGISTER**
> In everyday English, people usually say **do** or **carry out** rather than **conduct**: *They're* ***doing*** *a survey of opinions about organic food.*

2 MUSIC [I,T] to stand in front of a group of musicians or singers and direct their playing or singing → **conductor**: **conduct an orchestra/choir** *The orchestra is conducted by John Williams.* | *Who will be conducting?*
3 BEHAVE **conduct yourself** *formal* to behave in a particular way, especially in a situation where people judge you by the way you behave: *The players conducted themselves impeccably, both on and off the field.*
4 ELECTRICITY/HEAT [T] if something conducts electricity or heat, it allows electricity or heat to travel along or through it → **conductor**: *Aluminium, being a metal, readily* ***conducts heat****.*
5 SHOW SB STH [T always + adv/prep] *formal* to take or lead someone somewhere: **conduct sb to sth** *On arrival, I was conducted to the commandant's office.* | **conducted tour (of sth)** (=a tour of a building, city, or area with someone who tells you about that place) *a conducted tour of Berlin*

con·duct[2] /'kɒndʌkt $ 'kɑːn-/ ●●○ AWL *n* [U] *formal*
1 the way someone behaves, especially in public, in their job etc SYN **behaviour**: *The Senator's conduct is being investigated by the Ethics Committee.* | *an inquiry into the conduct of the police* | **ethical/professional etc conduct** *the Law Society's Code of Professional Conduct* | **improper/violent/offensive etc conduct** | *his arrest for* ***disorderly conduct*** (=noisy violent behaviour) **THESAURUS** BEHAVIOUR
2 conduct of sth the way in which an activity is organized and carried out: *complaints about the conduct of the elections* | *Disclosure of information would compromise the proper conduct of the investigation.*

con·duc·tion /kən'dʌkʃən/ *n* [U] the passage of electricity through wires, heat through metal, water through pipes etc

con·duc·tive /kən'dʌktɪv/ *adj* able to conduct electricity, heat etc OPP **non-conductive**: *Copper is a very conductive metal.* —**conductivity** /,kɒndʌk'tɪvəti $,kɑːn-/ *n* [U]

con·duc·tor /kən'dʌktə $ -ər/ ●●○ *n* [C]
1 someone who stands in front of a group of musicians or singers and directs their playing or singing
2 *BrE* someone whose job is to collect payments from passengers on a bus
3 *AmE* someone who is in charge of a train and collects payments from passengers or checks their tickets SYN **guard** *BrE*

4 something that allows electricity or heat to travel along it or through it: *Wood is a poor conductor of heat.* → LIGHTNING CONDUCTOR

con·duit /ˈkɒndjuət, -dɪt $ ˈkɑːnduɪt/ *n* [C] **1** *technical* a pipe or passage through which water, gas, a set of electric wires etc passes **2** *formal* a connection between two things that allows people to pass ideas, news, money, weapons, drugs etc from one place to another: **[+for]** *Drug traffickers have used the country as a conduit for shipments to the U.S.*

cone[1] /kəʊn $ koʊn/ ●○○ *n* [C]
1 a solid or hollow shape that is round at one end, has sloping sides, and has a point at the other end, or something with this shape → see picture at SHAPE[1]
2 an object shaped like a large cone that is put on a road to prevent cars from going somewhere or to warn drivers about something
3 the fruit of a PINE or FIR tree → **conifer** → see picture at TREE
4 a piece of thin cooked cake, shaped like a cone, that you put ICE CREAM in, or a cone like this with ice cream in it
5 *technical* a CELL in your eye that is shaped like a cone, that helps you see light and colour → **rod**

C

cone[2] *v*
cone sth ↔ **off** *phr v BrE* to put a row of orange CONES around an area to prevent people or cars from going there, for example during building work

cone·flow·er /ˈkəʊnˌflaʊə $ ˈkoʊnˌflaʊər/ *n* [C,U] a wild purple or white flower commonly found in the US. It is often used as a herb or as a medicine. SYN **echinacea**

con·fec·tion /kənˈfekʃən/ *n* [C] *formal* **1** a beautifully prepared sweet food **2** something, especially a piece of clothing or a building, that is very delicate and complicated, or has a lot of decoration: **[+of]** *a dreamy confection of pink beads and satin* **3** something such as a film or song that is not serious or important

con·fec·tion·er /kənˈfekʃənə $ -ər/ *n* [C] someone who makes or sells sweets, cakes etc

conˈfectioner's ˌsugar *n* [U] *AmE* a kind of sugar that is very powdery SYN **icing sugar** *BrE*

con·fec·tion·e·ry /kənˈfekʃənəri $ -neri/ *n* [U] sweets, chocolates etc

con·fed·e·ra·cy /kənˈfedərəsi/ *n* (*plural* **confederacies**) [C] a confederation

con·fed·e·rate /kənˈfedərət/ *n* [C] **1** *formal* someone who helps someone else do something, especially something secret or illegal SYN **accomplice**: *The young woman was his confederate, of course.* **2** a member of a confederacy —**confederate** *adj*

con·fed·e·ra·tion /kənˌfedəˈreɪʃən/ *n* [C] a group of people, political parties, or organizations that have united for political purposes or trade SYN **alliance**

con·fer /kənˈfɜː $ -ˈfɜːr/ ●○○ AWL *v* (**conferred**, **conferring**) *formal*
1 [I] to discuss something with other people, so that everyone can express their opinions and decide on something: **[+with]** *Franklin leant over and conferred with his attorneys.*
2 confer a title/degree/honour etc to officially give someone a title etc, especially as a reward for something they have achieved SYN **bestow**: **[+on/upon]** *An honorary degree was conferred on him by the University.* THESAURUS ▸ GIVE —**conferment** *n* [C,U]

con·fe·rence /ˈkɒnfərəns $ ˈkɑːn-/ ●●● S2 W1 AWL *n* [C]
1 a large formal meeting where a lot of people discuss important matters such as business, politics, or science, especially for several days: *Representatives from over 100 countries attended the International Peace Conference in Geneva.* | **[+on]** *a UN conference on the environment* → PRESS CONFERENCE
2 a private meeting for a few people to have formal discussions: **[+with]** *After a brief conference with his aides, he left for the airport.* | **conference room/table etc** *The meeting will be held in the conference room at 10 am.* | **in conference** *Mr Dickson is in conference.*
3 *AmE* a group of teams that play against each other to see who is the best: *the Western Conference finals*

COLLOCATIONS

VERBS

go to a conference (*also* **attend a conference** *formal*) *Hundreds of delegates are attending the conference.*
hold a conference (=have one) *Their annual conference was held in Chicago.*
host a conference (=have it in your country) *In June, Japan hosted a peace conference.*
organize a conference | **address a conference** (=give a speech at one)

ADJECTIVES/NOUN + conference

a peace/climate/sales etc conference *an international climate conference in Sweden*
a world/international conference *the world conference on human rights*
a national conference | **an annual conference** | **a party conference** (=for a particular political party) | **a summit conference** (=for the leaders of governments)

conference + NOUN

conference facilities *The hotel has conference facilities for 100 people.*
a conference centre (=a building or group of buildings used for conferences) | **a conference hall**

ˈconference ˌcall *n* [C] a telephone call in which several people in different places can all talk to each other

con·fess /kənˈfes/ ●●○ *v* [I,T]
1 to admit, especially to the police, that you have done something wrong or illegal → **confession**: **confess to (doing) sth** *Edwards confessed to being a spy for the KGB.* | *Occasionally people confess to crimes they haven't committed just to get attention.* | **confess (that)** *My husband confessed he'd been having an affair with a woman in his office.* | *Torture was used and Fian confessed.* THESAURUS ▸ ADMIT
2 to admit something that you feel embarrassed about → **confession**: **confess (that)** *Marsha confessed that she didn't really know how to work the computer.* | **confess to (doing) sth** *He confessed to having a secret admiration for his opponent.* | **I (have to/must) confess** (=used when admitting something you feel slightly embarrassed about) *I must confess I don't visit my parents as often as I should.*

REGISTER

In everyday English, people usually say **admit** rather than **confess**: *I know it was him – he* ***admitted*** *it.* | *I* ***admit*** *I'm not very good with money.*

3 to tell a priest or God about the wrong things you have done so that you can be forgiven → **confession**: *He knelt and* ***confessed*** *his* ***sin****.*

con·fessed /kənˈfest/ *adj* [only before noun] having admitted publicly that you have done something: *a confessed criminal* → SELF-CONFESSED

con·fes·sion /kənˈfeʃən/ ●●○ *n*
1 [C] a statement that you have done something wrong, illegal, or embarrassing, especially a formal statement: *Sanchez's confession was read out to the court.* | **[+of]** *a confession of adultery* | *At 3 a.m. Higgins broke down and* ***made*** *a* ***full confession****.* | *I* ***have a confession*** *– I like Britney Spears' music.*
2 [C,U] when you tell a priest or God about the bad things that you have done: *You must* ***go to confession****.* | *a priest who* ***hears confession***
3 [C] *formal* a statement of what your religious beliefs are: **[+of]** *a* ***confession of faith***

con·fes·sion·al[1] /kənˈfeʃənəl/ *n* [C] a place in a church, usually an enclosed room, where a priest hears people make their confessions

confessional² *adj* confessional speech or writing contains private thoughts or feelings that you would normally keep secret

con·fes·sor /kənˈfesə $ -ər/ *n* [C] *formal* the priest who someone regularly makes their confession to

con·fet·ti /kənˈfeti/ *n* [U] small pieces of coloured paper that you throw into the air over people who have just got married or at events such as parties, PARADES etc

con·fi·dant /ˈkɒnfədænt, ˌkɒnfəˈdænt, -ˈdɑːnt $ ˈkɑːnfədænt/ *n* [C] someone you tell your secrets to or who you talk to about personal things

con·fi·dante /ˈkɒnfədænt, ˌkɒnfəˈdænt, -ˈdɑːnt $ ˈkɑːnfədænt/ *n* [C] a female confidant

con·fide /kənˈfaɪd/ ●○○ *v* [T]
1 to tell someone you trust about personal things that you do not want other people to know: **confide to sb that** *He confided to his friends that he didn't have much hope for his marriage.*
2 *formal* to give something you value to someone you trust so they look after it for you: **confide sth to sb** *He confided his money to his brother's safekeeping.*

confide in sb *phr v* to tell someone about something very private or secret, especially a personal problem, because you feel you can trust them: *I've never felt able to confide in my sister.*

con·fi·dence /ˈkɒnfɪdəns $ ˈkɑːn-/ ●●● S2 W2 *n*
1 FEELING SB/STH IS GOOD [U] the feeling that you can trust someone or something to be good, work well, or produce good results: **[+in]** *Public confidence in the government is at an all-time low.* | *She had complete confidence in the doctors.* | *Opinion polls show that voters have lost confidence in the administration.*
2 BELIEF IN YOURSELF [U] the belief that you have the ability to do things well or deal with situations successfully: **[+in]** *I didn't have any confidence in myself.* | **confidence to do sth** *Good training will give a beginner the confidence to enjoy skiing.* | *I felt I was doing well and my confidence began to grow.* | **with confidence** *Our goal is to prepare students to go into the business world with confidence.*
3 FEELING STH IS TRUE [U] the feeling that something is definite or true: **say/speak/predict etc with confidence** *How can anyone say with confidence that the recession is over?* | **[+in]** *I have complete confidence in Mr Wright's analysis of the situation.* | **have confidence (that)** *I have **every confidence** that the job will be completed satisfactorily on time.*
4 KEEP INFORMATION SECRET [U] if you tell someone something in confidence, you tell them something on the understanding that they will not tell anyone else → **confide**: **in confidence** *I'll tell you about Moira – in confidence, of course.* | **in strict/the strictest confidence** *Any information given during the interview will be **treated in the strictest confidence**.* | **breach of confidence** (=when someone tells someone something that they were told in confidence) *Lawyers are satisfied that no breach of confidence took place.*
5 **take sb into your confidence** to tell someone your secrets or private or personal details about your life: *Elsa took me into her confidence and told me about some of the problems she was facing.*
6 A SECRET [C] a secret or a piece of information that is private or personal: **share/exchange confidences** *They spent their evenings drinking wine and sharing confidences.* | *I have never **betrayed** a **confidence**.* → VOTE OF CONFIDENCE, VOTE OF NO CONFIDENCE

COLLOCATIONS – MEANING 1

VERBS

have confidence in sb/sth *The people no longer have any confidence in their government.*
lose confidence in sb/sth *Employees are losing confidence in the company.*
gain/win sb's confidence *As team captain, he soon won the confidence of the players.*
inspire confidence (=make people have confidence) *Our education system should inspire public confidence.*
restore confidence (=make people have confidence again) *Interest rate reductions would restore business confidence.*
boost confidence (=make people have more confidence) | **shake sb's confidence** (=make them have less confidence)

PHRASES

have every/complete/absolute confidence in sb/sth *A manager must be able to have complete confidence in his staff.*
a lack of confidence | **a crisis of confidence** (=a situation in which people no longer trust a government, system etc)

ADJECTIVES/NOUN + confidence

public confidence *The changes should improve public confidence in the system.*
consumer confidence (=that ordinary people have when the economic situation is good) *Consumer confidence has fallen to its lowest for two years.*
business confidence (=that businesses have when the economic situation is good) | **investor confidence** (=that investors have when the economic situation is good)

COLLOCATIONS – MEANING 2

VERBS

have confidence *Young teenagers often don't have a lot of confidence.*
be full of confidence *The team are full of confidence.*
lack/be lacking in confidence *She lacked the confidence to talk to people.*
lose (your) confidence *He'd been out of work for six months and had lost all his confidence.*
give sb confidence *I had really good teachers who gave me a lot of confidence in myself.*
gain confidence (*also* **grow/gain in confidence**) (=become more confident) | **boost/increase sb's confidence** (=make someone feel more confident) | **build up sb's confidence** (=gradually increase it) | **undermine sb's confidence** (=gradually reduce it) | **dent/shake sb's confidence** (=make it less strong) | **destroy/shatter sb's confidence** | **sb's confidence grows/increases**

ˈconfidence-ˌbuilding *adj* a confidence-building event, activity etc increases your confidence: *the use of **confidence-building exercises** to assist adults to return to the labour market*

ˈconfidence ˌtrick *n* [C] a dishonest trick played on someone in order to get their money SYN **con** —**confidence trickster** *n* [C]

con·fi·dent /ˈkɒnfɪdənt $ ˈkɑːn-/ ●●● S3 W3 *adj*
1 [not before noun] sure that something will happen in the way that you want or expect: **confident (that)** *We are confident next year's profits will be higher.* | *He is **quietly confident** that there will be no problems this time.* | **[+of]** *The Prime Minister appeared relaxed and **confident of winning** an overall majority.* | *The company is **confident of success**.* | **[+about]** *I **feel** quite **confident** about the future.* THESAURUS ▶ SURE
2 sure that you have the ability to do things well or deal with situations successfully: *Despite her disability, Philippa is very confident.* | **[+about]** *I **feel** much more **confident** about myself and my abilities these days.* | **confident smile/voice/manner etc** *He began to read in a calm confident voice.*
3 sure that something is true: **confident (that)** *We are confident we have done nothing wrong.* | *He began to **feel confident** that Zaborski was only guessing.* | *It is not possible to give a confident answer to the question of whether the delay was unreasonable.* —**confidently** *adv* → SELF-CONFIDENT

GRAMMAR: Patterns with confident

• You are **confident about** something: *I'm quite confident about my English.* ✗ Don't say: *I'm quite confident of my English.*

C

• You are **confident of** victory or success, or **confident of doing** something: *The team is confident of victory.* | *The team is confident of winning.*

THESAURUS

confident sure that you have the ability to do something well or deal with situations successfully: *She seemed confident that she would pass.* | *his calm and confident manner*
self-confident/self-assured confident, and not shy or nervous in social situations: *Jess was only 12, but she was very self-confident.* | *He was very self-assured and spoke without notes.*
assertive confident enough to say what you think and want, so that people take notice of you: *The course helps women learn how to be more assertive in the workplace.*
sure of yourself confident that you are right, even when other people do not agree with you: *He sounded so sure of himself that I didn't bother to argue.*
extrovert *n* [C] someone who behaves in a confident way in social situations and likes talking and being with other people: *Most actors are natural extroverts.*

NOT CONFIDENT

lack confidence/be lacking in confidence to not be confident about your abilities or appearance: *Francine is lacking in confidence and needs a lot of encouragement.* | *I was fat, had no friends, and lacked confidence.*
shy not confident about meeting or speaking to people who you do not know: *Jane is a quiet shy person.* | *He had been* ***painfully shy*** (=very shy) *as a child.*
insecure not confident about yourself or your relationships, especially because you are worried that you are not good enough: *His childhood had left him very insecure.*
unsure of yourself not confident, especially because you are young or you do not have much experience: *At first, Chris seemed nervous and unsure of herself.*
discouraged /dɪsˈkʌrɪdʒd $ -ˈkɜːr-/ not confident that you can succeed, because you have had problems trying to do something: *Students can become discouraged very easily if they are not given the help they need.*
demoralized someone who is demoralized has lost all their confidence and wants to give up: *The team were completely demoralized after losing a series of games.* | *a demoralized work force*

con·fi·den·tial /ˌkɒnfɪˈdenʃəl◂ $ ˌkɑːn-/ ●●○ *adj* **1** spoken or written in secret and intended to be kept secret: *a confidential government report* | *Doctors are required to* ***keep*** *patients' records completely* ***confidential***. | *The information will be regarded as* ***strictly confidential*** (=completely confidential). **THESAURUS▸** SECRET **2** a confidential way of speaking or behaving shows that you do not want other people to know what you are saying: *His voice sank into a confidential whisper.* —**confidentially** *adv*

con·fi·den·ti·al·i·ty /ˌkɒnfədenʃiˈæləti $ ˌkɑːn-/ ●○○ *n* [U] a situation in which you trust someone not to tell secret or private information to anyone else: *The relationship between attorney and client is based on confidentiality.* | **breach of confidentiality** (=when someone gives away information they have promised to keep secret) *It's a breach of confidentiality for a priest to reveal what someone has said in the confessional.*

con·fid·ing /kənˈfaɪdɪŋ/ *adj* behaving in a way that shows you want to tell someone about something that is private or secret: *Her tone was suddenly confiding.* —**confidingly** *adv*: *He leant forward confidingly.*

con·fig·u·ra·tion /kənˌfɪgəˈreɪʃən, -gjə- $ -gjə-/ *n* [C,U] **1** *formal or technical* the shape or arrangement of the parts of something (SYN) **layout**: **[+of]** *the configuration of pistons in an engine* **2** *technical* the combination of equipment needed to run a computer system

con·fig·ure /kənˈfɪgə $ -gjər/ *v* [T] *technical* to arrange something, especially computer equipment, so that it works with other equipment

con·fine /kənˈfaɪn/ ●●○ (W3) (AWL) *v* [T]
1 LIMIT to keep someone or something within the limits of a particular activity or subject (SYN) **restrict**: **confine sth to sth** *The police cadet's duties were confined to taking statements from the crowd.* | *We confined our study to ten cases.* | **confine yourself to (doing) sth** *Owen did not confine himself to writing only one type of poem.*
2 KEEP SB IN A PLACE to keep someone in a place that they cannot leave, such as a prison: **confine sb to sth** *Any soldier who leaves his post will be confined to barracks* (=made to stay in the barracks). | **be confined in sth** *He was allegedly confined in a narrow dark room for two months.*
3 STOP STH SPREADING to stop something bad from spreading to another place: **confine sth to sth** *Firefighters managed to confine the fire to the living room.*
4 STAY IN ONE PLACE if you are confined to a place, you have to stay in that place, especially because you are ill: **be confined to sth** *Vaughan is* ***confined to*** *a* ***wheelchair***. | *She's* ***confined to bed*** *with flu.*

con·fined /kənˈfaɪnd/ (AWL) *adj* **1 be confined to sb/sth** to exist in or affect only a particular place or group: *The risk of infection is confined to medical personnel.* **2** a confined space or area is one that is very small (SYN) **restricted**: *It wasn't easy to sleep in such a confined space.*

con·fine·ment /kənˈfaɪnmənt/ *n* **1** [U] *formal* the act of putting someone in a room, prison etc that they are not allowed to leave, or the state of being there: *They were held in confinement for three weeks.* | *He visited prisoners at their place of confinement.* → SOLITARY CONFINEMENT **2** [C,U] *old-fashioned or formal* the time when a woman gives birth to a baby: *the pros and cons of home versus hospital confinement*

con·fines /ˈkɒnfaɪnz $ ˈkɑːn-/ *n* [plural] limits or borders: **within/beyond the confines of sth** *within the confines of the prison*

con·firm /kənˈfɜːm $ -ɜːrm/ ●●● (S2) (W2) (AWL) *v* [T]
1 to show that something is definitely true, especially by providing more proof (OPP) **refute**: *New evidence has confirmed the first witness's story.* | *To confirm my diagnosis I need to do some tests.* | **confirm that** *Research has confirmed that the risk is higher for women.* | **confirm what** *The new results confirm what most of us knew already.*

GRAMMAR

In more formal English, you say **it is confirmed that** something is true: *It was confirmed that the bone was broken.*

2 to say that something is definitely true (OPP) **deny**: *The president refused to confirm the rumor.* | *Managers have so far refused to* ***confirm or deny*** *reports that up to 200 jobs are to go.* | **confirm that** *Walsh confirmed that the money had been paid.* | **confirm what** *My brother will confirm what I have told you.*
3 to tell someone that a possible arrangement, date, or situation is now definite or official: *Could you confirm the dates we discussed?* | *Smith was confirmed as the club's new manager yesterday.* | **confirm a booking/reservation/appointment** *I am writing to confirm a booking for a single room for the night of 6 June.*
4 to make you believe that your idea or feeling is right: **confirm your fears/doubts/suspicions etc** *This just confirms my worst fears.* | **confirm you in your belief/opinion/view etc (that)** (=make you believe something more strongly) *The expression on his face confirmed me in my suspicions.*
5 be confirmed to be made a full member of the Christian Church in a special ceremony

con·fir·ma·tion /ˌkɒnfəˈmeɪʃən $ ˌkɑːnfər-/ ●●○ (AWL) *n* [C,U]
1 a statement, document etc that says that something is

definitely true: **[+of]** *There has still been no* ***official confirmation*** *of the report.* | **confirmation that** *verbal confirmation that payment has been made*
2 a letter etc that tells you that an arrangement, date, time etc is now definite: *Most hotels require confirmation from a prospective guest in writing.*
3 a religious ceremony in which someone is made a full member of the Christian Church

con·firmed /kən'fɜːmd $ -ɜːr-/ *adj* **a confirmed bachelor/atheist/vegetarian etc** someone who seems completely happy with the way of life they have chosen

con·fis·cate /'kɒnfəskeɪt $ 'kɑːn-/ ●○○ *v* [T] to officially take private property away from someone, usually as a punishment: *Miss Williams confiscated all our sweets.* | *Many opposition supporters had their goods confiscated.* —**confiscation** /ˌkɒnfə'skeɪʃən $ ˌkɑːn-/ *n* [C,U]: *the confiscation of pornographic material*

con·fla·gra·tion /ˌkɒnflə'greɪʃən $ ˌkɑːn-/ *n* [C] *formal* **1** a very large fire that destroys a lot of buildings, forests etc **THESAURUS** ▸ **FIRE** **2** a violent situation or war

con·flate /kən'fleɪt/ *v* [T] *formal* to combine two or more things to form a single new thing: *He conflates two images from Kipling's short stories in the film.* —**conflation** /-'fleɪʃən/ *n* [C,U]

con·flict[1] /'kɒnflɪkt $ 'kɑːn-/ ●●○ W3 AWL *n*
1 [C,U] a state of disagreement or argument between people, groups, countries etc: **[+over]** *conflicts over wage settlements* | **[+between]** *the conflict between tradition and innovation* | **in conflict (with sb)** *normal kids who are in conflict with their parents* | **political/social/industrial conflict** *social and political conflict in the 1930s* | *the threat of industrial conflict in the coalfields* | *Marx points out the potential conflicts below the surface of society.* | *His views on the literal truth of the Bible* ***brought*** *him* ***into conflict with*** *other Christian leaders.* | *Doctors exercise considerable power and often* ***come into conflict*** *with politicians.* | *a lawyer specializing in* ***conflict resolution***
2 [C,U] fighting or a war: **armed/military/violent conflict** *For years the region has been torn apart by armed conflicts.* | *UN troops intervened to avert a threat of violent conflict.* | *efforts to* ***resolve the conflict*** **THESAURUS** ▸ **WAR**
3 [C,U] a situation in which you have to choose between two or more opposite needs, influences etc: *As women increasingly went out to work, the possibility of a* ***conflict of loyalties*** *became stronger.* | **[+between]** *a conflict between the demands of one's work and one's family* | **in conflict (with sth)** *The principles of democracy are sometimes in conflict with political reality.*
4 [C,U] a situation in which you have two opposite feelings about something: *a state of inner conflict*
5 [C] *AmE* something that you have to do at the same time that someone wants you to do something else: *I've got a conflict on Friday. Can we make it Monday?*
6 conflict of interest/interests a) a situation in which you cannot do your job fairly because you will be affected by the decision you make: *There is a growing conflict of interest between her position as a politician and her business activities.* **b)** a situation in which different people want different things

con·flict[2] /kən'flɪkt/ ●●○ AWL *v* [I] if two ideas, beliefs, opinions etc conflict, they cannot exist together or both be true: **[+with]** *new evidence which conflicts with previous findings*

con·flict·ed /kən'flɪktɪd/ *adj* **be/feel conflicted (about sth)** *AmE* to be confused about what choice to make, especially when the decision involves strong beliefs or opinions: *Many mothers today feel conflicted about working outside the home.*

ˈconflict-free *adj* conflict-free DIAMONDS or other valuable stones have been obtained without using violence, doing things against human rights etc

con·flict·ing /kən'flɪktɪŋ/ ●○○ *adj* conflicting ideas, beliefs, opinions etc cannot exist together or both be true: **conflicting opinions/demands/interests etc** *It can be difficult to balance the conflicting demands on our time.* | *The scientific advice is conflicting.*

con·flu·ence /'kɒnfluəns $ 'kɑːn-/ *n* [singular] **1** *technical* the place where two or more rivers flow together **2** *formal* a situation in which two or more things combine or happen at the same time: **[+of]** *a confluence of unhappy events*

con·form /kən'fɔːm $ -ɔːrm/ ●○○ AWL *v* [I]
1 to behave in the way that most other people in your group or society behave → **conformist**: *the pressure on schoolchildren to conform* | **[+to/with]** *people who do not conform to traditional standards of behaviour*
2 to obey a law, rule etc: **[+to/with]** *Students can be expelled for refusing to conform to school rules.* | *All new buildings must conform with the regional development plan.* | *products which conform to international safety standards*
3 conform to a pattern/model/ideal etc to be similar to what people expect or think is usual: *Joseph does not conform to the stereotype of a policeman.*

con·for·ma·tion /ˌkɒnfɔː'meɪʃən $ ˌkɑːnfɔːr-/ AWL *n* [C,U] *technical* the shape of something or the way in which it is formed: *the conformation of the Earth*

con·form·ist /kən'fɔːmɪst $ -ɔːr-/ AWL *adj* thinking and behaving like everyone else, because you do not want to be different, or forcing people to do this - often used to show disapproval → **nonconformist**: *a country with a conformist education system* —**conformist** *n* [C]

con·for·mi·ty /kən'fɔːməti $ -ɔːr-/ AWL *n* [U] **1** behaviour that obeys the accepted rules of society or a group, and is the same as that of most other people OPP **non-conformity**: *an emphasis on conformity and control* | **[+to]** *conformity to social expectations* **2 in conformity with sth** *formal* in a way that obeys rules, customs etc: *We must act in conformity with local regulations.*

con·found /kən'faʊnd/ *v* [T] **1** to confuse and surprise people by being unexpected: *His amazing recovery confounded the medical specialists.* **2** to prove someone or something wrong: **confound the critics/pundits/experts etc** *United's new striker confounded the critics with his third goal in as many games.* **3** *formal* to defeat an enemy, plan etc **4** *formal* if a problem etc confounds you, you cannot understand it or solve it: *Her question completely confounded me.* **5 confound it/him/them etc** *old-fashioned* used to show that you are annoyed with someone or something

con·found·ed /kən'faʊndɪd/ *adj* [only before noun] *old-fashioned* used to show that you are annoyed: *That confounded dog has run away again!*

con·front /kən'frʌnt/ ●○○ *v* [T]
1 if a problem, difficulty etc confronts you, it appears and needs to be dealt with: *The problems confronting the new government were enormous.* | **be confronted with sth** *Customers are confronted with a bewildering amount of choice.*
2 to deal with something very difficult or unpleasant in a brave and determined way: *We try to help people* ***confront*** *their* ***problems***.
3 to face someone in a threatening way, as though you are going to attack them: *Troops were confronted by an angry mob.*
4 to ACCUSE someone of doing something, especially by showing them the proof: **confront sb with/about sth** *I confronted him with my suspicions, and he admitted everything.* | *I haven't confronted her about it yet.*

con·fron·ta·tion /ˌkɒnfrən'teɪʃən $ ˌkɑːn-/ ●○○ *n* [C,U]
1 a situation in which there is a lot of angry disagreement between two people or groups: *She had stayed in her room to avoid another confrontation.* | **[+with/between]** *an ideological confrontation between conservatives and liberals*
2 a fight or battle: **military/violent/armed confrontation** *Japan seemed unlikely to risk military confrontation with Russia.*

con·fron·ta·tion·al /ˌkɒnfrən'teɪʃənəl◂ $ ˌkɑːn-/ *adj* likely to cause arguments or make people angry: *a confrontational style of management*

con·fuse /kən'fjuːz/ ●●○ *v* [T]
1 to make someone feel that they cannot think clearly or do not understand: *I understand the text but the diagrams are confusing me.*
2 to think wrongly that a person or thing is someone or something else: *People might well confuse the two products.* | **confuse sb/sth with sb/sth** *I always confuse you with your sister – you look so alike.* | *Donald Regan, not to be confused with former President Ronald Reagan*
3 confuse the issue/matter/argument etc to make it even more difficult to think clearly about a situation or problem or to deal with it: *He kept asking unnecessary questions which only confused the issue.*

con·fused /kən'fjuːzd/ ●●● S3 *adj*
1 unable to understand or think clearly about what someone is saying or what is happening: *I'm totally confused. Could you explain that again?* | **[+about]** *If you're confused about anything, phone me.* | *All the roads looked the same and he felt thoroughly confused.*
2 not clear or not easy to understand: *Witness statements presented a confused picture of the incident.* | *a lot of confused ideas* —**confusedly** /-'fjuːzɪdli/ *adv*

THESAURUS

confused unable to understand what someone is saying or what is happening: *I was rather confused by his question.* | *She gave me a confused look.*
puzzled (*also* **perplexed** *formal*) confused because you cannot understand something, especially because it is different from what you expect: *The doctor was puzzled by the man's symptoms and ordered several further tests.* | *He had a puzzled expression on his face.* | *Ross looked perplexed when the audience laughed.*
baffled very confused and unable to understand something, even though you have tried hard for a long time: *Detectives admit they are baffled by the case.* | *a baffled expression*
bewildered /bɪ'wɪldəd $ -ərd/ very confused and surprised when something unusual and unexpected happens to you: *He was bewildered to find three policemen at the front door.* | *Bewildered train passengers watched as the man was arrested.*
bemused /bɪ'mjuːzd/ confused and surprised by what has happened, or by what someone has said: *Local residents seem bemused by the sudden arrival of all the tourists.* | *She told him to leave, but he just sat there with a bemused expression.*
can't think straight *spoken* to have difficulty thinking clearly, for example because you are too tired, too busy, or because a lot of things are happening around you: *I can't think straight with all this noise going on.*

con·fus·ing /kən'fjuːzɪŋ/ ●●● S3 *adj* unclear and difficult to understand: *The instructions were really confusing.* | *It was a very confusing situation.* —**confusingly** *adv*

con·fu·sion /kən'fjuːʒən/ ●●○ S3 W3 *n*
1 [C,U] when you do not understand what is happening or what something means because it is not clear: **[+about/over/as to]** *There was some confusion as to whether we had won or lost.* | **create/lead to confusion** *The diversion led to* ***considerable confusion***.
2 [C,U] a situation in which someone wrongly thinks that a person or thing is someone or something else: *To avoid confusion, the teams wore different colours.* | **[+between]** *There is a confusion in the public mind between psychology and psychiatry.*
3 [U] a feeling of not being able to think clearly about what you should say or do, especially in an embarrassing situation: *His confusion at meeting her there was quite apparent.* | **in confusion** *Matt stared at her in confusion.*
4 [C,U] a very confusing situation, that usually has a lot of noise and action, so that it is difficult for someone to understand it or control it SYN **chaos**: *a scene of indescribable confusion* | **[+of]** *There was a confusion of shouts and orders as the ship prepared to depart.*

con·fute /kən'fjuːt/ *v* [T] *formal* to prove that a person or an argument is completely wrong

con·ga /'kɒŋgə $ 'kɑːŋgə/ *n* [C] a dance in which people dance in a line, holding on to the person in front of them

con·geal /kən'dʒiːl/ *v* [I] if a liquid such as blood congeals, it becomes thick or solid: *The fat had slowly congealed in the pan.*

con·ge·ni·al /kən'dʒiːniəl/ *adj* **1** pleasant in a way that makes you feel comfortable and relaxed: **congenial atmosphere/surroundings/environment** *The department provides a congenial atmosphere for research.* | *Frank was a very congenial colleague.* | **[+to]** *The summers out here are not congenial to the average North European.* **2** suitable for something: *Compost provides congenial conditions for roots to develop.* —**congeniality** /kən,dʒiːni'æləti/ *n* [U]

con·gen·i·tal /kən'dʒenətl/ *adj* [usually before noun] **1** a congenital medical condition or disease has affected someone since they were born: *congenital abnormalities* | *a congenital defect* **2** a congenital quality is one that has always been part of your character and is unlikely to change: *He's a* ***congenital liar***. | *her congenital inability to make decisions* —**congenitally** *adv*

con·ger eel /,kɒŋgər 'iːl $ 'kɑːŋgər iːl/ *n* [C] a large fish that looks like a snake

con·ges·ted /kən'dʒestɪd/ ●○○ *adj*
1 full of traffic: *congested airspace* | *London's roads are* ***heavily congested*** (=very congested).
2 a part of your body that is congested is very full of liquid, usually blood or MUCUS

con·ges·tion /kən'dʒestʃən/ ●○○ *n* [U]
1 the problem of too much traffic in a place: *Councillors are looking at ways to reduce* ***traffic congestion*** *in the town centre.*
2 the condition of part of your body being very full of liquid, usually blood or MUCUS

con'gestion ,charging *n* [U] *BrE* a way of reducing traffic in city centres by charging drivers money to enter SYN **road pricing**: *Plans to introduce congestion charging were dropped until after the election.* —**congestion charge** *n* [C]

con·glom·e·rate /kən'glɒmərət $ -'glɑː-/ *n* **1** [C] a large business organization consisting of several different companies that have joined together: *an international conglomerate* | **industrial/financial/media etc conglomerate** THESAURUS▸ COMPANY **2** [C,U] *technical* a rock consisting of different sizes of stones held together by clay **3** [C] *formal* a group of things gathered together

con·glom·e·ra·tion /kən,glɒmə'reɪʃən $ -,glɑː-/ *n* [C] *formal* a group of different things gathered together: **[+of]** *the loose conglomeration of artists known as L'Ecole de Paris*

con·grats /kən'græts/ *n* [plural] *informal* CONGRATULATIONS

con·grat·u·late /kən'grætʃəleɪt/ ●●○ *v* [T]
1 to tell someone that you are happy because they have achieved something or because something nice has happened to them: *He never even stopped to congratulate me.* | **congratulate sb on sth** *She congratulated me warmly on my exam results.* | **congratulate sb for doing sth** *All three are to be congratulated for doing so well.* THESAURUS▸ PRAISE
2 congratulate yourself (on sth) to feel pleased and proud of yourself because you have achieved something or something good has happened to you: *I congratulated myself on my good fortune.* —**congratulatory** /kən,grætʃə'leɪtəri $ -'grætʃələtɔːri/ *adj*: *congratulatory messages*

GRAMMAR: Patterns with congratulate

- You **congratulate** someone **on** something: *I'd like to congratulate you on your new job.* ✗ Don't say: *I'd like to congratulate you for your new job.*
- You can also say: *Congratulations on your new job!*
- You **congratulate** someone **for doing** something: *She congratulated me for getting a new job.*

con·grat·u·la·tion /kən,grætʃə'leɪʃən/ ●●● S3 *n*
1 congratulations a) used when you want to congratulate

someone: *'I've just passed my driving test!' 'Congratulations!'* | **[+on]** *Congratulations on a superb performance!* **b)** words saying you are happy that someone has achieved something: *Give Oscar my congratulations.*
2 [U] when you tell someone that you are happy because they have achieved something or because something nice has happened to them: *letters of congratulation*

con·gre·gate /ˈkɒŋɡrɪɡeɪt $ ˈkɑːŋ-/ *v* [I] to come together in a group OPP **disperse**: *Crowds began to congregate to hear the president's speech.*

con·gre·ga·tion /ˌkɒŋɡrəˈɡeɪʃən $ ˌkɑːŋ-/ ●○○ *n* [C]
1 a group of people gathered together in a church: *The congregation knelt to pray.*
2 the people who usually go to a particular church: *Several members of the congregation are away.*

Con·gre·ga·tion·al·is·m /ˌkɒŋɡrəˈɡeɪʃənəlɪzəm $ ˌkɑːŋ-/ *n* [U] a type of Christianity in which each congregation is responsible for making its own decisions —**Congregational** *adj* —**Congregationalist** *n* [C]

con·gress /ˈkɒŋɡres $ ˈkɑːŋɡrɪs/ *n* **1** [C,U] a formal meeting of representatives of different groups, countries etc, to discuss ideas, make decisions etc: *a congress of the ruling Labor Party* **2** [C] the group of people chosen or elected to make the laws in some countries
3 Congress the group of people elected to make laws in the US, consisting of the Senate and the House of Representatives: *The president has lost the support of Congress.*
4 [singular] used in the names of political parties: *Gandhi's Congress Party* —**congressional** /kənˈɡreʃənəl/ *adj* [only before noun]: *a congressional committee*

con·gress·man /ˈkɒŋɡrəsmən $ ˈkɑːŋ-/ *n* (*plural* **congressmen** /-mən/) [C] a man who is a member of a congress, especially the US House of Representatives

con·gress·wom·an /ˈkɒŋɡrəsˌwʊmən $ ˈkɑːŋ-/ *n* (*plural* **congresswomen** /-ˌwɪmɪn/) [C] a woman who is a member of a congress, especially the US House of Representatives

con·gru·ent /ˈkɒŋɡruənt $ ˈkɑːŋ-/ *adj* **1** *formal* fitting together well **2** *technical* congruent TRIANGLEs are the same size and shape —**congruence** *n* [U]

con·i·cal /ˈkɒnɪkəl $ ˈkɑː-/ *adj* shaped like a CONE: *huts with conical roofs*

co·ni·fer /ˈkəʊnəfə, ˈkɒ- $ ˈkɑːnəfər/ *n* [C] a tree such as a PINE or FIR that has leaves like needles and produces brown CONEs that contain seeds. Most types of conifer keep their leaves in winter. —**coniferous** /kəˈnɪfərəs $ koʊ-, kə-/ *adj*: *coniferous forests*

conj. (*also* **conj** *BrE*) the written abbreviation of ***conjunction***

con·jec·ture¹ /kənˈdʒektʃə $ -ər/ *n formal* **1** [U] when you form ideas or opinions without having very much information to base them on: *What she said was **pure conjecture**.* | *There has been some conjecture about a possible merger.* **2** [C] an idea or opinion formed by guessing SYN **guess**, **hypothesis**: *My results show that this conjecture was, in fact, correct.* —**conjectural** *adj*

conjecture² *v* [I,T] *formal* to form an idea or opinion without having much information to base it on SYN **guess**: **conjecture that** *It seems reasonable to conjecture that these conditions breed violence.*

con·join /kənˈdʒɔɪn/ *v* [I,T] *formal* to join together, or to make things or people do this

con,joined 'twins *n* [plural] two people who are born with their bodies joined to each other

con·ju·gal /ˈkɒndʒəɡəl $ ˈkɑːn-/ *adj* [only before noun] *formal* **1** relating to marriage: *conjugal love* **2 conjugal visit** a private meeting between a prisoner and his or her wife or husband, during which they are allowed to have sex

con·ju·gate /ˈkɒndʒəɡeɪt $ ˈkɑːn-/ *v* **1** [I] if a verb conjugates, it has different forms to show different tenses etc: *The verb 'to go' conjugates irregularly.* **2** [T] if you conjugate a verb, you state the different forms that it can have

con·ju·ga·tion /ˌkɒndʒəˈɡeɪʃən $ ˌkɑːn-/ *n* [C] **1** the way that a particular verb conjugates **2** a set of verbs in languages such as Latin that conjugate in the same way

con·junc·tion /kənˈdʒʌŋkʃən/ ●○○ *n*
1 in conjunction with sb/sth working, happening, or being used with someone or something else: *The worksheets are designed to be used in conjunction with the new coursebooks.*
2 [C] a combination of different things that have come together by chance: **[+of]** *a happy conjunction of events*
3 [C] *technical* a word such as 'and', 'but', or 'because' which joins parts of a sentence

con·junc·ti·vi·tis /kənˌdʒʌŋktɪˈvaɪtɪs/ *n* [U] a painful and infectious disease of the eye that makes it red

con·junc·ture /kənˈdʒʌŋktʃə $ -ər/ *n* [C] *formal* a combination of events or situations, especially one that causes problems: *the historic conjuncture from which Marxism arose*

con·jure /ˈkʌndʒə $ ˈkɑːndʒər, ˈkʌn-/ ●○○ *v*
1 [I,T] to perform clever tricks in which you seem to make things appear, disappear, or change by magic: *The magician conjured a rabbit out of his hat.*
2 [T] to make something appear or happen in a way which is not expected: *He has conjured victories from worse situations than this.*
3 a name to conjure with the name of a very important person

conjure sth ↔ **up** *phr v*
1 to bring a thought, picture, idea, or memory to someone's mind: **conjure up images/pictures/thoughts etc (of sth)** *Dieting always seems to conjure up images of endless salads.*
2 to make something appear when it is not expected, as if by magic: *Somehow we have to conjure up another $10,000.*
3 to make the soul of a dead person appear by saying special magic words

con·jur·er, **conjuror** /ˈkʌndʒərə $ ˈkɑːndʒərər, ˈkʌn-/ *n* [C] someone who entertains people by performing clever tricks in which things seem to appear, disappear, or change by magic SYN **magician**

con·jur·ing /ˈkʌndʒərɪŋ $ ˈkɑːn-, ˈkʌn-/ *n* [U] the skill of performing clever tricks in which you seem to make things appear, disappear, or change by magic SYN **magic**: *He did **conjuring tricks** for the children.*

conk¹ /kɒŋk $ kɑːŋk, kɒːŋk/ *n* [C] *BrE informal* a nose

conk² *v* [T] *informal* to hit someone hard, especially on the head

conk out *phr v informal* **1** if a machine or car conks out, it suddenly stops working: *Our car conked out on the way home.* **2** if someone conks out, they fall asleep because they are very tired: *I got home from work and I just conked out on the sofa.*

con·ker /ˈkɒŋkə $ ˈkɑːŋkər/ *n* **1** [C] the large brown shiny seed of the HORSE CHESTNUT tree **2 conkers** [U] *BrE* a children's game in which conkers are hung from pieces of string and you try to break the other person's conker by hitting it with your own

con·man /ˈkɒnmæn $ ˈkɑːn-/ *n* (*plural* **conmen** /-men/) [C] *informal* someone who tries to get money from people by tricking them → **con**

con·nect /kəˈnekt/ ●●● S2 W2 *v*
1 JOIN THINGS [T] to join two or more things together: **connect sth to/with sth** *The railway link would connect Felixstowe with Fishguard.* | *Connect the speakers to the CD player.* | *We'd like two rooms with **connecting doors** (=doors that join the rooms).*
2 RELATIONSHIP [T] to realize or show that a fact, event, or person is related to something: *I didn't connect the two events in my mind.* | **connect sb/sth with sth** *There is no evidence to connect them with the attack.*
3 ELECTRICITY/TELEPHONE ETC [I,T] to join something to the main supply of electricity, gas, or water, or to a telephone or computer network OPP **disconnect**: **[+to]** *Click here to connect to the Internet.* | *Has the phone been connected yet?* | *The power supply should be connected by a qualified electrician.*
4 TRANSPORT [I] if one train, flight etc connects with another, it arrives just before the other one leaves so that you can continue your journey: *I missed the **connecting flight**.* | **[+with/to]** *This train connects with the one to*

Glasgow. | *From Toronto you can connect to all other Air Canada destinations.*
5 TELEPHONES [T] to join two telephone lines so that two people can speak: *Please hold the line. I'm trying to connect you.*
6 HIT STH [I] to succeed in hitting someone or something: *He swung at the ball, but didn't connect.*
7 UNDERSTAND PEOPLE [I] *especially AmE* if people connect, they feel that they like each other and understand each other: **[+with]** *They valued her ability to empathize and connect with others.*
connect sth ↔ **up** *phr v* to join something to the main supply of electricity, gas, or water, to the telephone network, or to another piece of equipment: *Is the washing machine connected up yet?* | **[+with]** *The autopilot can be connected up with the flight recorder.*

C

con·nect·ed /kəˈnektɪd/ ●●● S3 W3 *adj*
1 to be joined to something else or joined to a large system or network: **[+to]** *The light is connected to a timer.* | *a computer connected to the Internet* | **[+by]** *a series of artificial lakes connected by waterfalls*
2 if two facts, events, people etc are connected, there is some kind of relationship between them: **[+with]** *problems connected with drug abuse* | *everyone connected with the film industry* | *Mr Edelson was* ***closely connected*** *with Trinity College.* THESAURUS▸ RELATED
3 well connected having important or powerful friends or relatives

con·nect·ed·ness /kəˈnektədnəs/ *n* [U] **1** the feeling people have that they are members of a group in society and that they share particular qualities with other members of that group: *Human beings have a need for both independence and connectedness.* **2** the degree to which people are connected by electronic technology such as the Internet and email: **[+between/with]** *Computers have increased the connectedness between physicians and patients.*

con·nec·tion /kəˈnekʃən/ ●●● S3 W2 *n*
1 RELATIONSHIP [C] the way in which two facts, ideas, events etc are related to each other, and one is affected or caused by the other SYN **link**: **[+between]** *the* ***causal connection*** *between smoking and cancer* | ***There is a connection*** *between pollution and the death of trees.* | **[+with]** *Mr O'Hara* ***had*** *no known* ***connection*** *with terrorist activity.* | **[+to]** *Williams apparently* ***has*** *no* ***connection*** *to the case.* | *Police have so far failed to* ***establish*** *a* ***connection*** *between the two murders.* | *The evidence was there in the file but no one* ***made the connection.*** | *Students often* ***see*** *little* ***connection*** *between school and the rest of their lives.* | *He demonstrated* ***the close connection*** *between social conditions and health.*
2 JOINING [C,U] when two or more things are joined together or when something is joined to a larger system or network: *a digital telephone connection via satellite* | *They're offering free Internet connection.* | **[+to]** *The socket allows connection to a PC.* | *There's a £25 connection charge* (=money you pay to be connected to a service such as telephones, electricity etc).
3 in connection with sth concerning or involving something: **arrest/charge/question etc sb in connection with a crime** *Two men have been arrested in connection with the attack.* | *visits made to Spain in connection with her business* | *his work in connection with refugees*
4 ELECTRICAL WIRE [C] a wire or piece of metal joining two parts of a machine or electrical system: *an electrical connection* | *There's a* ***loose connection*** (=wires which are not joined correctly).
5 TRAIN/FLIGHT ETC [C] a train, bus, or plane which is arranged to leave at a time that allows passengers from an earlier train, bus, or plane to use it to continue their journey: **[+to]** *If this train gets delayed we'll miss our connection to Paris.*
6 ROAD/RAILWAY ETC [C] a road, railway etc that joins two places and allows people to travel between them: *Cheshunt has good rail connections to London.*
7 PEOPLE **connections** [plural] **a)** people who you know who can help you, especially because they are in positions of power: *connections in high places* | *We have good connections in the advertising industry.* **b)** people who are related to you, but not very closely: *He is English, but has Irish connections.* | *the network of* ***family connections*** *in Italy*

con·nect·ive /kəˈnektɪv/ *n* [C] a word that joins parts of a sentence

conˈnective ˌtissue *n* [U] parts of the body such as muscle or fat that exist between or join organs and other body parts

con·nec·tiv·i·ty /ˌkɒnekˈtɪvəti $ ˌkɑː-/ *n* [U] *technical* the ability of computers and other electronic equipment to connect with other computers or programs: *a growing demand for high-speed connectivity* | *Internet connectivity software*

con·nec·tor /kəˈnektə $ -ər/ *n* [C] an object which is used to join two pieces of equipment together

con·ne·xion /kəˈnekʃən/ *n* [C,U] a British spelling of CONNECTION

ˈconning ˌtower *n* [C] *technical* the structure on top of a SUBMARINE (=underwater ship)

con·nip·tion /kəˈnɪpʃən/ (*also* **conˈniption ˌfit**) *n* [C] *AmE old-fashioned* a way of behaving which shows that you are very angry: *My mother* ***threw a conniption fit*** *when I didn't come home till two in the morning.*

con·nive /kəˈnaɪv/ *v* [I] **1** to not try to stop something wrong from happening: **[+at]** *He would not be the first politician to connive at a shady business deal.* **2 connive (with sb) to do sth** to work secretly with someone to achieve something, especially something wrong SYN **conspire**: *They connived with their mother to deceive me.* —**connivance** *n* [U]: *We could not have escaped without the connivance of the guards.*

con·niv·ing /kəˈnaɪvɪŋ/ *adj* a conniving person secretly tries to gain something or harm someone - used to show disapproval

con·nois·seur /ˌkɒnəˈsɜː $ ˌkɑːnəˈsɜːr/ *n* [C] someone who knows a lot about something such as art, food, or music: *a wine connoisseur* | **[+of]** *Fry was a connoisseur of Renaissance art.* THESAURUS▸ EXPERT

con·no·ta·tion /ˌkɒnəˈteɪʃən $ ˌkɑː-/ ●○○ *n* [C] a quality or an idea that a word makes you think of that is more than its basic meaning → **denotation**: **[+of]** *The word 'professional' has connotations of skill and excellence.* | *a negative connotation* —**connotative** /ˈkɒnəteɪtɪv $ ˈkɑːn-, kəˈnoʊtətɪv/ *adj*

con·note /kəˈnəʊt $ -ˈnoʊt/ *v* [T] *formal* if a word connotes something, it makes you think of qualities and ideas that are more than its basic meaning → **denote**: *The word 'plump' connotes cheerfulness.*

con·nu·bi·al /kəˈnjuːbiəl $ -ˈnuː-/ *adj* **connubial bliss** *formal* the state of being happily married: *living in connubial bliss*

con·quer /ˈkɒŋkə $ ˈkɑːŋkər/ ●●○ *v*
1 [I,T] to get control of a country by fighting: *The Normans conquered England in 1066.* | *Egypt was conquered by the Persian King Kambyses.*
2 [I,T] to defeat an enemy: *The Zulus conquered all the neighbouring tribes.*
3 [T] to gain control over something that is difficult, using a lot of effort: **conquer your nerves/fear** *She was determined to conquer her fear of flying.* | *efforts to conquer inflation* | *drugs to conquer the disease*
4 [T] to succeed in climbing to the top of a mountain when no one has ever climbed it before: *an attempt to conquer the peaks of Everest*
5 [T] to become very successful in a place: *In the last few years, the company has succeeded in conquering the European market.* —**conqueror** *n* [C] —**conquering** *adj*: *conquering heroes*

con·quest /ˈkɒŋkwest $ ˈkɑːŋ-/ ●○○ *n*
1 [singular, U] the act of getting control of a country by fighting: *the Norman Conquest* (=the conquest of England by the Normans) | **[+of]** *the Spanish conquest of the Inca Empire* THESAURUS▸ VICTORY

2 [C] land that is won in a war: *French conquests in Asia*
3 [C] someone that you have persuaded to love you or to have sex with you – often used humorously: *He boasts about his many conquests.*
4 [C] when you gain control of or deal successfully with something that is difficult or dangerous: **[+of]** *the conquest of space*

con·quis·ta·dor /kɒnˈkwɪstədɔː $ kɑːnˈkiːstədɔːr/ *n* [C] one of the Spanish conquerors of Mexico and Peru in the 18th century

con·san·guin·i·ty /ˌkɒnsæŋˈɡwɪnəti $ ˌkɑːn-/ *n* [U] *formal* when people are members of the same family

con·science /ˈkɒnʃəns $ ˈkɑːn-/ ●●○ *n* [C,U]
1 the part of your mind that tells you whether what you are doing is morally right or wrong: **a guilty/troubled conscience** *It was his guilty conscience that made him offer to help.* | *Well, at least I can face them all with a* ***clear conscience*** (=the knowledge that you have done nothing wrong). | **prisoner of conscience** (=someone in prison because of their beliefs) | *I can't tell you what to do – it's a* ***matter of conscience*** (=something you must make a moral judgement about). | *a* ***crisis of conscience*** *among medical staff* (=a situation in which it is very difficult to decide what is the right thing to do) ⚠ Do not confuse with **consciousness** (=the condition of being awake and aware of things).
2 a guilty feeling that you have about something bad you have done: **twinge/pang of conscience** *Ian felt a pang of conscience at having misjudged her.* | **have no conscience (about sth)** (=not feel guilty about something) *They've no conscience at all about cheating.*
3 on your conscience if you have something on your conscience, it makes you feel guilty: *He didn't want somebody's death on his conscience.* | *Could you live with that on your conscience?*
4 not in (all/good) conscience *formal* if you cannot in all conscience do something, you cannot do it because you think it is wrong: *I couldn't in all conscience tell him that his job was safe.*

ˈconscience-ˌstricken *adj* feeling very guilty about something that you have done wrong: *I hurried home, conscience-stricken at leaving mother alone.*

con·sci·en·tious /ˌkɒnʃiˈenʃəs◂ $ ˌkɑːn-/ ●○○ *adj* careful to do everything that it is your job or duty to do: *A conscientious teacher may feel inclined to take work home.* | *a conscientious and hard-working student* —**conscientiously** *adv* —**conscientiousness** *n* [U]: *his conscientiousness and loyalty to the company*

ˌconscientious obˈjector *n* [C] someone who refuses to become a soldier because of their moral or religious beliefs → DRAFT DODGER

con·scious /ˈkɒnʃəs $ ˈkɑːn-/ ●●○ S3 W3 *adj*
1 AWARE [not before noun] noticing or realizing something SYN **aware**: **conscious of (doing) sth** *I became conscious of someone watching me.* | *I was very* ***conscious of the fact that*** *I had to make a good impression.* | **conscious that** *She was conscious that Marie was listening to every word.*
2 AWAKE awake and able to understand what is happening around you OPP **unconscious**: *The driver was still conscious when the ambulance arrived.*
3 conscious effort/decision/attempt etc an effort etc that is deliberate and intended: *Vivien had made a conscious effort to be friendly.*
4 CONCERNED thinking a lot about or concerned about something: **politically/environmentally/socially etc conscious** *environmentally conscious consumers* | **health-conscious/fashion-conscious etc** *Many employers are becoming more safety-conscious.* | **[+of]** *She was very conscious of security.* → SELF-CONSCIOUS
5 THOUGHTS conscious thoughts, memories etc are ones which you know about → **subconscious**: *the conscious mind* | *Without conscious thought, she instinctively placed a hand on his arm.* | *It affects the audience at a deeper, less conscious level.*

con·scious·ly /ˈkɒnʃəsli $ ˈkɑːn-/ ●○○ *adv* in a way that involves you noticing or realizing something: *She was probably not* ***consciously aware*** *of her true feelings.* | *I'm not consciously trying to flirt with people.*

con·scious·ness /ˈkɒnʃəsnəs $ ˈkɑːn-/ ●●○ W3 *n*
1 [U] the condition of being awake and able to understand what is happening around you: *David* ***lost consciousness*** (=went into a deep sleep) *at eight o'clock and died a few hours later.* | *She could faintly hear voices as she began to* ***regain consciousness*** (=wake up).
2 [C,U] your mind and your thoughts: *The painful memories eventually faded from her consciousness.* | *Hypnosis is an altered* ***state of consciousness***. | *research into* ***human consciousness***
3 [C] someone's ideas, feelings, or opinions about politics, life etc: *The experience helped to change her political consciousness.*
4 [U] when you know that something exists or is true SYN **awareness**: *This will increase* ***public consciousness*** *of the pollution issue.* → STREAM OF CONSCIOUSNESS

ˈconsciousness ˌraising *n* [U] the process of making people understand and care more about a moral, social, or political problem, especially by giving them information

con·script[1] /kənˈskrɪpt/ *v* [T] **1** to make someone join the army, navy etc SYN **draft** *AmE*: **conscript sb into sth** *Young Frenchmen were conscripted into the army and forced to fight in Algeria.* **2** to make someone become a member of a group or take part in a particular activity SYN **recruit**

con·script[2] /ˈkɒnskrɪpt $ ˈkɑːn-/ *n* [C] someone who has been made to join the army, navy etc SYN **draftee** *AmE*: *a young army conscript*

con·scrip·tion /kənˈskrɪpʃən/ *n* [U] when people are made to join the army, navy etc SYN **draft**

con·se·crate /ˈkɒnsəkreɪt $ ˈkɑːn-/ *v* [T] **1** to officially state in a special religious ceremony that a place or building is holy and can be used for religious purposes: *The bones will be reburied in* ***consecrated ground***. **2** to officially state in a special religious ceremony that someone is now a priest, BISHOP etc —**consecration** /ˌkɒnsəˈkreɪʃən $ ˌkɑːn-/ *n* [U]

con·sec·u·tive /kənˈsekjətɪv/ ●●○ *adj* consecutive numbers or periods of time follow one after the other without any interruptions OPP **non-consecutive**: *It had rained for four consecutive days.* | *Can they win the title for the third consecutive season?* —**consecutively** *adv*: *Number the pages consecutively.*

con·sen·su·al /kənˈsenʃuəl/ *adj formal* **1** involving the agreement of all or most people in a group: *a consensual style of management* **2** consensual sexual activity is wanted and agreed to by the people involved

con·sen·sus /kənˈsensəs/ ●○○ AWL *n* [singular, U] an opinion that everyone in a group agrees with or accepts SYN **agreement**: **[+on/about]** *a lack of consensus about the aims of the project* | **consensus that** *There is a consensus among teachers that children should have a broad understanding of the world.* | *The EU Council of Finance Ministers failed to* ***reach*** *a* ***consensus*** *on the pace of integration.* | *the current* ***consensus of opinion*** | *The* ***general consensus*** *was that technology was a good thing.* | *the* ***consensus politics*** *of the fifties*

con·sent[1] /kənˈsent/ ●●○ W3 AWL *n* [U]
1 permission to do something: *He took the car* ***without*** *the owner's* ***consent***. | *Her parents* ***gave*** *their* ***consent*** *to the marriage.* | *A patient can* ***refuse consent*** *for a particular treatment at any time.* | *Most owners are happy to have their names used for publicity if this is done with their* ***prior consent***. | ***Informed consent*** *was obtained from all participants before the study began.* → AGE OF CONSENT
2 agreement about something → **dissent**: *The chairman was elected* ***by common consent*** (=with most people agreeing). | *divorce* ***by mutual consent*** (=by agreement between both the people involved)

consent[2] ●○○ AWL *v* [I] to give your permission for something or agree to do something OPP **refuse**: **[+to]** *Her father reluctantly consented to the marriage.* | **consent to do sth** *He rarely consents to do interviews.*

con͵senting ˈadult *n* [C] *law* someone who is considered to be old enough to decide whether they want to have sex → AGE OF CONSENT

con·se·quence /ˈkɒnsəkwəns $ ˈkɑːnsə-kwens/ ●●○ W2 AWL *n*
1 [C] something that happens as a result of a particular action or set of conditions: **[+of]** *Many believe that poverty is a direct consequence of overpopulation.* | **[+for]** *Our findings have far-reaching consequences for researchers.* | **with ... consequences** *He ate some poisonous mushrooms, with fatal consequences.* THESAURUS RESULT
2 as a consequence (of sth)/in consequence (of sth) *formal* as a result of something: *Animals have died as a consequence of coming into contact with this chemical.* | *She was over the age limit and, in consequence, her application was rejected.*
3 of little/no/any etc consequence *formal* not very important or valuable: **[+to]** *Your opinion is of little consequence to me.* | *I don't suppose it is of any consequence now.*

COLLOCATIONS

VERBS

be a consequence of sth *Low energy may be a consequence of sleeping badly.*
have consequences *Taking financial risks can have serious consequences.*
accept/take the consequences (=understand and deal with them) *I'm prepared to accept the consequences of my decision.*
face/suffer the consequences (=accept the bad results of something you have done) *He broke the law, and he will have to face the consequences.*
consequences follow (=happen) *Once the decision has been made, consequences follow.*
consider the consequences (=think what might happen as a result of something) | **escape the consequences** (=avoid them)

ADJECTIVES

the possible/likely consequences *What are the likely consequences of these changes?*
an inevitable consequence (=that you cannot avoid) *Loss of mobility is not an inevitable consequence of old age.*
serious consequences (=bad and important) *Too much fishing in these seas has had serious consequences.*
disastrous/dire consequences (=very bad and damaging) *If temperatures continue to rise, it could have disastrous consequences for agriculture.*
social/political/economic consequences | **a direct consequence of sth** (=a consequence directly caused by something) | **a natural/logical consequence** (=that naturally/logically follows something) | **a negative consequence** (=a bad or unpleasant result) | **an adverse/unfortunate consequence** (=that affects your life, a situation etc badly) | **tragic consequences** (=very sad, usually involving death) | **far-reaching consequences** (=important and affecting many things) | **long-term consequences** (=results that last a long time, or appear after a long time)

con·se·quent /ˈkɒnsəkwənt $ ˈkɑːn-/ ●○○ AWL *adj* [usually before noun] *formal* happening as a result of a particular event or situation SYN **resulting**: *the rise in inflation and consequent fall in demand* → SUBSEQUENT

con·se·quen·tial /͵kɒnsəˈkwenʃəl◂ $ ͵kɑːn-/ *adj* [usually before noun] *formal* **1** happening as a direct result of a particular event or situation: *redundancy and the consequential loss of earnings* **2** important SYN **significant** OPP **inconsequential**: *a consequential decision* —**consequentially** *adv*

con·se·quent·ly /ˈkɒnsəkwəntli $ ˈkɑːnsə-kwentli/ ●●○ AWL *adv* [sentence adverb] as a result SYN **therefore**: *Most computer users have never received any formal keyboard training. Consequently, their keyboard skills are inefficient.* | *The molecules are absorbed into the bloodstream and consequently affect the organs.*

con·ser·van·cy /kənˈsɜːvənsi $ -ɜːr-/ *n formal* **1** [singular] a group of officials who control and protect an area of land, a river etc: *the Thames Conservancy* **2** [U] the protection of natural things such as animals, plants, forests etc SYN **conservation**

con·ser·va·tion /͵kɒnsəˈveɪʃən $ ͵kɑːnsər-/ ●●○ *n* [U]
1 the protection of natural things such as animals, plants, forests etc, to prevent them from being spoiled or destroyed SYN **preservation** → **conserve**: *wildlife conservation* | *a local conservation group* | **[+of]** *conservation of the countryside*
2 when you prevent something from being lost or wasted → **conserve**: *energy conservation* | **[+of]** *the conservation of resources through recycling*

͵conserˈvation ͵area *n* [C] **1** an area where animals and plants are protected **2** *BrE* an area where interesting old buildings are protected and new buildings are carefully controlled

con·ser·va·tion·ist /͵kɒnsəˈveɪʃənɪst $ ͵kɑːnsər-/ *n* [C] someone who works to protect animals, plants etc or to protect old buildings —**conservationism** *n* [U]

con·ser·va·tis·m /kənˈsɜːvətɪzəm $ -ɜːr-/ *n* [U] **1** dislike of change and new ideas: *people's innate conservatism in matters of language* **2** (*also* **Conservatism**) the political belief that society should change as little as possible **3 Conservatism** the political beliefs of the British Conservative Party

con·ser·va·tive¹ /kənˈsɜːvətɪv $ -ɜːr-/ ●●○ *adj*
1 not liking changes or new ideas: *a very conservative attitude to education* | *conservative views*
2 Conservative belonging to or concerned with the Conservative Party in Britain: *Conservative policies* | *a Conservative MP*
3 not very modern in style, taste etc SYN **traditional**: *a dark conservative suit*
4 a conservative estimate/guess a guess which is deliberately lower than what the real amount probably is: *At a conservative estimate, the holiday will cost about £1,500.* —**conservatively** *adv*: *a fortune conservatively estimated at 2 million dollars* | *He was conservatively dressed in a dark business suit.*

conservative² *n* [C] **1 Conservative** someone who supports or is a member of the Conservative Party in Britain **2** someone who does not like changes in politics, ideas, or fashion: *an argument between reformers and conservatives in the organization*

con·ser·va·toire /kənˈsɜːvətwɑː $ -ˈsɜːrvətwɑːr/ *n* [C] *BrE* a school where people are trained in music or acting SYN **conservatory** *AmE*

con·ser·va·to·ry /kənˈsɜːvətəri $ -ˈsɜːrvətɔːri/ *n* (*plural* **conservatories**) [C] **1** *BrE* a room with glass walls and a glass roof, where plants are grown, that is usually added on to a house **2** *AmE* a conservatoire

con·serve¹ /kənˈsɜːv $ -ɜːrv/ ●○○ *v* [T]
1 to protect something and prevent it from changing or being damaged SYN **preserve** → **conservation**: *We must conserve our woodlands for future generations.* | *efforts to conserve fish stocks*
2 to use as little water, energy etc as possible so that it is not wasted → **conservation**: *the need to conserve energy*

con·serve² /ˈkɒnsɜːv $ ˈkɑːnsɜːrv/ *n* [C,U] *formal* fruit that is preserved by being cooked with sugar SYN **jam**: *strawberry conserve*

con·sid·er /kənˈsɪdə $ -ər/ ●●● S1 W1 *v*
1 THINK ABOUT [I,T] to think about something carefully, especially before making a choice or decision: **consider doing sth** *I seriously considered resigning* (=almost actually resigned). | **consider the possibility of (doing) sth** *Have you considered the possibility of retraining?* | **consider whether (to do sth)** *We are considering whether to change our advice to tourists.* | **consider where/how/why etc** *We're still considering where to move to.* | *We will have to* **consider** *your offer*

carefully. | **be considering your position** *formal* (=be deciding whether or not to leave your job) **THESAURUS** THINK

GRAMMAR

Consider is followed by an **-ing** form, not an infinitive. You **consider doing** something: *I considered asking for my money back.* ✗ Don't say: *I considered to ask for my money back.*

GRAMMAR GUIDE VERBS

2 OPINION [T] to think of someone or something in a particular way or to have a particular opinion: **consider (that)** *The local authority considered that the school did not meet requirements.* | **consider sb/sth (to be) sth** *A further increase in interest rates is now considered unlikely.* | *Liz Quinn was considered an excellent teacher.* | *They consider themselves to be Europeans.* | **consider it necessary/important etc to do sth** *I did not consider it necessary to report the incident.* | *I consider it a great honour to be invited.* | **consider sb/sth to do sth** *The campaign was considered to have failed.* | **consider yourself lucky/fortunate** (=believe you are lucky etc) *Consider yourself lucky you weren't in the car at the time.* | **consider yourself (to be) sth** (=think of yourself as a particular type of person) *They consider themselves to be middle class.*

3 PEOPLE'S FEELINGS [T] to think about someone or their feelings, and try to avoid upsetting them → **considerate**: *You've got to learn to consider other people!* | *Have you considered my feelings?*

4 IMPORTANT FACT [I,T] to think about an important fact relating to something when making a judgment → **considering**: *It's not surprising* ***when you consider that*** *he only arrived six months ago.* | ***All things considered****, I'm sure we made the right decision.*

5 DISCUSS [T] to discuss something such as a report or problem, so that you can make a decision about it: *The committee has been considering the report.*

6 LOOK AT [T] *formal* to look at someone or something carefully: *Ben considered the statue with an expert eye.*

7 consider it done *spoken* used to say yes very willingly when someone asks you to do something for them: *'Could you drive me to the airport tomorrow?' 'Consider it done.'*

GRAMMAR: Using the progressive

- In meaning 1, **consider** is often used in the progressive. You say: *I am considering investing some money* (=I am thinking about it and may do it).
- In meaning 2, **consider** is not used in the progressive. You say: *I consider it a good investment* (=I believe that it is). ✗ Don't say: *I am considering it a good investment.*

GRAMMAR GUIDE VERBS

con·sid·er·a·ble /kənˈsɪdərəbəl/ ●●○ W3 AWL *adj* fairly large, especially large enough to have an effect or be important → **inconsiderable**: **considerable amount/number etc of sth** *We've saved a considerable amount of money.* | *Michael has already spent considerable time in Barcelona.* | *issues of considerable importance* | *The series has aroused considerable interest.* **THESAURUS** BIG

con·sid·er·a·bly /kənˈsɪdərəbli/ ●●○ W3 AWL *adv* much or a lot: *It's considerably colder today.* | *Conditions have improved considerably over the past few years.*

con·sid·er·ate /kənˈsɪdərət/ ●○○ *adj* always thinking of what other people need or want and being careful not to upset them OPP **inconsiderate**: *He was always kind and considerate.* | **it is considerate of sb (to do sth)** *It was very considerate of you to let us know you were going to be late.* | **[+towards]** *As a motorist, I try to be considerate towards cyclists.* **THESAURUS** KIND —**considerately** *adv*

con·sid·e·ra·tion /kənˌsɪdəˈreɪʃən/ ●●○ *n*

1 [U] *formal* careful thought and attention, especially before making an official or important decision: *proposals put forward for consideration* | **under consideration** *There are several amendments under consideration.* | **due/serious/proper etc consideration** *After due consideration, I have decided to tender my resignation.* | **give sth careful/full etc consideration** *We would have to give serious consideration to banning it altogether.* | **deserve/merit consideration** *These plans definitely merit further consideration.*

2 take sth into consideration to remember to think about something important when you are making a decision or judgment: *We will take your recent illness into consideration when marking your exams.* GRAMMAR ✗ Don't say: *take something in consideration* | *take something under consideration*

3 [C] a fact that you think about when you are making a decision: *Political rather than economic considerations influenced the location of the new factory.*

4 [U] the quality of thinking about other people's feelings and being careful not to upset them: **[+for]** *The murdered woman's name has not been released, out of consideration for her parents.* | *They've got no* ***consideration for others****.* | ***Show*** *some* ***consideration****!*

5 [singular, U] *formal* a payment for something, especially a service: *I might be able to help you,* ***for a small consideration****.* | *a payment* ***in consideration of*** (=as payment for) *their services*

con·sid·ered /kənˈsɪdəd $ -ərd/ *adj* [only before noun] a considered opinion, reply, judgment etc is one that you have thought about carefully: *He hadn't had time to form a* ***considered opinion****.* | *The committee is meeting to prepare a* ***considered response*** *to the problem.* → ILL-CONSIDERED

con·sid·er·ing¹ /kənˈsɪdərɪŋ/ ●●○ *prep, conjunction* used to say that you are thinking about a particular fact when you are giving your opinion: *Considering the strength of the opposition, we did very well to score two goals.* | **considering (that)** *I think we paid too much for the house, considering that we needed to get the roof repaired.* | **considering who/how etc** *John did quite well in his exams, considering how little he studied.*

considering² *adv spoken* used after you have given an opinion, to say that something is true in spite of a situation that makes it seem surprising: *He didn't look too tired, considering.*

con·sign /kənˈsaɪn/ *v* [T] *formal* to send something somewhere, especially in order to sell it

consign sb/sth **to** sth *phr v formal* **1** to make someone or something be in a particular situation, especially a bad one: *It was a decision which consigned him to political obscurity.* | **consign sb/sth to the dustbin/scrapheap/rubbish heap etc** *BrE*: *Many older people feel they have been consigned to the medical scrapheap.* **2** to put something somewhere, especially in order to get rid of it: *The shoes looked so tatty that I consigned them to the back of the cupboard.*

con·sign·ee /ˌkɒnsaɪˈniː, -sə- $ ˌkɑːn-/ *n* [C] *technical* the person that something is delivered to

con·sign·ment /kənˈsaɪnmənt/ *n* **1** [C] a quantity of goods that are sent somewhere, especially in order to be sold: **[+of]** *a large consignment of clothes* **2 on consignment** goods that are on consignment are being sold for someone else for a share of the profit **3** [U] when someone sends or delivers something

conˈsignment ˌshop *n* [C] *AmE* a shop where you take things you do not want, so the shop can sell them and give you a share of the profit

con·sign·or /kənˈsaɪnə $ -ər/ *n* [C] *technical* the person who sends goods to someone else

con·sist /kənˈsɪst/ ●●● W3 AWL *v*

consist in sth *phr v formal* to be based on or depend on something: *Happiness does not consist in how many possessions you own.*

consist of sth *phr v* to be formed from two or more things or people: *The buffet consisted of several different Indian dishes.* | **consist mainly/largely/primarily of sb/sth** *The audience consisted mainly of teenagers.* | **consist entirely/solely of sb/sth** *The area does not consist entirely of rich people, despite popular belief.*

GRAMMAR

Comparison

consist of

- You say: *My family consists of four people.* ✗ Don't say: *My family consists in four people.*

C

• **Consist** is not used in the passive. ✗ Don't say: *My family is consisted of four people.*

be made up of

• You say: *My family is made up of four people.*

be composed of

• You say: *My family is composed of four people.*

Using the progressive

• The verb **consist** is not used in the progressive. You say: *The building consists of four floors.* ✗ Don't say: *The building is consisting of four floors.*

• However, the participle form **consisting** is often used: *There is a large art collection, consisting of over 300 paintings.*

GRAMMAR GUIDE ▸ VERBS

C

THESAURUS

consist of/be made up of to be formed from two or more things or people: *Lunch consisted of sandwiches and fruit.* | *The apartment consisted of three rooms.* | *The audience was largely made up of families.*

be composed of to consist of something – used especially when saying which natural substances something contains, or what kind of people are in a group: *Every chemical element is composed of atoms.* | *Venus' atmosphere is mainly composed of carbon dioxide.* | *The team was composed of leading scientists from around the world.*

comprise /kəm'praɪz/ *formal* to consist of the things mentioned. **Comprise** can also be used to talk about the people or things which form something: *The event comprises a champagne reception, two-course lunch, and a fashion show.* | *Men still comprise the majority of people who have the disease.*

make up (*also* **constitute** *formal*) to be the things or people that form something: *Women constitute a significant part of the workforce.* | *Toys make up about 10% of the company's sales.*

con·sis·ten·cy /kən'sɪstənsi/ ●○○ AWL *n* (*plural* **consistencies**) [C,U]
1 the quality of always being the same, doing things in the same way, having the same standards etc – used to show approval OPP **inconsistency**: **[+in]** *Consumer groups are demanding greater consistency in the labelling of food products.* | **[+of]** *Consistency of performance depends on several factors.* | **[+between/among]** *There are checks to ensure consistency between interviewers.*
2 how thick, smooth etc a substance is: **[+of]** *Beat the mixture until it has the consistency of thick cream.*

con·sis·tent /kən'sɪstənt/ ●●○ S3 W3 AWL *adj*
1 always behaving in the same way or having the same attitudes, standards etc – usually used to show approval OPP **inconsistent**: *She's the team's most consistent player.* | **[+in]** *We need to be consistent in our approach.*
2 continuing to happen or develop in the same way: *a consistent improvement in the country's economy*
3 a consistent argument or idea does not have any parts that do not match other parts OPP **inconsistent**: *The evidence is not consistent.*
4 be consistent with sth if a fact, idea etc is consistent with another one, it seems to match it: *Her injuries are consistent with having fallen from the building.* | *The results are consistent with earlier research.* —**consistently** *adv*: *consistently high performance*

con·so·la·tion /ˌkɒnsə'leɪʃən $ ˌkɑːn-/ ●○○ *n* [C,U] something that makes you feel better when you are sad or disappointed: **[+for/to]** *The only consolation for the team is that they get a chance to play the game again.* | ***If it's any consolation**, things do get easier as the child gets older.* | *He **had the consolation of** knowing that he couldn't have done any better.* | **be little/no consolation** *The fact that there has been a reduction in crime is little consolation to victims of crime.*

ˌconsoˈlation prize *n* [C] a prize that is given to someone who has not won a competition: *Ten runners-up received a T-shirt as a consolation prize.*

con·sol·a·to·ry /kən'sɒlətəri, -'səʊlə- $ -'soʊlətɔːri, -'sɑː-/ *adj formal* intended to make someone feel better

con·sole¹ /kən'səʊl $ -'soʊl/ *v* [T] to make someone feel better when they are feeling sad or disappointed → **consolation**: *No one could console her when Peter died.* | **console yourself with sth** *She consoled herself with the fact that no one else had done well in the exam either.* | **console yourself that** *He consoled himself that he would see Kate again soon.*

con·sole² /'kɒnsəʊl $ 'kɑːnsoʊl/ *n* [C] **1** a flat board that contains the controls for a machine, piece of electrical equipment, computer etc **2** a special cupboard for a television, computer etc

con·sol·i·date /kən'sɒlədeɪt $ -'sɑː-/ ●○○ *v* [I,T]
1 to strengthen the position of power or success that you have, so that it becomes more effective or continues for longer: *The company has **consolidated** its **position** as the country's leading gas supplier.* | *The team consolidated their lead with a third goal.*
2 to combine things in order to make them more effective or easier to deal with: *We consolidate information from a wide range of sources.* | *They took out a loan to consolidate their debts.* | *The company is planning to consolidate its business activities at a new site in Arizona.* —**consolidation** /kənˌsɒlə'deɪʃən $ -ˌsɑː-/ *n* [C,U]: *the consolidation of political power*

con·som·mé /kən'sɒmeɪ, 'kɒnsəmeɪ $ ˌkɑːnsə'meɪ/ *n* [U] clear soup made from meat or vegetables

con·so·nant¹ /'kɒnsənənt $ 'kɑːn-/ ●●○ *n* [C]
1 a speech sound made by partly or completely stopping the flow of air through your mouth → **vowel**
2 a letter that represents a consonant sound. The letters 'a', 'e', 'i', 'o', 'u', and sometimes 'y' represent vowels, and all the other letters are consonants.

consonant² *adj* **1 be consonant with sth** *formal* to match or exist well with something else: *This policy is scarcely consonant with the government's declared aims.* **2** *technical* relating to a combination of musical notes that sounds pleasant OPP **dissonant** —**consonance** *n* [U]

con·sort¹ /'kɒnsɔːt $ 'kɑːnsɔːrt/ *n* [C] **1** the wife or husband of a ruler → PRINCE CONSORT **2** a group of people who play very old music, or the group of old-fashioned instruments they use **3 in consort (with sb)** *formal* doing something together with someone

con·sort² /kən'sɔːt $ -ɔːrt/ *v*
consort with sb *phr v formal* to spend time with someone that other people do not approve of: *a man who regularly consorted with prostitutes*

con·sor·ti·um /kən'sɔːtiəm $ -ɔːr-/ ●○○ *n* (*plural* **consortia** /-tiə/ *or* **consortiums**) [C] a group of companies or organizations who are working together to do something: *a consortium of oil companies* | *The aircraft will be built by a European consortium.*

con·spic·u·ous /kən'spɪkjuəs/ ●○○ *adj*
1 very easy to notice OPP **inconspicuous**: *The notice must be displayed in a conspicuous place.* | *a bird with conspicuous white markings* | *I felt very conspicuous in my red coat.*
THESAURUS ▸ OBVIOUS
2 conspicuous success, courage etc is very great and impressive: *He had represented Italy with conspicuous success.* | *The award is given for notable or conspicuous achievement in science.*
3 be conspicuous by your/its absence used to say that someone or something is not somewhere where they were expected to be: *a group that were conspicuous by their absence from the awards ceremony*

conˌspicuous conˈsumption *n* [U] the act of buying a lot of things, especially expensive things that are not necessary, in order to IMPRESS other people and show them how rich you are

con·spi·ra·cy /kən'spɪrəsi/ ●○○ *n* (*plural* **conspiracies**) [C,U]
1 a secret plan made by two or more people to do something that is harmful or illegal → **conspire**: **conspiracy to do**

sth *He was charged with conspiracy to commit criminal damage.* | **[+against]** *a conspiracy against the government* | *There were many* ***conspiracy theories*** (=beliefs that something is the result of a conspiracy) *surrounding Princess Diana's death.* THESAURUS ▸ PLAN
2 conspiracy of silence an agreement not to talk about something, even though it should not be a secret: *There's often a conspiracy of silence surrounding bullying in schools.*

con·spi·ra·tor /kənˈspɪrətə $ -ər/ *n* [C] someone who is involved in a secret plan to do something illegal

con·spi·ra·to·ri·al /kənˌspɪrəˈtɔːriəl/ *adj* **1** a conspiratorial expression, voice, or manner suggests you are sharing a secret with someone: *His voice became low and conspiratorial.* | *Pat whispered to Maggie in a conspiratorial tone.* | **conspiratorial whisper/smile/wink etc** *Britta gave him a conspiratorial smile.* **2** relating to a conspiracy —**conspiratorially** *adv*

con·spire /kənˈspaɪə $ -ˈspaɪr/ ●○○ *v* [I]
1 to secretly plan with someone else to do something illegal → **conspiracy**: **conspire (with sb) to do sth** *All six men admitted conspiring to steal cars.* | **[+against]** *There was some evidence that he had been conspiring against the government.*
2 if events conspire to do something, they happen at the same time and make something bad happen: **conspire to do sth** *Pollution and neglect have conspired to ruin the city.* | **[+against]** *Emily felt that everything was conspiring against her.*

con·sta·ble /ˈkʌnstəbəl $ ˈkɑːn-/ *n* [C] **1** a British police officer of the lowest rank **2** in the US, someone who has some of the powers of a police officer and can send legal documents that order someone to do something

con·stab·u·la·ry /kənˈstæbjələri $ -leri/ *n* (*plural* **constabularies**) [C] the police force of a particular area or country

con·stan·cy /ˈkɒnstənsi $ ˈkɑːn-/ AWL *n* [U] *formal* **1** the quality of staying the same even though other things change: **[+of]** *constancy of temperature* **2** loyalty and faithfulness to a particular person SYN **devotion**

con·stant¹ /ˈkɒnstənt $ ˈkɑːn-/ ●●○ S3 W3 AWL *adj*
1 happening regularly or all the time SYN **continual**: *There was a* ***constant stream of*** *visitors to the house.* | *Amy lived in constant fear of being attacked.* | *He kept in constant contact with his family while he was in Australia.*
2 staying the same OPP **inconstant**: *travelling at a constant speed*
3 *literary* loyal and faithful SYN **devoted**: *a constant friend*

constant² ●○○ AWL *n* [C]
1 *technical* a number or quantity that never changes
2 *formal* something that stays the same even though other things change → VARIABLE²

con·stant·ly /ˈkɒnstəntli $ ˈkɑːn-/ ●●○ S3 W3 AWL *adv* all the time, or very often SYN **continually**: *He talked constantly about his work.* | *The English language is* ***constantly changing***.

con·stel·la·tion /ˌkɒnstəˈleɪʃən $ ˌkɑːn-/ *n* [C] **1** a group of stars that forms a particular pattern and has a name: *a star in the constellation of Orion* **2 a constellation of sth** *literary* a group of people or things that are similar: *a constellation of ideas*

con·ster·na·tion /ˌkɒnstəˈneɪʃən $ ˌkɑːnstər-/ *n* [U] a feeling of worry, shock, or fear SYN **alarm**: *The government's plans have* ***caused*** *considerable* ***consternation*** *among many Americans.* | *A new power station is being built* ***much to the consternation of*** *environmental groups* (=they are very worried about it). | **in consternation** *He looked at her in consternation.*

con·sti·pa·tion /ˌkɒnstəˈpeɪʃən $ ˌkɑːn-/ *n* [U] the condition of having difficulty in getting rid of solid waste from your body → **diarrhoea** —**constipated** /ˈkɒnstɪpeɪtɪd $ ˈkɑːn-/ *adj*

con·sti·tu·en·cy /kənˈstɪtʃuənsi/ ●○○ AWL *n* (*plural* **constituencies**) [C]
1 *BrE* an area of a country that elects a representative to a parliament → **seat**: *a rural constituency* | *constituency boundaries* | *He represents the Essex constituency of Epping Forest.*
2 the people who live and vote in a particular area
3 any group that supports or is likely to support a politician or a political party: *The trade unions were no longer the constituency of the Labour Party alone.*

con·sti·tu·ent¹ /kənˈstɪtʃuənt/ ●○○ AWL *n* [C]
1 someone who votes in a particular area
2 one of the substances or things that combine to form something: **[+of]** *Sodium is one of the constituents of salt.*

constituent² ●○○ AWL *adj* [only before noun] *formal* being one of the parts of something: *the EU and its constituent members*

conˌstituent asˈsembly *n* [C] a group of elected representatives that have the power to write or change their country's constitution

con·sti·tute /ˈkɒnstɪtjuːt $ ˈkɑːnstɪtuːt/ ●●○ W3 AWL *v*
1 [linking verb] to be considered to be something: *Failing to complete the work constitutes a breach of the employment contract.* | *The rise in crime constitutes a threat to society.*
2 [linking verb] if several people or things constitute something, they are the parts that form it SYN **make up**: *We must redefine what constitutes a family.*

> **REGISTER**
> In everyday English, people usually say **make up** rather than **constitute**: *His letters to his wife* ***make up*** *the middle section of the book.*

> **GRAMMAR: Using the progressive**
> • In meanings 1 and 2, **constitute** is not used in the progressive. You say: *This constitutes a criminal offence.* ✗ Don't say: *This is constituting a criminal offence.*
> • However, the participle form **constituting** is often used: *Fish products are significant in Japan's imports, constituting 30% of the total.*
> GRAMMAR GUIDE ▸ VERBS

3 [T] *formal* to officially form a group or organization SYN **found**: *The Federation was constituted in 1949.* GRAMMAR **Constitute** is usually passive in this meaning.

con·sti·tu·tion /ˌkɒnstɪˈtjuːʃən $ ˌkɑːnstɪˈtuː-/ ●●○ AWL *n* [C]
1 (*also* **Constitution**) a set of basic laws and principles that a country or organization is governed by: *The right to speak freely is written into the Constitution of the United States.*
2 your health and your body's ability to fight illness: **(have) a strong/good/weak etc constitution** *She's got a strong constitution – she'll recover in no time.*
3 *formal* the parts or structure of something: **[+of]** *What's the chemical constitution of the dye?*

con·sti·tu·tion·al¹ /ˌkɒnstəˈtjuːʃənəl◂ $ ˌkɑːnstɪˈtuː-/ ●●○ AWL *adj*
1 officially allowed or limited by the system of rules of a country or organization: *a* ***constitutional right*** *to privacy* | *a* ***constitutional monarchy*** (=a country ruled by a king or queen whose power is limited by a constitution)
2 connected with the constitution of a country or organization: *a constitutional crisis* | **constitutional reform/change/amendment** *a proposal for constitutional reform*
3 relating to someone's health, physical ability, or character —**constitutionally** *adv*: *a constitutionally guaranteed right* | *He was constitutionally incapable of dealing with conflict.*

constitutional² *n* [C] *old-fashioned* a walk you take because it is good for your health

con·sti·tu·tion·al·is·m /ˌkɒnstəˈtjuːʃənəlɪzəm $ ˌkɑːnstɪˈtuː-/ *n* [U] the belief that a government should be based on a constitution —**constitutionalist** *n* [C]

con·sti·tu·tion·al·i·ty /ˌkɒnstətjuːʃəˈnæləti $ ˌkɑːnstətuː-/ *n* [U] the quality of being acceptable

C

according to a constitution: *A decision on the proposal's constitutionality still has to be made.*

con·strain /kən'streɪn/ ●○○ AWL *v* [T]
1 to stop someone from doing what they want to do SYN **restrict**: **constrain sb from doing sth** *Financial factors should not constrain doctors from prescribing the best treatment for patients.*
2 to limit something SYN **restrict**: *Poor soil has constrained the level of crop production.* | *Women's employment opportunities are often severely constrained by family commitments.*

con·strained /kən'streɪnd/ AWL *adj* **be/feel constrained to do sth** to feel that you must do something SYN **obliged**: *He felt constrained to accept the invitation.*

C

con·straint /kən'streɪnt/ ●○○ AWL *n*
1 [C] something that limits your freedom to do what you want SYN **restriction**: **[+on]** *Constraints on spending have forced the company to rethink its plans.* | *the constraints of family life* | **financial/environmental/political etc constraints** *There have been financial and political constraints on development.* | **impose/place constraints on sb/sth** *constraints imposed on teachers by large class sizes*
2 [U] control over the way people are allowed to behave, so that they cannot do what they want: *freedom from constraint*

con·strict /kən'strɪkt/ *v* **1** [I,T] to make something narrower or tighter, or to become narrower or tighter: *Caffeine constricts the blood vessels in your body.* | *Linda's throat constricted and she started to cry.* **2** [T] to limit someone's freedom to do what they want SYN **restrict**: *Fear of crime constricts many people's lives.* —**constricted** *adj* —**constriction** /-'strɪkʃən/ *n* [C,U]

con·struct¹ /kən'strʌkt/ ●●○ W3 AWL *v* [T]
1 to build something such as a house, bridge, road etc: *There are plans to construct a new road bridge across the river.* | **construct sth from/of/in sth** *skyscrapers constructed entirely of concrete and glass* → see picture at ASSEMBLE
2 to form something such as a sentence, argument, or system by joining words, ideas etc together: *Boyce has constructed a new theory of management.*
3 *technical* to draw a mathematical shape: *Construct a square with sides of 5 cm.*

con·struct² /'kɒnstrʌkt $ 'kɑːn-/ AWL *n* [C] *formal*
1 an idea formed by combining several pieces of information or knowledge **2** something that is built or made SYN **construction**

con·struc·tion /kən'strʌkʃən/ ●●○ AWL *n*
1 BUILDING STH [U] the process of building things such as houses, bridges, roads etc: **[+of]** *the construction of a new airport* | **under construction** (=being built) *The hotel is currently under construction.* | *a road construction project* | *construction workers*
2 MAKING STH FROM MANY PARTS [U] the process of making something using many parts: *Work out the exact design before you start construction.*
3 WAY STH IS MADE [U] the materials used to build or make something, or its design and structure: *The houses were partly timber in construction.* | *External doors should be of robust construction.*
4 A BUILDING/STRUCTURE [C] *formal* something that has been built: *a modern construction*
5 GRAMMAR [C] the way in which words are put together in a sentence, phrase etc: *difficult grammatical constructions*
6 IDEAS/KNOWLEDGE [U] the process of forming something from knowledge or ideas: *the construction of sociological theory*
7 put a construction on sth *formal* to think that a statement has a particular meaning or that something was done for a particular reason: *The judge put an entirely different construction on his remarks.* —**constructional** *adj*

con·struc·tive /kən'strʌktɪv/ ●○○ AWL *adj* useful and helpful, or likely to produce good results: *The meeting was very constructive.* | *We welcome any* ***constructive criticism.*** —**constructively** *adv*

con,structive dis'missal *n* [C,U] *BrE* when your employer changes your job or working conditions so you feel forced to leave your job

con·struc·tor /kən'strʌktə $ -ər/ *n* [C] a company or person that builds things

con·strue /kən'struː/ ●○○ *v* [T] to understand a remark or action in a particular way → **misconstrue**: **be construed as sth** *comments that could be construed as sexist* | *The term can be construed in two different ways.*

con·sul /'kɒnsəl $ 'kɑːn-/ *n* [C] a government official sent to live in a foreign city to help people from his or her own country who are living or staying there → **ambassador**: *the British Consul in Paris* —**consular** /'kɒnsjələ $ 'kɑːnsələr/ *adj*: *a consular official*

con·su·late /'kɒnsjələt $ 'kɑːnsələt/ *n* [C] the building in which a consul lives and works → **embassy**

con·sult /kən'sʌlt/ ●●○ S3 W3 AWL *v*
1 [I,T] to ask for information or advice from someone because it is their job to know something: *If symptoms persist, consult a doctor without delay.* | **consult sb about sth** *An increasing number of people are consulting their accountants about the tax laws.* | **[+with]** *I need to consult with my lawyer.*

> **REGISTER**
> In everyday English, people usually say **ask** someone, or **see** someone, rather than **consult** someone: *You need to* ***ask*** *your lawyer.* | *I think you should* ***go and see*** *your doctor.*

2 [I,T] to discuss something with someone so that you can make a decision together: *I can't believe you sold the car without consulting me!* | **[+with]** *The president consulted with European leaders before taking action.*
3 [T] to look for information in a book, map, list etc: *Have you consulted a dictionary?*

con·sul·tan·cy /kən'sʌltənsi/ ●○○ AWL *n* (*plural* **consultancies**)
1 [C] a company that gives advice on a particular subject: *a management consultancy* | *a consultancy firm*
2 [U] advice that a company is paid to provide: *consultancy fees*

con·sul·tant /kən'sʌltənt/ ●●○ AWL *n* [C]
1 someone whose job is to give advice on a particular subject: *a management consultant*
2 *BrE* a hospital doctor of a very high rank who has a lot of knowledge about a particular area of medicine THESAURUS ▸ DOCTOR

con·sul·ta·tion /ˌkɒnsəl'teɪʃən $ ˌkɑːn-/ ●○○ AWL *n*
1 [C,U] a discussion in which people who are affected by or involved in something can give their opinions: **[+with]** *The decision was reached after consultation with parents and teachers.* | **[+between]** *He's calling for urgent consultations between the government and the oil industry to resolve the problem.* | **in consultation with sb** *The plans were drawn up in consultation with engineers.* | **consultation process/exercise/period** *There will be a public consultation exercise to ask for people's views.* | **consultation paper/document**
2 [C] a meeting with a professional person, especially a doctor, for advice or treatment: *A follow-up consultation was arranged for two weeks' time.*
3 [U] the process of getting advice from a professional person: *Trained parenting experts are available for consultation by telephone.*
4 [U] the process of looking for information or help in a book: *Leaflets were regularly displayed for consultation by students.*

con·sul·ta·tive /kən'sʌltətɪv/ AWL *adj* [usually before noun] providing advice and suggesting solutions to problems: *a consultative document*

con·sult·ing¹ /kən'sʌltɪŋ/ *n* [U] the service of providing advice to companies

consulting² *adj* [only before noun] providing advice to companies: *a major international consulting firm*

conˈsulting ˌroom *n* [C] a room where a doctor sees patients

con·sum·a·ble /kənˈsjuːməbəl $ -ˈsuːm-/ *adj* consumable goods are intended to be used and then replaced

con·sum·a·bles /kənˈsjuːməbəlz $ -ˈsuːm-/ *n* [plural] goods that are intended to be used and then replaced: *consumables such as printing paper*

con·sume /kənˈsjuːm $ -ˈsuːm/ ●●○ AWL *v* [T]
1 to use time, energy, goods etc → **consumption**: *Only 27% of the paper we consume is recycled.* | *A smaller vehicle will consume less fuel.*
2 *formal* to eat or drink something → **consumer, consumption**: *Alcohol may not be consumed on the premises.* **THESAURUS** EAT
3 *literary* if a feeling or idea consumes you, it affects you very strongly, so that you cannot think about anything else: *She was scared by the depression which threatened to consume her.* | **be consumed with sth** *He was consumed with guilt after the accident.*
4 *formal* if fire consumes something, it destroys it completely → TIME-CONSUMING

con·sum·er /kənˈsjuːmə $ -ˈsuːmər/ ●●○ S3 W3 AWL *n* [C] someone who buys and uses products and services → **consumption, producer**: *Consumers will soon be paying higher airfares.* | *It will offer a wider choice of goods for* ***the consumer*** (=consumers in general). | ***Consumer demand*** *led to higher imports of manufactured goods.* | ***Consumer spending*** *was down by 0.1% last month.* | *sources of* ***consumer advice*** **THESAURUS** CUSTOMER

conˌsumer ˈconfidence *n* [U] the level of people's satisfaction with the economic situation, which is shown by how much money they spend: *Consumer confidence reached an all-time low in September.*

conˌsumer ˈdurables *n* [plural] *BrE* large things such as cars, televisions, or furniture that you do not buy often

conˈsumer ˌgoods *n* [plural] goods that people buy for their own use, rather than goods bought by businesses and organizations → **capital goods, brown goods**

conˈsumer ˌgroup *n* [C] an organization that makes sure that CONSUMERs are treated fairly and that products are safe

con·sum·er·ism /kənˈsjuːmərɪzəm $ -ˈsuː-/ *n* [U]
1 the belief that it is good to buy and use a lot of goods and services - often used to show disapproval: *the growth of consumerism* **2** actions to protect people from unfair prices, advertising that is not true etc —**consumerist** *adj*

conˌsumer ˈprice ˌindex *n* [C] a list of the prices of products that shows how much prices have increased during a particular period of time

conˈsumer soˌciety *n* [C] a society in which buying goods and services is considered to be very important

con·sum·ing /kənˈsjuːmɪŋ $ -ˈsuː-/ *adj* [only before noun] a consuming feeling is so strong that you think of little else: *a consuming hatred* | **consuming interest/passion** (=a strong feeling of interest, or something you are extremely interested in) *During this period, politics became his consuming interest.*

-consuming /kənsjuːmɪŋ $ -suː-/ *suffix* using a lot of something such as time, energy, or space: *a time-consuming job* | *energy-consuming labour*

con·sum·mate¹ /kənˈsʌmət, ˈkɒnsəmət $ ˈkɑːnsəmət/ *adj* [only before noun] *formal* **1** showing a lot of skill: *a great performance from a consummate actor* | *He won the race* ***with consummate ease*** (=very easily). | *De Gaulle conducted his strategy* ***with consummate skill.*** **2** used to emphasize how bad someone or something is: *his consummate lack of tact* | *The man's a consummate liar.* —**consummately** *adv*

con·sum·mate² /ˈkɒnsəmeɪt $ ˈkɑːn-/ *v* [T] *formal*
1 to make a marriage or relationship complete by having sex **2** to make something complete, especially an agreement

con·sum·ma·tion /ˌkɒnsəˈmeɪʃən $ ˌkɑːn-/ *n* [singular, U] *formal* **1** when people make a marriage or relationship complete by having sex **2** the point at which something is complete or perfect SYN **realization**: *the consummation of his ambitions*

con·sump·tion /kənˈsʌmpʃən/ ●●○ W3 AWL *n* [U]
1 AMOUNT USED the amount of energy, oil, electricity etc that is used → **consume**: **energy/fuel etc consumption** *dramatic rises in fuel consumption* | *Vigorous exercise increases oxygen consumption.*
2 FOOD/DRINK **a)** *formal* the act of eating or drinking → **consume**: **[+of]** *The consumption of alcohol on the premises is forbidden.* | **fit/unfit for human consumption** (=safe or not safe to eat) *The meat was declared unfit for human consumption.* **b)** the amount of a substance that people eat, drink, smoke etc: **alcohol/tobacco/caffeine etc consumption** *The Government wants to reduce tobacco consumption by 40%.*
3 BUYING the act of buying and using products → **consume, consumer**: *art intended for* ***mass consumption*** (=to be bought, seen etc by lots of people) | *China's austerity program has cut* ***domestic consumption*** (=when products are bought in the country where they were produced). | **conspicuous consumption** (=when people buy expensive products to prove they are rich)
4 for general/public/private etc consumption intended to be heard or read only by a particular group of people: *figures that are not for public consumption*
5 *old-fashioned* TUBERCULOSIS

con·sump·tive /kənˈsʌmptɪv/ *n* [C] *old-fashioned* someone with TUBERCULOSIS —**consumptive** *adj*

cont. a written abbreviation of ***continued***

con·tact¹ /ˈkɒntækt $ ˈkɑːn-/ ●●● S2 W2 AWL *n*
1 COMMUNICATION [U] communication with a person, organization, country etc: **[+with/between]** *There is very little contact between the two tribes.* | *Many of us have no direct contact with elderly people.* | **in contact** *We stay in contact by email.* | *The town is cut off from contact with the outside world.*
2 TOUCH [U] when two people or things touch each other: **[+with/between]** *Children need* ***physical contact*** *with a caring adult.* | *The disease spreads by* ***sexual contact*** *between infected animals.* | **in contact with sth** *For a second, his hand was in contact with mine.* | *When water* ***comes into contact with*** *air, carbon dioxide is released.* | **on contact (with sth)** *The bomb exploded on contact* (=at the moment it touched something).
3 EXPERIENCE [U] when you meet someone or experience a particular kind of thing: *Everyone who* ***came into contact with*** *Di felt better for knowing her.* | *Pat's job* ***brings*** *her* ***into contact with*** *the problems people face when they retire.*
4 PERSON [C usually plural] a person you know who may be able to help or advise you: *He* ***has*** *a lot of* ***contacts*** *in the media.* | *a worldwide* ***network of contacts*** | **business/personal contacts**
5 contacts [plural] a situation in which you can communicate easily with a group, country etc: **[+with/between]** *We have* ***good contacts*** *with the local community.* | *He goes to great lengths to maintain these contacts.* | *the establishment of diplomatic contacts*
6 point of contact a) a place you go to or a person you meet when you ask an organization for help: **first/initial point of contact** *Primary health care teams are the first point of contact for users of the service.* **b)** a way in which two different things are related: *finding a point of contact between theory and practice* **c)** the part of something where another thing touches it: *The sting causes swelling at the point of contact.*
7 ELECTRICAL [C] an electrical part that completes a CIRCUIT when it touches another part
8 EYES [C] *informal* a contact lens → **eye contact** at EYE¹(5)

COLLOCATIONS

VERBS

have contact with sb *I haven't had any contact with her for at least two years.*
be in contact (=have regular communication) *He's been in contact with his lawyer about the situation.*

C

get in contact (=manage to communicate) *Where can I get in contact with you while you are away?*
stay/keep in contact (*also* **maintain contact** *formal*) *We've stayed in contact since we met on holiday.*
lose contact (=no longer see someone or hear from them) *She moved to Spain and I lost contact with her.*
make contact *We'd like to make contact with other schools in the area.*
put sb in contact with sb (=give someone the name, telephone number etc of another person) *I can put you in contact with a friend of mine in Paris.*
come into contact with sb (=meet or spend time with someone) *It's good to come into contact with people from different cultures.*
bring sb into contact with someone | **establish contact** | **avoid contact**

ADJECTIVES/NOUN + contact
direct contact (=spending time with someone) *Our volunteers work in direct contact with people who need help.*
close contact (=communicating with someone often) *I like to stay in close contact with my parents.*
personal contact (=seeing and speaking to someone personally) *She never comes into personal contact with senior managers.*
social/human contact (=spending time with other people) | **regular contact** | **day-to-day/daily contact** | **face-to-face contact** (=talking to someone who is with you) | **radio contact** (=communication by radio)

contact² ●●● S2 W2 AWL *v* [T] to write to or telephone someone: *Give the name of someone who we can contact in an emergency.* | *Please do not hesitate to contact me if you have any queries.* —**contactable** *adj* [not before noun]: *A mobile phone makes you contactable wherever you are.*

REGISTER
In everyday English, people often say **get in touch with** someone rather than **contact** someone: *Is there a number where I can* ***get in touch with*** *you?*

GRAMMAR: Comparison
contact
• You **contact** someone: *Contact the sales department for details.* ✗ Don't say: *Contact with the sales department for details.*
make contact/get in contact
• You **make contact with** someone: *I've been trying to make contact with him.* ✗ Don't say: *make a contact with someone*
• You **get in contact with** someone: *You can get in contact with us on this number.* ✗ Don't say: *get in contact to someone*
• You can also say that two or more people **make contact** or **get in contact**: *They made contact as soon as they landed.*
get in touch
• You **get in touch with** someone: *I managed to get in touch with the owner.*
• You can also say that two or more people **get in touch**: *We got in touch and arranged to meet.*

contact³ AWL *adj* [only before noun] **1** **contact number/address/details** a telephone number or address where someone can be found if necessary: *If you are babysitting, make sure you have a contact number for the parents.* **2** contact explosives or chemicals become active when they touch something: *contact poisons*

ˈcontact ˌlens *n* [C] a small round piece of plastic that you put on your eye to help you see clearly

con·tact·less /ˈkɒntæktləs $ ˈkɑːn-/ *adj* a contactless DEBIT CARD or CREDIT CARD is one you can use to pay for things by waving it over a machine, without using a PIN NUMBER —**contactless** *n* [U]: *I asked if I could pay by contactless.*

ˈcontact ˌsport *n* [C] a sport such as AMERICAN FOOTBALL, RUGBY etc in which players have physical contact with each other

con·ta·gion /kənˈteɪdʒən/ *n* **1** [U] *technical* a situation in which a disease is spread by people touching each other: *There is some danger of contagion.* **2** [C] *technical* a disease that can be passed from person to person by touch **3** [singular] *formal* a feeling or attitude that spreads quickly between people or places: *a contagion of fear spread from city to city*

con·ta·gious /kənˈteɪdʒəs/ *adj* **1** a disease that is contagious can be passed from person to person by touch → **infectious 2** a person who is contagious has a disease that can be passed to another person by touch → **infectious**: *The patient is still highly contagious.* **3** if a feeling, attitude, or action is contagious, other people are quickly affected by it and begin to have it or do it → **infectious**: *her contagious enthusiasm* —**contagiousness** *n* [U]

con·tain /kənˈteɪn/ ●●● S2 W1 *v* [T]
1 CONTAINER/PLACE if something such as a bag, box, or place contains something, that thing is inside it: *The thieves stole a purse containing banknotes.* | *The museum contains a number of original artworks.*

GRAMMAR: Using the progressive
In meanings 1, 2, and 3, **contain** is not used in the progressive. You say: *What does this box contain?*
✗ Don't say: *What is this box containing?*
GRAMMAR GUIDE ▸ VERBS

2 WRITING/SPEECH if a document, book, speech etc contains something, that thing is included in it: *The letter contained information about Boulestin's legal affairs.* | **be contained in/within sth** *The proposed changes are contained in a policy statement.*
3 SUBSTANCE if a substance contains something, that thing is part of it: *This product may contain nuts.*

REGISTER
In everyday English, people often use different phrases to say that something **contains** something else: *The box* ***contained*** *books.* → *The box* ***had*** *books* ***in*** *it.* | *The essay* ***contained*** *a lot of mistakes.* → ***There were*** *a lot of mistakes* ***in*** *the essay.* | *Does this dish* ***contain*** *any meat?* → ***Is there*** *any meat* ***in*** *this dish?*

4 CONTROL FEELINGS to control strong feelings of anger, excitement etc: *Jane couldn't contain her amusement any longer.* | **contain yourself** *He was so excited he could hardly contain himself.*
5 STOP STH to stop something from spreading or escaping: *Doctors are struggling to contain the epidemic.* | *measures aimed at containing political opposition*
→ SELF-CONTAINED
6 MATHS *technical* to surround an area or an angle: *How big is the angle contained by these two sides?*

con·tain·er /kənˈteɪnə $ -ər/ ●●○ *n* [C]
1 something such as a box or bowl that you use to keep things in: *ice cream in plastic containers*
2 a very large metal box in which goods are packed to make it easy to lift or move them onto a ship or vehicle: *a container ship*

con·tain·ment /kənˈteɪnmənt/ *n* [U] *formal* the act of keeping something under control, stopping it becoming more powerful etc: *containment of public expenditure* | *political containment of member states*

con·tam·i·nant /kənˈtæmɪnənt/ *n* [C] *formal* a substance that makes something dirty: *environmental contaminants*

con·tam·i·nate /kənˈtæməneɪt/ ●○○ *v* [T]
1 to make a place or substance dirty or harmful by putting something such as chemicals or poison in it: *Drinking water supplies are believed to have been contaminated.*
2 to influence something in a way that has a bad effect: *He claims the poster ads have 'contaminated Berlin's streets'.* —**contamination** /kənˌtæməˈneɪʃən/ *n* [U]: *radioactive contamination*

CONTAINERS

a pot of yogurt

a grocery bag *AmE*

a tin of beans *BrE*/ a can of beans *AmE*

a box of matches

a milk carton

a can of cola

a bag of crisps *BrE*/ potato chips *AmE*

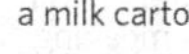

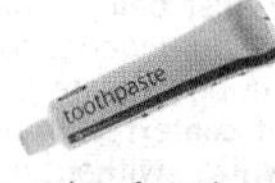

a tube of toothpaste

a wine barrel

a beer keg

a sachet of ketchup *BrE*/ a packet of ketchup *AmE*

a jar of pickles

an oil drum

a pot/jar of honey

con·tam·i·nat·ed /kən'tæmɪneɪtɪd/ *adj* water, food etc that is contaminated has had a harmful substance added to it → **tainted**: **contaminated food/blood/water supplies etc** *The infection was traced to contaminated food.* THESAURUS DIRTY

contd. a written abbreviation of ***continued***

con·tem·plate /'kɒntəmpleɪt $ 'kɑːn-/ ●○○ *v*
1 [T] to think about something that you might do in the future SYN **consider**: *He had even contemplated suicide.* | **contemplate doing sth** *Did you ever contemplate resigning?* THESAURUS THINK
2 [T] to accept the possibility that something is true: **too dreadful/horrifying etc to contemplate** *The thought that she might be dead was too terrible to contemplate.*
3 [I,T] to think about something seriously for a period of time SYN **consider**: *Jack went on vacation to contemplate his future.* | **contemplate what/whether/how etc** *She sat down and contemplated what she had done.* | **contemplate your navel** (=think so much about your own life that you do not notice other important things – used humorously)
4 [T] to look at someone or something for a period of time in a way that shows you are thinking: *He contemplated her with a faint smile.*

con·tem·pla·tion /ˌkɒntəm'pleɪʃən $ ˌkɑːn-/ *n* [U] quiet serious thinking about something → **meditation**: *The monks spend an hour in contemplation each morning.*

con·tem·pla·tive¹ /kən'templətɪv, 'kɒntəmpleɪtɪv $ kən-, 'kɑːntem-/ *adj* spending a lot of time thinking seriously and quietly → **reflective**: *a contemplative mood* —**contemplatively** *adv*

contemplative² *n* [C] *formal* someone who spends their life thinking deeply about religious matters

con·tem·po·ra·ne·ous /kənˌtempə'reɪniəs/ *adj formal* happening or done in the same period of time SYN **contemporary**: **[+with]** *Built in the 13th century, the chapels are contemporaneous with many of the great Gothic cathedrals.* —**contemporaneously** *adv* —**contemporaneity** /kənˌtempərə'niːəti/ *n* [U]

con·tem·po·ra·ry¹ /kən'tempərəri, -pəri $ -pəreri/ ●●○ AWL *adj*
1 belonging to the present time SYN **modern**: **contemporary music/art/dance etc** *an exhibition of contemporary Japanese prints* | *life in contemporary Britain*
2 happening or done in the same period of time: **[+with]** *The wall hangings are thought to be roughly contemporary with the tiled floors.*

contemporary² ●●○ AWL *n* (*plural* **contemporaries**) [C] someone who lived or was in a particular place at the same time as someone else: **sb's contemporaries** *Oswald was much admired by his contemporaries at the Academy.*

con·tempt /kən'tempt/ ●○○ *n* [U]
1 a feeling that someone or something is not important and deserves no respect: **[+for]** *The* ***contempt*** *he* ***felt*** *for his fellow students was obvious.* | **utter/deep contempt** *The report* ***shows*** *utter* ***contempt*** *for women's judgement.* | **open/undisguised contempt** *She looked at him with undisguised contempt.* | *The public is* ***treated with contempt*** *by broadcasters.* | *How could she have loved a man who so clearly* ***held*** *her* ***in contempt***? | **beneath contempt** *That sort of behaviour is simply beneath contempt* (=does not deserve respect or attention).
2 *law* disobedience or disrespect towards a court of law: *He was jailed for seven days for* ***contempt of court***. | **in contempt of sth** *He was found in contempt of the order.*
3 complete lack of fear about something: **[+for]** *his contempt for danger*

con·temp·ti·ble /kən'temptəbəl/ *adj literary* not deserving any respect at all SYN **despicable**: *They were portrayed as contemptible cowards.*

con·temp·tu·ous /kən'temptʃuəs/ *adj* showing that you think someone or something deserves no respect SYN **scornful**: *a contemptuous glance* | **[+of]** *He was* ***openly contemptuous*** *of his father.* —**contemptuously** *adv*

con·tend /kən'tend/ ●○○ *v*
1 [I] to compete against someone in order to gain something: **[+for]** *Three armed groups are contending for power.* | *Inevitably, fights break out between the members of contending groups.*
2 [T] to argue or state that something is true SYN **insist**: **contend (that)** *Some astronomers contend that the universe may be younger than previously thought.*

contend with sth *phr v* to have to deal with something difficult or unpleasant SYN **cope with**: *The rescue team also* ***had*** *bad weather conditions* ***to contend with***.

con·tend·er /kən'tendə $ -ər/ ●○○ *n* [C] someone or something that is in competition with other people or things: **[+for]** *a contender for the title* | **serious/strong/leading etc contender** *Her album is a strong contender for the Album of the Year award.*

con·tent¹ /'kɒntent $ 'kɑːn-/ ●●● S3 W2 *n*
1 contents [plural] **a)** the things that are inside a box, bag, room etc: **[+of]** *The customs official rummaged through the contents of his briefcase.* | *Most of the gallery's contents were damaged in the fire.* | **contents insurance** (=insurance for things such as furniture that you have in your house) **b)** the things that are written in a letter, book etc: **[+of]** *She kept the contents of the letter a secret.* | *The program automatically creates a* ***table of contents*** (=a list at the beginning of a document that shows the different parts into which it is divided). | *He cast his eye down the* ***contents page***.

2 [singular] the amount of a substance that is contained in something, especially food or drink: **fat/protein/alcohol etc content** *the fat content of cheese | water with a low salt content*
3 [singular, U] the ideas, facts, or opinions that are contained in a speech, piece of writing, film, programme etc: *The content of the media course includes scripting, editing, and camera work.*
4 [singular, U] the information contained in a website, considered separately from the software that makes the website work: *The graphics are brilliant. It's just a shame the content is so poor.*

con·tent² /kən'tent/ ●●○ *adj* [not before noun]
1 happy and satisfied: *Andy was a good husband, and Nicky was clearly very content.* | **[+with]** *We'll be content with a respectable result in tomorrow's match.* **THESAURUS** SATISFIED
2 content (for sb) to do sth willing to do or accept something, rather than doing more: *She sat quietly, content to watch him working.* | *He seemed* ***quite content*** *to let Steve do the talking.* | *Dr Belson had been* ***more than content*** *for them to deal with any difficulties.*
3 not content with sth used to emphasize that someone wants or does more than something: *Not content with her new car, Selina now wants a bike.*

content³ /kən'tent/ *n* [U] **1** *literary* a feeling of quiet happiness and satisfaction **2 do sth to your heart's content** to do something as much as you want: *She took refuge in the library, where she could read to her heart's content.*

content⁴ /kən'tent/ *v* [T] **1 content yourself with (doing) sth** to do or have something that is not what you really wanted, but is still satisfactory: *Mr Lal has been asking for more responsibility, but has* ***had to content*** *himself* ***with*** *a minor managerial post.* **2** *formal* to make someone feel happy and satisfied: *I was no longer satisfied with the life that had hitherto contented me.*

con·tent·ed /kən'tentɪd/ *adj* happy and satisfied because your life is good OPP **discontented**: *I felt warm, cosy, and contented.* | *They lapsed into a contented silence.* **THESAURUS** HAPPY —**contentedly** *adv*: *He smiled contentedly.*

con·ten·tion /kən'tenʃən/ ●○○ *n*
1 [C] *formal* a strong opinion that someone expresses: **sb's contention that** *Her main contention is that doctors should do more to encourage healthy eating.* **THESAURUS** CLAIM
2 [U] *formal* argument and disagreement between people: **source/area/point of contention** *The issue of hunting is a source of contention.* → **bone of contention** at BONE¹(5)
3 in contention having a chance of winning something: *Owen's goal* ***kept*** *England* ***in contention***.
4 out of contention no longer having a chance of winning something: *Injury has* ***put*** *him* ***out of contention*** *for the title.*

con·ten·tious /kən'tenʃəs/ ●○○ *adj*
1 causing a lot of argument and disagreement between people SYN **controversial**: **contentious issue/area/subject etc** *Animal welfare did not become a contentious issue until the late 1970s.*
2 someone who is contentious often argues with people SYN **argumentative** —**contentiously** *adv*

con·tent·ment /kən'tentmənt/ *n* [U] the state of being happy and satisfied OPP **discontent**: *He gave a* ***sigh of contentment****, and fell asleep.* | *a feeling of* ***deep contentment*** **THESAURUS** PLEASURE

con·test¹ /'kɒntest $ 'kɑːn-/ ●●○ W3 *n* [C]
1 a competition or a situation in which two or more people or groups are competing with each other: **[+for]** *the bitter contest for the Republican presidential nomination* | *Stone decided to* ***hold a contest*** *to see who could write the best song.* | *I only* ***entered*** *the* ***contest*** *for fun.* | *It is clear that the election will be a* ***close contest***. | **[+between/against]** *the 1960 contest between Kennedy and Nixon* | *the 1975 Liberal* ***leadership contest***
2 no contest *informal* **a)** *spoken* used to say that someone or something is the best of its kind: *I think you're the best rider here, no contest.* **b)** if a victory is no contest, it is very easy to achieve
3 plead no contest *law* to state that you will not offer a defence in a court of law for something wrong you have done

con·test² /kən'test/ ●●○ *v* [T] *formal*
1 to say formally that you do not accept something or do not agree with it: *His brothers are contesting the will.*
2 to compete for something or to try to win it: *His wife is contesting a seat on the council.*

con·tes·tant /kən'testənt/ *n* [C] someone who competes in a contest

con·text /'kɒntekst $ 'kɑːn-/ ●●○ W2 AWL *n* [C,U]
1 the situation, events, or information that are related to something and that help you to understand it: **political/social/historical etc context** *the political context of the election* | **place/put/see etc sth in context** *To appreciate what these changes will mean, it is necessary to* ***look at*** *them* ***in context***. | **in the context of sth** *These incidents are best understood in the* ***broader context*** *of developments in rural society.*
2 the words that come just before and after a word or sentence and that help you understand its meaning: *The meaning of 'mad' depends on its context.*
3 take/quote sth out of context to repeat part of what someone has said or written without describing the situation in which it was said, so that it means something quite different: *His comments, taken out of context, seem harsh.*

con·tex·tu·al /kən'tekstʃuəl/ AWL *adj* [usually before noun] relating to a particular context: **contextual information/factors etc** —**contextually** *adv*

con·tex·tu·al·ize (*also* **-ise** *BrE*) /kən'tekstʃuəlaɪz/ AWL *v* [T] *formal* to consider something together with the situation, events, or information related to it, rather than alone: *The essays seek to contextualise Kristeva's writings.*

con·tig·u·ous /kən'tɪgjuəs/ *adj formal* next to something, or next to each other: *America's 48 contiguous states* —**contiguously** *adv* —**contiguity** /ˌkɒntə'gjuːəti $ ˌkɑːn-/ *n* [U]

con·ti·nence /'kɒntənəns $ 'kɑːn-/ *n* [U] **1** *medical* the ability to control your BOWELS and BLADDER OPP **incontinence** **2** *old-fashioned* the ability to control your sexual desires

con·ti·nent¹ /'kɒntɪnənt $ 'kɑːn-/ ●●○ *n* [C]
1 a large mass of land surrounded by sea: *the continents of Asia and Africa*
2 the Continent *BrE old-fashioned* Western Europe, not including the British Isles

continent² *adj* **1** *medical* able to control your BOWELS and BLADDER OPP **incontinent** **2** *old-fashioned* able to control your sexual desires

con·ti·nen·tal /ˌkɒntə'nentl◂ $ ˌkɑːn-/ ●●○ *adj*
1 a) the continental United States all the states of the US except Alaska and Hawaii **b) continental Europe/Asia etc** all the countries of Europe, Asia etc that are not on islands
2 relating to a large mass of land: *the warming-up of continental interiors*
3 typical of the warmer countries in Western Europe: *a continental-style café*
4 *BrE old-fashioned* belonging to or in Europe, not including the British Isles: *continental holidays*

ˌcontinental 'breakfast *n* [C] a breakfast consisting of coffee and bread with butter and JAM → **English breakfast**

ˌcontinental 'drift *n* [U] the very slow movement of the CONTINENTS across the Earth's surface

ˌcontinental 'quilt *n* [C] *BrE* a DUVET

ˌcontinental 'shelf *n* (*plural* **continental shelves**) [C] *technical* the edge of a CONTINENT where it slopes down steeply to the bottom of the ocean

con·tin·gen·cy /kənˈtɪndʒənsi/ ●○○ *n* (*plural* **contingencies**) [C]
1 an event or situation that might happen in the future, especially one that could cause problems: *a* ***contingency plan*** | *Add up your outgoings, putting on a bit more for contingencies.*
2 contingency fee an amount of money that a lawyer in the US will be paid only if the person they are advising wins in court

con·tin·gent¹ /kənˈtɪndʒənt/ ●○○ *adj formal* depending on something that may happen in the future SYN **dependent**: **[+on/upon]** *Further investment is contingent upon the company's profit performance.*

contingent² *n* [C] **1** a group of people who all have something in common, such as their nationality, beliefs etc, and who are part of a larger group: *Has the Scottish contingent arrived yet?* **2** a group of soldiers sent to help a larger group: **[+of]** *A large* ***contingent of troops*** *was dispatched.*

con·tin·u·al /kənˈtɪnjuəl/ ●●○ *adj* [only before noun]
1 continuing for a long time without stopping SYN **constant**: *five weeks of continual rain* | *the Japanese business philosophy of continual improvement*
2 repeated many times, often in a way that is harmful or annoying SYN **constant**: *She has endured house arrest and continual harassment by the police.* —**continually** *adv*: *We are continually reassessing the situation.*

con·tin·u·ance /kənˈtɪnjuəns/ *n* [singular, U] *formal* the state of continuing for a long period of time: *the continuance in power of the Nationalist Party*

con·tin·u·a·tion /kənˌtɪnjuˈeɪʃən/ ●○○ *n*
1 [C] something that continues or follows something else that has happened before, without a stop or change: **[+of]** *The present economic policy is a continuation of the earlier one.*
2 [U] the continuation of something is the fact that it continues to exist or happen: **[+of]** *measures to ensure the continuation of food supplies*
3 [C] something that joins something else as if it were part of it: **[+of]** *The Baltic Sea is a continuation of the North Sea.*

continuˈation ˌschool *n* [C] *AmE* a school for children who cannot study at high school because they have social problems

This graph shows the main grammar patterns of the verb **continue**.

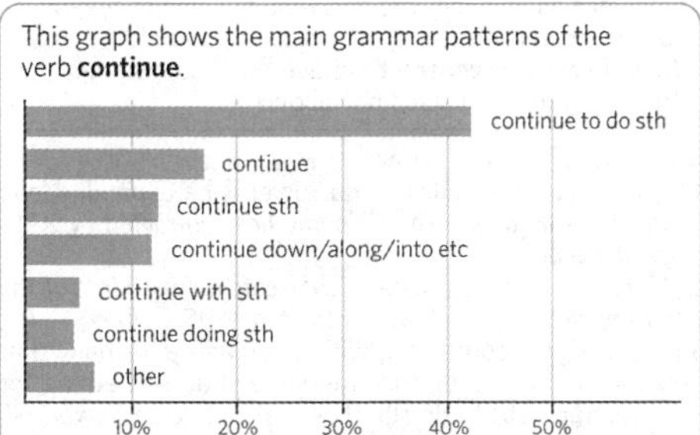

con·tin·ue /kənˈtɪnjuː/ ●●● S1 W1 *v*
1 [I,T] to not stop happening, existing, or doing something → **continuous**, **continual**, **discontinue**: **continue to do sth** *Sheila continued to work after she had her baby.* | *He will be continuing his education in the US.* | *I felt too sick to continue.* | **continue unabated/apace/unchecked** (=continue at the same high speed or level) *The flood of refugees continued unabated.* | **[+with]** *He was permitted to continue with his work while in prison.* | **[+for]** *The strike continued for another four weeks.* | **continue doing sth** *Most elderly people want to continue living at home for as long as they can.*
2 [I,T] to start again, or start doing something again, after an interruption SYN **resume**: *After a brief ceasefire, fighting continued.* | *Rescue teams will continue the search tomorrow.* | **continue doing sth** *He picked up his book and continued reading.*
3 [I] to go further in the same direction: **[+down/along/into etc]** *We continued along the road for some time.* | *The road continues northwards to the border.*
4 [I] to stay in the same job, situation etc: **[+as]** *Miss Silva will continue as publishing director.*
5 [I,T] to say more after an interruption: *'And so,' he continued, 'we will try harder next time.'*
6 to be continued used at the end of part of a story, a television show etc to tell people that the story has not finished yet

THESAURUS

TO CONTINUE DOING STH

continue to not stop doing something that you are already doing: *We need the money to continue our work.* | *They continued arguing for a long time.* | *Despite all the warnings, many people continue to smoke.*
go on (*also* **carry on** *especially BrE*) to continue doing something. **Go on** is less formal than **continue**, and is the phrase that people usually use in everyday English: *Dan went on talking but she was no longer listening.* | *He carried on with his day job.*
keep (on) doing sth [not in progressive] to continue doing something for a long time - especially so that you feel tired or annoyed: *We kept on walking until we got to the top of the hill.* | *The man kept staring at me.*
persevere /ˌpɜːsəˈvɪə $ ˌpɜːrsəˈvɪr/ to continue trying to do something in a very patient and determined way, in spite of difficulties. **Persevere** sounds rather formal: *He didn't know any English, but he persevered and became a good student.* | *Her health was rapidly declining but she persevered with her duties.*

TO CONTINUE TO HAPPEN

continue to happen without stopping: *The good weather seems likely to continue.* | *The review process is expected to continue for several weeks.*
last to continue - use this to say how long something continues for: *I know my good luck won't last forever.* | *The trial lasted for six days.* | *The meeting lasted until lunchtime.*
go on to continue, especially for a long time: *Disputes between neighbours can go on for years.*
carry on *BrE* to continue, especially when there are problems: *The game carried on despite the injury of two players.*
drag on to continue for much longer than necessary or for longer than you want: *The meeting dragged on for another hour.* | *The talks dragged on, with no apparent hope of achieving a peaceful solution.*
persist *formal* if something bad persists, it continues to exist or happen: *See your doctor if the symptoms persist.*

con·tin·ued /kənˈtɪnjuːd/ *adj* [only before noun] continuing to happen or exist for a long time, or happening many times: *threats to the continued existence of the species* | *continued press speculation*

conˌtinuing eduˈcation *n* [U] training and education for adults that takes place outside the formal education system, usually in classes in the evenings SYN **adult education**

con·ti·nu·i·ty /ˌkɒntəˈnjuːəti $ ˌkɑːntəˈnuː-/ ●○○ *n* [U]
1 the state of continuing for a period of time, without problems, interruptions, or changes: *We should ensure continuity of care between hospital and home.*
2 *technical* the organization of a film or television programme to make it seem that the action happens without pauses or interruptions

contiˈnuity anˌnouncer *n* [C] someone on the radio or television who says what programme is being broadcast next, or gives information about future programmes

con·tin·u·o /kənˈtɪnju-əʊ $ -oʊ/ *n* (*plural* **continuos**) [C] *technical* a musical part consisting of a line of low notes with figures showing the higher notes that are played with them

con·tin·u·ous /kən'tɪnjuəs/ ●●○ S3 W3 *adj*
1 continuing to happen or exist without stopping → **continue**: *continuous economic growth* | *a* **continuous flow** *of information*
2 something such as a line that is continuous does not have any spaces or holes in it OPP **broken**
3 continuous assessment *BrE* a way of judging a student's ability by looking at the work they have done during the year rather than by an examination
4 *technical* the continuous form of a verb shows that an action is continuing. In English, this is formed by the verb 'be', followed by a PRESENT PARTICIPLE, as in 'I was waiting for the bus.' → **simple** —**continuously** *adv*: *UMNO had ruled Malaysia continuously since independence.*

C

con·tin·u·um /kən'tɪnjuəm/ ●○○ *n* (*plural* **continuums** *or* **continua** /-njuə/) [C] *formal* a scale of related things on which each one is only slightly different from the one before: *The Creole language is really various dialects arranged on a continuum.* | *All the organisms in an ecosystem are part of an evolutionary continuum.*

con·tort /kən'tɔːt $ -ɔːrt/ *v* [I,T] if you contort something, or if it contorts, it twists out of its normal shape and looks strange or unattractive: **[+with/in]** *His face was contorted with rage.* | *His body contorted in agony.*

con·tor·tion /kən'tɔːʃən $ -ɔːr-/ *n* **1** [C] a twisted position or movement that looks surprising or strange: *I could not force my body into the contortions required by classical ballet.* | *facial contortions* **2** [U] when something is twisted so that it does not have its normal shape: *involuntary muscle contortion* **3** [C] something difficult you have to do in order to achieve something: *He* **went through** *a series of amazing* **contortions** *to get Karen a work permit.*

con·tor·tion·ist /kən'tɔːʃənɪst $ -ɔːr-/ *n* [C] someone who twists their body into strange positions in order to entertain people

con·tour /'kɒntʊə $ 'kɑːntʊr/ ●○○ *n* [C]
1 the shape of the outer edges of something such as an area of land or someone's body: *the contours of the hills* | *the contours of her face*
2 (*also* **contour line**) a line on a map that shows points that are of equal heights above sea level

con·toured /'kɒntʊəd $ 'kɑːntʊrd/ *adj* **1** a contoured surface or object has been made with curves in it: *contoured seats* **2** contoured land has some parts higher than others

contra- /kɒntrə $ kɑːn-/ *prefix* acting against something, or opposite to something: *contraceptive devices* (=against conception)

con·tra·band /'kɒntrəbænd $ 'kɑːn-/ *n* [U] goods that are brought into a country illegally, especially to avoid tax: *a cargo of contraband* —**contraband** *adj*: *contraband cigarettes*

con·tra·bass /ˌkɒntrə'beɪs $ ˌkɑːn-/ *n* [C] a DOUBLE BASS

con·tra·cep·tion /ˌkɒntrə'sepʃən $ ˌkɑːn-/ *n* [U] the practice of preventing a woman from becoming PREGNANT when she has sex, or the methods for doing this SYN **birth control**: *The pill is a popular method of contraception.*

con·tra·cep·tive /ˌkɒntrə'septɪv◂ $ ˌkɑːn-/ *n* [C] a drug, object, or method used to prevent a woman from becoming PREGNANT when she has sex: *free contraceptives* —**contraceptive** *adj* [only before noun]: *a contraceptive device*

con·tract¹ /'kɒntrækt $ 'kɑːn-/ ●●● S1 W1 AWL *n* [C]
1 an official agreement between two or more people, stating what each will do → **contractual**: **[+with/between]** *Tyler has agreed a seven-year contract with a Hollywood studio.* | **contract to do sth** *a three-year contract to* **provide pay telephones at local restaurants** | **on a contract/under contract** *The firm operates schools under contract to state education authorities.* | *Employees who refuse to relocate* **are in breach of contract** (=have done something not allowed by their contracts).
2 subject to contract if an agreement is subject to contract, it has not yet been agreed formally by a contract
3 *informal* an agreement to kill a person for money: *They* **put** *a* **contract out on** *him and he's in hiding.*

COLLOCATIONS

VERBS

have a contract *The company had a contract to build a new hotel there.*
sign a contract *He signed a contract to become vice president of the football club.*
enter (into) a contract *You will enter a two-year training contract with your chosen employer.*
agree to a contract (*also* **agree a contract** *BrE*) *Keane was reported to have agreed a contract for a further three years.*
make a contract *Did he know this when he made the contract?*
negotiate a contract (=agree the conditions of a contract with someone) *Your lawyer will assist you in negotiating a contract.*
break a contract (=do something that your contract does not allow) | **fulfil/honour a contract** (=do what you have agreed to do) | **draw up a contract** (=write one) | **win/get a contract** | **give sb a contract** | **award a company a contract** (=give them a contract) | **cancel/end/terminate a contract** | **renew sb's contract** (=give someone another contract when their old one ends)

ADJECTIVES

a one-year/two-year etc contract *He signed a five-year contract worth $2 million.*
a recording/building etc contract *The band was soon offered a recording contract with Columbia Records.*
a written contract

PHRASES

a contract of employment (*also* **an employment contract**) *Make sure you fully understand your contract of employment.*
the terms of a contract (=the conditions that are part of the contract) *He explained the terms of the contract.*
breach of contract (=an action that your contract does not allow) *They are suing the building company for breach of contract.*
be in breach of contract (=have done something that your contract does not allow)

con·tract² /kən'trækt/ ●○○ AWL *v*
1 [I] to become smaller or narrower OPP **expand**: *Metal contracts as it cools.* | *The economy has contracted by 2.5% since last year.*
2 [T] *formal* to get an illness SYN **catch**: *Two-thirds of the adult population there have contracted AIDS.*
3 [I,T] to sign a contract in which you agree formally that you will do something or someone will do something for you: **contract (sb) to do sth** *They are contracted to work 35 hours a week.* | *the company that had been contracted to build the models* | **contract (with) sb for sth** *Doctors control their budgets and contract with hospitals for services.* | **contract a marriage/alliance etc** (=agree to marry someone, form a relationship with them etc) *Most of the marriages were contracted when the brides were very young.*

contract³ /'kɒntrækt $ 'kɑːn-/
contract in *phr v BrE* **1 contract sb/sth ↔ in** to arrange for a person or company outside your own organization to come in and do a particular job: *We contract in cleaning services.* **2** *formal* to agree officially to take part in something: *The rules require all members to contract in.*
contract out *phr v* **1 contract sth ↔ out** to arrange to have a job done by a person or company outside your own organization: **[+to]** *We contracted the catering out to an outside firm.* **2** *BrE* to agree officially not to take part in something such as a PENSION PLAN

ˌcontract 'bridge *n* [U] a form of the card game BRIDGE, in which one of the two pairs says how many TRICKS they will try to win

con·trac·tion /kən'trækʃən/ *n* **1** [C] *medical* a very strong and painful movement of a muscle, especially the muscles around the WOMB during birth **2** [U] the process of becoming smaller or narrower: *the contraction of metal as it cools* **3** [C] a shorter form of a word or words: *'Haven't' is a contraction of 'have not'.*

con·trac·tor /kən'træktə $ 'kɑːntræktər/ ●○○ AWL *n* [C] a person or company that agrees to do work or provide goods for another company: *a roofing contractor*

con·trac·tu·al /kən'træktʃuəl/ *adj* [only before noun] agreed in a contract: *Tutors have a* ***contractual obligation*** *to research and publish.* —**contractually** *adv*

con·tra·dict /ˌkɒntrə'dɪkt $ ˌkɑːn-/ ●●○ AWL *v*
1 [I,T] to disagree with something, especially by saying that the opposite is true: *Deborah opened her mouth to contradict, but closed it again.* | *Dad just can't bear to be contradicted.* | *The article* ***flatly contradicts*** *their claims.*
2 [T] if one statement, story etc contradicts another, the facts in it are different so that both statements cannot be true: *The witness statements* ***contradict each other*** *and the facts remain unclear.*
3 contradict yourself to say something that is the opposite of what you said before: *Within five minutes he had contradicted himself twice.*

con·tra·dic·tion /ˌkɒntrə'dɪkʃən $ ˌkɑːn-/ ●●○ AWL *n*
1 [C] a difference between two statements, beliefs, or ideas about something that means they cannot both be true: ***apparent contradictions*** *in the defendant's testimony* | **[+between]** *a contradiction between the government's ideas and its actual policy*
2 [U] the act of saying that someone else's opinion, statement etc is wrong or not true: *You can say what you like without* ***fear of contradiction****.*
3 a contradiction in terms a combination of words that seem to be the opposite of each other, with the result that the phrase has no clear meaning: *'Permanent revolution' is a contradiction in terms.*
4 in (direct) contradiction to sth in a way that is opposite to a belief or statement: *Your behaviour is in direct contradiction to the principles you claim to have.*

con·tra·dic·to·ry /ˌkɒntrə'dɪktəri◂ $ ˌkɑːn-/ ●●○ AWL *adj* two statements, beliefs etc that are contradictory are different and therefore cannot both be true or correct: **contradictory messages/statements/demands etc** *The public is being fed contradictory messages about the economy.*

con·tra·dis·tinc·tion /ˌkɒntrədɪ'stɪŋkʃən $ ˌkɑːn-/ *n* [C] **in contradistinction to sth** *formal* in contrast to or compared to something: *plants in contradistinction to animals*

con·tra·flow /'kɒntrəfləʊ $ 'kɑːntrəfloʊ/ *n* [C,U] *BrE* a temporary arrangement on a road that is being repaired, that makes traffic travelling in both directions use only one side of the road: *A contraflow is in operation between Junctions 6 and 12.*

con·trail /'kɒntreɪl $ 'kɑːn-/ *n* [C] a line of white steam made in the sky by a plane

con·tra·in·di·ca·tion /ˌkɒntrəˌɪndɪ'keɪʃən $ ˌkɑːn-/ *n* [C] *medical* a medical reason for not giving someone a particular medicine or drug —**contraindicate** /ˌkɒntrə'ɪndɪkeɪt $ ˌkɑːn-/ *v* [T]: *In his case, steroids are contraindicated.*

con·tral·to /kən'træltəʊ $ -toʊ/ *n* (*plural* **contraltos**) **1** [C] the lowest female singing voice, or a woman with a voice like this **2** [singular] the part of a musical work that is written for a contralto voice

con·trap·tion /kən'træpʃən/ *n* [C] a piece of equipment or machinery that looks funny, strange, and unlikely to work well: *a bizarre contraption*

con·tra·ri·wise /kən'treəriwaɪz, 'kɒntrəriwaɪz $ 'kɑːntreri-/ *adv BrE* in the opposite way or direction SYN **conversely**

con·tra·ry¹ /'kɒntrəri $ 'kɑːntreri/ ●●○ AWL *n*
1 on the contrary/quite the contrary used to add to a negative statement, to disagree with a negative statement by someone else, or to answer no to a question: *It wasn't a good thing; on the contrary it was a huge mistake.* | *'I suppose your wife doesn't understand you.' 'On the contrary, she understands me very well.'* | *'Are they happy?' 'No, no, quite the contrary.'*
2 evidence/statements etc to the contrary something showing or saying the opposite: *Unless there is evidence to the contrary, we ought to believe them.* | *He continued to drink despite advice to the contrary.*
3 the contrary *formal* the opposite of what has been said or suggested

contrary² AWL *adj* **1** contrary ideas, opinions, or actions are completely different and opposed to each other SYN **opposing**: *Two contrary views emerged.* | *The men shouted contrary orders.* | **[+to]** *The government's actions are contrary to the public interest.* **2 contrary to popular belief/opinion** used to say that something is true even though people believe the opposite: *Contrary to popular belief, a desert can be very cold.* **3** *formal* a contrary wind is not blowing in the direction you want to sail

con·tra·ry³ /kən'treəri $ 'kɑːntreri, kən'treri/ *adj* someone who is contrary deliberately does different things from other people: *Evans was his usual contrary self.* —**contrariness** *n* [U]

con·trast¹ /'kɒntrɑːst $ 'kɑːntræst/ ●●○ W2 AWL *n*
1 [C,U] a difference between people, ideas, situations, things etc that are being compared: *While there are similarities in the two cultures, there are also great contrasts.* | **[+between]** *the economic and social contrasts between the poor and the rich* | **[+with]** *The marble is smooth and polished, making a strong contrast with the worn stonework around it.* | **by contrast (to/with)** *The birth rate for older women has declined, but, by contrast, births to teenage mothers have increased.* | **in contrast (to/with)** *The stock lost 60 cents a share, in contrast to last year, when it gained 21 cents.* | **(in) stark/marked/sharp etc contrast to sth** *The winter heat wave in California is a stark contrast to the below-freezing temperatures on the East Coast.* | *The spirited mood on Friday was in sharp contrast to the tense atmosphere last week.* | *The approach to learning at this school stands in marked contrast to the traditional methods used at other schools nearby.*
2 [C] something that is very different from something else: *The sauce is quite sweet, so add dried thyme as a contrast.* | **[+to]** *The red stems of this bush provide a contrast to the drab brown of the winter garden.*
3 [U] the degree of difference between the light and dark parts of a television picture, X-RAY, PHOTOCOPY etc: *This button adjusts the contrast.*
4 [U] the differences in colour, or between light and dark, that an artist uses in paintings or photographs to make a particular effect: *The artist has used contrast marvellously in his paintings.*

con·trast² /kən'trɑːst $ -'træst/ ●●○ AWL *v*
1 [I] if two things contrast, the difference between them is very easy to see and is sometimes surprising: **[+with]** *The snow was icy and white, contrasting with the brilliant blue sky.* | **contrast sharply/strikingly with sth** (=be extremely different from something) *These results contrast sharply with other medical tests carried out in Australia.*
2 [T] to compare two things, ideas, people etc to show how different they are from each other: **contrast sth with sth** *In another passage, Melville again contrasts the land with the sea.* | *an essay* ***comparing and contrasting*** (=showing how two things are similar and different) *Verdi and Wagner and their operas* **THESAURUS▸ COMPARE**

con·tras·ting /kən'trɑːstɪŋ $ -'træs-/ AWL *adj* two or more things that are contrasting are different from each other, especially in a way that is interesting or attractive: *a blue shirt with a contrasting collar*

con·tra·vene /ˌkɒntrə'viːn $ ˌkɑːn-/ *v* [T] *formal* to do something that is not allowed according to a law or rule SYN **violate**: *Some portions of the bill may contravene state law.* **THESAURUS▸ DISOBEY**

con·tra·ven·tion /ˌkɒntrə'venʃən $ ˌkɑːn-/ *n* [C,U] when someone does something that is not allowed by a law or rule SYN **violation**: **[+of]** *Sending the troops was a contravention of the treaty.* | **in contravention of sth** (=in a way not allowed by a rule or law) *Several of the girls were wearing trousers, in contravention of the school rules on dress.*

con·tre·temps /ˈkɒntrətɒŋ $ ˈkɑːntrətɑːn/ *n* (*plural* **contretemps**) [C] an argument or disagreement – often used humorously

con·trib·ute /kənˈtrɪbjuːt/ ●●○ S3 W2 AWL *v*
1 [I,T] to give money, help, ideas etc to something that a lot of other people are also involved in: **[+to/towards]** *City employees cannot contribute to political campaigns.* | **contribute sth to/towards sth** *The volunteers contribute their own time to the project.*
2 [I] to help to make something happen → **contributory**: *Stress is a* ***contributing factor*** *in many illnesses.* | **[+to]** *Alcohol contributes to 100,000 deaths a year in the US.* | **contribute substantially/significantly/greatly etc to sth** *His work contributed substantially to our knowledge of the disease and how to treat it.*
3 [I,T] to write articles, stories, poems etc for a newspaper or magazine → **contributor**: **[+to]** *one of several authors contributing to the book*

con·tri·bu·tion /ˌkɒntrəˈbjuːʃən $ ˌkɑːn-/ ●●○ W3 AWL *n*
1 [C] something that you give or do in order to help something be successful: **[+to/towards]** *Einstein was awarded the Nobel Prize for his contribution to Quantum Theory.* | *The school sees its job as preparing students to* ***make*** *a* ***contribution*** *to society.* | **significant/substantial/valuable etc contribution** *Wolko made outstanding contributions to children's medicine.*
2 [C] an amount of money that you give in order to help pay for something: *a campaign contribution* | **[+of]** *A contribution of £25 will buy 15 books.* | **[+to/towards]** *Contributions to charities are tax deductible.* | *You can* ***make*** *annual* ***contributions*** *of up to $1,000 in education savings accounts.*
3 [C] a regular payment that you make to your employer or to the government to pay for things that you will receive when you are no longer working, for example health care, a PENSION etc: *income tax and national insurance contributions* | **[+to]** *Have you been* ***making*** *regular* ***contributions*** *to a pension plan?*
4 [C] a piece of writing, a song, a speech etc that forms part of a larger work such as a newspaper, book, broadcast, recording etc: **[+from]** *a magazine with contributions from well-known travel writers* | *a Christmas album featuring contributions from Carly Simon, Amy Grant, and others*
5 [U] when you give money, time, help etc: *All the money has been raised by voluntary contribution.*

con·trib·u·tor /kənˈtrɪbjətə $ -ər/ ●○○ AWL *n* [C]
1 someone who gives money, help, ideas etc to something that a lot of other people are also involved in: *campaign contributors* | **[+to]** *Dr Win was a major contributor to the research.*
2 someone who writes a story, song, speech etc that forms part of a larger work such as a newspaper, book, broadcast, recording etc: **[+to]** *a regular contributor to 'Time' magazine*
3 *formal* someone or something that helps to cause something to happen: **[+to]** *Cars are still one of the principal contributors to air pollution.*

con·trib·u·to·ry /kənˈtrɪbjətəri $ -tɔːri/ *adj* **1** [only before noun] being one of the causes of a particular result: *Smoking is a* ***contributory factor*** *in lung cancer.* **2** a contributory PENSION or insurance plan is one that is paid for by the workers as well as by the company they work for OPP **noncontributory**

conˌtributory ˈnegligence *n* [U] *law* failure to take enough care to avoid or prevent an accident, so that you are partly responsible for any loss or damage caused

ˈcon trick *n* [C] a CONFIDENCE TRICK

con·trite /ˈkɒntraɪt $ ˈkɑːn-/ *adj formal* feeling guilty and sorry for something bad that you have done: *a contrite apology* —**contritely** *adv* —**contrition** /kənˈtrɪʃən/ *n* [U]

con·triv·ance /kənˈtraɪvəns/ *n formal* **1** [C] something that is artificial or does not seem natural, but that helps something else to happen – usually used to show disapproval: *A ridiculous series of plot contrivances moves the film along.* **2** [C,U] a plan or trick to make something happen or get something for yourself, or the practice of doing this: *Harriet's matchmaking contrivances* **3** [C] a machine or piece of equipment that has been made for a special purpose: *a steam-driven contrivance used in 19th century factories*

con·trive /kənˈtraɪv/ *v* [T] **1** *formal* to succeed in doing something in spite of difficulties: **contrive to do sth** *Schindler contrived to save more than 1,000 Polish Jews from the Nazis.* **2** to arrange an event or situation in a clever way, especially secretly or by deceiving people: *The lawsuit says oil companies contrived the oil shortage in the 1970s.* **3** to make or invent something in a skilful way, especially because you need it suddenly: *In 1862, a technique was contrived to take a series of photographs showing stages of movement.*

con·trived /kənˈtraɪvd/ *adj* seeming false and not natural: *The characters are as contrived as the plot.*

con·trol[1] /kənˈtrəʊl $ -ˈtroʊl/ ●●● S1 W1 *n*
1 MAKE SB/STH DO WHAT YOU WANT [U] the ability or power to make someone or something do what you want or make something happen in the way you want: *The disease robs you of muscle control.* | **[+of/over]** *Babies are born with very little control over their movements.* | *Artists like to* ***have*** *some* ***control over*** *where their works are hung in a gallery.* | *She's a good teacher who* ***has control of*** *her class.* | *Students are encouraged to* ***take control of*** *their own learning, rather than just depending on the teacher.* | *Excessive drinking can make you* ***lose control of*** *your own life.* | *'Do you need any help?' 'No. It's* ***under control****, thanks.'* | *Dogs are allowed on the trails if they are* ***kept under control****.* | *The car* ***spun out of control*** *and hit a tree.* | *Flight delays do occur, for reasons that are* ***outside our control****.*
2 POWER [U] the power to make the decisions about how a country, place, company etc is organized or what it does: *The press was freed from political control.* | **[+of]** *Jordan asked for editorial control of the project.* | **in control (of sth)** *Anti-government forces are still in control of the area.* | *By the end of the year, the rebels* ***had control over*** *the northern territories.* | *The Johnson family* ***has*** *effective* ***control of*** *the company, owning almost 60% of the shares.* | *China* ***gained control of*** *the island in 1683.* | *His son is being trained to* ***take control of*** *the family business.* | *The Democrats* ***lost control of*** *Congress in the last election.* | **under the control of sb** *The college was under the control of a group of trustees.* | *The whole of this area* ***came under*** *Soviet* ***control*** *after World War II.* | *The Conservatives are hoping to* ***regain control of*** *the city council.*
3 WAY OF LIMITING STH [C,U] an action, method, or law that limits the amount or growth of something, especially something that is dangerous: *pest control* | **[+of]** *the control of inflation* | **[+on]** *The authorities imposed strict controls on the movement of cattle.* | *an agreement on* ***arms control*** (=control of the amount of weapons a country has) | **under control** *Firefighters* ***had*** *the blaze* ***under control*** *by 9:44 p.m.* | *Shea used diet and exercise to* ***bring*** *her weight* ***under control****.* | *The Federal Reserve Bank raised interest rates to* ***keep*** *inflation* ***under control****.* | **rent/price/wage etc controls** *Rent controls ensured that no one paid too much for housing.* | **tight/rigid controls** (=strict controls) *the introduction of tighter controls on immigration* | *Police used fire hoses and dogs for* ***crowd control****.*
4 ABILITY TO STAY CALM [U] the ability to remain calm even when you feel very angry, upset, or excited: *There were sudden tears in his eyes and he paused, fighting for control.* | *Davidson* ***lost control of himself*** *and started yelling.* | *Small children can't be expected to have the same* ***self-control*** (=ability to control their emotions and behaviour) *as an adult.* | **under control** *Her voice is under control, but she is almost shaking with anger.* | **in control** *I felt calm and in control.*
5 MACHINE/VEHICLE [C] the thing that you press or turn to make a machine, vehicle, television etc work: *the TV*

remote control | *the volume control on the radio* | *a car with manual controls* | **at the controls** (=controlling a vehicle or aircraft) *Belton, at the controls, made a perfect landing.*
6 PEOPLE WHO ORGANIZE AN ACTIVITY [singular, U] the people who direct an activity or who check that something is done correctly, the place where this is done, or the process of doing it: *air-traffic control* | *Please stop at passport control.* | *computers used for stock control*
7 SCIENTIFIC TEST [C] **a)** a person, group etc against which you compare another person or group that is very similar, in order to see if a particular quality is caused by something or happens by chance: **control group/population/sample etc** *A control group of non-smoking women was compared to four groups of women smokers.* **b)** a thing that you already know the result for that is used in a scientific test, in order to show that your method is working correctly → CONTROLLED EXPERIMENT
8 COMPUTER [singular] (*also* **control key**) a particular button on a computer that allows you to do certain operations: *Press control and F2 to exit.* → BIRTH CONTROL, QUALITY CONTROL, REMOTE CONTROL

control² ●●● S2 W1 *v* (**controlled**, **controlling**) [T]
1 POWER to have the power to make the decisions about how a country, place, company etc is organized or what it does: *The Democrats continued to control the Senate until last year.* | *a huge company controlling half the world's coffee trade* | **Labour-/Republican-/Democrat- etc controlled**
2 LIMIT to limit the amount or growth of something, especially something that is dangerous: *a chemical used to control weeds* | *an economic plan to control inflation* | *Development in areas of outstanding natural beauty is strictly controlled.* | *Strict measures were taken to control the spread of foot and mouth disease.*
3 MAKE SB/STH DO WHAT YOU WANT to make someone or something do what you want, or make something happen in the way that you want: *Police had to be called in to control the crowds.* | *a skilled rider controlling a spirited horse*
4 EMOTION if you control your emotions, your voice, your expression etc, you succeed in behaving calmly and sensibly, even though you feel angry, upset, or excited: *Sarah took a deep breath, trying to control her anger.* | *He controlled the urge to laugh.* | **control yourself** *Newman controlled himself with an effort.*
5 MACHINE/PROCESS/SYSTEM to make a machine, process, or system work in a particular way: *a radio-controlled toy car* | *A thermostat controls the temperature in the building.* | **control how/what/which etc** *The valves in the heart control how quickly the blood is pumped around the body.*
6 CHECK STH to make sure that something is done correctly SYN **check**, **monitor**: *The company strictly controls the quality of its products.*

THESAURUS

control to have power over a country, place, company etc, and decide what happens there: *The Democrats controlled the US Congress.* | *Government forces now control the city.*
run to make the important everyday decisions concerning a company, organization, country etc, so that it can continue to operate: *He runs a software company in New York.* | *The parents want to run the school themselves.* | *The government is unfit to run the country.*
be in charge of sb/sth to have control over something, or responsibility for a group of people: *She is in charge of training new employees.* | *I left him in charge of the children while I was out.*
manage to be in charge of a company, especially one that someone else owns: *In 1963, she opened a furniture store, and her son has managed it since 1985.*
be in power if a group or leader is in power, they have political control of a country: *Abe resigned after less than a year in power.* | *It was the first time a democratically elected government had been in power.*
rule if a leader or political group rules a country, they have political control of that country: *President Assad ruled the country for almost 30 years.* | *The same party has ruled Japan for many years.*
supervise to be in charge of a group of workers or students and make sure that they do their work properly: *Professor Braude supervised the research team.* | *He's supervising the building work.*

con'trol ˌfreak *n* [C] *informal* someone who is too concerned about controlling all the details in every situation they are involved in

con'trol ˌkey *n* [C] a particular button on a computer that allows you to do certain operations

con·trol·la·ble /kənˈtrəʊləbəl $ -ˈtroʊl-/ *adj* able to be controlled: *Diabetes is a serious but controllable disease.*

con·trolled /kənˈtrəʊld $ -ˈtroʊld/ ●○○ *adj*
1 deliberately done in a particular way, or made to have particular qualities: *a test held under controlled conditions* | *a controlled explosion*
2 limited by a law or rule: *Access to the site is closely controlled.* | *a police search for* ***controlled drugs*** (=a drug that is illegal to have without permission from a doctor)
3 calm and not showing emotion, even if you feel angry, afraid etc: *a controlled authoritative voice*

conˌtrolled ex'periment *n* [C] a scientific test done in a place where you can control all the things that might affect the test: *a controlled experiment to determine the effects of light on plant growth*

conˌtrolled 'substance *n* [C] *law* a drug that is illegal to possess or use without permission from a doctor: *an arrest for the possession and sale of controlled substances*

con·trol·ler /kənˈtrəʊlə $ -ˈtroʊlər/ ●○○ *n* [C]
1 someone who is in charge of a particular system, organization, or part of an organization: *air-traffic controllers*
2 (*also* **comptroller**) *formal* someone who is in charge of the money received or paid out by a company or government department

con·trol·ling /kənˈtrəʊlɪŋ $ -ˈtroʊl-/ *adj* always trying to make someone do what you want – used to show disapproval: *She wanted to get away from her controlling parents.*

conˌtrolling 'interest *n* [C usually singular] if you have a controlling interest in a company, you own enough SHARES to be able to make decisions about what happens to the company: **[+in]** *The firm paid over $10 million for a controlling interest in five hotels.*

con'trol room *n* [C] the room that a process, service, large machine, factory etc is controlled from: *the submarine's control room*

con'trol ˌtower *n* [C] a tall building at an airport from which people direct the movement of aircraft on the ground and in the air

con·tro·ver·sial /ˌkɒntrəˈvɜːʃəl◂ $ ˌkɑːntrəˈvɜːr-/ ●●○ AWL *adj* causing a lot of disagreement, because many people have strong opinions about the subject being discussed: *the controversial issue of welfare reform* | *a* ***highly controversial*** (=very controversial) *plan to flood the valley in order to build a dam* | *He is a* ***controversial figure*** (=person who does controversial things) *in the art world.* —**controversially** *adv*

con·tro·ver·sy /ˈkɒntrəvɜːsi, kənˈtrɒvəsi $ ˈkɑːntrəvɜːrsi/ ●●○ AWL *n* (*plural* **controversies**) [C,U] a serious argument about something that involves many people and continues for a long time: *a political controversy* | *the* ***controversy surrounding*** *Skinner's theories* | **cause/provoke/arouse controversy** *The judges' decision provoked controversy.* | **[+over/about]** *the controversy over campaign-finance issues* | ***Controversy arose*** (=began) *over the use of the chemicals on crops.*

con·tu·sion /kənˈtjuːʒən $ -ˈtuː-/ *n* [C,U] *medical* a BRUISE or BRUISING —**contused** *adj*

co·nun·drum /kəˈnʌndrəm/ *n* [C] **1** a confusing and difficult problem: *the conundrum of our purpose on Earth* **2** a trick question asked for fun SYN **riddle**

con·ur·ba·tion /ˌkɒnɜːˈbeɪʃən $ ˌkɑːnɜːr-/ *n* [C] *formal* a group of towns that have spread and joined together to form an area with a high population, often with a large city as its centre

con·va·lesce /ˌkɒnvəˈles $ ˌkɑːn-/ *v* [I] to spend time getting well after an illness SYN **recover**: *the time needed to convalesce after an operation* THESAURUS RECOVER

con·va·les·cence /ˌkɒnvəˈlesəns $ ˌkɑːn-/ *n* [singular] the length of time a person spends getting well after an illness: *a long and painful convalescence*

con·va·les·cent /ˌkɒnvəˈlesənt◂ $ ˌkɑːn-/ *n* [C] someone who is spending time getting well after an illness —**convalescent** *adj*

ˌconvaˈlescent ˌhome (*also* **ˌconvaˈlescent ˌhospital**) *n* [C] a place where people stay when they need care from doctors and nurses, but are not sick enough to be in a hospital → **nursing home**

con·vect /kənˈvekt/ *v* [I] *technical* to move heat by convection

con·vec·tion /kənˈvekʃən/ *n* [U] *technical* the movement in a gas or liquid caused by warm gas or liquid rising, and cold gas or liquid sinking

conˈvection ˌoven *n* [C] a special OVEN that makes hot air move around inside it so that all the parts of the food get the same amount of heat

con·vec·tor /kənˈvektə $ -ər/ (*also* **conˈvector ˌheater**) *n* [C] *BrE* an electrical heater that uses hot air

con·vene /kənˈviːn/ ●○○ AWL *v* [I,T] if a group of people convene, or someone convenes them, they come together, especially for a formal meeting: *a report by experts convened by the National Institutes of Health*

con·ven·er, **convenor** /kənˈviːnə $ -ər/ *n* [C] **1** someone who arranges for people to meet at a formal meeting **2** *BrE* an important official for a TRADE UNION at a factory or office

con·ve·ni·ence /kənˈviːniəns/ ●●○ *n*

1 [U] the quality of being suitable or useful for a particular purpose, especially by making something easier or saving you time: *Ready meals sell well because of their convenience.* | **the convenience of doing sth** *Most of us like the convenience of using credit cards to buy things.* | **for convenience** *For convenience, the German translation is printed below.*

2 [U] what is easiest and best for a particular person: **at sb's convenience** (=at a time that is best and easiest for someone) *These meals can be prepared in advance, and served at your convenience.* | **for sb's convenience** *For your convenience, the bank is open until 7 p.m.* | *Services should be run to* ***suit the convenience of*** *the customer, not the staff.*

3 [C] something that is useful because it saves you time or means that you have less work to do: *The supermarket offers a bag-packing service, as a convenience to customers.* | *a hotel with all the* ***modern conveniences***

4 at your earliest convenience *formal* as soon as possible – used in letters: *We should be grateful if you would reply at your earliest convenience.*

5 [C usually plural] (*also* **public convenience**) *formal* a public toilet

6 a marriage of convenience a marriage that has been agreed for a particular purpose, not because the two people love each other: *In the past most royal marriages were marriages of convenience, arranged for political reasons.*

conˈvenience ˌfood *n* [C,U] food that is partly or completely prepared already and that is sold frozen or in cans, packages etc, so that it can be prepared quickly and easily: *We eat too little fresh food, relying instead on convenience foods.*

conˈvenience ˌstore ●●○ *n* [C] a shop where you can buy food, alcohol, magazines etc, that is often open 24 hours each day

con·ve·ni·ent /kənˈviːniənt/ ●●○ S3 *adj*

1 useful to you because it saves you time, or does not spoil your plans or cause you problems OPP **inconvenient**: *Mail-order catalogs are a convenient way to shop.* | *My secretary will call you to arrange a convenient time to meet.* | **[+for]** *Is three o'clock convenient for you?* | **convenient to do sth** *It is simple and convenient to use.*

> **REGISTER**
> In everyday English, people usually say **a good time/day** etc rather than **a convenient time/day** etc: *Is this* ***a good time*** *for you to talk?*

2 close and easy to reach OPP **inconvenient**: *The bus stop around the corner is probably the most convenient.* | **[+for]** *BrE* **[+to]** *AmE*: *restaurants convenient for shops and theatres* → INCONVENIENT

con·ve·ni·ent·ly /kənˈviːniəntli/ ●●○ *adv*

1 in a way that is useful to you because it saves you time or does not spoil your plans or cause you problems: *Conveniently, her parents are often willing to babysit.* | *At that time, ice cream couldn't be conveniently bought in a store.*

2 in a place that is close or easily reached: *The hotel is conveniently located near the airport.*

3 if someone has conveniently forgotten, ignored, lost etc something, they deliberately do this because it helps them to avoid a problem or to get what they want: *You conveniently forgot to tell me she was Nick's sister.*

con·ve·nor /kənˈviːnə $ -ər/ *n* [C] another spelling of CONVENER

con·vent /ˈkɒnvənt $ ˈkɑːnvent/ *n* [C] a building or set of buildings where NUNS live → **monastery** → CONVENT SCHOOL

con·ven·tion /kənˈvenʃən/ ●●○ AWL *n*

1 [C] a large formal meeting for people who belong to the same profession or organization or who have the same interests: *a teachers' convention* | *the city's new* ***convention center*** | *a convention for science fiction fans*

2 [C] a formal agreement, especially between countries, about particular rules or behaviour SYN **pact**, **treaty**: **[+on]** *the European convention on human rights*

3 [C,U] behaviour and attitudes that most people in a society consider to be normal and right SYN **custom**: *Playing together teaches children* ***social conventions*** *such as sharing.* | *They* ***defied*** *the* ***conventions*** *of the time by living together without being married.* | **by convention** *By convention, the bride's father gives her away at her wedding.*

4 [C] a method or style often used in literature, art, the theatre etc to achieve a particular effect: *the conventions of the 19th-century novel*

con·ven·tion·al /kənˈvenʃənəl/ ●●○ W3 AWL *adj*

1 [only before noun] a conventional method, product, practice etc has been used for a long time and is considered the usual type: *Internet connections through conventional phone lines are fairly slow.* | *Bake for 20 minutes in a conventional oven; 8 in a microwave.* THESAURUS NORMAL

2 always following the behaviour and attitudes that most people in a society consider to be normal, right, and socially acceptable, so that you seem slightly boring: *a strong believer in conventional morals* | **[+in]** *He is conventional in his approach to life.*

3 (the) conventional wisdom the opinion that most people consider to be normal and right, but that is sometimes shown to be wrong: *As traffic grew, the conventional wisdom was to widen the roads.*

4 [only before noun] conventional weapons and wars do not use NUCLEAR explosives or weapons: *conventional forces*

5 conventional medicine the usual form of medicine practised in most European and North American countries SYN **western medicine** —**conventionally** *adv* —**conventionality** /kənˌvenʃəˈnæləti/ *n* [U]

con·ven·tion·eer /kənˌvenʃəˈnɪə $ -ˈnɪr/ *n* [C] *especially AmE written* someone who attends a convention

ˈconvent ˌschool *n* [C] a school for girls that is run by Roman Catholic NUNS

con·verge /kənˈvɜːdʒ $ -ˈvɜːrdʒ/ ●○○ *v* [I]

1 to come from different directions and meet at the same point to become one thing OPP **diverge**: *The two rivers converge into one near Pittsburgh.*

2 if groups of people converge in a particular place, they come there from many different places and meet together to form a large crowd: **[+on]** *Reporters converged on the scene.*
3 if different ideas or aims converge, they become the same OPP **diverge**: *Cultural beliefs about the role of women converge with government policies.* —**convergent** *adj*: *The member states should start to have more convergent policies.*

con·ver·sant /kənˈvɜːsənt $ -ɜːr-/ *adj* [not before noun] **1** *formal* having knowledge or experience of something: **[+with]** *Staff members are conversant with the issues.* **2** *AmE* able to hold a conversation in a foreign language, but not able to speak it perfectly: **[+in]** *Kim was conversant in Russian.*

con·ver·sa·tion /ˌkɒnvəˈseɪʃən $ ˌkɑːnvər-/ ●●● S1 W2 *n* [C,U] an informal talk in which people exchange news, feelings, and thoughts: *a telephone conversation | Children quickly get bored by adult conversation.* | **[+with]** *a short conversation with the teacher* | **[+about]** *a conversation about family and friends | They* ***had*** *a short* ***conversation*** *in German and seemed to be disagreeing about something. | It's impossible to* ***carry on a conversation*** *with all this noise in the background. | 'Did you have a good journey?' he said, trying to* ***make conversation****. | He was silent, no matter how hard Sofia tried to* ***engage*** *him* ***in conversation****. | After a while, the* ***conversation turned to*** *a friend's coming wedding. | They were* ***deep in conversation****, relaxed and smiling. | He could hear* ***snatches of conversation*** *from across the room.*

con·ver·sa·tion·al /ˌkɒnvəˈseɪʃənəl◂ $ ˌkɑːnvər-/ *adj* **1** a conversational style, phrase etc is informal and commonly used in conversation: *The article was written in straightforward, almost conversational language.* **2** relating to conversation: *lessons in conversational German* —**conversationally** *adv*

con·ver·sa·tion·al·ist /ˌkɒnvəˈseɪʃənəlɪst $ ˌkɑːnvər-/ *n* [C] someone who talks about intelligent, amusing, and interesting things

ˌconverˈsation ˌpiece *n* [C] something that provides a subject for conversation - often used humorously about objects that seem very strange or ugly

con·verse¹ /kənˈvɜːs $ -ˈvɜːrs/ *v* [I] *formal* to have a conversation with someone SYN **talk**: **[+with]** *She enjoyed the chance to converse with another French speaker.*
THESAURUS ▸ TALK

con·verse² /ˈkɒnvɜːs $ ˈkɑːnvɜːrs/ *n* **the converse** *formal* the converse of a fact, word, statement etc is the opposite of it: *Some teachers welcomed the change; but for the majority of teachers,* ***the converse was true****.*

con·verse³ /ˈkɒnvɜːs $ kənˈvɜːrs/ AWL *adj formal* opposite: *a converse example*

con·verse·ly /kənˈvɜːsli, ˈkɒnvɜːsli $ kənˈvɜːrsli, ˈkɑːnvɜːrsli/ ●○○ AWL *adv* used when one situation is the opposite of another: *American consumers prefer white eggs; conversely, British buyers like brown eggs.*

con·ver·sion /kənˈvɜːʃən $ -ˈvɜːrʒən/ ●○○ AWL *n* [C,U]
1 when you change something from one form, purpose, or system to a different one: **[+into]** *The warehouse was undergoing conversion into apartments.* | **[+of]** *the conversion of waste into usable products* | **[+to]** *The British conversion to the metric system took place in the 1970s.* | **house/barn/loft etc conversion** *BrE* (=when you change the use of a house, barn etc, so that it becomes apartments, a house, a room etc)
2 when someone changes from one religion or belief to a different one: **[+to]** *a conversion to vegetarianism* | **[+from]** *Newman's conversion from Anglicanism to Catholicism*
3 a way of scoring extra points in RUGBY or AMERICAN FOOTBALL

conˈversion ˌcourse *n* [C] *BrE* a course for students who have some knowledge of a subject, but who need slightly different or more knowledge in order to do something: *A qualified pilot would still need a conversion course to fly microlight aircraft.*

con·vert¹ /kənˈvɜːt $ -ˈvɜːrt/ ●●○ W3 AWL *v*
1 a) [T] to change something into a different form, or to change something so that it can be used for a different purpose or in a different way → **convertible**: **convert sth to/into sth** *They converted the spare bedroom into an office. | The stocks can be easily converted to cash. | a 19th-century* ***converted barn*** (=barn changed into a house) **b)** [I] to change into a different form, or change into something that can be used for a different purpose or in a different way: **[+to/into]** *a sofa that converts into a bed | In the process, the light energy converts to heat energy.*
2 a) [T] to persuade someone to change to a different religion: **convert sb to sth** *European missionaries converted thousands to Christianity.* **b)** [I] to change to a different religion: **[+to]** *She converted to Catholicism.*
3 a) [I] to change to a different set of ideas, principles, or ways of doing something: **[+to]** *people who have recently converted to vegetarianism* **b)** [T] to persuade someone to change to a different set of ideas, principles, or ways of doing something: **convert sb to sth** *She succeeded in converting me to her point of view.* | **newly/freshly converted** *newly converted feminists*
4 [I,T] to make a conversion in RUGBY or AMERICAN FOOTBALL
→ **preach to the converted** at PREACH(4)

con·vert² /ˈkɒnvɜːt $ ˈkɑːnvɜːrt/ *n* [C] someone who has been persuaded to change their beliefs and accept a particular religion or opinion: **[+to]** *a convert to Christianity | recent converts to the cause*

con·vert·er, **convertor** /kənˈvɜːtə $ -ˈvɜːrtər/ *n* [C] a piece of equipment that changes the form of something, especially so that it can be more easily used: *a converter that allows you to view digital television on your old TV*
→ CATALYTIC CONVERTER

con·ver·ti·ble¹ /kənˈvɜːtəbəl $ -ɜːr-/ ●○○ AWL *adj*
1 an object that is convertible can be folded or arranged in a different way so that it can be used as something else: *a convertible sofa*
2 *technical* able to be exchanged for the money of another country: *a* ***convertible currency***
3 *technical* a financial document such as an insurance arrangement or a BOND that is convertible can be exchanged for money, STOCKS etc —**convertibility** /kənˌvɜːtəˈbɪləti $ -ɜːr-/ *n* [U]

convertible² *n* [C] a car with a soft roof that you can fold back or remove → **hardtop**, **cabriolet**

con·vex /ˌkɒnˈveks◂, kən-, ˈkɒnveks $ ˌkɑːnˈveks◂, kən-, ˈkɑːnveks/ *adj* curved outwards, like the surface of the eye OPP **concave**: *a convex lens | a convex mirror* → see picture at CONCAVE —**convexly** *adv* —**convexity** /kənˈveksəti/ *n* [C,U]

con·vey /kənˈveɪ/ ●○○ *v* [T]
1 to communicate or express something, with or without using words: *All this information can be conveyed in a simple diagram. | Ads* ***convey*** *the* ***message*** *that thin is beautiful. | He was sent to* ***convey*** *a* ***message*** *to the UN Secretary General.* | **convey sth to sb** *I want to convey to children that reading is one of life's greatest treats.* | **convey a sense/an impression/an idea etc** *You don't want to convey the impression that there's anything illegal going on.*
2 *formal* to take or carry something from one place to another: *Your luggage will be conveyed to the hotel by taxi.*
3 *law* to legally change the possession of property from one person to another

con·vey·ance /kənˈveɪəns/ *n* **1** [C] *formal* a vehicle: *Wheeled conveyances of any kind are not allowed in the park.* **2** [U] *formal* when you take something from one place to another: *the conveyance of goods* **3** [U] when you communicate or express something, with or without words: *Facial expressions are part of the conveyance of meaning.* **4** [C] *law* a legal document that gives land, property etc to one person from another

con·vey·anc·ing /kənˈveɪənsɪŋ/ *n* [U] *BrE* the work done, usually by a lawyer, to change the possession of property, especially a house, from one person to another —**conveyancer** *n* [C]

con·vey·or, **conveyer** /kənˈveɪə $ -ər/ *n* [C] **1** a person or thing that carries or communicates something: *the conveyer of good news* **2** a conveyor belt

con'veyor belt *n* [C] a long continuous moving band of rubber, cloth, or metal, used in a place such as a factory or an airport to move things from one place to another: *We lifted our baggage from the conveyor belt.*

con·vict¹ /kən'vɪkt/ ●○○ *v* [T] to prove or officially announce that someone is guilty of a crime after a TRIAL in a law court OPP **acquit**: **convict sb of sth** *She was convicted of shoplifting.* | **convict sb on sth** *He was* ***convicted on*** *fraud* ***charges***. | *a convicted murderer*

con·vict² /'kɒnvɪkt $ 'kɑːn-/ *n* [C] someone who has been proved to be guilty of a crime and sent to prison: *an escaped convict*

C

con·vic·tion /kən'vɪkʃən/ ●○○ *n*
1 [C] a very strong belief or opinion: **religious/political etc convictions** *a woman of strong political convictions* | **deep/strong conviction** *The Dotens have a deep conviction that marriage is for life.* | **conviction that** *The students possess the conviction that they can make a difference to their community.*
2 [U] the feeling of being sure about something and having no doubts: **with/without conviction** *He was able to say with conviction that he had changed.* | *'No,' she said, without conviction.* | *It was a reasonable explanation, but his voice* ***lacked conviction***. | *It took her so much effort to speak that what she said* ***carried*** *great* ***conviction*** (=showed she felt sure of what she said).
3 [C,U] a decision in a court of law that someone is guilty of a crime, or the process of proving that someone is guilty OPP **acquittal**: *They had no previous convictions.* | *Applicants are checked for criminal convictions.* | **[+for]** *This was her third conviction for theft.* | *the trial and conviction of Jimmy Malone* → **have the courage of your convictions** at COURAGE(2)

con·vince /kən'vɪns/ ●●○ S3 W3 AWL *v* [T]
1 to make someone feel certain that something is true: *Her arguments didn't convince everyone, but changes were made.* | **convince sb (that)** *Baker had to convince jurors that his client had been nowhere near the scene of the murder.* | **convince sb of sth** *The officials were eager to convince us of the safety of the nuclear reactors.*
2 to persuade someone to do something SYN **persuade**: **convince sb to do sth** *I've been trying to convince Jean to come with me.* **THESAURUS** PERSUADE

con·vinced /kən'vɪnst/ ●●○ AWL *adj*
1 [not before noun] feeling certain that something is true: *Molly agreed, but she did not sound very convinced.* | **be convinced (that)** *I was convinced that we were doing the right thing.* | **[+of]** *Researchers are convinced of a genetic cause for the disease.* | **firmly/totally/fully etc convinced** *Herschel was firmly convinced of the possibility of life on other planets.* **THESAURUS** SURE
2 convinced Muslim/Christian etc someone who believes very strongly in a particular religion

con·vinc·ing /kən'vɪnsɪŋ/ ●●○ AWL *adj*
1 making you believe that something is true or right: *convincing evidence of his guilt* | **wholly/utterly/totally etc convincing** *Courtenay played the role in an utterly convincing way.*
2 convincing victory/win an occasion when a person or team wins a game by a lot of points —**convincingly** *adv*

con·viv·i·al /kən'vɪviəl/ *adj formal* friendly and pleasantly cheerful: *a convivial atmosphere* —**convivially** *adv* —**conviviality** /kənˌvɪvi'æləti/ *n* [U]

con·vo·ca·tion /ˌkɒnvə'keɪʃən $ ˌkɑːn-/ *n* **1** [C usually singular] *formal* a large formal meeting of a group of people, especially church officials **2** [U] *formal* the process of arranging for a large meeting to be held **3** [C usually singular] *AmE* the ceremony held when students have finished their studies and are leaving a college or university

con·voke /kən'vəʊk $ -'voʊk/ *v* [T] *formal* to tell people that they must come together for a formal meeting: *Separate meetings had been convoked by the two opposing factions.*

con·vo·lut·ed /'kɒnvəluːtɪd $ 'kɑːn-/ *adj* **1** complicated and difficult to understand: *long paragraphs and convoluted sentences* | *The argument is rather convoluted.* **THESAURUS** COMPLICATED **2** *formal* having many twists and bends: *a tightly-coiled convoluted tube*

con·vo·lu·tion /ˌkɒnvə'luːʃən $ ˌkɑːn-/ *n* [C usually plural] **1** the complicated details of a story, explanation etc, which make it difficult to understand: **[+of]** *the endless convolutions of the plot* **2** a fold or twist in something which has many of them: **[+of]** *the many convolutions of the small intestine*

con·voy¹ /'kɒnvɔɪ $ 'kɑːn-/ ●○○ *n* [C] a group of vehicles or ships travelling together, sometimes in order to protect one another: **[+of]** *The British left in a convoy of 20 cars.* | **in convoy** *We drove in convoy.* | *a* ***military convoy*** | **aid/relief/food etc convoy**

convoy² *v* [T] to travel with something in order to protect it: *American destroyers helped to convoy much-needed supplies to Britain in 1917.*

con·vulse /kən'vʌls/ *v* **1** [I] if your body or a part of it convulses, it moves violently and you are not able to control it: *He sat down, his shoulders convulsing with sobs.* **2 be convulsed with laughter/anger etc** to be laughing so much or feel so angry that you shake and are not able to stop yourself **3** [T] if something such as a war convulses a country, it causes a lot of problems or confusion: *A wave of nationalist demonstrations convulsed the country in 1919.*

con·vul·sion /kən'vʌlʃən/ *n* [C] **1** a shaking movement of your body that you cannot control, which happens because you are ill SYN **seizure**: *His temperature was very high and he* ***went into convulsions***. **2** [usually plural] a great change that affects a country: *the 19th-century political convulsions in France* **3 be in convulsions** to be laughing a lot

con·vul·sive /kən'vʌlsɪv/ *adj* [usually before noun] a convulsive movement or action is sudden, violent, and impossible to control: *a convulsive sob* —**convulsively** *adv*: *Con's body jerked convulsively.*

coo¹ /kuː/ *v* **1** [I] when DOVES or PIGEONS coo, they make a low soft cry **2** [I,T] to make soft quiet sounds, or to speak in a soft quiet way: *'Darling,' she cooed.* | *a cooing voice* —**coo** *n* [C] → **bill and coo** at BILL²(3)

coo² *interjection BrE* used to express surprise: *Coo! That must have cost a lot!*

cook¹ /kʊk/ ●●● S1 W3 *v*
1 [I,T] to prepare food for eating by using heat: *Where did you learn to cook?* | *Cook the sauce over a low heat for ten minutes.* | **cook a meal/dinner/breakfast etc** *I'm usually too tired to cook an evening meal.* | **cook sth for supper/lunch/dinner etc** *He was cooking rice for supper.* | **cook sb sth** *She cooked them all a good dinner every night.* | **cook (sth) for sb** *I promised I'd cook for them.* | *slices of cooked ham* | *a cooked breakfast*
2 [I] to be prepared for eating by using heat: *He could smell something delicious cooking.* | *Hamburgers were cooking in the kitchen.*
3 cook the books to dishonestly change official records and figures in order to steal money or give people false information: *The Government was cooking the books and misleading the public.*
4 be cooking *informal* to be being planned in a secret way: *They've got something cooking, and I don't think I like it.*
5 be cooking (with gas) *spoken* used to say that someone is doing something very well: *The band's really cooking tonight.*

GRAMMAR

Cook belongs to a group of verbs where the same noun can be the subject of the verb or its object.
• You can say: *I'm cooking some pasta.* In this sentence, 'some pasta' is the object of **cook**.

• You can say: *Some pasta is cooking.* In this sentence, 'some pasta' is the subject of **cook**.
GRAMMAR GUIDE ▸ VERBS

THESAURUS

TO COOK SOMETHING

cook to prepare a meal or food for eating by using heat: *I offered to cook a meal for her.* | *Cook in a hot oven for 25 minutes.*
make to make a meal or a particular dish by cooking it or getting all the parts ready: *John was making dinner.* | *I think I'll make a salad for lunch.*
prepare to make a meal or a particular dish by getting all the parts ready. **Prepare** is more formal than **make**: *The children helped to prepare the evening meal.* | *The dish takes a long time to prepare.*
rustle up /ˈrʌsəl/ *informal* to cook a meal or dish quickly using whatever is available: *She soon rustled up a tasty soup.*
fix *especially AmE* to cook or prepare a meal – used about meals you make quickly: *Why don't you take a nap while I fix dinner?*
do *BrE informal* to make a particular type of food: *I could do you an omelette.* | *I was thinking of doing a fish pie when Michael comes.*

WAYS OF COOKING SOMETHING

bake to cook things such as bread or cakes in an oven: *Tom baked a cake for my birthday.*
roast to cook meat or vegetables in an oven: *Roast the potatoes for an hour.*
fry to cook food in hot oil: *She was frying some mushrooms.*
stir-fry to fry small pieces of food while moving them around continuously: *stir-fried tofu and bean sprouts*
sauté /ˈsəʊteɪ $ soʊˈteɪ/ to fry vegetables for a short time in a small amount of butter or oil: *Sauté the potatoes in butter.*
grill to cook food over or under strong heat: *grilled fish*
broil *AmE* to cook food under heat: *broiled fish*
boil to cook something in very hot water: *He doesn't even know how to boil an egg.* | *English people seem to love boiled vegetables.*
steam to cook vegetables over hot water: *Steam the rice for 15 minutes.*
poach to cook food, especially fish or eggs, slowly in hot water: *poached salmon*
toast to cook the outside surfaces of bread: *toasted muffins*
barbecue to cook food on a metal frame over a fire outdoors: *I thought we could barbecue some mackerel.*
microwave to cook food in a microwave oven: *The beans can be microwaved.*

cook sth ↔ **up** *phr v*
1 to prepare food, especially quickly: *Every night he cooked up a big casserole.*
2 *informal* to invent an excuse, reason, plan etc, especially one that is slightly dishonest or unlikely to work: *the plan that Graham and Dempster had cooked up*

cook² ●●● S2 *n* [C]
1 someone who prepares and cooks food as their job SYN **chef**: *He works as a cook in a local restaurant.*
2 be a good/wonderful/terrible etc cook to be good or bad at preparing and cooking food
3 too many cooks (spoil the broth) used when you think there are too many people trying to do the same job at the same time, so that the job is not done well → **chief cook and bottle-washer** at CHIEF¹(3)

cook·book /ˈkʊkbʊk/ *n* [C] *AmE* a book that tells you how to prepare and cook food SYN **cookery book** *BrE*

ˌcook-ˈchill *adj* [only before noun] *BrE* cook-chill foods have already been cooked when you buy them, and are stored at a low temperature, but not frozen

cook·er /ˈkʊkə $ -ər/ *n* [C] *BrE* **1** a large piece of equipment for cooking food on or in SYN **stove** *AmE*: *a gas cooker* **2** a fruit, especially an apple, that is suitable for cooking but not for eating raw

cook·e·ry /ˈkʊkəri/ *n* [U] *BrE* the art or skill of cooking: *a one-year cookery course* | *French cookery*

ˈcookery ˌbook *n* [C] *BrE* a book that tells you how to prepare and cook food SYN **cookbook** *AmE* → **recipe**

cook·house /ˈkʊkhaʊs/ *n* [C] *old-fashioned* an outdoor kitchen where you cook food, especially in a military camp

cook·ie /ˈkʊki/ ●●● S3 W3 *n* [C]
1 *especially AmE* a small flat sweet cake SYN **biscuit** *BrE*: *a glass of milk and a cookie* | *a chocolate chip cookie*
2 tough/smart cookie *informal* someone who is clever and successful, and knows how to get what they want
3 that's the way the cookie crumbles *informal* said when something bad has happened and you must accept things the way they are, even though you do not want to
4 *technical* information that a website leaves in your computer so that the website will recognize you when you use it again
5 *AmE old-fashioned* an attractive young woman

ˈcookie ˌcutter¹ *n* [C] *AmE* an instrument that cuts cookies into special shapes before you bake them

cookie cutter² *adj* [only before noun] *AmE* almost exactly the same as other things of the same type, and not very interesting: *the cookie cutter approach of the urban renewal programme*

ˈcookie sheet *n* [C] *AmE* a flat piece of metal that you bake food on SYN **baking tray** *BrE*

cook·ing¹ /ˈkʊkɪŋ/ ●●○ *n* [U]
1 the activity of preparing food so that it is ready to eat, usually by heating it: *My mother does all the cooking.* | *I love cooking.* THESAURUS ▸ FOOD
2 food made in a particular way or by a particular person: *My compliments on your cooking.* | *Indian cooking* | *simple basic* ***home cooking*** (=good food like the food you get in your own home)

cooking² *adj* [only before noun] suitable for or used in cooking: *The rooms all have* ***cooking facilities*** (=there is cooking equipment in the rooms). | **cooking pot/utensils/equipment etc** | *cooking apples*

ˈcooking ˌapple *n* [C] an apple that is usually cooked, rather than eaten raw → **eating apple**

ˈcooking oil *n* [U] oil from plants, such as SUNFLOWERS or OLIVES, used in cooking

cook·out /ˈkʊk-aʊt/ *n* [C] *AmE informal* a party or occasion when a meal is cooked and eaten outdoors: *a cookout on the beach*

cook·ware /ˈkʊkweə $ -wer/ *n* [U] containers and equipment used for cooking

cool¹ /kuːl/ ●●● S2 W3 *adj* (*comparative* **cooler**, *superlative* **coolest**)
1 TEMPERATURE low in temperature, but not cold, often in a way that feels pleasant: *She swam out into the cool water.* | *The evening air was cool.* | *Relax in the sun with a cool drink.* | *the cooler weather of September* THESAURUS ▸ COLD
2 CLOTHING clothing that is cool is made of thin material so that you do not become too hot: *a cool cotton dress*
3 CALM calm and not nervous, upset, or excited: **keep/stay cool** *his ability to keep cool in a crisis* | *She looks efficient and* ***as cool as a cucumber***. | *Outwardly she is* ***cool, calm, and collected***. | *a* ***cool customer*** (=someone who always behaves calmly) | *Keep a* ***cool head*** (=stay calm). THESAURUS ▸ CALM
4 APPROVAL *informal* very attractive, fashionable, interesting etc in a way that people admire – used in order to show approval: *She's pretty cool.* | *You* ***look cool*** *in denim.* | *Cool bike!* | *'I'm thinking of studying abroad.' 'Really? Cool.'* THESAURUS ▸ FASHIONABLE
5 AGREEMENT *spoken* used to say that you agree with something, that you understand it, or that it does not annoy you: *OK, Ryan,* ***that's cool***, *I can do it.* | *'I just have to*

C

go, you know.' 'It's all right, ***it's cool****.' | 'I'm finished.' 'Cool.'* | **[+about]** *My mum was cool about whatever I wore.* | **sth is cool with sb** *Is Friday cool with you guys?* | **sb is cool with sth** *'Do you want to come over and watch a video tonight?' 'I'm cool with that.'*

6 NOT FRIENDLY behaving in a way that is not as friendly as you expect: *My proposal met with a* ***cool response****.* | *Luke gave her a* ***cool look****.*

7 COLOUR a cool colour is one, such as blue or green, that makes you think of cool things

8 a cool million/hundred thousand etc *informal* a surprisingly large amount of money: *He earns a cool half million every year.* —**coolness** *n* [U]: *the coolness of the nights* —**coolly** *adv*: *She nodded coolly and walked out.*

cool² ●●○ S3 *v*

1 [I,T] (*also* **cool down**) to make something slightly colder, or to become slightly colder: *The air conditioning doesn't seem to be cooling the room much.* | *Allow the biscuits to cool for five minutes.* | *a cooling breeze*

2 [I] if a feeling, emotion, or relationship cools, it becomes less strong: *The affair had cooled, on her side at least.* | *When tempers had cooled, he apologized.*

3 cool it *spoken* **a)** used to tell someone to stop being angry, violent etc: *Come on now – calm down, cool it.* **b)** to stop putting as much effort into something, or pressure on someone, as you have been: *He was getting more serious about her. It was time to cool it.*

4 cool your heels to be forced to wait: *I'll put him in a cell to cool his heels for a bit.*

cool down *phr v*

1 to make something slightly colder, or to become slightly colder: *The air has cooled down a little now.* | **cool sb/sth ↔ down** *A cold beer will cool you down.*

2 to become calm after being angry: *After I cooled down I realized I had been wrong.*

cool off *phr v*

1 to return to a normal temperature after being hot: *Cool off with an iced drink.* | *By late autumn Mediterranean islands have cooled off, and can have rainy days.*

2 to become calm after being angry SYN **calm down**: *He slammed the door and went for a walk to cool off.*

cool³ *n* **1 the cool** a temperature that is pleasantly cold: **[+of]** *They went for a stroll* ***in the cool of the evening****.* **2 keep your cool** to remain calm in a frightening or difficult situation: *I must keep my cool, she thought; losing my temper isn't going to help.* **3 lose your cool** to stop being calm in an annoying or frightening situation: *Kenneth finally lost his cool with a photographer, and threatened to hit him.*

cool⁴ *adv* **play it cool** to behave in a calm way because you do not want someone to know that you are really nervous, angry etc: *She would not show him how upset she was. It was always smarter to play it cool.*

coo·lant /ˈkuːlənt/ *n* [C,U] *technical* a liquid or gas used to cool something, especially an engine

cool·box /ˈkuːlbɒks $ -bɑːks/ *n* [C] *BrE* a container that keeps food and drink cool and fresh, used on a PICNIC SYN **cooler** *AmE*

cool·er /ˈkuːlə $ -ər/ ●●○ *n* [C]

1 a container in which something, especially drinks, is cooled or kept cold: *Mike went to fetch a bottle of wine from the cooler.*

2 *AmE* a coolbox

3 *AmE* a machine that provides AIR CONDITIONING

4 the cooler *informal* prison

ˌcool-ˈheaded *adj* not easily excited or upset: *We need a quick-thinking, cool-headed person for the job.*

coo·lie /ˈkuːli/ *n* [C] *taboo old-fashioned* a very offensive word for an unskilled worker who is paid very low wages, especially in parts of Asia. Do not use this word.

ˌcooling-ˈoff ˌperiod *n* [C] **1** *BrE* a period of time after you have signed some types of sales agreement, when you can change your mind about buying something: *Customers signing new life policies will have a cooling-off period of 14 days in which to cancel.* **2** a period of time when two people or groups who are arguing about something can go away and think about how to improve the situation

ˈcooling ˌsystem *n* [C] a system for keeping the temperature in a machine, engine etc low: *a fault in the power station's cooling system*

ˈcooling ˌtower *n* [C] a large round tall building, used in industry for making water cool

coon /kuːn/ *n* [C] *informal* **1** *AmE* a RACCOON **2** *taboo* a very offensive word for a black person. Do not use this word.

coon·skin /ˈkuːnskɪn/ *adj* made from the skin of a RACCOON: *pictures of traders in coonskin caps*

coop /kuːp/ *n* [C] a building for small animals, especially chickens

co-op /ˈkəʊɒp $ ˈkoʊɑːp/ *n* [C] a COOPERATIVE

ˌcooped ˈup *adj* [not before noun] having to stay for a period of time in a place that is too small: *It isn't good for you to be cooped up in the house all day.*

coo·per /ˈkuːpə $ -ər/ *n* [C] someone who makes BARRELS

co·op·e·rate (*also* **co-operate** *BrE*) /kəʊˈɒpəreɪt $ koʊˈɑːp-/ ●●○ AWL *v* [I]

1 to work with someone else to achieve something that you both want: **[+in/on]** *The two universities are to cooperate in the development of a new industrial process.* | *They* ***agreed to co-operate*** *with Brazil on a programme to protect the rain forests.* | **[+with]** *Lions cooperate with each other when hunting game.* | *As chairman I was anxious to co-operate with Mr Baker as far as possible.* | *The church seeks to* ***cooperate closely*** *with local schools.* | **cooperate to do sth** *Both sides agreed to co-operate to prevent illegal fishing in the area.*

2 to do what someone wants you to do: **[+with]** *I advised my client to* ***cooperate fully*** *with the police.* | *If you* ***refuse to co-operate****, I'll kill you.*

co·op·e·ra·tion (*also* **co-operation** *BrE*) /kəʊˌɒpəˈreɪʃən $ koʊˌɑːp-/ ●●○ S3 W3 AWL *n* [U]

1 when you work with someone to achieve something that you both want: **[+with]** *political co-operation with Britain* | **in cooperation with sb** *A study was undertaken in co-operation with oil companies.* | *Burglar alarm companies claim they work in* ***close co-operation*** *with the police.* | **[+between]** *the lack of effective co-operation between industry and higher education* | *the need to strengthen* ***international co-operation***

2 willingness to do what someone asks you to do: *Have your passports ready, and thank you for your cooperation.* | *Your* ***full cooperation*** *is requested.*

co·op·e·ra·tive¹ (*also* **co-operative** *BrE*) /kəʊˈɒpərətɪv $ koʊˈɑːp-/ ●○○ AWL *adj*

1 willing to cooperate SYN **helpful** OPP **uncooperative**: *He was doing his best to be cooperative.* | *a cooperative witness*

2 made, done, or operated by people working together: *a co-operative venture between the City Council and the police*

3 a cooperative store, bank etc is operated by people working together as a cooperative: *a co-operative store in a provincial town* —**cooperatively** *adv*

cooperative² (*also* **co-operative** *BrE*) *n* [C] a business or organization owned equally by all the people working there SYN **co-op**: *a women-only housing co-operative* | *a workers' co-operative*

co-opt (*also* **co-opt** *BrE*) /kəʊˈɒpt $ koʊˈɑːpt/ *v* [T] *formal* **1** *BrE* to make someone a member of a group, committee etc, by the agreement of all the members: *The committee may co-opt additional members for special purposes.* | **coopt sb onto/into/to sth** *She was coopted onto the county education committee.* **2** to persuade someone to help or support you: **coopt sb to do sth** *Social scientists were co-opted to work with the development agencies.* | *Nan was coopted into the kitchen to make pastry.*

co·or·di·nate¹ (*also* **co-ordinate** *BrE*) /kəʊˈɔːdəneɪt $ koʊˈɔːr-/ ●○○ AWL *v*

1 [T] to organize an activity so that the people involved in it work well together and achieve a good result: *The agencies are working together to co-ordinate policy on food safety.*

2 [T] to make the parts of your body move and work together well: *Her movements were beautifully co-ordinated.* | *I couldn't get my brain to function or coordinate my muscles.*
3 [I,T] if clothes, decorations etc coordinate, or if you coordinate them, they look good together because they have similar colours and styles: *Don't be afraid to mix colours, as long as they co-ordinate.* | *You might coordinate your curtains and cushions.* | **[+with]** *The cooker is green, to co-ordinate with the kitchen.*

co·or·din·ate² (*also* **co-ordinate** *BrE*) /kəʊˈɔːdənət $ koʊˈɔːr-/ ●○○ AWL *n* [C]
1 *technical* one of a set of numbers which give the exact position of a point on a map, computer screen etc
2 **coordinates** [plural] things such as clothes that can be worn or used together because their colours match or their styles are similar: *Matching bag and accessories provide a complete ensemble of colour coordinates.*

coordinate³ AWL (*also* **co-ordinate** *BrE*) *adj technical* 1 equal in importance or rank in a sentence → **subordinate**: *coordinate clauses joined by 'and'* 2 involving the use of coordinates

coˌordinating conˈjunction *n* [C] a word such as 'and' or 'but' which joins two words, groups, or CLAUSES that are equal in importance or rank → **subordinating conjunction**

co·or·di·na·tion (*also* **co-ordination** *BrE*) /kəʊˌɔːdəˈneɪʃən $ koʊˌɔːr-/ ●○○ AWL *n* [U]
1 the way in which your muscles move together when you perform a movement: *Too much alcohol affects your coordination.*
2 the organization of people or things so that they work together well: **[+of]** *the coordination of our economic policies* | **[+between]** *co-ordination between central and local government*

co·or·di·na·tor /kəʊˈɔːdəneɪtə $ koʊˈɔːrdəneɪtər/ ●○○ AWL *n* [C] someone who organizes the way people work together in a particular activity

coot /kuːt/ *n* [C] 1 a small black and white water bird with a short beak 2 **old coot** *AmE informal* an old man who you think is strange or unpleasant: *a miserable mean old coot*

cop¹ /kɒp $ kɑːp/ ●●○ *n* [C]
1 *informal* a police officer: *the local cop* | *a narcotics cop* | *He pulled out his badge and said he was a cop.*
2 **not be much cop** *BrE informal* to not be very good: *They say he's not much cop as a coach.*
3 **it's a fair cop** *BrE spoken* used humorously when someone has discovered that you have done something wrong and you want to admit it

cop² *v* (**copped**, **copping**) [T] *spoken informal* 1 **cop it** *BrE* **a)** to be punished or spoken to angrily because you have done something wrong: *You'll cop it when Mum finds out!* **b)** to be killed 2 *BrE* to receive something, especially something that you do not want: *I copped all the blame for what happened.* 3 **cop hold of sth** *BrE* used to tell someone to hold something: *Cop hold of the other end, will you?* 4 **cop an attitude** *AmE* to behave in a way that is not nice, especially by showing that you think you are better or more intelligent than other people 5 **cop a feel** *AmE* to touch someone in a sexual way when they do not want you to 6 **cop a plea** *AmE* to agree to say you are guilty of a crime in order to receive a less severe punishment: *Dunn copped a plea to avoid going to jail.* 7 **cop a buzz** *AmE* to feel the effects of taking illegal drugs or drinking alcohol

cop off *phr v BrE informal* to meet someone and start a sexual relationship with them: **[+with]** *The hero eventually cops off with the princess.*

cop out *phr v informal* to not do something that someone thinks you should do: *As far as I'm concerned, she's copped out and joined the rat race.* → **COP-OUT**

cope¹ /kəʊp $ koʊp/ ●●○ S3 W3 *v* [I]
1 to succeed in dealing with a difficult problem or situation: *Sometimes I find it hard to cope.* | *He coped quite well as manager while still captaining the team.* | **[+with]** *She feared she wouldn't be able to cope with two new babies.* | *Local authorities have to cope with the problems of homelessness.*
2 if a system or machine copes with a particular type or amount of work, it does it: **[+with]** *No system is designed to cope with the floods we have had this year.* | *My computer can cope with huge amounts of data.*

cope² *n* [C] a long loose piece of clothing worn by priests on special occasions

cop·i·er /ˈkɒpiə $ ˈkɑːpiər/ *n* [C] a machine that makes exact copies of writing or pictures on paper by photographing them SYN **photocopier**

ˈco-ˌpi·lot *n* [C] a pilot who shares the control of an aircraft with the main pilot

cop·ing /ˈkəʊpɪŋ $ ˈkoʊ-/ *n* [C,U] a layer of rounded stones or bricks at the top of a wall or roof

co·pi·ous /ˈkəʊpiəs $ ˈkoʊ-/ *adj* [usually before noun] existing or being produced in large quantities: *He could drink* ***copious amounts*** *of beer without ill effect.* | *She listened to me and took* ***copious notes***. —**copiously** *adv*: *Then she wept copiously.*

ˈcop-out *n* [C] *informal* something you do or say in order to avoid doing or accepting something: *Ignoring the problem is a cop-out.*

cop·per /ˈkɒpə $ ˈkɑːpər/ ●●○ *n*
1 [U] a soft reddish-brown metal that allows electricity and heat to pass through it easily, and is used to make electrical wires, water pipes etc. It is a chemical ELEMENT: symbol Cu
2 **coppers** [plural] *BrE* money of low value made of copper or BRONZE: *He offered to do the job for a few coppers.*
3 [U] a reddish-brown colour: *her copper hair*
4 [C] *BrE informal* a police officer —**coppery** *adj*: *coppery skin*

ˌcopper ˈbeech *n* [C] a large European tree with purple-brown leaves

ˌcopper-ˈbottomed *adj* able to be depended on: *a copper-bottomed guarantee*

cop·per·head /ˈkɒpəhed $ ˈkɑːpər-/ *n* [C] a poisonous yellow and brown North American snake

cop·per·plate /ˈkɒpəpleɪt $ ˈkɑːpər-/ *n* [U] neat regular curving handwriting with the letters all joined together in a very specific style, used especially in the past

cop·pice¹ /ˈkɒpɪs $ ˈkɑː-/ *n* [C] a copse

coppice² *v* [T] to cut a tree down so that useful new wood will grow from the bottom

copse /kɒps $ kɑːps/ (*also* **coppice**) *n* [C] a group of trees or bushes growing close together **THESAURUS** **FOREST**

ˈcop shop *n* [C] *BrE informal* a POLICE STATION

cop·ter /ˈkɒptə $ ˈkɑːptər/ *n* [C] *AmE* a HELICOPTER

cop·u·la /ˈkɒpjələ $ ˈkɑːp-/ *n* [C] *technical* a type of verb that connects the subject of a sentence to its COMPLEMENT, for example 'seem' in the sentence 'The house seems big' SYN **linking verb**

cop·u·late /ˈkɒpjəleɪt $ ˈkɑːp-/ *v* [I + with] *technical* to have sex —**copulation** /ˌkɒpjəˈleɪʃən $ ˌkɑːp-/ *n* [U]

cop·y¹ /ˈkɒpi $ ˈkɑːpi/ ●●● S1 W2 *n* (*plural* **copies**)
1 [C] something that is made to be exactly like another thing: **[+of]** *She forwarded them a copy of her British passport.* | *This chair is a copy of an original design.* | *Be sure to* ***make copies*** *of all the documents.* | ***back-up copies*** *of your files*
2 [C] one of many books, magazines, records etc that are all exactly the same: **[+of]** *We have six copies of the movie to give away.* | *a copy of the local newspaper* | *The hardback costs £16.99 a copy.* | *The record sold a million copies.* | ***Free copies*** *are available on request.*
3 [U] *technical* something written in order to be printed in a newspaper, magazine, advertisement etc: *Now that I've seen the finished copy, I'm delighted.*
4 **good copy** *informal* interesting news: *The interviews* ***made good copy*** *and helped with the film's publicity.* → **FAIR COPY**, **HARD COPY**, **SOFT COPY**

copy² ●●● S2 *v* (**copied, copying, copies**)
1 [I,T] to deliberately make or produce something that is exactly like another thing: *Could you copy this letter and send it out, please?* | *To copy a file, press F3.* | **copy (sth) from sth** *a design copied from an 18th-century wallpaper* | *The pupils just copy from textbooks and learn facts.* | **copy sth into sth** *He copied the number into his notebook* (=wrote the same number there).
2 [T] to deliberately do something that someone else has done or behave like someone else: *Children often copy what they see on television.* | *I found myself copying him and his mannerisms.*
3 [I,T] to cheat in an examination, schoolwork etc by looking at someone else's work and writing the same thing as they have: **[+from]** *Jeremy had copied from the girl next to him.*

C

THESAURUS

copy to deliberately make or produce something that is exactly like another thing: *You could copy the files onto a CD.* | *Many people have tried to copy his paintings.*
photocopy to copy a piece of paper with writing or pictures on it, using a machine: *I'll photocopy the letter and give it to you.*
reproduce to print a copy of a picture or document, especially in a book or newspaper: *The image has been reproduced in many magazines and newspapers around the world.*
forge to illegally copy something written or printed: *He forged my signature.* | *forged £10 notes*
pirate to illegally copy and sell something such as a book, DVD, or computer program: *The survey suggests that 27% of software in the UK has been pirated.*

copy sth ↔ **down** *phr v* to write something down exactly as it was said or written: *I must have copied your number down wrong.*
copy sb **in** *phr v* to send someone a copy of an email message you are sending to someone else: **[+on]** *Can you copy me in on the memo you're sending to Chris?*
copy sth ↔ **out** *phr v* to write something again exactly as it is written in the document that you are looking at: *The monks copied their manuscripts out by hand.*
copy sth ↔ **up** *phr v BrE* to write something again in a better or neater form SYN **write up**: *It is important to copy up your notes soon after the lecture.*

cop·y·book /ˈkɒpibʊk $ ˈkɑː-/ *adj* [only before noun] completely suitable or correct SYN **textbook**: *a copybook answer*

cop·y·cat¹ /ˈkɒpikæt $ ˈkɑː-/ *n* [C] *informal* someone who copies other people's clothes, behaviour, work etc – used by children to show disapproval

copycat² *adj* **copycat crime/attack etc** a crime, attack etc which is similar to a famous crime that another person has committed: *Crime reports in newspapers often encourage copycat crimes.*

ˈcopy ˌeditor *n* [C] someone whose job is to make sure that the words in a book, newspaper etc are correct and ready to be printed —**copy-edit** *v* [I,T]

cop·y·ist /ˈkɒpi-ɪst $ ˈkɑː-/ *n* [C] someone who made written copies of documents, books etc in the past

cop·y·right /ˈkɒpiraɪt $ ˈkɑː-/ ●○○ *n* [C,U] the legal right to be the only producer or seller of a book, play, film, or record for a specific length of time: *Who owns the copyright of this book?* | *The database will be* ***protected by copyright***. | **infringement/breach of copyright** (=when you break the copyright laws) —**copyright** *adj*: *copyright material* —**copyright** *v* [T]

cop·y·writ·er /ˈkɒpiˌraɪtə $ ˈkɑːpiˌraɪtər/ *n* [C] someone who writes the words for advertisements

coq au vin /ˌkɒk əʊ ˈvæn $ ˌkoʊk oʊ-/ *n* [U] chicken cooked in red wine

coq·ue·try /ˈkɒkətri $ ˈkoʊ-/ *n* (*plural* **coquetries**) [C,U] *literary* behaviour that is typical of a coquette

co·quette /kəʊˈket, kɒ- $ koʊ-/ *n* [C] *literary* a woman who frequently tries to attract the attention of men without having sincere feelings for them SYN **flirt** —**coquettish** *adj* —**coquettishly** *adv*

cor /kɔː $ kɔːr/ *interjection BrE spoken* used when you are very surprised or impressed by something

cor- /kə, kɒ $ kə, kɔːr, kɑːr/ *prefix* the form used for CON- before the letter 'r': *to correlate* (=connect together)

cor·a·cle /ˈkɒrəkəl $ ˈkɔː-, ˈkɑː-/ *n* [C] a small round boat that you move with a PADDLE

cor·al¹ /ˈkɒrəl $ ˈkɔː-, ˈkɑː-/ *n* [U] a hard red, white, or pink substance formed from the bones of very small sea creatures, which is often used to make jewellery

coral² *adj* pink or reddish-orange in colour

ˌcoral ˈreef *n* [C] a line of hard rocks formed by coral, found in warm sea water that is not very deep

cor an·glais /ˌkɔːr ˈɒŋgleɪ $ -ɒːŋˈgleɪ/ *n* (*plural* **cors anglais** (*same pronunciation*)) [C] *BrE* a long wooden musical instrument which is like an OBOE but with a lower sound SYN **English horn** *AmE*

cor bli·mey /ˌkɔː ˈblaɪmi $ ˌkɔːr-/ (*also* **blimey**) *interjection BrE old-fashioned* used to express surprise

cord¹ /kɔːd $ kɔːrd/ ●●○ *n*
1 [C,U] a piece of thick string or thin rope: *The robe was held at the waist by a cord.* | *He pulled explosives and some tangled cord from his bag.* → see picture at BAG¹
2 cords [plural] trousers made from a thick strong cotton cloth with thin raised lines on it
3 [C,U] an electrical wire or wires with a protective covering, usually for connecting electrical equipment to the supply of electricity: *the phone cord* | *an extension cord*
4 [C] *AmE* a specific quantity of wood cut for burning in a fire: *We use three cords of wood in a winter.* → **cut the cord** at CUT¹(40), → COMMUNICATION CORD, SPINAL CORD, UMBILICAL CORD, VOCAL CORDS

cord² *adj* cord clothes are made from CORDUROY: *green cord trousers*

cord·age /ˈkɔːdɪdʒ $ ˈkɔːr-/ *n* [U] rope or cord in general, especially on a ship

cor·di·al¹ /ˈkɔːdiəl $ ˈkɔːrdʒəl/ *n* [C,U] **1** *BrE* sweet fruit juice that you add water to before you drink it: *lime cordial* **2** *AmE old-fashioned* a strong sweet alcoholic drink SYN **liqueur**: *an after-dinner cordial*

cordial² *adj* friendly but quite polite and formal: *The talks were conducted in a cordial atmosphere.* THESAURUS FRIENDLY —**cordiality** /ˌkɔːdiˈæləti $ ˌkɔːrdʒiˈæ-, kɔːrˈdʒæ-/ *n* [U]

cor·di·al·ly /ˈkɔːdiəli $ ˈkɔːrdʒəli/ *adv* **1** in a friendly but polite and formal way: *You are cordially invited to our wedding on May 9.* **2 cordially dislike/loathe etc** to dislike someone or something very strongly

cor·dite /ˈkɔːdaɪt $ ˈkɔːr-/ *n* [U] an explosive used in bullets and bombs

cord·less /ˈkɔːdləs $ ˈkɔːrd-/ *adj* a piece of equipment that is cordless is not connected to its power supply by wires: *a cordless phone* | *a cordless drill*

cor·don¹ /ˈkɔːdn $ ˈkɔːrdn/ *n* [C] a line of police officers, soldiers, or vehicles that is put around an area to stop people going there: **[+of]** *A cordon of police surrounded the building.* | **[+around]** *the* ***security cordon*** *around the capital*

cordon² *v*
cordon sth ↔ **off** *phr v* to surround and protect an area with police officers, soldiers, or vehicles: *Police cordoned off the street where the murder took place.*

cor·don bleu /ˌkɔːdɒn ˈblɜː $ ˌkɔːrdɒːn ˈbluː/ *adj* [only before noun] relating to cooking of very high quality: *a cordon bleu chef*

cor·du·roy /ˈkɔːdʒərɔɪ, -djə- $ ˈkɔːrdə-/ *n* [U] a thick strong cotton cloth with thin raised lines on it, used for making clothes: *a corduroy jacket*

core¹ /kɔː $ kɔːr/ ●●○ W3 AWL *n* [C]
1 FRUIT the hard central part of a fruit such as an apple: *Remove the cores, and bake the apples for 40 minutes.* → see picture at FRUIT¹

2 MOST IMPORTANT PART the most important or central part of something: **[+of]** *The core of the book focuses on the period between 1660 and 1857.* | *Debt is* ***at the core of*** *the problem.*
3 PEOPLE a number of people who form a group which is very important to an organization: *The business needs a new core of trained administrators.* | *a core group of clients* → HARD CORE
4 to the core extremely or completely: **shaken/shocked/thrilled to the core** *When I heard the news, I was shaken to the core.* | *That woman is* ***rotten to the core****!* | *He was a bureaucrat to the core.*
5 PLANET the central part of the Earth or any other PLANET → see picture at EARTH[1]
6 NUCLEAR REACTOR the central part of a NUCLEAR REACTOR

core² AWL *adj* **1 core curriculum/subjects/skills etc** subjects that have to be studied at a school or college: *the national core curriculum* | *the core subjects of English, maths, and science* | *Schools have to deliver the core skills.* THESAURUS MAIN **2 core business/activities/operations etc** the main business or activities of a company or organization: *The core business of airlines is flying people and cargo from place to place.* | *the company's core product* **3 core values/beliefs** the values or beliefs that are most important to someone: *the core values of American liberalism, such as taxing the rich to help the poor*

core³ AWL *v* [T] to remove the centre from a fruit

co·re·li·gion·ist /ˌkəʊrɪˈlɪdʒənɪst $ ˌkoʊ-/ *n* [C] *formal* someone who is a member of the same religion as you

cor·er /ˈkɔːrə $ -ər/ *n* [C] a specially shaped knife for taking the hard centres out of fruit

co·res·pon·dent /ˌkəʊrəˈspɒndənt $ ˌkoʊrəˈspɑːn-/ *n* [C] someone whose name is given in a DIVORCE because they have had sex with the wife or husband of the person who wants the divorce → **respondent**

cor·gi /ˈkɔːgi $ ˈkɔːrgi/ *n* [C] a small dog with short legs and a pointed nose

co·ri·an·der /ˌkɒriˈændə $ ˌkɔːriˈændər/ *n* [U] *BrE* a herb, used especially in Asian and Mexican cooking SYN **cilantro** *AmE*

co·rin·thi·an, **Corinthian** /kəˈrɪnθiən/ *adj* relating to AMATEURS who do a sport because they enjoy it, rather than for money: *The game evolved from a purely corinthian pastime to an internationally recognised entity.*

cork¹ /kɔːk $ kɔːrk/ *n* **1** [U] the BARK (=outer part) of a tree from southern Europe and North Africa, used to make things: *a cork bulletin board* **2** [C] a long round piece of cork or plastic which is put into the top of a bottle, especially a wine bottle, to keep liquid inside

CORK

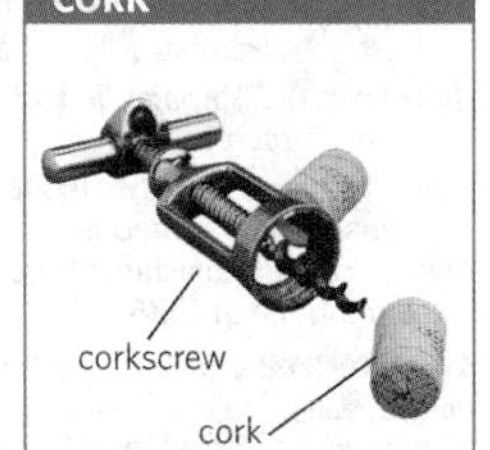

cork² *v* [T] to close a bottle by blocking the hole at the top tightly with a long round piece of cork or plastic OPP **uncork**

cork·age /ˈkɔːkɪdʒ $ ˈkɔːr-/ *n* [U] *BrE* the charge made by a hotel or restaurant for allowing people to bring in their own alcoholic drinks

corked /kɔːkt $ kɔːrkt/ *adj* corked wine tastes bad because a fault in the cork has allowed air into the bottle

cork·er /ˈkɔːkə $ ˈkɔːrkər/ *n* [C] *BrE old-fashioned* someone or something you think is very good —**corking** *adj*

cork·screw¹ /ˈkɔːkskruː $ ˈkɔːrk-/ *n* [C] a tool made of twisted metal that you use to pull a CORK out of a bottle → see picture at CORK

corkscrew² *adj* [only before noun] twisted or curly SYN **spiral**: *corkscrew curls*

cor·mo·rant /ˈkɔːmərənt $ ˈkɔːr-/ *n* [C] a large black seabird which has a long neck and eats fish

corn /kɔːn $ kɔːrn/ ●●○ S3 *n*
1 [U] *BrE* plants such as wheat, BARLEY, and OATS or their seeds: *fields of corn* | *an* ***ear of corn*** (=the top part of this plant where the seeds grow)
2 [U] **a)** *AmE* a tall plant with large yellow seeds that grow together on a COB (=long hard part), which is cooked and eaten as a vegetable or fed to animals SYN **maize** *BrE*: *All our chickens are fed on corn.* → CORN ON THE COB **b)** the seeds of this plant → SWEETCORN, see picture at VEGETABLE[1]
3 [C] a painful area of thick hard skin on your foot

corn·ball /ˈkɔːnbɔːl $ ˈkɔːrnbɒːl/ *adj* [only before noun] *AmE informal* cornball humour is extremely simple, old-fashioned, and silly: *Country and western songs always have such cornball titles.*

ˈcorn bread *n* [U] bread made from CORNMEAL

ˈcorn chip *n* [C] crushed MAIZE formed into a small flat piece, cooked in oil, and eaten cold, especially in the US

corn·cob /ˈkɔːnkɒb $ ˈkɔːrnkɑːb/ (*also* **cob**) *n* [C] the hard part of a corn plant that the yellow seeds grow on

corn·crake /ˈkɔːnkreɪk $ ˈkɔːrn-/ *n* [C] a European bird with a loud sharp cry

ˈcorn ˌdolly *n* [C] *BrE* a figure made in the past from wheat plants to celebrate the HARVEST

cor·ne·a /ˈkɔːniə $ ˈkɔːr-/ *n* [C] the transparent protective covering on the outer surface of your eye —**corneal** *adj*

corned beef /ˌkɔːnd ˈbiːf◂ $ ˌkɔːrnd-/ *n* [U] **1** *BrE* BEEF that has been cooked and preserved in a can **2** *AmE* BEEF that has been covered in salt water and spices to preserve it

cor·ner¹ /ˈkɔːnə $ ˈkɔːrnər/ ●●● S1 W2 *n*
1 WHERE TWO LINES/EDGES MEET [C] the point at which two lines or edges meet: *He pulled a dirty handkerchief out by its corner and waved it at me.* | **[+of]** *Their initials were sewn on the corner of every pillow.* | **in the corner (of sth)** *The TV station's name appears in the corner of the screen.* | **on the corner (of sth)** *Jessie sat on the corner of her bed.* | **three-cornered/four-cornered etc** *a three-cornered hat*
2 ROAD [C usually singular] **a)** the point where two roads meet: **[+of]** *Ruth walked with her as far as the corner of the road.* | **on the corner** *The hotel is on the corner of 5th and Maine.* | **at the corner** *Several women were standing at the corner, talking to two police officers.* | *kids hanging around on* ***street corners*** **b)** a point in a road where it turns sharply: *He had tried to* ***take*** *the* ***corner*** *too quickly, and had lost control of the car.* | *The petrol station is* ***around the corner****.*
3 CORNER OF A ROOM/BOX [C usually singular] the place inside a room or box where two walls or sides meet: **in the corner (of sth)** *There was an old piano in the corner of the living room.* | **corner table/seat** *I reserved a corner table in my favourite restaurant.*
4 MOUTH/EYE [C] the sides of your mouth or eyes: *A tear appeared in the corner of his eye.*
5 DIFFICULT SITUATION [singular] a difficult situation that you cannot easily escape from: **back/box/force/push sb into a corner** (=put someone into a situation where they do not have any choices about what to do) *Don't let your enemies back you into a corner.* | *The writers have* ***painted themselves into a corner*** *by killing off all the most popular characters in the first series.* | *He found himself in a* ***tight corner*** (=a very difficult situation) *looking for a way to get out.*
6 SPORTS [C] **a)** a kick or hit that one team is allowed to take from one of the corners of their opponent's end of the field **b)** any of the four corners of the area in which the competitors fight in BOXING or WRESTLING, especially one of the two corners where the competitors go in between ROUNDS
7 DISTANT PLACE [C] a distant place in another part of the world: **[+of]** *She's gone off to work in some remote corner of the world.* | *People came from* ***the four corners of the world*** (=from lots of different places) *to make America their new home.*
8 see sth out of the corner of your eye to notice something accidentally, without turning your head towards it or looking for it: *Out of the corner of her eye she saw the dog running towards her.*
9 (just) around/round the corner a) near: *There's a bus stop*

just around the corner. **b)** likely to happen soon: *Economic recovery is just around the corner.*
10 turn the corner to start to become successful or to feel better or happier, after a time when you have been unsuccessful, ill, or unhappy: *We knew Dad had turned the corner when he started complaining about the hospital food.*
11 fight your corner/fight sb's corner *BrE* to try very hard to defend yourself in a discussion or argument, or to do this for someone else: *My line manager supports me, and says she's willing to fight my corner.*
12 cut corners to save time, money, or energy by doing things quickly and not as carefully as you should: *Don't try to cut corners when you're decorating.*
13 cut a corner to go across the corner of something, especially a road, instead of staying next to the edges
14 have/get a corner on sth to be the only company, organization etc that has a particular product, ability, advantage etc: *London does not have a corner on film festivals.* | *The company admitted reducing prices to* ***get a corner on the market***. → KITTY-CORNER

C

corner² *v* **1** [T] to force a person or animal into a position from which they cannot easily escape: *Once the dog was cornered, he began to growl.* **THESAURUS** CATCH **2** [T] to go to someone who is trying to avoid you, and make them listen to you: *Later, he cornered Jenny on the stairs and asked her what was wrong.* **3 corner the market** to gain control of the whole supply of a particular kind of goods: *They've been trying to corner the market by buying up all the wheat in sight.* **4** [I] if a car corners, it goes around a corner or bend in the road

ˈcorner shop *n* [C] *BrE* a small shop near houses, that sells food, cigarettes, and other things needed every day → **convenience store**

cor·ner·stone /ˈkɔːnəstəʊn $ ˈkɔːrnərstoʊn/ *n* [C] **1** something that is extremely important because everything else depends on it: **[+of]** *The magazine became the cornerstone of McFadden's publishing empire.* **THESAURUS** BASIS **2** a stone at one of the bottom corners of a building, often put in place at a special ceremony SYN **foundation stone**

cor·net /ˈkɔːnɪt $ kɔːrˈnet/ *n* [C] **1** a musical instrument like a small TRUMPET → see picture at **BRASS 2** *BrE* a container made of very thin cake, that you hold in your hand and eat ICE CREAM from SYN **cone**

ˈcorn exˌchange *n* [C] *BrE* a place where CORN(1) used to be bought and sold

corn·flakes /ˈkɔːnfleɪks $ ˈkɔːrn-/ *n* [plural] small flat pieces of crushed CORN(1), usually eaten at breakfast with milk

corn·flour /ˈkɔːnflaʊə $ ˈkɔːrnflaʊr/ *n* [U] *BrE* fine white flour made from CORN(2), used in cooking to make soups and sauces thicker SYN **cornstarch** *AmE*

corn·flow·er /ˈkɔːnflaʊə $ ˈkɔːrnflaʊər/ *n* [C] a wild plant with blue flowers

cor·nice /ˈkɔːnɪs $ ˈkɔːr-/ *n* [C] wood or PLASTER that runs along the top edge of a wall, used for decoration: *A carved cornice runs around the high-ceilinged room.*

cor·niche /kɔːˈniːʃ $ kɔːr-/ *n* [C] a road built along a coast

Cor·nish pas·ty /ˌkɔːnɪʃ ˈpæsti $ ˌkɔːr-/ *n* [C] a folded piece of PASTRY, baked with meat and potatoes in it, for one person to eat

ˈcorn ˌliquor *n* [U] *AmE* CORN WHISKEY

corn·meal /ˈkɔːnmiːl $ ˈkɔːrn-/ *n* [U] a rough type of flour made from dried crushed CORN(2)

ˌcorn on the ˈcob *n* [U] the top part of a CORN(2) plant on which yellow seeds grow, cooked and eaten as a vegetable

corn pone /ˈkɔːn pəʊn $ ˈkɔːrn poʊn/ *n* [U] a kind of American bread made from cornmeal

corn·rows /ˈkɔːnrəʊz $ ˈkɔːrnroʊz/ *n* [plural] a way of having your hair in small tight PLAITS in lines along your head

corn·starch /ˈkɔːnstɑːtʃ $ ˈkɔːrnstɑːrtʃ/ *n* [U] *AmE* CORNFLOUR

ˌcorn ˈsyrup *n* [U] a very sweet thick liquid made from CORN(2), used in cooking

cor·nu·co·pi·a /ˌkɔːnjəˈkəʊpiə $ ˌkɔːrnəˈkoʊ-/ *n* [singular] **1** a container in the shape of an animal's horn, full of fruit and flowers, used to represent a time when there are large supplies of food **2** *literary* a lot of good things: **[+of]** *a cornucopia of delights*

ˈcorn ˌwhiskey (*also* **corn liquor**) *n* [U] *AmE* a strong alcoholic drink made from CORN(2)

corn·y /ˈkɔːni $ ˈkɔːrni/ *adj* too silly and repeated too often to be funny or interesting: *corny jokes* | *I know it sounds corny, but I dream about her every night.*

co·rol·la·ry /kəˈrɒləri $ ˈkɔːrəleri, ˈkɑː-/ ●○○ *n* (*plural* **corollaries**) [C] *formal* something that is the direct result of something else: **[+of/to]** *Is social inequality the inevitable corollary of economic freedom?*

co·ro·na /kəˈrəʊnə $ -ˈroʊ-/ *n* [C] the shining circle of light seen around the Sun when the Moon passes in front of it in an ECLIPSE

cor·o·na·ry¹ /ˈkɒrənəri $ ˈkɔːrəneri, ˈkɑː-/ *adj* relating to the heart SYN **cardiac**: *coronary disease*

coronary² *n* (*plural* **coronaries**) [C] *informal* if someone has a coronary, their heart suddenly stops working because the flow of blood to it has been blocked by a small piece of solid blood SYN **heart attack**

ˌcoronary ˈartery *n* [C] one of the two ARTERIES that supply blood to the heart

ˌcoronary thromˈbosis *n* [C,U] a disease which causes someone's heart to suddenly stop working, because the flow of blood to it has been blocked by a small piece of solid blood SYN **coronary**

cor·o·na·tion /ˌkɒrəˈneɪʃən◂ $ ˌkɔː-, ˌkɑː-/ *n* [C] the ceremony at which someone is officially made king or queen → **crown**

cor·o·ner /ˈkɒrənə $ ˈkɔːrənər, ˈkɑː-/ ●○○ *n* [C] an official whose job is to discover the cause of someone's death, especially if they died in a sudden or unusual way: *The coroner recorded a verdict of death by natural causes.* | *the* ***coroner's court***

cor·o·net /ˈkɒrənɪt $ ˌkɔːrəˈnet, ˌkɑː-/ *n* [C] a small CROWN worn by princes or other members of a royal family, especially on formal occasions

Corp. /kɔːp $ kɔːrp/ **1** the abbreviation of ***corporation***: *Microsoft Corp.* **2** the abbreviation of ***corporal***

cor·po·ra /ˈkɔːpərə $ ˈkɔːr-/ a plural of CORPUS

cor·po·ral /ˈkɔːpərəl $ ˈkɔːr-/ *n* [C] a low rank in the army, air force etc

ˌcorporal ˈpunishment *n* [U] punishment that involves hitting someone, especially in schools and prisons → **capital punishment**: *Corporal punishment was abolished in Britain in 1986.*

cor·po·rate /ˈkɔːpərət $ ˈkɔːr-/ ●●○ AWL *adj* [only before noun]
1 belonging to or relating to a corporation: *The company is moving its corporate headquarters* (=main offices) *from New York to Houston.* | *Vince is vice-president of corporate communications.* | *Corporate America is not about to be converted to the environmentalist cause.* | *changing the* ***corporate culture*** (=the way that people in a corporation think and behave) *to accept family-friendly policies* | *an advertising campaign intended to reinforce our* ***corporate identity*** (=the way a company presents itself to the public) | *the yacht can be hired for* ***corporate hospitality*** (=entertainment provided by companies for their customers)
2 shared by or involving all the members of a group: *corporate responsibility*
3 used to describe a group of organizations that form a single group: *The university is a* ***corporate body*** *made up of several different colleges.* —**corporately** *adv*

cor·po·ra·tion /ˌkɔːpəˈreɪʃən $ ˌkɔːr-/ ●○○ AWL *n* [C]
1 a big company, or a group of companies acting together as a single organization: *He works for a large American corporation.* | *multinational corporations* | *the Siemens*

Corporation | **corporation tax** (=tax that companies have to pay on their profits) **THESAURUS** ➤ **COMPANY**
2 an organization or group of organizations that work together for a particular purpose and are officially recognized as one: *the New Orleans Citywide Development Corporation* | *a housing corporation*
3 *BrE old use* a group of people elected to govern a town or city (SYN) **council**

cor·po·ra·tis·m /ˈkɔːpərətɪzəm $ ˈkɔːr-/ *n* [U] the power and influence that large corporations have

cor·po·re·al /kɔːˈpɔːriəl $ kɔːr-/ *adj formal* **1** relating to the body, rather than to the mind, feelings, or spirit (SYN) **physical**: *corporeal desires* **2** existing in a physical form and able to be touched

corps /kɔː $ kɔːr/ ●○○ *n* (*plural* **corps** /kɔːz $ kɔːrz/) [C]
1 a group in an army with special duties and responsibilities: *the medical corps* | *the U.S. Army Corps of Engineers*
2 a group of people who work together to do a particular job: *the president's press corps* | *the diplomatic corps*
3 *technical* a trained army unit made of two or more DIVISIONS (=groups of soldiers)

corpse /kɔːps $ kɔːrps/ ●●○ *n* [C] the dead body of a person (SYN) **body**: *The corpse was found by children playing in the woods.*

cor·pu·lent /ˈkɔːpjələnt $ ˈkɔːr-/ *adj formal* fat —**corpulence** *n* [U]

cor·pus /ˈkɔːpəs $ ˈkɔːr-/ *n* (*plural* **corpuses** *or* **corpora** /-pərə/) [C] **1** *formal* a collection of all the writing of a particular kind or by a particular person: *the entire corpus of Shakespeare's works* **2** *technical* a large collection of written or spoken language, that is used for studying the language: *a corpus of spoken English* → **HABEAS CORPUS**

cor·pus·cle /ˈkɔːpəsəl, kɔːˈpʌ- $ ˈkɔːrpə-/ *n* [C] one of the red or white cells in the blood

cor·ral¹ /kəˈrɑːl $ kəˈræl/ *n* [C] a fairly small enclosed area where cattle, horses etc can be kept temporarily, especially in North America

corral² *v* (**corralled**, **corralling** *BrE*, **corraled**, **corraling** *AmE*) [T] **1** to make animals move into a corral: *They corralled the cattle before loading them onto the truck.*
2 to keep people in a particular area, especially in order to control them: *Once at the airport, we were herded to the gate and corralled into a small room.*

cor·rect¹ /kəˈrekt/ ●●● (S1) (W2) *adj*
1 having no mistakes (SYN) **right** (OPP) **incorrect**: *If my calculations are correct, we're about ten miles from Exeter.* | *Score one point for each* ***correct answer****.* | *You are absolutely correct, the Missouri is the longest river in the US.* | **factually/grammatically/anatomically etc correct** *The sentence is grammatically correct, but doesn't sound natural.* **THESAURUS** ➤ **RIGHT**

> **REGISTER**
> In everyday English, people usually say **right** rather than **correct**: *Are you sure you've got the* ***right*** *address?*

2 suitable and right for a particular situation: *What's the correct procedure in cases like this?* | *The correct way to lift heavy weights is to make sure that your back is straight.*
3 correct behaviour is formal and polite (SYN) **proper**: *It was not considered correct for young ladies to go out on their own.* —**correctly** *adv*: *If I remember correctly, he's Spanish.* | *We must make sure that things are done correctly.* —**correctness** *n* [U]

correct² ●●○ (S3) *v* [T]
1 to make something right or to make it work the way it should: *Some eyesight problems are relatively easy to correct.* | *You have the right to see a copy of your file, and to correct any mistakes you may find.*

> **REGISTER**
> In everyday British English, people usually say **put** something **right** rather than **correct** something: *The problem should be fairly easy to* ***put right****.*

2 to show someone that something is wrong, and make it right: *Correct my pronunciation if it's wrong.* | *'She's in Ireland now.' 'She was,' Farrell corrected him.* | **correct yourself** *'I,' Lady Deverill corrected herself, 'we are very happy here.'*
3 if a teacher corrects a student's written work, he or she writes marks on it to show the mistakes in it
4 correct me if I'm wrong *spoken* used when you are not sure that what you are going to say is true or not: *Correct me if I'm wrong, but didn't you say you'd never met him before?*
5 I stand corrected *formal spoken* used to admit that something you have said is wrong after someone has told you it is wrong

cor·rec·tion /kəˈrekʃən/ ●●○ *n*
1 [C] a change made in something in order to make it right or better: *I just need to* ***make*** *a few* ***corrections****, and then we can send it to the printer.*
2 [U] *spoken* used to say that what you have just said is wrong and you want to change it: *That will basically cover 50 ... correction 60 percent of all charges.*
3 [U] the act of changing something in order to make it right or better: *Please hand in your papers for correction.*
4 [U] *old-fashioned* punishment for people who have done something wrong or illegal

cor·rec·tion·al /kəˈrekʃənəl/ *adj* [only before noun] *technical* relating to the punishment of criminals: **correctional facility/institution/centre** (=a prison)

corˈrection ˌfluid *n* [U] a special white liquid used for covering mistakes made when writing something → see picture at **STATIONERY**

cor·rec·ti·tude /kəˈrektɪtjuːd $ -tuːd/ *n* [U] *formal* correctness of behaviour

cor·rec·tive¹ /kəˈrektɪv/ *adj* [usually before noun] intended to make something right or better again: *corrective surgery* | **corrective action/measures** *corrective measures to deal with the country's serious economic decline*

corrective² *n* [C usually singular] *formal* something that is intended to correct a fault or mistake: **[+to]** *The biography is a useful corrective to the myths that have grown up around this man.*

cor·rel·ate¹ /ˈkɒrəleɪt $ ˈkɔː-, ˈkɑː-/ ●○○ *v* [I,T] if two or more facts, ideas etc correlate or if you correlate them, they are closely connected to each other or one causes the other: **[+with]** *Poverty and poor housing correlate with a shorter life expectancy.* | **correlate strongly/significantly/closely** *Lack of prenatal care correlates strongly with premature birth.*

cor·re·late² /ˈkɒrələt $ ˈkɔː-, ˈkɑː-/ *n* [C] either of two things that correlate with each other

cor·re·la·tion /ˌkɒrəˈleɪʃən $ ˌkɔː-, ˌkɑː-/ ●○○ *n* [C,U] a connection between two ideas, facts etc, especially when one may be the cause of the other: **[+between]** *a strong correlation between urban deprivation and poor health* | **strong/high/close/significant etc correlation** *There is a direct correlation between the best-known brands and the best-selling brands.* | **[+with]** *There's also some correlation with social class.*

cor·rel·a·tive /kəˈrelətɪv/ *adj formal* two or more facts, ideas etc that are correlative are closely related or dependent on each other (SYN) **related**: *rights and their correlative responsibilities* —**correlative** *n* [C]

cor·re·spond /ˌkɒrəˈspɒnd $ ˌkɔːrəˈspɑːnd, ˌkɑː-/ ●○○ (AWL) *v* [I]
1 if two things or ideas correspond, the parts or information in one relate to the parts or information in the other: *The two halves of the document did not correspond.* | **[+with/to]** *The numbers correspond to points on the map.*
2 to be very similar to or the same as something else: **[+to]** *The French 'baccalauréate' exam* ***roughly corresponds*** *to English A levels.* | **correspond closely/exactly/precisely to sth** *The description of these events corresponds closely to other accounts written at the time.*
3 to write letters to someone and receive letters from them: *For the next three years they corresponded regularly.* |

[+with] *She stopped corresponding with him after the death of her mother.*

cor·re·spon·dence /ˌkɒrəˈspɒndəns $ ˌkɔːrəˈspɑːn-, ˌkɑː-/ ●○○ AWL *n* [U]
1 the letters that someone sends and receives, especially official or business letters: *A secretary came in twice a week to deal with his correspondence.*
2 the process of sending and receiving letters: *The magazine is unable to* ***enter into*** *any* ***correspondence*** *on medical matters.* | **(be in) correspondence with sb** *He had been in correspondence with her for several years before they finally met.* | *All correspondence between us must cease.*
3 a relationship or connection between two or more ideas or facts: **[+between]** *There was no correspondence between the historical facts and Johnson's account of them.*

C

corre'spondence ˌcourse *n* [C] a course of lessons in which the student works at home and sends completed work to their teacher by post: *I'm taking a correspondence course in business studies.*

cor·re·spon·dent /ˌkɒrəˈspɒndənt $ ˌkɔːrəˈspɑːn-, ˌkɑː-/ ●○○ *n* [C]
1 someone who is employed by a newspaper or a television station etc to report news from a particular area or on a particular subject → **reporter**: **political/foreign/legal etc correspondent** *the political correspondent for 'The Times'* | *Our correspondent in South Africa sent this report.*
2 someone who writes letters: *I'm not a very good correspondent, I'm afraid.*

cor·re·spon·ding /ˌkɒrəˈspɒndɪŋ◂ $ ˌkɔːrəˈspɑːn-, ˌkɑː-/ ●○○ AWL *adj* [only before noun]
1 caused by or connected with something you have already mentioned: *The war and the corresponding fall in trade have had a devastating effect on the country.*
2 having similar qualities or a similar size, position etc to something else SYN **equivalent**: *Sales are up 10% on the corresponding period last year.* —**correspondingly** *adv*: *As his political power has shrunk, he has grown correspondingly more dependent on the army.*

cor·ri·dor /ˈkɒrədɔː $ ˈkɔːrədər, ˈkɑː-/ ●●○ S3 W3 *n* [C]
1 a long narrow passage on a train or between rooms in a building, with doors leading off it: **in the corridor** *We had to wait outside in the corridor until our names were called.* | **down/along the corridor** *She hurried down the corridor.* | *Go down here and the bathroom's at the end of the corridor.*
2 a narrow area of land between cities or countries that has different qualities or features from the land around it: *the industrial corridor that connects Querétaro with Mexico City*
3 corridors of power the places where important government decisions are made

cor·rie /ˈkɒri $ ˈkɔː- ˈkɑː-/ *n* [C] *BrE technical* a deep bowl-shaped area on a mountain

cor·rob·o·rate /kəˈrɒbəreɪt $ kəˈrɑː-/ *v* [T] *formal* to provide information that supports or helps to prove someone else's statement, idea etc SYN **back up**: *We now have new evidence to corroborate the defendant's story.* | *Experiments elsewhere corroborate these results.* —**corroboration** /kəˌrɒbəˈreɪʃən $ -ˌrɑː-/ *n* [U] —**corroborative** /kəˈrɒbərətɪv $ -ˈrɑːbəreɪ-/ *adj*: *corroborative evidence*

cor·rode /kəˈrəʊd $ -ˈroʊd/ *v* [I,T] **1** if metal corrodes, or if something corrodes it, it is slowly destroyed by the effect of water, chemicals etc: *Acidic water will corrode the pipes.* **2** *written* to gradually make something weaker or destroy it completely: *Corruption has corroded our confidence in the police force.*

cor·ro·sion /kəˈrəʊʒən $ -ˈroʊ-/ *n* [U] the gradual destruction of metal by the effect of water, chemicals etc or a substance such as RUST produced by this process: *They are sprayed with oil to prevent corrosion.* | *Check for signs of corrosion.*

cor·ro·sive /kəˈrəʊsɪv $ -ˈroʊ-/ *adj* **1** a corrosive liquid such as an acid can destroy metal, plastic etc: *a highly corrosive substance* **2** *written* gradually making something weaker, and possibly destroying it SYN **damaging**: *the corrosive effect of money in sport*

cor·ru·gated /ˈkɒrəgeɪtɪd $ ˈkɔː-, ˈkɑː-/ *adj* in the shape of waves or folds, or made like this in order to give something strength: *corrugated cardboard*

cor·rupt¹ /kəˈrʌpt/ ●●○ *adj*
1 using your power in a dishonest or illegal way in order to get an advantage for yourself OPP **incorruptible**: *Corrupt judges have taken millions of dollars in bribes.* **THESAURUS** DISHONEST
2 immoral or dishonest: *a corrupt society* | *officials engaged in corrupt practices*
3 something that is corrupt is not pure or has been damaged or partly ruined: *corrupt data* —**corruptly** *adv* —**corruptness** *n* [U]

corrupt² ●○○ *v* [T]
1 to encourage someone to start behaving in an immoral or dishonest way: *Young prisoners are being corrupted by the older, long-term offenders.*
2 to change the traditional form of something, such as a language, so that it becomes worse than it was: *The culture has been corrupted by Western influences.*
3 to change the information in a computer, so that the computer does not work properly anymore: *a virus which corrupts the data on your hard drive* —**corruptible** *adj* —**corruptibility** /kəˌrʌptəˈbɪləti/ *n* [U]

cor·rup·tion /kəˈrʌpʃən/ ●●○ *n*
1 [U] dishonest, illegal, or immoral behaviour, especially from someone with power: *officials charged with bribery and corruption* | *The investigation uncovered* ***widespread corruption*** *within the police force.* | **political/official corruption**
2 [C usually singular] *technical* a changed form of something, for example a word: *The word 'Thursday' is a corruption of 'Thor's Day'.*

CORSAGE

cor·sage /kɔːˈsɑːʒ $ kɔːr-/ *n* [C] a group of small flowers that a woman fastens to her clothes on a special occasion such as a wedding

cor·set /ˈkɔːsɪt $ ˈkɔːr-/ *n* [C] a piece of tight-fitting underwear that women wore especially in the past to make them look thinner

cor·tege /kɔːˈteɪʒ $ kɔːrˈteʒ/ *n* [C] a line of people or cars that move along slowly in a funeral

cor·tex /ˈkɔːteks $ ˈkɔːr-/ *n* (*plural* **cortices** /-təsiːz/) [C] the outer layer of an organ in your body, especially your brain —**cortical** /ˈkɔːtɪkəl $ ˈkɔːr-/ *adj*

cor·ti·sone /ˈkɔːtəzəʊn $ ˈkɔːrtəsoʊn/ *n* [U] a HORMONE that is used especially in the treatment of injuries and diseases such as ARTHRITIS: *a cortisone injection*

cor·us·ca·ting /ˈkɒrəskeɪtɪŋ $ ˈkɔː-, ˈkɑː-/ *adj literary* attractive and having a lot of energy, or shining brightly: *a play with scenes of coruscating brilliance*

cos¹, **'cos**, **coz** /kəz/ *conjunction BrE spoken informal* because: *I don't get out much now cos of the children.*

cos² *n* (*plural* **coses** *or* **cos**) [C,U] *BrE* a type of LETTUCE SYN **romaine**

cos³ /kɒz, kɒs $ kɑːs/ *technical* the written abbreviation of ***cosine***

cosh¹ /kɒʃ $ kɑːʃ/ *n* [C] **1** a heavy weapon in the shape of a short thick pipe **2 under the cosh** *BrE informal* in a difficult situation and under a lot of pressure: *A lot of people are under the cosh financially at present.*

cosh² *v* [T] to hit someone with a cosh

co·sig·na·to·ry /ˌkəʊˈsɪgnətəri $ ˌkoʊˈsɪgnətɔːri/ *n* (*plural* **cosignatories**) [C] one of a group of people who sign a legal document for their department, organization, country etc: *Both cosignatories must sign the cheque.*

co·sine /ˈkəʊsaɪn $ ˈkoʊ-/ *n* [C] *technical* the measurement of an ACUTE angle in a TRIANGLE with a RIGHT ANGLE, that is calculated by dividing the length of the side next to it by the length of the HYPOTENUSE → **sine**

cos·met·ic /kɒzˈmetɪk $ kɑːz-/ *adj* **1** dealing with the outside appearance rather than the important part of something SYN **superficial**: *We're making a few cosmetic changes to the house before we sell it.* | *Many MPs denounced the resolution as a* ***cosmetic exercise*** (=something which will look good, but have no real effect). **2** intended to make your hair, skin, body etc look more attractive: *the cosmetics industry* | *cosmetic products* | *Are you on the diet for health or cosmetic reasons?*

cos·met·ics /kɒzˈmetɪks $ kɑːz-/ ●○○ *n* [plural] creams, powders etc that you use on your face and body in order to look more attractive → **make-up**: *a range of cosmetics and toiletries*

cosˌmetic ˈsurgery *n* [U] medical operations that improve your appearance after you have been injured, or because you want to look more attractive SYN **plastic surgery**

cos·mic /ˈkɒzmɪk $ ˈkɑːz-/ ●○○ *adj*
1 relating to space or the universe
2 extremely large: *a scandal of cosmic proportions*
—**cosmically** /-kli/ *adv*

ˌcosmic ˈray *n* [C usually plural] a stream of RADIATION reaching the Earth from space

cos·mog·o·ny /kɒzˈmɒgəni $ kɑːzˈmɑː-/ *n* (*plural* **cosmogonies**) [C,U] the origin of the universe, or a set of ideas about this

cos·mol·o·gy /kɒzˈmɒlədʒi $ kɑːzˈmɑː-/ *n* [U] the science of the origin and structure of the universe, especially as studied in ASTRONOMY

cos·mo·naut /ˈkɒzmənɔːt $ ˈkɑːzmənɒːt/ *n* [C] an ASTRONAUT from the former Soviet Union

cos·mo·pol·i·tan¹ /ˌkɒzməˈpɒlətən◂ $ ˌkɑːzməˈpɑː-/ *adj* **1** a cosmopolitan place has people from many different parts of the world - use this to show approval: *a vibrant cosmopolitan city* | *a lively hotel with a cosmopolitan atmosphere* **2** a cosmopolitan person, belief, opinion etc shows a wide experience of different people and places: *Brigitta has such a cosmopolitan outlook on life.*

cosmopolitan² *n* [C] someone who has travelled a lot and feels at home in any part of the world

cos·mos /ˈkɒzmɒs $ ˈkɑːzməs, -moʊs/ *n* **the cosmos** the whole universe, especially when you think of it as a system → **cosmic**

cos·set /ˈkɒsɪt $ ˈkɑː-/ *v* [T] to give someone as much care and attention as you can, especially too much SYN **pamper**: *He cosseted her with flowers and champagne.*

cost¹ /kɒst $ kɒːst/ ●●● S1 W1 *n*
1 [C] the amount of money that you have to pay in order to buy, do, or produce something: **[+of]** *the cost of accommodation* | *I offered to* ***pay the cost of*** *the taxi.* | *Insurance to* ***cover the cost of*** *a funeral is possible.* | *This doesn't include* ***the cost of*** *repairing the damage.* | *The new building's going up* ***at a cost of*** *$82 million.* | ***low cost*** *housing* | *the* ***high cost*** *of production* | *Travel insurance is included* ***at no extra cost****.* | *The funds will just cover the museum's* ***running costs****.* → COST OF LIVING

> **REGISTER**
> In everyday English, people usually ask **how much did it cost?** or **how much was it?** rather than using the noun **cost**: *What was the* ***cost*** *of the accommodation?*
> → ***How much*** *did the accommodation* ***cost****?* | *I'll find out the* ***cost****.* → *I'll find out* ***how much*** *it* ***costs/is****.*

2 costs [plural] **a)** the money that you must regularly spend in order to run a business, a home, a car etc: **reduce/cut costs** *We have to cut costs in order to remain competitive.* | *At this rate we'll barely* ***cover*** *our* ***costs*** (=make enough money to pay for the things we have bought). | *the travel* ***costs incurred*** *in attending the meeting* (=money you have to spend) | *Because of the engine's efficiency the car has very low* ***running costs*** (=the cost of owning and using a car or machine). **b)** (*also* **court costs**) the money that you must pay to lawyers etc if you are involved in a legal case in court, especially if you are found guilty: *Bellisario won the case and was awarded costs.* | *He was fined £1,000 and ordered to pay costs of £2,200.*
3 [C,U] something that you lose, give away, damage etc in order to achieve something: **at (a) cost to sb** *She had kept her promise to Christine, but at what cost to herself?* | **social/environmental etc cost** *They need to weigh up the* ***costs and benefits*** (=disadvantages and advantages) *of regulation.* | *He's determined to win,* ***whatever the cost*** (=no matter how much work, money, risk etc is needed). | *We must avoid a scandal* ***at all costs*** (=whatever happens).
4 [singular] *especially AmE* the price that someone pays for something that they are going to sell SYN **cost price**: **at cost** *His uncle's a car dealer and let him buy the car at cost* (=without making a profit).
5 know/find out/learn etc sth to your cost to realize something is true because you have had a very unpleasant experience: *Driving fast in wet conditions is dangerous, as my brother discovered to his cost!* → **count the cost** at COUNT¹(11)

> **THESAURUS**
> **cost** the amount of money you need to buy or do something. **Cost** is usually used when talking in a general way about whether something is expensive or cheap rather than when talking about exact prices: *The cost of running a car is increasing.* | *the cost of raw materials*
> **price** the amount of money you must pay for something that is for sale: *They sell good-quality clothes at reasonable prices.* | *the price of a plane ticket to New York*
> **value** the amount of money that something is worth: *A new kitchen can increase the value of your home.*
> **charge** the amount that you have to pay for a service or to use something: *Hotel guests may use the gym for a small charge.* | *bank charges*
> **fee** the amount you have to pay to enter a place or join a group, or for the services of a professional person such as a lawyer or a doctor: *There is no entrance fee.* | *The membership fee is £125 a year.* | *legal fees*
> **fare** the amount you have to pay to travel somewhere by bus, plane, train etc: *I didn't even have enough money for my bus fare.* | *fare increases*
> **rent** the amount you have to pay to live in or use a place that you do not own: *The rent on his apartment is $800 a month.*
> **rate** a charge that is set according to a standard scale: *Most TV stations offer special rates to local advertisers.*
> **toll** the amount you have to pay to travel on some roads or bridges: *You have to pay tolls on many French motorways.*

cost² ●●● S1 W2 *v*
1 (*past tense and past participle* **cost**) [linking verb] to have a particular price: *A full day's activities will cost you £45.* | *His proposals could cost the taxpayer around £8 billion a year.* | *How much would it cost us to replace?* | **not cost sb a penny** (=cost nothing) *It won't cost you a penny for the first six months.* | **cost a (small) fortune/a pretty penny** (=have a very high price) *It's costing us a fortune in phone bills.* | **cost a bomb/a packet** *BrE* (=have a very high price) *What a fantastic dress. It must have cost a bomb!* | *Lighting can change the look of a room and needn't* ***cost the earth*** (=have a price which is too high). | *Getting that insured is going to* ***cost*** *you* ***an arm and a leg*** (=have a very high price).

> **GRAMMAR: Linking verbs**
> **Cost** is a linking verb that links the subject of the sentence with a noun, often an amount: *Tickets cost $15.* | *A second-hand car doesn't cost much.*

2 cost sb their job/life/marriage etc when something makes you lose your job etc: *Joe's brave action cost him his life.* | *His strong stand on the issue could have cost him his job.* | *Bad management could be costing this club a chance at the title.*
3 cost sb dear/dearly to make someone suffer a lot or to lose something important: *A couple of missed chances in the first half cost them dear.* | *The scandal has cost Nicholson dearly.*
4 (*past tense and past participle* **costed**) [T] to calculate the total price of something or decide how much the price of something should be: *We'll get the plan costed before presenting it to the board.* GRAMMAR **Cost** is often passive in this meaning.
5 it will cost you *spoken* used to say that something will be expensive: *Tickets are available, but they'll cost you!*

C

THESAURUS

cost to have a particular price: *The book costs $25.* | *A new kitchen will cost you a lot of money.*
be *especially spoken* to cost a particular amount of money: *These shoes were only £5.*
be priced at sth to have a particular price - used when giving the exact price that a shop or company charges for something: *Tickets are priced at $20 for adults and $10 for kids.*
retail at sth to be sold in shops at a particular price - used especially in business: *The scissors retail at £1.99 in department stores.*
sell/go for sth used for saying what people usually pay for something: *Houses in this area sell for around £200,000.*
fetch used for saying what people pay for something, especially at a public sale: *The painting fetched over $8,000 at auction.*
set sb back sth *informal* to cost someone a lot of money: *A good set of speakers will set you back around £150.*
come to if a bill comes to a particular amount, it adds up to that amount: *The bill came to £100 between four of us.*

Cos·ta del Sol, the /ˌkɒstə del ˈsɒl $ ˌkoʊstə del ˈsoʊl/ a name for part of the Mediterranean Sea coast in southern Spain, especially the areas in and around Malaga and Marbella. It is very popular with British tourists, especially those going on PACKAGE HOLIDAYS.

co-star¹ /ˈkəʊ stɑː $ ˈkoʊ stɑːr/ *n* [C] one of two or more famous actors who appear together in a film or play THESAURUS ACTOR

co-star² *v* (**co-starred**, **co-starring**) [I] to be working in a film or play with other famous actors: **[+with/in]** *She's co-starring in a TV version of the 1960s thriller.* | *He co-starred with Bruce Willis in the movie 'Die Hard'.*

ˈcost-ˌbenefit *n* **cost-benefit analysis/study/approach** *technical* a way of calculating the methods or plans that will bring you the most BENEFITS (=advantages or help) for the smallest cost, especially in business

ˈcost-efˌfective, **cost effective** *adj* bringing the best possible profits or advantages for the lowest possible costs: **cost-effective way of doing sth** *the most cost-effective way of reducing carbon dioxide emissions* | *The procedure is quick, easy to use, and cost effective.* —**cost-effectively** *adv* —**cost-effectiveness** *n* [U]

cos·ter·mon·ger /ˈkɒstəˌmʌŋgə $ ˈkɑːstərˌmɑːŋgər, -ˌmʌŋ-/ *n* [C] *BrE old-fashioned* someone who sells fruit and vegetables in the street

cost·ing /ˈkɒstɪŋ $ ˈkɒːst-/ *n* [C,U] the process of calculating the cost of a future business activity, product etc, or the calculation itself: *the planning and costing of staffing levels* | *We were asked to prepare detailed costings for the scheme.*

cost·ly /ˈkɒstli $ ˈkɒːstli/ ●●○ *adj*
1 very expensive, especially wasting a lot of money: *a complex and costly procedure* | *Such a database would be extremely costly to set up.* THESAURUS EXPENSIVE
2 something that is costly causes a lot of problems or trouble: *His delay in making a decision could* **prove costly** *in the long run.* —**costliness** *n* [U]

ˌcost of ˈliving *n* **the cost of living** the amount of money you need to pay for the food, clothes etc you need to live: *Average wages have increased in line with the cost of living.*

ˌcost ˈprice *n* [U] the price that someone pays for something that they are going to sell

cos·tume /ˈkɒstjʊm $ ˈkɑːstuːm/ ●●○ *n*
1 [C] a set of clothes worn by an actor or by someone to make them look like something such as an animal, famous person etc → **outfit**: *the film's lavish costumes and spectacular sets* | *Hallowe'en costumes*
2 [C,U] clothes that are typical of a particular place or period of time in the past: *The dancers were in* **national costume**. | *performers dressed in* **period costume** (=the clothes of a period of history)
3 [C] *BrE* a SWIMMING COSTUME

ˈcostume ˌdrama *n* [C] a play, TV programme, or film that is about a particular time in history, in which people wear costumes from that time

ˈcostume ˌjewellery *n* [U] cheap jewellery that is often designed to look expensive

co·sy¹ *BrE*, **cozy** *AmE* /ˈkəʊzi $ ˈkoʊzi/ ●●○ *adj*
1 a place that is cosy is small, comfortable, and warm: *The living room was* **warm and cosy**. THESAURUS COMFORTABLE
2 a situation that is cosy is comfortable and friendly: *a cosy chat*
3 having a close connection or relationship, especially one you do not approve of: *He was accused of being too cosy with some clients.* —**cosily** *adv* —**cosiness** *n* [U]

cosy² *BrE*, **cozy** *AmE* *v* (**cosied**, **cosying**, **cosies**)
cosy up *phr v* **1** to sit so that you are touching someone, because you love them or for warmth SYN **snuggle** **2** to get into a warm and comfortable position SYN **snuggle up**: *When it's cold outside, why not cosy up with a good book?*
cosy up to sb *phr v* to try to have a friendly relationship with someone, especially someone more powerful than you - used to show disapproval: *He was accused of cosying up to the dictator.*

cosy³ *n* (*plural* **cosies**) [C] *BrE* a covering for a TEAPOT that keeps the tea inside from getting cold too quickly: *a tea cosy*

cot /kɒt $ kɑːt/ *n* [C] **1** *BrE* a small bed with high sides for a baby or young child SYN **crib** *AmE* **2** *AmE* a CAMP BED

ˈcot ˌdeath *n* [C] *BrE* the sudden and unexpected death of a baby while it is sleeping SYN **crib death** *AmE*

co·te·rie /ˈkəʊtəri $ ˈkoʊ-/ *n* [C] *formal* a small group of people who enjoy doing the same things together, and do not like including others → **clique**

co·ter·mi·nous /kəʊˈtɜːmɪnəs $ koʊˈtɜːr-/ *adj technical* **1** *formal* having the same pattern or features **2** coterminous countries share the same border

cot·tage /ˈkɒtɪdʒ $ ˈkɑː-/ ●●○ S3 W3 *n* [C] a small house in the country: *a country cottage* | *We're staying in a holiday cottage in Dorset.* → see picture at **HOUSE¹**

ˌcottage ˈcheese / $ ˈ.. ./ *n* [U] soft white cheese made from sour milk

ˌcottage ˈhospital *n* [C] a small hospital, usually in a country area

ˌcottage ˈindustry *n* [C] an industry that consists of people working at home: *Hand weaving is a flourishing cottage industry in the region.*

cot·tag·er /ˈkɒtɪdʒə $ ˈkɑːtɪdʒər/ *n* [C] a person in the past who lived in a cottage

cot·tag·ing /ˈkɒtɪdʒɪŋ $ ˈkɑː-/ *n* [U] *BrE informal* when a HOMOSEXUAL man goes to a public toilet with the intention of meeting other men for sex

cot·ton¹ /ˈkɒtn $ ˈkɑːtn/ ●●● W3 *n* [U]
1 cloth or thread made from the white hair of the cotton plant: *a white cotton shirt* | *Made from 100% cotton.*
2 a plant with white hairs on its seeds that are used for making cotton cloth and thread
3 *BrE* thread used for sewing: *a needle and cotton* | *a cotton*

reel (=small round tube which cotton thread is wound around) → see picture at REEL[2]
4 *AmE* COTTON WOOL

cotton² *v*
cotton on *phr v informal* to begin to understand something → **realize**: *It took me a while to cotton on.* | **[+to]** *Sarah soon cottoned on to what he was trying to do.*
cotton to sb/sth *phr v AmE informal* to begin to like a person, idea etc SYN **take to**: *I didn't cotton to her at first, but she's really nice.*

'cotton bud *n* [C] *BrE* a small thin stick with COTTON WOOL at each end, used for cleaning places that are hard to reach, such as inside your ears SYN **Q-tip** *AmE*

'cotton ˌcandy *n* [U] *AmE* CANDYFLOSS

'cotton gin *n* [C] a machine that separates the seeds of a cotton plant from the cotton

'cotton-ˌpicking *adj* [only before noun] *especially AmE old-fashioned* used to emphasize that you are annoyed or surprised: *Mind your own cotton-picking business!*

cot·ton·wood /ˈkɒtnwʊd $ ˈkɑː-/ *n* [C,U] a North American tree with seeds that look like white cotton

ˌcotton 'wool *n* [U] *BrE* **1** a soft mass of cotton that you use especially for cleaning and protecting wounds: *She put some disinfectant on a piece of cotton wool and dabbed it on her cheek.* → see picture at FIRST AID KIT **2 wrap sb (up) in cotton wool** to protect someone completely from the dangers, difficulties etc of life: *You can't wrap those kids in cotton wool all their lives.*

couch¹ /kaʊtʃ/ ●●● S3 *n* [C]
1 a comfortable piece of furniture big enough for two or three people to sit on SYN **sofa**, **settee**: *Tom offered to sleep on the couch.*
2 a long narrow bed for a doctor's or PSYCHIATRIST's patients to lie on

couch² *v* **be couched in sth** *formal* to be expressed in a particular way: *The offer was couched in legal jargon.*

cou·chette /kuːˈʃet/ *n* [C] *BrE* a narrow bed that folds down from the wall in a train, or a comfortable seat on a night train or boat → **sleeping car**

'couch poˌtato *n* [C] someone who spends a lot of time sitting and watching television

'couch ˌsurfing (*also* **'sofa ˌsurfing**) *n* [U] the practice of staying for free at the homes of friends or other people and sleeping on their couches, when you do not have a permanent home of your own or when travelling

cou·gar /ˈkuːɡə, -ɡɑː $ -ɡər, -ɡɑːr/ *n* [C] **1** a large brown wild cat from the mountains of western North America and South America SYN **mountain lion** → see picture at BIG CAT **2** *AmE informal* an older woman in a romantic or sexual relationship with a younger man

cough¹ /kɒf $ kɔːf/ ●●● S3 W3 *v* [I]
1 to suddenly push air out of your throat with a short sound, often repeatedly: *Matthew coughed and cleared his throat.* | *I think I'm getting a cold or flu – I've been coughing and sneezing all day.*
2 to make a sudden sound like someone coughing: *The engine coughed and spluttered, then stopped altogether.*
cough up *phr v*
1 *informal* to give someone money, information etc when you do not really want to: *Come on, cough up.* | **cough sth ↔ up** *Insurance companies had to cough up £10 million in storm damage claims.*
2 cough sth ↔ up to push something out of your throat or lungs into your mouth: *You must go to the doctor if you're coughing up blood.*

cough² ●●● S3 W3 *n* [C]
1 a medical condition that makes you cough a lot: *He's got a bad cough.* | *Symptoms include a sore throat and a nasty cough.* | *cough medicine*
2 [C] the action or sound made when you cough: *Stuart* ***gave*** *an embarrassed* ***cough***.

COLLOCATIONS

VERBS
have (got) a cough *I've had a cough for weeks now.*
get/catch a cough *A lot of people get coughs at this time of year.*

ADJECTIVES
a bad cough *Jason's at home with a bad cough.*
a nasty/violent cough (=a very bad cough) | **a smoker's cough** (=one caused by smoking) | **a dry cough** (=one that does not produce any liquid) | **a loose cough** (=one that produces liquid) | **a chesty cough** *BrE* (=one that affects your chest) | **a hacking cough** (=a bad cough with an unpleasant sound) | **a slight cough** (=one that is not very serious) | **a tickly cough** (=one that keeps irritating your throat) | **a persistent cough** (=one that is difficult to cure)

cough + NOUN
cough medicine/cough mixture/cough syrup (=liquid containing medicine for a cough) *You should take some cough medicine.*
a cough drop (*also* **a cough sweet** *BrE*) (=a sweet you suck to make a cough less irritating) *He was sucking on a cough sweet.*

'cough ˌmixture (*also* **'cough ˌsyrup**, **'cough ˌmedicine**) *n* [U] a thick, usually sweet, liquid containing medicine that helps you to stop coughing

could /kəd; *strong* kʊd/ ●●● S1 W1 *modal verb* (*negative short form* **couldn't**)
1 PAST ABILITY used as the past tense of 'can' to say what someone was able to do or was allowed to do in the past: *By the time she was eight, she could read Greek and Latin.* | *In those days you could buy a box of cigars for a dollar.* | *Could you hear what I was saying?* | *I couldn't get tickets after all, they were sold out.* | *I knew I couldn't afford the rent.* | *The teacher said we could all go home.*
2 POSSIBILITY **a)** used to say that something is possible or might happen: *Most accidents in the home could be prevented.* | *It could be weeks before we get a reply.* | *If you're not careful, you could get into even worse trouble.* | *A faulty connection* ***could easily*** (=would be likely to) *cause a fire.* **b)** used to say that something was a possibility in the past, but did not actually happen: *Somebody could have been killed.* | *I could have warned you if I had known where you were.* | *He could have escaped, but he chose to fight.*
3 EMPHASIZING YOUR FEELINGS *spoken* used to emphasize how happy, angry etc you are by saying how you want to express your feelings: *He irritates me so much I could scream.* | *I was so angry I could have killed her.* | *I was so relieved I could have kissed them all.*
4 REQUESTING *spoken* used to make a polite request: *Could you help me with these boxes?* | *Could I have a drink of water, please?* | *How about Sam? Could he come along too?* | *I wonder if I could just ask you to sign this.*
5 SUGGESTING used to suggest doing something: *You could ask your doctor for a check-up.* | *You* ***could always*** *try phoning her at the office.* | *Maybe we could get together sometime next week?* | *Couldn't you get one of your friends to help you?*
6 ANNOYANCE *spoken* used to show that you are annoyed about someone's behaviour: *You could have told me you were going to be late* (=you should have told me but you did not)*!* | *You* ***could at least*** *say that you're sorry.* | *How could you be so stupid!*
7 couldn't be better/worse/more pleased etc used to emphasize how good, bad etc something is: *Their lifestyles couldn't be more different.* | *'How are things?' 'Fine! Couldn't be better.'* | *Ordering online couldn't be simpler.*
8 I couldn't *BrE spoken* used to politely say that you do not want any more food or drink: *'Would you like another piece of pie?' 'Oh, no thanks, I couldn't.'*
9 could do with sth *spoken* to need or want something:

C

I could do with a hot drink. → **could do worse (than)** at WORSE[1](5), → **couldn't care less** at CARE[2](5), → **couldn't agree more** at AGREE(1)

GRAMMAR: Patterns with could

- You use **could** with the base form of the verb (=the infinitive without 'to'): *The teacher said we could go home.* | *He could be in his office.*
- You say **Could I?** when asking for permission: *Could I use your phone?*
- You say that something **could have** happened: *The team could have won.* | *They could already have gone home.*
- You use **couldn't** or **could not** in negative sentences: *We couldn't see anything.* | *That could not be true.*

GRAMMAR GUIDE ▶ VERBS

C

couldst /kʊdst/ *v* **thou couldst** *old use* words meaning 'you could'

cou·lis /ˈkuːli/ *n* (*plural* **coulis** /ˈkuːliz/) [C] a thin fruit sauce

coun·cil /ˈkaʊnsəl/ ●●○ (S3) (W3) *n* [C]
1 a group of people that are chosen to make rules, laws, or decisions, or to give advice: *the council for civil liberties* | *the UN Security Council*
2 the organization that is responsible for local government in a particular area in Britain: ***local council** elections* | *He sent a letter to the council to complain about the noise.* | **County/District/City etc Council** *Northampton Borough Council* | **council leader/officer/worker etc** | **council chamber/offices**
3 a group of people elected to the government of a city in the US: *the Los Angeles city council*

ˈcouncil esˌtate *n* [C] *BrE* an area in a town or city with streets of council houses

ˈcouncil house *n* [C] *BrE* a house in Britain that is provided by the local council for a very low rent

coun·cil·lor *BrE*, **councilor** *AmE* /ˈkaʊnsələ $ -ər/ ●●○ *n* [C] a member of a council: *Write to your local councillor to complain.* ⚠ Do not confuse with **counsellor** (=someone whose job is to help people talk about and deal with their problems).

coun·cil·man /ˈkaʊnsəlmən/ *n* (*plural* **councilmen** /-mən/) [C] *AmE* a man who is a member of the government of a city in the US

ˌcouncil of ˈwar *n* (*plural* **councils of war**) [C] a meeting to decide how to deal with a particular problem – used humorously

ˈcouncil ˌtax *n* [singular, U] *BrE* a tax which every home in Britain has to pay to local government, based on the area and the value of the house, FLAT etc

coun·cil·wom·an /ˈkaʊnsəlˌwʊmən/ *n* (*plural* **councilwomen** /-ˌwɪmɪn/) [C] *AmE* a woman who is a member of the government of a city in the US

coun·sel[1] /ˈkaʊnsəl/ *n* [U] **1** a type of lawyer who represents you in court: **[+for]** *The judge asked counsel for the defence to explain.* **2 keep your own counsel** *written* to keep your plans, opinions etc secret **3** *literary* advice

counsel[2] *v* (**counselled, counselling** *BrE*, **counseled, counseling** *AmE*) [T] **1** *formal* to advise someone: **counsel sb to do sth** *She counselled them not to accept this settlement.* **2** to listen and give support to someone with problems: *a new unit to counsel alcoholics*

coun·sel·ling *BrE*, **counseling** *AmE* /ˈkaʊnsəlɪŋ/ ●○○ *n* [U] advice and support given by a counsellor to someone with problems, usually after talking to them: **group/bereavement/debt etc counselling** *a debt counselling service* | **[+for]** *She's been undergoing counseling for depression.*

coun·sel·lor *BrE*, **counselor** *AmE* /ˈkaʊnsələ $ -ər/ ●○○ *n* [C] someone whose job is to help and support people with problems: *Are you seeing a counsellor?* | **student/marriage guidance/stress etc counsellor**

count[1] /kaʊnt/ ●●● (S2) (W3) *v*
1 FIND THE TOTAL [T] (*also* **count up**) to calculate the total number of things or people in a group: *I was amazed at the number of plants – I counted 147.* | **count (up) how many** *Count up how many ticks are in each box.*
2 SAY NUMBERS [I] (*also* **count up**) to say numbers in order, one by one or in groups: **[+to]** *Sarah can count up to five now.* | **count by twos/fives etc** *It's quicker to count by tens* (=saying 10, 20, 30 ...).
3 BE ALLOWED [I,T] to be allowed or accepted, or to allow or accept something, according to a standard, set of ideas, or set of rules: *A linesman had his flag up so the kick did not count.* | **[+as]** *Locally produced sales by American firms in Japan do not count as exports.* | *Today's session is counted as training, so you will get paid.* | **[+towards]** *Results from the two rounds count towards championship points.*
4 INCLUDE [T] to include someone or something in a total: *There are more than two thousand of us, **not counting** the crew.* | **count sb/sth among sth** *I count Jules and Ady among my closest friends.*
5 CONSIDER STH [T] to consider someone or something in a particular way: **count sb/sth as sth** *I don't count him as a friend anymore.* | *You should **count** yourself **lucky** that you weren't hurt.*
6 IMPORTANT [I not in progressive] to be important or valuable: *First impressions really do count.* | **[+for]** *His promises don't count for much.* | *His overseas results **count for nothing**.*
7 I/you can count sb/sth on (the fingers of) one hand *spoken* used to emphasize how small the number of something is: *The number of cougar attacks on humans can be counted on the fingers of one hand.*
8 don't count your chickens (before they're hatched) *spoken* used to say that you should not make plans that depend on something good happening, because it might not: *I wouldn't count your chickens, Mr Vass. I've agreed to sign the contract, but that's all.*
9 count your blessings *spoken* used to tell someone to be grateful for the good things in their life
10 be counting (down) the minutes/hours/days to be waiting eagerly for something to happen: *I'm counting the days until I see you again.*
11 count the cost to start having problems as a result of your earlier decisions or mistakes: *We're now counting the cost of not taking out medical insurance.*
12 who's counting? used to say that you are not worried about the number of times something happens – often used humorously: *Apparently the next Star Trek film (number six, but who's counting?) will definitely be the last.*
13 and counting *especially spoken* used to say that an amount is continuing to increase: *At eight days and counting, this is the longest strike so far.*
14 count sheep to imagine a line of sheep jumping over a fence, one at a time, and count them as a way of getting to sleep → **stand up and be counted** at STAND[1](5), → **it's the thought that counts** at THOUGHT[2](12)

count sb **in** *phr v* to include someone in an activity: *When the game gets started, you can count me in.*

count on/upon sb/sth *phr v*
1 to depend on someone or something, especially in a difficult situation: *You can count on me.* | *With luck, you might cover your costs, but don't count on it.* | **count on (sb/sth) doing sth** *We're all counting on winning this contract.* | *They were counting on him not coming out of hospital.* | **count on sb/sth to do sth** *You can count on Dean to ruin any party.*
2 to expect something: *The presence of Paula was one thing he hadn't counted on.* | **count on (sb/sth) doing sth** *We didn't count on so many people being on vacation.*

count sb/sth **out** *phr v*
1 to not include someone or something in an activity: *I'm sorry, you'll have to count me out tonight.*
2 to decide that someone or something is not important or worth considering: *I wouldn't count him out. If anybody can make a comeback, he can.*
3 count sth ↔ out to put things down one by one as you count them: *The teller counted out ten $50 bills.*

count[2] ●●○ *n* [C]
1 TOTAL the process of counting, or the total that you get when you count things: *Hold your breath for a count of ten.*

2 MEASUREMENT a measurement that shows how much of a substance is present in a place, area etc that is being examined: *The* ***pollen count*** *is high today.*
3 lose count to forget a number you were calculating or a total you were trying to count: **[+of]** *There have been so many accidents here, the police have lost count of them.*
4 keep count to keep a record of the changing total of something over a period of time: **[+of]** *I never manage to keep count of what I spend on my credit card.*
5 on all/several/both etc counts in every way, in several ways etc: *It was important that they secured a large and widespread audience. They failed on both counts.*
6 at the last count according to the latest information about a particular situation: *At the last count, I had 15 responses to my letter.*
7 be out for the count a) to be in a deep sleep **b)** if a BOXER is out for the count, he has been knocked down for ten seconds or more
8 LAW *technical* one of the crimes that someone is charged with: *Davis was found not guilty* ***on all counts.*** | **count of theft/burglary/murder etc** *He was charged with two counts of theft.*
9 RANK/TITLE a European NOBLEMAN with a high rank

count·a·ble /ˈkaʊntəbəl/ *adj* a countable noun has both a singular and a plural form. In this dictionary countable nouns are marked [C] → **count noun** OPP **uncountable**

count·down /ˈkaʊntdaʊn/ *n* [C usually singular] **1** the period of time before something happens, such as a spacecraft being LAUNCHed, when someone counts backwards until the event happens **2** the period of time before an important event, when people become more and more excited about it: **[+to]** *the countdown to the World Cup*

coun·te·nance¹ /ˈkaʊntənəns/ *n* [C] *literary* your face or your expression: *All colour drained from her countenance.*

countenance² *v* [T] *formal* to accept, support, or approve of something: **countenance (sb) doing sth** *I will not countenance you being rude to Dr Baxter.*

coun·ter¹ /ˈkaʊntə $ -ər/ ●●● S3 *n* [C]
1 the place where you pay or are served in a shop, bank, restaurant etc: *He wondered if the girl behind the counter recognised him.*
2 *AmE* a long flat surface on top of a piece of furniture, especially in a kitchen SYN **worktop** *BrE*
3 over the counter drugs, medicines etc that are bought over the counter are ones that you can buy in a shop without a PRESCRIPTION from a doctor
4 under the counter if you buy something under the counter, you buy it secretly and usually illegally: *It's risky, but you can get alcohol under the counter.*
5 a small object that you use in some games that are played on a board → see picture at **BOARD GAME**
6 a piece of electrical equipment that counts something: *Set the video counter to zero before you press play.* → **GEIGER COUNTER**
7 a computer program that counts the number of people who have visited a website
8 an action that tries to prevent something bad from happening, or an argument that is used to prove that something is wrong: **[+to]** *The road blocks were a counter to terrorist attacks in that area.*

counter² ●○○ *v*
1 [I,T] to say something in order to try to prove that what someone said was not true or as a reply to something: *'I could ask the same thing of you,' she countered.* | **counter an argument/an allegation/a criticism etc** *He was determined to counter the bribery allegations.*
2 [T] to do something in order to prevent something bad from happening or to reduce its bad effects: *Exercise helps to counter the effects of stress.*

counter³ *adj, adv* **be/run/go counter to sth** to be the opposite of something: *Some actions by the authorities ran counter to the president's call for leniency.*

counter- /kaʊntə $ -tər/ *prefix* **1** the opposite of something: *a counterproductive thing to do* (=producing results opposite to what you wanted) | *It is not hard to find a counter-example* (=an example that shows the opposite). **2** done or given as a reaction to something, especially to oppose it: *claims and counterclaims* **3** matching something: *my counterpart in the American system* (=someone who has the same job as I have)

coun·ter·act /ˌkaʊntərˈækt/ ●○○ *v* [T] to reduce or prevent the bad effect of something, by doing something that has the opposite effect: *They gave him drugs to counteract his withdrawal symptoms.* —**counteraction** /-ˈækʃən/ *n* [C,U]

coun·ter·at·tack /ˈkaʊntərəˌtæk/ *n* [C] an attack you make against someone who has attacked you, in a war, sport, or argument —**counterattack** *v* [I,T]

coun·ter·bal·ance /ˌkaʊntəˈbæləns $ -tər-/ *v* [T] to have an equal and opposite effect to something such as a change, feeling etc: *Riskier investments tend to be counterbalanced by high rewards.* —**counterbalance** /ˈkaʊntəˌbæləns $ -tər-/ *n* [C]

coun·ter·charge /ˈkaʊntəˌtʃɑːdʒ $ -tərˌtʃɑːrdʒ/ *n* [C] a statement that says someone has done something wrong, made after they have said that you have done something wrong

coun·ter·clock·wise /ˌkaʊntəˈklɒkwaɪz◂ $ -tərˈklɑːk-/ *adv, adj AmE* ANTICLOCKWISE → **CLOCKWISE**

coun·ter·cul·ture /ˈkaʊntəˌkʌltʃə $ -tərˌkʌltʃər/ *n* [U] the art, beliefs, behaviour etc of people who are against the usual or accepted behaviour, art etc of society: *the counterculture revolution of the late 1960s*

ˌcounter-ˈespionage *n* [U] the process of trying to stop someone SPYing on your country

coun·ter·feit¹ /ˈkaʊntəfɪt $ -tər-/ *adj* made to look exactly like something else, in order to deceive people SYN **fake**: **counterfeit currency/money etc** *counterfeit £10 notes* | **counterfeit goods/software etc** THESAURUS **FALSE**

counterfeit² *v* [T] to copy something exactly in order to deceive people SYN **fake**: *They admitted counterfeiting documents.* —**counterfeiter** *n* [C]

coun·ter·foil /ˈkaʊntəfɔɪl $ -tər-/ *n* [C] the part of something such as a cheque that you keep as a record

coun·ter·in·sur·gen·cy /ˌkaʊntərɪnˈsɜːdʒənsi $ -ɜːr-/ *n* [U] military action against people who are fighting against their own country's government

coun·ter·in·tel·li·gence /ˌkaʊntərɪnˈtelədʒəns/ *n* [U] action that a country takes in order to stop other countries discovering its secrets

coun·ter·mand /ˌkaʊntəˈmɑːnd, ˈkaʊntəmɑːnd $ ˌkaʊntərˈmænd/ *v* [T] *formal* to officially tell people to ignore an order, especially by giving them a different one: *Terrorists tried to force him to countermand the order to attack.*

coun·ter·mea·sure /ˈkaʊntəmeʒə $ -tərmeʒər/ *n* [C usually plural] an action taken to prevent another action from having a harmful effect: *new countermeasures against terrorism*

coun·ter·pane /ˈkaʊntəpeɪn $ -ər-/ *n* [C] *old-fashioned* a BEDSPREAD

coun·ter·part /ˈkaʊntəpɑːt $ -tərpɑːrt/ ●○○ *n* [C] someone or something that has the same job or purpose as someone or something else in a different place: **sb's counterpart** *Belgian officials are discussing this with their French counterparts.*

coun·ter·point /ˈkaʊntəpɔɪnt $ -ər-/ *n* **1** [U] the combination of two or more tunes played together so that they sound like one tune: **in counterpoint to sth** *The viola is exactly in counterpoint to the first violin.* **2** [C] a tune that is one part of counterpoint **3** [C,U] when two things that are different are compared in an interesting or pleasant way: **[+to]** *I have used my interviews with parents as a counterpoint to a professional judgement.*

coun·ter·pro·duc·tive /ˌkaʊntəprəˈdʌktɪv◂ $ -tər-/ ●○○ *adj* achieving the opposite result to the one that you want: *Sending young offenders to prison can be counterproductive.*

ˌcounter-revoˈlution *n* [C,U] political or military actions taken to get rid of a government that is in power

C

because of a previous REVOLUTION —**counter-revolutionary** *n* [C] —**counter-revolutionary** *adj*

coun·ter·sign /ˈkaʊntəsaɪn $ -ər-/ *v* [T] to sign a paper that has already been signed by someone else: *The note must be countersigned by a doctor.*

coun·ter·ten·or /ˌkaʊntəˈtenə $ ˈkaʊntərˌtenər/ *n* [C] a man who is trained to sing with a very high voice

ˈcounter-ˌterrorist *adj* **counter-terrorist operation/team/unit etc** a plan or group that tries to prevent the activities of violent political groups —**counter-terrorism** *n* [U] —**counter-terrorist** *n* [C]

coun·ter·vail·ing /ˌkaʊntəˈveɪlɪŋ◂ $ -ər-/ *adj formal* with an equally strong but opposite effect

coun·tess /ˈkaʊntɪs/ *n* [C] a woman with the same rank as an EARL or a COUNT²(9)

ˈcounting house *n* [C] an office where accounts and money were kept in the past

count·less /ˈkaʊntləs/ ●●○ *adj* [usually before noun] too many to be counted: *a famous film clip which has been shown* ***countless times*** THESAURUS➤ MANY

ˈcount noun *n* [C] a noun that has both a singular and a plural form and can be used with 'a' or 'an' → **countable** → NOUN

coun·tri·fied /ˈkʌntrɪfaɪd/ *adj* typical of the countryside, or made to seem typical of the countryside: *the countrified existence of the newly rich*

coun·try¹ /ˈkʌntri/ ●●● S1 W1 *n* (*plural* **countries**)

1 [C] an area of land that is controlled by its own government, president, king etc → **nation**: *the Scandinavian countries | developing countries | travelling to a foreign country* → MOTHER COUNTRY

2 the country a) land that is outside towns and cities, including land used for farming SYN **the countryside**: **in the country** *I've always wanted to live in the country.* **b)** all the people who live in a particular country: *The president has the support of the country.*

3 [U] an area of land that is suitable for a particular activity, has particular features, or is connected with a particular person or people: *The Peak District is good walking country. | mountainous country | the rugged moors of Brontë country*

4 [U] country and western music: *I'm a big fan of country.*

5 go to the country *BrE* if a prime minister goes to the country, they ask for a GENERAL ELECTION to be held

COLLOCATIONS

ADJECTIVES/NOUN + country

a foreign country (=not your own country) *Have you ever worked in a foreign country?*

a European/African/Asian etc country *The president will be visiting four European countries.*

a democratic/capitalist/communist etc country *the former socialist countries of Eastern Europe*

your home/native country (=where you were born or live permanently) *After five years in America, she returned to her home country, Japan.*

a developing/Third World country (=poor and trying to increase its industry and trade) *Many developing countries receive some foreign aid.*

a developed country (=rich and where most people have a comfortable life) | **an underdeveloped country** (=poor and developing more slowly than others) | **an industrialized country** | **an advanced country** | **a Christian/Muslim/Catholic etc country** | **your adopted country** (=that you have chosen to live in permanently) | **an independent country** (=not controlled by another country) | **a free country** (=where people's actions are not too restricted) | **a member country** (=belonging to a particular international organization) | **the host country** (=where an event is held)

VERBS

run/govern the country (=officially control a country) *The government has the job of running the country.*

rule a country (=have complete control of a country) *For a long time the country was ruled by military dictators.*

flee the country (=leave it very quickly to avoid trouble) *At the outbreak of the war, many people fled the country.*

serve your country (=work for your country in an official way) *Remember those who are serving our country as soldiers, sailors, and airmen.*

lead the country | **represent your country** | **betray your country** (=be disloyal, especially by giving secrets to other countries)

PHRASES

sb's/sth's country of origin (=where you were born or live permanently, or where something was produced) *Please give your name, age, and country of origin.*

THESAURUS

country an area of land controlled by its own government, president, king etc: *Thailand is a beautiful country. | Which country would you most like to visit?*

nation a country, considered especially in relation to its people and its political and economic structure: *The events shocked the whole nation. | The US is the most powerful nation in the world. | Leaders of the world's major industrialized nations attended the meeting.*

state a country considered as a political organization with its own government: *They believe that Scotland should be an independent sovereign state. | Most European states joined the Council of Europe.*

power a country that is very strong and important: *a meeting of the* ***great powers*** *| Britain is still a* ***world power****.*

superpower one of the most powerful countries in the world: *During the Cuban Missile Crisis there was a real danger of conflict between the two world superpowers.*

land *literary* a country – used in stories: *He told them about his journeys to foreign lands. | a traveller from a far-off land*

country² *adj* [only before noun] **1** belonging to or connected with the countryside SYN **rural** OPP **urban**: *They much preferred country life to life in the city.* **2** relating to country and western music: *a country singer*

ˌcountry and ˈwestern *n* [U] *formal* popular music in the style of music from the southern and western US

ˌcountry ˈbumpkin *n* [C] someone who is considered to be stupid because they are from an area outside towns and cities SYN **yokel**

ˈcountry ˌclub *n* [C] a sports and social club, especially one for rich people

ˌcountry ˈcousin *n* [C] someone who does not have a lot of experience and is confused by busy city life

ˌcountry ˈdancing *n* [U] a traditional form of dance in which pairs of dancers move in rows and circles

ˌcountry ˈhouse *n* [C] *BrE* a large house in the countryside, especially one that is of historical interest → **stately home**

coun·try·man /ˈkʌntrimən/ *n* (*plural* **countrymen** /-mən/) [C] **1** **sb's countryman** someone from your own country SYN **compatriot**: *It was two years since I'd seen any* ***fellow countrymen****.* **2** *BrE* a man who lives in the country rather than in a town or city

ˈcountry ˌmusic *n* [U] COUNTRY AND WESTERN

ˌcountry ˈseat *n* [C] *BrE* the countryside house of someone who is rich and owns land

coun·try·side /ˈkʌntrisaɪd/ ●●● S3 W3 *n* [U] land that is outside cities and towns SYN **the country**: *The house had lovely views over* ***open countryside****.* | **in the countryside** *people who live in the countryside* THESAURUS➤ COUNTRY

THESAURUS

countryside *n* [U] an area away from towns and cities, where there are fields, forests etc – used especially when talking about the natural beauty of this kind of area: *The walk takes you through some beautiful countryside.* | *The countryside changes in winter.*
the country *n* [singular] the area away from towns and cities, where there are fields, forests etc: *Tired of city life, they moved to the country.* | *I've always wanted to live in the country.*
landscape *n* [C usually singular] a large area of countryside that you see from somewhere: *The house looks out over a peaceful rural landscape.* | *Adams is famous for his photographs of the American landscape.*
scenery *n* [U] the natural features of part of a country, such as mountains, forests etc, especially when these are attractive: *New Zealand has some spectacular scenery.*
wilderness *n* [C,U] a large area of land that has never been developed or farmed: *Yukon is a vast wilderness of mountains, lakes, and forests.*
the bush *n* [singular] wild country that has not been cleared, especially in Australia or Africa: *The camp is popular with tourists wishing to experience the African bush.*
rural *adj* relating to the country: *People are moving away from rural areas.* | *rural communities*

coun·try·wide /ˈkʌntriwaɪd/ *adj* happening or existing in all parts of a country SYN **nationwide** —**countrywide** *adv*

coun·try·wom·an /ˈkʌntriˌwʊmən/ *n* (*plural* **country-women** /-ˌwɪmɪn/) [C] *BrE* a woman who lives in the country rather than in a town or city

coun·ty /ˈkaʊnti/ ●●● W2 *n* (*plural* **counties**) [C] an area of a state or country that has its own government to deal with local matters: *Fairfax County, Virginia*

ˌcounty ˈcouncil *n* [C] a group of people who are elected to the local government of a county, especially in Britain: *Kent County Council*

ˌcounty ˈcourt *n* [C] a local court of law. In Britain, county courts deal with private quarrels between people rather than with serious crimes. In the US, they also deal with less important criminal cases. → **criminal court**

ˌcounty ˈfair *n* [C] *AmE* an event that happens each year in a particular county, with games and competitions for the best farm animals, cooking etc

ˌcounty ˈtown *BrE*, **ˌcounty ˈseat** *AmE n* [C] the town in a county where its government is

coup /kuː/ ●○○ *n* [C]
1 a sudden and sometimes violent attempt by citizens or the army to take control of the government SYN **coup d'état**: *Haiti's first elected president was deposed in a violent* ***military coup.*** | *a* ***coup attempt*** *by junior officers* | *He evaded capture after the* ***failed coup.*** THESAURUS ▸ REVOLUTION
2 an achievement that is extremely impressive because it was very difficult: *Beating Arsenal was a* ***major coup*** *for the club.*

coup de grâce /ˌkuː də ˈɡrɑːs/ *n* [singular] **1** an action or event that ends or destroys something that has gradually been getting weaker **2** a hit or shot that kills someone or something

coup d'état /ˌkuː deɪˈtɑː $ -deˈtɑː/ *n* (*plural* **coups d'état** (*same pronunciation*)) [C] a COUP

cou·pé /ˈkuːpeɪ $ kuːˈpeɪ/ *n* [C] a car with two doors and a sloping back → **sports car**

cou·ple¹ /ˈkʌpəl/ ●●● S1 W1 AWL *n*
1 a couple a) two things or people of the same kind SYN **a few**: **[+of]** *There are a couple of girls waiting for you.* **b)** a small number of things: *I just need to make a couple more calls.* | **[+of]** *You'll be all right in a couple of days.*
2 [C] two people who are married or having a sexual or romantic relationship: *a newly married couple* | *the couple next door*

couple² AWL *v* **1** [T] to join or fasten two things together: **couple sth to sth** *Each element is mathematically coupled to its neighbours.* **2** [I] *formal* to have sex
couple sth **with** sth *phr v* if one thing is coupled with another, the two things happen or exist together and produce a particular result SYN **combine**: *Lack of rain coupled with high temperatures caused the crops to fail.*

coup·let /ˈkʌplɪt/ *n* [C] two lines of poetry, one following the other, that are the same length: *rhyming couplets*

coup·ling /ˈkʌplɪŋ/ *n* [C] **1** something that connects two things together, especially two vehicles **2** when two things are joined or connected SYN **combination**: *an attractive coupling of two Slavonic Dances* **3** *formal* an act of having sex

cou·pon /ˈkuːpɒn $ -pɑːn/ ●●○ *n* [C]
1 a small piece of printed paper that gives you the right to pay less for something or get something free: *The coupon entitles you to ten cents off your next purchase.*
2 a printed form, used when you order something, enter a competition etc: *To order, fill in the coupon on page 154.*

cour·age /ˈkʌrɪdʒ $ ˈkɜːr-/ ●●○ *n* [U]
1 the quality of being brave when you are facing a difficult or dangerous situation, or when you are very ill → **bravery** OPP **cowardice**: *Sue showed great courage throughout her illness.* | **courage to do sth** *Gradually I lost the courage to speak out about anything.* | *He did not* ***have the courage*** *to tell Nicola that he was ending their affair.* | **summon/pluck up the courage (to do sth)** (=find the courage to do something) *I plucked up the courage to go out by myself.* | *Driving again after his accident must have* ***taken*** *a lot of* ***courage*** (=needed courage).
2 have the courage of your (own) convictions to continue to say or do what you think is right even when other people may not agree or approve → DUTCH COURAGE

cou·ra·geous /kəˈreɪdʒəs/ ●○○ *adj* brave: *He was wrong, and courageous enough to admit it.* | *a courageous decision* THESAURUS ▸ BRAVE —**courageously** *adv*

REGISTER
In everyday English, people usually say **brave** rather than **courageous**: *It was* ***brave*** *of you to tell him what you thought.*

cour·gette /kʊəˈʒet $ kʊr-/ *n* [C] a long vegetable with dark green skin SYN **zucchini** *AmE* → see picture at VEGETABLE¹

cou·ri·er¹ /ˈkʊriə $ -ər/ *n* [C] **1** a person or company that is paid to take packages somewhere **2** *BrE old-fashioned* a REP

courier² *v* [T] to send something somewhere using a courier

course¹ /kɔːs $ kɔːrs/ ●●● S1 W1 *n*
1 of course a) used to show that what you are saying is expected or already known and so not surprising: *You can pay by cheque, assuming of course you have a valid cheque card.* | *Of course there are exceptions to every rule.* **b)** (*also* **course** *informal*) *spoken* used to say yes or to give permission politely: *'Can I have a word with you?' 'Of course.'* | *'Can you give me a lift?' 'Course, no problem.'* **c)** (*also* **course** *informal*) *spoken* used to emphasize that what you are saying is true or correct: *Of course he'll come!* | **well/but of course** *Well of course I love you.*
2 of course not (*also* **course not** *informal*) *spoken* used to say very strongly that something is not true or correct: *He asked his father if it was true. 'Of course not,' Jack said.* | *'You don't mind if I call her?' 'No, course not.'*
3 EDUCATION [C] **a)** a series of lessons in a particular subject SYN **class** *AmE*: *Andy's doing a one-year journalism course.* | **[+on/in]** *a course on architecture* | *I'm taking a course in graphic design.* **b)** *BrE* a period of study in a particular subject, especially at university SYN **program** *AmE*: *a degree course in photography* ⚠ **Course** is never followed by 'of'. Don't say 'a course of Business Studies'. Say 'a course in Business Studies'.
4 TIME [singular] a period of time or process during which something happens: **during/in/throughout/over the course**

of sth *During the course of our conversation, it emerged that Bob had been in prison.* | *Over the course of the next few years, the steel industry was reorganized.* | **in the course of doing sth** *In the course of researching customer needs, we discovered how few families have adequate life insurance.*

5 DEVELOPMENT [singular] the usual or natural way that something changes, develops, or is done: **[+of]** *forces that shape the course of evolution* | *Meeting Sally changed the whole* ***course of*** *his* ***life***. | **in the normal/natural/ordinary course of events** *In the normal course of events, a son would inherit from his father.* | **take/run its course** (=develop in the usual way and reach a natural end) *Relax and* ***let*** *nature* ***take its course***. | *It seems the boom in World Music has run its course.* | *Gorbachev* ***changed the course of*** *Soviet history.*

6 PLANS [singular, U] the general plans someone has to achieve something or the general way something is happening: *They will go to any lengths to get the White House to* ***change course***. | *He will* ***steer a middle course*** *between pacifism and revolution.* | *As long as the economy* ***stays on course***, *the future looks rosy.*

7 ACTIONS [C usually singular] an action or series of actions that you could take in order to deal with a particular situation: *I agreed that this was the only sensible* ***course of action***. | **take/decide on a course** *The judge took the only course of action open to him.*

8 DIRECTION [C usually singular, U] the planned direction taken by a boat or plane to reach a place: *The plane* ***changed course*** *to avoid the storm.* | **on/off course** (=going in the right or wrong direction) *The ship was* ***blown off course***. | *The aircraft was almost ten miles off course.* | *She tightened the mainsail while* ***holding the course*** (=travelling in the same direction as planned).

9 on course likely to achieve something because you have already had some success: **[+for]** *If he wins today, he's on course for the Grand Slam.* | **on course to do sth** *We're* ***back on course*** *to qualify for the championship.*

10 MEAL [C] one of the separate parts of a meal: **three-course/five-course etc meal** *The ticket includes entry and a four-course meal.* | **first/second/main etc course** *We had fish for the main course.*

11 SPORT [C] an area of land or water where races are held, or an area of land designed for playing golf: *a particularly difficult course* | *an 18-hole course* → ASSAULT COURSE, OBSTACLE COURSE(1)

12 MEDICAL TREATMENT [C] *especially BrE* an amount of medicine or medical treatment that you have regularly for a specific period of time: **course of injections/drugs/treatment etc** *a course of antibiotics*

13 in (the) course of time after some or enough time has passed SYN **eventually**: *She'll get used to school in the course of time.*

14 RIVER [C] the direction a river moves in: *The course of the water was shown by a line of trees.*

15 WALL [C] a layer of bricks, stone etc in a wall: *a damp-proof course* → **as a matter of course** at MATTER[1](20), → **par for the course** at PAR(3), → **stay the course** at STAY[1](7), → **in due course** at DUE[1](4)

COLLOCATIONS – MEANING 3

VERBS

take a course (*also* **do a course** *BrE*) *I decided to do a course in Italian.*
go on a course *BrE My company wanted me to go on a course in management skills.*
pass/fail a course *If you pass the course, you get a diploma in psychology.*
apply for a course *The following year she applied for a nursing course.*
enrol on a course/put your name down for a course *BrE* (=to arrange to officially join a course) | **attend a course** *formal* (=take part in a course) | **withdraw from a course/drop out of a course** (=leave it without finishing it) | **teach a course** | **run a course**

ADJECTIVES/NOUN + course

a language/art/design etc course *The school runs ten-week language courses three times a year.*
a full-time/part-time course *There are also part-time courses for mature students.*
an elementary/intermediate/advanced course *an advanced course in art and design*
a one-year/two-year etc course *She did a one-year teacher training course.*
a short course | **an intensive course** (=in which you learn a lot in a short time) | **a crash course** *informal* (=in which you learn a great deal in a very short time) | **a training course** | **a vocational course** (=that trains you to do a particular job) | **a correspondence course** (=in which you work at home, sending work to a teacher by post) | **an introductory course** (=for people who have never done a particular subject or activity before) | **a refresher course** (=short and intended to teach you about new developments in a subject) | **a sandwich course** *BrE* (=that includes periods of work in industry or business)

course + NOUN

a course tutor *BrE: I discussed it with my course tutor.*
course material *Teachers are provided with course material.*
the course syllabus (=the plan of what is taught on a course)

COMMON ERRORS

⚠ Don't say 'make a course'. Say **do** or **take a course**.

course² *v* **1** [I always + adv/prep] *literary* if a liquid or electricity courses somewhere, it flows there quickly: *Tears coursed down his cheeks.* **2** [I always + adv/prep] *literary* if a feeling courses through you, you feel it suddenly and strongly: *His smile sent waves of excitement coursing through her.* **3** [I,T] to chase rabbits with dogs as a sport

course·book /ˈkɔːsbʊk $ ˈkɔːrs-/ ●●○ *n* [C] *BrE* a book that students use regularly during a set of lessons on a particular subject SYN **textbook**

course·ware /ˈkɔːsweə $ ˈkɔːrswer/ *n* [U] computer software that is designed to teach people a particular subject

course·work /ˈkɔːswɜːk $ ˈkɔːrswɜːrk/ *n* [U] work students do during a course of study rather than in examinations, and that forms part of their final mark

court¹ /kɔːt $ kɔːrt/ ●●● S1 W1 *n*

1 FOR DECIDING ABOUT A LEGAL CASE [C,U] the place where a trial is held, or the people there, especially the judge and the JURY who examine the evidence and decide whether someone is guilty or not guilty: *It could not be proved in a court of law.* | *The court case lasted six weeks.* | *Four people will appear in court today, charged with fraud.* | *The court ruled that no compensation was due.* | *She threatened to* ***take*** *the magazine* ***to court*** (=take legal action against them) *if they didn't publish an immediate apology.*

2 FOR PLAYING A SPORT [C] an area made for playing games such as tennis → **field**, **pitch**: **squash/tennis/basketball etc court** *Can you book a squash court for tomorrow?* | **on court** *The players are due on court in an hour.* → see picture at TENNIS

3 KING/QUEEN **a)** [C] the place where a king or queen lives and works: *the* ***royal courts*** *of Europe* **b) the court** the king, queen, their family, and their friends, advisers etc: *Several members of the court were under suspicion.* | *There was a taste in* ***court circles*** *for romantic verse.* | ***Court officials*** *denied the rumours.*

4 hold court *formal* to speak in an interesting, amusing, or forceful way so that people gather to listen: **[+to]** *Dylan was holding court upstairs to a group of fans.*

5 pay court to sb *old-fashioned* to give someone a lot of attention to try and make them like you

6 AREA NEXT TO A BUILDING [C] a COURTYARD → **the ball is in sb's court** at BALL[1](7), → **be laughed out of court** at LAUGH[1](6), → FOOD COURT

COLLOCATIONS

PHRASES

a court of law *You may be asked to give evidence before a court of law.*

court + NOUN

a court case (=a problem or crime that is dealt with in a court of law) *a recent court case involving the death of a baby*
a court order (=an instruction that someone must do something) *A court order specified that the money must be paid back over six months.*
a court ruling (=an official decision) *The company appealed against the court ruling.*
court action (=a court case) *He was threatened with court action.*
court proceedings (=the processes that are part of a court case) *The court proceedings were over in a day.*

VERBS

go to court (=take legal action) *The costs of going to court are very high.*
take sb to court (=take legal action against someone) *She took the company to court for sex discrimination.*
bring sb/sth to court (*also* **bring sb/sth before a court**) *Three teenage girls were brought before the court for robbing an elderly woman.*
appear in court *A man has appeared in court charged with cruelty to animals.*
a case comes to court/comes before the court *The case came to court 21 months later.*
a court hears a case *The county court will hear the case next month.*
settle sth out of court (=reach an agreement without using a court)
a court rules/orders/holds sth *The court ruled that the penalty was not excessive.*
a court clears/acquits sb (=says that they are not guilty) | **a court convicts sb** (=says that they are guilty) | **a court upholds sth** (=says that an earlier decision was right) | **a court quashes/overturns sth** (=says that an earlier decision was wrong) | **a court adjourns a case/trial etc** (=stops dealing with it for a period of time) | **a court dismisses/throws out sth** (=refuses to allow or consider something)

ADJECTIVES/NOUN + court

a criminal court (=for cases about crime) *Two French magistrates ruled that he should stand trial in a criminal court.*
a civil court (=for cases about disagreements) | **a Crown Court** (=a British court for cases about serious crimes) | **a High Court** (=an important court, with more power than an ordinary court) | **an appeals court/court of appeal** (=dealing with cases in which people are not satisfied with a decision) | **the Supreme Court** (=the most important court in some countries or US states) | **a federal court** (=a national court rather than a state court) | **a county court** (=a local court) | **a magistrates' court** (=a court in each area in England and Wales that deals with less serious crimes)
a kangaroo court (=an unofficial court that punishes people unfairly) *The army reportedly held kangaroo courts and executed alleged rebels.*

court[2] *v* [T] **1** to try hard to please someone, especially because you want something from them: *His campaign team have assiduously courted the media.* **2 court danger/death etc** *formal* to behave in a way that makes danger etc more likely: *To have admitted this would have* ***courted*** *political* ***disaster***. **3 be courting** *old-fashioned* if a man and a woman are courting, they are having a romantic relationship and may get married: *That was back in the 1960s when we were courting.* **4** *old-fashioned* if a man courts a woman, he spends time being nice to her because he hopes to marry her

ˈcourt card *n* [C] *BrE* the king, queen, or JACK in a set of playing cards SYN **face card** *AmE*

ˌcourt correˈspondent *n* [C] *BrE* someone who reports the news relating to a royal family for a newspaper or television company

ˈcourt ˌcosts *n* [plural] the costs of taking a case to court: *You could be ordered to pay court costs.*

cour·te·ous /ˈkɜːtiəs $ ˈkɜːr-/ ●○○ *adj* polite and showing respect for other people OPP **discourteous**: *The staff are always courteous and helpful.* | *a courteous reply*
THESAURUS ▸ POLITE

cour·te·san /ˌkɔːtɪˈzæn $ ˈkɔːrtɪzən/ *n* [C] a woman who had sex with rich or important men for money in the past → **prostitute**

cour·te·sy[1] /ˈkɜːtəsi $ ˈkɜːr-/ ●○○ *n* (*plural* **courtesies**)
1 [U] polite behaviour and respect for other people SYN **politeness** OPP **discourtesy**: *It's a matter of* ***common courtesy*** *to acknowledge letters.* | **have the courtesy to do sth** *He didn't even have the courtesy to call and say he couldn't come.*
2 [C] something you do or say to be polite: *The two men* ***exchanged courtesies*** *before getting down to business.*
3 (by) courtesy of sb by someone's permission or kindness, rather than by paying them: *photographs supplied courtesy of Blenheim Palace*
4 (by) courtesy of sth if one thing happens courtesy of another, the second thing caused the first: *Healy received a deep cut on his left hand, courtesy of Nicole's ice skate.*
5 do sb the courtesy of doing sth to be polite enough to do something for someone: *At least do me the courtesy of telling the truth.*

courtesy[2] *adj* [only before noun] **1** provided free to a customer by a company: **courtesy bus/taxi/car/phone etc** *The hotel runs a courtesy bus from the airport.* | *Most reviewers receive a courtesy copy of the book.* **2 courtesy visit/call** a visit etc done to be polite or show respect: *Our captain put in a courtesy visit during dinner.*

court·house /ˈkɔːthaʊs $ ˈkɔːrt-/ *n* [C] *AmE* a building containing law courts and government offices

court·ier /ˈkɔːtɪə $ ˈkɔːrtɪr/ *n* [C] someone in the past with an important position at a royal court

court·ly /ˈkɔːtli $ ˈkɔːrtli/ *adj* graceful and polite: *a tall man with courtly manners* —**courtliness** *n* [U]

ˌcourt-ˈmartial[1] / $ ˈ. ˌ../ *n* [C,U] a court that judges soldiers etc who may have broken military law, or an occasion when this judgment is made: *Navy commanders recommended that he be tried by court-martial.*

court-martial[2] *v* (**court-martialled**, **court-martialling** *BrE*, **court-martialed**, **court-martialing** *AmE*) [T] to hear and judge someone's case in a military court: *The drill instructor was court-martialled for having sex with a trainee.*

ˌCourt of Apˈpeal *n* [singular] the highest law court in Britain apart from the HOUSE OF LORDS

ˌCourt of Apˈpeals *n* [singular] one of 12 law courts in the US that deals with cases when people are not satisfied with the judgment given by a lower court → **appellate court**

ˌcourt of inˈquiry *n* (*plural* **courts of inquiry**) [C] *BrE* a group of people chosen to discover the facts about something such as a serious accident → **grand jury**

ˌcourt of ˈlaw (*also* **law court**) *n* (*plural* **courts of law**) [C] a place where law cases are judged SYN **court**

ˌcourt ˈorder *n* [C] an order or decision made by a law court: *His computer was seized under a court order.*

ˌcourt reˈporter *n* [C] someone whose job is to record everything that is said during a court case

court·room /ˈkɔːtruːm, -rʊm $ ˈkɔːrt-/ ●○○ *n* [C] a room in a law court where cases are judged

court·ship /ˈkɔːt-ʃɪp $ ˈkɔːrt-/ *n* **1** [C,U] the period of time during which a man and woman have a romantic relationship before marrying **2** [U] special behaviour used by animals to attract each other for sex: *courtship rituals*

ˈcourt shoe *n* [C] *BrE* a type of plain formal shoe worn by women SYN **pump** *AmE* → see picture at SHOE[1]

court·yard /ˈkɔːtjɑːd $ ˈkɔːrtjɑːrd/ ●○○ *n* [C] an open space that is completely or partly surrounded by buildings: *the castle courtyard*

C

cous·cous /ˈkʊskʊs/ *n* [U] a type of North African food made of crushed wheat

cous·in /ˈkʌzən/ ●●● S2 *n* [C]
1 the child of your UNCLE or AUNT → **FIRST COUSIN**, **KISSING COUSIN**, **SECOND COUSIN**
2 something that has the same origins as something else: **[+of/to]** *a drug that is a chemical cousin to amphetamines* | **close/distant cousin** *The Alaskan brown bear is a close cousin of the grizzly bear.*
3 someone or something that is similar to someone or something else: *His avant-garde music, sometime cousin to jazz, had limited appeal.*

cou·ture /kuːˈtjʊə $ -ˈtʊr/ (*also* **haute-couture**) *n* [U] the design and production of expensive and fashionable clothes, or the clothes themselves: *a couture collection*

cove /kəʊv $ koʊv/ *n* [C] **1** part of the coast where the land curves round so that the sea is partly surrounded by land → **bay**: *The last fishing boats left the cove.* **2** *BrE old-fashioned* a man

cov·en /ˈkʌvən/ *n* [C] a group or meeting of WITCHes

cov·e·nant /ˈkʌvənənt/ *n* [C] a legal agreement in which someone promises to pay a person or organization an amount of money regularly → **endowment** —**covenant** *v* [I,T]: *He covenanted to pay £30 a month into the fund.*

Cov·en·try /ˈkɒvəntri, ˈkʌv- $ ˈkʌv-, ˈkɑːv-/ **1** an industrial city in central England **2 send sb to Coventry** *BrE* to refuse to speak to someone in order to punish them, show disapproval etc

cov·er¹ /ˈkʌvə $ -ər/ ●●● S1 W1 *v* [T]
1 HIDE/PROTECT (*also* **cover up**) to put something over or be over something in order to hide, close, or protect it: *Cover the pot and bake for an hour.* | *She wore a low-cut dress, partly covered by a thin shawl.* | **cover sth with sth** *Dan covered his face with his hands.*
2 LAYER if something covers a surface, it forms a layer over it: *Grey mould covered the walls.* | *Much of the country is covered by snow.* | **cover sth with/in sth** *The bulletin board was covered with messages.* | *The eruption of the volcano covered states as far away as Montana in a fine layer of ash.*
3 INCLUDE to include or deal with a particular subject or group of things: *a course covering business law* | *Are there any areas you feel are not covered adequately in the book?* | *'Exercise' is a word which covers a vast range of activities.* | *We need more time to* **cover** *so much* **ground** (=include so many things). | *pollutants that are not covered by the Kyoto agreement*
4 DISTANCE to travel a particular distance: *They were hoping to cover 40 miles yesterday.* | *A leopard can* **cover** *a lot of* **ground** *very quickly.*
5 AREA to spread over an area: *The city covers 25 square miles.*
6 NEWS to report the details of an event for a newspaper or a television or radio programme: *I'd just returned from covering the Cambodian war.*
7 MONEY if a sum of money covers the cost of something, it is enough to pay for it: *The award should be enough to cover her tuition fees.* | *Airlines are raising fares to* **cover** *the rising* **costs** *of fuel.*
8 INSURANCE if your insurance covers you or your possessions, it promises to pay you money if you have an accident, something is stolen etc: *Most policies cover accidental damage to pipes.* | *The treatment wasn't covered by her health care insurance.* | **cover sb against/for sth** *Are we covered for theft?* | **cover sb to do sth** *He thought he was covered to drive the vehicle.*
9 GUNS **a)** to protect someone by being ready to shoot anyone who attacks them: *I'll make for the door – cover me, will you?* **b)** to aim a gun at a person or a place where people might be, in order to prevent them from moving or escaping: *He stepped into the doorway and swung the gun up to cover the corridor.*
10 SPORT to stay close to a member of the opposing team or a part of the field in order to prevent your opponents from gaining points
11 MUSIC to perform or record a song that was originally recorded by another artist: *They've covered several hits from the 1980s.*
12 cover (all) the bases to make sure you can deal with any situation or problem so that nothing bad happens: *Parents are already stressed trying to cover the bases at home and at work.*
13 cover yourself (against sth) (*also* **cover your back**, **cover your butt/ass** *AmE*) to do things in a way that will prevent people from blaming or criticizing you: *Doctors are concerned to cover themselves against charges of negligence.* | *He copied Stella in on the email just to cover his back.*
14 cover your tracks to try to hide something you have done so that other people do not find out: *He started to destroy documents to cover his tracks.*

cover for sb *phr v*
1 to do the work that someone else usually does, because they are not there: *Who's covering for you while you're away?*
2 to prevent someone from getting into trouble by lying for them, especially about where they are or what they are doing

cover sth ↔ **over** *phr v* to put something on top of something else so that it is completely hidden: *The female lays a single egg and covers it over.*

cover up *phr v*
1 cover sth ↔ up to put something over something else so that it cannot be seen: *Her legs were so swollen she had to cover them up.*
2 cover sth ↔ up to prevent people from discovering mistakes or unpleasant facts → **whitewash**: *The affair was covered up and never reached the papers.* | *Mum's worried, but she covers it up by joking.* → **COVER-UP**
3 cover up for sb to protect someone by hiding unpleasant facts about them: *They covered up for Kirk by refusing to answer any questions.*
4 to put clothes, BLANKETs etc over yourself in order to protect or hide your body, or to keep yourself warm: *Cover up, or stay out of the sun.* | **cover yourself up** *Hastily, she covered herself up with the towel.*

cover² ●●● S1 W2 *n*
1 PROTECTION [C] something that is put on top of something else to protect it → **lid**: *a blue duvet cover* | *a plastic cover* | *A* **dust cover** (=to keep dirt etc off) *hung over the painting.*
2 BOOKS [C] the outer front or back part of a magazine, book etc: *His photo's on the cover of 'Newsweek' again.* | **front/back cover** *an advertisement on the back cover* | *I* **read** *the magazine* **from cover to cover** (=all of it). | **cover photo/shot/picture** (=picture on the front cover) *The cover shot was of three guys in army kit.*
3 BED **the covers** [plural] the sheets etc that you put over yourself when you are in bed: *The covers had slipped off in the night.*
4 SHELTER [U] shelter or protection from bad weather or attack: **run/dive for cover** *He was shot in the head as he ran for cover.* | *We were forced to* **take cover** *in a barn.* | *Three soldiers* **broke cover** (=left the place where they were hiding).
5 INSURANCE [U] *BrE* the protection insurance gives you, so that it pays you money if you are injured, something is stolen etc SYN **coverage** *AmE*: *medical cover* | **[+against/for]** *cover against fire and theft*
6 WAR [U] military protection and support given to aircraft, ships etc that are likely to be attacked: *fighters used as cover for ground troops*
7 PLANTS [U] trees and plants that grow in large numbers on a piece of land: *Once the forest cover is felled, rains wash away the soil.* | *With its spreading stems, ivy makes good* **ground cover**.
8 WEATHER [U] clouds, snow etc that partly hide the sky or the ground: **cloud/snow/fog etc cover** *Cloud cover in the morning should clear later.*
9 WORK [U] an arrangement in which people do a job or provide a service, especially because the people who normally do it are not there → **backup**: *It's your responsibility to arrange adequate cover for holiday periods.* | *night-time ambulance cover*

10 MUSIC [C] (*also* **cover version**) a new recording of a song, piece of music etc that was originally recorded by a different artist: *She's opted to* **do** *a* **cover version** *for her first single.*
11 SECRET [C usually singular] behaviour or activities that seem normal or honest but are being used to hide something bad or illegal: **[+for]** *The gang used the shop as a cover for drug deals.* | *All that toughness is just a cover for his inability to show affection.*
12 under cover a) pretending to be someone else in order to do something secretly: *She was* **working under cover** *to get information on drug gangs.* **b)** under a roof or other structure: *The aircraft is displayed under cover in the USAF Gallery.*
13 under (the) cover of darkness/night *literary* hidden by the darkness of night: *They escaped under cover of darkness.*
14 under plain cover/under separate cover if a letter etc is sent under plain cover or under separate cover, it is sent in a plain envelope or a separate envelope: *The bill will be sent to you later under separate cover.*

cov·er·age /ˈkʌvərɪdʒ/ ●○○ *n* [U]
1 when a subject or event is reported on television or radio, or in newspapers: **media/press etc coverage** *The allegations received widespread media coverage.* | ***live coverage*** *of the match* (=the match is broadcast at the same time that it is happening)
2 *AmE* the protection an insurance company gives you, so that it pays you money if you are injured, something is stolen etc SYN **cover** *BrE*: *health care coverage*
3 the range of subjects and facts included in a book, programme, class etc: **[+of]** *Prestel's website provides good coverage of the subject.*
4 when something affects or covers a particular area or group of things: *More satellites are needed to provide telephone coverage in remote areas.*

cov·er·alls /ˈkʌvərɔːlz $ -ɒːlz/ *n* [plural] *AmE* a piece of clothing that you wear over all your clothes to protect them SYN **overalls** *BrE*

ˈcover charge *n* [C] money that you have to pay in a restaurant in addition to the cost of the food and drinks, especially when there is a band or dancing

cov·ered /ˈkʌvəd $ -ərd/ *adj* **1** having a roof: *a covered arena* **2** having a layer of something on top: *snow-covered hills*

ˈcover girl *n* [C] an attractive young woman whose photograph is on the front cover of a magazine

cov·er·ing /ˈkʌvərɪŋ/ *n* **1** [singular] something that covers or hides something: *a light covering of snow* **2 coverings** [plural] a layer of something such as paper, wood, or cloth used to cover walls, floors etc: *colourful wall coverings*

ˌcovering ˈletter *n* [C] *BrE* a letter that you send with documents or a package that gives information about its contents SYN **cover letter** *AmE*: *Send your CV and a covering letter to the address below.*

cov·er·let /ˈkʌvəlɪt $ -vər-/ *n* [C] *old-fashioned* a cloth cover for a bed SYN **bedspread**

ˈcover ˌletter *n* [C] *AmE* a covering letter

cov·er·mount /ˈkʌvəmaʊnt $ -ər-/ *adj* [only before noun] a covermount CD, DVD etc is one which is attached to the cover of a magazine, and which you get free when you buy the magazine —**covermount** *n* [C]

ˈcover note *n* [C] *BrE* a document that proves you have car insurance

ˈcover ˌprice *n* [C usually singular] the price printed on the front of a book, magazine etc: *Ten pence of the cover price goes directly to charity.*

ˈcover ˌstory *n* [C] **1** the main story that appears with a picture on the front cover of a newspaper or magazine **2** false information that you give people about who you are, what you are doing somewhere etc

cov·ert¹ /ˈkʌvət, ˈkəʊvɜːt $ ˈkoʊvərt/ *adj* secret or hidden OPP **overt**: *covert operations* THESAURUS ▸ SECRET

covert² *n* [C] a group of thick bushes where animals can hide

ˈcover-up *n* [C] an attempt to prevent the public from discovering the truth about something → **whitewash**: *He accused the government of a cover-up.* → COVER UP

cov·et /ˈkʌvɪt/ *v* [T] *formal* to have a very strong desire to have something that someone else has: *The Michelin Awards are coveted by restaurants all over the world.*

cov·et·ous /ˈkʌvɪtəs/ *adj formal* having a very strong desire to have something that someone else has: *They began to cast covetous eyes on their neighbours' fields.* —**covetously** *adv* —**covetousness** *n* [U]

cow¹ /kaʊ/ ●●● S2 *n* [C]
1 a large female animal that is kept on farms and used to produce milk or meat → **bull**
2 a male or female animal of this type → **bull**: *a herd of cows*
3 the female of some large animals, such as the ELEPHANT or the WHALE → **bull**
4 *BrE spoken not polite* an offensive word for a woman who you think is stupid or unpleasant
5 have a cow *informal* to be very angry or surprised about something
6 till the cows come home *informal* for a very long time, or for ever → CASH COW, MAD COW DISEASE, SACRED COW

cow² *v* [T] to frighten someone in order to make them do something: **be cowed into sth** *The protesters had been* ***cowed into submission*** *by the police.* GRAMMAR **Cow** is usually passive.

cow·ard /ˈkaʊəd $ -ərd/ *n* [C] someone who is not at all brave: *Try it. Don't be such a coward.* —**cowardly** *adj*: *a cowardly attack on a defenceless man*

cow·ard·ice /ˈkaʊədɪs $ -ər-/ (*also* **cow·ard·li·ness** /ˈkaʊədlinəs $ -ərd-/) *n* [U] lack of courage OPP **bravery**: *cowardice in the face of danger*

cow·bell /ˈkaʊbel/ *n* [C] a small bell → see picture at BELL

cow·boy /ˈkaʊbɔɪ/ ●●○ *n* [C]
1 in the US, a man who rides a horse and whose job is to care for cattle
2 *BrE* someone who is dishonest in business, or who produces very bad quality work: *a firm of cowboy builders*
3 cowboys and Indians a game played by children who fight while pretending to be cowboys and Native Americans

ˈcowboy ˌhat *n* [C] a hat with a wide circular edge and a soft round top → **Stetson**

cow·catch·er /ˈkaʊˌkætʃə $ -ər/ *n* [C] a piece of metal on the front of a train that pushes things off the track

ˈcow chip *n* [C] *AmE* a round flat mass of dry solid waste from a cow SYN **cowpat**

cow·er /ˈkaʊə $ -ər/ *v* [I] to bend low and move back because you are frightened: **[+back/against/under etc]** *He cowered against the wall.*

cow·girl /ˈkaʊgɜːl $ -gɜːrl/ *n* [C] in the US, a woman who rides a horse and whose job is to care for cattle

cow·hand /ˈkaʊhænd/ *n* [C] someone whose job is to care for cattle → **rancher**

cow·hide /ˈkaʊhaɪd/ *n* [C,U] the skin of a cow or the leather made from it

cowl /kaʊl/ *n* [C] **1** a large HOOD that covers your head and shoulders: *a monk in a dark habit and cowl* **2** a cover for a CHIMNEY

cow·lick /ˈkaʊˌlɪk/ *n* [C] hair that sticks up on your head

cow·ling /ˈkaʊlɪŋ/ *n* [C] a metal cover for an aircraft engine

ˌcowl ˈneck *n* [C] the neck on a piece of clothing that falls in folds at the front

co-work·er /ˌkəʊ ˈwɜːkə $ ˈkoʊ ˌwɜːrkər/ ●●○ *n* [C] someone who works with you and has a similar position SYN **colleague**

cow·pat /ˈkaʊpæt/ *n* [C] a round flat mass of solid waste from a cow SYN **cow chip** *AmE*

ˌcow ˈpie *n* [C] *AmE informal* a COW CHIP

cow·poke /ˈkaʊpəʊk $ -poʊk/ *n* [C] *AmE old-fashioned* a COWBOY

cow·rie /ˈkaʊri/ *n* [C] a small shiny shell that was used in the past as money in parts of Africa and Asia

cow·shed /ˈkaʊʃed/ *n* [C] a building where cows are kept

cow·slip /ˈkaʊˌslɪp/ *n* [C] a small European wild plant with sweet-smelling yellow flowers

cox /kɒks $ kɑːks/ *n* [C] someone who controls the direction of a rowing boat, especially in races —**cox** *v* [T]

cox·comb /ˈkɒkskəʊm $ ˈkɑːkskoʊm/ *n* [C] *old-fashioned* a stupid man who is too proud of his clothes and appearance

cox·swain /ˈkɒksən, -sweɪn $ ˈkɑːk-/ *n* [C] a cox

coy /kɔɪ/ *adj* **1** shy or pretending to be shy in order to attract people's interest: *She gave him a coy smile.* **2** unwilling to give information about something OPP **open**: **[+about]** *Tania was always coy about her age.* —**coyly** *adv* —**coyness** *n* [U]

coy·ote /ˈkɔɪ-əʊt, kɔɪˈəʊti $ ˈkaɪ-oʊt, kaɪˈoʊti/ *n* [C] a small wild dog that lives in North West America and Mexico

coy·pu /ˈkɔɪpuː/ *n* [C] an animal like a BEAVER, kept on farms for its fur

coz, **cos** /kʌz, kəz $ kɒːz, kəz/ *conjunction BrE informal* because

coz·en /ˈkʌzən/ *v* [T] *old-fashioned* to trick or deceive someone

co·zy /ˈkəʊzi $ ˈkoʊ-/ *adj* the usual American spelling of COSY

coz·zie /ˈkɒzi $ ˈkɑː-/ *n* [C] *BrE informal* a SWIMMING COSTUME

CPA /ˌsiː piː ˈeɪ/ *n* [C] *AmE* (***Certified Public Accountant***) an ACCOUNTANT who has passed all his or her examinations

CPR /ˌsiː piː ˈɑː $ -ˈɑːr/ *n* [U] (***cardiopulmonary resuscitation***) when you breathe into someone's mouth and press repeatedly on their chest in order to make them breathe again and make their heart start beating again after it has stopped

CPS, the /ˌsiː piː ˈes/ (***the Crown Prosecution Service***) the government organization in England and Wales which is responsible for bringing legal charges against criminals

CPU /ˌsiː piː ˈjuː/ *n* [C] *technical* (***central processing unit***) the part of a computer that controls what it does

crab /kræb/ ●●○ *n*
1 [C] a sea animal with a hard shell, five legs on each side, and two large CLAWS → **crustacean**
2 [U] the flesh of this animal that you can cook and eat: *crab meat | dressed crab* (=prepared for eating)
3 crabs [plural] *informal* a medical condition in which a type of LOUSE (=insect) is in the hair around sexual organs
4 [singular] *AmE informal* someone who becomes annoyed easily about unimportant things

ˈcrab ˌapple *n* [C] a small sour apple, or the tree it grows on

crab·bed /ˈkræbɪd/ *adj literary* writing which is crabbed is small, untidy, and difficult to read

crab·by /ˈkræbi/ *adj* easily annoyed by unimportant things SYN **bad-tempered**: *a crabby old man | You're a bit crabby this morning.*

crab·grass /ˈkræbgrɑːs $ -græs/ *n* [U] *AmE* a kind of rough grass

crab·wise /ˈkræbwaɪz/ (*also* **crab·ways** /-weɪz/) *adv* sideways: *I moved crabwise along the edge of the cliff.*

crack¹ /kræk/ ●●● S2 W2 *v*
1 BREAK [I,T] to break or to make something break, either so that it gets lines on its surface, or so that it breaks into pieces: *Don't put boiling water in the glass or it will crack. | Concrete is liable to crack in very cold weather. | He picked up a piece of rock and cracked it in half. | She fell and cracked a bone in her leg. | He cracked a couple of eggs into a pan.* THESAURUS ▸ BREAK
2 SOUND [I,T] to make a quick loud sound like the sound of something breaking, or to make something do this: *Thunder cracked overhead. | He cracked his whip and galloped off. | Dennis rubbed his hands together and* ***cracked*** *his* ***knuckles***.
3 HIT [T] to hit someone or something hard: **crack sth on sth** *I slipped and cracked my head on the door. | She* ***cracked*** *him* ***over the head*** *with a hammer.*
4 NOT BE ABLE TO CONTINUE [I] to be unable to continue doing something because there is too much pressure and you do not have the mental strength to continue: **[+under]** *Some young executives crack under the pressure of having to meet tough sales targets every month. | He cracked under interrogation and confessed.*
5 VOICE [I] if your voice cracks, it starts to sound different because you are feeling strong emotions: *His voice cracked slightly as he tried to explain.*
6 SOLVE/UNDERSTAND [T] to find the answer to a problem or manage to understand something that is difficult to understand SYN **solve**: *I think we've* ***cracked*** *the* ***problem*** *of the computer crashing all the time. | It took them nearly two months to* ***crack*** *the* ***code***. *| This new evidence could help detectives to* ***crack*** *the* ***case***.
7 STOP SB [T] *informal* to stop a person from being successful: *Political enemies have tried to crack me.*
8 OPEN A SAFE [T] to open a SAFE illegally in order to steal the things inside it
9 COMPUTER [T] to illegally copy computer software or change free software which may lack certain features of the full VERSION, so that the free software works in the same way as the full version: *You can find out how to crack any kind of software on the web.*
10 crack it *BrE informal* to manage to do something successfully: *I think we've cracked it! | He seems to have* ***got it cracked***.
11 crack a joke to tell a joke: *He kept cracking jokes about my appearance.*
12 crack a smile to smile, usually only slightly or unwillingly: *Even Mr Motts managed to crack a smile at that joke.*
13 crack open a bottle *BrE informal* to open a bottle of alcohol for drinking: *We cracked open a few bottles.*
14 get cracking *informal* to start doing something or going somewhere quickly: *I think we need to get cracking if we're going to catch this train.*
15 crack the whip *informal* to make people work very hard
16 sth is not all/everything it's cracked up to be *informal* used to say that something is not as good as people say it is: *I thought the film was OK, but it's not all it's cracked up to be.*

crack down *phr v* to become more strict in dealing with a problem and punishing the people involved: **[+on]** *The government is determined to crack down on terrorism. | The police are* ***cracking down hard*** *on violent crime.* → CRACKDOWN

crack into sth *phr v* to secretly enter someone else's computer system, especially in order to damage the system or steal the information stored on it → **hack**: *A teenager was accused of cracking into the company's network.*

crack on *phr v BrE informal* to continue working hard at something in order to finish it: **[+with]** *I need to crack on with my project work this weekend.*

crack up *phr v informal*
1 crack (sb) up to laugh a lot at something, or to make someone laugh a lot: *Everyone in the class just cracked up. | She's so funny. She cracks me up.*
2 to become unable to think or behave sensibly because you have too many problems or too much work: *I was beginning to think I was cracking up!*

crack² ●●● S3 *n*
1 GAP [C] a very narrow space between two things or two parts of something: **[+between]** *He squeezed into a crack between two rocks. |* **[+in]** *He could see them through a crack in the door. | She* ***opened*** *the door* ***a crack*** *and peeped into the room.* THESAURUS ▸ HOLE → see picture at HOLE¹
2 BREAK [C] a thin line on the surface of something when it is broken but has not actually come apart: **[+in]** *There were several small cracks in the glass.*

3 WEAKNESS [C] a weakness or fault in an idea, system, or organization: **[+in]** *The cracks in their relationship were starting to show.* | *The first **cracks** are beginning to **appear** in the economic policy.*
4 SOUND [C] a sudden loud sound like the sound of a stick being broken: **loud/sharp crack** *There was a sharp crack as the branch broke off.* | **[+of]** *We could hear the crack of gunfire in the distance.* | *a crack of thunder*
5 JOKE [C] *informal* a clever joke or rude remark: **[+about]** *I didn't like his crack about her being overweight.* | *He's always **making cracks** about how stupid I am.*
6 ATTEMPT [C] *informal* an attempt to do something SYN **shot**: **[+at]** *I'd like a crack at climbing that mountain.* | *The competition's open to anyone – why don't you **have a crack**?*
7 DRUG [U] an illegal drug that some people take for pleasure: *crack addicts*
8 BODY [C] *informal* the space between someone's BUTTOCKS
9 a crack on the head a hard hit on the head: *You've had a nasty crack on the head and you need to rest.*
10 a crack in sb's voice a change in someone's voice because they are feeling very upset: *He noticed the crack in her voice as she tried to continue.*
11 the crack of dawn very early in the morning: **at the crack of dawn** *We were up at the crack of dawn.*
12 COMPUTER [C] a piece of information or computer CODE that lets you illegally change free software which may lack certain features of the full VERSION, so that the free software works in the same way as the full version
13 a fair crack of the whip *BrE informal* the same chance as other people to do something: *They feel they haven't been **given a fair crack of the whip**.*
14 another spelling of CRAIC

crack[3] *adj* [only before noun] **1** with a lot of experience and skill: *crack troops* | *a crack regiment* | *a crack sportsman* **2 crack shot** someone who is able to shoot a weapon very well and hit the thing they are aiming at

crack·ber·ry /ˈkrækbəri $ -beri/ *n* (*plural* **crackberries**) [C] *informal* a BLACKBERRY™ – used humorously when someone uses their BlackBerry all the time, as if they are ADDICTED to it like a drug

crack·down /ˈkrækdaʊn/ *n* [C usually singular] action that is taken to deal more strictly with crime, a problem, protests etc: **[+on/against]** *a military crackdown on pro-democracy demonstrations* | *the government's crackdown against drugs* → **crack down** at CRACK[1]

cracked /krækt/ *adj* **1** something that is cracked has one or more lines on the surface because it is damaged but not completely broken: *The mirror was cracked and dirty.* | *dry cracked lips* | *He escaped with a cracked rib and bruising.* **2** someone's voice that is cracked sounds rough and uncontrolled **3** [not before noun] *informal* slightly crazy **4** cracked software has been changed by a user, for example so that they can continue to use it after a particular date or so that it can be used without a LICENCE

crack·er /ˈkrækə $ -ər/ *n* [C] **1** a hard dry type of bread in small flat shapes, that is often eaten with cheese **2** (*also* **Christmas cracker**) a decorated paper tube that makes a small exploding sound when you pull it apart. Crackers contain a small gift, a paper hat, and a joke, and are used at Christmas in Britain. **3** a FIRECRACKER **4** *BrE spoken* something that is very good or funny: *That was a cracker of a goal.* **5** someone who illegally breaks into a computer system in order to steal information or stop the system from working properly SYN **hacker**: *computer crackers* **6** *BrE old-fashioned informal* a very attractive woman

crack·ers /ˈkrækəz $ -ərz/ *adj* [not before noun] *informal* crazy: *You lent him all that money? You must be crackers!*

crack·head /ˈkrækhed/ *n* [C] *informal* someone who uses the illegal drug CRACK

ˈ**crack house** *n* [C] a place where the illegal drug CRACK is sold, bought, and smoked

crack·ing /ˈkrækɪŋ/ *adj* [only before noun] *BrE informal* very good, exciting etc SYN **great**: *We've got two cracking games to look forward to.*

crack·le /ˈkrækəl/ ●○○ *v* [I] to make repeated short sounds like something burning in a fire: *logs crackling on the fire* | *An announcement crackled over the tannoy.* —**crackle** *n* [C] —**crackly** *adj*

crack·ling /ˈkræklɪŋ/ *n* **1** [singular, U] the sound made by something when it crackles: *There was silence except for the crackling of the fire.* **2** [U] *BrE* the hard skin on a piece of pig meat when it has been cooked for a long time **3 cracklings** [plural] *AmE* pieces of skin, usually from a pig or chicken, that have been cooked in hot oil and are eaten cold

crack·pot /ˈkrækpɒt $ -pɑːt/ *n* [C] *informal* someone who is slightly crazy —**crackpot** *adj*: *crackpot schemes*

ˈ**crack-up** *n* [C] **1** a NERVOUS BREAKDOWN **2** *AmE* an accident involving one or more vehicles → **crack up** at CRACK[1]

cra·dle[1] /ˈkreɪdl/ *n* **1** [C] a small bed for a baby, especially one that moves gently from side to side → **cot**: *She **rocked** the **cradle** to quieten the child.* **2 the cradle of sth** *formal* the place where something important began: *Athens is often regarded as the cradle of democracy.* **3 from (the) cradle to (the) grave** all through your life: *From cradle to grave, the car marks every rite of American passage.* **4** [singular] the beginning of something: *Like most Catholic children, he had heard stories of Ireland **from the cradle**.* **5** [C] a structure that is used to lift something heavy up or down: *a window-cleaner's cradle* **6** [C] the part of a telephone where you put the RECEIVER when you are not using it: *She replaced the receiver on the cradle.* → CAT'S CRADLE, → **rob the cradle** at ROB(5)

cradle[2] *v* [T] **1** to hold something gently, as if to protect it: *John cradled the baby in his arms.* THESAURUS HUG **2** to hold a telephone RECEIVER by putting it between your ear and your shoulder: *She hunched over the desk, telephone cradled at her neck.*

ˈ**cradle-ˌrobber** (*also* ˈ**cradle-ˌsnatcher** *BrE*) *n* [C] someone who has a romantic relationship with someone who is much younger – used to show disapproval → **sugar daddy, toy boy** —**cradle-rob** (*also* **cradle-snatch** *BrE*) *v* [I]

craft[1] /krɑːft $ kræft/ ●●○ W3 *n*
1 (*plural* **crafts**) [C] a job or activity in which you make things with your hands, and that you usually need skill to do → **handicraft**: *traditional rural crafts* | *arts and crafts*
2 (*plural* **craft**) [C] **a)** a small boat **b)** an aircraft or spacecraft
3 [singular] *formal* the skills needed for a particular profession: *The musician spends years perfecting his craft.*
4 [U] skill in deceiving people: *Craft and cunning were necessary for the scheme to work.* → LANDING CRAFT

craft[2] *v* [T] to make something using a special skill, especially with your hands: *Each doll is crafted individually by specialists.* | *a **hand-crafted** silver cigar case*

-craft /krɑːft $ kræft/ *suffix* [in nouns] **1** a vehicle of a particular type: *a spacecraft* | *a hovercraft* | *several aircraft* **2** skill of a particular kind: *statecraft* (=skill in government) | *stagecraft* (=skill in acting, directing etc in plays)

ˈ**craft knife** *n* (*plural* **craft knives**) [C] *BrE* a very sharp knife used for cutting paper, thin wood etc → see picture at KNIFE[1]

crafts·man /ˈkrɑːftsmən $ ˈkræfts-/ ●○○ *n* (*plural* **craftsmen** /-mən/) [C] someone who is very skilled at a particular CRAFT

crafts·man·ship /ˈkrɑːftsmənʃɪp $ ˈkræfts-/ *n* [U] **1** very detailed work that has been done using a lot of skill, so that the result is beautiful: *The carving is a superb piece of craftsmanship.* **2** the special skill that someone uses to make something beautiful with their hands: *high standards of craftsmanship*

crafts·wom·an /ˈkrɑːftsˌwʊmən $ ˈkræfts-/ *n* (*plural* **craftswomen** /-ˌwɪmɪn/) [C] a woman who is very skilled at a particular CRAFT

craft·y /ˈkrɑːfti $ ˈkræf-/ ●○○ *adj* (*comparative* **craftier**, *superlative* **craftiest**) good at getting what you want by clever planning and by secretly deceiving people SYN **cunning**, **sly**: *He's a crafty old devil.* THESAURUS INTELLIGENT —**craftily** *adv* —**craftiness** *n* [U]

crag /kræg/ *n* [C] a high and very steep rough rock or mass of rocks

crag·gy /ˈkrægi/ *adj* **1** a mountain that is craggy is very steep and covered in rough rocks: *the craggy peaks of the Sierra Madre* **2** having a face with many deep lines on it: *his thin craggy face*

craic, **crack** /kræk/ *n* [singular, U] *informal* enjoyable conversation or fun with other people – used especially in Ireland

C

cram /kræm/ ●○○ *v* (**crammed**, **cramming**)
1 [T always + adv/prep] to force something into a small space: **cram sth into/onto etc sth** *Jill crammed her clothes into the bag.* | *A lot of information has been crammed into this book.* THESAURUS FILL → see picture at FILL[1]
2 [I always + adv/prep] if a lot of people cram into a place or vehicle, they go into it so it is then full: **[+in/into]** *We all crammed in and Pete started the car.* | *Thirty-six thousand spectators crammed into the stadium to see the game.*
3 [T] *especially AmE* if a lot of people cram a place, they fill it: *Thousands of people crammed the mall Sunday.*
4 [I] to prepare yourself for an examination by learning a lot of information quickly SYN **swot** *BrE*: *She's been cramming hard all week.* | **[+for]** *I have to cram for my chemistry test tomorrow.* THESAURUS STUDY
cram sth ↔ **in** (*also* **cram sth into sth**) *phr v* to do a lot of activities in a short period of time SYN **pack in**: *We crammed in as much sightseeing as possible during our stay in New York.*

crammed /kræmd/ *adj* **crammed with/crammed full of sth** completely full of things or people SYN **packed**: *The guide is crammed full of useful information.* | *The streets were crammed with people.* THESAURUS FULL

cram·mer /ˈkræmə $ -ər/ *n* [C] *BrE* a special school that prepares people quickly for examinations

cramp[1] /kræmp/ *n* **1** [C,U] a severe pain that you get in part of your body when a muscle becomes too tight, making it difficult for you to move that part of your body: *Several players were suffering from cramp.* | *muscle cramps* | **have/get (a) cramp** *One of the swimmers got cramp and had to drop out of the race.* → WRITER'S CRAMP **2 (stomach) cramps** [plural] severe pains in the stomach, especially the ones that women get when they MENSTRUATE

cramp[2] *v* **1** [T] to prevent the development of someone or something SYN **hinder**, **restrict**: *Stricter anti-pollution laws may cramp economic growth.* **2 cramp sb's style** *informal* to prevent someone from behaving in the way they want to: *Paul said he didn't want Sarah to come along because she cramps his style.* **3** [I,T] (*also* **cramp up**) to get or cause cramp in a muscle: *He cramped in the last 200 metres of the race.* | *Sitting still for so long had cramped her muscles.*

cramped /kræmpt/ ●○○ *adj*
1 a cramped room, building etc does not have enough space for the people in it → **crowded**: *The kitchen was small and cramped.* | *a cramped apartment* | *The troops slept in* ***cramped conditions*** *with up to 20 in a single room.* THESAURUS SMALL
2 (*also* **cramped up**) unable to move properly and feeling uncomfortable because there is not enough space: *cramped muscles*
3 writing that is cramped is very small and difficult to read

cram·pon /ˈkræmpɒn $ -pɑːn/ *n* [C usually plural] a piece of metal with sharp points that mountain climbers fasten under their boots to stop them slipping on ice or snow

cran·ber·ry /ˈkrænbəri $ -beri/ *n* (*plural* **cranberries**) [C] a small red sour fruit: *cranberry sauce* → see picture at FRUIT[1]

crane[1] /kreɪn/ ●●○ *n* [C]
1 a large tall machine used by builders for lifting heavy things → **hoist**
2 a tall water bird with very long legs

crane[2] *v* [I,T always + adv/prep] to look around or over something by stretching or leaning: **crane forward/over etc** *The children craned forward to see what was happening.* | *He* ***craned his neck*** *above the crowd to get a better view.*

ˈcrane fly *n* (*plural* **crane flies**) [C] *BrE* a flying insect with long legs SYN **daddy longlegs**

cra·ni·um /ˈkreɪniəm/ *n* (*plural* **craniums** *or* **crania** /-niə/) [C] *technical* the part of your head that is made of bone and covers your brain —**cranial** *adj*

crank[1] /kræŋk/ *n* [C] **1** a handle on a piece of equipment, that you can turn in order to move something **2** *informal* someone who has unusual ideas and behaves strangely: *Zoff was originally dismissed as a crank, but his theories later became very influential.* **3 crank call/letter** a telephone call or letter in which someone says annoying things **4** *AmE informal* someone who easily gets angry or annoyed with people

crank[2] (*also* **crank up**) *v* [T] to make something move by turning a crank: *Try* ***cranking*** *the* ***engine***.
crank sth ↔ **out** *phr v* to produce a lot of something very quickly: *He cranked out three novels last year.*
crank sth ↔ **up** *phr v informal* to make the sound of something, especially music, louder: *We* ***cranked up*** *the* ***volume***.

crank·shaft /ˈkræŋkʃɑːft $ -ʃæft/ *n* [C] a long piece of metal in a vehicle that is connected to the engine and helps to turn the wheels

crank·y /ˈkræŋki/ *adj* **1** *BrE informal* strange → **eccentric**, **weird**: *Organic farming is no longer thought of as cranky.* **2** *informal* bad-tempered: *I was feeling tired and cranky.* —**crankiness** *n* [U]

cran·ny /ˈkræni/ *n* (*plural* **crannies**) [C] a small narrow hole in a wall or rock: *The toad hid itself in a cranny in the wall.* → **nook and cranny** at NOOK(3)

crap[1] /kræp/ *n* **1** [U] *spoken not polite* something someone says that you think is completely wrong or untrue SYN **rubbish**: *You don't believe all that crap, do you?* | **load/pile of crap** (*also* **bunch of crap** *AmE*): *That's a bunch of crap! I never said that.* | *He came out with a load of crap about how he'd tried to call me yesterday.* | *Greg's* ***full of crap*** (=often says things that are completely wrong). | **cut the crap** (=used to tell someone to stop saying things that are completely wrong) *Just cut the crap and tell me what really happened.* **2** [U] *spoken not polite* something that is very bad or is of bad quality SYN **rubbish**: *They sell a lot of stuff cheap, but most of it is crap.* | **load/pile of crap** (*also* **bunch of crap** *AmE*): *The game was a load of crap.* **3** [U] *spoken not polite* things that are useless or unimportant: *What is all this crap doing on my desk?* **4** [U] *spoken not polite* bad or unfair treatment: **take/stand for/put up with crap** (=to allow someone to treat you badly) *I'm not going to take any more of this crap!* | *I* ***don't need this*** *kind of* ***crap*** (=used when you are angry about the way someone is behaving towards you).* | *I'm tired of you* ***giving*** *me* ***crap*** (=saying bad things) *about my long hair.* **5** [U] *spoken not polite* solid waste that is passed from your BOWELS **6** [singular] *spoken not polite* the act of passing solid waste from your BOWELS: **take a crap** (*also* **have a crap** *BrE*) **7 craps** [plural] *AmE* a game played for money in the US, using two DICE: **shoot craps** (=to play this game)

crap[2] *adj BrE spoken not polite* very bad: *a crap film* | *I've had such a crap day.* | **[+at]** *I'm really crap at tennis.*

crap[3] *v* (**crapped**, **crapping**) [I] *spoken not polite* to pass waste matter from your BOWELS

crap·per /ˈkræpə $ -ər/ *n* **the crapper** *spoken not polite* a toilet

crap·py /ˈkræpi/ *adj spoken not polite* very bad: *a crappy hotel*

crash[1] /kræʃ/ ●●● S3 W2 *v*
1 CAR/PLANE ETC [I,T] to have an accident in a car, plane etc by violently hitting something else → **collide**: *The jet crashed after take-off.* | **[+into/onto etc]** *The plane crashed into a mountain.* | **crash a car/bus/plane etc** *He was drunk when he crashed the car.*

GRAMMAR: Reciprocal verbs

Crash is a reciprocal verb. This type of verb is used when saying that two or more people or things do something that involves both or all of them: *Two planes crashed in midair.* You can also say: *Two planes crashed with each other in midair.* | *One plane crashed with another in midair.*

GRAMMAR GUIDE ▸ VERBS

2 HIT SB/STH HARD [I,T always + adv/prep] to hit something or someone extremely hard while moving, in a way that causes a lot of damage or makes a lot of noise: **[+into/through etc]** *A brick crashed through the window.* | *We watched the waves crashing against the rocks.* | *The plates **went crashing** to the ground.* | *A large branch **came crashing down**.*

3 LOUD NOISE [I] to make a sudden loud noise: *Thunder crashed and boomed outside.*

4 COMPUTER [I,T] if a computer crashes, or if you crash the computer, it suddenly stops working: *The system crashed and I lost three hours' worth of work.*

5 FINANCIAL [I] if a STOCK MARKET or SHARES crash, they suddenly lose a lot of value

6 SPORT [I] *BrE* to lose very badly in a sports event: *Liverpool **crashed to** their worst **defeat** of the season.*

7 SLEEP [I] *spoken* **a)** to stay at someone's house for the night: *Can I crash at your place on Saturday night?* **b)** (*also* **crash out**) to go to bed, or go to sleep very quickly, because you are very tired: *I crashed out on the sofa this afternoon.*

8 PARTY [T] *informal* to go to a party that you have not been invited to: *We crashed Joe's party yesterday.*

9 crashing bore *BrE old-fashioned* someone who is very boring

crash² ●●● S3 W2 *n* [C]

1 an accident in which a vehicle violently hits something else → **collision**: **plane/car/rail crash** *Forty-one people were killed in a plane crash.* | **a fatal crash** (=one in which someone is killed) | **[+between/with]** *She was involved in **a head-on crash** with a motorbike* (=in which the front of one vehicle directly hits the front of another). | *a motorway crash between a coach and a lorry* | *a **crash victim*** THESAURUS ▸ ACCIDENT

2 a sudden loud noise made by something falling, breaking etc: *I heard a **loud crash**.* | **with a crash** *The branch came down with a crash.* | **[+of]** *a crash of thunder* THESAURUS ▸ SOUND

3 an occasion when a computer or computer system suddenly stops working

4 an occasion on which the STOCKS and SHARES in a STOCK MARKET suddenly lose a lot of value: *the stock market crash of October 1987*

crash and burn, **crash-and-burn** *n* [C] *informal* an occasion when something fails very quickly or suddenly, especially in a DRAMATIC way: *His bid for the presidency finally did its crash-and-burn.* —**crash-and-burn** *adj* [only before noun]

ˈcrash ˌbarrier *n* [C] *BrE* a strong fence or wall built to keep cars apart or to keep them away from people, in order to prevent an accident → see picture at RAIL¹

ˈcrash course *n* [C] a course in which you learn a lot about a particular subject in a very short period of time: **[+in]** *a crash course in Spanish*

ˈcrash ˌdiet *n* [C] an attempt to lose a lot of weight quickly by strictly limiting how much you eat

ˈcrash ˌhelmet *n* [C] a very strong hard hat that protects your head, and is worn by racing car drivers, people riding MOTORCYCLES etc

ˌcrash ˈlanding, **crash-landing** *n* [C] an occasion when a pilot has to bring a plane down to the ground in a sudden and dangerous way because the plane has a problem: *He was forced to **make** a **crash-landing** in the desert.* —**crash-land** *v* [I,T]

crass /kræs/ *adj* behaving in a stupid and offensive way which shows that you do not understand or care about other people's feelings → **insensitive**: *a **crass remark*** | *an act of **crass stupidity*** —**crassly** *adv*

-crat /kræt/ *suffix* [in nouns] another form of the suffix -OCRAT

crate¹ /kreɪt/ ●○○ *n* [C]

1 a large box made of wood or plastic that is used for carrying fruit, bottles etc: **[+of]** *a crate of beer* → see picture at BOX¹

2 *old-fashioned* a very old car or plane that does not work very well

crate² (*also* **crate up**) *v* [T] to pack things into a crate

cra·ter /ˈkreɪtə $ -ər/ ●○○ *n* [C]

1 a round hole in the ground made by something that has fallen on it or by an explosion: *craters on the Moon's surface* THESAURUS ▸ HOLE

2 the round open top of a VOLCANO → see picture at VOLCANO

cra·vat /krəˈvæt/ *n* [C] a wide piece of loosely folded material that men wear around their necks → **tie**

crave /kreɪv/ *v* [I,T] to have an extremely strong desire for something: *an insecure child who **craves attention***

cra·ven /ˈkreɪvən/ *adj formal* completely lacking courage SYN **cowardly**: *He had a craven fear of flying.* —**cravenly** *adv*

crav·ing /ˈkreɪvɪŋ/ *n* [C] an extremely strong desire for something → **longing**: **[+for]** *She had a craving for some chocolate.*

craw /krɔː $ krɒː/ → **stick in your craw** at STICK¹(11)

craw·fish /ˈkrɔːˌfɪʃ $ ˈkrɒː-/ *n* (*plural* **crawfish**) [C] a CRAYFISH

crawl¹ /krɔːl $ krɒːl/ ●●○ *v* [I]

1 to move along on your hands and knees with your body close to the ground: **[+along/across etc]** *The baby crawled across the floor.*

2 if an insect crawls, it moves using its legs: **[+over/up etc]** *There's a bug crawling up your leg.*

3 crawl into/out of bed to get into or out of bed slowly because you are very tired: *We crawled into bed at 2 am.*

4 if a vehicle crawls, it moves forward very slowly: **[+by/along etc]** *The traffic was crawling along.*

5 *BrE informal* to be too pleasant or helpful to someone in authority, especially because you want them to help you - used to show disapproval: **[+to]** *She's always crawling to the boss.*

6 be crawling with sth to be completely covered with insects, people etc: *The floor was crawling with ants.* | *The whole place was crawling with cops.*

7 crawl the Net/web if a computer program crawls the Net, it quickly searches the Internet to find the particular information you need → **spider**: *robots that crawl the net searching out e-mail addresses for junk mailing*

crawl² *n* [singular] **1** a very slow speed: *The traffic had slowed to a crawl.* **2 the crawl** a way of swimming in which you lie on your stomach and move one arm, and then the other, over your head → **backstroke**, **breaststroke**, **butterfly** → see picture at SWIM

ˈcrawler ˌlane *n* [C] *BrE* a special part of a road that can be used by slow vehicles so that other vehicles can go past → **fast lane**

cray·fish /ˈkreɪˌfɪʃ/ *n* (*plural* **crayfish**) [C,U] a small animal like a LOBSTER that lives in rivers and streams, or the meat from this animal

cray·on¹ /ˈkreɪən, -ɒn $ -ɑːn, -ən/ ●○○ *n* [C] a stick of coloured WAX or CHALK that children use to draw pictures

crayon² *v* [I,T] to draw something with a crayon

craze /kreɪz/ *n* [C] a fashion, game, type of music etc that becomes very popular for a short time SYN **fad**: **[+for]** *She started a craze for this type of jewellery.* | *At that time, scooters were the **latest craze**.* | **fitness/dance/fashion etc craze** *The jogging craze began in the 1970s.*

crazed /kreɪzd/ *adj* behaving in a wild and uncontrolled way like someone who is mentally ill: **crazed with grief/pain/fear etc** *He was crazed with grief after the death of his*

C

mother. | The old woman had a **crazed expression** on her face. | a **crazed killer**

cra·zy[1] /ˈkreɪzi/ ●●● S2 *adj* (*comparative* **crazier**, *superlative* **craziest**)

1 STRANGE very strange or not sensible SYN **mad**: *The neighbours must think we're crazy.* | *It's an absolutely* ***crazy idea***. | *I know this idea* ***sounds crazy****, but it may be worth a try.* | **crazy to do sth** *It'd be crazy to go out in this rain.* | *I must have been crazy to agree to this.* | *He often works 12 hours a day –* ***it's crazy***. THESAURUS ▸ STUPID

2 crazy about sb/sth liking someone very much, or very interested in something: *He's crazy about her.* | *Dan's crazy about football.*

3 ANGRY angry or annoyed: *Turn that music down. It's* ***driving*** *me* ***crazy***! (=really annoying me) | *Dad will* ***go crazy*** *when he hears about this.*

4 like crazy very much or very quickly: *We're going to have to work like crazy to get this finished on time.*

5 go crazy to do something too much, in a way that is not usual or sensible, especially because you are excited: *Don't go crazy and spend it all at once.*

6 MENTALLY ILL mentally ill SYN **mad**: *I feel so alone, sometimes I wonder if I'm* ***going crazy***. —**crazily** *adv* —**craziness** *n* [U]

GRAMMAR

Crazy is not used with 'very'. You say: *You'd be absolutely crazy to agree.* ✗ Don't say: *You'd be very crazy to agree.*
GRAMMAR GUIDE ▸ ADJECTIVES

crazy[2] *n* (*plural* **crazies**) [C] *especially AmE informal* someone who is crazy

ˌcrazy ˈgolf *n* [U] *BrE* a golf game, played for fun outdoors, in which you hit a small ball through passages, over bridges and small hills etc SYN **miniature golf**

ˌcrazy ˈpaving *n* [U] *BrE* pieces of stone of different shapes fitted together to make a path or flat area

ˌcrazy ˈquilt *n* [C] a cover for a bed, made from small pieces of cloth of different shapes and colours that have been sewn together SYN **patchwork quilt**

creak /kriːk/ ●○○ *v* [I] if something such as a door, wooden floor, old bed, or stair creaks, it makes a long high noise when someone opens it, walks on it, sits on it etc: *The floorboards creaked as she walked across the room.* | *The door creaked open.* THESAURUS ▸ SOUND —**creak** *n* [C]

creak·y /ˈkriːki/ *adj* **1** something such as a door, floor, or bed that is creaky creaks when you open it, walk on it, sit on it etc, especially because it is old and not in good condition: *creaky stairs* **2** an organization, company etc that is creaky uses old-fashioned methods and does not work very well: *creaky state-owned factories* —**creakily** *adv* —**creakiness** *n* [U]

cream[1] /kriːm/ ●●● S2 *n*

1 [U] a thick yellow-white liquid that rises to the top of milk: *fresh cream* | *strawberries and cream*

2 [U] a pale yellow-white colour

3 [C,U] used in the names of foods containing cream or something similar to it: *cream of chicken soup*

4 [C,U] a thick smooth substance that you put on your skin to make it feel soft, treat a medical condition etc → **lotion**: *sun cream* | *face cream*

5 the cream of sth the best people or things from a group: *the cream of Europe's athletes* | *The students at this college are the* ***cream of the crop*** (=the best of all).

cream[2] *adj* pale yellow-white in colour: *a cream-coloured carpet*

cream[3] *v* [T] **1** to mix foods together until they become a thick soft mixture: *Cream the butter and sugar together.* **2** *AmE informal* to easily defeat someone in a game, competition etc: *We* ***got creamed*** *45–6.* **3** to hit a ball very hard, for example in a game of tennis or cricket **4** *AmE informal* to hit someone very hard

cream sb/sth ↔ **off** *phr v especially BrE* to choose the best people or things from a group, especially so that you can use them for your own advantage: *The best students are creamed off by the large companies.*

ˌcream ˈcheese / $ ˈ. ./ *n* [U] a type of soft white smooth cheese

ˌcream ˈcracker *n* [C] *BrE* a light BISCUIT often eaten with cheese

cream·er /ˈkriːmə $ -ər/ *n* **1** [U] a white liquid or powder that you can use instead of milk or cream in coffee or tea **2** [C] a small container for holding cream

cream·e·ry /ˈkriːməri/ *n* (*plural* **creameries**) [C] *old-fashioned* a place where milk, butter, cream, and cheese are produced or sold → **dairy**

ˌcream ˈtea *n* [C,U] *BrE* a small meal eaten in Britain, with small cakes and tea

cream·y /ˈkriːmi/ *adj* (*comparative* **creamier**, *superlative* **creamiest**) **1** thick and smooth like cream: *Beat the mixture until smooth and creamy.* | *a soft cheese with a creamy texture* **2** containing cream: *creamy milk* **3** pale yellow-white in colour

crease[1] /kriːs/ *n* **1** [C] a line on a piece of cloth, paper etc where it has been folded, crushed, or pressed: *She* ***smoothed*** *the* ***creases*** *from her skirt.* | *I'll have to iron out the creases.* **2** [C] a fold in someone's skin → **wrinkle**: *the creases on his forehead* **3** [singular] the line where the player has to stand to hit the ball in CRICKET

crease[2] *v* [I,T] to become marked with a line or lines, or to make a line appear on cloth, paper etc by folding or crushing it → **crumple**: *Don't sit on my newspaper. You'll crease it!* | *These trousers crease really easily.* | *A worried frown creased her forehead.* —**creased** *adj*: *This shirt is too creased to wear.*

crease (sb) **up** *phr v BrE spoken* to laugh a lot, or to make someone laugh a lot SYN **crack up**: *She really creases me up!*

cre·ate /kriˈeɪt/ ●●● S2 W1 AWL *v* [T]

1 to make something exist that did not exist before: *Some people believe the universe was created by a big explosion.* | *Her behaviour is creating a lot of problems.* | *The new factory is expected to create more than 400 new jobs.* THESAURUS ▸ MAKE

2 to invent or design something: *This dish was created by our chef Jean Richard.* | *Philip Glass created a new kind of music.* | *The software makes it easy to create colourful graphs.* THESAURUS ▸ INVENT

3 create sb sth *BrE* to officially give someone a special rank or title: *James I created him Duke of Buckingham.*

cre·a·tion /kriˈeɪʃən/ ●●○ W3 AWL *n*

1 [U] the act of creating something: **[+of]** *the creation of 2,000 new jobs* | *the creation of a single European currency* | *a* ***job creation*** *scheme*

2 [C] something that has been created: *The dress is a stunning creation in green, gold, and white.* | *Most countries have systems of government that are relatively modern creations.*

3 the Creation the act by God, according to the Bible, of making the universe, including the world and everything in it

4 [U] *literary* the whole universe and all living things

cre·a·tion·ist /kriˈeɪʃənɪst/ *n* [C] someone who believes that God created the universe in the way described in the Bible —**creationism** *n* [U] —**creationist** *adj*

cre·a·tive[1] /kriˈeɪtɪv/ ●●○ W3 *adj*

1 involving the use of imagination to produce new ideas or things: *This job is so boring. I wish I could do something more creative.* | *I teach* ***creative writing*** *at Trinity College.* | *the* ***creative process*** *of writing a poem* | *Diaghilev did his great* ***creative work*** *in France.* | *a* ***creative solution*** *to the problem*

2 someone who is creative is very good at using their imagination to make things → **inventive**: *You're so creative! I could never make my own clothes.* —**creatively** *adv* —**creativeness** *n* [U]

creative[2] *n* [C] *informal* someone such as a writer or artist who uses their imagination or skills to make things

creˌative acˈcounting *n* [U] the process of using

unusual but not illegal ways to change business accounts to make them look better than they really are

cre·a·tiv·i·ty /ˌkriːeɪˈtɪvəti/ ●●○ AWL *n* [U] the ability to use your imagination to produce new ideas, make things etc: *artistic creativity* | *Teachers have been attacked for stifling creativity in their pupils.* | *Editors complain about the lack of creativity in the ideas put to them.*

cre·a·tor /kriˈeɪtə $ -ər/ ●●○ AWL *n*
1 [C] someone who made or invented a particular thing → **inventor**: **[+of]** *Walt Disney, the creator of Mickey Mouse*
2 the Creator God

crea·ture /ˈkriːtʃə $ -ər/ ●●● W3 *n* [C]
1 LIVING THING anything that is living, such as an animal, fish, or insect, but not a plant: *all the **living creatures** in the sea* | **creatures of the deep** (=animals and fish that live in the ocean) THESAURUS ▸ ANIMAL
2 IMAGINARY OR STRANGE an imaginary animal or person, or one that is very strange and frightening: *creatures from outer space*
3 a creature of habit someone who always does things in the same way or at the same time
4 STH MADE OR INVENTED *formal* something, especially something bad, that was made or invented by a particular person or organization: **[+of]** *The poll tax was a creature of the government.*
5 SB CONTROLLED BY STH someone who is controlled or influenced a lot by something: **[+of]** *He was a creature of the military government.*
6 beautiful/stupid/adorable etc creature *literary* someone who has a particular character or quality: *He was the most beautiful creature Dot had ever seen.*

ˌcreature ˈcomforts *n* [plural] all the things that make life more comfortable and enjoyable, such as good food, a warm house, and comfortable furniture → **mod cons**

cre·che, **crèche** /kreʃ $ kreʃ, kreɪʃ/ *n* [C] **1** *BrE* a place where babies are looked after while their parents are at work SYN **day care center** *AmE* **2** *AmE* a model of the scene of Jesus Christ's birth, placed in churches and homes at Christmas SYN **crib** *BrE*

cre·dence /ˈkriːdəns/ *n* [U] *formal* the acceptance of something as true: **give credence to sth** (=to believe or accept something as true) *I don't give any credence to these rumors.* | **gain credence** (=to become more widely accepted or believed) *His ideas quickly gained credence among economists.* | **lend credence to sth** (=to make something more believable) *The DNA results lend credence to Hausmann's claims of innocence.*

cre·den·tialed /krɪˈdenʃəld/ *adj* someone who is credentialed is legally allowed to do a particular job, because they have done the right type of training SYN **qualified**: *a newly credentialed teacher*

cre·den·tials /krɪˈdenʃəlz/ ●○○ *n* [plural]
1 someone's education, achievements, experience etc that prove they have the ability to do something: **[+for/as]** *She had excellent credentials for the job.* | *There are doubts over his credentials as a future prime minister.* | *He spent the first part of the interview trying to **establish** his **credentials** as a financial expert.* | *Her **academic credentials** include an MA and a PhD.*
2 a letter or other document which proves your good character or your right to have a particular position: *The commissioner presented his credentials to the State Department.*

cred·i·bil·i·ty /ˌkredəˈbɪləti/ ●○○ *n* [U]
1 the quality of deserving to be believed and trusted: **damage/undermine sb's credibility (as sth)** *The scandal has damaged his credibility as a leader.* | **[+of]** *There are serious questions about the credibility of these reports.* | **gain/lose credibility** *Predictions of economic recovery have now lost all credibility.*
2 credibility gap the difference between what someone says and what they do: *a credibility gap between the government's promises and their achievements*

cred·i·ble /ˈkredəbəl/ ●○○ *adj* deserving or able to be believed or trusted → **incredible**: **credible explanation/story/account etc** *He was unable to give a credible explanation for his behaviour.* | *Her excuse was barely credible.* | **credible threat/challenge/force etc** *Can Thompson make a credible challenge for the party leadership?* | *a **credible alternative** to nuclear power* —**credibly** *adv*

cred·it¹ /ˈkredɪt/ ●●● S2 W2 AWL *n*
1 DELAYED PAYMENT [U] an arrangement with a shop, bank etc that allows you to buy something and pay for it later: **on credit** *Most new cars are bought on credit.* | *The store agreed to let him have credit.* | *What's the credit limit on your Visa card?*
2 PRAISE [U] approval or praise that you give to someone for something they have done: **[+for]** *Credit for this win goes to everybody in the team.* | *They never **give** Gene any **credit** for all the extra work he does.* | **take/claim/deserve etc (the) credit** *She deserves credit for trying her best.* | **to sb's credit** (=used to say that someone has done something good) *To Jamie's credit, he remained calm.* | *Credit must go to Fiona for making sure everything ran smoothly.*
3 be a credit to sb/sth (*also* **do sb/sth credit**) to behave so well or be so successful that your family, team etc are proud of you: *She's a credit to her profession.* | *Your children really do you credit.*
4 have sth to your credit to have achieved something: *She already has two successful novels to her credit.*
5 in credit if you are in credit, there is money in your bank account: *There are no bank charges if you stay in credit.*
6 the credits [plural] a list of all the people involved in making a film or television programme, which is shown at the beginning or end of it
7 on the credit side used to talk about the good things about someone or something: *On the credit side, the book is extremely well researched.*
8 (give) credit where credit is due used to say that someone deserves to be praised for the good things they have done
9 UNIVERSITY [C] a successfully completed part of a course at a university or college: *I don't have enough credits to graduate.*
10 AMOUNT OF MONEY [C] an amount of money that is put into someone's bank account or added to another amount OPP **debit**: *The company promised to provide credits to customers who had been charged too much.*
11 TRUE/CORRECT [U] the belief that something is true or correct: *The witness's story **gained credit** with the jury.*

COLLOCATIONS

VERBS

buy/get sth on credit *They bought all their furniture on credit.*
use credit *The survey showed only 15% of people had never used credit.*
get/obtain credit (=be allowed to buy something on credit) *The economic situation is making it more difficult for people to get credit.*
give/offer credit (=allow customers to buy things on credit) *A business may lose customers if it does not give credit.*
refuse sb credit *You may be refused credit if you have a bad financial record.*

credit + NOUN

a credit card (=a plastic card that you use to buy things and pay for them later) *Can I pay by credit card?*
credit facilities (=the opportunity to buy something on credit) *Credit facilities are available if you are over 18.*
a credit agreement (=an arrangement to allow or receive credit) | **credit terms** (=how much you must pay back and when) | **sb's credit rating** (=how likely a bank etc thinks someone is to pay their debts) | **a credit risk** (=a risk that a bank etc may not get back the money it lends) | **a credit limit** (=the most someone can spend using credit) | **a credit crunch/squeeze** (=a situation in which people are not allowed as much credit as before)

C

ADJECTIVES/NOUN + credit
consumer credit (=the amount of credit used by consumers) *Consumer credit has risen substantially during this period.*
interest-free credit (=with no interest added to it) *We offer interest-free credit for up to 50 weeks.*

credit² ●○○ AWL *v* [T]
1 to add money to a bank account OPP **debit**: **[+to]** *The cheque has been credited to your account.* | **[+with]** *For some reason my account's been credited with an extra $76.*
2 credit sb with (doing) sth to believe or admit that someone has a quality, or has done something good: *Do credit me with a little intelligence!* | *Evans is credited with inventing the system.*
3 be credited to sb/sth if something is credited to someone or something, they have achieved it or are the reason for it: *Much of Manchester United's success can be credited to their manager.*
4 *formal* to believe that something is true: **difficult/hard/impossible etc to credit** *We found his statement hard to credit.*

cred·it·a·ble /ˈkredətəbəl/ *adj* [usually before noun] deserving praise or approval: *The team produced a* ***creditable performance****.* | *She did a* ***creditable job*** *of impersonating the singer.* —**creditably** *adv*

ˈcredit acˌcount *n* [C] *BrE* an account with a shop which allows you to take goods and pay for them later SYN **charge account** *AmE*

ˈcredit card ●●● S2 *n* [C] a small plastic card that you use to buy goods or services and pay for them later: *We accept all major credit cards.*

ˈcredit crunch *n* [singular] a time when borrowing money becomes difficult because banks reduce the amount they lend and charge high INTEREST RATES

ˈcredit-ˌcrunched *adj* affected badly by the credit crunch: *credit-crunched companies*

ˈcredit ˌeasing *n* [U] a system by which a national bank makes it easier for businesses to get CREDIT

ˈcredit note *n* [C] *BrE* a document given to a customer who is owed money, for example because they have returned goods

cred·i·tor /ˈkredɪtə $ -ər/ AWL *n* [C] a person, bank, or company that you owe money to OPP **debtor**

ˈcredit ˌrating *n* [C] a judgment made by a bank or other company about how likely a person or business is to pay their debts

ˈcredit ˌvoucher *n* [C] a CREDIT NOTE

cred·it·wor·thy /ˈkredətˌwɜːði $ -ˌwɜːr-/ *adj formal* considered to be able to pay debts: *creditworthy borrowers* —**creditworthiness** *n* [U]

cre·do /ˈkriːdəʊ, ˈkreɪ- $ -doʊ/ *n* (*plural* **credos**) [C] a formal statement of the beliefs of a particular person, group, religion etc: *American Express is emphasizing its 'the customer is first' credo.*

cre·du·li·ty /krɪˈdjuːləti $ -ˈduː-/ *n* [U] *formal* willingness or ability to believe that something is true → **incredulity**: *Advertisers were accused of exploiting consumers' credulity.* | **strain/stretch credulity** (=seem very difficult to believe) *It strained credulity to believe that a nuclear war would not lead to the destruction of the planet.*

cred·u·lous /ˈkredjələs $ -dʒə-/ *adj formal* always believing what you are told, and therefore easily deceived SYN **gullible**: *Quinn charmed credulous investors out of millions of dollars.*

creed /kriːd/ *n* [C] **1** a set of beliefs or principles: *Marxism has never been weaker as a* ***political creed****.* | *a* ***religious creed*** | *people of all colours and creeds* **2 the Creed** a formal statement of belief spoken in certain Christian churches

creek /kriːk/ ●○○ *n* [C]
1 *AmE, AusE* a small narrow stream or river
2 *BrE* a long narrow area of water that flows from the sea into the land
3 be up the creek (without a paddle) (*also* **be up shit creek (without a paddle)** *not polite*) *spoken* to be in a very difficult situation: *If I don't get my passport by Friday, I'll be up the creek.*

creel /kriːl/ *n* [C] a FISHERMAN's basket for carrying fish

creep¹ /kriːp/ ●●○ *v* (*past tense and past participle* **crept** /krept/) [I always + adv/prep]
1 to move in a quiet, careful way, especially to avoid attracting attention: **[+into/over/around etc]** *Johann would creep into the gallery to listen to the singers.* | *He crept back up the stairs, trying to avoid the ones that creaked.* THESAURUS ▸ WALK
2 if something such as an insect, small animal, or car creeps, it moves slowly and quietly → **crawl**: **[+down/along/away etc]** *a caterpillar creeping down my arm*
3 to gradually enter something and change it: **[+in/into/over etc]** *Funny how religion is creeping into the environmental debate.*
4 if a plant creeps, it grows or climbs up or along a particular place: **[+up/over/around etc]** *ivy creeping up the walls of the building*
5 if mist, clouds etc creep, they gradually fill or cover a place: **[+into/over etc]** *Fog was creeping into the valley.*
6 *BrE informal* to be insincerely nice to someone, especially someone in authority, in order to gain an advantage for yourself: **creep (up) to sb** *I'm not the kind of person to creep to anybody.*
7 sb/sth makes my flesh creep used to say that someone or something makes you feel strong dislike or fear: *His glassy stare made my flesh creep.*

creep sb **out** *phr v informal* to make someone feel nervous, uncomfortable, and slightly frightened: *He's always staring at me - it creeps me out!*

creep up on sb/sth *phr v*
1 to surprise someone by walking up behind them silently: *Don't yell – let's creep up on them and scare them.*
2 if a feeling or idea creeps up on you, it gradually increases: *The feeling she had for Malcolm had crept up on her and taken her by surprise.*
3 to seem to come sooner than you expect: *Somehow, the end of term had crept up on us.*

creep² *n* [C] **1** *especially AmE informal* someone who you dislike extremely: *Get lost, you little creep!* **2** *BrE informal* someone who tries to make you like them or do things for them by being insincerely nice to you: *Don't try and flatter her – she doesn't approve of creeps.* **3 give sb the creeps** if a person or place gives you the creeps, they make you feel nervous and a little frightened, especially because they are strange: *That house gives me the creeps.* **4 mission/cost/grade etc creep** when something gradually starts to go beyond what it was intended to deal with or include: *He denied that giving civilian tasks to the NATO forces was a case of mission creep.*

creep·er /ˈkriːpə $ -ər/ *n* [C] a plant that grows up trees or walls, or along the ground → VIRGINIA CREEPER

creep·y /ˈkriːpi/ ●○○ *adj informal* making you feel nervous and slightly frightened: *There's something creepy about the way he looks at me.* | *The whole place feels creepy.* THESAURUS ▸ FRIGHTENING

ˌcreepy-ˈcrawly *n* (*plural* **creepy-crawlies**) [C] *informal* an insect, especially one that you are frightened of

cre·mate /krəˈmeɪt $ ˈkriːmeɪt/ *v* [T] to burn the body of a dead person at a funeral ceremony —**cremation** /krɪˈmeɪʃən/ *n* [C,U]

crem·a·to·ri·um /ˌkreməˈtɔːriəm $ ˌkriː-/ *n* (*plural* **crematoriums** *or* **crematoria** /-riə/) (*also* **crem·a·to·ry** /ˈkremətəri $ ˈkriːmətɔːri/) *AmE* [C] a building in which the bodies of dead people are burned at a funeral ceremony

crème car·a·mel /ˌkrem ˈkærəməl, -mel/ *n* (*plural* **crèmes caramels** (*same pronunciation*)) [C,U] *BrE* a sweet food made from milk, eggs, and sugar

crème de la crème, **creme de la creme** /ˌkrem də lɑː ˈkrem/ *n* [singular] the very best of a kind of thing or group of people: *Oxford and Cambridge are often seen as the crème de la crème of British universities.*

crème de menthe /ˌkrem də ˈmɒnθ $ -ˈmɑːnt/ *n* [U] a strong sweet green alcoholic drink

crème fraiche /ˌkrem ˈfreʃ/ *n* [U] a slightly sour thick cream

cre·ole /ˈkriːəʊl $ -oʊl/ *n* **1** [C,U] a language that is a combination of a European language with one or more other languages → **pidgin 2 Creole** [C] **a)** someone whose family were originally from both Europe and Africa **b)** someone whose family were originally French SETTLERS in the southern US **3** [U] food prepared in the spicy strong-tasting style of the southern US: *shrimp creole* —**creole** *adj*

cre·o·sote /ˈkriːəsəʊt $ -soʊt/ *n* [U] a thick brown oily liquid used for preserving wood —**creosote** *v* [T]

crepe, **crêpe** /kreɪp/ *n* **1** [U] a type of light soft thin cloth, with very small folded lines on its surface, made from cotton, silk, wool etc **2** [C] a very thin PANCAKE **3** [U] tightly pressed rubber used especially for making the bottoms of shoes: *crepe-soled shoes*

ˌcrepe ˈpaper / $ ˈ. ˌ../ *n* [U] a type of thin brightly coloured paper that stretches slightly and is used for making decorations

crept /krept/ the past tense and past participle of CREEP

cre·scen·do /krəˈʃendəʊ $ -doʊ/ *n* (*plural* **crescendos**) [C] **1** if a sound or a piece of music rises to a crescendo, it gradually becomes louder until it is very loud OPP **diminuendo**: *The shouting* ***rose to a*** *deafening* ***crescendo***. | *The curtains opened as the music* ***reached a crescendo***. **2** if an activity or feeling reaches a crescendo, it gradually becomes stronger until it is very strong SYN **climax**: *The campaign* ***reached its crescendo*** *in the week of the election.*

cres·cent /ˈkresənt, ˈkrez-/ *n* [C] **1** a curved shape that is wider in the middle and pointed at the ends: *a small crescent of pastry topped with cheese* | *a* ***crescent moon*** **2** the curved shape that is used as a sign of the Muslim religion **3** a street with a curved shape - often used in the names of streets

cress /kres/ *n* [U] a small plant with round green leaves that are eaten raw → **mustard**: *Sprinkle some finely chopped cress over the top.*

crest[1] /krest/ *n* [C] **1** the top or highest point of something such as a hill or a wave: **[+of]** *It took us over an hour to reach the crest of the hill.* **2** a special picture that is used as a sign of a family, town, school, or organization → **coat of arms**: **school/family crest 3** a group of feathers that stick up on the top of a bird's head: *exotic birds with colourful crests* **4** a decoration of long bright feathers that soldiers wore in the past on top of their hats **5 be on/riding the crest of a wave** to be very successful: *a young film director who is on the crest of a wave at the moment*

crest[2] *v* [T] *formal* to reach the top of a hill or mountain: *They* ***crested*** *a wooded* ***hill*** *shortly before sunset.*

crest·ed /ˈkrestɪd/ *adj* **1** a crested bird has a crest on its head **2** marked by the crest of a family, town, school, or organization: *crested notepaper*

crest·fal·len /ˈkrestˌfɔːlən $ -ˌfɒːl-/ *adj* looking disappointed and upset SYN **downcast**: *He came back* ***looking crestfallen***. THESAURUS ▶ DISAPPOINTED

Cre·ta·ceous /krəˈteɪʃəs/ *adj* the Cretaceous period was the time long ago when rocks containing CHALK were formed

cret·in /ˈkretɪn $ ˈkriːtn/ *n* [C] *informal not polite* an offensive word for someone who is extremely stupid

Creutz·feldt–Jak·ob dis·ease /ˌkrɔɪtsfelt ˈjækɒb dɪˌziːz $ -ˈjɑːkoʊb-/ *n* [U] (*abbreviation* **CJD**) a very serious disease that kills people and that may be caused by eating BEEF that is infected with BSE

cre·vasse /krɪˈvæs/ *n* [C] a deep open crack in the thick ice on a mountain

crev·ice /ˈkrevɪs/ *n* [C] a narrow crack in the surface of something, especially in rock: *small creatures that hide in crevices in the rock*

crew[1] /kruː/ ●●● S3 W3 *n*
1 [C] all the people who work on a ship or plane: *The plane crashed, killing two of the crew and four passengers.* | **[+of]** *He joined the crew of a large fishing boat.* | *a* ***crew member*** THESAURUS ▶ GROUP
2 [C] a group of people working together with special skills: *a TV camera crew* → **GROUND CREW**
3 [C] a team of people who compete in ROWING races: *Who will be on the college crew?*
4 [singular] a group of people or friends - often used to show disapproval: *The volunteers were a* ***motley crew*** (=very mixed group of people). | *Do you still hang out with* ***the same crew***?
5 [C] *informal* **a)** a group of musicians, especially ones playing HIP HOP, RAP, or GARAGE music **b)** a group of HIP HOP dancers
6 [C] *informal* a group of young people who spend time together, often one that is involved in crime, drugs, or violence SYN **gang**

crew[2] *v* [I,T] to be part of the crew on a boat: *The boat is crewed by ten men.*

ˈcrew cut *n* [C] a very short hairstyle for men → see picture at **HAIRSTYLE**

crew·man /ˈkruːmən/ *n* (*plural* **crewmen** /-mən/) [C] a member of the crew on a boat or ship

ˈcrew neck *n* [C] a plain round neck on a SWEATER or shirt, or a sweater or shirt with this type of neck → see picture at **NECK**[1]

crib[1] /krɪb/ *n* **1** [C] *AmE* a bed for a baby or young child, with bars on the side to stop the baby from falling out SYN **cot** *BrE* **2** [C] *BrE* a bed with high sides for a very young baby, which you can move gently from side to side SYN **cradle 3** [C] a wooden frame in which you put food for animals such as cows and horses **4** [C] *BrE* a model of the scene of Jesus Christ's birth, often placed in churches and homes at Christmas → **Nativity 5** [C] *BrE informal* a book or piece of paper with information or answers to questions, which students sometimes use dishonestly in examinations **6** [C] *AmE spoken* the place where someone lives: **sb's crib** *I'm not at my crib, I'm at Jed's house.* **7** [U] the card game of cribbage

crib[2] *v* (**cribbed**, **cribbing**) [I,T] *especially BrE* to copy school or college work dishonestly from someone else: **crib sth off/from sb** *He didn't want anyone to crib the answers from him.*

crib·bage /ˈkrɪbɪdʒ/ (*also* **crib**) *n* [U] a card game in which players show how many points they have by putting small pieces of wood in holes in a small board

ˈcrib death *n* [C] *AmE* the sudden and unexpected death of a baby while it is asleep SYN **cot death** *BrE*

crick[1] /krɪk/ *n* [C] a pain in the muscles in your neck or back that is caused by the muscles becoming stiff: **a crick in your back/neck** *He was getting a crick in his neck from leaning out of the window for so long.*

crick[2] *v* [T] to hurt your back or neck by bending or moving in a way that makes the muscles become stiff: *I cricked my back bending to pick up the suitcase.*

crick·et /ˈkrɪkɪt/ ●●○ *n*
1 [U] a game between two teams of 11 players in which players try to get points by hitting a ball and running between two sets of three sticks
2 [C] a small brown insect that can jump, and that makes a rough sound by rubbing its wings together

crick·et·er /ˈkrɪkɪtə $ -ər/ *n* [C] *BrE* someone who plays cricket → **batsman**, **bowler**, **fielder**: *Her father was a very good cricketer.*

cri·er /ˈkraɪə $ -ər/ *n* [C] a TOWN CRIER

cri·key /ˈkraɪki/ *interjection BrE spoken* used to show that you are surprised or annoyed: *Crikey, I'm late!*

crime /kraɪm/ ●●● S2 W2 *n*
1 [U] illegal activities in general: *We moved here because there was very little crime.* | *Police officers are being given new powers to help combat crime.* | *a police crackdown on car crime* | *a town with a relatively low crime rate*

GRAMMAR

Don't use 'the crime' when talking about illegal activities in general. You say: *Crime has increased*

dramatically. ✗ Don't say: *The crime has increased dramatically.*
GRAMMAR GUIDE ▸ NOUNS

2 [C] an illegal action, which can be punished by law: *He insisted that he had not committed any crime.* | *men who have been found guilty of violent crimes* | **[+against]** *Crimes against the elderly are becoming more common.* | *Police are still busy hunting for clues at* ***the scene of the crime*** (=where the crime happened).
3 a life of crime when someone spends their life stealing and committing crimes, in order to get money to live
4 the perfect crime a crime that no one knows has been committed, so no one can be punished for it
5 crime of passion a crime, especially murder, caused by sexual jealousy
6 crime against humanity a crime of cruelty against large numbers of people, especially in a war
7 crime doesn't pay used to say that crime does not give you any advantage, because you will be caught and punished - used when warning people not to get involved in crime
8 [singular] something that someone is blamed or criticized for doing - use this when you think someone is treated very unfairly → **sin**: ***My only crime*** *is that I fell in love with another girl.* | *Johnson's* ***biggest crime*** *was that he told the truth.*
9 it's a crime *spoken* said when you think something is very wrong, and someone should not do it: *It would be a crime to waste all that good food.* → **partners in crime** at PARTNER[1](5), → WHITE-COLLAR(2)

COLLOCATIONS - MEANINGS 1 & 2

VERBS
commit (a) crime *Most crime is committed by young men.*
carry out a crime *The boy admitted that he'd carried out the crime.*
fight/combat/tackle crime *There are a number of ways in which the public can help the police to fight crime.*
turn to crime (=start committing crimes) *Youngsters who are bored sometimes turn to crime.*
solve a crime *It took ten years for the police to solve the crime.*
report a crime *I immediately telephoned the police to report the crime.*

ADJECTIVES/NOUN + crime
(a) serious crime *Kidnapping is a very serious crime.*
(a) violent crime *Figures show a 19% rise in violent crime.*
a terrible/horrific crime (*also* **a dreadful crime** *BrE*) *What made him commit such a terrible crime?*
petty crime (=crime that is not very serious) *Immigrants were blamed for the increase in petty crime.*
juvenile/youth crime (=committed by children and teenagers) | **organized crime** (=committed by large organizations of criminals) | **car crime** *BrE* (=stealing cars) | **street crime** (=crimes such as robbery committed on the streets) | **corporate crime** (=involving businesses) | **property crime** (=stealing from or damaging property) | **computer crime** (=committed using computers) | **war crimes** (=serious crimes committed during a war) | **a sex crime** (=in which someone is sexually attacked) | **a hate crime** (=committed against someone because of their race, religion etc)

PHRASES
a victim of crime *Victims of crime do not always report the offence.*
a crackdown on crime (=strong action to fight crime) *The government has promised a crackdown on crime.*
the scene of the crime (*also* **the crime scene**) (=the place where a crime has happened) *Detectives were already at the scene of the crime.*
be tough on crime (=punish crime severely) *Politicians want to appear tough on crime.*

crime + NOUN
a crime wave (=a sudden increase in crime in an area) *Larger cities have been the worst hit by the crime wave.*
crime prevention *The police can give you advice on crime prevention.*
the crime rate *The crime rate has gone up.*
crime figures/statistics | **a crime writer** (=someone who writes stories about crimes, especially murder)

COMMON ERRORS
⚠ Don't say 'do a crime'. Say **commit a crime** or **carry out a crime**.

ˈcrime wave *n* [singular] a sudden large increase in the amount of crime in an area: *More police officers are being brought in to help tackle the current crime wave.*

crim·i·nal¹ /ˈkrɪmɪnəl/ ●●● S3 W2 *adj*
1 relating to crime: *Experts cannot agree on the causes of* ***criminal behaviour****.* | *I was sure he was involved in some kind of* ***criminal activity****.* | *She has not committed a* ***criminal offence*** (=a crime). | *He was arrested and charged with* ***criminal damage*** (=damaging someone's property illegally). | *The doctor was found guilty of* ***criminal negligence*** (=not taking enough care to protect people you are responsible for).
2 relating to the part of the legal system that is concerned with crime → **civil**: *The case will be tried in a* ***criminal court****.* | *We have no faith in the* ***criminal justice system****.* | *The police are investigating the matter, and he may face* ***criminal charges*** (=be officially accused of a crime). | *She usually deals with serious* ***criminal cases****.* | *a* ***criminal lawyer***
3 wrong, dishonest, and unacceptable SYN **wicked**: *It seems criminal that teachers are paid so little money.*
—**criminally** *adv*: *a hospital for the criminally insane*
—**criminality** /ˌkrɪməˈnæləti/ *n* [U]

criminal² ●●● W3 *n* [C] someone who is involved in illegal activities or has been proved guilty of a crime → **offender**: *Police have described the man as a violent and dangerous criminal.* | *a* ***convicted criminal*** (=someone who has been found guilty of a crime) | *The new law will ensure that* ***habitual criminals*** (=criminals who commit crimes repeatedly) *receive tougher punishments than first-time offenders.* | *Teenagers should not be sent to prison to mix with* ***hardened criminals*** (=criminals who have committed and will continue to commit a lot of crimes).

crim·i·nal·ize (*also* **-ise** *BrE*) /ˈkrɪmənəl-aɪz/ *v* [T] to make something illegal, or to say that someone is a criminal because of something they have done OPP **decriminalize**: *The government has introduced new legislation to criminalize computer hacking.*

ˌcriminal ˈlaw *n* [U] laws concerning crimes and their punishments → **civil law**, **common law**: *There was not enough evidence to bring a prosecution under criminal law.*

ˌcriminal ˈrecord *n* [C] an official record kept by the police of any crimes a person has committed: *He already* ***had a criminal record****.*

crim·i·nol·o·gy /ˌkrɪməˈnɒlədʒi $ -ˈnɑː-/ *n* [U] the scientific study of crime and criminals —**criminologist** *n* [C]

crimp /krɪmp/ *v* [T] **1** to press cloth, paper etc into small regular folds: *Use a hot iron to crimp the edges.* **2** to make your hair slightly curly by using a special heated tool: *crimped blonde hair*

Crimp·lene /ˈkrɪmpliːn/ *n* [U] *trademark BrE* a type of artificial cloth that does not easily get lines when it is folded or crushed

crim·son¹ /ˈkrɪmzən/ *adj* **1** deep red in colour: *The leaves turn crimson in autumn.* | *a crimson dress* **2** if you go crimson, your face becomes red because you are very angry or embarrassed: **go/turn/flush/blush crimson** *The boy blushed crimson.* | **[+with]** *Her face was crimson with embarrassment.* —**crimson** *n* [U]

crimson² *v* [I] *literary* if your face crimsons, it becomes red because you are embarrassed SYN **blush**: *Rachel crimsoned and sat down.*

cringe /krɪndʒ/ *v* [I] **1** to move away from someone or something because you are afraid: *A stray dog was cringing by the door.* | *She cringed away from him.* **2** to feel embarrassed by something you have said or done because you think it makes you seem silly → **wince**: **[+at]** *She cringed at the sound of her own voice.* | *It* ***makes*** *me* ***cringe*** *when I think how stupid I was.*

crin·kle¹ /ˈkrɪŋkəl/ (*also* **crinkle up**) *v* [I,T] **1** if you crinkle part of your face, or if it crinkles, you move it so that small lines appear on it: *His mouth crinkled into a smile.* | *He smiled boyishly, crinkling his eyes.* | *Her face crinkled up in disgust.* **2** to become covered with small folds, or make something do this: *The heat was beginning to make the cellophane crinkle.* —**crinkled** *adj*: *The pages were brown and crinkled.*

crinkle² *n* [C] a thin fold, especially in your skin or on cloth, paper etc → **crease**: *The first crinkles of age were beginning to appear round her eyes.*

ˈcrinkle-cut *adj* crinkle-cut vegetables have been cut into long pieces with gentle curves along the edges: *a bag of frozen crinkle-cut chips*

crin·kly /ˈkrɪŋkli/ *adj* **1** having a lot of small lines or folds: *She looked fondly at his crinkly face.* | *He smiled his nice crinkly smile.* | *The paper was brown and crinkly at the edges.* **2** hair that is crinkly is stiff and curly: *He had blue eyes and crinkly fair hair.*

crin·o·line /ˈkrɪnəlɪn/ *n* [C] a round frame that was worn in the past under a woman's skirt to support it and hold it away from her body

cripes /kraɪps/ *interjection old-fashioned* used to express surprise or anger

cripple¹ ●○○ *v* [T]

1 *old-fashioned* to hurt someone badly so that they cannot walk properly SYN **disable**: *She was crippled in a car accident.*

2 to damage something badly so that it no longer works or is no longer effective: *Industry is being crippled by high interest rates.* —**crippled** *adj*: *landing the crippled plane*

crip·ple² /ˈkrɪpəl/ *n* [C] **1** *old-fashioned* someone who is unable to walk properly because their legs are damaged or injured, now considered offensive → **disabled** **2 emotional cripple** *informal* someone who cannot express their feelings to other people – used to show disapproval

crip·pling /ˈkrɪplɪŋ/ *adj* **1** causing so much damage or harm that something no longer works or is no longer effective: *the crippling effects of war on the economy* **2** a crippling disease or condition causes severe pain and makes it difficult or impossible for someone to walk → **disabling**

cri·sis /ˈkraɪsɪs/ ●●○ S3 W3 *n* (*plural* **crises** /-siːz/) [C,U]

1 a situation in which there are a lot of problems that must be dealt with quickly so that the situation does not get worse or more dangerous → **emergency**: *The country now faces an* ***economic crisis****.* | *The prime minister was criticized for the way in which he* ***handled the crisis****.* | *the current* ***debt crisis*** | *a* ***major political crisis*** | *I was relieved that we had* ***averted*** *yet another financial* ***crisis****.* | *Oil companies were heavily criticized when they made large profits* ***during the*** *oil* ***crisis*** *of the 1970s.* | *The car industry* ***is now in crisis****.* | *He doesn't seem to be very good at* ***crisis management****.*

2 a time when a personal emotional problem or situation has reached its worst point: *an emotional crisis* | *In times of crisis, you find out who your real friends are.* | *He seems to be* ***going through*** *a* ***crisis****.* | *She has reached a* ***crisis point*** *in her career.* | *Both parties experienced an* ***identity crisis*** (=feeling of uncertainty about their purpose) *at the end of the '90s.*

3 crisis of confidence a situation in which people no longer believe that a government or an economic system is working properly, and will no longer support it or work with it: *There seems to be a crisis of confidence in the economy.*

4 crisis of conscience a situation in which someone feels worried or uncomfortable because they have done something which they think is wrong or immoral → MIDLIFE CRISIS

crisp¹ ●○○ *adj*

1 HARD something that is crisp is hard, and makes a pleasant sound when you break it or crush it: *She kicked at the crisp leaves at her feet.* | *He stepped carefully through the crisp deep snow.* THESAURUS HARD

2 FOOD food that is crisp is pleasantly hard or firm when you bite it SYN **crispy** OPP **soggy**: *a crisp green salad* | *a*

THESAURUS: crime

ILLEGAL ACTIONS

crime *n* [C,U] an illegal action or activity, or these actions in general: *The police need the public's help to solve crimes.* | *Crime is on the increase.* | *It was a horrific crime.*

offence *BrE*, **offense** *AmE* *n* [C] a crime, especially one that has a particular description and name in law: *It is an offence to drive while using a mobile phone.* | *a minor offence* (=one that is not serious) | *a parking offence*

misdemeanor *n* [C] *AmE law* a crime that is not very serious: *They pleaded guilty to a misdemeanor and were fined.*

felony *n* [C,U] *especially AmE law* a serious crime: *Fewer than 25 percent of the people arrested on felony charges are convicted.*

CRIMES OF STEALING

robbery *n* [C,U] the crime of stealing from a bank, shop etc: *Over £100,000 was stolen in the robbery.* | *The gang carried out a string of daring robberies.*

burglary *n* [C,U] the crime of breaking into someone's home in order to steal things: *There have been several burglaries in our area.*

theft *n* [C,U] the crime of stealing something: *Car theft is a big problem.* | *thefts of credit cards*

shoplifting *n* [U] the crime of taking things from shops without paying for them: *They get money for drugs from shoplifting.*

fraud *n* [C,U] the crime of getting money from people by tricking them: *He's been charged with tax fraud.* | *credit card fraud*

VIOLENT CRIMES

assault *n* [C,U] the crime of physically attacking someone: *He was arrested for an assault on a policeman.*

mugging *n* [C,U] the crime of attacking and robbing someone in a public place: *Muggings usually happen at night.*

murder *n* [C,U] the crime of deliberately killing someone: *He is accused of the murder of five women.*

homicide *n* [C,U] *especially AmE law* murder: *Homicide rates are rising fastest amongst teenagers.*

rape *n* [C,U] the crime of forcing someone to have sex: *In most cases of rape, the victim knows her attacker.*

CRIMES AGAINST PROPERTY

arson *n* [U] the crime of deliberately setting fire to a building: *The school was completely destroyed in an arson attack.*

vandalism *n* [U] the crime of deliberately damaging things, especially public property: *He often got into fights and committed acts of vandalism.*

crisp juicy apple | Cook the pastry until it is crisp and golden. | The meat should be nice and crisp on the outside.
3 PAPER/CLOTH paper or cloth that is crisp is fresh, clean, and new SYN **fresh**: *a crisp new five-dollar bill | crisp cotton sheets*
4 WEATHER weather that is crisp is cold and dry OPP **humid**: *The air was fresh and crisp. | a crisp clear autumn day | The weather remained crisp and dry.* THESAURUS ▸ COLD
5 PEOPLE if someone behaves or speaks in a crisp way, they are confident, polite, and firm, but not very friendly: *Her tone was crisp and businesslike.*
6 PICTURE/SOUND a picture or sound that is crisp is clear SYN **sharp**: *an old recording that still sounds remarkably crisp* —**crisply** *adv*: *'Take a seat,' she said crisply.* —**crispness** *n* [U]

crisp² /krɪsp/ *n* [C] *BrE* a very thin flat round piece of potato that is cooked in oil and eaten cold → **chip** SYN **potato chip** *AmE*: *a packet of crisps*

crisp³ *v* [I,T] to become crisp or make something become crisp by cooking or heating it: *Cook the chicken until the skin is nicely crisped.*

crisp·bread /ˈkrɪspbred/ *n* [C,U] a thin dry BISCUIT with a salty taste

crisp·y /ˈkrɪspi/ *adj* food that is crispy is pleasantly hard on the outside: *a piece of crispy fried bread* THESAURUS ▸ HARD

criss·cross¹, **criss-cross** /ˈkrɪskrɒs $ -krɒːs/ *v* **1** [I,T] to make a pattern of straight lines that cross each other: *Railway lines crisscross the countryside.* **2** [T] to travel many times from one side of an area to another: *They spent the next two years crisscrossing the country by bus.*

crisscross², **criss-cross** *n* [C] a pattern made up of a lot of straight lines that cross each other → **zigzag**: *Inside the box was a crisscross of wires.* —**crisscross** *adj*: *a crisscross pattern of streets*

cri·te·ri·on /kraɪˈtɪəriən $ -ˈtɪr-/ ●●○ W2 AWL *n* (*plural* **criteria** /-riə/) [C usually plural] a standard that you use to judge something or make a decision about something: *the criteria we use to select candidates* | **[+for]** *the criteria for measuring how good schools are | Academic ability is not the **sole criterion** for admission to the college. | a universal **set of criteria** for diagnosing patients* | **meet/satisfy/fulfil criteria** *To qualify for a grant, students must satisfy certain criteria.*

crit·ic /ˈkrɪtɪk/ ●●○ W3 *n* [C]
1 someone whose job is to make judgments about the good and bad qualities of art, music, films etc SYN **reviewer**: **music/art/film/theatre/literary critic** *a review by the theatre critic of the 'Sunday Times'*
2 someone who criticizes a person, organization, or idea: **[+of]** *Critics of the scheme have said that it will not solve the problem of teenage crime.* | **fierce/outspoken critic** *an outspoken critic of the government*
3 armchair critic someone who criticizes other people but who does not have any proper experience of the activity the other people are doing

crit·i·cal /ˈkrɪtɪkəl/ ●●○ S3 W2 *adj*
1 CRITICIZING if you are critical, you criticize someone or something: **[+of]** *Many economists are critical of the government's economic policies. | Many parents are **strongly critical** of the school. | He made some **highly critical** remarks.*
2 IMPORTANT something that is critical is very important because what happens in the future depends on it SYN **crucial**: **[+to]** *These talks are critical to the future of the peace process. | It is **absolutely critical** for us to know the truth. | Foreign trade is **of critical importance** to the economy.*
3 SERIOUS/WORRYING a critical time or situation is serious and worrying because things might suddenly become much worse: *The fighting has stopped, but the situation is still critical. | changes that took place during the critical period at the end of the war* THESAURUS ▸ SERIOUS
4 ILL so ill that you might die: *He is still **in a critical condition** in hospital. | She is in intensive care, where she remains critical but stable.*
5 the critical list a) the list of patients in a hospital who are so ill that they might die: **on the critical list** *Two of the victims were still on the critical list Sunday night.* | **take sb off the critical list** *He was taken off the critical list and is now in a stable condition.* **b)** if a system, plan, company etc is on the critical list, it is having severe problems and might fail soon
6 MAKING JUDGMENTS making careful judgments about how good or bad something is: *His book provides a critical analysis of the television industry in Britain. | She looked round the room **with a critical eye**.*
7 ART/LITERATURE according to critics who give judgments about art, films, theatre, and books: *The book came out last year **to** great **critical acclaim*** (=critics said it was very good). | *Her first play was a **critical success*** (=critics said it was good).

crit·i·cally /ˈkrɪtɪkli/ ●○○ *adv*
1 critically ill/injured so ill or so badly injured that you might die → **fatally**: *Ten people died and thirty were critically injured in a rail crash yesterday. | She is still critically ill in hospital.*
2 IMPORTANT in a way that is very important SYN **crucially**: *The success of the project depends critically on the continuation of this funding. | This is a **critically important** meeting.*
3 SERIOUS/WORRYING in a way that is very serious and worrying SYN **dangerously**: *Food supplies are at a critically low level.*
4 CRITICIZING in a way that shows you are criticizing someone or something: *Mike looked at her critically. | He has spoken critically of the government's refusal to support the industry.*
5 MAKING JUDGMENTS thinking about something and giving a careful judgment about how good or bad it is: *We teach students to **think critically** about the texts they are reading.*
6 ART/LITERATURE according to critics who give judgments about art, films, theatre, and books: *The play was **critically acclaimed*** (=praised by critics) *when it opened in London last month.*

ˌcritical ˈmass *n* [C,U] **1** the amount of a substance that is necessary for a NUCLEAR CHAIN REACTION to start **2** the smallest number of people or things that are needed in order for something to happen or be possible: *How can we get a critical mass of people involved to keep the club running?*

ˌcritical ˈpath *n* [C] a way of planning and organizing a large piece of work so that there will be few delays and the cost will be as low as possible: *Costs can be calculated once the critical path has been established.*

crit·i·cis·m /ˈkrɪtɪsɪzəm/ ●●○ S3 W2 *n* [C,U]
1 remarks that say what you think is bad about someone or something OPP **praise**: **[+of]** *My main criticism of the scheme is that it does nothing to help families on low incomes. | Despite **strong criticism**, the new system is still in place. | There has been **widespread criticism** of the decision. | We try to give students **constructive criticism**. | Another **criticism levelled at** him was that his teaching methods were old-fashioned. | The government's economic strategy has **attracted** a lot of **criticism**. | You must learn to **accept criticism**. | Many employees find it hard to **take** even mild **criticism**. | His actions **provoked** severe **criticism** from civil rights groups. | the **storm of criticism** that followed his announcement*
2 writing which expresses judgments about the good or bad qualities of books, films, music etc: *literary criticism*

crit·i·cize (*also* **-ise** *BrE*) /ˈkrɪtɪsaɪz/ ●●● W3 *v*
1 [I,T] to express your disapproval of someone or something, or to talk about their faults OPP **praise**: *Ron does nothing but criticize and complain all the time.* | **be strongly/sharply/heavily criticized** *The decision has been strongly criticized by teachers. | The new law has been **widely criticized**.* | **criticize sb/sth for (doing) sth** *He has been criticized for incompetence. | Doctors have criticized the government for failing to invest enough in the health service.* | **criticize sb/sth as sth** *The report has been criticized as inaccurate and incomplete.*
2 [T] *formal* to express judgments about the good and

bad qualities of something: *We look at each other's work and criticize it.*

THESAURUS

criticize to say what you think is bad about someone or something: *He was criticized for not being tough enough with the terrorists. | Stop criticizing my friends!*
be critical of sb/sth to criticize someone or something, especially by giving detailed reasons for this: *The report was highly critical of the police investigation. | The press have been critical of his leadership style.*
attack to criticize someone or something very strongly, especially publicly in the newspapers, on TV etc: *They attacked the government's decision to undertake nuclear weapons tests.*
lay into sb/tear into sb to criticize someone very strongly for something they have done, especially by shouting at them: *He started laying into one of his staff for being late.*
tear sb/sth to shreds to find a lot of things wrong with someone's arguments or ideas and make them seem very weak: *The prosecution will tear him to shreds.*
pan to strongly criticize a film, play etc in the newspapers, on TV etc: *Her first movie was panned by the critics.*
be pilloried *especially written* to be strongly criticized by a lot of people in the newspapers, on TV etc: *He was pilloried in the right-wing press.*
condemn to say very strongly in public that you do not approve of something or someone, especially because you think they are morally wrong: *Politicians were quick to condemn the bombing.*

TO CRITICIZE UNFAIRLY

find fault with sb/sth to criticize things that you think are wrong with something, especially small and unimportant things: *He's quick to find fault with other people's work.*
pick holes in sth *informal* to criticize something by finding many small faults in it, in a way that seems unreasonable and unfair: *Why are you always picking holes in my work?*
knock to criticize someone or something, in an unfair and unreasonable way: *I know it's fashionable to knock Tony Blair, but I think he did a good job.*

cri·tique[1] /krɪˈtiːk/ ●○○ *n* [C,U] a detailed explanation of the problems of something such as a set of political ideas → **evaluation**: **[+of]** *a major new critique of his work | a critique of modern economic theory*

critique[2] *v* [T] *formal* to say how good or bad a book, play, painting, or set of ideas is → **evaluate**: *He offered to critique our plans.*

crit·ter /ˈkrɪtə $ -ər/ *n* [C] *AmE spoken* a creature, especially an animal

croak[1] /krəʊk $ kroʊk/ *v* **1** [I] to make a deep low sound like the sound a FROG makes **2** [I,T] to speak in a low rough voice, as if you have a sore throat: *'Help!' she croaked, her throat dry with fear.* **3** [I] *informal* to die

croak[2] *n* [C] **1** the sound that a FROG makes **2** a low rough sound made in a person's or animal's throat: *The words came out as a dry croak.* —**croaky** *adj*

cro·chet /ˈkrəʊʃeɪ $ kroʊˈʃeɪ/ *v* [I,T] to make clothes etc from wool or cotton, using a special needle with a hook at one end → **knit** —**crochet** *n* [U] —**crocheting** *n* [U]

crock /krɒk $ krɑːk/ *n* [C] **1** *old use* a clay pot **2 crocks** *BrE informal old-fashioned* cups, dishes, plates etc **3 a crock (of shit)** *AmE spoken* something that is unbelievable, unfair, untrue etc

crocked /krɒkt $ krɑːkt/ *adj* [not before noun] **1** *BrE old-fashioned* injured or broken **2** *AmE spoken* drunk: *Kitty **got** totally **crocked** last night.*

crock·e·ry /ˈkrɒkəri $ ˈkrɑː-/ *n* [U] *BrE* cups, dishes, plates etc → **cutlery**: *a stack of dirty crockery*

croc·o·dile /ˈkrɒkədaɪl $ ˈkrɑː-/ ●●○ *n*
1 [C] a large REPTILE with a long mouth and many sharp teeth that lives in lakes and rivers in hot wet parts of the world → **alligator** → see picture at **REPTILE**
2 [U] the skin of this animal, used for making things such as shoes: *a crocodile briefcase*
3 [C] *BrE* a long line of people, especially school children, walking in pairs
4 crocodile tears if someone sheds crocodile tears, they seem sad, sorry, or upset, but they do not really feel this way

cro·cus /ˈkrəʊkəs $ ˈkroʊ-/ *n* [C] a small purple, yellow, or white flower that appears in early spring → see picture at **FLOWER**[1]

Croe·sus /ˈkriːsəs/ (?-546 BC) a king of Lydia in Asia Minor, known for being very rich. People sometimes say that someone is 'as rich as Croesus' to mean that they are extremely rich.

croft /krɒft $ krɒːft/ *n* [C] *BrE* a very small farm in Scotland

croft·er /ˈkrɒftə $ ˈkrɒːftər/ *n* [C] *BrE* someone who lives and works on a croft in Scotland

croft·ing /ˈkrɒftɪŋ $ ˈkrɒːf-/ *n* [U] *BrE* the system of farming on crofts in Scotland

crois·sant /ˈkwɑːsɒŋ $ krɒːˈsɑːnt/ *n* [C] a type of sweet bread, shaped in a curve and usually eaten for breakfast → see picture at **BREAD**

crone /krəʊn $ kroʊn/ *n* [C] *not polite* an ugly or unpleasant old woman

cro·ny /ˈkrəʊni $ ˈkroʊni/ *n* (*plural* **cronies**) [C usually plural] one of a group of people who spend a lot of time with each other – used to show disapproval: **sb's cronies** *the senator's political cronies* **THESAURUS** ▶ **FRIEND**

cro·ny·i·sm /ˈkrəʊni-ɪzəm $ ˈkroʊ-/ *n* [U] the practice of unfairly giving the best jobs to your friends when you are in a position of power – used to show disapproval

crook[1] /krʊk/ ●○○ *n* [C]
1 *informal* a dishonest person or a criminal: *The crooks got away across the park.*
2 a long stick with a curved end, used by people who look after sheep
3 the crook of your arm the part of your arm where it bends

crook[2] *v* [T] if you crook your finger or your arm, you bend it

crook·ed /ˈkrʊkɪd/ ●○○ *adj*
1 bent, twisted, or not in a straight line OPP **straight**: **crooked smile/grin** *His lips curled into a crooked smile. | Your tie's crooked. | narrow crooked streets* → see picture at **STRAIGHT**[2]
2 dishonest: *a crooked cop* —**crookedly** *adv* —**crookedness** *n* [U]

croon /kruːn/ *v* [I,T] to sing or speak in a soft gentle voice, especially about love: *Sinatra crooning mellow tunes | 'My child,' Sarah crooned.* —**crooner** *n* [C]

crop[1] /krɒp $ krɑːp/ ●●● W3 *n* [C]
1 a plant such as wheat, rice, or fruit that is grown by farmers and used as food → **GM**: *The main crops were oats and barley. | **crop production** | crops grown for market* → **CASH CROP**
2 the amount of wheat, rice, fruit etc that is produced in a season SYN **harvest**: **[+of]** *this season's crop of quality pears | Fruit growers are gathering in a **bumper crop*** (=a very large amount of something produced in a season). | *increased **crop yields***
3 crop of sb/sth a group of people who arrive or things that happen at the same time: **[+of]** *South Korea's present crop of elected politicians*
4 a short whip used in horse-riding
5 the part under a bird's throat where food is stored
6 a very short HAIRSTYLE
7 crop of dark hair/blonde curls etc hair that is short, thick, and attractive: *his reddish crop of shining hair*

crop[2] *v* (**cropped**, **cropping**) **1** [T] to cut someone's hair short: *Stella's had her hair **closely cropped**.* **2** [T] to cut a part off a photograph or picture so that it is a particular size or shape **3** [T] if an animal crops grass or other plants, it makes them short by eating them **4** [I] *BrE* if a plant crops, it produces fruit, grain etc: *My strawberries crop in June or July.*

crop up *phr v* **1** if a problem crops up, it happens or appears suddenly and in an unexpected way SYN **arise** **2** if something such as a name or a subject crops up, it appears in something you read or hear SYN **come up**: *Your name kept cropping up in conversation.*

ˈcrop ˌcircle *n* [C] a pattern that began appearing in the fields of farms in Britain during the 1980s and the 1990s.

ˈcrop-ˌdusting *n* [U] *AmE* CROP-SPRAYING

crop·per /ˈkrɒpə $ ˈkrɑːpər/ **come a cropper** *BrE informal* **a)** to fail in something, especially unexpectedly: *Swedish investors have come a cropper in London.* **b)** to accidentally fall from a horse, bicycle etc: *She came a cropper on the ski slopes.*

ˈcrop roˌtation *n* [U] the practice of changing the crops that you grow in a field each year to preserve the good qualities in the soil

ˈcrop-ˌspraying *n* [U] *BrE* the practice of dropping chemicals from a plane onto crops in order to kill insects SYN **crop-dusting** *AmE*

ˈcrop top *n* [C] a type of women's shirt that does not cover the stomach

cro·quet /ˈkrəʊkeɪ, -ki $ kroʊˈkeɪ/ *n* [U] a game played on grass in which players hit balls with wooden MALLETS (=long-handled hammers) so that they roll under curved wires called HOOPS

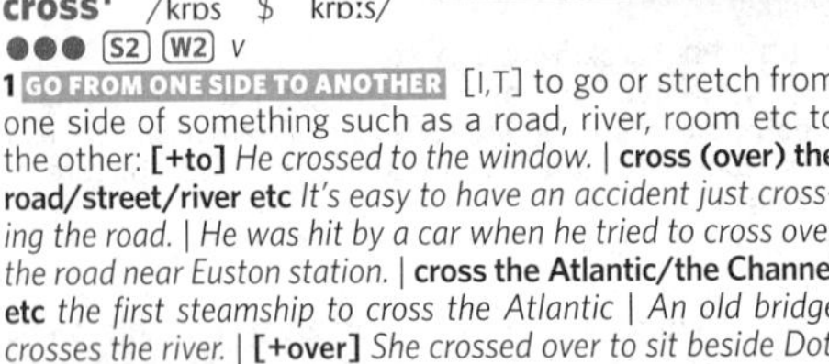

cro·quette /krəʊˈket $ kroʊ-/ *n* [C] a piece of crushed meat, fish, potato etc that is made into a small round piece, covered in BREADCRUMBS, and cooked in oil

cro·si·er /ˈkrəʊziə, -ʒə $ -ʒər/ *n* [C] a CROZIER

cross¹ /krɒs $ krɔːs/ ●●● S2 W2 *v*

1 GO FROM ONE SIDE TO ANOTHER [I,T] to go or stretch from one side of something such as a road, river, room etc to the other: **[+to]** *He crossed to the window.* | **cross (over) the road/street/river etc** *It's easy to have an accident just crossing the road.* | *He was hit by a car when he tried to cross over the road near Euston station.* | **cross the Atlantic/the Channel etc** *the first steamship to cross the Atlantic* | *An old bridge crosses the river.* | **[+over]** *She crossed over to sit beside Dot.*

THESAURUS ▸ TRAVEL

2 CROSS A LINE ETC [T] if you cross a line, track etc, you go over and beyond it: *He raised his arms in triumph as he crossed the line for his 100-metres win.*

3 TWO ROADS/LINES ETC [I,T] if two or more roads, lines, etc cross, or if one crosses another, they go across each other: *The by-pass crosses Wilton Lane shortly after a roundabout.*

4 LEGS/ARMS/ANKLES [T] if you cross your legs, arms, or ANKLES, you put one on top of the other: *She was sitting on the floor with her legs crossed.*

5 cross sb's mind [usually in negatives] if you say that an idea, thought etc never crossed your mind, you mean that you did not think of it SYN **occur to sb**: ***It didn't cross** her **mind that** she might be doing something illegal.* | **the thought has (never) crossed my mind** (=used to tell someone you have thought of the thing they are suggesting, or have never thought of it)

6 cross sb's face *written* if an expression crosses someone's face, it appears on their face: *A look of surprise crossed her face.*

7 cross your fingers used to say that you hope something will happen in the way you want: *She hung the washing out, then crossed her fingers for a dry day.* | *The exam's at two. Will you keep your fingers crossed for me?*

8 BREED OF PLANT/ANIMAL [T] to mix two or more different breeds of animal or plant to form a new breed → **crossbreed**: *a flower produced by crossing several different varieties* | **cross sth with sth** *These cattle were crossed with a breed from the highlands.*

9 sb's paths cross (*also* **cross paths**) if two people's paths cross, or if they cross paths, they meet, usually without expecting it: *If our paths crossed I usually ignored her.* | *We didn't cross paths again until 2001.*

10 cross that bridge when you come to it used to say that you will not think or worry about something until it actually happens

11 cross my heart (and hope to die) *spoken informal* used to say that you promise that you will do something, or that what you are saying is true

12 MAKE SB ANGRY [T] to make someone angry by opposing their plans or orders: *He hated anyone who crossed him.*

13 SPORT [I,T] to kick, throw, or hit the ball across the playing area in a sport such as football, HOCKEY etc

14 CHEQUE [T] *BrE* to draw two lines across a cheque to show that it must be paid into the bank account of the person whose name is on it

15 LETTERS [I] if two letters about the same subject cross in the post, each was sent before the other was received

16 cross swords (with sb) to argue with someone: *I've crossed swords with him on a number of issues.*

17 cross yourself to move your hand across your upper body in the shape of a cross as a sign of the Christian faith

18 cross sb's palm with silver *especially BrE* to give money to someone when you want them to tell your FORTUNE → **dot the i's and cross the t's** at DOT²(4), → **cross the Rubicon** at RUBICON

cross sth ↔ **off** (*also* **cross sth off sth**) *phr v* to draw a line through one or more things on a list because you have dealt with them or they are not needed anymore: *Whenever I buy something, I cross it off the list.*

cross sth ↔ **out** *phr v* to draw a line or lines through something you have written or drawn, usually because it is wrong: *I crossed out 'Miss' and wrote 'Ms'.*

cross over *phr v*

1 if an entertainer crosses over from one area of entertainment to another, they become successful in the second one as well as the first → CROSSOVER(2)

2 *BrE old use* to die

cross² ●●● S3 W3 *n* [C]

1 MIXTURE OF THINGS a mixture of two things, breeds, or qualities: **[+between]** *The tour manager's role is a cross between hostess and courier.* | *Their dog is a cross between two well-known breeds.*

2 MARK ON PAPER *especially BrE* **a)** a mark (x or +) used on paper, to represent where something is, or where something should be: *I've **put** a **cross** on the map to mark where our street is.* | *Please sign your name by the cross.* **b)** a mark (x) used on paper to show that something that has been written or printed is not correct: *My homework got a lot more ticks than crosses.* **c)** a mark (x or +) used by someone who cannot write, in order to sign their name

3 CHRISTIAN SIGN **a) the cross** the cross that Jesus Christ died on: *Christians believe that Jesus died on the cross for our sins.* **b)** an object, picture, or mark in the shape of a cross, used as a sign of the Christian faith or for decoration: *Pauline wore a tiny gold cross.*

4 PUNISHMENT an upright post of wood with another crossing it near the top, that people in the past were fastened to with nails and left to die on as a punishment

5 MILITARY AWARD a decoration in the shape of a cross that is given to someone as an honour, especially for military courage: *He was awarded the George Cross.*

6 SPORT **a)** a kick or hit of the ball in a sport such as football, HOCKEY etc, that goes across the field **b)** a way of hitting someone in the sport of BOXING, in which your arm goes over theirs as they try to hit you: *He caught his opponent with a **right cross** to the chin.*

7 PROBLEM if you describe something as the cross that

someone has to bear, you mean it is a problem that makes them very unhappy or worried, and that continues for a long time: *I feel sorry for you, but we all* ***have*** *our* ***crosses to bear.*** → **the sign of the Cross** at SIGN¹(10)

cross³ ●●● S2 *adj* [usually before noun] *especially BrE* angry or annoyed: **get/be cross (with sb)** *She gets cross when he goes out drinking.* | *Sometimes I get very cross with the children.* | **[+at/about]** *She was cross at being interrupted.* **THESAURUS** ANGRY —**crossly** *adv*

cross- /krɒs $ krɒːs/ *prefix* **1** going from one side to the other: *a cross-Channel ferry* (=sailing from Britain to France) **2** going between two things and joining them: *cross-cultural influences*

cross·bar /ˈkrɒsbɑː $ ˈkrɒːsbɑːr/ *n* [C] **1** a bar that joins two upright posts, especially two GOALPOSTS → see picture at **FOOTBALL** **2** the metal bar between the seat and the HANDLEBARS on a man's bicycle → see picture at **BICYCLE**

cross·bones /ˈkrɒsbəʊnz $ ˈkrɒːsboʊnz/ *n* [plural] → **SKULL AND CROSSBONES**

ˈcross-ˌborder *adj* [only before noun] relating to activity across a border between two countries: **cross-border trade/business etc** | **cross-border attack/raid**

cross·bow /ˈkrɒsbəʊ $ ˈkrɒːsboʊ/ *n* [C] a weapon like a small BOW attached to a longer piece of wood, used for shooting ARROWS with a lot of force

cross·breed¹ /ˈkrɒsbriːd $ ˈkrɒːs-/ *v* (*past tense and past participle* **crossbred** /-bred/) [I,T] if one breed of plant or animal crossbreeds with another, or if you crossbreed them, they breed, producing a new type of plant or animal —**crossbred** /-bred/ *adj*

crossbreed² *n* [C] an animal or plant that is a mixture of breeds → **hybrid**

ˌcross-ˈcheck *v* [I,T] to make certain that something is correct by using a different method to check it again —**ˈcross-check** *n* [C]

ˌcross-ˈcountry¹ *adj* [only before noun] **1** across fields or not along main roads: *cross-country running* | *We took a cross-country route instead of the motorway.* **2** from one part of the country to the other: *cross-country flights* —**cross-country** *adv*: *We rode cross-country to the village.*

cross-country² *n* (*plural* **cross-countries**) [C,U] a race that involves running or SKIING across countryside and fields, not on a track, or the sport of doing this

ˌcross-ˈcultural *adj* [only before noun] belonging to or involving two or more different societies, countries, or CULTURES → **multicultural**: *cross-cultural exchanges*

ˈcross-ˌcurrent *n* [C] a current in the sea, a river etc that moves across the general direction of the main current

ˌcross-ˈdressing *n* [U] *BrE* the practice of wearing the clothes of the opposite sex, especially for sexual pleasure → **transvestite** —**cross-dresser** *n* [C]

crossed /krɒst $ krɒːst/ *adj* if a telephone line is crossed, it is connected by mistake to two or more telephones, so that you can hear other people's conversations: *I phoned him up and got a* ***crossed line.***

ˌcrossed ˈcheque *n* [C] a cheque in Britain that has two lines across it showing that it must be paid into a bank account

ˌcross-exˈamine *v* [T] to ask someone questions about something that they have just said, to see if they are telling the truth, especially in a court of law **THESAURUS** ASK —**ˌcross-examiˈnation** *n* [C,U]: *He broke down* ***under cross-examination.***

ˌcross-ˈeyed / $ ˈ. ./ *adj* having eyes that both look in towards the nose

ˌcross-ˈfertilize (*also* **-ise** *BrE*) *v* [T] **1** to combine the male sex cells from one type of plant with female sex cells from another **2** to influence someone or something with ideas from other areas: *In a university students live together, encourage, support, and cross-fertilise each other.* —**ˌcross-fertiliˈzation** *n* [U]

cross·fire /ˈkrɒsfaɪə $ ˈkrɒːsfaɪr/ *n* [U] **1** bullets from two or more opposite directions that pass through the same area: *Doctors who tried to help the wounded were* ***caught in the crossfire.*** | **in crossfire** *Many civilians were killed in crossfire.* **2** a situation in which people are arguing, and the results of this affect other people who are not directly involved: *During a divorce, kids often get* ***caught in the crossfire.***

ˌcross-ˈgrained *adj* wood that is cross-grained has lines that go across it instead of along it

ˈcross-ˌhatching *n* [U] lines drawn across part of a picture, DIAGRAM etc to show that something is made of different material, or to produce the effect of shade

cross·ing /ˈkrɒsɪŋ $ ˈkrɒː-/ ●○○ *n* [C]
1 a place where you can safely cross a road, railway, river etc: *You must give way to any pedestrians on the crossing.* → **LEVEL CROSSING, PEDESTRIAN CROSSING, PELICAN CROSSING, ZEBRA CROSSING**
2 a place where two lines, roads, tracks etc cross: *Turn left at the first crossing.*
3 a journey across the sea, a lake, or a river: *The crossing was rough.* **THESAURUS** JOURNEY

CROSS-LEGGED

cross-legged
with your legs crossed

cross-legged /ˌkrɒs ˈlegəd◂, -ˈlegd◂ $ ˈkrɒːs ˌlegəd, -ˌlegd/ *adv* in a sitting position with your knees wide apart and one foot on top of the other: *We* ***sat cross-legged*** *on the floor.* —**cross-legged** *adj*

cross·o·ver /ˈkrɒsəʊvə $ ˈkrɒːsoʊvər/ *n* **1** [C] the change a popular performer makes from working in one area of entertainment to another: *J Lo has made a crossover from music to the movies.* **2** [C,U] the fact of liking, using, or supporting different types of things or groups: *There's some crossover between the musical genres.* **3** [C] (*also* **crossover car**) a car that has some of the features of a normal car and some of the features of an SUV or 4X4 → **CROSS OVER**

cross·piece /ˈkrɒspiːs $ ˈkrɒːs-/ *n* [C] something that lies across another thing, especially in a building, on a railway track etc

ˌcross-ˈpurposes *n* **at cross-purposes** if two people are at cross-purposes, they do not understand each other because they are talking about different things but fail to realize this: *I think we're talking at cross-purposes.*

ˌcross-ˈquestion *v* [T] *BrE* to ask someone many detailed questions about something: *Ministers were cross-questioned by the committee about their expenses.*

ˌcross-reˈfer *v* (**cross-referred**, **cross-referring**) [I,T] to tell a reader to look in another place in the book they are reading, so that they can get further information: **[+to/from]** *The author cross-refers to his other books.*

ˌcross-ˈreference / $ ˈ. ˌ.../ *n* [C,U] a note that tells the reader of a book to go to another place in the book, to get further information: *The book has clear cross-references and a good index.* —**cross-reference** *v* [T]

cross·roads /ˈkrɒsrəʊdz $ ˈkrɒːsroʊdz/ ●●○ *n* (*plural* **crossroads**) [C]
1 a place where two roads meet and cross each other

C

→ **junction**, **T-junction**: **at the crossroads** *Turn left at the next crossroads.* | *The car was approaching the crossroads.*
2 a time when someone has to make very important decisions which will affect their future: **at a crossroads** *Now farming is at a crossroads in the European Community.* | *a career crossroads*
3 an important or central place: **at the crossroads** *The city was ideally situated at the crossroads to the great trade centres of Europe.*

ˈcross-ˌsection *n* [C] **1** something that has been cut in half so that you can look at the inside, or a drawing of this: **[+of]** *a cross-section of a plant stem* | **in cross-section** *The roof beams were 50 centimetres square in cross-section.* **2** a group of people or things that is typical of a much larger group → **sample**: **[+of]** *a wide cross-section of the taxpaying population*

C

ˌcross-ˈselling *n* [U] when one company helps to sell another company's products by, for example, advertising the second company's products at the same time as its own

ˈcross-stitch *n* [C,U] a stitch in a cross shape used in decorative sewing

ˈcross street *n* [C] a smaller street that crosses another street

cross·town, **cross-town** /ˈkrɒstaʊn $ ˈkrɒːs-/ *adj* [only before noun] moving in a direction across a town or city: *a crosstown bus*

ˌcross-ˈtrainer *n* [C usually plural] a type of shoe that can be worn for playing different types of sports → see picture at **GYM**

ˌcross-ˈtraining *n* [U] **1** an exercise programme that includes many different kinds of exercise, so that all of your muscles are used **2** when people in a company learn about each other's jobs, so that they understand each other better and work together better as a team: *Cross-training is a vital part of job rotation.* —**cross-train** *v* [I]

cross·walk /ˈkrɒswɔːk $ ˈkrɒːswɒːk/ ●●○ *n* [C] *AmE* a specially marked place for people to walk across a street SYN **pedestrian crossing** *BrE*

cross·wind /ˈkrɒsˌwɪnd $ ˈkrɒːs-/ *n* [C] a wind that blows across the direction that you are moving in

cross·wise /ˈkrɒsˌwaɪz $ ˈkrɒːs-/ *adv* **1** from one corner of something to the opposite corner: *Halve the potatoes crosswise.* **2** two things that are placed crosswise are arranged to form the shape of an 'x'

cross·word /ˈkrɒswɜːd $ ˈkrɒːswɜːrd/ ●●○ (*also* **ˈcrossword ˌpuzzle**) *n* [C] a word game in which you write the answers to questions in a pattern of numbered boxes: *I like to sit down and* **do** *the* **crossword**.

crotch /krɒtʃ $ krɑːtʃ/ (*also* **crutch** *BrE*) *n* [C] the part of your body between the tops of your legs, or the part of a piece of clothing that covers this → **groin**

crotch·et /ˈkrɒtʃɪt $ ˈkrɑː-/ *n* [C] *BrE* a musical note which continues for a quarter of the length of a SEMIBREVE SYN **quarter note** *AmE* → **minim**, **quaver**

crotch·et·y /ˈkrɒtʃəti $ ˈkrɑː-/ *adj* easily annoyed or made slightly angry SYN **grumpy**: *a crotchety old man*

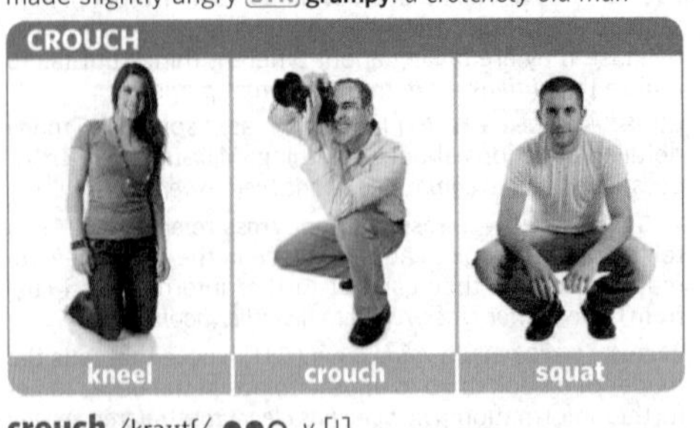

crouch /kraʊtʃ/ ●●○ *v* [I]
1 (*also* **crouch down**) to lower your body close to the ground by bending your knees completely → **squat**: *He crouched in the shadows near the doorway.* | *Paula crouched down and held her hands out to the fire.*
2 to bend over something so that you are very near to it → **lean**: **[+over]** *a young girl crouched over a book* —**crouch** *n* [C]: *She dropped to the ground in a crouch.*

croup /kruːp/ *n* [U] an illness in children which makes them cough and have difficulty breathing

crou·pi·er /ˈkruːpiə $ -ər/ *n* [C] someone whose job is to collect and pay out money where people play cards, ROULETTE etc for money at a CASINO

crou·ton /ˈkruːtɒn $ -tɑːn/ *n* [C usually plural] a small square piece of CRISP bread, served with soup or on SALAD

crow¹ /krəʊ $ kroʊ/ *n* **1** [C] a large shiny black bird with a loud cry **2** [singular] the loud sound a COCK makes **3** **as the crow flies** in a straight line: *ten miles from here as the crow flies* → **eat crow** at **EAT(7)**

crow² *v* [I] **1** if a COCK crows, it makes a loud high sound **2** to talk about what you have done in a very proud way – used to show disapproval: **[+over/about]** *He was crowing over winning the bet.* **3** *written* if someone, especially a baby, crows, they make a noise that shows they are happy: *Ben rushed to his father, crowing with pleasure.*

crow·bar /ˈkrəʊbɑː $ ˈkroʊbɑːr/ *n* [C] a heavy iron bar used to lift something or force it open

crowd¹ /kraʊd/ ●●● S3 W2 *n*
1 [C] a large group of people who have gathered together to do something, for example to watch something or protest about something: **[+of]** *a crowd of angry protesters* | *a crowd of 30,000 spectators* | *There were crowds of shoppers in the street.* | *A vast* **crowd gathered** *in the main square.* | *She* **mingled with the crowd** *of guests, exchanging greetings.* | *Saturday's game was watched by a* **capacity crowd** (=the maximum number of people that a sports ground etc can hold). | *Troops fired tear gas and shots to* **disperse** *a* **crowd** *of 15,000 demonstrators.*
THESAURUS ▸ GROUP
2 [singular] *informal* a group of people who know each other, work together etc: *I didn't know him; he wasn't one of the usual crowd.*
3 **the crowd** ordinary people, not unusual in any way: *You have to do things exceptionally well to* **stand out from the crowd** (=be different from ordinary people). | *He wanted to go unnoticed, to be* **one of the crowd**.

crowd² ●●○ *v*
1 [I always + adv/prep] if people crowd somewhere, they gather together in large numbers, filling a particular place: **[+into]** *Hundreds of people crowded into the church for the funeral.* | **[+round/around]** *We all crowded round the table.* | **be crowded together** *the rapid spread of infection in areas where people are crowded together*
2 [T] if people or things crowd a place, there are a lot of them there: *Holidaymakers crowded the beaches.* | *Range after range of mountains crowd the horizon.*
3 [T] if thoughts or ideas crowd your mind or memory, they fill it, not allowing you to think of anything else: *Strange thoughts and worries were crowding his mind.*
4 [T] **a)** to make someone angry by moving too close to them: *Stop crowding me – there's plenty of room.* **b)** *especially AmE* to make someone angry or upset by making too many unfair demands on them

crowd in *phr v* if problems or thoughts crowd in on you, you cannot stop thinking about them: **[+on]** *She shut her mind against the fears that crowded in on her.*

crowd sb/sth ↔ **out** *phr v* to force someone or something out of a place or situation: *Supermarket chains have crowded out the smaller shops.*

crowd·ed /ˈkraʊdɪd/ ●●● S3 *adj* too full of people or things → **empty**: *a crowded room* | *a crowded street* | *The train was very crowded, and we had to stand.* | **[+with]** *The narrow roads were crowded with holiday traffic.*

crowd·fund·ing /ˈkraʊdˌfʌndɪŋ/ *n* [U] a method of getting money for something, for example a new film or ALBUM, by asking many people to give part of the money needed, often on the Internet —**crowdfunded** *adj*

ˈcrowd ˌpleaser, **crowd-pleaser** *n* [C] an actor, politician, or sportsperson etc who always pleases an AUDIENCE (=people watching a performance)

ˈcrowd ˌpuller, **crowd-puller** *n* [C] a performer who a lot of people want to see, or something that a lot of people want to visit: *The exhibition has been a big crowd puller.*

crowd·sourc·ing /ˈkraʊdˌsɔːsɪŋ $ -ˌsɔːrs-/ *n* [U] *technical* the business practice of getting members of the public to do work or think of ideas for you, usually for little or no money —**crowdsource** *v* [I,T]

ˈcrowd-ˌsurfing *n* [U] the act of letting yourself be held up and moved along by a crowd holding their hands up high at a ROCK concert

crown[1] /kraʊn/ ●●○ W3 *n*

1 HAT FOR KING/QUEEN [C] **a)** a circle made of gold and decorated with jewels, worn by kings and queens on their heads **b)** a circle, sometimes made of things such as leaves or flowers, worn by someone who has won a special honour

2 COUNTRY'S RULER **the Crown** (*also* **the crown**) **a)** the position of being king or queen: *The treaty of Troyes made Henry V heir to the crown of France.* | *Questioning the authority of the Crown was considered an act of treason.* **b)** the government of a country such as Britain that is officially led by a king or queen: *He has retired from the service of the Crown.*

3 TOOTH [C] an artificial top for a damaged tooth

4 HEAD [usually singular] the top part of a hat or someone's head: **[+of]** *auburn hair piled high on the crown of her head* | *a hat with a high crown*

5 HILL [usually singular] the top of a hill or something shaped like a hill: **[+of]** *They drove to the crown of Zion hill and on into town.* | *The masonry at the crown of the arch is paler than on either curve.*

6 SPORTS [usually singular] the position you have if you have won an important sports competition: *Can she retain her Wimbledon crown?* | *He went on to win the* ***world crown*** *in 2001.*

7 MONEY [C] **a)** the standard unit of money in some European countries: *Swedish crowns* **b)** an old British coin. Four crowns made a pound.

8 PICTURE [C] a mark, sign, BADGE etc in the shape of a crown, used especially to show rank or quality

crown[2] *v* [T] **1** to place a crown on the head of a new king or queen as part of an official ceremony in which they become king or queen → **coronation**: *Louis was crowned at Reims in 814.* | **crown sb (as) king/queen etc** *In 1896 Nicholas was crowned as Tsar.* **2** to give someone a title for winning a competition: *She was crowned Wimbledon champion.* **3** to make something perfect or complete, by adding an achievement etc: **crown sb with sth** *a long career crowned with a peaceful retirement* **4 be crowned with sth** *literary* having something on top: *every hill is crowned with a walled village* **5** to put a protective top on a damaged tooth **6** *informal* to hit someone on the head

ˌcrown ˈcolony *n* [C] a COLONY controlled by the British government

ˈCrown Court *n* [C,U] a court of law in Britain that deals with serious criminal cases and is higher than a Magistrate's Court

ˌcrowned ˈhead *n* [C usually plural] a king or queen: *All the crowned heads of Europe were present.*

crown·ing /ˈkraʊnɪŋ/ *adj* [always before noun] used to describe something that makes something complete or perfect, or is the best feature of something: *The hotel's* ***crowning glory*** *was a stunning roof garden.* | *his* ***crowning achievement***

ˌcrown ˈjewel *n* [C] **1 the crown jewels** the crown, sword, jewels etc worn by a king or queen for official ceremonies **2** the best or most valuable thing that a person or place has: *Innsbruck's crown jewel is the old town centre.*

ˌCrown ˈPrince *n* [C] the son of a king or queen, who is expected to become the next king

ˌCrown Prinˈcess / $ ˌ. ˈ../ *n* [C] the daughter of a king or queen, who is expected to become the next queen

ˈcrow's feet *n* [plural] the very small lines that form in the skin near the eyes of older people

ˈcrow's nest *n* [C] a small box at the top of a ship's MAST from which someone can watch for danger, land etc

cro·zi·er, **crosier** /ˈkrəʊziə, -ʒə $ -ʒər/ *n* [C] a long stick with a decorative curved end, carried by a BISHOP

CRT /ˌsiː ɑː ˈtiː $ -ɑːr-/ *n* [C] the abbreviation of ***cathode ray tube***

cru·cial /ˈkruːʃəl/ ●●○ W2 AWL *adj* something that is crucial is extremely important, because everything else depends on it SYN **vital**: **[+to]** *This aid money is crucial to the government's economic policies.* | **crucial in/to doing sth** *The work of monks was crucial in spreading Christianity.* | **play a crucial role/part in sth** *The city of Mycenae played a crucial role in the history of Greece.* | *The conservation of tropical forests is* ***of crucial importance.*** THESAURUS IMPORTANT —**crucially** *adv*

cru·ci·ate lig·a·ment /ˈkruːʃieɪt ˌlɪgəmənt/ *n* [C] *medical* one of two LIGAMENTS (=bands of strong material) in the knee that cross each other and connect the bones above and below the knee: *The Chelsea player suffered a torn cruciate ligament.*

cru·ci·ble /ˈkruːsəbəl/ *n* [C] a container in which substances are heated to very high temperatures

cru·ci·fix /ˈkruːsəfɪks/ *n* [C] a cross with a figure of Christ on it

cru·ci·fix·ion /ˌkruːsəˈfɪkʃən/ *n* **1** [C,U] in past times, the act of killing someone by fastening them to a cross and leaving them to die **2 the Crucifixion** the death of Christ on the cross **3** [C] (*also* **Crucifixion**) a picture or other object representing Christ on the cross

cru·ci·form /ˈkruːsəfɔːm $ -fɔːrm/ *adj formal* shaped like a cross

cru·ci·fy /ˈkruːsɪfaɪ/ *v* (**crucified**, **crucifying**, **crucifies**) [T] **1** to kill someone by fastening them to a cross **2** to criticize someone severely and cruelly for something they have done, especially in public

crud /krʌd/ *n* [U] *informal* something unpleasant to look at, smell, taste etc: *I can't eat this crud!* —**cruddy** *adj*

crude[1] /kruːd/ ●●○ *adj*

1 not exact or without any detail, but generally correct and useful → **approximate**: *a crude estimate of the population available for work*

2 not developed to a high standard, or made with little skill: *a crude wooden bridge* | *crude workmanship*

3 offensive or rude, especially in a sexual way SYN **vulgar**: *crude pictures* | *His language was often crude.*

4 [only before noun] crude oil, rubber etc is in its natural or raw condition before it is treated with chemicals

5 in crude terms expressed in a simple way: *Private morality, in crude terms, is not the law's business.* —**crudely** *adv*: *crudely built shacks* —**crudeness** *n* [U] —**crudity** *n* [C,U]

crude[2] (*also* **ˌcrude ˈoil**) *n* [U] oil that is in its natural condition, as it comes out of an OIL WELL, before it is made more pure or separated into different products: *1,000 barrels of crude*

cru·el /ˈkruːəl/ ●●● S3 *adj*

1 making someone suffer or feel unhappy: *His death was a* ***cruel blow.*** | *Sometimes life seems unbearably cruel.* THESAURUS UNKIND

2 deliberately hurting people or animals OPP **kind**: *The prisoner was a hard cruel man.* | *cruel jokes about mothers-in-law* | *It was a cruel tactless thing to say.* | **[+to]** *She was often cruel to her sister.*

3 be cruel to be kind to do something to someone that will make them upset or unhappy in order to help them in another way —**cruelly** *adv*: *He was cruelly neglected by his parents.*

THESAURUS

cruel deliberately hurting people or making them suffer: *It was cruel to lock the dog in the garage all day.* | *Her father had been very cruel to her when she was a child.* | *a cruel, selfish woman*

C

heartless not feeling any pity and not caring about other people or their problems: *How could you be so heartless!* | *He was cold and heartless and had no concern for the welfare of his employees.*
sadistic getting pleasure from making other people suffer: *a sadistic killer* | *a sadistic thing to do*
barbaric extremely cruel, in a way that shocks people: *a barbaric punishment* | *a barbaric sport*
vicious very violent and cruel, especially by suddenly attacking someone and causing injury to them: *a vicious attack on an innocent man* | *Some dogs can be vicious.*
brutal very cruel and violent, in a way that shows no human feelings: *a brutal dictator* | *the brutal methods used by the secret police*
inhumane inhumane conditions, treatment etc are not considered acceptable because they cause too much suffering: *the inhumane treatment of prisoners*
cold-blooded a cold-blooded murder, attack etc is done without showing any feeling or pity for the person who is attacked. A cold-blooded killer kills people without showing any pity: *a woman's cold-blooded murder of her devoted husband* | *a cold-blooded psychopath*

cru·el·ty /ˈkruːəlti/ ●●○ *n* (*plural* **cruelties**)
1 [C,U] behaviour or actions that deliberately cause pain to people or animals OPP **kindness**: *The children had suffered cruelty and neglect.* | *There was a hint of cruelty in Brian's smile.* | **[+to]** *cruelty to animals* | **[+of]** *the cruelty of the slave trade* | *The deliberate cruelty of his words cut her like a knife.* | *the cruelties of war*
2 [U] the unfairness of something that happens: *the cruelty of life*

cru·et /ˈkruːɪt/ *n* [C] a thing that holds the containers for salt, pepper, oil, or VINEGAR on a table

cruise[1] /kruːz/ ●●○ *n* [C]
1 a holiday on a large ship: *a Mediterranean cruise* | **[+around]** *a cruise around the world* THESAURUS ▸ JOURNEY
2 a journey by boat for pleasure

cruise[2] ●○○ *v*
1 [I,T] to sail along slowly, especially for pleasure: *We were cruising in the Caribbean all winter.* | *an evening spent cruising the River Seine*
2 [I usually + adv/prep] to move at a steady speed in a car, aircraft etc: *We were cruising along at 50 miles per hour.* | *We fly at a* ***cruising speed*** *of 500 mph.*
3 [I,T] to drive a car slowly through a place with no particular purpose: *They cruised up and down the coast road.*
4 [I] *informal* to do something well or successfully, without too much effort: **[+to]** *The horse cruised to a three-length win.*
5 [I,T] *informal* to go to a bar or other public place, looking for a sexual partner: *We went cruising the singles bars.*

ˈcruise conˌtrol *n* [C] a piece of equipment in a car that makes it go at a steady speed

ˈcruise ˌliner *n* [C] a large ship for cruising

ˌcruise ˈmissile *n* [C] a large explosive weapon that flies close to the ground and can be aimed at something hundreds of kilometres away

cruis·er /ˈkruːzə $ -ər/ *n* [C] **1** a large fast ship used by the navy: *a* ***battle cruiser*** **2** a boat used for pleasure **3** *AmE* a police car

cruis·er·weight /ˈkruːzəweɪt $ -zər-/ *n* [C] a BOXER who weighs less than 86.18 kilograms, and who is heavier than a LIGHT HEAVYWEIGHT but lighter than a HEAVYWEIGHT

ˈcruise ship *n* [C] a large ship with restaurants, bars etc that people have holidays on

cruis·ing /ˈkruːzɪŋ/ *n* [U] **1** the activity of taking a holiday on a cruise ship **2** *AmE* when young people drive cars slowly down a particular street as a way of being with their friends: *a sign saying 'No cruising'* **3** when someone looks for sexual partners in bars, restaurants, on the street etc

crumb /krʌm/ *n* [C] **1** a very small piece of dry food, especially bread or cake: *She stood up to brush the crumbs off her uniform.* | *Coat with* ***bread crumbs*** *and bake.* THESAURUS ▸ PIECE **2** a very small amount of something: **crumb of comfort/hope/affection etc** *There was only one crumb of comfort – Alex hadn't said anything to Jeff.*

crum·ble[1] /ˈkrʌmbəl/ ●○○ *v*
1 [I] (*also* **crumble away**) if something, especially something made of stone or rock, is crumbling, small pieces are breaking off it: *The old stonework was crumbling away.* | *crumbling colonial buildings* THESAURUS ▸ BREAK
2 [I,T] to break apart into lots of little pieces, or make something do this: *The fall leaves crumbled in my fingers.* | *¼ cup crumbled goat's cheese*
3 [I] (*also* **crumble away**) to lose power, become weak, or fail SYN **disintegrate**: *The Empire began to crumble during the 13th century.* | *our crumbling economy* → **that's the way the cookie crumbles** at COOKIE(3)

crumble[2] *n* [U] *BrE* a sweet dish of fruit covered with a dry mixture of flour, butter, and sugar and baked: *apple crumble*

crum·bly /ˈkrʌmbli/ *adj* something that is crumbly breaks easily into small pieces: *a nice crumbly cheese* | *the garden's crumbly black soil*

crumbs /krʌmz/ *interjection BrE old-fashioned* used to express surprise

crum·my /ˈkrʌmi/ *adj informal* of bad quality or unpleasant: *a crummy hotel* | *a crummy job*

crum·pet /ˈkrʌmpɪt/ *n BrE* **1** [C] a small round bread with holes in one side, eaten hot with butter **2** [U] *informal not polite* an offensive word for someone who is sexually attractive

crum·ple /ˈkrʌmpəl/ *v* **1** [I,T] (*also* **crumple up**) to crush something so that it becomes smaller and bent, or to be crushed in this way: *Dan tore the page out, crumpled it, and threw it in the wastepaper basket.* **2** [I] if your face crumples, you suddenly look sad or disappointed, as if you might cry **3** [I] if your body crumples, you fall down in an uncontrolled way: **[+to]** *The blow hit him on the head and he crumpled to the ground.*

crum·pled /ˈkrʌmpəld/ *adj* **1** (*also* **crumpled up**) crushed into a smaller bent shape: *Tom flattened the crumpled paper against his knee.* **2** cloth or clothing that is crumpled has a lot of lines or folds in it: *an old man with untidy hair and a crumpled suit* **3** someone who is crumpled somewhere is lying still in a strange position after they have fallen

crunch[1] /krʌntʃ/ *n* **1** [singular] a noise like the sound of something being crushed: *The only sound was the crunch of tyres on gravel.* **2** [C, singular] *AmE* a difficult situation caused by a lack of something, especially money or time: *Three new teachers were hired to help ease the crunch.* | **cash/budget/financial etc crunch** *Cost cutting had enabled the organization to survive a previous cash crunch.* **3 the crunch** (*also* **crunch time** *AmE*) an important time, especially one when a difficult decision has to be made: ***The crunch came*** *when my bank asked for my credit card back.* | ***When it came to the crunch***, *she couldn't agree to marry him.* **4** [C] an exercise in which you lie on your back and lift your head and shoulders off the ground to make your stomach muscles strong SYN **sit-up**

crunch[2] *v* **1** [I] to make a sound like something being crushed: *Their boots crunched loudly on the frozen snow.* **2** [I always + adv/prep, T] to eat hard food in a way that makes a noise: **[+on]** *The dog was crunching on a bone.* **3 crunch (the) numbers** to do a lot of calculations in order to find an answer: *The computer will crunch all the numbers to determine the final score.*

crunch·y /ˈkrʌntʃi/ ●●○ *adj* food that is crunchy is firm and makes a noise when you bite it – usually used to show approval: *a delicious crunchy salad* THESAURUS ▸ HARD —**crunchiness** *n* [U]

cru·sade[1] /kruːˈseɪd/ ●○○ *n* [C]
1 a determined attempt to change something because you think you are morally right → **campaign**: **[+against/**

for] *He seems to be running a one-man crusade against cigarette smoking.*
2 (*also* **Crusade**) one of a series of wars fought in the 11th, 12th, and 13th centuries by Christian armies trying to take Palestine from the Muslims

crusade² *v* [I] to take part in a crusade SYN **campaign**: **[+against/for]** *He continued to crusade for free education for all.* —**crusader** *n* [C]

crush¹ /krʌʃ/ ●●○ *v* [T]

CRUSH

1 to press something so hard that it breaks or is damaged: *His leg was crushed in the accident.* | *Two people were **crushed to death** in the rush to escape.*
2 to press something in order to break it into very small pieces or into a powder: *Crush two cloves of garlic.*
3 crush a rebellion/uprising/revolt etc to use severe methods to stop people from fighting you or opposing you SYN **put down**: *The revolution was crushed within days.*
4 crush sb's hopes/enthusiasm/confidence etc to make someone lose all hope, confidence etc
5 to make someone feel extremely upset or shocked: *Sara was crushed by their insults.*
crush on sb *phr v AmE informal* to have a feeling of romantic love for someone, especially someone you do not know well: *a guy in my class that I'm crushing on*

crush² *n* **1** [singular] a crowd of people pressed so close together that it is difficult for them to move: *There's always such a crush on the train in the mornings.* **2** [C] a strong feeling of romantic love for someone, especially one that a young person has for someone older who they do not know well → **infatuation**: *She **had a** huge **crush on** her geography teacher.* | *It's just a **schoolgirl crush**.* **3** [C] *AmE informal* someone who you have a feeling of romantic love for, but who you do not know well: *a first date with your crush*

crush·ing /ˈkrʌʃɪŋ/ *adj* [usually before noun] **1** very hard to deal with, and making you lose hope and confidence: *The Eighth Army had suffered a **crushing defeat**.* | *Failing his final exams was a **crushing blow*** (=made him lose hope and confidence). | *the crushing burden of debt* **2** a crushing remark, reply etc contains a very strong criticism —**crushingly** *adv*: *'That's fairly obvious,' she replied crushingly.*

Crusoe, Robinson → ROBINSON CRUSOE

crust /krʌst/ ●●○ *n* [C,U]
1 the hard brown outer surface of bread: *sandwiches with the crusts cut off*
2 the baked outer part of foods such as PIES or PIZZAS: *a thin-crust pizza*
3 a thin hard dry layer on the surface of something: *A hard gray **crust** had **formed** on the bottom of the tea kettle.*
4 the hard outer layer of the Earth: *deep within the Earth's crust* → see picture at EARTH¹ → **earn a crust** at EARN(1), UPPER CRUST

crus·ta·cean /krʌˈsteɪʃən/ *n* [C] *technical* an animal such as a LOBSTER or a CRAB that has a hard outer shell and several pairs of legs, and usually lives in water —**crustacean** *adj*

crust·ed /ˈkrʌstɪd/ *adj* having a thin hard dry layer on the surface: **[+with]** *old boots crusted with mud*

crust·y¹ /ˈkrʌsti/ *adj* **1** bread that is crusty is pleasant to eat because it has a hard CRUST: *a crusty baguette* **2** *informal* someone who is crusty is bad-tempered SYN **grumpy**: *a crusty old man* **3** having a thin dry hard layer of something on the surface: *The lake was ringed by crusty salt deposits.*

crusty² *n* (*plural* **crusties**) [C] *BrE informal* a young person with a dirty and untidy appearance, usually one who has no permanent job or home and takes part in protests about protecting the environment

crutch /krʌtʃ/ *n* [C] **1** [usually plural] one of a pair of long sticks that you put under your arms to help you walk when you have hurt your leg: **on crutches** (=using crutches) *I was on crutches for three months after the operation.* **2** something that gives someone support or help, especially something that is not really good for them: *As things got worse at work, he began to use alcohol as a crutch.* **3** *BrE* the part of your body between the tops of your legs SYN **crotch**

crux /krʌks/ *n* **the crux** the most important part of a problem, question, argument etc: **[+of]** *The **crux of the matter** is how do we prevent a flood occurring again?* | *The **crux of the problem** lay in the lack of equipment.*

cry¹ /kraɪ/ ●●● S2 W2 *v* (**cried**, **crying**, **cries**)
1 PRODUCE TEARS [I,T] to produce tears from your eyes, usually because you are unhappy or hurt: *Don't cry, Laura. It'll be OK.* | *Upstairs, a baby began to cry.* | *Jamie looked like he'd been crying.* | *I just couldn't stop crying.* | *That film always **makes** me **cry**.* | **[+over/about]** *I am too old to be crying over some young guy.* | **[+with/in]** *She felt like crying with frustration.* | **[+for]** *She could hear him crying for his mother.* | **cry your eyes/heart out** (=be extremely sad and cry a lot) | *Oliver, alone, began to **cry bitterly*** (=cry a lot). | **cry yourself to sleep** (=cry until you fall asleep)
2 SAY LOUDLY [T] *written* to shout or say something loudly SYN **cry out**: *'Stop!' she cried.* | *It was painful, and made me **cry aloud**.* | **[+to]** *'Goodbye then!' he cried to her.* | **[+for]** *I could hear voices crying for help.*
3 cry over spilt milk to waste time feeling sorry about an earlier mistake or problem that cannot be changed: *It's **no use crying over spilt milk**.*
4 for crying out loud *spoken* used when you feel annoyed or impatient with someone: *For crying out loud, stop nagging!*
5 cry foul to protest because you think something is wrong or not fair: *When the ads appeared, it was the Democrats' turn to cry foul.*
6 ANIMALS/BIRDS [I] if animals or birds cry, they make a loud sound: *I could hear gulls crying and the soft whisper of the sea.*
7 cry wolf to ask for help when you do not need it, so that people do not believe you when you really need help
8 cry into your beer *informal* to feel too much pity for yourself, especially because you think you have been treated unfairly → **not know whether to laugh or cry** at LAUGH¹(3), → **cry for the moon** at MOON¹(4), → **a shoulder to cry on** at SHOULDER¹(5)

THESAURUS

cry to produce tears from your eyes: *Don't cry - everything will be all right!* | *Men aren't supposed to cry.*
cry your eyes out *especially spoken* to cry a lot and for a long time: *I cried my eyes out when I watched 'Titanic'.*
be in tears to be crying: *By the end of his story, we were all in tears.*
be close to tears to be almost crying: *You could see that she was close to tears.*
weep *literary* to cry, especially for a long time: *His mother put her head on the table and wept.*
sob to cry, taking sudden loud breaths: *I could hear someone sobbing in the next room.*
wail /weɪl/ to cry very loudly in a high voice: *The baby started wailing for its mother.*
whimper /ˈwɪmpə $ -ər/ to cry quietly and weakly: *She began rocking to and fro, whimpering softly.*
hold/fight back the tears to make a big effort not to cry: *She told her story, struggling to hold back the tears.*
your eyes water if your eyes water, they have tears in them, for example because of smoke, wind, or when you are cutting onions: *The onions were making my eyes water.*

TO START CRYING

burst into tears to suddenly start crying: *The man shouted at her and she burst into tears.*

break down to start crying after trying hard not to cry, especially when talking about something very upsetting: *He broke down and begged for forgiveness.*

cry off *phr v BrE* to say that you cannot do something that you have already promised to do → **cancel**: *Leah and I were going to go to Morocco together, but at the last moment she cried off.*

cry out *phr v*

1 to make a loud sound of fear, shock, pain etc: **[+in/with]** *Even the smallest movement made him cry out in pain.* | *John tightened his grip until she cried out.*

2 to shout or say something loudly: *'Why are you doing this?' she cried out suddenly.* | **[+for]** *I felt too terrified to even cry out for help.*

3 **be crying out for sth** *informal* to need something urgently: *The kitchen is crying out for a coat of paint.* | *My parents had divorced and I was crying out for love.*

C

cry² ●●○ W3 *n* (*plural* **cries**)

1 SOUND EXPRESSING EMOTION [C] a loud sound expressing a strong emotion such as pain, fear, or pleasure: *a baby's cry* | **cry of pain/alarm/delight etc** *Alice let out a cry of alarm.* | **let out/give a cry** *The stone hit him on the forehead and he gave a sharp cry.*

2 SHOUT [C] a shouted word or phrase: **[+of]** *At last, there was a cry of 'Silence!', and everyone looked towards the door.* | **[+for]** *Fortunately, a passerby heard his* ***cries for help***.

3 TEARS [singular] *especially BrE* a period of time during which tears come out of your eyes, usually because you are unhappy: *It's good to* ***have a cry*** *sometimes.* | *I felt much better after I'd had* ***a good cry*** (=cried for a long time).

4 **cry for help** something someone says or does that shows that they are very unhappy and need help: *I think taking the pills was a cry for help.*

5 PHRASE [C] a phrase that is used to unite people in support of a particular action or idea SYN **slogan**: *'Land and Liberty' was the* ***rallying cry*** *of revolutionary Mexico.* → BATTLE CRY(1), WAR CRY

6 ANIMAL/BIRD [C] a sound made by a particular animal SYN **call**: *the cries of seagulls overhead* → **be a far cry from sth** at FAR²(5), → **in full cry** at FULL¹(22), → HUE AND CRY

cry·ba·by /ˈkraɪˌbeɪbi/ *n* (*plural* **crybabies**) [C] someone, especially a child, who cries too often without good reason – used to show disapproval: *Don't be such a crybaby!*

cry·ing¹ /ˈkraɪ-ɪŋ/ *adj* **1 it's a crying shame** *spoken* used to say that something is very sad or upsetting: *It would be a crying shame if the village shop closed down.* **2 crying need for sth** a serious need for something: ***There is a crying need for*** *doctors.*

crying² *n* [U] when someone produces tears from their eyes, usually because they are unhappy or hurt: *As he neared her tent he heard the sound of crying.*

cry·o·gen·ics /ˌkraɪəˈdʒenɪks/ *n* [U] the scientific study of very low temperatures —**cryogenic** *adj*

crypt /krɪpt/ *n* [C] a room under a church, used in the past for burying people → **vault**

cryp·tic /ˈkrɪptɪk/ *adj* having a meaning that is mysterious or not easily understood: **cryptic remark/comment/statement etc** *a cryptic note at the end of the letter* —**cryptically** /-kli/ *adv*

crypto- /krɪptəʊ, -tə $ -toʊ, -tə/ *prefix formal* secret or hidden: *a crypto-Communist*

cryp·tog·ra·phy /krɪpˈtɒɡrəfi $ -ˈtɑː-/ *n* [U] the study of secret writing and CODES —**cryptographer** *n* [C]

crys·tal /ˈkrɪstl/ ●●○ *n*

1 [U] very high quality clear glass: *a set of six crystal glasses*

2 [C] a small regular-shaped piece of a substance, formed naturally when this substance becomes solid: *ice crystals* | *copper sulphate crystals*

3 [C,U] rock that is clear, or a piece of this

4 [C] *AmE* the clear cover on a clock or watch

ˌcrystal ˈball *n* [C] a glass ball that you can look into, which some people believe can show what is going to happen in the future

ˌcrystal ˈclear *adj* **1** very clearly stated and easy to understand: *I want to make one thing crystal clear – I do not agree with these proposals.* **2** completely clean and clear: *the crystal clear water of the lake*

crys·tal·line /ˈkrɪstəlaɪn, -liːn $ -lən/ *adj* **1** made of crystals **2** very clear or transparent, like crystal

crys·tal·lize (*also* **-ise** *BrE*) /ˈkrɪstəlaɪz/ *v* **1** [I,T] if a liquid crystallizes, it forms CRYSTALS: *The liquid will crystallize at 50 degrees centigrade.* **2** [I,T] if an idea, plan etc crystallizes or is crystallized, it becomes very clear in your mind: *Inside her a thought was crystallizing.* —**crystallization** /ˌkrɪstəlaɪˈzeɪʃən $ -lə-/ *n* [U]

crys·tal·lized (*also* **crystallised** *BrE*) /ˈkrɪstəlaɪzd/ *adj* crystallized fruit, GINGER, or flowers are made by a special process which covers them with sugar

crystal meth /ˌkrɪstl ˈmeθ/ *n* [U] *informal* the illegal drug METHAMPHETAMINE

CSA, the /ˌsiː es ˈeɪ/ (***the Child Support Agency***) a British government department which deals with CHILD SUPPORT. It can decide, for example, how much money a father should pay to support his children if he no longer lives with them.

CSE /ˌsiː es ˈiː/ *n* [C,U] (***Certificate of Secondary Education***) an examination in a range of subjects that was done by students in schools in England and Wales before 1988, usually at the age of 15 or 16 → **GCSE**

C-section /ˈsiː ˌsekʃən/ *n* [C] *AmE informal* a CAESAREAN

CS gas /ˌsiː es ˈɡæs/ *n* [U] *BrE* TEAR GAS

ct *BrE*, **ct.** *AmE* the written abbreviation of ***carat***: *a 24 ct gold necklace*

CT scan /ˌsiː ˈtiː skæn, ˈkæt skæn/ *n* [C] another name for a CAT SCAN

cu *BrE*, **cu.** *AmE* the written abbreviation of ***cubic***

cub /kʌb/ ●●○ *n* [C]

1 the baby of a wild animal such as a lion or a bear: *a five-month-old lion cub* | *a tiger and her cubs*

2 **the Cubs** the CUB SCOUT organization

3 a member of the CUB SCOUT organization → **CUB REPORTER**

Cu·ban mis·sile cri·sis, the /ˌkjuːbən ˈmɪsaɪl ˌkraɪsɪs $ -ˈmɪsəl-/ a dangerous situation which developed in 1962 when the Soviet Union began to build bases for NUCLEAR MISSILEs in Cuba, and US president John F. Kennedy threatened to take military action. It caused a lot of international anxiety until the Soviet Union agreed to remove the missile bases.

cub·by·hole /ˈkʌbihəʊl $ -hoʊl/ *n* [C] a very small space or room, used especially for storing things

cube¹ /kjuːb/ ●●○ *n* [C]

1 a solid object with six equal square sides: *a sugar cube* | *an ice cube* | *Cut the meat into small cubes.* THESAURUS PIECE → see picture at SHAPE¹

2 **the cube of sth** the number you get when you multiply a number by itself twice, for example 4 x 4 x 4 = 64, so the cube of 4 is 64

3 *AmE spoken* a CUBICLE

cube² *v* [T] **1** to multiply a number by itself twice: *4 cubed is 64* **2** to cut food into cubes

ˌcube ˈroot / $ ˈ. ./ *n* [C] the cube root of a particular number is the number that, when multiplied by itself twice, will give that number: *4 is the cube root of 64*

cu·bic /ˈkjuːbɪk/ ●○○ *adj* relating to a measurement of space which is calculated by multiplying the length of something by its width and height → **square**: **cubic centimetre/metre/inch etc** *75,000 million cubic metres of gas* | *the cubic capacity of an engine*

cu·bi·cle /ˈkjuːbɪkəl/ *n* [C] a small part of a room that is separated from the rest of the room: *a* ***shower cubicle*** | *office workers in their cubicles*

cub·is·m /ˈkjuːbɪzəm/ *n* [U] a 20th-century style of art, in which objects and people are represented by GEOMETRIC shapes —**cubist** *adj*: *cubist paintings* —**cubist** *n* [C]

cu·bit /ˈkjuːbɪt/ *n* [C] an ancient unit for measuring length, equal to the length of your arm between your wrist and your elbow

ˌcub reˈporter *n* [C] a young newspaper or television REPORTER without much experience

ˈCub ˌScout *n* [C] **1 the Cub Scouts** the part of the SCOUT organization for younger children **2** a young child who is a member of this organization → **Girl Scout**, **Boy Scout**

cuck·old¹ /ˈkʌkəld, ˈkʌkəʊld $ -kəld/ *n* [C] *old use* an insulting word for a man whose wife has been having sex with another man

cuckold² *v* [T] *old use* if a wife and her LOVER cuckold her husband, they have sex with each other

cuck·oo¹ /ˈkʊkuː $ ˈkuːkuː, ˈkʊ-/ *n* [C] a grey European bird that puts its eggs in other birds' NESTS and that makes a sound that sounds like its name

cuckoo² *adj* [not before noun] *informal* crazy or silly: *You're completely cuckoo!*

ˈcuckoo clock *n* [C] a clock with a wooden bird inside that comes out every hour and makes a sound

cu·cum·ber /ˈkjuːkʌmbə $ -ər/ ●●○ *n* [C,U] a long thin round vegetable with a dark green skin and a light green inside, usually eaten raw → **cool as a cucumber** at COOL¹(3)

cud /kʌd/ *n* [U] food that a cow or similar animal has chewed, swallowed, and brought back into its mouth to chew a second time: *a cow* ***chewing*** *its* ***cud***

cud·dle¹ /ˈkʌdl/ *v* [I,T] to hold someone or something very close to you with your arms around them, especially to show that you love them → **hug**: *Dawn and her boyfriend were cuddling on the sofa.* **THESAURUS** HUG

cuddle up *phr v* to lie or sit very close to someone or something: **[+to/together]** *The children cuddled up to each other for warmth.*

cuddle² *n* [singular] an act of cuddling someone → **hug**: *Come over here and let me* ***give*** *you a* ***cuddle***.

cud·dly /ˈkʌdli/ *adj* **1** a person or animal that is cuddly makes you want to cuddle them: *He is the most affectionate and cuddly dog I have ever known.* **2** [only before noun] cuddly toys are soft toys designed for children to cuddle

cud·gel /ˈkʌdʒəl/ *n* **1** [C] a short thick stick used as a weapon **2 take up the cudgels (on behalf of sb/sth)** *formal* to start to fight for an idea that you believe in

cue¹ /kjuː/ ●○○ *n* [C]

1 an action or event that is a signal for something else to happen: **[+for]** *Our success was the cue for other companies to press ahead with new investment.* | **sb's cue to do sth** *I think that's my cue to explain why I'm here.*

2 a word, phrase, or action in a play that is a signal for the next person to speak or act: *She stood nervously in the wings waiting for her cue.* | **miss your cue** (=not speak or act when you are supposed to)

3 (right/as if) on cue happening or done at exactly the right moment: *And then, on cue, the weather changed.* | *As if on cue, Sam arrived.*

4 take your cue from sb to use someone else's actions or behaviour to show you what you should do or how you should behave: *With interest rates, the smaller banks will take their cue from the Federal Bank.*

5 a long straight wooden stick used for hitting the ball in games such as BILLIARDS and POOL → see picture at **POOL¹**

cue² *v* [T] to give someone a sign that it is the right moment for them to speak or do something, especially during a performance: *The studio manager will cue you when it's your turn to come on.*

cue sth ↔ **up** *phr v* to make a record, CD, DVD etc be exactly in the position you want it to be in, so that you can play something immediately when you are ready: *The DVD player's cued up and ready to go!*

ˈcue ball *n* [C] the ball which a player hits with the cue in a game such as BILLIARDS → see picture at **POOL¹**

cuff¹ /kʌf/ *n* [C] **1** the end of a sleeve **2** *AmE* a narrow piece of cloth turned upwards at the bottom of a trouser leg SYN **turn-up** *BrE* **3** an action in which you hit someone lightly on the head with your hand open **4 cuffs** [plural] HANDCUFFS **5** a wide band of metal, leather, plastic etc, worn around the wrist as decoration → **OFF-THE-CUFF**

cuff² *v* [T] **1** to hit someone lightly, especially in a friendly way: *She cuffed him playfully on the side of the head.* **2** to put HANDCUFFS on someone

ˈcuff link *n* [C] a small piece of jewellery that a man can use to fasten his shirt cuffs → see picture at **JEWELLERY**

cui·sine /kwɪˈziːn/ ●○○ *n* [U]

1 a particular style of cooking: *French cuisine* | *vegetarian cuisine* | **[+of]** *the traditional cuisine of the Southwest* **THESAURUS** FOOD

2 the food cooked in a particular restaurant or hotel, especially when it is very good: *Enjoy the delicious cuisine created by our award-winning chef.* → **HAUTE CUISINE**

cul-de-sac /ˈkʌl də ˌsæk, ˈkʊl- $ ˌkʌl də ˈsæk, ˌkʊl-/ *n* [singular] **1** a road which is closed at one end, so that there is only one way in and out **2** an unhelpful situation in which you cannot make any more progress SYN **dead end**: *These ideas lead us into a philosophical cul-de-sac.*

cul·i·na·ry /ˈkʌlənəri $ ˈkʌləneri, ˈkjuːl-/ *adj* [only before noun] *formal* relating to cooking: *culinary skills* | *mushrooms dried for culinary use* | *the region's* ***culinary delights*** (=food that tastes very good)

cull¹ /kʌl/ *v* [T] **1** to kill animals so that there are not too many of them, or so that a disease does not spread **2** *formal* to find or choose information from many different places SYN **collate**: **cull sth from sth** *The data had been culled from a variety of sources.*

cull² *n* [C] the act of killing animals so that there are not too many of them, or so that a disease does not spread

cul·len·der /ˈkʌləndə $ -ər/ *n* [C] another spelling of COLANDER

cul·mi·nate /ˈkʌlmәneɪt/ ●○○ *v*

culminate in/with sth *phr v* if a process culminates in or with a particular event, it ends with that event: *A series of events for teachers and students will culminate in a Shakespeare festival next year.*

cul·mi·na·tion /ˌkʌlməˈneɪʃən/ *n* [U] **the culmination of sth** something, especially something important, that happens at the end of a long period of effort or development: *This little book represented the culmination of 15 years' work.*

cu·lottes /kjuːˈlɒts $ kjʊˈlɑːts/ *n* [plural] women's trousers which stop at the knee and are shaped to look like a skirt

cul·pa·ble /ˈkʌlpəbəl/ *adj* **1** *formal* deserving blame: *Both parties were held to be to some extent culpable.* **THESAURUS** GUILTY **2** *law* a culpable action is one that is considered criminal: **culpable homicide/negligence etc** *He pleaded guilty to culpable homicide.* —**culpably** *adv* —**culpability** /ˌkʌlpəˈbɪləti/ *n* [U]

cul·prit /ˈkʌlprɪt/ *n* [C] **1** the person who is guilty of a crime or doing something wrong → **victim**: *Police finally managed to catch the culprit.* **2** *informal* the reason for a particular problem or difficulty: *High production costs are* ***the main culprit***.

cult¹ /kʌlt/ ●●○ *n*

1 [C] an extreme religious group that is not part of an established religion

2 [C] a fashionable belief, idea, or attitude that influences people's lives: **[+of]** *Diet, exercise ... It's all part of this cult of self-improvement.*

3 [singular] a group of people who are very interested in a particular thing: *O'Brien has a cult of devoted readers.*

4 [C,U] *formal* a system of religious beliefs and practices → **PERSONALITY CULT**

cult² *adj* [only before noun] **cult film/band/figure etc** a film, music group etc that has become very popular but only among a particular group of people: *the 1980s cult movie 'The Gods Must Be Crazy'* | *The actor James Dean acquired the status of a cult hero.*

cul·ti·va·ble /ˈkʌltəvəbəl/ *adj* land which is cultivable can be used to grow crops

cul·ti·vate /ˈkʌltɪveɪt/ ●○○ *v* [T]

1 to prepare and use land for growing crops and plants: *The land was too rocky to cultivate.*

2 *formal* to plant and take care of a particular crop SYN **grow**: *We cultivated maize and watermelons.*

> **REGISTER**
> In everyday English, people usually say someone **grows** a crop rather than **cultivates** it: *They have been **growing** grapes there for hundreds of years.*

3 to work hard to develop a particular skill, attitude, or quality: *Try to cultivate a more relaxed and positive approach to life.* | *The company has been successful in cultivating a very professional image.*
4 to make an effort to develop a friendly relationship with someone, especially someone who can help you: *Professor Gladwyn would be an acquaintance worth cultivating.*

cul·ti·vat·ed /ˈkʌltɪveɪtɪd/ *adj* **1** someone who is cultivated is intelligent and knows a lot about music, art, literature etc: *a **highly cultivated** man* **2** cultivated land is land that is used for growing crops or plants: *cultivated fields* **3** [only before noun] cultivated crops or plants are ones grown by people OPP **wild**: *cultivated mushrooms*

cul·ti·va·tion /ˌkʌltəˈveɪʃən/ *n* [U] **1** the preparation and use of land for growing crops: *soil cultivation* | **under cultivation** *These fields have been under cultivation* (=used for growing crops) *for years.* **2** the planting and growing of plants and crops: *Terraces for rice cultivation covered the hillsides.* | **[+of]** *the cultivation of tobacco* **3** the deliberate development of a particular quality or skill

cul·ti·va·tor /ˈkʌltəveɪtə $ -ər/ *n* [C] **1** *formal* someone who grows crops or plants, especially a farmer **2** a tool or machine that is used to prepare land for growing crops

cul·tu·ral /ˈkʌltʃərəl/ ●●● W2 AWL *adj* [usually before noun]
1 belonging or relating to a particular society and its way of life → **multicultural**: *the very real historical and **cultural differences** between our two societies* | *the desire to maintain a distinct **cultural identity*** | *It is important to look at the political and **cultural context** in which the novel was written.* | *people who share the same **cultural background*** | **cultural heritage/traditions etc** (=ideas, customs etc that have existed in a particular society for a long time) *Japan's unique cultural heritage* → MULTICULTURAL
2 relating to art, literature, music etc: *the city's rich and varied **cultural life*** | *Students need to have time for relaxation and **cultural activities**, as well as for academic work.* | *In the later Middle Ages, Prague was an important **cultural centre*** (=a place, usually a big city, where a lot of artistic and musical events happen).

cul·tu·ral·ly /ˈkʌltʃərəli/ ●●○ AWL *adv*
1 in a way that is related to the ideas, beliefs, or customs of a society: *Teaching materials need to be culturally appropriate.* | [sentence adverb] *Historically and culturally, Britain has always been linked to the continent.*
2 in a way that is related to art, music, literature etc: *The French are a culturally sophisticated people.* | [sentence adverb] *Culturally, the city has a lot to offer.*

cul·ture¹ /ˈkʌltʃə $ -ər/ ●●● S2 W1 AWL *n*
1 IN A SOCIETY [C,U] the beliefs, way of life, art, and customs that are shared and accepted by people in a particular society: *We speak Danish at home so that the boys don't lose touch with their language and culture.* | *In our culture, it is rude to ask someone how much they earn.* | *I love working abroad and meeting people from different cultures.* | **Western/American/Japanese etc culture** *A brief history of Western culture.* | **modern/contemporary culture** *Business is one of the major forces in modern culture.*
2 IN A GROUP [C,U] the attitudes and beliefs about something that are shared by a particular group of people or in a particular organization: *Every government department has its own particular culture.* | **corporate/business/company culture** *Changing the corporate culture is a long and difficult process.* | **[+of]** *In the field of drug development, the culture of secrecy is deep and strong.* | *modern American **youth culture*** | *the **drug culture** that is destroying so many young lives today* | *the German political culture* → SUBCULTURE
3 ART/MUSIC/LITERATURE [U] activities that are related to art, music, literature etc: *If it's culture you're looking for, the city has plenty of museums and art galleries.* | *the Italian Ministry of Culture* | **popular culture** (=the music, books, films etc that are liked by a lot of people) | **culture vulture** *informal* (=someone who is very interested in art, music, literature etc)
4 SOCIETY [C] a society that existed at a particular time in history: *This technique was then adapted and refined by the more sophisticated cultures of the ancient world.* | *primitive cultures*
5 MEDICINE/SCIENCE [C,U] *technical* BACTERIA or cells grown for medical or scientific use, or the process of growing them: *It takes two to three weeks to grow the culture.* | ***tissue cultures***
6 CROPS [U] *technical* the practice of growing crops SYN **cultivation**: *clearing forest for rice culture*

culture² *v* [T] *technical* to grow BACTERIA or cells for medical or scientific use

cul·tured /ˈkʌltʃəd $ -ərd/ *adj* intelligent, polite, and interested in art, literature, music etc SYN **cultivated**: *a well-read and cultured woman* | *His voice was cultured and unmistakably English.*

ˌcultured ˈpearl *n* [C] a PEARL that has been grown artificially

ˈculture ˌshock ●○○ *n* [singular, U] the feeling of being confused or anxious that you get when you visit a foreign country or a place that is very different from the one you are used to: *India is where I first experienced real culture shock.* | *Moving to London was a bit of a culture shock after ten years of living in the country.*

cul·vert /ˈkʌlvət $ -ərt/ *n* [C] a pipe that takes a stream under a road, railway line etc

cum /kʊm, kʌm/ *prep* used between two nouns to show that something has two purposes: *a kitchen-cum-dining room* | *a lunch-cum-business meeting*

cum·ber·some /ˈkʌmbəsəm $ -bər-/ *adj* **1** a process or system that is cumbersome is slow and difficult: *Doctors are complaining that the system is cumbersome and bureaucratic.* | *cumbersome procedures* **2** heavy and difficult to move: *a large cumbersome machine* **3** words or phrases that are cumbersome are long or complicated

cum·in /ˈkʌmən, ˈkjuː- $ ˈkʌmən, ˈkuː-, ˈkjuː-/ *n* [U] the seeds of a plant that have a sweet smell and are used especially in Mexican and Indian cooking, or the plant that they grow on

cum lau·de /kʊm ˈlaʊdeɪ, kʌm ˈlɔːdi $ kʊm ˈlaʊdi/ *adv AmE* (**with honours**) if you GRADUATE cum laude, you finish a university degree and are given official praise for special achievement → MAGNA CUM LAUDE, SUMMA CUM LAUDE

cum·mer·bund /ˈkʌməbʌnd $ -ər-/ *n* [C] a wide piece of cloth that a man wears around his waist as part of a special suit worn on very formal occasions

cu·mu·la·tive /ˈkjuːmjələtɪv $ -leɪtɪv/ ●○○ *adj* increasing gradually as more of something is added or happens: *Learning is a cumulative process.* | **cumulative effect (of sth)** *Depression is often caused by the cumulative effects of stress and overwork.*

cu·mu·lus /ˈkjuːmjələs/ *n* [C,U] a thick white cloud with a flat bottom edge

cu·nei·form /ˈkjuːnɪfɔːm, ˈkjuːni-əfɔːm $ kjuːˈniːəfɔːrm/ *adj* relating to the writing used by the people of ancient Mesopotamia —**cuneiform** *n* [U]

cun·ni·lin·gus /ˌkʌnɪˈlɪŋgəs/ *n* [U] *technical* the act of touching the female sex organs with the lips and tongue in order to give sexual pleasure → **fellatio**

cun·ning¹ /ˈkʌnɪŋ/ ●●○ *adj*
1 someone who is cunning is clever and good at deceiving people in order to get what they want SYN **crafty**: *a cunning opponent* THESAURUS INTELLIGENT
2 behaviour or actions that are cunning are clever but dishonest and unfair, and are used to get what you want: *a cunning plan*
3 a cunning object or piece of equipment is clever and unusual: *a cunning little device for keeping out draughts*

4 *AmE old-fashioned* attractive: *a cunning little dress* —**cunningly** *adv*

cunning² *n* [U] the ability to achieve what you want by deceiving people in a clever way: *the tiger's ferocity and cunning* | *She would use* ***low cunning*** (=unpleasant dishonest methods) *to win people's sympathy.*

cunt /kʌnt/ *n* [C] *taboo informal* **1** a very offensive word for a stupid or unpleasant person. Do not use this word. **2** a very offensive word for a woman's VAGINA (=sex organ). Do not use this word.

cup¹ /kʌp/ ●●● S1 W1 *n*
1 FOR DRINKING [C] a small round container, usually with a handle, that you use to drink tea, coffee etc → **saucer**: *Mathew picked up the cup and sipped his coffee.* | *She put her* ***cup and saucer*** *down on the table.* | **tea/coffee cup** *Helen took the coffee cups into the kitchen.* | **paper/plastic/china etc cup** *They drank cheap wine from plastic cups.*
2 DRINK [C] the liquid contained inside a cup: **[+of]** *Let's go and have a cup of coffee.* | *Will you stay for a cup of tea?* | *Would you like another cup?*
3 AMOUNT OF LIQUID/FOOD [C] **a)** a unit used in the US for measuring food or liquid in cooking, equal to eight FLUID OUNCES or 237 MILLILITRES: *Mix the butter with one cup of powdered sugar until light and fluffy.* **b)** (*also* **cupful** /ˈkʌpfʊl/) the amount of liquid or food that a cup can hold: *Breakfast consisted of half a cup of milk and a dry biscuit.*
4 SPORT COMPETITION **a)** [C] a specially shaped silver container, often with two handles, that is given as a prize in a competition, especially a sports competition: *The president of the club came to* ***present*** *the* ***cup*** *to the winners.* **b)** [singular] a sports competition in which a cup is given as a prize: *They've* ***won the*** *European* ***Cup*** *twice.* | *Germany's World Cup team*
5 ROUND THING [C] something round and hollow that is shaped like a cup: *The flowers' white petals contrast handsomely with their lemon-yellow cups.* | *acorn cups* | **[+of]** *She held it in the cup of her hand.*
6 GOLF [C] *AmE* a hole in the ground that you have to try to hit the ball into in the game of golf
7 CLOTHING [C] **a)** the part of a BRA that covers a woman's breast **b)** *AmE* a JOCKSTRAP
8 ALCOHOL [C,U] *BrE* a mixed alcoholic drink: *He's gone to get me some* ***fruit cup****.*
9 not be your cup of tea *spoken* to not be the type of thing that you like: *Jazz just isn't my cup of tea – I prefer classical music.*
10 in your cups *BrE old-fashioned* drunk, or when drunk: *By the time Anthony arrived, Richard was already* ***deep in*** *his* ***cups****.* → EGGCUP

cup² *v* (**cupped**, **cupping**) [T] **1** to hold something in your hands, so that your hands form part of a circle around it: *He* ***cupped*** *her* ***face*** *in his hands and kissed her.* | *Luke was sitting at his desk, one hand* ***cupping*** *his* ***chin****.* **2 cup your hand(s)** to make a shape like a cup with your hand or hands: *He struck a match and cupped his hand around the flame.*

cup·board /ˈkʌbəd $ -ərd/ ●●● S2 *n* [C]
1 a piece of furniture with doors, and sometimes shelves, used for storing clothes, plates, food etc → **closet**, **wardrobe**, **cabinet**: *It's in the kitchen cupboard.* | *The cupboard doors were open.*
2 the cupboard is bare used to say that there is no money etc left that can be used: *The workers have been told not to expect a pay rise because the cupboard is bare.* → **AIRING CUPBOARD**, → **skeleton in the cupboard** at SKELETON(5)

cup·cake /ˈkʌpkeɪk/ *n* [C] a small round cake

ˈcup ˌfinal *n* [C] the last and most important game in a competition, especially a football competition

cup·ful /ˈkʌpfʊl/ *n* [C] the amount that a cup can hold

cu·pid /ˈkjuːpɪd/ *n* **1 Cupid** [singular] the Roman god of sexual love, represented as a beautiful boy with wings who is carrying a BOW and ARROW **2** [C] an image of this god, used to represent love **3 play cupid** to try to arrange for two people to fall in love with each other: *She vowed never to play cupid again.*

cu·pid·i·ty /kjʊˈpɪdəti/ *n* [U] *formal* very strong desire for something, especially money or property SYN **greed**: *the cupidity of some businessmen*

cu·po·la /ˈkjuːpələ/ *n* [C] a round structure on the top of a building, that is shaped like an upside down bowl: *a golden edifice with an onion-shaped cupola*

cup·pa /ˈkʌpə/ *n* [C] *BrE spoken* a cup of tea: *I'm dying for a cuppa!*

cup·ping /ˈkʌpɪŋ/ *n* [U] a medical treatment that involves putting special glass cups onto parts of the body and then heating the cup, causing the skin to rise gently upwards inside the cup. This treatment is done by an ACUPUNCTURIST or someone giving you a MASSAGE, not a doctor.

ˈcup tie *n* [C] a game between two teams in a competition in which only the winning team will play any more games: *Saturday's FA Cup tie against Spurs*

cur /kɜː $ kɜːr/ *n* [C] *old-fashioned* an unfriendly dog, especially one that is a mix of several breeds

cur·a·ble /ˈkjʊərəbəl $ ˈkjʊr-/ *adj* an illness that is curable can be cured OPP **incurable**

cu·ra·çao /ˈkjʊərəsəʊ $ ˈkjʊrəsoʊ/ *n* [U] a strong thick alcoholic drink that tastes of oranges

cu·ra·cy /ˈkjʊərəsi $ ˈkjʊr-/ *n* (*plural* **curacies**) [C] the job or position of a curate, or the period of time that someone has this position

cu·rate¹ /ˈkjʊərət $ ˈkjʊr-/ *n* [C] **1** a priest of the lowest rank, whose job is to help the priest who is in charge of an area **2 curate's egg** *BrE* something that has good and bad parts: *The book is something of a curate's egg.*

cu·rate² /kjʊˈreɪt $ kjʊˈreɪt, ˈkjʊreɪt/ *v* [T] to choose and organize the art, music, objects etc for an EXHIBITION, show, concert etc

cu·ra·tive /ˈkjʊərətɪv $ ˈkjʊr-/ *adj* able to or intended to cure illness → **heal**: *the spring's alleged* ***curative properties*** —**curative** *n* [C]: *This herb was once thought to be a curative.*

cu·ra·tor /kjʊˈreɪtə $ -ər/ ●○○ *n* [C] someone who is in charge of a MUSEUM or ZOO: *He's Curator of Prints at the Metropolitan.*

curb¹ /kɜːb $ kɜːrb/ ●○○ *v* [T] to control or limit something in order to prevent it from having a harmful effect: *measures to curb the spread of the virus*

curb² *n* [C] **1** an influence which helps to control or limit something: **[+on]** *We are trying to keep a curb on their activities.* **2** *AmE* the raised edge of a road, between where people can walk and cars can drive SYN **kerb** *BrE* → **pavement**, **sidewalk**

curd /kɜːd $ kɜːrd/ *n* [U] (*also* **curds** [plural]) the thick substance that forms in milk when it becomes sour → **whey**, **bean curd**

cur·dle /ˈkɜːdl $ ˈkɜːrdl/ *v* [I,T] **1** to become thicker or form curd, or to make a liquid do this: *Milk may curdle in warm weather.* **2 make your blood curdle** to make you very frightened → BLOODCURDLING

cure¹ /kjʊə $ kjʊr/ ●●○ *n* [C]
1 a medicine or medical treatment that makes an illness go away: **[+for]** *There is still no cure for AIDS.*
2 something that solves a problem, or improves a bad situation → **solution**: **[+for]** *There is no easy cure for loneliness.*
3 the act of making someone well again after an illness: *The new treatment effected a miraculous cure.*

cure² ●●○ *v* [T]
1 to make an illness or medical condition go away: *Many types of cancer can now be cured.* | *an operation that can cure short-sightedness in 15 minutes*
2 to make someone well again after they have been ill → **heal**: *She had some acupuncture treatment which seems to have cured her.* | **cure sb of sth** *90% of patients can be cured of the disease.*
3 to solve a problem, or improve a bad situation: *Attempts to cure unemployment have so far failed.*
4 cure sb of sth to make someone stop behaving in a particular way or stop them having a particular feeling or attitude: *Nothing could cure her of her impatience with Anna.*
5 to preserve food, tobacco etc by drying it, hanging it in smoke, or covering it with salt: *cured ham*

ˈcure-all *n* [C] something that people think will cure any problem or illness: **[+for]** *Investment is not a cure-all for every economic problem.*

cur·few /ˈkɜːfjuː $ ˈkɜːr-/ ●○○ *n* [C,U]
1 a law that forces people to stay indoors after a particular time at night, or the time people must be indoors: *The government **imposed** a night-time **curfew** throughout the country.* | *The **curfew** was **lifted** (=ended) on May 6th.* | *The whole town was **placed under curfew**.* | *Anyone found in the streets after curfew was shot.*
2 *AmE* the time, decided by a parent, by which a child must be home or asleep in the evening

cu·ri·o /ˈkjʊəriəʊ $ ˈkjʊrioʊ/ *n* (*plural* **curios**) [C] a small object that is interesting because it is beautiful or rare

cu·ri·os·i·ty /ˌkjʊəriˈɒsəti $ ˌkjʊriˈɑːs-/ ●●○ *n* (*plural* **curiosities**)
1 [singular, U] the desire to know about something: *I opened the packet just to **satisfy** my **curiosity**.* | *The news **aroused** a lot of **curiosity** among local people.* | *She decided to follow him **out of curiosity**.* | *Margaret looked at him **with curiosity**.* | **[+about]** *Children have a **natural curiosity** about the world around them.* | *a man of immense **intellectual curiosity*** | *It was **idle curiosity** that made me ask.*
2 [C] someone or something that is interesting because they are unusual or strange: *a house full of old maps and other curiosities* | *In the past, men who wanted to work with children were regarded as something of a curiosity.* | *It's not worth much, but I kept it for its **curiosity value**.*
3 curiosity killed the cat used to tell someone not to ask too many questions about something

cu·ri·ous /ˈkjʊəriəs $ ˈkjʊr-/ ●●○ W3 *adj*
1 wanting to know about something → **inquisitive**: *Puppies are naturally curious.* | **[+about]** *He was curious about how she would react.* | **curious to know/see/hear etc** *Mandy was curious to know what happened.* | **curious look/glance** *Her shouting attracted some curious glances from other people in the restaurant.*
2 strange or unusual: *He felt a curious mixture of excitement and panic.* | *a curious coincidence* | ***It's curious that** she left without saying goodbye.* **THESAURUS** ▸ STRANGE

cu·ri·ous·ly /ˈkjʊəriəsli $ ˈkjʊr-/ ●○○ *adv*
1 in a way that shows you want to know about something: *'What have you got in there?' Felix asked curiously.*
2 [sentence adverb] strangely or unusually: *Curiously, exactly the same thing happened to me a year ago.* | *She felt curiously calm.*

curl¹ /kɜːl $ kɜːrl/ ●●○ *v* [I,T]
1 to form a twisted or curved shape, or to make something do this: *Mary was busy curling her hair.* | **[+around/round]** *Ivy curled round the tree.*
2 [always + adv/prep] to move, forming a twisted or curved shape, or to make something do this: **[+across/along etc]** *Morning mists curled across the river.* | **curl sth around/round/over etc sth** *He curled his arm around Claudia's waist.*
3 if you curl your lip, or if your lip curls, you move it upwards and sideways, to show that you disapprove of someone or something: *Her lip curled in contempt.*
→ **make sb's toes curl** at TOE¹(5), → **make your hair curl** at HAIR(9)

curl up *phr v*
1 to move so that you are lying or sitting with your arms and legs bent close to your body: *I just wanted to curl up and go to sleep.* | *Sarah was curled up on the sofa.*
2 if something flat curls up, its edges start to become curved and point upwards: *The letter was now yellow and beginning to curl up.*

curl² ●●○ *n*
1 [C] a piece of hair that hangs in a curved shape: *a little boy with beautiful blonde curls*
2 [singular, U] the ability of your hair to form curls: *Use a diffuser to maximise the volume and curl of your hair.* | *hair that has a natural curl*
3 [C] something in the shape of a curve: *Decorate the cake with chocolate curls.* | **[+of]** *A curl of smoke rose from her cigarette.*
4 [C] an exercise in which you repeatedly bend your arms, legs, or stomach in order to make your muscles strong → see picture at GYM
5 curl of sb's lip/mouth a sideways and upwards movement of your lip or mouth, showing that you disapprove of someone or something

curl·er /ˈkɜːlə $ ˈkɜːrlər/ *n* [C] a small plastic or metal tube used for making hair curl SYN **roller**: *Her hair was in curlers.*

cur·lew /ˈkɜːljuː $ ˈkɜːrluː/ *n* [C] a bird with long legs and a long beak that lives near water

curl·ing /ˈkɜːlɪŋ $ ˈkɜːr-/ *n* [U] a sport played on ice, in which players slide flat heavy stones towards a marked place

ˈcurling ˌtongs *BrE* [plural], **ˈcurling ˌiron** *AmE* [C] *n* a piece of electrical equipment that you heat and use to put curls in your hair

curl·y /ˈkɜːli $ ˈkɜːrli/ ●●● S3 *adj*
1 having a lot of curls OPP **straight**: *long dark curly hair* → see picture at HAIRSTYLE
2 *BrE* curved in shape: *cows with curly horns* —**curliness** *n* [U]

cur·mud·geon /kɜːˈmʌdʒən $ kɜːr-/ *n* [C] *old-fashioned* someone who is often annoyed or angry, especially an old person

cur·rant /ˈkʌrənt $ ˈkɜːr-/ ●●○ *n* [C]
1 a small dried GRAPE used especially in baking cakes → **raisin, sultana**
2 a small round red or black BERRY → BLACKCURRANT, REDCURRANT

cur·ren·cy /ˈkʌrənsi $ ˈkɜːr-/ ●●○ W3 AWL *n* (*plural* **currencies**)
1 [C,U] the system or type of money that a country uses: *The bank can supply you with **foreign currency**.* | *The euro is the **single currency** for 12 of the European Union's 15 member states.* | *The **local currency** is the Swiss franc.* → HARD CURRENCY **THESAURUS** ▸ MONEY
2 [U] the state of being accepted or used by a lot of people: *The argument has received **wide currency**.* | *Marxism began to **gain currency**.* | *The idea was **common currency** in European political life.*

cur·rent¹ /ˈkʌrənt $ ˈkɜːr-/ ●●● S2 W2 *adj* [only before noun] happening or existing now SYN **present**: *the current president* | *In its current state, the car is worth £1,000.*

current² ●●○ W3 *n* [C]
1 a continuous movement of water in a river, lake, or sea → **tide**: **ocean/sea/tidal etc current** | ***Strong currents*** *can be very dangerous for swimmers.*
2 a continuous movement of air: *Some birds use warm* ***air currents*** *to help them fly.* | **[+of]** *currents of warm air rising from the plain*
3 a flow of electricity through a wire: *an* ***electrical current*** → ALTERNATING CURRENT, DIRECT CURRENT
4 an idea, feeling, or opinion that a particular group of people has: *The committee reflects the different political currents within the organization.* | **[+of]** *There was an underlying current of discontent among teachers.* ⚠ Do not confuse with **currant** (=a dried grape or a type of berry).

ˈcurrent acˌcount ●○○ *n* [C] *BrE* a bank account that you can take money out of at any time SYN **checking account** *AmE*

ˌcurrent afˈfairs *n* [U] important political events or other events in society that are happening now

cur·rent·ly /ˈkʌrəntli $ ˈkɜːr-/ ●●● S2 W2 *adv* at the present time: *the products that are currently available* | *He is currently working on his first novel.* THESAURUS ▸ NOW

cur·ric·u·lar /kəˈrɪkjələ $ -ər/ *adj* [only before noun] relating to the curriculum of a school: *curricular changes*

cur·ric·u·lum /kəˈrɪkjələm/ ●○○ *n* (*plural* **curricula** /-lə/ *or* **curriculums**) [C] the subjects that are taught by a school, college etc, or the things that are studied in a particular subject: *Languages are an essential part of the school curriculum.* | *curriculum planning* | **on the curriculum** *BrE*: *IT is now on the curriculum in most schools.* | **in the curriculum** *AmE*: *Students are exempt from some classes in the curriculum for religious reasons.* → **syllabus**

curriculum vi·tae /kəˌrɪkjələm ˈviːtaɪ/ *n* [C] **1** a formal British expression for CV SYN **resume** *AmE* **2** *AmE* a short written description of a university teacher's previous jobs and work, that they send when looking for a new teaching job

cur·ried /ˈkʌrid $ ˈkɜː-/ *adj* [only before noun] cooked with hot spices: *curried lamb*

cur·ry¹ /ˈkʌri $ ˈkɜːri/ ●●○ *n* (*plural* **curries**) [C,U] a type of food from India, consisting of meat or vegetables in a spicy sauce: *chicken curry*

curry² *v* (**curried**, **currying**, **curries**) **curry favour (with sb)** to try to make someone like you or notice you in order to get something that you want – used to show disapproval: *a businessman who made several attempts to curry favour with politicians*

ˈcurry ˌpowder *n* [U] a mixture of spices, used in cooking to give food a spicy taste

curse¹ /kɜːs $ kɜːrs/ ●○○ *v*
1 [I] to swear: *Gilbert was cursing under his breath.*
2 [T] to say or think bad things about someone or something because they have made you angry: *He cursed his bad luck in arriving just after she'd left.* | **curse sb/sth for (doing) sth** *Elsa cursed herself for believing his lies.*
3 [T] to ask God or a magical power to harm someone
curse sb ↔ **out** *phr v AmE informal* to swear at someone who has made you angry

curse² ●○○ *n* [C]
1 a swear word or words that you say because you are very angry: *He muttered a curse under his breath.*
2 a word or sentence used to ask God or a magical power to do something bad to someone or something: *He believed that someone had* ***put*** *a* ***curse on*** *the house.*
3 something that causes trouble, harm etc: **[+of]** *Noise is one of the curses of modern-day life.*
4 the curse *old-fashioned* a MENSTRUAL PERIOD

curs·ed /ˈkɜːsɪd $ ˈkɜːr-/ *adj* **1 be cursed with/by sth** to be affected by something bad: *The museum has been cursed by financial problems since it opened.* **2** *literary* suffering as a result of a punishment by God or a god

cur·sive /ˈkɜːsɪv $ ˈkɜːr-/ *adj* written in a style of writing with the letters joined together: *cursive script* —**cursively** *adv*

cur·sor /ˈkɜːsə $ ˈkɜːrsər/ ●●○ *n* [C] a mark that can be moved around a computer screen to show where you are working

cur·so·ry /ˈkɜːsəri $ ˈkɜːr-/ *adj* done very quickly without much attention to details: **cursory glance/look** *Even a cursory glance at the figures will tell you that sales are down.* | **cursory examination/inspection** *a cursory examination of the evidence* —**cursorily** *adv*

curt /kɜːt $ kɜːrt/ *adj* using very few words in a way that seems rude SYN **abrupt**: *With a curt nod, he turned away and sat down.* | *a curt note* —**curtly** *adv* —**curtness** *n* [U]

cur·tail /kɜːˈteɪl $ kɜːr-/ ●○○ *v* [T] *formal* to reduce or limit something SYN **cut**: *The new law will curtail police powers.* | **severely/drastically curtail** *Budget cuts have drastically curtailed training programs.* —**curtailment** *n* [C,U]

cur·tain¹ /ˈkɜːtn $ ˈkɜːrtn/ ●●● S3 W3 *n* [C]
1 a piece of hanging cloth that can be pulled across to cover a window, divide a room etc: *red velvet curtains* | **draw/close/pull the curtains** *Ella drew the curtains and switched the light on.* | **draw back/open the curtains** *Shall I open the curtains?* | **curtain rail/pole/rod** (=for hanging a curtain on)
2 a sheet of heavy material that comes down at the front of the stage in a theatre: **the curtain goes up/rises** *Before the curtain went up, the dancers took their places on stage.* | **the curtain comes down/falls** → see picture at THEATRE
3 *written* a thick layer of something that stops anything behind it from being seen: **[+of]** *a curtain of smoke*
4 bring down the curtain on sth *informal* to cause or mark the end of a situation or period of time: *The decision brought down the curtain on a 30-year career.*
5 (it'll) be curtains for sb/sth *informal* used to say that someone will die or that something will end

curtain² *v*
curtain sth ↔ **off** *phr v* to separate one area, room etc from another by hanging a curtain between them: *The room was curtained off by red drapes.*

ˈcurtain call *n* [C] the time at the end of a performance when the actors come to the front of the stage to receive APPLAUSE

cur·tained /ˈkɜːtnd $ ˈkɜːr-/ *adj* [only before noun] a curtained window or door has a curtain hanging across it

ˈcurtain hook *n* [C] a small hook that is joined to the top of a curtain so that you can hang it up

ˈcurtain ˌraiser *n* [C] an event such as a performance or sports event that happens before a more important one: *A local team are playing as a curtain raiser to the game between England and Italy.*

curt·sy, **curtsey** /ˈkɜːtsi $ ˈkɜːr-/ *v* (**curtsied**, **curtsying**, **curtsies**) [I] if a woman curtsies, she bends her knees with one foot in front of the other as a sign of respect for an important person → **bow** —**curtsy** *n* [C]

cur·va·ceous /kɜːˈveɪʃəs $ kɜːr-/ *adj* having an attractively curved body shape - used about women: *a tall curvaceous young woman*

cur·va·ture /ˈkɜːvətʃə $ ˈkɜːrvətʃər/ *n* [C,U] *technical* the state of being curved, or the degree to which something is curved: **[+of]** *the curvature of the Earth's surface* | *He suffered from curvature of the spine.*

curve¹ /kɜːv $ kɜːrv/ ●●○ S3 W3 *n* [C]
1 a line that gradually bends like part of a circle: **[+of]** *the curve of her hips* | *a sweeping curve of railroad track*
2 a line on a GRAPH that gradually bends and represents a change in the amount or level of something: *The curve illustrates costs per capita.* | **demand/supply curve** *The market demand curve has increased.*
3 a bend in a road, river etc: *The car took the curve much too quickly.*
4 in baseball, a ball that spins and moves in a curve when it is thrown, so that it is difficult to hit
5 throw sb a curve *AmE* to surprise someone with a question or problem that is difficult to deal with → CURVEBALL
6 ahead of/behind the curve *informal* more advanced than other people in what you do or think, or less advanced than other people → LEARNING CURVE

curve² ●●○ *v* [I,T] to bend or move in the shape of a curve, or to make something do this: *The track curved round the side of the hill.* | *A smile curved her lips.*

curve·ball /ˈkɜːvbɔːl $ ˈkɜːrvbɒːl/ *n* [C] **1** *AmE* in baseball, a ball that is difficult to hit because it does not move in a straight direction **2** *informal* a surprising and unexpected action or event: *When life throws you a curveball, you need to know how to handle it.*

CURVED

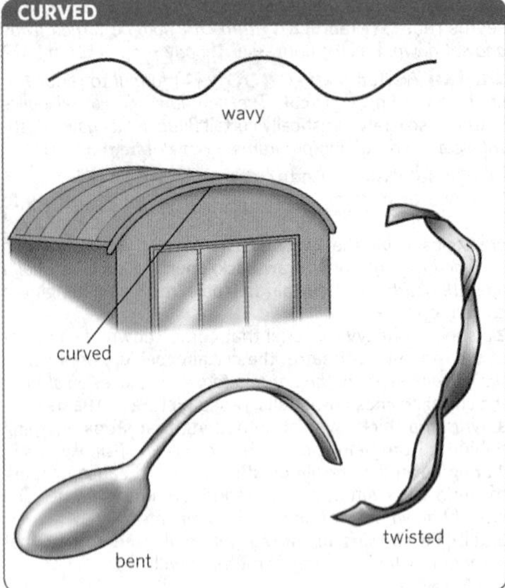

curved /kɜːvd $ kɜːrvd/ ●●○ *adj* having a shape that is like a curve and not straight: *a curved wall*

cur·vi·lin·e·ar /ˌkɜːvɪˈlɪniə $ ˌkɜːrvəˈlɪniər/ *adj formal* having curved lines or a curved shape: *curvilinear patterns*

curv·y /ˈkɜːvi $ ˈkɜːrvi/ *adj* **1** having a shape with several curves: *a curvy line* **2** a woman who is curvy is attractive because her body has a lot of curves

cush·ion¹ /ˈkʊʃən/ ●●● S3 *n* [C]
1 a cloth bag filled with soft material that you put on a chair or the floor to make it more comfortable → **pillow**: *a velvet cushion* | *a cushion cover*
2 something that stops one thing from hitting another thing: *Good sports shoes should provide a cushion when running.*
3 [usually singular] something, especially money, that prevents you from being immediately affected by a bad situation: **[+against]** *Savings can act as a cushion against unemployment.*
4 the soft rubber edge of the table used for playing BILLIARDS or SNOOKER → see picture at **POOL¹**

cushion² *v* [T] **1** to make the effect of a fall or hit less painful, for example by having something soft in the way: *His landing was cushioned by the fresh snow that had fallen.* **2** to protect someone from an unpleasant situation or the unpleasant effects of something: **cushion the blow/impact (of sth)** *generous leaving allowances to help cushion the blow of redundancy* | **cushion sb from/against sth** *Many parents try to cushion their children from the outside world.*

cush·ion·ing /ˈkʊʃənɪŋ/ *n* [U] something soft that protects someone or something when they hit a surface: *a lightweight cushioning material*

cush·y /ˈkʊʃi/ *adj* a cushy job or life is very easy and does not need much effort: *I wish I had a nice cushy job like her.* | *a very* ***cushy number*** (=an easy job or life) **THESAURUS** EASY

cusp /kʌsp/ *n* **1** [C] *technical* the point formed where two curves join **2 be on the cusp of sth** [singular] to be at the time when a situation or state is going to change: *The country was on the cusp of economic expansion.* **3 on the cusp** someone who was born on the cusp was born near the time when one STAR SIGN ends and another begins

cuss /kʌs/ *v* [I,T] *BrE old-fashioned, AmE spoken* to swear because you are annoyed by something

cuss sb ↔ **out** *phr v AmE spoken* to swear and shout at someone because you are angry: *She got mad and started cussing him out.*

ˈcuss word *n* [C] *old-fashioned* a rude word that you use because you are angry

cus·tard /ˈkʌstəd $ -ərd/ ●●○ *n*
1 [U] a sweet yellow sauce that is made with milk, sugar, eggs, and flour
2 [C,U] a soft baked mixture of milk, sugar, and eggs

ˌcustard ˈpie *n* [C] a PIE filled with a substance that looks like custard, which people throw at each other as a joke in films, on television etc

cus·to·di·al /kʌˈstəʊdiəl $ -ˈstoʊ-/ *adj* relating to the custody of someone, especially a child: *custodial care*

cusˌtodial ˈsentence *n* [C] *BrE* a period of time that someone has to spend in prison as a punishment

cus·to·di·an /kʌˈstəʊdiən $ -ˈstoʊ-/ *n* [C] **1** someone who is responsible for looking after something important or valuable: **[+of]** *Farmers are custodians of the land for the next generation.* **2** *especially AmE* someone who looks after a public building: *a custodian at the stadium* **3 custodian of tradition/moral values etc** someone who tries to protect a traditional set of beliefs, attitudes etc

cus·to·dy /ˈkʌstədi/ ●○○ *n* [U]
1 the right to take care of a child, given to one of their parents when they have DIVORCED: **[+of]** *He got custody of his son after the divorce.* | *The mother is usually* ***awarded custody*** (=legally allowed to have custody). | *a dispute over who should* ***have custody of*** *the children* | *The couple will retain* ***joint custody*** (=they will both have custody) *of their daughters.* | *Allen is fighting a bitter* ***custody battle*** *over his three children.*
2 when someone is kept in prison until they go to court, because the police think they have committed a crime: *The committee is looking at alternatives to custody.* | **in custody** *the death of a man in custody* | **hold/keep sb in custody** *A man is being held in police custody in connection with the murder.* | **remand sb in custody** *BrE* (=send someone to prison to wait until they go to court) *A man has been remanded in custody charged with the murder of a schoolgirl.* | *She was* ***taken into custody*** *as a suspect.*
3 *formal* when someone is responsible for keeping and looking after something: *Managers are responsible for the safe custody and retention of records.* | *The collection of art books is now* ***in the custody of*** *the university.*

cus·tom¹ /ˈkʌstəm/ ●●● W3 *n*
1 [C,U] something that is done by people in a particular society because it is traditional → **tradition**: **local/ancient/French etc custom** *The guide offers information on local customs.* | **it is the custom (for sb) to do sth** *It's the custom for the bride's father to pay for the wedding.* | **the custom of doing sth** *The custom of naming women after flowers is becoming less common.* **THESAURUS** HABIT
2 [singular] *formal* something that you usually do every day, or in a particular situation SYN **habit**: *He awoke early, as was his custom.*
3 customs [plural] **a)** the place where your bags are checked for illegal goods when you go into a country → **immigration**: *She was stopped at customs and questioned.* | *It took ages to* ***clear customs*** (=be allowed through customs) *but then we were out of the airport quite quickly.* | *You won't be able to take that* ***through customs***. **b)** the government department that checks goods coming into a country and collects any taxes on them: *customs officers* | *the US customs service*
4 [U] *formal* the practice of regularly using a particular shop or business: *an advertisement to attract more custom* | *Smaller shops lose a lot of custom when supermarkets open nearby.*

custom² *adj* [only before noun] *especially AmE* custom products or services are specially designed and made for a particular person SYN **bespoke**: *His son operates a custom furniture business.*

custom- /kʌstəm/ *prefix* **custom-made/custom-built/custom-designed etc** made, built etc for a particular person: *custom-made suit | custom-ordered vehicles*

cus·tom·a·ry /ˈkʌstəməri $ -meri/ ●○○ *adj*
1 something that is customary is normal because it is the way something is usually done SYN **usual**: **it is customary (for sb) to do sth** *In some cultures it is customary for the bride to wear white.*
2 [only before noun] someone's customary behaviour is the way they usually do things SYN **usual**: *Barbara answered with her customary enthusiasm.* —**customarily** /ˈkʌstəmərəli $ ˌkʌstəˈmerəli/ *adv*

cus·tom·er /ˈkʌstəmə $ -ər/ ●●● S1 W1 *n* [C]
1 someone who buys goods or services from a shop, company etc: *We aim to offer good value and service to all our customers. | We've had several letters from satisfied customers.* | **customer service/care** *Many of the banks offer a poor level of customer service. | He's one of our* ***regular customers.*** | **best/biggest/largest customer** (=the person or company who uses a shop or company the most)
2 awkward/tricky/tough etc customer someone who is difficult to deal with because they behave in a deliberately unhelpful way → **cool customer** at COOL[1](3)

THESAURUS

customer someone who buys goods or services from a shop or company: *Customers were waiting for the shop to open. | The bank is one of our biggest customers.*
client someone who pays for a service from a professional person or company: *He has a meeting with one of his clients. | The company buys and sells shares on behalf of their clients*
shopper someone who goes to the shops looking for things to buy: *The streets were full of Christmas shoppers.*
guest someone who pays to stay in a hotel: *Guests must leave their rooms by 10 am.*
patron /ˈpeɪtrən/ *formal* a customer of a particular shop, restaurant, or hotel – usually written on signs: *The notice said 'Parking for Patrons Only'.*
patient someone who is getting medical treatment from a doctor, or in a hospital: *He is a patient of Dr Williams.*
consumer anyone who buys goods or uses services – used when considering these people as a group who have particular rights, needs, or behaviour: *Consumers are demanding more environmentally-friendly products. | the rights of the consumer*
market the number of people who want to buy a product, or the type of people who want to buy it: *The market for organic food is growing all the time. | a magazine aimed at the youth market*
clientele /ˌkliːənˈtel $ ˌklaɪənˈtel, ˌkliː-/ *formal* the type of customers that a particular shop, restaurant etc gets: *The hotel has a very upmarket clientele. | They have a wealthy international clientele.*

ˈcustomer-ˌfacing *adj* dealing directly with customers: *customer-facing staff | customer-facing roles*

ˌcustomer ˈservices *n* [U] the part of a company or business that deals with questions, problems etc that customers have: *You should call customer services and complain. | He's customer services manager at the store.*

cus·tom·iz·a·ble (*also* **-isable** *BrE*) /ˈkʌstəmaɪzəbəl $ ˌkʌstəˈmaɪz-/ *adj* able to be changed in order to be suitable for a particular object or situation: *Download free customizable business forms from Entrepreneur.com.*

cus·tom·ize (*also* **-ise** *BrE*) /ˈkʌstəmaɪz/ *v* [T] to change something to make it more suitable for you, or to make it look special or different from things of a similar type: *a customized car*

ˌCustoms and ˈExcise *n* the former department of the British government that was responsible for collecting tax on goods that were being bought or sold, or on goods that had been brought into the country. The department MERGEd with the Inland Revenue to form Her Majesty's Revenue and Customs in 2005.

cut[1] /kʌt/ ●●● S1 W1 *v* (*past tense and past participle* **cut**, *present participle* **cutting**)
1 REDUCE [T] to reduce the amount of something: *They're introducing CCTV cameras in an attempt to cut street crime in the area. | You need to cut the amount of fat and sugar in your diet. | Scientists are warning that unless carbon emissions are cut, we could be heading for an environmental catastrophe. | Seven hundred jobs will be lost in order to* ***cut costs*** *and boost profits. | The major aviation companies need to* ***cut prices*** *if they are to compete with budget airlines.* | **cut sth by £1 million/$5 billion/half etc** *The welfare budget has been cut by $56 billion.* | **cut sth off sth** *A new direct service will cut two hours off the flying time between London and Seoul. | Staffing levels had already been* ***cut to the bone*** (=reduced to the lowest level possible). THESAURUS REDUCE
2 DIVIDE STH WITH A KNIFE, SCISSORS ETC [I,T] to divide something or separate something from its main part, using scissors, a knife etc: *Do you want me to cut the cake? | The telephone wires had been cut minutes before the assault.* | **cut sth with sth** *Jane cut the cord with a knife.* | **cut sb sth** *Can you cut me a piece of bread, please?* | **[+along/across/round etc]** *Using a pair of scissors, cut carefully along the dotted lines.* | **[+through]** *We'll need a saw that will cut through metal.* | **cut sth in half/in two** *Cut the orange in half.* | **cut sth into slices/chunks/pieces etc** (=make something into a particular shape by cutting) *Cut the carrots into thin strips.* | **cut sth to size/length** (=cut something so that it is the size you need) *The curtain pole can be cut to length.* → CUT OUT, CUT UP
3 MAKE STH SHORTER WITH A KNIFE ETC [T] to make something shorter with a knife, scissors etc, especially in order to make it neater: *For reasons of hygiene, we had to cut our fingernails really short.* | **cut the lawn/grass/hedge etc** *From outside came the sound of someone cutting the hedge.* | **have/get your hair cut** *It's about time you got your hair cut.*
4 REMOVE PARTS FROM FILM ETC [T] to remove parts from a film, book, speech etc, for example because it is too long or might offend people: *The original version was cut by more than 30 minutes.* THESAURUS REMOVE
5 MAKE A HOLE/MARK [I,T] to make a hole or mark in the surface of something, or to open it using a sharp tool: **[+into]** *The blade cut deep into the wood.* | **cut sth into sth** *Strange letters had been cut into the stone.* | ***Cut a hole*** *in the middle of the paper.* | ***Cut open*** *the chillies and remove the seeds.*
6 INJURE [T] to injure yourself on something sharp that breaks the skin and makes you bleed: **cut your finger/knee/hand etc** *I noticed he'd cut his finger quite badly.* | **cut yourself (on sth)** *Marcie said she'd cut herself on a broken glass. | That knife's extremely sharp! Mind you don't cut yourself. | On Eric's chin was a scrap of cotton wool where he'd* ***cut*** *himself* ***shaving****. | She fell and* ***cut*** *her head* ***open****.*
7 MAKE/FORM STH BY CUTTING [T] to make or form something from a solid piece of wood, metal etc using a sharp tool: *I'll get a spare key cut for you.* | **cut sth from sth** *The chair had been cut from the trunk of a tree.*
8 LET SB GET FREE [T] to cut something such as metal or rope in order to let someone escape from where they are trapped: **cut sb from sth** *She had to be cut from the wreckage of her car. | He was in the vehicle for an hour before he was* ***cut free****.*
9 TOOL/MATERIAL [I] if a tool cuts well, badly etc, it cuts things well or badly etc: *professional quality tools that cut efficiently and smoothly*
10 CLOTHES [T] if a piece of clothing is cut in a particular way, that is the way it is designed and made: *The T-shirt is cut fairly low at the neck.* GRAMMAR **Cut** is usually passive in this meaning.
11 ON COMPUTER [I,T] to remove something from a document or FILE on a computer: *To cut text, press Control + C.* | ***Cut and paste*** *the picture into a new file* (=remove it and then make it appear in a new file).
12 GO A QUICK WAY [I always + adv/prep] to get to somewhere by a quicker and more direct way than the usual

way → **shortcut**: **[+through/down/across etc]** *I usually cut through the car park to get to work.* | *Let's cut across the field.*

13 DIVIDE AN AREA [I,T] to divide an area into two or more parts: **cut sth in/into sth** *The river cuts the whole region in two.* | **[+through]** *The new road will cut through a conservation area.*

14 PLAYING CARDS [I,T] to divide a pack of cards into two: *First cut the pack, and then deal the cards*

15 MUSIC [T] to produce a CD, song etc for people to buy: *The band cut their first single in 2001.*

16 CROPS [T] to take the top part off crops such as wheat before gathering them

17 cut a deal to make a business deal: *A French company has reportedly cut a deal to produce software for government agencies.*

C

18 cut (sb) a check *AmE informal* to write a CHECK for a particular amount of money and give it to someone: *When the damage assessor called, he cut a check for $139.*

19 cut! *spoken* said by the DIRECTOR of a film to tell people to stop acting, filming etc

20 FILM a) [T] to put the parts of a film together so that they make a continuous story, and get rid of the parts you do not want **b)** [I always + adv/prep] in a film, if the camera cuts away or cuts to a different scene, the scene on the screen changes to a different one: *At the crucial moment, the camera cuts away and we don't see the murder.* | *The shark is shown moving through the water and then we cut to a shot of the beach.*

21 cut in line *AmE* to unfairly go in front of other people who are waiting to do something

22 cut class/school *AmE informal* to deliberately not go to a class that you should go to: *She started cutting classes.*

23 cut your teeth (on sth) to get your first experience of doing something and learn the basic skills: *Both reporters cut their journalistic teeth on the same provincial newspaper.*

24 cut corners to do something in a way that saves time, effort, or money, but that also results in it not being done properly: *There's a temptation to cut corners when you're pushed for time, but it's not worth it.*

25 cut sth short to stop doing something earlier than you planned: *The band has cut short its US concert tour.* | *Her athletic career was cut short by a leg injury.*

26 cut sb short to stop someone from finishing what they wanted to say: *I tried to explain, but he cut me short.*

27 cut the ... *spoken* an impolite way of telling someone to stop doing something because it is annoying you: *Cut the sarcasm, Jane, and tell me what really happened!* | ***Cut the crap*** (=stop saying something that is not true), *I saw his car outside your house!*

28 cut sb dead to deliberately ignore someone when you meet them: *I saw Ian in town but he cut me dead.*

29 cut your losses to stop doing something that is failing, so that you do not waste any more money, time, or effort: *He decided to cut his losses and sell the business.*

30 LINE [T] if a line cuts another line, they cross each other at a particular point

31 TOOTH [T] if a baby cuts a tooth, the tooth starts to grow

32 cut sb to the quick/bone *literary* to upset someone very much by saying something cruel: *His mockery frightened her and cut her to the bone.*

33 cut to the chase *informal* to immediately start dealing with the most important part of something

34 cut a fine/strange etc figure *literary* to have an impressive, strange etc appearance: *Mason cuts a battered but defiant figure.*

35 cut your own throat to behave in a way that will cause harm to yourself, especially because you are very offended or angry about something: *He'd just be cutting his own throat if he left now.*

36 (it) cuts both ways *spoken* used to say that something has two effects, especially a good effect and a bad one: *The higher the interest rate, the greater the financial risk – which, of course, cuts both ways.*

37 cut the ground from under sb's feet to make someone or their ideas seem less impressive by having better ideas yourself or doing something before they do

38 cut and run *informal* to avoid a difficult situation by leaving suddenly: *Although the company has faced financial difficulties, they do not intend to cut and run.*

39 cut no ice/not cut much ice if something cuts no ice with someone, it will not persuade them to change their opinion or decision: *It's unlikely that these arguments will cut much ice with Democrats.*

40 cut the (umbilical) cord to stop being too dependent on someone, especially your parents

41 not cut the mustard *informal* to not be good enough: *Other magazines have tried to copy the formula but have never quite cut the mustard.*

42 DRUGS [T] to mix an illegal drug such as HEROIN with another substance GRAMMAR **Cut** is often passive in this meaning.

43 cut your coat according to your cloth to spend only as much money as you can afford

44 to cut a long story short *spoken* used to say that you are only going to mention the main facts of something: *To cut a long story short, he threw them out of the house.*

45 cut it/things fine (*also* **cut it close** *AmE*) to leave yourself just enough time to do something: *Even in normal traffic, 20 minutes to get to the airport is cutting it fine.*

46 not cut it *informal* to not be good enough to do something: *Players who can't cut it soon quit the team.*

47 cut a swathe through sth *literary* to cause a lot of damage in a place or among a group of people: *A series of bribery scandals has cut a swathe through the government.*

48 you could cut the atmosphere with a knife *informal* used to say that everyone in a place is very annoyed or angry with each other and this is very easy to notice

THESAURUS

cut to divide something into two or more pieces, especially using a knife or SCISSORS: *Do you want me to cut the cake?* | *He cut off the lower branches.*

snip to quickly cut something, especially using SCISSORS: *I snipped the label off.* | *The hairdresser snipped away at her hair.*

slit to make a long narrow cut through something, especially using a knife: *He slit the envelope open with a penknife.* | *She slit through the plastic covering.*

slash to cut something quickly and violently with a knife, making a long thin cut: *Someone had slashed the tyres on his car.* | *He tried to slash his wrists.*

saw to cut wood, using a SAW (=a tool with a row of sharp points): *Saw the wood to the correct length.*

chop to cut wood, vegetables, or meat into pieces: *Bill was outside chopping up firewood with an axe.* | *They chopped down the old tree.* | *finely chopped onion*

slice to cut bread, meat, or vegetables into thin pieces: *I'll slice the cucumber.* | *Slice the bread thinly.*

dice to cut vegetables or meat into small square pieces: *First dice the apple into cubes.*

grate to cut cheese or a hard vegetable by rubbing it against a special tool: *Grate the cheese and sprinkle it over the vegetables.*

peel to cut the outside part off something such as a potato or apple: *I peeled the potatoes and put them in a saucepan.*

carve to cut thin pieces from a large piece of meat: *Uncle Ray carved the turkey.*

mow to cut the grass in a garden, park etc: *A gardener was mowing the lawn.*

trim (*also* **clip**) to cut a small amount off something, especially to make it look neater: *He was trimming his beard.* | *Trim the excess fat off the meat.*

cut across sth *phr v* if a problem or feeling cuts across different groups of people, they are all affected by it: *Domestic violence seems to cut across most social divisions.*

cut sth ↔ **away** *phr v* to remove unwanted or unnecessary parts from something by cutting it: *Cut away all the dead wood.*

cut back *phr v*

1 to reduce the amount, size, cost etc of something: **[+on]**

Several major hospitals are cutting back on staff at the moment. | **cut sth ↔ back** *Education spending cannot be cut back any further.* | *Richer countries must do more to cut back carbon emissions.* → CUTBACK
2 cut sth ↔ back to remove the top part of a plant in order to help it to grow: *Cut back the shoots in spring to encourage bushier growth.*
3 to eat, drink, or use less of something, especially in order to improve your health: **[+on]** *Try to cut back on foods containing wheat and dairy products.*
cut down *phr v*
1 REDUCE to reduce the amount of something: **cut sth ↔ down** *Installing double-glazing will cut down the noise from traffic.* | **[+on]** *By getting the design right, you can cut down on accidents.*
2 EAT/USE LESS to eat, drink, or use less of something, especially in order to improve your health: *I've always smoked, but I'm trying to cut down.* | **[+on]** *Cut down on fatty foods if you want to lose weight.*
3 TREE **cut sth ↔ down** to cut through the main part of a tree so that it falls on the ground
4 KILL **cut sb ↔ down** *literary* to kill or injure someone, especially in a battle: *Hundreds of men were cut down by crossbow fire.*
5 REDUCE LENGTH **cut sth ↔ down** to reduce the length of something such as a piece of writing: *Your essay's too long – it needs cutting down a little.*
6 cut sb down to size to make someone realize that they are not as important, successful etc as they think they are
cut in *phr v*
1 INTERRUPT to interrupt someone who is speaking by saying something: *'What shall I do?' Patrick cut in again.* | **[+on]** *Sorry to cut in on you, but there are one or two things I don't understand.*
2 DRIVING to suddenly drive in front of a moving car in a dangerous way: **[+on]** *She cut in on a red Ford, forcing the driver to brake heavily.*
3 MACHINE if a part of a machine cuts in, it starts to operate when it is needed: *The safety device cuts in automatically.*
4 INCLUDE SB **cut sb in** *informal* to allow someone to take part in a plan or to make money from it: **[+on]** *Come on, Joey, you promised to cut me in on this one!*
cut sb/sth **off** *phr v*
1 SEPARATE **cut sth ↔ off** to separate something by cutting it away from the main part: *One of his fingers was cut off in the accident.* | **cut sth off sth** *Cut the fat off the meat.*
2 STOP SUPPLY **cut sth ↔ off** to stop the supply of something such as electricity, gas, water etc: *The gas had been cut off.* | *The US has threatened to cut off economic and military aid.*
3 get cut off to suddenly not be able to hear someone that you were speaking to on the telephone: *I don't know what happened – we just got cut off.*
4 be cut off a) if a place is cut off, people cannot leave it or reach it: *In winter, the town is often cut off by snow.* **b)** to be a long way from other places and be difficult to get to: *Accessible only by air, the town is cut off from the rest of the country.* **c)** if someone is cut off, they are lonely and not able to meet many other people: *Many older people feel cut off and isolated.*
5 STOP BEING FRIENDLY **cut sb ↔ off** to stop having a friendly relationship with someone: *Julia had been completely cut off by all her family and friends.* | **cut yourself off (from sb)** *After his wife died, he cut himself off completely from the rest of the world.*
6 INTERRUPT to interrupt someone and stop them from finishing what they were saying: *Emma cut him off in mid-sentence.*
7 PREVENT STH **cut sb off from sth** to prevent someone from having something that they need or want: *The project aims to ensure that poorer people are not cut off from the benefits of computer technology.*
8 MONEY/PROPERTY to refuse to let someone receive your money or property, especially when you die: *My parents threatened to* ***cut*** *me* ***off without a penny*** *if I married him.*
9 DRIVING **cut sb ↔ off** *AmE* to suddenly drive in front of a moving car in a dangerous way: *A man in a station wagon cut me off on the freeway.*
10 cut off your nose to spite your face to do something because you are angry, even though it will harm you
cut out *phr v*
1 REMOVE STH **cut sth ↔ out** to remove something by cutting round it: *The cancerous cells had to be cut out.* | **[+of]** *Billy showed me the article he'd cut out of the magazine.*
2 CUT A SHAPE **cut sth ↔ out** to cut a shape from a piece of paper, cloth etc: *The children were cutting out squares from the scraps of material.*
3 STOP STH HAPPENING **cut sth ↔ out** to stop something from happening or existing: *The idea behind these forms is to cut out fraud.* | *A catalytic converter will cut out 90% of carbon monoxide emissions.*
4 STOP DOING/EATING STH **cut sth ↔ out** to stop doing or eating something, especially because it might be bad for your health: *The current advice to pregnant women is to cut out alcohol.*
5 FROM WRITING **cut sth ↔ out** to remove something from a piece of writing, especially because it might offend people: *Cut out the bit about racial prejudice.*
6 cut it/that out *spoken* used to tell someone to stop doing something because it is annoying you: *Hey, you guys, cut it out – Mom's trying to get some sleep.*
7 NOT INVOLVE SB **cut sb ↔ out** to stop someone from doing something or being involved in something: *The new rules will cut out 25% of people who were previously eligible to vote.*
8 be cut out for sth (*also* **be cut out to be sth**) [usually in questions and negatives] to have the qualities that you need for a particular job or activity: *In the end, I decided I wasn't cut out for the army.* | *Are you sure you're really cut out to be a teacher?*
9 ENGINE if an engine or machine cuts out, it suddenly stops working: *The engine cut out halfway across the lake.*
10 LIGHT/VIEW **cut sth ↔ out** to prevent light, sound etc from reaching somewhere: *You'll need sunglasses that will cut out harmful UV rays from the sun.*
11 cut sb out to prevent someone from getting something, especially your money after your death: *Em's father decided to* ***cut*** *her* ***out of*** *his* ***will***. → **have your work cut out** at WORK²(16), → **cut out the middleman** at MIDDLEMAN
cut through sth *phr v*
1 *written* to move or pass easily through water or air: *The boat cut effortlessly through the water.*
2 to quickly and easily deal with something that is confusing or difficult: *You need someone to help you cut through all the irritating legal jargon.*
3 *literary* if a sound cuts through silence or noise, it is heard because it is loud: *A piercing shriek cut through the silence.*
cut up *phr v*
1 CUT INTO PIECES **cut sth ↔ up** to cut something into small pieces: *Could you cut the pizza up, please?* | **[+into]** *He cut the paper up into little pieces.*
2 DRIVING **cut sb/sth ↔ up** *BrE* to suddenly drive in front of a moving vehicle in a dangerous way: *Some idiot cut me up on the motorway.*
3 BEHAVE BADLY *AmE informal* to behave in a noisy or rude way
4 cut up rough *BrE informal* to react in an angry or violent way: *Careful how you approach him – he can cut up a bit rough if he's got a mind to.*
5 CRITICIZE **cut sb ↔ up** *informal* to criticize someone in an unpleasant way → CUT UP

cut² ●●● S2 W2 *n* [C]
1 REDUCTION [usually plural] a reduction in the size or amount of something, especially the amount of money that is spent by a government or company: *There will be cuts across all levels of the company.* | **[+in]** *Cuts in public spending mean that fewer people can go on to higher education.* | *The decision to* ***make cuts*** *in health care provision has been widely criticized.* | **tax/pay/job etc cuts** *A shorter working week will mean pay cuts for millions of*

C

workers. | *The building plans could be hit by possible* ***spending cuts.*** | **[+of]** *A cut of 1% in interest rates was announced yesterday.*
2 SKIN WOUND a wound that is caused when something sharp cuts your skin: *That's quite a nasty cut – you ought to get it seen to by a doctor.* | *The driver escaped with minor* ***cuts and bruises.*** THESAURUS ▸ INJURY
3 HOLE/MARK a narrow hole or mark in the surface of something, made by a sharp tool or object: *Make a small cut in the paper.*
4 HAIR [usually singular] **a)** an act of cutting someone's hair SYN **haircut**: *How much do they charge for a cut and blow-dry?* **b)** the style in which your hair is cut SYN **haircut**: *a short stylish cut*
5 CLOTHES [usually singular] the style in which clothes have been made: *I could tell by the cut of his suit that he wasn't a poor man.*
6 SHARE OF STH [usually singular] someone's share of something, especially money: **[+of]** *She was determined to claim her cut of the winnings.*
7 REMOVAL FROM FILM an act of removing a part from a film, play, piece of writing etc, or a part that has been removed
8 FILM [usually singular] the process of putting together the different parts of a film and removing the parts that will not be shown: *Spielberg himself oversaw the final cut.*
9 MUSIC one of the songs or pieces of music on an ALBUM, CD etc
10 the cut and thrust of sth the exciting but sometimes difficult or unpleasant way that something is done: *the cut and thrust of political debate*
11 be a cut above sb/sth to be much better than someone else or something else: *The movie is a cut above recent thrillers.* | *He proved himself to be* ***a cut above the rest.***
12 MEAT a piece of meat that has been cut to a size suitable for cooking or eating: *Long slow cooking is more suitable for cheaper cuts of meat.*
13 ROAD *AmE* a road that has been made through a hill → COLD CUTS, POWER CUT, SHORT CUT

ˌcut and ˈdried *adj* a situation, decision, result etc that is cut and dried cannot now be changed: *I don't think the plan is as cut and dried as people think.*

cut·a·way[1] /ˈkʌtəweɪ/ *adj* a cutaway model, drawing etc is open on one side so that you can see the details inside it —**cutaway** *n* [C]

cutaway[2] *n* [C] a short part of a television programme or a film that shows something different from the main action, for example an image of someone listening to a person who is talking: *As he continued with his speech, cutaways showed the audience looking bored.*

cut·back /ˈkʌtbæk/ *n* [C usually plural] a reduction in something, such as the number of workers in a company or the amount of money a government or company spends: *The shortage of teachers was blamed on government cutbacks.* | **[+in]** *cutbacks in funding for libraries* | *A fall in donations has forced the charity to* ***make cutbacks.*** | **sharp/drastic/severe cutback** *sharp cutbacks in the military budget* → CUT BACK

cute /kjuːt/ ●●● S2 *adj*
1 very pretty or attractive: *a cute little puppy* | *The baby's so cute.* | *That's a really cute outfit.* THESAURUS ▸ BEAUTIFUL
2 *especially AmE* sexually attractive: *Tell us about this cute guy you met!*
3 *especially AmE* clever in a way that can seem rude: *Their lawyer tried a cute trick.* —**cutely** *adv* —**cuteness** *n* [U]

cute·sy /ˈkjuːtsi/ *adj* too pretty or clever in a way you think is annoying: *She spoke in a tiny cutesy voice.*

cute·y /ˈkjuːti/ *n* [C] another spelling of CUTIE

ˌcut ˈglass *n* [U] glass that has patterns cut into its surface: *a cut glass decanter*

cu·ti·cle /ˈkjuːtɪkəl/ *n* [C] the area of hard skin around the base of your nails

cut·ie, cutey /ˈkjuːti/ *n* [C] *spoken* someone who is attractive and nice: *Mark is such a cutie!*

cut·lass /ˈkʌtləs/ *n* [C] a short sword with a curved blade, used by SAILORS or PIRATES in the past

cut·ler /ˈkʌtlə $ -ər/ *n* [C] *old-fashioned* someone who makes or sells cutlery

cut·le·ry /ˈkʌtləri/ *n* [U] *especially BrE* knives, forks, and spoons that you use for eating and serving food → **crockery** SYN **silverware** *AmE*

cut·let /ˈkʌtlɪt/ *n* [C] **1** a small flat piece of meat on a bone: *a lamb cutlet* **2 vegetable/nut etc cutlet** *BrE* small pieces of vegetables, nuts etc that are pressed together into a flat piece and cooked

ˈcut-off, cut·off /ˈkʌtɒf $ -ɒːf/ *n* **1** [C usually singular] a limit or level at which you stop doing something → **deadline**: **cut-off date/point/score etc** (=the date etc when you stop doing something) *The cut-off date for registration is July 2.* **2** [C usually singular] when you completely stop doing something or supplying something: **[+of]** *A full-scale cut-off of US aid would be a disaster.* **3 cutoffs** (*also* **cut-off jeans/trousers etc**) [plural] short trousers that you make by cutting off the bottom part of a pair of trousers

cut·out /ˈkʌtaʊt/ *n* [C] **1** the shape of a person, object etc that has been cut out of wood or paper → **silhouette** **2** a piece of equipment that stops a machine that is not working properly

ˌcut-out-and-ˈkeep *adj* [only before noun] a cut-out-and-keep list of information, RECIPE etc is one that you can cut from a newspaper or magazine and keep to use later: *Here's a handy cut-out-and-keep guide to growing vegetables.*

ˌcut-ˈprice (*also* **ˌcut-ˈrate** *especially AmE*) *adj* **1** cut-price goods or services are cheaper than usual: *cut-price toys* | *a travel operator offering cut-price deals* **2** a cut-price shop sells goods at reduced prices: *cut-price supermarkets*

cut·ter /ˈkʌtə $ -ər/ *n* [C] **1** [often plural] a tool that is used for cutting something: *wire cutters* | *a pastry cutter* **2** someone whose job is to cut something: *a diamond cutter* **3** a small ship

ˈcut-throat, cut·throat /ˈkʌtθrəʊt $ -θroʊt/ *adj* [usually before noun] a cut-throat activity or business involves people competing with each other in an unpleasant way: *Cut-throat competition is keeping prices low.* | *the cut-throat world of advertising*

ˌcut-throat ˈrazor *n* [C] *BrE* a RAZOR with a very long sharp blade, used especially in the past

cut·ting[1] /ˈkʌtɪŋ/ *n* [C] **1** a stem or leaf that is cut from a plant and put in soil or water to grow into a new plant **2** *BrE* an article that has been cut from a newspaper or magazine SYN **clipping**: **press/newspaper cuttings** *Margot sent him some press cuttings about the wedding.* **3** *BrE* a passage that has been dug through high ground for a railway, road etc SYN **cut** *AmE*

cutting[2] *adj* unkind and intended to upset someone: *a cutting remark*

ˈcutting board *n* [C] *BrE* a piece of wood or plastic that you cut meat or vegetables on SYN **chopping board**

ˌcutting ˈedge *n* **1 the cutting edge (of sth)** the newest and most exciting stage in the development of something: **at the cutting edge (of sth)** *research that's at the cutting edge of genetic science* | *The deck represents the cutting edge in CD reproduction.* **2** [singular] an advantage over other people or things: *The team are relying on Gregg to* ***give*** *them* ***a cutting edge.*** —**ˈcutting-edge** *adj*: *cutting-edge scientific discoveries*

ˈcutting room *n* [C] a room where the different parts of a film are cut apart and put into the correct order, to make the final form of the film

cut·tle·fish /ˈkʌtlˌfɪʃ/ *n* (*plural* **cuttlefish**) [C] a sea creature with ten soft arms

ˌcut ˈup, cut-up *adj* [not before noun] **1** *informal* very upset about something that has happened: **[+about]** *He was very cut up about Stephen dying.* **2 be badly cut up** to have a lot of injuries because you have been in an accident or fight

ˈcut-up *n* [C] *AmE informal* someone who makes other people laugh by doing amusing things, especially in a situation when they should not do this

cuz /kəz, kʌz/ *conjunction AmE spoken* a short form of 'because' SYN **cos** *BrE*: *'Why?' 'Cuz I said so!'*

CV /ˌsiː ˈviː/ ●●○ *n* [C] (*curriculum vitae*) a short written document that lists your education and previous jobs, which you send to employers when you are looking for a job SYN **resume** *AmE*

c-word /ˈsiː wɜːd $ -wɜːrd/ *n* **the c-word** used when you are talking about the word CUNT but do not want to say it because it is offensive

cwt *BrE*, **cwt.** *AmE* the written abbreviation of ***hundredweight***

-cy /si/ *suffix* [in nouns] **1** the state or quality of being something: *accuracy* | *bankruptcy* **2** a particular rank or position: *a baronetcy*

cy·an /ˈsaɪən $ ˈsaɪ-æn, -ən/ *adj technical* having a dark greenish-blue colour —**cyan** *n* [U]

cy·a·nide /ˈsaɪənaɪd/ *n* [U] a very strong poison

cyber- /saɪbə $ -ər/ *prefix* relating to computers, especially to messages and information on the Internet: *cybershoppers*

cy·ber·at·tack /ˈsaɪbərəˌtæk/ *n* [C,U] the use of the Internet to illegally see or damage the information on someone's computer system

cy·ber·bul·ly·ing /ˈsaɪbəˌbʊliɪŋ $ -bər-/ *n* [U] the activity of sending Internet or TEXT MESSAGES that threaten or insult someone —**cyberbully** *n* [C]

cy·ber·café /ˈsaɪbəˌkæfeɪ $ -bərkæˌfeɪ/ *n* [C] an INTERNET CAFÉ

cy·ber·chon·dri·a /ˌsaɪbəˈkɒndriə $ -bərˈkɑːn-/ *n* [U] fear that you are seriously ill, which is caused or made worse by reading about illnesses on the Internet —**cyberchondriac** /-driæk/ *n* [C]

cy·ber·crime, **cyber crime** /ˈsaɪbəkraɪm $ -bər-/ *n* [C,U] criminal activity that involves the use of computers or the Internet

cy·ber·fraud /ˈsaɪbəfrɔːd $ -bərfrɒːd/ *n* [U] the illegal act of deceiving people on the Internet in order to gain money, power etc

ˈcyber ˌhygiene *n* [U] actions you can take to make sure that your use of the Internet is safe

cy·be·ri·a /saɪˈbɪəriə $ -ˈbɪr-/ *n* [U] CYBERSPACE

cy·ber·land /ˈsaɪbəlænd $ -bər-/ *n* [U] activity that involves the Internet and the people who use it

cy·ber·loaf·ing /ˈsaɪbəˌləʊfɪŋ $ -bərˌloʊ-/ *n* [U] *informal* the activity of wasting time looking on the Internet when you are at work and should be working

cy·ber·net·ics /ˌsaɪbəˈnetɪks $ -bər-/ *n* [U] the scientific study of the way in which information is moved and controlled in machines, the brain, and the NERVOUS SYSTEM —**cybernetic** *adj*

cy·ber·punk /ˈsaɪbəpʌŋk $ -bər-/ *n* [U] stories about imaginary events relating to computer science, usually set in the future —**cyberpunk** *adj* [only before noun]

cy·ber·se·cu·ri·ty /ˈsaɪbəsɪˌkjʊərəti $ -bərsɪˌkjʊr-/ *n* [U] things that are done to protect computer information and systems from crime: *He is responsible for cybersecurity.*

cy·ber·sick·ness /ˈsaɪbəˌsɪknəs $ -bər-/ *n* [U] a feeling of illness caused by using a computer for long periods of time or being in a room with a lot of computers – used humorously

cy·ber·space /ˈsaɪbəspeɪs $ -bər-/ *n* [U] all the connections between computers in different places, considered as a real place where information, messages, pictures etc exist: *Students are discovering the endless amount of information in cyberspace.*

cy·ber·squat·ter /ˈsaɪbəˌskwɒtə $ -bərˌskwɑːtər/ *n* [C] someone who officially records the names of companies that they do not own or work for as DOMAIN NAMES on the Internet in order to sell these names to companies for profit —**cybersquatting** *n* [U]

cy·ber·stalk·ing /ˈsaɪbəˌstɔːkɪŋ $ -bərˌstɒːk-/ *n* [U] the illegal use of the Internet, email, or other electronic communication systems to follow someone or threaten them: *The state's first cyberstalking laws went into effect a little over a year ago.* —**cyberstalker** *n* [C]

cy·ber·ter·ror·ist /ˈsaɪbəˌterərɪst $ -bər-/ *n* [C] someone who uses the Internet to damage computer systems, especially for political purposes: *Such a strategic attack, mounted by cyberterrorists, would shut down everything from power stations to air traffic control centres.* —**cyberterrorism** *n* [U]

cy·ber·threat /ˈsaɪbəθret $ -bər-/ *n* [C] the danger that someone will illegally see or use the information on a computer system

cy·ber·war·fare /ˈsaɪbəˌwɔːfeə $ -bərˌwɔːrfer/ *n* [U] the use of the Internet to attack a country, for example by causing problems in its transport system or power supplies

cy·ber·wid·ow /ˈsaɪbəˌwɪdəʊ $ -bərˌwɪdoʊ/ *n* [C] *informal* the wife of a man who spends a lot of time working or playing on his computer – used humorously

cy·borg /ˈsaɪbɔːg $ -bɔːrg/ *n* [C] a creature that is partly human and partly machine

cyc·la·men /ˈsɪkləmən/ *n* (*plural* **cyclamen**) [C] a plant with pink, red, or white flowers

cy·cle¹ /ˈsaɪkəl/ ●●○ S3 W3 AWL *n* [C]

1 a number of related events that happen again and again in the same order → **cyclic**: *a woman's menstrual cycle* | **[+of]** *the cycle of the seasons* | *Sometimes the only way to* ***break the cycle*** *of violence in the home is for the wife to leave.* → LIFE CYCLE, → **vicious cycle** at VICIOUS CIRCLE

2 *especially BrE* a bicycle or MOTORCYCLE: *cycle routes*

3 the period of time needed for a machine to finish a process: *This washing machine has a 50-minute cycle.*

4 a group of songs, poems etc that are all about a particular important event

cycle² ●●○ AWL *v*

1 [I] *especially BrE* to travel by bicycle SYN **bike** *AmE*: **[+to/down/home etc]** *Do you cycle to work?*

2 [I,T] *AmE* to go through a series of related events again and again, or to make something do this: *The water is cycled through the machine and reused.*

ˈcycle lane *n* [C] *BrE* a part of a wide road that only bicycles are allowed to use

ˈcycle path *n* [C] *BrE* a path for bicycles, for example beside a road or in a park

cy·cle·way /ˈsaɪkəlweɪ/ *n* [C] *BrE* a road or path, sometimes a long one, for bicycles

cy·clic /ˈsaɪklɪk/ AWL (*also* **cyc·li·cal** /ˈsɪklɪkəl, ˈsaɪ-/) *adj* happening in cycles: *cyclical changes in the economy* —**cyclically** /-kli/ *adv*

cy·cling /ˈsaɪklɪŋ/ *n* [U] *especially BrE* the activity of riding a bicycle

ˈcycling shorts *n* [plural] *especially BrE* a pair of short trousers made out of cloth that stretches

cy·clist /ˈsaɪklɪst/ ●●○ *n* [C] someone who rides a bicycle

cy·clone /ˈsaɪkləʊn $ -kloʊn/ *n* [C] a very strong wind that moves very fast in a circle → **hurricane**, **typhoon** THESAURUS STORM, WIND

Cy·clops /ˈsaɪklɒps $ -klɑːps/ *n* [singular] a very big man in ancient Greek stories who only had one eye in the middle of his forehead

cyg·net /ˈsɪgnɪt/ *n* [C] a young SWAN

cyl·in·der /ˈsɪləndə $ -ər/ ●●○ *n* [C]

1 a shape, object, or container with circular ends and long straight sides → **tube**: *The gases are stored in cylinders.* → see picture at SHAPE¹

2 the tube within which a PISTON moves forwards and backwards in an engine: *a four-cylinder engine*

3 be firing/running on all cylinders *informal* to be operating or performing very well: *The team is firing on all cylinders.*

cy·lin·dri·cal /səˈlɪndrɪkəl/ *adj* in the shape of a cylinder: *a cylindrical oil tank*

cym·bal /ˈsɪmbəl/ *n* [C] a musical instrument in the form of a thin round metal plate, which you play by

C

hitting it with a stick or by hitting two of them together: *the clash of cymbals*

cyn·ic /ˈsɪnɪk/ ●○○ *n* [C] someone who is not willing to believe that people have good, honest, or sincere reasons for doing something: *Even **hardened cynics** believe the meeting is a step towards peace.* —**cynicism** /-sɪzəm/ *n* [U]

cyn·i·cal /ˈsɪnɪkəl/ ●○○ *adj*
1 unwilling to believe that people have good, honest, or sincere reasons for doing something: *a cynical view of human nature* | **[+about]** *The public is cynical about election promises.*
2 not caring that something might not be morally right, might hurt someone etc, when you are trying to get something for yourself: *a cynical disregard for international agreements* —**cynically** /-kli/ *adv*

cy·pher /ˈsaɪfə $ -ər/ *n* [C,U] another spelling of CIPHER

cy·press /ˈsaɪprɪs/ *n* [C] a tree with dark green leaves and hard wood, which does not lose its leaves in winter

Cy·ril·lic /səˈrɪlɪk/ *adj* the Cyrillic alphabet is the one used for Russian, Bulgarian, and some other Slavonic languages

cyst /sɪst/ *n* [C] a lump containing liquid that grows in your body or under your skin, and that sometimes needs to be removed → **boil**

cystic fi·bro·sis /ˌsɪstɪk faɪˈbrəʊsɪs $ -ˈbroʊ-/ *n* [U] a serious medical condition, especially affecting children, in which breathing and DIGESTing food is very difficult

cyst·i·tis /sɪˈstaɪtɪs/ *n* [U] an infection of the BLADDER that especially affects women

cy·tol·o·gy /saɪˈtɒlədʒi $ -ˈtɑː-/ *n* [U] the scientific study of cells from living things —**cytologist** *n* [C]

cy·to·plasm /ˈsaɪtəʊˌplæzəm $ -toʊ-/ *n* [U] *technical* all the material in the cell of a living thing except the NUCLEUS (=central part)

czar /zɑː $ zɑːr/ *n* [C] **1** another spelling of TSAR **2 banking/drug/health etc czar** *AmE* someone who is very powerful in a particular job or activity

cza·ri·na /zɑːˈriːnə/ *n* [C] another spelling of TSARINA

Dd

D, **d** /diː/ (*plural* **D's**, **d's**) *n* **1** [C,U] the fourth letter of the English alphabet **2** [C,U] the second note in the musical SCALE of C MAJOR or the musical KEY based on this note **3** [C] a mark given to a student's work to show that it is not very good: *I got a D in history last semester.* **4** the number 500 in the system of ROMAN NUMERALS → **D AND C**

d. (*also* **d** *BrE*) **1** the written abbreviation of ***died***: *John Keats d. 1821* **2** the written abbreviation of ***penny*** or ***pence*** in the system of money used in Britain before 1971

d' /d/ the short form of 'do': *D'you know how many people are going to be there?*

-'d /d/ **1** the short form of 'would': *I asked if she'd be willing to help.* **2** the short form of 'had': *Nobody knew where he'd gone.* **3** the short form of 'did': *Where'd you get that?*

D.A. /ˌdiː ˈeɪ/ *n* [C] the abbreviation of ***district attorney***

dab¹ /dæb/ *n* [C] **1** a small amount of something that you put onto a surface: **[+of]** *a dab of butter* **2** a light touch with your hand, a cloth etc: *She wiped her tears away with a dab of her handkerchief.* **3 be a dab hand at/with sth** *BrE informal* to be very good at a particular activity **4** a small flat fish **5 dabs** [plural] *BrE old-fashioned* your FINGERPRINTS

DAB

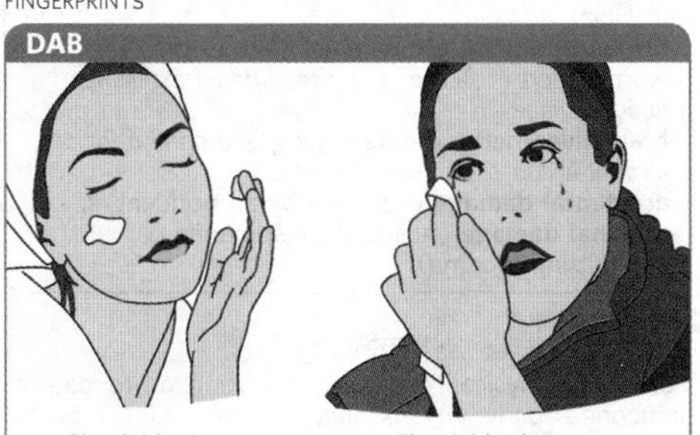

She dabbed some cream on her face. She dabbed her eyes with a handkerchief.

dab² *v* (**dabbed**, **dabbing**) **1** [I,T] to touch something lightly several times, usually with something such as a cloth: *She dabbed her eyes with a handkerchief.* | **[+at]** *He dabbed at his bleeding lip.* **2** [T] to put a substance onto something with quick light movements of your hand: **dab sth on/onto etc sth** *She dabbed some cream on her face.*

DAB /ˌdiː eɪ ˈbiː/ *n* [U] (***digital audio broadcasting***) a system of broadcasting radio programmes using DIGITAL technology

dab·ble /ˈdæbəl/ *v* **1** [I] to do something or be involved in something in a way that is not very serious: **[+in/at/with]** *people who dabble in painting as a way of relaxing* **2** [T] *BrE* to move your hands, feet etc about in water: **dabble sth in sth** *children dabbling their feet in the sea*

dach·a /ˈdætʃə $ ˈdɑː-/ *n* [C] a large country house in Russia

dachs·hund /ˈdæksənd, -sʊnd/ *n* [C] a type of small dog with short legs and a long body

Dac·ron /ˈdækrɒn $ ˈdeɪkrɑːn/ *n* [U] a type of cloth that is not made from natural materials

dac·tyl /ˈdæktɪl $ -tl/ *n* [C] a repeated sound pattern in poetry, consisting of one long sound followed by two short sounds, as in the word 'carefully' —**dactylic** /dækˈtɪlɪk/ *adj*

dad /dæd/ ●●● S1 W3 *n* [C] *informal* father: *She lives with her mom and dad.* | *Dad, will you help me?*

ˈdad ˌdancing *n* [U] *informal* dancing to popular music that looks silly or embarrassing, usually because it is done by an older person

dad·dy /ˈdædi/ ●●● S1 *n* (*plural* **daddies**) [C]
1 *informal* father – used especially by children or when speaking to children: *Daddy's home!*
2 the daddy/your daddy *informal* the best, most important, or most respected person: *Damon won the game for us – he's the daddy!* → **SUGAR DADDY**

daddy long·legs /ˌdædi ˈlɒŋlegz $ -ˈlɒːŋ-/ *n* [C] **1** *BrE* a flying insect with six long legs **2** *AmE* an insect with long legs that is similar to a SPIDER

da·do /ˈdeɪdəʊ $ -doʊ/ *n* (*plural* **dadoes**) [C] the lower part of a wall in a room, especially when it is decorated differently from the upper part of the wall

dae·mon /ˈdiːmən/ *n* [C] a creature in ancient Greek stories that is half a god and half a man → **demon**

daf·fo·dil /ˈdæfədɪl/ *n* [C] a tall yellow spring flower with a tube-shaped part in the middle → see picture at **FLOWER¹**

daf·fy /ˈdæfi/ *adj informal* silly or crazy in an amusing way

daft /dɑːft $ dæft/ *adj especially BrE* **1** silly: *a daft idea* | *Me, jealous?* ***Don't be daft*** (=that is a silly idea). | *She's* ***as daft as a brush*** (=extremely silly). THESAURUS ▸ STUPID
2 be daft about sth to be extremely interested in something: *Tony's still daft about cars!* —**daftness** *n* [U]

dag·ger /ˈdægə $ -ər/ *n* [C] **1** a short pointed knife used as a weapon **2 look daggers at sb** *informal* to look at someone angrily **3 be at daggers drawn** if two people are at daggers drawn, they are extremely angry with each other → **CLOAK-AND-DAGGER**

dag·gy /ˈdægi/ *adj AusE informal* **1** dirty or untidy **2** unfashionable

da·go /ˈdeɪgəʊ $ -goʊ/ *n* (*plural* **dagos**) [C] *taboo* a very offensive word for someone from Spain, Italy, or Portugal. Do not use this word.

da·guerre·o·type /dəˈgerəʊtaɪp $ -rə-/ *n* [C,U] an old type of photograph, or the process used to make it

dahl /dɑːl/ *n* [C,U] an Indian dish made with beans, PEAS, or LENTILS

dah·li·a /ˈdeɪliə $ ˈdæliə/ *n* [C] a large garden flower with a bright colour

dai·ly¹ /ˈdeɪli/ ●●● S3 W2 *adj* [only before noun]
1 happening or done every day: *daily flights to Miami*
2 daily life the ordinary things that you usually do or experience
3 relating to a single day: *the daily rate of pay*

daily² ●●○ *adv* happening or done every day: *The zoo is open daily.*

daily³ *n* (*plural* **dailies**) [C] **1** (*also* **ˌdaily ˈpaper**) a newspaper that is printed and sold every day, or every day except Sunday **2** *BrE old-fashioned* (*also* **ˌdaily ˈhelp**) someone, especially a woman, who is employed to clean someone's house **3 dailies** [plural] *AmE* the prints of a film as it is being made, which are looked at every day after filming ends SYN **rushes** *BrE*

dain·ty¹ /ˈdeɪnti/ *adj* (*comparative* **daintier**, *superlative* **daintiest**) **1** small, pretty, and delicate: *a dainty gold chain* | *a child with dainty features* **2** moving or done in a careful way, using small movements: *a dainty walk* —**daintily** *adv* —**daintiness** *n* [U]

dainty² *n* (*plural* **dainties**) [C] *old-fashioned* something small that is good to eat, especially something sweet such as a cake

dai·qui·ri /ˈdaɪkəri, ˈdæk-/ *n* [C] a sweet alcoholic drink made with RUM and fruit juice

dai·ry /ˈdeəri $ ˈderi/ ●●○ *n* (*plural* **dairies**) [C]
1 a place on a farm where milk is kept and butter and cheese are made
2 a company which sells milk and sometimes makes other things from milk, such as cheese
3 dairy products/produce milk, butter, cheese etc

'dairy ˌcattle *n* [plural] cattle that are kept to produce milk rather than for their meat

'dairy ˌfarm *n* [C] a farm that has cows and produces and sells milk

dai·ry·maid /ˈdeərimeɪd $ ˈder-/ *n* [C] a woman who worked in a dairy in the past

dai·ry·man /ˈdeərimən $ ˈderimən, -mæn/ *n* (*plural* **dairymen** /-mən $ -mən, -men/) [C] a man who works for a dairy

da·is /ˈdeɪəs, deɪs/ *n* [singular] a low stage in a room that you stand on when you are making a speech or performing, so that people can see and hear you

dai·sy /ˈdeɪzi/ *n* (*plural* **daisies**) [C] **1** a white flower with a yellow centre → see picture at FLOWER[1] **2 be pushing up (the) daisies** to be dead – used humorously → **as fresh as a daisy** at FRESH[1](11)

'daisy chain *n* [C] daisies attached together into a string that you can wear around your neck or wrist

Dal·ai La·ma, the /ˌdælaɪ ˈlɑːmə $ ˌdɑː-/ the leader of the Tibetan Buddhist religion

dale /deɪl/ *n* [C] a valley – used in the past or in the names of places, especially in the North of England: *the Yorkshire Dales National Park*

dal·li·ance /ˈdæliəns/ *n* [C,U] *literary* a romantic or sexual relationship between two people that is not considered serious SYN **fling**

dal·ly /ˈdæli/ *v* (**dallied**, **dallying**, **dallies**) [I] **1** to take too long to do something, especially to make a decision: *After months of dallying, the government has finally agreed to allow the plan to go ahead.* **2** to spend some time in a place, on your way to somewhere else: *He dallied in the Lake District for a while, then crossed to Belgium.*

dally with sb/sth *phr v* **1** to do something or think about something, but not in a very serious way: *They've dallied with the idea of touring round the world.* **2** *old-fashioned* to have a romantic relationship with someone, but not in a serious way

Dal·ma·tian, **dalmatian** /dælˈmeɪʃən/ *n* [C] a large dog with short white hair and black or brown spots

dam[1] /dæm/ ●●○ *n* [C]

1 a special wall built across a river or stream to stop the water from flowing, especially in order to make a lake or produce electricity

2 *technical* the mother of a four-legged animal, especially a horse

dam[2] *v* (**dammed**, **damming**) [T] (*also* **dam up**) **1** to stop the water in a river or stream from flowing by building a special wall across it **2** to stop something from being expressed or continuing: *Once she allowed her anger to show, it could not be dammed up again.*

dam·age[1] /ˈdæmɪdʒ/ ●●● S3 W2 *n*

1 PHYSICAL HARM [U] physical harm that is done to something or to a part of someone's body, so that it is broken or injured: **[+to]** *damage to property* | *These chemicals have been found to cause serious environmental damage.* | *There may be permanent brain damage.* | *His eyesight suffered irreparable damage.*

2 EMOTIONAL HARM [U] harm caused to someone's emotions or mind: *The death of a parent can cause long-lasting* ***psychological damage***.

3 BAD EFFECT [U] a bad effect on something: **[+to]** *The damage to his reputation was considerable.* | *The closure of the factory will cause severe damage to the local economy.* | **damage limitation/control** *the attempts at political damage control during the scandal*

4 damages [plural] *law* money that a court orders someone to pay to someone else as a punishment for harming them or their property → **compensation**: *The court awarded him £15,000 in damages.*

5 the damage is done used to say that something bad has happened which makes it impossible to go back to the way things were before it happened: *She immediately apologized, but the damage was done.*

6 what's the damage? *spoken* used humorously to ask how much you have to pay for something

COLLOCATIONS

VERBS

do damage *Too much sun can do severe damage to your skin.*
cause damage *We surveyed the damage caused by the bomb.*
suffer/sustain damage *formal She has suffered damage to her hearing.*
repair the damage *The cost of repairing the damage could be around £300 million.*
prevent/avoid damage *Young trees need protecting to prevent damage from the wind.*

ADJECTIVES/NOUN + damage

serious/severe *The earthquake caused severe damage to a number of buildings.*
extensive/widespread (=covering a large area) *Because of the size of the bomb, the damage was extensive.*
permanent/irreparable/irreversible damage (=that cannot be repaired) *By smoking for so long, she may have suffered irreversible damage to her health.*
minor damage *Fortunately, the fire caused only minor damage.*
physical damage *There is considerable evidence that the drug can cause physical damage.*
structural damage (=to the structure of a building) *The building was checked for structural damage.*
environmental damage *The programme will concentrate on reducing environmental damage and pollution.*
fire/storm/flood etc damage (=caused by fire, storm, flood etc) *The campsite suffered extensive flood damage.*
brain/liver/nerve etc damage *If you drink a lot of alcohol it can cause liver damage.*
accidental damage (=caused by an accident) | **criminal damage** (=caused by someone committing a crime)

damage[2] ●●● S3 W3 *v* [T]

1 to cause physical harm to something or to part of someone's body: *insects that damage crops* | **badly/severely/seriously damage** *Smoking can severely damage your health.* THESAURUS▸ HARM

2 to have a bad effect on something or someone in a way that makes them weaker or less successful: *The changes in share values have damaged investor confidence.*

THESAURUS

damage to cause physical harm to something or someone, or have a bad effect on them: *Several buildings were damaged by the earthquake.* | *The scandal could damage his career.*
harm to have a bad effect on something: *They use chemicals that will harm the environment.* | *The oil crisis could harm the economy.*
spoil to have a bad effect on something and make it less successful, enjoyable, useful etc: *We didn't let the rain spoil our holiday.* | *Local people say the new buildings will spoil the view.*
vandalize to deliberately damage buildings, vehicles, or public property: *All the public telephones in the area had been vandalized.*
sabotage /ˈsæbətɑːʒ/ to secretly damage machines or equipment so that they cannot be used, especially in order to harm an enemy: *There is evidence that the airplane was sabotaged.*
tamper with sth to deliberately and illegally damage or change a part of something in order to prevent it from working properly: *The car's brakes had been tampered with.*
desecrate to damage a church or other holy place: *The church had been desecrated by vandals.*

deface /dɪˈfeɪs/ to deliberately spoil the appearance of something by writing on it, spraying paint on it etc: *Someone had defaced the statue and painted it bright orange.*

damaged /ˈdæmɪdʒd/ ●●○ *adj*
1 something that is damaged has been harmed or injured: *a damaged leg | The ship is badly damaged. | a shampoo for dry or damaged hair* (=hair that is in bad condition)
2 a damaged person has emotional problems because of bad things that have happened to them in the past: *She works with emotionally damaged children.*

dam·ag·ing /ˈdæmɪdʒɪŋ/ ●●○ *adj*
1 causing physical harm to someone or something: *the damaging effects of sunlight* **THESAURUS** HARMFUL
2 affecting someone or something in a bad way: *damaging criticism of his policies* | **[+to]** *The loss of jobs was damaging to morale.*

dam·ask /ˈdæməsk/ *n* [U] a type of cloth with a pattern woven into it, often used to cover furniture: *a damask tablecloth*

dame /deɪm/ *n* [C] **1** *AmE old-fashioned informal* a woman **2** *BrE* a humorous female character in a PANTOMIME (=a special play at Christmas) who is played by a man

Dame *n* [C] a British title given to a woman as an honour for achievement or for doing good things, or a woman who has this title → **Sir**: *Dame Judi Dench | She was made a Dame in 1992.*

Dame·hood, **damehood** /ˈdeɪmhʊd/ *n* [C] the rank of being a Dame: *I think she should be given a Damehood.*

dam·mit /ˈdæmɪt/ *interjection not polite* a way of spelling 'damn it'

damn¹ /dæm/ *interjection not polite* **1** used when you are very annoyed or disappointed: *Damn! I've left my keys in the office.* **2** used when something is impressive or surprising: *Damn, she's old.*

damn² *adv* [+adj/adv] *informal not polite* **1** used to emphasize a statement: *Everything was so damn expensive. | The band sounded pretty damn good. | I'll* **damn well** *do as I please. | You* **know damn well** *what I'm talking about. | He* **damn near** (=almost) *drowned. | 'It isn't easy.' '***Damn right***, it's not.'* **2 damn all** *especially BrE* nothing at all: *He knows damn all about cars.*

damn³ *adj* [only before noun] *spoken not polite* **1** used when you are angry or annoyed with someone or something: *Turn off the damn TV!* **2** used to emphasize something negative: *It's a damn shame he left her.* **3 not a damn thing** nothing at all: *There's not a damn thing you can do about it.* **4 a damn sight more/better etc** a lot more, a lot better etc: *He's a damn sight tougher than you or me.*

damn⁴ *v* [T] **1 damn it/you etc!** *spoken not polite* used when you are extremely angry or annoyed with someone or something: *Damn it, be careful with that! | Stop, damn you! | Damn that telephone!* **2 (I'll be/I'm) damned if ...** *spoken not polite* used to make a negative statement in a strong way: *'Where's Wally?' 'Damned if I know.'* (=I don't know) | *I'll be damned if I can find my keys* (=I can't find them). | *I'll be damned if I let him in the house* (=I won't let him in). **3 I'll be damned** *spoken not polite* used when you are surprised: *Well, I'll be damned! I haven't seen him for years!* **4 damn the consequences/expense/calories etc** *spoken* used to say that you are going to do something, even though it might have bad results: *The time has come for me to speak out, and damn the consequences.* **5 be damned** to be given the punishment of going to HELL after you die **6** to state that something is very bad: *The critics damned the play on the first night.* | **damn (sb/sth) with faint praise** (=show that you think someone or something is not good by only praising them a little) **7 damned if you do, damned if you don't** *spoken* used to say that whatever you say or do will be considered wrong → **(as) near as damn it** at NEAR¹(8)

damn⁵ *n spoken not polite* **1 not give a damn (about sb/sth)** to not care at all about someone or something: *I don't give a damn about her.* **2 be not worth a damn** to have no value at all: *Her promise isn't worth a damn.*

dam·na·ble /ˈdæmnəbəl/ *adj old-fashioned* very bad or annoying: *This damnable heat!* —**damnably** *adv*

dam·na·tion¹ /dæmˈneɪʃən/ *n* [U] when someone is punished by being sent to HELL after their death, or the state of being in hell for ever → **Purgatory**

damnation² *interjection old-fashioned* used when you are very angry or annoyed

damned¹ /dæmd/ *adj, adv* another form of 'damn'

damned² *n* **the damned** [plural] the people who God will send to HELL when they die because they have been so bad

damned·est /ˈdæmdɪst/ *adj spoken not polite* **1 do/try your damnedest** to try very hard to do something: *I'll do my damnedest to fix it, but I can't promise anything.* **2** [only before noun] used to emphasize that something is unusual, surprising etc: *It was the damnedest thing you ever saw!*

ˈ**damn-fool** *adj* [only before noun] very stupid: *a damn-fool mistake*

damn·ing /ˈdæmɪŋ/ *adj* proving or showing that someone has done something very bad or wrong: *damning evidence of her treachery | a damning report*

Dam·o·cles /ˈdæməkliːz/ → **sword of Damocles** at SWORD(2)

damp¹ /dæmp/ ●●○ *adj*
1 slightly wet, often in an unpleasant way: *Wipe the leather with a damp cloth. | a cold, damp day* **THESAURUS** WET
2 damp squib *BrE informal* something that is intended to be exciting, effective etc, but which is disappointing —**dampness** *n* [U] —**damply** *adv*

THESAURUS

THINGS

damp slightly wet: *Iron the shirt while it is still damp. | a damp cloth*
moist slightly wet, especially when this is pleasant or how something should be: *a moist chocolate cake | The cream helps to keep your skin moist. | Make sure that the soil is moist.*
clammy slightly wet and sticky, in an unpleasant way - used especially about someone's skin: *His hands were cold and clammy.*

AIR/WEATHER

damp slightly wet, especially in a cold unpleasant way: *It was a cold damp morning.*
humid hot and damp in an unpleasant way: *Florida can be very humid in the summer.*
muggy warm and damp and making you feel uncomfortable: *This muggy weather gives me a headache.*
dank dank air is cold and damp and smells unpleasant - used especially about the air inside a room: *The dank air smelled of stale sweat.*

damp² *n* [U] *BrE* water in walls or in the air that causes things to be slightly wet: *Damp had stained the walls.*

damp³ *v* [T] to dampen something
damp sth ↔ **down** *phr v* to make a fire burn more slowly, often by covering it with ASH

ˈ**damp course** *n* [C] *BrE* a layer of material which is put into the bottom of a wall to prevent water rising through it

damp·en /ˈdæmpən/ *v* [T] **1** to make something slightly wet SYN **moisten 2** (*also* **dampen down** *BrE*) to make something such as a feeling or activity less strong: *The light rain dampened the crowd's enthusiasm. | Raising interest rates might dampen the economy.* **3** to make a sound or movement less loud or strong: *The spring dampens the shock of the impact.*

damp·er /ˈdæmpə $ -ər/ *n* [C] **1 put a damper on sth** to make something less enjoyable, active, or great than it could have been: *A couple of knee injuries put a damper on*

D

his football career. **2** a type of small metal door that is opened or closed in a STOVE or FURNACE, to control the air reaching the fire so that it burns more or less strongly **3** a piece of equipment that stops a movement from being too strong **4** a piece of equipment that stops a piano string from making a sound

ˈdamp-proof ˌcourse *n* [C] *BrE* a DAMP COURSE

dam·sel /ˈdæmzəl/ *n* [C] *old use* **1 damsel in distress** a young woman who needs help or protection – used humorously **2** a young woman who is not married, especially a pretty young woman in an old story

dam·son /ˈdæmzən/ *n* [C] a small bitter purple PLUM

dance¹ /dɑːns $ dæns/ ●●● S2 W3 *n*
1 [C] a special set of movements performed to a particular type of music: *The waltz is an easy dance to learn.* | **folk/traditional dance** *the traditional dances and music of Russia*
2 [C] a social event or party where you dance: *Are you going to the dance this weekend?* | *the school dance*
3 [C] an act of dancing: *Claire **did a** little **dance** of excitement.* | **have a dance** *especially BrE*: *Let's have another dance.*
4 [C] a piece of music which you can dance to: *The band was playing a slow dance.*
5 [U] the activity or art of dancing: *modern dance* | *dance and movement classes* → **song and dance about sth** at SONG(4), → **lead sb a dance** at LEAD¹(19)

dance² ●●● S2 W3 *v*
1 [I,T] to move your feet and body in a way that matches the style and speed of music: *Come on, let's dance.* | **[+to]** *They danced to Ruby Newman's orchestra* (=the orchestra was playing). | **[+with]** *The bride danced with her father.* | **dance a waltz/rumba/tango etc**
2 [I,T] to dance in performances, especially in BALLET: *He danced with the Boston Repertory Ballet.* | *Nakamura dances several solos in this production.*
3 [I] *literary* to move up, down, and around quickly: *Pink and white balloons danced in the wind.*
4 dance to sb's tune to do what someone wants you to do – used to show disapproval: *At that time, Eastern bloc countries danced to the Soviet tune.*
5 dance attendance on sb to do everything possible in order to please someone: *a movie star with several young men dancing attendance on her* —**dancing** *n* [U]: *the beauty of her dancing*

ˈdance band *n* [C] a group of musicians who play music that you dance to

ˈdance floor *n* [C] a special floor in a restaurant, hotel etc for people to dance on

ˈdance hall *n* [C] a large public room where people paid to go and dance in the past

danc·er /ˈdɑːnsə $ ˈdænsər/ ●●● W3 *n* [C]
1 someone who dances as a profession: *The dancer's technique is strong.* | **ballet/ballroom/flamenco etc dancer** *Margot Fonteyn, the famous British ballet dancer*
2 someone who dances: *the dancers on the floor* | **good/bad dancer** *Dave's a good dancer.*

D and C /ˌdiː ən ˈsiː/ *n* [C] a medical operation to clean out the inside of a woman's UTERUS

dan·de·li·on /ˈdændəlaɪən/ *n* [C] a wild plant with a bright yellow flower which later becomes a white ball of seeds that are blown away in the wind

ˈdandelion ˌclock *n* [C] *BrE* the soft ball of white seeds that grows on the dandelion plant

dan·der /ˈdændə $ -ər/ *n* **get sb's dander up** to make someone angry – often used humorously

dan·di·fied /ˈdændɪfaɪd/ *adj old-fashioned* a man who is dandified wears very fashionable clothes in a way that shows he cares too much about his appearance

dan·dle /ˈdændl/ *v* [T] *old-fashioned* to play with a baby or small child by moving them up and down in your arms or on your knee

dan·druff /ˈdændrəf, -drʌf/ *n* [U] small pieces of dead skin from someone's head that can be seen in their hair or on their shoulders

dan·dy¹ /ˈdændi/ *n* (*plural* **dandies**) [C] *old-fashioned* a man who spends a lot of time and money on his clothes and appearance

dandy² *adj informal especially AmE* very good – often used in a slightly humorous way: *We're at our hotel, and everything is **fine and dandy**.*

Dane /deɪn/ *n* [C] someone from Denmark

dang /dæŋ/ *interjection especially AmE* a word meaning DAMN that people use because it is less offensive —**dang** *adj, adv* —**dang** *v* [T]

dan·ger /ˈdeɪndʒə $ -ər/ ●●● S2 W2 *n*
1 [U] the possibility that someone or something will be harmed, destroyed, or killed: *Danger! No boats beyond this point.* | *The refugees believe that their lives are **in danger**.* | **[+of]** *The danger of a fire in the home increases during the holidays.* | **[+from]** *The public was not aware of the danger from nuclear tests in Nevada.*
2 [C,U] the possibility that something bad will happen: **be in danger of (doing) sth** *The party is in danger of being defeated in the next election.* | **danger that** *There is a danger that museums will attempt to entertain rather than educate.* | **the danger of (doing) sth** *to guard against the danger of becoming isolated* | **a danger sign/signal** *He didn't look pleased, but she ignored the danger signals.*
3 [C] something or someone that may harm or kill you: *the dangers that abound in the region* | **[+of]** *the dangers of drug use* | **be a danger to sb/sth** *The wreck is a danger to other ships.*
4 there's no danger of sth used to say that something will not happen: *There's no danger of confusion.* | *There's no danger of Darren ever getting up early.*
5 be on the danger list *BrE* to be so ill that you may die

COLLOCATIONS

PHRASES

be in danger *The public was not in danger at any time.*
be in danger of doing sth *It was clear that the ship was in grave danger of sinking.*
be out of danger (=no longer be in danger) *John is still in hospital but he is out of danger.*
put sb/sb's life in danger *Firemen put their own lives in danger as part of their job.*
be fraught with danger (=involve a lot of danger) *Their journey was long and fraught with danger.*

ADJECTIVES

great danger *I knew I was in great danger.*
grave/serious danger (=very great) *You have put us all in grave danger.*
mortal danger *literary* (=danger of death) *The plane's crew were now in mortal danger.*
immediate/imminent danger (=likely to happen very soon) *The passengers on the boat were not in immediate danger.*
potential danger (=possible but not definite) *Gloves should be worn because of the potential danger of infection.*
constant danger (=continuing all the time) *They are in constant danger of attack.*
physical danger (=danger to your body) *Many sports involve some physical danger.*

VERBS

face danger *Today's police officers face danger every day.*
sense danger (=feel that there is danger) *The animal lifted its head, sensing danger.*
danger threatens (=seems likely) *Most birds will warn other birds when danger threatens.*
danger passes (=there is no longer any danger) *At last the sound of bombing had stopped and the danger had passed.*

danger + NOUN

a danger area/zone (=an area that could be dangerous) *People living in the danger area have been told to leave.*

ˈ**danger ˌmoney** *BrE*, ˈ**danger ˌpay** *AmE n* [U] additional money that you are paid for doing dangerous work

dan·ger·ous /ˈdeɪndʒərəs/ ●●● S2 W2 *adj*
1 able or likely to harm or kill you → **harmful**: *laws about dangerous dogs | Some of these prisoners are extremely dangerous.* | **highly/very dangerous** *It was a highly dangerous situation.* | **[+for]** *The crumbling sidewalks are dangerous for old people.* | **[+to]** *The virus is probably not dangerous to humans.* | **it is dangerous for sb to do sth** *It's dangerous for a woman to walk alone at night.* | *The powdered milk was not as good as breast milk, and was* ***downright dangerous*** (=actually dangerous) *when it was mixed with unclean water.*
2 involving a lot of risk, or likely to cause problems SYN **risky**: *The business is in a dangerous financial position.* | *a politically dangerous strategy*
3 **dangerous ground/territory** a situation or subject that could make someone very angry or upset: *Teachers can be on dangerous ground if they discuss religion.*

THESAURUS

dangerous likely to cause death or serious harm, or cause something bad to happen: *Snow and ice are making driving conditions very dangerous.* | *dangerous drugs* | *a dangerous criminal*
risky if something is risky, something bad could easily happen or you could easily make a mistake: *Doctors said it was too risky to operate.* | *a risky situation*
hazardous /ˈhæzədəs $ -zər-/ *especially written* dangerous – used especially about substances, jobs, and journeys: *hazardous waste* | *hazardous chemicals* | *hazardous occupations* | *The expedition was extremely hazardous.*
unsafe dangerous because someone is very likely to be hurt – used especially about places or conditions: *The roads are unsafe for cyclists.* | *unsafe working conditions*
treacherous /ˈtretʃərəs/ *formal or literary* places or conditions that are treacherous are very dangerous for anyone who is walking, driving, climbing etc in them: *The snow turned to ice, making conditions treacherous for walkers.* | *the island's treacherous coastline*
perilous /ˈperələs/ *literary* a perilous journey, situation etc is very dangerous: *a perilous journey across the sea*
high-risk [only before noun] a high-risk job, situation, or behaviour is likely to be dangerous: *Drug users need to know that sharing needles is high-risk behaviour.*

dan·ger·ous·ly /ˈdeɪndʒərəsli/ ●○○ *adv* in a way that is dangerous: *The boat was* ***dangerously close*** *to the rocks.* | **dangerously high/low** *He's suffering from dangerously high blood pressure.* | *I am used to* ***living dangerously*** (=doing things that involve risks). | *She was found guilty of driving dangerously.*

DANGLE

Their legs are dangling from the ski lift.

dan·gle /ˈdæŋɡəl/ ●○○ *v*
1 [I,T] to hang or swing loosely, or to make something do this: **[+from]** *A light bulb dangled from a wire in the ceiling.* | **dangle sth in/over etc sth** *I dangled my feet in the clear blue water.*
2 **dangle sth in front of sb/before sb** to offer something good to someone, in order to persuade them to do something: *A good pay package and a company car were dangled in front of her.*

Da·nish¹ /ˈdeɪnɪʃ/ *n* **1** [U] the language used in Denmark **2** [C] a very sweet cake made of light PASTRY SYN **Danish pastry**

Danish² *adj* relating to Denmark, its people, or its language

ˌ**Danish** ˈ**pastry** *n* [C] a small fairly flat sweet cake, often with fruit inside

dank /dæŋk/ *adj* unpleasantly wet and cold: *a dank prison cell* THESAURUS DAMP —**dankness** *n* [U]

dap·per /ˈdæpə $ -ər/ *adj* a man who is dapper is nicely dressed, has a neat appearance, and is usually small or thin: *a dapper little man in a grey suit*

dap·ple /ˈdæpəl/ *v* [T] *literary* to mark something with spots of colour, light, or shade

dap·pled /ˈdæpəld/ *adj* marked with spots of colour, light, or shade: *the dappled shade of the trees*

ˌ**dapple-**ˈ**grey** *BrE*, **dapple-gray** *AmE n* [C] a horse that is grey with spots of darker grey

DAR /ˌdiː eɪ ˈɑː $ -ˈɑːr/ *n* [U] (***digital audio radio***) a system of broadcasting radio programmes using DIGITAL technology

dar·bou·ka /dɑːˈbuːkə $ dɑːr-/ *n* [C] a type of drum played in Northern Africa and the Middle East

Dar·by and Joan /ˌdɑːbi ən ˈdʒəʊn $ ˌdɑːrbi ən ˈdʒoʊn/ *n BrE* **like Darby and Joan** used humorously when talking about an old husband and wife who live very happily together

dare¹ /deə $ der/ ●●○ S3 W3 *v, modal verb*
1 [I] to be brave enough to do something that is risky or that you are afraid to do – used especially in questions or negative sentences: *He wanted to ask her, but he didn't dare.* | *'I'll tell Dad.' 'You wouldn't dare!'* | **dare (to) do sth** *I daren't go home.* | *Only a few journalists dared to cover the story.* | *She hardly dared hope that he was alive.* | *Dare we admit this?*
2 **how dare you** *spoken* said to show that you are very angry and shocked about what someone has done or said: *How dare you accuse me of lying!*
3 **don't you dare!** *spoken* said to warn someone not to do something because it makes you angry: *Don't you dare talk to me like that!*
4 [T] to try to persuade someone to do something dangerous or embarrassing as a way of proving that they are brave: **dare sb to do sth** *They dared Ed to steal a bottle of his father's whiskey.* | *So jump, then.* ***I dare you.***
5 **dare I say/suggest** *spoken formal* used when saying something that you think people may not accept or believe: *I thought the play was, dare I say it, boring.*
6 **I dare say** (*also* **I daresay**) *spoken especially BrE* used when saying or agreeing that something may be true: *I dare say things will improve.*

GRAMMAR

Patterns with dare

• You say that someone **dares to** do something: *Karen dared to ask why.* | *Not many people dared to argue.*
• **Dare** can also be used as a modal verb, followed by the base form (=infinitive without 'to'), especially in negatives and questions: *Not many people dared argue.* | *Dare we go back?*
• Don't use a 'to' infinitive with **daren't**. You say: *I daren't look.* ✗ Don't say: *I daren't to look.*

Using the progressive

Dare is not used in the progressive. You say: *I daren't say anything.* ✗ Don't say: *I am not daring say anything.*
GRAMMAR GUIDE VERBS

dare² *n* [C] something dangerous that you have dared someone to do: **for a dare** *BrE*, **on a dare** *AmE* (=because someone has dared you to) *She ran across a busy road for a dare.*

dare·dev·il /ˈdeədevəl $ ˈder-/ *n* [C] someone who likes doing dangerous things —**daredevil** *adj*

daren't /deənt $ dernt/ *especially BrE* the short form of 'dare not'

dare·say /ˌdeəˈseɪ $ ˈderseɪ/ → **I daresay** at DARE¹(6)

dar·ing¹ /ˈdeərɪŋ $ ˈder-/ ●●○ *adj*
1 involving a lot of risk or danger, or brave enough to do risky things: *a daring rescue attempt* THESAURUS▸ BRAVE
2 new or unusual in a way that may shock people: *a daring new building* —**daringly** *adv*

daring² *n* [U] courage that makes you willing to take risks: *a plan of great daring*

D

dark¹ /dɑːk $ dɑːrk/ ●●● S2 W1 *adj* (*comparative* **darker**, *superlative* **darkest**)
1 NO LIGHT if it is dark, there is little or no light OPP **light**: *The church was dark and quiet.* | *the dark winter days* | *Suddenly, the room* **went dark** (=became dark). | ***It gets dark*** (=night begins) *about ten o'clock.* | ***It was** still **dark*** (=was night) *when we boarded the train.* | *It was* **pitch dark** (=completely dark) *in the attic.*
2 COLOUR quite close to black in colour OPP **light**, **pale**: *There were dark clouds in the sky.* | *men in dark suits* | *a slightly darker colour* | **dark blue/green/pink etc** *a dark blue dress* THESAURUS▸ COLOUR
3 HAIR/EYES/SKIN someone who is dark has hair, eyes, or skin that is brown or black in colour OPP **fair**: *a tall, dark man* | *John's dark skin and eyes*
4 MYSTERIOUS mysterious or secret: *a dark secret* | **keep sth dark** *BrE* (=keep something secret) *Apparently, he has a son, but he's kept that very dark.*
5 EVIL evil or threatening: *There was a darker side to his character.* | *a place where so many dark deeds had been committed* | *the dark forces of the universe*
6 UNHAPPY TIME a dark time is unhappy or without hope: *the dark days of the war* | *Even in the darkest moments, I still had you, my love.*
7 FEELINGS/THOUGHTS if you have dark feelings or thoughts, you are very sad or worried: *a dark depression* | *her darkest fears*
8 HUMOUR dark humour deals with things that are bad or upsetting in a funny way SYN **black**: *the dark humor common in difficult situations*
9 darkest Africa/South America etc *old-fashioned* the parts of Africa etc about which we know very little – this use is now often considered offensive

THESAURUS

dark if a place is dark, there is little or no light: *The room was very dark.* | *It was a dark night with clouds covering the moon.*
dimly-lit a dimly-lit building or place is fairly dark because the lights there are not very bright: *a dimly-lit restaurant* | *The church was dimly lit.*
dim a dim light is fairly dark: *The camera can take good pictures even in dim lighting.* | *The evening sky grew dim.*
darkened a darkened room or building is darker than usual, especially because its lights have been turned off or the curtains have been drawn: *The prisoner lay in a darkened room.*
gloomy a gloomy place or room is not at all bright or cheerful: *The bar was gloomy and smelled of stale cigar smoke.*
murky dark and difficult to see through – used especially about water: *the murky waters of the lake*
pitch-dark/pitch-black completely dark, so that nothing can be seen: *It was pitch-dark inside the shed.*
shady a shady place is cooler and darker than the area around it, because the light of the sun cannot reach it: *It was nice and shady under the trees.* | *They found a shady spot for a picnic.*

dark² ●●● S3 W3 *n*
1 the dark when there is no light, especially because the sun has gone down: *my childish fear of the dark* | **in the dark** *I turned off the light and lay there in the dark.* | *We stood outside in the* ***pitch dark*** (=when there is no light at all). THESAURUS▸ COLOUR
2 after/before/until dark after, before, or until the sun goes down at night: *I want you home before dark.*
3 in the dark *informal* knowing nothing about something important, because you have not been told about it: *We're in the dark just as much as you are.* | *College officials were* ***kept in the dark*** *about the investigation.* → **a shot in the dark** at SHOT¹(10)

ˈDark ˌAges *n* **1 the Dark Ages** the period in European history from the 6th to the 10th centuries, after the end of the Roman Empire **2** a time when attitudes, knowledge, technology etc were not as modern or developed as they are now: *Ed is stuck in the Dark Ages when it comes to his attitudes towards women.*

dark·en /ˈdɑːkən $ ˈdɑːr-/ ●○○ *v*
1 [I,T] to become dark, or to make something dark: *The sky darkened and a few drops of rain fell.* | *a darkened theater* | *The evening shadows darkened the room.*
2 [I,T] to become less hopeful or positive, or to make something like this: *As he got drunker, his mood darkened.*
3 [I] if someone's face darkens, they start to look angry: *The captain's face darkened as he read.*
4 never darken my door again *old-fashioned* said when you do not want to see someone again – now used humorously

ˈdark ˌenergy *n* [U] *technical* a type of energy that scientists think is pushing things in the universe further apart

ˌdark ˈglasses *n* [plural] glasses with dark glass in them that you wear to protect your eyes from the sun or to hide your eyes → **sunglasses**

ˌdark ˈgreen *adj especially BrE* avoiding companies whose products or activities are thought to be morally unacceptable: *dark green consumers* | *dark green investments* → **light green**

ˌdark ˈhorse *n* [C] **1** someone who is not well known, and who surprises people by winning a competition: *In the 1955 golf championship, dark horse Jack Fleck defeated Ben Hogan.* **2** *BrE* someone who does not tell people much about themselves, but who has surprising qualities or abilities: *She's a dark horse. I didn't know she'd written a novel.*

dark·ie /ˈdɑːki $ ˈdɑːr-/ *n* [C] *taboo old-fashioned* a very offensive word for a black person. Do not use this word.

dark·ly /ˈdɑːkli $ ˈdɑːrk-/ *adv* **1** in a sad, angry, or threatening way: *Fred scowled darkly at her.* **2** having a dark colour: *a darkly handsome man* **3 darkly funny/humorous/comic** dealing with something that is bad or upsetting in a funny way: *a darkly comic look at illness*

ˈdark ˌmatter *n* [U] *technical* a type of matter that scientists think may exist. It cannot be seen but seems to affect the movements of stars

dark·ness /ˈdɑːknəs $ ˈdɑːrk-/ ●●● W3 *n* [U]
1 when there is no light: *the long hours of darkness during winter* | **in darkness** *The lamp suddenly went out, leaving us in darkness.* | **total/pitch/complete darkness** *The room was in total darkness.* | *We lit our campfire* ***as darkness fell*** (=it became night). | *He stared out the window at* ***the gathering darkness*** (=the night slowly coming).
2 evil or the devil: *His smooth manner covered a heart of darkness.* | **the forces/powers of darkness** (=the devil or evil people)
3 the dark quality of a colour: *the darkness of the lenses*

dark·room /ˈdɑːkruːm, -rʊm $ ˈdɑːrk-/ *n* [C] a special room with only red light or no light, where film from a camera is made into photographs

dar·ling¹ /ˈdɑːlɪŋ $ ˈdɑːr-/ ●●○ S3 *n*
1 *spoken* used when speaking to someone you love: *Look, darling, there's Mary.*

2 [C] someone who is very nice: *You really are a darling, Barney.*
3 the darling of sth the most popular person or thing in a particular group or area of activity: *She's the darling of the fashion world.*

darling² *adj* [only before noun] **1** used of someone you love very much: *my two darling daughters* **2** *spoken* used when you think someone or something is attractive: *What a darling little house!*

darn¹ /dɑːn $ dɑːrn/ (*also* **darn it/him/them etc**) *interjection AmE informal* used to show that you are annoyed or disappointed SYN **damn**: *Darn! I forgot my keys! | Darn it! I'll have to do it all myself!*

darn² (*also* **darned**) *adj spoken informal* **1** used to emphasize how bad, stupid, unfair etc someone or something is SYN **damn**: *The darn fool got lost on the way.* **2 a darn sight better/harder etc** a lot better, harder etc SYN **damn**: *He'd earn a darn sight more money there.* —**darn, darned** *adv*: *It was a darned good movie.*

darn³ *v* [T] to repair a hole in a piece of clothing by stitching wool over it: *Her cardigan had been darned at the elbows.* **THESAURUS** ▸ REPAIR

darn⁴ *n* [C] a place where a hole in a piece of clothing has been repaired neatly with wool

darned /dɑːnd $ dɑːrnd/ *adj spoken informal* **1 I'll be darned!** used when you are surprised about something: *Did they really? I'll be darned!* **2 I'll be darned if ...** used to emphasize that you will not allow something to happen **3 darned if I know** used to emphasize that you do not know something

dart¹ /dɑːt $ dɑːrt/ ●○○ *v*
1 [I always + adv/prep] to move suddenly and quickly in a particular direction: *Jill darted forward and pulled him away from the fire.*
2 [I,T] *literary* to look at someone or something very quickly: *Tom darted a terrified glance over his shoulder at his pursuers.*

dart² ●○○ *n*
1 [C] a small pointed object that is thrown or shot as a weapon, or one that is thrown in the game of darts: *a poisoned dart*
2 darts [U] a game in which darts are thrown at a round board with numbers on it
3 [singular] a sudden quick movement in a particular direction: *The prisoner* ***made a dart for*** *the door.*
4 dart of guilt/panic/pain etc a very sudden, sharp feeling: *It sent a dart of terror through her.*
5 [C] a small fold put into a piece of clothing to make it fit better

dart·board /ˈdɑːtbɔːd $ ˈdɑːrtbɔːrd/ *n* [C] a round board used in the game of darts

dash¹ /dæʃ/ ●●○ *v*
1 [I always + adv/prep] to go or run somewhere very quickly: *Olive dashed into the room, grabbed her bag, and ran out again.* **THESAURUS** ▸ HURRY, RUN
2 dash sb's hopes to disappoint someone by telling them that what they want is not possible: *Hopkins' hopes were dashed when his appeal was denied.*
3 (I) must dash/(I) have to dash *BrE spoken* used to tell someone that you must leave quickly: *Anyway, I must dash – I said I'd meet Daniel at eight.*
4 [I,T always + adv/prep] *written* to throw or push something violently against something, especially so that it breaks: **dash sth against/on sth** *The ship was dashed against the rocks.* | **[+against]** *Waves were dashing against the sea wall.*
5 dash it (all)! *BrE old-fashioned* used to show that you are slightly annoyed or angry about something
dash off *phr v*
1 to leave somewhere very quickly: *Harry dashed off before she had a chance to thank him.*
2 dash sth ↔ off to write or draw something very quickly: *She dashed off a quick letter.*

dash² ●●○ *n*
1 SMALL AMOUNT [singular] **a)** a small amount of a substance that is added to something else: **[+of]** *Add salt, pepper and a dash of vinegar.* **b)** a small amount of a quality that is added to something else: **[+of]** *Add a dash of romance to your life with a trip to Paris.*
2 RUN QUICKLY [C usually singular] an occasion when someone runs somewhere very quickly in order to get away from something or someone, or in order to reach them: **make a dash for sth** *He made a dash for the door. | The prisoners made a dash for freedom. | It's pouring with rain – we'll have to* ***make a dash for it****. | When the alarm went there was a* ***mad dash*** *for the exit.*
3 LINE [C] a line (–) used in writing to separate two closely related parts of a sentence, as for example, in the sentence 'Go home – they're waiting for you.'
4 SOUND [C] a long sound or flash of light used for sending messages in MORSE CODE → **dot**
5 CAR [C] *AmE* a DASHBOARD
6 STYLE [U] *old-fashioned* style, energy, and courage in someone such as a soldier
7 cut a dash *old-fashioned* to look very impressive and attractive in particular clothes: *With her new image, she'll certainly cut a dash on her holiday cruise.*

dash·board /ˈdæʃbɔːd $ -bɔːrd/ *n* [C] the part of a car in front of the driver, which has controls on it → see picture at **CAR**

dash·i /ˈdæʃi/ *n* [U] a clear liquid made with SEAWEED, dried TUNA, or MUSHROOMS which is used in Japanese cooking, for example to make soup

dash·ing /ˈdæʃɪŋ/ *adj* a man who is dashing wears nice clothes and is very attractive and confident: *a dashing young doctor* —**dashingly** *adv*

dast·ard·ly /ˈdæstədli $ -ərd-/ *adj old-fashioned* very cruel or evil: *tales of pirates and their dastardly deeds*

DAT /dæt/ *n* [U] (***digital audio tape***) a system used to record sound or information in DIGITAL form

da·ta /ˈdeɪtə, ˈdɑːtə/ ●●● S1 W1 AWL *n*
1 [plural,U] information or facts: *The research involves collecting data from two random samples.* | **[+on]** *data on pesticide use* | **experimental/historical/statistical etc data** *detailed research data*

> **GRAMMAR: Singular or plural verb?**
> • In everyday English, **data** is usually followed by a singular verb: *The data* ***is*** *collected by trained interviewers.*
> • In academic or very formal English, a plural verb is used: *These data* ***are*** *summarized in Table 5.*
> • When talking about one fact or piece of information, you say a **piece of data**: *This is a useful piece of data.* ✗ Don't say: *datas*

2 [U] information in a form that can be stored and used, especially on a computer: *It's possible to store a lot more data on a DVD.* | **data storage/transfer/retrieval**

ˈdata ˌbank *n* [C] a database

da·ta·base /ˈdeɪtəˌbeɪs/ ●●○ S3 W3 *n* [C] a large amount of data stored in a computer system so that you can find and use it easily: *customer details held on a database* | **database system/software/application etc**

ˈdata ˌmining *n* [U] the process of using a computer to examine large amounts of information, for example about customers, in order to discover things that are not easily seen or noticed

ˌdata ˈprocessing *n* [U] the use of computers to store and organize information, especially in business

ˈdata ˌroaming *n* [U] the process that a MOBILE PHONE uses when it is in a different country or area from usual, and connects to a different network

ˈdata stick *n* [C] *especially BrE* a small flat card that is used to store information electronically and that fits into machines such as computers

date¹ /deɪt/ ●●● S1 W1 *n* [C]
1 DAY a particular day of the month or year, especially

D

shown by a number: *The date on the letter was 30th August 1962.* | *What's today's date?* | **[+of]** *What's the date of the next meeting?* | *You should apply at least 8 weeks before your date of departure.* | **[+for]** *Have you set a date for the wedding yet?*
2 at a later/future date *formal* at some time in the future SYN **later**: *The details will be agreed at a later date.*
3 to date up to now: *The cost of the work to date has been about £150 million.* | *Her best performance to date was her third place at the World Junior Championships.*
4 ROMANTIC MEETING **a)** an occasion when you go out with someone that you like in a romantic way: **[+with]** *I've got a date with Andrea tomorrow night.* | *I felt like a teenager **going out on a** first **date**.* → BLIND DATE **b)** *AmE* someone that you have a date with: **sb's date** *Can I bring my date to the party?*
5 ARRANGEMENT TO MEET SB a time arranged to meet someone, especially socially: *Let's **make a date** to come over and visit.*
6 FRUIT a sweet sticky brown fruit with a long hard seed inside → CLOSING DATE, → **expiry date** at EXPIRY(2), → OUT-OF-DATE, SELL-BY DATE, UP-TO-DATE

D

COLLOCATIONS

ADJECTIVES/NOUN + date

the exact/precise date *I can't remember the exact date we moved into this house.*
the agreed date *BrE*, **agreed upon date** *AmE* (=one that people have agreed on) *The work was not finished by the agreed date.*
the closing date (=the last day you can officially do something) *The closing date for applications is April 30th.*
the due date (=the date by which something is due to happen) *Payment must be made by the due date.*
the delivery date (=a date on which goods will be delivered) *The delivery date should be around 23rd August.*
the publication date (=the date when something is published) *We are aiming at a publication date of mid-November.*
the departure date (=the date when someone leaves) *My departure date was only a few days away.*
the expiry date *BrE*, **expiration date** *AmE* (=a date on a product after which it cannot be used) *Check the expiry date on your credit card.*
the sell-by date *BrE* (=a date on a food product after which it should not be sold)

VERBS

decide on a date (=choose the date when something will happen) *Have you decided on a date for the wedding yet?*
set/fix a date (=decide the date when something will happen) *They haven't set a date for the election yet.*

PHRASES

today's date *Don't forget to put today's date at the top of the letter.*
sb's date of birth (*also* **sb's birth date**) (=the day and year when someone was born) *What's your date of birth?*
the date of publication/issue/departure etc *formal* *The insurance will only cover costs incurred on or after the date of departure.*

date² ●●○ S3 W3 *v*
1 WRITE DATE [T] to write or print the date on something: *a newspaper dated November 23, 1963* | *Make sure you sign and date it at the bottom.*
2 FIND AGE [T] to find out when something old was made or formed: *The rocks are dated by examining the fossils found in the same layer.* | *radiocarbon dating*
3 OLD-FASHIONED [I] if clothing, art etc dates, it begins to look old-fashioned: *His designs are so classic, they've hardly dated at all.* → DATED
4 RELATIONSHIP [I,T] *AmE* to have a romantic relationship with someone SYN **go out with**: *Is he still dating Sarah?* | *Are Chris and Liz dating?*
5 SHOW SB'S AGE [T] if something that you say, do, or wear dates you, it shows that you are fairly old: *Yes, I remember the Moon landings – that dates me, doesn't it?*
date from sth (*also* **date back to sth**) *phr v* to have existed since a particular time in the past: *The church dates from the 13th century.*

date·book /ˈdeɪtbʊk/ *n* [C] *AmE* a small book in which you write things you must do, addresses, telephone numbers etc SYN **diary**

dat·ed /ˈdeɪtɪd/ ●○○ *adj* old-fashioned → **out-of-date**: *That dress looks a bit dated now.* THESAURUS OLD-FASHIONED

date·line /ˈdeɪtlaɪn/ *n* [singular] the INTERNATIONAL DATE LINE

ˈ**date night** *n* [C] a night on which a husband and wife go out, for example for a meal, in order to spend time together: *She believes that having regular date nights will improve a couple's relationship.*

ˈ**date rape** *n* [C,U] a RAPE that is committed by someone the woman has met in a social situation

ˈ**date stamp** *n* [C] **a)** an object used for printing the date on documents **b)** the mark that it makes

ˈ**dating ˌagency** (*also* ˈ**dating ˌservice**) *n* [C] a business that helps people to meet other people in order to have a romantic relationship

da·tive /ˈdeɪtɪv/ *n* [C usually singular] a particular form of a noun in some languages such as Latin and German, which shows that the noun is the INDIRECT OBJECT of a verb

daub¹ /dɔːb $ dɒːb/ *v* [T] to put paint or a soft substance on something without being very careful: *soldiers' faces daubed with black mud*

daub² *n* **1** [C] a small amount of a soft or sticky substance: **[+of]** *a daub of paint* **2** [U] *technical* mud or clay used for making walls → **wattle and daub** at WATTLE(1)

daugh·ter /ˈdɔːtə $ ˈdɒːtər/ ●●● S1 W1 *n* [C] someone's female child → **filial**: *She's got two daughters and one son.* | *our eldest daughter* | **[+of]** *the daughter of an English king*

ˈ**daughter-in-law** ●●○ *n* (*plural* **daughters-in-law**) [C] your son's wife

daugh·ter·ly /ˈdɔːtəli $ ˈdɒːtər-/ *adj* behaving in a way that a daughter is expected to behave

daunt /dɔːnt $ dɒːnt/ *v* [T] **1** to make someone feel afraid or less confident about something: *He **felt** utterly **daunted** by the prospect of moving to another country.* | *Don't be daunted by all the technology.* **2 nothing daunted** *old-fashioned* used to say that someone continues or starts to do something in spite of difficulties: *It was steep but, nothing daunted, he started climbing.* GRAMMAR **Daunt** is usually passive.

daunt·ing /ˈdɔːntɪŋ $ ˈdɒːn-/ ●○○ *adj* frightening in a way that makes you feel less confident: *The trip seemed rather daunting for a young girl.* | *He's got the **daunting task** of following in Ferguson's footsteps.* | *the **daunting prospect** of asking for a loan* THESAURUS DIFFICULT

daunt·less /ˈdɔːntləs $ ˈdɒːnt-/ *adj* confident and not easily frightened: *dauntless optimism*

daw·dle /ˈdɔːdl $ ˈdɒː-/ *v* [I] to take a long time to do something or walk somewhere: *Don't dawdle – we're late already!* | **[+over]** *I dawdled over a second cup of coffee.* —**dawdler** *n* [C]

dawn¹ /dɔːn $ dɒːn/ ●●○ *n* [C,U]
1 the time at the beginning of the day when light first appears SYN **daybreak** → **dusk**: **at dawn** *The boats set off at dawn.* | *When **dawn broke** (=the first light of the day appeared), we were still 50 miles from Calcutta.* | *I was up **at the crack of dawn** (=very early in the morning) to get the plane.* | *We worked **from dawn to dusk** (=through the whole day while it is light).* | *the cold light of dawn*

2 the dawn of civilization/time etc the time when something began or first appeared: *People have been falling in love since the dawn of time.* THESAURUS ▸ BEGINNING
3 a false dawn something that seems positive or hopeful but really is not: *There was talk of share prices recovering, but that was just a false dawn.*

dawn² ●○○ *v* [I]
1 if day or morning dawns, it begins: *The morning dawned fresh and clear after the storm.*
2 if a period of time or situation dawns, it begins: *The age of Darwin had dawned.*
3 if a feeling or idea dawns, you have it for the first time: ***It** began to **dawn that** something was wrong.*
dawn on sb *phr v* if a fact dawns on you, you realize it for the first time: *The ghastly truth dawned on me.* | **it dawns on sb (that)** *It dawned on me that Jo had been right all along.*

ˌdawn ˈchorus *n* **the dawn chorus** the sound of many birds singing at dawn

ˌdawn ˈraid *n* [C] an attack or operation by soldiers or police that happens very early in the morning

day /deɪ/ ●●● S1 W1 *n*
1 24 HOURS [C] a period of 24 hours: *We spent three days in Paris.* | *'What day is it today?' 'Friday.'* | *He left two days ago.* | *I'll call you in a couple of days.* | **on a ... day** *We'll have to hold the party on a different day.* | **(on) that/the following/the previous day** (=during a particular day) *What really happened on that day so long ago?* | *Over 10,000 soldiers died on that one day in January.* | *The following day, a letter arrived.* | *I saw Jane **the day before yesterday**.* | *We're leaving for New York **the day after tomorrow**.* | *I got an email from Sue **the other day*** (=a few days ago). | *Women generally use up about 2,000 calories **a day*** (=each day).
2 NOT NIGHT [C,U] the period of time between when it gets light in the morning and when it gets dark OPP **night**: *She only leaves her house during the day.* | *It was a cold blustery day.* | *Kept in that dark cell, I could no longer tell whether it was day or night.* | **on a ... day** *She first met Steve on a cold but sunny day in March.* | **by day** (=during the day) *Owls usually sleep by day and hunt by night.* | *The **day dawned*** (=started) *bright and clear.*
3 WHEN YOU ARE AWAKE [C usually singular] the time during the day when you are awake and active: *His day begins at six.* | *Jackie starts the day with a few gentle exercises.* | *Sometimes I feel I just can't face another day.* | *It's been **a long day*** (=used when you have been awake and busy for a long time). | **all day (long)** *I've been studying all day. I'm beat!*
4 TIME AT WORK [C] the time you spend doing your job during a 24-hour period: *I work a ten-hour day.* | *Rail workers are campaigning for a shorter **working day**.* | *I've got a **day off*** (=a day when I do not have to go to work) *tomorrow.*
5 PAST [C] used to talk about a time in the past: *I knew him pretty well from his days as a DJ in the Bounty Club* (=from when he was a DJ). | *I always used to do the cooking in the **early days** of our marriage.* | *Not much was known about the dangers of smoking **in those days*** (=then). | *They were very much opposed to the government **of the day*** (=that existed then). | ***One day*** (=on a day in the past), *a mysterious stranger called at the house.* | ***From day one*** (=from the beginning), *I knew I wouldn't get on with him.* | ***In my day*** (=in the past, when I was young), *kids used to have some respect for their elders.* | **in sb's student/army/childhood etc days** (=in the past when someone was a student etc) *I used to run six miles a day in my army days.* | **those were the days** *spoken* (=used to talk about a time in the past you think was better than now) *We used to stay in bed all morning and party all night. Those were the days!*
6 NOW [C] used to talk about the situation that exists now: *I don't do much exercise **these days*** (=now). | *It's incredible that such attitudes still exist **in this day and age*** (=used to express disapproval that something still exists now). | ***To this day*** (=until and including now), *he denies any involvement in the crime.* | **up to/until/to the present day** (=until and including now) *This tradition has continued right up until the present day.*
7 FUTURE [C] used to talk about a time in the future: **one day/some day** (=some time in the future) *I'd like to go and visit the States one day.* | *Some day we might get him to see sense.* | ***One of these days*** (=some time soon) *I'm going to walk right out of here and never come back.* | *Kelly's expecting the baby **any day now*** (=very soon). | ***The day will come*** (=the time will come) *when he won't be able to care for himself anymore.*
8 sb's/sth's day a successful period of time in someone's life or in something's existence: *My uncle was a famous radio personality **in his day*** (=at the time he was most successful). | *Don't be too disappointed you didn't win – your **day will come*** (=you will be successful in the future). | *Game shows like that **have had** their **day*** (=were successful in the past, but are not anymore).
9 Independence/election/Christmas etc day a day on which a particular event or celebration takes place: *Rioting broke out just three days before polling day.*
10 five/three/nine etc years to the day exactly five years etc: *It's two years to the day since he died.*
11 sb's days someone's life: *She ended her days in poverty.*
12 sb's/sth's days are numbered used to say that someone or something will not exist for much longer: *It seems that the hospital's days are numbered.*
13 day after day (*also* **day in day out**) continuously for a long time in a way that is annoying or boring: *I couldn't stand sitting at a desk day after day.*
14 from day to day (*also* **from one day to the next**) if a situation changes from day to day or from one day to the next, it changes often: *I never know from day to day what I'm going to be doing.* | *His moods swung wildly from one day to the next.* → DAY-TO-DAY, → **live from day to day** at LIVE¹(5)
15 day by day slowly and gradually: *Her health was improving day by day.*
16 night and day (*also* **day and night**) all the time SYN **continuously**: *Being together night and day can put a great pressure on any relationship.*
17 day out *especially BrE* a trip you make for pleasure on a particular day: *A visit to the caves makes a fascinating and exciting day out for all the family.*
18 have an off day to be less successful or happy than usual, for no particular reason: *Even the greatest athletes have their off days.*
19 make sb's day to make someone very happy: *Hearing her voice on the phone really made my day.*
20 soup/dish/fish etc of the day a soup, meal etc that a restaurant serves on a particular day in addition to the meals they always offer
21 be all in a day's work if something difficult, unpleasant, or unusual is all in a day's work for someone, it is a normal part of their job
22 take each day as it comes (*also* **take it one day at a time**) to deal with something as it happens and not worry about the future: *Since I had the accident, I've learned to take each day as it comes.*
23 the day of reckoning a time when you have to deal with the bad results of something you did in the past

SPOKEN PHRASES

24 it's (just) one of those days used to say that everything seems to be going wrong
25 it's not sb's day used when several unpleasant things have happened to someone in one day: *It wasn't Chris's day – he overslept and then his car broke down.*
26 make a day of it *BrE* to spend all day doing something for pleasure: *If the weather's nice, we'll make a day of it and take a picnic.*
27 make my day used when warning someone that if they try to do something, you will enjoy stopping, defeating, or punishing them etc. This phrase was made popular by Clint Eastwood in the film 'Dirty Harry'.
28 that'll be the day used to say that you think something is very unlikely to happen: *'Bill says he's going to start going to the gym.' 'That'll be the day!'*
29 I/we don't have all day used to say that you want someone to do something faster because you do not

have enough time to wait for them to finish: *Hurry up! I haven't got all day!*
30 it's not every day (that) used to say that something does not happen often and is therefore very special: *Let's go out and celebrate. After all, it's not every day you get a new job.*
31 back in the day a long time ago, when you were much younger
32 be on days to work during the day at a job you sometimes have to do at night: *I'm on days this week.*
33 40/50/60 etc if he's/she's a day used to emphasize that someone is at least as old as you are saying: *She's ninety if she's a day.*

→ **at the end of the day** at END[1](11), → **call it a day** at CALL[1](10), → **carry the day** at CARRY[1](22), → **the early days** at EARLY[1](1), → **every dog (has) its day** at DOG[1](11), → **the good old days** at OLD(8), → HALF DAY, → **have a field day** at FIELD DAY(1), → **it's early days** at EARLY[1](3), → **it's (a little) late in the day** at LATE[1](8), → **it's sb's lucky day** at LUCKY(5), → **(live to) see the day** at SEE[1](22), → **name the day** at NAME[2](6), → OPEN DAY, → **save the day** at SAVE[1](12), → SPEECH DAY, SPORTS DAY

D

GRAMMAR: Patterns with day

on a day
• Something happens **on** a particular day: *We met on our first day at college.* ✗ Don't say: *in our first day*

in the day
• You use **in the day** when saying that something happens regularly during the time between dawn and sunset: *It gets very hot in the day.* | *She works at night and sleeps in the day.* ✗ Don't say: *She sleeps on the day.*

by day
• **By day** is very similar in meaning to **in the day**. It is used especially to make a contrast between the night and the day: *He's an office worker by day and a club DJ by night.*

all day
• If you do something **all day**, you do it during all or most of the time between dawn and sunset: *We've been driving all day.* | *The restaurant serves food all day.* ✗ Don't say: *all the day*

ˈday boy *n* [C] *BrE* a boy DAY PUPIL

day·break /ˈdeɪbreɪk/ *n* [U] the time of day when light first appears SYN **dawn**: *We arrived in Cairo at daybreak.*

ˈday camp *n* [C] *AmE* a place where children can go in the day during the school holidays to do sports, art etc

ˈday care, day-care /ˈdeɪkeə $ -ker/ *n* [U] when babies or young children, or sick or old people are looked after during the day, especially while their family members are at work: **day care centre/services/facilities** *subsidized day care facilities* | **[+for]** *Local authorities may provide day care for under fives.* | *a day care centre for the elderly*

ˈday ˌcentre *n* [C] *BrE* a place where sick or old people or people who have a particular problem can go during the day to be looked after, to meet other people, or to get help: **[+for]** *a local day centre for homeless people*

day·dream[1] /ˈdeɪdriːm/ ●○○ *v* [I] to think about something pleasant, especially when this makes you forget what you should be doing → **dream**: **[+about]** *What are you daydreaming about? There's work to be done.* THESAURUS IMAGINE —**daydreamer** *n* [C]

daydream[2] *n* [C] pleasant thoughts you have while you are awake that make you forget what you are doing → **dream**

ˈday girl *n* [C] *BrE* a girl DAY PUPIL

Day-Glo /ˈdeɪgləʊ $ -gloʊ/ *adj trademark* having a very bright orange, green, yellow, or pink colour: *Day-Glo orange posters*

ˈday job *n* [C] your normal job which you earn most of your money from doing, especially as opposed to another interest: *I'd love to be a professional writer, but I'm* ***not giving up my day job*** *just yet.*

day·light /ˈdeɪlaɪt/ ●●○ *n*
1 [U] the light produced by the sun during the day: **in daylight** *They're shy animals and don't often come out in daylight.* | *The park is open to the public during* ***daylight hours***. | *If possible, it's better to work in natural daylight.* → **in broad daylight** at BROAD[1](7)
2 (put) daylight between yourself and sb *informal* if you put daylight between yourself and someone else, you make the distance or difference between you larger: *Now the team need to put some daylight between themselves and their rivals for the championship.*
3 scare/frighten the (living) daylights out of sb *informal* to frighten someone a lot: *It scared the living daylights out of me when the flames shot out.*
4 beat/knock the (living) daylights out of sb *informal* to hit someone a lot and seriously hurt them
5 daylight robbery *BrE informal* a situation in which something costs you a lot more than is reasonable: *£2.50 for a cup of coffee? It's daylight robbery!*

ˌdaylight ˈsaving time (*also* **ˌdaylight ˈsavings**) *n* [U] the time during the summer when clocks are one hour ahead of standard time → BRITISH SUMMER TIME

ˈday ˌnursery *n* [C] a place where small children can be looked after while their parents are at work

ˌday ˈoff *n* (*plural* **days off**) [C] a day when you do not go to work, school etc because you have a holiday or because you are sick: *On my days off, you'll usually find me out in the back garden.* | **take/have a day off** *I'm taking a few days off before the wedding.*

ˌday of ˈjudgment *n* **the day of judgment** JUDGMENT DAY

day·pack /ˈdeɪpæk/ *n* [C] a small bag in which you carry things on your back

ˈday ˌpupil *n* [C] *BrE* a student who goes to a BOARDING SCHOOL but who lives at home

ˌday reˈlease *n* [U] *BrE* a system that allows workers to spend one day a week studying a subject at a college

ˌday reˈturn *n* [C] *BrE* a train or bus ticket that lets you go somewhere at a cheaper price than usual, if you go there and back on the same day

ˈday room *n* [C] a room in a hospital where patients can go to read, watch television etc

ˈday school *n* [C,U] a school where the students go home in the evening rather than one where they live → BOARDING SCHOOL

day·time /ˈdeɪtaɪm/ ●●○ *n* [U] the time during the day between the time when it gets light and the time when it gets dark: **in/during the daytime** *I can't sleep in the daytime.* | *Can I take your* ***daytime telephone number*** (=the number of the telephone you use during the day)? | *daytime television*

ˌday-to-ˈday ●○○ *adj* [usually before noun]
1 day-to-day work/business/life etc day-to-day jobs or activities are ones that you do every day as a normal part of your life, your job etc: *The manager is responsible for the* ***day-to-day running*** *of the hotel.*
2 planning for only one day at a time, usually because you are unable to plan for longer: *I see a counsellor and can now handle life on a* ***day-to-day basis***.

ˈday ˌtrading *n* [U] the activity of using a computer to buy and sell SHARES on the Internet, often buying and selling very quickly to make a profit out of small price changes —**day trader** *n* [C]

ˈday trip *n* [C] *BrE* a visit to an interesting place when you go there and come back the same day: **[+to]** *My grandparents took me on a day trip to Blackpool.* —**day tripper** *n* [C]

daze /deɪz/ *n* **in a daze** feeling confused and not able to think clearly: *She wandered round in a daze, not quite sure what to do.*

dazed /deɪzd/ *adj* unable to think clearly, especially because of a shock, accident etc: *Dazed survivors staggered from the wreckage.* | **dazed look/expression etc** *Her face was very pale and she wore a dazed expression.* THESAURUS SHOCKED

daz·zle /ˈdæzəl/ ●○○ *v* [T]
1 if a very bright light dazzles you, it stops you from seeing properly for a short time: *a deer dazzled by the headlights*
2 to make someone feel strong admiration: *As children, we were dazzled by my uncle's good looks and charm.* —**dazzle** *n* [U]

daz·zling /ˈdæzəlɪŋ/ *adj* **1** a light that is dazzling is very bright and makes you unable to see properly for a short time **THESAURUS** ▸ BRIGHT **2** very impressive and attractive: *a dazzling display of football skills*

dB the written abbreviation of ***decibel*** or ***decibels***

DC /ˌdiː ˈsiː/ the abbreviation of ***direct current*** → **AC**

D.C. the abbreviation of ***District of Columbia*** in the US

DD /ˌdiː ˈdiː/ **1** the written abbreviation of DIRECT DEBIT **2** (***Doctor of Divinity***) an advanced university degree in THEOLOGY (=religious studies) **3** (***darling daughter***) used on the Internet to refer to your daughter. You refer to your eldest daughter as DD1, your second daughter as DD2 etc: *DD1 came home from school in tears today.*

D-Day /ˈdiː deɪ/ 6th June, 1944; in World War II, the day the Allies landed in France to begin the spread of their forces through Europe, under the command of General Eisenhower. D-Day is sometimes used to describe the day on which an important operation or planned action will begin.

DDoS /ˈdiː dɒs $ -dɑːs/ *n* [U] (***distributed denial of service***) an attempt to slow down or block a website, for example by sending it many messages

DDT /ˌdiː diː ˈtiː/ *n* [U] a chemical formerly used to kill insects that harm crops

de- /diː, dɪ/ *prefix* **1** shows an opposite: *deindustrialization* (=becoming less industrial) **2** shows that something is removed: *Debone the fish* (=remove its bones). | *The king was dethroned* (=removed from power). **3** shows that something is reduced: *The government have devalued the currency.*

dea·con /ˈdiːkən/ *n* [C] a religious official, in some Christian churches, who is just below the rank of a priest

dea·con·ess /ˌdiːkəˈnes $ ˈdiːkənəs/ *n* [C] a female religious official, in some Christian churches, who is just below the rank of a priest

de·ac·ti·vate /diːˈæktɪveɪt/ *v* [T] to switch something off, especially a piece of equipment, or to stop it from being used anymore OPP **activate**: *You need to type in a code number to deactivate the alarm.*

dead¹ /ded/ ●●● S1 W1 *adj* [no comparative]
1 NOT ALIVE no longer alive: *Her mother had been dead for ten years.* | *Police are trying to contact the family of the dead man.* | *a pile of dead leaves* | *the* ***dead body*** *of a young soldier* | *Two men were* ***shot dead*** *by terrorists.* | *Magnus was* ***found dead*** *in his car.* | *One man is still missing,* ***presumed dead****.* | *He suddenly had a heart attack and* ***dropped dead****.* | *She was* ***pronounced dead on arrival*** *at the hospital.* | *His fellow climbers had* ***left*** *him* ***for dead*** *on the mountain.* | *We didn't know if she was dead or alive.* | *When they found him he was* ***more dead than alive****.* | *Her parents were* ***long dead****.*
⚠ Do not confuse **dead**, which is an adjective, with **died**, which is the past tense and past participle of the verb **die**: *The man was already dead (NOT The man was already died).*
2 NOT WORKING [not before noun] not working because there is no power: *I picked up the phone but discovered the* ***line*** *was* ***dead****.* | *Suddenly the radio* ***went dead****.* | *I think the* ***batteries*** *are* ***dead****.*
3 ALREADY USED already used: *a small pile of* ***dead matches*** | **dead glass/bottle** (=one that someone has finished drinking from in a bar or restaurant)
4 BORING [not before noun] a place that is dead is boring because there is nothing interesting or exciting happening there: *This place is dead after nine o'clock.*
5 NOT ACTIVE/USED not active or being used: *The luxury car market has been dead in recent months.*
6 ARM/LEG ETC a part of your body that is dead has no feeling in it, especially because the blood supply to it has been stopped: *When I got up my foot had* ***gone dead*** *where I'd been sitting on it.*
7 NO EMOTION [not before noun] showing no emotion or sympathy: *Jennie's eyes were cold and dead.*
8 TIRED [not before noun] *spoken* very tired: *I can't go out tonight. I'm absolutely dead!* | *She was* ***dead on*** *her* ***feet*** *and didn't have the energy to argue* (=used when someone keeps going even though they are very tired). **THESAURUS** ▸ TIRED
9 be dead to the world to be very deeply asleep or unconscious: *Better leave Craig – he's dead to the world.*
10 USED FOR EMPHASIS [only before noun] completely or exactly – used to emphasize what you are saying: *We all sat waiting in* ***dead silence*** (=complete silence). | *The train came to a* ***dead stop*** (=it stopped completely). | *The arrow hit the* ***dead centre*** *of the target* (=the exact centre). | *I've given the whole thing up as a* ***dead loss*** (=completely useless or a complete failure). | *John tells me it's a* ***dead cert****, we can't lose* (=something which will certainly happen, win, succeed etc). | *He fell to the floor* ***in a dead faint*** (=completely unconscious).
11 over my dead body *spoken* used to say that you are determined not to allow something to happen: *You'll marry him over my dead body!*
12 I wouldn't be seen/caught dead *spoken* used to say that you would never wear particular clothes, go to particular places, or do particular things, because you would feel embarrassed: **[+in/on/with etc]** *I wouldn't be seen dead in a dress like that!*
13 IN SERIOUS TROUBLE *informal* in serious trouble: **if ... I'm dead/you're dead etc** *If Mum finds out about this, I'm dead.* | *You're* ***in dead trouble*** *now* (=in very serious trouble)! | *One word of this to Sam and you're* ***dead meat*** (=you are in serious trouble and someone is very angry with you)!
14 be dead and buried an argument, problem, plan etc that is dead and buried is not worth considering again: *The old argument about whether the UK should be a member of the EU should now be dead and buried.*
15 be dead in the water *informal* if a plan or idea is dead in the water, it is unlikely to continue successfully
16 drop dead! *spoken* used to rudely and angrily tell someone to go away and leave you alone
17 dead language a dead language, for example Latin or Ancient Greek, is no longer used by ordinary people → **living language** at LIVING¹(1)
18 the dead hand of sth something which stops or slows your progress, especially a strong influence: *the dead hand of local government bureaucracy*
19 PLANET a dead PLANET has no life on it
20 IN SPORT when the ball is dead in some games, it is no longer on the playing area → **(as) dead as a dodo** at DODO(3), → DEAD RINGER —**deadness** *n* [U]

dead² *adv informal* **1** completely: **dead right/wrong** *'It's a crazy idea.' 'You're dead right!'* | **dead straight/flat** *The road was dead straight.* | **dead quiet/calm/still** *Everything suddenly went dead still.* | **be dead (set) against sth** (=completely disagree with something) *Her family were dead against the marriage.* | *He was obviously* ***dead drunk****.* | *When he saw her, he* ***stopped dead in his tracks*** (=suddenly stopped moving completely). **2** very: *He was dead good-looking.* | *It sounded dead boring.* | **dead beat/tired** (=very tired) **3** [+adj/adv] directly or exactly: *I stared* ***dead ahead*** *at the doorway.* | *The bus arrived* ***dead on time****.*

dead³ *n* **1 the dead** [plural] people who have died: *Families on both sides buried their dead.* | **the dead and injured/wounded/dying** *Most of the dead and injured had been passengers on the bus.* **2 the dead of night/winter** the middle of the night or the middle of the winter: *creeping around in the dead of night* **3 rise/come back/return from the dead** to become alive again after dying: *Christ rose from the dead.*

dead·beat /ˈdedbiːt/ *n* [C] **1** someone who is lazy and has no plans in life **2** someone who avoids paying their debts

dead·bolt /ˈdedbəʊlt $ -boʊlt/ *n* [C] a strong lock often used on doors → see picture at LOCK²

D

ˌdead ˈduck *n* **a dead duck** *informal* a plan, idea etc that is not worth considering because it is very likely to fail: *He admitted that the whole project was a dead duck.*

dead·en /ˈdedn/ *v* [T] to make a feeling or sound less strong: *medicine to deaden the pain*

ˌdead ˈend *n* [C] **1** a street with no way out at one end **2** a situation where no more progress is possible: **come to/reach a dead end** *The negotiations have reached a dead end.* **3 dead-end job** a job with low wages and no chance of progress

dead·head /ˈdedhed/ *v* [T] to remove the dead or dying flowers from a plant

ˌdead ˈheat *n* [C] a situation during or at the end of a race or competition in which two or more competitors have the same number of points etc, have reached the same level, or have taken the same time to complete a particular distance

ˌdead ˈletter *n* [C] **1** a law, idea etc that still exists but that people no longer obey **2** a letter that cannot be delivered or returned

D

dead·line /ˈdedlaɪn/ ●●○ *n* [C] a date or time by which you have to do or complete something: **[+for]** *He* ***missed the deadline*** *for applications.* | **[+of]** *It has to be in before the deadline of July 1st.* | *I'm always working under pressure to* ***meet deadlines*** (=finish something on time). | **set/impose a deadline** *They've set a deadline of 12 noon.* | **a tight/strict deadline** (=one that must be met but is difficult)

COLLOCATIONS

VERBS

have a deadline *It's easier to work hard if you have a deadline.*
work to a deadline (=have to finish something by a deadline) *We're all under pressure and working to deadlines.*
meet a deadline (=finish something by a deadline) *Everyone's working extremely hard to meet the deadline.*
miss a deadline (=fail to finish something by a deadline) *There will be penalties if the government misses the deadline to cut air pollution.*
set a deadline (=decide on a date when something must be finished) *The deadline has been set at January 31st.*
extend a deadline (=make the date or time later than it was before) *My editor agreed to extend the deadline by two weeks.*
a deadline approaches/looms *Things began to get more frantic as the deadline loomed.*
a deadline passes (=the date or time by which you must do something goes past) *The deadline had already passed for him to raise the money.*

ADJECTIVES/NOUN + deadline

a strict deadline (=a time or date when something must definitely be finished)
a tight deadline (=one that is difficult because it does not allow much time to do something) *As a journalist, you have to be able to work to tight deadlines.*
the Friday/December etc deadline *The project went on long after the December deadline.*

dead·lock /ˈdedlɒk $ -lɑːk/ *n* [singular, U] **1** a situation in which a disagreement cannot be settled SYN **stalemate**: *The talks have* ***reached a*** *complete* ***deadlock***. | *a last-ditch effort to* ***break the deadlock*** | *Negotiations ended in deadlock.* THESAURUS ▸ PROGRESS **2** *BrE* a DEADBOLT —**deadlocked** *adj*: *Talks between management and unions remain deadlocked.*

dead·ly¹ /ˈdedli/ ●●○ *adj*
1 VERY DANGEROUS likely to cause death SYN **lethal**: *a deadly poison* | *a deadly weapon* | **deadly disease/virus**
2 deadly enemy someone who will always be your enemy and will try to harm you as much as possible: *The two rapidly became deadly enemies.*
3 COMPLETE complete or total: *We sat in deadly silence.* | *He was* ***in deadly earnest*** (=completely serious).
4 VERY EFFECTIVE causing harm in a very effective way: *She hit the target with deadly accuracy.*
5 LIKE DEATH [only before noun] like death in appearance: *His face had a deadly paleness.* → **seven deadly sins** at SIN¹(1)

deadly² *adv* **deadly serious/dull/boring etc** very serious, dull etc: *I'm deadly serious, this isn't a game!*

ˌdeadly ˈnightshade *n* [C,U] a poisonous European plant SYN **belladonna**

dead·pan /ˈdedpæn/ *adj* sounding and looking completely serious when you are saying or doing something funny: **deadpan voice/expression etc** *deadpan humour*

ˌdead ˈreckoning *n* [U] calculating the position of a ship or aircraft without using the sun, moon, or stars

ˌdead ˈringer *n* [C] someone who looks exactly like someone else: **[+for]** *Dave's a dead ringer for Paul McCartney.*

dead·weight, **dead weight** /ˈdedweɪt/ *n* [singular] **1** something that is very heavy and difficult to carry **2** someone or something that prevents you from making progress or being successful

ˌdead ˈwood, **dead·wood** /ˈdedwʊd/ *n* [U] **1** people or things within an organization which are no longer useful or needed **2** branches of a tree which are no longer alive

deaf /def/ ●●○ W3 *adj*
1 physically unable to hear anything or unable to hear well → **hearing impaired**: *communication between deaf and hearing people* | *I think Mum's* ***going*** *a bit* ***deaf***. | *She's* ***deaf and dumb*** (=unable to hear or speak) *and communicates using sign language.* | *Tom was born* ***profoundly deaf*** (=having great difficulty hearing). | **stone deaf/deaf as a post** *informal* (=completely deaf) → HARD OF HEARING, TONE-DEAF
2 the deaf [plural] people who are deaf: *a school for the deaf*
3 be deaf to sth *literary* to be unwilling to hear or listen to something: *She was deaf to his pleas.*
4 turn a deaf ear (to sth) to be unwilling to listen to what someone is saying or asking: *The factory owners turned a deaf ear to the demands of the workers.*
5 fall on deaf ears if advice or a warning falls on deaf ears, everyone ignores it —**deafness** *n* [U]

deaf·en /ˈdefən/ *v* [T] **1** if a noise deafens you, it is so loud that you cannot hear anything else **2** to make someone go deaf GRAMMAR **Deafen** is often used in the passive.

deaf·en·ing /ˈdefənɪŋ/ *adj* **1** very loud: *a deafening roar* THESAURUS ▸ LOUD **2 deafening silence** a complete silence, when it is uncomfortable or you are expecting someone to say something

ˌdeaf ˈmute *n* [C] *old-fashioned, not polite* someone who is unable to hear or speak

deal¹ /diːl/ ●●● S1 W1 *n*
1 AGREEMENT [C] an agreement or arrangement, especially in business or politics, that helps both sides involved: *They made a deal to sell the land to a property developer.* | **[+with]** *rumors that the company had done a deal with Microsoft to market its products* | **[+between]** *Twelve US soldiers were released after a deal between the army and the guerillas.*
2 a great/good deal a large quantity of something SYN **a lot**: **[+of]** *It took a great deal of time and effort.* | *His work has been attracting a great deal of attention.* | **a great/good deal more/less etc** (=a lot more, less etc) *He knew a good deal more than I did.* | *She's married to a man a good deal older than herself.*

GRAMMAR: Comparison

a great/good deal of
• You use **a great deal of** or **a good deal of** with uncountable nouns: *a great deal of money* | *a good deal of work*
• **A great/good deal of** is not used with nouns in the plural. ✗ Don't say: *a great deal of people*

a lot of
• You can use **a lot of** with nouns in the plural or uncountable nouns: *a lot of people* | *a lot of trouble*

3 TREATMENT [C usually singular] treatment of a particular type that is given or received: **a better/fairer etc deal** *a better deal for nurses* | *The prime minister promised farmers a* ***new deal*** (=a new and fairer system). | **a rough/raw deal** (=unfair treatment) *Women tend to get a raw deal from employers.*
4 it's a deal *spoken* used to say that you agree to do something: *OK, it's a deal.*
5 what's the deal? *AmE spoken* used when you want to know about a problem or something strange that is happening: *So what's the deal? Why is he so mad?*
6 CARDS [singular] when you give out cards to players in a card game → **dealer**: *It's your deal, Alison.*
7 WOOD [U] *BrE* FIR or PINE wood used for making things: *a deal table*
8 a deal of sth *old-fashioned* a large amount of something → BIG DEAL

COLLOCATIONS

VERBS

do a deal *The two companies have recently done a major deal.*
make a deal *informal Why don't we make a deal to stay out of each other's way?*
reach/strike a deal (=agree a deal after a lot of discussions) *The US and North Korea reached a deal about North Korea's nuclear development program.*
sign a deal *The singer has signed a $20 million deal with an American TV network.*
negotiate a deal (=agree a deal by discussing over a long period) *We have negotiated a special deal with one of the world's leading car hire companies.*
close/conclude a deal *formal* (=agree a deal formally) *A deal between the two companies has now been concluded.*
clinch a deal (=finally agree on a deal, especially one that is good for you) *The salesman was eager to clinch the deal.*
cut a deal *informal* (=agree a deal, especially when it is difficult or you have to accept some things you would rather not accept) *In the end, they had to cut a deal with the Communists.*
have a deal *informal* (=have made or agreed on a deal) *Do we have a deal?*
get a good deal (=buy something at a good price) *He thought he had got a good deal.*
back out of/pull out of a deal (=decide not to make a deal after discussing one) *Twenty-five jobs were lost after their partner pulled out of the deal.*
a deal goes through/ahead (=it happens as arranged) *It's 99% certain that the deal will go through.*
a deal falls through (=does not happen as arranged) *The cost was simply too high, so the deal fell through.*

ADJECTIVES/NOUN + deal

a good deal (=a good price, offer, or arrangement) *You can buy two for £10, which sounds like a good deal.*
a business deal *He lost a fortune in an unwise business deal.*
a pay deal (=one that involves an agreement about how much people will be paid) *They are currently negotiating a new pay deal.*
a peace deal (=an agreement to end fighting between countries) *Hopes of a peace deal are fading.*
a financial/political etc deal *After weeks of negotiation the prospect of a political deal seemed increasingly unlikely.*
an arms/weapons deal (=one which involves selling weapons) *A number of recent arms deals have embarrassed the government.*
a record deal (=one between a singer or band and a recording company) *It's hard for a band to get a record deal.*
a one-year/two-year etc deal (=one that will be fixed for one year, two years etc) *The five-year deal is estimated to be worth $17.2 million.*
a shady deal (=dishonest or illegal) *Some senior members of the party were involved in shady deals and bribery.*

PHRASES

part of the deal *I got free accommodation as part of the deal.*
the terms of a deal (=the details or conditions in it) *The hotel group refused to release the financial terms of the deal.*
a done deal *informal* (=something that has been completely agreed) *The takeover has been described as a done deal.*

deal² ●●● S1 W1 *v* (*past tense and past participle* **dealt** /delt/)
1 [I,T] (*also* **deal sth ↔ out**) to give playing cards to each of the players in a game: *Whose turn is it to deal?*
2 [I] *informal* to buy and sell illegal drugs: *Many users end up dealing to support their habit.*
3 deal a blow (to sb/sth) to cause harm to someone or something – used in news reports: **deal a heavy/severe/serious etc blow** *The sanctions have dealt a severe blow to the local tourism industry.* | *This will deal a blow to consumer confidence.*

deal in *phr v*
1 deal in sth to buy and sell a particular type of product → **dealer**: **deal in shares/securities etc** *investors dealing in stocks and shares* | **deal in drugs/stolen goods etc** *He then began dealing in heroin.* | **deal in antiques/second-hand books etc**
2 deal in sth to be interested or involved in something: *As a scientist, I do not deal in speculation.*
3 deal sb in to include someone in a game of cards

deal sth **↔ out** *phr v*
1 to give playing cards to each of the players in a game: *I began dealing out the cards.*
2 to decide what kind of punishment someone will get

deal with sb/sth *phr v*
1 to take the necessary action, especially in order to solve a problem SYN **handle**: *a strategy for dealing with disruptive pupils* | *Don't worry, I'll deal with this.* | **deal with a problem/issue/matter etc** *The council has failed to deal with the problem of homelessness in the city.* | **deal effectively/adequately etc with sth** *They should deal properly and fairly with any complaint.*
2 if a book, speech etc deals with a particular subject, it is about that subject: *These ideas are dealt with more fully in Chapter Four.*
3 to do business with someone or have a business connection with someone: *Most travel agents do not deal directly with these companies.*
4 to succeed in controlling your feelings about an emotional problem so that it does not affect your life SYN **cope with**: *How's he dealing with the whole thing?*

THESAURUS

deal with sth to take the necessary action, especially in order to solve a problem: *We need to deal with problems like pollution and climate change.* | *I spend most of my day dealing with customer enquiries.*
handle to deal with a problem or difficult situation by making particular decisions – used especially when talking about how well or badly someone does this: *He handled the situation very well.* | *Most customers were happy with the way their complaints had been handled.*
tackle to start to deal with a problem, especially one that is complicated: *We need to tackle the issue of drugs in schools.* | *The government is introducing new measures to tackle online crime.*

D

see to/attend to sb/sth to deal with all the practical details of something that needs to be done or organized. **Attend to** is more formal than **see to**: *My son saw to all the funeral arrangements. | I have some business to attend to.*
take care of sth to do the work or make the arrangements that are necessary for something to happen – used especially when you do this for someone else so that they do not have to worry about it: *My secretary takes care of all the paperwork.*
process if a company or organization processes a letter, form etc, they do the things that are usually done as part of their official system, in order to deal with it: *It will take a minimum of 14 days to process your passport application.*

deal·break·er, **deal breaker** /ˈdiːlˌbreɪkə $ -ər/ *n* [C] *informal* something that makes you decide that you do not want a product, relationship, job etc, because you cannot accept that part of it: *The benefits package became a dealbreaker in the negotiations.*

deal·er /ˈdiːlə $ -ər/ ●●○ W3 *n* [C]
1 someone who buys and sells a particular product, especially an expensive one: **car/antique/art etc dealer** | **[+in]** *a dealer in modern art*
2 someone who sells illegal drugs
3 someone who gives out playing cards in a game

deal·er·ship /ˈdiːləʃɪp $ -ər-/ *n* [C] a business that sells a particular company's product, especially cars

deal·ing /ˈdiːlɪŋ/ ●○○ *n*
1 dealings [plural] the business activities or relationships that someone is involved in: *his financial dealings* | **[+with]** *She is ruthless in her dealings with competitors.* | *We've* ***had dealings with*** *him in the past.*
2 [U] the activity of buying, selling, or doing business with people: *penalties for drug dealing* | **plain/honest/fair dealing** (=a particular way of doing business) *a reputation for fair dealing* → **insider dealing** at INSIDER TRADING, WHEELING AND DEALING

dealt /delt/ the past tense and past participle of DEAL

dean /diːn/ *n* [C] **1** a priest of high rank in the Christian church who is in charge of several priests or churches **2** someone in a university who is responsible for a particular area of work: *the admissions dean* **3** *AmE* someone with a lot of experience of a particular job or subject SYN **doyen** *BrE*: **[+of]** *Neier is the dean of American human rights activism.*

dean·e·ry /ˈdiːnəri/ *n* (*plural* **deaneries**) [C] the area controlled by a dean or the place where a dean lives

ˈdean's list *n* [C] *AmE* a list of the best students at a university

dear[1] /dɪə $ dɪr/ ●●● S1 *interjection* **Oh dear!/Dear oh dear!** (*also* **Dear me!** *old-fashioned*) used to show that you are surprised, upset, or annoyed because something bad has happened: *Oh dear, I've broken the lamp.* | *'I think I'm getting a cold.' 'Dear oh dear!'*

dear[2] ●●● W1 *adj* (*comparative* **dearer**, *superlative* **dearest**)
1 Dear used before someone's name or title to begin a letter: *Dear Sir or Madam, ...* | *Dear Mrs. Wilson, ...* | *Dear Meg, ...*
2 *BrE* expensive OPP **cheap**: *Cars are 59% dearer in Britain than in Europe.* THESAURUS ▸ EXPENSIVE
3 *formal* a dear friend or relative is very important to you and you love them a lot: *Mark became a* ***dear friend***. | **be dear to sb** *His sister was very dear to him.*
4 hold sth dear to think that something is very important: *Household economy was something my mother held very dear.*
5 dear old ... *BrE spoken* used to describe someone or something in a way that shows your love or liking of them SYN **good old**: *Here we are, back in dear old Manchester!*
6 for dear life *written* if you run, fight, hold on etc for dear life, you do it as fast or as well as you can because you are afraid: *She grasped the side of the boat and* ***hung on for dear life***.
7 the dear departed *BrE literary* a person you love who has died

dear[3] ●●○ S3 *n* [C]
1 used when speaking to someone you love: *How did the interview go, dear?*
2 *spoken* used when speaking in a friendly way to someone, especially someone who is much younger or much older than you. This use can sometimes sound rather PATRONIZING: *Can I help you, dear?* | *Come along,* ***my dear***, *take a seat.*
3 *BrE spoken* someone who is kind and helpful: *Be a dear and make me a coffee.*
4 old dear *BrE* a fairly rude expression meaning an old woman

dear[4] *adv* **cost sb dear** *written* to cause a lot of trouble and suffering for someone: *Carolyn's marriage to Pete cost her dear.*

dear·est /ˈdɪərɪst $ ˈdɪr-/ *n spoken* used when speaking to someone you love

dear·ie, **deary** /ˈdɪəri $ ˈdɪr-/ *n old-fashioned informal* used when speaking in a friendly way to someone

dear·ly /ˈdɪəli $ ˈdɪrli/ *adv* **1** very much: *James* ***loved*** *her* ***dearly***. | *I* ***would dearly like*** *to know what she said.* **2** in a way that involves a lot of suffering, damage, trouble etc: *The weakness in their defense has already* ***cost*** *them* ***dearly*** *this season.* | *Ordinary people are* ***paying dearly for*** *the mistakes of this administration.* **3 dearly beloved** *spoken* used by a priest or minister at the beginning of a Christian service

dearth /dɜːθ $ dɜːrθ/ *n* [singular] a lack of something that people want or need: **[+of]** *a dearth of job opportunities*

dear·y /ˈdɪəri $ ˈdɪri/ *n* another spelling of DEARIE

death /deθ/ ●●● S1 W1 *n*
1 a) [U] the end of the life of a person or animal: **[+of]** *The death of his mother came as a tremendous shock.* | *Cancer is the leading* ***cause of death*** *in women.* | *How Danielle* ***met*** *her* ***death*** (=died) *will probably never be known.* | *His friend was* ***close to death***. | *His family are still* ***mourning*** *John's* ***tragic death***. | *the anniversary of Lenin's death* | **bleed/burn/starve etc to death** *a homeless man who froze to death* | **beat/stab/shoot etc sb to death** *The 76-year-old pensioner was beaten to death.* | **put/sentence/condemn sb to death** (=kill someone or decide they should be killed as an official punishment) *Legend has it that Sarah was put to death for practising witchcraft.* | *Members of the family have received* ***death threats***. | *He remained president until his* ***untimely death*** (=death at a surprisingly young age). | *Two of the passengers managed to* ***escape death*** (=avoid being killed). **b)** [C] a particular case when someone dies OPP **birth**: *a campaign to reduce the number of traffic deaths* | **[+from]** *deaths from cancer* | *I heard there'd been a* ***death in the family***.
2 the death of sth the permanent end of something OPP **birth**: *The latest bombing is the death of all our hopes.* | *These regulations could* ***spell the death*** (=lead to the end) *of the American car industry.*
3 to death *informal* **a)** used to emphasize that a feeling or emotion is very strong: **be bored/scared/frightened etc to death** *She was scared to death of what might happen next.* | *I'm absolutely* ***sick to death of*** *it* (=very angry, bored, or unhappy about something). | **bore/scare/love etc sb to death** *He drove at a speed which frightened Leonora to death.* | *She used to worry me to death.* **b)** used to say that an action is continued with a lot of effort and for as long as possible: *They just* ***work*** *you* ***to death*** *in that place.*
4 do sth to death *informal* to perform or present an idea, joke etc so often that people become tired of it: *Most of his material has been done to death by numerous comedians.*
5 to the death a) until someone is dead: *They will* ***fight to the death*** *rather than give an inch of ground.* | *soldiers locked in a struggle to the death* **b)** until you achieve something even if it means that you suffer: *The leadership election has become a fight to the death.*
6 Death a creature that looks like a human SKELETON, used in paintings, stories etc to represent the fact that people die

7 be at death's door to be very ill and likely to die
8 look/feel like death warmed up *BrE*, **look/feel like death warmed over** *AmE informal* to look or feel very ill or tired
9 you'll catch your death (of cold) *spoken old-fashioned* used to warn someone that they are likely to become ill because they are wet or cold
10 sb will be the death of me *spoken old-fashioned* used to say that someone is causing you a lot of worry and problems: *That boy will be the death of me!* → BLACK DEATH, THE, → **kiss of death** at KISS²(3), → **life and death** at LIFE(10)

death·bed /ˈdeθbed/ *n* [C usually singular] the bed on which someone dies or is dying: **on your deathbed** *On her deathbed, Miriam's mother reveals that she never knew her father.* | **deathbed confession/conversion etc** (=made when you are dying) *The disease allowed no time for a deathbed repentance.*

ˈdeath blow *n* [singular] an action or event that makes something fail or end → **death knell**: *His decision to leave the show has* ***delivered a death blow to*** *the series.*

ˈdeath camp *n* [C] a place where large numbers of prisoners are killed or die, usually in a war

ˈdeath cerˌtificate *n* [C] a legal document, signed by a doctor, that states the time and cause of someone's death → **birth certificate**

ˈdeath-deˌfying *adj* [only before noun] a death-defying action is very dangerous: *death-defying film stunts*

ˈdeath ˌduties *n* [plural] *BrE old-fashioned* INHERITANCE TAX

ˈdeath knell *n* [singular] a sign that something will soon fail or stop existing → **death blow**: **(sound/strike/toll) the death knell for/of sth** *The loss of Georgia would sound the death knell of Republican hopes.*

death·less /ˈdeθləs/ *adj* **deathless prose/verse/lines etc** writing that is very bad or boring - used humorously

death·ly /ˈdeθli/ *adj, adv* reminding you of death or of a dead body: **deathly cold/white/pale** *She was deathly pale, and looked as if she might faint.* | **a deathly hush/silence** (=complete silence) *A deathly hush fell over the room.*

ˈdeath mask *n* [C] a model of a dead person's face, made by covering their face with a soft substance and letting it become hard

ˈdeath ˌpenalty *n* [singular] the legal punishment of death → **capital punishment**: *Three Britons are facing the death penalty for spying.*

ˈdeath rate *n* [C] **1** the number of deaths for every 100 or every 1,000 people in a particular year and in a particular place → **birth rate 2** the number of deaths each year from a particular disease or in a particular group: *childhood death rates*

ˈdeath ˌrattle *n* [C] a noise that sometimes comes from the throat or chest of someone who is dying

death row /ˌdeθ ˈrəʊ $ -ˈroʊ/ *n* [U] the part of a prison where prisoners who will be punished by being killed are kept: **on death row** *a murderer on death row*

ˈdeath ˌsentence *n* [C] **1** the official punishment of death, ordered by a judge: *He* ***received*** *a* ***death sentence***. | *Premeditated murder* ***carries*** (=is punished by) ***the death sentence***. **2** something such as an illness that makes you sure you will die: *Cancer is no longer a death sentence.* **3** an action or decision that is very harmful to someone or something: *In 1987, the government* ***passed*** *a* ***death sentence on*** *the river by granting permission for the new dam.*

ˈdeath's head *n* [C] *literary* a human SKULL, used as a sign of death

ˈdeath squad *n* [C] a group of people who have been ordered to kill someone's political opponents

ˈdeath stare *n* [C] a way of looking at someone for a long time which shows you are angry with them or hate them

ˈdeath throes *n* [plural] **1** the final stages before something fails or ends: *The peace pact seems to be* ***in its death throes***. **2** sudden violent movements that people sometimes make when they are dying

ˈdeath toll *n* [C usually singular] the total number of people who die in an accident, war etc: *As the unrest continued, the* ***death toll rose***. | *The official* ***death toll stands at*** *53.*

ˈdeath trap *n* [C] *informal* a vehicle, building, piece of equipment etc that is in very bad condition and might injure or kill someone: *A car with tires in this condition is simply a death trap.*

ˈdeath ˌwarrant *n* [C] **1** an official document stating that someone is to be killed as a punishment **2** something that is likely to cause you very serious trouble, or even your death: *By indulging in casual sex, many teenagers could be* ***signing*** *their* ***own death warrants***.

ˈdeath wish *n* [singular] a desire to die: *Before I did the jump, people would ask if I* ***had a death wish***.

deb /deb/ *n* [C] *informal* a DEBUTANTE

de·ba·cle, **débâcle** /deɪˈbɑːkəl, dɪ-/ *n* [C] an event or situation that is a complete failure: *the debacle of the 1994 elections*

de·bar /dɪˈbɑː $ -ˈbɑːr/ *v* (**debarred, debarring**) [T] *formal* to officially prevent someone from doing something SYN **ban**: **be debarred from (doing) sth** *All five men were debarred from entering France for three years.* GRAMMAR **Debar** is usually passive.

de·bark /dɪˈbɑːk $ -ˈbɑːrk/ *v* [I] to DISEMBARK (=get off a ship): **[+from]** *I remember how glad I felt debarking from a ship in Bremerhaven after six days on the ocean.*

de·base /dɪˈbeɪs/ *v* [T] *formal* to make someone or something lose its value or people's respect: *The medical profession has been debased by these revelations.* | **debase yourself** *actors who debased themselves by participating in the show* | **debase a currency/coinage** (=reduce its value) —**debasement** *n* [C,U]: *currency debasement*

de·bat·a·ble /dɪˈbeɪtəbəl/ AWL *adj* things that are debatable are not certain because people have different opinions about them SYN **arguable**: *a* ***debatable point*** | **it is debatable whether/how etc** *It's debatable whether this book is as good as her last.* | *Whether the object was used for rituals is* ***highly debatable***.

de·bate¹ /dɪˈbeɪt/ ●●● S2 W2 AWL *n*
1 [C,U] discussion of a particular subject that often continues for a long time and in which people express different opinions: *the gun-control debate in the US* | *The new drug has become the subject of* ***heated debate*** *within the medical profession.* | **[+over/about]** *There has been* ***widespread public debate*** *over the introduction of genetically modified food.* | *There was much* ***lively debate*** *about whether women should spend more time in the home.* | *A fierce* ***debate raged*** *over which artist's work should be chosen for the prize.* | **[+between]** *the* ***ongoing debate*** *between environmentalists and the road-building lobby over the future of our countryside* | *Nuclear power has always been a topic that has* ***sparked off*** *considerable* ***debate***.
2 [C,U] a formal discussion of a particular problem, subject etc in which people express different opinions, and sometimes vote on them: **[+on/over/about]** *a debate on legalized gambling* | *a* ***televised debate*** | **have/hold/conduct a debate** *It would have been better to hold the debate during the day.* | **be under debate** *What topics are under debate in Congress this week?*
3 be open to debate (*also* **be a matter for debate**) if an idea is open to debate, no one has proved yet whether it is true or false SYN **debatable**: *Whether that would have made any difference is open to debate.*

debate² ●●○ AWL *v* [I,T]
1 to discuss a subject formally when you are trying to make a decision or find a solution: *The issue will be debated on Tuesday.* | **debate whether/what/how etc** *Meanwhile, philosophers debate whether it's right to clone an individual.* | **debate (sth) with sb** *an invitation to debate with William on the future of democracy* | *His conclusions* ***are hotly debated*** (=argued about strongly). THESAURUS TALK
2 to consider something carefully before making a decision: **debate with yourself** *I debated with myself whether I should tell anyone.* | **debate who/what/how etc** *I'm still*

D

debating what to do. | **debate doing sth** *For a moment Mary debated telling Rick the truth.*

de·bat·er /dɪˈbeɪtə $ -ər/ *n* [C] someone who speaks in a formal debate

de·bauched /dɪˈbɔːtʃt $ -ˈbɒːtʃt, -ˈbɑːtʃt/ *adj formal* someone who is debauched behaves in a bad or immoral way, for example by drinking too much alcohol, taking drugs, or having sex with many people

de·bauch·e·ry /dɪˈbɔːtʃəri $ dɪˈbɒː-, dɪˈbɑː-/ *n* [U] *formal* immoral behaviour involving drugs, alcohol, sex etc: *a life of debauchery*

de·ben·ture /dɪˈbentʃə $ -ər/ *n* [C] *technical* an official document produced by a company showing how much INTEREST it will pay on a LOAN

de·bil·i·tate /dɪˈbɪlɪteɪt/ *v* [T] *formal* **1** to make someone ill and weak: *He was debilitated by his illness.* **2** to make an organization or system less effective or powerful: *The state is debilitated by inefficiency and corruption.* —**debilitating** *adj*: *a debilitating disease*

de·bil·i·ty /dɪˈbɪləti/ *n* (*plural* **debilities**) [C,U] *formal* weakness, especially as the result of illness → **disability**: *physical and mental debility*

D

deb·it¹ /ˈdebɪt/ *n* [C] **1** *technical* a decrease in the amount of money in a bank account, for example because you have taken money out of it OPP **credit** → **direct debit** **2** *technical* a record in financial accounts that shows money that has been spent or that is owed OPP **credit** **3 on the debit side** used to say that something is a disadvantage in a particular situation, especially after you have described the advantages: *Bikes are easy to park, but on the debit side they can be dangerous in traffic.*

debit² *v* [T] *technical* **1** to take money out of a bank account OPP **credit**: **debit sth from sth** *The sum of £25 has been debited from your account.* **2** to record in financial accounts the money that has been spent or that is owed: **debit sth against/to sth** *Purchases are debited against the client's account.*

ˈdebit card ●●○ *n* [C] a plastic card with your signature on that you can use to pay for things. The money is taken directly from your bank account → CASH CARD, CHEQUE CARD, CREDIT CARD

ˈdebit note (*also* **ˈdebit reˌceipt** *AmE*) *n* [C] a written record showing that a customer owes money to a company

deb·o·nair /ˌdebəˈneə◂ $ -ˈner◂/ *adj old-fashioned* a man who is debonair is fashionable and confident

de·brief /ˌdiːˈbriːf/ *v* [T] to ask someone questions about a job they have just done or an experience they have just had, in order to gather information → **brief**: *The returning bomber crews were debriefed.* —**debriefing** *n* [U]: *a debriefing session*

deb·ris /ˈdebriː, ˈdeɪ- $ dəˈbriː, deɪ-/ ●○○ *n* [U] **1** the pieces of something that are left after it has been destroyed in an accident, explosion etc: *She was hit by **flying debris** from the blast.* **2** *technical* pieces of waste material, paper etc: **plant/garden/industrial etc debris** *Clean the ventilation ducts to remove dust and insect debris.*

debt /det/ ●●● S3 W2 *n*

1 [C] a sum of money that a person or organization owes: **[+of]** *She had debts of over £100,000.* | *He had enough money to pay off his outstanding debts.* | *students who run up huge debts*

2 [U] when you owe money to someone OPP **credit**: **in debt (to sb)** *Nearly half the students said they were in debt.* | *The band will be in debt to the record company for years.* | **£200/$1,000 etc in debt** *A rash business decision left him $600 in debt.* | **get/run/fall etc into debt** *The club **sank deeper into debt**.* | **be heavily/deeply in debt** (=owe a lot of money)

3 [C usually singular] the degree to which you have learned from or been influenced by someone or something else: **[+to]** *Braque **acknowledged** his **debt** to Impressionist painting.*

4 debt of gratitude/thanks the fact of being grateful to someone who has helped you: *I **owe a debt of gratitude** to my tutors.*

COLLOCATIONS

VERBS

have debts *Fortunately, I have no debts.*
run up debts (*also* **amass debts** *formal*) (=borrow more and more money) *At that time he was drinking a lot and running up debts.*
pay off a debt (=pay the money back) *The first thing I'm going to do is pay off my debts.*
repay/settle a debt *formal* (=pay the money back) *He was hoping he would soon have enough money to settle his debts.*
clear your debts (=repay all of them) *It took him three years to clear his bank debts.*
service a debt (=pay the interest on a debt, but not pay it back) *By then, she was borrowing more money just to service her debts.*
write off/cancel a debt (=say officially that it does not have to be paid) *The bank finally agreed to write off the debt.*
be burdened with/saddled with debts (=have big debts) *Many poor countries are saddled with huge debts.*
reduce a debt

ADJECTIVES/NOUN + debt

big/large *The debts got bigger and bigger.*
huge (=very big) *Young people often leave university with huge debts.*
unpaid/outstanding (=not yet paid) *The average outstanding debt on credit cards in Britain is now over £3,000.*
heavy debts (=big debts) *The company wanted to reduce its heavy debts.*
a bad debt (=one that is unlikely to be paid back) *Companies lose millions of pounds each year from having to write off bad debts.*
a bank debt (=one that you owe to a bank) | **the national debt** (=the total amount that is owed by the government of a country)

ˈdebt colˌlector *n* [C] someone whose job is to get back the money that people owe

debt·or /ˈdetə $ -ər/ *n* [C] *technical* a person, group, or organization that owes money OPP **creditor**

ˈdebt reˌlief *n* [U] an arrangement in which very poor countries do not have to pay back all the money that has been lent to them by richer countries

ˈdebt-ˌridden *adj* [usually before noun] debt-ridden countries or organizations owe so much money that they cannot pay the money back

de·bug /ˌdiːˈbʌg/ *v* (**debugged**, **debugging**) [T] **1** to remove the BUGS (=mistakes) from a computer program → **disinfect** **2** to remove secret listening equipment from a place —**debugging** *n* [U]

de·bunk /ˌdiːˈbʌŋk/ *v* [T] to show that an idea or belief is false: *His claims were later debunked by fellow academics.* —**debunker** *n* [C]

de·but¹ /ˈdeɪbjuː, ˈdeb- $ deɪˈbjuː, dɪ-/ ●○○ *n* [C] the first public appearance of an entertainer, sports player etc or of something new and important: **sb's debut** *He **made** his Major League **debut** as shortstop.* | **film/acting/directorial etc debut** *His Broadway debut was 'The Scarlet Pimpernel'.* | **debut album/CD/single etc** *Their debut album was recorded in 1991.* | **debut match/performance etc** *He scored in his debut match for the club.*

debut² *v* **1** [I] to appear in public or become available for the first time: *The show will debut next Monday at 8.00 pm.* **2** [T] to introduce a product to the public for the first time → **release** SYN **launch**: *Ralph Lauren debuted his autumn collection in Paris last week.*

deb·u·tante /ˈdebjʊtɑːnt/ (*also* **deb** *informal*) *n* [C] a young rich UPPER-CLASS woman who starts going to fashionable events as a way of being introduced to upper-class society

Dec. (*also* **Dec** *BrE*) the written abbreviation of ***December***

deca- /dekə/ *prefix* [in nouns] ten: *a decalitre* (=10 litres) | *the decathlon* (=a sports competition with 10 different events) → DECI-

dec·ade /ˈdekeɪd, deˈkeɪd/ ●●● W1 AWL *n* [C] a period of 10 years

dec·a·dence /ˈdekədəns/ *n* [U] behaviour that shows that someone has low moral standards and is more concerned with pleasure than serious matters

dec·a·dent /ˈdekədənt/ *adj* having low moral standards and being more concerned with pleasure than serious matters: *Pop music was condemned as decadent and crude.* —**decadently** *adv*

de·caf, **decaff** /ˈdiːkæf/ *n* [U] *informal* decaffeinated coffee

de·caf·fein·a·ted /diːˈkæfɪneɪtɪd/ *adj* coffee or tea that is decaffeinated does not contain CAFFEINE (=the substance that keeps you awake)

de·cal /ˈdiːkæl, ˈde- $ diːˈkæl, ˈdekəl/ *n* [C] *AmE* a piece of paper with a pattern or picture on it that you stick on a surface SYN **transfer** *BrE*

de·camp /dɪˈkæmp/ *v* [I] *formal* to leave a place quickly: **[+to/from]** *The wealthier inhabitants decamped to the suburbs.*

de·cant /dɪˈkænt/ *v* [T] to pour liquid, especially wine, from one container into another: **decant sth into sth** *Never decant cleaning products into old pop bottles.*

de·cant·er /dɪˈkæntə $ -ər/ *n* [C] a container used for serving alcoholic drinks: *a crystal decanter* → see picture at JUG

de·cap·i·tate /dɪˈkæpɪteɪt/ *v* [T] to cut off someone's head → **behead**: *a decapitated body* —**decapitation** /dɪˌkæpɪˈteɪʃən/ *n* [C,U]

de·cath·lon /dɪˈkæθlɒn, -lən $ -lɑːn, -lən/ *n* [singular] a sports competition with 10 different events → **pentathlon**, **triathlon**

de·cay[1] /dɪˈkeɪ/ ●●○ *v*

1 [I,T] to be slowly destroyed by a natural chemical process, or to make something do this: *Her body was already starting to decay.* | *Most archaeological finds are broken, damaged, or decayed.* | *decaying organic matter*

> REGISTER
> In everyday English, people usually say **rot** rather than **decay** when talking about food: *There was a smell of* ***rotting*** *vegetables.*

2 [I] if buildings, structures, or areas decay, their condition gradually becomes worse: *Hundreds of historic buildings are being allowed to decay.* | *Britain's decaying inner cities*

3 [I] if traditional beliefs, standards etc decay, people do not believe in them or support them anymore SYN **decline**: *In Orthodox Europe, mass religion seems to have decayed less.*

decay[2] ●●○ *n* [U]

1 the natural chemical change that causes the slow destruction of something: *old cars in various* ***stages of decay*** | ***tooth decay***

2 the gradual destruction of buildings, structures etc because they have not been cared for: *poverty and urban decay* | **fall into (a state of) decay** *During the war, the area fell into decay.*

3 the gradual destruction of ideas, beliefs, social or political systems etc: *moral decay*

de·cease /dɪˈsiːs/ *n* [U] *law* death: *On your decease, the house passes to your wife.*

de·ceased /dɪˈsiːst/ ●○○ *n law* **the deceased** someone who has died, especially recently: *The deceased left a large sum of money to his children.*

de·ceit /dɪˈsiːt/ *n* [C,U] behaviour that is intended to make someone believe something that is not true: *an atmosphere of hypocrisy and deceit* | **deliberate/calculated/outright deceit**

de·ceit·ful /dɪˈsiːtfəl/ *adj* someone who is deceitful tells lies in order to get what they want: *His manner was sly and deceitful.* —**deceitfully** *adv*: *His lawyer argued that his client had not* ***acted deceitfully***. —**deceitfulness** *n* [U]

de·ceive /dɪˈsiːv/ ●○○ *v* [T]

1 to make someone believe something that is not true → **deception**: *He had been deceived by a young man claiming to be the son of a millionaire.* | **deceive sb into doing sth** *He tried to deceive the public into thinking the war could still be won.* | **deceive sb about sth** *I wouldn't deceive you about anything as important as this.*

> REGISTER
> In everyday English, people usually say **trick** rather than **deceive**: *She thought they were trying to* ***trick*** *her.*

2 deceive yourself to refuse to believe that something is true because the truth is unpleasant: *I thought she loved me, but I was deceiving myself.* | **deceive yourself that** *He didn't deceive himself that he and Ruth could remain friends.*

3 to give someone a wrong belief or opinion about something: *Don't be deceived by the new cover – this is a rehash of old hits.* —**deceiver** *n* [C]

de·cel·e·rate /ˌdiːˈseləreɪt/ *v* [I] *formal* to go slower, especially in a vehicle SYN **slow down** OPP **accelerate** —**deceleration** /ˌdiːseləˈreɪʃən/ *n* [U]: *a deceleration in economic growth*

De·cem·ber /dɪˈsembə $ -ər/ ●●● S2 W2 *n* [C,U] (*written abbreviation* **Dec.**) the 12th month of the year, between November and January: **next/last December** *Last December they visited Prague.* | **in December** *We got married in December.* | **on December 6th** *Jake's birthday is on December 6th.* | **on 6th December** *BrE*: *The event was to take place on 6th December.* | **December 6** *AmE*: *Her letter arrived December 6.*

de·cen·cy /ˈdiːsənsi/ *n* **1** [U] polite, honest, and moral behaviour and attitudes that show respect for other people: *a judgment reflecting the decency and good sense of the American people* | **common/human/public decency** (=standards of behaviour that are expected of everyone) *The film was banned on the grounds of public decency.* | *Is there no* ***sense of decency*** *left in this country?* | *If they're going to charge people a fee, they ought to at least* ***have the decency to*** *tell them in advance.* **2 decencies** [plural] *old-fashioned* standards of acceptable behaviour

de·cent /ˈdiːsənt/ ●●○ S3 *adj*

1 [usually before noun] of a good enough standard or quality: *a decent salary* | *Don't you have a decent jacket?* | *a house with a* ***decent-sized*** *yard* | *Their in-flight magazine is* ***halfway decent*** (=quite good). THESAURUS ▶ SATISFACTORY

2 following moral standards that are acceptable to society → **decency**: **decent citizens/people/folk etc** *The majority of residents here are decent citizens.* | *a decent burial* | *Paul visited the local bars more frequently than was decent for a senior lecturer.* | *The chairman* ***did the decent thing*** (=did what people thought he ought to) *and resigned.*

3 [usually before noun] treating people in a fair and kind way: *I decided her father was a decent guy after all.* | ***It was decent of*** *you to show up today.*

4 wearing enough clothes so that you do not show too much of your body – used humorously: *Are you decent? Can I come in?* —**decently** *adv*

de·cen·tral·ize (*also* **-ise** *BrE*) /ˌdiːˈsentrəlaɪz/ *v* [I,T] to move parts of a government, organization etc from a central place to several different smaller ones OPP **centralize**: *Many firms are decentralizing their operations.* —**decentralized** *adj*: *a decentralized economy* —**decentralization** /diːˌsentrəlaɪˈzeɪʃən $ -lə-/ *n* [U]

de·cep·tion /dɪˈsepʃən/ ●○○ *n* [C,U] the act of deliberately making someone believe something that is not true → **deceive**: *She didn't have the courage to admit to her deception.* | *He was convicted of* ***obtaining money by deception***.

de·cep·tive /dɪˈseptɪv/ *adj* **1** something that is deceptive seems to be one thing but is in fact very different: *Some snakes move with deceptive speed* (=move faster

D

than you think or expect). | *Gwen's students may look angelic, but* ***appearances can be deceptive.*** **2** intended to make someone believe something that is not true: *misleading and deceptive adverts* | *deceptive practices* —**deceptively** *adv*

deci- /desɪ/ *prefix* [in nouns] a 10th part of a unit: *a decilitre* (=0.1 litres) → DECA-

dec·i·bel /ˈdesəbel, -bəl/ *n* [C] (*written abbreviation* **dB**) a unit for measuring the loudness of sound: *noise levels exceeding 85 decibels*

de·cide /dɪˈsaɪd/ ●●● S1 W1 *v*

1 [I,T] to make a choice or judgment about something, especially after considering all the possibilities or arguments → **decision**: *Has anything been decided yet?* | **decide to do sth** *Tina's decided to go to Rome for her holidays.* | **decide (that)** *It was decided that four hospitals should close.* | **decide who/what/whether etc** *I can't decide whether I like him or not.* | *People have a right to decide how to spend their own money.* | **decide between sth** *A meeting was called to decide between the three candidates.* | **decide for yourself** (=make your own decision) *You must decide for yourself.* | *The trainees decide among themselves what programs to take.* | **decide against/in favour of (doing) sth** *He eventually decided against telling her.* | *After a long discussion, they decided in favour of* (=chose) *the older applicant.*

GRAMMAR

In more formal English, you can say **it is decided that** something should be done: *It was decided that he should resign.*

2 [T] to influence a situation or event so that a particular result is produced: *It was the penalty kick that decided the match.*

3 [T] to be the reason for someone making a particular choice: *Taxes could be* ***the deciding factor*** *for millions of floating voters.* | **decide sb to do sth** *The look he gave her decided her not to ask.*

4 [I,T] *law* to make an official or legal judgment: *The Commission will have the power to decide disputes.* | **decide in favour of/against sb** *If the Parole Board decides in his favour, the prisoner will be released.*

decide on/upon sth *phr v* to choose something or someone after thinking carefully: *Have you decided on a date for the wedding?*

THESAURUS

decide to make a choice to do something: *We decided to send our son to a boarding school.* | *I decided to go home early.*

make up your mind to decide something, especially after thinking about it for a long time. **Make up your mind** is less formal than **decide** and is mainly used in spoken English: *Have you made up your mind about where you'll go on holiday?*

choose to do sth to decide to do something – especially when this is different from what people expect or tell you to do: *She chose to ignore my advice.* | *More young couples are choosing not to marry.*

make a decision to decide after thinking carefully about something, especially about something that is very important: *They made a decision not to have children.*

resolve *formal* to decide that you will definitely do something, especially because you think it will be better for you, or because of your past experiences: *She resolved to work hard at school.*

determine *formal* to officially decide what something shall be: *Each hospital can determine its own pay rates.*

come down in favour of sth *BrE*, **come down in favor of sth** *AmE* to decide to support a particular plan, argument etc – used especially about groups of people: *Eight of the ten committee members came down in favour of the changes.*

come to/reach a decision to officially decide about something important after discussing and carefully considering it – used especially about groups of people: *After two hours of discussion, the committee had still not come to a decision on any of the proposals.*

de·cid·ed /dɪˈsaɪdɪd/ *adj* [only before noun] *formal* definite and easily noticed: *a decided change for the better*

de·cid·ed·ly /dɪˈsaɪdɪdli/ ●○○ *adv*

1 [+adj/adv] definitely or in a way that is easily noticed: *Cole's style is decidedly more formal than the previous manager's.*

2 *BrE written* in a way that shows that you are very sure about a decision: *'I'm not going to do it,' said Margaret decidedly.*

de·cid·er /dɪˈsaɪdə $ -ər/ *n* [C usually singular] the last part of a game or competition, which will show who the winner is: *This next round will be the decider.*

de·cid·u·ous /dɪˈsɪdʒuəs/ *adj* deciduous trees lose their leaves in winter OPP **evergreen**

dec·i·mal¹ /ˈdesəməl/ *n* [C] a FRACTION (=a number less than 1) that is shown as a FULL STOP followed by the number of TENTHS, HUNDREDTHS etc. The numbers 0.5, 0.175, and 0.661 are decimals.

decimal² *adj* a decimal system is based on the number 10: *changing to a decimal system* | *calculations accurate to three* ***decimal places*** (=one of the numbers after the full stop in a decimal)

dec·i·mal·ization (*also* **-isation** *BrE*) /ˌdesəməlaɪˈzeɪʃən $ ˌdesəmələ-/ *n* [U] the process of changing to a decimal system of money or measurement —**decimalize** /ˈdesəməlaɪz $ ˈdesəmə-/ *v* [I,T]

ˌdecimal ˈpoint *n* [C] the FULL STOP in a decimal, used to separate whole numbers from TENTHS, HUNDREDTHS etc

dec·i·mate /ˈdesɪmeɪt/ *v* [T] to destroy a large part of something: *The population has been decimated by disease.* —**decimation** /ˌdesəˈmeɪʃən/ *n* [U]

de·ci·pher /dɪˈsaɪfə $ -ər/ *v* [T] **1** to find the meaning of something that is difficult to read or understand → **indecipherable**: *She studied the envelope, trying to decipher the handwriting.* **2** to change a message written in a CODE into ordinary language so that you can read it SYN **decode** —**decipherment** *n* [U]

de·ci·sion /dɪˈsɪʒən/ ●●● S1 W1 *n*

1 [C] a choice or judgment that you make after a period of discussion or thought: *Do you ever wonder if you made the right decision?* | **decision to do sth** *She refused to discuss her decision to quit the group.* | **[+about/on]** *We finally came to a firm decision on the matter.* | **[+as to which/whether/who etc]** *Viewers make the final decision as to who should be eliminated from the competition.* | *The judges'* ***decision*** *is* ***final*** (=it will not be changed).

2 [U] the quality someone has that makes them able to make choices or judgments quickly and confidently OPP **indecision**: *the ability to act with speed and decision*

3 [U] the act of deciding something: *The Court has the ultimate power of decision.*

COLLOCATIONS

VERBS

make a decision *I want to think about it a bit longer before I make a decision.*

take a decision *BrE* (=make an important or formal decision) *I fully accept the decision taken by the committee.*

reach/come to/arrive at a decision (=make a decision after a lot of thought) *We hope they will reach their decision as soon as possible.*

regret a decision (=wish you had not made a particular decision) *I was already regretting my decision to go on holiday with him.*

reconsider a decision (=think about changing a decision you have made) *He said he wasn't prepared to reconsider his decision.*

reverse a decision (=change a decision) *They want him to reverse his decision to quit.*

overrule/overturn a decision (=officially change a decision by another person or group) *A director of the company had overruled that decision.*

postpone a decision (=not make a decision until later) *The government has postponed its decision about when to hold the election.*

ADJECTIVES

an important decision *My father made all the important decisions.*
a big decision (=an important decision) *Marriage is a big decision.*
a major decision (=very important) *The government now has some major decisions to make.*
a difficult/hard/tough decision *In the end I took the difficult decision to retire early.*
a good decision *It was a good decision to change the name of the product.*
a bad decision *I think he made a bad decision.*
the right decision *She chose to study Engineering and it was definitely the right decision.*
the wrong decision *I thought I'd made the wrong decision marrying Jeff.*
a conscious/deliberate decision (=one that you have thought about clearly) *Belinda had made a conscious decision to have a baby.*
a clear/firm decision (=a definite one) *It's now time to come to a clear decision on this.*
a final decision (=one that will not be changed) *The council will make a final decision in four months.*
a snap decision (=one that you make extremely quickly) *Police officers often have to make snap decisions on how to act.*
a controversial decision (=that people disagree about) *The history of the law is full of controversial decisions.*
a hasty decision (=one that you make without enough thought) *Don't let yourself be forced into making hasty decisions.*
a joint decision (=one that two people make together) *Jo and I made a joint decision that we should separate.*

de'cision-ˌmaker *n* [C usually plural] a person in a large organization who is responsible for making important decisions: *the corporation's key decision-makers*

de'cision-ˌmaking *n* [U] the process of making important decisions: *attempts to involve workers in decision-making*

de·ci·sive /dɪˈsaɪsɪv/ ●○○ *adj*
1 an action, event etc that is decisive has a big effect on the way that something develops: **decisive factor/effect/influence etc** *Women can **play a decisive role** in the debate over cloning.* | **decisive action/steps** *We will **take decisive steps** towards political union with Europe.*
2 someone who is decisive is good at making decisions quickly and with confidence OPP **indecisive**: *a decisive leader* | *a talent for quick **decisive action***
3 definite and clear in a way that leaves no doubt OPP **indecisive**: **decisive victory/result/defeat etc** | *The answer was a decisive no.* —**decisively** *adv*: *Yet again, we have failed to **act decisively**.* —**decisiveness** *n* [U]: *military decisiveness* | *the speed and decisiveness of his victory*

deck[1] /dek/ ●●● S3 *n* [C]
1 ON A SHIP **a)** the outside top level of a ship that you can walk or sit on: *Let's **go up on deck**.* | **above/below deck** *Peter stayed below deck.* **b)** one of the different levels on a ship: **main/passenger/car etc deck** *a staircase leading to the passenger deck* THESAURUS ▸ FLOOR
2 ON A BUS, PLANE ETC one of the levels on a bus, plane etc: **lower/upper etc deck** *I managed to find a seat on the upper deck.* | *Eddie returned to the **flight deck*** (=the part of an aircraft where the pilot sits). → DOUBLE-DECKER(1), SINGLE-DECKER
3 AT THE BACK OF A HOUSE *AmE* a wooden floor built out from the back of a house, where you can sit and relax outdoors → **decking**: *deck furniture*
4 MUSIC a piece of equipment used for playing music tapes, records etc: **cassette/tape/record deck**
5 CARDS a set of playing cards SYN **pack** *BrE*: *Irene shuffled the deck.* | *a **deck of cards*** → **all hands on deck** at HAND[1](39), → **clear the decks** at CLEAR[2](17), → **hit the deck** at HIT[1](17)

deck[2] *v* [T] **1** (*also* **deck sth out**) to decorate something with flowers, flags etc: **be decked (out) with sth** *The street was decked with flags for the royal wedding.* GRAMMAR **Deck** is usually passive in this meaning. **2** *informal* to hit someone so hard that they fall over: *Gerry just swung round and decked him.*

deck·chair /ˈdektʃeə $ -tʃer/ *n* [C] *BrE* a folding chair with a long seat made of cloth, used especially on the beach → see picture at CHAIR[1]

deck·hand /ˈdekhænd/ *n* [C] someone who works on a ship, cleaning and doing small repairs

deck·ing /ˈdekɪŋ/ *n* [U] a wooden floor next to a house or in a garden

'deck shoe *n* [C] a flat shoe made of CANVAS (=heavy cloth)

de·claim /dɪˈkleɪm/ *v* [I,T] *written* to speak loudly, sometimes with actions, so that people notice you —**declamation** /ˌdekləˈmeɪʃən/ *n* [C,U]

de·clam·a·to·ry /dɪˈklæmətəri $ -tɔːri/ *adj* declamatory speech or writing expresses feelings and opinions very strongly: *a declamatory style*

dec·la·ra·tion /ˌdekləˈreɪʃən/ ●●○ *n* [C,U]
1 an important official statement about a particular situation or plan, or the act of making this statement: *a ceasefire declaration* | *Under Islamic law it was possible to divorce by simple declaration.* | **[+of]** *the declaration of war*
2 an official or serious statement of what someone believes: **[+of]** *the United Nations Declaration of Human Rights* | *declarations of undying love*
3 a statement in which you officially give information about yourself: *a declaration of taxable earnings*

de·clar·a·tive /dɪˈklærətɪv/ *adj* a declarative sentence has the form of a statement

de·clare /dɪˈkleə $ -ˈkler/ ●●○ W2 *v*
1 STATE OFFICIALLY [T] to state officially and publicly that a particular situation exists or that something is true: *A state of emergency has been declared.* | **declare that** *The court declared that Brown's case should be reviewed.* | **declare sb/sth (to be) sb/sth** *Several countries wanted Antarctica to be declared a 'world park'.* | *The city was declared to be in a state of siege.* | *I declare you man and wife.* | **declare sth illegal/invalid etc** *The war was declared illegal by the International Court of Justice.* | *Mr Steel has been **declared bankrupt*** (=it has been officially stated that he cannot pay his debts). | *We celebrate September 16, the day when Mexico **declared independence** from Spain* (=officially stated that it was no longer ruled by Spain). THESAURUS ▸ SAY
2 STATE WHAT YOU THINK [T] to say publicly what you think or feel: *'It's not fair,' Jane declared.* | *He **declared** his **intention** to stand for president.* | **declare that** *Carol held a press conference and declared that she was innocent.* | **declare yourself (to be) sth** *Edward declared himself angry and frustrated.*
3 declare war (on sb/sth) a) to state officially that you are at war with another country **b)** *informal* to say that something is wrong and that you will do everything you can to stop it: *Angry residents have declared war on the owners of the factory.*
4 MONEY/PROPERTY ETC [T] **a)** to state on an official government form how much money you have earned, what property you own etc: *All tips are counted as part of your earnings and must be declared.* **b)** to tell a CUSTOMS official that you are carrying goods on which you should pay tax when you enter a country
5 declare an interest to tell people that you are connected with something that is being discussed: *I should, at this point, declare an interest: I own shares in the company.*
6 CRICKET [I] to choose to end your team's turn before all your players have BATTED

declare against sb/sth *phr v* to state publicly that you oppose someone or something

D

declare for sb/sth *phr v* to state publicly that you support someone or something

de·clared /dɪˈkleəd $ -ˈklerd/ *adj* stated officially and publicly: **declared aim/objective/intention etc** *It is their declared intention to increase taxes.*

de·clas·si·fied /ˌdiːˈklæsɪfaɪd/ *adj* official information that is declassified was secret but is not secret anymore → **classified** —**declassify** *v* [T]

de·clen·sion /dɪˈklenʃən/ *n* [C] **1** the set of various forms that a noun, PRONOUN, or adjective can have according to whether it is the SUBJECT, OBJECT etc of a sentence in a language such as Latin or German **2** a particular set of nouns etc that all have the same set of forms

de·cline¹ /dɪˈklaɪn/ ●●○ W3 AWL *n* [singular, U] a decrease in the quality, quantity, or importance of something: **[+in]** *There has been a decline in the size of families.* | **[+of]** *the decline of manufacturing* | **rapid/sharp/steep/dramatic decline** *a rapid decline in unemployment* | **steady/gradual/long-term decline** *The island's population initially numbered 180, but there was a gradual decline until only 40 people were left.* | *the* ***economic decline*** *faced by many cities* | **in decline/on the decline** (=falling) *the widely held belief that educational standards are in decline* | **fall/go etc into decline** (=become less important, successful etc) *The port fell into decline in the 1950s.*

decline² ●●○ W3 AWL *v*

1 DECREASE [I] to decrease in quantity or importance: *Spending on information technology has declined.* | *Car sales have declined by a quarter.* | *After the war, the city declined in importance.* THESAURUS DECREASE

2 SAY NO [I,T] *formal* to say no politely when someone invites you somewhere, offers you something, or wants you to do something: *Offered the position of chairman, Smith declined, preferring to keep his current job.* | *Mary declined a hot drink and went to her room.* | **decline an offer/invitation etc** *Mary declined Jay's invitation to dinner.* | **decline to do sth** *The court declined to review her case.* | *The minister* ***declined to comment*** (=refused to speak to people who report the news) *about the progress of the peace talks.* THESAURUS REFUSE

3 BECOME WORSE [I] to become gradually worse in quality SYN **deteriorate**: *Her health has been declining progressively for several months.* | *Qualified staff are leaving and standards are declining.*

4 sb's declining years *formal* the last years of someone's life

5 GRAMMAR **a)** [I] if a noun, PRONOUN, or adjective declines, its form changes according to whether it is the SUBJECT, OBJECT etc of a sentence **b)** [T] if you decline a noun, PRONOUN, or adjective, you show the various forms that it can take —**declining** *adj*: *declining attendance at baseball games*

de·clut·ter /diːˈklʌtə $ -ər/ *v* [I,T] to make a place tidy by removing things you do not want or need: *I decided it was time to declutter my bedroom.*

de·code /ˌdiːˈkəʊd $ -ˈkoʊd/ *v* [T] **1** to discover the meaning of a message written in a CODE (=a set of secret signs or letters) SYN **decipher 2** if a computer decodes DATA, it receives it and changes it into a form that can be used by the computer or understood by a person OPP **encode**: *The software decodes the information embedded in the satellite broadcasts.* **3** to receive electronic or DIGITAL signals and change them into a picture and sound for a television or radio OPP **encode**: *decoding boxes for your TV set* **4** *technical* to understand the meaning of a word OPP **encode**

de·cod·er /diːˈkəʊdə $ -ˈkoʊdər/ *n* [C] a piece of electronic equipment that receives a signal and changes it for another machine to use, for example to put pictures and sound onto your television

dé·colle·tage /ˌdeɪkɒlˈtɑːʒ $ deɪˌkɑːləˈtɑːʒ/ *n* [U] the top edge of a woman's dress that is cut very low to show part of her shoulders and breasts —**décolleté** /deɪˈkɒlteɪ $ ˌdeɪkɑːləˈteɪ/ *adj*

de·col·o·nize (*also* **-ise** *BrE*) /ˌdiːˈkɒlənaɪz $ -ˈkɑː-/ *v* [T] to make a former COLONY politically independent —**decolonization** /diːˌkɒlənaɪˈzeɪʃən $ -ˌkɑːlənə-/ *n* [U]

de·com·miss·ion /ˌdiːkəˈmɪʃən/ *v* [T] to stop using a ship, weapon, or NUCLEAR REACTOR and to take it to pieces

de·com·pose /ˌdiːkəmˈpəʊz $ -ˈpoʊz/ *v* [I,T] **1** to decay or make something decay: *a partially decomposed body* **2** *technical* to divide into smaller parts, or to make something do this —**decomposition** /ˌdiːkɒmpəˈzɪʃən $ -kɑːm-/ *n* [U]

de·com·press /ˌdiːkəmˈpres/ *v* [T] **1** to reduce the pressure of air on something **2** *technical* to change the information in a computer document back into a form that can be easily read or used, when the information was stored on the computer in a special form that used less space in the computer's memory: *Most Macintosh computers can decompress files automatically.* —**decompression** /-ˈpreʃən/ *n* [U]

ˌdecomˈpression ˌchamber *n* [C] a special room where people go after they have been deep under the sea, so that their bodies can slowly return to normal air pressure

ˌdecomˈpression ˌsickness *n* [U] a dangerous medical condition that people get when they come up from deep under the sea too quickly SYN **the bends**

de·con·gest·ant /ˌdiːkənˈdʒestənt◂/ *n* [C,U] medicine that you can take if you have a cold, to help you breathe more easily

de·con·struc·tion /ˌdiːkənˈstrʌkʃən/ *n* [U] a method used in PHILOSOPHY and the criticism of literature which claims that there is no single explanation of the meaning of a piece of writing —**deconstruct** /-ˈstrʌkt/ *v* [T]

de·con·tam·i·nate /ˌdiːkənˈtæməneɪt/ *v* [T] to remove a dangerous substance from somewhere → **contamination**, **contaminate**: *It may cost over $5 million to decontaminate the whole site.* —**decontamination** /ˌdiːkəntæməˈneɪʃən/ *n* [U]

de·cor /ˈdeɪkɔː $ -kɔːr/ *n* [C usually singular, U] the way that the inside of a building is decorated: *The decor is a mix of antique and modern.*

DECORATE

decorating the home | decorating the Christmas tree

dec·o·rate /ˈdekəreɪt/ ●●○ *v*

1 [I,T] *BrE* to paint the inside of a room, put special paper on the walls etc: *The bathroom is decorated in green and yellow.* | *We plan to spend the weekend decorating.*

2 [T] to make something look more attractive by putting something pretty on it: *Children's pictures decorated the walls of the classroom.* | **decorate sth with sth** *an old-fashioned dress decorated with ribbons and lace*

3 [T] to give someone a MEDAL as an official sign of honour: **decorate sb for sth** *soldiers* ***decorated for bravery*** —**decorating** *n* [U]

dec·o·ra·tion /ˌdekəˈreɪʃən/ ●●○ *n*

1 [C usually plural] something pretty that you put in a place or on top of something to make it look attractive: *Christmas decorations* | *cake decorations*

2 [U] the style in which something is decorated: *He is an expert on Islamic decoration.* | **for decoration** *a box with paper flowers glued to it for decoration*

3 [U] *BrE* when you paint or put special paper on the inside walls, ceiling etc of a house or building
4 [C] something such as a MEDAL that is given to someone as an official sign of honour

dec·o·ra·tive /ˈdekərətɪv $ ˈdekərə-, ˈdekəreɪ-/ ●○○ *adj* pretty or attractive, but not always necessary or useful: *a decorative panel above the door* —**decoratively** *adv*

dec·o·ra·tor /ˈdekəreɪtə $ -ər/ *n* [C] *especially BrE* someone who paints houses and puts paper on the walls as their job

dec·o·rous /ˈdekərəs/ *adj formal* having the correct appearance or behaviour for a particular occasion —**decorously** *adv*: *A servant was hovering decorously behind them.*

de·co·rum /dɪˈkɔːrəm/ *n* [U] *formal* behaviour that shows respect and is correct for a particular situation, especially a formal occasion: *He was disciplined for breaching the Senate's rules of decorum.*

de·coy /ˈdiːkɔɪ/ *n* [C] **1** someone or something that is used to trick someone into going somewhere or doing something, so that you can catch them, attack them etc: *Officer Langley acted as a decoy to catch the rapist.* **2** a model of a bird used to attract wild birds so that you can watch them or shoot them —**decoy** /dɪˈkɔɪ/ *v* [T]

de·crease¹ /dɪˈkriːs/ ●●○ *v* [I,T] to become less or go down to a lower level, or to make something do this → **reduce** OPP **increase**: *The number of people who have the disease has* ***decreased significantly*** *in recent years.* | *They want to decrease their reliance on oil.* | **[+by]** *Average house prices decreased by 13% last year.* | **[+to]** *By 1881, the population of Ireland had decreased to 5.2 million.* | **[+from]** *The North's share of the world's energy consumption is expected to decrease from 70% to 60%.* | **[+in]** *Attacks of asthma decrease in frequency through early adult life.*

GRAMMAR

Decrease belongs to a group of verbs where the same noun can be the subject of the verb or its object.
- You can say: *They decreased the number of buses.* In this sentence, 'the number of buses' is the object of **decrease**.
- You can say: *The number of buses decreased.* In this sentence, 'the number of buses' is the subject of **decrease**.

GRAMMAR GUIDE ▸ VERBS

THESAURUS

decrease to become less in number or amount: *The average rainfall has decreased by around 30 percent.*
go down to decrease. **Go down** is less formal than **decrease** and is the usual word to use in conversation: *Unemployment has gone down in the past few months.*
decline *formal* to decrease – used with numbers or amounts, or about the level or standard of something: *The standard of living has declined.* | *Support for the government is steadily declining.* | *Salaries have declined by around 4.5%.*
diminish to become smaller or less important: *Union membership diminished from 30,000 at its height to just 2,000 today.*
fall/drop to decrease, especially by a large amount. **Fall** and **drop** are less formal than **decrease**: *The number of tigers in the wild has fallen to just over 10,000.* | *At night, the temperature drops to minus 20 degrees.*
plunge /plʌndʒ/, **plummet** /ˈplʌmət/ to suddenly decrease very quickly and by a very large amount: *Share prices have plummeted 29% in the last four months.* | *Climate change could cause global temperatures to plummet.*
slide if a price or value slides, it gradually decreases in a way that causes problems – used especially in news reports: *The dollar fell in late trading in New York yesterday and slid further this morning.*
dwindle /ˈdwɪndl/ to gradually decrease until there is very little left of something, especially numbers or amounts, popularity, or importance: *Support for the theory is dwindling.*
taper off /ˈteɪpə $ -ər/ if a number or the amount of an activity that is happening tapers off, it gradually decreases, especially so that it stops completely: *Political violence tapered off after the elections.*

de·crease² /ˈdiːkriːs/ ●●○ *n* [C,U] the process of becoming less, or the amount by which something becomes less OPP **increase** SYN **reduction**: **a decrease in sth** *Teachers reported decreases in drug use and verbal abuse of teachers.* | **a decrease of 50/5% etc** *There has been a decrease of 1 degree in average temperature.*

de·cree¹ /dɪˈkriː/ ●○○ *n* [C]
1 an official order or decision, especially one made by the ruler of a country: *The Emperor* ***issued*** *the* ***decree*** *repealing martial law.*
2 a judgment in a court of law

decree² *v* [T] to make an official judgment or give an official order: **decree (that)** *The King decreed that there should be an end to the fighting.*

de,cree 'absolute *n* [singular] *BrE* an order by a court of law which officially ends a marriage

decree ni·si /dɪˌkriː ˈnaɪsaɪ/ *n* [singular] *BrE* an order by a court of law that a marriage will end at a particular time in the future unless there is a good reason not to end it

de·crep·it /dɪˈkrepɪt/ *adj* old and in bad condition: *The buildings were in a decrepit state.* | *He was a rather decrepit old man.* —**decrepitude** *n* [U]

de·crim·in·a·lize (*also* **-ise** *BrE*) /diːˈkrɪmənəlaɪz/ *v* [T] to state officially that something is not illegal anymore: *a campaign to decriminalize cannabis* —**decriminalization** /diːˌkrɪmənəlaɪˈzeɪʃən $ -lə-/ *n* [U]

de·cry /dɪˈkraɪ/ *v* (**decried**, **decrying**, **decries**) [T] *formal* to state publicly that you do not approve of something SYN **condemn**

de·crypt /diːˈkrɪpt/ *v* [T] to change a message or information on a computer back into a form that can be read, when someone has sent it to you in a type of computer CODE → **encrypt**: *Only certain employees will be able to decrypt sensitive documents.* —**decryption** /diːˈkrɪpʃən/ *n* [U]

ded·i·cate /ˈdedɪkeɪt/ ●○○ *v* [T]
1 to give all your attention and effort to one particular thing: **dedicate yourself/your life to sth** *The actress now dedicates herself to children's charity work.*
2 to say at the beginning of a book or film, or before a piece of music, that it has been written, made, or performed for someone that you love or respect: **dedicate sth to sb** *The book was dedicated to her husband.*
3 to state in an official ceremony that a building will be given someone's name in order to show respect for them
4 to use a place, time, money etc only for a particular purpose: **dedicate sth to/for sth** *The company dedicated $50,000 for the study.*

ded·i·cat·ed /ˈdedɪkeɪtɪd/ ●○○ *adj*
1 someone who is dedicated works very hard at what they do because they care a lot about it: *a dedicated and thoughtful teacher* | *She is a dedicated socialist.* | **[+to]** *The Woodland Trust is dedicated to preserving our native woodland.*
2 [only before noun] made for or used for only one particular purpose: *a dedicated graphics processor*

ded·i·ca·tion /ˌdedɪˈkeɪʃən/ ●○○ *n*
1 [U] hard work or effort that someone puts into a particular activity because they care about it a lot: *To reach a high level of skill requires talent, dedication, and a lot of hard work.* | **[+to]** *I admire his dedication to the job.*
2 [C] an act of dedicating something to someone, or a ceremony where this is done
3 [C] the words used at the beginning of a book, film, or piece of music, thanking someone or saying that book etc has been written to show respect for them

D

de·duce /dɪˈdjuːs $ dɪˈduːs/ ●○○ AWL *v* [T] *formal* to use the knowledge and information you have in order to understand something or form an opinion about it: **deduce that** *From her son's age, I deduced that her husband must be at least 60.* | **[+from]** *What did Darwin deduce from the presence of these species?* —**deducible** *adj*

de·duct /dɪˈdʌkt/ ●○○ *v* [T] to take away an amount or part from a total SYN **subtract**: **deduct sth from sth** *The payments will be deducted from your salary.* —**deductible** *adj*: *Interest charges are* ***tax deductible***.

de·duc·tion /dɪˈdʌkʃən/ ●○○ AWL *n* [C,U]
1 the process of using the knowledge or information you have in order to understand something or form an opinion, or the opinion that you form: *Children will soon* ***make deductions*** *about the meaning of a word.*
2 the process of taking away an amount from a total, or the amount that is taken away: *After deductions for tax etc, your salary is about £700 a month.*

de·duc·tive /dɪˈdʌktɪv/ *adj* using the knowledge and information you have in order to understand or form an opinion about something: *deductive reasoning*

deed /diːd/ ●○○ *n* [C]
1 *formal* something someone does, especially something that is very good or very bad: *After the morning's* ***good deeds*** *he deserved a rest.* | *She tried to strangle her baby and her lover helped her finish the* ***evil deed***.
2 *law* an official paper that is a record of an agreement, especially an agreement concerning who owns property: *a mortgage deed*
3 in deed in what you do: *Everyone sins at some time, in thought if not in deed.*
4 your good deed for the day something kind or helpful that you do – used humorously

ˈdeed poll *n* [C,U] a legal document signed by only one person, for example in order to officially change your name: *Steve* ***changed*** *his* ***name by deed poll*** *to Elvis Presley-Smith.*

dee·jay /ˈdiːdʒeɪ/ *n* [C] *informal* a DISC JOCKEY —**deejay** *v* [I]

deem /diːm/ ●○○ *v* [T] *formal* to think of something in a particular way or as having a particular quality SYN **consider**: **deem that** *They deemed that he was no longer capable of managing the business.* | **deem sth necessary/appropriate etc** *They were told to take whatever action they deemed necessary.* | **be deemed to be sth** *They were deemed to be illegal immigrants.* | **be deemed to do sth** *UK plans were deemed to infringe EU law.*

deep¹ /diːp/ ●●● S2 W1 *adj* (*comparative* **deeper**, *superlative* **deepest**)
1 GOING FAR DOWN **a)** going far down from the top or from the surface OPP **shallow**: *The castle is on an island surrounded by a deep lake.* | *The swimming pool has a deep end and a shallow end for kids.* | *We'll take the boat out into* ***deep water*** *where we can dive.* | *a deep narrow valley* **b)** you use deep to say what distance something goes down from the top or surface: **2 metres/6 feet etc deep** *Dig a hole around 12 inches deep.* | **ankle-deep/waist-deep etc** *In places, the snow was waist-deep* (=deep enough to reach a person's waist). → KNEE-DEEP
2 GOING FAR IN going far in from the outside or from the front edge of something: *a deep wound* | *She was sitting in a deep leather chair.*
3 SERIOUS serious or severe: *Despite the peace process, there are deep divisions in the community.* | *The country is in a deep recession.* | *Evan will* ***be in deep trouble*** *if he is caught.*
4 BREATH a deep breath or SIGH is one in which you breathe a lot of air in or out: *She stopped and took a* ***deep breath***. | *Tom gave a deep sigh of relief.*
5 FEELING/BELIEF a deep feeling, belief etc is very strong and sincere SYN **profound**: *May I express my deepest sympathy.* | *The letters show her deep affection for him.* | *He has a deep understanding of the environment.*
6 SOUND a deep sound is very low: *Her laugh was deep and loud.* | *I love that deep bass line.*
7 COLOUR a deep colour is dark and strong OPP **light, pale**: *She gazed at him with wide deep blue eyes.* | *The berries are a deep red colour.* THESAURUS ▸ COLOUR
8 DIFFICULT TO UNDERSTAND important but complicated or difficult to understand: *These problems are too deep for me.* | *There is a deep issue of principle involved.*
9 SLEEP if someone is in a deep sleep, it is difficult to wake them: *He lay down and* ***fell into*** *a* ***deep sleep***.
10 deep in thought/conversation etc thinking so hard or paying attention to something so much that you do not notice anything else that is happening around you
11 deep in debt owing a lot of money
12 a deep impression a strong effect or influence that remains for a long time: *What he said* ***made a deep impression on*** *me.*
13 PERSON a deep person is serious and intelligent, but is hard to know well: *Henry has always been a* ***deep one***. *He keeps his views to himself.*
14 be in deep shit *spoken not polite* to be in a bad situation because of something you have done
15 be in deep water to be in trouble or in a difficult or serious situation: *The company is in deep water over their refusal to reduce prices.*
16 BALL GAMES a deep ball is hit, thrown, or kicked to a far part of the sports field
17 jump/be thrown in at the deep end to choose to do or be made to do a very difficult job without having prepared for it: *She decided to jump in at the deep end, buy a farm, and teach herself.*
18 go off at the deep end *informal* to become angry suddenly and violently, usually when there is not a good reason

deep² ●●● W3 *adv*
1 [always + adv/prep] a long way into or below the surface of something: *Some bones were hidden deep beneath the ground.* | *The tunnel led deep under the mountains.* | *We were deep in a tropical rainforest* (=far from the edge of the forest). | *Tom stared deep into her eyes.* | *They talked deep into the night* (=very late).
2 deep down a) if you know or feel something deep down, you secretly know or feel it even though you do not admit it: *He knew, deep down, that he would have to apologise.* **b)** if someone is good, evil etc deep down, that is what they are really like even though they usually hide it: *Deep down, she is a caring person.*
3 two/three etc deep if things or people are two deep, three deep etc, there are two, three etc rows or layers of things or people: *People were standing four deep at the bar.*
4 run/go deep if a feeling such as hatred or anger runs deep in someone, they feel it very strongly, especially because of something that has happened in the past: *The prejudice runs deep and we need to understand the fears behind it.*
5 be in (too) deep *informal* to be very involved in a situation, especially so that it causes you problems → **still waters run deep** at STILL²(5)

deep³ *n* **the deep** *literary* the sea THESAURUS ▸ COLOUR

deep ˈclean *n* [C] an extremely thorough clean of a place, especially a thorough clean of a hospital in order to reduce infection —**deep clean** *v* [T] —**deep cleaning** *n* [U]

deep·en /ˈdiːpən/ ●●○ *v*
1 GET WORSE [I] if a serious situation deepens, it gets worse – used especially in news reports: *The recession continues to deepen.* | *a deepening international crisis*
2 BECOME STRONGER [I,T] to become stronger or greater, or to make something stronger or greater: *Jeanne liked Simon as a friend but she did not want the relationship to deepen.* | *The idea only deepened his gloom.* | *The mystery deepened* (=became even more mysterious). | *Students explore new ideas as they deepen their understanding* (=understand more) *of the subject.*
3 EXPRESSION ON SB'S FACE [I] *literary* if someone's smile or FROWN deepens, they smile even more or frown even more: *Her worried frown deepened.*

4 WATER [I,T] if water deepens, or if someone deepens it, it becomes deeper: *The river deepens beyond the town.* | *The harbour was deepened to take bigger boats.*
5 COLOUR [I] *literary* if light or a colour deepens, it becomes darker: *The twilight deepened.*
6 SOUND [I] if a sound deepens, it becomes lower: *His voice deepened as he relaxed.*
7 BREATH [I] if your breathing deepens, you take more air into your lungs

ˌdeep ˈfreeze / $ '../ *n* [C] a large metal box in which food can be stored at very low temperatures for a long time SYN **freezer**

ˈdeep fry *v* [T] to cook food under the surface of hot fat or oil

deep·ly /ˈdiːpli/ ●●● W3 *adv*
1 used to emphasize that a belief, feeling, opinion etc is very strong, important, or sincere: *Her lies hurt my father deeply.* | *She is deeply upset.* | *He loves her deeply.* | *Teachers are deeply divided on this issue.* | ***deeply held** religious beliefs*
2 in a serious, careful way: *Most doctors **think deeply** about what their patients want.*
3 a long way into something: **[+into]** *John kept sinking more deeply into the mud.*
4 breathe deeply to take a large breath of air into your lungs
5 sleep deeply to be in a deep sleep, from which it is hard to wake up

ˌdeep-ˈrooted (*also* **ˌdeeply ˈrooted**) *adj* a deep-rooted habit, idea, belief etc is so strong in a person or society that it is very difficult to change or destroy it → **deep-seated**: *a deep-rooted suspicion of lawyers*

ˈdeep-sea *adj* [only before noun] deep-sea fishing or DIVING is done in the deep part of the sea, far away from land

ˌdeep-ˈseated *adj* a deep-seated attitude, feeling, or idea is strong and is very difficult to change → **deep-rooted**: *a deep-seated fear of failure*

ˌdeep-ˈset *adj* deep-set eyes seem to be further back into the face than most people's

ˌdeep ˈsix *v* [T] *AmE informal* to decide not to use something such as a plan

ˌdeep vein thromˈbosis *n* [U] *medical* (*abbreviation* **DVT**) a serious illness which happens when a small amount of blood becomes very thick and causes the heart to stop beating properly. This sometimes happens to people who have been on long plane journeys, because they have been sitting still for so long

ˌdeep ˈWeb *n* [singular] information available on the Internet that SEARCH ENGINES do not find

deer /dɪə $ dɪr/ ●●○ *n* (*plural* **deer**) [C] a large wild animal that can run very fast, eats grass, and has horns

deer·stalk·er /ˈdɪəˌstɔːkə $ ˈdɪrˌstɒːkər/ *n* [C] a type of soft hat with pieces of cloth that cover your ears

de·face /dɪˈfeɪs/ *v* [T] to spoil the surface or appearance of something, especially by writing on it or breaking it: *Most of the monuments had been broken or defaced.* THESAURUS ▸ DAMAGE —**defacement** *n* [U]

de fac·to /ˌdeɪ ˈfæktəʊ $ dɪ ˈfæktoʊ, ˌdeɪ-/ *adj formal* really existing although not legally stated to exist → **de jure**: *a de facto state of war* —**de facto** *adv*

def·a·ma·tion /ˌdefəˈmeɪʃən/ *n* [U] the act of defaming someone: *He sued the newspaper for **defamation of character**.*

de·fame /dɪˈfeɪm/ *v* [T] to write or say bad or untrue things about someone or something, so that people will have a bad opinion of them —**defamatory** /dɪˈfæmətəri $ -tɔːri/ *adj*

de·fault¹ /dɪˈfɔːlt $ -ˈfɒːlt/ ●○○ *n*
1 by default a) if you win a game, competition etc by default, you win it because your opponent did not play or because there were no other competitors **b)** if something happens by default, it happens because you did not do anything to change it
2 [C,U] *formal* failure to pay money that you owe at the right time: **in default** *The company is in default on its loan agreement.* | **[+in]** *The bank can seize the asset in the event of a default in payment.* | *the risk of default by borrowers*
3 [U] *law* failure to do something that you are supposed to do according to the law or because it is your duty
4 [C usually singular] *technical* the way in which things are arranged on a computer screen unless you decide to change them: *You can change the **default settings** to suit your needs.*
5 [singular] the usual and expected way in which something is done, unless you decide to do something different: *This way of working seems to be the default these days.*
6 in default of sth *formal* because of the lack or absence of something: *In default of any other instructions, they decided to use the same system as before.*

default² *v* [I] **1** to fail to pay money that you owe at the right time: **[+on]** *He defaulted on his child support payments.* **2** to not do something that you are supposed to do, especially that you are legally supposed to do —**defaulter** *n* [C]

de·feat¹ /dɪˈfiːt/ ●●● W3 *n* [C,U]
1 failure to win or succeed: **[+in]** *The socialist party suffered a crushing defeat in the elections.* | *She was a woman who hated to admit defeat.*
2 victory over someone or something: **[+of]** *The defeat of the army was followed by the establishment of constitutional government.*

COLLOCATIONS

VERBS

suffer a defeat (=be defeated) *The party suffered a defeat in the state elections.*
inflict a defeat on sb (=defeat someone, especially easily) *The army inflicted a heavy defeat on the English.*
admit defeat *If I left my job, I would be admitting defeat.*
accept defeat *It can be very hard to accept defeat.*
concede defeat (=formally accept that you have lost in a game, election etc) *His opponent conceded defeat.*
face defeat (=be likely to be defeated) *In May 1945 Germany faced defeat at the hands of the Allies.*

ADJECTIVES/NOUN + defeat

a big/bad defeat (*also* **a heavy defeat** *BrE*) (=by a large amount) *The polls were forecasting a heavy defeat for the president.*
a crushing/resounding defeat (=a complete defeat, by a very large amount) *He quit as prime minister following a crushing defeat in regional elections.*
a humiliating defeat (=very embarrassing) *They are still bitter about their humiliating defeat.*
a disastrous defeat (=very big, and with a very bad result) *The party suffered a disastrous defeat in the 2006 election.*
a narrow defeat (=by a small amount) *The goalkeeper was blamed for the team's narrow defeat.*
an election/electoral defeat *It was their worst general election defeat since 1982.*
a military defeat *The president resigned following a series of military defeats.*
a shock defeat *BrE* (=very unexpected) *Arsenal are now out of the competition, following their shock defeat by Torquay Town.*

defeat² ●●● W3 *v* [T]
1 to win a victory over someone in a war, competition, game etc SYN **beat**: *They hoped to defeat the enemy at sea.* | **defeat sb by sth** *We were defeated by 3 goals to 2.* THESAURUS ▸ BEAT

REGISTER
In everyday English, people usually say **beat** rather than **defeat** when talking about sport, games, or elections: *We were **beaten** by 3 goals to 2.*

D

2 if something defeats you, you cannot understand it and therefore cannot answer or deal with it SYN **beat**: *It was the last question on the paper that defeated me.*
3 to make something fail: **defeat the object/purpose (of the exercise)** *Don't let your arms relax as that would defeat the object of the exercise.*

de·feat·ed /dɪˈfiːtɪd/ *adj* sad and unable to deal with problems: *He looked lost and defeated.*

de·feat·ist /dɪˈfiːtɪst/ *n* [C] someone who believes that they will not succeed —**defeatist** *adj*: *a defeatist attitude* —**defeatism** *n* [U]

def·e·cate /ˈdefɪkeɪt/ *v* [I] *formal* to get rid of waste matter from your BOWELS —**defecation** /ˌdefɪˈkeɪʃən/ *n* [U]

de·fect[1] /dɪˈfekt, ˈdiːfekt/ ●●○ *n* [C] a fault or a lack of something that means that something or someone is not perfect: *All the cars are tested for defects before they leave the factory.* | *a genetic defect* THESAURUS► FAULT

defect[2] /dɪˈfekt/ *v* [I] to leave your own country or group in order to go to or join an opposing one: **[+to/from]** *a Russian actor who defected to the West* —**defector** *n* [C] —**defection** /dɪˈfekʃən/ *n* [C,U]

D

de·fec·tive /dɪˈfektɪv/ ●○○ *adj* not made properly, or not working properly SYN **faulty**: *The disease is caused by a defective gene.* | *defective products*

de·fence *BrE*, **defense** *AmE* /dɪˈfens/ ●●● S2 W1 *n*
1 PROTECTION **a)** [U] the act of protecting something or someone from attack: **[+of]** *In Britain, the defence of the country has historically been left to the navy.* | *a firm commitment to the defense of human rights* | *The first* ***line of defence*** *is a smoke detector.* **b)** [C] something that can be used to protect something or someone from attack: *The area's flood defences need repair.* | **[+against]** *The immune system is the body's defence against infection.* → SELF-DEFENCE
2 MILITARY **a)** [U] all the systems, people, materials etc that a country uses to protect itself from attack: *calls for a national debate on defence* | *the Defense Department* **b) defences** *BrE*, **defenses** *AmE* [plural] all the armies, weapons, structures etc that are available to defend a place: *The invading army easily overcame the town's defences.*
3 AGAINST CRITICISM [C,U] something that you say or do in order to support someone or something that is being criticized: **in sb's/sth's defence** *Jean wrote a letter to the paper in Angela's defense.* | **[+of]** *a philosophical defence of nationalism* | **come/leap to sb's defence** *Evelyn Waugh came to Wilson's defence and acknowledged the brilliance of the book's themes.*
4 IN A LAW COURT **a)** [C] the things that are said in a court of law to prove that someone is not guilty of a crime: *Major has a good defence and believes he will win the case.* | *a defence lawyer* **b) the defence** all the lawyers who try to prove in a court of law that someone is not guilty of a crime: *The defense called only one witness.* → PROSECUTION(2)
5 EMOTIONS [C] something you do or a way of behaving that prevents you from seeming weak or being hurt by others: *Liz dropped her defences and began to relax.*
6 SPORT [C] the players on a sports team whose main job is to try to prevent the other team from getting points

de·fence·less *BrE*, **defenseless** *AmE* /dɪˈfensləs/ *adj* weak and unable to protect yourself from attack or harm: *a defenceless old lady*

deˈfence ˌmechanism *BrE*, **defense mechanism** *AmE* *n* [C] **1** a process in your brain that makes you forget things that are painful for you to think about **2** a reaction in your body that protects you from an illness or danger

de·fend /dɪˈfend/ ●●● S3 W3 *v*
1 [I,T] to do something in order to protect someone or something from being attacked: *a struggle to defend our homeland* | **defend sth against/from sth** *the need to defend democracy against fascism* | **defend yourself (against/from sb/sth)** *advice on how women can defend themselves from sex attackers* | **[+against]** *We need to defend against military aggression.*
2 [T] to use arguments to protect something or someone from criticism, or to prove that something is right OPP **attack**: *She was always defending her husband in front of their daughter.* | *Students should be ready to explain and defend their views.* | **defend sb against/from sb/sth** *He defended his wife against rumours and allegations.* | **defend yourself (against/from sth)** | *Cooper wrote to the journal immediately, defending himself.*

> **REGISTER**
> In everyday English, people usually say **stand up for** someone rather than **defend** someone: *She was the only person who* ***stood up for*** *me at the meeting.*

3 [T] to do something in order to stop something from being taken away or in order to make it possible for something to continue: *the workers' attempts to* ***defend*** *their* ***interests*** | *We are* ***defending*** *the* ***right*** *to demonstrate.*
4 [I,T] to protect your own team's end of the field in a game such as football, in order to prevent your opponents from getting points OPP **attack**: *Bournemouth defended well throughout the game.*
5 [T] to take part in a competition that you won the last time it was held, and try to win it again: *The world champion was* ***defending*** *his* ***title***. | *the* ***defending champion*** | *He is defending a Labour majority of 5,000.*
6 [I,T] to be a lawyer for someone who has been charged with a crime OPP **prosecute**: *He had top lawyers to defend him.* | *Howard, defending, said Thompson had been drinking heavily.*

> **THESAURUS**
> **defend** to say something to support an idea or person when other people are criticizing them: *The mayor defended the action, saying that it was the best option.*
> **stand up for sb/sth** to strongly defend someone who is being criticized, or strongly defend your ideas or your rights: *My grandfather would always stand up for what was right.* | *I don't want him fighting, but I do want him to stand up for himself.*
> **stick up for sb** *informal* to strongly defend someone who is being criticized, especially when no one else will defend them: *The other kids tease her, but Sarah often sticks up for her.*
> **come to sb's defence** *BrE* (*also* **come to sb's defense** *AmE*) to say something to defend someone who is being criticized: *Aitken's colleagues quickly came to his defence.*

de·fen·dant /dɪˈfendənt/ *n* [C] the person in a court of law who has been ACCUSED of doing something illegal → **plaintiff** SYN **prisoner** *AmE*: *We find the defendant not guilty.*

de·fend·er /dɪˈfendə $ -ər/ ●●○ *n* [C]
1 one of the players in a game such as football who has to defend their team's GOAL from the opposing team: *It's his fourth season as an Arsenal defender.*
2 someone who defends a particular idea, belief, person etc: *He presented himself as a defender of democracy.*

de·fense[1] /dɪˈfens/ *n* [C,U] the American spelling of DEFENCE

de·fense[2] /dɪˈfens $ ˈdiːfens/ *n* [C,U] *AmE* the players in a game of football etc whose main job is to try to prevent the other team from getting points

de·fen·si·ble /dɪˈfensəbəl/ *adj* **1** a defensible opinion, idea, or action seems reasonable, and you can easily support it OPP **indefensible**: *a morally defensible prison system* **2** a defensible building or area is easy to protect against attack —**defensibly** *adv*

de·fen·sive[1] /dɪˈfensɪv/ ●○○ *adj*
1 used or intended to protect someone or something against attack OPP **offensive**: *The prince drew up his forces in a strong defensive position.* | *The rockets are a purely* ***defensive measure*** *against nuclear attack.*
2 behaving in a way that shows you think someone is criticizing you even if they are not: *She despised herself for sounding so defensive.* | *a reserved and defensive manner*

3 *AmE* relating to stopping the other team from getting points in a game OPP **offensive**: *defensive play* —**defensively** *adv* —**defensiveness** *n* [U]

defensive² *n* **1 on/onto the defensive** behaving in a way that shows that you think that someone is criticizing you even if they are not: *In his presence, she was constantly on the defensive.* **2 put/force sb on the defensive** if you put someone on the defensive in an argument, you attack them so that they are in a weaker position → **go on the offensive**: *an issue that put the White House on the defensive*

de·fer /dɪˈfɜː $ -ˈfɜːr/ ●○○ *v* (**deferred**, **deferring**) [T] to delay something until a later date SYN **put back**: **defer sth until/to sth** *Further discussion on the proposal will be deferred until April.* | *The committee **deferred** their **decision**.* THESAURUS DELAY —**deferment** *n* [C,U] —**deferral** *n* [C,U]

defer to sb/sth *phr v formal* to agree to accept someone's opinion or decision because you have respect for that person: *I will defer to your wishes.*

def·er·ence /ˈdefərəns/ *n* [U] *formal* polite behaviour that shows that you respect someone and are therefore willing to accept their opinions or judgment: **[+to]** *Lewis was annoyed that Adam did not show enough respect and deference to him.* | **out of/in deference to sth** (=because you respect someone's beliefs, opinions etc) *They were married in church out of deference to their parents' wishes.* —**deferential** /ˌdefəˈrenʃəl◂/ *adj*: *deferential treatment* —**deferentially** *adv*

def·fo /ˈdefəʊ $ -oʊ-/ *adv BrE informal* definitely

de·fi·ance /dɪˈfaɪəns/ ●○○ *n* [U] behaviour that shows you refuse to do what someone tells you to do, especially because you do not respect them → **defy**: **act/gesture of defiance** *Running away was an act of defiance against his parents.* | **in defiance (of sth)** *Many people were drinking in the streets, in flagrant defiance of the ban.* | *Her fists clenched in defiance.*

de·fi·ant /dɪˈfaɪənt/ *adj* clearly refusing to do what someone tells you to do: *Mark smashed a fist on the desk in a defiant gesture.* —**defiantly** *adv*

de·fib·ril·la·tor /diːˈfɪbrəleɪtə $ -ər/ *n* [C] a machine that gives the heart an electric shock to make it start beating again after a heart attack

de·fi·cien·cy /dɪˈfɪʃənsi/ ●○○ *n* (*plural* **deficiencies**) [C,U] *formal*

1 a lack of something that is necessary SYN **shortage**: **[+of]** *a deficiency of safe play areas for children* | **iron/vitamin etc deficiency** *Some elderly people suffer from iron deficiency in their diet.*

2 a weakness or fault in something: **[+in]** *There are deep deficiencies in this law.*

de·fi·cient /dɪˈfɪʃənt/ *adj formal* **1** not containing or having enough of something: *Women who are dieting can become iron deficient.* | **[+in]** *patients who were deficient in vitamin C* **2** not good enough: *Our prisons are our most deficient social service.*

def·i·cit /ˈdefɪsɪt/ ●○○ *n* [C] the difference between the amount of something that you have and the higher amount that you need → **shortfall**: *the country's widening **budget deficit*** | *the US's foreign **trade deficit*** | **[+of]** *a deficit of £2.5 million* | **[+in]** *Many countries have a big deficit in food supply.* | **in deficit** *The US balance of payments was in deficit.*

de·file¹ /dɪˈfaɪl/ *v* [T] *formal* to make something less pure and good, especially by showing no respect: *Hallam's tomb had been defiled and looted.*

de·file² /dɪˈfaɪl, ˈdiːfaɪl/ *n* [C] *formal* a narrow passage, especially through mountains

de·fine /dɪˈfaɪn/ ●●● S2 W2 AWL *v* [T]

1 to describe something correctly and thoroughly, and to say what standards, limits, qualities etc it has that make it different from other things: *the ability to define clients' needs* | *The duties of the post are difficult to define.* | **clearly/well defined** *The tasks will be clearly defined by the tutor.* | **define sth as sth** *70% of the workers can be defined as low-paid.*

2 to explain exactly the meaning of a particular word or idea → **definition**: *I'll now try to define the term 'popular culture'.* | **define sth as sth** *A budget is defined as 'a plan of action expressed in money terms'.* | *Define precisely what you mean by 'crime'.*

3 to show the edge or shape of something clearly → **definition**: *The bird has **sharply defined** black and rust markings.* —**definable** *adj*

def·i·nite /ˈdefɪnət, ˈdefənət/ ●●○ S3 AWL *adj*

1 clearly known, seen, or stated SYN **clear** OPP **indefinite**: *It's impossible for me to give you a definite answer.* | *We need to record sufficient data to enable definite conclusions to be reached.* | *He'd shown definite signs of resigning himself to the situation.* THESAURUS CERTAIN

2 a definite arrangement, promise etc will happen in the way that someone has said → **indefinite**: *Fix a definite date for the delivery of your computer.*

3 [not before noun] saying something very firmly so that people understand exactly what you mean: **[+about]** *She's not definite about retiring from the game.*

ˌdefinite ˈarticle *n* [C usually singular] **1** the word 'the' in English → INDEFINITE ARTICLE **2** a word in another language that is like 'the'

def·i·nite·ly /ˈdefɪnətli, ˈdefənətli/ ●●● S1 AWL *adv* without any doubt SYN **certainly**: *'Do you reckon Margot will be there?' '**Definitely not**.'* | *The hotel fitness centre is definitely worth a visit.* | *I definitely need a holiday.*

def·i·ni·tion /ˌdefəˈnɪʃən/ ●●○ S3 W2 AWL *n*

1 [C] a phrase or sentence that says exactly what a word, phrase, or idea means → **define**: *a dictionary definition* | **[+of]** *There are many definitions of the word 'feminism'.* | **definition of sth as sth** *the definition of God as infinite*

2 **by definition** if something has a particular quality by definition, it must have that quality because all things of that type have it: *People say that students are by definition idealistic and impatient.*

3 [U] the clear edges, shapes, or sound that something has: *technologies such as high definition television* | *good muscle definition*

de·fin·i·tive /dɪˈfɪnətɪv/ ●○○ AWL *adj*

1 [usually before noun] a definitive book, description etc is considered to be the best and cannot be improved: **definitive study/work/guide etc** *the definitive study of Victorian railway stations*

2 a definitive agreement, statement etc is one that will not be changed: *a definitive agreement to buy the company* —**definitively** *adv*

de·flate /ˌdiːˈfleɪt, dɪ-/ *v* **1** [I,T] if a tyre, BALLOON etc deflates, or if you deflate it, it gets smaller because the gas inside it comes out OPP **inflate** → **go down**, **let down**

> **REGISTER**
> In everyday British English, people usually say an object **goes down** rather than **deflates**: *It looks like the air bed has **gone down**.*

2 [T] to make someone feel less important or less confident: *She was deflated when Fen made no comment on her achievement.* **3** [T] to show that a statement, argument etc is wrong: *Simkin hoped to find a way to deflate his opponent's argument.* **4** [I,T] *technical* to change economic rules or conditions in a country so that prices fall or stop rising

de·fla·tion /diːˈfleɪʃən/ *n* [U] *technical* a reduction in the amount of money in a country's ECONOMY, so that prices fall or stop rising → **inflation** —**deflationary** *adj*: *the government's deflationary policies*

de·flect /dɪˈflekt/ ●○○ *v*

1 [I,T] if someone or something deflects something that is moving, or if it deflects, it turns in a different direction: *He **deflected** the **blow** with his forearm.*

2 [T] to do something to stop people paying attention to you, criticizing you etc: **deflect sth (away) from sth** *his attempts to **deflect attention** away from his private life* | *The committee is seeking to **deflect criticism** by blaming me.*

3 [T] to take someone's attention away from something:

deflect sb from (doing) sth *Nothing can deflect me from reaching my goal.*

de·flec·tion /dɪˈflekʃən/ *n* [C,U] **1** the action of making something change its direction: **[+of]** *the deflection of the missile away from its target* **2** *technical* the degree to which the moving part on a measuring instrument moves away from zero

de·flow·er /ˌdiːˈflaʊə, dɪ- $ -ər/ *v* [T] *literary* to have sex with a woman who has never had sex before

de·fog /diːˈfɒg $ -ˈfɑːg, -ˈfɔːg/ *v* (**defogged**, **defogging**) [T] *AmE* to remove mist from the windows inside a car, by using heat SYN **demist** *BrE*

de·fo·li·ant /diːˈfəʊliənt $ -ˈfoʊ-/ *n* [C,U] *formal* a chemical substance, used especially in war, that makes all the leaves of plants drop off

de·fo·li·ate /diːˈfəʊlieɪt $ -ˈfoʊ-/ *v* [T] *formal* to use defoliant on a plant or tree

de·for·es·ta·tion /diːˌfɒrəˈsteɪʃən $ -ˌfɔː-,-ˌfɑː-/ *n* [U] the cutting or burning down of all the trees in an area: *the deforestation of the tropics* —**deforest** /diːˈfɒrɪst $ -ˈfɔː-, -ˈfɑː-/ *v* [T]

D

de·form /dɪˈfɔːm $ -ɔːrm/ *v* [I,T] if you deform something, or if it deforms, its usual shape changes so that its usefulness or appearance is spoiled: *Wearing badly fitting shoes can deform your feet.*

de·for·ma·tion /ˌdiːfɔːˈmeɪʃən $ -ɔːr-/ *n* [C,U] *technical* a change in the usual shape of something, especially one that makes it worse, or the process of changing something's shape

de·formed /dɪˈfɔːmd $ -ɔːrmd/ *adj* something that is deformed has the wrong shape, especially because it has grown or developed wrongly: *deformed toe*

de·for·mi·ty /dɪˈfɔːməti $ -ɔːr-/ *n* (*plural* **deformities**) [C,U] a condition in which part of someone's body is not the normal shape: *a hip deformity*

DEFRA /ˈdefrə/ (***Department for Environment, Food, and Rural Affairs***) the British government department which is responsible for farming, food production, and the safety of food products. It is also responsible for protecting the environment in the UK.

de·frag·ment /ˌdiːfrægˈment $ diːˈfrægment, ˌdiːfrægˈment/ (*also* **de·frag** /diːˈfræg/ *informal*) *v* [T] to change the way in which the FILES on a computer's HARD DRIVE are stored and organized, by putting related information together so that the computer works more effectively: *It should start working faster after we defrag your disk.* —**defrag** /ˈdiːfræg/ *n* [C]

de·fraud /dɪˈfrɔːd $ -ˈfrɒːd/ *v* [T] to trick a person or organization in order to get money from them: **defraud sb of sth** *She defrauded her employers of thousands of pounds.* | *He faces charges of theft and* ***conspiracy to defraud*** (=a secret plan to cheat someone, made by two or more people).

de·fray /dɪˈfreɪ/ *v* **defray costs/expenses** *formal* to give someone back the money that they have spent on something: *The proceeds from the competition help to defray the expenses of the evening.*

de·friend /diːˈfrend/ *v* [T] to remove someone from your list of friends on a SOCIAL NETWORKING SITE: *I was really hurt when she defriended me.*

de·frock /ˌdiːˈfrɒk $ -ˈfrɑːk/ *v* [T] to officially remove a priest from his or her job because he or she did something wrong —**defrocked** *adj*

de·frost /ˌdiːˈfrɒst $ -ˈfrɒːst/ *v* **1** [I,T] if frozen food defrosts, or if you defrost it, it gets warmer until it is not frozen → **melt**, **thaw** **2** [I,T] if a FREEZER or REFRIGERATOR defrosts, or if you defrost it, it is turned off so that the ice inside it melts **3** [T] *AmE* to remove ice from inside the windows of a car by using heat or warm air

deft /deft/ *adj written* **1** a deft movement is skilful, and often quick: *He sketched her with quick, deft strokes.* | *deft footwork* **2** skilful at doing something SYN **adept**: *his deft chairmanship of the company* —**deftly** *adv* —**deftness** *n* [U]

de·funct /dɪˈfʌŋkt/ *adj formal* not existing anymore, or not useful anymore: *the* ***now-defunct*** *nuclear reactor*

de·fuse /ˌdiːˈfjuːz/ *v* [T] **1** to improve a difficult or dangerous situation, for example by making people less angry or by dealing with the causes of a problem: **defuse a situation/crisis/row etc** *Beth's quiet voice helped to defuse the situation.* | **defuse tension/anger etc** *The agreement was regarded as a means of defusing ethnic tensions.* **2** to remove the FUSE from a bomb in order to prevent it from exploding

de·fy /dɪˈfaɪ/ ●●○ *v* (**defied**, **defying**, **defies**) [T]

1 to refuse to obey a law or rule, or refuse to do what someone in authority tells you to do → **defiance**: *people who openly defy the law* **THESAURUS** ▸ DISOBEY

2 defy description/analysis/belief etc to be almost impossible to describe or understand: *The beauty of the scene defies description.*

3 defy logic/the odds etc to not happen according to the principles you would expect: *a 16-week premature baby who defied the odds and survived*

4 I defy sb to do sth *spoken formal* used when you ask someone to do something that you think is impossible: *I defy anyone to prove otherwise.*

deg. (*also* **deg** *BrE*) the written abbreviation of ***degree*** or ***degrees***

de·gen·e·rate¹ /dɪˈdʒenəreɪt/ *v* [I] to become worse: **[+into]** *The conference degenerated into a complete fiasco.* —**degeneration** /dɪˌdʒenəˈreɪʃən/ *n* [U]

de·gen·e·rate² /dɪˈdʒenərət/ *adj formal* morally unacceptable: *The painting was condemned as 'degenerate'.*

degenerate³ *n* [C] someone whose behaviour is considered to be morally unacceptable

de·gen·e·ra·tive /dɪˈdʒenərətɪv/ *adj* a degenerative illness gradually gets worse and cannot be stopped → **progressive**

deg·ra·da·tion /ˌdegrəˈdeɪʃən/ *n* **1** [C,U] an experience or situation that makes you feel ashamed and angry: *a life of poverty and degradation* **2** [U] the process by which something changes to a worse condition

de·grade /dɪˈgreɪd/ *v* **1** [T] to treat someone without respect and make them lose respect for themselves: *a movie that degrades women* | **degrade yourself (by doing sth)** *How can you degrade yourself by writing such trash?* **2** [T] to make a situation or the condition of something worse: *The dolphin's habitat is being rapidly degraded.* **3** [I,T] *technical* if a substance, chemical etc degrades, or if something degrades it, it changes to a simpler form —**degradable** *adj*

de·grad·ing /dɪˈgreɪdɪŋ/ *adj* a degrading experience, event etc is unpleasant and makes you lose respect for yourself: **[+to]** *Pornography is degrading to women and to the men that look at it.* | *the* ***degrading treatment*** *that the prisoners receive in jail*

de·gree /dɪˈgriː/ ●●● S2 W1 *n*

1 [C] (*written abbreviation* **deg.**) a unit for measuring temperature. It can be shown as a symbol after a number. For example, 70° means 70 degrees: *Preheat the oven to 425 degrees.* | **20 degrees Celsius/70 degrees Fahrenheit/1 degree Centigrade etc** *The temperature dropped to five degrees Centigrade.*

2 [C] (*written abbreviation* **deg.**) a unit for measuring the size of an angle. It can be shown as a symbol after a number. For example, 18° means 18 degrees: *Then the cylinder is rotated 180 degrees.*

3 [C,U] the level or amount of something: **[+of]** *1960s Britain was characterised by a greater degree of freedom than before.* | *Newspapers vary in* ***the degree to which*** *they emphasize propaganda rather than information.*

4 to a degree (*also* **to some degree/to a certain degree**) partly: *To a degree, it is possible to educate oneself.* | *We're all willing to support him to some degree.*

5 [C] a course of study at a university or college, or the QUALIFICATION that is given to you when you have successfully completed the course: **[+in]** *a degree in Economics* | *Applicants must* ***have a degree*** *in Engineering.* | *an Honours degree*

6 by degrees very slowly SYN **gradually**: *By degrees, he forced himself into a sitting position.*

de·hu·man·ize (*also* **-ise** *BrE*) /ˌdiːˈhjuːmənaɪz/ *v* [T] to treat people so badly that they lose their good human qualities: *War dehumanizes people.* —**dehumanizing** *adj* —**dehumanization** /diːˌhjuːmənaɪˈzeɪʃən $ -nə-/ *n* [U]

de·hy·drate /ˌdiːhaɪˈdreɪt $ diːˈhaɪdreɪt/ *v* **1** [T] to remove the liquid from a substance such as food or a chemical → **rehydrate**, **hydrate**: *The substance is dehydrated and stored as powder.* **2** [I,T] to lose too much water from your body, or to make this happen: *Alcohol dehydrates the body.* —**dehydrated** *adj* —**dehydration** /ˌdiːhaɪˈdreɪʃən/ *n* [U]

de-ice /ˌdiːˈaɪs/ *v* [T] to remove the ice from something, especially a car WINDSCREEN or the wings of an aircraft

de·i·fy /ˈdiːəfaɪ, ˈdeɪ-/ *v* (**deified**, **deifying**, **deifies**) [T] to treat someone or something with extreme respect and admiration —**deification** /ˌdiːəfəˈkeɪʃən, ˌdeɪ-/ *n* [U]

deign /deɪn/ *v* **deign to do sth** to do something that you think you are really too important to do - often used humorously: *Travis called after her, but she didn't deign to answer.*

de·is·m /ˈdeɪ-ɪzəm, ˈdiː-/ *n* [U] the belief in a god who made the world but has no influence on human lives

de·i·ty /ˈdeɪəti, ˈdiː-/ *n* (*plural* **deities**) [C] a god or GODDESS: *the deities of ancient Greece*

dé·jà vu /ˌdeɪʒɑː ˈvjuː $ -ˈvuː/ *n* [U] the feeling that what is happening now has happened before in exactly the same way: *a strange **sense of déjà vu***

de·jec·ted /dɪˈdʒektɪd/ *adj* unhappy, disappointed, or sad: *The unemployed stood at street corners, dejected.* **THESAURUS** SAD —**dejectedly** *adv* —**dejection** /dɪˈdʒekʃən/ *n* [U]

de ju·re /ˌdiː ˈdʒʊəri, ˌdeɪ ˈdʒʊəreɪ $ -ˈdʒʊr-/ *adj, adv technical* true or right because of a law → **de facto**

de·lay[1] /dɪˈleɪ/ ●●○ W3 *n*
1 [C] when someone or something has to wait, or the length of the waiting time: *Sorry for the delay, Mr Weaver.* | **[+in]** *Why was there a delay in warning the public?* | **[+of]** *a delay of about an hour* | **long/considerable/slight etc delay** *Long delays are expected on the motorways.*
2 [U] when something does not happen or start when it should do: **without delay** *They must restore normal services without delay.* | *There can be no excuse for any **further delay**.*

delay[2] ●●○ W3 *v*
1 [I,T] to wait until a later time to do something: *Don't delay - send off for the information now.* | *He **delayed** his **decision** on whether to call an election.* | **delay sth until sth** *The opening of this section of the road is delayed until September.* | **delay sth for sth** *Our meeting was delayed for ten minutes.* | **delay doing sth** *Big companies often delay paying their bills.*
2 [T] to make someone or something late: **seriously/badly/slightly etc delayed** *The flight was badly delayed because of fog.* —**delayed** *adj*

THESAURUS

delay to wait until a later time to do something: *He decided to delay his decision until he had seen the full report.*
postpone to change an event to a later time or date: *The meeting was postponed.*
put off to delay doing something. **Put off** is less formal than **delay** or **postpone**, and is the usual phrase to use in everyday English: *I used to put off making difficult decisions.* | *The game has been put off till next week.*
hold off to delay doing something, especially while you are waiting for more information or for something else to happen: *House buyers seem to be holding off until interest rates drop.*
defer *formal* to delay doing something until a later date, usually because something else needs to happen first: *The decision had been deferred until after a meeting of the directors.*
procrastinate /prəˈkræstəneɪt/ *formal* to delay doing something that you ought to do: *Don't procrastinate – make a start on your assignments as soon as you get them.*

deˌlayed-ˈaction *adj* [only before noun] designed to work or start only after a fixed period of time has passed: *a delayed-action bomb*

deˈlaying ˌtactic *n* [C usually plural] something you do deliberately in order to delay something so that you gain an advantage for yourself

de·lec·ta·ble /dɪˈlektəbəl/ *adj formal* **1** extremely pleasant to taste or smell SYN **delicious**: *Delectable smells rose from the kitchen.* **2** used, often humorously, to describe a very attractive woman —**delectably** *adv*

de·lec·ta·tion /ˌdiːlekˈteɪʃən/ *n* [U] *formal* if you do something for someone's delectation, you do it to give them enjoyment, pleasure, or amusement

del·e·gate[1] /ˈdeləgət/ ●○○ *n* [C] someone who has been elected or chosen to speak, vote, or take decisions for a group → **representative**: *Around 350 delegates attended the conference.*

del·e·gate[2] /ˈdelɪgeɪt/ ●○○ *v*
1 [I,T] to give part of your power or work to someone in a lower position than you: *A good manager knows when to delegate.* | *It takes experience to judge correctly how much power should be delegated.* | **delegate sth to sb** *Minor tasks should be delegated to your assistant.*
2 [T] to choose someone to do a particular job, or to be a representative of a group, organization etc: **delegate sb to do sth** *I was delegated to find a suitable conference venue.*

del·e·ga·tion /ˌdeləˈgeɪʃən/ ●○○ *n*
1 [C] a group of people who represent a company, organization etc: **[+to]** *the head of the American delegation to the United Nations* | **[+of]** *a delegation of government officials* | *A trade delegation will visit Kuwait.*
2 [U] the process of giving power or work to someone else so that they are responsible for part of what you normally do: **[+of]** *the delegation of authority*

de·lete /dɪˈliːt/ ●●○ *v* [T] to remove something that has been written down or stored in a computer: *His name was deleted from the list.* | *I deleted the file by mistake.* **THESAURUS** REMOVE

del·e·ter·i·ous /ˌdeləˈtɪəriəs◂ $ -ˈtɪr-/ *adj formal* damaging or harmful SYN **detrimental**: *the **deleterious effects** of smoking*

de·le·tion /dɪˈliːʃən/ *n* **1** [U] when you remove something from a piece of writing or from a computer's memory: **[+of]** *the deletion of unwanted files* **2** [C] a letter or word that has been removed from a piece of writing

del·i /ˈdeli/ *n* [C] a DELICATESSEN

de·lib·e·rate[1] /dɪˈlɪbərət/ ●●○ *adj*
1 intended or planned OPP **unintentional** SYN **intentional**: *a **deliberate attempt** to humiliate her* | *The attack on him was quite deliberate.*
2 deliberate speech, thought, or movement is slow and careful: *He approached her with slow, deliberate steps.* —**deliberateness** *n* [U]

de·lib·e·rate[2] /dɪˈlɪbəreɪt/ *v* [I] to think about something very carefully: *The jury deliberated for four days before acquitting him.* | **[+on/about/over]** *There was silence while she deliberated on his words.*

de·lib·er·ate·ly /dɪˈlɪbərətli/ ●●○ S3 *adv*
1 done in a way that is intended or planned: *He deliberately upset her.*
2 done or said in a slow careful way: *He shook his head slowly and deliberately.*

THESAURUS

deliberately if you do something deliberately, you do it because you want to: *He upset her deliberately.* | *I deliberately kept the letter short.*
on purpose *especially spoken* deliberately, especially in order to annoy someone or get an advantage for yourself: *I didn't push her on purpose; it was an accident.*

intentionally deliberately, especially in order to have a particular result or effect: *Very few teenagers become pregnant intentionally.*
consciously /ˈkɒnʃəsli/ done after thinking carefully about what you are doing, especially because you know what the results of your actions might be: *Parents pass their values to their children, though not always consciously.*
knowingly if you knowingly do something wrong or illegal, you do it even though you know it is wrong: *FBI agents arrested Dillon for 'knowingly making a false statement on a passport application'.*

de·lib·er·a·tion /dɪˌlɪbəˈreɪʃən/ *n* **1** [C,U] careful consideration or discussion of something: ***After much deliberation**, first prize was awarded to Derek Murray.* | **[+of]** *the deliberations of committee meetings* **2** [U] *formal* if you speak or move with deliberation, you speak or move slowly and carefully

de·lib·e·ra·tive /dɪˈlɪbərətɪv $ -bəreɪtɪv/ *adj formal* existing for the purpose of discussing or planning something

D

del·i·ca·cy /ˈdelɪkəsi/ *n* (*plural* **delicacies**) **1** [C] something good to eat that is expensive or rare: *Snails are considered a delicacy in France.* THESAURUS FOOD **2** [U] a careful and sensitive way of speaking or behaving so that you do not upset anyone SYN **tact**: *He carried out his duties with great delicacy and understanding.* **3** [U] the quality of being easy to harm or damage

del·i·cate /ˈdelɪkət/ ●●○ *adj*
1 needing to be dealt with carefully or sensitively in order to avoid problems or failure: *There's something I have to speak to you about – it's a **delicate matter**. | delicate negotiations* THESAURUS DIFFICULT
2 easily damaged or broken SYN **fragile**: *delicate hand-cut glass | The sun can easily damage a child's **delicate skin**.*
3 *old-fashioned* someone who is delicate is hurt easily or easily becomes ill: *a delicate child* THESAURUS ILL, WEAK
4 a part of the body that is delicate is attractive and graceful: *Her wrists and ankles were slim and delicate. | her **delicate features***
5 made skilfully and with attention to the smallest details: *a plate with a delicate pattern of leaves*
6 a taste, smell, or colour that is delicate is pleasant and not strong: *The wine has a dry delicate flavour. | a delicate pink* —**delicately** *adv* → INDELICATE

del·i·cates /ˈdelɪkəts/ *n* [plural] clothes that are made from material that needs careful treatment

del·i·ca·tes·sen /ˌdelɪkəˈtesən/ *n* [C] a shop that sells high quality cheeses, SALADS, cooked meats etc

de·li·cious /dɪˈlɪʃəs/ ●●● S2 *adj*
1 very pleasant to taste or smell: *'The meal was absolutely delicious,' she said politely. | the delicious smell of new-mown grass* THESAURUS TASTE
2 *literary* extremely pleasant or enjoyable —**deliciously** *adv*: *deliciously spicy meat*

de·light¹ /dɪˈlaɪt/ ●●○ *n*
1 [U] a feeling of great pleasure and satisfaction: **with/in delight** *The kids were screaming with delight.* | **to sb's delight/to the delight of sb** *To the delight of his proud parents, he has made a full recovery.* | **squeal/gasp/cry etc of delight** *She gave a little gasp of delight.* THESAURUS PLEASURE
2 [C] something that makes you feel very happy or satisfied: **the delights of sth** *a chance to sample the delights of nearby Vienna* | **it is a delight to do sth** *It was a delight to see him so fit and healthy.*
3 take delight in (doing) sth to enjoy something very much, especially something you should not do: *Chris takes great delight in teasing his sister.*

delight² ●○○ *v* [T] to give someone great satisfaction and enjoyment: *Her fabulous recipes will delight anyone who loves chocolate.* | **delight sb with sth** *He is delighting audiences with his wit and humour.*

delight in sth *phr v* [T] to enjoy something very much, especially something that other people think is not nice: *He delights in complicating everything.*

REGISTER
The verb **delight in** is not usually used to talk about things that people like doing. Use **enjoy** or **love** instead: *I really **enjoy** the countryside. | She **loves** watching old movies.*

de·light·ed /dɪˈlaɪtɪd/ ●●○ *adj* very pleased and happy: **delighted to do sth** *Sandy will be delighted to see you.* | **delighted (that)** *I'm delighted that we have settled the matter.* | **[+with/by/at]** *She was delighted with her new home. | I am delighted by the result. | Her screams of delighted laughter filled the air.* THESAURUS HAPPY —**delightedly** *adv*

GRAMMAR
Delighted is not used with 'very'. You say: *I'm absolutely delighted.* ✗ Don't say: *I'm very delighted.*
GRAMMAR GUIDE ADJECTIVES

de·light·ful /dɪˈlaɪtfəl/ ●○○ *adj* very pleasant: *a delightful little girl | The whole house is delightful.* THESAURUS NICE —**delightfully** *adv*: *a movie that's full of delightfully comic moments*

de·lim·it /dɪˈlɪmɪt/ *v* [T] *formal* to set or say exactly what the limits of something are —**delimitation** /dɪˌlɪmɪˈteɪʃən/ *n* [C,U]

de·lin·e·ate /dɪˈlɪnieɪt/ *v* [T] *formal* **1** to describe or draw something carefully so that people can understand it: *The document delineates your rights and your obligations.* **2** to make the borders between two areas very clear: *The boundaries of these areas should be **clearly delineated**.* —**delineation** /dɪˌlɪniˈeɪʃən/ *n* [U]

de·lin·quen·cy /dɪˈlɪŋkwənsi/ *n* (*plural* **delinquencies**) [C,U] illegal or immoral behaviour or actions, especially by young people: *the ever-rising statistics of delinquency and crime*

de·lin·quent¹ /dɪˈlɪŋkwənt/ *adj* **1** behaving in a way that is illegal or that society does not approve of → **criminal**: **delinquent girls/boys/children/teenagers 2** *technical* a delinquent debt, account etc has not been paid on time: *the recovery of delinquent loans*

delinquent² *n* [C] someone, especially a young person, who breaks the law or behaves in ways their society does not approve of: *Deanes writes and lectures about teenage delinquents.* → JUVENILE DELINQUENT

de·lir·i·ous /dɪˈlɪriəs/ *adj* **1** talking continuously in an excited or anxious way, especially because you are ill: *He suffered an attack of malaria and was delirious.* **2** extremely excited or happy: **[+with]** *He was delirious with joy.* —**deliriously** *adv*

de·lir·i·um /dɪˈlɪriəm/ *n* **1** [U] a state in which someone is delirious, especially because they are very ill: *Before she died she had fits of delirium.* **2** [singular, U] extreme excitement

delirium trem·ens /dɪˌlɪriəm ˈtremənz $ -ˈtriː-/ *n* [U] *medical* the DT's

de·liv·er /dɪˈlɪvə $ -ər/ ●●● S2 W2 *v*
1 TAKE STH SOMEWHERE [I,T] to take goods, letters, packages etc to a particular place or person: *The morning mail has just been delivered. | Do you deliver on Saturdays?* | **deliver sth to sb** *They set off to deliver supplies to an isolated village. | I'm **having** some flowers **delivered** for her birthday.* THESAURUS TAKE
2 deliver a speech/lecture/address etc to make a speech etc to a lot of people: *The king delivered a televised speech to the nation on November 5.*

REGISTER
In everyday English, people usually say **give a speech/lecture/talk** rather than **deliver a speech/lecture/talk**.

3 DO STH YOU SHOULD DO [I,T] to do or provide the things you are expected to, because you are responsible for

them or they are part of your job: *the costs of delivering adequate nursing care | the failure of some services to* ***deliver the goods*** (=do what they have promised) | *The company will* ***deliver on its promises.***
4 BABY [T] to help a woman give birth to her baby, or to give birth to a baby: *They rushed her to hospital where doctors delivered her baby.*
5 BLOW/SHOCK ETC [T] to give something such as a blow, shock, or warning to someone or something: *He delivered a strong warning about the dangers facing the government.*
6 deliver a judgment/verdict to officially state a formal decision or judgment: *The jury delivered a verdict of unlawful killing.*
7 PERSON [T] *formal* to put someone into someone else's control: **deliver sb to sb** *Sharett had betrayed him and delivered him to the enemy.*
8 VOTES [T] *especially AmE* to get the votes or support of a particular group of people in an election: *He cannot deliver the Latino vote.*
9 MAKE SB FREE OF STH [T] *literary or biblical* to help someone escape from something bad or evil: **deliver sb from sth** *'Deliver us from evil,' she prayed.* —**deliverer** *n* [C]
deliver sth ↔ **up** *phr v formal* to give something to someone else: *A bankrupt must deliver up all his books, papers and records.*

de·liv·er·a·ble /dɪˈlɪvərəbəl/ *n* [C usually plural] *technical* something that a company has promised to have ready for a customer, especially parts of computer systems: *software deliverables*

de·liv·er·ance /dɪˈlɪvərəns/ *n* [U + from] *formal* the state of being saved from harm or danger → **salvation**

de·liv·er·y /dɪˈlɪvəri/ ●●● S3 W3 *n* (*plural* **deliveries**)
1 [C,U] the act of bringing goods, letters etc to a particular person or place, or the things that are brought: *Most Indian restaurants offer free delivery. | You can expect delivery in a week to ten days. | fresh milk deliveries* | **[+of]** *deliveries of food and supplies* | **on delivery** (=when something is delivered) *The restaurant pays* ***cash on delivery*** *for fish, which the local fishermen like.*
2 take delivery of sth to officially accept something large that you have bought: *We expect to take delivery of the aircraft sometime in June.*
3 [C] the process of giving birth to a child → **labour**: *Mrs Howell had an easy delivery. | Liz was taken to the* ***delivery room*** (=a room in a hospital for births) *immediately.*
4 [U] the way in which someone speaks in public: *You'll have to work on your delivery.*

deˈlivery ˌman *n* [C] a man who delivers goods to people

dell /del/ *n* [C] *literary* a small valley with grass and trees

de·louse /ˌdiːˈlaʊs/ *v* [T] to remove lice (LOUSE) or similar animals from someone's hair, clothes etc

Del·phic or·a·cle, the /ˌdelfɪk ˈɒrəkəl $ -ˈɔː- -ˈɑː-/ a TEMPLE (=a holy building) in Delphi in ancient Greece where a PRIESTESS gave answers from the god Apollo to questions people asked him. The answer was often in the form of a mysterious RIDDLE (=a deliberately confusing question with a clever answer). Someone who is a respected authority on a particular subject is sometimes called a Delphic oracle: *Mrs Thatcher was regarded as the Delphic oracle of modern conservatism.*

del·ta /ˈdeltə/ *n* [C] **1** the fourth letter of the Greek alphabet **2** an area of low land where a river spreads into many smaller rivers near the sea: *the Nile delta*

de·lude /dɪˈluːd/ *v* [T] to make someone believe something that is not true SYN **deceive**: *I was angry with him for trying to delude me.* | **delude sb/yourself into doing sth** *It is easy to delude yourself into believing you're in love. | Don't be deluded into thinking your house is burglarproof.*

del·uge¹ /ˈdeljuːdʒ/ *n* [C] **1** [usually singular] a large amount of something such as letters or questions that someone gets at the same time SYN **flood**: **[+of]** *Viewers sent a deluge of complaints about the show.* **2** *formal* a large flood, or period when there is a lot of rain SYN **flood**

deluge² *v* [T] **1** to send a very large number of letters, questions etc to someone all at the same time SYN **flood**: **be deluged with sth** *He was deluged with phone calls from friends and colleagues, congratulating him.* GRAMMAR **Deluge** is usually passive in this meaning. **2** *formal* to cover something with a lot of water SYN **flood**

de·lu·sion /dɪˈluːʒən/ *n* **1** [C,U] a false belief about yourself or the situation you are in: **under a delusion (that)** *He is under the delusion that I am going to cheat him.* **2 delusions of grandeur** the belief that you are much more important or powerful than you really are —**delusive** /-sɪv/ *adj* —**delusional** *adj*

de·luxe /dəˈlʌks $ -ˈlʊks/ *adj* [usually before noun] of better quality and more expensive than other things of the same type → **luxury**: *a deluxe hotel | The deluxe model costs a lot more.*

delve /delv/ *v* [I] **1** to try to find more information about someone or something: **[+into]** *research that* ***delves deeply*** *into this issue* **2** [always + adv/prep] to search for something by putting your hand deeply into a bag, container etc: **[+into/in]** *He delved into his pocket and brought out a notebook.*

Dem. the written abbreviation of ***Democrat*** or ***Democratic***

de·mag·ne·tize (*also* **-ise** *BrE*) /ˌdiːˈmægnətaɪz/ *v* [T] to take away the MAGNETIC qualities of something

dem·a·gogue /ˈdeməgɒg $ -gɑːg/ *n* [C] a political leader who tries to make people feel strong emotions in order to influence their opinions - used to show disapproval —**demagogy, demagoguery** *n* [U] —**demagogic** /ˌdeməˈgɒgɪk◂ $ -ˈgɑː-/ *adj*

de·mand¹ /dɪˈmɑːnd $ dɪˈmænd/ ●●● S2 W1 *n*
1 [singular, U] the need or desire that people have for particular goods and services: *Production is increasing faster than demand.* | **[+for]** *the demand for new housing* | **in demand** (=wanted) *As a speaker he was always in demand.*
→ SUPPLY AND DEMAND
2 [C] a very firm request for something that you believe you have the right to get: *demonstrations in support of the nationalists' demands* | **[+for]** *their demand for higher salaries* | **demand that** *demands that he should resign*
3 demands [plural] the difficult, annoying, or tiring things that you need to do, or a skill you need to have: **[+of]** *the demands of modern life* | **[+on]** *The curriculum* ***makes*** *great* ***demands*** *on the teacher. | There are* ***heavy demands*** *on people's time these days.* | **place/put demands on/upon sb/sth** *the increased demands placed on police officers*
4 popular demand when a lot of people have asked for something to be done, performed etc: **by/due to popular demand** (=because of popular demand) *The exhibition will run for an extra week, due to popular demand.*
5 on demand *formal* whenever someone asks: *Should you feed your baby on demand, or stick to a timetable?*

COLLOCATIONS

ADJECTIVES/NOUN + demand

high (=a lot of people want something) *Demand for housing is higher than ever.*
low (=not many people want something) *Recently the demand for new cars has been relatively low.*
a big demand *There's always a big demand for photographs of celebrities.*
a great/huge demand (=very big) *There is a huge demand for business software and services.*
increased/increasing/growing demand *One of the problems is the growing demand for housing.*
falling demand (=decreasing) *the falling demand for coal*
consumer demand (=the desire of consumers to buy goods) *Consumer demand for new technology is strong.*

VERBS

meet/satisfy demand (=supply as much as people need or want) *There are reports that the company cannot produce enough to meet demand.*

keep up with demand (*also* **keep pace with demand**) (=satisfy the demand) *Public funding for higher education has not kept up with demand.*
cope with demand (=satisfy demand) *The existing services were not capable of coping with the demand for advice.*
increase/boost demand *A very hard winter boosted the demand for natural gas.*
reduce demand *Higher interest rates reduce the demand for credit.*
demand rises/increases *Demand for energy has continued to rise.*
demand falls (=becomes lower) *Demand for the products has fallen in the last six months.*

PHRASES

be much in demand (*also* **be in great demand**) (=be wanted by a lot of people) *Fuel-efficient cars are now much in demand.*
supply outstrips/exceeds demand (=more is available than people need or want) *In the 1980s, the supply of grain far exceeded the demand.*
a lack of demand *Many factories closed through lack of demand.*
a surge in demand (=a sudden increase) *There's often a surge in demand for the Internet at the weekend.*

D

demand² ●●● W2 *v* [T]
1 to ask for something very firmly, especially because you think you have a right to do this: *Angry demonstrators demanded the resignation of two senior officials.* | **demand to know/see/have etc sth** *I demand to know what's going on.* | **demand that** *They demanded that the military government free all political prisoners.* | **demand sth of sb** *It seemed that no matter what she did, more was demanded of her.* | *'Where are you going?' she demanded angrily.* THESAURUS ASK, INSIST
2 if one thing demands another, it needs that thing in order to happen or be done successfully: *Too many things demanded his* ***attention*** *at the same time.* | *It's a desperate situation demanding a desperate remedy.*

GRAMMAR: Patterns with demand

- You **demand** something: *I demand an explanation!*
- You **demand to do** something: *She demanded to see the manager.*
- In everyday English, you **demand that** someone **does** something: *I demand that he apologizes.*
- In formal English, you **demand that** someone **do** something, using the base form of the verb (=the infinitive without 'to'): *His opponents are demanding that he resign.* ✗ Don't say: *demand someone to do something*
- You use the base form of the verb when talking about the past: *They demanded that he* ***resign***. In everyday English, people also say: *They demanded that he* ***resigned***.
- You **demand that** someone **should do** something: *His opponents demanded that he should resign.* This pattern is often used in the past, when reporting what someone has demanded.

GRAMMAR GUIDE VERBS

de·mand·ing /dɪˈmɑːndɪŋ $ dɪˈmæn-/ ●●○ *adj*
1 needing a lot of ability, effort, or skill: *a* ***demanding job*** | **physically/emotionally/intellectually etc demanding** *Climbing is physically demanding.* THESAURUS DIFFICULT
2 expecting a lot of attention or expecting to have things exactly the way you want them, especially in a way that is not fair: *Her mother could be very demanding at times.*

de·mar·cate /ˈdiːmɑːkeɪt $ dɪˈmɑːr-/ *v* [T] *formal* to decide or mark the limits of an area, system etc

de·mar·ca·tion /ˌdiːmɑːˈkeɪʃən $ -ɑːr-/ *n* [U] *formal* **1** the point at which one area of work, responsibility etc ends and another begins: **[+between]** *traditional* ***lines of demarcation*** *between medicine and surgery* **2** the process of deciding on or marking the border between two areas of land: **[+of]** *the exact demarcation of the north-south boundary*

de·mean /dɪˈmiːn/ *v* [T] to do something that makes people lose respect for someone or something → **degrade**: *language that demeans women* | **demean yourself (by doing sth)** *I wouldn't demean myself by begging him for a job.*

de·mean·ing /dɪˈmiːnɪŋ/ *adj* showing less respect for someone than they deserve, or making someone feel embarrassed or ashamed → **degrading**: **[+to]** *policies demeaning to women* | *I refuse to do demeaning work.*

de·mea·nour *BrE*, **demeanor** *AmE* /dɪˈmiːnə $ -ər/ *n* [singular, U] *formal* the way someone behaves, dresses, speaks etc that shows what their character is like: *his quiet, reserved demeanour* THESAURUS BEHAVIOUR

de·men·ted /dɪˈmentɪd/ *adj* **1** crazy or behaving in a very strange way: *She was almost demented with grief.* **2** *old-fashioned* suffering from dementia

de·men·tia /dɪˈmenʃə, -ʃiə $ -tʃə/ *n* [U] an illness that affects the brain and memory, and makes you gradually lose the ability to think and behave normally

dem·e·ra·ra sug·ar /ˌdemərеərə ˈʃʊgə $ -rerə ˈʃʊgər/ *n* [U] *BrE* a type of rough brown sugar

de·merge /diːˈmɜːdʒ $ -ˈmɜːrdʒ/ *v* [I,T] *technical* to make one part of a large company into a separate company: *After the takeover, several subsidiary companies were demerged.*

de·merg·er /diːˈmɜːdʒə $ -ˈmɜːrdʒər/ *n* [C,U] the action of making one part of a large company into a separate company: *The demerger of the textile division is to go ahead.*

de·mer·it /diːˈmerɪt/ *n* [C] **1** *formal* a bad quality or feature of something: **[+of]** ***The merits and demerits*** (=the good and bad qualities) *of this argument have been explored.* **2** *AmE* a mark showing that a student has behaved badly at school → **merit**

de·mesne /dɪˈmeɪn/ *n* [C] in the past, a very big house and all the land that belonged to it

demi- /demɪ/ *prefix* half → **semi-**: *a demisemiquaver* (=very short musical note)

dem·i·god /ˈdemigɒd $ -gɑːd/ *n* [C] **1** someone who is so important and powerful that they are treated like a god **2** a man in ancient stories, who is half god and half human: *demigods such as Hercules*

dem·i·john /ˈdemidʒɒn $ -dʒɑːn/ *n* [C] *BrE* a large bottle with a short narrow neck, used for making wine

de·mil·i·ta·rize (*also* **-ise** *BrE*) /diːˈmɪlətəraɪz/ *v* [T] to remove the weapons, soldiers etc from a country or area so that there can be no fighting there: *the* ***demilitarized zone*** *between the two countries* —**demilitarization** /diːˌmɪlətəraɪˈzeɪʃən $ -rə-/ *n* [U]

de·min·ing /diːˈmaɪnɪŋ/ *n* [U] the process of removing LANDMINES from an area of land

de·mise /dɪˈmaɪz/ ●○○ *n* [U]
1 *formal* the end of something that used to exist: **[+of]** *the* ***imminent demise*** (=happening soon) *of the local newspaper*
2 *formal or law* death: *the mystery surrounding Elena's* ***untimely demise*** (=when death happens sooner than is normal or expected) —**demise** *v* [I]

de·mist /ˌdiːˈmɪst/ *v* [T] *BrE* to remove mist from a car window, by using heat SYN **defog** *AmE* —**demister** *n* [C]

dem·o¹ /ˈdeməʊ $ -moʊ/ *n* (*plural* **demos**) [C] **1** a recording containing an example of someone's music that is sent to a record company so that they can decide whether to produce it or not: *a demo tape* **2** *BrE informal* an event at which a large group of people publicly protest about something SYN **demonstration**: *pro-independence demos* **3** an explanation of how something works SYN **demonstration** **4 a)** *AmE* an example of a product that is used to show what it is like or how it works: *demo homes on the new development* **b)** a computer program that shows what a new piece of software will be able to do when it is ready to be sold: *Click here to download a demo of the new version of our personal finance software.*

demo² *v* [T] *informal* to show or explain how something works or is done, especially new computer equipment SYN **demonstrate**: *They're going to demo some of the new software at this year's Mac convention.*

de·mob /diːˈmɒb $ -ˈmɑːb/ *v* (**demobbed**, **demobbing**) [T] *BrE* to demobilize soldiers etc

ˌdemob ˈhappy *adj BrE informal* happy or behaving in a careless way because you are soon going to be leaving your job

de·mo·bi·lize (*also* **-ise** *BrE*) /diːˈməʊbəlaɪz $ -ˈmoʊ-/ *v* [T] to send home the members of an army, navy etc, especially at the end of a war: *programmes to help demobilized soldiers fit into civilian life* —**demobilization** /diːˌməʊbəlaɪˈzeɪʃən $ -ˌmoʊbələ-/ *n* [U]

de·moc·ra·cy /dɪˈmɒkrəsi $ dɪˈmɑː-/ ●●○ W3 *n* (*plural* **democracies**)
1 [U] a system of government in which every citizen in the country can vote to elect its government officials: *a return to democracy after 16 years of military rule* THESAURUS GOVERNMENT
2 [C] a country that has a government which has been elected by the people of the country: *a* ***parliamentary democracy*** | *Western democracies*
3 [U] a situation or system in which everyone is equal and has the right to vote, make decisions etc → **democratic**: *democracy within the trade unions*

dem·ocrat /ˈdeməkræt/ *n* [C] someone who believes in democracy, or works to achieve it

Democrat *n* [C] a member or supporter of the Democratic Party of the US

dem·o·crat·ic /ˌdeməˈkrætɪk◂/ ●●○ W3 *adj*
1 controlled by representatives who are elected by the people of a country: *a* ***democratic government*** | *the role of the media in the* ***democratic process***
2 organized according to the principle that everyone has a right to be involved in making decisions: *a democratic management style*
3 organized according to the principle that everyone in a society is equally important, no matter how much money they have or what social class they come from: *a democratic society*
4 (*also* **Democratic**) belonging to or supporting the Democratic Party of the US → **republican**: *the Democratic nominee for the presidency* —**democratically** /-kli/ *adv*: *democratically elected councils*

de·moc·ra·tize (*also* **-ise** *BrE*) /dɪˈmɒkrətaɪz $ dɪˈmɑː-/ *v* [T] to change the way in which a government, company etc is organized, so that it is more democratic: *efforts to democratize school management structures* —**democratization** /dɪˌmɒkrətaɪˈzeɪʃən $ dɪˌmɑːkrətə-/ *n* [U]

dem·o·graph·ic¹ /ˌdeməˈɡræfɪk◂/ ●○○ *adj* relating to the population and groups of people in it: *Demographic trends show that there are rising numbers of old people.* | *demographic changes*

demographic² *n* **1** **demographics** [plural] information about a group such as the people who live in a particular area: *the demographics of a newspaper's readership* **2** [C] a part of the population that is considered as a group, especially by advertisers who want to sell things to that group: *the 21–40 demographic*

de·mog·ra·phy /dɪˈmɒɡrəfi $ -ˈmɑː-/ *n* [U] the study of human populations and the ways in which they change, for example the study of how many births, marriages and deaths happen in a particular place at a particular time —**demographer** *n* [C]

de·mol·ish /dɪˈmɒlɪʃ $ dɪˈmɑː-/ ●○○ *v* [T]
1 to completely destroy a building: *The entire east wing of the building was demolished in the fire.* THESAURUS DESTROY
2 to prove that an idea or opinion is completely wrong: *He demolished my argument in minutes.*
3 to end or ruin something completely: *These ants can demolish large areas of forest.*
4 to defeat someone very easily: *Miami demolished Texas 46-3.*
5 *especially BrE informal* to eat all of something very quickly: *He demolished a second helping of pie.*

dem·o·li·tion /ˌdeməˈlɪʃən/ ●○○ *n* [C,U]
1 the complete destruction of a building: *Consent is required for the demolition of any building.* | *Demolition work has already begun at the site.*
2 an easy defeat: *50,000 fans watched the 7-0 demolition of Dynamo Kiev.*
3 a process in which something is ended or ruined completely: *The policies are intended to halt the demolition of the rural economy.*
4 the act of proving that an idea, opinion etc is wrong: *This is a legend that deserves demolition.*

ˌdemoˈlition ˌjob *n* [C] **1** an act of criticizing someone severely or telling other people things about them which may be unfair or untrue, in order to harm them or to cause people to have a bad opinion of them: *He accused opposition leaders of* ***doing a demolition job on*** *the president.*
2 an event, especially a sports event, in which one person or team defeats the other one very easily: **[+against]** *Currie led the team with 55 points in the demolition job against Ireland.*

de·mon /ˈdiːmən/ ●○○ *n* [C]
1 an evil SPIRIT or force: *He was speeding down the motorway as if pursued by a demon.*
2 [usually plural] something that makes you anxious and causes you problems: *She struggled with her husband's demons of addiction and alcoholism.*
3 someone who is very good at something - often used humorously: *a demon cook*
4 the demon drink *BrE* alcoholic drink - often used humorously → DAEMON

ˌde·mo·ni·a·cal /ˌdiːməˈnaɪəkəl◂/ (*also* **de·mo·ni·ac** /dɪˈməʊniæk $ -ˈmoʊ-/) *adj formal* wild, uncontrolled, and evil: *the demoniacal glint in his dark eyes* —**demoniacally** /-kli/ *adv*

de·mon·ic /dɪˈmɒnɪk $ dɪˈmɑː-/ *adj* **1** wild and cruel: *demonic laughter* **2** relating to a demon: *the demonic forces in the universe* —**demonically** /-kli/ *adv*

de·mon·stra·ble /dɪˈmɒnstrəbəl, ˈdemən- $ dɪˈmɑːn-/ AWL *adj formal* able to be shown or proved: *We must provide demonstrable improvements in health services.* —**demonstrably** *adv*: *These conclusions are demonstrably wrong.*

dem·on·strate /ˈdemənstreɪt/ ●●○ W2 AWL *v*
1 [T] to show or prove something clearly: *The study demonstrates the link between poverty and malnutrition.* | **demonstrate that** *Hitchcock's films demonstrate that a British filmmaker could learn from Hollywood.* | **demonstrate how/what/why etc** *This section will attempt to demonstrate how the Bank of England operates.* | *The government now has an opportunity to* ***demonstrate*** *its* ***commitment*** *to reform.*
2 [T] to show or describe how to do something or how something works: **demonstrate how** *They'll be demonstrating how to handle modern, high performance cars.* | *Instructors should demonstrate new movements before letting the class try them.* THESAURUS EXPLAIN, SHOW
3 [I] to protest or support something in public with a lot of other people: *Supporters demonstrated outside the courtroom during the trial.* | **[+against]** *What are they demonstrating against?*
4 [T] to show that you have a particular ability, quality, or feeling: *He has demonstrated an ability to meet deadlines.*

dem·on·stra·tion /ˌdemənˈstreɪʃən/ ●●○ W3 AWL *n* [C]
1 an event at which a large group of people meet to protest or to support something in public → **protest**: *Supporters staged a demonstration outside the US embassy.* | *Police opened fire on a peaceful demonstration.* | **[+against]** *a demonstration against the government's educational policies*
2 an act of explaining and showing how to do something or how something works: **[+of]** *He* ***gave*** *a practical* ***demonstration*** *of the boat's military potential.* | *a cookery demonstration*
3 *formal* an action that proves that someone or something

has a particular ability, quality, or feeling: **[+of]** *The high level of calls is a* ***clear demonstration of*** *the need for this service.* | *a physical demonstration of affection*

COLLOCATIONS

VERBS

hold/stage a demonstration (=organize and take part in one) *In April, students began holding demonstrations to demand more freedom.*
organize a demonstration *A large demonstration was organized by the opposition.*
take part in a demonstration (*also* **participate in a demonstration** *formal*) *As many as 400,000 people took part in the demonstration.*
go on a demonstration *BrE* (=take part in a demonstration) *I've never been on a demonstration before.*
join a demonstration *They were prevented by police from joining the demonstration.*
break up a demonstration (=prevent it from continuing) *Police moved in to break up the demonstration.*
provoke/spark a demonstration (=cause it) *The incident sparked a demonstration of 2,000 people.*
a demonstration takes place *Violent street demonstrations took place in the capital.*

ADJECTIVES/NOUN + demonstration

a big/large demonstration *Opponents of the new law are planning a big demonstration next week.*
a huge/massive demonstration (=very big) *a series of massive demonstrations against the war*
a mass demonstration (=involving a very large number of people) *There have been mass demonstrations in some American cities.*
a peaceful demonstration *Everyone has the right to take part in peaceful demonstrations.*
a violent demonstration *Nine people have been killed during violent demonstrations.*
a street demonstration (=in the streets of a city) *A street demonstration completely blocked the centre of the city.*
a student demonstration (=by students) *In France, student demonstrations were disrupting university teaching.*
a public demonstration (=by members of the public) *A series of public demonstrations have been held in cities across the country.*
a protest demonstration (=in which people protest against something) *The price increases were met by a series of strikes and protest demonstrations.*
a political demonstration (=to protest about the government or a political policy) *She was arrested twice for her part in political demonstrations.*
an anti-government/pro-democracy etc demonstration *There have been further violent anti-government demonstrations this week.*

PHRASES

a demonstration in support of sth/sb *public demonstrations in support of the rebels*
a demonstration in protest at sth *There were demonstrations in protest at the food shortages.*

de·mon·stra·tive /dɪˈmɒnstrətɪv $ dɪˈmɑːn-/ AWL *adj* willing to show that you care about someone: *My mother wasn't demonstrative; she never hugged me.* —**demonstratively** *adv*

deˌmonstrative ˈpronoun *n* [C] one of the words 'this', 'that', 'these', and 'those'

dem·on·stra·tor /ˈdemənstreɪtə $ -ər/ ●○○ AWL *n* [C]
1 someone who takes part in a demonstration: *anti-war demonstrators*
2 someone who shows people how to do something or how something works

de·mor·al·ize (*also* **-ise** *BrE*) /dɪˈmɒrəlaɪz $ dɪˈmɔː-, dɪˈmɑː-/ *v* [T] to reduce or destroy someone's courage or confidence: *The illness demoralized him and recovery took several weeks.* —**demoralized** *adj*: *The refugees were cold, hungry, and demoralized.* —**demoralizing** *adj*: *the demoralizing effects of unemployment* —**demoralization** /dɪˌmɒrəlaɪˈzeɪʃən $ -ˌmɔːrələ-, -ˌmɑː-/ *n* [U]

de·mote /dɪˈməʊt $ -ˈmoʊt/ *v* [T] to make someone's rank or position lower or less important OPP **promote**: **be demoted to sth** *The sergeant was demoted to private.* —**demotion** /-ˈməʊʃən $ -ˈmoʊ-/ *n* [C,U]

de·mot·ic /dɪˈmɒtɪk $ -ˈmɑː-/ *adj formal* used by or popular with most ordinary people

de·mo·ti·vat·ing /diːˈməʊtəveɪtɪŋ $ -ˈmoʊ-/ *adj* making someone less eager or willing to do their job: *Tasks that do not challenge you can be very demotivating.* —**demotivate** *v* [T]

de·mur¹ /dɪˈmɜː $ -ˈmɜːr/ *v* (**demurred**, **demurring**) [I] to express doubt about or opposition to a plan or suggestion: *They demurred politely, but finally agreed to stay.*

demur² *n* [U] disagreement or disapproval: **without demur** *I agreed to this without demur.*

de·mure /dɪˈmjʊə $ -ˈmjʊr/ *adj* **1** quiet, serious, and well-behaved - used especially about women in the past: *Old photos of Maggie show her young and demure.* **2** demure clothes do not show much of a woman's body: *a demure white dress* —**demurely** *adv*

de·mys·ti·fy /ˌdiːˈmɪstɪfaɪ/ *v* (**demystified**, **demystifying**, **demystifies**) [T] to make a subject that seems difficult or complicated easier to understand, especially by explaining it in simpler language: *This book demystifies the male worlds of plumbing and carpentry.* —**demystification** /diːˌmɪstəfɪˈkeɪʃən/ *n* [U]

den /den/ *n* [C] **1** the home of some animals, for example lions or FOXES **2** a place where secret or illegal activities take place: *corrupt gambling dens* | *a den of thieves* **3** an enclosed and secret place where children play **4** *especially AmE* a room in a house where people relax, watch television etc **5** *BrE old-fashioned* a small room in a house where people can work, read etc without being interrupted: *Father retreated to his den.* **6 den of iniquity** a place where activities that you think are immoral or evil happen - often used humorously: *Her mother was convinced that London was a den of iniquity.*

de·na·tion·al·ize (*also* **-ise** *BrE*) /diːˈnæʃənəlaɪz/ *v* [T] to sell a business or industry that is owned by the state, so that it is then owned privately SYN **privatize** OPP **nationalize** —**denationalization** /diːˌnæʃənəlaɪˈzeɪʃən $ -lə-/ *n* [U]

den·gue fe·ver /ˈdeŋgi ˈfiːvə $ ər/ *n* [U] an illness commonly found in hot countries, caused by the bite of a MOSQUITO which has been infected with a VIRUS. People with the illness have a fever and pain in their head, muscles, and joints.

de·ni·al /dɪˈnaɪəl/ ●○○ AWL *n*
1 [C,U] a statement saying that something is not true → **deny**: **[+of]** *The government* ***issued*** *an* ***official denial*** *of the rumour.* | **denial that** *denials that border security had not been strict enough*
2 [U] when someone refuses to allow someone else to have or to do something: **[+of]** *protests against the denial of human rights*
3 [U] a condition in which you refuse to admit or believe that something bad exists or has happened: **in denial** *His girlfriend is in denial, and refuses to admit that he will soon die.*

deˌnial of ˈservice atˌtack *n* [C] an attempt to make a company's website stop working. This is done by sending so much DATA to the website that the company's computers become unable to work properly. The result is that customers of the company cannot use the online services that the company provides.

den·i·er¹ /ˈdeniə $ -ər/ *n* [U] a unit for measuring how thin NYLON, silk etc thread is: **10-/15-/20- etc denier** *a pair of 15-denier tights*

de·ni·er² /dɪˈnaɪə $ -ər/ *n* [C] a person who says they do not believe something that most other people believe, especially that CLIMATE change is happening because of people's activities, or that the Holocaust happened – used to show disapproval: *How can we convince the climate change deniers that they are wrong?*

de·ni·grate /ˈdenəɡreɪt/ *v* [T] to say things to make someone or something seem less important or good: *people who denigrate their own country* —**denigration** /ˌdenɪˈɡreɪʃən/ *n* [U]

den·im /ˈdenɪm/ *n* [U] a type of strong cotton cloth used especially to make JEANS

den·i·zen /ˈdenɪzən/ *n* [C + of] *literary* an animal, plant, or person that lives or is found in a particular place

de·nom·i·nate /dɪˈnɒməneɪt $ dɪˈnɑː-/ *v* [T] *technical* to officially set the value of something according to one system or type of money: *bank deposits denominated in foreign currencies* GRAMMAR **Denominate** is usually passive.

de·nom·i·na·tion /dɪˌnɒməˈneɪʃən $ dɪˌnɑː-/ *n* [C] **1** a religious group that has different beliefs from other groups within the same religion: *Christians of all denominations* **2** *technical* the value shown on a coin, paper money, or a stamp

de·nom·i·na·tion·al /dɪˌnɒməˈneɪʃənəl $ dɪˌnɑː-/ *adj* relating or belonging to a particular religious denomination

de·nom·i·na·tor /dɪˈnɒməneɪtə $ dɪˈnɑːməneɪtər/ *n* [C] *technical* the number below the line in a FRACTION → **numerator** → **lowest common denominator** at **COMMON DENOMINATOR(2)**

de·note /dɪˈnəʊt $ -ˈnoʊt/ ●○○ AWL *v* [T] *formal*
1 to mean something → **connote**: *What does the word 'curriculum' denote that 'course' does not?*
2 to represent or be a sign of something SYN **indicate**: *Crosses on the map denote villages.* —**denotative** *adj* —**denotation** /ˌdiːnəʊˈteɪʃən $ -noʊ-/ *n* [C]

de·noue·ment /deɪˈnuːmɒŋ $ ˌdeɪnuːˈmɑːŋ/ *n* [C] *formal* the exciting last part of a story or play: *The plot takes us to Paris for the denouement of the story.*

de·nounce /dɪˈnaʊns/ ●○○ *v* [T]
1 to express strong disapproval of someone or something, especially in public → **denunciation**: *Amnesty International denounced the failure by the authorities to take action.* | **denounce sb/sth as sth** *He denounced the election as a farce.*
2 to give information to the police or another authority about someone's illegal political activities: **denounce sb to sb** *She denounced him to the police.*

dense /dens/ ●●○ *adj*
1 made of or containing a lot of things or people that are very close together SYN **thick**: **dense undergrowth/forest/woodland/jungle etc** *A narrow track wound steeply up through dense forest.* | *the city's* ***dense population***
2 difficult to see through or breathe in: **dense fog/smoke/cloud** *dense black smoke*
3 *informal* not able to understand things easily SYN **stupid**: *Am I being dense? I don't quite understand.*
4 a dense piece of writing is difficult to understand because it contains a lot of information or uses complicated language
5 *technical* a substance that is dense has a lot of MASS in relation to its size: *Water is eight hundred times denser than air.* —**densely** *adv*: *a* ***densely populated*** *area* —**denseness** *n* [U]

den·si·ty /ˈdensəti/ ●●○ *n* [U]
1 the degree to which an area is filled with people or things: **[+of]** *the size and density of settlements* | *areas of high* ***population density***
2 *technical* the relationship between the MASS of something and its size

dent¹ /dent/ *n* [C] **1** a hollow area in the surface of something, usually made by something hitting it: **[+in]** *There was a large dent in the passenger door.* **2** a reduction in the amount of something: **[+in]** *The trip* ***made a*** *big* ***dent*** *in our savings.* | *Eight years of effort have hardly* ***put a dent in*** *drug trafficking.*

dent² *v* **1** [I,T] if you dent something, or if it dents, you hit or press it so that its surface is bent inwards: *No one was injured, but the car was scratched and dented.* **2** [T] to damage or harm something: *The scandal has dented his reputation.*

den·tal /ˈdentl/ ●○○ *adj* [only before noun] relating to your teeth: **dental treatment/care** *Dental care was free in the 60s.* | **dental disease/problems/decay etc**

ˌdental ˈfloss *n* [U] thin strong string that you use for cleaning between your teeth

ˌdental ˈhygienist *n* [C] someone who works with a dentist and cleans people's teeth, or gives them advice about how to look after their teeth

ˈdental nurse *n* [C] someone whose job is to help a dentist

ˈdental ˌsurgeon *n* [C] a dentist who can perform operations in the mouth

den·tine /ˈdentiːn/ (*also* **den·tin** /ˈdentɪn/) *n* [U] the type of bone that your teeth are made of

den·tist /ˈdentɪst/ ●●● S3 *n* [C] someone whose job is to treat people's teeth: **the dentist/the dentist's** (=the place where a dentist works) *I'm* ***going to the dentist*** *this afternoon.*

den·tis·try /ˈdentəstri/ *n* [U] the medical study of the mouth and teeth, or the work of a dentist

den·tures /ˈdentʃəz $ -ərz/ *n* [plural] a set of artificial teeth worn by someone who does not have their own teeth any longer SYN **false teeth**

de·nude /dɪˈnjuːd $ dɪˈnuːd/ *v* [T] *formal* **1** to remove the plants and trees that cover an area of land: *a hillside denuded in a fire* **2** to take something away from someone or something: **denude sb/sth of sth** *The fact that people have left farm work has denuded many villages of their working populations.* —**denudation** /ˌdiːnjuːˈdeɪʃən $ -nuː-/ *n* [U]

de·nun·ci·a·tion /dɪˌnʌnsiˈeɪʃən/ *n* [C] a public statement in which you criticize someone or something → **denounce**

de·ny /dɪˈnaɪ/ ●●● S3 W2 AWL *v* (**denied**, **denying**, **denies**) [T]
1 SAY STH IS NOT TRUE to say that something is not true, or that you do not believe something → **denial**: **deny (that)** *I've never denied that there is a housing problem.* | *I can't deny her remarks hurt me.* | **deny doing sth** *Two men have denied murdering a woman at a remote picnic spot.* | **strongly/vehemently/strenuously etc deny sth** *Jackson vehemently denied the allegations.* | *The government* ***denied the existence of*** *poverty among 16- and 17-year-olds.* | **deny a charge/allegation/claim** *The men have denied charges of theft.*
2 NOT ALLOW to refuse to allow someone to have or do something: *Some landowners deny access to the countryside.* | **deny sb sth** *She could deny her son nothing.* | **deny sth to sb** *This is the only country in Europe to deny cancer screening to its citizens.* THESAURUS ▸ REFUSE
3 there's no denying (that/sth) *spoken* used to say that it is very clear that something is true: *There's no denying that this is an important event.*
4 FEELINGS to refuse to admit that you are feeling something: *Emotions can become destructive if they are suppressed and denied.*
5 deny yourself (sth) to decide not to have something that you would like, especially for moral or religious reasons: *He denied himself all pleasures and luxuries.*

de·o·do·rant /diːˈəʊdərənt $ -ˈoʊ-/ *n* [C,U] a chemical substance that you put on the skin under your arms to stop you from smelling bad → **antiperspirant**

de·o·do·rize (*also* **-ise** *BrE*) /diːˈəʊdəraɪz $ -ˈoʊ-/ *v* [T] to remove a bad smell or to make it less noticeable

de·part /dɪˈpɑːt $ -ɑːrt/ ●●○ *v*
1 [I,T] to leave, especially when you are starting a journey → **departure**: **[+from]** *ocean liners arriving at and departing from the island* | **[+for]** *Dorothy departed for*

Germany last week. | *Flights by Air Europe depart Gatwick on Tuesdays.*

> **REGISTER**
> In everyday English, people usually say **leave** or **go** rather than **depart**: *What time does the next plane* ***leave/go****?* | *She* ***left for*** *Germany last week.* | *Flights* ***leave*** *from Gatwick on Tuesdays.*

2 depart this life *formal* to die
3 [I] to start to use new ideas or do something in a different way → **departure**: **[+from]** *It's revolutionary music; it departs from the old form and structures.* | *In his speech, the president departed from his text only once.*
4 [I,T] to leave an organization or job → **departure**: *the company's departing chairman*

de·part·ed /dɪˈpɑːtɪd $ -ɑːr-/ *adj* [only before noun] dead – used in order to avoid saying the word 'dead': *his* ***dear departed*** *wife*

de·part·ment /dɪˈpɑːtmənt $ -ɑːr-/ ●●● S2 W1 *n* [C]
1 one of the groups of people who work together in a particular part of a large organization such as a hospital, university, company, or government: *the personnel department* | *the English department* | **[+of]** *the Department of the Environment*
2 an area in a large shop where a particular type of product is sold: *the toy department*
3 be sb's department *spoken* if something is someone's department, they are responsible for it or know a lot about it: *I'll see what I can do, but it's not really my department.*
4 *spoken* a particular part of someone's character, or a particular part of a larger activity or subject: *Dave was lacking in the trustworthiness department.* —**departmental** /ˌdiːpɑːtˈmentl◂ $ -ɑːr-/ *adj*: *a departmental meeting*

de·part·men·ta·lize (*also* **-ise** *BrE*) /ˌdiːpɑːtˈmentl-aɪz $ -ɑːr-/ *v* [T] to divide something into different departments

deˈpartment ˌstore ●●○ *n* [C] a large shop that is divided into separate departments, each selling a different type of goods

de·par·ture /dɪˈpɑːtʃə $ -ˈpɑːrtʃər/ ●●○ W3 *n*
1 [C,U] an act of leaving a place, especially at the start of a journey OPP **arrival**: **[+for]** *I saw Simon shortly before his departure for Russia.* | **[+of]** *There was a delay in the departure of our plane.* | **[+from]** *Mozart's departure from Paris in September 1778*
2 [C,U] an act of leaving an organization or position: **[+from]** *He refused to discuss his departure from the government.*
3 [C] a flight, train etc that leaves at a particular time: *There are several departures for New York every day.*
4 [C] a way of doing something that is different from the usual, traditional, or expected way: **[+from]** *Their new designs represent a departure from their usual style.* | **radical/major/significant etc departure** (=a big change) *This would be a radical departure from the subsidy system.*

deˈparture ˌlounge *n* [C] the place at an airport where people wait until their plane is ready to leave

deˈpartures ˌboard *n* [C] a big screen at an airport or station that shows the times at which planes or trains leave

de·pend /dɪˈpend/ ●●● S1 W2 *v* **it/that depends** *spoken* used to say that you cannot give a definite answer to something because your answer will be affected by something else: *'How long are you staying?' 'I don't know; it depends.'* | **it depends who/what/how/whether etc** *You may take several months to reach your target weight – it depends how much you want to lose.*

> **GRAMMAR**
> **Patterns with depend**
> • You say: *The cost depends on the time of year.*
> • You can also use the adjective **dependent**: *The cost is dependent on the time of year.* ✗ Don't say: *The cost is depend on the time of year.*
>
> **Using the progressive**
> • **Depend** is not used in the progressive. You say: *It depends (on) what you want.* ✗ Don't say: *It is depending (on) what you want.*
> • However, the present participle **depending** is often used: *It costs between $50 and $70, depending on what you want.*
> GRAMMAR GUIDE ▸ VERBS

depend on/upon sb/sth *phr v*
1 if something depends on something else, it is directly affected or decided by that thing: *The length of time spent exercising depends on the sport you are training for.* | **depend on how/what/whether etc** *Choosing the right bike depends on what you want to use it for.* | **depending on sth** *The expenses you claim can vary enormously, depending on travel distances involved.*
2 to need the support, help, or existence of someone or something in order to exist, be healthy, be successful etc SYN **rely on**: *The country* ***depends heavily*** *on its tourist trade.* | *We depend entirely on donations from the public.* | **depend on sb/sth for sth** *Many women have to depend on their husbands for their state pension.* | **depend on sb/sth to do sth** *I'm depending on you to tell me everything.* | **depend on sb/sth doing sth** *We're depending on him finishing the job by Friday.*
3 to trust or have confidence in someone or something: *You can depend on Jane – she always keeps her promises.*

de·pend·a·ble /dɪˈpendəbəl/ ●○○ *adj* able to be trusted to do what you need or expect: *our most dependable ally* | *a dependable source of income* —**dependably** *adv* —**dependability** /dɪˌpendəˈbɪləti/ *n* [U]

de·pen·dant *BrE*, **dependent** *AmE* /dɪˈpendənt/ *n* [C] someone, especially a child, who depends on you for food, clothes, money etc

de·pen·dence /dɪˈpendəns/ ●●○ (*also* **dependency**) *n* [U]
1 when you depend on the help and support of someone or something else in order to exist or be successful OPP **independence**: **[+on/upon]** *our dependence on oil as a source of energy* | *the financial dependency of some women on men*
2 drug/alcohol dependence when someone is ADDICTED to drugs or alcohol
3 *technical* when one thing is strongly affected by another thing: **[+of]** *the mutual dependence of profit and growth*

de·pen·den·cy /dɪˈpendənsi/ *n* (*plural* **dependencies**) **1** [U] DEPENDENCE: *drug dependency* **2** [C] a country that is controlled by another country → **colony**: *Britain's Caribbean dependencies*

de·pen·dent¹ /dɪˈpendənt/ ●●○ W3 *adj*
1 needing someone or something in order to exist, be successful, be healthy etc OPP **independent**: **[+on/upon]** *Norway's economy is* ***heavily dependent*** *on natural resources.* | *Jan's mother was* ***dependent on*** *her* ***for*** *physical care.* | *Do you have any* ***dependent children*** (=who you are still supporting financially)?
2 ADDICTED to drugs, alcohol etc: **[+on/upon]** *the needs of people dependent on drugs* | *a danger of becoming* ***alcohol dependent***
3 be dependent on/upon sth to be directly affected or decided by something else: *Your pay is dependent on how much you produce.*

> **GRAMMAR**
> Someone or something is **dependent on** something: *We are all dependent on computers.* ✗ Don't say: *dependent of something*
> GRAMMAR GUIDE ▸ ADJECTIVES

dependent² *n* [C] the American spelling of DEPENDANT

deˌpendent ˈclause *n* [C] a CLAUSE in a sentence that gives information related to the main clause, but cannot exist alone

de·pict /dɪˈpɪkt/ ●○○ *v* [T] *formal* to describe something or someone in writing or speech, or to show them in a painting, picture etc: *a book depicting life in pre-revolutionary Russia* | **depict sb/sth as sth** *The god is depicted as a bird with a human head.* THESAURUS▸ DESCRIBE —**depiction** /dɪˈpɪkʃən/ *n* [C,U]

de·pil·a·to·ry /dɪˈpɪlətəri $ -tɔːri/ *n* (*plural* **depilatories**) [C] *formal* a substance that gets rid of unwanted hair from your body —**depilatory** *adj* [only before noun]: *depilatory creams*

de·plane /diːˈpleɪn/ *v* [I] to get off a plane

de·plete /dɪˈpliːt/ *v* [T] to reduce the amount of something that is present or available: *Salmon populations have been* ***severely depleted****.* GRAMMAR **Deplete** is often passive in this meaning. —**depletion** /dɪˈpliːʃən/ *n* [U]: *the depletion of the ozone layer*

de·plor·a·ble /dɪˈplɔːrəbəl/ *adj formal* very bad, unpleasant, and shocking SYN **appalling**: *The prisoners were held in* ***deplorable conditions****.* | *His conduct was deplorable.* —**deplorably** *adv*

de·plore /dɪˈplɔː $ -ˈplɔːr/ *v* [T] *formal* to disapprove of something very strongly and criticize it severely, especially publicly: *The UN deplored the invasion as a 'violation of international law'.*

de·ploy /dɪˈplɔɪ/ ●○○ *v*

1 [I,T] to organize or move soldiers, military equipment etc so that they are in the right place and ready to be used: **deploy forces/troops/weapons etc** *NATO's decision to deploy cruise missiles*

2 [T] *formal* to use something for a particular purpose, especially ideas, arguments etc: *a job in which a variety of professional skills will be deployed* —**deployment** *n* [C,U]

de·po·lic·ing, **depolicing** /ˌdiːpəˈliːsɪŋ/ *n* [U] a way of keeping control over an area in which the police deliberately ignore small crimes by members of ethnic minorities (ETHNIC MINORITY) so that they are not ACCUSEd of RACISM (=treating members of a particular race unfairly)

de·po·lit·i·cize (*also* **-ise** *BrE*) /ˌdiːpəˈlɪtɪsaɪz/ *v* [T] to remove political influence or control from a situation —**depoliticization** /ˌdiːpəˌlɪtəsaɪˈzeɪʃən $ -sə-/ *n* [U]

de·pop·u·late /ˌdiːˈpɒpjəleɪt $ -ˈpɑːp-/ *v* [T] to greatly reduce the number of people living in a particular area: *Disease depopulated the whole region.* —**depopulation** /diːˌpɒpjəˈleɪʃən $ -ˌpɑːp-/ *n* [U]

de·port /dɪˈpɔːt $ -ɔːrt/ ●○○ *v* [T] to make someone leave a country and return to the country they came from, especially because they do not have a legal right to stay → **export**: **deport sb from/to sth** *He was deported from Ecuador when his visa expired.* —**deportation** /ˌdiːpɔːˈteɪʃən $ -pɔːr-/ *n* [C,U]: *the deportation of illegal immigrants*

de·por·tee /ˌdiːpɔːˈtiː $ -pɔːr-/ *n* [C] *formal* someone who has been deported or is going to be deported

de·port·ment /dɪˈpɔːtmənt $ -ɔːr-/ *n* [U] **1** *BrE* the way that someone stands and walks: *lessons in manners and deportment* **2** *old-fashioned especially AmE* the way that someone behaves in public

de·pose /dɪˈpəʊz $ -ˈpoʊz/ *v* [T] to remove a leader or ruler from a position of power

de·pos·it[1] /dɪˈpɒzɪt $ dɪˈpɑː-/ ●●○ S3 W3 *n* [C]

1 a part of the cost of something you are buying that you pay some time before you pay the rest of it: **[+of]** *A deposit of 10% is required.* | **put down a deposit (on sth)** (=pay a deposit) *We put down a deposit on a house.*

2 money that you pay when you rent something such as an apartment or car, which will be given back if you do not damage it: **[+of]** *We ask for one month's rent in advance, plus a deposit of $500.*

3 an amount of money that is paid into a bank account OPP **withdrawal**: **[+into]** *I'd like to* ***make a deposit*** (=pay some money) *into my savings account.*

4 a layer of a mineral, metal etc that is left in soil or rocks through a natural process: **[+of]** *rich deposits of gold in the hills*

5 an amount or layer of a substance that gradually develops in a particular place: *fatty deposits on the heart*

6 an amount of money paid by a CANDIDATE in a political election in Britain, that is returned to them if they get enough votes: **lose your deposit** (=not get enough votes)

deposit[2] ●○○ *v*

1 [T always + adv/prep] *formal* to put something down in a particular place: *The female deposits her eggs directly into the water.*

2 [T] to leave a layer of a substance on the surface of something, especially gradually: *As the river slows down, it deposits a layer of soil.*

3 [T] to put money or something valuable in a bank or other place where it will be safe: **deposit sth in sth** *You are advised to deposit your valuables in the hotel safe.* | **deposit sth with sb/sth** *The dollars are then deposited with banks outside the USA.*

> **REGISTER**
> In everyday English, people usually say they **put in** or **pay in** money, rather than **deposit** money: *I* ***paid/put*** *$100* ***into*** *his account.* | *You should* ***put*** *your valuables* ***in*** *the hotel safe.*

deˈposit acˌcount *n* [C] *especially BrE* a bank account that pays INTEREST on the money that you leave in it SYN **savings account** → CHECKING ACCOUNT, CURRENT ACCOUNT

dep·o·si·tion /ˌdepəˈzɪʃən, ˌdiː-/ *n* **1** [U] *technical* the natural process of depositing a substance on rocks or soil: *the deposition of marine sediments* **2** [C] *law* a statement written or recorded for a court of law, by someone who has promised to tell the truth **3** [C,U] the act of removing someone from a position of power

de·pos·i·tor /dɪˈpɒzɪtə $ dɪˈpɑːzɪtər/ *n* [C] someone who puts money in a bank or other financial organization

de·pos·i·to·ry /dɪˈpɒzətəri $ dɪˈpɑːzətɔːri/ *n* (*plural* **depositories**) [C] a place where something can be safely kept —**depository** *adj*

dep·ot /ˈdepəʊ $ ˈdiːpoʊ/ ●○○ *n* [C]

1 a place where goods are stored until they are needed: *the company's* ***distribution depot*** | *a fuel* ***storage depot***

2 **bus/tram etc depot** *BrE* a place where buses etc are kept and repaired

3 *AmE* a railway station or bus station, especially a small one

de·prave /dɪˈpreɪv/ *v* [T] *formal* to be an evil influence on someone, especially someone who is young or not very experienced

de·praved /dɪˈpreɪvd/ *adj* completely evil or morally unacceptable: *a killer's depraved mind* —**depravity** /dɪˈprævəti/ *n* [U]

dep·re·cate /ˈdeprɪkeɪt/ *v* [T] *formal* to strongly disapprove of or criticize something —**deprecation** /ˌdeprɪˈkeɪʃən/ *n* [U]

dep·re·cat·ing /ˈdeprəkeɪtɪŋ/ (*also* **dep·re·ca·to·ry** /ˈdeprəkeɪtəri $ ˈdeprəkətɔːri/) *adj formal* **1** expressing criticism or disapproval: *She glanced at me in a deprecating way.* **2** *BrE* intended to make someone feel less annoyed or disapproving: *a deprecating smile* → SELF-DEPRECATING —**deprecatingly** *adv*

de·pre·ci·ate /dɪˈpriːʃieɪt/ *v* **1** [I] to decrease in value or price OPP **appreciate**: *New cars* ***depreciate in value*** *quickly.* **2** [T] *technical* to reduce the value of something over time, especially for tax purposes: *Company computers are depreciated at 50% per year.* **3** [T] *formal* to make something seem unimportant: *those who depreciate the importance of art in education*

de·pre·ci·a·tion /dɪˌpriːʃiˈeɪʃən/ *n* [U] a reduction in the value or price of something: *the depreciation of the dollar*

dep·re·da·tion /ˌdeprəˈdeɪʃən/ *n* [C usually plural] *formal* an act of taking or destroying something

de·press /dɪˈpres/ AWL *v* [T] **1** to make someone feel very unhappy → **depression**: *The thought of taking the exam again depressed him.* | ***It depresses me that*** *nobody seems to care.* **2** to prevent an ECONOMY from being as active and successful as it usually is → **depression**: *Several factors combined to depress the American economy.*

D

3 *formal* to press something down, especially a part of a machine: *Depress the clutch fully.*

> **REGISTER**
> In everyday English, people usually say they **push (down)** or **press (down)** a button rather than **depress** it: ***Push** this button for cold water.* | ***Push** the clutch **down** fully.*

4 *formal* to reduce the value of prices or wages: *High interest rates may depress share prices.*

de·press·ant /dɪˈpresənt/ *n* [C] a substance or drug that makes your body processes slower and makes you feel very relaxed or sleepy → **stimulant** —**depressant** *adj*

de·pressed /dɪˈprest/ ●●○ *adj*
1 a) very unhappy: *She **felt** lonely and **depressed**.* | **[+about]** *Don't **get depressed** about it.* | *The divorce left him **deeply depressed**.* | *I was **depressed at the thought of** all the hard work ahead.* **b)** suffering from a medical condition in which you are so unhappy that you cannot live a normal life: *patients who are **clinically depressed*** THESAURUS ▸ SAD
2 an area, industry etc that is depressed does not have enough economic or business activity: *Britain's depressed housing market*
3 *formal* a depressed level or amount is lower than normal: *a depressed appetite*

de·press·ing /dɪˈpresɪŋ/ ●●○ *adj* making you feel very sad: *It's a depressing thought.* | *The whole experience was very depressing.* —**depressingly** *adv*: *depressingly poor results*

de·pres·sion /dɪˈpreʃən/ ●●○ W3 AWL *n*
1 [C,U] **a)** a medical condition that makes you very unhappy and anxious and often prevents you from living a normal life: *women who suffer from **post-natal depression*** (=that sometimes happens after the birth of a baby) **b)** a feeling of sadness that makes you think there is no hope for the future: *Lucy's mood was one of **deep depression**.*
2 the (Great) Depression the period during the 1930s when there was not much business activity and not many jobs
3 [C,U] a long period during which there is very little business activity and a lot of people do not have jobs → **recession**: *the devastating effects of **economic depression***
4 [C] a part of a surface that is lower than the other parts: *depressions in the ground*
5 [C] *technical* a mass of air under low pressure, that usually causes rain

de·press·ive[1] /dɪˈpresɪv/ *adj* relating to or suffering from DEPRESSION: *patients with depressive symptoms*

depressive[2] *n* [C] someone who suffers from DEPRESSION

dep·ri·va·tion /ˌdeprəˈveɪʃən/ ●○○ *n* [C usually plural, U] the lack of something that you need in order to be healthy, comfortable, or happy: ***Sleep deprivation** can result in mental disorders.* | **social/economic/emotional etc deprivation** *Low birth weight is related to economic deprivation.* | **[+of]** *the deprivations of prison life*

de·prive /dɪˈpraɪv/ ●○○ *v*
deprive sb **of** sth *phr v* to prevent someone from having something, especially something that they need or should have: *A lot of these children have been deprived of a normal home life.*

de·prived /dɪˈpraɪvd/ ●○○ *adj* not having the things that are necessary for a comfortable or happy life: ***Deprived children** tend to do less well at school.* | **deprived areas/neighbourhoods etc** (=where a lot of deprived people live) *our deprived inner cities* THESAURUS ▸ POOR

Dept. (*also* **Dept** *BrE*) the written abbreviation of ***department***

depth /depθ/ ●●● S3 W3 *n*
1 [C usually singular, U] **a)** the distance from the top surface of something such as a river or hole to the bottom of it → **deep**: *a sea with an average depth of 35 metres* | **to/at a depth of sth** *The cave descends to a depth of 340 feet.* | *Plant the beans at a depth of about six inches.* | **a metre/foot etc in depth** (=deep) *a channel of two feet in depth* **b)** the distance from the front to the back of an object: *The depth of the shelves is about 35 cm.* → see picture at DIMENSION
2 [U] how strong an emotion is or how serious a situation is: **[+of]** *the depth of public feeling on this issue* | *People need to realize the depth of the problem.*
3 [U] **a)** (*also* **depths**) the quality of having a lot of knowledge, understanding, or experience: **depth of knowledge/understanding/experience** *I was impressed by the depth of her knowledge.* | *a man of great depth and insight* | *She's quiet, but perhaps she has **hidden depths**.* **b)** when a lot of details about a subject are provided or considered: *Network news coverage often lacks depth.* | *The subject was discussed **in great depth**.*
4 be out of your depth a) to be involved in a situation or activity that is too difficult for you to understand or deal with: *I felt completely out of my depth at the meeting.* **b)** *BrE* to be in water that is too deep for you to stand in
5 the depths of sth when a bad feeling or situation is at its worst level: *She was **in the depths of despair**.* | *The country was recovering from **the depths of recession**.*
6 the depths of the ocean/countryside/forest etc the part that is furthest away from people, and most difficult to reach: *Astronomers may one day travel to the depths of space.*
7 the depths of winter the middle of winter, especially when it is very cold
8 the depths *literary* the deepest parts of the sea

ˈdepth charge *n* [C] a bomb that explodes at a particular depth under water

dep·u·ta·tion /ˌdepjəˈteɪʃən/ *n* [C] *formal* a small group of people who are sent to talk to someone in authority, as representatives of a larger group

de·pute /dɪˈpjuːt/ *v* **depute sb to do sth** *formal* to tell or allow someone to do something instead of you

dep·u·tize (*also* **-ise** *BrE*) /ˈdepjətaɪz/ *v* **1** [I] *BrE* to do the work of someone of a higher rank than you for a short time because they are unable to do it: **[+for]** *Jed could deputise for Stewart, if necessary.* **2** [T] *AmE* to give someone below you in rank the authority to do your work for a short time, usually because you are unable to do it → **delegate**

dep·u·ty /ˈdepjəti/ ●●○ *n* (*plural* **deputies**) [C]
1 (*also* **Deputy**) someone who is directly below another person in rank, and who is officially in charge when that person is not there: **deputy director/chairman/governor etc** *the Deputy Secretary of State*
2 someone whose job is to help a SHERIFF in the US
3 a member of parliament in some countries, for example France

de·rail /ˌdiːˈreɪl, dɪ-/ *v* **1** [I,T] if a train derails or something derails it, it goes off the tracks **2** [T] to spoil or interrupt a plan, agreement etc: *a mistake that might derail the negotiations* —**derailment** *n* [C,U]

de·ranged /dɪˈreɪndʒd/ *adj* someone who is deranged behaves in a crazy or dangerous way, usually because they are mentally ill: *a deranged gunman* —**derangement** *n* [C,U]

der·by /ˈdɑːbi $ ˈdɜːrbi/ *n* (*plural* **derbies**) [C] **1 Derby** used in the names of some well-known horse races: *the Kentucky Derby* | ***the Derby** BrE* (=a famous race in England) **2** *BrE* a sports match between two teams from the same area or city **3** *especially AmE* a man's hard round hat that is usually black SYN **bowler** *BrE* **4** a particular type of race or competition: *a donkey derby*

Derby, the a very important yearly horse race held at Epsom in England in May or June, on a day which is known as Derby Day

de·reg·u·late /ˌdiːˈregjəleɪt/ *v* [T] to remove government rules and controls from some types of business activity: *The decision to deregulate the banks was criticised.* | *industries that have been deregulated* GRAMMAR **Deregulate** is often used in the passive. —**deregulation** /diːˌregjəˈleɪʃən/ *n* [U]

der·e·lict[1] /ˈderəlɪkt/ *adj* a derelict building or piece of land is in very bad condition because it has not been used for a long time

derelict² *n* [C] someone who has no money or home, lives on the streets, and is very dirty – used to show disapproval

der·e·lic·tion /ˌderəˈlɪkʃən/ *n* **1 dereliction of duty** *formal* when someone fails to do what they should do as part of their job **2** [U] the state of being derelict: *areas of* ***industrial dereliction***

de·ride /dɪˈraɪd/ *v* [T] *formal* to make remarks or jokes that show you think someone or something is silly or useless SYN **mock** → **derisive**: *You shouldn't deride their efforts.* | **deride sb as sth** *The party was derided as totally lacking in ideas.*

de ri·gueur /də riːˈgɜː $ -ˈgɜːr/ *adj* [not before noun] considered to be necessary if you want to be accepted, fashionable etc – used humorously: *the gleaming white teeth that are de rigueur for movie stars*

de·ri·sion /dɪˈrɪʒən/ *n* [U] when you show that you think someone or something is stupid or silly: *His speech was* ***greeted with derision*** *by opposition leaders.*

de·ri·sive /dɪˈraɪsɪv/ *adj* showing that you think someone or something is stupid or silly: *derisive laughter* —**derisively** *adv*

de·ri·so·ry /dɪˈraɪsəri/ *adj* **1** an amount of money that is derisory is so small that it is not worth considering seriously: *Unions described the pay offer as derisory.* **2** DERISIVE

de·riv·a·ble /dɪˈraɪvəbəl/ *adj* [+from] something that is derivable can be calculated from something else

der·i·va·tion /ˌderəˈveɪʃən/ AWL *n* [C,U +of] *technical* the origin of something, especially a word

de·riv·a·tive¹ /dɪˈrɪvətɪv/ AWL *n* [C] **1** something that has developed or been produced from something else: **[+of]** *Heroin is a derivative of morphine.* **2** a type of financial INVESTMENT: *the derivatives market*

derivative² *adj* not new or invented, but copied or taken from something else – used to show disapproval: *a derivative text*

de·rive /dɪˈraɪv/ ●●○ W3 AWL *v*

1 [T] to get something, especially an advantage or a pleasant feeling, from something: **derive sth from sth** *Medically, we will* ***derive*** *great* ***benefit*** *from this technique.* | **derive pleasure/enjoyment etc** *Many students derived enormous satisfaction from the course.*

2 (*also* **be derived**) [I,T] to develop or come from something else → **derivation**: **[+from]** *This word is derived from Latin.* | *patterns of behaviour that derive from basic beliefs*

> **REGISTER**
> In everyday English, people usually say that something **comes from** something rather than **is derived from** something: *This word* ***comes from*** *Latin.*

3 [T] *technical* to get a chemical substance from another substance: **be derived from sth** *The enzyme is derived from human blood.*

derm·a·brade /ˈdɜːməbreɪd $ ˈdɜːr-/ *v* [T] *medical* to remove something from a surface, using the edge of a SCALPEL or knife etc SYN **scrape**

der·ma·bra·sion /ˌdɜːməˈbreɪʒən $ ˌdɜːr-/ *n* [C,U] *medical* a type of SURGERY that removes the top layers of someone's skin in order to make the skin below look smoother and to make new skin healthier. This is often done to repair SCARS caused by an accident or by previous surgery.

der·ma·ti·tis /ˌdɜːməˈtaɪtɪs $ ˌdɜːr-/ *n* [U] a disease of the skin that causes redness, swelling, and pain

der·ma·tol·o·gy /ˌdɜːməˈtɒlədʒi $ ˌdɜːrməˈtɑː-/ *n* [U] the part of medical science that deals with skin diseases and their treatment —**dermatologist** *n* [C]

de·rog·ate /ˈderəgeɪt/ *v law* to state officially that a part of a law or agreement has ended and that it no longer has any legal authority

derogate from sth *phr v formal* **1** to make something seem less important or less good: *Louis XIV clearly thought it derogated from his dignity as a ruler.* **2** to ignore a responsibility or duty

de·rog·a·to·ry /dɪˈrɒgətəri $ dɪˈrɑːgətɔːri/ *adj* derogatory remarks, attitudes etc are insulting and disapproving: *Their conversation contained a number of* ***derogatory*** *racial* ***remarks***.

der·rick /ˈderɪk/ *n* [C] **1** a tall machine used for lifting heavy weights, especially on ships **2** a tall tower built over an oil well, used to raise and lower the DRILL

der·rière /ˈderieə $ ˌderiˈer/ *n* [C] your BUTTOCKS – used humorously

der·ring-do /ˌderɪŋ ˈduː/ *n* **deeds/acts etc of derring-do** very brave actions like the ones that happen in adventure stories – used humorously

der·vish /ˈdɜːvɪʃ $ ˈdɜːr-/ *n* [C] a member of a Muslim religious group, some of whom dance fast and spin around as part of a religious ceremony

de·sal·i·na·tion /diːˌsæləˈneɪʃən/ *n* [U] *technical* the process of removing salt from sea water so that people can use it —**desalinate** /diːˈsæləneɪt/ *v* [T]

de·scale /ˌdiːˈskeɪl/ *v* [T] *BrE* to remove the white substance that forms on the inside of pipes, KETTLES etc

des·cant /ˈdeskænt/ *n* [C,U] a tune that is played or sung above the main tune in a piece of music

de·scend /dɪˈsend/ ●●○ *v*

1 [I,T] *formal* to move from a higher level to a lower one OPP **ascend** → **descent**: *Our plane started to descend.* | *I heard his footsteps descending the stairs.* | **[+to/from/into etc]** *The path continues for some way before descending to Garsdale Head.*

> **REGISTER**
> In everyday English, people usually say **go down** or **come down** rather than **descend**: *They* ***went down*** *into the lobby.* | *I heard his footsteps* ***coming down*** *the stairs.*

2 [I] *literary* if darkness, silence, a feeling etc descends, it becomes dark etc or you start to feel something, especially suddenly: **[+on/upon/over]** *Total silence descended on the room.* | *An air of gloom descended over the party headquarters.*

3 in descending order (of sth) numbers, choices etc that are in descending order are arranged from the highest or most important to the lowest or least important: *The hotels are listed in descending order of price.*

descend from sb/sth *phr v*

1 be descended from sb to be related to a person or group who lived a long time ago: *She claims to be descended from Abraham Lincoln.* | *The people here are descended from the Vikings.*

2 to have developed from something that existed in the past SYN **come from**: *ideas that descend from those of ancient philosophers*

descend on/upon sb/sth *phr v* if a large number of people descend on a person or a place, they come to visit or stay, especially when they are not very welcome: *Millions of tourists descend on the area every year.*

descend to sth *phr v* to behave or speak in an unpleasant way, which is not the way you usually behave SYN **stoop to**: *Surely he wouldn't descend to such a mean trick?* | **descend to sb's level** (=behave or speak as badly as someone else) *Other people may gossip, but don't descend to their level.*

de·scen·dant /dɪˈsendənt/ ●○○ *n* [C]

1 someone who is related to a person who lived a long time ago, or to a family, group of people etc that existed in the past → **ancestor**: **sb's descendants/the descendants of sb** *The coastal areas were occupied by the descendants of Greek colonists.* | *He was a* ***direct descendant*** *of Napoleon Bonaparte.* **THESAURUS** RELATIVE

2 something that has developed from something else: **[+of]** *Quechua is a descendant of the Inca language.*

de·scent /dɪˈsent/ ●○○ *n*

1 [C,U] *formal* the process of going down OPP **ascent**:

D

Passengers must fasten their seat belts prior to descent. | **[+from/to]** *The descent to Base Camp took about two days.*
2 [U] your family origins, especially your nationality or relationship to someone important who lived a long time ago: **of Russian/Italian etc descent** *young men and women of Asian descent* | **[+from]** *The emperor* ***claimed descent*** *from David.* | **by descent** *They're Irish by descent.*
3 [C] a path or road that goes down a slope (OPP) **ascent**: **[+from/to]** *There is no direct descent from the summit.*
4 [singular] a gradual change towards behaviour or a situation that is very bad: **descent into alcoholism/chaos/madness etc** *his descent into drug abuse*
5 [singular] *BrE* a sudden unwanted visit or attack: *the descent on the town by a motorcycle gang*

de·scribe /dɪˈskraɪb/ ●●● (S2) (W1) *v* [T]
1 to say what something or someone is like by giving details about them: *The police asked her to describe the man.* | *Another approach to the problem is described in Chapter 3.* | **describe sb/sth as (being/having) sth** *After the operation her condition was described as comfortable.* | *The youth is described as being 18 to 19 years old.* | **describe how/why/what etc** *It's difficult to describe how I feel.* | **describe sb/sth to sb** *So describe this new boyfriend to me!* | **describe doing sth** *He described finding his mother lying on the floor.*
2 describe a circle/an arc etc *formal* to make a movement which forms the shape of a circle etc: *Her hand described a circle in the air.*

D

THESAURUS

describe to talk or write about a person, place, event etc, in order to show what they are like: *Could you try and describe the man you saw?* | *In her book, she describes her journey across the Sahara.* | *Police described the attack as particularly violent.*
tell sb about sb/sth to describe someone or something to someone. This phrase is more commonly used than **describe** in everyday spoken English: *So, tell me about your holiday!* | *My friends have told me all about you!*
depict *formal* to describe someone or something in a piece of writing: *His stories depict life in Trinidad as seen through the eyes of a young boy.* | *In this new biography she is depicted as a lonely and unhappy woman.*
portray/represent *formal* to describe someone or something in a particular way: *College teachers are often represented on television shows as slightly eccentric.* | *The magazine has been criticized for the way it portrays women.*
characterize sb/sth as sth *formal* to describe someone or something by emphasizing one particular quality or feature about them: *He characterized himself as 'an average American'.* | *The successful schools were characterized as innovative and creative.*
paint sb/sth as sth to describe someone or something, especially in a way that makes people believe something that is not true: *Not all young people are as bad as they're painted in the press.* | *We won, yet the media is painting it as a victory for our opponents.*
paint a picture to describe a situation, so that people can get a general idea of what it is like: *Can you paint a picture of life in Japan for us?* | *My uncle's letters generally painted a rosy picture of how things were.*

de·scrip·tion /dɪˈskrɪpʃən/ ●●● (S2) (W2) *n* [C,U]
1 a piece of writing or speech that gives details about what someone or something is like: **[+of]** *an accurate description of the event* | *The booklet gives a brief description of each place.* | *Berlin sounds fascinating from your description.* → JOB DESCRIPTION
2 be beyond/past description to be too good, bad, big etc to be described easily: *The death and destruction were beyond description.*
3 of every/some/any etc description (*also* **of all descriptions**) people or things of every type, some type etc: *People of all descriptions came to see the show.*

COLLOCATIONS

VERBS

give (sb) a description *She was unable to give the police a description of her attacker.*
provide a description *formal The diary provides a clear description of farming life in the 1850s.*
issue a description (=formally give a description of someone to the public) *Police have issued a description of the two men they are looking for.*
fit/match a description (=be like the person in a police description) *The first man they arrested did not fit the description given by the victim.*
sb answering a description (=a person who looks like someone in a police description) *A young girl answering this description has been seen in Spain.*

ADJECTIVES

good *Her descriptions of the natural world are very good.*
clear *He gave us a clear description of the situation in the city.*
detailed *Some of his descriptions of the island are very detailed.*
accurate *I don't think the hotel's description of its facilities was very accurate.*
vivid (=very clear and interesting) *The book contains some vivid descriptions of his childhood.*
perfect *We have a perfect description of the man we are looking for.*
a full description *formal* (=detailed) *Please give a full description of your responsibilities in your present job.*
a long/lengthy description *I didn't want to hear a lengthy description of their holiday.*
a brief/short description *There's only a brief description of the hotel on the Internet.*
a general description (=not detailed) *He started by giving us a general description of the manufacturing process.*
a graphic description (=very clear and containing a lot of details, usually about something unpleasant) *The book has some graphic descriptions of life in the prison camp.*

de·scrip·tive /dɪˈskrɪptɪv/ ●○○ *adj*
1 giving a description of something: *the descriptive passages in the novel*
2 *technical* describing how the words of a language are actually used, rather than saying how they ought to be used (OPP) **prescriptive** —**descriptively** *adv*

des·e·crate /ˈdesɪkreɪt/ *v* [T] to spoil or damage something holy or respected THESAURUS▶ DAMAGE —**desecration** /ˌdesɪˈkreɪʃən/ *n* [U]

de·seg·re·gate /diːˈsegrɪgeɪt/ *v* [T] to end a system in which people of different races are kept separate → **integrate** (OPP) **segregate** —**desegregation** /ˌdiːsegrəˈgeɪʃən $ diːˌseg-/ *n* [U]

de·sel·ect /ˌdiːsəˈlekt/ *v* [T] **1** to remove something from a list of choices on a computer **2** *BrE* if members of a political party deselect an existing Member of Parliament, they refuse to choose him or her as a CANDIDATE at the next election —**deselection** /-ˈlekʃən/ *n* [U]

de·sen·si·tize (*also* **-ise** *BrE*) /diːˈsensətaɪz/ *v* [T] to make someone react less strongly to something by making them become used to it: **desensitize sb to sth** *Does TV desensitize people to violence?* —**desensitization** /diːˌsensətaɪˈzeɪʃən $ -tə-/ *n* [U]

des·ert[1] /ˈdezət $ -ərt/ ●●○ (W3) *n*
1 [C,U] a large area of land where it is always very dry, there are few plants, and there is a lot of sand or rocks: *the Sahara Desert* | *This area of the country is mostly desert.* | **in the desert** *The plane crash-landed in the desert.*
2 [C] a place where there is no activity or where nothing

interesting happens: *The railroad yard was a desert now.* ⚠ Do not confuse with **dessert** (=the sweet part of a meal).

de·sert² /dɪ'zɜːt $ -'zɜːrt/ ●○○ *v*
1 [T] to leave someone or something and no longer help or support them SYN **abandon**: *Helen was deserted by her husband.* | *Many of the party's traditional voters deserted it at the last election.* | *The price rise caused many readers to desert the magazine.* | **desert sb for sb** *He deserted her for another woman.*
2 [T] to leave a place so that it is completely empty SYN **abandon**: *The birds have deserted their nest.*
3 [I] to leave the army, navy etc without permission: *Several hundred soldiers have deserted.*
4 [T] if a feeling, quality, or skill deserts you, you no longer have it, especially at a time when you need it: *Mike's confidence seemed to have deserted him.*

de·sert·ed /dɪ'zɜːtɪd $ -ɜːr-/ ●○○ *adj*
1 empty and quiet because no people are there: *The streets were deserted.* | *The old mine now **stands** completely **deserted**.* THESAURUS ▸ EMPTY
2 deserted wife/husband/child etc a wife etc who has been left by her husband etc

de·sert·er /dɪ'zɜːtə $ -'zɜːrtər/ *n* [C] a soldier who leaves the army, navy etc without permission

de·sert·i·fi·ca·tion /dɪˌzɜːtɪfɪ'keɪʃən $ -ˌzɜːr-/ *n* [U] *technical* the process by which useful land, especially farmland, changes into desert

de·ser·tion /dɪ'zɜːʃən $ -ɜːr-/ *n* **1** [C,U] the act of leaving the army, navy etc without permission **2** [U] *law* the act of leaving your wife or husband because you do not want to live with them any longer

ˌdesert 'island *n* [C] a small tropical island that is far away from other places and has no people living on it

de·serts /dɪ'zɜːts $ -'zɜːrts/ *n* **get/receive your (just) deserts** to be punished in a way that you deserve: *Offenders should receive their just deserts.*

de·serve /dɪ'zɜːv $ -ɜːrv/ ●●● S3 W3 *v* [T]
1 to have earned something by good or bad actions or behaviour: *What have I done to deserve this?* | **deserve to do sth** *We didn't deserve to win.* | **richly/fully/thoroughly etc deserve sth** *the success he so richly deserves* | *I'm sorry for the kids. They **deserve better*** (=deserve to be treated in a better way). | **deserve a rest/break/holiday etc** *I think we deserve a rest after all that hard work.* | *Ledley **deserves** a **place** in the team.* | *Paula **deserves** a special **mention** for all the help she has given us.* | *I would never hit anyone, even if they deserved it.* | *What has he done to **deserve** this **punishment**?* | **deserve all/everything you get** (=deserve any bad things that happen to you) *He deserves all he gets for being so dishonest.* | *People who are sent to prison for drunk-driving **get what they deserve**.*

GRAMMAR: Using the progressive
Deserve is not used in the progressive. You say: *She deserves a prize.* ✗ Don't say: *She is deserving a prize.*
GRAMMAR GUIDE ▸ VERBS

2 deserve consideration/attention etc if a suggestion, idea, or plan deserves consideration, attention etc, it is good enough to be considered, paid attention to etc SYN **merit**: *This proposal deserves serious consideration.*
3 sb deserves a medal *spoken* used to say that you admire the way someone dealt with a situation or problem: **[+for]** *You deserve a medal for putting up with Ian's constant demands.*

de·served /dɪ'zɜːvd $ -'zɜːrvd/ *adj* earned because of good or bad behaviour, skill, work etc: *He has a **well-deserved** reputation as a reliable worker.* | **a deserved win/victory/success etc** *Larsson's goal gave Celtic a deserved victory.*

de·serv·ed·ly /dɪ'zɜːvɪdli $ -ɜːr-/ *adv* **1** in a way that is right or deserved: **deservedly popular/well-known/famous etc** *Bistro Roti is a deservedly popular restaurant.* | *Arsenal were **deservedly beaten** 2–1 by Leeds.* **2 (and) deservedly so** used to say that you agree that something is right and deserved: *She is widely respected in the music world, and deservedly so.*

de·serv·ing /dɪ'zɜːvɪŋ $ -ɜːr-/ *adj* **1** needing help and support, especially financial support: **deserving causes/cases** *The National Lottery provides extra money for deserving causes.* **2 be deserving of sth** *formal* to deserve something: *Some criminals are more deserving of their punishment than others.*

des·ic·cat·ed /'desɪkeɪtɪd/ *adj technical* **1** desiccated food has been dried in order to preserve it **2** completely dry: *desiccated soil*

des·ic·ca·tion /ˌdesɪ'keɪʃən/ *n* [U] *technical* the process of becoming completely dry

de·sid·e·ra·tum /dɪˌzɪdə'rɑːtəm, -'reɪ-, -ˌsɪd- $ dɪˌsɪdə'reɪtəm, -'rɑː-/ *n* (*plural* **desiderata** /-tə/) [C] *formal* something that is wanted or needed

de·sign¹ /dɪ'zaɪn/ ●●● S2 W1 AWL *n*
1 PROCESS OF PLANNING [U] the art or process of making a drawing of something to show how you will make it or what it will look like: *The new plane is in its final design stage.* | *the design process* | *the design team* | *a course in **graphic design*** | *computer-aided design*
2 ARRANGEMENT OF PARTS [C,U] the way that something has been planned and made, including its appearance, how it works etc: *The car's design has been greatly improved.* | **[+of]** *the design of the new building* | *Some changes have been made to the computer's basic design.* | *a **design fault*** | *The electric windows are an important **design feature** of this model.*
3 PATTERN [C] a pattern for decorating something: *a floral design* | *Vinyl flooring is available in a wide range of designs.*
4 DRAWING [C] a drawing that shows how something will be made or what it will look like: **[+for]** *the design for the new sports centre*
5 INTENTION [C,U] a plan that someone has in their mind: **by design** (=intentionally) *We shall never know whether this happened by accident or by design.* | *He has some **grand designs** for the company.*
6 have designs on sth to want something for yourself, especially because it will bring you money: *Several developers have designs on the property.*
7 have designs on sb *formal* to want a sexual relationship with someone: *He had designs on her.*

design² ●●● S3 W1 AWL *v* [T]
1 to make a drawing or plan of something that will be made or built: *The tower was designed by Gilbert Scott.* | **design sth for sth** *She designed a new logo for the company.* | **well/badly etc designed** *a badly designed office* | ***specially designed** software*
2 to plan or develop something for a specific purpose: **be designed to do sth** *These exercises are designed to strengthen muscles.* | **be designed for sb/sth** *The course is designed for beginners.* | **be designed as sth** *The book is designed as a reference manual.* GRAMMAR **Design** is usually passive in this meaning.

des·ig·nate¹ /'dezɪgneɪt/ ●○○ *v* [T]
1 to choose someone or something for a particular job or purpose: **be designated sth** *The lake was recently designated a conservation area.* | **be designated as/for sth** *Funds were designated for projects in low-income areas.* | **be designated to do sth** *She has been designated to take over the position of treasurer.*
2 to represent or refer to something using a particular sign, name etc: *Buildings are designated by red squares on the map.* GRAMMAR **Designate** is usually passive.

des·ig·nate² /'dezɪgnət,-neɪt/ *adj* [only after noun] *formal* used after the name of an official job to show that someone has been chosen for that job but has not yet officially started work: *the director designate*

ˌdesignated 'driver *n* [C] someone who agrees not to drink alcohol when a group of friends go out together to a party, bar etc so that he or she can drive the others safely home

D

ˌdesignated ˈhitter *n* [C] a baseball player who replaces the PITCHER when it is the pitcher's turn to hit the ball

des·ig·na·tion /ˌdezɪgˈneɪʃən/ *n formal* **1** [U] the act of choosing someone or something for a particular purpose, or of giving them a particular description: **[+as]** *the designation of Stansted as the third London airport* **2** [C] a name or title: *Her official designation is Systems Manager.*

de·sign·er¹ /dɪˈzaɪnə $ -ər/ ●●○ W3 *n* [C] someone whose job is to make plans or patterns for clothes, furniture, equipment etc: *an* ***interior designer*** | *a software designer* | **dress/fashion designer**

designer² *adj* [only before noun] made by a well-known and fashionable designer: **designer clothes/jeans/suits etc** | **designer label** (=an expensive brand from a well-known designer)

deˈsigner ˌbaby *n* [C] a baby whose GENES have been selected by GENETIC ENGINEERING, because its parents want to be able to choose things like the colour of its eyes or hair, or to be sure what sex the baby will be - used to show disapproval

D

ˈdesigner ˌdrug *n* [C] an illegal drug that has an exciting or relaxing effect, and is taken for pleasure

de·sir·a·ble /dɪˈzaɪərəbəl $ -ˈzaɪr-/ ●●○ *adj*
1 *formal* something that is desirable is worth having or doing: *The ability to speak a foreign language is* ***highly desirable***. | *a desirable neighborhood* | ***It is desirable that*** *you should have some familiarity with computers.* | *It is desirable to keep the cost as low as possible.*
2 *literary* sexually attractive: *a desirable young woman* —**desirably** *adv* —**desirability** /dɪˌzaɪrəˈbɪləti $ -ˌzaɪr-/ *n* [U]

de·sire¹ /dɪˈzaɪə $ -ˈzaɪr/ ●●● W2 *n*
1 [C,U] a strong hope or wish: **desire to do sth** *a* ***strong desire*** *to win* | **[+for]** *a desire for knowledge* | **desire that** *It was Harold's desire that he should be buried next to his wife.* | **express/show a desire** *She expressed a desire to visit us.* | **have no desire to do sth** (=used to emphasize that you do not want to do something) *I have no desire to cause any trouble.* | **overwhelming/burning desire** (=very strong desire) *Paul had a burning desire to visit India.*
2 [U] *formal* a strong wish to have sex with someone: *female* ***sexual desire*** | **[+for]** *He tried to hide his desire for her.* → **your heart's desire** at HEART¹(24)

desire² ●●○ *v* [T]
1 *formal* to want something very much: *The hotel has* ***everything you could*** *possibly* ***desire***. | **desire to do sth** *He desired to return to Mexico.* | *Add lemon juice* ***if desired***.

> **REGISTER**
> In everyday English, people usually say **want** rather than **desire,** although the meaning of **desire** is stronger than **want**: *You can have anything you* ***want***. | *I* ***wanted to*** *meet her.*

2 *literary* to want to have sex with someone —**desired** *adj*: *His remarks* ***had the desired effect***.

> **GRAMMAR: Using the progressive**
> **Desire** is not usually used in the progressive. You say: *He desires adventure.* ✗ Don't say: *He is desiring adventure.*
> GRAMMAR GUIDE ▸ VERBS

de·sir·ous /dɪˈzaɪərəs $ -ˈzaɪr-/ *adj* [not before noun] *formal* wanting something very much: **[+of]** *He became restless and desirous of change.*

de·sist /dɪˈzɪst, dɪˈsɪst/ *v* [I] *formal* to stop doing something: *We hope that the military regime will desist from its acts of violence.* → **cease and desist** at CEASE¹(2)

desk /desk/ ●●● S2 W2 *n* [C]
1 a piece of furniture like a table, usually with drawers in it, that you sit at to write and work: *Marie was sitting at her desk.* → see picture at TABLE¹
2 a place where you can get information or use a particular service in a hotel, airport etc: *the* ***reception desk*** | *the* ***check-in desk***
3 an office that deals with a particular subject, especially in newspapers or television: **the news/sports desk**

ˈdesk clerk *n* [C] someone who works at the main desk in a hotel

de·skill /ˌdiːˈskɪl/ *v* [T] to remove or reduce the need for skill in a job, usually by changing to machinery —**deskilling** *n* [U]

ˈdesk ˌjob *n* [C] a job that involves working mostly at a desk in an office

ˈdesk ˌjockey *n* [C] *AmE informal* someone who works in an office, sitting at a desk all or most of the day - used humorously

ˈdesk ˌtidy *n* (*plural* **desk tidies**) [C] *BrE* a container for putting pens, pencils etc in, that you keep on your desk

desk·top /ˈdesktɒp $ -tɑːp/ ●●○ *n* [C]
1 the main area on a computer where you can find the ICONS that represent programs, and where you can do things to manage the information on the computer
2 the top surface of a desk

ˌdesktop comˈputer *n* [C] a computer that is small enough to be used on a desk → LAPTOP

ˌdesktop ˈpublishing *n* [U] (*abbreviation* **DTP**) the work of arranging the writing and pictures for a magazine, small book etc, using a computer and special software

des·o·late¹ /ˈdesələt/ *adj* **1** a place that is desolate is empty and looks sad because there are no people there: *a desolate landscape* **2** someone who is desolate feels very sad and lonely —**desolately** *adv* —**desolation** /ˌdesəˈleɪʃən/ *n* [U]

des·o·late² /ˈdeseleɪt/ *v* [T] *literary* to make someone feel very sad and lonely SYN **devastate**: *David was desolated by his wife's death.* GRAMMAR **Desolate** is usually passive. —**desolated** *adj*

de·spair¹ /dɪˈspeə $ -ˈsper/ ●●○ *n* [U]
1 a feeling that you have no hope at all: **in despair** *She killed herself in despair.* | **the depths of despair** (=very strong feelings of despair) | *The noise from the neighbours used to* ***drive*** *him* ***to despair***. | **to the despair of sb** *To the despair of the workers, the company announced the closure of the factory.*
2 be the despair of sb *old-fashioned* to make someone feel very worried, upset, or unhappy: *She is the despair of her teachers.*

despair² *v* [I] *formal* to feel that there is no hope at all: *Despite his illness, Ron never despaired.* | **despair of (doing) sth** *He despaired of ever finding her.* | **despair of sb** *My teachers began to despair of me.*

de·spair·ing /dɪˈspeərɪŋ $ -ˈsper-/ *adj* showing a feeling that you have no hope at all: **despairing cry/look/sigh etc** *She gave me a last despairing look.* —**despairingly** *adv*

de·spatch /dɪˈspætʃ/ *n, v* another spelling of DISPATCH

des·pe·ra·do /ˌdespəˈrɑːdəʊ $ -doʊ/ *n* (*plural* **desperadoes** *or* **desperados**) [C] *old-fashioned* a violent criminal who is not afraid of danger

des·per·ate /ˈdespərət/ ●●○ S3 W3 *adj*
1 willing to do anything to change a very bad situation, and not caring about danger: *I had no money left and was desperate.* | *Time was running out and we were* ***getting desperate***. | *the missing teenager's desperate parents* | **[+with]** *She was desperate with fear.*
2 needing or wanting something very much: **[+for]** *The team is desperate for a win.* | *I was desperate for a cigarette.* | **desperate to do sth** *He was desperate to get a job.*
3 a desperate situation is very bad or serious: *a* ***desperate shortage*** *of doctors* | *We're* ***in desperate need of*** *help.* THESAURUS ▸ SERIOUS
4 a desperate action is something that you only do because you are in a very bad situation: **desperate attempt/bid/effort** *a desperate attempt to escape* | *We*

resorted to ***desperate measures****.* | **desperate battle/struggle/fight** *a desperate struggle to rescue the men*

des·pe·rate·ly /ˈdespərətli/ ●●○ *adv*
1 in a desperate way: *The doctors* ***tried desperately*** *to save her life.* | *He looked round desperately for someone to help him.*
2 very or very much: **desperately want/need** *The crops desperately need rain.* | **desperately poor/ill/tired etc** *He was desperately ill with a fever.* | **desperately unhappy/lonely/worried etc**

des·per·a·tion /ˌdespəˈreɪʃən/ ●○○ *n* [U] the state of being desperate: *a look of desperation* | **in/out of desperation** *She resorted to stealing food out of desperation.* | *In desperation, we had to borrow the money.*

des·pic·a·ble /dɪˈspɪkəbəl, ˈdespɪ-/ *adj* extremely bad, immoral, or cruel: *It's despicable the way he treats those kids.* | *a* ***despicable act*** *of terrorism* | *a* ***despicable crime*** —**despicably** *adv*

de·spise /dɪˈspaɪz/ ●○○ *v* [T] to dislike and have a low opinion of someone or something: *She despised her neighbours.* **THESAURUS** ▸ HATE

de·spite /dɪˈspaɪt/ ●●● S3 W1 AWL *prep*
1 used to say that something happens or is true even though something else might have prevented it SYN **in spite of**: *Despite all our efforts to save the school, the authorities decided to close it.* | **despite the fact (that)** *She went to Spain despite the fact that her doctor had told her to rest.*
2 despite yourself if you do something despite yourself, you do it although you did not intend to: *Liz realized that, despite herself, she cared about Edward.*

GRAMMAR: Patterns with despite

- You say **despite doing** something: *He won despite being injured.*
- You say **despite the fact that**: *He won despite the fact that he was injured.* ✗ Don't say: *He won despite he was injured.*
- Don't confuse **despite** and **in spite of**. ✗ Don't say: *despite of*

de·spoil /dɪˈspɔɪl/ *v* [T] *literary* **1** to make a place much less attractive by removing or damaging things → **spoil**
2 to steal from a place or people using force, especially in a war

de·spon·dent /dɪˈspɒndənt $ dɪˈspɑːn-/ *adj* extremely unhappy and without hope: *Gill had been out of work for a year and was getting very despondent.* | **[+about]** *He was becoming increasingly despondent about the way things were going.* —**despondency** *n* [U] —**despondently** *adv*

des·pot /ˈdespɒt, -ət $ ˈdespət, -ɑːt/ *n* [C] someone, especially a ruler, who uses power in a cruel and unfair way SYN **tyrant** —**despotic** /deˈspɒtɪk $ -ˈspɑː-/ *adj* —**despotically** /-kli/ *adv*

des·pot·is·m /ˈdespətɪzəm/ *n* [U] rule by a despot

des res /ˌdez ˈrez/ *n* [C] *BrE informal* a house that a lot of people admire and would like to live in – often used humorously. **Des res** is short for 'desirable residence'.

des·sert /dɪˈzɜːt $ -ɜːrt/ ●●● S2 *n* [C,U] sweet food served after the main part of a meal: **for dessert** *What are we having for dessert?*

des·sert·spoon /dɪˈzɜːtspuːn $ -ˈzɜːrt-/ *n* [C] *BrE*
1 a spoon that is larger than a TEASPOON but smaller than a TABLESPOON **2** (*also* **dessertspoonful** /-fʊl/) the amount that a dessertspoon can hold, used as a unit for measuring food or liquid in cooking: **[+of]** *Add a dessertspoonful of dry mustard.*

desˈsert wine *n* [C,U] a sweet wine served with dessert

de·sta·bil·ize (*also* **-ise** *BrE*) /diːˈsteɪbəlaɪz/ *v* [T] to make something such as a government or ECONOMY become less successful or powerful, or less able to control events: *an attempt to destabilize the government* —**destabilization** /diːˌsteɪbəlaɪˈzeɪʃən $ -lə-/ *n* [U]

DESSERTS

des·ti·na·tion /ˌdestəˈneɪʃən/ ●●○ *n* [C]
1 the place that someone or something is going to: **sb's destination** *Allow plenty of time to get to your destination.* | **holiday/tourist destination** *Maui is a popular tourist destination.*
2 destination hotel/resort a place to stay that is the reason for visiting a country or area because it is special or provides many services or activities

des·tined /ˈdestɪnd/ ●○○ *adj*
1 [not before noun] seeming certain to happen at some time in the future: **[+for]** *She seemed destined for a successful career.* | **destined to do sth** *We were destined never to meet again.*
2 destined for sth to be travelling to a particular place, or intended to go there: *The flight was destined for Cairo.*
3 [only before noun] *literary* a destined person or thing is one that you will have in the future: *the King's destined bride*

des·ti·ny /ˈdestɪni/ ●●○ *n* (*plural* **destinies**)
1 [C usually singular] the things that will happen to someone in the future, especially those that cannot be changed or controlled SYN **fate**: **sb's destiny** *Nancy wondered whether it was her destiny to live in England and marry Melvyn.* **THESAURUS** ▸ FUTURE
2 [U] the power that some people believe decides what will happen to them in the future: *She always had a strong* ***sense of destiny****.*

des·ti·tute /ˈdestɪtjuːt $ -tuːt/ *adj* **1** having no money, no food, no home etc: *The floods* ***left*** *many people* ***destitute****.* **THESAURUS** ▸ POOR **2 be destitute of sth** *literary* to be completely without something: *a man who is destitute of mercy* —**destitution** /ˌdestɪˈtjuːʃən $ -ˈtuː-/ *n* [U]

de·stress /diːˈstres/ *v* [I] to relax after a worrying or busy time

de·stroy /dɪˈstrɔɪ/ ●●● S2 W2 *v* [T]
1 to damage something so badly that it no longer exists or cannot be used or repaired → **destruction**: **completely/totally destroy** *The school was completely destroyed by fire.* | *companies that are polluting and destroying the environment* | **destroy sb's confidence/hope/faith etc**
2 if something destroys someone, it ruins their life completely: *The scandal destroyed Simmons and ended his political career.*
3 *informal* to defeat an opponent easily: *The Bears destroyed the Detroit Lions 35–3.*
4 to kill an animal, especially because it is ill or dangerous: *One of the bulls had to be destroyed.*

THESAURUS

destroy to damage something so badly that it no longer exists or cannot be used or repaired: *The earthquake almost completely destroyed the city.* | *The twin towers were destroyed in a terrorist attack.*

D

devastate to damage a large area very badly and destroy many things in it: *Allied bombings in 1943 devastated the city.*
demolish to completely destroy a building, either deliberately or by accident: *The original 15th century house was demolished in Victorian times.*
flatten to destroy a building or town by knocking it down, bombing it etc, so that nothing is left standing: *The town centre was flattened by a 500 lb bomb.*
wreck to deliberately damage something very badly, especially a room or building: *The toilets had been wrecked by vandals.*
trash *informal* to deliberately destroy a lot of the things in a room, house etc: *Apparently, he trashed his hotel room while on drugs.*
obliterate *formal* to destroy a place so completely that nothing remains: *The nuclear blast obliterated most of Hiroshima.*
reduce sth to ruins/rubble/ashes to destroy a building or town completely: *The town was reduced to rubble in the First World War.*
ruin to spoil something completely, so that it cannot be used or enjoyed: *Fungus may ruin the crop.*

D

de·stroy·er /dɪˈstrɔɪə $ -ər/ *n* [C] **1** a small fast military ship with guns **2** someone or something that destroys things or people

de·struc·tion /dɪˈstrʌkʃən/ ●●○ W3 *n* [U] the act or process of destroying something or of being destroyed → **destroy**: **[+of]** *the destruction of the rainforest* | ***weapons of mass destruction*** | *the* ***environmental destruction*** *caused by the road building programme* | *The floods brought* ***death and destruction*** *to the area.*

de·struc·tive /dɪˈstrʌktɪv/ ●○○ *adj* causing damage to people or things → **destroy**: *the* ***destructive power*** *of modern weapons* | **[+to]** *What is good for the individual can be destructive to the family.* —**destructively** *adv* —**destructiveness** *n* [U]

des·ul·to·ry /ˈdesəltəri, ˈdez- $ -tɔːri/ *adj formal* done without any particular plan or purpose: *They talked briefly in a desultory manner.* —**desultorily** /ˈdesəltərəli, ˈdez- $ -tɔːrəli/ *adv*

Det. (*also* **Det** *BrE*) **1** the written abbreviation of ***detective*** **2** the written abbreviation of ***determiner***

de·tach /dɪˈtætʃ/ ●○○ *v*
1 [I,T] if you detach something, or if it detaches, it becomes separated from the thing it was attached to OPP **attach**: **detach sth from sth** *You can detach the hood from the jacket.* | *Please detach and fill out the application form.*
2 detach yourself from sb/sth to try to be less involved in or less concerned about a situation: *Doctors have to detach themselves from their feelings.*

de·tach·a·ble /dɪˈtætʃəbəl/ *adj* able to be removed and put back SYN **removable**: *The coat has a detachable lining.*

de·tached /dɪˈtætʃt/ *adj* **1** not reacting to or becoming involved in something in an emotional way OPP **involved**: *Try to take a more* ***detached view.*** | **[+from]** *He appeared totally detached from the horrific nature of his crimes.* | **detached way/manner** *She described what had happened in a cold and detached manner.* **2** *especially BrE* a detached house or garage is not joined to another building → SEMI-DETACHED

de·tach·ment /dɪˈtætʃmənt/ *n* **1** [U] the state of not reacting to or being involved in something in an emotional way OPP **involvement**: **[+from]** *He felt a* ***sense of detachment*** *from what was happening around him.* **2** [C] a group of soldiers who are sent away from a larger group to do a special job **3** [singular, U] *formal* when something becomes separated from something else: **[+of]** *detachment of the retina*

de·tail¹ /ˈdiːteɪl $ dɪˈteɪl/ ●●● S2 W1 *n*
1 [C] a single feature, fact, or piece of information about something: **[+of]** *She told me every detail of her trip.* | **down to the smallest/last detail** (=completely) *Todd had planned the journey down to the smallest detail.*
2 [U] all the separate features and pieces of information about something: **in detail** *He described the process in detail* (=using a lot of details). | *This issue will be discussed* ***in more detail*** *in Chapter 5.* | *McDougal was reluctant to* ***go into detail*** (=give a lot of details) *about the new deal.* | *Editing requires great* ***attention to detail.*** | *the* ***fine detail*** *of the plan* | **have an eye for detail** (=be skilled at noticing details) *Photographers need to have an eye for detail.*
3 details [plural] information that helps to complete what you know about something: **[+of]** ***Full details*** *of the incident were recently revealed.* | **[+about]** *She refused to* ***give*** *any* ***details*** *about what had happened.* | *Details of the course can be found on our website.* | **further/more details** *For further details, contact the personnel department.*
4 [singular, U] *technical* a specific duty in the army, or the person or group with that duty: *the security detail*

detail² *v* [T] **1** to list things or give all the facts or information about something: *The report details the progress we have made over the last year.* **2 detail sb to (do) sth** to officially order someone, especially soldiers, to do a particular job: *Four soldiers were detailed to guard duty.* **3** *AmE* to clean a car very thoroughly, inside and out SYN **valet** *BrE*

de·tailed /ˈdiːteɪld $ dɪˈteɪld/ ●●● W2 *adj*
1 containing or including a lot of information or details: **detailed description/account/analysis etc** *a detailed study of crime in Seattle* | *More detailed information is available on request.*
2 having a lot of decorations or small features that are difficult to produce SYN **intricate**: *a beautifully detailed carving*

de·tail·ing /ˈdiːteɪlɪŋ $ dɪˈteɪlɪŋ/ *n* [U] **1** decorations that are added to something such as a car or piece of clothing **2** *AmE* the process of cleaning a car very thoroughly, inside and out SYN **valeting** *BrE*

de·tain /dɪˈteɪn/ ●○○ *v* [T]
1 to officially prevent someone from leaving a place: *Two suspects have been* ***detained*** *by the police* ***for questioning.*** | *She was detained in hospital with a suspected broken leg.*
2 *formal* to stop someone from leaving as soon as they expected SYN **delay**: *He was detained in Washington on urgent business.*

de·tain·ee /ˌdiːteɪˈniː/ *n* [C] *formal* someone who is officially kept in a prison, usually because of their political views

de·tect /dɪˈtekt/ ●●○ W3 AWL *v* [T] to notice or discover something, especially something that is not easy to see, hear etc: *Many forms of cancer can be cured if detected early.* | **difficult/impossible/easy/possible etc to detect** | **detect a change/difference** *Dan detected a change in her mood.* | **detect a note of sarcasm/irony/excitement etc** *Do I detect a note of sarcasm in your voice?* **THESAURUS** NOTICE —**detectable** *adj*

de·tec·tion /dɪˈtekʃən/ ●●○ AWL *n* [U] when something is found that is not easy to see, hear etc, or the process of looking for it: **[+of]** *Early detection of the disease is vital.* | **escape/avoid detection** *By flying low, the plane avoided detection by enemy radar.*

de·tec·tive /dɪˈtektɪv/ ●●○ AWL *n* [C]
1 a police officer whose job is to discover information about crimes and catch criminals → STORE DETECTIVE
2 (*also* **private detective**) someone who is paid to discover information about someone or something: *She hired a detective to find out if her husband was having an affair.*
3 detective work efforts to discover information, find out how something works, answer a difficult question etc: *It took a lot of detective work to discover the cause of the problem.*
4 detective story/novel etc a story etc about a crime, often a murder, and a detective who tries to find out who did it

de·tec·tor /dɪˈtektə $ -ər/ ●○○ AWL *n* [C] a machine or piece of equipment that finds or measures something: *a smoke detector* | *a metal detector* → LIE DETECTOR

dé·tente, **detente** /ˈdeɪtɒnt, deɪˈtɑːnt $ deɪˈtɑːnt/ *n* [U] a time or situation in which two countries that are not friendly towards each other agree to behave in a more friendly way

de·ten·tion /dɪˈtenʃən/ ●○○ *n*
1 [U] the state of being kept in prison: **in detention** *Willis was* ***held in detention*** *for five years.*
2 [C,U] a punishment in which children who have behaved badly are forced to stay at school for a short time after the others have gone home: **in detention** *She was always getting* ***put in detention***.

deˈtention ˌcentre *BrE*, **detention center** *AmE n* [C] a place where people are kept and prevented from escaping, especially people who have entered the country illegally, or young people who have committed crimes

de·ter /dɪˈtɜː $ -ˈtɜːr/ ●○○ *v* (**deterred**, **deterring**) [T] to stop someone from doing something, by making them realize it will be difficult or have bad results → **deterrent**: *The company's financial difficulties have deterred potential investors.* | **deter sb from (doing) sth** *The security camera was installed to deter people from stealing.*

> **REGISTER**
> In everyday English, people usually say **put** someone **off** rather than **deter** someone: *Don't let a few problems* ***put*** *you* ***off***.

de·ter·gent /dɪˈtɜːdʒənt $ -ɜːr-/ *n* [C,U] a liquid or powder used for washing clothes, dishes etc

de·te·ri·o·rate /dɪˈtɪəriəreɪt $ -ˈtɪr-/ ●●○ *v* [I]
1 to become worse: *Ethel's health has deteriorated.* | *America's deteriorating economy*
2 deteriorate into sth to develop into a bad or worse situation: *The argument deteriorated into a fight.*
—**deterioration** /dɪˌtɪəriˈreɪʃən $ -ˌtɪr-/ *n* [U]

de·ter·mi·nant /dɪˈtɜːmɪnənt $ -ɜːr-/ *n* [C] *formal* something that strongly influences what you do or how you behave: **[+of]** *Social class is a major determinant of consumer spending patterns.*

de·ter·mi·nate /dɪˈtɜːmənət $ -ɜːr-/ *adj formal* definite or with an exact limit OPP **indeterminate**: *a determinate prison sentence of five years*

de·ter·mi·na·tion /dɪˌtɜːməˈneɪʃən $ -ɜːr-/ ●●○ W3 *n*
1 [U] the quality of trying to do something even when it is difficult: **determination to do sth** *Yuri shows great determination to learn English.* | *his* ***dogged determination*** (=very strong determination) *to succeed*
2 [C,U] *formal* the act of deciding something officially: **[+of]** *the determination of government policy*
3 [C] *formal* the act of finding the exact level, amount, or cause of something: **[+of]** *accurate determination of the temperature*

de·ter·mine /dɪˈtɜːmɪn $ -ɜːr-/ ●●○ *v* [T]
1 to find out the facts about something SYN **establish**: *Investigators are still trying to determine the cause of the fire.* | **determine how/what/who etc** *The aim of the inquiry was to determine what had caused the accident.* | **determine that** *Experts have determined that the signature was forged.*
2 if something determines something else, it directly influences or decides it: *The amount of available water determines the number of houses that can be built.* | *The age of a wine is a* ***determining factor*** *as to how it tastes.* | **determine how/whether/what etc** *How hard the swimmers work now will determine how they perform in the Olympics.*
3 to officially decide something: *The date of the court case has not yet been determined.* | **determine how/what/who etc** *The tests will help the doctors determine what treatment to use.* THESAURUS DECIDE
4 determine to do sth *formal* to decide to do something: *We determined to leave at once.*

de·ter·mined /dɪˈtɜːmɪnd $ -ɜːr-/ ●●○ W3 *adj*
1 having a strong desire to do something, so that you will not let anyone stop you: *Gwen is a very determined woman.* | **determined to do sth** *She was determined to win.* | **determined (that)** *He was determined that the same mistakes would not be repeated.*
2 showing determination, especially in a difficult situation: **determined attempt/effort** *She was making a determined effort to give up smoking.* | *The library was closed down despite* ***determined opposition***.

de·ter·min·er /dɪˈtɜːmənə $ -ˈtɜːrmənər/ *n* [C] *technical* a word that is used before a noun in order to show which thing you mean. In the phrases 'the car' and 'some cars', 'the' and 'some' are determiners

de·ter·min·is·m /dɪˈtɜːmənɪzəm $ -ɜːr-/ *n* [U] the belief that what you do and what happens to you are caused by things that you cannot control —**deterministic** /dɪˌtɜːməˈnɪstɪk◂ $ -ɜːr-/ *adj*

de·ter·rent /dɪˈterənt $ -ˈtɜːr-/ ●○○ *n* [C]
1 something that makes someone less likely to do something, by making them realize it will be difficult or have bad results: *The small fines for this type of crime do not* ***act as much of a deterrent***. | **[+to/for/against]** *Window locks are an effective deterrent against burglars.* | *the* ***deterrent effect*** *of prison sentences*
2 nuclear deterrent the NUCLEAR weapons that a country has in order to prevent other countries from attacking it
—**deterrence** *n* [U]

THESAURUS: determined

determined if you are determined to do something, you have decided that you are definitely going to do it, and you will not let anything stop you. **Determined** is also used about someone's character, when they usually behave in this way: *I was determined to be a doctor.* | *She's a very determined woman.*
stubborn determined not to change what you are doing, especially when other people think you are behaving in an unreasonable way. **Stubborn** is often used when you disapprove of someone. It is also sometimes used when you admire them: *I wish you would stop being so stubborn!* | *Churchill's stubborn refusal to surrender*
single-minded someone who is single-minded works very hard in order to achieve one particular thing, and thinks that everything else is much less important: *During a war, a leader must be single-minded and, if necessary, ruthless.* | *her single-minded pursuit of power*
tough /tʌf/ determined to succeed, even if a situation is difficult or frightening: *In competitive sports, it is as important to be mentally tough as it is to be physically fit.* | *Gorelick is known as a tough manager.*
firm showing by your behaviour that you are determined not to change your mind, especially when you are telling someone what to do: *What this country needs is firm leadership.* | *You have to be firm with young children.*
feisty determined and full of energy, and not afraid to say what you think and argue with people – used especially when you admire this person. **Feisty** is often used about women: *In the film she plays a feisty young woman who is smarter than all the men put together.*
resolute *formal* doing something in a very determined way because you have very strong beliefs, aims etc: *the soldiers' resolute defence of the town*
tenacious *formal* determined and refusing to give up: *McTaggart was seen by many in the environment movement as a tenacious hero.* | *his tenacious grip on power*
dogged [only before noun] dogged behaviour shows that you are very determined and that you will not give up – used especially in the following phrases: **dogged determination/persistence/resistance/refusal**: *The team played with dogged determination.* | *his dogged refusal to admit defeat*
ruthless /ˈruːθləs/ someone who is ruthless is so determined to get what they want, that they do not care if they harm other people: *a ruthless dictator* | *He was ruthless in his ambition.*

D

de·test /dɪ'test/ *v* [T] to hate something or someone very much: *The two men detested each other.* THESAURUS HATE —**detestation** /ˌdiːte'steɪʃən/ *n* [U]

GRAMMAR: Using the progressive
Detest is not used in the progressive. You say: *I detest housework.* ✗ Don't say: *I am detesting housework.*
GRAMMAR GUIDE VERBS

de·test·a·ble /dɪ'testəbəl/ *adj* very bad, and deserving to be criticized or hated: *a detestable little man* —**detestably** *adv*

de·throne /dɪ'θrəʊn $ -'θroʊn/ *v* [T] **1** to remove a king or queen from power **2** to remove someone from a position of authority or importance: *an attempt to dethrone the senator | He dethroned Tyson in a fight that shook the boxing world.* —**dethronement** *n* [U]

det·o·nate /'detəneɪt/ *v* [I,T] to explode or to make something explode THESAURUS EXPLODE —**detonation** /ˌdetə'neɪʃən/ *n* [U]

det·o·na·tor /'detəneɪtə $ -ər/ *n* [C] a piece of equipment used to make a bomb etc explode

D

de·tour[1] /'diːtʊə $ -tʊr/ *n* [C] **1** a way of going from one place to another that is longer than the usual way: **make/take a detour** *We took a detour to avoid the town centre.* **2** *AmE* a different road for traffic when the usual road cannot be used SYN **diversion** *BrE*

detour[2] *v* [I,T] *AmE* to make a detour

de·tox[1] /'diːtɒks $ -tɑːks/ *n* [U] *informal* **1** special treatment to help people stop drinking alcohol or taking drugs SYN **rehab**: **in detox** *She spent a month in detox.* **2** when you do not eat solid food or only drink special liquids for a period of time, which is thought to remove harmful substances from your body

detox[2] *v* [I] *informal* **1** if someone detoxes, they are given special treatment at a hospital to help them stop drinking alcohol or taking drugs **2** to not eat solid food or only drink special liquids for a period of time, which is thought to remove harmful substances from your body

de·tox·i·fi·ca·tion /ˌdiːtɒksɪfɪ'keɪʃən $ -ˌtɑːk-/ *n* [U] **1** the process of removing harmful chemicals or poison from something **2** detox —**detoxify** /diː'tɒksɪfaɪ $ -'tɑːk-/ *v* [T]

de·tract /dɪ'trækt/ *v*
detract from sth *phr v* to make something seem less good OPP **enhance**: *One mistake is not going to detract from your achievement.*

de·trac·tor /dɪ'træktə $ -ər/ *n* [C] someone who says bad things about someone or something, in order to make them seem less good than they really are SYN **critic**: **sb's detractors** *Even the president's detractors admit that the decision was the right one.*

det·ri·ment /'detrəmənt/ *n* [U] *formal* harm or damage: **to the detriment of sth** (=resulting in harm or damage to something) *He worked very long hours, to the detriment of his marriage.*

det·ri·men·tal /ˌdetrə'mentl◂/ ●○○ *adj formal* causing harm or damage SYN **harmful, damaging**: **[+to]** *Smoking is detrimental to your health. | the **detrimental effect** of pollution on the environment* THESAURUS HARMFUL —**detrimentally** *adv*

de·tri·tus /dɪ'traɪtəs/ *n* [U] *formal* pieces of waste that remain after something has been broken up or used

deuce /djuːs $ duːs/ *n* **1** [U] the situation in tennis when both players have 40 points, after which one of the players must win two more points to win the game **2** [C] *AmE* a playing card with the number two on it **3 what/how etc the deuce ...?** *old-fashioned spoken* used to add force to a question: *What the deuce is going on?*

Deutsch·mark /'dɔɪtʃmɑːk $ -mɑːrk/ (*also* **mark**) *n* [C] the standard unit of money used in Germany before the EURO

de·val·ue /diː'væljuː/ *v* **1** [I,T] *technical* to reduce the value of one country's money when it is exchanged for another country's money: *Nigeria has just **devalued** its **currency**.* **2** [T] to make someone or something seem less important or valuable: *History has tended to devalue the contributions of women.* —**devaluation** /diːˌvælju'eɪʃən/ *n* [C,U]: *the devaluation of the pound*

dev·a·state /'devəsteɪt/ ●○○ *v* [T]
1 to make someone feel extremely shocked and sad: *Rob was devastated by the news of her death.*
2 to damage something very badly or completely: *The city centre was devastated by the bomb.* THESAURUS DESTROY —**devastation** /ˌdevə'steɪʃən/ *n* [U]

dev·a·stat·ed /'devəsteɪtɪd/ ●○○ *adj* feeling extremely shocked and sad: *She was left feeling totally devastated.* THESAURUS SAD, SHOCKED

dev·a·stat·ing /'devəsteɪtɪŋ/ ●○○ *adj*
1 badly damaging or destroying something: **devastating effect/impact** *Acid rain has a devastating effect on the forest.* | **devastating results/consequences** *The oil spill had devastating consequences for wildlife. | It will be a **devastating blow** for the town if the factory closes.*
2 making someone feel extremely sad or shocked: *He was in Nice when he heard the **devastating news**. | Long-term unemployment can be devastating.*
3 very impressive or effective: *In a devastating display of military muscle, soldiers seized the town.*
4 *literary* extremely attractive: *a devastating smile* —**devastatingly** *adv*: *a devastatingly attractive man*

de·vel·op /dɪ'veləp/ ●●● S2 W1 *v*
1 GROW [I,T] to grow or change into something bigger, stronger, or more advanced, or to make someone or something do this → **advance**: *Knowledge in the field of genetics has been developing very rapidly. | Corsica has developed its economy around the tourist industry.* | **[+into]** *Chicago developed into a big city in the late 1800s.* | **[+from]** *It's hard to believe that a tree can develop from a small seed. | exercises to **develop muscle** strength*
2 NEW IDEA/PRODUCT [T] to design or make a new idea, product, system etc over a period of time: *Scientists are developing new drugs to treat arthritis. | She should have developed her own style instead of copying him. | Researchers are developing technology for the US military.* THESAURUS MAKE
3 FEELING [T] to start to have a feeling or quality that then becomes stronger: *He had developed a certain affection for me.* | **develop a sense/awareness/knowledge of sth** *The children are beginning to develop a sense of responsibility. | It was in college that he **developed a taste for*** (=started to like) *rugby football.*
4 SKILL/ABILITY [I,T] if you develop a skill or ability, or if it develops, it becomes stronger or more advanced: *The course is designed to help students develop their speaking skills.*
5 DISEASE [I,T] if you develop a disease or illness, or if it develops, you start to have it: *Some alcoholics develop liver disease. | Pneumonia can develop very quickly.*
6 FAULT/PROBLEM [T] to begin to have a physical fault: *The oil tank had developed a small crack. | The plane developed engine trouble and was forced to land.*
7 PROBLEM/DIFFICULTY [I] if a problem or difficult situation develops, it begins to happen or exist, or it gets worse: *Trouble is developing in the cities.* | **[+into]** *Regional clashes could develop into larger quarrels.*
8 IDEA/ARGUMENT [T] to make an argument or idea clearer, by studying it more or by speaking or writing about it in more detail: *We will develop a few of these points in the seminar.*
9 LAND [T] to use land for the things that people need, for example by taking minerals out of it or by building on it: *The land was developed for low-cost housing.*
10 PHOTOGRAPHY [I,T] to make a photograph out of a photographic film, using chemicals: *Did you ever **get** the pictures **developed**?*

de·vel·oped /dɪ'veləpt/ ●●○ *adj*
1 a developed country is one of the rich countries of the world with many industries, comfortable living for most people, and usually an elected government → **developing**,

underdeveloped: *energy consumption in the* ***developed world*** | **developed countries/nations** | *The charity works with children in less developed countries.*
2 a developed sense, system etc, is better, larger, or more advanced than others: *Dogs have a* ***highly developed*** *sense of smell.* | *plants with* ***well-developed*** *root systems* | *Labour has a more* ***fully developed*** *programme for the unemployed.*

de·vel·op·er /dɪˈveləpə $ -ər/ ●●○ *n*
1 [C] a person or company that makes money by buying land and then building houses, factories etc on it: *a Florida* ***property developer***
2 [C] a person or an organization that works on a new idea, product etc to make it successful: *software developers*
3 [C,U] a chemical substance used for making images appear on film or photographic paper → **late developer** at LATE[1](7)

de·vel·op·ing /dɪˈveləpɪŋ/ ●●○ *adj*
1 a developing country is a poor country that is trying to increase its industry and trade and improve life for its people → **developed**, **underdeveloped**: **developing countries/nations** *aid to developing countries* | *poverty and hunger in the* ***developing world*** | **developing economies/markets** *the developing economies in Eastern Europe*
2 growing or changing: *the growth of the developing embryo* | *a developing crisis in Washington*

de·vel·op·ment /dɪˈveləpmənt/ ●●● S1 W1 *n*
1 GROWTH [U] the process of gradually becoming bigger, better, stronger, or more advanced: *child development* | **[+of]** *a course on the development of Greek thought* | **professional/personal development** *opportunities for professional development*
2 ECONOMIC ACTIVITY [U] the process of increasing business, trade, and industrial activity: **economic/industrial/business etc development** *economic development in Russia*
3 EVENT [C] a new event or piece of news that changes a situation: ***recent*** *political* ***developments*** *in the former Soviet Union* | *We will* ***keep*** *you* ***informed of developments.***
4 NEW PLAN/PRODUCT [U] the process of working on a new product, plan, idea etc to make it successful: *The funds will be used for marketing and* ***product development.*** | **under/in development** *Spielberg has several interesting projects under development.*
5 IMPROVEMENT [C] a change that makes a product, plan, idea etc better: *There have been significant computer developments during the last decade.*
6 BUILDING PROCESS [U] the process of planning and building new houses, streets etc on land: **for development** *The land was sold for development.*
7 HOUSES/OFFICES ETC [C] a group of new buildings that have all been planned and built together on the same piece of land: *a new* ***housing development***

de·vel·op·men·tal /dɪˌveləpˈmentl/ ●○○ *adj* relating to the development of someone or something: *the* ***developmental stages*** *of childhood* | *Higher education is a continuing* ***developmental process.*** —**developmentally** *adv*

de·vi·ance /ˈdiːviəns/ (*also* **de·vi·an·cy** /ˈdiːviənsi/) *n* [U] when something is different, especially in a bad way, from what is considered normal: *sexual deviance*

de·vi·ant /ˈdiːviənt/ *adj* different, in a bad way, from what is considered normal: *deviant behaviour* —**deviant** *n* [C]: *a sexual deviant*

de·vi·ate[1] /ˈdiːvieɪt/ AWL *v* [I] to change what you are doing so that you are not following an expected plan, idea, or type of behaviour: **[+from]** *The plane had to deviate from its normal flight path.*

de·vi·ate[2] /ˈdiːviət/ *adj formal* DEVIANT

de·vi·a·tion /ˌdiːviˈeɪʃən/ ●○○ AWL *n*
1 [C,U] a noticeable difference from what is expected or acceptable: **[+from]** *deviation from the normal procedure*
2 [C] *technical* the difference between a number or measurement in a SET and the average of all the numbers or measurements in that set → STANDARD DEVIATION

de·vice /dɪˈvaɪs/ ●●○ S3 W2 AWL *n* [C]
1 a machine or tool that does a special job SYN **gadget**: *modern labour-saving devices* | **device for doing sth** *a device for separating metal from garbage* | **device to do sth** *The company makes devices to detect carbon monoxide.*
2 a special way of doing something that makes it easier to do: **device for doing sth** *Testing yourself with information on cards is a useful device for studying.* | *a memory device*
3 a plan or trick, especially for a dishonest purpose: **device to do sth** *Their proposal was only a device to confuse the opposition.*
4 a bomb or other explosive weapon: **explosive/nuclear/incendiary etc device**
5 the special use of words in literature, or of words, lights etc in a play, to achieve an effect: *Metaphor is a common literary device.* → **leave sb to their own devices** at LEAVE[1](4)

dev·il /ˈdevəl/ ●●○ S3 *n*
1 the devil (*also* **the Devil**) the most powerful evil SPIRIT in some religions, especially in Christianity SYN **Satan**
2 [C] an evil SPIRIT SYN **demon**: *The villagers believed a devil had taken control of his body.*
3 speak of the devil (*also* **talk of the devil** *BrE*) *spoken* used when someone you have just been talking about walks into the room where you are
4 poor/lucky/handsome etc devil *spoken* used to talk about someone who you feel sorry for, who is lucky etc: *What on earth is wrong with the poor devil?*
5 little/old devil *spoken* used to talk about a child or an older man who behaves badly, but who you like: *He's a naughty little devil.* | *I really miss the old devil.*
6 be a devil *BrE spoken* used to persuade someone to do something they are not sure they should do: *Go on, be a devil, have another gin and tonic.*
7 what/who/why etc the devil? *old-fashioned spoken* used to show that you are surprised or annoyed: *How the devil should I know what she's thinking?*
8 a devil of a time/job etc *old-fashioned spoken* a difficult or unpleasant time, job etc: *We had a devil of a job trying to get the carpet clean again.*
9 go to the devil! *old-fashioned spoken* used to tell someone rudely to go away or stop annoying you
10 do sth like the devil *old-fashioned spoken* to do something very fast or using a lot of force: *They rang the bell and ran like the devil.*
11 better the devil you know (than the devil you don't) used to say that it is better to deal with someone or something you know, even if you do not like them, than to deal with someone or something new that might be worse
12 between the devil and the deep blue sea in a difficult situation because there are only two choices you can make and both of them are unpleasant
13 ... and the devil take the hindmost used to say that everyone in a situation only cares about what happens to themselves and does not care about other people
14 the devil makes/finds work for idle hands used to say that people who do not have enough to do will start to do bad things
15 the devil is in the detail used to say that the details of a plan, agreement etc are very important and may result in problems → DEVIL'S ADVOCATE

dev·il·ish /ˈdevəlɪʃ/ *adj* **1** *literary* very bad, difficult, or unpleasant: *devilish schemes to cheat people* **2** seeming likely to cause trouble, but in a way that is amusing or attractive: *Dalton looked at her with a devilish grin.*

dev·il·ish·ly /ˈdevəlɪʃli/ *adv* [+adj/adv] *old-fashioned* very – used to show that you think something is annoying or bad: *a devilishly difficult task*

dev·illed *BrE*, **deviled** *AmE* /ˈdevəld/ *adj* devilled food is cooked with very hot pepper: *deviled eggs*

ˌdevil-may-ˈcare *adj* happy and willing to take risks: *a* ***devil-may-care attitude*** *to life*

dev·il·ment /ˈdevəlmənt/ (*also* **dev·il·ry** /ˈdevəlri/) *n* [U] *literary* wild or bad behaviour that causes trouble: *eyes blazing with devilment*

ˌdevil's ˈadvocate *n* [C] someone who pretends to disagree with you in order to have a good discussion about something: *He would* ***play devil's advocate*** *with anyone.*

ˈdevil's food ˌcake *n* [C,U] *AmE* a type of chocolate cake

de·vi·ous /ˈdiːviəs/ ●○○ *adj*
1 using dishonest tricks and deceiving people in order to get what you want → **deceitful**: *a devious politician* THESAURUS ▸ DISHONEST
2 *formal* not going in the most direct way to get to a place SYN **circuitous**: *a devious route* —**deviously** *adv* —**deviousness** *n* [U]

de·vise /dɪˈvaɪz/ ●●○ *v* [T] to plan or invent a new way of doing something: *She* ***devised a method*** *for quicker communications between offices.* THESAURUS ▸ INVENT

de·void /dɪˈvɔɪd/ *adj formal* **be devoid of sth** to be completely lacking in something: *His face was devoid of any warmth or humour.*

de·vo·lu·tion /ˌdiːvəˈluːʃən/ *n* [U] when a national government gives power to a group or organization at a lower or more local level —**devolutionist** *adj* —**devolutionist** *n* [C]

de·volve /dɪˈvɒlv $ dɪˈvɑːlv/ *v formal* [I,T] **1** if you devolve responsibility, power etc to a person or group at a lower level, or if it devolves on them, it is given to them: **devolve sth to sb/sth** *The federal government has devolved responsibility for welfare to the states.* | **[+on/upon]** *Half of the cost of the study will devolve upon the firm.* **2** if land, money etc devolves to someone, it becomes their property when someone else dies SYN **pass**

D

de·vote /dɪˈvəʊt $ -ˈvoʊt/ ●●○ AWL *v* [T]
1 to use all or most of your time, effort etc in order to do something or help someone SYN **dedicate**: **devote your time/energy/attention etc to sth** *He devoted his energies to writing films.* | **devote yourself to sth** *She devoted herself full-time to her business.*

> **REGISTER**
> In everyday English, people usually say **put** time/energy etc **into** something rather than **devote** time/energy etc **to** something: *He* ***put a lot of time into*** *the project.*

2 to use a particular area, period of time, or amount of space for a specific purpose: **devote sth to sth** *The meeting will be devoted to health and safety issues.*

de·vot·ed /dɪˈvəʊtɪd $ -ˈvoʊ-/ ●●○ AWL *adj*
1 giving someone or something a lot of love and attention: *a devoted father* | **[+to]** *Isabella was devoted to her brother.*
2 dealing with, containing, or being used for only one thing SYN **dedicated**: **[+to]** *a museum devoted to photography*
3 strongly supporting someone or something because you admire or enjoy them: *Beckham's* ***devoted fans*** | *The journal had a* ***devoted following*** *of around 1,000 subscribers.* —**devotedly** *adv*

dev·o·tee /ˌdevəˈtiː/ *n* [C] **1** someone who enjoys or admires someone or something very much: **[+of]** *a devotee of 1930s films* **2** a very religious person: *a Sikh devotee*

de·vo·tion /dɪˈvəʊʃən $ -ˈvoʊ-/ ●○○ AWL *n*
1 [U] the strong love that you show when you pay a lot of attention to someone or something: **[+to]** *Alanna has always shown intense devotion to her children.*
2 [U] the loyalty that you show towards a person, job etc, especially by working hard → **dedication**: **[+to]** *the soldier's courage and* ***devotion to duty*** | *his integrity and devotion to his patients*
3 [U] strong religious feeling
4 devotions [plural] prayers and other religious acts

de·vo·tion·al /dɪˈvəʊʃənəl $ -ˈvoʊ-/ *adj* relating to or used in religious services: *devotional music*

de·vour /dɪˈvaʊə $ -ˈvaʊr/ ●○○ *v* [T]
1 to eat something quickly because you are very hungry: *The boys devoured their pancakes.* THESAURUS ▸ EAT
2 to read something quickly and eagerly, or watch something with great interest: *He devoured science fiction books.*
3 be devoured by sth to be filled with a strong feeling that seems to control you: *Cindy felt devoured by jealousy.*
4 *literary* to destroy someone or something: *Her body had been almost entirely devoured by the disease.*
5 to use up all of something: *a job that devours all my energy*

de·vout /dɪˈvaʊt/ *adj* **1** someone who is devout has a very strong belief in a religion: *a devout Catholic* THESAURUS ▸ RELIGIOUS **2** *formal* a devout hope or wish is one that you feel very strongly: *It is my devout hope that we can work together in peace.* —**devoutly** *adv*

dew /djuː $ duː/ *n* [U] the small drops of water that form on outdoor surfaces during the night

dew·drop /ˈdjuːdrɒp $ ˈduːdrɑːp/ *n* [C] a single drop of dew: *dewdrops sparkling in the morning sunlight*

dew·fall /ˈdjuːfɔːl $ ˈduːfɒːl/ *n* [U] *AmE* the forming of dew or the time when dew begins to appear

dew·y /ˈdjuːi $ ˈduːi/ *adj* wet with drops of DEW: *I walked barefoot through the dewy grass.*

ˌdewy-ˈeyed *adj* having eyes that are slightly wet with tears

dex·ter·i·ty /dekˈsterəti/ *n* [U] **1** skill and speed in doing something with your hands: *Computer games can improve children's* ***manual dexterity***. **2** skill in using words or your mind: *his charm and* ***verbal dexterity***

dex·ter·ous /ˈdekstərəs/ (*also* **dextrous**) *adj* **1** skilful and quick when using your hands: *dextrous use of the needle* **2** skilful in using words or your mind: *his dexterous accounting abilities* —**dexterously** *adv*

dex·trose /ˈdekstrəʊz, -strəʊs $ -stroʊz, -stroʊs/ *n* [U] a type of sugar that is in many sweet fruits

dex·trous /ˈdekstrəs/ *adj* another spelling of DEXTEROUS

dho·ti /ˈdəʊti $ ˈdoʊ-/ *n* [C] a piece of clothing worn by some Hindu men, consisting of a piece of cloth that is wrapped around the waist and between the legs

di- /daɪ, dɪ/ *prefix* two, twice, or double: *A diphthong is a vowel made up of two sounds.* → SEMI-, BI-, TRI-

di·a·be·si·ty /ˌdaɪəˈbiːsəti/ *n* [U] a type of diabetes that is caused by being very fat

di·a·be·tes /ˌdaɪəˈbiːtiːz, -tɪs/ *n* [U] a serious disease in which there is too much sugar in your blood

> **GRAMMAR: Singular or plural verb?**
> **Diabetes** is followed by a singular verb: ***Diabetes is*** *linked to obesity.*
> GRAMMAR GUIDE ▸ NOUNS

di·a·bet·ic¹ /ˌdaɪəˈbetɪk◂/ *adj* **1** having diabetes: *Sarah is diabetic.* **2** caused by diabetes: *a diabetic coma* **3** produced for people who have diabetes: *diabetic chocolate*

diabetic² *n* [C] someone who has diabetes

di·a·bol·i·cal /ˌdaɪəˈbɒlɪkəl◂ $ -ˈbɑː-/ *adj* **1** (*also* **di·a·bol·ic** /ˌdaɪəˈbɒ◂lɪk $ -ˈbɑː-/) evil or cruel: *diabolical abuse* **2** *BrE informal* extremely unpleasant or bad: *The toilets were in a diabolical state.* —**diabolically** /-kli/ *adv*

di·a·crit·ic /ˌdaɪəˈkrɪtɪk/ *n* [C] *technical* a mark placed over, under, or through a letter in some languages, to show that the letter should be pronounced differently from the same letter without a mark —**diacritical** *adj*: *diacritical marks*

di·a·dem /ˈdaɪədem/ *n* [C] *literary* a circle of jewels that a queen, princess etc wears on her head

di·ag·nose /ˈdaɪəgnəʊz $ -noʊs/ ●○○ *v* [T] to find out what illness someone has, or what the cause of a fault is, after doing tests, examinations etc: **diagnose sb as (having) sth** *Joe struggled in school before he was diagnosed as dyslexic.* | **diagnose sth as sth** *The illness was diagnosed as mumps.* | **diagnose sb with sth** *She was diagnosed with breast cancer.*

di·ag·no·sis /ˌdaɪəgˈnəʊsɪs $ -ˈnoʊ-/ ●○○ *n* (*plural* **diagnoses** /-siːz/) [C,U] the process of discovering exactly what is wrong with someone or something, by examining them closely → **prognosis**: **[+of]** *diagnosis of kidney disease* | *An exact* ***diagnosis*** *can only be* ***made*** *by obtaining a blood sample.*

di·ag·nos·tic /ˌdaɪəgˈnɒstɪk◂ $ -ˈnɑː-/ ●○○ *adj* relating to or used for discovering what is wrong with someone or something: **diagnostic tests/tools** *Doctors depend on accurate diagnostic tools.*

di·ag·o·nal /daɪˈæɡənəl/ ●○○ *adj*
1 a diagonal line is straight and joins two opposite corners of a flat shape, usually a square → **horizontal**, **vertical**
2 following a sloping angle: *diagonal parking spaces* —**diagonal** *n* [C] —**diagonally** *adv*: *The path goes diagonally across the field.*

di·a·gram¹ /ˈdaɪəɡræm/ ●●○ S3 *n* [C] a simple drawing or plan that shows exactly where something is, what something looks like, or how something works: **[+of]** *a diagram of the heating system* —**diagrammatic** /ˌdaɪəɡrəˈmætɪk◂/ *adj* —**diagrammatically** /-kli/ *adv*

diagram² *v* (**diagrammed**, **diagramming**) [T] to show or represent something in a diagram

dial¹ /daɪəl/ ●●○ *n* [C]
1 the round part of a clock, watch, machine etc that has numbers that show you the time or a measurement: *The lighted dial of her watch said 1.20.* | *She looked at the dial to check her speed.*
2 the part of a piece of equipment such as a radio or THERMOSTAT that you turn around to do something, such as find a different station or change the temperature: *The* ***dial*** *on the heater was* ***set to*** *'HOT'.*
3 the wheel on an older telephone with numbered holes for your fingers that you move around in order to make a call

dial² ●●○ *v* (**dialled**, **dialling** *BrE*, **dialed**, **dialing** *AmE*) [I,T] to press the buttons or turn the dial on a telephone in order to make a telephone call: *I think I dialed the wrong number.*

dial sth ↔ **back/down** *phr v AmE* to reduce something or make it less extreme: *The candidates have dialed back their attacks on each other, but they are still making their differences clear.*

dial sb/sth ↔ **up** *phr v*
1 to get a connection to a computer or telephone over a telephone line
2 *AmE* to increase something: *We are going to dial up our marketing efforts.*

di·a·lect /ˈdaɪəlekt/ ●●○ *n* [C,U] a form of a language which is spoken only in one area, with words or grammar that are slightly different from other forms of the same language → **accent**: **Chinese/Yorkshire etc dialect** *The people up there* ***speak*** *a Tibetan* ***dialect***. | *the* ***local dialect***

di·a·lec·tic /ˌdaɪəˈlektɪk/ (*also* **dialectics**) *n* [U] *formal* a method of examining and discussing ideas in order to find the truth, in which two opposing ideas are compared in order to find a solution that includes them both —**dialectical** *adj*

ˈdialling code *n* [C] *BrE* the numbers at the beginning of a telephone number that represent a specific area of a city or country SYN **area code** *AmE*

ˈdialling tone *n* [C] *BrE* the sound you hear when you pick up the telephone that lets you know that you can make a call SYN **dial tone** *AmE*

di·a·logue (*also* **dialog** *AmE*) /ˈdaɪəlɒɡ $ -lɒːɡ, -lɑːɡ/ ●●● S3 *n* [C,U]
1 a conversation in a book, play, or film: *a boring movie full of bad dialog* | *Students were asked to read simple dialogues out loud.*
2 *formal* a discussion between two groups, countries etc: **[+between/with]** *There is a need for constructive dialogue between leaders.* → **MONOLOGUE**

ˈdialogue ˌbox *BrE*, **dialog box** *AmE* *n* [C] a box that appears on your computer screen when the program you are using needs to ask you a question before it can continue to do something. You CLICK on one part of the box to give your answer.

ˈdial tone *n* [C] *AmE* the sound you hear when you pick up the telephone that lets you know that you can make a call SYN **dialling tone** *BrE*

ˈdial-up *adj* [only before noun] relating to a telephone line that is used to send information from one computer to another: *a dial-up connection* —**dial-up** *n* [C]

di·al·y·sis /daɪˈælɪsɪs/ *n* [U] the process of taking harmful substances out of someone's blood using a special machine, because their KIDNEYS do not work properly: ***a dialysis machine*** | **on dialysis** *He has been on dialysis for the past three years.*

di·a·mant·é /ˌdiːəˈmɒnteɪ◂ $ ˌdiːəmɑːnˈteɪ◂/ *adj* decorated with artificial DIAMONDS: *a diamanté necklace*

di·am·e·ter /daɪˈæmɪtə $ -ər/ ●●○ *n* [C] a straight line from one side of a circle to the other side, passing through the centre of the circle, or the length of this line: **3 inches/1 metre etc in diameter** *Draw a circle six centimetres in diameter.* | **[+of]** *The diameter of the Earth is about 13,000 km.* → see picture at **CIRCLE¹**

di·a·met·ri·cally /ˌdaɪəˈmetrɪkli/ *adv* **diametrically opposed/opposite** completely different and opposite: *The two ideas are diametrically opposed.*

di·a·mond /ˈdaɪəmənd/ ●●○ S3 *n*
1 [C,U] a clear, very hard valuable stone, used in jewellery and in industry: *a diamond engagement ring* → see picture at **JEWELLERY**
2 [C] a shape with four straight but sloping sides of equal length, with one point facing directly up and the other directly down: *Cut the cookie dough into diamonds.*
3 a) diamonds one of the four SUITS (=types of cards) in a set of playing cards, which has the design of a red diamond shape on it: **two/queen etc of diamonds** *the ace of diamonds* **b)** [C] a card from this suit: *You have to play a diamond.*
4 [C] **a)** the area in a baseball field that is within the diamond shape formed by the four BASES **b)** the whole playing field used in baseball

ˌdiamond anniˈversary *n* [C] the date that is exactly 60 years after the date when two people were married or after some other important date

ˌdiamond in the ˈrough *n* [C] *AmE* someone who behaves in a slightly rude way, but is really kind and generous SYN **rough diamond** *BrE*

ˌdiamond ˈjubilee *n* [C] the date that is exactly 60 years after the date of an important event, especially of someone becoming a king or queen → **GOLDEN JUBILEE**, **SILVER JUBILEE**

ˈdiamond ˌlane *n* [C] *AmE* a special LANE on a road or street that is marked with a diamond shape and can be used only by buses, taxis etc and sometimes private cars with more than one passenger

ˌdiamond ˈwedding *n* [C] *BrE* the date that is exactly 60 years after the date when two people were married

di·a·per /ˈdaɪəpə $ ˈdaɪpər/ *n* [C] *AmE* a piece of soft cloth or soft paper that is put between a baby's legs and fastened around its waist to hold liquid and solid waste SYN **nappy** *BrE*: *I* ***changed*** *her* ***diaper***.

ˈdiaper ˌrash *n* [U] *AmE* sore skin between a baby's legs and on its BUTTOCKS, caused by a wet diaper SYN **nappy rash** *BrE*

di·aph·a·nous /daɪˈæfənəs/ *adj literary* diaphanous cloth is so thin that you can almost see through it

di·a·phragm /ˈdaɪəfræm/ *n* [C] **1** the muscle that is between your lungs and your stomach, and that you use when you breathe **2** a round rubber object that a woman can put inside her VAGINA to stop her from getting PREGNANT **3** *technical* a thin round object, especially in a telephone or LOUDSPEAKER, that is moved by sound or that moves when it produces sound **4** *technical* a round flat part inside a camera that controls the amount of light that enters the camera

di·a·rist /ˈdaɪərɪst $ ˈdaɪr-/ *n* [C] someone who writes a diary, especially one that is later sold

di·ar·rhoea *BrE*, **diarrhea** *AmE* /ˌdaɪəˈrɪə/ *n* [U] an illness in which waste from the BOWELS is watery and comes out often

di·a·ry /ˈdaɪəri $ ˈdaɪri/ ●●○ S3 *n* (*plural* **diaries**) [C]
1 a book in which you write down the things that happen to you each day SYN **journal**: *Inge* ***kept*** *a* ***diary*** (=wrote in a diary) *during the war years.* | **diary entry** (=what you have written for a particular day)
2 *especially BrE* a book with separate spaces for each day of the year, in which you write down the meetings, events etc that are planned for each day SYN **calendar** *AmE*: *Did you* ***put*** *the meeting date* ***in*** *your* ***diary****?*

di·as·po·ra /daɪˈæspərə/ *n* [C] **1 the Diaspora** the movement of the Jewish people away from ancient Palestine, to settle in other countries **2** the spreading of people from a national group or culture to other areas: *the African diaspora*

di·a·ton·ic scale /ˌdaɪətɒnɪk ˈskeɪl $ -tɑː-/ *n* **the diatonic scale** a set of eight musical notes that uses a particular pattern of spaces between the notes

di·a·tribe /ˈdaɪətraɪb/ *n* [C] *formal* a long speech or piece of writing that criticizes someone or something very severely: **[+against]** *a diatribe against contemporary American civilization*

dibs /dɪbz/ *n* [plural] *AmE informal* the right to have, use, or do something: *Freshmen* ***have first dibs on*** *dormitory rooms.*

dice¹ /daɪs/ ●○○ *n* (*plural* **dice**)
1 [C] (*also* **die**) a small block of wood, plastic etc that has six sides with a different number of spots on each side, used in games: **throw/roll the dice** *It's your turn to roll the dice.* → see picture at BOARD GAME
2 [U] any game of chance that is played with dice
3 the dice are loaded the situation is arranged so that a particular person will win or gain an advantage
4 no dice *especially AmE old-fashioned spoken* used to refuse to do something or to say that something is not possible: *'Can I borrow some cash?' 'Sorry, no dice.'*
5 a throw of the dice something you do that you hope will have an effect on a situation, but is not certain to do so: *a* ***last*** *desperate* ***throw of the dice*** *to try and win his wife back*

dice² *v* **1** (*also* **dice sth ↔ up**) [T] to cut food into small square pieces: *diced carrots* THESAURUS CUT **2 dice with death** to put yourself in a very dangerous situation

dic·ey /ˈdaɪsi/ *adj informal* slightly dangerous and uncertain: *The future looks pretty dicey for small businesses.*

di·chot·o·my /daɪˈkɒtəmi $ -ˈkɑː-/ *n* (*plural* **dichotomies**) [C] *formal* the difference between two things or ideas that are completely opposite: **[+between]** *a dichotomy between his public and private lives*

dick¹ /dɪk/ *n* [C] **1** *informal not polite* a PENIS **2** *spoken not polite* an offensive word for a stupid annoying person, especially a man: *He's acting like a complete dick.* **3** *AmE old-fashioned* a PRIVATE DETECTIVE → **clever dick** at CLEVER(6), → SPOTTED DICK

dick² *v*
dick sb **around** *phr v AmE spoken not polite* to cause a lot of problems for someone, especially by changing your mind a lot or preventing them from getting what they want: *The phone company's been dicking me around for three months.*

dick·ens /ˈdɪkənz/ *n spoken old-fashioned* **1 what/who/where the dickens ...?** used when asking a question to show that you are very surprised or angry: *What the dickens is the matter with her?* **2 as pretty/smart etc as the dickens** *AmE* very pretty, clever etc: *Isn't she as cute as the dickens!*

Dic·ken·si·an /dɪˈkenziən/ *adj* Dickensian buildings, living conditions etc are poor, dirty, and unpleasant: *a single mother living in a Dickensian block of flats*

dick·er /ˈdɪkə $ -ər/ *v* [I] *informal especially AmE* to argue about or discuss the details of a sale, agreement etc: **[+about/over]** *Politicians in Washington are still dickering over the budget.*

dick·ey /ˈdɪki/ *n* [C] another spelling of DICKY²

dick·head /ˈdɪkhed/ *n* [C] *spoken not polite* an offensive word for a stupid annoying person, especially a man. Do not use this word.

dick·y¹ /ˈdɪki/ *adj BrE old-fashioned* weak, and likely to break or not work properly: **dicky heart/ticker** (=a heart that is weak and not very healthy)

dicky², **dickey** *n* [C] a false shirt front or collar worn under a suit or dress

dick·y·bird /ˈdɪkibɜːd $ -bɜːrd/ *n* [C] *BrE informal*
1 a small bird – used by or when speaking to children
2 not hear a dickybird to not hear any news about someone or something: *'Have you heard from them since they moved?' 'No, not a dickybird.'*

dic·ta /ˈdɪktə/ a plural of DICTUM

Dic·ta·phone /ˈdɪktəfəʊn $ -foʊn/ *n* [C] *trademark* an office machine on which you can record speech so that someone can listen to it and TYPE it later

dic·tate¹ /dɪkˈteɪt $ ˈdɪkteɪt/ ●○○ *v*
1 [I,T] to say words for someone else to write down: **dictate a letter/memo etc to sb** *She's dictating a letter to her secretary right now.*
2 [I,T] to tell someone exactly what they must do or how they must behave: **[+to]** *The media cannot be allowed to dictate to the government.* | **dictate who/what/how etc** *Can they dictate how the money will be spent?* | *Federal funds have to be used* ***as dictated by*** *Washington.* | **dictate that** *Islamic custom dictates that women should be fully covered.* | *The US government attempted to* ***dictate the terms*** *of the agreement.*
3 [T] to control or influence something SYN **determine**: **dictate what/how etc** *Funds dictate what we can do.* | **dictate that** *The laws of physics dictate that what goes up must come down.* | *The massive publicity dictated a response from the city government.*

dic·tate² /ˈdɪkteɪt/ *n* [C] an order, rule, or principle that you have to obey: **[+of]** *teenagers* ***following the dictates of*** *fashion*

dic·ta·tion /dɪkˈteɪʃən/ *n* **1** [U] when you say words for someone to write down: *There were no secretaries available to* ***take dictation*** (=write down what someone is saying). **2** [C] a piece of writing that a teacher reads out to test your ability to hear and write the words correctly: *I hate* ***doing*** *French* ***dictations***.

dic·ta·tor /dɪkˈteɪtə $ ˈdɪkteɪtər/ ●○○ *n* [C]
1 a ruler who has complete power over a country, especially one whose power has been gained by force: *the downfall of the hated dictator*
2 someone who tells other people what they should do, in a way that seems unreasonable: *a real little dictator*

dic·ta·to·ri·al /ˌdɪktəˈtɔːriəl◂/ *adj* **1** a dictatorial government or ruler has complete power over a country: *dictatorial regimes* **2** a dictatorial person tells other people what to do in an unreasonable way: *Professor Clement's dictatorial attitude* —**dictatorially** *adv*

dic·ta·tor·ship /dɪkˈteɪtəʃɪp $ -ˈteɪtər-/ ●○○ *n*
1 [C,U] government by a ruler who has complete power THESAURUS GOVERNMENT
2 [C] a country that is ruled by one person who has complete power

dic·tion /ˈdɪkʃən/ *n* [U] **1** the way in which someone pronounces words: **clear/perfect/good etc diction** *She had perfect diction.* **2** the choice and use of words and phrases to express meaning, especially in literature

dic·tion·a·ry /ˈdɪkʃənəri $ -neri/ ●●● S3 *n* (*plural* **dictionaries**) [C]
1 a book that gives a list of words in alphabetical order and explains their meanings in the same language, or another language: *a German – English dictionary*
2 a book that explains the words and phrases used in a particular subject: *a science dictionary*

dic·tum /ˈdɪktəm/ *n* (*plural* **dictums** *or* **dicta** /-tə/) [C]
1 a formal statement of opinion by someone who is respected or has authority **2** a short phrase that expresses a general rule or truth: *Descartes' famous dictum: 'I think; therefore, I am'*

did /dɪd/ *v* the past tense of DO

di·dac·tic /daɪˈdæktɪk, də-/ *adj* **1** speech or writing that is didactic is intended to teach people a moral lesson: *His* *novel has a didactic tone.* **2** someone who is didactic is too eager to teach people things or give instructions —**didactically** /-kli/ *adv*

did·dle /ˈdɪdl/ *v* [T] *BrE informal* to get money from someone by deceiving them SYN **swindle**: **diddle sb out of sth** *They'll diddle you out of your last penny if you let them.*

did·dly /ˈdɪdli/ (*also* **did·dly·squat** /ˌdɪdliˈskwɒt $ ˈdɪdliskwɑːt/) *AmE informal n* **not know/mean diddly** to know or mean nothing at all: *Brad? He doesn't know diddly about baseball.*

did·dums /ˈdɪdəmz/ *interjection BrE spoken* used humorously to show that you are not sympathetic and think someone is getting upset without good reason: *'I'll have to make my own dinner.' 'Ah, diddums!'*

did·ge·ri·doo /ˌdɪdʒəriˈduː/ *n* [C] a long wooden musical instrument, played especially in Australia

did·n't /ˈdɪdnt/ the short form of 'did not': *You saw him, didn't you? | I didn't want to go.*

didst /dɪdst/ **thou didst** *old use* you did

die¹ /daɪ/ ●●● S1 W1 *v* (**died, dying, dies**) [I]

1 BECOME DEAD to stop living and become dead: *He died in 1985 at the age of 76. | Her father died suddenly in an accident when she was only ten.* | **[+of/from]** *The animals died of starvation in the snow. | patients who are dying from cancer | She* ***died*** *peacefully* ***in her sleep*** *at the age of 98.* | **die for sth** (=be killed while fighting to defend something) *Do you believe in anything enough to die for it?* | **die young/happy/poor** *She died young, at the age of 27. | The bullet went straight through his head, and he* ***died instantly***. | **to your dying day/until the day you die** (=until you die) *It must remain a secret until the day I die.* | **sb's dying breath/wish** (=someone's last breath or wish) *It was his dying wish that the house be opened to the public.* | **die a hero/martyr/rich man etc** *My uncle died a hero.* | **die a natural/violent/agonizing death** *Did she die a natural death?* (=did she die naturally, or did someone kill her?)

GRAMMAR: Prepositions with die

- Someone **dies of** or **from** a disease or injury: *He died of a heart attack. | He died from a heart attack.* **Die of** is more common than **die from**. ✗ Don't say: *He died because of a heart attack.*
- Someone **dies in** an accident: *He died in a car crash.* ✗ Don't say: *He died by a car crash.*
- Someone **dies for** a person, place, or idea that they want to protect: *These men died for our freedom.*

2 DISAPPEAR to disappear or stop existing: *Our love will never die. | The family name will die with him* (=disappear when he dies). | *He's one of a* ***dying breed*** (=a type of person that is no longer common).

3 MACHINES *informal* to stop working SYN **break down**: *The engine spluttered and died.* | **die on sb** (=stop working while they are using it) *The mower just died on me.*

4 be dying for sth/to do sth *spoken* to want something very much: *I'm dying for a cup of tea. | She was dying to ask where he'd got it. | I'm dying to see what it is.*

5 be dying of hunger/thirst/boredom *spoken* to be very hungry, thirsty, bored etc: *Do you fancy a cup of tea? I'm dying of thirst.*

6 I nearly died/I could have died *spoken* used to say that you felt very surprised or embarrassed: *I nearly died when I saw it was my ex-husband!*

7 die of embarrassment/shame to be very embarrassed or ashamed: *The room was such a mess, I just died of embarrassment.*

8 I'd rather die *spoken* used to say very strongly that you do not want to do something: *I'd rather die than work for him!*

9 in the dying minutes/seconds/moments (of sth) during the last minutes or seconds before the end of something: *United scored an equaliser in the dying minutes of the game.*

10 old habits/traditions/customs die hard used to say that it takes a long time to change to a new way of doing something

11 never say die *spoken* used to encourage someone to continue doing something that is difficult

12 die a/the death *informal* to gradually fail or be forgotten: *The rumour gradually died a death.*

13 die laughing *spoken* to laugh a lot: *We* ***nearly died laughing*** *when he told us.*

14 to die for *informal* extremely nice, attractive, or desirable: *She had hair to die for.*

THESAURUS

die to stop being alive, as a result of old age or illness: *I want to see Ireland again before I die. | No wonder your plants always die – you don't water them enough.*

pass away to die – used when you want to avoid using the word 'die', in order to show respect or to avoid upsetting someone: *My wife had just passed away, and I didn't want to be around people.*

lose your life to be killed in a terrible event: *Hundreds of people lost their lives when the ship overturned in a storm.*

perish *literary* to die in a terrible event – used especially in literature and news reports: *Five children perished before firefighters could put out the blaze.*

give your life/lay down your life *formal* to die in order to save someone, or because of something that you believe in: *We honor the men and women who have given their lives in service of their country.*

drop dead *informal* to suddenly die, when people do not expect you to: *One day, he came home from work and dropped dead of a heart attack.*

die away *phr v* if sound, wind, or light dies away, it becomes gradually weaker until you cannot hear, feel, or see it: *Her voice died away as she saw the look on David's face. | She waited until the footsteps had died away.*

die back *phr v* if a plant dies back, it dies above the ground but remains alive at its roots

die down *phr v* if something dies down, it becomes less strong, active, or violent: *Don't worry, the gossip will soon die down. | when the excitement had died down*

die off *phr v* if a group of people or animals die off, they die one by one until there are no more of them

die out *phr v* to disappear or stop existing completely: *The wild population of koalas is in danger of dying out. | There will be outbreaks of rain, gradually dying out later.*

die² *n* [C] **1** a metal block used to press or cut something into a particular shape **2** a DICE **3 the die is cast** used to say that a decision has been taken and cannot now be changed

die·back /ˈdaɪbæk/ *n* [U] a condition that affects trees and bushes, in which the ends of branches die and then the whole branch dies

ˈdie ˌcasting *n* [U] the process of making metal objects by forcing liquid metal into a hollow container with a particular shape, and then allowing it to become hard

die·hard /ˈdaɪhɑːd $ -hɑːrd/ *n* [C] someone who opposes change and refuses to accept new ideas —**diehard** *adj*: *a few diehard fans* → **old habits die hard** at DIE¹(10)

die·sel /ˈdiːzəl/ ●●○ *n*

1 [U] a type of heavy oil used instead of petrol in engines, especially in trucks, buses, and trains: *a 1.9 litre* ***diesel engine*** | **diesel car/truck etc**

2 [C] *informal* a vehicle that uses diesel

ˈdiesel ˌfuel (*also* **ˈdiesel oil**) *n* [U] DIESEL

di·et¹ /ˈdaɪət/ ●●● S3 W2 *n*

1 [C] a way of eating in which you only eat certain foods, in order to lose weight, or to improve your health: *Lyn always seems to be on a diet. | a salt-free diet | Not all diets are good for you.*

2 [C,U] the kind of food that a person or animal eats each day: | *She doesn't eat a very* ***healthy diet***. | *It is important to have a* ***balanced diet***. | *the effects of* ***poor diet*** *and lack of exercise | Rice is* ***the staple diet*** (=the main food that a group of people usually eat). | *Studies have shown the benefits of* ***a vegetarian diet***. | **[+of]** *They exist on a diet of fish.* | **in sb's diet** *the importance of vitamins and minerals in your diet*

D

3 a diet of sth too much of an activity that you think is boring or has bad effects: *Kids today are raised on a constant diet of pop music and television.*
4 [C] *old-fashioned* an official meeting to discuss political or church matters

COLLOCATIONS

VERBS

be on a diet (=to only eat certain foods in order to lose weight) *No cake, thanks – I'm on a diet.*
go on a diet (=start eating less or only some types of food) *I really ought to go on a diet.*
follow a diet (=only eat certain types of food) *You will feel better if you follow a low-fat diet.*
stick to a diet (=continue to follow a diet)

ADJECTIVES

a strict diet (=in which you eat a very limited amount or range of food) *She followed a strict diet for several weeks.*
a crash diet (=a very sudden and strict attempt to lose weight) *It's better to lose weight gradually than to go on a crash diet.*
a low-calorie/low-fat etc diet

COMMON ERRORS

⚠ Don't say 'she's doing a diet'. Say **she's on a diet**. Don't say 'keep a diet'. Say **stick to a diet**.

diet² ●●○ *v* [I] to limit the amount and type of food that you eat, in order to become thinner SYN **slim**
diet³ *adj* [only before noun] diet drinks or foods contain less sugar or fat than ordinary ones: ***a diet soda***
di·e·ta·ry /ˈdaɪətəri $ -teri/ ●○○ *adj* related to the food someone eats → **nutritional**: *special dietary requirements*
di·et·er /ˈdaɪətə $ -ər/ *n* [C] someone who is trying to become thinner by controlling what they eat
di·e·tet·ics /ˌdaɪəˈtetɪks/ *n* [U] the science that is concerned with what people eat and drink and how this affects their health
di·e·ti·cian, **dietitian** /ˌdaɪəˈtɪʃən/ *n* [C] someone who is trained to give people advice about what it is healthy for them to eat and drink
dif·fer /ˈdɪfə $ -ər/ ●●○ W3 *v* [I]
1 to be different from something in some way: *The two systems differ in many respects.* | **[+from]** *People differ from one another in their ability to handle stress.* | **[+between]** *The symptoms did not differ between the two groups.* | **differ widely/greatly/significantly etc** *We soon found that prices differed enormously.* | *Experts have* ***differing views*** *on the subject.*
2 if two people or groups differ about something, they have opposite opinions SYN **disagree**: **[+about/on/over]** *The two lawyers differed about how to present the case.*
THESAURUS ▸ DISAGREE
3 agree to differ to stop arguing with someone and accept that you will never agree
4 I beg to differ *spoken formal* used to say that you disagree with someone
dif·fe·rence /ˈdɪfərəns/ ●●● S1 W1 *n*
1 [C,U] a way in which two or more people or things are not like each other OPP **similarity**: **[+between]** *There's a big difference between knowing that something is true, and being able to prove it.* | *There is very little difference between the parties on green issues.* | *Do children know the difference between right and wrong?* | **[+in]** *Researchers found a number of important differences in the way boys and girls learn.* | ***There's a world of difference*** (=there's a very big difference) *between being alone and being lonely.*
2 [singular, U] the amount by which one thing is greater or smaller than another: **difference in age/size etc** *There's not much difference in price.* | *There's a five-hour* ***time difference*** *between London and New York.* → **split the difference** at SPLIT¹(9)
3 make a/the difference to have an important effect or influence on something or someone: *Whatever she did, it made no difference.* | **[+to]** *One more person wouldn't make any difference to the arrangements.* | **[+between]** *It could make the difference between missing your train and getting to work on time.* | *Having a good teacher has* ***made all the difference*** *for Alex* (=had an important influence).
4 it makes no difference to sb used to say that it does not matter to someone which thing happens, is chosen etc: *Morning or afternoon. It makes no difference to me.*
5 our/your/their differences disagreements: *We've* ***had*** *our* ***differences*** *in the past.* | **settle/resolve your differences** (=agree not to argue anymore)
6 difference of opinion a slight disagreement: *There have been some differences of opinion as to exactly how the money should be spent.*
7 with a difference *informal* used to describe something which is interesting or unusual, especially in a good way: *an adventure holiday with a difference*

COLLOCATIONS

ADJECTIVES/NOUN + difference

a big/major/huge difference *I think you'll notice a big difference.*
an important/significant/crucial difference *A study of the two groups of students showed a significant difference.*
a slight/small/minor difference *There's only a slight difference between the male and the female bird.*
a marked/dramatic difference (=very noticeable) *There was a marked difference between the two sets of results.*
a subtle difference (=not obvious) | **an essential/fundamental difference** (=a very basic one) | **cultural/political/regional etc differences** | **class differences** (=between different classes of society) | **sex/gender differences** (=between men and women) | **individual differences** (=between one person and another)

VERBS

show a difference *Our data showed considerable national differences.*
know the difference (=know how two things are different) *If you don't know the difference between two words, your dictionary can help.*
can tell/see the difference (=can recognize how two things are different) *I can't really see the difference between these two colours.*
notice a difference | **spot the difference** (=see the difference)

dif·fe·rent /ˈdɪfərənt/ ●●● S1 W1 *adj*
1 not like something or someone else, or not like before OPP **similar**: **[+from]** *Our sons are* ***very different*** *from each other.* | **[+to]** *Her jacket's different to mine.* | **[+than]** *AmE: He seemed different than he did in New York.* | *The place looks* ***completely different*** *now.* | *They decided to try a* ***radically different*** *approach.* | *We found women had* ***significantly different*** *political views from men.* | *a* ***slightly different*** *way of doing things* | *What actually happened was* ***subtly different*** *from the PR people's version.* | *The show is* ***refreshingly different*** *from most exhibitions of modern art.* | *The publishing business is* ***no different*** *from any other business in this respect.* | *It's* ***a different world*** *here in London.*

GRAMMAR: Prepositions with different

- You usually say **different from**: *Their home is different from ours.*
- In American English, people also say **different than**: *Their home is different than ours.*
- In spoken British English, people also say **different to**: *Their home is different to ours.* ✗ Don't say: *Their home is different of ours.*

2 [only before noun] used to talk about two or more separate things of the same basic kind SYN **various**: *Different people reacted in* ***different ways***. | **different types/kinds etc** *There are many different types of fabric.* | *I looked in lots of different books but couldn't find anything about it.*

3 [only before noun] another: *I think she's moved to a different job now.*
4 *spoken* unusual, often in a way that you do not like: *'What did you think of the film?' 'Well, it was certainly different.'* —**differently** *adv*: *I didn't expect to be treated any differently from anyone else.* | *Things could have turned out quite differently.*

THESAURUS

different if something or someone is different, they are not like something or someone else, or they are not like they were before: *You look different. Have you had your hair cut?* | *We've painted the door a different colour.* | *The cultures of the two countries are very different.*
unique very different, special, or unusual and the only one of its kind. Don't use words such as **very** before **unique**: *The book is certainly very rare, and possibly unique.* | *the unique wildlife of the Galapagos Islands*
distinctive having a special feature or appearance that makes something different from other things, and makes it easy to recognize: *Male birds have distinctive blue and yellow markings.*
unlike [prep] completely different from a particular person or thing: *In Britain, unlike the United States, the government provides health care.*
have nothing in common if two people have nothing in common, they do not have the same interests or opinions and therefore cannot form a friendly relationship: *Apart from the fact that we went to the same school, we have absolutely nothing in common.*
there's no/little resemblance used when saying that two people or things seem very different: *There's no resemblance between the two sisters at all.* | *The final product* ***bore no resemblance to*** *the original proposal* (=it was very different).
dissimilar *formal* not the same as something else: *These four politically dissimilar states have all signed a treaty of friendship and cooperation.*
be like chalk and cheese *BrE informal* if two people are like chalk and cheese, they are completely different: *It's hard to believe that they're brothers – they're like chalk and cheese!*
be (like) apples and oranges *AmE informal* used when saying that two people or things are very different: *You can't compare residential and commercial real estate markets. It's apples and oranges.*

dif·fe·ren·tial¹ /ˌdɪfəˈrenʃəl◂/ *n* [C] **1** *formal* a difference between things, especially between the wages of people doing different types of jobs in the same industry or profession: **pay/wage/salary differential** **2** *technical* a differential gear

differential² *adj* based on or depending on a difference: *differential rates of pay* | *differential treatment of part-time and full-time staff*

ˌdifferential ˈcalculus *n* [U] a way of measuring the speed at which an object is moving at a particular moment

ˌdifferential ˈgear *n* [C] *technical* an arrangement of GEARS that allows one back wheel of a car to turn faster than the other when the car goes around a corner

dif·fe·ren·ti·ate /ˌdɪfəˈrenʃieɪt/ ●○○ AWL *v*
1 [I,T] to recognize or express the difference between things or people SYN **distinguish**: **[+between]** *It's important to differentiate between fact and opinion.* | **differentiate sth from sth** *It's sometimes hard to differentiate one sample from another.*
2 [T] to be the quality, feature etc that makes one thing or person clearly different from another SYN **distinguish**: *What differentiates these two periods of history?* | **differentiate sth from sth** *Its unusual nesting habits differentiate this bird from others.*
3 [I] to behave differently towards someone or something, especially in an unfair way SYN **discriminate**: **[+between]** *a policy which differentiates between men and women* —**differentiation** /ˌdɪfərenʃiˈeɪʃən/ *n* [U]: *socio-economic differentiation*

dif·fi·cult /ˈdɪfɪkəlt/ ●●● S1 W1 *adj*
1 hard to do, understand, or deal with OPP **easy**: *a difficult question* | *an immensely difficult task* | *Was the exam very difficult?* | ***It's difficult*** *to see how more savings can be made.* | **difficult (for sb) to understand/find/obtain etc** *That's rather difficult for me to explain.* | *He's* ***finding it difficult*** *to get a job.*
2 involving a lot of problems and causing a lot of trouble or worry: *a difficult situation* | *Things are a bit difficult at home at the moment.* | *There could be difficult times ahead.* | **make life/things difficult for sb** (=cause problems for someone) *She's doing everything she can to make life difficult for him.*
3 someone who is difficult never seems pleased or satisfied SYN **awkward**: *Don't be so difficult!* | *a difficult customer*

THESAURUS

difficult not easy to do, understand, or deal with: *a difficult question* | *The homework was really difficult.* | *It is difficult to see how peace can be achieved in the region.*
hard difficult. Hard is less formal than **difficult** and is very common in spoken English: *The test was really hard.* | *a hard decision* | *It was hard to forgive him.*
tough very difficult, because you have to use a lot of effort, or because it affects you emotionally: *a tough race* | *Doctors have to make tough decisions about who to treat first.*
tricky difficult because it is complicated and full of problems: *She had helped him out of a tricky situation.* | *Merging the two companies was bound to be tricky.*
awkward rather difficult to deal with – used especially when something could be embarrassing: *You've put me in a very awkward position.*
challenging difficult in an interesting or enjoyable way: *I wanted a job that was more challenging.* | *a challenging piece of music*
demanding difficult and tiring, because it takes a lot of effort: *Being a nurse in a busy hospital is a demanding job.*
daunting if something seems daunting, you think that it will be difficult and you do not feel confident about being able to do it: *a daunting challenge* | *The task seemed a little daunting at first.*
delicate needing to be dealt with carefully or sensitively, especially in order to avoid offending people or causing problems: *This is a very delicate subject, and it can be difficult to talk about it with your parents.*

COLLOCATIONS CHECK

difficult question/decision/situation/problem etc
hard question/decision/test
tough question/decision/job/game/race
tricky question/situation/position/moment
awkward question/situation/position/moment
challenging job
demanding work/schedule/course
daunting task/challenge/prospect
delicate subject/matter/issue

dif·fi·cul·ty /ˈdɪfɪkəlti/ ●●● S2 W1 *n* (*plural* **difficulties**)
1 [U] if you have difficulty doing something, it is difficult for you to do: **have/experience difficulty (in) doing sth** *They had* ***great difficulty*** *in finding a replacement.* | **with/without difficulty** *He got to his feet with difficulty.* ⚠ Do not say that someone 'has difficulty to do something'. Say that someone **has difficulty doing something** or **has difficulty in doing something**.
2 [C usually plural] a problem or something that causes trouble: **[+with]** *There are several difficulties with this theory.* | *If you have any difficulties, give me a call.* | *The*

project soon ran into difficulties. | *Difficulties can arise when there is more than one defendant.*
3 [U] if you are in difficulty, you are in a situation in which you have problems: **in difficulty** *The business is in financial difficulty.* | **get/run into difficulty** (=get into a difficult situation) *She soon got into difficulty with debt.*
4 [U] the quality of being difficult to do: **the difficulty of (doing) sth** *the difficulty of solving such problems*
5 [U] how difficult something is: *The tests vary in difficulty.*
→ LEARNING DIFFICULTIES

COLLOCATIONS – MEANING 2

VERBS

have difficulties *By the age of eight, Robbie was having difficulties at school.*
run into/get into difficulties (=find yourself in a difficult situation) *Three people were rescued from a boat that had got into difficulties.*
experience/encounter difficulties *formal* (=have difficulties) *Graduates often experience considerable difficulties in getting their first job.*
face difficulties *The hotel's owners were facing financial difficulties.*
overcome/resolve difficulties (=deal with them successfully) *We are confident that we can overcome these difficulties.*
present/pose difficulties *formal* (=be something that is difficult to deal with) *English spelling may present some difficulties for learners.*
be fraught with difficulties (=involve a lot of them) | **cause/lead to difficulties**
give rise to difficulties *formal* (=cause them) *The stormy weather gave rise to difficulties for many of the competitors in the yacht race.*
difficulties arise (=happen)

ADJECTIVES

major/serious/severe difficulties *By then, we were having serious financial difficulties.*
considerable difficulties (=a lot of problems) *They had considerable difficulties in getting funding for their research.*
technical difficulties *The flight was delayed due to technical difficulties.*
practical difficulties (=problems with doing something)
financial/economic difficulties *The company is facing serious financial difficulties.*
breathing difficulties

dif·fi·dent /ˈdɪfɪdənt/ *adj* shy and not wanting to make people notice you or talk about you: **diffident manner/smile/voice etc** | **[+about]** *He was diffident about his own success.* —**diffidently** *adv* —**diffidence** *n* [U]

dif·fract /dɪˈfrækt/ *v* [T] *technical* to bend light or sound waves as they pass around something or through a hole → **refract** —**diffraction** /dɪˈfrækʃən/ *n* [U]

dif·fuse¹ /dɪˈfjuːz/ *v* **1** [I,T] to make heat, light, liquid etc spread through something, or to spread like this: **[+through/into/across]** *The pollutants diffuse into the soil.* **2** [I,T] to spread ideas or information among a lot of people, or to spread like this: *Their ideas diffused quickly across Europe.* **3** [T] to make a bad feeling or situation less strong or serious: *an attempt to diffuse his anger* —**diffusion** /dɪˈfjuːʒən/ *n* [U]

dif·fuse² /dɪˈfjuːs/ *adj* **1** spread over a large area: *The organization is large and diffuse.* **2** using a lot of words and not explaining things clearly and directly: *His writing is diffuse and difficult to understand.* —**diffuseness** *n* [U]

dig¹ /dɪɡ/ ●●● S2 *v* (*past tense and past participle* **dug** /dʌɡ/, *present participle* **digging**)
1 [I,T] to move earth, snow etc, or to make a hole in the ground, using a SPADE or your hands: **dig a hole/trench/grave etc** *They dig a small hole in the sand to bury their eggs.* | **[+down]** *Dig down about 6 inches.* | **[+for]** *birds digging for worms*
2 [T] to remove something, especially vegetables, from the ground using a SPADE: *freshly dug carrots*
3 [I,T always + adv/prep] to put your hand into something, especially in order to search for something: *She dug around in her bag for a pen.* | *He dug his hands deep into his pockets.*
4 dig your heels in to refuse to do something in spite of other people's efforts to persuade you
5 dig deep to use something which you have, especially money or effort, which you would not normally need: *With one man sent off, the team had to dig deep and hang on for a draw.*
6 dig a hole for yourself (*also* **dig yourself into a hole**) to get yourself into a difficult situation by doing or saying the wrong thing
7 dig sb out of trouble/a mess/a hole etc to help a person or organization get out of trouble
8 dig your own grave to do something that will cause serious problems for you in the future
9 [T] *old-fashioned* to like something: *I dig that hat!*

THESAURUS

dig to make a hole in the ground using your hands, a tool, or a machine: *Some workmen were digging a trench at the side of the road.* | *In Africa, the people know where to dig for water.*
make a hole to dig a hole in the ground, using your hands or a tool: *Make a hole just big enough for the plant's roots.*
burrow /ˈbʌrəʊ $ ˈbɜːroʊ/ if an animal burrows, it makes a hole or a passage in the ground by digging the earth with its feet, nose etc: *The rabbits had burrowed a hole under the fence.*
plough *BrE*, **plow** *AmE* /plaʊ/ to turn over the soil using a machine or a tool pulled by animals, to prepare the soil for planting seeds: *The farmers here still plough their fields using buffaloes.*
excavate /ˈekskəveɪt/ *formal* to dig a large hole in the ground, especially as a preparation for building something: *The men began excavating the hole for the pool.*
bore to make a deep round hole in the ground using a special machine, especially in order to look for oil or water: *Companies need a special licence to bore for oil.*

dig in *phr v*
1 dig sth ↔ in (*also* **dig sth into sth**) to mix something into soil by digging: *Dig some fertilizer into the soil first.*
2 (*also* **dig (sth) into sth**) to push a hard or pointed object into something, especially someone's body, or to press into something: *She dug her fingernails into his arm.* | **dig sth ↔ in** *He dug his spurs in and urged his horse on.* | *I could feel one of the hooks digging in.*
3 if a group of people, especially soldiers, dig in, they make a protected place for themselves or prepare for a difficult situation: *The troops dug in along the defensive line.* | *We just have to dig in and hope we can turn things around.*
4 (*also* **dig into sth**) *informal* to start eating food that is in front of you: *Go on – dig in!* | *He was already digging into his pie and chips.*

dig into sth *phr v*
1 to start using a supply of something, especially money: *I'm going to have to dig into my savings again.*
2 to try to find out about something unknown or secret: *He had been digging into her past.* → DIG IN

dig sth ↔ **out** *phr v*
1 to get something out of earth, snow etc using a SPADE or your hands: **[+of]** *We had to dig the car out of a snow drift.*
2 to find something you have not seen for a long time, or that is not easy to find: *I must remember to dig out that book for you.*

dig sth ↔ **up** *phr v*
1 to remove something from the earth using a SPADE: *I'll dig up that plant and move it.*
2 to remove the surface of an area of ground, road etc, or

to make holes in it: *They're digging up the road just outside my flat.*
3 to find hidden or forgotten information by careful searching: *They tried to dig up something from his past to spoil his chances of being elected.*

dig² *n* [C] **1** a joke or remark that you make to annoy or criticize someone: **[+at]** *He couldn't resist a dig at the referee.* | *Here was a chance to* ***have a dig*** *at trade unionists.* **THESAURUS** ▸ COMMENT **2 give sb a dig** to push someone quickly and lightly with your finger or elbow: *Ginnie gave her sister a dig in the ribs.* **3** an organized process of digging in order to find ancient objects for study: *an* ***archaeological dig*** **4 digs** [plural] *BrE old-fashioned* a room that you pay rent to live in: **in digs** *He's 42 and still* ***living in digs***.

di·gest¹ /daɪˈdʒest, də-/ ●○○ *v* [T]
1 to change food that you have just eaten into substances that your body can use: *Most babies can digest a wide range of food easily.* → INGEST
2 to understand new information, especially when there is a lot of it or it is difficult to understand SYN **take in**: *I struggled to digest the news.*

di·gest² /ˈdaɪdʒest/ *n* [C] a short piece of writing that gives the most important facts from a book, report etc

di·gest·i·ble /daɪˈdʒestəbəl, də-/ *adj* food that is digestible can be easily digested OPP **indigestible**

di·ges·tion /daɪˈdʒestʃən, də-/ ●○○ *n*
1 [U] the process of digesting food
2 [C] your ability to digest food easily → **indigestion**: *Too much tea is bad for your digestion.*

di·ges·tive /daɪˈdʒestɪv, də-/ *adj* [only before noun] connected with the process of digestion: **digestive system/organs/juices etc**

diˌgestive ˈbiscuit (*also* **digestive**) *n* [C] a type of plain slightly sweet BISCUIT that is popular in Britain

dig·ger /ˈdɪgə $ -ər/ *n* [C] a large machine that digs and moves earth → GOLD DIGGER

dig·gings /ˈdɪgɪŋz/ *n* [plural] a place where people are digging holes in the ground

Di·gi·box /ˈdɪdʒibɒks $ -bɑːks/ *n* [C] *trademark* a piece of electronic equipment which people in Britain put on top of their televisions if they want to receive DIGITAL TV programmes → SET-TOP BOX

di·gi·cam /ˈdɪdʒɪkæm/ *n* [C] a type of camera that can store pictures in a DIGITAL form which can be put into a computer, rather than on film

di·gi·pack /ˈdɪdʒipæk/ *n* [C] a CARDBOARD container for a CD which folds out from the centre

di·git /ˈdɪdʒɪt/ ●○○ *n* [C]
1 one of the written signs that represent the numbers 0 to 9: **three-digit/four-digit etc number** *4305 is a four-digit number.*
2 *technical* a finger or toe

di·gi·tal /ˈdɪdʒətl/ ●●○ *adj*
1 using a system in which information is recorded or sent out electronically in the form of numbers, usually ones and zeros: *digital TV* | *a digital signal* | *a* ***digital camera*** | *digital recording* | **digital cassette/audiotape etc** *a recording on digital audiotape*
2 giving information in the form of numbers → **analogue**: *a* ***digital watch***
3 *formal* relating to the fingers and toes —**digitally** *adv*

ˌdigital diˈvide *n* [singular] the differences of opportunity that exist between people who can regularly and easily use the Internet and email, and people who cannot do this

ˌdigital ˈimmigrant *n* [C] someone who is not very good at using digital equipment such as computers and mobile phones because they have only recently started using them OPP **digital native**

ˌdigital inˈclusion *n* [U] the activity of making sure that everyone is able to use computers and the Internet

ˌdigital ˈnative *n* [C] someone who is very good at using digital equipment such as computers and mobile phones because they have used them since they were young OPP **digital immigrant**

ˌdigital ˈsignature *n* [C] information on an electronic message that proves who the person sending the message is

ˌdigital ˈtelevision *n* **1** (*also* **digital**) [U] a system of broadcasting using digital signals → **analogue**, **cable**
2 [C] a television which can receive digital broadcasts

di·gi·tize (*also* **-ise** *BrE*) /ˈdɪdʒətaɪz/ *v* [T] to put information into a digital form

dig·ni·fied /ˈdɪgnɪfaɪd/ ●●○ *adj* behaving in a calm and serious way, even in a difficult situation, which makes people respect you: *a dignified old lady* | *She made a dignified departure.*

dig·ni·fy /ˈdɪgnɪfaɪ/ *v* (**dignified, dignifying, dignifies**) [T] to make something or someone seem better or more important than they really are, especially by using a particular word to describe them: **dignify sb/sth with sth** *I cannot dignify him with the name 'physician'.*

dig·ni·ta·ry /ˈdɪgnətəri $ -teri/ *n* (*plural* **dignitaries**) [C] someone who has an important official position SYN **VIP**: *Flowers were presented to visiting dignitaries.*

dig·ni·ty /ˈdɪgnəti/ ●●○ *n* [U]
1 the ability to behave in a calm controlled way even in a difficult situation: **with dignity** *The family faced their ordeal with dignity.* | *an appearance of quiet dignity*
2 your dignity your sense of your own value or importance: **retain/lose your dignity** *Old people need to retain their dignity and independence.* | *Arguing* ***was beneath*** *her* ***dignity*** (=was something she thought she was too important to do).
3 the fact of being respected or deserving respect: **with dignity** *Patients should be allowed to die with dignity.* | *Prisoners should be treated with regard for* ***human dignity***.
4 a calm and serious quality: **[+of]** *the dignity of the occasion*
5 stand on your dignity *formal* to demand to be treated with proper respect

di·gress /daɪˈgres/ *v* [I] to talk or write about something that is not your main subject: *Do you mind if I digress for a moment?* —**digression** /daɪˈgreʃən/ *n* [C,U]: *After several long digressions he finally reached the interesting part of the story.*

dike /daɪk/ *n* [C] another spelling of DYKE

dik·tat /dɪkˈtæt/ *n* [C,U] an order that is forced on people by a ruler or government: *government by diktat*

di·lap·i·dat·ed /dɪˈlæpɪdeɪtɪd/ *adj* a dilapidated building, vehicle etc is old and in very bad condition → **derelict** —**dilapidation** /dəˌlæpəˈdeɪʃən/ *n* [U]

di·late /daɪˈleɪt/ *v* [I,T] if a hollow part of your body dilates or if something dilates it, it becomes wider OPP **contract**: *dilated pupils* —**dilation** /daɪˈleɪʃən/ *n* [U]

dilate on/upon sth *phr v formal* to speak or write a lot about something: *He dilated upon their heroism.*

dil·a·to·ry /ˈdɪlətəri $ -tɔːri/ *adj formal* slow in doing something

dil·do /ˈdɪldəʊ $ -doʊ/ *n* (*plural* **dildos**) [C] an object shaped like a male sex organ that a woman can use for sexual pleasure

di·lem·ma /dəˈlemə, daɪ-/ ●●○ *n* [C] a situation in which it is very difficult to decide what to do, because all the choices seem equally good or equally bad: *a moral dilemma* | **in a dilemma** *I'm in a dilemma about this job offer.* | *This* ***placed*** *Robert Kennedy* ***in a dilemma***. | *Many women are* ***faced with*** *the* ***dilemma*** *of choosing between work and family commitments.* → **be on the horns of a dilemma** at HORN¹(6)

dil·et·tan·te /ˌdɪləˈtænti $ -ˈtɑːnti/ *n* [C] someone who is not serious about what they are doing or does not study a subject thoroughly —**dilettante** *adj* [only before noun]

dil·i·gent /ˈdɪlədʒənt/ *adj* someone who is diligent

D

works hard and is careful and thorough: *a diligent student* —**diligently** *adv*: *They worked diligently all morning.* —**diligence** *n* [U]

dill /dɪl/ *n* [U] a type of herb

ˌdill ˈpickle *n* [C] a whole CUCUMBER which has been preserved in VINEGAR

dil·ly-dal·ly /ˈdɪli ˌdæli/ *v* (**dilly-dallied**, **dilly-dallying**, **dilly-dallies**) [I] to waste time, because you cannot decide about something: *Don't dilly-dally, just get on with it!*

di·lute¹ /daɪˈluːt $ dɪˈluːt, daɪ-/ ●○○ *v* [T]
1 to make a liquid weaker by adding water or another liquid → **water down**: *diluted fruit juice* | **dilute sth with/in sth** *Dilute the paint with a little oil.* **THESAURUS** MIX
2 to make a quality, belief etc weaker or less effective SYN **water down**: *an attempt to dilute the proposals* —**dilution** /daɪˈluːʃən/ *n* [C,U]: *Any dilution of standards must be resisted.*

di·lute² *adj* a dilute liquid has been made weaker by the addition of water or another liquid OPP **concentrated**: *dilute hydrochloric acid*

D

dim¹ /dɪm/ ●○○ *adj* (*comparative* **dimmer**, *superlative* **dimmest**)
1 DARK fairly dark or not giving much light, so that you cannot see well OPP **bright**: *in the dim light of the early dawn* | *a dim glow* **THESAURUS** DARK
2 SHAPE a dim shape is one which is not easy to see because it is too far away, or there is not enough light: *The dim outline of a building loomed up out of the mist.*
3 take a dim view of sth to disapprove of something: *Miss Watson took a dim view of Paul's behaviour.*
4 dim recollection/awareness etc a memory or understanding of something that is not clear in your mind SYN **vague**: *Laura had a dim recollection of someone telling her this before.*
5 EYES *literary* dim eyes are weak and cannot see well: *Isaac was old and his eyes were dim.*
6 FUTURE CHANCES if your chances of success in the future are dim, they are not good: *Prospects for an early settlement of the dispute are dim.*
7 in the dim and distant past a very long time ago - used humorously
8 NOT INTELLIGENT *informal* not intelligent: *You can be really dim sometimes!* —**dimly** *adv*: *a dimly lit room* | *She was only dimly aware of the risk.* —**dimness** *n* [U]

dim² *v* (**dimmed**, **dimming**) **1** [I,T] if a light dims, or if you dim it, it becomes less bright: *The lights in the theatre began to dim.* **2** [I,T] if a feeling, quality etc dims or is dimmed, it grows weaker or less: *Even the rain could not dim their enthusiasm.* | *Hopes of a peaceful settlement have dimmed.* **3 dim your headlights/lights** *AmE* to lower the angle of the front lights of your car, especially when someone is driving towards you SYN **dip** *BrE*

dime /daɪm/ *n* [C] **1** a coin of the US and Canada, worth one tenth of a dollar **2 a dime a dozen** *AmE informal* very common and not valuable SYN **ten a penny** *BrE*: *PhDs are a dime a dozen nowadays.*

ˈdime ˌnovel *n* [C] *AmE* a cheap book with a story that contains a lot of exciting events

di·men·sion /daɪˈmenʃən, də-/ ●●○ W3 AWL *n* [C]
1 a part of a situation or a quality involved in it SYN **aspect**: **[+of]** *the moral dimension of world politics* | **add a new/an extra/another etc dimension (to sth)** *His coaching has added another dimension to my game.* | **political/social/economic etc dimension** *It is important to keep in mind the historical dimension to these issues.* | *You can have a* ***spiritual dimension*** *to your life without being religious.*
2 [usually plural] the length, height, width, depth, or DIAMETER of something SYN **measurement**: *a rectangle with the dimensions 5cm x 2cm* | **[+of]** *We'll need to know the exact dimensions of the room.*
3 a direction in space that is at an angle of 90 degrees to two other directions: *A diagram represents things in only two dimensions.* → FOURTH DIMENSION, THREE-DIMENSIONAL(1), TWO-DIMENSIONAL(1)

DIMENSION

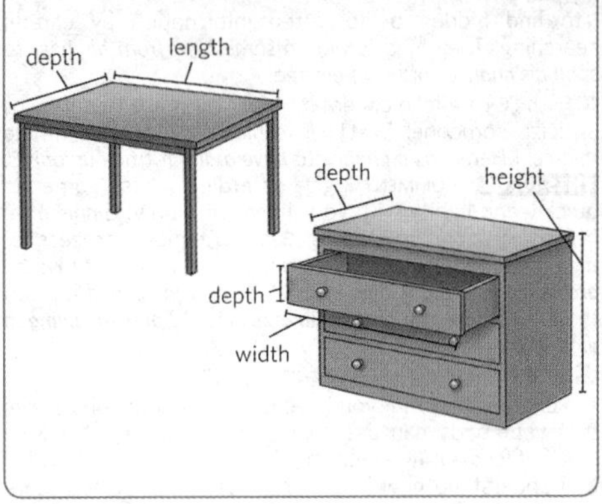

4 dimensions [plural] how great or serious a problem is: *a catastrophe of enormous dimensions*

ˈdime store *n* [C] *AmE* a shop that sells many different kinds of cheap goods, especially for the house

di·min·ish /dəˈmɪnɪʃ/ ●●○ AWL *v*
1 [I,T] to become or make something become smaller or less SYN **reduce**: *The party's share of the electorate has diminished steadily.* | *These drugs diminish blood flow to the brain.* **THESAURUS** DECREASE
2 [T] to deliberately make someone or something appear less important or valuable than they really are: *Don't let him diminish your achievements.* | *But that's not to diminish the importance of his discoveries.*
3 diminishing returns when the profits or advantages you are getting from something stop increasing in relation to the effort you are making

diˌminished responsiˈbility (*also* **diˌminished caˈpacity** *AmE*) *n* [U] *law* when someone is not considered to be responsible for their actions because they are mentally ill

di·min·u·en·do /dəˌmɪnjuˈendəʊ $ -doʊ/ *n* (*plural* **diminuendos**) [C] a part in a piece of music where it becomes gradually quieter OPP **crescendo** —**diminuendo** *adj, adv*

dim·i·nu·tion /ˌdɪməˈnjuːʃən $ -ˈnuː-/ AWL *n* [C,U] *formal* a reduction in the size, number, or amount of something: **[+of/in]** *a diminution in value*

di·min·u·tive¹ /dəˈmɪnjətɪv/ *adj* small: *a shy diminutive man* **THESAURUS** SHORT

diminutive² *n* [C] a word formed by adding a diminutive suffix

diˌminutive ˈsuffix *n* [C] *technical* an ending that is added to a word to express smallness, for example 'ling' added to 'duck' to make 'duckling'

dim·mer /ˈdɪmə $ -ər/ (*also* **ˈdimmer ˌswitch**) *n* [C] an electric light switch that can change the brightness of the light

dim·ple /ˈdɪmpəl/ *n* [C] **1** a small hollow place on your skin, especially one on your cheek or chin when you smile **2** a small hollow place in a surface —**dimpled** *adj*: *dimpled cheeks*

dim·wit /ˈdɪmwɪt/ *n* [C] *spoken* a stupid person —**dimwitted** *adj*

din¹ /dɪn/ *n* [singular] a loud unpleasant noise that continues for a long time: **[+of]** *The din of the engines was deafening.* | **above the din** *Ged was trying to make himself heard above the din.*

din² *v* (**dinned**, **dinning**)
din sth **into** sb *phr v* to make someone learn and remember something by saying it to them many times: *Respect for our elders was dinned into us at school.*

di·nar /ˈdiːnɑː $ dɪˈnɑːr, ˈdiːnɑːr/ *n* [C] the standard unit of money in Macedonia, Serbia and some North African and Middle Eastern countries

dine /daɪn/ ●●○ *v* [I] *formal* to eat dinner: *He was dining with friends at the Ritz.* → **wine and dine sb** at WINE[2]
dine on/off sth *phr v formal* to eat a particular kind of food for dinner, especially expensive food: *We dined on lobster and strawberries.*
dine out *phr v*
1 *formal* to eat dinner in a restaurant or in someone else's house → **eat out**: *They would dine out together once a month.*
2 dine out on sth *BrE informal* to keep using a story about something that has happened to you, in order to entertain people at meals

din·er /ˈdaɪnə $ -ər/ ●○○ *n* [C]
1 someone who is eating in a restaurant
2 *especially AmE* a small restaurant that serves cheap meals

di·nette /daɪˈnet/ *n* [C] *AmE* a small area, usually in or near the kitchen, where people eat meals

ding-a-ling /ˈdɪŋ ə lɪŋ/ (*also* **ding·bat** /ˈdɪŋbæt/) *n* [C] *AmE spoken* a stupid person: *Some ding-a-ling parked too close to us.*

ding-dong /ˈdɪŋ dɒŋ $ -dɒːŋ/ *n* **1** [U] the noise made by a bell **2** [singular] *BrE spoken* a noisy argument: *They were having a real ding-dong in the kitchen.* **3** [C] *AmE spoken* a stupid person

din·ghy /ˈdɪŋgi, ˈdɪŋi/ *n* (*plural* **dinghies**) [C] a small open boat used for pleasure, or for taking people between a ship and the shore → RUBBER DINGHY

din·go /ˈdɪŋgəʊ $ -goʊ/ *n* (*plural* **dingoes**) [C] an Australian wild dog

din·gy /ˈdɪndʒi/ *adj* (*comparative* **dingier**, *superlative* **dingiest**) dark, dirty, and in bad condition: *a dingy room | a dingy side-street* THESAURUS DIRTY —**dinginess** *n* [U]

ˈ**dining car** *n* [C] a carriage on a train where meals are served SYN **restaurant car**

ˈ**dining room** ●●● S3 *n* [C] a room where you eat meals in a house or hotel

ˈ**dining ˌtable** *n* [C] a table at which you eat meals → DINNER TABLE → see picture at TABLE[1]

din·kum /ˈdɪŋkəm/ *adj* **fair dinkum** *spoken informal* fair or honest – used in Australian English

din·ky /ˈdɪŋki/ *adj informal* **1** *BrE* small and attractive: *a dinky little bag* **2** *AmE* too small and often not very nice: *It was a really dinky hotel room.*

din·ner /ˈdɪnə $ -ər/ ●●● S1 W2 *n*
1 [C,U] the main meal of the day, eaten in the middle of the day or the evening: *What time do you usually have dinner? | We're having fish for dinner tonight. | What's for dinner?*
2 [C] a formal occasion when an evening meal is eaten, often to celebrate something: *the Club's annual dinner* → **dog's dinner** at DOG[1](9), → **more sth than you've had hot dinners** at HOT[1](30)

GRAMMAR: Patterns with dinner

for dinner
- You eat something **for dinner**: *We had fish for dinner.*
✗ Don't say: *We had fish at dinner.*

at dinner
- You use **at dinner** to talk about something that happens while you are eating dinner: *She told us at dinner that she was going away.*

COLLOCATIONS

VERBS

have/eat dinner *Why don't you come and have dinner with us?*
make/cook dinner *I offered to cook dinner.*
have sth for dinner *I thought we might have pasta for dinner tonight.*
have sb for/to dinner *We're having a few friends round to dinner.*
ask/invite sb to dinner *Let's ask Kate and Mike to dinner.*
come for/to dinner | go out for/to dinner (=go and eat in a restaurant) | **serve dinner** (=start giving people food)

ADJECTIVES/NOUN + dinner

a three-course/four-course etc dinner *The cost of the hotel includes a three-course dinner.*
Sunday/Christmas/Thanksgiving dinner (=a special meal eaten on Sunday etc) *We usually have a walk after Christmas dinner.*
a romantic dinner (=for two people in a romantic relationship) *Clive and Denise were enjoying a romantic dinner for two in a quiet French restaurant.*
a candle-lit dinner (=with only candles for lighting) *Chris treated his girlfriend to a candle-lit dinner.*
a black-tie dinner (=where people wear special formal clothes) *He was invited to a black-tie dinner at one of the Oxford colleges.*
school dinners *BrE* (=meals provided at school in the middle of the day) *School dinners are served in the canteen.*
TV dinners (=meals that you eat while watching TV) *TV dinners in aluminium containers can be found in the freezer departments of many supermarkets.*

dinner + NOUN

a dinner party (=when someone's friends are invited for a special evening meal) *We are having a dinner party on Saturday.*
a dinner guest *The dinner guests began arriving at about seven o'clock.*

ˈ**dinner ˌdance** *n* [C] a social event in the evening, that includes a formal meal and music for dancing

ˈ**dinner ˌjacket** *n* [C] *BrE* a black or white jacket worn by men on very formal occasions, usually with a BOW TIE SYN **tuxedo**

ˈ**dinner ˌlady** *n* [C] *BrE* a woman who serves meals to children at school

ˈ**dinner ˌparty** *n* [C] a social event when people are invited to someone's house for an evening meal

ˈ**dinner ˌservice** (*also* ˈ**dinner set**) *n* [C] a complete set of plates, dishes etc, used for serving a meal

ˈ**dinner ˌtable** *n* **the dinner table a)** an occasion when people are eating dinner together: *It wasn't a very suitable conversation for the dinner table.* **b)** the table at which people eat dinner → DINING TABLE

ˈ**dinner ˌtheater** *n* [C,U] *AmE* a restaurant in which you see a play after your meal, or this type of entertainment

din·ner·time /ˈdɪnətaɪm $ -ər-/ *n* [U] the time when you usually have dinner, especially in the middle of the day: *Do you want to go for a drink at dinnertime?*

di·no·saur /ˈdaɪnəsɔː $ -sɔːr/ ●○○ *n* [C]
1 one of a group of REPTILES that lived millions of years ago
2 *informal* someone or something that is old-fashioned and no longer effective or suitable for modern times: *lengthy speeches by some of the party's dinosaurs*

dint /dɪnt/ *n* **by dint of (doing) sth** by using a particular method: *By dint of hard work and persistence, she had got the job of manager.*

di·o·cese /ˈdaɪəsɪs/ *n* [C] the area under the control of a BISHOP in some Christian churches —**diocesan** /daɪˈɒsəsən $ -ˈɑː-/ *adj*

di·ode /ˈdaɪəʊd $ -oʊd/ *n* [C] *technical* a piece of electrical equipment that makes an electrical current flow in one direction

di·ox·ide /daɪˈɒksaɪd $ -ˈɑːk-/ *n* [C,U] a chemical COMPOUND that contains two atoms of oxygen and one atom of another chemical ELEMENT → CARBON DIOXIDE

di·ox·in /daɪˈɒksɪn $ -ˈɑːk-/ *n* [C,U] a very poisonous chemical used in industry and farming

dip[1] /dɪp/ ●●○ *v* (**dipped, dipping**)
1 PUT STH IN LIQUID [T] to put something into a liquid and lift it out again: **dip sth in/into sth** *He dipped his hand in the water.* | *Dip the strawberries into melted chocolate.* THESAURUS PUT

D

2 MOVE DOWN [I,T] to move down, or to make something move down, usually for just a short time: *We watched the **sun dip** below the horizon.* | *She **dipped** her **head** and spoke into the microphone.*
3 BECOME LESS [I] if an amount or level dips, it becomes less, usually for just a short time SYN **fall**: *Profits dipped slightly last year.* | *Temperatures dipped to -10°C last night.*
4 ROAD/PATH [C] if land or a road or path dips, it slopes down and then goes up again
5 dip your headlights/lights *BrE* to lower the angle of the front lights of your car when someone is driving towards you
6 ANIMALS [T] to put animals in a chemical that kills insects on their skin → SKINNY-DIPPING

dip into sth *phr v*
1 to read short parts of a book, magazine etc, but not the whole thing: *It's the kind of book you can dip into now and again.*
2 to use some of an amount of money that you have: *Medical bills forced her to **dip into** her **savings**.* | *Parents are being asked to **dip into** their **pockets** for new school books* (=use their own money to pay for them).
3 to put your hand into a bag or box in order to take out one of the things inside: *On her lap was a bag of candy which she kept dipping into.*

dip² ●●○ *n*
1 SWIM [C] *informal* a quick swim: *Are you coming in for a dip?* | **take/have a dip** *Let's take a dip in the lake.*
2 DECREASE [C] a slight decrease in the amount of something: **[+in]** *an unexpected dip in profits*
3 FOOD [C,U] a thick mixture that you can dip food into before you eat it: *sour cream and onion dip*
4 IN A SURFACE [C] a place where the surface of something goes down suddenly, then goes up again: **[+in]** *a dip in the road*
5 FOR ANIMALS [C,U] a chemical that kills insects on sheep and other animals: ***sheep dip***
6 PERSON [C] *AmE spoken* a stupid person
7 a dip into sth a quick look at information, a book, magazine etc: *People interested in history would enjoy a dip into this book.* → LUCKY DIP

Dip *BrE* the written abbreviation of ***diploma***

diph·ther·i·a /dɪfˈθɪəriə, dɪp- $ -ˈθɪr-/ *n* [U] a serious infectious throat disease that makes breathing difficult

diph·thong /ˈdɪfθɒŋ, ˈdɪp- $ -θɔːŋ/ *n* [C] *technical* a vowel sound made by pronouncing two vowels quickly one after the other. For example, the vowel sound in 'main' is a diphthong.

di·plo·ma /dəˈpləʊmə $ -ˈploʊ-/ ●●○ *n* [C]
1 *BrE* a document showing that someone has successfully completed a course of study or passed an examination: *I'm hoping to **get** my teaching **diploma** this year.* | **[+in]** *a diploma in catering*
2 *AmE* a document showing that a student has successfully completed their HIGH SCHOOL or university education: **high school/college diploma**

di·plo·ma·cy /dəˈpləʊməsi $ -ˈploʊ-/ ●○○ *n* [U]
1 the job or activity of managing the relationships between countries: *international diplomacy*
2 skill in dealing with people without upsetting them: *The job requires tact and diplomacy.* → **gunboat diplomacy** at GUNBOAT(2)

dip·lo·mat /ˈdɪpləmæt/ ●●○ *n* [C]
1 someone who officially represents their government in a foreign country → **ambassador**: *French diplomats*
2 someone who is good at dealing with people without upsetting them

dip·lo·mat·ic /ˌdɪpləˈmætɪk◂/ ●○○ *adj*
1 relating to or involving the work of diplomats: *Diplomatic efforts to end the fighting began on October 25.*
2 diplomatic relations/ties the arrangement between two countries that each should keep representatives at an EMBASSY in the other's country: **establish/break off diplomatic relations** *The two countries established diplomatic relations last year.*
3 dealing with people politely and skilfully without upsetting them SYN **tactful**: *They were always very diplomatic with awkward clients.* | *a diplomatic answer* —**diplomatically** /-kli/ *adv*: *Maria handled the situation very diplomatically.*

ˌdiplomatic ˈbag *n* [C] a bag or container used for sending official government documents to diplomats working abroad

diploˈmatic ˌcorps *n* [U] all the diplomats working in a particular country

ˌdiplomatic imˈmunity *n* [U] a diplomat's special rights in the country where they are working, which protect them from local taxes and PROSECUTION

Diploˈmatic ˌService *n* **the Diplomatic Service** the British government department that sends people to represent Britain in other countries

di·plo·ma·tist /dɪˈpləʊmətɪst $ -ˈploʊ-/ *n* [C] *old-fashioned* a DIPLOMAT

dip·per /ˈdɪpə $ -ər/ *n* [C] **1** a small bird that finds its food in streams **2** a large spoon with a long handle, used for taking liquid out of a container → BIG DIPPER

dip·py /ˈdɪpi/ *adj informal* silly or crazy

dip·shit /ˈdɪpʃɪt/ *n* [C] *AmE spoken not polite* an offensive word for a stupid person. Do not use this word.

dip·so·ma·ni·ac /ˌdɪpsəˈmeɪniæk/ *n* [C] *BrE old-fashioned* someone who has a very strong desire for alcohol, which they cannot control SYN **alcoholic**

dip·stick /ˈdɪpˌstɪk/ *n* [C] **1** a stick for measuring the amount of liquid in a container, especially the amount of oil in a car's engine **2** *spoken* a stupid person

dip·tych /ˈdɪptɪk/ *n* [C] a picture made in two parts which can be closed like a book → TRIPTYCH

dire /daɪə $ daɪr/ ●○○ *adj*
1 extremely serious or terrible: *warnings of **dire consequences** that often don't come true* | *The country is **in dire need of** food aid.* | *The situation looked dire.*
2 be in dire straits to be in an extremely difficult or serious situation: *Everyone agrees the sport is in dire straits.*
3 dire warning/prediction/forecast a warning about something terrible that will happen in the future: *Last night there were dire warnings of civil war.*

di·rect¹ /dəˈrekt, ˌdaɪˈrekt◂/ ●●● S2 W1 *adj*
1 WITHOUT INVOLVING OTHERS done without any other people, actions, processes etc coming between OPP **indirect**: *Experienced users have direct access to the main data files.* | *I'm not in **direct contact** with them.* | *Few policy-makers have had direct experience of business.* | **direct effect/impact/influence etc** *Educational level has a sizeable direct effect on income.* | **direct link/connection/relationship etc** *There is a direct link between poverty and ill-health.* | **direct result/consequence** *The decision to close the hospital is a direct result of Government health policy.*
2 FROM ONE PLACE TO ANOTHER going straight from one place to another without stopping or changing direction OPP **indirect**: *Which is the most **direct route** to London?* | ***a direct flight** to New York*
3 EXACT [only before noun] exact or total: *Weight increases **in direct proportion to** mass.* | *For Lawrence, **in direct contrast to** Adam, everything seemed to come so easily.* | *a **direct quote*** (=exact words) *from the book*
4 BEHAVIOUR/ATTITUDE saying exactly what you mean in an honest clear way OPP **indirect**: *Women often feel men are too direct and not sympathetic enough.* | *Now, let me ask you a **direct question**, and I expect a **direct answer**.*
THESAURUS HONEST
5 direct descendant someone who is related to someone else through their parents and grandparents, not through their AUNTS, UNCLES etc: **[+of]** *She claimed to be a direct descendant of Wordsworth.*
6 direct hit an occasion on which something such as a bomb hits a place exactly, causing a lot of damage: *During the war, the cathedral **suffered** many **direct hits**.* | *One of the bombers **scored a direct hit**.*

7 direct heat/sunlight strong heat or light that someone or something is not protected from OPP **indirect**: *Never change the film in direct sunlight.* → DIRECTLY[1], DIRECTNESS

direct² ●●● S3 W2 *v*

1 AIM [T always + adv/prep] to aim something in a particular direction or at a particular person, group etc: **direct sth at/towards etc sth** *The machine directs an X-ray beam at the patient's body.* | *The new route directs lorries away from the town centre.* | *I'd like to* **direct** *your* **attention** *to paragraph four.* | *I want to* **direct** *my* **efforts** *more towards my own projects.*

2 BE IN CHARGE [T] to be in charge of something or control it: *Mr Turner was directing the investigation from a very early stage.* | *The choir was directed by Sir David Willcocks.*

3 FILM/PLAY [I,T] to give the actors in a play, film, or television programme instructions about what they should do: *The play was directed by Frank Hauser.*

4 WAY/ROUTE [T] *formal* to tell someone how to get to a place: **direct sb to sth** *Could you direct me to Trafalgar Square, please?* THESAURUS LEAD

5 TELL SB TO DO STH [T] *formal* to tell someone what they should do SYN **order**: **direct sb to do sth** *The judge directed the jury to find Mr Baggs not guilty.* | **direct that** *He directed that his body should be buried in Upton.* THESAURUS ORDER

direct³ *adv* **1** without stopping or changing direction SYN **directly**: *Can we fly direct to Chicago, or do we stop in Salt Lake City first?* **2** without dealing with anyone else first SYN **directly**: *Esther decided to contact the manager direct.* | *It is usually cheaper to buy the goods direct from the wholesaler.*

di,rect 'access *n* [U] *technical* the ability to obtain DATA directly from a computer FILE without starting from the beginning

di,rect 'action *n* [U] an action such as a STRIKE or a protest that is intended to make a government or company change something immediately: *Peaceful direct action by pressure groups has a powerful effect on public opinion.*

di,rect 'current *n* [U] (*abbreviation* **DC**) a flow of electricity that moves in one direction only → **alternating current**

di,rect 'debit *n* [C,U] *BrE* an instruction you give your bank to pay money directly out of your account regularly to a particular person or organization

di,rect de'posit *n* [U] a method of paying someone's wages directly into their bank account —**direct deposit** *v* [T]

di,rect 'discourse *n* [U] *AmE technical* DIRECT SPEECH

di·rec·tion /də'rekʃən, daɪ-/ ●●● S1 W1 *n*

1 TOWARDS [C] the way something or someone moves, faces, or is aimed: *Which* **direction** *did they* **go in**? | **in the direction of sth** *The suspects were last seen heading in the direction of Miami.* | **in sb's direction** *Tony glanced in her direction and their eyes met.* | *The girls pointed* **in the opposite direction**. | *On seeing me, Maurice* **changed direction** *and went along the wharf instead.* | *As shots rang out, the crowd ran screaming* **in all directions**. | **from the direction of sth** *There was a loud scream from the direction of the children's pool.* | **in a southerly/easterly etc direction** *Continue in a southerly direction until you reach the road.*

> **REGISTER**
> In everyday English, people usually use **which way ...?** when asking where something is rather than using the noun **direction**: *Which* **direction** *did they go in?*
> → ***Which way*** *did they go?* | *Which* **direction** *is north?*
> → ***Which way*** *is north?*

2 directions [plural] **a)** instructions about how to get from one place to another: *A very helpful woman* **gave** *me* **directions** *to the police station.* **b)** instructions about what to do: *Be sure you* **read the directions** *before using any piece of equipment.*

3 WAY STH DEVELOPS [C] the general way in which someone or something changes or develops: *We are happy with the* **direction** *the club is* **taking**. | **move/head/go in the right direction** *I believe that things are heading in the right direction in South Africa.* | **new/different/exciting etc direction** *The company is hoping to extend its operations in new directions.*

4 CONTROL [U] control, management, or advice: **under sb's direction** *Under Thompson's direction, the college has developed an international reputation.*

5 WHERE FROM OR WHERE TO [C] where something comes from or where something leads: **in a direction** *The evidence all points in this direction.* | **from a direction** *Help came from a wholly unexpected direction.*

6 PURPOSE [U] a general purpose or aim: *Her mother felt that Rachel's life* **lacked direction**.

7 FILM/PLAY [U] the instructions given to the actors and other people working on a film, play etc → **a step in the right direction** at STEP[1](2)

di·rec·tion·al /də'rekʃənəl, daɪ-/ *adj technical* **1** relating to the direction in which something is pointing or moving **2** a directional piece of equipment receives or gives out radio signals from some directions more strongly than others

di·rec·tion·less /də'rekʃənləs, daɪ-/ *adj* lacking a clear direction or aim: *I felt directionless and lost.*

di·rec·tive¹ /də'rektɪv, daɪ-/ ●○○ *n* [C] an official order or instruction: **[+on]** *proposals for* **implementing** *the EU* **directive** *on paternity leave*

directive² *adj formal* giving instructions: *The team leader will have a less directive role.*

di·rect·ly¹ /də'rektli, daɪ-/ ●●● S2 W2 *adv*

1 with no other person, action, process etc between OPP **indirectly**: *The new property tax law won't* **directly affect** *us.* | *We hope to bring together the countries* **directly involved** *in the conflict.* | **[+to/from]** *Application for admission to this course should be made directly to the University.* THESAURUS EXACTLY

2 exactly in a particular position or direction SYN **right**: **directly in front of/behind/under etc sth** *It was a small house, directly behind the church.* | *The girl was sitting directly opposite him.* | *Have you noticed how he never looks directly at you?*

3 speak/ask/answer etc directly to say exactly what you mean without trying to hide anything: *Jeff has a job in mind, but refuses to say directly what it is.*

4 *BrE old-fashioned* very soon: *He should be here directly, if you don't mind waiting.*

5 *BrE old-fashioned* immediately

directly² *conjunction BrE old-fashioned* as soon as: *I came directly I got your message.*

di,rect 'mail *n* [U] advertisements that are sent by post to many people

di,rect 'marketing *n* [U] the business of selling things directly to people by post or telephone rather than in shops

di,rect 'method *n* [singular, U] a method of teaching a foreign language without using the student's own language

di·rect·ness /də'rektnəs, daɪ-/ *n* [U] the quality of being clear, plain, or easy to understand: *She has a child-like enthusiasm and directness.* | **[+of]** *The directness of the question startled me.*

,direct 'object *n* [C] *technical* in grammar, the person or thing that is affected by the action of a TRANSITIVE verb, for example 'Mary' in the statement 'I saw Mary' → INDIRECT OBJECT

di·rec·tor /də'rektə, daɪ- $ -ər/ ●●● S2 W1 *n* [C]

1 someone who controls or manages a company → **executive**: **[+of]** *a former director of Gartmore Pensions Ltd* | *The company is run by a* **board of directors** (=a group of directors).

2 someone who is in charge of a particular activity or organization: **[+of]** *the director of education* | **finance/marketing/sales etc director** (=the person in charge of the financial department etc)

3 the person who gives instructions to the actors and

D

other people working on a film or play → **producer** → MANAGING DIRECTOR, NON-EXECUTIVE DIRECTOR

di·rec·tor·ate /dəˈrektərət, daɪ-/ *n* [C] **1** the group of directors who run a company SYN **board** **2** a department of a government or large organization in charge of a particular area or activity: *the regional directorate of education*

di͵rector-ˈgeneral *n* [C] *BrE* the person in charge of a large public organization: *the Director-General of Fair Trading*

di·rec·to·ri·al /͵daɪrekˈtɔːriəl◂/ *adj* [only before noun] relating to the work of a film or theatre director: *De Niro's directorial debut*

Di͵rector of ˈStudies *n* [C] a teacher in a British university or language school who is in charge of organizing the students' programmes of study

diˈrector's ͵chair *n* [C] a folding wooden chair with arms, which has pieces of cloth as the seat and the back → see picture at CHAIR[1]

diˈrector's ͵cut *n* [C] a film containing all the parts that the director wanted to include, that usually appears after the film has been shown in cinemas without those parts

di·rec·tor·ship /dəˈrektəʃɪp, daɪ- $ -ər-/ *n* [C] the position of being a director of a company or organization: **under the directorship of sb** *The Institute was established under the directorship of Professor Gray.*

di·rec·to·ry /daɪˈrektəri, də-/ ●●○ S3 *n* (*plural* **directories**) [C]

1 a book or list of names, facts etc, usually arranged in alphabetical order: *I couldn't find your number in the telephone directory.* | *a new business directory*

2 a place in a computer where FILES or programs are organized

di͵rectory enˈquiries *BrE*, **di͵rectory asˈsistance** *AmE* *n* [U] a service on the telephone network that you can use to find out someone's telephone number

di͵rect ˈspeech *n* [U] *technical* speech reported using the actual words spoken: *She said, 'I'm not going if it rains.' is an example of direct speech.* → INDIRECT SPEECH, REPORTED SPEECH

di͵rect ˈtax *n* [C,U] a tax, such as income tax, which is collected from the person who pays it, rather than a tax on goods or services → **indirect tax** —**direct taxation** *n* [U]

di͵rect-to-conˈsumer *adj* [only before noun] direct-to-consumer advertising is aimed at the customer who will buy the product rather than the shops where it will be sold

dirge /dɜːdʒ $ dɜːrdʒ/ *n* [C] **1** a slow sad song sung at a funeral **2** a song or piece of music that is too slow and boring

dir·i·gi·ble /ˈdɪrədʒəbəl, dəˈrɪ-/ *n* [C] an AIRSHIP

dirk /dɜːk $ dɜːrk/ *n* [C] a heavy pointed knife used as a weapon in Scotland in the past

dirt /dɜːt $ dɜːrt/ ●●● S3 *n* [U]

1 any substance that makes things dirty, such as mud or dust: *You should have seen the dirt on that car!* | *His face and hands were black with dirt.* | *a patch of grass, covered in* **dog dirt** (=waste from a dog's bowels)

2 *especially AmE* earth or soil: *Michael threw his handful of dirt onto the coffin.* | **in (the) dirt** *The children had been sitting in the dirt.*

3 *informal* information about someone's private life or activities which could give people a bad opinion of them if it became known: *The newspapers had been* **digging up dirt on** *the president.*

4 talk, writing, a film etc that is considered bad or immoral because it is about sex → **dish the dirt** at DISH[2], → **hit/strike paydirt** at PAYDIRT, → **hit the dirt** at HIT[1](17), → **treat sb like dirt** at TREAT[1](1)

dirt·bag /ˈdɜːtbæg $ ˈdɜːrt-/ *n* [C] *informal especially AmE* someone who is very unpleasant and immoral

ˈdirt bike *n* [C] a small MOTORCYCLE for young people, usually ridden on rough paths or fields

͵dirt ˈcheap *adj, adv informal* extremely cheap or cheaply: *Such cheap goods obviously rely on dirt cheap labor.* | *I got these shoes dirt cheap.*

ˈdirt-͵disher *n* [C] *AmE informal* a DISHER

ˈdirt ͵farmer *n* [C] *AmE* a poor farmer who works to feed himself and his family, without paying anyone else to help

͵dirt ˈpoor *adj informal* extremely poor

ˈdirt road *n* [C] a road made of hard earth

ˈdirt track *n* [C] **1** a road or path made of hard earth **2** a track used for MOTORCYCLE races

dirt·y[1] /ˈdɜːti $ ˈdɜːr-/ ●●● S2 W3 *adj* (*comparative* **dirtier**, *superlative* **dirtiest**)

1 NOT CLEAN covered in or marked by an unwanted substance OPP **clean**: *a stack of* **dirty dishes** *in the sink* | *How did you get so dirty?* | **dirty clothes/washing/laundry** *She circled the bedroom, picking up dirty clothes.*

2 SEX relating to sex, in a way that is considered immoral or unpleasant: *kids telling* **dirty jokes** | *a dirty magazine* | *She looked at me as if I had said a* **dirty word**. | **have a dirty mind** *BrE* (=think about sex a lot) | **dirty weekend** *BrE* (=a weekend when a man and woman who are not married to each other go away to have sex)

3 BAD/IMMORAL used to emphasize that you think someone or something is bad, dishonest, or immoral: *You're a dirty liar!* | *a dirty fighter* | *you and your* **dirty little** *deals* | **do the dirty on sb** *BrE* (=treat someone in a way that is unfair or dishonest) | *What a dirty trick!*

4 sth is a dirty word if something is a dirty word, people believe it is a bad thing even if they do not know or think much about it SYN **swear word**: *'Liberal' has somehow become a dirty word in America.*

5 give sb a dirty look to look at someone in a very disapproving way: *Susan gave her brother a dirty look.*

6 dirty trick a dishonest or unfair action, especially done by a government, company, or organization: *political dirty tricks*

7 wash your dirty linen/laundry (*also* **air your dirty laundry** *AmE*) to discuss something embarrassing or bad about yourself where everyone can see, know, or hear: *The divorce has meant airing their dirty laundry in court.*

8 do sb's dirty work to do an unpleasant or dishonest action for someone, so that they do not have to do it themselves: *I'm not talking to him; you do your own dirty work!*

9 it's a dirty job, but someone has to do it used to say that something is unpleasant to do, but that it is necessary – often used humorously

10 DRUGS *AmE informal* containing or possessing illegal drugs

11 dirty bomb a bomb that contains a RADIOACTIVE substance which makes the bomb more dangerous than bombs containing only traditional explosives

12 SPORT a dirty sports event is one in which people competing in the event have illegally used drugs to improve their performance: *Many people think that the race has been a dirty event for years.*

13 ENVIRONMENT producing POLLUTION or CARBON DIOXIDE: *dirty forms of energy* —**dirtily** *adv*

THESAURUS

dirty not clean: *His clothes were untidy and he had dirty hands.*

filthy very dirty: *Each year filthy water causes millions of cases of illness.*

muddy covered with mud: *It had been raining hard and the path was muddy.*

dusty covered with dust: *the dusty shelves in the attic*

greasy covered with oil or grease: *Greasy food is bad for your health.*

grubby (*also* **mucky** *BrE*) *informal* fairly dirty and needing to be cleaned or washed: *He was wearing a grubby white T-shirt.* | *mucky fingers*

grimy covered with thick dirt or dirt that has been there a long time: *I couldn't see much out of the grimy windows of the train.*

dingy /ˈdɪndʒi/ looking dark, dirty, and unpleasant. Used about rooms, houses, and buildings: *We worked in a dingy little office behind the station.*
polluted used about land, water, or air that has been made dirty: *85% of city dwellers breathe heavily polluted air.*
contaminated made dirty by a dangerous substance or bacteria: *The virus is mainly spread through contaminated food.*
squalid /ˈskwɒləd $ ˈskwɑː-/ *formal* extremely dirty and unpleasant. Used about the place or conditions in which someone lives: *People are living in squalid conditions, with little water and no sanitation.*
unhygienic /ˌʌnhaɪˈdʒiːnɪk◂ $ -ˈdʒe-, -ˈdʒiː-/ *formal* used about dirty conditions that are likely to cause disease, especially conditions in kitchens, restaurants, and hospitals: *The food was prepared under unhygienic conditions.*
unsanitary (*also* **insanitary** *BrE*) *formal* used about dirty conditions that are likely to cause disease, especially because there is not a good system for getting rid of waste: *People's health is being threatened by overcrowded and insanitary homes.* | *They work for long hours in unsanitary conditions.*
soiled *formal* made dirty, especially by waste from your body: *Soiled nappies should be changed as quickly as possible.*

dirty² *adv informal* **1 play dirty** to behave in a very unfair and dishonest way, especially in a competition or game: *a team that plays dirty* **2 talk dirty** to talk about sex using offensive words **3 dirty great/dirty big** *BrE spoken* extremely big: *a dirty great snake*

dirty³ *v* (**dirtied**, **dirtying**, **dirties**) [I,T] **1** to make something dirty **2** to make someone feel or seem bad, dishonest, or immoral: *The army's actions dirtied its reputation.* **3 dirty your hands** to do hard physical work, in which your hands become dirty

ˌdirty old ˈman *n* [C] *informal* an older man who is too sexually interested in younger women – used to show disapproval

dis /dɪs/ *v* another spelling of DISS

dis- /dɪs/ *prefix* **1** shows an opposite or negative: *I disapprove* (=do not approve) | *dishonesty* (=lack of honesty) **2** [in verbs] shows the stopping or removing of a condition: *Disconnect the machine.* | *Disinfect the wound.*

dis·a·bil·i·ty /ˌdɪsəˈbɪləti/ ●●○ *n* (*plural* **disabilities**)
1 [C] a physical or mental condition that makes it difficult for someone to use a part of their body properly, or to learn normally: **with a disability** *Public places are becoming more accessible to people with disabilities.* | **learning/physical/mental etc disability** *children with* ***severe*** *learning* ***disabilities***
2 [U] when you have a physical or mental disability: *learning to cope with disability*
3 [U] *AmE* money that is given by the government to people who have physical disabilities: **on disability** *Evans lives on disability because of an accident that left her paralyzed.*

dis·a·ble /dɪsˈeɪbəl/ *v* [T] **1** to make someone unable to use a part of their body properly: *Carter was permanently disabled in the war.* GRAMMAR **Disable** is usually passive in this meaning. **2** to deliberately make a machine or piece of equipment impossible to use: *The virus will disable your computer.* —**disablement** *n* [C,U] —**disabling** *adj*: *a disabling injury*

dis·a·bled /dɪsˈeɪbəld/ ●●● S3 W3 *adj*
1 someone who is disabled cannot use a part of their body properly, or cannot learn easily → **handicapped**: *a support group for parents of disabled children* | *a* ***severely disabled*** *polio patient* | **physically/mentally disabled** *If you are elderly or physically disabled, massage can be beneficial.* | *teachers who work with* ***learning disabled*** *children* (=children who have problems learning) | **disabled parking/toilet/access etc** (=for physically disabled people)
2 the disabled [plural] people who are disabled: *The theatre has good access for the disabled.*

dis·a·buse /ˌdɪsəˈbjuːz/ *v* [T] *formal* to persuade someone that what they believe is not true: **disabuse sb of sth** *I tried to disabuse him of that notion.*

dis·ad·van·tage¹ /ˌdɪsədˈvɑːntɪdʒ $ -ˈvæn-/ ●●● W2 *n* [C,U] something that causes problems, or that makes someone or something less likely to be successful or effective OPP **advantage**: **[+of]** *The disadvantage of the material is that it fades in strong sunlight.* | **[+to]** *There are some big disadvantages to marriage – you do lose a lot of your freedom.* | *Criminal behaviour can be linked to economic disadvantage.*

COLLOCATIONS

ADJECTIVES
the main disadvantage *The main disadvantage of iron as a material is its weight.*
a big/great/major disadvantage *This method has one major disadvantage: its cost.*
a serious/severe disadvantage *Public transport is very bad here, which is a serious disadvantage.*
a slight/minor disadvantage | **a further/additional/added disadvantage** | **social/economic/educational disadvantage**

VERBS
have a disadvantage *Cheap air travel has considerable environmental disadvantages.*
suffer (from) a disadvantage *formal Working-class boys suffer disadvantages in the educational system.*
overcome a disadvantage (=succeed in spite of a disadvantage)

PHRASES
sb is at a disadvantage (=someone has a disadvantage) *The company was at a disadvantage compared with its competitors.*
put/place sb at a disadvantage (=make someone less likely to be successful than others) *Not speaking English might put you at a disadvantage.*
be/work to the disadvantage of sb (=make someone unlikely to be successful) *This system works to the disadvantage of women.*
advantages and disadvantages (=the good and bad features of something) | **the advantages outweigh the disadvantages** (=there are more advantages than disadvantages)

THESAURUS
disadvantage *n* [C] a bad feature that something has, which makes it less good or less useful than other things: *What do you think are the disadvantages of nuclear energy?*
drawback *n* [C] a bad feature that something has, although it has advantages that are usually more important: *One of the main drawbacks is the price.*
bad point *n* [C] *especially spoken* a bad feature that something has: *All of these designs have both their good points and bad points.*
the downside *n* [singular] the disadvantage of a situation that in most other ways seems good or enjoyable: *It's a great job. The only downside is that I don't get much free time.*

disadvantage² *v* [T] to make someone less likely to be successful or to put them in a worse situation than others

dis·ad·van·taged /ˌdɪsədˈvɑːntɪdʒd◂ $ -ˈvæn-/ ●○○ *adj*
1 having social problems, such as a lack of money or education, which make it difficult for you to succeed: *disadvantaged areas of the city* THESAURUS▸ POOR
2 the disadvantaged [plural] people who are disadvantaged: *health programs for the disadvantaged*

dis·ad·van·ta·geous /ˌdɪsædvənˈteɪdʒəs, -væn-/ *adj*

D

[+to/for] *formal* unfavourable and likely to cause problems for you OPP **advantageous** —**disadvantageously** *adv*

dis·af·fec·ted /ˌdɪsəˈfektɪd◂/ *adj formal* not satisfied with your government, leader etc, and therefore no longer loyal to them or no longer believing they can help you: *the disaffected youth from poor neighborhoods* —**disaffection** /-ˈfekʃən/ *n* [U]

dis·af·fil·i·ate /ˌdɪsəˈfɪlieɪt/ *v* [I,T + from] *formal* if an organization disaffiliates from another organization or is disaffiliated from it, it breaks the official connection it has with it OPP **affiliate** —**disaffiliation** /ˌdɪsəfɪliˈeɪʃən/ *n* [U]

dis·a·gree /ˌdɪsəˈgriː/ ●●● S3 *v* [I]
1 to have or express a different opinion from someone else OPP **agree**: **[+with]** *He is tolerant of those who disagree with him.* | **[+about/on/over]** *Experts disagree on how much the program will cost.* | *Barr* ***strongly disagreed*** *with Kronfeld's statement.*
2 if statements, numbers, or reports about the same event or situation disagree, they are different from each other OPP **agree**: *The statements of several witnesses disagree.*

disagree with sb *phr v* if something such as food or weather disagrees with you, it has a bad effect on you or makes you ill: *Seafood always disagrees with me.*

GRAMMAR

Reciprocal verbs

Disagree is a reciprocal verb. This type of verb is used when saying that two or more people or groups do something that involves both or all of them: *Kate and I often disagree.* You can also say: *Kate and I often disagree with each other.* | *I often disagree with Kate.*

Patterns with disagree

disagree with
• You **disagree with** someone: *I totally disagree with you.* ✗ Don't say: *I totally disagree you.*
• You **disagree with** an idea, or something that someone says: *I disagree with his views on the economy.* ✗ Don't say: *I disagree his views on the economy.*

disagree about/on/over
• People **disagree about/on/over** a subject: *Experts disagree about the answer to this question.* | *Parents often disagree on the best way to bring up children.* | *Scientists disagree over whether oil is unhealthy.*

I disagree
• You say **I disagree** when you do not agree with what someone says: *'Women are better drivers than men.' 'I disagree.'* ✗ Don't say: *I disagree you.*

Using the progressive

Disagree is not used in the progressive. You say: *I disagree with your analysis.* ✗ Don't say: *I am disagreeing with your analysis.*
GRAMMAR GUIDE ▶ VERBS

THESAURUS

disagree/not agree to have a different opinion from someone else about something: *Scholars disagree about the meaning of the poem.* | *I don't agree with a word of what she says.*
be divided/split if a group of people is divided or split on something, some of them have one opinion and others have a completely different opinion: *The party is divided on this issue.*
differ if two or more people differ about something, they have different opinions from each other about it: *The two men differed on how to handle the crisis.*
not see eye to eye used to say that two people have different opinions and ideas so that it is difficult for them to be friends or work together: *Some of the teachers don't see eye to eye with the principal of the school.*
be mistaken used to say that you disagree with someone's opinion and that you think they are wrong: *People are mistaken if they think that this problem will go away on its own.*
take issue with sb/sth *formal* to express strong disagreement with an idea or with what someone has said or done: *A number of people took issue with the mayor's decision.*
dissent *formal* to say publicly that you disagree with an official opinion or one that most people accept: *Two members of the jury dissented from the majority verdict.*

dis·a·gree·a·ble /ˌdɪsəˈgriːəbəl◂/ *adj formal* **1** not at all enjoyable or pleasant OPP **agreeable**: *a disagreeable job* | **[+to]** *The conversation was disagreeable to him.*

REGISTER

In everyday English, people usually say someone or something is **not very nice** rather than **disagreeable**: *It's* ***not*** *a* ***very nice*** *job.*

2 unfriendly and bad-tempered OPP **agreeable**: *a rude, disagreeable woman* —**disagreeably** *adv*

dis·a·gree·ment /ˌdɪsəˈgriːmənt/ ●●○ *n*
1 [C,U] a situation in which people express different opinions about something and sometimes argue OPP **agreement**: *We've* ***had*** *a few* ***disagreements****, but we're still good friends.* | **[+about/over/as to/on]** *disagreements about who will be allowed to vote* | **[+among/between]** *There were disagreements among doctors about the best way to treat the disease.* | **[+with]** *Connor's disagreements with school administrators* | **sharp/fundamental/profound etc disagreement** (=serious disagreement) | **be in disagreement** (=disagree) *Scientists are in disagreement about the significance of the data.* THESAURUS ▶ ARGUMENT
2 [U] differences between two statements, reports, numbers etc that ought to be similar OPP **agreement**: **[+between]** *There is disagreement between these two estimates.*

dis·al·low /ˌdɪsəˈlaʊ/ *v* [T] to officially refuse to accept something, because a rule has been broken OPP **allow**: *Manchester United had a goal disallowed.* THESAURUS ▶ REFUSE

dis·ap·pear /ˌdɪsəˈpɪə $ -ˈpɪr/ ●●● S2 W2 *v* [I]
1 to become impossible to see any longer SYN **vanish** OPP **appear**: **[+behind/under/into etc]** *The sun had disappeared behind a cloud.* | **disappear from view/sight** *David watched her car until it disappeared from view.* | *At this point the path seemed to* ***disappear altogether*** (=disappear completely).
2 to be lost, or to become impossible to find SYN **vanish**: *The two girls disappeared while walking home from school.* | *My keys have disappeared again.* | **disappear without trace** *BrE*, **without a trace** *AmE* (=without any way of finding them) *75,000 soldiers simply disappeared without trace.*
3 to stop existing: *The rain forest may disappear forever.*

THESAURUS

disappear if something disappears, you cannot see it any longer, or it does not exist any longer: *The sun slowly disappeared over the horizon.* | *Millions of people saw their savings disappear.*
vanish to completely disappear, especially suddenly: *The boat* ***vanished without trace*** *off the coast of Australia.* | *All hopes of finding the boy alive have vanished.*
go away to stop existing – used about something bad such as a pain or a problem: *I wish this headache would go away.* | *I'm afraid the problem won't just go away.*
fade away to gradually become less clear, strong, or bright, and finally disappear: *Her voice began to fade away.* | *His anger slowly faded away.*

melt away *especially literary* to disappear, especially gradually – used about feelings or groups of people: *The crowd began to melt away.* | *His initial excitement had melted away.*
die out to stop existing after gradually becoming more and more rare – used about a type of animal or plant, a disease, or a custom: *Wolves had died out in much of Europe.* | *Many of the old childhood diseases have almost died out.*
become extinct if a type of animal or plant becomes extinct, it stops existing: *Dinosaurs became extinct millions of years ago.*

dis·ap·pear·ance /ˌdɪsəˈpɪərəns $ -ˈpɪr-/ ●●○ *n* [C,U]
1 when someone or something becomes impossible to see or find: *Police are investigating the woman's disappearance.*
2 when something stops existing → **extinction**: *the disappearance of ancient forests*

dis·ap·point /ˌdɪsəˈpɔɪnt/ ●●● W3 *v* [I,T]
1 to make someone feel unhappy because something they hoped for did not happen or was not as good as they expected: *I hated to disappoint her.* | *Great things were expected of this band, and they didn't disappoint.*
2 disappoint sb's hopes/expectations/plans to prevent something from happening that someone hoped for or expected: *The Berlin settlement of 1878 disappointed Russian hopes in the Balkans.*

dis·ap·point·ed /ˌdɪsəˈpɔɪntɪd◂/ ●●● S3 W3 *adj* unhappy because something you hoped for did not happen, or because someone or something was not as good as you expected: *Dad seemed more disappointed than angry.* | *disappointed customers* | **disappointed (that)** *I was disappointed that we played so well yet still lost.* | **disappointed at/with/about sth** *Local residents were disappointed with the decision.* | **disappointed by sth** *People are disappointed by the lack of political change.* | **disappointed in sb** *I'm very disappointed in you.* | **disappointed to hear/see/find etc** *Visitors were disappointed to find the museum closed.* | **bitterly/deeply/terribly disappointed** *The girl's parents were bitterly disappointed at the jury's verdict.*

THESAURUS

disappointed unhappy because something you hoped for did not happen, or because something was not as good as you expected: *Hundreds of disappointed fans were unable to get tickets for the game.* | *I was disappointed with the grade I got in my Maths exam.*
feel let down to feel disappointed because something was not as good as you expected, or someone did not do what you expected them to do for you – a rather informal use: *I felt let down when I saw the film.* | *Nurses feel badly let down – they were promised a pay increase months ago.*
disillusioned /ˌdɪsəˈluːʒənd◂/ disappointed because you have lost your belief that an idea is right, or that something or someone is good: *Their leaders are deeply disillusioned with the peace process.* | *Disillusioned voters are turning against the government.*
disenchanted no longer feeling enthusiastic, especially so that you do not think you should be involved in something, or give someone your support: *Americans have grown increasingly disenchanted with politics.* | *a disenchanted workforce*
be/feel sorry *spoken* used when telling someone that you feel disappointed and wish that the situation was different: *I'm sorry you can't come to the party.* | *She always felt sorry that she hadn't got to know him better.*

VERY DISAPPOINTED

gutted [not before noun] *BrE informal* extremely disappointed, especially because you were unsuccessful: *I was gutted when we lost the game.*
crestfallen *literary* looking very disappointed and sad, especially when you suddenly realise that something you want cannot happen: *Gary looked crestfallen as they calculated how much money they would need.* | *a crestfallen look*

dis·ap·point·ing /ˌdɪsəˈpɔɪntɪŋ◂/ ●●○ *adj* not as good as you hoped or expected: *disappointing profit figures* | *The Lakers' loss in the playoffs was very disappointing.* THESAURUS ▸ BAD —**disappointingly** *adv*

dis·ap·point·ment /ˌdɪsəˈpɔɪntmənt/ ●●○ *n*
1 [U] a feeling of unhappiness because something is not as good as you expected, or has not happened in the way you hoped: *He could see the disappointment in her eyes.* | **to sb's (great) disappointment** *To Edward's disappointment, Gina never turned up at the party.* | **[+at/with/over etc]** *the managers' disappointment with the results* | *Several people* ***expressed disappointment*** *at the delay.* | **disappointment that** *her disappointment that she hadn't been picked* | *She hid her* ***bitter disappointment***.
2 [C] someone or something that is not as good as you hoped or expected: *The movie was kind of a disappointment.* | **great/bitter disappointment** *The loss was a bitter disappointment.* | **[+to]** *She felt she was a disappointment to her family.* | **[+for]** *The team's performance has been a disappointment for the fans.*

dis·ap·pro·ba·tion /ˌdɪsæprəˈbeɪʃən/ *n* [U] *formal* disapproval of someone or something because you think they are morally wrong OPP **approbation**

dis·ap·prov·al /ˌdɪsəˈpruːvəl/ ●●○ *n* [U] an attitude that shows you think that someone or their behaviour, ideas etc are bad or not suitable OPP **approval**: **[+of]** ***strong disapproval*** *of the country's human rights record* | **with/in disapproval** *Baxter eyed our clothes with obvious disapproval.* | *Clarissa shook her head in disapproval.*

dis·ap·prove /ˌdɪsəˈpruːv/ ●●○ *v*
1 [I] to think that someone or their behaviour, ideas etc are bad or wrong OPP **approve**: *I knew my parents would disapprove, but I went anyway.* | **[+of]** *I disapprove of diets; it's better to eat sensibly.* | *Her family* ***strongly disapproved*** *of her behaviour.*

REGISTER
In everyday English, people often say they **don't agree with** an idea rather than **disapprove of** it: ***I don't agree with*** *capital punishment.*

2 [T] *formal* to not agree to something that has been suggested OPP **approve**: *The board of directors disapproved the sale.*

dis·ap·prov·ing /ˌdɪsəˈpruːvɪŋ◂/ *adj* showing that you think someone or something is bad or wrong OPP **approving**: *a disapproving frown* —**disapprovingly** *adv*

dis·arm /dɪsˈɑːm $ -ˈɑːrm/ *v* **1** [I] to reduce the size of your army, navy etc, and the number of your weapons OPP **arm**: *Getting the rebels to disarm will not be easy.* **2** [T] to take away someone's weapons OPP **arm**: *Captured soldiers were disarmed and put into camps.* **3** [T] to make someone feel less angry or disapproving of you, and more friendly → **disarming**: *His tact and political skills disarmed his critics.* **4** [T] to take the explosives out of a bomb, MISSILE etc

dis·ar·ma·ment /dɪsˈɑːməmənt $ -ˈɑːr-/ *n* [U] when a country reduces the number of weapons it has, or the size of its army, navy etc: *a commitment to worldwide* ***nuclear disarmament***

dis·arm·ing /dɪsˈɑːmɪŋ $ -ˈɑːr-/ *adj* making you feel less angry or disapproving towards someone, and more friendly: *a disarming sense of humor* —**disarmingly** *adv*

dis·ar·range /ˌdɪsəˈreɪndʒ/ *v* [T] *formal* to make something untidy

dis·ar·ray /ˌdɪsəˈreɪ/ *n* [U] *formal* the state of being untidy or not organized: **in disarray** *This left the Liberal Party* ***in total disarray***. | **throw sth into disarray/fall into disarray** *The delay threw the entire timetable into disarray.*

dis·as·so·ci·ate /ˌdɪsəˈsəʊʃieɪt, -sieɪt $ -ˈsoʊ-/ *v* [T] another form of DISSOCIATE

D

di·sas·ter /dɪˈzɑːstə $ dɪˈzæstər/ ●●● S3 W3 *n* [C,U]
1 a sudden event such as a flood, storm, or accident which causes great damage or suffering → **catastrophe**: *One hundred and twenty people died in China's worst **air disaster**.* | *the economic consequences of the Chernobyl **nuclear disaster*** | **[+for]** *The oil spill was a disaster for Alaskan sea animals.* | *The 1987 hurricane was the worst **natural disaster** to hit England for decades.* | *Their expedition nearly **ended in disaster**, when one of the climbers slid off the mountain.* | *The drought could **spell disaster** for wildlife.* | ***Disaster struck** when two men were killed during their parachute jumps.* | *The peace process was **on the brink of disaster**.* | *Luckily the pilot saw the other plane just in time, and a **disaster** was narrowly **averted**.* THESAURUS ACCIDENT
2 something that is very bad or a failure, especially when this is very annoying or disappointing: **sth is a complete/total/disaster** *Because of the weather, the parade was a total disaster.* | *The evening was an **unmitigated disaster*** (=a complete failure). | **[+for]** *The cuts in funding will be a disaster for the schools.* | *Five small boys on skis **is a recipe for disaster*** (=is very likely to end badly).

diˈsaster ˌarea *n* [C] **1** a place where a flood, storm, fire etc has happened and caused a lot of damage: *The town was **declared a disaster area*** (=officially called a disaster area) *after the floods.* **2** *informal* a place that is very untidy or dirty: *The kitchen is a disaster area.*

diˈsaster reˌcovery *n* [U] a system or process that a company has and which it will use if something goes seriously wrong, for example if it loses large amounts of DATA from its computer system: *We need to increase the budget allocation for disaster recovery.*

di·sas·trous /dɪˈzɑːstrəs $ dɪˈzæ-/ ●●○ *adj* very bad, or ending in failure: *a disastrous first marriage* | **disastrous effects/consequences/results** *Climate change could have disastrous effects on Earth.* | *The move **proved disastrous*** (=was disastrous) *for the company.* —**disastrously** *adv*

dis·a·vow /ˌdɪsəˈvaʊ/ *v* [T] *formal* to say that you are not responsible for something, that you do not know about it, or that you are not involved with it —**disavowal** *n* [C,U]

dis·band /dɪsˈbænd/ *v* [I,T] to stop existing as an organization, or to make something do this

dis·bar /dɪsˈbɑː $ -ˈbɑːr/ *v* (**disbarred**, **disbarring**) [T] to make a lawyer leave the legal profession → **debar**

dis·be·lief /ˌdɪsbəˈliːf/ ●○○ *n* [U] a feeling that something is not true or does not exist → **unbelief**, **belief**: *The reaction to the murders was one of shock and disbelief.* | **in/with disbelief** *Rosie stared in disbelief.*

dis·be·lieve /ˌdɪsbəˈliːv/ *v* [I,T] *formal* to not believe something or someone → **doubt**: *I see no reason to disbelieve him.* —**disbelieving** *adj*

dis·burse /dɪsˈbɜːs $ -ɜːrs/ *v* [T] *formal* to pay out money, especially from a large sum that is available for a special purpose —**disbursement** *n* [C,U]

disc (*also* **disk** *especially AmE*) /dɪsk/ ●●○ S3 W3 *n* [C]
1 a round flat shape or object: *three keys attached to a metal disc*
2 a COMPACT DISC
3 a record that you play on a RECORD PLAYER
4 *BrE* a computer DISK: **on disc** *The report form is available on disc from Personnel.*
5 a flat piece of CARTILAGE between the bones of your back: *He retired early because of a **slipped disc*** (=one that has moved out of its correct place). → DISC BRAKES, DISC JOCKEY, DISK DRIVE, LASER DISK

dis·card¹ /dɪsˈkɑːd $ -ɑːrd/ ●○○ *v*
1 [T] to get rid of something SYN **throw away**: *Discard any old cleaning materials.* | *discarded paper*
2 [I,T] to put down unwanted cards in a card game

dis·card² /ˈdɪskɑːd $ -ɑːrd/ *n* [C] an unwanted card that is put down in a card game

ˈdisc brakes *n* [plural] BRAKES that work by two hard surfaces pressing against a DISC in the centre of a car wheel

dis·cern /dɪˈsɜːn $ -ɜːrn/ ●○○ *v* [T] *formal*
1 to notice or understand something by thinking about it carefully: **discern what/where/why etc** *Officials were keen to discern how much public support there was.* THESAURUS RECOGNIZE
2 to be able to see something by looking carefully SYN **perceive**: *We **could just discern** a town in the distance.* —**discernible** *adj* —**discernibly** *adv*

di·scern·ing /dɪˈsɜːnɪŋ $ -ɜːr-/ *adj* showing the ability to make good judgments, especially about art, music, style etc SYN **discriminating**: *an ideal tour for the discerning traveller* | **the discerning eye/ear** (=someone who can make good judgments about art or music)

di·scern·ment /dɪˈsɜːnmənt $ -ɜːr-/ *n* [U] *formal* **1** the ability to make good judgments about people or about art, music, style etc: *the woman's taste and discernment* **2** when you notice or understand something: *the discernment of opportunities*

dis·charge¹ /dɪsˈtʃɑːdʒ $ -ɑːr-/ ●○○ *v*
1 SEND SB AWAY [T] to officially allow someone to leave somewhere, especially the hospital or the army, navy etc, or to tell them that they must leave: *Hospitals now tend to discharge patients earlier than in the past.* | *The judge discharged the jury.* | **discharge sb from sth** *Several of the recruits were discharged from the Army due to medical problems.* | **discharge yourself** *BrE* (=leave hospital before your treatment is complete) | **conditionally discharge sb** *BrE* (=let someone leave prison if they obey particular rules) *Dunning was conditionally discharged for two years.*
2 GAS/LIQUID/SMOKE ETC [I always + adv/prep, T] to send out gas, liquid, smoke etc, or to allow it to escape: **discharge sth into sth** *Sewage is discharged directly into the sea.* | **[+into]** *Rainwater collects here and then discharges into the river Kennett.*
3 SHOOT [T] *formal* to fire a gun or shoot an ARROW etc: *A soldier accidentally discharged his weapon.*
4 DUTY/RESPONSIBILITY/DEBT ETC [T] *formal* to do or pay what you have a duty to do or pay: **discharge your duties/responsibilities/obligations etc** *The trustees failed to discharge their duties properly.*
5 ELECTRICITY [I,T] if a piece of electrical equipment discharges, or if it is discharged, it sends out electricity
6 A WOUND [I,T] if a wound or body part discharges a substance such as PUS (=infected liquid), the substance slowly comes out of it
7 GOODS/PASSENGERS [T] *formal* to take goods or passengers off a ship, plane etc

dis·charge² /ˈdɪstʃɑːdʒ $ -tʃɑːrdʒ/ *n formal* **1** [U] when you officially allow someone to leave somewhere, especially the hospital or their job in the army, navy etc: **[+from]** *Nurses visit the mother and baby for two weeks after their discharge from the hospital.* → DISHONOURABLE DISCHARGE, HONORABLE DISCHARGE **2** [C,U] when gas, liquid, smoke etc is sent out, or the substance that is sent out: **[+of]** *the discharge of toxic waste into the sea* **3** [C,U] when a substance slowly comes out of a wound or part of your body, or the substance that comes out **4** [C,U] electricity that is sent out by a piece of equipment, a storm etc **5** [U] when someone performs a duty or pays a debt: **[+of]** *the discharge of the college's legal responsibilities* **6** [U] when someone shoots a gun

di·sci·ple /dɪˈsaɪpəl/ ●○○ *n* [C]
1 someone who believes in the ideas of a great teacher or leader, especially a religious one: **[+of]** *He was also an avid reader and a disciple of Tolstoy.*
2 one of the first 12 men to follow Christ —**discipleship** *n* [U]

dis·ci·pli·nar·i·an /ˌdɪsəpləˈneəriən $ -ˈner-/ *n* [C] someone who believes people should obey orders and rules, and who makes them do this: *Dad was a **strict disciplinarian**.*

dis·ci·pli·na·ry /ˈdɪsəplɪnəri, ˌdɪsəˈplɪ- $ ˈdɪsəpləneri/ *adj* relating to the punishment of someone who has not obeyed rules, or to trying to make people obey rules: *The investigation led to **disciplinary action*** (=things you do to punish someone) *against two officers.* | **disciplinary**

hearing/committee (=a meeting or group that decides if someone should be punished)

dis·ci·pline¹ /ˈdɪsɪplɪn/ ●●○ S3 W3 *n*
1 [U] a way of training someone so that they learn to control their behaviour and obey rules: *The book gives parents advice on discipline.* | *serious* ***discipline problems*** *in the police force*
2 [U] the ability to control your own behaviour, so that you do what you are expected to do: *Working from home requires a good deal of discipline.* → SELF-DISCIPLINE
3 [C,U] a way of training your mind or learning to control your behaviour: *Martial arts teach respect, discipline, and cooperation.* | **[+for]** *Learning poetry is a good discipline for the memory.*
4 [C] an area of knowledge or teaching, especially one such as history, chemistry, mathematics etc that is studied at a university

discipline² ●○○ *v* [T]
1 to punish someone in order to keep order and control: *The officers were later disciplined.*
2 to teach someone to obey rules and control their behaviour: *Different cultures have different ways of disciplining their children.*
3 discipline yourself (to do sth) to control the way you work, how regularly you do something etc, because you know it is good for you: *Try to discipline yourself to write every day.*

dis·ci·plined /ˈdɪsɪplɪnd/ *adj* obeying rules and controlling your behaviour: *skilled and disciplined workers*

ˈdisc ˌjockey *n* [C] (*abbreviation* **DJ**) someone whose job is to play the music on a radio show or in a club where you can dance

dis·claim /dɪsˈkleɪm/ *v* [T] *formal* to state, especially officially, that you are not responsible for something, that you do not know about it, or that you are not involved with it SYN **deny**: **disclaim responsibility/knowledge etc** *Martin disclaimed any responsibility for his son's actions.*

dis·claim·er /dɪsˈkleɪmə $ -ər/ *n* [C] a statement that you are not responsible for or involved with something, or that you do not know about it - used especially in advertising or legal agreements

dis·close /dɪsˈkləʊz $ -ˈkloʊz/ ●○○ *v* [T] *formal*
1 to make something publicly known, especially after it has been kept secret SYN **reveal**: *Some companies have already voluntarily* ***disclosed*** *similar* ***information***. | *He* ***refused to disclose*** *the identity of the politician.* | **disclose that** *It was disclosed that £3.5 million was needed to modernize the building.* THESAURUS ▸ REVEAL
2 to show something by removing the thing that covers it SYN **reveal**

dis·clo·sure /dɪsˈkləʊʒə $ -ˈkloʊʒər/ ●○○ *n* [C,U] a secret that someone tells people, or the act of telling this secret: *the disclosure of private medical information*

dis·co /ˈdɪskəʊ $ -koʊ/ *n* (*plural* **discos**) **1** [C] a place or social event at which people dance to recorded popular music: *the school disco* **2** [U] a type of dance music that was first popular in the 1970s

dis·col·or /dɪsˈkʌlə $ -ər/ *v* [I,T] the American spelling of DISCOLOUR

dis·col·o·ra·tion /dɪsˌkʌləˈreɪʃən/ *n* **1** [U] the process of becoming discoloured **2** [C] a place on the surface of something where it has become discoloured

dis·col·our *BrE*, **discolor** *AmE* /dɪsˈkʌlə $ -ər/ *v* [I,T] to change colour, or to make something change colour, so that it looks unattractive: *Once cut, apples quickly discolour.*

dis·com·bob·u·lat·ed /ˌdɪskəmˈbɒbjəleɪtɪd $ -ˈbɑːb-/ *adj* completely confused - used humorously

dis·com·fit /dɪsˈkʌmfɪt/ *v* [T] *formal* to make someone feel slightly uncomfortable, annoyed, or embarrassed: *He was discomfited by her silence.* —**discomfiture** *n* [U]

dis·com·fort /dɪsˈkʌmfət $ -ərt/ ●○○ *n*
1 [U] a feeling of slight pain or of being physically uncomfortable: *If the exercise causes discomfort, stop immediately.* THESAURUS ▸ PAIN
2 [U] a feeling of embarrassment, shame, or worry: *To her discomfort, he laughed.*
3 [C] something that makes you feel uncomfortable or gives you a slight pain: *the discomforts of air travel*

dis·com·pose /ˌdɪskəmˈpəʊz $ -ˈpoʊz/ *v* [T] *formal* to make someone feel worried and no longer calm SYN **disturb** —**discomposure** /-ˈpəʊʒə $ -ˈpoʊʒər/ *n* [U]

dis·con·cert /ˌdɪskənˈsɜːt $ -ɜːrt/ *v* [T] to make someone feel slightly confused, embarrassed, or worried —**disconcerted** *adj*: *a disconcerted look*

dis·con·cert·ing /ˌdɪskənˈsɜːtɪŋ◂ $ -ɜːr-/ *adj* making you feel slightly confused, embarrassed, or worried: *a disconcerting question* —**disconcertingly** *adv*

dis·con·nect¹ /ˌdɪskəˈnekt/ ●●○ *v*
1 [T] to remove the supply of power, gas, water etc from a machine or piece of equipment OPP **connect**: **disconnect sth from sth** *Always disconnect the machine from the mains first.* | *The family agreed to disconnect her life support system.*
2 [I,T] to separate something from the thing it is connected to, or to become separated OPP **connect**: **[+from]** *Two freight cars disconnected from the train engine.* | **disconnect sth from sth** *Disconnect part A from part D.*
3 [T] to officially stop supplying a service, such as water, telephone, electricity, or gas, to a house or other building OPP **connect**: *Eleven percent of households were disconnected for non-payment of bills.*
4 [I,T] if you disconnect or become disconnected from your feelings, family, society etc, you no longer feel as though you belong or have a relationship with them: **[+from]** *Divorced men can too easily become disconnected from their children.*
5 [T] to break the telephone connection between two people OPP **connect** —**disconnection** /-ˈnekʃən/ *n* [C,U]

disconnect² *n* [singular] when two people or groups no longer understand or have a relationship with each other: *the disconnect between the ordinary public and the concerns of politicians*

dis·con·nect·ed /ˌdɪskəˈnektɪd◂/ *adj* disconnected thoughts or ideas do not seem to be related to each other SYN **unrelated**

dis·con·so·late /dɪsˈkɒnsələt $ -ˈkɑːn-/ *adj formal* extremely sad and hopeless: *He was disconsolate after his divorce.* —**disconsolately** *adv*

dis·con·tent /ˌdɪskənˈtent/ (*also* **dis·con·tent·ment** /-ˈtentmənt/) *n* [U] a feeling of being unhappy and not satisfied with the situation you are in OPP **contentment**: **[+with]** *Discontent with the current government is strong.* | **[+at/over]** *There is* ***widespread discontent*** *at the quality of education.* | *Perhaps she sensed my* ***growing discontent***.

dis·con·tent·ed /ˌdɪskənˈtentɪd◂/ *adj* unhappy or not satisfied with the situation you are in OPP **contented**: **[+with]** *She became increasingly discontented with her work.* —**discontentedly** *adv*

dis·con·tin·ue /ˌdɪskənˈtɪnjuː/ *v* [T] to stop doing, producing, or providing something: *Bus route 51 is being discontinued.* | *a discontinued china pattern* —**discontinuation** /ˌdɪskəntɪnjuˈeɪʃən/ *n* [U] —**discontinuance** /ˌdɪskənˈtɪnjuəns/ *n* [U]

dis·con·ti·nu·i·ty /ˌdɪskɒntəˈnjuːəti $ -kɑːntəˈnuː-/ *n* (*plural* **discontinuities**) **1** [C] a sudden change or pause in a process: **[+between]** *the policy discontinuities between the present and previous governments* **2** [U] when a process is not continuous: *discontinuity in economic development*

dis·con·tin·u·ous /ˌdɪskənˈtɪnjuəs◂/ *adj formal* not continuous

dis·cord /ˈdɪskɔːd $ -ɔːrd/ *n* **1** [U] *formal* disagreement or arguing between people: *marital discord* | *discord within NATO* **2** [C,U] an unpleasant sound made by a group of musical notes that do not go together well → **harmony**

dis·cord·ant /dɪsˈkɔːdənt $ -ɔːr-/ *adj* **1** *formal* a discordant sound is unpleasant because it is made up of musical notes that do not go together well **2** *literary* strange, wrong, or unsuitable in relation to everything around OPP **harmonious**: *The modern decor* ***strikes a discordant note*** *in this old building.* **3** *formal* not in agreement: *discordant results from the experiment*

dis·co·theque /ˈdɪskətek, ˌdɪskəˈtek/ *n* [C] *especially BrE* a DISCO

dis·count¹ /ˈdɪskaʊnt/ ●●○ S3 W3 *n* [C] a reduction in the usual price of something: **10% discount/discount of 25% etc** *Members* ***get*** *a 15%* ***discount***. | **at a discount** *Employees can buy books at a discount.* | **[+on]** *The Young Persons Railcard gives you a discount on rail travel.* | **offer/give sb a discount** | **discount price/fare** *discount airfares to Europe* | **discount store/shop/warehouse** (=a place where you can buy goods cheaply)

dis·count² /dɪsˈkaʊnt $ ˈdɪskaʊnt/ ●○○ *v* [T]
1 to regard something as unlikely to be true or important: *Experts discounted the accuracy of the polls.* | *General Hausken had not* ***discounted the possibility of*** *an aerial attack.*
2 to reduce the price of something: *Games were discounted to as little as $5.*

dis·count·er /ˈdɪskaʊntə $ -ər/ *n* [C] a shop or person that sells goods cheaply

ˈdiscount ˌrate *n* [C usually singular] the interest rate that a country's CENTRAL BANK charges to other banks

dis·cour·age /dɪsˈkʌrɪdʒ $ -ˈkɜːr-/ ●●○ *v* [T]
1 to persuade someone not to do something, especially by making it seem difficult or bad OPP **encourage**: *attempts to discourage illegal immigration* | **discourage sb from doing sth** *My father is a lawyer, and he discouraged me from entering the field.*

GRAMMAR

You say: *She discouraged me from going.* ✗ Don't say: *She discouraged me to go.*

GRAMMAR GUIDE ▸ VERBS

2 to make someone less confident or less willing to do something SYN **demoralize** OPP **encourage**: *You should not let one failure discourage you.*
3 to make something less likely to happen OPP **encourage**: *Aspirin may discourage tumour growth in some types of cancer.*

dis·cour·aged /dɪsˈkʌrɪdʒd $ -ˈkɜːr-/ ●●○ *adj* no longer having the confidence you need to continue doing something SYN **demoralized** OPP **encouraged**: *A lot of players* ***get discouraged*** *and quit.* THESAURUS ▸ CONFIDENT

dis·cour·age·ment /dɪsˈkʌrɪdʒmənt $ -ˈkɜːr-/ *n*
1 [U] when you no longer feel confident or willing to do something: *In research, times of discouragement alternate with times of great achievement.* **2** [U] when you try to persuade someone not to do something, especially by making it seem difficult or bad: *the discouragement of smoking* **3** [C] something that discourages you

dis·cour·a·ging /dɪsˈkʌrɪdʒɪŋ $ -ˈkɜːr-/ *adj* making you lose the confidence or determination you need to continue doing something OPP **encouraging**: *The results were discouraging.* —**discouragingly** *adv*

dis·course¹ /ˈdɪskɔːs $ -ɔːrs/ ●○○ *n formal*
1 [C] a serious speech or piece of writing on a particular subject: **[+on/upon]** *a discourse on art*
2 [U] serious conversation or discussion between people: *Candidates should engage in serious political discourse.*
3 [U] the language used in particular types of speech or writing: *a study of spoken discourse*

dis·course² /dɪsˈkɔːs $ -ɔːrs/ *v*
discourse on/upon sth *phr v formal* to make a long formal speech about something, or to discuss something seriously

dis·cour·te·ous /dɪsˈkɜːtiəs $ -ɜːr-/ *adj formal* not polite, and not showing respect for other people SYN **rude, impolite**: *It would be discourteous to ignore his request.* THESAURUS ▸ RUDE —**discourteously** *adv*

dis·cour·te·sy /dɪsˈkɜːtəsi $ -ɜːr-/ *n* (*plural* **discourtesies**) [C,U] *formal* an action or behaviour that is not polite or does not show respect

dis·cov·er /dɪsˈkʌvə $ -ər/ ●●● S2 W1 *v* [T]
1 to find someone or something, either by accident or because you were looking for them: *The body was discovered in a field.* | *Forest Service crews often discover campfires that have not been put out completely.* THESAURUS ▸ FIND
2 to find out something that you did not know about before: *The exercises let students discover math concepts on their own.* | **discover (that)** *She discovered that she was pregnant.* | **discover who/what/how etc** *His friends were shocked to discover how ill he was.*

GRAMMAR

In more formal English, you say **it is discovered that** something is true: *It was discovered that lightning was electrical.*

3 if someone discovers a new place, fact, substance etc, they are the first person to find it or know that it exists: *The Curies are best known for discovering radium.*
4 to notice or try something for the first time and start to enjoy it: *At fourteen, Louise discovered boys.*
5 to notice someone who is very good at something and help them to become successful and well known: *a band that's waiting to be discovered* —**discoverer** *n* [C]

dis·cov·er·a·ble /dɪsˈkʌvərəbəl/ *adj* able to be found easily on the Internet: *How can we make our business more discoverable?*

dis·cov·e·ry /dɪsˈkʌvəri/ ●●○ W3 *n* (*plural* **discoveries**)
1 [C] a fact or thing that someone finds out about, when it was not known about before: **[+about]** *The Hubble Telescope allowed astronomers to make significant discoveries about our galaxy.* | **discovery that** *the discovery that bees can communicate with each other*
2 [U] when someone discovers something: **[+of]** *the discovery of oil in Alaska*

COLLOCATIONS

VERBS

make a discovery *By making new discoveries we expand our understanding of the natural world.*
lead to a discovery *It was pure chance that led to the discovery.*

ADJECTIVES

a new discovery *New discoveries are being made all the time.*
a recent discovery *the recent discovery of frozen water on the moon*
a great/major/important discovery *The archaeologists had made an important discovery.*
a scientific/medical etc discovery *The book covers the major scientific discoveries of the last century.*
an exciting discovery | **a surprising/unexpected discovery**

dis·cred·it¹ /dɪsˈkredɪt/ ●○○ *v* [T]
1 to make people stop respecting or trusting someone or something: *The company's lawyers tried to discredit her testimony.*
2 to make people stop believing in a particular idea: *His theories have now been discredited.*

discredit² *n* [U] the loss of other people's respect or trust: **to sb's discredit** *To his discredit, he knew about the problem but said nothing.* | **bring discredit on/upon/to sb/sth** *The behaviour of fans has brought discredit on English football.*

dis·cred·it·a·ble /dɪsˈkredətəbəl/ *adj formal* bad or wrong, and making people lose respect for you or trust in you: *discreditable dealings*

di·screet /dɪˈskriːt/ ●○○ *adj*
1 careful about what you say or do, so that you do not

offend, upset, or embarrass people or tell secrets OPP **indiscreet**: *He assured her that he would be discreet.* | *I stood back at a discreet distance.*
2 small and showing good taste or judgment - use this to show approval: *discreet jewelry* —**discreetly** *adv*

di·screp·an·cy /dɪˈskrepənsi/ ●○○ *n* (*plural* **discrepancies**) [C,U] a difference between two amounts, details, reports etc that should be the same: **[+in]** *Police **found discrepancies** in the two men's reports.* | **[+between]** *There is a large discrepancy between the ideal image of motherhood and the reality.*

di·screte /dɪˈskriːt/ AWL *adj* clearly separate: *The change happens in a series of discrete steps.* —**discretely** *adv* —**discreteness** *n* [U]

di·scre·tion /dɪˈskreʃən/ ●○○ AWL *n* [U]
1 the ability and right to decide exactly what should be done in a particular situation: **at sb's discretion** (=according to someone's decision) *The awards are made at the discretion of the committee.* | *Promotions are **left to the discretion** of the supervisor.* | **[+over/as to]** *People want to have more discretion over their working hours.* | **use/exercise your discretion** *The judge exercised his discretion rightly to admit the evidence.* | **discretion to do sth** *The committee has the absolute discretion to refuse applications.*
2 the ability to deal with situations in a way that does not offend, upset, or embarrass people or tell any of their secrets → **indiscretion**: *British newspapers no longer feel they must treat the royal family with discretion.*
3 discretion is the better part of valour used to say that it is better to be careful than to take unnecessary risks

di·scre·tion·a·ry /dɪˈskreʃənəri $ -neri/ AWL *adj* not controlled by strict rules, but decided on by someone in a position of authority: *the court's **discretionary powers*** | **discretionary award/grant/fund etc**

disˌcretionary ˈincome *n* [U] the money remaining from your income after your bills have been paid, which can be spent on entertainment, holidays etc

di·scrim·i·nate /dɪˈskrɪməneɪt/ ●○○ AWL *v*
1 [I] to treat a person or group differently from another in an unfair way: **[+against]** *Under federal law, it is illegal to discriminate against minorities and women.* | **discriminate on the grounds/basis of sth** *It was found that the company still discriminated on the basis of race in promotions.*
2 [I,T] to recognize a difference between things SYN **differentiate**: **[+between]** *Newborn babies can discriminate between a man's and a woman's voice.* | **discriminate sth from sth** *the process of learning to discriminate fact from opinion*

di·scrim·i·nat·ing /dɪˈskrɪməneɪtɪŋ/ *adj* able to judge what is of good quality and what is not SYN **discerning**: *discriminating readers*

di·scrim·i·na·tion /dɪˌskrɪməˈneɪʃən/ ●●○ *n* [U]
1 the practice of treating one person or group differently from another in an unfair way: *laws to prevent discrimination* | **[+against]** *widespread discrimination against older people in the job market* | **[+in favour of]** *discrimination in favour of university graduates* | **racial/sex/religious etc discrimination** (=treating someone unfairly because of their race, sex etc) → POSITIVE DISCRIMINATION, REVERSE DISCRIMINATION THESAURUS ▸ PREJUDICE
2 the ability to recognize the difference between two or more things, especially the difference in their quality: *shape discrimination*

di·scrim·in·a·to·ry /dɪˈskrɪmənətəri $ -tɔːri/ *adj* treating a person or a group of people differently from other people, in an unfair way: *discriminatory hiring practices*

dis·cur·sive /dɪsˈkɜːsɪv $ -ɜːr-/ *adj formal* discussing many different ideas, facts etc, without always having a clear purpose: *a long, discursive article* —**discursively** *adv*

dis·cus /ˈdɪskəs/ *n* [C] **1** a heavy flat circular object which is thrown as far as possible as a sport **2 the discus** the sport of throwing this object

di·scuss /dɪˈskʌs/ ●●● S2 W1 *v* [T]
1 to talk about something with another person or a group in order to exchange ideas or decide something: *Littman refused to discuss the case publicly.* | *If you would like to **discuss the matter** further, please call me.* | **discuss sth with sb** *Pupils should be given time to discuss the book with their classmates.* | **discuss what/who/where etc** *Your accountant will discuss with you how to complete these forms.* THESAURUS ▸ TALK

> **REGISTER**
> In everyday English, people usually say **talk about** rather than **discuss**: *It's good to be able to **talk about** these things.*

2 to talk or write about something in detail and consider different ideas or opinions about it: *This topic will be discussed in Chapter 4.*

> **GRAMMAR**
> **Comparison**
> **discuss**
> • You **discuss** something with someone: *She discussed the idea with her parents.* ✗ Don't say: *discuss about something*
> **talk**
> • You **talk about** something with someone: *She talked about the idea with her parents.*
> **debate**
> • People **debate** something: *Congress will debate the bill.*
> **Patterns with discuss**
> • You **discuss what to** do: *We discussed what to pay him.*
> • You **discuss what** you **should** do: *We discussed what we should pay him.*
> • You **discuss whether to** do something: *The board discussed whether to go ahead with the plan.*
> • You **discuss whether** you **should** do something: *The board discussed whether they should go ahead with the plan.*
> • You **discuss how to** do something: *They discussed how to prevent terrorist attacks.*
> • You **discuss how** you **might** do something: *They discussed how they might prevent terrorist attacks.*
> GRAMMAR GUIDE ▸ VERBS

di·scus·sion /dɪˈskʌʃən/ ●●● S2 W1 *n* [C,U]
1 when you discuss something: *class discussions* | *the topics suggested for discussion* | **[+of]** *the discussion of important issues* | **[+about]** *high-level discussions about trade and commerce* | **[+with]** *The embassy will continue discussions with the Chinese government.* | *We have **had discussions** about her legal situation.* | **under discussion** (=being discussed) *The project is under discussion as a possible joint venture.*
2 a piece of writing about a subject that considers different ideas or opinions about it: **[+of]** *the report's discussion of the legislation*

diˈscussion ˌlist *n* [C] a place on the Internet where people can write and receive messages in order to share ideas and information about a particular subject: *the Mercedes-Benz discussion list*

dis·dain¹ /dɪsˈdeɪn/ *n* [U] *formal* a complete lack of respect that you show for someone or something because you think they are not important or good enough: **with disdain** *She watched me with disdain.* | *a look of complete disdain* | **[+for]** *his disdain for capitalism*

disdain² *v formal* **1** [T] to have no respect for someone or something, because you think they are not important or good enough: *Childcare was seen as women's work, and men disdained it.* **2 disdain to do sth** to refuse to do something because you are too proud to do it: *Butler disdained to reply.*

dis·dain·ful /dɪsˈdeɪnfəl/ *adj formal* showing that you do not respect someone or something, because you think that they are not important or good enough: *a disdainful look* | **[+of]** *professors who are disdainful of popular entertainment* —**disdainfully** *adv*

D

dis·ease /dɪˈziːz/ ●●● S3 W1 *n*
1 [C,U] an illness which affects a person, animal, or plant: **[+of]** *She suffers from a rare disease of the brain.* | *His father died of heart disease.* | *She contracted the disease while she was abroad on holiday.* **THESAURUS** ILLNESS
2 [C] something that is seriously wrong with society or with someone's mind, behaviour etc: *Loneliness is a disease of our urban communities.* —**diseased** *adj*: *diseased muscles* | *a diseased plant*

COLLOCATIONS

VERBS

have a disease *How long have you had the disease?*
suffer from a disease *About three million people suffer from the disease.*
catch/get a disease (*also* **contract a disease** *formal*) *He caught the disease while travelling in Africa.*
develop a disease *A few years ago, she developed a serious lung disease.*
pass on a disease (*also* **transmit a disease** *formal*) *They may pass the disease on to their children.*
cause a disease *Smoking is probably the major factor causing heart disease.*
prevent a disease | **treat a disease** | **cure a disease** | **fight (a) disease** (=try to stop it continuing) | **a disease spreads**

ADJECTIVES/NOUN + disease

common *common childhood diseases*
rare *She suffers from a rare bone disease.*
serious *vaccines against serious diseases like hepatitis and meningitis*
fatal/deadly (=that causes death) *If left untreated, the disease can be fatal.*
incurable (=that cannot be cured) *Diseases that were once thought incurable can be treated with antibiotics.*
infectious/contagious (=that spreads quickly from one person to another) *The disease is highly contagious.*
a skin/brain/lung etc disease *The fumes have caused skin diseases among the villagers.*
heart/liver/kidney disease *He is being treated for kidney disease.*
a hereditary/inherited disease (=that is passed from parent to child) | **a sexually-transmitted disease** (=that is spread by having sex)

PHRASES

a cure for a disease *There is no known cure for this disease.*
an outbreak of a disease (=when a disease appears in a number of people or animals) *There has been an outbreak of the disease in Wales.*
the spread of a disease *Knowing the facts about AIDS can prevent the spread of the disease.*
the symptoms of a disease (=physical signs that someone has a disease)

dis·em·bark /ˌdɪsəmˈbɑːk $ -ɑːrk/ *v* **1** [I] to get off a ship or aircraft OPP **embark** **2** [T] to put people or goods onto the shore from a ship —**disembarkation** /ˌdɪsembɑːˈkeɪʃən $ -bɑːr-/ *n* [U]

dis·em·bod·ied /ˌdɪsəmˈbɒdid◂ $ -ˈbɑː-/ *adj* **1** existing without a body or separated from a body: *disembodied spirits* **2** a disembodied sound or voice comes from someone who cannot be seen

dis·em·bow·el /ˌdɪsəmˈbaʊəl/ *v* (**disembowelled, disembowelling**) [T] to remove someone's BOWELS —**disembowelment** *n* [U]

dis·en·chant·ed /ˌdɪsɪnˈtʃɑːntɪd $ -ˈtʃænt-/ *adj* disappointed with someone or something, and no longer believing that they are good SYN **disillusioned**: **[+with]** *By that time I was becoming disenchanted with the whole idea.* **THESAURUS** DISAPPOINTED —**disenchantment** *n* [U]: *Voters expressed* ***growing disenchantment*** *with the government.*

dis·en·fran·chise /ˌdɪsɪnˈfræntʃaɪz/ *v* [T] to take away someone's rights, especially their right to vote —**disenfranchisement** /-tʃɪzmənt $ -tʃaɪz-/ *n* [U]

dis·en·fran·chised /ˌdɪsɪnˈfræntʃaɪzd/ *adj* not having any rights, especially the right to vote, and not feeling part of society

dis·en·gage /ˌdɪsənˈgeɪdʒ/ *v* **1** [T] to move so that you are not touching or holding someone: **disengage yourself** *Sally found it difficult to disengage herself from his embrace.* **2** [I,T] if you disengage something, especially a part of a machine, or if it disengages, you make it move away from another part that it was connected to OPP **engage**: *Disengage the gears when you park the car.* | *He tapped in the code and the lock disengaged.* **3** [I] to stop being involved or interested in something: **[+from]** *Too many young people disengage from learning.* **4** [I,T] if two armies disengage, they stop fighting OPP **engage** —**disengagement** *n* [U]

dis·en·gaged /ˌdɪsɪnˈgeɪdʒd/ *adj* not involved with or interested in something or someone, and feeling separate from them OPP **engaged**: *teenagers who are depressed or disengaged from their families*

dis·en·tan·gle /ˌdɪsənˈtæŋgəl/ *v* [T] **1** to separate different ideas or pieces of information that have become confused together: *It's very difficult to disentangle fact from fiction in what she's saying.* **2 disentangle yourself (from sb/sth)** to escape from a difficult situation that you are involved in: *She had just disentangled herself from a long relationship.* **3** to remove knots from ropes, strings etc that have become twisted or tied together **4** to separate something from the things that are twisted around it

dis·e·qui·lib·ri·um /ˌdɪsekwəˈlɪbriəm, ˌdɪsiː-/ *n* [U] a lack of balance in something

dis·es·tab·lish /ˌdɪsəˈstæblɪʃ/ AWL *v* [T] *formal* to officially decide that a particular church is no longer the official church of your country

dis·fa·vour *BrE*, **disfavor** *AmE* /dɪsˈfeɪvə $ -ər/ *n* [U] a feeling of dislike and disapproval OPP **favour**: **with disfavour** *The job creation programme is* ***looked upon with disfavour*** *by the local community.* | *Coal* ***fell into disfavour*** *because burning it caused pollution.*

dis·fig·ure /dɪsˈfɪgə $ -ˈfɪgjər/ *v* [T] to spoil the appearance that something naturally has: *His face had been disfigured in an accident.* —**disfigured** *adj* —**disfigurement** *n* [C,U] —**disfiguring** *adj*: *a disfiguring disease*

dis·fran·chise /dɪsˈfræntʃaɪz/ *v* [T] to DISENFRANCHISE someone

dis·gorge /dɪsˈgɔːdʒ $ -ɔːrdʒ/ *v* **1** [T] *literary* if a vehicle or building disgorges people, they come out of it in a large group: *Cars drew up to disgorge a wedding party.* **2** [T] if something disgorges what was inside it, it lets it pour out: *Chimneys were disgorging smoke into the air.* **3** [I,T] if a river disgorges, it flows into the sea: *The Mississippi disgorges its waters into the Gulf of Mexico.* **4** [T] *formal* to give back something that you have taken illegally **5** [T] *formal* to bring food back up from your stomach through your mouth

dis·grace[1] /dɪsˈgreɪs/ ●○○ *n*
1 [U] the loss of other people's respect because you have done something they strongly disapprove of: *Smith faced total public disgrace after the incident.* | **in disgrace** *Toranaga sent us away in disgrace.* | *His actions* ***brought disgrace on*** *the family.* | *There was* ***no disgrace*** *in finishing fourth.* **THESAURUS** SHAME
2 be a disgrace used to say that something or someone is so bad or unacceptable that the people involved with them should feel ashamed: *The UK rail system is a national disgrace.* | **[+to]** *You are a disgrace to the medical profession.* | **absolute/utter disgrace** ***It's an*** *absolute* ***disgrace****, the way he treats his wife.*

disgrace[2] *v* [T] to do something so bad that you make other people feel ashamed: *How could you disgrace us all like that?* | **disgrace yourself (by doing sth)** *I'm not the one who disgraced herself at the wedding!* | **be (publicly) disgraced** (=be made to feel ashamed, especially in public)

dis·grace·ful /dɪsˈgreɪsfəl/ ●○○ *adj* bad, embarrassing, or unacceptable: *It's a disgraceful waste of taxpayers' money.* | **absolutely/utterly etc disgraceful** *Their behaviour* *was absolutely disgraceful.* | ***It is disgraceful that** anyone should have to live in such conditions.* —**disgracefully** *adv*

dis·grun·tled /dɪsˈɡrʌntld/ *adj* annoyed or disappointed, especially because things have not happened in the way that you wanted: *a disgruntled client*

dis·guise¹ /dɪsˈɡaɪz/ ●●○ *v* [T]
1 to change someone's appearance so that people cannot recognize them: **disguise yourself as sb/sth** *Maybe you could disguise yourself as a waiter and sneak in there.* | *He escaped across the border disguised as a priest.* **THESAURUS** HIDE
2 to change the appearance, sound, taste etc of something so that people do not recognize it: *There's no way you can disguise that southern accent.* | **disguise sth as sth** *a letter bomb disguised as a musical greetings card*
3 to hide a fact or feeling so that people will not notice it: *Try as he might, Dan couldn't disguise his feelings for Katie.* | **disguise the fact (that)** ***There's no disguising the fact that** business is bad.* | *The speech was seen by many as a **thinly disguised** attack on the president.*

disguise² ●●○ *n*
1 [C,U] something that you wear to change your appearance and hide who you are, or the act of wearing this: *His disguise didn't fool anyone.* | *She wore dark glasses in an absurd attempt at disguise.*
2 in disguise a) wearing a disguise: *The woman in the park turned out to be a police officer in disguise.* **b)** made to seem like something else that is better: *'Tax reform' is just a tax increase in disguise.* → **blessing in disguise** at BLESSING(4)

dis·gust¹ /dɪsˈɡʌst, dɪz-/ ●○○ *n* [U]
1 a strong feeling of dislike, annoyance, or disapproval: **with disgust** *Joan looked at him with disgust.* | **in disgust** *Sam threw his books down in disgust and stormed out of the room.* | **to sb's disgust** ***Much to** my **disgust**, I found that there were no toilets for the disabled.* | **[+with]** *Nelson's disgust with US politics* | **[+at]** *The fans didn't hide their disgust at the umpire's decision.*
2 a very strong feeling of dislike that almost makes you sick, caused by something unpleasant: *He reached into the bin with a look of disgust on his face.* | **with disgust** *Edward tasted the thin, sour wines with disgust.*

disgust² ●○○ *v* [T]
1 to make someone feel very annoyed or upset about something that is not acceptable: *Many parents claimed to be disgusted by the amount of violence in the film.* | **be disgusted to find/hear/see etc** *Dear Sir, I was disgusted to see the picture on page one of Sunday's feature section.* | **it disgusts sb that/how/to do** *It disgusts me that he got away with it.*
2 to be so unpleasant that it makes you feel almost sick: *The thought of eating insects disgusts me.*

dis·gust·ed /dɪsˈɡʌstɪd, dɪz-/ ●●○ *adj* very annoyed or upset by something that is not acceptable: *Disgusted onlookers claimed the driver was more concerned about his car than about the victim.* | **[+at/by/with]** *Most locals are disgusted by the anti-foreigner violence.* | **disgusted that** *Animal welfare workers were disgusted that anyone could do this to a puppy.*

Dis,gusted of ,Tunbridge 'Wells *BrE* a humorous name for a typical old-fashioned MIDDLE-CLASS person living in the town of Tunbridge Wells in southeast England, who writes letters to newspapers strongly criticizing things about modern behaviour or modern life which they find shocking

dis·gust·ing /dɪsˈɡʌstɪŋ, dɪz-/ ●●● S2 *adj*
1 extremely unpleasant and making you feel sick SYN **revolting**: *Rubbish was piled everywhere – it was disgusting.* | *Smoking is a really disgusting habit.* **THESAURUS** BAD, HORRIBLE, TASTE
2 shocking and unacceptable: *Sixty pounds for a thirty-minute consultation. I think that's disgusting!* | *That's a disgusting thing to say.* —**disgustingly** *adv*: *They're disgustingly rich.*

dish¹ /dɪʃ/ ●●● S2 W2 *n* [C]
1 a flat container with low sides, for serving food from or cooking food in → **bowl**: *a serving dish* | *an ovenproof dish* | **[+of]** *a large dish of spaghetti*
2 the dishes all the plates, cups, bowls etc that have been used to eat a meal and need to be washed: **do/wash the dishes** *I'll just do the dishes before we go.* → see picture at CLEAN²

> **REGISTER**
> In everyday English, people often use the expression **do the washing-up** (BrE) or **do the dishes** (AmE), rather than **wash the dishes**.

3 a type of food that is cooked in a particular way and served as part of a meal: *a wonderful pasta dish* | *The menu includes a wide selection of vegetarian dishes.* | *This soup is substantial enough to serve as a **main dish*** (=the biggest part of a meal). **THESAURUS** FOOD
4 something that is shaped like a dish: *a soap dish*
5 *informal old-fashioned* someone who is sexually attractive → SIDE DISH, SATELLITE DISH

dish² *v* [I,T] *informal* to give a lot of information about something or someone, especially something that would usually be secret or private: **[+on]** *She's ready to dish on boys, beauty, and break-ups in her new column.* | **dish the dirt** (=tell people shocking things about someone's private life)

dish sth ↔ **out** *phr v* **1** to give something to various people in a careless way: *We dished out some leaflets there too.* | *Paul tends to dish out unwanted advice.* **2** to serve food to people: *Sam's dishing out sandwiches if you want one.* **3 sb can dish it out but they can't take it** used to say that someone often criticizes other people, but does not like being criticized

dish sth ↔ **up** *phr v* to put food for a meal into dishes, ready to be eaten: *Could you dish up the vegetables?*

dis·har·mo·ny /dɪsˈhɑːməni $ -ɑːr-/ *n* [U] disagreement about important things which makes people be unfriendly to each other

dish·cloth /ˈdɪʃklɒθ $ -klɒːθ/ *n* [C] a cloth used for washing dishes

dis·heart·ened /dɪsˈhɑːtnd $ -ɑːrtnd/ *adj formal* disappointed, so that you lose hope and the determination to continue doing something: *If young children don't see quick results they grow disheartened.* —**dishearten** *v* [T]

dis·heart·en·ing /dɪsˈhɑːtn-ɪŋ $ -ɑːr-/ *adj* making you lose hope and determination: **it is disheartening to hear/see etc sth** *It's disheartening to see what little progress has been made.* —**dishearteningly** *adv*

dish·er /ˈdɪʃə $ -ər/ (*also* **dirt-disher**) *n* [C] *AmE informal* someone who enjoys telling people a lot of information about other people's behaviour and private lives SYN **gossip**: *the movie role of the light-hearted Hollywood disher*

di·shev·elled *BrE*, **disheveled** *AmE* /dɪˈʃevəld/ *adj* if someone's appearance or their clothes, hair etc is dishevelled, they look very untidy: *Pam arrived late, dishevelled and out of breath.*

dis·hon·est /dɪsˈɒnɪst $ -ˈɑː-/ *adj* not honest, and so deceiving or cheating people OPP **honest**: *dishonest traders* | *People on welfare are wrongly seen as lazy or dishonest.* —**dishonestly** *adv*: *A person is guilty of theft if he or she dishonestly obtains property.*

> **THESAURUS**
> **dishonest** behaving in a way that is intended to deceive people, for example by lying, cheating, or stealing: *Are you accusing me of being dishonest?* | *The money was acquired through dishonest means.*
> **corrupt** using your power in a dishonest way for your own advantage – used about people in official positions: *corrupt politicians* | *Law and order has broken down, and most government officials are corrupt.*
> **devious** /ˈdiːviəs/ good at secretly thinking of clever plans to trick people in order to get what you want: *You have a very devious mind!* | *They use all kinds of devious methods to find out your personal details.*

underhand *BrE*, **underhanded** *AmE* underhand methods involve secretly deceiving people in order to get what you want: *In a series of underhand moves, Browne managed to gain control of the company.*
sneaky doing or saying things secretly, in a way that seems wrong because it is slightly dishonest or unfair: *It was pretty sneaky when the bank charged me interest on my account without telling me.*
sly deliberately behaving in a way that hides what you are really thinking or doing, in a way that is slightly dishonest: *Lucy decided not to tell him where she was going. She was often a bit sly like that.* | *He's a sly old fox.*
unscrupulous /ʌnˈskruːpjələs/ using dishonest and unfair methods to get what you want, without caring if you harm other people: *Some unscrupulous companies try to persuade people to borrow huge sums of money.*
fraudulent /ˈfrɔːdjələnt $ ˈfrɒːdʒə-/ *formal* deliberately deceiving people in an illegal way in order to gain money or power: *You will be prosecuted if you make a fraudulent claim on your insurance policy.*

D

dis·hon·est·y /dɪsˈɒnəsti $ -ˈɑː-/ *n* [U] behaviour in which you deceive or cheat people OPP **honesty**

dis·hon·our¹ *BrE*, **dishonor** *AmE* /dɪsˈɒnə $ -ˈɑːnər/ *n* [U] loss of respect from other people, because you have behaved in a morally unacceptable way OPP **honour**: *You've* ***brought*** *enough* ***dishonour on*** *your family already without causing any more trouble.* THESAURUS ▸ SHAME

dishonour² *BrE*, **dishonor** *AmE* *v* [T] **1** *formal* to make your family, country, profession etc lose the respect of other people: *He dishonored the uniform and did not deserve to be a marine.* **2** if a bank dishonours a cheque, it refuses to pay out money for it OPP **honour 3** to refuse to keep an agreement or promise OPP **honour**: *Union leaders accused management of dishonouring existing pay agreements.*

dis·hon·our·a·ble *BrE*, **dishonorable** *AmE* /dɪsˈɒnərəbəl $ -ˈɑː-/ *adj* not morally correct or acceptable OPP **honourable**: *Surrender was seen as dishonourable.*

dis͵honourable ˈdischarge *BrE*, **dishonorable discharge** *AmE* *n* [C,U] an order to someone to leave the army, navy etc, because they have behaved in a morally unacceptable way

dish·pan /ˈdɪʃpæn/ *n* [C] *AmE* a large bowl in which you wash dishes, plates etc

dish·rag /ˈdɪʃræg/ *n* [C] *AmE* a DISHCLOTH

ˈdish ͵towel *n* [C] *AmE* a cloth used for drying dishes

dish·wash·er /ˈdɪʃ͵wɒʃə $ -͵wɒːʃər, -͵wɑː-/ ●●○ *n* [C]
1 a machine that washes dishes
2 *especially AmE* someone whose job is to wash dirty dishes, plates etc, especially in a restaurant

dish·wash·ing liq·uid /ˈdɪʃwɒʃɪŋ ͵lɪkwɪd $ -wɒː-, -wɑː-/ *n* [U] *AmE* liquid soap used to wash dishes SYN **washing-up liquid** *BrE*

dish·wa·ter /ˈdɪʃ͵wɔːtə $ -͵wɒːtər, -͵wɑː-/ *n* [U] **1** dirty water that dishes have been washed in **2** *informal* if you say that tea or coffee tastes like dishwater, you mean that it tastes unpleasantly weak

dish·y /ˈdɪʃi/ *adj old-fashioned informal* sexually attractive

dis·il·lu·sion /͵dɪsəˈluːʒən/ *v* [T] to make someone realize that something which they thought was true or good is not really true or good: *I hate to disillusion you, but I don't think she's coming back.*

dis·il·lu·sioned /͵dɪsəˈluːʒənd◂/ *adj* disappointed because you have lost your belief that someone is good, or that an idea is right SYN **disenchanted**: **[+by/with]** *As she grew older, Laura* ***became*** *increasingly* ***disillusioned*** *with politics.* THESAURUS ▸ DISAPPOINTED —**disillusionment** (*also* **disillusion**) *n* [U]

dis·in·cen·tive /͵dɪsənˈsentɪv/ *n* [C] something that makes people less willing to do something OPP **incentive**: **disincentive to (doing/do) sth** *High interest rates can be a disincentive to expanding a business.*

dis·in·cli·na·tion /͵dɪsɪŋkləˈneɪʃən/ *n* [U] a lack of willingness to do something OPP **inclination**: *the increasing disinclination of farm workers' children to consider a job in farming*

dis·in·clined /͵dɪsɪnˈklaɪnd/ *adj* **be/feel disinclined to do sth** *formal* to be unwilling to do something SYN **reluctant**: *I was disinclined to talk to Sam about it.*

dis·in·fect /͵dɪsənˈfekt/ *v* [T] **1** to clean something with a chemical that destroys BACTERIA: *First use some iodine to disinfect the wound.* | *Disinfect the area thoroughly.* **2** to run a special computer program to get rid of a computer VIRUS

dis·in·fec·tant /͵dɪsənˈfektənt/ *n* [C,U] a chemical or a cleaning product that destroys BACTERIA → **antiseptic**

dis·in·for·ma·tion /͵dɪsɪnfəˈmeɪʃən $ -fər-/ *n* [U] false information which is given deliberately in order to hide the truth or confuse people, especially in political situations → **misinformation**: *government disinformation about the effects of nuclear testing*

dis·in·gen·u·ous /͵dɪsənˈdʒenjuəs◂/ *adj formal* not sincere and slightly dishonest OPP **ingenuous**: *Keeping the details of the tax changes vague is disingenuous.* —**disingenuously** *adv*

dis·in·her·it /͵dɪsɪnˈherɪt/ *v* [T] to take away from someone, especially your son or daughter, their legal right to receive your money or property after your death → **inherit**, **will**

dis·in·te·grate /dɪsˈɪntɪgreɪt/ *v* **1** [I,T] to break up, or make something break up, into very small pieces: *The plane just disintegrated in mid-air.* **2** [I] to become weaker or less united and be gradually destroyed: *a society disintegrating under economic pressures* —**disintegration** /dɪs͵ɪntɪˈgreɪʃən/ *n* [U]: *the disintegration of the Soviet empire into separate republics*

dis·in·ter /͵dɪsɪnˈtɜː $ -ˈtɜːr/ *v* (**disinterred**, **disinterring**) [T] *formal* **1** to dig and remove a dead body from a GRAVE OPP **inter 2** to find or use something that has been lost or not used for a long time: *She disinterred two frozen TV dinners from the freezer.*

dis·in·terest /dɪsˈɪntrɪst/ *n* [U] **1** a lack of interest: **[+in]** *The exception to Balfour's disinterest in social issues was education.* **2** when you are able to judge a situation fairly because you are not involved in it

dis·in·terest·ed /dɪsˈɪntrɪstɪd/ *adj* **1** able to judge a situation fairly because you are not concerned with gaining any personal advantage from it SYN **objective**, **impartial**, **unbiased**: *A lawyer should provide disinterested advice.* **2** not interested. Many teachers think that this is not correct English → **uninterested** —**disinterestedly** *adv*

dis·in·ter·me·di·a·tion /dɪs͵ɪntəmiːdiˈeɪʃən $ -tər-/ *n* [U] the practice of selling a product directly to customers using the Internet, rather than first selling the product to a shop

dis·in·vest·ment /͵dɪsənˈvestmənt/ *n* [C,U] *technical* the process of taking your money out of a company by selling your SHARES in it OPP **investment**

dis·joint·ed /dɪsˈdʒɔɪntɪd/ *adj* **1** something, especially a speech or piece of writing, that is disjointed has parts that do not seem well connected or are not arranged well: *disjointed fragments of information* **2** a disjointed activity or system is one in which the different parts do not work well together: *Burley was critical of his team's disjointed performance.*

dis·junc·tion /dɪsˈdʒʌŋkʃən/, **dis·junc·ture** /dɪsˈdʒʌŋktʃə $ -ər/ *n* [C usually singular] *formal* a difference between two things that you would expect to be in agreement: *a disjunction between the skills taught in schools and the skills demanded by employers*

dis·junc·tive /dɪsˈdʒʌŋktɪv/ *adj technical* a disjunctive CONJUNCTION expresses a choice or opposition between two ideas. For example, 'or' is a disjunctive conjunction.

disk /dɪsk/ ●●○ *n* [C]
1 a small flat piece of plastic or metal which is used for storing computer or electronic information
2 the usual American spelling of DISC → **COMPACT DISC**, **FLOPPY DISK**, **HARD DISK**, **LASER DISK**

ˈ**disk drive** *n* [C] a piece of equipment in a computer system that is used to get information from a disk or to store information on it

dis·kette /dɪsˈket $ ˈdɪsket/ *n* [C] a FLOPPY DISK

dis·like[1] /dɪsˈlaɪk/ ●●○ *v* [T] to think someone or something is unpleasant and not like them OPP **like**: *Why do you dislike her so much?* | **dislike doing sth** *I dislike being the centre of attention.*

REGISTER
In everyday English, people usually say **don't like** rather than **dislike**: *Why* ***don't you like*** *her?* | *He* ***doesn't like*** *being criticized.*

GRAMMAR

Patterns with dislike

Dislike is used with an **-ing** form, not an infinitive. You **dislike doing** something: *I dislike eating dinner alone.* ✗ Don't say: *I dislike to eat dinner alone.*

Using the progressive

Dislike is not used in the progressive. You say: *Tell us what you dislike about it.* ✗ Don't say: *Tell us what you are disliking about it.*

GRAMMAR GUIDE ▸ VERBS

THESAURUS

dislike to not like someone or something. **Dislike** is stronger than **not like**, and is used especially in written English: *She disliked him as soon as she met him.* | *Chemistry was the only subject he disliked at school.*

not like: *Why did you invite Claire? You know I don't like her.* | *I don't really like getting up in the morning when it's dark.*

not be very keen on sth *informal* (*also* **not be very fond of sth**) *especially BrE* used to say that you do not like something, but in a polite or gentle way: *I'm not very keen on Chinese food.* | *She's never been very fond of his books.*

not think much of sb/sth to not like someone or something because you do not have a good opinion of them: *We've tried that restaurant twice and we don't think much of it.* | *I worked with him for years and I didn't think much of him.*

not be sb's kind of thing (*also* **not be sb's cup of tea**) *informal* to not be the kind of thing you enjoy – used about activities, films, books etc: *Detective stories aren't really my kind of thing.*

go off sb/sth *BrE informal* to stop liking someone or something that you used to like: *Dan and I went out together for six months and then I just went off him.*

put sb off sb/sth *BrE* to make you stop liking someone or something: *I was terrible at sport at school and it totally put me off doing any kind of exercise.*

dis·like[2] /dɪsˈlaɪk, ˈdɪslaɪk/ ●●○ *n*
1 [C,U] a feeling of not liking someone or something OPP **liking**: **[+of]** *She shared her mother's dislike of housework.* | **[+for]** *Truman had a strong dislike for communism.* | **intense/acute/violent etc dislike** (=very strong dislike) *His colleagues regarded him with intense dislike.* | *They* ***took an instant dislike to*** *each other* (=they disliked each other immediately).
2 dislikes [plural] the things that you do not like: *A good hotel manager should know his regular guests'* ***likes and dislikes***.

dis·lo·cate /ˈdɪsləkeɪt $ -loʊ-/ *v* [T] **1** to move a bone out of its normal position in a joint, usually in an accident: *I dislocated my shoulder playing football.* THESAURUS ▸ HURT
2 *formal* to spoil the way in which a plan, system, or service is arranged, so that it cannot work normally SYN **disrupt**: *Communications were temporarily dislocated by the bad weather.* —**dislocated** *adj*: *a dislocated elbow* —**dislocation** /ˌdɪsləˈkeɪʃən $ -loʊ-/ *n* [C,U]: *a period of economic dislocation*

dis·lodge /dɪsˈlɒdʒ $ -ˈlɑːdʒ/ *v* [T] **1** to force or knock something out of its position: *Ian dislodged a few stones as he climbed up the rock.* **2** to make someone leave a place or lose a position of power: *the revolution that failed to dislodge the British in 1919*

dis·loy·al /dɪsˈlɔɪəl/ *adj* doing or saying things that do not support your friends, your country, or the group you belong to OPP **loyal**: **[+to]** *He felt he had been disloyal to his friends.* —**disloyalty** *n* [U]

dis·mal /ˈdɪzməl/ ●○○ *adj*
1 if a situation or a place is dismal, it is so bad that it makes you feel very unhappy and hopeless: *The future looks pretty dismal right now.* | *a dismal, grey afternoon*
2 bad and unsuccessful: *The team's record so far is pretty dismal.* | *Her scheme was a* ***dismal failure***. —**dismally** *adv*

dis·man·tle /dɪsˈmæntl/ ●○○ *v* [T]
1 to take a machine or piece of equipment apart so that it is in separate pieces: *Chris dismantled the bike in five minutes.*
2 to gradually get rid of a system or organization: *an election promise to dismantle the existing tax legislation*

dis·may[1] /dɪsˈmeɪ/ ●○○ *n* [U] the worry, disappointment, or unhappiness you feel when something unpleasant happens: **with/in dismay** *They stared at each other in dismay.* | **to sb's dismay** *I found to my dismay that I had left my notes behind.* | *The thought of leaving* ***filled*** *him* ***with dismay***.

dismay[2] *v* [T] to make someone feel worried, disappointed, and upset: *The poor election turnout dismayed politicians.*

dis·mayed /dɪsˈmeɪd/ *adj* worried, disappointed, and upset when something unpleasant happens: **dismayed to see/discover/learn etc** *Ruth was dismayed to see how thin he had grown.* | **[+at/by]** *They were dismayed at the cost of the repairs.* | **dismayed that** *We are dismayed that the demonstration was allowed to take place.*

dis·mem·ber /dɪsˈmembə $ -ər/ *v* [T] **1** to cut a body into pieces or tear it apart **2** *formal* to divide a country, area, or organization into smaller parts SYN **break up** —**dismemberment** *n* [U]

dis·miss /dɪsˈmɪs/ ●●○ W3 *v* [T]
1 to refuse to consider someone's idea, opinion etc, because you think it is not serious, true, or important: *The government has dismissed criticisms that the country's health policy is a mess.* | **dismiss sth as sth** *He just laughed and dismissed my proposal as unrealistic.* | *It's an idea that shouldn't be* ***dismissed out of hand*** (=dismissed immediately and completely).
2 to remove someone from their job SYN **fire**, **sack**: **dismiss sb from sth** *Bryant was* ***unfairly dismissed*** *from his post.* | **dismiss sb for sth** *Employees can be dismissed for sending obscene emails.*

REGISTER
In everyday British English, people usually say **sack** someone, and in everyday American English, people usually say **fire** someone, rather than use **dismiss**: *He was* ***sacked*** *(BrE)/****fired*** *(AmE) for being late all the time.*

3 *formal* to tell someone that they are allowed to go, or are no longer needed: *The class was dismissed early today.*
4 if a judge dismisses a court case, he or she stops it from continuing: *The case was dismissed owing to lack of evidence.*
5 to end the INNINGS of a player or team in the game of CRICKET

dis·miss·al /dɪsˈmɪsəl/ ●●○ *n*
1 [C,U] when someone is removed from their job: *Wilson was claiming compensation for* ***unfair dismissal***. | *No dismissals have been announced yet.*
2 [U] when someone decides or says that something is not important, serious, or true: *Gill's dismissal of the book as '386 pages of rubbish'.*
3 [C,U] a decision by a judge to stop a court case

dis·miss·ive /dɪsˈmɪsɪv/ *adj* refusing to consider someone or something seriously: **[+of]** *Some historians have been dismissive of this argument.* | **dismissive gesture/wave/shrug etc** *Cath spread both hands in a dismissive gesture.* —**dismissively** *adv*

dis·mount /dɪsˈmaʊnt/ *v formal* **1** [I + from] to get off a horse, bicycle, or MOTORCYCLE OPP **mount** **2** [T] to take something, especially a gun, out of its base or support

dis·o·be·di·ent /ˌdɪsəˈbiːdiənt◂, ˌdɪsəʊ- $ ˌdɪsə-, ˌdɪsoʊ-/ ●○○ *adj* deliberately not doing what you are told to do by your parents, teacher etc OPP **obedient** —**disobedience** *n* [U] → CIVIL DISOBEDIENCE

dis·o·bey /ˌdɪsəˈbeɪ, ˌdɪsəʊ- $ ˌdɪsə-, ˌdɪsoʊ-/ ●●○ *v* [I,T] to refuse to do what someone with authority tells you to do, or refuse to obey a rule or law OPP **obey**: *You disobeyed my orders.*

THESAURUS

disobey to not obey a person, order, rule, or law: *In the army, it is a crime to disobey a superior officer.* | *He had disobeyed the school rules.*
break a law/rule to not obey a law or rule: *Anyone who breaks the law must expect to be punished.*
defy *formal* to deliberately refuse to obey a rule or law, or what someone in authority tells you to do: *The police arrested the youth for defying a court order.*
flout /flaʊt/ *formal* to deliberately disobey a rule or law in a very public way: *Timber companies are continuing to flout environmental laws.*
violate *formal* to disobey a law, or do something that is against an agreement or principle: *Both countries have accused each other of violating the treaty.* | *Technically he had violated the law.*
contravene *formal* to be against a law, rule, or agreement, or to do something that is against a law, rule, or agreement: *The British government's actions contravened the European Convention on Human Rights.*

dis·or·der /dɪsˈɔːdə $ -ˈɔːrdər/ ●○○ *n*
1 [C] *medical* a mental or physical illness which prevents part of your body from working properly: **a disorder of the brain/liver/digestive system etc** *He **suffers from** a rare **disorder** of the liver.* | **a stomach/lung/heart etc disorder** | **a mental/psychiatric disorder** *people with mental disorders* | *severe **eating disorders** such as bulimia and anorexia* THESAURUS ▸ ILLNESS
2 [U] a situation in which a lot of people behave in an uncontrolled, noisy, or violent way in public: **civil/public/crowd disorder** *A number of stadiums were closed because of crowd disorder.*
3 [U] a situation in which things or people are very untidy or disorganized OPP **order**: **in/into disorder** *Everything was in disorder, but nothing seemed to be missing.* | *His whole system was **thrown into disorder**.*

dis·or·dered /dɪsˈɔːdəd $ -ˈɔːrdərd/ *adj* **1** not tidy, planned, or arranged in order: *her grey, disordered hair* **2** if someone is mentally disordered, their mind is not working in a normal and healthy way

dis·or·der·ly /dɪsˈɔːdəli $ -ˈɔːrdər-/ *adj formal* **1** untidy or without any order OPP **orderly**: *clothes left in a disorderly heap* **2** behaving in a noisy violent way and causing trouble in a public place: **disorderly conduct/behaviour** *He was arrested for disorderly conduct.* | *Bell denied being **drunk and disorderly**.*

dis·or·gan·ized (*also* **-ised** *BrE*) /dɪsˈɔːɡənaɪzd $ -ˈɔːr-/ ●○○ *adj*
1 not arranged or planned in a clear order, or lacking any kind of plan or system OPP **well-organized**: *The conference was completely disorganized.*
2 someone who is disorganized is very bad at arranging or planning things OPP **organized**: *He's an extremely disorganized person.* → UNORGANIZED

dis·or·i·ent·ed /dɪsˈɔːrientɪd/ (*also* **dis·or·i·en·tat·ed** /dɪsˈɔːriənteɪtɪd/ *BrE*) *adj* **1** confused and not understanding what is happening around you **2** confused about where you are or which direction you should go: *When he emerged into the street, he was completely disoriented.*

dis·or·i·en·ting /dɪsˈɔːrientɪŋ/ (*also* **dis·or·i·en·tat·ing** /dɪsˈɔːriənteɪtɪŋ/ *BrE*) *adj* **1** making someone not know where they are or which direction they should go: *a disorientating maze of corridors* **2** confusing you and making you not certain about what is happening around you: *Lack of sleep can be disorienting.* —**disorient** (*also* **disorientate** *BrE*) *v* [T] —**disorientation** /dɪsˌɔːriənˈteɪʃən/ *n* [U]

dis·own /dɪsˈəʊn $ -ˈoʊn/ *v* [T] to say that you no longer want to be connected with someone or something, especially a member of your family or something that you are responsible for: *Frankly, I'm not surprised her family disowned her.* | *Since 1960, Kubrick has virtually disowned the film.*

di·spar·age /dɪˈspærɪdʒ/ *v* [T] *formal* to criticize someone or something in a way that shows you do not think they are very good or important: *Matcham's theatres were widely disparaged by architects.* —**disparagement** *n* [C,U]

di·spar·a·ging /dɪˈspærədʒɪŋ/ *adj* criticizing someone or something, and showing that you do not think they are very good or important: **disparaging remarks/comments** *She made some disparaging remarks about the royal family.* —**disparagingly** *adv*

dis·pa·rate /ˈdɪspərət/ *adj formal* consisting of things or people that are very different and not related to each other: *a meeting covering many disparate subjects* | *the difficulties of dealing with disparate groups of people*

di·spar·i·ty /dɪˈspærəti/ ●○○ *n* (*plural* **disparities**) [C,U] *formal* a difference between two or more things, especially an unfair one → **parity**: **[+in/between]** *a disparity between the rates of pay for men and women*

dis·pas·sion·ate /dɪsˈpæʃənət/ *adj* not influenced by personal emotions and therefore able to make fair decisions SYN **impartial**: *a dispassionate view of the situation* —**dispassionately** *adv*

di·spatch[1], **despatch** /dɪˈspætʃ/ ●○○ *v* [T]
1 *formal* to send someone or something somewhere for a particular purpose: **dispatch sb/sth to sb/sth** *A reporter was dispatched to Naples to cover the riot.* | *Goods are normally dispatched within 24 hours.*
2 to deal with someone or to finish a job quickly and effectively: *She dispatched* (=beat) *her opponent 6–2, 6–1.*
3 *old-fashioned* to deliberately kill a person or animal

dispatch[2], **despatch** *n* **1** [C] a message sent between military or government officials: *a dispatch from headquarters* **2** [C] a report sent to a newspaper from one of its writers who is in another town or country **3** [singular] the act of sending people or things to a particular place: *the dispatch of warships to the region* **4 with dispatch** *formal* if you do something with dispatch, you do it well and quickly → **mentioned in dispatches** at MENTION[1](4)

diˈspatch box *n BrE* **1 the dispatch box** a box on a central table in the British Parliament, which important members of parliament stand next to when they make speeches **2** [C] a box for holding official papers

di·spatch·er /dɪˈspætʃə $ -ər/ *n* [C] *AmE* someone whose job is to send out vehicles such as taxis or AMBULANCES to places where they are needed

diˈspatch ˌrider *n* [C] *BrE* someone whose job is to take messages or packages by MOTORCYCLE

di·spel /dɪˈspel/ *v* (**dispelled**, **dispelling**) [T] to make something go away, especially a belief, idea, or feeling: *We want to **dispel** the **myth** that you cannot eat well in Britain.* | *Light poured into the hall, dispelling the shadows.*

di·spen·sa·ble /dɪˈspensəbəl/ *adj* not necessary or important and so easy to get rid of OPP **indispensable**: *Part-time workers are considered dispensable.*

di·spen·sa·ry /dɪˈspensəri/ *n* (*plural* **dispensaries**) [C] a place where medicines are prepared and given out, especially in a hospital → PHARMACY

dis·pen·sa·tion /ˌdɪspənˈseɪʃən, -pen-/ *n* **1** [C,U] special permission from someone in authority, especially a religious leader, to do something that is not usually allowed:

Caroline's marriage was annulled by ***special dispensation*** *from the church.* **2** [U] *formal* the act of providing people with something as part of an official process: **[+of]** *the dispensation of justice* **3** [C] *formal* a religious or political system that has control over people's lives at a particular time

di·spense /dɪˈspens/ ●○○ *v* [T] *formal*
1 to give something to people, especially in fixed amounts SYN **give out**: **dispense sth to sb** *Villagers dispensed tea to visitors.* | *a machine for dispensing cash*
2 to officially provide something for people: **dispense justice** (=decide whether or not someone is guilty of a crime and what punishment they should receive)
3 to officially prepare and give medicines to people
dispense with sth *phr v formal* to not use or do something that people usually use or do, because it is not necessary: *Ann suggested that they dispense with speeches altogether at the wedding.* | **dispense with sb's services** (=no longer employ someone) | *Let's* ***dispense with the formalities*** (=speak openly and directly), *shall we?*

di·spens·er /dɪˈspensə $ -ər/ *n* [C] a machine which provides a particular amount of a product or substance when you press a button or put money into it: *a paper towel dispenser* → CASH DISPENSER

diˈspensing ˌchemist *n* [C] *BrE* a CHEMIST or PHARMACIST

di·sper·sal /dɪˈspɜːsəl $ -ɜːr-/ *n* [C,U] the process of spreading things over a wide area or in different directions: *the role of birds in the dispersal of seeds*

di·sperse /dɪˈspɜːs $ -ɜːrs/ ●○○ *v* [I,T]
1 if a group of people disperse or are dispersed, they go away in different directions: *Police used tear gas to disperse the crowd.*
2 if something disperses or is dispersed, it spreads in different directions over a wide area: *The clouds dispersed as quickly as they had gathered.*

di·sper·sion /dɪˈspɜːʃən $ -ˈspɜːrʒən/ *n* [U] DISPERSAL

di·spir·it·ed /dɪˈspɪrɪtɪd/ *adj* someone who is dispirited does not feel as hopeful, eager, or interested in something as they were in the past SYN **discouraged**: *At last, dispirited and weary, they gave up the search.* —**dispiritedly** *adv*

dis·place /dɪsˈpleɪs/ ●○○ AWL *v* [T]
1 to take the place or position of something or someone SYN **replace**: *Coal has been displaced by natural gas as a major source of energy.* | *immigrants who displace US workers in the job market*
2 to make a group of people or animals have to leave the place where they normally live: *Fifty thousand people have been displaced by the fighting.*
3 to force something out of its usual place or position: *The water displaced by the landslides created a tidal wave.* —**displaced** *adj*

disˌplaced ˈperson *n* (*plural* **displaced persons**) [C] *technical* someone who has been forced to leave their country because of war or cruel treatment SYN **refugee**

dis·place·ment /dɪsˈpleɪsmənt/ AWL *n* **1** [U] *formal* when a group of people or animals are forced to leave the place where they usually live **2** [singular] *technical* the weight or VOLUME of liquid that something replaces when it floats in that liquid – used especially to describe how heavy something such as a ship is

di·splay¹ /dɪˈspleɪ/ ●●● S3 W2 AWL *n* [C]
1 OBJECTS an arrangement of things for people to look at or buy: **[+of]** *a superb display of African masks* | *a* ***dazzling display*** (=very good display) *of flowers* | *The* ***window display*** *caught her eye.* | ***display cases*** *containing old photographs*
2 ENTERTAINMENT a public performance of something that is intended to entertain people: *a fireworks display* | **[+of]** *a display of juggling*
3 on display a) something that is on display is in a public place where people can look at it SYN **on show**: *Mapplethorpe's photographs were first* ***put on display*** *in New York.* | **be/go on display** *One of the world's oldest cars has gone on display in Brighton today.* **b)** if a quality, feeling, or skill is on display, it is very clear and easy to notice: *The musical talent on display is extremely impressive.*
4 display of affection/emotion/aggression etc an occasion when someone clearly shows a particular feeling, attitude, or quality: *Unprovoked displays of aggression cannot be tolerated.*
5 ON EQUIPMENT a part of a piece of equipment that shows information, for example a computer screen: *This time the display flashed a red warning signal.*

display² ●●● W2 AWL *v*
1 [T] to show something to people, or put it in a place where people can see it easily: *shop windows displaying the latest fashions* | *All the exam results will be displayed on the noticeboard.*
2 [T] to clearly show a feeling, attitude, or quality by what you do or say: *She displayed no emotion on the witness stand.* | *ten piano pieces, each written to display the talents of individual players*
3 [T] if a computer or something similar displays information, it shows it on its screen: *I pressed 'return' and an error message was displayed.*
4 [I] if a male bird or animal displays, it behaves in a particular way as a signal to other birds or animals, especially to attract a female

dis·pleased /dɪsˈpliːzd/ *adj formal* annoyed or not satisfied OPP **pleased**: *He looked extremely displeased.* | **[+with]** *City officials are displeased with the lack of progress.* —**displease** *v* [T] —**displeasing** *adj*

dis·plea·sure /dɪsˈpleʒə $ -ər/ *n* [U] *formal* the feeling of being annoyed or not satisfied with someone or something SYN **annoyance**: **[+at/with]** *Their displeasure at being kept waiting was clear.* | **incur sb's displeasure** (=make someone displeased)

dis·port /dɪˈspɔːt $ -ɔːrt/ *v* [T] **disport yourself** *old-fashioned* to amuse yourself by doing things that are active and enjoyable – used humorously

dis·pos·a·ble /dɪˈspəʊzəbəl $ -ˈspoʊ-/ AWL *adj* **1** intended to be used once or for a short time and then thrown away: *disposable nappies* **2** available to be used: *disposable resources* —**disposable** *n* [C]

disˌposable ˈincome *n* [U] the amount of money you have left to spend after you have paid your taxes, bills etc

dis·pos·al /dɪˈspəʊzəl $ -ˈspoʊ-/ ●○○ AWL *n*
1 [U] when you get rid of something: **[+of]** *the safe disposal of radioactive waste* | ***bomb disposal*** *experts*
2 at sb's disposal available for someone to use: *Tanner* ***had*** *a lot of cash* ***at*** *his* ***disposal***. | **sb is at your (complete) disposal** (=someone is ready to help you in any way)
3 [C] *AmE* a small machine under the kitchen SINK which breaks vegetable waste into small pieces SYN **waste disposal**
4 [U] *technical* the sale of something you own such as a house, a business, or land: *The profit or loss on the disposal of an asset must be accounted for.*
5 [U] *formal* the way in which an amount of money is used: *They had complete control over the disposal of the funds.*

dis·pose /dɪˈspəʊz $ -ˈspoʊz/ ●○○ AWL *v* [T always + adv/prep] *formal* to arrange things or put them in their places: *Chinese vases are disposed around the gallery.*
dispose of sth *phr v*
1 to get rid of something, especially something that is difficult to get rid of: *an incinerator built to dispose of toxic waste*
2 to sell something, especially part of a business: *I am still not sure how best to dispose of the shares.*
3 *formal* to deal with something such as a problem or question successfully: *Your idea at least disposes of the immediate problem.*
4 to defeat an opponent: *Two goals by Raúl disposed of Barcelona.*
dispose sb **to/towards** sth *phr v formal* to make someone more likely to have particular feelings or thoughts: *The body releases a chemical that disposes you towards sleep.*

dis·posed /dɪˈspəʊzd $ -ˈspoʊzd/ *adj formal* **1 be well/**

D

favourably/kindly disposed (to/towards sb/sth) to like or approve of someone or something: *Management is favourably disposed to the idea of job-sharing.* **2 be/feel/seem etc disposed to do sth** to want or be willing to do something SYN **inclined**: *Jon disagreed, but did not feel disposed to argue.* **3 be disposed to sth** to have a tendency towards something SYN **inclined**: *a man disposed to depression*

dis·po·si·tion /ˌdɪspəˈzɪʃən/ ●○○ *n formal*
1 [C usually singular] a particular type of character which makes someone likely to behave or react in a certain way SYN **temperament**: **of a nervous/sociable/sensitive etc disposition** (=having a nervous etc character) *The film is not suitable for people of a nervous disposition.* | **have a cheerful/sunny etc disposition** (=have a happy character)
2 [singular] a tendency or willingness to behave in a particular way SYN **inclination**: **have/show a disposition to do sth** *Neither side shows the slightest disposition to compromise.* | **[+towards]** *Most children have a disposition towards obedience.*
3 [C usually singular] the position or arrangement of something in a particular place: **[+of]** *a map showing the disposition of American forces*
4 [U] *formal* the way in which something is dealt with or used: **[+of]** *A solicitor advised him as to the disposition of the money.*
5 [C,U] *law* the act of formally giving property to someone: *the disposition of assets on death*

dis·pos·sess /ˌdɪspəˈzes/ *v* [T] to take property or land away from someone: **be dispossessed of sth** *Many black South Africans had been dispossessed of their homes.* GRAMMAR **Dispossess** is usually passive. —**dispossession** /-ˈzeʃən/ *n* [U]

dis·pos·sessed /ˌdɪspəˈzest◂/ *n* **the dispossessed** people who have had property or land taken away

dis·pro·por·tion /ˌdɪsprəˈpɔːʃən $ -ɔːr-/ AWL *n* [C,U] *formal* a situation in which two or more things are not equal in amount, level etc SYN **imbalance**: *a dangerous disproportion between production and consumption*

dis·pro·por·tion·ate /ˌdɪsprəˈpɔːʃənət◂ $ -ɔːr-/ AWL *adj* too much or too little in relation to something else: *the disproportionate amount of money being spent on defence* —**disproportionately** *adv*

dis·prove /dɪsˈpruːv/ *v* [T] to show that something is wrong or not true OPP **prove**: *These figures disproved Smith's argument.* —**disproof** /-ˈpruːf/ *n* [C,U] *formal*

di·sput·a·ble /dɪˈspjuːtəbəl, ˈdɪspjə-/ *adj* something that is disputable is not definitely true or right, and therefore is something that you can argue about OPP **indisputable**

dis·pu·ta·tion /ˌdɪspjəˈteɪʃən/ *n* [C,U] *formal* a discussion about a subject which people cannot agree on

dis·pu·ta·tious /ˌdɪspjəˈteɪʃəs/ *adj formal* tending to argue SYN **argumentative**

dis·pute¹ /dɪˈspjuːt, ˈdɪspjuːt/ ●●○ W3 *n* [C,U]
1 a serious argument or disagreement: **[+with]** *The firm is involved in a legal dispute with a rival company.* | **[+over]** *He got into a dispute over a taxi fare.* | **[+between]** *the bitter border dispute between the countries* THESAURUS ▸ ARGUMENT
2 be beyond dispute if something is beyond dispute, everyone agrees that it is true or that it really happened: ***It is beyond dispute that*** *advances in medicine have enabled people to live longer.*
3 be open to dispute if something is open to dispute, it is not completely certain and not everyone agrees about it: *His interpretation of the poem is open to dispute.*
4 be in dispute if something is in dispute, people are arguing about it: *The facts of the case are still in dispute.*

COLLOCATIONS

VERBS

resolve/settle a dispute (=end it) *It is hoped that the dispute can be resolved peacefully.*
be involved in a dispute *The US government became involved in a dispute with China.*
get into a dispute (=become involved) *We don't want to get into a dispute with them.*
be in dispute with sb *He was in dispute with the company about his contract.*
be locked in a dispute (=be involved in one that is difficult to resolve) | **a dispute arises** (=starts)

ADJECTIVES/NOUN + dispute

a bitter/fierce dispute (=very angry) *It caused a bitter dispute between the neighbouring republics.*
a long-running dispute (=continuing for a long time) *India's long-running dispute with Pakistan*
an industrial dispute *BrE*, **a labor dispute** *AmE* (=between workers and employers) *A lot of working days are lost through industrial disputes.*
a pay dispute (=about how much money employees are paid) | **a political/legal dispute** | **a domestic dispute** *formal* (=between people who live together) | **a border dispute** (=about where the border between two countries is) | **a territorial dispute** (=about which country land belongs to)

dis·pute² /dɪˈspjuːt/ ●●○ *v*
1 [T] to say that something such as a fact or idea is not correct or true: *The main facts of the book have never been disputed.* | **dispute that** *Few would dispute that travel broadens the mind.*
2 [I,T] *formal* to argue or disagree with someone: **dispute (sth) with sb** *Hazlitt, though much younger, was soon disputing with Wordsworth on equal terms.* | *What happened next is* ***hotly disputed****.*
3 [T] to try to get control of something or win something: *Soviet forces disputed every inch of ground.*

dis·qual·i·fy /dɪsˈkwɒlɪfaɪ $ -ˈkwɑː-/ *v* (**disqualified, disqualifying, disqualifies**) [T] **1** to stop someone from taking part in an activity because they have broken a rule SYN **ban**: *They disqualified the team for fielding an underage player.* | **be disqualified from (doing) sth** *He was* ***disqualified from driving****.* GRAMMAR **Disqualify** is often passive in this meaning. **2** to unfairly prevent someone from doing a job or taking part in an activity SYN **exclude**: **disqualify sb from (doing) sth** *a system which disqualifies the poor from education* —**disqualification** /dɪsˌkwɒlɪfɪˈkeɪʃən $ -ˌkwɑː-/ *n* [C,U]: *automatic disqualification*

dis·qui·et /dɪsˈkwaɪət/ *n* [U] *formal* anxiety or unhappiness about something SYN **uneasiness**: **[+over/about/at]** ***public disquiet*** *over deaths in police custody* | **[+among]** *His appointment* ***caused disquiet*** *among members.* | **express/voice your disquiet** *The union has voiced its disquiet about the way the protest was handled.*

dis·qui·et·ing /dɪsˈkwaɪətɪŋ/ *adj formal* causing anxiety: *He found Jean's manner disquieting.*

dis·qui·si·tion /ˌdɪskwəˈzɪʃən/ *n* [C] *formal* a long speech or written report

dis·re·gard¹ /ˌdɪsrɪˈgɑːd $ -ɑːrd/ ●○○ *v* [T] to ignore something or treat it as unimportant: *He ordered the jury to disregard the witness's last statement.* | *Mark totally disregarded my advice.*

disregard² *n* [singular, U] when someone ignores something that they should not ignore: **[+for/of]** *his disregard for her feelings* | **total/reckless/complete/flagrant etc disregard** *Local councillors accused the terrorists of* ***showing*** *a complete* ***disregard for*** *human life.* | **in disregard of sth** *He said the bombing was in complete disregard of the Geneva Convention.*

dis·re·pair /ˌdɪsrɪˈpeə $ -ˈper/ *n* [U] buildings, roads etc that are in disrepair are in bad condition because they have not been cared for: *buildings allowed to* ***fall into disrepair*** | *The castle is* ***in a state of disrepair****.*

dis·rep·u·ta·ble /dɪsˈrepjətəbəl/ *adj* considered to be dishonest, bad, illegal etc OPP **reputable**: *disreputable behavior* | *a disreputable neighbourhood*

dis·re·pute /ˌdɪsrɪˈpjuːt/ *n* [U] a situation in which people no longer admire or trust someone or something: *He faces six charges of* ***bringing*** *the game* ***into disrepute****.* | *This theory* ***fell into disrepute*** *in the fifties.*

dis·re·spect¹ /ˌdɪsrɪˈspekt/ *n* [singular, U] lack of respect for someone or something OPP **respect**: **[+for]** *disrespect for the law | Damien has always had **a healthy disrespect*** (=that you think is good) *for media opinion. | It was said on the spur of the moment and I **meant no disrespect** to anybody. | **No disrespect to** Phil, but the team has performed better since he left* (=used to show you are not criticizing someone). —**disrespectful** *adj* —**disrespectfully** *adv*

disrespect² *v* [T] to say or do things that show a lack of respect for someone: *Hicks accused Williams of disrespecting him at a record company party.*

dis·robe /dɪsˈrəʊb $ -ˈroʊb/ *v* [I] *formal* to remove your clothes SYN **undress**

dis·rupt /dɪsˈrʌpt/ ●●○ *v* [T] to prevent something from continuing in its usual way by causing problems: *Traffic was disrupted by a hoax bomb. | Climate change could disrupt the agricultural economy.*

dis·rup·tion /dɪsˈrʌpʃən/ ●●○ *n* [C,U] a situation in which something is prevented from continuing in its usual way: *The strike **caused** widespread **disruption**.* | **[+to]** *There will be some disruption to traffic while the work is in progress.*

dis·rup·tive /dɪsˈrʌptɪv/ *adj* causing problems and preventing something from continuing in its usual way: **[+to]** *Night work can be very disruptive to home life. | Mike's parents thought I was **a disruptive influence*** (=a person who causes disruption). | *ways to handle **disruptive pupils*** —**disruptively** *adv*

diss, dis /dɪs/ *v* [T] *informal* to say unkind things about someone you know

dis·sat·is·fac·tion /dɪˌsætəsˈfækʃən, dɪsˌsæ-/ ●○○ *n* [U] a feeling of not being satisfied OPP **satisfaction**: **[+with]** *30% of customers **expressed dissatisfaction** with the service.*

dis·sat·is·fied /dɪˈsætəsfaɪd, dɪsˈsæ-/ ●○○ *adj* not satisfied because something is not as good as you had expected OPP **satisfied**: *dissatisfied clients* | **[+with]** *If you are dissatisfied with this product, please return it.*

dis·sect /dɪˈsekt, daɪ-/ *v* [T] **1** to cut up the body of a dead animal or person in order to study it **2** to examine something carefully in order to understand it: *books in which the lives of famous people are dissected* **3** to divide an area of land into several smaller pieces: *fields dissected by small streams* —**dissection** /-ˈsekʃən/ *n* [C,U]

dis·sem·ble /dɪˈsembəl/ *v* [I,T] *literary* to hide your true feelings, thoughts etc

dis·sem·i·nate /dɪˈseməneɪt/ *v* [T] *formal* to spread information or ideas to as many people as possible: *Her findings have been **widely disseminated**.* —**dissemination** /dɪˌseməˈneɪʃən/ *n* [U]: *the dissemination of information*

dis·sen·sion /dɪˈsenʃən/ *n* [C,U] disagreement among a group of people: **[+in/within/between/among]** *This move **sowed dissension** within the party ranks. | The Labour Party was torn by **internal dissensions**.*

dis·sent¹ /dɪˈsent/ ●○○ *n*
1 [U] refusal to agree with an official decision or accepted opinion SYN **opposition** → **consent**, **assent**: *the ruthless suppression of political dissent | These **voices of dissent** grew louder.*
2 [C] *law* a statement by a judge giving their reasons for disagreeing with the other judges in a law case

dissent² *v* [I] **1** to say that you disagree with an official decision or accepted opinion: **[+from]** *Few historians would dissent from this view. | There are some **dissenting voices*** (=people who do not agree) *among the undergraduates.* THESAURUS ▸ DISAGREE **2** *law* if a judge dissents, they say formally that they do not agree with the other judges in a law case

dis·sent·er /dɪˈsentə $ -ər/ *n* [C] **1** a person or organization that disagrees with an official decision or accepted opinion: *Political dissenters were imprisoned.* **2** (*also* **Dissenter**) someone in the past who did not accept the beliefs of the established Protestant church in Western Europe SYN **non-conformist**

dis·ser·ta·tion /ˌdɪsəˈteɪʃən $ ˌdɪsər-/ ●○○ *n* [C] a long piece of writing on a particular subject, especially one written for a university degree → **thesis**

dis·ser·vice¹ /dɪˈsɜːvəs, dɪsˈsɜː $ -ɜːr-/ *n* **do sb/sth a disservice** (*also* **do a disservice to sb/sth**) to do something that gives other people a bad opinion of someone or something: *The fans have done the game a great disservice.*

disservice² /dɪˈsɜːvɪs, dɪsˈsɜ- $ -ɜːr-/ *v* [T] to do something that gives other people a bad opinion of someone or something: *Hart's poems are disserviced by the decision to squeeze three or even four short pieces onto one page.*

dis·si·dent /ˈdɪsɪdənt/ *n* [C] someone who publicly criticizes the government in a country where this is punished: *a political dissident* —**dissident** *adj* [only before noun]: *dissident writers* —**dissidence** *n* [U]

dis·sim·i·lar /dɪˈsɪmələ, dɪsˈsɪ- $ -ər/ AWL *adj* not the same OPP **similar**: **[+to]** *Madonna's career is **not dissimilar to*** (=is quite similar to) *Cher's.* THESAURUS ▸ DIFFERENT —**dissimilarity** /dɪˌsɪməˈlærəti, dɪsˌsɪ-/ *n* [C,U]: *dissimilarities between the US and Britain*

dis·sim·u·late /dɪˈsɪmjəleɪt/ *v* [I,T] *formal* to hide your true feelings or intentions, especially by lying

dis·si·pate /ˈdɪsəpeɪt/ *v formal* **1** [I,T] to gradually become less or weaker before disappearing completely, or to make something do this: *As he thought it over, his anger gradually dissipated. | Little by little, the smoke was dissipated by the breeze.* **2** [T] to waste something valuable such as time, money, or energy: *His savings were soon dissipated.*

dis·si·pat·ed /ˈdɪsɪpeɪtɪd/ *adj formal* spending too much time enjoying physical pleasures such as drinking alcohol in a way that is harmful

dis·si·pa·tion /ˌdɪsəˈpeɪʃən/ *n* [U] *formal* **1** the process of making something gradually weaker or less until it disappears: *the dissipation of heat* **2** the enjoyment of physical pleasures in a way that is harmful: *a life of dissipation* **3** the act of wasting money, time, energy etc: *the dissipation of resources*

dis·so·ci·ate /dɪˈsəʊʃieɪt, -sieɪt $ -ˈsoʊ-/ *v* [T] **1** to do or say something to show that you do not agree with the views or actions of someone with whom you had a connection: **dissociate yourself from sth** *I wish to dissociate myself from Mr Irvine's remarks.* **2** *technical* to regard two things or people as separate and not connected to each other OPP **associate** —**dissociation** /dɪˌsəʊʃiˈeɪʃən -siˈeɪ- $ -ˌsoʊ-/ *n* [U]

dis·so·lute /ˈdɪsəluːt/ *adj* having an immoral way of life, for example drinking too much alcohol or having sex with many people SYN **debauched**

dis·so·lu·tion /ˌdɪsəˈluːʃən/ *n* [U] **1** the act of formally ending a parliament, business, or marriage → **dissolve**: *The president announced the dissolution of the National Assembly.* **2** the act of breaking up an organization, institution etc so that it no longer exists: *the dissolution of the monasteries* **3** the process by which something gradually becomes weaker and disappears: *the eventual dissolution of class barriers*

dis·solve /dɪˈzɒlv $ dɪˈzɑːlv/ ●●○ *v*
1 BECOME PART OF LIQUID [I,T] if a solid dissolves, or if you dissolve it, it mixes with a liquid and becomes part of it: *Stir until the sugar dissolves.* | **[+in]** *Sugar dissolves in water.* | **dissolve sth in sth** *Dissolve the tablet in water.*
2 END [T] to formally end a parliament, business arrangement, marriage etc: *The monarch had the power to dissolve parliament.*
3 EMOTION **dissolve into/in laughter/tears etc** to start laughing or crying: *She dissolved into fits of laughter.*
4 BECOME WEAKER [I,T] to gradually become smaller or weaker before disappearing, or to make something do this: *Her enthusiasm dissolved his shyness. | A few clouds formed briefly before dissolving again.*

dis·so·nance /ˈdɪsənəns/ *n* **1** [C,U] *technical* a combination of notes that sound strange because they are not in HARMONY OPP **consonance** **2** [U] *formal* lack of agreement —**dissonant** *adj*

D

dis·suade /dɪˈsweɪd/ *v* [T] to persuade someone not to do something OPP **persuade**: **dissuade sb from (doing) sth** *a campaign to dissuade young people from smoking* **THESAURUS** ➤ PERSUADE —**dissuasion** /dɪˈsweɪʒən/ *n* [U]

dis·taff /ˈdɪstɑːf $ -stæf/ *n* [C] a stick, used in the past for spinning wool

dis·tance¹ /ˈdɪstəns/ ●●● S2 W2 *n*
1 AMOUNT OF SPACE [C,U] the amount of space between two places or things: **[+from/between]** *the distance from Chicago to Detroit | Measure the distance between the two points.* | *The cottage is* **some distance** (=quite a long distance) *from the road.* | **at a distance of 2 feet/10 metres etc** *A shark can smell blood at a distance of half a kilometer.*

> **REGISTER**
> In everyday English, when talking about how far something is, people often use an expression such as **how far** or **a long/short way** rather than the noun **distance**: *What is the **distance** from Chicago to Detroit?* → ***How far** is it from Chicago to Detroit?* | *The cottage is some **distance** from the road.* → *The cottage is **a long way** from the road.*

D

2 FAR AWAY [singular] used to talk about a situation when something is far away from you in space or time: **in the distance** *Church bells rang in the distance* (=they were far away). | **at/from a distance** *We watched from a distance.*
3 UNFRIENDLY FEELING [singular] a situation in which two people do not have a close friendly relationship: **[+between]** *There was still a distance between me and my father.*
4 keep your distance a) to stay far enough away from someone or something to be safe: *A lighthouse on the cliff warns ships to keep their distance.* **b)** (*also* **keep sb at a distance**) to avoid becoming too friendly with someone: *The neighbours tend to keep their distance.*
5 go the (full) distance *informal* to finish something you have started: *Do you think Greg will go the distance this time?* → LONG-DISTANCE, MIDDLE DISTANCE

COLLOCATIONS

ADJECTIVES

a long/great/considerable distance *The sound of guns seemed a long distance away.*
a short distance *I quickly walked the short distance to the car.*
a safe distance (=enough space to be safe) *You should keep a safe distance from the car in front.*
some distance (=quite a long distance) *He heard a scream some distance away.*
vast distances | **the stopping/braking distance** (=how far you travel in a car after pressing the brakes)

VERBS

travel a great/long etc distance *In some countries children must travel great distances to school each day.*
measure the distance between things *Now we are able to measure the distances between the planets.*
judge distances (=judge how much space there is between things)

PHRASES

within (easy) walking distance (=near enough to walk to easily) *There are lots of restaurants within walking distance.*
within travelling/commuting/driving distance of sth (=near enough to make travel to or from a place possible) *The job was not within travelling distance of my home.*
within striking distance of sth (=not far from something, especially something you are going to attack) | **within spitting distance** *informal* (=very near something)

distance² *v* **distance yourself (from sth)** to say that you are not involved with someone or something, especially to avoid being connected with them: *The UNO has firmly distanced itself from the anti-government movement.*

ˈdistance ˌlearning *n* [U] a method of study that involves working at home and sending your work to your teacher

dis·tant /ˈdɪstənt/ ●●○ W3 *adj*
1 FAR AWAY far away in space or time: *the sound of distant gunfire | Her honeymoon seemed a* **distant memory**. | *That affair was* **in the dim and distant past** (=a long time ago). | *The president hopes to visit Ireland* **in the not too distant future** (=quite soon). | **[+from]** *stars that are distant from our galaxy* **THESAURUS** ➤ FAR
2 NOT FRIENDLY unfriendly: *After the quarrel Sue remained cold and distant.*
3 NOT CONCENTRATING thinking deeply about something private, rather than about what is happening around you: *Geri had a distant look in her eyes.*
4 RELATIVE [only before noun] not closely related to you OPP **close**: *a distant cousin*
5 distant from sth different from something or not closely connected with it: *The reality of independence was distant from the hopes they had had.* —**distantly** *adv*: *We are* ***distantly related***.

dis·taste /dɪsˈteɪst/ *n* [U] a feeling that something or someone is unpleasant or morally offensive: **[+for]** *her distaste for any form of compromise*

dis·taste·ful /dɪsˈteɪstfəl/ *adj* unpleasant or morally offensive: *What follows is John's story. Parts of it may seem distasteful, even shocking.*

dis·taste·ful·ly /dɪsˈteɪstfəli/ *adv written* feeling or showing distaste: *She looked distastefully at the overflowing bin.*

dis·tem·per /dɪˈstempə $ -ər/ *n* [U] **1** a serious infectious disease that affects animals, especially dogs **2** *BrE* a type of paint that you mix with water to paint walls

dis·tend /dɪˈstend/ *v* [I,T] *formal* to swell or make something swell because of pressure from inside —**distended** *adj*: *a distended stomach* —**distension** /-ˈtenʃən/ *n* [U] *technical*

dis·till, **distil** /dɪˈstɪl/ *v* (**distilled**, **distilling**) [T] **1** to make a liquid such as water or alcohol more pure by heating it so that it becomes a gas and then letting it cool. Drinks such as WHISKY are made this way: *distilled water* **2** to remove a chemical substance from a plant, for example by heating or pressing it **3** to get the main ideas or facts from a much larger amount of information: **distill sth into sth** *The notes I had brought back were waiting to be distilled into a book.* —**distillation** /ˌdɪstəˈleɪʃən/ *n* [C,U]

dis·til·ler /dɪˈstɪlə $ -ər/ *n* [C] a person or company that makes strong alcoholic drinks such as WHISKY

dis·til·le·ry /dɪˈstɪləri/ *n* (*plural* **distilleries**) [C] a factory where strong alcoholic drink such as WHISKY is produced

dis·tinct /dɪˈstɪŋkt/ ●●○ W3 AWL *adj*
1 clearly different or belonging to a different type: *two* ***entirely distinct*** *languages* | **distinct types/groups/categories etc** *There are four distinct types.* | **[+from]** *The learning needs of the two groups are* ***quite distinct*** *from each other.*
2 as distinct from sth used to make it clear that you are not referring to a particular kind of thing, but to something else: *a movie star, as distinct from an actor*
3 something that is distinct can clearly be seen, heard, smelled etc OPP **indistinct**: *The outline of the ship became more distinct.*
4 [only before noun] a distinct possibility, feeling, quality etc definitely exists and cannot be ignored: *I got the* ***distinct impression*** *he was trying to make me angry.* | ***There is a distinct possibility that*** *this will eventually be needed.* | *a* ***distinct lack of*** *enthusiasm*

dis·tinc·tion /dɪˈstɪŋkʃən/ ●●○ W3 AWL *n*
1 DIFFERENCE [C,U] a clear difference or separation between two similar things: **[+between]** *the distinction between formal and informal language* | **clear/sharp distinction** *There is often no clear distinction between an allergy and food intolerance.* | **make/draw a distinction** *The Act* ***makes no***

distinction *between children and adults* (=it treats them as if they were the same).

REGISTER
In written English, people often use **draw a distinction** rather than **make a distinction**, because it sounds more formal: *The law **draws a distinction** between temporary and permanent employees.*

2 EXCELLENCE [U] the quality of being excellent and important: *Eliot's distinction as a poet*
3 BEING SPECIAL [singular] the quality of being special in some way: **have/earn/achieve etc the distinction of doing sth** *At that time, it had the distinction of being the largest bridge in the UK.* | *The US enjoys the **dubious distinction** of being the lawsuit capital of the world.*
4 RESULT [C,U] a special mark given to a student whose work is excellent: **with distinction** *He obtained a law doctorate with distinction.*

dis·tinc·tive /dɪˈstɪŋktɪv/ ●●○ AWL *adj* having a special quality, character, or appearance that is different and easy to recognize: *a rock band with a distinctive sound* THESAURUS ▸ DIFFERENT —**distinctively** *adv* —**distinctiveness** *n* [U]

dis·tinct·ly /dɪˈstɪŋktli/ ●○○ AWL *adv*
1 clearly OPP **indistinctly**: *Speak clearly and distinctly.* | *He **distinctly remembered** the day his father left.*
2 very: *Paul was left **feeling distinctly** foolish.* | **distinctly uncomfortable/uneasy/unhappy etc**
3 used to say that something has a particular quality or character that is easy to recognize: *dishes with a distinctly Jewish flavor*

dis·tin·guish /dɪˈstɪŋgwɪʃ/ ●●○ S3 W3 *v*
1 [I,T] to recognize and understand the difference between two or more things or people SYN **differentiate**: **[+between]** *His attorney argued that Cope could not distinguish between right and wrong.* | **distinguish sb/sth from** *a method of distinguishing cancer cells from normal tissue* THESAURUS ▸ RECOGNIZE

REGISTER
In everyday English, people usually use the phrases **tell the difference between sb/sth** or **tell sb/sth from sb/sth**, rather than **distinguish**: *He can't **tell the difference between** right and wrong.* | *How do you **tell** cancer cells **from** healthy cells?*

2 [T not in progressive] to be the thing that makes someone or something different or special: **distinguish sb/sth from** *The factor that distinguishes this company from the competition is customer service.* | **distinguishing feature/mark/characteristic** *The main distinguishing feature of this species is the leaf shape.*
3 [T not in progressive] *written* to be able to see the shape of something or hear a particular sound: *The light was too dim for me to distinguish anything clearly.*
4 distinguish yourself to do something so well that people notice and remember you: *He distinguished himself on several occasions in the civil war.*

dis·tin·guish·a·ble /dɪˈstɪŋgwɪʃəbəl/ *adj* easy to recognize as being different from something else OPP **indistinguishable**: **[+from]** *The fake was barely distinguishable from the original painting.* | **barely/hardly/scarcely distinguishable** | **clearly/easily/readily distinguishable** *The cheese is easily distinguishable by its colour.*

dis·tin·guished /dɪˈstɪŋgwɪʃt/ ●●○ *adj*
1 successful, respected, and admired: *a long and distinguished career*
2 dressed in neat and attractive clothes that are worn by adults, not looking like a young person: *a tall distinguished figure in a dark suit*

dis·tort /dɪˈstɔːt $ -ɔːrt/ ●○○ AWL *v*
1 [I,T] to change the appearance, sound, or shape of something so that it is strange or unclear: *Tall buildings can distort radio signals.*
2 [T] to report something in a way that is not completely true or correct: *His account was badly distorted by the press.*
3 [T] to change a situation from the way it would naturally be: *an expensive subsidy which distorts the market* —**distorted** *adj*: *His face was distorted in anger.* —**distortion** /dɪˈstɔːʃən $ -ɔːr-/ *n* [C,U]: *a gross distortion of the facts*

dis·tract /dɪˈstrækt/ ●●○ *v* [T] to take someone's attention away from something by making them look at or listen to something else: *Try not to distract the other students.* | **distract sb/sth from sth** *Coverage of the war was used to **distract attention** from other matters.* —**distracting** *adj*

dis·tract·ed /dɪˈstræktɪd/ *adj* anxious and unable to think clearly —**distractedly** *adv*

disˌtracted ˈdriving *n* [U] *AmE* driving while your attention is on something else, for example a MOBILE PHONE

dis·trac·tion /dɪˈstrækʃən/ ●○○ *n*
1 [C,U] something that stops you paying attention to what you are doing: *I study in the library as there are too many distractions at home.* | **[+from]** *Demands for equality were seen as a distraction from more serious issues.*
2 drive sb to distraction to continue annoying or upsetting someone very much: *The baby's constant crying drove me to distraction.*
3 [C] *old-fashioned* a pleasant activity

dis·traught /dɪˈstrɔːt $ -ˈstrɒːt/ *adj* so upset and worried that you cannot think clearly: *Relatives are tonight comforting the distraught parents.* THESAURUS ▸ SAD

dis·tress¹ /dɪˈstres/ ●●○ *n* [U]
1 a feeling of extreme unhappiness: *Luke's behaviour caused his parents great distress.* | **in distress** *The girl was crying and clearly in distress.*
2 suffering and problems caused by a lack of money, food etc: *acute financial distress* | **in distress** *charities that aid families in distress*
3 *formal* great physical pain
4 a situation when a ship, aircraft etc is in danger and needs help: *We picked up a **distress signal** 6 km away.* | **in distress** *The ship is in distress.*

distress² ●○○ *v* [T] to make someone feel very upset: *The dream had distressed her greatly.*

dis·tressed /dɪˈstrest/ ●○○ *adj*
1 very upset: **deeply/visibly distressed** *Hannah was deeply distressed by the news.* | **[+at/by]** *My client is very distressed at the treatment she received from your officers.* | **distressed to find/hear/see/learn etc sth** *She was distressed to see he was crying.* THESAURUS ▸ SAD
2 *technical* in a lot of pain: *The animal was clearly distressed.*
3 distressed furniture or clothes have been made to look older than they really are
4 *formal* having very little money: *a family living in distressed circumstances*

dis·tress·ing /dɪˈstresɪŋ/ (*also* **dis·tress·ful** /dɪˈstresfəl/) *adj* making you feel very upset: *a distressing experience* —**distressingly** *adv*

dis·trib·ute /dɪˈstrɪbjuːt/ ●●○ W2 AWL *v* [T]
1 to share things among a group of people, especially in a planned way SYN **give out**: **distribute sth among/to sb** *Clothes and blankets have been distributed among the refugees.* | *a man distributing leaflets to passers-by* THESAURUS ▸ GIVE
2 to supply goods to shops and companies so that they can sell them: *Milk is distributed to the local shops by Herald's Dairies.*
3 to spread something over a large area: *Make sure the weight of the load is **evenly distributed**.*
4 be distributed to exist in different parts of an area or group: **be widely/evenly distributed** *This species of dolphin is widely distributed throughout the world.* | *The population is distributed in a very uneven pattern.*

dis·tri·bu·tion /ˌdɪstrəˈbjuːʃən/ ●●○ W3 AWL *n*
1 [U] the act of sharing things among a large group of

D

people in a planned way: **[+of]** *the distribution of aid supplies*
2 [U] when goods are supplied to shops and companies for them to sell: *a distribution centre*
3 [C,U] the way in which something exists in different amounts in different parts of an area or group: *population distribution* | **[+of]** *the highly unequal distribution of economic power*

dis·trib·u·tive /dɪˈstrɪbjətɪv/ AWL *adj* [usually before noun] connected with distribution: *distributive costs*

dis·trib·u·tor /dɪˈstrɪbjətə $ -ər/ ●●○ *n* [C]
1 a company or person that supplies shops and companies with goods
2 the part of an engine that sends an electric current to the SPARK PLUGS

dis·trib·u·tor·ship /dɪˈstrɪbjətəʃɪp $ -ər-/ *n* [C] a company that has an arrangement to sell the products of another company: *the UK distributorship for Sol lighting products*

dis·trict /ˈdɪstrɪkt/ ●●● S3 W2 *n* [C]
1 an area of a town or the countryside, especially one with particular features: **rural/financial/theatre etc district** *a house in a pleasant suburban district* THESAURUS ➤ AREA
2 an area of a country, city etc that has official borders: *a postal district*

ˌdistrict atˈtorney *n* [C] a lawyer in the US who works for the government in a particular area and who is responsible for bringing people who may be criminals to court

ˌdistrict ˈcouncil *n* [C] *BrE* a group of people elected to organize local services such as education, health services etc in a particular area

ˌdistrict ˈcourt *n* [C] a US court of law which deals with cases involving national rather than state law

ˌdistrict ˈnurse *n* [C] *BrE* a nurse who visits people in their own homes

dis·trust¹ /dɪsˈtrʌst/ ●○○ *n* [U] a feeling that you cannot trust someone → **mistrust**: *Local people regard the police with suspicion and distrust.* | **[+of]** *Dylan's* ***deep distrust*** *of journalists made him difficult to interview.* —**distrustful** *adj*

distrust² ●○○ *v* [T] to not trust someone or something OPP **trust**: *She had every reason to distrust him.*

dis·turb /dɪˈstɜːb $ -ɜːrb/ ●●○ W3 *v* [T]
1 INTERRUPT to interrupt someone so that they cannot continue what they are doing: ***Sorry to disturb you****, but I have an urgent message.* | *The thieves fled when they were disturbed by a neighbour.* | **Do not disturb** (=a sign you put on a door so that people will not interrupt you).
2 WORRY to make someone feel worried or upset: *What disturbs you most about this latest development?*
3 MOVE to move something or change its position: *If you find a bird's nest, never disturb the eggs.* | *I promise not to* ***disturb anything****.*
4 CHANGE to change a normal situation in a way that causes problems: *My hormone balance is disturbed by my pregnancy.* | *New procedures often disturb the comfortable habits of the workforce.*
5 disturb the peace *law* to behave in a noisy and unpleasant way in public

dis·turb·ance /dɪˈstɜːbəns $ -ɜːr-/ ●○○ *n*
1 [C,U] *formal* a situation in which people behave violently in public: *There were disturbances in the crowd as fans left the stadium.* | **create/cause a disturbance** | *army training on controlling* ***civil disturbance***
2 [C,U] something that interrupts what you are doing, or the act of making this happen: *We arrange the work so there's as little disturbance as possible.* | **[+to]** *When a helicopter lands, it can* ***cause*** *a* ***disturbance*** *to local residents.*
3 [U] a medical condition in which someone is mentally ill and does not behave normally: *a history of mental disturbance*

dis·turbed /dɪˈstɜːbd $ -ɜːrbd/ *adj* **1** not behaving normally because of a mental condition: **mentally/emotionally disturbed** *the care of emotionally* ***disturbed children*** | *while the balance of his mind was disturbed* **2** worried or upset: **[+by/about/at]** *Police are very disturbed about the latest trend.* | **seriously/deeply/greatly etc disturbed** | **disturbed to find/see/discover/learn etc** *She was disturbed to learn he had bought a motorbike.* | **disturbed that** *I'm disturbed that so many of the students appear to be illiterate.* **3 disturbed sleep** sleep that is interrupted

dis·turb·ing /dɪˈstɜːbɪŋ $ -ɜːr-/ ●●○ *adj* worrying or upsetting: *a disturbing increase in the crime rate* —**disturbingly** *adv*

dis·u·nited /ˌdɪsjuːˈnaɪtɪd/ *adj* people who are disunited are in the same organization, country, or group but cannot agree or work with each other

dis·u·ni·ty /dɪsˈjuːnəti/ *n* [U] a situation in which a group of people cannot agree or work with each other: *Disunity destroyed the Republicans at the polls.*

dis·use /dɪsˈjuːs/ *n* [U] a situation in which something is no longer used: *The building eventually* ***fell into disuse****.*

dis·used /ˌdɪsˈjuːzd◂/ *adj* [usually before noun] a disused building, railway, mine etc is no longer used

ditch¹ /dɪtʃ/ ●●○ *n* [C] a long narrow hole dug at the side of a field, road etc to hold or remove unwanted water → LAST-DITCH

ditch² *v* **1** [T] *informal* to stop having something because you no longer want it: *The government has ditched plans to privatise the prison.* **2** [T] *informal* to end a romantic relationship with someone: *Meg and Neil were due to marry, but she ditched him.* **3** [T] *AmE spoken informal* to not go to school, a class etc when you should SYN **skip** *BrE*: *Did you ditch class today?* **4** [T] *AmE spoken informal* to leave someone you are with in a place without telling them you are going **5** [I,T] to land an aircraft in a controlled crash into water: *Two balloonists had to ditch during the race.*

ditch·wa·ter /ˈdɪtʃwɔːtə $ -wɒːtər, -wɑː-/ *n* **as dull as ditchwater** *BrE* very boring

dith·er /ˈdɪðə $ -ər/ *v* [I] to keep being unable to make a final decision about something: **[+over/about/between]** *He accused the government of dithering over the deal.* | ***Stop dithering****, girl, and get on with it!* —**ditherer** *n* [C]

di·tran·si·tive /ˌdaɪˈtrænsətɪv, -zə-/ *adj* a ditransitive verb has an INDIRECT OBJECT and a DIRECT OBJECT. 'Give' in the sentence 'Give me the book' is ditransitive. → **intransitive**, **transitive**

dit·sy /ˈdɪtsi/ *adj* another spelling of DITZY

dit·to¹ /ˈdɪtəʊ $ -toʊ/ ●○○ *adv spoken informal*
1 used to say that you have exactly the same opinion as someone else: *'I hated school.' 'Ditto.'*
2 used to say that what is true of one thing is also true of another: *Where should she go? Mississippi? Too hot. Ditto Alabama.*

ditto² (*also* **ˈditto mark**) *n* (*plural* **dittoes**) [C] *written* a mark (") that you write immediately under a word in a list to show that the same word is repeated

dit·ty /ˈdɪti/ *n* (*plural* **ditties**) [C] a short simple poem or song – used humorously

dit·zy, **ditsy** /ˈdɪtsi/ *adj AmE informal* silly or stupid, and likely to forget things easily —**ditz** *n* [C]

di·u·ret·ic /ˌdaɪjʊˈretɪk◂/ *n* [C] *medical* a substance that increases the flow of URINE —**diuretic** *adj*

di·ur·nal /daɪˈɜːnəl $ -ˈɜːr-/ *adj technical* **1** happening or active in the daytime OPP **nocturnal** **2** happening every day

Div. (*also* **Div** *BrE*) *n* the written abbreviation of ***division***

di·va /ˈdiːvə/ *n* [C] **1** a very successful and famous female singer: *opera diva Jessye Norman* **2** a famous or important woman who behaves badly or gets angry when people do not give her the attention or treatment she thinks she deserves: *She's such a diva - she walked out of the interview because she thought the interviewer was rude.*

di·van /dɪˈvæn $ ˈdaɪvæn/ *n* [C] **1** a bed with a thick base **2** a long low soft seat without a back or arms

dive¹ /daɪv/ ●●○ *v* (*past tense* **dived** *also* **dove** /dəʊv $ doʊv/ *AmE, past participle* **dived**) [I]

1 JUMP INTO WATER to jump into deep water with your head and arms going in first: **[+into/off etc]** *She dived into a pool.* | *Diving off the cliffs is dangerous.* THESAURUS JUMP → see picture at JUMP[1]
2 SWIM UNDER WATER to swim under water using special equipment to help you breathe: *The first time you dive on a coral reef is an experience you will never forget.*
3 GO DEEPER/LOWER to travel down through the air or through water to a lower level: *The submarine began to dive.* | *The aircraft appeared to dive vertically towards the crowd.*
4 MOVE QUICKLY [always + adv/prep] to move or jump quickly in a particular direction or into a particular place: *Jackson dived after the ball.* | *We dived into a shop to avoid the rain.* | *The soldiers were* ***diving for cover*** (=to protect themselves behind something).
5 **dive into your bag/pocket etc** to put your hand quickly in your bag, pocket etc in order to get something out: *He dived into his pocket and produced a packet of cigarettes.*
6 NUMBERS if numbers, prices etc dive, they suddenly become much lower than before: *The dollar dived against the yen in Tokyo today.*
7 SOCCER to fall down deliberately in order to unfairly win a FREEKICK or a PENALTY
dive in *phr v* to start doing something eagerly: *Harvey dived in with several questions.*

dive² ●●○ *n* [C]
1 SUDDEN MOVEMENT a sudden movement in a particular direction or into a particular place: *She* ***made a dive for*** *the bathroom.*
2 SUDDEN FALL a sudden fall in the amount, value, or success of something: *The news* ***put*** *shares* ***in a dive***. | *The team's fortunes have* ***taken a dive*** *this year.*
3 MOVEMENT DOWNWARDS when something moves down through the air or water: *Thankfully, the pilot managed to* ***pull out of*** *the* ***dive*** *and regain control.* | **steep/vertical dive**
4 JUMP a jump into deep water with your head and arms going in first
5 SWIM the act of going under water to swim, using special equipment to help you breathe
6 PLACE *informal* a bar, club etc that is cheap and dirty
7 SOCCER the act of falling down deliberately in order to unfairly win a FREEKICK or a PENALTY

ˈdive-bomb *v* [I,T] if an aircraft dive-bombs a place, it drops bombs on it —**dive-bomber** *n* [C]

div·er /ˈdaɪvə $ -ər/ ●●○ *n* [C]
1 someone who swims or works under water using special equipment to help them breathe
2 someone who jumps into water with their head and arms first

di·verge /daɪˈvɜːdʒ, də- $ -ɜːrdʒ/ *v* [I] **1** if similar things diverge, they develop in different ways and so are no longer similar: *The two species diverged millions of years ago.* | *Global growth rates are diverging markedly.* **2** if opinions, interests etc diverge, they are different from each other: **[+from]** *Here his views diverged from hers.* **3** if two lines or paths diverge, they separate and go in different directions OPP **converge** —**divergence** *n* [C,U]: *divergence between the US and Europe* —**divergent** *adj*: ***divergent views***

di·verse /daɪˈvɜːs $ dəˈvɜːrs, daɪ-/ ●●○ AWL *adj* very different from each other: *subjects as diverse as pop music and archaeology* —**diversely** *adv*

di·ver·si·fy /daɪˈvɜːsɪfaɪ $ dəˈvɜːr-, daɪ-/ ●○○ AWL *v* (**diversified**, **diversifying**, **diversifies**)
1 [I,T] if a business, company, country etc diversifies, it increases the range of goods or services it produces: **[+(away) from]** *farmers forced to diversify away from their core business* | **[+into]** *The company is planning to diversify into other mining activities.* | *We need to diversify the economy.*
2 [I,T] to change something or to make it change so that there is more variety: *User requirements have diversified over the years.*
3 [I] *technical* to put money into several different types of INVESTMENT instead of only one or two: **[+into]** *Spread the risk by diversifying into dollar bonds.* —**diversification** /daɪˌvɜːsɪfɪˈkeɪʃən $ dəˌvɜːr-, daɪ-/ *n* [U]: *diversification of the rural economy*

di·ver·sion /daɪˈvɜːʃən, də- $ -ɜːrʒən/ ●○○ *n*
1 [C,U] a change in the direction or use of something, or the act of changing it: **[+of]** *the diversion of the river* | *the diversion of funds into the military budget*
2 [C,U] an enjoyable activity that you do to stop yourself from becoming bored
3 [C] something that stops you from paying attention to what you are doing or what is happening: *Two prisoners* ***created a diversion*** *to give the men time to escape.*
4 [C] *BrE* a different way that traffic is sent when the usual roads are closed

di·ver·sion·a·ry /daɪˈvɜːʃənəri, də- $ -ˈvɜːrʒəneri/ *adj written* intended to take someone's attention away from something: *Most children are skilled in* ***diversionary tactics***.

di·ver·si·ty /daɪˈvɜːsəti, də- $ -ɜːr-/ ●●○ AWL *n*
1 [U] the fact of including many different types of people or things: **cultural/ethnic/linguistic etc diversity** *The curriculum will take account of the ethnic diversity of the population.*
2 [singular] a range of different people, things, or ideas SYN **variety**: **[+of]** *a diversity of opinions*

di·vert /daɪˈvɜːt, də- $ -ɜːrt/ ●○○ *v* [T]
1 to change the use of something such as time or money: **divert sth into/to/(away) from etc sth** *The company should* ***divert*** *more* ***resources*** *into research.* | *Officials diverted revenue from arms sales to the rebels.*
2 to change the direction in which something travels: **divert a river/footpath/road etc** *Canals divert water from the Truckee River into the lake.* | *The high street is closed and* ***traffic*** *is being* ***diverted***.
3 if you divert your telephone calls, you arrange for them to go directly to another number, for example because you are not able to answer them yourself for some time: *Remember to divert your phone when you are out of the office.*
4 to deliberately take someone's attention from something by making them think about or notice other things: **divert (sb's) attention (away from sb/sth)** *The crime crackdown is an attempt to divert attention from social problems.* | *He'd been trying to* ***divert suspicion*** *away* ***from*** *himself.*
5 *formal* to amuse or entertain someone

di·vert·ing /daɪˈvɜːtɪŋ, daɪ- $ -ɜːr-/ *adj formal* entertaining and amusing: *a mildly diverting film*

di·vest /daɪˈvest, də-/ *v* [I,T] *technical* if a company divests, it sells some of its ASSETS, INVESTMENTS etc: *pressure on hospitals to divest tobacco-related stocks*
divest sb of sth *phr v formal* **1** **divest yourself of sth** to sell or give away something you own: *Dad had long since divested himself of anything valuable.* **2** **divest yourself of sth** to remove something you are wearing or carrying: *Pedro divested himself of his overcoat.* **3** to take something away from someone: *The king was divested of all his wealth and power.*

di·vest·ment /daɪˈvestmənt/ *n* [C,U] *technical* another word for DISINVESTMENT

di·vide¹ /dəˈvaɪd/ ●●● S2 W2 *v*
1 SEPARATE [I,T] if something divides, or if you divide it, it separates into two or more parts: **divide sth into sth** *Scientists traditionally divide the oceans into zones.* | *The book is divided into six sections.* | **[+into]** *Here, the river divides into three channels.* THESAURUS SEPARATE
2 KEEP SEPARATE (*also* **divide off**) [T] to keep two areas separate from each other: *The Wall used to divide East and West Berlin.* | **divide sth from sth** *Only a thin curtain divided her cabin from his.*
3 SHARE (*also* **divide up**) [T] to separate something into parts and share them between people: **divide sth between/among sb/sth** *The money will be* ***divided equally*** *among the charities.*
4 SPEND TIME/ENERGY [T] if you divide your time, energy etc between different activities or places, you spend part of your time doing each activity or in each place: **divide sth between sth/sb** *She divides her time between New York and Paris.*
5 MATHEMATICS **a)** [T] to calculate how many times one

D

number contains a smaller number → **multiply**: **divide sth by sth** *If you divide 21 by 3, you get 7.* | *'What's six divided by three?' 'Two'.* **b)** [I] to be contained exactly in a number one or more times: **[+into]** *8 divides into 64.*
6 DISAGREE [T] to make people disagree so that they form groups with different opinions: *The issue of cloning has* ***sharply divided*** *voters.*
7 divide and rule/conquer to defeat or control people by making them argue with each other instead of opposing you
8 divided loyalties a feeling you have when two people you like have argued and you are not sure which person you should support: *Divorce is an agony of divided loyalties for children.* —**divided** *adj*: *a* ***deeply divided*** *society* | *The committee was divided over the proposal.*

divide² *n* [C usually singular] **1** a strong difference between the beliefs or way of life of groups of people, that may make them hate each other: *The* ***North/South divide*** *is characteristic of Britain.* | **cultural/political/racial etc divide** *people on both* ***sides of the*** *political* ***divide*** **2** *AmE* a line of high ground between two river systems SYN **watershed**

di,vided 'highway *n* [C] *AmE* a main road with two lines of traffic travelling in each direction, separated by a piece of land SYN **dual carriageway** *BrE*

div·i·dend /ˈdɪvədənd, -dend/ *n* [C] **1** a part of a company's profit that is divided among the people with SHARES in the company **2** *BrE* prize money offered in a national competition called the FOOTBALL POOLS which people can win by correctly guessing the results of football games **3** *technical* a number that is to be divided by another number **4 pay/bring dividends** to be very useful and bring a lot of advantages, especially later in the future: *Good eating habits will pay dividends later on in life.*

di·vid·er /dəˈvaɪdə $ -ər/ *n* [C] **1** something that divides something else into parts: *a room divider* | *alphabetical file dividers* **2** *AmE* a piece of land that separates traffic travelling in opposite directions on a main road SYN **reservation** *BrE*: *Police saw his Mercedes speeding along the center divider.* **3 dividers** [plural] an instrument used for measuring or marking lines or angles, consisting of two pointed pieces of metal joined together at the top → see picture at **MATHEMATICS**

di'viding ,line *n* [C usually singular] the difference between two similar things: **[+between]** *What's the dividing line between normal drinking and addiction?*

div·i·na·tion /ˌdɪvəˈneɪʃən/ *n* [U] the ability to say what will happen in the future, or the act of doing this

di·vine¹ /dəˈvaɪn/ ●●○ *adj*
1 coming from or relating to God or a god: **divine intervention/providence/revelation/guidance etc** *faith in divine providence* | *divine power* | *divine love*
2 *old-fashioned* very pleasant or good —**divinely** *adv*: *a divinely inspired idea*

divine² *v* **1** [T] *literary* to discover or guess something: **divine that** *Somehow, the children had divined that he was lying.* **2** [I] to search for underground water or minerals using a Y-shaped stick: *a* ***divining rod*** (=the stick used for this) —**diviner** *n* [C]

di,vine 'right *n* [singular] **1** the right given to a king or queen by God to rule a country, that in former times could not be opposed **2** *informal* the right to do what you want without having to ask permission: *Being my wife doesn't* ***give*** *you* ***the divine right to*** *read my mail.*

div·ing /ˈdaɪvɪŋ/ *n* [U] **1** the sport of swimming under water using special equipment to help you breathe: *We* ***went diving*** *on the coral reef.* **2** the activity of jumping into water with your head and arms first → **SCUBA DIVING**

'diving bell *n* [C] a metal container that is open at the bottom and filled with air under pressure, in which people can work under water

'diving board *n* [C] a board above the edge of a SWIMMING POOL which people DIVE from

di·vin·i·ty /dəˈvɪnəti/ *n* (*plural* **divinities**) **1** [U] *AmE* the study of God and religious beliefs SYN **theology** *BrE*: *a graduate of Harvard divinity school* **2** [U] the quality or state of being a god **3** [C] a god → **divine**

di·vis·i·ble /dəˈvɪzəbəl/ *adj* [not before noun] able to be divided, for example by a number OPP **indivisible**: **[+by]** *6 is divisible by 3.* | **[+into]** *The story is divisible into three parts.*

di·vi·sion /dəˈvɪʒən/ ●●● S3 W1 *n*
1 SEPARATING [C,U] the act of separating something into two or more different parts, or the way these parts are separated or shared: **division of sth between/among/into sth** *the division of words into syllables* | *the traditional* ***division of labour*** (=the way that particular tasks are shared) *between husband and wife*
2 DISAGREEMENT [C,U] disagreement among the members of a group that makes them form smaller opposing groups: **division between/within/among sth** *Can he heal the* ***deep divisions*** *among Republican ranks?* | **racial/class/gender etc division** *The old class divisions had begun to break down.* | *The Army was plagued by* ***internal divisions.***
3 MATHEMATICS [U] the process of finding out how many times one number is contained in another → **multiplication**, **long division**
4 PART OF AN ORGANIZATION [C] a group that does a particular job within a large organization: *the Computer Services Division*
5 MILITARY [C] a large military group: *a tank division*
6 SPORT [C] one of the groups of teams that a sports competition is divided into, often based on the number of games they have won: **the Premier/First/Second/Third/Fourth Division** *a second-division club*
7 IN PARLIAMENT [C] a process in which members of the British parliament vote for something by dividing into groups: *MPs* ***forced a division*** *on the bill.* | *Some members supported the opposition in the* ***division lobbies*** (=the rooms where the vote takes place).

di·vi·sion·al /dəˈvɪʒənəl/ *adj* [only before noun] relating to one of the parts into which a large organization, group etc is divided: *divisional headquarters*

di·vi·sive /dəˈvaɪsɪv/ *adj* causing a lot of disagreement between people: *The strike was a* ***divisive issue*** *in the community.* | **socially/economically/politically etc divisive** *socially divisive policies*

di·vi·sor /dəˈvaɪzə $ -ər/ *n* [C] *technical* the number by which another number is to be divided

di·vorce¹ /dəˈvɔːs $ -ɔːrs/ ●●● S2 W2 *n*
1 [C,U] the legal ending of a marriage → **separation**: *Why doesn't she* ***get a divorce****?* | *One in three marriages* ***ends in divorce.*** | **file/sue/petition for divorce** (=start the legal divorce process) | *His wife has* ***started divorce proceedings.*** | *the rise in the* ***divorce rate*** | *She received the house as part of the* ***divorce settlement*** (=the amount of money, property etc each person receives in a divorce case). | *The Act extended the* ***grounds*** (=legal reasons) ***for divorce.***
2 [C usually singular] *formal* the fact of separating two related things: **[+between]** *the divorce between theory and method*

divorce² ●●● S2 W3 *v*
1 [I,T] if someone divorces their husband or wife, or if two people divorce, they legally end their marriage → **separate**: *David's parents divorced when he was six.* | *My father threatened to divorce her.*
2 [T] *formal* to separate two ideas, subjects etc completely: **divorce sth from sth** *It is difficult to divorce sport from politics.*
3 [T] to stop being involved in an activity, organization, situation etc: **divorce yourself from sth** *Our society has divorced itself from religion.*

di·vorced /dəˈvɔːst $ -ɔːrst/ ●●● S2 W3 *adj*
1 no longer married to your wife or husband: *Are you married, single, or divorced?* | *a divorced woman* | **[+from]** *Anne is divorced from Simon's father.* | *My parents are* ***getting divorced.*** THESAURUS ▸ MARRIED
2 separate from and not connected in any way to an idea, subject etc: **[+from]** *His ideas are completely* ***divorced from reality.***

di·vor·cée /dəˌvɔːˈsiː $ dəˌvɔːrˈseɪ/ *n* [C] **1** *AmE old-fashioned* a woman who is divorced **2** *BrE* a man or woman who is divorced

div·ot /ˈdɪvət/ *n* [C] a small piece of earth and grass that you dig out accidentally while playing a sport such as GOLF or POLO

di·vulge /daɪˈvʌldʒ, də-/ *v* [T] *formal* to give someone information that should be secret SYN **reveal**: **divulge information/secrets/details etc (to sb)** *It is not company policy to divulge personal details of employees.* | **divulge that** *Clare divulged that she was recovering from a nervous breakdown.* | **divulge what/where etc** *The Pentagon refused to divulge what type of plane it was.* THESAURUS ▸ REVEAL

div·vy[1] /ˈdɪvi/ *n* (*plural* **divvies**) [C] *BrE informal* a stupid person

divvy[2] *v* (**divvied, divvying, divvies**)

divvy sth ↔ **up** *phr v informal* to share something between several people: *We can divvy up the profits between us.*

Di·wa·li /dɪˈwɑːli/ (*also* **Di·va·li** /-ˈvɑːli/) *n* [U] a Hindu FESTIVAL that is celebrated in the autumn

Dix·ie /ˈdɪksi/ *n informal* the southern states of the US that fought against the northern states in the Civil War

Dix·ie·land /ˈdɪksilænd/ *n* [U] a type of traditional JAZZ music

DIY /ˌdiː aɪ ˈwaɪ/ *n* [U] *BrE* (***do-it-yourself***) the activity of making or repairing things yourself instead of buying them or paying someone else to do it

diz·zy /ˈdɪzi/ ●●○ *adj*

1 feeling unable to stand steadily, for example because you are looking down from a high place or because you are ill: *The heat and the champagne made him **feel dizzy**.* | *She started to suffer from **dizzy spells*** (=a short period when you feel dizzy). | **[+with]** *Ruth felt dizzy with relief.*

2 the dizzy heights (of sth) an important position – used humorously: *Naomi had **reached the dizzy heights of** manageress.*

3 *informal* stupid and forgetful: *a dizzy blonde*

4 very busy and exciting: *Hong Kong buzzes from dawn to dusk at a dizzy pace.* —**dizziness** *n* [U]: *headaches, dizziness, and vomiting* —**dizzily** *adv*

diz·zy·ing /ˈdizi-ɪŋ/ *adj* making you feel dizzy: *The riverbank rushed towards her with dizzying speed.*

DJ /ˌdiː ˈdʒeɪ◂/ *n* [C] (***disc jockey***) someone who plays records on a radio show or in a club where you can dance

djinn /dʒɪn/ *n* [C] an invisible creature with special powers in Islamic stories SYN **genie**

DNA /ˌdiː en ˈeɪ◂/ ●○○ *n* [U] (***deoxyribonucleic acid***) a substance that carries GENETIC information in the cells of the body: *A **DNA test** showed that he was not the baby's father.*

ˌDNA ˈprofiling (*also* **DNA fingerprinting**) *n* [U] the act of examining the DNA found where a crime has happened and the DNA of people who may have committed the crime, in order to find out who is responsible

ˌDNA ˈsequencing *n* [U] the act of finding out the order of the MOLECULES that some DNA consists of SYN **gene sequencing**

DNS park·ing /ˌdː en es ˈpɑːkɪŋ $ -pːr-/ *n* [U] the practice of putting a particular DOMAIN NAME (=name used as part of an Internet address) on the official list of domain names, but then not using it in an Internet address until some time in the future. This is done in order to stop the domain name being used by anyone else.

do[1] /duː/ ●●● S1 W1 *auxiliary verb* (*past tense* **did** /dɪd/, *past participle* **done** /dʌn/, *third person singular* **does** /dəz; *strong* dʌz/)

1 a) used with another verb to form questions or negatives: *Do you like bananas?* | *I don't feel like going out tonight.* | *Ian didn't answer.* | *Where do you live?* | *Doesn't Rosie look wonderful?* | *Don't listen to her!* **b)** *spoken* used to form QUESTION TAGS (=short questions that you add to the end of statements): *You know Tony, don't you?* | *She didn't understand, did she?*

2 used instead of repeating a verb that has already been used: *'Will Kay come?' 'She may do.'* | *So now you know as much as I do.* | *'You forgot all about it.' 'No, I didn't.'* | *'I want to go home.' 'So do I.'* | *I didn't believe the story and neither did he.*

3 used to emphasize the main verb in a sentence: *Do be careful.* | *You do look nice in that hat.* | *I do think she's behaved badly.* | *'You should have warned me.' 'But I did warn you.'* | *He owns, or did own* (=emphasizing past tense), *a yacht.*

4 *spoken* used when politely offering someone something: *Do have another sandwich.*

do[2] ●●● S1 W1 *v* (*past tense* **did**, *past participle* **done**, *third person singular* **does**)

1 ACTION/ACTIVITY [T] to perform an action or activity: *Have you done your homework yet?* | *You need to do more exercise.* | *It's a pleasure doing business with you.* | *I didn't know what to do.* | *All he does is sit in front of the television all day.* | **do something/nothing/anything etc** *We should do something to help him.* | *It all happened so quickly that I couldn't do anything about it.* | *bored teenagers with nothing to do* | **do the laundry/ironing/dishes etc** *It's your turn to do the dishes.*

> **REGISTER**
> In written English, people often use the verb **act** rather than the phrase **do something**, as it sounds more formal: *The government needs to **act** to help these people.*

2 SUCCEED [I] used to ask or talk about how successful someone is at something: **do well/badly** *Students are under considerable pressure to do well.* | **how sb/sth is doing (with/in sth)** *You should get promoted after about a year, depending on how you're doing.* | *How's he doing in trying to give up smoking?*

3 HAVE AN EFFECT [T] to have a particular effect on something or someone: *The scandal will do serious damage to his reputation.* | *This will **do nothing for*** (=will not improve) *Jamie's confidence.* | *The colour **does nothing for** her* (=does not improve her appearance). | *Getting the job has **done a lot for*** (=had a good effect on) *her self-esteem.* | *A week in the countryside will **do you good*** (=make you feel better). | *Exercise can **do wonders for*** (=have a very good effect on) *body, mind, and spirit.*

4 JOB [T] to have a particular job: *What do you want to do after you leave school?* | *What do you **do for a living*** (=as your job)? | *She's very good at what she does.*

5 ENOUGH/ACCEPTABLE [I,T not in progressive] used to say that something will be enough or be acceptable: *We don't have a lot of wine for the party, but it should just about do.* | *I can't find my black shoes so these **will have to do**.* | *A few sandwiches will **do me** for lunch.* | ***It won't do*** (=it is not acceptable) *to say that the situation couldn't have been avoided.*

6 what sb will do for sth used to talk about what arrangements someone has made to get something they need: *What will you do for money if you leave your job?* | *I'm not sure what we'll do for transport yet.*

7 what is sb/sth doing? *spoken* used to ask why someone or something is in a particular place or doing a particular thing, especially when you are surprised or annoyed by this: *What's my coat doing on the floor?* | *What are you doing walking around at this time of night?* | *What on earth do you **think** you're **doing**?*

8 do your/sb's hair/nails/make-up etc to do something that improves your appearance or someone else's appearance: *It must take her ages to do her make-up in the mornings.* | *Who does your hair?*

9 SPEND TIME [T] *informal* to spend a period of time doing something: *She did a year backpacking around the world.* | *Oh yes, I certainly **did** my **time** in the army* (=spent time in the army).

10 STUDY [T] *BrE* to study a particular subject in a school or university: *I did French for five years.* THESAURUS ▸ STUDY

D

11 COOK [T] to cook a particular type of food: *I was thinking of doing a casserole tonight.* THESAURUS ▸ COOK
12 do 10 miles/20 kms etc to achieve a particular distance, speed etc: *We did 300 kilometres on the first day.* | *The car can do 120 mph.*
13 PROVIDE A SERVICE [T] to provide a particular service or sell a particular product: *They do interior and exterior design.* | *We don't do food after two o'clock.*
14 PERFORM A PLAY [T] to perform a particular play, show etc: *We did 'Guys and Dolls' last year.*
15 DECORATE [T] to paint or decorate a room, house etc: *How are you going to do your living room?*
16 BEHAVE [I] to behave in a particular way: *In the evenings students are free to* ***do as they please*** (=do what they want). | *I wish you'd* ***do as you're told*** (=do what you are told to do)*!*
17 sb doesn't do nice/funny/sensible etc *spoken informal* used humorously to say that someone cannot or does not behave in a particular way: *Sensible? I don't do sensible.*
18 COPY BEHAVIOUR [T] to copy someone's behaviour or the way they talk, especially in order to entertain people: *He does a brilliant George Bush* (=copies him in a very funny way).
19 do lunch/do a movie etc *informal* to have lunch, go to see a film etc with someone: *Let's do lunch next week.*
20 DRUGS [T] *informal* to use an illegal drug: *He says he's never done hard drugs in his life.*
21 VISIT [T] to visit a particular place, especially as a tourist: *Let's do the Eiffel Tower today.*
22 that'll do! *spoken* used to tell a child to stop behaving badly
23 that does it! *spoken* used to say angrily that you will not accept a situation anymore: *Right, that does it! I'm not going to listen to any more of this!*
24 that should do it (*also* **that ought to do it**) *spoken* used to say that you will have finished doing something if you just do one more thing: *I've just got to prepare the dessert and that should do it.*
25 do it *informal* to have sex – used humorously or when you want to avoid saying the word 'sex'
26 sb would do well to do sth used to advise someone that they should do something: *Most people would do well to reduce the amount of salt in their diet.*
27 PUNISH [T] *BrE spoken* to punish or attack someone → **be/get done** at DONE²(8)
28 DECEIVE [T] *BrE informal* to deceive or trick someone → **be done** at DONE²(7)
29 what's doing ...? *spoken* used to ask what is happening: *What's doing at your place tonight?*
30 do or die used to say that someone is determined to do something very brave or dangerous even if they die attempting it
31 how (are) you doing? *spoken* used when you meet someone to ask them if they are well, happy etc: *Hi Bob, how you doing?*
32 what can I do you for? *spoken* used humorously to ask someone how you can help them, especially when you are trying to sell them something
33 do well by sb to treat someone well: *His relations always did pretty well by him.*
34 do one *spoken, informal* used to tell someone who is making you feel upset or angry to go away: *Oh, just go and do one!* → DOING, DONE², → **do your bit** at BIT²(8), → **how do you do** at HOW(11), → **nothing doing** at NOTHING¹(14), → **do sb proud** at PROUD(5), → **do sth to death** at DEATH(4), → CAN-DO

do away with sb/sth *phr v*
1 to get rid of something or stop using it: *People thought that the use of robots would do away with boring low-paid factory jobs.*
2 *informal* to kill someone

do sb ↔ **down** *phr v* to criticize someone, especially in an unfair way: *I know you don't like him, but there's no need to keep doing him down in front of the boss.*

do for sb/sth *phr v BrE informal* to kill someone or harm something or someone very badly: *Working 100 hours a week nearly did for me.* → **be done for** at DONE²(3)

do sb **in** *phr v informal*
1 to kill someone: *He was planning to do himself in.*
2 to make someone feel extremely tired: *That walk really did me in.* → **done in** at DONE²(4)

do sth ↔ **out** *phr v BrE*
1 to make a room look nice by decorating it: *The room was beautifully done out in pastel colours.*
2 *informal* to clean a room or cupboard thoroughly

do sb **out of** sth *phr v informal* to dishonestly stop someone from getting or keeping something, especially something they have a right to have: *Are you trying to do me out of a job?*

do sb/sth **over** *phr v*
1 do sth ↔ over *especially AmE* to make a place look attractive by decorating it: *The whole apartment had been done over in an Art Deco style.*
2 *AmE* to do something again, especially because you did it wrong the first time: *If you make too many mistakes, you'll have to do it over.*
3 do sth ↔ over *BrE spoken informal* to steal things from a building
4 *BrE spoken informal* to attack and injure someone

do up *phr v*
1 to fasten something, or to be fastened in a particular way: **do sth ↔ up** *Do up your coat or you'll get cold.* | *a skirt which does up at the back*
2 do sth ↔ up to repair an old building or car, or to improve its appearance: *They did up an old cottage in the Scottish Highlands.*
3 do sth ↔ up to decorate something in a particular way: *The apartment was done up in Viennese style.*
4 do sth ↔ up to wrap something in paper
5 do yourself up to make yourself look neat and attractive: *Sue spent ages doing herself up.*

do with sth *phr v*
1 could do with sth *spoken* to need or want something: *I could have done with some help this morning.*
2 have/be to do with sb/sth to be about something, be related to something, or be involved with something: *Their conversation had been largely to do with work.* | *I'm sorry about the accident, but it's* ***nothing to do with*** *me* (=I am not involved in any way). | *This question* ***doesn't have anything to do with*** *the main topic of the survey.* | *I'm sure her problems* ***have something to do with*** *what happened when she was a child.*
3 what to do with yourself how to spend your time: *She didn't know what to do with herself after she retired.*
4 what sb should do with sth/what to do with sth etc used to ask or talk about how someone should deal with something: *What shall I do with these papers?* | *I wouldn't know what to do with a newborn baby.*
5 what has sb done with sth? *spoken* used to ask where someone has put something: *What have you done with the remote for the TV?*
6 what is sb doing with sth? used to ask why someone has something: *What are you doing with my diary?*
7 I can't be doing with sth *BrE spoken* used to say that you are annoyed by something and do not want to have to think about it: *I can't be doing with all this right now.*

do without *phr v*
1 do without (sth) to live or do something without a particular thing: *I don't have any sugar so you'll have to do without.* | *You can do without a carpet but you've got to have somewhere to sit.*
2 can do without sth used to say that something is annoying you or causing you problems: *You can do without all that hassle.* | *Those are the type of stupid remarks I can do without.*

do³ *n* (*plural* **dos** *or* **do's**) [C] **1** *informal* a party or other social event: *We're having a do to celebrate his 30th birthday.* THESAURUS ▸ PARTY **2 dos and don'ts** (*also* **do's and don'ts**) things that you should and should not do in a particular situation: *The booklet lists the dos and don'ts of caring for dogs.* **3** *AmE informal* a HAIRDO

do⁴ /dəʊ $ doʊ/ *n* [singular, U] another spelling of doh

D.O.A. /ˌdiː əʊ ˈeɪ $ -oʊ-/ *adj* (***dead on arrival***) used when someone is said by a doctor to be dead when they are brought to a hospital

do·a·ble /ˈduːəbəl/ *adj* [not before noun] *spoken informal* able to be done or completed: *We've got to think first whether this plan is doable.* THESAURUS POSSIBLE

dob /dɒb $ dɑːb/ *v* (**dobbed**, **dobbing**)

dob sb **in** *phr v AusE, BrE informal* to tell someone, usually a person in authority, that someone else has done something wrong

d.o.b. the written abbreviation of ***date of birth***

doc /dɒk $ dɑːk/ *n* [C] *informal* a doctor

do·cent /dəʊˈsent $ doʊ-/ *n* [C] *AmE* someone who guides visitors through a MUSEUM, church etc

do·cile /ˈdəʊsaɪl $ ˈdɑːsəl/ *adj* quiet and easily controlled: *Labradors are gentle, docile dogs.* —**docilely** *adv* —**docility** /dəʊˈsɪləti $ dɑː-/ *n* [U]

dock¹ /dɒk $ dɑːk/ ●●○ *n*

1 [C] a place in a port where ships are loaded, unloaded, or repaired → **dry dock**: *A crowd was waiting at the dock to greet them.* | **in dock** *The ship is in dock for repairs.*

2 the docks [plural] the area of a port where there are docks: *James arrived at the docks expecting to see a luxury liner.*

3 [C] *AmE* a JETTY

4 the dock the part of a law court where the person who is charged with a crime stands: **in the dock** *Three defendants stood in the dock.*

5 in the dock *especially BrE* thought to have done something dishonest, harmful, or wrong: *These chemicals remain in the dock until we have more scientific evidence.*

6 [C,U] a plant with thick green leaves that grows wild in Britain: *a* ***dock leaf***

7 [C] a piece of equipment that connects a PORTABLE MEDIA PLAYER to a computer, television etc

dock² *v*

1 SHIPS [I,T] if a ship docks, or if the captain docks it, it sails into a dock so that it can unload: **[+at/in]** *We docked at Rangoon the next morning.*

2 dock sb's wages/pay/salary to reduce the amount of money you pay someone as a punishment: *The company has threatened to dock the officers' pay.*

3 COMPUTERS [T] to connect two computers using an electrical wire: **dock sth to/into/with sth** *Users can dock a laptop to their desktop setup.*

4 SPACECRAFT [I + with] if two spacecraft dock, they join together in space

5 ANIMALS [T] to cut an animal's tail short

dock·er /ˈdɒkə $ ˈdɑːkər/ *n* [C] *BrE* someone whose job is loading and unloading ships SYN **longshoreman** *AmE*

dock·et /ˈdɒkɪt $ ˈdɑː-/ *n* [C] **1** *technical* a short document giving details of goods that are delivered **2** *AmE law* a list of legal cases that will be heard in a particular court **3** *AmE* a list of things that are to be discussed or done SYN **agenda**: *What's* ***on the docket*** *for tomorrow's meeting?*

dock·ing sta·tion /ˈdɒkɪŋ ˌsteɪʃən $ ˈdɑːk-/ *n* [C] a piece of equipment that is used to connect a LAPTOP computer or a PORTABLE MEDIA PLAYER to other pieces of equipment

ˈdocking ˌsystem *n* [C] a piece of electronic equipment where you put other electronic equipment to play or RECHARGE

dock·land /ˈdɒklənd, -lænd $ ˈdɑːk-/ (*also* **docklands**) *n* [U] the area of a port where there are docks: *a dockland development*

dock·side /ˈdɒksaɪd $ ˈdɑːk-/ *n* [singular] the edge of the land that is next to the water in a port

dock·work·er /ˈdɒkˌwɜːkə $ ˈdɑːkˌwɜːrkər/ *n* [C] someone whose job is loading and unloading ships

dock·yard /ˈdɒkjɑːd $ ˈdɑːkjɑːrd/ *n* [C] a place where ships are repaired or built

doc·tor¹ /ˈdɒktə $ ˈdɑːktər/ ●●● S1 W1 *n* [C]

1 (*written abbreviation* **Dr**) someone who is trained to treat people who are ill → **GP**: *She was treated by her local doctor.* | *I'd like to make an appointment to see Dr Pugh.* | **the doctor's** *informal* (=the place where your doctor works) *'Where's Sandy today?' 'I think she's at the doctor's.'*

2 someone who holds the highest level of degree given by a university → **doctoral**: *a Doctor of Law*

3 be just what the doctor ordered *informal* to be exactly what someone needs or wants: *A 2-0 victory is just what the doctor ordered.* → see Thesaurus box on p. 524

COLLOCATIONS

VERBS

go to the doctor *I'd been having bad headaches so I went to the doctor.*
see a doctor (*also* **visit a doctor** *AmE*) (=go to the doctor) *Have you seen a doctor about it yet?*
ask a doctor (*also* **consult a doctor** *formal*) *If you have any of these symptoms, you should consult a doctor.*
call a doctor (=telephone one, especially to ask them to come to you) *His mother was very worried and called the doctor.*
get a doctor (=arrange for one to come to you) | **a doctor examines sb** | **a doctor prescribes sth** (=writes an order for medicine for someone)

ADJECTIVES/NOUN + doctor

a family doctor (=who treats all the members of a family) *We've had the same family doctor for fifteen years.*
sb's local doctor (=working near where you live) | **a hospital doctor** *BrE* (=working in a hospital)

doctor² *v* [T] **1** to dishonestly change something in order to gain an advantage: *He had doctored his passport to pass her off as his daughter.* | *There are concerns that some players have been doctoring the ball.* **2** to add something harmful to food or drink: *Paul suspected that his drink had been doctored.* **3** to remove part of the sex organs of an animal to prevent it from having babies SYN **neuter**: *You should* ***have*** *your cat* ***doctored***. **4** to give someone medical treatment, especially when you are not a doctor: *Bill doctored the horses with a strong-smelling ointment.*

doc·tor·al /ˈdɒktərəl $ ˈdɑːk-/ *adj* [only before noun] done as part of work for the university degree of doctor: *a doctoral thesis*

doc·tor·ate /ˈdɒktərət $ ˈdɑːk-/ *n* [C] a university degree of the highest level: **[+in]** *She received her doctorate in history in 1998.*

ˌDoctor of Phiˈlosophy *n* [C] a PHD

doc·tri·naire /ˌdɒktrəˈneə◂ $ ˌdɑːktrəˈner◂/ *adj formal* certain that your beliefs or opinions are correct and unwilling to change them: *The party followed an increasingly doctrinaire course.*

doc·trine /ˈdɒktrɪn $ ˈdɑːk-/ ●○○ *n*

1 [C,U] a set of beliefs that form an important part of a religion or system of ideas: *traditional doctrines of divine power* | *Marxist doctrine*

2 Doctrine [C] *AmE* a formal statement by a government about its future plans: *the announcement of the Truman Doctrine* —**doctrinal** /dɒkˈtraɪnl $ ˈdɑːktrɪnəl/ *adj*

doc·u·dra·ma /ˈdɒkjʊˌdrɑːmə $ ˈdɑːkjʊˌdrɑːmə,-ˌdræmə/ *n* [C] a film on television which shows real events in the form of a story

doc·u·ment¹ /ˈdɒkjəmənt $ ˈdɑːk-/ ●●● S2 W2 AWL *n* [C]

1 a piece of paper that has official information on it

2 a piece of written work that is stored on a computer

doc·u·ment² /ˈdɒkjəment $ ˈdɑːk-/ ●○○ AWL *v* [T]

1 to write about something, film it, or take photographs of it, in order to record information about it: **document how/what etc** *His research documents how the crisis occurred.*

2 to support an opinion, argument etc with recorded facts: **be well/extensively/poorly etc documented** *It is well documented that men die younger than women.*

doc·u·men·ta·rist /ˌdɒkjəˈmentərɪst $ ˌdɑːk-/ *n* [C] someone whose job is to make documentaries

D

doc·u·men·ta·ry[1] /ˌdɒkjəˈmentəri◂ $ ˌdɑːk-/ ●●○ *n* (*plural* **documentaries**) [C] a film or a television or radio programme that gives detailed information about a particular subject: **[+on/about]** *A local film crew is* ***making*** *a* ***documentary*** *about volcanoes.* **THESAURUS** ➜ **MOVIE, PROGRAMME**

documentary[2] *adj* [only before noun] **1** documentary films, programmes, photographs etc give or show information about a particular subject: *documentary films* **2** consisting of or written on documents: **documentary evidence/proof** *One of the most useful sources of documentary evidence is maps.*

doc·u·men·ta·tion /ˌdɒkjəmənˈteɪʃən, -men- $ ˌdɑːk-/ ●○○ AWL *n*
1 [U] official documents, reports etc that are used to prove that something is true or correct: *Applicants must provide* ***supporting documentation****.*
2 [C,U] the act of recording information in writing, on film etc: **[+of]** *a careful documentation of the costs*

doc·u·soap /ˈdɒkjʊsəʊp $ ˈdɑːkjʊsoʊp/ *n* [C] *BrE* a television programme that shows what happens in the daily lives of real people

dod·der·ing /ˈdɒdərɪŋ $ ˈdɑː-/ *adj* shaking slightly and walking with difficulty because of old age: *a doddering old man* —**dodder** *v* [I]

dod·dery /ˈdɒdəri $ ˈdɑː-/ *adj BrE* weak and not able to do things easily because of old age: *Some of the patients are a bit doddery.*

dod·dle /ˈdɒdl $ ˈdɑːdl/ *n* **be a doddle** *BrE informal* to be very easy: *The exam was a doddle!*

dodge[1] /dɒdʒ $ dɑːdʒ/ ●○○ *v*
1 [I,T] to move quickly to avoid someone or something: *He ran across the courtyard, dodging a storm of bullets.* | **[+between/through/into etc]** *Helen clutched Edward's arm as they* ***dodged*** *through the* ***traffic****.*
2 [T] to deliberately avoid discussing something or doing something SYN **evade**: **dodge an issue/question** *Senator O'Brian skillfully dodged the crucial question.* | **draft dodging** (=when someone avoids an order to join the army, navy etc)

dodge[2] *n* [C] *informal* something dishonest that is done to avoid a rule or law: *Businesses are investing in tree plantations as a* ***tax dodge*** (=a way of avoiding paying tax).

ˌDodge ˈCity a city in the US state of Kansas. In the 19th century, Dodge City was a place where many people came to drink and play cards for money, and there was a lot of fighting and shooting. Various WESTERNS have been set in Dodge City. If someone says that they 'have to get out of Dodge', they mean that they have to leave quickly. → **WILD WEST, THE**

dodg·em car /ˈdɒdʒəm ˌkɑː $ ˈdɑːdʒəm ˌkɑːr/ *n* [C] *BrE* a car used on the dodgems SYN **bumper car** *AmE*

dodg·ems /ˈdɒdʒəmz $ ˈdɑː-/ *n BrE* **the dodgems** a ride at a FUNFAIR in which people drive small electric cars in an enclosed area, trying to hit other cars

dodg·er /ˈdɒdʒə $ ˈdɑːdʒər/ *n* [C] **tax/fare dodger** someone who dishonestly avoids paying taxes or paying to travel on a bus or train → **DRAFT DODGER**

dodg·y /ˈdɒdʒi $ ˈdɑː-/ ●○○ *adj BrE informal*
1 not working properly or not in good condition: *Norton Disk Doctor can perform miracles on a dodgy hard disk.* | *Simon was rushed to hospital after eating what must have been dodgy prawns.*
2 seeming to be false, dishonest, or not to be trusted: *One girl thought the men looked dodgy.* | *dodgy share dealings*
3 involving risk or danger: *There were a few dodgy moments.*

do·do /ˈdəʊdəʊ $ ˈdoʊdoʊ/ *n* (*plural* **dodos**) [C] **1** a large bird that was unable to fly and no longer exists **2** *AmE informal* a stupid person **3 (as) dead as a dodo** completely dead or inactive, or no longer used

doe /dəʊ $ doʊ/ *n* [C] **1** a female rabbit or DEER → **buck, stag 2 doe eyes** large attractive eyes: *a pretty girl with big brown doe eyes*

do·er /ˈduːə $ -ər/ *n* [C] *informal* someone who does things instead of just thinking or talking about them: *Dole is a doer, not a talker.*

does /dəz; *strong* dʌz/ the third person singular of the present tense of DO

does·n't /ˈdʌzənt/ the short form of 'does not'

doff /dɒf $ dɑːf, dɒːf/ *v* [T] *old-fashioned* to remove the hat you are wearing as a sign of respect

dog[1] /dɒg $ dɒːg/ ●●● S1 W1 *n* [C]
1 ANIMAL a common animal with four legs, fur, and a tail. Dogs are kept as pets or trained to guard places, find drugs etc → **puppy**: *I could hear a* ***dog barking****.* | *He's* ***taken the dog for a walk****.* | *We used to* ***have a dog*** *when I was young.* | *the most popular* ***breed of dog***
2 MALE ANIMAL a male dog, FOX, or WOLF → **bitch**

THESAURUS: doctor

doctor someone who treats people who are ill, who has completed a long course of study at medical school: *If you have bad chest pains, you should see a doctor.*
GP *BrE* a doctor who is trained in general medicine and who treats the people who live in a local area: *My GP told me that I must lose weight.*
physician /fəˈzɪʃən/ *formal especially AmE* a doctor: *the American physician, Dr James Tyler Kent*
the medical profession doctors and nurses considered as a group: *This view is widely accepted among the medical profession.*
surgeon /ˈsɜːdʒən $ ˈsɜːr-/ a doctor who does operations in a hospital: *One of the world's top heart surgeons performed the operation.*
specialist a doctor with special knowledge about a particular illness, part of the body, or type of treatment: *The new drug is being tested by cancer specialists.* | *an eye specialist*
consultant *BrE* a very senior doctor in a hospital, with a lot of knowledge about a particular area of medicine: *The consultant said that he did not think it was cancer.*
paramedic someone who has been trained to treat sick or injured people, especially at the scene of an accident: *Paramedics treated him for shock.*
vet (*also* **veterinarian** *especially AmE*) a doctor who treats animals: *We took the cat to the vet.*

A DOCTOR WHO TREATS MENTAL ILLNESS

psychiatrist /saɪˈkaɪətrɪst $ sə-/ a doctor who is trained to treat people with mental illnesses: *In order to become a psychiatrist, you first need a medical degree.*
psychologist /saɪˈkɒlədʒɪst $ -ˈkɑː-/ a scientist who studies and is trained in PSYCHOLOGY (=the study of the mind): *Many psychologists believe that aggression is a learned behaviour.*
therapist a trained person whose job is to help people with their emotional problems, especially by talking to them and asking them to talk about their feelings

SOMEONE WHO IS STUDYING TO BE A DOCTOR

medical student a student who is studying medicine in order to be a doctor: *James is a medical student at Edinburgh university.*
intern *AmE* a student who has almost finished studying to be a doctor, and who is working in a hospital

3 WOMAN *informal not polite* an offensive word meaning an unattractive woman
4 dog eat dog when people compete against each other and will do anything to get what they want: *It's a **dog eat dog world** out there.*
5 be going to the dogs *informal* if a country or organization is going to the dogs, it is getting worse and will be difficult to improve
6 DISHONEST *informal not polite* an offensive word for an unpleasant or dishonest man: *You **dirty dog**!*
7 a dog's life *spoken* a life that is difficult and unpleasant, with very little pleasure: *His wife's a nag who **leads** him **a dog's life*** (=makes his life unpleasant).
8 make a dog's breakfast of sth *BrE informal* to do something very badly: *The orchestra made a complete dog's breakfast of the fourth movement.*
9 a dog's dinner *BrE informal* something that is meant to be impressive or fashionable but that other people think is not: *She was **dressed up like a dog's dinner**.*
10 not have a dog's chance *BrE informal* to have no chance of being successful
11 every dog has its/his day used to say that even the most unimportant person has a time in their life when they are successful and important
12 like a dog with two tails *BrE informal* very pleased and happy because something good has happened
13 a dog in the manger someone who cannot have or does not need something, but does not want anyone else to have it
14 FEET **dogs** [plural] *AmE informal* feet: *Boy, my dogs really hurt.*
15 POOR QUALITY *AmE informal* something that is of very poor quality
16 dog and pony show *AmE* an event that has only been organized so that people can admire it and think that it is impressive, not for any real purpose
17 be the dog's bollocks *BrE informal* a very rude expression used to say that something is very good
18 put on the dog *AmE old-fashioned* to pretend to be richer, more clever etc than you really are
19 the dogs *BrE informal* a sports event consisting of a series of races for dogs → **the hair of the dog** at HAIR(13), → SHAGGY DOG STORY, → **as sick as a dog** at SICK[1](1), → **let sleeping dogs lie** at SLEEP[1](7), → **the tail wagging the dog** at TAIL[1](11), → TOP DOG, → **treat someone like a dog** at TREAT[1](1)

dog² ●○○ *v* (**dogged, dogging**) [T]
1 if a problem or bad luck dogs you, it causes trouble for a long time: *He has been dogged by injury all season.*
2 to follow close behind someone

dog·cart /ˈdɒgkɑːt $ ˈdɒːgkɑːrt/ *n* [C] **1** a vehicle with two wheels and seats that is pulled by a horse **2** a small vehicle pulled by a dog

dog·catch·er /ˈdɒgˌkætʃə $ ˈdɒːgˌkætʃər/ *n* [C] a DOG WARDEN

ˈdog ˌcollar *n* [C] **1** a piece of thin leather that you fasten around a dog's neck **2** *informal* a stiff round white collar worn by priests

ˈdog days *n* [plural] **1** the hottest days of the year **2** a period of time when something is not successful: *Few opera houses survived the dog days of the 1980s.*

dog-eared /ˈdɒg ɪəd $ ˈdɒːg ɪrd/ *adj* dog-eared books or papers have been used so much that the corners are turned over or torn: *a dog-eared novel*

ˈdog-end *n* [C] *BrE* the small part of a cigarette left after it has been smoked

dog·fight /ˈdɒgfaɪt $ ˈdɒːg-/ *n* [C] **1** an organized fight between dogs **2** a fight between armed aircraft

dog·fish /ˈdɒgˌfɪʃ $ ˈdɒːg-/ *n* (*plural* **dogfish** *or* **dogfishes**) [C] a type of small SHARK

dog·ged /ˈdɒgɪd $ ˈdɒː-/ *adj* dogged behaviour shows that you are very determined to continue doing something: *a **dogged determination** to succeed* THESAURUS DETERMINED —**doggedly** *adv* —**doggedness** *n* [U]

dog·ge·rel /ˈdɒgərəl $ ˈdɒː-, ˈdɑː-/ *n* [U] poetry that is silly or funny and not intended to be serious

dog·gie /ˈdɒgi $ ˈdɒː-/ *n* [C] another spelling of DOGGY

dog·gone /ˈdɒgɒn $ ˈdɒːgɒːn/ *v* **doggone it** *AmE spoken old-fashioned* used when you are slightly annoyed about something —**doggone** *adj, adv*: *What are those doggone kids doing in my yard?*

dog·gy¹, **doggie** /ˈdɒgi $ ˈdɒːgi/ *n* (*plural* **doggies**) [C] a dog – used by or to children

doggy² *adj informal* **1** like or relating to dogs: *doggy smells* **2 doggy style/fashion** a way of having sex in which a man has a position behind his partner

ˈdoggy bag *n* [C] a small bag for taking home the food that is left over from a meal in a restaurant

ˈdoggy ˌpaddle *n* [singular, U] DOG PADDLE

dog·house /ˈdɒghaʊs $ ˈdɒːg-/ *n* **1 be in the doghouse** *informal* to be in a situation in which someone is annoyed with you because of something you have done **2** [C] *AmE* a small house outdoors for a dog to sleep in

dog·leg /ˈdɒgleg $ ˈdɒːg-/ *n* [C] a place where a road, path etc suddenly changes direction

dog·ma /ˈdɒgmə $ ˈdɒːgmə, ˈdɑːgmə/ *n* [C,U] a set of firm beliefs held by a group of people who expect other people to accept these beliefs without thinking about them: **religious/political/ideological etc dogma** *the rejection of political dogma*

dog·mat·ic /dɒgˈmætɪk $ dɒːg-, dɑːg-/ *adj* someone who is dogmatic is completely certain of their beliefs and expects other people to accept them without arguing: *Her staff find her bossy and dogmatic.* —**dogmatically** /-kli/ *adv* —**dogmatism** /ˈdɒgmətɪzəm $ ˈdɒːg-, ˈdɑːg-/ *n* [U]: *the narrow dogmatism of the past* —**dogmatist** *n* [C]

do-good·er /duː ˈgʊdə $ -ər/ *n* [C] someone who helps people who are in bad situations, but who is annoying because their help is not needed – used to show disapproval: *I've got very little time for those interfering do-gooders.*

ˈdog ˌpaddle (*also* **doggy paddle**) *n* [singular, U] a simple way of swimming by moving your legs and arms up and down

dogs·bod·y /ˈdɒgzˌbɒdi $ ˈdɒːgzˌbɑːdi/ *n* (*plural* **dogsbodies**) [C] *BrE* someone who has to do all the small boring jobs that no one else wants to do: *I spent the summer helping out as a **general dogsbody**.*

dog·sled /ˈdɒgsled $ ˈdɒːg-/ *n* [C] a SLEDGE (=a vehicle that travels over snow) that is pulled by dogs

ˈdog tag *n* [C] *AmE* a small piece of metal that soldiers wear on a chain around their necks with their name, blood type etc written on it

dog-ˈtired *adj informal* very tired

ˈdog ˌwarden *n* [C] *BrE* someone whose job is to collect dogs without owners

dog·whis·tle pol·i·tics /ˈdɒgwɪsəl ˌpɒlɪtɪks $ ˈdɒːg-, -ˌpɑːl-/ *n* [plural] *informal* in politics, the practice of expressing political opinions in a way that only a particular group of people understands, so that you do not become unpopular with people who do not have these opinions

doh, **do** /dəʊ $ doʊ/ *n* [singular, U] the first or eighth note in the SOL-FA musical SCALE

d'oh /dəʊ, dɜː $ dʌ, doʊ/ *interjection spoken* used humorously when you have just realized that you have done or said something stupid

DOH, the /ˌdiː əʊ ˈeɪtʃ $ -oʊ-/ (***the Department of Health***) a British government department which is responsible for health programmes in the UK and for the National Health Service

doi·ly /ˈdɔɪli/ *n* (*plural* **doilies**) [C] a circle of paper or cloth with a pattern of holes in it that you put under things to protect the surface below, or for decoration

do·ing /ˈduːɪŋ/ *n* **1 be sb's (own) doing** if something bad is someone's doing, they did or caused it: *If you fall into this trap, it will be all your own doing.* **2 take some doing** *informal* to be hard work: *We had to be on the parade ground for 5.30 a.m. and that took some doing.* **3 doings** [plural] events, activities etc that someone is

D

involved in: *Supper is a family get-together, where the doings of the day are talked about.*

ˌdo-it-yourˈself *n* [U] DIY

dol·drums /ˈdɒldrəmz $ ˈdoʊl-, ˈdɑːl-, ˈdɒːl-/ *n* [plural] *informal* **a)** if an industry, company, activity etc is in the doldrums, it is not doing well or developing: **in the doldrums** *The property market has been in the doldrums for months.* | *Recent economic doldrums have damaged the rural west.* **b)** if you are in the doldrums, you are feeling sad: *Fay is in the doldrums today.*

dole¹ /dəʊl $ doʊl/ *n* [U] *informal* **1** *BrE* money given by the government in Britain to people who are unemployed: **be/go on the dole** (=be unemployed and receiving money from the government) *Too many young people are still on the dole.* | *The number* ***claiming dole*** *went up by 3,500.* **2 the dole queue/dole queues** *BrE* the number of people who are unemployed and claiming money from the government, or a line of people waiting to claim this money each week: *As two factories closed today, 500 people* ***joined the dole queue***. | *Dole queues lengthened.* **3 the dole** *AmE* money given by the government in the US to people who need financial help SYN **welfare**: **on the dole** *How many people are on* ***the public dole***?

dole² *v*

dole sth ↔ **out** *phr v informal* to give something such as money, food, advice etc to more than one person: **[+to]** *Vera was doling out candy to all the kids.*

dole·ful /ˈdəʊlfəl $ ˈdoʊl-/ *adj formal* very sad: *a doleful song about lost love* —**dolefully** *adv*

doll¹ /dɒl $ dɑːl, dɒːl/ ●●● S3 *n*

1 [C] a child's toy that looks like a small person or baby: *a small wooden doll*

2 [C] *old-fashioned informal* a word meaning an attractive young woman - now usually considered offensive: *Hey, doll, why don't you get me a cup of coffee?*

3 [singular] *AmE informal* a very nice person: *Thanks, you're a doll.*

doll² *v*

doll yourself **up** *phr v informal* if a woman dolls herself up, she puts on attractive clothes and MAKE-UP, especially before going out to a party, club etc: *Maggie was in her room, dolling herself up.* | **be/get dolled up (for sth)** *The girls were all dolled up for a party.*

dol·lar /ˈdɒlə $ ˈdɑːlər/ ●●● S1 W2 *n* [C]

1 the standard unit of money in the US, Canada, Australia, and some other countries, divided into 100 CENTS: symbol $: *It cost three dollars.* | *a ten-dollar bill* | *You can pay in dollars or euros at the airport.*

2 the dollar the value of US money in relation to the money of other countries: *The pound has* ***risen against the dollar*** (=increased in value in relation to the dollar). → **you can bet your bottom dollar** at BET¹(6), → **feel/look like a million dollars** at MILLION(4)

dol·lar·i·za·tion /ˌdɒləraɪˈzeɪʃən $ -rə-/ *n* [U] *technical* a situation in which countries outside the US want to use the dollar rather than their own country's money

ˌdollars-and-ˈcents *adj* [only before noun] *AmE* financial: *From a dollars-and-cents point of view, this idea just won't work.*

doll·house /ˈdɒlhaʊs $ ˈdɑːl-, ˈdɒːl-/ *n* [C] *AmE* a DOLL'S HOUSE

dol·lop /ˈdɒləp $ ˈdɑː-/ *n* [C] *informal* **1** a small amount of soft food, usually dropped from a spoon: **[+of]** *a dollop of thick cream* **2** an amount of something: **[+of]** *You'll need a big dollop of luck.* —**dollop** *v* [T]

ˈdoll's house *n* [C] *BrE* a small toy house with furniture inside SYN **dollhouse** *AmE*

dol·ly /ˈdɒli $ ˈdɑːli, ˈdɒːli/ *n* (*plural* **dollies**) [C] **1** a DOLL – used especially by children **2** *technical* a flat frame on wheels used for moving heavy objects

ˈdolly bird *n* [C] *BrE old-fashioned informal* a pretty young woman, especially one who wears fashionable clothes

dol·men /ˈdɒlmen, -mən $ ˈdoʊlmən, ˈdɒːl-, ˈdɑːl-/ *n* [C] *technical* two or more large upright stones supporting a large flat piece of stone, built in ancient times

dol·our *BrE*, **dolor** *AmE* /ˈdɒlə $ ˈdoʊlər/ *n* [U] *literary* great sadness

dol·phin /ˈdɒlfɪn $ ˈdɑːl-, ˈdɒːl-/ ●●○ *n* [C] a very intelligent sea animal like a fish with a long grey pointed nose

ˈdolphin-safe *adj* dolphin-safe fish are caught in a way that does not harm or kill dolphins: *dolphin-safe tuna*

dolt /dəʊlt $ doʊlt/ *n* [C] *old-fashioned* a silly or stupid person —**doltish** *adj*

-dom /dəm/ *suffix* **1** [in U nouns] the state of being something: *freedom* | *boredom* **2** [in C nouns] **a)** an area ruled in a particular way: *a kingdom* **b)** a particular rank: *a dukedom* → OFFICIALDOM

do·main /dəˈmeɪn, dəʊ- $ də-, doʊ-/ ●○○ AWL *n* [C] *formal*

1 an area of activity, interest, or knowledge, especially one that a particular person, organization etc deals with: **outside/within the domain of sth/sb** *This problem is outside the domain of medical science.* | *Looking after the house was viewed as a woman's domain.* → PUBLIC DOMAIN

2 an area of land owned and controlled by one person or government, especially in the past: *the extent of the royal domain*

3 *technical* the set of possible quantities by which something can vary in mathematics

4 a domain name

doˈmain ˌname *n* [C] the first part of a website's address, which usually begins with 'www.' and ends with '.com', '.org', '.uk', or other letters that show which country the website is from

dome /dəʊm $ doʊm/ ●●○ *n* [C]

1 a round roof on a building

2 a shape or building like a ball cut in half

domed /dəʊmd $ doʊmd/ *adj* covered with a dome or shaped like a dome: *the domed roof of the church*

do·mes·tic¹ /dəˈmestɪk/ ●●○ W3 AWL *adj*

1 relating to or happening in one particular country and not involving any other countries → **foreign**: **domestic market/economy/demand etc** *the booming domestic economy* | *US foreign and* ***domestic policy*** | *our nation's* ***domestic affairs*** | ***Domestic flights*** (=flights that stay inside a particular country) *go from Terminal 1.*

2 [only before noun] relating to family relationships and life at home: *Unfortunately his* ***domestic life*** *wasn't very happy.* | **domestic tasks/chores/responsibilities etc** *Nowadays there is more sharing of domestic chores.* | *families that can afford* ***domestic help*** (=help with cleaning, washing etc) | *an organization that supports women facing* ***domestic violence*** (=violence in a family, especially from a husband to his wife)

3 used in people's homes: *a new tax on* ***domestic fuel*** | ***domestic appliances*** *such as washing machines*

4 someone who is domestic enjoys spending time at home and is good at cooking, cleaning etc: *No, I'm not very domestic.*

5 [only before noun] a domestic animal lives on a farm or in someone's home OPP **wild**: ***domestic pets*** —**domestically** /-kli/ *adv*: *domestically produced coal*

domestic² *n* [C] **1** *old-fashioned* a servant who works in a large house **2** *BrE informal* a fight between members of a family in their home: *It sounded like the neighbours were having a bit of a domestic.*

do·mes·ti·cate /dəˈmestɪkeɪt/ AWL *v* [T] to make an animal able to work for people or live with them as a pet → **tame** —**domestication** /dəˌmestɪˈkeɪʃən/ *n* [U]

do·mes·ti·cat·ed /dəˈmestɪˈkeɪtɪd/ AWL *adj* **1** domesticated animals are able to work for people or live with them as pets **2** someone who is domesticated enjoys spending time at home and doing work in the home: *Ray's very domesticated and even likes baking cakes.*

do·mes·tic·i·ty /ˌdəʊmeˈstɪsəti $ ˌdoʊ-/ *n* [U] life at home with your family: *a scene of happy domesticity*

doˌmestic ˈpartner *n* [C] *AmE* someone who you live

with and have a sexual relationship with, but who you are not married to

doˌmestic 'science *n* [U] *BrE old-fashioned* the study of cooking, sewing etc, taught as a subject at school SYN **home economics**

doˌmestic 'service *n* [U] *formal* the work of a servant in a large house

dom·i·cile /'dɒməsaɪl $ 'dɑː-, 'doʊ-/ *n* [C] *formal* the place where someone lives: *Military service entails frequent changes of domicile.*

dom·i·ciled /'dɒməsaɪld $ 'dɑː-,'doʊ-/ *adj formal* **1 be domiciled in** to live in a particular place **2** if a company is domiciled in a place, it is officially REGISTERED there

dom·i·cil·i·a·ry /ˌdɒmə'sɪliəri $ ˌdɑːmə'sɪlieri, ˌdoʊ-/ *adj* [only before noun] *formal* **domiciliary services/care/visits etc** services, care etc in someone's home

dom·i·nance /'dɒmənəns $ 'dɑː-/ ●○○ AWL *n* [U] the fact of being more powerful, more important, or more noticeable than other people or things → **dominate**: **[+of]** *the continuing dominance of the army in Uganda* | **political/economic/cultural etc dominance** *the economic and political dominance of Western countries* | **[+over]** *television's dominance over other media*

dom·i·nant¹ /'dɒmɪnənt $ 'dɑː-/ ●●○ W3 AWL *adj*
1 more powerful, important, or noticeable than other people or things → **dominate**: *The* ***dominant male*** *gorilla is the largest in the group.* | *Japan* ***became dominant*** *in the mass market during the 1980s.* | *its* ***dominant position*** *within the group* THESAURUS ▸ POWERFUL
2 controlling or trying to control other people or things – used to show disapproval SYN **domineering**: *a dominant personality*
3 *technical* a dominant GENE causes a child to have a particular physical feature or illness, even if it has been passed on from only one parent → **recessive**: *The disease is under the control of a single dominant gene.*

dominant² *n* [singular] *technical* the fifth note of a musical SCALE of eight notes

dom·i·nate /'dɒməneɪt $ 'dɑː-/ ●●○ W3 AWL *v*
1 [I,T] to control someone or something or to have more importance than other people or things: *The industry is dominated by five multinational companies.* | *New Orleans dominated throughout the game.* | *Her loud voice totally dominated the conversation.* | *Education issues dominated the election campaign.*
2 [T] to be larger and more noticeable than anything else in a place: *The cathedral dominates the city.* —**dominating** *adj*: *his dominating characteristic*

dom·i·na·tion /ˌdɒmɪ'neɪʃən $ ˌdɑː-/ ●●○ AWL *n* [U] control or power over someone or something: *the desire for political domination* | *The company is still aiming for world domination.*

dom·i·na·trix /ˌdɒmə'neɪtrɪks $ ˌdɑː-/ *n* [C] a woman who is the stronger partner in a SADOMASOCHISTIC sexual relationship

dom·i·neer·ing /ˌdɒmə'nɪərɪŋ◂ $ ˌdɑːmə'nɪr-/ *adj* someone who is domineering tries to control other people without considering their feelings or ideas – used to show disapproval: *a domineering mother* —**domineer** *v* [I]

Do·min·i·can /də'mɪnɪkən/ *n* [C] a member of a Christian religious group who leads a holy life —**Dominican** *adj*

do·min·ion /də'mɪnjən/ *n* **1** [U] *literary* the power or right to rule people or control something: **have/hold dominion over sb/sth** *The King held dominion over a vast area.* **2** [C] *formal* the land owned or controlled by one person or a government: *the king's dominions* **3** (*also* **Dominion**) [C] *old-fashioned* a country belonging to the British EMPIRE or COMMONWEALTH → **colony**, **protectorate**: *opinion at home and in* ***the dominions***

dom·i·no /'dɒmənəʊ $ 'dɑːmənoʊ/ *n* (*plural* **dominoes**) **1** [C] one of a set of small flat pieces of wood, plastic etc, with different numbers of spots, used for playing a game **2 dominoes** [U] the game played using dominoes **3 domino effect** a situation in which one event or action causes several other things to happen one after the other

don¹ /dɒn $ dɑːn/ *n* [C] **1** *BrE* a university teacher, especially one who teaches at the universities of Oxford or Cambridge **2** *informal* the leader of a Mafia organization

don² *v* (**donned**, **donning**) [T] *literary* to put on a hat, coat etc

do·nate /dəʊ'neɪt $ 'doʊneɪt/ ●●○ *v* [I,T]
1 to give something, especially money, to a person or an organization in order to help them → **donor**: **donate sth to sb/sth** *Last year he donated $1,000 to cancer research.* THESAURUS ▸ GIVE
2 to allow some blood or a body organ to be removed from your body so that it can be used in a hospital to help someone who is ill or injured → **donor**: *people who volunteer to donate blood*

do·na·tion /dəʊ'neɪʃən $ doʊ-/ ●●○ *n*
1 [C] something, especially money, that you give to a person or an organization in order to help them: **[+to/from]** *Would you like to* ***make*** *a* ***donation*** (=give money) *to our charity appeal?* | *There have been* ***generous donations*** *from EEC funds.*
2 [U] the act of giving something, especially money, to help a person or an organization: **[+of]** *the donation of a quarter of a million pounds* | **blood/organ donation**

done¹ /dʌn/ *v* the past participle of DO

done² *adj* [not before noun, no comparative]
1 FINISHED finished or completed SYN **finished**: *The job's nearly done.* | **sb is done (with sth)** (=someone has finished doing or using something) *As soon as I'm done, I'll give you a call.* | *Are you done with this magazine?* | *I'll be glad when the exams are* ***over and done with*** (=completely finished).
2 COOKED cooked enough to eat → **overdone**, **underdone**: *Is the pasta done yet?*
3 be done for *informal* to be in serious trouble or likely to fail: *If we get caught, we're done for.*
4 done in *informal* extremely tired: *You look done in.*
5 be done (*also* **be the done thing** *BrE*) to be socially acceptable: *Showing affection in public just isn't done in Japan.*
6 be done with it (*also* **have done with it** *BrE*) used to tell someone to stop thinking about or trying to decide something because they have already done this enough: *Just buy it and have done with it!*
7 be done *BrE informal* to be deceived or cheated: *If you paid £50, you were done, mate!*
8 be/get done *BrE informal* to be caught by the police for doing something illegal, but usually not too serious: **[+for]** *I got done for speeding last night.*
9 a done deal *informal* an agreement that has been made and cannot be changed: *The merger is far from a done deal.*
10 done and dusted *BrE informal* completely finished or completed: *It was all done and dusted within forty-five minutes.* → **be hard done by** at HARD²(6)

done³ *interjection* used to agree to and accept the conditions of a deal: *'I'll give you $90 for it.' 'Done!'*

don·gle /'dɒŋgəl $ 'dɑːŋ-/ *n* [C] *technical* a small piece of equipment that you must connect to a computer before you can use a particular piece of software

Don Juan /ˌdɒn 'hwɑːn, -'wɑːn, -'dʒuːən $ ˌdɑːn-/ *n* [C] a man who is good at persuading women to have sex with him

D

don·key /ˈdɒŋki $ ˈdɑːŋki/ ●○○ *n*
1 [C] a grey or brown animal like a horse, but smaller and with long ears
2 donkey's years *BrE spoken* a very long time: **for donkey's years** *I've had this jacket for donkey's years.*

ˈdonkey ˌjacket *n* [C] *BrE* a short thick coat, usually very dark blue, with a piece of leather or plastic across the shoulders

don·key·work /ˈdɒŋkiwɜːk $ ˈdɑːŋkiwɜːrk/ *n* [U] *BrE* the hard boring work that is part of a job or project: *Why do I always have to* ***do the donkeywork****?*

don·nish /ˈdɒnɪʃ $ ˈdɑːnɪʃ/ *adj BrE* clever, serious, and more interested in ideas than real life

do·nor /ˈdəʊnə $ ˈdoʊnər/ ●○○ *n* [C]
1 a person, group etc that gives something, especially money, to help an organization or country → **donate**: *We urgently need more assistance from* ***donor countries*** (=countries that give money, food etc to help in poor countries or disaster areas). | *An* ***anonymous donor*** (=whose name is unknown) *has given £500 towards the restoration fund.*
2 someone who gives blood or a body organ so that it can be used in the medical treatment of someone else → **donate**: *Some patients die before a* ***suitable donor*** *is found.* | **blood/organ/kidney etc donor** *the shortage of blood donors*

ˈdonor ˌcard *n* [C] a card that you carry to show that when you die a doctor can take parts of your body to use in the medical treatment of someone else

do-ˌnothing *adj* [only before noun] *BrE informal* lazy or unwilling to make any changes, especially in politics: *the do-nothing government of the last few years*

Don Quix·ote /ˌdɒn ˈkwɪksət,-kɪˈhəʊti $ ˌdɑːn-, -ˈhoʊti/ *n* someone who is determined to change what is wrong, but who does it in a way that is silly or not practical. This name comes from the main character in the humorous book *Don Quixote de la Mancha* by Miguel de Cervantes. Don Quixote wants to be a KNIGHT like the characters he admires in old stories, but when he tries to copy their adventures and behaviour, he makes many stupid mistakes.

don't /dəʊnt $ doʊnt/ **1** the short form of 'do not': *Don't worry!* | *You know him, don't you?* → **dos and don'ts** at DO³(2) **2** *spoken* an incorrect short form of 'does not': *She don't like it.*

do·nut /ˈdəʊnʌt $ ˈdoʊ-/ *n* [C] *especially AmE* another spelling of DOUGHNUT

doo·dah /ˈduːdɑː/ *BrE*, **doo·dad** /ˈduːdæd/ *AmE n* [C] *informal* a small object whose name you have forgotten or do not know: *Where's the doodah to turn off the TV?*

doo·dle /ˈduːdl/ *v* [I] to draw shapes, lines, or patterns without really thinking about what you are doing: *Brad was doodling on a sheet of paper.* **THESAURUS** ▸ DRAW
—**doodle** *n* [C]

doo·fus /ˈduːfəs/ *n* [C] *informal* a stupid person

doo·hick·ey /ˈduːˌhɪki/ *n* [C] *AmE informal* a small object whose name you have forgotten or do not know, especially a part of a machine

doo·lal·ly /duːˈlæli/ *adj BrE spoken* crazy

doom¹ /duːm/ ●○○ *v* [T] to make someone or something certain to fail, die, be destroyed etc: **be doomed to failure/defeat/extinction etc** *Many species are doomed to extinction.* | *The plan was* ***doomed from the start****.* | **be doomed to do sth** *We are all doomed to die in the end.* GRAMMAR **Doom** is usually passive. —**doomed** *adj*: *passengers on the doomed flight*

doom² ●○○ *n* [U] something very bad that is going to happen, or the fact that it is going to happen: *A sense of* ***impending doom*** (=coming very soon) *gripped her.* | **sense/feeling of doom** | **spell doom for sth** (=mean that something will be unable to continue or survive) *The recession spelled doom for many small businesses.* | *Thousands of soldiers* ***met their doom*** (=died) *on this very field.* | **doom and gloom/gloom and doom** (=when there seems to be no hope for the future) *Despite these poor figures,* ***it's not all doom and gloom****.*

ˈdoom-ˌladen *adj BrE* saying or making you feel that something very bad is going to happen soon: *documentaries full of doom-laden predictions*

doom·say·er /ˈduːmˌseɪə $ -ər/ *especially AmE* (*also* **doomster** *BrE*) *n* [C] someone who says that bad things are going to happen

Dooms·day /ˈduːmzdeɪ/ *n* [U] **1 till/until Doomsday** *informal* for a very long time: *You could wait till Doomsday and he'd never show up.* **2** the last day of the Earth's existence, when everything will be destroyed, according to some religions: **doomsday scenario** (=a description of a very bad and hopeless situation)

doom·ster /ˈduːmstə $ -ər/ *n* [C] *BrE informal* a DOOMSAYER

doom·y /ˈduːmi/ *adj informal* making you feel that bad things are going to happen, or thinking that bad things will happen: *doomy warnings* | *He's always doomy.*

door¹ /dɔː $ dɔːr/ ●●● S1 W1 *n* [C]
1 the large flat piece of wood, glass etc that you move when you go into or out of a building, room, vehicle etc, or when you open a cupboard → **gate**: *Could you open the door for me?* | *The door flew open and Ruth stormed in.* | *Don't forget to lock the garage door.* → FIRE DOOR, FRENCH DOORS, REVOLVING DOOR(1), SLIDING DOOR, STAGE DOOR, SWING DOOR, TRAPDOOR
2 the space made by an open door SYN **doorway**: **in/out (of)/through the door** *Rick turned and ran out of the door.* | *I glanced through the open door.*
3 at the door if someone is at the door, they are waiting for you to open the door of a building so they can come inside: *There's somebody at the front door.*
4 out of doors outside SYN **outdoors**: *I prefer working out of doors.*
5 show/see sb to the door to take someone to the main way out of a building: *My secretary will show you to the door.*
6 two/three etc doors away/down/up used to say how many houses or buildings there are between your house, office etc and another building: **[+from]** *Patrick lived two doors away from me.*
7 (from) door to door a) *especially BrE* from one place to another: *How long is the journey, door to door?* **b)** going to each house in a street or area to sell something, collect money, or ask for votes: *Joe sold vacuum cleaners door to door for years.* → DOOR-TO-DOOR
8 be on the door to work at the entrance to a theatre, club etc, collecting tickets
9 shut/close the door on sth to make something impossible: *The accident shut the door on her ballet career.* → **at death's door** at DEATH(7), → **behind closed doors** at CLOSED(5), → **get in through the back door** at BACK DOOR(2), → **lay sth at sb's door** at LAY²(19), → NEXT DOOR¹, → **open doors (for sb)** at OPEN²(16), → OPEN-DOOR POLICY, → **open the door to sth** at OPEN²(16), → **show sb the door** at SHOW¹(20)

COLLOCATIONS

VERBS

open/close/shut the door *I opened the door and Dad was standing there.*
slam/bang the door (=shut it loudly, usually because you are angry) *He strode from the room, slamming the door behind him.*
answer the door (=open it for someone who has knocked or pressed the bell) *Lucy ran downstairs to answer the door.*
a door leads somewhere (=used to say what place is on the other side of a door) *This door leads into the garden.*
a door opens/closes/shuts *We were still waiting for the train doors to open.*
a door slams/bangs (shut) (=shuts loudly) *I heard the front door slam.*
a door flies/bursts open (=opens very suddenly and quickly) | **a door swings open/shut** (=moves forward to open or backwards to shut) | **a door slides open/shut** (=moves smoothly to the side or back again) | **lock/unlock the door** | **bolt the door**

(=slide a metal bar across to fasten it) | **knock on/at the door** (=hit it with your hand to make someone open it) | **bang/hammer on the door** (=hit it very loudly and urgently) | **tap on/at the door** (=hit it very gently) | **get the door** (=open or close it for someone)

ADJECTIVES/NOUN + door

the front/back/side door (=of a house) *I heard someone knocking at the front door.*
the main door (=the door into a building that most people use) *The main door to the hotel is on Queen Street.*
the kitchen/bedroom/bathroom etc door | **the cupboard door** *BrE*, **the closet door** *AmE* | **the fridge/oven door** | **a car door** | **the passenger door** (=for the person in a car who sits beside the driver) | **a rear door** (=a door at the back of a vehicle)

door + NOUN

a door handle (=that you move up or down to open a door) | **a door knob** (=that you turn to open a door) | **a door key**

door² *v* [T] to hit someone with a car door when they are riding past on a bicycle: *I nearly got doored as I went past the flats in Camden Street.*

door·bell /'dɔːbel $ 'dɔːr-/ *n* [C] a button outside a house that makes a sound when you push it so that people inside know you are there: **ring the doorbell** (=push the button) → see picture at BELL

,do-or-'die *adj* [only before noun] very determined: *a do-or-die attitude*

door·jamb /'dɔːdʒæm $ 'dɔːr-/ *n* [C] *especially AmE* a DOORPOST

door·keep·er /'dɔːˌkiːpə $ 'dɔːrˌkiːpər/ *n* [C] someone who guards the main door of a large building and lets people in and out

door·knob /'dɔːnɒb $ 'dɔːrnɑːb/ *n* [C] a round handle that you turn to open a door

door·knock·er /'dɔːˌnɒkə $ 'dɔːrˌnɑːkər/ (*also* **knocker**) *n* [C] a heavy metal ring or bar on a door that you use to knock with

door·man /'dɔːmæn, -mən $ 'dɔːr-/ *n* (*plural* **doormen** /-men, -mən/) [C] a man who usually wears a uniform and works in a hotel, club etc letting people into the building, helping people find taxis etc → **porter**

door·mat /'dɔːmæt $ 'dɔːr-/ *n* [C] **1** a piece of material inside or outside a door for you to clean your shoes on **2** *informal* someone who lets other people treat them badly and never complains: *Don't let him* ***treat*** *you* ***like a doormat***.

door·nail /'dɔːneɪl $ 'dɔːr-/ *n* **(as) dead as a doornail** *informal* completely dead

door·post /'dɔːpəʊst $ 'dɔːrpoʊst/ *n* [C] one of two upright posts on either side of a doorway

'door prize *n* [C] *AmE* a prize given to someone who has the winning number on their ticket for a show, dance etc

door·step¹ /'dɔːstep $ 'dɔːr-/ ●○○ *n* [C]
1 a step just outside a door to a house or building: **on the doorstep** *He* ***stood on the doorstep***, *straightening his tie.* | *the* ***front doorstep***
2 on sb's/the doorstep a) very near someone's home: *Wow! You've got the beach* ***right on*** *your* ***doorstep***! **b)** at someone's home: *I got a shock when he just* ***turned up on the doorstep***.
3 *BrE informal* a very thick piece of bread

doorstep² *v* (**doorstepped**, **doorstepping**) [I,T] *BrE* if politicians or JOURNALISTS doorstep people, they visit people at their homes in order to get votes or information – often used to show disapproval: *Journalists had door-stepped the couple and their neighbours.*

door·stop /'dɔːstɒp $ 'dɔːrstɑːp/ (*also* **door·stop·per** /-ˌstɒpə $ -ˌstɑːpər/ *BrE*) *n* [C] **1** something you put under or against a door to keep it open **2** a rubber object fastened to a wall to stop a door hitting it when it opens

ˌdoor-to-'door *adj* [only before noun] visiting each house in a street or area, usually to sell something, collect money, or ask for votes: *a door-to-door salesman* → **door to door** at DOOR¹(7)

door·way /'dɔːweɪ $ 'dɔːr-/ ●●○ *n* [C] the space where a door opens into a room or building: **in the doorway** *There was Paolo,* ***standing in the doorway***.

doo·zy /'duːzi/ *n* (*plural* **doozies**) [C] *AmE informal* something that is extremely good, bad, strange, big etc: *I've heard lies before, but* ***that*** *one* ***was a*** *real* ***doozy***!

dope¹ /dəʊp $ doʊp/ *n informal* **1** [U] a drug that is not legal, especially MARIJUANA: *Jeff used to* ***smoke dope*** *all the time.* **2** [C] *spoken* a stupid person SYN **idiot**: *What a dope!* **3 dope test** a test given to people or animals taking part in a sport, to see if they have taken or have been given a drug to improve their performance **4 the dope (on sb/sth)** new information about someone or something, especially information that not many people know: *What's the dope on the new guy?*

dope² *v* [T] **1** (*also* **dope sb up**) to give a person or an animal a drug, often in their food or drink, to make them unconscious: *The girl had been doped and kidnapped.* **2** to give an animal a drug that makes it perform better in a race **3 be doped (up)** *BrE* to be unable to think or behave normally, because of the effects of drugs or alcohol: **[+on]** *She was doped up on drink and drugs most of the time.*

dope³ *adj AmE informal* very good: *a dope album*

dope·head /'dəʊphed $ 'doʊp-/ *n* [C] *informal* someone who takes a lot of illegal drugs

dop·ey (*also* **dopy** *BrE*) /'dəʊpi $ 'doʊpi/ *adj informal* **1** thinking or reacting slowly, as if you have taken a drug: *She's still a little dopey from the anaesthetic.* **2** slightly stupid: *a dopey grin*

dop·ing /'dəʊpɪŋ $ 'doʊ-/ *n* [U] the practice of using drugs to improve performance in a sport: **doping scandal/ban/test etc** *doping offences*

dop·pel·gang·er /'dɒpəlgæŋə, -geŋ- $ 'dɑːpəlgæŋər/ *n* [C] **1 sb's doppelganger** someone who looks exactly like someone else SYN **double 2** an imaginary spirit that looks exactly like a living person

do·py /'dəʊpi $ 'doʊpi/ *adj* a British spelling of DOPEY

Dor·ic /'dɒrɪk $ 'dɔː-, 'dɑː-/ *adj* in the oldest and simplest of the Greek building styles → **Ionic**: *a Doric column*

dork /dɔːk $ dɔːrk/ *n* [C] *informal* someone who you think is or looks stupid —**dorky** *adj*

dorm /dɔːm $ dɔːrm/ *n* [C] *informal* a DORMITORY

dor·mant /'dɔːmənt $ 'dɔːr-/ *adj* not active or not growing at the present time but able to be active later OPP **active**: **lie/remain dormant** *The seeds remain dormant until the spring.* | *a huge* ***dormant volcano*** —**dormancy** *n* [U]

dor·mer /'dɔːmə $ 'dɔːrmər/, **'dormer ˌwindow** *BrE n* [C] a window built into a roof, so that it sticks out from the roof → SKYLIGHT → see picture at WINDOW

dor·mi·to·ry /'dɔːmətəri $ 'dɔːrmətɔːri/ *n* (*plural* **dormitories**) [C] **1** *especially BrE* a large room for several people to sleep in, for example in a BOARDING SCHOOL or HOSTEL **2** *AmE* a large building at a college or university where students live SYN **hall of residence** *BrE*

'dormitory ˌtown *n* [C] *BrE* a town that is near a city with more work opportunities, so that many people who live there travel to work in the city every day SYN **bedroom community/suburb** *AmE*

dor·mouse /'dɔːmaʊs $ 'dɔːr-/ *n* (*plural* **dormice**) [C] a small European mouse with a long furry tail

dor·sal /'dɔːsəl $ 'dɔːr-/ *adj* [only before noun] on or relating to the back of an animal or fish: *a shark's* ***dorsal fin*** → see picture at FISH¹

do·ry /'dɔːri/ *n* (*plural* **dories**) **1** [C] a rowing boat that has a flat bottom and is used for fishing **2** [C,U] a flat sea fish that can be eaten, or the flesh of this fish

DOS /dɒs $ dɑːs/ *n* [U] *technical* (***Disk Operating System***) software that is loaded onto a computer system to make all the different parts work together

dos·age /ˈdəʊsɪdʒ $ ˈdoʊ-/ *n* [C usually singular] the amount of a medicine or drug that you should take at one time, especially regularly: **high/low dosage** | **[+of]** *He was recommended a high dosage of morphine.* | **increase/reduce the dosage** | *The **daily dosage** is steadily reduced over several weeks.*

dose¹ /dəʊs $ doʊs/ ●●○ *n* [C]
1 the amount of a medicine or a drug that you should take: **[+of]** *Never exceed the **recommended dose** of painkillers.* | **high/low dose** *Start with a low dose and increase it.*
2 an amount of something that you do or experience at one time, especially something unpleasant: **a bad/mild dose of flu** *BrE* (=making you feel very ill or only slightly ill) *Dave **had a bad dose of flu**.* | **lethal/fatal dose (of sth)** (=an amount that kills) *a lethal dose of radiation* | *I quite like Jamie **in small doses*** (=in limited amounts but not a lot or often).
3 like a dose of salts *BrE informal* very quickly and easily: *The cleaners **went through** the house **like a dose of salts**.*

dose² *v* [T] (*also* **dose up**) to give someone medicine or a drug: **dose sb/yourself with sth** *Sumi dosed herself up with aspirin and went to bed.*

dosh /dɒʃ $ dɑːʃ/ *n* [U] *BrE informal* money

do-si-do /ˌdəʊ si ˈdəʊ $ ˌdoʊ si ˈdoʊ/ *n* [singular] an action in COUNTRY DANCING in which partners move around each other with their backs towards each other —**do-si-do** *v* [I]

doss¹ /dɒs $ dɑːs/ *v* [I] *BrE informal* (*also* **doss down**) to sleep somewhere that is not your usual place, or not a real bed: *I dossed down on the couch downstairs.*

doss around/about *phr v* to spend your time in a lazy way, doing very little: *We just dossed around all day Saturday.*

doss² *n BrE informal* **a doss** work that does not need much effort: *This job's a real doss.*

doss·er /ˈdɒsə $ ˈdɑːsər/ *n* [C] *BrE informal* **1** someone who has nowhere to live, and sleeps in the street or in cheap HOSTELS **2** someone who is very lazy

ˈdoss house *n* [C] *BrE informal* a place where people who have nowhere to live can stay cheaply SYN **flophouse** *AmE*

dos·si·er /ˈdɒsieɪ $ ˈdɒːsjeɪ, ˈdɑː-/ *n* [C] a set of papers containing detailed, usually secret information about a person or subject SYN **file**: **[+on]** *A firm of detectives produced a dossier on his activities.*

dot¹ /dɒt $ dɑːt/ ●●● S2 *n* [C]
1 a small round mark or spot: *a pattern of dots*
2 on the dot *informal* exactly on time or at a particular time: *I'll be there on the dot.* | **at three o'clock/seven thirty etc on the dot** (=at exactly 3:00/7:30 etc) *Mr Green **arrived** at six **on the dot**.*
3 something that looks like a small spot because it is so far away: *The plane was just **a dot on the horizon**.*
4 a short sound or flash of light used when sending messages by MORSE CODE → **dash** → **the year dot** at **YEAR**(14)

dot² ●○○ *v* (**dotted**, **dotting**) [T]
1 to mark something by putting a dot on it or above it: *She never dots her i's.*
2 [usually passive] if an area is dotted with things, there are a lot of them there but they are spread far apart: **be dotted with sth** *The lake was dotted with sailboats.* | **be dotted about/around etc sth** *The company has over 20 stores dotted around the country.* | *Poppies dotted the field.*
3 to put a very small amount of something on a surface, especially in several places: **dot sth with sth** *Dot the apples with butter.*
4 dot the i's and cross the t's *informal* to pay careful attention to all the details when you are finishing something

do·tage /ˈdəʊtɪdʒ $ ˈdoʊ-/ *n* **in your dotage** in your old age

dot-com, **dot.com, dot com** /ˌdɒt ˈkɒm $ ˌdɑːt ˈkɑːm/ *adj* [only before noun] *informal* relating to a person or company whose business is done using the Internet or involves the Internet: *a dot-com company* | *dot-com millionaires* —**dot-com** *n* [C]: *Several of the leading dot-coms saw their share prices slide yesterday.*

dote /dəʊt $ doʊt/ *v*

dote on/upon sb *phr v* to love someone very much, and show this by your actions: *Everyone doted on Sally, the only girl in the family.* —**doting** *adj* [only before noun]: *a doting parent* —**dotingly** *adv*

doth /dʌθ/ *old use* a form of 'does'

ˌdot-matrix ˌprinter *n* [C] a machine connected to a computer that prints letters, numbers etc using many small DOTS

ˌdotted ˈline *n* [C] a series of printed or drawn DOTS that form a line → **sign on the dotted line** at **SIGN²**(4)

dot·ty /ˈdɒti $ ˈdɑːti/ *adj old-fashioned informal* **1** slightly crazy **2 dotty about sb/sth** liking or loving someone or something very much: *Gemma's dotty about horses.*

doub·le¹ /ˈdʌbəl/ ●●● S1 W2 *adj* [usually before noun]
1 OF TWO PARTS consisting of two parts that are similar or exactly the same: *a double sink* | *a double wardrobe* | *the great double doors of the cathedral* | *Don't park your car on double yellow lines.*
2 TWO DIFFERENT USES combining or involving two things of the same type: *a double murder case* | *A lot of the jokes were based on **double meaning**.*
3 TWICE AS BIG twice as big, twice as much, or twice as many as usual: *a double whisky* | *The city was enclosed by walls of double thickness.*
4 FOR TWO PEOPLE made for two people or things to use → **single**: *Do you need a double bed or two singles?* | *a double room* | *a double garage*
5 TWO LETTERS/NUMBERS *BrE spoken* used to say that a particular letter or number is repeated: *My name's Robbins with a double 'b'.* | *The number is 869 double 2* (=86922).
6 FLOWER a double flower has more than the usual number of PETALS → **DOUBLY**

double² ●●● S3 W3 *n*
1 TWICE THE SIZE [C,U] something that is twice as big, as much etc as usual or as something else: *Scotch and water, please – make it a double.* | *'They offered me £10,000.' 'I'll give you double.'*
2 ROOM [C] a room for two people in a hotel → **single**: *A double costs $95 a night.*
3 TENNIS **doubles** [U] a game played between two pairs of players, especially in tennis → **singles**: *the men's doubles* → **MIXED DOUBLES**
4 BASEBALL [C] a hit in baseball which allows the BATTER to reach second BASE: *Walker led the inning with a double.*
5 SIMILAR PERSON **sb's double** someone who looks very like someone else: *She's her mother's double.*
6 IN FILMS [C] an actor who takes the place of a more famous actor in a film, especially because the acting involves doing something dangerous: *I think they used a double in the shower scene.*
7 at the double *BrE*, **on the double** *AmE informal* very quickly and without any delay: *He was told to get back to Washington on the double.*
8 double or quits *BrE*, **double or nothing** *AmE* a situation in a game when you must do something that could either win you twice as much money or make you lose it all

double³ ●●● S3 *v*
1 [I,T] to become twice as big or twice as much, or to make something twice as big or twice as much: **double in size/number/value etc** *Within two years the company had doubled in size.* | *The church has doubled its membership in the last five years.* | **double the size/number/amount etc (of sth)** *A promise was given to double the number of police on duty.* THESAURUS ▸ INCREASE
2 [T] (*also* **double over/up**) to fold something in half: *Take a sheet of paper and double it over.*
3 [I] to hit the ball far enough to get to second BASE in a game of baseball

double as sb/sth *phr v* to have a second use, job, or

purpose as a particular thing: *The school doubled as a hospital during the war.*
double back *phr v* to turn around and go back the way you have come: *The driver doubled back and headed for Howard Bay.* | **double back on yourself** *We kept getting lost and having to double back on ourselves.*
double up *phr v*
1 (*also* **double over**) to suddenly bend over at the waist because you are laughing so much or are in pain: *Emilio doubled over, grabbing his leg.* | **be doubled up/over with laughter/pain etc** *Both the girls were doubled up with laughter.*
2 to share something, especially a bedroom: **[+with]** *You'll have to double up with Susie while your aunt is here.*

double[4] ●●○ *adv* **be bent double** to be bent over a long way: *The trees were almost bent double in the wind.* → **see double** at SEE[1](28)

double[5] ●●○ *predeterminer* twice as big, twice as much, or twice as many: **double the amount/number/size etc** *We'll need double this amount for eight people.* | *The value of the house is double what it was.*

ˈdouble act *n* [C] two actors, especially COMEDIANS, who perform together

ˌdouble ˈagent *n* [C] someone who finds out an enemy country's secrets for their own country but who also gives secrets to the enemy → **spy**

ˌdouble-ˈbarrelled *BrE*, **double-barreled** *AmE* **1** a double-barrelled gun has two places where the bullets come out **2** *BrE* a double-barrelled family name has two parts **3** *AmE* very strong or using a lot of force: *a double-barreled attack*

double bass /ˌdʌbəl ˈbeɪs/ (*also* **bass**) *n* [C] a very large musical instrument shaped like a VIOLIN that the musician plays standing up → see picture at **STRINGED INSTRUMENT**

ˌdouble ˈbed *n* [C] a bed made for two people to sleep in

ˌdouble ˈbill *n* [C] a cinema, theatre, concert etc performance in which you can see two films, plays etc, one after the other

ˌdouble ˈbind *n* [C usually singular] a situation in which any choice you make will have bad results

ˌdouble-ˈblind *adj technical* a double-blind scientific test or study compares two groups in which neither the scientists nor the people being studied know which group is being tested and which group is not

ˌdouble ˈbluff *n* [C] an attempt to deceive someone by telling them the truth, hoping that they will think you are lying

ˌdouble ˈboiler *n* [C] a pot for cooking food, consisting of one pan resting on top of another pan with hot water in it

ˌdouble-ˈbook *v* [I,T] to promise the same seat in a theatre, on a plane etc to more than one person by mistake —**double-booking** *n* [U]

ˌdouble-ˈbreasted *adj* a double-breasted jacket, coat etc has two sets of buttons → **single-breasted**

ˌdouble-ˈcheck *v* [I,T] to check something again so that you are completely sure it is correct, safe etc **THESAURUS** ▸ **CHECK**

ˌdouble ˈchin *n* [C] a fold of loose skin under someone's chin that looks like a second chin

ˌdouble ˈclick ●●○ *v* [I,T] to press a button on a computer mouse twice in order to send an instruction to the computer

ˌdouble ˈcream *n* [U] *BrE* very thick cream → **single cream**

ˌdouble-ˈcross *v* [T] to cheat someone, especially after you have agreed to do something dishonest with them —**double cross** *n* [C] —**double-crosser** *n* [C]

ˌdouble ˈdate *n* [C] *old-fashioned* an occasion when two COUPLES meet to go to a film, restaurant etc together —**double-date** *v* [I,T]

ˌdouble ˈdealer *n* [C] *BrE informal* someone who deceives other people —**double dealing** *n* [U]

double-deck·er /ˌdʌbəl ˈdekə◂ $ -ər◂/ *n* [C] **1** a bus with two levels → **single-decker** **2** a sandwich made with three pieces of bread and two layers of food —**double-decker** *adj* [only before noun]

ˌdouble-ˈdigit *adj* [only before noun] *especially AmE* relating to the numbers 10 to 99 SYN **double-figure** *BrE*: *double-digit inflation*

ˌdouble ˈdigits *n* [plural] *AmE* the numbers from 10 to 99 SYN **double figures**: *Sam's team* ***scored in the double digits*** *in nine out of ten games.*

ˌdouble-ˈdip *v* [I] *AmE* to get money from two places at once, usually in a way that is not legal or not fair

ˌdouble-dip reˈcession *n* [C] a situation in which an economy goes into RECESSION, begins to get better, then goes back into recession again

ˌdouble-ˈDutch *n* [U] **1** *BrE informal* speech or writing that you cannot understand SYN **nonsense** **2** *AmE* a game in which one child jumps over two long ropes that are being swung around by other children

ˌdouble ˈduty *n* **do double duty** to do more than one job or be useful for more than one thing at the same time: **[+as]** *The sofa does double duty as a guest bed.*

ˌdouble-ˈedged *adj* **1** **a double-edged sword/weapon** something that seems to be good, but that can have a bad effect: *Being famous is often a double-edged sword.* **2** having two different parts: *a double-edged attack on global warming* **3** a double-edged remark has two possible meanings, one of which is not very nice: *It sounded like a double-edged comment.* **4** with two cutting edges: *a double-edged knife*

double en·ten·dre /ˌduːblɒnˈtɒndrə $ -blɑːnˈtɑːn-/ *n* [C] a word or phrase that may be understood in two different ways, one of which is often sexual

ˌdouble ˈfault *n* [C] two mistakes, one after another, when you are SERVING in tennis, which make you lose a point

ˌdouble ˈfeature *n* [C] *AmE* **1** a cinema performance in which two films are shown one after the other SYN **double bill** *BrE* **2** a DVD with two films on it

ˌdouble-ˈfigure *adj* [only before noun] relating to the numbers 10 to 99 SYN **double-digit** *AmE*: *Almost all leading shares had double-figure gains.*

ˌdouble ˈfigures *n* [plural] the numbers from 10 to 99 SYN **double digits** *AmE*: **in double figures** *King's was the only other score in double figures.* | **approach/reach/go into etc double figures** *The death toll is thought to have reached double figures.*

ˌdouble ˈfirst *n* [C usually singular] a British university degree in which a student reaches the highest standard in two subjects

ˌdouble ˈglazing *n* [U] *BrE* glass on a window or door in two separate sheets with a space between them, used to keep noise out and heat in —**double-glaze** *v* [T]

ˌdouble-ˈheader *n* [C] two baseball games played one after the other

ˌdouble ˈhelix *n* [C] *technical* a shape consisting of two parallel SPIRALS that twist around the same centre, found especially in the structure of DNA

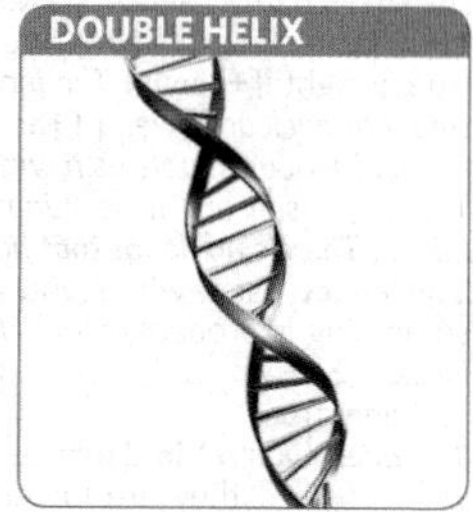

ˌdouble inˈdemnity *n* [U] *AmE law* a feature of a life insurance POLICY that allows double the value of the contract to be paid in the case of death by accident

ˌdouble ˈjeopardy *n* [U] *law* when someone is taken to court a second time for the same crime, in some unusual situations

D

ˌdouble-ˈjointed *adj* able to move the joints in your fingers, arms etc backwards as well as forwards

ˌdouble ˈlife *n* [C] if someone lives a double life, they deceive people by having two separate homes, families, or sets of activities, one of which they keep secret: **lead/live a double life** *Marje had no idea that her husband was leading a double life with another woman.*

ˌdouble ˈnegative *n* [C] two negative words used in one sentence when only one is needed in correct English grammar, for example in the sentence 'I don't want nobody to help me!'

ˌdouble-ˈpark *v* [I,T] to leave a vehicle on a road beside another vehicle that is already parked there

ˌdouble ˈplay *n* [C] the action of making two runners in a game of baseball have to leave the field by throwing the ball quickly from one BASE to another before the runners reach either one

ˌdouble ˈquick *adv BrE informal* as quickly as possible: *Call an ambulance double quick!* —**double-quick** *adj* [only before noun]: *Lunch was produced* ***in double-quick time***.

ˌdouble-ˈsided *adj* something such as tape or paper that is double-sided has something on both surfaces: *double-sided sticky tape*

doub·le·speak /ˈdʌbəlˌspiːk/ *n* [U] *BrE* speech that is complicated and can have more than one meaning, sometimes used deliberately to deceive or confuse people SYN **double-talk**

ˌdouble ˈstandard *n* [C] a rule, principle etc that is unfair because it treats one group of people more severely than another in the same situation

doub·let /ˈdʌblɪt/ *n* [C] a man's tight jacket, worn in Europe from about 1400 to the middle 1600s

ˌdouble ˈtake *n* [C] **do a double take** to look at someone or something again because you are very surprised by what you saw or heard

ˈdouble-talk *n* [U] speech that is complicated and can have more than one meaning, sometimes used deliberately to deceive or confuse people SYN **double-speak** *BrE*: *legal double-talk*

doub·le·think /ˈdʌbəlˌθɪŋk/ *n* [U] *BrE* a dishonest belief in two opposing ideas at the same time

ˌdouble ˈtime *n* [U] double pay given to someone when they work at a time when people do not normally work

ˈdouble-time *adj, adv especially AmE* very quick or as quickly as possible: *Get upstairs and clean your room – double-time!*

ˌdouble ˈvision *n* [U] a medical condition in which you see two objects instead of one all the time, for example after an accident

ˌdouble ˈwhammy *n* [C] two bad things that happen together or one after the other: *the double whammy of higher prices and more taxes*

dou·bloon /dʌˈbluːn/ *n* [C] a gold coin used in the past in Spain and Spanish America

doub·ly /ˈdʌbli/ *adv* **1** [+adj] much more than usual: *Be doubly careful when driving in fog.* **2** in two ways or for two reasons: *You are doubly mistaken.*

doubt[1] /daʊt/ ●●● S1 W1 *n*

1 [C,U] a feeling of being not sure whether something is true or right: **[+about]** *The incident raises doubts about the safety of nuclear power.* | **[+as to]** *Some government ministers had serious doubts as to whether the policy would work.* | *There was still one little nagging doubt at the back of his mind.* | ***There's no doubt that*** *he was a major artist.*

2 no doubt used when you are saying that you think something is probably true: *No doubt you'll have your own ideas.* | *She was a top student,* ***no doubt about it*** (=it is certainly true).

3 if/when (you're) in doubt used when advising someone what to do if they are uncertain about something: *If in doubt, consult your doctor.*

4 be in doubt if something is in doubt, it may not happen, continue, exist, or be true: *The future of the peace talks is in doubt.*

5 beyond doubt if something is beyond doubt, it is completely certain: *The prosecution must prove* ***beyond reasonable doubt*** *that the accused is guilty of the crime.* | **put the game/result/match beyond doubt** (=do something which makes it certain that a particular player or team will win a match) *Ferdinand's second goal put the game beyond doubt.*

6 without doubt used to emphasize an opinion: *Jo is without doubt one of the finest swimmers in the school.*

7 open to doubt something that is open to doubt has not been proved to be definitely true or real: *The authenticity of the relics is open to doubt.* → SELF-DOUBT, → **give sb/sth the benefit of the doubt** at BENEFIT[1](4)

COLLOCATIONS

VERBS

have doubts *Scientists still have some doubts about the theory.*

have your doubts (=have some doubts) *Everyone else thinks it's a good idea, but I have my doubts.*

have no/little doubt *I have no doubt that you are right.*

be in no/any doubt about sth *The government is in no doubt about the seriousness of the situation.*

leave no/little doubt (that) (=make people sure or almost sure about something) *The evidence left no doubt that he was the murderer.*

cast/throw doubt on sth (=make people unsure about something) *Research has cast doubt on the safety of mobile phones.*

raise doubts about sth (=make people unsure about something) | **call/throw sth into doubt** (=make people unsure about something) | **express/voice doubts** (=say that you have doubts)

ADJECTIVES

serious/grave doubts *They have some serious doubts as to his honesty.*

considerable doubts | **a lingering/nagging doubt** (=one that does not go away)

PHRASES

there is no/little/some doubt (=used to talk about how sure people are about something) *There is little doubt that he will play for England one day.*

without a shadow of a doubt (=without any doubt) *I knew without a shadow of a doubt that I was going to win.*

an element of doubt (=a slight doubt) | **not the slightest doubt** (=no doubt)

doubt[2] ●●● S2 *v* [T not in progressive]

1 to think that something may not be true or that it is unlikely: *Kim never doubted his story.* | **doubt (that)** *I doubt we'll ever see him again.* | **doubt if/whether** *You can complain, but I doubt if it'll make any difference.* | *'Do you think there'll be any tickets left?'* ***'I doubt it*** (=I don't think so).'

2 to not trust or have confidence in someone: *I never doubted myself. I always knew I could play tennis at this level.* | *She loved him, and had never doubted him.* | *I have no reason to* ***doubt*** *his* ***word*** (=think that he is lying). —**doubter** *n* [C]

GRAMMAR

Patterns with doubt

- You **doubt whether** someone **can** do something: *I doubt whether we can afford a new car.* | *She doubted whether she could trust him again.*
- You **doubt whether** something **will** happen: *I doubt whether the plan will work.* | *He doubted whether this would happen.*
- You can also say **doubt if** with the same meaning as **doubt whether**: *I doubt if we can afford a new car.* | *I doubt if the plan will work.*
- You can also say **doubt that**: *I doubt that we can afford a new car.* | *I doubt that the plan will work.*

✗ Don't say: *doubt about*

Using the progressive

The verb **doubt** is not usually used in the progressive. You say: *I doubt he'll come to the party.* ✗ Don't say: *I am doubting he'll come to the party.*

GRAMMAR GUIDE ▸ VERBS

THESAURUS

doubt to think that something may not be true or that it is unlikely: *'Do you think she really is eighteen?' 'I doubt it.' | There was so much noise that I doubt if anyone slept.*

be doubtful/dubious /ˈdjuːbiəs $ ˈduː- / to doubt that something will happen, is true, or is a good idea: *Economists are doubtful that the situation will improve this year. | 'You can eat the whole fish including the head.' Janey looked dubious.*

have reservations to feel that a plan or idea may not be good because you think there may be some problems with it: *Health care professionals had reservations about giving both vaccines together.*

have misgivings to feel worried about doing something, because it may have a bad result: *Ralph had serious misgivings about changing his career at the age of 50.*

have mixed feelings to be unsure exactly how you feel about something or someone because there are both good and bad things about them: *I have very mixed feelings about moving house – it's exciting but I'll miss this area.*

have second thoughts to start having doubts about whether a decision you have just made is the right one: *I liked the dress in the shop, but when I got it home I had second thoughts.*

doubt·ful /ˈdaʊtfəl/ ●●○ *adj*
1 probably not true or not likely to happen: *Prospects for a lasting peace remain doubtful.* | **it is doubtful if/whether** *It was doubtful whether the patient would survive the operation.* | **it is doubtful that** *It is doubtful that the missing airmen will ever be found.*
2 not sure that something is true or right: *'Everything's going to be all right, you'll see.' Jenny* ***looked doubtful****.* | **[+if/whether]** *I'm still doubtful whether I should accept this job.* | **doubtful about (doing) sth** *At first we were doubtful about employing Charlie.*
3 unlikely to be successful: *Already the whole scheme was looking increasingly doubtful.*
4 probably not good SYN **dubious**: *Here the tap water is of doubtful quality.* —**doubtfully** *adv*

doubt·ing Thom·as /ˌdaʊtɪŋ ˈtɒməs $ -ˈtɑːm-/ *n* [singular] someone who does not always believe things until they have seen proof of them. This expression comes from the story of the APOSTLE Thomas in the Bible. He doubted the truth of the RESURRECTION (=return to life) of Jesus Christ and demanded to feel Jesus' wounds before he would believe it.

doubt·less /ˈdaʊtləs/ ●○○ *adv* used when saying that something is almost certain to happen or be true: *Doubtless there would be lots of rumours.*

douche /duːʃ/ *n* [C usually singular] a mixture of water and something such as VINEGAR, that a woman puts into her VAGINA to wash it, or the object that she uses to do this —**douche** *v* [I,T]

dough /dəʊ $ doʊ/ ●○○ *n*
1 [singular, U] a mixture of flour and water ready to be baked into bread, PASTRY etc → see picture at **BREAD**
2 [U] *informal* money

dough·nut /ˈdəʊnʌt $ ˈdoʊ-/ *n* [C] a small round cake, often in the form of a ring

dough·ty /ˈdaʊti/ *adj* [only before noun] *literary* brave and determined

dough·y /ˈdəʊi $ ˈdoʊi/ *adj* **1** looking and feeling like dough **2** doughy skin is pale and soft and looks unhealthy

dou·la /ˈduːlə/ *n* [C] a woman whose job is to help and support a woman while she gives birth, and often before and after the birth too

dour /dʊə, ˈdaʊə $ daʊr, dʊr/ *adj* **1** serious, never smiling, and unfriendly **2** a dour place is one that is plain and dull, and where people do not have any fun —**dourly** *adv*

douse, dowse /daʊs/ *v* [T] **1** to stop a fire from burning by pouring water on it **2** [+with/in] to cover something in water or other liquid

dove¹ /dʌv/ *n* [C] **1** a kind of small white PIGEON (=bird) often used as a sign of peace **2** someone in politics who prefers peace and discussion to war OPP **hawk**

dove² /dəʊv $ doʊv/ *AmE* a past tense of DIVE

dove·cot, dove·cote /ˈdʌvkɒt $ -kɑːt/ *n* [C] a small house built for doves to live in

dove·tail¹ /ˈdʌvteɪl/ *v* **1** [I,T] to fit together perfectly or to make two plans, ideas etc fit together perfectly: **[+with]** *My vacation plans dovetail nicely with Joyce's.* **2** [T + together] to join two pieces of wood by means of dovetail joints

dovetail² (*also* ˌ**dovetail** ˈ**joint**) *n* [C] a type of JOINT fastening two pieces of wood together

dov·ish /ˈdʌvɪʃ/ *adj* preferring peace and discussion to war OPP **hawkish**

dow·a·ger /ˈdaʊədʒə $ -ər/ *n* [C] **1** a woman from a high social class who has land or a title from her dead husband: *the dowager Duchess of Devonshire* **2** *informal* a respected and impressive old lady

dow·dy /ˈdaʊdi/ *adj* **1** a dowdy woman is not attractive, because she wears dull and unfashionable clothes **2** dowdy things are dull, unattractive, and unfashionable: *a dowdy dress*

dow·el /ˈdaʊəl/ *n* [C] a wooden pin for holding two pieces of wood, metal, or stone together

dow·el·ling /ˈdaʊəlɪŋ/ *n* [U] wood in the shape of a round rod, cut up to make dowels

Dow Jones In·dex /ˌdaʊ ˈdʒəʊnz ˌɪndeks $ -ˈdʒoʊnz-/ (*also* ˌ**Dow** ˈ**Jones** ˌ**Average**) *n* **the Dow Jones Index** a daily list of prices of shares on the American Stock Exchange, based on the daily average prices of 30 industrial shares → **the FTSE Index**

down¹ /daʊn/ ●●● S1 W1 *adv, prep, adj*
1 TO A LOWER POSITION to or towards a lower place or position OPP **up**: *David bent down to tie his shoelace. | Get down off the table. | Tears were streaming down my face. | The sun was going down and it would soon be dark. | They came running down the stairs. | She stood on a balcony looking down into the courtyard. | Glancing down the list of runners, I noticed a familiar name. | Her hair came down to her waist. | Ken fell asleep* ***face down*** (=with his face towards the ground) *on the couch.*
2 IN A LOWER PLACE in a lower place or position OPP **up**: *We heard the sound of laughter down below. | The bathroom is down those stairs. | Halfway down the page, there was the item I was looking for.*
3 TO LIE/SIT into a sitting or lying position: *Please sit down. | I think I'll go and lie down for a while.*
4 ALONG at or to a place that is further along something such as a road or path: *A young man came hurrying down the street. | She looked down the road to see if anyone was coming. | There is a pleasant little cafe bar a hundred yards down the road. | The bus stop is a bit further down on the left-hand side.*
5 SOUTH in or towards the south OPP **up**: *They drove all the way down from Boston to Miami. | They sailed down the east coast of Africa. | Now he's bought a villa down south. | a trip down Mexico way*
6 SOMEWHERE LOCAL at or to a place that is not far away: *She's just gone down to the shops. | I saw her down at the station this morning.*
7 RIVER away from the place where a river starts OPP **up**: *Chunks of ice came floating down the river.*
8 FASTENED TO A SURFACE used with verbs that mean 'fasten' to show that something is fastened firmly to the surface or object below it: *The coffin lid had been nailed down.*

D

9 LESS at or towards a level or amount that is less OPP **up**: *Keep your speed down.* | *House prices have come down in recent months.* | *Turn the radio down.* | **[+to]** *Sharif cut his report down to only three pages.*
10 LOSING losing to an opponent by a certain number of points: **two goals down/three points down etc** *Swindon were six points down at one stage.*
11 WRITTEN used with verbs that mean 'write' to show that you write something on paper or in a book: *I'll write down the address for you.* | *Start by jotting down a few ideas.* | *Let's put you down as self-employed.*
12 ON A LIST if you are down for something, your name is on a list of people who want to do something or are intended to do something: **[+for]** *Purvis is down for the 200 metre freestyle event.* | *We've already put his name down for nursery school.* | **down to do sth** *I've got you down to do the table decorations.*
13 TO LATER TIMES from an earlier time in history to a later time or to people who are born in later times: *a person whose words and actions have inspired millions of people down the centuries* | *This knowledge was handed down in the family from father to son.* | *The story has been passed down the generations for a thousand years.* | **[+to]** *traditions that have come down to us from medieval times*
14 PAID IMMEDIATELY paid to someone immediately: *A top quality freezer for only £20 down and £5 a week for a year.*
15 EVERY PART from top to bottom: *I want you to wash my car down.*
16 SWALLOWED in or into your stomach as a result of swallowing: *Meg's been very ill and can't keep her food down.* | *He gulped down the coffee.*
17 SAD unhappy or sad: *Tim's been feeling down.* THESAURUS ▸ SAD
18 COMPUTER if a computer is down, it is not working OPP **up** THESAURUS ▸ BROKEN
19 be down to sb if an action or decision is down to you, it is your responsibility: *It's down to me to make sure that everyone is happy.* → **be up to sb** at UP[1]
20 be down to sb/sth to be the result of one person's actions or one particular thing: *Chris's success is all down to him.*
21 be down to your last pound/dollar/litre etc to be left with only a small amount of something: *We're down to our last five dollars.*
22 down to sth/sb including everything or everyone, even the smallest thing or the least important person: *Everyone uses the cafeteria, from the managing director down to the office boy.* | *The plans were all complete down to the last detail.*
23 be/go down with sth to have a particular illness: *Jane's gone down with flu.*
24 Down with sb/sth *spoken* used to say that you strongly oppose a government, leader etc and want them to lose their power: *Down with the government!*
25 be down on sb/sth *informal* to have a severe attitude towards someone or something, especially when this is unfair: *Why is Mark so down on her at the moment?*
26 LEAVING UNIVERSITY *BrE* used to say that someone leaves or has left a university at the end of a period of study: **[+from]** *Sarah came down from Oxford in 1966.*
27 COMPLETED already done or completed: *Well, you've passed your second test, so it's two down and four more to go.*
28 down under *informal* in or to Australia or New Zealand
29 Down! *spoken* used to tell a jumping dog to get down
30 be down with sb *spoken informal* to be friends with someone → **be down on your luck** at LUCK[1](17)

down² *v* [T] **1** to drink or eat something quickly: *He downed the coffee in one gulp.* **2** to knock or force someone to the ground: *O'Malley downed his opponent in the first round.* **3 down tools** *BrE* to stop working, especially because you are taking part in a STRIKE (=protest about pay or conditions by stopping work)

down³ *n* **1** [U] soft hair like a baby's **2** [U] the soft fine feathers of a bird **3** [C] one of the four chances that an American football team has to move forward when it is their turn to have the ball **4 the downs** low round hills covered with grass, as in the south of England **5 have a down on sb** *BrE informal* to dislike or have a bad opinion of someone: *For some reason, Malcolm had a down on the whole teaching profession.* → **ups and downs** at UP²(1)

down- /daʊn/ *prefix* **1** at or towards the bottom or end of something → **up-**: *downstairs* | *downriver* (=nearer to where it goes into the sea) **2** used to show that something is being made smaller or less important OPP **up-**: *to downgrade a job* (=make it less important) | *to downsize a company* (=reduce the number of jobs in it) **3** used to show that something is bad or negative OPP **up-**: *the downside of a situation* (=the negative part of it) | *downmarket products* (=low quality products)

ˌdown-and-ˈout¹ *adj* **1** having no luck or money: *a down-and-out actor* **2** having no home and living on the street

ˌdown-and-ˈout² *n* [C] *BrE* someone who has no home and who lives on the street

ˌdown-at-ˈheel *adj BrE* unattractive and not well cared for, because of a lack of money: *The town today is a shabby, down-at-heel place.*

down·beat¹ /ˈdaʊnbiːt/ *adj* not showing any strong feelings, especially not happy ones OPP **upbeat**: *Al was surprisingly downbeat about the party.*

downbeat² *n* [C] **1** the first note in a BAR of music **2** the movement a CONDUCTOR makes to show when this note is to be played or sung

down·cast /ˈdaʊnkɑːst $ -kæst/ *adj* **1** sad or upset because of something bad that has happened THESAURUS ▸ SAD **2** downcast eyes are looking down: *Penelope sat silently, her eyes downcast.*

down·er /ˈdaʊnə $ -ər/ *n informal* **1** [C] a drug that makes you feel very relaxed or sleepy → **upper** **2** [singular] a person or situation that stops you feeling happy: *The weather was a bit of a downer.* **3 be on a downer** *BrE* to be sad or experiencing a series of sad events: *What's up with Ruth? She's been on a downer all week.*

down·fall /ˈdaʊnfɔːl $ -fɒːl/ *n* [singular] **1** complete loss of your money, moral standards, social position etc, or the sudden failure of an organization: *the scandal that **led to** the president's **downfall*** **2** something that causes a complete failure or loss of someone's money, moral standards, social position etc: **be sb's downfall** *an addiction to gambling that proved to be her downfall*

down·grade /ˈdaʊngreɪd/ *v* [T] **1** to make a job less important, or to move someone to a less important job OPP **upgrade** **2** to make something seem less important or valuable than it is: *Police often downgrade the seriousness of violence against women in the home.* **3** to state that something is not as serious as it was: *Hurricane Bob has been downgraded to a tropical storm.*

down·heart·ed /ˌdaʊnˈhɑːtɪd◂ $ -ɑːr-/ *adj* feeling sad and disappointed, especially because you have tried to achieve something but have failed: *When no replies came, I began to feel downhearted.*

down·hill¹ /ˌdaʊnˈhɪl◂/ *adv* **1** towards the bottom of a hill or towards lower land OPP **uphill**: *I was going downhill and my brakes failed.* **2 go downhill** if a situation goes downhill, it gets worse SYN **deteriorate**: *Grandma fell and broke her leg, and she **went downhill** quite **rapidly** after that.*

downhill² *adj* **1** on a slope that goes down to a lower point OPP **uphill**: *downhill skiing* | *It's a long walk back, but at least it's all downhill.* **2 be all downhill (from here)/be downhill all the way (from here)** to be easy to do, because you have already done the hard part: *The worst is over – it's all downhill from here.*

ˈdown-home *adj* [only before noun] *AmE* typical of the simple values and customs of people who live in the country, especially in the southern US → **homely**: *down-home family recipes*

Dow·ning Street /ˈdaʊnɪŋ striːt/ *n* the government or prime minister of Great Britain: *Downing Street declined to comment on the allegations.*

down·light·er /ˈdaʊnˌlaɪtə $ -ər/ *n* [C] a small light, usually one of many, that is fitted into a ceiling and shines light down towards the ground

down·load[1] /ˌdaʊnˈləʊd $ ˈdaʊnloʊd/ ●●● S2 W2 *v* [T] to move information or programs from a computer network to a small computer: *games that can be downloaded free from the Internet*

down·load[2] /ˈdaʊnləʊd $ -loʊd/ *n* [C] a computer FILE or program that has been downloaded, or the process of downloading it: *We've got reviews and downloads of the latest business software.*

down·load·a·ble /ˌdaʊnˈləʊdəbəl $ ˈdaʊnloʊd-/ *adj* if a computer program or FILE is downloadable, you are allowed to copy it from a computer network onto your own computer

down·mar·ket[1] /ˌdaʊnˈmɑːkɪt◂ $ -ɑːr-/ *adj BrE* downmarket goods or services are cheap and not of very good quality SYN **downscale** *AmE* OPP **upmarket**: *downmarket tabloid newspapers | The company wanted to break away from its traditional, downmarket image.*

downmarket[2] *adv BrE* **1 go/move downmarket** to start buying or selling cheaper goods or services **2 take sth downmarket** to change a product or service so that it is cheaper and more popular – used to show disapproval: *He was accused of taking the radio station downmarket in order to compete with commercial stations.*

ˌdown ˈpayment *n* [C] a payment you make when you buy something that is only part of the full price, with the rest to be paid later: *We've almost got enough money to* ***make a down payment on*** *a house.*

down·play /ˌdaʊnˈpleɪ $ ˈdaʊnpleɪ/ *v* [T] to make something seem less important than it really is SYN **play down**: *White House officials attempted to downplay the president's role in the affair.*

down·pour /ˈdaʊnpɔː $ -pɔːr/ *n* [C usually singular] a lot of rain that falls in a short time **THESAURUS** ▸ RAIN

down·right /ˈdaʊnraɪt/ *adv* [+adj/adv] used to emphasize that something is completely bad or untrue: *Jed's downright lazy. | It's downright disgusting!* —**downright** *adj* [only before noun]: *That's a downright lie!*

down·riv·er /ˌdaʊnˈrɪvə $ -ər/ *adv* in the direction that the water in a river is flowing OPP **upriver** → **downstream**: *The bridge was another mile downriver.*

down·scale[1] /ˈdaʊnskeɪl/ *adj AmE* downscale goods or services are cheap and not of very good quality

down·scale[2] /ˌdaʊnˈskeɪl $ ˈdaʊnskeɪl/ *v* [I,T] *AmE* to sell or buy cheaper goods of lower quality

down·shift /ˌdaʊnˈʃɪft $ ˈdaʊnʃɪft/ *v* [I] **1** to put the engine of a vehicle into a lower GEAR in order to go slower **2** if someone downshifts, they choose to do a less important or difficult job, so that they do not have to worry about their work and have more time to enjoy their life —**downshifter** *n* [C] —**downshifting** *n* [U]

down·side /ˈdaʊnsaɪd/ *n* **the downside** the negative part or disadvantage of something OPP **upside**: *Digital cell phones offer more security, but the downside is that they have less power.* | **[+of]** *The downside of the book is that it is written in a rather boring style.*

down·size /ˈdaʊnsaɪz/ *v* [I,T] if a company or organization downsizes, it reduces the number of people it employs in order to reduce costs: *The airline has downsized its workforce by 30%.* **THESAURUS** ▸ REDUCE —**downsizing** *n* [U]

down·spout /ˈdaʊnspaʊt/ *n* [C] *BrE* a pipe that carries water away from the roof of a building

ˈDown's ˌsyndrome *n* [U] a condition that someone is born with, that stops them from developing in a normal way, both mentally and physically

down·stage /ˌdaʊnˈsteɪdʒ◂/ *adv* towards or near the front of the stage in a theatre OPP **upstage** —**downstage** *adj*

down·stairs[1] /ˌdaʊnˈsteəz◂ $ -ˈsterz/ ●●● S2 *adv* towards or on a lower floor of a building, especially a house OPP **upstairs**: *Rosie ran downstairs to answer the door. | Charles was downstairs in the kitchen.* —**downstairs** *adj*: *a downstairs bathroom*

down·stairs[2] *n* **the downstairs** the rooms on the ground floor in a house: *We have still got to paint the downstairs.*

down·state /ˈdaʊnsteɪt/ *adj* [only before noun] *AmE* in or from the southern part of a state OPP **upstate**: *A downstate judge was called in to hear the case.* —**down·state** /ˌdaʊnˈsteɪt/ *adv*

down·stream /ˌdaʊnˈstriːm◂/ *adv* in the direction that the water in a river or stream is flowing OPP **upstream** → **downriver**: *a boat drifting downstream*

down·time /ˈdaʊntaɪm/ *n* [U] **1** the time when a computer is not working **2** (*also* **down time**) *informal* a period of time when you have finished what you were doing, and you can relax or do something that you had not originally planned to do: *Often, during semesters, you have down time when you can do some exercise.* —**downtime** *adj*: *downtime activities for teachers*

ˌdown-to-ˈearth *adj* practical and direct in a sensible honest way: *Fran's a friendly, down-to-earth person. | a chef with a down-to-earth approach to cooking*

down·town /ˌdaʊnˈtaʊn◂/ ●●● S3 W3 *adv* to or in the centre or main business area of a town or city → **uptown**: *I have to* ***go downtown*** *later.* —**downtown** *adj* [only before noun]: *downtown restaurants | She works for a law firm in downtown Miami.*

down·trod·den /ˈdaʊnˌtrɒdn $ -ˌtrɑː-/ *adj* downtrodden people are treated badly and without respect by people who have power over them

down·turn /ˈdaʊntɜːn $ -tɜːrn/ *n* [C usually singular] a period or process in which business activity, production etc is reduced and conditions become worse OPP **upturn**: *America's current* ***economic downturn*** | **[+in]** *a downturn in the auto industry*

down·ward /ˈdaʊnwəd $ -wərd/ *adj* [only before noun] **1** moving or pointing towards a lower position OPP **upward**: *a gentle downward slope* **2** moving to a lower level OPP **upward**: *Share prices continued their* ***downward trend****. | She was caught in a* ***downward spiral*** *of drink and drugs.* → DOWNWARDS

ˌdownwardly comˈpatible *adj* computer software that is downwardly compatible can be used on older computers as well as very new ones

ˌdownwardly ˈmobile *adj* someone who is downwardly mobile is becoming poorer OPP **upwardly mobile**

down·wards /ˈdaʊnwədz $ -wərdz/ ●●○ (*also* **downward**) *adv*

1 towards a lower level or position OPP **upwards**: *Nina glanced downwards. | Hold out your hands with your palms facing downwards. | The body was lying* ***face downwards*** (=with the front of the body on the floor).

2 used when a number or amount becomes smaller OPP **upwards**: *The death toll was later revised downwards to 689.*

3 from the chairman/president/top etc downwards used to mean that people of all levels in an organization, country etc are affected by something: *Everyone from the chairman downwards is taking a pay cut.*

down·wind /ˌdaʊnˈwɪnd/ *adv* in the direction that the wind is moving OPP **upwind**

down·y /ˈdaʊni/ *adj* covered in or filled with soft fine hair or feathers: *the baby's downy head*

dow·ry /ˈdaʊəri $ ˈdaʊri/ *n* (*plural* **dowries**) [C] property and money that a woman gives to her husband when they marry in some societies

dowse[1] /daʊz/ *v* [I + for] to look for water or minerals under the ground using a special stick that points to where they are

dowse[2] /daʊs/ *v* [T] another spelling of DOUSE

dows·er /ˈdaʊzə $ -ər/ *n* [C] someone who dowses for water or minerals

dowsing rod /ˈdaʊzɪŋ ˌrɒd $ -ˌrɑːd/ *n* [C] a special stick in the shape of a Y used by a dowser

doy·en /ˈdɔɪən/ *n* [C] the oldest, most respected, or

most experienced member of a group: **[+of]** *the doyen of sports commentators*

doy·enne /dɔɪ'en/ *n* [C] the oldest, most respected, or most experienced woman in a group: **[+of]** *the doyenne of piano teachers in the city*

doz. (*also* **doz** *BrE*) *n* the written abbreviation of ***dozen***

doze /dəʊz $ doʊz/ *v* [I] to sleep lightly for a short time: *Grandad was dozing in his chair.* THESAURUS ▸ SLEEP —**doze** *n* [singular]

doze off *phr v* to go to sleep, especially when you did not intend to SYN **drop off**, **nod off**: *I must have dozed off.*

doz·en /'dʌzən/ ●●● S2 W3 *number* (*plural* **dozen** *or* **dozens**) (*written abbreviation* **doz.**)
1 twelve: ***a dozen*** *eggs* | **two/three/four etc dozen** (=24, 36, 48 etc) *The number of deaths has risen to more than two dozen.* | **dozens of people/companies/cars etc** (=but not hundreds or thousands) *Dozens of people were killed.* | *Chris, Helen, and* ***half a dozen*** *others went on holiday together.* | ***A dozen or so*** (=about 12) *cars were parked near the entrance.*
2 *informal* a lot of: **a dozen** *I've heard this story a dozen times before.* | **dozens of sth** *She's had dozens of boyfriends.* | *We collected* ***dozens and dozens*** *of shells on the beach.* → BAKER'S DOZEN, → **a dime a dozen** at DIME(2), → **nineteen to the dozen** at NINETEEN(2), → **six of one and half a dozen of another** at SIX(4)

doz·y /'dəʊzi $ 'doʊ-/ *adj* **1** not feeling very awake **2** *BrE informal* slow to understand things SYN **stupid**: *Those kids are really dozy sometimes!*

DP /ˌdiː 'piː/ *n* [U] *technical* the abbreviation of ***data processing***

D.Phil. (*also* **DPhil** *BrE*) /ˌdiː 'fɪl/ *n* [C] (***Doctor of Philosophy***) a university degree of a very high level, which involves doing advanced RESEARCH SYN **PhD**

dpi /ˌdiː piː 'aɪ/ (***dots per inch***) a way of measuring how much ink is put on the page by a PRINTER

DPP /ˌdiː piː 'piː/ *n* **the DPP** the abbreviation of ***the Director of Public Prosecutions***

Dr W2 *BrE*, **Dr.** *AmE* ●●●
1 the written abbreviation of ***doctor***
2 the written abbreviation of ***drive***: *88 Park Dr*

drab /dræb/ *adj* **1** not bright in colour, especially in a way that stops you from feeling cheerful SYN **dull**: *The walls were painted a drab green.* **2** boring SYN **dull**: *people forced to live grey, drab existences in ugly towns* —**drabness** *n* [U] → **DRIBS AND DRABS**

drach·ma /'drækmə/ *n* (*plural* **drachmas** *or* **drachmae** /-miː/) [C] the standard unit of money used in Greece before the EURO

dra·co·ni·an /drə'kəʊniən $ -'koʊ-/ *adj* very strict and cruel: **draconian measures/controls/penalties etc** *draconian measures to control population growth*

draft[1] /drɑːft $ dræft/ ●●○ S3 W3 AWL *n* [C]
1 PIECE OF WRITING a piece of writing or a plan that is not yet in its finished form: *the* ***rough draft*** *of his new novel* | *I read the* ***first draft*** *and thought it was very good.* | *All parties eventually approved the* ***final draft*** (=finished form) *of the peace treaty.*
2 MILITARY **the draft** *AmE* **a)** a system in which people are ordered to join the army, navy etc, especially during a war SYN **conscription b)** the group of people who are ordered to do this
3 MONEY *especially BrE* a written order for money to be paid by a bank, especially from one bank to another
4 SPORTS *AmE* a system in which professional teams choose players from colleges to join their teams
5 COLD AIR/BEER the American spelling of DRAUGHT

draft[2] AWL *v* [T]
1 PIECE OF WRITING to write a plan, letter, report etc that will need to be changed before it is in its finished form: *Eva's busy drafting her speech for the conference.*
2 MILITARY to order someone to join the army, navy etc, especially during a war SYN **conscript**: **be drafted into sth** *My dad was eighteen when he got drafted into the army.* GRAMMAR **Draft** is usually passive in this meaning.
3 SPORTS *AmE* to choose a college player to join a professional team: *Craigwell was drafted by the Chicago Blackhawks.*

draft sb ↔ **in** (*also* **draft sb into sth**) *phr v* to ask or order someone to work in a place where they do not normally work: *Extra staff were drafted in to deal with the Christmas rush.* | *Hundreds of police have been drafted into the area.*

draft[3] AWL *adj* **1 draft proposal/copy/version etc** a piece of writing that is not yet in its finished form **2** the American spelling of DRAUGHT

'draft board *n* [C] the committee that decides who will be drafted into the army, navy etc

'draft card *n* [C] a card sent to someone telling them they have been drafted into the army, navy etc

'draft ˌdodger *n* [C] someone who illegally avoids joining the army, navy etc, even though they have been ordered to join

draft·ee /drɑː'fiː $ dræf-/ *n* [C] someone who has been drafted into the army, navy etc

draft·er /'drɑːftə $ 'dræftər/ *n* [C] a draftsman

drafts·man /'drɑːftsmən $ 'dræfts-/ *n* (*plural* **draftsmen** /-mən/) [C] **1** (*also* **drafter**) someone who puts a suggested law or a new law into the correct words **2** the American spelling of DRAUGHTSMAN

draft·y /'drɑːfti $ 'dræfti/ *adj* the American spelling of DRAUGHTY

drag[1] /dræg/ ●●● S3 W3 *v* (**dragged**, **dragging**)
1 PULL STH [T] to pull something along the ground, often because it is too heavy to carry: **drag sth away/along/through etc** *Inge managed to drag the table into the kitchen.* THESAURUS ▸ PULL
2 PULL SB [T always + adv/prep] to pull someone somewhere where they do not want to go, in a way that is not gentle: *He grabbed her arm and dragged her into the room.*
3 drag yourself to/into/out of etc sth *informal* to move somewhere with difficulty, especially because you are ill, tired, or unhappy: *I dragged myself out of bed and into the bathroom.* | *Can you* ***drag yourself away from*** (=stop watching) *the TV for a minute?*
4 PERSUADE SB TO COME [T always + adv/prep] *informal* if you drag someone somewhere, you persuade or force them to come with you when they do not want to: *Mom dragged us to a classical music concert.*
5 COMPUTER [T] to move words, pictures etc on a computer screen by pulling them along with the MOUSE: *You can* ***drag and drop*** *text like this.*
6 BE BORING [I] if time or an event drags, it seems to go very slowly because nothing interesting is happening: *Friday afternoons always drag.*
7 TOUCH THE GROUND [I] if something is dragging along the ground, part of it is touching the ground as you move: **[+along/in/on]** *Your coat's dragging in the mud.*
8 drag your feet/heels *informal* to take too much time to do something because you do not want to do it: *The authorities are dragging their feet over banning cigarette advertising.*
9 drag a lake/river etc to look for something in a lake, river etc by pulling a heavy net along the bottom: *The police are dragging the lake for the missing girl's body.*
10 drag sb's name through the mud to tell people about the bad things that someone has done, so that they will have a bad opinion of them
11 drag sb through the courts to force someone to go to a court of law, especially in order to make them have a bad experience because you are angry with them
12 drag sb kicking and screaming into sth to force someone to do something that they do not want to - used humorously: *The party will have to be dragged kicking and screaming into the 21st century.*
13 look as if you've been dragged through a hedge backwards to look very untidy - used humorously
14 INJURED LEG/FOOT [T] if you drag your leg, foot etc, you cannot lift it off the ground as you walk because it is injured: *a bird dragging its broken wing*

drag sb/sth ↔ **down** *phr v*
1 to make someone feel unhappy and weak: *Joe's been ill for weeks now – it's really dragging him down.*
2 to make the price, level, or quality of something go down: *Declining prices for aluminium have dragged down the company's earnings.*
3 if someone or something bad drags you down, they make you become worse or get into a worse situation: *Don't let them **drag** you **down to** their **level**.*
drag sb/sth **into** sth (*also* **drag sb/sth ↔ in**) *phr v*
1 to make someone get involved in an argument, war, or other unpleasant situation that they do not want to be involved in: *I'm sorry to drag you into this mess.*
2 to talk about something when you are having a discussion or argument, even though it is not connected with it: *Don't drag my past into this!*
drag on *phr v* if an event or situation drags on, it continues for too long: **[+for]** *an expensive court battle that could drag on for years*
drag sth ↔ **out** *phr v* to make an event or situation last longer than is necessary: *Neither of them wanted to drag the divorce out longer than they had to.*
drag sth **out of** sb *phr v* to make someone tell you something when they had not intended to tell you or were not supposed to tell you: *Police finally dragged a confession out of him.*
drag sb/sth ↔ **up** *phr v*
1 to mention an unpleasant or embarrassing story from the past, even though it upsets someone: *Why do you have to drag that up again?*
2 be dragged up *BrE* if a child is dragged up, their parents do not teach them to behave properly – used humorously: *Those children have been dragged up, not brought up!*

drag² *n* **1 a drag** *informal* **a)** something or someone that is boring: *Don't be such a drag! Come to the party.* **b)** something that is annoying and continues for a long time: *It's a **real drag** having to travel so far to work every day.* **2 be a drag on sb/sth** to make it hard for someone to make progress towards what they want: *Any slowdown in the economy is going to be a drag on the president's re-election campaign.* **3** [C] the act of breathing in smoke from your cigarette: *Frank **took a drag** on his cigarette.* **4 in drag** wearing clothes worn by the opposite sex, especially to entertain people: *The whole performance is done in drag.* **5** [U] the force of air that pushes against an aircraft or a vehicle that is moving forward: *The car's rounded edges reduce drag.* **6 the main drag** *AmE informal* the biggest or longest street that goes through a town: *Our hotel is right on the main drag.*

drag·net /ˈdrægnet/ *n* [C] **1** a system in which the police look for criminals, using very thorough methods **2** a net that is pulled along the bottom of a river or lake, to bring up things that may be there

drag·on /ˈdrægən/ ●●○ *n* [C]
1 a large imaginary animal that has wings and a long tail and can breathe out fire
2 a woman who behaves in an angry, unfriendly way → **chase the dragon** at CHASE¹(7)

drag·on·fly /ˈdrægənflaɪ/ *n* (*plural* **dragonflies**) [C] a brightly-coloured insect with a long thin body and transparent wings which lives near water → see picture at INSECT

dra·goon¹ /drəˈguːn/ *n* [C] a soldier in past times who rode a horse and carried a gun and sword

dragoon² *v*
dragoon sb **into** sth *phr v* to force someone to do something they do not want to do: **dragoon sb into doing sth** *Monica was dragooned into being on the committee.*

ˈdrag queen *n* [C] *informal* a HOMOSEXUAL man who dresses as a woman, especially to entertain people

ˈdrag race *n* [C] a car race over a very short distance —**drag racing** *n* [U]

drag·ster /ˈdrægstə $ -ər/ *n* [C] a car used in drag races that is long, narrow, and low

drain¹ /dreɪn/ ●●○ *v*
1 LIQUID **a)** [T] to make the water or liquid in something flow away: *The swimming pool is drained and cleaned every winter.* | **drain sth from sth** *Brad drained all the oil from the engine.* | *Can you drain the spaghetti, please* (=pour away the water from the pan)? **b)** [I always + adv/prep] if liquid drains away, it flows away: **[+away/off/from]** *I watched the bath water drain away.* **c)** [I] if something drains, the liquid that is in it or on it flows away and it becomes dry: *Open ditches drain very efficiently.* | *She washed up and left the dishes to drain.* | **well-drained/poorly-drained soil** (=soil from which water flows away quickly or slowly) *This plant needs rich, well-drained soil.*
2 MAKE SB TIRED [T] to make someone feel very tired and without any energy: *Working with children all day really drains you.*
3 USE TOO MUCH [T] to use too much of something, especially money, so that there is not enough left: *Huge imports were draining the country's currency reserves.*
4 the colour/blood drains from sb's face/cheeks used to say that someone's face becomes very pale, because they are frightened or shocked: *When the verdict was read out, all the colour drained from Zelda's cheeks.*
5 drain a glass/cup etc *written* to drink all the liquid in a glass, cup etc: *Hannah drained her mug in one gulp.*
drain away *phr v* if something drains away, it is reduced until there is none left: *I watched the light drain away.* | **anger/confidence/tension/hope etc drains away** *Sally felt her anger drain away.*
drain sth ↔ **off** *phr v* to make water or a liquid flow off something, leaving it dry: *After cooking the meat, drain off the excess fat.*

drain² ●●○ *n* [C]
1 *especially BrE* a pipe that carries water or waste liquids away: *The flood was caused by a **blocked drain**.* | *There's a problem with **the drains**.*
2 *BrE* the frame of metal bars over a drain where water etc can flow into it SYN **grate** *AmE*
3 *AmE* the hole in the bottom of a bath or SINK that water flows out through SYN **plughole** *BrE* → see picture at PLUG¹
4 a drain on sth something that continuously uses a lot of time, money etc: *The war was an enormous **drain on** the country's **resources**.*
5 down the drain *informal* **a)** if time, effort, or money goes down the drain, it is wasted or produces no results: *Well that's it. 18 months' work down the drain.* **b)** if an organization, country etc goes down the drain, it becomes worse or fails: *That's why this country's going down the drain!* → BRAIN DRAIN, → **laugh like a drain** at LAUGH¹(1)

drain·age /ˈdreɪnɪdʒ/ ●○○ *n* [U] the process or system by which water or waste liquid flows away: *A handful of pebbles in the bottom of a flowerpot will help drainage.* | *a plan to improve the town's drainage system*

ˈdrain board *n* an American word for DRAINING BOARD

drained /dreɪnd/ *adj* very tired and without any energy: *Suddenly, she felt totally drained.* | *I felt depressed and completely **drained of energy**.* THESAURUS TIRED

ˈdraining board (*also* **drain board** *AmE*) *n* [C] a slightly sloping area next to a kitchen SINK where you put wet dishes to dry

drain·pipe /ˈdreɪnpaɪp/ *n* [C] **1** *BrE* a pipe that carries rainwater away from the roof of a building SYN **downspout** **2** *AmE* a pipe that carries waste water away from buildings SYN **drain**

ˌdrainpipe ˈtrousers *n* [plural] tight trousers with narrow legs

drake /dreɪk/ *n* [C] a male duck → DUCKS AND DRAKES

dram /dræm/ *n* [C] a small alcoholic drink, especially WHISKY – used especially in Scotland

dra·ma /ˈdrɑːmə $ ˈdrɑːmə, ˈdræmə/ ●●● W3 AWL *n*
1 [C,U] a play for the theatre, television, radio etc, usually a serious one, or plays in general → **comedy**: *the great traditions of ancient Greek drama* | **a TV/television/radio drama** *the award-winning TV drama 'Prime Suspect'* | *a new **drama series** for Saturday nights* | *a drama critic* | *a **courtroom drama*** (=one that takes place in a court of law) | *a*

D

lavish ***costume drama*** *(=one about events in a past century) | He plays a Russian spy in the* ***comedy drama*** *'Sleepers'.*
2 [U] acting – used when talking about it as a subject to study or teach: *young actors coming out of* ***drama school*** *| our drama teacher*
3 [C,U] an exciting event or set of events, or the quality of being exciting: *Maggie's life is always full of drama. | accidents, burst pipes, and other domestic dramas | a night of* ***high drama*** (=very exciting events) *| the drama of the moment*
4 make a drama out of sth to become upset about a small problem and make it seem worse than it really is: *Brian always makes such a drama out of everything.*
5 drama queen a woman or HOMOSEXUAL man who tends to behave as if situations are worse than they really are – used to show disapproval

dra·mat·ic /drəˈmætɪk/ ●●○ W3 AWL *adj*
1 great and sudden: **dramatic change/shift/improvement** *Computers have brought dramatic changes to the workplace.* | **dramatic increase/rise/fall/drop/reduction etc** *Universities have suffered a dramatic drop in student numbers.* | **dramatic effect/results** *A serious accident can have a dramatic effect on your family's finances.*
2 exciting or impressive: *A superb goal by Owen earned United a dramatic victory yesterday. | Some of the most* ***dramatic events*** *in American history happened here. | the* ***dramatic scenery*** *of the Grand Canyon* THESAURUS EXCITING
3 connected with acting or plays: *the amateur dramatic society | the dramatic arts*
4 intended to be impressive, so that people notice: *She needed a stunning dress to help her make a dramatic entrance. | Tristan threw up his hands in a* ***dramatic gesture****.*

dra·mat·i·cally /drəˈmætɪkli/ ●●○ AWL *adv*
1 in a great and sudden way: **increase/rise/fall/drop dramatically** *Output has increased dramatically. | Three years on, Jack's life has* ***dramatically changed****.*
2 in a way that is intended to be impressive, so that people notice: *She leaned forward dramatically.*

draˌmatic ˈirony *n* [U] when the people watching a play know something that the characters do not, and can understand the real importance or meaning of what is happening

dra·mat·ics /drəˈmætɪks/ *n* [plural] behaviour that shows too much emotion, and is annoying or does not seem sincere: *Rex had no time for her dramatics, and left the room.* → **amateur dramatics** at AMATEUR[1]

dram·a·tis per·so·nae /ˌdræmətəs pɜːˈsəʊnaɪ, pəˈsəʊniː $ -pərˈsoʊniː/ *n* [plural] *formal* the characters in a play → **cast**

dram·a·tist /ˈdræmətɪst/ AWL *n* [C] someone who writes plays, especially serious ones SYN **playwright**

dram·a·tize (*also* **-ise** *BrE*) /ˈdræmətaɪz/ AWL *v* [T]
1 to make a book or event into a play or film: *a novel dramatized for television* **2** to make a situation seem more exciting, terrible etc than it really is: *Why do you have to dramatize everything?* **3** to make something more noticeable SYN **highlight**: *This incident dramatized the difficulties involved in the project.* —**dramatization** /ˌdræmətaɪˈzeɪʃən $ -tə-/ *n* [C,U]

dra·me·dy /ˈdrɑːmədi $ ˈdrɑː-, ˈdræ-/ *n* [C] *especially AmE* a television programme or film which has some amusing parts and some more serious parts

drank /dræŋk/ *v* the past tense of DRINK

drape /dreɪp/ ●○○ *v* [T]
1 to put something somewhere so that it hangs or lies loosely: **drape sth over/around/across sth** *He took off his coat and draped it over a chair. | Mina lay back, her arms draped lazily over the cushions.*
2 to cover or decorate something with a cloth: **drape sth over/around sth** *Jack emerged with a towel draped around him.* | **drape sth with/in sth** *The soldiers' coffins were draped with American flags.*

drap·er /ˈdreɪpə $ -ər/ *n* [C] *BrE old-fashioned* someone who sells cloth, curtains etc

drap·er·y /ˈdreɪpəri/ *n* **1** [U] cloth arranged in folds: *a table covered with drapery* **2 draperies** [plural] *AmE* long heavy curtains **3** [U] *BrE* cloth and other goods sold by a draper: *a drapery business*

drapes /dreɪps/ *n* [plural] *AmE* long heavy curtains

dras·tic /ˈdræstɪk/ ●○○ *adj* extreme and sudden: **drastic action/measures** *NATO threatened drastic action if its terms were not met. |* ***drastic cuts*** *in government spending |* ***Drastic changes*** *are needed if environmental catastrophe is to be avoided.* —**drastically** /-kli/ *adv*: *The size of the army was drastically cut.*

drat /dræt/ *interjection old-fashioned* used to show you are annoyed —**dratted** *adj*

draught[1] /drɑːft $ dræft/ *n* [C] *BrE*
1 AIR cold air that moves through a room and that you can feel SYN **draft** *AmE*: *Can you close the window? I'm* ***in a draught****.* THESAURUS WIND
2 BEER **on draught** beer that is on draught is served from a large container rather than a bottle SYN **on draft** *AmE*
3 GAME **a) draughts** [U] a game played by two people, each with 12 round pieces, on a board of 64 squares SYN **checkers** *AmE* **b)** one of the round pieces used in the game of draughts SYN **checker** *AmE* → see picture at BOARD GAME
4 MEDICINE *old use* a medicine that you drink: *a sleeping draught*
5 SHIP *technical* the depth of water needed by a ship so that it will not touch the bottom of the sea, a river etc SYN **draft** *AmE*
6 SWALLOW *written* the act of swallowing liquid, or the amount of liquid swallowed at one time SYN **draft** *AmE*: *Mick took a long draught of lager.*

draught[2] *BrE*, **draft** *AmE adj* [only before noun] **1** draught beer is served from a large container rather than a bottle **2** a draught animal is used for pulling heavy loads

draught·board /ˈdrɑːftbɔːd $ ˈdræftbɔːrd/ *n* [C] *BrE* a board with 64 squares on which the game of draughts is played SYN **checkerboard** *AmE*

ˈdraught exˌcluder *n* [C,U] *BrE* material that you put around the edge of windows and doors to stop cold air from coming into the house

draughts·man *BrE*, **draftsman** *AmE* /ˈdrɑːftsmən $ ˈdræfts-/ *n* (*plural* **draughtsmen** /-mən/) [C] **1** someone whose job is to draw all the parts of a new building or machine that is being planned **2** someone who draws well

draughts·man·ship *BrE*, **draftsmanship** *AmE* /ˈdrɑːftsmənʃɪp $ ˈdræfts-/ *n* [U] the skill of drawing or the ability to draw well

draugh·ty *BrE*, **drafty** *AmE* /ˈdrɑːfti $ ˈdræfti/ *adj* a draughty room or building has cold air blowing through it: *a draughty old house* THESAURUS COLD

draw[1] /drɔː $ drɒː/ ●●● S1 W1 *v* (*past tense* **drew** /druː/, *past participle* **drawn** /drɔːn $ drɒːn/)
1 PICTURE [I,T] to produce a picture of something using a pencil, pen etc: *Katie had drawn a cottage with a little stream running next to it. | She asked the little girl to* ***draw a picture*** *of the man she'd spoken to. | Keith was drawing a complicated-looking graph. | I've never been able to draw very well.* | **draw sb sth** *Can you draw me a map of how to get there?*
2 draw (sb's) attention to make someone notice something: **[+to]** *I have been asked to draw your attention to the following points. | A dark house can* ***draw attention to the fact that*** *the house is empty.* | **draw attention to yourself** *He didn't want to draw attention to himself. | The case drew international attention.*
3 draw a conclusion to decide that a particular fact or principle is true according to the information you have been given: **[+from]** *It would be unwise to draw firm conclusions from the results of a single survey.*

REGISTER
In everyday English, people usually say **reach a conclusion** or **come to a conclusion**.

4 draw a comparison/parallel/distinction etc to compare two people or things and show how they are similar or different: **[+between]** *The author draws a comparison between East and West Germany and the North-South divide in England.* | *The report draws a distinction between various forms of health care.*

> REGISTER
> In everyday English, people usually say **make a comparison or distinction** (but NOT **make a parallel**).

5 GET A REACTION [T] to get a particular kind of reaction from someone: **draw sth from sb** *His remarks drew an angry response from Democrats.* | **draw praise/criticism** *The movie drew praise from critics.*
6 ATTRACT [T] to attract someone or make them want to do something: **draw sb to sth** *What first drew you to teaching?* | *Beth felt strangely drawn to this gentle stranger.* | *The festival is likely to* ***draw*** *huge* ***crowds****.*
7 GET STH YOU NEED [T] to get something that you need or want from someone or something: **draw sth from sth** *I drew a lot of comfort from her kind words.* | *Plants draw nourishment from the soil.*
8 GIVE INFORMATION **be drawn** [usually in negatives] to give information in reply to questions about something: *She refused to be drawn on the subject.*
9 MOVE [I always + adv/prep] to move in a particular direction: *She drew away, but he pulled her close again.* | *The boat drew alongside us and a man appeared on the deck.* | *I arrived just as the train was drawing into the station.*

> REGISTER
> In everyday English, people usually use **pull** rather than **draw**: *The train was* ***pulling*** *into the station.*

10 draw near/closer to become closer in time or space: *Maria grew anxious as the men drew closer.* | *Christmas is drawing near.*

> REGISTER
> In everyday English, people usually say **get nearer/closer**: *Christmas is* ***getting nearer****.*

11 draw level to move into a position where you are equal to someone else in a race, game, or competition: *Black drew level with the other runners.*
12 PULL SB/STH [T always + adv/prep] to move someone or something in a particular direction by pulling them gently: **draw sb/sth aside/up/across etc** *Bobby drew a chair up to the table.* | *Hussain drew me aside to whisper in my ear.* | **draw the curtains/a blind etc** (=close them by pulling them gently) THESAURUS ▶ PULL
13 PULL A VEHICLE [T] if an animal draws a vehicle, it pulls it along: *a carriage drawn by six horses* | *an ox-drawn cart* THESAURUS ▶ PULL
14 TAKE STH OUT [T] to take something out of a container, pocket etc: **draw sth out/from sth** *Ali reached into his pocket and drew out a piece of paper.* | **draw a gun/sword/weapon etc** *Maria drew her gun nervously and peered out into the gloom.*

> REGISTER
> In everyday English, people usually use **pull** something **out** or **take** something **out** rather than **draw** something **out**: *Ali reached into his pocket and* ***pulled out*** *a piece of paper.*

15 draw a line (between sth) to think or show that one thing is different from another: *Adolescents often use drugs simply to try to draw a line between their own and their parents' way of life.*
16 draw the line (at sth) to allow or accept something up to a particular point, but not beyond it: *I don't mind doing some gardening but I draw the line at digging.*
17 where do you draw the line? *spoken* used to say it is impossible to decide at which point an acceptable limit has been reached: *Some say 50 is too old to have a baby, but where do you draw the line?*
18 draw a line under sth to say that something is completely finished and you will not think about it again: *I just want to draw a line under the relationship.*
19 draw sb's eye (to sth) if something draws your eye, it makes you notice it: *My eye was drawn to a painting on the wall.*
20 FROM A BANK (*also* **draw out**) [T] to take money from your bank account SYN **withdraw**: *Hughes had drawn $8,000 in cash from a bank in Toronto.*
21 RECEIVE MONEY [T] to receive an amount of money regularly from a government or financial institution: *How long have you been drawing unemployment benefit?* | *I'll be* ***drawing*** *my* ***pension*** *before he'll ever get around to asking me to marry him!*
22 draw a cheque (on sth) *BrE*, **draw a check (on sth)** *AmE* to write a cheque for taking money out of a particular bank account
23 BREATHE [I,T] to take air or smoke into your lungs: *She* ***drew a deep breath****.* | *Ruth paused to* ***draw breath****, her voice barely hiding her excitement.* | *He lit his pipe and drew deeply.*
24 draw breath to find time to have a rest when you are busy: *I've hardly had a moment to draw breath.*
25 TAKE LIQUID FROM STH [T] **a)** to take a liquid from something such as a BARREL or TAP **b)** to take water from a WELL
26 FIRE [I] if a fire or CHIMNEY draws, it lets the air flow through to make the fire burn well
27 CHOOSE [I,T] to choose by chance a ticket etc that will win a prize: *The winning ticket will be drawn at the Christmas Party.*
28 draw lots/straws to decide who will do something by taking pieces of paper out of a container or choosing STRAWs of hidden lengths: *We drew lots to see who would go first.*
29 draw the short straw used to say that someone has been unlucky because they were chosen to do something that no one else wanted to do: *He drew the short straw and had to drive everyone to the party.*
30 GAME [I,T] *especially BrE* to finish without either side winning in a game such as football SYN **tie**: *They drew 3-3.* | **[+with]** *Liverpool drew with Juventus.*
31 be drawn against sb *BrE* to be chosen by chance to play or compete against someone: *England have been drawn against France in next month's game.*
32 draw a blank *informal* to be unsuccessful in finding information or the answer to a problem: *All his investigations have drawn a blank so far.*
33 draw to a halt/stop if a vehicle draws to a halt or stop, it slows down and stops
34 draw to a close/end to end: *Festival-goers began to drift off as the evening drew to an end.*
35 draw a veil over sth to deliberately keep something unpleasant or embarrassing from being known: *I'd rather draw a veil over what happened last night.*
36 draw blood a) to make someone bleed: *The dog bit her so hard that it drew blood.* **b)** to make someone angry or embarrass them in an argument, especially a public one: *Barker sought to draw blood by mentioning his rival's weakness of character.*
37 draw a bow to bend a BOW by pulling back the string in order to shoot an ARROW
38 SHIP [T] *technical* if a ship draws a particular depth, it needs that depth of water to float in → **be at daggers drawn** at DAGGER(3)

> **THESAURUS**
> **draw** to make a picture, pattern etc using a pen or pencil: *The children were asked to draw a picture of their families.* | *I'm going to art classes to learn how to draw.*
> **sketch** /sketʃ/ to draw a picture of something or someone quickly and without a lot of detail: *Roy took a pencil and sketched the bird quickly, before it moved.*
> **illustrate** to draw the pictures in a book: *It's a beautiful book, illustrated by Arthur Rackham.*
> **doodle** /ˈduːdl/ to draw shapes or patterns without really thinking about what you are doing: *He was on the phone, doodling on his notepad as he spoke.*

D

scribble to draw shapes or lines without making a definite picture or pattern. Small children do this before they have learned to draw or write: *At the age of two, she loved scribbling with crayons and coloured pencils.*
trace to copy a picture by putting a piece of thin paper over it and drawing the lines that you can see through the paper: *First trace the map, and then copy it into your workbooks.*

draw back *phr v*
1 to move backwards, especially because you are frightened or surprised: *Suddenly, she drew back, startled.* | **draw back in horror/shock/fear etc** *She peeped into the box and drew back in horror.*
2 to decide not to do something, especially because you think it would be bad for you SYN **withdraw**: **[+from]** *The government drew back from their extreme standpoint.*

draw sth ↔ **down** *phr v* to obtain money that it has been agreed that you can borrow, or to use money that has been saved: *He drew down the final $25 million of the loan.*

draw in *phr v*
1 *BrE* if the days or nights draw in, it starts to get dark earlier in the evening because winter is coming: *In October the nights start drawing in.*
2 draw sb ↔ in to get someone involved in something: *We should use the demonstration as an opportunity to draw more supporters in.* | *Despite himself, he found himself being drawn in by the man's warmth and ease.*
3 draw in your horns *BrE* to spend less money because you have financial problems

draw sb **into** sth *phr v* to make someone become involved in something, especially when they do not want to be involved: *He tried to draw her into conversation.* | *She found herself drawn into a disagreement between two of her neighbours.*

draw sth ↔ **off** *phr v* to remove some liquid from a larger supply: *The cold water is heated as it is drawn off.*

draw on *phr v*
1 draw on/upon sth to use information, experience, knowledge etc for a particular purpose: *His work* ***draws heavily on*** *learning theories of the 1980s.* | *She has 20 years' teaching experience to draw on.*
2 draw on sth to use part of a supply of something such as money: *I drew on my savings to pay for the repairs.*
3 draw on a cigarette/cigar etc to breathe in smoke from a cigarette etc
4 *BrE formal* if a period of time or an event draws on, it comes closer to its end: *Winter is drawing on.* | *As the journey drew on, he started to feel tired.*

draw out *phr v*
1 draw sth ↔ out to take money from your bank account
2 draw sb ↔ out to make someone feel less shy and more willing to talk: *She just needed someone to draw her out and take an interest in her.*
3 draw sth ↔ out *formal* to mention a particular piece of information and explain it clearly and in detail: *There are two major themes to be drawn out in this discussion.*
4 draw sth ↔ out to make an event last longer than usual: *The final question drew the meeting out for another hour.* → DRAWN-OUT
5 *BrE* if the days or nights draw out, it stays light until later in the evening because summer is coming

draw up *phr v*
1 draw sth ↔ up to prepare a written document, such as a list or contract: ***Draw up a list*** *of all the things you want to do.* | **draw up plans/proposals** *He was asked to draw up proposals for reforming the law.* | *The contract was drawn up last year.*
2 if a vehicle draws up, it arrives somewhere and stops: *A taxi drew up at the gate.*
3 draw up a chair to move a chair closer to someone or something
4 draw yourself up (to your full height) to stand up very straight because you are angry or determined about something: *He drew himself up and said, 'This has gone far enough.'*
5 draw your knees up to bring your legs closer to your body: *Ruth sat, knees drawn up under her chin, and waited.*

draw² ●●○ S3 *n* [C]
1 the final result of a game or competition in which both teams or players have the same number of points SYN **tie**: *The match* ***ended in a draw.***
2 an occasion when someone or something is chosen by chance, especially the winning ticket in a LOTTERY, or the teams who will play against each other in a competition: *England has been selected to play Germany in the draw for the first round of the World Cup.*
3 *BrE* a competition in which people whose names or tickets are chosen by chance win money or prizes: *Congratulations! You have been entered into our £100,000* ***prize draw!***
4 a performer, place, event etc that a lot of people come to see: *It is hoped that the new art gallery will be a big draw for visitors.*
5 when you breathe in smoke from a cigarette SYN **drag**: *Maltravers took a long draw on his cigarette.* → **the luck of the draw** at LUCK¹(18), → **quick on the draw** at QUICK¹(9)

draw·back /ˈdrɔːbæk $ ˈdrɒː-/ ●○○ *n* [C] a disadvantage of a situation, plan, product etc: *It's a great city – the only drawback is the weather.* | **drawback of/to (doing) sth** *The main drawback to these products is that they tend to be too salty.* **THESAURUS** DISADVANTAGE

draw·bridge /ˈdrɔːbrɪdʒ $ ˈdrɒː-/ *n* [C] **1** a bridge that can be pulled up to stop people from entering a castle, or to let ships pass **2 pull up the drawbridge a)** to stop being involved in something: *Perhaps we should just pull up the drawbridge and let them get on with it.* **b)** to stop more people coming into a country, joining an organization etc

drawer /drɔː $ drɒːr/ ●●● S3 *n* [C]
1 part of a piece of furniture, such as a desk, that you pull out and push in and use to keep things in: *She took a file from her* ***desk drawer.*** | *The scissors are in the* ***kitchen drawer*** (=drawer in a piece of kitchen furniture). | **top/bottom/right-hand/left-hand drawer** *He opened the top drawer of his desk, and took out a brown envelope.* | **sock/cutlery drawer** (=one for keeping socks, or knives, forks etc in) → BOTTOM DRAWER, CHEST OF DRAWERS, TOP-DRAWER
2 drawers [plural] *old-fashioned* underwear that women and girls wear between their waist and the tops of their legs SYN **knickers**

draw·ing /ˈdrɔːɪŋ $ ˈdrɒː-/ ●●● S3 W3 *n*
1 [C] a picture that you draw with a pencil, pen etc: **[+of]** *a drawing of Canterbury Cathedral*
2 [U] the art or skill of making pictures, plans etc with a pen or pencil: *I've never been very good at drawing.*
3 [C] *AmE* a competition in which people whose names or tickets are chosen by chance win money or prizes SYN **draw** *BrE*: *The church social will include a buffet dinner and a* ***prize drawing.***

ˈdrawing board *n* [C] **1 (go) back to the drawing board** if you go back to the drawing board, you start again with a completely new plan or idea, after the one you tried before has failed: *The current system just isn't working – we need to go back to the drawing board and start afresh.* **2 on the drawing board** if a plan or product is on the drawing board, it is in the process of being planned or prepared: *Other car manufacturers have similar projects on the drawing board.* **3** a large flat board that artists and DESIGNERS work on

ˈdrawing pin *n* [C] *BrE* a short metal pin with a round flat head, used especially for putting notices on boards or walls SYN **thumbtack** *AmE* → see picture at STATIONERY

ˈdrawing ˌpower *n* [U] an event's, performer's, place's etc ability to attract people to come and see them SYN **pulling power**

ˈdrawing room *n* [C] *formal* a room, especially in a large house, where you can entertain guests or relax → **sitting room**

drawl /drɔːl $ drɒːl/ *v* [I,T] to speak slowly, with vowel sounds that are longer than usual: *'Can't do that,' he* *drawled languidly.* **—drawl** *n* [singular]: *'What you got there?' he asked in a slow Texan drawl.*

drawn[1] /drɔːn $ drɒːn/ *v* the past participle of DRAW

drawn[2] *adj* someone who looks drawn has a thin pale face, because they are ill, tired, or worried

ˌdrawn-ˈout *adj* taking more time than usual or more time than you would like: *The government wants to avoid a* ***long drawn-out*** *war against the rebel forces.*

draw·string /ˈdrɔːstrɪŋ $ ˈdrɒː-/ *n* [C] a string through the top of a bag, piece of clothing etc that you can pull to make it tighter: *trousers with a drawstring waist*

dray /dreɪ/ *n* [C] a flat CART with four wheels that was used in the past for carrying heavy loads, especially BARRELs of beer

dread[1] /dred/ ●○○ *v* [T] to feel anxious or worried about something that is going to happen or may happen: *I've got an interview tomorrow and I'm dreading it.* | **dread doing sth** *I'm dreading going back to work.* | **dread sb doing sth** *Tim dreaded his parents finding out.* | **dread (that)** *I'm dreading that I'll be asked to make a speech.* | **dread the thought/prospect of (doing) sth** *He dreaded the prospect of being all alone in that house.* | ***I dread to think*** *what will happen if they get elected* (=I think it will be very bad).

dread[2] *n* [singular, U] a strong fear of something that is going to happen or may happen: **dread of (doing) sth** *the dread of losing those we love* | **with dread** *Bernice looked with dread at the end of the passage.* | *The prospect of flying* ***filled*** *me* ***with dread.*** | *She* ***lives in dread of*** (=is continuously very afraid of) *the disease returning.*

dread·ed /ˈdredɪd/ (*also* **dread** *literary*) *adj* [only before noun] making you feel afraid or anxious – often used humorously: *She couldn't put off the dreaded moment forever.*

dread·ful /ˈdredfəl/ ●●○ *adj*
1 extremely unpleasant SYN **terrible**: *We've had some dreadful weather lately.* | *Michelle felt absolutely dreadful* (=very ill). THESAURUS ▸ BAD, HORRIBLE
2 [only before noun] used to emphasize how bad something or someone is SYN **terrible**: *a dreadful mistake*

GRAMMAR

Dreadful is not used with 'very'. You say: *The food was absolutely dreadful.* ✗ Don't say: *The food was very dreadful.*

dread·ful·ly /ˈdredfəli/ *adv* **1** extremely or very much: *They're dreadfully busy at the moment.* | *Would you mind dreadfully if I didn't come?* **2** very badly: *The team played dreadfully.*

dread·locks /ˈdredlɒks $ -lɑːks/ *n* [plural] a way of arranging your hair, popular with Rastafarians, in which it hangs in thick pieces that look like rope → see picture at HAIRSTYLE

dream[1] /driːm/ ●●● S2 W2 *n* [C]
1 WHILE SLEEPING a series of thoughts, images, and feelings that you experience when you are asleep → **daydream**: *I had lots of dreams last night.* | **[+about]** *a dream about drowning* | **in a dream** *In my dream I flew to a forest of enormous trees.*
2 WISH a wish to do, be, or have something – used especially when this seems unlikely: *Her dream is to make a movie.* | **dream of (doing) sth** *She had dreams of university.* | **fulfil/realize a dream** *I fulfilled a childhood dream when I became champion.* | *I have just met* ***the man of my dreams*** (=the perfect man)! | **beyond your wildest dreams** (=better than anything you imagined or hoped for)
3 dream house/home/job etc something that seems perfect to someone: *I've finally found my dream house.* | *Win a dream holiday for two in San Francisco!*
4 in a dream having a state of mind in which you do not notice or pay attention to things around you: *Ruth went about her tasks in a dream.*
5 be a dream come true if something is a dream come true, it happens after you have wanted it to happen for a long time: *Marriage to her is a dream come true.*
6 like a dream extremely well or effectively: *The plan* ***worked like a dream.***
7 be/live in a dream world to have ideas or hopes that are not correct or likely to happen: *If you think that all homeless people have it as easy as me, then you are living in a dream world.*
8 be a dream be perfect or very desirable: *Her latest boyfriend is an absolute dream.* | *Some performers are a dream to work with; others are not.* | **sb's dream** (=something someone would really like) *She's every adolescent schoolboy's dream.*
9 in your dreams *spoken* used to say in a rude way that something is not likely to happen: *'I'm going to ask her to go out with me.' 'In your dreams!'*

COLLOCATIONS

VERBS

have a dream *I had a dream about you last night.*

ADJECTIVES

a bad dream (=unpleasant or frightening) *The movie gave the kids bad dreams.*
a strange/weird dream *Sometimes I have a strange dream in which I try to speak but I can't.*
a vivid dream (=very clear) | **a recurrent/recurring dream** (=that you have many times)

PHRASES

be/seem like a dream (=seem unreal) *That summer was so wonderful it seemed like a dream.*
Sweet dreams! (=said to someone who is going to bed)

dream[2] ●●● S3 W3 *v* (*past tense and past participle* **dreamed** *or* **dreamt** /dremt/)
1 WISH [I,T] to think about something that you would like to happen or have: **dream of/about (doing) sth** *She dreamed of becoming a chef.* | *He's got the sort of money that you and I can* ***only dream about.*** | **dream (that)** *She dreamed that one day she would be famous.*

GRAMMAR

You **dream of** doing something: *I've always dreamed of being an artist.* ✗ Don't say: *I've always dreamed to be an artist.*

GRAMMAR GUIDE ▸ VERBS

2 WHILE SLEEPING [I,T] to have a dream while you are asleep: **[+about]** *I dreamt about you last night.* | **dream (that)** *It's quite common to dream that you're falling.*
3 NOT PAY ATTENTION [I] to think about something else and not give your attention to what is happening around you SYN **daydream**: *She had been dreaming and had not followed the conversation.*
4 IMAGINE [I,T] to imagine that you have done, seen, or heard something that you have not: *I was sure I posted the letter but I* ***must have dreamt it.***
5 never dreamed (that) used to say that you did not think that something would happen: *We never dreamed that we would get through to the next round.*
6 wouldn't dream of (doing) sth *spoken* used to say that you would never do something because you think it is bad or wrong: *I wouldn't dream of letting strangers look after my own grandmother!*
7 who would have dreamt that ...? *spoken* used to express surprise about something that has happened: *Who would have dreamt that this would happen?*

dream sth ↔ **away** *phr v* to waste time by thinking about what may happen: *She would just sit in her room dreaming away the hours.*

dream on *phr v* [only in imperative] *spoken* used to tell someone that they are hoping for something that will not happen: *You think I'm going to help you move house? Dream on!*

dream sth ↔ **up** *phr v* to think of a plan or idea, especially an unusual one: *He was continually dreaming up new schemes to promote and enlarge the business.*

dream·er /ˈdriːmə $ -ər/ *n* [C] **1** someone who has ideas or plans that are not practical: *She was a dreamer –*

D

not pragmatic. **2** someone who dreams while they are asleep

dream·i·ly /ˈdriːməli/ *adv* thinking about something pleasant and not about what is happening around you: *'I'm coming,' he replied dreamily, without moving.*

dream·land /ˈdriːmlænd/ *n* [U] **1** a happy place or situation that exists only in your imagination **2** *informal* sleep: *The kids are both far away in dreamland.*

dream·less /ˈdriːmləs/ *adj* dreamless sleep is very deep and peaceful

dream·like /ˈdriːmlaɪk/ *adj* as if happening in a dream SYN **unreal**: *The film had a dreamlike quality.*

dreamt /dremt/ a past tense and past participle of DREAM

ˈ**dream ˌticket** *n* [singular] a combination of people who you think will be sure to win an election for a political party

dream·y /ˈdriːmi/ *adj* **1** looking as though you are thinking about something pleasant rather than what is happening around you: *a dreamy smile* **2** someone who is dreamy has a good imagination but is not very practical: *He was an artist, not particularly tidy, too dreamy to match her ways.* **3** pleasant, peaceful, and relaxing: *The windows cast a dreamy light in the room.* **4** *informal* very attractive and desirable: *a book of dreamy chocolate recipes* —**dreaminess** *n* [U]

D

drear·i·ly /ˈdrɪərəli $ ˈdrɪr-/ *adv* **1** sadly: *Laura stared drearily at herself in the mirror.* **2** dully: *a drearily predictable thriller*

drear·y /ˈdrɪəri $ ˈdrɪri/ (*also* **drear** /drɪə $ drɪr/ *literary*) *adj* dull and making you feel sad or bored: *the same dreary routine* | *a dreary winter's day* —**dreariness** *n* [U]

dreck /drek/ *n* [U] *AmE informal* something that is of very bad quality: *Readers for publishing houses see a lot of good stuff and a lot of dreck.*

dredge /dredʒ/ *v* **1** [I,T] to remove mud or sand from the bottom of a river, HARBOUR etc, or to search for something by doing this: *They dredged for oysters.* **2** [T + with] to cover food lightly with flour, sugar etc

dredge sth ↔ **up** *phr v* **1** to start talking again about something that happened a long time ago, especially something unpleasant: *Newsweek magazine dredged up some remarks which he made last year.* **2** to manage to remember something, or to feel or express an emotion, with difficulty: *Robertson tried to dredge up an image of her in his mind.* | *From somewhere she dredged up a brilliant smile.* **3** to pull something up from the bottom of a river, lake etc

dredg·er /ˈdredʒə $ -ər/ (*also* **dredge**) *n* [C] a machine or ship used for digging or removing mud and sand from the bottom of a river, lake etc

dregs /dregz/ *n* **1** [plural] a small amount of a drink, sometimes with bits in, left at the bottom of a cup, glass, or bottle **2 the dregs of society/humanity** *not polite* an offensive expression used to describe the people that you consider are the least important or useful in society

drei·del /ˈdreɪdl/ *n* [C] a TOP (=a toy that you spin) with a Hebrew letter on each of its four sides and a point at the bottom, used in a game played during Hanukkah

drench /drentʃ/ *v* [T] to make something or someone extremely wet: *In the early morning they had got drenched in the grass.* —**drenching** /ˈdrentʃɪŋ/ *adj*: *drenching rain*

drenched /drentʃt/ *adj* **1** covered with a lot of a liquid: *Come on in – you're drenched!* | **[+in/with]** *I was drenched in sweat.* | *chips drenched in vinegar* | **rain-drenched/sweat-drenched etc** *He changed out of his rain-drenched clothes.* THESAURUS▸ WET **2 drenched in/with light** *literary* something that is drenched with light has a lot of light shining on it

dress¹ /dres/ ●●● S2 W2 *n*

1 [C] a piece of clothing worn by a woman or girl that covers the top of her body and part or all of her legs → **skirt**: *Sheila wore a long red dress.* | *a summer dress* THESAURUS▸ CLOTHES

2 [U] clothes for men or women of a particular type or for a particular occasion: *a gentleman in* ***evening dress*** (=formal clothes worn especially at important social events) | *The play was performed in* ***modern dress*** (=clothes from the present time). | **dress code** (=a standard of what you should wear for a particular situation) *This restaurant has a strict dress code – no tie, no service.*

dress² ●●● S2 W2 *v*

1 PUT ON CLOTHES [I,T] to put clothes on yourself or someone else: *Can you wait a minute? I'm just* ***getting dressed.*** | *She dressed quickly and went out of the house.* | *I usually have to dress the kids in the mornings.* | **dress sb in sth** *She dressed Louis in his best blue shirt.*

2 WEAR CLOTHES [I] to wear a particular kind of clothes: *Dress warmly if you're going out for a walk.* | **dress casually/smartly** *I spend most of my time in the house with young children, so I dress casually.* | **[+for]** *How do you normally dress for work?* | *We usually* ***dress for dinner*** (=wear formal clothes for our evening meal).

3 MAKE/CHOOSE CLOTHES [T] to make or choose clothes for someone: *Versace dressed some of the most famous people in Hollywood.*

4 WOUND/CUT ETC [T] to clean, treat, and cover a wound

5 MEAT/FISH [T] to clean and prepare meat or fish so that it is ready to cook or eat: *dressed crab*

6 SALAD [T] to put oil, VINEGAR, salt etc onto a SALAD

7 WINDOW [T] to put an attractive arrangement in a shop window → WINDOW DRESSER

8 SOLDIERS [I,T] *technical* to stand in a straight line, or to make soldiers do this

9 HAIR [T] *formal* to arrange someone's hair into a special style

10 WOOD/STONE ETC [T] *technical* to prepare or put a special surface onto wood, stone, leather etc

dress down *phr v*

1 to wear clothes that are more informal than the ones you would usually wear: *In many offices, people dress down on Fridays.*

2 dress sb ↔ down to speak angrily to someone about something they have done wrong → DRESSING-DOWN

THESAURUS

TO PUT ON CLOTHES

get dressed to put on all your clothes: *You'd better get dressed! It's almost time to leave for school!*

dress *especially literary* to put on all your clothes. Dress is used especially in literature. In everyday English, people usually say **get dressed**: *That day she dressed with extra care, choosing a brown velvet jacket that matched her skirt.*

put sth on to put on a particular piece of clothing, jewellery etc: *Wait – I just have to put my shoes on!* | *She was putting on her earrings in front of the mirror.*

dress up to put on more formal clothes than you usually wear, or to put on special clothes for fun: *We always used to dress up to go to church.* | *Paul dressed up as a pirate for the party.*

dress yourself to put on your clothes – used when this is difficult for someone because they are very old, young, injured etc: *He's hurt his arm so badly that he can't dress himself.*

TO BE WEARING CLOTHES

wear to have a particular piece of clothing or a particular style of clothing on your body: *All visitors must wear a protective helmet.* | *She always wears black.*

have sth on to be wearing a particular piece of clothing, jewellery etc. **Have sth on** is more informal than **wear**: *I had my new blue top on.* | *He had on a red tie and a grey jacket.*

be dressed in sth *especially written* used especially in written descriptions when describing the clothes that someone is wearing: *Alistair was dressed in his best suit and tie.*

dress up *phr v*

1 to wear special clothes for fun, or to put special clothes on someone: **[+as]** *He went to the party dressed up as a*

Chicago gangster. | **[+in]** *I keep a box of old clothes for the children to dress up in.* | **dress sb ↔ up** *We dressed him up as a gorilla.*
2 to wear clothes that are more formal than the ones you would usually wear: *It's a small informal party – you don't have to dress up.*
3 dress sth ↔ up to make something more interesting or attractive: *It was the old offer dressed up as something new.*

dres·sage /ˈdresɑːʒ $ drəˈsɑːʒ/ *n* [U] a competition in which a horse performs a complicated series of movements in answer to signals from its rider

ˈdress ˌcircle *n* [C] *BrE* the lowest of the curved rows of seats upstairs in a theatre SYN **first balcony** *AmE*

ˌdress-down ˈFriday *n* [C,U] *BrE* a Friday when people who work for a company are allowed to wear informal clothes to work SYN **casual Friday** *AmE*

dressed /drest/ *adj* **1 get dressed** to put your clothes on: *Go and get dressed!* **2** having your clothes on or wearing a particular type of clothes: *Aren't you dressed yet?* | **half/fully dressed** *She lay down fully dressed on the bed.* | **smartly/well-/elegantly etc dressed** *a very well-dressed young man* | **[+in]** *She was dressed in a two-piece suit.* | **[+as]** *The children came dressed as animals.* **3 dressed to kill** *informal* wearing very attractive clothes so that everyone notices and admires you **4 dressed (up) to the nines** *informal* wearing your best or most formal clothes

dress·er /ˈdresə $ -ər/ *n* [C] **1** *BrE* a large piece of furniture with open shelves for storing plates, dishes etc SYN **Welsh dresser 2** *AmE* a piece of furniture with drawers for storing clothes, sometimes with a mirror on top SYN **chest of drawers** *BrE* **3 a fashionable/stylish/sloppy etc dresser** someone who dresses in a fashionable etc way: *Stanley was an impeccable dresser.* **4** someone who takes care of someone's clothes, especially an actor's in the theatre, and helps them to dress

dress·ing /ˈdresɪŋ/ ●●○ *n*
1 [C,U] a mixture of liquids, usually oil and VINEGAR, that you put on SALAD or raw vegetables: *a vinaigrette dressing*
→ **FRENCH DRESSING, SALAD DRESSING**
2 [C,U] *AmE* STUFFING(1)
3 [C] a special piece of material used to cover and protect a wound: *The nurse came to change his dressing.*
→ **CROSS-DRESSING, POWER DRESSING, WINDOW DRESSING**

ˌdressing-ˈdown *n* [singular] an occasion when you talk angrily to someone because they have done something wrong: **give sb/get a dressing-down** *The tobacco companies got a severe dressing-down.*

ˈdressing gown ●●○ *n* [C] *BrE, AmE formal* a piece of clothing like a long loose coat that you wear inside the house, usually over night clothes SYN **bathrobe, robe**

ˈdressing room *n* [C] **1** a room where an actor or performer can get ready before going on stage, appearing on television etc **2** *AmE* a room or area in a store where you can try on clothes SYN **changing room** *BrE* **3** a small room next to a bedroom in some houses where you can get dressed

ˈdressing ˌtable *n* [C] a piece of furniture like a table with a mirror on top, sometimes with drawers, that you use when you are doing your hair, putting on MAKE-UP etc → see picture at **TABLE**[1]

ˌdressing-ˈup *BrE*, **ˌdress-ˈup** *AmE* *n* [U] a children's game in which they put on special clothes and pretend that they are someone else

dress·mak·er /ˈdresˌmeɪkə $ -ər/ *n* [C] someone who makes their own clothes, or makes clothes for other people as a job —**dressmaking** *n* [U]

ˈdress reˌhearsal *n* [C] the final practice of a play, OPERA etc, using all the clothes, objects etc that will be used for the actual performance

ˈdress sense *n* [U] the ability to choose clothes that make you look attractive

ˈdress shirt *n* [C] a formal shirt, sometimes with a special decoration at the front, that a man wears under a DINNER JACKET

ˈdress ˌuniform *n* [C,U] a uniform that officers in the army, navy etc wear for formal occasions or ceremonies

dress·y /ˈdresi/ *adj* **1** dressy clothes are suitable for formal occasions: *Her outfit was smart but not too dressy.* **2** someone who is dressy likes to wear very fashionable or formal clothes

drew /druː/ *v* the past tense of DRAW

drib·ble[1] /ˈdrɪbəl/ ●○○ *v*
1 [I,T] to let liquid come out of your mouth onto your face: *Watch out, the baby is dribbling on your shirt!* | *He was dribbling tea onto his tie.*
2 [I always + adv/prep] if a liquid dribbles somewhere, it flows in a thin irregular stream: *Blood from the wound dribbled down the side of his face.*
3 [I,T] to move the ball along with you by short kicks, BOUNCES, or hits in a game of football, BASKETBALL etc: *He was trying to dribble the ball past his opponents.* → see pictures at **BASKETBALL, FOOTBALL**
4 [I always + adv/prep] if something such as money or news dribbles somewhere, it comes or goes in small irregular amounts: *Money is finally dribbling back into the country now.*
5 [T always + adv/prep] to pour something out slowly in an irregular way: *Dribble a few drops of olive oil over the pizza.*

dribble[2] *n* **1** [U] a small amount of liquid that has come out of your mouth: *He wiped the dribble from his chin.* **2 a dribble of sth** a small amount of liquid: *There was a dribble of brandy in the bottom of the bottle.* **3** [C] the act of moving the ball along with you by short kicks, BOUNCES or hits in a game of football, BASKETBALL etc

dribs and drabs /ˌdrɪbz ən ˈdræbz/ *n* **in dribs and drabs** in small irregular amounts or numbers over a period of time: *The guests arrived in dribs and drabs.*

dried /draɪd/ ●●○ *adj* dried substances, such as food or flowers, have had the water removed: *dried herbs*

ˌdried ˈfruit *n* [U] fruit, usually GRAPES, that has been dried and is often used in cooking

ˌdried ˈmilk *n* [U] milk that is made into a powder and can be used by adding water

dri·er /ˈdraɪə $ -ər/ *n* [C] another spelling of DRYER

drift[1] /drɪft/ ●●○ *v* [I]
1 MOVE SLOWLY to move slowly on water or in the air: **[+out/towards etc]** *The rubber raft drifted out to sea.* | *Smoke drifted up from the jungle ahead of us.*
2 WITHOUT PLAN to move, change, or do something without any plan or purpose: **[+around/along etc]** *Jenni spent the year drifting around Europe.* | **[+into]** *I just drifted into teaching, really.* | **[+away]** *The others drifted away. Melanie stayed.* | **drift from sth to sth** *The* ***conversation drifted*** *from one topic to another.* | **let your gaze/eyes/thoughts/mind etc drift** *Idly she let her eyes drift over his desk.*
3 CHANGE to gradually change from being in one condition, situation etc into another without realizing it: **[+into]** *She was just* ***drifting into sleep*** *when the alarm went off.* | *He* ***drifted in and out of consciousness***.
4 MONEY/PRICES if values, prices, SHARES etc drift, they gradually change: *The dollar drifted lower against the yen today.*
5 SNOW/SAND if snow, sand etc drifts, the wind blows it into large piles
6 let sth drift to allow something, especially something bad, to continue in the same way: *He couldn't let the matter drift for much longer.*

drift apart *phr v* if people drift apart, their relationship gradually ends: *Over the years my college friends and I have drifted apart.*

drift off *phr v* to gradually fall asleep: *I was just drifting off when the phone rang.* | *He felt himself* ***drifting off to sleep***.

drift[2] ●○○ *n*
1 SNOW/SAND [C] a large pile of snow or sand that has been blown by the wind: **[+of]** *The road is blocked with massive drifts of snow.* | *a snow drift*
2 CHANGE [singular] a slow change or development from one situation, opinion etc to another: **[+towards/to]** *a drift towards longer working hours*

D

3 MOVEMENT OF PEOPLE [singular, U] a slow movement of large numbers of people that has not been planned: **[+from/to/into]** *the drift from the countryside to the cities*
4 the drift (of sth) the general meaning of what someone is saying: *So what's the drift of the argument?* | **follow/get/catch sb's drift** (=understand the general meaning of what someone is saying) *She didn't quite get my drift, did she?*
5 SHIPS/PLANES [U] the movement of a ship or plane from its original direction because of the movement of the wind or water
6 SLOW MOVEMENT [U] very slow movement, especially over water or through the air

drift·er /ˈdrɪftə $ -ər/ *n* [C] **1** someone who is always moving from one job or place to another with no real purpose **2** a fishing boat that uses a floating net

drift·net /ˈdrɪftnet/ *n* [C] a large fishing net that floats behind a boat

drift·wood /ˈdrɪftwʊd/ *n* [U] wood floating in the sea or left on the shore

drill¹ /drɪl/ ●●○ *n*
1 [C] a tool or machine used for making holes in something: *an electric drill* | *a whine like a dentist's drill* → PNEUMATIC DRILL, see picture at TOOL¹
2 [C] a method of teaching students, sports players etc something by making them repeat the same lesson, exercise etc many times: *a pronunciation drill*
3 fire/emergency drill an occasion when people practise what they should do in a dangerous situation such as a fire
4 [U] military training in which soldiers practise marching, using weapons etc: *rifle drill*
5 the drill *BrE old-fashioned* the usual way that something is done: *'You know the drill?' 'Not really. Tell me again what to do.'*
6 [U] a type of strong cotton cloth
7 [C] **a)** a machine for planting seeds in rows **b)** a row of seeds planted by a machine

drill² ●●○ *v*
1 [I,T] to make a hole in something using a drill: *Drill a hole in each corner.* | **[+into/through]** *He accidentally drilled into a water pipe.* | **drill for oil/water/gas etc** *BP has been licensed to drill for oil in the area.*
2 [T] to teach students, sports players etc by making them repeat the same lesson, exercise etc many times: **drill sb in sth** *She was drilling the class in the forms of the past tense.* | **drill sb to do sth** *I acted instinctively because I had been trained and drilled to do just that.* | *The crew were* ***well drilled*** *in handling emergency situations.*
3 [T] to train soldiers to march or perform other military actions: *The sergeant was drilling the new recruits.*
4 [T] to plant seeds in rows using a machine

drill down *phr v technical* to get a more detailed level of information relating to something, when using a computer

drill sth **into** sb *phr v* to keep telling someone something until they know it very well: *Mother had drilled it into me not to talk to strangers.*

ˈdrilling ˌplatform *n* [C] a large structure in the sea used for drilling for oil, gas etc

dri·ly /ˈdraɪli/ *adv* another spelling of DRYLY

drink¹ /drɪŋk/ ●●● S1 W2 *v* (*past tense* **drank** /dræŋk/, *past participle* **drunk** /drʌŋk/)
1 [I,T] to take liquid into your mouth and swallow it: *You should drink plenty of water.* | *What would you like to drink?* | *Take a seat while I get you* ***something to drink***. | *She filled the glass and drank.*
2 [I] to drink alcohol, especially regularly or too much: *He's been* ***drinking heavily*** *since his wife died.* | *I don't drink.* | *Don't* ***drink and drive***. | *My flatmate Cherry* ***drinks like a fish*** (=regularly drinks a lot of alcohol).
3 drink yourself silly/into a stupor/to death etc to drink so much alcohol that you become very drunk or unconscious, or die: *If he goes on this way he'll drink himself to death.*
4 drink sb under the table to drink more alcohol than someone but not feel as ill as them: *He could drink nearly anyone under the table.*
5 What are you drinking? *spoken* used to offer to buy someone a drink, especially in a PUB
6 drink sb's health *BrE* to wish someone good health before having an alcoholic drink

THESAURUS

sip (*also* **take a sip**) to drink something very slowly
slurp *informal* to drink something in a noisy way
gulp sth down (*also* **down sth**) to drink all of something very quickly
knock sth back *informal* to drink all of an alcoholic drink very quickly
swig (*also* **take/have a swig**) *informal* to drink something quickly with large mouthfuls, especially from a bottle
swallow to make food or drink go down your throat and towards your stomach: *She swallowed the bitter medicine instead of spitting it out.*

drink sth ↔ **in** *phr v* to look at, listen to, feel, or smell something in order to enjoy it: *She just sat there, drinking in the atmosphere.*

drink to sth *phr v*
1 to wish someone success, good luck, good health etc before having an alcoholic drink: *Let's drink to your success in your new job.*
2 I'll drink to that! *spoken* used to agree with what someone has said

drink up *phr v* to drink all of something: **drink sth ↔ up** *Drink up your milk.*

drink² ●●● S1 W2 *n*
1 [C] an amount of liquid that you drink, or the act of drinking something: **[+of]** *Have a drink of water.* | *He took a drink of his coffee.*
2 [C,U] liquid that you can drink: *What's your favourite drink?* | *food and drink companies*
3 [C,U] an alcoholic drink: *He'd obviously had a few drinks.* | *Let's go for a drink.*
4 [U] the habit of drinking too much alcohol, in a way that is very bad for your health: *The marriage ended because of her husband's* ***drink problem*** (=he drank too much alcohol). | *They had* ***driven*** *him* ***to drink*** (=made him start drinking too much alcohol regularly). | *After her retirement from the stage she* ***took to drink*** (=started drinking too much alcohol).
5 drinks [plural] *BrE* a social occasion when you have alcoholic drinks and sometimes food: **for drinks** *Don't forget we're invited to the Jones' for drinks on Sunday.*
6 the drink *old-fashioned* the sea, a lake, or another large area of water

COLLOCATIONS – MEANINGS 1, 2, & 3

VERBS

have a drink (=drink something, especially an alcoholic drink) *Let's go and have a drink.*
take a drink *He took another long drink of water.*
go for a drink (=go to a pub or bar) *Why don't we go for a drink after work?*
buy/get sb a drink (=in a pub or a bar) | **pour (sb) a drink** | **make (sb) a drink** (=make tea or coffee) | **sip your drink** (=drink it in very small amounts) | **down your drink** (=drink it very quickly)

ADJECTIVES

a soft drink (=which does not contain alcohol) *Would you like some wine, or a soft drink?*
an alcoholic drink (=containing alcohol) | **a fizzy drink** *BrE*, **a carbonated drink** *AmE* (=with bubbles of gas) | **a hot/warm drink** | **a cool/cold drink** | **a refreshing drink** (=making you feel less tired or hot) | **a stiff/strong drink** (=a drink with a lot of strong alcohol)

THESAURUS

drink something that you drink: *'Would you like a drink?' 'Yes, I'll have a lemonade.'* | *They had a few drinks in a local bar.*

something to drink *especially spoken* a drink: *Can I get you something to drink?*
soft drink a cold drink that does not contain alcohol, especially one that is sweet and has bubbles in it: *Coca-Cola and other soft drinks*
toast a drink, usually of wine, that a group of people have on a special occasion, for example to celebrate something or wish someone luck in the future: *At midnight they all drank a toast to the New Year.*
beverage /ˈbevərɪdʒ/ *formal, especially written* a drink – often used on MENUs and signs: *Beer is the most popular alcoholic beverage.* | *the list of beverages*

drink·a·ble /ˈdrɪŋkəbəl/ *adj* **1** water that is drinkable is safe to drink **2** wine, beer etc that is drinkable is of good quality and tastes pleasant

ˌdrink-ˈdriving *n* [U] *BrE* driving a car after having drunk too much alcohol SYN **drunk-driving** *AmE* —**drink-driver** *n* [C]

drink·er /ˈdrɪŋkə $ -ər/ ●○○ *n* [C]
1 someone who regularly drinks alcohol: *Dave has always been a bit of a drinker.* | *He was a* ***heavy drinker*** (=he drank a lot).
2 coffee/wine/champagne etc drinker someone who regularly drinks coffee, wine etc

drink·ing /ˈdrɪŋkɪŋ/ *n* [U] the activity of drinking alcohol: *after a night of* ***heavy drinking*** (=drinking a lot of alcohol) | **drinking companion/buddy/partner etc**

ˈdrinking ˌchocolate *n* [U] *BrE* sweet COCOA powder, which is made into a drink with hot milk or water

ˈdrinking ˌfountain *n* [C] a piece of equipment in a public place that produces a stream of water for you to drink from

ˌdrinking-ˈup time *n* [U] *BrE* the time when people are allowed to finish their drinks in a PUB, but cannot buy any more drinks

ˈdrinking ˌwater ●○○ *n* [U] water that is pure enough for you to drink

ˈdrinks maˌchine *n* [C] *BrE* a machine that serves hot and cold drinks when you put money into it → **vending machine**

ˈdrinks ˌparty *n* [C] *BrE* a party at which alcoholic drinks are served and where you mainly talk to people SYN **cocktail party**

DRIP

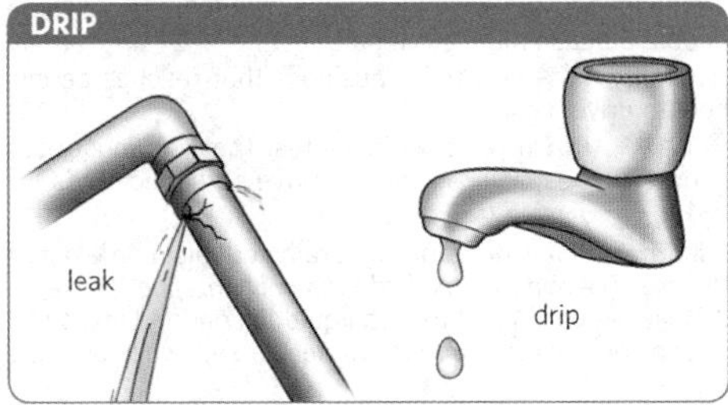

drip¹ /drɪp/ ●●○ *v* (**dripped**, **dripping**)
1 [I,T] to let liquid fall in drops: *The* ***tap's dripping.*** | *Her boots were muddy and her* ***hair was dripping.*** | **drip blood/water/sweat etc** *John came in, his arm dripping blood.* | **be dripping with blood/sweat etc** *The hand that held the gun was dripping with sweat.*
2 [I] to fall in drops: **[+down/from etc]** *The* ***rain dripped*** *down his neck.* | ***Water*** *was* ***dripping*** *through the ceiling.*
3 be dripping with sth to contain or be covered in a lot of something: **be dripping with jewels/gems/pearls etc** *All the princes were dripping with gems.* | *His tone was now* ***dripping with sarcasm.***

drip² ●●○ *n*
1 [C] one of the drops of liquid that fall from something: *I put some plastic buckets on the floor to catch the drips.*
2 [singular, U] the sound or action of a liquid falling in drops: *The silence was broken only by a regular drip, drip, drip.*
3 [C] a piece of equipment used in hospitals for putting liquids directly into your blood through a tube SYN **IV**: **be/put sb on a drip** *At the hospital they put me on a drip.*
4 [C] *informal* someone who is boring and weak
5 drip, drip, drip used to talk about something happening gradually or continually over a period of time: *the drip, drip, drip of new revelations every day*

ˌdrip-ˈdry *adj* drip-dry clothing does not need IRONing —**drip-dry** *v* [I,T]

ˈdrip-feed¹ *v* [T] **1** to put a liquid directly into a person's blood through a tube **2** to keep giving someone small amounts of information, money etc: *The public was drip-fed with news.*

ˈdrip-feed² *n* [C] a piece of equipment used in hospitals for putting liquids directly into your blood through a tube SYN **drip**

drip·ping¹ /ˈdrɪpɪŋ/ *n* [U] *BrE* the oily substance that comes out of meat when you cook it SYN **fat**

dripping² *adj* extremely wet SYN **soaking**: *Take off that jacket – you're* ***dripping wet.***

drip·py /ˈdrɪpi/ *adj informal* very emotional in a silly way: *The movie is nothing but a drippy melodrama.*

drive¹ /draɪv/ ●●● S1 W1 *v* (*past tense* **drove** /drəʊv $ droʊv/, *past participle* **driven** /ˈdrɪvən/)
1 VEHICLE **a)** [I,T] to make a car, truck, bus etc move along: **[+to/down/off etc]** *I am planning to drive to Morocco next year.* | *the man driving the car* | *Can you drive?* | *So when did you* ***learn to drive?*** | *Bye! Drive carefully!* | *He drives 12 miles to work.* | *He drives* (=has) *a BMW estate.* **b)** [I always + adv/prep] if a car, truck etc drives somewhere, it moves there: *After the accident, the other car just drove off.* **c)** [I] if people drive somewhere, they travel somewhere in a car: *Shall we drive or take the bus?* | **[+to/down/off etc]** *They drove back to Woodside.* **d)** [T always + adv/prep] to take someone somewhere in a car, truck etc: *She drove Anna to London.* | *I'll* ***drive*** *you* ***home.*** | **drive yourself** *I drove myself to hospital.*
2 MAKE SB MOVE [T] to force a person or animal to go somewhere: *Torrential rain drove the players off the course.* | *With a few loud whistles, they drove the donkeys out of the enclosure.*
3 MAKE SB DO STH [T] to strongly influence someone to do something: **drive sb to do sth** *The detective wondered what had driven Christine to phone her.* | **drive sb to/into sth** *The noises in my head have nearly driven me to suicide.* | *Phil, driven by jealousy, started spying on his wife.*
4 MAKE SB/STH BE IN A BAD STATE [T] to make someone or something get into a bad or extreme state, usually an emotional one: **drive sb crazy/nuts/mad/insane** (=make someone feel very annoyed) *This cough is driving me mad!* | **drive sb crazy/wild** (=make someone feel very sexually excited) | **drive sb up the wall/out of their mind** (=make someone feel very annoyed) | **drive sb to distraction/desperation** *The mosquitoes drive me to distraction.* | **drive sb/sth into sth** *The factory had been driven into bankruptcy.*
5 HIT/PUSH STH INTO STH [T] to hit or push something into something else: **drive sth into sth** *We watched Dad drive the posts into the ground.* | *She drove her heels into the sand.*
6 MAKE SB WORK [T] to make a person or animal work hard: **drive yourself** *Don't drive yourself too hard.*
7 SPORTS [I,T] **a)** to move a ball etc forward in a game of baseball, football, golf etc by hitting or kicking it hard and fast: *He drove the ball into the corner of the net.* **b)** to run with the ball towards the GOAL in sports such as BASKETBALL and American football → see picture at **GOLF**
8 PROVIDE POWER [T] to provide the power for a vehicle or machine: **petrol-driven/electrically-driven/battery-driven etc** *a petrol-driven lawn mower*
9 RAIN/WIND ETC [I always + adv/prep] if rain, snow, wind etc drives somewhere, it moves very quickly in that direction: *The rain was driving down hard.*
10 drive a coach and horses through sth to destroy an argument, plan etc completely: *The new bill will drive a coach and horses through recent trade agreements.*
11 MAKE A HOLE [T always + adv/prep] to make a large hole

in something using heavy equipment or machinery: *They drove a tunnel through the mountains.*
12 drive sth home to make something completely clear to someone: *He didn't have to* ***drive*** *the* ***point home****. The videotape had done that.*
13 drive a wedge between sb to do something that makes people disagree or start to dislike each other: *I don't want to drive a wedge between you and your father.* → **drive/strike a hard bargain** at HARD[1](18)
drive at sth *phr v* **what sb is driving at** the thing someone is really trying to say SYN **get at**: *I still couldn't understand what Toby was driving at.*
drive sb ↔ **away** *phr v* to behave in a way that makes someone leave: *He was cruel because he wanted to drive me away.*
drive sth ↔ **down** *phr v* to make prices, costs etc fall quickly: *We have to drive down costs.*
drive sb/sth ↔ **in** *phr v* to hit the ball so that another player can score a RUN in baseball
drive off *phr v*
1 to hit the ball to begin a game of golf
2 drive sb ↔ off to force a person or animal to go away from you: *We keep dogs in the yard to drive off intruders.*
drive sb/sth ↔ **out** *phr v*
1 to force someone or something to leave: *Downtown stores are being driven out by crime.*
2 *written* to make something stop existing: *As we went forward, our fear was driven out by horror.*
drive sth ↔ **up** *phr v* to make prices, costs etc rise quickly: *The oil shortage drove gas prices up by 20 cents a gallon.*

drive[2] ●●● S2 W2 *n*
1 IN A CAR [C] a journey in a car: **[+to/along etc]** *Let's* ***go for a drive*** *along the coast.* | *Taylor* ***took*** *me* ***for a drive*** *through the town.* | **an hour's/a two-hour etc drive** *It's a two-hour drive from Calais to Thiepval.* **THESAURUS** JOURNEY
2 NATURAL NEED [C] a strong natural need or desire: *The treatment will not affect your* ***sex drive****.*
3 OUTSIDE YOUR HOUSE [C] the hard area or road between your house and the street SYN **driveway**: **in/on the drive** *He parked his car in the drive.*
4 EFFORT [C] an effort to achieve something, especially an effort by an organization for a particular purpose: *a* ***recruitment drive*** *for new members* | *an* ***economy drive*** (=effort to reduce spending) | **drive to do sth** *a nationwide drive to crack down on crime*
5 DETERMINATION [U] determination and energy to succeed: *Brian* ***has*** *got tremendous* ***drive****.*
6 POWER [U] the power from an engine that makes the wheels of a vehicle go round: **front-wheel/rear-wheel/four-wheel drive**
7 COMPUTER [C] a piece of equipment in a computer that is used to get information from a DISK or to store information on it: **hard/floppy/A etc drive** → DISK DRIVE
8 SPORT [C] an act of hitting a ball hard, especially in tennis, baseball, or golf: *He hit a long, high drive to right field.*
9 MILITARY ATTACK [C] several military attacks: **[+into]** *a drive deep into enemy territory*
10 ANIMALS [C] when animals such as cows or sheep are brought together and made to move in a particular direction
11 Drive used in the names of roads: *141 Park Drive*

ˈ**drive-by** *adj* **drive-by shooting/killing** an occasion when someone is shot by someone in a moving car —**drive-by** *n* [C]

ˈ**drive-in** *n* [C] **1** a restaurant where you are served and eat in your car **2** a place where you can watch films outdoors while sitting in your car

driv·el /ˈdrɪvəl/ *n* [U] something that is said or written that is silly or does not mean anything: *Don't talk such drivel!* —**drivel** *v* [I]

driv·en[1] /ˈdrɪvən/ *v* the past participle of DRIVE

driven[2] *adj* trying extremely hard to achieve what you want: *He claims he is not a driven workaholic.* → **as pure as the driven snow** at PURE(11)

driv·er /ˈdraɪvə $ -ər/ ●●● S1 W2 *n* [C]
1 someone who drives a car, bus etc → **chauffeur**: *a taxi driver* | *Do you think you're a good driver?*
2 *technical* a piece of software that makes a computer work with another piece of equipment such as a printer or a mouse
3 a GOLF CLUB with a wooden head → **back seat driver** at BACK SEAT(2), → **Sunday driver** at SUNDAY(3)

driv·er·less /ˈdraɪvələs $ -vər-/ *adj* a driverless vehicle is controlled by equipment in the vehicle, rather than by a human driver

ˌ**driver's eduˈcation** (*also* ˌ**driver's ˈed**) *n* [U] *AmE* a course, usually taken in high school, that teaches you how to drive a car

ˈ**driver's ˌlicense** *n* [C] *AmE* an official document or card that says that you are legally allowed to drive SYN **driving licence** *BrE*

ˈ**drive shaft** *n* [C] *technical* a part of a vehicle that takes power from the GEARBOX to the wheels

ˈ**drive-through** (*also* **drive-thru**) *n* [C] a restaurant, bank etc where you can be served without getting out of your car

drive·time, **drive time** /ˈdraɪvtaɪm/ *n* [U] the time during the morning or afternoon when many people are driving to or from work → **rush hour**: *a morning drivetime radio show*

drive·way /ˈdraɪvweɪ/ ●●○ *n* [C] the hard area or road between your house and the street SYN **drive**

driv·ing[1] /ˈdraɪvɪŋ/ *n* [U] the activity of driving a car, truck etc: *driving lessons* | *He was charged with causing death by* ***dangerous driving****.* | *hazardous* ***driving conditions*** (=weather that makes driving dangerous) → **in the driving seat** at SEAT[1](11)

driving[2] *adj* **1 driving rain/snow** rain or snow that falls very hard and fast **2 driving force** someone or something that strongly influences people and makes them do something: **[+behind]** *Hawks was the driving force behind the project.* **3 driving ambition** a very great desire to do or achieve something

ˈ**driving ˌlicence** ●●○ *n* [C] *BrE* an official document or card that says that you are legally allowed to drive SYN **driver's license** *AmE*

ˈ**driving range** *n* [C] an open outdoor area where people practise hitting golf balls

ˈ**driving school** *n* [C] a business that teaches people how to drive a car

ˈ**driving test** *n* [C] the official test that you must pass in order to be legally allowed to drive on public roads

driz·zle[1] /ˈdrɪzəl/ ●○○ *v*
1 it drizzles if it is drizzling, light rain and mist come out of the sky: *The rain isn't too bad – it's only drizzling.*
2 [T always + adv/prep] to let a liquid fall on food in a small stream or in small drops: *Drizzle the soy sauce over the chicken.*

drizzle[2] *n* [singular, U] weather that is a combination of light rain and mist: *A light drizzle had started by the time we left.* **THESAURUS** RAIN —**driz·zly** /ˈdrɪzli/ *adj*

droll /drəʊl $ droʊl/ *adj* amusing in an unusual way

drom·e·da·ry /ˈdrɒmədəri $ ˈdrɑːməderi/ *n* (*plural* **dromedaries**) [C] a CAMEL with one HUMP on its back

drone[1] /drəʊn $ droʊn/ *v* [I] to make a continuous low dull sound: *An airplane droned overhead.*
drone on *phr v* to speak in a boring way, usually for a long time: **[+about]** *Tom was droning on about work.*

drone[2] *n* **1** [singular] a continuous low dull sound: **[+of]** *the steady drone of traffic* **2** [C] a male BEE that does no work **3** [C] someone who has a good life but does not work to earn it or give anything back to society **4** [C] *technical* an aircraft that does not have a pilot, but is operated by radio

drool /druːl/ *v* **1** [I,T] *BrE* to let SALIVA (=the liquid in your mouth) come out of your mouth → **slobber**: *The dog* *was drooling at the mouth.* **2** [I] to show in a silly way that you like someone or something a lot: **[+over]** *He was drooling over a Porsche.*

droop /druːp/ *v* **1** [I,T] to hang or bend down, or to make something do this: *The plant needs some water – it's starting to droop.* | *His eyelids began to droop* (=close, because he was sleepy). | *Jessie drooped her head.* **2** [I] to become sad or weak: *Our spirits drooped as we faced the long trip home.* —**droop** *n* [singular] —**droopy** *adj: a droopy moustache*

drop¹ /drɒp $ drɑːp/ ●●● S1 W2 *v* (**dropped**, **dropping**)

1 LET STH FALL [T] **a)** to stop holding or carrying something so that it falls: *He dropped his briefcase on a chair.* | *She screamed and dropped the torch.* **b)** to make something such as a bomb fall from a plane: *U.S. planes began dropping bombs on the city.* | *Supplies are being dropped for the refugees.*

2 FALL [I] to fall suddenly onto the ground or into something: **[+from/off]** *The apples are beginning to drop from the trees.* | *Your button has dropped off.*

3 MOVE YOUR BODY DOWN [I always + adv/prep, T] to lower yourself or part of your body suddenly: **[+down/onto/into]** *He dropped down onto the floor and hid under the table.* | *She* ***dropped*** *her* ***head*** *back against the cushion.*

4 BECOME LESS [I] to fall to a lower level or amount, especially a much lower level or amount: **drop suddenly/sharply/dramatically** *The number of deaths on the roads has dropped sharply.* | *Temperatures drop quite dramatically at night, so bring some warm clothing.* | **[+to]** *Their share of the market dropped to 50 percent this year.* THESAURUS DECREASE

5 REDUCE [T] to reduce the level or amount of something: *You might be able to get them to* ***drop*** *the* ***price****.* | *As soon as she saw the police car she* ***dropped*** *her* ***speed****.*

6 NOT INCLUDE [T] to decide not to include someone or something: *His name was dropped from the list.* | **drop sb from a team/side** *Taylor was bitterly disappointed to be dropped from the England side.*

7 STOP DOING STH [T] to stop doing something, discussing something, or continuing with something: *The proposal was dropped after opposition from civil liberties groups.* | **drop charges/drop a case** *New evidence was presented to the court and the case was dropped.* | **drop a subject at school/university** (=stop studying it) *Students are allowed to drop history in Year 9.* | *You can't expect me to* ***drop everything*** (=completely stop doing whatever I am doing) *whenever you're in town.* | *Oh, drop the 'Senator'* (=stop calling me 'Senator') *– just call me Gordon.* | *Some time later, the matter was quietly dropped.*

8 STOP TALKING ABOUT STH [I,T] to stop talking about something: **drop the subject** *To her relief, Julius* ***dropped the subject****.* | **drop it** (=stop talking about a subject) *Just* ***drop it, will you****? I don't want to talk about it anymore.* | *'What about the money?' 'We've agreed to* ***let it drop*** (=we have agreed not to talk about it anymore).'

9 TAKE SB SOMEWHERE (*also* **drop off**) [T] to take someone by car to a place and leave them there, especially on your way to another place: *Just drop me here – I can walk the rest of the way.* | **drop sb at sth** *She dropped Johnny at the school gates at about 8:30.*

10 TAKE STH SOMEWHERE [T] to take something to a place and leave it there: **drop sth round/in** *I've got your books – I'll drop them round to your place later.*

11 VISIT [I always + adv/prep] to visit someone you know, usually without arranging a particular time: **[+by/round]** *I just dropped by to see how you were getting on.* | *The kids drop round and see her from time to time.* | **[+into]** *Jan dropped into the office this morning to tell me her news.* | **drop in (on sb)** *Why don't you drop in for a drink one evening?*

12 SLOPE DOWNWARDS [I always + adv/prep] if a path, land etc drops, it goes down suddenly, forming a steep slope: **[+down]** *The cliff dropped down over a hundred feet to the sea below.* | **[+away]** *On the left the ground drops away, giving a view over the rooftops.*

13 END A RELATIONSHIP [T] *informal* to suddenly stop having a relationship with someone, especially a romantic relationship: *She dropped him as soon as she found out he had been seeing another woman.*

14 until/till you drop until you are too tired to continue doing something: *We're going to shop till we drop!*

15 drop a hint to suggest or ask for something in an indirect way, hoping that the person you are talking to will understand what you mean: *He dropped some big hints about what he wanted for his birthday.*

16 drop sb a line/note *informal* to write a short letter to someone: *Drop us a line to let us know how you're getting on.*

17 drop dead a) *informal* to die suddenly **b)** *spoken informal* an impolite expression which you say to someone when you are extremely angry with them

18 sb's jaw dropped used to say that someone was very surprised

19 drop your eyes/gaze to stop looking at someone and look down, usually because you feel embarrassed or uncomfortable: *Ben looked at me in horror for a moment and then dropped his gaze.*

20 the wind drops the wind stops: *They waited for the wind to drop.*

21 drop a bombshell *informal* to suddenly tell someone a shocking piece of news: *Finally she dropped the bombshell. She was pregnant and I was the father.*

22 drop sb in it *informal* to say or do something that gets someone else into trouble: *You told her where we went on Friday night! You've really dropped me in it now!*

23 drop $50/£2,000 etc [T] *informal* to lose money in a business deal, a game etc: *Phil dropped $200 playing poker yesterday.*

24 drop a catch to fail to catch a ball hit by a BATSMAN in CRICKET

25 drop a point to lose a point in a sports competition: *Real Madrid dropped a point at home yesterday.*

26 be dropping like flies *informal* if people are dropping like flies, they are getting ill or dying in large numbers

27 drop a clanger/brick *BrE* to say something embarrassing in a social situation

28 drop a stitch to let the wool fall off the needle when you are KNITTING

29 drop anchor to lower a boat's ANCHOR to the bottom of the sea, a lake etc so that the boat does not float away

30 drop acid *informal* to swallow LSD (=an illegal drug)

drop back (*also* **drop behind**) *phr v* to move more slowly than other people so that they get ahead of you: *He started out with the leaders but at the first fence he dropped back.* | *Ellen dropped behind to tie her shoelace.*

drop off *phr v*

1 to begin to sleep: *She kept dropping off at her desk.* | *I must have* ***dropped off to sleep****.*

2 drop sb/sth ↔ off to take someone or something to a place by car and leave them there on your way to another place: *I'll drop you off on my way home.*

3 to fall to a lower level or amount: *The number of graduates going into teaching has dropped off sharply.*

drop out *phr v*

1 to no longer do an activity or belong to a group: *The group gets smaller as members move away or drop out.*

2 to leave a school or university before your course has finished → **dropout**: **[+of]** *Bill dropped out of college after his first year.*

3 to refuse to take part in ordinary society because you do not agree with its principles → **dropout**: *In the 60s, Leary urged kids to 'Turn on, tune in and drop out.'*

4 if an Internet connection drops out, it suddenly stops, usually for a short time

drop² ●●● S2 W3 *n*

1 LIQUID [C] a very small amount of liquid that falls in a round shape: **[+of]** *As the first drops of rain began to fall, Michael started to run.* | *A single drop of blood splashed onto the floor.* | *A drop of sweat ran down her forehead and into her eye.* → **RAIN DROP**, **TEARDROP** THESAURUS PIECE

2 SMALL AMOUNT [usually singular] *informal* **a)** a small amount of liquid that you drink, especially alcohol: **[+of]**

She likes to add a drop of brandy to her tea. | *George hasn't **touched a drop*** (=drunk any alcohol) *for years.* **b)** a small amount of something: **[+of]** *I haven't got a drop of sympathy for him.*
3 REDUCTION [singular] a reduction in the amount, level, or number of something, especially a large or sudden one SYN **fall**: **[+in]** *Manufacturers report a big drop in new orders.* | *a drop in temperature* | **a sharp/dramatic/marked drop in sth** *The results showed a sharp drop in profits.*
4 DISTANCE TO GROUND [singular] a distance from a higher point down to the ground or to a lower point: *There was a steep drop on one side of the track.* | *a 20-metre drop* | *There was an almost **sheer*** (=vertical) ***drop** to the valley below.*
5 at the drop of a hat immediately and without pausing to think about what you are going to do: *Some of these corporations threaten to sue at the drop of a hat.*
6 DELIVERY [C] an act of delivering something somewhere, for example by dropping it from a plane SYN **delivery**: *Air drops* (=from a plane) *of food aid were made to the region yesterday.* | *My first drop of the day is usually somewhere in north London.* → MAIL DROP
7 lemon/fruit/chocolate etc drop a sweet that tastes of LEMON etc
8 a drop in the ocean *BrE*, **a drop in the bucket** *AmE* a very small amount of something compared to what is needed or wanted: *5,000 new schools are to be built, but this is just a drop in the ocean for such a vast country.*
9 eye/ear etc drops a type of medicine that you put in your eye, ear etc, one drop at a time

ˈdrop cloth *n* [C] *AmE* a large cloth for covering furniture or floors in order to protect them from dust or paint SYN **dustsheet** *BrE*

ˌdrop dead ˈdate *n* [C usually singular] *AmE informal* a date by which you must have completed something, because after this date it is no longer worth doing

ˌdrop-dead ˈgorgeous *adj informal* very attractive

ˈdrop-down ˌmenu *n* [C] a list of choices which appears on a computer screen when you CLICK on a place on the screen

ˈdrop goal *n* [C] a GOAL in RUGBY football made with a dropkick

ˈdrop-in *adj* [only before noun] a drop-in place is a place offering a service or support where you can go without having to make arrangements first: *a drop-in advice centre*

drop·kick /ˈdrɒpkɪk $ ˈdrɑːp-/ *n* [C] a kick in a game such as RUGBY football, made by dropping the ball and kicking it immediately

drop·let /ˈdrɒplɪt $ ˈdrɑːp-/ *n* [C] a very small drop of liquid: **[+of]** *tiny **droplets of water***

drop·out /ˈdrɒpaʊt $ ˈdrɑːp-/ *n* [C] **1** someone who leaves school or college before they have finished: *a high school dropout* **2** someone who refuses to take part in ordinary society because they do not agree with its social practices, moral standards etc

drop·per /ˈdrɒpə $ ˈdrɑːpər/ *n* [C] a short glass tube with a hollow rubber part at one end, that you use to measure liquid one drop at a time

drop·pings /ˈdrɒpɪŋz $ ˈdrɑː-/ *n* [plural] the solid waste that passes out of the bodies of animals or birds

ˈdrop shot *n* [C] a shot in a game such as tennis in which the ball is hit softly and falls quickly to the ground

dross /drɒs $ drɑːs, drɔːs/ *n* [U] **1** something that is of very low quality: *Most of the poems were pretentious dross.* **2** waste or useless substances: *gold with impurities or dross*

drought /draʊt/ ●●○ *n* [C,U] a long period of dry weather when there is not enough water for plants and animals to live

drove¹ /drəʊv $ droʊv/ *v* the past tense of DRIVE

drove² *n* [C] **1 droves** [plural] crowds of people: **in droves** *Tourists come in droves to see the White House.* **2** a group of animals that are being moved together: **[+of]** *a drove of cattle*

drov·er /ˈdrəʊvə $ ˈdroʊvər/ *n* [C] someone who moves cattle or sheep from one place to another in groups

drown /draʊn/ ●●○ *v*
1 [I,T] to die from being under water for too long, or to kill someone in this way: *Many people drowned when the boat overturned.* | *Jane was drowned in the river.* | **drown yourself** *Depressed, Peter tried to drown himself.*
2 (*also* **drown out**) [T] if a loud noise drowns out another sound, it prevents it from being heard: *A train blew its whistle and drowned his voice.* | *The noise of the battle was drowned out by his aircraft's engine.*
3 [T] to cover something, especially food, with more liquid than is necessary or nice: **drown sth in sth** *The fish was drowned in a rich sauce.*
4 [I,T] to have a very strong feeling or a serious problem that is difficult to deal with: **[+in]** *Relief agencies are drowning in frustration.* | *The country is drowning in debt.*
5 drown your sorrows to drink a lot of alcohol in order to forget your problems

drowse /draʊz/ *v* [I] to be in a light sleep or to feel as though you are almost asleep: *I was drowsing in front of the television when you called.*

drow·sy /ˈdraʊzi/ *adj* **1** tired and almost asleep SYN **sleepy**: *The drug can make you drowsy.* **2** so peaceful that you feel relaxed and almost asleep SYN **sleepy**: *a drowsy summer afternoon* —**drowsily** *adv* —**drowsiness** *n* [U]

drub·bing /ˈdrʌbɪŋ/ *n* [C] an occasion when one team easily beats another team in sport: *Ireland **gave** England **a drubbing** at Twickenham.*

drudge /drʌdʒ/ *n* [C] someone who does hard boring work —**drudge** *v* [I]

drudg·e·ry /ˈdrʌdʒəri/ *n* [U] hard boring work

drug¹ /drʌg/ ●●● S2 W1 *n* [C]
1 an illegal substance such as MARIJUANA or COCAINE, which some people take in order to feel happy, relaxed, or excited: *A lot of young people start taking drugs at school.* | *She always looks as though she's **on drugs*** (=taking drugs). | *Jimi Hendrix died of a drug overdose.*
2 a medicine, or a substance for making medicines: *a drug used in the treatment of cancer* | **[+for]** *new drugs for AIDS-related conditions* | ***Drugs prescribed*** (=ordered for people) *by doctors can be extremely hazardous if used in the wrong way.* | *The big **drug companies** make huge profits.*
3 a substance that people doing a sport sometimes take illegally to improve their performance: *She was banned from the Olympics after failing a **drug test*** (=a test that shows if you have taken drugs). | **performance-enhancing drugs**
4 [usually singular] a substance such as tobacco, coffee, or alcohol, that makes you want more and more of it
5 be (like) a drug if an activity is like a drug, you enjoy it so much that you want to do it more and more: *Athletics is like a drug – it keeps dragging you back for more.* → **miracle drug** at MIRACLE(3)

COLLOCATIONS

VERBS

take/use drugs *I think I took drugs to escape my problems.*
do drugs *informal* (=take drugs) *All my friends were doing drugs.*
be on drugs (=take drugs regularly) *It can be very hard to tell if your teenager is on drugs.*
be addicted to drugs/dependent on drugs (=be unable to stop taking drugs) *People who are addicted to drugs need help.*
be/get hooked on drugs *informal* (=be/get addicted) | **experiment with drugs** (=try taking drugs) | **come off/get off drugs** (=stop taking drugs permanently) | **deal (in) drugs** (*also* **supply drugs** *formal*) (=sell drugs) | **inject drugs** (=use a needle to put drugs into your body) | **be high on drugs** (=be experiencing the effects of a drug)

drug + NOUN

drug use/abuse (=taking drugs) *She is being treated for drug abuse.*

D

a drug user (=someone who takes drugs) *We set up a counselling service for drug users.*
drug addiction (=the problem of not being able to stop taking drugs) *his struggles with alcoholism and drug addiction*
a drug addict (=someone who cannot stop taking drugs) | **a drug problem** (=the problem of being addicted to drugs) | **a drug overdose** (=taking too much of a drug at one time) | **a drug dealer/pusher** (=someone who sells drugs) | **a drug trafficker/smuggler** (=someone involved in bringing drugs into a country) | **drug trafficking/smuggling** (=the crime of bringing drugs into a country) | **the war on drugs** (=a long struggle by the authorities to control drugs)

ADJECTIVES

illegal drugs *A lot of crime is connected to illegal drugs.*
hard drugs (*also* **class A drugs** *BrE*) (=strong drugs such as heroin, cocaine etc) | **soft drugs** (=less strong drugs such as marijuana) | **recreational drugs** (=taken for pleasure) | **designer drugs** (=produced artificially from chemicals)

COMMON ERRORS

⚠ Don't say 'light drugs'. Say **soft drugs**. Instead of 'heavy drugs', you usually say **hard drugs**.

drug² *v* (**drugged**, **drugging**) [T] **1** to give a person or animal a drug, especially in order to make them feel tired or go to sleep, or to make them perform well in a race: *Johnson drugged and attacked four women.* | *There was no evidence that the horse had been drugged.* **2** to put drugs in someone's food or drink in order to make them feel tired or go to sleep SYN **spike**: *The wine had been drugged.* **3 be drugged up to the eyeballs** *especially BrE* to have taken a lot of illegal drugs, or to have been given a lot of medicine: *She was in pain, despite being drugged up to the eyeballs.* —**drugged** *adj*

ˈdrug ˌaddict *n* [C] someone who cannot stop taking illegal drugs —**drug addiction** *n* [U]

ˈdrug ˌbaron *n* [C] someone who leads an organization that buys and sells large quantities of illegal drugs

ˈdrug czar *n* [C] an official employed by a government to try to stop the trade of illegal drugs

ˈdrug ˌdealer *n* [C] someone who sells illegal drugs SYN **dealer**

ˌdrug-ˈdriving *n* [U] *especially BrE* the crime of driving after having taken drugs —**drug drive** *v* [I]

drug·get /ˈdrʌgɪt/ *n* [C,U] rough heavy cloth used especially as a floor covering, or a piece of this cloth

drug·gie /ˈdrʌgi/ *n* [C] *informal* someone who often takes illegal drugs

drug·gist /ˈdrʌgɪst/ *n* [C] *AmE old-fashioned* someone who is trained to prepare medicines, and works in a shop SYN **pharmacist**

ˌdrug rehabiliˈtation (*also* **ˌdrug ˈrehab**) *n* [U] the process of helping someone to live without illegal drugs after they have been ADDICTed to them

ˈdrug ˌrunner *n* [C] someone who brings illegal drugs from one country to another

drug·store /ˈdrʌgstɔː $ -stɔːr/ ●●● S3 *n* [C] *especially AmE* a shop where you can buy medicines, beauty products etc SYN **chemist** *BrE*

dru·id /ˈdruːɪd/ *n* [C] a member of an ancient group of priests, in Britain, Ireland, and France, before the Christian religion

drum¹ /drʌm/ ●●● S3 *n* [C]
1 a musical instrument made of skin stretched over a circular frame, played by hitting it with your hand or a stick: *a big bass drum* | *1,000 people marched,* ***beating drums*** *and carrying flags.* | **on drums** *Trumpeter Red Rodney was playing with Kenny Clarke on drums* (=playing the drums). | *Jones* ***played the drums*** *in an all-girl band.*
2 a large round container for storing liquids such as oil, chemicals etc: *a 5-gallon oil drum* → see picture at CONTAINER
3 something that looks like a drum, especially part of a machine: *a brake drum*
4 bang/beat the drum for sb/sth to speak eagerly in support of someone or something: *The company is banging the drum for their new software.*
5 the drum of sth a sound like the sound a drum makes: *the drum of the rain on the window* → EARDRUM

drum² *v* (**drummed**, **drumming**) **1** [I] to play a drum **2** [I,T] to make a sound similar to a drum by hitting a surface again and again: *I could hear the rain drumming against the windows.* | *Lisa* ***drummed*** *her* ***fingers*** *impatiently on the table.* **3 drum sth home** to use repeated arguments or messages in order to make sure that people understand something: *An information booklet will be available and press advertisements will drum home the message.*

drum sth **into** sb *phr v* to keep telling someone something until they cannot forget it: *'Don't talk to strangers' is a* ***message drummed into*** *children.*

drum sb **out of** sth *phr v* to force someone to leave an organization, place, or job: *He was drummed out of the army.*

drum sth ↔ **up** *phr v* to get support, interest, attention etc from people by making an effort: *He travelled throughout Latin America* ***drumming up support*** *for the confederation.* | *The organization is using the event to* ***drum up business*** (=get more work and sales).

drum·beat /ˈdrʌmbiːt/ *n* [C] the sound made when someone hits a drum

ˈdrum kit *n* [C] a set of drums, used especially by professional musicians

ˈdrum maˌchine *n* [C] a piece of electronic equipment that makes patterns of sounds like drum music

ˌdrum ˈmajor / $ ˈ. ˌ../ *n* [C] the male leader of a MARCHING BAND

ˌdrum majorˈette / $ ˈ. ..ˌ./ *n* [C] a MAJORETTE

drum·mer /ˈdrʌmə $ -ər/ ●○○ *n* [C] someone who plays drums

drum·ming /ˈdrʌmɪŋ/ *n* [U] **1** when you play a drum, or the sound of a drum being played **2** the sound of something hitting a surface again and again: *the drumming of the horses' hooves*

drum 'n' bass /ˌdrʌm ən ˈbeɪs/ *n* [U] a type of electronic dance music with a very hard fast beat

ˈdrum-roll *n* [C] a quick continuous beating of a drum, used especially to introduce an important event

drum·stick /ˈdrʌmˌstɪk/ *n* [C] **1** the lower part of the leg of a chicken or other bird, cooked as food **2** a stick that you use to hit a drum

drunk¹ /drʌŋk/ *v* the past participle of DRINK

drunk² ●●○ S3 *adj*
1 [not before noun] unable to control your behaviour, speech etc because you have drunk too much alcohol OPP **sober**: *You're drunk.* | *David would* ***get drunk*** *and I would have to take him home and put him to bed.* | **[+on]** *He was drunk on beer and whisky.* | **blind drunk** *BrE* (=very drunk) *All she wants to do is get blind drunk.* | **drunk as a lord** (*also* **drunk as a skunk**) (=very drunk) *He turned up one morning, drunk as a lord.*
2 being drunk and disorderly *law* the crime of behaving in a violent noisy way in a public place when you are drunk
3 drunk on/with sth so excited by a feeling that you behave in a strange way: *drunk with happiness*
→ PUNCH-DRUNK, → **roaring drunk** at ROARING(5)

drunk³ (*also* **drunk·ard** /ˈdrʌŋkəd $ -ərd/) *n* [C] someone who is drunk or often gets drunk → **alcoholic**

ˌdrunk ˈdriving *n* [U] *AmE* driving a car after having drunk too much alcohol SYN **drink-driving** *BrE* —**drunk driver** *n* [C]

drunk·en /ˈdrʌŋkən/ *adj* [only before noun] **1** drunk or showing that you are drunk: *He was a drunken bully.* | *She was lying* ***in a drunken stupor*** (=nearly unconscious from being drunk) *on the sidewalk.* **2 drunken party/orgy/brawl etc** a party etc where people are drunk: *Tom got into a* *drunken brawl* (=fight) *in a bar.* —**drunkenly** *adv* —**drunkenness** *n* [U]

ˈ**drunk tank** *n* [C] *AmE informal* a cell in a prison for people who have drunk too much alcohol

dry[1] /draɪ/ ●●● S2 W2 *adj* (*comparative* **drier**, *superlative* **driest**)
1 NOT WET without water or liquid inside or on the surface OPP **wet**: *I need to change into some **dry clothes**.* | *Make sure that the surface is clean and dry before you start to paint.* | *You should store disks in a cool, dry place.* | **shake/rub/wipe etc sth dry** *Jean rubbed her hair dry.* | *The path is **dry as a bone*** (=very dry). → BONE DRY
2 WEATHER having very little rain or MOISTURE OPP **wet** → **arid**: *The weather was hot and dry.* | *Eastern areas should stay dry tomorrow.* | *the **dry season*** | *These plants do not grow well in **dry conditions*** (=when there is not much rain). | *a prolonged **dry spell*** (=period)
3 dry mouth/skin/lips/hair etc without enough of the liquid or oil that is normally in your mouth, skin etc → **parched**: *His heart was pounding and his mouth was dry.* | *Mary has dry, sensitive skin.* | *a shampoo for dry hair* | *She licked her dry lips.*
4 run/go dry if a lake, river etc runs dry, all the water gradually disappears, especially because there has been no rain: *The river ran dry last summer.*
5 HUMOUR someone with a dry sense of humour says funny and clever things while seeming to be serious: *He had a delightfully dry sense of humour.*
6 BORING boring, very serious, and without humour: *In schools, science is often presented in a dry and uninteresting manner.* | *a dry debate on policies* THESAURUS BORING
7 dry cough a cough which does not produce any PHLEGM
8 dry wine/sherry etc wine etc that is not sweet: *a glass of dry white wine*
9 WITHOUT ALCOHOL not drinking alcohol, or not allowing any alcohol to be sold: *Paula had been dry for a year before she started drinking again.* | *Kuwait's a dry country.*
10 VOICE showing no emotion when you speak: *'Good evening gentlemen,' he said, in a dry voice.*
11 dry bread/toast bread etc eaten on its own without anything such as butter or JAM spread on it
12 THIRSTY *informal* thirsty
13 not a dry eye in the house used to say that everyone was crying because something was very sad – often used humorously —**dryness** *n* [U] → DRIP-DRY, DRY ROT, → **home and dry** at HOME[2](6), → **leave sb high and dry** at HIGH[2](5), → DRYLY

dry[2] ●●● S2 W3 *v* (**dried**, **drying**, **dries**) [I,T]
1 to make something dry, or to become dry: *Mrs Brown hung the washing on the line to dry.* | *He was **drying** his **hair** with a towel.* | *Mary **dried** her **hands**.* | *Leave the first coat of paint to dry before adding another.* | *She stood up and **dried** her **eyes*** (=wiped away her tears). | **dry yourself** *He quickly dried himself on the thin towel.*
2 (*also* **dry up** *BrE*) to rub plates, dishes etc dry with a cloth after they have been washed: *You wash and I'll dry.* | *Shall I dry up these glasses?* → CUT AND DRIED, DRIED

GRAMMAR

Dry belongs to a group of verbs where the same noun can be the subject of the verb or its object.
- You can say: *I'm drying the washing on the line.* In this sentence, 'the washing' is the object of **dry**.
- You can also say: *The washing is drying on the line.* In this sentence, 'the washing' is the subject of **dry**.

GRAMMAR GUIDE VERBS

dry off *phr v* to become dry or to make something dry, especially on the surface: *We swam in the sea, then stretched out on the sand to dry off.* | **dry sth ↔ off** *He dried the camera off, hoping it would still work.*

dry out *phr v*
1 to become completely dry or to make something completely dry, especially after it has been very wet: *In summer, water the plants regularly and never let the soil dry out.* | **dry sth ↔ out** *The kitchen was flooded and it took ages to dry it out.*
2 dry (sb) out to stop drinking alcohol after you have become an ALCOHOLIC, or to make someone do this: *He's been drying out at a private clinic.* | *The hospital dried Michael out and sent him home.*

dry up *phr v*
1 COME TO AN END if a supply of something dries up, it comes to an end and no more is available: *Foreign investment may dry up.* | *The work soon dried up.*
2 RIVER/LAKE ETC if something such as a river dries up, the water in it disappears: *Across central and west Texas, waterholes and wells have dried up.* | **dry sth ↔ up** *Taking too much water for household use is drying up the river.*
3 STOP TALKING if someone dries up, they stop talking: *'It was -' She dried up again.* | *Everyone became embarrassed and conversation dried up.*
4 PLATES/DISHES ETC *BrE* to rub plates, dishes etc dry with a cloth after they have been washed: **dry sth ↔ up** *I'll just dry up these mugs and we can have a coffee.*

dry·ad /ˈdraɪæd/ *n* [C] a female spirit who lives in a tree, in ancient Greek stories

ˈ**dry** ˌ**battery** *n* [C] an electric BATTERY containing chemicals that are not in a liquid form

ˈ**dry** ˌ**cell** *n* [C] the type of cell used in a dry battery

ˌ**dry-ˈclean** / $ ˈ../ *v* [T] to clean clothes etc with chemicals instead of water —**dry cleaning** *n* [U]

ˌ**dry ˈcleaner's** *n* (*plural* **dry cleaner's**) [C] a shop where you can take clothes etc to be dry-cleaned

ˈ**dry dock** *n* [C] a place where a ship can be taken out of the water for repairs

dry·er, **drier** /ˈdraɪə $ -ər/ ●●○ *n* [C] a machine that dries things, especially clothes → HAIRDRYER, SPIN-DRYER, TUMBLE DRYER

ˌ**dry-ˈeyed** *adj* not crying

ˈ**dry goods** *n* [plural] **1** goods such as tobacco, tea, and coffee that do not contain liquid **2** *AmE* things that are made from cloth such as clothes, sheets, and curtains: *a dry goods store*

ˌ**dry ˈice** *n* [U] CARBON DIOXIDE in a solid form, which is used to make mist in a theatre or DISCO, or to keep food or other things cold

ˌ**dry ˈland** *n* [U] land rather than water: *After three weeks at sea we were glad to be back on dry land again.*

dry·ly, **drily** /ˈdraɪli/ *adv* if you say something dryly, you say something that is amusing but you appear to be completely serious: *'I hear you're a hero,' Philip said dryly.*

ˌ**dry-ˈroasted** *adj* dry-roasted nuts have been cooked without any oil

ˌ**dry ˈrot** *n* [U] a disease in wood that turns it into powder

ˌ**dry ˈrun** *n* [C] an event that is a practice for a more important event: *Both the parties are treating the local elections as a dry run.*

ˌ**dry-ˈshod** *adv* without getting your feet wet

ˌ**dry-stone ˈwall** *n* [C] in Britain, a wall built with pieces of stone that are fitted closely together without using CEMENT to hold them in place

ˌ**dry ˈwall** *n* [U] *AmE* a type of board made of two large sheets of CARDBOARD with PLASTER between them, used to cover walls and ceilings —**dry-wall** *v* [I,T]

DSL /ˌdiː es ˈel/ *n* [C] *technical* (***digital subscriber line***) a telephone line that has special equipment which allows it to receive information from the Internet, or send information at very high speeds

DTI /ˌdiː tiː ˈaɪ/ *n* **the DTI** the abbreviation of the former ***Department of Trade and Industry*** in Britain

DTP /ˌdiː tiː ˈpiː/ *n* [U] (***desktop publishing***) the work of arranging the writing and pictures for a magazine, small book etc, using a computer and special software

DT's *BrE*, **D.T.'s** *AmE* /ˌdiː ˈtiːz/ *n* **the DT's** a condition in which your body shakes and you see imaginary things, caused by drinking too much alcohol – used humorously

du·al /ˈdjuːəl $ ˈduːəl/ ●○○ *adj* [only before noun] having two of something or two parts → **single**: **dual role/purpose/function** *The bridge has a dual role, carrying both road and rail.* | *a **dual system** of education* | **dual citizenship/**

nationality *She* ***has dual nationality****, of Canada and Britain* (=she is a citizen of Canada and Britain). —**duality** /dju'æləti $ du-/ *n* [U]

'dual-band *adj* [only before noun] a dual-band MOBILE PHONE is able to work in at least two different countries because it can receive two different types of signals

,dual 'carriageway ●○○ *n* [C] *BrE* a main road that has two lines of traffic travelling in each direction, with a narrow part between them that has no traffic → **single carriageway** SYN **divided highway** *AmE*

'dual-core *adj technical* a dual-core PROCESSOR contains two independent processors

,dual-'heritage *adj* used to describe someone who has parents from two different races or CULTURES

du·a·lis·m /'dju:əlɪzəm $ 'du:-/ *n* [U] *technical* the idea that there are two opposite parts or principles in everything, for example body and soul, or the state of having two parts or principles

dub¹ /dʌb/ *v* (**dubbed**, **dubbing**) [T] **1** to give something or someone a name that describes them in some way → **label**, **name**: **be dubbed sth** *The body, thousands of years old, was found in the Alps and dubbed 'The Iceman'.* **2** to change the original spoken language of a film or television programme into another language: **be dubbed into sth** *a British film dubbed into French* GRAMMAR **Dub** is usually passive in meanings 1 and 2. **3** *especially BrE* to make a record out of two or more different pieces of music or sound mixed together **4** *AmE* to copy a recording from a tape or CD onto another tape **5** if a king or queen dubs someone, they give the title of KNIGHT to that person in a special ceremony

dub² *n* [U] a style of poetry or music from the West Indies with a strong regular beat

du·bi·ous /'dju:biəs $ 'du:-/ ●○○ *adj*

1 probably not honest, true, right etc: *The firm was accused of dubious accounting practices.* | *Many critics regard this argument as dubious or, at best, misleading.* | *The assumption that growth in one country benefits the whole world is* ***highly dubious****.*

2 [not before noun] not sure whether something is good or true SYN **doubtful**: *I can see you are dubious; take some time to think about it.* | **[+about]** *Some universities are dubious about accepting students over the age of 30.* | *'Are you sure you know what you are doing?' Andy said,* ***looking dubious****.*

3 the dubious honour/distinction/pleasure (of doing sth) a dubious honour etc is the opposite of an honour – used about something unpleasant that happens: *The Stephensons* ***had the dubious honor*** *of being the 100th family to lose their home in the fire.*

4 not good or not of good quality: *The room was decorated in dubious taste.* —**dubiously** *adv* —**dubiousness** *n* [U]

dub·step /'dʌbstep/ *n* [U] *BrE* a type of dance music with a heavy BASS beat

du·cal /'dju:kəl $ 'du:-/ *adj* like a DUKE or belonging to a duke

duc·at /'dʌkət/ *n* [C] a gold coin that was used in several European countries in the past

duch·ess /'dʌtʃɪs/ *n* [C] a woman with the highest social rank outside the royal family, or the wife of a DUKE: *the Duchess of York*

duch·y /'dʌtʃi/ *n* (*plural* **duchies**) [C] the land and property of a DUKE or DUCHESS SYN **dukedom**

duck¹ /dʌk/ ●●● S3 *n*

1 [C] a very common water bird with short legs and a wide beak, used for its meat, eggs, and soft feathers

2 [C] a female duck → **drake**

3 [U] the meat of a duck used as food: *roast duck with orange sauce*

4 take to something like a duck to water to learn how to do something very easily: *She took to dancing like a duck to water.*

5 (*also* **ducks**) *BrE spoken* used to speak to someone, especially a woman, in a friendly way: *What can I get you, ducks?*

6 [C] a SCORE of zero by a BATSMAN in a game of CRICKET → DEAD DUCK, LAME DUCK, → **like water off a duck's back** at WATER¹(8), → DUCKS AND DRAKES, SITTING DUCK

duck² *v* **1** (*also* **duck down**) [I,T] to lower your head or body very quickly, especially to avoid being seen or hit: *If she hadn't ducked, the ball would have hit her.* | **[+behind/under etc]** *Jamie saw his father coming and ducked quickly behind the wall.* | *Tim ducked down to comb his hair in the mirror.* | *She* ***ducked*** *her* ***head*** *to look more closely at the inscription.* **2** [I always + adv/prep] to move somewhere very quickly, especially to avoid being seen or to get away from someone: **[+into]** *The two men ducked into a block of flats and disappeared.* | **[+out of]** *She ducked out of the door before he could stop her.* | **[+back]** *'Wait a minute', he called, ducking back inside.* **3** [T] *informal* to avoid something, especially a difficult or unpleasant duty SYN **dodge**: *The ruling body wanted to* ***duck*** *the* ***issue*** *of whether players had been cheating.* | *Glazer* ***ducked*** *a* ***question*** *about his involvement in the bank scandal.* **4** [T] to push someone under water for a short time as a joke: **duck sb under sth** *Tom grabbed him from behind to duck him under the surface.*

DUCK

duck out of sth *phr v* to avoid doing something that you have to do or have promised to do: *I always ducked out of history lessons at school.*

duck-billed plat·y·pus /,dʌkbɪld 'plætəpəs/ *n* [C] a PLATYPUS

duck·boards /'dʌkbɔ:dz $ -bɔ:rdz/ *n* [plural] long boards used to make a path over muddy ground

'ducking stool *n* [C] a seat on the end of a long pole, used in the past to put a person under water as a punishment

duck·ling /'dʌklɪŋ/ *n* [C] a young duck

,ducks and 'drakes *n* [U] *BrE* a children's game in which you make flat stones jump across the surface of water

duck·weed /'dʌkwi:d/ *n* [U] a plant that grows on the surface of ponds

duck·y¹ /'dʌki/ *n BrE spoken* used to speak to someone in a friendly way, especially a woman or child

ducky² *adj old-fashioned informal* **1** *AmE* perfect or satisfactory: *Well, that's* ***just ducky****.* **2** attractive in an amusing or interesting way SYN **cute**

duct /dʌkt/ *n* [C] **1** a pipe or tube that liquids, air, CABLES etc pass through: *Air is heated and then circulated through large ducts to all parts of the house.* **2** a narrow tube in your body or in a plant that liquid passes through: *a tear duct*

duc·tile /'dʌktaɪl $ -tl/ *adj* ductile metals can be pressed or pulled into shape without needing to be heated —**ductility** /dʌk'tɪləti/ *n* [U]

duct·ing /'dʌktɪŋ/ *n* [U] a system of pipes or tubes that liquids, air, CABLES etc pass through

dud /dʌd/ *n* [C] **1** something that is useless, especially because it does not work correctly: *Several of the fireworks were duds.* **2 duds** [plural] *informal* clothes —**dud** *adj*: *a dud light bulb*

dude /dju:d $ du:d/ *n* [C] *AmE* **1** *informal* a man: *a real cool dude* **2** *old-fashioned* an American man from a city, who is living in or visiting a farm or RANCH

'dude ranch *n* [C] a holiday place in the US where you can ride horses and live like a COWBOY

dud·geon /'dʌdʒən/ *formal* **in high dudgeon** in an angry or offended way – often used humorously

due¹ /dju: $ du:/ ●●● S1 W1 *adj*

1 EXPECTED [not before noun] expected to happen or arrive at a particular time: **due to do sth** *The team are due to fly to Italy next month.* | *His new book is due to be published next*

D

year. | **[+in/on/at]** *She's pregnant and the baby's due in April.* | *The final results of the experiment are due on December 9.* | *I'm due at his office at 4.30.* | **[+for]** *The car is due for its annual service again.* | **[+back]** *When are the library books due back?* → DUE DATE

2 OWED owed to someone either as a debt or because they have a right to it: *Any money due you will be sent by cheque through the post.* | **[+to]** *Thanks are due to all those who took part.*

3 MONEY if an amount of money is due, it must be paid at a particular time: *The next income tax payment is due on 31 January.*

4 in due course at some time in the future when it is the right time, but not before: *Further details will be announced in due course.*

5 PROPER [only before noun] *formal* proper or suitable: *He was banned for six months for driving without due care and attention.* | **due regard/consideration** *We want the best for each individual child with due regard for the interests of the other children.*

6 with (all) due respect *spoken* used when you disagree with someone or criticize them in a polite way: *Dad, with all due respect, was not a very good husband.* → DULY, DUE TO

D

due² ●●○ *adv* **due north/south/east/west** directly to the north, south, east, or west

due³ *n* **1 your due** your due is what you deserve, or something it is your right to have: *He accepted all the praise he received as his due.* | *Freddy,* ***to give*** *him his* ***due*** (=to be fair to him), *always tried to be honest.* **2 dues** [plural] regular payments you make to an organization of which you are a member SYN **fees**: *Robert failed to* ***pay*** *his* ***dues*** *last year.*

ˌdue ˈdate *n* [C usually singular] the date on which something is supposed to happen: *Fewer than five percent of women have their babies on their due date.*

du·el¹ /ˈdjuːəl $ ˈduːəl/ *n* [C] **1** a fight with weapons between two people, used in the past to settle a quarrel: *The officer* ***challenged*** *him* ***to*** *a* ***duel***. **2** a situation in which two people or groups are involved in an angry disagreement: *a verbal duel*

duel² *v* (**duelled**, **duelling** *BrE*, **dueled**, **dueling** *AmE*) [I] to fight a duel

ˌdue ˈprocess *n* [U] *AmE law* the correct process that should be followed in law and is designed to protect someone's legal rights

du·et¹ /djuˈet $ duˈet/ *n* [C] a piece of music for two singers or players → **quartet**, **solo**, **trio**

duet² *v* (*past tense* **duetted**, *past participle* **duetting**) if one singer or musician duets with another, they sing or play together

ˈdue to *prep* because of something: *The court of inquiry ruled that the crash was due to pilot error.* | *She has been absent from work due to illness.* | *The restaurant's success was* ***due largely to*** *its new manager.* | *Attendance at the meeting was small,* ***due in part to*** (=partly because of) *the absence of teachers.*

> **REGISTER**
> **Due to** is mostly used in formal or official contexts. In everyday English, people usually use **because of**: *We cancelled the picnic* ***because of*** *the weather.*

duff¹ /dʌf/ *n* [C] *AmE informal* the part of your body that you sit on SYN **bottom**: *Get off your duff* (=stop sitting or stop being lazy) *and help me!*

duff² *adj BrE informal* bad or useless

duff³ *v*

duff sb ↔ **up** *phr v BrE informal* to fight someone and injure them

duf·fel bag, **duffle bag** /ˈdʌfəl bæg/ *n* [C] a bag made of strong cloth, with a round bottom and a string around the top

duffel coat, **duffle coat** /ˈdʌfəl kəʊt $ -koʊt/ *n* [C] a coat made of rough heavy cloth, usually with a HOOD and TOGGLEs (=buttons shaped like tubes)

duf·fer /ˈdʌfə $ -ər/ *n* [C] *informal* someone who is stupid or not very good at something

dug /dʌg/ the past tense and past participle of DIG

dug·out /ˈdʌgaʊt/ *n* [C] **1** a low shelter at the side of a sports field, where players and team officials sit **2** a shelter dug into the ground for soldiers to use → **trench** **3** a small boat made by cutting out a hollow space in a tree trunk: *a dugout canoe*

duh /dʌ/ *interjection AmE* used to say that what someone else has just said or asked is stupid

DUI /ˌdiː juː ˈaɪ/ *n* [C,U] *law AmE* (***driving under the influence***) the crime of driving when you have had too much alcohol to drink SYN **DWI**: *There were a large number of DUI arrests on New Year's Eve.*

du jour /djuː ˈʒʊə $ -ˈʒʊr/ *adv* **the actor/issue/crime etc du jour** the actor, issue, crime etc that is particularly popular or frequent at this time: *Alien invasions are the cinematic theme du jour.*

duke /djuːk $ duːk/ *n* [C] a man with the highest social rank outside the royal family → **duchess**: *the Duke of Norfolk*

duke·dom /ˈdjuːkdəm $ ˈduːk-/ *n* [C] **1** the rank of a duke **2** the land and property belonging to a duke SYN **duchy**

dul·cet /ˈdʌlsɪt/ *adj* **sb's dulcet tones** someone's voice – used humorously: *Basil's dulcet tones could be heard in the corridor.*

dul·ci·mer /ˈdʌlsəmə $ -ər/ *n* [C] **1** a musical instrument with up to 100 strings, played with light hammers **2** a small instrument with strings that is popular in American FOLK MUSIC, and is played across your knees

dull¹ /dʌl/ ●●○ S3 *adj* (*comparative* **duller**, *superlative* **dullest**)

1 BORING not interesting or exciting: ***Life is never dull when*** *Elizabeth is here.* | *a dull movie* | *It sounded pretty dull to me.* | *The weekly meeting tends to be* ***deadly dull*** (=very dull). | *Last week we had a hurricane.* ***Never a dull moment*** *running a hotel in the Caribbean* (=it's always interesting or exciting). THESAURUS ▸ BORING

> **REGISTER**
> In everyday English, people usually say **boring** rather than **dull**: *a long,* ***boring*** *film*

2 COLOUR/LIGHT not bright or shiny: *The bird is dull brown and gray in colour.* | *Her eyes were dull with dark shadows beneath them.* | *the dull afternoon light*

3 WEATHER not bright and with lots of clouds: *Outside the weather was hazy and dull.* | *a dull sky*

4 PAIN a dull pain is not severe but does not stop OPP **sharp**: *a* ***dull ache*** *in her lower back* | *The pain was dull but persistent.*

5 SOUND not clear or loud: *The gates shut with a* ***dull thud***.

6 KNIFE/BLADE not sharp SYN **blunt**

7 NOT INTELLIGENT *old-fashioned* not able to think quickly or understand things easily SYN **stupid**: *If you don't understand then you're duller than I thought.*

8 TRADE if business on the Stock Exchange is dull, few people are buying and selling OPP **brisk** —**dully** *adv*: *'Well Michael?' he said dully.* | *Her stomach ached dully.* —**dullness** *n* [U]

dull² *v* **1** [T] to make something become less sharp or clear: *He drank some alcohol to* ***dull*** *the* ***pain***. | *Her fear and anxiety dulled her mind.* **2** [I,T] to become less bright or loud, or to make something become less bright or loud: *His* ***eyes dulled*** *a little.* | *The constant rain dulled all sound.*

dull·ard /ˈdʌləd $ -ərd/ *n* [C] someone who is stupid and has no imagination

du·ly /ˈdjuːli $ ˈduːli/ *adv* **1** in the proper or expected way: *Here are your travel documents, all duly signed.* **2** at the proper time or as expected: *The Queen duly appeared on the balcony to wave to the crowds.*

dumb¹ /dʌm/ ●●○ S3 *adj*

1 *informal* stupid: *What a dumb question.* | *a bunch of dumb kids* | *'What is it?' I asked,* ***playing dumb*** (=pretending to be

stupid). | *She's no* **dumb blonde** (=a pretty woman with blonde hair who seems stupid). THESAURUS ▸ STUPID
2 unable to speak, because you are angry, surprised, shocked etc: *He stared at the burnt-out car in dumb disbelief.* | *She was* **struck dumb** *with terror.*
3 *old-fashioned* someone who is dumb is not able to speak at all. Many people think that this use is offensive → **mute** → **deaf and dumb** at DEAF(1)
4 dumb luck *informal* something good that happens in an unexpected way, especially when it is not deserved: *It was just dumb luck that we found the place at all.*
5 dumb animals/creatures used to talk about animals when you want to emphasize that humans often treat them badly and they cannot protect themselves —**dumbly** *adv*: *For a few seconds she gazed dumbly at him.* —**dumbness** *n* [U]

dumb² *v*
dumb sth ↔ **down** to present news or information in a simple and attractive way without many details so that everyone can understand it - used to show disapproval: *Have history textbooks been dumbed down over the past decade?* —**dumbing down** *n* [U]

dumb·bell /ˈdʌmbel/ *n* [C] **1** two weights connected by a short bar, that you can lift to strengthen your arms and shoulders SYN **weights** → see picture at GYM **2** *AmE informal* someone who is stupid

dumb·found·ed /dʌmˈfaʊndɪd/ *adj* extremely surprised: *He was completely dumbfounded by the incident.* THESAURUS ▸ SURPRISED —**dumbfound** *v* [T]

dum·bo /ˈdʌmbəʊ $ -boʊ/ *n* (*plural* **dumbos**) [C] *informal* someone who is stupid

ˈ**dumb show** *n* [C,U] the use of movements without words to express something → **mime**

dumb·struck /ˈdʌmstrʌk/ *adj* so shocked or surprised that you cannot speak

ˌ**dumb ˈwaiter** *n* [C] a small LIFT used to move food, plates etc from one level in a restaurant, hotel etc to another

dum-dum /ˈdʌm dʌm/ *n* [C] a soft bullet that causes serious wounds because it breaks into pieces when it hits you

dum·my¹ /ˈdʌmi/ *n* (*plural* **dummies**) [C]
1 FOR CLOTHES a model that is the shape and size of a person, especially used in order to show clothes in a shop or when you are making clothes: *a shop-window dummy* | *a tailor's dummy*
2 COPY an object that is made to look like a tool, weapon, vehicle etc but which you cannot use: *During practice runs, the warheads in the missiles will be dummies.*
3 DOLL a small model of a person, with a mouth that can be moved so that it looks as though it is talking, used for entertainment: *a ventriloquist's dummy*
4 SPORTS *BrE* a move in a sport such as football in which a player pretends to pass the ball but does not, in order to deceive the other team's players
5 FOR BABIES *BrE* a specially shaped rubber object that you put in a baby's mouth for it to suck SYN **pacifier** *AmE*
6 STUPID PERSON *especially AmE informal* someone who is stupid: *No, you dummy. The other hand.*
7 CARD GAME cards that are placed on the table by one player for all the other players to see in a game of BRIDGE → **spit the dummy** at SPIT¹

dummy² *adj* [only before noun] a dummy tool, weapon, vehicle etc is made to look like a real one but you cannot use it SYN **replica**: *a dummy rifle*

ˌ**dummy ˈrun** *n* [C] an occasion when you practise doing something in complete detail to see if it works SYN **dry run**: *Do a dummy run to see how long it will take.*

dump¹ /dʌmp/ ●●● S3 *v* [T]
1 PUT STH SOMEWHERE [always + adv/prep] to put something somewhere in a careless untidy way: *Merrill dumped her suitcase down in the hall.* | **dump sth on sth** *They dump tons of salt on icy road surfaces to make driving safer.* | **dump sth in/into sth** *He found a can of beef stew and dumped it in a saucepan to heat.* THESAURUS ▸ PUT
2 GET RID OF STH **a)** to get rid of something that you do not want: *Ellie dumped all the photos of her ex-husband.* | *He dumped her body into the sea.* **b)** to get rid of waste material by taking it from people's houses and burying it under the soil: *Britain dumps more of its waste than any other European country.*
3 END RELATIONSHIP *informal* to end a relationship with someone: *Vicky dumped Neil yesterday.*
4 SELL GOODS to get rid of goods by selling them in a foreign country at a much lower price: **[+in/on]** *a campaign to stop cheap European beef being dumped in West Africa*
5 COPY INFORMATION *technical* to copy information stored in a computer's memory on to something else such as a DISK or MAGNETIC TAPE → **DUMPING**

dump on sb *phr v informal*
1 dump sth on sb to unfairly give someone an unwanted job, duty, or problem to deal with: *Don't just dump the extra work on me.*
2 *AmE* to treat someone badly
3 *AmE* to criticize someone very strongly and often unfairly: *politicians dumping on their opponents*
4 dump (sth) on sb to tell someone all your problems and worries: *We all dump our troubles on Mike.*

dump² ●●○ *n* [C]
1 WASTE a place where unwanted waste is taken and left: **rubbish dump** *BrE*, **garbage dump** *AmE*: *The fire probably started in a rubbish dump.* | *Put the rest into a sack to take to* **the dump**. | *an underground nuclear* **waste dump** | *a dump site*
2 WEAPONS a place where military supplies are stored, or the supplies themselves: *There has been a series of explosions in an ammunition dump.*
3 UNPLEASANT PLACE *informal* a place that is unpleasant to live in because it is dirty, ugly, untidy etc: '**What a dump**,' *she added as they entered the village.* | *Why are you living in a dump like this?*
4 down in the dumps *informal* very sad and without much interest in life: *She's feeling a bit down in the dumps.*
5 COMPUTER *technical* the act of copying the information stored in a computer's memory onto something else, such as a DISK: *a screen dump*
6 take a dump *informal not polite* to pass solid waste from the BOWELS

ˈ**dumper truck** *n* [C] *BrE* a DUMP TRUCK

dump·ing /ˈdʌmpɪŋ/ *n* [U] the act of getting rid of dangerous waste material in a place that is not safe: *The government has promised to stop dumping by the state-owned chemical plants.*

ˈ**dumping ˌground** *n* [C] **1** a place where people get rid of waste material: **[+for]** *Rivers have always been a dumping ground for man's unwanted waste.* **2** a place where people are sent when no one knows how to deal with them: **[+for]** *The prison has been the dumping ground for difficult prisoners for years.*

dump·ling /ˈdʌmplɪŋ/ *n* [C] **1** a round lump of flour and fat mixed with water, cooked in boiling liquid and served with meat: *chicken and dumplings* **2** a sweet dish made of PASTRY filled with fruit: *apple dumplings*

Dump·ster /ˈdʌmpstə $ -ər/ *n* [C] *trademark* a large metal container used for waste in the US SYN **skip** *BrE*

ˈ**Dumpster ˌdiving** *n* [U] *AmE informal* the activity of looking through Dumpsters for clothes, food, furniture etc that other people have thrown away

ˈ**dump truck** *AmE n* [C] a vehicle with a large open container at the back that can move up to pour sand, soil etc onto the ground

dump·y /ˈdʌmpi/ *adj* someone who is dumpy is fat, short, and unattractive: *a dumpy little man* THESAURUS ▸ SHORT

dun /dʌn/ *n* [U] a brownish-grey colour —**dun** *adj*

dunce /dʌns/ *n* [C] *old-fashioned* someone who is slow at learning things: *the dunce of the class*

ˈ**dunce's cap** *n* [C] a tall pointed hat that a stupid student had to wear in school in the past

Dun·dee cake /dʌnˈdiː ˌkeɪk/ *n* [C,U] a British cake made with fruit and nuts

dun·der·head /ˈdʌndəhed $ -ər-/ *n* [C] *old-fashioned* someone who is stupid

dune /djuːn $ duːn/ *n* [C] a hill made of sand near the sea or in the desert SYN **sand dune**

ˈdune ˌbashing *n* [U] the sport of riding QUAD BIKES through sand dunes

ˈdune ˌbuggy *n* [C] a car with big wheels and no roof that you can drive across sand SYN **beach buggy**

dung /dʌŋ/ *n* [U] solid waste from animals, especially cows

dun·ga·rees /ˌdʌŋgəˈriːz/ *n* [plural] **1** *BrE* loose trousers that have a square piece of cloth that covers your chest, and long thin pieces that fasten over your shoulders SYN **overalls** *AmE* **2** *AmE old-fashioned* heavy cotton trousers used for working in SYN **jeans**

dun·geon /ˈdʌndʒən/ *n* [C] a dark underground prison, especially under a castle, that was used in the past

dunk /dʌŋk/ *v* **1** [T] to quickly put something into a liquid and take it out again, especially something you are eating: *Jill dunked her ginger biscuit in her tea.* | *I dunked my head under the water and scrubbed at my hair.* **THESAURUS** ▸ **PUT 2** [T] *AmE* to push someone under water for a short time as a joke SYN **duck** *BrE* **3** [I,T] to jump up by the basket and throw the ball down into it in BASKETBALL → **dunk for apples** at **APPLE(3)**, → **SLAM DUNK**, → see picture at **BASKETBALL** —**dunk** *n* [C]

ˌDunkirk ˈspirit, the a determination to succeed despite being in a difficult or impossible situation, which is believed to be a typical British quality. The expression comes from the events involving British soldiers during World War II at Dunkirk.

dun·no /dʌˈnəʊ $ -noʊ/ a way of saying 'I don't know'. Some people think that this use is not correct English: *'Do you want to come?' 'I dunno, I might.'*

du·o /ˈdjuːəʊ $ ˈduːoʊ/ ●○○ *n* (*plural* **duos**) [C]
1 two people who perform together or are often seen together: *the comedy duo Reeves and Mortimer*
2 a piece of music for two performers SYN **duet**

du·o·de·num /ˌdjuːəˈdiːnəm $ ˌduːəˈdiːnəm, duˈɑːdn-əm/ *n* [C] the top part of your BOWEL, below your stomach —**duodenal** /ˌdjuːəˈdiːnl◂ $ ˌduːəˈdiːnl◂, duˈɑːdn-əl/ *adj*: *a duodenal ulcer*

dupe¹ /djuːp $ duːp/ *n* [C] someone who is tricked, especially into becoming involved in something illegal

dupe² *v* [T] to trick or deceive someone: **be duped into doing sth** *Consumers are being duped into buying faulty electronic goods.* GRAMMAR **Dupe** is usually passive.

du·plex /ˈdjuːpleks $ ˈduː-/ *n* [C] *AmE* a type of house that is divided into two parts, so that it has two separate homes in it

du·pli·cate¹ /ˈdjuːplɪkeɪt $ ˈduː-/ ●○○ *v* [T]
1 to copy something exactly: *New copies of the form can be duplicated from a master copy.* | *The video was duplicated illegally.*
2 to repeat something in exactly the same way: *We don't want staff to duplicate each other's work.* —**duplication** /ˌdjuːplɪˈkeɪʃən $ ˌduː-/ *n* [U]

du·pli·cate² /ˈdjuːplәkәt $ ˈduː-/ ●○○ *adj* [only before noun] exactly the same as something, or made as an exact copy of something: *A* ***duplicate copy*** *should be made for the county record office.* | *a duplicate key*

duplicate³ ●○○ *n* [C]
1 an exact copy of something that you can use in the same way: **[+of]** *Locksmiths can* ***make duplicates*** *of most keys.* | *She kept both the duplicate and the original.*
2 in duplicate if something is in duplicate, there are two copies of it: *Copies of the proposal should be sent in duplicate.*

du·plic·i·ty /djuːˈplɪsəti $ duː-/ *n* [U] dishonest behaviour that is intended to deceive someone —**duplicitous** *adj*

dur·a·ble /ˈdjʊərəbəl $ ˈdʊr-/ *adj* **1** staying in good condition for a long time, even if used a lot SYN **hard-wearing**: *Wood is a durable material.* **THESAURUS** ▸ **STRONG 2** continuing for a long time SYN **long-lasting**: *His poetry has proved durable.* —**durably** *adv* —**durability** /ˌdjʊərəˈbɪləti $ ˌdʊr-/ *n* [U] → **CONSUMER DURABLES**

ˈdurable ˌgoods *n* [plural] *AmE* large things such as cars, televisions, and furniture, that you do not buy often SYN **consumer durables** *BrE*

du·ra·tion /djʊˈreɪʃən $ dʊ-/ ●○○ AWL *n* [U] the length of time that something continues: *The course is of three years' duration.* | **for the duration (of sth)** *The package includes cycle hire for the duration of your holiday.*

du·ress /djʊˈres $ dʊ-/ *n* [U] illegal or unfair threats: **under duress** *The confession was obtained under duress.*

Dur·ex /ˈdjʊəreks $ ˈdʊr-/ *n trademark* **1** [C] *BrE* a rubber CONTRACEPTIVE that a man wears over his PENIS during sex **2** [U] *AusE* clear narrow plastic that is sticky on one side and is used for fastening paper

dur·ing /ˈdjʊərɪŋ $ ˈdʊr-/ ●●● S1 W1 *prep*
1 from the beginning to the end of a period of time: *During the summer she worked as a lifeguard.* | *He slept calmly during the early part of the night.* | *Foxes remain hidden during the day.*
2 at some point in a period of time: *My father was killed during the war.* | *I mentioned the subject during our discussions at her Washington office.* ⚠ Don't say 'during doing something' or 'during someone does something'. Use **while**: *They chatted while waiting for the train (NOT during waiting for the train).* | *He stole her money while she slept (NOT during she slept).*

THESAURUS

during at one point in a period of time, or through the whole of a period of time: *Did you hear the storm during the night?* | *During the summer we spend a lot more time out of doors.*
all through (*also* **throughout**) /ɔːl ˈθruː, θruːˈaʊt/ during all of a period of time: *The cafe's closed all through the winter and opens again in April.* | *Throughout her career she has worked hard and achieved the highest standards.*
over at one point or at various different points during a period of time: *I'm going to redecorate my bedroom over the holidays.* | *She's been a great help to me over the past year.*
in the course of sth *formal* during a particular process or period of time: *In the course of the study we consulted with leading experts in global warming.* | *There was huge social change in the course of the 1960s.*
within during a period of time, or before the end of a period – used when you want to emphasize that it is a short or limited period: *There have been five serious accidents within the last few days.* | *Payment must be made within 30 days.*

durst /dɜːst $ dɜːrst/ *v old use* the past tense of DARE

dusk /dʌsk/ ●○○ *n* [U] the time before it gets dark when the sky is becoming less bright SYN **twilight** → **dawn, dusk**: *The street lights go on at dusk.*

dusk·y /ˈdʌski/ *adj* dark or not very bright in colour: *The room was filled with dusky shadows.* | **dusky pink/orange/blue etc** *a dusky pink room*

dust¹ /dʌst/ ●●● S3 W3 *n*
1 [U] dry powder consisting of extremely small bits of dirt that is in buildings on furniture, floors etc if they are not kept clean: *All the furniture was* ***covered in dust***. | *a thick* ***layer of dust*** | *There's not a* ***speck of dust*** *in the kitchen.* | **gather/collect dust** (=become covered with dust) *Her old trophies were collecting dust on the shelves.* | ***Dust particles*** *floated in the sunlight.* | *A sudden breeze sent* ***motes of dust*** (=small bits of dust) *dancing in the air.*
2 [U] dry powder consisting of extremely small bits of earth or sand: *The wind was blowing dust and leaves up from the ground.* | *A car sped past in a* ***cloud of dust***.

3 [U] powder consisting of extremely small bits of a particular substance: **coal/brick/chalk etc dust**
4 a dust *BrE* the act of dusting something: *I need to **give** the sitting room **a dust**.*
5 let the dust settle/wait for the dust to settle to allow or wait for a confused situation to become clear → **bite the dust** at BITE[1](8), → DUSTY, → **leave sb in the dust** at LEAVE[1](15), → **not see sb for dust** at SEE[1](35)

dust² ●●○ *v*
1 [I,T] to clean the dust from a surface by moving something such as a soft cloth across it: *Rachel dusted the books and the bookshelves.* | *I was dusting in the bedroom when the phone rang.* → see picture at CLEAN²
2 [T] (*also* **dust down, dust off**) to remove something such as dust or dirt from your clothes by brushing them with your hands: *He got to his feet and dusted his knees.* | **dust yourself (down/off)** *Corbett dusted himself down and walked off.*
3 [T] to put a fine powder over something: **dust sth with sth** *Dust the biscuits with icing sugar.*

dust sth ↔ **off** *phr v*
1 to remove something such as dust or dirt from your clothes by brushing them with your hands: *They were dusting off leaves and twigs.* | **dust yourself off** *He got to his feet and dusted himself off.*
2 to get something ready in order to use it again, after not using it for a long time: *The government is dusting off schemes for supporting creative industries.*

dust·bin /ˈdʌstbɪn/ *n* [C] *BrE* a large container outside your house, used for holding waste until it is taken away SYN **garbage can** *AmE* → see picture at BIN¹

ˈdustbin ˌman *n* [C] a DUSTMAN

ˈdust bowl *n* [C] an area of land that has DUST STORMS and very long periods without rain

ˈdust ˌbunny *n* [C] *AmE informal* a small ball of dust that forms in a place that is not cleaned regularly, such as under furniture

ˈdust cart *n* [C] *BrE* a large vehicle that goes from house to house to collect waste from dustbins SYN **garbage truck** *AmE*

ˈdust ˌcover *n* [C] *AmE* a paper cover of a book, which you can remove SYN **dust jacket**

dust·er /ˈdʌstə $ -ər/ *n* [C] **1** a cloth for removing dust from furniture **2** *AmE old-fashioned* a light coat that you wear to protect your clothes while you are cleaning the house **3** *AmE informal* a DUST STORM

ˈdust ˌjacket *n* [C] a paper cover of a book, which you can remove

dust·man /ˈdʌstmən/ *n* (*plural* **dustmen** /-mən/) [C] *BrE* someone whose job is to remove waste from DUSTBINS SYN **garbage collector** *AmE*

dust·pan /ˈdʌstpæn/ *n* [C] a flat container with a handle that you use with a brush to remove dust and waste from the floor: *Have you got a dustpan and brush?* → see picture at BRUSH¹

dust·sheet /ˈdʌst-ʃiːt/ *n* [C] *especially BrE* a large sheet of cloth used to protect furniture from dust or paint SYN **drop cloth** *AmE*

ˈdust storm *n* [C] a storm with strong winds that carries large amounts of dust

dust-up /ˈdʌst-ʌp/ *n* [C] *BrE informal* a fight

dust·y /ˈdʌsti/ ●●○ *adj*
1 covered with dust: *Adrian cycled along the dusty road.* | *Everything's really dusty.* THESAURUS ▸ DIRTY
2 dusty blue/pink etc blue etc that is not bright but is slightly grey: *The curtains had faded to a dusty pink.*

Dutch¹ /dʌtʃ/ *adj* **1** relating to the Netherlands, its people, or its language **2 go Dutch (with sb)** to share the cost of a meal in a restaurant **3 Dutch treat** *AmE* an occasion when you share the cost of something such as a meal in a restaurant

Dutch² *n* **1 the Dutch** [plural] people from the Netherlands **2** [U] the language used in the Netherlands and in some parts of Belgium → DOUBLE-DUTCH

ˌDutch ˈauction *n* [C,U] a public sale at which the price of something is gradually reduced until someone will pay it

ˌDutch ˈbarn *n* [C] a farm building with a curved roof on a frame that has no walls, used for storing HAY

ˌDutch ˈcap *n* [C] a round rubber CONTRACEPTIVE, that a woman wears inside her VAGINA during sex SYN **diaphragm, cap**

ˌDutch ˈcourage *n* [U] courage or confidence that you get when you drink alcohol

ˌDutch ˈelm disˌease *n* [U] a disease that affects and kills ELM trees

Dutch·man /ˈdʌtʃmən/ *n* (*plural* **Dutchmen** /-mən/) [C] **1** a man from the Netherlands **2 I'm a Dutchman** *BrE spoken* used to show that you do not believe something: ***If** that ball was out, **then I'm a Dutchman**.*

ˌDutch ˈoven *n* [C] a large cooking pot with a lid

Dutch·wom·an /ˈdʌtʃˌwʊmən/ *n* (*plural* **Dutchwomen** /-ˌwɪmɪn/) [C] a woman from the Netherlands

du·ti·a·ble /ˈdjuːtiəbəl $ ˈduː-/ *adj* dutiable goods are those that you must pay duty on

du·ti·ful /ˈdjuːtɪfəl $ ˈduː-/ *adj* doing what you are expected to do and behaving in a loyal and obedient way: *a dutiful son* | *Dutiful applause greeted his speech.*

dut·i·ful·ly /ˈdjuːtɪfəli $ ˈduː-/ *adv* if you do something dutifully, you do it because you think it is the correct way to behave: *I dutifully wrote down every word.*

du·ty /ˈdjuːti $ ˈduː-/ ●●● S2 W1 *n* (*plural* **duties**)
1 STH YOU MUST DO [C,U] something that you have to do because it is morally or legally right SYN **obligation**: *I promise I will **do** my **duty**.* | *We feel **it is our duty to** help her.* | *Local authorities **have a duty to** keep the streets clean.* | *You **have a duty to** your husband and to your children.* | *She has a strong **sense of moral duty**.* | *The unions have **failed in their duty** to female workers.* | *In the traditional Hindu family, the son is **duty-bound** to look after his mother.*
2 WORK [C usually plural, U] something you have to do as part of your job: **duties** *Martin's duties included cleaning the cars.* | *She works for her father doing part-time secretarial duties.* | *He will soon be fit enough to **carry out** his **duties*** (=do his job). | *He can only do **light duties**.* | *When Juliet **reported for duty*** (=arrived and said she was ready to start work) *she was sent to check on a new patient.* | *A teacher may be fired for **neglect of duty*** (=failing to do their job properly). | *He did three **tours of duty** in Vietnam* (=three periods working in a foreign country as a soldier, government officer etc).
3 be on/off duty to be working or not working at a particular time, especially when you are doing a job which people take turns to do, so that someone is always doing it: *He's **on night duty**.* | *Mary **goes on duty*** (=starts working) *tonight at half past ten.* | *What time do you **go off duty*** (=finish work)?
4 TAX [C,U] a tax you pay on something you buy: **[+on]** *the duty on cigarettes* | **customs duty** (=tax paid on goods coming into the country) → DEATH DUTIES, STAMP DUTY
5 do duty as sth to be used as something SYN **serve as sth**: *The living room also does duty as a home office.* → DOUBLE DUTY, HEAVY-DUTY, → **jury duty** at JURY SERVICE, → **on active duty** at ACTIVE SERVICE

ˌduty-ˈfree¹ *adj* duty-free goods can be brought into a country without paying tax on them: *duty-free cigarettes* | *the duty-free shop* —**duty-free** *adv*

duty-free² *n* [C,U] alcohol, cigarettes etc that you can bring into a country without having to pay tax on them

du·vet /ˈduːveɪ, ˈdjuː- $ duːˈveɪ/ ●●○ *n* [C] *especially BrE* a large cloth bag filled with feathers or similar material that you use to cover yourself in bed SYN **comforter** *AmE*

ˈduvet day / $.ˈ../ *n* [C] *informal* a day when you are supposed to go to work, but stay at home and relax instead

DVD /ˌdiː viː ˈdiː/ ●●● S3 W3 *n* [C,U] (***digital video disc*** *or* ***digital versatile disc***) a type of computer DISC that can store a large amount of information, sound, pictures, and video: *a DVD player* | *The film is now out on video and DVD.*

ˌDVD-ˈROM *n* [C,U] (***digital video disc read-only memory***) a type of computer DISC that can store more information than a CD-ROM

DVLA, the /ˌdiː viː el ˈeɪ/ (***the Driver and Vehicle Licensing Agency***) the British government department that is responsible for collecting road tax from people who own vehicles, for giving driving tests, and for giving people their DRIVING LICENCES

DVT /ˌdiː viː ˈtiː/ *n* [U] *medical* the abbreviation of ***deep vein thrombosis***

dwarf¹ /dwɔːf $ dwɔːrf/ *n* (*plural* **dwarfs** *or* **dwarves**) [C] **1** an imaginary creature that looks like a small man: *Snow White and the Seven Dwarfs* **2** a person who is a dwarf has not continued to grow to the normal height because of a medical condition. Many people think that this use is offensive. → **WHITE DWARF**

dwarf² *adj* [only before noun] a dwarf plant or animal is much smaller than the usual size: *a dwarf conifer*

dwarf³ *v* [T] to be so big that other things are made to seem very small: *The cathedral is dwarfed by the surrounding skyscrapers.* GRAMMAR **Dwarf** is usually passive.

dweeb /dwiːb/ *n* [C] *AmE informal* someone who is weak, slightly strange, and not popular or fashionable

dwell /dwel/ ●○○ *v* (*past tense and past participle* **dwelt** /dwelt/ *or* **dwelled**) [I always + adv/prep] *literary* to live in a particular place: *They dwelt in the forest.*

dwell on/upon sth *phr v* to think or talk for too long about something, especially something unpleasant: *That is not a subject I want to dwell on.*

dwel·ler /ˈdwelə $ -ər/ *n* [C] **city/town/cave etc dweller** a person or animal that lives in a particular place: *City dwellers suffer higher pollution levels.*

dwell·ing /ˈdwelɪŋ/ *n* [C] *formal* a house, apartment etc where people live

ˈdwelling house *n* [C] *formal especially BrE* a house that people live in, not one that is being used as a shop, office etc

dwelt /dwelt/ a past tense and past participle of DWELL

DWI /ˌdiː dʌbəljuː ˈaɪ/ *n* [C,U] *AmE law* (***driving while intoxicated***) the crime of driving when you have had too much alcohol to drink SYN **DUI**

dwin·dle /ˈdwɪndl/ ●○○ *v* [I] (*also* **dwindle away**) to gradually become less and less or smaller and smaller: *The elephant population is dwindling.* | *His money had dwindled away.* | **[+to]** *The stream has dwindled to a trickle.* THESAURUS▸ DECREASE —**dwindling** *adj*: *dwindling resources*

dye¹ /daɪ/ ●●○ *n*
1 [C,U] a substance you use to change the colour of your clothes, hair etc: *hair dye*
2 a dye job *informal* someone who has had a dye job has used a substance to change the colour of their hair

dye² ●●○ *v* [T] to give something a different colour using a dye: **dye sth black/blue/blonde etc** *Priscilla's hair was dyed jet black.* —**dyed** *adj*

ˌdyed-in-the-ˈwool *adj* having strong beliefs, likes, or opinions that will never change: *Even dyed-in-the-wool traditionalists were impressed by the changes.*

dy·ing¹ /ˈdaɪ-ɪŋ/ the present participle of DIE

dying² *adj* **1 dying moment/minutes/seconds** during the last minutes, seconds etc before something ends: *Chandler's goal was in the dying minutes of the game.* **2** [only before noun] happening just before someone dies: *It was her **dying wish** to have a simple burial.* **3 to your dying day** for the rest of your life: *He regretted the decision to his dying day.* **4** [only before noun] gradually decreasing until soon there will be none left: *Women who enjoy baking are a **dying breed**.* **5 the dying** [plural] people who are dying: *a hospice for the dying*

dyke, **dike** /daɪk/ *n* [C] **1** a wall or bank built to keep back water and prevent flooding **2** *taboo informal* an offensive word for a LESBIAN (=woman who is sexually attracted to women). Do not use this word. **3** *especially BrE* a narrow passage to carry water away SYN **ditch**

dy·nam·ic¹ /daɪˈnæmɪk/ ●●○ AWL *adj*
1 full of energy and new ideas, and determined to succeed: *dynamic and ambitious people* THESAURUS▸ ENERGETIC
2 continuously moving or changing: *a dynamic and unstable process*
3 *technical* relating to a force or power that causes movement —**dynamically** /-kli/ *adv*

dynamic² ●○○ AWL *n*
1 dynamics a) [plural] the way in which things or people behave, react, and affect each other: **[+of]** *the dynamics of the family* | *He did research on **group dynamics** and leadership styles.* **b)** [U] the science relating to the movement of objects and the forces involved in movement **c)** [plural] changes in how loudly music is played or sung
2 [singular] *formal* something that causes action or change: **[+of]** *She regards class conflict as a central dynamic of historical change.*

dy·na·mis·m /ˈdaɪnəmɪzəm/ *n* [U] energy and determination to succeed: *her entrepreneurial dynamism*

dy·na·mite¹ /ˈdaɪnəmaɪt/ *n* [U] **1** a powerful explosive used especially for breaking rock: *a dynamite blast* **2** something or someone that is likely to cause a lot of trouble: *If the proposals became public they would be dynamite.* **3** *old-fashioned informal* someone or something that is very exciting or impressive: *The band is dynamite.*

dynamite² *v* [T] to damage or destroy something with dynamite

dy·na·mo /ˈdaɪnəməʊ $ -moʊ/ *n* (*plural* **dynamos**) [C]
1 a machine that changes some other form of power directly into electricity: *bicycle lights powered by a dynamo*
2 someone who is excited about what they do and who puts a lot of energy into it: *the team's midfield dynamo*
3 something that has a strong effect on something else, and that makes things happen: *Oil is the dynamo of the country's economy.*

dyn·a·sty /ˈdɪnəsti $ ˈdaɪ-/ ●○○ *n* (*plural* **dynasties**) [C]
1 a family of kings or other rulers whose parents, grandparents etc have ruled the country for many years: *The Habsburg dynasty ruled in Austria from 1278 to 1918.*
2 a period of time when a particular family ruled a country or area
3 *informal* a group or family that controls a particular business or organization for a long time: *the Rothschild banking dynasty*

d'you /djʊ, dʒə/ the short form of 'do you': *D'you know what I mean?*

dys·cal·cu·li·a /ˌdɪskælkjəˈliːə/ *n* [U] a condition that makes it difficult for someone to recognize numbers correctly, so that they cannot do simple sums → **dyslexia** —**dyscalculic** *adj* —**dyscalculic** *n* [C]

dys·en·te·ry /ˈdɪsəntəri $ -teri/ *n* [U] a serious disease of your BOWELS that makes them BLEED and pass much more waste than usual

dys·func·tion·al /dɪsˈfʌŋkʃənəl/ *adj* **1** not following the normal patterns of social behaviour, especially with the result that someone cannot behave in a normal way or have a satisfactory life: *dysfunctional family relationships* **2** not working properly or normally OPP **functional**

dys·lex·i·a /dɪsˈleksiə/ *n* [U] a condition that makes it difficult for someone to read and spell —**dyslexic** *adj*: *Two of the children in the class are dyslexic.* —**dyslexic** *n* [C]

dys·pep·si·a /dɪsˈpepsiə, -ˈpepʃə/ *n* [U] a problem that your body has in dealing with the food you eat SYN **indigestion**

dys·pep·tic /dɪsˈpeptɪk/ *adj* **1** suffering from dyspepsia **2** *old-fashioned* bad-tempered

dys·prax·i·a /dɪsˈpræksiə/ *n* [U] a condition that makes it difficult for someone to control their movements accurately and can affect their learning

dys·to·pi·a /dɪsˈtəʊpiə $ -ˈtoʊ-/ *n* [C] an imaginary place where life is extremely difficult and a lot of unfair or immoral things happen OPP **utopia**

dys·tro·phy /ˈdɪstrəfi/ → **MUSCULAR DYSTROPHY**

D

Ee

E[1], **e** /iː/ *n* (*plural* **E's** *or* **e's**) **1** [C,U] the fifth letter of the English alphabet **2** [C,U] the third note in the SCALE of C MAJOR or the musical KEY based on this note **3** [C] a mark given to a student's work to show that it is of very low quality **4** [C,U] ECSTASY (=an illegal drug)

E[2] **1** *BrE technical* the written abbreviation of ***earth*** (=a connection between a piece of electrical equipment and the ground) **2** the abbreviation of ***E number*** **3** the written abbreviation of ***east*** or ***eastern***

e-, **E-** /iː/ *prefix* (***electronic***) used before another word to mean something that is done on or involves the Internet: *e-shopping | e-commerce*

each /iːtʃ/ ●●● (S1) (W1) *determiner, pron, adv*

1 every one of two or more things or people, considered separately → **every**: *She had a bottle in each hand. | Grill the fish for five minutes on each side. | Each member of the team is given a particular job to do. | We each have our own skills. | When the children arrive, you give them each a balloon. | There are four bedrooms, each with its own shower and WC. | The tickets cost £20 each* (=each ticket costs £20). *| You get two cookies each* (=every one of you gets two cookies). | **[+of]** *I'm going to ask each of you to speak for three minutes. | There are 250 blocks of stone, and* ***each one*** *weighs a ton.* | **each day/week/month etc** (=on each day, in each week etc) *a disease that affects about 10 million people each year*

2 each and every used to emphasize that you are talking about every person or thing in a group: *These are issues that affect* ***each and every one of*** *us. | Firemen face dangerous situations each and every day.*

3 each to his/their own used to say that we all have different ideas about how to do things, what we like etc, especially when you do not agree with someone else's choice: *I'd have chosen something more modern myself, but each to his own.*

GRAMMAR: Patterns with each

- **Each** is used before a singular noun with a singular verb: *Each item* ***was*** *thoroughly checked.*
- **Each** can also be used before 'of' and a plural noun. The verb should still be singular: *Each of these people* ***has*** *some useful talent or experience.*
- You usually use 'his', 'her', 'himself', or 'herself' after **each**: *Each boy is issued with his own locker. | Each of them tried it for herself.*
- However, you can use 'they', 'them', 'their' etc when you do not want to say whether people are male or female: *Each individual has a right to express their views.*
- Don't use **each** in negative clauses. Use **none**: *None of the answers was correct.* ✗ Don't say: *Each of the answers was not correct.*

USAGE: Each, every

- It is often correct to use either **each** or **every**, but they have slightly different meanings.
- Use **each** when you are thinking about the people or things in a group separately, one by one: *Each student came forward to receive a medal. | Each time you exercise, you get a little stronger.*
- Use **every** when you are thinking about the whole group of people or things together, with no exceptions: *Every student was given a prize. | You have to enter your password every time you log on.*
- Don't use **each** after words such as 'almost', 'nearly', or 'not'. Use **every**: *Almost every window was broken. | Not every child enjoyed the party.*

each ˈother ●●● (S1) (W1) *pron* [not used as the subject of a sentence] used to show that each of two or more people does something to the other or others → **one another**: *Susan and Robert kissed each other passionately. | The girls looked at each other. | They enjoy each other's company.* → **be at each other's throats** at THROAT(5)

ˌeach ˈway *adv BrE* if you BET (=try to win money by guessing the winner of a race) money each way, you will win if the horse or dog you choose comes first, second, or third —**each way** *adj*: *a £10 each way bet*

ea·ger /ˈiːɡə $ -ər/ ●●○ *adj*

1 very keen and excited about something that is going to happen or about something you want to do: **eager to do sth** *I was eager to get back to work as soon as possible. | He's a bright kid and eager to learn. | She's a very hard worker and very* ***eager to please****. | A crowd of eager young students were already waiting outside.* | **[+for]** *fans eager for a glimpse of the singer*

2 eager beaver *informal* someone who is too keen and works harder than they should —**eagerly** *adv*: *They're eagerly awaiting the big day.* —**eagerness** *n* [U]: *People were pushing each other out of the way* ***in their eagerness*** *to get to the front.*

ea·gle[1] /ˈiːɡəl/ ●●○ *n* [C]

1 a very large strong bird with a beak like a hook that eats small animals, birds etc → see picture at **BIRD OF PREY**

2 two STROKES less than PAR (=the usual number of strokes for a hole) in a game of golf

3 eagle eye used to say that someone is watching carefully or is likely to notice something: *They carried on working, under the eagle eye of the owner.*

eagle[2] *v* [T] to use two STROKES less than the usual number of strokes for a hole in a game of golf

ˌeagle-ˈeyed *adj* [only before noun] very good at seeing or noticing things: *One eagle-eyed passerby noticed that the window was slightly open.*

ea·glet /ˈiːɡlɪt/ *n* [C] a young EAGLE

EAL /ˌiː eɪ ˈel/ *n* [U] (***English as an Additional Language***) the teaching of English to people who live in an English-speaking country, but whose first language is not English (SYN) **ESL**

Ea·ling com·e·dy /ˌiːlɪŋ ˈkɒmədi $ -ˈkɑː-/ *n* [C] one of many humorous films, mostly in black and white, made at Ealing Studios in London during the 1940s and 1950s, in which many well-known British actors appeared

-ean /iən/ *suffix* [in adjectives and nouns] another form of the SUFFIX -AN: *Keynesean economics* (=according to the ideas of Keynes)

EAP /ˌiː eɪ ˈpiː/ *n* [U] (***English for Academic Purposes***) the teaching of English to people whose first language is not English and who need English for studying at a college or university

ear /ɪə $ ɪr/ ●●● (S2) (W2) *n*

1 PART OF YOUR BODY [C] one of the organs on either side of your head that you hear with: *She tucked her hair behind her ears.* | **long-eared/short-eared etc** *a long-eared rabbit*

2 GRAIN [C] the top part of a plant such as wheat that produces grain: **[+of]** *an ear of corn*

3 smile/grin etc from ear to ear to show that you are very happy or pleased by smiling a lot: *She came out of his office, beaming from ear to ear.*

4 reach sb's ears if something reaches someone's ears, they hear about it or find out about it: *The news eventually reached the ears of the king.*

5 to sb's ears used when saying how something sounds to someone: *It sounds odd to the ears of an ordinary English speaker.*

6 [singular] the ability to learn music, copy sounds etc: **[+for]** *She* ***has*** *no* ***ear*** *for languages at all. | a* ***good ear*** *for dialogue*

7 a sympathetic ear used to say that someone listens sympathetically to what someone is saying: *He's always prepared to* ***lend a sympathetic ear****.*

8 close/shut your ears to sth to refuse to listen to bad or unpleasant news: *You can't just close your ears to their* *warnings*. → **turn a deaf ear** at DEAF(4), → **fall on deaf ears** at DEAF(5)

9 be all ears *informal* to be very keen to hear what someone is going to tell you: *As soon as I mentioned money, Karen was all ears.*

10 be out on your ear *informal* to be forced to leave a job, organization etc, especially because you have done something wrong: *You'd better start working harder, or you'll be out on your ear.*

11 be up to your ears in work/debt/problems etc to have a lot of work etc

12 have sth coming out (of) your ears *informal* to have too much of something: *We've got pumpkins coming out our ears this time of year.*

13 keep your/an ear to the ground to make sure that you always know what is happening in a situation

14 keep your ears open to always be listening in order to find out what is happening or to hear some useful information: *I hope you'll all keep your eyes and ears open for anything unusual.*

15 go in (at) one ear and out (at) the other *informal* if information goes in one ear and out the other, you forget it as soon as you have heard it: *I don't know why I tell her anything. It just goes in one ear and out the other.*

16 give sb a thick ear *BrE informal* to hit someone on the ear: *Behave yourself or I'll give you a thick ear!*

17 have sb's ear to be trusted by someone so that they will listen to your advice, opinions etc: *He claimed to have the ear of several top ministers.*

18 play sth by ear to play music that you have heard without having to read written music → see also **play it by ear** at PLAY[1](11)

19 sb's ears are burning used to say that someone thinks that people are talking about them

20 sb's ears are flapping *BrE spoken* used to say that someone is trying to listen to your private conversation → DOG-EARED, → **bend sb's ear** at BEND[1](7), → **send sb off with a flea in their ear** at FLEA(2), → **make a pig's ear of** at PIG[1](5), → **prick (up) your ears** at PRICK[1](5), → **wet behind the ears** at WET[1](7)

COLLOCATIONS

ADJECTIVES

big *African elephants' ears are bigger than those of Indian elephants.*
floppy (=soft and hanging down loosely, rather than being stiff) *a rabbit with big floppy ears*
pointy/pointed *The dog has short pointy ears.*
sb's left/right ear *She is deaf in her right ear.*
inner/middle ear (=the parts inside your ear, which you use to hear sounds) *I've got an infection in my middle ear.*

VERBS

say/whisper sth into sb's ear *He whispered something into his wife's ear.*
have your ears pierced (=have a hole put into the skin, so that you can wear an earring) | **sb's ears stick out** (=they are noticeable because they do not lie flat against someone's head) | **sb's ears pop** (=the pressure in them changes suddenly, for example when you go up or down quickly in a plane)

ear·ache /ˈɪəreɪk $ ˈɪr-/ ●●○ *n* [singular, U] a pain inside your ear: *I've got terrible earache and a sore throat.*

ear·bash·ing /ˈɪəˌbæʃɪŋ $ ˈɪr-/ *n* [singular] *BrE informal* if someone gives you an earbashing, they criticize you in an angry way for a long time because you have done something wrong

ear·bud /ˈɪəbʌd $ ˈɪr-/ *n* [C usually plural] a small EARPHONE

ear·cuff /ˈɪəkʌf $ ˈɪr-/ *n* [C] a piece of jewellery that you wear around the outer edge of your ear

ˈear drops *n* [plural] liquid medicine to put in your ear

ear·drum /ˈɪədrʌm $ ˈɪr-/ *n* [C] a tight thin piece of skin over the inside of your ear which allows you to hear sound

ear·ful /ˈɪəfʊl $ ˈɪr-/ *n* **give sb an earful** *informal* to tell someone how angry you are about something they have done: *He gave me a real earful about being late so often.*

ear·hole /ˈɪəhəʊl $ ˈɪrhoʊl/ *n* [C] *BrE informal* your ear → **clip round the earhole** at CLIP[1](6)

earl /ɜːl $ ɜːrl/ *n* [C] a man with a high social rank: *the Earl of Warwick*

earl·dom /ˈɜːldəm $ ˈɜːrl-/ *n* [C] **1** the rank of an earl **2** the land or property belonging to an earl

ear·li·est /ˈɜːliəst $ ˈɜːr-/ *n* **at the earliest** no earlier than the time or date mentioned: *Work will begin in October at the very earliest.*

ˈear lobe *n* [C] the soft piece of flesh at the bottom of your ear

ear·ly[1] /ˈɜːli $ ˈɜːrli/ ●●● S1 W1 *adj* (*comparative* **earlier**, *superlative* **earliest**)

1 FIRST PART in the first part of a period of time, event, or process: *the* ***early morning*** *sunshine* | *an afternoon in* ***early spring*** | ***In the early days****, the railways mainly carried goods.* | *She is* ***in her early twenties****.* | *the recession of* ***the early 1980s*** | *The money could be paid* ***as early as*** *next week.* | *He spent* ***the early part of*** *his career at St John's Hospital.* | *the experiences of* ***early childhood*** | *the* ***early works*** *of Shakespeare* | *My* ***earliest memories*** *are of fruit trees.* | ***Early signs*** *are encouraging.*

2 BEFORE USUAL arriving or happening before the usual or expected time OPP **late**: **five minutes/three hours etc early** *The bus was ten minutes early.* | **[+for]** *I was a few minutes early for my appointment.* | *David decided to take* ***early retirement*** (=stop working before the normal age). | *She drank herself into an* ***early grave*** (=died younger than is normal).

3 BEGINNING used to emphasize that something has just begun, especially when you do not know how it will develop: ***It's too early*** *to say what will happen.* | ***It's early days*** *yet. I don't want to make any predictions.*

4 NEW THING [only before noun] being one of the first people, events, machines etc: *Early motor cars had very poor brakes.* | *fossil evidence of early man*

5 the early hours the time between MIDNIGHT and morning: *I didn't finally get to bed until the early hours.* | **in the early hours of sth** *The attack happened in the early hours of Sunday morning.*

6 an early start a start made very early in the day because you have a lot to do, far to go etc: *We need to* ***make an early start*** *tomorrow.*

7 at/from an early age when you are very young, or starting when you were very young: *She's played tennis from a very early age.*

8 an early night if you have an early night, you go to bed earlier than usual OPP **a late night**: **have/get an early night** *I think I'll get an early night.*

9 early bird/early riser someone who always gets up very early in the morning

10 the early bird catches the worm used to say that if you do something early or before other people, you will be successful

11 early potatoes/lettuces etc potatoes etc that are ready to be picked before any others

THESAURUS

early arriving or happening before the usual or expected time: *For once, the train arrived early.* | *Let's have an early lunch before we go.*
in good time *especially BrE* early enough, so that you do not have to rush, or so that you have time to get ready: *Everything was ready for the party in good time.*
on time arriving somewhere or happening at the right time: *The bus was on time.* | *The project was finished on time.*
ahead of time earlier than the time when you have arranged to do something or than when you need something: *The building work was completed ahead of time.* | *Some of the food can be prepared ahead of time.*
ahead of schedule earlier than the officially agreed time: *The prime minister called the elections early, five months ahead of schedule.*

with time to spare arriving somewhere or finishing something before the time when you have to arrive or finish: *We got to the airport with plenty of time to spare.* | *I finished the test with time to spare.*
first thing *especially spoken* immediately after you get up, or as soon as you start work: *I'll telephone her first thing tomorrow.*

early² ●●● S1 W1 *adv* (*comparative* **earlier**, *superlative* **earliest**)
1 before the usual, arranged, or expected time OPP **late**: *We arrived early.* | *They must have come home early.*
2 near the beginning of a period of time, event, process etc OPP **late**: **[+in]** *She went out early in the morning.* | *He was sent off early in the game.* | **early this/next/last year etc** *The building should be finished early next year.* | *The restaurant opened earlier this month.* | *We want to start* ***as early as possible.*** | *The disease is easy to treat if diagnosed early.*
3 early on at an early stage in a relationship, process etc: *I realized early on I'd never pass the exam.* | **[+in]** *We encountered problems early on in the project.*

ˈearly ˌdoors *adv BrE spoken informal* early in a football match or season; used especially by football players and managers when they are talking to JOURNALISTS on the radio or television: *We were well on top early doors.*

ˌearly ˈwarning *adj* **early warning system/device etc** a system or equipment which tells you that something bad, especially an enemy attack, is going to happen

ear·mark /ˈɪəmɑːk $ ˈɪrmɑːrk/ *v* [T] to decide that something will be used for a particular purpose or have something done to it in the future: **be earmarked for sth** *85% of foreign aid is earmarked by Congress for specific purposes.* | *schools earmarked for closure* | **be earmarked as sth** *He had been earmarked as a potential leader.*

ear·muffs /ˈɪəmʌfs $ ˈɪr-/ *n* [plural] two pieces of material joined by a band over the top of your head, which you wear to keep your ears warm

EARMUFFS

earn /ɜːn $ ɜːrn/ ●●● S2 W2 *v*
1 MONEY FOR WORK [I,T] to receive a particular amount of money for the work that you do: *He earns nearly £20,000 a year.* | *You don't* ***earn*** *much* ***money*** *being a nurse.* | *He did all sorts of jobs to* ***earn a living.*** | *I was the only person in the house who* ***was earning.*** | *She was* ***earning good money*** *at the bank.* | *Chris will pay – he's* ***earning a fortune.*** THESAURUS ▸ GET
2 PROFIT [T] to make a profit from business or from putting money in a bank etc: *The movie earned £7 million on its first day.* | *You could* ***earn*** *a higher rate of* ***interest*** *elsewhere.*
3 STH DESERVED [T] **a)** to do something or have qualities that make you deserve something: *I think you've earned a rest.* | *He soon earned the respect of the players.* | *He hopes to* ***earn*** *a* ***place*** *in the team.* | *The company has* ***earned*** *a* ***reputation*** *for reliability.* **b)** if your actions or qualities earn you something, they make you deserve to have it: **earn sb sth** *That performance earned her an Oscar as Best Actress.*
4 earn your/its keep a) to do jobs in return for being given a home and food: *We older children were expected to earn our keep.* **b)** to be useful enough to be worth the time or money spent: *These aircraft are still earning their keep.*

THESAURUS
earn to be paid a particular amount of money for your work. **Earn** is more formal than **get** or **make**: *A newly-qualified teacher can expect to earn about £20,000 a year.*
get to earn a particular amount of money every hour, week etc: *How much do you get an hour?* | *She gets more than I do.*
make to earn money, especially a lot of money, or money that is not from regular employment: *You can make a lot of money in banking.* | *Jo makes a bit of extra money by selling his paintings.*
be on sth *BrE* to earn a particular amount of money each year. This is the most common way of talking about someone's salary in British English: *How much are you on?* | *Some chief executives are on huge salaries.*
be/get paid to receive money for work that you do for an employer, not by working for yourself: *Workers are paid around $500 a month.* | *I get paid monthly.*
well-paid/badly-paid paid a lot of money/not much money for the work that you do: *well-paid lawyers working in the city* | *It was boring badly-paid work.*
take home to earn a particular amount of money after tax etc has been taken away from your pay: *After tax and other deductions, I only take home £200 a week.*

earn·er /ˈɜːnə $ ˈɜːrnər/ *n* [C] **1** someone who earns money for the job that they do: **high/low/average earner** *Private childcare is still too expensive for the average earner.* | *He is the only* ***wage earner*** *in the family.* **2** a business or activity which makes a profit: *the country's biggest export earner* **3 a nice little earner** *BrE informal* something that earns you a lot of money

ear·nest¹ /ˈɜːnɪst $ ˈɜːr-/ ●○○ *adj* very serious and sincere: *a rather earnest young man* | *Matthews was* ***in earnest conversation*** *with a young girl.* | *an* ***earnest desire*** *to offer something useful to society* | **earnest expression/look/voice etc** | **earnest attempt/effort etc** THESAURUS ▸ SERIOUS —**earnestly** *adv*: *earnestly discussing politics* —**earnestness** *n* [U]

earnest² *n* **1 in earnest** if something starts happening in earnest, it begins properly – used when it was happening in a small or informal way before: *On Monday your training* ***begins in earnest!*** **2 be in earnest** to really mean what you are saying, especially when expressing an intention or wish: *She wasn't sure whether he was in earnest or not.* | **be in dead/deadly/complete earnest** *Although he smiled, Ashley knew he was in deadly earnest.*

earn·ings /ˈɜːnɪŋz $ ˈɜːr-/ ●●○ *n* [plural]
1 the money that you receive for the work that you do → **salary, pay**: *an employee's average weekly earnings* | *He claimed compensation for* ***loss of earnings.*** THESAURUS ▸ SALARY
2 the profit that a company or country makes: *The company's earnings have dropped by 5% in the first quarter.* | *Oil provides 40% of Norway's* ***export earnings.***

ˌearnings-reˈlated *adj* relating to the amount of money that you earn: *an earnings-related pension scheme*

ear·phone /ˈɪəfəʊn $ ˈɪrfoʊn/ *n* [usually plural] a small piece of equipment connected by a wire to a radio, PERSONAL STEREO etc, which you put in or over your ears so that only you can listen to it

ear·piece /ˈɪəpiːs $ ˈɪr-/ *n* [C] **1** a small piece of equipment that you put into your ear to hear a recording, message etc **2** [usually plural] one of the two pieces at the side of a pair of glasses that go round your ears **3** the part of a telephone that you listen through

ear·plug /ˈɪəplʌg $ ˈɪr-/ *n* [C usually plural] a small piece of rubber that you put inside your ear to keep out noise or water

ear·ring /ˈɪərɪŋ $ ˈɪr-/ ●●● S3 *n* [C] a piece of jewellery that you wear on your ear: **gold/diamond/pearl etc earrings** | *She was wearing a* ***pair of*** *beautiful diamond* ***earrings.*** → see picture at JEWELLERY

ear·set /ˈɪəset $ ˈɪr-/ *n* [C] a piece of equipment that allows you to use a telephone without your hands. It has a part that fits into the ear and a MICROPHONE.

ear·shot /ˈɪəʃɒt $ ˈɪrʃɑːt/ *n* **1 within earshot** near enough to hear what someone is saying: *Everyone within earshot soon knew her opinion of Reggie.* **2 out of earshot** not near enough to hear what someone is saying: *I waited for her to get out of earshot before laughing.*

'ear-ˌsplitting *adj* very loud: *There was an ear-splitting crack.* THESAURUS LOUD

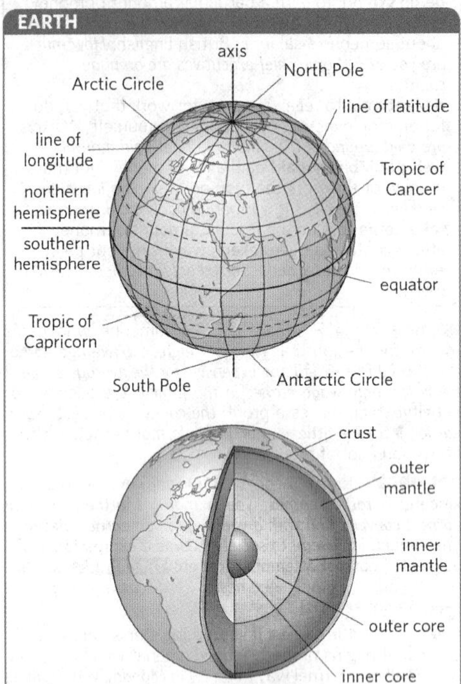

earth¹ /ɜːθ $ ɜːrθ/ ●●● S2 W2 *n*
1 WORLD (*also* **Earth**) [singular, U] the PLANET that we live on: *the planet Earth* | **the Earth** *The Earth revolves around the Sun.* | **the Earth's surface/atmosphere/crust etc** *71% of the Earth's surface is sea.* | **on Earth** *the origin of life on Earth*
2 SOIL [U] the substance that plants grow in SYN **soil**: **soft/bare/damp etc earth** *footprints in the wet earth* | *a lump of earth* THESAURUS GROUND
3 LAND [U] the hard surface of the world, as opposed to the sea or air SYN **ground**: *The earth shook.* | *They watched the kite fall back to earth.*
4 what/why/how etc on earth ...? *spoken* used to ask a question when you are very surprised or angry: *What on earth did you do that for?*
5 cost/pay/charge the earth *informal* to cost etc a very large amount of money: *It must have cost the earth!*
6 the biggest/tallest/most expensive etc ... on earth the biggest etc example of something that exists: *the most powerful man on earth*
7 RELIGION [U] used in religion to refer to the time when people are alive as opposed to being in HEAVEN or HELL: *Jesus' time on earth* → **move heaven and earth** at HEAVEN(9), → **hell on earth** at HELL¹(2)
8 come back/down to earth (with a bump) to stop behaving or living in a way that is not practical: *She soon brought him back down to earth.*
9 no ... /nothing on earth used to emphasize that you mean nothing at all: *Nothing on earth would have persuaded me to go.* | *There's no reason on earth why you should tell him.*
10 look/feel etc like nothing on earth *BrE* to look or feel very strange: *The next morning I felt like nothing on earth.*
11 ELECTRICITY [C usually singular] *BrE* a wire that makes a piece of electrical equipment safe by connecting it with the ground SYN **ground** *AmE*
12 ANIMAL'S HOME [C] the hole where a wild animal such as a FOX lives → **den, lair**
13 go to earth *BrE* to hide in order to escape from someone who is chasing you SYN **go to ground**
14 run sb/sth to earth *BrE* to find someone, especially by looking in many places → DOWN-TO-EARTH, → **promise sb the moon/the earth** at PROMISE¹(3), → **the salt of the earth** at SALT¹(2)

earth² *v* [T] *BrE* to make electrical equipment safe by connecting it to the ground with a wire SYN **ground** *AmE*: *Make sure that the machine is properly earthed.*

earth·bound /ˈɜːθbaʊnd $ ˈɜːrθ-/ *adj* **1** unable to move away from the surface of the Earth **2** having very little imagination and thinking too much about practical things

earth·en /ˈɜːθən, -ðən $ ˈɜːr-/ *adj* [only before noun] **1** an earthen floor or wall is made of soil **2** an earthen pot etc is made of baked clay

earth·en·ware /ˈɜːθənweə, -ðən- $ ˈɜːrθənwer, -ðən-/ *adj* an earthenware pot, bowl etc is made of very hard baked clay → **pottery** —**earthenware** *n* [U]

earth·ling /ˈɜːθlɪŋ $ ˈɜːrθ-/ *n* [C] a human - used in SCIENCE FICTION stories

earth·ly /ˈɜːθli $ ˈɜːrθli/ *adj* **1 no earthly reason/use etc** no reason, use etc at all: *I see no earthly reason why he shouldn't come.* **2** [only before noun] *literary* connected with life on Earth rather than in heaven: *our earthly pleasures* | *an earthly paradise*

'earth ˌmother *n* [C] a woman who has all the qualities expected of a mother and is especially interested in simple natural ways of living

earth·quake /ˈɜːθkweɪk $ ˈɜːrθ-/ ●●○ *n* [C] a sudden shaking of the Earth's surface that often causes a lot of damage → **seismic**: *An earthquake measuring 6.1 on the Richter scale struck southern California on June 28.* | *The city is in an earthquake zone.*

'earth ˌscience *n* [C usually plural] a science, such as GEOLOGY, which involves the study of the physical world

'earth-ˌshattering *adj* surprising or shocking and very important: *an earth-shattering event*

earth·wards /ˈɜːθwədz $ ˈɜːrθwərdz/ (*also* **earthward** /-wəd $ -wərd/) *adv* towards the earth's surface: *The missile fell earthwards.* —**earthward** *adj*

earth·work /ˈɜːθwɜːk $ ˈɜːrθwɜːrk/ *n* [C] a large long pile of earth, used in the past to stop attacks

earth·worm /ˈɜːθwɜːm $ ˈɜːrθwɜːrm/ *n* [C] a common type of long thin brown WORM that lives in soil

earth·y /ˈɜːθi $ ˈɜːrθi/ *adj* **1** tasting, smelling, or looking like earth or soil: *earthy colours* **2** talking about things that are often considered rude, especially sex and the human body, in a relaxed direct way: *earthy language* —**earthiness** *n* [U]

'ear ˌtrumpet *n* [C] a type of tube that is wide at one end, used by old people in the past to help them hear

ear·wig /ˈɪəˌwɪɡ $ ˈɪr-/ *n* [C] a long brown insect with two curved pointed parts at the back end of its body → see picture at INSECT

ear·worm /ˈɪəˌwɜːm $ ˈɪrwɜːrm/ *n* [C] *informal* a tune that you keep thinking about in your head, even when you do not want to

ease¹ /iːz/ ●●○ W3 *n* [U]
1 with ease if you do something with ease, it is very easy for you to do it SYN **easily**: *They won with ease.* | *The security codes could be broken* ***with relative ease.*** | *I was impressed by the ease with which the information could be retrieved.*
2 at ease feeling relaxed, especially in a situation in which people might feel a little nervous: **[+with]** *She* ***felt*** *completely* ***at ease*** *with Bernard.* | **put/set sb at (their) ease** (=make someone feel relaxed) *She had an ability to put people at their ease.*
3 ill at ease not relaxed: *You always look ill at ease in a suit.*
4 ease of application/use etc *written* how easy something is to use etc, or the quality of being easy to use etc: *It emphasizes the software's convenience and ease of use.* | **for ease of sth** *The bowl is removable for ease of cleaning.*
5 the ability to feel relaxed or behave in a natural relaxed way: *He had a natural ease which made him very popular.*
6 a life of ease a comfortable life, without problems or worries

7 (stand) at ease used to tell soldiers to stand in a relaxed way with their feet apart

ease² ●○○ *v*
1 IMPROVE [I,T] if something unpleasant eases, or if you ease it, it gradually improves or becomes less: **ease the pain/stress/tension** *He'll give you something to ease the pain.* | **ease the pressure/burden** *This should ease the burden on busy teachers.* | *measures to ease congestion in the city* | *Her breathing had eased.*
2 MAKE EASIER [T] to make a process happen more easily SYN **smooth**: *The agreement will* **ease the way for** *other countries to join the EU.*
3 MOVE [I,T always + adv/prep] to move yourself or something slowly and carefully into another place or position: *She eased her shoes off.* | **ease yourself into/through etc sth** *He eased himself into a chair.* | **ease your way past/through etc sth** *He eased his way through the crowd.* | *Jean eased back on the pillows and relaxed.*
4 ease your grip to hold something less tightly
5 ease sb's mind to make someone feel less worried about something: *It would ease my mind to know you had arrived safely.*
ease (sb) **into** sth *phr v* if you ease yourself or someone else into a new job etc, you start doing it gradually or help them to start: *After the baby, she eased herself back into work.*
ease off *phr v*
1 if something, especially something that you do not like, eases off, it improves or gets less SYN **ease up**: *The rain had eased off a bit.* | *Why don't you wait until the traffic eases off a little?*
2 ease off on sb to stop being unpleasant to someone or asking so much from them
ease out *phr v*
1 if a vehicle eases out, it slowly moves forward into the traffic
2 ease sb ↔ out to make someone leave a job, a position of authority etc, in a way that makes it seem as if they have chosen to leave
ease up *phr v*
1 to work less hard or do something with less energy than before: *Just relax and ease up a little.*
2 to start doing something less: **[+on]** *You should ease up on the whisky.*
3 to improve or get less SYN **ease off**: *The snow was easing up.*

ea·sel /ˈiːzəl/ *n* [C] a wooden frame that you put a painting on while you paint it → see picture at STAND²

eas·i·ly /ˈiːzəli/ ●●● S2 W1 *adv*
1 without problems or difficulties: *They won quite easily.* | *We found the house* **easily enough**. | **easily accessible/available etc** *The castle is easily accessible by road.* | **easily understood/identified etc** *It's easily recognised by its bright blue tail feathers.*
2 could/can/might easily used to say that something is possible or is very likely to happen: *The first signs of the disease can easily be overlooked.* | *Gambling can* **all too easily** *become an addiction* (=used to say that something bad is very possible).
3 easily the best/biggest etc definitely the best etc: *She is easily the most intelligent person in the class.*
4 in a relaxed way: *His son grinned easily back at him.*

eas·i·ness /ˈiːzinəs/ *n* [U] **1** a feeling of being relaxed and comfortable with someone **2** when something is not difficult

east¹, **East** /iːst/ ●●● S2 W1 *n* [singular, U] (*written abbreviation* **E**)
1 the direction from which the sun rises, and which is on the right if you are facing north: *Which way is east?* | **from/towards the east** *He turned and walked away towards the east.* | **to the east (of sth)** *To the east of the pier were miles of sandy beaches.*
2 the east the eastern part of a country or area: *housing problems in the east* | **[+of]** *the east of Scotland*

east², **East** ●●● S3 W3 *adj* [only before noun] (*written abbreviation* **E**)
1 in the east or facing the east: *I don't know the east coast well.* | *He was born in East Jerusalem.*
2 an east wind comes from the east

east³ ●●● S2 W2 *adv*
1 towards the east: *We drove east along Brooklyn Avenue.* | **[+of]** *a small farming community 18 miles east of Paris* | *an east-facing bedroom*
2 out east to or in the countries in Asia, especially China and Japan: *The drug is being used all the time out east.*

East *n* **1 the East a)** the countries in Asia, especially China and Japan: *Martial arts originated in the East.* **b)** the countries in the eastern part of Europe and Central Asia: *American relations with the East.* **c)** *AmE* the part of the US east of the Mississippi River, especially the states north of Washington DC: *She was born in the East but now lives in Atlanta.* | *He was born in Utah but went to college* **back East**. **2 East-West relations/trade etc** political relations etc between countries in eastern Europe and those in western Europe and North America → **Far East**, **Middle East**, **Near East**

east·bound /ˈiːstbaʊnd/ *adj* travelling or leading towards the east: *A crash on the eastbound side of the freeway is blocking traffic.*

ˌEast ˈCoast *n* **the East Coast** the part of the US that is next to the Atlantic Ocean, especially those states north of Washington DC

ˌEast ˈEnd *n* **the East End** the eastern part of London, north of the River Thames —**East Ender** *n* [C]

Eas·ter /ˈiːstə $ -ər/ ●●○ *n* [C,U]
1 a Christian holy day in March or April when Christians remember the death of Christ and his return to life: *on* **Easter Sunday** → GOOD FRIDAY
2 the period of time just before and after Easter Day: **at Easter** *We'll probably go away at Easter.* | **Easter holiday/weekend/break** *We spent the Easter holidays in Wales.*

ˌEaster ˈBunny *n* [singular] an imaginary rabbit that children believe brings chocolate eggs at Easter

ˈEaster egg *n* [C] **1** *BrE* a chocolate egg bought or given as a present at Easter **2** *AmE* an egg that has been coloured and decorated to celebrate Easter

eas·ter·ly¹ /ˈiːstəli $ -ərli/ *adj* **1** towards or in the east: *We drove off* **in an easterly direction**. **2** an easterly wind comes from the east

easterly² *n* (*plural* **easterlies**) [C] a wind that comes from the east

east·ern, **Eastern** /ˈiːstən $ -ərn/ ●●● S2 W2 *adj* (*written abbreviation* **E**)
1 in or from the east of a country or area: *the eastern shore of the island* | *farmers in eastern England*
2 in or from the countries in Asia, especially China and Japan: *Eastern religions*
3 in or from the countries in the east part of Europe, especially the countries that used to have Communist governments: *Eastern Europe*

East·ern·er /ˈiːstənə $ -ərnər/ *n* [C] *AmE* someone from the eastern US, north of Washington DC

east·ern·most /ˈiːstənməʊst $ -ərnmoʊst/ *adj* furthest east: *the easternmost part of the country*

east·wards /ˈiːstwədz $ -wərdz/ (*also* **east·ward** /-wəd $ -wərd/) *adv* towards the east: *The ship continued sailing eastwards.* —**eastward** *adj*: *We followed an eastward course up the river.*

eas·y¹ /ˈiːzi/ ●●● S1 W1 *adj* (*comparative* **easier**, *superlative* **easiest**)
1 NOT DIFFICULT not difficult to do, and not needing much effort OPP **difficult**, **hard**: *The test was easy.* | *Finishing the task will not be easy.* | *There must be an easier way to do that.* | **easy to do sth** *It's a great car, and very easy to drive.* | *instructions that are easy to follow* | *It would have been easy for the team to lose the game.* | **make it easier (to do sth)** *The software makes it easier to download music.* | *Having you here does* **make things** *a lot* **easier** *for me.* | **as easy as pie/ABC/falling off a log** (=very easy) | *The station is* **within**

E

easy reach** of* (=close to) *the town centre.* | *The park is **within easy** walking **distance (=close enough to walk to).
2 COMFORTABLE comfortable or relaxed, and without problems OPP **hard**: *On the whole, Dad has had an **easy** life.* | **easy day/week etc** *She had a nice easy day at home.* | *You can **have an easy time of it** now that the kids have all left home.* | *Why don't we **make life easy for ourselves** and finish it tomorrow?*
3 NOT WORRIED not feeling worried or anxious OPP **uneasy**: *We talk more openly when we feel easy and relaxed.* | *I can leave the children with my mother **with an easy mind**.*
4 FRIENDLY friendly and pleasant with other people: *She is gentle and **easy to be with**.*
5 EASILY ATTACKED able to be hunted or attacked without difficulty: *The soldiers on the streets are an **easy target** for terrorists.* | *Tourists are **easy prey** for thieves.*
6 take the easy way out to end a situation in a way that seems easy, but is not the best or most sensible way: *I just **took the easy way out** and gave him some cash.*
7 have an easy time (of it) to have no problems or difficulties: *She's not been having an easy time of it financially.*
8 easy money money that you do not have to work hard to get: *We can buy them for $10 and sell them for $25 – easy money.*
9 easy on the eye/ear pleasant to look at or listen to: *Soft colours are easy on the eye.*
10 it's/that's easy for you to say *spoken* used when someone has given you some advice that would be difficult for you to follow
11 there are no easy answers used when saying that it is difficult to find a good way of dealing with a problem
12 I'm easy *spoken* used to say that you do not mind what choice is made: *'What would you like to do now?' 'I don't know, I'm easy.'*
13 be (living) on easy street *especially AmE informal* to be in a situation in which you have plenty of money: *If I get this new job, we'll be living on easy street.*
14 on easy terms if you buy something on easy terms, you pay for it with several small payments instead of paying the whole amount at once: *New settlers in the west could buy land on relatively easy terms.*
15 eggs over easy *AmE* eggs cooked on a hot surface and turned over quickly before serving
16 woman/lady/girl of easy virtue *old-fashioned* a woman who has sex with a lot of men
17 SEX *informal* someone, especially a woman, who is easy has a lot of sexual partners → see also EASE[1], EASILY

THESAURUS

easy not difficult to do, and not needing much effort: *an easy task* | *The house was easy to find.*
simple easy and not complicated – used about things such as instructions and explanations, or about machines and systems: *The system is relatively simple to operate.* | *a simple recipe for chocolate cake*
straightforward easy to understand or do, and unlikely to cause you any problems: *a straightforward explanation* | *The calculation is fairly straightforward.*
user-friendly easy to use – used especially about computers or written information about how to do something: *Their website is very user-friendly.* | *a user-friendly guide to owning a dog*
undemanding easy because it does not take a lot of effort: *It was an undemanding role for someone of his experience.*
cushy /ˈkʊʃi/ *informal* a cushy job is easy to do and needs very little effort – often used when you are envious of the person who has it: *It's a pretty cushy job – all she has to do is drive a nice car around.*
mindless so easy that you can do it without thinking – used especially when it makes you feel bored: *mindless tasks*
painless without any difficulties or problems – used especially when you expected something to be much worse: *Finding the carhire place at the airport was relatively painless.*
be plain sailing *BrE*, **be smooth sailing** *AmE* to be easy and with no problems that you have to deal with: *Things should be plain sailing from now on.*

INFORMAL PHRASES MEANING VERY EASY

be a piece of cake *informal* to be very easy to do, especially compared to doing something else: *This test was a piece of cake compared to the last one.*
be child's play *informal* to be surprisingly easy, or much easier than something else which is very difficult or dangerous: *Getting people's credit card details is child's play when you know how to do it.* | *Climbing in England is child's play compared to climbing in the Himalayas.*
be a breeze *informal* (*also* **be a doddle** *BrE*) to be very easy to do: *The software is a doddle to use.*
it's not rocket science *informal* used when saying that something is very easy to do or understand, and you do not need to be intelligent to do it: *Making your PC run faster isn't exactly rocket science.*

easy² ●●● S2 *adv*
1 take it easy a) (*also* **take things easy**) to relax and not do very much: *Take things easy for a few days and you should be all right.* **b)** *spoken* used to tell someone to become less upset or angry: *Just take it easy and tell us what happened.* **c)** *AmE spoken* used to say goodbye
2 go easy on/with sth to not use too much of something: *Go easy on salty foods such as bacon.*
3 go easy on sb to be more gentle and less strict or angry with someone: *Go easy on Peter for a while – he's having a hard time at school.*
4 easier said than done *especially spoken* used to say that something would be very difficult to do: *Finding the perfect house was easier said than done.*
5 rest/breathe easy to stop worrying: *We can rest easy now – we've got everything under control.*
6 easy does it *spoken* used to tell someone to be more careful and slow, especially in moving
7 get off easy *informal* to escape severe punishment for something that you have done wrong: *The rich could hire good lawyers and get off easy.*
8 easy come, easy go *spoken* used when something, especially money, was easily obtained and is quickly used or spent
9 stand easy an order telling soldiers who are already standing at EASE to relax more

ˌeasy ˈchair *n* [C] a large comfortable chair → **armchair**
ˌeasy-ˈgoing *adj* not easily upset, annoyed, or worried OPP **uptight**: *Her easy-going nature made her popular.*
ˌeasy ˈlistening *n* [U] music that is relaxing to listen to and has nice tunes, but is not very interesting
easy-pea·sy /ˌiːzi ˈpiːzi◂/ *adj BrE* a word meaning very easy, used especially by children

eat /iːt/ ●●● S1 W1 *v* (*past tense* **ate** /et, eɪt $ eɪt/, *past participle* **eaten** /ˈiːtn/)
1 FOOD [I,T] to put food in your mouth and chew and swallow it: *Felix chatted cheerfully as he ate.* | *A small girl was eating an ice cream.* | *We had plenty to eat and drink.* | *It's important to **eat healthily** when you are pregnant.* | *I exercise and **eat right** and get plenty of sleep.* | *Would you like **something to eat**?* | *She can **eat like a horse** and never put on weight.* | *We stopped at McDonalds to get **a bite to eat**.* | *Good **eating habits** are the best way of preventing infection.* | ***ready-to-eat** foods such as deli meats and cheeses* | *'More cake?' 'No thanks, **I couldn't eat another thing**.'* | *No chicken for me. I don't eat meat* (=I never eat meat). | *Does Rob eat fish?*
2 MEAL [I,T] to have a meal: *Let's eat first and then go to a movie.* | *They're eating breakfast.* | **[+at]** *We could not afford to eat at Walker's very often.*
3 eat your words to admit that what you said was wrong: *I'm going to make you eat your words.*
4 eat your heart out a) used to say, especially humorously, that something is very good: *That's a great drawing. Pablo Picasso eat your heart out!* **b)** *BrE* to be unhappy about something or to want someone or something very much:

If you had any sense you'd forget him, but eat your heart out if you want to.
5 eat sb alive/eat sb for breakfast to be very angry with someone or to defeat them completely: *You can't tell him that – he'll eat you alive!*
6 USE [T] to use a very large amount of something: *This car eats petrol.*
7 eat humble pie (*also* **eat crow** *AmE*) to admit that you were wrong and say that you are sorry
8 I'll eat my hat used to emphasize that you think something is not true or will not happen: *If the Democrats win the election, I'll eat my hat!*
9 have sb eating out of your hand to have made someone very willing to believe you or do what you want: *He soon had the client eating out of his hand.*
10 eat sb out of house and home to eat a lot of someone's supply of food, so that they have to buy more – used humorously
11 what's eating sb? *spoken* used to ask why someone seems annoyed or upset: *What's eating Sally today?*
12 I could eat a horse *spoken* used to say you are very hungry
13 I/we won't eat you *spoken* used to tell someone that you are not angry with them and they need not be frightened
14 you are what you eat used to say that you will be healthy if the food you eat is healthy → EATS, → **have your cake and eat it** at CAKE[1](6)

eat sth ↔ **away** *phr v* to gradually remove or destroy something SYN **erode**: *The stones are being eaten away by pollution.*

eat away at sth/sb *phr v*
1 to gradually remove or reduce the amount of something: *His gambling was eating away at their income.*
2 to make someone feel very worried over a long period of time: *The thought of mother alone like that was eating away at her.*

eat in *phr v* to eat at home instead of in a restaurant

eat into sth *phr v*
1 to gradually reduce the amount of time, money etc that is available: *John's university fees have been eating into our savings.*
2 to gradually damage or destroy something: *Acid eats into the metal, damaging its surface.*

eat out *phr v* to eat in a restaurant instead of at home: *Do you eat out a lot?*

eat up *phr v*
1 to eat all of something: *Come on, eat up, there's a good girl.* | **eat sth ↔ up** *She's made a cake and wants us to help eat it up.*
2 eat sth ↔ up *informal* to use a lot of something, especially until there is none left: *Big cars just eat up money.*
3 be eaten up with/by jealousy/anger/curiosity etc to be very jealous, angry etc, so that you cannot think about anything else

eat·a·ble /ˈiːtəbəl/ *adj* in a good enough condition to be eaten → **EDIBLE**

eat·er /ˈiːtə $ -ər/ *n* [C] **big/light/fussy etc eater** someone who eats a lot, not much, only particular things etc: *I've never been a big eater.*

eat·e·ry /ˈiːtəri/ *n* (*plural* **eateries**) [C] *informal especially AmE* a restaurant or other place to eat: *one of the best eateries in town*

ˈeating ˌapple *n* [C] an apple that you eat raw rather than cooked → **cooking apple**

ˈeating disˌorder *n* [C] a medical condition in which you do not eat a normal amount of food and are ill because of this → **bulimia**

eats /iːts/ *n* [plural] *informal* food, especially for a party: *You get the drink, and I'll organize the eats.*

eau de co·logne /ˌəʊ də kəˈləʊn $ ˌoʊ də kəˈloʊn/ *n* [U] a sweet-smelling liquid used to make you feel fresh and smell nice

eau de toi·lette /ˌəʊ də twɑːˈlet $ ˌoʊ-/ *n* [C,U] a liquid containing a small amount of PERFUME, used by women to make them feel fresh and smell nice

eaves /iːvz/ *n* [plural] the edges of a roof that stick out beyond the walls: *Birds had nested under the eaves.*

eaves·drop /ˈiːvzdrɒp $ -drɑːp/ *v* (**eavesdropped, eavesdropping**) [I] to deliberately listen secretly to other people's conversations → **overhear**: *There was Helena eavesdropping outside the door.* —**eavesdropper** *n* [C]

EBacc /ˈiːbæk/ *n* [singular] (***the English Baccalaureate***) in English schools, the achievement of GRADE C or above in five subjects at GCSE level: English, mathematics, history or GEOGRAPHY, a science, and a language

THESAURUS: eat

eat to put food in your mouth and chew and swallow it: *Experts recommend eating plenty of fruit and vegetables.*
have to eat a particular food: *'What do you usually have for breakfast?' 'I usually just have coffee and toast.'* | *We had the set meal.*
feed on sth to eat a particular kind of food – used when talking about animals: *Foxes feed on a wide range of foods including mice, birds, insects, and fruit.*
consume *written* to eat or drink something – used especially in scientific or technical contexts: *Babies consume large amounts relative to their body weight.*
munch (on) sth to eat something with big continuous movements of your mouth, especially when you are enjoying your food: *He was munching on an apple.* | *They were sitting on a bench munching their sandwiches.*
nibble (on) sth to eat something by biting off very small pieces: *If you want a healthy snack, why not just nibble on a carrot?*
pick at sth to eat only a small amount of your food because you are not hungry or do not like the food: *Lisa was so upset that she could only pick at her food.*
stuff/gorge yourself to eat so much food that you cannot eat anything else: *He's always stuffing himself with cakes.* | *We gorged ourselves on my mother's delicious apple tart.*
slurp to eat soup, NOODLEs etc with a noisy sucking sound: *In England it's considered rude to slurp your soup, but in some countries it's seen as a sign of enjoyment.*

TO EAT SOMETHING QUICKLY

gobble sth up/down *informal* to eat something very quickly, especially because you like it very much or you are greedy: *You've gobbled up all the ice-cream!* | *The children gobbled it down in no time.*
wolf sth down *informal* to eat food quickly, especially because you are very hungry or in a hurry: *The boy wolfed down everything on his plate and asked for more.*
bolt sth down *BrE* to eat food very quickly, especially because you are in a hurry: *He bolted down his breakfast and was out of the door within 5 minutes.* | *You shouldn't bolt your food down like that.*
devour /dɪˈvaʊə $ -ˈvaʊr/ *especially written* to eat all of something quickly because you are very hungry: *In a very short time, the snake had devoured the whole animal.*

E

e-bank·ing /ˈiː ˌbæŋkɪŋ/ *n* [U] a service that allows people to pay money from one bank account to another, pay bills etc using the Internet

eBay /ˈiːbeɪ/ *trademark* a WEBSITE which people use to buy and sell things, especially by AUCTION

ebb[1] /eb/ *n* **1** [singular] (*also* **ebb tide**) the flow of the sea away from the shore, when the TIDE goes out OPP **flood tide** **2 be at a low ebb** to be in a bad state or condition: *His confidence is at a low ebb.* **3 ebb and flow** a situation or state in which something increases and decreases in a kind of pattern: *the ebb and flow of the conversation | the ebb and flow of passengers in the station*

ebb[2] *v* [I] **1** if the TIDE ebbs, it flows away from the shore **2** (*also* **ebb away**) to gradually decrease: *Linda's enthusiasm began to ebb away.*

e-bike /ˈiː baɪk/ *n* [C] an electrically powered MOTORBIKE

E·bo·la /ɪˈbəʊlə $ ɪˈboʊ-/ *n* [U] a VIRUS that causes bleeding from many parts of the body and usually causes death

E·bon·ics, **ebonics** /ɪˈbɒnɪks $ ɪˈbɑː-/ *n* [U] *especially AmE* BLACK ENGLISH

eb·o·ny[1] /ˈebəni/ *n* [U] a hard black wood

ebony[2] *adj literary* black: *her ebony hair*

e-book /ˈiː bʊk/ *n* [C] (***electronic book***) a book that you read on a computer screen or on a special small computer that you can hold in your hands, and that is not printed on paper

E

e·bul·li·ent /ɪˈbʌliənt, ɪˈbʊ-/ *adj formal* very happy and excited: *My father is a naturally ebullient personality.* —**ebullience** *n* [U]

e-cash /ˈiː kæʃ/ *n* [U] (***electronic cash***) money used to buy things on the Internet, but that does not exist in a physical form or belong to any particular country

ec·cen·tric[1] /ɪkˈsentrɪk/ ●○○ *adj*
1 behaving in a way that is unusual and different from most people: *His eccentric behaviour lost him his job. | Aunt Nessy was always a bit eccentric.* THESAURUS STRANGE, UNUSUAL
2 *technical* eccentric circles do not have the same centre point → **concentric** —**eccentrically** /-kli/ *adv*

eccentric[2] *n* [C] someone who behaves in a way that is different from what is usual or socially accepted: *I was regarded as something of an eccentric.*

ec·cen·tri·ci·ty /ˌeksenˈtrɪsəti, -sən-/ *n* (*plural* **eccentricities**) **1** [U] strange or unusual behaviour: *Kate's mother had a reputation for eccentricity.* **2** [C] an opinion or action that is strange or unusual: *I found his eccentricities amusing rather than irritating.*

Ec·cles cake /ˈekəlz keɪk/ *n* [C] *BrE* a round cake filled with CURRANTS (=type of dried fruit)

ec·cle·si·as·tic /ɪˌkliːziˈæstɪk◂/ *n* [C] *formal* a priest, usually in the Christian church

ec·cle·si·as·ti·cal /ɪˌkliːziˈæstɪkəl/ (*also* **ec·cle·sias·tic** /-ˈæstɪk/) *adj* relating to the Christian church or its priests: *ecclesiastical history*

ECG /ˌiː siː ˈdʒiː/ *n* [C] *especially BrE* **1** (***electrocardiograph***) a piece of equipment that records electrical changes in your heart **2** (***electrocardiogram***) a drawing produced by an ELECTROCARDIOGRAPH

ech·e·lon /ˈeʃəlɒn $ -lɑːn/ *n* [C] **1** (*also* **echelons** [plural]) a rank or level of authority in an organization, business etc, or the people at that level: **upper/higher/lower echelons** *the upper echelons of government | Their clients are drawn from the highest echelons of society.* **2** *technical* a line of ships, soldiers, planes etc arranged in a pattern that looks like a series of steps

ech·i·na·ce·a /ˌekɪˈneɪsiə/ *n* [C,U] a wild purple or white flower commonly found in the US. It is often used as a herb or as a medicine SYN **coneflower**

ech·o[1] /ˈekəʊ $ ˈekoʊ/ ●●○ *v*
1 [I] if a sound echoes, you hear it again because it was made near something such as a wall or hill: *The sound of an engine echoed back from the thick forest.* | **[+through/round]** *He could hear eerie noises echoing through the corridors.*
2 [I] if a place echoes, it is filled with sounds that are repeated or are similar to each other: **[+with]** *The house echoed with the sound of children's voices.*
3 [T] *literary* to repeat what someone else has just said: *'You bet,' she said, echoing his words.*
4 [T] to repeat an idea or opinion because you agree with it: *The article simply echoed the NRA's arguments against gun control.*

echo[2] ●●○ *n* (*plural* **echoes**) [C]
1 a sound that you hear again after a loud noise, because it was made near something such as a wall: *Her scream was followed by a loud echo.*
2 something that is very similar to something that has happened or been said before: **[+of]** *The article contains echoes of an earlier report. | This idea* ***finds*** *an* ***echo*** *in many African countries.*

e-cig·a·rette /ˈiː sɪgəˌret $ ˌsɪgəret/ *n* [C] a small piece of electronic equipment that is the same shape as a cigarette, and produces a mist containing NICOTINE that the user can breathe in

é·clair /ɪˈkleə, eɪ- $ ɪˈkler, eɪ-/ *n* [C] a long cake covered with chocolate and filled with cream

é·clat /eɪˈklɑː/ *n* [U] *literary* **1** praise and admiration: *Miller's new play has been greeted with great éclat.* **2** a way of doing something with a lot of style, especially in order to attract attention

e·clec·tic[1] /ɪˈklektɪk/ *adj* including a mixture of many different things or people, especially so that you can use the best of all of them SYN **diverse**: *galleries with an eclectic range of styles and artists | an eclectic mixture of 18th- and 19th-century furniture* —**eclectically** /-kli/ *adv* —**eclecticism** /-tɪsɪzəm/ *n* [U]

eclectic[2] *n* [C] *formal* someone who chooses the best or most useful parts from many different ideas, methods etc

e·clipse[1] /ɪˈklɪps/ ●○○ *n*
1 [C] an occasion when the Sun or the Moon cannot be seen, because the Earth is passing directly between the Moon and the Sun, or because the Moon is passing directly between the Earth and the Sun: *an eclipse of the Sun | a* ***total eclipse***
2 [singular] a situation in which someone or something loses their power or fame, because someone or something else has become more powerful or famous: *Many people expected the growth of television to mean the eclipse of radio.*
3 in eclipse *formal* less famous or powerful than you should be: *Mrs Bosanquet's novels are now in eclipse.*

eclipse[2] ●○○ *v* [T]
1 if the Moon eclipses the Sun, the Sun cannot be seen behind the Moon, and if the Earth eclipses the Moon, the Moon cannot be seen because the Earth is between the Sun and the Moon
2 to become more important, powerful, famous etc than someone or something else, so that they are no longer noticed → **overshadow**: *The economy had eclipsed the environment as an election issue. | He was eclipsed by his more famous sister.* GRAMMAR **Eclipse** is often passive in this meaning.

e·clip·tic /ɪˈklɪptɪk/ *n* [singular] *technical* the path along which the Sun seems to move → **orbit**

eco- /iːkəʊ $ iːkoʊ/ *prefix* relating to the environment: *eco-warriors* (=people who try to stop damage to the environment)

e·co·cide /ˈiːkəʊsaɪd $ ˈiːkoʊ-/ *n* [U] the gradual destruction of a large area of land, including all of the plants, animals etc living there, because of the effects of human activities such as cutting down trees, using PESTICIDES etc SYN **ecological genocide**

e·co-friend·ly /ˈiːkəʊ ˌfrendli $ ˈiːkoʊ-/ ●○○ *adj* not harmful to the environment: *eco-friendly products* THESAURUS ENVIRONMENTALLY FRIENDLY

e·co-home /ˈiːkəʊ həʊm $ -koʊ hoʊm/ *n* [C] a home

that is designed to harm the environment as little as possible and use as little energy as possible

E. co·li /ˌiː ˈkəʊlaɪ $ -ˈkoʊ-/ *n* [U] a type of BACTERIA that can make you very ill if it is in any food that you eat

e·co·lo·gi·cal /ˌiːkəˈlɒdʒɪkəl◂ $ -ˈlɑː-/ ●●○ *adj* [only before noun]
1 connected with the way plants, animals, and people are related to each other and to their environment → **environmental**: *an ecological disaster*
2 interested in preserving the environment → **environment**: *ecological groups* —**ecologically** /-kli/ *adv*: *This method of growing crops is effective and ecologically sound* (=not likely to harm the environment).

ˌecological ˈfootprint *n* [C] the amount of land needed by a person, group of people, or a society in order for them to have enough food or RESOURCES to live and continue to exist

e·col·o·gist /ɪˈkɒlədʒɪst $ -ˈkɑː-/ *n* [C] a scientist who studies ecology

e·col·o·gy /ɪˈkɒlədʒi $ ɪˈkɑː-/ ●●○ *n* [singular, U] the way in which plants, animals, and people are related to each other and to their environment, or the scientific study of this → **environment**: *the natural ecology of the Earth | plant ecology*

e-comm /ˈiː kɒm $ -kɑːm/ *n* [U] *informal* the abbreviation of ***e-commerce***

e-com·merce /ˈiː kɒmɜːs, $ -kɑːmɜːrs/ *n* [U] (***electronic commerce***) the activity of buying and selling goods and services and doing other business activities using a computer and the Internet: *e-commerce applications such as online ticketing and reservations*

ec·o·nom·ic /ˌekəˈnɒmɪk◂, ˌiː- $ -ˈnɑː-/ ●●● S2 W1 AWL *adj*
1 [only before noun] relating to trade, industry, and the management of money → **economy**: *Economic growth is slow. | the government's economic policy | Economic reform is needed. | In the current* ***economic climate*** (=conditions), *we must keep costs down.* THESAURUS FINANCIAL
2 an economic process, activity etc produces enough profit for it to continue SYN **profitable** OPP **uneconomic**: *It is no longer economic to run the service.* ⚠ Do not confuse with **economical** (=cheap or not wasteful).

ec·o·nom·i·cal /ˌekəˈnɒmɪkəl, ˌiː- $ -ˈnɑː-/ ●●○ AWL *adj*
1 using money, time, goods etc carefully and without wasting any → **economic**: *A small car is more economical to run. | good-quality clothes at economical prices* THESAURUS CHEAP
2 economical with the truth used humorously to say that someone is not telling the truth

ec·o·nom·i·cally /ˌekəˈnɒmɪkli, ˌiː- $ -ˈnɑː-/ ●●○ AWL *adv*
1 in a way that is related to systems of money, trade, or business: *In economically advanced countries, women marry later. |* [sentence adverb] *Economically, capitalism has transformed societies.*
2 in a way that uses money, goods, time etc without wasting any: *We produce food as economically as possible. | Small trees use space in the garden economically.*

ˌeconomic ˈmigrant *n* [C] someone who moves to a different country in order to get a better job

ec·o·nom·ics /ˌekəˈnɒmɪks, ˌiː- $ -ˈnɑː-/ ●●○ W3 AWL *n*
1 [U] the study of the way in which money and goods are produced and used → **economic**: *a Harvard professor of economics*
2 [plural] the way in which money influences whether a plan, business etc will work effectively: *the economics of the scheme* → HOME ECONOMICS

GRAMMAR: Singular or plural verb?
- In meaning 1, **economics** is followed by a singular verb: ***Economics is*** *often studied with politics.*
- In meaning 2, **economics** is followed by a plural verb: *The* ***economics do*** *not add up.*

e·con·o·mist /ɪˈkɒnəmɪst $ ɪˈkɑː-/ ●●○ AWL *n* [C] someone who studies the way in which money and goods are produced and used and the systems of business and trade

e·con·o·mize (*also* **-ise** *BrE*) /ɪˈkɒnəmaɪz $ ɪˈkɑː-/ *v* [I] to reduce the amount of money, time, goods etc that you use SYN **cut down**: **[+on]** *Higher taxes encourage people to economize on fuel.*

e·con·o·my[1] /ɪˈkɒnəmi $ ɪˈkɑː-/ ●●● S2 W1 AWL *n* (*plural* **economies**)
1 [C] the system by which a country's money and goods are produced and used, or a country considered in this way: *a successful economy | the slowdown in the Japanese economy*

GRAMMAR
You say **the economy** when talking about the economic system in a particular country: *Tourism is an important part of the economy.* ✗ Don't say: *Tourism is an important part of economy.*
GRAMMAR GUIDE NOUNS

2 [C] something that you do in order to spend less money: *The council must* ***make economies*** *to meet government spending targets. | Not insuring your belongings is a* ***false economy*** (=it is cheaper but could have bad results).
3 [U] the careful use of money, time, goods etc so that nothing is wasted: *The gas fire was turned low for reasons of economy. | The company announced that it would cut 500 jobs as part of an* ***economy drive*** (=a way to save money).
4 economies of scale *technical* the financial advantages of producing something in very large quantities → BLACK ECONOMY, MARKET ECONOMY, MIXED ECONOMY

COLLOCATIONS
ADJECTIVES/NOUN + economy
strong/healthy/sound *The new government inherited a strong economy.*
weak/ailing/depressed *The economy is weak and consumer confidence is low.*
fragile (=weak and likely to become worse)
stable (=steady, rather than being strong then weak) *The economy has been relatively stable for the last two or three years.*
stagnant (=bad and not progressing or improving)
a flagging economy (=starting to become weaker) *The government must take action to boost the flagging economy.*
a booming economy (=extremely strong and successful) *What can we learn from China's booming economy?*
the world/global economy *Rising oil prices threaten the world economy.*
the local/national/domestic economy (=in one particular country or area) *The new factory has given a massive boost to the local economy.*
a large/powerful economy *the world's two most powerful economies*
a small economy *Small economies like Kenya might struggle to survive in a global recession.*
an industrial economy (=one that is based mainly on industries producing goods or materials) *Expectations for growth in the main industrial economies remain low.*
an agricultural/a rural economy (=one that is based mainly on farming) *The early 1920s saw a rapid expansion in the American agricultural economy.*
a service economy (=one that is based mainly on selling services such as insurance or tourism) *Britain has shifted from a manufacturing to a service economy.*
a market/free-market economy (=based on companies producing and selling products freely, without restrictions) *Eastern European countries were gradually making the transition to a market economy.*
a capitalist/socialist economy (=based on a capitalist or socialist political system) *the large capitalist economies of western Europe*

E

the black economy *especially BrE* (=business activity in which people buy and sell goods illegally, without paying tax)

VERBS

manage/handle the economy *Governments are judged on how well they manage the economy.*
boost the economy (=make it stronger) *It is hoped that the Olympic Games will boost the country's economy.*
harm/damage the economy (=make it less successful) *Sanctions have damaged the economy.*
destroy the economy *The floods last year destroyed the region's economy.*
the economy develops/expands/grows (=becomes more successful) *The economy grew by 3% last year.*
the economy booms (=becomes very successful very quickly)
the economy slows down *The US economy is slowing down after a long period of growth.*
the economy recovers (=returns to normal condition after a period of trouble or difficulty)

USAGE: Economy, economics

Don't confuse **economy** (=a country's economic system) and **economics** (=the study of how money is produced and used). You say: *He is studying economics.* ✗ Don't say: *He is studying economy.*

E

economy² *adj* **economy size/pack** a product that is cheaper because you are buying a larger amount

e'conomy ˌclass *n* [U] the cheapest type of seats in a plane —**economy class** *adv*: *We flew economy class.*

e'conomy ˌclass ˌsyndrome *n* [U] *BrE* a serious illness in which people get blood CLOTs because they have been sitting for a long time in a very small space on a plane → **DVT**

e·co·sys·tem /ˈiːkəʊˌsɪstɪm $ ˈiːkoʊ-/ ●○○ *n* [C] all the animals and plants in a particular area, and the way in which they are related to each other and to their environment → **ecology**

e·co·ter·ror·is·m /ˈiːkəʊˌterərɪzəm $ ˈiːkoʊ-/ *n* [U] when someone tries to stop or harm organizations or companies that do things that are bad for the environment —**ecoterrorist** *n* [C]

e·co·tour·is·m /ˈiːkəʊˌtʊərɪzəm $ ˈiːkoʊˌtʊr-/ *n* [U] the business of organizing holidays to natural areas, especially areas that are far away such as the RAIN FOREST, where people can visit and learn about the area in a way that will not hurt the environment —**ecotourist** *n* [C]

e·co·town /ˈiːkəʊtaʊn $ -koʊ-/ *n* [C] a new town that the government builds in a way that makes it not harmful to the environment

e·co·vil·lage /ˈiːkəʊˌvɪlɪdʒ $ -koʊ-/ *n* [C] a small group of homes where people try not to harm the environment, for example by using RENEWABLE energy or living in a simple way

e·co-war·ri·or /ˈiːkəʊˌwɒriə $ ˈiːkoʊˌwɔːriər, -ˌwɑː-/ *n* [C] someone who takes action in order to stop damage to the environment: *Eco-warriors are trying to stop the new road being built.*

e·cru /ˈeɪkruː, ˈek-/ *n* [U] a pale brown colour —**ecru** *adj*

ec·sta·sy /ˈekstəsi/ ●○○ *n* (*plural* **ecstasies**)
1 [C,U] a feeling of extreme happiness: **in (an) ecstasy** *She was in an ecstasy of love.* | **go into ecstasies** (=become very happy and excited)
2 [U] an illegal drug that gives a feeling of happiness and energy. Ecstasy is especially used by people who go out to dance at clubs and parties.

ec·stat·ic /ɪkˈstætɪk, ek-/ ●○○ *adj*
1 feeling extremely happy and excited: *an ecstatic welcome from the thousands who lined the streets* THESAURUS ▸ HAPPY
2 ecstatic review/praise/applause a REVIEW (=an opinion about a film, play etc that appears in a newspaper or magazine), praise etc that says that something is very good: *The exhibition attracted thousands of visitors and ecstatic reviews.* —**ecstatically** /-kli/ *adv*

ECT /ˌiː siː ˈtiː/ *n* [U] electro-convulsive therapy; another word for ELECTRIC SHOCK THERAPY

ec·to·morph /ˈektəʊˌmɔːf $ ˈektoʊˌmɔːrf/ *n* [C] *technical* someone with a naturally thin body

-ectomy /ektəmi/ *suffix* [in nouns] *technical* the removing of a particular part of someone's body by an operation: *an appendectomy* (=removing the appendix)

ec·top·ic preg·nan·cy /ekˌtɒpɪk ˈpregnənsi $ -ˌtɑː-/ *n* [C,U] *medical* a PREGNANCY in which an unborn baby develops outside its mother's UTERUS, usually in a FALLOPIAN TUBE

e·cu·men·i·cal /ˌiːkjəˈmenɪkəl◂ $ ˌek-/ *adj* supporting the idea of uniting the different branches of the Christian religion —**ecumenically** /-kli/ *adv*

ec·ze·ma /ˈeksəmə $ ˈeksəmə, ˈegz-, ɪgˈziːmə/ *n* [U] a condition in which your skin becomes dry, red, and swollen

ed., **Ed.** /ed/ **1** the abbreviation of ***education***: *Higher Ed.* **2** the written abbreviation of ***edited***, ***edition***, or ***editor***

-ed /d, əd, t/ *suffix* **1** forms the regular past tense and past participle of verbs. The past participle form is often used as an adjective: *I want, I wanted, I have wanted* | *I show, I showed, I have shown* | *He walked away.* | *a sound that echoed through the room* | *a wanted criminal* **2** [in adjectives] having a particular thing: *a bearded man* (=a man with a beard) | *a kind-hearted woman*

E·dam /ˈiːdæm, -dəm/ *n* [U] a type of yellow cheese from the Netherlands

ed·a·ma·me bean /ˌedəˈmɑːmeɪ biːn/ *n* [C] a young SOYA BEAN

ed·dy¹ /ˈedi/ *n* (*plural* **eddies**) [C] a circular movement of water, wind, dust etc: *the racing river caused swirling eddies*

eddy² *v* (**eddied**, **eddying**, **eddies**) [I] if water, wind, dust etc eddies, it moves around with a circular movement: *Mist eddied round the house.*

E·den /ˈiːdn/ (*also* **the Garden of Eden**) *n* [singular] in the Bible story, the garden where Adam and Eve, the first humans lived, often seen as a place of happiness and INNOCENCE

EDGE

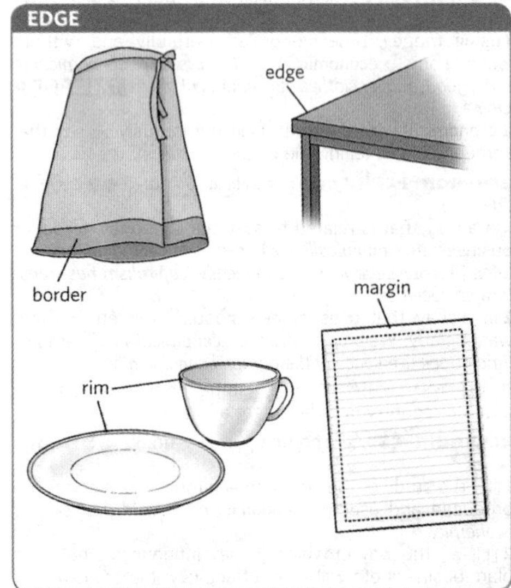

edge¹ /edʒ/ ●●● S2 W2 *n*
1 OUTSIDE PART [C] the part of an object that is furthest from its centre: *Put the eggs in the centre of the dish, with the vegetables and herbs around the edge.* | **the edge of sth** *the right hand edge of the page* | *Jennifer walked to the edge of the wood.* | *Billy sat on the edge of the bed.* | *He stood at*

the water's edge staring across the lake. | *A leaf was on the ground, curling up at the edges.*
2 BLADE [C] the thin sharp part of a blade or tool that cuts: *a knife with a sharp edge*
3 ADVANTAGE [singular, U] something that gives you an advantage over others: *Companies are employing more research teams to get an edge.* | *The next version of the software* ***will have*** *the* ***edge*** *over its competitors.*
4 on edge nervous, especially because you are expecting something unpleasant to happen: *Paul felt on edge about meeting Lisa.*
5 VOICE [singular] a quality in someone's voice that makes it sound slightly angry or impatient: *There was an edge of hostility in Jack's voice.* | *Desperation lent an edge to her voice.*
6 SLOPE [C] an area beside a very steep slope: *She walked almost to the edge of the cliff.*
7 on the edge of sth close to the point at which something different, especially something bad, will happen: *Their economy is on the edge of collapse.* | *She is on the edge of despair.*
8 QUALITY [singular] a special quality of excitement or danger: *The school's campaign has been given an extra edge by being filmed for television.*
9 take the edge off sth to make something less bad, good, strong etc: *Pascoe was drinking whisky to take the edge off the pain.*
10 on the edge of your seat giving all your attention to something exciting: *The film's ending had me on the edge of my seat.*
11 be on the edge *informal* to be behaving in a way that makes it seem as if you are going crazy → CUTTING EDGE

THESAURUS

edge the part of something that is furthest from its centre or nearest the place where it ends: *He got up quickly, knocking his plate off the edge of the table.* | *the outer edge of the village*
side the part of something that is near its left or right edge: *On the left side of the garden there was an old stone wall.* | *They parked by the side of the road.*
rim the edge of something circular, especially the top of a cup or glass, or the outside edge of a pair of glasses: *a white cup with a gold rim* | *She was looking at me over the rim of her spectacles.*
margin the empty space at the side of a page that has writing on it: *My teacher had marked my essay and made some comments in the margin.* | *Leave wide margins on both sides of the page.*
hem the edge of a piece of cloth that is turned under and stitched down, especially the lower edge of a skirt, trousers etc: *If you want the dress a bit shorter, I can easily turn up the hem.*
kerb *BrE*, **curb** *AmE* the edge of the pavement (=raised path) at the side of a road: *A big black car was parked at the kerb.*
outskirts the areas of a city that are furthest away from the centre: *The new station was built on the outskirts of the city.*
perimeter the outside edge around an enclosed area of land such as a military camp or a prison: *Security guards patrol the perimeter night and day.*

edge[2] *v*
1 MOVE [I,T always + adv/prep] to move gradually with several small movements, or to make something do this: *Tim was edging away from the crowd.* | *She edged closer to get a better look.* | *He edged her towards the door.* | **edge your way into/round/through etc sth** *Christine edged her way round the back of the house.*
2 PUT AT EDGE [T] to put something on the edge or border of something: *The city square was edged by trees.* | **be edged with sth** *The tablecloth is edged with lace.* GRAMMAR **Edge** is usually passive in this meaning.
3 CHANGE [I,T always + adv/prep] to change gradually, especially so as to get better or worse: **[+up/down]** *Profits have edged up.* | *The paper has* ***edged ahead*** *of (=been more successful than) its rivals.*
4 GRASS [T] to cut the edges of an area of grass so that they are tidy and straight

edge sb ↔ **out** *phr v*
1 to defeat someone by a small amount: *Italy edged out France by two points.*
2 to gradually force someone to leave their job or an area of activity

ˌedge ˈcity *n* [C] *AmE* an area at the edge of a large city that has its own businesses, shops, offices etc, so that many of the people who used to live there while working in the large city now both live and work in the edge city

edge·ways /ˈedʒweɪz/ (*also* **edge·wise** /-waɪz/) *adv* sideways → **get a word in edgeways** at WORD[1](27)

edg·ing /ˈedʒɪŋ/ *n* [C,U] something that forms an edge or border: *a white handkerchief with blue edging*

edg·y /ˈedʒi/ *adj* **1** nervous and worried: *She's been edgy lately, waiting for the test results.* THESAURUS ▸ NERVOUS
2 aware of the newest ideas and styles and therefore considered very fashionable: *The band has developed an edgy new image.*

EDI /ˌiː diː ˈaɪ/ *n* [U] *technical* the abbreviation of ***electronic data interchange***

ed·i·ble /ˈedəbəl/ *adj* something that is edible can be eaten OPP **inedible**: *These berries are edible, but those are poisonous.*

e·dict /ˈiːdɪkt/ *n* [C] *formal* **1** an official public order made by someone in a position of power SYN **decree**: *The emperor issued an edict forbidding anyone to leave the city.*
2 any order – used humorously

ed·i·fice /ˈedɪfɪs/ *n* [C] *formal* a building, especially a large one: *Their head office was an imposing edifice.*

ed·i·fy /ˈedɪfaɪ/ *v* (**edified**, **edifying**, **edifies**) [T] *formal* to improve someone's mind or character by teaching them something SYN **enlighten** —**edification** /ˌedɪfɪˈkeɪʃən/ *n* [U]: *For our edification, the preacher reminded us what 'duty' meant.*

ed·i·fy·ing /ˈedəfaɪ-ɪŋ/ *adj formal* an edifying speech, book etc improves your mind or moral character by teaching you something – sometimes used humorously: *a morally edifying film*

ed·it /ˈedɪt/ ●●○ *v*
1 [I,T] to prepare a book, piece of film etc for printing or broadcasting by removing mistakes or parts that are not acceptable: *The newspaper edits letters before printing them.*
2 [T] to prepare a book or article for printing by deciding what to include and in what order: *a collection of essays edited by John Gay*
3 [T] to prepare a film by deciding what to include and in what order
4 [T] to be responsible for the information that is included in a newspaper, magazine etc: *She used to edit the Observer.* —**edit** *n* [C]

edit sth ↔ **out** *phr v* to remove something when you are preparing a book, piece of film etc for printing or broadcasting SYN **cut**: *The interviewer's questions have been edited out.*

e·di·tion /ɪˈdɪʃən/ ●●○ W3 AWL *n* [C]
1 the form that a book, newspaper, magazine etc is produced in: *a paperback edition* | *the US edition of Marie Claire magazine*
2 the copies of a book, newspaper etc that are produced and printed at the same time: *The textbook was first published in 1858 and is now in its 39th edition.* | *A* ***limited edition*** *of 2,000 copies has been published.* | **first edition** (=the first copies of a particular book, that are often valuable)
3 a newspaper, magazine etc: *Martin was reading the early edition of the Evening News.*
4 a television or radio programme that is broadcast regularly or is part of a series: *the early evening edition of Scotland Today*

ed·i·tor /ˈedɪtə $ -ər/ ●●○ W2 AWL *n* [C]
1 the person who is in charge of a newspaper or magazine, or part of a newspaper or magazine, and decides

what should be included in it: **[+of]** *the editor of the Daily Telegraph* | **economics/sports/political etc editor**
2 someone who prepares a book or article for printing by deciding what to include and checking for any mistakes
3 someone who chooses what to include in a book on a particular subject: *the editor of a book of essays on modern poetry*
4 someone who prepares a film, television programme, or sound recording for broadcasting by deciding what to include and checking for any mistakes: *a TV script editor*
5 someone who reports on a particular subject for a radio or television news programme → **correspondent**: *Here is John Simmonds, our Diplomatic Editor, with the latest news.*
6 *technical* a computer program that allows you to make changes to saved information → COPY EDITOR, SUB-EDITOR

ed·i·to·ri·al¹ /ˌedəˈtɔːriəl◂/ ●○○ AWL *n* [C] a piece of writing in a newspaper that gives the editor's opinion about something, rather than reporting facts

ed·i·to·ri·al² AWL *adj* **1** relating to the preparation of a newspaper, book, television programme etc for printing or broadcasting: *an editorial assistant*
2 [usually before noun] expressing the opinion of a particular newspaper editor rather than just giving facts: *the paper's editorial column* —**editorially** *adv*: *The paper is editorially independent.*

ed·i·to·ri·a·lize (*also* **-ise** *BrE*) /ˌedəˈtɔːriəlaɪz/ *v* [I] to give your opinion and not just the facts about something, especially publicly: **[+on/about/against etc]** *The BBC is not supposed to editorialize about the news.*

ed·i·tor·ship /ˈedətəʃɪp $ -tər-/ *n* [U] the position of being the editor of a newspaper or magazine, or the time during which someone is an editor

EDT /ˌiː diː ˈtiː/ *n* [C,U] the abbreviation for ***eau de toilette***

.edu /dɒt iː diː ˈjuː/ the abbreviation for ***educational institution***, used in Internet addresses for schools, colleges etc

ed·u·ca·ble /ˈedjʊkəbəl $ ˈedʒə-/ *adj* able to learn or be educated: *At that time, deaf children were not considered educable.*

ed·u·cate /ˈedjʊkeɪt $ ˈedʒə-/ ●●○ *v* [T]
1 to teach a child at a school, college, or university: *The Ormerod School educates handicapped children.* | **be educated at sth** *He was educated at Bristol University.*
GRAMMAR **Educate** is often passive in this meaning.
THESAURUS ▸ TEACH
2 to give someone information about a particular subject, or to show them a better way to do something → **teach**: **educate sb about/in/on sth** *a campaign to educate teenagers about HIV*

ed·u·cat·ed /ˈedjʊkeɪtɪd $ ˈedʒə-/ ●●○ *adj*
1 having been well taught and learned a lot: *a **highly** educated woman*
2 university-educated/well educated/privately educated etc having had a particular type of education
3 educated guess a guess that is likely to be correct because it is based on some knowledge: *Investors must **make** an **educated guess** as to the company's potential.*

ed·u·ca·tion /ˌedjʊˈkeɪʃən $ ˌedʒə-/ ●●● S1 W1 *n*
1 [singular, U] the process of teaching and learning, usually at school, college, or university: *She also hopes her children will get a good education.* | *efforts to improve girls' access to education* → **formal education** at FORMAL¹(6)
2 [U] the teaching of a particular subject: **health/sex education**
3 [U] the institutions and people involved with teaching: *the local education authority*
4 [singular] an interesting experience which has taught you something - often used humorously: *Having Jimmy to stay has been quite an education!* → ADULT EDUCATION, FURTHER EDUCATION, HIGHER EDUCATION

COLLOCATIONS

ADJECTIVES/NOUN + education

a good education *All parents want a good education for their children.*
a poor education (=not very good) *She had a poor education, and left school without qualifications.*
an all-round education (=including a balance of lots of different subjects) *The school offers a good all-round education.*
full-time education (=spending every weekday in a school or college) *Children must stay in full-time education until the age of 16.*
state education *BrE*, **public education** *AmE* (=provided by the government of a country) *The state of California guarantees free public education to all children.*
private education (=that people have to pay for) *I don't agree with the principle of private education.*
formal education (=from teachers at school or college, rather than learning by yourself) *She had no formal education and was brought up by her grandmother.*
primary (school) education *BrE*, **elementary education** *AmE* (=for children aged between 5 and 11) *The government has announced plans to improve the quality of primary school education.*
secondary education (*also* **high school education** *AmE*) (=for children aged between 11 and 18) *She hopes to start a teaching career in secondary education.*
university/college education *Do you have a university education?*
further/higher education (=at a college or university) *I did a carpentry course at the further education college.*
adult education (=for adults) | **vocational education** (=relating to skills needed for a particular job) | **nursery/pre-school education** (=for children aged under 5)

VERBS

have an education *The women have had little education.*
get/receive an education *Some children grow up without receiving any education.*
give/provide an education *The school aims to provide a good general education.*
enter education (=start going to school, college etc) *The number of students entering higher education has risen.*
leave education *BrE* (=stop going to school, college etc) *She left full-time education at the age of 16.*
continue your education

education + NOUN

the education system (=the way education is organized and managed in a country) *Is the British education system failing some children?*
the education department (=the government organization that makes decisions about education) *Newcastle City Council's education department*
an education authority (=a government organization that makes official decisions about education in one particular area) | **the education service** (=all the government organizations that work together to provide education) | **education policy** (=political plans for managing an education system) | **education reform** (=changes that a government makes to the education system in a country)

ed·u·ca·tion·al /ˌedjʊˈkeɪʃənəl◂ $ ˌedʒə-/ ●●○ S3 W2 *adj*
1 relating to education: *the educational development of children*
2 teaching you something you did not know before: *educational games* —**educationally** *adv*

ed·u·ca·tion·al·ist /ˌedjʊˈkeɪʃənəlɪst $ ˌedʒə-/ (*also* **ed·u·ca·tion·ist** /-ʃənɪst/) *n* [C] *formal* someone who knows a lot about ways of teaching and learning

ed·u·cat·ive /ˈedjʊkətɪv $ ˈedʒəkeɪ-/ *adj* something that is educative teaches you something SYN **educational**: *The educative process needs to begin early in a child's life.*

ed·u·ca·tor /ˈedjʊkeɪtə $ ˈedʒəkeɪtər/ *n* [C] **1** *formal* a teacher or someone involved in the process of educating people THESAURUS TEACHER **2** *AmE* an EDUCATIONALIST

ed·u·tain·ment /ˌedjʊˈteɪnmənt $ ˌedʒə-/ *n* [U] films, television programmes, or computer SOFTWARE that educate and entertain at the same time

Ed·ward·i·an /edˈwɔːdiən $ -ˈwɔːr-/ *adj* relating to the time of King Edward VII of Britain (1901–1910): *an Edwardian house*

-ee /iː/ *suffix* [in nouns] **1** someone who is being treated in a particular way: *the payee* (=someone who is paid) | *a trainee* | *an employee* **2** someone who is in a particular state or who is doing something: *an absentee* (=someone who is absent) | *an escapee*

EEG /ˌiː iː ˈdʒiː/ *n* [C] **1** (***electroencephalograph***) a piece of equipment that records the electrical activity of your brain **2** (***electroencephalogram***) a drawing made by an electroencephalograph

eek /iːk/ *interjection* an expression of sudden fear and surprise: *Eek! A mouse!*

eel /iːl/ *n* [C] a long thin fish that looks like a snake and can be eaten → see picture at FISH[1]

e'en /iːn/ *adv literary* the short form of EVEN

e'er /eə $ er/ *adv literary* the short form of EVER

-eer /ɪə $ ɪr/ *suffix* [in nouns] someone who does or makes a particular thing: *an auctioneer* (=someone who runs auction sales) | *a profiteer* (=someone who makes unfair profits)

ee·rie /ˈɪəri $ ˈɪri/ *adj* strange and frightening: *the eerie sound of an owl hooting at night* THESAURUS FRIGHTENING —**eerily** *adv*

e-fa·tigue /ˈiː fəˌtiːg/ (*also* **electronic fatigue**) *n* [U] problems that people have as a result of using computers too much or for too long, for example tiredness at work or a lack of communication

eff /ef/ *v* [I] *BrE spoken informal* **1 effing and blinding** swearing: *Did you hear her effing and blinding at him?* **2 eff off!** used to tell someone to go away instead of saying FUCK OFF → **EFFING**

ef·face /ɪˈfeɪs/ *v* [T] *formal* **1** to destroy or remove something SYN **erase** → **deface**: *Nothing can efface the last picture I have of them from my mind.* **2 efface yourself** to behave in a quiet way so that people do not notice or look at you → SELF-EFFACING

ef·fect¹ /ɪˈfekt/ ●●● S1 W1 *n*

1 CHANGE/RESULT [C,U] a change that is caused by an event, action etc: **[+on]** *My parents' divorce* ***had*** *a big* ***effect*** *on me.* | **[+of]** *the* ***harmful effects*** *of modern farming practices* | *the* ***long-term effects*** *of the drug* | *I could* ***feel*** *the* ***effects*** *of the thin mountain air.* | *This ingredient also* ***has the effect of*** *making your skin look younger.* | *A system failure has a* ***knock-on effect*** *throughout the whole hotel.* | *the* ***cumulative effect*** *of human activities on the global environment* | *A much lower dose of the painkiller can still produce* ***the desired effect***. | *In mental illness, there is a complex relationship between* ***cause and effect***. → GREENHOUSE EFFECT, SIDE EFFECT

⚠ Do not confuse with the verb **affect** (=to have an effect on something).

2 put/bring sth into effect to make a plan or idea happen: *It won't be easy to put the changes into effect.*

3 take effect to start to produce results: *The morphine was starting to take effect and the pain eased.*

4 LAW/RULE **a) take effect/come into effect** if a law, rule, or system takes effect or comes into effect, it officially starts **b) be in effect** if a law, rule, or system is in effect, it is being used now

5 with immediate effect/with effect from *formal* starting to happen immediately, or from a particular date: *Hoskins is appointed manager, with immediate effect.*

6 in effect used when you are describing what you see as the real facts of a situation SYN **effectively**: *In effect, we'll be earning less than we were last year.*

7 to good/great/no etc effect used to show how successful an action is: *We tried to wake him, but to no effect.*

8 to this/that/the effect used when you are giving the general meaning of something, rather than the exact words: *Jim told me to go away, or* ***words to that effect***. | *The letter said something* ***to the effect that*** *she was no longer needed.*

9 IDEA/FEELING [C usually singular] an idea or feeling that an artist, speaker, book etc tries to make you think of or to feel SYN **impression**: **[+of]** *Turner's paintings give an effect of light.*

10 for effect if someone does something for effect, they do it in order to make people notice: *She paused for effect, then carried on speaking.*

11 PERSONAL POSSESSIONS **effects** [plural] *formal* the things that someone owns SYN **belongings**: *Don's few* ***personal effects*** *were in a suitcase under the bed.*

12 FILM [C usually plural] an unusual or impressive sound or image that is artificially produced for a film, play, or radio programme → SOUND EFFECTS, SPECIAL EFFECT

THESAURUS

effect a change that is caused by an event, action etc: *The people in this area are still suffering from the effects of the famine.* | *The treatment had little or no effect.*

impact an effect that happens as a result of something important, especially a big and permanent effect: *Changes in technology have had a massive impact on the way we work.* | *the environmental impact of industrial activity*

influence the effect that something has on people's opinions or behaviour, or on how something develops: *American television has had a big influence on popular culture in the west.* | *His ideas had a lot of influence at the time.*

side effect an unwanted and unplanned effect that something has - used especially about drugs and medical treatment: *Common side effects of the drug may include headaches and muscle pains.*

after-effects *BrE*, **aftereffects** *AmE* bad effects that continue for a long time after the thing that caused them: *A traumatic experience can have severe psychological after-effects.* | *the after-effects of the war*

repercussions /ˌriːpəˈkʌʃəns $ -pər-/ the effects that happen later as a result of an event or decision, especially a range of effects that continue for a long time: *The scandal could have serious repercussions for her career.* | *The judge's decision is likely to have important repercussions for future cases of this kind.*

a knock-on effect *BrE* used when something has an effect on something, which then has an effect on something else: *Higher oil prices have a knock-on effect on other fuels.*

footprint the effect that human activities have on the environment, caused by using up its natural resources, pollution, waste etc: *Businesses all over the world must attempt to reduce their environmental footprint.* | *The house has a low* ***carbon footprint*** (=it uses very little energy from carbon and therefore is good for the environment).

effect² *v* [T] *formal* to make something happen SYN **bring about**: *Many parents lack confidence in their ability to effect change in their children's behaviour.* ⚠ Do not confuse with the verb **affect** (=to have an effect on something).

ef·fec·tive /ɪˈfektɪv/ ●●● S2 W1 *adj*

1 successful, and working in the way that was intended OPP **ineffective**: *The cheaper drugs are just as effective in treating arthritis.* | *the painting's* ***highly effective*** *use of colour* | *Training is often much less effective than expected.* | *the most effective ways of reducing inner city congestion* THESAURUS SUCCESSFUL

REGISTER

In everyday English, people usually say that something **works (well)**, rather than say that it is **effective**: *The cheaper drugs* ***work just as well***.

2 [no comparative, not before noun] if a law, agreement, or system becomes effective, it officially starts: **[+from]** *The cut in interest rates is effective from Monday.*
3 [no comparative, only before noun] real rather than what is officially intended or generally believed: *The rebels are in effective control of the city.* —**effectiveness** *n* [U]

ef·fec·tive·ly /ɪˈfektɪvli/ ●●● S3 W2 *adv*
1 in a way that produces the result that was intended OPP **ineffectively**: *Children have to learn to communicate effectively.*
2 used to describe what you see as the real facts of the situation SYN **in effect**: [sentence adverb] *Effectively, it has become impossible for us to help.* | *Most of the urban poor are effectively excluded from politics.*

ef·fec·tu·al /ɪˈfektʃuəl/ *adj formal* producing the result that was wanted or intended SYN **effective** OPP **ineffectual**

ef·fem·i·nate /ɪˈfemənət/ *adj* a man who is effeminate looks or behaves like a woman —**effeminately** *adv* —**effeminacy** *n* [U]

ef·fer·vesce /ˌefəˈves $ ˌefər-/ *v* [I] *technical* a liquid that effervesces produces small bubbles of gas

ef·fer·vesc·ent /ˌefəˈvesənt◂ $ ˌefər-/ *adj* **1** someone who is effervescent is very happy, excited, and active: *an effervescent personality* **2** a liquid that is effervescent produces small bubbles of gas SYN **fizzy**, **sparkling** —**effervescence** *n* [U]

E

ef·fete /ɪˈfiːt $ e-/ *adj formal* **1** weak and powerless in a way that you dislike: *effete intellectuals* **2** an effete man looks or behaves like a woman SYN **effeminate**

ef·fi·ca·cious /ˌefəˈkeɪʃəs◂/ *adj formal* working in the way you intended SYN **effective**: *an equally efficacious method of treatment*

ef·fi·ca·cy /ˈefəkəsi/ *n* [U + of] *formal* the ability of something to produce the right result SYN **effectiveness** OPP **inefficacy**

ef·fi·cien·cy /ɪˈfɪʃənsi/ ●●○ W3 *n*
1 [U] the quality of doing something well and effectively, without wasting time, money, or energy OPP **inefficiency**: **[+of]** *the efficiency of the train service* | *considerable advancements in* ***energy efficiency***
2 **efficiencies** [plural] the amounts of money, supplies etc that are saved by finding a better or cheaper way of doing something: *operating efficiencies*

COLLOCATIONS

VERBS

improve/increase efficiency *The company is taking steps to improve efficiency and reduce costs.*
promote efficiency (=develop or encourage efficient ways of doing something)

ADJECTIVES/NOUN + efficiency

greater/increased efficiency *In a search for greater efficiency, the two departments have merged.*
maximum efficiency (=the most that is possible) *The boat's design helps it to move with maximum efficiency.*
fuel efficiency (=using fuel in an efficient way) *Better fuel efficiency can be achieved by driving more slowly.*
energy efficiency (=using energy in an efficient way) *Energy efficiency can play a huge role in reducing pollution.*

efficiency + NOUN

efficiency gains (=increases in efficiency) *New technology introduced by the company has brought efficiency gains.*
efficiency savings (=money saved by being more efficient) | **efficiency measures** (=changes introduced to make something more efficient)

ef·fi·cient /ɪˈfɪʃənt/ ●●● S3 W3 *adj* if someone or something is efficient, they work well without wasting time, money, or energy OPP **inefficient**: *a very efficient secretary* | *an efficient use of land* | *Lighting is now more* ***energy efficient***. —**efficiently** *adv*

ef·fi·gy /ˈefɪdʒi/ *n* (*plural* **effigies**) **1** [C] a STATUE of a famous person: **[+of]** *an effigy of Saint Francis* **2** [U] a roughly made, usually ugly, model of someone you dislike: *a threat to* ***burn*** *the president* ***in effigy***

ef·fing /ˈefɪŋ/ *adj* [only before noun] *BrE informal not polite* an offensive word used to emphasize that you are angry and to avoid saying the swear word ' FUCKING' directly: *She's gone to effing bingo again.* → **effing and blinding** at **EFF**

ef·flo·res·cence /ˌefləˈresəns/ *n* [U] *literary* the action of something forming and developing, or the period of time when this happens: *There was an efflorescence of scientific publication in the period 1645-1660.*

ef·flu·ent /ˈefluənt/ *n* [C,U] *formal* liquid waste, especially chemicals or SEWAGE

ef·fort /ˈefət $ ˈefərt/ ●●● S1 W1 *n*
1 PHYSICAL/MENTAL ENERGY [U] the physical or mental energy that is needed to do something: *Lou lifted the box easily, without using much effort.* | *Frank put a lot of effort into the party.* | *Learning to speak another language takes effort.*
2 ATTEMPT [C,U] an attempt to do something, especially when this involves a lot of hard work or determination: *Please make an effort to be polite.* | **sb's effort(s) to do sth** *Tom's efforts to stop smoking haven't been very successful.* | *Church leaders are prepared to meet the terrorists* ***in an effort to*** (=in order to try to) *find peace.* | **[+at]** *Further efforts at negotiation have broken down.* | **through sb's efforts** (=because of their efforts) *The money was raised largely through the efforts of parents.* | **despite sb's efforts** *Despite all our efforts we lost the game 1–0.*
3 **be an effort** to be difficult or painful to do: *I was so weak that even standing up was an effort.*
4 PARTICULAR SITUATION [C] work that people do to achieve something in a particular situation: *the fundraising effort* | *the international* ***relief effort*** | *Everyone did what they could to support the* ***war effort***.
5 **good/bad/poor etc effort** something that has been done well, badly etc: *Not a bad effort for a beginner!*

COLLOCATIONS – MEANINGS 1 & 2

VERBS

make an effort (=try) *She made an effort to change the subject of the conversation.*
put effort into (doing) sth (=try hard to do something) *Let's try again, only put more effort into it this time.*
take the effort out of sth (=make it easy) *An automatic car takes the effort out of driving.*
sth takes effort (*also* **it takes effort to do sth**) (=you have to try hard) *It takes a sustained effort to quit smoking.*
sth requires/involves effort *formal* (=it takes effort)

ADJECTIVES/NOUN + effort

successful *Their efforts were successful, and they won the contract.*
unsuccessful *Efforts to save the hospital from closure have been unsuccessful.*
futile (=having no chance of succeeding, and therefore not worth doing) *Doctors knew that any effort to save his life would be futile.*
a big/great effort *The government has made a big effort to tackle the problem of poverty.*
considerable effort (=a lot of effort) *The police put considerable effort into finding his car.*
a supreme/tremendous effort (=a very big effort) *It was only with a supreme effort that Roger controlled his temper.*
a special effort (=one that you do not normally make) *I made a special effort to be nice to the children.*
a sustained effort (=one that you continue making for a long time) | **a conscious/deliberate effort**

(=one that you concentrate on in order to achieve something) | **a determined effort** (=showing a lot of determination) | **a desperate effort** (=one you make when you are in a very bad situation) | **a concerted effort** (=involving a lot of different actions, or a lot of people working together) | **a joint/team effort** (=involving a group or team of people) | **physical/mental effort**

PHRASES

make the effort (=do something that requires some effort) *I felt too tired to go to a party, but decided to make the effort.*
make every effort to do sth (=try very hard) *I made every effort to see their point of view.*
make no effort to do sth (=not try at all) *They make no effort to speak the local language.*
be (well) worth the effort (=used to say that something is worth doing even though it is hard) *It's a difficult place to get to, but it's well worth the effort.*
an effort of will (=a big effort to do something that you find difficult because of the way you feel) *It took a huge effort of will not to cry.*
with effort *formal* (=trying very hard) *With great effort, he managed to keep quiet.*
without effort (=easily, without trying hard)

ef·fort·less /ˈefətləs $ ˈefərt-/ *adj* something that is effortless is done in a very skilful way that makes it seem easy: *Alexei rose to his feet with a single effortless movement.* —**effortlessly** *adv*: *He dived effortlessly into the turquoise water.*

ef·fron·te·ry /ɪˈfrʌntəri/ *n* [U] *formal* rude behaviour that shocks you because it is so confident SYN **nerve**: **have the effrontery to do sth** *She had the effrontery to ask me for more money.*

ef·ful·gent /ɪˈfʌldʒənt $ ɪˈfʊl-/ *adj literary* beautiful and bright —**effulgence** *n* [U]

ef·fu·sion /ɪˈfjuːʒən/ *n* [C,U] **1** *technical* a liquid or gas that flows out of something, or the act of flowing out: *a massive effusion of poisonous gas* **2** *formal* an uncontrolled expression of strong good feelings: *He greeted the guests with effusion.*

ef·fu·sive /ɪˈfjuːsɪv/ *adj* showing your good feelings in a very excited way: *Our host gave us an effusive welcome.* | **[+in]** *Dotty was effusive in her thanks.* —**effusively** *adv* —**effusiveness** *n* [U]

E-FIT /ˈiː fɪt/ *n* [C] *trademark BrE* a picture, made by using a computer, of a person who the police think was responsible for a crime, which they show on television or the Internet in order to try and catch the person

EFL /ˌiː ef ˈel/ *n* [U] (***English as a Foreign Language***) the teaching of English to people whose first language is not English, and who do not live in an English-speaking country

EFT /ˌiː ef ˈtiː/ *n* [C,U] *technical* the abbreviation of ***electronic funds transfer***

e.g. /ˌiː ˈdʒiː/ ●●○ the abbreviation of ***for example***: *citrus fruits, e.g. oranges and grapefruit* **THESAURUS** ▸ **EXAMPLE**

REGISTER
In formal contexts such as essays or business letters, people usually avoid using the abbreviation **e.g.**, and write **for example** in full: *They might use local health care facilities, **for example** clinics and district hospitals.*

e·gal·i·tar·i·an /ɪˌɡæləˈteəriən $ -ˈter-/ *adj* based on the belief that everyone is equal and should have equal rights: *an egalitarian society* —**egalitarianism** *n* [U]

EGGS

egg¹ /eɡ/ ●●● S1 W2 *n*
1 BIRD [C] a round object with a hard surface, that contains a baby bird, snake, insect etc and which is produced by a female bird, snake, insect etc: *Blackbirds **lay** their **eggs** in March.* | *an ostrich egg* | *The **eggs hatch** (=break open to allow the baby out) in 26 days.*
2 FOOD [C,U] an egg, especially one from a chicken, that is used for food: **fried/poached/boiled etc eggs** | *Joe always has **bacon and egg** for breakfast.* | *Whisk the **egg white** (=the white part) until stiff.* | *Beat in two of the **egg yolks** (=the yellow part).* → SCRAMBLED EGG
3 EGG SHAPE [C] something the same shape as an egg: *a chocolate Easter egg* → EASTER EGG
4 ANIMALS/PEOPLE [C] a cell produced by a woman or female animal that combines with SPERM (=male cell) to make a baby SYN **ovum**
5 (have) egg on your face if someone, especially someone in authority, has egg on their face, they have been made to look stupid by something embarrassing: *The Pentagon's been left with egg on its face.*
6 put all your eggs in one basket to depend completely on one thing or one course of action in order to get success, so that you have no other plans if this fails: *When planning your investments, it's unwise to put all your eggs in one basket.*
7 lay an egg *AmE informal* to fail or be unsuccessful at something that you are trying to do
8 good egg *old-fashioned* someone who you can depend on to be honest, kind etc → **kill the goose that lays the golden egg** at KILL¹(14), → NEST EGG

egg² *v*
egg sb ↔ **on** *phr v* to encourage someone to do something, especially something that they do not want to do or should not do: *Bob didn't want to jump, but his friends kept egging him on.*

egg·cup /ˈeɡ-kʌp/ *n* [C] a small container that holds a boiled egg while you eat it → see picture at CUP¹

egg·head /ˈeɡhed/ *n* [C] *informal* someone who is very intelligent, and only interested in ideas and books

egg·nog /ˈeɡnɒɡ $ -nɑːɡ/ *n* [U] a drink made from eggs, sugar, milk, and alcohol, drunk at Christmas

egg·plant /ˈeɡplɑːnt $ -plænt/ *n* [C,U] *AmE* a large vegetable with smooth purple skin SYN **aubergine** *BrE* → see picture at VEGETABLE¹

ˌegg ˈroll *n* [C] a SPRING ROLL

egg·shell /ˈeɡʃel/ *n* **1** [C,U] the hard outside part of a bird's egg **2** [U] a type of paint, used especially on wood, that is not shiny when dry

ˈegg-ˌtimer *n* [C] a small glass container with sand in it that runs from one part to the other in about three or five minutes, used for measuring the time it takes to boil an egg

e·go /ˈiːɡəʊ, ˈeɡəʊ $ -ɡoʊ/ ●○○ *n* (*plural* **egos**) [C]
1 the opinion that you have about yourself: **big/enormous etc ego** *Richard has the biggest ego (=thinks he is very*

clever and important) *of anyone I've ever met.* | *That promotion really* ***boosted*** *her* ***ego*** (=made her feel better about herself). | *I need someone to massage my* ***bruised ego*** (=when you feel less confident than before). | *a fragile ego* → ALTER EGO
2 *technical* the part of your mind with which you think and take action, according to Freudian PSYCHOLOGY → **ID, superego**

e·go·cen·tric /ˌiːɡəʊˈsentrɪk◂, ˌeɡ- $ -ɡoʊ-/ *adj* thinking only about yourself and not about what other people might need or want SYN **self-centred** —**egocentricity** /ˌiːɡəʊsenˈtrɪsəti, ˌeɡ- $ -ɡoʊ-/ *n* [C,U]

e·go·is·m /ˈiːɡəʊɪzəm, ˈeɡ- $ -ɡoʊ-/ *n* [U] EGOTISM —**egoist** *n* [C] —**egoistic** /ˌiːɡəʊˈɪstɪk◂, ˌeɡ- $ -ɡoʊ-/ *adj*

e·go·ma·ni·ac /ˌiːɡəʊˈmeɪniæk, ˌeɡ- $ -ɡoʊ-/ *n* [C] someone who thinks that they are very important, and does not care whether they upset other people in order to get what they want

e·go·surf /ˈiːɡəʊsɜːf, ˈeɡ- $ -ɡoʊsɜːrf/ *v* [I] to look on the Internet to see how many websites mention your name —**egosurfing** *n* [U]

e·go·tis·m /ˈiːɡətɪzəm, ˈeɡ-/ *n* [U] the belief that you are much better or more important than other people

e·go·tist /ˈiːɡətəst, ˈeɡ-/ *n* [C] someone who likes to talk about how great and important they think they are —**egotistic** /ˌiːɡəˈtɪstɪk◂, ˌeɡ-/ *adj*

e·go·tis·tic·al /ˌiːɡəˈtəstɪkəl◂, ˌeɡ-/ *adj* someone who is egotistical likes to talk about how great and important they think they are: *He's a selfish, egotistical individual!* —**egotistically** /-kli/ *adv*

ˈego ˌtrip *n* [C] if someone is on an ego trip, they think that what they do makes them more important than other people - used to show disapproval: *Their singer's on a real ego trip.*

e·gre·gious /ɪˈɡriːdʒəs/ *adj formal* an egregious mistake, failure, problem etc is extremely bad and noticeable —**egregiously** *adv*

e·gress /ˈiːɡres/ *n* [U] *formal or law* the act of leaving a building or place, or the right to do this

e·gret /ˈiːɡrət, -et/ *n* [C] a bird that lives near water and has long legs and long white tail feathers

E·gyp·tian¹ /ɪˈdʒɪpʃən/ *adj* relating to Egypt or its people

Egyptian² *n* [C] someone from Egypt

eh /eɪ/ *interjection spoken* **1** *BrE* used when you want someone to repeat something because you did not hear it: *Eh? She's got how many children?* **2** used when you want someone to reply to you or agree with something you have said: *Maybe teenagers aren't as clueless as everyone thought, eh?* **3** *BrE* used when you are surprised by something that someone has said

Eid /iːd/ *n* [U] one of two important holidays in the Muslim religion

ei·der·down /ˈaɪdədaʊn $ -dər-/ *n* [C] a thick warm cover for a bed, filled with duck feathers → **duvet**

Eid ul-Ad·ha /ˌiːd ʊl ˈɑːdə $ ˌɪd-/ *n* [U] a religious FESTIVAL that MUSLIMS celebrate at the end of the HAJ in order to remember that the Prophet Ibrahim was willing to kill his son for Allah

Eid ul-Fitr /ˌiːd ʊl ˈfɪtrə $ ˌɪd ʊl ˈfɪtər/ *n* [U] a religious FESTIVAL that MUSLIMS celebrate at the end of RAMADAN. Special prayers are said in the MOSQUE, and children and women are given presents.

eight /eɪt/ ●●● S2 W2 *number, n*
1 the number 8: *It's only eight days till Christmas.* | *They woke at eight* (=eight o'clock). | *My parents died when I was eight* (=eight years old).
2 [C] a team of eight people who row a racing boat, or the boat that they row

eigh·teen /ˌeɪˈtiːn◂/ ●●● S3 W2 *number* the number 18: *At least eighteen bullets were fired.* | *Jim was eighteen* (=18 years old). —**eighteenth** *adj, pron*: *in the eighteenth century* | *her eighteenth birthday* | *I'm planning to leave on* ***the eighteenth*** (=the 18th day of the month).

eighth¹ /eɪtθ/ ●●● S3 W3 *adj* coming after seven other things in a series: *in the eighth century* | *her eighth birthday* —**eighth** *pron*: *I'm planning to leave on* ***the eighth*** (=the eighth day of the month).

eighth² *n* [C] one of eight equal parts of something

ˈeighth note *n* [C] *AmE technical* a musical note that continues for an eighth of the length of a WHOLE NOTE SYN **quaver** *BrE*

eigh·ty /ˈeɪti/ ●●● W3 *number*
1 the number 80
2 the eighties [plural] (*also* **the '80s, the 1980s**) the years from 1980 to 1989: *The band was incredibly successful in the eighties.* | **the early/mid/late eighties** *Their troubles began in the mid eighties.*
3 be in your eighties to be aged between 80 and 89: **early/mid/late eighties** *Hilda Simpson was a woman in her early eighties.*
4 in the eighties if the temperature is in the eighties, it is between 80 degrees and 89 degrees: **in the low/mid/high eighties** *The temperature is expected to remain in the low eighties.* —**eightieth** *adj*: *her eightieth birthday*

ei·stedd·fod /aɪˈstedfəd $ -vɑːd/ *n* [C] an event in Wales at which there are competitions in singing, poetry, and music

ei·ther¹ /ˈaɪðə $ ˈiːðər/ ●●● S1 W1 *conjunction* **either ... or a)** used to begin a list of two or more possibilities: *You add either one or two cloves of garlic.* | *She's the kind of person you either love or hate.* **b)** used to say that if one thing does not happen then something else will have to: *It's your choice! Either she leaves or I will!* | *£75 seems a lot to pay for a starter motor, but it's either that or a new car!* **c) an either-or situation** a situation in which you cannot avoid having to make a decision or choice

either² ●●● S1 W1 *determiner, pron*
1 one or the other of two things or people → **any**: *There's tea or coffee - you can have either.* | *We can offer a comfortable home to a young person of either sex.* | **[+of]** *Could either of you lend me five pounds?*
2 used to show that a negative statement is true about both of two things or people → **neither**: *I've lived in New York and Chicago, but don't like either city very much.* | **[+of]** *There were two witnesses but I wouldn't trust either of them.*
3 either side/end/hand etc both sides, ends, hands etc SYN **each**: *He sat in the back of the car with a policeman on either side.* | *There are shops at either end of the street.*
4 either way a) used to say that something will be the same whichever of two things happens or is true: *You can get to Edinburgh by train or plane, but either way it's very expensive.* **b)** more or less than a certain amount or measurement: *A few marks either way can make the difference between a pass and a fail.* **c)** used to say that someone or something does not firmly support or want either one of two things: *'All right, let's do that,' said Camille, who didn't care either way.*
5 could go either way if a situation could go either way, both possible results are equally likely: *The latest opinion poll suggests the vote could go either way.*

GRAMMAR: Singular or plural verb?

- You use **either** before a singular noun, with a singular verb: *Either explanation* ***is*** *possible.*
- You use **either of** before a plural pronoun or a plural noun: *I don't believe either of them.*
- In formal speech and writing, you use a singular verb: ***Has*** *either of them called yet?*
- In informal speech and writing, people often use a plural verb: ***Have*** *either of them called yet?*

either³ ●●● S1 W2 *adv*
1 [in negatives] used to show that a negative statement is also true about another thing or person, or to add a different negative statement about something or someone → **neither**: *I haven't seen the movie and my brother hasn't either* (=he also has not seen it). | *'I can't swim.' 'I can't either.'* | *It's not an easy car to drive, and at $40,000 it's not cheap either.*

2 me either *AmE spoken* used to say that a negative statement is also true about you: *'I don't have any money right now.' 'Me either.'*

e·jac·u·late /ɪˈdʒækjəleɪt/ *v* [I,T] **1** when a man ejaculates, SEMEN comes out of his PENIS **2** *old-fashioned or literary* to suddenly shout or say something, especially because you are surprised —**ejaculation** /ɪˌdʒækjəˈleɪʃən/ *n* [C,U]

e·ject /ɪˈdʒekt/ ●○○ *v*
1 [T] to make someone leave a place or building by using force: **eject sb from sth** *The demonstrators were ejected from the hall.*
2 [T] to make someone leave a job or position very quickly: **eject sb from sth** *420 workers have been ejected from their jobs with no warning.*
3 [T] to suddenly send something out: *Two engines cut out and the plane started to eject fuel as it lost height.*
4 [I] if a pilot ejects, he or she escapes from a plane, using an ejector seat because it is going to crash
5 [I,T] if you eject a DISK or a tape, or if it ejects, it comes out of a machine after you have pressed a particular button —**ejection** /ɪˈdʒekʃən/ *n* [C,U]

eˈjector ˌseat *BrE*, **eˈjection ˌseat** *AmE n* [C] a special seat that throws the pilot out of a plane when it is going to crash

eke /iːk/ *v*
eke sth ↔ **out** *phr v* **1 eke out a living/existence** to manage to live with very little money or food: *They eke out a miserable existence in cardboard shacks.* **2** to make a small supply of something such as food or money last longer by carefully using small amounts of it: *How did she manage to eke out the food?*

EKG /ˌiː keɪ ˈdʒiː/ *n* [C] *AmE* an ECG

e·lab·o·rate¹ /ɪˈlæbərət/ ●●○ *adj*
1 having a lot of small parts or details put together in a complicated way SYN **intricate**: *pure silks embroidered with elaborate patterns* **THESAURUS** ▸ COMPLICATED
2 carefully planned and organized in great detail SYN **complex**: *a very elaborate telecommunications network* —**elaborately** *adv*: *an elaborately carved wooden statue*

e·lab·o·rate² /ɪˈlæbəreɪt/ *v* [I,T] to give more details or new information about something SYN **enlarge**: *He said he had new evidence, but refused to elaborate any further.* | **[+on]** *McDonald refused to elaborate on his reasons for resigning.* —**elaboration** /ɪˌlæbəˈreɪʃən/ *n* [C,U]

é·lan /ˈeɪlɒn $ eɪˈlɑːn/ *n* [U] *literary* a style that is full of energy and confidence: *The attack was planned and led with great élan.*

e·lapse /ɪˈlæps/ *v* [I] *formal* if a particular period of time elapses, it passes: *Several months elapsed before his case was brought to trial.* | *The assignment must be completed within an overall **elapsed time** of one week.*

> **REGISTER**
> In everyday English, people usually say that time **passes**: *We hardly notice how much time **passes**.*

e·las·tic¹ /ɪˈlæstɪk/ ●○○ *n* [U] a type of rubber material that can stretch and then return to its usual length or size: *a **piece of elastic***

elastic² *adj* **1** made of elastic: *an elastic cord* **2** a material that is elastic can stretch and then go back to its usual length or size: *the horny elastic pad in a horse's hoof* **3** a system or plan that is elastic can change or be changed easily: *Demand for this type of holiday will probably be fairly elastic.* **4** *AmE* if a piece of clothing is elastic, it is made with material that can stretch: *children's pants with an elastic waist*

e·las·ti·cat·ed /ɪˈlæstɪkeɪtɪd/ *adj BrE* if a piece of clothing is elasticated, it is made with material that can stretch: *skirts with elasticated waists*

eˌlastic ˈband *n* [C] *BrE* a thin circular piece of rubber used for fastening things together SYN **rubber band** → see picture at STATIONERY

e·las·tic·i·ty /ˌiːlæˈstɪsəti/ *n* [U] **1** the ability of something to stretch and go back to its usual length or size: *the skin's natural elasticity* **2 elasticity of demand** *technical* the degree to which a change in the price of something leads to a change in the amount of it that is sold

E·las·to·plast /ɪˈlæstəplɑːst $ -plæst/ *n* [C,U] *trademark BrE* a piece of thin material that is stuck to the skin to cover cuts and other small wounds SYN **Band-Aid** *AmE*

e·lat·ed /ɪˈleɪtɪd/ *adj* extremely happy and excited, especially because of something that has happened or is going to happen OPP **depressed**: *He **felt elated** and mildly drunk.* | **[+at/by]** *She was elated at the prospect of a holiday.*

e·la·tion /ɪˈleɪʃən/ *n* [U] a feeling of great happiness and excitement **THESAURUS** ▸ PLEASURE

el·bow¹ /ˈelbəʊ $ -boʊ/ ●●○ *n* [C]
1 the joint where your arm bends
2 the part of a shirt etc that covers your elbow
3 elbow grease *informal* hard work and effort, especially when cleaning or polishing something
4 give sb the elbow *BrE informal* to tell someone that you no longer like them or want them to work for you and that they should leave
5 elbow room enough space in which to move easily: *There's more elbow room in the restaurant since they extended it.*
6 a curved part of a pipe → **rub elbows with sb** at RUB¹(5)

elbow² *v* [T] to push someone with your elbows, especially in order to move past them: **elbow your way through/past/into etc sth** (=move through a group of people by pushing past them) *He elbowed his way to the bar and ordered a beer.* | *She pushed through the crowd, **elbowing** people **out of the way**.*

el·der¹ /ˈeldə $ -ər/ ●●○ *adj especially BrE* the elder of two people, especially brothers and sisters, is the one who was born first OPP **younger**: **elder brother/son/sister/daughter etc** *His elder son Liam became a lawyer.* | *Sarah is **the elder** of the two.* ⚠ Don't say 'elder than someone'. Say **older than someone**: *She was two years older than me.*

elder² ●○○ *n* [C]
1 be sb's elder *formal* to be older than someone else: **be two/ten etc years sb's elder** *Janet's sister was eight years her elder.*
2 sb's elders (and betters) people who are older than you and who you should respect
3 a member of a tribe or other social group who is important and respected because they are old: *a meeting of the village elders*
4 someone who has an official position of responsibility in some Christian churches
5 elder abuse the crime of harming an old person
6 a small wild tree that has white flowers and black BERRIES

el·der·ber·ry /ˈeldəbəri $ -dərberi/ *n* (*plural* **elderberries**) [C] the fruit of the elder tree

el·der·ly /ˈeldəli $ ˈeldərli/ ●●● S3 W2 *adj*
1 used as a polite way of saying that someone is old or becoming old: *a well-dressed elderly woman* **THESAURUS** ▸ OLD
2 the elderly people who are old: *a retirement village for the elderly*

ˌelder ˈstatesman *n* [C] someone old and respected, especially a politician, who people ask for advice because of his or her knowledge and experience

el·dest /ˈeldɪst/ ●●○ *adj especially BrE* the eldest of a group of people, especially brothers and sisters, is the one who was born first → **old**: **eldest son/daughter/brother/child etc** *My eldest daughter is 17.* | *He was **the eldest** of six children.*

El Do·ra·do, **Eldorado** /ˌel dəˈrɑːdəʊ/ a place of very great wealth, especially a place that people travel a long way to find, or an imaginary place that does not really exist. El Dorado comes from the ancient story of the king of a South American TRIBE who covered himself in gold dust and dived into a lake. Some people believed that the king's city, El Dorado, really existed and tried to find it.

e-learn·ing /ˈiː ˌlɜːnɪŋ $ -ˌlɜːr-/ *n* [U] a method of

E

learning that involves studying at home using a computer and the Internet

e·lect[1] /ɪˈlekt/ ●●○ S3 W3 *v* [T]
1 to choose someone for an official position by voting: *the country's first* ***democratically elected*** *government | a new method for electing the leader of the party* | **be elected to sth** *He was elected to a US state governorship.* | **be elected (as) president/leader/mayor etc** *In 1768, John Wilkes was elected as their Member of Parliament.* GRAMMAR **Elect** is often passive in this meaning. THESAURUS ▸ VOTE
2 elect to do sth *formal* to choose to do something: *You can elect to delete the message or save it.*

elect[2] *adj* **president-elect/governor-elect/prime minister-elect etc** the person who has been elected as president etc, but who has not yet officially started their job

e·lec·tion /ɪˈlekʃən/ ●●● S2 W1 *n*
1 [C] when people vote to choose someone for an official position: *The Labour Party won the 2001 election by a huge majority. | Elections for the state governorship will be on November 25.*
2 [singular] the fact of being elected to an official position: *Within three months of his election he was forced to resign.* | **sb's election to sth** *his election to Parliament* → GENERAL ELECTION

COLLOCATIONS

VERBS

have/hold an election *The government plans to hold an election in November.*
call an election (=arrange for an election to happen) *The prime minister would be unwise to call an election now.*
win an election *Who do you think will win the election?*
lose an election *If the party loses the election, they may decide they need a new leader.*
fight an election *BrE* (*also* **contest an election** *BrE formal*) (=take part in it and try to win) *Three independent candidates are also planning to contest the election.*
run for election (*also* **stand for election** *BrE*) (=try to become elected) *If you plan to stand for election to the committee, you must be nominated by three members.*

ADJECTIVES/NOUN + election

fair (=with no unfair advantage to one person or group) *The ruling party has promised that the elections will be fair.*
free (=with everyone allowed to vote for who they want) *These will be the country's first free multi-party elections.*
democratic *The unions are calling for democratic elections.*
a general/national election (=one in which the whole country votes to elect a government) *Labour's victory in the general election gave them a huge majority.*
a local/regional election *The Green Party increased its share of the vote in the French regional elections.*
a presidential election (=to elect a new president) | **a leadership election** (=to elect a new leader for a political party) | **a congressional/parliamentary election** (=to elect people to a congress or parliament) | **a federal election** (=to elect a federal government) | **a mayoral election** (=to elect a new mayor)

election + NOUN

an election victory/defeat *He became prime minister after a decisive election victory.*
the election results *The election results have been coming in all night.*
an election campaign *The election campaign got off to a bad start.*
an election candidate *BrE* (=someone trying to be elected in an election) *Local party members choose the election candidates.*
an election promise/pledge (=one that is made while a person or party is trying to be elected) *The government has broken all its election promises.*
an election broadcast *BrE* (=a programme by a party saying why people should vote for them in an election) | **an election rally** (=a public meeting to support a politician or party before an election) | **an election year** (=a year in which there is an election) | **election day/night** (=the day or night when people are voting and the votes are being counted) | **election time**

PHRASES

the run-up to the election (=the period of time before an election) *There have been violent street protests in the run-up to the elections.*

THESAURUS

election an occasion when people choose a government or leader by voting: *the American presidential election | South Africa held its first multi-racial elections in 1994.*
ballot /ˈbælət/ an occasion when the members of an organization vote by marking what they want on a piece of paper, especially to make sure that it is secret: *The result of the ballot showed that nurses were not in favour of a strike.*
referendum /ˌrefəˈrendəm/ an occasion when everyone in a country votes on an important political subject: *In the Danish referendum, the people voted 'no' to joining the European single currency.*
the polls the process of voting in a political election - used especially in news reports: *4,500,000 voters went to the polls in eight provinces to elect six governors.*
show of hands an act of voting informally for something by the people in a group raising their hands: *May I have a show of hands from all those in favour of the proposal?*

e·lec·tion·eer·ing /ɪˌlekʃəˈnɪərɪŋ $ -ˈnɪr-/ *n* [U] speeches and other activities that are intended to persuade people to vote for a particular person or political party

e·lec·tive[1] /ɪˈlektɪv/ *adj formal* **1** an elective position or organization is one for which there is an election: *the 34 elective seats in the National Assembly* **2** elective medical treatment is treatment that you choose to have, although you do not have to: ***elective surgery*** *such as hip replacements* **3** *AmE* an elective course is one that students can choose to take, although they do not have to take it in order to GRADUATE → **module**

elective[2] *n* [C] *AmE* a course that students can choose to take, but they do not have to take it in order to GRADUATE → **module**

e·lec·tor /ɪˈlektə $ -tər, -tɔːr/ *n* [C] someone who has the right to vote in an election: *Over 36% of electors did not vote at all.*

e·lec·to·ral /ɪˈlektərəl/ ●○○ *adj* [only before noun] relating to elections and voting: *Our* ***electoral system*** *strongly favours two-party government. | a campaign for* ***electoral reform*** —**electorally** *adv*

eˌlectoral ˈcollege *n* **the Electoral College** a group of people chosen by the votes of the people in each US state, who come together to elect the president, or a similar group in other countries

eˌlectoral ˈregister (*also* **eˌlectoral ˈroll**) *n* [C] an official list of the people who are allowed to vote in an election

e·lec·to·rate /ɪˈlektərət/ ●○○ *n* [singular] all the people in a country who have the right to vote: *A majority of the electorate oppose the law.*

e·lec·tric /ɪˈlektrɪk/ ●●● S2 W3 *adj*
1 needing electricity to work, produced by electricity, or used for carrying electricity: **electric light/kettle/cooker etc** *the heat from a small electric fire* | **electric current/power/**

charge (=a flow of electricity) | *an* ***electric blanket*** (=one with electric wires in it, used for making a bed warm)
2 making people feel very excited: *The* ***atmosphere*** *in the courtroom was* ***electric***.

e·lec·tri·cal /ɪˈlektrɪkəl/ ●●○ S3 *adj*
1 relating to electricity: *The fire was caused by an* ***electrical fault***. | *an* ***electrical engineer*** (=a person who designs and makes electrical equipment)
2 using electricity: **electrical equipment/goods/appliances etc** —**electrically** /-kli/ *adv*

eˌlectrical ˈstorm (*also* **eˌlectric ˈstorm**) *n* [C] a violent storm with a lot of LIGHTNING

eˌlectric ˌblue *n* [U] a very bright blue colour —**electric blue** *adj*

eˌlectric ˈchair *n* [C usually singular] a chair in which criminals are killed using electricity, especially in the US, in order to punish them for murder: *He faces death by the electric chair in a Florida state prison.*

el·ec·tri·cian /ɪˌlekˈtrɪʃən, ˌelɪk-/ ●●○ *n* [C] someone whose job is to connect or repair electrical wires or equipment

e·lec·tri·ci·ty /ɪˌlekˈtrɪsəti, ˌelɪk-/ ●●● S2 W3 *n* [U]
1 the power that is carried by wires, CABLES etc, and is used to provide light or heat, to make machines work etc: *The farm was very isolated, but it had electricity.*
2 a feeling of excitement: *There was electricity in the air between the two of them.*

COLLOCATIONS

VERBS

generate/produce electricity *We need to find cleaner ways of generating electricity.*
provide/supply electricity (=produce electricity and make it available to people) *The dam will provide water and electricity for 30 million people.*
use electricity *The system uses electricity to heat the water.*
be powered by electricity *In an emergency, the hospital can be powered by electricity from a generator.*
conduct electricity (=used of a substance - allow electricity to travel along or through it) | **cut off the electricity** (=stop the supply of electricity)

electricity + NOUN

the electricity supply (=electricity provided to homes and businesses) *The storms have disrupted the electricity supply to some areas.*
electricity demand (=the amount of electricity that is needed) *There has been a dramatic growth in electricity demand.*
electricity production (=the process of producing electricity, or the amount produced) | **electricity consumption** (=the amount of electricity that is used) | **an electricity bill** (=a bill you have to pay for electricity you have used) | **an electricity company** | **the electricity industry**

ADJECTIVES/NOUN + electricity

mains electricity *BrE* (=electricity supplied to a building from the national electricity supply) *The cottage has no mains electricity.*
static electricity (=electricity that collects on a surface, for example on your clothes or a balloon)

e·lec·trics /ɪˈlektrɪks/ *n* [plural] *BrE* the parts of a machine that use electrical power

eˌlectric ˈshock *n* [C] a sudden shock to your body, caused by electricity

eˌlectric ˈshock ˌtherapy *n* [U] a method of treatment for mental illness that involves sending electricity through someone's brain SYN **ECT**

e·lec·tri·fy /ɪˈlektrɪfaɪ/ *v* (**electrified**, **electrifying**, **electrifies**) [T] **1** if a performance or a speech electrifies people, it makes them feel very interested or excited: *She would sit at the piano and sing, electrifying us all.* **2** to change a railway so that it uses electrical power, or to supply a building or area with electricity: *The west coast main line has been electrified.* —**electrifying** *adj* —**electrified** *adj*: *electrified fences* —**electrification** /ɪˌlektrɪfɪˈkeɪʃən/ *n* [U]

e·lec·tro /ɪˈlektrəʊ $ -troʊ/ *n* [U] a type of music that uses electronic sounds

electro- /ɪlektrəʊ, -trə $ -troʊ, -trə/ *prefix technical* **1** relating to electricity or made to work by electricity: *electrocute* (=to hurt or kill someone by electricity) | *an electromagnet* **2** electric and something else: *electrochemical*

e·lec·tro·car·di·o·gram /ɪˌlektrəʊˈkɑːdiəgræm $ -troʊˈkɑːr-/ *n* [C] *technical* an ECG(2)

e·lec·tro·car·di·o·graph /ɪˌlektrəʊˈkɑːdiəgrɑːf $ -troʊˈkɑːrdiəgræf/ *n* [C] *technical* an ECG(1)

eˌlectro-conˌvulsive ˈtherapy *n* [U] ELECTRIC SHOCK THERAPY

e·lec·tro·cute /ɪˈlektrəkjuːt/ *v* [T usually passive] **1** *BrE* if someone is electrocuted, they are injured or killed by electricity passing through their body: *Last week a housewife was electrocuted by her washing machine.* **2** to kill someone using electricity —**electrocution** /ɪˌlektrəˈkjuːʃən/ *n* [U]

e·lec·trode /ɪˈlektrəʊd $ -troʊd/ *n* [C] a small piece of metal or a wire that is used to send electricity through a system or through a person's body: *The monkeys have electrodes implanted into the brain to measure their brain activity.*

e·lec·tro·en·ceph·a·lo·gram /ɪˌlektrəʊɪnˈsefələgræm, -trəʊen- $ -troʊ-/ *n* [C] *technical* an EEG(2)

e·lec·tro·en·ceph·a·lo·graph /ɪˌlektrəʊɪnˈsefələgrɑːf, -trəʊen- $ -troʊɪnˈsefələgræf, -troʊen-/ *n* [C] *technical* an EEG(1)

e·lec·trol·y·sis /ɪˌlekˈtrɒləsəs, ˌelɪk- $ -ˈtrɑː-/ *n* [U]
1 *technical* the process of separating a liquid into its chemical parts by passing an electric current through it
2 the process of using electricity to destroy hair roots and to remove unwanted hairs from your face etc

e·lec·tro·lyte /ɪˈlektrəlaɪt/ *n* [C] *technical* a liquid that allows electricity to pass through it

e·lec·tro·mag·net /ɪˌlektrəʊˈmægnɪt $ -troʊ-/ *n* [C] a piece of metal that becomes MAGNETIC (=able to attract metal objects) when an electric current is turned on

e·lec·tro·mag·net·ic /ɪˌlektrəʊmægˈnetɪk◂ $ -troʊ-/ *adj technical* relating to both electricity and MAGNETISM, or having both electrical and MAGNETIC qualities: *electromagnetic waves* | **the electromagnetic spectrum** (=different waves of energy, including light, heat, radio waves, and X-RAYS)

e·lec·tro·mag·ne·tis·m /ɪˌlektrəʊˈmægnətɪzəm $ -troʊ-/ *n* [U] *technical* the relationship between electricity and MAGNETISM, and the effect that they have on each other

e·lec·tron /ɪˈlektrɒn $ -trɑːn/ *n* [C] a very small piece of matter with a negative electrical CHARGE that moves around the NUCLEUS (=central part) of an atom → **proton**, **neutron** → see picture at **ATOM**

e·lec·tron·ic /ˌelɪkˈtrɒnɪk, ɪˌlek- $ -ˈtrɑː-/ ●●● S3 W3 *adj*
1 electronic equipment, such as computers and televisions, uses electricity that has passed through computer CHIPS, TRANSISTORS etc: *electronic games* | *an electronic organizer* (=a small piece of electronic equipment that you can use to record addresses, phone numbers etc)
2 using or produced by electronic equipment → **e-**: *electronic music* | *electronic banking* | *electronic publishing* (=a system of producing books, magazines etc in a form that can be read on a computer) —**electronically** /-kli/ *adv*: *electronically controlled gates* | *The information is recorded electronically.*

e·lec·tron·i·ca /ˌelɪkˈtrɒnɪkə, ɪˌlek- $ -ˈtrɑː-/ *n* [U] a general word for various different types of electronic dance and listening music → **drum 'n' bass**, **house music**, **techno**, **trance**

ˌelectronic ˈbanking *n* [U] a service provided by

banks that allows people to pay money from one account to another, pay bills etc using the Internet SYN **e-banking**

ˌelectronic ˈcash *n* [U] money that can be used to buy things on the Internet, but that does not exist in a physical form or belong to any particular country

ˌelectronic ˈdata ˌinterchange *n* [U] *technical* (*abbreviation* **EDI**) a way for companies and banks to send information to each other by computer using an agreed FORMAT so that the company receiving the documents can easily read them on their computer and print them out on paper

ˌelectronic ˈfunds ˌtransfer *n* [C,U] (*abbreviation* **EFT**) when money is moved from one bank account, business etc to another using only computer systems

ˌelectronic ˈink *n* [U] a type of technology used to show words on an E-READER

ˌelectronic ˈmail *n* [U] EMAIL

ˌelectronic ˈmoney *n* [U] money that can be used to buy things on the Internet, but that does not exist in a physical form or belong to any particular country

ˌelectronic ˈorganizer *n* [C] a small piece of electronic equipment that you can use to record addresses, telephone numbers, dates of meetings etc

ˌelectronic ˈpaper *n* [U] a thin sheet of special material, like a piece of paper, that is completely covered in very small round marks that can turn either black or white when attached to an electrical connection, and which then show up as words on the page

E

ˌelectronic ˈpublishing *n* [U] the business of producing books, magazines, or newspapers that are designed to be read using a computer

e·lec·tron·ics /ɪˌlekˈtrɒnɪks, ˌelɪk- $ -ˈtrɑː-/ ●●○ *n*
1 [U] the study or industry of making equipment, such as computers and televisions, that work electronically: **electronics company/industry/firm etc** *an electronics engineer*

> **GRAMMAR: Singular or plural verb?**
>
> In this meaning, **electronics** is followed by a singular verb: ***Electronics deals*** *with electrical circuits that have active components.*
>
> GRAMMAR GUIDE ▸ NOUNS

2 [plural] electronic equipment: *the market for consumer electronics*

ˌelectronic ˈsignature *n* [C] a type of CODE that is used in an electronic document to prove who wrote it

ˌelectronic ˈtagging *n* [U] a system of attaching a small piece of electronic equipment to a criminal, which allows the police to know where he or she is

ˌelectronic ˈticketing *n* [U] a service provided by AIRLINES that allows people to buy their tickets on the Internet and usually does not give them tickets in the form of paper

eˌlectron ˈmicroscope *n* [C] a very powerful MICROSCOPE (=scientific instrument used for looking at small objects) that uses ELECTRONS instead of light to make things look larger

e·lec·tro·plate /ɪˈlektrəʊpleɪt $ -troʊ-/ *v* [T] to put a very thin layer of metal onto the surface of an object, using ELECTROLYSIS

e·lec·tro·smog /ɪˈlektrəʊˌsmɒg $ -troʊˌsmɑːg, -ˌsmɒːg/ *n* [U] *informal* the waves or forces produced by electrical equipment such as MOBILE PHONES and computers, which some people believe make them ill

el·e·gant /ˈeləgənt/ ●●○ *adj*
1 beautiful, attractive, or graceful: *a tall, elegant young woman | You can dine in* ***elegant surroundings****.*
2 an idea or a plan that is elegant is very intelligent yet simple: *an elegant solution to the problem* —**elegantly** *adv* —**elegance** *n* [U]: *the style and elegance of the designs*

el·e·gi·ac /ˌeləˈdʒaɪək◂/ *adj literary* showing that you feel sad about someone who has died or something that no longer exists: *He spoke of her in elegiac tones.*

el·e·gy /ˈelɪdʒi/ *n* (*plural* **elegies**) [C] a sad poem or song, especially about someone who has died → **eulogy**

el·e·ment /ˈeləmənt/ ●●● S2 W1 AWL *n* [C]
1 PART one part or feature of a whole system, plan, piece of work etc, especially one that is basic or important: **[+of]** *Honesty is a vital element of her success.* | **[+in]** *the primary element in the country's economy* | **important/key/essential/vital etc element** *Besides ability, the other essential element in political success is luck.* | *Business and management elements are built into the course.*
2 element of surprise/truth/risk/doubt etc an amount, usually small, of a quality or feeling: *There is an element of truth in your argument.*
3 CHEMISTRY a simple chemical substance such as CARBON or oxygen that consists of atoms of only one kind → COMPOUND[1](1)
4 PEOPLE a group of people who form part of a larger group, especially when the rest of the group does not approve of them → **faction**: *the hard-line communist elements in the party*
5 the elements [plural] the weather, especially bad weather: *sailors battling against the elements*
6 HEATING the part of a piece of electrical equipment that produces heat
7 the elements of sth the most simple things that you have to learn first about a subject: *She doesn't even know the basic elements of politeness.*
8 EARTH/AIR/FIRE/WATER one of the four substances (earth, air, fire, and water) from which people used to believe that everything was made
9 be in your element to be in a situation that you enjoy, because you are good at it: *Graham was in his element, building a fire and cooking the steaks.*
10 be out of your element to be in a situation that makes you uncomfortable or unhappy: *She was out of her element in this dull little town.*

el·e·men·tal /ˌeləˈmentl◂/ *adj* **1** simple, basic, and important: *Love and fear are two of the most elemental human emotions.* **2** *technical* existing as a simple chemical element that has not been combined with anything else: *elemental sulphur*

el·e·men·ta·ry /ˌeləˈmentəri◂/ ●●○ *adj*
1 simple or basic: *the elementary principles of justice and democracy | You've made a very elementary mistake.*
2 [only before noun] concerning the first and easiest part of a subject → **intermediate**, **advanced**: *I'm only familiar with the subject at an elementary level. | I know a little elementary science.*
3 [only before noun] *AmE* relating to elementary school SYN **primary** *BrE*: ***elementary education***
4 Elementary, my dear Watson. people sometimes use this expression humorously to say how easy something is to solve. Some people think that the phrase comes from the Sherlock Holmes stories by Sir Arthur Conan Doyle. Holmes says this to his friend Watson when explaining how easy it is to understand something about a crime. In fact, the phrase does not appear in the books.

ˌelementary ˈparticle *n* [C] *technical* one of the types of pieces of matter including ELECTRONS, PROTONS, and NEUTRONS that make up atoms

eleˈmentary ˌschool *n* [C] a school in the US where basic subjects are taught for the first six years of a child's education

el·e·phant /ˈeləfənt/ ●●● W3 *n* [C]
1 a very large grey animal with four legs, two TUSKS (=long curved teeth) and a TRUNK (=long nose) that it can use to pick things up
2 the elephant in the (living) room an important subject or problem that everyone knows about but no one mentions: *The race issue is the elephant in the room in this election.* → WHITE ELEPHANT

el·e·phan·tine /ˌeləˈfæntaɪn◂ $ -tiːn◂/ *adj formal* slow, heavy, and awkward, like an elephant: *elephantine footsteps*

el·e·vate /ˈelɪveɪt/ ●○○ *v* [T]
1 *formal* to move someone or something to a more important level or rank, or make them better than before SYN **raise**: *Language has elevated humans above the other animals.* | **elevate sb/sth to sth** *Their purpose is to elevate AIDS to the top of government priorities.*
2 *technical* to lift someone or something to a higher position: *Gradually elevate the patient into an upright position.* **THESAURUS** LIFT
3 *technical* to increase the amount, temperature, pressure etc of something SYN **raise**: *These drugs may elevate acid levels in the blood.*

el·e·vat·ed /ˈelɪveɪtɪd/ *adj* **1** elevated thoughts, words etc seem to be intelligent or of high moral standard: *elevated philosophical language* **2** [only before noun] an elevated position or rank is very important and respected SYN **high** **3** raised off the ground or higher up than other things: *The train runs on an elevated track.* **4** *formal* elevated levels, temperatures etc are higher than normal SYN **high**: *elevated blood sugar levels*

ˌelevated ˈrailway *BrE*, **ˌelevated ˈrailroad** *AmE n* [C] a railway that is above the streets in a town

el·e·vat·ing /ˈeləveɪtɪŋ/ *adj formal* making you feel interested in intelligent or moral subjects - sometimes used humorously: *an elevating experience*

el·e·va·tion /ˌeləˈveɪʃən/ *n* **1** [singular] a height above the level of the sea: **[+of]** *The road climbs steadily to an elevation of 1,400 feet.* **2** [U] *formal* an act of moving someone to a more important rank or position: **[+to]** *her sudden elevation to international stardom* **3** [C,U] *formal* an increase in the amount or level of something: *a sudden elevation of blood pressure* **4** [C] *technical* an upright side of a building, as shown in a drawing done by an ARCHITECT (=person who plans buildings): *the front elevation of a house* **5** [C] *technical* the angle made with the HORIZON by pointing a gun: *The cannon was fired at an elevation of 60 degrees.*

el·e·va·tor /ˈeləveɪtə $ -ər/ ●●● S3 W3 *n* [C]
1 *AmE* a machine that takes people and goods from one level to another in a building SYN **lift** *BrE*: *We'll have to take the elevator.*
2 a machine with a moving belt and containers, used for lifting grain and liquids, or for taking things off ships

ˈelevator ˌmusic *n* [U] *informal* the type of music that is played in shops and public places, and is usually thought to be boring

e·lev·en /ɪˈlevən/ ●●● S3 W2 *number, n*
1 the number 11: *She was sent to jail for eleven months.* | *I never go to bed before eleven* (=11 o'clock). | *James had worked every summer since he was eleven* (=11 years old).
2 [C] a team of 11 players in football or CRICKET: *He plays regularly in* ***the first eleven*** (=the best team of 11 players).

eˌleven-ˈplus (*also* **11-plus**) *n* [singular] an examination that all children in Britain used to take at the age of 11 in order to decide what kind of SECONDARY SCHOOL they should go to. In some areas, children still take this examination.

e·lev·en·ses /ɪˈlevənzɪz/ *n* [U] *BrE old-fashioned* a cup of coffee or tea and a BISCUIT, that you have in the middle of the morning

e·lev·enth¹ /ɪˈlevənθ/ ●●● S3 W3 *adj*
1 coming after ten other things in a series: *in the eleventh century* | *her eleventh birthday*
2 **the eleventh hour** the last moment before something important happens: *At the eleventh hour the government decided that something had to be done.* —**eleventh** *pron*: *I'm planning to leave on* ***the eleventh*** (=the 11th day of the month).

eleventh² *n* [C] one of eleven equal parts of something

elf /elf/ *n* (*plural* **elves** /elvz/) [C] an imaginary creature like a small person with pointed ears and magical powers → **fairy**, **pixie**

ELF /ˌiː el ˈef/ *n* [U] (***English as a lingua franca***) the use of English as a means of communication by people whose first languages are different, and are not English

el·fin /ˈelfɪn/ *adj* someone who looks elfin is small and delicate: *She had an elfin face and wide grey eyes.*

e·li·cit /ɪˈlɪsɪt/ ●○○ *v* [T] to succeed in getting information or a reaction from someone, especially when this is difficult: *When her knock* ***elicited*** *no* ***response****, she opened the door and peeped in.* | **elicit sth from sb** *The test uses pictures to elicit words from the child.* —**elicitation** /ɪˌlɪsɪˈteɪʃən/ *n* [U]

e·lide /ɪˈlaɪd/ *v* [T] *technical* to leave out the sound of a letter or of a part of a word: *Most English speakers elide the first 'd' in 'Wednesday.'* —**elision** /ɪˈlɪʒən/ *n* [C,U]

el·i·gi·ble /ˈelɪdʒəbəl/ ●○○ *adj*
1 someone who is eligible for something is able or allowed to do it, for example because they are the right age: **[+for]** *Students on a part-time course are not eligible for a loan.* | **eligible to do sth** *Over 500,000 18-year-olds will become* ***eligible to vote*** *this year.*
2 [only before noun] an eligible man or woman would be good to marry because they are rich, attractive, and not married: *Stephen was regarded as an* ***eligible bachelor****.* —**eligibility** /ˌelɪdʒəˈbɪləti/ *n* [U]

e·lim·i·nate /ɪˈlɪməneɪt/ ●●○ AWL *v* [T]
1 to completely get rid of something that is unnecessary or unwanted → **eradicate**: **eliminate a need/possibility/risk/problem etc** *The credit card eliminates the need for cash or cheques.* | *There is no solution that will totally eliminate the possibility of theft.* | **eliminate sth/sb from sth** *Fatty foods should be eliminated from the diet.* **THESAURUS** REMOVE

> **REGISTER**
> In everyday English, people usually say **get rid of** rather than **eliminate**: *It is almost impossible to* ***get rid of*** *the problem.*

2 to defeat a team or person in a competition, so that they no longer take part in it SYN **knock out**: *Our team was eliminated in the first round.* GRAMMAR **Eliminate** is usually passive in this meaning.
3 to kill someone in order to prevent them from causing trouble: *a ruthless dictator who eliminated all his rivals* **THESAURUS** KILL
4 **eliminate sb from your enquiries** *BrE* if the police eliminate someone from their enquiries, they decide that that person did not commit a particular crime

e·lim·i·na·tion /ɪˌlɪməˈneɪʃən/ ●●○ AWL *n* [U]
1 REMOVAL OF STH the removal or destruction of something → **eradication**: **[+of]** *the elimination of lead in petrol*
2 DEFEAT the defeat of a team or player in a competition, so that they may no longer take part
3 KILLING the act of killing someone, especially to prevent them from causing trouble: **[+of]** *The killings are part of a campaign of elimination of the political opposition.*
4 BODY PROCESS *technical* the process of getting rid of substances that your body no longer needs: **[+of]** *the elimination of toxins from the body* → **process of elimination** at PROCESS¹(6)

elimiˈnation ˌdiet *n* [C] a special DIET used by doctors to discover whether certain foods are making someone ill. It involves not eating foods that might be causing the problem. Later you start to eat each of these foods again separately over a period of time until one of them makes you ill.

e·lite¹ /eɪˈliːt, ɪ-/ ●○○ *n* [C] a group of people who have a lot of power and influence because they have money, knowledge, or special skills: **political/social/economic etc elite** *the domination of power by a small political elite* | *a struggle for power within the* ***ruling elite***

elite² ●○○ *adj* an elite group contains the best, most skilled, or most experienced people or members of a larger group: *an elite group of artists* | *elite universities*

e·lit·ist /eɪˈliːtəst, ɪ-/ *adj* an elitist system, government etc is one in which a small group of people have more power and advantages than other people: *an elitist education system* —**elitism** *n* [U] —**elitist** *n* [C]

e·lix·ir /ɪ'lɪksə $ -ər/ *n* **1** [C] *literary* a magical liquid that is supposed to cure people of illness, make them younger etc: *the search for the* ***elixir of life*** **2** [C] something that is supposed to solve problems as if by magic: *The current new wave of technology should prove an economic elixir.*

E·liz·a·be·than /ɪˌlɪzə'bi:θən◂/ *adj* relating to the period 1558-1603 when Elizabeth I was queen of England: *Elizabethan drama* —**Elizabethan** *n* [C]: *The Earl of Essex was a famous Elizabethan.*

elk /elk/ *n* (*plural* **elk**) [C] **1** *BrE* a very large brown North American, European, and Asian animal with wide flat horns SYN **moose** *AmE* **2** *AmE* a large North American DEER

el·lipse /ɪ'lɪps/ *n* [C] a curved shape like a circle, but with two slightly longer and flatter sides → **oval**

el·lip·sis /ɪ'lɪpsɪs/ *n* (*plural* **ellipses** /-si:z/) *technical* **1** [C,U] when words are deliberately left out of a sentence, though the meaning can still be understood. For example, you may say 'He's leaving but I'm not' instead of saying 'He's leaving but I'm not leaving'. **2** [C] the sign (...) used in writing to show that some words have deliberately been left out of a sentence

el·lip·ti·cal /ɪ'lɪptɪkəl/ (*also* **el·lip·tic** /-tɪk/) *adj* **1** having the shape of an ellipse: *Kepler published his discovery of the elliptical orbits of planets in 1609.* **2** elliptical speech or writing is difficult to understand because more is meant than is actually said: *The language is often elliptical and ambiguous.*

elm /elm/ *n* [C,U] a type of large tree with broad leaves, or the wood from this tree

el·o·cu·tion /ˌelə'kju:ʃən/ *n* [U] good clear speaking in public, involving voice control, pronunciation etc: ***elocution lessons*** —**elocutionary** *adj* —**elocutionist** *n* [C]

e·lon·gate /'i:lɒŋgeɪt $ ɪ'lɒ:ŋ-/ *v* [I,T] to become longer, or make something longer than normal: *Her legs were elongated by the very high heels which she wore.* —**elongation** /ˌi:lɒŋ'geɪʃən $ ɪˌlɒ:ŋ-/ *n* [C,U]

e·lon·gat·ed /'i:lɒŋgeɪtɪd $ ɪ'lɒ:ŋ-/ *adj* longer than normal: *The picture shows two elongated figures dancing.*

e·lope /ɪ'ləʊp $ ɪ'loʊp/ *v* [I] to leave your home secretly in order to get married: *My parents didn't approve of the marriage, so we eloped.* —**elopement** *n* [C,U]

el·o·quent /'eləkwənt/ *adj* **1** able to express your ideas and opinions well, especially in a way that influences people: *an eloquent appeal for support* **2** showing a feeling or meaning without using words: *The photographs are an eloquent reminder of the horrors of war.* —**eloquently** *adv* —**eloquence** *n* [U]

else /els/ ●●● S1 W1 *adv*
1 [used after words beginning with 'some-', 'every-', 'any-', and 'no-', and after question words] **a)** besides or in addition to someone or something: *There's something else I'd like to talk about as well.* | *I'd like you to come, and anyone else who's free.* | *He was awake now, as was everyone else.* | *Who else was at the party?* | *'Two coffees, please.' 'Anything else?' 'No, thanks.'* | ***Above all else*** (=more than any other things) *she was seeking love.* **b)** used to talk about a different person, thing, place etc: *I'd like to live anywhere else but here.* | *If I can't trust you, who else can I trust?*
2 or else *spoken* **a)** used to say that there will be a bad result if someone does not do something: *Hurry up or else we'll miss the train.* **b)** used to say what another possibility might be: *The salesman will reduce the price or else include free insurance.* **c)** used to threaten someone: *Hand over the money, or else!*
3 *BrE spoken* used after a question word to say that the thing, person, or place you have mentioned is the only one possible: *'What are you doing?' 'Waiting for you, what else?'*
4 what else can sb do/say? *spoken* used to say that it is impossible to do or say anything apart from what has been mentioned: *'Will you really sell the house?' 'What else can I do? I can't live here.'* → **if nothing else** at NOTHING[1](11), → **be something else** at SOMETHING(9)

> **GRAMMAR**
> The possessive form of **someone/anyone else** is **someone/anyone else's**: *Don't use someone else's ideas.* | *Nobody else's cooking is as good as yours.*
> ✗ Don't say: *someone's else ideas* | *nobody's else cooking*

else·where /els'weə, 'elsweə $ 'elswer/ ●●● S3 W2 *adv* in, at, or to another place: *She is becoming famous in Australia and elsewhere.* | *Kerala has less crime and alcoholism than elsewhere in India.*

ELT /ˌi: el 'ti:/ *n* [U] *especially BrE* (***English Language Teaching***) the teaching of the English language to people whose first language is not English

e·lu·ci·date /ɪ'lu:sədeɪt/ *v* [I,T] *formal* to explain something that is difficult to understand by providing more information SYN **clarify**: *The full picture has not yet been elucidated.* —**elucidation** /ɪˌlu:sə'deɪʃən/ *n* [C,U] —**elucidatory** /ɪ'lu:sədətəri $ -dətɔ:ri/ *adj*

e·lude /ɪ'lu:d/ *v* [T] **1** to escape from someone or something, especially by tricking them SYN **avoid**: *He eluded his pursuers by escaping into a river.* **2** if something that you want eludes you, you fail to find or achieve it: *She took the exam again, but again success eluded her.* **3** if a fact or the answer to a problem eludes you, you cannot remember or solve it SYN **escape**: *The exact terminology eludes me for the moment.*

e·lu·sive /ɪ'lu:sɪv/ ●○○ *adj*
1 an elusive person or animal is difficult to find or not often seen: *She managed to get an interview with that elusive man.*
2 an elusive result is difficult to achieve: *She enjoys a firm reputation in this country but wider international success has been elusive.*
3 an elusive idea or quality is difficult to describe or understand: *For me, the poem has an elusive quality.* —**elusively** *adv* —**elusiveness** *n* [U]

elves /elvz/ *n* the plural of ELF

E·lys·i·um /ɪ'lɪziəm $ ɪ'lɪʒiəm, zi-/ (*also* **the Eˌlysian 'Fields**) *literary* a place of complete happiness. According to ancient Greek stories, Elysium is the place where good people go after their death.

em- /ɪm, em/ *prefix* the form used for EN- before b, m, or p: *embittered* (=made to feel extremely disappointed) | *empowerment* (=when someone is given control of something)

'em /əm/ *pron spoken* sometimes used as a short form of 'them': *Go on, Bill, you tell 'em!*

e·ma·ci·a·ted /ɪ'meɪʃieɪtəd, -si-/ *adj* extremely thin from lack of food or illness: *The prisoners were ill and emaciated.* THESAURUS THIN —**emaciation** /ɪˌmeɪʃi'eɪʃən, -si-/ *n* [U]

e·mail[1], **e-mail** /'i: meɪl/ ●●● S1 W1 *n*
1 [U] a system that allows you to send and receive messages by computer SYN **electronic mail**: *It's usually best to contact him by email.*
2 [C,U] a message that is sent from one person to another using the email system: *Send me an e-mail when you have any news.*

> **COLLOCATIONS – MEANINGS 1 & 2**
> **VERBS**
> **send (sb) an email** *Can you send me an email with all the details?*
> **get/receive an email** *Within seconds, I got an email confirming the booking.*
> **read an email** *It took most of the morning to read my emails.*
> **write an email** *Jack spent the evening writing emails and surfing the Internet.*
> **answer/reply to an email** *She did not bother replying to his email.*
> **check your email(s)** *The first thing I do every morning is check my email.*

delete an email | **forward an email** (=send an email you have received to someone else) | **fire off an email** *informal* (=send it quickly, especially because you are angry about something)

email + NOUN

an email address *What's your email address?*
an email message *I can send email messages on my phone.*
an email attachment (=a computer file sent in an email) *Don't open an email attachment unless you know who sent it.*

email², **e-mail** ●●● S1 W1 *v* [T]
1 to send someone an email SYN **mail**: *Will you e-mail me about it?*
2 to send someone a document using email SYN **mail**: *Can you email me the proposal by the end of today?*

em·a·nate /ˈeməneɪt/ *v* [T] *formal* to produce a smell, light etc, or to show a particular quality: *He emanates tranquility.* —**emanation** /ˌeməˈneɪʃən/ *n* [C,U]

emanate from sth *phr v formal* to come from or out of something: *Wonderful smells were emanating from the kitchen.*

e·man·ci·pate /ɪˈmænsəpeɪt/ *v* [T] *formal* to give someone the political or legal rights that they did not have before: *Slaves were emancipated in 1834.* —**emancipation** /ɪˌmænsəˈpeɪʃən/ *n* [U]

e·man·ci·pat·ed /ɪˈmænsɪpeɪtɪd/ *adj* **1** socially, politically, or legally free **2** *old-fashioned* an emancipated woman is not influenced by old-fashioned ideas about how women should behave

e·mas·cu·late /ɪˈmæskjəleɪt/ *v* [T] **1** to make a man feel weaker and less male: *Some men feel emasculated if they work for a woman.* **2** to make someone or something weaker or less effective: *The bill has been emasculated by Congress.* **3** *medical* to remove all or part of a male's sex organs SYN **castrate** —**emasculation** /ɪˌmæskjəˈleɪʃən/ *n* [U]

em·balm /ɪmˈbɑːm $ -ˈbɑːm, -ˈbɑːlm/ *v* [T] to treat a dead body with chemicals, oils etc to prevent it from decaying —**embalmer** *n* [C]

em·bank·ment /ɪmˈbæŋkmənt/ *n* [C] a wide wall of earth or stones built to stop water from flooding an area, or to support a road or railway

em·bar·go¹ /ɪmˈbɑːɡəʊ $ -ˈbɑːrɡoʊ/ ●○○ *n* (*plural* **embargoes**) [C] an official order to stop trade with another country SYN **boycott**, **sanctions**: **[+on/against]** *an embargo on wheat exports* | *an embargo against the country* | **impose/lift an embargo** (=start or end one) *Many allies are pushing to lift the embargo.* | **trade/arms/oil etc embargo**

embargo² *v* [T] **1** to officially stop particular goods being traded with another country SYN **boycott**: *Several countries embargoed arms shipments to Yugoslavia.* **2** to stop information from being made public until a particular date or until permission is given SYN **censor**

em·bark /ɪmˈbɑːk $ -ɑːrk/ ●○○ *v* [I,T] to go onto a ship or a plane, or to put or take something onto a ship or plane OPP **disembark** —**embarkation** /ˌembɑːˈkeɪʃən $ -bɑːr-/ *n* [C,U]

embark on/upon sth *phr v* to start something, especially something new, difficult, or exciting: *He embarked on a new career as a teacher.*

em·bar·rass /ɪmˈbærəs/ ●●○ *v* [T]
1 to make someone feel ashamed, nervous, or uncomfortable, especially in front of other people: *He didn't want to embarrass her by asking questions.*
2 to do something that causes problems for a government, political organization, or politician, and makes them look bad: *The revelations in the press have embarrassed the government.*

em·bar·rassed /ɪmˈbærəst/ ●●● S2 *adj*
1 feeling uncomfortable or nervous and worrying about what people think of you, for example because you have made a silly mistake, or because you have to talk or sing in public: *Lori* ***gets embarrassed*** *if we ask her to sing.* | *He* ***looked embarrassed*** *when I asked him where he'd been.* | **very/deeply/highly/acutely embarrassed** *Michelle was* ***acutely embarrassed*** (=very embarrassed) *at having to ask for money.* | **embarrassed smile/laugh/grin etc** *Ken gave her an embarrassed grin.* | *There was an embarrassed silence.* | **embarrassed to do sth** *He was embarrassed to admit making a mistake.* | **[+about/at]** *I felt embarrassed about how untidy the house was.*
2 financially embarrassed having no money or having debts

THESAURUS

embarrassed feeling uncomfortable or nervous and worrying about what people think of you, for example because you have made a silly mistake, or because you have to talk or sing in public: *I was really embarrassed when I arrived at the party an hour early.* | *There's no need to be embarrassed - you've got a lovely voice.*
self-conscious embarrassed about your body or the way you look or talk: *Paul had always been self-conscious about his big feet.*
uncomfortable unable to relax because you are embarrassed and not sure what to say or do: *There was a long silence and everyone at the table looked uncomfortable.*
awkward /ˈɔːkwəd $ ˈɒːkwərd/ feeling embarrassed because you are in a situation in which it is difficult to behave naturally: *Teenagers often feel awkward in formal social situations.* | *There were some awkward moments when neither of us knew what to say to each other.*
sheepish slightly embarrassed because you know that you have done something silly or because you feel a little guilty: *Nigel came in late looking sheepish and apologetic.*
red-faced embarrassed or ashamed - used mainly in newspaper reports: *A judge was left red-faced when his mobile phone rang in court.*
mortified [not before noun] extremely embarrassed and ashamed because you realize that you have done something very silly or wrong: *He said he was mortified at the way his comments had been reported in the papers.*

em·bar·ras·sing /ɪmˈbærəsɪŋ/ ●●● S3 *adj* making you feel ashamed, nervous, or uncomfortable: *She asked a lot of* ***embarrassing questions***. | *an* ***embarrassing situation*** | **[+for]** *This incident is deeply embarrassing for the government.* —**embarrassingly** *adv*: *an embarrassingly poor performance*

em·bar·rass·ment /ɪmˈbærəsmənt/ ●●○ *n*
1 [U] the feeling you have when you are embarrassed: **[+at]** *She suffered extreme embarrassment at not knowing how to read.* | *He could not* ***hide*** *his* ***embarrassment*** *at his children's rudeness.* | **to sb's embarrassment** *To her embarrassment, she couldn't remember his name.*
2 [C] an event that causes a government, political organization etc problems, and makes it look bad: **[+to/for]** *The allegations have been an* ***acute embarrassment*** (=serious and severe embarrassment) *to the prime minister.* | *The scandal was a further* ***source of embarrassment*** *to the government.*
3 [C] someone who behaves in a way that makes you feel ashamed, nervous, or uncomfortable: **[+to]** *Tim's drinking has made him an embarrassment to the whole family.*
4 financial embarrassment debts or a lack of money that causes problems for you
5 an embarrassment of riches so many good things that it is difficult to decide which one you want

em·bas·sy /ˈembəsi/ ●●○ *n* (*plural* **embassies**) [C] a group of officials who represent their government in a foreign country, or the building they work in → **ambassador**: *the American Embassy in Paris*

em·bat·tled /ɪmˈbætld/ *adj formal* **1** [only before noun]

E

an embattled person, organization etc has many problems or difficulties: *The embattled president had to resign.* **2** surrounded by enemies, especially in war or fighting: *The embattled army finally surrendered.*

em·bed¹ /ɪm'bed/ ●○○ *v* (**embedded, embedding**)
1 [I,T] to put something firmly and deeply into something else, or to be put into something in this way: **be embedded in sth** *A piece of glass was embedded in her hand.*
2 [T] if ideas, attitudes, or feelings etc are embedded, you believe or feel them very strongly: *Feelings of guilt are **deeply embedded** in her personality.*
3 [T] to put something such as a GRAPHIC into a computer program or page on the Internet: *embedded hyperlinks*
GRAMMAR **Embed** is usually passive when used as a transitive verb.

em·bed² /'embed/ *n* [C] an EMBEDDED JOURNALIST

em,bedded 'journalist (*also* **em,bedded re'porter**) *n* [C] a JOURNALIST who stays with a unit of the ARMED FORCES during a war in order to report directly about the fighting

em·bel·lish /ɪm'belɪʃ/ *v* [T] **1** to make something more beautiful by adding decorations to it SYN **decorate**: **embellish sth with sth** *The dress was embellished with gold threads.* **2** to make a story or statement more interesting by adding details that are not true SYN **embroider**: *She gave an embellished account of what had happened.* —**embellishment** *n* [C,U]

em·ber /'embə $ -ər/ *n* [C usually plural] a piece of wood or coal that stays red and very hot after a fire has stopped burning: *glowing embers*

em·bez·zle /ɪm'bezəl/ *v* [I,T] to steal money from the place where you work: *Two managers were charged with embezzling $400,000.* —**embezzlement** *n* [U] —**embezzler** *n* [C] THESAURUS ▸ STEAL

em·bit·tered /ɪm'bɪtə $ -ər/ *adj* angry, sad, or full of hate because of bad or unfair things that have happened to you SYN **bitter**: *a sick, embittered, and lonely old man* —**embitter** *v* [T]

em·bla·zoned /ɪm'bleɪzənd/ *adj* [not before noun] if something is emblazoned with a name, design etc, it has that design on it where it can easily be seen: **[+with]** *a T-shirt emblazoned with a political slogan* | **[+on/across]** *The sponsor's name is emblazoned on the players' shirts.* —**emblazon** *v* [T]

em·blem /'embləm/ *n* [C] **1** a picture, shape, or object that is used to represent a country, organization etc → **logo**: **[+of]** *The **national emblem** of Canada is a maple leaf.* **2** something that represents an idea, principle, or situation SYN **symbol**: **[+of]** *Expensive cars are seen as an emblem of success.*

em·ble·mat·ic /,emblə'mætɪk◂/ *adj formal* seeming to represent or be a sign of something SYN **representative**: **[+of]** *The Vespa scooter became emblematic of sophisticated urban culture across Europe.*

em·bod·i·ment /ɪm'bɒdɪmənt $ ɪm'bɑː-/ *n* **the embodiment of sth** someone or something that represents or is very typical of an idea or quality SYN **epitome**: *He is the embodiment of evil.*

em·bod·y /ɪm'bɒdi $ ɪm'bɑːdi/ ●○○ *v* (**embodied, embodying, embodies**) [T]
1 to be a very good example of an idea or quality SYN **represent**: *She embodies everything I admire in a teacher.*
2 *formal* to include something: *The latest model embodies many new improvements.*

em·bold·en /ɪm'bəʊldən $ -'boʊl-/ *v* [T] *formal* to give someone more courage: *Emboldened by her smile, he asked her to dance.*

em·bo·lis·m /'embəlɪzəm/ *n* [C] *medical* something such as a hard mass of blood or a small amount of air that blocks a tube carrying blood through the body

em·bos·sed /ɪm'bɒs $ ɪm'bɑːs, -'bɒːs/ *adj* having a surface that is decorated with a raised pattern: **[+with]** *She was given a Bible embossed with her name.* | *embossed stationery* —**emboss** *v* [T]

em·brace¹ /ɪm'breɪs/ ●○○ *v*
1 [I,T] to put your arms around someone and hold them in a friendly or loving way SYN **hug**: *Jack warmly embraced his son.* | *Maggie and Laura embraced.* THESAURUS ▸ HUG
2 [T] *formal* to eagerly accept a new idea, opinion, religion etc: *We hope these regions will embrace democratic reforms.* | *Most West European countries have embraced the concept of high-speed rail networks with enthusiasm.*
3 [T] *formal* to include something as part of a subject, discussion etc: *This course embraces several different aspects of psychology.*

embrace² ●○○ *n* [C] the act of holding someone close to you, especially as a sign of love: **in an embrace** *They held each other in a tender embrace.*

em·broi·der /ɪm'brɔɪdə $ -ər/ *v* **1** [I,T] to decorate cloth by sewing a pattern, picture, or words on it with coloured threads: **embroider sth with sth** *The dress was embroidered with flowers.* | **embroider sth on sth** *A colourful design was embroidered on the sleeve of the shirt.* | *a richly embroidered jacket* **2** [T] to make a story or report of events more interesting or exciting by adding details that are not true SYN **embellish**

em·broi·der·y /ɪm'brɔɪdəri/ *n* (*plural* **embroideries**) **1** [C,U] a pattern sewn onto cloth, or cloth with patterns sewn onto it **2** [U] the act of sewing patterns onto cloth **3** [U] imaginary details that are added to make a story seem more interesting or exciting SYN **embellishment**

em·broil /ɪm'brɔɪl/ *v* [T] to involve someone or something in a difficult situation: **embroil sb/sth in sth** *I became **embroiled in** an **argument** with the taxi driver.*

em·bry·o /'embriəʊ $ -brioʊ/ *n* (*plural* **embryos**) [C] **1** an animal or human that has not yet been born, and has just begun to develop → **foetus 2 in embryo** at a very early stage of development: *The system already exists in embryo.*

em·bry·ol·o·gy /,embri'ɒlədʒi $ -'ɑːl-/ *n* [U] the scientific study of embryos —**embryologist** *n* [C]

em·bry·on·ic /,embri'ɒnɪk◂ $ -'ɑːn-/ *adj* **1** at a very early stage of development: *The plans are still only in embryonic form.* **2** relating to an EMBRYO: *embryonic development* | *embryonic cells*

em·cee /,em 'siː/ *n* [C] *AmE* (***master of ceremonies***) someone who introduces the performers on a television or radio programme or at a social event: *a game show emcee* —**emcee** *v* [I,T]

e·mend /ɪ'mend/ *v* [T] *formal* to remove the mistakes from something that has been written → **amend** —**emendation** /,iːmen'deɪʃən/ *n* [C,U]

em·e·rald /'emərəld/ *n* **1** [C] a valuable bright green stone that is often used in jewellery **2** [U] a bright green colour —**emerald** *adj*

e·merge /ɪ'mɜːdʒ $ -ɜːrdʒ/ ●●○ W2 AWL *v* [I]
1 to appear or come out from somewhere: *The flowers emerge in the spring.* | **[+from]** *The sun emerged from behind the clouds.*
2 if facts emerge, they become known after being hidden or secret → **come out**: *Eventually the **truth emerged**.* | **it emerges that** *Later it emerged that the judge had employed an illegal immigrant.*
3 to come out of a difficult experience: **[+from]** *She emerged from the divorce a stronger person.*
4 to begin to be known or noticed: *a religious sect that emerged in the 1830s* | **[+as]** *Local government has recently emerged as a major issue.*

e·mer·gence /ɪ'mɜːdʒəns $ -ɜːr-/ ●○○ AWL *n* [U]
1 when something begins to be known or noticed: **[+of]** *the emergence of Japan as a world leader*
2 when someone or something comes out of a difficult experience: **[+from]** *the company's emergence from bankruptcy*

e·mer·gen·cy /ɪ'mɜːdʒənsi $ -ɜːr-/ ●●● S3 W3 *n* (*plural* **emergencies**) [C,U] an unexpected and dangerous situation that must be dealt with immediately → **crisis**: *Lifeguards are trained to **deal with emergencies**.* | **in an emergency** *The staff need to know what to do in an emergency.* | ***In case of emergency**, press the alarm button.* |

emergency exit/supplies etc (=used in an emergency) *$500,000 of* ***emergency aid*** *for the victims of the earthquake | The plane had to make an* ***emergency landing****. | The government called an emergency meeting to discuss the crisis.* → STATE OF EMERGENCY

e'mergency ˌbrake *n* [C] *AmE* a piece of equipment in a car that you pull up with your hand to stop the car from moving SYN **handbrake** → see picture at CAR

e'mergency ˌcord *n* [C] *AmE* a chain that a passenger pulls to stop a train in an emergency SYN **communication cord** *BrE*

e'mergency ˌroom *n* [C] *AmE* a part of a hospital that immediately helps people who have been hurt in an accident or who are extremely ill SYN **ER**, **casualty** *BrE*

e'mergency ˌservices *n* [plural] *BrE* official organizations such as the police or the fire service, that deal with crime, fires, and injuries

e·mer·gent /ɪ'mɜːdʒənt $ -ɜːr-/ AWL *adj* [only before noun] in the early stages of existence or development → **developing**: *the emergent nations of the world*

e·mer·ging /ɪ'mɜːdʒɪŋ $ -ɜːr-/ AWL *adj* [only before noun] in an early state of development: *the country's emerging oil industry*

e·mer·i·tus /ɪ'merɪtəs/ *adj* **emeritus professor/director etc** *or* **professor/director etc emeritus** a PROFESSOR, director etc who is no longer working but has kept his or her previous job title as an honour

em·e·ry /'eməri/ *n* [U] a very hard mineral that is used for polishing things and making them smooth

'emery board *n* [C] a narrow piece of stiff paper with emery on it, used for shaping your nails

e·met·ic /ɪ'metɪk/ *n* [C] *medical* something that you eat or drink in order to make yourself VOMIT (=bring up food from your stomach) —**emetic** *adj*

em·i·grant /'emɪgrənt/ *n* [C] someone who leaves their own country to live in another → **immigrant**

em·i·grate /'emɪgreɪt/ ●○○ *v* [I] to leave your own country in order to live in another country → **immigrate**: **[+to/from]** *He emigrated to Australia as a young man.* —**emigration** /ˌemɪ'greɪʃən/ *n* [C,U]

ém·i·gré /'eməgreɪ/ *n* [C] *formal* someone who leaves their own country to live in another, usually for political reasons: *Russian émigrés living in Paris*

em·i·nence /'emɪnəns/ *n* **1** [U] the quality of being famous and important: **of great/such etc eminence** *a scientist of great eminence* **2 Your/His Eminence** a title used when talking to or about a CARDINAL (=priest of high rank in the Roman Catholic Church) **3** [C] *literary* a hill or area of high ground

em·i·nence grise /ˌemɪnɒns 'griːz $ -nɑːns-/ *n* (*plural* **eminences grises**) [C] someone who has unofficial power, often secretly, through someone else: *Borusa had no wish to become president, instead preferring to operate as an eminence grise behind the scenes.*

em·i·nent /'emɪnənt/ ●○○ *adj* an eminent person is famous, important, and respected: *an eminent lawyer*

ˌeminent do'main *n* [U] *law* the right of the US government to take private land for public use

em·i·nent·ly /'emɪnəntli/ *adv formal* completely and without a doubt - use this to show approval SYN **highly**: *Woods is* ***eminently suitable*** *for the job.*

e·mir /e'mɪə $ e'mɪr/ *n* [C] a Muslim ruler, especially in the Middle East and parts of Africa → **sultan**: *the Emir of Kuwait*

e·mir·ate /'emɪrət $ ɪ'mɪrət/ *n* [C] the country ruled by an emir, or his position

em·is·sa·ry /'eməsəri $ -seri/ *n* (*plural* **emissaries**) [C] someone who is sent with an official message or to do official work SYN **envoy**: *Japan is sending two emissaries to Washington to discuss trade issues.*

e·mis·sion /ɪ'mɪʃən/ ●○○ *n*
1 [C usually plural] a gas or other substance that is sent into the air: *Britain agreed to cut emissions of nitrogen oxide from power stations.*
2 [U] the act of sending out light, heat, gas etc

e'mission ˌcredit *n* [C usually plural] official permission to produce a particular amount of a substance that can harm the environment, which is given to a company by a government or organization or bought by a company

e'missions ˌtrading *n* [U] the practice of buying or selling emission credits

e·mit /ɪ'mɪt/ ●○○ *v* (**emitted**, **emitting**) [T] to send out gas, heat, light, sound etc: *The kettle emitted a shrill whistle.*

e·mi·tter /ɪ'mɪtə $ -ər/ *n* [C] a person, organization, or country that produces a GREENHOUSE GAS such as CARBON DIOXIDE or a substance that POLLUTEs the environment: *Which country is the biggest emitter of greenhouse gases?*

Em·my /'emi/ (*also* **'Emmy Aˌward**) *n* [C] a US prize given each year for special achievements in television. There are Emmys for actors, writers, directors etc, and the prize is a small STATUE. → **OSCAR**

e·mo /'iːməʊ $ 'iːmoʊ/ *n* [U] a type of PUNK music whose song LYRICS (=words) are full of emotion

e·mo·ji /ɪ'məʊdʒi $ ɪ'moʊ-/ *n* [C] an ICON, similar to an EMOTICON, used in electronic messages and on websites, originally in Japan

e·mol·li·ent /ɪ'mɒliənt $ ɪ'mɑː-/ *adj formal* **1** making something, especially your skin, softer and smoother: *Almond oil is renowned for its soothing, emollient properties.* **2** making someone feel calmer when they have been angry: *an emollient reply* —**emollient** *n* [C]

e·mol·u·ment /ɪ'mɒljəmənt $ ɪ'mɑːl-/ *n* [C,U] *formal* money or another form of payment for work you have done SYN **remuneration**

e-mon·ey /'iː mʌni/ (*also* **e-cash**) *n* [U] ELECTRONIC MONEY

e·mote /ɪ'məʊt $ ɪ'moʊt/ *v* [I] to clearly show emotion, especially when you are acting: *Siskind encourages the children to emote to the music as they dance.*

e·mo·ti·con /ɪ'məʊtɪkɒn $ ɪ'moʊtɪkɑːn/ *n* [C] a special sign that is used to show an emotion in EMAIL and on the Internet, often by making a picture. For example, the emoticon :-) looks like a smiling face and means that you have made a joke.

e·mo·tion /ɪ'məʊʃən $ ɪ'moʊ-/ ●●● W3 *n* [C,U] a strong human feeling such as love, hate, or anger: *Her voice was* ***full of emotion****.* | **conflicting/mixed emotions** *Sara listened with mixed emotions. | She was good at* ***hiding*** *her* ***emotions****. | Kim received the news without showing any visible* ***sign of emotion****.*

e·mo·tion·al /ɪ'məʊʃənəl $ ɪ'moʊ-/ ●●● S3 W3 *adj*
1 [only before noun] relating to your feelings or how you control them: *She provided* ***emotional support*** *at a very distressing time for me. | Ann suffered from depression and a number of other* ***emotional problems****. | the physical and* ***emotional state*** *of the patient*
2 making people have strong feelings: *Abortion is a very* ***emotional issue****. | The funeral was a very* ***emotional experience*** *for all of us.*
3 having strong feelings and showing them to other people, especially by crying: **get/become emotional** *He became very emotional when we had to leave.*
4 influenced by what you feel, rather than what you know: *an* ***emotional response*** *to the problem* —**emotionally** *adv*: *Nursing is an emotionally and physically demanding job.*

e·mo·tion·al·is·m /ɪ'məʊʃənəlɪzəm $ ɪ'moʊ-/ *n* [U] a tendency to show or feel too much emotion

e·mo·tive /ɪ'məʊtɪv $ ɪ'moʊ-/ *adj* making people have strong feelings SYN **emotional**: **emotive issue/subject/word etc** *Child abuse is an emotive subject.* —**emotively** *adv*

em·pan·el /ɪm'pænl/ (**empanelled**, **empanelling** *BrE*, **empaneled**, **empaneling** *AmE*) *v* [T] to choose the members of a JURY in a court of law

em·pa·thize (*also* **-ise** *BrE*) /'empəθaɪz/ *v* [I] to be able to understand someone else's feelings, problems etc, especially because you have had similar experiences → **sympathize**: **[+with]** *My mother died last year so I can really empathize with what he's going through.*

em·pa·thy /ˈempəθi/ ●○○ *n* [U] the ability to understand other people's feelings and problems → **sympathy**: **[+with/for]** *She had great empathy with people.* —**empathetic** /ˌempəˈθetɪk◂/ (*also* **empathic** /emˈpæθɪk/) *adj*

em·pe·ror /ˈempərə $ -ər/ ●●○ *n* [C] the man who is the ruler of an EMPIRE

ˌemperor's new ˈclothes, the this expression is often used to describe a situation in which people are afraid to criticize something because everyone else seems to think it is good or important. It is the title of a FAIRY TALE by Hans Christian Andersen about an EMPEROR who pays a lot of money for some new magic clothes which can only be seen by wise people. The clothes do not really exist, but the emperor does not admit he cannot see them, because he does not want to seem stupid.

em·pha·sis /ˈemfəsɪs/ ●●○ W2 AWL *n* (*plural* **emphases** /-siːz/) [C,U]
1 special attention or importance: **[+on]** *In Japan there is a lot of emphasis on politeness.* | **put/place emphasis on sth** *The course places emphasis on practical work.* | *a* ***change of emphasis*** *in government policy*
2 special importance that is given to a word or phrase by saying it louder or higher, or by printing it in a special way → **stress**: **[+on]** *The emphasis should be on the first syllable.* | *'And I can assure you,' she* ***said with emphasis****, 'that he is innocent.'*

em·pha·size (*also* **-ise** *BrE*) /ˈemfəsaɪz/ ●●○ W2 AWL *v* [T]
1 to say something in a strong way SYN **stress**: *The report* ***emphasizes*** *the* ***importance*** *of improving safety standards.* | *Logan made a speech* ***emphasizing*** *the* ***need*** *for more volunteers.* | **emphasize that/how** *The prime minister emphasized that there are no plans to raise taxes.*
2 to say a word or phrase louder or higher than others to give it more importance SYN **stress**
3 to make something more noticeable SYN **accentuate**: *The dress emphasized the shape of her body.*

THESAURUS

emphasize to say strongly or show clearly that a fact, idea etc is especially important: *Our company emphasizes the need for good communication between staff.*
stress to emphasize something when you are talking about a subject: *Most schools stress the importance of parental involvement in their child's learning.* | *He stressed the need for parents to listen to their children.*
highlight to show that something is important, so that people will pay special attention to it: *This case highlights the need for tougher laws on gun ownership.* | *The report highlights the decline in the numbers of native plants and insects.*
underline/underscore to help to show clearly that a fact is true, especially a fact that is already known: *These attacks underline the fact that the security situation here remains fragile.*
accentuate to show something clearly and make it easier to notice: *The recent economic crisis has accentuated the gap between the rich and the poor.*
overemphasize to emphasize something too much: *The relation between food and health is often overemphasized in my view.*
play up to emphasize something and make it seem more important than it really is, especially to get advantages for yourself: *The story has been played up by the media.* | *The Labour party had a great time playing up the Conservatives' problems.*

em·phat·ic /ɪmˈfætɪk/ AWL *adj* **1** expressing an opinion, idea etc in a clear, strong way to show its importance: *an emphatic denial* | **emphatic that** *Wilde was emphatic that the event should go ahead.* | **[+about]** *He was pretty emphatic about me leaving.* **2 emphatic win/victory/defeat** a win etc in which one team or player wins by a large amount —**emphatically** /-kli/ *adv*

em·phy·se·ma /ˌemfəˈsiːmə/ *n* [U] *medical* a serious disease that affects the lungs, making it difficult to breathe

em·pire /ˈempaɪə $ -paɪr/ ●●○ W3 *n* [C]
1 a group of countries that are all controlled by one ruler or government: *the Roman empire*
2 a group of organizations controlled by one person: *a* ***business empire***

ˈempire-ˌbuilding *n* [U] attempts to get more power within the organization you work for

em·pir·i·cal /ɪmˈpɪrɪkəl/ ●○○ AWL *adj* [only before noun] based on scientific testing or practical experience, not on ideas OPP **theoretical**, **hypothetical**: ***empirical evidence*** —**empirically** /-kli/ *adv*

em·pir·i·cis·m /ɪmˈpɪrɪsɪzəm/ AWL *n* [U] the belief in basing your ideas on practical experience —**empiricist** *n* [C]

em·place·ment /ɪmˈpleɪsmənt/ *n* [C] a place where a large gun is put and fired: *a gun emplacement*

em·ploy¹ /ɪmˈplɔɪ/ ●●● S3 W2 *v* [T]
1 to pay someone to work for you: *The factory employs over 2,000 people.* | **employ sb as sth** *Kelly is employed as a mechanic.* | **employ sb to do sth** *We have been employed to look at ways of reducing waste.*

REGISTER
In everyday English, people usually say **give** someone a **job** rather than **employ** someone, and **have a job** rather than **be employed**: *They* ***gave him a job*** *delivering furniture.* | *He* ***has a job*** *at the factory.*

2 to use a particular object, method, skill etc in order to achieve something: **employ a method/technique/tactic etc** *The report examines teaching methods employed in the classroom.* **THESAURUS** ▸ USE

REGISTER
In everyday English, people usually say **use** a method rather than **employ** a method.

3 *formal* to spend your time doing a particular thing: **be employed in (doing) sth** *Her days are employed in gardening and voluntary work.*

employ² *n* **in sb's employ** *old-fashioned* working for someone: *He had a number of servants in his employ.*

em·ploy·a·ble /ɪmˈplɔɪəbəl/ *adj* having skills or qualities that are necessary to get a job: *The training scheme aims to make people more employable.*

em·ploy·ee /ɪmˈplɔɪ-iː, ˌemplɔɪˈiː/ ●●● S2 W2 *n* [C] someone who is paid to work for someone else SYN **worker**: *a government employee*

em·ploy·er /ɪmˈplɔɪə $ -ər/ ●●● S2 W2 *n* [C] a person, company, or organization that employs people: *The shoe factory is the largest employer in this area.*

em·ploy·ment /ɪmˈplɔɪmənt/ ●●● S2 W1 *n* [U]
1 the condition of having a paid job: *She was offered employment in the sales office.* | *terms and conditions of employment* | **employment opportunities/prospects** *The employment prospects for science graduates are excellent.* | *Steve's still looking for* ***full-time employment***. | *the needs of women who combine* ***paid employment*** *and care for their families* | **in employment** *21.7% of all those in employment were in part-time jobs.* **THESAURUS** ▸ JOB
2 the act of paying someone to work for you: **[+of]** *Mexican law prohibits the employment of children under 14.*
3 the number of people who have jobs OPP **unemployment**: *Nationwide employment now stands at 95%.* | **full employment** (=a situation in which everyone has a job) *Many economists consider full employment an unrealistic goal.*

4 *formal* the use of a particular object, method, skill etc to achieve something: **[+of]** *Was the employment of force justified?*

em'ployment ˌagency *n* [C] a business that makes money by finding jobs for people → **job centre**

em·po·ri·um /ɪm'pɔːriəm/ *n* (*plural* **emporiums** *or* **emporia** /-riə/) [C] *old-fashioned* a large shop

em·pow·er /ɪm'paʊə $ -'paʊr/ ●○○ *v* [T]
1 to give someone more control over their own life or situation: *The Voting Rights Act was needed to empower minority groups.*
2 *formal* to give a person or organization the legal right to do something: **be empowered to do sth** *The president is empowered to appoint judges to the Supreme Court.* —**empowerment** *n* [U]

em·press /'emprɪs/ *n* [C] a female ruler of an EMPIRE, or the wife of an EMPEROR

emp·ties /'emptiz/ *n* [plural] bottles or glasses that are empty: *The barman collected the empties.*

emp·ti·ness /'emptinəs/ *n* [U] **1** a feeling of great sadness and loneliness: *She felt an emptiness in her heart when he left.* **2** when there is nothing or nobody in a place: **[+of]** *the silence and emptiness of the desert*

emp·ty¹ /'empti/ ●●● S2 W2 *adj* (*comparative* **emptier**, *superlative* **emptiest**)
1 CONTAINER having nothing inside: *an empty box | an empty bottle | an* ***empty space*** *behind the desk | The fuel tank's almost empty.*
2 PLACE an empty place does not have any people in it: *I hate coming home to an empty house. | The hall was* ***half-empty****. | The streets were empty. | The building* ***stood empty*** *for several years.*
3 NOT USED not being used by anyone: *I spotted an empty table in the corner. | He put his feet on an empty chair.*
4 PERSON/LIFE unhappy because nothing in your life seems interesting or important: *The divorce left him* ***feeling empty*** *and bitter. | Her life felt empty and meaningless.*
5 empty of sth not containing a particular type of thing, or not having a particular quality: *The beach was almost empty of people.*
6 empty words/gestures/promises etc words etc that are not sincere, or have no effect: *His repeated promises to pay them back were just empty words.*
7 do sth on an empty stomach to do something without having eaten any food first: *I can't work properly on an empty stomach.*
8 empty nest (*also* **empty nest syndrome**) a situation in which parents become sad because their children have grown up and moved out of their house
9 empty suit *especially AmE* a politician or manager who does not achieve much or does not have much ability
10 be running on empty to continue doing something even though you no longer have supplies of something you need in order to do it properly: *With the country running on empty, the president has no hope of winning the election.*
—**emptily** *adv*

THESAURUS

WITH NOTHING IN IT OR ON IT

empty used about something that has nothing inside: *an empty can of hair spray | The fridge is almost empty.*
blank used about a computer screen or a piece of paper that has no writing or pictures on it, or a CD, DVD etc with nothing recorded on it: *a blank sheet of paper | He stared at the blank screen for a few minutes. | a blank tape*
bare used about a room or cupboard that has very little in it: *His room was bare except for a bed and a wardrobe.*
hollow used about something that has an empty space inside: *a hollow tree | The suitcase had a hollow bottom.*

WITH NO PEOPLE

empty used about a place that has no one in it or no one using it: *There were no lights on and the house looked empty. | the empty streets*
free used about a seat, space, or room that is available to use because no one else is using it: *Is this seat free? | There are never any parking spaces free at this time of day.*
vacant used about a room or building that is available for people to pay to use: *a vacant apartment | The next guesthouse we tried had a couple of rooms vacant.*
deserted used about a place that is quiet because there is no one there, or because the people who used to be there have left: *a deserted village | It was three o'clock in the morning and the streets were deserted.*
uninhabited /ˌʌnɪn'hæbətəd◂/ used about a place that has no people living in it, especially permanently: *an uninhabited island*
unoccupied /ʌn'ɒkjəpaɪd $ -'ɑːk-/ *especially written* used about a house, room, or office that no one is living in or using at the moment: *unoccupied buildings | Burglaries frequently happen when people are on holiday and their house is unoccupied.*

empty² ●●○ *v* (**emptied**, **emptying**, **empties**)
1 (*also* **empty out**) [T] to remove everything that is inside something: *Did you empty the dishwasher?* | **empty sth onto/into sth** *Elinor emptied the contents of the envelope onto the table. | He emptied out the ashtray. | Ruth* ***emptied her glass*** (=drank all the liquid left in it) *in one gulp.*
2 [I] if a place empties, everyone leaves it: *The stores were closing, and the streets began to empty.*
empty into sth *phr v* if a river empties into a larger area of water, it flows into it: *The Mississippi River empties into the Gulf of Mexico.*

ˌempty-'handed *adj* without getting what you hoped or expected to get: **return/come back etc empty-handed** *I spent all morning looking for a suitable present, but came home empty-handed.*

ˌempty-'headed *adj informal* silly and not intelligent

EMS /ˌiː em 'es/ *n* [U] (***enhanced messaging service***) a service for sending messages, images etc between MOBILE PHONES

e·mu /'iːmjuː/ *n* (*plural* **emus** *or* **emu**) [C] a large Australian bird that can run very fast but cannot fly

em·u·late /'emjəleɪt/ ●○○ *v* [T] to do something or behave in the same way as someone else, especially because you admire them SYN **imitate**: *He hoped to* ***emulate*** *the* ***success*** *of Wilder.* —**emulation** /ˌemjə'leɪʃən/ *n* [U]

e·mul·si·fi·er /ɪ'mʌlsəfaɪə $ -ər/ *n* [C] a substance that is added, especially to food, to prevent liquids and solids from separating

e·mul·si·fy /ɪ'mʌlsɪfaɪ/ *v* (**emulsified**, **emulsifying**, **emulsifies**) [I,T] to combine to become a smooth mixture, or to make two liquids do this

e·mul·sion /ɪ'mʌlʃən/ *n* [C,U] **1** a mixture of liquids that do not completely combine, such as oil and water **2** *technical* the substance on the surface of photographic film or paper that makes it react to light **3** *BrE* (*also* **emulsion paint**) a type of paint used inside buildings on walls or ceilings that is not shiny when it dries → **gloss**, **eggshell**

en- /ɪn, en/ *prefix* [in verbs] **1** to make someone or something be in a particular state or have a particular quality: *enlarge* (=make something bigger) | *endanger* (=put someone in danger) **2** to go completely around something, or include all of it: *encircle* (=surround everything)

-en /ən/ *suffix* **1** [in adjectives] made of a particular material or substance: *a golden crown | wooden seats* **2** [in verbs] to make something have a particular quality: *darken* (=make or become dark) | *strengthen* (=make or become stronger)

E

en·a·ble /ɪˈneɪbəl/ ●●● S3 W1 AWL *v* [T] to make it possible for someone to do something, or for something to happen: **enable sb/sth to do sth** *The loan enabled Jan to buy the house.* | *There are plans to enlarge the runway to enable jumbo jets to land.* —**enabler** *n* [C]

-enabled /ɪneɪbəld/ *suffix* [in adjectives] **Internet-enabled/Java-enabled etc** a computer PROGRAM that is Internet-enabled, Java-enabled etc can be used with that program or includes it as one of its features: *Find out more about our free Internet-enabled software.*

en·a·bling /ɪˈneɪblɪŋ/ AWL *adj* [only before noun] *law* an enabling law is one that makes something possible or gives someone special legal powers

en·act /ɪˈnækt/ *v* [T] **1** *formal* to act in a play, story etc: *a drama enacted on a darkened stage* **2** *law* to make a proposal into a law: *Congress refused to enact the bill.* —**enactment** *n* [C,U]

e·nam·el[1] /ɪˈnæməl/ *n* [U] **1** a hard shiny substance that is put onto metal, clay etc for decoration or protection **2** the hard smooth outer surface of your teeth **3** a type of paint that produces a shiny surface when it is dry —**enamel** *adj*

enamel[2] *v* (**enamelled**, **enamelling** *BrE*, **enameled**, **enameling** *AmE*) [T] to cover or decorate with enamel

en·am·oured *BrE*, **enamored** *AmE* /ɪˈnæməd $ -ərd/ *adj* **1** [not before noun] liking something very much: **[+of/with]** *You don't seem very enamoured with your job.* **2** *formal* in love with someone: **[+of/with]** *He was greatly enamoured of Elizabeth.*

en bloc /ɒn ˈblɒk $ ɑːn ˈblɑːk/ *adv* all together as a single unit, rather than separately: *You cannot dismiss these stories en bloc.*

en·camp /ɪnˈkæmp/ *v* [I,T] *formal* to make a camp or put people, especially soldiers, in a camp: *The army was encamped near Damascus.*

en·camp·ment /ɪnˈkæmpmənt/ *n* [C] a large temporary camp, especially of soldiers: *a military encampment*

en·cap·su·late /ɪnˈkæpsjəleɪt $ -sə-/ *v* [T] **1** to express or show something in a short way SYN **sum up**: *The words of the song neatly encapsulate the mood of the country at that time.* | **encapsulate sth in sth** *Her whole philosophy can be encapsulated in this one sentence.* **2** to completely cover something with something else, especially in order to prevent a substance getting out: **encapsulate sth in sth** *The leaking fuel rods will be encapsulated in lead.* —**encapsulation** /ɪnˌkæpsjəˈleɪʃən $ -sə-/ *n* [C,U]

en·case /ɪnˈkeɪs/ *v* [T] to cover or surround something completely: **encase sth in sth** *His broken leg was encased in plaster.*

-ence /əns/ *suffix* [in nouns] another form of the suffix -ANCE: *existence* | *occurrence*

en·ceph·a·li·tis /ɪnˌkefəˈlaɪtɪs $ -ˌsef-/ *n* [U] *medical* swelling of the brain

en·chant /ɪnˈtʃɑːnt $ ɪnˈtʃænt/ *v* [T] **1** *formal* if something that you see or hear enchants you, you like it very much: *I was enchanted by the way she smiled.* | *The garden enchanted her.* **2** *literary* to use magic on something or someone

en·chant·ed /ɪnˈtʃɑːntɪd $ ɪnˈtʃæn-/ *adj* **1** someone who is enchanted with someone or something likes them very much: **[+with]** *She was enchanted with the flowers you sent her.* **2** an enchanted object or place has been changed by magic so that it has special powers → **bewitched**: *an enchanted castle*

en·chant·er /ɪnˈtʃɑːntə $ ɪnˈtʃæntər/ *n* [C] *literary* someone who uses magic on people and things → **wizard**

en·chant·ing /ɪnˈtʃɑːntɪŋ $ ɪnˈtʃæn-/ *adj* very pleasant or attractive: *an enchanting place* | *an enchanting story* | *The child* ***looked enchanting*** *in a pale blue dress.* —**enchantingly** *adv*

en·chant·ment /ɪnˈtʃɑːntmənt $ ɪnˈtʃænt-/ *n* **1** [U] the quality of being very pleasant or attractive: *the enchantment of poetry* **2** [C,U] *literary* a change caused by magic, or the state of being changed by magic

en·chant·ress /ɪnˈtʃɑːntrɪs $ ɪnˈtʃæn-/ *n* [C] *literary* **1** a woman who uses magic on people and things → **witch** **2** a woman who men think is very attractive and interesting

en·chi·la·da /ˌentʃəˈlɑːdə/ *n* **1** [C] a Mexican food consisting of a TORTILLA (=flat piece of bread) that is rolled up and filled with meat or cheese, and covered with a spicy sauce **2 the big enchilada** *AmE informal* something that is the most important or biggest of its type: *We're aiming our products at the big enchilada – the home computer market.* **3 the whole enchilada** *AmE informal* all of something: *Come on. Let's hear it – the whole enchilada.*

en·cir·cle /ɪnˈsɜːkəl $ -ɜːr-/ *v* [T] to surround someone or something completely: *The island was encircled by a dusty road.* —**encirclement** *n* [U]

en·clave /ˈenkleɪv, ˈeŋ-/ *n* [C] a small area that is within a larger area where people of a different kind or nationality live: *the former Portuguese enclave of East Timor*

en·close /ɪnˈkləʊz $ -ˈkloʊz/ ●●○ *v* [T]
1 to put something inside an envelope as well as a letter: *Please enclose a cheque with your order.* | **please find enclosed** (=used in business letters to say that you are sending something with a letter) *Please find enclosed an agenda for the meeting.*
2 to surround something, especially with a fence or wall, in order to make it separate: *The pool area is enclosed by a six-foot wall.* | *an enclosed area* GRAMMAR **Enclose** is usually passive in this meaning.

en·clo·sure /ɪnˈkləʊʒə $ -ˈkloʊʒər/ *n* **1** [C] an area surrounded by a wall or fence, and used for a particular purpose: *the bear enclosure at the zoo* **2** [U] the act of making an area separate by putting a wall or fence around it: *the enclosure of arable land for pasture* **3** [C] something that is put inside an envelope with a letter

en·code /ɪnˈkəʊd $ -ˈkoʊd/ *v* [T] to put a message or other information into CODE OPP **decode**, **decipher**

en·co·mi·um /ɪnˈkəʊmiəm $ -ˈkoʊ-/ *n* (*plural* **encomiums** *or* **encomia** /-miə/) [C] *formal* the expression of a lot of praise

en·com·pass /ɪnˈkʌmpəs/ ●○○ *v* [T] *formal*
1 to include a wide range of ideas, subjects, etc: *The study encompasses the social, political, and economic aspects of the situation.*
2 to completely cover or surround something: *The houses encompassed about 100 square metres.*

en·core[1] /ˈɒŋkɔː $ ˈɑːŋkɔːr/ *n* [C] an additional or repeated part of a performance, especially a musical one: *The band came back onstage for an encore.*

encore[2] *interjection* said when you have enjoyed a musical performance very much and want the performer to sing or play more

en·coun·ter[1] /ɪnˈkaʊntə $ -ər/ ●●○ W3 AWL *v* [T]
1 to experience something, especially problems or opposition: **encounter problems/difficulties** *They encountered serious problems when two members of the expedition were injured.* | **encounter opposition/resistance** *The government has encountered strong opposition to its plans to raise income tax.* | *The doctor had encountered several similar cases in the past.*

> **REGISTER**
> In everyday English, people usually say **come across problems/difficulties** rather than **encounter problems/difficulties** and **come up against opposition/resistance** rather than **encounter opposition/resistance**: *Did you* ***come across*** *any problems?* | *We* ***came up against*** *quite a lot of opposition from local people.*

2 *formal* to meet someone without planning to: *I first encountered him when studying at Cambridge.*

encounter[2] ●○○ AWL *n* [C]
1 an occasion when you meet someone, or do something with someone you do not know: *She didn't remember our encounter last summer.* | **[+with]** *His* ***first encounter*** *with Wilson was back in 1989.* | *Bernstein began training the*

young musician after a ***chance encounter*** *at a concert* (=a meeting that happened by chance). | *casual* ***sexual encounters*** (=occasions when people have sex) | **[+between]** *hostile encounters between supporters of rival football teams*
2 an occasion when you meet or experience something: **[+with]** *a child's first encounter with books* | *a* ***close encounter*** *with a snake* (=a frightening situation in which you get too close to something)

en·cour·age /ɪnˈkʌrɪdʒ $ ɪnˈkɜːr-/ ●●● S2 W1 *v* [T]
1 to give someone the courage or confidence to do something OPP **discourage**: *I want to thank everyone who has encouraged and supported me.* | **encourage sb to do sth** *Cooder was encouraged to begin playing the guitar by his father.* | **encourage sb in sth** *Fleur encouraged Dana in her ambition to become a model.*
2 to persuade someone to do something OPP **discourage**: *Cantor didn't mind if they worked late; in fact, he* ***actively encouraged*** *it.* | **encourage sb to do sth** *A 10p rise in cigarette prices is not enough to encourage smokers to stop.*
THESAURUS ▸ PERSUADE
3 to make something more likely to exist, happen, or develop: *Violent TV programmes encourage anti-social behaviour.* —**encouraged** *adj* [not before noun]: *She felt encouraged by the many letters of support.*

en·cour·age·ment /ɪnˈkʌrɪdʒmənt $ ɪnˈkɜː-/ ●●○ *n* [U] when you encourage someone or something, or the things that encourage them OPP **discouragement**: *With encouragement, Sally is starting to play with the other children.* | ***words of encouragement*** | **encouragement to do sth** *She* ***needed no encouragement*** *to continue* (=did not need any encouragement).

en·cour·ag·ing /ɪnˈkʌrədʒɪŋ $ ɪnˈkɜːr-/ ●●○ S3 *adj* giving you hope and confidence SYN **reassuring** OPP **discouraging**: *The* ***encouraging news*** *is that typhoid is on the decrease.* | *The* ***signs*** *are* ***encouraging*** *— but there's a long way to go.* —**encouragingly** *adv*

en·croach /ɪnˈkrəʊtʃ $ -ˈkroʊtʃ/ *v* [I always + adv/prep]
1 to gradually take more of someone's time, possessions, rights etc than you should: **[+on/upon]** *Bureaucratic power has encroached upon the freedom of the individual.*
2 to gradually cover more and more land: **[+into]** *The fighting encroached further east.* —**encroachment** *n* [C,U]: *foreign encroachment*

en·crust·ed /ɪnˈkrʌstɪd/ *adj* covered with a hard layer of something: **[+with/in]** *a gold crown encrusted with diamonds* | **mud-encrusted/jewel-encrusted etc** —**encrustation** /ˌɪnkrʌˈsteɪʃən/ *n* [C,U]

en·crypt /ɪnˈkrɪpt/ *v* [T] to protect information by putting it into a special CODE that only some people can read, especially information that is on a computer → **decrypt** —**encryption** /ɪnˈkrɪpʃən/ *n* [U]: *secure encryption of data* —**encrypted** *adj*: *files stored in encrypted form*

en·cum·ber /ɪnˈkʌmbə $ -ər/ *v* [T] *formal* to make it difficult for you to do something or for something to happen SYN **burden**: *He died in 1874,* ***heavily encumbered*** *by debt.* | **be encumbered with sth** *The whole process was encumbered with bureaucracy.* —**encumbrance** *n* [C]

en·cyc·li·cal /ɪnˈsɪklɪkəl/ *n* [C] a letter sent by the Pope to all Roman Catholic BISHOPS

en·cy·clo·pe·di·a (*also* **encyclopaedia** *BrE*) /ɪnˌsaɪkləˈpiːdiə/ ●○○ *n* [C] a book or CD, or a set of these, containing facts about many different subjects, or containing detailed facts about one subject: *the Encyclopedia of Music*

en·cy·clo·pe·dic (*also* **encyclopaedic** *BrE*) /ɪnˌsaɪkləˈpiːdɪk◂/ *adj* having a lot of knowledge or information about a particular subject: *an* ***encyclopedic knowledge*** *of medieval literature*

end¹ /end/ ●●● S1 W1 *n*
1 LAST PART [singular] the last part of a period of time, event, activity, or story OPP **beginning**, **start**: **[+of]** *Costs are expected to double by the end of 2012.* | **at the end** *What would she find at the end of her journey?* | *Hooker's death marked* ***the end of an era.*** | *I played the tape* ***from beginning to end.***
2 FINISHED [singular] a situation in which something is finished or no longer exists: **put/bring an end to sth** *It's hoped the talks may bring an end to the violence.* | **call for/demand an end to sth** *The EU is demanding an end to the ivory trade.* | *At last it seemed the war might be* ***coming to an end.*** | *The spacecraft is nearing the* ***end of*** *its useful* ***life.*** | **be at an end** *He rose to indicate that the conversation was at an end.* | *Well, I hope that's* ***the end of the matter.*** | *Another year has passed, with* ***no end in sight*** *to the suffering.*
3 FURTHEST PART [C] the part of a place or object that is furthest from its beginning or centre: **[+of]** *We sat at* ***opposite ends*** *of the table.* | *He wore spectacles perched on* ***the very end*** *of his nose.* | *The end of the pencil snapped.* | *Jo joined the end of the line.* | **the far end** (=furthest from you) *of the room* | *The channel measures 20 feet* ***from end to end.*** | **stand/place sth on end** (=in an upright position) *He stood the box on end to open it.* | **lay/place sth end to end** (=in a line, with the ends touching) *bricks laid end to end*
4 SCALE [C usually singular] one of the two points that begin or end a scale: **lower/cheaper etc end** *the cheaper end of the price range* | *At the* ***opposite end of the*** *political* ***spectrum*** *are the Marxist theories.* | *Some teenagers are just a nuisance, but* ***at the other end of the scale*** *there are kids who pose a real threat.*
5 CONNECTION [C usually singular] one of two places that are connected by a telephone call, journey etc: **the end of the phone/line** *Sometimes, all you need is a calm voice on the end of the phone.* | *We'll get a bus connection* ***at the other end.*** | *Any problems at your end* (=where you are)?
6 REMAINING PIECE [C] *especially BrE* a small piece of something that is left after you have finished with it: *cigarette ends*
7 AIM [usually plural] an aim or purpose, or the result you hope to achieve: **political/military etc ends** *40% of all research is undertaken for military ends.* | *She'll do anything to* ***achieve*** *her* ***own ends.*** | *Every task has a clear* ***end in view.*** | **to that end** *formal*: *He wants to cut costs, and to that end is looking at ways of cutting the company's operations.* | **an end in itself** (=something you do because you want to, not in order to get other advantages) *IT is a tool for learning, not merely an end in itself.* | **the end justifies the means** (=used to say that doing bad things is acceptable if they achieve an important result)
8 PART OF AN ACTIVITY [singular] *informal* part of a job, activity, or situation that involves or affects one person or group of people: *She works in the sales end of things.*
9 SPORT [C] one of the two halves of a sports field
10 DEATH [C usually singular] a word meaning death – used to avoid saying this directly: *He* ***met*** *his* ***end*** (=died) *in a car accident.*
11 at the end of the day *spoken* used to give your final opinion after considering all the possibilities: *At the end of the day, it's his decision.*
12 for days/weeks etc on end for many days, weeks etc without stopping: *He was tortured for days on end.*
13 in the end after a period of time, or after everything has been done: *What did you decide in the end?*
14 end of (story) *spoken informal* used to mean that you will not say any more about something, or that the situation cannot be changed: *I'm not going – end of story.*
15 the end of your tether/rope the point at which you are so angry and tired of a situation that you can no longer deal with it: *Frustrated and bitter, Hogan had* ***reached the end of*** *his* ***tether*** *with politics.*
16 the end of the road/line the end of a process, activity, or state: *Our marriage had* ***reached the end of the line.***
17 make ends meet to have only just enough money to buy the things you need: *When Mike lost his job, we could barely make ends meet.*
18 it's not the end of the world *spoken* used to tell someone that a problem is not as bad as they think
19 hold/keep your end up *BrE informal* to stay brave and hopeful in a difficult situation
20 no end *spoken informal* very much: *Your letter cheered me up no end.*
21 no end of trouble/problems etc *spoken informal* a lot of trouble etc: *This will cause no end of trouble.*

E

22 the living end *AmE spoken* used as an expression of slight disapproval – often used humorously: *What will she do next? She's the living end!*
23 go to the ends of the earth *literary* to do everything possible to achieve something: *I'd go to the ends of the earth to be with him.*
24 to the end of time *literary* forever → DEAD END, ODDS AND ENDS, → **be-all and end all** at BE²(15), → **to the bitter end** at BITTER¹(6), → **burn the candle at both ends** at BURN¹(19), → **jump/be thrown in at the deep end** at DEEP¹(17), → **go off at the deep end** at DEEP¹(18), → **be at a loose end** at LOOSE¹(14), → **make sb's hair stand on end** at HAIR(8), → **be on/at the receiving end (of sth)** at RECEIVE(5), → **be on the sharp end of** at SHARP¹(19), → **come to a sticky end** at STICKY(6), → **the tail end of sth** at TAIL¹(6), → **at your wits' end** at WIT(7), → **get the wrong end of the stick** at WRONG¹(16)

GRAMMAR: Prepositions with end

- You use **at the end** when talking about the last part of a story, book, film, game etc: *At the end, the hero dies.| There is a summary at the end of the chapter.*
- You often use **at the end of** when talking about the last part of a period of time: *Marco Polo travelled through Asia at the end of the 13th century.* ✗ Don't say: *in the end of the 13th century*
- **In the end** means the same as 'eventually'. You use it when saying that something happens or after a long period of time or a lot of other things have happened: *In the end, she got her money back. | I'm sure we'll win in the end.*

end² ●●● S1 W1 *v*
1 a) [I] if an event, activity, or story ends, it stops happening OPP **start, begin**: *World War II ended in 1945.* | **[+with]** *The festival will end with a spectacular laser show.* **b)** [T] to make something stop happening OPP **start, begin**: *The talks are aimed at ending the conflict.*
2 [I] to finish what you are doing OPP **start, begin**: *I think we'll end there for today.* | **end by doing sth** *I'd like to end by inviting questions from the audience.*
3 [I] if a road, path, line etc ends, it reaches its final point OPP **start, begin**: *This is where the line ends.*
4 [T] to reach the final point in a period of time in a particular condition OPP **start, begin**: *They ended the game with a score of 63-42.* | *The company ended the year with record profits.*
5 end your days to spend the last part of your life in a particular place or doing a particular thing: *He ended his days in prison.*
6 end your life/end it all to kill yourself
7 the ... to end all ... used to describe something that is the best, most important, or most exciting of its kind: *the movie with the car chase to end all car chases*
8 the year/week etc ending sth used to refer to the year etc that ends on a particular date: *the financial results for the year ending 31 Dec 2008*

GRAMMAR

End belongs to a group of verbs where the same noun can be the subject of the verb or its object.
- You can say: *We will end the session with questions.* In this sentence, 'the session' is the object of **end**.
- You can say: *The session will end with questions.* In this sentence, 'the session' is the subject of **end**.

GRAMMAR GUIDE ▸ VERBS

THESAURUS

end if a event, activity, or story ends, it stops happening: *How does the story end? | The school year ends in June.*
finish to end – use this about an organized event such as a meeting, party, or lesson, especially when saying what time it ends: *The meeting will finish at 5.30. | What time does your Spanish class finish?*
be over if an event, activity, or period of time is over, it has ended: *I can't wait for our exams to be over. | The long summer vacation was almost over.*
come to an end to finally end – used about a period of time, a situation, or an activity that has continued for a long time: *The war finally came to an end six years later.*
draw to an end/to a close *written* to end gradually over a period of time – used in written descriptions: *These problems still remained as the twentieth century drew to an end.*
time is up if time is up, you are not allowed any more time to do something: *I wasn't able to finish the test before the time was up.*
time runs out if time runs out, there is no more time available to do something, especially something important: *The desperate search for survivors continues, but time is running out.*
expire *formal* if a ticket, bank card, legal document etc expires, the period of time during which you can use it has ended: *I'm afraid we can't accept this credit card – it expired last week.*
be at an end if something is at an end, it has ended: *We both knew that our marriage was at an end. | The long wait was at an end.*

end in sth *phr v*
1 to finish in a particular way: *One in three marriages ends in divorce.*
2 it'll (all) end in tears *BrE spoken* used to say that something will have a bad result or not be successful

end up *phr v* to be in a particular situation, state, or place after a series of events, especially when you did not plan it: *He came round for a coffee and we ended up having a meal together. | I wondered where the pictures would end up after the auction.* | **end up doing sth** *Most slimmers end up putting weight back on.* | **[+with]** *Anyone who swims in the river could end up with a nasty stomach upset.* | **[+as]** *He could end up as president.* | **[+like]** *I don't want to end up like my parents.*

en·dan·ger /ɪnˈdeɪndʒə $ -ər/ ●○○ *v* [T] to put someone or something in danger of being hurt, damaged, or destroyed: *Smoking during pregnancy* ***endangers*** *your baby's* ***life***. —**endangerment** *n* [U] *law*: *charges of child endangerment*

en·dan·gered /ɪnˈdeɪndʒəd $ -ərd/ ●○○ *adj* an endangered animal, bird etc is one that may soon no longer exist because there are so few of them: *The lizards are classed as an* ***endangered species***.

en·dear /ɪnˈdɪə $ ɪnˈdɪr/ *v*
endear sb **to** sb *phr v* to make someone popular and liked: **endear yourself to sb** *The emperor saw an opportunity to endear himself to the Athenians.*

en·dear·ing /ɪnˈdɪərɪŋ $ ɪnˈdɪr-/ *adj* making someone love or like you: **endearing qualities/traits etc** *Shyness is one of her most endearing qualities. | an endearing smile* —**endearingly** *adv*

en·dear·ment /ɪnˈdɪəmənt $ ɪnˈdɪr-/ *n* [C,U] actions or words that express your love for someone: *nicknames and other* ***terms of endearment***

en·deav·our¹ *BrE*, **endeavor** *AmE* /ɪnˈdevə $ -ər/ ●○○ *v* [I] *formal* to try very hard: **endeavour to do sth** *We always endeavor to please our customers.* THESAURUS ▸ TRY

endeavour² *BrE*, **endeavor** *AmE* *n* [C,U] *formal* an attempt to do something new or difficult: **scientific/creative etc endeavour** | *an outstanding example of* ***human endeavor*** | **endeavour to do sth** *They* ***made every endeavour*** *to find the two boys. | Despite our* ***best endeavours***, *we couldn't start the car.*

en·dem·ic /enˈdemɪk, ɪn-/ *adj* an endemic disease or problem is always present in a particular place, or among a particular group of people → **epidemic, pandemic**: *Violent crime is now endemic in parts of Chicago.*

ˈend game, end·game /ˈendgeɪm/ *n* [C usually singular] the final stage of a war, disagreement etc when everyone is trying to gain an advantage for themselves

end·ing /ˈendɪŋ/ ●●○ *n*
1 [C] the way that a story, film, activity etc finishes:

happy/perfect/surprise etc ending *a story with a happy ending* | **[+to]** *Coffee is the perfect ending to a meal.*
2 [U] when a process stops or is finished, or when you finish it: **[+of]** *the first elections since the ending of the dictatorship*
3 [C] the last part of a word: *Verbal nouns have the ending -ing.* → NEVER-ENDING

en·dive /ˈendɪv $ ˈendaɪv/ *n* [C,U] **1** *BrE* a vegetable with curly green leaves that you eat raw **2** *AmE* a vegetable with long white bitter-tasting leaves that you eat raw or cooked SYN **chicory** *BrE*

end·less /ˈendləs/ ●●○ *adj*
1 very large in amount, size, or number: *an* ***endless stream of*** *visitors* | *The* ***possibilities*** *are* ***endless****.* | *He's been in a lot of trouble – drugs, guns, blackmail –* ***the list is endless****.*
2 something that is endless seems to continue forever: *an* ***endless round of*** *boring meetings* —**endlessly** *adv*: *This city is endlessly fascinating.*

en·do·crine /ˈendəʊkrɪn $ -doʊ-/ *adj medical* relating to the system in your body that produces HORMONES: *the endocrine glands*

en·dor·phin /enˈdɔːfɪn $ -ˈdɔːr-/ *n* [C usually plural] a chemical produced by your body that reduces pain and can make you feel happier

en·dorse /ɪnˈdɔːs $ -ɔːrs/ ●○○ *v* [T]
1 to express formal support or approval for someone or something: **endorse a proposal/an idea/a candidate etc** *The prime minister is unlikely to endorse this view.* THESAURUS SUPPORT
2 if a famous person endorses a product or service, they say in an advertisement that they use and like it THESAURUS RECOMMEND
3 to sign your name on the back of a cheque to show that it is correct
4 *BrE* if your DRIVING LICENCE is endorsed for a driving offence, an official record is made on it to show that you are guilty of the offence

en·dorse·ment /ɪnˈdɔːsmənt $ -ɔːrs-/ ●○○ *n*
1 [C,U] an expression of formal support or approval for someone or something: *the official endorsement of his candidacy* | *To say it is the least bad system is hardly a* ***ringing endorsement*** (=a statement showing strong support).
2 [C,U] a statement made by a famous person in an advertisement saying that they like and use a particular product: *celebrity endorsements*
3 [C] *BrE* an official record made on someone's DRIVING LICENCE to show that they are guilty of a driving offence

en·do·scope /ˈendəskəʊp $ -skoʊp/ *n* [C] *medical* an instrument used by doctors who are performing a medical OPERATION on someone. It is a very small camera with a powerful LENS, which is pushed into the body through a very small hole and sends pictures back to the doctor.

en·dos·co·py /enˈdɒskəpi $ -ˈdɑː-/ *n* [U] *medical* the medical examination of the inside of the body, using an endoscope

en·dow /ɪnˈdaʊ/ *v* [T] to give a college, hospital etc a large sum of money that provides it with an income
endow sb/sth **with** sth *phr v formal* **1** to make someone or something have a particular quality, or to believe that they have it: *Her resistance to the Nationalists endowed her with legendary status.* **2 be endowed with sth** to naturally have a good feature or quality: *She was endowed with good looks.* **3** to give someone something → WELL-ENDOWED

en·dow·ment /ɪnˈdaʊmənt/ *n* **1** [C,U] a sum of money given to a college, hospital etc to provide it with an income, or the act of giving this money **2** [C] a natural quality or ability that someone has

enˈdowment ˌpolicy *n* [C] *BrE technical* an insurance arrangement that pays you a sum of money after an agreed period of time

ˈend ˌproduct *n* [C usually singular] something that is produced by a particular process or activity → **by-product**: *a high-quality end product* | *the end product of years of practice*

ˌend reˈsult *n* [C usually singular] the final result of a process or activity: *If tasks are too challenging, the end result is that learners are discouraged.*

en·dur·a·ble /ɪnˈdjʊərəbəl $ ɪnˈdʊr-/ *adj formal* if a bad situation is endurable, you can accept it, even though it is difficult or painful SYN **bearable**

en·dur·ance /ɪnˈdjʊərəns $ ɪnˈdʊr-/ *n* [U] the ability to continue doing something difficult or painful over a long period of time: **physical/mental endurance** | *She was pushed* ***beyond*** *her* ***powers of endurance****.* | *The marathon is a* ***test of endurance****.* | **endurance sports/training** (=designed to test or improve your endurance)

en·dure /ɪnˈdjʊə $ ɪnˈdʊr/ ●○○ *v*
1 [T] to be in a difficult or painful situation for a long time without complaining: *It seemed impossible that anyone could endure such pain.* | **endure doing sth** *He can't endure being apart from me.*

> **REGISTER**
> In everyday English, people usually say **stand** rather than **endure**: *I couldn't* ***stand*** *the pain.*

2 [I] to remain alive or continue to exist for a long time: *friendships which endure over many years*

en·dur·ing /ɪnˈdjʊərɪŋ $ ɪnˈdʊr-/ *adj* continuing for a very long time: *the* ***enduring appeal*** *of Shakespeare's plays* | *enduring hatred* THESAURUS LONG —**enduringly** *adv*: *an enduringly popular performer*

ˈend ˌuser *n* [C] the person who uses a particular product, rather than the people who make or develop it

ˈend zone *n* [C] one of the areas at each end of an American football field where you carry or catch the ball to score → see picture at AMERICAN FOOTBALL

en·e·ma /ˈenəmə/ *n* [C] a liquid that is put into someone's RECTUM to make their BOWELs empty

en·e·my /ˈenəmi/ ●●● W2 *n* (*plural* **enemies**) [C]
1 someone who hates you and wants to harm you: *She's a dangerous enemy to have.* | *Cats and dogs have always been* ***natural enemies****.* | *an* ***old enemy*** *of her father* | **make an enemy (of sb)** *a ruthless businessman who made a lot of enemies* | *the unforgettable sight of the president shaking hands with his* ***sworn enemy*** (=an enemy you will always hate) | **sb's worst enemy** (=the person they hate most) *I* ***wouldn't wish*** *this* ***on*** *my* ***worst enemy****.*
2 someone who opposes or competes against you: *political enemies* | *He was imprisoned for being 'an enemy of the revolution'.*
3 (*also* **the enemy**) the country against which your country is fighting in a war: *He was accused of collaboration with the enemy.* | **enemy forces/aircraft/territory etc** *a town behind* ***enemy lines***

> **GRAMMAR: Singular or plural verb?**
> • **The enemy** is usually followed by a singular verb: *The enemy* ***was*** *defeated.*
> • In British English, you can also use a plural verb: *The enemy* ***were*** *defeated.*
> GRAMMAR GUIDE NOUNS

4 something that people think is harmful or damaging: *The usual enemies, cigarettes and alcohol, are targeted for tax rises.* | *The* ***common enemy*** *that united them was communism.*
5 be your own worst enemy to behave in a way that causes problems for yourself
6 public enemy number one *informal* someone famous who has done something bad and who a lot of people do not like: *His views made him public enemy number one in the eyes of the media.*
7 the enemy within people in a society etc that other people think are trying to secretly destroy or damage it: *efforts to label environmentalists as the enemy within*
8 if one thing is the enemy of another, the second thing cannot exist because the first thing destroys it: *Boredom is the enemy of learning.*

E

en·er·get·ic /ˌenəˈdʒetɪk◂ $ -ər-/ ●●○ AWL *adj* having or needing a lot of energy or determination: *an energetic man | an energetic drive to get more customers |* **energetic in doing sth** *We need to be more energetic in promoting ourselves abroad.* —**energetically** /-kli/ *adv*: *He fought energetically against apartheid.*

THESAURUS

energetic having a lot of energy: *If you're feeling energetic, we could go out for a run.*
full of energy/bursting with energy energetic and ready to work hard or do a lot of things: *I admire her because she's so full of energy and enthusiasm.*
dynamic very energetic and always wanting to do new things: *What this country needs is a dynamic new leader.*
hyperactive having more energy than is normal or good, because you cannot keep still or quiet for very long - used especially about children: *Our youngest daughter was hyperactive, and it had a damaging effect on the whole family.*
tireless working with a lot of energy in a determined way, especially to achieve a particular thing: *She was a tireless campaigner against apartheid in South Africa.*
full of beans *informal* feeling energetic and happy and showing this in the way you behave: *He's one of those people who leap out of bed full of beans every morning.*

en·er·gize (*also* **-ise** *BrE*) /ˈenədʒaɪz $ -ər-/ *v* [T] **1** to make someone feel more determined and energetic: *The charity hopes the campaign will energise its volunteers.* **2** *technical* to make a machine work GRAMMAR **Energize** is usually passive in this meaning. —**energizing** *adj*

en·er·gy /ˈenədʒi $ -ər-/ ●●● S2 W1 AWL *n* (*plural* **energies**)
1 [U] power that is used to provide heat, operate machines etc: *The water is heated using energy from the sun. | The problem with nuclear energy is dealing with the waste.*
2 [U] the physical and mental strength that makes you able to do things: *Where do those kids get their energy from? | Are you suffering from* **a lack of energy**? *| The city is full of* **creative energy**. *| I really* **put** *a lot of* **energy into** *what I do. | He wants to* **conserve** *his* **energy** *for next week's game* (=use as little energy as possible now, so that you have more energy to use later).
3 [U] a special power that some people believe exists in their bodies and in some buildings: *There was a lot of energy in the room this morning - did you feel it?*
4 [U] *technical* in physics, the ability that something has to work or move: *kinetic energy*
5 sb's energies the effort and interest that you use to do things: **apply/devote/channel your energies into/to sth** *She's devoting all her energies to the wedding plans.*

COLLOCATIONS

VERBS

generate/produce energy *a power plant that generates energy from household waste*
supply/provide energy *The wind farm will provide enough energy for 100,000 homes.*
store energy *Batteries store the energy from the solar panels.*
use energy *Washing machines use a lot of energy.*
conserve energy (=not waste any energy) *An efficient boiler will conserve energy and save you money.*

ADJECTIVES/NOUN + energy

solar energy *The water pump is powered by solar energy.*
nuclear/atomic energy *a report on the cost of nuclear energy*
wind/wave energy *The windmill uses wind energy to crush grain and pump water.*
renewable energy (=energy such as solar or wind energy that can be replaced naturally) *Switching to sources of renewable energy will reduce carbon emissions.*
alternative energy (=energy from sources other than oil, coal, or nuclear energy) *It is the first form of public transport to be powered by alternative energy.*
clean energy (=which does not cause pollution) *Iceland possesses sufficient quantities of clean energy sources that it does not need to rely on fossil fuels.*

energy + NOUN

energy use *30% of all our energy use is in the home.*
energy efficiency *This guide provides advice on ways of improving energy efficiency.*
energy consumption *We all need to reduce our energy consumption.*
energy needs/requirements *65% of the country's energy needs are met by imported oil.*
energy production *hydro-electricity and other methods of energy production*
energy resources *The world's energy resources are being used up at an alarming rate.*
an energy shortage | an energy crisis | energy supplies | an energy company | the energy industry | an energy bill | energy prices

PHRASES

a source/form of energy *Coal is more expensive than other sources of energy.*
the demand for energy *The demand for energy in developing countries will continue to grow.*

ˌenergy-efˈficient *adj* using as little energy as possible: *How can we make our homes more energy-efficient?*

en·er·vate /ˈenəveɪt $ -ər-/ *v* [T] *formal* to make you feel tired and weak: *The hot sun enervated her to the point of collapse.* —**enervated** *adj* [not before noun]: *David felt too enervated to resist.* —**enervating** *adj*

en·fant ter·ri·ble /ˌɒnfɒn teˈriːblə $ ˌɑːnfɑːn-/ *n* [C] a young successful person who behaves in a way that is shocking but also amusing

en·fee·bled /ɪnˈfiːbəld/ *adj literary* very weak or ill —**enfeeble** *v* [T]

en·fold /ɪnˈfəʊld $ -ˈfoʊld/ *v* [T] *formal* to cover or surround someone or something completely: *The wizard screamed as the darkness enfolded him. | He reached out to enfold her in his arms.*

en·force /ɪnˈfɔːs $ -ɔːrs/ ●○○ AWL *v* [T]
1 to make people obey a rule or law: **enforce a law/ban etc** *Governments make laws and the police enforce them. | Parking restrictions will be* **strictly enforced**.
2 to make something happen or force someone to do something: **enforce sth on sb** *It is unlikely that a record company would enforce its views on an established artist.* —**enforceable** *adj*: *The recommendations are not* **legally enforceable**.

en·forced /ɪnˈfɔːst $ -ɔːrst/ AWL *adj* made to happen, especially by things you cannot control: **enforced absence/separation etc** *a period of enforced isolation*

en·force·ment /ɪnˈfɔːsmənt $ -ɔːr-/ ●○○ AWL *n* [U] when people are made to obey a rule, law etc: ***law enforcement***

en·forc·er /ɪnˈfɔːsə $ -ˈfɔːrsər/ *n* [C] someone whose job is to make sure people do the things they should: *a law enforcer | an enforcer for a drugs gang*

en·fran·chise /ɪnˈfræntʃaɪz/ *v* [T] to give a group of people the right to vote OPP **disenfranchise** —**enfranchisement** /-tʃɪz- $ -tʃaɪz-/ *n* [U]: *the enfranchisement of EU citizens* —**enfranchised** *adj*: *newly enfranchised shareholders*

en·gage /ɪnˈɡeɪdʒ/ ●○○ *v formal*
1 [I always + prep] to be doing or to become involved in an activity: **[+in/on/upon]** *Only 10% of American adults engage in regular exercise. | The two parties engaged upon an escalating political struggle. | Mr Armstrong was engaged*

in prayer. | **engage in doing sth** *Despite her illness, she remains* ***actively engaged*** *in shaping policy.*
2 [T] to attract someone's attention and keep them interested: **engage sb's interest/attention** *The toy didn't engage her interest for long.* | **engage sb in conversation** (=start talking to them)
3 engage with sb/sth to get involved with other people and their ideas in order to understand them: *Are you so tired you don't have the energy to engage with your kids?*
4 [T] *formal* to employ someone to do a particular job: **engage sb to do sth** *Her father engaged a tutor to improve her maths.* | **engage sb as sth** *We'd be able to engage local people as volunteers.*
5 [I,T] if you engage part of a machine, or if it engages, it moves so that it fits into another part of the machine OPP **disengage**: *She engaged the clutch and the car moved.* | **[+with]** *The wheel engages with the cog and turns it.*
6 [I,T] to begin to fight an enemy: *American forces did not directly engage.*

en·gaged /ɪnˈgeɪdʒd/ ●●○ *adj*
1 if two people are engaged, they have agreed to marry: *Have you heard? Sally and Ray are* ***getting engaged****.* | *She is* ***engaged to be married****.* | **[+to]** *Kate's engaged to Mark.*

> **GRAMMAR**
> You are or get **engaged to** someone: *He is engaged to a lovely woman.* ✗ Don't say: *He is engaged with a lovely woman.*
> GRAMMAR GUIDE ▸ ADJECTIVES

THESAURUS ▸ MARRIED
2 *BrE* if you call someone on the telephone and their line is engaged, they are already speaking to someone else SYN **busy** *AmE*: *She rang Mrs Tavett but the* ***line*** *was* ***engaged****.* | **engaged tone/signal** (=the sound you hear when the phone is engaged)
3 *BrE written* a public toilet that is engaged is being used OPP **vacant**
4 be otherwise engaged *formal* to be unable to do something because you are doing something else

en·gage·ment /ɪnˈgeɪdʒmənt/ ●●○ *n*
1 BEFORE MARRIAGE [C] an agreement between two people to marry, or the period of time they are engaged: **[+of/to]** *Their* ***engagement*** *was* ***announced*** *in the paper.* | *Tony was stunned when Lisa suddenly* ***broke off*** *their* ***engagement*** (=finished it). | **engagement ring** (=a ring that a man gives a woman to show that they are engaged)
2 ARRANGEMENT TO DO STH [C] an official arrangement to do something, especially one that is related to your work: **official/public/royal etc engagement** *The princess will continue to* ***carry out*** *royal* ***engagements****.* | *This is his only public* ***speaking engagement*** *on the tour.* | *His excuse of a* ***prior engagement*** *was accepted.*
3 INVOLVEMENT [U] when you become involved with someone or something in order to understand them: **[+with/in]** *a strategy of engagement and cooperation with China* | *Many students pass without any real engagement in learning.*
4 FIGHTING [C,U] *technical* fighting between armies etc: *military* ***rules of engagement***
5 EMPLOYMENT [C,U] *formal* an official arrangement to employ or pay someone to do a particular job: *Please sign to indicate your acceptance of the* ***terms of engagement****.*
6 MACHINE PARTS [U] the fitting together of the working parts of a machine

en·gag·ing /ɪnˈgeɪdʒɪŋ/ *adj* pleasant and attracting your interest: *an* ***engaging smile*** THESAURUS ▸ NICE —**engagingly** *adv*

en·gen·der /ɪnˈdʒendə $ -ər/ *v* [T] *formal* to be the cause of a situation or feeling: *the changes in society engendered by the war* | **engender sth in sb** *relationships that engender trust in children*

en·gine /ˈendʒɪn/ ●●● S2 W2 *n* [C]
1 the part of a vehicle that produces power to make it move → **motor**: **start/switch on an engine** *The engine won't start.* | **stop/turn off/switch off an engine** *He switched off the car's engine and waited.* | *Is the* ***engine running*** *smoothly?* | **diesel/petrol etc engine** *an old steam engine* | *We were stranded with* ***engine trouble*** *on a deserted highway.* → see picture at MOTORBIKE
2 a vehicle that pulls a railway train
3 [usually singular] *formal* something powerful that causes great changes in society: **engine of change/growth etc** *The Marshall Plan was the engine of post-war economic growth.* | *Rome's deadly* ***war engine*** → FIRE ENGINE

en·gi·neer¹ /ˌendʒəˈnɪə $ -ˈnɪr/ ●●● S3 W3 *n* [C]
1 someone whose job is to design or build roads, bridges, machines etc: **mechanical/electrical/software etc engineer** | *He trained as a* ***civil engineer*** (=one who designs and builds roads, bridges etc).
2 someone whose job is to take care of the engines on a ship or aircraft
3 *BrE* someone whose job is to repair electrical equipment or machines: **service/maintenance engineer**
4 *AmE* someone whose job is driving a train

engineer² *v* [T] **1** to make something happen by skilful secret planning: *powerful enemies who engineered his downfall* | *Perhaps she could engineer a meeting between them?* **2** to change the GENETIC structure of a plant, animal etc SYN **genetically modify**: *the dangers of engineering native plants* | ***genetically engineered*** *crops* **3** *technical* to design and plan the building of roads, bridges, machines, etc: *The car is engineered to drive smoothly at high speeds.* GRAMMAR **Engineer** is often passive in this meaning.

en·gi·neer·ing /ˌendʒəˈnɪərɪŋ $ -ˈnɪr-/ ●●○ S3 W3 *n* [U] the work involved in designing and building roads, bridges, machines etc → CIVIL ENGINEERING, GENETIC ENGINEERING

En·glish¹ /ˈɪŋglɪʃ/ *n* **1** [C,U] the language used in Britain, the US, Australia, and some other countries: *Do you speak English?* | *leaflets written in* ***plain English*** (=English that is easy to understand) **2 the English** [plural] people from England **3** [U] literature written in English, studied as a subject at school or university: *She decided to major in English.*

English² *adj* **1** relating to England or its people: *the English countryside* | *under English law* **2** relating to the language used in Britain, the US, Australia, and some other countries: *English grammar*

ˌEnglish ˈbreakfast *n* [C usually singular] a large cooked breakfast consisting of BACON, eggs, TOAST etc → **continental breakfast**

ˌEnglish ˈhorn *n* [C] *AmE* a long wooden musical instrument which is like an OBOE but with a lower sound SYN **cor anglais** *BrE*

En·glish·man /ˈɪŋglɪʃmən/ *n* (*plural* **Englishmen** /-mən/) [C] **1** a man from England **2 an Englishman's home is his castle** *BrE* used to say that your home is a place where you can feel safe and do whatever you want

ˌEnglish ˈmuffin *n* [C] *AmE* a round thick flat piece of bread with small holes inside

En·glish·wom·an /ˈɪŋglɪʃˌwʊmən/ *n* (*plural* **Englishwomen** /-ˌwɪmɪn/) [C] a woman from England

en·gorged /ɪnˈgɔːdʒd $ -ɔːr-/ *adj formal* swollen and full of liquid

en·grave /ɪnˈgreɪv/ *v* [T]
1 to cut words or designs on metal, wood, glass etc: **engrave sth on sth** *Their names are engraved on a stone tablet.* | **engrave sth with sth** *a pendant engraved with a simple design*
2 be engraved in/on your memory/mind/heart *literary* to be impossible to forget —**engraver** *n* [C]

ENGRAVE

an engraved box

E

en·grav·ing /ɪnˈɡreɪvɪŋ/ *n* **1** [C] a picture made by cutting a design into metal, putting ink on the metal, and then printing it **2** [U] the skill of engraving things

en·gross /ɪnˈɡrəʊs $ -ˈɡroʊs/ *v* [T] if something engrosses you, it interests you so much that you do not notice anything else: *The scene was stunning, and for a time engrossed all our attention.* | **engross yourself in sth** *Take your mind off it by engrossing yourself in a good book.* —**engrossed** *adj*: *Dad was* **engrossed in** *the paper.* | *Who's that guy Ally's been* **engrossed in conversation with** *all night?* —**engrossing** *adj*

en·gulf /ɪnˈɡʌlf/ *v* [T] **1** if an unpleasant feeling engulfs you, you feel it very strongly: *despair so great it* **threatened to engulf** *him* **2** to completely surround or cover something: *The building was* **engulfed in flames**.

en·hance /ɪnˈhɑːns $ ɪnˈhæns/ ●●○ W3 AWL *v* [T] to improve something: *Good lighting will enhance any room.* | *The publicity has* **enhanced** *his* **reputation**. —**enhancer** *n* [C]: *flavor enhancers* —**enhancement** *n* [C,U]

en·hanced /ɪnˈhɑːnst $ -ˈhænst/ ●○○ AWL *adj written* improved or better: *enhanced access to information*

e·nig·ma /ɪˈnɪɡmə/ *n* [C] someone or something that is strange and difficult to understand SYN **mystery**: *The neighbours regarded him as something of an enigma.*

en·ig·mat·ic /ˌenɪɡˈmætɪk◂/ *adj* mysterious and difficult to understand: **enigmatic smile/expression etc** —**enigmatically** /-kli/ *adv*: *'You'll see,' he replied enigmatically.*

E

en·join /ɪnˈdʒɔɪn/ *v* [T] **1** *formal* to order or try to persuade someone to do something: **enjoin sb to do sth** *The organisation has been enjoined to end all restrictions.* **2** *law* to legally prevent someone from doing something: **enjoin sb from doing sth** *The defendant was enjoined from using the patent.*

en·joy /ɪnˈdʒɔɪ/ ●●● S1 W1 *v* [T]
1 to get pleasure from something: *Sandra enjoys her job in the city.* | *I* **enjoyed every minute** *of it.* | **enjoy doing sth** *Young children enjoy helping around the house.* | **enjoy yourself** (=be happy in a particular situation) *Julia was just starting to enjoy herself.*
2 *formal* to have a particular ability or advantage: *These workers enjoy a high level of job security.*
3 enjoy! *spoken* used to say that you hope someone gets pleasure from something you give them: *Here's your steak - enjoy!*

GRAMMAR: Patterns with enjoy

- **Enjoy** is usually transitive. You **enjoy** something: *I enjoyed the game.* | *Did you enjoy it?* ✗ Don't say: *I enjoyed.* | *Did you enjoy?*
- You **enjoy doing** something: *I enjoyed watching the game on TV.*
- **Enjoy** is never followed by an infinitive. ✗ Don't say: *I enjoyed to watch the game on TV.*
- In informal English, you sometimes use **Enjoy!** on its own, when saying that you hope someone enjoys something: *Here's your pizza. Enjoy!*

GRAMMAR GUIDE ▶ VERBS

en·joy·a·ble /ɪnˈdʒɔɪəbəl/ ●●○ *adj* something enjoyable gives you pleasure: *Games can make learning more enjoyable.* | *an enjoyable experience* **THESAURUS** ▶ NICE —**enjoyably** *adv*

en·joy·ment /ɪnˈdʒɔɪmənt/ ●●○ *n*
1 [C,U] the feeling of pleasure you get from having or doing something, or something you enjoy doing: *Acting has* **brought** *me enormous* **enjoyment**. | *Unfortunately, a small minority want to* **spoil** *everyone else's* **enjoyment**. **THESAURUS** ▶ FUN
2 [U] *formal* the fact of having something

en·large /ɪnˈlɑːdʒ $ -ɑːrdʒ/ ●○○ *v* [I,T] if you enlarge something, or if it enlarges, it increases in size or scale: *an operation to enlarge her breasts* | *Police will have the pictures enlarged in an attempt to identify the thief.* | **enlarge sb's understanding/knowledge etc** *A good way to enlarge your vocabulary is to read a daily newspaper.*

enlarge on/upon sth *phr v formal* to provide more information about something you have already mentioned: *Mrs Maughan did not enlarge on what she meant.*

en·large·ment /ɪnˈlɑːdʒmənt $ -ɑːr-/ *n* **1** [C] a photograph that has been printed again in a bigger size **2** [C,U] an increase in size or amount: *enlargement of the EU*

en·lar·ger /ɪnˈlɑːdʒə $ -ˈlɑːrdʒər/ *n* [C] a piece of equipment used to make photographs bigger

en·light·en /ɪnˈlaɪtn/ *v* [T] *formal* to explain something to someone: **enlighten sb as to/on/about sth** *Baldwin enlightened her as to the nature of the experiment.* —**enlightening** *adj*

en·light·ened /ɪnˈlaɪtənd/ *adj* **1** someone with enlightened attitudes has sensible modern views and treats people fairly and kindly: **enlightened attitude/approach etc** | *'Empowerment' is the new buzz-word in enlightened management circles.* **2** showing a good understanding or knowledge of something SYN **informed**: *We don't actually know, but I can make an enlightened guess.*

en·light·en·ment /ɪnˈlaɪtnmənt/ *n* [U] **1** *formal* when you understand something clearly, or when you help someone do this: *Isabel looked to Ron for enlightenment.* **2** the final stage reached in the Buddhist and Hindu religions when you no longer suffer or feel desire and you are at peace with the universe: *the quest for* **spiritual enlightenment**

en·list /ɪnˈlɪst/ ●○○ *v*
1 [T] to persuade someone to help you to do something: **enlist sb's help/services etc** *He has enlisted the help of a sports psychologist for the team.* | *The public are being enlisted to help.*
2 [I,T] to join the army, navy etc: **[+as]** *He enlisted as a private.* | **[+in]** *At the outbreak of war, he was enlisted in the army.* —**enlistment** *n* [C,U]

en·list·ed /ɪnˈlɪstɪd/ *adj* [usually before noun] having a rank below that of an officer in the army, navy etc: *officers and* **enlisted men**

en·liv·en /ɪnˈlaɪvən/ *v* [T] to make something more interesting SYN **liven up**: *Humour can help enliven a dull subject.*

en masse /ˌɒn ˈmæs $ ˌɑːn-/ *adv* if people do something en masse, they do it together: *The management team resigned en masse.*

en·meshed /ɪnˈmeʃt/ *adj* [not before noun] very involved in an unpleasant or complicated situation: **[+in/with]** *Congress worried about becoming enmeshed in a foreign war.*

en·mi·ty /ˈenməti/ *n* (*plural* **enmities**) [C,U] *formal* a feeling of hatred towards someone → **enemy**: **[+between/towards]** *the enmity between the two communities*

en·no·ble /ɪˈnəʊbəl $ ɪˈnoʊ-/ *v* [T] *formal* **1** to improve your character: *art which ennobles the human race* **2** to make someone a member of the NOBILITY (=the people in society who have a high rank, such as princes etc) —**ennoblement** *n* [U] —**ennobling** *adj*

en·nui /ɒnˈwiː $ ɑːn-/ *n* [U] *formal* a feeling of being tired, bored, and unsatisfied with your life

e·nor·mi·ty /ɪˈnɔːməti $ -ɔːr-/ AWL *n* (*plural* **enormities**) **1** [singular] the great size, seriousness, or difficulty of a situation, problem, event etc: **[+of]** *Even now, the full enormity of his crimes has not been exposed.* | *the enormity of the task* **2** [C usually plural] *formal* a very evil and cruel act SYN **atrocity**

e·nor·mous /ɪˈnɔːməs $ -ɔːr-/ ●●● S2 W3 AWL *adj* very big in size or in amount SYN **huge**: *an enormous bunch of flowers* | *an* **enormous amount of** *money* | *The team made an* **enormous effort**. **THESAURUS** ▶ BIG

GRAMMAR

Enormous is not used with 'very'. You say: *Their garden is absolutely enormous.* ✗ Don't say: *Their garden is very enormous.*

GRAMMAR GUIDE ▸ ADJECTIVES

e·nor·mous·ly /ɪˈnɔːməsli $ ˈɔːr-/ ●○○ AWL *adv* very or very much SYN **hugely**: *an enormously successful actor | The project has benefited enormously from Jan's knowledge.*

e·nough¹ /ɪˈnʌf/ ●●● S1 W1 *adv* [always after a verb, adjective, or adverb]

1 to the degree that is necessary or wanted: *Are the carrots cooked enough? | He just hadn't thought enough about the possible consequences. | You can go to school when you're old enough.* | **[+for]** *Is the water warm enough for you?* | **enough to do sth** *Will Evans be fit enough to play? | The rooms are all large enough to take a third bed. | Surely no one would be foolish enough to lend him the money? | You're late. It's just* ***not good enough*** (=not satisfactory or acceptable).
2 fairly but not very: *I was happy enough in Bordeaux, but I missed my family. | He's a nice enough young man.*
3 bad/difficult/hard etc enough used to say that a situation is already bad and you do not want it to get any worse: *Life's difficult enough without you interfering all the time.*
4 lucky/unfortunate etc enough to be/do sth used to say that someone is lucky or unlucky that something happens to them: *They were unlucky enough to be caught in the storm.*
5 would you be good/kind enough to do sth? *spoken* used to ask someone politely to do something for you: *Would you be good enough to hold the door open?*
6 strangely/oddly/curiously etc enough used to say that a fact or something that happens is strange or surprising: *Strangely enough, I didn't feel at all nervous when I faced the audience.*
7 near enough *BrE spoken* used when you are guessing a number, amount, time etc because you cannot be exact: *The full cost comes to £3,000, near enough.* → **fair enough** at FAIR¹(14), → **sure enough** at SURE²(1)

GRAMMAR: Word order

You use **enough** after an adjective or adverb: *It's small enough to fit in your pocket. | We're not going fast enough.* ✗ Don't say: *It's enough small to fit in your pocket. | We're not going enough fast.*

enough² ●●● S1 W2 *determiner, pron*

1 as many or as much as is needed or wanted: *Have I given you enough money? | Not enough is known about what happened.* | **[+for]** *There aren't enough chairs for everyone.* | **enough to do/eat etc** *Erica was worried that the children weren't getting enough to eat.* | **enough (sth) to do sth** *The police didn't have enough evidence to convict him. | He didn't even earn enough to pay the rent. | You've had* ***more than enough*** *time to make all the preparations.* | **enough to go round** (=enough of something for everyone to have some) *Do you think we've got enough pizza to go round?* | **not nearly/nowhere near enough** *informal* (=much less than you need) *We only had $500, and that was nowhere near enough to buy a new camcorder.* | **time/reason/trouble etc enough** *old-fashioned*: *Come on – there'll be time enough to chat later.*
2 used to say that a situation is already bad and you do not want it to get any worse: *She has enough problems without you two getting into fights. | I don't want to bother him – he has enough to worry about.*
3 have had enough (of sth) *spoken* used to say you are tired or angry about a situation and want it to stop: *When I got home I just sat down and cried. I'd had enough. | I've just about had enough of your stupid remarks.*
4 enough is enough *spoken* used to say that something that is happening should stop: *There comes a point when you say enough is enough.*
5 that's (quite) enough (*also* **enough already** *AmE*) *spoken* used to tell someone to stop doing something: *Now, you two, that's quite enough. Sit down and be quiet.*
6 enough said *spoken* used to tell someone that they do not need to say any more because you understand the point they are making: *'He's the sort of man who wears a lot of jewellery.' 'Enough said.'*
7 can't get enough of sth/sb *informal* to enjoy something so much that you want more and more of it: *Her millions of fans can't get enough of her.*

GRAMMAR

You use **enough** before uncountable and plural nouns: *There isn't enough time. | There aren't enough books.*

THESAURUS

enough /ɪˈnʌf/ as much or as many as necessary, or as you want: *My family never had enough money for holidays abroad. | Have you had enough to eat?*
sufficient *formal* enough for a particular purpose: *The police did not have sufficient evidence to justify a charge. | The accuracy of the older technique was sufficient for our needs.*
adequate *formal* enough in quantity or good enough in quality for a particular purpose: *All staff must be given adequate training in health and safety. | The heating system was barely adequate.*
ample more than enough for what is needed: *Local residents will be given ample opportunity to express their views. | People used to think that 1 GB of memory was ample for the average personal computer.*
plenty an amount that is enough or more than enough: *Allow yourself plenty of time to get to the airport. | Your daughter won't need much cash at camp ($20-$25 will be plenty).*
sth will do/sth should do *spoken* used to say that a particular number or amount will be enough for what you need: *'How many envelopes do you want?' 'Ten should do.'*

en·quire /ɪnˈkwaɪə $ -ˈkwaɪr/ *v* [I,T] *especially BrE* another spelling of INQUIRE THESAURUS ▸ ASK

en·qui·ry /ɪnˈkwaɪəri $ ɪnˈkwaɪri, ˈɪŋkwəri/ *n* (*plural* **enquiries**) *especially BrE* another spelling of INQUIRY

en·rage /ɪnˈreɪdʒ/ *v* [T] to make someone very angry → **anger**: *Many readers were enraged by his article.* GRAMMAR **Enrage** is usually passive.

en·rap·tured /ɪnˈræptʃəd $ -ərd/ *adj formal* enjoying something so much that you can think of nothing else SYN **enthralled**: *The orchestra played before an enraptured audience.*

en·rich /ɪnˈrɪtʃ/ ●○○ *v* [T]
1 to improve the quality of something, especially by adding things to it: *Add fertilizer to enrich the soil. | Education can greatly* ***enrich*** *your* ***life***.
2 to make someone richer
3 *technical* to increase the number of atoms in a NUCLEAR FUEL so that it produces more power —**enrichment** *n* [U]: *curriculum enrichment* —**enriched** *adj*: *enriched uranium*

en·rol *BrE*, **enroll** *AmE* /ɪnˈrəʊl $ -ˈroʊl/ ●○○ *v* (**enrolled**, **enrolling**) [I,T] to officially arrange to join a school, university, or course, or to arrange for someone else to do this: **[+on/for]** *BrE*: *I decided to enrol for 'Art for Beginners'.* | **[+in]** *especially AmE*: *Californians are rushing to enroll in special aerobics classes.*

en·rol·ment *BrE*, **enrollment** *AmE* /ɪnˈrəʊlmənt $ ɪnˈroʊl-/ *n* **1** [U] the process of arranging to join a school, university, course etc: *Enrolment will take place in September.* **2** [C] the number of people who have arranged to join a school, university, course etc: *Student enrolments have more than doubled.*

en route /ˌɒn ˈruːt $ ˌɑːn-/ *adv* on the way: **[+from/to]** *a flight en route from Tokyo to Sydney* | **[+for]** *BrE*: *We stayed there en route for London. | Why don't we stop for lunch en route?*

en·sconce /ɪnˈskɒns $ ɪnˈskɑːns/ *v* [T] to settle yourself in a place where you feel comfortable and safe: **be ensconced in/at/on etc** *Nick was* ***comfortably ensconced*** *in* *front of the TV set.* | **ensconce yourself** *Agnes had ensconced herself in the best bedroom.*

en·sem·ble /ɒnˈsɒmbəl $ ɑːnˈsɑːm-/ *n* **1** [C] a small group of musicians, actors, or dancers who perform together regularly: **instrumental/string/brass etc ensemble** | **[+of]** *an ensemble of Mexican artistes* **2** [C usually singular] a set of things that go together to form a whole **3** [C usually singular] a set of clothes that are worn together: *an attractive ensemble*

en·shrine /ɪnˈʃraɪn/ *v* [T] *formal* if something such as a tradition or right is enshrined in something, it is preserved and protected so that people will remember and respect it: **be enshrined in sth** *The right of free speech is enshrined in the Constitution.*

en·shroud /ɪnˈʃraʊd/ *v* [T] *formal* to cover or surround something so that it is not possible to see, understand, or explain it SYN **shroud**: *hills enshrouded in mist* | *the mystery that enshrouds their disappearance*

en·sign /ˈensaɪn, -sən $ ˈensən/ *n* [C] **1** a flag on a ship that shows what country the ship belongs to: *the Russian ensign* **2** a low rank in the US navy, or an officer who has this rank

en·slave /ɪnˈsleɪv/ *v* [T] **1** to make someone a slave: *enslaved peoples* **2** *formal* if you are enslaved by something, it completely controls your life and your actions: *She seemed enslaved by hatred.* GRAMMAR **Enslave** is usually passive. —**enslavement** *n* [U]

en·snare /ɪnˈsneə $ -ˈsner/ *v* [T] **1** *formal* to trap someone in an unpleasant or illegal situation, from which they cannot escape: **[+in]** *Young girls were ensnared in prostitution rings.* **2** to catch an animal in a trap

en·sue /ɪnˈsjuː $ ɪnˈsuː/ ●○○ *v* [I] *formal* to happen after or as a result of something SYN **follow**: **[+from]** *problems that ensue from food and medical shortages*

en·su·ing /ɪnˈsjuːɪŋ $ -ˈsuː-/ *adj* [only before noun] happening after a particular action or event, especially as a result of it SYN **following**: **the ensuing battle/conflict/debate etc** *In the ensuing fighting, two students were killed.* | **the ensuing days/months/years etc** (=the days, months etc after an event) *The situation deteriorated over the ensuing weeks.*

en suite¹ /ɒn ˈswiːt $ ɑːn-/ *adj, adv BrE* **a)** an en suite bathroom is joined onto a bedroom: *Both bedrooms have en suite bathrooms.* **b)** an en suite bedroom has a bathroom joined onto it: *57 bedrooms, all en suite*

en suite², **ensuite** *n* [C] *BrE* **a)** a bathroom that is joined onto a bedroom, especially in a hotel: *Each room has an ensuite and a balcony.* **b)** a bedroom that has a bathroom joined onto it, especially in a hotel: *All the en suites have a log fire and a private garden or terrace.*

en·sure *especially BrE* (*also* **insure** *AmE*) /ɪnˈʃʊə $ -ˈʃʊr/ ●●● S2 W1 AWL *v* [T] to make certain that something will happen properly SYN **make sure**: *facilities to ensure the safety of cyclists* | **ensure (that)** *The hospital tries to ensure that people are seen quickly.*

> **REGISTER**
> In everyday English, people usually say **make sure** rather than **ensure**: *Please* ***make sure*** *all the windows are closed.*
> **Make sure** is followed by a clause (with or without **that**), never a direct object: *regulations to* ***ensure their safety*** → *regulations to* ***make sure (that) they are safe***

-ent /ənt/ *suffix* [in adjectives and nouns] someone or something that does something, or that has a particular quality: *local residents* → **-ANT**

en·tail /ɪnˈteɪl/ *v* [T] **1** to involve something as a necessary part or result: *A new computer system entails a lot of re-training.* | *Some foreign travel is entailed in the job.* | **entail doing sth** *The journey will entail changing trains twice.* **2** *old use* if you entail property, you arrange for it to be given to a specific person, usually your oldest son, when you die

en·tan·gle /ɪnˈtæŋɡəl/ *v* [T always + adv/prep] **1** to make something become twisted and caught in a rope, net etc: **be/get entangled in/with sth** *Small animals can* ***get entangled*** *in the net.* **2** to involve someone in an argument, a relationship, or a situation that is difficult to escape from OPP **disentangle**: **be/get etc entangled in sth** *fears that the US could* ***get entangled*** *in another war* | **be/get etc entangled with sb** *I didn't want to* ***become entangled*** *with my best friend's wife.* —**entangled** *adj*

en·tan·gle·ment /ɪnˈtæŋɡəlmənt/ *n* **1** [C] a difficult situation or relationship that is hard to escape from: *She had always been afraid of any emotional entanglements.* **2** [U] when something becomes entangled in something **3** [C often plural] a fence made of BARBED WIRE that prevents enemy soldiers from getting too close

entendre *n* → **DOUBLE ENTENDRE**

en·tente /ɒnˈtɒnt $ ɑːnˈtɑːnt/ *n* [C,U] a situation in which two countries have friendly relations with each other → **détente**: *the Anglo-Russian entente*

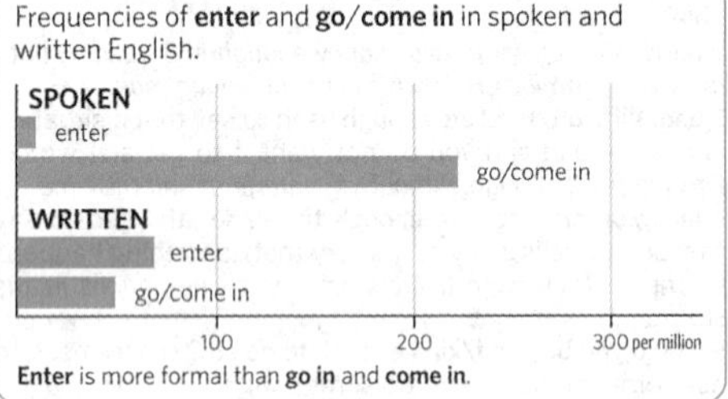

en·ter /ˈentə $ -ər/ ●●● S2 W1 *v*

1 GO INTO **a)** [I,T] to go or come into a place: *Silence fell as I entered the room.* | *Few reporters dared to enter the war zone.* **b)** [T] if an object enters part of something, it goes inside it: *The bullet had entered his brain.*

2 START WORKING [I,T] to start working in a particular profession or organization, or to start studying at a school or university: *Both the boys entered the army.* | *She* ***entered politics*** *in 1996.* | *He* ***entered the Church*** (=became a priest) *as a young man.*

3 START AN ACTIVITY [T] to start to take part in an activity, or become involved in a situation: *He entered the election as the clear favourite.* | *The rebels were prepared to* ***enter negotiations*** (=start discussing something).

4 COMPUTER **a)** [T] to put information into a computer by pressing the keys: *Press the return key to enter the information.* | **enter sth into sth** *The names are entered into a database.* **b)** [I,T] if you enter a computer system, you are given permission to use it by the computer: *It won't let you enter without a password.* THESAURUS ▸ WRITE

5 WRITE INFORMATION [T] to write information on a particular part of a form, document etc: *Don't forget to enter your postcode.* | **[+in/into]** *Enter your name in the space provided.*

6 COMPETITION/EXAMINATION [I,T] to arrange to take part in a race, competition, examination etc, or to arrange for someone else to take part: *At least 30 schools entered the competition.* | **[+for]** *Decisions about when he or she is entered for an examination should be taken very carefully.*

7 PERIOD OF TIME [T] to begin a period of time when something happens: *The economy has entered a period of recession.* | **enter its third week/sixth day/second year etc** *The talks have now entered their third week.*

8 START TO EXIST [T] if a new idea, thought etc enters your head, or a new quality enters something, it suddenly starts to exist there: *A note of panic entered her voice.* | **it never entered sb's head/mind** (=used to say that someone never considered a particular idea, especially when this is surprising) *It never entered his head that she might be seeing someone else.*

9 enter sb's life if someone or something enters your life, you start to know them or be affected by them: *By the time Angie entered his life, he was almost 30.*

10 OFFICIAL STATEMENT [T] *formal* to make an official statement: *Wilson* ***entered*** *a* ***plea*** *of not guilty* (=said that he was not guilty at the beginning of a court case). | *Residents entered a number of objections to the scheme.*

GRAMMAR: Comparison

enter

- You **enter** a place: *They entered the building through the front door.* ✗ Don't say: *They entered into the building.*
- You usually use **enter into** when talking about starting agreements or discussions with someone.

go

- You **go into** a place: *They went into the building through the front door.*

THESAURUS

enter to go or come into a place. **Enter** is more formal than **go in**: *It appears the burglars entered the house through a back window.* | *Occupying troops entered the town on 8th April.*

go in/into sth to enter a place. **Go in/into** is the usual phrase to use in everyday English: *It was getting cold so we went in.* | *He went into the cafe and ordered a drink.*

come in/into sth to enter a place - used when you are already in that place: *Come in and sit down.* | *When you come into the village, you'll see the church on your right.*

get in/into sth to succeed in entering a place, especially when it is difficult or it takes a long time: *I'd lost my key so I couldn't get in.* | *You can't get into the club if you are under 18.*

break in/into sth to enter a building using force, for example in order to steal something: *If anyone tries to break in, the alarm will go off.*

burst in/into sth to enter a room or building very suddenly and noisily: *Two men with guns burst in and told us to lie on the floor.* | *He burst into my office laughing and screaming like a maniac.*

barge in/into sth to suddenly enter a room where you are not wanted because you are interrupting someone or you were not invited: *She just barged into my room without knocking.* | *You can't just go barging in.*

sneak in/into sth to enter a place quietly and secretly hoping that no one will notice you: *If you're late, just try and sneak into the back of the class.*

slip in/into sth to enter a place quietly and quickly: *Maggie opened the door silently and slipped in.*

trespass *formal* to enter an area of land that belongs to someone else without permission: *The sign said 'Trespassers will be prosecuted'.* | *Trespassing on the railway is a criminal offence in the UK.*

enter into sth *phr v*
1 enter into an agreement/contract etc to make an official agreement to do something: **[+with]** *Some local authorities have entered into partnership with private companies.*
2 to start discussing or dealing with something: *It could be a problem, but we don't need to enter into that just yet.* | **enter into discussions/negotiations (with sb)** *The government refused to enter into discussions with the opposition.*
3 [usually in negatives] to affect a situation and be something that you consider when you make a choice: *He always buys the best – money doesn't enter into it.*
4 enter into the spirit of it/things to take part in a game, party etc in an eager way

enter upon sth *phr v formal* to start doing something or being involved in it: *countries newly entering upon industrialization*

en·te·ri·tis /ˌentəˈraɪtɪs/ *n* [U] a painful infection in your INTESTINES

en·ter·prise /ˈentəpraɪz $ -tər-/ ●●○ W3 *n*
1 [C] a company, organization, or business: ***commercial enterprises*** *such as banks and food manufacturers* | **state/public enterprise** *especially BrE* (=one owned by the government)
2 [U] the activity of starting and running businesses: *the management of* ***state enterprise*** (=done by the government) → FREE ENTERPRISE, PRIVATE ENTERPRISE
3 [C] a large and complicated project, especially one that is done with a group of other people SYN **initiative**: *The programme is a* ***joint enterprise*** *with the London Business School.*
4 [U] the ability to think of new activities or ideas and make them work: *We're looking for young people with enterprise and creativity.*

ˈenterprise ˌculture *n* [C,U] a society or attitude which encourages people to start new businesses and be successful

ˈenterprise ˌzone *n* [C] an area where the government is encouraging business activity. New businesses there usually pay lower taxes and companies are given money to encourage them to move to the area.

en·ter·pris·ing /ˈentəpraɪzɪŋ $ -tər-/ *adj* having the ability to think of new activities or ideas and make them work: *Some enterprising students are designing software.* | *an enterprising scheme to provide interest-free loans* —**enterprisingly** *adv*

en·ter·tain /ˌentəˈteɪn $ -tər-/ ●●○ *v*
1 [I,T] to amuse or interest people in a way that gives them pleasure: **entertain sb with sth** *She entertained the children with stories, songs and drama.* | *A museum should aim to entertain as well as educate.*
2 [I,T] to invite people to your home for a meal, party etc, or to take your company's customers somewhere to have a meal, drinks etc: *Mark usually does the cooking when we entertain.* | *Do you get an allowance for* ***entertaining clients****?*
3 entertain an idea/hope/thought etc *formal* to consider an idea etc, or allow yourself to think that something might happen or be true: *She could never entertain the idea of living in the country.*

en·ter·tain·er /ˌentəˈteɪnə $ -tərˈteɪnər/ *n* [C] someone whose job is to tell jokes, sing etc in order to entertain people: *Sinatra remains one of the top entertainers of all time.* | *street entertainers*

en·ter·tain·ing[1] /ˌentəˈteɪnɪŋ◂ $ -tər-/ ●●○ *adj* amusing and interesting: *Children's TV nowadays is much more entertaining.* | *an entertaining evening*

entertaining[2] *n* [U] when you invite people for meals or to parties, at home or for business reasons: *simple recipes for easy entertaining* | *The hotel is used for* ***corporate entertaining*** (=for business reasons).

en·ter·tain·ment /ˌentəˈteɪnmənt $ -tər-/ ●●● S3 W3 *n*
1 [C,U] things such as films, television, performances etc that are intended to amuse or interest people: *The town provides a wide choice of entertainment.* | *There will be* ***live entertainment*** (=performed then, not recorded) *throughout the day.* | **light entertainment** (=comedy) | *The dolphins give good* ***entertainment value*** (=a lot of amusement and interest). | **the entertainment industry/business/world** THESAURUS ▸ FUN
2 [U] *formal* when you entertain someone at home, or for business: *the entertainment of friends*

en·thral *BrE*, **enthrall** *AmE* /ɪnˈθrɔːl $ -ˈθrɒːl/ *v* (**enthralled**, **enthralling**) [T] to make someone very interested and excited, so that they listen or watch something very carefully: **be enthralled by/with sb/sth** *The children were enthralled by the story she was telling.* —**enthralled** *adj*

en·thrall·ing /ɪnˈθrɔːlɪŋ $ -ˈθrɒːl-/ *adj* extremely interesting: *an enthralling experience* THESAURUS ▸ INTERESTING

en·throne /ɪnˈθrəʊn $ -ˈθroʊn/ *v* [T] if a king or queen is enthroned, there is a ceremony to show that they are starting to rule —**enthronement** *n* [C,U]

en·thuse /ɪnˈθjuːz $ ɪnˈθuːz/ *v* **1** [I] to talk about something in a very interested or excited way: **[+about/over]** *Rick was there, enthusing about life in Australia.* **2** [T] to make someone interested in something or excited by it: **be enthused by/with sth** *The owners were certainly enthused by the offer.* GRAMMAR **Enthuse** is usually passive in this meaning.

en·thu·si·as·m /ɪnˈθjuːziæzəm $ ɪnˈθuː-/ ●●○ W3 *n*
1 [U] a strong feeling of interest and enjoyment about something and an eagerness to be involved in it: *Gillian and Darren greeted the speakers* ***with great enthusiasm****.* | *We went along to the local diving club,* ***full of enthusiasm****.* | *They go about their tasks* ***with little enthusiasm****.* | **[+for]** *Britain's apparent* ***lack of enthusiasm*** *for such a scheme* | *Employers* ***showed little enthusiasm*** *for the new regulations.* | *He* ***shares*** *your* ***enthusiasm*** *for jazz.* | *I left university* ***fired with enthusiasm*** *for work.* | *A delay of two hours did not* ***dampen*** *their* ***enthusiasm****.*
2 [C] *formal* an activity or subject that someone is very interested in

en·thu·si·ast /ɪnˈθjuːziæst $ ɪnˈθuː-/ ●○○ *n* [C] someone who is very interested in a particular activity or subject: **baseball/outdoors/sailing etc enthusiast** *a keep-fit enthusiast* | **[+for]** *an enthusiast for the latest management thinking*

en·thu·si·as·tic /ɪnˌθjuːziˈæstɪk◂ $ ɪnˌθuː-/ ●●○ S3 *adj* feeling or showing a lot of interest and excitement about something: **enthusiastic about (doing) sth** *All the staff are enthusiastic about the project.* | *The singer got an enthusiastic reception.* | *an enthusiastic supporter of reform* —**enthusiastically** /-kli/ *adv*

en·tice /ɪnˈtaɪs/ *v* [T] to persuade someone to do something or go somewhere, usually by offering them something that they want: **[+into/away/from etc]** *The birds were enticed back into Britain 40 years ago.* | **entice sb/sth to do sth** *Our special offers are intended to entice people to buy.* —**enticement** *n* [C,U]

en·ti·cing /ɪnˈtaɪsɪŋ/ *adj* something that is enticing attracts or interests you a lot SYN **tempting**: *It was a hot day and the water looked enticing.* —**enticingly** *adv*

en·tire /ɪnˈtaɪə $ -ˈtaɪr/ ●●● S3 W2 *adj* [only before noun] used when you want to emphasize that you mean all of a group, period of time, amount etc SYN **whole**: *It was the worst day in my entire life.* | *The entire staff agreed.* | *Have you drunk the entire bottle?*

en·tire·ly /ɪnˈtaɪəli $ -ˈtaɪr-/ ●●● S2 W2 *adv* completely and in every possible way → **partially**: *Our situation is entirely different.* | *The ridge consists entirely of volcanic rock.* | *Her reasons were not entirely clear.*

en·tir·e·ty /ɪnˈtaɪərəti $ -ˈtaɪr-/ *n formal* **1 in its/their entirety** including every part: *The film has been shown in its entirety for the first time.* **2 the entirety of sth** the whole of something: *We stayed in the hotel throughout the entirety of the weekend.*

en·ti·tle /ɪnˈtaɪtl/ ●●○ S3 W3 *v* [T]
1 to give someone the official right to do or have something: **be entitled to (do) sth** *Full-time employees are entitled to receive health insurance.* | **entitle sb to sth** *Membership entitles you to the monthly journal.* GRAMMAR **Entitle** is often passive in this meaning. THESAURUS ALLOW
2 be entitled sth if a book, play etc is entitled something, that is its name: *a documentary entitled 'The Price of Perfection'*

en·ti·tle·ment /ɪnˈtaɪtlmənt/ ●○○ *n* [C,U] the official right to have or do something, or the amount that you have a right to receive: **[+to]** *Do you need advice on your entitlement to state benefits?* | **benefit/holiday/pension etc entitlement** *The paid holiday entitlement is 25 days.*

enˈtitlement ˌprogram (*also* **entitlement**) *n* [C] a US government programme or system that gives money or help to people who need it

en·ti·ty /ˈentəti/ ●○○ AWL *n* (*plural* **entities**) [C] *formal* something that exists as a single and complete unit → **being**: *The mind exists as a* ***separate entity****.* | *Good design brings a house and garden together as a* ***single entity****.*

en·tomb /ɪnˈtuːm/ *v* [T] *formal* to bury or trap someone in something or under the ground: *They were entombed in rubble.* GRAMMAR **Entomb** is usually passive.

en·to·mol·o·gy /ˌentəˈmɒlədʒi $ -ˈmɑː-/ *n* [U] the scientific study of insects —**entomologist** *n* [C] —**entomological** /ˌentəməˈlɒdʒɪkəl◂ $ -ˈlɑː-/ *adj*

en·tou·rage /ˈɒntʊrɑːʒ $ ˈɑːn-/ *n* [C usually singular] a group of people who travel with an important person: *the president and his entourage*

en·trails /ˈentreɪlz/ *n* [plural] the inside parts of an animal's or person's body, especially their INTESTINES

en·trance¹ /ˈentrəns/ ●●● S3 W3 *n*
1 [C] a door, gate etc that you go through to enter a place OPP **exit**: **[+to/of]** *the* ***main entrance*** *to the school* | **front/back/side entrance** | *the station entrance* | **entrance hall/foyer/gate etc**
2 [C usually singular] the act of entering a place or room, especially in a way that people notice: *Bridget* ***made*** *a dramatic* ***entrance*** *into the room.*
3 [U] the right or ability to go into a place: **[+to]** *Entrance to the museum is free.* | *Reporters even managed to* ***gain entrance*** *to her hotel.* | *How much is the* ***entrance fee*** (=money you pay to get in somewhere)*?*
4 [U] permission to become a member of or become involved in a profession, university, society etc: *the initial interview for entrance to the Civil Service* | ***entrance examinations***
5 [C] when a person, country, organization etc first becomes involved in a particular area of activity: **[+into]** *The referendum blocked Switzerland's entrance into the European Economic Area.*
6 make your/an entrance to come onto the stage in a play

en·trance² /ɪnˈtrɑːns $ -ˈtræns/ *v* [T] *literary* if you are entranced by someone or something, you give them all your attention because they are so beautiful, interesting etc: *I was entranced by the sweetness of her voice.* —**entranced** *adj*: *She stopped, entranced.* —**entrancing** *adj*: *entrancing stories*

en·trant /ˈentrənt/ *n* [C] **1** someone who takes part in a competition **2** *especially BrE* someone who has recently started studying at university, or working: **[+to]** *new entrants to higher education*

en·trap /ɪnˈtræp/ *v* (**entrapped**, **entrapping**) [T] *formal* to trap someone or something, or make it impossible for them to escape from a situation, especially by tricking them: *He felt that she was trying to entrap him.*

en·trap·ment /ɪnˈtræpmənt/ *n* [U] the practice of trapping someone by tricking them, especially to show that they are guilty of a crime

en·treat /ɪnˈtriːt/ *v* [T] *formal* to ask someone, in a very emotional way, to do something for you SYN **beg**: **entreat sb to do sth** *His friends entreated him not to go.*

en·trea·ty /ɪnˈtriːti/ *n* (*plural* **entreaties**) [C,U] *formal* a serious request in which you ask someone to do something for you

en·trée /ˈɒntreɪ $ ˈɑːn-/ *n* **1** [C] the main dish of a meal, or a dish served before the main course – used in restaurants or on formal occasions: *an entrée of roast duck* **2** [C,U] *formal* the right or freedom to enter a place or to join a social group: **[+to/into]** *My family name* ***gave*** *me an* ***entrée*** *into upper-class Boston society.*

en·trenched /ɪnˈtrentʃt/ *adj* strongly established and not likely to change – often used to show disapproval: **[+in]** *Ageism is entrenched in our society.* | **entrenched attitudes/positions/interests etc** *a* ***deeply entrenched*** *belief in male superiority* —**entrench** *v* [T]

en·trench·ment /ɪnˈtrentʃmənt/ *n* **1** [U] when an attitude, belief etc becomes firmly established **2** [C] a system of TRENCHES (=long deep holes) dug by soldiers for defence or protection

en·tre nous /ˌɒntrə ˈnuː $ ˌɑːn-/ *adv BrE spoken* used humorously to tell someone that what you are going to say is secret and they must not tell anyone else

en·tre·pre·neur /ˌɒntrəprəˈnɜː $ ˌɑːntrəprəˈnɜːr/ ●○○ *n* [C] someone who starts a new business or arranges business deals in order to make money, often in a way that involves financial risks —**entrepreneurial** *adj*

en·tro·py /ˈentrəpi/ *n* [U] *technical* a lack of order in a system, including the idea that the lack of order increases over a period of time

en·trust /ɪnˈtrʌst/ ●○○ *v* [T] to make someone

responsible for doing something important, or for taking care of someone: **entrust sth/sb to sb** *She entrusted her son's education to a private tutor.* | **be entrusted with sth/sb** *I was entrusted with the task of looking after the money.*

en·try /'entri/ ●●● S3 W2 *n (plural* **entries**)
1 ACT OF ENTERING [C,U] the act of going into something OPP **exit**: **[+into]** *It was dark and their entry into the camp had gone unnoticed.* | *Harry **made** his **entry** into the village.* | *There was no sign of a **forced entry**.* | *How did the thieves **gain entry*** (=get in)?
2 BECOMING INVOLVED [U] when someone starts to take part in a system, a particular kind of work etc, or the permission they need in order to do this: **[+into/to]** *Britain's entry into the European Union* | *the minimum height for entry into the police force* | *This enabled European banks to **gain entry** into new markets.* | *the entry requirements for a degree course*
3 RIGHT TO ENTER [U] the right to enter a place, building etc: **[+to/into]** *Entry to the gardens is included in the price of admission.* | *The refugees were repeatedly **refused entry** into* (=not allowed in) *the country.* | **no entry** (=written on signs to show that you are not allowed to go somewhere) | *an **entry visa***
4 COMPETITION [C] **a)** something that you write, make, do etc in order to try and win a competition: *The **winning entry** will be published in our April issue.* | *What's the closing date for entries?* **b)** [usually singular] the number of people or things taking part in a competition: *We've attracted a record entry this year.*
5 STH WRITTEN [C] a piece of writing in a DIARY, or in a book containing information such as a dictionary: *a dictionary entry*
6 COMPUTER [U] the act of putting information into a computer: *data entry*
7 DOOR [C] (*also* **entryway** *AmE*) a door, gate, or passage that you go through to enter a place → ENTRANCE[1](1)

'entry ˌlevel, **entry-level** *adj* **entry level product/model/computer etc** a product etc that is the most basic or simple of its kind, making it suitable for people who do not have much money to spend or who do not have experience using the product

En·try·phone /'entrifəʊn $ -foʊn/ *n* [C] *trademark* a type of telephone outside a building that allows visitors to ask someone inside to open the door

en·try·way /'entriweɪ/ *n* [C] *AmE* a door, gate, room, or passage that you go through to enter a place SYN **entry**

en·twine /ɪn'twaɪn/ *v* [I,T] **1** to twist two things together or to wind one thing around another: *They walked together with their arms entwined.* GRAMMAR **Entwine** is usually passive when used as a transitive verb. **2 be entwined (with sth)** to be closely connected with something in a complicated way: *Our views of leadership are entwined with ideas of heroism.*

E num·ber /'iː ˌnʌmbə $ -ər/ *n* [C] *BrE* a number representing a chemical that has been added to a food, shown on the outside of a container

e·nu·me·rate /ɪ'njuːməreɪt $ ɪ'nuː-/ *v* [T] *formal* to name a list of things one by one

e·nun·ci·ate /ɪ'nʌnsieɪt/ *v* **1** [I,T] to pronounce words clearly and carefully **2** [T] *formal* to express an idea clearly and exactly: *ideas that he was to enunciate decades later* —**enunciation** /ɪˌnʌnsi'eɪʃən/ *n* [U]

e·nure /ɪ'njʊə $ ɪ'njʊr/ *v* another spelling of INURE

en·vel·op /ɪn'veləp/ *v* [T] *formal* to cover or wrap something or someone up completely: **[+in]** *mountain peaks enveloped in mist* | *the enveloping darkness*

en·ve·lope /'envələʊp $ -loʊp/ ●●● S3 *n* [C]
1 a thin paper cover in which you put and send a letter: *envelopes and stamps* | *She tore open the envelope and frantically read the letter.* | *He got a job **stuffing envelopes*** (=filling them with letters) *at the campaign headquarters.* → SAE, SASE
2 a layer of something that surrounds something else: **[+of]** *an envelope of gases around the planet*
3 push the envelope *especially AmE* to try to go beyond the normal limits of something: *a musician who pushes the envelope of improvisation*

en·vi·a·ble /'enviəbəl/ *adj* an enviable quality, position, or possession is good and other people would like to have it: *Now he was in the enviable position of not having to work for a living.* —**enviably** *adv*

en·vi·ous /'enviəs/ ●●○ *adj* wanting something that someone else has → **jealous**: **[+of]** *Colleagues were envious of her success.* | *envious looks* THESAURUS JEALOUS —**enviously** *adv*

en·vi·ron·ment /ɪn'vaɪrənmənt/ ●●● S1 W1 AWL *n*
1 the environment the air, water, and land on Earth, which is affected by man's activities: *Some of these chemicals are very damaging to the environment.* | *legislation to protect the environment* | *the effects of acid rain on the environment* | *the government minister for the environment*

GRAMMAR
You always say **the environment** in this meaning: *Pollution from cars is bad for the environment.* ✗ Don't say: *Pollution from cars is bad for environment.*
GRAMMAR GUIDE NOUNS

2 [C,U] the people and things that are around you in your life, for example the buildings you use, the people you live or work with, and the general situation you are in: *The company had failed to provide a safe environment for its workers.*
3 [C] the natural features of a place, for example its weather, the type of land it has, and the type of plants that grow in it → **habitat**: *a forest environment* | *a very adaptable creature that will eat different foods in different environments*

COLLOCATIONS

VERBS
protect the environment *We need to take drastic steps to protect the environment.*
conserve the environment *formal* (=protect it and prevent it from changing or being damaged) *People need to live in harmony with nature and conserve the environment.*
harm/damage the environment *The government insists that the dam will not harm the environment.*
destroy the environment *We need to find ways of producing energy without destroying the environment.*
pollute the environment *Nuclear waste will pollute the environment for centuries.*
clean up the environment *It's about time that we started cleaning up the environment.*

ADJECTIVES
the natural environment *Current methods of farming are damaging the natural environment.*
the marine environment (=the sea and the creatures that live there)

PHRASES
be good/bad for the environment *Plastic bags are bad for the environment.*
be harmful to the environment *Emissions from cars are harmful to the environment.*
protection of the environment *In developing countries, protection of the environment is not a primary concern.*
conservation of the environment *There are many organizations dedicated to conservation of the environment.*
damage/harm to the environment *A lot of chemicals used in industry cause harm to the environment.*
the destruction of the environment *Logging has led to the destruction of the natural environment.*
pollution of the environment *The waste material must be stored safely to avoid pollution of the environment.*
the effect/impact on the environment *The building's design will minimize its impact on the environment.*

E

COMMON ERRORS

⚠ Don't say 'hurt the environment'. Say **harm the environment** or **damage the environment**.

en·vi·ron·men·tal /ɪnˌvaɪrənˈmentl◂/ ●●● S2 W2 AWL *adj*
1 concerning or affecting the air, land, or water on Earth → **ecological**: *the environmental damage caused by the chemical industry* | *an international meeting to discuss* ***environmental issues*** | *the environmental impact of pollution from cars* | *an* ***environmental group*** (=group of people who want to protect the environment)
2 concerning the people and things around you in your life, for example the buildings you use, the people you live or work with, and the general situation you are in: *environmental risks to employees' health* —**environmentally** *adv*: *environmentally damaging projects*

enˌvironmental ˈfootprint *n* [C] the harmful effects of your activities on the environment: *You can* ***reduce*** *your* ***environmental footprint*** *by recycling as much as you can.*

en·vi·ron·men·tal·ist /ɪnˌvaɪrənˈmentəlɪst/ ●○○ AWL *n* [C] someone who is concerned about protecting the environment

enˌvironmentally ˈfriendly ●○○ (*also* **enˌvironment ˈfriendly**) *adj* not harmful to the environment

en·vi·rons /ɪnˈvaɪrənz/ *n* [plural] *formal* the area surrounding a place: *people living in Geneva and its environs* | *outside the environs of the college*

en·vis·age /ɪnˈvɪzɪdʒ/ ●○○ *v* [T] to think that something is likely to happen in the future: *The scheme cost a lot more than we had originally envisaged.* | **envisage doing sth** *I don't envisage working with him again.* THESAURUS ▸ IMAGINE

en·vi·sion /ɪnˈvɪʒən/ *v* [T] to imagine something that you think might happen in the future, especially something that you think will be good SYN **envisage**: *I envisioned a future of educational excellence.* THESAURUS ▸ IMAGINE

en·voy /ˈenvɔɪ/ ●○○ *n* [C] someone who is sent to another country as an official representative SYN **emissary**: *The United Nations is sending a special envoy to the area.*

en·vy¹ /ˈenvi/ ●●○ *v* (**envied**, **envying**, **envies**) [T]
1 to wish that you had someone else's possessions, abilities etc: *I really envy you and Ian, you seem so happy together.* | *She has a lifestyle which most people would envy.* | **envy sb sth** *He envied Rosalind her youth and strength.*
2 I don't envy you/her etc *spoken* used to say that you are glad that you are not in the bad situation that someone else is in

envy² ●○○ *n* [U]
1 the feeling of wanting something that someone else has → **jealousy**: **with envy** *He watched the others with envy.* | **[+of]** *his envy of the young man's success* | **twinge/pang of envy** *I felt a twinge of envy when I saw them together.* | *She could see that all the other girls were* ***green with envy*** (=feeling a lot of envy).
2 be the envy of sb to be something that other people admire and want to have very much: *an education system that is the envy of all European countries*

en·zyme /ˈenzaɪm/ *n* [C] a chemical substance that is produced in a plant or animal, and helps chemical changes to take place in the plant or animal

e·on /ˈiːən/ *n* [C] another spelling of AEON

e-pa·per /ˈiː ˌpeɪpə $ -ər/ *n* [U] ELECTRONIC PAPER

ep·au·lette, **epaulet** /ˌepəˈlet/ *n* [C] a small piece of cloth attached to the shoulder of a coat or shirt, especially on a military uniform

é·pée /ˈeɪpeɪ, ˈep- $ eɪˈpeɪ, ˈepeɪ/ *n* [C] a narrow sword with a sharp point, used in the sport of FENCING

e-pe·ti·tion /ˈiː pəˌtɪʃən/ *n* [C] a proposal on a website that people can show their support for by adding their name and email address: *More than 20,000 people have signed an e-petition calling for the hospital to remain open.*

e·phem·e·ra /ɪˈfemərə/ *n* [plural] small cheap things that people use in their ordinary life: *a collection of sporting ephemera*

e·phem·e·ral /ɪˈfemərəl/ *adj* existing or popular for only a short time SYN **transitory**: *Fashion is by nature ephemeral.* THESAURUS ▸ SHORT

ep·ic¹ /ˈepɪk/ ●○○ *n* [C] a book, poem, or film that tells a long story about brave actions and exciting events: *a Hollywood epic* THESAURUS ▸ STORY

epic² *adj* **1** an epic book, poem, or film tells a long story about brave actions and exciting events: *an epic tale of mutiny on the high seas* | *epic poetry* **2** an epic event continues for a long time and involves brave or exciting actions: *his epic journey to South America* **3** very large and impressive: *He had produced a meal* ***of epic proportions***.

ep·i·cen·tre *BrE*, **epicenter** *AmE* /ˈepɪˌsentə $ -ər/ *n* [C]
1 the place on the surface of the Earth that is right above the point where an EARTHQUAKE begins inside the Earth
2 the place where the most important things happen and important decisions are made: *London became the epicentre of the world fashion industry.*

ep·i·cure /ˈepɪkjʊə $ -kjʊr/ *n* [C] *formal* someone who enjoys good food and drink SYN **gourmet**

ep·i·cu·re·an /ˌepɪkjʊˈriːən/ *adj formal* gaining pleasure from the senses, especially through good food and drink

ep·i·dem·ic /ˌepəˈdemɪk◂/ ●●○ *n* [C]
1 a large number of cases of a disease that happen at the same time → **pandemic**: *Over 500 people died during last year's flu epidemic.* | **[+of]** *an epidemic of cholera*
2 a sudden increase in the number of times that something bad happens: **[+of]** *Britain is suffering an epidemic of petty crime.* —**epidemic** *adj* [only before noun]: *Violent crime is reaching* ***epidemic proportions*** *in some cities.*

ep·i·de·mi·ol·o·gy /ˌepədiːmiˈɒlədʒi $ -ˈɑːl-/ *n* [U] the study of the way diseases spread, and how to control them —**epidemiologist** *n* [C] —**epidemiological** /ˌepɪdiːmiəˈlɒdʒɪkəl $ -ˈlɑː-/ *adj*

ep·i·der·mis /ˌepɪˈdɜːmɪs $ -ɜːr-/ *n* [C,U] *technical* the outside layer of your skin

ep·i·dur·al /ˌepɪˈdjʊərəl◂ $ -ˈdʊr-/ *n* [C] a drug that is put into your back using a needle, done to prevent you feeling pain, especially when having a baby

ep·i·ge·net·ics /ˈepɪdʒəˈnetɪks/ *n* [U] *technical* the scientific study of changes in the behaviour of GENES that are caused by things that a living thing experiences

ep·i·glot·tis /ˌepɪˈglɒtɪs $ -ˈglɑː-/ *n* [C] the piece of flesh that hangs down at the back of your throat

ep·i·gram /ˈepɪgræm/ *n* [C] a short sentence that expresses an idea in a clever or amusing way —**epigrammatic** /ˌepɪgrəˈmætɪk◂/ *adj*

epi·graph /ˈepɪgrɑːf $ -græf/ *n* [C] a short sentence written on a STATUE, or used as an introduction to a book

ep·i·lep·sy /ˈepəlepsi/ *n* [U] a medical condition affecting your brain, that can make you suddenly become unconscious or unable to control your movements for a short time

ep·i·lep·tic¹ /ˌepəˈleptɪk◂/ *adj* caused by epilepsy: *He had an* ***epileptic fit***.

epileptic² *n* [C] someone who has epilepsy

ep·i·logue (*also* **epilog** *AmE*) /ˈepəlɒg $ -lɒːg, -lɑːg/ *n*
1 [C] a speech or piece of writing that is added to the end of a book, film, or play and discusses or explains the ending **2** [singular] *literary* something that happens at the end of a series of events → **prologue**: *a disastrous epilogue to his career*

E

Ep·i·Pen /ˈepɪpen/ *n* [C] *trademark* a medical instrument shaped like a large thick pen with a needle at one end, designed so that someone can INJECT a special drug into their body quickly and easily if they are having a severe ALLERGIC REACTION (=are extremely ill because of eating or touching a particular substance) or an ASTHMA attack that might kill them.

epiphany *n* [C] *literary* an occasion when you suddenly understand something

E·piph·a·ny /ɪˈpɪfəni/ *n* [U] a Christian holy day on January 6th that celebrates the day when the Three Kings came to see the baby Jesus

e·pis·co·pal /ɪˈpɪskəpəl/ *adj* relating to a BISHOP: *his episcopal duties*

Eˌpiscopal ˈChurch *n* [singular] a group of Christians in the US and Scotland

ep·i·sode /ˈepəsəʊd $ -soʊd/ ●●○ *n* [C]
1 an event or a short period of time during which something happens: *She decided she would try to forget the episode by the lake.* | *one of the most interesting episodes in his career*
2 a television or radio programme that is one of a series of programmes in which the same story is continued each week → **series**: *Watch next week's thrilling episode!* | **[+of]** *the first episode of a new drama series* **THESAURUS** PART

ep·i·sod·ic /ˌepəˈsɒdɪk◂ $ -ˈsɑː-/ *adj formal* **1** something that is episodic happens from time to time and then stops for a while, rather than happening all the time: *his episodic involvement in politics* **2** an episodic story or memory is one in which a lot of different events happen that do not follow on from each other

e·pis·te·mol·o·gy /ɪˌpɪstəˈmɒlədʒi $ -ˈmɑː-/ *n* [U] the part of PHILOSOPHY that deals with how we know things, how firmly we can know things etc —**epistemological** /ɪˌpɪstəməˈlɒdʒɪkəl $ -ˈlɑː-/ *adj*

e·pis·tle /ɪˈpɪsəl/ *n* [C] *formal* a long or important letter

Epistle /ɪˈpɪsəl/ *n* [C] one of the letters in the New Testament of the Bible

e·pis·to·la·ry /ɪˈpɪstələri $ -leri/ *adj formal* written in the form of a letter or a series of letters: *an epistolary novel*

ep·i·taph /ˈepətɑːf $ -tæf/ *n* [C] a short piece of writing on the stone over someone's GRAVE (=place in the ground where someone is buried)

ep·i·thet /ˈepəθet/ *n* [C] a word or short phrase used to describe someone, especially when praising them or saying something unpleasant about them: *He hardly deserves the epithet 'fascist'.*

e·pit·o·me /ɪˈpɪtəmi/ *n* **the epitome of sth** the best possible example of something: *She looked the epitome of elegance.* | *He was* ***the very epitome of*** *evil.*

e·pit·o·mize (*also* **-ise** *BrE*) /ɪˈpɪtəmaɪz/ *v* [T] to be a very typical example of something: *This building epitomizes the spirit of the nineteenth century.*

e·poch /ˈiːpɒk $ ˈepək/ *n* [C] a period of history SYN **era**: *the Victorian epoch* | *The king's death marked* ***the end of*** *an* ***epoch***. | ***the beginning of*** *a new* ***epoch*** **THESAURUS** PERIOD

ˈepoch-ˌmaking *adj* very important in changing the way people live or the way a society is organized: *the epoch-making social changes of the 1960s*

e-poll /ˈiː pəʊl $ -poʊl/ *n* [C] a POLL that is done on the Internet, in order to find out what people think or do

e·pon·y·mous /ɪˈpɒnɪməs $ ɪˈpɑː-/ *adj* [only before noun] the eponymous character in a book, film, or play is the character whose name is in its title: *Hester, the book's eponymous heroine*

e·pox·y res·in /ɪˌpɒksi ˈrezɪn $ ɪˌpɑː-/ *n* [U] a type of glue

Ep·som salts /ˌepsəm ˈsɔːlts $ -ˈsɒːlts/ *n* [plural] a white powder that can be mixed with water and used as a medicine

e-pub·lish·ing /ˈiː ˌpʌblɪʃɪŋ/ *n* [U] (***electronic publishing***) the business of producing books, magazines, or newspapers that are designed to be read using a computer —**e-publisher** *n* [C]

eq·ua·ble /ˈekwəbəl/ *adj* **1** *formal* someone who is equable remains calm and happy and does not often get annoyed: *a young man with a naturally equable temperament* **2** *technical* equable weather is neither too hot nor too cold SYN **temperate**: *a place with a pleasant, equable climate* —**equably** *adv*: *She smiled equably.*

e·qual¹ /ˈiːkwəl/ ●●● S1 W2 *adj*
1 SAME the same in size, number, amount, value etc as something else → **equivalent**: **equal number/amount (of sth)** *Both candidates received an equal number of votes.* | **(of) equal value/importance** *They believe that all work is of equal value.* | **equal in size/length/height etc** *The two towns are roughly equal in size.* | **of equal size/length/height etc** | **[+to]** *The rent was equal to half his monthly income.* **THESAURUS** SAME
2 SAME RIGHTS/CHANCES having the same rights, opportunities etc as everyone else, whatever your race, religion, or sex: *Our constitution states that all men are equal.* | *Our education system should provide* ***equal opportunities*** *for all children.* | *The government is committed to achieving* ***equal rights*** *for women.*
3 be equal to sth a) to have the ability to deal with a problem, piece of work etc successfully SYN **be up to**: *I'm not sure he's* ***equal to the task***. | *Are you* ***equal to*** *this* ***challenge***? **b)** to be as good as something else: *The architecture here is equal to any in the world.*
4 on equal terms/on an equal footing with neither side having any advantage over the other: *This law will help small businesses to compete on equal terms with large multinational corporations.*
5 all (other) things being equal *spoken* if things are as you normally expect them to be: *All things being equal, a small car will cost less than a larger one.*

equal² ●●○ S3 W3 *v* (**equalled, equalling** *BrE*, **equaled, equaling** *AmE*)
1 [linking verb] to be exactly the same in size, number, or amount as something else: *Two plus two equals four.* | *Prices become more stable when supply equals demand.*
2 [T] to be as good as something else, or get to the same standard as someone or something else: *Thompson equalled the world record.*
3 be equalled (only) by sth used to say that two things are as strong or as important as each other: *Her distaste for books was equalled only by her dislike of people.*
4 [T] to produce a particular result or effect: *A highly-trained workforce equals high productivity.*

equal³ ●○○ *n* [C]
1 someone who is as important, intelligent etc as you are, or who has the same rights and opportunities as you do: *He treats all his staff as equals.* | *a friendship between equals* | **[+in]** *She wasn't his equal in intelligence.*
2 be the equal of sb/sth to be as good as someone or something else: *The company proved to be the equal of its US rivals.*
3 be without equal (*also* **have no equal**) *formal* to be better than everyone or everything else of the same type: *His paintings are without equal.*

e·qual·i·ty /ɪˈkwɒləti $ ɪˈkwɑː-/ ●●○ *n* [U] a situation in which people have the same rights, advantages etc OPP **inequality**: **[+of]** *All people have the right to equality of opportunity.* | **[+with]** *Women have yet to achieve full equality with men in the workplace.* | **[+between]** *equality between men and women* | **racial/sexual equality** *The government must promote racial equality.*

e·qual·ize (*also* **-ise** *BrE*) /ˈiːkwəlaɪz/ *v* **1** [T] to make two or more things the same in size, value, amount etc: *We have tried to equalize the workload between the different teachers.* **2** [I] *BrE* to get a point in a game, so that you have the same number of points as your opponent: *England equalized ten minutes later.*

E

e·qual·iz·er (*also* **-iser** *BrE*) /ˈiːkwəlaɪzə $ -ər/ *n* [C] **1** *BrE* a point that you score in a game, that gives you the same number of points as your opponent: *England scored the equalizer with only ten minutes to go.* **2** something that makes all people equal because everyone experiences it in the same way: *Sport is a great equalizer in schools.*

e·qual·ly /ˈiːkwəli/ ●●○ W2 *adv*
1 [+adj/adv] to the same degree or amount: *You must have a good education, but practical training is equally important.*
2 in equal parts or amounts: *We agreed to divide the money equally between everyone.*
3 [sentence adverb] used when introducing a second idea or statement that is as important as your first one: *We want the economy to grow, but equally we want low inflation.*

ˈ**equals sign** *BrE*, ˈ**equal sign** *AmE n* [C] the sign (=) that you use in mathematics to show that two things are the same size, number, or amount

e·qua·nim·i·ty /ˌiːkwəˈnɪməti, ˌekwə-/ *n* [U] *formal* calmness in the way that you react to things, which means that you do not become upset or annoyed: *He received the news with surprising equanimity.*

e·quate /ɪˈkweɪt/ ●○○ AWL *v* [T] to consider that two things are similar or connected: **equate sth with sth** *Most people equate wealth with success.*

equate to sth *phr v* to be equal to something: *a rate of pay which equates to £6 per hour*

e·qua·tion /ɪˈkweɪʒən/ ●●○ AWL *n*
1 [C] a statement in mathematics that shows that two amounts or totals are equal → **algebra**: *In the equation 2x + 1 = 7, what is x?*
2 [C usually singular] the set of different facts, ideas, or people that all affect a situation and must be considered together: *The tourist industry forms a crucial* ***part of*** *the region's economic* ***equation***. | *The question of cost has now* ***entered the equation***.
3 [singular] when you consider that two things are similar or connected: *the equation of violence with power*

e·qua·tor, **Equator** /ɪˈkweɪtə $ -ər/ *n* **the equator** an imaginary line drawn around the middle of the Earth that is exactly the same distance from the North Pole and the South Pole: **on/at/near the equator** *a small village near the equator* → see picture at EARTH[1]

e·qua·to·ri·al /ˌekwəˈtɔːriəl◂/ *adj* **1** near the equator: *equatorial rain forests* **2** equatorial weather is very hot and wet: *an equatorial climate*

e·ques·tri·an /ɪˈkwestriən/ *adj* relating to horse-riding: *equestrian sports*

e·qui·dis·tant /ˌiːkwəˈdɪstənt◂/ *adj* at an equal distance from two places SYN **halfway**: **[+from/between]** *The city is equidistant between London and Glasgow.*

e·qui·lat·e·ral tri·an·gle /ˌiːkwəlætərəl ˈtraɪæŋɡəl/ *n* [C] *technical* a TRIANGLE whose three sides are all the same length → see picture at TRIANGLE

e·qui·lib·ri·um /ˌiːkwəˈlɪbriəm/ ●○○ *n* [singular, U]
1 a balance between different people, groups, or forces that compete with each other, so that none is stronger than the others and a situation is not likely to change suddenly: *The government is anxious not to upset the economic equilibrium.*
2 a state in which you are calm and not angry or upset: *She struggled to recover her equilibrium.*

e·quine /ˈekwaɪn, ˈiː-/ *adj* relating to horses, or looking like a horse

e·qui·nox /ˈiːkwənɒks, ˈe- $ -nɑːks/ *n* [C] one of the two times in a year when night and day are of equal length → **solstice**: *the spring equinox*

e·quip /ɪˈkwɪp/ ●●○ AWL *v* (**equipped**, **equipping**) [T]
1 to provide a person or place with the things that are needed for a particular kind of activity or work: **equip sb/sth with sth** *They spent a lot of money equipping the school with new computers.* | *He equipped himself with a hammer and nails.* | **be equipped with sth** *The rooms are equipped with video cameras.* | **be equipped to do sth** *The emergency services are equipped to deal with disasters of this kind.* | **well/poorly/fully etc equipped** *a well equipped hospital*
2 to give someone the information and skills that they need to do something: **equip sb with sth** *We equip students with the skills they will need once they leave college.* | **equip sb for sth** *training that will equip you for the job* | **equip sb to do sth** *We must equip young teachers to deal with difficult children.*

e·quip·ment /ɪˈkwɪpmənt/ ●●● S2 W2 AWL *n*
1 [U] the tools, machines etc that you need to do a particular job or activity: *a shop selling camping equipment* | *some brand new computer equipment* | *a very useful* ***piece of equipment***

> **REGISTER**
> In everyday English, people usually say **stuff** or, in British English, **things** rather than **equipment**: *Have you got your tennis* ***stuff***?

> **GRAMMAR: Countable or uncountable?**
> • **Equipment** is an uncountable noun and is not used in the plural. You say: *The laboratory has all the latest equipment.* ✗ Don't say: *The laboratory has all the latest equipments.*
> • **Equipment** is always followed by a singular verb: *All our equipment* ***has*** *been carefully tested.*
> • When talking about one machine or tool, you say **a piece/an item of equipment**: *A good compass is an essential piece of equipment when you are hiking.*

2 [singular] the process of equipping someone or something: **[+of]** *A lot of money was spent on the equipment of the new hospital.*

eq·uit·a·ble /ˈekwətəbəl/ ●○○ *adj formal* treating all people in a fair and equal way OPP **inequitable**: *an equitable distribution of food supplies* THESAURUS ▸ FAIR —**equitably** *adv*: *The work should be shared more equitably.*

eq·ui·ty /ˈekwəti/ *n* **1** [U] *formal* a situation in which all people are treated equally and no one has an unfair advantage OPP **inequity**: *a society run on the principles of equity and justice* **2** [U] *technical* the amount of money that you would have left if you sold your house and paid off the money you borrowed to buy the house **3 equities** [plural] *technical* SHARES in a company from which the owner of the shares receives some of the company's profits rather than a fixed regular payment **4** [U] *law* the principle that a fair judgment must be made in a situation where the existing laws do not provide an answer

e·quiv·a·lent[1] /ɪˈkwɪvələnt/ ●●○ W3 AWL *adj* having the same value, purpose, job etc as a person or thing of a different kind: **[+to]** *a qualification which is equivalent to a degree* | *I had no dollars, but offered him an equivalent amount of sterling.* —**equivalence** *n* [U]

equivalent[2] ●●○ AWL *n* [C] something that has the same value, purpose, job etc as something else: *The word has no equivalent in English.* | **[+of]** *He had drunk the equivalent of 15 whiskies.*

e·quiv·o·cal /ɪˈkwɪvəkəl/ *adj* **1** if you are equivocal, you are deliberately unclear in the way that you give information or your opinion SYN **ambiguous**: *His answer was equivocal.* | *She was rather equivocal about her work.* **2** information that is equivocal is difficult to understand or explain because it contains different parts which suggest that different things are true: *The results of the police enquiry were equivocal.*

e·quiv·o·cate /ɪˈkwɪvəkeɪt/ *v* [I] *formal* to avoid giving a clear or direct answer to a question —**equivocation** /ɪˌkwɪvəˈkeɪʃən/ *n* [C,U]

er /ɜː, ə $ ɜːr, ər/ *interjection BrE* a sound you make when you do not know exactly what to say next: *Well, er – I'm not really sure.*

-er[1] /ə $ ər/ *suffix* forms the comparative of many short adjectives and adverbs: *hot, hotter* | *dry, drier* | *fast, faster* → -EST

-er² *suffix* [in nouns] **1** someone who does something or is doing something: *a dancer* | *a driver* **2** something that does something: *a scraper* (=a tool you use for scraping) → **-AR, -OR**

ER /ˌiː ˈɑː $ -ˈɑːr/ *n* [C usually singular] *AmE informal* EMERGENCY ROOM

e·ra /ˈɪərə $ ˈɪrə/ ●●○ W3 *n* [C] a period of time in history that is known for a particular event, or for particular qualities: **[+of]** *We live in an era of instant communication.* | *a* ***new era*** *of world peace* | *His death marked* ***the end of an era.*** | *the Victorian era* **THESAURUS** PERIOD

e·rad·i·cate /ɪˈrædɪkeɪt/ ●○○ *v* [T] to completely get rid of something such as a disease or a social problem: **eradicate sth from sth** *We can eradicate this disease from the world.* | *an attempt to eradicate inflation* | *This problem has now been completely eradicated.* **THESAURUS** REMOVE —**eradication** /ɪˌrædɪˈkeɪʃən/ *n* [U]

e·rase /ɪˈreɪz $ ɪˈreɪs/ ●●○ *v* [T]
1 to remove information from a computer memory or recorded sounds from a tape: *The computer crashed, and all our records were erased.* **THESAURUS** REMOVE
2 to remove writing from paper: *Some of the names had been accidentally erased.*
3 to get rid of something so that it has gone completely and no longer exists: *Their dream is to erase poverty and injustice from the world.* | **erase sth from your mind/memory** *He couldn't erase the image from his mind.* | *She had tried to* ***erase the memory*** *of that day.*

e·ras·er /ɪˈreɪzə $ -sər/ ●●● *n* [C] a small piece of rubber that you use to remove pencil or pen marks from paper SYN **rubber** *BrE* → see picture at STATIONERY

e·ra·sure /ɪˈreɪʒə $ -ʃər/ *n* [U] *formal* when you erase something, or when something is erased: *a way to avoid accidental erasure of data from your computer*

-erati /ərɑːti/ *suffix* [in nouns] used to form nouns referring to people who have a lot of knowledge or influence in a particular subject: *the jazzerati* (=people who know a lot about jazz) | *the digerati* (=people who are skilled at using computers)

ere /eə $ er/ *prep, conjunction old use or literary* before

e-read·er /ˈiː ˌriːdə $ -ər/ *n* [C] a small piece of electronic equipment for reading E-BOOKS

erect¹ ●●○ *v* [T]
1 *formal* to build something such as a building or wall: *an imposing town hall, erected in 1892* | *Police have erected barriers across the main roads into the town.*
2 to fix all the pieces of something together, and put it in an upright position SYN **put up**: *It took a couple of hours to erect the tent.*
3 to establish something such as a system or institution

e·rect² /ɪˈrekt/ *adj* **1** in a straight upright position: *Martin* ***stood erect*** *on the platform.* **2** an erect PENIS or NIPPLE is stiff and bigger than it usually is because a person is sexually excited

e·rec·tion /ɪˈrekʃən/ *n* **1** [C] if a man has an erection, his PENIS increases in size and becomes stiff and upright because he is sexually excited: **have/get an erection** **2** [U] the act of building something or putting it in an upright position: **[+of]** *the erection of a new temple*

e-res·u·me (*also* **e-résumé**) /ˈiː ˌrezjʊmeɪ $ -rezʊˌmeɪ/ *n* [C] (***electronic resume***) an electronic written record of your education and previous jobs that you send to an employer over the Internet when you are looking for a new job

er·ga·tive /ˈɜːgətɪv $ ˈɜːr-/ *adj technical* an ergative verb can be either TRANSITIVE or INTRANSITIVE, with the same word used as the object of the transitive form and as the subject of the intransitive form, such as 'cooked' in the sentences 'He cooked the potatoes' and 'The potatoes cooked quickly'.

er·go /ˈɜːgəʊ $ ˈɜːrgoʊ/ *adv formal* [sentence adverb] therefore

er·go·nom·ics /ˌɜːgəˈnɒmɪks $ ˌɜːrgəˈnɑː-/ *n* [U] the way in which the careful design of equipment helps people to work better and more quickly: *We were very impressed with the machine's ergonomics.* —**ergonomic** *adj*: *a new ergonomic design* —**ergonomically** /-kli/ *adv* —**ergonomist** /ɜːˈgɒnəmɪst $ ɜːrˈgɑː-/ *n* [C]

ERM /ˌiː ɑːr ˈem/ *n* [singular, U] the abbreviation of ***exchange rate mechanism***

er·mine /ˈɜːmɪn $ ˈɜːr-/ *n* **1** [U] an expensive white fur, used especially for the formal clothes of judges, kings, and queens **2** [C] a small animal whose fur is white in winter

e·rode /ɪˈrəʊd $ ɪˈroʊd/ ●○○ AWL (*also* **erode away**) *v* [I,T]
1 if the weather erodes rock or soil, or if rock or soil erodes, its surface is gradually destroyed: *The cliffs are being constantly eroded by heavy seas.* | *The rocks have gradually eroded away.*
2 to gradually reduce something such as someone's power or confidence: *Our personal freedom is being gradually eroded away.* | *Repeated exam failure had eroded her confidence.*

e·ro·ge·nous zone /ɪˌrɒdʒənəs ˈzəʊn $ ɪˌrɑːdʒənəs ˈzoʊn/ *n* [C] a part of your body that gives you sexual pleasure when it is touched

e·ro·sion /ɪˈrəʊʒən $ ɪˈroʊ-/ ●○○ AWL *n* [U]
1 the process by which rock or soil is gradually destroyed by wind, rain, or the sea: *the problem of soil erosion* | *the erosion of the coastline*
2 the process by which something is gradually reduced or destroyed: **[+of]** | *the gradual erosion of our civil liberties*

e·rot·ic /ɪˈrɒtɪk $ ɪˈrɑː-/ *adj* **1** an erotic book, picture, or film shows people having sex, and is intended to make people reading or looking at it have feelings of sexual pleasure **2** erotic thoughts, feelings, or experiences involve sexual excitement: *an erotic dream* —**erotically** /-kli/ *adv*

e·rot·i·ca /ɪˈrɒtɪkə $ ɪˈrɑː-/ *n* [plural] erotic pictures, films, and writing → **pornography**

e·rot·i·cis·m /ɪˈrɒtɪsɪzəm $ ɪˈrɑː-/ *n* [U] a style or quality that expresses strong feelings of sexual love and desire, especially in works of art: *the eroticism of his early love poems*

err /ɜː $ ɜːr/ *v* [I] **1** **err on the side of sth** to be more careful or safe than is necessary, in order to make sure that nothing bad happens: *It's always best to* ***err on the side of caution.*** **2** *old use* to make a mistake

er·rand /ˈerənd/ *n* [C] a short journey in order to do something for someone, for example delivering or collecting something for them: *I seemed to spend my life* ***running errands*** *for people.* | *She was always* ***sending*** *me* ***on errands.*** | **on an errand** *I couldn't stop because I was on an errand.* | *He quickly set out on his* ***errand of mercy*** (=journey to help someone in danger). → **(send sb on) a fool's errand** at FOOL¹(11)

er·rant /ˈerənt/ *adj* [only before noun] *old-fashioned* behaving badly, usually by not obeying your parents or not being faithful to your husband or wife: *an errant wife* | *their errant son*

er·rat·ic /ɪˈrætɪk/ *adj* something that is erratic does not follow any pattern or plan but happens in a way that is not regular: *His breathing was becoming erratic.* | *his erratic behaviour* —**erratically** /-kli/ *adv*: *He always drives erratically.*

er·ra·tum /eˈrɑːtəm/ *n* (*plural* **errata** /-tə/) [C] *technical* a mistake in a book, shown in a list added after the book is printed

er·ro·ne·ous /ɪˈrəʊniəs $ ɪˈroʊ-/ AWL *adj formal* erroneous ideas or information are wrong and based on facts that are not correct SYN **incorrect**: *His economic predictions are based on some erroneous assumptions.* —**erroneously** *adv*

Frequencies of the nouns **error** and **mistake** in spoken and written English.

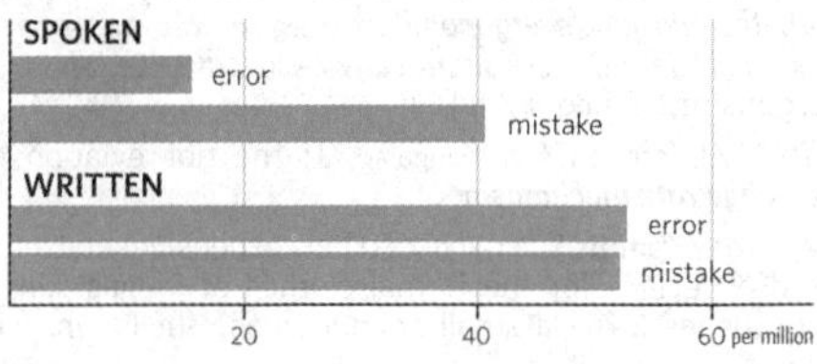

This graph shows that the word **mistake** is more common in spoken English than the word **error**. This is because **error** is not used in a very general way. It is used when describing particular types of mistake, for example in the expressions **computer error** or **error of judgement**, and sounds formal when used on its own. It is therefore more common in written English.

er·ror /ˈerə $ ˈerər/ ●●● S3 W2 AWL *n*
1 [C,U] a mistake: **[+in]** *There must be an error in our calculations.* THESAURUS▸ MISTAKE

REGISTER
Error is rather formal and is mainly used when talking about computers or in some fixed expressions such as **human error**. In everyday English, people usually use **mistake**: *There must be a* ***mistake*** *somewhere.*

2 [C] a mistake when you are working on a computer, which means that the computer program cannot do what you want it to do: *an* ***error message***
3 **error of judgment** a mistake in the way that you examine a situation and decide what to do: *The decision to expand the company was an error of judgment.*
4 **be in error** to have made a mistake, especially when making an official decision: *The doctor has admitted that he was in error.*
5 **do sth in error** if you do something in error, you do it by mistake: *The wrong man was arrested in error.*
6 **see the error of your ways** *literary* to realize that you have been behaving badly and decide to stop → **trial and error** at TRIAL[1](4)

COLLOCATIONS – MEANINGS 1 & 2

VERBS

make an error *We made too many errors, and that cost us the game.*
commit an error *formal* (=make an error, especially a serious one) *He knew he had committed a grave error of judgement.*
have/contain an error *If the data contains errors, the results will be wrong.*
find/spot/notice an error *His accountant spotted several errors in his tax return.*
realize your error *By the time she realized her error, it was too late.*
correct an error (*also* **rectify an error** *formal*) *We will rectify the error as soon as possible.*
avoid errors | **compound an error** (=make it worse) | **an error arises/occurs** *formal* (=happens)

ADJECTIVES/NOUN + error

a common error *a common error which students often make when writing essays*
a serious/bad error *The police made a serious error, which resulted in a young man's death.*
a small/minor error *The letter contained some minor spelling errors.*
a glaring error (=very bad and very noticeable) *There is a glaring error on page 10, where his date of death is given as 2053, not 1003.*
a huge/monumental error (=very serious) | **a grave error** (=extremely serious, with serious results) | **a fatal error** (=extremely serious, so that you are certain to fail) | **a grammatical/spelling/typing error** | **a clerical/administrative error** | **a factual error** (=which includes a fact that is wrong) | **a tactical error** (=one that may cause a plan to fail) | **a random error** (=one that is not like others or part of a pattern)
human error (=errors made by people) *Automatic checks reduce the danger of human error.*
computer error *An on-board computer error meant that the plane's systems shut down for a few vital seconds.*
pilot/driver error | **sb's past errors** *formal*

PHRASES

a margin of error (=the degree to which a calculation might be wrong) *We have to allow for a small margin of error in the calculations.*

er·satz /ˈeəzæts $ ˈerzɑːts/ *adj* [usually before noun] artificial, and not as good as the real thing: *ersatz coffee*

erst·while /ˈɜːstwaɪl $ ˈɜːrst-/ *adj* [only before noun] *formal* former or in the past: *She found herself ostracized by erstwhile friends.* | *his erstwhile allies*

er·u·dite /ˈerədaɪt/ *adj* showing a lot of knowledge based on careful study SYN **learned** —**eruditely** *adv* —**erudition** /ˌerəˈdɪʃən/ *n* [U]

e·rupt /ɪˈrʌpt/ ●○○ *v* [I]
1 if fighting, violence, noise etc erupts, it starts suddenly SYN **break out**: *Violence erupted after police shot a student during the demonstration.* | *A political row erupted over the MP's comments.*
2 if a VOLCANO erupts, it explodes and sends smoke, fire, and rock into the sky THESAURUS▸ EXPLODE
3 if a place or situation erupts, there is a sudden increase in activity or emotion: **[+into]** *They were angry to the point of erupting into riot.* | *Their conversations often erupted into squabbles.*
4 **erupt into laughter/shouting etc** to suddenly start laughing, shouting etc: *He erupted into loud, desperate sobs.*
5 if spots erupt on your body, they suddenly appear on your skin —**eruption** /ɪˈrʌpʃən/ *n* [C,U]: *a volcanic eruption* | *the eruption of violence*

-ery /əri/ (*also* **-ry**) *suffix* [in nouns] **1** a quality or condition: *bravery* (=the quality of being brave) | *slavery* (=the condition of being a slave) **2** things of a particular kind: *machinery* (=different types of machines) | *all her finery* (=beautiful clothes) **3** a place where a particular activity happens: *a bakery* (=where bread is baked) | *an oil refinery*

es·ca·late /ˈeskəleɪt/ ●○○ *v* [I,T]
1 if fighting, violence, or a bad situation escalates, or if someone escalates it, it becomes much worse: **[+into]** *Her fear was escalating into panic.* | *The fighting on the border is escalating.* | *We do not want to escalate the war.*
2 to become higher or increase, or to make something do this: *The costs were escalating alarmingly.* | *policies that escalate their own costs* | *escalating crime* THESAURUS▸ INCREASE —**escalation** /ˌeskəˈleɪʃən/ *n* [C,U]: *the escalation of fighting in June* | *a rapid escalation in value*

es·ca·la·tor /ˈeskəleɪtə $ -ər/ ●●○ *n* [C] a set of moving stairs that take people to different levels in a building

es·ca·lope /ˈeskəlɒp $ ɪˈskæləp/ *n* [C] *BrE* a thin piece of meat with no bones in it, especially VEAL (=meat from a young cow), cooked in hot oil

es·ca·pade /ˈeskəpeɪd/ *n* [C] **1** an adventure or series of events that are exciting or contain some risk: *their dangerous escapades in the Great War* **2** *AmE* a sexual relationship that is exciting or risky, but that is not considered serious

es·cape[1] /ɪˈskeɪp/ ●●● S3 W2 *v*
1 PERSON/PLACE [I] to leave a place when someone is trying to catch you or stop you, or when there is a dangerous situation: *He broke down the locked door and escaped.* | **[+from/through/over etc]** *He escaped from prison in October.* | **[+to]** *She escaped to Britain in 1938.*
2 DANGER [I,T] to get away from a dangerous or bad situation: **[+with]** *He escaped with minor injuries.* | **escape unhurt/unscathed/unharmed etc** *A boy escaped unhurt*

when the fire in his room exploded. | *They went to the hills to escape the summer heat.* | **escape sb's clutches** (=escape from someone) *The youth was trying to escape the clutches of two drunken female companions.*
3 AVOID [I,T] to avoid something bad or that you do not want to happen: *He* ***narrowly escaped*** *death in an avalanche.* | *The two passengers* ***escaped*** *serious* ***injury***. | *They must not be allowed to* ***escape justice***. | *It seemed impossible he would* ***escape detection***.
4 GAS/LIQUID ETC [I] if gas, liquid, light, heat etc escapes from somewhere, it comes out: *Vents allow any steam to escape if the system overheats.*
5 SOUND [I,T] *literary* if a sound escapes from someone, they accidentally make that sound: *A small laugh escaped her.* | **[+from]** *Holman let a weary sigh escape from his lips.*
6 escape sb's attention/notice if something escapes your attention or notice, you do not see it or realize that it is there
7 the name/date/title etc escapes sb used to say that someone cannot remember something: *For some reason which escapes me, we had to take a taxi.*
8 there's no escaping (the fact) used to emphasize that something is definitely important or will definitely happen: *There's no escaping the fact that work has profound effects on emotions and health.*

THESAURUS

escape to leave a place when someone is trying to catch you or stop you, or when there is a dangerous situation: *The thief escaped through an upstairs window.* | *She managed to escape from her attacker and call the police.*
get away to escape from someone who is chasing you, especially when there is no chance that you will be caught. **Get away** is more informal than **escape**: *The robbers got away but left plenty of clues at the scene.* | *Don't let him get away!*
break free/break away to escape from someone who is holding you: *She broke free and started running.*
flee *written* to leave somewhere very quickly in order to escape from danger: *Many people were forced to flee the country.* | *The two men fled before police arrived.*
get out to escape from a building or room: *I was locked in the room and couldn't get out.*
break out to escape from prison: *The jail is so secure that no one has ever broken out of it.*
abscond *formal* to escape from a prison or institution where you are supposed to stay: *Three prisoners who absconded have still not been found.* | *He absconded from a psychiatric hospital.*

escape² ●●○ S3 *n*
1 [C,U] the act of getting away from a place, or a dangerous or bad situation: *The girl had no chance of escape.* | *Christina hoped it wouldn't be too long before she could* ***make*** *her* ***escape***. | **[+from]** *the firm's* ***narrow escape*** *from bankruptcy* | *an* ***escape route*** | *They* ***had*** *a* ***lucky escape*** (=were lucky not to be hurt or killed) *when a car crashed into the front of their house.*
2 [singular, U] a way of forgetting about a bad or boring situation for a short time: **[+from]** *Travel can be an escape from the routine drudgery of life.*
3 [C,U] an amount of gas, liquid etc that accidentally comes out of the place where it is being kept, or an occasion when this happens: *The lid prevents the escape of poisonous gases.* → FIRE ESCAPE

es·caped /ɪ'skeɪpt/ *adj* [only before noun] an escaped person or animal has escaped from somewhere: *an* ***escaped prisoner***

es·cap·ee /ˌeskeɪ'piː, ɪˌskeɪ'piː/ *n* [C] *literary* someone who has escaped from somewhere

es'cape veˌlocity *n* [C,U] the speed at which a ROCKET must travel in order to get into space

es·cap·is·m /ɪ'skeɪpɪzəm/ *n* [U] activities or entertainment that help you forget about bad or boring things for a short time: *Books were* ***a form of escapism*** *from the real world.* —**escapist** *adj*: *pure escapist entertainment*

es·ca·pol·o·gist /ˌeskə'pɒlədʒɪst $ -'pɑː-/ *n* [C] *BrE* someone who escapes from ropes, chains, a cage etc to entertain people

e·scarp·ment /ɪ'skɑːpmənt $ -ɑːr-/ *n* [C] a high steep slope or cliff between two levels on a hill or mountain

es·cheat /ɪs'tʃiːt/ *n* [C] *AmE law* a legal process in which someone's money and property are given to the state after they die if they do not have a WILL, or if there is nobody else with a legal right to receive their money or property

es·chew /ɪs'tʃuː/ *v* [T] *formal* to deliberately avoid doing or using something: *I had eschewed politics in favour of a life practising law.*

e·scort¹ /ɪ'skɔːt $ -ɔːrt/ ●○○ *v* [T]
1 to take someone somewhere, especially when you are protecting or guarding them: *The shipment was escorted by guards.* | **escort sb back/through/to etc (sth)** *Two Marines escorted Benny inside.* | *I escorted her to the door.*
THESAURUS ▸ LEAD, TAKE
2 to go with someone and show them a place: **escort sb around (sth)** *The company escorts prospective buyers around the property.*
3 *old-fashioned* to go with someone to a social event: *Bill escorted Ellie to the opera.*

es·cort² /'eskɔːt $ -ɔːrt/ *n* [C] **1** a person or a group of people or vehicles that go with someone in order to protect or guard them: *a* ***police escort*** | ***under escort*** *He was driven away to prison under armed escort* (=protected or guarded by an escort). **2** someone who goes with someone to a formal social event **3** someone who is paid to go out with someone socially: *an escort agency* **4** *AmE* a PROSTITUTE, especially one who goes to social events or on trips with the person who pays them

es·cri·toire /ˌeskrə'twɑː $ -'twɑːr/ *n* [C] *formal* a small writing desk

es·crow /'eskrəʊ $ -kroʊ/ *n* [U] *law* money, land, or a written contract etc that is held by someone who is not directly involved in an agreement while the agreement is being achieved: *a property* ***held in escrow***

es·cu·do /e'skuːdəʊ $ -doʊ/ *n* (*plural* **escudos**) [C] the standard unit of money used in Portugal before the EURO

e·scutch·eon /ɪ'skʌtʃən/ *n* [C] *formal* a SHIELD on which someone's COAT OF ARMS (=family sign) is painted

-ese /iːz/ *suffix* **1** [in nouns] the people or language of a particular country or place: *the Viennese* (=people from Vienna) | *I'm learning Japanese* (=the language of Japan). **2** [in adjectives] belonging to a particular country or place: *Chinese music* **3** [in nouns] *informal* language or words used by a particular group, especially when it sounds ugly or is difficult to understand: *journalese* (=language used in newspapers) | *officialese* (=language used in official or legal writing)

e-sig·na·ture /'iː ˌsɪgnətʃə $ -ər/ *n* [C] ELECTRONIC SIGNATURE

Es·ki·mo /'eskəməʊ $ -moʊ/ *n* (*plural* **Eskimo** *or* **Eskimos**) [C] *old-fashioned* an INUIT (=someone who belongs to a race of people living in the very cold northern areas of North America). Many people now consider this word offensive.

ESL /ˌiː es 'el/ *n* [U] (***English as a Second Language***) the teaching of English to people who are living in an English-speaking country but whose first language is not English

ESOL /'iːsɒl $ -sɔːl/ *n* [U] the abbreviation of ***English for Speakers of Other Languages***

e·soph·a·gus /ɪ'sɒfəgəs $ ɪ'sɑː-/ *n* [C] the American spelling of OESOPHAGUS

es·o·ter·ic /ˌesə'terɪk◂, ˌiːsə-/ *adj* known and understood by only a few people who have special knowledge about something: *the esoteric world of scientific supercomputing* —**esoterically** /-kli/ *adv*

esp. the written abbreviation of ***especially***

ESP /ˌiː es 'piː/ *n* [U] **1** (***extra-sensory perception***) the

E

ability to know what will happen in the future, or to know what another person is thinking **2** (***English for Specific Purposes*** *or* ***English for Special Purposes***) the teaching of English to business people, scientists etc whose first language is not English

es·pa·drille /ˌespəˈdrɪl $ ˈespədrɪl/ *n* [C] a light shoe that is made of cloth and rope

es·pe·cial /ɪˈspeʃəl/ *adj BrE formal* SPECIAL

es·pe·cial·ly /ɪˈspeʃəli/ ●●● S1 W1 *adv*
1 [sentence adverb] used to emphasize that something is more important or happens more with one particular thing than with others SYN **particularly**: *I never liked long walks, especially in winter.* | *Art books are expensive to produce, especially if they contain colour illustrations.*
2 [+adj/adv] to a particularly high degree or much more than usual SYN **particularly**: *I was especially fond of chocolate biscuits.* | *Feedback is especially important in learning skills.* | *A depreciation of the dollar would make US exports cheaper and* ***especially so*** *in Japan.* | *Graphics are especially well handled in the book.*
3 for a particular person, purpose etc: **[+for]** *She bought a new pair of trainers especially for the trip.*
4 **not especially** not very, or not very much: *Accidents aren't especially common, but you never know.* | *He didn't especially want to learn to dance.*

GRAMMAR: Word order
- **Especially** is not used at the start of a sentence before the subject.
- You say: *I like Thai food especially.* | *I especially like Thai food.* ✗ Don't say: *Especially I like Thai food.*
- You say: *Young people especially are being affected by the economic crisis.* ✗ Don't say: *Especially young people are being affected.*

Es·pe·ran·to /ˌespəˈræntəʊ $ -ˈrɑːntoʊ/ *n* [U] an artificial language invented in 1887 to help people from different countries in the world speak to each other

es·pi·o·nage /ˈespiənɑːʒ/ *n* [U] the activity of secretly finding out secret information and giving it to a country's enemies or a company's competitors SYN **spying** → **spy**: *a campaign of* ***industrial espionage*** *against his main rival* → COUNTER-ESPIONAGE

es·pla·nade /ˌespləˈneɪd $ ˈesplənɑːd/ *n* [C] *especially BrE* a wide street next to the sea in a town

es·pouse /ɪˈspaʊz/ *v* [T] *formal* to support an idea, belief etc, especially a political one: **espouse a cause/policy etc** *He espoused a variety of scientific, social and political causes.* —**espousal** *n* [singular, U]: *her espousal of liberal reforms*

es·pres·so /eˈspresəʊ, ɪˈspre- $ -soʊ/ *n* (*plural* **espressos**) [C,U] strong black Italian coffee, or a cup of this coffee

es·prit de corps /eˌspriː də ˈkɔː $ -ˈkɔːr/ *n* [U] *formal* feelings of loyalty towards people who are all involved in the same activity as you SYN **team spirit**

es·py /ɪˈspaɪ/ *v* (**espied**, **espying**, **espies**) [T] *literary* to suddenly see someone or something SYN **spy**

Esq. **1** *especially BrE* (**esquire**) a title that is sometimes written after a man's name in the address on an official letter instead of using MR before the name **2** *AmE* a title of respect that is sometimes put after a lawyer's name: *Franklin Taylor Esq.*

-esque /esk/ *suffix* [in adjectives] **1** in the manner or style of a particular person, group, or place: *Kafkaesque* (=in the style of the writer Franz Kafka) **2** having a particular quality: *picturesque* (=pleasant to look at)

es·quire /ɪˈskwaɪə $ ˈeskwaɪr, ɪˈskwaɪr/ *n* [singular] a formal title that can be written after a man's name, especially in the address on an official letter

-ess /es, ɪs/ *suffix* [in nouns] a female: *an actress* (=a female actor) | *two lionesses*

es·say¹ /ˈeseɪ/ ●●● S3 *n* [C]
1 a short piece of writing about a particular subject by a student as part of a course of study: **[+on/about]** *an essay on Bernard Shaw*
2 a short piece of writing giving someone's ideas about politics, society etc: **[+on]** *Rousseau's 'Essay on the Origin of Languages'*
3 *formal* an attempt to do something

COLLOCATIONS - MEANINGS 1 & 2

VERBS
write/do an essay *I've got a 3,000 word essay to write before Friday.*
give in/hand in an essay *Half the class failed to hand in their essay on time.*
mark an essay *BrE*, **grade an essay** *AmE*: | **read an essay**

ADJECTIVES/NOUN + essay
an English/history/politics etc essay *He got a good grade for his English essay.*
a critical essay (=one that judges how good a book, writer etc is) | **an academic essay**

essay + NOUN
an essay question *We practised essay questions from previous exam papers.*
an essay title | **an essay topic**

PHRASES
a collection of essays *She published a collection of essays on philosophy.*

es·say² /eˈseɪ/ *v* [T] *formal* to attempt to do something

es·say·ist /ˈeseɪ-ɪst/ *n* [C] someone who writes essays giving their ideas about politics, society etc

es·sence /ˈesəns/ ●●○ *n*
1 [singular] the most basic and important quality of something: **[+of]** *The essence of Arsenal's style of football was speed.* | *She seems* ***the very essence of*** *kindness* (=she seems very kind).
2 **in essence** used when talking about the most basic and important part of something, especially an idea, belief, or argument: *In essence his message was very simple.*
3 [C,U] a liquid obtained from a plant, flower etc that has a very strong smell or taste and is used especially in cooking: *vanilla essence*
4 **sth is of the essence** used to say that something is very important: *Good communications are of the essence to remain competitive.* | **time/speed is of the essence** (=it is very important to do something quickly)

es·sen·tial¹ /ɪˈsenʃəl/ ●●● S3 W2 *adj*
1 extremely important and necessary: **[+for/to]** *A good diet is essential for everyone.* | **it is essential (that)** *It is essential that our pilots be given the best possible training.* | **it is essential to do sth** *It is essential to book in advance.* | *Window locks are fairly cheap and* ***absolutely essential****.* | *Even in small companies, computers are an essential tool.* THESAURUS IMPORTANT, NECESSARY
2 the essential part, quality, or feature of something is the most basic one SYN **fundamental**: *The* ***essential difference*** *between Sam and me was the fact that I took life seriously.* | *The* ***essential point*** *of relay racing is that it is a team effort.*

essential² *n* **1** [C usually plural] something that is necessary to do something or in a particular situation SYN **necessity**: *She packed a few essentials.* | *We only had the* ***bare essentials*** (=the most necessary things).
2 **the essentials** [plural] the basic and most important information or facts about a particular subject: **[+of]** *We have no reason to doubt the essentials of the girl's story.*

es·sen·tial·ly /ɪˈsenʃəli/ ●●○ S3 W3 *adv* used when stating the most basic facts about something SYN **basically**: *Ballet is essentially a middle-class interest.* | *Suicide rates have remained essentially unchanged.* | [sentence adverb] *Essentially, we are talking about the cold war period.*

esˌsential ˈoil *n* [C] an oil from a plant that has a strong smell and is used for making PERFUME or in AROMATHERAPY

est. **1** the written abbreviation of ***established***: *H. Perkins and Company, est. 1869* **2** the written abbreviation of ***estimated***

-est /ɪst/ *suffix* forms the SUPERLATIVE of many short adjectives and adverbs: *cold, colder, coldest* | *early, earlier, earliest* → **-ER**[1]

es·tab·lish /ɪˈstæblɪʃ/ ●●● S2 W1 AWL *v* [T]
1 to start a company, organization, system, etc that is intended to exist or continue for a long time SYN **found**: *The city of Boerne was established by German settlers in the 1840s.* | *Our goal is to establish a new research centre in the North.*
2 to begin a relationship with someone or a situation that will continue: **establish relations/links/contact etc (with sb)** *Hungary established diplomatic relations with Chile in 1990.* | *I wondered why he should bother to try and establish contact with me.*
3 to find out facts that will prove that something is true: *The police must establish the facts of the case before proceeding.* | **establish that** *The autopsy established that he had been murdered.* | **establish whether/if** *I was never able to establish whether she was telling the truth.*
4 to make people accept that you can do something, or that you have a particular quality: **establish yourself (as/in)** *He had three years in which to establish himself as prime minister.* | *He'd already begun to establish quite a reputation as a journalist.*

THESAURUS

establish to start a company or organization, especially one that exists for a long time: *The company was established in 1899.* | *He established a new research centre in Dublin.*
set up to start a new company or organization. **Set up** is less formal than **establish**, and is the usual phrase to use in everyday English: *Kate and her partner are setting up their own printing business.*
open to start a business that provides services to the public, such as a shop, restaurant, or hotel: *He opened his first restaurant in 1995.*
found to start a company or an organization such as a school or a hospital, especially by providing the money for it - used about something that was started a long time ago: *Who originally founded the college?* | *The bank was founded 60 years ago in Munich.*
inaugurate /ɪˈnɔːɡjəreɪt $ -ˈnɒː-/ *formal* to start an organization with an official ceremony: *Twenty years after the airport was inaugurated, it introduced its first transatlantic flights.*

es·tab·lished /ɪˈstæblɪʃt/ ●●○ AWL *adj* [only before noun]
1 already in use or existing for a long period of time: *Competition from established businesses can be formidable.* | ***well-established*** *teaching methods* | *By 1969 the civil rights movement was already an* ***established fact***. | *Every once in a while, the* ***established order*** (=people who rule) *is overthrown.*
2 known to do a particular job well, because you have done it for a long time: *an established professor of French literature*
3 established church/religion *especially BrE* the official church or religion in a particular country

es·tab·lish·ment /ɪˈstæblɪʃmənt/ ●●○ W3 AWL *n*
1 [C] *formal* an organization or institution, especially a business, shop etc: *a first-class training establishment*
2 the establishment the group of people in a society or profession who have a lot of power and influence and are often opposed to any kind of change or new ideas: *Young people are supposed to rebel against the Establishment.* | **the medical/legal/military etc establishment** *The public is treated with contempt by the art establishment.*
3 [U] the act of starting an organization, relationship, or system: **[+of]** *the establishment of NATO in 1949*

es·tate /ɪˈsteɪt/ ●●○ AWL *n*
1 [singular] *law* all of someone's property and money, especially everything that is left after they die: **sb's estate** *The property is part of the deceased's estate.*
2 [C] a large area of land in the country, usually with one large house on it and one owner: *a country estate* THESAURUS ▸ LAND
3 [C] *BrE* an area where houses or buildings of a similar type have all been built together in a planned way: **council/industrial/housing etc estate** → FOURTH ESTATE, REAL ESTATE

esˈtate ˌagent ●○○ *n* [C] *BrE* someone whose business is to buy and sell houses or land for people SYN **real estate agent, realtor** *AmE* —**estate agency** *n* [C]

esˈtate car (*also* **estate**) *n* [C] *BrE* a car with a door at the back, folding back seats, and a lot of space at the back SYN **station wagon** *AmE*

esˈtate tax *n* [C,U] a tax in the US on the money and possessions of a dead person → **inheritance tax**

es·teem[1] /ɪˈstiːm/ *n* [U] a feeling of respect for someone, or a good opinion of someone: **hold sb in high/great esteem** *The critics held him in high esteem as an actor.* | **token/mark of sb's esteem** (=a sign of their respect) *Please accept the small gift we enclose as a mark of our esteem.* | **[+for]** *my father's complete lack of esteem for actors* → SELF-ESTEEM

esteem[2] *v* [T] *formal* to respect and admire someone or something: *Peden was greatly esteemed by the people of Ayrshire.* | *He was esteemed as a literary wit.*

es·teemed /ɪˈstiːmd/ *adj* [usually before noun] *formal* respected and admired: *the esteemed French critic Olivier Boissiere* | ***highly esteemed*** *scholars*

es·thete /ˈiːsθiːt $ ˈes-/ *n* [C] an American spelling of AESTHETE —**esthetic** /iːsˈθetɪk $ es-/ *adj* —**esthetical** *adj* —**esthetically** /-kli/ *adv* —**esthetics** *n* [U]

es·ti·ma·ble /ˈestəməbəl/ *adj formal* deserving respect and admiration → **inestimable**

es·ti·mate[1] /ˈestəmət/ ●●○ W2 AWL *n* [C]
1 a calculation of the value, size, amount etc of something made using the information that you have, which may not be complete: *We just need an estimate of the number of people who will come.*
2 a statement of how much it will probably cost to build or repair something: **[+for]** *The garage said they'd send me an estimate for the work.*

COLLOCATIONS - MEANINGS 1 & 2

VERBS

make an estimate *Insurers have to make an estimate of the risk involved.*
give an estimate *The builder gave me an estimate of £10,000.*
provide (sb with) an estimate *Could you ask him if he can provide us with an estimate?*
put an estimate on sth (=say the amount that you think something is) *It is impossible to put an estimate on the value of the manuscript.*
an estimate puts sth at sth *Independent estimates put the number of refugees at 50,000.*
base an estimate on sth (=use something as information to give an estimate)

ADJECTIVES

a rough/approximate estimate (=not exact) *Can you give me a rough estimate of how much the repairs will cost?*
an accurate/reliable estimate (=fairly exact) *It's hard to put an accurate estimate on the number of people affected.*
a conservative estimate (=deliberately low) *By conservative estimates, 2.5 million people die each year from smoking cigarettes.*
an official estimate (=accepted by people in authority) *According to official army estimates, more than 500 rebels had been killed.*
current/recent estimates (=ones that are accepted now) | **the latest estimates** (=the most recent

E

ones) | **earlier/previous estimates** | **the original estimate** (=the one given at the beginning of a process)

PHRASES

according to an estimate *According to some estimates, an acre of forest is cleared every minute.*
estimates range/vary from ... to ... *Estimates of the number of homeless people in the city range from 6,000 to 10,000.*

es·ti·mate² /ˈestɪmeɪt/ ●●○ S3 W2 AWL *v* [T] to try to judge the value, size, speed, cost etc of something, without calculating it exactly: **be estimated to be/have/cost etc** *The tree is estimated to be at least 700 years old.* | **estimate sth at sth** *Organizers estimated the crowd at 50,000.* | **estimate that** *Scientists estimate that smoking reduces life expectancy by around 12 years on average.* | **estimate how many/what etc** *It is not easy to estimate how many people have the disease.*

REGISTER
In everyday English, people often say **put sth at** an amount rather than **estimate sth at**: *The damage **was put at** thousands of dollars.*

GRAMMAR
In more formal English, you say **it is estimated that** something is true: *It is estimated that the statue weighs 60 tons.*

—**estimated** *adj*: *heroin with an estimated street value of £50,000* —**estimator** *n* [C]

es·ti·ma·tion /ˌestəˈmeɪʃən/ ●○○ AWL *n*
1 [singular] a judgment or opinion about someone or something: **in sb's estimation** *In your estimation, who's going to win?* | **go up/come down in sb's estimation** (=be respected or admired more or less by someone)
2 [C] a calculation of the value, size, amount etc of something: *Estimations of total world sales are around the 50 million mark.*

es·tranged /ɪˈstreɪndʒd/ *adj* **1 sb's estranged husband/wife** someone's husband or wife whom they are no longer living with, used especially in newspaper reports **2** no longer seeing or talking to a relative or good friend, because of an argument: **[+from]** *Mill became estranged from his family after the marriage.* **3** no longer feeling any connection with something that used to be important in your life SYN **alienated**: **[+from]** *young adults who feel estranged from the church* —**estrangement** *n* [C,U]

es·tro·gen /ˈiːstrədʒən $ ˈes-/ *n* [U] the usual American spelling of OESTROGEN

es·tu·a·ry /ˈestʃuəri, -tʃəri $ -tʃueri/ *n* (*plural* **estuaries**) [C] the wide part of a river where it goes into the sea → **source**: *the Thames estuary*

ETA /ˌiː tiː ˈeɪ/ *n* [U] (***estimated time of arrival***) the time when a plane, ship etc is expected to arrive

e·tail·er /ˈiː ˌteɪlə $ -ər/ *n* [C] (***electronic retailer***) a business that sells products or services on the Internet, instead of in a shop —**e-tail** *n* [U]

et al /ˌet ˈæl/ *adv* written after a list of names to mean that other people are also involved in something: *Boers et al, 2001*

etc. (*also* **etc** *BrE*) /et ˈsetərə/ ●●● W2 *adv* (***et cetera***) used in writing after a list to show that there are many other similar things or people that you could have added: *a shop which sells cards, calendars, wrapping paper etc* | **etc. etc.** (=used when you are rather bored or annoyed by the list you are giving) *The letter says pay at once, they've reminded us before etc. etc.*

THESAURUS

etc. used when you want to say that there are many other examples of things of the same kind. The full form is **et cetera**, but this is rarely used. Don't use etc. in essays or formal writing: *They asked me about my past experience, qualifications etc.* | *Precise details of times, dates etc. should be recorded.*
such as used before one or more nouns to say that there are many other examples of the same kind. It is better to use **such as** rather than **etc.** in essays and formal writing: *It is best to avoid drinks such as tea, coffee or alcohol.* | *a distressing event such as the break-up of a marriage*
to name (but) a few used after examples of something when saying that there are many more you could have mentioned: *Our daily activities include tennis, swimming, darts, snooker to name but a few.*
and so on *spoken* used in spoken English when you want to say that there are other examples of things of the same kind. Don't use **and so on** in essays or formal writing – it sounds too vague: *You can do things to look after yourself in the way of diet, exercise, not smoking and so on.*
and many others and many other people or things: *The book includes poems by Christina Rossetti, William Blake and many others.*

et cet·e·ra /etˈsetərə/ *adv* the full form of **etc.**

etch /etʃ/ *v* **1** [I,T] to cut lines on a metal plate, piece of glass, stone etc to form a picture or words: **[+on]** *a gravestone with three names etched on it* | *A laser is used to etch a pattern in the smooth surface of the disc.* **2 be etched on/in your memory/mind** *literary* if an experience, name etc is etched on your memory or mind, you cannot forget it and you think of it often: *The island remained etched in my memory.* **3** [T] if someone's face is etched with pain, sadness etc, you can see these feelings from their expression: **be etched with sth** *Her face was etched with tiredness.* | *Craig saw lines of pain etched around her mouth.* **4** [T] to make lines or patterns appear on something very clearly: *etched glass*

etch·ing /ˈetʃɪŋ/ *n* [C] a picture made by printing from an etched metal plate

e·ter·nal /ɪˈtɜːnəl $ -ɜːr-/ ●●○ *adj*
1 continuing for ever and having no end: *the Christian promise of eternal life* | *She's an **eternal optimist*** (=she always expects that good things will happen). THESAURUS ▸ PERMANENT
2 seeming to continue for ever, especially because of being boring or annoying SYN **never-ending**: *the eternal arguments between mother and son*
3 eternal truths principles that are always true

e·ter·nal·ly /ɪˈtɜːnəl-i $ -ɜːr-/ *adv* **1** for ever: *I'll be **eternally grateful*** (=very grateful) *to you for this.* **2** *informal* always or very often SYN **constantly**: *He's a player who's eternally arguing with the referee.*

eˌternal ˈtriangle *n* [singular] *literary* the difficult situation that occurs when two people have a sexual relationship with the same person

e·ter·ni·ty /ɪˈtɜːnəti $ -ɜːr-/ *n* **1 an eternity** a period of time that seems very long because you are annoyed, anxious etc: *Here she waited for **what seemed like an eternity**.* | *That week was an eternity of solitude and boredom.* **2** [U] the whole of time without any end: *a little animal preserved **for all eternity** as a fossil* **3** [U] the state of existence after death that some people believe continues for ever

eˈternity ˌring *n* [C] a ring, usually with many jewels, that someone gives their wife or partner as a symbol of lasting love

-eth /əθ/ (*also* **-th**) *suffix old use or biblical* forms the third person singular of verbs: *he giveth*

eth·a·nol /ˈeθənɒl, ˈiː- $ -noʊl/ *n* [U] *technical* the type of alcohol in alcoholic drinks, which can also be used as a FUEL for cars SYN **ethyl alcohol**

e·ther /ˈiːθə $ -ər/ *n* **1** [U] a clear liquid used in the past as an ANAESTHETIC to make people sleep before an operation **2 the ether a)** the space through which radio waves or computer signals travel: *voices coming through the ether* **b)** (*also* **aether** *BrE*) *literary* the upper part of the sky

e·the·re·al /ɪˈθɪəriəl $ ɪˈθɪr-/ *adj* very delicate and light, in a way that does not seem real: *ethereal beauty* | *His music is ethereal.* —**ethereally** *adv*

E·ther·net /ˈiːθənet $ -ər-/ *n* [U] *trademark* a system used for connecting computer networks

eth·ic /ˈeθɪk/ ●●○ AWL *n*
1 [C] a general idea or belief that influences people's behaviour and attitudes: *The old ethic of hard work has given way to a new ethic of instant gratification.* → WORK ETHIC
2 ethics [plural] moral rules or principles of behaviour for deciding what is right and wrong: *a report on the ethics of gene therapy* | **professional/business/medical ethics** (=the moral rules relating to a particular profession) *public concern about medical ethics* | *a* ***code of ethics***

eth·i·cal /ˈeθɪkəl/ ●●○ AWL *adj* [no comparative]
1 relating to principles of what is right and wrong SYN **moral**: **ethical issues/questions/problems** *The use of animals in scientific tests raises difficult ethical questions.* | *The president must have the highest* ***ethical standards***.
2 morally good or correct OPP **unethical**: *I don't think it's ethical for you to accept a job you know you can't do.* | ***ethical investment*** *policies* (=investing only in businesses that are considered morally acceptable) → UNETHICAL —**ethically** /-kli/ *adv*

eth·nic¹ /ˈeθnɪk/ ●●○ W3 AWL *adj*
1 relating to a particular race, nation, or tribe and their customs and traditions: *The school teaches pupils from different* ***ethnic groups***. | *ethnic Russians in Estonia* | **ethnic violence/divisions/strife etc** (=violence etc between people from different races or cultures) | **ethnic background/origin** *The students are from a variety of ethnic backgrounds.* | *plans to partition the republic* ***along ethnic lines*** (=in a way that keeps different ethnic groups apart)
2 ethnic cooking/fashion/design etc cooking, fashion etc from countries that are far away, which seems very different and unusual: *ethnic music* —**ethnically** /-kli/ *adv*: *Surinam is culturally and ethnically diverse.*

ethnic² AWL *n* [C] someone who comes from a group of people who are a different race, religion etc or who have a different background from most other people in that country: *In that neighborhood of New York, we were all ethnics.*

ˌethnic ˈcleansing *n* [U] the action of forcing people to leave an area or country because of their RACIAL or national group

ˌethnic miˈnority *n* [C] a group of people of a different race from the main group in a country: *racial discrimination against doctors from ethnic minorities*

eth·no·cen·tric /ˌeθnəʊˈsentrɪk◂ $ -noʊ-/ *adj* based on the idea that your own race, nation, group etc is better than any other – used to show disapproval: *ethnocentric history textbooks* —**ethnocentrism** *n* [U] —**ethnocentricity** /ˌeθnəʊsenˈtrɪsəti $ -noʊ-/ *n* [U]

eth·nog·ra·phy /eθˈnɒɡrəfi $ eθˈnɑː-/ *n* [U] the scientific description of different races of people —**ethnographer** *n* [C] —**ethnographic** /ˌeθnəˈɡræfɪk◂/ *adj* —**ethnographically** /-kli/ *adv*

eth·nol·o·gy /eθˈnɒlədʒi $ eθˈnɑː-/ *n* [U] the scientific study and comparison of different races of people → **anthropology**, **sociology** —**ethnologist** *n* [C] —**ethnological** /ˌeθnəˈlɒdʒɪkəl◂ $ -ˈlɑː-/ *adj* —**ethnologically** /-kli/ *adv*

e·thos /ˈiːθɒs $ ˈiːθɑːs/ *n* [singular] the set of ideas and moral attitudes that are typical of a particular group: *a community in which people lived according to an ethos of sharing and caring*

eth·yl al·co·hol /ˌeθəl ˈælkəhɒl, ˌiːθaɪl- $ -hɒːl/ *n* [U] *technical* ETHANOL

E-tick·et /ˈiː ˌtɪkɪt/ *n* [C] (***electronic ticket***) a ticket, especially for a plane journey, that is stored in a computer and is not given to you in the form of paper

e·ti·o·lat·ed /ˈiːtiəleɪtɪd/ *adj* **1** *literary* pale and weak **2** *technical* a plant that is etiolated is weak and not very green because it has not received enough light —**etiolation** /ˌiːtiəˈleɪʃən/ *n* [U]

et·i·ol·o·gy /ˌiːtiˈɒlədʒi, $ -ˈɑːlə-/ *n* [C,U] *technical* the cause of a disease or the scientific study of this —**etiological** /ˌiːtiəˈlɒdʒɪkəl◂ $ -ˈlɑː-/ *adj* —**etiologically** /-kli/ *adv*

et·i·quette /ˈetɪket $ -kət/ *n* [U] the formal rules for polite behaviour in society or in a particular group: *strict rules of professional etiquette*

-ette /et/ *suffix* [in nouns] **1** a small thing of a particular type: *a kitchenette* (=small kitchen) | *a snackette* (=a very small meal) **2** a woman who is doing a particular job: *an usherette* (=female usher) **3** something that is not real, but is IMITATION(2): *flannelette* | *chairs covered with leatherette*

et·y·mol·o·gy /ˌetəˈmɒlədʒi $ -ˈmɑː-/ *n* **1** [U] the study of the origins, history, and changing meanings of words **2** [C] a description of the history of a word —**etymologist** *n* [C] —**etymological** /ˌetəməˈlɒdʒɪkəl◂ $ -ˈlɑː-/ *adj* —**etymologically** /-kli/ *adv*

eu·ca·lyp·tus /ˌjuːkəˈlɪptəs/ *n* [C,U] a tall tree that produces an oil with a strong smell, used in medicines

Eu·cha·rist /ˈjuːkərɪst/ *n* **the Eucharist** the holy bread and wine, representing Christ's body and blood, used during a Christian ceremony, or the ceremony itself

eu·gen·ics /juːˈdʒenɪks/ *n* [U] the study of methods to improve the mental and physical abilities of the human race by choosing who should become parents – used to show disapproval

eu·lo·gize (*also* **-ise** *BrE*) /ˈjuːlədʒaɪz/ *v* [I,T] to praise someone or something very much: *The poem does not eulogize the dead soldiers.* | *Commentators are eulogizing about the 17-year-old left-hander.* —**eulogist** *n* [C] —**eulogistic** /ˌjuːləˈdʒɪstɪk◂/ *adj*

eu·lo·gy /ˈjuːlədʒi/ *n* (*plural* **eulogies**) [C,U] a speech or piece of writing in which you praise someone or something very much, especially at a funeral: *The minister delivered a long eulogy.*

eu·nuch /ˈjuːnək/ *n* [C] a man whose TESTICLES have been removed, especially someone who guarded a king's wives in some Eastern countries in the past

eu·phe·mis·m /ˈjuːfəmɪzəm/ *n* [C] a polite word or expression that you use instead of a more direct one to avoid shocking or upsetting someone: *'Pass away' is a euphemism for 'die'.*

eu·phe·mis·tic /ˌjuːfəˈmɪstɪk◂/ *adj* euphemistic language uses polite words and expressions to avoid shocking or upsetting people —**euphemistically** /-kli/ *adv*

eu·pho·ri·a /juːˈfɔːriə $ jʊ-/ *n* [U] an extremely strong feeling of happiness and excitement which usually only lasts for a short time: *There was a general atmosphere of pessimism after the euphoria of last year.* THESAURUS PLEASURE

eu·phor·ic /juːˈfɒrɪk $ jʊˈfɔːrɪk, -ˈfɑː-/ *adj* feeling very happy and excited: *Scientists are euphoric at the success of the test.* —**euphorically** /-kli/ *adv*

Eu·ra·sian¹ /jʊˈreɪʒən, -ʃən/ *adj* **1** relating to both Europe and Asia **2** *old-fashioned* having one European parent and one Asian parent

Eurasian² *n* [C] *old-fashioned* someone who has one European parent and one Asian parent

eu·re·ka /jʊˈriːkə/ *interjection humorous* used to show how happy you are that you have discovered the answer to a problem, found something etc

eu·ro /ˈjʊərəʊ $ ˈjʊroʊ/ ●●● S2 W2 *n* (*plural* **euros**) [C] a unit of money that can be used in most countries of the European Union: *the value of the euro against the dollar* | *Prices are given in pounds and euros.*

Euro *adj* [only before noun] European, especially relating to the European Union: *next month's Euro elections*

Euro- /ˈjʊərəʊ $ ˈjʊroʊ/ *prefix* [in nouns and adjectives] **a)** relating to Europe, especially western Europe or the European Union: *Euro-MPs* | *Europop* **b)** European and something else: *the Euro-Asiatic area*

E

Eu·ro·crat /ˈjʊərəʊkræt $ ˈjʊroʊ-/ *n* [C] *informal* a word meaning a government official of the European Union, often one who makes decisions you do not like – used especially in newspapers

Eu·ro·dol·lar /ˈjʊərəʊˌdɒlə $ ˈjʊroʊˌdɑːlər/ *n* [C usually plural] *technical* a US dollar that has been put in a European bank or lent to a European customer to help trade and provide an international money system

Eu·rope /ˈjʊərəp $ ˈjʊr-/ *n* **1** the CONTINENT that is north of the Mediterranean and goes as far east as the Ural Mountains in Russia: *eastern Europe* **2** *BrE* the European Union: *the prime minister's stated aim of keeping Britain at the heart of Europe* **3** *BrE* the CONTINENT of Europe not including Britain and Ireland: *British exports to Europe*

Eu·ro·pe·an[1] /ˌjʊərəˈpiːən◂ $ ˌjʊrə-/ *n* [C] someone from Europe

European[2] *adj* relating to Europe or its people: *European languages | our European partners*

ˌEuropean ˈUnion *n* **the European Union** (*abbreviation* **EU**) a European political and economic organization that encourages trade and friendship between the countries that are members

Eu·ro·scep·tic /ˈjʊərəʊˌskeptɪk $ ˈjʊroʊ-/ *n* [C] *BrE* someone, especially a politician, who is against the EU and closer relations with other European countries: *Conservative Eurosceptics* —**Eurosceptic** *adj*

eu·tha·na·si·a /ˌjuːθəˈneɪziə $ -ˈneɪʒə/ *n* [U] the deliberate killing of a person who is very ill and going to die, in order to stop them suffering SYN **mercy killing**

eu·tha·nize /ˈjuːθənaɪz/ (*also* **eu·tha·nase** /-neɪz/ *BrE*) *v* [T] to kill an animal in a painless way, usually because it is very sick or old SYN **put down**: *The decision to euthanase a pet is heartbreaking.*

e·vac·u·ate /ɪˈvækjueɪt/ ●○○ *v*
1 [T] to send people away from a dangerous place to a safe place: **evacuate sb from/to sth** *Several families were evacuated from their homes. | During the war he was evacuated to Scotland.*
2 [I,T] to empty a place by making all the people leave: *Police evacuated the area. | The order was given to evacuate.*
3 [T] *formal* to empty your BOWELS —**evacuation** /ɪˌvækjuˈeɪʃən/ *n* [C,U]: *the evacuation of British troops from the area | Police ordered the evacuation of the building.*

e·vac·u·ee /ɪˌvækjuˈiː/ *n* [C] someone who is sent away from a place because it is dangerous, for example because there is a war

e·vade /ɪˈveɪd/ ●○○ *v* [T]
1 NOT TALK ABOUT STH to avoid talking about something, especially because you are trying to hide something → **evasion**: *I could tell that he was trying to* ***evade*** *the* ***issue***. *| The minister* ***evaded*** *the* ***question***.
2 NOT DO STH to not do or deal with something that you should do → **evasion**: *You can't go on* ***evading*** *your* ***responsibilities*** *in this way. | You're simply trying to* ***evade the problem***. THESAURUS AVOID
3 NOT PAY to avoid paying money that you ought to pay, for example tax → **evasion**: *Employers will always try to find ways to evade tax.*
4 ESCAPE to escape from someone who is trying to catch you: *She managed to evade the police. | So far he has* ***evaded capture***.
5 NOT ACHIEVE/UNDERSTAND *formal* if something evades you, you cannot do it or understand it SYN **elude**: *The subtleties of his argument evaded me.*

e·val·u·ate /ɪˈvæljueɪt/ ●○○ AWL *v* [T] to judge how good, useful, or successful something is SYN **assess**: *You should be able to evaluate your own work. | We need to evaluate the success of the campaign. | It can be difficult to evaluate the effectiveness of different treatments.*

e·val·u·a·tion /ɪˌvæljuˈeɪʃən/ ●○○ AWL *n* [C,U] a judgment about how good, useful, or successful something is SYN **assessment**: *We need to* ***carry out*** *a proper* ***evaluation*** *of the new system. | They took some samples of products for evaluation.*

ev·a·nes·cent /ˌevəˈnesənt, ˌiː- $ ˌev-/ *adj literary* something that is evanescent does not last very long

e·van·gel·i·cal /ˌiːvænˈdʒelɪkəl◂/ *adj* **1** evangelical Christians believe that they should persuade as many people as possible to become Christians: *the evangelical church | evangelical missionaries* **2** very eager to persuade people to accept your ideas and beliefs: *He spoke with evangelical fervour.*

e·van·ge·list /ɪˈvændʒɪlɪst/ *n* [C] **1** someone who travels to different places and tries to persuade people to become Christians **2 Evangelist** one of the four writers of the books in the Bible called the Gospels —**evangelism** *n* [U] —**evangelistic** /ɪˌvændʒəˈlɪstɪk◂/ *adj*: *his evangelistic work*

e·van·ge·lize (*also* **-ise** *BrE*) /ɪˈvændʒəlaɪz/ *v* [I,T] to try to persuade people to become Christians: *an attempt to evangelize the whole nation*

e·vap·o·rate /ɪˈvæpəreɪt/ ●○○ *v*
1 [I,T] if a liquid evaporates, or if heat evaporates it, it changes into a gas: *Most of the water had evaporated. | The sun evaporates moisture on the leaves.*
2 [I] if a feeling evaporates, it slowly disappears: *Hopes of achieving peace are beginning to evaporate. | His courage had evaporated away.* —**evaporation** /ɪˌvæpəˈreɪʃən/ *n* [U]

eˌvaporated ˈmilk *n* [U] milk which has been made thicker and sweeter by removing some of the water from it

e·va·sion /ɪˈveɪʒən/ *n* **1** [U] when you deliberately avoid doing something that you should do, or paying an amount of money that you should pay → **evade**: *He is in prison for* ***tax evasion***. *|* **[+of]** *She accused him of evasion of his responsibilities.* **2** [C,U] when you deliberately avoid talking about something or answering a question → **evade**: *I'm tired of his lies and evasions.*

e·va·sive /ɪˈveɪsɪv/ *adj* **1** not willing to answer questions directly: **[+about]** *Paul's being a bit evasive about this job. | an evasive reply* **2 take evasive action** to move or do something quickly to avoid someone being hurt: *Both pilots took evasive action and a collision was avoided.* —**evasively** *adv*: *She answered evasively.* —**evasiveness** *n* [U]

eve /iːv/ *n* **1** [C usually singular] the night or day before an important day: **[+of]** *on the eve of the election | We're arriving on* ***Christmas Eve***. *| a* ***New Year's Eve*** *party* **2** [C] *literary* evening: *one summer's eve*

e·ven[1] /ˈiːvən/ ●●● S1 W1 *adv*
1 used to emphasize something that is unexpected or surprising in what you are saying: *Most companies have suffered a drop in their profits, even very large companies. | It was quite difficult to see, even with the light on. | He became quite successful and even appeared on a television show once. | She did not even bother to phone us. | He never even acknowledged my letter.*
2 even bigger/better/brighter etc used to emphasize that someone or something is bigger, better etc: *This will make our job even more difficult. | The news was even worse than we expected. | The new version is even better than the old one.*
3 used to add a stronger, more exact word to what you are saying: *Some patients become depressed, even suicidal.*
4 even so *spoken* used to introduce something that is true although it is different from something that you have just said: *I know he's only a child, but even so he should have known that what he was doing was wrong.*
5 even if used to emphasize that something will still be true if another thing happens: *She's going to have problems finding a job even if she gets her A levels.*
6 even though used to emphasize that something is true although something else has happened or is true: *Even though he's 24 now, he's still like a little child. | I can still remember, even though it was so long ago.*
7 even now/then in spite of what has happened: *Even now I find it hard to believe that he lied. | They invested in new machinery and equipment, but even then the business was still losing money.*
8 even as used to emphasize that something happens at

the same moment as something else: *He realized, even as he spoke, that no one would ever believe him.*

GRAMMAR

Word order

• You use **even** before a person, thing, or phrase, when you want to emphasize what you are saying: ***Even young children** know the difference between right and wrong.* | *Poverty exists **even in rich countries**.*
• You use **even** before a verb: *He **even offered** to buy me a drink.*
• You use **even** after an auxiliary verb: *He **has even** offered to buy me a drink.* | *You **can even** see tigers.*

Even though/even if

• You use **even though** and **even if** when saying that something happens or is true in spite of another thing: *Even though she was tired, she carried on walking.* | *We're still going to the concert, even if it rains.* ✗ Don't say: *even she was tired* | *even it rains*
• You can use **even though** and **even if** with **still**: ***Even though** we're completely different, we're **still** friends.* ✗ Don't say: *Even though we're completely different, yet we're friends.* | *Even though we're completely different, but we're friends.*

even² ●●○ *adj*
1 LEVEL flat and level, with no parts that are higher than other parts OPP **uneven**: *The floor must be completely even before we lay the tiles.* | *You need a flat, **even surface** to work on.* | *He had lovely white, even teeth.* THESAURUS ▸ FLAT
2 NOT CHANGING an even rate, speed, or temperature is steady and does not change: *The room is kept at an even temperature.* | *Wood burns at a fairly even rate.*
3 DIVIDED EQUALLY divided equally, so that there is the same amount of something in each place, for each person etc: *Divide the dough into three even amounts.* | *an even distribution of wealth*
4 NUMBER an even number can be divided exactly by two OPP **odd**: *2, 4, 6 and 8 are even numbers.*
5 COMPETITION having teams or competitors that are equally good so that everyone has a chance of winning: *The first half was very even, and neither side scored.* | *an even contest*
6 SCORES if the score in a game is even, two teams or players have the same number of points: *At the end of the first half the score is even.*
7 be even *informal* to no longer owe someone something, especially money: *If you give me $5, we'll be even.*
8 CALM calm and controlled, and not extreme: *He read most of the speech in an even tone.*
9 an even chance a situation in which it is just as likely that something will happen as not happen: *I think we **have an even chance** of winning.* | *We knew there was an even chance that the operation would fail.*
10 get even (with sb) *informal* to do something unpleasant to someone to punish them for something that they did to you SYN **get revenge (on sb)**: *I'll get even with him one day.*
11 break even to neither make a profit nor lose money: *We're hoping that we'll at least break even, and perhaps make a small profit.* → EVEN-TEMPERED —**evenness** *n* [U]

even³ ●○○ *v*
even out *phr v* if things even out, or if you even them out, the differences between them become smaller SYN **level out**: *The differences in their income should even out over time.* | **even sth ↔ out** *Use a brush to even out the variations in colour.*
even sth ↔ **up** *phr v* to make a situation or competition more equal: *We put on a couple of more experienced players to even things up a bit.*

ˌeven-ˈhanded *adj* giving fair and equal treatment to everyone SYN **fair**: *He was very even-handed in the way he treated his employees.* THESAURUS ▸ FAIR

eve·ning¹ /ˈiːvnɪŋ/ ●●● S1 W1 *n*
1 [C,U] the early part of the night between the end of the day and the time you go to bed: *I do most of my studying **in the evening**.* | *I'm usually out **on Friday evenings**.* | *What are you doing **tomorrow evening**?* | *Peter left **yesterday evening**.* | *I'll see you **this evening**.* | *It was **early evening** by the time we got home.* | *We had just finished our **evening meal** when the doorbell rang.* | *a broadcast on the **evening news***
2 [C] a social event that takes place in the evening: *a musical evening* | *an evening of music and poetry*
3 good evening used to greet someone when you meet them in the evening

GRAMMAR: Patterns with evening

in the evening
• You do something **in the evening**: *I watched TV in the evening.* ✗ Don't say: *I watched TV on the evening.*

on Monday/Tuesday etc evening
• You do something **on Monday/Tuesday etc evening**: *We had a barbecue on Sunday evening.* ✗ Don't say: *We had a barbecue in Sunday evening.*

on the evening of sth
• Something happens **on the evening of** a particular date or event: *The accident happened on the evening of January 23.* | *On the evening of my birthday we planned to go out for dinner.*

evening² *interjection informal* used to greet someone when you meet them in the evening: *Evening, Joe. Everything all right?*

ˈevening class *n* [C] a class where adults can go to study in the evening

ˈevening dress *n* **1** [U] formal clothes that people wear for formal meals, parties, and social events in the evening
2 (*also* **evening gown**) *especially AmE* [C] an attractive dress that a woman wears to a formal meal, party, or social event in the evening

ˌevening ˈprimrose *n* [C,U] a plant with small flowers, whose seeds are used to make medicines

e·ven·ly /ˈiːvənli/ ●○○ *adv*
1 covering or affecting all parts of something equally: *Make sure the surface is evenly covered with paint.* | ***Spread** the butter **evenly** over the toast.* | *Support for the Liberals is fairly evenly spread across the country.* | *Make sure the weight is evenly distributed.*
2 divided in an equal way: *The profits will be split evenly between the three of us.* | *Government ministers are fairly evenly divided on this issue.* | *The prospects for the country are fairly **evenly balanced** between peaceful reform and revolution.*
3 in a regular or steady way: *He was breathing more evenly now.* | *rows of **evenly spaced** desks*
4 evenly matched if two competitors are evenly matched, they are as good as each other and so have an equal chance of winning: *The two teams are very evenly matched.*
5 if you say something evenly, you say it in a calm way without getting angry or upset SYN **calmly**

e·vens /ˈiːvənz/ *n* [U] *BrE technical* when there is an equal chance that an animal or person will win or lose a race, and the money that someone can win by BETTING on the race is the same as the amount they risk —**evens** *adj*: *the evens favourite*

e·ven·song /ˈiːvənsɒŋ $ -sɔːŋ/ *n* [U] the evening religious ceremony in the Church of England

e·vent /ɪˈvent/ ●●● S1 W1 *n*
1 INTERESTING/EXCITING [C] something that happens, especially something important, interesting or unusual: *one of the most important events in the history of mankind*
2 SOCIAL GATHERING [C] a performance, sports competition, party etc at which people gather together to watch or take part in something: *The conference was an important **social event*** (=an event at which people can meet each other). | *one of the major **sporting events** of the year* | **charity/fundraising etc event** *The school raises money by organizing fundraising events.*
3 RACE/COMPETITION [C] one of the races or competitions that are part of a large sports competition: *The next*

event will be the 100 metres. | *The 800 metres is not his best event.* → FIELD EVENT, THREE-DAY EVENT
4 in any/either event (*also* **at all events**) used to say that something will definitely happen or be true in spite of anything else that may happen SYN **in any case**: *I might see you tomorrow, but I'll phone in any event.*
5 in the event used to emphasize what actually happened in a situation as opposed to what you thought might happen SYN **as it happened**: *Extra police officers were brought in, although in the event the demonstration passed off peacefully.*
6 in the event of sth (*also* **in the event that sth happens**) used to tell people what they should do if something happens: *He left a letter for me to read in the event of his death.*
7 in the normal course of events if things happen in the normal way SYN **normally**: *In the normal course of events, the money is released within about three months.*

COLLOCATIONS

ADJECTIVES

a big/major event (=important) *Getting married is a major event in anyone's life.*
an important/significant event *It's natural to be nervous before such an important event.*
a momentous event (=very important) *the momentous events of 9/11*
a historic event (=very important in a country's history) *The signing of the peace treaty was a historic event.*
a dramatic event (=very exciting) | **a tragic event** (=very sad) | **a traumatic event** (=very upsetting) | **a rare/unusual event**
recent events *Recent events in the country have caused great concern.*
the latest events *We will be bringing you news of all the latest events.*
current events *There are some similarities between what happened in the 1920s and current events in the US.*

VERBS

an event happens/takes place (*also* **an event occurs** *formal*) *The event took place last year.*
events unfold (=happen, usually in an exciting or unexpected way) *I watched the dramatic events unfold from my window.*
events lead (up) to sth (=cause something) *His assassination was one of the events that led to the First World War.*
the events surrounding sth (=the events that are closely related to a situation) *The events surrounding her death remain a mystery.*
celebrate/commemorate/mark an event (=do something to show that you remember it) | **witness an event** (=see it happen) | **record an event** (=write down or photograph what happened)

PHRASES

a series/sequence of events (=related events that happen one after the other) *The incident was the first in a series of events that finally led to his arrest.*
a chain of events (=a series of events where each one causes the next) *He set in motion a chain of events that he couldn't control.*
the course of events (=the way in which a series of events happens) *Nothing you could have done would have changed the course of events.*

THESAURUS

event something that happens, especially something important, interesting, or unusual: *He spoke of the tragic event in which more than 100 people died.* | *recent political events*
occurrence /əˈkʌrəns $ əˈkʌrəns/ *formal* something that happens – used especially when saying how often something happens: *Storms like this one are fortunately a rare occurrence.* | *Accidents are almost a daily occurrence on this road.*
incident something that happens, especially something that is unusual or unpleasant, or something that is one of several events: *He died after a violent incident outside a nightclub.* | *This latest incident could put an end to his career.*
occasion an important social event or celebration: *She only wore the dress for special occasions.* | *It was his 100th birthday, and friends and family gathered to mark the occasion.*
affair [usually singular] something that happens, especially something shocking in political or public life which involves several people and events: *The affair has caused people to lose confidence in their government.*
phenomenon /fɪˈnɒmənən $ fɪˈnɑːmənɑːn, -nən/ something that happens or exists in society, science, or nature, especially something that is studied because it is difficult to understand: *natural phenomena such as earthquakes* | *Homelessness is not a new phenomenon.*

ˌeven-ˈtempered *adj* someone who is even-tempered is calm and does not easily become angry SYN **placid**

e·vent·ful /ɪˈventfəl/ *adj* full of interesting or important events: *She's led an eventful life.* | *an eventful day*

e·ven·tide /ˈiːvəntaɪd/ *n* [U] *literary* evening

e·vent·ing /ɪˈventɪŋ/ (*also* **three-day eventing**) *n* [U] a sport in which horses do three different sorts of competition, usually over three days

e·ven·tu·al /ɪˈventʃuəl/ ●●○ AWL *adj* [only before noun] happening at the end of a long period of time or after a lot of other things have happened: *Sweden were the eventual winners of the tournament.* | *Both sides were happy with the eventual outcome of the talks.*

e·ven·tu·al·i·ty /ɪˌventʃuˈæləti/ AWL *n* (*plural* **eventualities**) [C] *formal* something that might happen, especially something bad: **any/every eventuality** *We are prepared for every eventuality.* | *That is an unlikely eventuality.*

e·ven·tu·al·ly /ɪˈventʃuəli, -tʃəli/ ●●● S1 W2 AWL *adv* after a long time, or after a lot of things have happened: *He eventually escaped and made his way back to England.* | *Eventually, she got a job and moved to London.*

ev·er /ˈevə $ ˈevər/ ●●● S1 W1 *adv*
1 a word meaning at any time; used mostly in questions, negatives, comparisons, or sentences with 'if': *Nothing ever seems to upset him.* | *Have you ever been to Paris?* | *I don't think I've ever been here before.* | *If you're ever in Seattle, come and see me.*
2 *formal* always: *Ever optimistic, I decided to take the exam again.*
3 hardly ever not very often: *We hardly ever go out.*
4 never ever *spoken* never: *You never ever offer to help!*
5 for ever for all time: *Nothing lasts for ever.*
6 as ever as always happens: *As ever, Joe was late.*
7 ever since continuously since: *My back has been bad ever since I fell and hurt it two years ago.*
8 ever after for all time after something: *I suppose they'll get married and live happily ever after.*
9 hotter/colder/better etc than ever even hotter etc than before: *Last night's show was better than ever.*
10 as friendly/cheerful/miserable etc as ever as friendly etc as someone or something usually is: *George was as miserable as ever.* | *The food was as bad as ever!*
11 ever so cold/wet/nice etc *BrE spoken* very cold, wet etc: *The assistant was ever so helpful.* | *Thanks ever so much.*
12 ever such a *BrE* used to emphasize what someone or something is like: *She's ever such a nice girl.*
13 ever-increasing/ever-present etc increasing, present etc all the time: *the ever-increasing problem of drugs in the inner cities*
14 Yours ever/Ever yours *informal* used at the end of a letter above the signature
15 if ever there was one *informal* used to say that someone or something is a typical example of something: *He's a natural comedian if ever there was one.*

ev·er·green¹ /ˈevəgriːn $ -ər-/ *adj* **1** an evergreen tree or bush does not lose its leaves in winter OPP **deciduous** **2** an evergreen sportsman, singer etc is still good and popular even though they are fairly old: *the evergreen Cliff Richard*

evergreen² *n* [C] a tree or bush that does not lose its leaves in winter

ev·er·last·ing /ˌevəˈlɑːstɪŋ◂ $ ˌevərˈlæ-/ *adj formal* continuing for ever, even after someone has died SYN **eternal**: *everlasting fame | a symbol of God's everlasting love | a belief in life everlasting* THESAURUS PERMANENT

ev·er·more /ˌevəˈmɔː $ ˌevərˈmɔːr/ *adv* **for evermore** *literary* for ever: *I will love you for evermore.*

ev·ery /ˈevri/ ●●● S1 W1 *determiner* [always followed by a singular countable noun]

1 used to refer to all the people or things in a particular group or all the parts of something: *We looked carefully at every car that drove past. | Every child will receive a certificate at the end of the course. | I enjoyed every minute of the film. | I listened carefully to every word he said.* | **every single** (=used to emphasize that you mean 'all') *He seems to know every single person in the school.* | **every last drop/bit/scrap etc** (=all of something, including even the smallest amount of it) *They made us pick up every last scrap of paper.*

2 a) used to say how often something happens: **every day/week/month etc** (=at least once on each day, in each week etc) *They see each other every day. | Richard visits his mother every week.* | **every few seconds/ten days etc** *Re-apply your sunscreen every two hours. | Freda had to stop to rest every hundred metres or so* (=each time she had gone 100 metres). **b)** used to say how much distance there is between the things in a line: **every few feet/ten yards etc** *There were traffic lights every ten yards.*

3 every time whenever: *The roof leaks every time it rains.*

4 every now and then/again (*also* **every so often**) sometimes, but not often or regularly: *I still see her every now and then.*

5 every other the first, third, fifth etc or the second, fourth, sixth etc: *You only need to water plants every other day. | I visit my parents every other weekend.*

6 one in every three/two in every hundred etc used to show how common something is: *In Britain, one in every three marriages now ends in divorce.*

7 the strongest or greatest possible: *We wish you every happiness in your new home. | There is **every chance** that he will recover. | We have **every reason** to believe that the operation will be a success. | We have **every intention** of winning this competition.*

8 in every way in all ways: *The school's much better now in every way.*

9 every bit as good/important etc used to emphasize that something is equally as good, important etc as something else: *Taking regular exercise is every bit as important as having a healthy diet. | I loved him **every bit as much as** she did.*

10 every Tom, Dick, and Harry *spoken* used to mean 'everyone' or 'anyone', especially when you disapprove because there is no limit on who can be included: *I didn't want every Tom, Dick and Harry knowing about my private life.*

11 every which way *AmE informal* in every direction: *The kids ran off every which way.* → **every inch** at INCH¹(3), → usage note EACH

GRAMMAR: Patterns with every

- You use **every** with a singular noun and a singular verb: *Every person has the right to a fair trial.*
- Don't use **every** with a plural noun. ✗ Don't say: *every people*
- You usually use 'his', 'her', 'himself', or 'herself' after **every**: *Every player did his best. | Every woman can speak for herself.*
- However, you can use 'their', 'they', 'them' etc when you do not want to say whether the people are male or female: *Every child has their own room.*

ev·ery·bod·y /ˈevribɒdi $ -bɑːdi/ ●●● S1 W3 *pron* everyone

ev·ery·day /ˈevrideɪ/ ●●○ *adj* [only before noun] ordinary, usual, or happening every day: *the problems of **everyday life** | wearing everyday clothes | a simple, everyday object | Describe it in ordinary **everyday language**.* ⚠ Do not confuse with **every day** (=each day): *I see him every day.* THESAURUS NORMAL

Ev·ery·man /ˈevrimæn/ *n* [singular] *literary* a typical, ordinary person who is not very rich and has the problems and difficulties that all people have

ev·ery·one /ˈevriwʌn/ ●●● S1 W1 *pron* every person SYN **everybody**: *If everyone is ready, I'll begin. | Send my best wishes to everyone in the family. | Of course **everyone else** thought it was hilarious! | Not everyone enjoys sport.*

GRAMMAR: Singular or plural verb?

Use a singular verb after **everyone**: *Everyone likes her.* ✗ Don't say: *Everyone like her.*

USAGE: Everyone, every one

- You use **everyone** when you mean 'all of the people in a group'. You write it as one word: *Everyone enjoyed the concert.*
- You use **every one** when you mean 'every person or thing in a group, considered as separate people or things'. You write it as two words: *There are no chocolates left – someone has eaten every one.*
- You say **every one of** a group of people or things: *I wish to thank every one of you.* ✗ Don't write: *everyone of*

ev·ery·place /ˈevripleɪs/ *adv AmE spoken* everywhere

ev·ery·thing /ˈevriθɪŋ/ ●●● S1 W1 *pron*

1 each thing or all things: *Everything was covered in a thick layer of dust. | I decided to tell her everything. | Apart from the bus arriving late, **everything else** seemed to be going according to plan.*

2 all the things in your life, work etc: *Everything's fine at the moment. | I felt that everything was going wrong.*

3 be/mean everything (to sb) to be the most important thing in someone's life: *Money isn't everything. | His children mean everything to him.*

4 have everything to have all the things that people want in their lives: *What do you buy for the man who has everything?*

5 and everything *spoken* and a lot of other similar things: *Tina's worried about her work and everything.*

6 have everything going for you to have all the qualities that are likely to make you succeed: *You shouldn't worry so much – you've got everything going for you.*

7 everything but the kitchen sink *informal* all the equipment that you need and also a lot of things that you do not need – used humorously: *I think we've packed everything but the kitchen sink!*

GRAMMAR: Singular or plural verb?

You use a singular verb after **everything**: *Everything was the same.* ✗ Don't say: *Everything were the same.*

ev·ery·where /ˈevriweə $ -wer/ ●●● S2 W3 (*also* **everyplace** *AmE spoken*) *adv*

1 in or to every place: *I've looked everywhere but I can't find the map. | He's travelled everywhere in Europe. | The south should remain dry, but **everywhere else** will have heavy rain.*

2 be everywhere to be very common: *You must have seen the posters, they're everywhere.*

Eve's pud·ding /ˌiːvz ˈpʊdɪŋ/ *n* [C,U] a sweet DESSERT food, consisting of cooked apples with a layer of SPONGE cake on top

e·vict /ɪˈvɪkt/ *v* [T] to tell someone legally that they must leave the house they are living in: **evict sb from sth** *They were unable to pay the rent, and were evicted from their home.* | **be/get evicted** *They refused to leave and were **forcibly evicted** (=evicted by force). | attempts to have them evicted* —**eviction** /ɪˈvɪkʃən/ *n* [C,U]: *The family now faces eviction from their home.*

E

ev·i·dence¹ /ˈevɪdəns/ ●●● S2 W1 AWL *n*

1 [U] facts or signs that show clearly that something exists or is true: **[+of]** *At present we have no evidence of life on other planets.* | **[+for]** *There is no evidence for these claims.* | **evidence that** *Do you have evidence that this treatment works?* **THESAURUS** ▶ SIGN

2 [U] information that is given in a court of law in order to prove that someone is guilty or not guilty: *Murrow's evidence was enough to convict Hayes of murder.* | *He refused to give evidence at the trial.* | **[+against]** *There was very little evidence against the two men.* | **in evidence** *The documents may be used in evidence at the trial.*

3 be in evidence *formal* to be present and easily seen or noticed: *The police are always in evidence at football matches.* → KING'S EVIDENCE, QUEEN'S EVIDENCE, STATE'S EVIDENCE

GRAMMAR: Countable or uncountable?

- **Evidence** is an uncountable noun and is not used in the plural. You say: *The judge listened to all the evidence.* ✗ Don't say: *The judge listened to all the evidences.*
- **Evidence** is always followed by a singular verb: *The evidence **is** very clear.*
- When talking about one fact or sign, you say a **piece of evidence**: *The police found a vital piece of evidence.*

E

COLLOCATIONS – MEANINGS 1 & 2

VERBS

have evidence *Do the police have any evidence against him?*

find evidence (*also* **obtain evidence** *formal*) *The authorities failed to obtain enough evidence to convict him.*

gather/collect evidence *Police experts are still collecting evidence at the scene of the crime.*

look for/search for evidence *The investigation will look for evidence of financial mismanagement.*

hide evidence *The killer may have tried to burn the bodies in an attempt to hide the evidence.*

plant evidence (=deliberately put evidence somewhere to make someone look guilty) *He claims the evidence was planted there by the police.*

produce evidence (=find evidence and prepare it for a court case) *The case was adjourned to allow the police time to produce further evidence.*

give evidence (=tell a court about what you have seen or know to be true) *Ms White has agreed to give evidence at their trial.*

consider/examine/study the evidence *Having considered all the evidence, the court found him not guilty.*

ADJECTIVES

good/clear/strong evidence *There is clear evidence that smoking causes heart disease.*

hard evidence (=very clear evidence which proves that something is true) *They have no hard evidence to support their claim.*

fresh evidence (=new evidence) *The police say they may have found fresh evidence which proves Tilly was at the scene of the crime.*

medical/scientific evidence *There isn't any medical evidence to support the claim.*

reliable/credible (=which people can trust or believe) *Do you think their evidence is reliable?*

flimsy (=not good enough to make you believe something) *Their conclusions are drawn from some very flimsy evidence.*

convincing/compelling (=making you feel sure that something is true) *The data provides compelling evidence that the climate is changing.*

overwhelming (=when there is so much evidence that you are sure that something is true) *The evidence against him was overwhelming.*

conclusive/incontrovertible/irrefutable evidence (=very strong evidence which cannot be disproved) | **conflicting evidence** (=pieces of evidence that support different conclusions) | **circumstantial evidence** (=evidence which makes something seem likely, but does not prove it) | **anecdotal evidence** (=based on what people believe, rather than on facts) | **empirical evidence** (=based on scientific testing or practical experience)

PHRASES

a piece of evidence *The study produced one interesting piece of evidence.*

not a scrap/shred of evidence (=no evidence at all) *There is not one scrap of evidence against our client.*

COMMON ERRORS

⚠ Don't say 'true evidence'. Say **reliable evidence**.

evidence² *v* [T] *formal* to show that something exists or is true: **as (is) evidenced by** *The volcano is still active, as evidenced by the recent eruption.*

ev·i·dent /ˈevɪdənt/ ●●○ AWL *adj* easy to see, notice, or understand SYN **obvious**, **clear**: **evident that** *It was evident that she was unhappy.* | *It soon **became evident** that she was seriously ill.* | *It was **clearly evident** that the company was in financial difficulties.* | **[+to]** *It was evident to me that he was not telling the truth.* | **[+in]** *The growing popularity of the subject is evident in the numbers of students wanting to study it.* | *Bob ate his lunch with evident enjoyment.* → SELF-EVIDENT

ev·i·den·tial /ˌevɪˈdenʃəl◂/ AWL *adj* able to be used as evidence, or relating to evidence: *All jury members should have a copy of the evidential data.* —**evidentially** *adv*

ev·i·dent·ly /ˈevədəntli $ -dənt-, -dent-/ ●●○ AWL *adv*

1 used to say that something is true because you can see that it is true SYN **clearly**: *She was evidently a heavy smoker.* | *He was evidently in pain.* | *She was evidently upset by what she saw.* | [sentence adverb] *Evidently, the builders had finished and gone home early.*

2 used to say that you have been told that something is true SYN **apparently**: *He was evidently a rude, unpleasant child.* | [sentence adverb] *Evidently, the local authority are planning to close the school.*

e·vil¹ /ˈiːvəl/ ●●○ S3 W3 *adj*

1 BAD someone who is evil deliberately does very cruel things to harm other people: *an evil dictator responsible for the deaths of millions* | *his evil deeds*

2 WRONG something that is evil is morally wrong because it harms people SYN **wicked**: *They condemned slavery as evil.*

3 UNPLEASANT very unpleasant: *an evil smell* | *a puddle of evil black liquid*

4 DEVIL connected with the Devil and having special powers to harm people: *evil spirits* | *an evil spell*

5 the evil eye the power, which some people believe exists, to harm people by looking at them: *He claimed to have the power of the evil eye.*

6 the evil hour/day etc a time when you expect something unpleasant or difficult to happen: *Don't delay, you're only putting off the evil hour.* —**evilly** *adv*: *Jeff grinned evilly as he picked up the phone.*

evil² ●●○ *n*

1 [C] something that is very bad or harmful: *She wanted to protect her children from the evils of the outside world.* | *Poverty is one of the greatest social evils of our time.* | *the evils of capitalism*

2 [U] cruel or morally bad behaviour in general OPP **good**: *There is too much evil in the world.* | *the eternal struggle between good and evil* → **the lesser of two evils** at LESSER(2), → **necessary evil** at NECESSARY¹(3)

ˈevil-ˌdoer *n* [C] *old-fashioned* someone who commits crimes or does evil things

ˌevil-ˈminded *adj* immoral and cruel, and likely to cause a lot of harm or damage: *an evil-minded dictator*

e·vince /ɪ'vɪns/ *v* [T] *formal* to show a feeling or have a quality in a way that people can easily notice: *She evinced no surprise at seeing them together.*

e·vis·ce·rate /ɪ'vɪsəreɪt/ *v* [T] *formal or technical* to cut the organs out of a person's or animal's body

e·voc·a·tive /ɪ'vɒkətɪv $ ɪ'vɑː-/ *adj* making people remember something by producing a feeling or memory in them: **[+of]** *a picture that is wonderfully evocative of a hot, summer's day* | *evocative music*

e·voke /ɪ'vəʊk $ ɪ'voʊk/ ●○○ *v* [T] to produce a strong feeling or memory in someone: *The photographs evoked strong memories of our holidays in France.* | *His appearance is bound to evoke sympathy.* | *Her speech evoked a hostile response.* —**evocation** /ˌevə'keɪʃən, ˌiːvəʊ- $ ˌevə-, ˌiːvoʊ-/ *n* [C,U]: *The poem is an evocation of lost love.*

ev·o·lu·tion /ˌiːvə'luːʃən, ˌevə- $ ˌevə-/ ●○○ AWL *n* [U]
1 the scientific idea that plants and animals develop and change gradually over a long period of time: **[+of]** *the evolution of mammals* | *the* ***theory of evolution***
2 the gradual change and development of an idea, situation, or object: **[+of]** *the evolution of the computer*

ev·o·lu·tion·a·ry /ˌiːvə'luːʃənəri◂, ˌevə- $ ˌevə'luːʃəneri◂/ ●○○ AWL *adj*
1 relating to the way in which plants and animals develop and change gradually over a long period of time: *the evolutionary development of birds* | *Some scientists have rejected evolutionary theory.*
2 relating to the way in which ideas or situations gradually change and develop over a long period of time: *He is in favour of gradual, evolutionary social change.*

e·volve /ɪ'vɒlv $ ɪ'vɑːlv/ ●●○ AWL *v* [I,T]
1 if an animal or plant evolves, it changes gradually over a long period of time → **evolution**: **[+from]** *Fish evolved from prehistoric sea creatures.* | *Animals have evolved camouflage to protect themselves from predators.*
2 to develop and change gradually over a long period of time: *The school has evolved its own style of teaching.* | *Businesses need to evolve rapidly.* | **[+out of]** *The idea evolved out of work done by British scientists.* | **[+into]** *The group gradually evolved into a political party.*

e-vot·ing /'iː ˌvəʊtɪŋ $ -ˌvoʊ-/ *n* [U] voting using the Internet

ewe /juː/ *n* [C] a female sheep → **ram**

ew·er /'juːə $ 'juːər/ *n* [C] a large container for water, that was used in the past

eww /'iːu/ *interjection informal* used to show that you think something is extremely unpleasant: *She kissed him? Eww!*

ex /eks/ *n* [C usually singular] *informal* someone's former wife, husband, GIRLFRIEND, or BOYFRIEND: *I bumped into my ex in town.*

ex- /eks/ *prefix* former and still living: *his ex-wife* | *an ex-England cricketer*

ex·a·cer·bate /ɪg'zæsəbeɪt $ -sər-/ ●○○ *v* [T] to make a bad situation worse: *The recession has exacerbated this problem.* | *I don't want to exacerbate the situation.* —**exacerbation** /ɪgˌzæsə'beɪʃən $ -sər-/ *n* [U]

ex·act¹ /ɪg'zækt/ ●●● S2 W3 *adj*
1 completely correct in every detail: *Police are still investigating the exact cause of the accident.* | *What were his exact words?* | *The timing had to be exact.* | **exact location/position/spot etc** *The exact location of the hostages is unknown.* | **exact date/time/number/amount etc** *I know her birthday's in July, but I can't remember the exact date.* | **exact copy/replica etc** *It's not an exact copy, but most people wouldn't notice the difference.* | *Some concepts in Chinese medicine have no exact equivalent in Western medicine.*
THESAURUS ▸ RIGHT
2 to be exact *formal* used to emphasize that what you are saying is exact: *She has worked at the bank for many years, nine to be exact.*
3 the exact colour/moment/type etc used to emphasize that the same thing is involved: *the exact colour I was looking for* | *He came into the room at the exact moment I mentioned his name.* | *That's the* ***exact same*** *thing my dad said.*
4 the exact opposite (of sb/sth) someone or something that is as different as possible from another person or thing: *Gina's the exact opposite of her little sister.*
5 sth is not an exact science if you say that an activity is not an exact science, you mean that it involves opinions, guessing etc: *Predicting the weather is not an exact science.*
6 someone who is exact is very careful and thorough in what they do SYN **precise** —**exactness** *n* [U]

exact² *v* [T] **1** *formal* to demand and get something from someone by using threats, force etc: **exact sth from sb** *I exacted a promise from Ros that she wouldn't say a word.*
2 exact revenge (on sb) if someone exacts revenge, they punish a person who has harmed them: *Leonard was determined to exact revenge on his wife's killer.* **3 exact a high/heavy price** if something exacts a high or a heavy price, it has a very bad effect on a person or on a situation: *The years of conflict have exacted a heavy price.*

ex·act·ing /ɪg'zæktɪŋ/ *adj* demanding a lot of effort, careful work, or skill SYN **demanding**: *She was an exacting woman to work for.* | **exacting standards/demands/requirements etc** *He could never live up to his father's exacting standards.*

ex·act·i·tude /ɪg'zæktɪtjuːd $ -tuːd/ *n* [U] *formal* the state of being exact

ex·act·ly /ɪg'zæktli/ ●●● S1 W2 *adv*
1 used when emphasizing that something is no more and no less than a number or amount, or is completely correct in every detail: *It's exactly half past five.* | *The figures may not be exactly right, but they're close enough.* | **exactly where/what/when etc** *I can't remember exactly what she said.* | *It's a tragic situation and no one will ever know exactly what happened.* | **why/what/where etc exactly ...?** *Where exactly did you stay in Portugal?*
2 used to emphasize that something is the same or different SYN **precisely**: *That's exactly what we've been trying to tell you.* | *It's exactly the kind of work I've been looking for.* | *She tries to be* ***exactly like*** *her older sister.* | *Kevin's teachers saw him as quiet and serious, but with his friends he was* ***exactly the opposite***. | *The two candidates responded to the question in* ***exactly the same*** *way.*
3 not exactly *spoken* **a)** used as a reply to show that what someone has said is not completely correct or true: *'You hate Lee, don't you?' 'Not exactly. I just think he's a bit annoying, that's all.'* **b)** used to show that you mean the complete opposite, either humorously, or when you are annoyed SYN **hardly**: *I wouldn't bother asking Dave – he's not exactly Einstein* (=he is stupid).
4 *spoken* used as a reply to show that you think what someone has said is completely correct or true: *'So you think we should sell the house?' 'Exactly.'*

THESAURUS

exactly used when emphasizing that something is no more and no less than a number or amount, or is completely correct in every detail: *The bill came to exactly $1,000.* | *Police are still trying to find out exactly how the accident happened.*
precisely exactly – used when it is important to be sure that something is completely correct in every detail: *We need to know precisely how much this is going to cost.* | *Can you tell us precisely where he is?*
just *especially spoken* exactly – used especially when saying that things are exactly right, exactly the same, or exactly in a particular position: *The frame is just the right size for the picture.* | *He and his brother are just the same.* | *The hotel is just next to the station.*
right exactly in a particular position or direction: *The ball hit me right in the eye!* | *There's the house, right in front of you.*
directly exactly in a particular position or direction Directly is more formal than **right**: *Amy was sitting directly opposite me.*
on the dot *informal* at exactly a particular time, and no earlier or later than that time: *She always leaves the office at 5.30 p.m. on the dot.*

E

bang *BrE informal* exactly – used especially in the following very informal expressions: *The train was* ***bang on time****.* | *The shot was* ***bang on target****.* | *Cockatoo Island is right* ***bang in the middle of*** *Sydney harbour.*

ex·ag·ge·rate /ɪɡˈzædʒəreɪt/ ●●○ *v* [I,T] to make something seem better, larger, worse etc than it really is: *I couldn't sleep for three days – I'm not exaggerating.* | **it's easy/difficult/impossible to exaggerate sth** *It's difficult to exaggerate the importance of sleep.*

ex·ag·ge·rat·ed /ɪɡˈzædʒəreɪtɪd/ *adj* **1** if something is exaggerated, it is described as better, larger etc than it really is: *The revenue figures may be* ***slightly exaggerated****.* | **grossly/greatly/wildly exaggerated** *The danger had been greatly exaggerated.* **2** an exaggerated sound or movement is emphasized to make people notice: *an exaggerated sigh* | *He made an exaggerated bow.* | *He spoke with an exaggerated New York accent.* —**exaggeratedly** *adv*

ex·ag·ge·ra·tion /ɪɡˌzædʒəˈreɪʃən/ ●●○ *n* [C,U] a statement or way of saying something that makes something seem better, larger etc than it really is OPP **understatement**: *It would be an exaggeration to say that we were close friends.* | *It is* ***no exaggeration*** *to say that everyone will be affected by the new policy.* | *The situation can be described, without exaggeration, as disastrous.* | **slight/gross exaggeration** *That sounds like a slight exaggeration.*

E

ex·alt /ɪɡˈzɔːlt $ -ˈzɒːlt/ *v* [T] *formal* **1** to put someone or something into a high rank or position **2** to praise someone, especially God: *Exalt ye the Lord.*

ex·al·ta·tion /ˌeɡzɔːlˈteɪʃən, ˌeksɔːl- $ -ɒːl-/ *n* [U] *formal* **1** a very strong feeling of happiness **2** the state of being put into a high rank or position

ex·alt·ed /ɪɡˈzɔːltɪd $ -ɒːl-/ *adj* **1** having a very high rank and highly respected: *I felt shy in such exalted company.* **2** *formal* filled with a great feeling of joy

ex·am /ɪɡˈzæm/ ●●● S1 *n* [C]
1 a spoken or written test of knowledge, especially an important one: *At the end of each level, there's an exam.* | *How did you do* ***in your exams****?* THESAURUS ▸ TEST
2 *AmE* the paper on which the questions for an exam are written: *Do not open your exams until I tell you.*
3 *AmE* a set of medical tests: *an eye exam*

COLLOCATIONS

VERBS

take/do an exam (*also* **sit an exam** *BrE*) *We have to take exams at the end of each year.*
pass an exam (=succeed in it) *Did you pass your final exam?*
fail an exam *If you fail the exam, you can retake it.*
do well/badly in an exam *BrE*, **do well/badly on an exam** *AmE*: *Maria always did well in her exams at school.*
study for an exam (*also* **revise for an exam** *BrE*) *She has to study for her exams.*
sail though an exam (=pass it easily) *Don't worry - I'm sure you'll sail through all your exams.*
scrape through an exam (=only just pass it) | **flunk an exam** *AmE informal* (=fail it) | **cheat in an exam** *BrE*, **cheat on an exam** *AmE*: | **retake an exam** (*also* **resit an exam** *BrE*) (=take it again because you did not do well the first time)

ADJECTIVES/NOUN + exam

a chemistry/French etc exam *I knew I wouldn't pass the German exam.*
a written exam *There is a written exam at the end of the course.*
an oral exam (=in which you answer questions by speaking) *I have my French oral exams next week.*
a mock exam *BrE* (=one that you do to practise for the real exams) *He did well in the mock exams.*
a practical exam (=in which you have to make or do things) | **a final exam** (=at the end of a course) | **the end of year/term exam** *BrE*: | **high school exams** | **an entrance exam** (=in order to enter a school or university) | **a professional exam** (=to qualify in a profession, for example to be an accountant) | **the bar exam** (=in order to become a lawyer) | **board exams** *AmE* (=in order to become a nurse or doctor)

exam + NOUN

exam results *The school achieves consistently good exam results.*
an exam paper *I've still got dozens of exam papers to mark.*
an exam question *Read the exam questions carefully before writing your answers.*
exam revision *BrE*: | **exam practice** | **exam technique** (=good ways to succeed in exams)

COMMON ERRORS

⚠ Don't say 'make an exam'. Say **take an exam** or **do an exam**.

ex·am·i·na·tion /ɪɡˌzæməˈneɪʃən/ ●●○ W2 *n*
1 [C] *formal* a spoken or written test of knowledge, especially an important one SYN **exam**: *The examination results will be announced in September.* | *He's already taken the* ***entrance examination****.*
2 [C,U] the process of looking at something carefully in order to see what it is like: **[+of]** *a* ***detailed examination*** *of population statistics* | **under examination** *The proposals are still under examination.* | *The issues need* ***further examination****.* | **on examination** ***On closer examination*** *the vases were seen to be cracked.*
3 [C] a set of medical tests: *All patients had a complete physical examination.* | *A* ***post-mortem examination*** (=an examination on a dead body) *showed that he died from head injuries.*
4 [C,U] *law* the process of asking questions to get specific information, especially in a court of law → CROSS-EXAMINE

Frequencies of the verbs **examine**, **take/have a look at**, and **inspect** in spoken and written English.

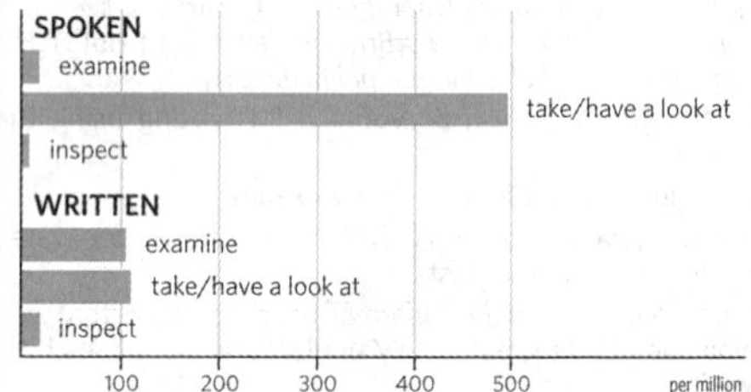

This graph shows that the expressions **have a look at** and **take a look at** are much more common in spoken English than the words **examine** or **inspect**. This is because **have a look at** and **take a look at** are much more general than **examine** or **inspect**, which mean 'to look at something carefully in order to find out about it or check if it is satisfactory'. They are more common in written English.

ex·am·ine /ɪɡˈzæmɪn/ ●●● S3 W2 *v* [T]
1 to look at something carefully and thoroughly because you want to find out more about it: *A team of divers was sent down to examine the wreck.* | *Hegel's philosophy will be examined in detail in Chapter 4.* | **examine how/whether/what etc** *In the course, we will examine how and why Spain became a democracy in 1931.* | **examine sth for sth** *The police will have to examine the weapon for fingerprints.* THESAURUS ▸ CHECK
2 if a doctor examines you, they look at your body to check that you are healthy
3 *formal* to ask someone questions to test their knowledge of a subject SYN **test**: **examine sb in/on sth** *You will be examined on American history.*
4 *law* to officially ask someone questions in a court of law → CROSS-EXAMINE

THESAURUS

examine to look at something carefully and thoroughly because you want to find out more about

it: *Experts who examined the painting believe it is genuine.*
have a look at/take a look at *especially spoken* to quickly examine something to find out what is wrong with it or to find out more about it. **Have a look at** is less formal than **examine**, and is the usual phrase to use in everyday English: *I'll have a look at your car if you like.*
inspect to examine something carefully to make sure that it is correct, safe, or working properly, especially when it is your job to do this: *The building is regularly inspected by a fire-safety officer.*
analyze (*also* **analyse** *BrE*) to examine something carefully, especially detailed information about something, so that you can understand it: *Researchers analyzed the results of the survey.* | *We're still analysing all the data.*
study to spend a lot of time examining something very carefully, for example a problem or situation: *A team of scientists has been studying the effects of global warming on Antarctica.*
review to examine something such as a situation or process to see if any changes are necessary: *The bank will review its security procedures after last week's attack.*
scrutinize (*also* **scrutinise** *BrE*) to examine something very carefully to find out if there is anything wrong with it: *Congress is currently scrutinizing the deal.*

ex·am·in·er /ɪɡˈzæmɪnə $ -ər/ *n* [C] someone from a university, college, or professional institution who tests students' knowledge or ability

ex·am·ple /ɪɡˈzɑːmpəl $ ɪɡˈzæm-/ ●●● S1 W1 *n* [C]
1 a specific fact, idea, person, or thing that is used to explain or support a general idea, or to show what is typical of a larger group: **[+of]** *Can anyone give me an example of a transitive verb?*
2 for example used before mentioning a specific thing, person, place etc in order to explain what you mean or to support an argument: *Many countries, for example Mexico and Japan, have a lot of earthquakes.* | *Car prices can vary a lot. For example, in Belgium the VW Golf costs $1,000 less than in Britain.*
3 someone whose behaviour is very good and should be copied by others, or this type of behaviour: **[+to]** *Her courage is an example to us all.* | *Parents should* ***set an example*** *for their children.* | *I suggest you* ***follow*** *Rosie's* ***example*** (=copy her behaviour) *and start doing regular exercise.* | *The team captain* ***leads by example****.* | *She's a* ***shining example*** (=a very good example) *of what a mother should be.*
4 make an example of sb to punish someone so that other people are afraid to do the same thing

COLLOCATIONS

ADJECTIVES

a good/typical example *This painting is a good example of his early work.*
a fine/excellent example *The house is a fine example of a medieval building.*
an outstanding example (=extremely good) *The garden is one of the most outstanding examples of traditional Japanese garden design.*
a classic/perfect/prime example (=very typical) *This is a classic example of how not to run a business.*
an obvious example *Our climate is changing at an alarming rate. The melting of the polar ice caps is an obvious example of this.*
a blatant/glaring example (=very obvious and very bad) *His case is a blatant example of the unfairness of the current system.*
an extreme example | **a notable example** *formal* (=important and worth mentioning) | **a graphic example** (=very clear and full of unpleasant details)

VERBS

give (sb) an example *Let me give you an example of how this might happen.*
provide an example *Our brochure provides examples of the different villas on offer.*
take an example (=consider it or talk about it) *Let's take the example of a family with two school-age children.*
use an example *He used several examples to illustrate his point.*
cite an example (=mention an example) *The report cites the example of Sweden, where there is a complete ban on advertising on children's television.*
find an example *We found examples of people being overcharged by as much as 50%.*
contain/include an example *The exhibition also contains some examples of his book illustrations.*
an example shows/illustrates sth *These examples show how the disease can be passed on to humans.*

THESAURUS

WHAT YOU SAY WHEN GIVING EXAMPLES

for example used when giving an example: *Prices have risen sharply. The price of gasoline, for example, has risen by over 50%.* | *Nepal has many attractions for visitors. For example, you can go trekking in the Himalayas, or see tigers in Chitwan National Park.*
for instance used when giving an example. **For instance** is slightly less formal than **for example** and is used more in spoken English: *There were many unanswered questions. For instance, where was the money going to come from?* | *Some people are really good at languages.* ***Take*** *Katie,* ***for instance****.*
eg/e.g. *written* used when giving an example or a list of examples. Don't use **eg** in formal writing - use the full phrase **for example**: *Make sure you eat foods that contain protein, e.g. meat, fish, eggs, milk, or cheese.*
such as *especially written* used when giving one or two typical examples when there are many others: *It is difficult to get even basic foods such as bread and sugar.*
take *spoken* used when giving a particular example as a way of proving that what you are saying is correct: *Take John - he has a good job but he didn't go to university.* | *It is possible to recover from some types of cancer.* ***Take*** *skin cancer,* ***for example****.*
be a case in point used when emphasizing that someone or something is a good or typical example of what you have just mentioned: *Some birds have returned to Britain after once being extinct here. The return of the osprey is a case in point.*

ex·as·pe·rate /ɪɡˈzɑːspəreɪt $ ɪɡˈzæ-/ *v* [T] to make someone very annoyed by continuing to do something that upsets them: *It exasperates me to hear comments like that.*

ex·as·pe·rat·ed /ɪɡˈzɑːspəreɪtɪd $ -ˈzæs-/ ●○○ *adj* very annoyed and upset: **[+with]** *He was becoming exasperated with the child.* | *an exasperated look* —**exasperatedly** *adv*

ex·as·pe·rat·ing /ɪɡˈzɑːspəreɪtɪŋ $ -ˈzæs-/ ●○○ *adj* extremely annoying: *You have this exasperating habit of never looking at me!* —**exasperatingly** *adv*

ex·as·pe·ra·tion /ɪɡˌzɑːspəˈreɪʃən $ ɪɡˌzæs-/ *n* [U] when you feel annoyed because someone continues to do something that is upsetting you: *Carol sighed in exasperation.*

ex·ca·vate /ˈekskəveɪt/ *v* [I,T] **1** if a scientist or ARCHAEOLOGIST excavates an area of land, they dig carefully to find ancient objects, bones etc: *Schliemann excavated the ancient city of Troy.* THESAURUS DIG **2** *formal* to make a hole in the ground by digging up soil etc —**excavation** /ˌekskəˈveɪʃən/ *n* [C,U]

ex·ca·va·tor /ˈekskəveɪtə $ -ər/ *n* [C] **1** *BrE* a large

E

machine that digs and moves earth and soil SYN **steam shovel** *AmE* **2** someone who digs to find things that have been buried under the ground for a long time

ex·ceed /ɪk'siːd/ ●●○ AWL v [T] *formal*
1 to be more than a particular number or amount: *Working hours must not exceed 42 hours a week.* | *His performance* ***exceeded*** *our* ***expectations****.*
2 to go beyond what rules or laws say you are allowed to do: *He was fined for exceeding the speed limit.* | *The riot police had* ***exceeded*** *their* ***authority****.*

ex·ceed·ing·ly /ɪk'siːdɪŋli/ *adv formal* extremely: *Thank you. You've been exceedingly kind.*

ex·cel /ɪk'sel/ v (**excelled**, **excelling**) **1** [I, not in progressive] to do something very well, or much better than most people: **[+at/in]** *Rick has always excelled at foreign languages.* **2 excel yourself** *BrE* to do something better than you usually do: *You have excelled yourself with the new exhibition.*

ex·cel·lence /'eksələns/ ●●○ n [U] the quality of being excellent: **[+of]** *the excellence of the performance* | **[+in]** *the university's reputation for excellence* | *centres of academic excellence* → PAR EXCELLENCE

Ex·cel·len·cy /'eksələnsi/ n **Your/His/Her Excellency** a way of talking to or about people who hold high positions in the state or the church: *His Excellency the Spanish ambassador*

E

ex·cel·lent /'eksələnt/ ●●● S1 W2 adj
1 extremely good or of very high quality: *an excellent suggestion* | *His car is in excellent condition.* | *Second-hand computers can be excellent value.* THESAURUS ▸ GOOD
2 *spoken* said when you approve of something SYN **great**: *'I'll bring the books over tonight.' 'Excellent.'* —**excellently** *adv*

GRAMMAR

Excellent is not used with 'very'. You say: *It's an excellent idea.* | *It's a really excellent idea.* ✗ Don't say: *It's a very excellent idea.*
GRAMMAR GUIDE ▸ ADJECTIVES

ex·cept¹ /ɪk'sept/ ●●● S2 W2 *conjunction, prep*
1 used to introduce the only person, thing, action, fact, or situation about which a statement is not true: *The office is open every day except Sundays.* | *You can have any of the cakes except this one.* | **[+for]** *Everyone went except for Scott and Dan.* | *She felt fine except for being a little tired.* | **except (that)** *Clarissa could think of nothing to say except that she was so sorry.* | **[+in/by/to etc]** *Staff are not permitted to make personal phone calls except in an emergency.* | **except when/where/if** *Benson kept the studio locked except when he was working there.* | **except do sth** *She had nothing to do except spend money.* | **except to do sth** *He wouldn't talk about work, except to say that he was busy.*
2 used to give the reason why something was not done or did not happen: **except (that)** *Liz would have run, except that she didn't want to appear to be in a hurry.*
3 *spoken* used to mention a fact that makes what you have just said seem less true: **except (that)** *I have earrings just like those, except they're blue.* | *A date book would make a great gift, except that a lot of people already have one.*

GRAMMAR: Patterns with except

• You use **except** before a noun: *The shop is open every day except Sunday.* | *She invited everyone except Tom.*
• You can also say **except for** someone or something: *The shop is open every day except for Sunday.* | *She invited everyone except for Tom.* ✗ Don't say: *except of*
• You say **except (that)**: *The twins look very similar, except one is taller than the other.* **That** is often omitted in spoken English.
• You say **except when/where/if**: *I cycle to work, except when it rains.* | *You have to attend, except if you're ill.* **When/where/if** are not omitted. ✗ Don't say: *I cycle to work, except it rains.* | *You have to attend, except you're ill.*

THESAURUS

except used when saying that a statement does not include a particular person or thing. At the beginning of a sentence, you must use **except for**, not just **except**, before a noun: *The office is open every day except Sundays.* | *Except for a man walking his dog, the park was empty.*
apart from/aside from used when mentioning one or two things that do not fit the main thing that you are saying: *Aside from one or two minor errors, this is an excellent piece of research.* | *The films were all made in Hollywood, apart from one, which was made in the UK.*
excluding/not including used when saying that something, especially a total number or amount, does not include a particular thing or person. **Excluding** is more formal than **not including**: *The software costs $49.95, not including tax.* | *Excluding students, the total number of unemployed rose from 2 million to 2.3 million.*
with the exception of *formal* except for one particular person or thing: *Denmark has more wind turbines than any other place in the world, with the exception of California.*
but used especially after words such as **nothing, all, any, anyone, everything** or **everyone** when saying that something is the only thing, or someone is the only person: *There is nothing but trees, for mile after mile.* | *The garment covers everything but the eyes.*
save *formal* used for mentioning the only person or thing which is not included in what you are saying: *Every man she had ever loved, save her father, was now dead.*

except² v [T] *formal* to not include something: **except sth from sth** *High technology equipment would be excepted from any trade agreement.*

ex·cept·ed /ɪk'septɪd/ *adv* **sb/sth excepted** used to say that you are not including a particular person or thing in a statement about something: *History excepted, Peter has made good progress in all subjects this term.* → **present company excepted** at PRESENT¹(6)

ex·cept·ing /ɪk'septɪŋ/ *prep formal* used to introduce the only thing or person in a group about which a statement is not true SYN **except (for)**: *O'Rourke answered all the questions excepting the last one.*

ex·cep·tion /ɪk'sepʃən/ ●●● S3 W2 n [C,U]
1 something or someone that is not included in a general statement or does not follow a rule or pattern: *It's been cold, but today's an exception.* | **with the exception of sb/sth** *We all laughed, with the exception of Maggie.* | **without exception** *Each plant, without exception, contains some kind of salt.* | **notable/important/significant exception** *With one or two* ***notable exceptions****, there are few women conductors.* | **minor/major exception** *With a few minor exceptions, the new edition is much like the previous one.* | *The law applies to all EU countries; Britain is* ***no exception****.* | *We don't usually accept checks, but for you we'll* ***make an exception*** (=not include you in this rule). | *The spelling of this word is an interesting* ***exception to the rule****.* | *Successful two-career couples are still* ***the exception, not the rule*** (=used to emphasize that something is unusual).
2 sb/sth is the exception that proves the rule *spoken* used to say that the fact that something is not true or does not exist in one situation emphasizes the fact that it is true or exists in general: *Most people here are very dedicated; I'm afraid Rhea's the exception that proves the rule.*
3 take exception to sth to be angry or upset because of something: *Tom took great exception to my remark about Americans.*

ex·cep·tion·al /ɪk'sepʃənəl/ ●●○ *adj*
1 unusually good SYN **outstanding**: *an exceptional student* | *exceptional bravery* THESAURUS ▸ GOOD
2 unusual and likely not to happen often: *This is an exceptional case; I've never seen anything like it before.* | *Promotion*

in the first year is only given ***in exceptional circumstances****.*
THESAURUS ▸ UNUSUAL

ex·cep·tion·al·ly /ɪkˈsepʃənəli/ ●○○ *adv* [+adj/adv] extremely SYN **outstandingly**: *She defended her position exceptionally well.* | *an exceptionally talented player*

ex·cerpt /ˈeksɜːpt $ -ɜːrpt/ ●○○ *n* [C] a short piece taken from a book, poem, piece of music etc SYN **extract**: **[+of/from]** *An excerpt of the speech appeared in the Sunday paper.* —**excerpt** *v* [T]

ex·cess¹ /ɪkˈses, ˈekses/ ●●○ *n*
1 [singular, U] a larger amount of something than is allowed or needed: *After you apply the oil, wait 20 minutes before wiping off any excess.* | **[+of]** *It was an excess of enthusiasm that caused the problem.*
2 in excess of sth more than a particular amount: *The car reached speeds in excess of 100 miles per hour.*
3 do sth to excess to do something too much or too often, so that it may harm you: *Drinking is OK as long as you don't do it to excess.*
4 excesses [plural] harmful actions that are socially or morally unacceptable: **[+of]** *The government was unable to* ***curb*** *the* ***excesses*** *of the secret police.* | *the* ***worst excesses*** *of journalism*
5 [U] behaviour which is not acceptable because it is too extreme: *a long sermon against the dangers of excess*

ex·cess² /ˈekses/ ●●○ *adj* [only before noun]
1 additional and not needed because there is already enough of something: *Cut any excess fat from the meat.*
2 excess baggage/luggage bags or cases that weigh more than the legal limit that you can take on a plane

ex·ces·sive /ɪkˈsesɪv/ ●●○ *adj* much more than is reasonable or necessary: *his excessive drinking* | *$15 for two beers seems a little excessive.* —**excessively** *adv*: *excessively high taxes*

ex·change¹ /ɪksˈtʃeɪndʒ/ ●●○ S3 W3 *n*
1 GIVING/RECEIVING [C,U] the act of giving someone something and receiving something else from them: **[+of]** *an exchange of political prisoners* | **in exchange for sth** *I've offered to paint the kitchen in exchange for a week's accommodation.* | *Four of my cassettes for your Madonna CD is a* ***fair exchange****.* → PART EXCHANGE
2 ARGUMENT/DISCUSSION [C] a short conversation, usually between two people who are angry with each other: *a quiet exchange between the judge and the clerk* | *The DJ was fired after a* ***heated exchange*** (=a very angry conversation) *on air with a call-in listener.*
3 exchange of ideas/information etc when people discuss or share ideas, information etc: *The organization is dedicated to the free exchange of information.*
4 STH YOU BUY [C] the act of giving something you have bought back to the store where you bought it, for example because it does not work, fit etc, and taking something else instead: *The store's policy is not to allow returns or exchanges.*
5 MONEY [U] a process in which you change money from one CURRENCY to another: *Most capital cities have extensive exchange facilities.*
6 STUDENTS/TEACHERS [C] an arrangement in which a student, teacher etc visits another school or university to work or study: **on an exchange (with sb)** *I'm here for one term, on an exchange with Dr. Fisher.*
7 JOBS/HOMES ETC [C] an arrangement in which you stay in someone's home, do someone's job etc for a short time while that person stays in your home, does your job etc: *Kate's in New York on an employee exchange so she can get some more training.*
8 FIGHT [C] an event during a war or fight when two people, armies etc shoot or fire MISSILES at each other: **exchange of fire/gunfire**
9 BUILDING **corn/wool/cotton etc exchange** a large building in a town that was used in the past for buying and selling corn, wool etc → LABOUR EXCHANGE, STOCK EXCHANGE

exchange² ●●○ *v* [T]
1 a) to give someone something and receive the same kind of thing from them at the same time: *We exchange gifts at Christmas.* | *At the end of the game, players traditionally exchange shirts with each other.* | *We exchanged phone numbers.* **b)** to give someone something and receive something different from them SYN **change**: **exchange sth for sth** *Where can I exchange my dollars for pounds?*

> **REGISTER**
> In everyday British English, people usually say **swap** or, in everyday American English, **trade**, rather than **exchange**: *Do you want to* ***swap*** *(BrE)/****trade*** *(AmE) seats with me?*

2 to replace one thing with another SYN **swap**: **exchange sth for sth** *He exchanged the black jacket for a blue one.*
3 exchange words/looks etc (with sb) if two people exchange words, looks etc, they talk to each other, look at each other etc: *Until this evening I had never so much as exchanged a word with him.* | *The two women exchanged glances and laughed.* | *I went over and exchanged greetings with everyone.*
4 exchange blows (with sb) if two people exchange blows, they hit each other
5 exchange information/ideas etc to discuss something or share information, ideas etc: *It's a place where people can chat and exchange ideas.*
6 exchange contracts *especially BrE* to complete the final stage of buying a house by signing a contract with the person you are buying it from —**exchangeable** *adj*

exˈchange rate *n* [C] the value of the money of one country compared to the money of another country: *a more favourable exchange rate*

exˈchange rate ˌmechanism *n* [U] (*abbreviation* **ERM**) a system for controlling the exchange rate between the money of one country and that of another

exˈchange ˌstudent *n* [C] a student who goes to a foreign country to study, usually as a part of a programme: *an 18-year-old exchange student from France*

Ex·cheq·uer /ɪksˈtʃekə $ ˈekstʃekər/ *n* **the Exchequer** the British government department that is responsible for collecting taxes and paying out public money SYN **treasury**

ex·cise¹ /ˈeksaɪz/ *n* [C,U] the government tax that is put on the goods that are produced and used inside a country: **excise officer** (=someone who collects excise) | **excise duty/tax** (=the money paid as excise) *excise duty on tobacco* → CUSTOMS AND EXCISE

ex·cise² /ɪkˈsaɪz/ *v* [T] *formal* to remove or get rid of something, especially by cutting it out: *The tumour was excised.* —**excision** /ɪkˈsɪʒən/ *n* [C,U]

ex·cit·a·ble /ɪkˈsaɪtəbəl/ *adj* becoming excited too easily: *A puppy is naturally affectionate and excitable.* —**excitability** /ɪkˌsaɪtəˈbɪləti/ *n* [U]

ex·cite /ɪkˈsaɪt/ ●●○ *v* [T]
1 [not in progressive] to make someone feel happy, interested, or eager: *His playing is technically brilliant, but it doesn't excite me.*
2 *formal* to cause a particular feeling or reaction SYN **arouse**: **excite interest/curiosity/sympathy etc** *The court case has excited a lot of public interest.* | *He tried not to do anything to excite the suspicion of the police.* | **excite comment/speculation/a reaction** *The book excited very little comment.*
3 to make someone feel sexual desire SYN **arouse**
4 *technical* to make an organ, nerve etc in your body react or increase its activity

ex·cit·ed /ɪkˈsaɪtɪd/ ●●● S2 *adj*
1 happy, interested, or hopeful because something good has happened or will happen: *Steve flies home tomorrow – we're all really excited.* | **[+about]** *Maria's starting to* ***get*** *pretty* ***excited*** *about the wedding.* | **[+by/at]** *We're all excited by the prospect of a party.* | **excited to do sth** *Michelle sounded excited to hear from him.* | **excited (that)** *I'm so excited that we're going to New York.* | *The food was* ***nothing to get excited about*** (=not very good or special). | *excited crowds of shoppers*
2 very nervous and upset about something so that you

E

cannot relax: **[+about]** *There's no point getting excited about it. We can't change things.*
3 feeling sexual desire —**excitedly** *adv*: *People had gathered and were talking excitedly.*

THESAURUS

excited feeling happy, especially about something good that has happened or is going to happen: *He's excited about his new job.* | *The kids always get excited on their birthday.*
thrilled /θrɪld/ [not before noun] very excited and pleased: *She was thrilled to hear that you were in London.* | *I was thrilled when they told me that I'd got a place on the course.*
exhilarated /ɪɡˈzɪləreɪtɪd/ [not before noun] very excited and full of energy, especially because you are experiencing something new or something that involves risks: *She felt exhilarated by her new freedom.* | *The climb left him feeling exhilarated.*
look forward to sth to feel excited about something good that is going to happen and to think about it a lot: *The kids are looking forward to their vacation – they've never been to California before.*
can't wait to do sth *especially spoken* to be very excited about something good that is going to happen: *I can't wait to see him again.*
on the edge of your seat extremely excited and interested when you are watching a film, game etc, because you do not know what is going to happen next: *I was on the edge of my seat throughout the movie.*
on tenterhooks /ˈtentəhʊks $ -ər-/ very excited and nervous because you are waiting to find out what has happened: *Don't keep us on tenterhooks! Did you pass your test?*

ex·cite·ment /ɪkˈsaɪtmənt/ ●●○ S3 W3 *n*
1 [U] the feeling of being excited: **[+of]** *the excitement of becoming a parent* | **[+at]** *The children were filled with excitement at the thought of visiting Disneyland.* | **in the excitement/in your excitement** *In all the excitement, I left my wallet behind.* | *In his excitement he couldn't remember her name.*
2 [C] an exciting event or situation: *We were both new to the excitements of life in the big city.*

COLLOCATIONS

VERBS

cause/generate excitement *The arrival of a stranger caused some excitement in the village.*
hide/conceal your excitement *He tried to hide his excitement, but his voice was shaking.*
control/contain your excitement *She could hardly control her excitement when I told her the news.*
be trembling with excitement (=to be shaking slightly because you are so excited) *Her hands were trembling with excitement as she opened the letter.*
sb's excitement grows (=it increases) *Her excitement grew as the day of the wedding came nearer.*
the excitement wears off (=it gradually becomes less) | **the excitement dies down** (=people stop feeling excited)

ADJECTIVES

great/enormous/tremendous excitement *There is great excitement about the Pope's visit.*
growing/mounting excitement *The children waited with growing excitement.*
sheer excitement (=a very strong feeling of excitement) *Nothing can beat driving a racing car for sheer excitement.*
real/genuine excitement | **intense excitement** (=a very strong feeling of excitement) | **youthful/childlike excitement**

PHRASES

be full of/filled with excitement *They were full of excitement at the thought of meeting a real movie star.*
a sense/feeling of excitement *He woke up that morning with a feeling of excitement.*
a state of excitement *It seemed that the whole country was in a state of excitement.*
an air of excitement (=a general feeling of excitement among a group of people) *There was a real air of excitement before the game.*
a surge/buzz of excitement (=a sudden feeling of excitement) | **a flurry of excitement** (=an occasion when there is suddenly a lot of excitement about something) | **a ripple of excitement** (=a feeling of excitement that spreads through a group of people) | **a flicker of excitement** (=a feeling of excitement that lasts a very short time)

ex·cit·ing /ɪkˈsaɪtɪŋ/ ●●● S2 W3 *adj* making you feel excited: *an exciting discovery* | *'Julia and Paul are getting married!' 'Oh, how exciting!'* | *I've got some very exciting news for you.* | *Let's do something exciting.* | *Melanie finds her work exciting and rewarding.* | **exciting opportunity/possibility/prospect etc** *exciting job opportunities* —**excitingly** *adv*: *the most excitingly original movie of the year*

THESAURUS

thrilling /ˈθrɪlɪŋ/ very exciting
gripping a gripping film, story etc is very exciting and interesting
dramatic used about something that is exciting to watch or hear about as it happens: *the dramatic events of the past week*
exhilarating /ɪɡˈzɪləreɪtɪŋ/ making you feel happy, excited, and full of energy: *an exhilarating ride*
nail-biting very exciting, especially because you do not know what is going to happen next: *a nail-biting finish*

ex·claim /ɪkˈskleɪm/ ●○○ *v* [I,T] *written* to say something suddenly and loudly because you are surprised, angry, or excited: *'No!' she exclaimed in shock.*
THESAURUS SAY

ex·cla·ma·tion /ˌekskləˈmeɪʃən/ ●○○ *n* [C] a sound, word, or short sentence that you say suddenly and loudly because you are surprised, angry, or excited: **[+of]** *horrified exclamations of disgust*

ˌexclaˈmation mark *BrE*, **ˌexclaˈmation point** *AmE* ●●○ *n* [C] the mark (!) that you write after a sentence or word that expresses surprise, anger, or excitement

ex·clude /ɪkˈskluːd/ ●●○ W3 AWL *v* [T]
1 to deliberately not include something OPP **include**: *a special diet that excludes dairy products* | *The judges decided to exclude evidence which had been unfairly obtained.* | **exclude sth from sth** *Some of the data was specifically excluded from the report.*

REGISTER

In everyday English, people usually say **leave** something or someone **out** rather than **exclude** something or someone: *Some information was **left out** of the report.* | *We didn't mean to **leave** you **out**.*

2 to not allow someone to take part in something or not allow them to enter a place, especially in a way that seems wrong or unfair OPP **include**: *a mainstream exhibition that excluded women artists* | **exclude sb from (doing) sth** *The press had been deliberately excluded from the event.* | *Sarah heard the other girls talking and laughing and felt excluded.*
3 *BrE* to officially make a child leave their school because of their bad behaviour
4 to decide that something is not a possibility SYN **rule out**: *Social workers have excluded sexual abuse as a reason for the child's disappearance.* | *At this stage we cannot entirely **exclude the possibility** of staff cuts.*

ex·clud·ing /ɪkˈskluːdɪŋ/ ●●○ AWL *prep* not including – used especially when you are making a list or calculating a total OPP **including**: *Television is watched in 97 per cent of American homes (excluding Alaska and Hawaii).*

ex·clu·sion /ɪkˈskluːʒən/ ●○○ AWL *n*
1 [C,U] when someone is not allowed to take part in something or enter a place OPP **inclusion**: **[+from]** *the country's exclusion from the United Nations*
2 [C,U] *BrE* when a child is officially made to leave their school because of their bad behaviour
3 do sth to the exclusion of sth to do something so much that you do not do, include, or have time for other things: *Your essays tend to concentrate on one theme to the exclusion of everything else.*
4 [C] something that is excluded from a contract OPP **inclusion**: *You will be sent full details of the exclusions of your insurance policy.* —**exclusionary** *adj*: *exclusionary business practices*

exˈclusion ˌzone *n* [C] an area that people are not allowed to enter because it is dangerous or because secret things happen there: *the military exclusion zone*

ex·clu·sive[1] /ɪkˈskluːsɪv/ ●○○ AWL *adj*
1 available or belonging only to particular people, and not shared: **exclusive access/rights/use etc** *Our figure skating club has exclusive use of the rink on Mondays.* | **exclusive report/interview/coverage etc** *Tune in to our exclusive coverage of Wimbledon.* | **[+to]** *This offer is exclusive to readers of 'The Sun'.*
2 exclusive places, organizations, clothes etc are so expensive that not many people can afford to use or buy them: *Bel Air is an exclusive suburb of Los Angeles.* | *an exclusive girls' school*
3 deliberately not allowing someone to do something or be part of a group: *a racially exclusive hiring policy*
4 mutually exclusive if two things are mutually exclusive, you cannot have or do both of them: *Lesbianism and motherhood are not mutually exclusive.*
5 exclusive of sth not including something OPP **inclusive of sth**: *Our prices are exclusive of sales tax.*
6 concerned with only one thing OPP **inclusive**: *The committee's exclusive focus will be to improve public transportation.* —**exclusivity** /ˌeksklυːˈsɪvəti/ (*also* **exclusiveness**) *n* [U]: *the exclusivity of private education*

exclusive[2] *n* [C] an important or exciting story that is printed in only one newspaper, because that newspaper was the first to find out about it: *a New York Post exclusive about the Kennedy marriage*

ex·clu·sive·ly /ɪkˈskluːsɪvli/ ●○○ AWL *adv* only: *This offer is available exclusively to people who call now.*

ex·com·mu·ni·cate /ˌekskəˈmjuːnɪkeɪt/ *v* [T] to punish someone by no longer allowing them to be a member of the Roman Catholic church —**excommunication** /ˌekskəmjuːnɪˈkeɪʃən/ *n* [C,U]

ˌex-ˈcon *n* [C] *informal* a criminal who has been in prison but who is now free

ex·co·ri·ate /ɪkˈskɔːrieɪt/ *v* [T] *formal* to express a very bad opinion of a book, play etc: *an excoriating review in 'The Times'*

ex·cre·ment /ˈekskrəmənt/ *n* [U] *formal* the solid waste material that you get rid of through your BOWELS

ex·cres·cence /ɪkˈskresəns/ *n* [C] *formal* **1** something that is bad, unnecessary, or ugly - used to show disapproval: *The new museum is nothing but an excrescence on the urban landscape.* **2** an ugly growth on an animal or plant

ex·cre·ta /ɪkˈskriːtə/ *n* [plural, U] *formal* the solid or liquid waste material that people and animals produce and get rid of from their bodies

ex·crete /ɪkˈskriːt/ *v* [I,T] *formal* to get rid of waste material from your body through your BOWELS, your skin etc → **secrete**

ex·cre·tion /ɪkˈskriːʃən/ *n* **1** [U] the process of getting rid of waste material from your body **2** [C,U] the waste material that people or animals get rid of from their bodies

ex·cru·ci·at·ing /ɪkˈskruːʃieɪtɪŋ/ *adj* **1** extremely painful SYN **painful**: *When I bend my arm, the pain is excruciating.* **2** if something is excruciating, it is extremely unpleasant, for example because it is boring or embarrassing SYN **agonizing**: *Helen described the events of the night before in excruciating detail.* —**excruciatingly** *adv*: *His poetry is excruciatingly bad.*

ex·cul·pate /ˈekskʌlpeɪt/ *v* [T] *formal* to prove that someone is not guilty of something —**exculpation** /ˌekskʌlˈpeɪʃən/ *n* [U]

ex·cur·sion /ɪkˈskɜːʃən $ ɪkˈskɜːrʒən/ ●○○ *n* [C]
1 a short journey arranged so that a group of people can visit a place, especially while they are on holiday: **[+to]** *Included in the tour is an excursion to the Grand Canyon.* | **on an excursion** *We went on an excursion to the Pyramids.*
THESAURUS ▸ JOURNEY
2 a short journey made for a particular purpose SYN **trip**: *a shopping excursion*
3 excursion into sth *formal* an attempt to experience or learn about something that is new to you: *the company's excursion into new markets*

ex·cus·a·ble /ɪkˈskjuːzəbəl/ *adj* behaviour that is excusable can be forgiven SYN **forgivable** OPP **inexcusable**: *an excusable reaction of anger*

ex·cuse[1] /ɪkˈskjuːz/ ●●● S1 *v* [T]
1 excuse me *spoken* **a)** used when you want to get someone's attention politely, especially when you want to ask a question: *Excuse me, can you tell me the way to the museum please?* **b)** used to say that you are sorry for doing something rude or embarrassing: *Oh, excuse me. I didn't know anyone was here.* **c)** used to ask someone politely to move so that you can walk past: *Excuse me, could I just squeeze past?* **d)** used to politely tell someone that you are leaving a place: *Excuse me a moment. I'll be right back.* **e)** used when you disagree with someone but want to be polite about it SYN **I'm sorry**: *Excuse me, but I don't think that's what he meant at all.* **f)** *AmE* used to show that you disagree with someone or are very surprised or upset by what they have just said: *'You're going to pay, right?' 'Excuse me?'* **g)** *especially AmE* used to ask someone to repeat something that they have just said SYN **pardon me**: *'What time is it?' 'Excuse me?' 'I asked you what time it is.'*
2 FORGIVE to forgive someone for doing something that is not seriously wrong, such as being rude or careless: *I'll excuse you this time, but don't be late again.* | *Please excuse my bad handwriting.* | **excuse sb for (doing) sth** *Please excuse me for being so late today.* | *Smith* ***can be excused*** *for his lack of interest in the course* (=his lack of interest is reasonable).

> **REGISTER**
> In informal situations, people often say **sorry about ...**, **sorry for doing ...** or **sorry I ...** rather than asking someone to **excuse** something: ***Sorry about*** *my handwriting.* | ***Sorry for being*** *so late, or* ***Sorry I'm*** *so late.*

3 FROM A DUTY to allow someone not to do something that they are supposed to do: **be excused from (doing) sth** *Can I be excused from swimming today? I have a cold.* GRAMMAR **Excuse** is usually passive in this meaning.
4 EXPLAIN to be or give a good reason for someone's careless or offensive behaviour: *Nothing can excuse that kind of rudeness.*
5 FROM A PLACE to give someone permission to leave a place: *May I please be excused from the table?* GRAMMAR **Excuse** is usually passive in this meaning.
6 excuse yourself to say politely that you need to leave a place: *Richard excused himself and went to his room.*
7 excuse me (for living)! *spoken* used to show that you are annoyed when someone has told you that you have done something wrong

ex·cuse[2] /ɪkˈskjuːs/ ●●● S3 *n* [C]
1 a reason that you give to explain careless or offensive behaviour: **excuse for (doing) sth** *What's your excuse for being late this time?* | *I'm tired of listening to his excuses.*
THESAURUS ▸ REASON
2 a reason that you invent to explain an action and to hide your real intentions: **excuse to do sth** *I need an excuse to call*

her. | **[+for]** *The conference is just an excuse for a holiday in New York.*
3 there is no excuse for sth used to say that someone's behaviour is too bad to be explained or accepted: *There is no excuse for such rudeness.*
4 make your excuses to explain why you are not able to do something: *Please make my excuses at the meeting tomorrow.*
5 a poor/rotten etc excuse for sth used when you think someone or something is very bad: *He's a rotten excuse for a lawyer. Why on earth did you hire him?*
6 *AmE* a note written by your doctor or one of your parents saying that you were ill on a particular day SYN **sick note** *BrE*

COLLOCATIONS – MEANINGS 1 & 2

VERBS

make up/think up/invent an excuse *I made up some excuse about my car breaking down.*
make excuses for sb/sth (=give reasons which try to explain why someone has made a mistake or behaved badly) *His mother was always making excuses for her son's behaviour.*
use sth as an excuse *She never complained or used her illness as an excuse.*
look for an excuse *I began to look for excuses to avoid seeing him.*
give an excuse *I'll have to give my boss some kind of excuse.*
believe/accept an excuse *She didn't believe his excuse for one minute.*
have an excuse *Companies have no excuse for breaking the law.*

ADJECTIVES

a good excuse *A sunny day is a good excuse to go to the beach.*
a reasonable/plausible excuse (=one that other people will believe) *If your train was cancelled, that is a perfectly reasonable excuse.*
a legitimate/valid excuse (=one that is true and that other people cannot criticize) *He didn't have a legitimate excuse for being late.*
the perfect excuse *The phone call gave me the perfect excuse to leave.*
a feeble/flimsy/weak excuse (=one that is difficult to believe) *Joe muttered some feeble excuse about having a headache.*
a pathetic/lame excuse (=very weak) | **the usual excuse/the same old excuse** | **a convenient excuse**

PHRASES

use every excuse in the book (=use every possible excuse) *He used every excuse in the book to avoid seeing the doctor.*
at the slightest excuse (=for any reason, however unimportant) *She comes to our house at the slightest excuse.*

ˌex-diˈrectory *adj BrE* a person or telephone number that is ex-directory is not in the public telephone book SYN **unlisted** *AmE*: *The number is ex-directory.* | *After several threatening calls, we decided to* **go ex-directory**.

ex·ec /ɪɡˈzek/ *n* [C] an informal word for EXECUTIVE

ex·e·cra·ble /ˈeksəkrəbəl/ *adj formal* extremely bad SYN **terrible**

ex·e·crate /ˈeksəkreɪt/ *v* [T] *literary* to express strong disapproval or hatred for someone or something

ex·e·cu·ta·ble /ˈeksəkjuːtəbəl/ *n* [C] a computer FILE that can be run as a program —**executable** *adj*

ex·e·cute /ˈeksəkjuːt/ ●○○ *v* [T]
1 KILL SB to kill someone, especially legally as a punishment: **execute sb for sth** *Thousands have been executed for political crimes.* | *13 people were* **summarily executed** (=killed without any trial or legal process) *by the guerrillas.* **THESAURUS** ▶ **KILL**
2 DO STH *formal* to do something that has been carefully planned SYN **implement**: *The job involves drawing up and executing a plan of nursing care.*
3 PERFORM AN ACTION *formal* to perform a difficult action or movement: **beautifully/skilfully/poorly etc executed** *The skaters' routine was perfectly executed.*
4 COMPUTER *technical* if a computer executes a program or COMMAND (=instruction), it makes the program or command happen or work
5 LEGAL DOCUMENT *law* to make sure that the instructions in a legal document are followed
6 PRODUCE STH *formal* to produce a painting, book, film etc: *a boldly executed story*

ex·e·cu·tion /ˌeksəˈkjuːʃən/ ●○○ *n*
1 [C,U] when someone is killed, especially as a legal punishment: *a* **public execution** | *The two men* **face execution** (=they will be killed as a punishment). | *Torture and* **summary execution** (=execution without a trial or any legal process) *are common.* | *He was granted* **a stay of execution** (=delay in carrying out an execution).
2 [U] *formal* a process in which you do something that has been carefully planned SYN **implementation**: **[+of]** *the formulation and execution of urban policy*
3 [U] *law* the process of making sure that the instructions in a legal document are followed: *the execution of a will*
4 [U] *formal* the performance of a difficult action or movement
5 [U] *formal* the process of producing something such as a painting, film, book etc, or the way it is produced: *art that is unusual in design and execution*
6 [C,U] *technical* when you make a computer program work, or a COMMAND (=instruction) happen

ex·e·cu·tion·er /ˌeksəˈkjuːʃənə $ -ər/ *n* [C] someone whose job is to execute criminals

ex·ec·u·tive¹ /ɪɡˈzekjətɪv/ ●●○ W3 *n* [C]
1 a manager in an organization or company who helps make important decisions: *a marketing executive* | **senior/top executive** *top executives on high salaries* → **CHIEF EXECUTIVE**
2 the executive the part of a government that makes sure decisions and laws work well → **JUDICIARY, LEGISLATURE**
3 *BrE* a group of people who are in charge of an organization and make the rules: *the union's executive*

executive² ●●○ *adj* [only before noun]
1 relating to the job of managing a business or organization and making decisions: *a commission with* **executive powers** | **executive body/committee etc** (=a group of people who have the power to make decisions)
2 for the use of people who have important jobs in a company: *the executive dining-room*
3 expensive and designed for people who earn a lot of money: **executive cars/homes etc** | **executive toys** (=objects to play with at work)

exˌecutive ˈprivilege *n* [C] *AmE* the right of a president or other government leader to keep official records and papers secret

ex·ec·u·tor /ɪɡˈzekjətə $ -ər/ *n* [C] someone who deals with the instructions in someone's WILL

ex·e·ge·sis /ˌeksɪˈdʒiːsɪs/ *n* (*plural* **exegeses** /-siːz/) [C,U] *formal* a detailed explanation of a piece of writing, especially a religious piece of writing

ex·em·plar /ɪɡˈzemplə, -plɑː $ -plər, -plɑːr/ *n* [C] *formal* a good or typical example: **[+of]** *Milt's career is an exemplar of survival in difficult times.*

ex·em·pla·ry /ɪɡˈzempləri/ *adj* **1** excellent and providing a good example for people to follow: *a company with an exemplary record on environmental issues* **2** [only before noun] an exemplary punishment is very severe and is intended to stop other people from committing the same crime

ex·em·pli·fy /ɪɡˈzemplɪfaɪ/ ●○○ *v* (**exemplified, exemplifying, exemplifies**) [T] *formal*
1 to be a very typical example of something: *The building exemplifies the style of architecture which was popular at the time.*

E

2 to give an example of something: *Problems are exemplified in the report.* —**exemplification** /ɪɡˌzemplɪfɪˈkeɪʃən/ *n* [C,U]

ex·empt¹ /ɪɡˈzempt/ ●○○ *adj* not affected by something, or not having to do it or pay it: **[+from]** *The interest is* ***exempt from*** *income* ***tax****.* | *Children are exempt from the charges.*

exempt² *v* [T] to give someone permission not to do or pay something: **exempt sb from sth** *Charities are* ***exempted from*** *paying the* ***tax****.* | *a document that exempts the owner from liability in case of accidents*

> **REGISTER**
> In everyday British English, people usually say **let sb off (doing) sth** rather than **exempt sb from (doing) sth**: *Living abroad doesn't necessarily* ***let*** *you* ***off*** *paying tax.*

ex·emp·tion /ɪɡˈzempʃən/ ●○○ *n*
1 [C] an amount of money that you do not have to pay tax on: *You qualify for a* ***tax exemption*** *on the loan.*
2 [C,U] permission not to do or pay something that you would normally have to do or pay: **[+from]** *exemption from customs duties* | *The commission* ***granted*** *temporary* ***exemptions****.*

ex·er·cise¹ /ˈeksəsaɪz $ -ər-/ ●●● S2 W2 *n*
1 FOR HEALTH [U] physical activities that you do in order to stay healthy and become stronger: *Try to fit some regular exercise into your daily routine.* | *Working in an office, I don't* ***get*** *much* ***exercise****.* | **do/take exercise** *Most people need to do more exercise.* | **gentle/light exercise** *Gentle exercise can be beneficial for older people.* | **vigorous/strenuous exercise** *After the operation, you should avoid strenuous exercise.*
2 MOVEMENT [C] a movement or set of movements that you do regularly to keep your body healthy: *stretching exercises* | *You can* ***do exercises*** *to strengthen your stomach muscles.*
3 FOR A SKILL [C usually plural] an activity or process that helps you practise a particular skill: *relaxation exercises* | *role-play exercises*
4 IN A BOOK [C] a set of questions in a book that test a student's knowledge or skill: *Do Exercises 3 and 4 on page 51 for homework.*
5 FOR A PARTICULAR RESULT [singular] an activity or situation that has a particular quality or result: *closing libraries as part of a cost-cutting exercise* | *It's a pointless exercise.* | **[+in]** *Buying a house can be an exercise in frustration.*
6 ARMY/NAVY ETC [C,U] a set of activities for training soldiers etc: *a military exercise* | **on exercise** *Half the unit was away on exercise.*
7 the exercise of sth *formal* the use of a power or right: *the exercise of political leadership*

> **COLLOCATIONS**
> **VERBS**
> **do some exercise** (*also* **take some exercise** *BrE*) *He ought to do more exercise.*
> **get some exercise** *I don't get enough exercise.*
> **ADJECTIVES**
> **good exercise** *Swimming is very good exercise for your muscles.*
> **regular/daily exercise** *Taking regular exercise is the best way to improve your overall health.*
> **physical exercise** *Physical exercise keeps you fit and helps to reduce stress.*
> **hard/strenuous/vigorous exercise** (=involving a lot of physical effort) *Pregnant women should avoid strenuous exercise.*
> **gentle/light/moderate exercise** (=not involving too much physical effort) *Try to do some gentle exercise as part of your daily routine.*
> **aerobic exercise** (=in which you breathe deeply and your heart beats faster)
> **PHRASES**
> **a type/form of exercise** *This type of exercise is excellent for losing weight.*
> **lack of exercise** *Children are becoming overweight through lack of exercise.*
> **exercise + NOUN**
> **an exercise programme/routine/regime** *BrE*, **an exercise program** *AmE* (=a plan that includes different types of exercise) *The athletes follow an intensive exercise programme.*
> **an exercise class**

exercise² ●●○ S3 W2 *v*
1 USE STH [T] *formal* to use a power, right, or quality that you have: *There are plans to encourage people to exercise their right to vote.* | *People who can* ***exercise*** *some* ***control*** *over their surroundings feel less anxious.*
2 DO PHYSICAL ACTIVITY [I] to do sports or physical activities in order to stay healthy and become stronger: *It's important to exercise regularly.*
3 USE PART OF YOUR BODY [T] to make a particular part of your body move in order to make it stronger: *Swimming exercises all the major muscle groups.*
4 ANIMAL [T] to make an animal walk or run in order to keep it healthy and strong: *people exercising their dogs in the park*
5 MAKE SB THINK [T] *formal* **a)** to make someone think about a subject or problem and consider how to deal with it: *It's an issue that's* ***exercised*** *the* ***minds*** *of scientists for a long time.* **b)** *BrE* if something exercises someone, they think about it all the time and are very anxious or worried - often used humorously: *It was clear that Flavia had been exercised by this thought.*

ˈexercise ˌbike *n* [C] a bicycle that does not move and is used for exercising indoors → see picture at **GYM**

ˈexercise ˌbook *n* [C] a book that students use for writing in

ex·ert /ɪɡˈzɜːt $ -ɜːrt/ ●○○ *v* [T]
1 to use your power, influence etc in order to make something happen: *They exerted considerable influence within the school.* | *Environmental groups are* ***exerting pressure on*** *the government to tighten pollution laws.*
2 exert yourself to work very hard and use a lot of physical or mental energy: *He has exerted himself tirelessly on behalf of the charity.*

ex·er·tion /ɪɡˈzɜːʃən $ -ɜːr-/ *n* [C,U] **1** a lot of physical or mental effort: *The afternoon's exertions had left us feeling exhausted.* | *mental exertion* **2** the use of power, influence etc to make something happen: *the exertion of authority*

ex·e·unt /ˈeksiʌnt/ *v* [I] a word written in the instructions of a play to tell two or more actors to leave the stage

ex·fo·li·ate /eksˈfəʊlieɪt $ -ˈfoʊ-/ *v* [I,T] to remove dead cells from your skin in order to make it smoother —**exfoliation** /eksˌfəʊliˈeɪʃən $ -ˌfoʊ-/ *n* [U]

ex gra·tia /ˌeks ˈɡreɪʃə/ *adj formal* an ex gratia payment is one that is made as a gift, and not as a legal duty: *an ex gratia payment of £15,000*

ex·hale /eksˈheɪl/ *v* [I,T] to breathe air, smoke etc out of your mouth OPP **inhale**: *Take a deep breath, then exhale slowly.* —**exhalation** /ˌekshəˈleɪʃən/ *n* [C,U]

ex·haust¹ /ɪɡˈzɔːst $ -ˈzɒːst/ ●○○ *v* [T]
1 to make someone feel extremely tired: *A full day's teaching exhausts me.* | **exhaust yourself** *He'd exhausted himself carrying all the boxes upstairs.*
2 to use all of something SYN **use up**: *We are in danger of* ***exhausting*** *the world's oil* ***supply****.* | *Having* ***exhausted*** *all other* ***possibilities****, I asked Jan to look after the baby.*
3 exhaust a subject/topic etc to talk about something so much that you have nothing more to say about it: *Once we'd exhausted the subject of Jill's wedding, I didn't know what to say.*

exhaust² ●○○ *n*
1 (*also* **exhaust pipe**) [C] a pipe on a car or machine that

waste gases pass through → see pictures at CAR, MOTORBIKE
2 [U] the gas produced when an engine is working: *exhaust fumes*

ex·haust·ed /ɪɡˈzɔːstɪd $ -ˈzɒːs-/ ●●○ *adj*
1 extremely tired SYN **worn out**: *You look absolutely exhausted.* | **[+from/by]** *I was exhausted by the journey.* THESAURUS ▸ TIRED

> **REGISTER**
> In everyday English, people often say **worn out** rather than **exhausted**: *You look* ***worn out***.

2 having or containing no more of a particular thing or substance: *an exhausted coal mine*

ex·haust·ing /ɪɡˈzɔːstɪŋ $ -ˈzɒːs-/ ●●○ *adj* making you feel extremely tired: *an exhausting process* | *It had been an exhausting day.* THESAURUS ▸ TIRING

ex·haus·tion /ɪɡˈzɔːstʃən $ -ˈzɒːs-/ ●○○ *n* [U]
1 extreme tiredness: **with exhaustion** *He collapsed with exhaustion.* | ***Sheer exhaustion*** *forced him to give up.* | *Many runners were suffering from* ***heat exhaustion*** (=when you become tired and ill because you are too hot). | **nervous exhaustion** (=when you become ill because you have been working too hard or have been very worried)
2 when all of something has been used: **[+of]** *the exhaustion of oil supplies*

ex·haus·tive /ɪɡˈzɔːstɪv $ -ˈzɒːs-/ *adj* extremely thorough and complete: *an exhaustive investigation* | *The* ***list*** *is by no means* ***exhaustive***. —**exhaustively** *adv*

ex·hib·it[1] /ɪɡˈzɪbɪt/ ●●○ AWL *v*
1 [I,T] to show something in a public place so that people can go to see it SYN **show**: *Her paintings have been exhibited all over the world.*
2 [T] *formal* to clearly show a particular quality, emotion, or ability SYN **display**: **exhibit signs/symptoms/behaviour etc** *a patient who is exhibiting classic symptoms of mental illness*

exhibit[2] ●●○ AWL *n* [C]
1 something, for example a painting, that is put in a public place so that people can go to see it: *The exhibits date from the 17th century.*
2 an object that is shown in court to prove whether someone is guilty or not: *Exhibit A is the hammer found next to the victim.*
3 *AmE* an exhibition: *a big exhibit in Milan*

ex·hi·bi·tion /ˌeksəˈbɪʃən/ ●●● W2 AWL *n*
1 [C] *especially BrE* a show of paintings, photographs, or other objects that people can go to see: **[+of]** *an exhibition of black and white photographs* | **stage/mount/hold etc an exhibition** *The museum is staging an exhibition of Picasso's work.*
2 [U] when something such as a painting is shown in a public place: **[+of]** *She never agreed to the public exhibition of her sculptures while she was still alive.* | **on exhibition** *A collection of paintings by David Hockney is on exhibition at the Museum of Art.*
3 exhibition of sth a situation in which someone shows a particular skill, feeling, or type of behaviour SYN **display**: *I've never seen such an exhibition of jealousy.*
4 make an exhibition of yourself to behave in a silly or embarrassing way SYN **make a fool of yourself**

ex·hi·bi·tion·is·m /ˌeksəˈbɪʃənɪzəm/ *n* [U] **1** behaviour that is intended to make people notice or admire you - used to show disapproval **2** *medical* a medical condition that makes someone want to show their sexual organs in public places

ex·hi·bi·tion·ist /ˌeksɪˈbɪʃənɪst/ *n* [C] **1** someone who likes to make other people notice them - often used to show disapproval **2** *medical* someone who has a medical condition that makes them want to show their sexual organs in public places —**exhibitionist** *adj*

ex·hib·i·tor /ɪɡˈzɪbɪtə $ -ər/ *n* [C] a person or company who is showing their work or products to the public: *an exhibitor at a trade show*

ex·hil·a·rate /ɪɡˈzɪləreɪt/ *v* [T] to make someone feel very excited and happy

ex·hil·a·rat·ed /ɪɡˈzɪləreɪtɪd/ *adj* feeling extremely happy, excited, and full of energy: *Dan felt strangely exhilarated by the day's events.* THESAURUS ▸ EXCITED

ex·hil·a·rat·ing /ɪɡˈzɪləreɪtɪŋ/ *adj* making you feel happy, excited, and full of energy: *an exhilarating experience* | *an exhilarating walk* THESAURUS ▸ EXCITING

ex·hil·a·ra·tion /ɪɡˌzɪləˈreɪʃən/ *n* [U] a feeling of being happy, excited, and full of energy: **[+of]** *She enjoyed the exhilaration of jet-skiing.*

ex·hort /ɪɡˈzɔːt $ -ɔːrt/ *v* [T] *formal* to try very hard to persuade someone to do something SYN **urge**: **exhort sb to do sth** *Police exhorted the crowd to remain calm.* —**exhortation** /ˌeksɔːˈteɪʃən $ -ɔːr-/ *n* [C,U]

ex·hume /ɪɡˈzjuːm, eksˈhjuːm $ ɪɡˈzuːm, ɪkˈsjuːm/ *v* [T] *formal* to remove a dead body from the ground, especially in order to check the cause of death SYN **dig up** —**exhumation** /ˌekshjʊˈmeɪʃən $ ˌekshjʊ-, ˌegzjʊ-/ *n* [C,U]

ex·i·gen·cies /ˈeksədʒənsiz, ɪɡˈzɪdʒ-/ *n* [plural] *formal* the things you must do in order to deal with a difficult or urgent situation SYN **demands**: **[+of]** *the exigencies of war*

ex·i·gent /ˈeksədʒənt, ˈegzə-/ *adj formal* **1** demanding a lot of attention from other people in a way that is unreasonable **2** an exigent situation is urgent, so that you must deal with it very quickly

ex·ig·u·ous /ɪɡˈzɪɡuəs/ *adj formal* very small in amount: *exiguous earnings*

ex·ile[1] /ˈeksaɪl, ˈegzaɪl/ ●○○ *n*
1 [singular, U] a situation in which you are forced to leave your country and live in another country, especially for political reasons: **in exile** *a writer now living in exile* | *He* ***went into exile*** *to escape political imprisonment.* | **force/drive sb into exile** *The house was raided and the family was forced into exile.* | *He spent many years in* ***enforced exile***. | **voluntary/self-imposed exile** *She had been in voluntary exile since 1990.*
2 [C] someone who has been forced to live in exile: *political exiles* → TAX EXILE

exile[2] *v* [T] to force someone to leave their country, especially for political reasons: **be exiled to sth** *Several of the leaders were arrested and exiled to France.* | **be exiled from sth** *a dictator who was exiled from his home country* | *the exiled former president* GRAMMAR **Exile** is usually passive.

ex·ist /ɪɡˈzɪst/ ●●● S2 W1 *v* [I]
1 to happen or be present in a particular situation or place: *The custom of arranged marriages still exists in many countries.* | *Opportunities exist for students to gain sponsorship.* | *Stop pretending that the problem doesn't exist.* | *The club will* ***cease to exist*** *if financial help is not found.*
2 to be real or alive: *Do fairies really exist?* | *Tom acts as if I don't exist at times.*
3 to stay alive, especially in a difficult situation when you do not have enough money, food etc SYN **survive**: **[+on]** *The hostages existed on bread and water.*

> **GRAMMAR: Using the progressive**
> • **Exist** is not used in the progressive in meanings 1 and 2. You say: *No company of that name exists.*
> ✗ Don't say: *No company of that name is existing.*
> • **Exist** can be used in the progressive in meaning 3. You can say: *At the moment they are existing on a few dollars a day.*
> GRAMMAR GUIDE ▸ VERBS

ex·ist·ence /ɪɡˈzɪstəns/ ●●○ W2 *n*
1 [U] the state of existing: **[+of]** *It is impossible to prove the existence of God.* | **in existence** *The organization has been in existence for 25 years.* | *Scientists have many theories about how the universe first* ***came into existence*** (=started to exist). | **[+of]** *The* ***very existence*** *of the museum is threatened by lack of funding.* | *the* ***continued existence*** *of economic inequalities*
2 [C usually singular] the type of life that someone has,

especially when it is bad or unhappy: *Pablo* ***led a*** *miserable* ***existence*** *when he first moved to San Juan.* → **eke out a living/existence** at EKE

ex·ist·ent¹ /ɪɡˈzɪstənt/ *adj formal* existing now OPP **nonexistent**: *existent differences*

existent² *n* [C] *technical* something that is real and exists

ex·is·ten·tial /ˌeɡzɪˈstenʃəl◂/ *adj* [only before noun] *formal* relating to the existence of humans or to existentialism

ex·is·ten·tial·is·m /ˌeɡzɪˈstenʃəlɪzəm/ *n* [U] *technical* the belief in PHILOSOPHY that people are responsible for their own actions and experiences, and that the world has no meaning —**existentialist** *adj* —**existentialist** *n* [C]

ex·ist·ing /ɪɡˈzɪstɪŋ/ ●●○ S3 W2 *adj* [only before noun] present or being used now: *the existing laws* | *The service is available to all existing customers.*

ex·it¹ /ˈeɡzɪt, ˈeksɪt/ ●●● S3 W3 *n* [C]
1 a door or space through which you can leave a public room, building etc: *We made for the nearest exit.* | *an exit door* | *Two men were blocking her exit.* | **emergency/fire exit** (=a special door used only when there is a fire etc)
2 [usually singular] when you leave a room or building: *They* ***made*** *a quick* ***exit*** *when they saw the police approaching.*
3 a place where vehicles can leave a road such as a MOTORWAY, and join another road: *Take the next exit for Lynchburg.*
4 [usually singular] when someone stops being involved in a competition or business, especially because they have not been successful SYN **departure**: *France's early exit from the World Cup*

exit² ●○○ *v* [I,T]
1 *formal* to leave a place: **[+from/through]** *I exited through a side window.* | *He exited the courtroom in a fury.*
2 to stop using a computer program: *Press F3 to exit.*
3 used in the instructions of a play to tell an actor to leave the stage: *Exit Hamlet, bearing the body of Polonius.*

ˈexit ˌpoll *n* [C] the activity of asking people how they have voted in an election in order to discover the likely result

ˈexit ˌstrategy *n* [C] a plan for ending your INVOLVEMENT (=taking part) in an activity, such as a war or a business, in a way that causes no damage or problems: *The president convinced people that he had a workable exit strategy to free his forces from the conflict.*

ex·o·dus /ˈeksədəs/ *n* [singular] a situation in which a lot of people leave a particular place at the same time: **[+of]** *A massive exodus of doctors is forcing the government to recruit from abroad.* | **[+from/to]** *the exodus from the countryside to the towns in the 19th century* | *I joined the* ***mass exodus*** *for drinks during the interval.*

ex-of·fi·ci·o /ˌeks əˈfɪʃiəʊ $ -ʃioʊ/ *adj formal* an ex-officio member of an organization is only a member because of their rank or position —**ex officio** *adv*

ex·on·e·rate /ɪɡˈzɒnəreɪt $ ɪɡˈzɑː-/ *v* [T] to state officially that someone who has been blamed for something is not guilty: **exonerate sb from/of sth** *He was totally exonerated of any blame.* —**exoneration** /ɪɡˌzɒnəˈreɪʃən $ -ˌzɑː-/ *n* [U]

ex·o·plan·et /ˈeksəʊˌplænɪt $ -soʊ-/ *n* [C] *technical* a PLANET that is not in the SOLAR SYSTEM

ex·or·bi·tant /ɪɡˈzɔːbətənt $ -ɔːr-/ ●○○ *adj* an exorbitant price, amount of money etc is much higher than it should be SYN **astronomical**: **exorbitant rent/prices etc** *exorbitant rates of interest* THESAURUS EXPENSIVE —**exorbitantly** *adv*

ex·or·cis·m /ˈeksɔːsɪzəm $ -ɔːr-/ *n* [C,U] **1** a process during which someone tries to make an evil SPIRIT leave a place by saying special words, or a ceremony when this is done **2** *literary* the process of making yourself forget a bad memory or experience

ex·or·cist /ˈeksɔːsɪst $ -ɔːr-/ *n* [C] someone who tries to make evil SPIRITS leave a place

ex·or·cize (*also* **-ise** *BrE*) /ˈeksɔːsaɪz $ -ɔːr-/ *v* [T] **1** to force evil SPIRITS to leave a place by using special words and ceremonies **2** to make yourself forget a bad memory or experience: *trying to exorcise the past*

ex·o·skel·e·ton /ˈeksəʊˌskelətən $ -soʊ-/ *n* [C] *technical* the hard parts on the outside of the body of creatures such as insects and CRABS

ex·ot·ic /ɪɡˈzɒtɪk $ ɪɡˈzɑː-/ ●●○ *adj* something that is exotic seems unusual and interesting because it is related to a foreign country - use this to show approval: *exotic birds* | *exotic places* —**exotically** /-kli/ *adv*

ex·ot·ic·a /ɪɡˈzɒtɪkə $ ɪɡˈzɑː-/ *n* [plural] things that are unusual and exciting, especially because they come from foreign countries

exˌotic ˈdancer *n* [C] a dancer who takes off her clothes while dancing → STRIPTEASE

ex·pand /ɪkˈspænd/ ●●○ S3 W3 AWL *v*
1 [I,T] to become larger in size, number, or amount, or to make something become larger → **expansion** OPP **contract**: *Water expands as it freezes.* | *Sydney's population* ***expanded rapidly*** *in the 1960s.* | *exercises that expand the chest muscles* | *his expanding waistline* THESAURUS INCREASE
2 [I,T] if a company, business etc expands, or if someone expands it, they open new shops, factories etc → **expansion**: *The computer industry has expanded greatly over the last decade.* | *The hotel wants to expand its business by adding a swimming pool.* | *the* ***rapidly expanding*** *field of information technology* | **[+into]** *We have plans to expand into the U.S. market.*
3 [I] *literary* to become more confident and start to talk more: *After a few whiskies he started to expand a little.*

expand on/upon sth *phr v* to add more details or information to something that you have already said: *Payne later expanded on his initial statement.*

ex·pand·a·ble /ɪkˈspændəbəl/ *adj* able to be increased or made larger: *a computer with 2 GB RAM expandable to 4 GB RAM*

ex·panse /ɪkˈspæns/ *n* [C] a very large area of water, sky, land etc: **[+of]** *an expanse of blue sky* | **vast/wide/large etc expanse** *the vast expanse of the ocean*

ex·pan·sion /ɪkˈspænʃən/ ●●○ W3 AWL *n*
1 [C,U] when something increases in size, range, amount etc SYN **growth** → **expand**: **[+of]** *The* ***rapid expansion*** *of cities can cause social and economic problems.* | **[+in]** *an expansion in student numbers*
2 [C,U] when a company, business etc becomes larger by opening new shops, factories etc → **expand**: *The industry underwent a period of* ***rapid expansion***.
3 [C] an idea, story etc that is based on one that is simpler or more general: *The novel is an expansion of a short story he wrote about forty years ago.*

ex·pan·sion·a·ry /ɪkˈspænʃənəri $ -ʃəneri/ *adj formal* encouraging a business or ECONOMY to become bigger and more successful: *expansionary fiscal policy*

exˈpansion ˌcard *n* [C] a CIRCUIT BOARD that fits into a computer and makes it possible for the computer to do more things, for example produce sounds, play CD ROMS, or use a telephone line

ex·pan·sion·is·m /ɪkˈspænʃənɪzəm/ AWL *n* [U] when a country or group increases the amount of land or power that they have - used especially to show disapproval: *military expansionism* —**expansionist** *adj* —**expansionist** *n* [C]

exˈpansion ˌslot *n* [C] a place on a computer system CIRCUIT BOARD that can hold an EXPANSION CARD

ex·pan·sive /ɪkˈspænsɪv/ AWL *adj* **1** very friendly and willing to talk a lot: *Hauser was in an* ***expansive mood***. **2** very large in area, or using a lot of space: *expansive beaches* | *She flung her arms out in an* ***expansive gesture***. **3** including a lot of information and using a lot of words: *an expansive definition* | *It was written in an expansive style.* **4** relating to a business or ECONOMY becoming bigger or more successful: *expansive economic policies* —**expansively** *adv* —**expansiveness** *n* [U]

E

ex·pat /ˌeksˈpæt/ *n* [C] *informal* an expatriate

ex·pa·ti·ate /ɪkˈspeɪʃieɪt/ *v*

expatiate on/upon sth *phr v formal* to speak or write in detail about a particular subject

ex·pat·ri·ate /eksˈpætriət, -trieɪt $ -ˈpeɪ-/ *n* [C] someone who lives in a foreign country: *British expatriates living in Spain* —**expatriate** *adj* [only before noun]: *expatriate workers*

This graph shows how common the different grammar patterns of the verb **expect** are.

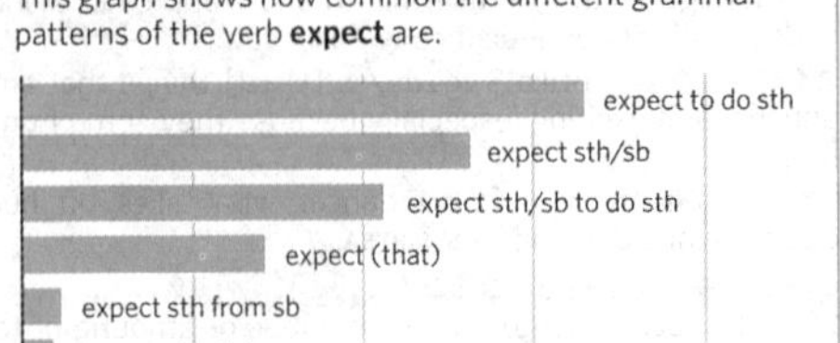

ex·pect /ɪkˈspekt/ ●●● S1 W1 *v* [T]

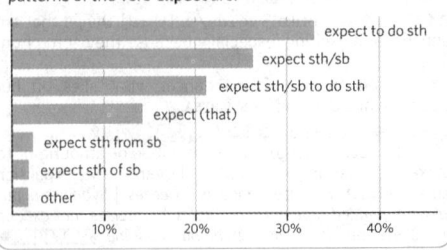

1 THINK STH WILL HAPPEN to think that something will happen because it seems likely or has been planned: **expect to do sth** *I expect to be back within a week.* | *The company expects to complete work in April.* | **expect sb/sth to do sth** *Emergency repairs were expected to take three weeks.* | *I didn't expect him to stay so long.* | **expect (that)** *There's the doorbell – I expect it'll be my mother.* | *He will be hard to beat. I* ***fully expect*** (=am completely sure about) *that and I'm ready.* | *'Who are you?' he murmured, only* ***half expecting*** (=thinking it was possible, but not likely) *her to answer.* | *He didn't get his expected pay rise.* | **as expected** (=in the way that was planned or thought likely to happen) *As expected, the whole family was shocked by the news.* | **sth is (only) to be expected** (=used to say that you are not surprised by something, especially something unpleasant) *A little nervousness is only to be expected when you are starting a new job.*

2 DEMAND to demand that someone does something because it is a duty or seems reasonable: **expect sth from sb** *The officer expects complete obedience from his troops.* | **expect sb to do sth** *I can't expect her to be on time if I'm late myself.* | **expect a lot of sb/expect too much of sb** (=think someone can do more than may be possible) *The school expects a lot of its students.*

3 THINK SB/STH WILL ARRIVE to believe that someone or something is going to arrive: *We're expecting Alison home any minute now.* | *Snow is expected by the weekend.* | *an expected crowd of 80,000 people*

4 THINK to think that you will find that someone or something has a particular quality or does a particular thing: *I expected her to be taller than me, not shorter.*

5 be expecting (a baby) if a woman is expecting, she is going to have a baby

6 what can/do you expect? *spoken* used to say that you are not surprised by something unpleasant or disappointing: *He was late, but what do you expect?*

7 how do/can you expect ...? *spoken* used to say that it is unreasonable to think that something will happen or be true: *If I can't help her, how can you expect to?*

8 I expect *BrE spoken* used to introduce or agree with a statement that you think is probably true: *I expect you're right.* | *'Do you think they're going to attack?'* ***'I expect so.'***

GRAMMAR: Patterns with expect

- You **expect to do** something: *The team expects to win.*
- You **expect** someone **to do** something: *We didn't expect them to come.*
- You **expect that** something **will** happen: *We expect that we will arrive at about midday.*
- You say that you **expected that** something **would** happen: *They had not expected that there would be so much traffic.*
- You say that something **is expected to** happen: *Sales are expected to reach $10 million.*
- In more formal English, you can also say **it is expected that** something **will** happen: *It is expected that sales will reach $10 million.*
- You can say you **are expecting** something. **Expect** is often used in the progressive: *I'm expecting a call from the hospital.*
- You can use the phrases **I expect so** or **I don't expect so**, usually to give a short answer: *'Were they surprised?' 'I expect so.'* | *'Will it take long?' 'I don't expect so.'* ✗ Don't say: *I expect it.*

GRAMMAR GUIDE ▸ VERBS

ex·pec·tan·cy /ɪkˈspektənsi/ *n* [U] the feeling that something pleasant or exciting is going to happen: *I saw the look of expectancy in the children's eyes.* → LIFE EXPECTANCY

ex·pec·tant /ɪkˈspektənt/ *adj* [usually before noun] **1** hopeful that something good or exciting will happen, or showing this: *a row of expectant faces* **2 expectant mother/father** a mother or father whose baby will be born soon —**expectantly** *adv*: *He looked expectantly at Sarah, but she didn't speak.*

ex·pec·ta·tion /ˌekspekˈteɪʃən/ ●●○ *n*

1 [C,U] what you think or hope will happen: **expectation that** *For some time he lived with the expectation that he was going to die.* | **in (the) expectation of sth** *Anne left Germany in the expectation of seeing her family again before very long.* | **against/contrary to (all) expectations** *Against all expectations, getting up at five is actually easier in winter.* | *Having* ***raised expectations*** (=made people more hopeful), *he went on to help only a few people.* | **above/below expectations** *Profits are below expectations.* | **beyond (sb's) expectations** *Gina has succeeded beyond our expectations.* | *The show* ***exceeded all expectations*** (=was much better than expected). | **come/live up to (sb's) expectations** *His performance did not live up to our expectations* (=was not as good as we expected). | *The number of people who attended* ***fell short of expectations*** (=was lower than expected).

2 [C usually plural] a feeling or belief about the way something should be or how someone should behave: **[+of]** *Women who have* ***high expectations*** *of marriage are often disappointed.* | *Some people* ***have*** *totally unrealistic* ***expectations*** *of both medical and nursing staff.*

3 expectation of life the number of years that someone is likely to live SYN **life expectancy**

ex·pec·to·rant /ɪkˈspektərənt/ *n* [U] *medical* a type of medicine that you take to help you cough up PHLEGM (=a sticky substance) from your lungs

ex·pec·to·rate /ɪkˈspektəreɪt/ *v* [I] *formal* to force liquid out of your mouth SYN **spit**

ex·pe·di·en·cy /ɪkˈspiːdiənsi/ (*also* **ex·pe·di·ence** /-diəns/) *n* (*plural* **expediencies**) [C,U] action that is quickest or most effective in a particular situation, even if it is morally wrong: *the ethics of* ***political expediency***

ex·pe·di·ent¹ /ɪkˈspiːdiənt/ *adj* helping you to deal with a problem quickly and effectively although sometimes in a way that is not morally right OPP **inexpedient**: *This solution is* ***politically expedient*** *but may well cause long-term problems.* | **expedient to do sth** *We think it is expedient to make a good-will gesture to the new administration.*

expedient² *n* [C] a quick and effective way of dealing with a problem: *Moore escaped* ***by the simple expedient of*** *lying down in a clump of grass.*

ex·pe·dite /ˈekspədaɪt/ *v* [T] to make a process or action happen more quickly SYN **speed up**: *strategies to expedite the decision-making process*

ex·pe·di·tion /ˌekspəˈdɪʃən/ ●●○ *n*

1 [C] a long and carefully organized journey, especially to a dangerous or unfamiliar place, or the people that make this journey: *an expedition to the North Pole* | *another Everest expedition* | **on an expedition** *He* ***went on*** *an* ***expedition*** *to Borneo.* THESAURUS ▸ JOURNEY

2 [C] a short journey, usually made for a particular purpose SYN **trip**: *a shopping expedition | a fishing expedition*

ˌexpeˈditionary force *n* [C] a group of soldiers that is sent to another country to fight in a war

ex·pe·di·tious·ly /ˌekspəˈdɪʃəsli/ *adv formal* in a quick and effective way SYN **efficiently**: *All issues presented to the court are considered as fairly and expeditiously as possible.* —**expeditious** *adj*: *an expeditious system for examining claims for refugee status*

ex·pel /ɪkˈspel/ ●○○ *v* (**expelled, expelling**) [T]
1 to officially force someone to leave a school or organization → **expulsion**: **expel sb from sth** *Two girls were expelled from school for taking drugs. | The main opposition leader was expelled from her party.* | **expel sb for doing sth** *He was expelled for making racist remarks.*
2 to force a foreigner to leave a country, especially because they have broken the law or for political reasons: **expel sb from sth** *Foreign priests were expelled from the country.* | **expel sb for sth** *Three diplomats were expelled for spying.*
3 to force air, water, or gas etc out of your body or out of a container → **expulsion**

ex·pend /ɪkˈspend/ *v* [T] to use or spend a lot of energy etc in order to do something: **expend energy/effort/time/resources etc** *People of different ages expend different amounts of energy. | Manufacturers have expended a lot of time and effort trying to improve computer security.* | **expend sth in/on (doing) sth** *A great deal of time and money has been expended on creating a pleasant office atmosphere.*

ex·pend·a·ble /ɪkˈspendəbəl/ *adj* not needed enough to be kept or saved: *It's a sad moment when a man loses his job and discovers that he is expendable.*

ex·pen·di·ture /ɪkˈspendɪtʃə $ -ər/ ●○○ *n*
1 [C,U] the total amount of money that a government, organization, or person spends during a particular period of time → **income**: **[+on]** *expenditure on research and development | huge cuts in* ***public expenditure*** (=the amount of money a government spends on services for the public) | ***government expenditure*** *on education* | ***capital expenditure*** (=spending by a company on buildings, machinery, equipment etc) | **[+of]** *an expenditure of £1 million*
2 [U] the action of spending or using time, money, energy etc: *the expenditure of time and money on your house or garden*

ex·pense /ɪkˈspens/ ●●○ *n*
1 [C,U] the amount of money that you spend on something: *He borrowed £150,000 and used the money for legal expenses. | Conference rooms were equipped at great expense.*
2 expenses money that you spend on things such as travel and food while you are doing your job, and which your employer then pays to you: **on expenses** *Can you claim this meal on expenses?*
3 at the expense of sb/sth if something is done at the expense of someone or something else, it is only achieved by doing something that could harm the other person or thing: *the growth in short breaks, at the expense of longer package holidays*
4 at sb's expense a) if you do something at someone's expense, they pay for you to do it: *Her mansion was refurnished at taxpayers' expense.* **b)** if you make jokes at someone's expense, you laugh about them and make them seem stupid or silly: *Louis kept making jokes at his wife's expense.*
5 all expenses paid having all of your costs for hotels, travel, meals etc paid for by someone else: *The prize is an all-expenses-paid trip to Rio.*

COLLOCATIONS

ADJECTIVES/NOUN + expense

the extra/additional expense *Is it worth the extra expense to get a room with a sea view?*
an unnecessary expense *Paying extra for leather seats seemed like an unnecessary expense.*
living expenses (=money that you spend on rent, food, and things such as electricity, gas etc) *She receives £80 a week, from which she must pay for all her living expenses.*
operating expenses (=money that a company spends on running its business) *We must reduce our operating expenses.*
legal/medical expenses *We had to get a loan to pay for my husband's medical expenses.*
household expenses (=money spent looking after a house and the people in it) | **funeral expenses** (=the cost of arranging a funeral)

PHRASES

at great/huge/considerable/vast expense (=used when saying that something costs a lot of money) *The tiles were imported at great expense from Italy.*
at your own expense (=used when saying that you pay for something yourself) *He had copies of the book printed at his own expense.*
at (the) public expense (=paid for by the public through taxes) *The bridge was built at public expense.*
go to the expense of doing sth (=do something that costs a lot of money) *The council must now decide whether to go to the expense of appealing through the courts.*
spare no expense (in doing sth) (=spend a lot of money to buy the best things) *Her parents spared no expense in arranging the wedding.*

VERBS

incur an expense *formal* (=have to pay for something) *Potential buyers incur the expense of a survey and legal fees.*

exˈpense acˌcount *n* [C] money that is available to someone who works for a company so that they can pay for meals, hotels etc when travelling or entertaining people for work: *I have an expense account and spend about £10,000 a year on entertaining.*

ex·pen·sive /ɪkˈspensɪv/ ●●● S1 W2 *adj* costing a lot of money OPP **cheap**: *the most expensive restaurant in town | Petrol is becoming more and more expensive. | Photography is an expensive hobby.* | **expensive to buy/run/produce/maintain etc** *The house was too big and expensive to run. | For low-income families, children's safety equipment can be* ***prohibitively expensive*** (=so expensive that most people cannot afford it). | *Employing the wrong builder can be a horribly* ***expensive mistake****. | Her husband* ***had expensive tastes*** (=liked expensive things). —**expensively** *adv*: *She's always expensively dressed.*

THESAURUS

expensive costing a lot of money: *an expensive car | Apartments in the city are very expensive.*
high costing a lot of money. You use **high** about rents/fees/prices/costs. Don't use **expensive** with these words: *Rents are very high in this area. | Lawyers charge high fees. | the high cost of living in Japan*
dear [not before noun] *BrE spoken* expensive compared to the usual price: *£3.50 seems rather dear for a cup of coffee.*
pricey /ˈpraɪsi/ *informal* expensive: *The clothes are beautiful but pricey.*
costly expensive in a way that wastes money: *Upgrading the system would be very costly. | They were anxious to avoid a costly legal battle.*
cost a fortune *informal* to be very expensive: *The necklace must have cost a fortune!*
exorbitant /ɪɡˈzɔːbətənt $ -ɔːr-/ much too expensive: *Some accountants charge exorbitant fees.*
astronomical astronomical prices, costs, and fees are extremely high: *the astronomical cost of developing a new spacecraft*
overpriced too expensive and not worth the price: *The DVDs were vastly overpriced.*

E

sb can't afford sth someone does not have enough money to buy or do something: *Most people can't afford to send their children to private schools.*

ex·pe·ri·ence¹ /ɪk'spɪəriəns $ -'spɪr-/ ●●● S1 W1 *n*
1 KNOWLEDGE/SKILL [U] knowledge or skill that you gain from doing a job or activity, or the process of doing this: **[+of/in/with]** *You've got a lot of experience of lecturing.* | *my experience in many areas of the music business* | *He had no* ***previous experience*** *of managing a farm.* | *The advice in the booklet reflects the* ***practical experience*** *we have gained* (=experience gained by actually doing something, rather than knowledge from books etc). | *I* ***had*** *some* ***experience*** *in fashion design.* | *She was turned down on the grounds of* ***lack of experience***. | *I have* ***first-hand experience*** (=experience gained by doing something myself) *of running a school.* | **gain/get experience** *The programme enables pupils to gain some experience of the world of work.*
2 KNOWLEDGE OF LIFE [U] knowledge that you gain about life and the world by being in different situations and meeting different people, or the process of gaining this: **in sb's experience** *In his experience, women did not like getting their feet wet and muddy.* | **know/learn/speak from experience** *Being a parent isn't easy, as I know from experience.* | *All animals appear to have some capacity to learn from experience.* | *I speak from* ***bitter experience*** (=having learnt something because something unpleasant happened). | **personal/previous/past experience** *From personal experience, she knew and understood the problems of alcohol addiction.* | **experience shows/suggests that** *Beth's experience suggests that people don't really change deep down.*
3 STH THAT HAPPENS [C] something that happens to you or something you do, especially when this has an effect on what you feel or think: ***childhood experiences*** | **[+of/with]** *This was my first experience of living with other people.* | **[+for]** *Failing an exam was a new experience for me.* | *I* ***had*** *a similar* ***experience*** *last year.* | *The two children in this story have been through a lot of* ***bad experiences***. | *Parachuting is quite an experience.* | **memorable/unforgettable experience** *This romantic evening cruise is a memorable experience.* | **religious experience** (=a situation in which you feel, hear, or see something that affects you strongly and makes you believe in God) *This kind of religious experience was a sign of God's special favour.*
4 the black/female/Russian etc experience events or knowledge shared by the members of a particular society or group of people: *No writer expresses the black experience with such passion as Toni Morrison.*
5 work experience *BrE* a system in which a student can work for a company in order to learn about a job, or the period during which a student does this: *Ella is about to do work experience with a clothing manufacturer.* | **on work experience** *students on work experience*

experience² ●●○ S3 W2 *v* [T]
1 if you experience a problem, event, or situation, it happens to you or affects you: **experience problems/difficulties** *Many old people will experience problems as the result of retirement.* | *Children need to experience things for themselves in order to learn from them.*
2 to feel a particular emotion, pain etc: *Many women experience feelings of nausea during pregnancy.*

ex·pe·ri·enced /ɪk'spɪəriənst $ -'spɪr-/ ●●○ S3 *adj* possessing skills or knowledge because you have done something often or for a long time OPP **inexperienced**: *an experienced pilot* | *an experienced public speaker* | *She is experienced and self-assured.* | **[+in]** *Blake's very experienced in microsurgery.*

ex·per·i·en·tial /ɪkˌspɪəri'enʃəl◂ $ -ˌspɪr-/ *adj informal* based on experience or related to experience: *experiential approaches to learning*

ex·per·i·ment¹ /ɪk'sperəmənt/ ●●● S3 W2 *n* [C]
1 a scientific test done to find out how something reacts under certain conditions, or to find out if a particular idea is true: **[+with/in/on]** *experiments with alcohol-fuelled cars* | *experiments on sleep deprivation* | **by experiment** *Many small birds guide themselves by the stars, as has been verified by experiment.*
2 a process in which you test a new idea or method to see if it is useful or effective: **[+with/in/on]** *an experiment in state socialism*

COLLOCATIONS

VERBS

do/carry out an experiment *They carried out a series of experiments to test the theory.*
perform/conduct an experiment *formal* (=do an experiment) *The laboratory began conducting experiments on rats.*
an experiment shows/proves/demonstrates sth *His experiment showed that lightning was a kind of electricity.*

ADJECTIVES/NOUN + experiment

a scientific experiment *Astronauts performed scientific experiments during the flight.*
animal experiments (=experiments using animals) *I think most animal experiments are cruel and unnecessary.*
a laboratory experiment (=one that takes place in a laboratory) *They did a series of laboratory experiments on human sleep patterns in the 1960s.*
a field experiment (=one that takes place in the real world, not in a laboratory) | **a controlled experiment** (=one that is done using correct scientific methods) | **a practical experiment** (=one that relates to real situations or events, not scientific theories)

PHRASES

an experiment to test/measure/find out sth *We did an experiment to test the acidity of the soil.*

COMMON ERRORS

⚠ Don't say 'make an experiment'. Say **carry out an experiment** or **do an experiment**.

ex·per·i·ment² /ɪk'sperəment/ ●●○ *v* [I]
1 to try using various ideas, methods etc to find out how good or effective they are: **[+with/on/in]** *He experimented with lighter-than-air flight.* | *The teacher provided some different materials and left the children to experiment.*
2 to do a scientific test to find out if a particular idea is true or to obtain more information: **[+with/on]** *I would defend the right of scientists to experiment on animals.*
3 to try doing something to find out what it feels like, for example having sex or using illegal drugs: **[+with]** *She admitted she had experimented with cocaine.*
—**experimenter** *n* [C]

ex·per·i·men·tal /ɪkˌsperə'mentl◂/ ●●○ W3 *adj*
1 used for, relating to, or resulting from experiments: **experimental evidence/results/data** *A hypothesis is tested by finding experimental evidence for it.* | **experimental work/studies** *experimental studies on birds and animals* | *experimental animals*
2 using new ideas or methods: *an experimental theatre group*

ex·per·i·men·tal·ly /ɪkˌsperə'mentl-i/ *adv* **1** relating to experiments: *data obtained experimentally* **2** in a way that involves using new ideas or methods: *The drugs are being used experimentally on patients suffering from breast cancer.* **3** if you do something experimentally, you do it in order to see or feel what something is like: *He moved his shoulder experimentally; it still hurt.*

ex·pe·ri·men·ta·tion /ɪkˌsperəmen'teɪʃən/ *n* [U]
1 the process of testing various ideas, methods etc to find out how good or effective they are: **[+with/in]** *experimentation with computer-assisted language learning* **2** the process of performing scientific tests to find out if a particular idea is true or to obtain more information: *The issue of animal experimentation is an emotive subject.* **3** when you try doing something to find out what it feels like, for example having sex or using illegal drugs: **[+with]**

experimentation with cannabis | *There is often a period of sexual experimentation during adolescence.*

ex·pert[1] /ˈekspɜːt $ -ɜːrt/ ●●● S3 W2 AWL *n* [C] someone who has a special skill or special knowledge of a subject, gained as a result of training or experience: **[+on]** *He's a world expert on marine mammals.* | **[+in]** *an expert in statistics* | **medical/technical/financial etc expert** *Tests should be administered by a medical expert.*

GRAMMAR: Prepositions with expert

- Someone is an **expert on** a subject or issue: *He's an expert on the Cold War.* ✗ Don't say: *He's an expert of the Cold War.*
- Someone is an **expert in** a field of study or an activity: *She's an expert in family law.* ✗ Don't say: *She's an expert of family law.*

THESAURUS

expert someone who has a lot of knowledge about something or skill at doing something: *a computer expert* | *an expert on beetles* | *It's best to ask an expert.*
specialist an expert who has studied a particular medical or technical subject for a long time and knows much more about it than other people: *She is a specialist in corporate finance.* | *My doctor sent me to see a heart specialist.*
authority an expert whose knowledge and opinions are greatly respected: *The professor is one of the world's leading authorities on African art.*
connoisseur /ˌkɒnəˈsɜː $ ˌkɑːnəˈsɜːr/ an expert on food, art, literature, or design, who has had a lot of experience and knows when something is of very good quality: *He was a connoisseur of fine wines.*
buff /bʌf/ *informal* someone who is very interested in a subject and knows a lot about it: *a wine buff* | *Jazz buffs will be familiar with the band's first album.*
virtuoso /ˌvɜːtʃuˈəʊsəʊ $ ˌvɜːrtʃuˈoʊsoʊ/ an expert player or performer: *The piece was played by violin virtuoso Pavel Sporcl.* | *a virtuoso pianist*

expert[2] ●●● W3 AWL *adj*
1 having a special skill or special knowledge of a subject OPP **inexpert**: **[+on/in/at]** *The police are expert at handling situations like this in strict confidence.* | *He cast his* ***expert eye*** *on the gardener's work.* THESAURUS▸ SKILFUL
2 relating to or coming from an expert: *Ministers depend on civil servants for* ***expert advice****.* —**expertly** *adv* —**expertness** *n* [U]

ex·per·tise /ˌekspɜːˈtiːz $ -ɜːr-/ ●●○ AWL *n* [U] special skills or knowledge in a particular subject, that you learn by experience or training: **technical/financial/medical etc expertise** *What he's bringing to the company is financial expertise.* | *trainee engineers with varying degrees of computer expertise* | **[+in]** *expertise in the management of hotels* THESAURUS▸ KNOWLEDGE, SKILL

ˌexpert ˈsystem *n* [C] a computer system containing a lot of information about one particular subject, so that it can help someone find an answer to a problem

ˌexpert ˈwitness *n* [C] someone with special knowledge about a subject who is asked to give their opinion about something relating to that subject in a court of law: *He appeared as an expert witness before several government inquiries.*

ex·pi·ate /ˈekspieɪt/ *v* [T] *formal* to show you are sorry for something you have done wrong by accepting your punishment willingly, or trying to do something to improve what you did: *She expiated her crime by becoming a nun.* —**expiation** /ˌekspiˈeɪʃən/ *n* [U]

ex·pir·a·tion /ˌekspəˈreɪʃən/ *n* [U] **1** the ending of a fixed period of time **2 expiration date** the American form of EXPIRY date

ex·pire /ɪkˈspaɪə $ -ˈspaɪr/ ●●○ *v* [I]
1 if an official document expires, it can no longer be legally used SYN **run out**: *My passport expires next week.* | *players whose contracts expire this summer* | **[+in/on/at]** *My driving licence expires in March.* | *The lease on the flat expired on June 14th.* THESAURUS▸ END
2 if a period of time when someone has a particular position of authority expires, it ends: *The chairman's term of office has already expired.*
3 *literary* if someone expires, they die: *Ophelia expires in Act IV of Hamlet.*

ex·pir·y /ɪkˈspaɪəri $ -ˈspaɪri/ *n* [U] *BrE* **1** the end of a period of time during which an official document can legally be used, or the end of a period of authority SYN **expiration** *AmE*: **[+of]** *the formal expiry of the presidential term in September* | *Only seven minutes remained before the expiry of the noon deadline.* **2 expiry date** the date after which something is not safe to eat or can no longer be used SYN **expiration date** *AmE*: *Check the expiry date on your passport.* | *Eggs must be marked with an expiry date that is ten days from the date of packing.* → SELL-BY DATE

ex·plain /ɪkˈspleɪn/ ●●● S1 W1 *v* [I,T]
1 to tell someone about something in a way that is clear or easy to understand: *He carefully explained the procedure.* | **explain (to sb) why/how/what etc** *The librarian will explain how to use the catalogue system.* | *Let me explain what I mean.* | **explain that** *He explained that it had been a difficult film to make.* | **explain sth to sb** *I explained the situation to my bank manager.*
2 to give a reason for something or to be a reason for something: *Wait! I can explain everything.* | *How can you explain that sort of behaviour?* | **explain that** *She explained that she had been ill.* | **explain why/how/what etc** *I'll explain why I don't believe your story.* | *That still doesn't explain how he was able to hide the body.*
3 explain yourself a) to tell someone who is angry or upset with you the reasons why you did something: *I'm going to give you five seconds to explain yourself.* **b)** to say clearly what you mean: *Sorry, I'm not explaining myself very well.*

explain sth ↔ **away** *phr v* to make something seem less important or bad by giving reasons for it: *The difference in the treatment they receive is hard to explain away.*

GRAMMAR

You **explain** something **to** someone: *Alan explained the system to me.* ✗ Don't say: *Alan explained me the system.* | *Alan explained to me the system.*

THESAURUS

explain to give someone the information they need to understand something: *She explained how to use the software.* | *Doctors usually explain the risks of the treatment to patients.*
tell to explain something. People often use **tell** instead of **explain** in everyday conversation: *He told me how to get to his house.* | *The book tells you how to improve your health through diet.*
show to explain to someone how to do something by doing it while they watch you: *Ellen showed me how to work the coffee maker.*
demonstrate /ˈdemənstreɪt/ to explain to someone how to do something by doing it while they watch you, especially when it is part of your job: *The cabin crew demonstrated the safety procedures to the passengers.* | *A qualified instructor will demonstrate how to use the equipment properly.*
go through sth to explain something carefully, especially one step at a time: *Mrs. Riddell went through the homework assignment.*
set out sth to explain a series of ideas, reasons or opinions in an organized way in writing or in a speech: *In his speech, he intended to set out the party's policies on education.*

ex·pla·na·tion /ˌekspləˈneɪʃən/ ●●● S3 W2 *n*
1 [C,U] the reasons you give for why something happened or why you did something: **[+of/for]** *Can you think of any explanation for this failure?* | **without explanation** *The concert was cancelled without explanation.* THESAURUS▸ REASON
2 [C] a statement or piece of writing intended to describe how something works or make something easier to

E

understand: **provide/give an explanation** *The ability to give clear explanations is the most important quality of the ideal teacher.* | **[+of]** *I'll try and give you a quick explanation of how the machine works.*

COLLOCATIONS

VERBS

have an explanation *Does the hospital have any explanation for why he died?*
give an explanation *The police gave no explanation for their actions.*
provide/offer an explanation *This theory may provide an explanation for the origins of the universe.*
ask for/demand an explanation *When I asked for an explanation, the people at the office said they didn't know.*
find/think of/come up with an explanation *Scientists have been unable to find an explanation for this phenomenon.*
owe (sb) an explanation *I think you owe me some kind of explanation.*
accept an explanation (=believe that it is true or correct) *The court accepted her explanation.*

ADJECTIVES

a possible explanation *Can anyone think of a possible explanation for why this is happening?*
the most likely/probable explanation (=one that is probably true) *The most likely explanation is that John missed the bus.*
an obvious explanation (=one that is easy to see or notice) *There is no obvious explanation for his strange behaviour.*
a reasonable/plausible explanation (=one that is easy to believe) *Pilot error is the most plausible explanation for the crash.*
a satisfactory/adequate explanation (=one that explains something completely) | **a convincing/credible explanation** (=one that you can believe is true) | **a logical/rational explanation** (=one that is based on facts) | **further explanation** (=additional reasons)

ex·plan·a·to·ry /ɪkˈsplænətəri $ -tɔːri/ ●○○ *adj* giving information about something or describing how something works, in order to make it easier to understand: *There are **explanatory notes** at the end of each chapter.* → SELF-EXPLANATORY

ex·ple·tive /ɪkˈspliːtɪv $ ˈeksplətɪv/ *n* [C] *formal* a rude word that you use when you are angry or in pain, for example 'shit' SYN **swear word**

ex·pli·ca·ble /ekˈsplɪkəbəl/ *adj* able to be easily understood or explained OPP **inexplicable**: *The success of the Revolution is explicable in terms of the weakness of the king's government.*

ex·pli·cate /ˈeksplɪkeɪt/ *v* [T] *formal* to explain an idea in detail: *It is essentially a simple notion, but explicating it is difficult.* —**explication** /ˌeksplɪˈkeɪʃən/ *n* [C,U]

ex·pli·cit /ɪkˈsplɪsɪt/ ●○○ AWL *adj*
1 expressed in a way that is very clear and direct → **implicit**: *The contrast could not have been **made** more **explicit**.* | ***explicit knowledge** of grammar* | *The kidnappers gave us **explicit instructions** not to involve the police.* | *Be explicit when you talk about money with your family.* | **[+about]** *He made the rules without being explicit about them.*
2 language or pictures that are explicit describe or show sex or violence very clearly: *The film contains some very explicit love scenes.* | ***sexually explicit** language* —**explicitly** *adv* —**explicitness** *n* [U]

ex·plode /ɪkˈspləʊd $ -ˈsploʊd/ ●●● W3 *v*
1 BURST [I,T] to burst, or to make something burst, into small pieces, usually with a loud noise and in a way that causes damage → **explosion**: *The device was thrown at an army patrol but failed to explode.* | *Far sooner than anyone thought possible, the Russians exploded an atomic bomb.*
2 INCREASE SUDDENLY [I] to suddenly increase greatly in number, amount, or degree SYN **rocket** → **explosion**: *Florida's population exploded after World War II.*
3 STRONG FEELINGS [I] to suddenly express strong feelings such as anger → EXPLOSION: *Paul exploded. 'What has it got to do with you?' he yelled.* | **[+with]** *She exploded with grief and anger.* | *He told a joke which made Hank explode with laughter.* | **[+into]** *He exploded into a screaming, kicking rage.*
4 BECOME DANGEROUS [I] if a situation explodes, it is suddenly no longer controlled, and is often violent SYN **blow up**: *Riots may explode at any time.* | **[+into]** *The continued tension could explode into more violence.*
5 **explode the myth** to prove that something that is believed by many people is actually wrong or not true: *The programme sets out to explode the myth that some delicate tropical fish are impossible to keep.*
6 MAKE A LOUD NOISE [I] to make a very loud noise → **explosion**: *A clap of thunder exploded overhead.*

THESAURUS

TO EXPLODE

explode *v* [I] if a bomb explodes, it bursts suddenly and violently with a loud noise: *A bomb exploded in a crowded metro station this morning, killing five people.*
go off *phr v* if a bomb goes off, it explodes. **Go off** is less formal than **explode** and is the usual phrase to use in everyday English: *Luckily the station was empty when the bomb went off.*
blow up *phr v* if a building, car, plane etc blows up, it bursts suddenly and violently into pieces, causing a lot of damage: *The plane blew up in mid-air, killing all the passengers and crew.* | *In early 1986, a US space shuttle blew up shortly after launch.*
erupt /ɪˈrʌpt/ *v* [I] if a VOLCANO erupts, it explodes and sends smoke and rock into the sky: *The volcano has erupted at least fifteen times since 1883.*
burst *v* [I] if something that has air or liquid inside it bursts, it explodes and the air or liquid comes out: *One of the water pipes had burst.* | *The plane caught fire after its tyre burst on landing.*

TO MAKE SOMETHING EXPLODE

explode *v* [T] to make a bomb burst suddenly and violently with a loud noise: *The terrorists planned to explode a car bomb outside the US embassy.*
set off *phr v* to make a bomb explode, either deliberately or accidentally. **Set off** is less formal than **explode** and is the usual phrase to use in everyday English: *The group set off a bomb outside a crowded cafe in Izmir last September.*
detonate /ˈdetəneɪt/ *v* [T] to make a bomb explode, especially by using special equipment. **Detonate** is a more technical word than **set off**: *Army experts detonated the bomb safely in a nearby field.*
let off *phr v BrE* to deliberately make a bomb explode: *Terrorists let off a bomb in the city centre.*
blow up *phr v* to make a building, car, plane etc explode: *He was involved in a plot to blow up a passenger jet.*

ex·plod·ed /ɪkˈspləʊdɪd $ -ˈsploʊ-/ *adj technical* an exploded drawing, model etc shows the parts of something separately but in a way that shows how they are related or put together → **unexploded**: *an exploded diagram of an engine*

ex·ploit¹ /ɪkˈsplɔɪt/ ●○○ AWL *v* [T]
1 to treat someone unfairly by asking them to do things for you, but giving them very little in return – used to show disapproval: *Homeworkers can easily be exploited by employers.*
2 to try to get as much as you can out of a situation, sometimes unfairly: *The violence was blamed on thugs exploiting the situation.*
3 to use something fully and effectively: *The new TV companies are fully exploiting the potential of satellite transmission.* THESAURUS USE
4 to develop and use minerals, forests, oil etc for business

E

or industry: *the urgent need to exploit the resources of the Irish Sea* —**exploitable** *adj* —**exploiter** *n* [C]

ex·ploit² /ˈeksplɔɪt/ *n* [C usually plural] a brave and exciting adventure that someone has had: **[+of]** *the daring exploits of the British Parachute Regiment*

ex·ploi·ta·tion /ˌeksplɔɪˈteɪʃən/ ●○○ AWL *n* [U]
1 a situation in which you treat someone unfairly by asking them to do things for you, but give them very little in return – used to show disapproval: **[+of]** *The film industry thrives on the* ***sexual exploitation*** *of women.*
2 the development and use of minerals, forests, oil etc for business or industry: **[+of]** *the controlled exploitation of resources* | **commercial/economic exploitation**
3 the full and effective use of something: **[+of]** *greater exploitation of these data*
4 an attempt to get as much as you can out of a situation, sometimes unfairly: **[+of]** *the exploitation of religion for political ends*

ex·ploit·a·tive /ɪkˈsplɔɪtətɪv/ *adj* taking as much as possible from someone or something and giving very little in return: *the exploitative nature of multinational companies*

ex·plo·ra·tion /ˌekspləˈreɪʃən/ ●●○ *n* [C,U]
1 the act of travelling through a place in order to find out about it or find something such as oil or gold in it: *oil exploration facilities in the North Sea* | *You can then use this hut as a base for explorations into the mountains around.* | **[+of]** *the exploration of space*
2 when you try to find out more about something by discussing it, thinking about it etc: **[+into/of]** *an exploration into how an abused child becomes an abuser* | *the exploration of literary texts*

ex·plor·a·to·ry /ɪkˈsplɒrətəri $ ɪkˈsplɔːrətɔːri/ *adj* done in order to find out more about something: *He's going to have exploratory surgery on his knee.*

ex·plore /ɪkˈsplɔː $ -ˈsplɔːr/ ●●● S3 W2 *v*
1 [T] to discuss or think about something carefully SYN **look at**: *Management need to explore ways of improving office security.* | *I'm going to* ***explore the possibility of*** *a part-time job.*
2 [I,T] to travel around an area in order to find out about it: *Venice is a wonderful city to explore.*
3 explore (sth) for oil/minerals/gold etc to look for something such as oil, minerals etc
4 [T] *written* to feel something with your hand or another part of your body to find out what it is like: *Gingerly she explored the bump on her head with her fingers.*

ex·plo·rer /ɪkˈsplɔːrə $ -ər/ ●○○ *n* [C] someone who travels through an unknown area to find out about it THESAURUS ▸ TRAVEL

ex·plo·sion /ɪkˈspləʊʒən $ -ˈsploʊ-/ ●●● W3 *n*
1 [C] a loud sound and the energy produced by something such as a bomb bursting into small pieces → **explode**: **bomb/gas/nuclear explosion** | *Several people were injured in a bomb explosion.* | *We heard a* ***loud explosion***. | **huge/massive etc explosion** *A massive explosion ripped through the building.*
2 [C,U] a process in which something such as a bomb is deliberately made to explode: *Police carried out a* ***controlled explosion*** *of the device.*
3 [C] a sudden or quick increase in the number or amount of something: *the* ***population explosion*** *in India* | **[+of]** *the recent explosion of interest in Latin music and dance*
4 [C] a sudden expression of emotion, especially anger SYN **outburst**
5 [C] a sudden very loud noise: **[+of]** *an explosion of laughter*

ex·plo·sive¹ /ɪkˈspləʊsɪv $ -ˈsploʊ-/ ●○○ *adj*
1 able or likely to explode: *Because the gas is* ***highly explosive****, it needs to be kept in high-pressure containers.* | *A small* ***explosive device*** (=bomb) *was set off outside the UN headquarters today.*
2 [usually before noun] relating to or like an explosion: *the* ***explosive force*** *of volcanoes*
3 likely to become violent or to cause feelings of violence: *He's good at defusing* ***potentially explosive*** *situations.* | *the explosive issue of uncontrolled immigration*
4 showing sudden strong or angry emotion: *Both men suddenly spoke in the same explosive tone of voice.*
5 [usually before noun] increasing suddenly or quickly in amount or number: *the explosive growth of microcomputers*
6 an explosive sound is sudden and loud —**explosively** *adv* —**explosiveness** *n* [U]

explosive² ●○○ *n* [C,U] a substance that can cause an explosion → PLASTIC EXPLOSIVE

ex·po /ˈekspəʊ $ -poʊ/ *n* (*plural* **expos**) [C] *informal* an EXPOSITION(2)

ex·po·nent /ɪkˈspəʊnənt $ -ˈspoʊ-/ *n* [C] **1** an exponent of an idea, belief etc tries to explain it and persuade others that it is good or useful: **[+of]** *a* ***leading exponent*** *of desktop publishing* **2** an exponent of a particular skill, idea, or activity is someone who is good at it: **[+of]** *The most famous exponent of this approach to art was probably Charles Rennie Mackintosh.* **3** *technical* a sign written above and to the right of a number or letter to show how many times that quantity is to be multiplied by itself

ex·po·nen·tial /ˌekspəˈnenʃəl◂/ *adj technical*
1 exponential growth/increase etc exponential growth, increase etc becomes faster as the amount of the thing that is growing increases: *an exponential increase in travel*
2 using a small number or letter slightly above and to the right of a number or letter that shows how many times a quantity is to be multiplied by itself —**exponentially** *adv*

ex·port¹ /ˈekspɔːt $ -ɔːrt/ ●●○ W3 AWL *n*
1 [U] the business of selling and sending goods to other countries OPP **import**: **[+of]** *a ban on the export of toxic waste* | **for export** *bales of cloth for export to the continent*
2 [C usually plural] a product that is sold to another country OPP **import**: *Wheat is one of the country's main exports.* THESAURUS ▸ PRODUCT

COLLOCATIONS – MEANINGS 1 & 2

export + NOUN

an export market *The US is Scotland's second largest export market after France.*
export trade *Most of its export trade is with Russia.*
export earnings/revenue (=the money a company or country makes from exports) *Oil and gas provide 40% of Norway's export earnings.*
export sales/figures (=the total number of products that are sold to other countries) *Export sales exceeded 50% of the company's total turnover.*
an export licence (=an official document giving you permission to sell something to another country) |
export controls/restrictions/quotas (=official limits on the number of exports) | **an export ban** (*also* **a ban on exports**)

ADJECTIVES/NOUN + export

the major/main/principal export *Agricultural products are the country's principal exports.*
oil/agricultural/manufacturing exports *Oil exports from Iraq have resumed.*
British/US etc exports *Higher tariffs will affect a wide range of British exports.*
invisible exports (=services that are exported, such as banking or insurance, rather than a product)

VERBS

boost exports (=increase them) *The measures should boost exports and create employment.*
encourage exports (=make them more likely to exist) *Kenya used subsidies to encourage exports.*
reduce exports *OPEC has threatened to reduce exports of oil to the West.*
restrict exports (=limit or control them) *The government threatened to restrict exports because of weak demand.*
ban exports (=stop them completely) | **exports increase/rise/grow** | **exports fall/decline/drop**

E

PHRASES
a growth/rise/increase in exports *The electronics sector has seen a 16% growth in exports.*
a fall/decline/drop in exports

ex·port² /ɪk'spɔːt $ -ɔːrt/ ●●○ W3 AWL *v*
1 [I,T] to sell goods to another country OPP **import**: **export sth (from sb) to sb** *The company exports tuna to the US.* THESAURUS SELL
2 [T] to introduce an activity, idea etc to another place or country: *Italian food has been exported all over the world.*
3 [T] *technical* to move computer information from one computer to another, from one computer document to another, or from one piece of software to another OPP **import** —**exportation** /ˌekspɔː'teɪʃən $ -ɔːr-/ *n* [U]

ex·port·er /ɪk'spɔːtə $ -'spɔːrtər/ AWL *n* [C] a person, company, or country that sells goods to another country OPP **importer**: **[+of]** *With the expanded production of North Sea oil and gas, the UK has become a* ***net exporter of fuel*** (=it exports more fuel than it imports). | **major/leading exporter** *Japan is a leading exporter of textiles.*

ex·pose /ɪk'spəʊz $ -'spoʊz/ ●●○ W3 AWL *v* [T]
1 SHOW to show something that is usually covered or hidden: *He lifted his T-shirt to expose a jagged scar across his chest.* | **expose sth to sth** *Potatoes turn green when exposed to light.* THESAURUS SHOW
2 TO STH DANGEROUS to put someone in a situation where they are not protected from something dangerous or unpleasant: **expose sb to sth** *The report revealed that workers had been exposed to high levels of radiation.* | **expose yourself to ridicule/criticism etc** (=say or do something that may make people laugh at you, criticize you etc)
3 TELL THE TRUTH to show the truth about someone or something, especially when it is bad: *The film exposes the utter horror of war.* | *The report* ***exposes*** *the* ***weaknesses*** *of modern medical practice.* | **expose sb as sth** *The baron was exposed as a liar and a cheat.*
4 SEE/EXPERIENCE to make it possible for someone to experience new ideas, ways of life etc: **expose sb to sth** *Some children are never exposed to classical music.*
5 expose yourself if a man exposes himself, he shows his sexual organs to someone he does not know in a public place, usually because he is mentally ill
6 PHOTOGRAPH to allow light onto a piece of film in a camera in order to take a photograph
7 FEELINGS to show other people feelings that you usually hide, especially when this is not planned: *I'm afraid I might expose my real feelings for him.*

ex·po·sé /ek'spəʊzeɪ $ ˌekspə'zeɪ/ *n* [C] a story in a newspaper or on television that shows the truth about something, especially something dishonest or shocking: **[+of]** *an exposé of corrupt practices by lawyers*

ex·posed /ɪk'spəʊzd $ -'spoʊzd/ AWL *adj* **1** not protected from the weather OPP **sheltered**: *an exposed coastline* | *the side of the garden most exposed to wind* **2** not covered: *All exposed skin should be covered with protective cream.* **3** not protected from attack SYN **vulnerable**: *The old fort was very exposed.* | *These developments leave the British government in an* ***exposed position****.*

ex·po·si·tion /ˌekspə'zɪʃən/ *n* **1** [C,U] *formal* a clear and detailed explanation: **[+of]** *a lucid exposition of educational theories* **2** [C] a large public event at which you show or sell products, art etc

ex post fac·to law /ˌeks pəʊst 'fæktəʊ ˌlɔː $ -poʊst 'fæktoʊ ˌlɒː/ *n* [C] *law* a law that makes a particular action into a crime, and then punishes people who took that action before it had legally become a crime

ex·pos·tu·late /ɪk'spɒstʃəleɪt $ -'spɑː-/ *v* [I] *formal* to express strong disapproval, disagreement, or annoyance with someone —**expostulation** /ɪkˌspɒstʃə'leɪʃən $ -ˌspɑː-/ *n* [C,U]

ex·po·sure /ɪk'spəʊʒə $ -'spoʊʒər/ AWL *n*
1 TO DANGER [U] when someone is in a situation where they are not protected from something dangerous or unpleasant: **[+to]** *Prolonged exposure to the sun can cause skin cancer.*
2 TRUTH [U] the action of showing the truth about someone or something, especially when it is bad: **[+of]** *the exposure of his underground political activity* | **[+as]** *her fear of exposure as a spy*
3 PUBLIC ATTENTION [U] the attention that someone or something gets from newspapers, television etc SYN **publicity**: *The failure of their marriage has* ***got*** *a lot of* ***exposure*** *recently.*
4 EXPERIENCE [singular, U] the chance to experience new ideas, ways of life etc: **[+to]** *The visit to Germany gave them exposure to the language.* | *her brief exposure to pop stardom*
5 BE VERY COLD [U] the harmful effects on your body of being outside in very cold weather without protection: *We nearly died of exposure on the mountainside.*
6 PHOTOGRAPHY [C] **a)** a length of film in a camera that is used to take a photograph: *I have three exposures left on this roll.* **b)** the amount of time that light is allowed to enter the camera when taking a photograph
7 SHOW [C] the act of showing something that is usually hidden
8 BUSINESS [C,U] the amount of financial risk that a company or person has
9 DIRECTION [singular] the direction in which a building, hill etc faces: *My bedroom has a southern exposure.* → INDECENT EXPOSURE

ex·pound /ɪk'spaʊnd/ *v* [I,T] *formal* to explain or talk about something in detail: **[+on]** *She's always expounding on the latest dogmas of feminism.*

ex·press¹ /ɪk'spres/ ●●● S2 W1 *v* [T]
1 FEELING to tell or show what you are feeling or thinking by using words, looks, or actions: **express your views/opinions** *Bill's not afraid to express his opinions.* | *Parents have* ***expressed*** *their* ***concerns about*** *their children's safety.* | *She* ***expressed*** *an* ***interest in*** *seeing York.* | **express sth in/by/through sth** *Express your reasons for applying in simple terms.* | **express sympathy/fear/anger etc** *She doesn't express her emotions as much as he does.* | **express thanks/gratitude (for sth) (to sb)** (=thank someone in a speech or by writing a letter) *Finally, I'd like to express my sincere thanks to all those who have helped today.* | **express doubts/reservations** *The USA expressed reservations before agreeing to sign the agreement.* | *Many people have* ***expressed*** *their* ***opposition to*** *the proposals.* | **express yourself** (=say what you think or feel) *Young children often have difficulty expressing themselves.* | *He first learnt to* ***express*** *himself* ***through*** *movement at his dance classes.* | *Words* ***can't express*** (=it is impossible to describe) *how angry we felt.* THESAURUS SAY
2 PARTICULAR EMOTION to show or describe a particular feeling: *Many of Munch's paintings express a deep feeling of despair.*
3 sth expresses itself if something expresses itself, it becomes noticeable SYN **sth reveals itself**: *Religious faith expresses itself in a variety of ways.*
4 MATHEMATICS *technical* to change an amount or quantity into a different form, especially in mathematics: **express sth as/in sth** *Express three-quarters as a decimal.* | *The value of the coffee becomes significantly higher when expressed in foreign currency.*
5 FEEDING BABIES if a woman expresses milk, she presses milk out of her breast in order to feed it to her baby later

express² ●●○ *adj* [only before noun]
1 deliberate and for a specific situation: *The school was founded with the* ***express purpose*** *of teaching deaf children.*
2 clear and definite: **express agreement/consent/authority etc** *He is not to leave without my express permission.* | *Matthew left express instructions to keep all doors locked.*
3 express train/coach/bus a train or bus that does not stop at many places and can therefore travel more quickly
4 express post/mail a system that delivers letters and packages very quickly
5 *AmE* designed to help you move through a place more quickly: *express lanes on the freeway* | *an express line at a*

supermarket (=where people with only a few things to buy go to pay)

express³ ●●○ *n*
1 [C usually singular] a train or bus that does not stop in many places and therefore travels quickly: **London-Gatwick Express/Orient Express** (=a fast train or bus which does a particular journey regularly)
2 [U] a post service that delivers letters and packages very quickly: *Send these books by express.*

express⁴ *adv* **send/deliver sth express** to send or deliver a letter, package etc quickly using a special post service

ex·pres·sion /ɪk'spreʃən/ ●●● S2 W2 *n*
1 STRONG FEELINGS/THOUGHTS [C,U] something you say, write, or do that shows what you think or feel: **[+of]** *I decided to go to the meeting as an expression of support.* | **expression of sympathy/thanks/regret etc** *The letter was a genuine expression of sympathy.* | *Student leaders are demanding greater* ***freedom of expression*** (=the right to say what you think without being punished). | **give (political/religious/artistic) expression to sth** *The Socialist Party was founded to give political expression to the working classes.* | *Another writer who seeks to give expression to popular oral culture is José María Arguedas.*
2 ON SB'S FACE [C,U] a look on someone's face that shows what they are thinking or feeling: **[+of]** *an expression of surprise* | *There was a* ***blank expression on*** *her* ***face*** (=no expression on her face). | *In the photograph he seemed* ***devoid of*** *facial* ***expression*** (=having no expression on his face). | *A* ***pained*** (=worried) ***expression*** *crossed her face.*
3 WORD/PHRASE [C] a word or group of words with a particular meaning: *The old-fashioned expression 'in the family way' means 'pregnant'.* | **pardon/forgive/excuse the expression** (=used when you think you may offend someone by using particular words) *After the climb we were absolutely knackered, if you'll pardon the expression.* THESAURUS▶ PHRASE, WORD
4 MUSIC/ACTING [U] when you put feeling or emotion into the music that you are making or into your acting
5 MATHEMATICS [C] *technical* a sign or group of signs that represent a mathematical idea or quantity

ex·pres·sion·is·m /ɪk'spreʃənɪzəm/ *n* [U] a style of painting, writing, or music that expresses feelings rather than describing objects and experiences —**expressionist** *n* [C] —**expressionist** *adj* [only before noun]: *the expressionist movement*

ex·pres·sion·less /ɪk'spreʃənləs/ *adj* an expressionless face or voice does not show what someone thinks or feels OPP **expressive**: *a blank expressionless stare* —**expressionlessly** *adv*

ex·pres·sive /ɪk'spresɪv/ *adj* **1** showing very clearly what someone thinks or feels OPP **expressionless**: *her wonderfully expressive eyes* **2 be expressive of sth** *formal* showing a particular feeling or influence: *Her poem is expressive of calm days and peace of mind.* —**expressively** *adv* —**expressiveness** *n* [U]

ex·press·ly /ɪk'spresli/ ●○○ *adv formal*
1 if you say something expressly, you say it very clearly and firmly SYN **specifically**: *He was* ***expressly forbidden*** *to speak to the girl.*
2 deliberately or for a specific purpose SYN **specifically**: *The building is expressly designed to conserve energy.*

ex'press ˌmail *n* [U] *AmE* a post service that delivers letters and packages very quickly

ex·press·way /ɪk'spresweɪ/ *n* [C] *AmE* a wide road in a city on which cars can travel very quickly without stopping → FREEWAY, MOTORWAY

ex·pro·pri·ate /ɪk'sprəʊprieɪt $ -'sproʊ-/ *v* [T] *formal*
1 if a government or someone in authority expropriates your private property, they take it away for public use
2 to take something from someone illegally in order to use it —**expropriation** /ɪkˌsprəʊpri'eɪʃən $ -ˌsproʊ-/ *n* [C,U]

ex·pul·sion /ɪk'spʌlʃən/ *n* [C,U] **1** the act of forcing someone to leave a place → **expel**: **[+of]** *the expulsion of the protesters* | **[+from]** *his expulsion from the Soviet Union in 1964* **2** the act of stopping someone from going to the school where they were studying or from being part of the organization where they worked → **expel**: *The headmaster threatened the boys with expulsion.* | **[+of]** *the expulsion from the party of its former leader* **3** the act of forcing air, water, gas etc out of something → **expel**

ex·punge /ɪk'spʌndʒ/ *v* [T] *formal* **1** to remove a name from a list, piece of information, or book **2** to make someone forget something unpleasant: **expunge sth from sth** *I wanted to expunge the memory of that first race from my mind.*

ex·pur·gat·ed /'ekspəgeɪtɪd $ -ər-/ *adj* an expurgated book, play etc has had some parts removed because they are considered harmful or offensive: *an expurgated version of her writings* —**expurgate** *v* [T]

ex·qui·site /ɪk'skwɪzət, 'ekskwɪ-/ ●○○ *adj*
1 extremely beautiful and very delicately made: *the most exquisite craftsmanship* THESAURUS▶ BEAUTIFUL
2 very sensitive and delicate in the way you behave or do things: *She has exquisite taste in art.*
3 *literary* exquisite pain or pleasure is felt very strongly —**exquisitely** *adv* —**exquisiteness** *n* [U]

ˌex-'serviceman *n* (*plural* **ex-servicemen**) [C] *BrE* a man who used to be in the army, navy, or air force

ˌex-'servicewoman *n* (*plural* **ex-servicewomen**) [C] *BrE* a woman who used to be in the army, navy, or air force

ext. the written abbreviation of ***extension*** when you mean a particular telephone line

ex·tant /ɪk'stænt/ *adj formal* still existing in spite of being very old: *Few of the manuscripts are still extant.*

ex·tem·po·ra·ne·ous /ɪkˌstempə'reɪniəs◂/ *adj formal* spoken or done without any preparation or practice SYN **impromptu**: *an extemporaneous speech* —**extemporaneously** *adv*

ex·tem·po·re /ɪk'stempəri/ *adj formal* spoken or done without any preparation or practice SYN **impromptu**: *an extempore speech* —**extempore** *adv*

ex·tem·po·rize (*also* **-ise** *BrE*) /ɪk'stempəraɪz/ *v* [I] *formal* to speak or perform without preparation or practice —**extemporization** /ɪkˌstempəraɪ'zeɪʃən $ -rə-/ *n* [C,U]

ex·tend /ɪk'stend/ ●●○ S3 W2 *v*
1 TIME [I + adv/prep,T] to continue for a longer period of time, or to make something last longer: *Management have agreed to extend the deadline.* | **[+for/into/over etc]** *Some of our courses extend over two years.* | **extend sth for/by/until sth** *The government has extended the ban on the import of beef until June.* THESAURUS▶ INCREASE
2 AREA/DISTANCE [I always + adv/prep] to continue for a particular distance or over a particular area: **across/over/through etc** *The River Nile extends as far south as Lake Victoria.* | **extend 100 km/30 yards etc (from sth)** *The shelf extends 20 cms from the bookcase.*
3 SIZE [T] to make a room, building, road etc bigger or longer: *We plan to extend the kitchen by six feet.*
4 INCLUDE/AFFECT **a)** [I always + adv/prep] to affect or include people, things, or places: **[+to/beyond etc]** *My duties at the school extend beyond just teaching.* | *The vote was extended to all women aged 21 and over in 1928.* **b)** [T] to make something affect more people, situations, areas etc than before: *British Coal is planning to extend its operations in Wales.* | **extend sth to sb/sth** *We can extend our insurance cover to travel abroad.*
5 OFFER HELP/THANKS [T] *formal* to officially offer someone help, sympathy, thanks etc: **extend sth to sb** *We'd like to* ***extend a warm welcome*** *to our French visitors.* | *I'd like to* ***extend*** *my* ***thanks*** *to all the catering staff.* | *The Coroner* ***extended*** *his* ***sympathy*** *to the victim's family.* | *The Headteacher has* ***extended*** *an* ***invitation*** *to the prime minister to visit the school.* | *The banks have decided to* ***extend credit*** *to the company* (=allow them to borrow more money).
6 ARMS/LEGS [T] to stretch out a hand or leg: *George* ***extended*** *his* ***hand*** (=offered to shake hands).
7 CONTINUE WINNING [T] to increase the number of points, games etc by which one person or team is ahead of other competitors: *Manchester United* ***extended*** *their* ***lead*** *at the top of the table to 10 points.*

E

8 FURNITURE [I,T] if a table or ladder extends, it can be made longer → **fold**

ex·tend·ed /ɪk'stendɪd/ ●○○ *adj* [only before noun]
1 made longer or bigger: *an extended business trip* | *The computer uses extended memory.* THESAURUS ▸ LONG
2 long or longer than expected or planned: *If you are going abroad for an* ***extended period of time****, you should consider renting your house out.*
3 long and detailed: *an extended analysis of the film*

ex,tended 'family *n* [C] a family group that consists not only of parents and children but also of grandparents, AUNTS etc → **nuclear family**

ex·ten·sion /ɪk'stenʃən/ ●●○ S3 W3 *n*
1 MAKING STH BIGGER OR LONGER [C,U] the process of making a road, building etc bigger or longer, or the part that is added: **[+of]** *the extension of the Jubilee underground line*
2 EXTRA ROOMS [C] *BrE* another room or rooms which are added to a building: **[+to]** *the planned extension to the National Museum* | *a loft extension*
3 EXTRA TIME [C usually singular] an additional period of time allowed for something: *Donald's been given an extension to finish his thesis.* | *The pub's got an extension tonight* (=it will stay open longer than usual).
4 INCLUDE/AFFECT MORE THAN BEFORE [singular, U] the development of something in order to make it affect more people, situations, areas than before: **[+of]** *the extension of the copyright laws to cover online materials* | *an extension of the powers of the European Parliament*
5 TELEPHONE [C] **a)** one of many telephone lines connected to a central system in a large building, which all have different numbers: *Can I have extension 316, please?* | *Do you know Mr Brown's* ***extension number****?* **b)** one of the telephones in a house that all have the same number
6 **by extension** used when you want to mention something that is naturally related to something else: *My primary responsibility is to the pupils, and by extension to the teachers and parents.*
7 **extensions** [plural] long pieces of artificial hair that can be attached to your hair to make it look longer: **hair extensions**
8 COMPUTER [C] *technical* a set of three letters that follow the name of a computer FILE to show what it is. For example, the extension '.doc' shows that a file is a written document.
9 ELECTRIC WIRE [C] *BrE* an EXTENSION LEAD
10 STRETCH ARM/LEG [C,U] the position of a part of the body when it is stretched, or the process of stretching it
11 UNIVERSITY/COLLEGE [U] part of a university or college that offers courses to people who are not full-time students

ex'tension ,lead *BrE*, **ex'tension ,cord** *AmE* *n* [C] an additional piece of electric wire that you attach to another wire to make a very long one SYN **extension** → see picture at PLUG[1]

ex·ten·sive /ɪk'stensɪv/ ●●○ W3 *adj*
1 large in size, amount, or degree: *The house stands in extensive grounds.* | *Fire has caused extensive damage to the island's forests.* | *the extensive use of pesticides*
2 containing or dealing with a lot of information and details: *Extensive research is being done into the connection between the disease and poor living conditions.* | *The exhibition has received* ***extensive coverage*** *in the national press.* —**extensively** *adv*: *As a student, he travelled extensively in the Middle East.*

ex·tent /ɪk'stent/ ●●● S2 W1 *n*
1 **to ... extent** used to say how true something is or how great an effect or change is: **to a certain extent/to some extent/to an extent** (=partly) *We all to some extent remember the good times and forget the bad.* | *I do agree with him to an extent.* | **to a great/large extent** *Its success will depend to a large extent on local attitudes.* | **to a lesser/greater extent** (=less or more) *It will affect farmers in Spain and to a lesser extent in France.* | *They examined* ***the extent to which*** (=how much) *age affected language-learning ability.* | ***To what extent*** (=how much) *did she influence his decision?* | **to such an extent that/to the extent that** (=so much that) *Violence increased to the extent that residents were afraid to leave their homes.*
2 [U] how large, important, or serious something is, especially something such as a problem or injury: **[+of]** *Considering the extent of his injuries, he's lucky to be alive.* | *It's too early to assess* ***the full extent of*** *the damage.*
3 [U] the length or size of something: *They opened out the nets to their* ***full extent****.* | **in extent** *The region is over 10,000 square kilometres in extent.* THESAURUS ▸ SIZE

COLLOCATIONS – MEANING 2

ADJECTIVES

the full extent *He refused to reveal the full extent of his debts.*
the actual/true extent *Rescue workers still do not know the true extent of the disaster.*

VERBS

know/realize the extent of sth *We do not yet know the extent of the damage.*
understand the extent of sth *Other people didn't seem to understand the extent of his disability.*
discover/find out the extent of sth *We were shocked when we discovered the extent of the fraud.*
assess/establish/determine the extent of sth *We are still trying to assess the extent of the problem.*
show/reveal the extent of sth *These pictures show the extent of the devastation caused by the earthquake.*

ex·ten·u·at·ing /ɪk'stenjueɪtɪŋ/ *adj* **extenuating circumstances/factors etc** *formal* facts or reasons which make you feel that it was reasonable for someone to break the usual rules, or make you have sympathy for someone who did something wrong or illegal —**extenuation** /ɪk,stenju'eɪʃən/ *n* [U]

ex·te·ri·or[1] /ɪk'stɪəriə $ -'tɪriər/ ●●○ *n* [C]
1 [usually singular] the outside of something, especially a building OPP **interior**: **[+of]** *the exterior of the factory* | *The dome is tiled* ***on the exterior****.*
2 **calm/cool etc exterior** behaviour that seems calm, unfriendly etc but which often hides a different feeling or attitude: *Beneath that calm exterior, he has a fierce will to win.*

exterior[2] *adj* [usually before noun] **1** on the outside of something OPP **interior**: *The* ***exterior walls*** *need a new coat of paint.* **2** exterior scenes in a film are filmed outdoors **3** coming from or relating to facts, situations etc other than the one you are considering: *information that is exterior to the text itself*

ex·ter·mi·nate /ɪk'stɜːməneɪt $ -ɜːr-/ *v* [T] to kill large numbers of people or animals of a particular type so that they no longer exist: *Staff use the poison to exterminate moles and rabbits.* THESAURUS ▸ KILL —**exterminator** *n* [C] —**extermination** /ɪk,stɜːmə'neɪʃən $ -ɜːr-/ *n* [C,U]: *the extermination of the indigenous peoples*

ex·tern /'ekstɜːn $ -ɜːrn/ *n* [C] *AmE* a university student who works in a particular type of job for a short time in order to gain experience of that type of work: *a finance major who was an extern with Merrill Lynch* —**extern** *v* [I]

ex·ter·nal /ɪk'stɜːnl $ -ɜːr-/ ●●○ W2 AWL *adj*
1 OUTSIDE PART relating to the outside of something or of a person's body OPP **internal**: *the external appearance of the building* | **For external use only** (=written on medicines which must be put on your skin and not swallowed)

REGISTER
In everyday English, people usually say **outside** rather than **external**: *The* ***outside*** *walls of the building were painted yellow.*

2 EFFECT relating to your environment or situation, rather than to your own qualities, ideas etc SYN **outside**: *Low birth weight may be caused by* ***external factors****, such as smoking during pregnancy.* | *influences from the external environment*

3 ORGANIZATION coming from or happening outside a particular place or organization OPP **internal**: *information from external sources*
4 FOREIGN relating to foreign countries OPP **internal**: *China will not tolerate any external interference in its affairs.* | **external affairs/relations** *the Minister of External Affairs*
5 INDEPENDENT *BrE* coming from outside a particular school, university, or organization, and therefore independent OPP **internal**: **external examination/examiner** | **external auditors** (=someone from outside who looks at an organization's finances) —**externally** *adv*: *The job should be advertised internally and externally.*

ex·ter·nal·ize (*also* **-ise** *BrE*) /ɪkˈstɜːnəlaɪz $ -ɜːr-/ AWL *v* [T] *formal* to express inner feelings → **internalize** —**externalization** /ɪkˌstɜːnəlaɪˈzeɪʃən $ -ˌstɜːrnələ-/ *n* [C,U]

ex·ter·nals /ɪkˈstɜːnlz $ -ɜːr-/ *n* [plural] the outer appearance of a situation

ex·tern·ship /ˈekstɜːnʃɪp $ -tɜːrn-/ *n* [C] *AmE* a job that a university student does in order to gain experience in a particular area of work. Externships are usually not paid and usually last only a short time → **extern**, **internship**: *an externship in a law firm*

ex·tinct /ɪkˈstɪŋkt/ ●●○ *adj*
1 an extinct type of animal or plant does not exist anymore: *Dinosaurs have been extinct for millions of years.* | *Pandas could* ***become extinct*** *in the wild.* | *an extinct species*
2 if a type of person, custom, skill etc is extinct, it does not exist in society anymore
3 an extinct VOLCANO does not ERUPT anymore OPP **active**

ex·tinc·tion /ɪkˈstɪŋkʃən/ ●○○ *n* [U]
1 when a particular type of animal or plant stops existing: *species* ***in danger of extinction*** | **on the verge/edge/brink of extinction** (=nearly extinct) *The breed was on the verge of extinction.* | *They were* ***hunted*** *almost* ***to extinction***. | *Conservationists are trying to* ***save*** *the whale* ***from extinction***. | **face extinction/be threatened with extinction** *Many endangered species now face extinction.*
2 when a type of person, custom, skill etc stops existing: *Their traditional way of life seems doomed to extinction.*

ex·tin·guish /ɪkˈstɪŋgwɪʃ/ *v* [T] *formal* **1** to make a fire or light stop burning or shining SYN **put out**: *Please extinguish all cigarettes.* | *Firemen were called to extinguish the blaze.* THESAURUS ▸ BURN **2** to make an idea or feeling stop: *All hope was almost extinguished.*

ex·tin·guish·er /ɪkˈstɪŋgwɪʃə $ -ər/ *n* [C] a FIRE EXTINGUISHER

ex·tir·pate /ˈekstɜːpeɪt $ -ɜːr-/ *v* [T] *formal* to completely destroy something that is unpleasant or unwanted

ex·tol /ɪkˈstəʊl $ -ˈstoʊl/ *v* (**extolled**, **extolling**) [T] *formal* to praise something very much: **extol the virtues/benefits etc of sth** *a speech extolling the merits of free enterprise*

ex·tort /ɪkˈstɔːt $ -ɔːrt/ *v* [T] to illegally force someone to give you something, especially money, by threatening them → **blackmail**: **extort sth from sb** *Rebels* ***extorted money*** *from local villagers.* —**extortion** /ɪkˈstɔːʃən $ -ɔːr-/ *n* [U]: *He faces charges of kidnapping and extortion.* —**extortionist** *n* [C]

ex·tor·tion·ate /ɪkˈstɔːʃənət $ -ɔːr-/ *adj* an extortionate price, demand etc is unreasonably high SYN **exorbitant**: *Many local taxi drivers charge extortionate rates.* —**extortionately** *adv*

ex·tra[1] /ˈekstrə/ ●●● S1 W2 *adj*
1 [only before noun] more of something, in addition to the usual or standard amount or number: *Could you get an extra loaf of bread?* | *Allow extra time for your journey.* | *Drivers are advised to take* ***extra care***. | *Residents can use the gym* ***at no extra cost***. | **an extra ten minutes/three metres etc** *I asked for an extra two weeks to finish the work.* THESAURUS ▸ MORE
2 [not before noun] if something is extra, it is not included in the price of something and you have to pay more for it OPP **included**: *Dinner costs $15 but wine is extra.*

extra[2] ●●○ *adv*
1 in addition to the usual things or the usual amount: *They need to offer something extra to attract customers.* | **one/a few etc extra** *I got a few extra in case anyone else decides to come.* | *I'll be making $400 extra a month.*
2 [+adj/adv] used to emphasize an adjective or adverb: *You're going to have to work extra hard to pass the exam.* | *an extra special effort*

extra[3] *pron* an amount of something, especially money, in addition to the usual, basic, or necessary amount SYN **more**: **pay/charge/cost etc extra** *I earn extra for working on Sunday.*

extra[4] *n* [C] **1** something which is added to a basic product or service that improves it and often costs more: *Tinted windows and a sunroof are* ***optional extras*** (=something that you can choose to have or not). | *Be careful, there may be* ***hidden extras*** (=additional charges which you are not told about). | *It's got lots of useful* ***little extras***.
2 an actor in a film who does not say anything but is part of a crowd: *He started his acting career as an extra.* THESAURUS ▸ ACTOR

extra- /ekstrə/ *prefix* **1** outside or beyond: *extragalactic* (=outside our galaxy) | *extracellular* (=outside a cell) **2** *informal* very or more than normal: *extra-large* | *extra-strong* | *extra-special*

ex·tract[1] /ɪkˈstrækt/ ●●○ AWL *v* [T]
1 *formal* to remove an object from somewhere, especially with difficulty SYN **pull out**: *You'll have to have that* ***tooth extracted***. | **extract sth from sth** *He extracted an envelope from his inside pocket.*
2 to carefully remove a substance from something which contains it, using a machine, chemical process etc: **extract sth from sth** *Oils are extracted from the plants.*
3 to get something which you want from someone, such as information, money, help etc, especially when they do not want to give it to you: **extract sth from sb** *She had extracted a promise from him.* | *They used torture to* ***extract information*** *about their families.*
4 to take information or a short piece of writing from a book: *We need to extract the relevant financial data.*
5 to get an advantage or good thing from a situation: **extract sth from sth** *They aim to extract the maximum political benefit from the Games.*

ex·tract[2] /ˈekstrækt/ ●●○ AWL *n*
1 [C] a short piece of writing, music etc taken from a particular book, piece of music etc SYN **excerpt**: **[+from]** *I've only seen short extracts from the film.*
2 [C,U] a substance obtained from something by using a special process: **vanilla/malt/plant etc extract** *Add one teaspoon of vanilla extract.*

ex·trac·tion /ɪkˈstrækʃən/ AWL *n* **1** [C,U] the process of removing or obtaining something from something else: **[+of]** *the extraction of salt from seawater* | *the extraction of information from appropriate reference sources* | **mineral/oil etc extraction 2 be of French/Russian/Italian etc extraction** to be from a French, Russian etc family even though you were not born in that country

ex·trac·tor /ɪəˈstræktə $ -ər/ (*also* **exˈtractor ˌfan**) *n* [C] a machine for removing air that is hot or smells unpleasant from a kitchen, factory etc

ex·tra·cur·ric·u·lar /ˌekstrəkəˈrɪkjələ◂ $ -ər◂/ *adj* [only before noun] extracurricular activities are not part of the course that a student is doing at a school or college → **curriculum**

ex·tra·dit·a·ble /ˈekstrədaɪtəbəl/ *adj* an extraditable crime is one for which someone can be extradited: *Possession of explosives is an extraditable offence.*

ex·tra·dite /ˈekstrədaɪt/ *v* [T] to use a legal process to send someone who may be guilty of a crime back to the country where the crime happened in order to judge them in a court of law: **extradite sb to/from Britain/the US etc** *They are expected to be extradited to Britain to face trial.* —**extradition** /ˌekstrəˈdɪʃən/ *n* [C,U]: *an extradition order*

ex·tra·ju·di·cial /ˌekstrədʒuːˈdɪʃəl◂/ *adj* [only before noun] beyond or outside the ordinary powers of the law

ex·tra·mar·i·tal /ˌekstrəˈmærətl◂/ *adj* [only before noun] an extramarital sexual relationship is one that a married person has with a person who is not their husband or wife

ex·tra·mu·ral /ˌekstrəˈmjʊərəl◂ $ -ˈmjʊr-/ *adj* [only before noun] **1** relating to a place or organization but happening or done outside it: *extramural activities* **2** *especially BrE* extramural courses are for people who are not FULL-TIME students

ex·tra·ne·ous /ɪkˈstreɪniəs/ *adj formal* **1** not belonging to or directly related to a particular subject or problem SYN **irrelevant**: **[+to]** *Such details are extraneous to the matter in hand.* **2** coming from outside: *extraneous noises*

ex·tra·net /ˈekstrənet/ *n* [C] a computer system in a company that allows better communication between the company and its customers by combining Internet and INTRANET systems, so that some customers can view some of the company's private information that is not normally available on the Internet

ex·traor·di·naire /ɪkˌstrɔːdəˈneə $ -ˌstrɔːrdnˈer/ *adj* [only after noun] used, often humorously, to describe someone who is very good at doing something: **gardener/cakemaker/chef etc extraordinaire**

ex·traor·di·na·ri·ly /ɪkˈstrɔːdənərəli $ ɪkˌstrɔːrdnˈerəli, ˌekstrəˈɔːrdn-erəli/ ●○○ *adv especially BrE*
1 [+adj/adv] extremely: *We were extraordinarily lucky.*
2 in a way that seems strange: *Why had James behaved so extraordinarily?*

ex·traor·di·na·ry /ɪkˈstrɔːdənəri $ ɪkˈstrɔːrdn-eri, ˌekstrəˈɔːr-/ ●●○ S3 W3 *adj*
1 very unusual or surprising: *It took an extraordinary amount of work.* | ***It's extraordinary that** he should make exactly the same mistake again.* | **quite/most extraordinary** *BrE: Chris's behaviour that morning was quite extraordinary.* | **extraordinary thing to do/say/happen** *What an extraordinary thing to do!* | **how extraordinary!** *BrE spoken* (=used to express surprise) **THESAURUS** ▸ SURPRISING
2 very much greater or more impressive than usual SYN **incredible**: *a woman of extraordinary beauty* | *an extraordinary talent*
3 extraordinary meeting/session etc a meeting which takes place in addition to the usual ones
4 envoy/ambassador/minister extraordinary an official employed for a special purpose, in addition to the usual officials

exˌtraordinary renˈdition *n* [U] the practice by a government of arranging for someone who is thought to be a TERRORIST to be taken to another country where more severe ways of getting information, for example TORTURE, can be used

ex·trap·o·late /ɪkˈstræpəleɪt/ *v* [I,T] to use facts about the present or about one thing or group to make a guess about the future or about other things or groups: **extrapolate (sth) from sth** *It is possible to extrapolate future developments from current trends.* | *You're extrapolating from your own feelings to mine.* | **extrapolate (sth) to sth** *These results cannot, however, be extrapolated to other patient groups.* —**extrapolation** /ɪkˌstræpəˈleɪʃən/ *n* [C,U]

ˌextra-ˌsensory perˈception *n* [U] ESP

ex·tra·ter·res·tri·al[1] /ˌekstrətəˈrestriəl◂/ *n* [C] a creature that people think may exist on another PLANET

extraterrestrial[2] *adj* relating to things that exist outside the Earth

ex·tra·ter·ri·to·ri·al /ˌekstrəterəˈtɔːriəl◂/ *adj formal* happening outside a particular country

ˌextra ˈtime *n* [U] *especially BrE* a period, usually of 30 minutes, added to the end of a football game in some competitions if neither team has won after normal time SYN **overtime** *AmE*: **in extra time** *Beckham scored in extra time.* | *The match **went into extra time**.*

ex·trav·a·gant /ɪkˈstrævəgənt/ ●●○ *adj*
1 spending or costing a lot of money, especially more than is necessary or more than you can afford: *Would it be too extravagant to buy both?* | *an extravagant lifestyle*
2 doing or using something too much or more than is necessary: **[+with]** *Don't be too extravagant with the wine.* | *an extravagant display of loyalty*
3 if someone makes extravagant claims, promises etc, they make big claims or promises that are not true or real: *extravagant claims about the drug's effectiveness*
4 very impressive because of being very expensive, beautiful etc: *extravagant celebrations* —**extravagantly** *adv* —**extravagance** *n* [C,U]: *the extravagance of the Royal Palace* | *His only extravagance* (=the only expensive thing he bought) *was fine wine.*

ex·trav·a·gan·za /ɪkˌstrævəˈgænzə/ *n* [C] a very large and expensive entertainment: *a musical extravaganza*

ex·tra·vert /ˈekstrəvɜːt $ -ɜːrt/ *n* [C] another spelling of EXTROVERT

ˌextra virgin *adj* extra virgin OLIVE OIL comes from OLIVES that are pressed for the first time, and is considered to be the best quality olive oil

ex·treme[1] /ɪkˈstriːm/ ●●○ S3 W3 *adj*
1 [only before noun] very great in degree: *Extreme poverty still exists in many rural areas.* | **extreme care/caution** *It is necessary to use extreme caution with chemicals.* | *extreme cold* | *He had extreme difficulty getting hold of the ingredients.*
2 very unusual and severe or serious: **extreme example/case** *an extreme case of cruelty* | *Force is only justified **in extreme circumstances**.* | **extreme weather/conditions etc**
3 extreme west/end/left etc the part furthest to the west, nearest the end etc: *on the extreme edge of the cliff*
4 extreme opinions, beliefs, or organizations, especially political ones, are considered by most people to be unacceptable and unreasonable: *extreme right-wing nationalists*
5 [only before noun] **extreme sports/surfing/skiing etc** an extreme sport is one that is done in a way that has much more risk and so is more dangerous than an ordinary form of the sport
6 extreme athlete/surfer/skier etc someone who does extreme sports: *Extreme surfers will ride waves that reach heights of more than fifty feet.*

extreme[2] ●●○ *n* [C]
1 a situation, quality etc which is as great as it can possibly be - used especially when talking about two opposites: **[+of]** *The bacteria can withstand extremes of heat and cold.* | *In fact, the truth lies **between the two extremes**.* | **at the other/opposite extreme** *At the other extreme is a country like Switzerland with almost no unemployment.* | *Advertisements seem to **go from one extreme to the other*** (=change from one extreme thing to something totally opposite).
2 in the extreme to a very great degree: *This kind of experiment seems cruel in the extreme.*
3 to extremes if someone does something to extremes, they do it to a point beyond what is normal or acceptable: **take/carry sth to extremes** *Problems only occur when this attitude is taken to extremes.* | *She had **gone to extremes** to avoid seeing him.*

exˌtreme ˈfighting *n* [U] a competition, similar to BOXING, in which two people are allowed to hit or kick each other and in which there are almost no rules

ex·treme·ly /ɪkˈstriːmli/ ●●● S2 W2 *adv* [+adj/adv] to a very great degree: *Earthquakes are extremely difficult to predict.* | *I'm extremely sorry to have troubled you.*

extremis → IN EXTREMIS

ex·trem·is·m /ɪkˈstriːmɪzəm/ *n* [U] opinions, ideas, and actions, especially political or religious ones, that most people think are unreasonable and unacceptable

ex·trem·ist /ɪkˈstriːmɪst/ ●○○ *n* [C] someone who has extreme political opinions and aims, and who is willing to do unusual or illegal things in order to achieve them: *The bomb was planted by right-wing extremists.* —**extremist** *adj*

ex·trem·i·ty /ɪkˈstreməti/ *n* (*plural* **extremities**)
1 [C usually plural] one of the parts of your body that is furthest away from the centre, for example your fingers and toes **2** [U] the degree to which something goes beyond what is usually thought to be acceptable: *The committee was uncomfortable about the extremity of the proposal.* **3** [C] the part that is furthest away from the

centre of something: **eastern/southern etc extremity of sth** *the southern extremity of New Zealand*

ex·tri·cate /ˈekstrɪkeɪt/ *v* [T] **1** to escape from a difficult or embarrassing situation, or to help someone escape: **extricate yourself/sb from sth** *How was he going to extricate himself from this situation?* **2** to remove someone from a place in which they are trapped: **extricate sb/yourself from sth** *Firemen had to extricate the driver from the wreckage.*

ex·trin·sic /ekˈstrɪnsɪk, -zɪk/ *adj formal* coming from outside or not directly relating to something OPP **intrinsic**: *Staff who complete extra qualifications receive no* ***extrinsic rewards*** (=no extra money etc). | *a combination of intrinsic and extrinsic factors*

ex·tro·vert, **extravert** /ˈekstrəvɜːt $ -ɜːrt/ ●○○ *n* [C] someone who is active and confident, and who enjoys spending time with other people OPP **introvert**: *Her sister was always more of an extrovert.* THESAURUS ▸ CONFIDENT —**extrovert** *adj*: *a friendly, extrovert young Australian*

ex·tro·vert·ed /ˈekstrəvɜːtɪd $ -vɜːr-/ (*also* **extrovert**) *adj* having a confident character and enjoying the company of other people OPP **introverted** —**extroversion** /ˌekstrəˈvɜːʃən $ -ˈvɜːrʒən/ *n* [U]

ex·trude /ɪkˈstruːd/ *v* [T] **1** *formal* to push or force something out through a hole **2** *technical* to force plastic or metal through a hole so that it has a particular shape —**extrusion** /ɪkˈstruːʒən/ *n* [C,U]

ex·u·be·rant /ɪɡˈzjuːbərənt $ ɪɡˈzuː-/ *adj* **1** happy and full of energy and excitement: *an exuberant personality* **2** exuberant decorations, patterns etc are exciting and complicated or colourful: *exuberant carvings* —**exuberance** *n* [U]: *She needs to try and control her natural exuberance.* —**exuberantly** *adv*

ex·ude /ɪɡˈzjuːd $ ɪɡˈzuːd/ *v* **1** [T] if you exude a particular quality, it is easy to see that you have a lot of it: *She exudes self-confidence.* | *He exuded an air of wealth and power.* **2** [I,T] *formal* to flow out slowly and steadily, or to make something do this: *The plant exudes a sticky liquid.*

ex·ult /ɪɡˈzʌlt/ *v* [I,T] *formal* to show that you are very happy and proud, especially because you have succeeded in doing something: **[+at/in/over]** *She exulted in her new discovery.* | *'We made the front page!' Jos exulted.* —**exultation** /ˌeɡzʌlˈteɪʃən/ *n* [U]: *a sense of exultation*

ex·ul·tant /ɪɡˈzʌltənt/ *adj formal* very happy or proud, especially because you have succeeded in doing something: *an exultant mood* | *Ralph was exultant.* —**exultantly** *adv*

-ey /i/ *suffix* [in adjectives] the form used for -Y, especially after y: *clayey soil*

EYE

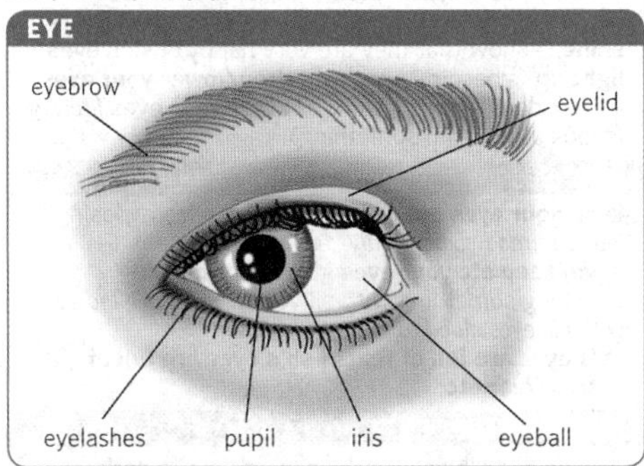

eye¹ /aɪ/ ●●● S1 W1 *n*

1 FOR SEEING WITH [C] one of the two parts of the body that you use to see with: *He's got beautiful eyes.* | *There were tears in her eyes as she listened to the story.* | *Ow! I've got something in my eye!* | **blue-eyed/one-eyed/bright-eyed etc** *a brown-eyed girl* → WIDE-EYED

2 WAY OF SEEING/UNDERSTANDING [C usually singular] a particular way of seeing, judging, or understanding something: *Go through your shopping list with* ***a critical eye*** *for foods with a high fat content.* | **with the eye of sb** *The magazine combines the accuracy of the scientist with the eye of the artist.* | **to sb's eye(s)** *The picture quality, to my eye, is excellent.* | **through the eyes of sb** (=from the point of view of a particular person) *The story is told through the eyes of a refugee child.* | **in the eyes of sb** (=according to a particular person or group) *Carl could do no wrong in the eyes of his parents.*

3 keep an eye on sth/sb to look after someone or something and make sure that they are safe: *Mary will keep an eye on the kids this afternoon.* | *We keep a watchful eye on our elderly neighbors.*

4 have/keep your eye on sb to carefully watch everything that someone does, especially because you do not trust them: *We want Taylor in jail where we can keep an eye on him.*

5 eye contact when you look directly at someone at the same time as they are looking at you: *People who are lying tend to avoid eye contact.* | *In a formal interview, try to maintain good eye contact with the interviewers.*

6 keep/have one eye/half an eye on sb/sth to be watching someone or something at the same time that you are doing something else: *Louise was stirring the soup with half an eye on the baby.*

7 have your eye on sth to want something that you think might become available: *He has his eye on the bigger apartment next door.*

8 the naked eye if you can see something with the naked eye, you can see it without using any artificial help such as a TELESCOPE or MICROSCOPE: **with the naked eye** *It's just about possible to see the planet with the naked eye on a clear night.* | **visible/invisible to the naked eye** *Dust mites are tiny creatures, invisible to the naked eye.*

9 before your very eyes (*also* **(right) in front of your eyes**) *especially spoken* if something happens before your very eyes, it happens where you can clearly see it: *The murder had apparently taken place before our very eyes.*

10 can't take your eyes off sb/sth to be unable to stop looking at someone or something, especially because they are extremely interesting or attractive: *She looked stunning. I couldn't take my eyes off her all evening.*

11 under the (watchful/stern etc) eye of sb while being watched by someone who is making sure that you behave properly or do something right: *We went to dances, but only under the watchful eye of our father.*

12 run/cast your eye over sth to look at something quickly: *She cast her eye over the front page of the paper.*

13 set/lay/clap eyes on sb/sth *spoken* to see something or meet someone, especially for the first time: *I loved that house from the moment I clapped eyes on it.*

14 keep an eye open/out (for sb/sth) to watch carefully so that you will notice when someone or something appears: *Keep an eye out for rabbits in the field.*

15 with an eye to (doing) sth if you do something with an eye to doing something else, you do it in order to make the second thing more likely to happen: *Most novels are published with an eye to commercial success.*

16 close/shut your eyes to sth to ignore something or pretend that you do not know it is happening: *Most governments know that we're heading for an environmental catastrophe but they shut their eyes to it.*

17 have an eye/a good eye for sth to be good at noticing a particular type of thing, especially something attractive, valuable, of good quality etc: *Ernest has an eye for detail.* | *She's definitely got a good eye for a bargain.*

18 keep your eyes peeled/skinned *spoken* to watch carefully and continuously for something: **[+for]** *She stumbled along, keeping her eyes peeled for a phone box.*

19 with your eyes open knowing fully what the problems, difficulties, results etc of a situation might be: *I've no one to blame but myself – I went into this deal with my eyes open.*

20 can do sth with your eyes shut/closed to be able to do something very easily: *Believe me, you could run that place with your eyes closed.*

21 make eyes at sb/give sb the eye *informal* to look at someone in a way that shows you think they are sexually attractive: *Don't look now, but that guy over there is really giving you the eye.*

22 an eye for/on/to the main chance if you have an eye for

E

the main chance, you will take advantage of any possible opportunity to get what you want - used to show disapproval
23 one in the eye for sb *BrE spoken* something that will annoy someone or give them a disadvantage - used especially when you think this is a good thing: *This latest judgment will definitely be one in the eye for the fast food corporations.*
24 an eye for an eye the idea that if someone does something wrong, you should punish them by doing the same thing to them: *An eye for an eye is no way to run a civilised justice system.*
25 for sb's eyes only used to say that something is secret and must only be seen by one particular person or group: *The information is for police eyes only.*
26 have eyes in the back of your head to know what is happening all around you, even when this seems impossible: *We'll have to be really careful - old Jonesey has eyes in the back of his head.*
27 get/keep your eye in *BrE informal* to practise or to continue practising an activity so that you become good at it
28 have eyes like a hawk to notice every small detail or everything that is happening, and therefore be very difficult to deceive: *We never got away with anything in Mrs. Podell's class - she had eyes like a hawk.*
29 his/her etc eyes were popping (out of his/her etc head) *BrE especially spoken* to be very surprised, shocked, or excited by something you see
30 be up to your eyes in sth *BrE informal* to be very busy doing something: *He's up to his eyes in paperwork.*
31 have eyes bigger than your belly *spoken* used to say that you have taken more food than you are able to eat
32 only have eyes for sb if someone only has eyes for someone, they love and are interested in that person only
33 my eye! *old-fashioned spoken* used to say that you do not believe something
34 all eyes are on/watching/fixed on etc a) used to say that everyone is looking at someone or something: *All eyes were on the speaker, and nobody noticed me slip into the hall.* **b)** used to say that a lot of people are paying attention to a particular person or situation: *For the time being, all eyes are on the White House.*
35 in a pig's eye! *AmE spoken* used to show that you do not believe what someone is saying
36 CAMERA [singular] the eye of the camera is the way that you appear in photographs: *Fashion models are completely comfortable with the eye of the camera.*
37 NEEDLE [C] the hole in a needle that you put the thread through
38 FOR FASTENING CLOTHES [C] a small circle or U-shaped piece of metal used together with a hook for fastening clothes
39 STORM [singular] the calm centre of a storm such as a HURRICANE
40 POTATO [C] a dark spot on a potato that a new plant can grow from → BIRD'S-EYE VIEW, BLACK EYE, CATSEYE, PRIVATE EYE, RED EYE, → **the apple of sb's eye** at APPLE(2), → **not bat an eye** at BAT[2](2), → **turn a blind eye (to sth)** at BLIND[1](3), → **see sth out of the corner of your eye** at CORNER[1](8), → **the evil eye** at EVIL[1](5), → **give sb the glad eye** at GLAD(6), → **look sb in the eye/face** at LOOK[1](7), → **in your mind's eye** at MIND[1](40), → **here's mud in your eye** at MUD, → **open sb's eyes (to)** at OPEN[2](17), → **in the public eye** at PUBLIC[1](4), → **make sheep's eyes at** at SHEEP(3), → **a sight for sore eyes** at SIGHT[1](14), → **in the twinkling of an eye** at TWINKLING, → **keep a weather eye on** at WEATHER[1](5), → **pull the wool over sb's eyes** at WOOL(4)

COLLOCATIONS

COLOUR

brown/blue/grey/green *Both their children have blue eyes.*
dark brown/pale brown *His eyes are dark brown.*
deep blue/pale blue *She looked into his deep blue eyes.*
hazel (=pale brown and slightly green or golden)

SHAPE/POSITION

big *She looked at me with those big brown eyes.*
small *His small cold eyes seemed full of menace.*
round/wide *The children gazed at the screen, their eyes wide with excitement.*
narrow *He has a thin face and narrow eyes.*
bulging (=round and sticking far out) | **beady eyes** (=small round and bright, and noticing a lot of things) | **deep-set** (=far back in someone's face) | **close-set** (=close together) | **wide-set** (=wide apart) | **sunken** (=having fallen inwards, especially because of age or illness)

SHOWING YOUR FEELINGS/CHARACTER

sleepy/tired *His eyes looked sleepy.*
sad *Her beautiful eyes suddenly looked sad.*
tearful/moist/misty (=feeling that you want to cry) *As she left a village, people waved at her with tearful eyes.*
bright (=happy or excited) *the bright eyes of the children*
cold (=unfriendly and not showing any emotion) *Her eyes were cold and uncaring.*
red/bloodshot (=red because you are upset, tired, ill etc) *My mother's eyes were red from crying.*
puffy (=swollen because you are ill or upset) *The girl's eyes were puffy and full of tears.*
soulful eyes (=showing strong emotions, especially sadness) *The dog looked up at her with big soulful eyes.*
wild/mad eyes (=very angry, afraid etc) *He stared at them with wild eyes.*
hungry/greedy eyes (=showing that you want something very much) *The men looked around the room with their greedy eyes.*

VERBS

open your eyes *I slowly opened my eyes.*
sb's eyes open *Suddenly his eyes opened.*
close/shut your eyes *Joe closed his eyes and tried to get back to sleep.*
sb's eyes close *She let her eyes close for just a moment.*
rub your eyes *Anna rubbed her eyes wearily.*
shade/shield your eyes (=protect them from a bright light or the sun) | **narrow your eyes** (=partly close them, especially to show that you do not trust someone) | **sb's eyes narrow** (=become half closed, especially because someone does not trust another person) | **sb's eyes widen** (=become more open because they are surprised) | **sb's eyes sparkle/shine** (=show that they are very happy) | **sb's eyes light up** (=become excited) | **drop/lower your eyes** (=look down at the ground) | **avert your eyes** *literary* (=look away from something)

PHRASES

keep your eyes open (=prevent them from closing) *I was so tired I could hardly keep my eyes open.*
have/keep etc your eyes glued to sth (=be watching something with all your attention) *Ted sat with his eyes glued to the television.*
sb's eyes are full of tears | **sb's eyes are full of hatred/fear etc**

COMMON ERRORS

⚠ Don't say 'black eyes' when you mean **dark brown eyes**. You normally use 'black eye' when someone has a bruise around their eye, after being hit by someone.

eye² *v* (*present participle* **eyeing** *or* **eying**) [T] to look at someone or something carefully, especially because you do not trust them or because you want something: *The man behind the desk eyed us suspiciously.* | *A crowd of local children gathered around, eying us in silence.*
eye sb ↔ **up** *phr v informal* to look at someone in a way that shows you think they are sexually attractive: *There*

was a group of lads at the bar, eyeing up every girl who walked in.

eye·ball¹ /ˈaɪbɔːl $ -bɒːl/ *n* [C] **1** the round ball that forms the whole of your eye, including the part inside your head → see picture at EYE¹ **2 eyeball to eyeball** if two people are eyeball to eyeball, they are directly facing each other, especially in an angry or threatening way **3 up to the/your eyeballs in sth** *informal* if someone is up to their eyeballs in something, they have more than they can deal with: *She's up to her eyeballs in debt.* **4 drugged/doped up to the eyeballs** if someone is drugged up to the eyeballs, they have taken a lot of drugs so that their behaviour is severely affected

eyeball² *v* [T] *informal* to look directly and closely at something or someone: *They eyeballed each other suspiciously.*

eye·brow /ˈaɪbraʊ/ ●●○ *n* [C]
1 the line of hair above your eye: *thick bushy eyebrows* → see picture at EYE¹
2 raise your eyebrows to move your eyebrows upwards in order to show surprise or disapproval: *'Really?' she said, raising her eyebrows.* | *This decision caused a few raised eyebrows* (=surprised some people).
3 be up to your eyebrows in sth *spoken* to have more of something than you can deal with: *I'm absolutely up to my eyebrows in work.*

ˈeyebrow ˌpencil *n* [C,U] a special pencil you can use to make your eyebrows darker

ˈeye ˌcandy *n* [U] *informal* someone or something that is attractive to look at, but is not serious or important

ˈeye-ˌcatching *adj* something eye-catching is unusual or attractive in a way that makes you notice it: *an eye-catching design*

ˈeye drops *n* [plural] special liquid which you put into your eyes because they are sore or dry, or as a medical treatment

eye·ful /ˈaɪfʊl/ *n* [C] **1 an eyeful** *informal* **a)** if you get an eyeful of something interesting or shocking, you see it **b)** *old-fashioned* something or someone, especially a woman, who is very attractive to look at **2** an amount of liquid, dust, or sand that has got into someone's eye

eye·glass /ˈaɪglɑːs $ -glæs/ *n* **1** [C] a LENS for one eye, worn to help you see better with that eye SYN **monocle** **2 eyeglasses** [plural] *old-fashioned or AmE* a pair of GLASSES

eye·lash /ˈaɪlæʃ/ *n* [C] **1** one of the small hairs that grow along the edge of your EYELIDS → see picture at EYE¹ **2 flutter your eyelashes** if a woman flutters her eyelashes, she moves them up and down very quickly, in order to look sexually attractive

eye·less /ˈaɪləs/ *adj* having no eyes

eye·let /ˈaɪlɪt/ *n* [C] a hole surrounded by a metal ring that is put in leather or cloth so that a string can be passed through it

ˈeye ˌlevel *n* [U] a height equal to the level of your eyes: **at/above/below eye level** *Your screen should be at eye level.* | *an eye-level grill*

eye·lid /ˈaɪlɪd/ ●●○ *n* [C] a piece of skin that covers your eye when it is closed: *His* ***eyelids*** *began to* ***droop*** (=close, because he was sleepy). | *The room spun. Her* ***eyelids fluttered*** (=moved up and down quickly) *and she fainted.* → **not bat an eyelid** at BAT²(2) → see picture at EYE¹

eye·lin·er /ˈaɪˌlaɪnə $ -ər/ *n* [C,U] coloured MAKE-UP that you put along the edges of your eyelids to make your eyes look bigger or more noticeable: *She was wearing thick, black eyeliner.* | *an eyeliner pencil*

ˈeye-ˌopener *n* [C usually singular] an experience from which you learn something surprising or new: *The whole trip has been a real eye-opener.*

ˈeye patch *n* [C] a piece of material worn over one eye, usually because that eye has been damaged → see picture at PATCH¹

eye·piece /ˈaɪpiːs/ *n* [C] the glass piece that you look through in a MICROSCOPE or TELESCOPE → see picture at MICROSCOPE

eye·ro·bics /aɪˈrəʊbɪks $ -ˈroʊ-/ *n* [U] eye exercises that are meant to improve how well you see

ˈeye scan *n* [C] an examination of someone's eye using special computer equipment in order to IDENTIFY them. Eye scans are done by the police and IMMIGRATION officials at some airports to check the information on someone's PASSPORT or ID CARD SYN **iris scan**

ˈeye ˌshadow *n* [C,U] coloured MAKE-UP that you put on your EYELIDS to make your eyes look more attractive → see picture at MAKE-UP

eye·sight /ˈaɪsaɪt/ *n* [U] your ability to see SYN **vision**: **poor/good/failing etc eyesight** *Eagles have very keen eyesight.* | *He had a problem with his eyesight.*

eye·sore /ˈaɪsɔː $ -sɔːr/ *n* [C] something that is very ugly, especially a building surrounded by other things that are not ugly: *The factory is an eyesore.*

ˈeye strain *n* [U] a pain you feel in your eyes, for example because you are tired or have been reading a lot

ˈeye tooth *n* [C] **1 sb would give their eye teeth for sth** *spoken* used to say that someone wants something very much: *I'd give my eye teeth to be able to play the piano like that.* **2** one of the long pointed teeth at the corner of your mouth SYN **canine tooth**

eye·wash /ˈaɪwɒʃ $ -wɒːʃ, -wɑːʃ/ *n* [U] *BrE spoken old-fashioned* something that you do not believe is true

eye·wa·ter·ing /ˈaɪˌwɔːtərɪŋ $ -ˌwɒː-, -ˌwɑː-/ *adj* an eye-watering amount of money is an extremely large one: *He is on an eyewatering salary of £4 million a year.*

eye·wear /ˈaɪweə $ -wer/ *n* [U] glasses, SUNGLASSES etc – used especially by companies who make them

eye·wit·ness /ˈaɪˌwɪtnəs/ ●○○ *n* [C] someone who has seen something such as a crime happen, and is able to describe it afterwards: **eyewitness account/report/testimony** *According to eyewitness accounts, soldiers opened fire on the crowd.* | *One eyewitness said he saw her talking to a man in a blue car.*

ey·ing /ˈaɪ-ɪŋ/ a present participle of EYE²

eyot /eɪt, ˈeɪət/ *n* [C] *BrE* a small island in a river

ey·rie (*also* **eyry** *BrE*) /ˈɪəri, ˈeəri, ˈaɪəri $ ˈɪri, ˈeri, ˈaɪri/ *n* [C] **1** the NEST of a large bird, especially an EAGLE, that is usually built high up in rocks or trees **2** *literary* a room or building that is very high up

e-zine /ˈiː ziːn/ *n* [C] a website that is like a magazine SYN **webzine**

F¹, **f** /ef/ (*plural* **F's, f's**) *n* **1** [C,U] the sixth letter of the English alphabet **2** [C,U] the fourth note in the musical SCALE¹(8) of C MAJOR or the musical KEY based on this note **3** [C] a mark given to a student's work to show that it is not good enough: *I got an F in chemistry.* → F-WORD

F² **1** the written abbreviation of ***Fahrenheit***: *Water boils at 212° F.* **2** the written abbreviation of ***female*** **3** the written abbreviation of ***false***

f. (*also* **f** *BrE*) **1** the written abbreviation of ***forte***, used in music to show that a part should be played or sung loudly **2** the written abbreviation of ***female***

fa /fɑː/ *n* [U] the fourth note in a musical SCALE¹(8) according to the SOL-FA system

FA /ˌef ˈeɪ◂/ *n* **1 the FA** (***the Football Association***) the organization that is in charge of professional and amateur football in England and Wales: *the FA Cup* **2 sweet FA** *BrE not polite* nothing

FAA, the /ˌef eɪ ˈeɪ/ (***the Federal Aviation Administration***) a US government organization which is responsible for making sure that aircraft and airports are safe for people to use

fab /fæb/ *adj BrE informal* extremely good: *a fab new car*

fa·ble /ˈfeɪbəl/ *n* **1** [C] a traditional short story that teaches a moral lesson, especially a story about animals: *the fable of the fox and the crow* THESAURUS ▸ STORY **2** [U] fables or other traditional stories: *monsters of fable*

fa·bled /ˈfeɪbəld/ *adj literary* famous and often mentioned in traditional stories SYN **legendary**: *the fabled 'Fountain of Youth'*

fab·ric /ˈfæbrɪk/ ●●○ *n*
1 [C,U] cloth used for making clothes, curtains etc SYN **material**: *our new range of fabrics and wallpapers* | **cotton/silk/synthetic etc fabric** *printed cotton fabric*
2 [singular] the fabric of a society is its basic structure, way of life, relationships, and traditions: **[+of]** *Drug abuse poses a major threat to the* ***fabric of*** *our* ***society***. | *The country's* ***social fabric*** *is disintegrating.*
3 the fabric of sth the fabric of a building is its basic structure, including walls and the roof: *the need to preserve the fabric of the church*

fab·ri·cate /ˈfæbrɪkeɪt/ *v* [T] **1** to invent a story, piece of information etc in order to deceive someone: *The police were accused of* ***fabricating evidence***.

> **REGISTER**
> **Fabricate** is used mainly in writing, for example in journalism and legal contexts. In everyday English, people usually say **make** something **up**: *They accused him of* ***making*** *the whole thing* ***up***.

2 *technical* to make or produce goods or equipment SYN **manufacture**: *The discs are expensive to fabricate.*

fab·ri·ca·tion /ˌfæbrɪˈkeɪʃən/ *n* **1** [C,U] a piece of information or story that someone has invented in order to deceive people: **complete/total/pure fabrication** *Of course, it might all be complete fabrication.* **2** [U] *technical* the process of making or producing something SYN **manufacture**

ˈfabric ˌsoftener (*also* **ˈfabric conˌditioner** *BrE*) *n* [C,U] a liquid that you put in water when washing clothes in order to make them feel softer

fab·u·lous /ˈfæbjələs/ ●●○ *adj*
1 extremely good or impressive SYN **wonderful**: *You look fabulous!* | *a fabulous meal* | *The room has fabulous views across the lake.*
2 [only before noun] very large in amount or size SYN **huge**: *the Duke's* ***fabulous wealth***
3 [only before noun] fabulous creatures, places etc are mentioned in traditional stories, but do not really exist → **fable**

fab·u·lous·ly /ˈfæbjələsli/ *adv* **fabulously rich/expensive/successful etc** extremely rich, expensive etc

fa·cade, **façade** /fəˈsɑːd, fæ-/ *n* [C] **1** the front of a building, especially a large and important one: **[+of]** *the facade of the cathedral* | *an impressive building with a red brick facade* **2** [usually singular] a way of behaving that hides your real feelings: ***Behind*** *her cheerful* ***facade***, *she's a really lonely person.* | **[+of]** *She managed to* ***maintain*** *a* ***facade*** *of bravery.*

face¹ /feɪs/ ●●● S1 W1 *n* [C]
1 FRONT OF YOUR HEAD the front part of your head, where your eyes, nose, and mouth are: *She had a beautiful face.* | *Her face was white with fear.* | *A big smile spread across his face.* | *I felt like punching him in the face.* ⚠ You say that something is **on sb's face**, not 'in sb's face': *You've got a mark on your face.*
2 EXPRESSION an expression on someone's face: *I'll never forget my father's face – I'd never seen him so upset before.*
3 keep a straight face to not laugh or smile, even though something is funny
4 pale-faced/round-faced etc having a face that has a particular colour or shape: *a pale-faced youth* → RED-FACED
5 grim-faced/serious-faced etc showing a particular expression on your face: *Negotiators emerged grim-faced after the day's talks.* → BAREFACED, PO-FACED, POKER-FACED, STONY-FACED
6 PERSON a person: **new/different face** (=someone who you have not seen before) *There are a few new faces in class this year.* | *Gordon is a* ***familiar face*** (=someone who you know or have seen many times before) *at the Shrewsbury Flower Show.* | *It's* ***the same old faces*** (=people who you see often, especially too often) *at our meetings every week.* | **famous/well-known face** (=someone who is famous from television, magazines, films etc) | *She looked around at the* ***sea of faces*** (=lots of people seen together) *in the cafeteria.*
7 face to face a) if two people are standing face to face, they are very close and are looking at each other: **meet sb/talk to sb/explain sth etc face to face** (=to meet someone and talk to them, instead of just hearing about them, talking to them on the phone etc) *I've never met her face to face.* | *'You could have just phoned.' 'I wanted to explain things face to face.'* | **come face to face/find yourself face to face (with sb)** (=to meet someone, especially in a way that surprises or frightens you) *At that moment he came face to face with Sergeant Burke.* | *The two men stood face to face without a word.* **b)** if you come face to face with something difficult, you experience it and have to deal with it: *It was the first time he'd ever* ***come face to face with*** *death.* | **bring sb face to face with sth** *Sometimes one is brought face to face with facts which cannot be ignored.* → FACE-TO-FACE
8 say sth/tell sb sth to their face if you say something unpleasant to someone's face, you say it to them directly, rather than to other people: *I told him to his face just what I thought of him.*
9 face down/downwards with the face or front towards the ground: *Keith was* ***lying face down*** *on the bed.*
10 face up/upwards with the face or front towards the sky: *The body was* ***lying face up*** *in the rain.*
11 in the face of sth in a situation where there are many problems, difficulties, or dangers: *It is amazing how Daniels has survived in the face of such strong opposition from within the party.*
12 on the face of it used to say that something seems true but that you think there may be other facts about it which are not yet clear: *It looks, on the face of it, like a minor change in the regulations.* | *On the face of it, his suggestion makes sense.*
13 the face of sth a) the nature or character of an organization, industry, system etc, and the way it appears to people: *technology that has* ***changed the face of*** *society* | *Is this the new face of the Tory party?* | **the ugly/unacceptable/acceptable face of sth** (=the qualities of an organization,

F

industry etc which people find unacceptable or acceptable) *the unacceptable face of capitalism* **b)** the general appearance of a particular place: *the changing face of the landscape*
14 MOUNTAIN/CLIFF the face of a mountain, cliff etc is a steep vertical surface or side: **[+of]** *He fell and died while attempting to climb the* ***north face*** *of Mont Blanc.* | *The* ***cliff face*** *was starting to crumble into the sea.* | *a sheer* (=very steep) ***rock face***
15 CLOCK the front part of a clock or watch, where the numbers and hands are → see picture at CLOCK
16 lose face if you lose face, you do something which makes you seem weak, stupid etc, and which makes people respect you less: *He doesn't want to back down* (=accept defeat in an argument) *and risk losing face.*
17 save face if you do something to save face, you do it so that people will not lose their respect for you: *Both countries saved face with the compromise.*
18 disappear/vanish from/off the face of the earth used to say that you have no idea where someone is and have not seen them in a very long time: *I haven't seen Paul in ages; he seems to have vanished off the face of the earth.*
19 on the face of the earth used when you are emphasizing a statement to mean 'in the whole world': *If she were the last woman on the face of the earth, I still wouldn't be interested!*
20 sb's face doesn't fit used to say that someone will not get or keep a particular job because they are not the kind of person that the employer wants
21 set your face against sth *especially BrE* to be very determined that something should not happen: *The local Labour Party has set its face against the scheme.*
22 MINE the part of a mine from which coal, stone etc is cut → COALFACE
23 OUTSIDE SURFACE one of the outside surfaces of an object or building: *A cube has six faces.*
24 SPORT the part of a RACKET or BAT etc that you use to hit the ball
25 in your face *spoken informal* behaviour, criticisms, remarks etc that are in your face are very direct and often shocking or surprising: *Bingham has a very 'in your face' writing style.*
26 get in sb's face *spoken informal* if someone gets in your face, they really annoy you
27 get out of my face *spoken informal* used to tell someone in an impolite way to go away because they are annoying you
28 what's his face/what's her face *spoken informal* used as a way of talking about someone when you cannot remember their name: *I saw old what's his face in school yesterday.*
29 put your face on *informal* to put MAKE-UP on: *I just need to run upstairs and put my face on.* → **blow up in sb's face** at BLOW UP, → **put on a brave face** at BRAVE[1](3), → **do sth till you're blue in the face** at BLUE[1](4), → **have egg on your face** at EGG[1](5), → FACE-TO-FACE, → **fly in the face of** at FLY[1](18), → **laugh in sb's face** at LAUGH[1](11), → **long face** at LONG[1](12), → **not just a pretty face** at PRETTY[2](4), → **show your face** at SHOW[1](15), → **shut your face** at SHUT[1](2), → **a slap in the face** at SLAP[2](2), → **be staring sb in the face** at STARE[1](2), → **a straight face** at STRAIGHT[2](8), → **wipe sth off the face of the earth** at WIPE[1](8), → **wipe the smile/grin off sb's face** at WIPE[1](7), → **have sth written all over your face** at WRITE(10)

COLLOCATIONS – MEANINGS 1 & 2

ADJECTIVES

pretty/beautiful/handsome etc *Her face was beautiful in the morning light.*
round/oval/square *Her face was round and jolly.*
thin/narrow *Tears rolled down her thin face.*
pale/dark *His face suddenly became pale and I thought he was going to faint.*
sad/serious *Maggie looked at him with a sad face.*
happy/smiling *Shelley looked at the children's happy faces.*
angry | **worried/anxious** | **puzzled** | **blank/impassive** (=showing no emotion or thoughts) | **wrinkled/lined** (=with a lot of small lines, especially because of old age) | **scowling** (=showing that you are not pleased about something) | **a long face** (=an unhappy expression)

VERBS

sb's face goes/turns red (=becomes red) *His face went red with embarrassment.*
sb's face goes/turns pale (=becomes pale) *I saw her face go pale when he walked in.*
sb's face lights up/brightens (=they start to look happy) | **sb's face darkens** (=they start to look angry or threatening) | **sb's face falls** (=they look sad or disappointed) | **pull/make a face** (=to change your expression to make people laugh or to show you are angry, disappointed etc)

PHRASES

a look/expression on sb's face *She had a rather surprised look on her face.*
a smile/grin/frown on sb's face *There was a mischievous grin on her face.*
you can see sth in sb's face (=you know what someone is feeling from the expression on their face) *She could see the despair in his face.*
sth is written all over sb's face (=their feelings can be seen very clearly in their expression)

face² ●●● S1 W1 *v* [T]
1 DIFFICULT SITUATION if you face or are faced with a difficult situation, or if a difficult situation faces you, it is going to affect you and you must deal with it: *Emergency services are* ***facing*** *additional* ***problems*** *this winter.* | *The president* ***faces*** *the difficult* ***task*** *of putting the economy back on its feet.* | *McManus is* ***facing*** *the biggest* ***challenge*** *of his career.* | *As the project comes to an end, many workers now* ***face*** *an uncertain* ***future****.* | *He must* ***face*** *the* ***prospect*** *of financial ruin.* | **be faced with sth** *I was faced with the awful job of breaking the news to the girl's family.* | *the difficulties faced by the police* | *If he is found guilty, he faces up to 12 years in jail.* | **face charges/prosecution** (=have legal charges brought against you) *He was the first member of the former government to face criminal charges.*
2 ADMIT A PROBLEM EXISTS (*also* **face up to sth**) to accept that a difficult situation or problem exists, even though you would prefer to ignore it: *Many couples refuse to* ***face the fact that*** *there are problems in their marriage.* | *You've got to* ***face facts****, Rachel. You can't survive on a salary that low.* | *He had to* ***face the*** *awful* ***truth*** *that she no longer loved him.* | ***Face it,*** *kid. You're never going to be a rock star.*
3 can't face if you can't face something, you feel unable to do it because it seems too unpleasant or difficult: *I don't want to go back to college – I just* ***can't face it****.* | *I* ***can't face the thought of*** *going into town when it's this hot.* | *She* ***couldn't face the prospect of*** *another divorce.* | **can't face doing sth** *He couldn't face driving all the way to Los Angeles.*
4 TALK/DEAL WITH SB to talk or deal with someone, when this is unpleasant or difficult for you: *You're going to* ***have to face*** *him sooner or later.* | *I don't know how I'm going to face her after what happened.* | *The accident left her feeling depressed and unable to* ***face the world*** (=be with people and live a normal life).
5 BE OPPOSITE to be opposite someone or something, or to be looking or pointing in a particular direction: *The two men stood facing each other, smiling.* | *When he* ***turned to face*** *her, he seemed annoyed.* | *Lunch is served on the terrace facing the sea.* | **south-facing/west-facing etc** *a south-facing garden* | **face north/east etc** *The dining room faces east.*
6 OPPONENT/TEAM to play against an opponent or team in a game or competition: *Martinez will face Robertson in tomorrow's final.*
7 face the music *informal* to accept criticism or punishment for something you have done
8 BUILDING **be faced with stone/concrete etc** a building that is faced with stone, CONCRETE etc has a layer of that material on its outside surfaces
face sb ↔ **down** *phr v especially AmE* to deal in a strong and confident way with someone who opposes you: *Harrison successfully faced down the mob of angry workers.*

F

face off *phr v AmE* to fight, argue, or compete with someone, or to get into a position in which you are ready to do this: *The two candidates will face off in a televised debate on Friday.*

face up to sth *phr v* to accept and deal with a difficult fact or problem: *They'll never offer you another job; you might as well* ***face up to it***. | *She had to* ***face up to the fact that*** *he was guilty.*

Face·book[1] /ˈfeɪsbʊk/ *n trademark* a SOCIAL NETWORKING WEBSITE started in 2004

Face·book[2] *v* [T] *trademark* to use the SOCIAL NETWORKING website Facebook to find information about someone or communicate with someone —**Facebooking** *n* [U]

ˈface card *n* [C] *AmE* the king, queen, or JACK in a set of playing cards SYN **court card** *BrE*

face·cloth /ˈfeɪsklɒθ $ -klɒːθ/ *n* [C] *BrE* a small square cloth used to wash your face or hands SYN **washcloth** *AmE*

ˈface cream *n* [C,U] a thick cream used to keep the skin on your face soft and smooth

face·less /ˈfeɪsləs/ *adj* [usually before noun] **1** a faceless person, organization, or building has nothing that makes them special, interesting, or different – used to show disapproval: *He had become just another* ***faceless bureaucrat***. | *faceless modern office blocks* **2** faceless communication does not involve seeing the person you are communicating with: *Faceless communication, online or in text messages, can lead to misunderstandings.*

face·lift /ˈfeɪslɪft/ *n* [C] **1** if you have a facelift, you have an operation in which doctors remove loose skin from your face in order to make you look younger **2** work or repairs that make a building or place look newer or better: *The new owner had* ***given*** *the pub a* ***facelift***.

ˈface-off *n* [C] **1** *informal especially AmE* a fight or argument: *a face-off between police and rioters* **2** the start of a game of ICE HOCKEY

ˈface pack *n* [C] *BrE* a thick cream that you spread over your face and leave on for a short time, in order to clean and improve your skin

ˈface-palm *v* [I,T] *informal* to put the PALM of your hand on your face, or put your face down on your hand, when you are embarrassed, disappointed, shocked at someone's stupidity etc —**face-palm** *n* [C]

ˈface-plant *v* [I] *AmE informal* to accidentally fall, face first —**face-plant** *n* [C]

face·plate /ˈfeɪspleɪt/ *n* [C] a cover, usually made of metal or plastic, used on a piece of electronic equipment such as a MOBILE PHONE or an IPOD

ˈface ˌpowder *n* [U] powder that you put on your face in order to make it look less shiny

ˈface ˌsaver *n* [C] an action or arrangement that prevents you from losing other people's respect

ˈface-ˌsaving *adj* [only before noun] a face-saving action or arrangement prevents you from losing other people's respect: *a face-saving compromise*

fac·et /ˈfæsɪt/ ●○○ *n* [C]

1 one of several parts of someone's character, a situation etc SYN **aspect**: **[+of]** *He has travelled extensively in China, recording every facet of life.*

2 multi-faceted/many-faceted consisting of many different parts: *The issues are complex and multi-faceted.*

3 one of the flat sides of a cut jewel

ˈface time *n* [U] *AmE* **1** time that you spend at your job because you want other people, especially your manager, to see you there, whether or not you are actually doing good work: *Here we reward performance, not face time.* **2** time that you spend talking to someone when you are with them, rather than on the telephone: **[+with]** *In return for his donation, he wanted face time with the president.*

fa·ce·tious /fəˈsiːʃəs/ *adj* saying things that are intended to be clever and funny but are really silly and annoying: *Don't be so facetious!* | *facetious comments* —**facetiously** *adv* —**facetiousness** *n* [U]

ˌface-to-ˈface *adj* [only before noun] a face-to-face meeting, conversation etc is one where you are with another person and talking to them: *a face-to-face interview* → **face to face** at FACE[1](7)

ˌface ˈvalue *n* **1 take sth at face value** to accept a situation or accept what someone says, without thinking there may be a hidden meaning: *You shouldn't always take his remarks at face value.* **2** [singular, U] the value or cost shown on the front of something such as a stamp or coin

fa·cial[1] /ˈfeɪʃəl/ ●○○ *adj* on your face or relating to your face: *Victor's facial expression didn't change.* | *facial hair* → see picture at MASK —**facially** *adv*: *Facially the boys are similar.*

facial[2] *n* [C] if you have a facial, you have a beauty treatment in which your face is cleaned and creams are rubbed into it

ˌfacial ˈscrub *n* [C] a thick substance which you use to clean the skin on your face thoroughly

fa·cile /ˈfæsaɪl $ ˈfæsəl/ *adj* **1** a facile remark, argument etc is too simple and shows a lack of careful thought or understanding: *facile generalizations* **2** [only before noun] *formal* a facile achievement or success has been obtained too easily and has no value: *a facile victory* —**facilely** *adv* —**facileness** *n* [U]

fa·cil·i·tate /fəˈsɪlɪteɪt/ ●○○ AWL *v* [T] *formal* to make it easier for a process or activity to happen: *Computers can be used to facilitate language learning.* —**facilitation** /fəˌsɪlɪˈteɪʃən/ *n* [U]

fa·cil·i·tat·or /fəˈsɪləteɪtə $ -ər/ AWL *n* [C] **1** someone who helps a group of people discuss things with each other or do something effectively **2** *technical* something that helps a process to take place

fa·cil·i·ty /fəˈsɪləti/ ●●○ W3 AWL *n* (*plural* **facilities**)

1 facilities [plural] rooms, equipment, or services that are provided for a particular purpose: *All rooms have* ***private facilities*** (=private bathroom and toilet). | *The hotel has its own pool and* ***leisure facilities***. | ***toilet facilities*** | *childcare facilities*

2 [C usually singular] a special part of a piece of equipment or a system which makes it possible to do something: *Is there a call-back facility on this phone?* | *a bank account with an overdraft facility*

3 [C] a place or building used for a particular activity or industry, or for providing a particular type of service: *a top-secret research facility* | *the finest indoor sports facility in the US*

4 [singular] a natural ability to do something easily and well SYN **talent**: **[+for]** *She has an amazing facility for languages.*

5 the facilities *AmE spoken* the toilet, used to be polite: *Excuse me, I have to use the facilities.*

fac·ing /ˈfeɪsɪŋ/ *n* [C,U] **1** an outer surface of a wall or building made of a different material from the rest in order to make it look attractive **2** material fastened to the inside of a piece of clothing to strengthen it **3 facings** [plural] parts of a jacket, coat etc around the neck and wrists which have a different colour from the rest

fac·sim·i·le /fækˈsɪməli/ *n* [C] **1** an exact copy of a picture, piece of writing etc **2** *formal* a FAX

fact /fækt/ ●●● S1 W1 *n*

1 TRUE INFORMATION [C] a piece of information that is known to be true: **[+about]** *The book is full of facts about the World Cup.* | **[+of]** *First of all, we need to know the facts of the case.* | **it's a fact/that's a fact** (=used to emphasize that something is definitely true or that something definitely happened) *The divorce rate is twice as high as in the 1950s – that's a fact.* | **is that a fact?** (=used to reply to a statement that you find surprising, interesting, or difficult to believe) *'She used to be a professional singer.' 'Is that a fact?'*

2 the fact (that) used when talking about a situation and saying that it is true: *Our decision to build the museum in Hartlepool was influenced by the fact that there were no national museums in the North East.* | *He refused to help me,*

***despite the fact that** I asked him several times.* | **given the fact (that)/in view of the fact (that)** (=used when saying that a particular fact influences your judgment about something or someone) *Given the fact that this is their first game, I think they did pretty well.* | **due to the fact (that)/owing to the fact (that)** (=because) *The school's poor exam record is largely due to the fact that it is chronically underfunded.* | *The fact we didn't win when we were so close is very disappointing.*

3 in (actual) fact a) used when you are adding something, especially something surprising, to emphasize what you have just said: *I know the mayor really well. In fact, I had dinner with her last week.* **b)** used to emphasize that the truth about a situation is the opposite of what has been mentioned: *They told me it would be cheap but in fact it cost me nearly $500.* | *Her teachers said she was a slow learner, whereas in actual fact she was partially deaf.*

4 the fact (of the matter) is *spoken* used when you are telling someone what is actually true in a particular situation, especially when this may be difficult to accept, or different from what people believe: *The fact of the matter is that he's just not up to the job.*

5 the fact remains used to emphasize that what you are saying about a situation is true and people must realize this: *The fact remains that the number of homeless people is rising daily.*

6 REAL EVENTS/NOT A STORY [U] situations, events etc that really happened and have not been invented OPP **fiction**: *Much of the novel is based on fact.* | *It's a news reporter's job to separate **fact from fiction**.*

7 facts and figures [plural] the basic details, numbers etc concerning a particular situation or subject: *Here are a few facts and figures about the country.*

8 the facts speak for themselves used to say that the things that have happened or the things someone has done show clearly that something is true

9 after the fact after something has happened or been done, especially after a mistake has been made → **as a matter of fact** at MATTER[1](4), → **face facts** at FACE[2](2), → **in point of fact** at POINT[1](17)

COLLOCATIONS

ADJECTIVES

the basic/key facts *The report outlines the basic facts concerning the case.*
a well-known fact *It is a well-known fact that new cars lose a lot of their value in the first year.*
a little-known fact | **an interesting fact** | **a curious/remarkable fact** | **hard facts** (=information that is definitely true and can be proven) | **a historical/scientific fact** | **the bare facts** (=only the basic general facts of a situation)

VERBS

give sb/provide the facts *Newspapers have a duty to give their readers the facts.*
establish/piece together the facts (=find out what actually happened in a situation) *The police are still piecing together the facts.*
examine the facts | **state the facts** (=say what you know is true) | **stick to the facts** (=say only what you know is true)

PHRASES

know for a fact (=used to say that something is definitely true) *I know for a fact that she is older than me.*
get your facts right/straight (=make sure that what you say or believe is correct) *You should get your facts straight before making accusations.*
get your facts wrong

ˈfact-ˌfinding *adj* **fact-finding trip/visit/mission etc** an official trip, visit etc during which you try to find out facts and information about something for your organization, government etc

fac·tion /ˈfækʃən/ *n* **1** [C] a small group of people within a larger group, who have different ideas from the other members, and who try to get their own ideas accepted: *struggles between the different factions within the party* | *the leaders of the **warring factions*** **2** [U] *formal* disagreements and arguments between different groups within an organization: *jealousy and faction* —**factional** *adj*: *factional conflict*

fac·tion·al·is·m /ˈfækʃənəlɪzəm/ *n* [U] disagreements between different groups within an organization

fac·ti·tious /fækˈtɪʃəs/ *adj formal* made to happen artificially by people rather than happening naturally

ˌfact of ˈlife *n* (*plural* **facts of life**) [C] **1** an unpleasant situation that exists and that must be accepted: *Mass unemployment seems to be a fact of life nowadays.* | *Persuading others to accept the hard financial facts of life is not a very popular job.* **2 the facts of life** the details about sex and how babies are born: *Mum **told** me **the facts of life** when I was twelve.*

fact·oid /ˈfæktɔɪd/ *n* [C] *informal* a small and quite interesting piece of information that is not important: *The Web is a prime source of insignificant factoids.*

fac·tor[1] /ˈfæktə $ -ər/ ●●● S3 W1 AWL *n* [C]

1 CAUSE/INFLUENCE one of several things that influence or cause a situation: *The rise in crime is mainly due to social and economic factors.* | **[+in]** *The vaccination program has been a major factor in the improvement of health standards.* | **important/major/key/crucial factor** *The weather could be a crucial factor in tomorrow's game.* | **deciding/decisive/determining factor** (=the most important factor) *We liked both houses, but price was the deciding factor.*

2 LEVEL ON A SCALE a particular level on a scale that measures how strong or effective something is: *factor 15 suntan oil* | *Even in July the **wind chill factor** (=the degree to which the air feels colder because of the wind) can be intense.*

3 by a factor of five/ten etc if something increases or decreases by a factor of five, ten etc, it increases or decreases by five times, ten times etc

4 MATHEMATICS *technical* a number that divides into another number exactly: *3 is a factor of 15.*

factor[2] AWL *v* [T] *AmE technical* to divide a number into factors

factor sth ↔ **in** (*also* **factor sth into sth**) *phr v* to include a particular thing in your calculations about how long something will take, how much it will cost etc

factor sth ↔ **out** *phr v* to not include something in your calculations about how long something will take, how much it will cost etc

fac·to·ri·al /fækˈtɔːriəl/ *n* [C] *technical* the result when you multiply a whole number by all the numbers below it: *factorial 3 = 3 x 2 x 1*

fac·to·ry /ˈfæktəri/ ●●● S2 W2 *n* (*plural* **factories**) [C] a building or group of buildings in which goods are produced in large quantities, using machines: *a car factory* | *factory workers*

ˈfactory ˌfarming *n* [U] a type of farming in which animals are kept inside, in small spaces or small CAGES, and made to grow or produce eggs very quickly —**factory farm** *n* [C]

ˌfactory ˈfloor *n* **the factory floor a)** the area in a factory where goods are made **b)** the ordinary workers in a factory, rather than the managers: **on the factory floor** *There's been a lot of talk on the factory floor* (=among the ordinary workers) *about more layoffs.*

fac·to·tum /fækˈtəʊtəm $ -ˈtoʊ-/ *n* [C] *formal* a servant or worker who has to do many different kinds of jobs for someone

ˈfact sheet *n* [C] a piece of paper giving all the most important information about something

fac·tu·al /ˈfæktʃuəl/ ●○○ *adj* based on facts or relating to facts: *Try to keep your account of events as factual as possible.* | **factual information/knowledge/statements etc** *Libraries are stores of factual information.* | *The report contained a number of **factual** errors.* THESAURUS TRUE —**factually** *adv*: *The document is factually correct.*

F

fac·ul·ty /ˈfækəlti/ ●○○ *n* (*plural* **faculties**)
1 [C] a department or group of related departments within a university → **school**: **[+of]** *the Faculty of Law | the Engineering Faculty*
2 [C,U] *AmE* all the teachers in a university: *Both faculty and students oppose the measures.*
3 [C usually plural] a natural ability, such as the ability to see, hear, or think clearly: *the patient's mental faculties* | **in full possession of all your faculties** (=able to see, hear, think etc in the normal way) | **[+of]** *the faculty of sight*
4 [C] *formal* a particular skill that someone has SYN **talent**: **[+for]** *She had a great faculty for absorbing information.*

FA Cup, the /ˌef eɪ ˈkʌp/ a football competition open to all AMATEUR and professional football teams in the FA in England and Wales. It is the most important football competition in England: *Liverpool won the FA Cup.*

fad /fæd/ *n* [C] something that people like or do for a short time, or that is fashionable for a short time: *Interest in organic food is not a fad, it's here to stay.* —**faddish** *adj* —**faddishness** *n* [U]

fad·dy /ˈfædi/ *adj* someone who is faddy dislikes many kinds of food - used to show disapproval SYN **picky**: *Jackie's a terribly faddy eater.*

fade /feɪd/ ●●○ *v*
1 [I] (*also* **fade away**) to gradually disappear: *Hopes of a peace settlement are beginning to fade. | Over the years her beauty had faded a little.*
2 [I,T] to lose colour and brightness, or to make something do this: *the fading evening light | a pair of faded jeans | The sun had faded the curtains.*
3 [I] (*also* **fade away**) to become weaker physically, especially so that you become very ill or die
4 [I] if a team fades, it stops playing as well as it did before
5 fade into insignificance to seem unimportant: *Our problems fade into insignificance when compared with those of the people here.*

fade in *phr v* to appear slowly or become louder, or to make a picture or sound do this: **fade sth ↔ in** *Additional background sound is faded in at the beginning of the shot.* —ˈ**fade-in** *n* [C]

fade out *phr v* to disappear slowly or become quieter, or to make a picture or sound do this: **fade sth ↔ out** *He slid a control to fade out the music.* —ˈ**fade-out** *n* [C]

fae·ces (*also* **feces** *AmE*) /ˈfiːsiːz/ *n* [plural] *formal* solid waste material from the BOWELS —**faecal** /ˈfiːkəl/ *adj*

fae·ry, **faerie** /ˈfeəri $ ˈferi/ *n* (*plural* **faeries**) [C] *old use* a FAIRY

faff /fæf/ *v*

faff about/around *phr v BrE informal* to waste time doing unnecessary things: *Stop faffing around!*

fag /fæg/ *n* [C] **1** *BrE informal* a cigarette **2** *AmE taboo informal* a very offensive word for a HOMOSEXUAL man. Do not use this word. **3 be a fag** *BrE informal* to be a boring or difficult thing to do **4** a young student in some British PUBLIC SCHOOLS who has to do jobs for an older student

ˈ**fag end** *n* [C] *BrE informal* the end of a cigarette that someone has finished smoking

fagged /fægd/ *adj BrE informal* **1** (*also* **fagged out**) [not before noun] extremely tired **2 I can't be fagged** *spoken* used to say that you are too tired or bored to do something SYN **I can't be bothered**

fag·got /ˈfægət/ *n* [C] **1** *BrE* a ball made of meat mixed with bread, which is cooked **2** *AmE taboo informal* a very offensive word for a HOMOSEXUAL man. Do not use this word. **3** *old-fashioned* small sticks that are tied together, used for burning on a fire

ˈ**fag hag** *n* [C] *informal* a woman who likes to spend a lot of time with HOMOSEXUAL male friends - used to show disapproval

Fah·ren·heit /ˈfærənhaɪt/ *n* [U] (*written abbreviation* **F**) a scale of temperature in which water freezes at 32° and boils at 212°: *72° Fahrenheit* (=72 degrees on the Fahrenheit scale) —**Fahrenheit** *adj*

fail[1] /feɪl/ ●●● S2 W1 *v*
1 NOT SUCCEED [I] to not succeed in achieving something: *It looks likely that the peace talks will fail.* | **[+in]** *He* ***failed in*** *his* ***attempt*** *to regain the world title.* | **fail to do sth** *Doctors failed to save the girl's life. | Millions of people have tried to quit smoking and* ***failed miserably*** (=been completely unsuccessful). | *his efforts to save his* ***failing marriage*** | ***If all else fails****, you may be advised to have an operation.*
2 NOT DO STH [I] to not do what is expected, needed, or wanted: **fail to do sth** *The letter failed to arrive. | Firms that fail to take advantage of the new technology will go out of business. | The government are* ***failing*** *in their* ***duty*** *to protect people.*

> **REGISTER**
> **Fail to do** something is used mainly in writing and in formal contexts. In everyday English, people usually say **do not do** something instead: *The letter* ***failed*** *to arrive.* → *The letter* ***didn't*** *arrive.*

3 EXAM/TEST **a)** [I,T] to not pass a test or examination: *I failed my driving test the first time I took it. | He failed maths but passed all his other subjects.* **b)** [T] to decide that someone has not passed a test or examination: *Her work was so bad that I had no choice but to fail her.*
4 I fail to see/understand *formal* used to show that you are annoyed by something that you do not accept or understand: *I fail to see why you find it so amusing.*
5 COMPANY/BUSINESS [I] if a company or business fails, it is unable to continue because of a lack of money
6 MACHINE/BODY PART [I] if a part of a machine or an organ in your body fails, it stops working: *The engine failed on take-off. | The hospital said that his kidneys were failing.*
7 HEALTH [I] if your sight, memory, health etc is failing, it is gradually getting weaker or is not as good as it was: ***Failing eyesight*** *forced him to retire early.*
8 never fail to do sth to do something or happen so regularly that people expect it: *My grandson never fails to phone me on my birthday.*
9 your courage/will/nerve fails (you) if your courage etc fails, or if it fails you, you suddenly do not have it when you need it: *She had to leave immediately, before her courage failed her.*
10 fail sb to not do what someone has trusted you to do SYN **let sb down**: *I feel I've failed my children by not spending more time with them.*
11 CROPS [I] if crops fail, they do not grow or produce food, for example because of bad weather
12 RAINS [I] if the RAINS (=a lot of rain that falls at a particular time each year) fail, they do not come when expected or it does not rain enough → **words fail me** at WORD[1](29)

> **THESAURUS**
> **fail** to not succeed - used about people, plans, methods etc: *The plan failed. | They failed to persuade her to change her mind.*
> **go wrong** if something you do goes wrong, it fails after starting well: *The experiment went wrong when the chemicals combined to form a poisonous gas.*
> **not work** if something does not work, it does not do what you want it to do: *The drugs don't work. | I tried to fix it with glue, but that didn't work.*
> **be unsuccessful** /ˌʌnsəkˈsesfəl◂/ to not have the result you wanted: *His first attempt to get a teaching job was unsuccessful. | The search was unsuccessful.*
> **be a failure** to be unsuccessful, with the result that you have wasted your efforts: *The government's 5-year plan to modernize the economy was a* ***complete failure****.*
> **backfire** if a plan or action backfires, it does the opposite of what it was intended to do: *His plan to get attention backfired, and instead of being promoted he lost his job.*
> **in vain** if you try to do something in vain, you fail to do it: *They tried in vain to save him. | All her efforts had been in vain.*

F

fail² *n* **1 without fail a)** if you do something without fail, you always do it: *Tim visits his mother every day without fail.* **b)** used to tell someone very firmly that they must do something: *I want that work finished by tomorrow, without fail!* **2** [C] an unsuccessful result in a test or examination OPP **pass**: *I got a fail in history.* **3** [C] *informal* an occasion when someone is not successful or does something badly: *My parenting has included some spectacular fails.*

fail³ *interjection informal* used for saying that someone has failed or done something badly

failed /feɪld/ *adj* **a failed actor/writer etc** someone who wanted to be an actor etc but was unsuccessful

fail·ing¹ /ˈfeɪlɪŋ/ *n* [C] a fault or weakness: *I love him, despite his failings.*

failing² *prep* **failing that/this** used to say that if your first suggestion is not successful or possible, there is another possibility that you could try: *We will probably have the conference at the Hyatt Hotel or, failing that, at the Fairmont.*

ˈfail-safe *adj* **1** a fail-safe machine, piece of equipment etc contains a system that makes the machine stop working if one part of it fails **2** a fail-safe plan is certain to succeed

fail·ure /ˈfeɪljə $ -ər/ ●●● S3 W2 *n*
1 LACK OF SUCCESS [C,U] a lack of success in achieving or doing something OPP **success**: *Successful people often aren't very good at dealing with failure.* | **failure to do sth** *the conference's failure to reach an agreement*
2 UNSUCCESSFUL PERSON/THING [C] someone or something that is not successful OPP **success**: *I always felt a bit of a failure at school.*
3 failure to do sth an act of not doing something which should be done or which people expect you to do: *Failure to produce proof of identity could result in prosecution.*
4 BUSINESS [C,U] a situation in which a business has to close because of a lack of money: *Business failures in Scotland rose 10% last year.*
5 MACHINE/BODY PART [C,U] an occasion when a machine or part of your body stops working properly: *The cause of the crash was engine failure.* | **heart/kidney/liver etc failure** *He died from kidney failure.* | **[+in]** *a failure in the computer system*
6 CROPS [C,U] an occasion when crops do not grow or produce food, for example because of bad weather: *a series of* ***crop failures***

COLLOCATIONS – MEANINGS 1 & 2

VERBS

end in/result in failure *A series of rescue attempts ended in failure.*
be doomed to failure (=be certain to fail) *The rebellion was doomed to failure from the start.*
admit failure *He was too proud to admit failure.*
accept failure | **avoid failure**

ADJECTIVES

complete/total/utter failure *The project ended in total failure.*
abject/dismal failure (=used to emphasize how bad a failure is) *The experiment was considered a dismal failure.*
a personal failure (=a failure that is someone's personal fault) | **economic failure**

PHRASES

fear of failure *Fear of failure should not deter you from trying.*
the risk/possibility of failure *The risk of failure for a new product is very high.*
an admission of failure *Dropping out of college would be an admission of failure.*
a history of failure (=a situation in which someone has failed many times in the past) *Some children have a history of failure at school.*
a string of failures (=a series of failures) | **a sense of failure**

failure + NOUN

a failure rate *There is a high failure rate in the restaurant industry.*

faint¹ /feɪnt/ ●●○ *adj*
1 difficult to see, hear, smell etc: *She gave a faint smile.* | *a very faint noise* | *the* ***faint light*** *of dawn* THESAURUS▸ QUIET
2 a faint hope/possibility/chance etc a very small or slight hope etc: *a faint hope that they might be alive*
3 not have the faintest idea to not know anything at all about something: *I don't have the faintest idea what you're talking about.*
4 feeling weak and as if you are about to become unconscious because you are very ill, tired, or hungry: *The heat made him* ***feel*** *quite* ***faint***. | **[+with]** *I was faint with hunger.*
—**faintly** *adv*: *Everyone looked faintly surprised.* | *The sun shone faintly through the clouds.* —**faintness** *n* [U] → **damn sb/sth with faint praise** at DAMN⁴(6)

faint² ●●○ *v* [I]
1 to suddenly become unconscious for a short time SYN **pass out**: *Several fans fainted in the blazing heat.*
2 I nearly/almost fainted *spoken* used to say that you were very surprised by something: *I nearly fainted when they told me the price.*

faint³ *n* [singular] an act of becoming unconscious: **in a (dead) faint** *She fell down in a faint.*

faint-heart·ed /ˌfeɪnt ˈhɑːtɪd $ -ɑːr-/ *adj* **1** not trying very hard, because you do not want to do something, or you are not confident that you can succeed SYN **half-hearted**: *She made a rather faint-hearted attempt to stop him from leaving.* **2 sth is not for the faint-hearted** used humorously to say that something is difficult and needs a lot of effort

fair¹ /feə $ fer/ ●●● S1 W2 *adj*
1 REASONABLE AND ACCEPTABLE a fair situation, system, way of treating people, or judgment seems reasonable, acceptable, and right OPP **unfair**: *All we are asking for is a fair wage.* | *£150 is a fair price.* | **fair trial/hearing** *the right to a fair trial* | *What do you think is the fairest solution?* | *The report is a fair summary of the issues facing us.* | **it is fair to do sth** *It seems fair to give them a second chance.* | **it's only fair (that)** (=used to say that it is right to do something) *It's only fair that we tell him what's happening.* | **it's fair to say (that)** (=used when you think what you are saying is correct or reasonable) *It's fair to say that by then he had lost the support of his staff.* | **it's not fair on sb** *I can't carry on working such long hours. It's not fair on my family.*
2 TREATING EVERYONE EQUALLY treating everyone in a way that is right or equal OPP **unfair**: *Why does Eric get to go and I don't?* ***It's not fair!*** | *Life isn't always fair.* | **[+to]** *The old law wasn't fair to women.* | **it's only fair (that)** *You pay him $10 an hour - it's only fair that I should get the same.* | *My boss expects a lot - but he's very fair.*
3 QUITE LARGE **a fair size/amount/number/bit/distance etc** *especially BrE* quite a large size, number etc: *I've still got a fair amount of work left to do.* | *We had travelled a fair way* (=quite a long distance) *by lunch time.* | **there's a fair chance (that)/of sth** (=it is quite likely that something will happen) *There's a fair chance we'll be coming over to England this summer.*
4 HAIR/SKIN someone who is fair, or who has fair hair or skin, has hair or skin that is very light in colour OPP **dark**
5 ACCORDING TO THE RULES a fair fight, game, or election is one that is played or done according to the rules OPP **unfair**
6 LEVEL OF ABILITY neither particularly good nor particularly bad SYN **average**: *Her written work is excellent but her practical work is only fair.*
7 WEATHER weather that is fair is pleasant and not windy, rainy etc SYN **fine**: *It should be generally fair and warm for the next few days.*
8 have had more than your fair share of sth to have had more of something, especially something unpleasant, than seems reasonable: *Poor old Alan! He's had more than his fair share of bad luck recently.*

F

9 give sb a fair crack of the whip *BrE informal* to give someone the opportunity to do something, especially so that they can show that they are able to do it
10 give sb/get a fair shake *AmE informal* to treat someone, or to be treated, in a way that gives everyone the same chances as everyone else: *Women don't always get a fair shake in business.*
11 by fair means or foul using any method to get what you want, including dishonest or illegal methods
12 all's fair in love and war used to say that in some situations any method of getting what you want is acceptable
13 PLEASANT/ATTRACTIVE *old use or literary* pleasant and attractive: *a fair maiden*

SPOKEN PHRASES
14 fair enough *especially BrE* used to say that you agree with someone's suggestion or that something seems reasonable SYN **OK**: *'I think we should split the bill.' 'Fair enough.'*
15 to be fair used when adding something after someone has been criticized, which helps to explain or excuse what they did SYN **in fairness**: *She should have phoned to tell us what her plans were although, to be fair, she's been very busy.*
16 be fair! *especially BrE* used to tell someone not to be unreasonable or criticize someone too much: *Now Pat, be fair, the poor girl's trying her hardest!*
17 fair's fair used when you think it is fair that someone should do something, especially because of something that has happened earlier: *Come on, fair's fair – I paid last time so it's your turn.*
18 fair comment *BrE* used to say that a remark or criticism seems reasonable
19 you can't say fairer than that *BrE* used to say that an offer you are making to someone is the best and fairest offer they can possibly get: *I'll give you £25 for it – you can't say fairer than that, can you?*
20 it's a fair cop *BrE* used humorously to admit that you should not be doing something that someone has caught you doing
21 with your own fair hands *BrE* if you do something with your own fair hands, you do it yourself without any help – used humorously → **have a fair idea of sth** at IDEA

THESAURUS

fair treating people equally or in the way that is right: *It's not fair that she gets paid more than me.* | *Everyone has the right to a fair trial.*
just *formal* morally right and fair: *a just punishment* | *a just cause* | *a just society* | *Do you think it was a just war?*
reasonable fair and sensible according to most people's standards: *a reasonable request* | *Lateness, without a reasonable excuse, will not be tolerated.*
balanced giving fair and equal treatment to all sides of an argument or subject: *Balanced reporting of the news is essential.*
even-handed giving fair and equal treatment to everyone, especially when it would be easy to favour one particular group: *The drama takes an even-handed look at the consequences of violent crime, both on attackers and their victims.*
equitable /ˈekwətəbəl/ *formal* giving equal treatment to everyone involved: *We need an equitable solution to this problem.* | *a more equitable distribution of wealth*

fair² ●●○ *n* [C]
1 (*also* **funfair** *BrE*) a form of outdoor entertainment, at which there are large machines to ride on and games in which you can win prizes SYN **carnival** *AmE*
2 *AmE* an outdoor event, at which there are large machines to ride on, games to play, and sometimes farm animals being judged and sold: **state/county fair**
3 book/antiques/craft/trade etc fair an event at which people or businesses show and sell their products: *the Frankfurt Book Fair* | *an antiques fair* | *a trade fair* (=where companies show their newest products) | *a craft fair* (=where people sell handmade products such as jewellery, paintings etc)
4 job/careers fair an event where people go to get information about different kinds of jobs
5 *BrE* an outdoor event with games and things to eat and drink, usually organized to get money for a school, club etc SYN **fête**
6 *BrE old-fashioned* a market where animals and farm products are sold: *a horse fair*

fair³ *adv* **1 win (sth)/beat sb fair and square** to win a competition, sports match etc honestly and without cheating **2 play fair** to do something in a fair and honest way: *In international trade, very few countries play fair.*

ˌfair ˈcopy *n* [C] *BrE* a neat copy of a piece of writing

fair din·kum /ˌfeə ˈdɪŋkəm $ ˌfer-/ *adj AusE spoken* real or true

ˌfair ˈgame *n* [U] if someone or something is fair game, it is acceptable, reasonable, or right to criticize them: *The young star's behavior made her fair game for the tabloid press.*

fair·ground /ˈfeəgraʊnd $ ˈfer-/ *n* [C] an open space on which a FAIR²(1) takes place

ˌfair-haired ˈboy *n* [C] *AmE old-fashioned informal* someone who is likely to succeed because someone in authority likes them SYN **blue-eyed boy** *BrE*: *the boss's fair-haired boy*

fair·ly /ˈfeəli $ ˈferli/ ●●● S1 W2 *adv*
1 [+adj/adv] more than a little, but much less than very → **quite**: *The house had a fairly large garden.* | *She speaks English fairly well.* | *The instructions seem fairly straightforward.*
2 in a way that is fair, honest, and reasonable: *I felt I hadn't been treated fairly.*
3 *BrE old-fashioned* used to emphasize the degree, force etc of an action: *He fairly raced past us on his bike.*

ˌfair-ˈminded / $ ˈ. ˌ../ *adj* able to understand and judge situations fairly and always considering other people's opinions: *He's a fair-minded man – I'm sure he'll listen to what you have to say.*

fair·ness /ˈfeənəs $ ˈfer-/ ●●○ *n* [U]
1 the quality of being fair: *the basic fairness of the judicial system*
2 in fairness (to sb) used after you have just criticized someone, in order to add something that explains their behaviour or performance SYN **to be fair**: *Tardelli had a poor match, although in fairness he was playing with a knee injury.*

ˌfair ˈplay *n* [U] **1** playing according to the rules of a game without cheating: *rules designed to* ***ensure fair play*** **2** fair treatment of people without cheating or being dishonest: *the British tradition of fair play* | *This kind of behavior violates many people's* ***sense of fair play***. **3 fair play to sb** *BrE spoken* used to say that you think what someone did was right: *He has to earn money somehow, so fair play to him.* → **turnabout is fair play** at TURNABOUT

ˌfair ˈsex *n* **the fair sex** (*also* **the fairer sex**) *old-fashioned* women

fair ˈtrade *n* [U] the activity of making, buying, and selling goods in a way that is morally right, for example by making sure that international LABOUR laws are obeyed, that the environment has not been damaged by making the goods, and that the people who grow or make a product have been paid a fair price for it: *fair trade bananas*

fair·way /ˈfeəweɪ $ ˈfer-/ *n* [C] the part of a GOLF COURSE that you hit the ball along towards the hole → see picture at **GOLF**

ˌfair-weather ˈfriend *n* [C] someone who only wants to be your friend when you are successful

fai·ry /ˈfeəri $ ˈferi/ ●●○ *n* (*plural* **fairies**) [C]
1 a small imaginary creature with magic powers, which looks like a very small person
2 *old-fashioned not polite* an offensive word for a HOMOSEXUAL man

ˈfairy ˌcake *n* [C] *BrE* a very small cake

ˌfairy ˈgodmother *n* [C] **1** a woman with magic powers who saves someone from trouble, in a story **2** someone who helps people when they are in trouble

fai·ry·land /ˈferilænd $ ˈferi-/ *n* **1** [U] an imaginary place where fairies live **2** [singular] a place that looks very beautiful and special: *At night, the harbor is a fairyland.*

ˈfairy lights *n* [plural] *BrE* small coloured lights used especially to decorate a Christmas tree

ˈfairy tale (*also* **ˈfairy ˌstory**) *n* [C] **1** a children's story in which magical things happen **2** a story that someone has invented and is difficult to believe

fai·ry·tale /ˈfeəriteɪl $ ˈferi-/ *adj* [only before noun] extremely happy, lucky etc in a way that usually only happens in children's stories: *a fairytale romance* | *The kiss was a* ***fairytale ending*** *to the evening.*

fait ac·com·pli /ˌfeɪt əˈkɒmpli $ -ˌækɑːmˈpliː/ *n* [singular] something that has already happened or been done and cannot be changed

faith /feɪθ/ ●●● S3 W2 *n*

1 TRUST/CONFIDENCE IN SB/STH [U] a strong feeling of trust or confidence in someone or something: **have faith (in sb/sth)** *I still have faith in him.* | *'Have faith, Alexandra,' he said.* | **lose faith (in sb/sth)** *The public has lost faith in the government.* | **destroy/restore sb's faith (in sb/sth)** *It's really helped restore my faith in human nature.*

2 RELIGION **a)** [U] belief and trust in God: *deep religious faith* | **[+in]** *my faith in God* **b)** [C] one of the main religions in the world: *People from all faiths are welcome.* | **the Jewish/Muslim/Hindu etc faith** *members of the Jewish faith*

3 break faith with sb/sth to stop supporting or believing in a person, organization, or idea: *How could he tell them the truth without breaking faith with the Party?*

4 keep faith with sb/sth to continue to support or believe in a person, organization, or idea

5 good faith honest and sincere intentions: *He proposed a second meeting as a sign of his good faith.* | *The woman who sold me the car claimed she had* ***acted in good faith*** (=had not meant to deceive me).

6 bad faith intentions that are not honest or sincere

7 an act of faith something you do that shows you trust someone completely: *Allowing Ken to be in charge of the project was a total act of faith.*

ˈfaith-based *adj* involving ideas that are based on religious beliefs: *faith-based schools* | *faith-based government initiatives*

ˈfaith comˌmunity *n* [C] a group of people who share a particular set of religious beliefs: *In any faith community there are varying levels of commitment.*

faith·ful¹ /ˈfeɪθfəl/ ●●○ *adj*

1 [usually before noun] remaining loyal to a particular person, belief, political party etc and continuing to support them: *a* ***faithful friend*** | *years of* ***faithful service*** *to the company* | *our faithful family dog, Bogey* | *a faithful member of the church* | **[+to]** *He* ***remained faithful*** *to his principles to the last.*

2 [usually before noun] representing an event or an image in a way that is exactly true or that looks exactly the same SYN **exact**: *a faithful account of what had happened* | *a* ***faithful reproduction*** *of the original picture*

3 if you are faithful to your wife, boyfriend etc, you do not have a sexual relationship with anyone else: **[+to]** *Do you think Bob's always been faithful to you?*

4 [only before noun] able to be trusted or depended on SYN **reliable**: *my faithful old Toyota* —**faithfulness** *n* [U]

faithful² *n* **1 the faithful** [plural] **a)** the people who are very loyal to a leader, political party etc and continue to support them: *Hess still has the support of* ***the party faithful.*** **b)** the people who believe in a religion: *church bells calling the faithful to evening prayer* **2** [C] a loyal follower, supporter, or member: *A handful of* ***old faithfuls*** *came to the meeting.*

faith·ful·ly /ˈfeɪθfəl-i/ *adv* **1** in a loyal way: *He had served the family faithfully for 40 years.* | *Ann faithfully promised never to tell my secret.* **2** in a regular way: *She wrote faithfully in her journal every day.* | *Every year, we faithfully make a trip up there to see him.* **3 Yours faithfully** *BrE* the usual polite way of ending a formal letter, which you have begun with Dear Sir or Dear Madam → **Yours sincerely** at SINCERELY

ˈfaith ˌhealing *n* [U] a method of treating illnesses by praying —**faith healer** *n* [C]

faith·less /ˈfeɪθləs/ *adj formal* someone who is faithless cannot be trusted SYN **untrustworthy**: *a faithless friend* —**faithlessness** *n* [U]

ˈfaith school *n* [C] *BrE* a school run by, and usually for, members of a particular religion

fa·ji·ta /fæˈhiːtə, fə-/ *n* [C] a type of Mexican food consisting of pieces of cooked meat or vegetables, wrapped in a TORTILLA

fake¹ /feɪk/ ●●○ *n* [C]

1 a copy of a valuable object, painting etc that is intended to deceive people OPP **original**: *The painting was judged a fake.* | *Jones can spot a fake from 20 feet away.*

2 someone who is not what they claim to be or does not have the skills they say they have: *Her psychologist turned out to be a fake.*

fake² ●●○ *adj* [usually before noun]

1 made to look like a real material or object in order to deceive people OPP **genuine**: *fake fur* | *a fake ID card* | *a fake 20 dollar bill* THESAURUS ARTIFICIAL, FALSE

2 not real and seeming to be something it is not, in order to deceive people SYN **false**: *I gave a fake name.* | *She was speaking with a fake German accent.* | *a fake smile of friendliness*

fake³ *v* **1** [T] to make something seem real in order to deceive people: *She faked her father's signature on the cheque.* | *The insurance company suspected that he had faked his own death.* | *The results of the experiments were faked.* **2** [I,T] to pretend to be ill, interested etc when you are not: *I thought he was really hurt but he was* ***faking it.*** **3** [I,T] to pretend to move in one direction, but then move in another, especially when playing sport: *He faked a pass.*

fake sb ↔ **out** *phr v AmE* to deceive someone by making them think you are planning to do something when you are really planning to do something else

fa·kie /ˈfeɪki/ *n* [U] the practice of riding a SKATEBOARD backwards

fa·kir /ˈfeɪkɪə, ˈfæ-, fæˈkɪə $ fəˈkɪr, fæ-/ *n* [C] a travelling Hindu or Muslim holy man

fa·laf·el /fəˈlæfəl, ˈlɑː- $ -ˈlɑː-/ *n* [C,U] fried balls of an Arabic food made with CHICKPEAS

fal·con /ˈfɔːlkən $ ˈfæl-/ *n* [C] a bird that kills and eats other animals and can be trained to hunt → see picture at BIRD OF PREY

fal·con·er /ˈfɔːlkənə $ ˈfælkənər/ *n* [C] someone who trains falcons to hunt

fal·con·ry /ˈfɔːlkənri $ ˈfæl-/ *n* [U] the skill or sport of using falcons to hunt

ˌFalklands ˈWar, the a war in the Falkland Islands between the UK and Argentina in 1982. The war started when Argentina sent soldiers to take control of the Falklands from the UK. The British prime minister, Margaret Thatcher, sent a TASK FORCE of ships and aircraft to the islands, which took control of them again.

fall¹ /fɔːl $ fɒːl/ ●●● S1 W1 *v* (*past tense* **fell** /fel/, *past participle* **fallen** /ˈfɔːlən $ ˈfɒːl-/)

1 MOVE DOWNWARDS [I] to move or drop down from a higher position to a lower position: *The tree was about to fall.* | *The book fell from his hands.* | *Enough rain had fallen to flood the grounds.* | **[+down]** *Rob fell down the stairs.* | *She flushed and her* ***eyes fell*** (=she looked down).

2 STOP STANDING/WALKING ETC [I] to suddenly go down onto the ground after you have been standing, walking, or running, especially without intending to: *I fell and hit my head.* | **slip/stumble/trip etc and fall** *He slipped and fell on the ice.* | **[+down]** *Lizzie fell down and hurt her knee.* | *Peter was playing by the river when he* ***fell in*** (=fell into the water). | **fall to/on your knees** (=move down to the ground

F

so that your body is resting on your knees) *She fell to her knees beside his body.* → **fall flat on your face** at FLAT³(5)

3 DECREASE [I] to go down to a lower level, amount, price etc, especially a much lower one OPP **rise**: *The rate of inflation was falling.* | *The island is warm all year round and winter temperatures never fall below 10 degrees.* | *He believes that educational standards are falling.* | **[+from]** *Advertising revenue fell from $98.5 million to $93.3 million.* | **[+to]** *The number of subscribers had fallen to 1,000.* | **fall sharply/steeply** (=by a large amount) *London share prices fell sharply yesterday.* THESAURUS DECREASE

> **REGISTER**
> In everyday English, people often say an amount or level **goes down** rather than **falls**: *House prices have **gone down** again.*

4 BECOME [I, linking verb] to start to be in a new or different state: **[+adj]** *I'll stay with her until she **falls asleep**.* | *I think that I've **fallen in love** with Angela.* | *She fell ill with flu.* | *Albert fell silent and turned his attention to his food.* | **[+into]** *The house was empty for many years and fell into disrepair.* | *One false step can mean falling into debt.* | *He fell into despair.*

5 BELONG TO A GROUP [I always + prep] to belong to or be part of a particular group, area of responsibility, range of things, or type of things: **[+into]** *Many illnesses fall into the category of stress-related illnesses.* | *Leaders fall into two categories.* | **[+within]** *The judge said that this matter did not fall within the scope of the auditor's duties.* | **[+under]** *The job falls under the heading of 'sales and marketing'.* | *Meat production **falls under the control** of the Agriculture Department.*

6 fall short of sth to be less than the amount or standard that is needed or that you want: *This year's profit will fall short of 13%.* | *He would sack any of his staff who fell short of his high standards.*

7 fall victim/prey to sth/sb to get a very serious illness or be attacked or deceived by someone: *Breastfed babies are less likely to fall victim to stomach disorders.* | *people who fall victim to violence*

8 night/darkness/dusk falls if night etc falls, it starts to become dark at the beginning of the night: *It grew colder as night fell.* | *Darkness had fallen by the time we reached home.*

9 silence/a hush/sadness etc falls *literary* used to say that a person, group, or place becomes quiet, sad etc: *A long silence fell between us.*

10 START DOING STH [I] to start doing something or being involved with something, often without intending to: *I **fell into conversation** with some guys from New York.* | *He had **fallen into the habit of** having a coffee every time he passed the coffee machine.*

11 fall into place a) if parts of a situation that you have been trying to understand fall into place, you start to understand how they are connected with each other: *Suddenly, all the details started falling into place.* **b)** if the parts of something that you want to happen fall into place, they start to happen in the way that you want: *I was lucky because everything fell into place at exactly the right time.*

12 fall to pieces/bits a) to break into many pieces SYN **fall apart**: *The book had been well used and finally fell to pieces.* **b)** if something such as a plan or a relationship falls to pieces, it stops working properly SYN **fall apart**: *The family is falling to pieces.*

13 be falling to pieces/bits if something is falling to pieces, it is in very bad condition, especially because it is very old SYN **be falling apart**: *The house is falling to pieces.*

14 fall flat if a joke, remark, or performance falls flat, it fails to interest or amuse people: *Marlow's attempts at jokes fell flat.*

15 fall foul of sb/sth to do something which makes someone angry or which breaks a rule, with the result that you are punished: *He is worried that his teenage kids will **fall foul of the law**.*

16 fall by the wayside to fail, or to stop being done, used, or made: *Health reform was one of his goals that fell by the wayside.* | *Luxury items fall by the wayside during a recession.*

17 fall from grace/favour to stop being liked by people in authority: *He fell from grace for the first time when he was convicted of drink-driving.*

18 fall from a great height to be forced to leave an important job or position, or lose the respect that people had for you

19 fall into the hands/clutches of sb if something or someone falls into the hands of an enemy or dangerous person, the enemy etc gets control or possession of them: *He wants to prevent the business falling into the hands of a competitor.* | *We must not let these documents **fall into the wrong hands**.*

20 fall into a trap/pitfall to make a mistake that many people make: *Don't fall into the trap of feeling guilty.*

21 fall into step a) to start to walk next to someone else, at the same speed as them: **[+beside/with]** *Holly slowed her pace and fell into step with the old man.* **b)** to start doing something in the same way as the other members of a group: **[+with]** *The other countries on the Council are expected to fall into step with the US.*

22 fall into line to obey someone or do what other people want you to do, especially when you do not want to do it at first: *Most countries have signed the treaty but some are reluctant to fall into line.*

23 HANG DOWN [I always + adv/prep] to hang down loosely: **[+over]** *His dark hair fell over his face.*

24 LIGHT/SHADOW [I always + adv/prep] to shine on a surface or go onto a surface: *The last rays of sunlight were falling on the fields.* | *Arthur's shadow fell across the doorway.*

25 SPECIAL EVENT/CELEBRATION [I always + adv/prep] to happen on a particular day or at a particular time: *I'd like to dedicate this record to all whose anniversaries fall at this time of year.* | **[+on]** *Her birthday will fall on a Friday this year.*

26 LOSE POWER [I] if a leader or a government falls, they lose their position of power: *The previous government fell after only 6 months in office.*

27 BE TAKEN BY AN ENEMY [I] if a place falls in a war or an election, a group of soldiers or a political party takes control of it: **[+to]** *The city fell to the advancing Russian armies.*

28 BE KILLED [I] to be killed in a war SYN **die**

29 HIT [I always + adv/prep] to hit a particular place or a particular part of someone's body: **[+on]** *The first punch fell on his nose.*

30 VOICE/SOUND [I] if someone's voice or a sound falls, it becomes quieter or lower OPP **rise**

31 it's as easy as falling off a log *spoken* used to say that something is very easy to do

32 fall between two stools *BrE* to be neither one type of thing nor another, or be unable to choose between two ways of doing something

33 fall on stony ground *BrE* if a request, suggestion, joke etc falls on stony ground, it is ignored or people do not like it

34 fall from sb's lips *literary* if words fall from someone's lips, they say them

35 fall into sb's lap if an opportunity falls into someone's lap, they get it without having made any effort to get it

36 the stress/accent/beat falls on sth used to say that a particular part of a word, phrase, or piece of music is emphasized or is played more loudly than the rest: *In the word 'report', the stress falls on the second syllable.* → **be/fall under a spell** at SPELL²(3), → **fall on your feet** at FOOT¹(19), → **sb's face fell** at FACE¹(2), → **stand or fall by/on** at STAND¹(33)

> **THESAURUS**
> **fall** (*also* **fall over, fall down**) to suddenly go down onto the floor when standing, walking, or running: *She fell on the stairs and broke her ankle.* | *Children are always falling over.*
> **trip on/over sth** to fall or almost fall when you hit your foot against something: *Someone might trip over those toys.* | *I tripped on a piece of wood.*

F

slip to fall or almost fall when you are walking on a wet or very smooth surface: *She slipped and hurt her ankle.* | *I was scared I would slip on the highly polished floor.*
stumble to almost fall when you put your foot down in an awkward way: *He stumbled and almost fell.* | *One of our porters stumbled on the rough ground.*
collapse to fall suddenly and heavily to the ground, especially when you become unconscious: *One of the runners collapsed halfway through the race.*
lose your balance to become unsteady so that you start to fall over: *She lost her balance on the first step and fell down the stairs.*
fall flat on your face to fall forwards so you are lying on your front on the ground: *She fell flat on her face getting out of the car.*

fall about *phr v BrE* to laugh a lot about something: *It was so funny everyone just **fell about laughing**.*
fall apart *phr v*
1 if an organization, system, relationship etc falls apart, it stops being effective or successful: *Don't be reckless or your plans may fall apart.* | *The health service is **falling apart at the seams**.*
2 be falling apart to be in very bad condition: *Tommy's old bicycle was rusty and falling apart.*
3 to break into pieces: *The book fell apart in my hands.*
4 to be unable to deal with your personal or emotional problems: *She had to get some rest or she was going to fall apart.*
5 sb's world/life falls apart if someone's world or life falls apart, something very bad and serious happens which changes their life: *When his wife left him, his world fell apart.*
fall away *phr v*
1 to slope down: *From where we stood, the ground fell away sharply to the valley floor.*
2 to become separated from something after being fixed to it: *The paint was falling away in patches.*
3 if a feeling falls away, you stop having it, usually suddenly: *The view from the top was wonderful and our tiredness fell away.*
4 *BrE* to decrease SYN **fall** OPP **rise**: *Demand for our more theoretical courses has fallen away.*
fall back *phr v*
1 if soldiers fall back, they move back because they are being attacked SYN **retreat**: *He yelled for his men to fall back.*
2 to move backwards because you are very surprised, frightened etc: *Scott fell back a pace in astonishment.*
3 *BrE* to decrease SYN **fall** OPP **rise**: *When inflation started to rise, house prices fell back.*
fall back into sth *phr v* to go back to doing something or behaving in a way which you did before: *I was amazed at how easily I fell back into the old routine.*
fall back on sb/sth *phr v* to use something or depend on someone's help when dealing with a difficult situation, especially after other methods have failed: **have sb/sth to fall back on** *She has no relatives to fall back on.* | *Where negotiation fails, they must fall back on the law.* → FALLBACK
fall behind (sb/sth) *phr v*
1 to go more slowly than other people so that they gradually move further ahead of you: *His mother was chatting and didn't notice that he had fallen behind.* | *She hurt her ankle and had fallen behind the others.*
2 to become less successful than other people, companies, countries etc: *After her time in hospital, Jenny's parents are afraid she has fallen behind educationally.* | *Companies that are not market-driven risk falling behind the competition.*
3 to fail to finish a piece of work or pay someone money that you owe them at the right time: **[+with/on]** *After losing his job, he fell behind with his mortgage payments.* | *The project has **fallen behind schedule**.*
fall down *phr v*
1 be falling down if a building is falling down, it is in very bad condition: *The bridge is falling down and will need a million dollars to repair it.*
2 to fail because of a particular reason or in a particular way: *That's where the whole argument falls down.* | **[+on]** *He is falling down on the supervisory aspects of his job.* | *The local authority is **falling down on the job** of keeping the streets clean.*
fall for sb/sth *phr v informal*
1 to be tricked into believing something that is not true: *He is too smart to fall for that trick.*
2 to start to love someone: *That was the summer I worked at the fairground, and met and fell for Lucy.*
3 to like a place as soon as you see it
fall in *phr v*
1 if the roof, ceiling etc falls in, it falls onto the ground SYN **collapse**
2 to start walking or forming a line of people behind someone else: **[+behind]** *His men fell in behind him.*
fall into sth *phr v*
1 to move somewhere quickly by relaxing your body and letting it fall on something: *She turned and fell into his arms.* | *We fell into bed, exhausted.*
2 to start doing something by chance: *I fell into the job really.*
fall in with sb/sth *phr v*
1 to accept someone's ideas, decisions etc and not disagree with them: *Once she explained her problem, he was happy to fall in with her plans.*
2 to become friendly with a person or group of people after meeting them by chance SYN **get in with**: *She fell in with the wrong crowd in her teens.*
fall off *phr v*
1 fall off (sth) if part of something falls off, it becomes separated from the main part: *The door handle keeps falling off.* | *A button had fallen off her jacket.*
2 if the amount, rate, or quality of something falls off, it decreases SYN **fall** OPP **rise**: *Audience figures fell off during the second series of the programme.*
3 sb nearly/almost fell off their chair *spoken* used to say that someone was very surprised when something happened: *When I saw my brother on the stage I nearly fell off my chair.*
→ **fall off the back of a lorry** at LORRY
fall on/upon sb/sth *phr v*
1 if a duty or job falls on someone, they are responsible for doing it: *The responsibility usually falls on the mother.*
2 *literary* to eagerly start eating or using something: *She fell on the food as if she hadn't eaten for days.*
3 *literary* to suddenly attack or get hold of someone: *Some of the older boys fell on him and broke his glasses.*
4 sb's eyes/gaze/glance fall(s) on sth if your eyes etc fall on something, you notice it: *His eyes fell on her bag. 'Are you going somewhere?'*
5 fall on hard/bad times to experience difficulties and problems in your life such as not having enough money: *The aim is to raise money for workers who have fallen on hard times.*
6 fall on your sword to leave your job because your organization has done something wrong, and you are taking responsibility for it: *It was clear that the prime minister wanted her to fall on her sword.* → **fall on deaf ears** at DEAF(5)
fall out *phr v*
1 to have a quarrel: **[+with]** *Carrie's always falling out with people.*
2 if a tooth or your hair falls out, it is then no longer attached to your body: *The drugs made her hair fall out.*
3 if soldiers fall out, they stop standing in a line and move away to different places
fall over *phr v*
1 to fall onto the ground or to fall from an upright position: *Tommy fell over and cut his knee badly.* | *Her bike fell over.*
2 fall over sth to hit your foot against something by mistake and fall to the ground SYN **trip over**: *She fell over the dog and broke her front teeth.*
3 fall over yourself to do sth to be very eager to do something, especially something you do not usually do: *People were falling over themselves to help her.*
fall through *phr v* if an agreement, plan, sale etc falls through, it is not completed successfully: *The studio*

planned to make a movie of the book but the deal fell through.

fall to sb/sth *phr v*

1 if a duty or job falls to someone, they are responsible for doing it, especially when this is difficult or unpleasant: ***It fell to** me **to** give her the bad news.*

2 *written* to start doing something: *They fell to work with a will.* | **fall to doing sth** *He fell to thinking about how nice a warm bath would be.*

fall² ●●● S2 W2 *n*

1 MOVEMENT DOWN [C] movement down towards the ground or towards a lower position: *the first fall of autumn leaves* | *The **rise and fall** of the dancers' bodies creates a pattern.* | *Mrs Evans **had** a **fall*** (=fell to the ground) *and broke her leg.* | *He stretched out his hands to **break** his **fall*** (=prevent himself from falling too quickly and hurting himself).

2 REDUCTION [C] a reduction in the amount, level, price etc of something OPP **rise**: **[+in]** *There has been a fall in oil prices.* | **sharp/steep fall** *the sharp fall in the birth rate in European countries* | **[+of]** *Their industrial output went down again in December, which meant a fall of 2.2% over the year.*

3 SEASON [singular] *AmE* the season between summer and winter, when leaves change colour and the weather becomes slightly colder SYN **autumn**: *Eleanor plans to go to Southwestern Community College this fall.* | *The area is beautiful in the fall.*

4 LOSS OF POWER/SUCCESS [singular] a situation in which someone or something loses their position of power or becomes unsuccessful: **[+from]** *The president lived on for twenty years after his fall from power.* | *the story of Napoleon's **rise and fall*** (=period of success followed by failure) | *Rumours are that the company is **heading for a fall*** (=is likely to fail soon).

5 fall from grace a situation in which someone stops being respected by other people or loses their position of authority, especially because they have done something wrong: *He was the head of the intelligence service until his fall from grace.*

6 DEFEAT [singular] a situation in which a country, city etc is defeated by an enemy: **[+of]** *the fall of Jerusalem in AD70*

7 falls (*also* **Falls**) [plural] a place where a river suddenly goes straight down over a cliff: *The spray from the falls is so dense that you can hardly see.* | *Niagara Falls*

8 SPORT [C] an act of forcing your opponent onto the ground in WRESTLING or JUDO

9 SNOW/ROCKS [C] an amount of snow, rocks etc that falls onto the ground: **[+of]** *Fresh falls of snow were forecast.* | *The road is blocked by a rock fall.*

10 the Fall (*also* **the fall**) the occasion in the Bible when God punished Adam and Eve by making them leave the Garden of Eden

GRAMMAR: Patterns with fall (meaning 3)

in the fall/in fall

• You use **in the fall** or **in fall** when talking about something that happens during the fall season: *He visited them in the fall.*

in the fall of

• You use **in the fall of** with a year when saying when something happens: *The project will be completed in the fall of 2018.*

last fall/this fall etc

Don't use **in** with these words:

• You say **last fall**: *She started college last fall.* ✗ Don't say: *She started college in last fall.*

• You say **this fall**: *This fall the leaves are really beautiful.* ✗ Don't say: *In this fall the leaves are really beautiful.*

• You say **next fall**: *The book will come out next fall.* ✗ Don't say: *The book will come out in next fall.*

• You say **that fall**: *That fall I went to Kyoto.* ✗ Don't say: *In that fall I went to Kyoto.*

fal·la·cious /fəˈleɪʃəs/ *adj formal* containing or based on false ideas: *Such an argument is misleading, if not wholly fallacious.* —**fallaciously** *adv*

fal·la·cy /ˈfæləsi/ *n* (*plural* **fallacies**) **1** [C] a false idea or belief, especially one that a lot of people believe is true SYN **misconception**: *It's a common fallacy that a neutered dog will become fat and lazy.* **2** [C,U] *formal* a weakness in someone's argument or ideas which is caused by a mistake in their thinking SYN **flaw** → PATHETIC FALLACY

fall·back /ˈfɔːlbæk $ ˈfɒːl-/ *n* [C] something that can be used or done if a supply, method etc fails SYN **backup**: *It's wise to have an extra video player as a fallback.* | *Do you have a fallback option?* → **fall back on sb/sth** at FALL¹

fall·en¹ /ˈfɔːlən $ ˈfɒːl-/ *v* the past participle of FALL¹

fallen² *adj* **1** [only before noun] on the ground after falling down: *The road was blocked by a fallen tree.* | *fallen leaves* **2 a fallen woman** *old-fashioned* a woman who has had a sexual relationship with someone she is not married to **3 the fallen** [plural] *formal* soldiers who have been killed in a war

ˈfall guy *n* [C] *especially AmE informal* **1** someone who is punished for someone else's crime or mistake SYN **scapegoat**: *Browne claims that the company was simply looking for a fall guy.* **2** someone who is easily tricked or made to seem stupid

fal·li·ble /ˈfæləbəl/ *adj formal* able to make mistakes or be wrong OPP **infallible**: *Humans are fallible.* | *These surveys are often a rather fallible guide to public opinion.* —**fallibility** /ˌfæləˈbɪləti/ *n* [U]

ˌfalling-ˈout *n* **have a falling-out (with sb)** *informal* to have a bad quarrel with someone

ˌfalling ˈstar *n* [C] a SHOOTING STAR

ˈfall-off (*also* **ˌfalling-ˈoff** *BrE*) *n* [singular] a decrease in the level, amount, or number of something SYN **fall** OPP **rise**: **[+in]** *a fall-off in profits*

fal·lo·pi·an tube /fəˌləʊpiən ˈtjuːb $ fəˈloʊpiən tuːb/ *n* [C] *medical* one of the two tubes in a female through which eggs move to the UTERUS

fall·out /ˈfɔːlaʊt $ ˈfɒːl-/ *n* [U] **1** the dangerous RADIOACTIVE dust which is left in the air after a NUCLEAR explosion and which slowly falls to earth: *protection against **radioactive fallout*** **2** the results of a particular event, especially when they are unexpected: *The **political fallout** of the affair cost him his job.*

ˈfallout ˌshelter *n* [C] a building under the ground in which people can shelter from a NUCLEAR attack

fal·low /ˈfæləʊ $ -loʊ/ *adj* **1** fallow land is dug or PLOUGHed but is not used for growing crops: *They let the land **lie fallow** for a year.* **2 fallow period** a time when nothing is done or achieved: *The band went through a fallow period in the late 90s.*

ˈfallow deer *n* [C] a small European DEER which is yellowish brown with white spots

false /fɔːls $ fɒːls/ ●●● W3 *adj*

1 UNTRUE a statement, story etc that is false is completely untrue: *Please decide whether the following statements are **true or false**.* | *false accusations*

REGISTER

In everyday English, people usually say **not true** rather than **false**, apart from in the fixed expression **true or false**: *What he said was **false**.* → *What he said was **not true**.*

2 WRONG based on incorrect information or ideas: *I don't want to give you any **false hopes**.* | *The statement gives us a **false impression** that we understand something when we do not.* | ***false assumptions** about people of other cultures* | ***a false sense of security*** (=a feeling of being safe when you are not really safe) THESAURUS WRONG

3 NOT REAL **a)** not real, but intended to seem real and deceive people: *The drugs were hidden in a suitcase with a false bottom.* | *The man had given a false name and address.* **b)** artificial: **false teeth/hair/eyelashes etc** THESAURUS ARTIFICIAL

4 NOT SINCERE not sincere or honest, and pretending to

have feelings that you do not really have: *She's so false.* | *a false laugh* | *'You played brilliantly.' 'Not really,' Ian replied with **false modesty**.*
5 false economy something that you think will save you money but which will really cost you more: *It's a false economy not to have travel insurance.*
6 under false pretences if you get something under false pretences, you get it by deceiving people: *He was accused of obtaining money under false pretences.*
7 false move/step a small movement or action that will result in harm: ***One false move** and you're dead.*
8 false imprisonment/arrest the illegal act of putting someone in prison or ARRESTing them for a crime they have not committed

THESAURUS

false not real, but intended to seem real and deceive people: *He uses a false name.*
fake made to look or seem like something else, especially something worth a lot more money: *fake fur* | *a fake Rolex watch* | *fake designer goods*
forged a forged official document or bank note has been illegally made to look like a real one: *a forged passport* | *a forged £50 note*
counterfeit /ˈkaʊntəfɪt $ -tər-/ counterfeit money or goods have been illegally made to look exactly like something else: *How do you detect counterfeit currency?* | *counterfeit drugs*
imitation made to look real – used especially about guns, bombs etc or about materials: *The two men used an imitation firearm to carry out the robbery.* | *imitation leather/silk/silver*
phoney/phony / ˈfəʊni $ ˈfoʊ-/ *disapproving informal* false – used when you think someone is deliberately trying to deceive people: *She put on a phoney New York accent.* | *The doctors were accused of supplying phoney medical certificates.*
spurious /ˈspjʊəriəs $ ˈspjʊr-/ false and giving a wrong impression about someone or something: *spurious claims* | *That's a spurious argument.* | *The company was trying to get some spurious respectability by using our name.*

ˌfalse aˈlarm *n* [C] a situation in which people wrongly think that something bad is going to happen: *Fire fighters responded to a false alarm at one of the college dormitories.* | *The patient was okay – it was a false alarm.*
ˌfalse ˈdawn *n* [C] *formal* a situation in which something good seems likely to happen, but it does not: *The ceasefire turned out to be another false dawn.*
ˌfalse ˈfriend *n* [C] **1** a word in a foreign language that is similar to one in your own, so that you wrongly think they both mean the same thing **2** someone who seems to be your friend but is not
false·hood /ˈfɔːlshʊd $ ˈfɒːls-/ *n formal* **1** [C] a statement that is untrue SYN **lie**: *Saunders is deliberately telling a falsehood.* **2** [U] the practice of telling lies SYN **lying**: *No one had accused me of falsehood before.* **3** [U] the state of not being true OPP **truth**: *Most people believe in right and wrong, truth and falsehood.*
ˌfalse ˈmemory *n* [C] a memory which you seem to have of something that in fact did not happen
ˌfalse ˈpositive *n* [C] something that is wrongly thought or shown to be a particular thing, especially after a scientific test or RESEARCH: *50% of the 170 compounds were judged to be carcinogenic, but some of these might be false positives.* | *Many substances give false positive reactions in allergy skin testing.*
ˌfalse ˈstart *n* [C] **1** an unsuccessful attempt to begin a process or event: *After several false starts, the concert finally began.* **2** a situation at the beginning of a race when one competitor starts too soon and the race has to start again
ˌfalse ˈteeth *n* [plural] a set of artificial teeth worn by someone who has lost their natural teeth SYN **dentures**
fal·set·to /fɔːlˈsetəʊ $ fɒːlˈsetoʊ/ *n* (*plural* **falsettos**) [C] a very high male voice —**falsetto** *adv*

fals·ies /ˈfɔːlsiz $ ˈfɒːl-/ *n* [plural] *informal* pieces of material inside a BRA used to make a woman's breasts look larger
fal·si·fy /ˈfɔːlsɪfaɪ $ ˈfɒːl-/ *v* (**falsified, falsifying, falsifies**) [T] to change figures, records etc so that they contain false information: *The file was altered to falsify the evidence.* —**falsification** /ˌfɔːlsɪfɪˈkeɪʃən $ ˌfɒːl-/ *n* [C,U]: *the falsification of records*
fal·si·ty /ˈfɔːlsəti $ ˈfɒːl-/ *n* [U] *formal* the quality of being false or not true OPP **truth**
Fal·staff·i·an /fɔːlˈstɑːfiən $ fɒːlˈstæf-/ *adj* a Falstaffian person is fat, friendly, enjoys having fun, and drinks too much. This word comes from Falstaff, a character in some of Shakespeare's plays.
fal·ter /ˈfɔːltə $ ˈfɒːltər/ *v* **1** [I] to become weaker and unable to continue in an effective way: *The economy is showing signs of faltering.* | *My mother's grip upon the household never faltered.* **2** [I,T] to speak in a voice that sounds weak and uncertain, and keeps stopping: *Laurie's **voice faltered** as she tried to thank him.* | *'I can't,' she faltered.* **3** [I] to become less certain and determined that you want to do something: *We must not falter in our resolve.* **4** [I] to stop walking or to walk in an unsteady way because you suddenly feel weak or afraid: *She faltered for a moment.*
fal·ter·ing /ˈfɔːltərɪŋ $ ˈfɒːl-/ *adj* **1** nervous and uncertain or unsteady: *a baby's first faltering steps* **2** becoming less effective or successful: *the faltering Mideast peace talks* —**falteringly** *adv*
fame /feɪm/ ●●○ *n* [U] the state of being known about by a lot of people because of your achievements: *He claims he is not really interested in fame.* | **of ... fame** (=used to show what someone is famous for) *Muhammad Ali, of boxing fame*

COLLOCATIONS

VERBS

win/gain fame *He won fame when he appeared in the film 'The Graduate'.*
achieve/find fame *Amy Johnson found fame as a pilot.*
bring/win sb/sth fame *Chomsky's theories about language brought him fame.*
rise to fame (=become famous) *She rose to fame during the early Sixties.*
shoot to fame (=become famous very suddenly) | **seek fame** (=try to become famous)

ADJECTIVES

international/worldwide fame *Edinburgh achieved international fame as a centre of medical education.*
lasting fame (=being famous for a long time) | **brief fame** (=being famous for a short time) | **instant fame** | **great fame**

PHRASES

sb's/sth's rise to fame *Her rise to fame has been astonishingly rapid.*
at the height of sb's/sth's fame (=when someone was most famous) *At the height of his fame, he could earn $5,000 a day.*
sb's/sth's claim to fame (=reason for being famous) *One of his main claims to fame is having invented the electric light bulb.*
fame and fortune (=being rich and famous)

famed /feɪmd/ *adj written* well-known SYN **famous**: *the famed literary critic Nathan Hall* | **[+for]** *the island of Lontar, famed for its nutmeg and cloves*
fa·mil·i·al /fəˈmɪliəl/ *adj* [only before noun] *formal* connected with a family or typical of a family → **family**: *familial obligations* | *familial relationships*
fa·mil·i·ar¹ /fəˈmɪliə $ -ər/ ●●○ S3 W2 *adj*
1 someone or something that is familiar is well-known to you and easy to recognize: *a familiar tune* | **look/sound familiar** *The voice on the phone sounded familiar.* | **be familiar to sb** *The signs of drug addiction are familiar to most*

F

doctors. | *It was a relief to be back in* ***familiar surroundings***. | *Beggars on the street are becoming a* ***familiar sight***. | *This kind of situation was* ***all too familiar*** (=very familiar) *to John.* | *Her face seems* ***vaguely familiar****, but I can't quite place her.*

> **REGISTER**
> In everyday English, people often say that they **know** something rather than saying it **is familiar**: *The name of the restaurant* ***was not familiar*** *to me.* → *I* ***didn't know*** *the name of the restaurant.*

2 be familiar with sth to have a good knowledge or understanding of something: *Are you familiar with this type of machine?* | *I'm not familiar with her poetry.*
3 be on familiar terms with sb to know someone well and be able to talk to them in an informal way: *He's on familiar terms with all the teachers.*
4 talking to someone as if you know them well although you do not: **[+with]** *I thought he was being a bit familiar with my wife.*
5 informal and friendly in speech, writing etc: *The novel is written in an easy familiar style.* → FAMILIARLY

familiar² *n* [C] a cat or other animal that lives with a WITCH and has magical powers

fa·mil·iar·ise /fəˈmɪliəraɪz/ *v* a British spelling of FAMILIARIZE

fa·mil·i·ar·i·ty /fəˌmɪliˈærəti/ ●○○ *n* [U]
1 a good knowledge of a particular subject or place: **[+with]** *In fact his familiarity with the Bronx was pretty limited.*
2 the quality of being well-known to you: *I miss the familiarity of home.*
3 a relaxed way of speaking to someone or behaving with someone: *He treated her with the easy familiarity of an equal.*
4 familiarity breeds contempt an expression meaning that if you know someone too well, you find out their faults and respect them less

fa·mil·i·ar·ize (*also* **-ise** *BrE*) /fəˈmɪliəraɪz/ *v* **familiarize yourself/sb with sth** to learn about something so that you understand it, or to teach someone else about something so that they understand it: *Employees must familiarize themselves with the health and safety manual.* —**familiarization** /fəˌmɪliəraɪˈzeɪʃən $ -rə-/ *n* [U]: *a one-day familiarization course*

fa·mil·i·ar·ly /fəˈmɪliəli $ -liərli/ *adv* in an informal or friendly way: *Charles, familiarly known as Charlie*

fam·i·ly /ˈfæməli/ ●●● S1 W1 *n* (*plural* **families**)
1 CLOSELY RELATED GROUP [C] a group of people who are related to each other, especially a mother, a father, and their children: *Do you know the family next door?* | *The Webb family still has its farm over there.* | *This house isn't big enough for a family of seven.*
2 ALL YOUR RELATIONS [C,U] all the people you are related to, including those who are now dead: *I'm moving to Detroit because I have some family there.* | **in sb's family** *That painting has been in our family* (=been owned by our family) *for 200 years.* | *Asthma* ***runs*** *in the* ***family*** (=is common in the family).

> **GRAMMAR: Singular or plural verb?**
> • In senses 1 and 2, **family** is usually followed by a singular verb: *The family now* ***lives*** *in London.* | *My family* ***comes*** *from Scotland originally.*
> • In British English, you can also use a plural verb: *The family now* ***live*** *in London.* | *My family* ***come*** *from Scotland originally.*
> GRAMMAR GUIDE ▸ NOUNS

3 CHILDREN [C] children: *Couples with* ***young families*** *wouldn't want to live here.* | *They're getting married next year, and hope to* ***start a family*** (=have children) *straight away.* | **bring up/raise a family** *the problems of bringing up a family on a very low income*
4 family size/pack etc a container or package containing a large amount of a product
5 GROUP OF ANIMALS/THINGS [C] *technical* a group of related animals, plants, languages etc: **the cat/parrot/squirrel etc family** *The cat family includes lions and tigers.* | *Spanish and Italian are part of the Romance language family.*
6 she's/he's family *informal* used to emphasize your connection with someone who is related to you
7 in the family way *old-fashioned* PREGNANT

> **COLLOCATIONS – MEANINGS 1 & 2**
>
> **ADJECTIVES**
> **the whole family** *We invited the whole family round.*
> **all the family** *This is a game which all the family can enjoy.*
> **sb's immediate family** (=closest relations) *What if one of your immediate family were disabled?*
> **sb's extended family** (=including not only parents and children, but also grandparents, aunts etc) *She gets a lot of help from her extended family.*
> **a large/small family** *She came from a large family of seven children.*
> **a one-parent/single-parent family** | **the nuclear family** (=a family consisting of a mother, a father, and their children) | **close/close-knit family** (=a family that spends a lot of time together and gives each other support)
>
> **family + NOUN**
> **a family member/a member of the family** *The event was attended by many of his family members, including his children and grandchildren.*
> **sb's family background** *He comes from a stable family background.*
> **a family history** *Is there a family history of heart disease?*
> **family life** *Some people believe that television is destroying family life.*
> **a family unit** | **sb's family home** (=where someone's family live and where they lived as a child) | **a family business** (=one run by members of a family) | **a family car** (=one designed for families with children) | **a family holiday** *BrE*, **a family vacation** *AmE*: | **a family resemblance** (=when members of the same family look like each other)
>
> **COMMON ERRORS**
> ⚠ Don't say 'my family is five', 'my family is five members/people', or 'my family is of five members/people'. Say **there are five people in my family**.

ˌfamily ˈcircle *n* [C usually singular] a group of people who are closely related to each other – used especially when emphasizing that someone does or does not belong to this group

ˌfamily ˈdoctor *n* [C] a doctor trained to treat the general health problems of people of all ages SYN **GP**

ˌfamily-ˈfriendly *adj* suitable and enjoyable for families with young children: *family-friendly museums*

ˈfamily ˌman *n* [C] **1** a man who enjoys being at home with his wife or partner and children **2** a man with a wife or partner and children

ˈfamily ˌname *n* [C] the name someone shares with all the members of their family SYN **surname**, **last name**

ˌfamily ˈplanning *n* [U] the practice of controlling the number of children that are born by using CONTRACEPTION: *a family planning clinic*

ˌfamily ˈpractice *n* [U] a part of medical practice in the US in which doctors learn to treat general health problems of people of all ages

ˌfamily pracˈtitioner *n* [C] *especially BrE* a GP

ˈfamily ˌroom *n* [C] **1** a room in a house where the family can play games, watch television etc **2** a hotel room which has enough space for several people, especially parents and children, to sleep **3** a room in a PUB in Britain where children are allowed to sit

ˌfamily ˈtree *n* [C] a drawing that gives the names of all the members of a family over a long period of time, and shows how they are related to each other → **genealogy**

F

ˌfamily ˈvalues *n* [plural] traditional ideas about what a family should be like, which emphasize the importance of marriage - used especially when talking about politics: *The party places great emphasis on family values.*

fam·ine /ˈfæmɪn/ ●○○ *n* [C,U] a situation in which a large number of people have little or no food for a long time and many people die: *the great potato famine in Ireland* | **severe/widespread famine** *Widespread famine had triggered a number of violent protests.* | *A million people are* ***facing famine****.*

fam·ished /ˈfæmɪʃt/ *adj* [not before noun] *informal* extremely hungry SYN **starving**: *What's for supper? I'm famished.*

fa·mous /ˈfeɪməs/ ●●● S2 W2 *adj*
1 a) known about by many people in many places: *a famous actor* | *Many famous people have stayed in the hotel.* | *The Eiffel Tower is a* ***famous landmark*** (=a famous place or building that is easy to recognize). | **[+for]** *France is famous for its wine.* | **[+as]** *Virginia is famous as the birthplace of several US presidents.* | *Da Vinci's* ***world-famous*** *portrait of the Mona Lisa* **b) the famous** [plural] people who are famous: *a nightclub used by* ***the rich and famous***
2 famous last words *spoken* used when someone has said too confidently that they can do something or that something will happen

THESAURUS

famous known about by a lot of people in many places, often all over the world: *She always wanted to be famous.* | *The Mona Lisa is Da Vinci's most famous painting.*
well-known known about by a lot of people, especially in a particular place: *Shilpa Shetty was well-known in India, but few people in the UK had heard of her.* | *a well-known brand of cat food*
celebrated *written* very well-known and admired: *Dalí is one of Spain's most celebrated artists.* | *Martin Luther King's celebrated speech*
renowned/noted famous, especially for a particular thing or activity. **Noted** is more formal than **renowned**: *The British are renowned for their love of animals.* | *The area is noted for its wines.*
legendary very famous and greatly admired - used especially about people who have been doing something for a long time or who have died: *the legendary blues guitarist, BB King* | *Her stage performances were legendary.*

FAMOUS BECAUSE OF SOMETHING BAD

notorious /nəʊˈtɔːriəs, nə- $ noʊ-, nə-/ famous because of doing something bad: *a notorious criminal* | *a notorious legal case*
infamous famous because of doing something very bad, which seems immoral or evil: *the infamous attack on the World Trade Center* | *the infamous Jack the Ripper*

fa·mous·ly /ˈfeɪməsli/ *adv* **1 get on/along famously** *old-fashioned* to have a friendly relationship with someone **2** in a way that is famous: *The trouble with common sense, as Voltaire famously observed, is that it is not very common.*

FANS

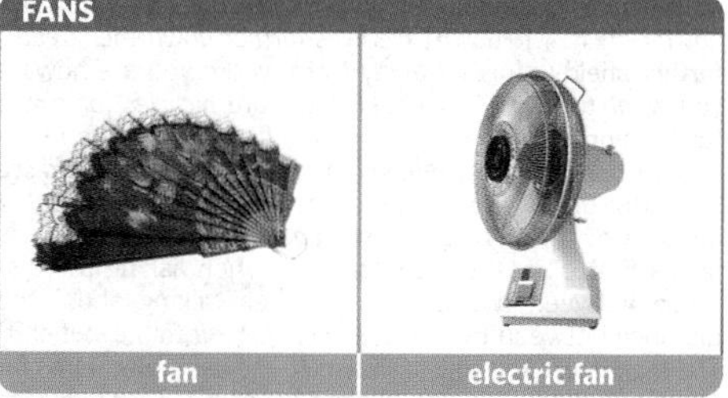

fan | electric fan

fan¹ /fæn/ ●●● S3 W2 *n* [C]
1 someone who likes a particular sport or performing art very much, or who admires a famous person: *Groups of football fans began heading towards the ground.* | **[+of]** *He's a* ***big fan*** *of Elvis Presley.* | **fan mail/letters** (=letters sent to famous people by their fans)
2 a) a machine with turning blades that is used to cool the air in a room by moving it around: *a ceiling fan* **b)** a flat object that you wave with your hand which makes the air cooler

fan² ●○○ *v* [T] (**fanned**, **fanning**)
1 to make air move around by waving a fan, piece of paper etc so that you feel cooler: **fan yourself** *People in the audience were fanning themselves with their programmes.*
2 *literary* to make someone feel an emotion more strongly SYN **fuel**: *Her resistance only fanned his desire.* | **fan the flames (of sth)** *The book will serve to fan the flames of debate.*
3 fan a fire/flame etc to make a fire burn more strongly by blowing or moving the air near it: *The wind rose, fanning a few sparks in the brush.*

fan out *phr v*
1 if a group of people fan out, they walk forwards while spreading over a wide area
2 fan sth ↔ out to spread out a group of things that you are holding so that they make a half-circle: *Fan the cards out, then pick one.*
3 if something such as hair or clothing fans out, it spreads out in many directions

fa·nat·ic /fəˈnætɪk/ *n* [C] **1** someone who has extreme political or religious ideas and is often dangerous SYN **extremist**: *fanatics who represent a real danger to democracy* | *a* ***religious fanatic*** **2** someone who likes a particular thing or activity very much SYN **enthusiast**: *a health food fanatic* | *a* ***fitness*** *fanatic* —**fanatical** *adj*: *a fanatical sportsman* | *He was fanatical about tidiness.* —**fanatically** /-kli/ *adv*

fa·nat·i·cis·m /fəˈnætɪsɪzəm/ *n* [U] extreme political or religious beliefs - used to show disapproval SYN **extremism**: *The bombing symbolizes the worst of* ***religious fanaticism****.*

ˈfan belt *n* [C] the belt that operates a FAN which keeps a car engine cool

fan·boy /ˈfænbɔɪ/ *n* [C] *especially AmE* a boy or young man who is very interested in a particular computer game, COMIC, television programme etc and spends a lot of time discussing it → **fangirl**

fan·ci·a·ble /ˈfænsiəbəl/ *adj BrE* sexually attractive

fan·ci·er /ˈfænsiə $ -ər/ *n* [C] **pigeon/horse etc fancier** someone who breeds or is interested in a particular kind of animal or plant

fan·ci·ful /ˈfænsɪfəl/ *adj* **1** imagined rather than based on facts - often used to show disapproval: *a fanciful story* | *The suggestion that there was a conspiracy is not entirely fanciful.* **2** full of unusual and very detailed shapes or complicated designs: *fanciful decorations* —**fancifully** *adv*

ˈfan club *n* [C] an organization for FANS of a particular team, famous person etc

fan·cy¹ /ˈfænsi/ ●●○ S3 *v* (**fancied**, **fancying**, **fancies**) [T]
1 LIKE/WANT *BrE informal* to like or want something, or want to do something SYN **feel like**: *Fancy a quick drink, Emma?* | **fancy doing sth** *Sorry, but I don't fancy going out tonight.*
2 SEXUAL ATTRACTION *BrE informal* to feel sexually attracted to someone: *All the girls fancied him.*
3 fancy yourself *BrE informal* to behave in a way that shows you think you are very attractive or clever: *That bloke on the dance floor really fancies himself.*
4 fancy yourself (as) sth *BrE* to believe, usually wrongly, that you have particular skills or are a particular type of person: *He fancies himself an artist.* | *She fancies herself as another Madonna.*
5 THINK STH WILL BE SUCCESSFUL *BrE* to think someone or something is likely to be successful in something: *Which team do you fancy this year?* | *I don't* ***fancy*** *our* ***chances*** *of getting a ticket this late.*

F

6 fancy!/fancy that! *BrE spoken* used to express your surprise or shock about something: *'The Petersons are getting divorced.' 'Fancy that!' | Fancy seeing you here!*
7 THINK/BELIEVE *literary* to think or believe something without being certain: **fancy (that)** *She fancied she heard a noise downstairs.*

fancy² ●○○ *n* (*plural* **fancies**)
1 LIKING/WISH [singular] *especially BrE* **a)** a feeling, especially one that is not particularly strong or urgent, that you like someone or want to have something: **take a fancy to sb/sth** (=decide that you like someone or want to have something) *Mr Hill took a real fancy to Clara. | Wanting to go to Mexico was just a **passing fancy*** (=the feeling did not last long). *| Because of its high cost, a carpet is not an item that you change **as the fancy takes you*** (=whenever you want). **b) take/catch your fancy** if something takes or catches your fancy, you like it or want to have it: *Did you see anything that took your fancy?*
2 tickle sb's fancy *informal* to seem attractive or amusing to someone: *The idea of playing a joke on her tickled his fancy.*
3 IDEA [C] *old-fashioned* an idea or opinion that is not based on fact: *Oh, that was just a fancy of his.*
4 IMAGINATION [U] *literary* imagination or something that you imagine → **flight of fancy** at FLIGHT(6)

fancy³ ●○○ *adj* (*comparative* **fancier**, *superlative* **fanciest**)
1 fancy hotels, restaurants, cars etc are expensive and fashionable SYN **swanky**: *Harry took me to a fancy restaurant for our anniversary.* | **fancy prices** *BrE* (=very high and often unreasonable prices)
2 having a lot of decoration or bright colours, or made in a complicated way: *fancy soaps in seashell shapes | I just want a basic sports coat – **nothing fancy**.*
3 complicated and needing a lot of skill OPP **straightforward**: *I can't do all that fancy stuff on the computer. | Negotiating a deal can take some **fancy footwork*** (=skill at making deals).
4 [only before noun] *AmE* fancy food is of a high quality

ˌfancy ˈdress *n* [U] *BrE* clothes that you wear, especially to parties, that make you look like a famous person, a character from a story etc: *an invitation to a **fancy-dress party***

ˌfancy-ˈfree *adj* able to do anything you like because you do not have a family or other responsibilities: *Ten years ago I was **footloose and fancy-free**.*

ˈfancy man *n* [C] *old-fashioned* a man that a married woman has a sexual relationship with, who is not her husband

ˈfancy ˌwoman *n* [C] *old-fashioned* a woman that a married man has a sexual relationship with, who is not his wife

fan·cy·work /ˈfænsiwɜːk $ -wɜːrk/ *n* [U] decorative sewing SYN **embroidery**

fan·dan·go /fænˈdæŋgəʊ $ -goʊ/ *n* (*plural* **fandangos**) [C] a fast Spanish or South American dance, or the music for this dance

fan·fare /ˈfænfeə $ -fer/ *n* **1** [C] a short loud piece of music played on a TRUMPET to introduce an important person or event **2** [U] a lot of activity, advertising, or discussion relating to an event: *The deal was announced with much fanfare.*

fan·fic /ˈfænfɪk/ (*also* **ˈfan ˌfiction** *or* **ˈfanˌfiction**) *n* [U] stories, usually on the Internet, written by FANS of a TV series, film, book etc (=people who like it a lot) about the characters that appear in it

fang /fæŋ/ *n* [C] a long sharp tooth of an animal such as a snake or wild dog

fan·girl /ˈfæŋgɜːl $ -gɜːrl/ *n* [C] *especially AmE* a girl or young woman who is very interested in a particular computer game, COMIC, television programme etc and spends a lot of time discussing it → **fanboy**

fan·light /ˈfænlaɪt/ *n* [C] **1** *especially BrE* a small window above a door or a larger window SYN **transom** *AmE* **2** *AmE* a window shaped like a half-circle

fan·ny /ˈfæni/ *n* (*plural* **fannies**) [C] *informal* **1** *AmE* the part of your body that you sit on SYN **bottom** **2** *BrE informal not polite* a woman's outer sex organs SYN **genitals**

fan·ta·si·a /fænˈteɪziə, ˌfæntəˈziːə $ fænˈteɪʒə/ *n* [C] a piece of music that does not have a regular form or style

fan·ta·size (*also* **-ise** *BrE*) /ˈfæntəsaɪz/ *v* [I,T] to imagine that you are doing something which is very pleasant or exciting, but which is very unlikely to happen SYN **dream**: **[+about]** *Sometimes she fantasized about buying a boat and sailing around the world.* | **fantasize that** *I used to fantasize that my real parents were famous movie stars.* THESAURUS ▸ IMAGINE

fan·tas·tic /fænˈtæstɪk/ ●●● S3 *adj*
1 extremely good, attractive, enjoyable etc: *You look fantastic! | It's a fantastic place, really beautiful!* THESAURUS ▸ GOOD
2 *spoken* used when someone has just told you something good SYN **excellent**, **wonderful**: *'I've passed my driving test.' 'Fantastic!' | That's fantastic news!*
3 a fantastic amount is extremely large SYN **huge**: *Kids spend fantastic amounts of money on CDs.*
4 a fantastic plan, suggestion etc is not likely to be possible: *fantastic schemes for making money*
5 [only before noun] a fantastic story, creature, or place is imaginary and is very strange and magical SYN **fantastical** → **fantasy (3)**: *fantastic tales of dragons and fairy queens*
—**fantastically** /-kli/ *adv*

fan·tas·ti·cal /fænˈtæstɪkəl/ *adj* strange, unreal, and magical SYN **fantastic**: *fantastical creatures with golden wings and lions' faces*

fan·ta·sy /ˈfæntəsi/ ●●○ *n* (*plural* **fantasies**)
1 [C,U] an exciting and unusual experience or situation that you imagine happening to you, but which will probably never happen: *I used to **have fantasies about** living in Paris with an artist. | sexual fantasies | Young children sometimes can't distinguish between fantasy and reality. | He **lived in** a **fantasy world** of his own, even as a small boy.*
2 [singular, U] an idea or belief that is based only on imagination, not on real facts: *Memories can sometimes be pure fantasy, rather than actual recollections.*
3 [C] a story, film etc that is based on imagination and not facts: *a surrealist fantasy set in a South American village*

ˌfantasy ˈfootball *n* [U] a game in which lots of people make imaginary football teams by choosing real players. They get points according to how well the players do in real games, and the winner is the person whose team gets the most points.

fan·zine /ˈfænziːn/ *n* [C] a magazine written by and for people who admire and support a popular musician, a sports team etc

FAQ /fæk, ˌef eɪ ˈkjuː/ *n* [C usually plural] the abbreviation of ***frequently asked question***

far¹ /fɑː $ fɑːr/ ●●● S1 W1 *adv* (*comparative* **farther** /ˈfɑːðə $ ˈfɑːrðər/ *or* **further** /ˈfɜːðə $ ˈfɜːrðər/, *superlative* **farthest** /ˈfɑːðɪst $ ˈfɑːr-/ *or* **furthest** /ˈfɜːðɪst $ ˈfɜːr-/)
1 DISTANCE **a)** a long distance: *Have you driven far? | Since I changed jobs, I have to travel further to get to work. | Let's see who can jump the furthest!* | **[+from]** *The children don't go far from home.* | **[+away]** *She wants to move as far away from here as possible. | They could hear the sound of water not far away.* | **[+down]** *He lives further down the street.* | **further afield** (=further away from where you are now) *If you want to go further afield, there are bicycles for hire.* | **further north/south etc** *Many birds fly further south in the autumn. | The plains stretched for **as far as the eye could see*** (=all the distance you could see). *| The lake is about 4 miles away, but we probably **won't get that far*** (=won't go as far as that place). **b) how far** used when asking the distance between two places, or when talking about the distance between two places: *How far is it to the station? | The man didn't say how far it was to the next town.* **c) as far as sth** to a place or point, but not beyond it: *They managed to get as far as the Spanish border.*
2 A LOT/VERY MUCH very much, or to a great degree: **far better/easier etc** *The new system is far better than the old*

one. | *There are a far greater number of women working in television than twenty years ago.* | **far more/less** *I enjoyed it far more than I expected.* | **far too much/long/busy etc** *That's far too much to pay.* | *It would take me far too long to explain.* | **[+above/below/beyond]** *He bought it for a price that was far beyond* (=much more than) *its real value.* | *The teacher said that her writing skills were far below average.* | *We've kept the original features of the house* ***as far as possible*** (=as much as possible). | ***How far*** *do those old, outdated laws affect today's legislation?* | *His style was* ***far removed*** (=very different) *from that of Picasso.* | **not far off/out/wrong** (=close to being correct) *I guessed it would cost $100 and it was $110, so I was not far out.*

3 PROGRESS used to talk about how much progress someone makes, or how much effect something has: *He started to explain, but he didn't* ***get far*** (=he did not succeed in saying very much) *before Mary interrupted him.* | **get as far as doing sth** *They had got as far as painting the kitchen.* | *Many people felt that the new law did not* ***go far enough*** (=did not have a big enough effect, so that more needed to be done).

4 TIME a long time in the past or the future, or a long time into a particular period: **[+into]** *We talked far into the night.* | **[+ahead]** *They want to plan much further ahead than the next few years.* | *The first petrol-driven car was produced* ***as far back as*** *1883.* → FAR-OFF

5 go too far (*also* **take/carry sth too far**) to do something too extreme: *One day she will go too far.* | *Some people thought he had gone too far in his criticism of the police.*

6 go so far/as far as to do sth *spoken* to do or say something extreme: *The government went so far as to try to arrest opposition leaders.* | *I wouldn't go so far as to say that we agreed on the subject.*

7 so far (*also* **thus far** *formal*) until now: *So far we have not had to borrow any money.* | *They're delighted with the replies they've received from the public thus far.*

8 so far so good *spoken* used to say that things have been happening successfully until now: *We've reached the semi-finals. So far so good.*

9 far from sth used to say that something very different is true or happens: *Conditions are still far from ideal.* | **far from doing/being sth** *Far from helping the situation, you've just made it worse.*

10 far from it *spoken* used to say that the opposite of what has just been said is true: *'Are you bored?' 'Far from it. I could listen all night.'* | *Local people aren't objecting – far from it.*

11 far and wide over a large area: *His fame spread far and wide.* | *People* ***came from far and wide*** (=came from many places) *to see the concert.*

12 by far/far and away used to say that something is much better, worse etc than anything else: *Watching sport was by far the most popular activity on Saturday afternoons.* | *Spring is far and away the best time to visit the islands.*

13 sb will/would/should etc go far used to say that you think someone will be successful in the future: *He was the best student in his year, and everyone was sure he would go far.*

14 as/so far as I'm concerned *spoken* used when giving your opinion about something: *As far as I'm concerned she can come home whenever she likes.*

15 as/so far as sth is concerned *spoken* used when you want to talk about a particular thing: *As far as money's concerned, there shouldn't be a problem.*

16 as/so far as I know/I can remember/I can tell/I can see etc *spoken* used to say that you think that something is true, although it is possible that you do not know all the facts or cannot remember completely: *There weren't any buildings there at all, as far as I can remember.* | *As far as I can see, there's nothing else to discuss.*

17 far be it from me to do sth *spoken* used when saying that you do not want to criticize someone or say what they should do, especially when this is what you are really about to do: *Far be it from me to teach you your job, but don't you think you should have been more careful?*

18 as far as it goes used to say that an idea, suggestion, plan etc is satisfactory, but only to a limited degree: *His theories are fine, as far as they go.*

19 not go far a) if money does not go far, you cannot buy very much with it: *My salary doesn't go very far these days.* **b)** if a supply of something does not go far, it is not enough: *The coffee won't go far if everyone wants a cup.*

20 in so far as/insofar as/in as far as *formal* to the degree that: *The research suggests that the drug will be successful, in so far as one can draw conclusions from such a small sample size.*

THESAURUS

far *adv* a long distance – used mainly in negatives and questions, or after 'too', 'so', and 'as': *It's not far to the airport from here.* | *Have you driven far?* | *The ship was so* ***far away*** *we could hardly see it.*

a long way *adv* a long distance from somewhere. This is the most common way of talking about long distances, except in negatives and questions when far is also common: *You must be tired – you've come a long way.* | *It's a long way down from the top of the cliff.*

miles *adv informal* a very long way: *We hiked miles.* | *The school is* ***miles away*** *from where I live.*

in the distance *adv* a long way from where you are now – used when talking about things that seem small or sounds that seem quiet because they are a long way away: *Dogs were barking somewhere in the distance.*

distant *adj especially written* used about something that is a long distance from where you are now, and looks small or sounds quiet: *By now, the plane was just a distant speck in the sky.* | *the rumble of distant thunder*

faraway *adj especially written* a very long distance from where you are now: *a traveller from a faraway land* | *His voice sounded faraway.*

remote *adj* a remote place is a long distance from other places, and few people go there: *The helicopter crashed in a remote part of the country.* | *remote holiday destinations*

isolated *adj* an isolated place is a long distance from other towns, buildings, or people, and there is very little communication with surrounding places: *isolated rural areas of Nepal* | *Occasionally we passed through a small isolated village.*

off the beaten track (*also* **off the beaten path** *AmE*) *adv* a place that is off the beaten track is a long distance from the places where people usually go, and often seems interesting and different because of this: *She likes to go to places that are a bit off the beaten track.*

far² ●●● S1 W1 *adj* (*comparative* **farther** *or* **further**, *superlative* **farthest** *or* **furthest**)

1 a long distance away OPP **near**: *We can walk to my house from here. It isn't far.* | *You could see the mountains in the far distance.*

2 the far side/end/corner etc the side, end etc that is furthest from you OPP **near**: *They crossed the bridge and walked along the far side of the stream.* | *There was a piano in the far corner of the room.*

3 the far north/south etc the part of a country or area that is furthest in the direction of north, south etc: *It will become windy in the far north and west.*

4 the far left/right people who have extreme LEFT-WING or RIGHT-WING political opinions: *The candidate for the far right got ten percent of the vote.*

5 be a far cry from sth to be very different from something: *The company lost £3 million, which is a far cry from last year's £60 million profit.*

6 a bridge too far (*also* **a step/cut/adventure etc too far**) something that is too extreme: *An amendment to the constitution would be regarded as a step too far.*

far·a·way /ˈfɑːrəweɪ/ *adj* **1** [only before noun] *literary* a long distance away SYN **distant**: *She dreamed of flying away to exotic faraway places.* | *faraway noises* THESAURUS FAR **2 a faraway look** an expression on your face which shows that you are not paying attention but thinking

F

about something very different: *His eyes had a distant faraway look, like a sailor staring out to sea.*

farce /fɑːs $ fɑːrs/ *n* **1** [singular] an event or a situation that is very badly organized or does not happen properly, in a way that is silly and unreasonable: *She admitted that the interview had been a complete farce from start to finish.* **2** [C,U] a humorous play or film in which the characters are involved in complicated and silly situations, or the style of writing or acting that is used

far·ci·cal /ˈfɑːsɪkəl $ ˈfɑːr-/ *adj* **1** a situation or event that is farcical is very silly and badly organized: *Opposition leaders described the government's plans as 'farcical'.* **2** a farcical play or film is a humorous one in which the characters become involved in silly and complicated situations —**farcically** /-kli/ *adv*

fare¹ /feə $ fer/ ●●○ *n*
1 [C] the price you pay to travel somewhere by bus, train, plane etc: **bus/train/air/cab fare** *Air fares have shot up by 20%.* | **half-fare/full-fare** *Children under 14 travel half-fare.* **THESAURUS** COST
2 [U] *written* food, especially food served in a restaurant or eaten on a special occasion: *traditional Christmas fare* **THESAURUS** FOOD
3 [C] a passenger in a taxi
4 [U] something that is offered to the public, especially as entertainment: *The movie is suitable **family fare**.*

fare² *v* **fare well/badly/better etc** to be successful, unsuccessful etc: *Although Chicago has fared better than some cities, unemployment remains a problem.* | *He wondered how Ed had fared in the interview.*

ˌFar ˈEast *n* **the Far East** the countries in the east of Asia, such as China, Japan, Korea etc —**Far Eastern** *adj* → MIDDLE EAST, NEAR EAST

F

fare·well¹ /ˌfeəˈwel◂ $ ˌfer-/ ●○○ *n*
1 [C,U] *old-fashioned* the action of saying goodbye: *Mourners gathered to **bid farewell to** the victims of the plane tragedy.* | *a farewell speech*
2 farewell party/dinner/drink etc a party or dinner that you have because someone is leaving a job, city etc: *40 of her colleagues gathered for her farewell presentation.*

farewell² *interjection old use* goodbye

ˌfar-ˈfetched *adj* extremely unlikely to be true or to happen: *All this may sound a bit far-fetched, but companies are already developing 'intelligent' homes.*

ˌfar-ˈflung *adj* **1** very distant: **far-flung corners/places/regions etc** *expeditions to far-flung corners of the globe* | *people flying to far-flung destinations* **2** spread out over a very large area: *Email enables far-flung friends to keep in touch.*

ˌfar ˈgone *adj* [not before noun] *informal* very sick, drunk, crazy etc: *She's pretty far gone – can you drive her home?*

farm¹ /fɑːm $ fɑːrm/ ●●● S2 W2 *n* [C]
1 an area of land used for growing crops or keeping animals: *a 300-hectare farm* | *farm workers* | *farm animals* | *Joe had **worked on** the **farm** all his life.* | **a pig/dairy/cattle etc farm** *He runs a pig farm in Lincolnshire.* ⚠ Say **on a farm** not 'in a farm'.
2 the main house on a farm where the farmer lives → **factory farm** at FACTORY FARMING, FISH FARM, FUNNY FARM

farm² ●●○ *v* [I,T]
1 to use land for growing crops or keeping animals: *The family has farmed here for generations.* | *The land has been farmed organically since 1995.*
2 farmed salmon/fish/rabbits etc fish and animals that have been raised on farms, and not caught from the wild

farm sb/sth ↔ **out** *phr v*
1 to send work to other people instead of doing it yourself: **[+to]** *The processing will be farmed out to people in local villages.*
2 to send someone to a different place where they will be looked after – used to show disapproval: **[+to]** *At the age of 16 she was farmed out to family friends.*

farm·er /ˈfɑːmə $ ˈfɑːrmər/ ●●● S2 W2 *n* [C] someone who owns or manages a farm

ˈfarmers' ˌmarket *n* [C] a place where farmers bring their fruit, vegetables, meat, and other products to sell directly to people in a town or city

farm·hand /ˈfɑːmhænd $ ˈfɑːrm-/ *n* [C] someone who works on a farm

farm·house /ˈfɑːmhaʊs $ ˈfɑːrm-/ ●○○ *n* [C] the main house on a farm, where the farmer lives

farm·ing /ˈfɑːmɪŋ $ ˈfɑːr-/ ●●○ *n* [U] the practice or business of growing crops or keeping animals on a farm → **agriculture**: **sheep/dairy/livestock etc farming** | **organic/intensive farming** | *the farming industry*

farm·land /ˈfɑːmlænd, -lənd $ ˈfɑːrmlænd/ *n* [U] land used for farming **THESAURUS** LAND

ˈfarm shop *n* [C] a shop selling things produced on a particular farm, such as vegetables, eggs, and meat

farm·stead /ˈfɑːmsted $ ˈfɑːrm-/ *n* [C] a farmhouse and the buildings around it

farm·yard /ˈfɑːmjɑːd $ ˈfɑːrmjɑːrd/ *n* [C] an area surrounded by farm buildings

ˌfar-ˈoff *adj literary* **1** a long way from where you are SYN **distant**: **a far-off land/country/place etc** *visitors from a far-off land* | *far-off galaxies* **2** a long time ago: *in those far-off days when we were young*

ˌfar-ˈout *adj* very strange or unusual SYN **weird**: *Tim's designs were just far-out.*

ˌfar-ˈreaching ●○○ *adj* having a great influence or effect: **far-reaching reforms/proposals/changes** *The country carried out far-reaching reforms to modernize its economy.* | **far-reaching implications/impact/effects** *Tourism has had far-reaching effects on the island's culture.*

far·ri·er /ˈfæriə $ -ər/ *n* [C] someone who makes shoes for horses' feet → **blacksmith**

Far·si /ˈfɑːsi $ ˈfɑːr-/ *n* [U] the language of Iran SYN **Persian**

ˌfar-ˈsighted / $ ˈ. ˌ../ *adj* **1** far-sighted people, ideas, or plans are wise because they show an understanding of what will happen in the future: *far-sighted investments* | *a far-sighted politician* **2** *especially AmE* able to see or read things clearly only when they are far away from you OPP **short-sighted** SYN **long-sighted** *BrE* —**far-sightedness** *n* [U]

fart¹ /fɑːt $ fɑːrt/ *v* [I] *not polite* to make air come out of your BOWELS SYN **break wind**

fart about/around *phr v informal* to waste time not doing very much: *Stop farting around and get on with your work!*

fart² *n* **1** [C] *not polite* an act of making air come out of your BOWELS **2 old fart** *informal* a stupid and uninteresting older person

far·ther¹ /ˈfɑːðə $ ˈfɑːrðər/ *adv* **1** a greater distance than before or than something else; a COMPARATIVE form of 'far' SYN **further**: *We decided not to go any farther.* | **farther away/apart/down/along etc** *The boats were drifting **farther and farther** apart.* | *a resort town farther up the coast* | **farther south/north etc** *Two miles farther south is the village of Santa Catarina.* | *Most of them were locals, but some had come from **farther afield*** (=a greater distance away). **2** if you do something farther, you do it more or to a greater degree SYN **further**: *We'd better investigate farther.* | *The police decided not to **take** the matter any **farther*** (=do more about it).

> **REGISTER**
> In everyday English, people usually say **further** rather than **farther**, and **furthest** rather than **farthest**: *We decided not to take it any **further**.* | *This was the **furthest** away from home I'd ever been.*

farther² *adj* [only before noun] more distant; a COMPARATIVE form of 'far' SYN **further**: *A table stood at the farther end of the kitchen.*

far·thest¹ /ˈfɑːðɪst $ ˈfɑːr-/ *adv* at or to the greatest distance away; a SUPERLATIVE form of 'far' SYN **furthest**: *My sister was the one who travelled farthest.* | **farthest away/apart etc** *She lived farthest away from school of all of us.*

farthest² *adj* the most distant; a SUPERLATIVE form of 'far' SYN **furthest**: *the farthest corners of the globe*

far·thing /ˈfɑːðɪŋ $ ˈfɑːr-/ *n* [C] an old British coin that was worth one quarter of a PENNY

fa·scia /ˈfeɪʃə/ *n* [C] *BrE* **1** a DASHBOARD **2** a long board above a shop with the shop's name on it **3** a cover for a MOBILE PHONE

fas·ci·nate /ˈfæsəneɪt/ ●●○ *v* [T] if someone or something fascinates you, you are attracted to them and think they are extremely interesting: *The idea of travelling through time fascinated him.*

GRAMMAR: Using the progressive

- The verb **fascinate** is not used in the progressive. You say: *Dolphins fascinate me.* ✗ Don't say: *Dolphins are fascinating me.*
- **Fascinating** is used as an adjective: *a fascinating subject*

GRAMMAR GUIDE ▶ VERBS

fas·ci·nat·ed /ˈfæsɪneɪtɪd/ ●●○ *adj* [not before noun] extremely interested by something or someone: *I was fascinated by her voice.* | **fascinated to see/hear/learn etc** *Ed was fascinated to see gorillas in the wild.*

fas·ci·nat·ing /ˈfæsəneɪtɪŋ/ ●●○ S3 *adj* extremely interesting: *a fascinating book* | *That sounds* ***absolutely fascinating.*** | **find sb/sth fascinating** *I found him quite fascinating.* THESAURUS ▶ INTERESTING —**fascinatingly** *adv*

fas·ci·na·tion /ˌfæsəˈneɪʃən/ ●○○ *n*
1 [singular, U] the state of being very interested in something, so that you want to look at it, learn about it etc → **obsession**: **[+for/with]** *Police knew of his fascination with guns.* | **in fascination** *The children watched in fascination.*
2 [C,U] something that interests you very much, or the quality of being very interesting: **hold/have a fascination for sb** *India will always hold a great fascination for me.* | *The fascination lay in the mystery of what was inside the box.*

fas·ci·na·tor /ˈfæsəneɪtə $ -tər/ *n* [C] a small pretty object, usually made of feathers, that a woman wears on her head at a special occasion such as a wedding

fas·cis·m /ˈfæʃɪzəm/ *n* [U] a RIGHT-WING political system in which people's lives are completely controlled by the state and no political opposition is allowed

fas·cist /ˈfæʃɪst/ *n* [C] **1** someone who supports fascism: *The fascists came to power in 1933.* **2** *informal* someone who is cruel and unfair and does not like people to argue with them: *My last boss was a real fascist.* **3** *informal* someone who has extreme RIGHT-WING opinions —**fascist** *adj*: *Mussolini's fascist regime*

fash·ion¹ /ˈfæʃən/ ●●● S3 W2 *n*
1 [C,U] something that is popular or thought to be good at a particular time: **[+for]** *the fashion for 'discovery methods' of learning* | **[+in]** *The emerging science of photography was already changing fashions in art.* | **in fashion** *Bright colours are in fashion this summer.* | **out of fashion** *Their music will never go out of fashion.* | *His ideas are* ***coming back into fashion*** (=they are becoming popular again). | *Eastern religions used to* ***be the fashion*** *in the 60s.* | *Self-help books are* ***all the fashion*** (=they are very fashionable). GRAMMAR ✗ Don't say: *on fashion*
2 [C,U] a style of clothes, hair etc that is popular at a particular time: *Young people are very concerned with fashion.* | *The store has all the latest fashions.*
3 [U] the business or study of making and selling clothes, shoes etc in new and changing styles: *magazines about fashion and beauty* | *the London College of Fashion*
4 in a ... fashion in a particular way: *Please leave the building in an orderly fashion.* | *Perhaps they could sit down and discuss things in a civilised fashion.* | *She will be working out her problems* ***in her own fashion*** (=in the way that she usually does this).
5 after a fashion not very much, not very well, or not very effectively: *'Can you speak Russian?' 'After a fashion.'*
6 after the fashion of sb in a style that is typical of a particular person: *Her early work is very much after the fashion of Picasso and Braque.*
7 like it's going out of fashion *informal* use this to emphasize that someone does something a lot or uses a lot of something: *Danny's been* ***spending money like it's going out of fashion.*** → **parrot fashion** at PARROT¹(2)

COLLOCATIONS

PHRASES

be in fashion *Belted jackets are in fashion this winter.*
be out of fashion *Flared trousers were out of fashion in the 1980s.*
go out of fashion (=stop being fashionable) *Long evening dresses are going out of fashion.*
come back into fashion (=become fashionable again) *Short skirts are coming back into fashion this year.*
be the height of fashion (=be very fashionable) | **keep up with fashion** (=make sure that you know about the most recent fashions) | **fashion-conscious** (=very interested in the latest fashions, and always wanting to wear fashionable clothes)

ADJECTIVES

the latest fashion *They sell all the latest fashions.*
men's/women's fashions *Men's fashions have not changed much in 50 years.*

fashion + NOUN

the fashion industry *London is the centre of the British fashion industry.*
the fashion world *Small women are often overlooked by the fashion world.*
a fashion show | **a fashion model** | **a fashion designer** | **fashion design** | **a fashion house** (=a company that produces new and expensive styles of clothes) | **a fashion magazine** | **fashion photography** | **a fashion photographer** | **a fashion shoot** (=an occasion when photographs are taken of fashion models) | **a fashion shop**

COMMON ERRORS

⚠ Don't say 'the last fashion'. Say **the latest fashion**.

fashion² ●○○ *v* [T]
1 to shape or make something, using your hands or only a few tools: **fashion sth from sth** *He fashioned a box from a few old pieces of wood.* | **fashion sth into sth** *Jamie could take a piece of wood and fashion it into a wonderful work of art.*
2 to influence and form someone's ideas and opinions: *We are all unique human beings, fashioned by life experiences.* GRAMMAR **Fashion** is usually passive in this meaning.

-fashion /fæʃən/ *suffix* [in adverbs] like something, or in the way that a particular group of people does something: *They ate Indian-fashion, using their fingers.*

fash·ion·a·ble /ˈfæʃənəbəl/ ●●● S3 W2 *adj*
1 popular, especially for a short period of time OPP **unfashionable**: *Strong colours are very fashionable at the moment.* | **it is fashionable (for sb) to do sth** *It suddenly became fashionable for politicians to talk about green issues.*
2 popular with, or used by, rich people OPP **unfashionable**: **a fashionable resort/area/address etc** *He runs a fashionable restaurant near the Harbor.* —**fashionably** *adv*: *fashionably dressed women*

THESAURUS

fashionable popular at a particular time: *fashionable clothes* | *It was fashionable to have red hair.* | *His theories were fashionable in the 1980s.*
trendy *informal* modern and fashionable - often used in a slightly disapproving or joking way: *a trendy tie* | *a trendy restaurant* | *The area has become very trendy and a lot of artists live there.*
stylish fashionable and well-designed in an attractive way: *She was wearing a stylish two-piece suit.* | *The furniture looked very stylish and modern.*
cool *informal* fashionable - used especially when you think someone or something looks good: *Michael looked very cool in his dark jacket and sunglasses.* | *a cool shirt*

F

happening [only before noun] *informal* a happening place is fashionable and lively: *London has always been a happening place.*
be in fashion *v phrase* to be fashionable at a particular time: *The Sixties look is back in fashion.*
in *informal* fashionable at a particular time. **In** is not used before a noun, except in the phrases below: *Pale colours are in.* | *New York was the* ***in place to be.*** | *Yoga has become* ***the in thing to do.***

ˌfashion ˈforward *adj* wearing or having the newest styles of clothes – used especially in magazines

ˈfashion house *n* [C] a company that produces new and expensive styles of clothes

fash·ion·ist·a /ˌfæʃəˈniːstə/ *n* [C] *informal* someone who is very interested in fashion and who likes the very newest styles

ˈfashion plate *n* [C] *informal* someone who likes to wear very fashionable clothes

ˈfashion show *n* [C] an event at which new styles of clothes are shown to the public

ˈfashion ˌstatement *n* [C] something that you own or wear that is considered new or different, and that is intended to make other people notice you: *Mobile phones make a big fashion statement.*

ˈfashion ˌvictim *n* [C] *informal* someone who always wears what is fashionable, even if it makes them look bad

fast[1] /fɑːst $ fæst/ ●●● S2 W2 *adj*
1 MOVING QUICKLY moving or able to move quickly: *a fast car* | *He's one of the fastest runners in the world.*
2 IN A SHORT TIME doing something or happening in a short time: *The subway is the fastest way to get downtown.* | *The company must give a faster response to clients' requests.* | *The rain forests are being chopped down at an alarmingly fast rate.* | *I'm a fast learner.*
3 CLOCK [not before noun] a clock that is fast shows a later time than the real time: *That can't be the time – my watch must be fast.* | **five minutes/an hour etc fast** *I always keep my watch 15 minutes fast.*
4 fast track a way of achieving something more quickly than is normally done: **on the fast track** *a young actress on the fast track to fame and success*
5 fast road a road on which vehicles can travel very quickly
6 fast film/lens a film or LENS(2) that can be used when there is little light, or when photographing something that is moving very quickly
7 COLOUR a colour that is fast will not change when clothes are washed → COLOURFAST
8 SPORTS a fast surface is one on which a ball moves very quickly
9 fast and furious done very quickly with a lot of effort and energy, or happening very quickly with a lot of sudden changes: *Arsenal's opening attack was fast and furious.*
10 sb is a fast worker *informal* used to say that someone can get what they want very quickly, especially in starting a sexual relationship with another person
11 fast talker someone who talks quickly and easily but is often not honest or sincere
12 WOMAN *old-fashioned* becoming involved quickly in sexual relationships with men: *fast cars and fast women*
13 fast friends *literary* two people who are very friendly for a long time → **FAST FOOD, FAST-FORWARD, FAST LANE,** → **make a fast buck** at BUCK[1](1), → **pull a fast one** at PULL[1](10)

THESAURUS

fast moving or able to move quickly: *The cheetah is the fastest animal in the world.* | *a fast car*
quick moving fast or doing something in a short time: *He was much quicker than I was over the first 100 metres.* | *Do I have time for a quick shower?*
high-speed [only before noun] designed to travel or operate very quickly: *a high-speed train* | *high-speed Internet access*
rapid *especially written* happening in a short period of time – used about changes, increases, improvements etc: *a rapid increase in the population* | *the rapid expansion of the firm's business in the Middle East*
swift *written* moving quickly or happening after only a short time: *The horses ran along the track at a swift trot.* | *He received a swift response to his letter.*
brisk quick and energetic: *a brisk walk in the countryside* | *His manner was very brisk.*
speedy [only before noun] happening after only a short time: *Everyone wishes you a speedy recovery.* | *a speedy resolution to the problem*
hurried done more quickly than usual, because you do not have much time: *She ate a hurried breakfast in the cafe before catching her train.* | *We made a hurried departure.*
hasty deciding or doing something very quickly, especially when this has bad results: *It was a hasty decision, which he later regretted.* | *Let's not be too hasty.*

fast[2] ●●● S2 W3 *adv*
1 MOVING QUICKLY moving quickly: *Slow down – you're driving too fast.* | *a* ***fast-moving*** *river* | *Johnny ran off* ***as fast as*** *his* ***legs could carry*** *him* (=running as quickly as he could). THESAURUS ▸ QUICKLY
2 IN A SHORT TIME happening in a short time: *Kids grow up fast these days.* | *The survivors needed help fast.* | *How fast can you get the job done?* | **fast becoming/disappearing/approaching etc** *Access to the Internet is fast becoming a necessity.* | ***It*** *all* ***happened so fast*** *I didn't even notice I was bleeding.*
3 fast asleep sleeping very deeply: *Nick was lying on the sofa, fast asleep.*
4 be stuck/held fast to become or be firmly fixed and unable to move: *The boat was stuck fast in the mud.* | *She tried to pull her hand free, but it was held fast.*
5 be getting/be going nowhere fast *informal* to not succeed in making progress or achieving something: *I kept asking her the same question, but I was getting nowhere fast.*
6 not so fast *spoken* used to tell someone not to be too eager to do or believe something: *Not so fast. We've got to prove it first, haven't we?*
7 make sth fast to tie something such as a boat or tent firmly to something else
8 fast by sth *literary* very close to something: *fast by the river* → **play fast and loose with sb** at PLAY[1](32), → **stand fast** at STAND[1](25), → **thick and fast** at THICK[2](2)

fast[3] *v* [I] to eat little or no food for a period of time, especially for religious reasons: *Muslims fast during Ramadan.*

fast[4] *n* [C] a period during which someone does not eat, especially for religious reasons: *Gandhi drank some orange juice to* ***break*** (=end) *his three-week* ***fast.***

fast·ball /ˈfɑːstbɔːl $ ˈfæstbɒːl/ *n* [C] a ball that is thrown very hard and quickly towards the BATTER in a game of BASEBALL

ˌfast ˌbreeder reˈactor (*also* **fast ˈbreeder**) *n* [C] a NUCLEAR REACTOR (=large machine that produces nuclear energy) which turns some of the URANIUM used in the process into PLUTONIUM

ˈfast ˌday *n* [C] a day when you do not eat any food, especially for religious reasons

fas·ten /ˈfɑːsən $ ˈfæ-/ ●●○ *v*
1 CLOTHES/BAG ETC (*also* **fasten up**) **a)** [T] to join together the two sides of a coat, shirt, bag etc so that it is closed SYN **do up** OPP **unfasten**: *'I'm going now,' she said, fastening her coat.* | *Fasten your seat belt.* **b)** [I] to become joined together with buttons, hooks etc SYN **do up**: *I was so fat that my skirt wouldn't fasten.*

REGISTER
In everyday British English, people usually say **do up** rather than **fasten**: ***Do up*** *your jacket – it's cold.*

2 WINDOW/GATE ETC [I,T] to firmly close a window, gate etc so that it will not open, or to become firmly closed OPP **unfasten**: *Make sure all the windows are securely fastened before you leave.*
3 ATTACH STH TO STH [T] to attach something firmly to

another object or surface: **fasten sth with sth** *Fasten the edges of the cloth together with pins.* | **fasten sth to sth** *They fastened the rope to a tree.*
4 HOLD STH TIGHTLY [I,T] to hold something firmly with your hands, legs, arms, or teeth: **fasten sth around/round sth** *She fastened her arms around his neck.* | **[+around/round]** *A strong hand fastened round her wrist.* | **[+on/onto]** *Their long claws allow them to fasten onto the rocks and hold firm.*
5 fasten your eyes/gaze on sb/sth to look at someone or something for a long time: *He rose, his eyes still fastened on the piece of paper.*
6 fasten your attention on sb/sth to think a lot about one particular thing or person: *He was working quietly, all his attention fastened on the task.*

GRAMMAR

Fasten belongs to a group of verbs where the same noun can be the subject of the verb or its object.
- You can say: *You fasten the dress at the back.* In this sentence, 'the dress' is the object of **fasten**.
- You can say: *The dress fastens at the back.* In this sentence, 'the dress' is the subject of **fasten**.

GRAMMAR GUIDE ▸ VERBS

fasten on/upon sth *phr v* to give particular attention to something because you think it is important or interesting: *My mother fastened on the word 'unsafe'.*
fasten onto sb/sth (*also* **fasten on to sb/sth**) *phr v*
1 to give particular attention to something because you think it is important or interesting
2 to follow someone and stay with them, especially when they do not want you to SYN **latch onto sb**: *The dog seemed lost and fastened onto us.*

FASTENERS

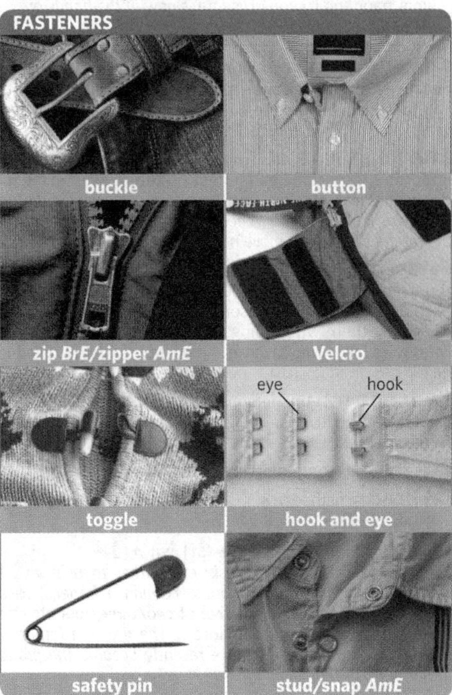

buckle | button | zip *BrE*/zipper *AmE* | Velcro | toggle | hook and eye | safety pin | stud/snap *AmE*

fas·ten·er /ˈfɑːsənə $ ˈfæsənər/ (*also* **fas·ten·ing** /ˈfɑːsənɪŋ $ ˈfæ-/) *n* [C] **1** something that you use to join something together, such as a button on a piece of clothing: *shoes with velcro fasteners* **2** something that is used to keep a door, window etc firmly shut SYN **latch**

ˈfast food *n* [U] food such as HAMBURGERS which is prepared quickly and that you can take away with you

ˌfast-ˈforward *v* [I,T] **1** to wind a tape or video forwards quickly in a machine without playing it **2** to move quickly to a later point in a story: **[+to]** *Fast-forward to York at the turn of the century.* —**fast-forward** *n* [U]

fas·tid·i·ous /fæˈstɪdiəs/ *adj* very careful about small details in your appearance, work etc SYN **meticulous**: *people who are fastidious about personal hygiene* —**fastidiously** *adv* —**fastidiousness** *n* [U]

ˈfast lane *n* **1 the fast lane** *informal* an exciting way of life that involves dangerous and expensive activities: *Brenda is a lady who loves* ***life in the fast lane***. **2** [C usually singular] the part of a big road where people drive fastest OPP **slow lane**: *I broke down in the fast lane of the M6.*

fast·ness /ˈfɑːstnəs $ ˈfæst-/ *n* [C] *literary* a place that is safe because it is difficult to reach SYN **stronghold**: *mountain fastnesses*

ˈfast track *n* [singular] the fast track to something is the fastest way of achieving it: *Many saw independence as the fast track to democracy.*

ˈfast-track¹ *adj* [only before noun] happening or making progress more quickly than is usual: *a fast-track procedure for adoption*

ˈfast-track² *v* [T] to help something happen or make progress more quickly than usual: *Your application can be fast-tracked for a fee.*

fat¹ /fæt/ ●●● S1 W2 *adj* (*comparative* **fatter**, *superlative* **fattest**)
1 FLESH weighing too much because you have too much flesh on your body OPP **thin**: *Are you suggesting I'm too fat?* | *a short fat man in his early fifties* | *You'll* ***get fat*** *if you eat all that chocolate.* | *He looks much fatter than in his photo.*
2 OBJECT thick or wide OPP **thin**: *Dobbs was smoking a fat cigar.* | *a big fat book* → see picture at THICK
3 MONEY [only before noun] *informal* containing or worth a large amount of money: *a* ***fat cheque*** | *Of course the supermarkets' aim is to make* ***fat profits***.
4 fat chance *informal* used to say that something is very unlikely to happen: **[+of]** *'You can go to bed now and sleep easy.' 'Fat chance of that!'*
5 (a) fat lot of good/use *spoken* not at all useful or helpful: *Fat lot of use you are in the kitchen.*
6 fat cat *informal* someone who has too much money, especially someone who is paid too much for their job - used to show disapproval: *the fat cats at the top who have recently been given obscene pay increases*
7 in fat city *AmE old-fashioned* having plenty of money
8 grow fat on sth to become rich because of something - used to show disapproval: *The finance men had grown fat on managing other people's money.*
9 a fat lip *informal* a lip that is swollen because it has been hit: *My friend was badly injured with bruised ribs and a fat lip.*
10 APPROVAL *informal* another spelling of PHAT - used to show approval, especially of someone or something that is fashionable, interesting, or attractive: **fat/phat beats** (=music that sounds good) *Check out these fat beats.*
—**fatness** *n* [U]: *a rise in fatness in children*

THESAURUS

fat having too much flesh on your body. It is rude to tell someone that they are fat. It is also better not to use any of these words when talking directly to someone about their body: *She thinks she's fat.* | *He looks the same, just a little fatter.*
overweight weighing more than you should: *Many medical conditions are caused by being overweight.* | *She was several kilos overweight.*
big/large used when saying that someone has a big body. **Large** is more common than **big** in written English: *My father was a big man.* | *two large ladies*
obese extremely fat in a way that is dangerous to your health: *He went to a summer camp for obese teenagers.*
chubby slightly fat in a nice-looking way - used especially about babies and children: *A chubby little baby was playing on the rug.*

plump a woman or child who is plump is slightly fat, especially in a pleasant way: *Her mother was a plump cheerful woman.*
flabby having soft loose skin that looks unattractive: *a flabby stomach | Her body was getting old and flabby.*
portly *literary* fat and round – used especially about fairly old men: *The bishop was a portly middle-aged gentleman.*

fat² ●●● S2 W2 *n*
1 [U] a substance that is stored under the skin of people and animals, that helps to keep them warm: *Rolls of fat bulged over his collar. | I didn't like the meat – there was too much fat on it.*
2 [C,U] an oily substance contained in certain foods: *Cream has a high* ***fat content****.* | **high/low in fat** *This cheese is relatively low in fat. | You should think about reducing your* ***fat intake*** (=the amount of fat you eat). | **high-fat/low-fat** *a low-fat diet* → SATURATED FAT
3 [C,U] an oily substance taken from animals or plants and used in cooking: *Place the chicken in the hot fat.*
4 the fat is in the fire used to say that there will be trouble because of something that has happened
5 live off the fat of the land to get enough money to live comfortably without doing much work
6 run to fat to start to become fat, especially because you are getting older or do not do much exercise → **chew the fat** at CHEW¹(4), → PUPPY FAT

fa·tal /ˈfeɪtl/ ●●○ *adj*
1 resulting in someone's death: *potentially fatal diseases* | **fatal accident/illness/injury etc** *a fatal climbing accident | If it is not treated correctly, the condition can* ***prove fatal*** (=be fatal).
2 having a very bad effect, especially making someone fail or stop what they are doing: **[+to]** *Disunity finally* ***proved fatal*** *to the rebels' cause. | There was one* ***fatal flaw*** (=serious weakness) *in his argument. | His presidential hopes suffered a* ***fatal blow*** *in New Hampshire.* | **fatal mistake/error** *Telling your employees they're unimportant is a fatal error.*

fa·tal·is·m /ˈfeɪtl-ɪzəm/ *n* [U] the belief that there is nothing you can do to prevent events from happening → **fate** —**fatalist** *n* [C]

fa·tal·is·tic /ˌfeɪtlˈɪstɪk◂/ *adj* believing that there is nothing you can do to prevent events from happening → **fate**: *a fatalistic approach to life* —**fatalistically** /-kli/ *adv*

fa·tal·i·ty /fəˈtæləti/ *n* (*plural* **fatalities**) **1** [C] a death in an accident or a violent attack: *a 50% increase in the number of traffic fatalities* **2** [U] *formal* the fact that a disease is certain to cause death: *The most serious form of skin cancer has a 30 percent fatality rate.* **3** [U] *formal* the feeling that you cannot control what happens to you

fa·tal·ly /ˈfeɪtəl-i/ *adv* **1** in a way that causes death: **fatally injured/wounded** *Two officers were fatally injured in the explosion.* **2** in a way that will make something fail or be unable to continue: **fatally flawed/weakened/damaged etc** *Bolton's idea was fatally flawed. | He has been fatally undermined by his own finance minister.*

ˈfat camp *n* [C] *informal* a place where children who are fat go to lose weight and to exercise, especially in the summer

fate /feɪt/ ●○○ *n*
1 [C usually singular] the things that happen to someone or something, especially unpleasant things that end their existence or end a particular period: *I wouldn't wish such a fate on my worst enemy.* | **[+of]** *No one knows what the fate of the hostages will be.* THESAURUS ▸ FUTURE
2 [U] a power that is believed to control what happens in people's lives: *Fate plays cruel tricks sometimes.* | **a twist/quirk of fate** (=something unexpected that happens) *By a* ***strange twist of fate****, Smith's first match is against the team that gave him the sack last season.*
3 a fate worse than death something terrible that might happen to you – often used humorously: *He had rescued an innocent girl from a fate worse than death.* → **tempt fate** at TEMPT(3)

COLLOCATIONS

VERBS

suffer a fate *We must prevent other children from suffering the same fate.*
meet a fate *The beautiful old building met a sad fate when it was sold off to property developers.*
decide/settle sb's/sth's fate *The meeting will decide the fate of the factory.*
seal sb's fate (=make it certain that something bad will happen to someone, especially that they will die) *Engine failure sealed the pilot's fate.*
leave/abandon sb to their fate (=leave someone in a bad situation) | **discover/find out sb's fate** | **resign yourself to/accept your fate** | **a fate awaits sb** *formal* (=a fate will happen to someone) | **a fate befalls sb** *formal* (=someone suffers a particular fate)

ADJECTIVES

the same fate *He did not intend to meet the same fate as his companion.*
a similar fate *The project suffered a similar fate to many of its predecessors.*
sb's ultimate fate (=what finally happens to someone) *The ultimate fate of the refugees is in our hands.*
a terrible/horrible/grim fate *The crew of the ship met a terrible fate.*
a sad/tragic fate | **a cruel fate** | **an uncertain fate** (=not clear, definite, or decided)

PHRASES

your fate is in sb's hands (=someone will decide what happens to you) *His fate is now in the hands of the judge.*

fat·ed /ˈfeɪtɪd/ *adj* certain to happen or to do something because a mysterious force is controlling events SYN **destined**: **be fated to do sth** *I'm fated to spend my last years in an old folks' home.* → ILL-FATED

fate·ful /ˈfeɪtfəl/ *adj* [usually before noun] having an important, especially bad, effect on future events: **fateful day/night/year etc** *The goalkeeper on that fateful day in 1954 was Fred Martin. | When his rent was raised, he made the fateful decision to move north.* —**fatefully** *adv*

Fates, the /feɪts/ in Greek and Roman MYTHOLOGY, the three goddesses who decided what should happen in each person's life. People sometimes say the Fates are for or against them when things are going well or badly: *The Fates were conspiring to make it impossible for him to win the race.*

ˈfat farm *n* [C] *AmE informal* a place where people who are fat can go to lose weight and improve their health → HEALTH FARM

ˌfat-ˈfree *adj* containing no fat: *fat-free yoghurt*

fat·head /ˈfæthed/ *n* [C] *informal* a stupid person SYN **idiot** —**ˌfat-ˈheaded** *adj*

fa·ther¹ /ˈfɑːðə $ -ər/ ●●● S1 W1 *n* [C]
1 PARENT a male parent: *Ask your father to help you. | Andrew was very excited about becoming a father. | He's been like a father to me.* | **a father of two/three/four etc** (=a man with two, three etc children) *The driver, a father of four, escaped uninjured. | Steve recently became the proud father of a 7lb 12oz baby girl.*
2 PRIEST **Father** a priest, especially in the Roman Catholic Church: *I have sinned, Father. | Father Devlin* → HOLY FATHER
3 fathers [plural] people related to you who lived a long time ago SYN **ancestors**: *Our fathers were exiles from their native land.* → FOREFATHER
4 GOD **Father** a way of talking to or talking about God, used in the Christian religion: *our* ***Heavenly Father***
5 the father of sth the man who was responsible for starting something: *Freud is the father of psychoanalysis.*
6 from father to son if property or skill passes from father to son, children receive it or learn it from their parents:

This is a district where old crafts are handed down from father to son.
7 like father like son used to say that a boy behaves like his father, especially when this behaviour is bad
8 a bit of how's your father *BrE informal* the act of having sex – used humorously → CITY FATHERS, FOUNDING FATHER
father[2] *v* [T] **1** to become the father of a child by making a woman PREGNANT: *Hodgkins fathered seven children.* **2** *formal* to start an important new idea or system: *Bevan fathered the concept of the National Health Service.*
father sth **on** sb *phr v BrE formal* to claim that someone is responsible for something when they are not: *A collection of Irish stories was fathered on him.*
ˌFather 'Christmas *n* [singular] *BrE* an imaginary man who wears red clothes, has a long white beard, and is said to bring presents to children at Christmas SYN **Santa Claus**
'father ˌfigure *n* [C] an older man who you trust and respect: **[+to/for]** *Ken was a father figure to all of us.*
fa·ther·hood /ˈfɑːðəhʊd $ -ðər-/ *n* [U] the state of being a father SYN **paternity**: *The idea of fatherhood frightens me.*
fa·ther·ing /ˈfɑːðərɪŋ/ *n* [U] the skills and activities involved in being a father → **mothering**: *Don't get me wrong, fathering certainly has changed.*
'father-in-ˌlaw ●●○ *n* (*plural* **fathers-in-law**) [C] the father of your husband or wife
fa·ther·land /ˈfɑːðəlænd $ -ðər-/ *n* [singular] the place where someone or their family was born → MOTHER COUNTRY, MOTHERLAND
fa·ther·ly /ˈfɑːðəli $ -ðər-/ *adj* [only before noun] kind and gentle in a way that is considered typical of a good father → **motherly**: *He took my arm in a fatherly way.* | *fatherly advice*
'Father's Day *n* [C] a day on which people give cards and presents to their father
fath·om[1] /ˈfæðəm/ *n* [C] a unit for measuring the depth of water, equal to six feet or about 1.8 metres
fathom[2] (*also* **fathom out**) *v* [T] to understand what something means after thinking about it carefully SYN **work out**: *I still can't fathom out what she meant.* | **[+how/why/where etc]** *Mark couldn't fathom why she resented him so much.* THESAURUS ▸ UNDERSTAND
fath·om·less /ˈfæðəmləs/ *adj literary* impossible to measure or understand: *the fathomless depths of the sea*
fa·tigue /fəˈtiːɡ/ ●○○ *n*
1 [U] very great tiredness SYN **exhaustion**: **with fatigue** *Sam's face was grey with fatigue.* | **from fatigue** *He's suffering from physical and mental fatigue.*
2 [U] *technical* a weakness in metal or wood, caused when it is bent or stretched many times, which is likely to make it break: ***metal fatigue***
3 fatigues [plural] loose-fitting army clothes
fa·tigued /fəˈtiːɡd/ *adj formal* extremely tired SYN **exhausted**: *Sara looked white and fatigued.*
fa·tigu·ing /fəˈtiːɡɪŋ/ *adj formal* extremely tiring SYN **exhausting**
fat·so /ˈfætsəʊ $ -soʊ/ *n* (*plural* **fatsoes**) [C] *informal* an insulting word for someone who is fat
'fat tax *n* [C] *informal* a tax on foods that are likely to make people fat
fat·ted /ˈfætɪd/ *adj* → **kill the fatted calf** at KILL[1](15)
fat·ten /ˈfætn/ *v* **1** [I,T] to make an animal become fatter so that it is ready to eat, or to become fat and ready to eat **2** [T] to make an amount larger: *These projects simply serve to fatten the pockets of developers.*
fatten sb/sth ↔ **up** *phr v* to make a person or animal fatter: *My parents are always trying to fatten me up.*
fat·ten·ing /ˈfætn-ɪŋ/ ●○○ *adj* likely to make you fat: *Fats are the most fattening foods of all.*
fat·tist /ˈfætɪst/ *adj informal* having or showing unkind attitudes towards people who are fat: *fattist jokes*
fat·ty[1] /ˈfæti/ *adj* containing a lot of fat: *fatty foods*
fatty[2] *n* (*plural* **fatties**) [C] *informal* an insulting word for someone who is fat
ˌfatty 'acid *n* [C] *technical* an acid that the cells in your body need to use food effectively
fat·u·ous /ˈfætʃuəs/ *adj* very silly or stupid SYN **idiotic**: *fatuous questions* —**fatuously** *adv* —**fatuousness** *n* [U]
fat·wa /ˈfætwɑː/ *n* [C] an official order made by an important Islamic religious leader
fau·cet /ˈfɔːsɪt $ ˈfɒː-/ ●●○ *n* [C] *AmE* the thing that you turn on and off to control the flow of water from a pipe SYN **tap** *BrE*
fault[1] /fɔːlt $ fɒːlt/ ●●● S2 W3 *n* [C]
1 RESPONSIBLE FOR MISTAKE if something bad that has happened is your fault, you should be blamed for it, because you made a mistake or failed to do something: *I'm really sorry – it's all my fault.* | **be sb's fault (that)** *It's your fault we're late.* | *I didn't sleep well that night, but it was my* ***own fault***. | **be sb's fault for doing sth** *It's my fault for not making your new job clearer.*
2 at fault if someone is at fault, they are responsible for something bad that has happened: *The police said that the other driver was at fault.* | *Some people claim that it is the UN that is at fault.*
3 STH WRONG WITH STH **a)** something that is wrong with a machine, system, design etc, which prevents it from working properly: *a design fault* | **[+in]** *It sounds as if there's a fault in one of the loudspeakers.* **b)** something that is wrong with something, which could be improved SYN **flaw**: *There are two serious faults in Hobsbawm's discussion of nationalism.* | ***For all*** *its* ***faults*** (=in spite of its faults) *we love this city.* **c)** a mistake in the way that something was made, which spoils its appearance: **[+in]** *The sweater had a fault in it and I had to take it back.*
4 SB'S CHARACTER a bad or weak part of someone's character: *His worst fault is his arrogance.* | *I may* ***have*** *my* ***faults***, *but ingratitude is not one of them.* | ***For all*** *his* ***faults*** (=in spite of his faults) *he was a good father.*
5 through no fault of her/my etc own used to say that something bad that happened to someone was not caused by them: *Through no fault of our own we are currently two players short.*
6 CRACK a large crack in the rocks that form the Earth's surface: *the San Andreas fault*
7 generous/loyal/honest etc to a fault extremely generous, loyal etc: *Barry's kind, caring and generous to a fault.*
8 TENNIS a mistake made when a player is SERVING the ball in tennis → DOUBLE FAULT, LOYAL, → **find fault with sb/sth** at FIND[1](14)

THESAURUS – MEANING 3
SOMETHING WRONG

fault a problem in a machine, system, design etc that causes damage or makes it not work properly: *The fire was caused by an electrical fault.* | *a fault in the engine*
defect a fault in something such as a product or machine, resulting from the way it was made or designed: *Cars are tested for defects before they leave the factory.*
weakness a part of a plan, system, or argument that is not as good as the other parts, and makes it likely to fail: *What are the strengths and weaknesses of each method?*
flaw a fault in a plan, system, argument etc, especially one that makes it useless or not effective: *Your argument has a fundamental flaw.* | *There was one major flaw in his suggestion – we didn't have enough money.*
bug a fault in a computer program: *A bug in the system was quickly fixed.*
glitch a small fault in the way something works, that can usually be easily corrected: *I noticed a small glitch when installing the software.*
mistake something that is wrong in someone's spelling, grammar, calculations etc: *The article was full of spelling mistakes.*

there's something wrong with sth used when saying that there is a problem in a machine, car etc, but you do not know what it is: *There's something wrong with the computer – it won't close down.*

fault² *v* [T] to criticize someone or something for a mistake: **be faulted on/for sth** *The judge **cannot be faulted** on his decision.* | **it is hard/difficult to fault sb/sth** *You might not like O'Donnel's arrogance, but it's hard to fault what he does on the field.*

fault·less /ˈfɔːltləs $ ˈfɒːlt-/ *adj* having no mistakes SYN **perfect**: *a faultless performance* —**faultlessly** *adv*

ˈfault-ˌtolerant *adj* **fault-tolerant computer/machine** a computer or machine that continues working even if it has a fault or when there is a fault in a program

fault·y /ˈfɔːlti $ ˈfɒːlti/ ●○○ *adj*
1 not working properly, or not made correctly: *Customers may ask for a refund if the goods are faulty.* | *a faulty gene that causes breast cancer*
2 a faulty way of thinking about something contains a mistake, so that you make a wrong decision OPP **correct**: *an idea based on a faulty understanding of biology*

faun /fɔːn $ fɒːn/ *n* [C] an ancient Roman god with the body of a man and the legs and horns of a goat

fau·na /ˈfɔːnə $ ˈfɒː-/ *n* [C,U] *technical* all the animals living in a particular area or period in history → FLORA

fauv·is·m /ˈfəʊvɪzəm $ ˈfoʊ-/ *n* [U] a style of painting that uses pure bright colours, which was developed in the early 20th century

faux /fəʊ $ foʊ/ *adj* [only before noun] *especially AmE* artificial, but made to look real SYN **false**: *faux pearls*

faux pas /ˌfəʊ ˈpɑː, ˈfəʊ pɑː $ ˌfoʊ ˈpɑː/ *n* (*plural* **faux pas** /-ˈpɑːz/) [C] an embarrassing mistake in a social situation

F

fa·va bean /ˈfɑːvə biːn/ *n* [C] *AmE* a large flat pale green bean SYN **broad bean** *BrE*

fave /feɪv/ *n* [C] *informal* a favourite person or thing: *a band that's a college fave* —**fave** *adj*

fav·i·con /ˈfævɪkɒn $ -kɑːn/ *n* [C] a small square image that is a sign for a website, for example in a list of favourite websites

fa·vor /ˈfeɪvə $ -ər/ *n, v* the American spelling of FAVOUR

fa·vor·a·ble /ˈfeɪvərəbəl/ *adj* the American spelling of FAVOURABLE

fa·vored /ˈfeɪvəd $ -vərd/ *adj* the American spelling of FAVOURED

fa·vo·rite /ˈfeɪvərət/ *adj, n* [C] the American spelling of FAVOURITE

fa·vo·rit·is·m /ˈfeɪvərətɪzəm/ *n* [U] the American spelling of FAVOURITISM

fa·vour¹ *BrE*, **favor** *AmE* /ˈfeɪvə $ -ər/ ●●● S2 W3 *n*
1 HELP [C] something that you do for someone in order to help them or be kind to them: *Could you **do** me **a favour** and tell Kelly I can't make it?* | *He hired John **as a favour to** his father.* | *Paul, can I **ask** you **a favor**?* | *I **owed** him **a favour** so I couldn't say no.* | *She helps me out when I have too much to do, and I **return the favour** when I can.* | ***Do yourself a favour** and make sure you get some time to yourself.*
2 SUPPORT/APPROVAL [U] support, approval, or agreement for something such as a plan, idea, or system: **in favour of sth** *Senior ministers spoke in favour of the proposal.* | *I talked to Susie about it, and she's **all in favor*** (=completely approves) *of going.* | **find/gain/win favour** *The idea may find favor with older people.* | **in sb/sth's favour** *The vote was 60–59 in the government's favor.* | *In Sweden and other countries, nuclear power has **lost favor**.* | **look on/view/regard sth with favour** *formal* (=support something, and want to help it succeed) *Employers are more likely to look with favour on experienced candidates.* | ***All in favour*** (=used when asking people to vote on something by raising a hand)? | **vote/decide in favour of sth** (=vote or decide to support something) *288 members voted in favor of the ban.* | **find/rule in favour of sb** *formal* (=make a legal decision that supports someone)
3 POPULAR/UNPOPULAR [U] when someone or something is liked or approved of by people, or not liked or approved of: **be in favour (with sb)** *The island is very much in favour as a holiday destination.* | **be out of favour (with sb)** *The stock is currently out of favor with investors.* | **find/gain/win favour** *Radcliffe's books began to find favour with the reading public.* | **come/be back in favour** (=become popular again) *Fountain pens have come back in favour.* | **fall/go out of favour** (=stop being approved of) *Grammar-based teaching methods went out of favour in the 60s and 70s.*
4 ADVANTAGE **in sb's favour** if something is in someone's favour, it gives them an advantage over someone else: *Conditions on court are very much in Williams' favour.* | *The new rules should actually **work in your favor**.* | *Duncan **had** his height and weight **in his favour** during the fight.* | **the odds are (stacked) in sb's favour** (=someone has a big advantage)
5 CHOOSE STH INSTEAD **do sth in favour of sth** if you decide not to use one thing in favour of another, you choose the other one because you think it is better: *Plans for a tunnel were rejected in favour of a bridge.*
6 do sb/sth no favours, not do sb/sth any favours to do something that makes someone or something look worse than they are, or that does not help at all: *Low interest rates don't do savers any favours.*
7 UNFAIR SUPPORT [U] support that is given to one person or group and not to others, in a way that does not seem fair: *Teachers should not **show favour to** any pupil.*
8 do me/us a favour! *BrE spoken* used when you are annoyed because someone has asked a silly question or done something to upset people: *Do us a favour, Mike, and shut up!* | *'Did you like it?' 'Do me a favour!'*
9 GIFT [C] *AmE* a PARTY FAVOR
10 SEX **favours** [plural] *old-fashioned* when you allow someone to have sex with you: *She shared her **sexual favors** with many men.* → **curry favour (with sb)** at CURRY², → **without fear or favour** at FEAR¹(6), → **be thankful/grateful for small favours** at SMALL¹(13)

favour² *BrE*, **favor** *AmE* ●●○ W3 *v* [T]
1 PREFER to prefer someone or something to other things or people, especially when there are several to choose from: *Both countries seem to favour the agreement.* | *loose clothing of the type favoured in Arab countries* | **favour sb/sth over sb/sth** *Florida voters favored Bush over Gore by a very small margin.*
2 GIVE AN ADVANTAGE to treat someone much better than someone else, in a way that is not fair: *a tax cut that favours rich people* | **favour sb over sb** *a judicial system that favours men over women*
3 HELP to provide suitable conditions for something to happen: *The current economy does not favour the development of small businesses.*
4 be favoured to do sth to be expected to win or be the one that is successful: *Silva is favoured to win a medal in the marathon.*
5 LOOK LIKE *old-fashioned* to look like one of your parents or grandparents
favour sb **with** sth *phr v formal* to give someone something such as a look or reply: *McIntosh favoured her with a smile.*

fa·vour·a·ble *BrE*, **favorable** *AmE* /ˈfeɪvərəbəl/ ●○○ *adj*
1 a favourable report, opinion, or reaction shows that you think that someone or something is good or that you agree with them: *favourable film reviews* | *The response has been overwhelmingly favorable.*
2 suitable and likely to make something happen or succeed: *The disease spreads quickly under **favourable conditions**.* | **[+for/to]** *a financial environment that is favorable to job creation*
3 if a LOAN, agreement, rate etc is favourable, the conditions of it are reasonable and not too expensive or difficult: *a favourable interest rate* | *the **favorable terms** of the settlement*
4 making people like or approve of someone or something: *A smart appearance makes a **favourable impression** at an interview.* —**favourably** *adv*

fa·voured *BrE*, **favored** *AmE* /ˈfeɪvəd $ -ərd/ *adj* [only before noun] **1** receiving special attention, help, or treatment, sometimes in an unfair way: *favoured customers | China's* ***most-favored-nation*** *trading status with the US* **2** chosen or preferred by many people SYN **popular**: *Brittany is a favoured holiday destination for families.* **3** a favoured team, player etc is one that is expected to win → **favourite**: **be favoured to do sth** *Silva is favoured to win a medal in the marathon.* **4** having desirable qualities SYN **desirable**: *a house in a favoured position on a hill*

fa·vou·rite¹ BrE, **favorite** AmE /ˈfeɪvərət/ ●●● S2 W2 *adj* [only before noun]
1 your favourite person or thing is the one that you like the most: *a child's favourite toy | What's your favourite colour? | a favorite spot for picnickers*
2 favourite son a politician, sports player etc who is popular with people in the place that they come from

favourite² BrE, **favorite** AmE ●●● S2 W2 *n* [C]
1 something that you like more than other things of the same kind: *Can we have strawberries? They're my favourite.* | **an old/firm/particular favourite** *a sweater that's an old favorite* | **[+with]** *Dahl's books are firm favourites with children.*
2 someone who is liked and treated better than others by a teacher or parent: *You always were Dad's favourite.* | **play favorites** AmE (=treat one person better than others) *The manager insisted he doesn't play favorites.* → FAVOURITISM
3 the team, player etc that is expected to win a race or competition: **favourite to do sth** *Italy were the favourites to win the World Cup. | He was the* ***hot favourite*** *for the Booker Prize.*
4 favourites [plural] a list of your favourite websites on your BROWSER: *Put our website in your favourites.*

favourite³ BrE, **favorite** AmE *v* [T] to mark a website as a favourite on your BROWSER: *Favourite our website and keep checking for the latest bargains!*

fa·vou·ri·tis·m BrE, **favoritism** AmE /ˈfeɪvərətɪzəm/ *n* [U] when you treat one person or group better than others, in an unfair way → **favourite**: *their favouritism towards their first son*

fawn¹ /fɔːn $ fɒːn/ *n* **1** [C] a young DEER **2** [U] a pale yellow-brown colour

fawn² *adj* having a pale yellow-brown colour

fawn³ *v* [I] to praise someone and be friendly to them in an insincere way, because you want them to like you or give you something: **[+on/over]** *I refused to fawn over her or flatter her.* —**fawning** *adj*

fax¹ /fæks/ *n* **1** [C] a letter or message that is sent in electronic form down a telephone line and then printed using a special machine: *Did you get my fax?* **2** [C] (*also* **fax machine**) a machine used for sending and receiving faxes: *What's your fax number?* **3** [U] the system of sending letters and messages using a fax machine: **by fax** *You can book tickets by fax or online.*

fax² *v* [T] to send someone a letter or message using a fax machine: **fax sb sth** *She asked me to fax her the details.* | **fax sth (through/on) to sb** *The contract should be faxed to him today.*

fay /feɪ/ *n* [C] *literary* a FAIRY(1) - used especially in poetry

faze /feɪz/ *v* [T] *informal* if a new or difficult situation fazes you, it makes you feel confused or shocked, so that you do not know what to do: *John was embarrassed, but it didn't faze Mike a bit.*

FBI, the /ˌef biː ˈaɪ/ (***the Federal Bureau of Investigation***) the police department in the US that is controlled by the central government, and that deals with crimes that break national laws rather than state laws → **CIA**

FC /ˌef ˈsiː/ BrE the abbreviation of ***football club***, used in the names of teams: *Liverpool FC*

FCO, the /ˌef siː ˈəʊ/ (***the Foreign and Commonwealth Office***) the official name of the British Foreign Office

FDA, the /ˌef diː ˈeɪ/ (***the Food and Drug Administration***) a US government organization which makes sure that foods and drugs are safe enough to be sold. It decides which chemicals can legally be added to food, which medical drugs are safe, and how information about food and drugs should be shown on containers.

FE /ˌef ˈiː/ *n* [U] BrE the abbreviation of ***further education***

fe·al·ty /ˈfiːəlti/ *n* [U] *old-fashioned* loyalty to a king, queen etc

fear¹ /fɪə $ fɪr/ ●●● S3 W1 *n*
1 [C,U] the feeling you get when you are afraid or worried that something bad is going to happen: **[+of]** *a fear of flying* | **[+that]** *There are fears that share prices could decrease still further.* | **[+for]** *The girl's parents expressed fears for her safety.* | **in fear** *The children looked at her in fear.* | **without fear** *People must be able to express their views without fear of criticism.*
2 for fear (that), for fear of sth because you are worried that you will make something happen: *She finally ran away for fear that he would kill her.* | **for fear of doing sth** *He got to the station early, for fear of missing her.*
3 no fear! BrE *informal* used humorously to say that you are definitely not going to do something: *'Are you going to Bill's party tonight?' 'No fear!'*
4 [U] the possibility or danger that something bad might happen: ***There's no fear of*** *revolt now.*
5 put the fear of God into sb *informal* to make someone feel that they must do something, by making sure they know what will happen if they do not do it: *The Italian manager must have put the fear of God into his team.*
6 without fear or favour BrE *formal* in a fair way: *The law must be enforced without fear or favour.*

COLLOCATIONS

ADJECTIVES

sb's worst/greatest fear *Her worst fear was never seeing her children again.*
an irrational fear (=one that is not reasonable) *He grew up with an irrational fear of insects.*
a deep-seated fear (=very strong and difficult to change) | **groundless** (=without any reason)

VERBS

conquer/overcome your fear (=stop being afraid) *She managed to conquer her fear of flying.*
shake/tremble with fear *He was shaking with fear after being held at gunpoint.*
be gripped by fear (=be very afraid) *We were gripped by fear as the boat was tossed around by the waves.*
be paralysed with fear (=be so afraid that you cannot move) | **confirm sb's fears** (=show that what you were afraid of has actually happened) | **ease/allay/dispel sb's fears** (=help someone stop being afraid)

PHRASES

be in fear of/for your life (=be afraid that you may be killed) *Celia was in fear of her life when she saw the truck coming toward her.*
be full of fear *The residents are too full of fear to leave their houses.*
be/live in fear of sth (=be always afraid of something) *They were constantly in fear of an enemy attack.*
have no fear of sth *He had no fear of death.*
sb's hopes and fears

COMMON ERRORS

⚠ Do not say that someone 'has fear'. Say that someone **is frightened** or **is afraid**.

THESAURUS

fear a feeling of being frightened: *He was trembling with fear. | Fear of failure should not stop you trying.*
terror a feeling of great fear, because you think that something terrible is about to happen: *She let out a scream of pure terror.*
fright a sudden feeling of fear, or a situation that makes you feel this: *My body was shaking with fright. | You gave me a fright!*

F

panic a sudden feeling of fear or nervousness that makes you unable to think clearly or behave sensibly: *She was in such a panic that she hardly knew what she was doing!*
alarm a feeling of fear or worry which shows in your voice or behaviour, because you think something bad might happen: *When I mentioned her name, he looked up at me in alarm.* | *The streets were calm and there was no sign of alarm.*
foreboding /fɔːˈbəʊdɪŋ $ fɔːrˈboʊ-/ a feeling that something bad or unpleasant might happen although there is no obvious reason why it should: *She felt the same sense of foreboding she had before her father died.*
phobia /ˈfəʊbiə $ ˈfoʊ-/ a permanent strong unreasonable fear of something: *I had a phobia about going to the dentist.*

fear² ●●○ W2 *v*
1 [I,T] to feel afraid or worried that something bad may happen: *Fearing violence, the group asked for police protection.* | **fear (that)** *Police fear that there may be further terrorist attacks.* | **fear to do sth** *formal*: *Women feared to go out at night.* | **fear for sb** *His wife seemed depressed, and he feared for his children.* | **fear for sb's safety/life** *a terrifying ordeal in which she feared for her life* | *Hundreds of people are* ***feared dead*** *in the ferry disaster.*

GRAMMAR
In more formal English, you say **it is feared that** something is true: *It is feared that the child has been abducted.*

2 fear the worst to think that the worst possible thing has happened or might happen: *When Tom heard about the accident he immediately feared the worst.*
3 [T] to be afraid of someone and what they might do: *As a leader, he was distrusted and even feared.*
4 I fear *formal* used when telling someone that you think that something bad has happened or is true: **I fear (that)** *I fear that there is little more we can do.* | **I fear so/I fear not** *'Were they satisfied?' 'I fear not.'*
5 fear not/never fear *formal* used to tell someone not to worry: *Never fear, he'll be with us soon.* → GOD-FEARING

fear·ful /ˈfɪəfəl $ ˈfɪr-/ ●○○ *adj*
1 *formal* frightened that something bad might happen: *a shy and fearful child* | **[+of]** *People are fearful of rising crime in the area.* | **fearful that** *Officials are fearful that the demonstrations will cause new violence.* THESAURUS ▸ FRIGHTENED
2 *BrE* extremely bad SYN **awful**, **terrible**: *The room was in a fearful mess.*
3 [only before noun] *written* very frightening SYN **terrifying**: *a fearful creature* —**fearfulness** *n* [U]

fear·ful·ly /ˈfɪəfəli $ ˈfɪr-/ *adv* **1** in a way that shows you are afraid: *She glanced fearfully over her shoulder.* **2** [+adj/adv] *BrE old-fashioned* extremely: *She's fearfully clever.*

fear·less /ˈfɪələs $ ˈfɪr-/ *adj* not afraid of anything: *These dogs are absolutely fearless.* | *a fearless explorer* THESAURUS ▸ BRAVE —**fearlessly** *adv* —**fearlessness** *n* [U]

fear·some /ˈfɪəsəm $ ˈfɪr-/ *adj* very frightening: *a fearsome weapon*

fea·si·ble /ˈfiːzəbəl/ ●○○ *adj* a plan, idea, or method that is feasible is possible and is likely to work SYN **possible**: *a feasible solution* | **economically/technically/politically etc feasible** *It was no longer financially feasible to keep the community centre open.* THESAURUS ▸ POSSIBLE —**feasibly** *adv* —**feasibility** /ˌfiːzəˈbɪləti/ *n* [U]: *a feasibility study*

feast¹ /fiːst/ ●●○ *n* [C]
1 a large meal where a lot of people celebrate a special occasion → **banquet**: *a* ***wedding feast*** | *The king promised to* ***hold*** *a great* ***feast*** *for all his people.*
2 a very good large meal: *all the ingredients for a spaghetti feast* | **midnight feast** (=a meal eaten secretly at night by children)
3 an occasion when there are a lot of enjoyable things to see or do: **[+for]** *Next week's film festival should be a real feast for cinema-goers.* | *The play is also a* ***visual feast****.*
4 a day or period when there is a religious celebration: *the* ***feast day*** *of St. Francis* → MOVABLE FEAST

feast² ●○○ *v*
1 feast on/upon sth to eat a lot of a particular food with great enjoyment: *We feasted on chicken and roast potatoes.*
2 feast your eyes on sb/sth to look at someone or something with great pleasure: *If you like luxury cars, feast your eyes on these.*
3 [I] to eat and drink a lot to celebrate something

feat /fiːt/ ●○○ *n* [C] something that is an impressive achievement, because it needs a lot of skill, strength etc to do: **remarkable/considerable/incredible etc feat** *They climbed the mountain in 28 days, a remarkable feat.* | **[+of]** *an incredible feat of engineering* | **perform/accomplish/achieve a feat** *the woman who performed the feat of sailing around the world alone* | **no mean feat** (=something that is difficult to do) *It is no mean feat to perform such a difficult piece.*

feath·er¹ /ˈfeðə $ -ər/ ●●○ *n* [C]
1 one of the light soft things that cover a bird's body: *an ostrich feather* | **feather bed/pillow etc** (=a bed etc that is filled with feathers)
2 a feather in your cap something you have done that you should be proud of → **light as a feather** at LIGHT²(4), → **birds of a feather** at BIRD(5), → **ruffle sb's feathers** at RUFFLE¹(2)

feather² *v* [T] **1 feather your nest** to get money by dishonest methods **2** to put feathers on an ARROW → **tar and feather sb** at TAR²(3)

ˌfeather ˈbedding *n* [U] the practice of letting workers keep their jobs even if they are not needed or do not work well

ˌfeather ˈboa *n* [C] a long SCARF made of feathers and worn around a woman's neck

feath·er·brained /ˈfeðəbreɪnd $ -ər-/ *adj* extremely silly

ˌfeather ˈduster *n* [C] a stick with feathers on the end that you use to remove dust

feath·ered /ˈfeðəd $ -ərd/ *adj* **1** having feathers, or made from feathers **2 feathered friend** *informal* a bird – used humorously

feath·er·weight /ˈfeðəweɪt $ -ər-/ *n* [C] a BOXER who weighs less than 57.15 kilograms, and who is heavier than a BANTAMWEIGHT but lighter than a LIGHTWEIGHT

feath·er·y /ˈfeðəri/ *adj* looking or feeling light and soft, like a feather: *The plant has feathery leaves.*

fea·ture¹ /ˈfiːtʃə $ -ər/ ●●● S2 W1 AWL *n* [C]
1 a part of something that you notice because it seems important, interesting, or typical: *Air bags are a standard feature in most new cars.* | **[+of]** *An important feature of Van Gogh's paintings is their bright colours.* | *Striped tails are a* ***common feature*** *of many animals.* | *The hotel's only* ***redeeming features*** (=things that make it acceptable) *were that it was cheap and near the city centre.* | **main/important/significant etc feature** *The most distinctive feature of the dinosaurs was their size.* | *One of the* ***distinguishing features*** (=features that are different from other things of the same sort) *of modern banking is its dependence on computers.*
2 a piece of writing about a subject in a newspaper or a magazine, or a special report on television or on the radio: **[+on]** *a feature on holidaying with your dog*
3 [usually plural] a part of someone's face, such as their eyes, nose etc: *He had fine delicate features.* | *Her eyes were her best feature.*
4 a part of the land, especially a part that you can see: *Hedges are an important* ***feature of the landscape*** *in Britain.*
5 a film being shown at a cinema: *There were a couple of short cartoons before the main feature.* | **double feature** (=when two films are shown together)

feature² ●●○ W3 AWL *v*
1 [I,T] to include or show something as a special or important part of something, or to be included as an

important part: *The exhibition features paintings by Picasso.* | *a cruise ship featuring extensive spa facilities* | **[+in]** *A study of language should feature in an English literature course.* | **be featured in sth** *Pupils visited some of the websites featured in the article.* | **feature prominently/strongly/heavily etc** *Violence seems to feature heavily in all of his books.* | **feature sb as sth** *The film featured Brando as the Godfather.*
2 [T] to show a film, play etc: *The Retro Theatre is featuring films by Frank Capra this week.*

'feature creep *n* [U] *informal* the tendency to keep adding extra features onto a piece of electronic equipment, so that the original product gets more complicated and more difficult to use rather than better - used to show disapproval

'feature ˌfilm *n* [C] a full-length film that has a story and is acted by professional actors, and which is usually shown in a cinema

fea·ture·less /ˈfiːtʃələs $ -tʃər-/ *adj* a featureless place has no interesting parts to notice: *featureless plains*

Feb. (*also* **Feb** *BrE*) the written abbreviation of ***February***

fe·brile /ˈfiːbraɪl $ ˈfebrəl/ *adj* **1** *literary* full of nervous excitement or activity: *a febrile imagination* **2** *medical* relating to or caused by a fever

Feb·ru·a·ry /ˈfebruəri, ˈfebjʊri $ ˈfebjueri/ ●●● S2 W2 *n* [C,U] (*written abbreviation* **Feb.**) the second month of the year, between January and March: **next/last February** *Mum died last February.* | **in February** *We can do it in February.* | **on February 6th** *She was allowed home on February 6th.* | **on 6th February** *BrE*: *Francis was born on 6th February 1928.* | **February 6** *AmE*: *I finally arrived February 6.*

fe·ces /ˈfiːsiːz/ *n* [plural] the American spelling of FAECES —**fecal** /ˈfiːkəl/ *adj*

feck·less /ˈfekləs/ *adj* lacking determination, and not achieving anything in your life: *Alice's feckless younger brother* —**fecklessly** *adv* —**fecklessness** *n* [U]

fec·und /ˈfekənd, ˈfiːkənd/ *adj formal* able to produce many children, young animals, or crops SYN **fertile** —**fecundity** /fɪˈkʌndəti/ *n* [U]

fed¹ /fed/ the past tense and past participle of FEED¹ → FED UP

fed² *n* [C] *AmE informal* a police officer in the FBI

fed·e·ral /ˈfedərəl/ ●●● W1 AWL *adj*
1 a federal country or system of government consists of a group of states which control their own affairs, but which are also controlled by a single national government which makes decisions on foreign affairs, defence etc: *Switzerland is a federal republic.*
2 relating to the central government of a country such as the US, rather than the government of one of its states: *federal law* | *federal taxes*

ˌFederal ˌBureau of Invest'igation *n* the FBI

fed·e·ral·is·m /ˈfedərəlɪzəm/ *n* [U] belief in or support for a federal system of government

fed·e·rate /ˈfedəreɪt/ *v* [I + with] if a group of states federate, they join together to form a federation

fed·e·ra·tion /ˌfedəˈreɪʃən/ AWL *n* **1** [C] a group of organizations, clubs, or people that have joined together to form a single group → **confederation**: *the National Federation of Women's Institutes* **2** [C] a group of states that have joined together to form a single group: *the Russian Federation* **3** [U] when groups of people, states etc join together to form a larger group

fe·do·ra /fəˈdɔːrə/ *n* [C] a soft hat with a BRIM that curls upwards slightly

ˌfed 'up *adj informal* annoyed or bored, and wanting something to change: *She felt tired and a bit fed up.* | **[+with]** *I'm really fed up with this constant rain.* | *Anna* ***got fed up*** *with waiting.*

fee /fiː/ ●●● S3 W3 AWL *n* [C] an amount of money that you pay to do something or that you pay to a professional person for their work: *You can use the gym and pool for a fee of £35 a month.* THESAURUS ▸ COST

COLLOCATIONS

ADJECTIVES

small/low *Some companies will sell the items for you, for a small fee.*
high/large/big *The school fees are extremely high.*
a hefty/fat fee *informal* (=a very large fee) *Customers are being charged a hefty fee for their telephone service.*
an annual/a monthly fee | **an entrance/entry fee** (=a fee to enter a place) | **a membership fee** (=a fee to become a member of a club or organization) | **school/college/university fees** | **tuition fees** (=money paid for being taught) | **doctor's/lawyer's/accountant's etc fees** | **legal/medical fees** | **a booking fee** (*also* **a service fee** *AmE*) (=a charge you pay when buying a ticket) | **a licence fee** *BrE* (=the money a television licence costs)

VERBS

charge a fee *The accountant charged a big fee for his services.*
pay a fee *You have to pay a small fee to rent a locker.*

fee·ble /ˈfiːbəl/ ●○○ *adj*
1 extremely weak OPP **strong**: *His voice sounded feeble and far away.* | *She was too feeble to leave her room.* THESAURUS ▸ WEAK
2 not very good or effective SYN **weak**: *a feeble excuse* | *a rather feeble committee*

ˌfeeble-'minded *adj* **1** stupid or not sensible: *a feeble-minded policy* **2** *old use* having much less than average intelligence —**feeble-mindedness** *n* [U]

feed¹ /fiːd/ ●●● S1 W2 *v* (*past tense and past participle* **fed** /fed/)
1 GIVE FOOD [T] **a)** to give food to a person or animal: *Have you fed the cat?* | **feed yourself** *She was too weak to feed herself.* | **feed sth to sb** *Several children were feeding bread to the ducks.* | **feed sb on/with sth** *They were fed well on her mother's home cooking.* **b)** to provide enough food for a group of people: *groceries to feed a family of five* | *The prison is required to feed and clothe the prisoners.*
2 PLANT [T] to give a special substance to a plant, which helps it grow: *Feed the tomatoes once a week.* | **feed sth with sth** *Feed houseplants with a liquid fertilizer.*
3 ANIMAL/BABY [I] if a baby or an animal feeds, they eat: *Frogs generally feed at night.* | *Let your baby feed as long as she wants.*
4 well-fed/under-fed/poorly-fed having plenty of food or not enough food: *a well-dressed, well-fed woman*
5 COMPUTER [T always + adv/prep] to put information into a computer over a period of time: **feed sth into sth** *Figures are fed into the computer, which then predicts the likely profit.*
6 SUPPLY STH [T] to supply something, especially a liquid, gas, or electricity: *The public baths are fed by natural springs.* | **feed sth to sth** *The sound is fed directly to the headphones.* | **feed sth with sth** *Laura crouched by the fire, feeding it with dry sticks.*
7 PUT STH INTO STH [T] to put something into something else, especially gradually and through a small hole: **feed sth into/through sth** *A tube was fed down the patient's throat into her stomach.* | **feed sth into sth** *She fed her last two coins into the machine for a cup of coffee.* | *Shelton* ***fed*** *the electricity* ***meter***.
8 INCREASE EMOTION [T] to increase the strength of an emotion, desire etc: *Her depression grew, fed by her bitter experiences.*
9 feed an addiction/need etc to satisfy a strong need, such as a need for a drug: *He committed both crimes to feed his addiction to heroin.*
10 INFORMATION [T] to give someone information or ideas over a period time: **feed sb with sth** *She feeds the media with stories, which is a way of getting free advertising.* | **feed sth to sb** *US intelligence had been feeding false information to a KGB agent.*

11 SPORT [T] to throw or hit a ball to someone else on your team, especially so that they can make a point: **feed sth to sb** *He fed the ball to Jol, who scored.*
12 feed lines/jokes to sb to say things to another performer so that they can make jokes
13 feed your face *informal* to eat a lot of food SYN **stuff yourself**
14 TV/RADIO [T] to send a television or radio programme somewhere so that it can be broadcast
15 feed sb a line *informal* to tell someone something which is not true, so that they will do what you want → BREAST-FEED, FORCE-FEED, SPOON-FEED, → **mouth to feed** at MOUTH[1](10)

feed back *phr v* to give advice or criticism to someone about something they have done: **[+on]** *We're just waiting for the manager to feed back on it.* | **feed sth ↔ back (to sb)** *I am grateful to all those who fed back their comments.* | *They feed back to the government the reactions of the people affected.*

feed into sth *phr v* to have an effect on something or help to make it happen: *The influence of Italian designer fashion feeds into sports fashion.*

feed off sth *phr v*
1 if an animal feeds off something, it gets food from it: *birds that feed off the seeds from trees*
2 to use something to increase, become stronger, or succeed – sometimes used to show disapproval: *fad diets that feed off our desire to be thin*

feed on sth *phr v*
1 if an animal feeds on a particular food, it usually eats that food: *Owls feed on mice and other small animals.*
2 if a feeling or process feeds on something, it becomes stronger because of it: *Prejudice feeds on ignorance.*

feed sb **up** *phr v BrE* to give someone a lot of food to make them more healthy SYN **fatten up** *AmE*

F

feed² *n*
1 BABY [C] *BrE* one of the times when you give milk to a small baby: *the two a.m. feed*
2 ANIMAL FOOD [U] food for animals: *fish feed*
3 SUPPLY [C] a tube or piece of equipment which supplies a machine with something, especially FUEL
4 TV/RADIO/COMPUTER [C,U] when a television or radio signal, computer information etc is sent somewhere, or the connection that is used to do this: *a live satellite feed from the space station*
5 MEAL [C] *old-fashioned* a big meal

feed·back /ˈfiːdbæk/ ●●○ S3 W3 *n* [U]
1 advice, criticism etc about how successful or useful something is: *How can I **provide feedback** without making someone angry?* | **[+on]** *Try to **give** each student some **feedback** on the task.*
2 a very unpleasant high noise, caused when a MICROPHONE is too close to an AMPLIFIER

feed·bag /ˈfiːdbæg/ *n* [C] *AmE* a bag put around a horse's head containing food SYN **nosebag**

feed·er /ˈfiːdə $ -ər/ *n* [C] **1** a container with food for animals or birds: *a bird feeder* **2** something that provides supplies for something else: *The Shyok River is a major feeder of the Indus River.* | *The length of the feeder pipe is 50m.* **3** a piece of equipment that supplies something to a machine: *the printer's paper feeder* **4** a person or animal that eats in a particular way: *Catfish are bottom feeders* (=they feed at the bottom of rivers). **5** a small road, railway line, or AIRLINE service that takes traffic to a main road, line, or service

ˈfeeder ˌschool *n* [C] a school from which many students go to a SECONDARY SCHOOL in the same area

ˈfeeding-ˌbottle *n* [C] a plastic bottle used for giving milk to a baby or young animal → see picture at **BOTTLE**

ˈfeeding ground *n* [C] a place where a group of animals or birds find food to eat

ˈfeed-in ˌtariff *n* [C] money that you are paid for RENEWABLE energy that you produce, for example with SOLAR PANELS or WIND TURBINES

feel¹ /fiːl/ ●●● S1 W1 *v* (*past tense and past participle* **felt** /felt/)
1 FEELING/EMOTION [linking verb, T] to experience a particular physical feeling or emotion: *Do you still feel hungry?* | *You can never tell what he's feeling.* | *Stop exercising if you feel any pain.* | **feel fine/good/comfortable etc** *I'm feeling a little better today.* | *Marie immediately felt guilty.* | **feel as if/as though** *When his dad left, he felt as though his world had turned upside-down.* | *I **felt like** I'd really achieved something.*
2 NOTICE [T not in progressive] to notice something that is happening to you, especially something that is touching you: *She felt his warm breath on her cheek.* | *The earthquake was felt as far south as San Diego.* | **feel sb/sth do sth** *She felt his arms go round her.* | **feel yourself doing sth** *I felt myself blushing.*
3 FEEL SMOOTH/DRY ETC [linking verb] to give you a particular physical feeling, especially when you touch or hold something: **feel smooth/cold/damp etc** *Her hands felt rough.* | *The house felt hot and stuffy.* | **feel as if/as though** *My leg feels as if it's broken.* | *It's nice fabric – it **feels like** velvet.*
4 FEEL GOOD/STRANGE/EXCITING ETC [linking verb] if a situation, event etc feels good, strange etc, that is the emotion or feeling that it gives you: *After twenty years, seeing him again felt very strange.* | **feel ... to be/do sth** ***It felt** wonderful to be wearing clean clothes again.* | *How does **it feel** to be 40?* | *It's been a year since her daughter died, but to her, **it** still **feels like** yesterday.*
5 HAVE AN OPINION [T] to have a particular opinion, especially one that is based on your feelings, not on facts: **feel (that)** *Some of the parents felt the school wasn't doing enough about bullying.* | **[+about]** *How would you feel about working with Nicole for a while?* | *What does your partner feel about all this?* | **feel sure/certain** (=think that something is definitely true) *She felt sure she'd made the right decision.* **THESAURUS** ▸ THINK

GRAMMAR

Using the progressive

Feel is not usually used in the progressive in this meaning. You say: *I feel this is probably the right decision.* ✗ Don't say: *I'm feeling this is probably the right decision.*

Using the passive

In more formal English, you say **it is felt that** when saying what many people think: *It was felt that the experiment should be stopped.*

6 feel like (doing) sth *spoken* to want to have something or do something: *He didn't feel like going to work.* | *Do you feel like another drink?*
7 TOUCH [T] to touch something with your fingers to find out about it: *She felt his forehead. Perhaps he had a temperature.* | *Mum, feel this stone. Isn't it smooth?* | **feel how hard/soft/rough etc sth is** *He could feel how damp his shirt was against his chest.* **THESAURUS** ▸ TOUCH
8 feel around/on/in etc sth (for sth) to search for something with your fingers: *She felt in her bag for a pencil.*
9 feel the force/effects/benefits etc of sth to experience the good or bad results of something: *The local economy is beginning to feel the effects of the recession.*
10 feel the need to do sth to believe that you need to do something: *Children who can talk to their parents feel less need to try drugs.*
11 feel your way a) to move carefully, with your hands out in front of you, because you cannot see properly: *Silently, she felt her way across the room.* **b)** to do things slowly and carefully, because you are not completely sure about a new situation: **[+towards]** *The European Union is still feeling its way towards common policies.*
12 feel free *spoken* used to tell someone that they can do something if they want to: *'Could I use your phone for a minute?' 'Feel free.'* | **feel free to do sth** *Please feel free to make suggestions.*
13 I know (just/exactly) how you feel *spoken* used to express sympathy with someone or with a remark they

have just made: *I know how you feel, Mark, but maybe it's better not to confront him.*
14 not feel yourself *spoken* to not feel as healthy or happy as usual: *I don't know what's wrong. I just don't feel quite myself.*
15 feel your age to realize that you are not as young or active as you used to be: *Looking at his grandson made him really feel his age.*
16 feel the cold/heat to suffer because of cold or hot weather: *Old people tend to feel the cold more.*
17 feel a death/a loss etc to react very strongly to a bad event, especially someone's death: *Susan felt her grandmother's death more than the others.*

GRAMMAR: Linking verbs

Feel is a linking verb. This type of verb links the subject of the sentence with an adjective or noun: *She felt tired at the end of the day.* | *I feel such an idiot.*

feel for sb *phr v* to feel sympathy for someone: *At the Center, the other mothers know what it's like, and they really feel for you.*

feel sb ↔ **out** *phr v AmE informal* to find out what someone's opinions or feelings are, without asking them directly: *I thought I'd feel out some of my colleagues before the meeting.*

feel sb ↔ **up** *phr v informal* to touch someone sexually, without their permission

feel up to sth *phr v* [usually in questions and negatives] *informal* to have the strength, energy etc to do something: *I just didn't feel up to going.*

feel² ●○○ *n*
1 [singular] a quality that something has that makes you feel or think a particular way about it: *Despite their age, the photographs have a modern feel.* | **[+about]** *The restaurant has a nice relaxed feel about it.*
2 [singular] the way that something feels when you touch it: **[+of]** *I like the feel of this cloth.* | *a soft feathery feel*
3 have/get/give a feel for sth *informal* to have or develop an understanding of something and skill in doing it: *exercises that give a child a feel for numbers*
4 [U] when you use your hands, body etc to feel something SYN **touch**: **by feel** *She found the light switch by feel.*

feel·er /ˈfiːlə $ -ər/ *n* [C usually plural] **1** one of the two long things on an insect's head that it uses to feel or touch things. Some sea animals also have feelers. **2 put out feelers** to carefully try to discover what people think about something that you want to do: *They seem interested in a peace settlement and have begun putting out feelers.*

ˈfeel-good *adj* **1 feel-good film/programme/music etc** a film etc whose main purpose is to make you feel happy **2 feel-good factor** *especially BrE* a feeling among ordinary people that everything is going well, and that they do not need to worry about losing their jobs or spending money

feel·ing¹ /ˈfiːlɪŋ/ ●●● S1 W1 *n*
1 ANGER/SADNESS/JOY ETC [C] an emotion that you feel, such as anger, sadness, or happiness: *Knowing we'd won was a wonderful feeling.* | **[+of]** *a terrible feeling of guilt*
2 WAY SB THINKS/FEELS **feelings** [plural] someone's feelings are their thoughts, emotions, and attitudes: *He's considerate of other people's feelings.*
3 OPINION [C] a belief or opinion about something, especially one that is influenced by your emotions: *My personal feeling is that not enough has been done.* | **[+on]** *She has* ***strong feelings*** *on the issue of abortion.* | **[+about]** *a survey on people's feelings about the candidates* | *His* ***gut feeling*** (=opinion based on emotion) *was that Burns was probably guilty.* | *I had this* ***funny feeling*** (=not easily explained) *that something was wrong.*
4 have/get the feeling (that) to think that something is probably true, or will probably happen: **[+(that)]** *Leslie suddenly got the feeling that somebody was watching her.* | *He had a* ***sneaking feeling*** (=a slight feeling that something is true, without being sure) *that they were laughing at him.* | *Gary* ***had a sinking feeling*** (=had a sudden bad feeling that something was true) *that he was making a mistake.* | **[+about]** *I have a* ***good feeling*** *about this. I think it's going to work.*
5 GENERAL ATTITUDE [U] a general attitude among a group of people about a subject: *the anti-American feeling in the region* | **[+against/in favour of]** *Johnson underestimated the strength of* ***public feeling*** *against the war.* | *the* ***depth of feeling*** *against nuclear weapons*
6 HEAT/COLD/PAIN ETC [C] something that you feel in your body, such as heat, cold, tiredness etc: *I keep getting this* *funny feeling* (=a strange feeling) *in my neck.* | **[+of]** *feelings of dizziness*
7 ABILITY TO FEEL [U] the ability to feel pain, heat etc in part of your body: *Harry had lost all feeling in his toes.*
8 EFFECT OF A PLACE/BOOK ETC [singular] the effect that a place, book, film etc has on people and the way it makes them feel: **[+of]** *the town's strong feeling of history* | *It* ***gives a feeling*** *of eating outdoors, without having to worry about being rained on.*
9 I know the feeling *spoken* said when you understand how someone feels because you have had the same experience: *'It's so embarrassing when you can't remember someone's name.' 'I know the feeling.'*
10 the feeling is mutual *spoken* said when you have the same feeling about someone as they have towards you: *My dad hated my boyfriend, and the feeling was mutual.*
11 bad/ill feeling anger, lack of trust etc between people, especially after an argument or unfair decision: *The changes have caused a lot of ill feeling among the workforce.*
12 with feeling in a way that shows you feel very angry, happy etc: *Chang spoke with great feeling about the injustices of the regime.*
13 a feeling for sth a) an ability to do something or understand a subject, which you get from experience: *an orchestra that has always shown a special feeling for Brahms' music* **b)** a natural ability to do something SYN **talent**: *He has a natural feeling for mathematical ideas.*
14 EMOTIONS NOT THOUGHT [U] a way of reacting to things using your emotions, instead of thinking about them carefully: *The Romantic writers valued feeling above all else.* → **no hard feelings** at HARD¹(19), → **hurt sb's feelings** at HURT¹(4)

COLLOCATIONS – MEANINGS 1 & 2

ADJECTIVES

a good/great/wonderful etc feeling *It's a great feeling when you try something new and it works.*
deep *A deep feeling of sadness came over her.*
strong/intense *There was a strong feeling of anger among the workers.*

VERBS

experience a feeling *I remember experiencing a feeling of tremendous excitement.*
give sb a feeling *My work gives me a feeling of achievement.*
arouse a feeling (=cause it) | **hurt sb's feelings** (=make someone feel upset) | **hide your feelings** | **show your feelings** | **express your feelings** (*also* **put your feelings into words**) (=tell other people what you are feeling or thinking)

PHRASES

have mixed feelings (=have both positive and negative feelings) *Her parents had mixed feelings about the marriage.*
feelings are running high (=people have strong feelings, especially of anger)

feeling² *adj* showing strong feelings: *a feeling look* —**feelingly** *adv*

ˈfee-ˌpaying *adj BrE* **1 fee-paying school** a school which you have to pay to go to **2 fee-paying student/patient** a student or PATIENT who pays for their education or medical treatment

feet /fiːt/ *n* the plural of FOOT → **get/have cold feet** at COLD¹(6), → **feet of clay** at FOOT¹(26), → **have itchy feet** at ITCHY(3)

F

feign /feɪn/ *v* [T] *formal* to pretend to have a particular feeling or to be ill, asleep etc: *Feigning a headache, I went upstairs to my room.*

feint¹ /feɪnt/ *n* [C] a movement or an attack that is intended to deceive an opponent, especially in BOXING

feint² *v* [I,T] to pretend to hit someone in BOXING

feist·y /ˈfaɪsti/ *adj* having a strong determined character and being willing to argue with people – use this to show approval: *DiFranco charmed the audience with her feisty spirit.* **THESAURUS** DETERMINED

fe·laf·el /fəˈlæfəl, -ˈlɑː- $ -ˈlɑː-/ *n* [C,U] another spelling of FALAFEL

feld·spar /ˈfeldspɑː $ -ɑːr/ *n* [U] a type of grey or white mineral

fe·li·ci·ta·tions /fɪˌlɪsəˈteɪʃənz/ *interjection formal* said to wish someone happiness

fe·li·ci·tous /fɪˈlɪsɪtəs/ *adj formal or literary* well-chosen and suitable OPP **infelicitous**: *a felicitous choice of candidate*

fe·li·ci·ty /fɪˈlɪsəti/ *n formal* **1** [U] happiness: *domestic felicity* **2** [U] the quality of being well-chosen or suitable: *a felicity of language* **3 felicities** [plural] *BrE formal* suitable or well-chosen remarks or details

fe·line¹ /ˈfiːlaɪn/ *adj* **1** relating to cats or other members of the cat family, such as lions **2** looking like or moving like a cat: *She moves with feline grace.*

feline² *n* [C] *technical* a cat or a member of the cat family, such as a tiger

fell¹ /fel/ *v* the past tense of FALL

fell² *n* [C usually plural] a mountain or hill in the north of England

fell³ *v* [T] **1** to cut down a tree: *More than 100 trees were felled in just over an hour.* **2** *written* to knock someone down with great force: *The goalkeeper was felled by a coin thrown from the crowd.* GRAMMAR **Fell** is often used in the passive.

fell⁴ *adj* **in one fell swoop** (*also* **at one fell swoop** *BrE*) doing a lot of things at the same time, using only one action SYN **in one go**: *A single company can close a factory, eliminating 74,000 jobs in one fell swoop.*

fel·la /ˈfelə/ *n* [C] *spoken informal* **1** a man: *There's a fella outside who wants to see you.* **2** *especially BrE* a BOYFRIEND: *What do you think of Janet's new fella?*

fel·la·ti·o /fəˈleɪʃiəʊ $ -ʃioʊ/ *n* [U] the practice of touching a man's PENIS with the lips and tongue to give sexual pleasure → **cunnilingus**

fel·ler /ˈfelə $ -ər/ *n* [C] *spoken old-fashioned* a man

fellow¹ ●●○ W3 *adj*
1 fellow workers/students/countrymen etc people that you work with, study with, or who are in the same situation as you
2 our fellow man/men other people in general: *We all have obligations to our fellow men.*

fel·low² /ˈfeləʊ $ -loʊ/ *n* [C] **1** *old-fashioned* a man: *Paul's an easy-going sort of fellow.* **2 sb's fellows** *BrE old-fashioned* people that you work with, study with, or who are in the same situation as you: *Wooderson's courage earned him the respect of his fellows.* **3** *AmE* a GRADUATE student who has a fellowship in a university **4** *especially BrE* a member of an important society or a college: *She is a Fellow of the Royal College of Surgeons.* → BEDFELLOW

ˌfellow ˈfeeling *n* [U] *literary* a feeling of sympathy and friendship towards someone because they are like you: *As an only child myself, I had a fellow feeling for Laura.*

fel·low·ship /ˈfeləʊʃɪp $ -loʊ-/ ●○○ *n*
1 [U] a feeling of friendship resulting from shared interests or experiences: *Regular outings contribute to a sense of fellowship among co-workers.*
2 [C] a group of people who share an interest or belief, especially Christians who have religious ceremonies together
3 [C] *BrE* a job at a university which involves making a detailed study of a particular subject
4 [C] **a)** *especially AmE* money given to a student to allow them to continue their studies at an advanced level → **scholarship**: *Florian came to the United States on a Fulbright fellowship.* **b)** *AmE* a group of officials who decide which students will receive this money: *He received a gold medal from the Artists' Fellowship in New York.*

ˌfellow ˈtraveller *BrE*, **fellow traveler** *AmE n* [C] someone who supports and agrees with the beliefs of an organization, such as the Communist Party, but does not belong to it – used to show disapproval

fel·on /ˈfelən/ *n* [C] *law* someone who is guilty of a serious crime SYN **criminal**: *By law,* ***convicted felons*** (=criminals who are sent to prison) *may not own or use guns.*

fel·o·ny /ˈfeləni/ *n* (*plural* **felonies**) [C,U] *law* a serious crime such as murder → **misdemeanour** **THESAURUS** CRIME

felt¹ /felt/ the past tense and past participle of FEEL

felt² *n* [U] a thick soft material made of wool, hair, or fur that has been pressed flat

ˌfelt-tip ˈpen (*also* **ˌfelt-tipped ˈpen**, **ˈfelt-tip** *BrE*) *n* [C] a pen that has a hard piece of felt at the end that the ink comes through → see picture at STATIONERY

fem. **1** the written abbreviation of ***female*** **2** the written abbreviation of ***feminine***

fe·male¹ /ˈfiːmeɪl/ ●●● S3 W2 *adj*
1 relating to women or girls OPP **male** → **feminine**: *female voters* | *Over half of the staff are female.*
2 belonging to the sex that can have babies or produce eggs OPP **male**: *a female spider*
3 a female plant or flower produces fruit OPP **male**
4 *technical* a female part of a piece of equipment has holes into which the male part can be fitted OPP **male**

female² ●●● W3 *n* [C]
1 an animal that belongs to the sex that can have babies or produce eggs OPP **male**
2 a woman or girl OPP **male**: *As a group, females performed better on the test than males.* **THESAURUS** WOMAN
3 a plant that produces flowers or fruit OPP **male**

ˌfemale ˈcondom *n* [C] a loose rubber tube with one end closed, that fits inside a woman's VAGINA when she is having sex, so that she will not have a baby

fem·i·nine /ˈfemɪnɪn/ ●○○ *adj*
1 having qualities that are considered to be typical of women, especially by being gentle, delicate, and pretty: *Dianne loved pretty feminine things.* **THESAURUS** WOMAN
2 relating to being female SYN **female**: *traditional feminine roles* | *Amelia's report describes the experience from a feminine point of view.*
3 a feminine noun, PRONOUN etc belongs to a class of words that have different INFLECTIONS from MASCULINE or NEUTER words → **masculine**

fem·i·nin·i·ty /ˌfeməˈnɪnəti/ *n* [U] qualities that are considered to be typical of women, especially qualities that are gentle, delicate, and pretty → **masculinity**: *You don't have to lose your femininity to be an independent, successful woman.*

fem·i·nis·m /ˈfemənɪzəm/ *n* [U] the belief that women should have the same rights and opportunities as men

fem·i·nist /ˈfemɪnɪst/ ●○○ *n* [C] someone who supports the idea that women should have the same rights and opportunities as men: *She's been an outspoken feminist for over twenty years.* —**feminist** *adj* [only before noun]: *feminist literature*

fem·i·nize (*also* **-ise** *BrE*) /ˈfemənaɪz/ *v* [T] to change something so that it includes women, is suitable for women, or is considered typical of women: *women who resist cultural attempts to feminize them*

femme fa·tale /ˌfæm fəˈtɑːl $ ˌfem-/ *n* (*plural* **femmes fatales**) [C] a beautiful woman who men find very attractive, even though she may make them unhappy

fe·mur /ˈfiːmə $ -ər/ *n* [C] *medical* the THIGH bone → see picture at SKELETON —**femoral** /ˈfemərəl/ *adj* [only before noun]

fen /fen/ (*also* **fenland**) *n* [C,U] an area of low flat wet land, especially in eastern England

FENCES

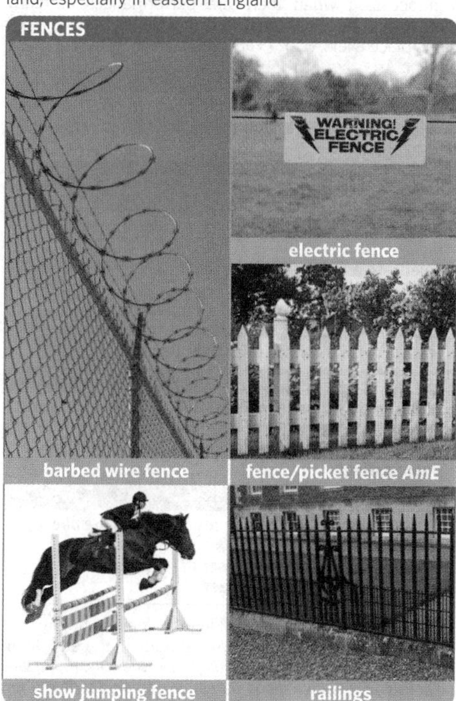

electric fence

barbed wire fence

fence/picket fence *AmE*

show jumping fence

railings

fence¹ /fens/ ●●● S3 *n* [C]
1 a structure made of wood, metal etc that surrounds a piece of land
2 a wall or other structure that horses jump over in a race or competition
3 *informal* someone who buys and sells stolen goods
4 sit/be on the fence to avoid saying which side of an argument you support → **mend (your) fences** at MEND¹(4)

fence² *v* **1** [T] to put a fence around something: *old farmhouses and fenced gardens* **2** [I] to fight with a long thin sword as a sport **3** [I + with] to answer someone's questions in a clever way in order to get an advantage in an argument

fence sb/sth ↔ **in** *phr v* **1** to surround a place with a fence: *The yard was fenced in to keep out wolves.* **2** to make someone feel that they cannot leave a place or do what they want: *Young mothers often feel fenced in at home.*

fence sth ↔ **off** *phr v* to separate one area from another area with a fence: *a planting area fenced off from the main garden*

ˈfence-ˌmending *adj* [only before noun] **fence-mending measures/talks/trips etc** fence-mending trips, talks etc are between countries who have a disagreement about something, and are meant to try to improve relations between them —**fence-mending** *n* [U]

fenc·er /ˈfensə $ -ər/ *n* [C] someone who fights with a long thin sword as a sport

fenc·ing /ˈfensɪŋ/ *n* [U] **1** the sport of fighting with a long thin sword **2** fences or the pieces of wood, metal etc used to make them

fend /fend/ *v* **fend for yourself** to look after yourself without needing help from other people: *The kids had to fend for themselves while their parents were away.*

fend sb/sth **off** *phr v* **1** to defend yourself against someone who is attacking you SYN **fight sb ↔ off**: *Tabitha threw up an arm to fend her attacker off.* **2** to defend yourself from something such as difficult questions, competition, or a situation you do not want to deal with: *She uses her secretary to fend off unwanted phone calls.* | *The company managed to fend off the hostile takeover bid.*

fend·er /ˈfendə $ -ər/ *n* [C] **1** *AmE* the side part of a car that covers the wheels SYN **wing** *BrE* → see picture at CAR **2** a low metal wall around a FIREPLACE that prevents burning wood or coal from falling out **3** *AmE* a curved piece of metal over the wheel of a bicycle that prevents water and mud from flying up SYN **mudguard** *BrE* → see pictures at MOTORBIKE, BICYCLE

ˈfender-ˌbender *n* [C] *AmE informal* a car accident in which little damage is done

feng shui¹ /ˌfʌŋ ˈʃweɪ/ *n* [U] a Chinese system of organizing the furniture and other things in a house or building in a way that people believe will bring good luck and happiness

feng shui² *v* [T] **feng shui a room/house etc** to place the furniture and other things in a room or house in a particular position so that it is arranged according to the feng shui system

fen·land /ˈfenlənd, -lænd/ *n* [C,U] a FEN

fen·nel /ˈfenl/ *n* [U] a pale green plant whose seeds are used to give a special taste to food and which is also used as a vegetable → see picture at VEGETABLE

fer·al /ˈferəl, ˈfɪərəl $ ˈferəl, ˈfɪrəl/ *adj* **1** feral animals used to live with humans but have become wild: *feral cats* **2** feral children or young people behave badly in public and commit crimes, because they are not controlled by anyone and have no respect for authority: *The riots were blamed on feral teenagers.*

fer·ment¹ /fəˈment $ fər-/ *v* [I,T] if fruit, beer, wine etc ferments, or if it is fermented, the sugar in it changes to alcohol: *fermented fruit juice* —**fermentation** /ˌfɜːmenˈteɪʃən $ ˌfɜːrmən-/ *n* [U]

fer·ment² /ˈfɜːment $ ˈfɜːr-/ *n* [U] a situation of great excitement or trouble in a country, especially caused by political change SYN **turmoil**: **in ferment** *In the 1960s, American society was in ferment.* | **political/intellectual/cultural etc ferment** *the artistic ferment of the late sixth century*

fern /fɜːn $ fɜːrn/ *n* [C] a type of plant with green leaves shaped like large feathers, but no flowers —**ferny** *adj*

fe·ro·cious /fəˈrəʊʃəs $ -ˈroʊ-/ ●○○ *adj*
1 violent, dangerous, and frightening SYN **fierce**: *a ferocious, hungry lion* | *a ferocious battle* | *The storm grew more and more ferocious with each second.* THESAURUS VIOLENT
2 very strong, severe, and unpleasant SYN **fierce**: *The congressman is one of the president's most ferocious critics.* | *The heat was ferocious.* | *He is famous for his ferocious temper.*
3 relating to an emotion that is felt very strongly SYN **fierce**: *Parker was driven by a ferocious determination to succeed.* —**ferociously** *adv*

fe·ro·ci·ty /fəˈrɒsəti $ fəˈrɑː-/ *n* [U] the state of being extremely violent and severe: **[+of]** *Detectives were shocked by the ferocity of the attack.*

FERRET

fer·ret¹ /ˈferɪt/ *n* [C] a small animal with a pointed nose, used to hunt rats and rabbits

ferret² *v* [I] **1** [always + adv/prep] *informal* to search for something that is lost or hidden among a lot of things or inside a drawer, box etc: **[+around/round/about]** *He started ferreting around in his desk.* | **[+for]** *She ferreted in her bag for a pen.* **2** to hunt rats and rabbits using a ferret

F

ferret sb/sth ↔ **out** *phr v* **1** to succeed in finding something such as a piece of information, that is difficult to find: *It's been difficult for reporters to ferret out the facts in this case.* | *Uncle Vernon ferreted out the laundry box from under the stairs.* **2** *AmE* to find and usually get rid of someone who is causing a problem: *The new program is meant to ferret out problem cops.*

Fer·ris wheel /ˈferəs ˌwiːl/ *n* [C] *especially AmE* a very large upright wheel with seats on it for people to ride on in an AMUSEMENT PARK SYN **big wheel** *BrE* → see picture at AMUSEMENT PARK

fer·rous /ˈferəs/ *adj technical* containing or relating to iron: *ferrous metals*

fer·rule /ˈferuːl, ˈferəl $ ˈferəl/ *n* [C] *technical* a piece of metal or rubber put on the end of a stick to make it stronger

fer·ry¹ /ˈferi/ ●●○ *n* (*plural* **ferries**) [C] a boat that carries people or goods across a river or a narrow area of water

ferry² *v* (**ferried, ferrying, ferries**) [T always + adv/prep] to carry people or things a short distance from one place to another in a boat or other vehicle: **ferry sb/sth (from sth) to sth** *The ship was used to ferry supplies to Russia during the war.* | **ferry sb/sth across sth** *ferrying passengers across the Channel*

fer·ry·boat /ˈferibəʊt $ -boʊt/ *n* [C] a ferry

fer·tile /ˈfɜːtaɪl $ ˈfɜːrtl/ ●○○ *adj*
1 fertile land or soil is able to produce good crops: *800 acres of fertile cropland*
2 able to produce babies, young animals, or new plants OPP **infertile**: *Most men remain fertile into old age.*
3 a fertile imagination/mind/brain an imagination, mind etc that is able to produce a lot of interesting and unusual ideas
4 [only before noun] a fertile situation is one in which something can easily develop and succeed: *the fertile Philadelphia music scene*

fer·til·i·ty /fɜːˈtɪləti $ fɜːr-/ ●○○ *n* [U]
1 the ability of the land or soil to produce good crops
2 the ability of a person, animal, or plant to produce babies, young animals, or seeds OPP **infertility**

ferˈtility ˌdrug *n* [C] a drug given to a woman to help her have a baby

fer·ti·lize (*also* **-ise** *BrE*) /ˈfɜːtəlaɪz $ ˈfɜːrtl-aɪz/ *v* [T] **1** to make new animal or plant life develop: *After the egg has been fertilized, it will hatch in about six weeks.* **2** to put fertilizer on the soil to make plants grow —**fertilization** /ˌfɜːtəlaɪˈzeɪʃən $ ˌfɜːrtl-əˈzeɪ-/ *n* [U]

fer·ti·liz·er /ˈfɜːtəlaɪzə $ ˈfɜːrtl-aɪzər/ *n* [C,U] a substance that is put on the soil to make plants grow

fer·vent /ˈfɜːvənt $ ˈfɜːr-/ *adj* believing or feeling something very strongly and sincerely SYN **strong**: *a fervent appeal for peace* | **fervent admirer/believer etc** *a fervent supporter of human rights* —**fervently** *adv*

fer·vid /ˈfɜːvɪd $ ˈfɜːr-/ *adj formal* believing or feeling something too strongly —**fervidly** *adv*

fer·vour *BrE*, **fervor** *AmE* /ˈfɜːvə $ ˈfɜːrvər/ *n* [U] very strong belief or feeling: *religious fervour* | *revolutionary fervour* | *patriotic fervor*

fess /fes/ *v*
fess up *AmE informal* to admit that you have done something wrong, although it is not very serious SYN **own up**: *Come on, fess up! Who ate that last cookie?*

fest /fest/ *n* **a beer/song/food etc fest** an informal occasion when a lot of people do a fun activity together, such as drinking beer, singing songs, or eating food → SLUGFEST

-fest /fest/ *suffix* [in nouns] *informal* used to form nouns referring to events that have a lot of a particular thing or have a very great effect of a particular kind: *a talkfest* | *a snoozefest* (=a very boring event)

fes·ter /ˈfestə $ -ər/ *v* [I] **1** if an unpleasant feeling or problem festers, it gets worse because it has not been dealt with: *The dispute can be traced back to resentments which have festered for centuries.* **2** if a wound festers, it becomes infected: *festering sores* **3** if rubbish or dirty objects fester, they decay and smell bad

fes·ti·val /ˈfestəvəl/ ●●● S3 W3 *n* [C]
1 an occasion when there are performances of many films, plays, pieces of music etc, usually happening in the same place every year: **[+of]** *the Swansea Festival of Music and the Arts*
2 a special occasion when people celebrate something such as a religious event, and there is often a public holiday: *Christmas is one of the main festivals in the Christian calendar.*

COLLOCATIONS

VERBS

have/hold a festival *Tucson had a film festival last month.*
celebrate a festival *The festival is celebrated each July.*
go to a festival (*also* **attend a festival** *formal*) | **appear/play/speak at a festival** (=perform at a festival) | **take part in a festival** (=perform there)

ADJECTIVES/NOUN + festival

a film/music/dance/arts festival *The movie won an award at the Cannes Film Festival.*
a rock/pop/jazz/folk festival | **a literary festival** | **a beer festival**

festival + NOUN

festival events *Many of the festival events are already sold out.*
a festival programme (=a series of events at a festival) | **a festival organizer**

fes·tive /ˈfestɪv/ *adj* **1** looking or feeling bright and cheerful in a way that seems suitable for celebrating something: *The atmosphere was festive and jolly.* | *John was obviously in a* ***festive mood.*** **2 festive occasion** a day when you celebrate something special such as a birthday **3 the festive season/period/holiday** the period around CHRISTMAS **4** [only before noun] relating to Christmas: ***festive cheer*** | *festive gifts*

fes·tiv·i·ty /feˈstɪvəti/ *n* **1 festivities** [plural] things such as drinking, eating, or dancing that are done to celebrate a special occasion: *The festivities started with a procession through the town.* **2** [U] a happy feeling that exists when people celebrate something: *There was an air of festivity in the village.*

fes·toon¹ /feˈstuːn/ *v* [T usually passive] to cover something with flowers, long pieces of material etc, especially for decoration: **be festooned with/in sth** *Malaga was festooned with banners and flags in honour of the king's visit.*

festoon² *n* [C] *formal* a long thin piece of material, flowers etc, used especially for decoration

fet·a cheese /ˌfetə ˈtʃiːz/ (*also* **feta**) *n* [U] a white cheese from Greece made from SHEEP's milk or GOAT's milk

fe·tal /ˈfiːtl/ *adj* the usual American spelling of FOETAL

fetch¹ /fetʃ/ ●●● S3 *v* [T]
1 *especially BrE* to go and get something or someone and bring them back: *Quick! Go and fetch a doctor.* | *Shannon went upstairs to fetch some blankets.* | **fetch sb/sth from sth** *Would you mind going to fetch the kids from school?* | **fetch sb sth/fetch sth for sb** *Fetch me some coffee while you're up.*
2 to be sold for a particular amount of money, especially at a public sale – used especially in news reports: *The painting is expected to fetch at least $20 million.* THESAURUS ▸ COST
3 fetch and carry to do simple and boring jobs for someone as if you were their servant: *Am I supposed to fetch and carry for him all day?*
4 *BrE* to make people react in a particular way: *This announcement fetched a huge cheer from the audience.*

fetch up *phr v BrE informal* [always + adv/prep] to arrive somewhere without intending to SYN **end up**: *I fell asleep on the train and fetched up in Glasgow.*

F

fetch² *n* **play fetch** if you play fetch with a dog, you throw something for the dog to bring back to you

fetch·ing /ˈfetʃɪŋ/ *adj* attractive, especially because the clothes you are wearing suit you: *Your sister* ***looks*** *very* ***fetching*** *in that dress.*

fête¹ /feɪt/ *n* [C] **1** *BrE* an outdoor event where there are competitions and things to eat and drink, usually organized to get money: *the church fête* **2** *AmE* a special occasion to celebrate something: *a farewell fête in honor of the mayor*

fête² *v* [T] to honour someone by holding public celebrations for them: *The team was fêted from coast to coast.*

fet·id /ˈfetɪd/ *adj formal* having a strong bad smell SYN **stinking**: *the black fetid water of the lake | the dog's fetid breath*

fet·ish /ˈfetɪʃ/ *n* [C] **1** a desire for sex that comes from seeing a particular type of object or doing a particular activity, especially when the object or activity is considered unusual: *a leather fetish* **2** something you are always thinking about or spending too much time doing → **obsession**: **[+for/about]** *Sue* ***has*** *a real* ***fetish*** *about keeping everything tidy.*

fet·ish·ist /ˈfetɪʃɪst/ *n* [C] someone who gets sexual pleasure from unusual objects or activities —**fetishism** *n* [U]

fet·lock /ˈfetlɒk $ -lɑːk/ *n* [C] the back part of a horse's leg, just above the HOOF

fet·ter /ˈfetə $ -ər/ *v* [T] *literary* **1** to restrict someone's freedom and prevent them from doing what they want: *fettered by family responsibilities* **2** to put chains around a prisoner's hands or feet SYN **chain**

fet·ters /ˈfetəz $ -ərz/ *n* [plural] *literary* **1** the things that prevent someone from being free SYN **constraints**: **[+of]** *breaking the fetters of convention* **2** chains that were put around a prisoner's feet in past times

fet·tle /ˈfetl/ *n* **in fine/good fettle** *old-fashioned* healthy or working properly

fe·tus /ˈfiːtəs/ *n* [C] the usual American spelling of FOETUS

feud¹ /fjuːd/ *n* [C] an angry and often violent quarrel between two people or groups that continues for a long time: **[+over]** *a bitter feud over territory* | **[+with/between]** *a feud between rival drug organizations* THESAURUS ARGUMENT

feud² *v* [I] to continue quarrelling for a long time, often in a violent way: **feud (with sb) over sth** *The neighboring states are feuding over the rights to the river.*

feud·al /ˈfjuːdl/ *adj* [only before noun] relating to feudalism: *the feudal system | feudal society*

feu·dal·is·m /ˈfjuːdl-ɪzəm/ *n* [U] a system which existed in the Middle Ages, in which people received land and protection from a lord when they worked and fought for him → **serfdom**

feu·dal·is·tic /ˌfjuːdlˈɪstɪk◂/ *adj* based on a system in which only a few people have all the power in a way that seems very old-fashioned

fe·ver /ˈfiːvə $ -ər/ ●●○ *n*

1 [C,U] an illness or a medical condition in which you have a very high temperature: *Andy* ***has a fever*** *and won't be coming into work today. | I woke up this morning with a fever and an upset stomach. | She's* ***running a fever*** (=has a fever). | **a high/low/slight fever** *The usual symptoms are a pink rash with a slight fever.* → HAY FEVER, SCARLET FEVER, YELLOW FEVER, GLANDULAR FEVER, RHEUMATIC FEVER

> **REGISTER**
> In everyday English, people usually use **fever** to talk about a very high temperature. If someone's temperature is just high, they say that someone **has a temperature** rather than **has a fever**: *He stayed home from school because he* ***had a temperature****.*

2 [singular] a situation in which many people feel very excited or feel very strongly about something: **[+of]** *a fever of excitement on Wall Street* | **election/carnival etc fever** (=great interest or excitement about a particular activity or event) *Soccer fever has been sweeping the nation as they prepare for the World Cup.*

3 (at) fever pitch *BrE* if people's feelings are at fever pitch, they are extremely excited: *The nation was at fever pitch in the days leading up to the election. | After a night of rioting, tensions in the city* ***reached fever pitch****.* → CABIN FEVER

ˈfever ˌblister *n* [C] *AmE* a COLD SORE

fe·vered /ˈfiːvəd $ -ərd/ *adj* [only before noun] *literary* **1** extremely excited or worried SYN **feverish**: *the child's fevered cries* **2** suffering from a fever SYN **feverish**: *his* ***fevered brow*** (=a hot forehead caused by a fever) **3 a fevered imagination/mind/brain** a mind that imagines strange things that are not real: *These stories are merely a product of her fevered imagination.*

fe·ver·ish /ˈfiːvərɪʃ/ *adj* **1** suffering from a fever: *She lay in bed, too feverish to sleep. | There was a feverish blush to his cheeks.* THESAURUS HOT **2** very excited or worried about something: *They waited in a state of feverish anxiety for their mother to come home. | The show was about to begin and backstage there were signs of* ***feverish activity*** (=activity that is done very quickly because there is not much time). —**feverishly** *adv*: *Congress is* ***working feverishly*** *to pass the bill.*

few /fjuː/ ●●● S1 W1 *determiner, pron, adj* (*comparative* **fewer**, *superlative* **fewest**)

1 [no comparative] a small number of things or people: **a few** *I have to buy a few things at the supermarket. | Pam called to say she's going to be a few minutes late. | There were a few people sitting at the back of the hall. | There are* ***a few more*** *things I'd like to discuss.* | **[+of]** *I've read a few of her books. | I could suggest many different methods, but anyway, here are* ***just a few****. | There are* ***only a very few*** (=not many) *exceptions.* | **the last/next few** *The office has been closed for the last few days.* | **every few days/weeks etc** *The plants need to be watered every few days.* | **the/sb's few days/weeks etc** *She had enjoyed her few days in Monaco.*

2 quite a few/a good few/not a few a fairly large number of things or people: *She must have cooked a good few dinners over the years.* | **[+of]** *There were hundreds of protesters, not a few of whom were women.*

3 not many or hardly any people or things OPP **many**: *low-paid jobs that few people want | Many people expressed concern, but few were willing to help. | The team that makes the fewest mistakes usually wins.* | **[+of]** ***Very few*** *of the staff come from the local area. | Mr Wingate was full of explanations, but* ***precious few*** (=hardly any) *of them made sense.* | **the few** *The cathedral was one of the few buildings not destroyed in the war. | This hospital is one of the few that are equipped to provide transplant surgery.* | **sb's few belongings/friends etc** *I gathered together my few possessions.*

4 no fewer than used to emphasize that a number is large: *I tried to contact him no fewer than ten times.*

5 as few as 5/10 etc used to emphasize how surprisingly small a number is: *Sometimes as few as 20 out of 500 or more candidates succeed in passing all the tests.*

6 to name/mention but a few used when you are mentioning only a small number of people or things as examples of a large group: *This is a feature of languages such as Arabic, Spanish and Portuguese, to name but a few.*

7 the (privileged/chosen) few the small number of people who are treated better than others and have special advantages: *Such information is made available only to the chosen few. | The needs of the many have been ignored – instead, the priority has been to bring benefits only to the few.*

8 be few and far between to be rare: *Jobs are few and far between at the moment.*

9 have had a few (too many) *informal* to have drunk too much alcohol: *He looks as if he's had a few!*

> **GRAMMAR: Comparison**
> **a few**
> • **A few** means 'a small number, for example two or three people or things'.
> • You use **a few** before plural nouns: *A few people were waiting. | He called me a few days later.*

F

• You say **a few of the**: *A few of the people were getting annoyed.* ✗ Don't say: *A few of people were getting annoyed.*
• You say **a few of my/her/his etc** or **a few of them/us/ you**: *A few of my friends came too.* | *A few of us left early.*

few
• **Few** means 'not many or hardly any'. It emphasizes how small the number is.
• In formal English, you use **few** before plural nouns, without 'a': *Few people knew he was ill.*
• In everyday English, people usually say **not many** instead: *Not many people knew he was ill.*

fey /feɪ/ *adj* very sensitive and behaving or talking in a strange way: *a fey and delicate child*

fez /fez/ *n* [C] a round red hat with a flat top and no BRIM

ff (*and following*) used in writing to refer to the pages after the one you have mentioned: *pages 17ff*

fi·an·cé /fiˈɒnseɪ $ ˌfiːɑːnˈseɪ/ ●●○ *n* [C] the man who a woman is going to marry **THESAURUS▸ MARRIED**

fi·an·cée /fiˈɒnseɪ $ ˌfiːɑːnˈseɪ/ ●●○ *n* [C] the woman who a man is going to marry **THESAURUS▸ MARRIED**

fi·as·co /fiˈæskəʊ $ -koʊ/ *n* (*plural* **fiascoes** *or* **fiascos**) [C] an event that is completely unsuccessful, in a way that is very embarrassing or disappointing SYN **disaster**: *The first lecture I ever gave was **a complete fiasco**.*

fi·at /ˈfiːæt, ˈfaɪæt/ *n* [C] *formal* an official order given by someone in a position of authority, without considering what other people want: **by fiat** *The matter was settled by presidential fiat.*

fib¹ /fɪb/ *n* [C] *spoken* a small unimportant lie → **white lie**: *He's been known to **tell fibs**.*

fib² *v* (**fibbed**, **fibbing**) [I] *spoken* to tell a small unimportant lie: *I think you're fibbing.* —**fibber** *n* [C]

fi·ber /ˈfaɪbə $ -ər/ *n* [C,U] the American spelling of FIBRE

fi·ber·board /ˈfaɪbəbɔːd $ -bərbɔːrd/ *n* [U] the American spelling of FIBREBOARD

fi·ber·glass /ˈfaɪbəglɑːs $ -bərglæs/ *n* [U] the American spelling of FIBREGLASS

fi·bre *BrE*, **fiber** *AmE* /ˈfaɪbə $ -ər/ ●●○ *n*
1 [U] the parts of plants that you eat but cannot DIGEST. Fibre helps to keep you healthy by moving food quickly through your body: *Fruit and vegetables are high in **fibre content**.* | *food that is high in **dietary fibre***
2 [C,U] a mass of threads used to make rope, cloth etc: **natural/synthetic/man-made etc fibre** *Nylon is a man-made fibre.*
3 [C] a thin thread, or one of the thin parts like threads that form natural materials such as wood or CARBON
4 nerve/muscle fibres the thin pieces of flesh that form the nerves or muscles in your body
5 with every fibre of your being *literary* if you feel something with every fibre of your being, you feel it very strongly: *He wanted her with every fibre of his being.* → **moral fibre** at MORAL¹(2), **OPTICAL FIBRE**

fi·bre·board *BrE*, **fiberboard** *AmE* /ˈfaɪbəbɔːd $ -bərbɔːrd/ *n* [U] board made from wood fibres pressed together

fi·bre·glass *BrE*, **fiberglass** *AmE* /ˈfaɪbəglɑːs $ -bərglæs/ *n* [U] a light material made from small glass threads pressed together, used for making sports cars, small boats etc

ˌfibre ˈoptics *BrE*, **fiber optics** *AmE n* [U] the process of using very thin threads of glass or plastic to carry information in the form of light, especially on telephone lines: *fibre optic cables*

fi·brous /ˈfaɪbrəs/ *adj* consisting of many fibres or looking like fibres: *The coconut has a fibrous outer covering.*

fib·u·la /ˈfɪbjələ/ *n* [C] *medical* the outer bone of the two bones in your leg below your knee → see picture at SKELETON

fick·le /ˈfɪkəl/ *adj* **1** someone who is fickle is always changing their mind about people or things that they like, so that you cannot depend on them - used to show disapproval OPP **faithful**: *an unpredictable and fickle lover* **2** something such as weather that is fickle often changes suddenly OPP **reliable** —**fickleness** *n* [U]: *the fickleness of fame*

fic·tion /ˈfɪkʃən/ ●●○ *n*
1 [U] books and stories about imaginary people and events OPP **non-fiction**: *romantic fiction* | *historical fiction* **THESAURUS▸ BOOK**
2 [C] something that people want you to believe is true but which is not true OPP **fact**: *preserving the fiction of his happy childhood*

fic·tion·al /ˈfɪkʃənəl/ ●○○ *adj* fictional people, events etc are imaginary and from a book or story OPP **factual**: *fictional characters* | *The novel is set in the fictional German town of Kreiswald.*

fic·tion·al·ize (*also* **-ise** *BrE*) /ˈfɪkʃənəlaɪz/ *v* [T] to make a film or story about a real event, changing some details and adding some imaginary characters: *a fictionalized account of his life in Berlin*

fic·ti·tious /fɪkˈtɪʃəs/ ●○○ *adj* not true, or not real SYN **imaginary**: *a fictitious address* | *fictitious characters*

fic·tive /ˈfɪktɪv/ *adj AmE* imaginary and not real: *the fictive world of James Bond*

fid·dle¹ /ˈfɪdl/ *n* [C] *informal* **1** a VIOLIN **2** *BrE* a dishonest way of getting money: *an insurance fiddle* | **on the fiddle** *They suspected he was on the fiddle* (=getting money dishonestly or illegally) *all along.* **3 be a fiddle** to be difficult to do and involve complicated movements of your hands: *This blouse is a bit of a fiddle to do up.* → **fit as a fiddle** at FIT²(1), → **play second fiddle (to sb)** at PLAY¹(22)

fiddle² *v* **1** [I] to keep moving and touching something, especially because you are bored or nervous: *Stop fiddling, will you!* | *I sat and fiddled at the computer for a while.* | **[+with]** *She was at her desk in the living room, fiddling with a deck of cards.* **2** [T] *BrE informal* to give false information about something, in order to avoid paying money or to get extra money: *Bert had been fiddling his income tax for years.* | **fiddle the books** (=give false figures in a company's financial records) **3** [I] to play a VIOLIN

fiddle around (*also* **fiddle about** *BrE*) *phr v* to waste time doing unimportant things

fiddle around with sth (*also* **fiddle about with sth** *BrE*) *phr v* **1** to move the parts of a machine in order to try to make it work or repair it: *I've been fiddling around with this old car for months but I still can't get it to work.* **2** to make small unnecessary changes to something - used to show disapproval SYN **mess around with**: *Why did you let her fiddle about with the remote control?* | *The bus company is always fiddling around with the schedules.*

fiddle with sth *phr v* **1** to move part of a machine in order to make it work, without knowing exactly what you should do: *After fiddling with the tuning I finally got JFM.* **2** to move or touch something that does not belong to you, in an annoying way: *Don't let him fiddle with my bag.*

fid·dler /ˈfɪdlə $ -ər/ *n* [C] **1** someone who plays the VIOLIN, especially if they play FOLK MUSIC **2** someone who gives false information, especially on official documents, in order to pay less money or get more than they should: *tax fiddlers* —**fiddling** *n* [U]

fid·dle·sticks /ˈfɪdlˌstɪks/ *interjection old-fashioned* said when you disagree with someone, or are slightly annoyed about something

fid·dling /ˈfɪdlɪŋ/ *adj* [only before noun] unimportant and annoying: *fiddling little jobs around the house*

fid·dly /ˈfɪdli/ *adj BrE informal* difficult to do, especially because you have to deal with very small objects: *Fixing the TV was a **fiddly job**.*

fi·del·i·ty /fɪˈdeləti/ *n* [U] *formal* **1** when you are loyal to your husband, girlfriend etc, by not having sex with anyone else SYN **loyalty** OPP **infidelity**: *the importance of **marital fidelity*** (=in marriage) **2** when you are loyal to a person, an organization, or something that you believe in SYN **loyalty**: **[+to]** *his fidelity to the company over 25 years* **3** *formal* how much a film, a piece of written work etc remains unchanged from an earlier piece of work, or the facts that are known SYN **faithfulness**: **[+to]** *the movie's fidelity to the original book* → **HIGH FIDELITY**

fid·get¹ /ˈfɪdʒɪt/ *v* [I] to keep moving your hands or feet, especially because you are bored or nervous: *The kids had started to fidget.* | **[+with]** *Stop fidgeting with your pens!* **THESAURUS** ▸ **MOVE**

fidget² *n* [C] *informal* someone who is unable to sit or stand still

fid·get·y /ˈfɪdʒəti/ *adj informal* unable to stay still, especially because of being bored or nervous: *The boys* ***get fidgety*** *if they can't play outside.*

fie /faɪ/ *interjection old use* **fie on sb** used to express anger or disapproval towards someone

fief·dom /ˈfi:fdəm/ *n* [C] **1** an area, organization, or part of an organization that someone has complete control over: *He regarded the company as his* ***personal fiefdom***. **2** in history, a small area that was ruled by a king or lord

field¹ /fi:ld/ ●●● S1 W1 *n* [C]

1 FARM an area of land in the country, especially one where crops are grown or animals feed on grass: *a view of green fields and rolling hills* | **[+of]** *a field of wheat* | **corn/rice/wheat etc field** *working in the cotton fields*

2 SUBJECT a subject that people study or an area of activity that they are involved in as part of their work: **[+of]** *her work in the field of human rights* | *Peter's an expert* ***in his field***. | *He's the best-known American* ***outside the field of*** (=not connected with) *politics.*

3 SPORT an area of ground where sports are played: **a baseball/football/cricket etc field** *the local soccer field* | **on/off the field** *The team have had a bad year, both on and off the field.* | *Fans cheered as the players* ***took the field*** (=went onto the field). → see picture at **FOOTBALL**

4 PRACTICAL WORK work or study that is done in the field is done in the real world rather than in a class or LABORATORY: **in the field** *His theories have not yet been tested in the field.* | **field trials/testing/research etc** → **FIELD TRIP**, **FIELDWORK**

5 COMPETITORS **a)** all the people, companies, products etc that are competing against each other: *the field of candidates for the election* | **be ahead of/lead the field** (=be doing better than the others) *Germany was leading the field with a figure of 53%.* **b)** all the horses or runners in a race: *Prince* ***led the field*** (=was ahead of the others) *as they came around the final bend.*

6 magnetic/gravitational/force field the area in which a natural force is felt or has an effect: *the Earth's magnetic field*

7 coal/oil/gas field a large area of land where coal, oil, or gas is found: *North Sea oil fields*

8 the field (of battle) the time or place where there is fighting in a war: *The new tank has yet to be tested in the field.* | *medals won* ***on the field of battle***

9 field of vision/view the whole area that you are able to see without turning your head

10 snow/ice field a large area of land covered with snow or ice

11 field of fire the area that you can hit when you shoot from a particular position

12 leave the field clear for sb to make it possible for someone to do something or to be successful at something, by not competing with them: *Josh left the company, leaving the field clear for me.*

13 COMPUTERS in a computer document, an amount of space made available for a particular type of information: *an empty field* (=not yet written in) → **have a field day** at **FIELD DAY**, → **play the field** at **PLAY¹**(31)

field² ●○○ *v* [T]

1 if you field a team, an army etc, they represent you or fight for you in a competition, election, or war: *The Ecology Party* ***fielded*** *109* ***candidates***. | *We* ***fielded*** *a* ***team*** *of highly talented basketball players.*

2 to answer questions, telephone calls etc, especially when there are a lot of them or the questions are difficult: *The Minister* ***fielded questions*** *on the Middle East.* | *The press office* ***fielded*** *numerous* ***calls*** *from the media.*

3 be fielding the team that is fielding in a game of CRICKET or baseball is the one that is throwing and catching the ball, rather than the one hitting it OPP **be batting**

4 if you field the ball in a game of CRICKET or baseball, you stop it after it has been hit

ˈfield corn *n* [U] *AmE* a type of corn grown to feed to animals, rather than to be eaten by people → **SWEETCORN**

ˈfield day *n* **1 have a field day** *informal* to have a chance to do a lot of something you want, especially the chance to criticize someone: *The newspapers had a field day when the trial finished.* **2** [C] *AmE* a day when students at a school have sports competitions and parents watch SYN **sports day** *BrE*

field·er /ˈfi:ldə $ -ər/ (*also* **fieldsman** *BrE*) *n* [C] one of the players who tries to catch the ball in a game of CRICKET or baseball

ˈfield ˌevent *n* [C] a sport such as jumping or throwing the JAVELIN in an outdoor competition → **TRACK EVENT**

ˈfield ˌglasses *n* [plural] BINOCULARS

ˈfield ˌgoal *n* [C] **1** the act of kicking the ball over the GOAL in American football **2** the act of putting the ball through the net to get points in BASKETBALL

ˈfield ˌhockey *n* [U] *AmE* HOCKEY played on grass

ˈfield ˌhospital *n* [C] a temporary hospital for soldiers that is near where the fighting is

ˈfield ˌmarshal *n* [C] an officer of the highest rank in the British army

field·mouse /ˈfi:ldmaʊs/ *n* (*plural* **fieldmice** /-maɪs/) [C] a mouse that has a long tail and lives in fields

ˈfield ˌofficer *n* [C] **1** *BrE* someone who works for an organization whose job involves practical outdoor work, especially work connected with the countryside **2** an officer of high rank in the British army

fields·man /ˈfi:ldzmən/ *n* (*plural* **fieldsmen** /-mən/) [C] *BrE* FIELDER

ˈfield ˌsports *n* [plural] *BrE* sports that happen in the countryside, such as hunting, shooting, and fishing

ˈfield test *n* [C] a test of a new piece of equipment, done in the place where it will be used rather than in a LABORATORY —**field-test** *v* [T]

ˈfield trip *n* [C] an occasion when students go somewhere to learn about a particular subject, especially one connected with nature or science: *a geography field trip*

field·work /ˈfi:ldwɜ:k $ -wɜ:rk/ *n* [U] the study of scientific or social subjects, done outside the class or LABORATORY —**fieldworker** *n* [C]

fiend /fi:nd/ *n* [C] **1** a very cruel, evil, or violent person: *a heartless fiend* | *Both of them were fighting like fiends.* | **a sex/rape fiend** (=one who commits very unpleasant sex attacks) **2 television/sports/fresh-air etc fiend** someone who likes watching television, doing sports etc a lot, or more than is normal SYN **fanatic** **3 drug/dope/cocaine etc fiend** someone who takes a lot of illegal drugs **4** an evil spirit

fiend·ish /ˈfi:ndɪʃ/ *adj* **1** cruel and unpleasant: *a particularly fiendish practical joke* **2** very clever in an unpleasant way: *a fiendish plan* **3** extremely difficult or complicated: *several fiendish exam questions* —**fiendishly** *adv* —**fiendishness** *n* [U]

fierce /fɪəs $ fɪrs/ ●●○ *adj*

1 done with a lot of energy and strong feelings, and sometimes violence: *fierce fighting in the city* | **fierce attack/opposition/criticism etc** *The government's policies came under fierce attack.* | *a fierce debate* | ***fierce competition*** *between the companies* **THESAURUS** ▸ **VIOLENT**

2 a fierce person or animal is angry or ready to attack, and looks very frightening: *fierce guard dogs* | *She turned round, looking fierce.*

3 fierce emotions are very strong and often angry: *These people take fierce pride in their independence.*

4 fierce cold, heat, or weather is much colder, hotter etc than usual: *a fierce wind*

F

5 *informal* looking very good and fashionable SYN **fabulous**
6 something fierce *AmE spoken* more loudly, strongly etc than usual: *It was snowing something fierce.* —**fierceness** *n* [U]

fierce·ly /ˈfɪəsli $ ˈfɪrs-/ ●●○ *adv*
1 strongly or severely: *The idea was* ***fiercely opposed*** *by nationalists.* | *It is a* ***fiercely competitive*** *market.* | *Maria was* ***fiercely independent****.*
2 in an angry way: *He stared fiercely into my eyes.* | *'Don't you dare laugh!' she said fiercely.*

fi·er·y /ˈfaɪəri $ ˈfaɪri/ ●○○ *adj*
1 very red or orange, and looking like fire: *a fiery sunset* | *leaves that turn* ***fiery red*** *in autumn*
2 becoming angry or excited very quickly: *He has a* ***fiery temper****.*
3 showing or encouraging anger or excitement: *a fiery speech*
4 fiery food or drink tastes very strong, making part of your body feel hot

fi·es·ta /fiˈestə/ *n* [C] a religious holiday with dancing, music etc, especially in Spain and South America

fife /faɪf/ *n* [C] a musical instrument like a small FLUTE, often played in military bands

fif·teen /ˌfɪfˈtiːn◂/ ●●● S3 W3 *number, n*
1 the number 15: *a coastal village fifteen miles south of Tourane* | *They met when she was fifteen* (=15 years old).
2 [C] a team of 15 players in RUGBY UNION —**fifteenth** *adj, pron*: *in the fifteenth century* | *her fifteenth birthday* | *I'm planning to leave on* ***the fifteenth*** (=the 15th day of the month).

fifth¹ /fɪfθ/ ●●● S3 W3 *adj*
1 coming after four other things in a series: *in the fifth century* | *her fifth birthday*
2 fifth wheel *AmE informal* someone who is not wanted in a particular group of people: *They'd made her feel like a fifth wheel.* —**fifth** *pron*: *I'm planning to leave on* ***the fifth*** (=the fifth day of the month). —**fifthly** *adv*

fifth² *n* [C] **1** one of five equal parts of something **2** *AmE* an amount of alcohol equal to 1/5 of an American GALLON(1), sold in bottles: *a fifth of bourbon*

ˌfifth ˈcolumn *n* [C] a group of people who work secretly to help the enemies of the country where they live or the organization in which they work —**fifth columnist** *n* [C]

fif·ty /ˈfɪfti/ ●●● S3 W3 *number, n*
1 the number 50
2 the fifties [plural] (*also* **the '50s, the 1950s**) the years between 1950 and 1959: *Standards of living rose in the fifties.* | **the early/mid/late fifties** *The play was written in the late fifties.*
3 be in your fifties to be aged between 50 and 59: **early/mid/late fifties** *He must be in his early fifties by now.*
4 in the fifties if the temperature is in the fifties, it is between 50 degrees and 59 degrees: **in the low/mid/high fifties** *sunny, with temperatures in the mid fifties*
5 [C] a piece of paper money that is worth 50 dollars or 50 pounds: *I can give you five tens for that fifty if you want.* —**fiftieth** *adj*: *her fiftieth birthday*

ˌfifty-ˈfifty *adv, adj spoken* **1** if you divide something fifty-fifty, you divide it equally between two people, companies etc: **divide/split/share sth fifty-fifty** *The companies split the profits fifty-fifty.* | *We'll share it on* ***a fifty-fifty basis****.* | **go fifty-fifty (on sth)** (=share the cost of something equally) *We went fifty-fifty on a new TV set.* **2** if there is a fifty-fifty chance of something happening, it is as equally likely to happen as not to happen SYN **equal**: ***a fifty-fifty chance*** *of winning*

fig /fɪg/ *n* [C] **1** a soft sweet fruit with a lot of small seeds, often eaten dried, or the tree on which this fruit grows **2 not give a fig/not care a fig (about/for sth/sb)** *old-fashioned informal* to not be at all concerned about or interested in something or someone

fig. **1** the written abbreviation of ***figure*** **2** the written abbreviation of ***figurative***

fight¹ /faɪt/ ●●● S1 W1 *v* (*past tense and past participle* **fought** /fɔːt $ fɒːt/)
1 WAR [I,T] to take part in a war or battle: **[+in]** *the families of those who fought in the war* | **[+against/with]** *rebel forces fighting against the Russians* | **[+about/over/for]** *They fought for control of the islands.* | *Neither country is capable of* ***fighting*** *a long* ***war****.* | *Later the Indians fought the Anglo settlers.*

GRAMMAR: Reciprocal verbs

Fight is a reciprocal verb. This type of verb is used when saying that two or more people or groups do something that involves both or all of them. It does not need to have an object: *The Republicans and the Nationalists fought.* In this sentence, **fight** is intransitive and does not have an object.
You can also say: *The Republicans and the Nationalists fought each other.* | *The Republicans fought the Nationalists.* In these sentences, **fight** is transitive.
GRAMMAR GUIDE ▸ VERBS

2 HIT PEOPLE [I,T] if someone fights another person, or if two people fight, they hit and kick the other person in order to hurt them: **[+with]** *Two guys were fighting with each other in the street.* | **[+about/over/for]** *They were fighting over a girl.* | *She fought him desperately, kicking and biting.*
3 TRY TO DO STH [I,T] to try hard to do or get something: **[+for]** *The men were fighting for higher wages.* | *Stockley is* ***fighting for*** *his* ***life*** (=trying to stay alive), *with serious head injuries.* | *She* ***fought*** *her* ***way*** *back into the first team.* | **fight to do sth** *The president was fighting to survive.*
4 PREVENT STH [I,T] to try very hard to prevent something or to get rid of something unpleasant that already exists: **[+against]** *People are fighting against repression and injustice.* | *We will fight terrorism, wherever it exists.*
5 COMPETE [I,T] to take part in an election or compete strongly for something, especially a job or political position: **fight an election/a campaign** *The prime minister decided to fight an early general election.* | **fight (sb) for sth** *He had to fight several other applicants for the job.* | *Both men were used to fighting for power.*
6 ARGUE [I] to argue about something: **[+with]** *I heard her fighting with the boss.* | **[+about/over]** *They're fighting about who should do the dishes.*
7 SPORT [I,T] to take part in a BOXING match: *Ali fought Foreman for the heavyweight title.*
8 EMOTION [I,T] to try very hard not to have or show a feeling: *She fought her fear.* | **[+with]** *She was clearly fighting with her emotions.*
9 LAW [T] to try to get something or prevent something in a court of law: *The insurance company are fighting the claims in court.*
10 fight your way (through/past etc sb/sth) to move somewhere with difficulty, for example because there are so many people around you: *We fought our way through the crowd.*
11 fight a losing battle to try to do something that you probably cannot succeed in doing: *I'm fighting a losing battle on this diet.*
12 have a fighting chance to have a chance to do something or achieve something if you try very hard: *Lewis has a fighting chance to win the gold medal.*
13 fight tooth and nail (for sth)/fight sth tooth and nail to try very hard to do or achieve something, or to prevent something: *He's rich now, but he had to fight tooth and nail for it.*
14 fight to the death/finish to fight until one person or group is dead or completely defeated
15 fight your own battles to fight for what you want, without needing help from other people: *Mum, I can fight my own battles now.*
16 fighting spirit the desire to fight or win: *In the second half the team showed their true fighting spirit.*
17 fighting words/talk something you say that shows that you want to fight hard for something
18 fight fire with fire to use the same methods as your opponents in an argument, competition etc

19 fight like cat and dog if two people fight like cat and dog, they argue a lot because they dislike each other or disagree: *I didn't get on with her at work either – we fought like cat and dog.*
20 fighting fit *BrE* extremely fit and healthy
21 fight your corner *BrE* to try to persuade people that your ideas about something are right and should be accepted: *The prime minister made it clear that Britain would fight its corner on Europe.*
22 fight shy of (doing) sth *BrE* to try to avoid doing something or being involved in something: *Many women fight shy of motherhood.*
fight back *phr v*
1 to work hard to achieve or oppose something, especially in a situation where you are losing: *United fought back and scored a last-minute goal.* | **[+against]** *She was fighting back against the cancer.*
2 to use violence or arguments against someone who has attacked you or argued with you: *The rebels are fighting back.*
3 fight sth ↔ back to try hard not to have or show a feeling: *She looked away,* ***fighting back*** *her* ***tears****.* | *He fought back the impulse to slap her.*
fight sth ↔ **down** *phr v* to try hard not to have or show a feeling: *Doug fought down a feeling of panic.*
fight sb/sth ↔ **off** *phr v*
1 to keep someone away, or stop them doing something to you, by fighting or opposing them: *Bodyguards had to fight off the crowds.* | *The company managed to fight off a takeover attempt.*
2 to succeed in stopping other people getting something, and to get it for yourself: *Allan fought off stiff competition from throughout the UK to win one of only four places at the college.*
3 to try hard to get rid of something, especially an illness or a feeling: *Elaine's fighting off a cold.*
fight sth **out** *phr v* to argue or fight until a disagreement is settled: *We left them to* ***fight it out****.*

fight² ●●● S2 W3 *n*
1 PEOPLE HIT EACH OTHER [C] a situation in which two people or groups hit, push etc each other: *Her son was always getting into fights at school.* | **[+with]** *They ended up having a fight with each other.* | **[+between]** *A fight broke out between the fans.* | **[+over/about]** *fights over territory*
2 TO ACHIEVE/PREVENT STH [singular] the process of trying to achieve something or prevent something: **[+for]** *the fight for justice and democracy* | *The little girl lost her* ***fight for life*** (=fight to stay alive) *last night.* | **[+against]** *the fight against crime* | **fight to do sth** *the fight to get financial aid* | *You'll* ***have a fight on*** *your* ***hands*** (=it will be difficult) *to convince the committee.*
3 ARGUMENT [C] an argument: **[+with]** *They've* ***had*** *a* ***fight*** *with the neighbours.* | **[+over/about]** *fights over money*
4 BOXING [C] a BOXING match: *Are you going to watch the big fight tonight?*
5 BATTLE [C] a battle between two armies: **[+for]** *the fight for Bunker Hill*
6 ENERGY [U] energy or the desire to keep fighting for something you want: *There's plenty of fight left in your grandmother.*
7 put up a good fight to work very hard to fight or compete in a difficult situation: *Our team put up a good fight.*
8 a fight to the death/finish a fight that continues until one side is completely defeated

COLLOCATIONS
VERBS
have a fight *I didn't want to have a fight with him.*
get into a fight (=become involved in a fight) *The two men got into a fight over a girl.*
start a fight *They started a fight in the crowded bar.*
pick a fight (=deliberately start a fight) *The guy tried to pick a fight with Jack.*
stop a fight/break up a fight | **win/lose a fight** | **be spoiling for a fight** (=be very eager to fight with someone) | **a fight breaks out/erupts** (=suddenly starts) | **a fight takes place** (=happens)

ADJECTIVES/NOUN + fight
a big fight *They ended up having a big fight in the pub.*
a fair fight *It was a fair fight, just two on two.*
a fierce fight *There was a fierce fight with rebel forces and several soldiers were killed.*
a street fight | **a fist fight** (=a fight in which people hit each other with their closed hands) | **a knife/sword fight**

fight·back /ˈfaɪtbæk/ *n* [C] *BrE* an attempt by someone to get back to a position of strength after they have lost it, especially in sport: *Arsenal staged a spirited fightback in the second half.*

fight·er /ˈfaɪtə $ -ər/ ●●○ *n* [C]
1 (*also* **ˈfighter plane/aircraft/jet**) a small fast military plane that can destroy other planes: *He was shot down by* ***enemy fighters****.* | *a* ***fighter pilot***
2 someone who fights, especially as a sport
3 someone who keeps trying to achieve something in difficult situations: *James is a fighter – he never gives up.*
→ FIREFIGHTER, FREEDOM FIGHTER

fight·ing /ˈfaɪtɪŋ/ ●●○ *n* [U] when people or groups fight each other in a war, in the street etc: **[+between]** ***heavy fighting*** *between government and rebel forces* | ***Fighting broke out*** *in the crowds.* THESAURUS ▸ WAR

ˈfig leaf *n* [C] the large leaf of the fig tree, sometimes shown in paintings as covering people's sex organs

fig·ment /ˈfɪɡmənt/ *n* **a figment of sb's imagination** something that you imagine is real, but does not exist

fig·u·ra·tive /ˈfɪɡjərətɪv, -ɡə-/ ●○○ *adj*
1 a figurative word or phrase is used in a different way from its usual meaning, to give you a particular idea or picture in your mind → **literal**: *He's my son,* ***in the figurative sense*** *of the word.*
2 *technical* figurative art shows objects, people, or the countryside as they really look → **abstract** —**figuratively** *adv*: *They have a taste –* ***figuratively speaking*** *– for excitement.*

fig·ure¹ /ˈfɪɡə $ ˈfɪɡjər/ ●●● S1 W1 *n* [C]
1 NUMBER **a)** [usually plural] a number representing an amount, especially an official number: **unemployment/sales/trade figures** *Ohio's unemployment figures for December* | *Government figures underestimate the problem.* | *It's about 30,000* ***in round figures*** (=to the nearest 10, 20, 100 etc). **b)** a number from 0 to 9, written as a character rather than a word: *the figure '2'* | *executives with salaries* ***in six figures*** (=more than £99,999) | **a four/five/six figure number** (=a number in the thousands, ten thousands, hundred thousands etc) → DOUBLE FIGURES, SINGLE FIGURES
2 AMOUNT OF MONEY a particular amount of money: **[+of]** *an estimated figure of $200 million*
3 PERSON **a)** someone who is important or famous in some way: **a leading/key/central figure** *Several leading figures resigned from the party.* | *the outstanding* ***political figure*** *of his time* **b)** someone with a particular type of appearance or character, especially when they are far away or difficult to see: *a tall figure in a hat* | *Through the window I could see the commanding figure of Mrs Bradshaw.* → **cult figure** at CULT²
4 WOMAN'S BODY the shape of a woman's body: *She* ***has a good figure****.* | **keep/lose your figure** (=stay thin or become fat) | *Most women have to* ***watch*** *their* ***figure*** (=be careful not to get fat).
5 father/mother/authority figure someone who is considered to be like a father etc, or to represent authority, because of their character or behaviour
6 figures [plural] *BrE* the activity of adding, multiplying etc numbers SYN **arithmetic**: *a natural ability* ***with figures*** | **have a head for figures** (=be good at arithmetic)
7 MATHEMATICAL SHAPE a GEOMETRIC shape: *A hexagon is a six-sided figure.*
8 PAINTING/MODEL a person in a painting or a model of a person: *the figure in the background* → FIGURINE
9 DRAWING (*written abbreviation* **fig.**) a numbered drawing or a DIAGRAM in a book
10 put a figure on it/give an exact figure to say exactly how

F

much something is worth, or how much or how many of something you are talking about: *It's worth a lot but I couldn't put a figure on it.*
11 a fine figure of a man/woman someone who is tall and has a good body
12 a figure of fun someone who people laugh at
13 ON ICE a pattern or movement in FIGURE SKATING

figure² ●●● S1 W3 *v*
1 [I] to be an important part of a process, event, or situation, or to be included in something: **[+in/among]** *Social issues* ***figured prominently*** *in the talks.* | *My wishes didn't figure among his considerations.* | *Reform now* ***figures high*** *on the agenda.*
2 [T] *informal* to form a particular opinion after thinking about a situation: **figure (that)** *From the way he behaved, I figured that he was drunk.* | *It was worth the trouble, I figured.*
3 that figures/(it) figures *spoken especially AmE* **a)** used to say that something that happens is expected or typical, especially something bad: *'It rained the whole weekend.' 'Oh, that figures.'* **b)** used to say that something is reasonable or makes sense: ***It figures that*** *she'd be mad at you, after what you did.*
4 go figure *AmE spoken* said to show that you think something is strange or difficult to explain: *'He didn't even leave a message.' 'Go figure.'*
5 [T] *AmE* to calculate an amount SYN **work out**: *I'm just figuring my expenses.*
figure on sth *phr v informal especially AmE* to expect something or include it in your plans: *She was younger than any of us had figured on.*
figure sb/sth ↔ **out** *phr v*
1 to think about a problem or situation until you find the answer or understand what has happened SYN **work out**: **figure out how/what/why etc** *Can you figure out how to do it?* | *If I have a map, I can figure it out.* | *Don't worry, we'll figure something out* (=find a way to solve the problem).
2 to understand why someone behaves in the way they do SYN **work out**: *Women. I just can't figure them out.*

fig·ured /ˈfɪɡəd $ ˈfɪɡjərd/ *adj* [only before noun] *formal* decorated with a small pattern

fig·ure·head /ˈfɪɡəhed $ ˈfɪɡjər-/ *n* [C] **1** someone who seems to be the leader of a country or organization but who has no real power → **puppet**: *The Queen is merely a figurehead.* THESAURUS▸ LEADER **2** a wooden model of a woman that used to be placed on the front of ships

ˌfigure of ˈeight *BrE*, **ˌfigure ˈeight** *AmE* *n* [C] the pattern or shape of a number eight, as seen in a knot, dance etc

ˌfigure of ˈspeech *n* [C] a word or expression that is used in a different way from the normal meaning, to give you a picture in your mind

ˈfigure ˌskating *n* [U] a kind of SKATING in which you move in patterns on the ice —**figure skater** *n* [C]

fig·u·rine /ˌfɪɡjəˈriːn, ˈfɪɡjəriːn $ ˌfɪɡjəˈriːn/ *n* [C] a small model of a person or animal used as a decoration

fil·a·ment /ˈfɪləmənt/ *n* [C] a very thin thread or wire: *an electric filament*

fil·bert /ˈfɪlbət $ -bərt/ *n* [C] *especially AmE* a HAZELNUT

filch /fɪltʃ/ *v* [T] *informal* to steal something small or not very valuable SYN **pinch, nick** *BrE*: *He filched a bottle of wine from the cellar.*

file¹ /faɪl/ ●●● S1 W2 AWL *n* [C]
1 a set of papers, records etc that contain information about a particular person or subject: **[+on]** *Mendoza read over the file on the murders.* | *The FBI* ***keeps files on*** *former White House employees.* | *We will* ***keep*** *your details* ***on file*** (=store them for later use). | **police/case/medical etc file** *a copy of the court file*
2 a box or piece of folded card in which you store loose papers: *She pulled a blue file from the shelf.*
3 information on a computer that you store under a particular name: *a list of all the files and folders on your hard disk*
4 a metal tool with a rough surface that you rub on something to make it smooth → NAIL FILE, see picture at TOOL¹
5 a line of people who are standing or walking one behind the other: **[+of]** *a file of soldiers marching in step* | **in file** *It was dark as we set off in file.* → SINGLE FILE, RANK AND FILE

COLLOCATIONS – MEANING 3

VERBS

open a file *Click on the icon to open the file.*
close a file *You may need to close the file and restart the computer.*
save a file *Save the file under a different filename.*
create a file *I created a file of useful contacts.*
delete a file (=remove it) | **access a file** (=open or read it) | **edit a file** (=make changes to it) | **copy a file** | **move a file** | **transfer a file** (=move it from one computer system to another) | **download a file** (=move a copy of it from the Internet or another computer to your computer) | **upload a file** (=move a copy of it from your computer to the Internet or another computer) | **load a file** (=put it onto a computer) | **send sb a file** (=send it using email) | **attach a file** (=send it with an email)

NOUN + file

a computer file *Delete some of the old computer files and create some space on the hard drive.*
a backup file (=a copy of a file, which is made in case the original becomes lost or damaged) *You can burn your backup file to CD or DVD.*

file² ●●○ S3 W3 AWL *v*
1 [T] to keep papers, documents etc in a particular place so that you can find them easily: *The contracts are* ***filed alphabetically.*** | **file sth under sth** *I looked to see if anything was filed under my name.* | **file sth away** *The handbooks are filed away for future reference.*
2 [T] to give or send an official report or news story to your employer: *The officer left the scene without filing a report.*
3 [I always + adv/prep, T] *law* to give a document to a court or other organization so that it can be officially recorded and dealt with: **file a complaint/lawsuit/petition etc (against sb)** *Mr Genoa filed a formal complaint against the department.* | **[+for]** *The Morrisons have* ***filed for divorce.*** | *Today is the deadline for Americans to* ***file*** *their* ***tax returns.***
4 [I always + adv/prep] if people file somewhere, they walk there in a line: *We began to file out into the car park.* | *The mourners filed past the coffin.*
5 [I always + adv/prep, T] to use a metal or wooden tool to rub something in order to make it smooth: *File down the sharp edges.* | *She sat filing her nails.*

ˈfile ˌcabinet *n* [C] *AmE* a piece of office furniture with drawers for storing letters, reports etc SYN **filing cabinet** *BrE*

ˈfile exˌtension *n* [C] the letters, for example .doc, at the end of the name of a computer file that show what type of file it is

file·name /ˈfaɪlneɪm/ *n* [C] the name you give to a particular computer file

ˈfile ˌsharing, **file-sharing** *n* [U] the act of sharing computer files, such as music files, with other people using the Internet

fil·et /ˈfɪlɪt $ ˈfɪlət, -leɪ, fɪˈleɪ/ *n, v* an American spelling of FILLET

fi·li·al /ˈfɪliəl/ *adj formal* relating to the relationship of a son or daughter to their parents → **parental**: *her filial duty*

fil·i·bus·ter /ˈfɪləbʌstə $ -ər/ *v* [I,T] to try to delay action in Congress or another law-making group by making very long speeches: *Opponents of the bill tried to filibuster its final stages.* —**filibuster** *n* [C]

fil·i·gree /ˈfɪləɡriː/ *n* [U] delicate designs or decorations made of gold or silver wire: *silver filigree jewellery*

fil·ing /ˈfaɪlɪŋ/ AWL *n* **1** [U] the work of arranging documents in the correct FILES **2 filings** [plural] small sharp bits that come off when a piece of metal is cut or FILEd: *iron*

F

filings **3** [C] a document, report etc that is officially recorded: *a bankruptcy filing*

ˈfiling ˌcabinet *n* [C] *BrE* a piece of office furniture with drawers for storing letters, reports etc SYN **file cabinet** *AmE*

FILL

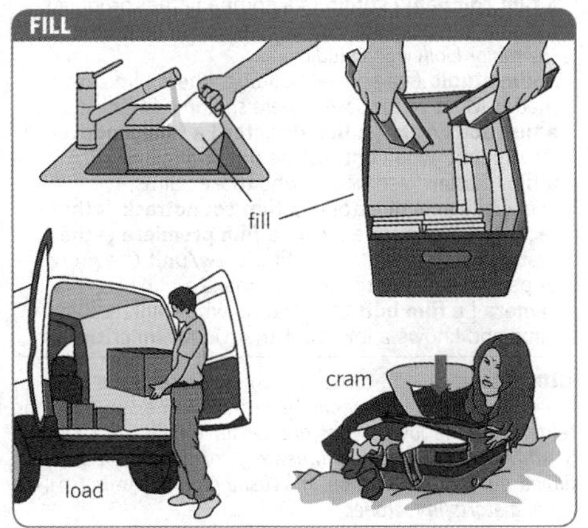

fill¹ /fɪl/ ●●● S1 W1 *v*

1 BECOME/MAKE FULL [I,T] (*also* **fill up**) if a container or place fills, or if you fill it, enough of something goes into it to make it full: *He poured her a drink, then filled his own glass.* | *My job was filling the flour sacks.* | *Take a deep breath and allow your lungs to fill.* | **fill (sth) with sth** *Her* **eyes filled with tears**. | **fill sth to the brim/to overflowing** (=fill something completely) *a bucket filled to the brim with ice* | *There was just enough wind to fill the sails.* | *Miller's band was filling dance halls* (=attracting a lot of people) *all over the country.*

2 LARGE THING/NUMBER [T] if a thing or group fills something, there is no space left: *Crowds of well-wishers filled the streets.* | *His wartime experiences would fill a book!* | *All the seats were filled and a number of people were standing.* | *Numerous pictures* **fill** *every available* **space**.

3 SOUND/SMELL/LIGHT [T] if a sound, smell, or light fills a place, you notice it because it is very loud or strong: *The smell of freshly baked bread filled the room.* | **be filled with sth** *The air was filled with the sound of children's laughter.*

4 EMOTIONS [T] if you are filled with an emotion, or if it fills you, you feel it very strongly: **be filled with admiration/joy/happiness etc** *I was filled with admiration for her.* | **be filled with horror/fear/anger/doubt/remorse** *Their faces were suddenly filled with fear.* | **fill sb with sth** *The prospect filled him with horror.*

5 PROVIDE STH [T] to provide something that is needed or wanted but which has not been available or present before: **fill a need/demand** *Volunteers fill a real need for teachers in the Somali Republic.* | **fill a gap/hole/niche etc** *I spent most of the summer filling the gaps in my education.* | *The company has moved quickly to fill the niche in the overnight travel market.*

6 SPEND TIME [T] if you fill a period of time with a particular activity, you spend that time doing it: **fill your time/the days etc (with sth)** *I have no trouble filling my time.*

7 PERFORM A JOB [T] to perform a particular job, activity, or purpose in an organization, or to find someone or something to do this: **fill a post/position/vacancy etc** *Women fill 35% of senior management positions.* | *Thank you for your letter. Unfortunately, the vacancy has already been filled.* | *The UK should find another weapon to* **fill** *the same* **role**.

8 CRACK/HOLE [T] (*also* **fill in**) to put a substance into a hole, crack etc to make a surface level: *Fill in any cracks before starting to paint.* | *materials developed to fill tooth cavities*

9 **fill yourself (up)/fill your face** *informal* to eat so much food that you cannot eat any more

10 **fill an order** to supply the goods that a customer has ordered: *The company is struggling to fill $11 million in back orders.*

11 **fill the bill** *AmE* to have exactly the right qualities SYN **fit the bill** *BrE*: *We needed an experienced reporter and Willis fills the bill.*

12 **fill sb's shoes** to do the work that someone else normally does, especially when this is difficult because they have set a high standard

GRAMMAR

Fill belongs to a group of verbs where the same noun can be the subject of the verb or its object.

- You can say: *She filled the bath with water.* In this sentence, 'the bath' is the object of **fill**.
- You can say: *The bath filled with water.* In this sentence, 'the bath' is the subject of **fill**.

GRAMMAR GUIDE ▸ VERBS

THESAURUS

fill to put enough of something into a container to make it full: *Jenny filled the kettle and put it on to boil.* | *Party balloons can be filled with helium.*

fill up to fill something completely – used especially about putting petrol in the tank of a car: *I need to fill up the car.* | *The waiter filled up everyone's glasses.*

load/load up to fill a vehicle with goods, furniture etc: *Two men were loading a truck with boxes of melons.*

stuff/cram to quickly fill something such as a bag or pocket by pushing things into it tightly: *She hurriedly stuffed some things into an overnight bag and left.*

refill to fill a container again, after what was in it has been used: *I'm just going to refill this bottle from the tap.*

top up *BrE*, **top off** *AmE* to fill a glass or cup that still has some liquid in it: *Can I top up your glass of wine?*

replenish *formal* to make something full again, especially with a supply of something such as water or food: *The lake is fed by springs that are eternally replenished by the rain.*

fill in *phr v*

1 DOCUMENT **fill sth ↔ in** to write all the necessary information on an official document, form etc: *Don't forget to fill in your boarding cards.*

2 TELL SB NEWS **fill sb ↔ in** to tell someone about recent events, especially because they have been away from a place: **[+on]** *I think you'd better fill me in on what's been happening.*

3 CRACK/HOLE **fill sth ↔ in** to put a substance into a hole, crack etc so it is completely full and level

4 **fill in time** to spend time doing something unimportant because you are waiting for something to happen: *She flipped through a magazine to fill in the time.*

5 SPACE **fill sth ↔ in** to paint or draw over the space inside a shape

6 DO SB'S JOB to do someone's job because they are not there: **[+for]** *I'm filling in for Joe for a few days.*

fill out *phr v*

1 **fill sth ↔ out** to write all the necessary information on an official document, form etc

2 if you fill out, or your body fills out, you become slightly fatter: *Eric has filled out around the waist.*

3 if a young person fills out, their body becomes more like an adult's body, for example by having bigger muscles, developing breasts etc: *At puberty, a girl's body begins to fill out.*

4 **fill sth ↔ out** to add more details to a description or story

fill up *phr v*

1 if a container or place fills up, or if you fill it up, it becomes full: **[+with]** *Her* **eyes filled up with tears**. | **fill sth ↔ up** *Shall I fill the car up* (=with petrol)?

2 **fill (yourself) up** *informal* to eat so much food that you cannot eat any more: **[+with/on]** *Don't fill yourself up with cookies.* | *He filled up on pecan pie.*

3 **fill sb up** *informal* food that fills you up makes you feel as

F

though you have eaten a lot when you have only eaten a small amount

fill² *n* **1 have had your fill of sth** *informal* to have done something or experienced something, especially something unpleasant, so that you do not want any more: *I've had my fill of screaming kids for one day.* **2 eat/drink your fill** *old-fashioned* to eat or drink as much as you want or need

fill·er /ˈfɪlə $ -ər/ *n* [C,U] **1** *BrE* a substance used to fill cracks in wood, walls etc, especially before you paint them **2** stories, information, pictures etc that are not important but are used to fill a page in a newspaper or magazine **3** a substance that is put under a person's skin to make lines on their skin less deep or to make their lips bigger

ˈfiller cap *n* [C] *BrE* the lid that fits over the hole in a car that you pour a liquid into, especially oil or petrol

fil·let¹ (*also* **filet** *AmE*) /ˈfɪlɪt $ ˈfɪlət, -leɪ, fɪˈleɪ/ *n* [C] a piece of meat or fish without bones: **[+of]** *a fillet of sole*

fillet² (*also* **filet** *AmE*) *v* [T] to remove the bones from a piece of meat or fish: *filleted fish*

ˈfill-in *n* [singular] *BrE informal* someone who does someone else's job because that person is not there SYN **stand-in**: *I'm here as a fill-in while Robert's away.*

fill·ing¹ /ˈfɪlɪŋ/ *adj* food that is filling makes your stomach feel full: *Pasta and rice are both very filling.*

filling² *n* **1** [C] a small amount of metal or other substance that is put into your tooth to cover a hole: *gold fillings* **2** [C,U] the food that you put inside a PIE, sandwich etc: *cherry filling* **3** [C,U] the soft material inside a CUSHION, PILLOW etc

ˈfilling ˌstation *n* [C] a place where you can buy petrol for your car SYN **petrol station** *BrE*, **gas station** *AmE*

fil·lip /ˈfɪlɪp/ *n* [singular] something that improves a situation or adds excitement or interest to something SYN **boost**: *A cut in lending rates would* ***give a fillip to*** *the housing market.* | *British athletics* ***received a*** *tremendous* ***fillip*** *when Wells won the Gold.*

fil·ly /ˈfɪli/ *n* (*plural* **fillies**) [C] a young female horse → **colt**, **foal**

film¹ /fɪlm/ ●●● S1 W1 *n*

1 [C] a story that is told using sound and moving pictures, shown at a cinema or on television SYN **movie** *AmE*: *Have you seen any good films recently?* | **[+about]** *a film about a young dancer* **THESAURUS** ▸ MOVIE

2 [U] moving pictures of real events that are shown on television or at a cinema: *newsreel film* | *the race to be first with* ***film footage*** (=pictures) *of news events*

3 [U] the work of making films, considered as an art or a business: *I'm interested in photography and film.* | *the film industry* | *a background in film and animation*

4 [C,U] the thin plastic used in a camera for taking photographs or recording moving pictures: *I* ***shot*** *five* ***rolls of film*** *on vacation.* | **record/capture/preserve sth on film** *The whole incident was recorded on film.* → see picture at REEL²

5 [singular] a very thin layer of liquid, powder etc on the surface of something: **[+of]** *a film of oil on the surface of the water* → CLINGFILM

COLLOCATIONS

VERBS

watch a film *He stayed in and watched a film on TV.*
see a film *We saw a good film last night at the cinema.*
appear in a film *She once appeared in a film with Al Pacino.*
star in a film (=be one of the main characters in a film) | **direct a film** | **make/shoot a film** | **show/screen a film** | **a film stars/features sb** | **a film is released/comes out** (=it is made available for people to see) | **a film is showing** (*also* **a film is on** *BrE*) (=it is being shown at a cinema)

ADJECTIVES/NOUN + film

a horror/adventure/war film *He likes watching horror films.*
a cowboy/gangster etc film *John Wayne was best-known for his roles in cowboy films.*
a feature film (=a full-length film shown in the cinema) | **a documentary film** | **a low-budget film**

film + NOUN

the film industry *Scorsese is a highly respected figure in the film industry.*
a film company/studio (=a company that produces films) *a European film company trying to compete with the major Hollywood studios*
a film studio (=a special building where films are made) *Many of the scenes were shot in a film studio.*
a film actor/star | **a film director** | **a film producer** (=someone who controls the preparation of a film) | **a film maker** (=someone who makes films, especially as a director) | **a film soundtrack** (=the recorded music for a film) | **a film premiere** (=the first showing of a film) | **a film crew/unit** (=a group of people working together to make a film) | **a film camera** | **a film buff** (=someone who is interested in films and knows a lot about them) | **a film critic**

film² ●●○ *v* [I,T] to use a camera to record a story or real events so that they can be shown in the cinema or on television: *The love scenes are sensitively filmed.* | *She's in South Africa filming a documentary for the BBC.* | *a thriller* ***filmed*** *entirely* ***on location*** *in Washington* —**filming** *n* [U]: *Filming starts in October.*

film over *phr v* if your eyes film over, they become covered with a thin layer of liquid

film·go·er /ˈfɪlmgəʊə $ -goʊər/ *n* [C] *BrE* someone who goes to see films, especially regularly SYN **moviegoer** *AmE* → **theatregoer**

film·ic /ˈfɪlmɪk/ *adj formal* relating to films or the art of making films: *a new filmic style*

ˈfilm-ˌmaker, **film·mak·er** /ˈfɪlmˌmeɪkə $ -ər/ ●○○ *n* [C] someone who makes films, especially a DIRECTOR or PRODUCER —**film-making** *n* [U]

film noir /ˌfɪlm ˈnwɑː $ -ˈnwɑːr/ *n* (*plural* **films noirs** (*same pronunciation*)) [C,U] a film that deals with subjects such as evil, moral problems etc, often using a story about people involved in a crime and filmed in a way that seems dark or filled with shadows

ˈfilm star *n* [C] *BrE* a famous actor or actress in cinema films SYN **movie star** *AmE*

film·strip /ˈfɪlmˌstrɪp/ *n* [C] a photographic film that shows photographs, pictures etc one at a time, not as moving pictures: *an educational filmstrip*

film·y /ˈfɪlmi/ *adj* very thin, so that you can almost see through it: *a filmy nightdress*

fi·lo /ˈfiːləʊ $ -oʊ/ (*also* **ˈfilo ˌpastry**) *n* [U] a type of very thin PASTRY which is used by placing many layers together

Fi·lo·fax /ˈfaɪləfæks/ *n* [C] *trademark* a small book for writing addresses, things you must do etc, which has pages you can add or remove → **personal organizer**

fil·ter¹ /ˈfɪltə $ -ər/ ●●○ *n* [C]

1 something that you pass water, air etc through in order to remove unwanted substances and make it clean or suitable to use: **water/air/oil etc filter** *a pond filter* | *coffee filter papers* | *filter cigarettes* (=with a filter at the end)

2 a piece of equipment or computer program that only allows certain sounds, images, signals, types of information etc to pass through it: *a UVA light filter* | *The firm uses electronic filters to prevent workers from accessing the Internet.*

3 *BrE* a traffic light that shows car drivers when they can turn right or left

filter² ●○○ *v*

1 [T] to remove unwanted substances from water, air etc by passing it through a special substance or piece of equipment: *The water in the tank is constantly filtered.* | *The ozone layer filters harmful UV rays from the sun.*

2 [I always + adv/prep] if people filter somewhere, they move gradually to that place: *Chattering noisily, the crowd began to filter into the auditorium.*

3 [I always + adv/prep] if news, information etc filters somewhere, people gradually hear about it from each

F

other: *The news gradually filtered through from Bombay last night.*
4 [I always + adv/prep] if light or sound filters into a place, it can be seen or heard only slightly: *Moonlight filtered in through the frosted window.* | *The familiar notes of Beethoven's 'Für Elise' filtered from the bar.*
5 [I,T] *BrE* if traffic filters, or if a system filters it, cars can turn left or right while other vehicles going straight ahead must wait

filter sth ↔ **out** *phr v*
1 to remove something, using a filter: *The pump filters out mud.*
2 to remove words, information etc that you do not need or want: *Net users can filter out unwanted emails with software.*

'filter tip *n* [C] a filter at one end of a cigarette that removes some of the harmful substances from the smoke —**filter-tipped** *adj*

filth /fɪlθ/ *n* **1** [U] very offensive language, stories, or pictures about sex: *I don't know how you can watch that filth!* **2** [U] dirt, especially a lot of it: *a mound of filth and rubbish* | *people living in filth* | *Passing cars covered his shoes with filth.* **3 the filth** *BrE informal* an offensive word for the police

filth·y[1] /'fɪlθi/ ●●○ S3 *adj* (*comparative* **filthier**, *superlative* **filthiest**)
1 very dirty: *The house was filthy, with clothes and newspapers strewn everywhere.* THESAURUS ▸ DIRTY
2 showing or describing sexual acts in a very rude or offensive way: **filthy language/story/joke etc** | *Your problem is you've got a **filthy mind*** (=you are always thinking about sex).
3 showing anger or annoyance: **filthy mood/temper** *Simon had been drinking and was in a filthy temper.* | *She gave him a **filthy look**.*
4 filthy weather/night/day the weather, a night etc that is very cold and wet: *It's a filthy night to be out.*

filthy[2] *adv informal* **1 filthy dirty** very dirty **2 filthy rich** very rich – usually used to say you think someone has too much money

fil·trate /'fɪltreɪt/ *n* [C,U] *technical* a liquid from which a substance has been removed using a FILTER

fil·tra·tion /fɪl'treɪʃən/ *n* [U] the process of cleaning a liquid by passing it through a FILTER

fin /fɪn/ ●○○ *n* [C]
1 one of the thin body parts that a fish uses to swim → see picture at FISH[1]
2 part of a plane that sticks up at the back and helps it to fly smoothly
3 (*also* **tail fin**) a thin piece of metal that sticks out from a car or bomb at the back
4 a FLIPPER

fi·na·gle /fə'neɪgəl/ *v* [T] *AmE informal* to obtain something that is difficult to get by using unusual or unfair methods: *How he finagled four front row seats to the game I'll never know.* —**finagling** *n* [U]

fi·nal[1] /'faɪnəl/ ●●● S1 W1 AWL *adj*
1 [only before noun] last in a series of actions, events, parts of a story etc: *The final episode will be shown tonight.* | *students preparing for their final examinations* | *Stone is filming the final instalment of his Vietnam trilogy.* | *the **final stages** in their relationship* | *They scored in the **final minutes** of the game.* | *The **final whistle*** (=blown at the end of a game) *was only seconds away when Redknapp equalised.* | **final demand** *BrE* (=the last bill you receive for money you owe before court action is taken against you) THESAURUS ▸ LAST
2 [only before noun] being the result at the end of a process: *the quality of the final product* | *Does anyone know the final score?* | **final result/outcome** *I do not know what the final outcome will be.*
3 if a decision, offer, answer etc is final, it cannot or will not be changed: *The judge's **decision** is **final**.* | **final decision/say/approval etc** *We can advise the client, but in the end it is he who **has the final say**.* | *Is that your **final answer**?* | **and that's final!** (=used to say forcefully that you will not change your decision) *She's not coming with us, and that's final!*
4 [only before noun] happening at or near the end of an event or process SYN **last**: *In the final years of his life, Hervey achieved high office in the church.*
5 used to emphasize that the last thing in a series of events is very severe or damaging SYN **ultimate**: **final indignity/humiliation** *The vote of no confidence was the final humiliation for a government that had been clinging to office.*
→ **in the final analysis** at ANALYSIS(4)

final[2] ●●○ AWL *n* [C]
1 the last and most important game, race, or set of games in a competition: **be through to/reach the final** *He's through to the men's tennis final for the first time.* | **the finals** (=the last few games or races in a competition) *the NBA finals*
2 finals [plural] *BrE* the set of examinations that students take at the end of their time at university SYN **final exams**: **sit/take your finals** *Anna sat her finals last summer.*
3 *AmE* an important test that you take at the end of a particular class in high school or college THESAURUS ▸ TEST

fi·na·le /fɪ'nɑːli $ fɪ'næli/ *n* [C] the last part of a piece of music or of a show, event etc: *the finale of a Broadway show* | *a game with a dramatic finale* | **grand finale** (=very impressive end to a show) *The fireworks were the grand finale of the ceremonies.*

fi·nal·ist /'faɪnəl-ɪst/ *n* [C] one of the people or teams that reaches the final game in a competition

fi·nal·i·ty /faɪ'næləti/ AWL *n* [U] the quality something has when it is finished or complete and cannot be changed: **a sense/air of finality** *The word 'retirement' has a terrible air of finality about it.*

fi·nal·ize (*also* **-ise** *BrE*) /'faɪnəl-aɪz/ ●○○ AWL *v* [T] to finish the last part of a plan, business deal etc: *Jo flew out to Thailand to finalize the details of the deal.* THESAURUS ▸ FINISH —**finalization** /ˌfaɪnəlaɪ'zeɪʃən $ -nl-ə-/ *n* [U]

fi·nal·ly /'faɪnəl-i/ ●●● S2 W1 AWL *adv*
1 after a long time SYN **eventually**: *After several delays we finally took off at six o'clock.* | *Finally, Karpov cracked under the pressure.*
2 [sentence adverb] used to introduce the last in a series of things SYN **lastly** → **firstly** OPP **firstly**: *And finally, I'd like to thank the crew.*
3 used when talking about the last in a series of actions: *She drove off at great speed, hit several parked cars, and finally crashed into a lamp-post.*
4 in a way that does not allow changes: *The matter was not finally settled until 1475.*

fi·nance[1] /'faɪnæns, fə'næns $ fə'næns, 'faɪnæns/ ●●○ W3 AWL *n*
1 [U] the management of money by governments, large organizations etc: *leasing and other forms of business finance* | *Russia's finance minister* | *the world of **high finance*** (=financial activities involving very large amounts of money)
2 finances [plural] the money that an organization or person has, and the way that they manage it: *concerns about the company's finances* | *She refused to answer questions about her personal finances.*
3 [U] money provided by a bank or other institution to help buy or do something SYN **funding/funds**: **[+for]** *We need to **raise finance** for further research.*

finance[2] ●●○ AWL *v* [T] to provide money, especially a lot of money, to pay for something SYN **fund**: *The concerts are financed by the Arts Council.* —**financing** *n* [U]: *The financing for the deal has been approved in principle.*

'finance ˌcompany / $ '.. ˌ.../ (*also* **'finance ˌhouse** / $ '../ *BrE*) *n* [C] a company that lends money, especially to businesses

fi·nan·cial /fə'nænʃəl, faɪ-/ ●●● W1 AWL *adj* [usually before noun] relating to money or the management of money: *financial transactions* | *financial assistance* | *a financial advisor* | *Organic farmers should be encouraged with financial incentives.* | *It was a wonderful film, but not exactly **a financial success*** (=something that makes a profit). |

F

financial difficulties/problems/crisis —**financially** *adv*: *He was successful and* **financially secure**. | *Is the project* **financially viable**?

THESAURUS

financial relating to money or the management of money: *businesses that provide personal financial services* | *the financial problems of old age*
economic relating to the money of a country, area, or society, and the way it is earned, spent, and controlled: *American voters were anxious for a change in economic policy.* | *an economic crisis*
fiscal [only before noun] *formal* relating to the money, debts, tax etc that are owned and managed by the government: *fiscal control* | *The Indian government is trying to reduce the fiscal deficit.*
monetary [only before noun] *formal* relating to money, especially all the money in a country, and how it is managed: *The Bank of Thailand has retained a tight monetary policy.*
budgetary [only before noun] *formal* relating to the official plan of how the money of a country or organization is spent: *City officials are facing tough budgetary decisions.*

fi,nancial 'aid *n* [U] *AmE* money given or lent to students at college or university to pay for their education

fi,nancial insti'tution *n* [C] *technical* a business organization that lends and borrows money, for example a bank: *All the big financial institutions cut their interest rates today.*

fi,nancial 'year *n* [singular] *especially BrE* the 12-month period over which a company's accounts are calculated SYN **fiscal year** *AmE*

fi·nan·cier /fəˈnænsɪə, faɪˈnæn- $ ˌfɪnənˈsɪr/ AWL *n* [C] someone who controls or lends large sums of money

finch /fɪntʃ/ *n* [C] a small bird with a short beak

find[1] /faɪnd/ ●●● S1 W1 *v* (*past tense and past participle* **found** /faʊnd/) [T]

1 GET BY SEARCHING to discover, see, or get something that you have been searching for: *I can't find the car keys.* | *Hold on while I find a pen.* | *Her body was later found hidden in the bushes.* | *I have to find somewhere else to live.* | *She had almost given up hope of finding a husband.* | **find sb sth** *Tony asked us to find him office facilities in New York.* | *Her mother went to the shops, and on her return, Kathleen was* **nowhere to be found** (=could not be found).

2 SEE BY CHANCE to discover something by chance, especially something useful or interesting: *I found a purse in the street.* | *We found a nice pub near the hotel.*

3 DISCOVER STATE OF SB/STH to discover that someone or something is in a particular condition or doing a particular thing when you see or touch them: *I'm sure we'll find her hard at work when we get home.* | *He tried the door and found it unlocked.* | *She* **woke to find** *a man by her bed.* | **find sb/sth doing sth** *Often he found her quietly weeping alone.* | **find (that)** *She looked at her glass and was amazed to find it was empty.*

4 DO STH WITHOUT MEANING TO to be in a particular state or do a particular thing, or to realize that this is happening, especially when you did not expect or intend it: *After wandering around, we found ourselves back at the hotel.* | **find yourself/your mind etc doing sth** *When he left, Karen found herself heaving a huge sigh of relief.* | *She tried to concentrate, but found her mind drifting back to Alex.* | **find (that)** *He found he was shivering.*

5 LEARN STH BY STUDY to discover or learn something by study, tests, sums etc: *The federal government isn't doing enough to find a cure.* | *How do you find the square root of 20?* | **be found to do sth** *The liquid was found to contain 7.4g of phenylamine.* | **find that** *His study found that married men and women had similar spending patterns.*

GRAMMAR

In more formal English, you say **it was found that** something was true: *It was found that over 50% of children had seen the ad.*

6 THINK/FEEL to have a particular feeling or opinion, or to have a particular feeling or opinion about someone or something: *Will Gary and Gail find happiness together?* | **find sth/sb easy/useful/interesting etc** *She found the work very dull.* | *Lots of women I know find him attractive.* | *I found them quite easy to use.* | **find it hard/easy/difficult etc (to do sth)** *Hyperactive children find it difficult to concentrate.*

7 EXPERIENCE to have the experience of discovering that something happens or is true: **find (that)** *You might find that his work improves now he's at a new school.* | *I find people are often surprised at how little it costs.* | **find sb/sth doing sth** *I think you'll find more women entering the film business now.* | **find sb/sth to be sth** *I found the people to be charming and very friendly.*

8 EXIST IN A PLACE **be found somewhere** if something is found somewhere, it lives or exists there naturally: *This species is only found in West Africa.*

9 GET ENOUGH MONEY/TIME ETC to succeed in getting enough of something, especially money, time, or energy, to be able to do something: *He's struggling to find the money for the trip.* | *Where are we going to find the time, the support, and the resources to do all this?*

10 IN A COURT OF LAW to make an official decision in a court of law: **find sb guilty/not guilty (of sth)** *Both men were found guilty of illegally entering the country.* | **find in sb's favour** *The tribunal found in favour of the defendant.*

11 find your way (somewhere) to reach a place by discovering the right way to get there: *Will you be able to find your way back?*

12 find its way somewhere *informal* if something finds its way somewhere, it arrives or gets there after some time: *Her invention has found its way into the shops.*

13 find comfort/pleasure/fulfilment etc in sth to experience a good feeling because of something: *He eventually* **found solace in** *religion.*

14 find fault with sb/sth to criticize someone or something, often unfairly and frequently: *He could always find fault with something, either in my writing or in my personality.*

15 find it in your heart/yourself to do sth *literary* to feel able or willing to do something: *Seb could not find it in his heart to tell Nahum.*

16 find yourself *informal* to discover what you are really like and what you want to do – often used humorously: *She went to India to find herself.*

17 find favour (with sb/sth) *formal* to be liked or approved of by someone: *The recipes rapidly found favour with restaurant owners.*

18 find your feet to become confident in a new situation, especially one that is difficult at first: *Rob is still finding his feet as a coach.*

19 find its mark/target a) if a bullet, ARROW etc finds its mark etc, it hits what it is supposed to hit **b)** if a remark, criticism etc finds its mark etc, it has the effect that you intended it to have: *She soon saw that her accusation had found its mark.*

20 find your voice a) (*also* **find your tongue**) to manage to say something after being too nervous to talk **b)** if a writer, musician etc finds their voice, they are able to express their views, ideas, art etc in the way they want to: *a young film-maker who has finally found his voice*

21 be found wanting *formal* to not be good enough: *Their defence was found wanting.*

THESAURUS

find to get or see something that you have been searching for: *Have you found your passport yet?* | *Police later found the car abandoned in a wood.*
discover to find something that was hidden or that people did not know about before: *A second bomb has been discovered in south London.*
locate *formal* to find the exact position of something: *The airline are still trying to locate my luggage.*
come across sth to find something unexpectedly when you are not looking for it: *I came across some old letters from my father in my drawer.*
stumble on/across sth to find something unexpectedly, especially something very important: *They may have stumbled across some vital evidence.*

trace to find someone or something that has disappeared, especially by a careful process of collecting information: *She had given up all hope of tracing her missing daughter.*
track sb/sth down to find someone or something that is difficult to find by searching in different places: *I've been trying to track down a book that's out of print.* | *The police managed to track down the killer.*
unearth to find something that has been hidden or lost for a long time, by digging or searching for it: *In 1796, a carved stone was unearthed near the burial mound.*

find against sb *phr v law* to judge that someone is wrong or guilty: *The inspectors are likely to find against the company.*
find for sb *phr v law* to judge that someone is right or not guilty: *The judge found for the plaintiff.*
find out *phr v*
1 to get information, after trying to discover it or by chance: **find out who/what/how etc** *Has anyone bothered to find out how much all this is going to cost?* | **find out if/whether** *Did you find out whether there are any seats left?* | **find out (that)** *I found out that my parents had never been married.* | **find sth ↔ out** *To find out more, visit our website.* | **find out (sth) about sth** *I need to find out more about these night courses.* | **[+from]** *We could find out from the local council.* | *I thought it best to let you* ***find out for yourself***.

REGISTER
In written English, people usually say that someone **discovers** something rather than **finds out** something: *Scientists soon* ***discovered*** *that this was false.*

2 find sb out if you are found out, someone discovers that you have been doing something dishonest or illegal → **catch**: *What happens if we get found out?* GRAMMAR **Find out** is usually passive in this meaning.

find² ●○○ *n* [C]
1 a find something very good or useful that you discover by chance: *That restaurant was a real find!*
2 something that someone finds, especially by digging or by searching under water: *important archaeological finds*

find·er /ˈfaɪndə $ -ər/ *n* [C] **1** someone who finds something that was lost or stolen: *The finder usually receives a reward.* **2 finders keepers (losers weepers)** *spoken* used to say that if someone finds something, they have the right to keep it

fin de siè·cle /ˌfæn də ˈsjekləˌ/ *adj* [only before noun] typical of the end of the 19th century, especially its art, literature, and attitudes

find·ing /ˈfaɪndɪŋ/ ●●○ W3 *n* [C]
1 [usually plural] the information that someone has discovered as a result of their study, work etc: *Surveys conducted in other countries reported similar findings.*
2 *law* a decision made by a judge or JURY

fine¹ /faɪn/ ●●● S1 W1 *adj*
1 ACCEPTABLE [not before noun] *especially spoken* satisfactory or acceptable SYN **OK**: *'We're meeting at 8.30.' 'Okay, fine.'* | **looks/seems/sounds fine** *In theory, the scheme sounds fine.* | *If you want to use cheese instead of chicken,* ***that's fine***. | *'Do you want chili sauce on it?' 'No,* ***it's fine as it is****, thanks.'* | **I'm fine (thanks/thank you)** *spoken* (=used when telling someone that you do not want any more when they offer you something) *'More coffee?' 'No,* ***I'm fine****, thanks.'* | **that's fine by me/that's fine with me etc** *spoken* (=used when saying that you do not mind about something) *If Scott wanted to keep his life secret, that was fine by her.*
2 HEALTHY in good health SYN **OK**: *'How are you?' 'Fine, thanks, how are you?'* | *I* ***feel fine****, really.* THESAURUS HEALTHY
3 VERY GOOD [usually before noun] very good or of a very high standard: *Many people regard Beethoven's fifth symphony as his finest work.* | *He's a very fine player.* | *It's a fine idea.* | *Hatfield House is a* ***fine example of*** *Jacobean architecture.* | *The restaurant was chosen for its good food and* ***fine wines***. THESAURUS GOOD
4 WEATHER bright and not raining: *If it's fine tomorrow we'll go out.* | **a fine day/morning/evening** | *I hope it* ***stays fine*** *for you.*
5 NARROW very thin or narrow: *Fine needles are inserted in the arm.* | *a fine thread* | *very fine hairs* → see picture at THIN¹
6 DELICATE [usually before noun] attractive, neat, and delicate: *fine china* | *Her dark hair accentuates her* ***fine features*** (=nose, eyes, cheeks etc).
7 SMALL **a)** fine details, changes, differences etc are very small and therefore difficult to understand or notice: *We stayed up discussing the* ***finer points*** *of Marxist theory.* **b)** in small grains, pieces, or drops: *A fine drizzle started falling.* | *a mixture of fine and coarse breadcrumbs* **c)** fine material is made so that the spaces between the threads are very small: *fine netting* | *scarlet cloth with a very fine weave*
8 BAD [only before noun] *especially spoken* used humorously to say that someone or something is bad in some way: *That's another* ***fine mess*** (=bad situation) *he's got himself into.* | *You're* ***a fine one to talk*** (=you are criticizing someone for something you do yourself).
9 SPEECH/WORDS sounding important and impressive, but probably not true or honest: *Only time will tell whether these fine sentiments will translate into action.*
10 a fine man/woman etc a good person that you respect: *Your father is a fine man, a real gentleman.*
11 a fine line between sth and sth if you say that there is a fine line between two different things, you mean that they are so similar that one can easily become the other: *There's a fine line between bravery and recklessness.*
12 get sth down to a fine art to practise something so often that you become very skilled at it: *Mike had got the breakfast routine down to a fine art.*
13 not to put too fine a point on it *spoken* used when you are criticizing something in a plain and direct way: *The restaurant was terrible, not to put too fine a point on it.*
14 finer feelings someone's finer feelings are the moral values they have, such as love, honour, loyalty etc: *You can hardly expect such finer feelings in a thief.*
15 a fine figure of a man/woman *literary* someone who looks big, strong, and physically attractive: *In his portrait, Donlevy is a fine figure of a man.*
16 sb's finest hour a time when someone is very successful, brave etc: *The tournament proved to be Gascoigne's finest hour.* → **chance would be a fine thing** at CHANCE¹(11)

fine² ●●● S3 *adv*
1 *especially spoken* in a way that is satisfactory or acceptable: *'How's it going?' 'Fine, thanks.'* | *The dress fitted me fine.* | *If I had a good job and my boyfriend stayed at home, that'd* ***suit*** *me* ***fine*** (=be very acceptable to me).
2 do fine *spoken* **a)** to be satisfactory or acceptable: *'Something very light,' he ordered. 'An omelette will do fine.'* **b)** to do something well or in a satisfactory way: *Don't worry, you're doing fine. Keep at it.* **c)** to be healthy and well: *'How's your husband?' 'He's doing fine, thank you.'*
3 if you cut something fine, you cut it into very small or very thin pieces SYN **finely**
4 cut it/things fine *informal* to leave yourself only just enough time to do something

fine³ ●●○ *v* [T] to make someone pay money as a punishment: **fine sb for (doing) sth** *She was fined for speeding.* | **fine sb £200/$500 etc** *The club was fined £50,000 for financial irregularities.*

fine⁴ ●●○ *n* [C] money that you have to pay as a punishment: *a £40 fine* | **pay a fine/pay £100/$50 etc in fines** *She was ordered to pay £150 in parking fines, plus court costs.* | *Councils will get sweeping powers to* ***impose fines*** *on drivers who park illegally.* | **heavy/hefty fine** (=a large fine) *If convicted, the men face heavy fines.* THESAURUS PUNISHMENT

ˌfine ˈart *n* **the fine arts** forms of art, especially paintings or SCULPTURE, that are produced and admired for their

F

beauty and high quality OPP **applied art**: *Can photography be considered fine art?* | *the faculty of fine arts*

fine·ly /ˈfaɪnli/ ●●○ *adv*
1 into very thin or very small pieces: *finely chopped onion*
2 in a very careful, delicate, or exact way: *Saunders' finely crafted drawings* | *These instruments are very finely tuned.*
3 beautifully or impressively: *He wore a silk cloak over a finely embroidered robe.* | *high-quality, finely carved statues*

ˌfine ˈprint *n* [U] *AmE* SMALL PRINT

fi·ne·ry /ˈfaɪnəri/ *n* [U] *literary* clothes and jewellery that are beautiful or very expensive, and are worn for a special occasion: *The guests arrived in all their finery.*

fi·nesse¹ /fəˈnes/ *n* [U] if you do something with finesse, you do it with a lot of skill and style: *Dario played the sonata with great finesse.*

finesse² *v* [T] **1** to handle a situation well, but in a way that is slightly deceitful **2** *AmE* to do something with a lot of skill and style

ˌfine-tooth ˈcomb *n* **go through/over sth with a fine-tooth comb** to examine something very carefully and thoroughly: *The police went over the scene of the crime with a fine-tooth comb.*

ˌfine-ˈtune *v* [T] to make very small changes to something such as a machine, system, or plan, so that it works as well as possible: *Over the next few days, we fine-tuned the scheme and made some useful improvements.* —**fine tuning** *n* [U]

fin·ger¹ /ˈfɪŋɡə $ -ər/ ●●● S2 W2 *n* [C]
1 PART OF YOUR HAND one of the four long thin parts on your hand, not including your thumb: *The woman had a ring on her finger, so I assumed she was married.* | *We ate with our fingers.* | **run your fingers through/over/along etc sth** *She ran her fingers through his hair.* → INDEX FINGER, LITTLE FINGER, FOREFINGER, MIDDLE FINGER, RING FINGER

FINGER

cross your fingers

2 cross your fingers a) to hope that something will happen the way you want: *We're* ***keeping*** *our* ***fingers crossed*** *that she's going to be OK.* **b)** to secretly put one finger over another finger, because you are telling a lie – done especially by children: *'He's nice,' said Laura, crossing her fingers under the table.*
3 not lift/raise a finger to not make any effort to help someone with their work: *I do all the work around the house – Frank never lifts a finger.*
4 put your finger on sth to know or be able to explain exactly what is wrong, different, or unusual about a situation: *There was something about the man that worried Wycliffe, but he couldn't put his finger on it.*
5 not lay a finger on sb to not hurt someone at all, especially to not hit them: *Don't lay a finger on me, or I'll call the police!*
6 have/keep your finger on the pulse (of sth) to always know about the most recent changes or developments in a particular situation or activity: *people who have their finger on the pulse of fashion and pop culture*
7 have a finger in every pie/in many pies to be involved in many activities and to have influence over a lot of people, used especially when you think someone has too much influence
8 twist/wrap/wind sb around your little finger to be able to persuade someone to do anything that you want: *Ed could wrap his mother around his little finger.*
9 the finger of blame/suspicion: *The* ***finger of suspicion*** *immediately* ***fell on*** *Broderick.*
10 OF A GLOVE the part of a GLOVE that covers your finger
11 SHAPED LIKE A FINGER anything that is long and thin, like the shape of a finger, especially a piece of land, an area of water, or a piece of food: *fish fingers* | *chocolate fingers* | **[+of]** *the long finger of Chile*
12 pull/get your finger out *BrE informal* used to tell someone to work harder
13 put two fingers up at sb *BrE informal* to show someone you are angry with them in a very offensive way by holding up your first two fingers with the back of your hand facing them
14 give sb the finger *AmE informal* to show someone you are angry with them in a very offensive way by holding up your middle finger with the back of your hand facing them
15 be all fingers and thumbs *BrE* to use your hands in an awkward or careless way, so that you drop or break things
16 long-fingered/slim-fingered etc having long fingers, slim fingers etc: *lovely long-fingered hands*
17 DRINK an amount of an alcoholic drink that is as high in the glass as the width of someone's finger: *two fingers of whiskey* → BUTTERFINGERS, FISH FINGER, → **have your hands/fingers in the till** at TILL²(3), → **count sth on the fingers of one hand** at COUNT¹(7), → **have green fingers** at GREEN¹(10), → **burn your fingers/get your fingers burnt** at BURN¹(16), → **point the/a finger at sb** at POINT²(9), → **let sth slip through your fingers** at SLIP¹(15), → **snap your fingers** at SNAP¹(7), → **have sticky fingers** at STICKY(6), → **work your fingers to the bone** at WORK¹(29)

finger² *v* [T] **1** to touch or handle something with your fingers: *She fingered the beautiful cloth.* THESAURUS TOUCH **2** *informal* if someone, especially a criminal, fingers another criminal, they tell the police what that person has done

fin·ger·board /ˈfɪŋɡəbɔːd $ -gərbɔːrd/ *n* [C] the long part of a STRINGED INSTRUMENT which the player presses the strings onto

ˈfinger bowl *n* [C] a small bowl in which you wash your fingers during a meal

fin·ger·ing /ˈfɪŋɡərɪŋ/ *n* [U] the positions in which a musician puts his or her fingers to play a piece of music, or the order in which he or she uses the fingers

fin·ger·mark /ˈfɪŋɡəmɑːk $ -gərmɑːrk/ *n* [C] a mark made by dirty fingers on something clean THESAURUS MARK

fin·ger·nail /ˈfɪŋɡəneɪl $ -gər-/ ●●○ *n* [C] the hard flat part that covers the top end of your finger SYN **nail** → see picture at HAND¹

ˈfinger-paints *n* [plural] special paints that children use to paint with, using their fingers —**finger painting** *n* [U]

ˈfinger-ˌpointing *n* [U] when people blame other people for something that has gone wrong, instead of trying to solve the problem: *There followed months of name-calling and finger-pointing.*

FINGERPRINT

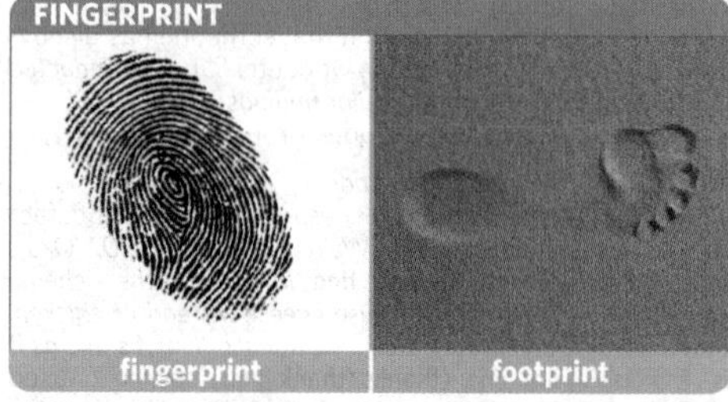

fingerprint footprint

fin·ger·print /ˈfɪŋɡəˌprɪnt $ -gər-/ ●○○ *n* [C] a mark made by the pattern of lines at the end of a person's finger, which is used by the police to find out who has committed a crime: *His fingerprints were all over the gun.* | *He was careful not to* ***leave*** *any* ***fingerprints.*** | *The police questioned Beresford and* ***took*** *his* ***fingerprints*** (=made a record of them). THESAURUS MARK —**fingerprint** *v* [T]

fin·ger·print·ing /ˈfɪŋɡəˌprɪntɪŋ $ -gər-/ *n* [U] the practice of making a record of people's fingerprints, and using them to try and find out who has committed a crime → GENETIC FINGERPRINTING

fin·ger·spell·ing /ˈfɪŋɡəˌspelɪŋ $ -gər-/ *n* [U] a system of speaking to people who are DEAF by touching their hand with your fingers and making the shapes of letters

fin·ger·tip /ˈfɪŋɡəˌtɪp $ -ɡər-/ *n* [C] **1** the end of your finger that is furthest away from your hand: *She touched his cheek gently with her fingertips.* **2 have sth at your/their etc fingertips** to have knowledge or information ready and available to use very easily: *We have all the facts and figures at our fingertips.* **3 to his/her fingertips** *BrE* in all ways; completely: *She's British to her fingertips.*

fin·i·cky /ˈfɪnɪki/ *adj* **1** too concerned with unimportant details and small things that you like or dislike SYN **fussy**: *She's very finicky about what she eats.* **2** needing to be done very carefully, while paying attention to small details SYN **fiddly**: *a finicky job*

fin·ish¹ /ˈfɪnɪʃ/ ●●● S1 W2 *v*

1 STOP DOING STH (*also* **finish off**) [I,T] to complete the last part of something that you are doing: *You can't go anywhere until you've finished your homework.* | *Have you finished that book yet?* | **finish doing sth** *I finished typing the report just minutes before it was due.* | *'How's the decorating going?' 'We've nearly finished.'*

2 END [I] *especially BrE* when an event, activity, or period of time finishes, it ends, especially at a particular time: *The football season finishes in May.* | *What time does school finish?*

3 EAT/DRINK (*also* **finish up/off**) [T] to eat or drink all the rest of something, so there is none left: *I'll just finish my coffee.*

4 END STH BY DOING STH (*also* **finish off**) [I,T] to complete an event, performance, piece of work etc by doing one final thing: **[+with]** *The party finished with a sing-song.* | **finish (sth) by doing sth** *I would like to finish by thanking you all for your help.*

5 RACE [I,T] to be in a particular position at the end of a race, competition etc: **finish first/second/third etc** *He finished second in the 100 metres, behind Ben Johnson.*

6 TAKE AWAY SB'S STRENGTH (*also* **finish off**) [T] to take away all of someone's strength, energy etc SYN **do sb in**: *Another run like that would just about finish me.*

7 USE ALL OF STH [I,T] *BrE* to completely use up the supply of something, especially food: *The ice cream's finished – can you get some more?*

8 put/add the finishing touches (to sth) to add the final details that make your work complete: *The band are putting the finishing touches to their new album.*

9 SURFACE [T] to give the surface of something, especially wood, a smooth appearance by painting, polishing, or covering it: *The furniture had been attractively finished in a walnut veneer.*

GRAMMAR: Patterns with finish

• **Finish** is followed by an **-ing** form, not an infinitive. You say: *He finished cleaning the kitchen.* ✗ Don't say: *He finished to clean the kitchen.*
• **Finish** belongs to a group of verbs where the same noun can be the subject of the verb or its object.
• You can say: *He finished his speech with a joke.* In this sentence, 'his speech' is the object of **finish**.
• You can say: *His speech finished with a joke.* In this sentence, 'his speech' is the subject of **finish**.

GRAMMAR GUIDE ▸ VERBS

THESAURUS

finish to complete the last part of something that you are doing: *Have you finished your homework?* | *The builders say they should have finished by Friday.*
complete to finish making or doing something that has taken a long time to finish: *The new bridge will be completed in two years' time.* | *She has just completed her PhD.*
finalize to do the last things that are necessary in order to settle a plan or agreement in a satisfactory way: *A spokesman said that they were hoping to finalize an agreement in the near future.*
conclude *formal* to officially finish something: *The police have now concluded their investigations.*
wrap sth up *informal* to finish something successfully – used especially about agreements or sports competitions: *Negotiators are meeting on Friday to wrap up the deal.*
round sth off *BrE*, **round sth out** *AmE* to do something as a way of ending a day, an evening, an event etc in an enjoyable or suitable way: *They rounded off the day with a barbecue at the beach.*
get it over with/get it over and done with to do something that you have to do now, so that it is finished and you can stop worrying about it: *Let's go and do the shopping now and get it over with.*
be done/be through *informal* if you are done, you have finished – used especially when other people are waiting for you: *We're nearly done.*
be through with sth/be done with sth *informal* to have finished using something – used especially when other people are waiting to use it: *I'm done with the file.*

finish off *phr v*

1 finish sth ↔ off to complete the last part of something that you are doing: *It'll take me a couple of hours to finish this job off.*

2 finish sth ↔ off to use or eat all of something, so there is none left: *Who finished off the cake?*

3 to complete an event, performance, piece of work etc by doing one final thing: **[+with]** *We'll finish off with a track from Adam's new album.* | **finish sth ↔ off** *She finished off her speech by thanking her sponsors.* | **finish off/finish sth ↔ off by doing sth** *Finish off by cleaning the monitor and the keyboard.*

4 finish sb/sth ↔ off to kill a person or animal when they are already weak or wounded

5 finish sb ↔ off to take away all of someone's strength, energy etc: *The walk up the hill really finished me off.*

finish up *phr v*

1 *BrE informal* to arrive at a particular place, after going to other places first SYN **end up**: *I took a long holiday in Italy and finished up in Rome.*

2 *BrE informal* to get into a particular state or situation as the result of what you have done, especially without planning or expecting it SYN **end up**: *He tried to bribe a police officer and finished up in jail.* | **[+with]** *Brett got into a fight and finished up with a broken wrist.*

3 finish sth ↔ up to eat or drink all the rest of something, so there is none left: *Come on, finish up your drinks!*

finish with sth/sb *phr v*

1 have/be finished with sth to no longer need to use something: *Have you finished with the scissors?*

2 have/be finished with sb to have finished talking to someone or dealing with them, especially when you are angry with them or want to punish them: *Don't go. I haven't finished with you yet.* | *'When I'm finished with you,' he said, 'you'll be lucky if you're still alive.'*

3 to end a romantic or sexual relationship with someone: *So I told him I wanted to finish with him.*

finish² ●●○ S3 *n*

1 [C] the end or last part of something: *I was watching the race but I didn't get to see the finish.* | *The day was a disaster* ***from start to finish*** (=from the beginning until the end). | *I won't walk out – I like to see things through* ***to the finish***. | **a close finish** (=an end of a race where two competitors are very close to each other)

2 a fight to the finish a fight or game in which the teams or competitors struggle until one is completely defeated

3 [C,U] the appearance of the surface of an object after it has been painted, polished etc: *That table has a beautiful finish.*

fin·ished /ˈfɪnɪʃt/ *adj* **1** [not before noun] no longer doing, dealing with, or using something SYN **done**: *I'm almost finished.* | **[+with]** *Are you finished with my tools yet?* **2** [only before noun] fully and properly made or completed: *It took a long time to do, but the* ***finished product*** *was worth it.* | **finished article** *BrE*: *The painting began to look like the finished article.* **3** [not before noun] no longer successful,

F

effective, or able to continue: *If the bank refuses to increase our loan, we're finished!*

ˈfinishing ˌline (*also* **ˈfinish line** *AmE*) *n* **the finishing line** the line at which a race ends: *James* ***crossed the finish line*** *in just under four minutes.* → STARTING LINE

ˈfinishing ˌschool *n* [C] a private school where rich girls go to learn social skills

fi·nite /ˈfaɪnaɪt/ ●○○ AWL *adj*
1 having an end or a limit OPP **infinite**: *the Earth's* ***finite resources***
2 *technical* a finite verb form shows a particular time. 'Am', 'was', and 'are' are examples of finite verb forms, but 'being' and 'been' are not OPP **non-finite**

fink¹ /fɪŋk/ *n* [C] *AmE informal old-fashioned* **1** someone who tells the police, a teacher, or a parent when someone else breaks a rule or a law **2** a person who you do not like or respect

fink² *v* [I +on] *AmE informal old-fashioned* to tell the police, a teacher, or a parent that someone has broken a rule or a law SYN **squeal on sb**

fi·ord /ˈfiːɔːd, fjɔːd $ fiːˈɔːrd, fjɔːrd/ *n* [C] another spelling of FJORD

fir /fɜː $ fɜːr/ *n* [C] a tree with leaves shaped like needles that do not fall off in winter: *a fir tree*

FIR

ˈfir cone *n* [C] the hard brown fruit that contains the seeds of a fir tree

fire¹ /faɪə $ faɪr/ ●●● S1 W1 *n*
1 FLAMES THAT DESTROY THINGS [C,U] uncontrolled flames, light, and heat that destroy and damage things: *The warehouse was completely destroyed by fire.* | *Thirty people died in a fire in downtown Chicago.* | *Police think that the fire was started deliberately.* | *Rioters* ***set fire to*** *a whole row of stores* (=made them start burning). | **on fire** (=burning) *Within minutes, the entire building was on fire.* GRAMMAR ✗ Don't say: *in fire*
2 FLAMES FOR HEATING/COOKING ETC [C] burning material used to heat a room, cook food etc, or get rid of things you do not want: *You put up the tent and I'll* ***make a fire***. | *Can you help me* ***light the fire***? | *The* ***fire*** *has almost* ***gone out*** (=stopped burning). | *They all sat around the* ***camp fire****, singing songs.* | *The* ***fire*** *was still* ***smouldering*** *in the grate* (=there was a little smoke and it had almost stopped burning). | **by the fire/in front of the fire** *Come and sit by the fire.* | *They dried their clothes in front of an* ***open fire***.
3 HEATING EQUIPMENT [C] *BrE* a machine that produces heat to warm a room, using gas or electricity as power: *a gas fire* | *an electric fire* | **turn the fire on/off** *Turn on the fire, I'm cold.* | **turn the fire up/down** (=make it hotter or colder)
4 SHOOTING [U] shots fired from a gun, especially many guns at the same time: *Troops* ***opened fire on*** (=started shooting at) *the demonstrators.* | *These women did vital work, often under* ***enemy fire***. | *The rebels agreed to* ***hold*** *their* ***fire*** (=not shoot). → **be in the line of fire** at LINE¹(35)
5 BE ATTACKED **be/come under fire a)** to be severely criticized for something you have done – used in news reports: *Rail chiefs came under fire after raising train fares.* **b)** to be shot at: **[+from]** *Our patrol came under fire from rooftop gunmen.*
6 EMOTION [U] a very strong emotion that makes you want to think about nothing else: **[+of]** *the fire of religious fanaticism*
7 fire in your belly a strong desire to achieve something: *Ali returned to boxing with a new fire in his belly.*
8 SICK/INJURED **be on fire** *literary* a part of your body that is on fire feels very painful
9 light a fire under sb *AmE spoken* to do something that makes someone who is being lazy start doing their work
10 go through fire (and water) (for sb) *old-fashioned* to do something very difficult and dangerous for someone
11 fire and brimstone a phrase describing Hell, used by some religious people → CEASEFIRE, → **add fuel to the fire/flames** at ADD(9), → **fight fire with fire** at FIGHT¹(18), → **get on like a house on fire** at HOUSE¹(13), → **hang fire** at HANG¹(12), → **play with fire** at PLAY¹(26), → **set the world on fire** at WORLD¹(22), → **there's no smoke without fire** at SMOKE¹(5)

COLLOCATIONS

VERBS

start a fire *The fire may have been started by a cigarette.*
set fire to sth/set sth on fire (=make something start burning) *A candle fell over, setting fire to the curtains.*
sth catches fire (=it starts burning) *The boat caught fire and sank.*
put out a fire (*also* **extinguish a fire** *formal*) (=stop a fire burning) *Firemen successfully extinguished the fire.*
fight a fire (=try to make a fire stop burning) *Further attempts to fight the fire were abandoned.*
a fire burns *The fire was burning more strongly every minute.*
a fire breaks out (=it starts suddenly) *A fire broke out in the engine room.*
a fire goes out (=it stops burning) *After several hours, the fire eventually went out.*
a fire rages/blazes (=it burns strongly for a long time over a large area) | **a fire spreads** | **sth is damaged/destroyed by fire**

PHRASES

be on fire (=be burning) *The whole house was on fire within minutes.*
bring a fire under control *Firefighters took more than an hour to bring the fire under control.*

ADJECTIVES/NOUN + fire

a big/major fire *A big fire was raging at the fuel depot.*
a forest fire (=a very large fire in a forest) | **a house fire** (=a fire that starts inside a house)

THESAURUS

fire flames that burn in an uncontrolled way and destroy or damage things: *In April, a fire at the school destroyed the science block.* | *a forest fire*
flames the bright parts of a fire that you see burning in the air: *The flames from the burning building were lighting up the night sky.*
blaze *written* a large and dangerous fire – used especially in news reports: *Firemen fought to keep the blaze under control.*
inferno *written* an extremely large and dangerous fire which is out of control – used especially in news reports: *The entire building was on fire and hundreds of people were trapped in the inferno.*
conflagration /ˌkɒnfləˈɡreɪʃən $ ˌkɑːn-/ *formal* a very large fire that destroys a lot of buildings, trees etc: *The conflagration spread rapidly through the old town.*

fire² ●●○ S3 W3 *v*
1 SHOOT [I,T] to shoot bullets or bombs: **[+at/on/into]** *Soldiers fired on the crowd.* | **fire sth at sb** *The police* ***fired*** *two* ***shots*** *at the suspects before they surrendered.* | **fire a gun/weapon/rifle etc** (=make it shoot) *the sound of a gun being fired* | **fire bullets/missiles/rockets etc** *Guerrillas fired five rockets at the capital yesterday, killing 23 people.* THESAURUS SHOOT
2 JOB [T] to force someone to leave their job SYN **sack** *BrE*: **be/get fired** *She didn't want to get fired.* | **fire sb from sth** *I've just been fired from my job, and I don't know what to do.* | **fire sb for sth** *The airline fired him for being drunk.*

REGISTER
In written English, people usually say that someone is **dismissed** rather than **fired**, which is slightly informal: *He was dismissed for being drunk.*

3 EXCITE [T] to make someone feel interested in something and excited about it SYN **inspire**: **be fired with enthusiasm** *I was fired with enthusiasm to go traveling in Asia.* | **fire sb's enthusiasm/imagination** *stories of magic and adventure that fire children's imaginations*
4 QUESTIONS fire questions at sb to ask someone a lot of questions quickly, often in order to criticize them
5 wood-fired/gas-fired/coal-fired using wood, gas, or coal as FUEL: *a gas-fired stove* | *a coal-fired boiler*
6 CLAY [T] to bake bricks, clay pots etc in a KILN: *fired earthenware*
7 ENGINE [I] if a vehicle's engine fires, the petrol is lit to make the engine work
8 be firing on all cylinders *informal* to be thinking or doing something well, using all your mental abilities and energy: *When the team's firing on all cylinders, they can beat the best in the league.*
fire away *phr v spoken* used to tell someone that you are ready to answer questions: *'Do you mind if I ask you something, Woody?' 'Fire away.'* GRAMMAR **Fire away** is usually used in the imperative.
fire back *phr v* to quickly and angrily answer a question or remark: **[+at]** *President Bush has fired back at his critics.*
fire sth ↔ **off** *phr v*
1 to shoot a bullet, bomb etc into the air: *Chuck reloaded and fired off both barrels.* | *Mexicans have a tradition of firing off guns to welcome in the new year.*
2 to quickly send an angry letter to someone: *I fired off a furious letter to the editor.*
fire sb ↔ **up** *phr v* to make someone become very excited, interested, or angry: *It was alarming the way she got so fired up about small things.* GRAMMAR **Fire up** is usually passive.

ˈfire aˌlarm ●●○ *n* [C] a piece of equipment that makes a loud noise to warn people of a fire in a building: *We were in the middle of an exam when the* ***fire alarm went off***. | *Someone* ***set off*** *the* ***fire alarm***.

ˈfire ant *n* [C] a type of insect that lives in groups. They build large piles of earth to live in, and can give a very painful bite.

fire·arm /ˈfaɪərɑːm $ ˈfaɪrɑːrm/ ●○○ *n* [C] *formal* a gun: *He was charged with illegal possession of a firearm.*

fire·ball /ˈfaɪəbɔːl $ ˈfaɪrbɒːl/ *n* [C] a ball of fire, especially one caused by an explosion: *The jet exploded in midair and turned into a fireball.*

fire·bomb¹ /ˈfaɪəbɒm $ ˈfaɪrbɑːm/ *n* [C] a bomb that makes a fire start burning when it explodes

firebomb² *v* [T] to attack a place with firebombs: *His home was firebombed by animal rights activists.* —**firebombing** *n* [U]

fire·brand /ˈfaɪəbrænd $ ˈfaɪr-/ *n* [C] someone who tries to make people angry about a law, government etc so that they will try to change it: *an idealistic young firebrand from the valleys*

fire·break /ˈfaɪəbreɪk $ ˈfaɪr-/ *n* [C] a narrow piece of land where all the plants and trees have been removed, made to prevent fires from spreading

fire·brick /ˈfaɪəˌbrɪk $ ˈfaɪr-/ *n* [C] a brick that is not damaged by heat, used in chimneys

ˈfire briˌgade ●●○ *n* [C]
1 *BrE* the FIRE SERVICE SYN **fire department** *AmE*
2 *AmE* a group of people who work together to stop fires burning, but are not paid to do this

fire·bug /ˈfaɪəbʌg $ ˈfaɪr-/ *n* [C] *informal* someone who deliberately starts fires to destroy property SYN **arsonist**

ˈfire ˌchief *n* [C] someone who is in charge of all the FIRE STATIONS in a city or area

fire·crack·er /ˈfaɪəˌkrækə $ ˈfaɪrˌkrækər/ *n* [C] a small FIREWORK that explodes loudly

ˈfire deˌpartment *n* [C] *AmE* the organization that works to prevent fires and stop them burning SYN **fire service** *BrE*

ˈfire ˌdoor *n* [C] a heavy door in a building that is kept closed to help to prevent a fire from spreading

ˈfire drill *n* [C,U] an occasion when people pretend that a building is burning and practise leaving it, so that they learn what to do if there is a real fire

ˈfire-ˌeater *n* [C] an entertainer who puts burning sticks into their mouth —**fire-eating** *n* [U]

ˈfire ˌengine *n* [C] a special large vehicle that carries equipment and the people that stop fires burning, especially the equipment that shoots water at a fire SYN **fire truck** *AmE* → see picture at TRUCK¹

ˈfire esˌcape *n* [C] metal stairs or a metal LADDER on the outside of a tall building, that people can use to escape if there is a fire

ˈfire ˌexit *n* [C] a door that is used to let people out of a building such as a cinema, hotel, restaurant etc when there is a fire

ˈfire exˌtinguisher *n* [C] a metal container with water or chemicals in it, used for stopping small fires

ˈfire fight *n* [C] *technical* a short gun battle, involving soldiers or the police

fire·fight·er, fire fighter /ˈfaɪəˌfaɪtə $ ˈfaɪrˌfaɪtər/ ●●● W3 *n* [C] someone whose job is to stop fires burning → **fireman**

ˈfire ˌfighting *n* [U] **1** the work of stopping fires burning **2** *BrE* the actions that are taken to find out what has caused a sudden problem in an organization, machine etc, and to correct it

fire·fly /ˈfaɪəflaɪ $ ˈfaɪr-/ *n* (*plural* **fireflies**) [C] an insect with a tail that shines in the dark

fire·guard /ˈfaɪəgɑːd $ ˈfaɪrgɑːrd/ *n* [C] *BrE* a large wire or metal screen that is put in front of a FIREPLACE to protect people SYN **firescreen** *AmE*

fire·house /ˈfaɪəhaʊs $ ˈfaɪr-/ *n* [C] *AmE* a small FIRE STATION, especially in a small town

ˈfire ˌhydrant *n* [C] a water pipe in a street used to get water to stop fires burning

ˈfire ˌiron *n* [C] a metal tool used to move or put coal or wood on a fire in a FIREPLACE

fire·light /ˈfaɪəlaɪt $ ˈfaɪr-/ *n* [U] the light produced by a small fire: *The room glowed in the firelight.*

fire·light·er /ˈfaɪəˌlaɪtə $ ˈfaɪrˌlaɪtər/ *n* [C] *BrE* a piece of a substance that burns easily and helps to light a coal fire

fire·man /ˈfaɪəmən $ ˈfaɪr-/ *n* (*plural* **firemen** /-mən/) [C] a man whose job is to stop fires burning SYN **firefighter**

fire·place /ˈfaɪəpleɪs $ ˈfaɪr-/ ●○○ *n* [C] a special place in the wall of a room, where you can make a fire

fire·pow·er /ˈfaɪəˌpaʊə $ ˈfaɪrˌpaʊr/ *n* [U] **1** *technical* the number of weapons that an army, military vehicle etc has available **2** the amount of something important or necessary that is available: *There is no shortage of financial firepower to fund atomic research.*

fire·proof /ˈfaɪəpruːf $ ˈfaɪr-/ *adj* a building, piece of cloth etc that is fireproof cannot be badly damaged by flames: *fireproof clothing* —**fireproof** *v* [T]

ˈfire-ˌraising *n* [U] *BrE* the crime of starting a fire deliberately SYN **arson** —**fire-raiser** *n* [C]

ˈfire reˌtardant (*also* **fire-retardant**) *adj* fire retardant materials or substances do not burn easily and are put on things to stop them from burning quickly: *furniture treated with fire-retardant chemicals*

ˈfire sale *n* [C] a sale of goods at a lower price because they have been slightly damaged by a fire, or of goods that cannot be stored because of a fire

fire·screen /ˈfaɪəskriːn $ ˈfaɪr-/ *n* [C] *AmE* a large wire or metal screen that is put in front of a FIREPLACE to protect people SYN **fireguard** *BrE*

ˈfire ˌservice (*also* **fire brigade**) *n* [C usually singular] *BrE* the organization that works to prevent fires and stop them from burning SYN **fire department** *AmE*

fire·side /ˈfaɪəsaɪd $ ˈfaɪr-/ *n* [C usually singular] the area close to or around a small fire, especially in a home: *a cat dozing by the fireside*

F

ˈfire ˌstation ●●○ *n* [C] a building where the equipment used to stop fires burning is kept, and where FIREFIGHTERS stay until they are needed

fire·storm /ˈfaɪəstɔːm $ ˈfaɪrstɔːrm/ *n* [C] **1** a very large fire that is kept burning by the high winds that it causes **2** a lot of protests, complaints, or arguments that happen suddenly and all at once SYN **storm**: **[+of]** *Green's proposal provoked a firestorm of protests.*

fire·trap /ˈfaɪətræp $ ˈfaɪr-/ *n* [C] a building that would be very difficult to escape from if a fire started there

ˈfire truck *n* [C] *AmE* a FIRE ENGINE

fire·wall /ˈfaɪəwɔːl $ ˈfaɪrwɒːl/ *n* [C] **1** a special wall that prevents fires from spreading to other parts of a building **2** a system that protects a computer NETWORK from being used or looked at by people who do not have permission to do so **3** a system that is used by large financial or law companies to stop secret information from being passed from one department to another

fire·wa·ter /ˈfaɪəˌwɔːtə $ ˈfaɪrˌwɔːtər, -ˌwɑː-/ *n* [U] *informal* a strong alcoholic drink, such as WHISKY

fire·wood /ˈfaɪəwʊd $ ˈfaɪr-/ *n* [U] wood that has been cut or collected in order to be burned in a fire

fire·work /ˈfaɪəwɜːk $ ˈfaɪrwɜːrk/ ●●○ *n* [C usually plural]
1 a small container filled with powder that burns or explodes to produce coloured lights and noise in the sky: *a New Year's Eve* ***fireworks display*** | *Jeff and David were in the back yard* ***setting off fireworks****.*
2 *spoken* used to say that someone will be angry: ***There'll be fireworks*** *if I get home late again.*
3 something that is exciting or impressive: *The real fireworks are provided by Shakespeare's poetry.*

ˈfiring line *n* **(be) in the firing line** to be in a position or situation in which you can be attacked or blamed for something, often unfairly

ˈfiring squad *n* [C] a group of soldiers whose duty is to punish prisoners by shooting and killing them

firm¹ /fɜːm $ fɜːrm/ ●●● S1 W1 *n* [C] a business or company, especially a small one: **electronics/advertising/law etc firm** *She works for an electronics firm.* | **a firm of accountants/solicitors/builders etc** *Kevin is with a firm of accountants in Birmingham.* THESAURUS ▸ COMPANY

firm² ●●● S3 W2 *adj*
1 not completely hard, but not soft, and not easy to bend into a different shape OPP **soft**: *The sofa cushions are fairly firm.* | *a firm green apple* | *Most doctors recommend sleeping on a firm mattress.* THESAURUS ▸ HARD
2 strongly fixed in position, and not likely to move SYN **secure**: *Make sure the ladder feels firm before you climb up.* | *A concrete foundation was poured after digging down to firm ground.* | *Mount the tanks side by side on* ***a firm base****.*
3 not likely to change: **firm conviction/commitment/belief etc** *Our client hasn't reached a firm decision on the matter yet.* | *Blackpool remains a* ***firm favourite*** *with holidaymakers from Northern Ireland.* | *Corey was always a* ***firm believer*** *in prayer.* | *They made a* ***firm offer*** (=offered to pay a particular amount) *on the house over the weekend.* | *Diana and Laura have been* ***firm friends*** (=close friends) *since their early teens.*
4 showing in the way that you behave or speak that you are the person in control and that you are not likely to change your answer, belief etc: *Cal replied with a polite but firm 'no'.* | *What this country needs is firm leadership.* | **be firm with sb** *You need to be firm with her or she'll try to take advantage of you.* THESAURUS ▸ DETERMINED, STRICT
5 HAND **a firm grip/hold/grasp etc** if you have something in a firm grip etc, you are holding it tightly and strongly: *He took a firm grip of my arm and marched me towards the door.* | *a firm handshake*
6 take a firm stand/line to state your opinion clearly and not be persuaded to change it
7 stand/hold firm to not change your actions or opinions: **[+against]** *Jones is urging Christians to stand firm against abortion.*
8 a firm hand a strict way of dealing with someone: *These children* ***need a firm hand****.*
9 MONEY [not before noun] if the value of a particular country's money is firm, it does not fall in value SYN **steady**: **[+against]** *The pound is still firm against the dollar.* —**firmly** *adv* —**firmness** *n* [U]

firm³ *v* [T] to press down on soil to make it harder or more solid

firm sth ↔ **up** *phr v* **1** to make arrangements, ideas etc more definite and exact: *We're hoping to firm up the deal later this month.* **2** to make a part of your body have more muscle and less fat by exercising

fir·ma·ment /ˈfɜːməmənt $ ˈfɜːr-/ *n* **the firmament** *literary* the sky or heaven

firm·ware /ˈfɜːmweə $ ˈfɜːrmwer/ *n* [U] *technical* instructions to computers that are stored on CHIPS rather than in programs → HARDWARE(1), SOFTWARE

first¹ /fɜːst $ fɜːrst/ ●●● S1 W1 *adj*
1 IN A SERIES coming before all the other things or people in a series: *Ella was his first girlfriend.* | **the first thing/time/day etc** *The first time I flew on a plane I was really nervous.* | *In the first year, all students take five courses.* | *He said the first thing that came into his head.* | *the first step towards achieving a peace agreement* | *There's a meeting on the first Monday of every month.* | **the first two/three/few etc** *I only read the first two chapters of the book.* | *It rained during the first few days of the trip.* | *The* ***first and last*** *mountain I climbed was Mount Rundle* (=it was the only mountain I ever climbed).
2 for the first time used to say that something has never happened or been done before: *For the first time in his life he felt truly happy.* | *The survey revealed that, for the first time, there are more women in the workplace than men.* | **Not for the first time** *she wondered how he coped with so many children.*
3 MAIN most important: *Our first priority is to maintain the standard of work.* | *As I see it, my first responsibility is to my family.*
4 in the first place a) used to talk about the beginning of a situation, or the situation before something happened: *Why did you agree to meet her in the first place?* | *He wouldn't have given you the job in the first place if he didn't think you could do it.* **b)** *written* used to give the first in a list of reasons or points: *Her success was secured by two factors. In the first place, she had the support of managers.*
5 in the first instance *formal* at the start of a situation or series of actions: *The appointment of research officer will be for two years in the first instance.* | *Enquiries should be made in the first instance to the Human Resources Director.*
6 at first glance/sight the first time that you look at someone or something, before you notice any details: *At first glance the twins look identical.* | *At first sight, there didn't appear to be much damage.* → **love at first sight** at LOVE²(2)
7 first things first used to say that something should be done or dealt with first because it is the most important
8 (at) first hand if you see, experience, hear etc something at first hand, you see, experience etc it yourself, not through other people: *Many people have seen the horrors of war at first hand.* → FIRST-HAND
9 first prize/place the prize that is given to the best person or thing in a competition: **win/take first prize** *She won first prize in a painting competition.* | **[+of]** *There is a first prize of £10,000.*
10 first choice the thing or person you like best: *John was our first choice as a name for the baby.*
11 first thing as soon as you get up in the morning, or as soon as you start work: *I'll call you first thing tomorrow.* | *We're leaving first thing.*
12 at first light *literary* very early in the morning: *The search will resume at first light tomorrow.*
13 make the first move to be the person who starts to do something when someone else is too nervous, embarrassed etc to do it: *He was glad she had made the first move and kissed him.*
14 not have the first idea about sth (*also* **not know/understand the first thing about sth**) to not know anything about

a subject, or not know how to do something: *I wouldn't have the first idea about what to do in that situation.* | *I don't know the first thing about cars.*
15 the first flush of sth the beginning of a good period of time when you are young, successful etc: **be in the first flush of passion/youth etc** *He was no longer in the first flush of youth.* | *The first flush of enthusiasm had passed.*
16 JOB TITLE used in the title of someone's job or position to show that they have a high rank: *the first officer* | *the First Lord of the Admiralty*
17 first among equals officially on the same level as other people but really having more power
18 of the first water *old-fashioned* of the highest quality

first² ●●● S1 W2 *adv*
1 before anything or anyone else: *Cindy and Joe arrived first.* | *An extra five points will be given to the team that finishes first.* | ***First of all*** *we'd better make sure we've got everything we need.*
2 before doing anything else, or before anything else happens: *I'll join you in a minute but I need to make a phone call first.*
3 done for the first time: *The book was first published in 2000.*
4 at the beginning of a situation or activity: *When we were first married we lived in Toronto.* | *We first became friends when we worked together.*
5 [sentence adverb] (*also* **first of all**) used before saying the first of several things you want to say SYN **firstly**: *First, I'd like to thank everyone for coming.*
6 first off *informal* **a)** before doing anything else: *First off I'd like you all to fill in an evaluation sheet.* **b)** used before saying the first of several things you want to say, especially when you are annoyed: *First off I didn't agree with the comments in your email.*
7 first up *BrE spoken informal* used to introduce the first thing you are going to talk about, or the first thing that is going to happen: *First up is the Blues song 'Mississippi Lad'.*
8 put sb/sth first to consider someone or something as the most important person or thing: *We need to choose energy policies that put the environment first.* | *Businesses should always put the customer first.*
9 come first a) to be the most important person or thing to someone: *The care and well-being of patients should always come first.* | *As far as I'm concerned, the children come first.* | **[+with]** *Business always came first with Luke.* **b)** to win a competition: **[+in]** *The choir came first in all sections of the competition.*
10 first and foremost used to emphasize the most important quality, purpose, reason etc: *Dublin is thought of first and foremost for its literary heritage.*
11 first and last used to emphasize that something is the most important thing or quality: *She regarded herself as a teacher first and last, not a writer.*
12 first come, first served used to say that something will be given to the people who ask for it first, when there is not enough for everyone: *Tickets will be allocated* ***on a first come, first served basis.***

GRAMMAR

Choosing the right tense

First is used with the simple past: *We first met in 2005.* ✗ Don't say: *We have first met in 2005.*

Word order

- **First** usually comes before a main verb: *I* ***first went*** *to Paris two years ago.*
- **First** comes after 'be' when it is the main verb: *I* ***was first*** *in Paris two years ago.*
- **First** comes after the first auxiliary: *When* ***did*** *you* ***first*** *realize you wanted to be a doctor?*

THESAURUS

first/firstly used when mentioning the first in a list of reasons, arguments, or questions to consider: *I want you to consider these three points in your essay: first, what is the writer's attitude to the war in this poem ...* | *There are several reasons for this conclusion. Firstly ...*
first of all used especially to emphasize that the first of several things you are going to say is the most important thing: *The content of the article must, first of all, be accurate.* | *First of all, a huge thank you to everyone who has supported us over the last two years.*
in the first place *spoken* (*also* **for a start** *BrE*) *spoken* used when giving the first and most important reason or example, especially when you are arguing or discussing something with someone: *Our main priority should be better public transport – in the first place to reduce the amount of traffic on our roads.* | *He's not the right person for the job. For a start he's too young.*
to begin with/to start with *spoken* used when telling someone the first and most important thing that you want to say: *There are numerous activities on offer. To start with there are over 60 miles of walks with splendid views.*

first³ ●●● S2 W2 *n*
1 at first used to talk about the beginning of a situation, especially when it is different now: *At first, Gregory was shy and hardly spoke.* | *I felt quite disappointed at first.*
2 [C usually singular] something that has never happened or been done before: **[+for]** *The 3-0 defeat was a first for the team.* | *These results are firsts in the history of women's athletics.* | *'I think he'll agree to it.'* ***'That will be a first.'***
3 from the (very) first from the beginning of a situation: *I was against the idea from the first.* | *I should have known from the first that the relationship would never work.*
4 [C] the highest mark you can get in a university DEGREE in Britain: *Helen* ***got a first in*** *Law.*
5 [U] the lowest GEAR in a car or other vehicle, that you use when moving slowly SYN **first gear**: **in first** *You should be in first on a hill like this.* | *He* ***put*** *the car* ***into first*** *and roared away.*

first⁴ ●●● S2 W2 *pron*
1 the first the first person to do something, or the first thing to happen: *There are now many similar housing projects but this was the first.* | *We hope this year's festival will be* ***the first of many.*** | **the first to do sth** *I always thought my sister would be the first to get married.* | *James was the first to arrive.*
2 the first I knew/heard used when you have just discovered something that other people already know, and you are slightly annoyed: *The first I knew he was in York was when I got an email from him.* | **[+of/about]** *The first I knew about it was when Tony called me.*
3 the First *spoken* used after the name of a king, queen, or pope when other later ones have the same name: *Queen Elizabeth the First* (=written as Queen Elizabeth I)

ˌfirst ˈaid ●●○ *n* [U] simple medical treatment that is given as soon as possible to someone who is injured or who suddenly becomes ill: *Being* ***given first aid*** *at the scene of the accident probably saved his life.*

ˌfirst ˈaider *n* [C] *BrE* someone who is trained to give first aid

ˌfirst ˈaid kit *n* [C] a special bag or box containing BANDAGES and medicines to treat people who are injured or become ill suddenly → see picture on *p. 684*

ˌfirst ˈbase *n* [C] **1 a)** the first of the four places in a game of baseball that a player must touch before gaining a point **b)** the position of a defending player near this place: *He plays first base for the Red Sox.* **2 get to/reach first base a)** *AmE informal* to reach the first stage of success in an attempt to achieve something: *You've gotten to first base if you've landed an interview.* **b)** *old-fashioned informal* to kiss someone in a sexual way, used especially by young men to talk about the first stage in a sexual relationship

first·born /ˈfɜːstbɔːn $ ˈfɜːrstbɔːrn/ *n* [singular] your first child —**firstborn** *adj*: *her firstborn son*

F

FIRST AID KIT

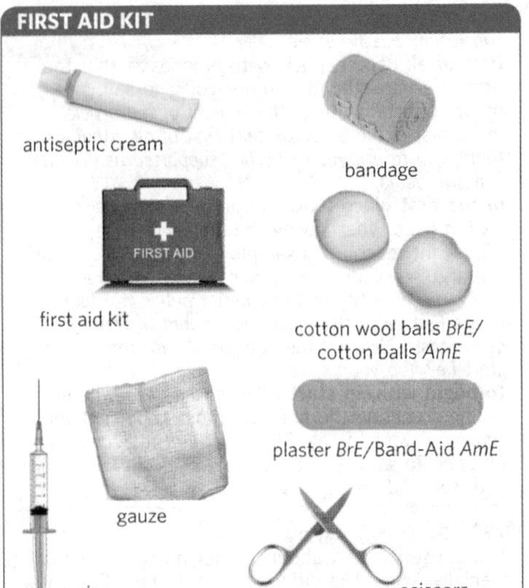

ˌfirst ˈclass *n* **1** [U] the best and most expensive seats on a plane or train, or rooms in a hotel: *We prefer to travel in first class.* → BUSINESS CLASS, CABIN CLASS, ECONOMY CLASS, TOURIST CLASS **2** [U] **a)** the class of post used in Britain for letters and parcels, that is quicker and more expensive than second-class post → **second class b)** the class of post used in the US for ordinary business and personal letters **3** [C] the highest class of degree from a British university

ˌfirst-ˈclass ●○○ *adj*
1 of very good quality, and much better than other things of the same type: *This is a first-class wine.* | *His writing is first-class.* THESAURUS GOOD
2 relating to the class of post that is the most expensive and quickest to arrive: **first-class stamp/mail/post etc**
3 relating to the best and most expensive class of seats on a plane or train, or rooms in a hotel: **first-class passenger/seat/compartment etc** —**first class** *adv*: *If I send the letter first class it should arrive tomorrow.* | *travel first class*

ˌfirst ˈcousin *n* [C] a child of your AUNT or UNCLE SYN **cousin**

ˌfirst deˈgree *n* **1** [C usually singular] *BrE* used to talk about a university degree such as a BA or a BSc, obtained by people who do not already have a degree **2 murder in the first degree** *AmE* first-degree murder

ˌfirst-deˈgree *adj* [only before noun] **1 first-degree burn** a burn that is not very serious **2 first-degree murder** *AmE* murder of the most serious type, in which someone deliberately kills someone else → **manslaughter**

ˌfirst eˈdition *n* [C] one of the first copies of a book, which is often valuable: *an impressive collection of 19th century first editions*

ˌfirst-ˈever *adj* [only before noun] happening for the first time: *her first-ever television interview* | *the first-ever visit to China by an American president*

ˌfirst ˈfamily, **First Family** *n* **the first family** the family of the president of the US

ˌfirst ˈfloor *n* **1 the first floor** *BrE* the floor of a building just above the one at the bottom level → **ground floor**: *a flat on the first floor* **2 the first floor** *AmE* the floor of a building at the bottom level: *Fire broke out on the first floor of the apartment building.*

ˌfirst ˈfruits *n* [plural] *BrE* the first good result of something: **[+of]** *the first fruits of the government's privatization policy*

ˌfirst ˈgear *n* [U] the lowest GEAR in a car or other motor vehicle, used when starting to move or when going up or down a very steep hill

ˌfirst geneˈration *n* [singular] **1** people who have moved to live in a new country, or the children of these people **2** the first type of a machine to be developed: **[+of]** *the first generation of hand-held computers* **3** the first people to do something: **[+of]** *the first generation of radical feminists in the US* —**first-generation** *adj*: *first-generation Americans*

ˌfirst ˈhalf *n* [C] the first of two equal periods of time that a sports match is divided into

ˌfirst-ˈhand (*also* **first·hand**) /ˌfɜːstˈhænd $ ˌfɜːrst-/ *adj* [only before noun] **first-hand experience/knowledge/account etc** experience etc that has been learned or gained by doing something yourself or by talking to someone yourself → **second-hand**: *journalists with first-hand experience of working in war zones* —**first-hand** *adv*: *experience gained first-hand* → **(at) first hand** at FIRST¹(8)

ˌfirst ˈlady *n* **1 the first lady** the wife of the president of the US, or of the GOVERNOR of a US state **2** [C usually singular] a woman who is considered to be the very best at a particular thing: **[+of]** *the first lady of jazz, Billie Holiday*

ˌfirst ˈlanguage *n* [C] the language that you first learn as a child SYN **native language/tongue**, **mother tongue** → **second language**

ˌfirst lieuˈtenant *n* [C] a middle rank in the US army, Marines, or Air Force, or someone who has this rank

ˌfirst ˈlight *n* [U] the time at the beginning of day when light first appears SYN **dawn**, **daybreak**

first·ly /ˈfɜːstli $ -ɜːr-/ ●●○ S3 *adv* [sentence adverb] used to say that the fact or reason that you are going to mention is the first one and will be followed by others OPP **lastly** → **finally**, **lastly**: *Firstly, I would like to thank everyone who has contributed to this success.* THESAURUS FIRST

ˌfirst ˈmate (*also* **first officer**) *n* [C] an officer who has the rank just below captain on a ship that is not a military ship

ˈfirst name ●●● S2 *n* [C]
1 the name or names that come before your family name SYN **Christian name** → **surname**, **last name**: *Her first name's Helen, but I don't know her surname.*
2 be on first name terms (with sb) *BrE*, **be on a first name basis** *AmE* to know someone well enough to call them by their first name

ˌfirst ˈnight *n* [C] the evening when the first public performance of a show, play etc is given

ˌfirst ofˈfender *n* [C] someone who is guilty of breaking the law for the first time

ˌfirst ˈofficer *n* [C] FIRST MATE

ˌfirst-past-the-ˈpost *adj* [only before noun] *BrE* (*abbreviation* **FPTP**) a first-past-the-post system of electing a politician, a government etc is one in which the person or party who gets the most votes wins: *Britain's first-past-the-post electoral system* | **first-past-the-post voting**

ˌfirst ˈperson *n* **1 the first person** *technical* a form of a verb or a pronoun that is used to show that you are the speaker. For example, 'I', 'me', 'we', and 'us' are first person pronouns, and 'I am' is the first person singular of the verb 'to be' → **second person**, **third person 2** [singular] a way of telling a story in which the writer or speaker tells it as though they were involved in the story → **third person**: *a first person narrative* | **in the first person** *'The Great Gatsby' is written in the first person.*

ˌfirst-person ˈshooter *n* [C usually singular] a computer or video game in which the person playing the game is the main character and has to shoot the other characters in the game

ˌfirst-ˈrate *adj* of the very best quality SYN **excellent**: *He's a first-rate surgeon.*

ˌfirst reˈfusal *n BrE* **have/give sb first refusal on sth** to let someone decide whether to buy something before you offer to sell it to other people: *I'll let you have first refusal on the car.*

ˌfirst reˈsponder *n* [C] *AmE* a member of the police,

fire, or medical services who has been specially trained to be the first person to go to a very serious accident or to an extremely dangerous and unexpected situation that must be dealt with quickly

ˌfirst ˈstrike *n* [C] an attack made on your enemy before they attack you, especially an attack made using NUCLEAR weapons

ˌfirst-ˈstring *adj* [only before noun] a first-string player in a team plays when the game begins because they are the most skilled → **second-string**

ˌfirst-time ˈbuyer *n* [C] someone who is buying a house or an apartment for the first time

ˌFirst ˈWorld *n* **the First World** the rich industrial countries of the world —**first world** *adj* [always before noun]: *first world economies* → **Third World**

ˌFirst World ˈWar *n* **the First World War** the big war fought in Europe between 1914 and 1918, which involved many different countries SYN **World War I**

firth /fɜːθ $ fɜːrθ/ *n* [C] a narrow area of sea between two areas of land, or the place where a river flows into the sea - used especially in Scotland: *the Firth of Forth*

fis·cal /ˈfɪskəl/ *adj formal* relating to money, taxes, debts etc that are owned and managed by the government: *a **fiscal crisis** | Sound (=good) **fiscal policies** are required to combat inflation. | a **fiscal matter*** THESAURUS ▸ FINANCIAL —**fiscally** *adv*: *fiscally conservative*

ˌfiscal ˈyear *n* [C] **1** the 12 month period used by governments to calculate spending and how much tax a person or business must pay: **last/current/coming/next fiscal year** **2** *AmE* the 12 month period over which a company calculates its profits or losses SYN **financial year** *BrE*

FISH

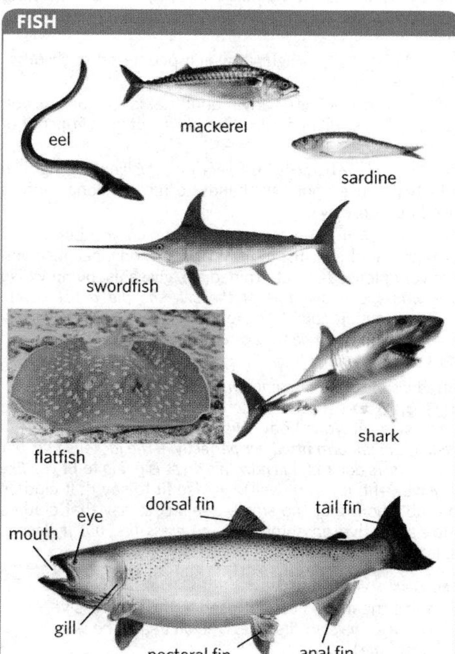

fish¹ /fɪʃ/ ●●● S1 W1 *n* (*plural* **fish** *or* **fishes**)
1 [C] an animal that lives in water, and uses its FINS and tail to swim: *Over 1,500 different species of fish inhabit the waters around the reef. | The stonefish is the most deadly of all fishes. | The lake is well stocked with fish* (=it contains a lot of fish).
2 [U] the flesh of a fish used as food → **seafood**: *You usually drink white wine with fish. | In Japan, people eat **raw fish**. | **Oily fish*** (=fish that contains a lot of oil) *is supposed to be good for you.* ⚠ You say **fish and chips**, not 'chips and fish'.
3 (be/feel) like a fish out of water to feel uncomfortable because you feel you do not belong in a place or situation: *I felt like a fish out of water in my new school.*
4 there are plenty more fish in the sea used to tell someone whose relationship has ended that there are other people they can have a relationship with
5 neither fish nor fowl neither one thing nor another
6 have other/bigger fish to fry *informal* to have other things to do, especially more important things
7 odd fish/queer fish *BrE old-fashioned* someone who is slightly strange or crazy
8 cold fish an unfriendly person who seems to have no strong feelings
9 a big fish in a little/small pond someone who is important in or who has influence over a very small area → **drink like a fish** at DRINK¹(2), → **another/a different kettle of fish** at KETTLE(3)

COLLOCATIONS

ADJECTIVES/NOUN + fish
freshwater fish (=that live in rivers or lakes) *The pools are home to frogs, newts, and freshwater fish.*
saltwater fish (=that live in the ocean) *saltwater fish such as cod and tuna*
river/sea fish *Pike are river fish.*
tropical fish | **farmed fish** (=fish that are from a fish farm)

VERBS
catch/land a fish *Pete caught a really big fish.*
breed fish *He has been breeding tropical fish for many years.*
keep fish (=have them as pets or for breeding) *We used to keep tropical fish when I was young.*
a fish swims *Red fish swam on either side of the boat.*
a fish bites (=it takes food from a hook and gets caught) *The fish aren't biting today.*

fish + NOUN
fish stocks (=the quantity of fish in the sea) *Fish stocks have declined dramatically.*
fish species (*also* **species of fish**) (=the group of fish that are similar and can breed together) *74 of California's 113 native fish species are in need of protection.*
a fish tank (=for keeping fish indoors, usually as pets) | **a fish pond** (=for keeping fish outdoors, in a garden) | **fish food** (=for feeding fish)

PHRASES
a shoal/school of fish (=a large group swimming together) *Shoals of little fish were swimming around her.*

fish² ●●○ S3 *v*
1 [I] to try to catch fish → **fishing**: *Dad really loves to fish.* | **[+for]** *a Japanese vessel fishing for tuna in the Eastern Pacific*
2 [I always +adv/prep] *informal* to search for something in a bag, pocket etc: **[+about/around]** *She fished around in her purse and pulled out a photo.* | **[+for]** *Chris fished in his pocket for a coin.*
3 [T] to try to catch fish in a particular area of water → **fishing**: *Other nations are forbidden to fish the waters within 200 miles of the coast.*
4 fish for compliments to try to make someone say something nice about you, usually by first criticizing yourself - used to show disapproval: *It's sickening the way he's always fishing for compliments.*
5 [I] to try to find out information, without asking directly: *'Are you here with your wife?' she asked, fishing.*

fish sb/sth **↔ out** *phr v* **a)** to pull someone or something out of water: **[+of]** *The body was fished out of the East River a week later.* **b)** to find something after searching through a bag, pocket etc, and take it out: **[+of]** *Eric fished a peppermint out of the bag.*

ˌfish and ˈchips *n* [U] a meal consisting of fish covered with BATTER (=a mixture of flour and milk) and cooked in oil, served with long thin pieces of potato also cooked in oil: *Get some fish and chips on your way home.* | *a fish and chip shop*

fish·bowl /ˈfɪʃbəʊl $ -boʊl/ *n* [C] **1** a glass bowl that you can keep fish in **2** a place or situation in which you cannot do anything in private: *Being in a small town like this is like living in a fishbowl.*

fish·cake /ˈfɪʃkeɪk/ *n* [C] a small round flat food consisting of cooked fish mixed with cooked potato

fish·er·man /ˈfɪʃəmən $ -ʃər-/ ●●○ *n* (*plural* **fishermen** /-mən/) [C] someone who catches fish as a sport or as a job → ANGLER

fish·e·ry /ˈfɪʃəri/ *n* (*plural* **fisheries**) [C] **1** a part of the sea where fish are caught in large numbers **2** a FISH FARM

ˌfish-eye ˈlens *n* [C] a type of curved LENS (=piece of glass on the front of a camera) that allows you to take photographs of a wide area

ˈfish ˌfarm (*also* **fishery**) *n* [C] an area of water used for breeding fish as a business —**fish farming** *n* [U]

ˌfish ˈfinger *n* [C] *BrE* a long piece of fish covered with BREADCRUMBS or BATTER and cooked SYN **fish stick** *AmE*

ˈfish fry *n* (*plural* **fish fries**) [C] *AmE* an outdoor event held to raise money for an organization, at which fish is cooked and eaten

fish·hook /ˈfɪʃhʊk/ *n* [C] a small hook with a sharp point at one end, that is fastened to the end of a long string in order to catch fish

FISHING

fish·ing /ˈfɪʃɪŋ/ ●●● S3 *n* [U]

1 the sport or business of catching fish: *Fishing is one of his hobbies.* | *Terry's* ***going fishing*** *at Lake Arrowhead next weekend.* | **deep sea/freshwater/saltwater fishing** | **salmon/trout/bass etc fishing** → FLYFISHING

2 be on a fishing expedition *AmE informal* to try to find out secret information by asking a lot of questions about different things

ˈfishing line *n* [U] very long string made of strong material and used to catch fish

ˈfishing rod (*also* **ˈfishing pole**) *n* [C] a long thin pole with a long string and a hook attached to it, used to catch fish → see picture at FISHING

ˈfishing ˌtackle *n* [U] equipment used for fishing → see picture at FISHING

ˈfish ˌkettle *n* [C] *BrE* a long deep dish used for cooking whole fish

ˈfish meal *n* [U] dried fish crushed into a powder and put on the land to help plants grow

fish·mon·ger /ˈfɪʃmʌŋgə $ -mɑːŋgər, -mʌŋ-/ *n* [C] *BrE* **1** someone who sells fish **2** (*also* **fishmonger's**) a shop that sells fish

fish·net stock·ings /ˌfɪʃnet ˈstɒkɪŋz $ -ˈstɑː-/ (*also* **ˌfishnet ˈtights**, **fish·nets** /ˈfɪʃnets/ *BrE*) [plural] *n* STOCKINGS with a pattern of small holes that make them look like a net

ˈfish slice *n* [C] *BrE* a kitchen tool used especially for turning food when cooking, with a wide flat part and a handle SYN **spatula**

ˈfish stick *n* [C] *AmE* a FISH FINGER

fish·tail /ˈfɪʃteɪl/ *v* [I] *AmE* if a vehicle or aircraft fishtails, the back end of it slides from side to side, usually because the tyres are sliding on water or ice

fish·wife /ˈfɪʃwaɪf/ *n* (*plural* **fishwives** /-waɪvz/) [C] *especially BrE* an insulting word for a woman who shouts a lot and is often in a bad temper

fish·y /ˈfɪʃi/ *adj* **1** *informal* seeming bad or dishonest SYN **suspicious**: *There's something very fishy about him.* **2** tasting or smelling of fish: *a fishy smell*

fis·sile /ˈfɪsaɪl $ -səl/ *adj technical* able to be split by atomic fission

fis·sion /ˈfɪʃən/ *n* [U] *technical* **1** the process of splitting an atom to produce large amounts of energy or an explosion → **fusion** **2** the process of dividing a cell into two or more parts

fis·sure /ˈfɪʃə $ -ər/ *n* [C] a deep crack, especially in rock or earth

fist /fɪst/ ●●○ *n* [C]

1 the hand when it is tightly closed, so that the fingers are curled in towards the PALM. People close their hand in a fist when they are angry or are going to hit someone: *She held the money tightly in her fist.* | *Malcolm* ***clenched*** *his* ***fist*** (=held his fist very tightly closed) *angrily.* | *Dooley stood up and* ***shook*** *his* ***fist*** *in her face.* | *Varney slammed his fist down onto the table so hard the dishes jumped.* → HAM-FISTED, TIGHT-FISTED, → **hand over fist** at HAND¹(35)

2 make a good/bad fist of sth *BrE informal* to make a successful or unsuccessful attempt to do something

ˈfist bump (*also* **ˈfist pound**) *n* [C] the action of hitting someone's closed hand with your own, as a greeting or celebration

ˈfist fight *n* [C] a fight in which people hit each other with their BARE fists

fist·ful /ˈfɪstfʊl/ *n* [C] an amount that is as much as you can hold in your hand: **[+of]** *a child clutching a fistful of toffees*

fis·ti·cuffs /ˈfɪstɪkʌfs/ *n* [plural] *old-fashioned* a fight in which you use your BARE hands to hit someone - often used humorously

ˈfist pump *n* [C] a movement in which you bend your arm and hold your fist in front of your body, because you are very pleased or determined: **do/give a fist pump** *When she won the final game of the set, she did a fist pump.* —**fist-pumping** *noun* [U]: *He is often seen enthusiastically fist-pumping when he wins a race.*

fit¹ /fɪt/ ●●● S1 W2 *v* (*past tense and past participle* **fitted** *also* **fit** *AmE*, *present participle* **fitting**)

1 CLOTHES **a)** [I,T] if a piece of clothing fits you, it is the right size for your body: *His clothes did not* ***fit*** *him very* ***well***. | *The uniform* ***fitted*** *her* ***perfectly***. | *The jacket's fine, but the trousers don't fit.* | *I know this dress is going to* ***fit*** *you* ***like a glove*** (=fit you very well). ⚠ Use **fit** to say that clothes are not too big or too small. Use **suit** to say that clothes look attractive on someone: *The dress fits, but it doesn't suit me.*

GRAMMAR: Using the progressive

In this meaning, **fit** is not used in the progressive. You say: *The skirt fits (me).* ✗ Don't say: *The skirt is fitting (me).*

GRAMMAR GUIDE ▸ VERBS

b) [T] to try a piece of clothing on someone to see if it is the right size for them, or to make sure a special piece of equipment is right for them: **be fitted for sth** *I'm being fitted for a new suit tomorrow.* | **be fitted with sth** *He may need to be fitted with a hearing aid.* GRAMMAR **Fit** is usually passive in this meaning.

2 RIGHT SIZE/SHAPE **a)** [I,T] if something fits in a place, it is the right size or shape to go there: *I couldn't find a key which fitted the lock.* | *Most cookers are designed to fit level with your worktops.* | **[+in/into/under etc]** *The plastic cover*

fits neatly over the frame. **b)** [T always + adv/prep] to put something carefully into a place that is the right size or shape for it: *She fitted the last piece into the jigsaw puzzle.*
3 ENOUGH SPACE [I,T] if something fits into a place, there is enough space for it: *I wanted to put the wardrobe behind the door, but I don't think it'll fit.* | *You might be able to fit some small flowering plants between the larger bushes.* | **fit sb/sth in/into sth** *I don't think we'll be able to fit any more people into the car.* | *We should be able to fit one more in.*
4 EQUIPMENT/PART [T] to put a piece of equipment into a place, or a new part onto a machine, so that it is ready to be used: **fit sth on/to etc sth** *I need to fit a lock on the door.* | *Anti-theft devices are fitted to all our cars.* | **be fitted with sth** *The windows are all fitted with security locks.*
5 MATCH/BE SUITABLE [I,T] if something fits another thing, it is similar to it or suitable for it: *The punishment should fit the crime.* | *Police said the car fits the description of the stolen vehicle.* | *Scientists often select facts to fit their theories.* | *He didn't fit the conventional image of a banker.* | **[+with]** *The rhythm should fit with the meaning of a poem.*
6 fit sb for sth *formal* to make someone suitable for something or able to do something: *His natural authority fitted him for a senior position.*
7 fit the bill to be the type of person or thing that you want: *We wanted an experienced sportscaster, and Waggoner fit the bill.*
8 if the cap fits (, wear it) *BrE*, **if the shoe fits (, wear it)** *AmE spoken* used to tell someone that you think a criticism of them is true: *'So you think I'm a liar.' 'Well, if the cap fits ...'*
→ **sb's face doesn't fit** at FACE[1](20)

fit in *phr v*
1 if someone fits in, they are accepted by the other people in a group: *I never really fitted in at school.* | **[+with]** *I wasn't sure if she would fit in with my friends.*
2 fit sth/sb ↔ in to manage to do something or see someone, even though you have a lot of other things to do SYN **squeeze sth/sb ↔ in**: *The doctor said he can fit me in at 4:30.* | *I wanted to fit in a swim before breakfast.*
3 if something fits in with other things, it is similar to them or goes well with them: *I don't know quite how this new course will fit in.* | **[+with]** *A new building must fit in with its surroundings.* | *You can't expect a baby to fit in with your existing routine.*

fit into sth *phr v*
1 to be part of a group or system: *Some of the patients we see do not fit neatly into any of the existing categories.* | *How does this fit into the company's overall marketing strategy?*
2 to be accepted by the people in a group or organization: *She fitted into the team very well.*

fit sb/sth ↔ **out** *phr v BrE* to provide a person or place with the equipment, furniture, or clothes that they need: *The office had been fitted out in style.* | **[+with]** *The new recruits were fitted out with uniforms and weapons.*

fit together *phr v*
1 if something fits together or you fit it together, different pieces can be joined to make something: *Look, the tubes fit together like this.* | **fit sth together** *The pictures show you how to fit it together.*
2 if a story, set of facts, set of ideas etc fit together, they make sense when considered together: *Telecom and computer businesses fit together well.*

fit sb/sth ↔ **up** *phr v BrE*
1 to provide a place with the furniture or equipment that it needs SYN **fit sb/sth ↔ out**: **[+with]** *The rooms are now fitted up with electric lights.*
2 *informal* to make someone seem guilty of a crime when they are really not guilty: *I knew that I had been fitted up.*

fit² ●●● S2 W3 *adj* (*comparative* **fitter**, *superlative* **fittest**)
1 STRONG someone who is fit is strong and healthy, especially because they exercise regularly OPP **unfit**: *You must be very fit if you do so much running.* | *He was young, good-looking, and* ***physically fit***. | *I swim twice a week to try and* ***keep fit***. | **[+for]** *He may not be fit for Saturday's match.* | **fit to do sth** *I don't know if I'll be fit enough to take part in the race.* | *Psychiatrists said he was fit to stand trial* (=he was mentally healthy enough). | *She's over eighty now, but still* ***as fit as a fiddle*** (=very fit). | **fighting fit** *BrE* (=very fit) *I had just come back from holiday and was fighting fit.* THESAURUS▸ HEALTHY
2 SUITABLE suitable or good enough for something OPP **unfit**: **[+for]** *We made sure the land was fit for drilling.* | *The food was not fit for human consumption.* | *This book is not fit for publication!* | **fit to do sth** *He is not fit to govern this country!* | *This room is not fit to be seen!*
3 see/think fit (to do sth) to decide that something is the best thing to do, especially when other people do not agree with you: *The government saw fit to ignore our advice.* | *Sort out the problem in any way you think fit.*
4 in a fit state (to do sth) *especially BrE* healthy enough or in good enough condition for something: *I was still very shocked and* ***in no fit state*** *to work.* | *We'll have to make sure the house is in a fit state to receive visitors.*
5 fit for a king of very good quality: *The meal they provided was fit for a king.*
6 ATTRACTIVE *BrE* sexually attractive
7 fit to drop *BrE informal* extremely tired SYN **exhausted**: *It was getting late and most of us were fit to drop.*
8 fit to burst *BrE informal* if you are laughing, shouting etc fit to burst, you are doing it a lot: *The girls were laughing fit to burst.*
9 fit to be tied *AmE* very angry, anxious, or upset: *I was fit to be tied when she didn't come home until 2 a.m.*

fit³ ●●○ *n*
1 EMOTION [C] a time when you feel an emotion very strongly and cannot control your behaviour: **[+of]** *She killed him in a fit of temper.* | *He quit his job in a fit of drunken depression.*
2 LOSE CONSCIOUSNESS [C] a short period of time when someone loses consciousness and cannot control their body because their brain is not working properly: *She used to* ***have fits*** *as a baby.* | *people who suffer from* ***epileptic fits***
3 LAUGH/COUGH [C] a short time during which you laugh or cough a lot in a way that you cannot control: *He had a violent* ***coughing fit***. | **[+of]** *The girls collapsed into a fit of the giggles.* | *We were all* ***in fits of laughter*** *trying to clear up the mess.* | *Carl* ***had*** *us all* ***in fits*** (=made us laugh a lot) *with his stories.*
4 have/throw a fit *informal* to be very angry or shocked: *If your mother finds out about this, she'll have a fit.*
5 RIGHT SIZE [singular] the way in which something fits on your body or fits into a space: *The dress was a* ***perfect fit***. | *I managed to get everything into the suitcase, but it was a* ***tight fit***.
6 SUITABLE [singular] *formal* if there is a fit between two things, they are similar to each other or are suitable for each other: **[+between]** *We must be sure that there's a fit between the needs of the children and the education they receive.*
7 in/by fits and starts if something happens in fits and starts, it does not happen smoothly, but keeps starting and then stopping again: *Technology advances by fits and starts.* | *He spoke in fits and starts.*

fit⁴ *v* (**fitted, fitting**) [I] *BrE* to have a SEIZURE (=a sudden condition in which someone cannot control the movements of their body): *The patient was fitting.*

fit·ful /ˈfɪtfəl/ *adj* not regular, and starting and stopping often: *John awoke from a* ***fitful sleep***. | *The peace talks only seem to be making fitful progress.* —**fitfully** *adv*: *She slept fitfully.*

fit·ment /ˈfɪtmənt/ *n* [C usually plural] *BrE* a piece of furniture or equipment that is made especially for a particular space in a room: *bathroom fitments*

fit·ness /ˈfɪtnəs/ ●●○ *n* [U]
1 when you are healthy and strong enough to do hard work or play sports: *an exercise programme to improve your fitness* | *Running marathons requires a high level of* ***physical fitness***.
2 the degree to which someone or something is suitable or good enough for a particular situation or purpose: **[+for]** *He questioned McNeil's fitness for high office.* | **fitness**

to do sth *The doctor will first determine your fitness to receive the anaesthetic.*

fit·ted /ˈfɪtɪd/ *adj* **1 be fitted with sth** to have or include something as a permanent part: *Is your car fitted with an alarm?* **2** *BrE* [only before noun] built, made, or cut to fit a particular space: *a fitted wardrobe | a fitted kitchen | fitted carpets* **3** [only before noun] fitted clothes are designed so that they fit closely to someone's body OPP **loose**: *a fitted black jacket* **4** *BrE* [not before noun] having the right qualities or experience for a particular job SYN **suited**: *Elinor is* ***well fitted*** *to be the sales manager.*

fit·ter /ˈfɪtə $ -ər/ *n* [C] *BrE* someone who puts together or repairs machines or equipment: *a gas fitter*

fit·ting¹ /ˈfɪtɪŋ/ *n* **1** [C, usually plural] *BrE* a piece of equipment in a house, for example a COOKER or a FRIDGE, that can be moved or taken with you when you sell the house → **fixtures and fittings** at FIXTURE(2) **2** [C, usually plural] an outside part of a piece of equipment that makes it possible to use or handle it: *a sink with chrome fittings* (=handle and taps) | *new light fittings* **3** [U] an occasion when you put on a piece of clothing that is being made for you, to see if it fits properly

fitting² *adj formal* right for a particular situation or occasion SYN **appropriate**: *I thought the memorial was a* ***fitting tribute*** *to the president.* | *a* ***fitting end*** *to what was a memorable trip* | **it is only fitting (that)** *It is only fitting that Simon should propose the first toast tonight.*

ˈfitting room *n* [C] an area in a shop where you can put on clothes to see how they look SYN **dressing room** *AmE*

five /faɪv/ ●●● S2 W2 *number, n*

1 the number 5: *There is also a golf course five miles away.* | *I'll be back by five* (=five o'clock). | *The family moved to Canada when he was five* (=five years old).

2 [C] a piece of paper money that is worth five dollars or five pounds → **fiver**: *Do you have two fives for a ten?*

3 give sb (a) five *informal* to hit the inside of someone's hand with your hand to show that you are very pleased about something

4 take five *spoken* used to tell people to stop working for a few minutes

5 fives [U] a British ball game in which the ball is hit with the hand against any of three walls → **handball**

6 five a day *BrE* the five amounts of fruit and vegetables that you should eat every day: *Beans count as* ***one of your five a day***. → HIGH FIVE, NINE TO FIVE

ˌfive-and-ˈten (*also* **ˌfive-and-ˈdime**) *n* [C] *AmE old-fashioned* a shop that sells many types of inexpensive goods, especially for the house SYN **dime store**

ˌfive-a-ˈside *adj* [only before noun] *BrE* five-a-side football is played with five players on each side, usually indoors

ˌfive o'clock ˈshadow *n* [singular] the dark colour on a man's chin where the hair has grown during the day

fiv·er /ˈfaɪvə $ -ər/ *n* [C] *BrE informal* a piece of paper money worth five pounds: *Lend me a fiver, mate?*

ˈfive-spot *n* [C] *AmE old-fashioned* a piece of paper money worth five dollars: *It only costs a five-spot.*

ˈfive-star *adj* [only before noun] a five-star hotel, restaurant etc has been judged to be of the highest standard

ˌfive-star ˈgeneral *n* [C] *AmE* a GENERAL of the highest rank, who controls an army

fix¹ /fɪks/ ●●● S2 W2 *v*

1 REPAIR [T] to repair something that is broken or not working properly: *He's outside fixing the brakes on the car.* | *Ellis was able to quickly find and fix the problem.* THESAURUS ▸ REPAIR

2 LIMIT [T] **a)** to decide on a limit for something, especially prices, costs etc, so that they do not change SYN **set**: **fix sth at sth** *The interest rate has been fixed at 6.5%.* | *Rent was fixed at $1,750 per month.* **b)** if two or more companies fix the price for a particular product or service, they secretly agree on the price they will charge for it, in order to keep the price high and make more profit. This practice is illegal: *The government accused the two companies of fixing petrol prices.*

3 fix a time/date/place etc to decide on a particular time etc when something will happen: *Have you fixed a date for the wedding yet?*

4 ARRANGE (*also* **fix up**) [I,T] *spoken* to make arrangements for something: *'So when do I get to meet them?' 'Tomorrow, if I can fix it.'* | **fix (it) for sb to do sth** *I've fixed for you to see him this afternoon at four.*

5 ATTACH [T] to attach something firmly to something else, so that it stays there permanently: **fix sth to/on sth** *The shelves should be fixed to the wall with screws.*

6 PREPARE FOOD [T] *informal especially AmE* to prepare a meal or drinks SYN **get**: *I'll watch the kids and you* ***fix dinner***. | **fix sb sth** *Can I fix you a snack?* | *Terry* ***fixed*** *herself a cold* ***drink*** *and sat out on the balcony.* THESAURUS ▸ COOK

7 SOLVE [T] to find a solution to a problem or bad situation: *The government seems confident that environmental problems can be fixed.*

8 fix your attention/eyes/mind etc on sb/sth to think about or look at someone or something carefully: *Aziz tried to fix his mind on the job at hand.* | *Every eye was fixed on the new girl.*

9 fix sb with a stare/glare/look etc *literary* to look directly at someone for a long time: *Rachel fixed him with an icy stare.*

10 HAIR/FACE [T] *especially AmE* to make your hair or MAKE-UP look neat and attractive: *Who fixed your hair for the wedding?* | *Hold on. Let me just* ***fix*** *my* ***face*** (=put on make-up) *before we go out.*

11 CAT/DOG [T] *AmE informal* to do a medical operation on a cat or dog so that it cannot have babies SYN **neuter**

12 RESULT [T] to arrange an election, game etc dishonestly, so that you get the result you want: *Many suspected that the deal had been fixed in advance.*

13 PAINTINGS/PHOTOGRAPHS [T] *technical* to use a chemical process on paintings, photographs etc that makes the colours or images permanent

14 PUNISH [T] *informal* used to say that you will punish someone you are angry with: *If anybody did that to me, I'd fix him good.*

15 be fixing to do sth *AmE spoken* to be preparing to do something – used in some parts of the US: *I'm fixing to go to the store. Do you need anything?*

fix on sb/sth *phr v* to choose a suitable thing or person, especially after thinking about it carefully: *We've finally fixed on a place to have the concert.*

fix sb/sth ↔ **up** *phr v*

1 to arrange a meeting, event etc: *I fixed up an interview with him.* | *We'll have to fix up a time to meet.*

2 to decorate or repair a room or building SYN **do up**: *We fixed up the guest bedroom before he came to stay.*

3 to provide someone with something they want: **[+with]** *Can you fix me up with a bed for the night?*

4 to find a suitable romantic partner for someone: **[+with]** *I asked my best friend to fix me up with someone.*

fix² *n* **1** [C] something that solves a problem: *Robinson called the proposal a* ***quick fix*** (=a temporary or easy solution) *of limited value.* **2 (be) in a fix** to have a problem that is difficult to solve SYN **(be) in a mess**: *We're going to be in a real fix if we miss that bus.* | *That's put us in a fix.* **3** [singular] an amount of something, especially an illegal drug such as HEROIN, that you often use and badly want: *addicts looking for a fix* | *I need my fix of caffeine in the morning or I can't think.* **4 get a fix on sb/sth a)** to find out exactly where someone or something is: *He peered out, trying to get a fix on the enemy's position.* **b)** to understand what someone or something is really like: *I couldn't seem to get a fix on the situation.* **5** [singular] something that has been dishonestly arranged: *People think the election was a fix.*

fix·a·ted /fɪkˈseɪtɪd/ *adj* always thinking or talking about one particular thing: **[+on]** *He never used to be so fixated on losing weight.*

fix·a·tion /fɪkˈseɪʃən/ *n* [C] **1** a very strong interest in or love for someone or something, that is not natural or healthy: **[+on/with/about]** *Carlo has an absolute fixation with the royal family.* | *a mother fixation* **2** *technical* a kind of mental illness in which someone's mind or emotions stop developing

fix·a·tive /ˈfɪksətɪv/ *n* [C,U] **1** a substance used to stick things together or to hold things such as false teeth in place **2** a chemical used on a painting or photograph so that the colours do not change

fixed /fɪkst/ ●●○ S3 W3 *adj*
1 [not before noun] firmly fastened to a particular position: **[+to/in/on]** *a mirror fixed to the bathroom wall*
2 fixed times, amounts, meanings etc cannot be changed SYN **set**: *The classes begin and end at fixed times.* | *fixed prices* | *My contract was for a fixed term of five years.* | *interest at 10%, fixed for 5 years*
3 have fixed ideas/opinions to have very definite ideas or opinions that you will not change – often used to show disapproval: **[+about/on]** *He has very fixed ideas about how a wife should behave.*
4 how are you fixed for sth? *spoken* used to ask someone how much of something they have, or to ask about an arrangement: *How are you fixed for cash?* | *How are we fixed for Monday?*
5 a fixed smile, expression etc does not show any emotion or does not show how someone really feels
6 be of/have no fixed abode/address *BrE law* to not have a permanent place to live

ˌfixed ˈassets *n* [plural] *technical* land, buildings, or equipment that a business owns and uses

ˌfixed ˈcapital *n* [U] *technical* buildings or machines that a business owns and that can be used for a long time to produce goods

ˌfixed ˈcosts *n* [plural] *technical* costs, such as rent, that a business has to pay even when it is not producing anything → **variable costs**

ˌfixed ˈincome *n* [C] an amount of money that you receive to live on that does not change: *pensioners living on a fixed income*

fix·ed·ly /ˈfɪksɪdli/ *adv* without looking at or thinking about anything else: **stare/gaze/look fixedly at sth** *Ann stared fixedly at the screen.*

ˈfixed-rate *adj* [only before noun] a fixed-rate LOAN or MORTGAGE is one in which the amount of interest you pay remains the same for a specific period of time → **capped**

ˈfixed-term *adj* [only before noun] lasting for an agreed period of time: *a fixed-term contract*

fix·er /ˈfɪksə $ -ər/ *n* [C] someone who is good at arranging things and solving problems for other people, sometimes by using dishonest methods: *a political fixer*

ˌfixer-ˈupper *n* [C] *AmE* a house that you buy or sell that needs repairs

fix·ings /ˈfɪksɪŋz/ *n* [C] **1 the fixings** *AmE* the vegetables, bread etc that are eaten with meat at a large meal SYN **the trimmings** *BrE*: *turkey with all the fixings* **2** [plural] *BrE* things that are used to hold other things together, for example SCREWS

fix·i·ty /ˈfɪksəti/ *n* [U] *formal* when something does not change: **[+of]** *fixity of purpose*

fix·ture /ˈfɪkstʃə $ -ər/ *n* [C] **1** *BrE* a sports match that has been arranged for a particular time and place: *a list of this season's fixtures* **2** [usually plural] a piece of equipment that is fixed inside a house or building and is sold as part of the house: *light fixtures* | **fixtures and fittings** *BrE* (=all the equipment that is normally included as part of a house or building when it is sold) **3 be a (permanent) fixture** to be always present and not likely to move or go away: *Gerrard soon became a permanent fixture in the Liverpool team.*

fizz¹ /fɪz/ *v* [I] if a liquid fizzes, it produces a lot of bubbles and makes a continuous sound: *champagne fizzing out of the bottle*

fizz² *n* [singular, U] **1** the bubbles of gas in some kinds of drinks, or the sound that they make **2** *BrE informal* CHAMPAGNE

fiz·zle /ˈfɪzəl/ *v*
fizzle out *phr v informal* to gradually stop happening, especially because people become less interested: *Their romance just fizzled out.*

fiz·zy /ˈfɪzi/ *adj* **1** a fizzy liquid contains bubbles of gas → **sparkling**, **flat**: *fizzy water* **2 fizzy drink** *BrE* a sweet non-alcoholic drink with bubbles of gas → see picture at STILL²

fjord, **fiord** /ˈfiːɔːd, fjɔːd $ fiːˈɔːrd, fjɔːrd/ *n* [C] a narrow area of sea between high cliffs, especially in Norway

flab /flæb/ *n* [U] *informal* soft loose flesh on a person's body – used to show disapproval: *simple advice to help you **fight the flab*** (=lose weight)

flab·ber·gas·ted /ˈflæbəgɑːstɪd $ -bərgæs-/ *adj informal* extremely surprised or shocked: *When I heard how much money we'd made, I was flabbergasted.* THESAURUS SURPRISED

flab·by /ˈflæbi/ ●○○ *adj informal*
1 having unattractive soft loose flesh rather than strong muscles: *a flabby stomach* THESAURUS FAT
2 used to describe something that is weak or not effective OPP **powerful**: *intellectually flabby arguments* | *The band's performance was tired and flabby.* —**flabbiness** *n* [U]

flac·cid /ˈflæsɪd, ˈflæksɪd/ *adj technical* soft and weak instead of firm: *a flaccid penis* —**flaccidity** /flæˈsɪdəti, flæk-/ *n* [U]

flack /flæk/ *n* **1** [U] another spelling of FLAK **2** [C] *AmE informal* someone whose job is to represent an organization and answer questions about it, especially when something bad has happened: *They spent millions on lobbyists and flacks to improve their image.*

flag¹ /flæg/ ●●● S2 W2 *n* [C]
1 a piece of cloth with a coloured pattern or picture on it that represents a country or organization: *Children **waving flags** greeted the Russian leader.* | *the flag of Kenya* | *the Spanish flag* | **a flag is flying** (=a flag is shown on a pole) ***Flags** were **flying at half-mast** because of the death of the Premier.*
2 a coloured piece of cloth used in some sports as a signal or as a sign showing the position of something: *The flag went down, and the race began.* | *a free kick near the **corner flag*** (=flag on a football pitch)
3 the flag an expression meaning a country or organization and its beliefs, values, and people: *loyalty to the flag*
4 keep the flag flying to achieve success on behalf of your country in a competition: *Bristol kept the flag flying for English rugby with this win.*
5 a FLAGSTONE → **fly the flag** at FLY¹(13)

flag² *v* (**flagged**, **flagging**) **1** [T] to make a mark against some information to show that it is important: *I've flagged the parts I want to comment on.* **2** [I] to become tired or weak: *By the end of the meeting we had begun to flag.*
flag sb/sth ↔ **down** *phr v* to make the driver of a vehicle stop by waving at them: *I flagged down a taxi.*

fla·gel·lant /ˈflædʒələnt, fləˈdʒelənt/ *n* [C] *formal* someone who whips themselves, especially as a religious punishment

fla·gel·late /ˈflædʒəleɪt/ *v* [T] *formal* to whip yourself or someone else, especially as a religious punishment —**flagellation** /ˌflædʒəˈleɪʃən/ *n* [U]

ˈflag ˌfootball *n* [U] *AmE* a game like American football in which players tear off small pieces of cloth called flags from around other players' waists instead of knocking them down → **touch football**

flagged /flægd/ *adj* covered with FLAGSTONES

flag·ging /ˈflægɪŋ/ *adj* becoming tired or losing strength: **flagging spirits/energy/morale** *By now the wine had lifted her flagging spirits.* | *He presents himself as the man to revive the party's **flagging fortunes**.* | *concern for the country's **flagging economy***

flag·on /ˈflægən/ *n* [C] a large container for liquids, especially beer or wine

flag·pole /ˈflægpəʊl $ -poʊl/ *n* [C] a tall pole on which a flag hangs SYN **flagstaff**

fla·grant /ˈfleɪgrənt/ *adj* a flagrant action is shocking because it is done in a way that is easily noticed and shows no respect for laws, truth etc: **flagrant abuse/violation/breach etc** *flagrant violations of human rights* | *a **flagrant disregard** for the law* —**flagrantly** *adv*

F

flag·ship /ˈflæɡʃɪp/ *n* [C] **1** the most important ship in a group of ships belonging to the navy **2** [usually singular] the best and most important product, building etc that a company owns or produces: *the flagship of the new Ford range | The firm has just opened a* ***flagship store*** *in Las Vegas. | the company's* ***flagship product***

flag·staff /ˈflæɡstɑːf $ -stæf/ *n* [C] a tall pole on which a flag hangs SYN **flagpole**

flag·stone /ˈflæɡstəʊn $ -stoʊn/ *n* [C] a smooth flat piece of stone used for floors, paths etc

ˈflag-ˌwaving *n* [U] the expression of strong national feelings, especially when these feelings seem too extreme

flail[1] /fleɪl/ *v* **1** [I,T] to wave your arms or legs in an uncontrolled way: *He flailed wildly as she tried to hold him down. |* **[+around/about]** *James flailed about in the shallow water.* **2** [T] to beat someone or something violently, usually with a stick **3** [I,T] to beat grain with a flail

flail[2] *n* [C] a tool consisting of a stick that swings from a long handle, used in the past to separate grain from wheat by beating it

flair /fleə $ fler/ *n* **1** [singular] a natural ability to do something very well SYN **talent**: *Jo* ***has a flair for*** *languages.* THESAURUS ➜ SKILL **2** [U] a way of doing things that is interesting and shows imagination: **artistic/creative flair** *a job for which artistic flair is essential | Irwin has real entrepreneurial flair.*

flak, **flack** /flæk/ *n* [U] **1** *informal* strong criticism: *Lilley has* ***taken*** *a lot of* ***flak*** *for his views on drugs.* **2** bullets or SHELLS that are shot from the ground at enemy aircraft → **FLAK JACKET**

flake[1] /fleɪk/ *n* [C] **1** a small thin piece that breaks away easily from something else: **[+of]** *flakes of snow | chocolate flakes* → **SNOWFLAKE** **2** *AmE informal* someone who seems strange or who often forgets things SYN **space cadet**

flake[2] *v* **1** (*also* **flake off**) [I] to break off in small thin pieces: *The paint is beginning to flake off. | Use a moisturising cream to stop your skin flaking.* **2** [I,T] to break fish or another food into small thin pieces, or to break in this way: *Poach the fish until it flakes easily. | Remove the skin and flake the flesh.*

flake out *phr v informal* **1** *BrE* to fall asleep because you are extremely tired: *Phil's flaked out on the sofa.* **2** *AmE* to do something strange, or to not do what you said you would do: **[+on]** *Kathy said she'd help but she flaked out on us.*

ˈflak ˌjacket *n* [C] a special coat made of strong heavy material to protect soldiers and policemen from bullets

flak·y /ˈfleɪki/ *adj* **1** tending to break into small thin pieces: *flaky pastry | flaky skin* **2** *informal especially AmE* a flaky person is slightly strange or often forgets things: *Carrie's pretty flaky but she's fun to be with.* —**flakiness** *n* [U]

flam·bé /ˈflɒmbeɪ $ flɑːmˈbeɪ/ (*also* **flam·béed** /ˈflɒmbeɪd $ flɑːmˈbeɪd/) *adj* food that is flambéed has an alcoholic drink such as BRANDY poured over it to produce flames

flam·boy·ant /flæmˈbɔɪənt/ *adj* **1** behaving in a confident or exciting way that makes people notice you: **flamboyant style/character/personality** *his flamboyant style of play | He lifted his arms in a* ***flamboyant gesture.*** **2** brightly coloured and easily noticed: *flamboyant clothes | She has red hair and a rather flamboyant appearance.* —**flamboyantly** *adv* —**flamboyance** *n* [U]

flame[1] /fleɪm/ ●●○ *n*

1 [C,U] hot bright burning gas that you see when something is on fire: *Flames poured out of the windows of the building. | They rushed past us with buckets of water and tried to* ***douse*** *the* ***flames****. | They sat around the campfire, watching the* ***flickering flames****. |* ***Flames*** *quickly* ***engulfed*** *the building. | a candle flame*

2 in flames burning in a way that is difficult to control: *When we reached Mandalay it was in flames. | They escaped just as the house was* ***engulfed in flames****.*

3 go up in flames/burst into flames to suddenly begin burning in a way that is difficult to control: *The helicopter burst into flames after hitting a power line.*

4 a flame of anger/desire/passion etc *literary* a strong feeling: *Flames of desire shot through her.*

5 [C] an angry or rude email → **old flame** at OLD(4), → **naked flame** at NAKED(5), → **fan the flames** at FAN[2](2), → **add fuel to the fire/flames** at ADD(9)

flame[2] *v* [I] **1** *literary* to become suddenly bright with light or colour, especially red or orange: *Erica's cheeks flamed with anger.* **2** *literary* to burn brightly: *A great fire flamed in an open fireplace.* **3** to send someone an angry or rude message in an email or on a BULLETIN BOARD

fla·men·co /fləˈmeŋkəʊ $ -koʊ/ *n* (*plural* **flamencos**) [C,U] a fast exciting Spanish dance, or the music that is played for this dance

flame·proof /ˈfleɪmpruːf/ (*also* **ˈflame reˌsistant**) *adj* **1** made of or covered with substances that will not burn easily **2** flameproof cooking dishes can be used in very hot places, such as in an OVEN

ˈflame ˌthrower *n* [C] a machine like a gun that shoots flames or burning liquid, used as a weapon or for clearing plants

flam·ing /ˈfleɪmɪŋ/ *adj* [only before noun] **1 a flaming row/temper** a very angry argument or temper: *They seem to have a flaming row at least once a week.* **2** covered with flames: *Residents panicked as flaming petrol poured down the street.* **3** *BrE informal* used to emphasize what you are saying, especially when you feel annoyed: *You flaming idiot!* **4** orange or bright red in colour: *flaming red hair*

fla·min·go /fləˈmɪŋɡəʊ $ -ɡoʊ/ *n* (*plural* **flamingos** or **flamingoes**) [C] a large pink tropical bird with very long thin legs and a long neck

FLAMINGO

flam·ma·ble /ˈflæməbəl/ *adj* something that is flammable burns easily → **inflammable**, **nonflammable**: *Caution!* ***Highly flammable*** *liquid.*

flan /flæn/ *n* [C] **1** *especially BrE* a round PIE or cake that is filled with fruit, cheese etc **2** *AmE* a sweet baked food made with eggs, milk, and sugar → **pie**, **quiche**

flange /flændʒ/ *n* [C] the flat edge that stands out from an object such as a railway wheel, to keep it in the right position or strengthen it

flank[1] /flæŋk/ *n* [C] **1** the side of an animal's or person's body, between the RIBS and the HIP → see picture at HORSE[1] **2** the side of an army in a battle, or a sports team when playing: *We were attacked on our left flank.* **3** the side of a hill, mountain, or very large building

flank[2] *v* [T] to be on both sides of someone or something: *Lewis entered flanked by two bodyguards. | mountains flanking the road*

flan·nel[1] /ˈflænl/ *n* **1** [U] soft cloth, usually made of cotton or wool, used for making clothes: *a flannel shirt* **2** [C] *BrE* a piece of cloth you use to wash yourself SYN **facecloth**, **washcloth** *AmE* **3** [U] *BrE informal* something that someone says that has no real meaning or does not tell you what you want to know **4 flannels** [plural] *BrE* men's trousers made of flannel

flannel[2] *v* (**flannelled**, **flannelling**) [I,T] *BrE* to say things that have no real meaning in order to avoid answering a question directly or to hide your lack of knowledge

flan·nel·ette /ˌflænəlˈet/ *n* [U] soft cotton cloth used especially for making nightclothes and sheets

flap[1] /flæp/ ●○○ *n*

1 FLAT PIECE OF SOMETHING [C] a thin flat piece of cloth, paper, skin etc that is fixed by one edge to a surface, which you can lift up easily: *the tent flap | A loose flap of skin covered the wound.* → **CAT FLAP**

2 MOVEMENT [singular] the noisy movement of something such as cloth in the air: *the flap of the sails*
3 EXCITEMENT/WORRY **a flap** *informal* a situation in which people feel very excited or worried about something: **be in a flap** *Rafi's in a bit of a flap over the wedding plans.* → UNFLAPPABLE
4 PART OF AIRCRAFT [C] a part of the wing of an aircraft that can be raised or lowered to help the aircraft go up or down

flap² ●○○ *v* (**flapped**, **flapping**)
1 [I,T] if a bird flaps its wings, it moves them up and down in order to fly
2 [I,T] to move quickly up and down or from side to side, often making a noise: *The flags were flapping in the breeze.* | *Flap your arms to keep warm.*
3 [I] *BrE informal* to behave in an excited or nervous way: *There's no need to flap!*

flap·jack /ˈflæpdʒæk/ *n* [C] **1** *BrE* a cake made of OATS, sugar, SYRUP, and butter **2** *AmE* a PANCAKE

flap·per /ˈflæpə $ -ər/ *n* [C] a fashionable young woman in the late 1920s

flare¹ /fleə $ fler/ ●○○ *v*
1 (*also* **flare up**) [I] to suddenly begin to burn, or to burn more brightly for a short time: *The fire flared up again.*
2 (*also* **flare up**) [I] if strong feelings flare or flare up, people suddenly become angry, violent etc: *Rioting has flared up in several towns.* | ***Tempers flared*** *during the debate.*
3 (*also* **flare up**) [I] if a disease or illness flares up, it suddenly becomes worse: *The injury has flared up again, keeping him out of today's game.*
4 [I,T] if a person or animal flares their NOSTRILS (=the openings at the end of the nose), or if their nostrils flare, their nostrils become wider because they are angry: *The bull flared its nostrils.*
5 [I always + adv/prep] if a piece of clothing flares out, it becomes wider at one end: **[+out]** *The dress flares out from the hips.* —**flared** *adj*: *flared jeans*

flare² *n* **1** [C] a piece of equipment that produces a bright flame, or the flame itself, used outdoors as a signal: *The distress flares were spotted by another ship.* **2** [C usually singular] a sudden bright flame: *There was a brief flare as the match was lit.* **3 flares** [plural] trousers that become wide below the knee

FLARES

ˈflare-up *n* [C] **1** a situation in which someone suddenly becomes angry or violent: *Apart from one or two flare-ups the match went fairly smoothly.* **2** a situation in which someone suddenly has problems because of a disease or illness after not having any problems for a long time: *a flare-up of her arthritis*

flash¹ /flæʃ/ ●●○ S3 *v*
1 SHINE [I,T] to shine suddenly and brightly for a short time, or to make something shine in this way: *Lightning flashed overhead.* | **flash sth into/at/towards sb/sth** *Why is that guy flashing his headlights at me?* | *Red warning lights* ***flashed on and off*** (=shone for a short time and then stopped shining). THESAURUS ▸ SHINE
2 PICTURES [I always + adv/prep] to be shown quickly on television, on a computer, or on a film: **[+across/onto/past etc]** *Images of the war flashed across the screen.*
3 flash through sb's mind/head/brain if thoughts, images, memories etc flash through your mind, you suddenly think of them or remember them: *The possibility that Frank was lying flashed through my mind.*
4 flash a smile/glance/look etc (at sb) to smile or look at someone quickly and for a short time: *'I love this city,' he said, flashing a big smile.*
5 SHOW STH QUICKLY [T] to show something to someone for only a short time: *He flashed his identification card.* THESAURUS ▸ SHOW
6 NEWS/INFORMATION [T always + adv/prep] to send news or information somewhere quickly by radio, computer, or SATELLITE: **flash sth across/to sth** *Reporters at the scene flashed the news to their offices.*
7 MOVE QUICKLY [I always + adv/prep] to move very quickly: **[+by/past/through]** *A meteor flashed through the sky.*
8 EYES [I] *literary* if your eyes flash, they look very bright for a moment, especially because of a sudden emotion: **[+with]** *Janet's blue eyes flashed with anger.*
9 SEX ORGANS [I,T] if a man flashes, or if he flashes someone, he shows his sexual organs in public → **flasher**
10 sb's life flashes before their eyes if someone's life flashes before their eyes, they suddenly remember many events from their life because they are in great danger and might die
11 TIME PASSING QUICKLY [I always + adv/prep] if a period of time or an event flashes by or flashes past, it seems to end very quickly: **[+by/past]** *Our vacation seemed to just flash by.*

flash sth ↔ **around** *phr v* to use or show something in a way that will make people notice you and think you have a lot of money: *He's always flashing his money around.*

flash back *phr v* to suddenly think about or show something that happened in the past, especially in a film, book etc: **[+to]** *From here the movie flashes back to Billy's first meeting with Schultz.* → FLASHBACK

flash forward *phr v* if a film, book etc flashes forward, it shows what happens in the future: **[+to]** *The movie then flashes forward to their daughter's fifth birthday.*

flash² ●●○ *n*
1 LIGHT [C] a bright light that shines for a short time and then stops shining: *Two flashes mean danger.* | **[+of]** *A* ***flash of lightning*** *lit up the night sky.* | **brilliant/blinding flash** *a brilliant flash of light*
2 CAMERA [C,U] a special bright light used when taking photographs indoors or when there is not much light: *Did the flash go off?*
3 in/like a flash (*also* **quick as a flash**) very quickly: *Just wait here. I'll be back in a flash.*
4 flash of inspiration/brilliance/insight/anger etc if someone has a flash of BRILLIANCE, anger etc, they suddenly have a clever idea or a particular feeling
5 a flash in the pan a sudden success that ends quickly and is unlikely to happen again: *Beene's new novel proves he isn't just a flash in the pan.*
6 BRIGHT COLOUR/STH SHINY [C] if there is a flash of something brightly coloured or shiny, it appears suddenly for a short time: **[+of]** *The bird vanished in a flash of blue.*
7 COMPUTER [U] *trademark* a system of instructions for a computer that is used especially to make pictures on a website appear to move: *Flash animation*
8 LOOK [C] *BrE* a quick look – used humorously SYN **glimpse**
9 MILITARY [C] *BrE* a small piece of coloured cloth worn on the shoulder of a military uniform → **NEWSFLASH**

flash³ *adj* **1 flash flood/fire** a flood or fire that happens very quickly or suddenly, and continues for only a short time **2** *BrE informal* looking very new, bright, and expensive – used to show disapproval: *a big flash car* **3** *BrE informal* liking to have expensive clothes and possessions so that other people notice you – used to show disapproval: *Chris didn't want to seem flash in front of his mates.*

flash·back /ˈflæʃbæk/ *n* **1** [C,U] a scene in a film, play, book etc that shows something that happened before that point in the story: *The events of the hero's childhood are shown as a series of flashbacks.* **2** [C] a sudden very clear memory of something that happened to you in the past: *Eaton still* ***has flashbacks*** *of the crash.* **3** [C] an occasion when someone has the same bad feeling that they had when they took an illegal drug in the past: *Many users of this drug experience flashbacks.* **4** [C] *technical* a burning gas or liquid that moves back into a tube or container

F

ˈflash bulb *n* [C] a small object that produces a bright light, used when taking photographs indoors or when there is not much light

flash·card /ˈflæʃkɑːd $ -kɑːrd/ *n* [C] a card with a word or picture on it, used in teaching

ˈflash drive *n* [C] a small piece of electronic equipment that uses FLASH MEMORY to store information and can be fitted into a computer SYN **USB drive**

flash·er /ˈflæʃə $ -ər/ *n* [C] a man who shows his sexual organs to women in public → **flash**

flash·gun /ˈflæʃgʌn/ *n* [C] a piece of equipment that lights a special bright light when you press the button on a camera to take a photograph

flash·light /ˈflæʃlaɪt/ ●●○ *n* [C] *AmE* a small electric light that you can carry in your hand SYN **torch** *BrE* → see picture at LAMP

ˈflash ˌmemory *n* [U] a type of computer memory that can continue storing information without a power supply. It is used, for example, in MEMORY CARDS.

flash·mob /ˈflæʃmɒb $ -mɑːb/ *n* [C] a sudden and planned gathering of many people at a particular place that has been arranged earlier on an Internet website. All of the people do or say something that has also been planned earlier and then separate and leave quickly in different directions. —**flashmob** *v* [T]: *The store was flash-mobbed by about a hundred people.* —**flashmobbing** *n* [U]

flash·point /ˈflæʃpɔɪnt/ *n* [C] **1** a place where trouble or violence might easily develop suddenly and be hard to control: *Hebron has been a flashpoint for years.* **2** [usually singular] *technical* the lowest temperature at which a liquid such as oil will produce enough gas to burn if a flame is put near it

flash·y /ˈflæʃi/ *adj informal* **1** big, bright, or expensive, and intended to be impressive – used to show disapproval: *large flashy cars* **2** someone who is flashy wears expensive clothes, JEWELLERY etc in a way that is intended to be impressive – used to show disapproval: *a flashy dresser*

FLASKS

hip flask | flask | Thermos/flask

flask /flɑːsk $ flæsk/ *n* [C] **1** *BrE* a special type of bottle that you use to keep liquids either hot or cold, for example when travelling SYN **Thermos 2** a HIP FLASK **3** a glass bottle with a narrow top, used in a LABORATORY

flat¹ /flæt/ ●●● S2 W2 *adj* (*comparative* **flatter**, *superlative* **flattest**)

1 SURFACE smooth and level, without raised or hollow areas, and not sloping or curving: *houses with flat roofs | a **perfectly flat** sandy beach | The countryside near there is **flat as a pancake*** (=very flat). *| Work on a clean, flat surface.*

2 MONEY a flat rate, amount of money etc is fixed and does not change or have anything added to it: *Clients are charged a **flat rate** of £250 annually. | We charge a **flat fee** for car hire.*

3 TYRE/BALL a flat tyre or ball has no air or not enough air in it

4 NOT DEEP not very deep, thick, or high, especially in comparison to its width or length: *The cake came out of the oven flat, not fluffy.*

5 DRINK a drink that is flat does not taste fresh because it has no more bubbles of gas in it OPP **fizzy**

6 NOT INTERESTING [not before noun] a performance, book etc that is flat lacks interest, excitement, or energy: *Arsenal looked flat for large parts of the game.*

7 BATTERY *BrE* a flat BATTERY has lost its electrical power SYN **dead** *AmE*: *Have you checked that the batteries haven't **gone flat*** (=become flat)?

8 BUSINESS/TRADE if prices, economic conditions, trade etc are flat, they have not increased or improved over a period of time: *Analysts are expecting flat sales in the coming months.*

9 E flat/B flat/A flat etc a musical note that is one SEMITONE lower than the note E, B, A etc → **sharp**, **natural**

10 MUSICAL SOUND if a musical note is flat, it is played or sung slightly lower than it should be OPP **sharp**

11 VOICE not showing much emotion, or not changing much in sound as you speak: *'He's dead,' she said in a flat voice.*

12 a flat refusal/denial etc a refusal etc that is definite and which someone will not change: *Our requests were met with a flat refusal.*

13 be flat on your back a) to be lying down so that all of your back is touching the floor **b)** to be very ill so that you have to stay in bed for a period of time: *I've been flat on my back with the flu all week.*

14 SHOES flat shoes have very low heels

15 LIGHT having little variety of light and dark: *Flat lighting is typical of Avedon's portraits.*

16 and that's flat! *BrE spoken old-fashioned* used to say that you will definitely not change what you have just said SYN **and that's that**: *I won't go, and that's flat!* —**flatness** *n* [U] → **in/into a flat spin** at SPIN²(6), → FLAT FEET

THESAURUS

flat on one level, without any holes or raised areas, and not sloping or curving: *a flat roof | a flat screen | Before you lay the tiles, make sure that the ground is completely flat.*

level not sloping in any direction, so that every part is at the same height: *Is the top of this picture level? | After four hours coming down the mountain, I was glad to be back on level ground.*

smooth without any holes or raised areas – used especially when saying how something feels when you touch it: *her lovely smooth skin | I ran my hand across the animal's smooth fur.*

even without any holes or raised areas: *Apply the paint to an even surface. | Be careful – the path is not very even here.*

horizontal going straight across and not sloping: *a horizontal line | Raise both arms to a horizontal position.*

flat² ●●● S2 W3 *n* [C]

1 PLACE TO LIVE *especially BrE* a place for people to live that consists of a set of rooms that are part of a larger building SYN **apartment**: *They have a flat in Crouch End. | a two-bedroom flat | The building was knocked down to make way for a **block of flats*** (=a large building with many flats in it). → GRANNY FLAT

2 TYRE *especially AmE* a tyre that does not have enough air inside SYN **flat tyre**: *Damn, the car **has a flat**. | He stopped to **change a flat**.*

3 MUSIC **a)** a musical note that is one SEMITONE lower than a particular note **b)** the sign (♭) in written music that shows that a note is one SEMITONE lower than a particular note → **sharp**, **natural**

4 LAND **flats** [plural] an area of land that is at a low level, especially near water: *mud flats*

5 SHOES **flats** [plural] a pair of women's shoes with very low heels

6 the flat of sb's hand/a knife/a sword etc the flat part or flat side of something

7 on the flat *BrE* on ground that is level and does not slope

flat³ ●●○ *adv*

1 FLAT POSITION in a position in which the surface of something is against another surface without curving or sloping: *The bed can be folded flat for storage. | He **lay flat** on the floor. | That night I **lay flat on** my **back** and stared up at the ceiling.*

2 three minutes/ten seconds etc flat *informal* in exactly three minutes, ten seconds etc – used to emphasize that

something happens or is done very quickly: *I was dressed in five minutes flat.*
3 fall flat *informal* if a joke, story etc falls flat, it does not achieve the effect that is intended: *Unfortunately, what could have been a powerful drama fell flat.*
4 MUSIC if you sing or play music flat, you sing or play slightly lower than the correct note so that the sound is unpleasant OPP **sharp**
5 fall flat on your/sth's face a) to fall so that you are lying on your chest on the ground: *Babe slipped and fell flat on her face.* **b)** *informal* to not have the result you want or expect, especially when this is embarrassing: *The theory falls flat on its face when put into practice.*
6 flat out *informal* **a)** as fast as possible: *Everyone's working flat out to finish on time.* **b)** *AmE* in a direct and complete way SYN **straight out**: **ask/tell sb flat out** *She asked him flat out if he was seeing another woman.*
7 tell sb flat *BrE spoken* to tell someone something directly and definitely SYN **straight out**: *I told him flat that I didn't want to see him again.* → **flat broke** at BROKE[2](1)

flat·bed /ˈflætbed/ *adj* [only before noun] having a flat surface to put something on: *a flatbed scanner | a flatbed truck* —**flatbed** *n* [C]

flat·bread /ˈflætbred/ *n* [C] a general name for any type of flat bread, for example PITTA BREAD, or the base for a PIZZA

ˌflat ˈcap *n* [C] *BrE* a cap made of cloth, with a stiff piece that sticks out at the front

flat·car /ˈflætkɑː $ -kɑːr/ *n* [C] *AmE* a railway carriage without a roof or sides, used for carrying goods

ˌflat-ˈchested *adj* a woman who is flat-chested has small breasts

ˌflat ˈfeet *n* [plural] a medical condition in which someone's feet rest flat on the ground because the middle of each foot is not as curved as it should be

flat·fish /ˈflætˌfɪʃ/ *n* (*plural* **flatfish**) [C] a type of sea fish with a thin flat body, such as COD or PLAICE → see picture at **FISH[1]**

ˌflat-ˈfooted *adj* **1** having flat feet **2** *informal* moving in an awkward way SYN **clumsy**: *The defence looked flat-footed as Sutton scored easily.* **3 catch sb flat-footed** *AmE* to surprise someone so that they cannot do something in the way they ought to SYN **catch sb off guard**: *The president's announcement seemed to catch Democrats flat-footed.*

flat·forms /ˈflætfɔːmz $ -fɔːrmz/ *n* [plural] shoes that have a thick layer under the whole shoe, so that the heel is not much higher than the rest of the shoe

flat·let /ˈflætlɪt/ *n* [C] *BrE* a small apartment

flat·line /ˈflætlaɪn/ *v* **be flatlining** to be at a low level or standard that is neither increasing nor decreasing: *The Tories have been flatlining in the polls.*

flat·ly /ˈflætli/ *adv* **1 flatly refuse/deny/oppose etc sth** to say something in a direct and definite way that is not likely to change: *He flatly denied ever having met the woman.* **2** without showing any emotion: *'Aunt Alicia has changed her will,' she said flatly.*

flat·mate /ˈflætmeɪt/ *n* [C] *BrE* someone who shares a flat with one or more other people SYN **roommate** *AmE*

ˈflat-pack (*also* **ˈflat pack**) *n* [C] *BrE* furniture that is sold as parts in a box and has to be put together: *flat-pack furniture*

ˈflat-panel *adj* a flat-panel television or computer MONITOR has a flat screen —**flat-panel** *n* [C]

ˈflat ˌracing *n* [U] *BrE* horse racing on flat ground without any fences → **steeplechase**

flat·screen /ˈflætˌskriːn/ *adj* a flatscreen television or computer MONITOR is very thin

flat·ten /ˈflætn/ ●○○ *v*
1 (*also* **flatten out**) [I,T] to make something flat or flatter, or to become flat or flatter: *Use a rolling pin to flatten the dough. | The land flattened out as we neared the coast.*
2 [T] to destroy a building or town by knocking it down, bombing it etc SYN **level**: *Hundreds of homes were flattened by the tornado.* THESAURUS ▸ DESTROY
3 flatten yourself against sth to press your body against something: *I flattened myself against the wall.*
4 [T] *informal* to defeat someone completely and easily in a game, argument etc: *We flattened them 6–0.*
5 [T] *informal* to hit someone very hard

flat·ter /ˈflætə $ -ər/ ●○○ *v* [T]
1 to praise someone in order to please them or get something from them, even though you do not mean it: *Perry would always flatter Mrs. Mitchell by praising her cooking.* THESAURUS ▸ PRAISE
2 to make someone look as attractive as they can SYN **suit**: *That dress really flatters your figure.*
3 to make something look or seem more important or better than it is: *Lewis's novel doesn't flatter Midwestern attitudes and morals.*
4 flatter yourself if you flatter yourself that something is true about your abilities or achievements, you make yourself believe it is true, although it is not: **flatter yourself that** *She flatters herself that she could have been a model.* —**flatterer** *n* [C]

flat·tered /ˈflætəd $ -ərd/ *adj* [not before noun] pleased because someone has shown you that they like or admire you: *We were flattered by all the attention.*

flat·ter·ing /ˈflætərɪŋ/ *adj* clothes, pictures etc that are flattering make someone look as attractive as they can or make something as good as possible, even if it is not really very good: *That colour is very flattering.*

flat·ter·y /ˈflætəri/ *n* [U] **1** praise that you do not really mean **2 flattery will get you everywhere/nowhere** used humorously when someone has praised you and you want to say that you will help them or not help them

flat·top /ˈflæt-tɒp $ -tɑːp/ *n* [C] a type of hair style that is very short and looks flat on top → see picture at HAIRSTYLE

flat·u·lence /ˈflætjələns $ -tʃə-/ *n* [U] the condition of having too much gas in the stomach —**flatulent** *adj*

flat·ware /ˈflætˌweə $ -ˌwer/ *n* [U] *AmE* knives, forks, and spoons SYN **cutlery**

flat ˈwhite *n* [C] a cup of coffee made with ESPRESSO (=strong black Italian coffee) and hot milk without any bubbles in it

flaunt /flɔːnt $ flɒːnt, flɑːnt/ *v* [T] **1** to show your money, success, beauty etc so that other people notice it - used to show disapproval: *The rich flaunted their wealth while the poor starved on the streets.* **2 if you've got it, flaunt it** *spoken* used humorously to tell someone not to hide their beauty, wealth, or abilities

flau·tist /ˈflɔːtɪst $ ˈflɒː-/ *n* [C] *BrE* someone who plays the FLUTE SYN **flutist** *AmE*

fla·va /ˈfleɪvʌ/ *n* [U] *informal* a quality that something has that makes you feel or think a particular way about it SYN **flavour**: *music with a little bit of Caribbean flava*

fla·vour[1] *BrE*, **flavor** *AmE* /ˈfleɪvə $ -ər/ ●●● S2 W2 *n*
1 [C] the particular taste of a food or drink: *Which flavour do you want - chocolate or vanilla?* | **[+of]** *a dry wine with flavors of honey and apricot*
2 [U] the quality of tasting good: *I prefer this one because it has more flavour.*
3 [C,U] a substance used to give something a particular taste SYN **flavouring**: *artificial flavours*
4 [singular] a quality or feature that makes something have a particular style or character: *The stories have a strong regional flavour.* | **[+of]** *Critics claim the building would destroy the flavor of the neighborhood.*
5 [singular] an idea of what the typical qualities of something are: **[+of]** *Marston's book* **gives** *you a* **flavour of** *life in the 16th century.*
6 flavour of the month an idea, person, style etc that is very popular at a particular time

COLLOCATIONS - MEANINGS 1 & 2

ADJECTIVES/NOUN + flavour

delicious *Mango has a delicious flavour.*
sweet/spicy/bitter/salty etc *The flavor was like peaches, but not as sweet.*

strong *The flavour of the sauce was quite strong.*
rich (=strong and pleasant) *The brown sugar makes the flavour especially rich.*
mild *I prefer a sausage with a milder flavour.*
mellow/smooth (=pleasant and not strong or bitter) | **delicate/subtle** (=pleasant and not strong) | **distinctive/unique** (=very different from other foods or drinks) | **chocolate/strawberry etc flavour**

VERBS

have a sweet/strong etc flavour *These biscuits have a very distinctive flavour.*
add/give flavour *Herbs add flavor to a salad.*
bring out the flavour (=make the flavour more noticeable) | **improve/enhance the flavour**

PHRASES

be full of flavour *The beef is tender and full of flavour.*

flavour² *BrE*, **flavor** *AmE* *v* [T] to give something a particular taste or more taste

fla·voured *BrE*, **flavored** *AmE* /ˈfleɪvəd $ -vərd/ *adj* **1 strawberry-flavoured/chocolate-flavoured etc** tasting of STRAWBERRIES, chocolate etc **2** having had a flavour added: *flavored coffees*

fla·vour·ful *BrE*, **flavorful** *AmE* /ˈfleɪvəfʊl $ -vər-/ *adj* having a strong pleasant taste: *flavourful cheese*

fla·vour·ing *BrE*, **flavoring** *AmE* /ˈfleɪvərɪŋ/ *n* [C,U] a substance used to give something a particular flavour or increase its flavour: *artificial flavourings*

fla·vour·some /ˈfleɪvəsəm $ -vər-/ *BrE*, **flavorful** *AmE* *adj* having a strong pleasant taste OPP **bland**: *a flavorful Mexican dish*

F

flaw /flɔː $ flɒː/ ●○○ *n* [C]
1 a mistake, mark, or weakness that makes something imperfect SYN **defect**: **[+in]** *a flaw in the software* | **serious/major/basic/minor etc flaw** *a slight flaw in the glass* | *A **design flaw** (=a mistake or weakness in the way something was made) caused the engine to explode.* THESAURUS ▸ FAULT
2 a mistake or problem in an argument, plan, set of ideas etc: **[+of]** *Beautiful scenery does not make up for the flaws of this film.* | **[+in]** *There is a **fundamental flaw** in Walton's argument.* | **fatal flaw** (=a weakness that makes something certain to fail)
3 a fault in someone's character: *Jealousy is Othello's major flaw.* | *the president's character flaws*

flawed /flɔːd $ flɒːd/ ●○○ *adj* spoiled by having mistakes, weaknesses, or by being damaged: *a flawed concept* | **fatally/fundamentally/deeply etc flawed** *The research behind this report is seriously flawed.*

flaw·less /ˈflɔːləs $ ˈflɒː-/ *adj* having no mistakes or marks, or not lacking anything SYN **perfect**: *Adrian's flawless French* —**flawlessly** *adv*

flax /flæks/ *n* [U] **1** a plant with blue flowers, used for making cloth and oil **2** the thread made from this plant, used for making LINEN

flax·en /ˈflæksən/ *adj literary* flaxen hair is light yellow in colour SYN **blond**

flay /fleɪ/ *v* [T] **1** *formal* to criticize someone very severely: *She was well-known for flaying public officials in her daily column.* **2** *literary* to whip or beat someone very severely **3** *formal* to remove the skin from an animal or person, especially one that is dead

flea /fliː/ *n* [C] **1** a very small insect without wings that jumps and bites animals and people to eat their blood: *Are you sure the dog **has fleas**?* **2 send sb off with a flea in their ear** *BrE* to talk angrily to someone, especially because they have done something you disapprove of

flea·bag /ˈfliːbæg/ *n* [C] *informal* **1** *BrE* a dirty animal or person that you dislike **2** *AmE* (*also* **fleabag hotel**) a cheap dirty hotel

ˈflea ˌcollar *n* [C] a special collar, worn by a dog or cat, that contains chemicals to keep fleas away from them

ˈflea ˌmarket *n* [C] a market where old or used goods are sold

flea·pit /ˈfliːˌpɪt/ *n* [C] *old-fashioned* a cheap dirty cinema or theatre - used humorously

fleck /flek/ *n* [C] **1** a small mark or spot SYN **speck**: **[+of]** *a black beard with flecks of gray* **2** a small piece of something SYN **speck**: **[+of]** *flecks of sawdust*

flecked /flekt/ *adj* [not before noun] having small marks or spots, or small pieces of something, covering a surface: **[+with]** *red cloth flecked with white*

fledged /fledʒd/ *adj* → FULLY-FLEDGED

fledg·ling¹, **fledgeling** /ˈfledʒlɪŋ/ *n* [C] a young bird that is learning to fly

fledgling², **fledgeling** *adj* [only before noun] a fledgling state or organization has only recently been formed and is still developing → **infant**: *a fledgling republic*

flee /fliː/ ●●○ *v* (*past tense and past participle* **fled** /fled/) [I,T] *written* to leave somewhere very quickly, in order to escape from danger: *His attackers turned and fled.* | *Masaari spent six months in prison before **fleeing** the **country**.* | **[+to/from/into]** *Many German artists fled to America at the beginning of World War II.* THESAURUS ▸ ESCAPE

fleece¹ /fliːs/ *n* **1** [C] the woolly coat of a sheep, especially the wool and skin of a sheep when it has been made into a piece of clothing **2** [U] an artificial soft material used to make warm jackets **3** [C] *BrE* a jacket made of this artificial material

fleece² *v* [T] *informal* to charge someone too much money for something, especially by tricking them

flee·cy /ˈfliːsi/ *adj* soft and woolly, or looking soft and woolly: *fleecy white towels*

fleet¹ /fliːt/ ●●○ *n* [C]
1 a group of ships, or all the ships in a navy: *the US seventh fleet*
2 a group of vehicles that are controlled by one company: **[+of]** *a fleet of taxis*

fleet² *adj literary* fast or quick: *Atalanta was **fleet of foot*** (=able to run quickly).

ˈfleet ˌadmiral *n* [C] the highest rank in the US navy, or someone who holds this rank

fleet·ing /ˈfliːtɪŋ/ *adj* [usually before noun] lasting for only a short time SYN **brief**: *a fleeting smile* | *For one **fleeting moment**, Paula allowed herself to forget her troubles.* | *I caught a **fleeting glimpse** of them as they drove past.* | *Carol was paying a **fleeting visit** to Paris.* THESAURUS ▸ SHORT —**fleetingly** *adv*

ˈFleet Street a street in London where many important newspaper offices used to be, often used as a name for the British newspaper industry

Flem·ish /ˈflemɪʃ/ *n* [U] a language like German spoken in northern Belgium → **Dutch**

flesh¹ /fleʃ/ ●●○ W3 *n* [U]
1 the soft part of the body of a person or animal that is between the skin and the bones: *a freshwater fish with firm white flesh*
2 the skin of the human body: *His flesh was red and covered in sores.*
3 the soft part of a fruit or vegetable that can be eaten: *Cut the melon in half and scoop out the flesh.*
4 in the flesh if you see someone in the flesh, you see someone who you previously had only seen in pictures, films etc: *He looked much shorter in the flesh than on television.*
5 make sb's flesh creep/crawl to make someone feel frightened, nervous, or uncomfortable: *The way he stared at her made her flesh creep.*
6 your own flesh and blood someone who is part of your family: *How can he treat his own flesh and blood that way?*
7 the flesh *literary* the physical human body, as opposed to the mind or spirit: **the pleasures/desires/temptations of the flesh** (=things such as drinking, eating a lot, or having sex)

8 put flesh on sth to give more details about something to make it clear, more interesting etc SYN **flesh sth ↔ out**: *I'll try to put some flesh on the plan Margaret has outlined.*
9 go the way of all flesh *literary* to die → **get your pound of flesh** at POUND[1](5), → **press the flesh** at PRESS[2](14), → **the spirit is willing but the flesh is weak** at SPIRIT[1](16)

flesh² *v*
flesh sth **↔ out** *phr v* to add more details to something in order to make it clear, more interesting etc SYN **put flesh on sth**: *You need to flesh out your argument with a few more examples.*

ˈflesh-ˌcoloured *BrE*, **flesh-colored** *AmE adj* having a pinkish colour like the colour of white people's skin: *flesh-coloured tights*

flesh·pots /ˈfleʃpɒts $ -pɑːts/ *n* [plural] areas in a city or town where there are many places that people go to for pleasure, especially sexual pleasure – used humorously

ˈflesh wound *n* [C] a wound that cuts the skin but does not injure the organs and bones inside the body

flesh·y /ˈfleʃi/ *adj* **1** having a lot of flesh: *the fleshy part of your hand* **2** having a soft thick inner part: *a plant with fleshy leaves*

flew /fluː/ *v* the past tense of FLY

flex¹ /fleks/ *v* [T] **1** to tighten your muscles or bend part of your body **2 flex your muscles** to show your ability to do something, especially your skill or power: *The role will allow her to flex her acting muscles.*

flex² *n* [C] *BrE* an electrical wire covered with plastic, used to connect electrical equipment to an electricity supply SYN **cord** *AmE* → **lead**

flex·i·bil·i·ty /ˌfleksəˈbɪləti/ ●●○ AWL *n* [U]
1 the ability to change or be changed easily to suit a different situation: *Employees expect flexibility in the workplace.*
2 the ability to bend or be bent easily SYN **suppleness**: *Stretching exercises will help your flexibility.*

flex·i·ble /ˈfleksəbəl/ ●●○ AWL *adj*
1 a person, plan etc that is flexible can change or be changed easily to suit any new situation OPP **inflexible**: *We can be flexible about your starting date.* | **extremely/highly/fairly etc flexible** *Our new computer software is extremely flexible.* | *The government needs a more* ***flexible approach*** *to education.*
2 something that is flexible can bend or be bent easily OPP **rigid**: *shoes with flexible rubber soles* —**flexibly** *adv*

flex·i·time /ˈfleksitaɪm/ *BrE*, **flex·time** /ˈflekstaɪm/ *AmE n* [U] a system in which people work a particular number of hours each week or month, but can change the times at which they start and finish each day

flick¹ /flɪk/ ●○○ *v*
1 [T usually + adv/prep] to make something move away by hitting or pushing it suddenly or quickly, especially with your thumb and finger: *Papa flicked the ash from his cigar.*
2 [I,T always + adv/prep] to move with a sudden quick movement, or to make something move in this way: **[+from/up/down]** *The cow's tail flicked from side to side.* | **flick sth up/down etc** *Jackie flicked her long hair back.*

FLICK

3 [T] to move a switch so that a machine or piece of electrical equipment starts or stops SYN **flip**: *I felt inside the doorway and* ***flicked*** *the light* ***switch***. | **flick sth on/off** *Sandra flicked the TV on.*
4 flick a glance/look at sb/sth *BrE* to look very quickly at someone or something: *Leith flicked a glance at her watch.*
5 [T] if you flick something such as a TOWEL or rope, you move it so that the end moves quickly away from you: *The old man flicked his whip and the horses moved off.*

flick through sth *phr v* to look at a book, magazine, set of photographs etc quickly: *Will flicked through Carla's photo album.*

flick² *n* **1** [C] a short quick sudden movement or hit with a part of your body, whip etc: *With* ***a flick of the wrist****, Frye sent the ball into the opposite court.* **2 the flick of a switch** used to emphasize how easy it is to start a machine and use it: *I can shut off all the power in the building* ***at the flick of a switch****.* **3** [C usually singular] *especially AmE* a film: *an action flick* **4 the flicks** *BrE old-fashioned* the cinema **5 have a flick through sth** *BrE* to look at a book, magazine, set of pictures etc very quickly: *I had a quick flick through your report.*

flick·er¹ /ˈflɪkə $ -ər/ ●○○ *v* [I]
1 to burn or shine with an unsteady light that goes on and off quickly: *The overhead lights flickered momentarily.*
THESAURUS ▸ SHINE
2 [always + adv/prep] if an emotion or expression flickers on someone's face or through their mind, it exists or is shown for only a short time: **[+across/through/on etc]** *A puzzled smile flickered across the woman's face.*
3 to quickly make a sudden small movement or series of movements: *Polly's eyelids flickered, then she slept.*

flicker² *n* [C] **1** an unsteady light that goes on and off quickly: **[+of]** *the flicker of the firelight* **2 a flicker of emotion/uncertainty/excitement etc** a feeling or expression that continues for a very short time: *She saw a flicker of doubt in his eyes.* **3** a quick sudden movement or series of movements

ˈflick knife *n* [C] *BrE* a knife with a blade inside the handle that moves quickly into position when you press a button SYN **switchblade** *AmE* → see picture at KNIFE[1]

fli·er /ˈflaɪə $ -ər/ *n* [C] another spelling of FLYER

flies /flaɪz/ a FLY[3](2)

flight /flaɪt/ ●●● S3 W2 *n*
1 TRAVEL [C] a journey in a plane or space vehicle, or the plane or vehicle that is making the journey → **fly**: *He immediately booked a flight to Toulouse.* | *There are only three flights a day to Logan Airport from Heathrow.*
THESAURUS ▸ JOURNEY
2 FLYING [U] when something flies through the air: **in flight** *pelicans in flight* | *In 1968, the first supersonic airliner* ***took flight*** (=began flying).
3 MOVEMENT THROUGH AIR [U] an object's or bird's movement through the air: *During its flight, the weapon twists and turns.*
4 STAIRS [C] a set of stairs between one floor and the next: *Bert lives two flights down from here.* | **a flight of stairs/steps** *She fell down a whole flight of stairs.*
5 ESCAPE [U] when you leave a place in order to try and escape from a person or a dangerous situation: **[+from]** *Donald Woods' hasty flight from South Africa early in 1978* | **take flight** (*also* **take to flight** *BrE*): *When the alarm sounded, the whole gang took flight.* | **put sb to flight** (=make someone run away especially by fighting or threatening them)
6 flight of fancy/imagination/fantasy thoughts, ideas etc that are full of imagination but that are not practical or sensible
7 BIRDS [C] a group of birds all flying together SYN **flock**: **[+of]** *a flight of swallows* → IN-FLIGHT, TOP-FLIGHT

COLLOCATIONS

VERBS

book a flight (=reserve a seat on a particular plane) *I booked the flight over the Internet.*
get a flight (=book it) *I'll be there tomorrow morning if I can get a flight.*
catch a flight (=be in time to get on a plane) *They caught a flight that night to Frankfurt.*
board a flight (=get on a flight) *We arrived at the departure lounge to board the flight to Madrid.*
miss a flight (=arrive too late for a flight) *Jack overslept and missed his flight.*
charter a flight (=pay a company for the use of their aircraft) | **a flight is cancelled** (=a flight that was

F

due to go somewhere does not go) | **a flight is delayed** (=it is late leaving) | **a flight is bound for London/New York etc** (=it is going there)

ADJECTIVES

good/pleasant/comfortable *Have a good flight!*
smooth (=with no problems or sudden movements) *The flight had been smooth all the way.*
bumpy (=uncomfortable because the plane moved up and down a lot) *The flight was very bumpy, and we really wondered whether we would make it.*
long/short *I was very tired after the long flight.*
cheap flights *Environmental groups are calling for an end to cheap flights.*
a direct/non-stop flight (=a flight going straight from one place to another without stopping) *the first direct flight to Tokyo*
an international flight (=a flight between one country and another) | **a domestic/internal flight** (=a flight within a country) | **a long-haul flight** (=a flight over a very long distance) | **a scheduled flight** (=a plane service that flies at the same time every day or every week)
a charter flight (=a plane service that is arranged for a particular group or purpose) *The company is operating charter flights to Crete.*
a connecting flight (=a flight that arrives before another one leaves) | **an intercontinental flight** (=a flight that goes from one continent to another, for example from Europe to Asia) | **a routine flight** (=a normal flight)

flight + NOUN

the flight time (=how long it takes to fly somewhere) *Our estimated flight time is three hours and fifteen minutes.*
the flight path (=the route taken by an aircraft) | **the flight number**

ˈflight atˌtendant ●●○ *n* [C] someone who serves food and drinks to passengers on a plane, and looks after their comfort and safety

ˈflight crew *n* [C] the people, such as the pilot and flight attendants, who work on a plane during a flight

ˈflight deck *n* [C] **1** the room in a plane where the pilot sits to control the plane **2** the flat surface of a ship which military aircraft use to fly into the air from

flight·less /ˈflaɪtləs/ *adj* unable to fly: *a flightless bird*

ˌflight lieuˈtenant *n* [C] a middle rank in the British air force, or someone who holds this rank

ˈflight path *n* [C] the course that a plane or space vehicle travels along

ˈflight reˌcorder *n* [C] a piece of equipment in an aircraft that records details such as the plane's speed and direction SYN **black box**

ˈflight ˌsergeant *n* [C] a middle rank in the British air force, or someone who holds this rank

ˈflight ˌsimulator *n* [C] a machine used to train pilots that copies closely the movements and conditions that exist when flying an aircraft

flight·y /ˈflaɪti/ *adj disapproving* someone who is flighty changes their ideas and opinions often, and only remains interested in people or things for a short time – used especially about women

flim·flam /ˈflɪmflæm/ *n* [U] *old-fashioned informal* information or ideas that are not true or seem very stupid: *I was sick of his intellectual flimflam.*

flim·sy /ˈflɪmzi/ ●○○ *adj*
1 flimsy cloth or clothing is light and thin: *a flimsy cotton dress*
2 something that is flimsy is not strong or well-made, and will break easily: *a flimsy wooden building* THESAURUS WEAK
3 a flimsy agreement is weak and can easily be damaged or broken: *a flimsy alliance between the two tribal groups*
4 a flimsy argument or excuse does not seem very likely and people do not believe it OPP **convincing**: *The **evidence** against him is extremely **flimsy**.* | *a **flimsy excuse*** —**flimsily** *adv* —**flimsiness** *n* [U]

flinch /flɪntʃ/ (*also* **flinch away**) *v* [I] **1** to move your face or body away from someone or something because you are in pain, frightened, or upset: **[+at]** *She flinched at the touch of his hand.* | **[+from]** *The boy flinched away from him.* **2** to feel embarrassed or upset: **[+at]** *Jo flinched at her sister's insensitivity.* **3 not flinch from (doing) sth** to be willing to do something even though it is difficult or unpleasant: *He never flinched from doing his duty.* → **unflinching**

fling¹ /flɪŋ/ ●●○ *v* (*past tense and past participle* **flung** /flʌŋ/) [T always + adv/prep]
1 THROW STH to throw something somewhere using a lot of force: **fling sth into sth** *He flung the box into the river.* | *People cheered and flung their hats into the air.* THESAURUS THROW
2 MOVE STH to throw or move something roughly and carelessly: *He flung his coat over the back of a chair.* | *She flung back the covers and got up.* | *He flung the books aside angrily.*
3 PUSH SB to push someone roughly, especially so that they fall to the ground SYN **throw**: *He grabbed her arm and flung her to the ground.*
4 MOVE YOUR BODY to move yourself or part of your body quickly, using a lot of force SYN **throw**: *He **flung himself** down on the bed.* | *She **flung** her **arms** round Louise.*
5 SAY STH to say something to someone in an angry way SYN **throw**: **fling sth at sb** *People were flinging all sorts of accusations at her.* | *His own words were flung back at him.*
6 fling sth open to open a door or window roughly, using a lot of force: *The door was flung open and Selkirk entered.*
7 fling sb in/into prison/jail to put someone in prison, often without having a good reason: *Opposition leaders were flung into jail.*
8 fling yourself into sth to start doing something with a lot of energy: *After the divorce he flung himself into his work to forget her.*
9 fling yourself at sb a) to move suddenly towards someone in order to attack them or hold them: *He flung himself at her and snatched the bag.* | *The children flung themselves at him, squealing with joy.* **b)** *informal* to show in a very clear open way that you want to have a sexual relationship with someone – used to show disapproval

fling sth ↔ **off** *phr v* to quickly remove a piece of clothing SYN **tear off**: *He flung off his coat.*

fling sb/sth ↔ **out** *phr v BrE informal*
1 to make someone leave a place when they do not want to SYN **throw sb/sth out**: **[+of]** *He was flung out of school for swearing at a teacher.*
2 to get rid of something you no longer want or need SYN **throw sth out**: *If it doesn't work, just fling it out.*

fling² *n* [C usually singular] **1** a short and not very serious sexual relationship: *They **had** a **brief fling** a few years ago.* **2** a short period of time during which you enjoy yourself without worrying about anything: *He sees this as his **final fling** before he retires.*

flint /flɪnt/ *n* **1** [U] a type of smooth hard stone that makes a small flame when you hit it with steel **2** [C] a piece of this stone or a small piece of metal that makes a small flame when you hit it with steel

flint·y /ˈflɪnti/ *adj* **1** *literary* not showing any emotions SYN **hard**, **icy**: **flinty look/stare** *Duvall gave him a flinty stare.* **2** like flint or containing flint

flip¹ /flɪp/ ●○○ *v* (**flipped**, **flipping**)
1 MOVE [I,T always + adv/prep] to move something with a quick sudden movement so that it is in a different position: *He flipped the top off the bottle and poured himself a drink.* | *She **flipped** the lid of the box **open** and looked inside.* | **[+over]** *He flipped the paper over and started writing on the back.*
2 TURN IN THE AIR [T] to make a flat object such as a coin go upwards and turn over in the air SYN **toss**: *We **flipped** a **coin** to see who would go first.* | *There's quite an art to flipping pancakes.*

3 ANGRY [I] *informal* to suddenly become very angry or upset SYN **lose it**: *I just flipped and started shouting.*
4 TURN A SWITCH [T] to move a switch so that a machine or piece of electrical equipment starts or stops SYN **flick**: *Anna* ***flipped*** *the* ***switch*** *that opened the front gate.* | **flip sth on/off** *Josie flipped on the radio.*
5 TURN PAGES [I,T] to turn the pages of a book or newspaper quickly, especially because you are looking for something: *He picked up the newspaper and flipped straight to the sports pages.* | **[+through]** *I flipped through my address book but couldn't find her phone number.*
6 [T] *AmE* to buy a house and then sell it again quickly for a profit, usually after improving it
7 flip your lid *informal* to suddenly become very angry SYN **go crazy**: *Mom flipped her lid when she found out I was pregnant.*
flip sb ↔ **off** *phr v AmE informal* (*also* **flip sb the bird**) to make a rude sign at someone by lifting up your middle finger and keeping your other fingers down

flip² *n* [C] **1** an action in which you make a flat object such as a coin go upwards and turn over in the air SYN **toss**: *In the end the decision was made by the* ***flip of a coin.*** **2** a movement in which you jump up and turn over in the air, so that your feet go over your head SYN **somersault**: *I tripped and almost did a backward flip down the stairs.* **3** an action in which you turn the pages of a book or newspaper quickly, especially because you are looking for something SYN **flick**: **[+through]** *I had a quick flip through my cookery books and found a recipe that sounded quite nice.*

flip³ *adj informal* not said or meant seriously SYN **flippant**: *I was fed up with his flip comments.*

ˈflip chart *n* [C] a set of large pieces of paper that are connected at the top so that you can turn the pages over to present information to people

ˈflip chip *n* [C] a computer CHIP on which the electrical connections that store, use etc information face towards the computer's CIRCUIT BOARD (=the part that carries electricity to all the electrical connections), making it unnecessary to have electrical connections on both sides of the chip: *flip-chip technology*

ˈflip-flop *v* (**flip-flopped, flip-flopping**) [I] *AmE informal* to change your opinion about something —**flip-flop** *n* [C]: *an incredible political flip-flop*

ˈflip-flops *n* [plural] open summer shoes, usually made of rubber, with a V-shaped band across the front to hold your feet SYN **thongs** *AmE* → see picture at SHOE¹

flip·pant /ˈflɪpənt/ *adj* not being serious about something that other people think you should be serious about: *a rather flippant remark* | **[+about]** *You shouldn't be flippant about such things.* —**flippantly** *adv* —**flippancy** *n* [U]: *This is no time for flippancy.*

flip·per /ˈflɪpə $ -ər/ *n* [C] **1** a flat part on the body of some large sea animals such as SEALs, that they use for swimming **2** a large flat rubber shoe that you wear to help you swim faster → see picture at SPORT¹

ˈflip phone *n* [C] a MOBILE PHONE that has a cover which opens upwards

flip·ping /ˈflɪpɪŋ/ *adj, adv BrE spoken* used to show that you are slightly annoyed about something: *It's flipping cold outside!* | *This flipping pen doesn't work!*

ˈflip side *n* [singular] **1** the bad effects of something that also has good effects: *The flip side of the treatment is that it can make patients feel very tired.* **2** *old-fashioned* the side of a record that does not have the main song on

flirt¹ /flɜːt $ flɜːrt/ *v* [I] to behave towards someone in a way that shows that you are sexually attracted to them, although you do not really want a relationship with them: **[+with]** *She accused him of flirting with other women.* | *She was* ***flirting outrageously*** (=a lot) *with some of the managers.*
flirt with sth *phr v* **1** to consider doing something, but not be very serious about it: *He had flirted with the idea of emigrating.* **2** to do something that is dangerous or could cause problems for you: *Climbers enjoy* ***flirting with danger***.

flirt² *n* [C] someone who flirts with people: **a terrible/dreadful etc flirt** (=someone who flirts a lot) *She's an incorrigible flirt!*

flir·ta·tion /flɜːˈteɪʃən $ flɜːr-/ *n* **1** [C] a short period of time during which you are interested in something: **[+with]** *He started his own business last year, after a* ***brief flirtation*** *with political life.* **2** [U] behaviour that shows you are attracted to someone sexually: *She had no objection to a little* ***mild flirtation***. **3** [C] a short sexual relationship which is not serious SYN **fling**: **[+with]** *She* ***had*** *a* ***brief flirtation*** *with Tim.*

flir·ta·tious /flɜːˈteɪʃəs $ flɜːr-/ *adj* behaving in a way that deliberately tries to attract sexual attention: *She gave him a flirtatious smile.* | *a flirtatious giggle* —**flirtatiously** *adv* —**flirtatiousness** *n* [U]

flit /flɪt/ *v* (**flitted, flitting**) [I always + adv/prep] to move lightly or quickly and not stay in one place for very long: *Birds flitted about in the trees above them.* | *She seemed to spend her life flitting from one country to another.* | *His eyes flitted to his watch.*

float¹ /fləʊt $ floʊt/ ●●● S3 W2 *v*
1 ON WATER **a)** [I] to stay or move on the surface of a liquid without sinking: *I wasn't sure if the raft would float.* | *She spent the afternoon floating on her back in the pool.* | **[+along/down/past etc]** *A couple of broken branches floated past us.* **b)** [T] to put something on the surface of a liquid so that it does not sink: *The logs are trimmed and then floated down the river.*
2 IN THE AIR [I always + adv/prep] if something floats, it moves slowly through the air or stays up in the air: *I looked up at the clouds floating in the sky.* | *Leaves floated gently down from the trees.*
3 MUSIC/SOUNDS/SMELLS ETC [I always + adv/prep] if sounds or smells float somewhere, people in another place can hear or smell them: *The sound of her voice came floating down from an upstairs window.*
4 WALK GRACEFULLY [I] to walk in a slow light graceful way SYN **glide**: *Rachel floated around the bedroom in a lace nightgown.*
5 IDEAS [T] to suggest an idea or plan in order to see if people like it: *We first floated the idea back in 1992.*
6 MONEY [T] *technical* if the government of a country floats its money, the value of the money is allowed to change freely in relation to money from other countries: *Russia decided to float the rouble on the foreign exchange market.*
7 COMPANY [T] to sell SHARES in a company or business to the public for the first time: **float sth on sth** *The company will be floated on the stock market next year.* → FLOTATION(1)
8 CHEQUE [T] *AmE* to write a cheque when you do not have enough money in the bank to pay it
9 whatever floats your boat *informal* used to say that someone can do or use whatever they like: *You can add raisins, nuts, chocolate chips – whatever floats your boat.*
float around *phr v informal* to be present in a place: *There's a lot of cash floating around in the economy at the moment.*

float² ●○○ *n* [C]
1 VEHICLE a large vehicle that is decorated to drive through the streets as part of a special event: *We stood and watched the Carnival floats drive past.*
2 DRINK *AmE* a sweet drink that has ice cream floating in it
3 FOR FISHING a small light object that floats on the surface of the water, used by people trying to catch fish to show where their line is → see picture at FISHING
4 FOR SWIMMING a flat light object that you can rest part of your body on in water to help you learn to swim
5 MONEY a small amount of money that someone in a shop keeps so that they have enough money to give change to people
6 BUSINESS a time when SHARES in a company are made available for people to buy for the first time SYN **flotation**
7 RELAXATION a time when you sit in a FLOTATION TANK in order to treat illness or injury, or to relax

F

floa·ta·tion /fləʊˈteɪʃən $ floʊ-/ *n* [C,U] a British spelling of FLOTATION

float·ing¹ /ˈfləʊtɪŋ $ ˈfloʊ-/ *adj* [only before noun] often changing, and not staying the same: *You can choose either a fixed or floating interest rate for the loan.* | *The area has a large floating population.*

floating² *n* [U] the activity of sitting in a FLOTATION TANK in order to relax, or to treat illness or injury

ˌfloating ˈvoter *n* [C] someone who does not always vote for the same political party at elections

flock¹ /flɒk $ flɑːk/ ●●○ *n*
1 [C] a group of sheep, goats, or birds: **[+of]** *a flock of small birds* THESAURUS ▸ GROUP
2 [C usually singular] a large group of people SYN **crowd**: **[+of]** *a flock of children*
3 [C usually singular] a priest's flock is the group of people who regularly attend his or her church
4 [U] small pieces of wool or cotton that are used for filling CUSHIONS
5 (*also* **flocking** /ˈflɒkɪŋ $ ˈflɑː-/ *AmE*) [U] a soft substance that is used to make patterns on the surface of WALLPAPER, curtains etc

flock² *v* [I always +adv/prep] if people flock to a place, they go there in large numbers because something interesting or exciting is happening there: **[+to/into/down etc]** *People have been flocking to the exhibition.* | **flock to do sth** *Tourists flock to see the town's medieval churches and buildings.*

floe /fləʊ $ floʊ/ *n* [C] an ICE FLOE

flog /flɒg $ flɑːg/ *v* (**flogged**, **flogging**) [T] **1** to beat a person or animal with a whip or stick: *He was publicly flogged and humiliated.* **2** *informal* to sell something: *I'm going to flog all my old video tapes.* THESAURUS ▸ SELL **3 be flogging a dead horse** *spoken* to be wasting time or effort by trying to do something that is impossible **4 flog sth to death** *BrE informal* to repeat a story or use an idea etc so often that people become bored with it: *They take a good idea and flog it to death.*

flog·ging /ˈflɒgɪŋ $ ˈflɑːgɪŋ/ *n* [C] a punishment in which someone is severely beaten with a whip or stick

flood¹ /flʌd/ ●●○ W3 *v*
1 COVER WITH WATER [I,T] to cover a place with water, or to become covered with water: *Towns and cities all over the country have been flooded.* | *The houses down by the river flood quite regularly.*
2 RIVER [I,T] if a river floods, it is too full, and spreads water over the land around it: *There are now fears that the river could flood.*
3 GO/ARRIVE IN LARGE NUMBERS [I always + adv/prep] to arrive or go somewhere in large numbers SYN **pour**, **flow**: *Refugees are still flooding across the border.* | *Donations have been flooding in since we launched the appeal.*
4 flood sth with sth to send a very large number of things to a place or organization: *a plan to flood the country with forged banknotes*
5 be flooded with sth to receive so many letters, complaints, or inquiries that you cannot deal with them all easily: *We've been flooded with offers of help.*
6 flood the market to produce and sell a very large number of one type of thing, so that the price goes down: **[+with]** *Car manufacturers have been accused of flooding the market with cheap cars.*
7 LIGHT [I,T] if light floods a place or floods into it, it makes it very light and bright: **[+into]** *Light flooded into the kitchen.* | **flood sth with sth** *The morning sun flooded the room with a gentle light.*
8 FEELING [I always + adv/prep,T] if a feeling or memory floods over you or floods back, you feel or remember it very strongly: **[+over/back]** *I felt happiness and relief flooding over me.* | *Memories of my time in Paris flooded back.*
9 ENGINE [I,T] if an engine floods or if you flood it, it has too much petrol in it, so that it will not start

flood sb ↔ **out** *phr v* to force someone to leave their home because of floods

flood² ●●○ *n*
1 [C,U] a very large amount of water that covers an area that is usually dry: *The village was cut off by floods.* | *the worst floods for over fifty years*
2 [C] a very large number of things or people that arrive at the same time: **[+of]** *The UN appealed for help with the* ***flood of refugees*** *crossing the border.*
3 in floods of tears crying a lot: *She came downstairs in floods of tears.*
4 in flood a river that is in flood has much more water in it than usual → **flash flood** at FLASH³(1)

flood·gate /ˈflʌdgeɪt/ *n* [C] **1 open the floodgates a)** if something opens the floodgates, or if the floodgates open, it suddenly becomes possible for a lot of things to happen which were prevented from happening before: *If this case is successful it could open the floodgates for thousands of similar claims.* | *There are fears that the floodgates will open and large numbers of parents will take their children out of school.* **b)** if the floodgates open, or if something opens the floodgates, someone begins to cry and show their emotions after keeping them hidden: *His display of kindness to her opened the floodgates again, and she began to sob loudly.* **2** a gate that is used to control the flow of water from a large lake or river

flood·ing /ˈflʌdɪŋ/ *n* [U] a situation in which an area of land becomes covered with water, for example because of heavy rain: *The heavy rain has led to* ***serious flooding*** *in some areas.* | *The river banks have been built up to prevent flooding.*

flood·light /ˈflʌdlaɪt/ *n* [C] a very bright light that is used to light the outside of a building or sports ground at night: *The church was lit up by floodlights.* | **under floodlights** *The game will be played under floodlights.*

FLOODLIGHTS

flood·lit /ˈflʌdlɪt/ *adj* surrounded by floodlights so that people can see at night: *a floodlit football pitch*

ˈflood plain *n* [C] the large area of flat land on either side of a river that is sometimes covered with water when the river becomes too full

ˈflood tide *n* [C] the flow of the sea in towards the land → **ebb tide**

flood·wa·ter /ˈflʌdwɔːtə $ -wɒːtər, -wɑː-/ *n* [plural, U] water that covers an area during a flood

floor¹ /flɔː $ flɔːr/ ●●● S1 W1 *n* [C]
1 IN A BUILDING the flat surface that you stand on inside a building: *a polished wooden floor* | *a puddle of water on the kitchen floor* | *a warehouse that has 410,000 square feet of* ***floor space***
2 IN A CAR *BrE* the part of a car that forms its inside floor SYN **floorboard** *AmE*
3 LEVEL IN BUILDING one of the levels in a building: *a ground floor flat* | **on the top/first/tenth etc floor** *Our office is on the top floor.* | **[+of]** *We are located on the seventh floor of the building.*
4 OCEAN/FOREST/CAVE FLOOR ETC the ground at the bottom of the ocean, the forest etc: *creatures that live on the ocean floor*
5 FOR DANCING an area in a room where people can dance: *There were two or three couples already on the* ***dance floor***. | **take (to) the floor** (=begin dancing) *Everyone took to the floor for the last waltz.*
6 WHERE PEOPLE WORK a large area in a building where a lot of people do their jobs: *He wasn't keen on the idea of working on the* ***shop floor*** (=the part of a factory where people make things using machines). | *the busy* ***trading***

floor (=area where STOCKS and SHARES are bought and sold)
7 LIMIT an officially agreed limit below which something cannot go → **ceiling**: *Manufacturers have tried to* ***put a floor under*** *the price of their products.*
8 the floor a) the people attending a public meeting: *Are there any questions from the floor?* **b)** the part of a parliament, public meeting place etc where people sit: *The delegates crowded the floor of the House.*
9 take the floor to begin speaking at an important public meeting: *The chairman then took the floor.*
10 have the floor to be speaking or have the right to speak at an important public meeting: *He stepped aside to allow other speakers to have the floor.*
11 go through the floor if a price, amount etc goes through the floor, it becomes very low OPP **go through the roof**: *Share prices have gone through the floor.*

THESAURUS

floor one of the levels in a building: *She lives in an apartment on the eighteenth floor.*
storey *BrE*, **story** *AmE* used when saying how many levels a building has: *a five-storey car park | The school is a single storey building.*
the ground floor (*also* **the first floor** *AmE*) the floor of a building that is at ground level: *There is a shop on the ground floor.*
deck one of the levels on a ship, bus, or plane: *The Horizon Lounge is on the top deck of the ship.*

floor² *v* [T] **1** to surprise or shock someone so much that they do not know what to say or do: *A couple of the questions completely floored me.* **2** to hit someone so hard that they fall down: *He was floored in the first round of the fight.* **3** *AmE informal* to make a car go as fast as possible: *I got into the car and* ***floored it***.

floor·board /ˈflɔːbɔːd $ ˈflɔːrbɔːrd/ *n* [C] **1** a board in a wooden floor: *I lifted the carpet to check the floorboards for woodworm.* **2** *AmE* the floor in a car

floor·ing /ˈflɔːrɪŋ/ *n* [U] any material that is used to make or cover floors: *We've chosen wood flooring for the hall.* | *vinyl flooring*

ˈfloor lamp *n* [C] *AmE* a tall lamp that stands on the floor SYN **standard lamp** *BrE* → see picture at LAMP

ˈfloor-length *adj* [only before noun] long enough to reach the floor: *floor-length curtains | a floor-length skirt*

ˈfloor plan *n* [C] a drawing of the shape of a room or building and the position of things in it, as seen from above SYN **ground plan**

ˈfloor show *n* [C] a performance by singers, dancers etc at a NIGHTCLUB

floor·time /ˈflɔːtaɪm $ ˈflɔːr-/ *n* [U] when an adult gets down onto the floor in order to play with a child. People do this so that the child will feel more comfortable playing with an adult, and some people also believe that it can help a child's mental abilities to develop fully.

floo·zy, **floozie** /ˈfluːzi/ *n* (*plural* **floozies**) [C] *old-fashioned* a woman who has sexual relationships with a lot of different men, in a way that you disapprove of

flop¹ /flɒp $ flɑːp/ *v* (**flopped**, **flopping**) [I] **1** [always + adv/prep] to sit or lie down in a relaxed way, by letting all your weight fall heavily onto a chair etc: *He flopped down onto the bed.* | *I got home and flopped in front of the TV.* **2** [always + adv/prep] to hang or fall loosely, in an uncontrolled way: *His head flopped back pathetically.* **3** *informal* if something such as a product, play, or idea flops, it is not successful because people do not like it

flop² *n* **1** [C] *informal* a film, play, product etc that is not successful OPP **hit**: **disastrous/spectacular etc flop** *The film was a complete flop.* **2** [singular] the movement or noise that something makes when it falls heavily: *He fell with a flop into the water.* → BELLY FLOP

flop·house /ˈflɒphaʊs $ ˈflɑːp-/ *n* [C] *AmE informal* a very cheap hotel where people can stay when they have very little money and nowhere to live SYN **doss house** *BrE*

flop·py /ˈflɒpi $ ˈflɑːpi/ *adj* something that is floppy is soft and hangs down loosely rather than being stiff: *a floppy hat | a dog with long floppy ears*

ˌfloppy ˈdisk (*also* **floppy**) *n* [C] a square piece of plastic that you can store computer information on, and which you can remove from and put into a computer → **hard disk**

flo·ra /ˈflɔːrə/ *n* [U] all the plants that grow in a particular place or country: *Tourism is damaging the* ***flora and fauna*** (=plants and animals) *of the island.*

flo·ral /ˈflɔːrəl/ *adj* made of flowers or decorated with flowers or pictures of flowers: *a scarf with a bold floral pattern | a pretty floral dress | a light floral fragrance | There were* ***floral tributes*** (=flowers sent as a sign of respect after someone has died) *from his colleagues.* → see picture at PATTERN¹

flor·et /ˈflɒrət $ ˈflɔːr-/ *n* [C usually plural] one of the parts that a vegetable such as BROCCOLI or CAULIFLOWER can be divided into

flor·id /ˈflɒrɪd $ ˈflɔː-, ˈflɑː-/ *adj literary* **1** a florid face is red in colour: *a middle-aged man with a florid complexion* **2** florid language, music, or art has a lot of extra unnecessary details or decorations: *a book written in a very florid style*

flor·in /ˈflɒrɪn $ ˈflɔː-, ˈflɑː-/ *n* [C] a coin that was used in Britain before 1971, worth about 10p

flor·ist /ˈflɒrɪst $ ˈflɔː-/ *n* [C] **1** someone who owns or works in a shop that sells flowers and indoor plants for the home **2** (*also* **florist's**) a shop that sells flowers and indoor plants for the home

floss¹ /flɒs $ flɑːs, flɔːs/ *n* [U] **1** a type of thin thread that you use for cleaning between your teeth SYN **dental floss** **2** a type of thin thread that you use for sewing

floss² *v* [T] to clean between your teeth using floss

flo·ta·tion /fləʊˈteɪʃən $ floʊ-/ *n* [C,U] **1** a time when SHARES in a company are made available for people to buy for the first time: *The company has decided to postpone its flotation on the stock market.* **2 flotation chamber/compartment etc** a container filled with air or gas, fixed to something to make it float

floˈtation ˌtank *n* [C] a large container full of warm salty water, often with a cover on it to make it dark inside, that you float in so that you can relax, or to treat illness or injury

flo·til·la /fləˈtɪlə $ floʊ-/ *n* [C] a group of small ships

flot·sam /ˈflɒtsəm $ ˈflɑː-/ *n* [U] **1** broken pieces of wood and other things from a wrecked ship, floating in the sea or scattered on the shore: *He would walk along the beach collecting the* ***flotsam and jetsam*** *that had been washed ashore.* **2** things that people no longer want and so throw away: *works of art made from the* ***flotsam and jetsam*** *of everyday life* **3** people who are very poor and do not have jobs or homes: *Camps were set up to shelter the* ***flotsam and jetsam*** *of the war.*

flounce¹ /flaʊns/ *v* [I always + adv/prep] to walk in a quick determined way without looking at people because you are angry: *She flounced out of the room.*

flounce² *n* **1** [C] a wide band of cloth with folds, which is stitched onto the edge of a skirt, dress, shirt, or curtain as a decoration: *The dress had red satin flounces at the bottom.* **2** [singular] a way of walking in a quick determined way without looking at people, because you are angry: *She walked off with a flounce.*

FLOUNCE

flounced /flaʊnst/ *adj* decorated with flounces: *a flounced skirt*

floun·der¹ /ˈflaʊndə $ -ər/ *v* [I] **1** to not know what to say or do because you feel confused or upset: *I found myself floundering as I tried to answer her questions.* | *'I'm sorry,' she* ***floundered helplessly***. **2** to have a lot of problems and be likely to fail completely: *More and more firms are floundering because of the recession.* **3** [always + adv/prep] to be unable to move easily because you are in deep water or mud, or cannot see very well: *They were floundering chest-deep in the freezing water.* | **[+around]** *I could hear them floundering around in the dark.*

flounder² *n* (*plural* **flounder** *or* **flounders**) [C,U] a type of small fish that you can eat

flour¹ /flaʊə $ flaʊr/ ●●● S3 W3 *n* [U] a powder that is made by crushing wheat or other grain and that is used for making bread, cakes etc: **white/wholemeal/rice/wheat etc flour** → PLAIN FLOUR, SELF-RAISING FLOUR

flour² *v* [T] to cover a surface with flour when you are cooking: *Roll the pastry out on a lightly floured board.*

flour·ish¹ /ˈflʌrɪʃ $ ˈflɜːrɪʃ/ ●○○ *v*
1 [I] to develop well and be successful SYN **thrive**: *The economy is booming and small businesses are flourishing.*
2 [I] to grow well and be very healthy → **thrive**: *Most plants will flourish in the rich deep soils here.*
3 [T] to wave something in your hand in order to make people notice it: *She walked quickly to the desk, flourishing her cheque book.*

flour·ish² *n* **1 with a flourish** with a large confident movement that makes people notice you: *He opened his wallet with a flourish and took out a handful of notes.* **2** [C usually singular] a special or impressive part of something: *There's nothing like a luxurious dessert to give a menu a* ***final flourish***. | **with a flourish** *They finished the season with a flourish, winning their last three matches.* **3** [C] a loud part of a piece of music, played especially when an important person enters: *a flourish of trumpets* **4** [C] a curved line that you use to decorate writing

flour·y /ˈflaʊəri $ ˈflaʊri/ *adj* **1** covered with flour or tasting of flour: *She wiped her floury hands on her apron.* **2** floury potatoes become very soft and break easily when they are cooked

flout /flaʊt/ *v* [T] to deliberately disobey a law, rule etc, without trying to hide what you are doing: *Some companies flout the rules and employ children as young as seven.* | **deliberately/openly flout sth** *The union had openly flouted the law.* THESAURUS DISOBEY

flow¹ /fləʊ $ floʊ/ ●●● S3 W2 *n*
1 LIQUID/GAS/ELECTRICITY [C usually singular] a smooth steady movement of liquid, gas, or electricity: **[+of]** *He struggled to swim against the flow of the water.* | *I tied a towel round his leg to try to* ***stem*** *the* ***flow*** *of blood.*
2 TRAFFIC [C usually singular, U] the steady movement of traffic: *a new road system to improve traffic flow through the city centre*
3 GOODS/PEOPLE/INFORMATION [C usually singular] the movement of goods, people, or information from one place to another: **[+of]** *the flow of funds from the US to Europe* | *There has been a* ***steady flow*** *of people leaving the area.* | *They have accused the government of trying to block the* ***free flow*** *of information.* | *an attempt to* ***stem*** *the* ***flow*** *of refugees across the border*
4 SPEECH/WRITING [U] the continuous stream of words or ideas when someone is speaking, writing, or thinking about something: *I didn't want to* ***interrupt*** *her* ***flow***, *so I said nothing.*
5 OF THE SEA [singular] the regular movement of the sea towards the land: *the* ***ebb and flow*** *of the tide*
6 in full flow *informal* if someone is in full flow, they are busy talking about something and seem likely to continue for a long time
7 go with the flow to agree that you will do the thing that most people want to do: *I don't mind, I'll just go with the flow.*
8 go against the flow to do something very different from what other people are doing → CASH FLOW, → **ebb and flow** at EBB¹(3)

flow² ●●● W3 *v* [I]
1 LIQUID/GAS/ELECTRICITY when a liquid, gas, or electricity flows, it moves in a steady continuous stream: **[+over/down/through etc]** *These gates regulate the amount of water flowing into the canal.* | *If the windows are shut, air cannot* ***flow freely*** *through the building.*
2 GOODS/PEOPLE/INFORMATION [always + adv/prep] if goods, people, or information flow from one place to another, they move there in large numbers or amounts SYN **pour, flood**: *Money has been flowing into the country from Western aid agencies.* | *The number of refugees flowing into the area is still increasing.*
3 TRAFFIC if traffic flows, it moves easily from one place to another: *The new one-way system should help the traffic to flow better.*
4 ALCOHOL if alcohol flows at a party, people drink a lot and there is a lot available: *Beer and whisky* ***flowed freely*** *as the evening wore on.*
5 WORDS/IDEAS if conversation or ideas flow, people talk or have ideas steadily and continuously, without anything stopping or interrupting them: *Everyone was relaxed and the conversation* ***flowed freely***.
6 SEA when the sea flows, it moves towards the land: *We watched the tide* ***ebb and flow***.
7 FEELINGS if a feeling flows through you or over you, you feel it strongly: **[+through/over]** *She felt hot rage flowing through her.*
8 CLOTHES/HAIR if clothing or hair flows, it falls or hangs loosely and gracefully: *Her long hair flowed down her back.*
9 flow from sth to happen as a result of something: *the political consequences that flowed from this decision*

ˈflow chart (*also* **ˈflow ˌdiagram**) *n* [C] a drawing that uses shapes and lines to show how the different stages in a process are connected to each other → see picture at CHART¹

flow·er¹ /ˈflaʊə $ -ər/ ●●● S2 W2 *n* [C]
1 a coloured or white part that a plant or tree produces before fruit or seeds → **floral**: *a lovely rose bush with delicate pink flowers* | *fields full of beautiful* ***wild flowers***
2 a small plant that produces beautiful flowers: *He wasn't interested in growing flowers in the garden.* | *She bent down and* ***picked*** *a* ***flower***. | **bunch/bouquet of flowers** *The first night we met he gave me a bunch of flowers.* | *a beautiful* ***flower arrangement*** (=flowers arranged together in an attractive way) → see picture at BOUQUET
3 in flower a plant or tree that is in flower has flowers on it SYN **in bloom**: *It was May, and the apple trees were all in flower.* | *Roses start to* ***come into flower*** *in June.*
4 the flower of sth *literary* the best part of something: *young men killed in the flower of their youth*

flower² ●●○ *v* [I]
1 to produce flowers: *Bulbs that you plant in the autumn should flower the following spring.*
2 *literary* to develop in a very successful way SYN **flourish**: *the economic and social conditions that will allow democracy to flower*

ˈflower arˌranging *n* [U] the skill of arranging flowers in an attractive way

flow·er·bed /ˈflaʊəbed $ -ər-/ *n* [C] an area of ground, for example in a garden, in which flowers are grown

ˈflower child *n* (*plural* **flower children**) [C] a young person in the 1960s and 70s who was against war and wanted peace and love in society

flow·ered /ˈflaʊəd $ -ərd/ *adj* decorated with a pattern of flowers SYN **floral, flowery**: *a flowered silk dress*

ˈflower girl *n* [C] *AmE* a young girl who carries flowers at a wedding ceremony

flow·er·ing /ˈflaʊərɪŋ/ *n* **the flowering of sth** *formal* when something develops in a very successful way: *The 19th century saw a flowering of science and technology.*

flow·er·pot /ˈflaʊəpɒt $ -ərpɑːt/ *n* [C] a plastic or clay pot in which you grow plants → see pictures at POT¹, GARDEN

ˈflower ˌpower *n* [U] the ideas of young people in the

F

1960s and 70s who believed that peace and love were the most important things in life

flow·er·y /ˈflaʊəri/ *adj* **1** decorated with a pattern of flowers SYN **floral**, **flowered**: *a flowery cotton dress* **2** a flowery place has a lot of flowers growing in it: *a flowery meadow* **3** a flowery smell or taste is strong and sweet, like flowers: *her flowery perfume* **4** flowery speech or writing uses complicated and rare words instead of simple clear language: *flowery language*

flow·ing /ˈfləʊɪŋ $ ˈfloʊ-/ *adj* **1** hanging or moving in a smooth graceful way: *She had pale skin and dark, flowing hair.* | *long, flowing robes* **2** continuing in a smooth graceful way, with no sudden changes: *a flowing melody* | *flowing curves*

flown /fləʊn $ floʊn/ *v* the past participle of FLY[1]

fl oz *BrE*, **fl. oz.** *AmE* the written abbreviation of ***fluid ounce*** or fluid ounces

flu /fluː/ ●●● S2 *n* [U] a common illness that makes you feel very tired and weak, gives you a sore throat, and makes you cough and have to clear your nose a lot SYN **influenza**: *Steven's still **in bed with flu**.* | *She's **got the flu**.* | *I couldn't go because I **had flu**.* | ***a flu virus/bug** the spread of the flu virus* | *Doctors now fear a **flu epidemic**.*

flub /flʌb/ *v* (**flubbed**, **flubbing**) [T] *AmE informal* to make a mistake or do something badly SYN **fluff**, **mess sth ↔ up**: *Several of the actors flubbed their lines.*

fluc·tu·ate /ˈflʌktʃueɪt/ ●○○ AWL *v* [I] if a price or amount fluctuates, it keeps changing and becoming higher and lower SYN **vary**: **[+between]** *Prices were volatile, fluctuating between $20 and $40.* | **[+around]** *The number of children in the school fluctuates around 100.* | *Insect populations **fluctuate wildly** from year to year.*

fluc·tu·a·tion /ˌflʌktʃuˈeɪʃən/ ●○○ AWL *n* [C,U] a change in a price, amount, level etc SYN **variation**: **[+in]** *the fluctuation in interest rates* | *Prices are subject to fluctuation.*

flue /fluː/ *n* [C] a metal pipe or tube that lets smoke or heat from a fire out of a building

flu·ent /ˈfluːənt/ ●●○ *adj*
1 able to speak a language very well: **[+in]** *She was fluent in English, French, and German.*
2 fluent French/Japanese etc someone who speaks fluent French etc speaks it like a person from that country: *He spoke in fluent Italian.*
3 fluent speech or writing is smooth and confident, with no mistakes: *He was a fluent and rapid prose writer.*
4 fluent movements are smooth and gentle, not sudden and sharp: *She rose with the fluent movement of an athlete.*
—**fluently** *adv*: *He spoke French fluently.* —**fluency** *n* [U]

fluff¹ /flʌf/ *n* [U] **1** soft light bits of thread that have come from wool, cotton, or other materials: *He was picking bits of fluff off his trousers.* | *a ball of carpet fluff* **2** soft light hair or feathers, especially on a young bird or animal: *The chicks were just balls of yellow fluff.* **3** news, music, writing, work etc that is not serious or important: *a magazine full of pop and fashion fluff*

fluff² *v* [T] **1** *informal* to make a mistake or do something badly SYN **mess sth ↔ up**: *He fluffed his shot and missed the goal.* | *She fluffed her lines in the first scene.* **2** (*also* **fluff sth ↔ up/out**) to make something soft become larger by shaking it: *She fluffed up the pillows for me.* **3** (*also* **fluff sth ↔ up/out**) if a bird fluffs its feathers, it raises them and makes itself look bigger

fluff·y /ˈflʌfi/ *adj* **1** very light and soft to touch: *a fluffy little kitten* | *fluffy towels* **2** food that is fluffy is made soft and light by mixing it quickly so that a lot of air is mixed into it: *Cream the butter and sugar until the mixture is light and fluffy.* **3** fluffy clouds look light and soft **4** not serious or important: *Her new book is a fluffy romantic fantasy.*

FLOWERS

flu·id[1] /ˈfluːɪd/ ●●○ *n* [C,U] *technical* a liquid → **gas**, **solid**: *He is not allowed solid food yet, only fluids.* | *a powerful cleaning fluid*

fluid[2] *adj* **1** a situation that is fluid is likely to change **2** fluid movements are smooth, relaxed, and graceful: *a loose, fluid style of dancing* **3** a fluid substance is a liquid —**fluidity** /fluˈɪdəti/ *n* [U] → **gaseous**, **solid**

ˌfluid ˈounce *n* [C] (*written abbreviation* **fl oz**) a unit for measuring liquid, equal to 1/20 PINT or 0.028 litres in Britain, and 1/16 pint or 0.030 litres in the US

fluke /fluːk/ *n* [C] *informal* something good that happens because of luck: *He agreed that the second goal was a fluke.* —**fluky, flukey** *adj*: *a fluky win*

flume /fluːm/ *n* [C] a long narrow structure built for water to slide down, which is used to move water or wood, or which people slide down for fun: *a log flume*

flum·moxed /ˈflʌməkst/ *adj* completely confused by something SYN **bewildered**: *I was completely flummoxed by the whole thing.* —**flummox** *v* [T]

flung /flʌŋ/ the past tense and past participle of FLING[1]

flunk /flʌŋk/ *v informal especially AmE* **1** [I,T] to fail a test: *Tony flunked chemistry last semester.* **2** [T] to give someone low marks on a test so that they fail it SYN **fail**: *She hadn't done the work so I flunked her.*

flunk out *phr v informal especially AmE* to be forced to leave a school or college because your work is not good enough: **[+of]** *Ben flunked out of college.*

flun·key, **flunky** /ˈflʌŋki/ *n* [C] *informal* someone who does small jobs for an important person, especially someone who does this because they are trying to please the person – used to show disapproval: *One of his flunkeys let me in.*

flu·o·res·cent /flʊəˈresənt $ flʊ-, flɔː-/ *adj* **1** fluorescent colours are very bright and easy to see, even in the dark: *a fluorescent pink T-shirt* **2** a fluorescent light contains a tube filled with gas, which shines with a bright light when electricity is passed through it —**fluorescence** *n* [U]

flu·o·ri·date /ˈflʊərədeɪt $ ˈflʊr-,ˈflɔːr-/ *v* [T] to add fluoride to the water supply —**fluoridation** /ˌflʊərəˈdeɪʃən $ ˌflʊr-, ˌflɔːr-/ *n* [U]

flu·o·ride /ˈflʊəraɪd $ -ˈflʊr-/ *n* [U] a chemical which is believed to help protect teeth against decay

flu·o·rine /ˈflʊəriːn $ ˈflʊr-/ *n* [U] a chemical substance that is usually in the form of a poisonous pale yellow gas. It is a chemical ELEMENT: symbol F

fluo·ro·car·bon /ˌflʊərəʊˈkɑːbən $ ˌflʊroʊˈkɑːr-/ *n* [C] any chemical that contains fluorine and CARBON: *the problem of pollution from fluorocarbons* → **CFC**

flur·ried /ˈflʌrid $ ˈflɜːrid/ *adj* confused and nervous or excited SYN **flustered**: *Jack never seemed to be flurried, even when they were very busy.*

flur·ry /ˈflʌri $ ˈflɜːri/ *n* (*plural* **flurries**) **1** [singular] a time when there is suddenly a lot of activity and people are very busy: **[+of]** *After a quiet spell there was a sudden flurry of phone calls.* | *The day started with a* ***flurry of activity***. **2** [C] a small amount of snow or rain that is blown by the wind: **[+of]** *He opens the door and a flurry of snow blows in.* | *Snow flurries are expected overnight.*

flush[1] /flʌʃ/ ●○○ *v*

1 BECOME RED [I] to become red in the face, for example when you are angry or embarrassed SYN **blush**: *Susan* ***flushed deeply*** *and looked away.* | *He* ***flushed angrily***. | **flush red/crimson/scarlet** *Robyn felt her cheeks flush scarlet.* | **[+with]** *Mrs Cooper flushed with indignation.*

2 TOILET [I,T] if you flush a toilet, or if it flushes, you make water go through it to clean it: *Why do children never remember to flush the loo?* | *She* ***flushed*** *the rest of her drink* ***down the toilet***.

3 CLEAN STH [T] to force water through a pipe in order to clean it: **flush sth through sth** *They flush clean water through the pipes once a day.*

flush sb/sth ↔ **out** *phr v*

1 to make someone leave a place where they are hiding: *The government is determined to flush out the terrorists.*

2 to clean something by forcing water through it: *The heating system needs to be flushed out once a year.* | *Drinking water helps flush out toxins from the body.*

flush[2] *n*

1 REDNESS ON FACE [singular] a red colour that appears on your face when you are angry or embarrassed SYN **blush**: *His words brought a warm flush to her face.* → **HOT FLUSH**

2 FEELINGS **a flush of anger/embarrassment/excitement etc** a sudden feeling of anger, embarrassment etc SYN **surge**: *She felt a sudden flush of anger.*

3 TOILET [C] **a)** the part of a toilet that cleans it with a sudden flow of water: *The flush isn't working properly.* **b)** the act of cleaning a toilet by forcing water through it

4 CARDS [C] a set of cards that someone has in a card game that are all of the same SUIT

5 the first flush of youth/manhood the beginning of a period of time when you are young etc: *a group of adolescent boys in the first flush of manhood*

6 a flush of sth a large number of things that happen or arrive at the same time: *The spring brings a flush of young animals to the farm.*

flush[3] *adj* **1** if two surfaces are flush, they are at exactly the same level, so that the place where they meet is flat: **[+with]** *Make sure that the cupboard is flush with the wall.* **2** [not before noun] *informal* if someone is flush, they have plenty of money to spend: *I'm feeling flush at the moment.*

flushed /flʌʃt/ *adj* **1** red in the face: *He looked hot and rather flushed.* | *Her* ***cheeks*** *were* ***flushed***, *her expression angry.* | **[+with]** *He leaned forward, his face flushed with anger.* **2 flushed with success/excitement/pleasure etc** excited because you have achieved something: *The team are still flushed with success after their weekend victory.*

flus·ter[1] /ˈflʌstə $ -ər/ *v* [T] to make someone nervous and confused by making them hurry or interrupting them: *Don't fluster me, or I'll never be ready on time.*

fluster[2] *n BrE* **in a fluster** nervous and confused because you are trying to do things quickly

flus·tered /ˈflʌstəd $ -ərd/ *adj* confused and nervous: *Paul was looking flustered and embarrassed.* | *I always get flustered in interviews.*

flute /fluːt/ ●●○ *n* [C]

1 a musical instrument like a thin pipe, that you play by holding it across your lips, blowing over a hole, and pressing down buttons with your fingers → **flautist** → see picture at **WOODWIND**

2 a tall narrow glass, used especially for drinking CHAMPAGNE → see picture at **GLASS**[1]

flut·ed /ˈfluːtɪd/ *adj* something that is fluted has hollow or rounded lines down it: *fluted stone columns*

flut·ist /ˈfluːtɪst/ *n* [C] *AmE* someone who plays the flute SYN **flautist** *BrE*

flut·ter[1] /ˈflʌtə $ -ər/ ●○○ *v*

1 [I,T] if a bird or insect flutters, or if it flutters its wings, it flies by moving its wings lightly up and down: *A small bird fluttered past the window.*

2 [I] to make small gentle movements in the air: *Dead leaves fluttered slowly to the ground.* | *The flag fluttered in the light breeze.*

3 [I] if your heart or your stomach flutters, you feel very excited or nervous

4 [I] if your eyelids flutter, they move slightly when you are asleep: *Her eyelids fluttered but did not open.*

5 flutter your eyelashes (at sb) if a woman flutters her eyelashes at a man, she looks at him and moves her eyes to make herself attractive to him

flutter[2] *n* [singular] **1** a feeling of being nervous, confused, or excited: **in a flutter** *She was all in a flutter.* | *His sudden resignation caused quite a flutter.* **2 a flutter of sth** a sudden feeling that is not very strong: *She felt a flutter of curiosity.* **3** a light gentle movement: **[+of]** *a flutter of wings* **4 have a flutter** *BrE informal* to risk a small amount of money on the result of something such as a horse race SYN **have a bet**

flu·vi·al /ˈfluːviəl/ *adj technical* relating to rivers or caused by rivers

flux /flʌks/ *n* [U] a situation in which things are changing a lot and you cannot be sure what will happen: *Everything is in flux at the moment.* | *The education system is still* ***in a state of flux***.

fly¹ /flaɪ/ ●●● S1 W1 *v* (*past tense* **flew** /fluː/, *past participle* **flown** /fləʊn $ floʊn/)
1 TRAVEL BY PLANE [I] to travel by plane: *She's flying back to the States tomorrow.* | *Will you take the train there or fly?* | *Maurice is nervous about flying, so he usually travels overland.* | **[+to]** *The prime minister will be flying to Delhi later today for a three-day visit.* | **[+from/out of/in etc]** *He was arrested at Heathrow after flying from Brussels airport.* | *Lewis stopped off in Jamaica before flying on to Toronto.*
2 MOVE THROUGH THE AIR [I] if a plane, spacecraft etc flies, it moves through the air: *The plane was attacked as it flew over restricted airspace.*
3 CONTROL A PLANE [I,T] to be at the controls of a plane and direct it as it flies: *She was the first woman to fly Concorde.* | *The pilot was instructed to fly the plane to Montreal airport.* | *Sonny learnt to fly when he was 15.*
4 SEND SB/STH BY PLANE [T] to take goods or people somewhere by plane: *The injured boy was flown by air ambulance to the Royal London Hospital.* | **fly sth into/out of etc sth** *US planes have been flying food and medical supplies into the area.* THESAURUS ▸ TAKE
5 USE AIR COMPANY/SERVICE [I,T] to use a particular AIRLINE or use a particular type of ticket when you travel by plane: *We usually fly economy class.* | *Millions of passengers fly British Airways every year.*
6 CROSS SEA BY PLANE [T] to cross a particular ocean or area of sea in a plane: *Who was the first person to fly the Atlantic?*
7 BIRDS/INSECTS [I] to move through the air using wings: *The mother bird will feed her chicks until they are able to fly.* | *The evening air was clouded with mosquitoes and other flying insects.* | **[+away/off/in etc]** *At that moment, a wasp flew in through the open window.* | *The robin shook its feathers and flew away.*
8 MOVE SOMEWHERE QUICKLY [I] **a)** to move somewhere quickly and suddenly: **[+down/across/out of etc]** *Ellen flew across the room and greeted her uncle with a kiss.* | *Rachel's hand flew to her mouth.* | **[+open/shut]** *The door flew open and a child rushed out.* **b)** to move quickly and suddenly through the air: *There was a loud explosion, and suddenly there was glass flying everywhere.* | *William hit Jack on the head and* ***sent*** *his glasses* ***flying***. | *The ball bounced off the wall and* ***went flying*** *into the garden next door.*
9 KITE [T] to make a KITE fly in the air: *In the park people were walking their dogs or flying their kites.*
10 (I) must fly *spoken* used to say that you must leave quickly
11 MOVE FREELY [I] to move freely and loosely in the air: *Harriet ran after him, her hair flying behind her.*
12 FLAG [I,T] if a flag flies, or if you fly it, it is fixed to the top of a tall pole so that it can be easily seen: *After the invasion, people were forbidden to fly their national flag.* | *The flags were flying cheerfully in the breeze.* | *The government ordered that all flags should be flown* ***at half mast*** (=halfway down the pole, in order to express public sadness at someone's death).
13 fly the flag to behave in a way that shows that you are proud of your country, organization etc
14 time flies (*also* **the hours/the days etc fly**) used to say that a period of time seems to pass very quickly: *'Is it midnight already?' 'Well, you know what they say –* ***time flies when you're having fun!***' | **[+by]** *The following weeks flew by, and soon it was time to leave.*
15 fly into a rage/temper/panic etc to suddenly get extremely angry, extremely worried etc: *Rebecca flew into a rage when she realized no-one had been listening to her.*
16 fly off the handle *informal* to suddenly get very angry: *Calm down – there's no need to fly off the handle.*
17 let fly (sth) a) to suddenly start shouting angrily at someone SYN **let loose**: *The prisoner let fly with a torrent of abuse.* **b)** to suddenly attack someone, especially with bullets or a weapon that is thrown: **[+with]** *The soldiers let fly with a hail of machine-gun fire.*
18 fly in the face of sth to be the opposite of what most people think is reasonable, sensible, or normal: *He likes to fly in the face of convention.*
19 ESCAPE [T] *formal* to leave somewhere in order to escape SYN **flee**: *By the time the police arrived, the men had flown.*
20 be flying high to be having a lot of success: *The architectural firm has been flying high recently.*
21 fly the nest a) if a young bird flies the nest, it has grown old enough to look after itself and is no longer dependent on its parents **b)** if a young person flies the nest, he or she moves out of their parents' home in order to live independently: *Now that the kids have flown the nest, I'm thinking about taking a job abroad.*
22 PLAN [I] *AmE* a plan that will fly will be successful and useful: *News is that the plan for the new hotel isn't* ***going to fly***.
23 fly a kite to tell people about an idea, plan etc in order to get their opinion: *In my latest book, I wanted to fly the kite for an unfashionable theory.* → KITE-FLYING(2)
24 go fly a kite *AmE spoken* used to tell someone to go away, stop saying something, or stop annoying you
25 rumours/accusations etc are flying when a lot of people are talking about something, saying someone has done something wrong etc: *Rumours were flying as to how the fire started.*
26 fly the coop *AmE informal* to leave or escape: *All my children have flown the coop now.*
27 fly by the seat of your pants *informal* to have to deal with a situation by guessing what to do, because you know very little about it SYN **wing it**: *Sometimes you'll get back and find that things have changed, so you'll be flying by the seat of your pants for a while.* → **the bird has flown** at BIRD(8), → **as the crow flies** at CROW¹(3), → **sparks fly** at SPARK¹(6)

GRAMMAR

Fly belongs to a group of verbs where the same noun can be the subject of the verb or its object.
• You can say: *He flew the plane across the desert.* In this sentence, 'the plane' is the object of **fly**.
• You can say: *The plane flew across the desert.* In this sentence, 'the plane' is the subject of **fly**.
GRAMMAR GUIDE ▸ VERBS

fly at sb (*also* **fly into sb**) *AmE phr v* to suddenly rush towards someone and try to hit them because you are very angry with them

fly² ●●● S3 W3 *n* (*plural* **flies**) [C]
1 INSECT a small flying insect with two wings: *There were flies buzzing all around us.* → see picture at INSECT
2 TROUSERS *especially AmE* (*also* **flies** [plural] *BrE*) the part at the front of a pair of trousers which you can open: *He quickly did up his fly.* | *Your flies are undone.*
3 sb wouldn't hurt/harm a fly *informal* used to say that someone is very gentle and is not likely to hurt anyone
4 be dying/dropping etc like flies *informal* used to say that a lot of people are dying or becoming ill
5 a fly in the ointment *informal* the only thing that spoils something and prevents it from being successful: *The only fly in the ointment was Jacky.*
6 be a fly on the wall to be able to watch what happens without other people knowing that you are there: *I wish I'd been a fly on the wall during that conversation.* → FLY-ON-THE-WALL
7 there are no flies on sb *BrE spoken* used to say that someone is not stupid and cannot be tricked
8 on the fly a) *technical* while a computer program is actually running: *The code is translated on the fly.* **b)** while dealing with a situation, rather than before dealing with it: *So far, policy is being made on the fly.*
9 FISHING a hook that is made to look like a fly and is used for catching fish → see picture at FISHING
10 BASEBALL a fly ball

fly³ *v* (**flied**, **flying**, **flies**) [I] to hit a ball in baseball high into the air

fly⁴ *adj* **1** *informal* very fashionable and attractive: *Wear something really fly for your Friday date.* **2** *BrE old-fashioned* clever and not easily tricked: *He's a bit of a fly character.*

fly·a·way /ˈflaɪəweɪ/ *adj* **flyaway hair** hair that is soft and thin and becomes untidy easily

ˈfly ball *n* [C] a ball that has been hit high into the air in a game of BASEBALL

fly·blown /ˈflaɪbləʊn $ -bloʊn/ *adj BrE* **1** old, dirty, and in bad condition **2** meat that is flyblown has flies' eggs in it and is not suitable for eating

fly·boy /ˈflaɪbɔɪ/ *n* [C] *AmE informal* someone who flies a plane, especially in the US ARMED FORCES → **pilot**

fly·by /ˈflaɪbaɪ/ *n* (*plural* **flybys**) [C] an occasion when a spacecraft flies close to a PLANET etc in order to gather information about it

ˈfly-by-ˌnight *adj* [only before noun] *informal* a fly-by-night company or businessman is one that you cannot trust because they have only been in business for a short time and are only interested in making quick profits

ˈfly-by-ˌwire *n* [U] a system in an aircraft which uses computers and electrical signals to help control the aircraft

fly·catch·er /ˈflaɪˌkætʃə $ -ər/ *n* [C] a type of small bird that catches flies and other insects in the air

ˌfly-drive ˈholiday *n* [C] a holiday arranged at a fixed price that includes your flight to a place, a car to drive while you are there, and a place to stay

fly·er, **flier** /ˈflaɪə $ -ər/ *n* [C] **1** a small sheet of paper advertising something: *People were giving out flyers advertising the event.* **THESAURUS** ▸ **ADVERTISEMENT** **2** *informal* a pilot: *She was one of the first solo flyers.* **3** someone who travels in an aircraft: *Delays are familiar to all regular flyers.*

fly·fish·ing /ˈflaɪˌfɪʃɪŋ/ *n* [U] the sport of fishing in a river or lake with special hooks that are made to look like flies

ˌfly ˈhalf *n* [C] a player in a game of RUGBY. A fly half has to be able to run quickly.

fly·ing¹ /ˈflaɪ-ɪŋ/ *adj* **1** [only before noun] able to fly SYN **winged**: *a story about a flying horse* **2 with flying colours** if you pass a test with flying colours, you are very successful in it **3 a flying visit** a quick visit because you do not have much time **4 a flying start** a very good or successful start: *The appeal has **got off to a flying start**, with over £200,000 raised in the first week.* **5 a flying jump/leap** a long high jump made while you are running: *He **took a flying leap** and just managed to clear the stream.*

flying² *n* [U] the activity of travelling by plane: *Quite a lot of people are still nervous about flying.*

ˌflying ˈbuttress *n* [C] a curved line of stones or bricks that are joined to the outside wall of a large building such as a church, and help to support it

ˌflying ˈdoctor *n* [C] a doctor, especially in Australia, who goes by plane to visit sick people who live a long way from the nearest town

ˌflying ˈfish *n* [C] a type of sea fish that can jump out of the water and move along in the air for a short way

ˌflying ˈfox *n* [C] a type of BAT that lives in hot countries and eats fruit

ˈflying ˌofficer *n* [C] an officer in the British air force

ˌflying ˈpicket *n* [C] someone who travels to different factories during a STRIKE and tries to persuade workers to stop working

ˌflying ˈsaucer *n* [C] a large round spacecraft from somewhere else in space, that some people believe they have seen in the sky → **UFO**

ˈflying squad *n* [C] a special group of police officers in Britain whose job is to travel quickly to the place where there has been a serious crime: *the head of Scotland Yard's Flying Squad*

ˌflying ˈtackle *n* [C] a way of stopping someone from running by putting your arms around their legs and making them fall over

ˈfly leaf *n* [C] a page at the beginning or end of a book, on which there is no printing

ˌfly-on-the-ˈwall *adj* [only before noun] a fly-on-the-wall television programme shows people's daily lives in a very natural way, because they forget that they are being filmed → **be a fly on the wall** at FLY²(6)

fly·o·ver /ˈflaɪ-əʊvə $ -oʊvər/ *n* [C] **1** *BrE* a bridge that takes one road over another road SYN **overpass** *AmE* → see picture at **BRIDGE¹** **2** *AmE* a flight by a group of planes on a special occasion for people to watch SYN **flypast** *BrE*

ˈflyover ˌcountry *n* [U] the middle part of the US, considered as a place that rich, famous, or fashionable people living on the East or West coast of America would never visit, but which they often fly over on journeys to the other coast – used humorously: *I feel happy at 20,000 feet, approaching flyover country, far above that wasteland between Manhattan and California.*

fly·pa·per /ˈflaɪˌpeɪpə $ -ər/ *n* [C,U] paper covered with a sticky substance that is hung up in a room in order to catch flies

fly·past /ˈflaɪpɑːst $ -pæst/ *n* [C] *BrE* a flight by a group of planes on a special occasion for people to watch SYN **flyover** *AmE*

fly·sheet /ˈflaɪʃiːt/ (*also* **fly**) *n* [C] a sheet of material that is put over a tent to protect it from the rain

fly·swat·ter /ˈflaɪˌswɒtə $ -ˌswɑːtər/ *n* [C] a piece of plastic that you use for hitting and killing flies

ˈfly-ˌtipping *n* [U] the crime of putting waste material or unwanted things on land somewhere, for example beside a road, rather than taking them to an official place for waste

fly·weight /ˈflaɪweɪt/ *n* [C] a BOXER who weighs less than 50.80 kilograms, and who is heavier than a STRAWWEIGHT but lighter than a BANTAMWEIGHT

fly·wheel /ˈflaɪwiːl/ *n* [C] a heavy wheel that keeps a machine working at a steady speed

FM /ˌef ˈem◂/ *n* [U] (***frequency modulation***) a system used for broadcasting radio programmes → **AM**

FO, the /ˌef ˈəʊ $ -ˈoʊ/ (*also* **the FCO**) (***the Foreign Office***) the British government department responsible for foreign affairs. It is officially called the Foreign and Commonwealth Office.

foal¹ /fəʊl $ foʊl/ *n* [C] a young horse → **colt, filly**

foal² *v* [I] to give birth to a foal

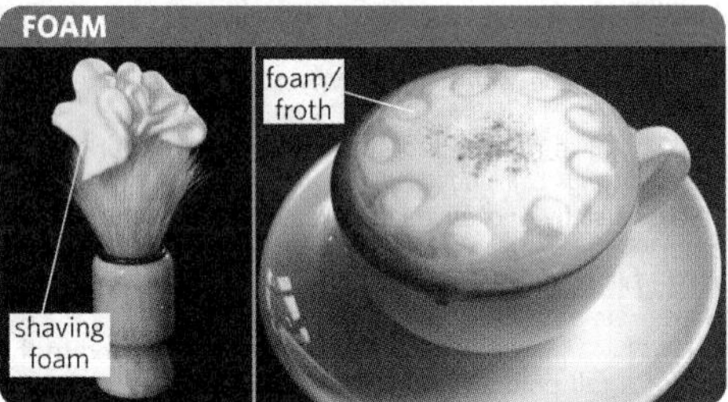

foam¹ /fəʊm $ foʊm/ ●○○ *n* [U]
1 (*also* **foam rubber**) a type of soft rubber with a lot of air in it, used in furniture: *a foam mattress*
2 a mass of very small bubbles on the surface of a liquid SYN **froth**: *The sea was covered in foam.*
3 a substance which is like a very thick soft liquid with a lot of bubbles in it: *Firefighters using water and foam are still tackling the blaze.* | *shaving foam* —**foamy** *adj*

foam² *v* [I] **1** to produce foam: *The green water splashed and foamed over the rocks.* **2 be foaming at the mouth a)** to have bubbles coming out of your mouth because you are very ill **b)** *informal* to be very angry

fob¹ /fɒb $ fɑːb/ *v* (**fobbed, fobbing**) *informal*

fob sb ↔ **off** *phr v* **1** to tell someone something that is not true in order to stop them from complaining: **[+with]** *She fobbed him off with a promise to pay him the money next week.* **2** to give someone something that is not very good instead of the thing they really want: **[+with]** *They tried to fob me off with a cheap camera.*

fob² *n* [C] a small object that is fixed to a key ring as a decoration

ˈ**fob watch** *n* [C] a watch that fits into a pocket, or is pinned to a woman's dress

fo·cac·ci·a /fəʊˈkætʃiə $ foʊˈkɑːtʃə/ *n* [U] a type of Italian bread

fo·cal /ˈfəʊkəl $ ˈfoʊ-/ *adj* [only before noun] the focal thing is the one that people pay most attention to → **focus**: *This issue has now become the focal centre of interest.*

ˈ**focal length** *n* [C] *technical* the distance between the centre of a lens and the focal point

ˈ**focal point** *n* [C] **1** the person or thing that you pay most attention to: **[+of]** *The pool is the focal point of the hotel.* | **[+for]** *The new tax has been the focal point for much discussion.* **2** *technical* the point at which beams of light meet after they have been through a LENS

fo'c'sle /ˈfəʊksəl $ ˈfoʊ-/ *n* [C] *BrE* the front part of a ship, where the sailors live SYN **forecastle** *AmE*

fo·cus¹ /ˈfəʊkəs $ ˈfoʊ-/ ●●○ S3 W2 AWL *v* (**focused** *or* **focussed**, **focusing** *or* **focussing**)

1 GIVE ATTENTION TO STH [I,T] to give special attention to one particular person or thing, or to make people do this SYN **concentrate**: **[+on]** *He needs to focus more on his career.* | **focus your attention/mind/efforts on sth** *She tried to focus her mind on her work.* | **focus (sb's) mind/attention (on sth)** (=make people give their attention to something) *We need to focus public attention on this issue.*

2 CAMERA/TELESCOPE [I,T] to point a camera or TELESCOPE at something, and change the controls slightly so that you can see that thing clearly: **[+on]** *She turned the camera and focussed on Martin's face.* | **focus sth on sth** *He focused his binoculars on the building opposite.*

3 EYES [I,T] if your eyes focus, or if you focus your eyes, you look at something and can see it clearly: **[+on]** *All eyes focussed on her.* | *His eyes were focussed straight ahead.*

4 LIGHT [T] if you focus beams of light, you aim them onto a particular place

focus² ●●○ S3 W2 AWL *n*

1 [singular] the thing, person, situation etc that people pay special attention to → **focal**: *The* **focus** *of recent research has* **been on** *environmental issues.* | **[+of]** *The war in Afghanistan had become* **the focus of** *media* **attention**. | **The focus of interest** *in the series is what goes on in everyday life.* | *Another* **focus of** *feminist* **debate** *has been the film industry.* | *I shall now turn to the* **main focus of** *this essay.* | *Eggs* **became the focus for** *the food poisoning scare.* | **The focus** *of the conference* **shifted from** *population growth to the education of women.*

2 [U] if your focus is on something, that is the thing you are giving most attention to: **[+on]** *Our main focus is on helping people get back into work.* | *a* **shift of focus**

3 come into focus/bring sth into focus if something comes into focus, or you bring it into focus, people start to talk about it and pay attention to it: *These issues have recently come into* **sharp focus** (=people have started to talk about them a lot).

4 in focus/out of focus if a photograph or an instrument such as a camera is in focus, you can see the picture clearly. If it is out of focus, you cannot see the picture clearly.

5 [U] the clearness of the picture seen through an instrument such as a camera: *He raised his binoculars and adjusted the focus.*

ˈ**focus group** *n* [C] a small group of people that a company, political party etc asks questions in order to find out what they think of their products, actions etc

fo·cussed *BrE*, **focused** *AmE* /ˈfəʊkəst $ ˈfoʊ-/ ●○○ AWL *adj* paying careful attention to what you are doing, in a way that shows you are determined to succeed: *I've got to stay focussed if I want to win this competition.*

fod·der /ˈfɒdə $ ˈfɑːdər/ *n* [U] **1** food for farm animals **2** something or someone that is useful only for a particular purpose – used to show disapproval: **[+for]** *The murders made prime fodder for newspapers.* → **CANNON FODDER**

foe /fəʊ $ foʊ/ *n* [C] *literary* an enemy: *Britain's friends and foes*

foe·tal, **fetal** /ˈfiːtl/ *adj* [only before noun] belonging or related to a foetus: *a test to detect foetal abnormalities*

ˈ**foetal poˌsition** *n* [C] the body position of an unborn child inside its mother, in which the body is curled and the legs are pulled up against the chest

foe·tus, **fetus** /ˈfiːtəs/ *n* [C] a baby or young animal before it is born → **embryo**

fog¹ /fɒg $ fɑːg, fɔːg/ ●●● S3 W3 *n*

1 [C,U] cloudy air near the ground which is difficult to see through SYN **mist**: **thick/dense/freezing fog** *We got lost in the thick fog.* | *It will be a cold night, and there may be* **fog patches**. | *A* **blanket of fog** *covered the fields.* | *The* **fog lifted** (=disappeared) *in the afternoon.*

2 [singular] *informal* a state in which you feel confused and cannot think clearly: *My mind was* **in a fog**. | **[+of]** *the fog of tiredness*

fog² *v* (**fogged**, **fogging**) **1** [I,T] (*also* **fog up**) if something made of glass fogs or becomes fogged, it becomes covered in small drops of water that make it difficult to see through SYN **mist up**, **steam up**: *The windscreen had fogged up.* **2** [T] to make something less clear SYN **cloud**

fog·bound /ˈfɒgbaʊnd $ ˈfɑːg-, ˈfɔːg-/ *adj* unable to travel or work normally because of fog: *The airport was fogbound.*

fo·gey, **fogy** /ˈfəʊgi $ ˈfoʊ-/ *n* (*plural* **fogeys** *or* **fogies**) [C] someone who has old-fashioned ideas and does not like change: *You're turning into a real* **old fogey**!

fog·gy /ˈfɒgi $ ˈfɑːgi, ˈfɔːgi/ ●●● S3 *adj*

1 if the weather is foggy, there is fog: *a foggy day in November* | *driving in foggy conditions*

2 not have the foggiest (idea) *spoken* to not know at all: *None of us had the foggiest idea about how to put the tent up.*

3 if your mind is foggy, you cannot think or remember things clearly

fog·horn /ˈfɒghɔːn $ ˈfɑːghɔːrn, ˈfɔːg-/ *n* [C] **1** a loud horn on a ship, used in fog to warn other ships of its position **2 a voice like a foghorn** *informal* a very loud unpleasant voice

ˈ**fog lamp** *BrE*, ˈ**fog light** *AmE* *n* [C] a strong light on the front of a car that helps drivers to see when there is FOG → see picture at **CAR**

foi·ble /ˈfɔɪbəl/ *n* [C] a small weakness or strange habit that someone has, which does not harm anyone else SYN **peculiarity**: *We all have our* **little foibles**.

foie gras /ˌfwɑː ˈgrɑː/ *n* [U] a smooth food made from the LIVER of a GOOSE

foil¹ /fɔɪl/ ●○○ *n*

1 [U] metal sheets that are as thin as paper, used for wrapping food: **silver/aluminium/kitchen foil** *Cover the chicken with silver foil and bake.* → **TINFOIL**

2 [U] paper that is covered with very thin sheets of metal: *chocolates in foil wrappers*

3 be a foil to/for sb/sth to emphasize the good qualities of another person or thing, by being very different from them: *The simple stone floor is the* **perfect foil** *for the brightly coloured furnishings.*

4 [C] a light narrow sword used in FENCING

foil² *v* [T] to prevent something bad that someone is planning to do: *A massive arms-smuggling plan has been foiled by the CIA.*

foist /fɔɪst/ *v*

foist sth **on/upon** sb *phr v* to force someone to accept or have to deal with something that they do not want: *I keep getting extra work foisted on me.*

F

FOLD

fold your arms fold clothes

fold¹ /fəʊld $ foʊld/ ●●○ W3 *v*
1 BEND [T] to bend a piece of paper, cloth etc by laying or pressing one part over another: *Fold the paper along the dotted line.* | *It'll fit in if you* **fold** *it* **in half**. | **fold sth over/under/down etc** *Spoon the filling onto the dough, fold it over, and press down the edges.*
2 SMALLER/NEATER [T] (*also* **fold up**) to fold something several times so that it makes a small neat shape → **unfold**: *I wish you kids would fold up your clothes!* | *He folded the map neatly.*
3 FURNITURE ETC [I,T] if something such as a piece of furniture folds, or you fold it, you make it smaller or move it to a different position by bending it: *The chairs fold flat for storage.* | **fold (sth) away/up/down etc** *a useful little bed that folds away when you don't need it* | *Can you fold the shutters back?* → FOLDING
4 fold your arms to bend your arms so that they rest together against your body: *George stood silently with his arms folded.*
5 BUSINESS [I] (*also* **fold up**) if an organization folds, it closes because it does not have enough money to continue
6 COVER [T always + adv/prep] to cover something, especially by wrapping it in material or putting your hand over it: **fold sth in sth** *a silver dagger folded in a piece of white cloth*
7 fold sb in your arms *literary* to hold someone closely by putting your arms around them
fold sth ↔ **in** (*also* **fold sth into sth**) *phr v* to gently mix another substance into a mixture when you are preparing food: *Next, fold in the sugar.*

fold² ●○○ *n* [C]
1 LINE a line made in paper or material when you fold one part of it over another: *Bend back the card and cut along the fold.*
2 SKIN/MATERIAL [usually plural] the folds in material, skin etc are the loose parts that hang over other parts of it: *Her dress* **hung in** *soft* **folds**.
3 the fold the group of people that you belong to and share the same beliefs and ideas as: **return to/come back into the fold** *The Church will welcome him back into the fold.* | **stray from/leave the fold** *a former advocate of free market economics who had strayed from the fold*
4 SHEEP a small area of a field surrounded by a wall or fence where sheep are kept for safety SYN **pen** → **corral**
5 ROCK *technical* a bend in layers of rock, caused by underground movements in the earth

-fold /fəʊld $ foʊld/ *suffix* **1** [in adjectives] of a particular number of kinds: *The government's role in health care is twofold: first, to provide the resources and, second, to make them work better for patients.* **2** [in adverbs] a particular number of times: *The value of the house has increased fourfold* (=it is now worth four times as much as before).

fold·a·way /ˈfəʊldəweɪ $ ˈfoʊld-/ *adj* [only before noun] a foldaway bed, table etc can be folded up so it uses less space → **folding**

fold·er /ˈfəʊldə $ ˈfoʊldər/ ●●● S2 W2 *n* [C]
1 a container for keeping loose papers in, made of folded card or plastic → see picture at STATIONERY
2 a group of related documents that you store together on a computer

fold·ing /ˈfəʊldɪŋ $ ˈfoʊl-/ *adj* [only before noun] a folding bicycle, bed, chair etc has parts that you can bend or fold together to make it easier to carry or store → **foldaway** → see picture at CHAIR¹

fo·li·age /ˈfəʊli-ɪdʒ $ ˈfoʊ-/ *n* [U] the leaves of a plant: *dark green foliage*

fo·lic acid /ˌfəʊlɪk ˈæsəd, ˌfɒ- $ ˌfoʊ-, ˌfɑː-/ *n* [U] a VITAMIN found especially in green vegetables, used by the body to produce red blood cells

fo·li·o /ˈfəʊliəʊ $ ˈfoʊlioʊ/ *n* (*plural* **folios**) [C] *technical* **1** a book made with very large sheets of paper **2** a single numbered sheet of paper from a book

folk¹ /fəʊk $ foʊk/ ●●● S2 W3 *n*
1 [plural] (*also* **folks**) *especially AmE* people: *I'm sure there are some folk who would rather they weren't here.* | *Thanks to the folks at NBC.* | *Wait till the folks back home hear about this!* | **young/old folk** *BrE old-fashioned*: *Young folk these days don't know the meaning of work.*
2 folks [plural] **a)** *especially AmE* your parents and family: *Is it OK if I call my folks?* **b)** used when talking to a group of people in a friendly way: *That's all for now, folks.*
3 country/farming etc folk [plural] (*also* **country etc folks** *AmE*) *literary* people who live in a particular area or do a particular kind of work: *simple country folk*
4 [U] FOLK MUSIC: *a folk singer*

folk² *adj* [only before noun] **1** folk art, stories, customs etc are traditional and typical of the ordinary people who live in a particular area: *folk tales* | *an Irish folk song* **2 folk science/psychology/wisdom etc** science etc that is based on the ideas or beliefs that ordinary people have, and does not involve a high level of technical knowledge **3 folk medicine/remedy** a traditional type of medical treatment that uses plants or simple treatments rather than scientific methods

ˈfolk dance *n* [C] a traditional dance from a particular area, or a piece of music for this dance —**folk dancer** *n* [C]

ˈfolk ˌhero *n* [C] someone who people in a particular place admire very much because of something they have done: *Casey Jones is an American folk hero.*

folk·lore /ˈfəʊklɔː $ ˈfoʊklɔːr/ *n* [U] the traditional stories, customs etc of a particular area or country

folk·lor·ist /ˈfəʊklɔːrɪst $ ˈfoʊk-/ *n* [C] someone who studies folklore

ˈfolk ˌmusic (*also* **folk**) *n* [U] **1** traditional music that has been played by ordinary people in a particular area for a long time **2** a style of popular music in which people sing and play GUITARS, without any electronic equipment

folk·sy /ˈfəʊksi $ ˈfoʊ-/ *adj informal* **1** *especially AmE* friendly and informal: *The town had a certain folksy charm.* **2** in a style that is typical of traditional countryside styles or customs

fol·li·cle /ˈfɒlɪkəl $ ˈfɑː-/ *n* [C] one of the small holes in the skin that hairs grow from

fol·low /ˈfɒləʊ $ ˈfɑːloʊ/ ●●● S1 W1 *v*
1 GO AFTER [I,T] to go, walk, drive etc behind or after someone else: *Are those men following us?* | *The patrol car followed the BMW for a few miles and then lost it.* | *Tom's already gone out to Rome and his wife and children will follow shortly.* | **follow sb into/to etc sth** *Peggy followed her out onto the landing.*
2 HAPPEN AFTER [I,T] to happen or do something after something else: *The agreement followed months of negotiation.* | *The assassination of Martin Luther King in 1968 was followed by that of Robert Kennedy.* | **there follows sth** *After weeks of intense fighting, there followed a brief*

FOLLOW

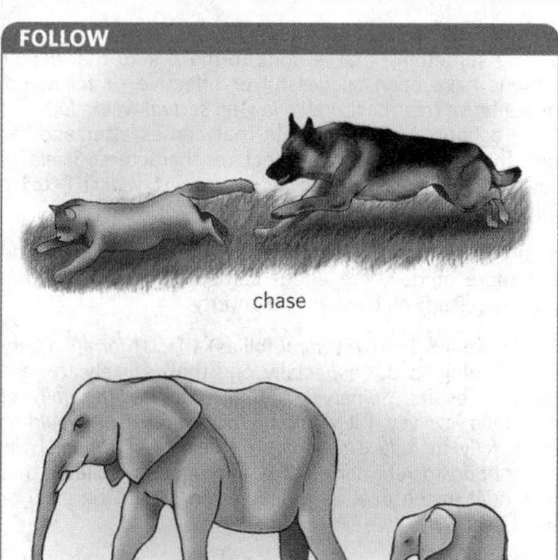

period of calm. | *Most EU countries have signed the agreement and the US is expected to* ***follow shortly*** (=soon). → FOLLOWING[3]

3 COME AFTER [I,T] to come directly after something else in a series, list, or order → **following**: *The chapters that follow deal mainly with mathematics.* | *In English, the letter Q is always followed by U.* | *We had vegetable casserole with a fruit salad to follow* (=as part of a meal). | **there follows sth** *There followed several pages of incomprehensible statistics.*

4 as follows used to introduce a list of things that you will mention next: *The winners are as follows: in third place, Mandy Johnson; in second place ...*

5 DO WHAT SB SAYS [T] to do something in the way that someone has told or advised you to do it: *He* ***followed*** *the doctor's* ***advice*** *and had no further trouble.* | ***Follow*** *the* ***instructions*** *very carefully when filling in the form.* | *They followed the plan that Elizabeth had worked out.*

6 follow the signs/sb's directions to go somewhere by a particular way according to road signs or to what someone has told you: *Just follow the signs for the airport.* | *I followed Brown's directions and found the farm quite easily.*

7 DO THE SAME THING [I,T] to do the same thing as someone else: *Some state schools* ***follow the example*** *of private schools in asking parents to donate money.* | *Environmentalists are urging the government to* ***follow the lead*** *of Scandinavian countries in this matter.* | *She's just like any young woman who enjoys following the latest fashions* (=wearing fashionable clothes). | **follow sb into sth** (=do the same job as someone else) *He does not want to follow his father into a scientific career.*

8 BELIEVE IN STH [T] to believe in and obey a particular set of religious or political ideas

9 GO IN PARTICULAR DIRECTION [T] **a)** to continue along a particular road, river etc: *I followed the main road up the mountain.* | *Tom followed the track that leads to the old Roman road.* **b)** to go in the same direction as something else, or to go parallel to something else: *The road follows the line of the river.*

10 UNDERSTAND [I,T] to understand something such as an explanation or story SYN **grasp**: *I didn't quite follow what he was saying.* | **easy/difficult/hard etc to follow** *The plot is a little difficult to follow.* THESAURUS ▶ UNDERSTAND

11 BE A RESULT [I] to be true as a result of something else that is true: **[+from]** *The conclusion that follows from these findings is that inner city schools need more investment, not less.* | ***It*** *doesn't necessarily* ***follow that*** *you're going to do well academically even if you're highly intelligent.*

12 BE INTERESTED [T] to be interested in something and in the way it develops: *Have you been following that crime series on TV?* | *I've been following his progress very closely.* | *She just doesn't understand people who follow football or any other kind of sport.*

13 follow a pattern/course/trend etc to continue to happen or develop in a particular way, especially in a way that is expected: *In Australia, the weather follows a fairly predictable pattern.*

14 follow suit to do the same as someone else has done: *Budget companies have been so successful that other airlines have had to follow suit and lower their fares.*

15 follow in sb's footsteps to do the same job or to work or live in the same way as someone else before you, especially someone in your family: *He is a doctor and expects his son to follow in his footsteps.*

16 BE ABOUT [T] to show or describe someone's life or a series of events, for example in a film or book: *The book follows the plight of an orphaned Irish girl who marries into New York society.*

17 be a hard act to follow to be so good or successful at something that it will be difficult for the next person, team etc to be as good: *We're looking for a replacement for Sue, but she's going to be a hard act to follow.*

18 WATCH CAREFULLY [T] to carefully watch someone do something: *She* ***followed*** *Simon* ***with*** *her* ***eyes*** *as he walked to the gate.*

19 THINK ABOUT/STUDY [T] to study or think about a particular idea or subject and try to learn something from it: *It turned out we were both following the same line of research.* | *If you follow that idea to its logical conclusion, we'd have to ban free speech altogether.*

20 follow your instincts/feelings/gut reaction etc to do the thing that you immediately feel is best without needing to stop and think about it

21 follow the herd/crowd to do the same thing that most other people are doing, without really thinking about it for yourself – used to show disapproval

22 follow your nose *informal* **a)** to go straight forward or continue in the same direction: *Just follow your nose until you come to a small bridge.* **b)** to go to the place from where there is a particular smell coming: *I followed my nose to the kitchen, where Marcie was making coffee.* **c)** to do something in the way that you feel is right: *After a few years in the detective game, you learn to follow your nose.*

23 follow a profession/trade/way of life etc to do a particular job or have a particular way of life

24 [T] to look at the messages sent by a particular person using the SOCIAL NETWORKING service Twitter

THESAURUS

follow to walk, drive etc behind or after someone, for example in order to see where they are going: *The man had followed her home to find out where she lived.*

chase to quickly run or drive after someone or something in order to catch them when they are trying to escape: *Police chased the car along the motorway at speeds of up to 90 mph.*

run after sb/go after sb to quickly follow someone or something in order to stop them or talk to them: *I ran after him to say sorry, but he'd already got on the bus.*

stalk /stɔːk $ stɒːk/ to secretly follow an animal in order to kill it, or to secretly follow a person in order to attack them: *a tiger stalking its prey* | *He had a long history of stalking women in his neighbourhood.*

pursue /pəˈsjuː $ pərˈsuː/ *written* to chase someone in a very determined way: *The ship was being pursued by enemy submarines.*

give chase *written* to chase someone or something who is trying to escape from you: *One of the officers gave chase and arrested the man.* | *The calf ran away and the lion gave chase.*

tail to secretly follow someone in order to watch what they do and where they go: *Apparently, the police had been tailing the terrorists for months.*

track to follow and find a person or animal by looking at the marks they leave on the ground: *The bushmen were tracking antelope in the Kalahari desert.*

F

follow sb **around** (*also* **follow sb about** *BrE*) *phr v* to follow someone everywhere they go, especially when this is annoying: *She told him to go away and stop following her around.*

follow on *phr v*
1 to happen after something else and be connected with it → **follow-on**: **[+from]** *The discussion sessions are supposed to follow on from this morning's lecture.*
2 to go to the same place as someone else at a later time: *You go ahead – I'll follow on later.*

follow through *phr v*
1 to do what needs to be done to complete something or make it successful: *The project went wrong when the staff failed to follow through.* | **follow sth ↔ through** *If you have followed through all the exercises in this book, you should be ready for the second year course.*
2 to continue moving your arm after you have hit the ball in tennis, GOLF etc → **follow-through**

follow sth ↔ **up** *phr v*
1 to find out more information about something and take action if necessary: *The police take people's statements and then follow them up.*
2 to do something in addition to what you have already done in order to make it more likely to succeed → **follow-up**: **[+with]** *If there is no response to your press release, follow it up with a phone call.* | *This experiment was quickly followed up by others using different forms of the drug.* → FOLLOW-UP²

fol·low·er /ˈfɒləʊə $ ˈfɑːloʊər/ ●●○ *n* [C]
1 someone who believes in a particular system of ideas, or who supports a leader who teaches these ideas → **disciple, supporter**: *Marx and his followers were convinced that capitalism would destroy itself.* | **[+of]** *followers of Sun Myung Moon, better known as Moonies*
2 someone who looks at the messages sent by a particular person using the SOCIAL NETWORKING service Twitter: *He currently has over 5000 followers on Twitter.* → CAMP FOLLOWER

F

fol·low·ing¹ /ˈfɒləʊɪŋ $ ˈfɑːloʊ-/ ●●● S3 W1 *adj*
1 the following afternoon/month/page/chapter etc the next afternoon, month etc OPP **preceding**: *He was sick in the evening, but the following day he was better.*
2 the following example/way etc the example, way etc that will be mentioned next: *Payment may be made in any of the following ways: cheque, cash, or credit card.*
3 a following wind a wind that is blowing in the same direction as a ship, and helps it to move faster

following² ●●○ *n* [C]
1 [usually singular] a group of people who support or admire someone: *The band has a big following in Europe.*
2 the following the people or things that you are going to mention: *The following have been selected to play in tomorrow's game: Louise Carus, Fiona Douglas ...*

following³ ●●○ *prep* after an event or as a result of it OPP **before**: *Following the president's speech, there will be a few minutes for questions.* | *Thousands of refugees left the country following the outbreak of civil war.*

ˌfollow-my-ˈleader *BrE*, **ˌfollow-the-ˈleader** *AmE n* [U] a children's game in which one of the players does actions which all the other players must copy

ˈfollow-on *n* [C] something that is done or made in addition to something else, or done to continue something that was done before → **follow on**: **[+to/from]** *The inspection was a follow-on from the review process.* | *a follow-on product*

ˈfollow-through *n* [singular] **1** the continued movement of your arm after you have hit the ball in tennis, golf etc → **follow through 2** the things that someone does in order to complete a plan → **follow through**: *The budget has to cover not only the main project but the follow-through.*

ˈfollow-up¹ ●○○ *n*
1 [C,U] something that is done to make sure that earlier actions have been successful or effective → **follow up**: *preventative treatment and follow-up several weeks later*
2 [C] a book, film, article etc that comes after another one that has the same subject or characters: *Spielberg says he's planning to do a follow-up next year.* | **[+to]** *a follow-up to their hit album*

follow-up² *adj* [only before noun] done in order to find out more or do more about something → **follow up**: *a follow-up study on children and poverty*

fol·ly /ˈfɒli $ ˈfɑːli/ *n* (*plural* **follies**) **1** [C,U] *formal* a very stupid thing to do, especially one that is likely to have serious results: *Somerville bitterly regretted his folly at becoming involved.* | **it would be folly to do sth** *It would be **sheer folly** to reduce spending on health education.* | *the follies of aristocratic society* **2** [C] an unusual building that was built in the past as a decoration, not to be used or lived in

fo·ment /fəʊˈment $ foʊ-/ *v* **foment revolution/trouble/discord etc** *formal* to cause trouble and make people start fighting each other or opposing the government SYN **stir up**: *They were accused of fomenting rebellion.* —**fomentation** /ˌfəʊmenˈteɪʃən, -mən- $ ˌfoʊ-/ *n* [U]

FOMO /ˈfəʊməʊ $ ˈfoʊmoʊ/ *n* [U] (***fear of missing out***) a feeling of anxiety or unhappiness you have because you think that other people are doing more exciting things than you are

fond /fɒnd $ fɑːnd/ ●●○ *adj*
1 be fond of sb to like someone very much, especially when you have known them for a long time and almost feel love for them: *Joe's quite fond of her, isn't he?* | *Over the years we've **grown** very **fond of** each other.*
2 be fond of (doing) sth to like something, especially something you have liked for a long time: *I'm not overly fond of cooking.* | *I'd **grown fond of** the place and it was difficult to leave.*
3 be fond of doing sth to do something often, especially something that annoys other people: *My grandfather was very fond of handing out advice to all my friends.*
4 [only before noun] a fond look, smile, action etc shows you like someone very much SYN **affectionate**: *He gave her a fond look.* | *As we parted we said a **fond farewell**.*
5 have fond memories of sth/sb to remember someone or something with great pleasure: *Marie still had fond memories of their time together.*
6 a fond hope/belief a belief or hope that something will happen, which seems silly because it is very unlikely to happen: **in the fond hope/belief that** *They sent him to another school in the fond hope that his behaviour would improve.* —**fondness** *n* [U]: *a **fondness for** expensive clothes* → FONDLY

fon·dant /ˈfɒndənt $ ˈfɑːn-/ *n* **1** [U] a soft mixture made from sugar and water, used for covering cakes: *a cake decorated with **fondant icing*** **2** [C] a soft sweet made of fondant

fon·dle /ˈfɒndl $ ˈfɑːndl/ *v* [T] to gently touch and move your fingers over part of someone's body in a way that shows love or sexual desire: *She fondled his neck.* THESAURUS ▸ TOUCH

fond·ly /ˈfɒndli $ ˈfɑːndli/ *adv* **1 fondly imagine/believe/hope etc** to believe something that is untrue, hope for something that will probably not happen etc: *Some people still fondly believe that modern science can solve all the world's problems.* **2** in a way that shows you like someone very much SYN **lovingly**: *He turned to see her smiling fondly at him.*

fon·due /ˈfɒndjuː $ fɑːnˈduː/ *n* [C,U] a dish made of melted cheese, hot oil, or chocolate into which you put small pieces of bread, meat, fruit etc using a long fork

FONT

italic large
bold small

font /fɒnt $ fɑːnt/ ●○○ *n* [C]
1 *technical* a set of letters of a particular size and style, used for printing books, newspapers etc or on a computer screen
2 a large stone container in a church, that holds the water used for the ceremony of BAPTISM

food /fuːd/ ●●● S1 W1 *n*
1 [C,U] things that people and animals eat, such as vegetables or meat: *The restaurant serves good food at affordable prices.* | *I love Italian food, especially pasta.* | *He was told to cut down on salty and fatty foods.* → see Thesaurus box on *p.710*
2 food for thought something that makes you think carefully: *The teacher's advice certainly gave me food for thought.*

GRAMMAR: Countable or uncountable?
• **Food** is usually uncountable: *There was not enough food for everyone.* ✗ Don't say: *enough foods*
• **Food** is used as a countable noun when talking about particular types of food: *The doctor advised her to avoid fatty foods.* | *Butter is a healthy food.*

COLLOCATIONS

ADJECTIVES
good/excellent *The hotel was nice and the food was really good.*
delicious/tasty *Thanks for dinner – the food was delicious.*
fresh *The food is all so fresh.*
healthy *We try to give the kids good healthy food.*
nourishing/nutritious (=making you strong and healthy) | **plain/simple** (=without anything added or without decoration) | **spicy** (=with a hot taste) | **hot food** | **cold food** | **Italian/French/Chinese etc food** | **exotic food** (=unusual because of being from a foreign country) | **fatty foods**

VERBS
have food *The family hadn't had any food for days.*
eat food *He sat in the corner and ate his food.*
cook/prepare food *I have to cook some food for this evening.*
serve food (=give food to someone, especially in a restaurant) | **enjoy your food** | **chew food** | **swallow food** | **digest food** | **food tastes good/delicious etc** | **food smells good**

PHRASES
be off your food *BrE* (=not want to eat) *The baby is off his food.*
go off your food *BrE* (=to stop wanting to eat) *Since becoming ill, he has gone off his food.*

NOUNS
a food supply *The government must ensure an adequate food supply.*
the food industry *The food industry has responded to consumer concerns about health.*
food production (=the process of making or growing food to be sold) *Farmers have increased food production to meet demand.*
food products | **food prices** | **a food shortage** | **a food scare** (=when people are afraid to eat a particular food) | **food colouring** *BrE*, **food coloring** *AmE* | **food additives** (=substances added to food in order to improve its taste or appearance)

'food bank *n* [C] a place that gives food to poor people

FOOD CHAIN

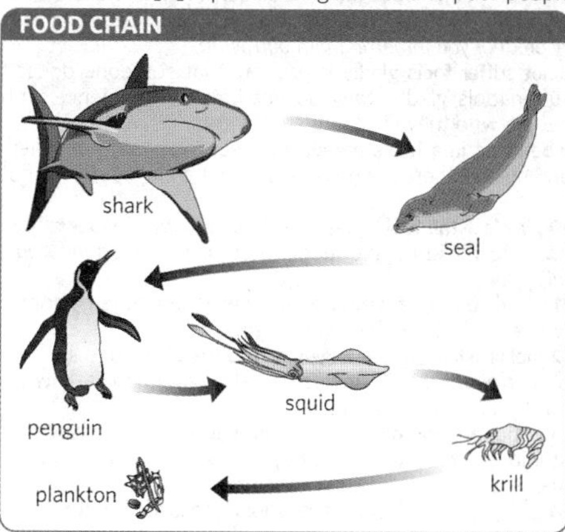

'food chain *n* **the food chain** all animals and plants considered as a group in which a plant is eaten by an insect or animal, which is then eaten by another animal and so on: *Pollution is affecting many creatures lower down the food chain.*
'food ˌcoupon *n* [C] *AmE* a FOOD STAMP
'food court *n* [C] the area in a shopping centre where there are many small restaurants
'food group *n* [C] one of the groups that types of food are divided into, such as meat, vegetables, or milk products
food·ie /ˈfuːdi/ *n* [C] *informal* someone who is very interested in cooking and eating food → **gourmet**
'food miles *n* [plural] the distance between the place where food is produced and the place where it is eaten, which is a way of measuring its harmful effect on the environment: *Reducing food miles would reduce carbon dioxide emissions.*
'food ˌpoisoning *n* [U] a stomach illness caused by eating food that contains harmful BACTERIA, so that you VOMIT
'food ˌprocessor *n* [C] a piece of electrical equipment used to prepare food by cutting and mixing it
'food seˌcurity *n* [U] the ability to get enough food to be healthy: *the impact of population growth on food security*
'food stamp (*also* **food coupon**) *n* [C] an official piece of paper that the US government gives to poor people so they can buy food
food·stuff /ˈfuːdstʌf/ *n* [C usually plural, U] food – used especially when talking about the business of producing or selling food: *a shortage of basic foodstuffs*

fool¹ /fuːl/ ●●○ *n*
1 STUPID PERSON [C] a stupid person or someone who has done something stupid SYN **idiot**: ***What a fool** she had been to think that he would stay.* | ***Like a fool**, I accepted straight away.* | *You **silly old fool**!*
2 make a fool of yourself to do something stupid that you feel embarrassed about afterwards and that makes you seem silly: *Sorry I made such a fool of myself last night. I must have been drunk.*
3 make a fool of sb to deliberately do something to make someone else seem stupid: *I suddenly realised that I was being made a fool of.*
4 any fool can do sth *spoken* used to say that it is very easy to do something or to see that something is true: *Any fool could have seen what would happen.*
5 be no/nobody's fool to be difficult to trick or deceive, because you have a lot of experience and knowledge about something: *Katherine was nobody's fool when it came to money.*

F

6 gooseberry/strawberry etc fool *BrE* a sweet food made of soft cooked fruit mixed with cream
7 more fool you/him etc *BrE spoken* used to say that you think someone was stupid to do something, and it is their own fault if this causes trouble: *'Jim smashed up my car.' 'More fool you for letting him borrow it!'*
8 not suffer fools gladly if you say that someone doesn't suffer fools gladly, they do not have any patience with people who they think are stupid
9 be living in a fool's paradise to feel happy and satisfied, and believe there are no problems, when in fact this is not true
10 play/act the fool to behave in a silly way, especially in order to make people laugh: *Stop playing the fool! You'll fall.*
11 (send sb on) a fool's errand to make someone go somewhere or do something for no good reason
12 fools rush in (where angels fear to tread) used to say that people are stupid if they do something immediately without thinking about it first
13 a fool and his money are soon parted used to say that stupid people spend money quickly without thinking about it
14 ENTERTAINER [C] a man whose job was to entertain a king or other powerful people in the past, by doing tricks, singing funny songs etc SYN **jester** → APRIL FOOL

fool² ●○○ *v*
1 [T] to trick someone into believing something that is not true: *Even art experts were fooled.* | **you don't/can't fool me** *You can't fool me with that old excuse.* | **be fooled by sth** *Don't be fooled by appearances.* | **fool sb into doing sth** *I was fooled into believing their promises.*
2 fool yourself to try to make yourself believe something that you know is not really true: *It's no good fooling yourself. He's not coming back.*
3 you could have fooled me *spoken* used to show that you do not believe what someone has told you: *'Look, we're doing our best to fix it.' 'Well, you could have fooled me.'*
4 sb is just fooling *spoken* used to say that someone is not serious and is only pretending that something is true SYN **sb is just kidding**: *Don't pay any attention to Henry. He's just fooling.*

fool around (*also* **fool about** *BrE*) *phr v*
1 to waste time behaving in a silly way or doing things that are not important SYN **mess around**: *He always used to fool around in class.*
2 to behave in a way which is careless and not responsible SYN **mess around**: **[+with]** *Some idiot's been fooling around with the electricity supply!*
3 *AmE* to spend time doing something that you enjoy, but that does not have a particular purpose SYN **mess around**: *The boys were out in the yard, just fooling around.*
4 to have a sexual relationship with someone else's wife, boyfriend etc SYN **mess around**: *She found out that he'd been fooling around behind her back.*

fool with sth *phr v AmE informal*
1 to touch or play with something, especially when you should not SYN **mess with sth**: *Who's been fooling with the radio dial?*
2 to become involved in something which could cause damage or be dangerous SYN **mess with sth**

fool³ *adj* [only before noun] *AmE informal* silly or stupid SYN **foolish**: *What did you say a fool thing like that for?*

fool·e·ry /ˈfuːləri/ *n* [U] *BrE old-fashioned* silly or stupid behaviour

fool·har·dy /ˈfuːlhɑːdi $ -ɑːr-/ *adj* taking stupid and unnecessary risks SYN **reckless**: *a foolhardy attempt to capture more territory* —**foolhardiness** *n* [U]

F

THESAURUS: food

food *n* [C,U] things that people and animals eat: *You can buy good fresh food in the market.* | *Do you like Japanese food?*
dish *n* [C] a type of food that is cooked in a particular way: *a traditional English dish* | *They also offer vegetarian dishes.*
speciality *BrE*, **specialty** *AmE n* [C] a type of food that a restaurant or place is famous for: *Fish dishes are a specialty of the region.* | *Home made pies are one of the hotel's specialities.*
delicacy *n* [C] an unusual food which people in a particular place like to eat: *The local delicacies include laverbread (boiled seaweed).*
diet *n* [C] the type of food that someone usually eats: *You shouldn't have too much salt in your diet.* | *In the Andes, the main diet is beans, potatoes, and corn.*
cooking *n* [U] food made in a particular way, or by a particular person: *Herbs are used a lot in French cooking.* | *I love my Mum's home cooking.*
cuisine /kwɪˈziːn/ *n* [C] *formal* the food you can eat in a particular restaurant, country, or area: *Italian cuisine* | *Trying the local cuisine is all part of the fun of travelling.*
nutrition *n* [U] food considered as something that is necessary for good health and growth: *a book on nutrition* | *Many homeless people suffer from poor nutrition.*
nourishment /ˈnʌrɪʃmənt $ ˈnɜː-, ˈnʌ-/ *n* [U] goodness that you get from food, which helps your body to stay healthy: *There's not much nourishment in fast food.*
fare *n* [U] *formal* the kind of food that is served in a place - used especially when saying how interesting it is: *In China you can feast on bird's nest soup and other exotic fare.*

TYPES OF FOOD

fast food food such as HAMBURGERS, which is prepared quickly and which you can take away with you to eat: *He ballooned to 300lbs on a diet of fast food.*
junk food food that is full of sugar or fat, and is bad for your health: *I used to eat loads of junk food.*
GM food *BrE* food made from vegetables and animals that have had their genetic structure changed: *There has been a lot of research into the safety of GM food.*
organic food food that is produced without using harmful chemicals: *Shoppers are willing to pay more for organic food.*
health food food that is thought to be good for your health: *You can buy the ingredients in any good health food shop.*
superfood a type of food that is believed to be good for your health because it contains a lot of a particular type of VITAMIN, MINERAL etc
vegetarian food food that does not contain meat
processed food food that has chemicals in it to make it last a long time
canned food (*also* **tinned food** *BrE*) food that is sold in cans
frozen food food that is kept at a very low temperature to make it last a long time
convenience food food that is sold in cans, packages etc, so that it can be prepared quickly and easily
baby food special food for babies
pet/dog/cat/bird etc food food for animals that you keep as pets

fool·ish /ˈfuːlɪʃ/ ●●○ *adj*
1 a foolish action, remark etc is stupid and shows that someone is not thinking sensibly SYN **silly**: *I've never heard anything so foolish in all my life.* | ***It** would **be foolish to** ignore his advice.* | **be foolish enough to do sth** *I was foolish enough to believe him.* **THESAURUS** ▶ STUPID

> **REGISTER**
> In everyday English, people usually say **silly** or **stupid** rather than **foolish**: *It was a **silly** thing to say.* | *I felt a bit **stupid** when she said no.*

2 a foolish person behaves in a silly way or looks silly SYN **stupid**: *I was young and foolish at the time.* | *a foolish grin* | **look/feel foolish** *He'd been made to look foolish.* —**foolishly** *adv*: *She foolishly agreed to go with them.* —**foolishness** *n* [U]

fool·proof /ˈfuːlpruːf/ ●○○ *adj* a foolproof method, plan, system etc is certain to be successful SYN **infallible**: *a foolproof way of preventing credit card fraud*

fools·cap /ˈfuːlskæp/ *n* [U] a large size of paper, especially paper for writing on

ˌfool's ˈgold *n* [U] **1** a kind of yellow metal that exists in some rocks and looks like gold **2** something that you think will be very exciting, very attractive etc but in fact is not

foos·ball /ˈfuːzbɔːl $ -bɒːl/ (*also* **foos** /fuːs/) *n* [U] *informal* TABLE FOOTBALL, especially played as a sport rather than a game

foos·er /ˈfuːzə $ -ər/ *n* [C] *informal* someone who plays foosball

foot¹ /fʊt/ ●●● S1 W1 *n* (*plural* **feet** /fiːt/) [C]
1 BODY PART the part of your body that you stand on and walk on: *My foot hurts.* | *I had blisters on **the soles of my feet**.* | *I dropped a glass earlier, so don't walk around **in bare feet**.* | *The vet examined the horse's **hind feet**.* | *Don't **wipe your feet** on the carpet!* | *She stood on the platform, her suitcase **at her feet**.*
2 MEASUREMENT (*plural* **feet** *or* **foot**) (*written abbreviation* **ft**) a unit for measuring length, equal to 12 INCHES or about 30 centimetres: *He's six **feet tall**, with blonde hair.* | *Mark was standing just a few feet away from me.* | *I'd say she's about **five foot three*** (=five feet and three inches). | **a one-/two-/three- etc foot sth** *a four-foot wall* | **square feet/cubic feet** *15,000 square feet of office space*
3 BOTTOM PART **the foot of sth** the lowest or bottom part of something: **the foot of the stairs/ladder etc** *He walked to the foot of the stairs.* | **the foot of a mountain/cliff etc** *a small cottage at the foot of the hill* | **at the foot of sth** *a large wooden trunk at the foot of his bed* | *The date is shown **at the foot of the page**.*
4 on foot if you go somewhere on foot, you walk there: *It takes about 30 minutes on foot, or 10 minutes by car.* GRAMMAR ✗ Don't say: *by foot*
5 get/jump/rise etc to your feet to stand up after you have been sitting: *He leapt to his feet and ran outside.*
6 on your feet a) to be standing for a long time without having time to sit down: *The worst thing about working in the shop is that you're on your feet all day.* → **dead on your feet** at DEAD¹(8) **b)** to be standing up: *As soon as the bell rang the class were on their feet and out of the door.* **c)** to feel better again after being ill and in bed: *We'll soon have you on your feet again.*
7 be/get back on your feet to have enough money again, or to be successful again after having problems: *I need to get back on my feet again and forget all this.*
8 off your feet sitting or lying down, rather than standing or walking: *The doctor told me to stay off my feet for a few days.*
9 knock/lift etc sb off their feet to make someone fall over: *They were blown off their feet by the force of the explosion.*
10 be rushed/run off your feet to be very busy: *Before Christmas, most salespeople are rushed off their feet.*
11 set foot in sth to go to or enter a place: *She swore she would never set foot in his house again.*
12 be/get under your feet to annoy you by always being in the same place as you and preventing you from doing what you want: *I hate summer vacation. The kids are under my feet all day long.*
13 put your foot down a) to say very firmly that someone must do something or must stop doing something: *You'll just have to put your foot down and tell him he can't stay out on school nights.* **b)** *informal* to make a car go faster
14 put your feet up *informal* to relax, especially by sitting with your feet supported on something
15 put your foot in it *especially BrE*, **put your foot in your mouth** *especially AmE* to say something without thinking carefully, so that you embarrass or upset someone: *I've really put my foot in it this time. I didn't realize that was her husband!*
16 start/get off on the wrong/right foot to start a relationship badly or well: *Simon and I got off on the wrong foot but we're good friends now.*
17 not put a foot wrong *BrE* to do everything right and make no mistakes, especially in your job
18 have/keep your feet on the ground to think in a sensible and practical way and not have ideas or aims that will be impossible to achieve: *It was a great result, but we have to keep our feet firmly on the ground.*
19 fall/land on your feet to get into a good situation because you are lucky, especially after being in a difficult situation: *Don't worry about Nina, she always falls on her feet.*
20 get/have/keep your foot in the door to get your first opportunity to work in a particular organization or industry
21 have a foot in both camps to be involved with or connected with two opposing groups of people
22 at your feet used to say that people admire or respect someone very much: *All Paris was at his feet.* → **have the world at your feet** at WORLD¹(24)
23 have two left feet *informal* to be very CLUMSY
24 have one foot in the grave to be very old or very ill – used humorously
25 ... my foot! *BrE old-fashioned* used to show that you do not believe something that someone has just said: *£50 my foot! It'll cost £200 at least.*
26 leave feet first to die before you leave a place or job – used humorously: *If you keep fooling around with that gun you'll be leaving this camp feet first.*
27 feet of clay someone that you admire who has feet of clay has faults and weaknesses that you did not realize they had
28 foot soldier/patrol a soldier or group of soldiers that walks and does not use a horse or a vehicle
29 foot passenger a passenger on a ship who has not brought a car with them
30 a) left-footed/right-footed using your left foot or right foot when you kick a ball **b) flat-footed/four-footed** having a particular type or number of feet
31 foot pedal/brake/pump etc a machine or control that you operate using your feet
32 SOCK **the foot** the part of a sock that covers your foot
33 POETRY *technical* a part of a line of poetry in which there is one strong BEAT and one or two weaker ones
→ **the boot is on the other foot** at BOOT¹(6), → **get/have cold feet** at COLD¹(6), → UNDERFOOT, → **drag your feet/heels** at DRAG¹(8), → **find your feet** at FIND¹(18), → **from head to foot** at HEAD¹(1), → **stand on your own (two) feet** at STAND¹(31), → **sweep sb off their feet** at SWEEP¹(14), → **have itchy feet** at ITCHY(3), → **not let the grass grow under your feet** at GRASS¹(6), → **vote with your feet** at VOTE¹(8)

foot² *v* **foot the bill** to pay for something, especially something expensive that you do not want to pay for: *He ordered drinks and then left me to foot the bill!*

foot·age /ˈfʊtɪdʒ/ ●○○ *n* [U] cinema film showing a particular event: *old footage from the First World War*

ˌfoot and ˈmouth disˌease *n* [U] a serious disease that kills cows and sheep

foot·ball /ˈfʊtbɔːl $ -bɒːl/ ●●● S1 W2 *n*
1 [U] *BrE* a game played by two teams of eleven players who try to kick a round ball into the other team's GOAL

SYN **soccer** *AmE*: *Which* ***football team*** *do you support?* | *kids* ***playing football*** *in the street* | *My Dad took me to watch my first* ***football match***. | *a football club* | **football fan/supporter** *a group of Scottish football fans* | **football boots/kit/shirt** (=clothes worn to play football) | **football pitch/ground/stadium** → see picture at SHOE[1]
2 [U] *AmE* a game played by two teams of eleven players who try to carry or kick an OVAL ball into the other team's GOAL SYN **American football** *BrE*: *college* ***football games*** | *a football field* | *He* ***played football*** *in high school.*
3 football hooligan *BrE* someone who behaves in a noisy or violent way at a football match
4 [C] a ball used in these games → **FLAG FOOTBALL**, → **political football** at POLITICAL(4)

foot·bal·ler /ˈfʊtbɔːlə $ -bɒːlər/ ●○○ *n* [C] *BrE* someone who plays football, especially a professional player SYN **soccer player** *AmE*

foot·bal·ling /ˈfʊtbɔːlɪŋ $ -bɒːl-/ *adj* [only before noun] *BrE* relating to football: *It was the high point of his footballing career.*

ˈfootball ˌpools *n* [plural] another word for the POOLS

foot·bridge /ˈfʊtˌbrɪdʒ/ *n* [C] a narrow bridge used by people who are walking → see picture at **BRIDGE**[1]

ˈfoot-ˌdragging *n* [U] when someone is deliberately being slow to do something → **drag your feet/heels** at DRAG[1](8)

foot·er /ˈfʊtə $ -ər/ *n* **1 six-footer/eighteen-footer etc** someone or something that measures six feet tall, eighteen feet long etc **2** [C] a line of writing which appears at the bottom of each page of a document which is printed by a computer → **header**

foot·fall /ˈfʊtfɔːl $ -fɒːl/ *n* **1** [C] *literary* the sound of each step when someone is walking SYN **footstep**: *heavy footfalls* **2** [U] *BrE technical* the number of people who visit a shop or shopping area – used in business

ˈfoot fault *n* [C] a mistake in tennis when the person who SERVES is not standing behind the line

foot·hill /ˈfʊtˌhɪl/ *n* [C usually plural] one of the smaller hills below a group of high mountains: *the foothills of the Himalayas*

foot·hold /ˈfʊthəʊld $ -hoʊld/ *n* [C] **1** a position from which you can start to make progress and achieve your aims: **gain/establish a foothold** *Extreme right-wing parties gained a foothold in the latest European elections.* **2** a small hole or crack where you can safely put your foot when climbing a steep rock

foot·ie /ˈfʊti/ *n* [U] *BrE informal* football

foot·ing /ˈfʊtɪŋ/ *n* **1** [singular] the conditions or arrangements on which something is based: **put/place sth on a ... footing** *He wanted to put their relationship on a permanent footing.* | **a financial/commercial/legal etc footing** *The firm started the new year on a stronger financial footing.* | **on an equal footing (with sb/sth)/on the same footing (as sb/sth)** (=in the same state or condition as other people or things) *The new law puts women on an equal legal footing with men.* | *Many of the old polytechnics are now on the same footing as universities.* | **a sound/firm/secure footing** *They managed to get the business onto a more secure footing.* | *The whole country was* ***on a war footing*** (=ready to go to war at any time). **2** [singular] a firm hold with your feet when you are standing on a dangerous surface: *Seb struggled to* ***keep*** *his* ***footing*** *on the slippery path.* | **lose/miss your footing** (=be unable to keep standing or balancing) *The girl lost her footing and fell about 150 feet.* **3** [C usually plural] the solid base of bricks, stone etc that is under a building to support it and fasten it to the ground SYN **foundation**

foot·lights /ˈfʊtlaɪts/ *n* [plural] a row of lights along the front of the stage in a theatre → **spotlight**

ˈfoot ˌlocker *n* [C] *AmE* a large strong box that you keep your things in, used especially by soldiers

foot·loose /ˈfʊtluːs/ *adj* free to do exactly what you want because you have no responsibilities, for example when you are not married or do not have children: *footloose students traveling around Europe* | *When the kids leave home, you'll be* ***footloose and fancy-free*** (=free and without worries).

foot·man /ˈfʊtmən/ *n* (*plural* **footmen** /-mən/) [C] a male servant in the past who opened the front door, announced the names of visitors etc

foot·note /ˈfʊtnəʊt $ -noʊt/ ●○○ *n* [C]
1 a note at the bottom of the page in a book, which gives more information about something
2 a piece of additional information that is not very important but is interesting or helps you understand something: **[+to]** *There was an interesting footnote to the story.*

foot·path /ˈfʊtpɑːθ $ -pæθ/ ●●○ *n* [C] *especially BrE* a narrow path for people to walk along, especially in the country SYN **trail** *AmE*

foot·plate /ˈfʊtpleɪt/ *n* [C] *BrE* the place on a steam train where the driver stood

foot·print /ˈfʊtˌprɪnt/ *n* [C] **1** (*also* **footmark**) a mark made by a foot or shoe: *We followed the footprints of a deer in the snow.* → see picture at **FINGERPRINT** THESAURUS **EFFECT 2** *technical* the amount of space on a desk that a computer uses: *PCs with a 50% smaller footprint than other models* **3** the effect that a person's or organization's activities have on the environment: *Answer these questions to calculate your business's environmental footprint.*

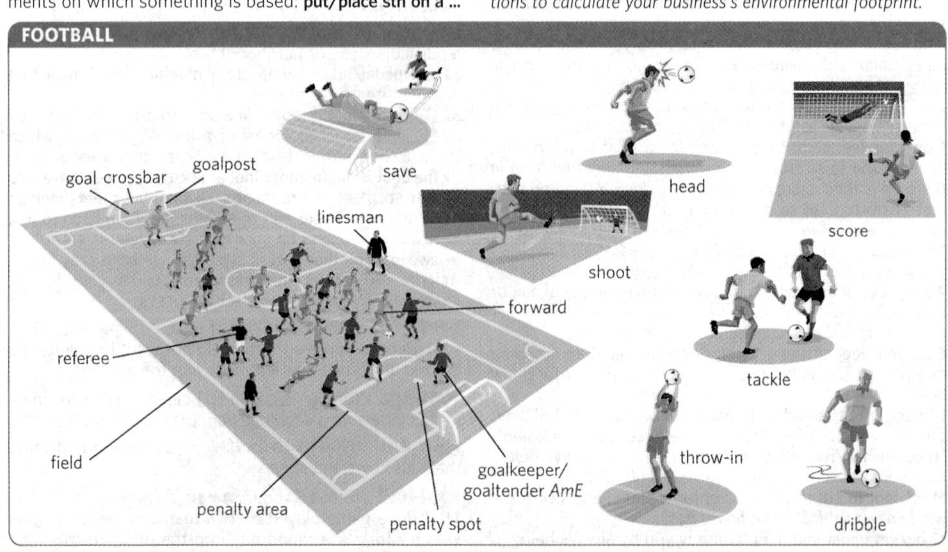

F

foot·rest /ˈfʊt-rest/ *n* [C] something that supports your feet when you are sitting, for example a small piece of furniture or the part of a MOTORCYCLE where you put your feet

foot·sie /ˈfʊtsi/ *n* **play footsie (with sb)** *informal* **a)** to secretly touch someone's feet with your feet under a table to show that you think they are sexually attractive **b)** *AmE* to work together and help each other in a dishonest way: *politicians playing footsie with each other*

foot·sore /ˈfʊtsɔː $ -sɔːr/ *adj* having feet that hurt because you have walked a long distance

foot·step /ˈfʊtstep/ ●●○ *n* [C] the sound each step makes when someone is walking: *He* ***heard*** *someone's* ***footsteps*** *in the hall.* → **follow (in) sb's footsteps** at FOLLOW(15)

foot·stool /ˈfʊtstuːl/ *n* [C] a low piece of furniture used to support your feet when you are sitting down

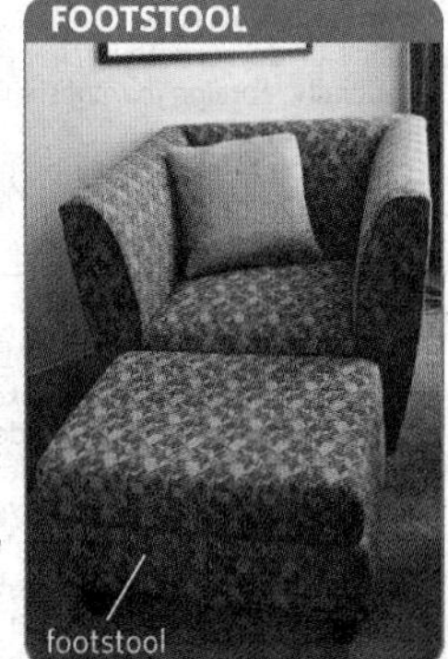

foot·wear /ˈfʊtweə $ -wer/ *n* [U] things that people wear on their feet, such as shoes or boots: *outdoor footwear*

foot·work /ˈfʊtwɜːk $ -wɜːrk/ *n* [U] **1** skilful use of your feet when dancing or playing a sport: **good/neat/fancy etc footwork** *The England keeper revealed some fancy footwork in the victory over Nottingham Forest.* **2** skilful methods that you use to achieve something: **fancy/deft/nifty etc footwork** *It took a bit of deft footwork to get them to agree.*

foot·y /ˈfʊti/ *n* [U] *BrE informal* football: *footy fans*

fop /fɒp $ fɑːp/ *n* [C] *old-fashioned* a man who is very interested in his clothes and appearance – used to show disapproval —**foppish** *adj* —**foppishness** *n* [U]

for¹ /fə; *strong* fɔː $ fər *strong* fɔːr/ ●●● S1 W1 *prep*
1 used to say who is intended to get or use something, or where something is intended to be used: *I've got a present for you.* | *Someone left a message for Vicky.* | *an English course for foreign students* | *We need a new battery for the radio.* | *These chairs are for the office.*
2 in order to help someone or something: *I looked after the kids for them.* | *Let me carry that bag for you.* | *The doctor knew that there was nothing he could do for her.* | *Charles died fighting for his country.* | *What can I do for you* (=used to ask a customer if you can help them)?
3 used to say what the purpose of an object, action etc is: **for doing sth** *a knife for cutting bread* | *What did you do that for?* | *I've bought him a watch for his birthday.* | *the documents prepared for his defence*

GRAMMAR: Comparison

for doing sth
• You say that something is **for doing** a particular thing: *This is for pulling up weeds.* ✗ Don't say: *This is for to pull up weeds.*

in order to do sth
• You say that someone does something **in order to do** a particular thing: *They borrowed money in order to build up the business.* ✗ Don't say: *They needed money for to build up the business.*

to do sth
• You say that someone does something **to do** a particular thing: *She went downtown to do some shopping.* ✗ Don't say: *She went downtown for to do some shopping.*

4 in order to have, do, get, or obtain something: *Are you waiting for the bus?* | *the qualifications necessary for a career in broadcasting* | *Mother was too ill to get up for dinner.* | *I paid $3 for a ticket.* | *For further details, write to this address.* | *Let's go for a walk.*
5 used to say how long an action or situation continues for: *Bake the cake for 40 minutes.* | *We had been talking for a good half hour.* | *He's been off work for a while.*
6 used to talk about distance: *We walked for miles.* | *Factories stretch for quite a way along the canal.*
7 if something is arranged for a particular time, it is planned that it should happen then: *I've invited them for 9 o'clock.* | *A meeting was arranged for 18th May.*
8 used to say where a person, vehicle etc is going: *I set off for work.* | *the train for Manchester* | *A few days later she would be leaving for New York.*
9 used to say what the price or value of something is: *a cheque for a hundred pounds* | *The diamond was insured for two thousand dollars.*
10 because of or as a result of something: *If, for any reason, you cannot attend, please inform us.* | *We could hardly see for the mist.* | *You'll feel better for a break.* | **for doing sth** *a reward for making good progress* | *Campbell was arrested for dangerous driving.*
11 used to say which thing or person your statement or question is related to: *I'm sure she's the ideal person for the job.* | *The questions on this paper are too difficult for 10-year-olds.* | *Are you all right for money?* | *Fortunately for him, he can swim.*
12 used to say which person or thing your feelings are directed towards: *I came away feeling sorry for poor old George.* | *My deep love for him still remains.* | *They show no respect for authority.*
13 used to say at which meal you eat something: *We had pasta for lunch.*
14 used to say which company, team etc you belong to: *I've worked for the BBC ever since I left university.* | *Deborah used to play for the A team.* | *He writes for a weekly paper.*
15 supporting or in agreement with something or someone: *We have studied the arguments for and against nuclear energy.* | *How many people voted for the proposal?* | *Three cheers for the captain.* | **be all for (doing) sth** (=support something very much) *I'm all for giving people more freedom.*
16 used to say what a word or sign means: *What's the French word for 'happy'?* | *Red is for danger.*
17 used to say that a particular quality of someone or something is surprising when you consider what they are: *She looks young for her age.* | *It's cold for July.*
18 as a representative of other people: *Paisley claims to speak for the majority of local people.*
19 used to say what is possible, difficult, necessary, unusual etc: **for sb/sth to do sth** *It's unusual for Donald to be so bad-tempered.* | *There is an urgent need for someone to tackle this problem.* | *Here is a chance for everyone to learn new skills.* | *There's nothing worse than for a parent to ill-treat a child.* | *It was too far for her to walk in high-heeled shoes.*
20 for each/every used to say that there is a relationship between one amount and another: *For each mistake, you'll lose half a point.* | *For every three people who agree, you'll find five who don't.*
21 sth is not for sb used to say that something is not the kind of thing that someone likes or will enjoy: *City life is not for me.* | *This book is not for everyone.*
22 it is (not) for sb to do sth used to say whether it is someone's right or duty to do something: *It's not for me to tell you what to do.* | *It will be for you to decide what action you should take.*
23 if it wasn't/weren't for sb/sth (*also* **if it hadn't been for sb/sth**) used to say who or what prevents or prevented something from happening: *If it hadn't been for you, I should have drowned.*
24 that's/there's sb/sth for you! *spoken* **a)** used to say that a particular kind of behaviour or situation is typical of someone or something, especially when you do not expect anything better from that person or thing: *I know it's outrageous, but that's Melissa for you.* **b)** used when you are annoyed or disappointed to say that something is the opposite of the quality you are mentioning: *Well, there's*

gratitude for you! Here am I trying to help and you tell me not to interfere!
25 be (in) for it *spoken* to be likely to be blamed or punished: *You'll be in for it if she finds out what you've done!*

for² ●●○ *conjunction formal* used to introduce the reason for something SYN **because**: *I cannot tell whether she is old or young, for I have never seen her.* | *He found it increasingly difficult to read, for his eyesight was beginning to fail.*

for·age¹ /ˈfɒrɪdʒ $ ˈfɑː-, ˈfɔː-/ *v* [I] **1** to go around searching for food or other supplies: **[+for]** *People are being forced to forage for food and fuel.* | *In the summer, the goats forage freely* (=in any place they want to go). **2** to search for something with your hands in a bag, drawer etc SYN **ferret around**: **[+around/through/among etc]** *She foraged around in her purse and produced her ticket.* —**forager** *n* [C]

forage² *n* **1** [U] food supplies for horses and cattle **2** [singular] *BrE* an act of searching for something

for·ay /ˈfɒreɪ $ ˈfɔː-, ˈfɑː-/ *n* [C] **1** a short attempt at doing a particular job or activity, especially one that is very different from what you usually do: **[+into]** *It will be my **first foray** into local government.* | *Wright is about to **make** his first **foray** into the music business.* **2** a short sudden attack by a group of soldiers, especially in order to get food or supplies → **raid**: **[+into]** *their nightly forays into enemy territory* **3** a short journey somewhere in order to get something or do something SYN **trip**: **[+into/to]** *We **make** regular **forays** to France to buy wine.* —**foray** *v* [I]

for·bade /fəˈbæd, -ˈbeɪd $ fər-/ *v* the past tense of FORBID

for·bear¹ /fɔːˈbeə, fə- $ fɔːrˈber, fər-/ *v* (*past tense* **forbore** /-ˈbɔː $ -ˈbɔːr/, *past participle* **forborne** /-ˈbɔːn $ -ˈbɔːrn/) [I] *literary* to not do something you could or would like to do because you think it is wiser not to: **[+from]** *He decided to forbear from interfering.* | **forbear to do sth** *Clara forbore to mention his name.*

for·bear² /ˈfɔːbeə $ ˈfɔːrber/ *n* [C] a FOREBEAR

for·bear·ance /fɔːˈbeərəns $ fɔːrˈber-/ *n* [U] *formal* the quality of being patient, able to control your emotions, and willing to forgive someone who has upset you SYN **patience**

for·bear·ing /fɔːˈbeərɪŋ $ fɔːrˈber-/ *adj formal* patient and willing to forgive

for·bid /fəˈbɪd $ fər-/ ●●○ *v* (*past tense* **forbade** /-ˈbæd, -ˈbeɪd/, *past participle* **forbidden** /-ˈbɪdn/, *present participle* **forbidding**) [T]
1 to tell someone that they are not allowed to do something, or that something is not allowed OPP **permit**: **forbid sb to do sth** *He was forbidden to leave the house, as a punishment.* | **forbid sb from doing sth** *Women are forbidden from going out without a veil.* | **strictly/expressly/explicitly etc forbid** *The law strictly forbids racial or sexual discrimination.*

> **REGISTER**
> In everyday English, people usually say that someone **is not allowed to do** something rather than **is forbidden to do** something: *He was **not allowed to** leave the house.*

2 God/Heaven forbid *spoken* used to emphasize that you hope that something will not happen: *'Supposing I had an accident.' 'God forbid!'*
3 *formal* to make it impossible for someone to do something SYN **prevent**: *Lack of space forbids listing the names of all those who contributed.*

> **THESAURUS**
> **forbid** to tell someone in a very strong way that they must not do something or that something is not allowed: *His doctor had strictly forbidden him to drink alcohol.* | *It is forbidden to say such things.*
> **not allow** to say that someone must not do or have something, and stop them doing or having it: *The company does not allow smoking inside the building.* | *Mobile phones are not allowed in school.*
> **not let** [not in passive] to not allow someone to do something. **Not let** is more informal than **not allow**: *My parents won't let me stay out later than 11 o'clock.*
> **not permit** [usually passive] if something is not permitted, a rule or law says that you must not do it. **Not permit** is more formal than **not allow**: *Candidates are not permitted to use dictionaries in this examination.* | *Parking is not permitted here after 8 am.*
> **ban** to say officially that people must not do or have something: *Parliament decided to ban fox-hunting.* | *The book was banned in many countries.*
> **prohibit** /prəˈhɪbət $ proʊ-/ to say officially that an action is illegal and make a law or rule about this: *Acts of vandalism are prohibited.*
> **bar** [usually passive] to not allow someone to enter a place or do something, especially by preventing it officially: *Foreign journalists were barred from entering the country.*
> **proscribe** *formal* to say officially that people are not allowed to do something: *The law proscribes discrimination in the workplace.*

for·bid·den /fəˈbɪdn $ fər-/ *adj* **1** not allowed, especially because of an official rule → **banned**: **it is forbidden (to do sth)** *It is forbidden to smoke at school.* | **be strictly/expressly/absolutely etc forbidden** *Alcohol is strictly forbidden in Saudi Arabia.* **2** a forbidden place is one that you are not allowed to go to: **[+to]** *The Great Mosque is forbidden to Christians.* **3** a forbidden activity, subject etc is one that people think that you should not do, talk about etc SYN **taboo**: *Sex was always a forbidden topic.* | **forbidden fruit** (=something that you should not have, but that you want) *Forbidden fruit is always more attractive.*

for·bid·ding /fəˈbɪdɪŋ $ fər-/ *adj* having a frightening or unfriendly appearance: **forbidding place/land/landscape etc** *We sailed past the island's rather dark and forbidding cliffs.* | *His face was forbidding, even hostile.* **THESAURUS** UNFRIENDLY —**forbiddingly** *adv*

for·bore /fɔːˈbɔː, fə- $ fɔːrˈbɔːr, fər-/ *v* the past tense of FORBEAR

for·borne /fɔːˈbɔːn, fə- $ fɔːrˈbɔːrn, fər-/ *v* the past participle of FORBEAR

force¹ /fɔːs $ fɔːrs/ ●●● S2 W1 *n*
1 MILITARY **a)** [C usually plural] a group of people who have been trained to do military work for a government or other organization: **government/military/defence etc forces** *The riots were suppressed by government forces.* | *He strengthened US forces in the Gulf.* | *a plan to disarm the **rebel forces*** (=those fighting against the government) **b) the forces** *BrE* the army, navy, and air force: **in the forces** *Both her sons are in the forces.* **c) nuclear/conventional forces** NUCLEAR weapons or ordinary weapons: *short-range nuclear forces* → AIR FORCE, ARMED FORCES, GROUND FORCES, → **peacekeeping force** at PEACEKEEPING, → **security forces** at SECURITY(1), TASK FORCE(2)
2 MILITARY ACTION [U] military action used as a way of achieving your aims: *Peace cannot be imposed **by force**.* | *The UN will allow **the use of force** against aircraft violating the zone.*
3 VIOLENCE [U] violent physical action used to get what you want: *The police used force to overpower the demonstrators.* | **by force** *In the end he had to be thrown out of the house by force.* | *They kicked the door down using sheer **brute force**.*
4 PHYSICAL POWER [U] the amount of physical power with which something moves or hits another thing → **strength**: **[+of]** *The force of the explosion blew out all the windows.* | **with great/considerable/increasing etc force** *He raised his hand and struck her with terrifying force.*
5 NATURAL POWER [C,U] a natural power or event: *the force of gravity* | *powerful **natural forces** such as earthquakes, floods, and drought* | *the **forces of nature***
6 ORGANIZED GROUP [C usually singular] a group of people who have been trained and organized to do a particular

job: *the company's **sales force** | the quality of the **teaching force*** → POLICE FORCE

7 STRONG INFLUENCE [C] something or someone who is powerful and has a lot of influence on the way things happen: **the driving force (behind sth/sb)** (=the person or thing that makes something happen) *Betty Coward was the driving force behind the project.* | **a force for change/peace/democracy etc** (=someone or something that makes change, peace etc more likely to happen) *Healthy competition is a force for innovation.* | *He's a quick and decisive player – **a force to be reckoned with*** (=a person, team, company etc that influences what happens). | *The fall in prices was due to **forces beyond** their **control**.* → MARKET FORCES

8 POWERFUL EFFECT [U] the powerful effect that something has on you: *Even after 30 years, the play has lost none of its force.* | *the force of his personality*

9 join/combine forces (with sb/sth) to work together so that you can deal with a problem, be more powerful etc: **join forces to do sth** *Local schools have joined forces with each other to share facilities.*

10 in force a) if a law, rule etc is in force, it already exists: *The trade embargo has been in force for a year.* **b)** in a large group, especially in order to protest about something SYN **in large numbers**: *Villagers **turned out in force** to protest about the new road.*

11 come into force/bring sth into force if a new law, rule, change etc comes or is brought into force, it starts to exist: *Parking restrictions in the town centre came into force last month.*

12 by/through/out of force of habit because you have always done a particular thing and it is difficult to change: *I get up at 6 o'clock every day out of force of habit.*

13 by/through force of circumstance(s) *BrE* if something happens by force of circumstance, events outside your control make it happen

14 WIND **a) force 8/9/10 etc** a unit for measuring the strength of the wind **b) gale/hurricane force wind** extremely strong wind that does a lot of damage

15 POLICE **the force** a word meaning the POLICE FORCE, used especially by police officers

16 the forces of good/evil etc *literary* people or things that increase the amount of good or bad in the world: *the battle against the forces of evil* → LABOUR FORCE, TOUR DE FORCE, WORKFORCE

force² ●●● S2 W1 *v* [T]

1 MAKE SB DO STH to make someone do something they do not want to do → **persuade**: **force sb to do sth** *Government troops have forced the rebels to surrender.* | *Due to the high cost of borrowing, many companies have been forced to close.* | **force yourself to do sth** *I had to force myself to get up this morning.* | **force sb/sth into (doing) sth** *women who are forced into arranged marriages* | *Bad health forced him into taking early retirement.*

2 MAKE SB/STH MOVE [always + adv/prep] to make someone or something move in a particular direction or into a different position, especially through or using great strength SYN **push**: *Strong winds forced the ship off course.* | *Firemen tried to enter the building, but were forced back by the flames.* | *She tried to keep the door shut but the man **forced** it **open**.*

3 force your way through/into etc sth (*also* **force your way in/out/past etc**) to push very hard in order to get somewhere: *The doctor forced his way through the crowd.* | *Demonstrators forced their way past.*

4 MAKE STH HAPPEN to make something happen or change, especially more quickly than planned or expected: *the unfortunate events that forced his resignation* | *We need to **force the pace** on alternative energy policies.* | **force prices/interest rates etc down/up** *The effect will be to increase unemployment and force down wages.*

5 force a door/lock/window to open a door etc using physical strength, often causing damage: *I forced the lock on the cupboard to see what was inside.*

6 force the issue to do something that makes it necessary for someone to make decisions or take action, instead of waiting to see what happens: *Polly decided to force the issue by demanding an explanation.*

7 force sb's hand to make someone do something unwillingly or earlier than they had intended: *They're reluctant to sell the house yet but the right offer could force their hand.*

8 force a smile/laugh etc to make yourself smile, laugh etc even though you feel upset or annoyed

GRAMMAR: Comparison

force

- You **force** someone **to do** something: *The robbers forced him to hand over the money.*
- **Force** is often used in the passive: *The minister **was forced to** resign because of the scandal.*

make

- You **make** someone **do** something: *The robbers made him hand over the money.* ✗ Don't say: *make someone to do something*

compel

- You **compel** someone **to do** something: *The court can compel witnesses to give evidence.*
- **Compel** is very often used in the passive: *He became seriously ill and **was compelled to** retire two years later.*

oblige

- You say that someone **is obliged to do** something. **Oblige** is almost always used in the passive: *Hotels **are obliged** by law **to** install smoke alarms.*

THESAURUS

force to make someone do something they do not want to do. Used when people or situations make you do something: *They were beaten and forced to confess to crimes they had not committed.* | *The drought forced millions of farmers to sell their cattle.*

make to force someone to do something by using pressure, threats, or violence. **Make sb do sth** is more common than **force sb to do sth** in everyday English: *Her parents disapproved of Alex and they made her stop seeing him.* | *Two men with guns made the staff hand over the money.*

pressure (*also* **pressurize** *BrE*) to try to force someone to do something by making them feel that they should do it: *Some employers pressure their staff into working very long hours.* | *She felt they were trying to pressurize her into getting married.*

blackmail to force someone to give you money or do what you want by threatening to tell embarrassing secrets about them: *She tried to blackmail him with photographs of them together at the hotel.*

compel *formal* to force someone to do something using official power or authority. Also used when someone has to do something because of their situation: *The town was surrounded and compelled to surrender.* | *I felt compelled to offer them some kind of explanation.*

coerce /kəʊˈɜːs $ ˈkoʊɜːrs/ *formal* to force someone to do something by threatening them: *Local people were coerced into joining the rebel army.*

be obliged to do sth *formal* if someone is obliged to do something, they must do it because it is the law or the rule, or because of the situation they are in: *You are not obliged to say anything which may harm your defence in court.* | *They were obliged to sell the land.*

force sth ↔ **back** *phr v* to stop yourself from showing that you are upset or frightened, especially with difficulty: *Janet **forced back** her **tears**.*

force sth ↔ **down** *phr v*

1 to make yourself eat or drink something, although you do not want it: *I forced down a piece of stale bread.*

2 to make a plane land by threatening to attack it: *The hijacked plane was forced down by military jets.*

force sth **on/upon** sb *phr v* to make someone do or accept something even though they do not want to: *It's no good trying to force a diet on someone.* | *people who try to force their own views on you*

F

force sth ↔ **out of** sb *phr v* to make someone tell you something by asking them many times, threatening them etc: *I wasn't going to tell Matt but he forced it out of me.*

forced /fɔːst $ fɔːrst/ *adj* **1** a forced smile, laugh etc is not natural or sincere: *'Oh, hello,' said Eileen, with forced brightness.* **2** [only before noun] done suddenly and quickly because the situation makes it necessary, not because it was planned or wanted: *The plane had to make a **forced landing** in a field.* | *the **forced repatriation** of thousands of refugees*

ˌforced ˈentry *n* [C,U] an occasion when someone gets into a building illegally by breaking a door, window etc: *The police found no signs of forced entry.*

ˌforced ˈlabour *BrE*, **forced labor** *AmE n* [U] when prisoners or SLAVES are forced to do very hard physical work, or a system in which this happens: *Two million suffered imprisonment or forced labour.*

ˈforce-feed *v* (*past tense and past participle* **force-fed**) [T] to force someone to eat by putting food down their throat

force·ful /ˈfɔːsfəl $ ˈfɔːrs-/ *adj* **1** a forceful person expresses their opinions very strongly and clearly and people are easily persuaded by them SYN **strong**: **a forceful personality/character/opponent etc** *He gained a reputation as a forceful member of the party.* **2** forceful arguments, reasons etc are strongly and clearly expressed SYN **powerful**: *a forceful attack on government policy* **3** having a powerful effect that is likely to change a situation: *The president hasn't been forceful enough in changing the judicial system.* | *Governments should adopt a more forceful approach to improve the environment.* **4** using physical force —**forcefully** *adv* —**forcefulness** *n* [U]

F

force ma·jeure /ˌfɔːs mæˈʒɜː $ ˌfɔːrs mɑːˈʒɜːr/ *n* [U] *law* unexpected events, for example a war, that prevent someone from doing what they had officially planned or agreed to do. An event like this can legally allow an agreement or contract to be changed or ended.

for·ceps /ˈfɔːseps, -səps $ ˈfɔːr-/ *n* [plural] a medical instrument used for picking up and holding things: *a pair of forceps*

for·ci·ble /ˈfɔːsəbəl $ ˈfɔːr-/ *adj* done using physical force: *the forcible overthrow of the government* | *signs of forcible entry into the building*

for·ci·bly /ˈfɔːsəbli $ ˈfɔːrs-/ *adv* **1** using physical force: *The police threatened to have protestors **forcibly removed**.* **2** in a way that has a strong clear effect SYN **powerfully**: *The case was forcibly put by the speaker.*

ford /fɔːd $ fɔːrd/ *n* [C] a place where a river is not deep, so that you can walk or drive across it —**ford** *v* [T]

fore[1] /fɔː $ fɔːr/ *n* **to the fore** to or in a position of importance or influence: *Environmental issues **came to the fore** in the 1980s.* | *The case **brought to the fore** a lot of racial tensions.*

fore[2] *adj* [only before noun] *technical* the fore parts of a ship, plane, or animal are the parts at the front —**fore** *adv*

fore- /fɔː $ fɔːr/ *prefix* **1** before: *The enemy had been forewarned.* → **forewarned is forearmed** at FOREWARN(2) **2** placed at the front: *her forenames* | *a horse's forelegs* **3** the front part of something: *his forehead*

fore·arm /ˈfɔːrɑːm $ -ɑːrm/ *n* [C] the lower part of the arm, between the hand and the elbow

fore·bear /ˈfɔːbeə $ ˈfɔːrber/ *n* [C usually plural] *formal* someone who was a member of your family a long time in the past SYN **ancestor**

fore·bod·ing /fɔːˈbəʊdɪŋ $ fɔːrˈboʊ-/ *n* [U] a strong feeling that something bad is going to happen soon: *She waited for news with a grim **sense of foreboding**.* THESAURUS▸ FEAR

fore·cast[1] /ˈfɔːkɑːst $ ˈfɔːrkæst/ ●●○ *n* [C] a description of what is likely to happen in the future, based on the information that you have now → **prediction**: *The **weather forecast** is good for tomorrow.* | **profit/sales/growth forecast** *the company's annual sales forecast*

forecast[2] ●●○ *v* (*past tense and past participle* **forecast** *or* **forecasted**) [T] to make a statement saying what is likely to happen in the future, based on the information that you have now SYN **predict**: *Rain was forecast for the weekend.* | **forecast (that)** *The Federal Reserve Bank forecasts that the economy will grow by 2% this year.* THESAURUS▸ PREDICT

fore·cast·er /ˈfɔːˌkɑːstə $ ˈfɔːrˌkæstər/ *n* [C] someone whose job is to say what is likely to happen in the future, especially what kind of weather is expected: *the **weather forecaster*** | ***Economic forecasters** think that the stock market is set to fall.*

fore·castle /ˈfəʊksəl $ ˈfoʊk-/ *n* [C] *AmE technical* the front part of a ship, where the sailors live SYN **fo'c'sle** *BrE*

fore·close /fɔːˈkləʊz $ fɔːrˈkloʊz/ *v* [I] *technical* if a bank forecloses, it takes away someone's property because they have failed to pay back the money that they borrowed from the bank to buy it: **[+on]** *Building societies may **foreclose on** a **mortgage** if payments are not kept up.* —**foreclosure** /-ˈkləʊʒə $ -ˈkloʊʒər/ *n* [C,U]: *housing foreclosures*

fore·court /ˈfɔːkɔːt $ ˈfɔːrkɔːrt/ *n* [C] *BrE* a large open area in front of a building such as a garage or hotel

fore·doomed /fɔːˈduːmd $ fɔːr-/ *adj formal* intended by FATE (=the power that is believed to control people's lives) to be unsuccessful or unhappy SYN **doomed**

fore·fa·ther /ˈfɔːˌfɑːðə $ ˈfɔːrˌfɑːðər/ *n* [C usually plural] **1** the people, especially men, who were part of your family a long time ago in the past SYN **ancestor**: **sb's forefathers** *What would our forefathers have thought?* **2** someone in the past who did something important that influences your life today: *Two hundred years ago our forefathers established this nation.*

fore·fin·ger /ˈfɔːˌfɪŋgə $ ˈfɔːrˌfɪŋgər/ *n* [C] the finger next to your thumb SYN **index finger**

fore·foot /ˈfɔːfʊt $ ˈfɔːr-/ *n* (*plural* **forefeet** /-fiːt/) [C] *BrE* one of the two front feet of an animal with four legs

fore·front /ˈfɔːfrʌnt $ ˈfɔːr-/ ●○○ *n*
1 be at/in/to the forefront (of sth) to be in a leading position in an important activity that is trying to achieve something or develop new ideas: *The company has always been at the forefront of science and technology.* | *Prison conditions have been pushed to the forefront of public debate.* **2 be in/at/to the forefront of sb's mind/attention etc** to be what someone is thinking about most, because it is very important to them → **at the back of sb's mind**: *Fear of unemployment was at the forefront of everyone's minds.*

fore·gath·er, **forgather** /fɔːˈgæðə $ fɔːrˈgæðər/ *v* [I] *formal* to meet in a group SYN **gather**

fore·go /fɔːˈgəʊ $ fɔːrˈgoʊ/ *v* [T] another spelling of FORGO

fore·go·ing /fɔːˈgəʊɪŋ $ fɔːrˈgoʊ-/ *adj, n formal* **the foregoing (sth)** something that has just been mentioned, read, dealt with etc OPP **following**: *The foregoing examples illustrate this point.* | *The foregoing helps to explain these results.*

ˌforegone conˈclusion *n* **be a foregone conclusion** if something is a foregone conclusion, its result is certain, even though it has not happened yet: *The election result was a foregone conclusion.*

fore·ground /ˈfɔːgraʊnd $ ˈfɔːr-/ *n* **1 the foreground** the part of the view in a picture or a photograph that is closest to you when you are looking at it OPP **background**: *There were three figures in the foreground.* → see picture at BACKGROUND **2 be in the foreground** to be regarded as important and receive a lot of attention: *Education has been very much in the foreground recently.*

fore·hand /ˈfɔːhænd $ ˈfɔːr-/ *n* [singular] a way of hitting the ball in tennis and some other games, with the flat part of your hand facing the direction of the ball OPP **backhand** → see picture at TENNIS —**forehand** *adj*

fore·head /ˈfɒrəd, ˈfɔːhed $ ˈfɔːrəd, ˈfɑː-, ˈfɔːrhed/ ●●○ *n* [C] the part of your face above your eyes and below your hair

for·eign /ˈfɒrɪn $ ˈfɔː-, ˈfɑː-/ ●●● S3 W1 *adj*
1 from or relating to a country that is not your own: *foreign students | Can you speak any foreign languages? | the success of foreign companies in various industries | I thought she sounded foreign. | transactions in foreign currencies*
2 [only before noun] involving or dealing with other countries OPP **domestic**: *America's **foreign policy** |* **foreign investment/trade etc** *Foreign competition provides consumers with a greater variety of goods. | our budget for **foreign aid*** (=financial help to countries in need) | *the Chinese Foreign Minister*
3 be foreign to sb *formal* **a)** to seem strange to someone as the result of not being known or understood SYN **be alien to sb**: *The language of finance is quite foreign to me.* **b)** to be not typical of someone's usual character: *Aggression is completely **foreign to** his **nature**.*
4 foreign body/matter/object *formal* a piece of dirt, glass, or other material that has got inside something, especially someone's body, and that should not be there: *cells that are designed to attack and destroy foreign bodies* —**foreignness** *n* [U]

ˌforeign afˈfairs *n* [plural] politics, business matters etc that affect or concern the relationship between your country and other countries

for·eign·er /ˈfɒrənə $ ˈfɔːrənər, ˈfɑː-/ ●●● W3 *n* [C] someone who comes from a different country: *Some of the local people are suspicious of foreigners.*

> REGISTER
> The word **foreigner** can sound negative and not very friendly. In everyday English, people often say **people from other countries**: *I like meeting **people from other countries**.*

ˌforeign exˈchange *n* **1** [U] used to talk about buying and selling foreign money: **foreign exchange markets/rates/transactions etc** *The dollar is expected to fall in the foreign exchange markets.* **2** [U] foreign money, especially money obtained by selling goods to a foreign country: *foreign exchange earned through exports* **3** (*also* **exchange**) [C] an arrangement through which a student exchanges homes, schools etc with a student from another country for a particular length of time, especially in order to learn a language: *The school organizes a foreign exchange to France.*

ˈForeign ˌOffice, the (*also* **the Foreign and Commonwealth Office**) the British government department that is responsible for dealing with matters concerning other countries

ˌForeign ˈSecretary *n* [C] the British Government minister who is in charge of the Foreign Office

fore·knowl·edge /fɔːˈnɒlɪdʒ $ fɔːrˈnɑːl-/ *n* [U] *formal* knowledge that something is going to happen before it actually does

fore·leg /ˈfɔːleg $ ˈfɔːr-/ *n* [C] one of the two front legs of an animal with four legs

fore·lock /ˈfɔːlɒk $ ˈfɔːrlɑːk/ *n* [C] **1** a piece of hair that falls over someone's forehead **2** the hair on a horse's head that grows between its ears and hangs forward on its face **3 tug/touch your forelock** *BrE* to show too much respect towards someone in authority - used to show disapproval

fore·man /ˈfɔːmən $ ˈfɔːr-/ ●○○ *n* (*plural* **foremen** /-mən/) [C]
1 a worker who is in charge of a group of other workers, for example in a factory
2 the leader of a JURY, who announces their decision in court

fore·most /ˈfɔːməʊst $ ˈfɔːrmoʊst/ ●○○ *adj*
1 the best or most important SYN **leading**, **top**: *one of the country's **foremost authorities** on chemical warfare | Rostropovich was long considered the world's foremost cellist.*
2 in a leading position among a group of people or things: **[+among/amongst]** *Sharpton was foremost among the protesters. | Economic concerns are foremost on many voters' minds.* → **first and foremost** at FIRST[2](10)

fore·name /ˈfɔːneɪm $ ˈfɔːr-/ *n* [C] *BrE formal* someone's FIRST NAME SYN **Christian name** → **surname**

fo·ren·sic /fəˈrensɪk, -zɪk/ ●○○ *adj* [only before noun] relating to the scientific methods used for finding out about a crime: **forensic evidence/science/medicine etc** *Forensic experts found traces of blood in the car. | a career in forensic science | a forensic pathologist*

fo·ren·sics /fəˈrensɪks, -zɪks/ *n* [U] the use of scientific tests to solve crimes

> **GRAMMAR: Singular or plural verb?**
> **Forensics** is followed by a singular verb: ***Forensics is** widely used in criminal cases.*
> GRAMMAR GUIDE ▶ NOUNS

fore·play /ˈfɔːpleɪ $ ˈfɔːr-/ *n* [U] sexual activity, such as kissing and touching the sexual organs, that happens before having sex

fore·run·ner /ˈfɔːˌrʌnə $ -ər/ *n* [C] **1** someone or something that existed before something similar that developed or came later: **[+of]** *Babbage's engine was the forerunner of the modern computer.* **2** a sign or warning that something is going to happen

fore·see /fɔːˈsiː $ fɔːr-/ ●○○ *v* (*past tense* **foresaw** /-ˈsɔː $ -ˈsɒː/, *past participle* **foreseen** /-ˈsiːn/) [T] to think or know that something is going to happen in the future → **predict**: *I've put your name on the list and I don't foresee any problems. | The disaster could not have been foreseen.* | **foresee that** *Few analysts foresaw that oil prices would rise so steeply.* | **foresee what/how etc** *No one foresaw what he was planning.* THESAURUS ▶ PREDICT

fore·see·a·ble /fɔːˈsiːəbəl $ fɔːr-/ *adj* **1 for/in the foreseeable future** for as long as it is possible to know what is likely to happen: *The situation is likely to continue for the foreseeable future.* **2 in the foreseeable future** fairly soon: *There is a possibility of water shortages in the foreseeable future.* **3** foreseeable difficulties, events etc should be planned for because they are very likely to happen in the future: *The judge found that **it was** not **foreseeable that** the fuel would catch fire. | foreseeable risk*

fore·shad·ow /fɔːˈʃædəʊ $ fɔːrˈʃædoʊ/ *v* [T] to show or say that something will happen in the future: *The revolution foreshadowed an entirely new social order.*

fore·shore /ˈfɔːʃɔː $ ˈfɔːrʃɔːr/ *n* [C usually singular, U] *BrE* **1** the part of the shore between the highest and lowest levels that the sea reaches **2** the part of the shore between the edge of the sea and the part of the land that has houses, grass etc

fore·short·ened /fɔːˈʃɔːtnd $ fɔːrˈʃɔːrtnd/ *adj formal* **1** objects, places etc that are foreshortened appear to be smaller, shorter, or closer together than they really are: *Viewed from high up, their bodies were oddly foreshortened.* **2** ended before the usual or expected time: *a foreshortened career* —**foreshorten** *v* [T]

fore·sight /ˈfɔːsaɪt $ ˈfɔːr-/ *n* [U] the ability to imagine what is likely to happen and to consider this when planning for the future → **forethought**: *It was an example of the authorities' **lack of foresight**.* | **foresight to do sth** *Luckily I'd **had the foresight** to get in plenty of food.*

fore·skin /ˈfɔːˌskɪn $ ˈfɔːr-/ *n* [C] a loose fold of skin covering the end of a man's PENIS

for·est /ˈfɒrɪst $ ˈfɔː-, ˈfɑː-/ ●●● S2 W2 *n* [C,U] a large area of land that is covered with trees → **wood**: **thick/dense forest** *Much of Scandinavia is covered in dense forest. | a **tropical forest** | the danger of **forest fires*** → RAIN FOREST, → **not see the forest for the trees** at SEE[1](40)

> **THESAURUS**
> **forest** a very large area of land with a lot of trees growing closely together: *In 1500, most of the country was forest. | the Black Forest in Germany*
> **woods** (*also* **wood** *BrE*) an area of land covered with a lot of trees, that is smaller than a forest: *Behind the house were the woods that we used to play in.*
> **woodland** an area of land that is covered with trees - used especially for describing the type of land in

F

an area: *The site covers 74 acres of beautiful ancient woodland.*
rainforest a thick forest with tall trees, in tropical parts of the world that have a lot of rain: *Tropical rainforests are home to over half of the planet's plant and animal species.* | *the Indonesian rainforest*
jungle an area of tropical forest where trees and large plants grow very closely together: *the jungles of Borneo* | *The palace was hidden for centuries in Guatemala's dense jungle.*
grove a small group of trees, or an area of land planted with a particular type of fruit tree: *The temple was built in the centre of a small grove of trees.* | *the olive groves of southern Spain*
copse /kɒps $ kɑːps/ a small area of trees or bushes growing closely together: *At the top of the field was a copse full of rabbits.*
plantation a large area of trees planted for their wood, fruit etc: *a rubber plantation*
thicket /ˈθɪkət/ a small group of bushes, plants, or small trees growing closely together: *Tall bamboo thickets fringed the narrow river.*

fore·stall /fɔːˈstɔːl $ fɔːrˈstɒːl/ *v* [T] *formal* to prevent something from happening or prevent someone from doing something by doing something first: *a measure intended to forestall further attacks*

for·est·ed /ˈfɒrɪstɪd $ ˈfɔː-, ˈfɑː-/ *adj* forested areas are covered in forests SYN **wooded**: **thickly/heavily/densely etc forested** *heavily forested terrain*

for·est·er /ˈfɒrɪstə $ ˈfɔːrəstər, ˈfɑː-/ *n* [C] someone who works in a forest taking care of, planting, and cutting down the trees

for·est·ry /ˈfɒrəstri $ ˈfɔː-, ˈfɑː-/ *n* [U] the science or skill of looking after large areas of trees

fore·taste /ˈfɔːteɪst $ ˈfɔːr-/ *n* **be a foretaste of sth** to be a sign of something more important, more impressive etc that will happen in the future: *Two wins at the start of the season were **a foretaste of things to come**.*

fore·tell /fɔːˈtel $ fɔːr-/ *v* (*past tense and past participle* **foretold** /-ˈtəʊld $ -ˈtoʊld/) [T] *formal* to say what will happen in the future, especially by using special magical powers SYN **predict**: *the birth of Christ, foretold by prophets* THESAURUS ▸ PREDICT

fore·thought /ˈfɔːθɔːt $ ˈfɔːrθɒːt/ *n* [U] careful thought or planning before you do something → **foresight**: **the forethought to do sth** *No one **had the forethought** to bring a map.*

fore·told /fɔːˈtəʊld $ fɔːrˈtoʊld/ the past tense and past participle of FORETELL

for·ev·er (*also* **for ever** *BrE*) /fərˈevə $ -ər/ ●●● S2 W3 *adv*
1 for all future time: *I wanted that moment to **last forever**.* | *Many valuable works of art were lost forever.* THESAURUS ▸ ALWAYS
2 *especially spoken* for a very long time: *Once built, stone walls last forever.* | *It **took forever** to clean up after the party.* | *The meeting seemed to go on **forever and a day**.*
3 be forever doing sth *spoken* to do something often, especially in a way that annoys people SYN **be always doing sth**: *He's forever making comments about my weight.*
4 forever and ever a phrase meaning forever, used especially in stories
5 go on forever *AmE* to be extremely long or large: *The road just went on forever.*

fore·warn /fɔːˈwɔːn $ fɔːrˈwɔːrn/ *v* [T] **1** to warn someone about something dangerous, unpleasant, or unexpected before it happens: **be forewarned of/about sth** *We'd been forewarned of the dangers of travelling at night.* GRAMMAR **Forewarn** is often used in the passive. THESAURUS ▸ WARN **2 forewarned is forearmed** used to say that it is better to know about something before it happens, so that you can be prepared for it —**forewarning** *n* [C,U]

fore·wom·an /ˈfɔːˌwʊmən $ ˈfɔːr-/ *n* (*plural* **forewomen** /-ˌwɪmɪn/) [C] **1** a female worker who is in charge of a group of other workers, especially in a factory **2** a woman who is the leader of a JURY and announces their decision in court

fore·word /ˈfɔːwɜːd $ ˈfɔːrwɜːrd/ ●○○ *n* [C] a short piece of writing at the beginning of a book that introduces the book or its writer

for·feit¹ /ˈfɔːfɪt $ ˈfɔːr-/ *v* [T] to lose a right, position, possession etc or have it taken away from you because you have broken a law or rule: *By being absent from the trial, he **forfeited** the **right** to appeal.* | *She was fined £3,000 and ordered to forfeit her car.*

forfeit² *n* [C] something that is taken away from you or something that you have to pay, because you have broken a rule or made a mistake

forfeit³ *adj* **be forfeit** *formal* to be legally or officially taken away from you as a punishment: *The company's property may even be forfeit.*

for·feit·ure /ˈfɔːfətʃə $ ˈfɔːrfətʃər/ *n* [C,U] *formal* when someone has their property or money officially taken away because they have broken a law or rule: *Refusal to sign meant forfeiture of property and exile.*

for·gath·er /fɔːˈgæðə $ fɔːrˈgæðər/ *v* [I] another spelling of FOREGATHER

for·gave /fəˈgeɪv $ fər-/ *v* the past tense of FORGIVE

forge¹ /fɔːdʒ $ fɔːrdʒ/ ●●○ *v*
1 [T] to develop something new, especially a strong relationship with other people, groups, or countries SYN **form**: **forge a relationship/alliance/link etc (with sb)** *In 1776 the United States forged an alliance with France.* | *The two women had forged a close bond.* | *Back in the 1980s, they were attempting to forge a new kind of rock music.*
2 [T] to illegally copy something, especially something printed or written, to make people think that it is real → **counterfeit**: *Someone stole my credit card and forged my signature.* | *a forged passport* THESAURUS ▸ COPY
3 [I always + adv/prep] *written* to move somewhere or continue doing something in a steady determined way: **[+into/through]** *Crowds of people forged through the streets towards the embassy.* | *He **forged into the lead** in the fourth set.* | **[+on]** | *Her speech wasn't going down too well, but she forged on.*
4 [T] to make something from a piece of metal by heating the metal and shaping it

forge ahead *phr v* to make progress, especially quickly: **[+with]** *Jo's forging ahead with her plans to write a film script.*

forge² *n* [C] **1** a place where metal is heated and shaped into objects **2** a large piece of equipment that produces high temperatures, used for heating and shaping metal objects

forg·er /ˈfɔːdʒə $ ˈfɔːrdʒər/ *n* [C] someone who illegally copies documents, money, paintings etc and tries to make people think they are real

for·ge·ry /ˈfɔːdʒəri $ ˈfɔːr-/ *n* (*plural* **forgeries**) **1** [C] a document, painting, or piece of paper money that has been copied illegally SYN **fake**: *The painting was a very clever forgery.* **2** [U] the crime of copying official documents, money etc

for·get /fəˈget $ fər-/ ●●● S1 W1 *v* (*past tense* **forgot** /-ˈgɒt $ -ˈgɑːt/, *past participle* **forgotten** /-ˈgɒtn $ -ˈgɑːtn/)
1 FACTS/INFORMATION [I,T] to not remember facts, information, or people or things from the past: *I'm sorry, I've forgotten your name.* | *I know you told me, but I forgot.* | *What happened that day will never be forgotten.* | **[+about]** *Karl says he forgot about our date.* | *She forgot all about their anniversary.* | **forget (that)** *I forgot that there's a speed limit here.* | **forget how/what/when/why etc** *How can you forget where you've parked the car?* | *He's someone who never **forgets a face*** (=forgets who someone is). | **I was forgetting ...** (=said when you have just remembered or been reminded about something) *spoken*: *Oh yes, I was forgetting she was pregnant.*
2 STH YOU MUST DO [I,T] to not remember to do something that you should do: *'Did you remember to post that letter?' 'Oh, sorry, I forgot.'* | *Give me your phone number*

F

before I forget (=forget to get it). | **forget to do sth** *Someone's forgotten to turn off their headlights.* | **clean forget** *AmE* (=completely forget) *He meant to invite Monica, but he clean forgot.*

3 LEAVE STH SOMEWHERE [T] to not remember to bring something that you need with you: **forget your keys/money/cigarettes etc** *Oh no, I've forgotten my wallet.*

4 STOP THINKING ABOUT [I,T] to stop thinking or worrying about someone or something: *Forget him, he's not worth it.* | *At my age, I think I can forget fashion.* | **forget (that)** *After a while you'll forget you're wearing contact lenses.* | **[+about]** *I'll never be able to forget about the accident.*

5 NOT CARE ABOUT [I,T] to not care about or give attention to someone or something any longer: **[+about]** *Don't forget about your old friends when you go off to college, okay?* | *You can't afford to forget your relationship with your husband.*

6 STOP A PLAN [I,T] to stop planning to do something because it is no longer possible or sensible: **[+about]** *We'll have to forget about going on holiday.* | *If we can't get any funding we might as well* ***forget the whole thing****.*

7 not forgetting sth *BrE* used to add something to a list of things you have mentioned: *You'll have to pay for the packaging and transportation costs, not forgetting airport taxes.*

8 forget yourself a) to do something stupid or embarrassing, especially by losing control of your emotions: *Lisa forgot herself and reached out to touch his knee.* **b)** *BrE* to become so involved in something that you do not think about or notice anything else SYN **lose yourself**: **forget yourself in sth** *Often he would forget himself in his work for hours.*

SPOKEN PHRASES

9 don't forget a) used to remind someone to do something: *We need bread, milk, and eggs – don't forget.* | **don't forget to do sth** *Don't forget to lock up when you leave.* **b)** used to remind someone about an important fact or detail that they should consider: **don't forget (that)** *But don't forget that you have to pay interest on the loan.* | *Don't forget, I'll be home late tonight.* **c)** used to remind someone to take something with them: *Don't forget your sandwiches.*

10 forget it a) used to tell someone that something is not important and they do not need to worry about it: *'Sorry I didn't phone.' 'Forget it.'* **b)** used to tell someone to stop asking or talking about something, because it is annoying you: *I'm not coming with you, so forget it.* **c)** (also **forget that!** *AmE*) used to tell someone that you refuse to do something or that it will be impossible to do something: *'Can you lend me $10.' 'Forget it, no way.'* | *If you're thinking of getting Roy to help, you can forget it!* **d)** used when someone asks you what you just said and you do not want to repeat it: *'What did you say?' ' Nothing, just forget it.'*

11 I'll never forget sth used to say that you will always remember something from the past, because it was sad, funny, enjoyable etc: *I'll never forget the look on his face when he opened the door.*

12 aren't you forgetting ...?/haven't you forgotten ...? used to remind someone about something, often humorously: *Aren't you forgetting that you're already married?*

13 I forget used to say that you cannot remember a particular detail about something: **I forget what/where/how etc** *I forget what he said exactly but it was very rude.* | **I forget the name/details etc** *I forget the name of the street, but it's the first on the left.*

14 and don't you forget it! used to remind someone angrily about an important fact that should make them behave differently: *I'm the boss around here, and don't you forget it!*

THESAURUS

forget to not remember something or someone: *I'm sorry, I've forgotten your name.* | *It was an experience she would never forget.*

don't remember/can't remember used when saying that you have forgotten something: *I know I needed something at the shops, but I can't remember what it was.*

have no recollection of sth *formal* to not remember anything about something that happened in the past: *He told the jury that he had no recollection of the accident.*

slip your mind *especially spoken* if something that you must do slips your mind, you forget to do it because you are busy thinking about other things: *I'm sorry I didn't call. There was so much going on that it completely slipped my mind.*

it goes in one ear and out the other *spoken* used to say that someone forgets what you tell them very quickly because they are not interested or do not listen properly: *With kids you have to say everything twice. It all goes in one ear and out the other.*

my mind goes blank *especially spoken* used to say that you are suddenly unable to remember something at a time when you need it: *I was so nervous that my mind went blank as soon as they asked me a question.*

TO TRY TO FORGET SOMETHING

forget to deliberately try not to think about something sad or unpleasant: *After the divorce came through, I just wanted to forget about it all.*

put sth out of your mind to make yourself stop thinking about something that stops you concentrating or makes you angry, sad, or nervous: *When I'm competing I put everything out of my mind and concentrate on winning.*

put sth behind you to stop thinking about something sad or unpleasant that happened to you in the past, so that you can continue with your life and be happy: *It can take a long time to put a traumatic experience like that behind you.*

take/keep your mind off sth to do something that helps you stop thinking about a problem for a short time: *Sara went out for a walk to try and take her mind off things.*

blot sth out to forget an unpleasant memory or thought, by deliberately stopping yourself from thinking about it: *He started drinking heavily in an effort to blot out the thought of what he had done.*

shut sb/sth out to deliberately forget someone or something and not let them be part of your thoughts and feelings: *The marriage was a disaster, and her husband shut her out of his life completely.*

for·get·ful /fəˈgetfəl $ fər-/ *adj* often forgetting things —**forgetfully** *adv* —**forgetfulness** *n* [U]

forˈget-me-ˌnot *n* [C] a small plant with pale blue flowers

for·get·ta·ble /fəˈgetəbəl $ fər-/ *adj* not very interesting or good – often used humorously OPP **unforgettable**: *He'd had a role in one or two forgettable movies.*

for·giv·a·ble /fəˈgɪvəbəl $ fər-/ *adj* if something bad is forgivable, you can understand how it happened and you can easily forgive it OPP **unforgivable**: *It was an easily forgivable mistake.*

for·give /fəˈgɪv $ fər-/ ●●○ *v* (*past tense* **forgave** /-ˈgeɪv/, *past participle* **forgiven** /-ˈgɪvən/) [I,T]

1 to stop being angry with someone and stop blaming them, although they have done something wrong: **forgive sb for (doing) sth** *I've tried to forgive him for what he said.* | *He never forgave her for walking out on him.* | **forgive myself/yourself etc** *If anything happened to the kids* ***I'd never forgive myself****.* | **you're forgiven** *spoken* (=used to tell someone that you are not angry with them) *'I'm really sorry.' 'It's okay, you're forgiven.'* | **forgive sb sth** *God forgives us our sins.* | *He didn't look the sort of man to* ***forgive and forget*** (=forgive someone and no longer think about it).

GRAMMAR: Patterns with forgive

- You **forgive** someone: *Alright, I forgive you.*
- You **forgive** something: *Please forgive his rudeness.*
- You **forgive** someone **for** something or **for doing**

something: *She lied and I can't forgive her for that.* | *Forgive me for not writing.*
• In literary or formal English, you can **forgive someone something**: *Forgive us our trespasses.* This pattern is not used in everyday English.

2 forgive me *spoken* used when you are going to say or do something that might seem rude or offensive and you want it to seem more polite: ***Forgive me, but*** *I don't think that is relevant.* | **forgive me for asking/saying etc sth** (*also* **forgive my asking/saying etc**) ***Forgive me for saying so***, *but that's nonsense.* | *Forgive my phoning you so late.*
3 sb can be forgiven for thinking/believing/feeling etc sth used to say that it is easy to understand why someone might think or do something: *You could be forgiven for thinking football is a religion here.*
4 forgive a debt/loan *formal* if a country or organization forgives a debt, it says that the money does not have to be paid back SYN **write off**: *Saudi Arabia's decision to forgive the debt owed by the poorest Islamic countries*

for·give·ness /fəˈɡɪvnəs $ fər-/ ●○○ *n* [U] when someone forgives another person → **absolution**: **ask/beg/pray etc for (sb's) forgiveness** *He never admitted his guilt or asked for forgiveness.*

for·giv·ing /fəˈɡɪvɪŋ $ fər-/ *adj* willing to forgive: *My father was a kind and forgiving man.*

for·go /fɔːˈɡəʊ $ fɔːrˈɡoʊ/ *v* (*past tense* **forwent** /-ˈwent/, *past participle* **forgone** /-ˈɡɒn $ -ˈɡɒːn/, *present participle* **forgoing**) [T] to not do or have something pleasant or enjoyable SYN **go without**: *I had to forgo lunch.*

for·got /fəˈɡɒt $ fərˈɡɑːt/ *v* the past tense of FORGET

for·got·ten¹ /fəˈɡɒtn $ fərˈɡɑːtn/ *v* the past participle of FORGET

forgotten² *adj* [usually before noun] that people have forgotten about or do not pay much attention to: *a forgotten corner of the churchyard*

FORKS

garden fork | fork | a fork of lightning | a fork in the road | tuning fork

fork¹ /fɔːk $ fɔːrk/ ●●● S3 *n* [C]
1 a tool you use for picking up and eating food, with a handle and three or four points: *Put the* ***knives and forks*** *on the table.*
2 a garden tool used for digging, with a handle and three or four points → PITCHFORK¹
3 a place where a road, river, or tree divides into two parts, or one of the parts it divides into: *the north fork of the Sacramento river* | *Take the left fork then go straight on.*
4 fork of lightning a sudden flash of LIGHTNING with two or more lines of light
5 one of the two metal bars between which the front wheel of a bicycle or MOTORCYCLE is fixed → **TUNING FORK** → see pictures at **BICYCLE**, **MOTORBIKE**

fork² *v* **1** (*also* **fork off**) [I] if a road, river etc forks, it divides into two parts → **divide**, **split**: *The path forked off in two directions.* **2 fork (off) left/right** to go left or right when a road divides into two parts SYN **turn**: *Fork left at the bottom of the hill.* **3** [T always + adv/prep] to put food into your mouth or onto a plate using a fork: **fork sth into/onto etc sth** *He forked some bacon into his mouth.* **4** [T always + adv/prep] to put MANURE into soil or to move soil around using a large garden fork: **fork sth in/over etc** *In November, the soil should be forked over.*

fork out (sth) *phr v informal* to spend a lot of money on something, not because you want to but because you have to: **[+for/on]** *I had to fork out £600 on my car when I had it serviced.* | *We don't want to have to fork out for an expensive meal.*

fork sth ↔ **over** *phr v especially AmE informal* to give money to someone or something, or spend money on something: *The arena won't be finished until private donors fork over more money.*

forked /fɔːkt $ fɔːrkt/ *adj* having one end divided into two or more parts: *Snakes have forked tongues.*

ˌforked ˈlightning *n* [U] lightning that looks like a line of light that divides into several smaller lines near the bottom → **sheet lightning**

fork·ful /ˈfɔːkfʊl $ ˈfɔːrk-/ *n* [C] an amount of food on a fork: **[+of]** *huge forkfuls of food*

ˌfork-lift ˈtruck (*also* **ˈfork-lift**) *n* [C] a vehicle with special equipment on the front for lifting and moving heavy things → see picture at **TRUCK¹**

ˌforklift ˈupgrade *n* [C] an UPGRADE to a computer system (=something done to the computer system that makes it better or able to do more) that involves buying a lot of new equipment: *We had to choose between an expensive forklift upgrade and keeping our old machines.*

for·lorn /fəˈlɔːn $ fərˈlɔːrn/ *adj* **1** seeming lonely and unhappy: *a* ***forlorn figure*** *sitting all by herself* | *Ana sat with a bowed head and spoke in a forlorn voice.* **2** a place that is forlorn seems empty and sad, and is often in bad condition: *The house looked old and forlorn.* **3** [only before noun] a forlorn hope, attempt, or struggle etc is not going to be successful: *the* ***forlorn hope*** *of finding a peace formula* —**forlornly** *adv*

Form 1040 /fɔːm ˌten ˈfɔːti $ ˌfɔːrm-, -ˈfɔːrti/ *n* [C] a form which people in the US use to give information to the IRS (Internal Revenue Service) so that their INCOME TAX can be calculated

Form 1099 /fɔːm ˌten ˌnaɪnti ˈnaɪn $ ˌfɔːrm-/ *n* [C] the form which people in the US use to give information to the IRS (Internal Revenue Service) about money that they have earned during the year apart from their salaries (SALARY)

form¹ /fɔːm $ fɔːrm/ ●●● S1 W1 *n*
1 TYPE [C] a particular type of something that exists in many different varieties: **[+of]** *a severe form of cancer* | *The bicycle is an environment-friendly form of transport.* | *the art forms of the twentieth century*
2 WAY STH IS/APPEARS [C] the way something is or appears to be: *We oppose racism in all its forms.* | **in the form of sth** *People are bombarded with information in the form of TV advertising.* | *Vitamin C can be taken* ***in*** *capsule or tablet* ***form***. | *A typical training programme* ***takes the form of*** *a series of workshops.*
3 SHAPE [C] a shape: **[+of]** *the shadowy forms of the divers swimming below the boat* | **in the form of sth** *The main staircase was in the form of a big 'S'.* | *The* ***female form*** *is a thing of beauty.*
4 DOCUMENT [C] an official document with spaces where you write information, especially about yourself: ***Application forms*** *are available from the college.* | *Just* ***complete*** *the* ***entry form*** (=write the answers to the questions on a form) *and return it.* | **fill in/out a form** (=write the answers to the questions on a form) *Fill in the form and send it back with your cheque.*
5 ART/LITERATURE [U] the structure of a work of art or piece of writing, rather than the ideas it expresses, events it describes etc: *the distinction between form and content*
6 PERFORMANCE [U] how well a sports person, team, musician etc is performing, or has performed recently: *I have been greatly encouraged by the team's recent form.* | **on present/current/past etc form** *On current form he's one of the top three players in the country.* | **in good/fine/great form**

He's been in good form all this season. | *He had no qualms about dropping players he thought were off form* (=not performing well).
7 SCHOOL [C] *BrE* a class in a school: **first/second/sixth etc form** *examinations taken in the fourth form* → FORM TEACHER
8 GRAMMAR [C] a way of writing or saying a word that shows its number, tense etc. For example, 'was' is a past form of the verb 'to be'.
9 CRIMINAL RECORD [U] *BrE informal* if someone has form, they are known to the police because they have committed crimes in the past
10 bad form *old-fashioned* behaviour that is considered to be socially unacceptable SYN **bad manners**: *It used to be considered bad form to talk about money.*
11 form of words a way of expressing something official SYN **wording**: *The precise form of words has been agreed by the 12 heads of government.*
12 be in good/fine/great etc form (*also* **be on good/fine/great etc form** *BrE*) to be full of confidence and energy, so that you do something well or talk in an interesting or amusing way: *Michelle was in great form at last week's conference.*
13 take form a) to begin to exist or develop: *The womb represents the very first place in which life takes form.* **b)** to start to become a particular shape: *As the men worked, I watched the ship's hull take form.* → **true to form** at TRUE¹(7)

form² ●●● S2 W1 *v*
1 ESTABLISH [T] to establish an organization, committee, government etc → **formation**: *The winning party will form the government.* | *CARE was formed in 1946 and helps the poor in 38 countries.*
2 BE PART OF STH [linking verb] to be the thing, or one of the things, that is part of something else, often having a particular use: *Love and trust should* ***form the basis of*** *a marriage.* | *The project* ***forms part of*** *a larger project investigating the history of the cinema.* | *The river formed a natural boundary between the two countries.*

GRAMMAR: Linking verbs
Form is a linking verb that links the subject of the sentence with a noun: *The changes form part of a new curriculum.*

3 START TO EXIST [I,T] to start to exist, or make something start to exist, especially as the result of a natural process → **formation**: *The rocks were formed more than 4,000 million years ago.* | *By midnight ice was already forming on the roads.* | *Sulphur dioxide and nitrogen oxide combine to form acid rain.* **THESAURUS** MAKE
4 MAKE/PRODUCE [T] to make something by combining two or more parts: *In English the past tense of a verb is usually formed by adding 'ed'.*
5 SHAPE/LINE [I,T] to come together in a particular shape or line, or to make something have a particular shape SYN **make**: *Film-goers began to form a line outside the cinema.* | *Cut off the corners of the square to form a diamond.*
6 RELATIONSHIP [T] to establish and develop a relationship with someone: *She seemed incapable of forming any relationships.* | *On returning to Boston, she formed a close friendship with her aunt.*
7 form an opinion/impression/idea to use available information to develop or reach an opinion or idea: *She formed the opinion that one of the pupils was bullying the other.*
8 INFLUENCE [T] to have a strong influence on how someone's character develops and the type of person they become SYN **mould** → **formative**: *Events in early childhood often help to form our personalities in later life.*

form·al¹ /ˈfɔːməl $ ˈfɔːr-/ ●●● S2 W2 *adj*
1 OFFICIAL [usually before noun] made or done officially or publicly OPP **informal**: ***formal recognition*** *of the reformed church* | *a* ***formal agreement*** *between the countries* | *There is no* ***formal structure*** *for negotiating pay increases.* | **make/lodge a formal complaint** *Mr Kelly has lodged a formal complaint against the police.*
2 BEHAVIOUR formal behaviour is very polite, and is used in official or important situations, or with people you do not know well OPP **informal**: *Over the years, teaching methods have changed and become less formal.*
3 LANGUAGE formal language is used in official or serious situations OPP **informal**: *'Yours sincerely' is a formal way of ending a letter.*
4 EVENT/OCCASION a formal event is important, and people who go to it wear special clothes and behave very politely OPP **informal**: *I've met her twice but only on* ***formal occasions.*** | *a formal dinner*
5 CLOTHES formal dress is clothing such as a TUXEDO for men or a long dress for women, that is worn to formal events OPP **casual, informal**: *We insist on formal dress for dinner.*
6 formal education/training/qualifications education etc in a subject or skill, that you receive in a school, college etc rather than practical experience of it: *knowledge and wisdom gained from experience rather than from formal education*
7 ORGANIZED done in a very organized way OPP **informal**: *The course includes formal lectures.*
8 GARDEN/PARK a formal garden, park, or room is arranged in a very organized way OPP **informal**: *the palace's beautifully restored formal gardens* → FORMALLY

formal² *n* [C] *AmE* **1** a dance at which you have to wear formal clothes **2** an expensive and usually long dress that women wear on formal occasions

for·mal·de·hyde /fɔːˈmældəhaɪd $ fɔːr-/ *n* [U] a strong-smelling gas that can be mixed with water and used for preserving things such as dead animals to be used in science etc: *frogs preserved in formaldehyde*

for·mal·ise /ˈfɔːməlaɪz $ ˈfɔːr-/ *v* [T] a British spelling of FORMALIZE

form·al·is·m /ˈfɔːməlɪzəm $ ˈfɔːr-/ *n* [U] a style or method in art, religion, or science that pays a lot of attention to the rules and correct forms of something, rather than to inner meanings —**formalist** *n* [C] —**formalistic** /ˌfɔːməˈlɪstɪk◂ $ ˌfɔːr-/ *adj*

for·mal·i·ty /fɔːˈmæləti $ fɔːr-/ ●○○ *n* (*plural* **formalities**)
1 [C usually plural] something that you must do as a formal or official part of an activity or process: *the formalities necessary for a valid marriage*
2 [C usually singular] something you must do even though it has no practical importance or effects: **just/only/merely etc a formality** *Getting a gun license here seems to be just a formality.*
3 [U] careful attention to polite behaviour and language in formal situations OPP **informality**: *There is always some* ***degree of formality*** *when one speaks to a stranger.* | *The loan was arranged with little formality.*

for·mal·ize (*also* **-ise** *BrE*) /ˈfɔːməlaɪz $ ˈfɔːr-/ *v* [T] to make a plan, decision, or idea official, especially by deciding and clearly describing all the details: *Final arrangements for the takeover have yet to be formalized.* —**formalization** /ˌfɔːməlaɪˈzeɪʃən $ ˌfɔːrmələ-/ *n* [U]

for·mal·ly /ˈfɔːməli $ ˈfɔːr-/ ●●○ W3 *adv*
1 officially OPP **informally**: *We announced a decision formally recognizing the new government.*
2 in a polite way OPP **informally**: *He put his hand out formally, and Liza took it.* | *'I apologize, Captain,' she said formally.*

for·mat¹ /ˈfɔːmæt $ ˈfɔːr-/ ●○○ AWL *n* [C]
1 the way in which something such as a television show or meeting is organized or arranged: *The courses were run to a consistent format.*
2 the size, shape, design etc in which something such as a book or magazine is produced: *a large-format book for the partially-sighted*
3 the way in which information is stored on a computer
4 the type of equipment that an MP3 file, DVD, or piece of computer SOFTWARE etc is designed to use

format² AWL *v* (**formatted, formatting**) [T] **1** *technical* to organize the space on a computer DISK so that information can be stored on it **2** to arrange the pages of a book or the information on a computer etc into a particular design: *better ways to format your spreadsheets* —**formatting** *n* [U] —**formatted** *adj*

for·ma·tion /fɔːˈmeɪʃən $ fɔːr-/ ●●○ W3 *n*
1 [U] the process of starting a new organization or group SYN **creation**: **[+of]** *the formation of a new government*
2 [U] the process by which something develops into a particular thing or shape: **[+of]** *the substances which lead to the formation of ozone | We now know a lot more about the early stages of planetary formation.*
3 [C] the way in which a group of things are arranged to form a pattern or shape: *troop formations*
4 in formation if a group of planes, ships, soldiers etc are moving in formation, they are flying, marching etc in a particular order or pattern: *a squadron of aircraft, flying in formation*
5 [C,U] rock or cloud that is formed in a particular shape, or the shape in which it is formed: **rock/cloud formation** *the canyon's impressive rock formations*
6 [C,U] *technical* society, politics etc seen as a system of practices and beliefs: **social/political/cultural etc formation** *Marx founded a new science: the science of the history of social formations.*

for·ma·tive /ˈfɔːmətɪv $ ˈfɔːr-/ *adj* [only before noun] having an important influence on the way someone or something develops: **formative years/period/stages etc** (=the period when someone's character develops) *He exposed his children to music throughout their formative years.* | **formative influence/effect etc** *International politics were a formative influence on the party.*

for·mer¹ /ˈfɔːmə $ ˈfɔːrmər/ ●●● S2 W1 *adj* [only before noun]
1 happening or existing before, but not now → **present**, **previous**: *the former Soviet Union | Their farm has been reduced to half its former size.* THESAURUS ▸ LAST
2 having a particular position in the past SYN **ex-** → **present**: *my former husband | former President Clinton*
3 in former times/years in the past
4 sb/sth's former self what someone or something was like before they were changed by age, illness, trouble etc: *She seems more like her former self.* | **be a shadow/ghost of your former self** (=be much less confident, healthy, energetic etc than you used to be) *The team's a shadow of its former self.*

former² *n* **1 the former** *formal* the first of two people or things that you have just mentioned OPP **the latter**: *Of the two possibilities, the former seems more likely.* **2 first/second/sixth etc former** *BrE* used in some schools to show which class a student is in, according to how many years they have been in school

for·mer·ly /ˈfɔːməli $ ˈfɔːrmərli/ ●●○ *adv* in earlier times SYN **previously**: *Kiribati, **formerly known as** the Gilbert Islands | This elegant hotel was formerly a castle.*

For·mi·ca /fɔːˈmaɪkə $ fɔːr-/ *n* [U] *trademark* strong plastic made in thin sheets, used especially for covering the surfaces of tables and kitchen COUNTERS

for·mi·da·ble /ˈfɔːmədəbəl, fəˈmɪd- $ ˈfɔːr-/ ●○○ *adj*
1 very powerful or impressive, and often frightening: *The building is grey, formidable, not at all picturesque. | The new range of computers have formidable processing power.*
2 difficult to deal with and needing a lot of effort or skill: **formidable task/challenge** *the formidable task of local government reorganization* —**formidably** *adv*

form·less /ˈfɔːmləs $ ˈfɔːrm-/ *adj* without a definite shape: *To the listener, this music is incoherent and formless. | formless horrors that await you in the fog* —**formlessly** *adv* —**formlessness** *n* [U]

ˈform ˌletter *n* [C] a standard letter that is sent to a number of people

ˈform ˌteacher *n* [C] *BrE* the teacher who is responsible for all the students in the same class at a school

for·mu·la /ˈfɔːmjələ $ ˈfɔːr-/ ●●○ S3 W3 AWL *n* (*plural* **formulas** *or* **formulae** /-liː/)
1 [singular] a method or set of principles that you use to solve a problem or to make sure that something is successful: *We're still searching for a peace formula.* | **[+for]** *a formula for the withdrawal of US forces from the area | There is no **magic formula*** (=a method that is certain to be successful) *that will transform sorrow into happiness. | With viewing figures up a million, the programme has a **winning formula**.*
2 [C] a series of numbers or letters that represent a mathematical or scientific rule: *the formula for calculating distance | Sugar is represented by the simple formula CHO.*
3 [C] a list of the substances used to make a medicine, FUEL, drink etc, showing the amounts of each substance that should be used: *Our products are handmade from traditional formulas.*
4 Formula One/Two/Three etc a type of car racing, in which the different types are based on the size of the cars' engines: *a Formula One car*
5 [U] a type of liquid food for babies that is similar to a woman's breast milk
6 [C] a fixed and familiar series of words that seems meaningless or insincere: *a speech full of the usual formulas and clichés*

for·mu·la·ic /ˌfɔːmjəˈleɪ-ɪk◂ $ ˌfɔːr-/ *adj formal* containing or made from ideas or expressions that have been used many times before and are therefore not very new or interesting: *Children love jokes and riddles that are heavily formulaic.*

for·mu·late /ˈfɔːmjəleɪt $ ˈfɔːr-/ ●○○ AWL *v* [T]
1 to develop something such as a plan or a set of rules, and decide all the details of how it will be done: **formulate a policy/plan/strategy etc** *He formulated Labour Party education policy in 1922.* | **formulate an idea/theory** *Darwin formulated the theory of natural selection.*
2 to think carefully about what to say, and say it clearly: *We are studying the situation but have not formulated any response yet.* —**formulation** /ˌfɔːmjəˈleɪʃən $ ˌfɔːr-/ *n* [C,U]: *the formulation of clear objectives*

for·ni·cate /ˈfɔːnɪkeɪt $ ˈfɔːr-/ *v* [I] a word meaning to have sex with someone who you are not married to - used to show strong disapproval —**fornication** /ˌfɔːnɪˈkeɪʃən $ ˌfɔːr-/ *n* [U]

for·sake /fəˈseɪk $ fər-/ *v* (*past tense* **forsook** /-ˈsʊk/, *past participle* **forsaken** /-ˈseɪkən/) [T] *formal* **1** to leave someone, especially when you should stay because they need you SYN **abandon**: *children forsaken by their parents* **2** to stop doing, using, or having something that you enjoy SYN **give up**: *She will never forsake her vegetarian principles.* **3** to leave a place, especially when you do not want to: *He has forsaken his native Finland to live in Britain.* → GODFORSAKEN

for·sooth /fəˈsuːθ $ fər-/ *adv old use* certainly

for·swear /fɔːˈsweə $ fɔːrˈswer/ *v* (*past tense* **forswore** /-ˈswɔː $ -ˈswɔːr/, *past participle* **forsworn** /-ˈswɔːn $ -ˈswɔːrn/) [T] *formal* to stop doing something or promise that you will stop doing something SYN **renounce**: *We are forswearing the use of chemical weapons for any reason.*

fort /fɔːt $ fɔːrt/ ●●○ *n* [C] a strong building or group of buildings used by soldiers or an army for defending an important place → **hold the fort** at HOLD¹(33)

for·te¹ /ˈfɔːteɪ $ fɔːrt/ *n* **1 be sb's forte** to be something that you do well or are skilled at: *He found that running long distances was **not** his **forte**. | As a writer, her forte is comedy.* **2** [C] a note or line of music played or sung loudly

for·te² /ˈfɔːteɪ $ ˈfɔːr-/ *adj, adv technical* played or sung loudly OPP **piano**

forth /fɔːθ $ fɔːrθ/ ●○○ *adv*
1 and so forth used to refer to other things of the type you have already mentioned, without actually naming them SYN **et cetera**: *She started telling me about her bad back, her migraines, and so forth.*
2 [only after verb] *formal* going out from a place or point, and moving forwards or outwards: *The house was still burning, pouring forth thick black smoke.* → **back and forth** at BACK¹(11), → **hold forth** at HOLD¹, → **put forth** at PUT, → **sally forth** at SALLY², → **set forth** at SET¹

ˌForth ˈBridge, the a famous metal railway bridge

built in 1889 over the River Forth in Scotland, which is considered to be a fine example of 19th century engineering. People sometimes say that a job is 'like painting the Forth Bridge' when they mean that it seems to never end, because the metal bridge takes a long time to paint, and when the job is finished it has to start again.

forth·com·ing /ˌfɔːθˈkʌmɪŋ◂ $ ˌfɔːrθ-/ ●○○ AWL *adj*
1 [only before noun] a forthcoming event, meeting etc is one that has been planned to happen soon: *the* ***forthcoming elections*** | *Keep an eye on the noticeboards for* ***forthcoming events****.*
2 willing to give information about something OPP **unforthcoming**: **[+about]** *IBM is usually pretty forthcoming about the markets for its products.*
3 [not before noun] if something is forthcoming, it is given or offered when needed – often used to say that this does not happen: *When no reply was forthcoming, she wrote again.*

forth·right /ˈfɔːθraɪt $ ˈfɔːrθ-/ *adj* direct and honest – used in order to show approval SYN **straightforward**: *She answered in her usual* ***forthright manner****.*

forth·with /fɔːθˈwɪð, -ˈwɪθ $ fɔːrθ-/ *adv formal* immediately: *He was fined £40, with 28 days' imprisonment if the money was not produced forthwith.*

for·ti·fi·ca·tion /ˌfɔːtɪfɪˈkeɪʃən $ ˌfɔːr-/ *n* **1** [U] the process of making something stronger or more effective **2 fortifications** [plural] towers, walls etc built around a place in order to protect it or defend it: *a site of ancient fortifications dating from about 500 B.C.*

ˌfortified ˈwine *n* [C,U] wine such as SHERRY or PORT that has strong alcohol added

for·ti·fy /ˈfɔːtɪfaɪ $ ˈfɔːr-/ *v* (**fortified**, **fortifying**, **fortifies**) [T] **1** to build towers, walls etc around an area or city in order to defend it: *The town was heavily fortified.* **2** to encourage an attitude or feeling and make it stronger SYN **strengthen**: *Her position was fortified by election successes and economic recovery.* **3** *written* to make someone feel physically or mentally stronger: **fortify yourself (with sth)** *We fortified ourselves with a breakfast of bacon and eggs.* **4** to make food or drinks more healthy by adding VITAMINS to them: *fortified breakfast cereals* | **be fortified with sth** *foods fortified with vitamin B* GRAMMAR **Fortify** is usually passive in this meaning.

for·tis·si·mo /fɔːˈtɪsəməʊ $ fɔːrˈtɪsəmoʊ/ *adj, adv* music that is fortissimo is played or sung very loudly OPP **pianissimo** → **forte**

for·ti·tude /ˈfɔːtɪtjuːd $ ˈfɔːrtɪtuːd/ *n* [U] *formal* courage shown when you are in great pain or experiencing a lot of trouble SYN **strength**: *Winnie is a woman of quiet fortitude who has endured a lot of suffering.*

ˌFort ˈKnox people often use the name 'Fort Knox' when talking about a place that is extremely well guarded or impossible to enter without permission. It comes from a military building in the US state of Kentucky which holds the government's store of gold: *His house is like Fort Knox.*

fort·night /ˈfɔːtnaɪt $ ˈfɔːrt-/ ●●○ S3 *n* [C usually singular] *BrE* two weeks: *a fortnight's holiday* | *in a fortnight's time* | *a fortnight ago*

fort·night·ly /ˈfɔːtnaɪtli $ ˈfɔːrt-/ *adj, adv BrE* happening every fortnight or once a fortnight: *We used to dread my uncle's fortnightly visits.*

for·tress /ˈfɔːtrɪs $ ˈfɔːr-/ ●○○ *n* [C] a large strong building used for defending an important place

for·tu·i·tous /fɔːˈtjuːɪtəs $ fɔːrˈtuː-/ *adj formal* happening by chance, especially in a way that has a good result: *The meeting with Jack was fortuitous.* THESAURUS ▸ LUCKY —**fortuitously** *adv*

for·tu·nate /ˈfɔːtʃənət $ ˈfɔːr-/ ●●○ *adj*
1 someone who is fortunate has something good happen to them, or is in a good situation SYN **lucky**: **fortunate to do sth** *I've been fortunate to find a career that I love.* | *I was* ***fortunate enough*** *to obtain a research studentship at Stanford.* | **fortunate in doing sth** *She felt fortunate in being able to please herself where she lived.* | **fortunate that** *I'm fortunate that I have such an understanding wife.* | **more/less fortunate than sb** *We've been more fortunate than a lot of farmers.* THESAURUS ▸ LUCKY
2 a fortunate event is one in which something good happens by chance, especially when this saves you from trouble or danger SYN **lucky**: *By a fortunate coincidence, a passer-by heard her cries for help.*
3 the less fortunate people who are poor: *We should all consider the plight of the less fortunate.*

for·tu·nate·ly /ˈfɔːtʃənətli $ ˈfɔːr-/ ●●○ *adv* [sentence adverb] happening because of good luck SYN **luckily**: *Fortunately, everything worked out all right in the end.*

> **REGISTER**
> In everyday English, people usually say **luckily** rather than **fortunately**: ***Luckily,*** *no one was hurt.*

for·tune /ˈfɔːtʃən $ ˈfɔːr-/ ●●○ S3 W3 *n*
1 MONEY [C] a very large amount of money: *He* ***made a fortune*** *selling property in Spain.* | *My first painting sold for £25,* ***a small fortune*** *then for an art student.* | *He died in poverty in 1947, but his art is* ***worth a fortune****.* | *The carpet must have* ***cost a fortune****.* | *It is quite easy to decorate your house without* ***spending a fortune****.* | *Her* ***personal fortune*** *was estimated at £37 million.*
2 CHANCE [U] chance or luck, and the effect that it has on your life: *I* ***had the good fortune to*** *work with a brilliant head of department.* | *Sickness or ill fortune could reduce you to a needy situation.* | *I felt it was useless to struggle against fortune.*
3 WHAT HAPPENS TO YOU [C usually plural] the good or bad things that happen in life: *a downturn in the company's fortunes* | *This defeat marked a change in the team's fortunes.* | *The geographical position of the frontier fluctuated with* ***the fortunes of war*** (=the things that can happen during a war). THESAURUS ▸ FUTURE
4 tell sb's fortune to tell someone what will happen to them in the future by looking at their hands, using cards etc → SOLDIER OF FORTUNE, → **fame and fortune** at FAME, → **a hostage to fortune** at HOSTAGE(3), → **seek your fortune** at SEEK(4)

FORTUNE COOKIE

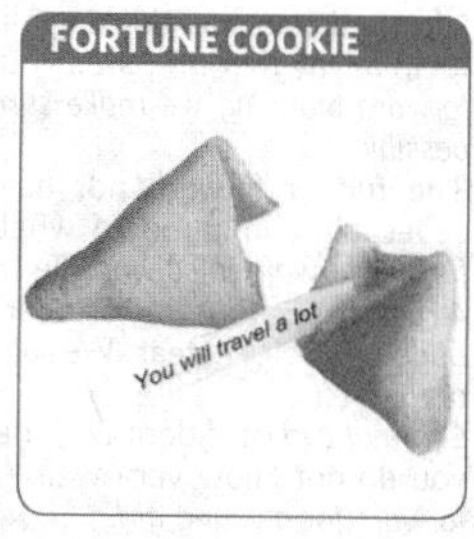

ˈfortune ˌcookie *n* [C] a BISCUIT served in Chinese restaurants, containing a piece of paper that says what is supposed to happen to you in the future

ˈfortune-ˌteller *n* [C] someone who uses cards or looks at people's hands in order to tell them what is supposed to happen to them in the future —**fortune telling** *n* [U]

for·ty /ˈfɔːti $ ˈfɔːrti/ ●●● S3 W3 *number*
1 the number 40
2 the forties (*also* **the '40s, the 1940s**) [plural] the years from 1940 to 1949: *The place was built as a casino in the forties.* | **the early/mid/late forties** *He spent several years in Paris in the late forties.*
3 be in your forties to be aged between 40 and 49: **early/mid/late forties** *The woman was probably in her mid forties.*
4 in the forties if the temperature is in the forties, it is between 40 degrees and 49 degrees: **in the low/mid/high forties** *The temperature was up in the high forties.* —**fortieth** *adj*: *her fortieth birthday*

ˌforty-ˈfive *n* [C] **1** (*also* **45**) a small record with one song on each side **2** (*also* **.45**, **Colt 45**) *trademark* a small gun

ˌforty ˈwinks *n* [U] *informal* a very short sleep: *I felt a lot better after I had forty winks.*

for·um /ˈfɔːrəm/ ●○○ *n* [C]
1 an organization, meeting, TV programme etc where people have a chance to publicly discuss an important subject: **[+for]** *The journal aims to provide a forum for discussion and debate.* | **[+on]** *the new national forum on the environment*

F

2 a group of computer users who are interested in a particular subject and discuss it using EMAIL or the Internet
3 a large outdoor public place in ancient Rome used for business and discussion

for·ward[1] /ˈfɔːwəd $ ˈfɔːrwərd/ ●●● S1 W1 (*also* **forwards** /-wədz $ -wərdz/) *adv*
1 towards a place or position that is in front of you OPP **backwards**: *He **leaned forward**, his elbows resting on the table. | The crowd surged forwards. | She took another small step forward.*
2 towards greater progress, improvement, or development: *We agreed that the sensible **way forward** was for a new company to be formed. | After the Labour Party conference, he stated that we could now **go forward** as a united party. | Britain is now ready to **move forward**.*
3 towards the future in a way that is hopeful OPP **backwards**: *I felt that at last I could begin to **look forward**.*
4 from that/this day/time/moment etc forward beginning on that day or at that time: *They never met again from that day forward.*
5 go forward to/into to successfully complete one stage of a competition so that you are able to compete in the next stage: *South Korea went forward into the next round of the World Cup.*
6 if you put a clock or a watch forward, you change it so that it shows a later time, for example when the time changes to BRITISH SUMMER TIME OPP **back**: *We **put our watches forward** by 2 hours. | **The clocks go forward** this weekend.*
7 in or towards the front part of a ship → **FAST-FORWARD**, → **look forward to sth** at LOOK[1], → **backwards and forwards** at **BACKWARDS(5)**

forward[2] ●●○ S3 W3 *adj*
1 [only before noun] closer to a person, place, or position that is in front of you OPP **backward**: *Army roadblocks prevented any further **forward movement**. | Always enter or leave a helicopter from a forward direction.*
2 forward planning/thinking plans, ideas etc that are helpful in a way that prepares you for the future: *With a bit of forward planning we make sure your budget goes as far as possible.*
3 no further forward not having made much progress, especially compared to what was expected: *We are no further forward in solving the crime.*
4 [only before noun] at or near the front of a ship, vehicle, building etc OPP **rear**: *We sat in one of the forward sections of the train.*
5 *formal* too confident and friendly in dealing with people you do not know very well: *My father thinks she's far too forward for a young girl.*

forward[3] ●○○ *v* [T]
1 to send letters, goods etc to someone when they have moved to a different address SYN **send on**: *Would you make sure that you forward my mail promptly?*
2 to send letters, information etc to someone: **forward sth to sb** *Flight times will be forwarded to you with your travel documentation.*
3 *formal* to help something to develop so that it becomes successful SYN **further**: *a good chance to forward my career*

forward[4] *n* [C] an attacking player on a team in sports such as football and BASKETBALL → **back**, **defender** → see pictures at **BASKETBALL**, **FOOTBALL**

ˈforwarding adˌdress / $ ˈ... ˌ../ *n* [C] an address that you leave for someone when you move to a new place so that they can send your letters etc to you: *Did she **leave** a **forwarding address**?*

ˈforward-ˌlooking *adj* planning for and thinking about the future in a positive way, especially by being willing to use modern methods or ideas → **backward-looking**: *a forward-looking Russian statesman*

for·ward·ness /ˈfɔːwədnəs $ ˈfɔːrwərd-/ *n* [U] behaviour that is too confident or friendly

ˌforward ˈroll *n* [C] *BrE* a movement in GYMNASTICS in which you roll over forwards onto your back so that your feet go over your head SYN **somersault**

for·wards /ˈfɔːwədz $ ˈfɔːrwərdz/ *adv* FORWARD

ˈforward slash *n* [C] *BrE* a line (/) used in writing to separate words, numbers, or letters SYN **slash**

fos·sick /ˈfɒsɪk $ ˈfɑː-/ *v* [I always + adv/prep] *BrE, AusE informal* to search for something in a group of things or a container SYN **rummage**: *She fossicked in her bag and took out a notepad.*

fos·sil /ˈfɒsəl $ ˈfɑː-/ ●●○ *n* [C]
1 an animal or plant that lived many thousands of years ago and that has been preserved, or the shape of one of these animals or plants that has been preserved in rock: *fossils of early reptiles | Marine sponges have a long **fossil record*** (=their development has been recorded over a long period). → see pictures at **STONE[1]**, **LIVING FOSSIL**
2 *informal* an insulting word for an old person

ˈfossil ˌfuel ●○○ *n* [C,U] a FUEL such as coal or oil that is produced by the very gradual decaying of animals or plants over millions of years: *Environmentalists would like to see fossil fuels replaced by renewable energy sources.*

fos·sil·ize (*also* **-ise** *BrE*) /ˈfɒsəlaɪz $ ˈfɑː-/ *v* **1** if people, ideas, systems etc fossilize or are fossilized, they never change or develop, even when there are good reasons why they should change: *Most couples, however fossilized their relationship, have some interests in common.* **2** [I,T] to become or form a FOSSIL by being preserved in rock: *fossilized dinosaur bones* GRAMMAR **Fossilize** is usually passive. —**fossilization** /ˌfɒsəlaɪˈzeɪʃən $ ˌfɑːsələ-/ *n* [U]

fos·ter[1] /ˈfɒstə $ ˈfɑːstər/ ●○○ *v*
1 [T] to help a skill, feeling, idea etc develop over a period of time SYN **encourage**, **promote**: *The bishop helped foster the sense of a community embracing all classes.*
2 [I,T] to take someone else's child into your family for a period of time but without becoming their legal parent → **adopt**: *The couple wanted to adopt a black child they had been fostering.*

foster[2] ●○○ *adj*
1 foster mother/father/parents the people who foster a child: *It is sometimes difficult to find suitable foster parents.*
2 foster child/son/daughter a child who is fostered
3 foster brother/sister someone who has different parents from you, but who is being brought up in the same family
4 foster home a private home where a child is fostered

fought /fɔːt $ fɒːt/ the past tense and past participle of FIGHT

foul[1] /faʊl/ ●●○ *adj*
1 SMELL/TASTE a foul smell or taste is very unpleasant SYN **disgusting**: *He woke up with a foul taste in his mouth. | a pile of **foul-smelling** garbage | He put down his mug of **foul-tasting** coffee.* THESAURUS▸ **HORRIBLE**
2 in a foul mood/temper *BrE* in a very bad temper and likely to get angry: *The argument with his mother left Putt in a foul mood.*
3 AIR/WATER very dirty: *Refugees in the camps are short of food and at risk from foul water. | extractor fans to remove foul air from the tunnel*
4 foul language rude and offensive words: *She claimed she had been subjected to abuse and foul language.*
5 WEATHER *especially BrE* foul weather is stormy and windy, with a lot of rain or snow: *Always carry foul weather gear when you go out walking.* —**foully** *adv* —**foulness** *n* [U] → **by fair means or foul** at **FAIR[1](11)**, → **fall foul of sb/sth** at **FALL[1](15)**

foul[2] *v* **1 a)** [T] if a sports player fouls another player, they do something that is not allowed by the rules **b)** [I,T] to hit a ball outside the limit of the playing area in baseball **2** (*also* **foul up**) [T] *formal* to make something very dirty, especially with waste: *rivers and lakes fouled almost beyond recovery by pollutants*

foul up *phr v informal* **1** to do something wrong or spoil something by making mistakes → **foul-up**: *We can't afford to foul up this time.* | **foul sth ↔ up** *Glen completely fouled up* *the seating arrangements.* **2 foul sth ↔ up** to make something very dirty, especially with waste: *He lit a cigarette and started to foul up the air with stinging yellow smoke.*

foul³ *n* [C] **1** an action in a sport that is against the rules: *Wright was booked for a foul on the goalkeeper.* **2** a hit in baseball which goes outside the limits of the playing area

ˈfoul line *n* [C] a line marked on a sports field outside of which a ball cannot be legally played

ˌfoul-ˈmouthed *adj* swearing too much: *Harry was a nasty foul-mouthed old devil.* —**ˈfoul mouth** *n* [C]

ˌfoul ˈplay *n* [U] **1** if the police think someone's death was caused by foul play, they think that person was murdered: *The police said they had no reason to* ***suspect foul play****.* | *Detectives have not* ***ruled out foul play****.* **2** an action that is dishonest, unfair, or illegal, especially one that happens during a sports game

ˈfoul-up *n* [C] *informal* a problem caused by a stupid or careless mistake → **foul up**: *a computer system foul-up*

found¹ /faʊnd/ the past tense and past participle of FIND

found² ●●○ AWL *v* [T]

1 to start something such as an organization, company, school, or city, often by providing the necessary money SYN **establish**: *Founded in 1935 in Ohio, Alcoholics Anonymous is now a world-wide organization.* | *Eton College was founded by Henry VI in 1440.* **THESAURUS** ESTABLISH

2 be founded on/upon sth a) to be the main idea, belief etc that something else develops from SYN **be based on sth**: *The British parliamentary system is founded on debate and opposition* **b)** to be the solid layer of CEMENT, stones etc that a building is built on: *The castle is founded on solid rock.*

3 *technical* to melt metal and pour it into a MOULD (=a hollow shape), to make things such as tools and parts for machines —**founding** *n* [U]: *the founding of the University of Chicago* → WELL-FOUNDED

foun·da·tion /faʊnˈdeɪʃən/ ●●○ AWL *n*

1 BUILDING [C] the solid layer of CEMENT, bricks, stones etc that is put under a building to support it: *It took the builders three weeks to* ***lay*** *the* ***foundations****.* | *The earthquake* ***shook*** *the* ***foundations*** *of the house.*

2 BASIC IDEA [C] a basic idea, principle, situation etc that something develops from: **[+of]** *All theories should be built on a foundation of factual knowledge.* | **solid/firm foundation** *The course gives students a solid foundation in the basics of computing.* **THESAURUS** BASIS

3 ORGANIZATION [C] an organization that gives or collects money to be used for special purposes, especially for CHARITY or for medical RESEARCH: *the British Heart Foundation*

4 ESTABLISHMENT [U] the establishment of an organization, business, school etc SYN **founding**: *The school has served the community since its foundation in 1835.*

5 be without foundation (*also* **have no foundation**) *formal* if a statement, idea etc is without foundation, there is no proof that it is true SYN **be groundless**: *Davis dismissed the allegations as being without foundation.*

6 lay/provide the foundation(s) for sth to provide the conditions that will make it possible for something to be successful: *Careful planning laid the foundations for the nation's economic miracle.*

7 SKIN [U] a cream in the same colour as your skin that you put on before the rest of your MAKE-UP → see picture at MAKE-UP

8 shake/rock the foundations of sth (*also* **shake/rock sth to its foundations**) to completely change the way something is done or the way people think by having a completely new idea: *Darwin's theory rocked the scientific establishment to its foundations.*

founˈdation ˌcourse *n* [C] *BrE* a general course of study that introduces students to a subject, and is taught in the first year at some universities in Britain

founˈdation ˌstone *n* [C] **1** a large stone that is placed at the base of a new building, usually by an important person as part of a ceremony **2** the facts, ideas, principles etc that form the base from which something else develops: *Greek and Latin were once viewed as the foundation stones of a good education.*

found·er¹ /ˈfaʊndə $ -ər/ ●○○ AWL *n* [C] someone who establishes a business, organization, school etc

founder² *v* [I] *formal* **1** to fail after a period of time because something has gone wrong: *Their marriage began to founder soon after the honeymoon.* | **[+on]** *The talks foundered on disagreements between the two parties.* **2** if a ship or boat founders, it fills with water and sinks: **[+on]** *The ship foundered on the rocks.*

ˌfounder ˈmember *n* [C] *BrE* someone who has helped to establish a new organization, club etc and is one of its first members SYN **charter member** *AmE*

ˌfounding ˈfather *n* [C] someone who begins something such as a new way of thinking, or a new organization: **[+of]** *Saint Basil, one of the founding fathers of the Greek Orthodox Church*

found·ling /ˈfaʊndlɪŋ/ *n* [C] *old use* a baby who has been left by its parents, and is found and looked after by other people

foun·dry /ˈfaʊndri/ *n* (*plural* **foundries**) [C] a place where metals are melted and poured into MOULDS (=hollow shapes) to make parts for machines, tools etc: *an* ***iron foundry***

fount /faʊnt/ *n* **the fount of all knowledge/wisdom etc** *literary* the place, person, idea etc that all knowledge, WISDOM etc comes from SYN **source**

foun·tain /ˈfaʊntɪn $ ˈfaʊntn/ ●○○ *n* [C]

1 a structure from which water is pushed up into the air, used for example as decoration in a garden or park

2 a flow of liquid, or of something bright and colourful that goes straight up into the air: **[+of]** *A fountain of blood was pouring from his chest.* | *A fountain of sparks shot high into the sky.*

3 fountain of sth *written* a SOURCE or supply of something: *He was a fountain of information on Asian affairs.* → DRINKING FOUNTAIN, SODA FOUNTAIN

foun·tain·head /ˈfaʊntənhed $ ˈfaʊntn-/ *n* [singular] the origin of something SYN **source**

ˈfountain pen *n* [C] a pen that you fill with ink → **ballpoint** → see picture at STATIONERY

four /fɔː $ fɔːr/ ●●● S2 W1 *number, n*

1 the number 4: *She is married with four children.* | *They arrived just after four* (=four o'clock). | *Luke will soon be four* (=four years old).

2 on all fours supporting your body with your hands and knees: *He was down on all fours playing with the puppy.*

3 in fours in groups of four people or things: *The boxes were stacked in fours.* → FOURSOME

4 [C] a hit in CRICKET that scores four RUNS because it goes over the edge of the playing area

5 [C] a team of four people who row a racing boat, or the boat that they row

6 the four corners of the Earth/world *literary* places or countries that are very far away from each other: *People from the four corners of the world have come to Ontario to make it their home.* → **four ply** at PLY²

four·fold /ˈfɔːfəʊld $ ˈfɔːrfoʊld/ *adj, adv* four times as much or as many: *a fourfold increase in price* | *Profits rose fourfold.*

ˌfour-leaf ˈclover (*also* **ˌfour-leaved ˈclover** *BrE*) *n* [C] a CLOVER plant that has four leaves instead of the usual three, and is considered to be lucky

ˌfour-letter ˈword *n* [C] a word that is considered very rude and offensive, especially one relating to sex or body waste SYN **swearword**

ˌfour-poster ˈbed (*also* **four-ˈposter**) *n* [C] a bed with four tall posts at the corners, a cover fixed at the top of the posts, and curtains around the sides

four·some /ˈfɔːsəm $ ˈfɔːr-/ *n* [C] a group of four people, especially two men and two women, who come together for a social activity or sport: *Jim and Tina* ***made up a foursome*** *with Jean and Bruce.*

F

ˈfour-square¹, **foursquare** /ˈfɔːskweə $ ˈfɔːrskwer/ *adj* **1** a building that is four-square is strongly built and square in shape **2** *BrE old use* firm and determined

four-square², **foursquare** *adv* **1** if you stand four-square behind someone, you support them completely: *He stood four-square behind the prime minister in the dispute.* **2** firmly and solidly: *The hut stood four-square in a corner of the garden.*

ˈfour-star¹ *adj* [only before noun] a four-star hotel, restaurant etc is of a very high standard

ˈfour-star² *n* [U] *BrE* a type of petrol with LEAD in it

ˌfour-star ˈgeneral *n* [C] *AmE* a GENERAL of a high rank in the US army

ˌfour-stroke ˈengine *n* [C] an engine that works with two up and down movements of a PISTON

four·teen /ˌfɔːˈtiːn◂ $ ˌfɔːr-/ ●●● S3 W3 *number* the number 14: *He used to work fourteen hours a day.* | *I started playing the guitar when I was fourteen* (=14 years old). —**fourteenth** *adj, pron*: *in the fourteenth century* | *my fourteenth birthday* | *I'm planning to leave on* ***the fourteenth*** (=the 14th day of the month).

fourth¹ /fɔːθ $ fɔːrθ/ ●●● S3 W3 *adj* coming after three other things in a series: *in the fourth century* | *her fourth birthday* —**fourthly** *adv*

fourth² ●●● S3 W3 *pron* the fourth thing in a series: *the fourth of July*

fourth³ *n* [C] ¼; one of four equal parts: **one-fourth/three-fourths** → QUARTER¹(1)

ˌfourth diˈmension *n* **the fourth dimension** an expression meaning 'time', used especially by scientists and writers of SCIENCE FICTION

ˌfourth esˈtate *n* **the fourth estate** newspapers, news magazines, television and radio news, the people who work for them, and the political influence that they have SYN **press**

ˌFourth of Juˈly, the a national holiday in the US that celebrates the beginning of the United States as a nation SYN **Independence Day**: *a Fourth of July picnic*

ˌfour-wheel ˈdrive *n* [C,U] a system which gives the power of the engine to all four wheels in a vehicle, or a vehicle that has this type of system

fowl /faʊl/ *n* (*plural* **fowl** *or* **fowls**) [C,U] **1** a bird, such as a chicken, that is kept for its meat and eggs, or the meat of this type of bird **2** *old use* any bird

fox¹ /fɒks $ fɑːks/ ●●○ *n*
1 [C] a wild animal like a dog with reddish-brown fur, a pointed face, and a thick tail
2 [C] *informal* someone who is clever and good at deceiving people: *He was a sly old fox.*
3 [U] the skin and fur of a fox, used to make clothes
4 [C] *AmE informal* someone who is sexually attractive

fox² *v* [T] *BrE informal* **1** to be too difficult for someone to do or understand: *We were foxed by the problem.* **2** to confuse or deceive someone in a clever way

fox·glove /ˈfɒksglʌv $ ˈfɑːks-/ *n* [C] a tall plant with many bell-shaped flowers → see picture at FLOWER¹

fox·hole /ˈfɒkshəʊl $ ˈfɑːkshoʊl/ *n* [C] **1** a hole in the ground that soldiers use to fire from or hide from the enemy **2** a hole in the ground where a fox lives

fox·hound /ˈfɒkshaʊnd $ ˈfɑːks-/ *n* [C] a dog with a very good sense of smell, trained to hunt and kill foxes

fox·hunt·ing /ˈfɒksˌhʌntɪŋ $ ˈfɑːks-/ *n* [U] the sport of hunting FOXES with dogs while riding on a horse —**foxhunt** *n* [C]

ˌfox ˈterrier *n* [C] a small dog with short hair

fox·trot /ˈfɒkstrɒt $ ˈfɑːkstrɑːt/ *n* [C] a formal dance which combines short quick steps with long slow steps, or a piece of music for this dance —**foxtrot** *v* [I]

fox·y /ˈfɒksi $ ˈfɑːksi/ *adj* **1** *informal especially AmE* sexually attractive SYN **sexy**: *a* ***foxy lady*** **2** like a FOX in appearance: *a* ***foxy face*** **3** skilful at deceiving people SYN **cunning**

foy·er /ˈfɔɪeɪ $ ˈfɔɪər/ *n* [C] **1** a room or hall at the entrance to a public building SYN **lobby**: **hotel/theatre/cinema etc foyer** **2** *AmE* a small room or hall at the entrance to a house or apartment

FPO /ˌef piː ˈəʊ $ -ˈoʊ/ the written abbreviation of ***field post office*** or ***fleet post office***, used as part of the address of someone in the American navy or army

Fr *BrE*, **Fr.** *AmE* **1** a written abbreviation of ***Father***, used before the name of a priest **2** the written abbreviation of ***French*** **3** the written abbreviation of ***France***

fra·cas /ˈfrækɑː $ ˈfreɪkəs/ *n* [singular] a short noisy fight involving several people SYN **affray**: *Eight people were injured in the fracas.*

frack·ing /ˈfrækɪŋ/ *n* [U] (***hydraulic fracturing***) a way of getting natural gas from underground rock by pumping a liquid at high pressure into the rock to make breaks in it that allow the gas to come up

frac·tal /ˈfræktəl/ *n* [C] *technical* a pattern, usually produced by a computer, that is made by repeating the same shape many times in smaller and smaller sizes

frac·tion /ˈfrækʃən/ ●●○ *n* [C]
1 a very small amount of something: **[+of]** *I got these shoes at a fraction of the original price.* | *She paused for a fraction of a second.*
2 a part of a whole number in mathematics, such as ½ or ¾

frac·tion·al /ˈfrækʃənəl/ *adj* **1** very small in amount SYN **tiny**: *a* ***fractional increase*** | *a* ***fractional hesitation*** *before he said yes* **2** *technical* happening or done in a series of steps **3** *technical* relating to fractions, in mathematics —**fractionally** *adv*

frac·tious /ˈfrækʃəs/ *adj* someone who is fractious becomes angry very easily SYN **irritable**: *Children become fractious when they are tired.* | **fractious baby/child etc** —**fractiousness** *n* [U]

frac·ture¹ /ˈfræktʃə $ -ər/ ●○○ *v* [I,T]
1 if a bone or other hard substance fractures, or if it is fractured, it breaks or cracks: *The immense pressure causes the rock to fracture.* | **fracture your leg/arm/hip etc** *He fractured his right leg during training.* THESAURUS ▸ BREAK
2 if a group, country etc fractures, or if it is fractured, it divides into parts in an unfriendly way because of disagreement SYN **split**: *The opposition has been fractured by bitter disputes.*

fracture² ●○○ *n* [C] a crack or broken part in a bone or other hard substance: *a* ***stress fracture*** *in his left knee* | *a* ***hairline fracture*** (=very thin crack) | *a fractured shoulder* → COMPOUND FRACTURE, SIMPLE FRACTURE THESAURUS ▸ INJURY

frac·tured /ˈfræktʃəd $ -ərd/ *adj* broken or cracked: **fractured skull/jaw/rib etc** *She suffered a fractured skull in the accident.*

frag /fræg/ *n* [C] *informal* a GRENADE that explodes into very small pieces

fra·gile /ˈfrædʒaɪl $ -dʒəl/ ●●○ *adj*
1 easily broken or damaged OPP **strong**: *Be careful with that vase – it's very fragile.* | *fragile bones* THESAURUS ▸ WEAK
2 a fragile situation is one that is weak or uncertain, and likely to become worse under pressure OPP **strong**: *the country's* ***fragile economy*** | *Relations between the two countries are in a* ***fragile state***. | *the party's fragile unity*
3 fragile health a weak physical condition because of illness
4 thin and delicate: *fragile beauty*
5 *BrE* if someone feels fragile they feel ill, especially because they have drunk too much alcohol —**fragility** /frəˈdʒɪləti/ *n* [U]

frag·ment¹ /ˈfrægmənt/ ●●○ *n* [C] a small piece of something that has broken off or that comes from something larger: *glass fragments* | **[+of]** *fragments of broken pottery* → see picture at PIECE¹ THESAURUS ▸ PIECE

frag·ment² /frægˈment $ ˈfrægment, frægˈment/ *v* [I,T] to break something, or be broken into a lot of small separate parts – used to show disapproval: *the dangers of* *fragmenting the Health Service* —**fragmented** *adj*: *a fragmented society* —**fragmentation** /ˌfræɡmənˈteɪʃən, -men-/ *n* [U]

frag·ment·a·ry /ˈfræɡməntəri $ -teri/ *adj* consisting of many different small parts: *a fragmentary account of the incident*

fra·grance /ˈfreɪɡrəns/ ●○○ *n*
1 [C,U] a pleasant smell SYN **scent**: **[+of]** *the rich fragrance of a garden flower* THESAURUS ▸ SMELL
2 [C] a liquid that you put on your body to make it smell pleasant SYN **perfume**, **scent**

fra·grant /ˈfreɪɡrənt/ *adj* having a pleasant smell: *fragrant flowers* —**fragrantly** *adv*

frail /freɪl/ ●○○ *adj*
1 someone who is frail is weak and thin because they are old or ill: ***frail elderly people*** | *her* ***frail health*** | **frail body/physique** | **mentally/physically frail** THESAURUS ▸ WEAK
2 something that is frail is easily damaged or broken SYN **fragile**: *It seemed impossible that these frail boats could survive in such a storm.* | *the country's frail economy*

frail·ty /ˈfreɪlti/ *n* (*plural* **frailties**) **1** [U] the lack of strength or health SYN **weakness**: **[+of]** *the frailty of her thin body* **2** [C,U] something bad or weak in your character SYN **weakness**: ***human frailties***

frame¹ /freɪm/ ●●● S3 W3 *n*
1 BORDER [C] a structure made of wood, metal, plastic etc that surrounds something such as a picture or window, and holds it in place: *They removed the picture from its wooden frame.* | **door/window/picture frame**
2 STRUCTURE [C] the structure or main supporting parts of a piece of furniture, vehicle, or other object: *a* ***bicycle frame*** | *the frame of the chair*
3 BODY [C] the general shape formed by the bones of someone's body: **large/thin/slight etc frame**
4 GLASSES [C usually plural] the metal or plastic part of a pair of GLASSes that holds the LENSes
5 MAIN FACTS/IDEAS [C usually singular] the main ideas, facts etc that something is based on: *A clear explanation of the subject provides a frame on which a deeper understanding can be built.* | *Some comments may or may not be understood as harassment, depending on your* ***frame of reference*** (=knowledge and beliefs that influence the way you think).
6 be in/out of the frame (for sth) to have or not have the chance to take part in something SYN **be in/out of the running (for sth)**: *Liverpool are in the frame for a place in the Cup Final.*
7 FILM [C] an area of film that contains one photograph, or one of the series of separate photographs that make up a film or video
8 SPORT [C] a complete part in the games of SNOOKER or BOWLING: *I won the next three frames.*
9 INTERNET [C] one of the areas into which a WEBPAGE is divided → CLIMBING FRAME, COLD FRAME, → **frame of mind** at MIND¹(15)

frame² ●○○ *v* [T]
1 to surround something with something else so that it looks attractive or can be seen clearly: *Sarah's face was framed by her long dark hair.* | *She stood there, framed against the doorway.*
2 to put a picture in a structure that will hold it firmly: *I'm going to* ***get*** *the picture* ***framed***. | *a* ***framed photograph***
3 to deliberately make someone seem guilty of a crime when they are not guilty, by lying to the police or in a court of law SYN **set up**: *Needham's lawyers claimed that he had been framed by the police.* | **frame sb for sth** *The two men were framed for murder.*
4 *formal* to carefully plan the way you are going to ask a question, make a statement etc: *She wondered how she was going to frame the question.*
5 *formal* to organize and develop a plan, system etc: *Newman played a central role in framing the new law.*
6 gilt-framed/wood-framed etc having a frame or frames of a particular colour or material: *wire-framed spectacles*

ˈframe-up *n* [C] a plan to make someone seem guilty of a crime which they did not do SYN **set-up**

frame·work /ˈfreɪmwɜːk $ -wɜːrk/ ●●○ AWL *n* [C]
1 [usually singular] a set of ideas, rules, or beliefs from which something is developed, or on which decisions are based: **[+of/for]** *This paper provides a framework for future research.*
2 social/legal/political etc framework the structure of a society, a legal or political system etc: *We have to act within the existing legal framework.*
3 the main supporting parts of a building, vehicle, or object: *the metal framework of the roof*

franc /fræŋk/ *n* [C] the standard unit of money in various countries, and used in France and Belgium before the EURO

fran·chise¹ /ˈfræntʃaɪz/ ●○○ *n*
1 a) [C,U] permission given by a company to someone who wants to sell its goods or services: *a* ***franchise holder*** | *a* ***franchise agreement*** | **under (a) franchise** *The beer is brewed under franchise.* **b)** [C] a business, shop etc that is run under franchise
2 [C] *AmE* a professional sports team
3 [U] *formal* the legal right to vote in your country's elections

franchise² *v* [T] to give or sell a franchise to someone

fran·chi·see /ˌfræntʃaɪˈziː/ *n* [C] someone who is given or sold a franchise to sell a company's goods or services

fran·chi·sor, **franchiser** /ˈfræntʃaɪzə $ -ər/ *n* [C] a company that sells a franchise

Franco- /fræŋkəʊ $ -koʊ/ *prefix* [in nouns and adjectives]
1 relating to France: *a Francophile* (=someone who loves France) **2** French and something else: *the Franco-Belgian border*

Fran·co·phone, **francophone** /ˈfræŋkəʊˌfəʊn $ -koʊˌfoʊn/ *adj* having French as a first or main language: **Francophone countries/nations/communities** —**Francophone** *n* [C]

Fran·glais /ˈfrɒŋɡleɪ $ ˌfrɑːŋˈɡleɪ/ *n* [U] *informal* a mixture of the French and English languages

frank¹ /fræŋk/ ●●○ *adj*
1 honest and truthful: **be frank with sb** *He was completely frank with her about what happened.* | **be frank about sth** *She was quite frank about the whole thing.* | **frank discussion/interview/exchange of views etc** THESAURUS ▸ HONEST
2 to be frank *spoken* used when you are going to say something that is true, but which other people may not like: *To be perfectly frank, I think it's a bad idea.* —**frankness** *n* [U]

frank² *v* [T] to print a sign on an envelope showing that the cost of sending it has been paid → **franking machine**

frank³ *n* [C] *AmE* a frankfurter

frank·en·food /ˈfræŋkənfuːd/ (*also* **Frank·en·stein foods** /ˈfræŋkənstaɪn ˌfuːdz/) *n* [C usually plural] *informal* food that has been produced by plants that were GENETICALLY MODIFIED – used when you disapprove of this process

Fran·ken·stein /ˈfræŋkənˌstaɪn/ a novel by Mary Shelley which was PUBLISHed in 1818 and tells the story of a scientist called Frankenstein who makes a creature by joining together bits of dead bodies and then brings it to life by passing an electric current through its body. The creature is gentle at first, but later becomes violent and attacks its maker. People sometimes mistakenly call the creature Frankenstein, instead of the scientist who made it. The story is very popular and has been made into many films.

frank·fur·ter /ˈfræŋkfɜːtə $ -fɜːrtər/ (*also* **frank** *AmE*) *n* [C] a long reddish smoked SAUSAGE

frank·in·cense /ˈfræŋkənsens/ *n* [U] a substance that is burnt to give a sweet smell, especially at religious ceremonies

ˈfranking maˌchine *n* [C] *BrE* a machine used by businesses that puts a mark on letters and packages to show that POSTAGE has been paid SYN **postage meter** *AmE* → **frank**

F

frank·ly /ˈfræŋkli/ ●●○ S3 *adv*
1 used to show that you are saying what you really think about something: *Frankly, I think the Internet is overrated.* | *His behaviour was frankly disgraceful.*
2 honestly and directly: *She answered all our questions frankly.* | *Nicholas* ***frankly admitted*** *that the report was a pack of lies.*

fran·tic /ˈfræntɪk/ ●○○ *adj*
1 extremely worried and frightened about a situation, so that you cannot control your feelings: **get/become frantic** *There was still no news of Jill, and her parents were getting frantic.* | **[+with]** *Your mother's been frantic with worry wondering where you've been.*
2 extremely hurried and using a lot of energy, but not very organized SYN **hectic**: *I spent three frantic days trying to get everything ready.* | **frantic effort/attempt** *Despite our frantic efforts, we were unable to save the boy's life.* | **frantic pace/rush/haste etc** *There was a frantic rush to escape from the building.* | *a day of* ***frantic activity*** | *a* ***frantic search*** *for her father* —**frantically** /-kli/ *adv*: *He* ***frantically searched*** *for the key.*

frat /fræt/ *n* [C] *AmE informal* a FRATERNITY: *a* ***frat boy*** (=member of a fraternity)

fra·ter·nal /frəˈtɜːnl $ -ɜːr-/ *adj formal* **1** showing a special friendliness to other people because you share interests or ideas with them: *fraternal solidarity amongst union members* | **fraternal association/organization/society** **2** relating to brothers: *fraternal loyalty* —**fraternally** *adv*

fraˌternal ˈtwin *n* [C usually plural] *technical* one of two children born at the same time to the same mother, who developed from different eggs rather than from the same egg, and who do not look alike SYN **non-identical twin** → **identical twin**

fra·ter·ni·ty /frəˈtɜːnəti $ -ɜːr-/ *n* (*plural* **fraternities**) **1 the teaching/scientific/criminal etc fraternity** all the people who work in a particular profession or share a particular interest **2** [C] a club at an American college or university that has only male members → **sorority** **3** [U] *formal* a feeling of friendship between members of a group: *fraternity between nations*

frat·er·nize (*also* **-ise** *BrE*) /ˈfrætənaɪz $ -ər-/ *v* [I] to be friendly with someone, especially if you have been ordered not to be friendly with them: **[+with]** *The troops were forbidden to fraternize with the enemy.* —**fraternization** /ˌfrætənaɪˈzeɪʃən $ -tərnə-/ *n* [U]

ˈfrat house *n* [C] *AmE informal* a house where members of a fraternity live when they are in college

frat·ri·cid·al /ˌfrætrəˈsaɪdl◂/ *adj* [only before noun] a fratricidal war or struggle is one in which people kill members of their own society or group

frat·ri·cide /ˈfrætrɪsaɪd/ *n* [C,U] the crime of murdering your brother or sister

fraud /frɔːd $ frɒːd/ ●●○ *n*
1 [C,U] the crime of deceiving people in order to gain something such as money or goods: **tax/insurance/credit card etc fraud** *He's been charged with tax fraud.* | ***electoral fraud*** | *She was found guilty of fraud.* THESAURUS CRIME
2 [C] someone or something that is not what they claim to be: *I felt like a fraud.* | *The police exposed the letter as a fraud.*

fraud·ster /ˈfrɔːdstə $ ˈfrɒːdstər/ *n* [C] someone who has committed a fraud

fraud·u·lent /ˈfrɔːdjələnt $ ˈfrɒːdʒə-/ *adj* intended to deceive people in an illegal way, in order to gain money, power etc: *a* ***fraudulent*** *insurance* ***claim*** | *a* ***fraudulent statement*** | **fraudulent activity/behaviour/conduct** THESAURUS DISHONEST —**fraudulently** *adv*: *He was accused of fraudulently using a stolen credit card.* —**fraudulence** *n* [U]

fraught /frɔːt $ frɒːt/ *adj* **1 fraught with problems/difficulties/danger etc** full of problems etc: *Their marriage has been fraught with difficulties.* **2** full of anxiety or worry SYN **tense**: *a* ***fraught atmosphere*** | *a* ***fraught situation*** | *Julie sounded rather fraught.*

fray¹ /freɪ/ *v* [I,T]

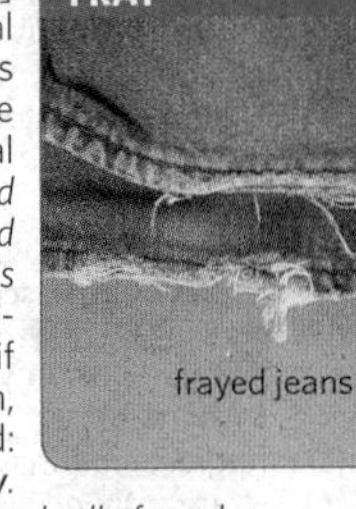

frayed jeans

1 if cloth or other material frays, or if something frays it, the threads become loose because the material is old: *The collar had started to fray on Ed's coat.* | *He had frayed the bottom of his jeans.* **2** if someone's temper or nerves fray, or if something frays them, they become annoyed: ***Tempers*** *soon began to* ***fray***. —**frayed** *adj*: *The carpet was badly frayed.*

fray² *n* **the fray** an argument or fight: *Three civilians were injured during the fray.* | **into the fray** *He launched himself into the fray.* | **join/enter the fray** *The other soldiers quickly joined the fray, launching missile attacks in the city.*

fraz·zle /ˈfræzəl/ *n BrE informal* **1 be burnt to a frazzle** to be completely burnt **2 be worn to a frazzle** to feel very tired and anxious

fraz·zled /ˈfræzəld/ *adj informal* feeling tired and anxious, for example after a journey or because you are very busy: *The meeting left me feeling completely frazzled.*

freak¹ /friːk/ ●○○ *n* [C]
1 *informal* someone who is extremely interested in a particular subject so that other people think they are strange or unusual: *a* ***fitness freak*** | *a* ***religious freak*** | *a* ***computer freak***
2 someone who is considered to be very strange because of the way they look, behave, or think SYN **weirdo**: *These glasses make me look like a freak.* | *Women who studied engineering used to be considered freaks.*
3 a control freak someone who always wants to control situations and other people
4 (*also* **freak of nature**) something in nature that is very unusual: *Due to some freak of nature, it snowed in June.*
5 an unexpected and very unusual event: *By some freak of fate, he walked away from the crash completely unhurt.* | *April's sales figures were a freak.*

freak² ●○○ *adj* [only before noun] unexpected and very unusual: *a* ***freak result*** | *He was crushed to death in a* ***freak accident***. | **freak wind/wave/storm etc** *The men drowned when a freak wave sank their boat.* THESAURUS UNUSUAL

freak³ *v* [I] *informal* to become suddenly angry or afraid, especially so that you cannot control your behaviour SYN **flip**: *When Ben heard about the accident, he just freaked.*
freak out *phr v informal* to become very anxious, upset, or afraid, or make someone very anxious, upset, or afraid: *People just freaked out when they heard the news.* | **freak sb out** *The whole idea freaked me out.*

freak·ish /ˈfriːkɪʃ/ *adj* very unusual and strange, and sometimes frightening SYN **weird**: *freakish weather* —**freakishly** *adv* —**freakishness** *n* [U]

freak·y /ˈfriːki/ *adj spoken* strange or unusual and a bit frightening SYN **weird**: *The movie was kind of freaky.*

freck·le /ˈfrekəl/ *n* [C usually plural] freckles are small brown spots on someone's skin, especially on their face, which the sun can cause to increase in number and become darker → **mole**

freck·led /ˈfrekəld/ *adj* having freckles: **freckled face/skin**

free¹ /friː/ ●●● S1 W1 *adj*
1 NO COST something that is free does not cost you any money: *Admission is free for children under 9.* | *All students are offered free accommodation.* | *Send for our free information pack for more details.* | *There's a special* ***free gift*** *with this month's magazine.*
2 NOT A PRISONER not held, tied up, or kept somewhere as a prisoner: *He knew he could be free in as little as three years.* | *With one leap he was free!* | *He walked out of the courtroom* ***a free man***. | *They have called on the government*

F

to **set** *all political prisoners* **free**. | *He was found not guilty and* **walked free** *from the court.* | *The animals are allowed to* **run free** *in the park.* | *Hundreds of dogs* **roam free** *on the streets.* | **break/pull/struggle free** *She broke free from her attacker.*

3 NOT CONTROLLED allowed to do or say whatever you want, or allowed to happen, without being controlled or restricted by anyone or anything: *We had a free and open discussion about religion.* | **free to do sth** *Remember, you are free to say no.* | **[+from]** *Newspapers today are entirely free from government control.* | *Women are struggling to* **break free** *from tradition.* | **[+of]** *I longed to be free of my family.* | *He became president following the country's first* **free elections** *last year.* | *We would all support the principle of* **free speech**. | *For the first time in its history, the country has a* **free press**. | *Patients are now allowed* **free access** *to their medical records.* | *The legislation will allow the* **free movement** *of goods through all the countries in Europe.*

4 NOT BUSY if you are free, or have some free time, you have no work, and nothing else that you must do → **available**: *I'm free next weekend.* | **[+for]** *Are you free for lunch tomorrow?* | **free to do sth** *At last I was free to concentrate on my own research.* | **a free day/morning/half-hour etc** *I haven't got a free day this week.* | *Children these days have very little* **free time**.

5 NOT BEING USED something that is free is available to use because it is not already being used: *Is this seat free?* | *I'm afraid we don't have any free tables this evening.* | *He used his* **free hand** *to open the door.* THESAURUS ▸ EMPTY

6 NOT SUFFERING not suffering from something: **[+of]** *At last she was free of pain.* | **[+from]** *A lot of the patients are now free from symptoms.* | **pain-free/trouble-free etc** *a stress-free life*

7 NOT CONTAINING STH not containing something: **[+from/of]** *All our drinks are free from artificial colourings.* | **fat-free/dairy-free etc** *a fat-free yoghurt*

8 TAX if something is free of tax, you do not have to pay tax on it: **[+of]** *This income should be free of tax.* | **tax-free/duty-free etc** *tax-free earnings* | *an opportunity to buy duty-free goods*

9 feel free *spoken* used to tell someone that they can do something: *Feel free to ask questions.* | *'Can I use your bathroom?' 'Yes, feel free.'*

10 free and easy relaxed, friendly, and without many rules: *I knew that life wasn't going to be so free and easy now.* | *the free and easy atmosphere of university life*

11 free spirit someone who lives as they want to rather than in the way that society considers normal

12 give sb a free hand/rein to let someone do whatever they want or need to do in a particular situation: *The producer was given a free rein with the script.*

13 there's no free lunch (*also* **there's no such thing as a free lunch**) used to say that you should not expect to get something good without having to pay for it or make any effort

14 it's a free country *BrE* used, usually humorously, to say that you are or should be allowed to do something, after someone has said that you should not do it: *It's a free country. You can't stop me.*

15 get/take a free ride *informal* to get something without paying for it or working for it, because other people are paying or working for it: *They are encouraging all workers to join the union rather than just taking a free ride on those who do join.*

16 be free with sth to be very generous with something: *He seems to be very free with other people's money.* | *She is always free with her advice.*

17 make free with sth *informal* to use something that belongs to someone else when you should not: *I knew that they had been making free with our food.*

18 NOT RESTRICTED something that is free is not held, blocked, or restricted: *We opened both doors to allow a free flow of air through the building.*

19 CHEMICALS *technical* a free chemical substance is not combined with any other substance: *the amount of free oxygen in the atmosphere*

THESAURUS

free something that is free does not cost you any money: *Parking is free after 6 pm.* | *They were giving away free tickets for the concert.*

for nothing/for free without having to pay for something that you would normally have to pay for: *He offered to fix the car for nothing.* | *Children under five can see the show for free.*

at no extra cost if a shop or company provides an additional service at no extra cost, they do it without asking you for any more money: *The shop will install the cooker for you at no extra cost.*

complimentary [only before noun] free - use this about things that a company, theatre, hotel etc gives people: *Honeymooners receive a complimentary bottle of champagne in their hotel room.*

be on the house if food or drinks are on the house, the owner of a bar or restaurant says you do not have to pay for them: *These drinks are on the house.*

free² ●●● W3 *v* (**freed**, **freeing**) [T]

1 RELEASE to allow someone to leave prison or somewhere they have been kept as a prisoner SYN **release**: *He expects to be freed quite soon.* | *The terrorists have at last agreed to free the hostages.* | **free sb from sth** *She was freed from prison last week.*

2 NOT CONTROL to allow someone to say and do what they want, after controlling or restricting them in the past: **free sb from/of sth** *The press has now been freed from political control.* | *She longed to be freed of her responsibilities.* | *Art frees the imagination.*

3 ALLOW SB/STH TO MOVE to move someone or something so that they are no longer held, fixed, or trapped SYN **release**: *He struggled to free himself, but the ropes were too tight.* | *I couldn't free the safety catch.* | **free sb/sth from sth** *All the victims have now been freed from the wreckage.*

4 STOP SB SUFFERING to stop someone suffering from something by removing it: **free sb from sth** *new drugs that can free people from pain* | *At last the country has been freed from its enormous debts.*

5 MAKE AVAILABLE (*also* **free sth ↔ up**) to make something available so that it can be used: *I need to free up some of the disk space on my computer.* | *This should free some money for investment.*

6 GIVE SB MORE TIME (*also* **free sb ↔ up**) to give someone time to do something by taking away other jobs that they have to do: **free sb (up) to do sth** *Taking away the burden of administration will free teachers to concentrate on teaching.* | *We have freed up some staff to deal with the backlog of work.*

free³ ●●● S3 *adv*

1 without payment: *Children under four can travel free.* | *You can get advice free from your local library.* | **for free** *He offered to do the work for free.* | *All these services are available to the public* **free of charge**.

2 not fixed or held in a particular place or position: *The ropes were now hanging free.* | *A gold chain swung free around his neck.* → FREELY, SCOT-FREE

free⁴ *n* [C] *BrE informal* a FREE TRANSFER; the process by which a player moves from one football club to another, but the new club does not pay any money for him: *We got Kevin on a free from Manchester United.*

-free /friː/ *suffix* [in adjectives and adverbs] without something that you do not want: *a trouble-free journey* | *duty-free cigarettes* | *a salt-free diet* | *They live in the house rent-free.*

ˌfree ˈagent *n* [C] someone who is not responsible to anyone else and can do what they want

ˌfree and ˈeasy (*also* **free-and-easy** *BrE*) *adj* very informal and relaxed: *the free-and-easy atmosphere of the local pub*

free·base /ˈfriːbeɪs/ *v* [I,T] to smoke a pure form of the illegal drug COCAINE —**freebasing** *n* [U]

free·bie /ˈfriːbiː/ *n* [C] *informal* something that you are given free, usually by a company: **on a freebie** *The company paid for the minister to fly out to Australia on a freebie.* |

F

freebie holiday/hotel/flight etc *A waiter was handing round freebie glasses of wine.*

free·birth /ˈfriːbɜːθ $ -bɜːrθ/ (*also* **free·birth·ing** /-bɜːθɪŋ $ -bɜːr-/) *n* [U] a method of giving birth to a baby in which a woman chooses to be at home without medical help —**freebirther** *n* [C]

free·boot·er /ˈfriːbuːtə $ -ər/ *n* [C] someone who joins in a war in order to steal other people's goods and money

free·born /ˌfriːˈbɔːn◂ $ -ˈbɔːrn◂/ *adj old use* not born as a slave

ˌfree colˌlective ˈbargaining *n* [U] *BrE* talks between TRADE UNIONS and employers about pay or working conditions that are not controlled by law

free·dom /ˈfriːdəm/ ●●● S3 W2 *n*

1 [C,U] the right to do what you want without being controlled or restricted by anyone → **liberty**: *People here like their freedom and privacy.* | *the rights and freedoms of citizens* | **freedom to do sth** *We do not have the freedom to do just what we like.* | *the freedom to vote* | **[+of]** *Tighter security measures are restricting our* ***freedom of movement*** (=the right to travel). | *The First Amendment guarantees* ***freedom of expression***.

2 [U] the state of being free and allowed to do what you want: *He thinks children have too much freedom these days.* | **freedom to do sth** *The wheelchair gives him the freedom to go out on his own.* | *Tracksuits are designed to give you* ***freedom of movement*** (=the ability to move your body freely).

3 [U] the state of being free because you are not in prison OPP **captivity, imprisonment**: *The prisoner was recaptured after only 48 hours of freedom.*

4 freedom from sth the state of not being affected by something that makes you worried, unhappy, afraid etc: **freedom from fear/pain/worry etc** *The contraceptive pill gave women freedom from the fear of pregnancy.*

5 freedom of choice the right or ability to choose whatever you want to do or have: *The new satellite TV channels offer viewers greater freedom of choice.*

6 freedom of information the legal right of people in some countries to see information which the government has about people and organizations

7 freedom of the city in Britain, an honour given by a city to someone who has done something special

COLLOCATIONS – MEANINGS 1 & 2

ADJECTIVES

total/complete freedom *Riding a motorbike gives me a feeling of total freedom.*
great/considerable freedom *Teachers are given considerable freedom to choose their teaching methods.*
personal/individual freedom *Our personal freedom is being restricted more and more.*
political/religious freedom (=freedom to have any political/religious beliefs) | **academic freedom** (=freedom to teach or study any ideas)

VERBS

have the freedom to do sth *We have the freedom to travel nearly anywhere in the world.*
enjoy freedom *Filmmakers today enjoy more freedom than in the past.*

PHRASES

the struggle/fight for freedom *The student movement played an important role in the struggle for political freedom.*
freedom of speech/expression (=the legal right to say what you want) *We will defend freedom of speech and oppose censorship.*
freedom of religion/worship (=the right to hold/practise any religious belief) | **freedom of assembly** (=the right of people to meet as a group for a particular purpose) | **the freedom of the press** (=the right of newspapers to publish what they like, free from political control)

ˈfreedom ˌfighter *n* [C] someone who fights in a war against an unfair or dishonest government, army etc → **guerrilla, terrorist**

free ˈenterprise *n* [U] the principle and practice of allowing private business to operate without much government control → **private enterprise**

ˈfree fall, free-fall *n* [singular, U] **1** the movement of someone or something through the air without engine power, for example before a PARACHUTE opens after someone has jumped out of a plane: **in/into free fall** *The spacecraft is now in free fall towards the Earth.* **2** a very fast and uncontrolled fall in the value of something: *the free-fall in housing prices* | **in/into free fall** *The economy is in free fall.* —**free-falling** *adj*

ˈfree-ˌfloating *adj* not connected to or influenced by anything: *a free-floating exchange rate* | *a free-floating currency*

Free·fone /ˈfriːfəʊn $ -foʊn/ *n* [U] *trademark* another spelling of FREEPHONE

ˌfree-for-ˈall *n* [singular] *informal* **1** a situation in which there is total freedom and anything can happen – used to show disapproval: *the free-for-all of sexual activity in the 1970s* **2** a noisy quarrel or fight involving a lot of people: *A controversial penalty decision sparked a free-for-all at the end of the match.*

free·form /ˈfriːfɔːm $ -fɔːrm/ *adj* [only before noun] freeform music or art does not have a standard structure or form, and uses new ideas or methods

free·hand /ˈfriːhænd/ *adj* [only before noun] drawn by hand without using any special tools: **freehand drawing/sketch** —**freehand** *adv*

free·hold /ˈfriːhəʊld $ -hoʊld/ *n* [C,U] *BrE law* when you completely own a building or piece of land for an unlimited time OPP **leasehold**: *They* ***bought*** *the* ***freehold*** *of their house.* —**freehold** *adj*: *a* ***freehold property*** —**freehold** *adv*: *The property will be sold freehold.*

free·hold·er /ˈfriːhəʊldə $ -hoʊldər/ *n* [C] *BrE* an owner of freehold land or property OPP **leaseholder**

ˌfree ˈhouse *n* [C] in Britain, a PUB that can buy beer from different BREWERIES (=a company that makes beer etc), rather than being controlled by one brewery

ˌfree ˈkick *n* [C] a chance for a player on one football team to kick the ball freely from a position shown by the REFEREE, given because the other team has done something wrong

free·lance /ˈfriːlɑːns $ -læns/ ●○○ *adj, adv* working independently for different companies rather than being employed by one particular company: *She works freelance from home.* | **freelance journalist/writer/photographer etc** —**freelance** *v* [I]: *He's freelancing for several translation agencies.* —**freelance** (*also* **freelancer**) *n* [C]

free·load·er /ˈfriːləʊdə $ -loʊdər/ *n* [C] *informal* someone who takes food, drink, or other things from other people, without giving anything in return – used to show disapproval —**freeload** *v* [I]

ˌfree ˈlove *n* [U] *old-fashioned* the practice or principle of having sex with people without being faithful to one person or without being married

free·ly /ˈfriːli/ ●●○ *adv*

1 without anyone stopping or limiting something: *the country's first* ***freely elected*** *president* | *EU members are allowed to* ***travel freely*** *between member states.* | **talk/speak/write etc freely** *In France he could write freely, without fear of arrest.* | *We went outside so that we could talk freely without being overheard.*

2 if something moves freely, it moves smoothly and nothing prevents it from doing this: *She was* ***breathing freely***. | *If your muscles are tense, blood cannot* ***circulate freely***. | *The injury prevented him from* ***moving freely***.

3 freely available very easy to obtain: *Information is freely available on the Internet.*

4 freely admit/acknowledge sth to agree that something is true, even though telling the truth is difficult or embarrassing: *They freely admitted using the drug.*

5 generously and willingly: *She* ***gave freely*** *to charity.*

free·man /ˈfriːmən/ *n* (*plural* **freemen** /-mən/) [C] someone who is not a slave

ˌfree ˈmarket *n* [C] an economic system in which prices are not controlled by the government: *a free market economy*

ˌfree marketˈeer *n* [C] someone who thinks that prices should be allowed to rise and fall naturally and should not be fixed by the government

Free·ma·son /ˈfriːˌmeɪsən, ˌfriːˈmeɪsən/ (*also* **Mason**) *n* [C] a man who belongs to a secret society in which each member helps the other members to become successful

Free·ma·son·ry, freemasonry /ˈfriːmeɪsənri, ˌfriːˈmeɪ-/ *n* [U] the system and practices of Freemasons

free·mi·um /ˈfriːmiəm/ *adj* [only before noun] a freemium service is a service, for example on the Internet, with a basic level that is free and a better level that people can choose to pay for - used in business —**freemium** *n* [C,U]

ˌfree ˈpardon *n* [C] *BrE law* the official act of forgiving someone for a crime

ˌfree ˈperiod *n* [C] *BrE* a period of time in a school day when a student does not have a class

Free·phone, Freefone /ˈfriːfəʊn $ -foʊn/ *n* [U] *trademark BrE* an arrangement by which a company or organization pays the cost of telephone calls made to it → **toll-free**

ˌfree ˈport *n* [C] a port or airport in one country where goods from other countries can be brought in and taken out without being taxed

Free·post /ˈfriːpəʊst $ -poʊst/ *n* [U] *trademark BrE* an arrangement by which a company or organization pays the cost of letters that you send to it by post

ˌfree ˈradical *n* [C] *technical* an atom or group of atoms with at least one free ELECTRON, which combines with other atoms very easily: *It is thought that free radicals can damage cells.*

ˌfree-ˈrange *adj* relating to a type of farming which allows animals such as chickens and pigs to move around and eat naturally, rather than being kept in a restricted space → **battery**: *free-range eggs*

free·run·ning /ˈfriːrʌnɪŋ/ *n* [U] the sport of running through city streets and jumping between buildings SYN **parkour** —**freerunner** *n* [C]

ˈfree school *n* [C] a school in England that is independent and not part of the main school system, but receives money from the government. It may be started by a group of parents or teachers, or an organization such as a CHARITY, a business, or a university.

free·sheet /ˈfriːʃiːt/ *n* [C] *BrE* a free newspaper

free·si·a /ˈfriːziə $ -ʒə/ *n* [C] a plant with pleasant-smelling yellow, white, pink, or purple flowers

free·stand·ing /ˌfriːˈstændɪŋ◂/ *adj* **1** not fixed to a frame, wall, or other support: *a freestanding bookcase* **2** able to exist on its own and not as part of something bigger: *The modules can be offered as freestanding courses.*

free·style /ˈfriːstaɪl/ *n* **1** [U] a swimming race in which swimmers can use any style they choose, usually CRAWL: *the 100m freestyle* **2** [U] a sports competition in which competitors can use any movements they choose: *freestyle wrestling* **3** [C] a RAP song in which the singer says words directly from their imagination, without planning or writing them first

free·think·er /ˌfriːˈθɪŋkə $ -ər/ *n* [C] someone who has their own opinions, ideas, and beliefs, rather than accepting other people's - used to show approval —**freethinking** *adj*

ˌfree-to-ˈair *adj BrE* free-to-air television or television programmes do not cost extra money to watch: *free-to-air television coverage of rugby league matches*

ˌfree ˈtrade *n* [U] a situation in which the goods coming into or going out of a country are not controlled or taxed

ˌfree ˈverse *n* [U] poetry that does not have a fixed structure and does not RHYME → **blank verse**

ˌfree ˈvote *n* [C] *BrE* a situation in which members of the British parliament can choose how to vote rather than following the choice of their political party

free·ware /ˈfriːweə $ -wer/ *n* [U] free computer software, often available on the Internet → **shareware**

free·way /ˈfriːweɪ/ ●●● S2 W3 *n* [C] *AmE* a very wide road in the US, built for fast travel → **motorway, expressway, highway**: *the Central Freeway*

free·wheel /ˌfriːˈwiːl/ *v* [I] to ride a bicycle or drive a vehicle down a hill, without using power from your legs or the engine

free·wheel·ing /ˌfriːˈwiːlɪŋ◂/ *adj* [only before noun] *informal* not worried about rules or what will happen in the future: *A lot of the girls envied me my independent, freewheeling life.*

ˌfree ˈwill *n* [U] **1 do sth of your own free will** to do something because you want to, not because someone else has forced you to: *He came of his own free will.* **2** the ability to make your own decisions about what to do, rather than being controlled by God or Fate

freeze¹ /friːz/ ●●● S3 W3 *v* (*past tense* **froze** /frəʊz $ froʊz/, *past participle* **frozen** /ˈfrəʊzən $ ˈfroʊ-/)

1 LIQUID [I,T] if a liquid or something wet freezes or is frozen, it becomes hard and solid because the temperature is very cold → **melt, thaw**: *The lake had frozen overnight.*

2 FOOD [I,T] to preserve food for a long time by keeping it at a very low temperature, or to be preserved in this way: *I think I'll freeze that extra meat.* | *Tomatoes don't freeze well.*

3 MACHINE/ENGINE [I] if a machine, engine, pipe etc freezes, the liquid inside it becomes solid with cold, so that it does not work properly: *The water pipes have frozen.*

4 WEATHER it freezes if it freezes outside, the temperature falls to or below FREEZING POINT: *Do you think it'll freeze tonight?*

5 FEEL COLD [I] to feel very cold: *I nearly* ***froze to death*** *watching that football match.*

6 WAGES/PRICES [T] if a government or company freezes wages, prices etc, they do not increase them for a period of time: *The government has been forced to cut spending and freeze public-sector wages.*

7 MONEY/PROPERTY [T] to legally prevent money in a bank from being spent, property from being sold etc: *The court* ***froze*** *their* ***assets.***

8 STOP MOVING [I] to stop moving suddenly and stay completely still and quiet: *I froze and listened; someone was in my apartment.* | **[+with]** *She* ***froze with horror.***

9 FILM [T] to stop a DVD or video in order to be able to look at a particular part of it → **freeze-frame**: *He froze the picture on the screen.*

10 sb's blood freezes used to say that someone is very frightened or shocked: *I heard his scream and felt my blood freeze.*

freeze sb ↔ **out** *phr v* to deliberately prevent someone from being involved in something, by making it difficult for them, being unkind to them etc: *Why did you freeze me out?*

freeze over *phr v* if an area or pool of water freezes over, its surface turns into ice: *The lake has frozen over.*

freeze up *phr v*

1 if a machine, engine, or pipe freezes up, the liquid inside becomes solid with cold so that it does not work properly SYN **freeze**

2 to suddenly be unable to speak or act normally: *I wouldn't know what to say. I'd just freeze up.*

freeze² ●○○ *n*

1 [C] a time when people are not allowed to increase prices or pay: **a price/pay/wage freeze** | **[+on]** *a freeze on pay rises*

2 [C] the stopping of some activity or process: **[+on]** *The government have imposed a freeze on civil service appointments.*

3 [singular] *BrE* a period of extremely cold weather

4 [C usually singular] *AmE* a short period of time, especially at night, when the temperature is extremely low → DEEP FREEZE

ˌfreeze-ˈdried / $ '../ *adj* freeze-dried food has been frozen and dried very quickly in order to preserve it

ˈfreeze-frame *n* [U] when you stop the action on a DVD or video at one particular place → **freeze**: *Press the freeze-frame button.* —**freeze-frame** *v* [T]

freez·er /ˈfriːzə $ -ər/ ●●● S3 *n* [C]
1 a large piece of electrical kitchen equipment in which food can be stored at very low temperatures for a long time SYN **deep freeze** → **fridge**
2 *AmE* a part of a FRIDGE in which food can be stored at very low temperatures for a long time SYN **freezer compartment** *BrE*

ˈfreezer comˌpartment *n* [C] *BrE* a part of a FRIDGE in which food can be stored at very low temperatures for a long time SYN **freezer** *AmE*

freezing[1] /ˈfriːzɪŋ/ ●●● S3 *adj, adv*
1 extremely cold: *It's freezing in this house. Can't I turn on the heating?* | *We were* ***freezing cold*** *in the tent last night.*
2 below the temperature at which water turns to ice: *freezing fog*

freez·ing[2] ●●○ *n* [U] **above/below freezing** above or below the temperature at which water freezes: *It was well below freezing last night.*

ˈfreezing ˌpoint *n* **1** [U] the temperature at which water turns into ice → **boiling point 2** [C usually singular] the temperature at which a particular liquid freezes: *Alcohol has a lower freezing point than water.*

freight[1] /freɪt/ ●●○ *n*
1 [U] goods that are carried by ship, train, or aircraft, and the system of moving these goods: *freight services* | *We'll send your personal belongings by* ***air freight*** *and your furniture by* ***sea freight****.*
2 [C] *AmE* a FREIGHT TRAIN

freight[2] *v* [T] to send goods by air, sea, or train

ˈfreight car *n* [C] part of a train which carries goods

freight·er /ˈfreɪtə $ -ər/ *n* [C] a ship or aircraft that carries goods

ˈfreight train *n* [C] a train that carries goods

French[1] /frentʃ/ *adj* relating to France, its people, or its language: *an excellent French wine*

French[2] *n* **1 the French** [plural] people from France **2** [U] the language used in France, and some other countries: *How do you ask for directions in French?* **3 pardon/excuse my French** *spoken* used to say sorry for swearing

ˌFrench ˈbean *n* [C] *BrE* a long thin green vegetable that is usually cooked and eaten whole SYN **green bean** → see picture at **VEGETABLE**

ˌFrench ˈbread *n* [U] a long thin LOAF of white bread

ˌFrench ˈdoors *n* [plural] *especially AmE* FRENCH WINDOWS → see picture at **WINDOW**

ˌFrench ˈdressing *n* [U] a mixture of oil and VINEGAR that is put on SALADS

ˌFrench ˈfry (*also* **fry**) *n* (*plural* **French fries**) [C usually plural] *especially AmE* a long thin piece of potato that has been cooked in hot oil SYN **chip** *BrE*

ˌFrench ˈhorn (*also* **horn** *especially BrE*) *n* [C] a musical instrument made of BRASS, that is curved round into a circle with a wide opening at one end → see picture at **BRASS**

ˌFrench ˈkiss *n* [C] a kiss made with your mouths open and with your tongues touching

ˌFrench ˈletter *n* [C] *BrE old-fashioned informal* a CONDOM

ˌFrench ˈloaf *n* [C] *BrE* a long thin LOAF of white bread SYN **baguette**

French·man /ˈfrentʃmən/ *n* (*plural* **Frenchmen** /-mən/) [C] a man from France

ˌFrench ˈplait *n* [C] a hairstyle in which the hair is put into a PLAIT that starts from the top of the head at the back → see picture at **HAIRSTYLE**

ˌFrench ˈpleat *n* [C] a hairstyle in which the hair is combed across at the back of the head, rolled under, and pinned

ˌFrench ˈpolish *n* [U] a clear liquid put on wooden furniture to protect it and make it shine

ˌFrench ˈstick *n* [C] a long thin LOAF of white bread SYN **baguette**

ˌFrench ˈtoast *n* [U] pieces of bread put into a mixture of egg and milk and then cooked in hot oil

ˌFrench ˈwindows *n* [plural] a pair of doors made mostly of glass, usually opening onto a garden or BALCONY → see picture at **WINDOW**

French·wom·an /ˈfrentʃˌwʊmən/ *n* (*plural* **Frenchwomen** /-ˌwɪmɪn/) [C] a woman from France

fren·e·my /ˈfrenəmi/ *n* (*plural* **frenemies**) [C] *informal* someone who you have a friendly relationship with but is really an enemy or competitor: *The office is full of frenemies.*

fre·net·ic /frəˈnetɪk/ *adj* frenetic activity is fast and not very organized SYN **frantic**: *She rushes from job to job at a frenetic pace.*

fren·zied /ˈfrenzid/ *adj* frenzied activity is fast and uncontrolled, usually because it is done by someone feeling very anxious or excited: *A woman was stabbed to death in a* ***frenzied attack*** *on her home tonight.* | *frenzied efforts to find a solution* —**frenziedly** *adv*

fren·zy /ˈfrenzi/ ●○○ *n* (*plural* **frenzies**)
1 [C,U] a state of great anxiety or excitement, in which you cannot control your behaviour: **[+of]** *a frenzy of religious feeling* | **in a frenzy** *The women were screaming and in a frenzy to get home.* | *Doreen had* ***worked*** *herself* ***into a frenzy****.*
2 [C] a time when people do a lot of things very quickly: **[+of]** *a frenzy of activity* | *a selling frenzy*
3 a feeding frenzy a) an occasion when a lot of people get involved in an activity in an uncontrolled way: *The film put America's moviegoers into a feeding frenzy.* **b)** an occasion when a lot of wild animals, especially SHARKS, eat something in a very excited way

fre·quen·cy /ˈfriːkwənsi/ ●●○ *n* (*plural* **frequencies**)
1 [U] the number of times that something happens within a particular period of time or within a particular group of people: **[+of]** *the frequency of serious road accidents* | **the high/low frequency (of sth)** *the higher frequency of diabetes in older people* | *Side effects from prescribed drugs are being reported* ***with increasing frequency*** (=more and more often). | *The* ***relative frequency*** *of fraternal twins has halved since 1950.*
2 [U] the fact that something happens a lot SYN **regularity**: *Businesses come and go* ***with alarming frequency****.*
3 [C,U] *technical* the number of radio waves, sound waves etc that pass any point per second: *This station broadcasts on three different frequencies.* | **high/low frequency** *Dolphins produce a high frequency sound.* | *the* ***frequency range*** *of the human ear*

fre·quent[1] /ˈfriːkwənt/ ●●○ W3 *adj* happening or doing something often OPP **infrequent**: **more/less frequent** *Her headaches are becoming less frequent.* | *Trains rushed past at* ***frequent intervals****.* | *She was a* ***frequent visitor*** *to the house.*

fre·quent[2] /frɪˈkwent $ frɪˈkwent, ˈfriːkwənt/ *v* [T] *formal* to go to a particular place often: *The bar was frequented by actors from the nearby theatre.*

fre·quent·ly /ˈfriːkwəntli/ ●●● S3 W2 *adv* very often or many times: *He was frequently drunk.*

> **REGISTER**
> In everyday English, people usually say that something **often** happens, or that something happens **a lot**, rather than say it happens **frequently**:
> *I* ***often*** *see him. OR I see him* ***a lot****.*

fres·co /ˈfreskəʊ $ -koʊ/ *n* (*plural* **frescoes** *or* **frescos**) [C] a painting made on a wall while the PLASTER is still wet → **mural**

fresh[1] /freʃ/ ●●● S2 W2 *adj*
1 NEW adding to or replacing something: *I'll just make*

some fresh coffee. | The report provides fresh evidence about the way the business was run. | You'll have to start again on a fresh sheet of paper. **THESAURUS** NEW
2 NEW AND INTERESTING good or interesting because it has not been done, seen etc before: *Ryan will bring a* ***fresh approach*** *to the job. | We need some* ***fresh ideas****. | Let's take a* ***fresh look*** *at the problem.*
3 RECENT done, experienced, or having happened recently: *There were fresh fox tracks around the hen huts. | The accident was still* ***fresh in her mind****.*
4 a fresh start when you start something again in a completely new and different way after being unsuccessful: *I hope Jim and I can get back together and* ***make a fresh start****.*
5 FOOD/FLOWERS **a)** fresh food has recently been picked or prepared, and is not frozen or preserved: **fresh fruit/vegetables/fish/bread etc** *The beans are fresh from the garden.* **b)** fresh flowers have recently been picked
6 fresh air air from outside, especially clean air: *Let's open the windows and have some fresh air in here!* → **breath of fresh air** at BREATH(2)
7 fresh water fresh water contains no salt and comes from rivers and lakes → **saltwater**
8 TASTE/SMELL ETC [usually before noun] pleasantly clean or cool: *a fresh minty taste | It's a light, fresh wine.*
9 APPEARANCE pleasant, bright, and clean OPP **dull**: *The kitchen is decorated in fresh blues and greens. | She has brown hair, hazel eyes and a* ***fresh complexion****.*
10 WEATHER if the wind is fresh, it is quite cold and strong: *a* ***fresh breeze***
11 NOT TIRED [not usually before noun] full of energy because you are not tired: *She always seems fresh and lively, even at the end of the day. | Despite his busy day he arrived looking* ***as fresh as a daisy*** (=not tired and ready to do things).
12 fresh from sth a) (*also* **fresh out of sth** *AmE*) having just finished your education or training, and not having a lot of experience: *He's fresh out of law school.* **b)** having just come from a particular place or experience: *The team is fresh from their victory over the French.*
13 get/be fresh with sb *old-fashioned* to behave rudely in a way which shows sexual interest, or lack of respect —**freshness** *n* [U]: *the freshness of the early morning | the freshness and vitality of youth*

fresh² *adv* **1 fresh-made/fresh-cut/fresh-grated etc** *especially AmE* recently made, cut etc: *fresh-ground coffee* **2 be fresh out of sth** *AmE spoken* to have just used your last supplies of something: *I'm fresh out of beer. Will you take a cola instead?*

fresh·en /ˈfreʃən/ *v* **1** (*also* **freshen up**) [T] to make something look or feel clean, new, attractive, cool etc SYN **brighten (up)**: *I'm going to buy some white paint to freshen up the bathroom walls.* **2** [I] if the wind freshens, it gets colder and stronger **3** (*also* **freshen up**) [T] to add more liquid to a drink: *The waitress freshened our coffee.*

freshen up *phr v* to wash your hands and face in order to feel clean and comfortable: **freshen yourself up** *Fiona's gone to freshen herself up.*

fresh·er /ˈfreʃə $ -ər/ *n* [C] *BrE* a student who has just started at a college or university

ˈfresh-faced *adj* fresh-faced people have a face that looks young and healthy: *a fresh-faced youth*

fresh·ly /ˈfreʃli/ ●●○ *adv* **freshly ground/picked/made etc** recently ground, picked etc: *freshly ground pepper* **THESAURUS** RECENTLY

fresh·man /ˈfreʃmən/ ●○○ *n* (*plural* **freshmen** /-mən/) [C] *AmE* a student in the first year of HIGH SCHOOL or university

fresh·wa·ter /ˈfreʃwɔːtə $ -wɔːtər, -wɑː-/ *adj* [only before noun] **1** having water that contains no salt → **saltwater**: *freshwater lakes* **2** living in water that contains no salt → **saltwater**: *freshwater crabs*

fret¹ /fret/ *v* (**fretted, fretting**) [I] to worry about something, especially when there is no need: *Don't fret – everything will be all right.* | **[+about/over]** *She's always fretting about the children.* | **fret that** *men of fifty, fretting that they're no longer young*

fret² *n* [C] one of the raised lines on the fretboard of a GUITAR etc

fret·board /ˈfretbɔːd $ -bɔːrd/ *n* [C] the long piece of wood on the NECK (=straight part) of a GUITAR against which the fingers press the strings to change the note

fret·ful /ˈfretfəl/ *adj* anxious and complaining, and unable to relax: *The child was tired and fretful.* —**fretfully** *adv* —**fretfulness** *n* [U]

fret·saw /ˈfretsɔː $ -sɒː/ *n* [C] a tool for cutting patterns in wood

fret·ted /ˈfretɪd/ *adj* cut or shaped into complicated patterns as decoration

fret·work /ˈfretwɜːk $ -wɜːrk/ *n* [U] patterns cut into thin wood, metal etc or the activity of making these patterns

Freud·i·an /ˈfrɔɪdiən/ *adj* **1** relating to Sigmund Freud's ideas about the way the mind works, and the way it can be studied **2** a Freudian remark or action is connected with the ideas about sex that people have in their minds but do not usually talk about

ˌFreudian ˈslip *n* [C] something you say that is different from what you intended to say, and shows your true thoughts

Fri. (*also* **Fri** *BrE*) the written abbreviation of ***Friday***

fri·a·ble /ˈfraɪəbəl/ *adj technical* friable rocks or soil are easily broken into very small pieces or into powder

fri·ar /ˈfraɪə $ -ər/ *n* [C] a member of a religious group of Catholic men, who travelled around in the past teaching about Christianity and who were very poor → **monk**

fri·a·ry /ˈfraɪəri/ *n* (*plural* **friaries**) [C] a place where friars live → **monastery**

fric·as·see /ˈfrɪkəseɪ $ ˌfrɪkəˈsiː/ *n* [C,U] food consisting of small pieces of meat in a thick white sauce: *chicken fricassee*

fric·a·tive /ˈfrɪkətɪv/ *n* [C] *technical* a sound, such as /f/ or /z/, made by forcing your breath through a narrow opening between your lips and teeth, or your tongue and teeth

frick·ing /ˈfrɪkɪŋ/ *adj, adv informal* used to emphasize what you are saying, in a slightly rude way: *It's a fricking miracle!*

fric·tion /ˈfrɪkʃən/ ●○○ *n*
1 [C,U] disagreement, angry feelings, or unfriendliness between people SYN **tension**: **cause/create friction** *Having my mother living with us causes friction at home.* | **[+between]** *the usual frictions between parents and their teenage children* | **[+with]** *His independent attitude was a constant* ***source of friction*** *with his boss.*
2 [U] *technical* the natural force that prevents one surface from sliding easily over another surface: *Putting oil on both surfaces reduces friction.*
3 [U] when one surface rubs against another: *Check your rope frequently, as friction against the rock can wear it away.*

Fri·day /ˈfraɪdi, -deɪ/ ●●● S2 W2 *n* [C,U] (*written abbreviation* **Fri.**) the day between Thursday and Saturday: **on Friday** *It's Kate's birthday on Friday. | Diane won't be here Friday. AmE* | **Friday morning/afternoon etc** *Can you meet me Friday morning?* | **last Friday** *I had a terrible time last Friday.* | **this Friday** *We're flying to Vienna this Friday.* | **next Friday** (=Friday of next week) *Her appointment is next Friday.* | **a Friday** (=one of the Fridays in the year) *We got married on a Friday.*

fridge /frɪdʒ/ ●●● S2 *n* [C] a large piece of electrical kitchen equipment, used for keeping food and drinks cool SYN **refrigerator** → **freezer**

ˌfridge-ˈfreezer *n* [C] *BrE* a large piece of electrical kitchen equipment, of which one part is a fridge and one part is a FREEZER

ˈfridge ˌmagnet *n* [C] a MAGNET with a picture on it or in an interesting shape, used for decorating the outside of a FRIDGE

F

fried /fraɪd/ *adj* **1** having been cooked in hot oil: *fried chicken* → see picture at EGG[1] **2** *AmE informal* unable to think clearly, because you are tired, anxious etc: *My brain is just totally fried.*

friend[1] /frend/ ●●● S1 W1 *n* [C]
1 PERSON YOU LIKE someone who you know and like very much and enjoy spending time with: *Jerry, this is my friend Sue.* | *She's always out with her friends.* | *One of her closest friends died at the weekend.* | *I met Jim through a friend.*
2 be friends (with sb) to be someone's friend: *I've been friends with the Murkets for twenty years.*
3 a) make friends to become friendly with people: *Jenny has always found it easy to make friends at school.* **b) make friends with sb** to become friendly with someone: *He made friends with an old fisherman.*
4 be just (good) friends used to say that you are not having a romantic relationship with someone: *I'm not going out with Nathan – we're just good friends.*
5 SUPPORTER someone who supports an organization such as a theatre, ART GALLERY, CHARITY etc by giving money or help: **[+of]** *the Friends of the Tate*
6 NOT AN ENEMY someone who has the same beliefs, wants to achieve the same things etc as you, and will support you: *our friends and allies around the world* | *She shot him a quick glance as if unsure whether he was friend or foe.* | *Don't worry, you're among friends.*
7 someone who has created a link with you on a SOCIAL NETWORKING SITE on the Internet, by visiting your WEBPAGE and clicking on it: *She has thousands of friends on MySpace.*
8 PARLIAMENT/COURT OF LAW *BrE* **a) my honourable friend** used by a member of parliament when speaking about another member of parliament **b) my learned friend** used by a lawyer when speaking about another lawyer in a court of law
9 be no friend of sth to not like or be a supporter of something: *I'm no friend of socialism, as you know.*
10 Friend a member of the Society of Friends SYN **Quaker**
11 our/your friend *spoken* used humorously to talk about someone you do not know, who is doing something annoying: *Our friend with the loud voice is back.*
12 have friends in high places to know important people who can help you
13 a friend in need someone who helps you when you need it
14 be in the friend zone *informal* to be regarded as a friend by someone for whom you have romantic feelings

COLLOCATIONS

ADJECTIVES/NOUN + friend

sb's best friend (=the friend you like the most) *Fiona was her best friend.*
a good/close friend (=one of the friends you like the most) *She's a good friend of mine.*
a dear friend (=a friend who is very important to you) *I'd like you to meet a dear friend of mine.*
an old friend (=someone who has been your friend for a long time) *We went to see some old friends who had moved to Harlow.*
a childhood friend (=someone who was your friend when you were a child) | **a school friend** | **a family friend** | **a personal friend** | **a mutual friend** (=someone who is a friend of both you and someone else) | **a firm friend** (=a friend you like a lot and intend to keep) | **a trusted friend** | **male/female friends**

VERBS

have a friend *Suzie has plenty of friends.*
become friends *Liz and Vanessa soon became friends.*
remain friends

PHRASES

a friend of mine/yours/Bill's etc *A friend of mine is going to Tokyo next week.*
a friend of a friend *I managed to get tickets from a friend of a friend.*
sb's circle of friends (=all the friends someone has)

THESAURUS

friend someone who you know and like very much and enjoy spending time with: *She's going to Palm Springs with some friends.* | *Amy's a close* ***friend of mine.***
acquaintance /əˈkweɪntəns/ someone who you know and see sometimes, but who is not one of your close friends: *We borrowed the money from one of Paul's business acquaintances.*
mate *BrE informal* a friend – used especially about boys or men: *He always goes to the pub with his mates on Friday night.*
buddy *AmE informal* a friend – used especially about men or young people: *He's out playing basketball with some of his high school buddies.*
pal *informal* a friend – **pal** sounds rather old-fashioned: *They met at school and have remained close pals.*
crony [usually plural] *disapproving* a friend – used about powerful people who will help each other even if it is slightly dishonest: *He's one of the president's cronies.*
companion *written* someone who spends time with you, doing the same things as you – used about animals as well as people: *travelling companions* | *His dog was his constant companion.*
the girls *informal* a woman's female friends
the lads *BrE informal* a man's male friends: *a night out with the lads*

friend[2] *v* [T] to add someone to your list of friends on a SOCIAL NETWORKING SITE: *I never friend someone I haven't met in real life.*

friend·less /ˈfrendləs/ *adj literary* having no friends and no one to help you

friend·ly[1] /ˈfrendli/ ●●● S2 W3 *adj* (*comparative* **friendlier**, *superlative* **friendliest**)
1 behaving towards someone in a way that shows you like them and are ready to talk to them or help them OPP **unfriendly**: *a friendly smile* | *I've found a great pub – good beer and a friendly atmosphere.* | **[+to/towards]** *Why is he suddenly so friendly towards you, Charlotte?*
2 be friendly with sb to be friends with someone: *Betty's very friendly with the Jacksons.*
3 not at war with your own country, or not opposing you OPP **hostile**: *friendly nations*
4 *BrE* a friendly game is played for pleasure or practice, and not because it is important to win: *a friendly match against AC Milan*
5 user-friendly/customer-friendly etc not difficult for particular people to understand or use: *a user-friendly computer program* | *a customer-friendly shopping mall*
6 environmentally-friendly/ozone-friendly/eco-friendly etc not harmful to the environment, OZONE LAYER etc: *eco-friendly washing powder*
7 friendly fire bombs, bullets etc that accidentally kill people who are fighting on the same side —**friendliness** *n* [U]

THESAURUS

friendly behaving towards someone in a way that shows you like them and are ready to talk to them or help them: *a friendly smile* | *The local people are very friendly.*
warm [usually before noun] friendly and caring about other people, in a way that makes people like you and feel comfortable: *He was such a warm caring person and everyone loved him.* | *We received a very* ***warm welcome.***
nice *especially spoken* friendly and kind: *Chris is a nice guy. I'm sure you'll get on with him.* | *He wasn't very nice to the other children.*
amiable /ˈeɪmiəbəl/ *formal* friendly and easy to like: *Tom was an amiable young man.*
welcoming friendly to someone who has just arrived somewhere: *a welcoming smile* | *The group are very welcoming to new members.*

F

hospitable friendly and eager to make visitors comfortable: *I found Japanese people to be very hospitable.*
genial *formal* behaving in a cheerful and friendly way: *a genial host | She was in a genial mood.*
cordial *formal* friendly and polite but formal: *The two nations have always maintained cordial relations.*
approachable friendly and easy to talk to – used especially about people in important positions: *The head teacher is very approachable.*

friendly² *n* (*plural* **friendlies**) [C] *BrE* a game played for pleasure or practice, and not because it is important to win

ˈfriendly soˌciety *n* [C] an association in Britain that people regularly pay small amounts of money to, which then provides them with money when they become old or ill

friend·ship /ˈfrendʃɪp/ ●●○ W3 *n*
1 [C] a relationship between friends: **[+between]** *The friendship between father and youth deepened.* | **[+with]** *his friendship with Sam | her* ***close friendship*** *with her aunt | a* ***lifelong friendship*** *| The two boys* ***formed*** *a deep and lasting* ***friendship****. | He and Bob* ***struck up a friendship*** (=began to be friends).
2 [U] the feelings and behaviour that exist between friends: *I could always rely on Gary for friendship and support. | The Indians have* ***extended the hand of friendship*** (=shown that they want to be friends with another country).

fri·er /ˈfraɪə $ -ər/ *n* [C] another spelling of FRYER

fries /fraɪz/ *n* [plural] long thin pieces of potato that have been cooked in hot oil SYN **chips** *BrE*

Frie·si·an /ˈfriːziən $ -ʒən/ *n* [C] *especially BrE* a type of cow that is black and white

frieze /friːz/ *n* [C] a decoration that goes along the top of the walls of a room or a building

frig·ate /ˈfrɪgət/ *n* [C] a small fast ship used especially for protecting other ships in wars

frig·ging /ˈfrɪgɪŋ/ *adj* [only before noun], *adv spoken not polite* used to emphasize something you are saying when you are angry, annoyed etc: *I can't open the frigging door!*

fright /fraɪt/ ●●○ *n*
1 [singular, U] a sudden feeling of fear: *You* ***gave*** *me such* ***a fright*** *creeping up on me like that!* | **get/have a fright** *I got an awful fright when I realised how much money I owed.* | **with fright** *He was shaking with fright.* | **in fright** *Several of the children cried out in fright.* THESAURUS ▸ FEAR
2 take fright to be very afraid of something, especially so that you run away from it or do not do something that you were going to do: *The bird took fright and flew away. | She had promised to marry him, but took fright at the last moment.*
3 look a fright *old-fashioned* to look untidy or unattractive
→ STAGE FRIGHT

fright·en /ˈfraɪtn/ ●●● S3 W3 *v* [T] to make someone feel afraid SYN **scare**: *Don't stand so near the edge! You're frightening me. | She was frightened by the anger in his eyes. | Computers used to frighten me, but not now.* | **frighten sb to death/frighten the life out of sb** (=make someone feel extremely afraid) *He drove at a speed which frightened Lara to death.*

frighten sb ↔ **away** *phr v* to make a person or animal go away by making them feel afraid: *Terrorist activity in the area has frightened most tourists away.*

frighten sb **into** sth *phr v* to force someone to do something by making them afraid: **frighten sb into doing sth** *He frightened me into staying silent.*

frighten sb/sth ↔ **off** *phr v* to make a person or animal so nervous or afraid that they go away or do not do something they were going to do: *The investors were frightened off by the company's low profits that year.*

fright·ened /ˈfraɪtnd/ ●●● S3 *adj* feeling afraid SYN **scared**: *Don't be frightened. We're not going to hurt you.* | **[+of]** *I was frightened of being left by myself in the house. | Her father had an awful temper and she was always frightened of him.* | **frightened to do sth** *The boy was frightened to speak.* | **frightened that** *She's frightened that her ex-husband will find her. | To tell the truth, I was* ***frightened to death*** (=very frightened). | *a frightened horse* ⚠ Do not confuse **frightened,** which describes a feeling, and **frightening,** which describes something that makes you feel frightened: *a frightened child | a frightening experience*

THESAURUS

frightened feeling worried because you might get hurt or because something bad might happen: *I was too frightened to say anything. | Many animals are frightened of fireworks.*
scared [not before noun] *especially spoken* frightened. Scared is less formal than **frightened** and is the usual word to use in everyday English: *I'm scared of dogs. | Old people are too scared to go out of their homes.*
afraid [not before noun] frightened. **Afraid** sounds more formal than **frightened** or **scared**: *Children are often afraid of the dark. | I was afraid that I might say the wrong thing.*
alarmed frightened and worried that something bad might happen: *She was alarmed at the thought of performing in front of an audience.*
fearful *formal* frightened that something bad might happen: *They are fearful of another terrorist attack.*

VERY FRIGHTENED

terrified very frightened: *He looked terrified as the plane took off. | James was absolutely terrified of losing his only child.*
petrified very frightened – used especially when you are so frightened that you cannot think or move: *She's absolutely petrified of spiders.*
scared stiff/scared to death *informal* very frightened: *I had to make a speech, and I was scared stiff. | She was scared to death of her father.*
in terror *written* if you do something in terror, you do it because you are very frightened: *People fled in terror as the building went up in flames.*

fright·en·ers /ˈfraɪtn-əz $ -ərz/ *n* [plural] *BrE informal* **put the frighteners on sb** to make someone do what you want by threatening them

fright·en·ing /ˈfraɪtn-ɪŋ/ ●●● S3 *adj* making you feel afraid or nervous SYN **scary**: *Going into hospital can be very frightening for a child. | It was the most frightening experience of my life.* | **it is frightening (to do sth)** *It's frightening to think what could happen if terrorists did get hold of nuclear materials.* —**frighteningly** *adv*: *a frighteningly real possibility.*

THESAURUS

frightening making you feel frightened: *Being held at gunpoint had been the most frightening moment of his life. | The experience was very frightening.*
scary *especially spoken* frightening. **Scary** is less formal than **frightening** and is very common in everyday English: *The movie was really scary. | There were some scary moments.*
chilling frightening, especially because violence, cruelty, or danger is involved: *a chilling tale of revenge, murder and madness | The court heard chilling details about the attack.*
spooky frightening and strange, especially because something involves ghosts or powers that people do not understand: *The forest is really spooky in the dark. | a spooky coincidence | spooky stories*
creepy *informal* frightening in a way that makes you feel nervous, especially when you are not sure exactly why – used especially about places, people, and feelings: *This place is really creepy. Let's get out of here. | a creepy guy*
eerie *especially literary* strange and frightening: *There was an eerie silence immediately after the bomb went off. | an eerie light | an eerie feeling*

F

intimidating making you feel frightened, nervous, or lacking in confidence: *Big schools can be an intimidating place for young children.* | *Giving evidence in court is often a rather intimidating experience.* | *the intimidating presence of a large number of soldiers*
menacing frightening because you think someone is going to hurt you, even though they have not said or done anything violent – used especially about someone's expression or voice: *The woman had a very menacing look.* | *'I'd like to have a word with you outside,' he said in a menacing tone.*

VERY FRIGHTENING

terrifying extremely frightening: *a terrifying thought* | *The experience was absolutely terrifying.* | *She spoke of the terrifying ordeal* (=a very bad experience) *when three armed men burst into her house.*
hair-raising very frightening and involving danger, in a way that is exciting: *hair-raising stories* | *a hair-raising motorcycle ride through the streets of Havana*
spine-chilling very frightening – used about films, stories etc that involve frightening or cruel events: *a spine-chilling novel by Stephen King*
blood-curdling *especially literary* [only before noun] very frightening – used especially about sounds: *a blood-curdling scream* | *a blood-curdling growl*

fright·ful /ˈfraɪtfəl/ *adj old-fashioned especially BrE* **1** unpleasant or bad SYN **awful**, **terrible**: *There's been a frightful accident.* **2** used to emphasize how bad something is SYN **awful**, **terrible**: *Her hair was a frightful mess.*

fright·ful·ly /ˈfraɪtfəli/ *adv BrE old-fashioned* very: *I'm frightfully sorry about the delay.*

fri·gid /ˈfrɪdʒɪd/ *adj* **1** a woman who is frigid does not like having sex **2** *literary* not friendly or kind SYN **cold**, **icy**, **frosty**: *The guard looked at us with a frigid stare.* **3** *formal* very cold SYN **icy**: *the frigid air* —**frigidly** *adv* —**frigidity** /frɪˈdʒɪdəti/ *n* [U]

frill /frɪl/ *n* [C] **1** a decoration that consists of a narrow piece of cloth that has many small folds in it → **flounce**: *She was wearing a white blouse with frills at the cuffs.* **2 frills** [plural] attractive but unnecessary features: **without/with no frills** *It was just a comfortable flat with no frills.* | *We supply basic,* ***no-frills*** *tractors at low prices.*

frill·y /ˈfrɪli/ *adj* decorated with lots of frills: *a frilly skirt*

FRINGE

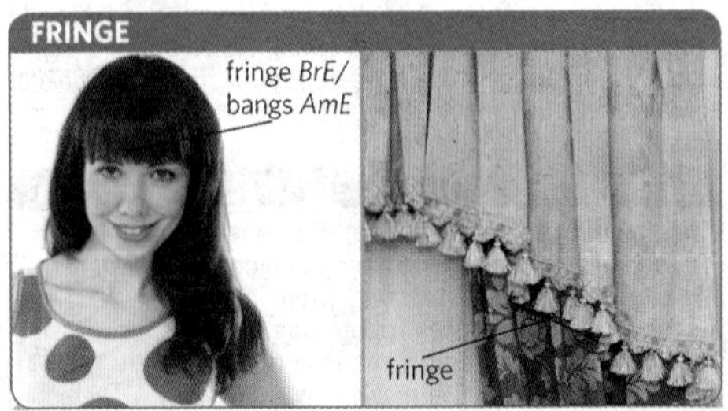

fringe¹ /frɪndʒ/ ●●○ *n* [C]
1 *BrE* if you have a fringe, your hair is cut so that it hangs down over your forehead SYN **bangs** *AmE*: *a tall girl with straight brown hair and a fringe*
2 a decorative edge of hanging threads on a curtain, piece of clothing etc
3 on the fringes (of sth) a) not completely belonging to or accepted by a group of people who share the same job, activities etc: *a small group on the fringes of the art world* **b)** (*also* **on the fringe**) at the part of something that is farthest from the centre SYN **on the edge of sth**: *Nina remained on the fringe of the crowd.* → **the lunatic fringe** at LUNATIC(3)

fringe² *adj* [only before noun] **fringe group/event/issue etc** a group, event etc that is less important or popular than the main group etc, or whose opinions are not accepted by most other people involved in the same activity OPP **mainstream**: *He used a party conference fringe meeting to defend terrorism.* | *The environment is no longer a fringe issue.* | *a fringe religious sect*

fringe³ *v* [T] to be around the edge of something: *A line of trees fringed the pool.*

ˈfringe ˌbenefit *n* [C usually plural] an additional service or advantage given with a job besides wages: *A competitive salary with fringe benefits will be offered.*

ˌfringe ˈtheatre *n* [U] *BrE* plays by new writers, often on difficult subjects or written in unusual ways, that are not performed in the main theatres

frip·pe·ry /ˈfrɪpəri/ *n* (*plural* **fripperies**) [C usually plural] an unnecessary and useless object or decoration

Fris·bee /ˈfrɪzbi/ *n* [C,U] *trademark* a piece of plastic shaped like a plate that you throw to someone else to catch as a game. The game is also called Frisbee.

frisk /frɪsk/ *v* **1** [T] to search someone for hidden weapons, drugs etc by feeling their body with your hands: *We were frisked at the airport.* **2** [I] if a young animal frisks, it runs and jumps playfully SYN **skip**: *The lambs were frisking around the pen.*

frisk·y /ˈfrɪski/ *adj* **1** full of energy and fun: *a frisky horse* **2** *informal* feeling sexually excited SYN **horny** —**friskily** *adv* —**friskiness** *n* [U]

fris·son /ˈfriːsɒn $ friːˈsoʊn/ *n* [C usually singular] a sudden feeling of excitement or fear SYN **shiver**: **[+of]** *A frisson of alarm went through her.*

frit·ter¹ /ˈfrɪtə $ -ər/ *v*
fritter sth ↔ **away** *phr v* to waste time, money, or effort on something small or unimportant: **[+on]** *He frittered away a fortune on fast cars and gambling.*

fritter² *n* [C] a thin piece of fruit, vegetable, or meat covered with a mixture of eggs and flour and cooked in hot fat: **apple/corn/banana etc fritter**

fritz /frɪts/ *n AmE informal* **be/go on the fritz** if something is or goes on the fritz, it is not working correctly SYN **be/go on the blink**: *My TV is on the fritz.*

fri·vol·i·ty /frɪˈvɒləti $ -ˈvɑː-/ *n* (*plural* **frivolities**) **1** [C,U] behaviour or activities that are not serious or sensible, especially when you should be serious or sensible: *I don't think such frivolity helps the organization's public image.* **2** [C] something that is silly and unimportant: *Try not to be distracted by the frivolities of the world.*

friv·o·lous /ˈfrɪvələs/ *adj* **1** not serious or sensible, especially in a way that is not suitable for a particular occasion: *The court discourages frivolous lawsuits.* **2** a frivolous person likes having fun rather than doing serious or sensible things – used to show disapproval OPP **serious** —**frivolously** *adv*

frizz /frɪz/ *v* [I,T] *informal* if your hair frizzes, or if you frizz it, it curls very tightly —**frizz** *n* [U]: *how to give your hair more shape and less frizz*

frizz·y /ˈfrɪzi/ *adj* frizzy hair is very tightly curled → see picture at HAIRSTYLE

fro /frəʊ $ froʊ/ *adv* → TO AND FRO¹

frock /frɒk $ frɑːk/ *n* [C] **1** *old-fashioned* a woman's or girl's dress: *a party frock* **2** a long loose piece of clothing worn by some Christian MONKS

ˌfrock ˈcoat / $ ˈ../ *n* [C] a knee-length coat for men, worn in the 19th century

frog /frɒg $ frɑːg, frɒːg/ ●●○ *n* [C]
1 a small green animal that lives near water and has long legs for jumping → **toad**
2 have a frog in your throat *informal* to have difficulty in speaking, especially because of a sore throat
3 Frog *taboo* a very offensive word for someone from France. Do not use this word.

frog·man /ˈfrɒgmən $ ˈfrɑːg-, ˈfrɒːg-/ *n* (*plural* **frogmen** /-mən/) [C] *BrE* someone who swims under water using special equipment to help them breathe, especially as a job SYN **diver**: *Police frogmen have been searching the lake looking for a weapon.*

frog·march /ˈfrɒgmɑːtʃ $ ˈfrɑːgmɑːrtʃ, ˈfrɔːg-/ *v* [T always + adv/prep] *BrE* to force someone to walk somewhere by holding their arms very tightly by their side or behind their back

frog·spawn /ˈfrɒgspɔːn $ ˈfrɑːgspɒːn, ˈfrɔːg-/ *n* [U] *BrE* frog's eggs

froi·deur /frwɑːˈdɜː $ -ˈdɜːr/ *n* [U] *formal* unfriendliness, or an unfriendly way of behaving: **[+between]** *There was a certain froideur between the president and the prime minister after the incident.*

frol·ic¹ /ˈfrɒlɪk $ ˈfrɑː-/ *v* (**frolicked, frolicking**) [I] *written* to play in an active happy way: *Lambs frolicked in the next field.*

frolic² *n* [C,U] *written* a fun enjoyable game or activity: *Everyone joined in the Saturday night frolics.*

from /frəm; *strong* frɒm $ frəm *strong* frʌm, frɑːm/ ●●● S1 W1 *prep*

1 WHERE SB/STH STARTS starting at a particular place or position: *How do you get from here to Colchester? | an empire stretching from Syria to Spain | The hotel is on the main road from Newport. | Ernest twice ran away from home.*

2 DISTANCE AWAY used when talking about the distance between places or people to mention one of the places or people: *We live about five miles from Boston. | a large Victorian house only fifty yards from my workplace | He was standing only a few feet away from me.*

3 WHEN STH STARTS starting at a particular time: *He'll be here tomorrow from about seven o'clock onwards. | We're going to tell her on her birthday – that's two weeks from today. | From now on, I will only be working in the mornings. | housewives who work* ***from morning to night*** (=without stopping)

4 ORIGINAL CONDITION used to say what condition or situation something is in before it changes: *translating from French into English | When she arrived, things just* ***went from bad to worse*** (=got even worse)*!*

5 from place to place/house to house etc to a number of places: *She went from house to house asking if anyone had seen the child.*

6 from day to day/from minute to minute etc used to say that something continues or keeps changing: *My health is improving from day to day.*

7 vary/change etc from sth to sth to change or be different according to the person, situation, time etc involved: *The treatment will vary from patient to patient.*

8 RANGE used to mention the two ends of a range: **from sth to sth** *Prices range from £10,000 to over £100,000. | a place where you can buy anything from a handgun to a rocket launcher*

9 POSITION WHEN WATCHING used to say where someone is when they see or watch something: *From the top of the hill, you can see for miles. | There's a man watching us from behind that fence.*

10 BEING REMOVED used to say where something is before it is removed: *She pulled her chair away from her desk. | Philip snatched the book from my hand. | He took a knife from his pocket. | Subtract three from fifteen.*

11 ABSENT used to say where someone would normally be, when they are not there: *The boy's absence from class has been noted. | I have a brother, but he's away from home at present.*

12 ORIGIN used to say where something was or who had it before you obtained it: *I got the idea from Colin. | Do you know where the information came from? | Gray caught smallpox from his nephew. | I'll show you a short extract from one of our training videos. | We usually buy our cheese from a shop in the market. | You have to choose the right answer from a list.*

13 SENT/GIVEN BY SB used to say who sends or gives something: *He had received a bill for nineteen dollars from St Peter's hospital. | I had a phone call from John. | You need to get permission from the owner. | with lots of love from Elaine* (=used at the end of a letter or on a card)

14 PLACE OF BIRTH/WORK used to say where someone was born, where they live, or where they work: *We invited speakers from all the regions. | Students from all faculties will have access to the machines. | There's a man from the tax office on the phone. | I'm from Yorkshire* (=I was born in Yorkshire).

15 CAUSE used to state the cause of something: *mothers who are exhausted from all the sleepless nights | Death rates from accidents have been on the increase. | a patient suffering from stomach pains | The community benefits from having an excellent health service.*

16 FORMING OPINIONS **a)** used to say what made you form a particular opinion: *From what I've read, the company seems to be in difficulties. | It's obvious from a quick glance that the plan has changed dramatically.* **b)** used to say how a subject is being considered: *These changes are ideal from my point of view. | We have spent a lot of time looking at the problem from all angles.*

17 MADE OF STH used to say what substance is used to make something: *Bread is made from flour, water, and yeast. | a cabinet constructed from chipboard*

18 PREVENTED used to say what is prevented or forbidden: **from doing sth** *These problems have prevented me from completing the work. | people who have been disqualified from driving | Tourist coaches will be banned from entering the city centre.*

19 HARM used to mention something bad that you do not want to affect someone or something: *ways of protecting yourself from attack | I will keep you safe from harm.*

20 DIFFERENCE used when you are comparing things or people to mention one of the things or people: *She's quite different from her sister. | Our two cats are so alike, I can never tell one from the other.*

from·age frais /ˌfrɒmɑːʒ ˈfreɪ $ frəˌmɑːʒ-/ *n* [U] *BrE* a thick creamy food made from milk and similar to YOGHURT

frond /frɒnd $ frɑːnd/ *n* [C] a leaf of a FERN or PALM¹(2)

front¹ /frʌnt/ ●●● S1 W1 *n*

1 PART THAT IS FURTHEST FORWARD **the front** the part of something that is furthest forward in the direction that it is facing or moving OPP **back**: **[+of]** *Ricky stepped forward to the front of the stage and began to sing. |* **the front of the line/queue** *It took ages to get to the front of the queue. |* **at/in the front (of sth)** *She always sits at the front of the class. | I found a good place on the bus, on the top deck, right at the front.*

2 SIDE THAT FACES FORWARD **the front** the front of something is the side or surface that faces forward OPP **back**: **[+of]** *Harvey ran quickly round the front of the car to try and open the other door. | the control panel on the front of the machine | He wore an old sweater with a coffee stain down the front.*

3 MOST IMPORTANT SIDE **the front** the most important side or surface of something, that you look at first OPP **back**: **on the front** *Dean sent me a lovely postcard with a picture of Bolton Abbey on the front. |* **[+of]** *She's on the front* (=a picture of her is on the front) *of this month's magazine. | There's an introduction at the front of the book* (=in the first pages).

4 BUILDING **the front** the most important side of a building, where you go in OPP **back**: **[+of]** *Ben had just finished painting the front of the house.*

5 in front of sb/sth a) further forward than someone or something OPP **behind**: *He was standing in front of her in the lunch queue, and they just got talking. | He walked along in front of me, holding the lantern. | Suddenly, something ran across the road in front of the car. | An old wooden desk stood in front of the window.* **b)** facing someone or something: *The door opened and Harriet stood in front of him. | She sat down in front of the mirror and brushed her hair carefully. | Billy crouched in front of the fire to warm his hands.* **c)** outside a building, near its entrance: *There was a small garden in front of the house. | It was raining as we parked in front of the hotel.* **d)** if you say or do something in front of someone, you do it where they can see or hear you: *Don't swear in front of the children! | The match was played in front of a crowd of 8,000.* **e)** if you have problems or difficulties in front of you, you will soon need to deal with them → **in front of your eyes** at EYE¹(9)

F

USAGE: In front of, opposite

- **In front of** a building means directly outside the front of it and on the same side of the street: *The car stopped in front of our hotel.*
- **Opposite** a building means outside the front of it on the other side of a street, area of land etc: *There are some shops opposite the school.*

6 in front a) ahead of something or someone OPP **behind**: *He drove straight into the car in front.* **b)** winning something such as a sports match or competition SYN **ahead** OPP **behind**: *His goal put Leeds back in front.* **c)** in the area nearest the most forward part of something, or nearest the entrance to a building

7 on a ... front in a particular area of activity: **on the economic/political etc front** *On the technical front, there have been a number of important developments.* | *Excellent teamwork from our staff has brought improvement* ***on all fronts***. | **on the domestic/international front** *On the domestic front, de Gaulle's priority was to secure his government's authority.* | **on a wide/broad/limited front** *Schemes of this kind enjoyed success only on a limited front.*

8 out front (*also* **out the front/out in front** *BrE*) the area near the entrance to a building: *Hurry up! The taxi is out front.*

9 in (the) front/up front in the front part of a car, next to the driver or where the driver sits: *Mom, can I sit in the front?*

10 in front of the television/TV/computer etc watching a television or using a computer: *The average child spends three to four hours in front of the TV.* | *I spend most of my time* ***sitting in front of*** *a computer.*

11 up front *informal* **a)** money that is paid up front is paid before work is done, or before goods are supplied: *We need two hundred pounds up front.* **b)** directly and clearly from the start: *It's important to tell potential clients this up front.* → UPFRONT[1]

12 WEATHER [C] *technical* the place where two areas of air of different temperatures meet, often shown as a line on weather maps: **warm/cold front** (=an area of warm or cold air)

13 SEA **the front** *BrE* a wide road next to the beach where people can walk for pleasure: *We could always go for a stroll along the front.*

14 BODY **your front** your chest, or the part of your body that faces forward: *You've spilled juice all down your front!* | *He was asleep, lying on his front with his head turned to one side.*

15 ILLEGAL ACTIVITIES [C] a legal business that someone operates in order to hide the illegal activities that they are involved in: **[+for]** *The casino was used as a front for cross-border smuggling operations.*

16 HIDE FEELINGS [singular] if you put on a front, you behave in a way that is happier, braver etc than you really feel: **put on/show a front** *Jenny didn't want Adam to see how worried she was. So she put on a* ***brave front***. | *His arrogance is just a front. Deep down he's really insecure.* | *When disciplining children, it is important that parents* ***present a united front*** (=show that they both feel the same about a situation).

17 ORGANIZATION [singular] used in the name of a political party or unofficial military organization: *the People's Liberation Front*

18 WAR [C] the area where fighting happens in a war SYN **front line**: *He joined the army, and was immediately* ***sent to the front***. | *Her husband was shot down over the Western Front.* → HOME FRONT

19 CHURCH [C] a side of a large important church building: *the west front of Rouen cathedral*

front² ●●● S1 W2 *adj* [only before noun]
1 at, on, or in the front of something OPP **back**: *Two of his front teeth had been knocked out.* | *the front cover of 'Hello!' magazine* | *the front wheel of his bicycle* | *the dog's front legs* | **front door/garden/porch etc** (=at the front of a house) *We walked up the front steps and into the reception area.* | **front seat/row** *We got there an hour early in order to get seats in the front row.*
2 a front organization is a legal one that is run in order to hide a secret or illegal activity: *a front organization for importing heroin* → FRONT MAN(1)
3 *technical* a front vowel sound is made by raising your tongue at the front of your mouth, such as the vowel sound in 'see' → **back**

front³ *v* **1** [T] *especially BrE* if someone fronts something such as a musical group or a television programme, they lead it and are the person that the public sees most: *Fronted by Alan Hull, the band had a number of memorable hits.* **2** [T] (*also* **front onto sth** *BrE*) if a building or area of land is fronted by something, or fronts onto it, it faces that thing: *The house was fronted by a large ornamental lake.* | *The hotel entrance fronted onto a busy road.* **3 be fronted by/with sth** to be covered or decorated at the front with something: *a large building fronted with marble*

front·age /ˈfrʌntɪdʒ/ *n* [U] the part of a building or piece of land that is along a road, river etc

front·al /ˈfrʌntl/ *adj* [only before noun] *formal* **1** at or relating to the front part of something: *the frontal armour of the new tanks* **2 frontal attack/assault a)** a direct attack on the front of an army: *The minefields make an all-out frontal attack impossible.* **b)** an attack or criticism that is very strong and direct: *After the election, the party launched into a frontal assault on the British media.* **3** *medical* relating to the front part of the head: *the* ***frontal lobes*** *of the brain* → FULL FRONTAL

ˈfrontal ˌsystem *n* [C] *technical* a weather FRONT[1](12)

ˌfront and ˈcenter *adj, adv AmE* in a very important position, where it will receive attention: *Prayer in schools has become a front-and-center issue.*

ˌfront ˈbench *n* [C] the front row of seats on each side of the British parliament, on which the leaders of the political parties sit → **back bench**

front·bench·er /ˌfrʌntˈbentʃə◂ $ -ər◂/ *n* [C] someone who sits on a front bench in the British parliament → **backbencher**

ˌfront ˈdesk *n* [U] the desk where visitors go when they arrive at a hotel or organization SYN **reception**

ˌfront ˈdoor *n* [C usually singular] the main entrance door to a house, at the front → **back door**

fron·tier /ˈfrʌntɪə $ frʌnˈtɪr/ ●●○ *n*
1 [C] *especially BrE* the border of a country: **[+between/with]** *Lille is close to the frontier between France and Belgium.* | **on/at the frontier** *Troops established a road block on the frontier.* | **frontier town/area/post etc** (=a town etc on a frontier) THESAURUS▸ BORDER
2 the frontier an area where people have never lived before, that not much is known about, especially in the western US before the 20th century: *a novel about a family's struggle on the American frontier* | *space, the final frontier*
3 the frontiers of knowledge/physics etc the limits of what is known about something: **push back the frontiers** (=discover new things)

fron·tiers·man /ˈfrʌntɪəzmən $ frʌnˈtɪrz-/ *n* (*plural* **frontiersmen** /-mən/) [C] a man who lived on the American frontier, especially in the 19th century

fron·tis·piece /ˈfrʌntəspiːs/ *n* [C] a picture or photograph at the beginning of a book, usually opposite the page with the title on it

ˌfront ˈline *n* **1** [C usually singular] the place where fighting happens in a war SYN **front**: **in/on the front line** *troops who had served in the front line at Magdeburg* | *three miles behind the front line* **2 in the front line a)** doing something that has not been done before: *in the front line of the fight against cancer* **b)** likely to be blamed for an organization's mistakes —**ˈfront-line** *adj* [only before noun]: *front-line troops*

ˈfront man *n* [C usually singular] **1** a person who speaks for an organization, for example an illegal one, but is not the leader of it **2** (*also* **frontman**) the leader, and usually the singer, of a musical group

ˈfront ˌmatter *n* [U] all the pages at the very beginning of a book, including the page with the title on it

ˌfront ˈoffice *n* [singular] the people in a business who manage things or who deal directly with the public → **back office**

ˌ**front of ˈhouse** *n* [U] *BrE* the areas in a theatre or hotel which are used by the public —**front-of-house** *adj*: *the front-of-house manager*

ˈ**front-page** *adj* [only before noun] **front-page news/article/story etc** something that is printed on the first page of a newspaper because it is very important or exciting

ˌ**front ˈroom** *n* [C] the main room in a house where you usually sit SYN **living room**

ˌ**front-ˈrunner** *n* [C] the person or thing that is most likely to succeed in a competition: *the front-runner in June's presidential election*

frost¹ /frɒst $ frɒːst/ ●●○ *n*
1 [C,U] very cold weather, when water freezes: **late/early/first frost** *Even in May we can sometimes get a late frost.* | **hard/heavy/sharp/severe frost** (=extremely cold weather) *three continuous nights of hard frost* | *the risk of* ***frost damage*** *to crops*
2 [U] ice that looks white and powdery and covers things that are outside when the temperature is very cold: *The grass and trees were white with frost.*

frost² *v* [T] *especially AmE* to cover a cake with a mixture of powdery sugar and liquid SYN **ice** *BrE*
frost over/up *phr v* to become covered in frost: *Overnight all the windowpanes had frosted over.*

frost·bite /ˈfrɒstbaɪt $ ˈfrɒːst-/ *n* [U] a condition caused by extreme cold, that makes your fingers and toes swell, become darker, and sometimes fall off: *I nearly* ***got frostbite***. —**frostbitten** /-bɪtn/ *adj*

frost·ed /ˈfrɒstɪd $ ˈfrɒːstɪd/ *adj*
1 GLASS **frosted glass/window etc** frosted glass has been given a rough surface, so that it is not transparent: *the frosted glass of the bathroom window*
2 COLD WEATHER *literary* covered with frost SYN **frosty**: *the frosted garden*
3 CAKE *especially AmE* covered with frosting SYN **iced** *BrE*: *chocolate frosted cupcakes*
4 HAIR *AmE* frosted hair has parts that have been made much lighter than others by using chemicals

frost·ing /ˈfrɒstɪŋ $ ˈfrɒːstɪŋ/ *n* [U] *especially AmE* a sweet substance put on cakes and made from powdery sugar and butter SYN **icing** *BrE*

frost·y /ˈfrɒsti $ ˈfrɒːsti/ *adj* **1 a)** extremely cold: *a beautiful* ***frosty morning*** | *frosty air* **b)** covered with FROST: *the frosty ground* THESAURUS ▸ **COLD** **2** unfriendly SYN **icy**: **frosty stare/look/tone** *He gave me a frosty stare.* | *the frosty silence that followed her announcement* | *My words got a frosty reception.* THESAURUS ▸ **UNFRIENDLY** —**frostily** *adv*

froth¹ /frɒθ $ frɒːθ/ *n* **1** [singular, U] a mass of small BUBBLES on the top of a liquid SYN **foam**: *'Excellent beer,' he said, wiping the froth from his mouth.* **2** [singular, U] small white BUBBLES of SALIVA around a person's or animal's mouth **3** [U] talk or ideas that are attractive but have no real value or meaning: *The book has too much froth and not enough fact.*

froth² *v* [I] **1** (*also* **froth up**) if a liquid froths, it produces or contains a lot of small BUBBLES on top: *When you first open the bottle the beer will froth for a few seconds.* **2** if someone's mouth froths, SALIVA comes out as small white BUBBLES **3 froth at the mouth a)** to have SALIVA coming out of your mouth as small white BUBBLES **b)** *informal* to be extremely angry

froth·y /ˈfrɒθi $ ˈfrɒːθi/ *adj* **1** a liquid that is frothy has lots of small BUBBLES on top: *a mug of frothy coffee* **2** a frothy book, film etc is enjoyable but not serious or important **3** a frothy market is one in which prices of something are rising and beginning to be higher than the thing's real value – used in business —**frothily** *adv*

frown¹ /fraʊn/ ●●○ *v* [I] to make an angry, unhappy, or confused expression, moving your EYEBROWS together: *She frowned as she read the letter.* | **[+at]** *Mattie frowned at him disapprovingly.*
frown on/upon sb/sth *phr v* to disapprove of someone or something, especially someone's behaviour: *Even though divorce is legal, it is still frowned upon.*

frown² ●●○ *n* [C usually singular] the expression on your face when you move your EYEBROWS together because you are angry, unhappy, or confused: **with a frown** *He looked at her with a puzzled frown.*

froze /frəʊz $ froʊz/ *v* the past tense of FREEZE¹

fro·zen¹ /ˈfrəʊzən $ ˈfroʊ-/ *v* the past participle of FREEZE¹

frozen² ●●● S2 W2 *adj*
1 FOOD frozen food has been stored at a very low temperature in order to preserve it → **freeze**: *You can use fresh or frozen fish.* | *frozen peas* THESAURUS ▸ **COLD**
2 be frozen (stiff) *spoken* to feel very cold: *You must be frozen! Come and sit by the fire.*
3 EARTH earth that is frozen is so cold it has become very hard: *The ground is frozen for most of the year.* | *the frozen wastes of Siberia*
4 AREA OF WATER a river, lake etc that is frozen has a layer of ice on the surface
5 be frozen with fear/terror/fright to be so afraid, shocked etc that you cannot move

fruc·tose /ˈfrʌktəʊs $ -oʊs/ *n* [U] a type of natural sugar in fruit juices and HONEY

fru·gal /ˈfruːɡəl/ *adj* **1** careful to buy only what is necessary OPP **extravagant**: *As children we were taught to be frugal and hard-working.* | *He led a remarkably frugal existence.* **2** a frugal meal is a small meal of plain food SYN **simple** OPP **extravagant**: *a frugal breakfast* —**frugally** *adv* —**frugality** /fruːˈɡæləti/ *n* [U]

fruit¹ /fruːt/ ●●● S2 W2 *n* (*plural* **fruit** *or* **fruits**)
1 [C,U] something that grows on a plant, tree, or bush, can be eaten as a food, contains seeds or a stone, and is usually sweet: *Try to eat plenty of* ***fresh fruit***. | ***fruit and vegetables*** | *a glass of* ***fruit juice*** | *a large garden with* ***fruit trees*** → **DRIED FRUIT**, **SOFT FRUIT**, see picture on *p. 740*

> **GRAMMAR: Countable or uncountable?**
> • **Fruit** is usually uncountable: *I love fruit.* ✗ Don't say: *I love fruits.*
> • **Fruit** is used as a countable noun when talking about particular types of fruit: *They grow mainly citrus fruits.*

2 [C,U] *technical* the part of a plant, bush, or tree that contains the seeds
3 the fruit(s) of sth the good results that you have from something, after you have worked very hard: *I'm looking forward to retirement and having time to enjoy* ***the fruits of my labour*** (=the results of my hard work).
4 in fruit *technical* trees, plants etc that are in fruit are producing their fruit
5 the fruits of the earth *literary* all the natural things that the earth produces, such as fruit, vegetables, or minerals → **bear fruit** at **BEAR¹**(9)

fruit² *v* [I] *technical* if a tree or a plant fruits, it produces fruit

ˈ**fruit bat** *n* [C] a large BAT (=small animal like a flying mouse) that lives in hot countries and eats fruit

fruit·cake /ˈfruːtkeɪk/ *n* **1** [C,U] a cake that has dried fruit in it **2** [C] *informal* someone who is mentally ill or behaves in a strange way: *He's an absolute fruitcake.* | *You really are nutty as a fruitcake* (=crazy).

fruit·er·er /ˈfruːtərə $ -tərər/ *n* [C] *BrE old-fashioned* someone who sells fruit

ˈ**fruit fly** *n* [C] a small fly that eats fruit or decaying plants

fruit·ful /ˈfruːtfəl/ ●○○ *adj*
1 producing good results OPP **fruitless**: *Today's meeting proved more fruitful than last week's.* | *a busy and fruitful time* | *a fruitful source of information*
2 *literary* land that is fruitful produces a lot of crops SYN **fertile** —**fruitfully** *adv* —**fruitfulness** *n* [U]

fru·i·tion /fruˈɪʃən/ *n* [U] *formal* if a plan, project etc comes to fruition, it is successfully put into action and completed, often after a long process: **come to/bring to/**

F

Fruit

apple

pip *BrE*/ seed *AmE*

core

apricot

avocado

blackberries

peel

banana

coconut

stalk

cherries

cranberries

grapefruit

pith

segment

grapes

flesh

kiwi fruit

lychees

lemon

lime

mango

nectarine

plum

seeds

melon

starfruit

stone *BrE*/ pit *AmE*

peach

pears

pineapple

strawberry

raspberries

satsuma

figs

pith

segment

oranges

clementine

blueberries

watermelon

blackcurrants

passion fruit

papaya

reach fruition *His proposals only came to fruition after the war.* | *Many people have worked together to bring this scheme to fruition.*

fruit·less /ˈfruːtləs/ *adj* failing to achieve what was wanted, especially after a lot of effort OPP **fruitful**: **fruitless attempt/exercise** *a fruitless attempt to settle the dispute* | *So far, their search has been fruitless.* —**fruitlessly** *adv*

ˈfruit maˌchine *n* [C] *BrE* a machine which you put money into, and which gives you more money back if three of the same pictures appear on a screen SYN **slot machine**

ˌfruit ˈsalad *n* [C,U] a dish of many different types of fruit cut into small pieces

fruit·y /ˈfruːti/ *adj* **1** tasting or smelling strongly of fruit: *a very fruity wine* **2** *BrE* a voice or laugh that is fruity sounds deep and pleasant

frump /frʌmp/ *n* [C] a woman who is frumpy

frump·y /ˈfrʌmpi/ (*also* **frump·ish** /ˈfrʌmpɪʃ/) *adj* a woman who is frumpy looks unattractive because she dresses in old-fashioned clothes

frus·trate /frʌˈstreɪt $ ˈfrʌstreɪt/ ●○○ *v* [T]
1 if something frustrates you, it makes you feel annoyed or angry because you are unable to do what you want: *The fact that he's working with amateurs really frustrates him.*
2 to prevent someone's plans, efforts, or attempts from succeeding SYN **foil**: *Their attempts to speak to him were frustrated by the guards.* GRAMMAR **Frustrate** is usually passive in this meaning.

frus·trat·ed /frʌˈstreɪtɪd $ ˈfrʌstreɪtɪd/ ●●○ *adj*
1 feeling annoyed, upset, and impatient, because you cannot control or change a situation, or achieve something: *He **gets frustrated** when people don't understand what he's trying to say.* | **[+with/at]** *She had become increasingly frustrated with her life.* | **sexually frustrated** (=feeling dissatisfied because you do not have any opportunity to have sex)
2 a frustrated artist/actor/poet etc someone who wants to develop a particular skill but has not been able to do this

frus·trat·ing /frʌˈstreɪtɪŋ $ ˈfrʌstreɪtɪŋ/ ●●○ *adj* making you feel annoyed, upset, or impatient because you cannot do what you want to do: *My job can be very frustrating sometimes.* | *This is an immensely frustrating experience for the student.*

frus·tra·tion /frʌˈstreɪʃən/ ●●○ *n*
1 [C,U] the feeling of being annoyed, upset, or impatient, because you cannot control or change a situation, or achieve something: *People often feel a **sense of frustration** that they are not being promoted quickly enough.* | **in/with frustration** *I was practically screaming with frustration.* | *In spite of his frustrations, he fell in love with the country.*
2 [U] the fact of being prevented from achieving what you are trying to achieve: **[+of]** *The frustration of his ambitions made him a bitter man.*

fry[1] /fraɪ/ ●●● S2 W3 *v* (**fried**, **frying**, **fries**)
1 [I,T] to cook something in hot fat or oil, or to be cooked in hot fat or oil: *Fry the potatoes, covered, for about 20 minutes.* | *I could smell onions frying.* → DEEP FRY, STIR-FRY[1]
THESAURUS ▸ COOK
2 [I,T] *AmE informal* to kill someone in an ELECTRIC CHAIR, or to be killed in an electric chair, as a punishment

GRAMMAR

Fry belongs to a group of verbs where the same noun can be the subject of the verb or its object.
- You can say: *I'm frying some fish.* In this sentence, 'some fish' is the object of **fry**.
- You can say: *Some fish is frying.* In this sentence, 'some fish' is the subject of **fry**.

GRAMMAR GUIDE ▸ VERBS

fry[2] ●●● S2 (*also* **french fry**) *n* (*plural* **fries**) [C usually plural] *especially AmE* a long thin piece of potato that has been cooked in fat SYN **chip** *BrE*

fry[3] *n* [plural] very young fish → SMALL FRY

fry·er, **frier** /ˈfraɪə $ -ər/ *n* [C] **1 deep (fat) fryer** a big deep pan for frying food **2** *AmE* a chicken that has been specially bred to be fried

ˈfrying ˌpan ●●○ *n* [C]
1 a round flat pan with a long handle, used for frying food → see picture at PAN
2 out of the frying pan and into the fire to go from a bad situation to one that is even worse

ˈfry-up *n* [C] *BrE informal* a meal of fried food such as eggs, BACON, potatoes etc

ft *BrE*, **ft.** *AmE* the written abbreviation of ***foot*** or ***feet***: *a board 6ft x 4ft*

Ft. the written abbreviation of ***fort***, used in the names of places: *Ft. Lauderdale*

FT, **F/T** the written abbreviation of ***full-time*** → **PT**

FTM /ˌef tiː ˈem/ *n* [C] (***female-to-male***) someone who has had an operation to change their sex from female to male → **MTF**

ftp (*also* **FTP**) /ˌef tiː ˈpiː/ *n* [U] file transfer protocol; a set of rules that allow you to send documents from one computer to another —**ftp** *v* [T]

FTSE In·dex /ˈfʊtsi ˌɪndeks/ (*also* **FT 100 Share Index** /ˌef tiː wʌn hʌndrəd ˈʃeər ˌɪndeks $ -ˈʃer-/, **FTSE 100**) *n* **the FTSE Index** (***the Financial Times Stock Exchange Index***) a daily list of prices of shares on the London Stock Exchange, based on the daily average prices of shares in the top 100 companies → **the Dow Jones Index**

fuch·sia /ˈfjuːʃə/ *n* **1** [C,U] a garden bush with hanging bell-shaped flowers that are red, pink, or white **2** [U] a bright pink colour

fuck[1] /fʌk/ *v taboo spoken* **1 fuck you/it/them etc** used to show that you are very angry at something or someone, or that you do not care about them at all: *Well, fuck you then. I'll go on my own.* **2** [I,T] to have sex with someone **3 fuck me** *especially BrE* used when you think something is surprising or impressive **4 go fuck yourself/himself/themselves etc** used to show you are very angry with someone: *Why don't you go fuck yourself!*

fuck around *phr v* **1** to waste time or behave in a silly or careless way: *Will you two stop fucking around!* **2 fuck sb around/about** *BrE* to make someone angry or annoyed by wasting their time: *Don't fuck me around, OK?*

fuck off *phr v* to go away – used especially to tell someone to go away in an extremely rude way

fuck sb ↔ **over** *phr v AmE* to treat someone very badly: *They'll just fuck you over if you let them.*

fuck up *phr v* **1 fuck sb ↔ up** to make someone very unhappy and confused so that they cannot live normally or have normal relationships → **mess sb up**: *Heroin fucks you up.* **2** to make a mistake or do something badly → **mess up**: *You really fucked up this time.* | **fuck sth ↔ up** *I'm scared of fucking things up.*

fuck with sb *phr v* to annoy someone or make them angry → **mess with sb**: *I wouldn't fuck with Alfie if I were you.*

fuck[2] *interjection taboo* used when you are very annoyed about something: *Fuck! I've forgotten my keys!*

fuck[3] *n taboo spoken* **1 the fuck** used when you are angry or surprised to emphasize what you are saying: *Get the fuck off my property!* | *Shut the fuck up!* | **what/how/who etc the fuck** *What the fuck do you think you're doing?* **2** [C usually singular] the act of having sex **3 not give a fuck** (*also* **not give a flying fuck** *AmE*) to not care at all what happens

ˌfuck ˈall *n* [U] *BrE taboo spoken* nothing: *Most of the time he sat around **doing fuck all**.*

fucked /fʌkt/ *adj taboo spoken* **1** (*also* **ˌfucked ˈup**) completely broken or in a very bad condition: *The engine's completely fucked.* **2** in a very bad situation which will not improve: *If she can't lend me the money, I'm fucked.*

ˌfucked ˈup *adj taboo spoken* **1** very unhappy and confused, so that you cannot control your life properly → **messed up**: *After three years with Johnny, I was completely fucked up.* **2** (*also* **fucked**) completely broken or in a very bad condition: *These speakers are fucked up.*

F

3 *AmE* having drunk too much alcohol or taken illegal drugs

fuck·er /ˈfʌkə $ -ər/ (*also* **fuck**) *n* [C] *taboo spoken* someone who you dislike very much or think is stupid. Do not use this word.

fuck·head /ˈfʌkhed/ *n* [C] *AmE taboo spoken* someone who you dislike very much or think is stupid. Do not use this word.

fuck·ing /ˈfʌkɪŋ/ *adj* [only before noun], *adv taboo spoken* **1** used to emphasize that you are angry or annoyed: *It's none of your fucking business!* | *I know fucking well you're lying to me.* | *What the fucking hell are you staring at?* **2** used to emphasize your opinion of something: *That's fucking good coffee.* | *What a fucking idiot!*

fuck·wit /ˈfʌkwɪt/ *n* [C] *taboo spoken* someone you dislike very much or think is stupid. Do not use this word.

fud·dle /ˈfʌdl/ *v* [T] *BrE informal* if something, especially alcohol or drugs, fuddles you or your mind, it makes you unable to think clearly —**fuddled** *adj*: *her fuddled mind*

fud·dy-dud·dy /ˈfʌdi ˌdʌdi/ *n* (*plural* **fuddy-duddies**) [C] someone who has old-fashioned ideas and attitudes: *You're such an* ***old fuddy-duddy****!* —**fuddy-duddy** *adj*

fudge[1] /fʌdʒ/ *n* **1** [U] a soft creamy brown sweet food **2** **a fudge** *BrE* an attempt to deal with a situation that does not solve its problems completely, or only makes it seem better

fudge[2] *v* **1** [I,T] to avoid giving exact details or a clear answer about something: *He tried to* ***fudge*** *the* ***issue*** *by saying that he did not want to specify periods.* **2** [T] to change important figures or facts to deceive people SYN **fiddle**: *Sibley has been fudging his data for years now.*

fu·el[1] /ˈfjuːəl/ ●●● S3 W2 *n* [C,U] a substance such as coal, gas, or oil that can be burned to produce heat or energy: *Coal is one of the cheapest fuels.* → **add fuel to the fire/flames** at ADD(9)

COLLOCATIONS

ADJECTIVES/NOUN + fuel

a fossil fuel (=a fuel such as coal or oil, produced by the gradual decaying of plants and animals) *Global warming may be caused by burning fossil fuels.*
nuclear fuel *What do we do with the spent nuclear fuel?*
solid fuel (=a solid substance, such as coal, that is used as a fuel) | **domestic/household fuel** (=used in a house) | **smokeless fuel** (=that burns without producing smoke) | **unleaded fuel** (=that does not contain lead) | **a green fuel** (=a fuel that harms the environment as little as possible)

VERBS

use fuel *People need to learn how to use fuel more efficiently.*
run on fuel (=use fuel as the source of power) *Will this engine run on unleaded fuel?*
run out of fuel (=use all the fuel available and have none left) | **fill up with fuel** (=put fuel in a vehicle's fuel tank) | **save fuel** | **waste fuel**

fuel + NOUN

fuel costs/prices *The increase in fuel costs is severely affecting pensioners.*
a fuel bill *Insulating your house will cut your fuel bill.*
a fuel tank (=a container for storing fuel) | **a fuel gauge** (=an instrument for measuring fuel) | **a fuel pump** (=a machine that forces fuel into an engine) | **fuel consumption** (=amount used) | **fuel economy/efficiency** (=how well a vehicle uses fuel, without wasting any)

PHRASES

sth is running low on fuel (=it does not have much fuel left) *The plane was running low on fuel.*

fuel[2] ●○○ *v* (**fuelled**, **fuelling** *BrE*, **fueled**, **fueling** *AmE*) **1** [T] to make something, especially something bad, increase or become stronger SYN **provoke**: *His words fuelled her anger still more.* | **fuel speculation/rumours/controversy etc** *Progress was slow, fueling concerns that the stadium would not be finished on time.* **2** (*also* **fuel up**) [I,T] if you fuel a vehicle, or if it fuels up, fuel is put into it SYN **fill up**: *We'd better fuel up at the next town.* | *The van was fuelled and waiting in the basement car park.*

ˈfuel cell *n* [C] a piece of equipment that combines two different ELEMENTS, such as OXYGEN and HYDROGEN, to produce electricity in order to supply power to a vehicle or machine

ˈfuel-efˌficient *adj* a fuel-efficient engine or vehicle burns fuel in a more effective way than usual, so that it loses less fuel

ˈfuel inˌjection *n* [U] a method of putting liquid fuel directly into an engine, which allows a car to ACCELERATE more quickly

ˈfuel poor *adj* **1** not having enough money for gas, electricity etc to keep your home warm **2** **the fuel poor** [plural] people who are fuel poor

ˈfuel ˌpoverty *n* [U] the state of not having enough money for gas, electricity etc to keep your home warm

fug /fʌɡ/ *n* [singular] *BrE informal* air inside a room that feels heavy and unpleasant because of smoke, heat, or too many people: *the fug of the bar*

fu·gi·tive[1] /ˈfjuːdʒətɪv/ *n* [C] someone who is trying to avoid being caught by the police: **[+from]** *a fugitive from US justice*

fugitive[2] *adj* [only before noun] **1** trying to avoid being caught by the police **2** *literary* lasting for a very short time: *rare and fugitive visits*

fugue /fjuːɡ/ *n* [C,U] a piece of music with a tune that is repeated regularly in different KEYS by different voices or instruments

-ful[1] /fəl/ *suffix* [in adjectives] **1** full of something: *an eventful day* **2** having the quality of something or causing something: *restful colours* | *Is it painful?* —**-fully** /fəli/ *suffix* [in adverbs]: *shouting cheerfully*

-ful[2] /fʊl/ *suffix* [in nouns] **1** the amount of a substance needed to fill a particular container: *two cupfuls of milk* **2** as much as can be carried by or contained in a particular part of the body: *an armful of flowers*

ful·crum /ˈfʊlkrəm, ˈfʌl-/ *n* (*plural* **fulcrums** *or* **fulcra** /-krə/) [C] the point on which a LEVER (=bar) turns, balances, or is supported in turning or lifting something

ful·fil *BrE*, **fulfill** *AmE* /fʊlˈfɪl/ ●●○ W3 *v* (**fulfilled**, **fulfilling**) [T]

1 if you fulfil a hope, wish, or aim, you achieve the thing that you hoped for, wished for etc: *Visiting Disneyland has* ***fulfilled*** *a boyhood* ***dream****.* | *Being deaf hasn't stopped Karen* ***fulfilling*** *her* ***ambition*** *to be a hairdresser.* | *It was then that the organization finally began to* ***fulfill*** *the* ***hopes*** *of its founders.* | **fulfil an aim/a goal/an objective** *an analysis of how different countries are attempting to fulfill their political goals*

2 to do or provide what is necessary or needed: **fulfil a role/duty/function etc** *A good police officer is not fulfilling his role if he neglects this vital aspect.* | **fulfil a requirement/condition/obligation etc** *Britain was accused of failing to fulfil its obligations under the EU Treaty.* | *Much of the electrical equipment failed to fulfill safety requirements.* | *There is little doubt that the scheme* ***fulfils*** *a* ***need*** *for our community.*

3 **fulfil a promise/pledge etc** *formal* to do what you said you would do SYN **keep** OPP **break**: *I'd like to see him fulfil his promise to reorganize the army.*

4 **fulfil your potential/promise** to be as successful as you possibly can be: *We want to make sure that all children are able to fulfil their potential.*

5 if your work fulfils you, it makes you feel satisfied because you are using all your skills, qualities etc

6 **fulfil yourself** to feel satisfied because you are using all your skills, qualities etc: *She succeeded in fulfilling herself both as an actress and as a mother.*

7 **fulfil a prophesy** if a PROPHESY is fulfilled, something happens that someone said would happen

ful·filled /fʊlˈfɪld/ *adj* happy and satisfied because your life is interesting and you are doing useful or important things: *Adult education helps people achieve more fulfilled lives.* THESAURUS ▸ SATISFIED

ful·fil·ling /fʊlˈfɪlɪŋ/ ●○○ *adj* making you feel happy and satisfied because you are doing interesting, useful, or important things SYN **satisfying**: *Nursing is still one of the most fulfilling careers.*

ful·fil·ment *BrE*, **fulfillment** *AmE* /fʊlˈfɪlmənt/ *n* [U]
1 the feeling of being happy and satisfied with your life because you are doing interesting, useful, or important things: *Are you looking for greater fulfillment and satisfaction in your work?* | *a deep* ***sense of fulfilment*** *that makes life worthwhile* | **seek/find fulfilment** *The real joy of the priesthood is helping people find* ***personal fulfilment.***
2 when something you wanted happens or is given to you SYN **achievement**: **[+of]** *the fulfillment of a long-held dream*
3 the act of doing something that you promised or agreed to do: **fulfilment of a promise/duty/condition etc** *People are wondering if they will ever see the fulfillment of the government's campaign pledges.*

full¹ /fʊl/ ●●● S1 W1 *adj*
1 NO SPACE containing as much or as many things or people as possible, so there is no space left → **empty**: *The train was completely full.* | *Don't talk with your mouth full.* | *The class is full, but you can register for next term.* | **[+of]** *The kitchen was full of smoke.* | **be crammed/stuffed/packed etc full of sth** *Ted's workshop was crammed full of old engines.* | **half-full/three-quarters full etc** *McQuaid filled his glass until it was three-quarters full.* | *The bath was* ***full to the brim*** (=completely full) *with hot water.* | **full (up) to bursting** *BrE informal* (=completely full) *The filing cabinet was full to bursting.*

> **REGISTER**
> In everyday English, people often say that a place is **packed** when it is full of people: *The trains are always* ***packed*** *in the rush hour.*

2 INCLUDING EVERYTHING [only before noun] complete and including all parts or details: *Please write your* ***full name*** *and address on the form.* | *The Health Centre offers a* ***full range of*** *services.* | *Lotus will not reveal* ***full details*** *until the Motor Show.* | *The BBC promised a* ***full investigation.*** | *I don't think he's telling us* ***the full story*** (=everything he knows about the matter).
3 HIGHEST AMOUNT/LEVEL [only before noun] the greatest amount or highest level of something that is possible SYN **maximum**: *rising prosperity and* ***full employment*** | *The charity helps disabled children reach their* ***full potential.*** | *Few customers* ***take full advantage*** *of off-peak fares.* | *Parker was driving* ***at full speed*** *when he hit the wall.* | **in full leaf/bloom** *The roses were now in full bloom.*
4 HAVING A LOT OF STH **be full of sth a)** to contain many things of the same kind: *a garden full of flowers* | *His essay was full of mistakes.* | *The music papers were full of gossip about the band.* | *Life's full of surprises, isn't it?* **b)** to feel, express, or show a lot of a particular emotion or quality: **full of excitement/energy/hope etc** *Lucy was a happy child, always* ***full of life.*** | *He was* ***full of praise*** *for the work of the unit.* **c)** to talk or think a lot about a particular thing: *She was full of plans for the wedding.*
5 FOOD (*also* **full up** *BrE*) [not before noun] having eaten so much food that you cannot eat any more: *No more, thanks. I'm full.*
6 EMPHASIS [only before noun] used to emphasize an amount, quantity, or rate: **three/six etc full days/years/pages etc** *We devote five full days a month to training.* | *His pants rose a full three inches off his shoes.*
7 BUSY busy and involving lots of different activities: *Before her illness, Rose enjoyed* ***a full life.*** | *Go to bed. You've a full day tomorrow.*
8 RANK having or giving all the rights, duties etc that belong to a particular rank or position: **full professor/member/colonel etc** *Only full members have the right to vote.* | *a full driving licence*
9 be full of yourself to have a high opinion of yourself – used to show disapproval: *My first impression was that he was a bit full of himself.*
10 be full of crap/shit/it *not polite* a rude expression used to say that someone often says things that are wrong or stupid: *Don't listen to Jerry. He's full of it.*
11 CLOTHES made using a lot of material and fitting loosely: *a dress with a full skirt*
12 BODY large and rounded in an attractive way: **full figure/face/breasts etc** *clothes for the* ***fuller figure***
13 TASTE having a strong satisfying taste: *Now you can enjoy Nescafé's* ***fuller flavour*** *in a decaffeinated form.* → FULL-BODIED
14 SOUND pleasantly loud and deep: *the rich full sound of the cello*
15 full price not a reduced price: *If you're over 14, you have to pay full price.*
16 in full view of sb so that all the people in a place can see, especially when this is embarrassing or shocking: *The argument happened on stage in full view of the audience.*
17 be in full swing if an event or process is in full swing, it has reached its highest level of activity: *By 8.30, the party was in full swing.*
18 full speed/steam ahead doing something with as much energy and effort as possible: *With last season's misery behind them, it's full steam ahead for the Bears.*
19 be full of beans to be excited and have lots of energy
20 (at) full blast *informal* as strongly, loudly, or quickly as possible: *The heater was on full blast but I was still cold.* | *a car stereo playing Wagner at full blast*
21 (at) full tilt/pelt moving as fast as possible: *She* ***ran full tilt*** *into his arms.*
22 be in full cry if a group of people are in full cry, they are criticizing someone very strongly: *Anyone who's seen the world's press in full cry can understand how Diana felt.*
23 to the full (*also* **to the fullest** *AmE*) in the best or most complete way: *Ed believes in* ***living life to the full.***
24 come/go/turn full circle to be in the same situation in which you began, even though there have been changes during the time in between: *Fashion has come full circle and denim is back.* → FULLY, → **have your hands full** at HAND¹(29), → **draw yourself up to your full height** at DRAW UP

> **THESAURUS**
> **full** containing as much or as many things or people as possible, so there is no space left: *The train was nearly full.* | *The cupboard was full of clothes.*
> **filled with sth** full of something – use this about a container when a lot of things have been put into it: *The envelopes were filled with cash.*
> **stuffed full of sth** completely full of something – use this about a container when lots of things have been put into it, often in an untidy way: *The case was stuffed full of clothes.*
> **packed** completely full of people – use this about a room, train etc: *a packed restaurant* | *The courtroom will be packed with journalists.*
> **bursting (with sth)** extremely full of something: *Her wardrobe was bursting with coats and shoes.* | *a small garden bursting with fruit and flowers*
> **crammed** so full that you cannot fit anyone or anything else in – often used when you think there are too many people or things: *In summer, the hotels are crammed with tourists.*
> **teeming (with sth)** /ˈtiːmɪŋ/ full of people, animals etc that are all moving around: *The rivers are teeming with fish.*
> **overflowing** used about a container that is so full that the liquid or things inside it come out over the top: *an overflowing bathtub* | *The drawers were overflowing with magazines.*
> **overloaded** used about a vehicle or a ship which has too many people or things in it: *an overloaded fishing boat*

full² *n* **in full** including the whole of something: *The debt must be* ***paid in full.*** | *His statement on the handling of prisoners is worth quoting in full.*

full³ *adv* directly: **[+on/in]** *She looked him full in the face as she spoke.*

full·back /ˈfʊlbæk/ *n* [C] a player in a football team who plays in defence, stopping opponents from getting the ball SYN **defender**

ˌfull ˈbeam *n BrE* **on full beam** car HEADLIGHTS (=the main lights at the front) that are on full beam are switched to a position that makes them shine very brightly and straight ahead SYN **high beam** *AmE* → **dipped**

ˌfull-ˈblooded *adj* [only before noun] **1** done with a lot of energy or in a complete way: *The conflict could escalate into a full-blooded war.* **2** having parents, grandparents etc from only one race of people: *Her father is a full-blooded Cherokee.*

ˈfull-blown *adj* [only before noun] having all the qualities of something that is at its most complete or advanced stage: *The drop in shares could develop into a full-blown crisis.* | *full-blown AIDS*

ˌfull ˈboard *n* [U] a hotel offering full board provides guests with all their meals → **half board**: *A two-night break costs £125 full board.*

ˌfull-ˈbodied *adj* **1** a full-bodied wine or other drink has a pleasantly strong taste → **light 2** a full-bodied sound is complicated and interesting

ˌfull ˈbore *adv AmE* fast and with a lot of energy: *Kate took a huge slice and was going at it full bore.*

ˌfull-ˈcolour *BrE*, **full-color** *AmE adj* [only before noun] printed using coloured inks rather than only black and white: *a full-colour brochure*

ˌfull-court ˈpress *n* [singular] **1** a method of defending in a strong way in BASKETBALL **2** *AmE informal* the use of pressure or influence by several groups on someone: *The DEA and the Justice Department put a full-court press on the drug barons.*

ˌfull-ˈcream *adj BrE* full-cream milk is ordinary milk without any of the fat removed → **skimmed**, **semi-skimmed**

ˌfull ˈdress *n* [U] special clothes worn for official occasions: *officers in full dress uniform*

ful·ler's earth /ˌfʊləz ˈɜːθ $ -ərz ˈɜːrθ/ *n* [U] dried clay made into a powder that is used to clean cloth or oil

ˌfull ˈface *adj* **1** showing the whole of someone's face → **profile**: *In portraits, chiefs were invariably shown full face.* **2** covering or protecting your whole face: *a full face helmet*

ˌfull-ˈfat *adj BrE* full-fat milk, cheese etc contains all the fat that is naturally in it → **low-fat**

ˌfull-ˈfledged *AmE*, **ˌfully-ˈfledged** *BrE adj* [only before noun] completely developed, trained, or established: *India has the potential to become a full-fledged major power.*

ˌfull ˈfrontal *adj* [only before noun] **1** showing the whole of the front of someone's body without clothes on: *scenes of **full frontal nudity*** **2** done in a direct and strong way: *a **full frontal attack** on the government*

ˌfull-ˈgrown *AmE*, **ˌfully-grown** *BrE adj* a full-grown animal, plant, or person has developed to their full size and will not grow any bigger: *A full-grown elephant may weigh 2,000 pounds.*

ˌfull ˈhouse *n* [C usually singular] **1** an occasion at a cinema, concert hall, sports field etc when there are no empty seats: *Billy Graham is a speaker who can be sure of **playing to a full house**.* **2** three cards of one kind and a pair of another kind in a game of POKER

ˌfull-ˈlength¹ *adj* **1 full-length mirror/photograph/portrait etc** a mirror etc that shows all of a person, from their head to their feet **2 full-length skirt/dress/coat etc** a skirt etc that reaches the ground, or is the longest possible for that particular type of clothing: *a full-length evening dress* **3 full-length play/book/film etc** a play etc that is the normal length: *Stravinsky's only full-length opera*

full-length² *adv* someone who is lying full-length is lying flat with their legs straight out: *Ali was stretched out full-length on the couch.*

ˌfull ˈlock *n* [U] *BrE* if you turn the STEERING WHEEL of a car to full lock, you turn it as far as it can be turned

ˌfull ˈmarks *n* [plural] **1** if you give someone full marks, you praise them for doing something well: **full marks to sb (for sth)** *Not the most stylish mobile, but full marks to Marconi for originality.* **2** *BrE* the highest number of points you can get for school work

ˌfull ˈmonty *n* **the full monty** *informal* the whole amount of something that people want and expect: *The ice cream was covered in sauce, nuts, chocolate – the full monty.*

ˌfull ˈmoon *n* [singular] the moon when you can see all of it as a complete circle → **new moon**, **half moon**, **crescent moon**

ful·ness /ˈfʊlnəs/ *n* [U] **1 in the fullness of time** *formal* after a period of time, when a situation has developed SYN **in due course**: *I'm sure he'll tell us what's bothering him in the fullness of time.* **2** the quality of being large and round in an attractive way: *Use a red gloss on your bottom lip to give it fullness.* **3** the quality of being complete **4** the quality of having a pleasantly strong taste or deep sound: *This recording has a fullness and warmth that brings out the brilliance of the piece.* **5** the condition of being full: *Do you have a feeling of fullness after even a small meal?*

ˌfull-ˈon *adj* [only before noun] extreme: *If you're going for full-on glamour, add some sparkly jewellery.*

ˌfull-ˈpage *adj* [only before noun] covering all of one page in a newspaper or magazine: *a full-page advert*

ˌfull-ˈscale *adj* [only before noun] **1** as complete or thorough as possible: **full-scale attack/war/riot etc** | **full-scale study/review etc** *The government will conduct a **full-scale** inquiry into the crash.* **2** a full-scale drawing, model etc is the same size as the thing it represents SYN **life-size**

ˌfull-ˈsize *adj* of the largest possible size: *The battery can run a full-size laptop for 12 hours.* | *a full-size basketball court*

ˌfull ˈstop¹ ●●○ *n* [C] *BrE* a point (.) that marks the end of a sentence or the short form of a word SYN **period** *AmE*: *Put a full stop at the end of the sentence.*

full stop² *interjection BrE informal* used at the end of a sentence to emphasize that you do not want to say any more about a subject SYN **period** *AmE*: *I don't have a reason. I just don't want to go, full stop.*

ˌfull-ˈterm *adj* [only before noun] a full-term baby is born after a PREGNANCY of the normal length → **premature**

ˌfull ˈtime *n* [U] *BrE* the end of the normal period of playing time in a sports game → **half time**: *As the ball went in, the referee blew his whistle for full time.*

ˌfull-ˈtime ●●○ *adj, adv*
1 for all the hours of a week during which it is usual for people to work, study etc → **part-time**: **work/study etc full-time** *She works full-time and has two kids.* | *The success of the series enabled her to concentrate full-time on writing.* | **full-time staff/student etc** *They're looking for full-time staff at the library.* | **full-time job/education etc** *We aim to double the number of young people in **full-time study**.*
2 be a full-time job to be very hard work and take a lot of time: *Keeping pace with changes is a full-time job.*

ful·ly /ˈfʊli/ ●●● S2 W2 *adv* completely: *The restaurant is **fully booked** this evening.* | *Elisa has not **fully recovered** from the incident.* | *I am **fully aware** of your problems.* | *The changes in policy are **fully described** in the review.* | *I **fully accept** that what he says is true.* | *This concept is **discussed more fully** in Chapter 9.*

ˌfully ˈdressed *adj* [not before noun] wearing clothes, including things such as shoes: *She collapsed fully dressed on the bed.*

ˌfully-ˈfledged *BrE*, **ˌfull-fledged** *AmE adj* [only before noun] completely developed, trained, or established: *After seven years of training she's now a fully-fledged doctor.*

ˌfully-ˈgrown *BrE*, **ˌfull-grown** *AmE adj* a fully-grown animal, plant, or person has developed to their full size and will not grow any bigger: *After six weeks, the larva emerges as a fully-grown beetle.*

ful·mi·nate /ˈfʊlməneɪt, ˈfʌl-/ *v* [I] *formal* to criticize someone or something angrily: **[+at/against/about]** *Mick was fulminating against the unfairness of it all.* —**fulmination** /ˌfʊlməˈneɪʃən, ˌfʌl-/ *n* [C,U]

ful·some /ˈfʊlsəm/ *adj formal* a fulsome speech or piece of writing sounds insincere because it contains too much praise, expressions of thanks etc: **fulsome gratitude/praise/tribute etc** *The book contains a fulsome dedication to his wife.* —**fulsomely** *adv*: *a fulsomely congratulatory message* —**fulsomeness** *n* [U]

fum·ble /ˈfʌmbəl/ *v* **1** (*also* **fumble around**) [I,T] to try to hold, move, or find something with your hands in an awkward way: **[+at/in/with]** *She dressed, her cold fingers fumbling with the buttons.* | **[+for]** *I fumbled around in my bag for a cigarette.* | *She reached round to fumble the light on.* **2** [I,T] if you fumble with your words when you are speaking, you have difficulty saying something: **[+for]** *Asked for an explanation, Mike had fumbled for words.* | *The second candidate fumbled her lines.* **3** [I,T] to drop a ball after catching it: *Quarterback Rattay was hit and fumbled the ball.* → see picture at AMERICAN FOOTBALL —**fumble** *n* [C] —**fumbling** *n* [C]

fume /fjuːm/ *v* **1** [I,T] to be angry about something: **[+at/over/about]** *She sat in the car, silently fuming about what he'd said.* | *'You've no right to be here,' he fumed.* **2** [I] to give off smoke or gases

fumes /fjuːmz/ ●●○ *n* [plural] strong-smelling gas or smoke that is unpleasant to breathe in: *paint fumes*

fu·mi·gate /ˈfjuːmɪgeɪt/ *v* [T] to remove disease, BACTERIA, insects etc from somewhere using chemicals, smoke, or gas —**fumigation** /ˌfjuːməˈgeɪʃən/ *n* [U]

fun[1] /fʌn/ ●●● S2 W3 *n* [U]

1 an experience or activity that is very enjoyable and exciting: *There's plenty of fun for all the family.* | *The children were having so much fun, I hated to call them inside.*

2 for fun (*also* **just for the fun of it**) if you do something for fun, you do it because you enjoy it and not for any other reason: *I simply believe that killing animals for fun is wrong.* | *Like most people her age, Deborah struck up relationships **just for the fun of it**.*

3 sb is (great/good) fun *BrE* used to say that someone is enjoyable to be with because they are happy and amusing: *You'll like her, darling, she's great fun.*

4 behaviour that is not serious and shows happiness and enjoyment: *Jan's always so cheerful and **full of fun**.* | *Her **sense of fun** made her very popular at college.* | *Evelyn would tease her, but only **in fun**.*

5 fun and games activities, behaviour etc that are not serious – often used to show disapproval

6 make fun of sb/sth to make unkind insulting remarks about someone or something: *I'm not making fun of you. I admire what you did.*

7 like fun *AmE spoken old-fashioned* used to say that something is not true or will not happen: *'I'm going to Barbara's house.' 'Like fun you are! Come and finish your chores first.'*

→ **figure of fun** at FIGURE[1](12), → **poke fun at** at POKE[1](6)

COLLOCATIONS

VERBS

have fun *Did you have fun at the party?*
join in the fun *The whole village joined in the fun.*
sth sounds (like) fun (=seems to be enjoyable) *The picnic sounded like fun.*

ADJECTIVES

good fun *BrE I never realized what good fun fishing could be.*
great fun *The show is great fun for all the family.*
harmless fun (=not likely to upset or offend anyone)

PHRASES

sth is no fun (*also* **sth is not much fun**) (=something is not at all enjoyable) *Being stuck in a traffic jam for three hours was no fun.*
be sb's idea of fun (=be what someone enjoys doing – used especially when this seems strange to you) *Camping in this rainy weather is not my idea of fun.*
be half the fun (=be a very enjoyable part of doing something) *Planning a vacation is half the fun.*
a lot of fun (*also* **lots of fun**) *The kids had a lot of fun singing and dancing.*

THESAURUS

fun *n* [U] *especially spoken* an experience or activity that is very enjoyable and exciting: *Have you ever been windsurfing? It's really good fun.* | *I just want to relax and have some fun.*
enjoyment *n* [U] the feeling you get when you enjoy doing something: *I get a lot of enjoyment out of working with young children.*
pleasure *n* [C] an experience or activity that makes you feel happy and satisfied: *The game was a pleasure to watch.* | *One of her greatest pleasures was walking in the mountains.*
good/great time *n* [C] *especially spoken* a time when you enjoyed yourself: *The kids all **had a great time**.* | *I remember the good times in Japan.*
entertainment *n* [U] things such as performances and films which are intended to be enjoyable: *Three musicians provided the entertainment.* | *What do you do for entertainment around here?*
relaxation *n* [U] a way of resting and enjoying yourself: *I play the piano for relaxation.* | *Her work left little time for relaxation.*
leisure *n* [U] the time when you are not working, when you can enjoy yourself – used especially in compounds: *leisure activities* | *the leisure industry* | *People have more leisure time.*
recreation *n* [C,U] *formal* activities that you do to enjoy yourself: *recreation facilities* | *The park is not just a place for recreation.*

fun[2] ●●● S2 W3 *adj*

1 enjoyable and amusing: *Try snowboarding – it's a really fun sport.* | **a fun day/evening etc** THESAURUS NICE

2 a fun person is enjoyable to be with because they are happy and amusing: *She's a really fun person to be around.*

GRAMMAR

Fun is not used with 'very'. You say: *It was really fun.*
✗ Don't say: *It was very fun.*

func·tion[1] /ˈfʌŋkʃən/ ●●● S3 W1 AWL *n*

1 [C,U] the purpose that something has, or the job that someone or something does: **perform/fulfil a function** *In your new job you will perform a variety of functions.* | *The church fulfils a valuable social function.* | *The nervous system regulates our **bodily functions*** (=eating, breathing, going to the toilet etc). | *Bauhaus architects thought that function was more important than form.*

2 [C] a large party or official event: *This room may be hired for weddings and other functions.* THESAURUS PARTY

3 [C usually singular] *technical* a quantity or quality whose value changes according to another quantity or quality that is related to it: *The degree of drought is largely a function of temperature and drainage.*

4 [C] one of the basic operations performed by a computer

function[2] ●●○ AWL *v* [I]

1 to work in the correct or intended way SYN **operate**: **function normally/correctly/properly etc** *Flights in and out of Taipei are functioning normally again.* | *Her legs have now **ceased to function**.* | *You know I **can't function*** (=cannot perform normal activities) *without a coffee in the morning.*

REGISTER

In everyday English, people usually say that something **works** rather than **functions**: *If the system is **working** as it should, you'll be paid within two weeks.*

2 if something functions in a particular way, it works in that way: *an understanding of how the economy functions*

function as sth *phr v* if something functions as a particular thing, it does what that type of thing normally does, or is used as that thing: *A library is functioning as a temporary hospital to cope with casualties.*

func·tion·al /ˈfʌŋkʃənəl/ ●●○ AWL *adj*
1 designed to be useful rather than beautiful or attractive OPP **decorative**: *buildings that are sensitively designed, not* ***purely functional***
2 something that is functional is working correctly SYN **operational**: *By 2004, the Supertram is expected to be* ***fully functional***.
3 relating to the purpose of something: *The two departments have slight functional differences.* —**functionally** *adv*

ˈfunctional ˌfood *n* [C,U] food that is designed to improve health and lower the risk of disease, for example by increasing the amount of VITAMINS in it, or removing some of the FAT SYN **nutraceuticals**

func·tion·al·is·m /ˈfʌŋkʃənəlɪzəm/ *n* [U] the idea that the most important thing about a building, piece of furniture etc is that it is useful —**functionalist** *n* [C] —**functionalist** *adj*

func·tion·al·i·ty /ˌfʌŋkʃəˈnæləti/ *n* (*plural* **functionalities**) [C,U] one or all of the operations that a computer, software program, or piece of equipment is able to perform

func·tion·a·ry /ˈfʌŋkʃənəri $ -neri/ *n* (*plural* **functionaries**) [C] someone who has a job doing unimportant or boring official duties: *Liberal Party functionaries*

ˈfunction key *n* [C] *technical* a key on a computer KEYBOARD that tells the computer to do something

ˈfunction word *n* [C] a word that does not mean anything on its own, but shows the relationship between other words in a sentence, for example words such as 'but' or 'if'

fund¹ /fʌnd/ ●●○ W3 AWL *n*
1 [C] an amount of money that is collected and kept for a particular purpose: *The fund was set up to try to save the cathedral.* | **pension/investment/memorial etc fund** → FUNDING, TRUST FUND
2 funds [plural] money that an organization needs or has: *A sale is being held to* ***raise funds*** *for the school.* | **government/public funds** *claims that ministers had misused public funds* | *The park remains unfinished due to* ***lack of funds***. | *The Museum is so* ***short of funds*** (=has so little money) *it may have to sell the painting.*
3 [singular] an organization that collects money, for example to help people who are ill, old etc → **charity**: *We give to the Children's Fund every Christmas.*
4 a fund of sth a large supply of something: *He had a fund of stories about his boyhood.*
5 in funds *formal* having enough money to do something

fund² ●●○ W3 AWL *v* [T] to provide money for an activity, organization, event etc: *The project is jointly funded by several local companies.* | *government-funded research*

fun·da·men·tal /ˌfʌndəˈmentl◂/ ●●○ W2 AWL *adj*
1 relating to the most basic and important parts of something: *We have to tackle the fundamental cause of the problem.* | **fundamental change/difference/distinction/shift etc** *a fundamental difference in opinion* | **fundamental mistake/error** *Novice programmers sometimes make fundamental errors.* | *the* ***fundamental principles*** *of liberty and equality*
2 very necessary and important: ***fundamental human rights*** | **[+to]** *Water is fundamental to survival.*

fun·da·men·tal·ist /ˌfʌndəˈmentəlɪst/ *n* [C] **1** someone who follows religious laws very strictly: *religious fundamentalists* **2** a Christian who believes that everything in the Bible is completely and actually true —**fundamentalism** *n* [U] —**fundamentalist** *adj*: *a fundamentalist doctrine*

fun·da·men·tal·ly /ˌfʌndəˈmentəli/ ●●○ AWL *adv* in every way that is important or basic: *The conclusions of the report are* ***fundamentally wrong***. | *The political culture of the US is* ***fundamentally different***.

fun·da·men·tals /ˌfʌndəˈmentlz/ *n* [plural] **the fundamentals (of sth)** the most important ideas, rules etc that something is based on: *an introduction to the fundamentals of design and print production*

fund·ing /ˈfʌndɪŋ/ ●●○ AWL *n* [U] money that is provided by an organization for a particular purpose: *College directors have called for more government funding.*

fund·rais·er /ˈfʌudˌreɪzə $ -ər/ *n* [C] **1** someone who collects money for a CHARITY, political party etc, for example by arranging social events that people pay to attend **2** an event that is organized to collect money for a CHARITY, political party etc

fund·rais·ing /ˈfʌndˌreɪzɪŋ/ *n* [U] the activity of collecting money for a specific purpose, especially in order to help people who are ill, old etc: *an Action Pack full of fundraising ideas*

fu·ne·ral /ˈfjuːnərəl/ ●●● S3 W3 *n* [C]
1 a religious ceremony for burying or CREMATING (=burning) someone who has died → **burial**, **cremation**: *The* ***funeral*** *will be* ***held*** *at St. Martin's Church.* | *Hundreds of mourners* ***attended*** *the* ***funeral*** *of the two boys.* | *the minister who conducted the* ***funeral service*** | *Nelson's* ***funeral procession*** *down the Thames* | *Ramdas set fire to the* ***funeral pyre***. | **funeral expenses/costs**
2 it's your funeral *spoken* used to warn someone that they, and no one else, must deal with the results of their actions

ˈfuneral diˌrector *n* [C] someone who is paid to organize a funeral SYN **undertaker** *BrE*

ˈfuneral home (*also* **ˈfuneral ˌparlour**) *n* [C] the place where a body is kept before a funeral

fu·ne·ra·ry /ˈfjuːnərəri $ -nəreri/ *adj* [only before noun] relating to a funeral or the place where someone is buried: *a funerary monument*

fu·ne·re·al /fjʊˈnɪəriəl $ -ˈnɪr-/ *adj* sad, slow, and suitable for a funeral: *funereal music* | *moving at a funereal pace*

fun·fair /ˈfʌnfeə $ -fer/ *n* [C] *BrE* a noisy outdoor event where you can ride on machines, play games to win prizes etc SYN **fair**

fun·gal /ˈfʌŋgəl/ *adj* connected with or caused by a FUNGUS: *a fungal infection*

fun·gi·cide /ˈfʌndʒəsaɪd, ˈfʌŋgə-/ *n* [C,U] a chemical used for destroying fungus

fun·gus /ˈfʌŋgəs/ ●○○ *n* (*plural* **fungi** /-dʒaɪ, -gaɪ/ *or* **funguses**) [C,U] a simple type of plant that has no leaves or flowers and that grows on plants or other surfaces. MUSHROOMS and MOULD are both fungi.

fu·nic·u·lar /fjʊˈnɪkjələ $ -ər/ *n* [C] a small railway that carries people up and down a steep hill or mountain, pulled by a thick metal rope

funk¹ /fʌŋk/ *n* [U] **1** a style of music with a strong RHYTHM that is based on JAZZ and African music **2 in a (blue) funk** *AmE informal* very unhappy, worried, or afraid: *She's in a funk about giving her talk on Sunday.* **3** *AmE informal* a strong smell that comes from someone's body

funk² *v* [T] *BrE old-fashioned* to avoid doing something because it is difficult, or because you are afraid

funk·y /ˈfʌŋki/ *adj informal* **1** modern, fashionable, and interesting: *Add a touch of style with these functional yet funky wall lights.* **2** funky music is simple with a strong RHYTHM that is easy to dance to **3** *AmE* having a bad smell or a dirty appearance

fun·nel¹ /ˈfʌnl/ *n* [C] **1** a thin tube with a wide top that you use for pouring liquid into a container with a narrow opening, such as a bottle **2** *BrE* a metal CHIMNEY that allows smoke from a steam engine or steamship to get out

funnel² *v* (**funnelled**, **funnelling** *BrE*, **funneled**, **funneling** *AmE*) **1** [I,T always + adv/prep] if you funnel something somewhere, or if it funnels there, it goes there by passing through a narrow opening: *Police at the barriers funnelled the crowd into the arena.* | *Incoming tides funnel up the channel with enormous power.* **2** [T always + adv/prep] to send money, information etc from various places to someone SYN **channel**: *His office funneled millions of dollars in secret contributions to the re-election campaign.*

F

fun·nies /ˈfʌniz/ *n* **the funnies** *AmE informal* a number of different CARTOONS in a newspaper or magazine

fun·ni·ly /ˈfʌnəli/ *adv* **1 funnily enough** *spoken* used to say that something is unexpected or strange: *Funnily enough, I was just about to call you when you called me.* **2** in an amusing or strange way

Frequencies of the adjective **funny** in spoken and written English.

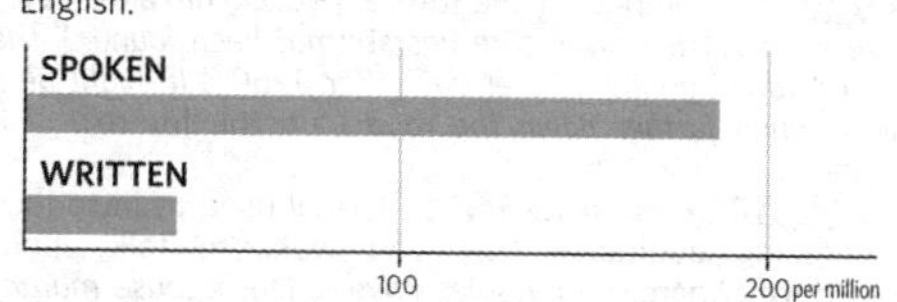

This graph shows that the adjective **funny** is much more common in spoken English than in written English. This is because it is used in a lot of common spoken phrases.

fun·ny /ˈfʌni/ ●●● S1 W3 *adj* (*comparative* **funnier**, *superlative* **funniest**)

1 AMUSING making you laugh: **funny story/joke/film etc** *Do you remember any funny stories about work?* | **hilariously/hysterically/wickedly funny** *a wickedly funny scene from the film* | *the funniest man in Britain* | *If this is your idea of a joke, I don't* ***find*** *it at all* ***funny****.* | *Luckily, when I explained the situation, he* ***saw the funny side*** (=recognized that it was partly funny). | *His laughter stopped her mid-sentence.* ***'What's so funny?'*** *she demanded.* | ***It's not funny*** (=don't laugh)*, Paul; poor Teresa was nearly in tears.* ⚠ Do not use **funny** to mean 'enjoyable'. Use **fun**: *The picnic was really fun.*

2 STRANGE unusual, strange, or difficult to explain: *I had a* ***funny feeling*** *something was going to happen.* | *What's that funny smell?* | ***It's funny how*** *you remember the words of songs, even ones you don't really like.* | **It's funny (that)** *It's funny that the kids are so quiet.* | ***That's funny****. I was sure I had $5 in my purse, but it's not there now.* | *People tell me I ran the greatest race of my life, but* ***the funny thing is*** *I can't remember much about it.* | ***It's a funny old world*** (=strange or unusual things happen in life). THESAURUS ▸ STRANGE

3 DISHONEST appearing to be illegal, dishonest, or wrong: *There's* ***something funny going on*** *here.* | *Remember, Marvin, no* ***funny business*** *while we're out.*

4 a funny look if you give someone a funny look, you look at them in a way that shows you think they are behaving strangely: *I hunkered down, ignoring the funny looks from passers-by.*

5 ILL feeling slightly ill: *I always* ***feel funny*** *after a long car ride.*

6 CRAZY *BrE informal* slightly crazy: *After his wife died he* ***went*** *a bit* ***funny****.*

7 go funny *informal* if a machine, piece of equipment etc goes funny, it stops working properly: *I just turned it on and the screen went all funny.*

8 very funny! *spoken* used when someone is laughing at you or playing a trick and you do not think it is amusing: *Very funny! Who's hidden my car keys?*

9 I'm not being funny (but) *BrE spoken* used when you are serious or do not want to offend someone: *I'm not being funny, but we haven't got much time.*

10 funny little sth used to describe something you like because it is small, unusual, or interesting: *The town centre is crammed with funny little shops.* | *his funny little grin*

11 funny peculiar or funny ha-ha? *BrE*, **funny weird/strange or funny ha-ha?** *AmE* used when someone has described something as funny and you want to know whether they mean it is strange or amusing: *'Tim's a funny guy.' 'Funny weird or funny ha-ha?'*

THESAURUS

funny making you laugh: *John told me a really funny joke.* | *She's very talented and funny.*

amusing *especially written* funny and enjoyable. Amusing is more formal than **funny**. It is often used when something is a little funny and makes you smile, rather than laugh: *an amusing anecdote* | *He* ***found*** *the whole incident rather* ***amusing****.*

humorous intended to be funny – used about stories, films, articles etc that have situations that are a little funny: *humorous stories* | *The movie is meant to be humorous.*

witty using words in a funny and clever way: *witty remarks* | *How witty!*

hilarious /hɪˈleəriəs $ -ˈler-/ (*also* **hysterical** *informal*) extremely funny: *The children thought it was hilarious.*

comical funny in a strange or silly way – often used when something is not intended to be funny: *It was quite comical watching him trying to dance.*

comic [only before noun] a comic film, play, novel etc is intended to be funny: *a comic drama*

light-hearted done for amusement or enjoyment, and not intended to be serious: *The programme is a light-hearted look at recent political events.*

comedy *n* [C] a film, play, or television programme that is intended to be funny: *a comedy by Shakespeare*

ˈfunny bone *n* [singular] the soft part of your elbow that particularly hurts when you hit it

ˈfunny farm *n* [C] *informal* an expression meaning a PSYCHIATRIC hospital that some people consider offensive – used humorously

fun·ny·man /ˈfʌnimæn/ *n* (*plural* **funnymen** /-men/) [C] a man who works as a COMEDIAN – used in newspapers etc: *the nation's best-loved funnyman*

ˈfunny ˌmoney *n* [U] *informal* money that has been printed illegally → **counterfeit**

ˈfunny ˌpapers *n* [plural] *AmE informal* another expression for the FUNNIES

fun·ny·wom·an /ˈfʌniˌwʊmən/ *n* (*plural* **funnywomen** /-ˌwɪmɪn/) [C] a woman who works as a COMEDIAN – used in newspapers etc

ˈfun ˌrun *n* [C] an event in which people run a long distance in order to collect money for CHARITY

fur[1] /fɜː $ fɜːr/ ●●○ *n*

1 [U] the thick soft hair that covers the bodies of some animals, such as cats, dogs, and rabbits → FURRY(1)

2 [C,U] the skin of a dead animal with the fur still attached: *a fur coat* | *a fur-lined jacket* | *a ban on* ***fur farming*** (=keeping and killing animals for their fur)

3 [C] a coat or piece of clothing made of fur: *Lady Yolanda was swathed in elegant furs.*

4 [U] a material that looks and feels like fur: **imitation/fake/artificial etc fur** *a pair of gloves trimmed with fake fur*

5 [U] a harmful or unpleasant substance that sometimes forms on surfaces that are always wet, such as water pipes SYN **scale**

6 the fur flies used to say that an angry argument or fight starts: *If you're both feeling frustrated, the fur may fly.*

fur[2] (*also* **fur up** *BrE*) *v* (**furred**, **furring**) [I] to become covered with an unwanted substance —**furred** *adj*: *Symptoms include dry lips and a furred tongue.*

fu·ri·ous /ˈfjʊəriəs $ ˈfjʊr-/ ●●○ *adj*

1 very angry: **[+at/about]** *Residents in the area are furious at the decision.* | **[+with]** *She was furious with herself for letting things get out of hand.* | **furious that** *Her family are furious that her name has been published by the press.* | *She was* ***absolutely furious****.* THESAURUS ▸ ANGRY

2 [usually before noun] done with a lot of energy, effort, or speed: *Neil set off at a* ***furious pace****.* | **furious debate/argument etc** *There was a* ***furious row*** *over the proposals.* | *The action is* ***fast and furious****.* —**furiously** *adv* → **fury**

furled /fɜːld $ fɜːrld/ *adj* a furled newspaper, flag etc has been rolled or folded neatly: *He held a furled umbrella in one hand.* —**furl** *v* [T]

fur·long /ˈfɜːlɒŋ $ ˈfɜːrlɔːŋ/ *n* [C] a unit for measuring length, equal to about 201 metres, which is used in horse racing. There are eight furlongs in a mile.

fur·lough /ˈfɜːləʊ $ ˈfɜːrloʊ/ *n* [C,U] **1** a period of time when a soldier or someone working in another country can return to their own country SYN **leave**: *a young soldier* home **on furlough** **2** *AmE* a period of time when workers are told not to work, especially because there is not enough money to pay them → **layoff**: *workers forced to take a long, unpaid furlough* **3** *AmE* a short period of time during which a prisoner is allowed to leave prison before returning: *Morton stabbed the man while* **on furlough**. —**furlough** *v* [T] *AmE*: *280,000 federal workers have been furloughed.*

fur·nace /ˈfɜːnɪs $ ˈfɜːr-/ ●○○ *n* [C]
1 a large container for a very hot fire, used to produce power, heat, or liquid metal
2 a piece of equipment used to heat a building

fur·nish /ˈfɜːnɪʃ $ ˈfɜːr-/ ●●○ *v* [T]
1 to put furniture and other things into a house or room: *Having bought the house, they couldn't afford to furnish it.* | **furnish sth with sth** *a room furnished with a desk and swivel chair*
2 *formal* to supply or provide something: *Will these finds furnish more information on prehistoric man?* | **furnish sb/sth with sth** *John was furnished with a list of local solicitors.* —**furnished** *adj*: *The bedrooms are elegantly furnished.* | *a* **fully furnished** *flat*

fur·nish·ings /ˈfɜːnɪʃɪŋz $ ˈfɜːr-/ *n* [plural] the furniture and other things, such as curtains, in a room: *a home furnishings store*

fur·ni·ture /ˈfɜːnɪtʃə $ ˈfɜːrnɪtʃər/ ●●● S2 W3 *n* [U] large objects such as chairs, tables, beds, and cupboards: *I helped him choose the furniture for his house.* | *I can't think of a single* **piece of furniture** *in my house that I bought new.* | *office furniture*

GRAMMAR: Countable or uncountable?

- **Furniture** is an uncountable noun and is not used in the plural. You say: *The house has some beautiful old furniture.* ✗ Don't say: *The house has some beautiful old furnitures.*
- **Furniture** is always followed by a singular verb: *The furniture* **was** *in good condition.*
- When talking about one chair or table, you say a **piece of furniture** or an **item of furniture**: *There was only one piece of furniture in the room.*

fu·ro·re /fjʊˈrɔːri, ˈfjʊərɔː $ ˈfjʊrɔːr/ *BrE*, **fu·ror** /ˈfjʊərɔː $ ˈfjʊrɔːr/ *AmE n* [singular] a sudden expression of anger among a large group of people about something that has happened SYN **row**: **cause/create a furore** *The security leaks have caused a widespread furore.* | **[+over/about]** *the furor over the oil embargo*

fur·ri·er /ˈfʌriə $ ˈfɜːriər/ *n* [C] someone who makes or sells fur clothing

fur·row¹ /ˈfʌrəʊ $ ˈfɜːroʊ/ *n* [C] **1** a deep line or fold in the skin of someone's face, especially on the forehead → **wrinkle**: *A deep furrow appeared between his brows.* **2** a wide deep line made in the surface of something, especially the ground: *the regular furrows of a plowed field* | *The river cuts a long straight furrow between the hills.*

furrow² *v* **1** [I,T] to make the skin on your face form deep lines or folds, especially because you are worried or thinking hard: *Quin's* **brow furrowed** *in concentration.* **2** [T] to make a wide deep line in the surface of something —**furrowed** *adj*: *a furrowed brow*

fur·ry /ˈfɜːri/ *adj* **1** covered with fur or short threads → **fluffy**: *furry kittens* | *pink furry slippers* | *furry leaves* **2 furry friends** *informal* used humorously to talk about animals in general → **feathered friend**

fur·ther¹ /ˈfɜːðə $ ˈfɜːrðər/ ●●● S1 W1 *adv*
1 MORE more, or to a greater degree: *A spokesman declined to comment until the evidence could be studied further.* | *The flavour of the wine is further improved during the aging period.* | *Whaling in Australia was stopped. But the Australian government* **went further** (=said or did something more extreme) *and proposed a global ban.* | **[+into/away etc]** *Marcus sank* **further and further** *into debt.* THESAURUS ▶ MORE
2 take sth further to take action at a more serious or higher level, especially in order to get the result you want: *The police do not propose to* **take** *the* **matter further**. | **take sth a stage/step further** *Critics want the government to take this a stage further and ban the film altogether.*
3 DISTANCE (*also* **farther**) a greater distance, or beyond a particular place: *They walked a little further.* | **[+up/away/along etc]** *His farm is located further away from Riobamba than his brother's.* | *His hands moved further down her back.* | *They've never been further south than San Diego.*
4 TIME into the past or the future: **[+back/on/ahead etc]** *Five years further on, a cure has still not been found.* | *The records don't go any further back than 1960.* | *It might be a sign, much* **further down the road** (=in the future), *of a change in policy.*
5 IN ADDITION [sentence adverb] *formal* used to introduce something additional that you want to talk about SYN **furthermore**: *Butter sales have fallen because margarine has improved in flavor. Further, butter consumption has decreased because of links to heart disease.*
6 further to sth *written formal* used in letters to mention a previous letter, conversation etc about the same matter SYN **following**: *Further to your letter of February 5th, we can confirm your order.*
7 nothing could be further from the truth used when you want to say that something is completely untrue: *People often described him as a bitter academic, but nothing could be further from the truth.*
8 nothing could be/is further from sb's mind/thoughts used to emphasize that someone is not thinking about or intending something
9 sth must not go any further used to say that something you are telling someone is secret or private

further² ●●○ *adj* [only before noun]
1 more or additional: *Are there any further questions?* | *We have decided to take* **no further action**. | **further details/information etc** *Visit our website for further details.* | **a further 10 miles/5 minutes etc** *Cook gently for a further 10 minutes.* THESAURUS ▶ MORE
2 until further notice until you are told that something has changed: *Lacunza ordered the suspension of the elections until further notice.*

further³ ●○○ *v* [T] to help something progress or be successful → **promote**: *He dedicated his life to furthering the cause of world peace.* | *Alan had been using her to* **further** *his* **career**.

fur·ther·ance /ˈfɜːðərəns $ ˈfɜːr-/ *n* [U] *formal* the act or process of helping something progress or be done: **[+of]** *the furtherance of science* | **in furtherance of sth** *Staff are encouraged to use information resources in furtherance of their own professional interests.*

ˌfurther eduˈcation *n* [U] *BrE* (*abbreviation* **FE**) education for adults after leaving school, that is not at a university → **higher education**

fur·ther·more /ˌfɜːðəˈmɔː $ ˈfɜːrðərmɔːr/ ●○○ AWL *adv* [sentence adverb] *formal* in addition to what has already been said SYN **moreover**: *He is old and unpopular. Furthermore, he has at best only two years of political life ahead of him.*

fur·ther·most /ˈfɜːðəməʊst $ ˈfɜːrðərmoʊst/ *adj formal* most distant SYN **furthest**: *In the furthermost corner sat a tall thin man.*

fur·thest /ˈfɜːðɪst $ ˈfɜːr-/ *adj, adv* **1** at the greatest distance from a place or point in time SYN **farthest**: *There was a huge tapestry on the furthest wall.* | **[+away/from]** *He walked slowly toward the end of the jury box furthest from the judge.* **2** more or to a greater degree than other people or things, or than before: *Maltby's book has probably gone furthest in explaining these events.*

fur·tive /ˈfɜːtɪv $ ˈfɜːr-/ *adj* behaving as if you want to keep something secret SYN **secretive**: *There was something furtive about his actions.* | **furtive glances/looks** *Chris kept stealing furtive glances at me.* —**furtively** *adv*: *She opened the door and looked furtively down the hall.* —**furtiveness** *n* [U]

fu·ry /ˈfjʊəri $ ˈfjʊri/ ●●○ *n*
1 [U] extreme, often uncontrolled anger SYN **rage**: *I was*

F

shaking with fury. | *Jo stepped forward, her* **eyes blazing with fury**. | *The report was leaked to the press, much to the president's fury.*
2 [singular] a feeling of extreme anger: *'Go on then!' shouted Jamie* **in a fury**. *'See if I care!'*
3 a fury of sth a state of very busy activity or strong feeling: *She was listening with such a fury of concentration that she did not notice Arthur had left.* | *In a fury of frustration and fear Nina bit his hand.*
4 like fury *informal* with great effort or energy: *We went out and played like fury.*
5 [U] *literary* used to describe very bad weather conditions: *At last the* **fury of the storm** *lessened.*
6 Fury one of the three snake-haired goddesses in ancient Greek stories who punished crime → **furious**

furze /fɜːz $ fɜːrz/ *n* [U] a wild bush with sharp stems and bright yellow flowers

fuse[1] /fjuːz/ *n* [C] **1** a short thin piece of wire inside electrical equipment which prevents damage by melting and stopping the electricity when there is too much power: *two 13 amp fuses* | *I taught him how to* **change** *a* **fuse**. | **blow a fuse** (=make it melt by putting too much electricity through it) **2** (*also* **fuze** *AmE*) a thing that delays a bomb, FIREWORK etc from exploding until you are a safe distance away, or makes it explode at a particular time **3 a short fuse** if someone has a short fuse, they get angry very easily → **blow a fuse** at BLOW[1](16)

fuse[2] *v* [I,T] **1** to join together physically, or to make things join together, and become a single thing: **fuse (sth) together** *The egg and sperm fuse together as one cell.* **2** to combine different qualities, ideas, or things, or to be combined SYN **merge**: *Their music fuses elements as diverse as Cajun, bebop and Cuban waltzes.* | **fuse (sth) with sth** *Leonard takes Carver-style dirty realism and fuses it with the pace of a detective story.* | **fuse (sth) into sth** *We intend to fuse the companies into a single organization.* **THESAURUS** MIX **3** *BrE* if electrical equipment fuses, or if you fuse it, it stops working because a fuse has melted: *The lights have fused again.* **4** *technical* if a rock or metal fuses, or if you fuse it, it becomes liquid by being heated: *Lead fuses at quite a low temperature.* → FUSION

'fuse box *n* [C] a box that contains the fuses of the electrical system of a house or other building

fused /fjuːzd/ *adj BrE* if a piece of electrical equipment is fused, it is fitted with a fuse

fu·se·lage /ˈfjuːzəlɑːʒ $ -sə-/ *n* [C] the main part of a plane, in which people sit or goods are carried → see picture at PLANE[1]

fu·si·lier /ˌfjuːzəˈlɪə $ -ˈlɪr/ *n* [C] a soldier in the past who carried a light gun called a MUSKET

fu·sil·lade /ˌfjuːzəˈleɪd $ -sə-/ *n* [C usually singular] **1** a quick series of shots fired from a gun, or a quick series of other objects that are thrown: **[+of]** *a fusillade of bullets* **2** a quick series of questions or remarks

fu·sion /ˈfjuːʒən/ *n* [C,U] **1** a combination of separate qualities or ideas: *Her work is a fusion of several different styles.* | *the best fusion cuisine in the whole of Vancouver* **2** a physical combination of separate things → **fission**: *the energy that comes from the fusion of hydrogen atoms* → NUCLEAR FUSION **3** a type of music which mixes JAZZ with other types of music, especially ROCK → FUSE[2]

'fusion ˌbomb *n* [C] another word for a HYDROGEN BOMB

fuss[1] /fʌs/ ●○○ *n* [singular, U]
1 anxious behaviour or activity that is usually about unimportant things: *James said he'd better be getting back or there'd* **be a fuss**. | *The Steamatic enables you to clean any carpet* **with** *the* **minimum of fuss**.
2 attention or excitement that is usually unnecessary or unwelcome: *They wanted a quiet wedding without any fuss.* | *Until I heard her sing I couldn't see* **what all the fuss was about** (=why people liked it so much).
3 make a fuss/kick up a fuss (about sth) to complain or become angry about something, especially when this is not necessary: *Josie kicked up a fuss because the soup was too salty.* | *I don't know why you're* **making such a fuss** *about it.*
4 make a fuss of sb/sth *BrE*, **make a fuss over sb/sth** *AmE* to pay a lot of attention to someone or something, to show that you are pleased with them or like them: *Make a fuss of your dog when he behaves properly.*

fuss[2] *v* [I] **1** to worry a lot about things that may not be very important: *I wish you'd stop fussing – I'll be perfectly all right.* **2** to pay too much attention to small unimportant details: **[+with/around/about]** *Paul was fussing with his clothes, trying to get his tie straight.* **3** *AmE* to behave in an unhappy or angry way: *The baby woke up and started to fuss.*

fuss over sb/sth *phr v* to pay a lot of attention or too much attention to someone or something, especially to show that you are pleased with them or like them: *His aunts fussed over him all the time.*

fussed /fʌst/ *adj* **not be fussed (about sth)** *BrE spoken* to not mind what happens or is done SYN **bothered**: *'Where do you want to go?' 'I'm not fussed.'*

fuss·pot /ˈfʌsˌpɒt $ -ˌpɑːt/ *BrE*, **fuss·bud·get** /ˈfʌsˌbʌdʒɪt/ *AmE old-fashioned n* [C] *informal* someone who worries about unimportant things

fuss·y /ˈfʌsi/ (*comparative* **fussier**, *superlative* **fussiest**) *adj* **1** very concerned about small, usually unimportant details, and difficult to please: **[+about]** *Sue was fussy about her looks.* | *A lot of small children are fussy eaters* (=they dislike many types of food). | *'Do you want to go out or just rent a movie?' 'I'm not fussy'* (=I don't mind). **2** fussy clothes, objects, buildings etc are very detailed and decorated – used to show disapproval OPP **plain**, **simple**: *The furniture looked comfortable, nothing fussy or too elaborate.* **3** with small, exact, and careful actions, sometimes showing nervousness: *She patted her hair with small fussy movements.* —**fussily** *adv* —**fussiness** *n* [U]

fus·ti·an /ˈfʌstiən $ -tʃən/ *n* [U] **1** a type of rough heavy cotton cloth, worn especially in the past **2** *literary* words that sound important but have very little meaning —**fustian** *adj*

fus·ty /ˈfʌsti/ *adj* **1** if rooms, clothes, buildings etc are fusty, they have an unpleasant smell, because they have not been used for a long time SYN **musty** **2** *informal* ideas or people that are fusty are old-fashioned: *fusty old academics* —**fustiness** *n* [U]

fu·tile /ˈfjuːtaɪl $ -tl/ ●○○ *adj* actions that are futile are useless because they have no chance of being successful SYN **pointless** OPP **worthwhile**: **a futile attempt/effort** *a futile attempt to save the paintings from the flames* | *My efforts to go back to sleep proved futile.* | **it is futile to do sth** *It was futile to continue the negotiations.* —**futility** /fjuːˈtɪləti/ *n* [U]: *This sums up Owen's thoughts on the futility of war.*

fu·ton /ˈfuːtɒn $ -tɑːn/ *n* [C] a MATTRESS used for sleeping on, especially in Japan

fu·ture[1] /ˈfjuːtʃə $ -ər/ ●●● S1 W1 *adj* [only before noun]
1 likely to happen or exist at a time after the present: *We are now more able to predict future patterns of climate change.* | *We've been able to save this land from development and preserve it for* **future generations**. | *the debate over the* **future development** *of the European Union* | **future wife/husband/son-in-law etc** (=someone who will be your wife, husband, son-in-law etc)
2 *technical* the form of a verb used for talking about things that are going to happen: *the future tense*
3 for future reference something kept for future reference is kept in order to be used or looked at in the future

future[2] ●●● S1 W1 *n*
1 the future a) the time after the present: *What are your plans for the future?* | *It may be useful at some time in the future.* **b)** *technical* the form of a verb that shows that something will happen or exist at a later time. In the sentence, 'I will leave tomorrow,' the verb is in the future.
2 [C] what someone or something will do or what will happen to them in the future: *The islands should have the right to decide their own future.* | **[+of]** *Ferguson is optimistic about the future of the business.* | *a leader who will shape the organization's future*

3 in future *BrE* from now: *In future, staff must wear identity badges at all times.*
4 have a/no future to have a chance or no chance of being successful or continuing: *Does this school have a future?*
5 there's a/no future in sth used to say that something is likely or not likely to be successful: *He felt there was no future in farming.*
6 futures [plural] *technical* goods, money, land etc that will be supplied or exchanged in the future at a time and price that has already been agreed

COLLOCATIONS – MEANINGS 1 & 2

VERBS

predict the future (=say what will happen in the future) *No-one can predict the future of boxing.*
foretell the future (=say or show what will happen in the future) *Some people think that dreams can foretell the future.*
see/look into the future (=know what will happen in the future) *I wish I could see into the future.*
look to the future (=think about or plan for the future) *She could now look to the future with confidence.*
plan for the future (*also* **make plans for the future**) (=think carefully about the future and decide what you are going to do) | **sb's/sth's future lies in/with sth** (=it is in a particular thing) | **the future looks good/bright etc**

ADJECTIVES

great/good *The country has a great future.*
bright/promising (=showing signs of being successful) *Her future as a tennis player looks promising.*
uncertain (=not clear or decided) *The college's future is now uncertain.*
bleak/grim/dark (=without anything to make you feel hopeful) *The theatre is losing money and its future looks bleak.*

PHRASES

the immediate future (=very soon) *There will be no major changes in the immediate future.*
the near future (=soon) *A new product launch is planned for the near future.*
the distant future (=a long time from now) *I don't worry about what might happen in the distant future.*
for/in the foreseeable future (=as far into the future as you can possibly know) *The population is expected to keep growing for the foreseeable future.*
in the not too distant future (=quite soon) *We're planning to go there again in the not too distant future.*
sb's hopes/fears/plans for the future *What are your hopes for the future?*
what the future holds (=what will happen)

THESAURUS

THE TIME AFTER NOW

the future the time after now: *What will life be like in the future?* | *The company is hoping to expand* ***in the near future*** (=soon).
from now on used when saying that something will always happen in the future, starting from now: *The meetings will be held once a month from now on.*
years/days etc to come for a long time in the future: ***In years to come****, people will look back on the 20th century as a turning point in history.* | *Nuclear power stations will still be needed* ***for a long time to come****.*
in the long/short/medium term use this to talk about what will happen over a period from now until a long, short etc time in the future: *We don't know what will happen in the long term.* | *In the short term, things look good.*
on the horizon used when talking about what is likely to happen in the future: *There are some big changes on the horizon.*

WHAT WILL HAPPEN TO SB/STH

sb's/sth's future what will happen to someone or something: *He knew that his future was in films.* | *Shareholders will meet to decide the company's future.*
fate someone or something's future – used especially when you are worried that something bad could happen: *The fate of the hostages remains uncertain.*
destiny what will happen to someone in their life, especially something important: *Sartre believed that everyone is in charge of their own destiny.* | *He thinks that it is his destiny to lead the country.*
the outlook what will happen, especially concerning business, the economy, or the weather: *The economic outlook looks good.* | *Here is the weather outlook for tomorrow.*
prospect the idea or possibility that something will happen: *the awful prospect of another terrorist attack* | *Prospects for a peace settlement don't look too good.*
fortune what will happen to a person, organization etc in the future – used especially when talking about whether or not they will be successful: *Fans are hoping for a change in the club's fortunes.*

ˌfuture ˈperfect *n technical* **the future perfect** the form of a verb that shows that the action described will be complete before a particular time in the future, formed in English by 'will have' or 'shall have', as in 'I will have finished by 5 o'clock.' —**future perfect** *adj*

ˈfuture-proof¹, **fu·ture·proof** /ˈfjuːtʃəpruːf $ -tʃər-/ *v* [T] to make or plan something in such a way that it will not become ineffective or unsuitable for use in the future: *plans to future-proof the company's network*

future-proof² *adj* if something is future-proof, it will not become ineffective or unsuitable for use in the future: *future-proof software*

ˈfutures ˌmarket *n* [C] *technical* a market where FUTURES are bought and sold

fu·tur·is·m /ˈfjuːtʃərɪzəm/ *n* [U] a style of art, music, and literature in the early 20th century which emphasized the importance of modern things, especially technology and machines —**futurist** *n* [C]

fu·tur·is·tic /ˌfjuːtʃəˈrɪstɪk◂/ *adj* **1** something which is futuristic looks unusual and modern, as if it belongs in the future instead of the present: *The futuristic sports stadium is the pride of the city.* **2** futuristic ideas, books, films etc imagine what may happen in the future, especially through scientific developments: *Orwell's disturbing futuristic novel, '1984'*

fu·tu·ri·ty /fjʊˈtjʊərəti $ -ˈtʊr-/ *n* [U] *formal* the time after the present SYN **future**

fu·tu·rol·o·gy /ˌfjuːtʃəˈrɒlədʒi $ -ˈrɑː-/ *n* [U] the activity of trying to say correctly what will happen in the future —**futurologist** *n* [C]

futz /fʌts/ *v*

futz around *phr v AmE informal* to waste time, especially by doing small unimportant jobs slowly: *I spent the entire day just futzing around.*

fuze /fjuːz/ *n* [C] an American spelling of FUSE¹(2)

fuzz /fʌz/ *n* **1** [singular, U] thin soft hair or a substance like hair that covers something: *When Jack was born he had a fuzz of black hair on his head.* **2** [U] *AmE* a small amount of soft material that has come from clothing etc SYN **fluff** **3 the fuzz** *informal* an insulting way of talking to or about the police, used especially in the 1960s and 1970s

fuzz·y /ˈfʌzi/ *adj* **1** if a sound or picture is fuzzy, it is unclear → **blurred**: *Some of the photos were so fuzzy it was hard to tell who was who.* **2** unclear or confused OPP **clear**: *There's a fuzzy line between parents' and schools' responsibilities.* **3** covered with soft short hair or fur: *I stroked the kitten's fuzzy back.* **4** fuzzy hair is very curly and sticks straight up —**fuzzily** *adv* —**fuzziness** *n* [U]

ˌfuzzy ˈlogic *n* [U] *technical* a type of LOGIC which is used to try to make computers think like humans

fwd the written abbreviation of ***forward***

FWIW for what it is worth; an abbreviation used in emails, to say that you are not sure if what you are writing is very useful

f-word /ˈef wɜːd $ -wɜːrd/ *n* [C] used when you are talking about the word FUCK but do not want to say it because it is offensive: *Mommy, Billy said the f-word.*

fwy. *AmE* the written abbreviation of ***freeway***

FX /ˌef ˈeks/ **1** the abbreviation of ***foreign exchange*** **2** the abbreviation of ***special effects***

-fy /faɪ/ *suffix* [in verbs] another form of the suffix -IFY

FY *AmE* the abbreviation of ***fiscal year***

FYI, **fyi** (***for your information***) used especially in short business notes and emails, when you are telling someone something they need to know

F

Gg

G, **g** /dʒiː/ *n* (*plural* **G's**, **g's**) **1** [C,U] the seventh letter of the English alphabet **2** [C,U] the fifth note in the musical SCALE of C MAJOR or the musical KEY based on this note **3** [singular, U] *AmE* used to describe a film that has been officially approved as suitable for people of any age SYN **U** *BrE* → **PG 4** [C] *technical* a unit for measuring the force caused by GRAVITY on an object as it starts to move faster and faster: *Astronauts endure a force of several G's during take-off.* | *high* ***g-forces*** **5** [U] *AmE* a GRAND (=$1,000)

g a written abbreviation of ***gram*** or ***grams***

gab /gæb/ *v* (**gabbed**, **gabbing**) [I + about] *informal* to talk continuously, usually about things that are not important: *You two were gabbing so much you didn't even see me!* —**gabby** *adj* → **the gift of the gab** at **GIFT**[1](5)

gab·ar·dine, **gaberdine** /ˈgæbədiːn, ˌgæbəˈdiːn $ ˈgæbərdiːn/ *n* **1** [U] a strong material which does not allow water to go through and is often used for making coats **2** [C] a coat made from gabardine

gab·ble[1] /ˈgæbəl/ *v* (**gabbled**, **gabbling**) [I,T] to say something so quickly that people cannot hear you clearly or understand you properly: *Just calm down, stop gabbling, and tell me what has happened.*

gabble[2] *n* [singular, U] a lot of talking that is difficult to understand, especially when several people are talking at the same time SYN **babble**: *a gabble of voices*

gab·er·dine /ˈgæbədiːn, ˌgæbəˈdiːn $ ˈgæbərdiːn/ *n* [C,U] another spelling of GABARDINE

gab·fest /ˈgæbfest/ *n* [C] *especially AmE informal* an occasion when people talk to each other a lot

ga·ble /ˈgeɪbəl/ *n* [C] the upper end of a house wall where it joins with a sloping roof and makes a shape like a TRIANGLE: *the gable end of the barn* → see picture at **ROOF**[1]

ga·bled /ˈgeɪbəld/ *adj* having one or more gables: *a gabled cottage* | *gabled roofs*

gad /gæd/ *v* (**gadded**, **gadding**)

gad about/around *phr v informal* to go out and enjoy yourself, going to many different places, especially when you should be doing something else: *While I'm at home cooking, he's gadding about with his friends.*

gad·a·bout /ˈgædəbaʊt/ *n* [C] *informal* someone who goes out a lot or travels a lot in order to enjoy themselves

gad·fly /ˈgædflaɪ/ *n* (*plural* **gadflies**) [C] **1** someone who annoys other people by criticizing them **2** a fly that bites cattle and horses

gad·get /ˈgædʒɪt/ *n* [C] a small, useful, and cleverly-designed machine or tool: *a neat gadget for sharpening knives*

gad·get·ry /ˈgædʒətri/ *n* [U] modern gadgets in general - sometimes used to show disapproval: *I don't understand how all this electronic gadgetry works.*

Gae·lic /ˈgeɪlɪk, ˈgælɪk/ *n* [U] one of the Celtic languages, especially spoken in parts of Scotland and in Ireland —**Gaelic** *adj*: *Gaelic poetry*

ˌGaelic ˈfootball *n* [U] a game played in Ireland between two teams of 15 players, using a round ball that can be kicked or hit with the hands

gaff /gæf/ *n* [C] **1** *BrE informal* the place where someone lives: *a wretched dirty gaff* **2** a stick with a hook at the end, used to pull big fish out of the water

gaffe /gæf/ *n* [C] an embarrassing mistake made in a social situation or in public SYN **faux pas**: *The consul's comments were a major diplomatic gaffe.* **THESAURUS** ▸ **MISTAKE**

gaf·fer /ˈgæfə $ -ər/ *n* [C] **1** the person who is in charge of the lighting in making a cinema film **2** *BrE informal* an old man - used humorously **3** *BrE informal* a man who is in charge of people, especially in a factory SYN **boss**

gag[1] /gæg/ *v* (**gagged**, **gagging**) **1** [I] to be unable to swallow and feel as if you are about to bring up food from your stomach: *The foul smell made her gag.* | **[+on]** *He almost gagged on his first mouthful of food.* **2** [T] to put a piece of cloth over someone's mouth to stop them making a noise: *Thugs gagged her and tied her to a chair.* | *He left his victim* ***bound and gagged*** (=tied up and with something over their mouth that stops them speaking). **3** [T] to stop people saying what they want to say and expressing their opinions: *an attempt to gag political activists* → **GAG ORDER**, **GAG RULE 4 be gagging to do sth/be gagging for sth** *BrE informal* to be very eager to do or have something: *They were gagging to sign the contract.* **5 be gagging for it** *BrE informal* to be very eager to have sex

gag[2] *n* [C] **1** *informal* a joke or funny story: *He told a few gags.* | *It was a bit of a* ***running gag*** (=a joke which is repeated) *in the show.* **2** a piece of cloth put over someone's mouth to stop them making a noise

ga·ga /ˈgɑːgɑː/ *adj* [not before noun] *informal* **1** an insulting word used to describe someone who is confused because they are old: *Sid keeps forgetting my name. I think he's going a bit gaga.* **2** having a strong but often temporary feeling of love for someone SYN **infatuated**: **[+about/over]** *I can't imagine why Susan is so gaga about him.*

gage /geɪdʒ/ *n* [C] an American spelling of GAUGE

gag·gle /ˈgægəl/ *n* **1 a gaggle of tourists/children etc** a noisy group of people: *a gaggle of teenage girls* **2 a gaggle of geese** a group of GEESE

ˈgag ˌorder *n* [C] an order made by the court to prevent any public reporting of a case which is still being considered by a court of law

ˈgag rule *n* [C] a rule or law that stops people from talking about a subject during a particular time or in a particular place

gai·e·ty /ˈgeɪəti/ *n old-fashioned* **1** [U] when someone or something is cheerful and fun: *Lars enjoyed the warmth and gaiety of these occasions.* → **GAY**[1](3) **2 gaieties** [plural] enjoyable events or activities: *Elaine missed the gaieties of life in Paris.*

gai·ly /ˈgeɪli/ *adv* **1** in a happy way SYN **cheerfully**: *'Morning, Albert,' she called gaily.* **2** in a way that shows you do not care about, or do not realize, the effects of your actions: *They gaily went on talking after the film had started.* **3 gaily coloured/painted/decorated etc** having bright cheerful colours: *gaily coloured tropical birds*

gain[1] /geɪn/ ●●● S3 W1 *v*

1 GET STH [T] to obtain or achieve something you want or need: **gain control/power** *Radical left-wing parties gained control of local authorities.* | *After gaining independence in 1957, it was renamed 'Ghana'.* | **gain a degree/qualification etc** *He gained a doctorate in Chemical Engineering.*

> **REGISTER**
> In everyday English, people usually say **get** rather than **gain**: *She* ***got*** *a degree in English.*

2 GET GRADUALLY [I,T] to gradually get more and more of a quality, feeling etc, especially a useful or valuable one: *She has* ***gained*** *a* ***reputation*** *as a good communicator.* | *Many of his ideas have* ***gained*** *popular* ***support***. | *an opportunity to* ***gain experience*** *in a work environment* | *The youngsters gradually* ***gain confidence*** *in their abilities.* | **[+in]** *The sport has* ***gained in popularity*** *in recent years.* **THESAURUS** ▸ **GET**

3 ADVANTAGE [I,T] to get an advantage from a situation, opportunity, or event: **gain (sth) from (doing) sth** *There is much to be gained from seeking expert advice early.* | *an attempt to gain a competitive advantage over their rivals* | *Who really* ***stands to gain*** (=is likely to get an advantage) *from these tax cuts?* | ***There's nothing to be gained*** (=it will not help you) *by losing your temper.*

4 INCREASE [T] to increase in weight, speed, height, or value: *Carrie's* ***gained*** *a lot of* ***weight*** *recently.* | *The dollar has gained 8% against the yen.*

5 gain access/entry/admittance etc (to sth) to manage to

enter a place, building, or organization: *New ramps will help the disabled gain better access.* | *methods used by burglars to gain entry to houses*
6 gain an understanding/insight/impression etc to learn or find out about something: **[+of]** *We are hoping to gain a better understanding of the underlying process.* | *This enabled me to gain an overall impression of the school.*
7 gain ground to make steady progress and become more popular, more successful etc: *The anti-smoking lobby has steadily gained ground in the last decade.*
8 gain time to deliberately do something to give yourself more time to think OPP **lose time**
9 CLOCK [I,T] if a clock or watch gains, or if it gains time, it goes too fast OPP **lose**
10 ARRIVE [T] *literary* to reach a place after a lot of effort or difficulty: *The swimmer finally gained the river bank.*
→ **nothing ventured, nothing gained** at VENTURE²(3)
gain on sb/sth *phr v* to gradually get closer to a person, car etc that you are chasing: *Quick – they're gaining on us!*

gain² ●●○ W3 *n*
1 ADVANTAGE [C] an advantage or improvement, especially one achieved by planning or effort: *The party* ***made*** *considerable* ***gains*** *at local elections.* | **[+in]** *substantial gains in efficiency* | **[+from]** *the potential gains from improved marketing* | **[+to/for]** *There are obvious gains for the student.*
2 INCREASE [C,U] an increase in the amount or level of something OPP **loss**: **[+in]** *a gain in weekly output* | **[+of]** *Retail sales showed a gain of 0.4%.* | *The Democratic Party needed a* ***net gain*** *of only 20 votes.* | *Eating too many fatty foods could cause* ***weight gain****.*
3 PROFIT [U] financial profit, especially when this seems to be the only thing someone is interested in OPP **loss**: **financial/economic/capital etc gain** *They are seeking to realize the maximum financial gain.* | **[+of]** *a pre-tax gain of $20 million* | **for gain** *Such research should not be for personal gain.* → CAPITAL GAINS
4 ill-gotten gains money or advantages obtained dishonestly – used humorously

gain·ful /ˈɡeɪnfəl/ *adj* **gainful employment/work/activity** *formal* work or activity for which you are paid —**gainfully** *adv*: *gainfully employed*

gain·say /ˌɡeɪnˈseɪ/ *v* (*past tense and past participle* **gainsaid** /-ˈsed/) [T usually in negatives] *formal* to say that something is not true, or to disagree with someone SYN **contradict**: *No one dared to gainsay him.*

gait /ɡeɪt/ *n* [singular] the way someone walks: *a slow shuffling gait*

gai·ter /ˈɡeɪtə $ -ər/ *n* [C usually plural] a cloth or leather covering worn below the knee by men in the past, or now by walkers to keep their legs dry

gal¹ /ɡæl/ *n* [C] *AmE informal* a girl or woman – used especially by older people: *She's a great gal.*

gal² *BrE*, **gal.** *AmE* the written abbreviation of ***gallon*** or ***gallons***

ga·la /ˈɡɑːlə $ ˈɡeɪlə, ˈɡælə/ *n* [C] **1** a public entertainment or performance to celebrate a special occasion: **gala dinner/performance/night etc** *the Society's Gala Dinner* | *a charity gala evening* **2** *BrE* a sports competition, especially in swimming

ga·lac·tic /ɡəˈlæktɪk/ *adj* relating to a galaxy → **intergalactic**

gal·ax·y /ˈɡæləksi/ ●○○ *n* (*plural* **galaxies**)
1 [C] one of the large groups of stars that make up the universe
2 the Galaxy the large group of stars which our Sun and its PLANETS belong to
3 [singular] a large number of things that are similar: **[+of]** *a galaxy of British artistic talent*

gale /ɡeɪl/ ●○○ *n* [C]
1 a very strong wind: *a severe gale* | **it's blowing a gale** *BrE* (=it's very windy) THESAURUS WIND
2 a gale/gales of laughter a sudden loud sound of laughter: *The bar erupted into gales of laughter.*

ˈgale force, **gale-force** *adj* a gale force wind is strong enough to be dangerous or cause damage —**gale-force** *adv*: *blowing gale-force*

gall¹ /ɡɔːl $ ɡɒːl/ *n* **1 have the gall to do sth** to do something rude and unreasonable that most people would be too embarrassed to do: *He even had the gall to blame Lucy for it.* **2** [U] *old-fashioned* anger and hate that will not go away SYN **resentment** **3** [U] *old-fashioned* BILE **4** [C] a swelling on a tree or plant caused by damage from insects or infection **5** [C] a painful place on an animal's skin, caused by something rubbing against it

gall² *v* [T] to make someone feel upset and angry because of something that is unfair: *It really galled him to see Anita doing so well now.* → GALLING

gal·lant¹ /ˈɡælənt/ *adj old-fashioned* **1** a man who is gallant is kind and polite towards women: *a gallant young man* **2** brave: *a gallant attempt to save lives*

gal·lant² /ɡəˈlænt, ˈɡælənt $ ɡəˈlænt, ɡəˈlɑːnt/ *n* [C] *old-fashioned* a well-dressed young man who is kind and polite towards women

gal·lan·try /ˈɡæləntri/ *n* [U] *formal* **1** courage, especially in a battle: *a medal for gallantry* **2** polite attention given by men to women

ˈgall ˌbladder *n* [C] the organ in your body in which BILE is stored

gal·le·on /ˈɡæliən/ *n* [C] a sailing ship used mainly by the Spanish from the 15th to the 17th century

gal·le·ry /ˈɡæləri/ ●●○ W3 *n* (*plural* **galleries**) [C]
1 a) a large building where people can see famous pieces of art: *an exhibition of African art at the Hayward Gallery* **b)** a small privately owned shop or STUDIO where you can see and buy pieces of art
2 a) an upper floor or BALCONY built on an inner wall of a hall, theatre, or church, from which people can watch a performance, discussion etc: *the* ***public gallery*** *in Congress* | **in the gallery** *We could only afford seats up in the gallery.* **b) the gallery** the people sitting in a gallery
3 play to the gallery to do or say something just because you think it will please people and make you popular
4 a level passage under the ground in a mine or CAVE
→ PRESS GALLERY, SHOOTING GALLERY

gal·ley /ˈɡæli/ *n* [C] **1** a kitchen on a ship: *The fire extinguishers are stored in the galley.* **2** a long low Greek or Roman ship with sails which was rowed by SLAVEs in the past **3** *technical* **a)** a TRAY used in the process of printing books etc which holds TYPE **b)** (*also* **galley proof**) a sheet of paper on which a new book is printed, so that mistakes can be put right before it is divided into pages

Gal·lic /ˈɡælɪk/ *adj* relating to or typical of France or French people: *Gallic charm*

gal·ling /ˈɡɔːlɪŋ $ ˈɡɒː-/ *adj* making you feel upset and angry because of something that is unfair SYN **annoying**: *The most galling thing is that the guy who got promoted is less qualified than me.*

gal·li·vant /ˈɡæləvænt/ *v* [I] *informal* to spend time enjoying yourself and going from place to place for pleasure – used humorously in order to show disapproval SYN **gad**: **[+about/around]** *She should be home with the children, not gallivanting around.*

gal·lon /ˈɡælən/ ●●● S3 W3 *n* [C]
1 (*written abbreviation* **gal**) a unit for measuring liquids, equal to eight PINTs. In Britain this is 4.55 litres, and in the US it is 3.79 litres: *a 20-gallon fish tank* | *The car does about 50* ***miles per gallon****.*
2 *informal* a lot of a liquid: *We drank gallons of coffee.*

gal·lop¹ /ˈɡæləp/ ●●○ *v*
1 [I] if a horse gallops, it moves very fast with all its feet leaving the ground together → **canter**, **trot**: *A neighbour's horse came galloping down the road, riderless.* | *a galloping horse* THESAURUS RUN
2 [I,T] if you gallop, you ride very fast on a horse or you make it go very fast: **[+along/off/towards etc]** *I watched as Jan galloped away.*
3 [I always + adv/prep] to move very quickly SYN **run**: *Ian came galloping down the stairs.*

gallop² *n* **1 a)** [singular] the movement of a horse at its

G

fastest speed, when all four feet leave the ground together → **canter**, **trot**: *The horses* ***broke into a gallop*** (=begin to go very fast). | **at a/full gallop** *Mounted police charged at full gallop.* **b)** [C] a ride on a horse when it is galloping **2** [singular] a very fast speed: **at a/full gallop** *The project began at full gallop.*

gal·lop·ing /ˈɡæləpɪŋ/ *adj* [only before noun] increasing or developing very quickly SYN **runaway**: **galloping inflation/consumption etc** *galloping inflation of 20 to 30%*

gal·lows /ˈɡæləʊz $ -loʊz/ *n* (*plural* **gallows**) [C] a structure used for killing criminals by hanging them from a rope

ˈgallows ˌhumour *BrE*, **gallows humor** *AmE* *n* [U] humour which makes very unpleasant or dangerous things seem funny

gall·stone /ˈɡɔːlstəʊn $ ˈɡɒːlstoʊn/ *n* [C] a hard stone which can form in your GALL BLADDER

ga·loot /ɡəˈluːt/ *n* [C] *AmE old-fashioned* someone who is not at all graceful and does not dress neatly: *You clumsy galoot!*

ga·lore /ɡəˈlɔː $ -ˈlɔːr/ *adj* [only after noun] in large amounts or numbers: *bargains galore in the sales*

ga·losh·es /ɡəˈlɒʃɪz $ -ˈlɑː-/ *n* [plural] *old-fashioned* rubber shoes worn over ordinary shoes when it rains or snows

gal·pal /ˈɡælpæl/ *n* [C] *AmE informal* a female friend

ga·lumph /ɡəˈlʌmf/ *v* [I always + adv/prep] *informal* to move in a noisy, heavy, and awkward way

gal·van·ic /ɡælˈvænɪk/ *adj* **1** *formal* making people react suddenly with strong feelings or actions: *The bomb warning had a galvanic effect.* **2** *technical* relating to the production of electricity by the action of acid on metal

gal·va·nise /ˈɡælvənaɪz/ *v* [T] a British spelling of GALVANIZE

gal·va·nis·m /ˈɡælvənɪzəm/ *n* [U] *technical* the production of electricity by the use of chemicals, especially as in a BATTERY

gal·va·nize (*also* **-ise** *BrE*) /ˈɡælvənaɪz/ *v* [T] to shock or surprise someone so that they do something to solve a problem, improve a situation etc: **galvanize sb into (doing) sth** *The possibility of defeat finally* ***galvanized*** *us* ***into action***. | *The report galvanized world opinion.*

gal·va·nized (*also* **-ised** *BrE*) /ˈɡælvənaɪzd/ *adj* **galvanized iron/metal etc** metal that has had a covering of ZINC put on it so that it does not RUST

gam·bit /ˈɡæmbɪt/ *n* [C] **1** something that you do or say which is intended to give you an advantage in an argument: *a clever debating gambit* | *These questions are often an* ***opening gambit*** (=the thing you say first) *for a negotiation.* **2** a planned series of moves at the beginning of a game of CHESS

gam·ble¹ /ˈɡæmbəl/ ●●○ *v* [I,T]
1 to risk money or possessions on the result of something such as a card game or a race, when you do not know for certain what the result will be → **bet**: *Their religion forbids them to drink or gamble.* | **[+on]** *Jack loves gambling on the horses.*
2 to do something that involves a lot of risk, and that will not succeed unless things happen the way you would like them to: **[+on]** *They're gambling on Johnson being fit for Saturday's game.* | **gamble sth on sth** *Potter gambled everything on his new play being a hit.* | **gamble that** *She was gambling that he wouldn't read it too carefully.* | **[+with]** *We can't relax our safety standards – we'd be gambling with people's lives.* —**gambler** *n* [C]: *Stevens was a* ***compulsive gambler***.

gamble sth ↔ **away** *phr v* to lose the whole of an amount of money by gambling: *Nielsen gambled his inheritance away.*

gamble² *n* [singular] an action or plan that involves a risk but that you hope will succeed: ***It was a*** *big* ***gamble*** *for her to leave the band and go solo.* | **[+on]** ***The gamble*** *on the harvest had paid off* (=succeeded). | *Ellen had to admit the* ***gamble*** *had* ***paid off*** (=succeeded). | *In a depressed market, we cannot afford to* ***take a gamble*** *on a new product.*

gam·bling /ˈɡæmblɪŋ/ ●●○ *n* [U] when people risk money or possessions on the result of something which is not certain, such as a card game or a horse race → **betting**: *The lottery is probably the most popular form of gambling.* | *gambling debts* | *The police raided a number of illegal* ***gambling dens*** (=places for illegal gambling).

gam·bol /ˈɡæmbəl/ *v* (**gambolled**, **gambolling** *BrE*, **gamboled**, **gamboling** *AmE*) [I] *literary* to jump or run around in a lively active way SYN **frolic**: *lambs gambolling in a field* —**gambol** *n* [C]

game¹ /ɡeɪm/ ●●● S1 W1 *n*
1 ACTIVITY OR SPORT [C] **a)** an activity or sport in which people compete with each other according to agreed rules: *We used to love playing games like chess or backgammon.* **b)** an occasion when a game is played → **match**: *Did you see the game on TV last night?* | **a game of tennis/football etc** *Would you like to have a game of tennis?* | **[+against/with]** *England's World Cup game against Holland* → BALL GAME, BOARD GAME, VIDEO GAME, WAR GAME
2 games [plural] **a)** a large organized sports event: *the Olympic Games* **b)** *BrE* organized sports as a school subject or lesson SYN **PE**: *We have games on Thursdays.* | *a games lesson*
3 PART OF A MATCH [C] one of the parts into which a single match is divided, for example in tennis or BRIDGE¹(4): *Graf leads, two games to one.*
4 CHILDREN [C] a children's activity in which they play with toys, pretend to be someone else etc: **[+of]** *a game of hide-and-seek* | *The boys were* ***playing*** *a* ***game*** *in the backyard.*
5 SKILL sb's game how well someone plays a particular game or sport: **improve/raise your game** *Liam's taking lessons to improve his game.* | *the strongest aspect of his game*
6 give the game away to spoil a surprise or secret by doing or saying something that lets someone guess what the secret is: *Lynn gave the game away by laughing when Kim walked in.*
7 beat sb at their own game (*also* **play sb at their own game** *BrE*) to beat someone or fight back against them by using the same methods that they use
8 NOT SERIOUS be a game to be something that you do to enjoy yourself rather than for a serious purpose: ***It's*** *just* ***a game*** *to them. They don't care what happens.*
9 play games (with sb) a) to behave in a dishonest or unfair way in order to get what you want: *Are you sure he's really interested, and not just* ***playing silly games*** *with you?* **b)** to not be serious about doing something: *We want a deal. We're not interested in playing games.*
10 ANIMALS/BIRDS [U] wild animals, birds, and fish that are hunted for food, especially as a sport: *game birds* → BIG GAME
11 the only game in town used to say that something is the only possible choice in a situation: *The Church of England is no longer the only game in town.*
12 BUSINESS [singular] *informal* an area of work or business: *I've been in this game for over ten years.*
13 what's her/your etc game? *BrE spoken* used to ask what the true reason for someone's behaviour is: *Reg is being very nice all of a sudden. What's his game?*
14 the game's up *spoken* used to tell someone that something wrong or dishonest that they have done has been discovered: *Come out, Don. The game's up.*
15 a game of chance a game in which you risk money on the result: *Poker is a game of chance.*
16 sb got game *AmE informal* used to say that someone is very skilful at doing something, especially a sport
17 be on the game *BrE informal* to be a PROSTITUTE
18 game on *spoken* said when the balance of a sports match or competition changes, and both sides suddenly have a chance of winning
19 game over *informal* said to emphasize that an event or activity is completely finished
20 make game of sb *old-fashioned* to make fun of someone → FAIR GAME, → **fun and games** at FUN¹(5), → **the name of the game** at NAME¹(10), → **a mug's game** at MUG¹(5)

G

COLLOCATIONS

VERBS

play a game *They explained how to play the game.*
see/watch a game *Did you see the game last night?*
have a game *BrE They were having a game of pool.*
win/lose a game *A.C. Milan won the game with a last-minute goal.*
the game is tied (=both teams or players had the same score) *The game was tied 10-10 at halftime.*
draw a game *BrE* (=end the game with the same score as the opposing team or player)

NOUN + game

a computer/video game *He was up all night playing computer games.*
a card game *Bridge is a card game for four people.*
a board/ball game *board games such as Monopoly and Scrabble*
a team game *I wasn't very good at team games when I was at school.*
a party game *What's your favourite party game?*
a basketball/baseball etc game | **a home game** (=played at a team's own sports field) | **an away game** (=played at an opposing team's sports field) | **a league game** (=played as part of a league competition) | **a cup game** (=played as part of a cup competition)

PHRASES

the rules of the game *It's against the rules of the game to pick up the ball.*

game² *adj* **1** willing to try something dangerous, new, or difficult: *Okay. I'm game if you are.* | **[+for]** *He's always game for a laugh.* | **game to do sth** *'Who's game to have a try?'* **2 game leg** *old-fashioned* an injured or painful leg —**gamely** *adv*

game³ /geɪm/ *v AmE* **game the system** to use rules or laws to get what you want in an unfair but legal way

game·chang·er /ˈgeɪmˌtʃeɪndʒə $ -ər/ *n* [C] *informal* something that completely changes a situation or activity: *This new electric car could be a real gamechanger for the industry.* —**game-changing** *adj*: *The economic crisis demands game-changing business strategies.*

game·keep·er /ˈgeɪmkiːpə $ -ər/ *n* [C] someone whose job is to look after wild animals and birds that are kept to be hunted on private land

gam·e·lan /ˈgæməlæn/ *n* [C] a group of Indonesian musicians who mainly play PERCUSSION instruments such as drums and GONGS

game·pad /ˈgeɪmpæd/ *n* [C] a piece of equipment held with both hands that you use to control a computer game or video game

ˈgame park *n* [C] a GAME RESERVE

ˈgame plan *n* [C] a plan for achieving success, especially in business or sports: *He has his game plan all worked out.*

game·play /ˈgeɪmpleɪ/ *n* [U] the way that a computer game is designed and the skills that you need to play it: *This is packed with brilliant graphics and gameplay.*

ˈgame ˌpoint *n* [C,U] the situation in a game such as tennis in which one player will win the game if they win the next point → **match point**

gam·er /ˈgeɪmə $ -ər/ *n* [C] *informal* **1** someone who plays computer games **2** *AmE* a person who is very good at a sport and helps their team to win games

ˈgame reˌserve (*also* **ˈgame preˌserve** *AmE*) *n* [C] a large area of land that is designed for wild animals to live in safely

ˈgames ˌconsole, **game console** *n* [C] an electronic machine that is used for playing games on a screen: *They're bringing out a new games console this Christmas.*

ˈgame show *n* [C] a television programme in which people play games or answer questions to win prizes

games·man·ship /ˈgeɪmzmənʃɪp/ *n* [U] the ability to succeed by using the rules of a game or activity to your own advantage

gam·ete /ˈgæmiːt/ *n* [C] *technical* a type of cell which joins with another cell, starting the development of a baby or other young creature

ˈgame ˌwarden *n* [C] someone whose job is to look after wild animals in a GAME RESERVE

gam·ey, **gamy** /ˈgeɪmi/ *adj* having the strong taste of wild animals that are hunted for food

gam·i·fi·ca·tion /geɪməfəˈkeɪʃən/ *n* [U] the designing of an activity such as learning, solving a problem, or being a customer so that it is like a game

ga·mine /ˈgæmiːn/ *n* [C] *literary* a small thin girl or woman who looks like a boy —**gamine** *adj*: *a gamine hairstyle*

gam·ing /ˈgeɪmɪŋ/ *n* [U] **1** *informal* the activity of playing computer games: *online gaming* **2** *old-fashioned* the activity of playing cards or other games of chance for money SYN **gambling**: *gaming tables*

gam·ma /ˈgæmə/ *n* [C] the third letter of the Greek alphabet

ˈgamma ray *n* [C usually plural] a beam of light with a short WAVELENGTH, that can pass through solid objects —**ˌgamma radiˈation** *n* [U]

gam·mon /ˈgæmən/ *n* [U] *BrE* meat from a pig's leg, preserved using salt → **bacon**: *gammon steak*

gam·my /ˈgæmi/ *adj BrE old-fashioned* a gammy leg or knee is injured or painful

gam·ut /ˈgæmət/ *n* [singular] the complete range of possibilities: **[+of]** *College life opened up a* ***whole gamut*** *of new experiences.* | *Her feelings that day* ***ran the gamut*** *of emotions* (=included all the possibilities between two extremes).

gam·y /ˈgeɪmi/ *adj* another spelling of GAMEY

gan·der /ˈgændə $ -ər/ *n* [C] **1** a male GOOSE¹ **2 have/take a gander at sth** *spoken* to look at something

G & T /ˌdʒiː ən ˈtiː/ *n* [C,U] (***gin and tonic***) a popular alcoholic drink served with ice and a thin piece of LEMON

gang¹ /gæŋ/ ●●● S3 *n* [C]

1 a) a group of young people who spend time together, and who are often involved in crime or drugs and who often fight against other groups: *two rival* ***street gangs*** | **gang member/member of a gang** *The parents have denied that their son is a gang member.* | *the problem of inner-city gang violence* | *a victim of* ***gang warfare*** **b)** a group of young people together in one place, especially young people who might cause trouble: **[+of]** *There were always gangs of kids hanging around the mall.* THESAURUS ▸ GROUP

2 a group of criminals who work together: *Several gangs were operating in the area.* | ***Armed gangs*** *have hijacked lorries.* | **[+of]** *a gang of smugglers*

3 *informal* a group of friends, especially young people: *The whole gang will be there next weekend.*

4 a group of workers or prisoners doing physical work together → **CHAIN GANG**

gang² *v*

gang together *phr v* if people gang together, they form a group in order to do something together, especially to oppose something: *The smaller shopkeepers ganged together to beat off competition from the supermarkets.*

gang up on/against sb *phr v* if people gang up on someone, they join together to attack, criticize, or oppose them, especially in a way that seems unfair: *Schoolchildren are quick to gang up on anyone who looks or behaves differently.*

ˈgang-ˌbang *n* [C] **1** *informal* an occasion when several people have sex with each other at the same time **2** a GANG RAPE —**gang-bang** *v* [I,T]

gang·bust·ers /ˈgæŋˌbʌstəz $ -ərz/ *n* **like gangbusters** *AmE informal* very eagerly and with a lot of energy, or very quickly: *They were going like gangbusters, then all of a sudden everything went wrong.*

gang·land /ˈgæŋlænd, -lənd/ *adj* **a gangland killing/murder/shooting etc** a killing etc relating to the world of organized and violent crime: *Sharp may have been the victim of a gangland revenge killing.*

gan·gling /ˈgæŋglɪŋ/ *adj* unusually tall and thin, and not able to move gracefully SYN **lanky**: *an awkward gangling teenager*

gan·gli·on /ˈgæŋgliən/ *n* [C] *technical* **1** a painful raised area of skin that is full of liquid, often on the back of your wrist **2** a mass of nerve cells

gan·gly /ˈgæŋgli/ *adj* another form of GANGLING

gang·mas·ter /ˈgæŋˌmɑːstə $ -ˌmæstər/ *n* [C] *BrE* someone who is in charge of a large group of foreign LABOURERS (=people who work outdoors, using their physical strength), especially labourers who do not have official permission to work in Britain

gang·plank /ˈgæŋplæŋk/ *n* [C] a board for walking on between a boat and the shore, or between two boats

ˈgang ˌrape *n* [C] an occasion when several men attack a woman and force her to have sex with them

gan·grene /ˈgæŋgriːn/ *n* [U] a condition in which your flesh decays in part of your body, because blood has stopped flowing there as a result of illness or injury —**gangrenous** /-grɪnəs/ *adj*

gang·sta /ˈgæŋstʌ/ *n* [C] *AmE informal* someone who is a member of a GANG: *gangstas in South Central L.A.*

ˈgangsta ˌrap *n* [U] a type of RAP music with words about drugs, violence, and life in poor areas of cities —**gangsta rapper** *n* [C]

gang·ster /ˈgæŋstə $ -ər/ ●○○ *n* [C] a member of a violent group of criminals

gang·way /ˈgæŋweɪ/ *n* [C] **1** a space between two rows of seats in a theatre, bus, or train SYN **aisle 2** a large board or steps between a boat and the shore for people to walk down **3 gangway!** *spoken* used to tell people in a crowd to let someone go through

gan·ja /ˈgændʒə/ *n* [U] *informal* MARIJUANA

gan·net /ˈgænɪt/ *n* [C] **1** a large sea bird that lives in large groups on cliffs **2** *BrE informal* someone who eats a lot

gan·try /ˈgæntri/ *n* (*plural* **gantries**) [C] a large metal frame which is used to support heavy machinery or railway signals

gaol /dʒeɪl/ *n, v* a British spelling of JAIL THESAURUS PRISON

gaol·bird /ˈdʒeɪlbɜːd $ -bɜːrd/ *n* [C] a British spelling of JAILBIRD

gaol·er /ˈdʒeɪlə $ -ər/ *n* [C] a British spelling of JAILER

gap /gæp/ ●●● S2 W2 *n* [C]

1 A SPACE a space between two objects or two parts of an object, especially because something is missing: **[+in]** *The neighbors' dog got in through a gap in the hedge.* | *a gap in the traffic* | **[+between]** *the gap between the two rows of seats* → see picture at HOLE THESAURUS HOLE

2 DIFFERENCE a big difference between two situations, amounts, groups of people etc → **gulf**: **[+between]** *the widening gap between the rich and the poor* → GENERATION GAP

3 STH MISSING something missing that stops something else from being good or complete: **[+in]** *There are huge gaps in my knowledge of history.* | *Frank's death has left a big gap in my life.* | **fill/plug the gap** *He filled the gap left by Hirst's retirement.*

4 IN TIME a period of time when nothing is happening, that exists between two other periods of time when something is happening: **[+in]** *an awkward gap in the conversation* | **[+between]** *The gaps between his visits got longer and longer.* → GAP YEAR

5 IN A MOUNTAIN a low place between two higher parts of a mountain

6 gap in the market a product or service that does not exist, so that there is an opportunity to develop that product or service and sell it

COLLOCATIONS – MEANING 2

ADJECTIVES/NOUN + gap

a big/large/wide gap *There's a big gap between the two test scores.*
a narrow gap *There's only a narrow gap between the two candidates in the polls.*
a yawning gap (=a very big difference) | **a growing/widening gap** | **a trade gap** (=the difference between the amount a country imports and exports) | **the generation gap** (=the difference in attitudes, tastes etc between older and younger people) | **an age gap** (=a difference in age between two people)

VERBS

bridge/close/narrow the gap (=reduce the amount or importance of a difference) *The book aims to bridge the gap between theory and practice.*
the gap narrows *Polls show the gap between the two candidates has narrowed.*
widen the gap | **the gap widens**

gape /geɪp/ *v* [I] **1** to look at something for a long time, especially with your mouth open, because you are very surprised or shocked SYN **stare**: **[+at]** *What are all these people gaping at?* THESAURUS LOOK **2** (*also* **gape open**) to open widely or be wide open: *Dan stood at the door, his shirt gaping open.*

gap·ing /ˈgeɪpɪŋ/ *adj* [only before noun] a gaping hole, wound, or mouth is very wide and open

ˌgap-ˈtoothed *adj* [usually before noun] having wide spaces between your teeth: **gap-toothed smile/grin**

ˈgap year *n* [C] *BrE* a year between leaving school and going to university, which some young people use as an opportunity to travel, earn money, or get experience of working: *Some students choose to work in high-tech industries during their gap year.*

gar·age¹ /ˈgærɪdʒ, -ɑːʒ $ gəˈrɑːʒ/ ●●● S2 *n*

1 [C] a building for keeping a car in, usually next to or attached to a house → **carport**: *I'll just go and put the car in the garage.* | **a double/single/two-car/one-car garage** *Their house had a **double garage**.* | *an automatic garage door*

2 [C] (*also* **parking garage** *especially AmE*) a building in a public place where cars can be parked: *We parked in an **underground garage** near the hotel.*

3 [C] a place where motor vehicles are repaired: *My car's at the garage.*

4 [C] *BrE* a place where you buy petrol SYN **petrol station, gas station** *AmE*

5 [U] a type of popular music played on electronic instruments, with a strong fast beat and singing: *a collection of the latest dance and garage hits*

garage² *v* [T] to put or keep a vehicle in a garage

ˈgarage ˌband / $.ˈ. ˌ./ *n* [C] a group of musicians who play ROCK music and practise in a garage

ˈgarage ˌsale / $.ˈ. ˌ./ *n* [C] *AmE* a sale of used furniture, clothes etc from people's houses, usually held in or near someone's garage

ga·ram ma·sa·la /ˌgɑːrəm məˈsɑːlə, -mɑː-/ *n* [U] a mixture of SPICES which gives a hot taste to food, used especially in Indian cooking

garb /gɑːb $ gɑːrb/ *n* [U] *formal* a particular style of clothing, especially clothes that show your type of work or look unusual: *priestly garb*

gar·bage /ˈgɑːbɪdʒ $ ˈgɑːr-/ ●●● S3 *n* [U]

1 *especially AmE* waste material, such as paper, empty containers, and food thrown away SYN **rubbish** *BrE*: *Can you **take out the garbage** when you go?*

2 stupid words, ideas etc SYN **rubbish** *BrE*: *You're talking garbage.*

3 garbage in, garbage out used to say that if the DATA (=information) you put into a computer is bad, the results you get back will be bad, even if the computer program you use works properly

ˈgarbage ˌcan *n* [C] *AmE* a container with a lid for

G

holding waste until it can be taken away SYN **dustbin** *BrE* → see picture at BIN

ˈgarbage colˌlector *n* [C] *AmE* someone whose job is to remove waste from garbage cans SYN **dustman** *BrE*

ˈgarbage disˌposal *n* [C] *AmE* a small machine in the kitchen SINK which breaks vegetable waste into small pieces so that it washes down the DRAIN of the sink SYN **waste disposal** *BrE*

ˈgarbage man *n* [C] *AmE* a garbage collector

ˈgarbage ˌtruck *n* [C] *AmE* a large vehicle which goes from house to house to collect the contents of garbage cans SYN **dust cart** *BrE*

gar·ban·zo /ɡɑːˈbænzəʊ $ ɡɑːrˈbɑːnzoʊ/ (*also* **garˈbanzo ˌbean**) *n* (*plural* **garbanzos**) [C] *AmE* a CHICKPEA

garbed /ɡɑːbd $ ɡɑːrbd/ *adj* **be garbed in sth** *literary* to be dressed in a particular type of clothing: *singers garbed in costumes of gold*

gar·bled /ˈɡɑːbəld $ ˈɡɑːr-/ *adj* a garbled statement or report is very unclear and confusing SYN **confused**: *The papers had some garbled version of the story.* | *a garbled phone message* —**garble** *v* [T] —**garble** *n* [U]

gar·çon /ˈɡɑːsɒn $ ɡɑːrˈsoʊn/ *n* [C] *BrE* a waiter in a French restaurant

GARDEN EQUIPMENT

gar·den¹ /ˈɡɑːdn $ ˈɡɑːr-/ ●●● S1 W1 *n*
1 [C] *BrE* the area of land next to a house, where there are flowers, grass, and other plants, and often a place for people to sit SYN **yard** *AmE*: *He's outside in the garden.* | *Grace brought us some flowers from her garden.* | **back/front garden** (=at the back or front of the house)
2 [C] a part of the area next to a house, which has plants and flowers in it: *The house has a beautiful herb garden.*
3 gardens [plural] a large area of land where plants and flowers are grown so that the public can go and see them: *the **Botanical Gardens** at Kew*
4 Gardens *BrE* used in the name of streets: *211 Roland Gardens* → KITCHEN GARDEN, MARKET GARDEN, → **lead sb up the garden path** at LEAD¹(12)

garden² *v* [I] to work in a garden, keeping it clean, growing plants etc

ˈgarden ˌcentre *n* [C] *BrE* a place that sells plants, flowers, and equipment for gardens SYN **nursery** *AmE*

ˌgarden ˈcity *n* [C] *BrE* a town that has been designed to have a lot of trees, areas of grass, and open spaces

gar·den·er /ˈɡɑːdnə $ ˈɡɑːrdnər/ ●●○ *n* [C]
1 someone whose job is to work in gardens
2 someone who enjoys growing flowers and plants: *Mom has always been a good gardener.*

gar·de·ni·a /ɡɑːˈdiːniə $ ɡɑːr-/ *n* [C] a large white pleasant-smelling flower that grows on a bush

gar·den·ing /ˈɡɑːdnɪŋ $ ˈɡɑːr-/ *n* [U] the activity of working in a garden, growing plants, cutting a LAWN etc → **horticulture**: *I might **do** a bit of **gardening** this afternoon.* | **gardening gloves/tools/equipment etc** → see picture at GLOVE

ˌGarden of ˈEngland, the a name for the COUNTY of Kent in southeast England, because of the fruit and vegetables it produces

ˈgarden ˌparty *n* [C] *BrE* a formal party for a lot of people which is held in a large garden in the afternoon

ˈgarden-vaˌriety *adj* [only before noun] *especially AmE* very ordinary and not very interesting: *This is not one of your garden-variety cases of fraud.*

gar·gan·tu·an /ɡɑːˈɡæntʃuən $ ɡɑːr-/ *adj written* extremely large SYN **gigantic**: *a meal of gargantuan proportions* | *gargantuan task*

gar·gle¹ /ˈɡɑːɡəl $ ˈɡɑːr-/ *v* [I] to clean the inside of your mouth and throat by blowing air through water or medicine in the back of your throat: **[+with]** *Gargling with salt water may help your sore throat.*

gargle² *n* **1** [C,U] liquid that you gargle with SYN **mouthwash 2 a gargle** the act of gargling

gar·goyle /ˈɡɑːɡɔɪl $ ˈɡɑːr-/ *n* [C] a stone figure of a strange and ugly creature, that carries rain water from the roof of an old building, especially a church

gar·ish /ˈɡeərɪʃ $ ˈɡer-/ *adj* very brightly coloured in a way that is unpleasant to look at SYN **brash** OPP **subtle**: *Many of the rugs are too garish for my taste.* | *garish colors* THESAURUS COLOUR —**garishly** *adv*: *a garishly painted house* —**garishness** *n* [U]

gar·land¹ /ˈɡɑːlənd $ ˈɡɑːr-/ *n* [C] a ring of flowers or leaves, worn on your head or around your neck for decoration or for a special ceremony → **wreath**: **[+of]** *garlands of flowers* → see picture at BOUQUET

garland² *v* [T] *literary* to decorate someone or something, especially with flowers SYN **festoon**: **be garlanded with sth** *The tree was garlanded with strings of coloured lights.*

gar·lic /ˈɡɑːlɪk $ ˈɡɑːr-/ ●●○ S3 *n* [U] a plant like a small onion, used in cooking to give a strong taste: *Add a crushed **clove of garlic*** (=single section of it). —**garlicky** *adj*: *his garlicky breath* → see picture at VEGETABLE

ˈgarlic ˌpress *n* [C] a tool used to crush garlic

gar·ment /ˈɡɑːmənt $ ˈɡɑːr-/ ●●○ *n* [C] *formal* a piece of clothing: *She pulled the garment on and zipped it up.* | **garment industry/factory/district etc** *She works in the garment district of Manhattan.* | **outer/upper garment** | *The outer garment was a loose-fitting robe.* → UNDERGARMENT

REGISTER
Garment is used in business contexts, especially in American English, to talk about the business of making and selling clothes. In everyday English, people usually say **clothes** (plural): *What kind of **clothes** was she wearing?*

ˈgarment ˌbag *n* [C] a special bag used to carry clothes such as suits and dresses: *I packed the dresses in a black garment bag.*

gar·ner /ˈɡɑːnə $ ˈɡɑːrnər/ *v* [T] *formal* to take or collect something, especially information or support → **glean**: *The party garnered 70 percent of the vote.*

gar·net /ˈɡɑːnɪt $ ˈɡɑːr-/ *n* **1** [C] a dark red stone used as a jewel **2** [U] a dark red colour

gar·nish¹ /ˈɡɑːnɪʃ $ ˈɡɑːr-/ *n* [C] a small amount of food such as SALAD or fruit that you place on food to decorate it

G

garnish² *v* [T] to add something to food in order to decorate it: **garnish sth with sth** *Garnish each dish with a slice of lemon.*

gar·ret /ˈgærɪt/ *n* [C] a small uncomfortable room at the top of a house, just under the roof → **attic**

gar·ri·son¹ /ˈgærəsən/ *n* [C] **1** a group of soldiers living in a town or FORT and defending it: *The garrison was called out when news of the enemy's advance was received.* | *a garrison town* **2** the buildings where a garrison of soldiers live

garrison² *v* [T] to send a group of soldiers to defend or guard a place: *Our regiment will garrison the town.*

gar·rotte /gəˈrɒt $ gəˈrɑːt/ *v* [T] to kill someone by pulling a metal collar or wire tightly around their neck → **strangle** —**garrotte** *n* [C]

gar·ru·lous /ˈgærələs/ *adj* always talking a lot SYN **talkative**: *Ian isn't normally this garrulous!* —**garrulously** *adv* —**garrulousness** *n* [U]

gar·ter /ˈgɑːtə $ ˈgɑːrtər/ *n* [C] **1** a band of ELASTIC (=material that stretches) worn around your leg to keep a sock or STOCKING up **2** *AmE* one of four pieces of elastic fixed to a woman's underwear and to her stockings to hold them up SYN **suspender** *BrE*

ˈgarter ˌbelt *n* [C] *AmE* a piece of women's underwear with garters hanging down from it which fasten onto STOCKINGS and hold them up SYN **suspender belt** *BrE*

ˈgarter ˌsnake *n* [C] a harmless American snake with lines of colour along its back

gas¹ /gæs/ ●●● S1 W2 *n* (*plural* **gases** *or* **gasses**)
1 [C,U] a substance such as air, which is not solid or liquid, and usually cannot be seen: *hydrogen gas* | **toxic/poisonous/noxious gases** *a cloud of toxic gas* | **a gas cylinder/bottle** (=for storing gas) → **GREENHOUSE GAS**
2 [U] a clear substance like air that is burned for heating or cooking: **gas cooker/stove/oven** *Can you light the gas for me?* | *The explosion was caused by a* ***gas leak*** *from the water heater.*
3 gas mark 4/5/6 etc *BrE* a measurement of the temperature of a gas OVEN
4 [U] *AmE* (*also* **gasoline**) a liquid made from PETROLEUM, used mainly for producing power in the engines of cars, trucks etc SYN **petrol** *BrE*: *I probably spend over $200 a month on gas.* | *The mechanic found a hole in the* ***gas tank***.
5 the gas *AmE* the gas PEDAL of a car SYN **accelerator**: *We* ***stepped on the gas*** (=pushed down the gas pedal and made the car go faster) *and sped away.*
6 [U] a clear substance like air that is used for medical reasons, for example to make people feel less pain or make them sleep during an operation: *an anaesthetic gas* → **LAUGHING GAS**
7 [U] a type of gas used as a weapon, because it harms or kills people when they breathe it in: *mustard gas* → **NERVE GAS, POISON GAS, TEAR GAS**
8 [U] *AmE informal* the condition of having a lot of air in your stomach SYN **wind** *BrE*
9 a gas *AmE old-fashioned spoken* something that is fun and makes you laugh a lot

gas² *v* (**gassed**, **gassing**) **1** [T] to poison or kill someone with gas **2** [I] *BrE informal* to talk for a long time about unimportant or boring things SYN **chat**: *They were just gassing away.*
gas up *phr v AmE* to put petrol in a car: *We'd better gas up before we go.* | **gas sth ↔ up** *George gassed up the car.*

gas·bag /ˈgæsbæg/ *n* [C] *informal* someone who talks too much SYN **windbag**

ˈgas ˌchamber *n* [C] a large room in which people or animals are killed with poisonous gas

gas·e·ous /ˈgæsiəs $ ˈgæsiəs, -ʃəs/ *adj* like gas or in the form of gas

ˈgas-fired *adj especially BrE* using gas as a fuel: *a gas-fired central heating system*

ˈgas-ˌguzzler *n* [C] *AmE informal* a car that uses a lot of petrol —**gas-guzzling** *adj*

gash /gæʃ/ *n* [C] a large deep cut or hole in something, for example in a person's skin: *Blood poured from a* ***deep gash*** *in her forehead.* **THESAURUS** ▸ **INJURY** —**gash** *v* [T]: *One day Frank gashed his hand on a bit of broken glass.*

gas·hold·er /ˈgæsˌhəʊldə $ -ˌhoʊldər/ *n* [C] *BrE* a very large round metal container or building from which gas is carried in pipes to buildings

gas·ket /ˈgæskɪt/ *n* [C] **1** a flat piece of material, often rubber, placed between two surfaces so that steam, oil, gas etc cannot escape **2 blow a gasket a)** if a vehicle blows a gasket, steam or gas escapes from the engine **b)** *informal* to become very angry

gas·light /ˈgæs-laɪt/ *n* **1** [U] the light produced from burning gas **2** [C] (*also* **gas lamp**) a lamp in a house or on the street which gives light from burning gas

gas·man /ˈgæsmæn/ *n* (*plural* **gasmen** /-men/) [C] *BrE informal* someone whose job is to come to your home to see how much gas you have used or to repair your gas system

ˈgas mask *n* [C] a piece of equipment worn over your face to protect you from poisonous gases → see picture at **MASK**

ˈgas ˌmeter *n* [C] a piece of equipment that measures how much gas is used in a building

gas·o·hol /ˈgæsəhɒl $ -hɒːl/ *n* [U] *AmE* petrol with a small amount of alcohol in it, which can be used in cars and is cheaper than petrol

gas·o·line /ˈgæsəliːn/ ●●○ S3 W3 *n* [U] *AmE* a liquid obtained from PETROLEUM, used mainly for producing power in the engines of cars, trucks etc SYN **petrol** *BrE*

gas·om·e·ter /gæˈsɒmɪtə $ -ˈsɑːmɪtər/ *n* [C] *BrE* a GASHOLDER

gasp¹ /gɑːsp $ gæsp/ ●○○ *v*
1 [I,T] to breathe in suddenly in a way that can be heard, especially because you are surprised or in pain: **[+in/with]** *Ollie gasped with pain and slumped forward.* | **[+at]** *The audience gasped at the splendour of the costumes.* | *'My leg!' he gasped. 'I think it's broken!'* **THESAURUS** ▸ **BREATHE**
2 [I] to breathe quickly in a way that can be heard because you are having difficulty breathing → **pant**: **gasp for air/breath** *Brendan climbed slowly, gasping for breath.*
3 be gasping (for sth) *BrE spoken* to feel that you urgently need something such as a drink or cigarette: *I'm gasping for a pint!*

gasp² ●○○ *n* [C]
1 when you take in a breath suddenly in a way that can be heard, especially because you are surprised or in pain: **[+of]** *With a gasp of pure horror, Lewis jumped up and ran.* | *She* ***gave a*** *little* ***gasp*** *and clutched George's hand.*
2 when you breathe in air quickly because you are having difficulty breathing: *Her breath came in shallow gasps.*
3 sb's/sth's last gasp the time when someone is about to die, or when something is about to stop happening or existing: *the last gasp of an industry in decline*

ˈgas ˌpedal *n* [C] *AmE* the thing that you press with your foot to make a car go faster SYN **accelerator** → see picture at **CAR**

ˈgas ring *n* [C] *BrE* a metal ring that gets hot when gas passes through it, used for cooking food SYN **burner** *AmE*

ˈgas ˌstation *n* [C] *AmE* a place where you can buy petrol and oil for motor vehicles SYN **petrol station** *BrE*

gas·sy /ˈgæsi/ *adj BrE* a gassy drink has too much gas in it → **fizzy**: *This beer is really gassy.*

gas·tric /ˈgæstrɪk/ *adj* [only before noun] *technical* **1** relating to your stomach: *gastric ulcers* **2 gastric juices** the acids in your stomach that break food into smaller parts **3 gastric flu** an illness that makes you VOMIT and gives you DIARRHOEA **4 gastric bypass** a medical operation done to treat a fat person, in which the top part of the stomach is divided from the rest of it and connected to the middle of the SMALL INTESTINE **5 gastric band** a band that is put around someone's stomach, so that they feel full and eat less

gas·tri·tis /gæˈstraɪtɪs/ *n* [U] *medical* an illness which makes the inside of your stomach become swollen, so that you feel a burning pain

gas·tro·en·te·ri·tis /ˌgæstrəʊ-entəˈraɪtɪs $ -troʊ-/ *n* [U] *medical* a painful illness which makes your stomach and INTESTINE become swollen

gas·tro·in·tes·tin·al /ˌgæstrəʊɪnˈtestɪnəl $ -troʊ-/ *adj* *medical* of or relating to the stomach and INTESTINES

gas·tro·nom·ic /ˌgæstrəˈnɒmɪk◂ $ -ˈnɑː-/ *adj* [only before noun] *formal* relating to the art of cooking good food or the pleasure of eating it: *the gastronomic delights of Thailand* —**gastronomically** /-kli/ *adv*

gas·tron·o·my /gæˈstrɒnəmi $ gæˈstrɑː-/ *n* [U] *formal* the art and science of cooking and eating good food

gas·tro·pub /ˈgæstrəʊpʌb $ -troʊ-/ *n* [C] *BrE* a PUB that serves very good food

ˌgas ˈturbine *n* [C] an engine in which a wheel of special blades is driven round at high speed by hot gases, producing a lot of power: *the ship's four gas turbine engines*

gas·works /ˈgæswɜːks $ -wɜːrks/ *n* (*plural* **gasworks**) [C] a place where gas is made from coal so that it can be used to produce heat and energy

gate¹ /geɪt/ ●●● (S2) (W2) *n*
1 [C] the part of a fence or outside wall that you can open and close so that you can enter or leave a place → **door**: *We went through the gate into the orchard.* | *the wrought-iron gates of the palace* | **open/close/shut a gate** *I left the engine running and ran back to close the gate.* | **front/back/main gate** *Make sure that the back gate is locked, please.* | **garden/farm/school gate** *The children poured out of the school gates.*
2 [C] the place where you leave an airport building to get on a plane: *Air France flight 76 leaves from gate 6A.*
3 a) [C] *BrE* the number of people who go in to see a sports event, especially a football match **b)** [U] *BrE* (*also* **gate money**) the amount of money that these people pay

gate² *v* [T] *BrE* to prevent a student from leaving a school as a punishment for behaving badly

-gate /geɪt/ *suffix* used after the name of a place, person, or thing to give a name to an event involving dishonest behaviour by a politician or other public official: *Irangate* (=when members of the US government sold weapons to Iran in exchange for the return of American hostages)

gâ·teau /ˈgætəʊ $ gæˈtoʊ/ *n* (*plural* **gâteaux** /-təʊz $ -ˈtoʊz/) [C,U] *BrE* a large sweet cake, often filled and decorated with cream, fruit, chocolate etc → see picture at DESSERT

gate·crash /ˈgeɪtkræʃ/ *v* [I,T] to go to a party that you have not been invited to —**gatecrasher** *n* [C]

ˌgated comˈmunity *n* [C] *AmE* an area of houses and sometimes also shops, tennis courts etc, where a fence or wall surrounds the area and the entrance is guarded

gate·house /ˈgeɪthaʊs/ *n* [C] a small building next to the gate of a park or at the entrance to the land surrounding a big house

gate·keep·er /ˈgeɪtˌkiːpə $ -ər/ *n* [C] **1** someone whose job is to open and close a gate, and to allow or not allow people to go through it **2** someone in an organization who has a lot of influence over what products the organization buys, who it buys them from etc **3** someone in an organization who tells customers or people with questions which people in the organization should be able to help them

gate·post /ˈgeɪtpəʊst $ -poʊst/ *n* [C] **1** one of two strong upright poles set in the ground to support a gate **2 between you, me, and the gatepost** *BrE spoken* used to say that you are going to tell someone your opinion, but you want it to be a secret

gate·way /ˈgeɪt-weɪ/ ●○○ *n*
1 [C] the opening in a fence, wall etc that can be closed by a gate
2 gateway to sth a) a place, especially a city, that you can go through in order to reach another much bigger place: *St. Louis is the gateway to the West.* **b)** a way of achieving something: *To me a home in the country is a gateway to happiness.*
3 [C] a way of connecting two computer NETWORKS

ˈgateway ˌdrug *n* [C] a drug such as CANNABIS which is not very dangerous, but which some people believe leads to the use of more dangerous drugs such as HEROIN

gath·er¹ /ˈgæðə $ -ər/ ●●● (S3) (W2) *v*
1 COME TOGETHER [I,T] to come together and form a group, or to make people do this: *A* ***crowd gathered*** *to watch the fight.* | *Thousands of people gathered outside the embassy.* | **[+around/round]** *Gather round, everyone, so that you can see the screen.* | *During the air raids, we gathered the children around us and sang songs.* | **[+together]** *Could the bride's family all gather together for a photo?* | **be gathered** *Dozens of photographers were gathered outside Jagger's villa.* **THESAURUS▸** MEET
2 KNOW/THINK [I,T not in progressive] to believe that something is true because of what you have seen or heard (SYN) **understand**: *You two know each other, I gather.* | **gather (that)** *I gather you've had some problems with our sales department.* | **from what I can gather/as far as I can gather** (=this is what I believe to be true) *She's his niece, from what I can gather.*
3 COLLECT [I,T] to get things from different places and put them together in one place: *The researcher's job is to gather information about people.* | *They had gathered 440,000 signatures to support their demand.* | **[+up/together]** *Debbie gathered up the clothes.* **THESAURUS▸** COLLECT
4 gather speed/force/momentum etc to move faster, become stronger, get more support etc: *The cart gathered speed as it coasted down the hill.* | *The international relief effort appears to be gathering momentum.*
5 gather dust if something gathers dust, it is not being used: *books just gathering dust on the shelf*
6 CLOTH [T] **a)** to pull material into small folds: *The skirt is gathered at the waist.* **b)** to pull material or a piece of clothing closer to you: *Moira gathered her skirts round her and climbed the steps.*
7 gather yourself/your strength/your thoughts to prepare yourself for something you are going to do, especially something difficult: *I took a few moments to gather my thoughts before going into the meeting.*
8 CLOUDS/DARKNESS [I] *literary* to gradually become more cloudy or get darker: *Storm* ***clouds*** *were* ***gathering*** *so we hurried home.* | **the gathering darkness/dusk/shadows etc** *the evening's gathering shadows*
9 gather sb to you/gather sb up *literary* to take someone into your arms and hold them in order to protect them or show them love

gather² *n* [C] a small fold produced by pulling cloth together

gath·er·er /ˈgæðərə $ -ər/ *n* [C] someone who gathers something: *information gatherers*

gath·er·ing /ˈgæðərɪŋ/ ●○○ *n* [C]
1 a meeting of a group of people: *a select gathering of 20 or 30 people*
2 intelligence/information etc gathering the process of collecting information from many different places
3 a fold or group of folds in cloth

ga·tor /ˈgeɪtə $ -ər/ *n* [C] *AmE informal* an ALLIGATOR

gauche /gəʊʃ $ goʊʃ/ *adj* doing or saying wrong or impolite things, especially because you do not know the right way to behave: *It would be gauche to mention the price.* —**gaucheness** *n* [U]

gau·cho /ˈgaʊtʃəʊ $ -tʃoʊ/ *n* (*plural* **gauchos**) [C] a South American COWBOY

gau·dy /ˈgɔːdi $ ˈgɒːdi/ *adj* clothes, colours etc that are gaudy are too bright and look cheap – used to show disapproval: *gaudy jewelry* **THESAURUS▸** COLOUR —**gaudily** *adv* —**gaudiness** *n* [U]

gauge¹ (*also* **gage** *AmE*) /geɪdʒ/ ●○○ *n* [C]
1 INSTRUMENT an instrument for measuring the size or amount of something: **fuel/temperature/pressure etc gauge** *The petrol gauge is still on full.*
2 WIDTH/THICKNESS a measurement of the width or thickness of something such as wire or metal: *a 27-gauge needle* | *heavy-gauge black polythene*

GAUGE

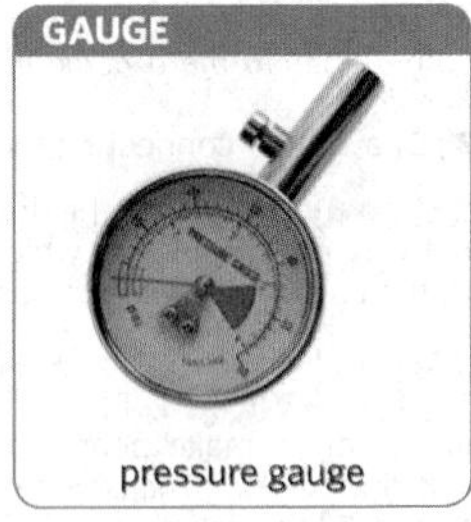

pressure gauge

3 a gauge of sth something that helps you make a judgment about a person or situation: *Retail sales are a gauge of consumer spending.* | *The tests will give parents a gauge of how their children are doing.*
4 RAILWAY the distance between the lines of a railway or between the wheels of a train: *a* ***standard gauge*** *railway* | **broad/narrow gauge** (=with more/less than the standard distance between the rails)
5 GUN the width of the BARREL of a gun: *a 12-gauge shotgun*

gauge² ●○○ *v* [T]
1 to judge how people feel about something or what they are likely to do: **[+whether/what/how etc]** *It is difficult to gauge what the other party's next move will be.* | *I looked at Chris, trying to gauge his reaction.*
2 to measure or calculate something by using a particular instrument or method: *The thermostat will gauge the temperature and control the heat.*

gaunt /gɔːnt $ gɒːnt/ *adj* **1** very thin and pale, especially because of illness or continued worry SYN **drawn**: *the old man's gaunt face* THESAURUS THIN **2** *literary* a building, mountain etc that is gaunt looks very plain and unpleasant: *a gaunt cathedral* —**gauntness** *n* [U]

gaunt·let /ˈgɔːntlɪt $ ˈgɒːnt-/ *n* **1 throw down the gauntlet** to invite someone to fight or compete over a disagreement **2 pick up/take up the gauntlet** to accept the invitation to fight or compete over a disagreement **3 run the gauntlet** to be criticized or attacked by a lot of people: *The foreign secretary ran the gauntlet of demonstrators.* **4** [C] a long GLOVE that covers someone's wrist and protects their hand, for example in a factory **5** [C] a GLOVE covered in metal, used for protection by soldiers in the past

gauze /gɔːz $ gɒːz/ *n* [U] **1** very thin transparent material with very small holes in it **2** (*also* **gauze bandage** *AmE*) thin cotton with very small holes in it that is used for tying around a wound: *His hands were wrapped in gauze bandages.* → see picture at FIRST AID KIT **3** a material made of thin threads of metal or plastic: *They covered the tubes with wire gauze.* —**gauzy** *adj*: *a gauzy white dress*

gave /geɪv/ *v* the past tense of GIVE

gav·el /ˈgævəl/ *n* [C] a small hammer that the person in charge of a meeting, court of law, AUCTION etc hits on a table in order to get people's attention

gawd /gɔːd $ gɒːd/ *interjection informal* used in writing to represent the word 'God' when it is said in this way as an expression of surprise, fear etc

gawk /gɔːk $ gɒːk/ *v* [I] *informal* to look at something for a long time, in a way that looks stupid SYN **stare**: **[+at]** *Don't just stand there gawking at those girls!*

gaw·ky /ˈgɔːki $ ˈgɒːki/ *adj* someone who is gawky moves or behaves in an awkward way SYN **clumsy**: *a gawky long-legged teenager* —**gawkiness** *n* [U]

gawp /gɔːp $ gɒːp/ *v* [I] *BrE informal* to look at something for a long time, especially with your mouth open because you are surprised → **gape**: **[+at]** *I was carried out on a stretcher, with everyone gawping at me.*

gay¹ /geɪ/ ●●○ S3 W3 *adj*
1 if someone, especially a man, is gay, they are sexually attracted to people of the same sex SYN **homosexual** → **straight**, **lesbian**: *the* ***gay community*** *in London* | *gay men and lesbians* | *a gay bar* | *a campaigner for* ***gay rights*** (=equal treatment for gay people)
2 *old-fashioned* bright or attractive: *gay colours*
3 *old-fashioned* cheerful and excited: *She felt excited and quite gay.*
4 with gay abandon in a careless way, without careful thought
5 *informal* stupid or not good. Some people think that this word is offensive.: *That was a gay thing to do!* —**gayness** *n* [U] → GAILY, GAIETY

gay² ●○○ *n* [C] someone who is HOMOSEXUAL, especially a man

gay·dar /ˈgeɪdɑː $ -dɑːr/ *n* [U] *informal* your natural ability to know whether a man that you meet or see is GAY (=sexually attracted to people of the same sex), based on your feelings rather than what you already know about the person

gaze¹ /geɪz/ ●●○ *v* [I always + adv/prep] to look at someone or something for a long time, giving it all your attention, often without realizing you are doing so SYN **stare**: **[+into/at etc]** *Nell was still gazing out of the window.* | *Patrick sat* ***gazing into space*** (=looking straight in front, not at any particular person or thing). THESAURUS LOOK

gaze² ●○○ *n* [singular] a long steady look: *She felt embarrassed under his steady gaze.* | **lower/drop your gaze** *Ellen smiled uncomfortably and lowered her gaze.* | **meet sb's gaze** (=look directly at someone who is looking at you) *He didn't dare to meet her gaze.*

ga·ze·bo /gəˈziːbəʊ $ -ˈzeɪboʊ-, -ˈziː-/ *n* (*plural* **gazebos**) [C] a small building with open sides in a garden, where you can sit and look at the view

GAZEBO

ga·zelle /gəˈzel/ *n* [C] a type of small DEER, which jumps very gracefully and has large beautiful eyes

ga·zette /gəˈzet/ *n* [C] **1** *BrE* an official newspaper, especially one from the government giving important lists of people who have been employed by them etc **2** used in the names of some newspapers: *the 'Phoenix Gazette'*

gaz·et·teer /ˌgæzəˈtɪə $ -ˈtɪr/ *n* [C] a list of names of places, printed as a dictionary or as a list at the end of a book of maps

ga·zil·lion /gəˈzɪljən/ *number informal* an extremely large number: **a gazillion** *I have a gazillion things to do.* | **gazillions of sth** *gazillions of dollars*

ga·zump /gəˈzʌmp/ *v* [T] *BrE informal* if you are gazumped, the person who is selling you a house sells it to another person who offers them more money: *We were gazumped at the last minute.* GRAMMAR **Gazump** is usually passive. —**gazumping** *n* [U]

ga·zun·der /gəˈzʌndə $ -ər/ *v* [T] *BrE informal* **be gazundered** if you are gazundered, someone who has agreed to buy your house says that they will only buy it for less than the amount originally agreed

GB 1 the written abbreviation of ***Great Britain*** **2** (*also* **Gb**) the written abbreviation of ***gigabyte*** *or* ***gigabytes***

GBH /ˌdʒiː biː ˈeɪtʃ/ *n* [U] *BrE law* (***grievous bodily harm***) the serious crime of attacking someone and injuring them

GCE /ˌdʒiː siː ˈiː◂/ *n* [C,U] (***General Certificate of Education***) an examination in a range of subjects, formerly done by students in schools in England and Wales at O LEVEL and A LEVEL. In 1988, GCE O levels were replaced by GCSEs: *two GCE A level passes*

GCHQ /ˌdʒiː siː eɪtʃ ˈkjuː/ (***Government Communication Headquarters***) a British government organization based in Cheltenham, which collects information about countries that may be enemies. This is done especially by listening to radio broadcasts and telephone calls from all over the world.

GCSE /ˌdʒiː siː es ˈiː/ *n* [C,U] (***General Certificate of Secondary Education***) an examination in a range of subjects, done by students in schools in England and Wales, usually at the age of 15 or 16 → **O level**, **A level**, **GNVQ**: **do/take (your) GCSEs** *Adam* ***took*** *his* ***GCSEs*** *last year.* **GCSE exam/course/coursework/results etc**

GDP /ˌdʒiː diː ˈpiː/ *n* [singular] (***gross domestic product***) the total value of all goods and services produced in a country, in one year, except for income received from abroad → **GNP**

gear¹ /gɪə $ gɪr/ ●●○ S3 *n*

1 IN CARS ETC [C,U] the machinery in a vehicle such as a car, truck, or bicycle that you use to go comfortably at different speeds: *His mountain bike had 18 gears.* | *Andy drove cautiously along* ***in third gear***. | *Does this thing have a* ***reverse gear***? | *Any cyclist can climb a difficult hill; you just* ***change gear***. | *Don't turn off the engine while you're still* ***in gear***. | *It's a good habit to take the car* ***out of gear*** *while you're at a stoplight.*

2 [C,U] used to talk about the amount of effort and energy that someone is using in a situation: *During this period, Japan's export industries were in* ***top gear*** (=were as active as they could be). | *The Republican's propaganda machine moved into* ***high gear***. | **step up a gear** *BrE* (=increase the level of effort) *United stepped up a gear in the second half.*

3 change gear *BrE*, **change/switch/shift gears** *AmE* to start doing something in a different way, especially using more or less energy or effort: *The boss expects us to be able to change gear just like that.*

4 EQUIPMENT [U] a set of equipment or tools you need for a particular activity: *He's crazy about photography – he's got all the gear.* | *We'll need some camping gear.*

5 CLOTHES [U] a set of clothes that you wear for a particular occasion or activity: *Bring your rain gear.* | *police in riot gear* **THESAURUS** ▸ CLOTHES

6 MACHINERY [U] a piece of machinery that performs a particular job: *the landing gear of a plane* | *heavy lifting gear*

7 DRUGS [U] *BrE informal* a word meaning illegal drugs, used by people who take drugs

8 get your ass in gear *AmE informal* used to tell someone to hurry SYN **move your ass**: *You'd better get your ass in gear – you're late.*

gear² *v* [T] **be geared to sb/sth** to be organized in a way that is suitable for a particular purpose or situation: *The typical career pattern was geared to men whose wives didn't work.* | **be geared to do sth** *The course curriculum is geared to span three years.*

gear up *phr v* to prepare for something: **[+for]** *The organization is gearing up for a convention in May.* | **gear up/be geared up to do sth** *Fast food restaurants are geared up to serve thousands of people daily.*

gear·box /ˈgɪəbɒks $ ˈgɪrbɑːks/ *n* [C] the system of gears in a vehicle

gear·ing /ˈgɪərɪŋ $ ˈgɪr-/ *n* [U] *technical* the relationship between the amount of money that a company is worth and the amount that it owes in debts

ˈgear ˌlever *n* [C] a metal rod that you move in order to control the gears of a vehicle

ˈgear shift *n* [C] *AmE* a gear lever → see picture at CAR

ˈgear stick *n* [C] *BrE* a gear lever → see picture at CAR

geck·o /ˈgekəʊ $ -koʊ/ *n* (*plural* **geckos** *or* **geckoes**) [C] a type of small LIZARD

gee¹ /dʒiː/ *interjection especially AmE* used to show that you are surprised or annoyed → **wow**: *Aw, gee, Mom, do we have to go?*

gee² *v*

gee up *phr v BrE* **1 gee sb ↔ up** *informal* to encourage someone to try harder: *The team needs a captain who can gee them up a bit.* **2 gee up!** used to tell a horse to go faster

ˈgee-gee *n* [C] *BrE* a horse – used especially by children or when you are talking to children

geek /giːk/ *n* [C] *informal* someone who is not popular because they wear unfashionable clothes, do not know how to behave in social situations, or do strange things SYN **nerd**: *a computer geek* —**geeky** *adj*

geese /giːs/ the plural of GOOSE

ˌgee ˈwhiz *interjection AmE old-fashioned* used to show that you are surprised or annoyed

gee-ˈwhiz *adj AmE informal* very good, in a way that is impressive and exciting: *gee-whiz graphics*

geez /dʒiːz/ *interjection* another spelling of JEEZ

gee·zer /ˈgiːzə $ -ər/ *n* [C] *informal* **1** *BrE* a man: *I know this geezer.* **2** *AmE* an old man

Gei·ger count·er /ˈgaɪgə ˌkaʊntə $ -gər ˌkaʊntər/ *n* [C] an instrument that finds and measures RADIOACTIVITY

G8 /dʒiː ˈeɪt/ *n* **the G8** eight of the most important industrial nations in the world (Britain, Canada, France, Germany, Italy, Japan, Russia, and the US) who meet regularly to discuss the world economic situation

gei·sha /ˈgeɪʃə/ (*also* **ˈgeisha girl**) *n* [C] a Japanese woman who is trained in the art of dancing, singing, and providing entertainment, especially for men

gel¹ /dʒel/ ●○○ *n* [C,U] a thick wet substance that is used in beauty or cleaning products: *hair gel* | *shower gel*

gel² *v* (**gelled**, **gelling**) **1** (*also* **jell** *especially AmE*) [I] if a thought, plan etc gels, it becomes clearer or more definite: *Don't start writing until the idea has gelled in your mind.* **2** (*also* **jell** *especially AmE*) [I] if two or more people gel, they start working well together as a group: **[+with]** *He did not gel with Chapman.* | *After two days, the group gelled into a team.* **3** (*also* **jell** *especially AmE*) [I] if a liquid gels, it becomes firmer or thicker **4** [T] to put gel into your hair: ***gelled hair***

gel³ /dʒel/ *n* [C] *BrE old-fashioned* used to represent the word 'girl', when it is said in this way

gel·a·tin, **gel·a·tine** /ˈdʒelətɪn $ -tn/ *n* [U] a clear substance obtained from boiled animal bones, used for making JELLY

ge·lat·i·nous /dʒɪˈlætɪnəs $ -ˈlætn-əs/ *adj* in a state between solid and liquid, like a gel

geld /geld/ *v* [T] to remove the TESTICLES of a horse

geld·ing /ˈgeldɪŋ/ *n* [C] a horse that has been gelded

gel·id /ˈdʒelɪd/ *adj written* very cold

gel·ig·nite /ˈdʒelɪgnaɪt/ *n* [U] a powerful explosive

gem /dʒem/ ●○○ *n* [C]

1 (*also* **gem stone**) a beautiful stone that has been cut into a special shape SYN **jewel**: *precious gems*

2 something that is very special or beautiful: *Every single ad in the campaign has been a gem.* | *The Fortune is* ***a*** *tiny* ***gem of a*** *theatre.* | **[+of]** *little gems of advice*

3 a very helpful or special person: *Ben, you're a real gem!*

Gem·i·ni /ˈdʒemənaɪ $ -ni/ *n* **1** [U] the third sign of the ZODIAC, represented by TWINS, which some people believe affects the character and life of people born between May 22 and June 21 **2** [C] someone who was born between May 22 and June 21

gen¹ /dʒen/ *n* [U] *BrE informal* information: **[+on]** *She has* ***all the gen*** *on cheap flights.*

gen² *v* (**genned**, **genning**)

gen up *phr v BrE informal* to learn a lot of information about something for a particular purpose: **[+on]** *Gen up on the company's product before the interview.*

Gen. (*also* **Gen** *BrE*) the written abbreviation of ***General***: *Gen. Philippe Morillon*

gen·darme /ˈʒɒndɑːm $ ˈʒɑːndɑːrm/ *n* [C] a French police officer

gen·der /ˈdʒendə $ -ər/ ●○○ AWL *n*

1 [C,U] the fact of being male or female: *people of the same gender* | *Discrimination on grounds of race or gender is forbidden.* | *There may be* ***gender differences*** *in attitudes to paid work.* | *traditional* ***gender roles*** | ***gender biases*** *in books* | *toys that do not reinforce* ***gender stereotypes*** | *a science fiction story dealing with* ***gender issues***

2 [C] males or females, considered as a group SYN **sex**: *differences between the genders*

3 a) [U] the system in some languages of marking words

G

such as nouns, adjectives, and PRONOUNS as being MASCULINE, FEMININE, or NEUTER **b)** [C] a group such as FEMININE into which words are divided in this system

ˈgender ˌbender *n* [C] *informal* someone who behaves or dresses in a way typical of the opposite sex

ˈgender ˌbias *n* [C,U] when men and women are treated differently, in a way that is unfair

ˈgender reasˌsignment *n* [U] the medical process of changing someone's body so that a man becomes a woman or a woman becomes a man

ˌgender-speˈcific *adj* relating only to males or only to females: *gender-specific language*

gene /dʒiːn/ ●●○ S3 W3 *n* [C] a part of a cell in a living thing that controls what it looks like, how it grows, and how it develops. People get their genes from their parents. → **genetic**: *human genes | the genes that regulate cell division*

ge·ne·al·o·gy /ˌdʒiːniˈælədʒi/ *n* (*plural* **genealogies**) **1** [U] the study of the history of families **2** [C] a drawing or description that explains how each person in a family is related to the others → **family tree** —**genealogist** *n* [C] —**genealogical** /ˌdʒiːniəˈlɒdʒɪkəl◂ $ -ˈlɑː-/ *adj*: *a useful source of genealogical information*

ˈgene ˌdoping *n* [U] the use of GENETIC changes to improve the performance of an ATHLETE such as a runner

ˈgene ˌmapping *n* [U] the act of finding out the position of one or more GENES on a CHROMOSOME (=the part of every living cell that contains genes)

ˈgene pool *n* [C] all of the genes available to a particular SPECIES

gen·e·ra /ˈdʒenərə/ the plural of GENUS

gen·e·ral¹ /ˈdʒenərəl/ ●●● S1 W1 *adj* [usually before noun]

1 NOT DETAILED describing or relating to only the main features or parts of something, not the details: *a general introduction to computing | I skimmed through it to get a general impression of the text. | I have a* ***general idea*** *of what I want to express. | He spoke* ***in general terms*** *about greater competitiveness.*

2 in general a) usually or in most situations: *In general, about 10% of the candidates are eventually offered positions.* **b)** used when talking about the whole of a situation, group, or thing, rather than specific parts of it: *a feeling of dissatisfaction with life in general | These policies are unpopular with politicians and people in general. | We're trying to raise awareness about the environment* ***in general and*** *air pollution* ***in particular***.

3 RELATING TO WHOLE involving the whole of a situation, group, or thing, rather than specific parts of it: *There has been a general decline in standards. | ways to improve your general health*

4 ORDINARY ordinary or usual: *general cooking and cleaning | I hate paperwork* ***as a general rule***.

5 MOST PEOPLE shared by or affecting most people, or most of the people in a group: *These courses are based around topics of* ***general interest***. *| How soon can the drug be made available for general use?*

6 NOT LIMITED not limited to one use, activity, subject etc: *The next ten minutes passed in general conversation. | It's a good general fertilizer. | Watford* ***General Hospital*** *| This type of microphone is suitable for general use.*

7 APPROXIMATE used to talk about an approximate area or direction: *Pat and his friend were in the* ***general area*** *of the crime when it happened. | They started walking* ***in the general direction of*** *the pub.*

8 JOB used in the name of a job to show that the person who does it has complete responsibility: *the* ***general manager*** *| the Attorney General*

general² *n* [C] an officer of very high rank in the army or air force

ˌgeneral anaesˈthetic *BrE*, **general anesthetic** *AmE n* [C,U] a medicine that makes you unconscious during an operation so that you do not feel any pain → **local anaesthetic**: *I had the operation done under general anaesthetic.*

ˌgeneral ˈcounsel *n* [C] **1** the legal officer of a US company with the highest rank **2** a firm of US lawyers that gives general legal advice

ˌgeneral deˈlivery *n* [U] *AmE* a post office department that keeps someone's letters until that person comes to get them SYN **poste restante** *BrE*

ˌgeneral eˈlection *n* [C] an election in which all the people in a country who can vote elect a government: *during the 1987* ***general election campaign*** *| an attempt to persuade the government to* ***hold*** *a* ***general election*** (=have a general election)

ˌgeneral ˈheadquarters *n* [plural] the place from which the actions of an organization, especially a military one, are controlled

gen·e·ral·ise /ˈdʒenərəlaɪz/ *v* [I,T] a British spelling of GENERALIZE

gen·e·ral·ist /ˈdʒenərəlɪst/ *n* [C] a person who knows about many different things and can do many things well OPP **specialist** —**generalist** *adj*

gen·e·ral·i·ty /ˌdʒenəˈræləti/ *n* (*plural* **generalities**) **1** [C usually plural] a very general statement that avoids mentioning details or specific cases: *The Secretary of State has given us nothing today but bland generalities.* **2 the generality of sth** *BrE formal* most of a group of people or things: *Temporary workers are considerably younger than the generality of workers.* **3** [U] *formal* the quality of being true or useful in most situations

gen·e·ral·i·za·tion (*also* **-isation** *BrE*) /ˌdʒenərəlaɪˈzeɪʃən $ -lə-/ ●○○ *n*

1 [C] a statement about all the members of a group that may be true in some or many situations but is not true in every case: *You can't* ***make generalizations*** *about what men and women are like.* | **broad/sweeping/gross generalization** *a sweeping generalization based on speculation*

2 [U] the act of making generalizations

gen·e·ral·ize (*also* **-ise** *BrE*) /ˈdʒenərəlaɪz/ ●○○ *v*

1 [I] to form a general principle or opinion after considering only a small number of facts or examples: **[+from]** *She has a tendency to generalize from her husband to all men.*

2 [I] to make a general statement about the whole of a group or thing: **[+about]** *It is difficult to generalise about the kind of people who come on these courses.*

3 [T] *formal* to say that an idea, result etc is related to a larger group: *Can we generalise this principle?* | **generalize sth to sth** *Can the research findings be generalized to a wider population?*

gen·e·ral·ized (*also* **-ised** *BrE*) /ˈdʒenərəlaɪzd/ *adj* [usually before noun] involving or relating to many things, people, or parts: *generalized statements | generalized anxiety*

ˌgeneral ˈknowledge *n* [U] knowledge of facts about many different subjects: *a general knowledge quiz*

gen·er·al·ly /ˈdʒenərəli/ ●●● S2 W1 *adv*

1 considering or relating to the whole of a thing or group, rather than to details or specific cases or parts SYN **broadly**: *It was generally a positive conversation. | She's not really ill, just generally run-down. |* [sentence adverb] *Generally, part-timers work in low-status, low-wage occupations. | The second survey was concerned with working-class culture more generally.*

2 by or to most people SYN **widely**: **generally regarded/accepted/known etc** *The plants are generally regarded as weeds. | a generally accepted view | It could be five years before the drug is* ***generally available***.

3 usually or most of the time SYN **usually**: *I generally get in to work by 8.00.*

4 generally speaking used to introduce a statement that is true in most cases but not always: *Generally speaking, the more expensive the stereo, the better it is.*

ˌgeneral ˈpractice *n* **1** [U] the work of a doctor or lawyer who deals with all the ordinary types of illnesses or legal cases, rather than one specific type **2** [C] a group of lawyers or doctors who do all types of work

ˌgeneral pracˈtitioner *n* [C] a doctor who is trained in general medicine SYN **GP**

G

ˌgeneral ˈpublic *n* **the general public** the ordinary people in a country, rather than people belonging to a particular group: *The information is not available to the general public.*

GRAMMAR: Singular or plural verb?

- **The general public** is usually followed by a singular verb: *The general public* ***is*** *not at any risk from the gas leak.*
- In British English, you can also use a plural verb: *The general public* ***are*** *not at any risk from the gas leak.*

GRAMMAR GUIDE ▸ NOUNS

ˌgeneral-ˈpurpose *adj* [only before noun] suitable for most situations or jobs, or having a wide range of uses: *a general-purpose computer*

gen·er·al·ship /ˈdʒenərəlʃɪp/ *n* [U] the skill or position of being a general

ˌgeneral ˈstaff *n* **the general staff** the group of military officers who work for a military leader

ˈgeneral ˌstore *n* [C] a shop that sells a wide variety of goods, especially one in a small town

ˌgeneral ˈstrike *n* [C] a situation when most of the workers in a country refuse to work in order to protest about working conditions, wages etc

gen·e·rate /ˈdʒenəreɪt/ ●●○ W2 AWL *v* [T]
1 to produce or cause something SYN **create**: *a useful technique for generating new ideas | The program would generate a lot of new jobs.* | **generate revenue/profits/income etc** *Tourism generates income for local communities.* | **generate excitement/interest/support etc** *The project generated enormous interest.* THESAURUS ▸ MAKE
2 to produce heat, electricity, or another form of energy: *Wind turbines generate electricity for the local community.*

gen·e·ra·tion /ˌdʒenəˈreɪʃən/ ●●● S3 W2 AWL *n*
1 [C] all people of about the same age: *Like most of my generation, I had never known a war. | In my generation the divorce rate is very high. | the need to preserve the planet for* ***future generations*** | **[+of]** *the post-war generation of writers* | **the younger/older generation** (=the younger or older people in society) *The younger generation don't know what hard work is. | The story has been handed down* ***from generation to generation.***

GRAMMAR: Singular or plural verb?

- In this meaning, **generation** is usually followed by a singular verb: *This generation* ***has*** *grown up using Internet technology.*
- In British English, you can also use a plural verb: *This generation* ***have*** *grown up using Internet technology.*

GRAMMAR GUIDE ▸ NOUNS

2 [C] all the members of a family of about the same age: *In those days it was common for three generations of the same family to live together.* | **first-generation/second-generation etc** (=being a member of the first, second etc generation to live or be born in a country) *first-generation immigrants | a third-generation American*
3 [C] the average period of time between the birth of a person and the birth of that person's children: **for generations** *Some families have lived here for generations. | The country's attitude toward government is harsher than it was a generation ago.*
4 [C] a group of things that were developed from something else, or from which better things were developed: **[+of]** *the* ***new generation*** *of mobile phones | the first generation of nuclear power stations* | **first-generation/second-generation etc** *second-generation computers*
5 [U] the process of producing something or making something happen SYN **production**: **[+of]** *the generation of electricity*

generation 1.5 /ˌdʒenəreɪʃən ˌwʌn pɔɪnt ˈfaɪv/ *n* [U] *AmE* people born and living in the US, whose parents originally come from a foreign country and have not learnt to speak English properly. Generation 1.5 children are able to speak English well, but talk in the language spoken by their parents when they are at home.

gen·e·ra·tion·al /ˌdʒenəˈreɪʃənəl/ *adj* [usually before noun] connected with a particular generation or the relationship between different generations: *generational conflict | generational divisions*

ˌgeneˈration ˌgap *n* [singular] the lack of understanding or the differences between older people and younger people

Generation X /ˌdʒenəreɪʃən ˈeks/ *n* [U] the group of people who were born during the late 1960s and the 1970s in the US

Generation Y /ˌdʒenəreɪʃən ˈwaɪ/ *n* [U] the group of people who were born during the 1980s and 1990s in the US

gen·e·ra·tive /ˈdʒenərətɪv/ *adj formal* **1** able to produce something: *the generative power of the life force*
2 generative grammar/linguistics/phonology the description of a language using rules that produce all the possible correct sentences of the language

gen·e·ra·tor /ˈdʒenəreɪtə $ -ər/ ●○○ *n* [C]
1 a machine that produces electricity: *an emergency generator*
2 a company that produces electricity
3 something that produces something else: **[+of]** *good generators of income*

ge·ner·ic /dʒəˈnerɪk/ ●○○ *adj* [usually before noun]
1 relating to a whole group of things rather than to one thing: **generic term/name (for sth)** *Fine Arts is a generic term for subjects such as painting, music, and sculpture.*
2 a generic product does not have a special name to show that it is made by a particular company: **generic drugs** —**generically** /-kli/ *adv*

gen·e·ros·i·ty /ˌdʒenəˈrɒsəti $ -ˈrɑː-/ ●○○ *n* [U] a generous attitude, or generous behaviour: *an act of great generosity* | **[+to/towards]** *his generosity to the poor | I shall never forget the* ***generosity shown*** *by the people of Bataisk.* | **acts of generosity**

gen·e·rous /ˈdʒenərəs/ ●●○ W3 *adj*
1 someone who is generous is willing to give money, spend time etc, in order to help people or give them pleasure OPP **mean**: **generous to sb** *She's always very generous to the kids.* | **generous with sth** *Jim is very generous with his time.* | **it/that is generous (of sb)** *It was generous of them to ask Anna along.* | **generous offer/support/donation etc** *my employer's generous offer to pay the bill* THESAURUS ▸ KIND
2 larger or more than the usual size or amount OPP **measly**: *a generous glass of wine* | **generous amount/helping/measure etc** *a generous helping of pasta | He had a well-shaped generous mouth.*
3 sympathetic in the way you deal with people, and tending to see the good qualities in someone or something OPP **mean**: *She was generous enough to overlook my little mistake.* —**generously** *adv: Please* ***give generously*** *to the refugee fund.*

ˈgene ˌsequencing *n* [U] DNA SEQUENCING

gen·e·sis /ˈdʒenɪsɪs/ *n* [singular] *formal* the beginning or origin of something: **[+of]** *the genesis of the myth*

ˈgene ˌtherapy *n* [U] a way of treating certain diseases by using GENETIC ENGINEERING

ge·net·ic /dʒəˈnetɪk/ ●○○ *adj* relating to GENES or GENETICS: *genetic defects | each person's genetic make-up | genetic research* —**genetically** /-kli/ *adv: genetically determined characteristics*

geˌnetically ˈmodified (*also* **geˌnetically enginˈeered**) *adj* (*abbreviation* **GM**) genetically modified foods or plants have had their genetic structure changed so that they are not affected by particular diseases or harmful insects

geˌnetic ˈcode *n* [C] the arrangement of GENES that controls the way a living thing develops

geˌnetic enginˈeering *n* [U] the science of changing the genetic structure of an animal, plant, or human,

G

usually to make them stronger or healthier —**genetic engineer** *n* [C]

ge,netic 'fingerprinting *n* [U] the process of examining the pattern of someone's GENES, especially in order to find out if they are guilty of a crime

ge·net·ics /dʒə'netɪks/ ●○○ *n* [U] the study of how the qualities of living things are passed on in their GENES —**geneticist** /-tɪsɪst/ *n* [C]

GRAMMAR: Singular or plural verb?

Genetics is followed by a singular verb: ***Genetics is** the study of genes.*

GRAMMAR GUIDE ▶ NOUNS

ge·ni·al /'dʒiːniəl/ *adj* friendly and happy: *a genial smile* THESAURUS ▶ FRIENDLY —**genially** *adv* —**geniality** /ˌdʒiːni'æləti/ *n* [U]

ge·nie /'dʒiːni/ *n* [C] **1** a magical creature in old Arabian stories that will do what you want when you call it **2 let the genie out of the bottle** to do something that has a great and often bad effect on a situation, which can then never return to its previous state

gen·i·tal /'dʒenətl/ *adj* [only before noun] relating to or affecting the outer sex organs: *the genital area* | *genital mutilation*

gen·i·tals /'dʒenətlz/ (*also* **gen·i·ta·li·a** /ˌdʒenə'teɪliːə/) *n* [plural] *formal or technical* the outer sex organs

gen·i·tive /'dʒenətɪv/ *n* [C] *technical* a form of a noun in some languages which shows a relationship of possession or origin between one thing and another —**genitive** *adj*

ge·ni·us /'dʒiːniəs/ ●●○ *n*
1 [U] a very high level of intelligence, mental skill, or ability, which only a few people have: *The film reveals Fellini's genius.* | **work/writer/man etc of genius** *Wynford was an architect of genius.* | **a stroke of genius** (=a very clever idea) *At the time, his appointment seemed a stroke of genius.* | *a work of **pure genius*** THESAURUS ▶ SKILL
2 [C] someone who has an unusually high level of intelligence, mental skill, or ability: *Freud was a genius.* | **musical/comic/mathematical etc genius** | **a genius at (doing) sth** *My father was a genius at storytelling.*
3 a genius for (doing) sth special skill at doing something: *That woman **has a genius for** organization.* | *Warhol's genius for publicity*

G

gen·o·cide /'dʒenəsaɪd/ ●○○ *n* [U] the deliberate murder of a whole group or race of people → **ethnic cleansing**: *The military leaders were accused of genocide.* —**genocidal** /ˌdʒenə'saɪdl◂/ *adj*: *a genocidal regime*

ge·nome /'dʒiːnəʊm $ -noʊm/ *n* [C] *technical* all the GENES in one type of living thing → **DNA**: *the human genome*

ge·no·mic /dʒiː'nəʊmɪk $ -'nɑː-/ *adj technical* relating to all the GENES that are found in one type of living thing

ge·nom·ics /dʒə'nəʊmɪks $ -'noʊ-/ *n* [U] *technical* the study of GENOMES

gen·o·type /'dʒenətaɪp, 'dʒiː-/ *n* [C] *technical* the GENETIC nature of one type of living thing

gen·re /'ʒɒnrə $ 'ʒɑːnrə/ ●○○ *n* [C] *formal* a particular type of art, writing, music etc, which has certain features that all examples of this type share: **[+of]** *a new genre of film-making* | *a literary genre*

gent /dʒent/ *n* [C] **1** *especially BrE informal* a GENTLEMAN: *a well-dressed elderly gent* | *I've always prided myself on being a perfect gent.* **2 the gents** *BrE* a public toilet for men SYN **men's room** *AmE*

gen·teel /dʒen'tiːl/ *adj* **1** polite, gentle, or graceful: *She broke into a genteel run.* **2** *old-fashioned* from or relating to a good social class —**genteelly** *adv*

gen·tian /'dʒenʃən/ *n* [C] a small plant with blue or purple flowers that grows in mountain areas

gen·tile, **Gentile** /'dʒentaɪl/ *n* [C] someone who is not Jewish —**gentile** *adj* [only before noun]

gen·til·i·ty /dʒen'tɪləti/ *n* [U] *formal* the quality of being polite, gentle, or graceful, and of seeming to belong to a high social class: *The hotel had an air of discreet gentility.*

gen·tle /'dʒentl/ ●●○ S3 W3 *adj*
1 kind and careful in the way you behave or do things, so that you do not hurt or damage anyone or anything OPP **rough**: *Arthur was a very gentle, caring person.* | **gentle voice/smile/touch** *'Where does it hurt?' she asked in a gentle voice.* | **[+with]** *Be gentle with the baby.*
2 not extreme, strong, or violent: **gentle exercise/walk/stroll etc** *a program of regular gentle exercise* | *the **gentle pressure** of Jill's hand* | *After a little **gentle persuasion**, she agreed to go back to her family.* | *Melt the butter over a **gentle heat*** (=low heat).
3 a gentle wind or rain is soft and light: *a **gentle breeze***
4 a gentle hill or slope is not steep or sharp: *the gentle slopes of Mt Pelée* —**gentleness** *n* [U] → GENTLY

gen·tle·folk /'dʒentlfəʊk $ -foʊk/ *n* [plural] *old use* people belonging to the higher social classes

gen·tle·man /'dʒentlmən/ ●●● S2 W2 *n* (*plural* **gentlemen** /-mən/) [C]
1 a polite word for a man, used especially when talking to or about a man you do not know → **lady**: *Could you serve this gentleman please, Miss Bath?* | *Good morning, **ladies and gentlemen**.* | *An elderly gentleman was asleep next to the fire.* THESAURUS ▶ MAN
2 a man who is always polite, has good manners, and treats other people well → **lady**: *Martin – always the **perfect gentleman** – got to his feet when my mother walked in.* | *Mr Field was a **real gentleman**.*
3 *old-fashioned* a man from a high social class, especially one whose family owns a lot of property → **lady**: *an English **country gentleman***

ˌgentleman 'farmer *n* [C] *especially BrE* a man belonging to a high social class who owns and runs a farm, but who usually hires people to do the work

gen·tle·man·ly /'dʒentlmənli/ *adj* a man who is gentlemanly speaks and behaves politely, and treats other people with respect

ˌgentleman's a'greement *n* [C] an agreement that is not written down, made between people who trust each other

gen·tle·wo·man /'dʒentlˌwʊmən/ *n* (*plural* **gentlewomen** /-ˌwɪmɪn/) [C] *old use* a woman who belongs to a high social class

gent·ly /'dʒentli/ ●●○ W3 *adv*
1 in a gentle way: *'You go back to bed now,' he said gently.* | *She kissed me gently on the cheek.* | *Gently cook the peppers for 10–15 minutes.* | *Rain pattered gently on the roof above.* | *The road curved gently upwards.*
2 gently/gently does it! *BrE spoken* used to tell someone to be careful when they are handling something, moving something etc: *Gently, Sammy, you don't want to break it.*

gen·tri·fi·ca·tion /ˌdʒentrɪfɪ'keɪʃən/ *n* [U] a gradual process in which an area in bad condition where poor people live is changed by people with more money coming to live there and improving it —**gentrify** /'dʒentrɪfaɪ/ *v* [T]

gen·try /'dʒentri/ *n* [plural] *old-fashioned* people who belong to a high social class: *a member of the **landed gentry*** (=gentry who own land)

gen·u·flect /'dʒenjəflekt/ *v* [I] *formal* **1** to bend one or both knees when in church or a holy place as a sign of respect **2** to show too much respect towards someone or something – used to show disapproval SYN **kowtow**: **[+to]** *He was a man of principle, refusing to genuflect to the party leadership.* —**genuflection** /ˌdʒenjə'flekʃən/ *n* [C,U]

gen·u·ine /'dʒenjuɪn/ ●●○ S3 W3 *adj*
1 a genuine feeling, desire etc is one that you really feel, not one you pretend to feel SYN **sincere**: **genuine interest/concern/desire etc** *The reforms are motivated by a genuine concern for the disabled.* | *a genuine fear of invasion* | *'Did he really?' Her surprise seemed genuine.*
2 something genuine really is what it seems to be SYN **real**: *We need laws that will protect genuine refugees.* | *The strap is genuine leather.*

3 someone who is genuine is honest and friendly and you feel you can trust them OPP **false**: *She is the most genuine person I've ever met.*
4 the genuine article a) *informal* a person or thing that is a true example of their type: *If you want to meet a real Southerner, Jake is the genuine article.* **b)** something that is real and is not a copy intended to deceive people: *Some fake designer clothes are so good that people have no idea they're not buying the genuine article.* —**genuineness** *n* [U]

THESAURUS

genuine used about a feeling, thing, or person that really is what they seem to be: *genuine concern | Experts believe that the painting is genuine. | genuine refugees*
real not false or artificial: *real wood | His real name is Reginald. | It looks just like* ***the real thing****.*
authentic authentic food, music, clothes etc are correct for the place or the period in history that they are supposed to be from: *It's a friendly restaurant offering authentic Greek food. | authentic medieval instruments*
bona fide /ˌbəʊnə ˈfaɪdi $ ˈbəʊnə faɪd/ [usually before noun] bona fide people or things are really what they say they are, especially when this can be checked by looking at official documents: *a bona fide medical qualification | a bona fide company*
hard evidence/facts evidence or facts that are genuine and can be proved: *There was no hard evidence to support the theory.*

gen·u·ine·ly /ˈdʒenjuɪnli/ ●●○ *adv*
1 in a real and sincere way: **genuinely concerned/interested/surprised** *He was genuinely concerned for the children. | His victims* ***genuinely believed*** *that he was helping them.*
2 used for emphasizing a particular quality: *genuinely new information | Matisse is a genuinely popular artist.*

ge·nus /ˈdʒiːnəs, ˈdʒen-/ *n* (*plural* **genera** /ˈdʒenərə/) [C] *technical* one of the groups into which scientists divide animals or plants, in which the animals or plants are closely related but cannot produce babies together. A genus includes fewer members than a FAMILY and more members than a SPECIES.

ge·o- /dʒiːəʊ, dʒɪə $ dʒiːoʊ, dʒɪə/ *prefix technical* relating to the Earth or its surface: *geophysics | geopolitical*

ge·o·cache /ˈdʒiːəʊkæʃ $ ˈdʒiːoʊ-/ *n* [C] a container that people try to find in the activity of geocaching

ge·o·cach·ing /ˈdʒiːəʊˌkæʃɪŋ $ ˈdʒiːoʊ-/ *n* [U] an activity in which people use GPS to find hidden boxes that contain a book that they sign and small objects that they can take in exchange for objects they have brought

ge·o·da·ta /ˈdʒiːəʊˌdeɪtə, -ˌdɑː- $ ˈdʒiːoʊ-/ *n* [plural,U] information about where something or someone is: *Your mobile phone is constantly sending back geodata.*

ge·o·des·ic /ˌdʒiːəʊˈdesɪk◂, -ˈdiː- $ ˌdʒiːoʊ-/ *adj* [only before noun] having a shape or structure made from small flat pieces, usually TRIANGLES or PENTAGONS, that are put together to form curves: *a geodesic dome*

ge·o·en·gi·neer·ing /ˌdʒiːəʊendʒeˈnɪərɪŋ $ -ovendʒəˈnɪr-/ *n* [U] the activity of building structures that remove CARBON DIOXIDE from the air or cool the Earth by sending back light from the sun, in order to reduce GLOBAL WARMING

ge·o·fence /ˈdʒiːəʊfens $ ˈdʒiːoʊ-/ *n* [C] a limit that you set using GPS so that you get a warning if someone or something moves into or out of a particular area

ge·og·ra·pher /dʒiˈɒɡrəfə, ˈdʒɒɡ- $ -dʒiˈɑːɡrəfər/ *n* [C] someone who has studied geography to a high level

ge·o·graph·i·cal /ˌdʒiːəˈɡræfɪkəl◂/ ●○○ (*also* **ge·o·graph·ic**) *adj*
1 relating to the place in an area, country etc where something or someone is: **geographical area/location/position** *a large geographical area | their geographical proximity to Japan* (=nearness to Japan)
2 relating to geography: *geographical research work* —**geographically** /-kli/ *adv*

ge·og·ra·phy /dʒiˈɒɡrəfi, ˈdʒɒɡ- $ dʒiˈɑːɡ-/ ●●● W3 *n* [U]
1 the study of the countries, oceans, rivers, mountains, cities etc of the world: *a geography lesson* → PHYSICAL GEOGRAPHY, POLITICAL GEOGRAPHY
2 the geography of a building, city etc is the way all its parts are arranged: **[+of]** *The geography of the flats made it hard to get to know our neighbours.*

ge·o·lo·ca·tion /ˌdʒiːəʊləʊˈkeɪʃən $ ˌdʒiːoʊloʊ-/ *n* [U] the ability a computer or a MOBILE PHONE has to find out and show where it is being used

ge·ol·o·gy /dʒiˈɒlədʒi $ -ˈɑːlə-/ ●○○ *n* [U] the study of the rocks, soil etc that make up the Earth, and of the way they have changed since the Earth was formed —**geologist** *n* [C] —**geological** /ˌdʒiːəˈlɒdʒɪkəl◂ $ -ˈlɑː-/ *adj* —**geologically** /-kli/ *adv*

ge·o·man·cer /ˈdʒiːəˌmænsə/ *n* [C] an expert in geomancy

ge·o·man·cy /ˈdʒiːəˌmænsi/ *n* [U] the belief that arranging your home, house, office etc in a particular way will bring you good or bad luck → **feng shui**

ge·o·met·ric /ˌdʒiːəˈmetrɪk◂/ (*also* **ge·o·met·ri·cal** /-trɪkəl/) *adj* **1** having or using the shapes and lines in GEOMETRY, such as circles or squares, especially when these are arranged in regular patterns: *a geometric design*
2 relating to GEOMETRY —**geometrically** /-kli/ *adv*

ˌgeoˌmetric proˈgression *n* [C] a set of numbers in order, in which each is multiplied by a specific number to produce the next number in the series (as in 1, 2, 4, 8, 16, ...) → **arithmetic progression**

ge·om·e·try /dʒiˈɒmətri $ -ˈɑːm-/ ●○○ *n* [U] the study in MATHEMATICS of the angles and shapes formed by the relationships of lines, surfaces, and solid objects in space → **geometric**

ge·o·phys·ics /ˌdʒiːəʊˈfɪzɪks $ ˌdʒiːoʊ-/ *n* [U] the study of the movements of parts of the Earth, and the forces involved with this, including the weather, the oceans etc —**geophysical** *adj* —**geophysicist** /-zɪsɪst/ *n* [C]

ge·o·pol·i·tics /ˌdʒiːəʊˈpɒlətɪks $ ˌdʒiːoʊˈpɑː-/ *n* [U] ideas and activities relating to the way that a country's position, population etc affect its political development and its relationship with other countries, or the study of this —**geopolitical** /ˌdʒiːəʊpəˈlɪtɪkəl◂ $ ˌdʒiːoʊ-/ *adj*

Geor·die /ˈdʒɔːdi $ ˈdʒɔːr-/ *n BrE informal* **1** [C] someone from Tyneside in northeast England **2** [U] a way of speaking that is typical of people from Tyneside

Geor·gian /ˈdʒɔːdʒən, -dʒiən $ ˈdʒɔːrdʒən/ *adj* Georgian buildings, furniture etc come from the 18th century, when Britain was ruled by the Kings George I, George II, and George III: *Georgian townhouse*

ge·o·sta·tion·a·ry or·bit /ˌdʒiːəʊsteɪʃənəri ˈɔːbɪt $ -oʊˌsteɪʃəneri ˈɔːrbɪt/ *n* [C,U] *technical* if something such as a SATELLITE is in geostationary orbit, it is moving around the Earth in a way that means it stays above the same point on the Earth's surface

ge·o·tag·ging /ˈdʒiːəʊˌtæɡɪŋ $ ˈdʒiːoʊ-/ *n* [U] the ability to add information about where someone or something is to DIGITAL photographs, videos, messages etc

ge·o·ther·mal /ˌdʒiːəʊˈθɜːməl◂ $ -oʊˈθɜːr-/ *adj* relating to or coming from the heat inside the Earth: *a geothermal energy plant*

ge·ra·ni·um /dʒəˈreɪniəm/ *n* [C] a plant with red, pink, or white flowers and round leaves

ger·bil /ˈdʒɜːbəl $ ˈdʒɜːr-/ *n* [C] a small animal with fur, a tail, and long back legs, that is often kept as a pet

ge·ri·at·ric /ˌdʒeriˈætrɪk◂/ *adj* **1** [only before noun] relating to the medical care and treatment of old people: *a specialist in geriatric medicine* THESAURUS ▸ OLD
2 *informal* too old to work well: *a geriatric rock star*

ge·ri·at·rics /ˌdʒeriˈætrɪks/ *n* [U] the medical treatment and care of old people → **gerontology** —**geriatrician** /ˌdʒeriəˈtrɪʃən/ *n* [C]

G

germ /dʒɜːm $ dʒɜːrm/ ●●○ *n* [C]
1 a very small living thing that can make you ill → BACTERIA: *Put disinfectant down the toilet to kill any germs.*
2 the germ of an idea/theory/feeling etc the early stage of an idea, feeling etc that may develop into something bigger and more important: *The germ of a story began to form in his mind.*
3 *technical* the part of a plant or animal that can develop into a new plant or animal: *germ cells containing DNA* → WHEATGERM, GERM WARFARE

Ger·man¹ /ˈdʒɜːmən $ ˈdʒɜːr-/ *adj* relating to Germany, its people, or its language: *German history*

German² *n* **1** [C] someone from Germany **2** [U] the language used in Germany, Austria, and parts of Switzerland

ger·mane /dʒɜːˈmeɪn $ dʒɜːr-/ *adj formal* an idea, remark etc that is germane to something is related to it in an important and suitable way SYN **relevant**: **[+to]** *an article which is germane to the subject being discussed*

Ger·man·ic /dʒɜːˈmænɪk $ dʒɜːr-/ *adj* **1** relating to the language family that includes German, Dutch, Swedish, and English **2** relating to or typical of Germany or German people

ˌGerman ˈmeasles *n* [U] an infectious disease that causes red spots on your body, and can damage an unborn child SYN **rubella**

ˌGerman ˈshepherd *n* [C] a large dog rather like a WOLF that is often used by the police, for guarding property etc SYN **Alsatian** *BrE*

ger·mi·nate /ˈdʒɜːməneɪt $ ˈdʒɜːr-/ *v* **1** [I,T] if a seed germinates, or if it is germinated, it begins to grow SYN **sprout** **2** [I] if an idea, feeling etc germinates, it begins to develop: *The idea of setting up his own company began to germinate in his mind.* —**germination** /ˌdʒɜːməˈneɪʃən $ ˌdʒɜːr-/ *n* [U]

ˌgerm ˈwarfare *n* [U] the use of harmful BACTERIA in war to cause illness and death among the enemy

ger·on·tol·o·gy /ˌdʒerɒnˈtɒlədʒi $ ˌdʒerənˈtɑː-/ *n* [U] the scientific study of old age and its effects on the body → **geriatrics** —**gerontologist** *n* [C] —**gerontological** /dʒəˌrɒntəˈlɒdʒɪkəl◂ $ -ˌrɑːntəˈlɑː-/ *adj*

ger·ry·man·der·ing /ˈdʒerimændərɪŋ/ *n* [U] when politicians change the size and borders of an area before an election, so that one person, group, or party has an unfair advantage —**gerrymander** *v* [I,T]

ger·und /ˈdʒerənd/ *n* [C] *technical* a noun in the form of the PRESENT PARTICIPLE of a verb, for example 'shopping' in the sentence 'I like shopping'

ge·stalt /gəˈʃtɑːlt/ *n* [C] *technical* a whole thing that is different from all its parts, and has qualities that are not present in any of its parts by themselves: *gestalt psychology*

Ge·sta·po /ˈgestɑːpəʊ $ -poʊ/ *n* **the Gestapo** the secret police force used by the state in Germany during the Nazi period

ges·ta·tion /dʒeˈsteɪʃən/ *n* [singular, U] **1** *medical* the process by which a child or young animal develops inside its mother's body before birth, or the period of time when this happens → **pregnancy**: *The **gestation period** of a horse is about 11 months.* **2** *formal* the process by which a new idea, piece of work etc is developed, or the period of time when this happens SYN **development**: **in gestation** *The report was a very long time in gestation.*

ges·tic·u·late /dʒeˈstɪkjəleɪt/ *v* [I] to make movements with your arms and hands, usually while speaking, because you are excited, angry, or cannot think of the right words to use SYN **gesture**: *Jane **gesticulated wildly** and shouted 'Stop! Stop!'* —**gesticulation** /dʒeˌstɪkjəˈleɪʃən/ *n* [C,U]

ges·ture¹ /ˈdʒestʃə $ -ər/ ●●○ *n*
1 [C,U] a movement of part of your body, especially your hands or head, to show what you mean or how you feel: **in a … gesture (of sth)** *Jim raised his hands in a despairing gesture.* | *Luke **made** an obscene **gesture** with his finger.* | **[+of]** *She shook her head with a gesture of impatience.*
2 [C] something that you say or do, often something small, to show how you feel about someone or something: *They decided it would be a **nice gesture** to send her a card.* | *Tearing up the price list was simply a **symbolic gesture**.* | **[+of]** *As a **gesture of goodwill**, we have decided to waive the charges on this occasion.* | **[+towards]** *The Queen has now **made** a **gesture** towards public opinion.* —**gestural** *adj*

gesture² ●○○ *v* [I] to move your hand, arm, or head to tell someone something, or show them what you mean: **[+to/towards/at]** *Brad gestured towards the door. 'Get out.'* | **gesture for sb to do sth** *He gestured for her to take a seat.*

ge·sund·heit /gəˈzʊndhaɪt/ *interjection AmE* used to wish someone good health when they have just SNEEZED SYN **bless you**

get /get/ ●●● S1 W1 *v* (*past tense* **got**, *past participle* **got** /gɒt $ gɑːt/ *BrE*, **gotten** /ˈgɒtn $ ˈgɑːtn/ *AmE*, *present participle* **getting**)
1 RECEIVE [T] to receive something that someone gives you or sends you: *She got loads of presents.* | *What did you get for Christmas?* | *We get a lot of junk mail.* | **get sth from sb** *We got a letter from Pam this morning.* | **get sth off sb** *spoken informal*: *I got it off my Dad.* | *I **got** a few games **free** when I bought my computer.*
2 OBTAIN [T] to obtain something by finding it, asking for it, or paying for it: *We need to get help quickly!* | *It would be a good idea to get professional advice.* | *You may be able to get a grant from the local authority.* | *He cleared his throat to get our attention.* | **get sth for sb** *I want you to get some information for me.* | **get sb sth** *His father managed to get him a job at the local factory.*
3 BRING [T] to bring someone or something back from somewhere: *Run upstairs and get a pillow.* | *I went back into the office to get a pen.* | *Shall I **go and get** the phone book?* | **get sb/sth from sth** *She's just gone to get the kids from school.* | **get sth for sb** *I'll get a towel for you.* | **get sb sth** *I'll get you a chair.* THESAURUS BRING
4 BUY [T] **a)** to buy something: *Where did you get that jacket?* | **get sth for sb** *Joe's going to get tickets for all of us.* | **get sb sth** *While you're out, could you get me some batteries?* | **get yourself sth** *He's just got himself a new van.* | **get sth from sth** *I usually get vegetables from the supermarket.* | **get sth for $20/£100/50p etc** *You can get a decent PC for about £500 now.* | *It's a lovely coat, and I managed to **get** it **cheap** in the sales.* **b)** *spoken* to pay for something for someone else: *I'll get these drinks.* **c)** to buy a newspaper regularly: *My parents always used to get the 'Daily Telegraph'.* THESAURUS BUY
5 MONEY [T] **a)** to receive money for doing work: *Hospital doctors get a minimum of £50,000 a year.* | **get £2,000/$4,000 etc for doing sth** *He gets £4 an hour for stacking shelves.* **b)** to receive money when you sell something: **get £100/$200 etc for sth** *You should get a couple of hundred pounds for your old car.* | *Did you **get a good price for** it?* THESAURUS EARN
6 HAVE A FEELING/IDEA [T] to start to have a feeling or an idea: *She began to get an uncomfortable feeling that she was being watched.* | *I got a terrible shock when I saw how ill he looked.* | *I got the impression that everyone was fed up with us.* | **get pleasure from/out of sth** *She gets a lot of pleasure from her garden.*
7 HAVE/EXPERIENCE [T] to have, do, or experience something: *You don't get enough exercise.* | *I never get time to read these days.* | *The west of the country gets quite a lot of rain.* | *We might get the chance to go to America this year.*
8 ILLNESS [T not in passive] to catch an illness: *I got flu last winter and was in bed for three weeks.* | *She was worried she might get food poisoning.*
9 ACHIEVE [T] to achieve something: *I got 98% in my last maths test.* | *the person who gets the highest score*
10 RECEIVE A PUNISHMENT [T] to receive something as a punishment: *He got ten years in prison for his part in the robbery.*

11 ARRIVE [I always + adv/prep] to arrive somewhere: *What time will we get there?* | *We didn't get home until midnight.* | **[+to]** *We got to Paris that evening.* THESAURUS ARRIVE

12 REACH A POINT [I always + adv/prep] to reach a particular point or stage of something: *I've got as far as chapter 5.* | *I couldn't wait to get to the end of the book.* | *Where have you got up to in the story?* | *It was disappointing to lose, having got this far in the competition.*

13 get (sb) somewhere/anywhere/nowhere if you get somewhere, or if an action gets you somewhere, you make progress: *I think we're getting somewhere at last.* | *We didn't seem to be getting anywhere.* | *I've tried arguing, but it got me nowhere.*

14 MOVE [I always + adv/prep] to move or go somewhere: *Get out of my house!* | *We managed to get past the guards.* | *They shouted at us to get back.* | *Peter* ***got to*** *his* ***feet*** (=stood up).

15 MAKE STH MOVE [T always + adv/prep] to make something or someone move to a different place or position, especially with some difficulty: *I couldn't get the disk out of the computer.* | *Could you help me get the wardrobe up the stairs?* | *We must get food and emergency aid into the area as quickly as possible.*

16 TRAVEL [T] to travel somewhere on a train, bus etc: *You can get a bus to the station.* | *I got the 9.15 from London to Edinburgh.*

17 BECOME [linking verb] to change to a new feeling, situation, or state SYN **become**: *Don't get upset.* | *She soon got bored with the job.* | *He calmed down as he got older.* | *Eat your dinner before it gets cold.* | *This is getting silly.* | **get to be sth** *informal*: *It's getting to be a problem.* THESAURUS BECOME

GRAMMAR: Linking verbs

In this meaning, **get** is used as a linking verb. It links the subject of the sentence with an adjective: *I'm getting tired now.* | *It soon got dark.*

18 MAKE SB/STH BECOME STH [T] to make someone or something change to a new feeling, situation, or state: *Sometimes she gets me so angry!* | *Don't get the children too excited.* | *He was terrified of getting her pregnant.* | *It took them 15 minutes to get the boat ready.*

19 BE HURT/BROKEN ETC [linking verb, T] used to say that something, especially something bad, happens to someone or something: **get hurt/broken/stolen etc** *You might get hurt if you stand there.* | *Mind the camera doesn't get broken.* | *My dad got killed in a car crash.* | *I knew I would get shouted at if I was late home.* | *This is a question we very often get asked.* | **get sth caught/stuck etc** *She got her foot caught in the wire.*

20 MAKE STH HAPPEN TO SB/STH [T] **a)** to accidentally make someone or something experience something: *You're going to get us all killed!* | *Mind you don't get yourself burned.* **b)** to do something, or arrange for it to be done: *I need to get the washing machine fixed.* | *We must get this work finished on time.*

21 MAKE STH DO STH [T] to make something do a particular thing: **get sth to do sth** *I couldn't get the engine to start.* | **get sth doing sth** *We got the lawn mower working again eventually.*

22 MAKE SB DO STH [T] to persuade or force someone to do something: **get sb to do sth** *I'll get Terry to check the wiring for me.* | *We couldn't get him to sign the agreement.* | **get sb doing sth** *In the end, we got the children clearing the playground.*

23 UNDERSTAND [T] *informal* to understand something: *I don't think she got the joke.* | *I don't* ***get it*** *– it doesn't make sense.* | **get what/how/who etc** *I still don't get how she knew about the meeting.* THESAURUS UNDERSTAND

24 COOK [T] to prepare food or a meal: *She's just getting lunch.* | **get sb sth** *Shall I get you a sandwich?*

25 RADIO/TELEVISION [T] to be able to receive a particular radio signal, television station etc: *Can you get satellite TV here?*

26 ANSWER THE DOOR/TELEPHONE [T] *informal* to answer the door or telephone: *Can you get the phone?*

27 CATCH SB [T] to catch someone: *The police got him in the end.*

28 HURT/KILL SB [T] *informal* to attack, hurt, or kill someone: *The other gang members threatened to get him if he went to the police.* | *I'll get you for this!*

29 TRICK SB [T] *informal* to deceive or trick someone: *I got you that time!*

30 ON THE TELEPHONE [T] if you get someone on the telephone, they answer the telephone when you have made a call, and so you talk to them: *I tried phoning him at work, but I just got his secretary.*

31 get doing sth to begin doing something: *We got talking about the old days.* | *I think we should get going quite soon.* | *What are we all waiting for? Let's get moving!*

32 get to do sth *informal* to have the opportunity to do something: *We got to meet all the stars after the show.* | *She gets to travel all over the place with her job.*

33 get to like/know/understand sb/sth to gradually begin to like, know, or understand someone or something: *It'll take a while for you to get to know everyone.* | *After a while, I got to like him.* → **have got** at HAVE[1]

SPOKEN PHRASES

34 you get sth used to say that something happens or exists: *I didn't know you got tigers in Europe.*

35 you've got me (there) used to say you do not know the answer to something

36 it/what gets me used to say that something really annoys you: *It really gets me the way he leaves wet towels on the bathroom floor.* | *What gets me is their attitude.*

37 get this *especially AmE* used to draw attention to something surprising or interesting that you are about to mention: *And the whole thing only cost – get this – $12.95.*

THESAURUS

get [not in passive] to get something by finding it, asking for it, or paying for it: *I've been trying to get some information.* | *She went to the bank to get some money.*

obtain *formal* to get something: *Maps and guides can be obtained from the tourist office.* | *The newspaper has obtained a copy of the letter.*

acquire *formal* to get something – used about knowledge, skills, or something big or expensive: *The course helps older people to acquire computing skills.* | *He acquired the property in 1985.*

inherit to get someone's money or property after they die: *Jo inherited a lot of money from her mother.*

gain to get something useful or necessary, such as knowledge or experience: *I've gained a lot of useful experience.* | *The research helped us gain an insight into how a child's mind works.*

earn to get something because you deserve it: *He had earned a reputation as a peacemaker.* | *She earned a lot of respect from her colleagues.*

get hold of sth *informal* to get something that is rare or difficult to find: *I'm trying to get hold of a ticket for the game.*

lay your hands on sth *informal* to get something that you want very much or that you have spent a lot of time looking for: *I read every book I could lay my hands on.*

get about *phr v BrE*
1 to go or travel to different places: *She's 80 now, and doesn't get about much anymore.* | *He's got an old van which he uses for getting about.*
2 if news or information gets about, it is told to a lot of people: *I don't really want this to get about.*

get across *phr v* to succeed in communicating an idea or piece of information to someone, or to be communicated successfully: **get sth ↔ across** *It took him ages to get his point across.* | *We must get across the simple fact that drugs are dangerous.* | *The message isn't getting across.* | **[+to]** *It is important that we get this message across to voters.*

get ahead *phr v* to be successful and do better than other people in a job or work: *She soon found that it wasn't easy to get ahead in the movie business.*

G

get along *phr v*
1 if two or more people get along, they have a friendly relationship: *We've always got along quite well.* | **[+with]** *They seem to get along with each other.*
2 to deal with a job or situation or to make progress: *How's Sam getting along at university?* | **[+without]** *Don't worry, we'll get along without you.*
3 I must/I'd better be getting along *spoken* used to say that it is time for you to leave, for example because you have something else to do
get around *phr v*
1 get around (sth) to go or travel to different places: *We had to use public transport to get around.* | *It's quite easy to get around London.*
2 if news or information gets around, it is told to a lot of people: *News of the accident soon got around.* | *Word got around that the department might be closed.*
3 get around sth to avoid something that is difficult or causes problems for you: *I think we should be able to get around most of these problems.* | *She was always very clever at getting around the rules.*
get around to sth *phr v* to do something that you have been intending to do for some time: *I meant to phone her yesterday, but I never got around to it.* | **get around to doing sth** *We finally got around to clearing out the garage.*
get at sb/sth *phr v*
1 CRITICIZE to keep criticizing someone in an unkind way: *Why is he always getting at me?* | *He felt he was being got at by the other students.*
2 be getting at sth to be trying to say something in a way that is difficult for other people to understand: *What are you getting at, Helen?* | *Do you see the point I'm getting at?*
3 REACH to be able to reach something: *We had to move the washing machine out to get at the wiring behind it.*
4 INFORMATION to discover information, especially the truth about a situation: *I was determined to get at the truth.*
5 THREATEN *informal* to use threats to influence the decision of people who are involved in a court case: *Do you think some of the jury have been got at?*
get away *phr v*
1 LEAVE to leave a place, especially when this is not easy: *The meeting dragged on, and I didn't get away until seven.* | **[+from]** *I like to get away from London at the weekend.*
2 ON HOLIDAY *informal* to take a holiday away from the place you normally live: *Will you manage to get away this summer?* | **[+to]** *We're hoping to get away to Scotland for a few days.*
3 ESCAPE to escape from someone who is chasing you or trying to catch you: *The three men got away in a stolen car.* | **[+from]** *We knew it wouldn't be easy to get away from the police.* | **[+with]** *The thieves got away with jewellery worth over £50,000.*
4 get away! *BrE spoken* used to say you are very surprised by something or do not believe it
5 the one that got away something good that you nearly had or that nearly happened
get away from sb/sth *phr v*
1 to avoid something that is difficult or unpleasant for you, or something that limits what you can do in some way: *I needed to get away from the pressures of work.* | *She wanted to get away from the traditional ideas of what theatre is about.* | ***There is no getting away from** this fact* (=you cannot avoid or deny this fact).
2 to begin to talk about other things rather than the subject you are supposed to be discussing: *I think we're getting away from the main issue.*
3 get away from it all to have a relaxing holiday: *You need to get away from it all for a couple of weeks.*
get away with sth *phr v*
1 to not be caught or punished when you have done something wrong: *Watch Frank – he'll cheat if he thinks he can get away with it.* | *No one insults my family and gets away with it!*
2 get away with murder *informal* to not be punished for doing something wrong: *Some of those children get away with murder!*
3 to receive only a small punishment for something: *The charge was reduced to manslaughter, and she got away with three years in prison.*
4 to do something without experiencing any problems or difficulties, even though it is not the best thing to do: *At school he had always got away with doing the bare minimum amount of work.* | *The colour's not quite right, but I think you'll get away with it.*
get back *phr v*
1 RETURN to return to a place: *I'll talk to you when I get back.* | **[+to]** *He got back to the office just before lunchtime.*
2 DO STH AGAIN to start doing something again or talking about something again: **[+to]** *Let's get back to the main point of the discussion.* | *Well, I must get back to work.* | **[+into]** *Have you ever thought about getting back into teaching?*
3 BE IN A STATE AGAIN to change to a previous state or condition again: **[+to]** *Life was beginning to **get back to normal**.* | *I couldn't **get back to sleep**.* | **[+together]** *Do you think they'll get back together* (=start having a relationship again)?
4 GET STH AGAIN **get sth ↔ back** to get something again after you have lost it or someone else has taken it: *Did you get your books back?*
5 PUNISH SB **get sb back** *informal* to do something to hurt or harm someone who has hurt or harmed you: **[+for]** *I'll get you back for this!*
get back at sb *phr v* to do something to hurt or harm someone who has hurt or harmed you: *He'll probably go out with her just to get back at me.*
get back to sb *phr v informal* to talk to someone or telephone them later in order to answer a question or give them information: *I'll find out the prices and get back to you.*
get behind *phr v*
1 if you get behind with a job, payments, rent etc, you do not do or pay as much of it as you should have by a particular time: **[+with]** *I don't want to get behind with my work.* | *You can always catch up later if you get behind.*
2 get behind sb *informal* to support someone: *The crowd really got behind them and cheered them on.*
get by *phr v* to have enough money to buy the things you need, but no more: *I don't earn a huge salary, but we get by.* | **[+on]** *Sometimes they had to get by on very little.*
get down *phr v*
1 MAKE SB SAD **get sb down** to make someone feel unhappy and tired: *His lack of social life was beginning to get him down.*
2 WRITE STH DOWN **get sth ↔ down** to write something, especially something that someone is saying: *He was followed by a group of reporters trying to get down every word he said.* | *It's important to get things down on paper.*
3 EAT/DRINK **get sth down (sb)** to eat or drink something, or persuade someone else to eat or drink something: *I knew I'd feel better once I'd got some food down.* | *Get that tea down you.* | *He still says he's not hungry, and I can't get anything down him.*
4 AFTER A MEAL *BrE* to leave the table after a meal – used by children or when you are talking to children: *Please may I get down?*
get down to sth *phr v* to start doing something that is difficult or needs a lot of time or energy: *It's time we got down to work.* | *We need to get down to some serious talking.* | **get down to doing sth** *I always find it hard to get down to revising.*
get in *phr v*
1 ENTER to enter a place, especially when this is difficult: *We managed to get in through a window.* | *The theatre was already full, and we couldn't get in.*
2 ARRIVE if a train, plane etc gets in at a particular time, it arrives at that time: *What time does the bus get in?* | **[+to]** *We get in to Heathrow at ten o'clock.*
3 GET HOME to arrive home: *We didn't get in until late.* | *What time do the boys get in from school?*
4 BE ELECTED to be elected to a position of political power: *The Conservatives have promised to increase spending on health and education if they get in.*
5 COLLEGE/UNIVERSITY to be allowed to be a student at a

G

university, college etc: *I applied to Bristol University, but I didn't get in.*
6 BUY A SUPPLY **get sth ↔ in** to buy a supply of something: *I must remember to get some food in for the weekend.*
7 CROPS **get sth ↔ in** to gather a crop and bring it to a sheltered place: *The whole village was involved with getting the harvest in.*
8 ASK FOR WORKER **get sb ↔ in** to ask someone to come to your home to do a job, especially to repair something: *We'll have to get a plumber in.*
9 GIVE STH TO SB **get sth in** to send something to a particular place or give it to a particular person: *Please can you get your essays in by Thursday.* | *It's best to get your insurance claim in as quickly as possible.*
10 DO STH **get sth ↔ in** to manage to do something even though you do not have much time: *We're hoping to get in a game of golf over the weekend.*
get in on sth *phr v informal* to become involved in something that other people are doing or planning: *Quite a few companies would like to get in on the project.* | *The scheme has proved very successful, and now other local authorities are keen to* ***get in on the act*** (=become involved in something exciting or interesting).
get in with sb *phr v informal* to become friendly with someone: *He got in with a bad crowd and started getting into trouble.*
get into sth
1 ENTER to enter a place, especially when this is difficult: *The door was locked and we couldn't get into the house.*
2 ARRIVE to arrive at a place: *What time do we get into New York?*
3 BE ELECTED to be elected to a Parliament: *He first got into Parliament in 1982.*
4 COLLEGE/UNIVERSITY to be allowed to be a student at a university, college etc: *She got into UCLA.*
5 TEAM to be made a member of a team: *Do you think you might get into the Olympic team this year?*
6 START DOING STH to start doing or feeling something, or being in a particular situation: *He's started getting into trouble at school.* | *My parents were always terrified of getting into debt.* | *She got into the habit of going for long walks by herself.* | *He got into a terrible temper and started throwing things around.*
7 BECOME INVOLVED to begin to be involved in doing something: *How did you first get into script writing?* | *She was starting to get into politics.*
8 ENJOY *informal* to begin to enjoy something or be interested in it: *I first got into jazz when I was at college.*
9 CLOTHING *informal* to put on a piece of clothing, especially when this is difficult because the piece of clothing is too small for you: *I don't know how she managed to get into those trousers.*
10 what's got into sb? *spoken* used to express surprise that someone is behaving very differently from the way they usually behave: *I don't know what's got into Sally recently.*
get off *phr v*
1 LEAVE to leave a place, or to help someone to leave a place: *We'll try and get off straight after lunch.* | **get off sth** *Get off my land!* | **get sb off** *I'll phone you as soon as I've got the children off to school.*
2 FINISH WORK **get off (sth)** to finish work and leave the place where you work at the end of the day: *I usually get off at six o'clock.* | *What time do you* ***get off work****?*
3 SEND STH **get sth off** to send a letter or package by post: *I'll have to get this letter off by tonight.* | **[+to]** *I'll get the forms off to you today.*
4 CLOTHING **get sth off** to remove a piece of clothing: *Why don't you get those wet clothes off?*
5 NOT BE PUNISHED if someone gets off, they are not punished for doing something wrong, or they receive only a small punishment: *In the end he got off because there wasn't enough evidence against him.* | *The police felt he had got off very lightly.* | **[+with]** *If you're lucky, you'll get off with a fine.*
6 HELP SB NOT BE PUNISHED **get sb off** to help someone avoid being punished for a crime: *Her lawyers were confident that they could get her off.*
7 SLEEP **get (sb) off** to go to sleep, or to help a child go to sleep: *I went to bed but couldn't* ***get off to sleep****.* | *It took us ages to get the baby off.*
8 get off to a good/bad etc start to start in a particular way: *The day had got off to a bad start.*
9 STOP TALKING ABOUT STH **get off sth** to stop talking about a subject: *Can we get off the subject of death, please?*
10 STOP TOUCHING STH **get off (sth/sb)** *informal* used to tell someone to stop touching something or someone: *Get off me!* | *Get off those cakes, or there'll be trouble.* | *Get off* (=stop touching me)*!*
11 tell sb where to get off *informal* to tell someone that they are asking you for too much or are behaving in a way you will not accept: *He wanted £50, but I told him where to get off.*
12 get off your butt/ass *AmE spoken not polite* used to tell someone that they should stop being lazy and start doing something useful
get off on sth *phr v informal* to become excited by something, especially sexually excited
get off with sb *phr v informal* to start a sexual relationship with someone: *She spent the whole evening trying to get off with Phil.*
get on *phr v*
1 LIKE SB *especially BrE* if people get on, they like each other and have a friendly relationship with each other: **[+with]** *I've always got on well with Henry.* | *The two boys get on well most of the time.*
2 PROGRESS to deal with a job or situation or to make progress: *How is George getting on at school?* | **[+with]** *How are you getting on with your essay?* | **[+without]** *I don't know how we'll get on without Michael.*
3 CONTINUE DOING STH to continue doing something: **[+with]** *Be quiet and get on with your work!*
4 BE SUCCESSFUL to be successful in your job: *You'll have to work hard if you want to get on.*
5 CLOTHING **get sth on** to put a piece of clothing on: *I can't get my boots on!*
6 be getting on a) if time is getting on, it is quite late: *Come on, it's getting on and we ought to go home.* | *I realized that time was getting on and we would have to hurry.* **b)** *informal* if someone is getting on, they are quite old
7 getting on for 90/10 o'clock/2,000 etc almost a particular age, time, number etc: *Mrs McIntyre must be getting on for 90 by now.* | *The total cost was getting on for $100,000.*
8 get it on *AmE informal* to have sex
9 get on with it! *spoken* used to tell someone to hurry: *Will you lot stop messing around and get on with it!*
10 let sb get on with it *informal* to let someone do something on their own, and not help them or tell them what to do: *She wanted to decorate her room, so I just let her get on with it.*
get onto sb/sth *phr v*
1 SPEAK/WRITE TO SB *informal* to speak or write to someone: *I'll get onto my lawyer about this.*
2 LEARN ABOUT SB *informal* to find out about someone who has been doing something wrong: *How did the police get onto him?*
3 BE ELECTED to be elected as a member of a committee, a political organization etc: *She was quite keen to get onto the management committee.*
4 TALK ABOUT STH to begin to talk about a subject after you have been discussing something else: *After a few minutes they got onto the subject of the election.*
5 DO STH *informal* to start dealing with something: *Right, I'll get onto it straight away.*
get out *phr v*
1 LEAVE to leave a room or building: *You ought to get out into the fresh air.* | *Mary screamed at me to get out.* | **[+of]** *Get out of the kitchen!*
2 ESCAPE to escape from a place: *Some of the animals had got out.* | **[+of]** *He was determined to get out of prison.*
3 HELP SB ESCAPE **get sb out** to help someone leave a place or escape from a place: *It's important to get these people out as soon as possible.* | **[+of]** *We knew it was going to be difficult to get him out of the country.*
4 TAKE STH FROM A PLACE **get sth ↔ out** to take something

G

from the place where it is kept: *She got out her violin and started to play.*
5 INFORMATION if information gets out, a lot of people then know it although it is meant to be secret: *We have to make absolutely certain that none of this gets out.* | *It's bound to get out that he's retiring soon.*
6 PRODUCE STH **get sth ↔ out** to produce a book or other product that can be sold to people: *We're hoping to get the new catalogue out next week.*
7 SAY STH **get sth ↔ out** to succeed in saying something, especially when this is very difficult: *I wanted to tell him I loved him, but couldn't get the words out.*
get out of sth *phr v*
1 AVOID DOING STH to avoid doing something you have promised to do or are supposed to do: *See if you can get out of that meeting tomorrow.* | **get out of doing sth** *He's trying to get out of tidying his room.*
2 STOP DOING STH to stop doing something or being involved in something: *I wanted to get out of teaching.*
3 MAKE SB GIVE/TELL YOU STH **get sth out of sb** to force or persuade someone to tell you something or give you something: *I was determined to get the truth out of her.*
4 ENJOY STH **get sth out of sth** to enjoy something you do or experience, or to learn something as a result: *I hope he got something out of his visit.* | **get sth out of doing sth** *Children can get a lot out of being involved in community projects.*
get over
1 ILLNESS **get over sth** to become well again after an illness: *It's taken me ages to get over the flu.*
2 UNPLEASANT EXPERIENCE **get over sth** to begin to feel better after a very upsetting experience: *She never got over the death of her son.*
3 IDEAS/INFORMATION **get sth ↔ over** to succeed in communicating ideas or information to other people: **[+to]** *It's important that we get this message over to young people.*
4 FINISH STH **get sth over** (*also* **get sth over with**) to do and finish something difficult that you have to do: *I'll be in touch once I've got my exams over.* | *I can't wait to get the interview over with.*
5 PROBLEM/DIFFICULTY **get over sth** to successfully deal with a problem or difficulty: *I don't know how we're going to get over this problem.* | *Once we've got over the first few months, we should be making a reasonable profit.*
6 can't/couldn't get over sth *spoken* used to say that you are very surprised, shocked, or amused by something: *I can't get over how well you look.*
7 get over yourself *informal* to stop being so sensitive or proud: *Get over yourself! Nobody cares if you've made a mistake.*
get round *phr v BrE*
1 if news or information gets round, it is told to a lot of people: *News like this soon gets round.*
2 get round sth to avoid something that is difficult or causes problems for you: *Most companies manage to get round the restrictions.*
3 get round sb to gently persuade someone to do what you want by being nice to them: *I know how to get round Chris.*
get round to sth *phr v BrE* to do something that you have been intending to do for some time: *I keep meaning to put a lock on it, but I never get round to it.* | **get round to doing sth** *I haven't got round to unpacking from my holiday yet.*
get through *phr v*
1 DO WORK **get through sth** to do an amount of work: *We got through half the application forms this morning.* | *We've got a lot of work to get through.*
2 USE STH **get through sth** *informal* to use a lot of something: *You wouldn't believe the amount of food children can get through in a week!*
3 SPEND MONEY **get through sth** *informal* to spend a lot of money: *He can get through £100 in one evening.*
4 DIFFICULT TIME **get (sb) through sth** to come successfully to the end of an unpleasant experience or period of time, or to help someone do this: *I don't know how we're going to get through the winter.* | *It was their love that got me through those first difficult months.*
5 TEST/COMPETITION **get (sb/sth) through (sth)** to be successful in a test or competition, or to make sure that someone or something is successful: *I finally managed to get through my driving test.* | *I knew it was going to be difficult to get the car through its MOT test.* | **[+to]** *Liverpool have got through to the final of the FA Cup.*
6 REACH A PERSON/PLACE to reach a place or person that is difficult to reach: **[+to]** *Aid agencies have been unable to get through to the thousands of refugees stranded on the border.*
7 BY TELEPHONE to succeed in speaking to someone on the telephone: *I tried phoning her office, but I couldn't get through.* | **[+to]** *At last I managed to get through to one of the managers.*
8 NEW LAW **get (sth) through (sth)** if a new law gets through parliament, or if someone gets it through, it is officially approved: *Anti-hunting legislation will never get through the House of Lords.* | *Once again we failed to get the Bill through Parliament.*
get (sth) **through to** sb *phr v* to succeed in making someone understand something, especially when this is difficult: *I couldn't seem to get through to her.* | *How can I* ***get it through to*** *him* ***that*** *this is really important?*
get to sb/sth *phr v informal*
1 to make someone feel annoyed or upset: *I'm under a lot of pressure at work, and sometimes it gets to me a bit.* | *Don't let things get to you.*
2 get to thinking/wondering sth *informal* to start thinking something: *He got to thinking how disappointed his parents would be.*
get together *phr v*
1 if people get together, they meet in order to spend time with each other: *We must get together for a drink.*
2 if two people get together, they start a romantic or sexual relationship
3 get sth ↔ together to collect things together: *I need to get some paperwork together for the meeting.*
4 get sb ↔ together to bring people together to make a group: *He got together a group of local businessmen to discuss the problem.*
5 get sth ↔ together to succeed in getting enough money to do or buy something: *We're trying to get together enough money to buy a flat.*
6 get sth together *informal* to change your life so that it is organized and you are in control of it: *He's just trying to get his life together at the moment.* | **get yourself together** *I'm staying with my parents for a while, until I've got myself together a bit.*
7 get it together *spoken* to be organized and successful in your life, job etc: *The government can't seem to get it together on the environment.*
get up *phr v*
1 get (sb) up to get out of your bed after sleeping, or to make someone get out of their bed: *We didn't get up until lunchtime.* | *Get me up at seven, would you?*
2 to stand up: *He got up and walked over to the window.*
3 if a wind or storm gets up, it starts and gets stronger
4 be got up as/in sth *BrE informal* to be dressed in particular clothes: *He arrived at the party got up as Count Dracula.* | *The men were all got up in suits.*
5 get it up *informal* to get an ERECTION(1)
get up to sth *phr v* to do something, especially something slightly bad: *Go upstairs and see what the kids are getting up to.* | *What did you get up to at the weekend?*

get·a·way /ˈɡetəweɪ/ *n* [C] **1** an escape from a place or unpleasant situation, especially after committing a crime: *The gunmen* ***made a getaway*** *on foot.* | **getaway car/vehicle/van** (=a car etc used by criminals to escape after a crime) **2** *especially AmE* a short holiday away from home, or a place where people go for a short holiday: *Big Bear Lake is a popular* ***weekend getaway***.

ˈget-go *n* **from the get-go** *AmE informal* from the beginning: *From the get-go, I knew these tapes were special.*

ˈget-toˌgether *n* [C] a friendly informal meeting or party: *a family get-together* THESAURUS ▸ PARTY

get·up /ˈgetʌp/ *n* [C] *informal* a set of clothes, especially strange or unusual clothes: *I hardly recognized him in that getup!*

ˌget-up-and-ˈgo *n* [U] *informal* energy and determination to do things: *He was the only candidate who had any get-up-and-go.*

gey·ser /ˈgiːzə $ ˈgaɪzər/ *n* [C] **1** a natural spring that sends hot water and steam suddenly into the air from a hole in the ground **2** *BrE* a machine fixed to a wall over a bath or SINK and used for heating water

GEYSER

ghast·ly /ˈgɑːstli $ ˈgæstli/ ●○○ *adj*
1 very bad or unpleasant SYN **horrible**: *a ghastly little hotel | The whole thing was a ghastly mistake. | The weather was ghastly.* THESAURUS BAD
2 making you very frightened, upset, or shocked: *a ghastly accident*
3 look/feel ghastly to look or feel ill, upset, or unhappy: *Are you all right? You look ghastly!* —**ghastliness** *n* [U]

ghee /giː/ *n* [U] melted butter made from the milk of a cow or BUFFALO, used in Indian cooking

gher·kin /ˈgɜːkɪn $ ˈgɜːr-/ *n* [C] a small type of CUCUMBER that has been preserved in VINEGAR to make a type of PICKLE

ghet·to /ˈgetəʊ $ -toʊ/ ●○○ *n* (*plural* **ghettos** *or* **ghettoes**) [C]
1 a part of a city where people of a particular race or class, especially people who are poor, live separately from the rest of the people in the city. This word is sometimes considered offensive. → **slum**: *unemployment in the ghetto* THESAURUS AREA
2 a part of a city where Jews were forced to live in the past: *the Warsaw ghetto*

ˈghetto ˌblaster *n* [C] *informal* a large radio and CD PLAYER that can be carried around, and is often played very loudly in public places. This word is sometimes considered offensive in American English. SYN **boom box** *AmE*

ghet·to·ize *v* (*also* **-ise** *BrE*) /ˈgetəʊaɪz $ -toʊ-/ [T] **1** to force people to live in a ghetto **2** to make part of a town become a ghetto

ghost[1] /gəʊst $ goʊst/ ●●● S3 *n* [C]
1 SPIRIT the spirit of a dead person that some people think they can feel or see in a place: **[+of]** *the ghost of Old Tom Morris | They say the young girl's* ***ghost*** *still* ***haunts*** (=often appears in) *the house. | He looked as if he'd* ***seen a ghost*** (=he looked very frightened). → HOLY GHOST, THE
2 MEMORY/EFFECT the memory or effect of someone or something bad that lived, existed, or happened in the past: **[+of]** *The ghost of Stalinism still affects life in Russia today.*
3 the ghost of a smile/sound etc a smile etc that is so slight you are not sure it happened: *The ghost of a smile flitted across her sad features.*
4 TELEVISION/COMPUTER a second image that is not clear on a television or computer screen
5 give up the ghost a) if a machine gives up the ghost, it does not work anymore and cannot be repaired – used humorously: *Unfortunately, my car's just given up the ghost.* **b)** to die
6 (not) a ghost of a chance not even a slight chance of doing something, or of something happening: *They* ***don't stand a ghost of a chance*** *of winning.*

ghost[2] *v* [T] to write something as a GHOST WRITER

ghost·ly /ˈgəʊstli $ ˈgoʊst-/ *adj* slightly frightening and seeming to be related to ghosts or spirits: *a ghostly figure in a white dress*

ˈghost ˌstory *n* [C] a story about ghosts that is intended to frighten people

ˈghost town *n* [C] a town that used to have a lot of people living and working in it, but now has very few or none

ˈghost train *n* [C] a small train ride at a FUNFAIR, that is designed to frighten you by taking you through a dark place full of SKELETONS and things that jump out at you

ˈghost ˌwriter *n* [C] someone who is paid to write a book or story for another person, who then says it is their own work —**ghost-write** *v* [T]

ghoul /guːl/ *n* [C] **1** an evil spirit in stories that takes bodies from GRAVES (=place in the ground where dead people are buried) and eats them **2** someone who gets pleasure from unpleasant things such as accidents that shock other people —**ghoulish** *adj*

GHQ /ˌdʒiː eɪtʃ ˈkjuː/ *n* [U] (***general headquarters***) the place that a large military operation is controlled from

GI /ˌdʒiː ˈaɪ/ *n* [C] a soldier in the US army, especially during the Second World War

gi·ant[1] /ˈdʒaɪənt/ ●●● S3 W2 *adj* [only before noun] extremely big, and much bigger than other things of the same type: *a giant electronics company | a giant tortoise*

giant[2] ●●● W3 *n* [C]
1 an extremely tall strong man, who is often bad and cruel, in children's stories
2 a very large successful company: *the German chemicals giant, BASF* THESAURUS COMPANY
3 a very big man, animal, or plant
4 someone who is very good at doing something: **[+of]** *Miles Davis, truly one of the giants of jazz*

gi·ant·ess /ˈdʒaɪəntes/ *n* [C] an extremely tall strong woman, who is often bad and cruel, in children's stories

ˈgiant ˌkiller *n* [C] *BrE* a person, sports team etc that defeats a much stronger opponent

ˌgiant ˈpanda *n* [C] a PANDA(1)

gib·ber /ˈdʒɪbə $ -ər/ *v* [I] to speak quickly in a way that is difficult to understand, especially because you are very frightened or shocked → **jabber**: **[+with]** *'It was her,' said Ruth, gibbering with fear.* —**gibbering** *adj BrE*: ***a gibbering wreck*** (=someone who is very shocked or frightened)

gib·ber·ish /ˈdʒɪbərɪʃ/ *n* [U] something you write or say that has no meaning, or is very difficult to understand SYN **nonsense**: *You're* ***talking gibberish****!*

gib·bet /ˈdʒɪbɪt/ *n* [C] a wooden frame on which criminals were HANGED in the past with a rope around their neck SYN **gallows**

gib·bon /ˈgɪbən/ *n* [C] a small animal like a monkey, with long arms and no tail, that lives in trees in Asia

gibe /dʒaɪb/ *n* [C] another spelling of JIBE

gib·lets /ˈdʒɪbləts/ *n* [plural] organs such as the heart and LIVER, that you remove from a chicken or other bird before you cook it

gid·dy /ˈgɪdi/ *adj* **1** feeling slightly sick and unable to balance, because everything seems to be moving SYN **dizzy**: *Greg stared down from the seventh floor and began to* ***feel giddy****.* **2** feeling silly, happy, and excited, or showing this feeling: **[+with]** *Sheila felt giddy with excitement.* **3 giddy heights** a situation in which you have a lot of success: *Although she had been quite a successful model, she had never reached the giddy heights of the Paris fashion world.* **4** *old-fashioned* silly and not interested in serious things: *Fiona's very pretty but a bit giddy.* —**giddily** *adv* —**giddiness** *n* [U]

GIF /gɪf/ *n* [C] *technical* (***graphics interchange format***) a type of computer FILE that contains images and is used on the Internet

gift[1] /gɪft/ ●●● S2 W2 *n* [C]
1 something that you give someone, for example to thank them or because you like them, especially on a special occasion SYN **present**: *The earrings were a gift from my aunt. |* **[+of]** *a generous gift of £50 | The clock was* ***given*** *as*

G

a retirement ***gift*** *when he left the police.* | *expensive* ***wedding gifts*** | *Enjoy a* ***free gift*** *with any purchase of $20 or more.* | *This excellent cookbook would* ***make an ideal gift*** *for anyone just going away to college.* **THESAURUS▸ PRESENT**

> **REGISTER**
> In everyday English, especially in British English, people usually say **present** rather than **gift**: *These were a* ***present*** *from my boyfriend.*

2 a) a natural ability SYN **talent**: **[+for]** *a gift for languages* | *He was a kind man, with a gift for forming lasting friendships.* | **[+of]** *She has the* ***rare gift*** *of being able to laugh at herself.* **b)** an ability that is given to you by God: **[+of]** *He was said to have possessed the gift of prophecy.* | *the use of* ***spiritual gifts*** → GIFTED **THESAURUS▸ SKILL**
3 a gift *BrE informal* something that is easier or cheaper than you expected: *The third goal was an absolute gift.*
4 gift (from God) something good you receive or something good that happens to you, even though you might not deserve it: *This opportunity was a gift from God.*
5 the gift of the gab *BrE*, **the gift of gab** *AmE informal* an ability to speak confidently and to persuade people to do what you want: *Jo has always* ***had the gift of the gab.***
6 be in sb's gift *BrE formal* if something is in your gift, you have the power to decide who it should be given to: *All appointments to military and administrative posts were in the gift of the King.*
7 never/don't look a gift horse in the mouth *spoken* used to tell someone to be grateful for something that has been given to them, instead of asking questions about it or finding something wrong with it → **God's gift to sb/sth** at GOD(3)

gift² *v* [T] to give something to someone as or like a present: **gift sb sth** *The local team was gifted victory as their opponents made a series of errors.* | **gift sth to sb** *The painting was gifted to the nation by its owner.*

G

ˈgift cerˌtificate *n* [C] *AmE* a special piece of paper that is worth a particular amount of money when it is exchanged for goods in a shop, often given as a present SYN **gift token** *BrE*

gift·ed /ˈɡɪftɪd/ ●○○ *adj* having a natural ability to do one or more things extremely well → **talented**: **gifted musician/artist/teacher etc** *She was an extremely gifted poet.* | **academically/musically/athletically etc gifted** *his musically gifted son* | **gifted child** (=one who is extremely intelligent) | **[+with]** *Gifted with a superb voice, she became the Opera's leading soprano.* **THESAURUS▸ INTELLIGENT, SKILFUL**

ˈgift shop *n* [C] a shop that sells small things that are suitable for giving as presents

ˈgift ˌtoken (*also* **ˈgift ˌvoucher**) *n* [C] *BrE* a special piece of paper that is worth a particular amount of money when it is exchanged for goods in a shop, often given as a present SYN **gift certificate** *AmE*

ˈgift wrap (*also* **ˈgift ˌwrapping**) *n* [U] attractive coloured paper used for wrapping presents in SYN **wrapping paper**

ˈgift-wrap, **gift wrap** *v* (**gift-wrapped**, **gift-wrapping**) [T] to wrap a present with gift wrap, especially in a shop: *Would you like that gift-wrapped, sir?*

gig¹ /ɡɪɡ/ *n* [C] **1** a performance by a musician or a group of musicians playing modern popular music or JAZZ, or a performance by a COMEDIAN: **do/play/have a gig** *The band are doing a gig in Sheffield on Nov 12.* **2** *informal* a job, especially one that does not last for a long time: *That's a nice gig if you can get it!* **3** *informal* a gigabyte

gig² *v* (**gigged**, **gigging**) [I] to give a performance of modern popular music or JAZZ

giga- /ɡɪɡə/ *prefix* [in nouns] a BILLION – used with units of measurement

gig·a·byte /ˈɡɪɡəbaɪt/ *n* [C] (*written abbreviation* **GB** *or* **Gb**) a unit for measuring computer information, equal to 1,024 MEGABYTES, and used less exactly to mean a BILLION bytes

gi·gan·tic /dʒaɪˈɡæntɪk/ ●●○ *adj* extremely big SYN **huge**: *a gigantic skyscraper* **THESAURUS▸ BIG** —**gigantically** /-kli/ *adv*

gig·a·pix·el /ˈɡɪɡəˌpɪksəl/ *n* [C] a BILLION PIXELS. Images with one or more gigapixels show a very large amount of detail.

gig·gle¹ /ˈɡɪɡəl/ ●○○ (**giggled**, **giggling**) *v* [I] to laugh quickly, quietly, and in a high voice, because something is funny or because you are nervous or embarrassed: *If you can't stop giggling you'll have to leave the room.* **THESAURUS▸ LAUGH**

giggle² ●○○ *n*
1 [C] a quick, quiet, high-sounding laugh: *'Catch me if you can,' she said with a giggle.* | *Vicky suppressed a* ***nervous giggle.*** | *He looked so ridiculous I* ***got the giggles*** (=started to giggle). | *Soon the whole group* ***had the giggles.*** | *Margaret was seized by* ***a fit of the giggles*** (=she could not stop giggling). | **give sb the giggles** (=make someone start giggling)
2 a giggle *BrE informal* something that you think is fun to do that will not hurt anyone or anything: *Go on, it'll be a giggle!*

gig·gly /ˈɡɪɡli/ *adj* giggling a lot: *a giggly schoolgirl*

gig·o·lo /ˈʒɪɡələʊ, ˈdʒɪ- $ -loʊ/ *n* (*plural* **gigolos**) [C] a man who is paid by a rich woman, especially an older woman, to have sex with her

gild /ɡɪld/ *v* [T] **1** to cover something with a thin layer of gold or with something that looks like gold: *a gilded frame* **2** *literary* to make something look as if it is covered in gold: *The autumn sun gilded the lake.* **3 gild the lily** to spoil something by trying to improve it when it is already good enough

gill¹ /ɡɪl/ *n* [C] **1** one of the organs on the sides of a fish through which it breathes → see picture at FISH **2 full/packed/stuffed etc to the gills** *informal* completely full: *The bar was packed to the gills on Monday.*

gill² /dʒɪl/ *n* [C] a unit for measuring liquid, equal to ¼ PINT. In Britain this is 0.14 litres, and in the US it is 0.12 litres.

gilt¹ /ɡɪlt/ *n* **1** [U] a thin shiny material, such as gold or something similar, used to cover objects for decoration **2** [C] a STOCK or SHARE that is GILT-EDGED

gilt² *adj* [only before noun] covered with gilt: *gilt lettering*

ˌgilt-ˈedged *adj technical* gilt-edged STOCKS or SHARES do not give you much INTEREST (=additional money) but are considered very safe as they are sold mainly by governments

gim·let /ˈɡɪmlɪt/ *n* [C] **1** a tool that is used to make small holes in wood so that you can put screws in easily **2 gimlet-eyed/gimlet eyes** if someone is gimlet-eyed, or has gimlet eyes, they look at things very hard and notice every detail

gim·me¹ /ˈɡɪmi/ a way of writing the non-standard spoken short form of 'give me': *Gimme the ball!*

gimme² *n* [C] *AmE informal* something that is so easy to do or succeed at that you do not even have to try: *The victory was a gimme for the New York Yankees.*

gim·mick /ˈɡɪmɪk/ *n* [C] *informal* a trick or something unusual that you do to make people notice someone or something – used to show disapproval → **stunt**: *advertising gimmicks* —**gimmicky** *adj* —**gimmickry** *n* [U]

gin /dʒɪn/ ●○○ *n*
1 [C,U] a strong alcoholic drink made mainly from grain, or a glass of this drink
2 [U] GIN RUMMY → **COTTON GIN, PINK GIN**

ˌgin and ˈtonic *n* [C,U] an alcoholic drink made with gin and TONIC (=a special type of bitter-tasting water), served with ice and a thin piece of LEMON or LIME

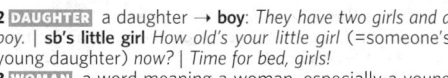

gin·ger¹ /ˈdʒɪndʒə $ -ər/ ●●○ *n* [U]
1 a root with a very strong hot taste, or the powder made from this root, that is used in cooking
2 the plant that this root comes from
3 a bright orange-brown colour → **gingery**

GINGER

ginger² *adj* **1** *BrE* hair or fur that is ginger is bright orange-brown in colour: *a ginger cat* **2** [only before noun] flavoured with ginger

ginger³ *v BrE*
ginger sth ↔ **up** *phr v* to make something more exciting

ˌginger ˈale / $ ˈ.../ *n* [C,U] a non-alcoholic drink that tastes of ginger and is often mixed with alcohol

ˌginger ˈbeer / $ ˈ.../ *n* [C,U] a non-alcoholic drink with a strong taste of ginger

gin·ger·bread /ˈdʒɪndʒəbred $ -dʒər-/ *n* [U] **1** a heavy sweet cake or a BISCUIT with ginger in it: **gingerbread man** (=a piece of gingerbread in the shape of a man) **2** *AmE* complicated decorations on the outside of a house, especially near the roof

ˈginger group *n* [C] *BrE* a group of people within a political party or organization who try to persuade the other members to support their ideas → **lobby**

gin·ger·ly /ˈdʒɪndʒəli $ -ər-/ *adv, adj* if you move gingerly, or touch something gingerly, you do it in a slow careful way, because you are afraid it will be dangerous or painful SYN **carefully**: *He gingerly felt his way along the dark tunnel.*

ˈginger nut *BrE*, **ˈginger snap** *AmE n* [C] a hard BISCUIT with ginger in it

gin·ger·y /ˈdʒɪndʒəri/ *adj* [usually before noun] gingery hair or fur is bright orange-brown in colour: *his gingery beard*

ging·ham /ˈɡɪŋəm/ *n* [U] cotton cloth that has a pattern of small white and coloured squares on it: *a red and white gingham tablecloth*

gin·gi·vi·tis /ˌdʒɪndʒɪˈvaɪtɪs/ *n* [U] a medical condition in which your GUMS are red, swollen, and painful

gi·nor·mous /dʒaɪˈnɔːməs $ -ˈnɔːr-/ *adj BrE informal* extremely large SYN **huge** —**ginormously** *adv*

ˌgin ˈrummy *n* [U] a type of RUMMY (=card game for two people)

gin·seng /ˈdʒɪnseŋ $ -sæŋ, -seŋ/ *n* [U] medicine made from the root of a Chinese plant, that some people think keeps you young and healthy

gip·sy /ˈdʒɪpsi/ *n* [C] another spelling of GYPSY

gi·raffe /dʒəˈrɑːf $ -ˈræf/ ●●○ *n* [C] a tall African animal with a very long neck and legs and dark spots on its yellow-brown fur

gird /ɡɜːd $ ɡɜːrd/ *v* (*past tense and past participle* **girded** *or* **girt** /ɡɜːt $ ɡɜːrt/) **1 gird (up) your loins** to get ready to do something difficult - used humorously **2** [I,T] if you gird for something, or gird yourself for something, especially something difficult, you prepare for it: **gird (yourself) for sth** *By midsummer both police and protesters were girding for confrontation.*

gir·der /ˈɡɜːdə $ ˈɡɜːrdər/ *n* [C] a strong beam, made of iron or steel, that supports a floor, roof, or bridge

gir·dle¹ /ˈɡɜːdl $ ˈɡɜːr-/ *n* [C] a piece of women's underwear which fits tightly around her stomach, bottom, and HIPS and makes her look thinner

girdle² *v* [T] *literary* to surround something: *the formal garden that girdled the house*

girl /ɡɜːl $ ɡɜːrl/ ●●● S1 W1 *n* [C]
1 CHILD a female child → **boy**: *Both* **boys and girls** *can apply to join the choir.* | **little/small/young girl** *I've known Mollie ever since I was a little girl.* | **five-year-old girl/girl of ten etc** *The patient was a girl of 12.* | *Girls! Please be quiet.* | *a teenage girl* THESAURUS ▸ WOMAN
2 DAUGHTER a daughter → **boy**: *They have two girls and a boy.* | **sb's little girl** *How old's your little girl* (=someone's young daughter) *now?* | *Time for bed, girls!*
3 WOMAN a word meaning a woman, especially a young woman, which is considered offensive by some women: *I'll invite some of the girls from the office.* | *Steve's married to a lovely Dutch girl.*
4 the girls *informal* a group of women who are friends and often go out together: *I'm going out with the girls tonight.*
5 ANIMAL used when speaking to a female animal, especially a dog, cat, or horse → **boy**: *Bring me the stick. Good girl!*
6 girl *AmE spoken informal* used by a woman when she is speaking to another woman she knows well: *Hey, girl. What's up?*
7 (you) go, girl! *AmE spoken informal* used to encourage a girl or woman, or to say that you agree with what she is saying
8 GIRLFRIEND *old-fashioned* a word for a woman who you are having a romantic relationship with SYN **girlfriend**
9 my girl *old-fashioned* used by an older person when speaking to a girl or woman who is younger than they are, or when they are annoyed: *Listen to me, my girl!*
10 factory girl/shop girl/office girl *old-fashioned* a young woman who works in a factory, shop, office etc
11 SERVANT *old-fashioned* a woman servant → OLD GIRL

ˌgirl ˈFriday *n* [C] *BrE old-fashioned* a girl or woman worker who does several different jobs in an office

girl·friend /ˈɡɜːlfrend $ ˈɡɜːrl-/ ●●● S3 *n* [C]
1 a girl or woman that you are having a romantic relationship with → **boyfriend**: *He's never* **had** *a* **girlfriend**. | **sb's girlfriend** *He lives in Chicago with his girlfriend.* | **split up/break up with your girlfriend** (=stop having a romantic relationship) | *one of my* **ex-girlfriends** (=former girlfriends) | *I didn't have a* **steady girlfriend** (=one you have a long relationship with).
2 *especially AmE* a woman or girl's female friend: *She's out with one of her girlfriends.*

girl·hood /ˈɡɜːlhʊd $ ˈɡɜːrl-/ *n* [U] the period of her life when a woman is a girl → **boyhood**

girl·ie¹, **girly** /ˈɡɜːli $ ˈɡɜːrli/ *adj informal* **1 girlie magazine/calendar etc** a magazine etc with pictures of women with no clothes on **2** *BrE* a girl or woman who is girlie behaves in a silly way, for example by pretending to be shy or always thinking about how she looks **3** *BrE spoken* suitable only for girls rather than men or boys: *Pink's a girlie colour!*

girlie² *n* [C] *old-fashioned not polite* an offensive word used by men when talking to a woman who they think is less sensible or intelligent than a man

girl·ish /ˈɡɜːlɪʃ $ ˈɡɜːr-/ *adj* behaving like a girl, looking like a girl, or suitable for a girl → **boyish**: *a peal of girlish laughter* —**girlishly** *adv*

ˈgirl ˌpower *n* [U] *informal* **1** the idea that women should take control over their own lives or situations **2** the social or political influence that women have

ˈGirl Scout *n* [C] a SCOUT (=member of the Girl Scouts Association in the US) → **Boy Scout**

girl·y /ˈɡɜːli $ ˈɡɜːrli/ *adj* another spelling of GIRLIE¹ THESAURUS ▸ WOMAN

gi·ro /ˈdʒaɪərəʊ $ ˈdʒaɪroʊ/ *n* (*plural* **giros**) *BrE* **1** [C] a cheque paid by the government to someone who is unemployed **2** [U] a system of BANKING in Britain in which a central computer can send money from one BANK ACCOUNT to another electronically

girt /ɡɜːt $ ɡɜːrt/ a past participle of GIRD

girth /ɡɜːθ $ ɡɜːrθ/ *n* [C] **1** the size of something or someone large when you measure around them rather than measuring their height: *the enormous girth of the tree* | *He was a tall man, of considerable girth* (=he was fat). **2** a band of leather which is passed tightly around the middle of a horse to keep a SADDLE or load firmly in position

gist /dʒɪst/ *n* **the gist** the main idea and meaning of what someone has said or written: **[+of]** *The gist of his*

G

argument is that full employment is impossible. | *Don't worry about all the details as long as you* ***get the gist*** (=understand the main meaning) *of it.*

git /gɪt/ *n* [C] *BrE spoken not polite* an offensive word for an unpleasant and annoying person, especially a man: *You miserable git!*

give[1] /gɪv/ ●●● S1 W1 *v* (*past tense* **gave** /geɪv/, *past participle* **given** /ˈgɪvən/)

1 PRESENT OR MONEY [I,T] to let someone have something as a present, or to provide something for someone: **give sb sth** *What did Bob give you for your birthday?* | *Researchers were given a £10,000 grant to continue their work.* | *I've got some old diaries that my grandmother gave me years ago.* | **give sth to sb** *a ring which was given to him by his mother* | *I didn't steal it! Maria gave it to me!* | *Most people are willing to* ***give to charity***. | *The situation is now desperate, so* ***please give generously***. ⚠ Don't say 'give to someone something': *He gave me a card (NOT He gave to me a card).* | *They gave a prize to the best chef (NOT They gave to the best chef a prize).*

2 PUT STH IN SB'S HAND [T] to put something in someone's hand: **give sb sth** *Give me the letter, please.* | **give sth to sb** *He poured some wine into a glass and gave it to her.*

3 LET SB DO STH [T] to allow or make it possible for someone to do something: **give sb sth** *He finally* ***gave*** *us* ***permission*** *to leave.* | *These meetings* ***give*** *everyone* ***a chance*** *to express their opinions.* | *Students are given the freedom to choose their own topics.* | *Language gives us the ability to communicate at a much higher level than any other animal.* | *Women were given the vote in the early 1900s.* | **give sb control/authority/responsibility etc** *She was given absolute control over all recruitment decisions.* | **give sth to sb** *This bill will give more power to local authorities.*

4 TELL SB STH [T] to tell someone information or details about something, or to tell someone what they should do: *She gave me some information on university courses.* | *My secretary will be able to give you more details.* | *Let me* ***give*** *you some* ***advice***. | **give orders/instructions** *She certainly likes giving orders.* | *They were given strict instructions not to tell anyone.* | *Can you* ***give*** *me* ***directions*** *to the station* (=tell me how to go there)*?* | *He* ***gave*** *the following* ***example***. | *You may have to* ***give evidence*** *in court* (=tell a court about what you have seen or know to be true). | **give an account/description** *He gave a disturbing account of the murder.*

5 MAKE A MOVEMENT/DO AN ACTION [T] to do something by making a movement with your hand, face, body etc: **give a smile/laugh/grin/frown/yawn etc** *She gave a little frown.* | *Joel gave me a smile as I walked in.* | *He gave her a big hug.* | **give a wave/movement/signal** *He gave a wave of his hand.* | *Don't move until I give the signal.* | **give sth a shake/rattle/tug etc** *She picked up the envelope and gave it a shake.*

6 SPEECH/TALK/PERFORMANCE [T] to make a speech, perform a piece of music etc for a group of people: **give a talk/speech/lecture** *He's giving a talk on early Roman pottery.* | **give a performance/display** *They gave one of their best performances to date.*

7 MAKE SB HAVE A FEELING [T] to make someone have a feeling: **give sb sth** *He* ***gave us*** *quite* ***a shock***. | *The course has* ***given*** *me a lot more* ***confidence***. | *His job did not give him much sense of fulfilment.* | **give sth to sb** *Their music has given pleasure to a lot of people over the years.* | **give sb a headache/hangover** *Keep the noise down – you're giving me a headache!*

8 MAKE SB HAVE PROBLEMS [T] to make someone have problems: **give sb problems/trouble/difficulties** *The new software has given us quite a few problems.*

9 MAKE SB ILL [T] to infect someone with the same illness that you have: **give sb sth** *Don't come too close – I don't want you to give me your cold!* | **give sth to sb** *It's very unlikely a doctor could give HIV to a patient.*

10 ORGANIZE A SOCIAL EVENT [T] to organize a social event such as a party SYN **hold**, **put on**: *We're* ***giving*** *a small* ***party*** *for dad's birthday next week.*

11 MAKE SB DO STH [T] to tell someone to do a job or piece of work: **give sb work/homework etc** *How much homework are you given in a week?* | *He's always giving us chores to do around the house.*

12 MAKE SB/STH HAVE A QUALITY [T] to make someone or something have a particular quality SYN **lend**: **give sb/sth sth** *The ginger gives the dish a wonderful spicy flavour.* | *His grey hair gave him an air of distinction.* | *Its association with the movie industry has given the place a certain glamor.*

13 PAY FOR [T] to pay a particular amount of money for something: *They say they're not willing to give any more than they've already offered.* | **give sb sth for sth** *They gave us £700 for our old car.* | *How much will you give me for these two games?* **THESAURUS▸ PAY**

14 BEHAVE TOWARDS [T] to behave towards someone in a way that shows you have a particular attitude or feeling towards them: **give sb loyalty/obedience/respect** *The people were expected to give their leader absolute obedience and loyalty.*

15 PUNISHMENT [T] to officially say that someone must have a particular punishment: **give sb a fine/a sentence** *If you don't pay on time, you could be given a fine of up to $1,000.* | **give sb six months/three years etc** (=in prison) *The judge gave her two years in prison.*

16 give (sb) an impression/a sense/an idea to make someone think about something in a particular way: *I didn't want to give him the wrong idea about the job.* | *The report gives us a very accurate picture of life in the inner cities.*

17 give sth thought/attention/consideration etc (*also* **give thought/attention/consideration etc to sth**) to spend some time thinking about something carefully: *Congress has been giving the crime bill serious consideration.* | *I'll give the matter some thought and let you know my decision next week.*

18 give (sb) a hand *spoken* to help someone do something: *Can you give me a hand?* | **[+with]** *Shall I give you a hand with that bag?*

19 give sb a call/buzz (*also* **give sb a ring/bell** *BrE*) *informal* to telephone someone: *I'll give you a call about seven, okay?*

20 give sth a try/shot/whirl (*also* **give sth a go** *BrE*) *informal* to try to do something, especially something you have not done before: *I'm not usually much good at this sort of game, but I'll give it a go.*

21 give sb time/a few weeks/all day etc to allow time for someone to do something, or for something to happen: *I've asked him to give me a couple more days to finish my essay.* | *Flexible working hours could give working parents more time to spend with their children.*

22 I give it six weeks/a month etc *spoken* used to say that you do not think something will continue successfully for very long: *I give the project six months at the most before it all falls apart.*

23 not give sth a second thought/another thought to not think or worry about something at all: *The matter didn't seem important, and I hardly gave it a second thought.*

24 BE LESS STRICT [I] to be willing to change what you think or do according to what else happens: *I think that both sides need to give a little.*

25 STATE A DECISION [T] *BrE* to state what your official decision or judgment is, for example in a game: *The referee has given a penalty.* | *The jury will be* ***giving*** *its* ***verdict*** *within the next couple of days.*

26 GIVE A MARK/SCORE [T] to decide that someone should have a particular score or mark for something that they have done: *She only gave me a B for my last essay.* | *The judges have given him top marks for this performance.*

27 BEND/STRETCH [I] if a material gives, it bends or stretches when you put pressure on it: *New shoes often feel tight, but the leather should give a little after a few days.*

28 BREAK/MOVE [I] if something gives, it breaks or moves away suddenly because of weight or pressure on it: *The branch suddenly gave beneath him.* | *I pushed against the door with all my might, but it still wouldn't give.*

29 give me sth (any day/time) *spoken* used to say that you like something much more than something else: *Give me good old-fashioned rock 'n' roll any day!*

G

30 would give anything/a lot/your right arm etc for sth *spoken* used when you would like something very much: *I'd give my right arm for a figure like that.*
31 not give a damn/shit etc *spoken not polite* used to say that you do not care at all about something: *I don't give a damn what you think.*
32 don't give me that *spoken* used to say that you do not believe someone's excuse or explanation: *Don't give me that! I know exactly where you've been!*
33 give sb what for *spoken* to tell someone angrily that you are annoyed with them: *I'll give that boy what for when I see him!*
34 give as good as you get to fight or argue with someone using the same amount of skill or force that they are using: *I don't worry about Emma because I know she can give as good as she gets.*
35 give and take *informal* to help other people and do things for them as well as expecting them to do things for you: *You have to learn to give and take in any relationship.*
36 give or take a few minutes/a penny/a mile etc *spoken* used to say that the amount or figure that you have just mentioned is nearly correct, but not exactly: *It'll be a £1,000, give or take £50 or so.*
37 I'll give you that *spoken* used to admit that someone is right about something: *I was wrong to trust him, I'll give you that.*
38 give sb to understand/think/believe sth *formal* to make someone think that a particular thing is true: *I was given to understand that I would be offered a permanent job.*
39 give it to sb straight *informal* to tell someone something in a clear direct way: *There's no point in beating about the bush, so I'll give it to you straight.*
40 I give you the chairman/prime minister/groom etc *BrE spoken* used at the end of a formal speech to invite people to welcome a special guest
41 SEX [T] *old-fashioned* if a woman gives herself to a man, she has sex with him

THESAURUS

give to let someone have something, without expecting to be paid for it: *He was always giving me gifts.* | *They gave a free drink to all their customers.*
donate to give money to an organization that helps people or protects something, or to give your blood or part of your body to save someone's life: *The company donates 1 per cent of its profits to charity.* | *70% of people wanted to donate their organs after death.*
award to officially give money or a prize to someone: *She was awarded a million dollars in damages.* | *Hollywood awarded him an Oscar for his performance.*
present to formally or officially give something to someone by putting it in their hands, especially at a formal ceremony: *They presented her with a bouquet of flowers.*
leave (*also* **bequeath** /bɪˈkwiːð, bɪˈkwiːθ/ *formal*) to officially arrange for someone to have something that you own after your death: *He left most of his property to his wife.*
lavish sb with sth/lavish sth on sb *formal* to give someone a lot of something, especially praise, attention, or gifts: *After his team won, the press lavished him with praise.*
confer *formal* to give someone an honour, a university degree, or the right or power to do something: *the powers conferred on him by Parliament*

TO GIVE SOMETHING TO A GROUP OF PEOPLE

hand sth out/give sth out to give something to each of the people in a group: *The teacher handed out the test papers.*
distribute to give things to a large number of people, especially in the streets: *Anti-war protesters were distributing leaflets.*
share (*also* **share sth out** *BrE*) to divide something into equal parts and give a part to each person: *They shared the profits among the staff.*

give sb/sth **away** *phr v*
1 to give something to someone because you do not want or need it for yourself: *I gave most of my books away when I left college.* | **[+to]** *Give your old clothes away to a thrift shop.*
2 to give something to someone without asking for any money, rather than selling it to them: *We're giving away a free diary with tomorrow's newspaper.* | **[+to]** *We have 1,000 CDs to give away to our readers.*
3 to show where someone is or what they are doing or thinking when they are trying to keep this a secret: *Don't worry, I won't give you away.* | *Sue tried to smile, but her voice gave her away.* | **give yourself away** *I knew that if I moved I would give myself away.* | *The look on his face* ***gave the game away*** (=showed something that he was trying to keep secret).
4 to tell someone something that you should keep secret: *He gave away as little information as possible.* | *I don't want to give away exactly how the system works.* | *I don't want to* ***give the game away*** (=give information that should be secret) *by saying too much.*
5 to lose in a game or competition by doing something badly or making mistakes: *We gave away two goals in the first half.* | *The Democrats are now in danger of giving the whole election away.*
6 to give formal permission for a woman to marry a man as part of a traditional wedding ceremony
give sth ↔ **back** *phr v*
1 to give something to the person it belongs to or the person who gave it to you: *This isn't your money and you must give it back.* | *Of course you can have a look at it, as long as you give it back.* | **give sth back to sb** *I'll give the keys back to you tomorrow morning.* | **give sb sth ↔ back** *Her ex-husband refused to give her back any of her old photos and letters.*
2 to make it possible for someone to have or do something again SYN **restore**: **give sb sth ↔ back** *He underwent an expensive operation to give him back his sight.* | *The company finally agreed to give the women their old jobs back.* | **give sth back to sb** *This legislation will give more power back to local authorities.*
give in *phr v*
1 to finally agree to do or accept something that you had at first opposed, especially because someone has forced or persuaded you to: *Eventually I gave in and accepted the job on their terms.* | *Bob's wife went on at him so much that eventually he gave in.* | **[+to]** *The government refused to give in to their demands.*
2 to accept that you are defeated in a game, fight, competition etc → **surrender**: *The rebels were eventually forced to give in.* | *We will carry on fighting to the end. We will never give in.*
3 give sth ↔ in *BrE* to give a piece of work or something you have written to someone in authority SYN **hand in**: *You were supposed to give this work in four days ago.* | *Rose decided to* ***give in*** *her* ***notice*** (=officially say she was going to leave her job). | **[+to]** *All assignments must be given in to your teacher by Friday.*
give in to sth *phr v* to no longer try to stop yourself from doing something you want to do: *Don't give in to the temptation to argue back.* | *If you feel the urge for a cigarette, try not to give in to it.*
give of sth *phr v formal* if you give of yourself, your time, your money etc, you do things for other people without expecting anything in return: *Retired people are often willing to give of their time to help with community projects.*
give off sth *phr v* to produce a smell, light, heat, a sound etc: *The wood gave off a sweet, perfumed smell as it burned.*
give onto sth *phr v* if a window, door, or building gives onto a particular place, it leads to that place or you can see that place from it: *the garden gate that gives onto the main road* | *a small balcony giving onto fields*
give out *phr v*
1 give sth ↔ out to give something to each person in a group SYN **hand out**: *Can you give the drinks out, please?* | **[+to]** *Students were giving out leaflets to everyone on the street.*

2 if part of your body gives out, it stops working properly or becomes much weaker: *Just as I approached the town, my legs finally gave out.*
3 if a supply of something gives out, there is none left: *My money was beginning to give out and there were no jobs to be found.* | *After two hours her patience gave out.*
4 give out sth to produce something such as light, heat, or a signal SYN **emit**: *A gas lamp gave out a pale yellowish light.*
5 give sth ↔ out *BrE formal* to announce something, especially officially: *It was given out that the government was to enter into negotiations with the rebels.*
give over *phr v BrE spoken informal* to stop doing or saying something that is annoying other people: *I wish you lot would just give over!* | **give over doing sth** *Oh, give over complaining, we're nearly there.*
give sth **over to** sb/sth *phr v*
1 be given over to sth to be used for a particular purpose: *The land surrounding the village was given over to vineyards.* | *The whole day was given over to cooking and preparing for the celebrations.*
2 give yourself over to sth to spend all your time doing something: *In his youth he had given himself over to pleasure.*
3 to give responsibility for or control over something to a particular person, organization etc: *The running of internal affairs was given over to the Chancellor.*
give up *phr v*
1 give sth ↔ up to stop doing something, especially something that you do regularly: *Darren has decided to give up football at the end of this season.* | *She gave up her job and started writing poetry.* | **give up doing sth** *I gave up going to the theatre when I moved out of London.* | *Why don't you give up smoking?*
2 to stop trying to do something: *We spent half an hour looking for the keys, but eventually gave up and went home.* | *I give up. What's the answer?* | *You shouldn't* ***give up*** *so* ***easily***. | **give up doing sth** *I gave up trying to persuade him to continue with his studies.* | **give sth ↔ up** *She has still not given up the search.* | *The ground was too hard to dig so I* ***gave it up as a bad job*** (=stopped trying because success seemed unlikely).
3 give yourself/sb up to allow yourself or someone else to be caught by the police or enemy soldiers: *The siege ended peacefully after the gunman gave himself up.* | **[+to]** *In the end, his family gave him up to the police.*
4 give up sth to use some of your time to do a particular thing: *I don't mind giving up a couple of hours a week to deal with correspondence.*
5 give sth/sb ↔ up to give something that is yours to someone else: *The family refused to give up any of their land.* | *She was put under tremendous pressure to give the baby up.* | **[+to]** *I would always give my seat up to an elderly person on the bus.*
6 give sb ↔ up to end a romantic relationship with someone, even though you do not really want to: *I knew deep down that I should give him up.*
7 give sb up for dead/lost etc to believe that someone is dead and stop looking for them: *The ship sank and the crew were given up for dead.*
8 give it up for sb *spoken informal* used to ask people to APPLAUD someone → **give up the ghost** at **GHOST[1](5)**
give up on sb/sth *phr v* to stop hoping that someone or something will change or improve: *He'd been in a coma for six months, and doctors had almost given up on him.* | *At that point, I hadn't completely given up on the marriage.*
give yourself **up to** sth *phr v* to allow yourself to feel an emotion completely, without trying to control it: *He gave himself up to despair.*

give[2] *n* [U] the ability of a material or substance to bend or stretch when put under pressure: *The rope* ***has*** *quite a bit of* ***give*** *in it.*

ˌgive-and-ˈtake *n* [U] a willingness between two people or groups to understand each other, and to let each other have or do some of the things they want SYN **compromise**: *In any relationship there has to be some give-and-take.*

give·a·way[1] /ˈɡɪvəweɪ/ *n* **1** [singular] something that makes it easy for you to guess something: **be a clear/dead giveaway** (=make it very easy to guess something) *He'd been smoking dope; his glazed eyes were a dead giveaway.* **2** [C] something that is given away free, especially something that a shop gives you when you buy a product

giveaway[2] *adj* [only before noun] giveaway prices are extremely cheap

giv·en[1] /ˈɡɪvən/ *v* the past participle of GIVE

given[2] ●○○ *adj* [only before noun]
1 any/a given ... any particular time, situation, amount etc that is being used as an example: *On any given day in the Houston area, half the hospital beds are empty.* | *The rules are to be followed in any given situation.* | **at any given time/moment** *There are thought to be around 10,000 young homeless Scots in London at any given time.*
2 previously arranged SYN **specific**: *The wrapping machine was pre-set to wrap a given number of biscuits.* | *Candidates will have to give a presentation on a given topic.* | *a game in which, at a given signal, everyone has to stand still*
3 be given to (doing) sth *formal* to tend to do something, especially something that you should not do: *He was a quiet man, not usually given to complaining.*
4 take sth as given to accept that something is true or exists, especially when you are developing an idea or argument: *The fact that people find change difficult is taken as given.*

given[3] *prep* taking something into account SYN **considering**: *Given the circumstances, you've done really well.* | **given that** *Given that the patients have some disabilities, we still try to enable them to be as independent as possible.*

given[4] *n* [C] a basic fact that you accept as being true: *Sandra will be at least 15 minutes late – that's a given.* | *The concept is* ***taken as a given*** *in social studies.*

ˈgiven name *n* [C] *AmE* your FIRST NAME

giv·ing /ˈɡɪvɪŋ/ *adj* kind, caring, and generous OPP **mean**: *She's a very giving person.*

giz·mo /ˈɡɪzməʊ $ -moʊ/ *n* (*plural* **gizmos**) [C] *informal* a small piece of equipment – used when you cannot remember or do not know its correct name SYN **gadget**

giz·zard /ˈɡɪzəd $ -ərd/ *n* [C] a part of a bird's stomach that breaks down food into smaller pieces

gla·cé /ˈɡlæseɪ $ ɡlæˈseɪ/ *adj* [only before noun] *BrE* glacé fruits, especially CHERRIES, have been covered in sugary liquid SYN **candied**

ˌglacé ˈicing / $ ˌ.. ˈ../ *n* [U] *BrE* a type of ICING used to decorate cakes

gla·cial /ˈɡleɪʃəl/ *adj* **1** relating to ice and glaciers, or formed by glaciers: *a glacial valley* | *glacial deposits* **2** a glacial look or expression is extremely unfriendly SYN **icy** **3** extremely slow: *Change was coming, but at a glacial pace.* **4** extremely cold SYN **icy**: *a glacial wind* —**glacially** *adv*

gla·ci·a·tion /ˌɡleɪsiˈeɪʃən/ *n* [U] *technical* the process in which land is covered by glaciers, or the effect this process has

gla·ci·er /ˈɡlæsiə $ ˈɡleɪʃər/ ●○○ *n* [C] a large mass of ice which moves slowly down a mountain valley → **glacial**

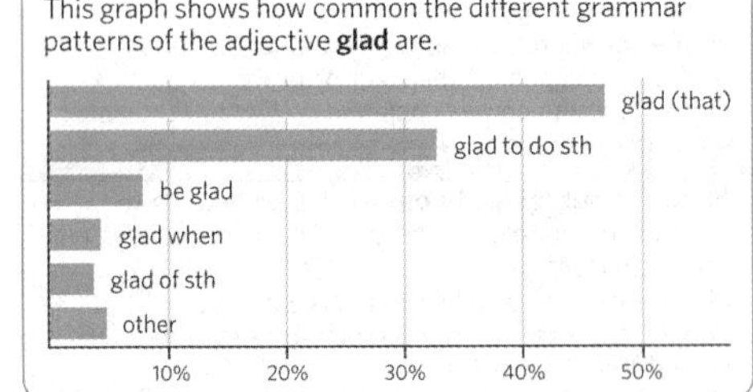

glad /ɡlæd/ ●●● S2 W3 *adj* [no comparative]
1 [not before noun] pleased and happy about something:

glad (that) *I'm really glad I don't have to go back there again.* | *We're so glad you came.* | **glad to do sth** *I am glad to be back home.* | **glad to see/hear etc** *I'm glad to see you looking so well.* | *'I've decided to accept the job.' 'I'm glad.'* | **glad when** *I'll be glad when the war is over.* | **[+about]** *She wasn't leaving after all. He was glad about that.* | **[+for]** *'Jamie's been accepted for medical school!' 'I'm so glad for him.'* → GLADLY **THESAURUS** HAPPY
2 be glad of sth to be grateful for something: *Thanks Marge, I'll be glad of the help.* | **be glad of an opportunity/chance/excuse to do sth** *They were glad of the chance to finally get some sleep.* | *It was cold outside, and she was glad of her coat.*
3 be glad to (do sth) to be very willing and eager to do something: *We will be glad to send you any information you may need.* | *I'm sure he'd be* ***only too glad to*** (=extremely willing to) *help you.* | *'Would you give me a hand?'* ***'I'd be glad to.'***
4 I would be glad if *formal* used in formal situations or letters to ask someone to do something for you: *I'd be glad if you'd let me know when the funeral is.*
5 glad tidings/news *old-fashioned* good news
6 give sb the glad eye *BrE old-fashioned* to look at someone in a way that shows you are sexually attracted to them
7 glad rags *old-fashioned informal* your best clothes that you wear for special occasions —**gladness** *n* [U] → GLAD-HAND

glad·den /ˈɡlædn/ *v* [T] *old-fashioned* to make someone feel pleased and happy: *It will* ***gladden*** *the* ***hearts*** *of my friends to see you.*

glade /ɡleɪd/ *n* [C] *literary* a small open space in a wood or forest

ˌglad-ˈhand *v* [I,T] to talk to or welcome people in a very friendly way, especially when this is not sincere: *He moved among the guests, glad-handing well-wishers.*

glad·i·a·tor /ˈɡlædieɪtə $ -ər/ *n* [C] a soldier who fought against other men or wild animals as an entertainment in ancient Rome —**gladiatorial** /ˌɡlædiəˈtɔːriəl◂/ *adj*: *gladiatorial combat*

ˈgladiator ˌsandal (*also* **gladiator**) *n* [C] a light flat shoe with several bands of leather that go across the foot and one or more bands that go around the ANKLE

glad·i·o·lus /ˌɡlædiˈəʊləs $ -ˈoʊ-/ *n* (*plural* **gladioli** /-laɪ/) [C] a tall garden plant with long leaves and large brightly-coloured flowers

glad·ly /ˈɡlædli/ *adv* **1** willingly or eagerly: *I would gladly have done it for him.* **2** happily: *'Here's Michelle!' he said gladly.* → **not suffer fools gladly** at SUFFER(5)

glam /ɡlæm/ *adj informal* attractive, exciting, and connected with wealth and success SYN **glamorous**: *glam young film directors*

glam·or /ˈɡlæmə $ -ər/ *n* [U] an American spelling of GLAMOUR

glam·o·rize (*also* **-ise** *BrE*) /ˈɡlæməraɪz/ *v* [T] to make something seem more attractive than it really is: *TV has been accused of glamorizing crime.* —**glamorization** /ˌɡlæməraɪˈzeɪʃən $ -rə-/ *n* [U]

glam·or·ous /ˈɡlæmərəs/ ●○○ *adj* attractive, exciting, and related to wealth and success: *She led an exciting and glamorous life.* | *the most glamorous neighborhood in the city* | *On television, she looks so glamorous.*

glam·our (*also* **glamor** *AmE*) /ˈɡlæmə $ -ər/ ●○○ *n* [U]
1 the attractive and exciting quality of being connected with wealth and success: **[+of]** *Forget all you read about the glamour of television.*
2 a style or attractiveness that suggests wealth: *Designer clothes are not a passport to instant glamour.*
3 glamour girl/boy a performer who is more noticeable for their attractiveness than for their skill or ability

glamp·ing /ˈɡlæmpɪŋ/ *n* [U] camping in a tent that is more comfortable and has better equipment than is usual - used especially in newspapers and magazines —**glamper** *n* [C]

glance¹ /ɡlɑːns $ ɡlæns/ ●●○ *v* [I always + adv/prep]
1 to quickly look at someone or something: **[+at/up/down etc]** *The man glanced nervously at his watch.* | *Wyatt glanced around the restaurant.* | *Emily glanced over her shoulder.* **THESAURUS** LOOK
2 to read something very quickly: **[+at/through etc]** *Can you glance through these figures for me?*

> **REGISTER**
> In everyday English, people often say **take a quick look at/through** etc something rather than **glance at/through** etc something: *I* ***took a quick look at*** *my watch.*

glance off (sth) *phr v*
1 to hit a surface at an angle and then move away from it in another direction SYN **ricochet**: *The bullet had crushed his helmet and glanced off.*
2 *literary* if light glances off a surface, it flashes or shines back from it SYN **reflect off**: *The sun was glancing off the icy tips of gleaming rock.*

glance² ●●○ *n* [C]
1 a quick look: *He* ***gave*** *her a quick* ***glance*** *and smiled.* | **sidelong/sideways glance** *She couldn't resist a sidelong glance* (=a look that is not direct) *at him.* | **take/shoot/throw/cast a glance (at sb)** (=look at someone or something quickly) *The couple at the next table cast quick glances in our direction.* | *The brothers* ***exchanged glances*** (=looked at each other quickly).
2 at a glance a) if you know something at a glance, you know it as soon as you see it: *He saw at a glance what had happened.* **b)** in a short form that is easy to read and understand: *Here are our top ten ski resorts at a glance.*
3 at first glance/sight when you first look at something: *At first glance, the place seemed deserted.*

glanc·ing /ˈɡlɑːnsɪŋ $ ˈɡlæn-/ *adj* **1 a glancing blow** a hit that partly misses so that it does not have its full force **2 a glancing reference/mention** a short or indirect reference to something or someone —**glancingly** *adv*

gland /ɡlænd/ ●○○ *n* [C] an organ of the body which produces a substance that the body needs, such as HORMONES, SWEAT, or SALIVA: *the pituitary gland*

glan·du·lar /ˈɡlændjələ $ -dʒələr/ *adj* related to the glands, or produced by the glands

ˌglandular ˈfever *n* [U] *BrE* an infectious disease which makes your LYMPH NODES swell up and makes you feel weak for a long time afterwards

glare¹ /ɡleə $ ɡler/ ●○○ *v* [I]
1 to look angrily at someone for a long time → **stare**: **[+at]** *She glared at him accusingly.* | **[+into/across/round etc]** *He glared round the room as if expecting a challenge.* **THESAURUS** LOOK
2 [always + adv/prep] to shine with a very strong bright light which hurts your eyes: *The sun glared down on us.* **THESAURUS** SHINE

glare² ●○○ *n*
1 [singular, U] a bright unpleasant light which hurts your eyes: **the glare of sth** *the harsh glare of the desert sun* | *a special screen to reduce glare*
2 [C] a long angry look → **stare**: *She gave him a hostile glare.*
3 the glare of publicity/the media/public scrutiny etc the full attention of newspapers, television etc, especially when you do not want it

glar·ing /ˈɡleərɪŋ $ ˈɡler-/ *adj* **1** very bad and very noticeable SYN **obvious**: *The book's most* ***glaring omission*** *is the lack of an index.* | *a* ***glaring example*** *of political corruption* **2** too bright and difficult to look at SYN **dazzling**: *the* ***glaring light*** *of high noon*

glar·ing·ly /ˈɡleərɪŋli $ ˈɡler-/ *adv* in a way that is very clear and easy to notice: *Some of the clues were* ***glaringly obvious.***

glas·nost /ˈɡlæznɒst $ ˈɡlɑːsnoʊst/ *n* [U] the POLICY begun by Mikhail Gorbachev in the USSR in the 1980s of allowing discussion of the country's problems

G

GLASSES

glass¹ /glɑːs $ glæs/ ●●● S1 W1 *n*
1 TRANSPARENT MATERIAL [U] a transparent solid substance used for making windows, bottles etc: *a glass bowl | a piece of* ***broken glass*** | **pane/sheet of glass** (=a flat piece of glass with straight edges) | *the cathedral's* ***stained glass*** *windows*
2 FOR DRINKING [C] a container used for drinking made of glass → **cup**: **wine/brandy/champagne etc glass** *Nigel* ***raised*** *his* ***glass*** *in a toast to his son.*
3 AMOUNT OF LIQUID [C] the amount of a drink contained in a glass: **[+of]** *She poured a glass of wine.*
4 FOR EYES **glasses** [plural] two pieces of specially cut glass or plastic in a frame, which you wear in order to see more clearly SYN **spectacles**: *He was clean-shaven and* ***wore glasses****. | I need a new* ***pair of glasses****.* | **distance/reading glasses** → DARK GLASSES, FIELD GLASSES

GRAMMAR
Glasses is plural, even when it refers to a single object: *She's got nice glasses.* ✗ Don't say: *She's got a nice glasses.*

5 GLASS OBJECTS [U] objects which are made of glass, especially ones used for drinking and eating: *a priceless collection of Venetian glass*
6 people in glass houses shouldn't throw stones used to say that you should not criticize someone for having a fault if you have the same fault yourself
7 sb sees the glass as half-empty/half-full used to say that a particular person is more likely to notice the good parts or the bad parts of a situation
8 under glass plants that are grown under glass are protected from the cold by a glass cover
9 MIRROR [C] *old-fashioned* a mirror
10 the glass *old-fashioned* a BAROMETER → **CUT GLASS, GROUND GLASS, LOOKING GLASS, MAGNIFYING GLASS, PLATE GLASS, STAINED GLASS, SAFETY GLASS,** → **raise your glass** at RAISE¹(16)

glass² *v* [T] to hit someone with a glass or bottle: *He was glassed in a pub fight.*

glass sth ↔ **in** *phr v BrE* to cover something with glass, or to build a glass structure around something

ˌglass ˈceiling *n* [singular] the attitudes and practices that prevent women or particular groups from getting high-level jobs, even though there are no actual laws or rules to stop them: *Goodhue shattered the glass ceiling as the first female publisher at Time Inc.*

ˌglassed-ˈin *adj* surrounded by a glass structure: *a glassed-in porch*

ˌglass ˈfibre *n* [U] FIBREGLASS

glass·ful /ˈglɑːsfʊl $ ˈglæs-/ *n* [C] the amount of liquid a glass will hold SYN **glass**

glass·house /ˈglɑːshaʊs $ ˈglæs-/ *n* [C] *BrE* **1** a building made mainly of glass which is used for growing plants SYN **greenhouse** **2 the glasshouse** *informal* a military prison

glass·ware /ˈglɑːsweə $ ˈglæswer/ *n* [U] glass objects, especially ones used for drinking and eating SYN **glass**

glass·y /ˈglɑːsi $ ˈglæsi/ *adj* **1** smooth and shining, like glass: *the glassy surface of the lake* **2** glassy eyes show no feeling or understanding, and do not move

ˌglassy-ˈeyed *adj* having eyes that do not move or show any expression

Glas·ton·bur·y /ˈglæstənbəri $ -beri/ a town in south-west England with one of the oldest ABBEYS (=type of religious building) in England. According to some old stories, it is the place where King Arthur is buried. A festival of modern music is held at Glastonbury every summer. When it rains, conditions can become very muddy at the festival, especially for people staying in tents.

glau·co·ma /glɔːˈkəʊmə $ glɒːˈkoʊ-/ *n* [U] an eye disease in which increased pressure inside your eye gradually makes you lose your sight

glaze¹ /gleɪz/ *v* **1** [I] (*also* **glaze over**) if your eyes glaze over, they show no expression, usually because you are very bored or tired: *Sometimes his eyes would glaze over for a second or two.* **2** [T] to cover plates, cups etc made of clay with a thin liquid that gives them a shiny surface **3** [T] to cover food with a liquid which gives it an attractive shiny surface: *Glaze the rolls with egg white.* **4** [T] to fit glass into window frames in a house, door etc

glaze² *n* [C,U] **1** a liquid that is used to cover plates, cups etc made of clay to give them a shiny surface **2** a liquid which is put onto food to give it an attractive shiny surface **3** a transparent covering of oil paint spread over a painting

glazed /gleɪzd/ *adj* **glazed look/eyes/expression etc** if you have a glazed look, your eyes show no expression, usually because you are very bored or tired

gla·zi·er /ˈgleɪziə $ -ʒər/ *n* [C] someone whose job is to fit glass into window frames

glaz·ing /ˈgleɪzɪŋ/ *n* [U] glass that has been used to fill windows → DOUBLE GLAZING

gleam¹ /gliːm/ ●○○ *v* [I]
1 to shine softly SYN **glimmer**: *His teeth gleamed under his moustache.* | **[+with]** *The wooden panelling was gleaming with wax polish.* THESAURUS ▸ SHINE
2 if your eyes or face gleam with a feeling, they show it SYN **glint**: **[+with]** *He laughed, his eyes gleaming with amusement.* —**gleaming** *adj*: *gleaming white walls*

gleam² *n* [C] **1** a small pale light, especially one that shines for a short time SYN **glimmer**: **[+of]** *They saw a sudden gleam of light.* **2** the brightness of something that shines SYN **glint**: **[+of]** *the gleam of gold and diamonds* **3** an emotion or expression that appears for a moment on someone's face: **[+of]** *She saw a gleam of amusement in his eyes. | Rose looked at me with a furious gleam in her eyes.* **4 sth is a gleam in sb's eye** used to say that something is being planned or thought about, but does not yet exist: *In those days, CD-ROMs were still just a gleam in the eye of some young engineer.*

glean /gliːn/ *v* **1** [T] to find out information slowly and with difficulty: **glean sth from sb/sth** *Additional information was gleaned from other sources.* **2** [I,T] to collect grain that has been left behind after the crops have been cut

glean·ings /ˈgliːnɪŋz/ *n* [plural] small pieces of information that you have found out with difficulty

glee /gliː/ *n* [U] a feeling of satisfaction and excitement, often because something bad has happened to someone else SYN **delight**: *Manufacturers are* ***rubbing*** *their* ***hands with glee*** *as they prepare to cash in.*

ˈglee club *n* [C] *AmE* a group of people who sing together for enjoyment

glee·ful /ˈgliːfəl/ *adj* very excited and satisfied: *a gleeful laugh* —**gleefully** *adv*

glen /glen/ *n* [C] a deep narrow valley in Scotland or Ireland

glib /glɪb/ *adj* **1** said easily and without thinking about all the problems involved – used to show disapproval: *glib generalizations* **2** speaking easily but without thinking carefully – used to show disapproval: *glib politicians* —**glibly** *adv* —**glibness** *n* [U]

glide¹ /glaɪd/ *v* [I] **1** [always + adv/prep] to move smoothly and quietly, as if without effort: **[+across/over/down etc]** *couples gliding over the dance floor* **2 a)** if a bird glides, it flies without moving its wings **b)** if a plane glides, it flies without using an engine **3** [always + adv/prep] to do or achieve things easily: **[+through]** *Kennedy seemed to glide through life.*

glide² *n* [C] **1** a smooth quiet movement that seems to take no effort **2** *technical* the act of moving from one musical note to another without a break in sound **3** *technical* a vowel which is made by moving your tongue from one position to another → **diphthong**

glid·er /ˈglaɪdə $ -ər/ *n* [C] a light plane that flies without an engine

glid·ing /ˈglaɪdɪŋ/ *n* [U] the sport of flying in a glider → HANG-GLIDING

glim·mer¹ /ˈglɪmə $ -ər/ *n* [C] **1** a small sign of something such as hope or understanding: **[+of]** ***a glimmer of hope*** *for the future* **2** a light that is not very bright SYN **gleam**: **[+of]** *the first glimmer of dawn*

glimmer² *v* [I] to shine with a light that is not very bright SYN **gleam**: *a weak glimmering light*

glim·mer·ing /ˈglɪmərɪŋ/ *n* [C often plural] a small sign of thought or feeling: *The glimmerings of an idea began to come to him.*

glimpse¹ /glɪmps/ ●○○ *n* [C]
1 a quick look at someone or something that does not allow you to see them clearly: **[+of]** *They* ***caught a glimpse*** *of a dark green car.* | **brief/fleeting/quick glimpse** (=a very short look) *We only had* ***a*** *fleeting glimpse* ***of*** *the river.*
2 a short experience of something that helps you begin to understand it: **[+of/into/at]** *a glimpse of what life might be like in the future*

glimpse² *v* [T] **1** to see someone or something for a moment without getting a complete view of them SYN **catch sight of**: *I glimpsed a figure at the window.*

> **REGISTER**
> In everyday English, people often say **catch sight of sb/sth** rather than **glimpse sb/sth**: *I* ***caught sight of*** *him as he was getting into his car.*

2 to begin to understand something for a moment: *For the first time she glimpsed the truth about her sister.*

glint¹ /glɪnt/ *v* [I] **1** if a shiny surface glints, it gives out small flashes of light SYN **sparkle**: *The gold rims of his spectacles glinted in the sun.* **THESAURUS** SHINE **2** if light glints off a surface, it shines back off it: *Sunlight glinted off the windows of a tall apartment building.* **3** if your eyes glint, they shine and show an unfriendly feeling

glint² *n* [C] **1** a look in someone's eyes which shows a particular feeling SYN **gleam**: *a humorous glint in her eyes* **2** a flash of light from a shiny surface

glis·ten /ˈglɪsən/ *v* [I] to shine and look wet or oily: **[+with]** *The boy's back was glistening with sweat.* | *glistening black hair* **THESAURUS** SHINE

glitch /glɪtʃ/ *n* [C] a small fault in a machine or piece of equipment, that stops it working: *a software glitch* **THESAURUS** FAULT

glit·ter¹ /ˈglɪtə $ -ər/ ●○○ *v* [I]
1 to shine brightly with flashing points of light SYN **sparkle**: *The river glittered in the sunlight.* **THESAURUS** SHINE
2 if someone's eyes glitter, they shine very brightly and show a particular strong emotion: **[+with]** *His blue eyes glittered with anger.*

glitter² *n* [U] **1** brightness consisting of many flashing points of light: *the glitter of his gold cigarette case* **2** *literary* a bright shining expression in someone's eyes that shows a particular emotion SYN **gleam**: *There was no mistaking the mocking glitter in his eyes.* **3** the exciting attractive quality of a place or a way of life which is connected with rich or famous people: *The glamour and glitter of London was not for him.* **4** very small pieces of shiny paper that are used for decoration —**glittery** *adj*: *glittery earrings*

glit·te·ra·ti /ˌglɪtəˈrɑːti/ *n* [plural] people who are rich, famous, and fashionable

glit·ter·ing /ˈglɪtərɪŋ/ *adj* [usually before noun] **1** giving off many small flashes of light SYN **sparkling**: *glittering jewels* **2** very successful: *a glittering career* **3** connected with rich, famous, and fashionable people: *a glittering Hollywood premiere*

glitz /glɪts/ *n* [U] the exciting attractive quality which is connected with rich, famous, and fashionable people SYN **glamour**: *show business glitz*

glitz·y /ˈglɪtsi/ *adj* exciting and attractive because of being connected with rich, famous, and fashionable people SYN **glamorous**: *glitzy London parties*

gloam·ing /ˈgləʊmɪŋ $ ˈgloʊ-/ *n* **the gloaming** *literary* the time in the early evening when it is becoming dark SYN **dusk**

gloat /gləʊt $ gloʊt/ *v* [I] to show in an annoying way that you are proud of your own success or happy about someone else's failure: **[+over]** *The fans are still gloating over Scotland's victory.* —**gloat** *n* [singular]

glob /glɒb $ glɑːb/ *n* [C] *informal* a small amount of something soft or liquid that has a round shape SYN **dollop**: *globs of paint*

glo·bal /ˈgləʊbəl $ ˈgloʊ-/ ●●○ W2 *adj*
1 affecting or including the whole world → **universal**: *global climate change* | *the global economy*
2 considering all the parts of a problem or situation together: *We are taking a global view of our business.*
3 affecting a whole computer system, program, or FILE —**globally** *adv*

glo·bal·ism /ˈgləʊbəl-ɪzəm $ ˈgloʊ-/ *n* [U] the idea that countries should consider the whole world when taking action, or the fact that events in one part of the world affect other parts of the world

glo·bal·i·za·tion (*also* **-isation** *BrE*) /ˌgləʊbəlaɪˈzeɪʃən $ ˌgloʊbələ-/ ●○○ AWL *n* [U] the process of making something such as a business operate in a lot of different countries all around the world, or the result of this: *the increasing globalization of world trade*

glo·bal·ize (*also* **-ise** *BrE*) /ˈgləʊbəlaɪz $ ˈgloʊ-/ *v* [I,T] if a company, industry, or ECONOMY globalizes or is globalized, it has business activities all over the world

ˌglobal ˈvillage *n* [singular] a name for the world, used to emphasize the degree to which everything is connected and each part depends on the others

ˌglobal ˈwarming ●●○ *n* [U] a general increase in world temperatures caused by increased amounts of CARBON DIOXIDE around the Earth → **greenhouse effect**

globe /gləʊb $ gloʊb/ ●●○ AWL *n* [C]
1 a round object with a map of the Earth drawn on it
2 the globe the world: *We export our goods all over the globe.*
3 an object shaped like a ball SYN **sphere**

ˌglobe ˈartichoke *n* [C] *BrE* an ARTICHOKE

globe·trot·ter /ˈgləʊbtrɒtə $ ˈgloʊbtrɑːtər/ *n* [C] *informal* someone who spends a lot of their time travelling to many different countries —**globe-trotting** *adj* —**globe-trotting** *n* [U]

glob·u·lar /ˈglɒbjələ $ ˈglɑːbjələr/ *adj* in the shape of a globule or a globe

glob·ule /ˈglɒbjuːl $ ˈglɑː-/ *n* [C] a small drop of a liquid, or of a solid that has been melted: *globules of fat*

glo·cal /ˈgləʊkəl $ ˈgloʊ-/ *adj* relating to the connections or relationships between GLOBAL and local businesses,

G

problems etc: *a glocal approach to crime* —**glocalization** /ˌɡləʊkəlaɪˈzeɪʃən $ ˌɡloʊkələ-/ *n* [U]

glock·en·spiel /ˈɡlɒkənspiːl $ ˈɡlɑː-/ *n* [C] a musical instrument consisting of many flat metal bars of different lengths, that you play with special hammers → **xylophone**

glom /ɡlɒm $ ɡlɑːm/ *v* (**glommed**, **glomming**)

glom onto sth *phr v AmE informal* **1** to become attached to someone or something so strongly that it is difficult to break the attachment: *The antibodies glom onto the virus and destroy it.* **2** to be very attracted to an idea, opinion, style etc: *College students have glommed onto the new African styles.*

gloom /ɡluːm/ ●○○ *n* [singular, U]
1 *literary* almost complete darkness: *He peered into the gathering* (=increasing) *gloom.*
2 a feeling of great sadness and lack of hope: *a time of high unemployment and economic gloom* → **doom and gloom** at DOOM²

gloom·y /ˈɡluːmi/ ●○○ (*comparative* **gloomier**, *superlative* **gloomiest**) *adj*
1 making you feel that things will not improve SYN **depressing** OPP **bright**: *The report **paints a gloomy picture** of the economy.*
2 sad because you think the situation will not improve SYN **depressed** OPP **cheerful**: *Anne dismissed these gloomy thoughts from her mind.* THESAURUS ▸ SAD
3 dark, especially in a way that makes you feel sad OPP **bright**: *It was a gloomy room with one small window.* THESAURUS ▸ DARK —**gloomily** *adv*

glop /ɡlɒp $ ɡlɑːp/ *AmE*, **gloop** /ɡluːp/ *BrE n* [U] *informal* a thick soft wet mass of something —**gloppy** *adj*

glo·ri·fied /ˈɡlɔːrɪfaɪd/ *adj* [only before noun] made to seem like something more important: *Many bosses view secretaries as no more than glorified typists.*

glo·ri·fy /ˈɡlɔːrɪfaɪ/ *v* (**glorified**, **glorifying**, **glorifies**) [T]
1 to make someone or something seem more important or better than they really are: *films which glorify violence*
2 to praise someone or something, especially God —**glorification** /ˌɡlɔːrɪfɪˈkeɪʃən/ *n* [U]: *the glorification of war*

glo·ri·ous /ˈɡlɔːriəs/ ●●○ *adj*
1 having or deserving great fame, praise, and honour: *a truly glorious future | a glorious victory* THESAURUS ▸ GOOD
2 very beautiful or impressive: ***glorious views** of the coast | a glorious red sky*
3 glorious weather is sunny and hot: *glorious sunshine*

> **REGISTER**
> In everyday English, people usually say **great** rather than **glorious**: *He's got a **great** future ahead of him. | The house has **great** views. | The weather's been **great**.*

4 extremely enjoyable SYN **wonderful**: *We had a glorious afternoon of sailing.* —**gloriously** *adv*

glo·ry¹ /ˈɡlɔːri/ ●●○ *n* (*plural* **glories**)
1 [U] the importance, honour, and praise that people give someone they admire a lot: *She dreamt of future glory as an Olympic champion. | Goran's **moment of glory** came when he defeated Rafter. | He began the season in a **blaze of glory**, scoring seven goals in as many games.*
2 [C] an achievement that is greatly admired or respected, or makes you very proud: **[+of]** *one of the finest artistic glories of Florence | monuments to **past glories** | Becoming a Supreme Court judge was the **crowning glory*** (=most successful part) *of her career.*
3 [U] when something is beautiful and impressive in appearance: *They spent $10 million restoring the theatre to its **former glory**.* | **in all its/their etc glory** *The sun emerged from behind the clouds in all its glory.*
4 bask/bathe in sb's/sth's (reflected) glory to share some of the importance and praise that belongs to someone close to you
5 glory days a time in the past when someone was admired: *the team's glory days in the late '80s*
6 to the (greater) glory of sb/sth *formal* in order to increase the honour that is given to someone or something: *The cathedral was built to the greater glory of God.*
7 glory (be) to God/Jesus etc *spoken* used to say that God deserves praise, honour, and thanks

glory² *v* (**gloried**, **glorying**, **glories**)

glory in sth *phr v* to enjoy or be proud of something: *She didn't like to glory in her past victories.*

gloss¹ /ɡlɒs $ ɡlɒːs, ɡlɑːs/ *n* **1** [singular, U] a bright shine on a surface: *This gel will add gloss to even the dullest hair.* | **polish/shine to a high gloss** *The silverware had been polished to a high gloss.* **2** [singular, U] an attractive appearance on the surface of something that may hide something less pleasant SYN **veneer**: *Beneath the gloss of success was a tragic private life. | The injury to Keane **took the gloss off** Manchester United's victory.* **3** [C] a note in a piece of writing that explains a difficult word, phrase, or idea **4** [singular] a description or explanation that makes something seem more attractive or acceptable than it really is → **spin**: *The minister was accused of **putting a gloss on** the government's poor performance.* **5 gloss finish/print** a surface or photograph that has been made shiny **6** (*also* **gloss paint**) [U] paint that looks shiny after it dries → **matt**

gloss² *v* [T] to provide a note in a piece of writing, explaining a difficult word, phrase, or idea

gloss over sth *phr v* to avoid talking about something unpleasant, or to say as little as possible about it SYN **skirt**: *She glossed over the details of her divorce.*

glos·sa·ry /ˈɡlɒsəri $ ˈɡlɒː-, ˈɡlɑː-/ ●○○ *n* (*plural* **glossaries**) [C] a list of special words and explanations of their meanings, often at the end of a book

gloss·y¹ /ˈɡlɒsi $ ˈɡlɒːsi, ˈɡlɑːsi/ ●○○ *adj*
1 shiny and smooth: *her glossy black hair | the glossy surface of the leaves*
2 glossy magazine/brochure etc a magazine etc printed on good-quality shiny paper, usually with lots of colour pictures
3 something that is glossy has an attractive appearance on the surface that may hide something less pleasant: *a glossy election campaign* —**glossiness** *n* [U]

glossy² *n* (*plural* **glossies**) [C usually plural] **1** (*also* **glossy magazine**) *BrE* a magazine that is printed on good-quality shiny paper, usually with lots of colour pictures
2 a photograph printed on shiny paper

ˌglottal ˈstop *n* [C] *technical* a speech sound made by completely closing and then opening your glottis, which in some forms of spoken English may take the place of a /t/ between vowel sounds or may be used before a vowel sound

glot·tis /ˈɡlɒtɪs $ ˈɡlɑː-/ *n* [C] *technical* the space between your VOCAL CORDS which helps to make the sound of your voice. When this space is opened and closed, the movement produces a sound. —**glottal** *adj*

glove /ɡlʌv/ ●●● S3 W3 *n* [C]
1 a piece of clothing that you wear on your hand in order to protect it or keep it warm → **mitten**: *a **pair of gloves** | boxing gloves* | **rubber/leather etc gloves** → see picture at SPORT
2 the gloves are off used to say that people are ready to begin a fight or argument → **fit (sb) like a glove** at FIT¹(1), → **hand in glove** at HAND¹(34)

ˈglove comˌpartment (*also* **ˈglove box**) *n* [C] a small cupboard in a car in front of the passenger seat, where things such as maps can be kept → see picture at CAR

gloved /ɡlʌvd/ *adj* wearing a glove

ˈglove ˌpuppet *n* [C] *BrE* a PUPPET that you put over your hand SYN **hand puppet** *AmE* → see picture at MARIONETTE

glow¹ /ɡləʊ $ ɡloʊ/ ●●○ *n* [singular]
1 a soft steady light: **[+from]** *the glow from the dying fire |* **[+of]** *the dim glow of the lightbulb | the warm glow of the setting sun | the green glow of the computer monitor*
2 the pink colour in your face or body that you have when you are healthy, have been doing exercise, or are excited: *She had a **healthy glow** in her cheeks.*

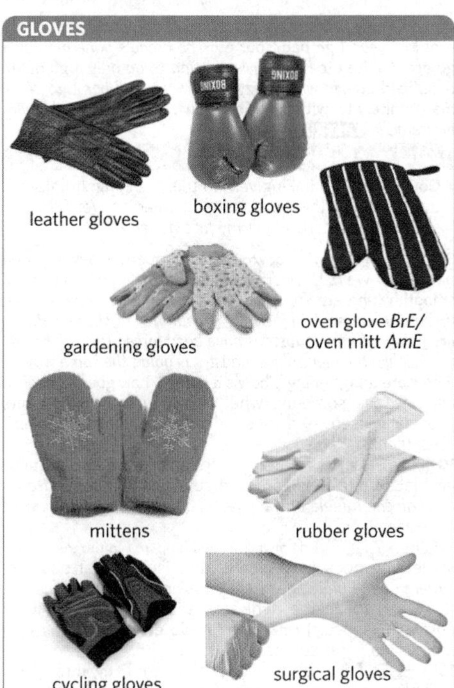

3 a glow of pleasure/satisfaction/happiness etc a strong feeling of pleasure etc: *Sophie **felt a glow of** pride.*

glow² ●●○ *v* [I]
1 to produce or REFLECT a soft steady light SYN **shine**: *The bedside lamp glowed dimly. | The fireplace was still glowing with the remains of last night's fire. | The red tip of his cigarette was glowing in the dark.* THESAURUS ▸ SHINE
2 if your face or body glows, it is pink or hot because you are healthy, have been doing exercise, or are feeling a strong emotion: **[+with]** *She looked exceptionally well, **glowing with health**.*
3 glow with pride/joy/pleasure etc to look very happy because you feel proud etc: *She gazed up at him, glowing with happiness.*
4 if something glows with a quality or colour, it is attractive and has strong colours: **[+with]** *The interior of the house glowed with colour, warmth, and life.*

glow·er /ˈglaʊə $ -ər/ *v* [I] to look at someone in an angry way SYN **glare**: **[+at]** *She glowered at him disapprovingly.* —**glower** *n* [C]

glow·ing /ˈgləʊɪŋ $ ˈgloʊ-/ *adj* **1 glowing report/account/description etc** a report etc that is full of praise: *I've had glowing reports from Neil about your work.* **2 in glowing terms** using a lot of praise: *He speaks of you in glowing terms.* —**glowingly** *adv*

glow·stick /ˈgləʊstɪk $ ˈgloʊ-/ *n* [C] a small plastic stick with chemicals inside that produce a coloured light when they are mixed together SYN **lightstick**: *Dancers were waving glowsticks.*

ˈglow-worm *n* [C] an insect that produces a small amount of light from its body

glu·cose /ˈgluːkəʊs $ -koʊs/ *n* [U] a natural form of sugar that exists in fruit

glue¹ /gluː/ ●●○ *n* [C,U] a sticky substance used for joining things together

glue² *v* (*present participle* **gluing** *or* **glueing**) [T] **1** to join two things together using glue SYN **stick**: **glue sth (back) together** *The sheets are glued together with strong adhesive.* | **glue sth in place/position** *Check that you have glued everything in place properly.* **2 be glued to sth** *informal* **a)** to look at something with all your attention: *He was glued to the TV when the Olympics were on.* **b)** to not move because you are very interested, surprised, frightened etc: *We were glued to our chairs, listening intently to every word.* | **be glued to the spot** *BrE*: *Sarah was glued to the spot, terrified by the scene in front of her.*

ˈglue-ˌsniffing *n* [U] the habit of breathing in gases from glues in order to produce a state of pleasure —**glue sniffer** *n* [C]

glue·y /ˈgluːi/ *adj* **1** sticky like glue **2** covered with glue

glum /glʌm/ *adj* (*comparative* **glummer**, *superlative* **glummest**) if someone is glum, they feel unhappy and do not talk a lot SYN **gloomy**: *Anna **looked glum**. | After dinner, Kate lapsed into a **glum silence**.* —**glumly** *adv*: *She **stared glumly** at her plate.* —**glumness** *n* [U]

glut¹ /glʌt/ *n* [C usually singular] a supply of something, especially a product or crop, that is more than is needed OPP **shortage**: **[+of]** *a glut of oil on the world market*

glut² *v* (**glutted**, **glutting**) [T] to cause something to have too much of something: *the **glutted** property **market***

glu·ten /ˈgluːtn/ *n* [U] a sticky PROTEIN substance that is found in wheat flour

glu·ti·nous /ˈgluːtɪnəs $ -tn-əs/ *adj* very sticky: *glutinous mud*

glut·ton /ˈglʌtn/ *n* [C] **1** someone who eats too much **2 a glutton for punishment** someone who seems to enjoy working hard or doing something unpleasant —**gluttonous** *adj*

glut·ton·y /ˈglʌtəni/ *n* [U] *formal* the bad habit of eating and drinking too much SYN **greed**

gly·ce·mic in·dex (*also* **glycaemic index** *BrE*) /glaɪˌsiːmɪk ˈɪndeks/ *n* [singular] *medical* a measure of the rate at which the level of sugar in the blood increases after eating a particular food

gly·ce·rine, **glycerin** /ˈglɪsərɪn/ *n* [U] a thick sweet transparent liquid made from fats and used in medicines, explosives, and foods

Glynde·bourne /ˈglaɪndbɔːn $ -bɔːrn/ a 16th-century COUNTRY HOUSE in East Sussex in the south of England, known for the Glyndebourne Festival that takes place there every year, when OPERAs are performed in its opera house. It is attended especially by rich people from the highest social class.

gm (*plural* **gm** *or* **gms**) the written abbreviation of ***gram*** or ***grams***

GM /ˌdʒiː ˈem/ *adj BrE* (***genetically modified***) GM foods or plants have had their GENETIC structure changed so that they are not affected by particular diseases or harmful insects

GMO /ˌdʒiː em ˈəʊ $ -ˈoʊ/ *n* [C] (***genetically modified organism***) a plant or other living thing whose GENEs have been changed by scientists, especially in order to make it less likely to get diseases or be harmed by insects etc —**GMO** *adj* [only before noun]: *GMO crops*

GMS /ˌdʒiːem ˈes/ *n* [U] a piece of equipment, like a small computer, that has special software which is able to produce an image of the natural features that exist in a particular area, such as the rocks and the water flowing under the rocks

GMT /ˌdʒiː em ˈtiː/ *n* [U] *BrE* (***Greenwich Mean Time***) the time as measured at Greenwich in London, that is used as an international standard for measuring time

gnarled /nɑːld $ nɑːrld/ *adj* **1** a gnarled tree or branch is rough and twisted with hard lumps **2** gnarled hands or fingers are twisted, rough, and difficult to move, usually because they are old

gnarl·y /ˈnɑːli $ ˈnɑːr-/ *adj* **1** a gnarly tree or branch is rough and twisted with hard lumps SYN **gnarled** **2** gnarly hands or fingers are twisted, rough, and difficult to move, usually because they are old SYN **gnarled** **3** *AmE spoken* a word meaning very good or excellent, used by young people: *'Look at the size of that wave.' 'Gnarly!'* **4** *AmE spoken* a word meaning very bad, used by young people: *a gnarly car wreck*

gnash /næʃ/ *v* **gnash your teeth** to be very angry or unhappy about something, or to move your teeth against each other so that they make a noise, especially because you are unhappy or angry

gnash·ers /ˈnæʃəz $ -ərz/ *n* [plural] *BrE informal* teeth

gnat /næt/ *n* [C] a small flying insect that bites

gnaw /nɔː $ nɒː/ *v* [I,T always + adv/prep] to keep biting something hard SYN **chew**: *Dexter gnawed his pen thoughtfully.* | *A rat had gnawed a hole in the box.* | **[+at/on]** *The puppy was gnawing on a bone.* THESAURUS ▶ BITE

gnaw (away) at sb/sth *phr v* to make someone feel worried or frightened, over a period of time: *Something was gnawing at the back of his mind.* | *Doubt was gnawing away at her confidence.*

gnaw·ing /ˈnɔːɪŋ $ ˈnɒː-/ *adj* [only before noun] worrying or painful, especially for a long time: *gnawing doubts*

gnome /nəʊm $ noʊm/ *n* [C] **1** a creature in children's stories who looks like a little old man. Gnomes have pointed hats, live under the ground, and guard gold, jewels etc. **2** a stone or plastic figure representing one of these creatures: *a* ***garden gnome***

gno·mic /ˈnəʊmɪk $ ˈnoʊ-/ *adj written* gnomic remarks are short, clever, and difficult to understand

GNP /ˌdʒiː en ˈpiː/ *n* [singular] (***gross national product***) the total value of all the goods and services produced in a country, usually in a single year → **GDP**

gnu /nuː/ *n* (*plural* **gnu** *or* **gnus**) [C] a large African animal with a tail and curved horns SYN **wildebeest**

GNVQ /ˌdʒiː en viː ˈkjuː/ *n* [C,U] (***General National Vocational Qualification***) a course of study and examination in practical subjects such as business, information technology, ENGINEERING etc, done by some students in schools in England and Wales, usually at the age of 16 → **BTEC**, **A level**, **GCSE**

go¹ /gəʊ $ goʊ/ ●●● S1 W1 *v* (*past tense* **went** /went/, *past participle* **gone** /gɒn $ gɒːn/, *third person singular* **goes** /gəʊz $ goʊz/)

1 MOVE/TRAVEL **a)** [I always + adv/prep] (*also* **been**) to travel or move to a place that is away from where you are or where you live → **come**: *There's nothing more we can do here. Let's* ***go home***. | ***Have you ever been to*** (=have you ever travelled to) *Japan?* | *I* ***have been to*** (=have travelled to) *Germany several times.* | *Where are you going?* | *We're going to Canada in the summer.* | *Dinah went into the kitchen.* | *She went over and put her arm around him.* | *I'm going round to her house to find out what's wrong.* | *I'll just go up* (=go upstairs) *and ask him what he wants.* **b)** [I,T] to move or travel in a particular way or for a particular distance: *It took us over an hour to go ten miles.* | *The car was going much too fast.* | *We went a different way from usual that day.* | **go by bus/train/car etc** *It'll be quicker to go by train.* **c) go and do sth** (*also* **go do sth** *AmE*) [not in past tenses] to move to a particular place in order to do something: *Go wash your hands.* | *I went and spoke to the manager.* THESAURUS ▶ TRAVEL

2 go flying/laughing/rushing etc to move in a particular way, or to do something as you are moving: *The plate went crashing to the floor.* | *The bullet went flying over my head.* | *John went rushing off down the corridor.*

3 ATTEND **a)** [I] to be at a concert, party, meeting etc: **[+to]** *Are you going to Manuela's party?* | *I first went to a rock concert when I was 15.* **b) go to school/church/work etc** to regularly attend school, a church etc: *He doesn't go to the synagogue these days.*

4 LEAVE [I] to leave a place: *What time does the last train go?* | *Right, let's go!* | *She turned to go.* | **be/get going** *It's late! I must get going.*

5 DO A PARTICULAR ACTIVITY [I,T] to leave the place where you are, in order to do something: **go for a walk/swim etc** *Let's go for a walk.* | **go shopping/swimming/skiing etc** *I need to go shopping this afternoon.* | **go on a trip/tour/cruise etc** *My parents are going on a cruise.*

6 be going to do sth a) to intend to do something: *I'm going to tell Dad what you said.* **b)** used to talk about what will happen in the future: *He looked as if he was going to cry.* | *It's going to rain later.* → GONNA

7 CHANGE [linking verb] to change in some way, especially by becoming worse than before: *The company went bankrupt last year.* | **go bad/sour etc** *The bread's gone mouldy.* | **go grey/white etc** *Her hair is starting to go grey.* | **go mad/deaf/bald etc** *He went crazy and tried to kill her.* | **go wild/mad/white etc with sth** *The crowd was going wild with excitement.* THESAURUS ▶ BECOME

> **GRAMMAR: Linking verbs**
>
> **Go** is used as a linking verb in this meaning. It links the subject of the sentence with an adjective: *The sky went very dark.* | *I felt my face go red.*

8 HAPPEN [I always + adv/prep] to happen or develop in a particular way: *How did your French test go?* | **go well/smoothly/fine etc** *The party went well.* | *Everything's going fine at the moment.* | *I feel very encouraged by* ***the way things are going***. | *Many industries have been forced to cut jobs and it looks like the electronics industry is* ***going the same way***.

9 how are things going?/how's it going?/how goes it? *spoken* used to ask someone what is happening in their life, especially used as a greeting: *'Hi Jane. How's it going?' 'Fine, thanks.'*

10 REACH [I always + adv/prep] to reach as far as a particular place or to lead to a particular place: *The road goes through the middle of the forest.* | *The belt won't go around my waist.*

11 USUAL POSITION [I always + adv/prep, not in progressive] if something goes somewhere, that is its usual position: *Where do the plates go?* | *The book goes on the top shelf.*

12 FIT [I] to be the right size, shape, or amount for a particular space: **[+in/under/inside etc]** *I don't think all that will go in the suitcase.*

13 BE SENT [I] to be sent or passed on: **[+by/through/to etc]** *The email went to everyone in the company.* | *That letter should go by special delivery.* | *Complaints must go through the proper channels.*

14 BE IN A PARTICULAR STATE/CONDITION [linking verb] to be in a particular state or condition, especially a bad one: *Many families are forced to* ***go hungry***.

15 go unanswered/unnoticed/unrewarded etc to not be answered, noticed etc: *All my letters went unanswered.* | *He hoped that his nervousness would go unnoticed.*

16 START [I] to start doing something: *The preparations have been completed and we're ready to go.* | *Generally the action doesn't* ***get going*** (=start) *until after midnight.* | *I'm going to* ***get going on*** (=start doing) *the decorating next week.*

17 WORK WELL [I] if a clock, watch, or machine goes, it moves and works as it should do: *My watch isn't going.* | *I couldn't* ***get*** *the pump* ***going*** (=make it work).

18 MAKE MOVEMENT [I always + adv/prep] used when you are telling someone about what movement someone or something made: *She went like this with her hand.*

19 SAY [T] *spoken informal* to say something: *I asked her what she meant and she just went, 'Don't ask!'*

20 MAKE A SOUND [T] to make a particular sound: *The balloon suddenly went bang.*

21 don't go doing sth *spoken* used to tell someone not to do something, especially something that is wrong or bad: *It's a secret, so don't go telling everyone.*

22 have gone and done sth *spoken* used when you are surprised or annoyed by what someone has done: *Kay's gone and lost the car keys!*

23 to go a) still remaining before something happens: *Only ten days to go to Christmas!* **b)** still having to be done or dealt with before you have finished: *Laura's sat six exams and has two more to go.* **c)** still to travel before you reach the place you are going to: *only another five miles left to go* **d)** used for saying that you want to take food away from a restaurant and eat it somewhere else: *Two chicken dinners with corn to go.*

24 don't go there *spoken informal* used to say that you do not want to think or talk about something: *'John and Clare having children?' 'Don't go there!'* | *'What if the two of them ...?'* ***'Don't even go there!'***

25 STORY/DISCUSSION/SONG ETC [I always + adv/prep, T] used to talk about what something such as a story or song consists of: *The argument goes like this.* | *We need to*

'spread a little happiness', as the song goes. | ***The story goes that*** *my grandfather saved his captain's life in battle.*
26 WHISTLE/BELL ETC [I] to make a noise as a warning or signal: *A bell goes to mark the end of each class.*
27 here/there sb goes again *spoken* used when someone has annoyed you by doing something they know you do not like: *There you go again, jumping to conclusions.*
28 DISAPPEAR [I] to no longer exist or no longer be in the same place SYN **disappear**: *Has your headache gone yet?* | *The door was open and all his things had gone.*
29 GET INTO WORSE CONDITION [I] if one of your senses such as sight, hearing etc is going, it is getting worse: *Dad's eyesight is starting to go.* | *I'd forgotten that. My mind must be going.*
30 TO BE OBEYED [I] if what someone says goes, that person is in authority and what they say should be obeyed: *Phil's in charge, and what he says goes.*
31 BE DAMAGED [I] to become weak, damaged etc, or stop working properly: *The bulb's gone in the bathroom.* | *My jeans are starting to go at the knee.*
32 DIE [I] to die – use this when you want to avoid saying the word 'die': *Now that his wife's gone, he's all on his own.* | *When I go, I'd like to have my ashes scattered at sea.* → **dead and gone** at DEAD[1](1)
33 BE SPENT [I] to be spent: *I don't know where all my money goes!* | **[+on]** *Half her salary goes on the rent.*
34 BE SOLD [I] to be sold: **[+for/at]** *A house like this would go for £250,000.* | **[+to]** *The jewels will go to the highest bidder.* | *He bought me some CDs which* ***were going cheap*** (=were being sold at a low price).
35 PAY MONEY [I] to offer a particular amount of money for something: *I'll give you $500 for it but I can't go any higher than that.* | **[+to]** *I think we could probably go to £15,000.*
36 going, going, gone! *spoken* used to say that something has been sold at an AUCTION
37 TIME [I always + adv/prep] used to say how quickly or slowly time passes: *The day seemed to go so slowly.*
38 there/bang goes sth *spoken* used to say that you are disappointed because something has stopped you doing or getting what you wanted: *Well, there goes my chance of fame!*
39 go to show/prove/indicate etc sth to help to prove something: ***It just goes to show*** *how much people judge each other by appearances.*
40 be going *informal* to be available: *Are there any jobs going at the café?* | *I'll take that if it's* ***going spare***.
41 COLOURS/STYLES/TASTES [I] if colours, tastes, styles etc go, they look, taste etc good together: *I don't think pink and yellow really go.* | **[+with]** *Do you think this shirt will go with the skirt I bought?* | **[+together]** *Pork and apple go especially well together.*
42 as sb/sth goes used for comparing someone or something with the average person or thing of that type: *As marriages go, it certainly wasn't dull.*
43 go all out to try very hard to do or get something: **[+for]** *We're going all out for victory in this afternoon's game.* | **go all out to do sth** *The company will be going all out to improve on last year's sales.*
44 have nothing/not much/a lot etc going for sb/sth used to talk about how many advantages and good qualities someone or something has: *It's a town that's got a lot going for it.*
45 where does sb/sth go from here? *spoken* used to ask what should be done next, especially when there is a problem: *So where do you think we should go from here?*
46 going forward in the future – used especially in business: *Going forward, we will increase our focus on customer service.*
47 LEAVE A JOB [I] to leave your job, especially because you are forced to: *He was becoming an embarrassment to the government and had to go.* | *If Jill goes, who will take her place?*
48 GET RID OF STH [I] if something goes, someone gets rid of it: *The policies will have to go if the party is to win the next election.* | *A hundred jobs are expected to go following the merger.*
49 TOILET [I] *informal* to make waste come out of your body

go about *phr v*
1 go about sth to start to do something: *I want to learn German but I don't know the best way to go about it.* | **go about doing sth** *The leaflet tells you how to go about making a will.*
2 go about sth to do something in the way that you usually do: *The villagers were* ***going about their business*** *as usual.* | *She went about her preparations in a quiet businesslike way.*
3 *BrE* if a ship goes about, it turns to go in the opposite direction

go after sth/sb *phr v*
1 to follow or chase someone or something because you want to catch them: *Joe went after her to make sure she was unhurt.*
2 to try to get something: *I can't decide whether to go after the job or not.*

go against sb/sth *phr v*
1 if something goes against your beliefs, principles etc, it is opposite to them: *This goes against everything I've been brought up to believe in.* | *I often have to make decisions that* ***go against the grain*** (=are not what I would normally choose to do).
2 to do the opposite of what someone wants or advises you to do: *She was scared to go against her father's wishes.*
3 if a decision, judgment etc goes against you, you do not get the result you want: *His lawyer hinted that the case might go against him.* | *The vote went against the government.*

go ahead *phr v*
1 to start to do something, especially after planning it or asking permission to do it: **[+with]** *They've decided to go ahead with plans to build 50 new houses on the site.* | **go ahead and do sth** *I went ahead and arranged the trip anyway.*
2 if an event or process goes ahead, it happens: *A judge has ruled that the music festival can go ahead.*
3 *spoken* used to give someone permission to do something, or let them speak before you: *'Do you mind if I open the window?' 'No, go ahead.'* | *If you want to leave,* ***go right ahead***.
4 (*also* **go on ahead**) to go somewhere before the other people in your group: *You go ahead and we'll catch you up later.* | **[+of]** *He stood back to let Sue go ahead of him.*
5 to start to be winning a game or competition: *Dulwich went ahead after 22 minutes.* → GO-AHEAD[1]

go along *phr v*
1 if you do something as you go along, you do it without planning or preparing it: *He was* ***making*** *the story* ***up as*** *he* ***went along***. | *I never had formal training, I just learned the job as I went along.*
2 to go to an event or a place where something is happening: **[+to]** *I might go along to the meeting tonight.*
3 to happen or develop in a particular way: *Things seem to be going along nicely.*

go along with sb/sth *phr v*
1 to agree with or support someone or something: *I would be happy to go along with the idea.* | *Often it was easier to go along with her rather than risk an argument.*
2 go along with you! *BrE spoken old-fashioned* used to tell someone that you do not believe what they are saying

go around (*also* **go round** *BrE*) *phr v*
1 DRESS/BEHAVE (*also* **go about** *BrE*) to behave or dress in a particular way: **go around doing sth** *You can't go around accusing people like that.* | *He goes around in a T-shirt even in winter.*
2 ILLNESS **go around (sth)** (*also* **go about (sth)** *BrE*) if an illness is going around, a lot of people get it: *He had a bad dose of the flu virus that was going around.* | *There are a lot of nasty bugs going around the school.*
3 NEWS/STORY **go around (sth)** (*also* **go about (sth)** *BrE*) if news, a story, a joke etc is going around, a lot of people hear it and are talking about it: *A rumour was going around that I was having an affair with my boss.* | *There was a lot of gossip going around the village.*
4 go around with sb/go around together (*also* **go about with**

sb *BrE*) to meet someone often and spend a lot of time with them: *I used to go around with a bad crowd.*
5 enough/plenty to go around enough for each person: *Is there enough ice cream to go around?* | *There were never enough textbooks to go around.*
6 what goes around comes around used to say that if someone does bad things now, bad things will happen to them in the future
7 go around in your head if words, sounds etc go around in your head, you keep remembering them for a long time: *That stupid song kept going around in my head.* → **go around/round in circles** at CIRCLE[1](5)

go at sth/sb *phr v informal*
1 to attack someone or argue with someone in a noisy way: *The two dogs went at each other.*
2 to do something, or start to do something, with a lot of energy: *Mary went at the task with great enthusiasm.*

go away *phr v*
1 to leave a place or person: *Go away and leave me alone!* | *I went away wondering if I'd said the wrong thing.*
2 to travel to a place and spend some time there, for example for a holiday: *Are you going away this year?* | **[+for]** *We're going away for the weekend.* | **[+to]** *He's going away to college next year.* | **[+on]** *I'm going away on a business trip next week.*
3 if a problem, unpleasant feeling etc goes away, it disappears: *Ignoring the crime problem won't make it go away.*

go back *phr v*
1 to return to a place that you have just come from: *I think we ought to go back now.* | **[+to/into/inside etc]** *I felt so sick I just wanted to go back to bed.* | **[+for]** *I had to go back for my passport* (=to get my passport).
2 there's no going back *spoken* used to say that you cannot make a situation the same as it was before: *I realized that once the baby was born there would be no going back.*
3 [always + adv/prep] to have been made, built, or started at some time in the past: *It's a tradition that goes back at least 100 years.* | **[+to]** *The building goes back to Roman times.*
4 if people go back a particular length of time, they have known each other for that length of time: *Peter and I go back 25 years.* | *We* ***go back a long way*** (=we have been friends for a long time).
5 to think about a particular time in the past or something that someone said before: *If you go back 20 years, most people didn't own a computer.* | **[+to]** *I'd like to go back to the point that was made earlier.*
6 the clocks go back when the clocks go back in the autumn, the time officially changes so that the clock shows one hour earlier than it was before: *The clocks go back in October.*

go back on sth *phr v* to not do something that you promised or agreed to do: **go back on your word/promise/decision** *Delors claimed that the president had gone back on his word.*

go back to sth *phr v* to start doing something again after you have stopped for a period of time: *He went back to sleep.* | **go back to doing sth** *She went back to watching TV.*

go before *phr v*
1 to happen or exist before something else: *In some ways this program improves on what has gone before.*
2 go before sb/sth if something goes before a judge, group of people in authority etc, they consider it before making a decision: *The case will go before the court.* | *The proposal is likely to go before the committee.*

go beyond sth *phr v* to be much better, worse, more serious etc than something else: *Their relationship had gone beyond friendship.* | *This goes beyond all limits of acceptable behaviour.*

go by *phr v*
1 if time goes by, it passes: *Things will get easier* ***as time goes by***. | **as the days/weeks/years go by** *As the weeks went by, I became more and more worried.* | **hardly a day/week/month etc goes by** *Hardly a week goes by without some food scare being reported in the media.* | **in days/times/years etc gone by** (=in the past) *These herbs would have been grown for medicinal purposes in days gone by.*
2 go by sth to form an opinion about someone or something from the information or experience that you have: *You can't always go by appearances.* | ***If*** *his past plays* ***are anything to go by***, *this should be a play worth watching.*
3 go by sth to do things according to a set of rules or laws: *Only a fool goes by the rules all the time.* | *There was no doubt that the referee* ***had gone by the book*** (=had obeyed all the rules). → **go by the board** at BOARD[1](8), → **go by the name of sth** at NAME[1](1)

go down *phr v*
1 GET LOWER to become lower in level, amount etc: *His income went down last year.* | *Computers have gone down in price.* | **go down by 10%/250/$900 etc** *Spending has gone down by 2%.*
2 STANDARD if something goes down, its quality or standard gets worse: *This neighbourhood has really gone down in the last few years.*
3 go down well/badly/a treat etc a) to get a particular reaction from someone: *His suggestion did not go down very well.* | *The movie went down very well in America.* | *The speech* ***went down a treat*** *with members* (=members liked it very much). | *The idea* ***went down like a lead balloon*** (=was not popular or successful). **b)** if food or drink goes down well, you enjoy it: *I'm not that hungry so a salad would go down nicely.*
4 GO FROM ONE PLACE TO ANOTHER to go from one place to another, especially to a place that is further south: **[+to]** *We're going down to Bournemouth for the weekend.* | *He's gone down to the store to get some milk.*
5 go down the shops/club/park etc *BrE spoken informal* to go to the shops, a club etc: *Does anyone want to go down the pub tonight?*
6 SHIP if a ship goes down, it sinks: *Ten men died when the ship went down.*
7 PLANE if a plane goes down, it suddenly falls to the ground: *An emergency call was received shortly before the plane went down.*
8 BECOME LESS SWOLLEN to become less swollen: *The swelling will go down if you rest your foot.*
9 LOSE AIR if something that is filled with air goes down, air comes out and it becomes smaller and softer: *Your tyre's gone down.*
10 BE REMEMBERED [always + adv/prep] to be recorded or remembered in a particular way: **[+as]** *The talks went down as a landmark in the peace process.* | *The carnival will* ***go down in history*** (=be remembered for many years) *as one of the best ever.*
11 COMPETITION/SPORT **a)** to lose a game, competition, or election: *The Hawkers went down 5-9.* | **[+by]** *The government went down by 71 votes.* | **[+to]** *Liverpool went down to Juventus.* **b)** to move down to a lower position in an official list of teams or players: **[+to]** *United went down to the second division.*
12 COMPUTER if a computer goes down, it stops working for a short time: *If one of the file servers goes down, you lose the whole network.*
13 LIGHTS if lights go down, they become less bright: *The lights went down and the curtain rose on an empty stage.*
14 SUN when the sun goes down, it appears to move down until you cannot see it anymore
15 WIND if the wind goes down, it becomes less strong: *The wind had gone down but the night had turned chilly.*
16 PRISON *informal* to be sent to prison: *He went down for five years.*
17 HAPPEN *spoken informal* to happen: *the type of guy who knows what's going down* | *What's going down?*
18 LEAVE UNIVERSITY *BrE formal old-fashioned* to leave Oxford or Cambridge University at the end of a period of study

go down on sb *phr v* to touch someone's sexual organs with the lips and tongue in order to give them sexual pleasure

go down with sth *phr v BrE informal* to become ill, especially with an infectious disease: *Half the team had gone down with flu.*

go for sb/sth *phr v*
1 ATTACK *BrE* to attack or criticize someone: *The dog suddenly went for me.*
2 TRY TO GET STH to try to get or win something: *Jackson is going for his second gold medal here.* | **go for it** *spoken* (=used to encourage someone to try to achieve something) *If you really want the job, go for it!* → **go for broke** at BROKE²(3)
3 CHOOSE *BrE* to choose something: *I think I'll go for the chocolate cake.*
4 I could/would go for sth *spoken* used to say that you would like to do or have something: *A full meal for less than five bucks! I could go for that!*
5 LIKE *informal* to like a particular type of person or thing: *Annie tends to go for older men.*
6 the same goes for sb/sth (*also* **that goes for sb/sth too**) *spoken* used to say that a statement you have just made is true about someone or something else too: *Close all doors and lock them when you go out. The same goes for windows.*
go forward *phr v*
1 if something that is planned to happen goes forward, it starts to happen or starts to make progress: *The trial is expected to go forward next week as planned.* |*The project can only go forward if we can get enough financial support.*
2 to compete in the next stage of a competition: *The team will go forward into the next round of the World Cup.*
3 the clocks go forward when the clocks go forward in the spring, the time officially changes so that the clock shows one hour later than it was before: *The clocks go forward this weekend.*
4 going forward in the near future – used especially in business and economic contexts: *Going forward, we will be able to deliver better products to our customers and better returns for our shareholders.* | *There are a number of concerns going forward and some areas are likely to face difficult times.* | *Analysts are predicting a gloomy picture for the U.S. economy going forward.*
go in *phr v* when the sun or the moon goes in, cloud moves in front of it so that it cannot be seen
go in for sth *phr v*
1 to do an examination or take part in a competition: *I go in for all the competitions.*
2 to do or use something often because you enjoy it or like it: *I never really went in for sports.*
3 to choose something as your job: *I suppose I could go in for advertising.*
go in with sb *phr v* to join with someone else to start a business or organization: *Ellie's going in with a friend who's just started a café.*
go into sth *phr v*
1 JOB to start to do a particular type of job: *I always wanted to go into nursing.* | *She's thinking of* ***going into business*** (=starting a business).
2 TIME/MONEY/EFFORT to be spent or used to get, make, or do something: *Years of research have gone into this book.* | **go into doing sth** *A great deal of time and effort has gone into ensuring that the event runs smoothly.*
3 EXPLAIN to explain, describe, or examine something in detail: *I don't want to go into the matter now.* | *I don't want to* ***go into details*** *now.*
4 COMPUTER to open a particular computer program, WINDOW, or FILE: *Go into your D drive.*
5 BE IN A PARTICULAR STATE to start to be in a particular state or condition: *She went into labour at midnight and the baby was born at 8 am.* | *The company went into liquidation.*
6 HIT if a vehicle goes into a tree, wall, or another vehicle, it hits it: *His car went into a lamppost in the high street.*
7 DIVIDE if a number goes into another number, the second number can be divided by the first: *12 goes into 60 five times.*
8 BEGIN TO MOVE IN A PARTICULAR WAY if a vehicle goes into a particular movement, it starts to do it: *The plane had gone into a steep descent.*
go off *phr v*
1 LEAVE to leave a place, especially in order to do something: *John decided to go off on his own.* | **[+to]** *He went off to work as usual.* | **go off to do sth** *Geoff went off to play golf.*
2 EXPLODE to explode or fire: *The bomb went off at 6.30 this morning.* | *Fireworks were going off all over the city.* | *The gun went off and the bullet went flying over his head.*
3 MAKE A NOISE if an ALARM goes off, it makes a noise to warn you about something: *The thieves ran away when the alarm went off.* | *I've set the alarm clock to go off at 7 am.*
4 STOP LIKING **go off sb/sth** *BrE informal* to stop liking something or someone: *Many women go off coffee during pregnancy.* | **go off doing sth** *I've gone off cooking lately.*
5 STOP WORKING if a machine or piece of equipment goes off, it stops working: *The central heating goes off at 9 o'clock.* | *Suddenly, all the lights went off.*
6 go off well/badly etc to happen in a particular way: *The party went off very well.*
7 HAPPEN *BrE spoken informal* to happen SYN **go on**: *There was a blazing row going off next door.*
8 DECAY *BrE* if food goes off, it becomes too bad to eat: *The milk's gone off.*
9 SLEEP to go to sleep: *I'd just* ***gone off to sleep*** *when the phone rang.*
10 GET WORSE *BrE informal* to get worse: *He's a singer whose talent has gone off in recent years.*
go off on sb *phr v AmE informal*
1 to criticize or speak to someone in a very angry way
2 go off on one *BrE informal* to suddenly start speaking and behaving in a very angry way: *When I told him I wouldn't be back till midnight, he went off on one.*
go off with sth/sb *phr v informal*
1 to leave your usual sexual partner in order to have a relationship with someone else: *She's gone off with her husband's best friend.*
2 to take something away from a place without having permission: *Who's gone off with my pen?*
go on *phr v*
1 CONTINUE **a)** to continue doing something or being in a situation: **go on doing sth** *He went on working until he was 91.* | **[+with]** *One of the actors was unwell and couldn't go on with the performance.* | *I* ***can't go on like this*** *for much longer.* **b)** to continue without stopping: *The noise goes on 24 hours a day.* | *The screaming* ***went on and on*** (=continued for a long time). → ONGOING
2 HAPPEN to happen: *I don't know what's going on.* | *What were the children doing while all this was going on?* | *Like all good resorts, there is plenty going on.* → GOINGS-ON
3 DO STH NEXT to do something after you have finished doing something else: **go on to do sth** *She went on to become a successful surgeon.* | **[+to]** *Go on to the next question when you've finished.*
4 CONTINUE TALKING to continue talking, especially after stopping or changing to a different subject: *Go on, I'm listening.* | *'But,' he went on, 'we have to deal with the problems we're facing.'* | **[+with]** *After a short pause Maria went on with her story.*
5 go on *spoken* **a)** used to encourage someone to do something: *Go on, have another piece of cake.* **b)** used when you are agreeing to do something or giving permission for something: *'Are you sure you won't have another drink?' 'Oh, go on then.'* | *'Can I go outside, Dad?' 'Yeah, go on then.'* **c)** (*also* **go on with you**) *BrE old-fashioned* used to tell someone that you do not believe them
6 USE AS PROOF **go on sth** to base an opinion or judgment on something: *Police haven't much to go on in their hunt for the killer.*
7 START TO WORK if a machine or piece of equipment goes on, it starts to work: *The heat goes on automatically at 6 o'clock.*
8 TIME to pass: *As time went on, I grew fond of him.*
9 BEHAVE *BrE informal* the way someone goes on is the way they behave: *The way she's going on, she'll have a nervous breakdown.*
10 be going on (for) 5 o'clock/60/25 etc to be nearly a particular time, age, number etc: *Nancy must be going on for 60.* | *She's one of those wise teenagers who's 16 going on 70* (=she behaves as though she is older than she is).
11 GO IN FRONT (*also* **go on ahead**) to go somewhere

before the other people you are with: *Bill went on in the car and I followed on foot.*
12 TALK TOO MUCH *informal* to talk too much: *I really like Clare but she does go on.* | **[+about]** *I got tired of him going on about all his problems.* | *He just* ***went on and on about*** *his new girlfriend.*
13 CRITICIZE *BrE informal* to continue to criticize someone or ask them to do something in a way that annoys them: *The way she went on, you would have thought it was all my fault.* | **[+at]** *Stop going on at me!* | **go on at sb to do sth** *My wife's always going on at me to dress better.* | **go on at sb about sth** *He's always going on at me about fixing the door.*
14 DEVELOP *BrE spoken informal* to develop or make progress
15 to be going on with/to go on with *BrE informal* if you have enough of something to be going on with, you have enough for now: *Have you got enough money to be going on with?*

go out *phr v*
1 LEAVE YOUR HOUSE to leave your house, especially in order to enjoy yourself: *Are you going out tonight?* | **[+for]** *We went out for a meal and then on to a movie.* | **go out doing sth** *Liam goes out drinking every Friday.* | **go out to do sth** *Can I go out to play now?* | **go out and do sth** *You should go out and get some fresh air.*
2 RELATIONSHIP to have a romantic relationship with someone: *They've been going out for two years now.* | **[+with]** *Tina used to go out with my brother.* | **[+together]** *How long have you been going out together?*
3 FIRE/LIGHT to stop burning or shining: *Suddenly the candle went out.*
4 TV/RADIO *BrE* to be broadcast on television or radio: *The programme goes out live at 5 o'clock on Mondays.*
5 BE SENT to be sent: *A copy of the instructions should go out with the equipment.* | *The magazine goes out to all members at the end of the month.*
6 GAME/SPORT to stop playing in a competition because you have lost a game: *He went out in the first round.*
7 MOVE ABROAD to travel to another country in order to live and work there: **[+to]** *They are looking for nurses to go out to Saudi Arabia.*
8 NO LONGER FASHIONABLE to stop being fashionable or used: *Hats like that went out years ago.* | *This kind of entertainment* ***went out with the ark*** (=is very old-fashioned).
9 SEA when the TIDE goes out, the sea moves away from the land OPP **come in**
10 MAKE PUBLIC if news or a message goes out, it is officially announced to everyone: *The appeal went out for food and medicines.*
11 your heart/thoughts go out to sb used to say that you feel sympathy for someone and are thinking about them: *Our hearts go out to the victim's family.*
12 TIME [always + adv/prep] *literary* to end: *March went out with high winds and rain.*

go over *phr v*
1 THINK ABOUT **go over sth** to think very carefully about something: *I had gone over and over what happened in my mind.*
2 EXAMINE **go over sth** to search or examine something very carefully: *In the competition, the judge goes over each dog and assesses it.*
3 REPEAT **go over sth** to repeat something in order to explain it or make sure it is correct: *Once again I went over exactly what I needed to say.*
4 CLEAN **go over sth** to clean something
5 go over well (*also* **go over big** *AmE*) if something goes over well, people like it: *That kind of salesman talk doesn't go over very well with the scientists.*

go over to sth *phr v*
1 to change to a different place or person for the next part of a television or radio programme: *We're going over to the White House for an important announcement.*
2 to change to a different way of doing things: *They went over to a computerized records system.*
3 to change to a different political party or religion: *the Labour MP who went over to the Conservatives last year*

go round *phr v BrE* → GO AROUND

go through *phr v*
1 DIFFICULT/UNPLEASANT SITUATION **go through sth** to experience a difficult or unpleasant situation, feeling etc: *When you're going through a crisis, it often helps to talk to someone.* | *He's going through a divorce at the moment.* | *It is devastating for a parent to watch a child go through misery.*
2 PROCESS **go through sth** to experience a particular process: *Candidates must go through a process of selection.* | *Caterpillars go through several stages of growth.*
3 USE **go through sth** to use up money or a supply of something: *We went through five pints of milk last week.*
4 LAW **go through (sth)** if a law goes through, or goes through Parliament, it is officially accepted
5 DEAL/AGREEMENT if a deal or agreement goes through, it is officially accepted and agreed: *He accepted the offer and the deal went through.* | *The sale of the land went through.*
6 PRACTISE **go through sth** to practise something, for example a performance: *Let's go through the whole thing again, from the beginning.*
7 SEARCH **go through sth** to search something in order to find something in particular: *Dave went through his pockets looking for the keys.* | *Customs officers went through all my bags.*
8 READ/DISCUSS **go through sth** to read or discuss something in order to make sure it is correct: *We'll go through the details later on.* | *Do you want me to go through this and check your spellings?*

go through with sth *phr v* to do something you had promised or planned to do, even though it causes problems or you are no longer sure you want to do it: *He bravely went through with the wedding ceremony even though he was in a lot of pain.* | *I had no choice but to go through with it.*

go to sb/sth *phr v* [not in passive]
1 to begin to experience or do something, or begin to be in a particular state: *I lay down and went to sleep.* | *Britain and Germany went to war in 1939.*
2 to be given to someone or something: *All the money raised will go to local charities.*

go together *phr v*
1 if two things go together, they exist together or are connected in some way: *Alcohol abuse and eating disorders often go together.*
2 *old-fashioned* if two people are going together, they are having a romantic relationship

go towards sth *phr v* if money goes towards something, it is used to pay part of the cost of that thing: *The money will go towards a new hospice.* | **go towards doing sth** *All money raised will go towards renovating the building.*

go under *phr v*
1 if a business goes under, it has to stop operating because of financial problems: *More than 7,000 businesses have gone under in the last three months.*
2 to sink beneath the surface of water: *The Titanic finally went under.* | *She went under, coughing and spluttering.*

go up *phr v*
1 INCREASE to increase in price, amount, level etc: *Train fares have gone up.* | *Blood-sugar levels go up as you digest food.* | **go up by 10%/250/£900 etc** *Unemployment in the country has gone up by a million.* | **go up from sth to sth** *Spending on research went up from $426 million to $461 million.*
2 BUILDING/SIGN if a building or sign goes up, it is built or fixed into place: *It was a lovely place before all these new houses went up.*
3 EXPLODE/BURN to explode, or be destroyed in a fire: *He had left the gas on and the whole kitchen went up.* | *The whole building* ***went up in flames.*** → **go up in smoke** at SMOKE[1](3)
4 SHOUT if a shout or a CHEER goes up, people start to shout or CHEER: **[+from]** *A great cheer went up from the audience.*
5 TO ANOTHER PLACE *BrE* to go from one place to another, especially to a place that is further north, or to a town or

city from a smaller place: **[+to]** *We're going up to Scotland next weekend.* | *He went up to the farm to get some eggs.*
6 LIGHTS if lights go up, they become brighter: *when the lights went up at the end of the performance*
7 UNIVERSITY *BrE formal old-fashioned* to begin studying at a university, especially Oxford or Cambridge University
go with sb/sth *phr v*
1 BE PART OF to be included as part of something: *The house goes with the job.* | *He had fame, money, and everything that goes with it.* | **go with doing sth** *Responsibility goes with becoming a father.*
2 EXIST TOGETHER to often exist with something else or be related to something else: *Ill health often goes with poverty.*
3 RELATIONSHIP *old-fashioned* to have a romantic relationship with someone
4 HAVE SEX *informal* to have sex with someone
5 AGREE to accept someone's idea or plan: *Let's go with John's original proposal.*
go without *phr v*
1 go without (sth) to not have something that you usually have: *I like to give the children what they want even if I have to go without.* | *It is possible to go without food for a few days.*
2 it goes without saying (that) used to say that something is so clearly true that it does not need to be said: *The Internet, too, it goes without saying, is a good source of information.*
go² ●●● S1 *n* (*plural* **goes**)
1 TRY [C] an attempt to do something: *'I can't open this drawer.' 'Here, let me **have a go**.'* | *On the tour, everyone can **have a go at** making a pot.* | *I'd thought about it for some time and decided to **give it a go*** (=try to do something). | *I **had a good go*** (=tried hard) *at cleaning the silver.* | **at/in one go** *Ruby blew out all her candles at one go.* | *I'm not sure it will work but **it's worth a go**.*
2 YOUR TURN [C] someone's turn in a game or someone's turn to use something: *Whose go is it?* | *It's your go.* | *Can I **have a go on** your guitar?* | *Don't I **get a go**?*
3 make a go of sth *informal* to make something succeed, especially a business or marriage: *Nikki was determined to make a go of the business.* | *Many businesses are struggling hard to **make a go of it**.*
4 £3/$50 etc a go *informal* used for saying how much it costs to do something or buy something: *At £3 a go, the cards are not cheap.*
5 on the go *informal* **a)** if you have something on the go, you have started it and are busy doing it: *Even with three top films on the go, Michelle is reluctant to talk about herself.* | *He **has** at least two other projects **on the go**.* **b)** very busy doing a lot of things: *Children are always on the go.*
6 sth is a go *AmE spoken* used to say that things are working correctly or that you have permission to do something: *The trip to London is a go.*
7 sth is (a) no go *spoken* used to say that something is not allowed or will not happen: *The hotel is no go for dogs.* → NO-GO AREA
8 it's all go *BrE spoken* it is very busy: *It's all go around here.* | *It's all go in the commercial property market.*
9 have a go *BrE spoken* **a)** to criticize someone: *You're always having a go.* | **[+at]** *Will you stop having a go at me!* | **have a go at sb for/about sth** *Mum had a go at me for not doing my homework.* **b)** to attack someone: *A whole gang of yobs were standing around, just waiting to have a go.* **c)** to try to catch someone who you see doing something wrong, rather than waiting for the police: *The public should not be encouraged to have a go.*
10 ENERGY [U] *BrE* energy and a desire to do things: *There's plenty of go in him yet.*
11 all the go *old-fashioned* very fashionable
goad¹ /gəʊd $ goʊd/ *v* [T] **1** to make someone do something by annoying or encouraging them until they do it → **provoke**: **goad sb into (doing) sth** *Kathy goaded him into telling her what he had done.* | **goad sb on** *They goaded him on with insults.* **2** to push animals ahead of you with a sharp stick
goad² *n* [C] **1** something that forces someone to do something: *The offer of economic aid was a goad to political change.* **2** a sharp stick for making animals move forward
ˈgo-ahead¹ *n* **give (sb) the go-ahead/get the go-ahead** to give or be given permission to start doing something: *The company has been given the go-ahead to build a new supermarket.*
go-ahead² *adj* [only before noun] *BrE* using new methods or ideas and therefore likely to succeed: *a **go-ahead company***
goal /gəʊl $ goʊl/ ●●● S2 W1 AWL *n* [C]
1 something that you hope to achieve in the future SYN **aim**: *Your goal as a parent is to help your child become an independent adult.* THESAURUS ▸ AIM, PURPOSE

> **REGISTER**
> In everyday British English, people often talk about what someone **is aiming to do** rather than talk about someone's **goal**: ***His goal is to** set up his own business.*
> → ***He's aiming to** set up his own business.*

2 the area between two posts where the ball must go in order to score in games such as football or HOCKEY: **be in goal/keep goal** *BrE* (=be the goalkeeper) → see picture at FOOTBALL
3 the action of making the ball go into a goal, or the score gained by doing this: *I **scored** the first **goal**.*

> **COLLOCATIONS**
>
> **ADJECTIVES**
> **sb's main/primary goal** *My main goal was to get the team to the finals.*
> **sb's ultimate goal** (=what they eventually and most importantly hope to achieve) *The ultimate goal is a freer, more democratic society.*
> **an immediate goal** (=that you need to achieve very soon) *Our immediate goal is to cut costs.*
> **a long-term goal** (=that you hope to achieve after a long time) | **a short-term goal** (=that you hope to achieve after a short time) | **sb's personal goal** | **a common goal** (=an aim shared by more than one person or organization) | **a realistic/achievable goal** | **an ambitious goal** (=an aim that will be difficult to achieve)
>
> **VERBS**
> **have a goal** *She had one goal in life: to accumulate a huge fortune.*
> **work towards a goal** *We are all working towards similar goals.*
> **achieve/attain/reach your goal** *They're hoping to reach their goal of raising £10,000 for charity.*
> **set (yourself/sb) a goal** (=decide what you or someone else should try to achieve)

goal·ie /ˈgəʊli $ ˈgoʊ-/ *n* [C] *informal* a goalkeeper
goal·keep·er /ˈgəʊlˌkiːpə $ ˈgoʊlˌkiːpər/ ●●○ *n* [C] the player in a sports team whose job is to try to stop the ball going into the goal SYN **goaltender** *AmE* → see picture at FOOTBALL
goal·kick /ˈgəʊlkɪk $ ˈgoʊl-/ *n* [C] a kick in football taken by a goalkeeper after the attacking team has kicked the ball over the goal line
goal·less /ˈgəʊl-ləs $ ˈgoʊl-/ *adj* a goalless match is one in which no goals are scored
ˈgoal line *n* [C] a line at either end of the playing area in sports such as football or HOCKEY, along which the goal is placed → see picture at AMERICAN FOOTBALL
goal·mouth /ˈgəʊlmaʊθ $ ˈgoʊl-/ *n* [C] the area directly in front of a GOAL
goal·post /ˈgəʊlpəʊst $ ˈgoʊlpoʊst/ *n* [C usually plural] **1** one of the two posts, with a bar along the top or across the middle, that form the GOAL in games such as football and HOCKEY SYN **post** → see pictures at AMERICAN FOOTBALL, FOOTBALL **2 move/shift the goalposts** *BrE informal* to change the rules, limits etc for something while someone is trying to do something, making it more difficult for them – used to show disapproval

G

goal·ten·der /ˈɡəʊlˌtendə $ ˈɡoʊlˌtendər/ *n* [C] *AmE* a GOALKEEPER → see picture at **FOOTBALL**

goat /ɡəʊt $ ɡoʊt/ ●●○ *n* [C]

1 an animal that has horns on top of its head and long hair under its chin, and can climb steep hills and rocks. Goats live wild in the mountains or are kept as farm animals.

2 get sb's goat *spoken informal* to make someone extremely annoyed

3 old goat *informal* an unpleasant old man, especially one who annoys women in a sexual way

4 act/play the goat *BrE informal* to behave in a silly way → **BILLY GOAT**, **NANNY GOAT**

GOATS

goa·tee /ɡəʊˈtiː $ ɡoʊ-/ *n* [C] a small pointed BEARD on the end of a man's chin

goat·herd /ˈɡəʊthɜːd $ ˈɡoʊthɜːrd/ *n* [C] someone who looks after a group of goats

gob¹ /ɡɒb $ ɡɑːb/ *n* [C] *informal* **1** *BrE* an impolite word for someone's mouth: *Jean told him to* ***shut*** *his* ***gob***. | *She's always stuffing her gob with food.* **2** a mass of something wet and sticky: **[+of]** *There's a gob of gum on my chair.* **3 gobs** *AmE* a large amount of something: **[+of]** *gobs of money*

gob² *v* (**gobbed**, **gobbing**) [I] *BrE informal* to blow a small amount of liquid out of your mouth SYN **spit**

gob·bet /ˈɡɒbɪt $ ˈɡɑː-/ *n* [C] *old use* a small piece of something, especially food

gob·ble /ˈɡɒbəl $ ˈɡɑː-/ *v informal* **1** (*also* **gobble up/down**) [I,T] to eat something very quickly, especially in an impolite or GREEDY way SYN **wolf**: *Don't gobble your food!* | *She gobbled down her lunch.* **2** [I] to make a sound like a TURKEY —**gobble** *n* [C]

gobble sth↔ **up** *phr v informal* **1** if one company gobbles up a smaller company, it buys it and takes control of it: *Air France gobbled up its main French rivals, Air Inter and UTA.* **2** to quickly use a lot of a supply of something such as money or land: *Inflation has gobbled up our wage increases.* **3** to eat something very quickly, especially in an impolite or GREEDY way: *We gobbled up all of the cake in one evening.*

gob·ble·dy·gook (*also* **gobbledegook** *BrE*) /ˈɡɒbəldiɡuːk $ ˈɡɑːbəldiɡʊk, -ɡuːk/ *n* [U] *informal* complicated language, especially in an official or technical document, that is impossible or difficult to understand – used to show disapproval

gob·bler /ˈɡɒblə $ ˈɡɑːblər/ *n* [C] *AmE informal* a male TURKEY

ˈgo-between *n* [C] someone who takes messages from one person or group to another because the two sides cannot meet or do not want to meet SYN **intermediary**: **act/serve as a go-between** *A UN representative will act as a go-between for leaders of the two countries.*

gob·let /ˈɡɒblɪt $ ˈɡɑːb-/ *n* [C] a cup made of glass or metal, with a base and a stem but no handle

gob·lin /ˈɡɒblɪn $ ˈɡɑːb-/ *n* [C] a small ugly creature in children's stories that likes to trick people

gob·smacked /ˈɡɒbsmækt $ ˈɡɑːb-/ *adj BrE spoken informal* very surprised or shocked

ˈgo-cart *n* [C] another spelling of GO-KART

god /ɡɒd $ ɡɑːd/ ●●● S1 W1 *n*

1 God the spirit or BEING who Christians, Jews, Muslims etc pray to, and who they believe created the universe: *Prayer is a way of talking to God.* ⚠ In this sense, **God** is written with a capital letter and without 'the': *We asked God (NOT the God) to help us.* Expressions containing the word God such as **oh my God** are common in spoken English but can offend religious people.

2 [C] a male spirit or BEING who is believed by some religions to control the world or part of it, or who represents a particular quality → **goddess**: **[+of]** *Mars, the god of war* | **Roman/Greek etc god** *Zeus was one of the most well-known Greek gods.*

3 God's gift to sb/sth someone who thinks they are perfect or extremely attractive – used to show disapproval: *Paul thinks he's God's gift to women.*

4 [C] someone who is admired very much: *To his fans he is a god.*

5 [C] something which you give too much importance or respect to: *Money became his god.*

6 the gods a) the force that some people believe controls their lives, bringing them good or bad luck: *The gods are against us.* **b)** *BrE informal old-fashioned* the seats high up and at the back of a theatre

7 God/oh (my) God/good God/God almighty *spoken* used to emphasize what you are saying, when you are surprised, annoyed, or amused: *Oh God, how embarrassing!*

8 for God's sake *spoken* used to emphasize something you are saying when you are annoyed: *For God's sake, shut up!*

9 I swear/hope/wish/pray to God *spoken* used to emphasize that you promise, hope etc that something is true: *I hope to God nothing goes wrong.*

10 God forbid (that) *spoken* used to say that you very much hope that something will not happen: *God forbid that this should ever happen again.*

11 God (only) knows *spoken* **a)** used to show that you are annoyed because you do not know something, or because you think that something is unreasonable: **God (only) knows who/what/how etc** *God knows what she's doing in there.* **b)** used to emphasize what you are saying: *God knows, it hasn't been easy.*

12 what/how/where/who in God's name *spoken* used to emphasize a question when you are angry or surprised: *Where in God's name have you been?*

13 God help you/him etc *spoken* used to warn someone that something bad will happen: *God help you if you spill anything on the carpet.*

14 God help us *spoken* said humorously when you think that something bad is going to happen: *'Simon's doing the cooking.' 'God help us!'*

15 honest to God *spoken* used to emphasize that you are not lying or joking: *Honest to God, I didn't tell her!*

16 God willing *spoken* used to say that you hope there will be no problems: *We'll be moving next month, God willing.*

17 God bless *spoken* used to say that you hope someone will be safe and happy, especially when you are saying goodbye: *Good night and God bless.*

18 God give me strength! *spoken* used when you are becoming annoyed

19 there is a God! *spoken* said when someone is explaining that something very good happened to them at a time when they thought that their situation was very bad: *In walked four gorgeous, blond Swedish boys, and I thought, 'There is a God!'*

20 God rest his/her soul (*also* **God rest him/her**) *spoken old use* used to show respect when speaking about someone who is dead

21 by God *spoken old use* used to emphasize how determined or surprised you are → **there but for the grace of God** at GRACE¹(6), → **in the lap of the gods** at LAP¹(6), → **play God** at PLAY¹(8), → **thank God/goodness/heavens** at THANK(2)

COLLOCATIONS

VERBS

believe in God *Do you believe in God?*
pray to God *They prayed to God for forgiveness.*
worship God (=show love and respect for God) | **praise God**

PHRASES

belief/faith in God *About one-third of the population has no belief in God.*

G

God's will/the will of God (=what God wants to happen) *He believed it was God's will that they should suffer.*
Almighty God/God Almighty (=used to emphasize God's power) *He swore by Almighty God to tell the truth.*
the word of God (=what God says) | **a gift from God** | **God's existence/the existence of God**

ˌgod-ˈawful, God-awful, god·aw·ful /ˈɡɒdɔːfəl $ ˈɡɑːdɒː-/ *adj* [only before noun] *informal* very bad or unpleasant. Some Christian people find this word offensive: *What's that god-awful smell?*

ˈgod-ˌbotherer *n* [C] *BrE informal* a very religious Christian – used to show disapproval

god·child /ˈɡɒdtʃaɪld $ ˈɡɑːd-/ *n* (*plural* **godchildren** /-tʃɪldrən/) [C] the child that a GODPARENT promises to help and to teach Christian values to. This promise is made at a BAPTISM ceremony.

god·dam·mit, God ˈdamn it /ɡɒˈdæmɪt $ ˌɡɑːdˈdæm-/ *interjection* a word used to express annoyance, anger etc. Some Christian people consider this word offensive.

god·damn, goddam /ˈɡɒdæm $ ˌɡɑːdˈdæm◂/ (*also* **god·damned** /-dæmd/) *adj* [only before noun] *spoken* a word used to show that you are angry or annoyed, considered offensive by some Christians: *Where's the goddamn key?* —**goddamn, goddam, goddamned** *adv*: *I just did something so goddamned stupid.*

god·daugh·ter /ˈɡɒdˌdɔːtə $ ˈɡɑːdˌdɒːtər/ *n* [C] a female godchild

god·dess, Goddess /ˈɡɒdɪs $ ˈɡɑː-/ ●●○ *n* [C]
1 a female BEING who is believed to control the world or part of it, or represents a particular quality: *Aphrodite, goddess of love*
2 screen goddess an attractive female film star

god·fa·ther /ˈɡɒdˌfɑːðə $ ˈɡɑːdˌfɑːðər/ *n* [C] **1** a male GODPARENT **2** *informal* the head of a criminal organization such as the MAFIA **3 the godfather of sth** someone who began or developed something such as a type of music: *Afrika Bambaataa, the Godfather of hip hop*

ˈGod-ˌfearing *adj old use* leading a good life and following the rules of the Christian religion

god·for·sak·en, Godforsaken /ˈɡɒdfəseɪkən $ ˈɡɑːdfər-/ *adj* [only before noun] a godforsaken place is far away from where people live and contains nothing interesting, attractive, or cheerful: *How can you stand living in this godforsaken town?*

ˈGod-given *adj* [usually before noun] received from God: *She has a God-given talent for singing.* | **a God-given right** (=the right to do something without asking anyone else's opinion) *The protesters have no God-given right to disrupt the life of the city.*

God·head /ˈɡɒdhed $ ˈɡɑːd-/ *n* **the Godhead** *formal* a word that Christians use to mean the Father, the Son, and the Holy Spirit, who they consider to be one God in three parts

god·less /ˈɡɒdləs $ ˈɡɑːd-/ *adj old use* not respecting God or not believing in a god —**godlessness** *n* [U]

god·like /ˈɡɒdlaɪk $ ˈɡɑːd-/ *adj* having a quality like God or a god SYN **divine**: *godlike powers*

god·ly /ˈɡɒdli $ ˈɡɑːdli/ *adj old use* obeying God and leading a good life —**godliness** *n* [U]

god·moth·er /ˈɡɒdˌmʌðə $ ˈɡɑːdˌmʌðər/ *n* [C] a female GODPARENT

god·pa·rent /ˈɡɒdˌpeərənt $ ˈɡɑːdˌper-/ *n* [C] someone who promises at a BAPTISM ceremony to help a child, and to teach him or her Christian values

ˌGod ˌSave the ˈQueen the NATIONAL ANTHEM (=the official national song) of the UK. The title of the song changes to *God Save the King* when the MONARCH is a king.

god·send /ˈɡɒdsend $ ˈɡɑːd-/ *n* [singular] something good that happens to you when you really need it: **[+for/to]** *The hot weather has been a godsend for ice-cream sellers.*

god·son /ˈɡɒdsʌn $ ˈɡɑːd-/ *n* [C] a male GODCHILD

god·speed, Godspeed /ˌɡɒdˈspiːd $ ˈɡɑːdspiːd, ˌɡɑːdˈspiːd/ *n* [U] *spoken old use* used to wish someone good luck, especially before a journey

ˈGod squad *n* **the God squad** an insulting way of describing Christians who try to persuade other people to become Christians

go·er /ˈɡəʊə $ ˈɡoʊər/ *n* [C] **1** *BrE spoken old-fashioned* a woman who often has sex with different men: *She's a bit of a goer.* **2** (*also* **-goer**) used after words such as party, church, and theatre to form nouns that refer to people who regularly go to parties, church etc: *cinema-goers*

go·fer /ˈɡəʊfə $ ˈɡoʊfər/ *n* [C] *informal* someone who carries messages etc for their employer

ˌgo-ˈgetter / $ ˈ. ˌ../ *n* [C] someone who is likely to be successful because they are very determined and have a lot of energy —**go-getting** *adj*

gog·gle /ˈɡɒɡəl $ ˈɡɑː-/ *v* [I] *old-fashioned* to look at something with your eyes wide open in surprise or shock SYN **gape**: **[+at]** *They were goggling at us as if we were freaks.*

ˌgoggle-ˈeyed *adj* with your eyes wide open and looking directly at something, especially in surprise or shock

GOGGLES

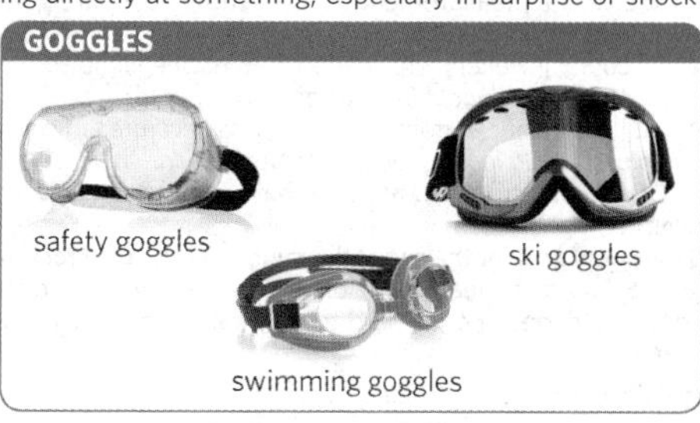

safety goggles

ski goggles

swimming goggles

gog·gles /ˈɡɒɡəlz $ ˈɡɑː-/ *n* [plural] a pair of GLASSES made of glass or plastic with a rubber or plastic edge that fit against your skin and protect your eyes

ˈgo-go *adj AmE informal* **1** a go-go period of time is one in which prices and the amount workers are paid increase very quickly: *the go-go 1980s* **2** go-go STOCKS increase in value very quickly in a short period of time, but involve a lot of risk

ˈgo-go ˌdancer *n* [C] a woman who dances with sexy movements in a bar or NIGHTCLUB —**go-go dancing** *n* [U]

go·ing¹ /ˈɡəʊɪŋ $ ˈɡoʊ-/ ●○○ *n* [U]
1 the difficulty or speed with which something is done: **hard/rough/slow etc going** *I'm getting the work done, but it's slow going.* | **good going/not bad going** *We climbed the mountain in three hours, which wasn't bad going.*
2 the act of leaving a place SYN **departure**: *His going will be no great loss to the company.*
3 heavy going if a book, play etc is heavy going, it is boring and difficult to understand
4 while the going's good *spoken* if you suggest doing something while the going's good, you think it should be done before it becomes difficult or impossible: *Let's leave while the going's good.*
5 when the going gets tough, the tough get going when the conditions become difficult, strong people begin to do something in a determined way
6 the going *BrE* the condition of the ground, especially for a horse race → **comings and goings** at COMING¹(2)

going² *adj* **1 the going rate/price/salary etc** the usual amount you pay or receive as payment for something: **[+for]** *Thirty dollars an hour is the going rate for a math tutor.* **2 the biggest/best/nicest etc sth going** the biggest, best etc of a particular thing: *It's some of the best beer going.* **3** [not before noun] *BrE informal* available: *Are there any jobs going where you work?* **4 have a lot going for you** to have many advantages and good qualities that will bring success: *Stop being so depressed. You have a lot going for you.* **5 a going concern** a business which is making a profit

G

and is expected to continue to do so **6** (*also* **-going**) used after words such as cinema and theatre to form adjectives that describe people who regularly go to the cinema, theatre etc: *the cinema-going public*

ˌgoing-ˈover *n* [singular] *informal* **1** a thorough examination of something to make sure it is all right → **once-over**: *The media gave his personal life a pretty firm going-over.* **2 give sth a going-over** to improve the condition of something, for example by cleaning it thoroughly: *You ought to give the place a going-over with the Hoover once in a while.* **3 give sb a going-over** *BrE* to hit someone and hurt them

ˌgoings-ˈon *n* [plural] activities or events that are strange or interesting, and often illegal: *She was shocked by some of the goings-on at the school.*

go·ji ber·ry /ˈɡəʊdʒi ˌberi $ ˈɡoʊ-/ *n* [C] a red fruit, grown especially in China, that is often dried before being eaten

ˈgo-kart, **go-cart** *n* [C] a small vehicle with an open frame and four wheels, used in races —**go-karting** *n* [U]

gold[1] /ɡəʊld $ ɡoʊld/ ●●● S2 W2 *n*
1 [U] a valuable soft yellow metal that is used to make coins, jewellery etc. It is a chemical ELEMENT: symbol Au: *a gold ring* | **pure/solid gold** *solid gold watches* | **9/18/22/24 carat gold** (=a measurement used to show how pure gold is) → **strike gold** at STRIKE[1](14)
2 [U] coins, jewellery etc made of gold: *She came to the party* ***dripping with gold*** (=wearing a lot of gold).
3 [C,U] the colour of gold: *The room was decorated in golds and blues.* | *Gold looks good on people with dark hair.*
4 [C] *informal* a GOLD MEDAL → **have a heart of gold** at HEART[1](2)
5 the pot of gold (at the end of the rainbow) (*also* **the crock of gold** *BrE*) great wealth or something very good which someone hopes or tries hard to get, but is not very likely to get

gold[2] ●●● S3 W3 *adj*
1 made of gold: **gold watch/chain/ring etc**
2 having the colour of gold: *a gold jacket* → **golden**

gold·brick /ˈɡəʊldbrɪk $ ˈɡoʊld-/ (*also* **gold·brick·er** /-brɪkə $ -ər/) *n* [C] *AmE informal* someone who stays away from their work, especially by pretending that they are ill —**goldbrick** *v* [I]

ˌgold ˈcard *n* [C] *BrE* a type of CREDIT CARD that gives you special advantages such as a high spending limit

ˈgold ˌdigger *n* [C] *informal* an attractive woman who uses her looks to get money from rich men

ˈgold dust *n* [U] **1** gold in the form of a fine powder **2 be like gold dust** *BrE* to be very valuable and difficult to find: *Cup final tickets are like gold dust.*

gold·en /ˈɡəʊldən $ ˈɡoʊl-/ ●●● W3 *adj*
1 having a bright yellow colour like gold: *golden hair* | *golden sand*
2 a golden opportunity a good chance to get something valuable or to be very successful: *He wasted a golden opportunity when he missed from the penalty spot.*
3 golden boy/girl someone who is popular and successful: *Hollywood's golden girl, Julia Roberts*
4 [only before noun] a golden period of time is one of great happiness or success: **golden years/days etc** *the golden years of childhood* | *the* ***golden age*** *of radio*
5 sb is golden *AmE spoken informal* used to say that someone is in a very good situation and is likely to be successful: *If the right editor looks at your article, you're golden.*
6 *literary* made of gold: *a golden crown*

ˌgolden anniˈversary *n* (*plural* **golden anniversaries**) [C] *especially AmE* the date that is exactly 50 years after the beginning of something, especially a wedding SYN **golden wedding, golden jubilee** *BrE* → **diamond anniversary, silver anniversary**

ˌgolden ˈeagle *n* [C] a large light brown bird that lives in northern parts of the world

ˈgolden ˌgoal *n* [C] *BrE* in some games of football, the first goal scored in EXTRA TIME. The team that scores the goal wins the game.

ˌgolden ˈhandcuffs *n* [plural] *informal* things such as a large SALARY or a good PENSION that make important workers want to continue working for an organization, rather than leave to work for a competing organization

ˌgolden ˈhandshake *n* [C] *BrE* a large amount of money given to someone when they leave their job

ˌgolden helˈlo *n* [C] *BrE informal* a large amount of money that is given to a new employee, in order to persuade them not to go to work for another organization: *New teachers are given golden hellos.*

ˌgolden ˈjubilee *n* [C] *BrE* the date that is exactly 50 years after an important event, such as the occasion when someone became king or queen SYN **golden anniversary** *AmE* → **diamond jubilee, silver jubilee**: *the Queen's golden jubilee celebrations*

ˌgolden ˈoldie *n* [C] *informal* a song, film etc that is old, but which many people still like

ˌgolden ˈparachute *n* [C] *informal* part of a business person's contract which states that they will be paid a large amount of money if they lose their job, for example if the company is sold

ˌgolden ˈraisin *n* [C] *AmE* a small pale RAISIN (=dried fruit) used in baking SYN **sultana** *BrE*

ˌgolden reˈtriever *n* [C] a large dog with light brown fur

ˌgolden ˈrule *n* [C] a very important principle, way of behaving etc that should be remembered: *The golden rule of cooking is to use fresh ingredients.*

ˌgolden ˈsyrup *n* [U] *BrE* a sweet thick liquid made from sugar that is used in cooking

ˌgolden ˈwedding *BrE n* [C] the date that is exactly 50 years after a wedding SYN **golden anniversary** → **diamond wedding, silver wedding**

gold·field /ˈɡəʊldfiːld $ ˈɡoʊld-/ *n* [C] an area of land where gold can be found

gold·finch /ˈɡəʊldˌfɪntʃ $ ˈɡoʊld-/ *n* [C] a small singing bird with yellow feathers on its wings

gold·fish /ˈɡəʊldˌfɪʃ $ ˈɡoʊld-/ *n* (*plural* **goldfish**) [C] a small shiny orange fish often kept as a pet

ˈgoldfish ˌbowl *n* **1** [C] a round glass bowl in which fish are kept as pets **2** [singular] a situation in which people know about everything that happens in your life: *Pop stars have to live their life in a goldfish bowl.*

Gold·i·locks /ˈɡəʊldilɒks $ ˈɡoʊldilɑːks/ *adj* [only before noun] exactly right - used especially to describe a place that has physical conditions that are exactly right for the existence of life: *In our solar system, only Earth lies in* ***the Goldilocks zone***.

ˌgold ˈleaf *n* [U] gold which has been beaten into extremely thin sheets and is used to cover things such as picture frames for decoration

ˌgold ˈmedal *n* [C] a prize made of gold that is given to someone for winning a race or competition → **bronze medal, silver medal** —**gold medallist** *BrE*, **gold medalist** *AmE*

gold·mine, **gold mine** /ˈɡəʊldmaɪn $ ˈɡoʊld-/ *n* [C] **1** *informal* a business or activity that produces large profits: *The nightclub turned out to be a goldmine.* **2** a place where gold is dug out from a hole in the ground **3 be sitting on a goldmine** to own something very valuable, especially without realizing it

ˌgold-ˈplated *adj* something that is gold-plated has a layer of gold on top of another metal —**gold plate** *n* [U]

ˌgold-ˈrimmed *adj* having a gold edge or border: *gold-rimmed glasses*

ˈgold rush *n* [C] a situation when a lot of people hurry to a place where gold has just been discovered

gold·smith /ˈɡəʊldˌsmɪθ $ ˈɡoʊld-/ *n* [C] someone who makes or sells things made from gold

ˈgold ˌstandard *n* **the gold standard** *technical* the use of the value of gold as a fixed standard on which to base the value of money

golf /gɒlf $ gɑːlf, gɒːlf/ ●●● S2 W3 *n* [U] a game in which the players hit a small white ball into holes in the ground with a set of golf clubs, using as few hits as possible: *He* ***plays golf*** *on Sundays.* | *a* ***round of golf*** (=complete game of golf) —**golfer** *n* [C] —**golfing** *n* [U]

ˈgolf ball *n* [C] a small hard white ball used in the game of golf

ˈgolf club *n* [C] **1** a long wooden or metal stick used for hitting the ball in the game of golf → see picture at SPORT **2** an organization of people who play golf, or the land and buildings they use

ˈgolf course *n* [C] an area of land where golf is played

ˈgolf links *n* (*plural* **golf links**) [C] a golf course, especially by the sea

Go·li·ath /gəˈlaɪəθ/ a person or organization that is very large and powerful. This name comes from a story in the Bible. A GIANT (=a very big, strong man) called Goliath was killed by a boy called David, who later became King David: *How can a small computer company compete with the Goliaths of the industry?*

gol·li·wog /ˈgɒliwɒg $ ˈgɑːliwɑːg/ *n* [C] a child's DOLL made of cloth, which looks like a man with a black face, white eyes, and short black hair. Golliwogs are considered offensive to black people and you should not use this word.

gol·ly¹ /ˈgɒli $ ˈgɑːli/ *interjection spoken old-fashioned* used to express surprise SYN **gosh**

golly² *n* (*plural* **gollies**) [C] *informal* a golliwog

go·nad /ˈgəʊnæd $ ˈgoʊ-/ *n* [C] *technical* the male or female sex organ in which the SPERM or eggs are produced

gon·do·la /ˈgɒndələ $ ˈgɑːn-, gɑːnˈdoʊlə/ *n* [C] **1** a long narrow boat with a flat bottom and high points at each end, used on the CANALS in Venice in Italy **2** the place where passengers sit that hangs beneath an AIRSHIP or BALLOON¹(2) **3** the enclosed part of a CABLE CAR where the passengers sit

gon·do·lier /ˌgɒndəˈlɪə $ ˌgɑːndəˈlɪr/ *n* [C] someone whose job is to take people for rides in a gondola

gone¹ /gɒn $ gɒːn/ *v* the past participle of GO

gone² *adj* **1 be gone a)** to be no longer in a particular place: *The door slammed and he was gone.* | *I turned round for my bag and it was gone.* **b)** to be dead or to no longer exist: *His wife's been gone for several years.* | *Many of the old houses are gone now.* → **dead and gone** at DEAD¹(1) **2 be gone on sb** *BrE informal* to be very attracted to someone of the opposite sex: *Kate's really gone on that boy next door.* **3 be five/six/seven etc months gone** *BrE informal* to have been PREGNANT for five, six etc months → **going, going, gone** at GO¹(36)

gone³ *prep BrE informal* later than a particular time or older than a particular age SYN **past**: *When we got home it was gone midnight.*

gon·er /ˈgɒnə $ ˈgɒːnər/ *n informal* **be a goner** if someone is a goner, they are soon going to die, fall, be caught etc: *Someone hit me from behind and I thought I was a goner.*

gong /gɒŋ $ gɒːŋ, gɑːŋ/ *n* [C] **1** a round piece of metal that hangs in a frame and which you hit with a stick to give a deep ringing sound. It is used as a musical instrument or to announce that a meal is ready. **2** *BrE informal* a MEDAL, title, or prize that someone is given

gon·na /ˈgɒnə, gənə $ ˈgɒːnə, gənə/ *spoken informal* a way of saying 'going to': *This isn't gonna be easy.*

gon·or·rhe·a, **gonorrhoea** /ˌgɒnəˈriːə $ ˌgɑː-/ *n* [U] a disease of the sex organs that is passed on during sex

gon·zo jour·nal·is·m /ˈgɒnzəʊ ˌdʒɜːnəlɪzəm $ ˈgɑːnzoʊ ˌdʒɜːr-/ *n* [U] *AmE informal* newspaper reporting that is concerned with shocking or exciting the reader and not with giving serious news —**gonzo journalist** *n* [C]

goo /guː/ *n* [U] *informal* an unpleasantly sticky substance → **gooey**: *My wash bag's covered in goo.*

good¹ /gʊd/ ●●● S1 W1 *adj* (*comparative* **better** /ˈbetə $ -ər/, *superlative* **best** /best/)

1 OF A HIGH STANDARD of a high standard or quality OPP **bad, poor**: *a good hotel* | *good quality cloth* | *The train service is not very good.* | *My French is better than my Spanish.* | *You'll receive the best medical treatment.* | *His qualifications aren't* ***good enough.*** THESAURUS▸ BRIGHT

2 SKILFUL able to do something well: *She's a very good player.* | *Do you know a good builder?* | **good at (doing) sth** *Alex is very good at languages.* | *She's good at making things.* | **[+with]** *As a politician, you need to be* ***good with words*** (=skilful at using words). | *He's very* ***good with people*** (=skilful at dealing with people). | **do/make a good job (of doing sth)** (=do something well) *Mike's done a good job of painting the windows.*

3 WHAT YOU WANT used about something that is what you want or happens in the way that you want OPP **bad**: *That's* ***good news!*** | *I need a bit of* ***good luck.***

4 PLEASANT/ENJOYABLE pleasant and enjoyable: **it's good to do sth** *It's good to see you again.* | **have a good time/day/weekend etc** *Did you have a good vacation?* | *That was* ***good fun.***

5 SUCCESSFUL/CORRECT likely to be successful or correct: *She's full of* ***good ideas.*** | *Well, can you think of a better plan?* | *What's* ***the best way*** *to deal with this?* | *The police have a* ***pretty good idea*** *who did it.* | *I'm not sure, but I could make* ***a good guess.***

6 SUITABLE suitable or convenient: *Is this a* ***good time*** *to talk to you?* | *It was a good place to rest.* | **good for (doing)**

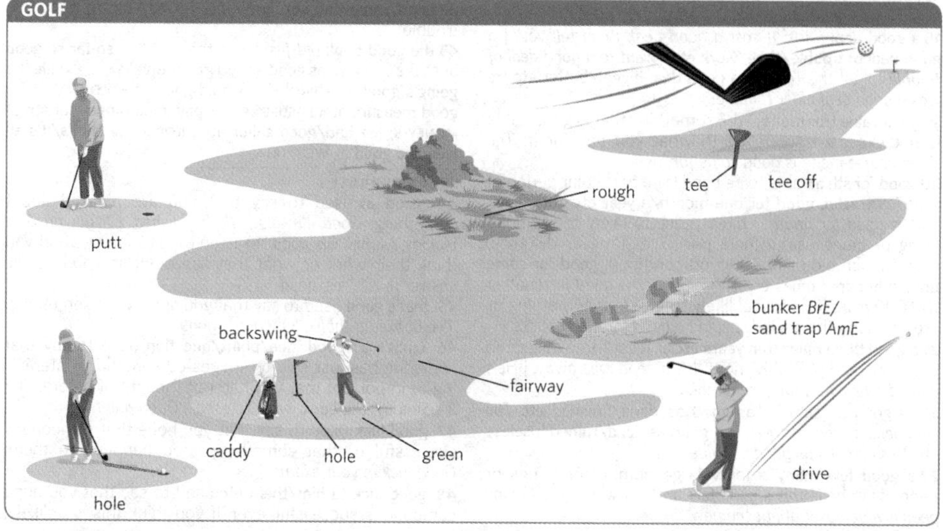

sth *It's a good day for going to the beach.* | **be good for sb** *especially AmE*: *Ten o'clock is good for me.*

7 USEFUL useful or helpful OPP **bad**: *Do you want some **good advice**?* | ***The best thing** you can do is wait here.* | *You should **make good use of** your time.*

8 BEHAVING WELL behaving well and not causing any trouble – used especially about a child SYN **well-behaved** OPP **naughty**: *She's such a good baby.* | *The kids were **as good as gold*** (=very good). → **be on your best behaviour** at BEHAVIOUR(2)

9 MAKING YOU HEALTHY likely to make you healthy, either physically or mentally OPP **bad**: **[+for]** *Fresh fruit and vegetables are good for you.* | *Watching too much TV isn't good for you.* | **good to eat/drink** *They have to learn which wild foods are good to eat.*

10 IMPROVING STH likely to improve the condition of something OPP **bad**: **[+for]** *products that are good for the environment* | *The publicity has been good for business.*

11 PHYSICALLY WELL [used especially in negatives and comparatives] healthy or well: *'How are you?' 'Better, thanks.'* | *Lyn's not **feeling** too **good** today.*

12 NOT DAMAGED OR WEAK if the condition of something is good, it is not damaged or weak: **in good condition/shape** *It's in pretty good condition for an old car.* | *Boris had always kept his body in good shape.* | *The Chancellor announced that the economy is in good shape.* | *Once the boat's repaired, it'll be **as good as new*** (=in perfect condition). | **sb's good eye/arm/leg etc** (=the one that is not damaged) *He sat up, supporting himself on his good arm.*

13 KIND kind and understanding about what other people need or want: **[+about]** *Dad lent me the money. He was very good about it.* | **it/that/this is good of sb** *It was good of him to offer you a lift.* | *The company's always **been** very **good to** me.* THESAURUS KIND

14 MORALLY RIGHT behaving correctly or being right according to accepted moral standards OPP **bad**: *a good man* | *I try to be good, but it isn't always easy.* | *Well, that's my **good deed for the day*** (=something good you try to do for someone else every day). | *I'm on the side of the **good guys*** (=people who behave in a morally right way, for example in a film).

15 LARGE large in amount, size, range etc → **goodish**: *We've had a good crop of apples.* | *There's a good range of leisure facilities.* | *I'd been waiting **a good while*** (=a fairly long time). | *Our team has **a good chance** of winning* (=is fairly likely to win).

16 REASONABLE PRICE a good price is reasonable and not expensive: *Thirty dollars sounds like a good price to me.*

17 COMPLETELY/THOROUGHLY [only before noun] doing something for a long time, so that you do it completely and thoroughly: *You need **a good rest**.* | ***Take a good look** at it.* | *She sat down and **had a good cry**.* | *This time he waited until he was **good and ready*** (=completely ready).

18 a good deal a lot: *It cost a good deal, I can tell you.* | **a good deal of trouble/time/work etc** *I went to a good deal of trouble to get this ticket.* | **a good deal bigger/better etc** *He was a good deal older than her.*

19 good value (for money) *BrE* something that is good value is not expensive, or is worth what you pay for it: *The three-course menu is good value for money.*

20 good for sth a) able to be used for a particular period of time SYN **valid**: **good for one month/a year etc** *Your passport is good for another three years.* **b)** likely to continue living or being useful for a particular time or distance, even though old or not in good condition: **good for some time/a hundred miles etc** *This old truck is good for another 100,000 miles.* **c)** *informal* likely to give you something or provide something: *Dad should be good for a few bucks.*

21 a good three miles/ten years etc at least three miles, ten years etc, and probably more: *It's a good mile away.* | *He's a good ten years younger than her.*

22 as good as almost: **as good as done/finished etc** *The summer's as good as over.* | **as good as dead/ruined/useless etc** *This carpet's as good as ruined.*

23 a good few/many a fairly large number of things or people: *I've done this a good few times now.* | *A good many people were upset about the new tax.*

24 too good to be true/to last *informal* so good that you cannot believe it is real, or you expect something bad to happen: *Their relationship had always seemed too good to be true.*

25 sb's too good for sb used to say that you think the second person does not deserve to have a relationship with the first: *George is a good lad, too good for you!*

26 in your own good time *informal* if you do something in your own good time, you do it only when you are ready to do it, rather than when other people want you to: *I'll tell him in my own good time.*

27 in good time (for sth/to do sth) *BrE* if you do something in good time, you do it early enough to be ready for a particular time or event: *Ben arrived in good time for dinner.*

28 hanging/shooting etc is too good for sb *spoken* used to say that someone has done something so bad that they deserve the most severe punishment available

29 as good a time/place etc as any used to say that although a time etc is not perfect, there will probably not be a better one: *I suppose this is as good a place as any to stay.*

30 be as good as your word to do something that you promised to do

31 a good word for sb/sth something good that you say about someone or something: *Dan **put in a good word** for you at the meeting.* | **have/find a good word (to say)** *No one had a good word to say for her.*

32 be in sb's good books *informal* if you are in someone's good books, they are pleased with you or your work: *I'll ask my boss for the day off – I'm in her good books just now.*

33 have a good thing going to have or be doing something that is successful: *They've got a good thing going with that little shop of theirs.*

34 be onto a good thing *BrE informal* to have found an easy way of being successful or getting what you want: *Andrew knew when he was onto a good thing.*

35 make good (*also* **make it good**) to become successful and rich after being poor – used especially in newspapers: *a country boy who made good in New York*

36 make good a debt/loss etc to pay someone money that you owe, or to provide money to replace what has been lost – used especially in business: *The loss to the company was made good by contributions from its subsidiaries.*

37 make good your escape *literary* to succeed in escaping

38 the good life an expensive way of living with good food, fast cars etc: *his weakness for women and the good life*

39 the good old days the good times in the past: *We talked for hours about the good old days.*

40 good works things that someone does to help other people, especially people with problems

41 sb's good offices *formal* help that someone provides, especially someone in a position of power

42 good Samaritan someone who gives help to people in trouble

43 the good book *old-fashioned* the Bible → **so far so good** at FAR[1](8), → **give as good as you get** at GIVE[1](34), → **while the going's good** at GOING[1](4), → **hold good** at HOLD[1](14), → **for good measure** at MEASURE[2](8), → **pay good money for sth** at MONEY(5), → **bad/good sailor** at SAILOR(2), → **that's/it's all well and good** at WELL[3](4)

SPOKEN PHRASES

44 good a) used to say that you are pleased about something: *Good. I'm glad that's finished.* | *'I got an A in biology, Mum.' '**Oh, good**.'* **b)** used to tell someone that you think their work or what they are doing is good: *'Is the answer five?' 'Yes, good.'*

45 that's good used to say that you approve of something: *'I've booked a table.' 'Oh, that's good.'*

46 (that's a) good idea/point/question used to say that someone has just said or suggested something interesting or important that you had not thought of before: *'But it's Sunday, the bank will be closed.' 'Good point.'*

47 good luck used to say that you hope that someone is successful or that something good happens to them: *Good luck in your exams.*

48 good luck to him/them etc used to say that you hope someone is successful, even if you think this is unlikely:

'They're hoping to finish it by November.' 'Good luck to them.'
49 good for sb used to say that you approve of something that someone has done: *'I've decided to accept the job.' 'Good for you.'*
50 it's a good thing (*also* **it's a good job** *BrE*) used to say that you are glad something happened, because there would have been problems if it had not happened: *It's a good thing you're at home. I've lost my keys.* | **and a good thing/job too** *BrE*: *She's gone, and a good thing too.*
51 that's/it's not good enough used to say that you are not satisfied with something and that you are annoyed about it: *It's just not good enough. I've been waiting an hour!*
52 be good and ready to be completely ready: *We'll go when I'm good and ready and not before.*
53 that's a good one used to tell someone that you do not believe something they have said and think it is a joke or a trick: *You won $50,000? That's a good one!*
54 be good for a laugh (*also* **be a good laugh** *BrE*) to be enjoyable or amusing: *It's Hazel's party tomorrow. Should be good for a laugh.*
55 good old John/Karen etc used to praise someone, especially because they have behaved in the way that you expect them to: *Good old Ed! I knew he wouldn't let us down.*
56 good grief/God/Lord/heavens/gracious! used to express surprise or anger: *'It's going to cost us £500.' 'Good grief!'*
57 good job *AmE* used to tell someone that they have done something well
58 good girl/boy/dog etc used to tell a child or animal that they have behaved well or done something well: *Sit! Good dog.*
59 if you know what's good for you used in a threatening way to tell someone to do something or something bad will happen to them: *Do as he says, if you know what's good for you!*
60 would you be good enough to do sth? (*also* **would you be so good as to do sth?**) *formal* used to ask someone very politely to do something: *Would you be good enough to help me with my bags?*
61 all in good time *BrE* used when someone wants to do something soon but you want to wait a little: *'When can we open our presents, Mum?' 'All in good time, Billy.'*
62 have a good one *AmE* used to say goodbye and to wish someone a nice day
63 be good to go *AmE informal* to be ready to do something: *I've got my shoes and I'm good to go.*
64 be as good as it gets if a situation is as good as it gets, it is not going to improve: *Enjoy yourself while you can. This is as good as it gets.*
65 it's all good *especially AmE informal* used to say that a situation is good or acceptable, or that there is not a problem: *Don't worry about it, man – it's all good.*
66 very good *BrE old-fashioned* used to tell someone in a position of authority that you will do what they have asked: *'Tell the men to come in.' 'Very good, sir.'*
67 (jolly) good show *BrE old-fashioned* used to say that you approve of something someone has done

USAGE: Good, well

• **Good** is an adjective in standard English. **Well** is an adverb: *She's a good player.* | *The team played well.*
• You will sometimes hear people say 'The team played good', especially in American English, but this is a non-standard use.
• The comparative form of both **good** and **well** is **better**: *His first book was better.* | *We'll play better next time.*
• The superlative form of both **good** and **well** is **best**: *Who is the best singer?* | *How could this best be achieved?*

good² ●●● S3 W2 *n*
1 no good/not much good/not any good a) not useful or suitable: *One lesson's not much good – you need five or six.* | *'I could come next week.' 'That's no good. I'll be away.'* | **[+for]** *The land here isn't any good for agricultural crops.* | **[+to]** *You're no good to me if you can't drive a car.* **b)** of a low standard or level of ability: *The movie wasn't much good.* | *Is the new headteacher any good?* | **no good at (doing) sth** *I'm no good at speaking in public.* **c)** morally bad: *Stay away from Jerry – he's no good.*
2 it's no good (doing sth) used to say that an action will not achieve what it is intended to achieve: *It's no good telling him – he won't listen.*
3 do some good/do sb good to have a useful effect: *She works for a small charity where she feels she can do some good.* | *I'll talk to him but I don't think it will do any good.* | *A bit more exercise would do you good.* → **do more harm than good** at HARM¹(1)
4 what's the good of ...?/what good is ...? used to say that it is not worth doing or having something in a particular situation: ***What's the good of*** *buying a boat* ***if*** *you're too busy to use it?* | ***What good is*** *money* ***when*** *you haven't any friends?*
5 for good permanently: *The injury may keep him out of football for good.*
6 for the good of sb/sth in order to help someone or improve a situation: *We must work together for the good of the community.* | *Take the medicine – it's* ***for*** *your* ***own good****!*
7 [U] behaviour, attitudes, forces etc that are morally right: *She is definitely an influence for good on those boys.* | *There's a lot of good in him, in spite of his rudeness.* | *the struggle between* ***good and evil*** → DO-GOODER
8 be up to no good *informal* to be doing or planning something wrong or dishonest: *Those guys look like they're up to no good.*

THESAURUS: good

good of a high standard or quality: *I've just read a really good book.* | *My French is not very good.*
nice pleasant and enjoyable. Nice is very common in spoken English. In written English, it is better to use other words: *I hope you have a nice vacation.* | *It will be nice to see you again.*
good quality/high quality well made from good materials: *If you buy good quality shoes, they last much longer.*
fine used for describing things of a very high quality, or weather with no rain and clear skies: *The restaurant serves the finest food in Florence.* | *If it's fine tomorrow, we'll go for a walk.*
neat *AmE spoken* good – used when you like something: *That's a neat idea.*
attractive an attractive offer, course of action etc seems good and makes you want to accept it or do it: *Going home for dinner was a more* ***attractive proposition*** *than completing his run.*
impressive something that is impressive is good in a way that makes people admire it: *an impressive achievement*

EXTREMELY GOOD

excellent/superb extremely good: *Your English is excellent.* | *She's a superb teacher.*
great/wonderful/terrific/fantastic *especially spoken* extremely good: *It's a great film.* | *Her cooking is wonderful.*
brilliant *BrE especially spoken* extremely good: *The play was absolutely brilliant.*
amazing/incredible extremely good, in a surprising and exciting way: *New York is an amazing place.*
beautiful/glorious used about weather that is very pleasant and sunny: *It's a beautiful day.* | *The weather was just glorious.*
outstanding/first-class/top-quality much better than other places, people etc: *an outstanding performance* | *The service is always first-class.*
exceptional unusually good: *Occasionally, we get a student with exceptional talent.*
be out of this world *spoken* to be extremely good: *Their chocolate cake is just out of this world!*

9 the common/general good *formal* the advantage of everyone in society or in a group: *countries united for the common good*
10 be (all) to the good used to say that something that happens is good, especially when it is in addition to or as the result of something else: *If further improvements can be made, that would be all to the good.*
11 three goals/£200 etc to the good used to say that someone has more of something than before or than someone else: *With United two goals to the good, the result seemed a certainty.*

good³ *adv informal spoken especially AmE* well. Many teachers think this is not correct English: *The business is* ***doing good*** *now.* | *Listen to me good!*

good ˌafterˈnoon ●●● S3 *formal* used to say hello when you are greeting someone in the afternoon, especially someone you do not know → **good evening**, **good morning**

> REGISTER
> In informal everyday English, people often just say **Afternoon**. If you don't want to sound formal or informal, you can just say **Hello**: *Afternoon, everyone.*

good·bye /gʊdˈbaɪ/ ●●● S3 used when you are leaving someone, or when they are leaving → **hello**: *Goodbye, John, see you tomorrow.* | *I just have to* ***say goodbye*** *to Jane.* | **say your goodbyes** (=say goodbye to several people or everyone) *We said our goodbyes and left.*

ˈgood choˌlesterol (*also* **HDL**) *n* [U] a type of CHOLESTEROL (=chemical substance found in your blood) that carries bad cholesterol away from your arteries (ARTERY) and back to your LIVER, helping to protect you against heart disease → **BAD CHOLESTEROL**

good ˈday *especially BrE old-fashioned* used to say hello or goodbye, especially in the morning or afternoon: *I must get back.* ***Good day to you.***

good ˈevening ●●● S3 *formal* used to say hello when you are greeting someone in the evening, especially someone you do not know → **good afternoon**, **good morning**, **good night**

> REGISTER
> In informal everyday English, people often just say **Evening**. If you don't want to sound formal or informal, you can just say **Hello**: *Evening, Tom.*

ˌgood ˈfaith *n* [U] when a person, country etc intends to be honest and sincere and does not intend to deceive anyone: **in good faith** *The company had* ***acted in good faith.*** | **sign/show/gesture etc of good faith** *A ceasefire was declared as a sign of good faith.*

ˌgood-for-ˈnothing *adj* a good-for-nothing person is lazy and useless: *an idle good-for-nothing drunk* —**ˈgood-for-nothing** *n* [C]: *Ian's a stupid good-for-nothing.*

ˌGood ˈFriday *n* [C,U] the Friday before the Christian holiday of Easter, that Christians remember as the day Jesus Christ was CRUCIFIED

good-heart·ed /ˌgʊd ˈhɑːtɪd $ -ˈhɑːr-/ *adj* kind and generous

ˌgood ˈhumour *BrE*, **good humor** *AmE n* [U] a happy friendly character or attitude to life: *At 80 her eyes still sparkled with good humour.* —**good-humoured** *adj*: *He was patient and good-humoured.* —**good-humouredly** *adv*

good·ie, **goody** /ˈgʊdi/ *n* [C] *BrE informal* someone in a book or film who is good and does things you approve of OPP **baddie**: *the goodies and the baddies*

good·ish /ˈgʊdɪʃ/ *adj BrE informal* **1** fairly good but not very good: *'Is the pay good?' 'Goodish.'* **2 a goodish distance/number etc** a fairly long way, a fairly large number etc

ˌgood-ˈlooking ●●● S2 *adj* someone who is good-looking is attractive: *a really good-looking guy* THESAURUS▸ **BEAUTIFUL** —**good-looker** *n* [C]

ˌgood ˈlooks *n* [plural] the attractive appearance of someone's face: *his natural good looks*

good·ly /ˈgʊdli/ *adj* [only before noun] **1 a goodly number/sum/amount etc** *old-fashioned* a large amount: *£1,500 is still a goodly sum.* **2** *old use* pleasant in appearance or good in quality

good ˈmorning ●●● S2 *interjection formal* used to say hello when you are greeting someone in the morning → **good afternoon**, **good evening**

> REGISTER
> In informal everyday English, people often just say **Morning**. If you don't want to sound formal or informal, you can just say **Hello**: *Morning, Joe.*

ˌgood ˈname *n* [singular] the good opinion that people have of someone or something SYN **reputation**: **[+of]** *It threatened to damage the good name of the firm.*

ˌgood ˈnature *n* [U] a naturally kind and helpful character or attitude to people: *He had his father's good looks and his mother's good nature.*

good-na·tured /gʊd ˈneɪtʃəd $ -ərd/ *adj* naturally kind and helpful and not easily made angry THESAURUS▸ **NICE** —**good-naturedly** *adv*

ˌgood ˈneighbourliness *n* [U] *BrE* when countries or people try to have friendly and helpful relationships with others that are near them

good·ness /ˈgʊdnəs/ ●●○ S3 *n* [U]
1 my goodness!/goodness (gracious) me! *spoken* said when you are surprised or sometimes angry: *My goodness, you have spent a lot!*
2 for goodness' sake *spoken* said when you are annoyed or surprised, especially when telling someone to do something: *For goodness' sake stop arguing!*
3 goodness (only) knows *spoken* used to emphasize that you are not sure about something, or to make a statement stronger: *That bar's been closed for goodness knows how long.* | *Goodness knows, I tried to help him!*
4 BEING GOOD the quality of being good: *the desire to see goodness and justice in the world*
5 BEST PART the part of food which is good for your health: *All the goodness of an egg is in the yolk.*
6 have the goodness to do sth *old-fashioned formal* used when asking someone to do something in an extremely polite way: *Please have the goodness to wait.*
7 out of the goodness of sb's heart used when someone has done something in order to be kind or helpful to other people: *He did it out of the goodness of his heart.*

good ˈnight ●●● S3 used to say goodbye when you are leaving someone or they are leaving at night, or before going to sleep → **good evening**: *Good night. Sleep well.*

> REGISTER
> In informal everyday English, people often just say **Night** or, especially to children, **Night night**: *Night night, darling. See you in the morning.*

goods /gʊdz/ ●●○ W3 *n* [plural]
1 things that are produced in order to be sold: **electrical/industrial/agricultural etc goods** *furniture and other household goods* | *the large market for* ***consumer goods*** (=televisions, washing machines etc) | *Britain's leading exporter of* ***manufactured goods*** (=things that are made, not grown) | *There will be tax increases on a range of* ***goods and services.*** → **DRY GOODS** THESAURUS▸ **PRODUCT**
2 things that someone owns and that can be moved: *They were charged with handling* ***stolen goods.*** | *We collected up our goods and left.*
3 *BrE* things which are carried by road, train etc SYN **freight**: *a goods train*
4 come up with the goods/deliver the goods *informal* to do what is needed or expected: *He's a great player. He always comes up with the goods on the day.*
5 have/get the goods on sb *AmE* to have or find proof that someone is guilty of a crime: *Face it, Bukowski, we got the goods on you!*
6 damaged goods someone whose actions mean that they no longer have a good effect or influence on something:

After the scandal, he was considered damaged goods by the party. → **worldly goods** at WORLDLY(1)

ˌgoods and ˈchattels *n* [plural] *BrE law* personal possessions

ˌgood ˈsense *n* [U] the quality someone has when they are able to make sensible decisions about what to do → **judgment**: *Mrs Booth showed a lot of good sense.* | **have the good sense to do sth** *Mark had the good sense not to argue.* | *It **makes good sense*** (=is sensible) *to do some research before buying.*

ˌgood-ˈtempered *adj* pleasant, kind, and not easily made angry OPP **bad-tempered**

good·will /ˌgʊdˈwɪl◂/ ●○○ *n* [U]
1 kind feelings towards or between people and a willingness to be helpful: *A fund was set up as a **goodwill gesture** to survivors and their families.* | **the season of goodwill** (=Christmas)
2 the value that a company has because it has a good relationship with its customers: *The sale price also covers the goodwill of the business.*

good·y¹ /ˈgʊdi/ *n* (*plural* **goodies**) [C usually plural] *informal* **1** something that is nice to eat: *We bought lots of goodies for the picnic.* **2** something attractive, pleasant, or desirable: *The competition gives you the chance to win all sorts of goodies.* **3** *BrE* a GOODIE

goody² *interjection* a word used by children to express pleasure or excitement

ˈgoody-ˌgoody *n* (*plural* **goody-goodies**) (*also* **ˌgoody-ˈtwo-shoes** *AmE*) [C] someone who tries hard to be very good and helpful in order to please their parents, teachers etc - used especially by children to show disapproval

goo·ey /ˈguːi/ *adj* (*comparative* **gooier**, *superlative* **gooiest**) *informal* **1** sticky and soft: *gooey cakes* | *gooey mud* **2** showing your love for someone in a way that other people think is silly SYN **soppy**: *Babies make her **go all gooey**.*

goof¹ /guːf/ (*also* **goof up**) *v* [I,T] *especially AmE informal* to make a silly mistake: *Somebody goofed and entered the wrong amount.* | *The restaurant totally goofed up our reservations.*

goof around *phr v AmE informal* to spend time doing silly things or not doing very much SYN **mess about** *BrE*: *We spent the afternoon just goofing around on our bikes.*

goof off *phr v AmE informal* to waste time or avoid doing any work: *He's been goofing off at school.*

goof² *n* [C] *especially AmE informal* **1** (*also* **goof up**) a silly mistake: *The goof could cost the city $5 million.* **2** (*also* **goofball**) someone who is silly

goof·ball /ˈguːfbɔːl $ -bɒːl/ *n* [C] *AmE* someone who is silly or stupid

goof·y /ˈguːfi/ *adj informal* stupid or silly: *A goofy grin spread across her face when she saw the card.*

ˌgoofy ˈfooted (*also* **ˌgoofy ˈfoot**) *adj* if you ride a SKATEBOARD or SNOWBOARD goofy footed, you ride with your right foot at the front of the board and your left foot at the back → **regular footed**

google *v* [I,T] to put a word or words into the Google™ SEARCH ENGINE in order to search for information on the Internet: *I googled her name and found out she runs her own company.*

Goo·gle /ˈguːgəl/ *trademark* a very popular SEARCH ENGINE (=computer program that allows you to search for information on the Internet). Google also provides other Internet services including e-mail, maps, SOCIAL NETWORKING, and video sharing.

goo·gle·whack /ˈguːgəlwæk/ (*also* **whack**) *n* [C] a single result when you search for a combination of two words on the SEARCH ENGINE Google. You do the search as a game. —**googlewhacking** *n* [U] —**googlewhack** *v* [I]

goo·gly /ˈguːgli/ *n* (*plural* **googlies**) [C] **1** a ball in the game of CRICKET that is thrown to an opponent so that it looks as if it will go in one direction but goes in the other **2 bowl sb a googly** *BrE informal* to ask someone a question that is intended to trick them

goo·gol /ˈguːgɒl $ -gɒːl/ *n* [C] *technical* the number that is written as the number 1 followed by 100 zeros, or 10 to the power 100

goo·gol·plex /ˈguːgəlpleks $ -gɒːl-/ *n* [C] *technical* the number that is written as the number 1 followed by a googol of zeros, or 10 to the power googol

goo·lie, **gooly** /ˈguːli/ *n* [C usually plural] *BrE informal* a rude or humorous word meaning a TESTICLE

goon /guːn/ *n* [C] *informal* **1** *especially BrE* a silly or stupid person **2** *especially AmE* a violent criminal who is paid to frighten or attack people

goop /guːp/ *n* [U] *AmE informal* a thick slightly sticky substance

GOOSE

goose¹ /guːs/ ●●○ *n* (*plural* **geese** /giːs/)
1 a) [C] a bird that is like a duck but is larger and makes loud noises **b)** [C] a female goose → **gander**
2 [U] the cooked meat of this bird
3 [singular] *old-fashioned informal* a silly person → **WILD GOOSE CHASE**, → **wouldn't say boo to a goose** at BOO²(3), → **kill the goose that lays the golden egg** at KILL¹(14), → **what's sauce for the goose is sauce for the gander** at SAUCE(3)

goose² *v* [T] *AmE informal* to touch or press someone on their bottom as a joke

goose·ber·ry /ˈgʊzbəri, ˈguːz-, ˈguːs- $ ˈguːsberi/ *n* (*plural* **gooseberries**) [C] **1** a small round green fruit that grows on a bush and has a sour taste **2 be a gooseberry** (*also* **play gooseberry** *BrE*) *informal* to be with two people who are having a romantic relationship and who want to be alone together

ˈgoose ˌpimples *especially BrE*, **goose·bumps** /ˈguːsbʌmps/ *especially AmE n* [plural] (*also* **goose·flesh** /ˈguːsfleʃ/ *especially BrE* [U]) small raised spots on your skin that you get when you are cold or frightened

goose·step /ˈguːs-step/ *n* **the goosestep** a way of marching by soldiers, in which they lift their legs quite high and do not bend their knees —**goosestep** *v* [I]

go·pher /ˈgəʊfə $ ˈgoʊfər/ *n* [C] **1** a North and Central American animal like a large rat that lives in holes in the ground **2** (*also* **Gopher**) *trademark* a computer program that helps people find and use information quickly on the Internet

Gor·di·an knot /ˌgɔːdiən ˈnɒt $ ˌgɔːrdiən ˈnɑːt/ *n* **cut/untie the Gordian knot** to quickly solve a difficult problem by determined action: *In recent years, governments have tried to cut the Gordian knot by imposing cuts in state support to the railways.*

gore¹ /gɔː $ gɔːr/ *v* [T] if an animal gores someone, it wounds them with its horns or TUSKS: *He was attacked and gored by a bull.*

gore² *n* [U] *literary* thick dark blood that has flowed from a wound → **gory**: *He likes movies with plenty of **blood and gore*** (=violence).

gorge¹ /gɔːdʒ $ gɔːrdʒ/ *n* [C] **1** a deep narrow valley with steep sides **2 feel your gorge rise** *BrE* to feel very sick or angry, especially when you see or smell something very unpleasant

gorge² *v* **1 gorge yourself (on sth)** to eat until you are too full to eat any more SYN **stuff yourself**: *We gorged ourselves on ripe plums.* **2 be gorged with sth** to be completely full of something: *The insect sucks until it is gorged with blood.*

G

gorge³ *adj BrE spoken informal* extremely beautiful or attractive

gor·geous /ˈɡɔːdʒəs $ ˈɡɔːr-/ ●●○ S3 *adj informal*
1 extremely beautiful or attractive: *'What do you think of my new flatmate?' 'He's* ***absolutely gorgeous****!' | You look gorgeous, Maria.* THESAURUS ▸ BEAUTIFUL
2 extremely pleasant or enjoyable SYN **lovely**: *a gorgeous cake | The hotel room had a gorgeous view.* —**gorgeously** *adv*

gor·gon /ˈɡɔːɡən $ ˈɡɔːr-/ *n* [C] **1 Gorgon** one of the three sisters in ancient Greek stories who had snakes on their heads that made anyone who looked at them change into stone **2** *BrE informal* an ugly frightening woman

go·ril·la /ɡəˈrɪlə/ *n* [C] **1** a very large African monkey that is the largest of the APES **2** a man who is very large and who looks as if he might become violent

gorm·less /ˈɡɔːmləs $ ˈɡɔːrm-/ *adj BrE informal* very stupid: *a gormless grin* —**gormlessly** *adv*

gorse /ɡɔːs $ ɡɔːrs/ *n* [U] a PRICKLY bush with bright yellow flowers, which grows in the countryside in Europe

gor·y /ˈɡɔːri/ *adj* **1** *informal* clearly describing or showing violence, blood, and killing: *a gory horror movie | gory tales of murder* THESAURUS ▸ VIOLENT **2 (all) the gory details** all the details about an unpleasant or interesting event – often used humorously: *Come on, I want to hear all the gory details.* **3** *literary* covered in blood

gosh /ɡɒʃ $ ɡɑːʃ/ *interjection informal* used to express surprise: *Gosh, it's cold.*

gos·ling /ˈɡɒzlɪŋ $ ˈɡɑːz-, ˈɡɒːz-/ *n* [C] a young GOOSE

ˌgo-ˈslow *n* [C] *BrE* a protest against an employer in which the workers work as slowly as possible SYN **slowdown** *AmE* → **work-to-rule, strike**

gos·pel /ˈɡɒspəl $ ˈɡɑːs-/ *n* **1 Gospel** [C] one of the four books in the Bible about Christ's life: ***the Gospel according to*** *St Luke* **2** (*also* **Gospel**) [singular] the life of Christ and the ideas that he taught: **preach/spread the gospel** (=tell people about it) *Missionaries were sent to preach the Gospel. | gospel stories* **3** [C usually singular] a set of ideas that someone believes in very strongly and tries to persuade other people to accept: **spread/preach the gospel** *spreading the gospel of science* **4** (*also* **gospel truth**) [U] something that is completely true: *Don't* ***take*** *everything she says* ***as gospel*** (=don't believe everything she says). **5** (*also* **gospel music**) [U] a type of Christian music in which religious songs are sung very loudly: *a gospel choir*

gos·sa·mer /ˈɡɒsəmə $ ˈɡɑːsəmər/ *n* [U] **1** *literary* a very light thin material **2** the light silky thread which SPIDERS leave on grass and bushes

gos·sip¹ /ˈɡɒsɪp $ ˈɡɑː-/ ●●○ *n*
1 [U] information that is passed from one person to another about other people's behaviour and private lives, often including unkind or untrue remarks: **[+about]** *Here's an interesting* ***piece of gossip*** *about Mrs Smith. | What's* ***the latest gossip****? | Do you want to hear some* ***juicy gossip****? | She had no time for* ***idle gossip****. | It was* ***common gossip*** *how he felt about her. | You miss a lot of* ***office gossip*** *when you have a day off work. | On Sundays all the men gather in the square to* ***exchange*** *local* ***gossip****.*
2 [C usually singular] a conversation in which you exchange information with someone about other people's lives and things that have happened: *Phil's in there, having a gossip with Maggie.*
3 [C] someone who likes talking about other people's private lives – used to show disapproval: *Rick's a terrible gossip.*

gossip² ●●○ *v* [I] to talk about other people's behaviour and private lives, often including remarks that are unkind or untrue: **[+about]** *The whole town was gossiping about them.* THESAURUS ▸ TALK

ˈgossip ˌcolumn *n* [C] a regular article in a newspaper or magazine about the behaviour and private lives of famous people —**gossip columnist** *n* [C]

gos·sip·y /ˈɡɒsəpi $ ˈɡɑː-/ *adj informal* **1** a gossipy conversation, letter etc is informal and full of gossip **2** a gossipy person likes to gossip: *gossipy secretaries*

got /ɡɒt $ ɡɑːt/ the past tense and a past participle of GET

> **GRAMMAR**
>
> In standard English, you say that someone **has** something or **has got** something: *I think he's got an idea.* ✗ Don't say: *I think he got an idea.*

got·cha /ˈɡɒtʃə $ ˈɡɑː-/ *interjection* **1** a word meaning 'I've got you', used when you catch someone or trick them in some way **2** a word meaning 'I understand': *'Yeah, 5 o'clock, gotcha.'*

goth /ɡɒθ $ ɡɑːθ/ *n* **1** [U] a type of slow sad popular music that is played on electric GUITARS and KEYBOARDS **2** [C] someone who likes goth music

Goth·ic /ˈɡɒθɪk $ ˈɡɑː-/ *adj* **1** the Gothic style of building was common in Western Europe between the 12th and 16th centuries and included tall pointed ARCHes and windows and tall PILLARS: *a Gothic church* **2** a Gothic story, film etc is about frightening things that happen in mysterious old buildings and lonely places, in a style that was popular in the early 19th century **3** Gothic writing, printing etc has thick decorated letters

ˈgo-to *adj* [only before noun] *informal* the go-to person is someone who people always ask for help with a particular problem, because of their great skill or knowledge: *He's the* ***go-to guy*** *for questions about spreadsheets.*

got·ta /ˈɡɒtə $ ˈɡɑːtə/ *spoken informal* a short form of 'have got to', 'has got to', 'have got a', or 'has got a', which most people think is incorrect: *We gotta go now.*

got·ten /ˈɡɒtn $ ˈɡɑːtn/ *v AmE* the past participle of GET → **ILL-GOTTEN GAINS**

> **USAGE: Gotten or got?**
>
> • In American English, **gotten** is the usual past participle of **get**: *I'd gotten an A on the test. | They have gotten divorced.*
> • In British English, the past participle of **get** is **got**: *I had got a letter from my sister in Australia.*

gou·ache /ɡʊˈɑːʃ, ɡwɑːʃ/ *n* **1** [U] a method of painting using colours that are mixed with water and made thicker with a type of glue **2** [C] a picture painted in this way

gouge¹ /ɡaʊdʒ/ *v* [T] to make a deep hole or cut in the surface of something: *He took a knife and gouged a hole in the bottom of the boat.*

gouge sth ↔ **out** *phr v* **1** to form a hole, space etc by digging into a surface and removing material, or to remove material by digging: **[+of]** *A rough road had been gouged out of the rock. | Every week 30,000 tonnes of slate are gouged out of the mountains.* **2 gouge sb's eyes out** to remove someone's eyes with a pointed weapon

gouge² *n* [C] a hole or cut made in something, usually by a sharp tool or weapon

gou·lash /ˈɡuːlæʃ $ -lɑːʃ, -læʃ/ *n* [C,U] a dish of meat cooked in liquid with a hot-tasting pepper, originally from Hungary

gourd /ɡʊəd $ ɡɔːrd, ɡʊrd/ *n* [C] a round fruit whose outer shell can be used as a container, or the container made from this fruit

gour·mand /ˈɡʊəmənd $ ˈɡʊr-/ *n* [C] someone who likes to eat and drink a lot

gour·met¹ /ˈɡʊəmeɪ $ ˈɡʊr-, ɡʊrˈmeɪ/ *adj* [only before noun] producing or relating to very good food and drink: *a gourmet cook | gourmet dinners*

gourmet² *n* [C] someone who knows a lot about food and wine and who enjoys good food and wine

gout /ɡaʊt/ *n* [U] a disease that makes your toes, fingers, and knees swollen and painful

gov **1 Gov.** the written abbreviation of ***governor*** **2 .gov** used in Internet addresses for government websites

gov·ern /ˈɡʌvən $ -ərn/ ●●○ W3 *v*
1 [I,T] to officially and legally control a country and make all the decisions about taxes, laws, public services etc SYN **rule**: *the leaders who govern the country | The party had been governing for seven months.*
2 [T] if rules, principles etc govern the way a system or situation works, they control how it happens: *legislation governing the export of live animals | The universe is governed by the laws of physics.*

gov·er·nance /ˈɡʌvənəns $ -ər-/ *n* [U] *formal* the act or process of governing

gov·ern·ess /ˈɡʌvənəs $ -ər-/ *n* [C] a female teacher in the past, who lived with a rich family and taught their children at home THESAURUS▸ TEACHER

gov·ern·ing /ˈɡʌvənɪŋ $ -ər-/ *adj* **1** [only before noun] having the power and authority to control an organization, country etc SYN **ruling**: *FIFA is the* ***governing body*** *of world soccer* (=the group of people who control it). | *The Democrats are now the governing party* (=the party in power) *in the country.* | *the governing class of ancient Rome*
2 governing principle a principle that has the most important influence on something: *Freedom of speech is one of the governing principles in a democracy.* → **self-governing**

gov·ern·ment /ˈɡʌvəmənt, ˈɡʌvənmənt $ ˈɡʌvərn-/ ●●● S2 W1 *n*
1 (*also* **Government**) [C usually singular] the group of people who govern a country or state: *The Government are planning further cuts in public spending. | The US government has tightened restrictions on firearms. | Neither party had the majority necessary to form a government.* | **under a government** (=during the period of a government) *Structural reforms are unlikely under the present government.*

GRAMMAR: Singular or plural verb?
- In this meaning, **government** is usually followed by a singular verb: *The government* ***is*** *planning to increase taxes.*
- In British English, you can also use a plural verb: *The government* ***are*** *planning to increase taxes.*

GRAMMAR GUIDE▸ NOUNS

2 [U] a form or system of government: *Most people in the country support the return to democratic government.* → LOCAL GOVERNMENT, CENTRAL GOVERNMENT
3 [U] the process or way of governing: **in government** *What would the opposition do if they were in government* (=governing the country)? | *the importance of good government in developing countries*
4 [U] *AmE* the degree to which the government controls economic and social activities: *The protest march was really about* ***big government*** (=when the government controls many activities).

COLLOCATIONS

ADJECTIVES/NOUN + government

the UK/French/Thai etc government *The UK government has offered to send aid.*
the Labour/Conservative/Social Democratic etc government *In August 1931, the Labour government collapsed.*
the Thatcher/Blair etc government | **a coalition government** (=government made up of members of more than one political party) | **a minority government** (=that does not have enough politicians to control parliament) | **a left-wing/right-wing government** | **central/national government** (=that deals with national rather than local things) | **federal government** (=in the US, the government of the whole country rather than of the individual states) | **local/state/city government**

government + NOUN

government spending *Government spending on health care totals about $60 billion a year.*
a government minister *A government minister said that there would be an inquiry.*
a government official (=someone who works for a government in an official position) | **a government body** (*also* **a government agency** *AmE*) (=an organization run by the government) | **a government department**

VERBS

elect a government (=vote to choose a government) *A new government was elected last October.*
form a government (=become the government) | **bring down a government** (=force it to lose power)

THESAURUS

government [C,U] the group of people who govern a country or the system they use to govern it: *The French government did not sign the agreement. | a democratic system of government*
administration [C] the government of a country, especially one such as the US, which is led by a president: *the Kennedy administration | the problems left by the previous administration*
regime [C] a government, especially one that was not elected fairly or that you disapprove of: *Most people opposed the apartheid regime.*
democracy [C,U] a political system in which everyone can vote to choose the government, or a country that has this system: *The transition to democracy has not been easy. | In a democracy, people have freedom of speech.*
republic [C] a country that has an elected government, and is led by a president, not a king or queen: *Mauritius became a republic in 1992.*
monarchy [C,U] /ˈmɒnəki $ ˈmɑːnərki/ the system of having a king or queen as the head of state, or a country that has this system: *Some monarchies have elected governments. | controversy about the institution of monarchy*

AN UNDEMOCRATIC GOVERNMENT

dictatorship [C,U] a political system or country that has a DICTATOR (=a leader who has complete power and who has not been elected): *Argentina was a military dictatorship until 1983. | Hungary's years of dictatorship*
totalitarian *adj* [only before noun] used for describing countries in which ordinary people have no power and the government has complete control over everything: *totalitarian states such as Nazi Germany | a totalitarian dictatorship*
police state [C] a country where the government strictly controls people's freedom, for example to travel or to talk about politics: *It's like living in a police state.*

gov·ern·men·tal /ˌɡʌvəˈmentl◂, ˌɡʌvən- $ ˌɡʌvərn-/ ●○○ *adj* of a government, or relating to government: *an attempt to restrict governmental power* | **governmental body** (=organization controlled by the government)

ˌgovernment ˈhealth ˈwarning *n* [C] *BrE* a notice that must be put on products such as cigarettes, to warn people that they are dangerous to their health

gov·er·nor, **Governor** /ˈɡʌvənə $ -vərnər/ ●●● W3 *n* [C]
1 a) the person in charge of governing a state in the US **b)** the person in charge of governing a country that is under the political control of another country
2 *BrE* a member of a committee that controls an organization or institution: *a school governor | the hospital's* ***board of governors***
3 *BrE* the person in charge of an institution: *the* ***prison governor*** | **[+of]** *the governor of the central bank*
4 *BrE* a GUVNOR

ˌGovernor-ˈGeneral *n* [C] someone who represents the king or queen of Britain in other Commonwealth countries which are not REPUBLICS: *the governor-general of Australia*

G

gov·ern·or·ship /ˈɡʌvənəʃɪp $ -vərnər-/ *n* [U] the position of being governor, or the period during which someone is governor

govt. the written abbreviation of ***government***

gown /ɡaʊn/ ●○○ *n* [C]
1 a long dress that a woman wears on formal occasions: **wedding/evening/ball gown** *a white silk wedding gown*
2 a long loose piece of clothing worn for special ceremonies by judges, teachers, lawyers, and members of universities SYN **robe**
3 a long loose piece of clothing worn in a hospital by someone doing or having an operation: *a hospital gown* → DRESSING GOWN

GP *BrE*, **G.P.** *AmE* /ˌdʒiː ˈpiː/ *n* [C] (***general practitioner***) a doctor who is trained in general medicine and treats people in a particular area or town → **consultant**: *I've got an appointment with my GP at five o'clock.* THESAURUS DOCTOR

GPA /ˌdʒiː piː ˈeɪ/ *n* [C] (***grade point average***) the average of a student's marks over a period of time in the US education system

GPS /ˌdʒiː piː ˈes/ *n* [U] (***Global Positioning System***) a system that uses radio signals from SATELLITES to show your exact position on the Earth on a special piece of equipment

grab¹ /ɡræb/ ●●● S1 W3 *v* (**grabbed**, **grabbing**) [T]
1 WITH YOUR HAND to take hold of someone or something with a sudden or violent movement SYN **snatch**: *I grabbed my bag and ran off.* | *Two men grabbed her and pushed her to the ground.* | *Kay* ***grabbed hold of*** *my arm to stop herself falling.* | **grab sth from sb/sth** *I managed to grab the gun from Bowen.* THESAURUS HOLD
2 FOOD/SLEEP *informal* to get some food or sleep quickly because you are busy SYN **snatch**: *Why don't you go and grab some sleep?* | *Hang on while I grab a cup of coffee.* | *Let's grab a bite to eat before we go.*
3 GET STH FOR YOURSELF to get something for yourself, sometimes in an unfair way: *Try to get there early and grab good seats.* | *Bob tried to grab all the profit.*
4 CHANCE/OPPORTUNITY (*also* **grab at sth**) *informal* to take an opportunity, accept an invitation etc immediately: *I think you should* ***grab*** *your* ***chance*** *to travel while you're young.* | *She* ***grabbed*** *the* ***opportunity*** *to go to America.* | *Melanie grabbed at the invitation to go.* | *This is our chance to grab a slice of this new market.*
5 GET ATTENTION to get someone's attention: *The book is full of good ideas to grab your students' attention.* | *The plight of the refugees immediately* ***grabbed the headlines*** (=was the most important story in the newspapers).
6 INFORMATION to take information on a computer, website etc
7 how does sth grab you? *spoken* used to ask someone if they would be interested in doing a particular thing: *How does the idea of a trip to Spain grab you?*

grab at/for sth *phr v* to quickly and suddenly put out your hand to try and catch or get something: *I grabbed at the glass just before it fell.* | *Lucy grabbed for the money.*

grab² *n* **1 make a grab for/at sth** to suddenly try to take hold of something: *As soon as he turned his back, I made a grab for the revolver.* **2 be up for grabs** *informal* if a job, prize, opportunity etc is up for grabs, it is available for anyone who wants to try to have it **3** [C] the act of getting something quickly, especially in a dishonest way: *a shameless power grab to eliminate opposition* | *Officials denounced the settlers'* ***land grab***.

ˈgrab ˌbag *n AmE* **1** [C] a container filled with small presents that you put your hand in to pick one out SYN **lucky dip** *BrE* **2** [singular] a mixture of different things or styles: **[+of]** *The treaty covers a grab bag of issues.* **3** [singular] *informal* a situation in which things are decided by chance

grace¹ /ɡreɪs/ ●●○ *n*
1 WAY OF MOVING [U] a smooth way of moving that looks natural, relaxed, and attractive SYN **gracefulness**: *Lena moved with the grace of a dancer.*
2 BEHAVIOUR **a)** [U] polite and pleasant behaviour: *The hotel maintains traditional standards of elegance, style, and grace.* | **have the grace to do sth** *He didn't even have the grace to apologize* (=he was not polite enough to apologize). **b) graces** [plural] the skills needed to behave in a way that is considered polite and socially acceptable: *Max definitely lacked* ***social graces***.
3 MORE TIME [U] (*also* **grace period** *AmE*) more time that is allowed to someone to finish a piece of work, pay a debt etc: **a day's/week's etc grace** *I got a few days' grace to finish my essay.*
4 with (a) good/bad grace in a willing and pleasant way, or an unwilling and angry way: *Kevin smiled and accepted his defeat with good grace.* | *With typical bad grace, they refused to come to the party.*
5 GOD'S KINDNESS [U] *formal* God's kindness that is shown to people: *We are saved by God's grace.*
6 there but for the grace of God (go I) used to say that you feel lucky not to be in the same bad situation as someone else
7 PRAYER [U] a prayer thanking God, said before a meal: *My father* ***said grace***.
8 SOUL [U] the state of someone's soul when it is free from evil, according to Christian belief: *He died* ***in a state of grace*** (=when God has forgiven you for the wrong things you have done).
9 Your/His etc Grace used as a title when talking to or about a DUKE, DUCHESS, or ARCHBISHOP
10 the Graces three beautiful Greek goddesses who often appear in art → **airs and graces** at AIR¹(9), → **fall from grace** at FALL¹(17), → **saving grace** at SAVE¹(14)

grace² *v* [T] **1 grace sth/sb with your presence** to bring honour to an occasion or group of people by coming to something - said humorously when someone comes late or does not often come to meetings etc: *Ah, so you've decided to grace us with your presence!* **2** *formal* to make a place or an object look more attractive: *His portrait graces the wall of the drawing room.*

grace·ful /ˈɡreɪsfəl/ ●●○ *adj*
1 moving in a smooth and attractive way, or having an attractive shape or form: *Her movements were graceful and elegant.* | *The branches formed a graceful curve.*
2 behaving in a polite and pleasant way: *Her father was a quiet man with graceful manners.* —**gracefully** *adv*: *She rose gracefully to her feet.* —**gracefulness** *n* [U]

grace·less /ˈɡreɪsləs/ *adj* **1** not being polite, especially when someone has been kind to you: *He was bad-tempered and graceless in defeat.* **2** moving or doing something in a way that seems awkward OPP **graceful**: *The soldiers were graceless with their heavy packs and helmets.* **3** something that is graceless is unattractive and unpleasant to look at OPP **graceful**: *graceless architecture* —**gracelessly** *adv*

gra·cious /ˈɡreɪʃəs/ *adj* **1** behaving in a polite, kind, and generous way, especially to people of a lower rank: *Sibyl was the most gracious, helpful, and generous person to work with.* | *a gracious apology* **2** having the kind of expensive style, comfort, and beauty that only rich people can afford: *a gracious manor house* | *a magazine about* ***gracious living*** **3 gracious (me)!/good gracious!/goodness gracious!** *old-fashioned* used to express surprise or to emphasize 'yes' or 'no': *Good gracious! What on earth has happened to your feet?* | *'Did you ever go back?' 'Good gracious, no.'* **4** a gracious act by or gift from God is kind and forgiving **5** [only before noun] used as a polite way of describing a royal person: *our gracious Queen* —**graciously** *adv* —**graciousness** *n* [U]

grad /ɡræd/ *n* [C] *AmE informal* a GRADUATE

grad·a·ble /ˈɡreɪdəbəl/ *adj* an adjective which is gradable can be used in the COMPARATIVE or SUPERLATIVE forms, or with words such as 'very' or 'fairly' —**gradability** /ˌɡreɪdəˈbɪləti/ *n* [U]

gra·da·tion /ɡrəˈdeɪʃən/ *n* [C] *formal* a small change or difference between points on a scale: *There are many gradations of colour between light and dark blue.*

grade¹ /ɡreɪd/ ●●● S2 W3 AWL *n* [C]
1 STANDARD a particular level of quality that a product,

material etc has: *The best grades of tea are expensive.* | *industrial grade diamonds* | **high/low grade** *low grade products*
2 RANK a particular level of job: *There are lots of jobs in junior grades.*
3 MARK IN SCHOOL a mark that a student is given for their work or for an examination: *He got a grade A in maths.* | *Tim worked hard and got good grades.*
4 make the grade to succeed or reach the necessary standard: *What does it take to make the grade as a top golfer?*
5 SCHOOL YEAR one of the 12 years that students are at school in the American school system, or the students in a particular year → **year**: **second/eleventh etc grade** *My brother is in sixth grade.* | *a fifth-grade teacher*
6 SLOPE *AmE* a slope or a degree of slope, especially in a road or railway SYN **gradient** *BrE*

grade² ●●○ AWL *v* [T]
1 to say what level of a quality something has, or what standard it is: **grade sth according to sth** *Pencils are graded according to softness.* | *All the parks are regularly checked and graded by tourist board inspectors.*
2 *especially AmE* to give a mark to an examination paper or to a piece of school work SYN **mark**: *Ted is grading papers in his office.*
3 to give a particular rank and level of pay to a job

ˈgrade ˌcrossing *n* [C] *AmE* a place where a road and railway cross each other, usually with gates that shut the road while the train passes SYN **level crossing** *BrE*

grad·ed /ˈgreɪdɪd/ AWL *adj* designed to suit different levels of learning: *graded coursebooks*

ˈgrade inˌflation *n* [U] the way in which the GRADES given for work in examinations get better each year, although the quality of the work does not

ˈgrade point ˌaverage *n* [C] *AmE* GPA

-grader /greɪdə $ -ər/ *suffix* [in nouns] **first-grader/fourth-grader etc** a student in one of the 12 years in an American school

ˈgrade ˌschool *n* [C,U] *AmE* an ELEMENTARY SCHOOL

gra·di·ent /ˈgreɪdiənt/ *n* [C] a slope or a degree of slope, especially in a road or railway SYN **grade** *AmE*: *a steep gradient*

ˈgrad school *n* [C,U] *AmE informal* a GRADUATE SCHOOL

grad·u·al /ˈgrædʒuəl/ ●●○ *adj*
1 happening slowly over a long period of time OPP **sudden**: *There has been a gradual change in climate.* | *the gradual decline in manufacturing industry* | *Education is a gradual process.* THESAURUS ▸ SLOW
2 a gradual slope is not steep

grad·u·al·ly /ˈgrædʒuəli/ ●●● S3 W3 *adv* slowly, over a long period of time OPP **suddenly**: *Jill gradually became aware of an awful smell.* | *Gradually, my ankle got better.* THESAURUS ▸ SLOWLY

grad·u·ate¹ /ˈgrædʒuət/ ●●● S2 W2 *n* [C]
1 someone who has completed a university degree, especially a first degree → **undergraduate**: *a Harvard graduate* | **[+of]** *a graduate of Edinburgh University* | *university graduates* | *a history graduate* | **[+in]** *He's a graduate in philosophy.*
2 *AmE* someone who has completed a course at a college, school etc: *a* ***high-school graduate***

grad·u·ate² /ˈgrædʒueɪt/ ●●● S2 W2 *v*
1 [I] to obtain a degree, especially a first degree, from a college or university: **[+from]** *Kate graduated from medical school last year.* | **[+in]** *He graduated in physics from Cambridge University.*
2 [I] *AmE* to complete your education at HIGH SCHOOL: **[+from]** *Jerry graduated from high school last year.*
3 graduate (from sth) to sth to start doing something that is bigger, better, or more important SYN **progress**: *As an actress she has graduated from small roles to more substantial parts.*
4 [T] *especially AmE* to give a degree or DIPLOMA to someone who has completed a course

grad·u·ate³ /ˈgrædʒuət/ *adj* [only before noun] *especially AmE* relating to or involved in studies done at a university after completing a first degree → **undergraduate** SYN **postgraduate** *BrE*: *a graduate student*

grad·u·at·ed /ˈgrædʒueɪtɪd/ *adj* **1** divided into different levels: *graduated rates of taxation* **2** a tool or container that is graduated has small marks on it showing measurements

ˈgraduate ˌschool *n* [C,U] *AmE* a college or university where you can study for a MASTER'S DEGREE or a DOCTORATE after receiving your first degree, or the period of time when you study for these degrees

grad·u·a·tion /ˌgrædʒuˈeɪʃən/ ●●● S3 *n*
1 [U] the time when you complete a university degree course or your education at an American HIGH SCHOOL: *After graduation, Neil returned to Ohio.* | *On graduation* (=after completing a first degree), *Nancy became an art teacher.*
2 [U] a ceremony at which you receive a university degree or a DIPLOMA from an American HIGH SCHOOL: *graduation day*
3 [C] a mark on an instrument or container used for measuring

Graeco- /griːkəʊ, grekəʊ $ -koʊ/ *prefix* another spelling of GRECO-

GRAFFITI

graf·fi·ti /græˈfiːti, grə-/ ●○○ *n* [U] rude, humorous, or political writing and pictures on the walls of buildings, trains etc: *The walls are daubed with graffiti.*

graft¹ /grɑːft $ græft/ *n* **1** [C] a piece of healthy skin or bone taken from someone's body and put in or on another part of their body that has been damaged: *Martha had to have several* ***skin grafts***. **2** [C] a piece cut from one plant and tied to or put inside a cut in another, so that it grows there **3** [U] *especially BrE informal* hard work: *Our success has been due to sheer* ***hard graft***. **4** [U] *especially AmE* the practice of obtaining money or advantage by the dishonest use of influence or power: *He promised to end graft in public life.*

graft² *v* **1** [T] to remove a piece of skin, bone etc from part of someone's body and put it onto or into a part of their body that has been damaged: **graft sth onto/to sth** *The technique involves grafting a very thin slice of bone onto the damaged knee.* **2** [T + on/onto] to join a part of a plant or tree onto another plant or tree **3** [T] to add something very different to something, so that it becomes part of it: **graft sth onto sth** *New elements are being grafted onto our traditional form of government.* | **graft sth on** *It is a 17th-century farmhouse with some Victorian additions grafted on.*
4 [I] *especially BrE informal* to work hard

graft off sb *phr v AmE* to get money or advantages from someone by the dishonest use of influence, especially political influence

Grail /greɪl/ *n* → **HOLY GRAIL**

grain /greɪn/ ●●○ *n*
1 FOOD **a)** [U] the seeds of crops such as corn, wheat, or rice that are gathered for use as food, or these crops themselves: *big sacks of grain* | *Last year's grain harvest was the biggest ever.* **b)** [C] a single seed of corn, wheat etc: *grains of rice*
2 LINES IN WOOD ETC [singular] the natural lines you can see in a substance such as wood, which are the result of its structure: **along the grain** (=in the same direction as the grain) *Cut along the grain of the wood.* | **across the grain** (=at 90 degrees to the grain)

3 SMALL PIECE [C] a single very small piece of a substance such as sand or salt: **[+of]** *a grain of sand | There were crumbs and grains of sugar on the table.* → see picture at PIECE
4 a grain of sth a very small amount of something: *The story wouldn't have fooled anyone with a grain of sense. | There is a **grain of truth** in all folklore and legend.*
5 against the grain if something goes against the grain, it is not what you would naturally or normally do: *Mary is always honest and **it went against the grain** to tell lies.*
6 MEASURE [C] the smallest unit for measuring weight, equal to about 0.06 grams. It is used for weighing medicines. → **take sth with a pinch/grain of salt** at SALT[1](3)

grain·y /ˈgreɪni/ *adj* a photograph that is grainy has a rough appearance, as if the images are made up of spots

gram (*also* **gramme** *BrE*) /græm/ ●●● S3 *n* [C] (*written abbreviation* **g** *or* **gm**) the basic unit for measuring weight in the METRIC SYSTEM

-gram /græm/ *suffix* [in nouns] a message delivered as an amusing surprise: *On his birthday we sent him a kissagram* (=a woman who was paid to give him a message and kiss him).

gram·mar /ˈgræmə $ -ər/ ●●● S3 W3 *n*
1 [U] the rules by which words change their forms and are combined into sentences, or the study or use of these rules: *Check your spelling and grammar. | the rules of English grammar*
2 [C] a particular description of grammar or a book that describes grammar rules: *A dictionary lists the words, a grammar states the rules.*

gram·mar·i·an /grəˈmeəriən $ -ˈmer-/ *n* [C] someone who studies and knows about grammar

ˈgrammar ˌschool *n* [C,U] **1** a school in Britain for children over the age of 11 who have to pass a special examination to go there → **comprehensive school** **2** *AmE old-fashioned* an ELEMENTARY SCHOOL

gram·mat·i·cal /grəˈmætɪkəl/ ●○○ *adj*
1 [only before noun] concerning grammar: *grammatical rules*
2 correct according to the rules of grammar OPP **ungrammatical** —**grammatically** /-kli/ *adv*

gramme /græm/ *n* [C] a British spelling of GRAM

Gram·my /ˈgræmi/ *n* [C] an AWARD given by the US National Academy of Recording Arts and Sciences for special achievement in the record industry

gram·o·phone /ˈgræməfəʊn $ -foʊn/ *n* [C] *old-fashioned* a RECORD PLAYER

gran /græn/ *n* [C] *BrE informal* grandmother

gran·a·ry /ˈgrænəri $ ˈgreɪ-, ˈgræ-/ *n* (*plural* **granaries**) [C] a place where grain, especially wheat, is stored

Granary *adj* [only before noun] *trademark BrE* Granary bread is bread which contains whole grains of wheat

grand¹ /grænd/ ●●○ S3 W3 *adj*
1 big and very impressive OPP **humble**: *a grand country house | The party was a grand affair. | New Yorkers build on a grand scale.*
2 aiming or intended to achieve something impressive: *Henry Luce had a grand design for America's future. | The company's grand ambition was to become the first and biggest global airline.*
3 important and rich: *He looked very grand in his ceremonial uniform. | the grand end of West Avenue*
4 Grand a) used in the titles of buildings or places that are big and impressive: *the Grand Hotel | Grand Central Station* **b)** used in the titles of some people who belong to the highest social class: *the Grand Duke of Baden*
5 *BrE informal* excellent: *We all had a grand time. | Thank you, Shirley, that's grand.*
6 a grand total the final total you get when you add up several numbers or amounts: **[+of]** *You could add the £15,000 Bonus to the First Prize and win a grand total of £125,000!*
7 grand (old) age an age when someone is quite old: *She had reached the grand old age of 80.*
8 the Grand Old Man of sth a man who has been involved in an activity or a profession for a long time and is highly respected: *the Grand Old Man of British theatre* —**grandly** *adv*: *'I am training her to cook for royalty,' Auguste said grandly.*

grand² *n* [C] *informal* **1** (*plural* **grand**) a thousand pounds or dollars: *The car cost him 15 grand.* **2** a GRAND PIANO → see picture at **PIANO**

gran·dad *especially BrE* (*also* **granddad**) /ˈgrændæd/ ●●● S3 *n informal* [C] grandfather

gran·dad·dy, **granddaddy** /ˈgrændædi/ *n* (*plural* **grandaddies**) [C] *AmE informal* **1** grandfather **2 the grandaddy of sth** the first or greatest example of something: *Louis Armstrong, the grandaddy of all jazz trumpeters*

ˌGrand Central ˈStation the main railway station in New York City. Grand Central Station is a very busy place, and in the US people often mention it humorously to say how busy another place is: *Our house was like Grand Central Station last night!*

grand·child /ˈgræntʃaɪld/ ●●● S3 W3 *n* (*plural* **grandchildren** /-tʃɪldrən/) [C] the child of your son or daughter

grand·dad /ˈgrændæd/ *n* [C] the usual American spelling of GRANDAD

grand·dad·dy /ˈgrændædi/ *n* [C] *AmE* another spelling of GRANDADDY

grand·daugh·ter /ˈgrænˌdɔːtə $ -ˌdɒːtər/ ●●● S3 W3 *n* [C] the daughter of your son or daughter

gran·dee /grænˈdiː/ *n* [C] **1** a politician of the highest social class who has a lot of influence **2** a Spanish or Portuguese NOBLEMAN of the highest rank, in the past

gran·deur /ˈgrændʒə $ -ər/ *n* [U] impressive beauty, power, or size: *the grandeur of the mountains* → **delusions of grandeur** at **DELUSION**(2)

grand·fa·ther /ˈgrændˌfɑːðə $ -ər/ ●●● S2 W3 *n* [C] the father of your father or mother

> **REGISTER**
> People usually say **grandad** (especially in British English) or **grandpa** when talking to or about their own grandfather: *I used to stay at my **grandpa**'s house.*

ˈgrandfather ˌclock *n* [C] an old-fashioned tall clock which stands on the floor → see picture at **CLOCK**

ˌgrand fiˈnale *n* [C] the last and most impressive or exciting part of a show or performance

gran·dil·o·quent /grænˈdɪləkwənt/ *adj formal* using words that are too long and formal in order to sound important SYN **pompous** —**grandiloquence** *n* [U]

gran·di·ose /ˈgrændiəʊs $ -oʊs/ *adj* grandiose plans sound very important or impressive, but are not practical: **grandiose scheme/plan/idea etc** *grandiose schemes of urban renewal*

ˌgrand ˈjury *n* [C] *law* a group of people in the US who decide whether someone charged with a crime should be judged in a court of law —**grand juror** *n* [C]

ˌgrand ˈlarceny *n* [U] *AmE law* the crime of stealing very valuable goods

grand·ma /ˈgrænmɑː/ ●●● S2 *n* [C] *informal* grandmother

grand mal /ˌgrɒn ˈmæl $ ˌgrɑːn-/ *n* [U] *technical* a serious form of EPILEPSY → **petit mal**

ˌgrand ˈmaster *n* [C] a CHESS player of a very high standard

grand·moth·er /ˈgrænˌmʌðə $ -ər/ ●●● S2 W2 *n* [C] the mother of your mother or father

> **REGISTER**
> People usually say **gran** (in British English) or **grandma** when talking to or about their own grandmother: *My **grandma** used to make lovely cakes.*

ˌGrand ˈNational, the a horse race that takes place every year at the Aintree racecourse near Liverpool, England

Grand Ole Op·ry, the /ˌgrænd əʊl ˈɒpri $ -ˈɑːpri/ a centre for COUNTRY music in Nashville, Tennessee, known especially for the radio and television broadcasts made there for many years. In 1974, it moved to Opryland, USA, near Nashville, and it is still an important centre for country and western music.

ˌgrand ˈopera *n* [C,U] an OPERA with a serious subject in which all the words are sung

grand·pa /ˈgrænpɑː/ ●●● S2 *n* [C] *informal* grandfather

grand·par·ent /ˈgrænˌpeərənt $ -ˌper-/ ●●● W3 *n* [C usually plural] one of the parents of your mother or father: *My grandparents live in Sussex.*

ˌgrand piˈano (*also* **grand**) *n* [C] the type of large piano often used in concerts, with strings in a horizontal position → **upright piano** → see picture at **PIANO**

Grand Prix /ˌgrɒn ˈpriː $ ˌgrɑːn-/ *n* (*plural* **Grands Prix** /-ˈpriː, -ˈpriːz/) [C] one of a set of international races, especially a car race

ˌgrand ˈslam *n* [C] **1** (*also* **Grand Slam** *trademark*) the winning of all of a set of important sports competitions in the same year: *Wales won the Grand Slam.* **2** a hit in BASEBALL which gets four points because it is a HOME RUN and there are players on all the bases **3** the winning of all of the TRICKS possible in one game of cards, especially in BRIDGE

grand·son /ˈgrænsʌn/ ●●● S3 W3 *n* [C] the son of your son or daughter

grand·stand /ˈgrændstænd/ *n* [C] **1** a large structure that has many rows of seats where people sit and watch sports competitions, games, or races **2 a grandstand view (of sth)** a very good view of something: *We had a grandstand view of the fireworks from our house.*

grand·stand·ing /ˈgrændstændɪŋ/ *n* [U] *AmE* an action that is intended to make people notice and admire you: *His opening the new school is just a piece of political grandstanding.*

ˌgrand ˈtour *n* [C] **1 the grand tour** a trip round Europe made in the past by young British or American people from rich families as part of their education **2** an occasion when someone takes you around a building to show it to you – used humorously: *They took us on a grand tour of their new house.*

grange /greɪndʒ/ *n* [C] a large country house with farm buildings

gra·ni·ta /grəˈniːtə/ *n* [C,U] an Italian sweet food that consists of water and coffee or fruit juice that is frozen and crushed into small pieces

gran·ite /ˈgrænət/ *n* [U] a very hard grey rock, often used in building

gran·ny¹, **grannie** /ˈgræni/ ●●○ S3 *n* (*plural* **grannies**) [C] *informal* grandmother

granny², **grannie** *adj* [only before noun] *BrE* of a style typically used by old women: *granny shoes*

ˈgranny ˌflat *n* [C] *BrE* a separate place inside or next to someone's house that is designed for an old relative to live in

ˈgranny ˌknot *n* [C] a knot that is like a REEF KNOT but is tied wrongly so that it is not firm

gra·no·la /grəˈnəʊlə $ -ˈnoʊ-/ *n* [U] *AmE* breakfast food made from mixed nuts, grains, and seeds

grant¹ /grɑːnt $ grænt/ ●●○ W3 AWL *v* [T]
1 *formal* to give someone something or allow them to have something that they have asked for: *Britain could* ***grant*** *Spain's* ***request****.* | *I would love to be able to grant her wish.* | **grant sb sth** *The council have* ***granted*** *him* ***permission*** *to build on the site.* | **grant sth to sb** *A licence to sell alcohol was granted to the club.* | **grant that** (=used in prayers) *Grant that we may know your presence and love.*

> **REGISTER**
> In everyday English, people usually say **give permission** rather than **grant permission**: *They* ***gave*** *him permission to stay.*

2 to admit that something is true although it does not make much difference to your opinion → **concede**: *He's got talent,* ***I grant you****, but he doesn't work hard enough.*
3 take it for granted (that) to believe that something is true without making sure: *He just took it for granted that he would pass the exam.*
4 take sb/sth for granted to expect that someone or something will always be there when you need them and never think how important or useful they are: *Bridget was careful not to take him for granted.*

grant² ●●○ W3 AWL *n* [C] an amount of money given to someone, especially by the government, for a particular purpose: *The university gets a government grant.* | *Anyone wishing to* ***apply for a grant*** *should write to the Treasurer.* | **[+of]** *a grant of £50,000* | **[+from]** *These studios are funded by a grant from the Kress Foundation.*

grant·ed /ˈgrɑːntɪd $ ˈgræn-/ *adv* [sentence adverb] used when you admit that something is true SYN **admittedly**: *Granted, the music is not perfect, but the flaws are outweighed by the sheer joy of the piece.*

ˌgrant-mainˈtained *adj* a grant-maintained school in Britain receives its money directly from the central government rather than from the local government

gran·u·lar /ˈgrænjələ $ -ər/ *adj* consisting of granules

gran·u·lar·i·ty /ˌgrænjəˈlærəti/ *n* [U] *formal* the amount of detail that is included in something such as a system: *The database should have an appropriate level of granularity.*

gran·u·lat·ed /ˈgrænjəleɪtɪd/ *adj* granulated sugar is in the form of small white grains

gran·ule /ˈgrænjuːl/ *n* [C] a small hard piece of something: *coffee granules*

grape /greɪp/ ●●● S3 *n* [C] one of a number of small round green or purple fruits that grow together on a VINE. Grapes are often used for making wine: *a* ***bunch of grapes*** | *grape juice* | *red seedless grapes* → **sour grapes** at **SOUR¹**(5)

grape·fruit /ˈgreɪpfruːt/ ●●● S3 *n* [C,U] a round yellow CITRUS fruit with a thick skin, like a large orange → see picture at **FRUIT**

grape·vine /ˈgreɪpvaɪn/ *n* [C] **1 hear sth on the grapevine** to hear about something because the information has been passed from one person to another in conversation: *I heard about his resignation on the grapevine.* **2** a climbing plant on which grapes grow SYN **vine**

graph /grɑːf $ græf/ ●●● S3 W2 *n* [C] a drawing that uses a line or lines to show how two or more sets of measurements are related to each other → **chart**: *Martin showed me a graph of their recent sales.* → see picture at **CHART¹**

graph·ene /ˈgræfiːn/ *n* [U] a strong, light material that is a sheet of CARBON one atom thick

graph·ic /ˈgræfɪk/ ●○○ *adj*
1 a graphic account or description of an event is very clear and gives a lot of details, especially unpleasant ones SYN **vivid**: *a graphic account of her unhappy childhood* | *His illness is described* ***in graphic detail****.*
2 [only before noun] connected with or including drawing, printing, or designing → **graphics**: *a graphic artist* | *the graphic arts*

graph·i·cal /ˈgræfɪkəl/ *adj* [usually before noun] relating to or containing graphics, especially on a computer: *a simple graphical representation of the problem*

graph·i·cally /ˈgræfɪkli/ *adv* **1** if you describe something graphically, you describe it very clearly with a lot of detail SYN **vividly** **2** *formal* using a graph: *statistics represented graphically*

ˌgraphical ˈuser ˌinterface *n* [C] (*abbreviation* **GUI**) a way of showing and organizing information on a computer screen that is easy to use and understand

ˌgraphic deˈsign *n* [U] the art of combining pictures, words, and decoration in the production of books, magazines etc —**graphic designer** *n* [C]

graph·ics /ˈgræfɪks/ *n* [plural] pictures or images that are designed to represent objects or facts, especially in a computer program

ˈgraphics ˌcard (*also* **ˈgraphics aˌdapter**) *n* [C] a CIRCUIT

G

BOARD that connects to a computer and allows the computer to show images, such as video images, on its screen

graph·ite /ˈɡræfaɪt/ *n* [U] a soft black substance that is a kind of CARBON, used in pencils, paints, and electrical equipment

gra·phol·o·gy /ɡræˈfɒlədʒi $ -ˈfɑː-/ *n* [U] the study of HANDWRITING in order to understand people's characters —**graphologist** *n* [C]

ˈgraph ˌpaper *n* [U] paper with many squares printed on it, used for drawing GRAPHS

-graphy /ɡrəfi/ *suffix* used in nouns to mean a way of making pictures or of writing: *radiography | photography | calligraphy*

grap·ple /ˈɡræpəl/ *v* [I] to fight or struggle with someone, holding them tightly SYN **wrestle**: **[+with]** *Two men grappled with a guard at the door.*

grapple with sth *phr v* to try hard to deal with or understand something difficult: *The Government has to grapple with the problem of unemployment. | Molly's upstairs grappling with her maths homework.*

ˈgrappling ˌiron (*also* **ˈgrappling ˌhook**) *n* [C] an iron tool with several hooks that you tie to a rope and use to hold a boat still, look for objects on the bottom of a river etc

grasp¹ /ɡrɑːsp $ ɡræsp/ ●●○ *v* [T]
1 to take and hold something firmly SYN **grip**: *I grasped his arm firmly and led him away. | Alan grasped the handle and pulled it.* THESAURUS ▸ HOLD
2 [not in progressive] to completely understand a fact or an idea, especially a complicated one: *At that time, we did not fully grasp the significance of what had happened. | Some people find the idea of relativity difficult to grasp.* | **grasp what/how etc** *A short opening paragraph enables the reader to quickly grasp what the article is about.* | **grasp that** *Nick had grasped that something was wrong.* THESAURUS ▸ UNDERSTAND
3 grasp an opportunity to eagerly and quickly use an opportunity to do something: *She is ready to grasp any opportunity to expand the business.*
4 grasp the nettle *BrE* to deal with an unpleasant situation firmly and without delay: *We need to grasp the nettle of prison reform.*

grasp at sth *phr v* to try to hold on to something: *His foot slipped and he grasped at the top of the wall.*

grasp² ●○○ *n* [singular]
1 the way you hold something or your ability to hold it SYN **grip**: *Luke took her arm in a firm grasp and led her through the gate. | He had allowed the ball to slip from his grasp.* THESAURUS ▸ KNOWLEDGE
2 your ability to understand a complicated idea, situation, or subject SYN **understanding**: **[+of]** *Her grasp of the issues was impressive.* | **a good/firm/thorough etc grasp of sth** *Steve has a good grasp of the European legal system.* | **[+on]** *After two months, his grasp on the subject was improving.*
3 your ability to achieve or gain something: **within sb's grasp** *An agreement to end the war seemed within their grasp.* | **beyond sb's grasp** *Many families are finding suitable housing beyond their grasp.*
4 *literary* control or power: *The king was determined not to let Scotland slip from his grasp.*

grasp·ing /ˈɡrɑːspɪŋ $ ˈɡræs-/ *adj* too eager to get money and unwilling to give any of it away or spend it: *Hanson was a hard, grasping man.*

grass¹ /ɡrɑːs $ ɡræs/ ●●● S2 W2 *n*
1 IN FIELDS AND GARDENS **a)** [U] a very common plant with thin leaves that covers the ground in fields and gardens and is often eaten by animals: *She enjoyed the feel of grass beneath her feet. | a* ***blade of grass*** (=single leaf) **b)** [C] a particular kind of grass: *All grasses need light to grow well.*
2 the grass an area of grass, especially an area where the grass is kept cut short: *I walked across the grass. | Keep off the grass.*
3 DRUG [U] *informal* MARIJUANA
4 CRIMINAL [C] *BrE informal* someone, usually a criminal, who gives information about other criminals to the police - used to show disapproval SYN **informer**, **stoolpigeon** *AmE* → SUPERGRASS
5 the grass is greener (on the other side) used to say that other places or situations seem better than yours, although they may not really be better
6 not let the grass grow under your feet to not waste time or delay starting something
7 put sb out to grass *informal* to make someone leave their job because they are too old to do it effectively → GRASS ROOTS, → **snake in the grass** at SNAKE¹(2)

grass² *v* [I] (*also* **grass sb up**) *BrE informal* to tell the police about a criminal's activities: **[+on]** *Burton grassed on other prisoners.*

grass sth ↔ **over** *phr v* to cover land with grass

ˈgrass ˌcourt *n* [C] a tennis court which has a grass surface for the players to play on → **hard court**

grass·hop·per /ˈɡrɑːsˌhɒpə $ ˈɡræsˌhɑːpər/ *n* [C] an insect that has long back legs for jumping and that makes short loud noises → **knee-high to a grasshopper** at KNEE-HIGH(2), → see picture at INSECT

grass·land /ˈɡrɑːslænd $ ˈɡræs-/ *n* [U] (*also* **grasslands** [plural]) a large area of land covered with wild grass SYN **prairie**

ˌgrass ˈroots *n* **the grass roots** the ordinary people in an organization, rather than the leaders —**grass roots** *adj*: *We are hoping for full participation at grass roots level.*

ˈgrass snake *n* [C] a common snake that is not poisonous

gras·sy /ˈɡrɑːsi $ ˈɡræsi/ *adj* covered with grass: *a grassy bank*

grate¹ /ɡreɪt/ *n* [C] the metal bars and frame that hold the wood, coal etc in a FIREPLACE

grate² *v* **1** [T] to rub cheese, vegetables etc against a rough or sharp surface in order to break them into small pieces: *grated cheese | Peel and grate the potatoes.* THESAURUS ▸ CUT **2** [T] *written* to talk in a low rough voice → **hiss**: *'Let me go,' he grated harshly.* **3** [I] to annoy someone: **[+on]** *Mr Fen had a loud voice that grated on her ears.* **4** [I,T] to make an unpleasant sound by rubbing, or to make something do this: *The stones beneath her shoes grated harshly.*

grate·ful /ˈɡreɪtfəl/ ●●○ S3 W3 *adj*
1 feeling that you want to thank someone because of something kind that they have done, or showing this feeling OPP **ungrateful**: **[+for]** *I'm so grateful for all your help.* | **[+to]** *I am very grateful to all those who took the trouble to write to me.* | **grateful (that)** *She should be grateful that he was making things easier for her.* | **extremely/deeply/eternally etc grateful** *I am extremely grateful for the assistance your staff have provided. | Our* ***grateful thanks*** *go to all who participated. | She gave me a grateful look.*

> **REGISTER**
> In everyday English, people usually say **I appreciate it** rather than **I'm grateful**: *Thanks,* ***I'm really grateful.***
> → *Thanks,* ***I really appreciate it.*** | ***I'm grateful for*** *everything you've done.* → ***I appreciate*** *everything you've done.*

2 I would be grateful if you could/would ... *formal* used to make a request: *I would be most grateful if you could send me an invoice in due course.* —**gratefully** *adv*: *All contributions will* ***be gratefully received****. | The authors gratefully acknowledge your financial support.*

grat·er /ˈɡreɪtə $ -ər/ *n* [C] a tool used for grating food: *a cheese grater*

grat·i·fy /ˈɡrætɪfaɪ/ *v* (**gratified**, **gratifying**, **gratifies**) [T] *formal* **1** to make someone feel pleased and satisfied: *He was gratified by Lucy's response.* | **be gratified to see/hear/learn etc** *John was gratified to see the improvement in his mother's health.* **2** to satisfy a desire, need etc: *She did not propose to gratify Gloria's curiosity any further.* —**gratification** /ˌɡrætɪfɪˈkeɪʃən/ *n* [C,U]: *sexual gratification*

grat·i·fy·ing /ˈɡrætəfaɪ-ɪŋ/ *adj* pleasing and satisfying:

G

it's gratifying to do sth *It's gratifying to note that already much has been achieved.* | *The support was considerable and very gratifying.* —**gratifyingly** *adv*

grat·in /ˈɡrætæn $ ˈɡrɑːtn/ *n* [C,U] a dish containing vegetables or fish, covered in cheese or cheese sauce and cooked in an OVEN

grat·ing¹ /ˈɡreɪtɪŋ/ *n* [C] a metal frame with bars across it, used to cover a window or hole: *Leaves clogged the grating over the drain.*

grating² *adj* a grating sound is hard and unpleasant: *a harsh grating voice* —**gratingly** *adv*

grat·is /ˈɡrætəs, ˈɡreɪ-/ *adj, adv* done or given without payment SYN **free**: *Medical advice was provided gratis.*

grat·i·tude /ˈɡrætɪtjuːd $ -tuːd/ ●○○ *n* [U] the feeling of being grateful OPP **ingratitude**: *Tears of gratitude filled her eyes.* | **[+to/towards]** *She had a* ***deep gratitude*** *towards David, but she did not love him.* | **[+for]** *The committee* ***expressed*** *its* ***gratitude*** *for the contribution he had made.* | **in gratitude for sth** *Will you let me take you out to dinner tomorrow in gratitude for what you've done?* | **with gratitude** *She accepted his offer with gratitude.* → **debt of gratitude** at DEBT(4)

gra·tu·i·tous /ɡrəˈtjuːɪtəs $ -ˈtuː-/ *adj* said or done without a good reason, in a way that offends someone SYN **unnecessary**: *children's books which include* ***gratuitous violence*** —**gratuitously** *adv*: *There is no point in gratuitously antagonizing people.*

gra·tu·i·ty /ɡrəˈtjuːəti $ -ˈtuː-/ *n* (*plural* **gratuities**) [C] *formal* **1** a small gift of money given to someone for a service they provided SYN **tip** **2** *especially BrE* a large gift of money given to someone when they leave their job, especially in the army, navy etc

grave¹ /ɡreɪv/ ●●○ *n* [C]
1 the place in the ground where a dead body is buried → **tomb**: *At the head of the grave there was a small wooden cross.*
2 the grave *literary* death: *He took that secret to the grave.*
3 sb would turn in their grave used to say that someone who is dead would strongly disapprove of something happening now: *The way Bill plays that piece would have Mozart turning in his grave.* → **dig your own grave** at DIG¹(8), → **from (the) cradle to (the) grave** at CRADLE¹(3), → **have one foot in the grave** at FOOT¹(24), → **silent as the grave** at SILENT(3), → **a watery grave** at WATERY(4)

grave² ●●○ *adj*
1 grave problems, situations, or worries are very great or bad → **serious**: *Matthew's life is in* ***grave danger****.* | *The report expressed* ***grave concern*** *over the technicians' lack of training.* | *I have* ***grave doubts*** *about his ability.* | *The situation is becoming very grave.* THESAURUS ▸ SERIOUS

> **REGISTER**
> In everyday English, people usually use **serious** rather than **grave**, and **seriously** rather than **gravely**: *I have* ***serious doubts*** *about whether he's up to the job.* | *I'm* ***seriously worried*** *about her.*

2 looking or sounding quiet and serious, especially because something important or worrying has happened SYN **sombre**: *Turnbull's face was grave as he told them about the accident.* —**gravely** *adv*: *Adam nodded gravely.* | *We are gravely concerned* (=very concerned) *about these developments.* → GRAVITY

grave³ /ɡrɑːv/ *adj* a grave ACCENT is a mark put above a letter in some languages such as French to show the pronunciation, for example è → **acute**, **circumflex**

grave·dig·ger /ˈɡreɪvˌdɪɡə $ -ər/ *n* [C] someone whose job is to dig graves

grav·el /ˈɡrævəl/ ●●○ *n* [U] small stones, used to make a surface for paths, roads etc: *a gravel path* | **gravel pit** (=a place where gravel is dug out of the ground)

grav·elled /ˈɡrævəld/ *adj* a gravelled path or road has a surface made of gravel

grav·el·ly /ˈɡrævəli/ *adj* **1** a gravelly voice has a low rough sound **2** covered with or mixed with gravel: *gravelly soil*

grave·side /ˈɡreɪvsaɪd/ *n* **at the graveside** beside a GRAVE, especially when someone is being buried there —**graveside** *adj* [only before noun]

grave·site /ˈɡreɪvsaɪt/ *n* [C] **1** a place where there is a grave **2** an old website which is no longer looked after by the people who started it **3** a website which not many people visit and so does not make much money

grave·stone /ˈɡreɪvstəʊn $ -stoʊn/ *n* [C] a stone above a GRAVE showing details of the person buried there SYN **tombstone**

grave·yard /ˈɡreɪvjɑːd $ -jɑːrd/ ●●○ *n* [C]
1 an area of ground where people are buried, often next to a church → **cemetery**, **churchyard**
2 a place where things that are no longer wanted are left: *a graveyard for old cars*
3 a place where people or things fail

ˈgraveyard ˌshift *n* [C] *especially AmE* a regular period of working time that begins late at night and continues until the early morning, or the people who work during this time

grav·i·tas /ˈɡrævɪtæs/ *n* [U] *formal* a seriousness of manner that people respect

grav·i·tate /ˈɡrævɪteɪt/ *v* [I always + adv/prep] *formal* to be attracted to something and therefore move towards it or become involved with it: **[+to/towards]** *Most visitors to London gravitate to Piccadilly Circus and Leicester Square.*

grav·i·ta·tion /ˌɡrævɪˈteɪʃən/ *n* [U] *technical* the force that causes two objects such as PLANETS to move towards each other because of their MASS → **gravity**: *Newton's law of gravitation*

grav·i·ta·tion·al /ˌɡrævəˈteɪʃənəl◂/ *adj* [usually before noun] *technical* related to or resulting from the force of gravity: *the Moon's* ***gravitational field*** | *the* ***gravitational pull*** *of the Moon*

grav·i·ty /ˈɡrævəti/ ●○○ *n* [U]
1 *technical* the force that causes something to fall to the ground or to be attracted to another PLANET → **gravitation**: *the* ***force of gravity***
2 *formal* the extreme and worrying seriousness of a situation: **[+of]** *I could not hide from her the gravity of the situation.* | *The penalties should be proportionate to the gravity of the offence.*
3 an extremely serious way of behaving or speaking: *The Consul spoke slowly and with great gravity.* → CENTRE OF GRAVITY

gra·vy /ˈɡreɪvi/ ●●● S3 *n* [U]
1 a sauce made from the juice that comes from meat as it cooks, mixed with flour and water
2 *AmE informal* something good that is more than you expected to get

ˈgravy boat *n* [C] a long JUG that you pour gravy from

ˈgravy ˌtrain *n* **the gravy train** *informal* an organization, activity, or business from which many people can make money or profit without much effort: *Privatization is not always the gravy train that governments promise.*

gray /ɡreɪ/ *n, adj* the usual American spelling of GREY

graze¹ /ɡreɪz/ ●○○ *v*
1 [I,T] if an animal grazes, or if you graze it, it eats grass that is growing: **[+on]** *Groups of cattle were grazing on the rich grass.* | *fields where they used to graze their sheep*
2 [T] to accidentally break the surface of your skin by rubbing it against something: *I fell on the gravel, severely grazing my knee.*
3 [T] to touch something lightly while passing it, sometimes damaging it: *A bullet grazed his arm.*
4 [I] *informal* to eat small amounts of food all through the day instead of having regular meals

graze² *n* [C] a wound caused by rubbing that slightly breaks the surface of your skin: *Adam walked away from the crash with just a graze on his left shoulder.* THESAURUS ▸ INJURY

G

GRE /ˌdʒiː ɑːr ˈiː/ *n* [C] *trademark* (***Graduate Record Examination***) an examination that is done by students in the US who have completed a first DEGREE and want to go to GRADUATE SCHOOL

grease¹ /griːs/ *n* [U] **1** a fatty or oily substance that comes off meat when it is cooked, or off food made using butter or oil **2** a thick oily substance that is put on the moving parts of a car, machine etc to make it run or move smoothly **3** an oily substance that is produced by your skin → **elbow grease** at ELBOW¹(3)

grease² *v* [T] **1** to put butter, grease etc on a pan etc to prevent food from sticking to it: *Grease the pan before you pour the batter in.* | *a greased baking tray* **2 grease sb's palm** to give someone money in a secret or dishonest way in order to persuade them to do something: *Joseph was able to grease a few palms, thus helping his brother to escape.* **3 like greased lightning** *informal* extremely fast

grease·paint /ˈgriːs-peɪnt/ *n* [U] a thick soft kind of paint that actors use on their face or body

grease·proof pa·per /ˌgriːs-pruːf ˈpeɪpə $ -ər/ *n* [U] *BrE* a kind of paper that butter, GREASE etc cannot pass through, used in cooking and for wrapping food SYN **waxed paper** *AmE*

greas·er /ˈgriːsə, -zə $ -ər/ *n* [C] *old-fashioned* a young man who is very interested in MOTORCYCLES and cars, and who behaves in a rough way

greas·y /ˈgriːsi, -zi/ *adj* **1** covered in grease or oil SYN **oily**: *a shampoo for greasy hair* | *The food was heavy and greasy.* THESAURUS▸ DIRTY **2** slippery: *Police say the rain's making the roads greasy.* **3** too polite and friendly in a way that seems insincere or unpleasant SYN **smarmy** **4 the greasy pole** used to refer to the difficult process of moving up in rank to a more important position: *a politician* ***climbing up the greasy pole*** —**greasily** *adv* —**greasiness** *n* [U]

ˌgreasy ˈspoon *n* [C] a small cheap restaurant that mainly serves FRIED food

great¹ /greɪt/ ●●● S1 W1 *adj* (*comparative* **greater**, *superlative* **greatest**)

1 LARGE [usually before noun] very large in amount or degree: *The movie was a great success.* | *The news came as possibly the greatest shock of my life.* | *The paintings cost* ***a great deal*** (=a lot) *of money.* | *John always takes* ***great care*** *over his work.* | ***It gives me great pleasure*** (=I am very pleased) *to introduce tonight's speaker.* | ***It's a great pity that*** *none of his poems survive.* | *The temptation was too great to resist.* THESAURUS▸ BIG

2 EXCELLENT *especially spoken* very good SYN **wonderful**, **fantastic**: *The weather here is great.* | *It's great to be home.* | *a great day out for all the family* | **sound/taste/smell/feel etc great** *I worked out this morning and I feel great.* | *You look great in that dress.* | **great for doing sth** *Email's great for keeping in touch.* | **the great thing about sb/sth** (=the very good thing about someone or something) *The great thing about Alex is that he's always willing to explain things to you.* THESAURUS▸ GOOD, NICE

GRAMMAR

Great is not used with 'very' in this meaning. You say: *You did a really great job.* ✗ Don't say: *You did a very great job.*

GRAMMAR GUIDE▸ ADJECTIVES

3 IMPORTANT **a)** [usually before noun] important or having a lot of influence: *one of the greatest scientific achievements of our time* | *What makes a novel* ***truly great***? | *great historical events* **b)** used in the title of a person or event that was very important in the past: **Peter/Catherine etc the Great** *I'm reading a biography of Alexander the Great.* | *the Great Depression* | **the Great War** *old-fashioned* (=World War I)

4 GENEROUS very good or generous in a way that people admire: *a great humanitarian gesture*

5 EXTREMELY SKILFUL famous for being able to do something extremely well: *Ali was undoubtedly one of the greatest boxers of all time.* | *a book about the lives of the great composers*

6 BIG *written* very big SYN **huge**: *A great crowd had gathered.* | *A great iron stove filled half the room.*

7 great big *spoken* very big: *Get your great big feet off my table!*

8 DOING STH A LOT used to emphasize that someone does something a lot: **a great talker/reader/admirer etc** *Anthony's a great talker – sometimes you just can't get a word in.* | *Len was* ***a great believer in*** *the power of positive thinking.* | **be a great one for doing sth** *She's a great one for telling stories about her schooldays.*

9 to a greater or lesser extent used to emphasize that something is always true, even though it is more true or noticeable in some situations than others: *Most companies operate in conditions that are to a greater or lesser extent competitive.*

10 be no great shakes *informal* to not be very good, interesting, or skilful: *The work's no great shakes, but at least I'm earning.*

11 be going great guns *informal* to be doing something extremely well: *After a slow start, the Tigers are going great guns.*

12 BAD *spoken informal* used when you are disappointed or annoyed about something: *'Daniel's cancelled the party.' 'Oh great!'*

13 ANIMAL/BIRD/PLANT ETC used in the names of some animals or plants, especially when they are bigger than other animals or plants of the same type: *the Great Crested Grebe*

14 the great outdoors *informal* the countryside, considered as enjoyable and healthy: *He had a taste for adventure and the great outdoors.*

15 great minds (think alike) *spoken* used humorously when you and another person have had the same idea

16 the greater good a general advantage that you can only gain by losing or harming something that is considered less important: *Some wars are fought for the greater good.*

17 the great apes the different types of animals that are similar to large monkeys, considered as a group: *Alone of the great apes, the gorilla is not very efficient at using tools.*

18 the great divide a situation in which there is a big difference between groups in society, areas of a country etc, for example a big difference between their wealth or attitudes: *The great divide between north and south seems to be as unbridgeable as ever.*

19 Greater London/Los Angeles/Manchester etc London, Los Angeles etc and its outer areas

20 huge/enormous great *BrE spoken* used to emphasize how big something is

21 great Scott!/great Heavens! *spoken old-fashioned* used to express shock or surprise

22 great with child *literary* very soon to have a baby —**greatness** *n* [U]: *She was destined for greatness.*

great² *n* **1** [C usually plural] a very successful and famous person in a particular sport, profession etc: *Jack Nicklaus is one of golf's* ***all-time greats***. | *I think his show's OK, but I wouldn't call him one of the greats.* THESAURUS▸ STAR **2 the great and the good** people who are considered important – used humorously

great- /greɪt/ *prefix* **1 great-grandfather/great-grandmother/great-aunt/great-uncle** the GRANDFATHER, GRANDMOTHER etc of your parents **2 great-grandchild/great-granddaughter etc** the GRANDCHILDREN of your child

great·coat /ˈgreɪtkəʊt $ -koʊt/ *n* [C] a long heavy coat

ˌGreat ˈDane *n* [C] a very large short-haired dog

great·ly /ˈgreɪtli/ ●●○ W3 *adv formal* extremely or very much: **greatly increased/reduced** *The cost of repairs has greatly increased in recent years.* | *All offers of help will be* ***greatly appreciated***. | *The quality of health care* ***varies greatly***.

ˌGreat ˈWar, the an old-fashioned name for World War I

grebe /griːb/ *n* [C] a water bird similar to a duck

Gre·cian /ˈgriːʃən/ *adj literary* from ancient Greece, or having a style or appearance that is considered typical of ancient Greece: *a Grecian urn*

Greco-, **Graeco-** /griːkəʊ, grekəʊ $ -koʊ/ *prefix* [in nouns and adjectives] ancient Greek and something else: *Greco-Roman art*

greed /griːd/ ●○○ *n* [U] a strong desire for more food, money, power, possessions etc than you need SYN **avarice**: *people motivated by jealousy and greed*

greed·y /ˈgriːdi/ ●●○ *adj* (*comparative* **greedier**, *superlative* **greediest**)
1 always wanting more food, money, power, possessions etc than you need: *a greedy and selfish society | He looked at the gold with greedy eyes. | Have you eaten them all, you greedy pig?* | **[+for]** *They are greedy for profits.*
2 greedy guts *BrE spoken* someone who is greedy: *Hey, greedy guts, leave some cake for me!* —**greedily** *adv*: *He grabbed the bottle and drank greedily.* —**greediness** *n* [U]

Greek¹ /griːk/ *adj* relating to Greece, its people, or its language: *Greek yoghurt*

Greek² *n* **1** [C] someone from Greece **2** [U] the language used in modern or ancient Greece **3** [C] *AmE* a member of a SORORITY or FRATERNITY at an American college or university **4 it's all Greek to me** *informal* used to say that you cannot understand something

green¹ /griːn/ ●●● S1 W2 *adj*
1 COLOUR having the colour of grass or leaves: *beautiful green eyes | Raw coffee beans are green in colour.* | **dark/light/pale/bright green** *a dark green dress* → **BOTTLE GREEN**, **LIME GREEN**, **PEA GREEN**, → **olive green** at **OLIVE(3)**
2 GRASSY covered with grass, trees, bushes etc: *green fields*
3 FRUIT/PLANT not yet ready to be eaten, or very young: *The bananas are still green. | tiny green shoots of new grass*
4 ENVIRONMENT **a)** (*also* **Green**) [only before noun] connected with the environment or its protection: *green issues such as the greenhouse effect and global warming | He was an early champion of green politics.* **b)** harming the environment as little as possible: *We need to develop greener cleaning products. | The industry has promised to* **go green** (=change so that it harms the environment less).
THESAURUS ENVIRONMENTALLY FRIENDLY
5 WITHOUT EXPERIENCE *informal* young and lacking experience SYN **naive**: *I was pretty green then; I had a lot of things to learn.*
6 ILL *informal* looking pale and unhealthy because you are ill: *George looked a bit green the next morning.* | **look green about/around the gills** (=look pale and ill)
7 green with envy wishing very much that you had something that someone else has
8 the green-eyed monster *literary* JEALOUSY - often used humorously
9 have green fingers *BrE*, **have a green thumb** *AmE* to be good at making plants grow
10 the green stuff *AmE informal* money —**greenness** *n* [U]

green² ●●● S2 W3 *n*
1 [C,U] the colour of grass and leaves: *a room decorated in pale blues and greens | different shades of green*
2 greens [plural] *informal* vegetables with large green leaves: *Eat your greens.*
3 [C] a level area of grass, especially in the middle of a village: *I walked home across the green.* → **VILLAGE GREEN**
4 [C] a smooth flat area of grass around each hole on a GOLF COURSE: *the 18th green* → see picture at **GOLF**
5 Green [C] someone who belongs to or supports a political party which thinks the protection of the environment is very important: *The Greens have 254 candidates in the election.*

green³ *v* [T] **1** to fill an area with growing plants in order to make it more attractive: *Existing derelict land is needed for greening the cities.* **2** to make a person or organization realize the importance of environmental problems

ˌgreen ˈaudit *n* [C] an examination of the activities of an organization in order to see how much it harms the environment and how much energy it uses

green·back /ˈgriːnbæk/ *n* [C] *AmE informal* an American BANKNOTE

ˌgreen ˈbean *n* [C] a long thin green vegetable which is picked before the beans inside it grow SYN **French bean** *BrE* → see picture at **VEGETABLE**

ˈgreen belt *n* [C,U] an area of land around a city where building is not allowed, in order to protect fields and woods

ˌgreen ˈcard *n* [C] **1** a document that a foreigner must have in order to work legally in the US **2** a British motor insurance document that you need when you drive in a country that is not a member of the European Union

ˌgreen-ˈcollar *adj* [only before noun] green-collar workers have jobs making or doing things that reduce damage to the environment or damage the environment as little as possible: *These clean energy projects could create thousands of new green-collar jobs.*

green·e·ry /ˈgriːnəri/ *n* [U] green leaves and plants: *the rich greenery of grass and trees*

green·field site /ˈgriːnfiːld ˌsaɪt/ *n* [C] a piece of land that has never been built on before → **brownfield site**

green·fly /ˈgriːnflaɪ/ *n* (*plural* **greenflies** *or* **greenfly**) [C] a very small green insect that feeds on and damages young plants SYN **aphid**

green·gage /ˈgriːngeɪdʒ/ *n* [C] a juicy greenish-yellow PLUM

green·gro·cer /ˈgriːnˌgrəʊsə $ -ˌgroʊsər/ *n* [C] *especially BrE* **1** someone who owns or works in a shop selling fruit and vegetables **2 greengrocer's** a greengrocer's shop

green·horn /ˈgriːnhɔːn $ -hɔːrn/ *n* [C] *informal especially AmE* someone who lacks experience of something

green·house /ˈgriːnhaʊs/ *n* [C] a glass building used for growing plants that need warmth, light, and protection

ˈgreenhouse efˌfect ●●○ *n* [singular] the gradual warming of the air surrounding the Earth as a result of heat being trapped by POLLUTION → **global warming**

ˈgreenhouse ˌgas *n* [C] a gas, especially CARBON DIOXIDE or METHANE, that is thought to trap heat above the Earth and cause the greenhouse effect

green·ing /ˈgriːnɪŋ/ *n* **the greening of sb/sth** when a person or organization starts to think and know more about environmental problems

green·ish /ˈgriːnɪʃ/ *adj* slightly green

ˌgreen ˈlight *n* [C] **1** a TRAFFIC LIGHT that shows cars they can go forward **2 give sb/sth the green light** to allow a project, plan etc to begin: *The government has given the green light to Sunday trading.*

ˌgreen ˈonion *n* [C] *AmE* an onion with a small white round part and a long green stem, usually eaten raw SYN **spring onion** *BrE* → see picture at **VEGETABLE**

ˌgreen ˈpaper *n* [C] a document produced by the British government containing proposals to be discussed, which may later be used in making laws → **white paper**, **bill**

ˌgreen ˈpepper *n* [C] a hollow green vegetable that you can cook or eat raw in SALADS → **capsicum**

ˌgreen revoˈlution *n* [singular] **1** a large increase in the amount of crops, such as wheat or rice, that are produced because of improved scientific methods of farming **2** the interest in protecting the environment that has developed in many parts of the world

ˈgreen room *n* **the green room** the room in a theatre, television STUDIO etc in which performers wait when they are not on stage performing

ˌgreen ˈsalad *n* [C] a SALAD made with LETTUCE and other raw green vegetables

ˌgreen ˈtax *n* [C] a tax, for example a tax on FUEL, that is intended to reduce harm to the environment

ˌgreen ˈtea *n* [U] light-coloured tea made from leaves that have been heated with steam, especially popular in eastern Asia

green·wash /ˈgriːnwɒʃ $ -wɔːʃ, -wɑːʃ/ *n* [U] when a company hides the true effects of its products or actions on the environment, by making it seem as though the company is very concerned about the environment —**greenwash** *v* [T]

ˌ**Green ˈWellie Briˌgade, the** *BrE* a humorous or insulting name for rich people who live in the country and enjoy country life, especially hunting and horse-riding. The name comes from the green WELLINGTONS (=rubber boots) that some of them wear.

Green·wich Mean Time /ˌgrenɪtʃ ˈmiːn taɪm, ˌgrɪ-, -nɪdʒ-/ *n* [U] (*abbreviation* **GMT**) the time as measured at Greenwich in London

greet /griːt/ ●●○ *v* [T]
1 to say hello to someone or welcome them: *Belinda greeted her warmly.* | **greet sb with sth** *Bill opened the door to Harold and greeted him with cries of welcome.*

> **REGISTER**
> In everyday English, people usually use **say hello (to sb)** rather than **greet sb**: *She came out to* ***greet*** *us.*
> → *She came out to* ***say hello****.*

2 to react to something in a particular way: **be greeted with/by sth** *His statement was greeted with cries of astonishment and indignation.* GRAMMAR **Greet** is usually passive in this meaning.
3 to be the first thing you see or hear when you arrive somewhere: *Complete silence greeted us as we entered the room.*

greet·er /ˈgriːtə $ -ər/ *n* [C] someone who greets people politely as they enter a place, especially someone who does this as a job

greet·ing /ˈgriːtɪŋ/ ●○○ *n* [C,U]
1 something you say or do when you meet someone: **in greeting** *She raised her hand in greeting.* | *I smiled a polite greeting, but the woman hardly acknowledged me.* | *The two cousins* ***exchanged greetings*** (=greeted each other).
2 birthday/Christmas etc greetings a message saying that you hope someone will be happy and healthy on their BIRTHDAY, at Christmas etc
3 greetings! *old use* used to say hello to someone

ˈ**greetings ˌcard** *BrE*, ˈ**greeting card** *AmE n* [C] a card that you send to someone on their BIRTHDAY, at Christmas etc

gre·gar·i·ous /grɪˈgeəriəs $ -ˈger-/ *adj* **1** friendly and preferring to be with other people SYN **sociable** OPP **solitary** **2** *technical* gregarious animals tend to live in a group OPP **solitary** —**gregariously** *adv* —**gregariousness** *n* [U]

Gre·go·ri·an cal·en·dar /grɪˌgɔːriən ˈkæləndə $ -dər/ *n* [singular] the system of arranging the 365 days of the year in months and giving numbers to the years from the birth of Christ, used in the West since 1582

Gre·go·ri·an chant /grɪˌgɔːriən ˈtʃɑːnt $ -ˈtʃænt/ *n* [C,U] a kind of church music for voices alone

grem·lin /ˈgremlɪn/ *n* [C] an imaginary evil spirit that is blamed for problems in machinery

gre·nade /grəˈneɪd/ *n* [C] a small bomb that can be thrown by hand or fired from a gun: *a hand grenade*

gren·a·dier /ˌgrenəˈdɪə◂ $ -ˈdɪr◂/ *n* [C] a soldier in a famous REGIMENT of the British army

gren·a·dine /ˈgrenədiːn, ˌgrenəˈdiːn/ *n* [U] a sweet liquid made from POMEGRANATES that is used in drinks

Gret·na Green /ˌgretnə ˈgriːn/ a village in southern Scotland on the border with England. Until 1940, the marriage laws were less strict in Scotland than in England, and many young English couples, whose parents did not want them to marry, ran away to get married in Gretna Green.

grew /gruː/ *v* the past tense of GROW

grey¹ *BrE*, **gray** *AmE* /greɪ/ ●●● S2 W2 *adj*
1 COLOUR having the colour of dark clouds, neither black nor white: *an old lady with grey hair* | *a grey sky* | **dark/light grey** *dark grey trousers* → BATTLESHIP GREY, IRON-GREY, → **slate grey** at SLATE¹(3)
2 HAIR having grey hair: **go/turn grey** *She was a tall thin woman who had gone grey early.*
3 FACE looking pale because you are tired, frightened, or ill: **[+with]** *As he listened, his face went grey with shock.*
4 BORING boring and unattractive OPP **colourful**: *the grey anonymous men in government offices* | *visions of a grey and empty world*
5 WEATHER if the weather is grey, the sky is full of clouds and the sun is not bright OPP **bright**: *a grey day*
6 OF OLD PEOPLE [only before noun] *BrE* connected with old people: *the grey vote*
7 grey area used to talk about a situation in which something is not clearly a particular thing, so that people are not sure how to deal with it: *people in the grey area between loyalty and opposition to the government* —**greyness** *n* [U]

grey² *BrE*, **gray** *AmE* ●●● S3 W3 *n* [C,U] the colour of dark clouds, neither black nor white: *Do you have these skirts in grey?* | *dull greys and browns*

grey³ *BrE*, **gray** *AmE v* [I] if someone greys, their hair becomes grey: *Jim was greying a little at the temples.* | *a full head of greying hair*

grey·hound /ˈgreɪhaʊnd/ *n* [C] a type of thin dog that can run very fast and is used in races

ˌ**Greyhound ˈBus** *trademark* a type of bus service, connecting cities in the US. Greyhound Buses are a popular way of travelling in the US, because they are cheaper than renting a car or going by plane.

grey·ing *BrE*, **graying** *AmE* /ˈgreɪ-ɪŋ/ *n* **the greying of sth** the situation in which the average age of a population increases, so that there are more old people than there were in the past: *the graying of classical music audiences*

grey·ish *BrE*, **grayish** *AmE* /ˈgreɪ-ɪʃ/ *adj* slightly grey: *The stone was a greyish colour.*

ˈ**grey ˌmarket** *BrE*, **gray market** *AmE n* [C] **1** the system by which people buy and sell goods that are hard to find, in a way that is legal but not morally good or correct → **black market** **2** *technical* a situation in which people are buying and selling SHARES just before they are officially made available to be sold for the first time

ˈ**grey ˌmatter** *BrE*, **gray matter** *AmE n* [U] *informal* your intelligence, or your brain

ˌ**grey ˈpound** *n BrE* **the grey pound** the money that older people have available to spend, especially after their children have grown up and left home

grid /grɪd/ ●●○ *n* [C]
1 a metal frame with bars across it → CATTLE GRID
2 a pattern of straight lines that cross each other and form squares: *Its streets were laid out in a grid pattern.*
3 a set of numbered lines printed on a map so that the exact position of any place can be referred to: *The pilots were just given a* ***grid reference*** (=number referring to a point on a map) *of the target.*
4 the network of electricity supply wires that connects POWER STATIONS and provides electricity to buildings in an area: *the* ***national grid*** (=the electricity supply in a country)
5 (*also* **starting grid**) a set of starting positions for all the cars in a motor race

ˈ**grid comˌputing** *n* [U] a system of running a computer program using a lot of small computers that are connected together in order to do very complicated jobs

grid·dle /ˈgrɪdl/ *n* [C] a round iron plate that is used for cooking meat, vegetables, or cakes on top of a STOVE or over a fire → see picture at PAN

grid·dle·cake /ˈgrɪdlˌkeɪk/ *n* [C] *AmE* a PANCAKE

grid·i·ron /ˈgrɪdaɪən $ -ərn/ *n* [C] **1** an open frame of metal bars for cooking meat or fish over a very hot fire **2** *AmE* a field marked in white lines for American football

grid·lock /ˈgrɪdlɒk $ -lɑːk/ *n* [U] *especially AmE* **1** a situation in which streets in a city are so full of cars that they cannot move **2** a situation in which nothing can happen, usually because people disagree strongly SYN **stalemate**: *The battle over spending led to gridlock.* —**gridlocked** *adj*

G

grief /griːf/ ●●○ *n*
1 [U] extreme sadness, especially because someone you love has died: **[+over/at]** *The grief she felt over Helen's death was almost unbearable.* | **with grief** *Charles was overcome with grief.*
2 [C] something that makes you feel extremely sad: *Every change in our lives brings with it griefs.*
3 good grief! *spoken* used when you are slightly surprised or annoyed: *Good grief! What a mess!*
4 come to grief to fail, or to be harmed or destroyed in an accident: *candidates who come to grief in exams*
5 give sb grief *informal* to criticize someone in an annoying way
6 [U] *informal* trouble or problems: *You'll save yourself a lot of grief if you check the measurements first.*

grief·ing /ˈgriːfɪŋ/ *n* [U] the activity of deliberately annoying other players in a game played on the Internet, or doing things that spoil the game for them —**griefer** *n* [C]

ˈgrief-ˌstricken *adj* feeling very sad because of something that has happened SYN **distraught**: *The grief-stricken widow refused to leave her dead husband's side.*

griev·ance /ˈgriːvəns/ ●○○ *n* [C,U] a belief that you have been treated unfairly, or an unfair situation or event that affects and upsets you: *anyone who* ***has a*** *legitimate* ***grievance against*** *the company* | *a means of overcoming* ***genuine grievances*** | *There must be an opportunity for both sides to* ***air*** *their* ***grievances***. | *The teachers' contract established a* ***grievance procedure***. | *the* ***sense of grievance*** *which characterized him as a young man*

grieve /griːv/ ●○○ *v*
1 [I,T] to feel extremely sad, especially because someone you love has died: **[+over/for]** *He died, and every day since then I have grieved for him.* | *People need time to grieve after the death of a loved one.* | *She grieved the loss of her only son.*
2 [T] if something grieves you, it makes you feel very unhappy SYN **upset**: *My aunt,* ***it grieves*** *me to say, gets things confused.*

grieved /griːvd/ *adj literary* very sad and upset: **[+at]** *King George V had been very grieved at the outbreak of the Great War.*

griev·ous /ˈgriːvəs/ *adj formal* very serious and causing great pain or suffering: *a grievous shortage of hospital beds* —**grievously** *adv*: *He was grievously hurt by their betrayal.*

ˌgrievous ˌbodily ˈharm *n* [U] *BrE law* serious injury caused by a criminal attack SYN **GBH**

grif·fin, gryphon /ˈgrɪfən/ *n* [C] an imaginary animal that has a lion's body and an EAGLE's wings and head

grif·ter /ˈgrɪftə $ -ər/ *n* [C] *AmE informal* someone who dishonestly obtains something, especially money —**grift** *v* [T]

grill¹ /grɪl/ ●●● S3 W3 *v*
1 [I,T] if you grill something, or if it grills, you cook it by putting it on a flat metal frame with bars across it, above or below strong direct heat SYN **barbecue**: *Grill the bacon until crisp.* | *swordfish grilled over charcoal* THESAURUS ▸ COOK
2 [T] to ask someone a lot of questions about something SYN **question**: **grill sb about/on sth** *She never grilled her husband about his work.*

grill² ●●● S3 W3 *n* [C]
1 *BrE* a part of a COOKER in which strong heat from above cooks food on a metal shelf below SYN **broiler** *AmE*: *Pop it under the grill for five minutes.*
2 a flat frame with metal bars across it that can be put over a fire, so that food can be cooked on it
3 a place where you can buy and eat grilled food: *the Tribeca Bar and Grill* → **MIXED GRILL**
4 a grille

grille, grill /grɪl/ *n* [C] **1** a frame with metal bars or wire across it that is put in front of a window or door for protection **2** the metal bars at the front of a car that protect the RADIATOR

gril·ling /ˈgrɪlɪŋ/ *n* [C] when you ask someone a lot of questions about something → **interrogation**: *The three party leaders each endured a 20-minute television grilling from voters.*

ˈgrill pan *n* [C] *BrE* a square flat pan, used under a GRILL

grim /grɪm/ ●●○ *adj*
1 making you feel worried or unhappy SYN **harsh**: *the grim reality of rebuilding the shattered town* | *When he lost his job, his future looked grim.* | *Millions of Britons face the grim prospect (=something bad that will probably happen) of dearer home loans.* | *We received the grim news in silence.*
2 looking or sounding very serious: *'I'll survive,' he said with a grim smile.* | *The child hung on to her arm with* ***grim determination***. | *The police officers were silent and grim-faced.*
3 *BrE informal* very bad, ugly, or unpleasant: *The weather forecast is pretty grim.* | *They painted a grim picture of what life used to be like there.* | *a grim industrial town*
4 [not before noun] *informal* ill: *Juliet felt grim through the early months of her pregnancy.*
5 hold/hang on for/like grim death *BrE informal* to hold something very tightly because you are afraid —**grimly** *adv*: *Arnold smiled grimly.* —**grimness** *n* [U]

gri·mace¹ /grɪˈmeɪs, ˈgrɪməs/ *v* [I] to twist your face in an ugly way because you do not like something, because you are feeling pain, or because you are trying to be funny: **[+at]** *She grimaced at her reflection in the mirror.* | *She sipped the whisky and grimaced.*

grimace² *n* [C] *written* an expression you make by twisting your face because you do not like something or because you are feeling pain: *His face twisted in a grimace of pain.* | *a grimace of disgust*

grime /graɪm/ *n* [U] **1** a lot of dirt SYN **filth**: *The walls were black with grime.* **2** (*also* **grime music**) a type of British popular music with a fast beat. It is related to several other types of music such as GARAGE and HIP HOP.

grim·y /ˈgraɪmi/ *adj* covered with dirt SYN **filthy**: *grimy windows* THESAURUS ▸ DIRTY

grin¹ /grɪn/ ●●○ *v* (**grinned, grinning**) [I]
1 to smile widely: **[+at]** *She grinned at me, her eyes sparkling.* | **grin broadly/widely** *He walked out of the pool, grinning widely.* | **[+like]** *He was grinning like an idiot* (=grinning in a silly way). | **grin from ear to ear** (=grin very widely)
2 grin and bear it to accept an unpleasant or difficult situation without complaining, usually because you realize there is nothing you can do to make it better

grin² ●●○ *n* [C] a wide smile: *He came into the room with a friendly* ***grin on*** *his* ***face***. | **wide/broad/big etc grin** *'Of course,' he agreed with a wide grin.* → **wipe the grin off sb's face** at WIPE¹(7)

grind¹ /graɪnd/ ●○○ *v* (*past tense and past participle* **ground** /graʊnd/)
1 INTO SMALL PIECES [T] **a)** (*also* **grind up**) to break something such as corn or coffee beans into small pieces or powder, either in a machine or between two hard surfaces: ***freshly ground*** *pepper* **b)** *AmE* to cut food, especially raw meat, into very small pieces by putting it through a machine SYN **mince** *BrE*: *ground beef*
2 SMOOTH/SHARP [T] to make something smooth or sharp by rubbing it on a hard surface or by using a machine: *a stone for grinding knives and scissors* | *The lenses are ground to a high standard of precision.*
3 PRESS **a)** [T always + adv/prep] to press something onto a surface and rub it with a strong twisting movement: **grind sth into sth** *He dropped a cigar butt and ground it into the carpet with his heel.* | *He* ***ground out*** *his* ***cigarette*** *on the window ledge.* **b)** [I always + adv/prep] to press hard against something: **[+against/together]** *as these plates (=large areas of land) grind against each other*
4 grind your teeth to rub your upper and lower teeth together, making a noise
5 grind to a halt (*also* **come to a grinding halt**) **a)** if a vehicle grinds to a halt, it stops gradually: *Traffic ground to a halt as it approached the accident site.* **b)** if a country, organization, or process grinds to a halt, its activity or the process

gradually stops: *After two days the talks had ground to a halt.*

6 PERFORM A MOVEMENT to perform a special movement in SKATEBOARDING or ROLLERBLADING, which involves moving sideways along the edge of something, so that the bar connecting the wheels of the SKATEBOARD or ROLLERBLADE presses hard against the edge → **have an axe to grind** at AXE[1](4)

grind sb ↔ **down** *phr v* to treat someone in a cruel way for such a long time that they lose all courage and hope SYN **oppress**: *I've never let male colleagues grind me down.*

grind on *phr v* to continue for an unpleasantly long time: *As the negotiations grind on, time is passing towards the deadline.*

grind sth ↔ **out** *phr v*

1 to produce information, writing, music etc in such large amounts that it becomes boring SYN **churn out**: *Frank just keeps grinding out detective stories.*

2 *written* to say something in a rough, angry, or emotional way: *'You don't love him,' he ground out.*

grind[2] *n* **1** [singular] something that is hard work and physically or mentally tiring: *I find the journey to work a real grind.* | *workers emerging from their* ***daily grind*** *in the factory* **2** [C] *AmE informal* a student who never does anything except study SYN **swot** *BrE* **3** [C] a movement in SKATEBOARDING or ROLLERBLADING, which involves moving sideways along the edge of something, so that the bar connecting the wheels of the SKATEBOARD or ROLLERBLADE presses hard against the edge

grind·er /ˈgraɪndə $ -ər/ *n* [C] a machine for crushing coffee beans, PEPPERCORNS etc into powder

grind·ing /ˈgraɪndɪŋ/ *adj* [only before noun] **1** very difficult and unpleasant, and never seeming to improve: *a country devastated by civil war and* ***grinding poverty*** **2** a grinding noise is the continuous unpleasant noise of machinery parts rubbing together

grind·stone /ˈgraɪndstəʊn $ -stoʊn/ *n* [C] a large round stone that turns like a wheel, and is used for making tools and knives sharp when they are rubbed against it → **keep your nose to the grindstone** at NOSE[1](11)

G

grin·go /ˈgrɪŋgəʊ $ -goʊ/ *n* (*plural* **gringos**) [C] *taboo* a very offensive word used in Latin America to refer to a foreigner, especially a white English-speaking person. Do not use this word.

gri·ot /ˈgriːəʊ $ -oʊ/ *n* [C] a STORYTELLER from West Africa who teaches people about their history and culture

grip[1] /grɪp/ ●●○ *n*

1 FIRM HOLD [C usually singular] the way you hold something tightly, or your ability to do this: *Hold the microphone in a* ***firm grip*** *and keep it still.* | *She felt her wrist caught in a* ***vice-like grip***. | *Don't* ***loosen*** *your* ***grip*** *on the rope or you'll fall.* | *He* ***released*** *his* ***grip*** *and stepped back.*

2 POWER [singular] power and control over someone or something: **have/keep a grip on sth** *Stalin's determination to keep an iron grip on Eastern Europe* | **tighten/loosen/relax your grip (on sth)** *By 1979 South Africa was tightening its grip on Namibia.* | **tight/firm/strong/iron etc grip** *The recession could be avoided if business keeps a firm grip on its costs.*

3 UNDERSTANDING [singular] an understanding of something: **have/get a grip on sth** *I'm just trying to get a grip on what's happening.* | *She was* ***losing*** *her* ***grip*** *on reality.*

4 come/get to grips with sth to understand or deal with something difficult: *I've never really got to grips with this new technology.*

5 lose your grip to become less confident and less able to deal with a situation: *I don't know what's the matter; I think I'm losing my grip.*

6 get/take a grip on yourself to start to improve your behaviour or control your emotions when you have been very upset: *Stop being hysterical and get a grip on yourself.*

7 get a grip *spoken* used in order to tell someone to control their emotions: *For God's sake get a grip!*

8 be in the grip of sth to be experiencing a very unpleasant situation that cannot be controlled or stopped: *a country in the grip of famine*

9 STOP STH SLIPPING **a)** [C] a special part of a handle that has a rough surface so that you can hold it firmly without it slipping: *My racquet needs a new grip.* **b)** [singular, U] the ability of something to stay on a surface without slipping: *boots which give a good grip*

10 FOR HAIR [C] *BrE* a HAIRGRIP

11 CAMERAMAN [C] *technical* someone whose job is to move the cameras around while a television show or film is being made

12 BAG [C] *old-fashioned* a bag or case used for travelling

grip[2] ●●○ *v* (**gripped**, **gripping**)

1 HOLD TIGHTLY [T] to hold something very tightly: *I gripped the rail and tried not to look down.* | **grip sth tightly/firmly** *The woman moved closer to Beth, gripping her arm tightly.*

2 HAVE A STRONG EFFECT [T] to have a strong effect on someone or something: *a country gripped by economic problems* | *Panic suddenly gripped me when it was my turn to speak.*

3 INTEREST SB [T] to hold someone's attention and interest: *a story that really grips you*

4 NOT SLIP [I,T] if something grips a surface, it stays on it without slipping: *Radial tires grip the road well.* → GRIPPING

gripe[1] /graɪp/ *v* [I] *informal* to complain about something in an annoying way SYN **whinge**: **[+about]** *Joe came in griping about how cold it was.*

gripe[2] *n informal* **1** [C] something unimportant that you complain about SYN **complaint**: *My main gripe was the price of refreshments.* **2 the gripes** *old-fashioned* sudden bad stomach pains

ˈgripe ˌwater *n* [U] *BrE* a liquid medicine which is given to babies when they have stomach pains

grip·ing /ˈgraɪpɪŋ/ *adj* a griping pain is a sudden severe pain in your stomach

grip·ping /ˈgrɪpɪŋ/ ●○○ *adj* a gripping film, story etc is very exciting and interesting: *Collins' gripping detective novel* THESAURUS EXCITING, INTERESTING

gris·ly /ˈgrɪzli/ *adj* extremely unpleasant and involving people being killed or injured: *a series of grisly murders*

grist /grɪst/ *n* **(all) grist to the mill** *BrE*, **(all) grist for the mill** *AmE* something that is useful in a particular situation: *Any publicity is good – it's all grist to the mill.*

gris·tle /ˈgrɪsəl/ *n* [U] the part of meat that is not soft enough to eat —**gristly** *adj*

grit[1] /grɪt/ *n* [U] **1** very small pieces of stone or sand: *Make sure both surfaces are free from dust and grit.* | *The council is responsible for putting grit on icy roads.* **2** *informal* determination and courage SYN **guts** **3 grits** *AmE* a type of grain that is roughly crushed and cooked, and often eaten for breakfast

grit[2] *v* (**gritted**, **gritting**) [T] **1** to scatter grit on a frozen road to make it less slippery **2 grit your teeth a)** to use all your determination to continue in spite of difficulties: *Just grit your teeth and hang on – it'll be over soon.* **b)** to bite your teeth together, especially when you are in pain, angry, or under pressure: *Ben gritted his teeth, hoping Sasha wouldn't notice his fear.* | *'No, that's alright,' she said through gritted teeth.*

grit·ter /ˈgrɪtə $ -ər/ *n* [C] *BrE* a large vehicle that puts salt or sand on the roads in winter to make them less icy SYN **salt truck** *AmE*

grit·ty /ˈgrɪti/ *adj* **1** showing determination and courage: *Henin gave a typically gritty performance, coming back from 4–0 down.* | *her gritty determination* **2** showing a difficult or unpleasant situation as it really is: *Billingham's pictures have a* ***gritty realism*** *which can be almost upsetting.* **3** containing grit or covered in grit: *Gritty soil had got under her nails.*

griz·zle /ˈgrɪzəl/ *v* [I] *BrE informal* **1** if a baby or child grizzles, they cry quietly for a long time **2** to complain in an annoying way SYN **moan**: *Ben was grizzling about being tired.*

griz·zled /ˈgrɪzəld/ *adj literary* having grey or greyish hair: **grizzled hair/head/beard etc** *a grizzled old man*

ˌgrizzly ˈbear / $ ˈ.../ (*also* **grizzly**) *n* [C] a very large bear that lives in the northwest of North America

groan[1] /grəʊn $ groʊn/ ●○○ *v*
1 [I] to make a long deep sound because you are in pain, upset, or disappointed, or because something is very enjoyable SYN **moan**: *The kids all groaned when I switched off the TV.* | **[+with]** *As she kissed him, Gary groaned with pleasure.* | *Richard's jokes make you groan rather than laugh.*
2 [I,T] to complain about something SYN **moan**: *I'm tired of him* ***moaning and groaning*** *all the time.* | *'It's too hot!' he groaned.*
3 [T] to make a low deep sound SYN **moan**: *The old tree groaned in the wind.*
4 [I] if a table groans with food, there is a very large amount of food on it

groan[2] *n* [C] **1** a long deep sound that you make when you are in pain or do not want to do something SYN **moan**: *Casey let out a groan of protest.* **2** *literary* a long low deep sound: *The door opened with a groan.*

groat /grəʊt $ groʊt/ *n* [C] a former British coin that had a low value

gro·cer /ˈgrəʊsə $ ˈgroʊsər/ *n* [C] **1** someone who owns or works in a shop that sells food and other things used in the home **2 grocer's** a grocer's shop

gro·cer·y /ˈgrəʊsəri $ ˈgroʊ-/ ●●● S3 *n*
1 groceries [plural] food and other goods that are sold by a grocer or a SUPERMARKET
2 (*also* ˈ**grocery store**) [C] *AmE* a SUPERMARKET

grog /grɒg $ grɑːg/ *n* [U] **1** a strong alcoholic drink, especially RUM mixed with water **2** *informal* any alcoholic drink

grog·gy /ˈgrɒgi $ ˈgrɑːgi/ *adj* weak and unable to move well or think clearly because you are ill or very tired: *I* ***felt*** *really* ***groggy*** *after 15 hours on the plane.*

groin /grɔɪn/ *n* [C] **1** the place where the tops of your legs meet the front of your body **2** a GROYNE

grom·met /ˈgrɒmɪt $ ˈgrɑː-/ *n* [C] **1** a small metal ring that is used around a hole in cloth or leather to make it stronger **2** *BrE* a small piece of plastic that a doctor puts into a child's ear in order to remove liquid from it

groom[1] /gruːm, grʊm/ ●●○ *n* [C]
1 a BRIDEGROOM
2 someone whose job is to feed, clean, and take care of horses

groom[2] ●○○ *v*
1 [T] to clean and brush an animal, especially a horse
2 [T] to prepare someone for an important job or position in society by training them over a long period: **groom sb for sth** *Tim was being groomed for a managerial position.* | **groom sb to do sth** *Clare's been groomed to take her father's place when he retires.*
3 [T] to take care of your own appearance by keeping your hair and clothes clean and tidy: *Her hair is always perfectly groomed.* → **WELL-GROOMED**
4 [T] to develop a friendship with a child, with the intention of starting a sexual relationship. This is done by adults, and is illegal when the child is younger than 16.
5 [I,T] if an animal grooms itself or another animal, it cleans its own fur and skin or that of the other animal

groom·ing /ˈgruːmɪŋ/ *n* [U] **1** the process in which an adult develops a friendship with a child, with the intention of having a sexual relationship. This is illegal when the child is younger than 16. **2** the process of cleaning and brushing an animal, especially a horse

grooms·man /ˈgruːmzmən, ˈgrʊms-/ *n* (*plural* **groomsmen** /-mən/) [C] *AmE* a friend of a BRIDEGROOM who has special duties at a wedding SYN **best man** *BrE*

groove /gruːv/ ●○○ *n* [C]
1 a thin line cut into a hard surface: *The bolt slid easily into the groove.* | *a shallow groove cut into the cliff*
2 be stuck in a groove to do something in the same way for a long time so that it becomes boring: *Our product range was stuck in a groove.*
3 *informal* the beat of a piece of popular music: *a hypnotic dub groove*

grooved /gruːvd/ *adj* having a groove or several grooves: *a slightly grooved surface*

groov·y /ˈgruːvi/ *adj old-fashioned informal* a word meaning fashionable, modern, and fun, used especially in the 1960s

grope[1] /grəʊp $ groʊp/ *v* **1** [I] to try to find something that you cannot see by feeling with your hands: **[+for]** *Ginny groped for her glasses on the bedside table.* | **[+around]** *We groped around in the darkness.* **2** [I,T] to go somewhere by feeling the way with your hands because you cannot see: **grope your way along/across etc** *I was groping my way blindly through the trees.* | *Ally groped steadily towards the door.* **3 grope for sth** to try hard to find the right words to say or the right solution to a problem but without any real idea of how to do this: *She hesitated, seeming to grope for words.* **4** [T] *informal* to move your hands over someone's body to get sexual pleasure, especially when they do not want you to do this

grope[2] *n* [C usually singular] *informal* touching someone's body to get sexual pleasure, especially when they do not want you to do this

gross[1] /grəʊs $ groʊs/ ●●○ S3 *adj*
1 TOTAL [only before noun] **a)** a gross sum of money is the total amount before any tax or costs have been taken away → **net**: *a gross profit of $5 million* | **gross income/salary/pay etc** *a family with gross earnings of just £75 per week* **b)** a gross weight is the total weight of something, including its wrapping THESAURUS PROFIT
2 VERY BAD [only before noun] clearly wrong and unacceptable: **gross negligence/misconduct etc** *soldiers accused of gross violations of human rights* | *The company described reports of environmental disaster as gross exaggeration.* | **gross indecency** (=the crime of doing something that is sexually offensive)
3 NASTY *spoken* very unpleasant to look at or think about SYN **disgusting**: *Ooh, gross! I hate spinach!*
4 FAT *informal* extremely fat and unattractive —**grossly** *adv* [+adj/adv]: *Lambert was* ***grossly overweight***. | *Medical records were found to be grossly inadequate.* —**grossness** *n* [U]

gross[2] *adv* **earn £20,000/$30,000 etc gross** to earn £20,000 etc before tax has been taken away → **net**: *a junior executive earning $50,000 gross*

gross[3] *v* [T] to gain an amount as a total profit, or earn it as a total amount, before tax has been taken away → **net**: *The movie has already grossed over $10 million.*

gross sb ↔ **out** *phr v AmE spoken* to make someone wish they had not seen or been told about something because it is so unpleasant SYN **disgust**: *His dirty fingernails really gross me out.* —**grossed out** *adj*

gross[4] *n* (*plural* **gross**) [C] a quantity of 144 things: **[+of]** *two gross of candles*

ˌ**gross doˌmestic ˈproduct** *n* [singular] GDP

ˌ**gross ˈmargin** *n* [C] *technical* the difference between what something costs to produce and what it is sold for

ˌ**gross ˌnational ˈproduct** *n* [singular] GNP

ˈ**gross-out** *adj* [only before noun] *informal* a gross-out film or part of a film is intended to shock viewers and is very unpleasant to watch, for example because it involves waste from the body: *gross-out comedies*

ˌ**gross ˈprofit** *n* [C] GROSS MARGIN

gro·tesque[1] /grəʊˈtesk $ groʊ-/ ●○○ *adj*
1 unpleasant, shocking, and offensive: *It's grotesque to portray peace campaigners as unpatriotic.* | *By modern standards, the treatment of prisoners was grotesque.*
2 extremely ugly in a strange or unnatural way: *a grotesque figure with a huge head* —**grotesquely** *adv*

grotesque[2] *n* **1** [C] a picture, SCULPTURE etc of someone who is strangely ugly **2 the grotesque** a grotesque style in art

grot·to /ˈgrɒtəʊ $ ˈgrɑːtoʊ/ *n* (*plural* **grottos** *or* **grottoes**) [C] a small attractive CAVE

grot·ty /ˈgrɒti $ ˈgrɑːti/ *adj BrE informal* **1** nasty, dirty, or unpleasant SYN **manky**: *a grotty little bar* **2** ill: *The next day I* ***felt*** *a bit* ***grotty***.

grouch[1] /graʊtʃ/ *n informal* **1** [C] someone who is

G

always complaining: *an old grouch* **2** [C] something unimportant that you complain about

grouch² *v* [I] *informal* to complain in a slightly angry way SYN **moan**: **[+about]** *He's always grouching about something!*

grouch·y /ˈgraʊtʃi/ *adj informal* in a bad temper, especially because you are tired SYN **bad-tempered** —**grouchiness** *n* [U]

ground¹ /graʊnd/ ●●● S1 W1 *n*

1 EARTH [U] **a)** the surface of the Earth: **the ground** *The leaves were slowly fluttering to the ground.* | *He lay on the ground and stared up at the sky.* | *The ground was frozen solid.* | **above/below/under ground** *At night, badgers feed above ground.* | *These youngsters work 70 metres* ***below ground level***. | *A raised platform stood two metres off the ground.* | *The air raids were followed by military action* ***on the ground*** (=on land). | ***ground troops*** (=soldiers who fight on land) **b)** the soil on and under the surface of the Earth: *Dig the ground over in the autumn.* | *Plant the seeds 2 cm deep in the ground.* | *The ground was dry, far too dry for growing corn.*

2 AREA OF LAND **a)** [U] an area of land without buildings, fences, woods etc: *The landscape is a mixture of* ***open ground*** *and woodland.* | *They were standing on the* ***waste ground*** (=land in a town that is not being used) *behind the car park.* **b)** [C] (*also* **grounds** [plural]) an area of land or sea that is used for a particular purpose: *fishing grounds* | **parade/hunting/burial etc ground** *These fields served as a hunting ground for the local people.* | *The rivers are used as* ***dumping grounds*** *for industrial waste.* | *He is buried in sacred ground.* → PLAYGROUND(1) **c) grounds** [plural] the land or gardens surrounding a large building: *We decided to take a stroll in the hotel grounds.*

3 REASON **grounds** [plural] a good reason for doing, believing, or saying something: **grounds for (doing) sth** *Mental cruelty can be* ***grounds for divorce***. | *There are* ***strong grounds*** *for believing his statement.* | **have grounds to do sth** *Did the police have* ***reasonable grounds*** *to arrest him?* | **on moral/legal/medical etc grounds** *The proposal was rejected on environmental grounds.* | **on (the) grounds of sth** *Flying was ruled out on grounds of cost.* | *'You're under arrest.' 'On what grounds?'* | **on the grounds that** *We oppose the bill, on the grounds that it discriminates against women.*

4 SUBJECT [U] a subject or area of knowledge: *At meetings, we just keep* ***going over the same ground*** (=talking about the same things). | *His latest movie looks set to* ***break new ground*** (=introduce new and exciting ideas). | **familiar/home ground** (=a subject etc that you know something about) *In his latest book, McManus returns to more familiar ground.*

5 OPINION [U] a general opinion or set of attitudes: *Often parents and teenagers find they have little* ***common ground*** (=they do not share the same attitudes etc). | **the middle/centre ground** (=opinions that are not extreme that most people would agree with) *Both parties are battling to* ***occupy the centre ground***. | *Careful, Laura. You could be* ***treading on dangerous ground*** (=expressing opinions etc that might offend someone). | *Each side was unwilling to* ***give ground*** (=change their opinion).

6 SPORT [C] *BrE* the place where a particular sport is played → **stadium**: *a new football ground* | *It's their first defeat at their* ***home ground*** (=the ground that belongs to a particular team) *all season.*

7 hold/stand your ground a) to stay where you are when someone threatens you, in order to show them that you are not afraid: *The men threatened him, but he stood his ground and they fled.* **b)** to refuse to change your mind about something, even though people are opposing you: *Jason vowed to stand his ground, even if it meant losing his job.*

8 get off the ground to start to be successful: *Her show never really got off the ground in the UK.*

9 gain ground a) to become more successful: *It was feared that the extreme right would gain ground in the election.* **b)** if an idea, belief etc gains ground, more people start to accept it: *His theories gradually gained ground among academics.* **c)** to get closer to someone or something that you are competing with

10 lose ground to become less successful compared with someone or something you are competing with: *The Indian team seem determined to regain the ground they lost in the last game.*

11 breeding/fertile/proving ground a situation in which something develops quickly or successfully: *The region, with its widespread poverty, provided fertile ground for revolutionary activists.* | **prepare/lay the ground** (=to provide the situation or conditions in which something can develop successfully) | **[+for]** *My task was to prepare the ground for the recruitment of support workers.*

12 burn/raze sth to the ground to destroy a city, building etc completely by fire, bombs etc: *The city of Tortona was burnt to the ground.*

13 work/drive/run yourself into the ground to work so hard that you become very tired or ill: *Kay's working herself into the ground trying to meet her deadlines.*

14 on the ground in the place or situation where something important is happening, rather than somewhere else – used especially in news reports: *While the politicians talk of peace, the situation on the ground remains tense.*

15 stamping ground *BrE*, **stomping ground** *AmE informal* someone's stamping ground is an area where they are known or have a lot of influence: *I guess he'll try to reach his* ***old stomping ground*** *to drum up support.*

16 ELECTRICAL [singular] *AmE* a wire that connects a piece of electrical equipment to the ground for safety SYN **earth** *BrE*

17 grounds [plural] small pieces of solid material that sink to the bottom of a liquid: *coffee grounds*

18 go to ground *BrE* to make it hard for people to find you: *The man has gone to ground since his photograph was published in a national newspaper.*

19 run sb/sth to ground *BrE* to succeed in finding someone or something after a long search

20 BACKGROUND [C] *technical* the colour used as the background for a design → **cut the ground from under sb's feet** at CUT¹(37), → **have/keep both feet on the ground** at FOOT¹(18), → **suit sb down to the ground** at SUIT²(1), → **be thin on the ground** at THIN¹(12), → **hit the ground running** at HIT¹(24)

THESAURUS

the ground the surface of the Earth, or the soil on its surface: *He collapsed and fell to the ground.* | *The ground was wet and muddy.*

the ocean/forest/cave etc floor the ground at the bottom of the ocean, a forest, a cave etc: *Many wonderful creatures live on the ocean floor.*

land used when talking about an area of ground that is owned by someone, or is used for an activity. Also used when talking about the part of the Earth's surface that is not covered with water: *His family owns a lot of land.* | *agricultural land* | *She got off the ferry, happy to be back on* ***dry land***.

terrain a type of land – used when talking about how easy an area of land is to cross, and whether it is rocky, flat etc: *The Land Rover is built to go over rough terrain.* | *The terrain gets flatter when you go further south.*

earth/soil the substance that plants grow in: *The vegetables were still covered in black soil.*

mud wet earth: *Your shoes are covered in mud.*

ground² ●○○ *v*

1 AIRCRAFT [T] to stop an aircraft or pilot from flying: *All planes are grounded until the fog clears.* GRAMMAR **Ground** is usually passive in this meaning.

2 BOAT [I,T] if you ground a boat or if it grounds, it hits the bottom of the sea so that it cannot move: *Both boats grounded on a mud bank.*

3 be grounded in/on sth to be based on something: *Lewis' ideas were grounded in his Christian faith.*

4 CHILD [T] *informal* to stop a child going out with their

G

friends as a punishment for behaving badly: *I got home at 2 am and Dad grounded me on the spot.*
5 ELECTRICITY [T] *AmE* to make a piece of electrical equipment safe by connecting it to the ground with a wire SYN **earth** *BrE* → WELL-GROUNDED
ground sb **in** sth *phr v* to teach someone the basic things they should know in order to be able to do something: *Most seven-year-olds are grounded in the basics of reading and writing.*

ground³ *adj* [only before noun] ground coffee or nuts have been broken up into powder or very small pieces, using a special machine → **grind**

ground⁴ the past tense and past participle of GRIND¹

ˈground bait *n* [U] food that you throw onto a river, lake etc when you are fishing in order to attract fish

ˌground ˈbeef *n* [U] *AmE* BEEF that has been cut up into very small pieces, often used to make HAMBURGERS SYN **mince** *BrE*

ground·break·ing /ˈgraʊndˌbreɪkɪŋ/ *adj* groundbreaking work involves making new discoveries, using new methods etc: *groundbreaking research*

ˈground cloth *n* [C] *AmE* a piece of material that water cannot pass through, which people sleep on when they are camping SYN **groundsheet** *BrE*

ˈground conˌtrol *n* [U] the people on the ground who are responsible for guiding the flight of spacecraft or aircraft

ˈground crew *n* [C] the group of people who work at an airport looking after the aircraft SYN **ground staff** *BrE*

ground·ed /ˈgraʊndɪd/ *adj* **1** reasonable and in control of your emotions, even when this is difficult **2** someone who is grounded understands their own character and knows what is really important: *Simmons says that her family* ***keeps*** *her* ***grounded****.* **3** someone, especially a child, who is grounded is kept indoors as a punishment

ground·er /ˈgraʊndə $ -ər/ *n* [C] a ball that is hit along the ground in a game of BASEBALL

ˌground ˈfloor *n* **1** [C] *especially BrE* the floor of a building that is at ground level SYN **first floor** *AmE*: *a ground floor flat* | *The dining room is on the ground floor.* → FLOOR¹(3) **2 be/get in on the ground floor** to become involved in a plan, business activity etc from the beginning

ˈground ˌforces (*also* **ˈground ˌtroops**) *n* [plural] soldiers who fight on the ground rather than at sea or in the air

ˌground ˈglass *n* [U] **1** glass that has been made into a powder **2** glass that has been rubbed on its surface so that you cannot see through it, but light passes through it – used for example on a camera

ground·hog /ˈgraʊndhɒg $ -hɑːg, -hɒːg/ *n* [C] a small North American animal that has thick brown fur

ˈGroundhog ˌDay *n* If one day seems very like another, people sometimes say that it is like *Groundhog Day*, a film in which the main character has to live the same day (2nd February) many times. In the US, according to old stories, the groundhog comes out of its hole on this day for the first time since winter began. If it sees its shadow, it is frightened back into its hole and there will be six more weeks of winter, but if it is cloudy and there is no shadow, there will be an early spring.

ground·ing /ˈgraʊndɪŋ/ *n* **1** [singular] a training in the basic parts of a subject or skill: **[+in]** *A basic grounding in math is essential for the economics course.* | **get/have a grounding in sth** *Applicants must have a good grounding in human resources management.* | **a good/thorough/solid etc grounding** *The aim of the course is to give students a thorough grounding in English pronunciation.* **2** [C] *AmE* a punishment for a child's bad behaviour in which they are not allowed to go out with their friends for a period of time **3** [C,U] the process of officially stopping an aircraft from flying, especially because it is not safe to fly **4** [U] when someone knows what their own character is like and understands what is really important and what is not: *a sense of grounding*

ground·less /ˈgraʊndləs/ *adj* not based on facts or reason OPP **well-founded**: *Fortunately my suspicions* ***proved groundless****.* | *Mr Kay's lawyer said the accusations were groundless.*

ˈground ˌlevel *n* [U] the same level as the surface of the Earth, rather than above it or below it: *The flats are set around a courtyard with shops at ground level.*

ground·nut /ˈgraʊndnʌt/ *n* [C] *BrE technical* a PEANUT or peanut plant

ˈground plan *n* [C] **1** a drawing of how a building is arranged at ground level, showing the size, position, and shape of walls, rooms etc SYN **floor plan 2** a plan for doing something in the future: *documents which formed the ground plan for the welfare state*

ˈground rent *n* [C,U] rent that you pay to the person who owns the land that your house, office etc is built on

ˈground rules *n* [plural] the basic rules or principles on which future actions or behaviour should be based: **lay down/establish ground rules for sth** *Our book lays down the ground rules for building a patio successfully.*

ground·sheet /ˈgraʊndʃiːt/ *n* [C] *BrE* a piece of material that water cannot pass through which people sleep on when they are camping SYN **ground cloth** *AmE*

grounds·man /ˈgraʊndzmən/ *n* (*plural* **groundsmen** /-mən/) [C] *especially BrE* a man whose job is to take care of a large garden or sports field SYN **groundskeeper** *AmE*

ˈground ˌsquirrel *n* [C] a GOPHER

ˈground staff *n* [C] *BrE* **1** the people who take care of the grass and equipment at a sports ground **2** the group of people who work at an airport looking after the aircraft SYN **ground crew**

ˈground ˌstroke *n* [C] a way of hitting the ball after it has hit the ground in tennis and similar games

ground·swell /ˈgraʊndswel/ *n* [singular] a sudden increase in a particular feeling among people: **[+of]** *There is a* ***groundswell of opinion*** *that tougher laws are needed.* | *a* ***groundswell of support*** *for the prime minister*

ground·wa·ter /ˈgraʊndˌwɔːtə $ -ˌwɒːtər, -ˌwɑː-/ *n* [U] water that is below the ground: *There are fears that groundwater might become contaminated.*

ground·work /ˈgraʊndwɜːk $ -wɜːrk/ *n* [U] something that has to happen before an activity or plan can be successful: *His speech* ***laid*** *the* ***groundwork*** *for independence.* | *Much of* ***the groundwork has*** *already* ***been done****.*

ˌground ˈzero *n* [U] the exact place where a bomb explodes: *Buildings within 25 km of ground zero would be flattened.*

group¹ /gruːp/ ●●● S1 W1 *n* [C]
1 several people or things that are all together in the same place: **[+of]** *a group of children* | *a small group of islands* | *Get into groups of four.* | *He was surrounded by a group of admirers.* | **in groups** *Dolphins travel in small groups.* | *A group of us are going to London.*
2 several people or things that are connected with each other: *a left-wing terrorist group* | **[+of]** *She is one of a group of women who have suffered severe side-effects from the drug.* | **age/ethnic/income etc group** (=people of the same age, race etc) *Minority groups are encouraged to apply.*
3 several companies that all have the same owner → **chain**: *a giant textiles group* | **[+of]** *He owns a group of hotels in southern England.*
4 a number of musicians or singers who perform together, playing popular music SYN **band** → BLOOD GROUP, FOCUS GROUP, INTEREST GROUP, PLAYGROUP, PRESSURE GROUP, WORKING GROUP

GRAMMAR: Singular or plural verb?

• **Group** is usually followed by a singular verb: *This group* ***has*** *a higher risk of heart disease.* | *His group* ***plays*** *jazz.*

G

• In British English, you can also use a plural verb: *This group **have** a higher risk of heart disease.* | *His group **play** jazz.*
GRAMMAR GUIDE ▸ NOUNS

THESAURUS

OF PEOPLE

group several people together in the same place: *A group of boys stood by the school gate.*
crowd a large group of people who have come to a place to do something: *There were crowds of shoppers in the streets.* | *The crowd all cheered.*
mob a large, noisy, and perhaps violent crowd: *An angry mob of demonstrators approached.*
mass a large group of people all close together in one place, so that they seem like a single thing: *The square in front of the station was a solid mass of people.*
bunch *informal* a group of people who are all similar in some way: *They're a nice bunch of kids.*
gang a group of young people, especially a group that often causes trouble and fights: *He was attacked by a gang of youths.*
rabble a noisy group of people who are behaving badly: *He was met by a rabble of noisy angry youths.*
horde a very large group of people who all go somewhere: *In summer hordes of tourists flock to the island.*
crew a group of people who all work together, especially on a ship or plane: *the ship's crew* | *The flight crew will serve drinks shortly.*
party a group of people who are travelling or working together: *A party of tourists stood at the entrance to the temple.*

OF ANIMALS

herd a group of cows, deer, or elephants: *A herd of cows was blocking the road.*
team a group of animals that work together: *The carriage was pulled by a team of horses.*
flock a group of sheep or birds: *a flock of seagulls* | *The farmer has over 100 sheep in his flock.*
pack a group of dogs or wolves
litter a group of kittens or puppies born at one time to a particular mother
school/shoal a group of fish or dolphins

OF THINGS

bunch a group of things held or tied together, especially flowers or keys: *He handed me a bunch of daffodils.*
bundle several papers, clothes, or sticks held or tied together in an untidy pile: *Bundles of papers and files filled the shelves.*
cluster a group of things of the same kind that are close together in a place: *a cluster of stars*

group² ●●○ *v*
1 [I,T] to come together and form a group, or to arrange things or people together in a group: **group (sth) together/round/into etc** *The photo shows four men grouped round a jeep.* | *Different flowers can be grouped together to make a colourful display.* | *small producers who group together to sell their produce*
2 [T always + adv/prep] to divide people or things into groups according to a system: *We were grouped into six age bands.* | *We've grouped the questions under three headings.*

ˌgroup ˈcaptain *n* [C] a fairly high rank in the British air force, or someone who has this rank

ˌgroup dyˈnamics *n* [plural] the way in which people in a group behave towards each other when they are working together or doing an activity together

group·ie /ˈgruːpi/ *n* [C] a young woman who follows popular musicians or other famous people around, hoping to meet them

group·ing /ˈgruːpɪŋ/ *n* **1** [C] a number of people, things, or organizations that do something together or have the same interests, qualities, or features: **[+of]** *a grouping of eight opposition parties* | **political/social/economic etc grouping** *During this period the family unit becomes the natural social grouping.* | *a loose grouping* (=informal and not well organized) *of anti-capitalist protesters* **2** [U] the act of putting people or things into groups: *the grouping of students by ability*

ˌgroup ˈpractice *n* [C,U] a group of several doctors who all work in the same building

ˌgroup ˈtherapy *n* [U] a method of treating people with emotional problems by getting them to meet and talk as a group

grouse¹ /graʊs/ *n* **1** [C,U] (*plural* **grouse**) a small bird that is hunted and shot for food and sport, or the flesh of this bird: *the grouse shooting season* | *roast grouse* **2** [C] *informal* a complaint: *His main grouse is that he isn't paid enough.*

grouse² *v* [I] *informal* to complain about something SYN **moan**: **[+about]** *I haven't really got much to grouse about.*

grout /graʊt/ *n* [U] a mixture of sand, water and CEMENT or LIME that you spread between TILES when you fix them to a wall —**grout** *v* [I,T]

grove /grəʊv $ groʊv/ ●○○ *n*
1 [C] a piece of land with trees growing on it: **[+of]** *a small **grove** of beech **trees*** | **olive/lemon/palm etc grove** *He owns an orange grove near Tel Aviv.* THESAURUS ▸ FOREST
2 Grove used in the names of roads: *Lisson Grove*

grov·el /ˈgrɒvəl $ ˈgrɑː-, ˈgrʌ-/ *v* (**grovelled**, **grovelling** *BrE*, **groveled**, **groveling** *AmE*) **1** [I] to praise someone a lot or behave with a lot of respect towards them because you think that they are important and will be able to help you in some way – used to show disapproval SYN **crawl**: **[+to]** *I had to really grovel to the bank manager to get a loan.* **2** [I always + adv/prep] to move along the ground on your hands and knees: *I saw him grovelling in the road for his hat.* —**grovelling** *adj*: *a grovelling apology*

grow /grəʊ $ groʊ/ ●●● S1 W1 *v* (*past tense* **grew** /gruː/, *past participle* **grown** /grəʊn $ groʊn/)
1 INCREASE **a)** [I] to increase in amount, size, number, or strength OPP **shrink**: *Support for Mr Thompson is growing.* | **[+by]** *Sales of new cars grew by 10% last year.* | **[+from/to]** *The number of students at the college has grown from 200 to over 500.* | ***A growing number** of people are taking part-time jobs.* | **grow rapidly/slowly/steadily** *The economy has grown steadily.* | *Fears are growing for the crew's safety.* | **[+in]** *a city that is still growing in size* | *Skiing has really grown in popularity.* | *There is growing concern about climate change.* | *my growing interest in China* **b)** [T] to make a business or part of a business bigger and more successful: *We want to grow the export side of the business.*

REGISTER
In everyday English, people usually say an amount or level **goes up** rather than **grows**: *Sales **went up** by 10% last year.* | *The population of the town has **gone up** to almost a million.*

THESAURUS ▸ BECOME, INCREASE

2 PERSON/ANIMAL [I] to become bigger, taller etc over a period of time in the process of becoming an adult OPP **shrink**: *You've really grown since I last saw you.* | *Victor seemed to **grow taller** every day.* | **grow 2 inches/5 cm etc** *Stan grew two inches in six months.*
3 PLANTS **a)** [I] if plants grow, they exist and develop in a natural way: *a tree which will grow well in most types of soil* | *The plants **grow wild*** (=grow without anyone looking after them) *by the river.* **b)** [T] to make plants or crops develop and produce fruit or flowers → **raise**: *Many families own plots of land to grow food.* | *Britain grows 6,000,000 tonnes of potatoes a year.* | *The **growing season** is from April to September.*
4 HAIR/NAILS **a)** [T] if you grow your hair or nails, you do not cut them: *I've decided to **grow** my hair **long**.* | **grow a beard/moustache** **b)** [I] when hair or nails grow, they become longer

5 BECOME **a)** [I always + adj] to change and become different quite slowly: *The sound was growing louder.* | *Her tastes have changed as she's grown older.* | *Donna has grown tired of being a model.* | *Gradually, Fiona's eyes grew used to the darkness* (=she gradually became able to see a little better). **b)** [I] to gradually change your opinions and have a feeling that you did not have before: **grow to like/hate/respect etc** *After a while the kids grew to like Mr Cox.* | *the city he had grown to love*

> **REGISTER**
> In everyday English, people usually say **get older/tired/angry** etc rather than **grow older/tired/angry** etc, which sounds rather literary: *The sound was* ***getting*** *louder.*

6 IMPROVE [I] to gradually become better, bigger etc: **[+as]** *She's grown tremendously as a musician.*

7 it/money doesn't grow on trees *spoken* used to say that you should not waste money

grow apart *phr v* if two people grow apart, their relationship becomes less close: *The couple had been growing apart for years.*

grow into sb/sth *phr v*
1 to develop over time and become a particular kind of person or thing: *Sue grew into a lovely young woman.* | *The two-part show has grown into a full-fledged series.*
2 to gradually learn how to do a job or deal with a situation successfully: *She will grow into her new role over the next few months.*
3 if a child grows into clothes, he or she becomes big enough to wear them

grow on sb *phr v* if something grows on you, you gradually like it more and more: *I hated his music at first, but it grows on you.*

grow out *phr v* if you grow out a hairstyle, or if it grows out, you gradually grow your hair until the style disappears: **grow sth ↔ out** *I'm growing my fringe out.*

grow out of sth *phr v*
1 if a child grows out of clothes, he or she becomes too big to wear them SYN **outgrow**
2 if someone grows out of something, they stop doing it as they get older SYN **outgrow**: *Mike finally seems to be growing out of his rebelliousness.*
3 to develop or happen as a result of something else that happened or existed: *His art grew out of his love of nature.* | *legislation which grew out of concern over the increasing crime rate*

grow up *phr v*
1 to develop from being a child to being an adult: *What do you want to be when you grow up?* | *I grew up in Chicago.*
2 grow up! *spoken* used to tell someone to behave in a more responsible way, like an adult
3 to start to exist or develop gradually: *Trading settlements grew up by the river.*

grow·bag /ˈɡrəʊbæɡ $ ˈɡroʊ-/ *n* another spelling of GRO-BAG

Growbag /ˈɡrəʊbæɡ $ ˈɡroʊ-/ *n* [C] *trademark BrE* a large plastic bag containing specially prepared earth for growing vegetables

grow·er /ˈɡrəʊə $ ˈɡroʊər/ *n* [C] **1** a person or company that grows fruit or vegetables in order to sell them: **fruit/vegetable/tobacco etc grower** *apple growers* **2** a plant that grows and develops in a particular way: **fast/slow etc grower** *Bamboo is a very vigorous grower.*

ˈgrowing ˌpains *n* [plural] **1** problems and difficulties that happen when an organization or system is new: *the growing pains of a new republic* **2** pain that children who are growing feel in their arms and legs

growl /ɡraʊl/ ●○○ *v*
1 [I] if an animal growls, it makes a long deep angry sound → **bark**, **snarl**: **[+at]** *The dog growled at me.*
2 [I,T] to say something in a low angry voice SYN **snarl**: *'Get out of my way,' he growled.* | **[+at]** *'Who are you?' he growled at me.* THESAURUS SAY —**growl** *n* [C]: *He heard a low growl behind him.*

grown¹ /ɡrəʊn $ ɡroʊn/ *v* the past participle of GROW

grown² *adj* **1 grown man/woman** an adult man or woman, used especially when you think someone is not behaving as an adult should: *Who ever heard of a grown man being scared of the dark?* **2 grown children/daughter/son** children etc who are now adults: *I've got two grown daughters and a son.*

ˌgrown-ˈup¹ ●●○ *adj*
1 fully developed as an adult: *Before you know it, the children will be grown-up and leaving home.* | *I've got two grown-up sons.*
2 behaving in a responsible way, like an adult SYN **mature** → **childish**: *I expect more grown-up behaviour of you.*

ˈgrown-up² ●●○ *n* [C] an adult – used by or to children: *If you're frightened, tell one of the grown-ups.*

growth /ɡrəʊθ $ ɡroʊθ/ ●●● S3 W1 *n*
1 INCREASE [singular, U] an increase in amount, number, or size OPP **decline**: **[+in/of]** *We've seen an enormous growth in the number of businesses using the Web.* | *the rapid growth of world population* | *the recent growth of interest in African music*
2 BUSINESS/ECONOMY [singular, U] an increase in the value of goods or services produced and sold by a business or a country OPP **decline**: *measures to stimulate* ***economic growth*** | **strong/rapid/slow etc growth** *a period of rapid growth in the economy* | *The company is preparing for* ***zero growth*** (=no growth) *this year.* | **growth area/industry** *Debt collection is a huge growth industry.*
3 SIZE/STRENGTH [singular, U] the development of the physical size, strength etc of a person, animal, or plant over a period of time: *Vitamins are essential for healthy growth.* | *a means of stimulating* ***plant growth*** | ***a growth hormone*** (=substance in the body that causes you to grow)
4 IMPORTANCE [singular, U] a gradual increase in the importance or influence that something has: **[+of]** *Cinemas declined with the growth of television.*
5 PERSONAL DEVELOPMENT [U] the development of someone's character, intelligence, or emotions: *A loving home is essential for a child's* ***personal growth.*** | **emotional/intellectual/spiritual etc growth** *the journey toward spiritual growth*
6 DISEASE [C] a swelling on or inside a person, animal, or plant, caused by disease → **tumour**: *a cancerous growth* | **[+on]** *a growth on his lung*
7 GROWING THING [C,U] something that has grown: *Feed the plants to encourage new growth.* | *His chin bore a thick growth of stubble.*

groyne, groin /ɡrɔɪn/ *n* [C] a low wall built out into the sea to prevent the sea from removing sand and stones from the shore

grub¹ /ɡrʌb/ *n* **1** [U] *informal* food: *Let's get some grub.* **2** [C] an insect when it is in the form of a small soft white worm

grub² *v* (**grubbed**, **grubbing**) [I always + adv/prep] *informal* to look for something on the ground or just under the ground, especially by moving things around: *Jake got on the floor and grubbed about under the desk.* | **[+for]** *chickens grubbing for worms*

grub sth **↔ up/out** *phr v* to dig plants out of the ground: *Farmers were encouraged to grub up hedgerows.*

grub·by /ˈɡrʌbi/ *adj* **1** fairly dirty: *a grubby handkerchief* | *a gang of grubby kids* THESAURUS DIRTY **2** grubby behaviour or activity is morally unpleasant: *the grubby details of his financial dealings* **3 grubby hands/paws/mitts** *informal* used to talk about someone touching something or becoming involved in it when you do not want them to: *Keep your grubby paws to yourself!* | *I bet he can't wait to get his grubby hands on my money!* —**grubbiness** *n* [U]

grub·stake /ˈɡrʌbˌsteɪk/ *n* [U] *AmE informal* an amount of money that is provided to develop a new business in return for a share of the profits

grudge¹ /ɡrʌdʒ/ *n* [C] **1** a feeling of dislike for someone because you cannot forget that they harmed you in the

G

past: **[+against]** *Is there anyone who might have* ***had a grudge against*** *her?* | *Mr Gillis was not normally a man to* ***bear grudges***. | *I'm not* ***harbouring*** *some secret* ***grudge*** *against you.* | *It could be the work of* ***someone with a grudge*** *against the company.* | *You let nasty little* ***personal grudges*** *creep in.* **2 grudge fight/match** a fight or sports competition between two people who dislike each other a lot

grudge² *v* [T] to do or give something very unwillingly: **grudge doing sth** *I really grudge paying for poor service.* | **grudge sb sth** *I don't grudge him his success.* —**grudging** *adj* [usually before noun]: *a grudging apology* —**grudgingly** *adv*: *He grudgingly admitted he'd been wrong.*

gru·el /ˈɡruːəl/ *n* [U] a food made of OATS cooked in water or milk, which poor people ate in the past

gru·el·ling *BrE*, **grueling** *AmE* /ˈɡruːəlɪŋ/ *adj* very difficult and tiring: *The cast took a break from their gruelling schedule.* | *a grueling journey* **THESAURUS** TIRING

grue·some /ˈɡruːsəm/ ●○○ *adj* very unpleasant or shocking, and involving someone being killed or badly injured: *Police described it as a particularly gruesome attack.* | *Spare me the gruesome details.* —**gruesomely** *adv*

gruff /ɡrʌf/ *adj* speaking in a rough unfriendly voice: *His manner can be rather gruff.* | *a gruff reply* | *His voice became gruff.* —**gruffly** *adv* —**gruffness** *n* [U]

grum·ble /ˈɡrʌmbəl/ ●○○ *v*
1 [I,T] to keep complaining in an unhappy way SYN **moan**: **[+about/at]** *Farmers are always grumbling about the weather.* | **grumble that** *A few passengers grumbled that their cabins were too small.* | *'This is boring,' Kathleen grumbled.* **THESAURUS** COMPLAIN
2 [I] to make a low continuous sound SYN **rumble**: *Thunder grumbled overhead.*
3 mustn't/can't grumble *BrE spoken* used to say that you are fairly healthy and happy: *'How are you today?' 'Mustn't grumble.'* —**grumble** *n* [C]: *the usual grumbles about pay*

grum·bling /ˈɡrʌmblɪŋ/ *n* **1** [U] (*also* **grumblings** [plural]) a complaint about something: *She paid up, with some grumbling.* | *Soon, the grumblings turned to open discontent.* **2** [U] a low continuous sound: *the grumbling of distant thunder*

grump¹ /ɡrʌmp/ *n* [C] *informal* someone who complains a lot: *'I hate Mondays.' 'I wish you would stop being such an old grump.'*

grump² *v* [I] *informal* to complain about something: **[+about]** *He was grumping about how cold the house was.*

grump·y /ˈɡrʌmpi/ ●○○ *adj* bad-tempered and easily annoyed SYN **irritable**: *Mina's always a bit grumpy first thing in the morning.* —**grumpily** *adv* —**grumpiness** *n* [U]

grunge /ɡrʌndʒ/ *n* [U] **1** a style of fashion and music popular with young people in the 1990s, involving loud electric music and dirty clothes, hair etc: *grunge rock* **2** *AmE informal* unpleasant dirt: *What's all that grunge in the bathtub?* —**grungy** *adj*: *a pair of grungy trainers*

grunt¹ /ɡrʌnt/ ●○○ *v*
1 [I,T] to make short sounds or say a few words in a rough voice, when you do not want to talk: *He just grunted and carried on reading his book.*
2 [I] if a person or animal grunts, they make short low sounds in their throat: *Grunting with effort, she lifted me up.*

grunt² *n* [C] **1** a short low sound that a person or animal makes in their throat: *Chris gave a grunt and went back to sleep.* **2** *AmE informal* someone who does hard physical work for low pay: *The grunts move the crates.* **3** *AmE informal* a soldier in the INFANTRY

ˈgrunt work *n* [U] *AmE informal* the difficult and uninteresting part of a job: *These guys do the grunt work in preparing tax returns.*

gryph·on /ˈɡrɪfən/ *n* [C] another spelling of GRIFFIN

G-spot /ˈdʒiː spɒt $ -spɑːt/ *n* [C] *informal* the place in a woman's VAGINA where she is thought to feel the most sexual pleasure

G-string /ˈdʒiː strɪŋ/ *n* [C] a very small piece of underwear that covers only the sexual organs

Gt. (*also* **Gt** *BrE*) *adj* [only before noun] the written abbreviation of **Great**, used in names: *Gt Britain*

gua·ca·mo·le /ˌɡwɑːkəˈməʊli $ -ˈmoʊ-/ *n* [U] a cold Mexican dish made with crushed AVOCADO

gua·no /ˈɡwɑːnəʊ $ -noʊ/ *n* [U] solid waste from sea birds, put on soil to help plants grow

guar·an·tee¹ /ˌɡærənˈtiː/ ●●○ S3 W3 AWL *v* [T]
1 a) to promise to do something or to promise that something will happen: **guarantee (that)** *I guarantee you'll love this film.* | **guarantee sb sth** *If you send the application form in straight away, I can guarantee you an interview.* | **guarantee to do sth** *I cannot guarantee to work for more than a year.* | *The law guarantees equal rights for men and women.* **b)** to make a formal written promise to repair or replace a product if it breaks within a specific period of time: *All our products are* ***fully guaranteed***. | **guarantee sth against sth** *The stereo is guaranteed against failure for a year.* **THESAURUS** PROMISE
2 to promise that you will pay back money that someone else has borrowed, if they do not pay it back themselves: *The bank will only lend me money if my parents guarantee the loan.*
3 to make it certain that something will happen: *In movies, talent by no means guarantees success.* | **guarantee that** *The built-in thermostat guarantees that the water remains at the same temperature all the time.* | **be guaranteed to do sth** *This latest incident is guaranteed to make the situation worse.* | **be guaranteed sth** *Even if you complete your training, you aren't guaranteed a job.*

guarantee² ●●○ AWL *n* [C]
1 a formal written promise to repair or replace a product if it breaks within a specific period of time SYN **warranty**: *They offer a two-year guarantee on all their electrical goods.* | **come with/carry a guarantee** *Our computers come with a one-year guarantee.* | **under guarantee** *Is your TV under guarantee* (=protected by a guarantee)? | *a* ***money-back guarantee***
2 a formal promise that something will be done: **[+of]** *I'm afraid there's no guarantee of success.* | **guarantee that** *I cannot* ***give*** *a* ***guarantee*** *that there will be no redundancies.*
3 a) a promise that you will pay back money that someone else has used or borrowed, if they do not pay it themselves **b)** something valuable that you give to someone to keep until you have done something you promised to do: *The bank is holding the airline's assets as guarantees.*

guar·an·tor /ˌɡærənˈtɔː $ -ˈtɔːr/ *n* [C] *law* someone who promises to pay a debt if the person who should pay it does not

guard¹ /ɡɑːd $ ɡɑːrd/ ●●● S2 W2 *n*
1 PERSON [C] **a)** someone whose job is to protect a place or person: *There were two* ***security guards*** *on duty outside the building.* | *We were stopped by* ***border guards***. | ***Armed guards*** *were posted by the exit.* **b)** someone whose job is to prevent prisoners from escaping: *The* ***prison guards*** *were reasonably friendly.*
2 PROTECTION [U] the act or duty of protecting places or people, or of preventing prisoners from escaping: **be on guard** *Who was on guard the night the fire broke out?* | **keep/stand guard (over sb/sth)** *Gunmen stood guard at the camp entrance.* | **be under (police/armed etc) guard** (=to be guarded by a group of people) *He was taken to hospital, where he is now under police guard.*
3 SOLDIERS a) [singular] a group of soldiers who guard someone or something: *The president has called in the National Guard.* **b) the Guards** *BrE* a group of soldiers who protect the king or queen
4 EQUIPMENT [C] something that is used to protect someone or something from damage or injury: *a face guard* | *a fire guard*
5 ON A TRAIN [C] *BrE* a person whose job is to be in charge of a train SYN **conductor** *AmE*
6 on your guard to be paying attention to what is happening in order to avoid danger, being tricked etc: *These men are dangerous so you'll need to* ***be on*** *your* ***guard***. | *Something in his tone* ***put*** *her* ***on*** *her* ***guard***.
7 catch/throw sb off guard to surprise someone by doing

G

something that they are not ready to deal with: *Senator O'Hare was caught off guard by the question.*
8 guard of honour a group of people who walk or stand together at a special occasion in order to show respect: *Police colleagues formed a guard of honour at her funeral.*
9 the old guard a group of people in an organization who want to do things in the way they were done in the past: *the Communist old guard*
10 FIGHTING [singular] the position of holding your arms or hands up in a fight in order to defend yourself: *He swung at me and I brought my guard up.*
11 SPORT [C] **a)** one of two players on a BASKETBALL team who is responsible for moving the ball to help their team gain points **b)** one of two players on an American football team who plays either side of the centre → see picture at **BASKETBALL**

guard² ●●● W2 *v* [T]
1 to protect a person, place, or object by staying near them and watching them: *The Sergeant told Swift to guard the entrance.* | *a lioness guarding her cubs* | **guard sb/sth against sth** *There is no one to guard these isolated farms against attack.* THESAURUS ▸ **PROTECT**
2 to watch a prisoner to prevent them from escaping
3 to protect something such as a right or a secret by preventing other people from taking it away, discovering it etc: *chiefs who* ***jealously guarded*** *their independence* | *a* ***closely guarded secret***
4 to prevent another sports player from gaining points, getting the ball etc
guard against sth *phr v* to prevent something from happening: *Exercise can guard against a number of illnesses.* | **guard against doing sth** *Nurses should guard against becoming too attached to their patients.*

ˈguard dog *n* [C] a dog that is trained to guard a place

guard·ed /ˈgɑːdɪd $ ˈgɑːr-/ *adj* not giving very much information or showing your feelings about something SYN **cautious**: *The minister was quite guarded in his comments.* | *He gave the proposal a guarded welcome.* —**guardedly** *adv*

guard·house /ˈgɑːdhaʊs $ ˈgɑːrd-/ *n* [C] a building for soldiers who are guarding the entrance to a military camp

guard·i·an /ˈgɑːdiən $ ˈgɑːr-/ ●○○ *n* [C]
1 someone who is legally responsible for looking after someone else's child, especially after the child's parents have died: **sb's guardian** *His aunt is his* ***legal guardian***.
2 *formal* someone who guards or protects something: **[+of]** *The US sees itself as the guardian of democracy.*

ˌguardian ˈangel *n* [C] **1** a good SPIRIT who is believed to protect a person or place **2** someone who helps or protects someone else when they are in trouble

guard·i·an·ship /ˈgɑːdiənʃɪp $ ˈgɑːr-/ *n* [U] *law* the position of being legally responsible for someone else's child

guard·rail /ˈgɑːd-reɪl $ ˈgɑːrd-/ *n* [C] **1** a bar that is intended to prevent people from falling from a bridge, cliff etc **2** *AmE* a bar that is intended to prevent cars from going off the road in an accident SYN **crash barrier** *BrE* → see picture at **RAIL**

guard·room /ˈgɑːd-rʊm, -ruːm $ ˈgɑːrd-/ *n* [C] a room for soldiers who are guarding a military camp

guards·man /ˈgɑːdzmən $ ˈgɑːr-/ *n* (*plural* **guardsmen** /-mən/) [C] a soldier who is a member of a GUARD

ˈguard's van *n* [C] *BrE* the part of a train where the person in charge of it travels SYN **caboose** *AmE*

gua·va /ˈgwɑːvə/ *n* [C] a tropical fruit with pink flesh and a lot of seeds

gub·bins /ˈgʌbɪnz/ *n* [U] *BrE informal* a group of things that you do not need, do not know much about, or do not know the exact name of SYN **stuff**: *I want a nice simple camera without all that gubbins.*

gu·ber·na·to·ri·al /ˌguːbənəˈtɔːriəl◂ $ -bər-/ *adj formal* relating to the position of being a GOVERNOR: *gubernatorial elections*

guer·ril·la /gəˈrɪlə/ ●○○ *n* [C] a member of a small unofficial military group that fights in small groups: **guerrilla war/warfare** *American troops found themselves fighting a guerrilla war.* | *left-wing guerrillas*

guerˈrilla ˌgardening *n* [U] the activity of growing plants or vegetables on any piece of land in a city that you do not own, especially land that is in bad condition because it has not been used for a long time. People do this so that cities will have more green areas and be better places to live. —**guerrilla gardener** *n* [C]: *Guerrilla gardeners came late in the night and turned the area outside the building into a vegetable patch.*

guerˈrilla ˌmarketing *n* [U] MARKETING (=the activity of deciding how to advertise a product, what price to charge for it etc) that uses new, clever, and unusual methods to sell a product, rather than spending a lot of money to sell it

guess¹ /ges/ ●●● S1 W3 *v*
1 [I,T] to try to answer a question or form an opinion when you are not sure whether you will be correct: *I'd say he's around 50, but I'm only guessing.* | **guess right/correctly/wrong** *If you guess correctly, you have another turn.* | **guess what/who/how etc** *You can guess what happened next.* | **[+at]** *We can only guess at the cause of the crash.* | *What star sign are you? No,* ***let*** *me* ***guess***. | **difficult/hard/easy etc to guess** *It's hard to guess his age because he dyes his hair.*
2 [I,T] to realize that something is true even though you do not know for certain: **guess (that)** *I guessed that you must be related because you look so similar.* | **[+from]** *I guessed from his expression that he already knew about the accident.* | *Can you guess the identity of this week's special guest?*
3 keep sb guessing to make someone feel excited or not sure about what will happen next: *a thriller that keeps audiences guessing*
4 I guess *spoken* **a)** used to say that you think something is true or likely, although you are not sure: *His light's on, so I guess he's still up.* **b)** used to say that you will do something even though you do not really want to: *I'm tired, so I guess I'll stay home tonight.*
5 I guess so/not *spoken* used to agree or disagree with a statement or question: *'You're one lucky guy.' 'I guess so.'* | *'I don't really have any choice, do I?' 'I guess not.'*
6 guess what/you'll never guess who/what etc *spoken* used before you tell someone something that will surprise them: *Guess what! Bradley's resigned.* | *You'll never guess who I saw today.* → **SECOND-GUESS**

guess² ●●● S3 *n* [C]
1 an attempt to answer a question or make a judgment when you are not sure whether you will be correct: *I'd say she's about 35, but that's only a guess.*
2 be anybody's guess to be something that no one knows: *What she's going to do with her life now is anybody's guess.*
3 your guess is as good as mine *spoken* used to tell someone that you do not know any more than they do about something

COLLOCATIONS

VERBS

make a guess *I didn't know the answer to question 7, so I just had to make a guess.*
have a guess *BrE*, **take a guess** *AmE*: *Go on, have a guess at how much it cost.*
hazard a guess (=guess something, when you feel very uncertain) *No one at this stage is prepared to hazard a guess about the outcome of the elections.*

ADJECTIVES

a rough guess (=one that is not exact) *This is just a rough guess, but I think it would cost about $50.*
a wild guess (=one made without much thought or information) *I made a wild guess and I got the answer right first time.*
a lucky guess *'How did you know?' 'It was just a lucky guess.'*
a good guess (=one that is likely to be right) *I'm not sure how old she is, but I can make a good guess!*

G

sb's best guess (=one that you think is most likely to be right) | **an educated/informed guess** (=a guess based on things that you know are correct)

PHRASES

my guess is (that) *My guess is there won't be many people there.*
at a guess *BrE* (=used when saying that you are making a guess) *I'd say it was built around the turn of the century, at a guess.*
I'll give you three guesses (=used to tell someone that it should be easy for them to guess the answer to their question)

guess·ti·mate /ˈgestəmət/ *n* [C] *informal* an attempt to judge a quantity by guessing it → **estimate**: *Could you give us a guesstimate of the numbers involved?* —**guesstimate** /-tɪmeɪt/ *v* [I,T]

guess·work /ˈgeswɜːk $ -wɜːrk/ *n* [U] the method of trying to find the answer to something by guessing: *There's a lot of guesswork in these calculations.*

guest¹ /gest/ ●●● S3 W2 *n* [C]
1 AT AN EVENT someone who is invited to an event or special occasion: *a banquet for 250 distinguished guests* | **as sb's guest** *You are here as my guests.* | **dinner/wedding etc guests** *Most of the wedding guests had left.* | *Among the invited guests were Jerry Brown and Elihu Harris.* | *The actress was* ***guest of honour*** (=the most important guest) *at the launch.* | *I've nearly finished the* ***guest list*** *for the wedding.*

REGISTER
In everyday English, people usually talk about **having friends/people over** (for a meal, short visit etc) or **having friends/people to stay** rather than saying that they **have guests**: *We're* ***having*** *some* ***people over*** *for dinner this evening.*

2 IN A HOUSE someone you have invited to stay in your home for a short time: *We have guests staying right now.* → HOUSE GUEST
3 IN A HOTEL someone who is paying to stay in a hotel: *Use of the sauna is free to guests.* THESAURUS▸ CUSTOMER
4 ON A SHOW someone famous who is invited to take part in a show, concert etc, in addition to those who usually take part: *We have some great guests for you tonight.* | *Fontaine* ***appeared as a guest*** *on the show.*
5 be my guest *spoken* used to give someone permission to do what they have asked to do: *'Do you mind if I look at your notes?' 'Be my guest.'*

guest² *adj* [only before noun] **1** for guests to use: *He was still asleep in the guest bedroom.* **2** a guest star, speaker etc is someone famous or important who is invited to take part in an event, in addition to the people who usually take part: *Camfield was lucky in getting Cage and Rampling as guest stars.* | *He will* ***make*** *a special* ***guest appearance*** *on next week's show.*

guest³ *v* [I] to take part in a show, concert etc as a guest: **[+on]** *She guested on a comedy show last year.*

ˈguest book *n* [C] a book in which everyone who comes to a formal occasion or stays at a hotel signs their name

guest·house /ˈgesthaʊs/ *n* [C] a private house where people can pay to stay and have meals THESAURUS▸ HOTEL

ˈguest room *n* [C] a bedroom for a visitor or visitors to use SYN **spare room**

ˈguest ˌworker *n* [C] a worker from one country who works in another country for a short time

guff /gʌf/ *n* [U] *informal* remarks that are stupid and untrue SYN **nonsense**: *I don't believe any of that guff!*

guf·faw /gəˈfɔː $ -ˈfɒː/ *v* [I] to laugh loudly: *We guffawed at what Graham had written.* THESAURUS▸ LAUGH —**guffaw** *n* [C]: *The announcement was greeted with loud guffaws.*

GUI /ˈguːi/ *n* [C] *technical* (***graphical user interface***) a way of showing and organizing information on a computer screen that is easy to use and understand

guid·ance /ˈgaɪdəns/ ●●○ S3 W3 *n* [U]
1 help and advice that is given to someone about their work, education, or personal life: **[+on/about]** *I went to a counselor for guidance on my career.* | **under sb's expert guidance** *I was looking forward to working under her expert guidance.* | **parental/spiritual etc guidance** *Children need moral guidance.*
2 the process of directing a MISSILE while it is flying through the air: *a missile with a sophisticated electronic guidance system*

guide¹ /gaɪd/ ●●● S3 W2 *n* [C]
1 FOR DECIDING/JUDGING something that provides information and helps you to form an opinion or make a decision: *The polls are not a reliable guide of how people will vote.* | *The figures are only a* ***rough guide***.
2 PERSON **a)** someone whose job is to take tourists to a place and show them around: *a* ***tour guide*** | *an experienced* ***mountain guide*** **b)** someone who advises you and influences the way you live: *my* ***spiritual guide***
3 INSTRUCTIONS **a)** a book or piece of writing that provides information on a particular subject or explains how to do something: **[+to]** *a guide to North American birds* | *Follow our* ***step-by-step guide***. | *Details of how to use the various programs are in the* ***user guide***. **b)** a guidebook
4 GIRL *BrE* **a) the Guides** the Guides Association, which teaches girls practical skills → **scout b)** a member of the Guides Association

guide² ●●○ W3 *v* [T]
1 to take someone to a place SYN **lead**: **guide sb along/through etc** *He guided us through the narrow streets to the central mosque.* THESAURUS▸ LEAD, TAKE
2 to help someone or something to move in a particular direction: **guide sb/sth into/towards etc** *He guided her firmly towards the sofa.* | *Searchlights were used to guide the ship into the harbour.*
3 to influence someone's behaviour or ideas: *Teenagers need adults to guide them.*
4 to show someone the right way to do something, especially something difficult or complicated: **guide sb through sth** *Guide your students through the program one section at a time.*

guide·book /ˈgaɪdbʊk/ *n* [C] a book about a city, country etc: *travel guidebooks* THESAURUS▸ BOOK

ˌguided ˈmissile *n* [C] a MISSILE that is controlled electronically while it is flying

ˈguide dog *n* [C] a dog trained to guide a blind person SYN **seeing eye dog** *AmE*

ˌguided ˈtour *n* [C] if someone takes you on a guided tour, they show you around a place of interest and tell you all about it: **[+of/around/round]** *You will be taken on a guided tour of the palace.*

guide·line /ˈgaɪdlaɪn/ ●●○ AWL *n* [C usually plural]
1 rules or instructions about the best way to do something: **[+for]** *a new set of guidelines for teachers* | **[+on]** *guidelines on the employment of children* | **draw up/issue guidelines** *The hospital has issued new guidelines on the treatment of mentally ill patients.* | *This chapter* ***gives*** *you some* ***guidelines*** *to help you in your work.* | **clear/strict guidelines** *Today most planning authorities enforce fairly strict guidelines on new houses.*
2 something that helps you form an opinion or make a decision: *When starting a new business, try to* ***follow*** *these general* ***guidelines***. | **within ... guidelines** *Teachers can choose books within certain broad guidelines.*

guid·ing /ˈgaɪdɪŋ/ *adj* **1 guiding principle** something that helps you decide what to do in a difficult situation: *Fairness, rather than efficiency, is the guiding principle.* **2 guiding light/hand/star** someone whose ideas and advice people follow: *Eddie was his hero – his guiding light.* | *He really needed a guiding hand.*

guild /gɪld/ *n* [C] an organization of people who do the same job or have the same interests: *the Women's Guild*

guil·der /ˈgɪldə $ -ər/ *n* [C] the standard unit of money used in the Netherlands before the EURO

guild·hall /ˌgɪldˈhɔːl, ˈgɪldhɔːl $ ˈgɪldhɒːl/ *n* [C] a large building in which members of a guild met in the past

guile /gaɪl/ *n* [U] *formal* the use of clever but dishonest methods to deceive someone SYN **cunning**: *With a little guile she might get what she wanted.* —**guileful** *adj*

guile·less /ˈgaɪl-ləs/ *adj* behaving in an honest way, without trying to hide anything or deceive people SYN **open**

guil·le·mot /ˈgɪləmɒt $ -mɑːt/ *n* [C] a black and white sea bird with a narrow beak

guil·lo·tine¹ /ˈgɪlətiːn/ *n* [C] **1** a piece of equipment used to cut off the heads of criminals, especially in France in the past **2** *BrE* a piece of equipment used to cut large sheets of paper **3** *BrE* the setting of a time limit on a discussion in the British Parliament: *Opposition leaders accused the government of introducing a guillotine motion to stifle debate.*

guillotine² *v* [T] **1** to cut off someone's head using a guillotine **2** *BrE* to limit the period of time allowed for the discussion of a possible new law in the British Parliament

guilt¹ /gɪlt/ ●●○ *n* [U]

1 a strong feeling of shame and sadness because you know that you have done something wrong: *He used to buy them expensive presents, out of guilt.* | **[+about/at/over]** *Don't you have any* ***feelings of guilt*** *about leaving David?* | *He felt an enormous* ***sense of guilt*** *when he thought about how he'd treated her.* | *I was* ***racked with guilt*** *at my part in making her this unhappy.* | *Sometimes I felt little* ***pangs of guilt****.*

2 the fact that you have broken an official law or moral rule OPP **innocence**: *He did not deny his guilt.*

3 responsibility and blame for something bad that has happened: **[+for]** *Guilt for poorly behaved children usually lies with the parents.*

4 be on a guilt trip *informal* to have a feeling of guilt about something when it is unreasonable

5 lay a guilt trip on sb *AmE informal* to make someone feel bad about something: *I wish my parents would stop laying a guilt trip on me for not going to college.*

guilt² *v*

guilt sb **into** sth *phr v AmE informal* to make someone feel guilty, so they will do what you want: **guilt sb into doing sth** *Her parents guilted her into not going to the concert.*

guilt·less /ˈgɪltləs/ *adj formal* not responsible for a crime or for having done something wrong SYN **innocent**

ˈguilt-ˌridden *adj* feeling so guilty about something that you cannot think about anything else

ˈguilt-trip *v* [T] *informal* to make someone feel guilty: *My mother tried to guilt-trip me by crying.*

guilt·y /ˈgɪlti/ ●●● S2 W3 *adj*

1 ASHAMED feeling very ashamed and sad because you know that you have done something wrong: **[+about/for/at]** *I* ***feel*** *really* ***guilty*** *about forgetting her birthday again.* | *She looked self-conscious and guilty.* | *It was his* ***guilty conscience*** *that made him offer to help.*

> **REGISTER**
> In everyday English, people often say that they **feel bad about** something rather than say that they **feel guilty about** it: *I* ***feel bad about*** *leaving him on his own.*

2 OF A CRIME having done something that is a crime OPP **innocent**: **[+of]** *The jury* ***found*** *her* ***guilty*** *of murder.* | *He was found* ***not guilty*** *of the death of PC Jones.* | *He* ***pleaded guilty*** *to two charges of theft.*

3 responsible for behaviour that is morally or socially unacceptable: **be guilty of doing sth** *Some journalists are guilty of reporting scandal in order to sell papers.*

4 the guilty party *formal* the person who has done something illegal or wrong —**guiltily** *adv*

> **GRAMMAR: Prepositions with guilty**
> • You feel **guilty about/for/at** something you have done: *She felt guilty about what had happened.* | *I feel guilty for not doing more to help.*
> • Someone is **guilty of** a crime or doing something wrong: *They were guilty of murder.* | *The government is guilty of mismanaging the economy.*

> **THESAURUS - MEANING 2**
> **guilty** if someone is guilty of a crime or doing something wrong, they did it, and they should be punished for it: *She was* ***found guilty of*** *murder.* | *He was guilty of serious misconduct.*
> **responsible** [not before noun] used when saying who should be blamed for something bad that has happened: *Police believe a local gang is responsible for the burglaries.* | *As manager, he is ultimately responsible for the failure of the project.*
> **be to blame** if someone is to blame for a bad situation, they are responsible: *The government is partly to blame for the crisis.*
> **culpable** /ˈkʌlpəbəl/ *formal* responsible for something bad or illegal, so that you deserve to be blamed or punished: *The people who helped the terrorists are equally culpable for what happened on July 7th.* | *He pleaded guilty to* ***culpable homicide*** (=being guilty of causing someone's death).
> **negligent** /ˈneglɪdʒənt/ [not usually before noun] responsible for something bad that has happened, because you did not take enough care, or you did not try to stop it from happening: *The court decided that the railway company was negligent.*
> **be in the wrong** to be responsible for an accident, mistake etc - used when deciding which person, group etc should be blamed: *The other driver was clearly in the wrong.* | *She always thinks it's me who is in the wrong.*
> **incriminating** used about things which seem to show that someone is guilty of a crime: *incriminating evidence* | *incriminating documents* | *He didn't want to say anything incriminating.*

guin·ea /ˈgɪni/ *n* [C] a British gold coin or unit of money used in the past, worth one pound and one SHILLING (£1.05). Prices are sometimes still given in guineas when buying or selling RACEHORSES.

ˈguinea fowl *n* [C] a grey bird that is often eaten as food

ˈguinea pig *n* [C] **1** a small furry animal with short ears and no tail, which is often kept as a pet **2** someone who is used in a scientific test to see how successful or safe a new product, system etc is

guise /gaɪz/ *n* [C] *formal* the way someone or something appears to be, which hides the truth or is only temporary: **in/under the guise of sth** *They operated a drug-smuggling business under the guise of an employment agency.* | *It's the same idea in a different guise.*

gui·tar /gɪˈtɑː $ -ˈtɑːr/ ●●● S3 W3 *n* [C] a musical instrument usually with six strings that you play by pulling the strings with your fingers or with a PLECTRUM (=small piece of plastic, metal etc): **an acoustic/an electric/a classical guitar** → BASS GUITAR, STEEL GUITAR → see pictures at STRINGED INSTRUMENT, ACOUSTIC

gui·tar·ist /gɪˈtɑːrɪst/ ●○○ *n* [C] someone who plays the guitar

gu·lag /ˈguːlæg $ -lɑːg/ *n* [C] one of a group of prison camps in the former USSR, where conditions were very bad

gulch /gʌltʃ/ *n* [C] *AmE* a narrow deep valley formed in the past by flowing water, but usually dry now

gulf /gʌlf/ ●○○ *n* [C]

1 a large area of sea partly enclosed by land: *the Gulf of Mexico*

2 the Gulf the Arabian Gulf, or the countries next to it: *the smaller* ***Gulf states***

3 a great difference and lack of understanding between two groups of people, especially in their beliefs, opinions, and way of life SYN **gap**: **[+between]** *the huge gulf between management and unions* | *a growing gulf between old and young*

G

ˈGulf Stream *n* **the Gulf Stream** a current of warm water that flows across the Atlantic Ocean from the Gulf of Mexico towards Europe

gull /gʌl/ *n* [C] a large common black and white sea bird that lives near the sea SYN **seagull**

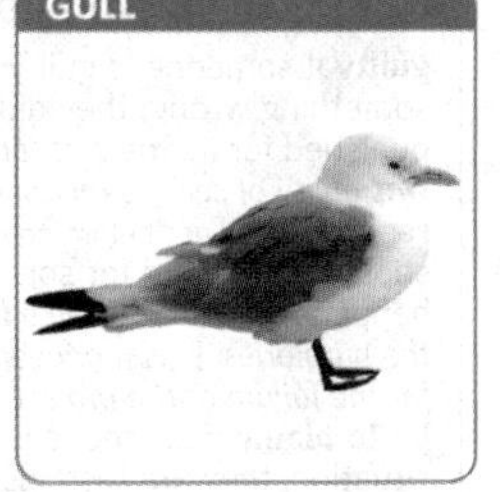

gul·let /ˈgʌlɪt/ *n* [C] the tube at the back of your mouth through which food goes down your throat

gul·ley /ˈgʌli/ *n* [C] another spelling of GULLY

gul·li·ble /ˈgʌləbəl/ *adj* too ready to believe what other people tell you, so that you are easily tricked: *Plastic replicas of the Greek pottery are sold to gullible tourists.* —**gullibility** /ˌgʌləˈbɪləti/ *n* [U]

gul·ly, **gulley** /ˈgʌli/ *n* (*plural* **gullies**) [C] **1** a small narrow valley, usually formed by a lot of rain flowing down the side of a hill **2** a deep DITCH

gulp¹ /gʌlp/ *v* **1** (*also* **gulp down**) [T] to swallow large quantities of food or drink quickly SYN **bolt**: *She gulped down her breakfast and ran for the bus.* **2** [I] to swallow suddenly because you are surprised or nervous: *I gulped when I saw the bill.* **3** (*also* **gulp in**) [T] to breathe in large amounts of air quickly: *We rushed outside and gulped in the sweet fresh air.* **4 be gulping for air** to breathe in large amounts of air quickly because you do not have enough air in your body

gulp sth ↔ **back** *phr v* to stop yourself from expressing your feelings: *Sandra tried to gulp back her tears.*

gulp² *n* [C] **1** a large amount of something that you swallow quickly, or the action of swallowing: **[+of]** *He* ***took*** *a huge* ***gulp*** *of brandy.* | **in one gulp/at a gulp** *Charlie drank the whisky in one gulp.* **2** a large amount of air that you breathe in quickly: *gulps of fresh air*

gum¹ /gʌm/ ●●● S3 *n*
1 [C usually plural] your gums are the two areas of firm pink flesh at the top and bottom of your mouth, in which your teeth are fixed
2 [U] CHEWING GUM
3 [U] *BrE* a type of glue used to stick light things such as paper together
4 [U] a sticky substance found in the stems of some trees
5 [C] a GUM TREE
6 by gum! *spoken old-fashioned* used to express surprise

gum² *v* (**gummed**, **gumming**) [T always + adv/prep] *BrE old-fashioned* to stick things together using glue SYN **glue**: **gum sth to sth** *A large label had been gummed to the back of the photograph.*

gum sth ↔ **up** *phr v informal* to prevent a machine from moving and working properly: *Dirt had got inside the watch and gummed up the works.*

gum·ball /ˈgʌmbɔːl $ -bɒːl/ *n* [C] *AmE* CHEWING GUM in the form of a small round brightly coloured sweet

gum·bo /ˈgʌmbəʊ $ -boʊ/ *n* [U] **1** a thick soup made with meat, fish, and OKRA (=a small green vegetable) **2** a word used in some parts of the US for OKRA

gum·boot /ˈgʌmbuːt/ *n* [C] *BrE old-fashioned* a tall boot made of rubber that you wear to keep your feet dry SYN **wellington boot**

gum·drop /ˈgʌmdrɒp $ -drɑːp/ *n* [C] a small sweet that you chew

gum·my /ˈgʌmi/ *adj* **1** sticky or covered in glue **2** a gummy smile shows the GUMS in someone's mouth when they have no teeth

gump·tion /ˈgʌmpʃən/ *n* [U] the ability and determination to decide what needs to be done and to do it: *At least she* ***had*** *the* ***gumption*** *to phone me.*

gum·shoe /ˈgʌmʃuː/ *n* [C] *AmE old-fashioned* a DETECTIVE

gum·shoe·ing /ˈgʌmˌʃuːɪŋ/ *n* [U] *AmE informal* when you try to find out information about something SYN **detective work**

ˈgum tree *n* [C] **1** a tall tree which produces a strong-smelling oil that is used in medicine SYN **eucalyptus** **2 be up a gum tree** *BrE informal* to be in a very difficult situation

gun¹ /gʌn/ ●●● S2 W2 *n* [C]
1 a metal weapon which shoots bullets or SHELLS: **have/hold/carry a gun** *I could see he was carrying a gun.* | *I've never* ***fired*** *a* ***gun*** *in my life.* | *Jake was* ***pointing*** *a* ***gun*** *at the door.* | *Two policemen were killed in a* ***gun battle***.
2 put/hold a gun to sb's head a) to put a gun very close to someone's head to shoot them or to force them to do something: *He put a gun to her head and told the cashier to hand over the money.* **b)** to force someone to do something they do not want to do: *You chose to live here. Nobody put a gun to your head.*
3 a tool that forces out small objects or a liquid by pressure: *a paint gun* | *a nail gun* → **FLASHGUN, SPRAY GUN**
4 (*also* **starting pistol**) a gun which is fired into the air at the start of a race
5 big/top gun *AmE informal* someone who is very important within an organization: *Jed wanted to impress a Harvard professor and some other big guns.*
6 hired gun *AmE informal* someone who is paid to shoot someone else
7 with all guns blazing if you do something with all guns blazing, you do it with a lot of energy, determination, and noise → **SON OF A GUN**, → **stick to your guns** at **STICK**¹, → **jump the gun** at **JUMP**¹(11), → **be going great guns** at **GREAT**¹(11), → **spike sb's guns** at **SPIKE**²(6)

gun² *v* (**gunned**, **gunning**) **1 be gunning for sb** *informal* to be trying to find an opportunity to criticize or harm someone: *Why is he gunning for me?* **2 be gunning for sth** *informal* to be trying very hard to obtain something: *He's gunning for your job.* **3** [T] *AmE informal* to make the engine of a car go very fast by pressing the ACCELERATOR very hard

gun sb ↔ **down** *phr v* to shoot someone and badly injure or kill them, especially someone who cannot defend themselves: *A policeman was gunned down as he left his house this morning.*

gun·boat /ˈgʌnbəʊt $ -boʊt/ *n* [C] **1** a small ship that carries several large guns **2 gunboat diplomacy** the practice of threatening to use force against another country to make them agree to your demands

ˈgun ˌcarriage *n* [C] a frame with wheels on which a large heavy gun is moved around

ˈgun conˌtrol *n* [U] *law* laws that limit the ways in which guns can be sold, owned, and used

ˈgun dog *n* [C] a dog that is trained to find and bring back dead birds that have been shot for sport SYN **bird dog** *AmE*

gun·fight /ˈgʌnfaɪt/ *n* [C] a fight between people using guns —**gunfighter** *n* [C]

gun·fire /ˈgʌnfaɪə $ -faɪr/ *n* [U] the repeated shooting of guns, or the noise made by this: *I heard a* ***burst of*** *distant* ***gunfire***. | *Two men were shot in an* ***exchange of gunfire*** *with the police.*

gunge¹ /gʌndʒ/ *n* [U] *BrE informal* any substance that is dirty, sticky, or unpleasant SYN **gunk** *AmE* —**gungy** *adj*

gunge² *v* **be gunged up with sth** *BrE informal* to be blocked with a dirty sticky substance: *The waste pipe is all gunged up.*

gung-ho /ˌgʌŋ ˈhəʊ $ -ˈhoʊ/ *adj informal* very eager to do something dangerous or violent: *The sporting opportunities here should suit the most gung-ho of tourists.*

gunk¹ /gʌŋk/ *n* [U] *AmE informal* any substance that is dirty, sticky, or unpleasant SYN **gunge** *BrE* —**gunky** *adj*

gunk² *v* **be gunked up (with sth)** *AmE informal* to be blocked with a dirty sticky substance: *Here's your problem. The fuel line's all gunked up.*

gun·man /ˈgʌnmən/ ●●○ *n* (*plural* **gunmen** /-mən/) [C] a criminal who uses a gun

gun·met·al /ˈgʌnˌmetl/ *n* [U] **1** a dull grey-coloured metal which is a mixture of COPPER, TIN, and ZINC **2** a dull blue-grey colour

gun·nel /ˈɡʌnl/ *n* [C] a GUNWALE

gun·ner /ˈɡʌnə $ -ər/ *n* [C] **1** a soldier, sailor etc whose job is to aim or shoot a large gun **2** a soldier in the British ARTILLERY (=part of the army which uses heavy guns): *Gunner Smith*

gun·ner·y /ˈɡʌnəri/ *n* [U] the skill of shooting with large heavy guns: *a gunnery officer*

gun·ny·sack /ˈɡʌnisæk/ *n* [C] *AmE* a large bag made from rough material and used for storing grain, coal, potatoes etc

gun·point /ˈɡʌnpɔɪnt/ *n* **at gunpoint** while threatening someone or being threatened with a gun: *She was held at gunpoint for 37 hours.*

gun·pow·der /ˈɡʌnˌpaʊdə $ -ər/ *n* [U] an explosive substance used in bombs and FIREWORKS

ˈgun-ˌrunning *n* [U] the activity of taking guns into a country secretly and illegally, especially so that they can be used by people who want to fight against their government —**gun-runner** *n* [C]

gun·ship /ˈɡʌnʃɪp/ *n* [C] a military HELICOPTER used to protect other helicopters and to destroy enemy guns

gun·shot /ˈɡʌnʃɒt $ -ʃɑːt/ *n* **1** [C] the action of shooting a gun, or the sound that this makes: *She says she heard a gunshot at about midnight.* **2** [U] the bullets fired from a gun: ***gunshot wounds***

gun·sling·er /ˈɡʌnˌslɪŋə $ -ər/ *n* [C] *AmE informal* someone who is very skilful at using guns, especially a criminal

gun·smith /ˈɡʌnˌsmɪθ/ *n* [C] someone who makes and repairs guns

ˈgun-ˌtoting *adj* [only before noun] carrying a gun: *gun-toting gangs on the street*

gun·wale (*also* **gunnel**) /ˈɡʌnl/ *n* [C] the upper edge of the side of a boat or small ship

gup·py /ˈɡʌpi/ *n* (*plural* **guppies**) [C] a small brightly coloured tropical fish

gur·gle¹ /ˈɡɜːɡəl $ ˈɡɜːr-/ *v* [I] **1** if water gurgles, it flows along gently with a pleasant low sound SYN **burble**: *We could hear the stream gurgling down in the valley.* **2** if a baby gurgles, it makes a happy low sound in its throat

gurgle² *n* [C] **1** the happy low sound that someone makes in their throat: *a gurgle of laughter* **THESAURUS** SOUND **2** the pleasant low sound of water moving along gently

gur·ney /ˈɡɜːni $ ˈɡɜːr-/ *n* [C] *AmE* a long narrow table with wheels used for moving sick people in a hospital

gu·ru /ˈɡʊruː/ *n* [C] **1** *informal* someone who knows a lot about a particular subject, and gives advice to other people: *a management guru* | *a fashion guru* **2** a Hindu religious teacher or leader

gush¹ /ɡʌʃ/ *v* **1 a)** [I always + adv/prep] if a liquid gushes, it flows or pours out quickly and in large quantities SYN **spurt**: **[+out/from/down etc]** *Water gushed from the broken pipe.* | *He opened the door and smoke gushed out.* **b)** [T] if something gushes a liquid, the liquid pours out quickly and in large quantities SYN **spurt**: *The wound gushed blood.* **2** [I,T] to express your praise, pleasure etc in a way that other people think is too strong: *'I simply loved your book,' she gushed.* **3** (*also* **gush out**) [I] if words or emotions gush out, you suddenly express them very strongly: *All that pent-up frustration gushed out in a torrent of abuse.*

gush² *n* **1** [C usually singular] a large quantity of something, usually a liquid, that suddenly pours out of something SYN **spurt**: *a gush of ice-cold water* **2 a gush of relief/self-pity etc** a sudden feeling or expression of emotion

gush·er /ˈɡʌʃə $ -ər/ *n* [C] a place in the ground where oil or water comes out very forcefully, so that a pump is not needed

gush·ing /ˈɡʌʃɪŋ/ (*also* **gush·y** /ˈɡʌʃi/) *adj informal* expressing praise, pleasure etc in a way that other people think is too strong: *the gushing praise of the New York critics* —**gushingly** *adv*

gus·set /ˈɡʌsɪt/ *n* [C] a piece of material that is stitched into a piece of clothing to make it stronger, wider, or more comfortable in a particular place

gus·sy /ˈɡʌsi/ *v* (**gussied**, **gussying**, **gussies**)

gussy sb/sth ↔ **up** *phr v AmE informal* to make someone look attractive by dressing them in their best clothes, or to make something look attractive by decorating it: *All the girls will be gussied up for the party.*

gust¹ /ɡʌst/ *n* [C] **1** a sudden strong movement of wind, air, rain etc: **[+of]** *A sudden gust of wind blew the door shut.* | *Gusts of up to 200 kph may be experienced.* **2 gust of laughter** a sound of loud laughter

gust² *v* [I] if the wind gusts, it blows strongly with sudden short movements: *winds gusting at up to 45 miles per hour*

gus·to /ˈɡʌstəʊ $ -toʊ/ *n* [U] **with gusto** if you do something with gusto, you do it with a lot of eagerness and energy: *They sang hymns with great gusto.*

gust·y /ˈɡʌsti/ *adj* with wind blowing in strong sudden movements: *a cold gusty October night*

gut¹ /ɡʌt/ ●●○ *n*

1 gut reaction/feeling/instinct *informal* a reaction or feeling that you are sure is right, although you cannot give a reason for it: *He had a gut feeling that Sarah was lying.*

2 COURAGE **guts** [plural] *informal* the courage and determination you need to do something difficult or unpleasant: *It **takes guts** to start a new business on your own.* | **have the guts (to do sth)** *No one had the guts to tell Paul what a mistake he was making.*

3 INSIDE YOUR BODY **a) guts** [plural] all the organs in someone's body, especially when they have come out of their body: *There were blood and guts all over the place.* **b)** [C] the tube through which food passes from your stomach SYN **intestine**: *It can take 72 hours for food to pass through the gut.*

4 STOMACH [C] *informal* someone's stomach, especially when it is large SYN **belly**: *He felt as if someone had just kicked him in the gut.* | *Phil has a huge **beer gut*** (=unattractive fat stomach caused by drinking too much beer).

5 STRING [U] a type of strong string made from the INTESTINE of an animal, and used for musical instruments such as VIOLINS → CATGUT

6 MACHINE/EQUIPMENT **guts** [plural] *informal* the parts inside a machine or piece of equipment

7 MOST IMPORTANT PARTS **guts** [plural] *informal* the most important or basic parts of something: **[+of]** *the guts of the problem*

8 work/sweat your guts out (*also* **slog your guts out** *BrE*) *informal* to work very hard

9 at gut level if you know something at gut level, you feel sure about it, though you could not give a reason for it: *She knew at gut level that he was guilty.*

10 I'll have sb's guts for garters *BrE informal* used to say that you would like to punish someone severely for something they have done → BLOOD-AND-GUTS, → **bust a gut** at BUST¹(3), → **hate sb's guts** at HATE¹(2), → **spill your guts** at SPILL¹(4)

gut² *v* (**gutted**, **gutting**) [T] **1** to completely destroy the inside of a building, especially by fire: *The building was gutted by fire.* GRAMMAR **Gut** is often passive in this meaning. **2** to remove the organs from inside a fish or animal in order to prepare it for cooking **3** to change something by removing some of the most important or central parts → GUTTED

gut·less /ˈɡʌtləs/ *adj informal* lacking courage or determination SYN **spineless**: *I should have had the support of my team, but they were really gutless.*

guts·y /ˈɡʌtsi/ *adj informal* **1** if someone's behaviour is gutsy, it is brave and determined: *It was a gutsy performance by McTaggart.* **2** if something is gutsy, it is strong and interesting: *a gutsy full-bodied wine*

gut·ted /ˈɡʌtɪd/ *adj* **1** seriously damaged or completely destroyed: *We drove slowly past the gutted buildings.*

G

2 *BrE spoken* very shocked or disappointed SYN **devastated**: *I was gutted when I lost my job.* **THESAURUS** DISAPPOINTED

gut·ter¹ /ˈɡʌtə $ -ər/ ●○○ *n*
1 [C] the low part at the edge of a road where water collects and flows away: *The gutters were blocked and overflowing.*
2 [C] an open pipe fixed to the edge of a roof to collect and carry away rainwater → see picture at ROOF¹
3 the gutter the bad social conditions of the lowest and poorest level of society: *Men like him usually ended up in jail – or the gutter.*
4 the gutter press *BrE* the newspapers that print shocking stories about people's personal lives – used to show disapproval → **tabloid**

gutter² *v* [I] *literary* if a CANDLE gutters, it burns with an unsteady flame

gut·ter·ing /ˈɡʌtərɪŋ/ *n* [U] *BrE* the open pipes that are fixed to the edge of the roof of a house to collect and carry away rainwater

gut·ter·snipe /ˈɡʌtəsnaɪp $ -ər-/ *n* [C] *old-fashioned* a dirty untidy badly behaved child from a poor home

gut·tur·al /ˈɡʌtərəl/ *adj* a guttural voice or sound is or seems to be produced deep in someone's throat SYN **throaty**

ˈgut-ˌwrenching *adj* making you feel very upset or anxious: *a gut-wrenching description of life in the war zone*

guv /ɡʌv/ *n BrE spoken* used by men, as a way of talking to a male customer in a shop, taxi etc: *Where to, guv?*

guv·nor, **guv'nor** /ˈɡʌvnə $ -ər/ *n BrE spoken old-fashioned informal* **1** [C] a man who is in a position of authority over you, usually your employer: *You'll have to speak to the guvnor about that.* **2** used as a way of talking to a man of a higher social class than you

guy /ɡaɪ/ ●●● S1 W3 *n* [C]
1 *informal* a man SYN **bloke**: *Dave's a nice guy when you get to know him. | Jake's a real tough guy.* **THESAURUS** MAN
2 *BrE* a model of a man burnt every year on Guy Fawkes Night, in Britain
3 (*also* **guy rope**) a rope that stretches from the top or side of a tent or pole to the ground to keep it in the right position
4 guys [plural] *AmE spoken* used when talking to or about a group of people, male or female: *Hey you guys! Where are you going?*
5 no more Mr Nice Guy! *spoken* used to say that you will stop trying to behave honestly and fairly → **wise guy** at WISE¹(5)

Guy Fawkes Night /ˌɡaɪ ˈfɔːks naɪt $ -ˈfɒːks-/ *n BrE* November 5th, when people in Britain light FIREWORKS and burn a GUY on a fire SYN **Bonfire Night**

guz·zle /ˈɡʌzəl/ *v* [I,T] *informal* **1** to eat or drink a lot of something, eagerly and quickly – usually showing disapproval → **scoff**: *They've been guzzling beer all evening.* **2** if a vehicle guzzles petrol, it uses a lot of it in a wasteful way → GAS-GUZZLER

gym /dʒɪm/ ●●● S3 *n*
1 [C] a special building or room that has equipment for doing physical exercise SYN **gymnasium**: **at/in a gym** *I try and work out at the local gym once a week. | I* **go to the gym** *as often as I can.*
2 [U] exercises that people do indoors for physical development and as a sport, especially at school: *We've got gym this afternoon. | Where's my* **gym kit**?

ˈgym ˌbunny *n* [C] *informal* someone who spends a lot of time exercising at the gym in order to look attractive

gym·kha·na /dʒɪmˈkɑːnə/ *n* [C] *BrE* a sporting event at which people on horses compete in races and jumping competitions

G

gym·na·si·um /dʒɪmˈneɪziəm/ *n* (*plural* **gymnasiums** *or* **gymnasia**) [C] *formal* a GYM

gym·nast /ˈdʒɪmnæst, -nəst/ *n* [C] someone who is good at gymnastics and competes against other people in gymnastics competitions

gym·nas·tics /dʒɪmˈnæstɪks/ ●●○ *n*
1 [U] a sport involving physical exercises and movements that need skill, strength, and control, and that are often performed in competitions: *a gymnastics display | We don't do gymnastics at school.*

GRAMMAR: Singular or plural verb?
In this meaning, **gymnastics** is followed by a singular verb: ***Gymnastics is*** *one of the most popular Olympic events.*
GRAMMAR GUIDE ▸ NOUNS

2 mental/intellectual/moral gymnastics [plural] very clever thinking
3 verbal/linguistic gymnastics [plural] using words in a very clever way —**gymnastic** *adj*: *The girls went through their gymnastic routine.*

ˈgym rat *n* [C] *informal* someone who spends a lot of time exercising at the GYM

ˈgym shoe *n* [C] a light shoe with a cloth top and a flat rubber bottom that children wear for games and sport at school SYN **plimsoll** *BrE*

gym·slip /ˈdʒɪmˌslɪp/ *n* [C] *BrE* a type of dress without sleeves that girls wore in the past over a shirt as a part of their school uniform

ˈgymslip ˌmother *n* [C] *BrE informal* a schoolgirl who has a baby – used in newspapers: *The video is intended to deter schoolgirls from becoming gymslip mothers.*

gy·nae·col·o·gy *BrE*, **gynecology** *AmE* /ˌɡaɪnəˈkɒlədʒi $ -ˈkɑː-/ *n* [U] the study and treatment of medical conditions and illnesses that affect only women, and usually relating to a woman's ability to have babies —**gynaecologist** *n* [C] —**gynaecological** /ˌɡaɪnəkəˈlɒdʒɪkəl◂ $ -ˈlɑː-/ *adj*

gyp¹ /dʒɪp/ *n informal* **1 give sb gyp** *BrE* **a)** to be painful: *My bad leg is really giving me gyp today.* **b)** to punish someone or be angry with them because of something they have done **2** [singular] *AmE* **a)** something that you were tricked into buying **b)** a situation in which you feel you have been cheated: *What a gyp!*

gyp² *v* (**gypped**, **gypping**) [T] *AmE informal* to cheat someone: *Ten bucks? You've been gypped!*

gyp·sum /ˈdʒɪpsəm/ *n* [U] a soft white substance that is used to make PLASTER OF PARIS

gyp·sy, **gipsy** /ˈdʒɪpsi/ ●○○ *n* (*plural* **gypsies**) [C]
1 a member of a group of people originally from India, who traditionally live and travel around in CARAVANS, and who now live all over the world. Most gypsies prefer to be called ROMANIES. → **traveller**
2 someone who does not like to stay in the same place for a long time

gy·rate /dʒaɪˈreɪt $ ˈdʒaɪreɪt/ *v* **1** [I,T] to turn around fast in circles SYN **spin**: *The dancers gyrated wildly to the beat of the music.* **2** [I] if the value of money in business gyrates, it moves up and down a lot → **fluctuate**: *Stock and bond markets have gyrated in recent weeks.* —**gyration** /dʒaɪˈreɪʃən/ *n* [C,U]

gy·ro·scope /ˈdʒaɪrəskəʊp $ -skoʊp/ *n* [C] a wheel that spins inside a frame and is used for keeping ships and aircraft steady. It can also be a child's toy. —**gyroscopic** /ˌdʒaɪrəˈskɒpɪk◂ $ -ˈskɑː-/ *adj*

G

Hh

H, h /eɪtʃ/ *n* (*plural* **H's, h's**) [C,U] the eighth letter of the English alphabet → **AITCH, H-BOMB**

ha, hah /hɑː/ *interjection* used when you are surprised or have discovered something interesting: *Ha! I thought it might be you hiding there!*

ha·be·as cor·pus /ˌheɪbiəs ˈkɔːpəs $ -ˈkɔːr-/ *n* [U] *law* a law which says that a person can only be kept in prison following a court's decision

hab·er·dash·er /ˈhæbədæʃə $ -bərdæʃər/ *n* [C] *old-fashioned* a shopkeeper who sells haberdashery

hab·er·dash·er·y /ˈhæbədæʃəri $ -bər-/ *n* (*plural* **haberdasheries**) **1** [C] *BrE* a shop or part of a large store where things used for making clothes are sold **2** [C] *AmE old-fashioned* a shop or part of a large store where men's clothes, especially hats, are sold **3** [U] the goods sold in these shops

hab·it /ˈhæbɪt/ ●●● S3 W3 *n*

1 USUAL/REGULAR [C,U] something that you do regularly or usually, often without thinking about it because you have done it so many times before: *Regular exercise is a good habit.* | *Thinking negatively can become a habit.* | *She has a habit of playing with her hair when she's nervous.* | *Some people drink alcohol as much from habit as from desire.* | **by/out of/from habit** (=because this is what you usually do in this situation) *I did it out of habit.*

2 DRUGS [C] a strong physical need to keep taking a drug regularly: *A lot of drug addicts get into petty crime to support their habit.* | **heroin/cocaine etc habit** *His cocaine habit ruined him physically and financially.*

3 not make a habit of (doing) sth *spoken* used to say that someone does not usually do something bad or wrong, or should not do it again: *You're ten minutes late. I hope you're not going to make a habit of this.*

4 I'm not in the habit of doing sth *spoken* used when you are annoyed, to say that you would not do something: *I'm not in the habit of lying to my friends.*

5 have a habit of doing sth if something has a habit of doing something, it usually or often does it - used humorously: *Life has a habit of springing surprises.*

6 old habits die hard used to say that it is difficult to make people change their attitudes or behaviour: *She knew it probably wasn't necessary anymore, but old habits die hard.*

7 habit of thought/mind the way someone usually thinks about something, or their usual attitudes

8 CLOTHING [C] a long loose piece of clothing worn by people in some religious groups: *a nun's habit* → **a creature of habit** at **CREATURE(3)**

COLLOCATIONS

VERBS

have a habit (of doing sth) *He has a habit of being late.*
sth becomes a habit *Once you have been driving for a few weeks, it becomes a habit.*
get into a habit (=start doing something regularly or often) *Try to get into the habit of walking for 30 minutes each day.*
get out of a habit (=stop doing something regularly or often) *She couldn't get out of the habit of saying 'sorry'.*
break/kick a habit (=stop doing something that is bad for you) *I've smoked for years, but I really want to kick the habit.*
develop/form a habit | **change your habits**

ADJECTIVES

a good/bad habit *Eating healthy food as snacks is a good habit to get into.*
eating/drinking habits (=the kinds of things you eat or drink regularly) *You need to change your eating habits.*
buying/spending habits (=the kinds of things you buy regularly) | **viewing habits** (=the kinds of television shows you regularly watch) | **personal habits** (=the things you normally do each day, for example keeping yourself clean or whether you smoke) | **an annoying/unpleasant/nasty habit** | **a strange/peculiar/odd habit**

PHRASES

be in the habit of doing sth *On Friday evenings, Carrie was in the habit of visiting her parents.*
(by/from) force of habit (=used about a habit that is difficult to change) *I still walk by his house each day - force of habit, I suppose.*
change/break the habits of a lifetime (=stop doing the things you have done for many years)

THESAURUS

habit something you do regularly, often without thinking about it: *Biting your nails is a bad habit.* | *I always go to the same supermarket, out of habit.*
custom something that people in a particular society do because it is traditional or the accepted thing to do: *In Japan, it is the custom to take off your shoes when you enter a house.*
tradition a belief, custom, or way of doing something that has existed for a long time: *The tradition of giving Easter eggs goes back hundreds of years.*
practice something that people often do, especially as part of their work or daily life: *The hotel has ended the practice of leaving chocolates in guests' rooms.*

hab·it·a·ble /ˈhæbətəbəl/ *adj* good enough for people to live in: *It would cost a fortune to make the place habitable.*

hab·i·tat /ˈhæbətæt/ ●○○ *n* [C,U] the natural home of a plant or animal: *watching monkeys in their* ***natural habitat*** | *The grassland is an important habitat for many wild flowers.*

hab·i·ta·tion /ˌhæbɪˈteɪʃən/ *n formal* **1 unfit for human habitation** a building that is unfit for human habitation is not safe or healthy for people to live in **2** [U] the act of living in a place: *There was no sign of habitation as far as the eye could see.* **3** [C] a house or place to live in

ˈhabit-ˌforming *adj* a drug or activity that is habit-forming makes you want to keep taking it, keep doing it etc

ha·bit·u·al /həˈbɪtʃuəl/ *adj* **1** [only before noun] doing something from habit, and unable to stop doing it: **habitual criminal/offender** | **habitual drinker/smoker/gambler** **2** done as a habit that you cannot stop: *His drinking had become habitual.* **3** [only before noun] usual or typical of someone: *James took his habitual morning walk around the garden.* —**habitually** *adv*: *men who are habitually violent*

ha·bit·u·ate /həˈbɪtʃueɪt/ *v* **be/become habituated to (doing) sth** *formal* to be used to something or gradually become used to it: *Over the centuries, these animals have become habituated to living in a dry environment.*

ha·bit·u·é /həˈbɪtʃueɪ/ *n* [C + of] *formal* someone who regularly goes to a particular place or event SYN **regular**

ha·ci·en·da /ˌhæsiˈendə/ *n* [C] a large farm in Spanish-speaking countries

hack[1] /hæk/ ●○○ *v*

1 [I,T] to cut something roughly or violently: **hack (away) at sth** *She hacked away at the ice, trying to make a hole.* | **hack sth off/down etc** *Whole forests have been hacked down.* | **hack your way through/into sth** *He hacked his way through the undergrowth.* | *Both men had been* ***hacked to death*** (=killed using large knives).

2 [I,T] to secretly find a way of getting information from someone else's computer or changing information on it:

H

[+into] *Somebody hacked into the company's central database.* | *He managed to hack the code.* → HACKER
3 can't hack sth *informal* to feel that you cannot continue to do something that is difficult or boring: *I've been doing this job for years, but I just can't hack it anymore.*
4 [I always + adv/prep] *BrE* to ride a horse along roads or through the country
5 [I] to cough in a loud unpleasant way
hack sb **off** *phr v BrE informal* to annoy someone: *His attitude really hacks me off!*

hack² /hæk/ *n* [C] **1** a writer who does a lot of low-quality work, especially writing newspaper articles: *A Sunday newspaper hack uncovered the story.* **2** an unimportant politician: *The meeting was attended by the usual old party hacks.* **3** a way of using a computer to get into someone else's computer system without their permission **4** *AmE informal* a taxi, or a taxi driver **5** an act of hitting something roughly with a cutting tool: *One more hack and the branch was off.* **6** an old tired horse **7** a horse you can pay money to ride on **8** *BrE* a ride on a horse: *a long hack across the fields*

ˌhacked ˈoff *adj BrE informal* extremely annoyed: *I'm getting really hacked off about the whole thing.*

hack·er /ˈhækə $ -ər/ *n* [C] *informal* someone who secretly uses or changes the information in other people's computer systems: *A hacker had managed to get into the system.* —**hacking** *n* [U]: *the threat of hacking and computer viruses*

ˌhacking ˈcough *n* [usually singular] a repeated painful cough with an unpleasant sound

hack·les /ˈhækəlz/ *n* [plural] **1 sb's hackles rise** if someone's hackles rise, they begin to feel very angry, because someone's behaviour or attitude offends them: *Laura heard his remark, and felt her hackles rising.* | **raise sb's hackles** (=make someone angry) *His tactless remarks were enough to raise anyone's hackles.* **2** the long feathers or hairs on the back of the neck of some animals and birds, which stand up straight when they are frightened or ready to fight

hack·ney car·riage /ˈhækni ˌkærɪdʒ/ *n* [C] *BrE* **1** a carriage pulled by a horse, used in the past like a taxi **2** (*also* **hackney cab** *formal*) a taxi

hack·neyed /ˈhæknid/ *adj* a hackneyed phrase is boring and does not have much meaning because it has been used so often

hack·saw /ˈhæksɔː $ -sɒː/ *n* [C] a cutting tool with small teeth on its blade, used especially for cutting metal → see picture at TOOL¹

hack·ti·vist /ˈhæktɪvɪst/ *n* [C] *informal* a HACKER who HACKS into other computers for political reasons —**hacktivism** *n* [U]

had /d, əd, həd; *strong* hæd/ the past tense and past participle of HAVE

had·dock /ˈhædək/ *n* (*plural* **haddock**) [C,U] a common fish that lives in northern seas and is often used as food

Ha·des /ˈheɪdiːz/ *n* [U] the land of the dead in the stories of ancient Greece SYN **hell**

had·n't /ˈhædnt/ short for 'had not': *If I hadn't seen it myself, I'd never have believed it.*

hae·ma·tol·o·gy *BrE*, **hematology** *AmE* /ˌhiːməˈtɒlədʒi $ -ˈtɑː-/ *n* [U] the scientific study of blood

hae·mo·glo·bin *BrE*, **hemoglobin** *AmE* /ˌhiːməˈgləʊbɪn $ -ˈgloʊ-/ *n* [U] a red substance in the blood that contains iron and carries oxygen

hae·mo·phil·i·a *BrE*, **hemophilia** *AmE* /ˌhiːməˈfɪliə/ *n* [U] a serious disease that prevents a person's blood from becoming thick, so that they lose a lot of blood easily if they are injured

hae·mo·phil·i·ac *BrE*, **hemophiliac** *AmE* /ˌhiːməˈfɪliæk/ *n* [C] a person who suffers from haemophilia

hae·mor·rhage¹ *BrE*, **hemorrhage** *AmE* /ˈhemərɪdʒ/ *n* [C,U] **1** a serious medical condition in which a person BLEEDs a lot, sometimes inside their body: *He died of a massive* ***brain haemorrhage***. **2** when a company or country loses a lot of money or people very quickly: **[+of]** *a haemorrhage of jobs from the region*

haemorrhage² *BrE*, **hemorrhage** *AmE v* **1** [I] to lose a lot of blood in a very short time **2** [T] to lose a lot of something over a short period of time, such as money or jobs: *The once prosperous town has hemorrhaged manufacturing jobs over the last 15 years.*

hae·mor·rhoids *BrE*, **hemorrhoids** *AmE* /ˈhemərɔɪdz/ *n* [plural] painfully swollen BLOOD VESSELS near a person's ANUS SYN **piles**

haft /hɑːft $ hæft/ *n* [C] *technical* a long handle on an AXE¹ or other weapon

hag /hæg/ *n* [C] *old-fashioned* an ugly or unpleasant woman, especially one who is old or looks like a WITCH

hag·gard /ˈhægəd $ -ərd/ *adj* someone who looks haggard has lines on their face and dark marks around their eyes, especially because they are ill, worried, or tired: *Sam looked tired and haggard.* | *a haggard face*

hag·gis /ˈhægɪs/ *n* [C,U] a food eaten in Scotland, made from the heart and other organs of a sheep, cut up and boiled in a skin made from the sheep's stomach

hag·gle /ˈhægəl/ *v* [I] to argue when you are trying to agree about the price of something: **[+over]** *tourists haggling over the price of souvenirs* | **[+with]** *Ted was haggling with the street vendors.* —**haggling** *n* [U]

hag·i·og·ra·phy /ˌhægiˈɒgrəfi $ -ˈɑːg-/ *n* (*plural* **hagiographies**) [C,U] **1** a book about the lives of SAINTS **2** a book about someone that praises them too much

hah /hɑː/ *interjection* another spelling of HA

ˌha-ˈha *interjection* **1** used in writing to represent a shout of laughter **2** *spoken* used, sometimes angrily, to show that you do not think something is funny: *Oh, very funny, John, ha-ha.*

hai·ku /ˈhaɪkuː/ *n* (*plural* **haiku** *or* **haikus**) [C] a type of Japanese poem with three lines consisting of five, seven, and five SYLLABLES

hail¹ /heɪl/ ●○○ *v*
1 [T] to describe someone or something as being very good: **hail sb/sth as sth** *Lang's first film was immediately hailed as a masterpiece.* | **be hailed sth** *The new service has been* ***hailed a success***. | *A young man is being* ***hailed a hero*** *tonight after rescuing two children.*
2 [T] to call to someone in order to greet them or try to attract their attention: *She leaned out of the window and hailed a passerby.* | **hail a cab/taxi** *The hotel doorman will hail a cab for you.*
3 it hails if it hails, small balls of ice fall like rain: *It's windy and hailing outside.*
hail from sth *phr v old-fashioned* to have been born in a particular place: *And where do you hail from?*

hail² *n* **1** [U] frozen raindrops which fall as hard balls of ice: *heavy showers of rain and hail* THESAURUS ▸ RAIN **2 a hail of bullets/stones etc** a large number of bullets, stones etc that are thrown or fired at someone: *The aircraft were met by a hail of gunfire.* **3 a hail of criticism/abuse etc** a lot of criticism etc: *The proposals met with a hail of criticism.*

Hail Ma·ry /ˌheɪl ˈmeəri $ -ˈmeri/ *n* [C] a special Roman Catholic prayer to Mary, the mother of Jesus

ˌHail ˈMary pass (*also* **ˌHail ˈMary play**) *n* [C] *AmE* **1** in American football, a long throw forward that you hope will be caught successfully, although it is unlikely, so that your team will score a point when you do not have much time to do this **2** an action you take that is unlikely to succeed, and which you only take because there is no other way of achieving something

hail·stone, **hail stone** /ˈheɪlstəʊn $ -stoʊn/ *n* [C] a small ball of frozen rain

hail·storm /ˈheɪlstɔːm $ -ɔːrm/ *n* [C] a storm when a lot of HAIL falls

hair /heə $ her/ ●●● S1 W1 *n*
1 [U] the mass of things like fine threads that grows on your head: *Her hair was short and dark.* | *a short fat man with no hair on his head* | **fair-haired/dark-haired/long-haired etc** *He's a tall fair-haired guy.*

GRAMMAR: Countable or uncountable?

Hair is only used as an uncountable noun in this meaning: *He has black hair.* ✗ Don't say: *He has black hairs.*

2 [C] one of the long fine things like thread that grows on people's heads and on other parts of their bodies, or similar things that grow on animals: *The cat has left white hairs all over the sofa.* | *I'm starting to get a few grey hairs.* | **long-haired/short-haired** *long-haired cats*
3 be tearing/pulling your hair out to be very worried or angry about something, especially because you do not know what to do: *Anyone else would have been tearing their hair out trying to follow these instructions.*
4 let your hair down *informal* to enjoy yourself and start to relax, especially after working very hard: *The party gave us all a chance to really let our hair down.*
5 bad hair day a day when your hair does not look tidy or neat even when you try to arrange it carefully – used humorously: *I'm* ***having*** *a bit of* ***a bad hair day***.
6 keep your hair on *BrE spoken* used to tell someone to keep calm and not get annoyed: *All right, all right, keep your hair on! I'm sorry.*
7 get in sb's hair *informal* to annoy someone, especially by always being near them
8 make sb's hair stand on end to make someone very frightened
9 make sb's hair curl if a story, experience etc makes your hair curl, it is very surprising, frightening, or shocking: *tales that would make your hair curl*
10 not have a hair out of place to have a very neat appearance
11 not turn a hair to remain completely calm when something bad or surprising suddenly happens
12 not harm/touch a hair of/on sb's head to not harm someone in any way
13 the hair of the dog (that bit you) alcohol that you drink to cure a headache caused by drinking too much alcohol the night before – used humorously → **have a good/fine/thick etc head of hair** at HEAD[1](14), → **not see hide nor hair of** at HIDE[2](5), → **split hairs** at SPLIT[1](8)

COLLOCATIONS

COLOUR

dark *He's about six feet tall, with dark hair and blue eyes.*
black | **jet black** *literary* (=completely black)
fair *Her long fair hair fell untidily over her shoulders.*
blond/blonde (=yellowish-white in colour) | **golden**
brown *Her hair was pale brown.*
chestnut *literary* (=dark brown) | **sandy** (=yellowish-brown) | **mousy** (=an unattractive dull brown)
red *The whole family had red hair.*
ginger *BrE* (=orange-brown in colour) | **auburn** *literary* (=orange-brown in colour)
white *an old man with white hair*
grey *BrE*, **gray** *AmE* | **silver**

LENGTH

short *I like your hair when it's short like that.*
long *A few of the boys had long hair.*
shoulder-length/medium-length *He had shoulder-length reddish hair.*

TYPE

straight *a girl with long straight hair*
curly *When he was young, his hair was thick and curly.*
frizzy (=tightly curled) | **wavy** (=with loose curls) | **thick** | **fine** (=thin) | **spiky** (=stiff and standing up on top of your head)

CONDITION

in good/bad/terrible etc condition *How do you keep your hair in such perfect condition?*
out of condition (=no longer in good condition)
glossy/shiny *She combed her hair until it was all glossy.*
lustrous *literary* (=very shiny and attractive) | **dull** (=not shiny)
greasy (=containing too much oil) *This shampoo is ideal for greasy hair.*
dry (=lacking oil) | **lank** *especially literary* (= thin, straight, and unattractive) | **thinning** (=becoming thinner because you are losing your hair) | **receding** (=gradually disappearing, so that it is high on your forehead)

VERBS

have ... hair *She has beautiful blonde hair.*
brush/comb your hair *He cleaned his teeth and brushed his hair.*
wash your hair *He showered and washed his hair.*
do your hair (*also* **fix your hair** *AmE*) (=arrange it in a style) *She's upstairs doing her hair.*
have your hair cut/done/permed (*also* **get your hair cut etc**) (=by a hairdresser) *I need to get my hair cut.*
cut sb's hair *My mum always cuts my hair.*
dye your hair (blonde/red etc) (=change its colour, especially using chemicals) | **wear your hair long/in a ponytail etc** (=have that style of hair) | **grow your hair (long)** (=let it grow longer)
lose your hair (=become bald) *He was a small, round man who was losing his hair.*
run your fingers through sb's hair (=touch someone's hair in a loving way) | **ruffle sb's hair** (=rub it in a kind friendly way)

hair + NOUN

hair loss *The drug can cause hair loss.*
hair colour *BrE*, **hair color** *AmE* *Genes control characteristics such as hair colour and eye colour.*
hair dye

PHRASES

a strand/wisp of hair (=a thin piece of hair) *She brushed away a strand of hair from her eyes.*
a lock of hair (=a fairly thick piece of hair) | **a mop of hair** (=a large amount of thick untidy hair)

COMMON ERRORS

⚠ Don't say 'I cut my hair' if another person cut your hair for you. Say **I had my hair cut**.

hair·brush /ˈheəbrʌʃ $ ˈher-/ *n* [C] a brush you use on your hair to make it smooth

hair·care, **hair care** /ˈheəkeə $ ˈherker/ *n* [U] the act of washing and drying your hair and shaping it into a style: *advice on make-up and hair care* —**haircare** *adj* [only before noun]: *haircare products*

hair·cloth /ˈheəklɒθ $ ˈherklɒːθ/ *n* [U] a type of rough material made from animal hair

hair·cut /ˈheəkʌt $ ˈher-/ ●●○ *n* [C]
1 when you have a haircut, someone cuts your hair for you: **have/get a haircut** *I haven't had a haircut for months!*
2 the style your hair is cut in: *Do you like my new haircut?*
3 take a haircut *informal* to agree to accept less money for something: *They may have to take a haircut on their investment.*

hair·do /ˈheədu: $ ˈher-/ *n* (*plural* **hairdos**) [C] *informal* the style in which someone's hair is cut or shaped SYN **hairstyle**

hair·dress·er /ˈheəˌdresə $ ˈherˌdresər/ ●●○ *n* [C]
1 a person who cuts, washes, and arranges people's hair in particular styles → **barber**
2 the hairdresser's *BrE* the hairdresser's shop SYN **salon** → **barber's**: *an appointment at the hairdresser's* —**hairdressing** *n* [U]

hair·dry·er, **hairdrier** /ˈheəˌdraɪə $ ˈherˌdraɪər/ ●●○ *n* [C] a machine that blows out hot air for drying hair SYN **blow-dryer**

hair·grip /ˈheəgrɪp $ ˈher-/ *n* [C] *BrE* a small thin piece

H

of metal that a woman uses to hold her hair in place SYN **bobby pin** *AmE*

hair·less /ˈheələs $ ˈher-/ *adj* with no hair SYN **bald**: *Young rabbits are born blind and hairless.*

hair·line /ˈheəlaɪn $ ˈher-/ *n* [C] **1** the line around your head, especially at the front, where your hair starts growing: *He had put on weight, and his hairline was beginning to recede.* **2 a hairline crack/fracture** a very thin crack: *a hairline fracture in a bone*

hair·net /ˈheənet $ ˈher-/ *n* [C] a very thin net that stretches over your hair to keep it in place → see picture at NET[1]

hair·piece /ˈheəpiːs $ ˈher-/ *n* [C] a piece of false hair that you wear on your head to make your own hair look thicker → **wig**, **toupée**

hair·pin /ˈheəˌpɪn $ ˈher-/ *n* [C] a pin made of wire bent into a U-shape to hold long hair in position

ˌhairpin ˈbend (*also* **ˌhairpin ˈturn** *AmE*) *n* [C] a very sharp U-shaped curve in a road

ˈhair-raising *adj* frightening and dangerous in a way that is exciting: *a hair-raising car chase* **THESAURUS** FRIGHTENING

ˈhair's breadth *n* [singular] a very small amount or distance: *The bullet missed me by a hair's breadth.*

ˌhair ˈshirt *n* [C] a shirt made of rough uncomfortable cloth containing hair, worn in the past by some religious people to punish themselves

ˈhair slide *n* [C] *BrE* a small attractive metal or plastic object that a woman uses to fasten her hair in place SYN **barrette** *AmE*

ˈhair-splitting *n* [U] when people pay too much attention to small differences and unimportant details, especially in an argument → **split hairs** at SPLIT[1](8)

hair·spray /ˈheəspreɪ $ ˈher-/ *n* [U] a sticky liquid that you SPRAY on your hair to keep it in place

hair·style /ˈheəstaɪl $ ˈher-/ ●●○ *n* [C] the style in which someone's hair has been cut or shaped: *Do you like my new hairstyle?*

ˌhair ˈtrigger *n* [C] a TRIGGER[1] on a gun that needs very little pressure to fire the gun

ˈhair-trigger *adj* [only before noun] easily made angry: *his hair-trigger temperament*

hair·y /ˈheəri $ ˈheri/ *adj* (*comparative* **hairier**, *superlative* **hairiest**) **1** a hairy person or animal has a lot of hair on their body: *a skinny guy with hairy legs* | *a hairy caterpillar* **2** *informal* dangerous or frightening, often in a way that is exciting: *It was pretty hairy climbing down the cliff.* | *a few hairy moments* —**hairiness** *n* [U]

haj, **hajj** /hædʒ/ *n* [C] a journey to Makkah (Mecca) for religious reasons, that all Muslims try to make at least once in their life

haj·ji /ˈhædʒi/ *n* [C] used as a title for a Muslim who has made a haj

hake /heɪk/ *n* (*plural* **hake**) [C,U] a sea fish, used as food

ha·kim /hɑːˈkiːm/ *n* [C] a Muslim doctor

ha·lal /hɑːˈlɑːl/ *adj* halal meat is meat from an animal that has been killed in a way that is approved by Muslim law

hal·berd /ˈhælbəd $ -ərd/ *n* [C] a type of sword that was used as a weapon in the past

hal·cy·on /ˈhælsiən/ *adj* **halcyon days** *literary* a time in the past when you were very happy

hale /heɪl/ *adj* **hale and hearty** someone, especially an old person, who is hale and hearty is very healthy and active: *She's still hale and hearty at 74.*

half[1] /hɑːf $ hæf/ ●●● S1 W1 *predeterminer, pron, adj* [only before noun]

1 50% exactly or about 50% (½) of an amount, time, distance, number etc: **[+of]** *Over half of the children live in one-parent families.* | *Only half the guests had arrived by seven o'clock.* | *If you look at our members, at least half are women.* | **half a mile/pound/hour etc** *half a pound of butter* | *It's about half a mile down the road.* | *She drank half a bottle of wine.* | ***half a million*** *dollars* | **a half hour/mile etc** *You can't just waltz in a half hour late.* | *It's about a half mile down the road.* | *a half day excursion to the island* | *He demanded a half share of the money.* | **half the price/size/length etc** *It's only half the size of a normal violin.* | *They offered to pay half the cost of repairs.*

2 MOST OF the largest part of something: **[+of]** *We missed half of what he said because someone was talking.* | *She seems to be asleep **half the time**.* | *Getting covered in mud is **half the fun**.*

3 TIME **half past one/two/three etc** *especially BrE* (*also* **half one/two/three etc** *BrE spoken*) 30 minutes after the hour mentioned: *I got home at about half past one.* | *I rang at about half six.* | *We'll be there by seven or half past* (=half past seven).

4 half a dozen a) six: *half a dozen eggs* **b)** a small number of people or things: *There were half a dozen other people in front of me.*

5 half a/the chance a small opportunity to do something, especially one which someone would take eagerly: *I'd go to university if I **got half the chance**.* | *Many kids would sleep till noon **given half a chance**.*

6 half an eye/ear if you have half an eye on something, or if you are listening with half an ear, you are giving only part of your attention to it: *He listened with only half an ear*

and his thoughts wandered. | *The teacher kept half an eye on them all through the lesson.*
7 be half the battle *spoken* used to say that when you have done the most difficult part of an activity, the rest is easy: *Getting the audience to like you is half the battle.*
8 half a minute/moment/second etc *spoken* a very short time: *Hold on, this will only take half a second.*
9 only half the story an explanation that is not complete, used especially to say that someone is trying to keep something secret: *Journalists are convinced that she was only telling them half the story.*
10 have half a mind to do sth *spoken* used to say that you would like to do something but you probably will not do it: *He had half a mind to ask for his money back.* | *I have half a mind to tell your mother about this.*
11 half measures actions or methods that are not strong enough, and so are not effective in dealing with a difficult problem: *This is no time for half measures.*
12 half a loaf (is better than none) something that is less than what you wanted or asked for, but that you might accept because it is better than nothing

GRAMMAR

Numbers with half

• You say **one and a half, two and a half** etc: *She is two and a half.* ✗ Don't say: *one and half* | *two and half*
• The phrases **one and a half, two and a half** etc are followed by a plural noun: *We were there for one and a half days.* ✗ Don't say: *We were there for one and a half day.*

Singular or plural verb?

• You can use **half (of)** with a plural noun and a plural verb: *Only half the citizens* ***vote***.
• You can use **half (of)** with an uncountable noun and a singular verb: *Half the food* ***was*** *wasted.*

Word order

You say **half (of) the**: *I've only read half the story.*
✗ Don't say: *I've only read the half story.*

half² ●●● S1 W2 *n* (*plural* **halves** /hɑːvz $ hævz/) [C]
1 50% one of two equal parts of something: *Two halves make a whole.* | **one/two etc and a half** (=1½, 2½ etc) *My son's three and a half now.* | *an hour and a half later* | *two and a half thousand people* | **first/second/other half (of sth)** *in the first half of the 19th century* | *He kept the other half of the cake for himself.* | **top/bottom/northern etc half (of sth)** *A veil covered the lower half of her face.* | *the southern half of the country* | **break/cut/tear etc sth in half** (=into two equal parts) *She tore the piece of paper in half.* | **reduce/cut sth by half** (=make something 50% smaller) *a plan to cut European forces by half*
2 SPORT one of the two parts into which a sports event is divided: **first/second half** *France played very well in the first half.*
3 PLAYER a player who plays in the middle part of the field in sports like football, RUGBY etc: *the 23-year-old Newcastle* ***centre half***
4 BEER *BrE* a half of a PINT of beer: **[+of]** *Can I have a half of lager, please?*
5 TICKET *BrE* a child's ticket, for example on a bus or train, that is cheaper than an adult's ticket: *One and a half to Waterloo, please.*
6 a ... and a half *informal* used when you think that something is very unusual or surprising, or very good: *That was a meal and a half!*
7 the half of it *spoken* used to emphasize that a situation is more difficult, complicated, or unpleasant than people realize: *Everyone knows she's a difficult girl, but they* ***don't know the half of it***.
8 your better half/other half *old-fashioned* used humorously to mean your husband, wife, or partner
9 not do sth by halves to do something very eagerly and using a lot of care and effort: *I'm sure it will be a fantastic wedding. Eva never does anything by halves.*
10 go halves (on sth) to share something, especially the cost of something, equally between two people: *Do you want to go halves on a pizza?*
11 too clever/rich/good etc by half *BrE informal* very clever, rich etc in an annoying way: *That boy's too arrogant by half.*
12 how the other half lives how people who are much richer or much poorer than you manage their lives, work, money etc

half³ ●●● S2 *adv*
1 partly, but not completely: *He was half in the water and half out.* | *She was standing there half dressed, putting on her make-up.* | *The door was only half closed.* | *The jug was still* ***half full***. | *a* ***half-empty*** *wine bottle* | *I was only* ***half awake***. | *He looked* ***half asleep***. | *I was half expecting her to say 'no'.* | *I half hoped that they wouldn't come.* | *I said it half jokingly.*
2 if something is half one thing and half something else, it is a combination of those two things: *He's half English, half Swiss.*
3 used to emphasize something bad, to say that it is almost an extremely bad thing: *The kitten looked half starved.* | *He was half dead with exhaustion.* | *I had been driven half out of my mind with worry.*
4 a) half as much/big etc half the size, amount etc of something else: *The new machine has all the same functions, but is only half as large.* **b) half as much/big etc again** larger by an amount that is equal to half the original size: *A flat in London costs almost half as much again as a flat in Glasgow.*
5 not half as/so good/interesting etc (as sb/sth) much less good, less interesting etc than someone or something else: *The movie wasn't half as entertaining as the book.* | *She can't love you half as much as I do.*
6 not half *BrE spoken* used when you want to emphasize an opinion or statement: *She doesn't half talk once she gets started.*
7 not half bad *spoken* an expression meaning good, used especially when you are rather surprised that something is good: *Actually, the party wasn't half bad.*
8 half and half partly one thing and partly another: *The group was about half and half, complete beginners and people with some experience.*

ˌhalf-and-ˈhalf *n* [U] *AmE* a mixture that is half milk and half cream, used in coffee or tea

half-arsed /ˌhɑːf ˈɑːst◂ $ ˈhæf ɑːrst/ *BrE*, **half-assed** /ˌhɑːf ˈæst $ ˈhæf æst/ *AmE adj* [only before noun] *informal*
1 doing something without making much effort: *He made a half-arsed attempt to clean up after the party.*
2 completely stupid: *What a half-assed idea!*

half·back /ˈhɑːfbæk $ ˈhæf-/ *n* [C] **1** a player in a game of football, RUGBY, HOCKEY etc who plays in the middle part of the field **2** a player in American football who, at the start of play, is behind the front line of players and next to the FULLBACK

ˌhalf-ˈbaked *adj informal* a half-baked idea, suggestion, plan etc has not been properly planned: *He's always coming out with these half-baked ideas which will never work.*

ˌhalf ˈboard, half-board *n* [U] *BrE* the price of a room in a hotel that includes breakfast and dinner: *half board accommodation* → **FULL BOARD**

ˈhalf-breed *n* [C] *taboo* a very offensive word for someone whose parents are of different races, especially one white parent and one Native American parent. Do not use this word. → **mixed race** —**half-breed** *adj*

ˈhalf-ˌbrother ●●○ *n* [C] a brother who is the son of only one of your parents → **half-sister**

ˈhalf-caste *n* [C] *taboo* a very offensive word for someone whose parents are of different races. Do not use this word. → **mixed race** —**half-caste** *adj*

ˌhalf ˈcocked (*also* **ˌhalf ˈcock** *BrE*) **go off half cocked** (*also* **go off at half cock** *BrE*) to do something without enough thought or preparation, so that it is not successful

ˌhalf-ˈcrazed *adj* behaving in a slightly crazy uncontrolled way: **[+with]** *She was half-crazed with pain.*

ˌhalf ˈcrown *n* [C] a coin used in Britain before 1971. There were eight half crowns in a pound.

H

ˌhalf-ˈcut *adj BrE old-fashioned* drunk

ˈhalf day, half-day *n* [C] a day when you work or go to school either in the morning or the afternoon, but not all day: *Friday is my half day off.*

ˈhalf-day *adj* [only before noun] a half-day event takes place in either the morning or the afternoon: *half-day courses on study skills*

ˌhalf ˈdollar *n* [C] an American or Canadian coin worth 50 cents

half-heart·ed /ˌhɑːf ˈhɑːtɪd◂ $ ˌhæf ˈhɑːr-/ ●○○ *adj* done without much effort and without much interest in the result: *Congress has made half-hearted attempts at finance reform.* —**half-heartedly** *adv*

ˌhalf-ˈholiday *n* [C] *BrE old-fashioned* an afternoon in which children do not have to go school SYN **half day**

ˌhalf-ˈhour, half hour *n* [C] a period of time that is 30 minutes long: *Fay had been in her room for a good half-hour.* —**half-hour** *adj*: *a half-hour TV show*

ˌhalf-ˈhourly *adj, adv BrE* done or happening every half hour: *Trains depart at half-hourly intervals.*

ˌhalf-ˈlength *adj* a half-length painting or picture shows the top half of someone's body → FULL-LENGTH[1](1)

ˈhalf-life *n* [C] the length of time it takes a RADIOACTIVE substance to lose half of its RADIOACTIVITY

ˈhalf-light *n* [U] the dull grey light you see when it is almost dark but not completely dark: *the cold half-light of the early morning*

ˌhalf-ˈmast *n* **at half-mast a)** if a flag is flying at half-mast, it has been raised to the middle of the pole in order to show respect and sadness for someone who has died **b)** *BrE humorous* if a piece of clothing is at half-mast, it is lower down the body than is usual

ˈhalf ˌmeasures, half-measures *n* [plural] *BrE* actions or methods that are not effective in dealing with the whole of a difficult problem: *Half measures will not fix the health care system.*

ˌhalf ˈmoon *n* [C] the shape of the moon when only half of it is showing → FULL MOON, NEW MOON(1)

half nel·son /ˌhɑːf ˈnelsən $ ˌhæf-/ *n* [C] a way of holding your opponent's arm behind their back in the sport of WRESTLING

ˈhalf note *n* [C] *AmE* a musical note which continues for half the length of a WHOLE NOTE SYN **minim** *BrE* → **quarter note**

half·pen·ny, ha'penny /ˈheɪpni/ *n* (*plural* **halfpennies, ha'pennies**) [C] a small coin worth half of one PENNY, used in Britain in the past

ˈhalf pipe, half-pipe /ˈhɑːfpaɪp $ ˈhæf-/ *n* [C] **1** a CONCRETE structure which has a rounded bottom and sides and is used for SKATEBOARDING **2** a structure which has a rounded bottom and sides, is made from snow, and is used for SNOWBOARDING

HALF PIPE

ˌhalf ˈprice *n* [U] half the usual price → **full price**: **at half price** *Many shoes are at half price or less.* —**half-price** *adj*: *Half-price tickets will be sold on the day.* —**half price** *adv*: *Children aged 2–14 go half price.*

ˈhalf-ˌsister ●●○ *n* [C] a sister who is the daughter of only one of your parents → **half-brother**

ˈhalf step *n* [C] *AmE* the difference in PITCH between any two notes that are next to each other on a piano SYN **semitone**

ˌhalf-ˈterm *n* [C] *BrE* a short holiday from school in the middle of a TERM

half-tim·bered /ˌhɑːf ˈtɪmbəd◂ $ ˌhæf ˈtɪmbərd◂/ *adj* a half-timbered house is usually old and shows the wooden structure of the building on the outside walls

ˌhalf-ˈtime, half time *n* [U] a short period of rest between two parts of a game, such as football or BASKETBALL: **at half-time** *The score at half-time was 34-7.* | *a half-time lead* → **FULL TIME**

half-tone /ˌhɑːfˈtəʊn◂ $ ˈhæftoʊn/ *n* **1** [U] a method of printing black and white photographs that shows different shades of grey by changing the number of black DOTS in an area of the photograph **2** [C] a photograph printed by this method

ˈhalf-truth *n* [C] a statement that is only partly true, especially one that is intended to keep something secret: *His replies were full of evasions and half-truths.*

half·way /ˌhɑːfˈweɪ◂ $ ˌhæf-/ ●●○ S3 *adj, adv*

1 at a middle point in space or time between two things SYN **partway**: **[+through/up/down/between etc]** *He chased Kevin halfway up the stairs.* | *It was a terrible film – I left halfway through.* | *traffic queues stretching back halfway to London* | **the halfway stage/mark/point** *They've just reached the halfway stage of the project.*

2 be halfway there to have done something that will allow you to achieve something else: *Establish the right relationships at work and you're halfway there.*

3 be/come/go halfway to doing sth to achieve something partly but not completely: *We're still only halfway to finishing the job.*

4 halfway decent/normal/successful etc *informal* reasonably good, normal, successful etc: *the only halfway decent hotel here* → **meet sb halfway** at MEET[1](19)

ˌhalfway ˈhouse *n* **1** [singular] *BrE* something which is a combination of the qualities of two different things: *Belief is a kind of halfway house between non-belief and absolute proof.* **2** [C] a place for former prisoners or people who have had problems such as mental illness, where they can live until they are ready to live on their own

ˈhalf-wit *n* [C] *informal* a stupid person —**ˌhalf-ˈwitted** *adj*: *I'm not half-witted, you know.*

ˌhalf-ˈyearly *adj, adv* done or happening every six months: *half-yearly meetings* | *The interest you earn will be paid half-yearly in June and December.*

hal·i·but /ˈhæləbət/ *n* (*plural* **halibut**) [C] a large flat sea fish used as food

hal·i·to·sis /ˌhælɪˈtəʊsɪs $ -ˈtoʊ-/ *n* [U] *technical* a condition in which someone's breath smells very bad SYN **bad breath**

hall /hɔːl $ hɒːl/ ●●● S2 W2 *n* [C]

1 ENTRANCE the area just inside the door of a house or other building, that leads to other rooms SYN **hallway**: **in the hall** *We hung our coats in a cupboard in the hall.* | *a huge tiled* ***entrance hall***

2 CORRIDOR a passage in a building or house that leads to many of the rooms SYN **corridor, hallway**: *Each floor had ten rooms on both sides of the hall.*

3 PUBLIC BUILDING a building or large room for public events such as meetings or dances: **sports/exhibition/banqueting etc hall** *The school has a new sports hall.* | *Five hundred people filled the lecture hall.* | **church/village hall** (=used by people who live in a place) *A coffee morning is to be held in the village hall.* | *a concert at Carnegie Hall* → CITY HALL(2), CONCERT HALL, DANCE HALL, MUSIC HALL(2), TOWN HALL

4 FOR STUDENTS *especially BrE* a college or university building where students live SYN **hall of residence, dorm** *AmE*: **in hall** *For a brief time Tom and Dave had shared a room in hall.*

hal·le·lu·jah /ˌhæləˈluːjə◂/ *interjection* used to express thanks, JOY, or praise to God —**hallelujah** *n* [C]

hall·mark[1] /ˈhɔːlmɑːk $ ˈhɒːlmɑːrk/ *n* [C] **1** an idea, method, or quality that is typical of a particular person or thing: **[+of]** *These hotels still offer the sort of service which was the hallmark of the grand days of travel.* | *The explosion* ***had all the hallmarks of*** *a terrorist attack.* | *Their performance did not* ***bear the hallmark of*** *European champions.* **2** a mark put on silver, gold, or PLATINUM that shows the quality of the metal, and where and when it was made

hallmark[2] *v* [T] to put a hallmark on silver, gold, or PLATINUM

H

hal·lo /həˈləʊ, hæ- $ -ˈloʊ/ *interjection BrE* an old-fashioned spelling of HELLO

ˌHall of ˈFame *n* [C] in the US, a list of famous sports players or a building where their uniforms, equipment, and information about them are shown

ˌhall of ˈresidence *n* [C] *BrE* a college or university building where students live SYN **dorm** *AmE*

hal·lowed /ˈhæləʊd $ -loʊd/ *adj* **1** holy or made holy by religious practices → **sacred**: *The bones will be buried in **hallowed ground**.* **2** important and respected by a lot of people: *the **hallowed halls** of government | hallowed traditions*

Hal·low·een, **Hallowe'en** /ˌhæləʊˈiːn◂ $ -loʊ-/ ●●● S3 *n* [U] the night of October 31st, which is now celebrated by children, who dress in COSTUMES and go from house to house asking for sweets, especially in the US and Canada. In the past, people believed the souls of dead people appeared on Halloween. → **trick or treat**

hal·lu·ci·nate /həˈluːsəneɪt/ *v* [I] to see or hear things that are not really there THESAURUS▸ IMAGINE

hal·lu·ci·na·tion /həˌluːsəˈneɪʃən/ *n* [C,U] something which you imagine you can see or hear, but which is not really there, or the experience of this: *The patients suffered hallucinations caused by the drug.*

hal·lu·ci·na·to·ry /həˈluːsənətəri $ -tɔːri/ *adj formal* **1** causing hallucinations or resulting from hallucinations: *hallucinatory drugs* **2** using strange images, sounds etc like those experienced in a hallucination: *hallucinatory poetry*

hal·lu·cin·o·gen /həˈluːsənədʒən/ *n* [C] a substance that causes hallucinations

hal·lu·cin·o·gen·ic /həˌluːsənəˈdʒenɪk◂/ *adj* hallucinogenic drugs make people experience hallucinations

hall·way /ˈhɔːlweɪ $ ˈhɒːl-/ ●○○ *n* [C]
1 the area just inside the door of a house or other building, that leads to other rooms SYN **hall**
2 a passage in a building or house that leads to many of the rooms SYN **hall**, **corridor**

ha·lo /ˈheɪləʊ $ -loʊ/ *n* (*plural* **halos**) [C] **1** a bright circle that is often shown above or around the heads of holy people in religious art **2** a circle of light or something bright: **[+of]** *a halo of sunlight | a halo of blonde curls*

hal·o·gen /ˈhælədʒən/ *n* **1** [U] a halogen light uses halogen gas to produce light: **halogen bulb/lamp/light etc**
2 [C,U] one of a group of five simple chemical substances that make COMPOUNDS easily

ha·lon /ˈheɪlɒn $ -lɑːn/ *n* [U] *technical* a COMPOUND gas that damages the OZONE LAYER

halt¹ /hɔːlt $ hɒːlt/ ●○○ *n*
1 [singular] a stop or pause: *Heavy snowfalls **brought** traffic **to a halt*** (=made it stop moving). | *The World Championship was **brought to a** temporary **halt*** (=was stopped from continuing). | **come/grind/screech etc to a halt** (=stop moving or continuing) *The whole peace process seems to have ground to a halt.* | *The car skidded to a halt.* | *The president has **called for a halt to** the wave of emigration.*
2 call a halt (to sth) to stop an activity from continuing: *I urge those responsible to call a halt to the violence.*
3 [C] *BrE* a place in the countryside where a train stops to let passengers get off, but where there is no station

halt² ●○○ *v*
1 [T] to prevent someone or something from continuing – used especially in news reports SYN **stop**: *The government has failed to halt economic decline.* | *Safety concerns have led them to halt work on the dam.*

> REGISTER
> **Halt** is mainly used in journalism. In everyday English, people usually say **stop**: *They had to **stop** the building work.*

2 [I] to stop moving: *The parade halted by a busy corner.*
3 halt! used as a military order to tell someone to stop moving or soldiers to stop marching: *Company halt!* | *Halt! Who goes there?*

hal·ter /ˈhɔːltə $ ˈhɒːltər/ *n* [C] **1** a rope or leather band that fastens around a horse's head, usually used to lead the horse **2** (*also* **halter top**, **halterneck**) a type of clothing for women that ties behind the neck and across the back, so that the arms and back are not covered: *Jen was wearing black shorts and a halter.*

halt·ing /ˈhɔːltɪŋ $ ˈhɒːl-/ *adj* if your speech or movements are halting, you stop for a moment between words or movements, especially because you are not confident SYN **hesitant**: *We carried on a rather halting conversation.* —**haltingly** *adv*

halve /hɑːv $ hæv/ ●○○ *v* [T]
1 to reduce something by a half: *Cash cuts have halved the number of places available on training courses.*
2 to cut or divide something into two equal pieces: *Halve the potatoes lengthwise.*

halves /hɑːvz $ hævz/ **1** the plural of HALF **2 go halves (with sb)** *BrE* if you go halves with someone, you divide something equally between you, especially money

hal·yard /ˈhæljəd $ -ərd/ *n* [C] *technical* a rope used to raise or lower a flag or sail

ham¹ /hæm/ ●●● S3 *n*
1 [C,U] the upper part of a pig's leg, or the meat from this that has been preserved with salt or smoke → **gammon**: *a ham sandwich | a seven-pound ham*
2 [C] someone who receives and sends radio messages for fun rather than as their job
3 [C] *informal* an actor who performs with too much false emotion

ham² *v* (**hammed**, **hamming**) **ham it up** *informal* to perform with too much false emotion when acting

ham·burg·er /ˈhæmbɜːgə $ -bɜːrgər/ ●●● S3 *n*
1 [C] a flat round piece of finely cut BEEF (=meat from a cow) which is cooked and eaten in a bread BUN
2 [U] *AmE* beef that has been cut into very small pieces SYN **mince** *BrE*

ham-fist·ed /ˌhæm ˈfɪstɪd◂/ (*also* **ˌham-ˈhanded**) *adj informal* **1** not at all skilful or careful in the way that you deal with people SYN **inept**: *They made several ham-fisted attempts to spy on her.* **2** not at all skilful with your hands SYN **clumsy**

ham·let /ˈhæmlɪt/ *n* [C] a very small village

ham·mer¹ /ˈhæmə $ -ər/ ●●○ *n* [C]
1 TOOL **a)** a tool with a heavy metal part on a long handle, used for hitting nails into wood **b)** a tool like this with a wooden head used to make something flat, make a noise etc: *an auctioneer's hammer* → see picture at TOOL¹
2 come/go under the hammer to be offered for sale at an AUCTION
3 hammer blow *BrE* an event that damages something very seriously: **[+for]** *The decision is a hammer blow for the coal industry.*
4 hammer and tongs *informal* **a)** if people go at each other hammer and tongs, they fight or argue very loudly **b)** if someone does something hammer and tongs, they do it with all their energy
5 GUN the part of a gun that hits the explosive CHARGE that fires a bullet
6 SPORT a heavy metal ball on a wire with a handle at the end, which you throw as far as possible as a sport
7 PIANO a wooden part of a PIANO that hits the strings inside to make a musical sound

hammer² ●○○ *v*
1 HIT WITH A HAMMER [I,T] to hit something with a hammer in order to force it into a particular position or shape: **hammer sth in/into sth** *Hammer the nails into the back of the frame.* | **hammer away (at sth)** *All afternoon, Martin had been hammering away in the conservatory.* | *the sound of hammering and sawing* THESAURUS▸ HIT
2 HIT REPEATEDLY [I] to hit something many times, especially making a loud noise SYN **pound**, **bang**: **[+at]** *Daniella hammered at the door.* | *The rain was hammering against the window.*
3 HURT WITH PROBLEMS [T] to hurt someone or something by causing them a lot of problems: *British industry was being hammered by the recession.*

4 HIT HARD [T] *informal* to hit or kick something very hard: *Robinson hammered the ball into the goal.*
5 CRITICIZE [T] to strongly criticize or attack someone for something they have said or done: *The president has been hammered for his lack of leadership.*
6 **hammer sth home** to make sure that people understand something by repeating it many times: *The message must be hammered home that crime doesn't pay.*
7 HEART [I] if your heart hammers, you feel it beating strongly and quickly SYN **pound**: *She stood outside the door, her heart hammering.*
8 DEFEAT [T] *informal* to defeat someone completely at a sport: *Arsenal hammered Manchester United 5-0.*

hammer away *phr v*
1 to keep saying something because you want people to understand or accept it: **[+at]** *I keep hammering away at this point because it's important.*
2 to work hard and continuously at something: **[+at]** *Keep on hammering away at achieving your goals.*

hammer sth ↔ **in** (*also* **hammer sth into sb**) *phr v* to keep saying something until people completely understand it: *The coach hammered his message into the team.*

hammer sth ↔ **out** *phr v* to decide on an agreement, contract etc after a lot of discussion and disagreement: *Leading oil producers tried to hammer out a deal.*

ˌhammer and ˈsickle *n* [singular] **1** the sign of a hammer crossing a SICKLE on a red background, used as a sign of COMMUNISM **2** the flag of the former Soviet Union

ham·mered /ˈhæməd $ -ərd/ *adj* [not before noun] *informal* very drunk

ham·mer·ing /ˈhæmərɪŋ/ *n* [singular, U] **1 take a hammering/be given a hammering** to be attacked or defeated very severely: *The city took a real hammering during the war.* **2** the sound of someone hitting something with a hammer or with their hands: *There was a loud hammering at the door.*

ham·mock /ˈhæmək/ *n* [C] a large piece of cloth that is hung between two trees or posts, which you can sleep in

ham·my /ˈhæmi/ *adj* if a performance by an actor is hammy, it is done with too much false emotion

ham·per¹ /ˈhæmpə $ -ər/ ●○○ *v* [T] to make it difficult for someone to do something: *She tried to run, but was hampered by her heavy suitcase.* | *An attempt to rescue the men has been hampered by bad weather.*

hamper² *n* [C] **1** *BrE* a basket with a lid, which is used for carrying food or sending it to someone as a present: *a picnic hamper* | *They sent us a lovely Christmas hamper.* **2** *AmE* a large basket that you put dirty clothes in until they can be washed SYN **laundry basket** *BrE*

ham·ster /ˈhæmstə $ -ər/ *n* [C] a small animal that looks like a mouse with no tail

ham·string¹ /ˈhæmˌstrɪŋ/ *n* [C] a TENDON behind your knee, which sometimes gets injured when you do sport: *He* ***pulled a hamstring*** *in training.* | **hamstring injury/problem/strain etc**

hamstring² *v* (*past tense and past participle* **hamstrung** /-strʌŋ/) [T] to make someone unable to take the action they want or need to take, especially by restricting them: *The president feels he is hamstrung by Congress.*

hand¹ /hænd/ ●●● S1 W1 *n*
1 PART OF BODY [C] the part of your body at the end of your arm, including your fingers and thumb, that you use to hold things: *Steve gripped the steering wheel tightly with both hands.* | *In her hand was a tattered old photograph.*
2 HELP **a hand** help with something – used in the following phrases: **need/want a hand** *Do you need a hand packing?* | **give/lend (sb) a hand** *Can you give me a hand to lift this?* | *If you get stuck, Denise is always willing to lend a hand.* | **I could do with a hand/use a hand** (=it would be useful to have some help) *We could certainly do with a hand.* → **a helping hand** at HELP¹(9)
3 CONTROL [singular, U] control, power, or influence that someone has: *The president has* ***strengthened the hand of*** *the gun lobby.* | *This matter is too important to be left* ***in the hands of*** (=in the control of) *an inexperienced lawyer.* | *a manager with* ***a firm hand*** (=who controls things strictly)

HAND

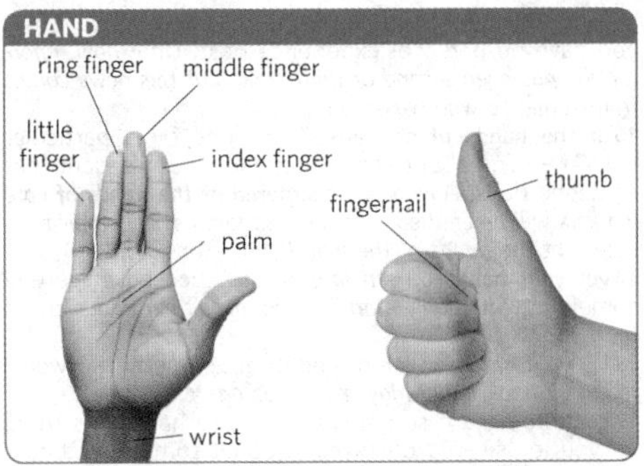

4 **get out of hand** if a situation or person gets out of hand, they become impossible to control any longer: *The demonstration was getting out of hand.*
5 **on the other hand** (*also* **on the one hand ... on the other hand**) used to give another opinion or fact that should be considered as well as the one you have just given: *I'd like to eat out, but on the other hand I should be trying to save money.* ⚠ Don't say 'on one hand'. Say **on the one hand**.
6 **hands off** *spoken* used to say that someone cannot have, take, or touch something: *Hey! Hands off that CD! It's mine!* | *Tell your little brother to* ***keep*** *his* ***hands off*** *my car.* → HANDS-OFF
7 **in hand a)** if something is in hand, it is being done or dealt with: *Plans are in hand to perform 'Oz' next semester.* | *Lisa seemed to* ***have*** *things* ***in hand*** *by the time he returned.* | **job/task/matter etc in hand** *Our officers have to concentrate 100 per cent on the task in hand.* | **take sb in hand** (=begin to deal with someone's problems etc) **b)** *BrE* if you work a week, a month etc in hand, you do not get paid until after you have worked two weeks, two months etc **c)** *BrE* if you have time, money etc in hand, you have it available: *I usually have a few days' leave in hand at the end of the year.* **d)** *BrE* if a team or player has a game in hand in a competition, they still have another game to play in which they could gain more points
8 **in the hands of sb/in sb's hands** being dealt with or cared for by someone: *The matter is in the hands of the police.* | **in good/safe/capable etc hands** *You can be sure your children are in good hands.* | *The fear is that nuclear secrets could* ***fall into the wrong hands.*** ⚠ Don't say 'in the hand of someone'. Say **in the hands of someone**. → **a safe pair of hands** at SAFE¹(12)
9 **hands up a)** with your arms straight up in the air – used especially to tell someone to do this as a sign that they will not attack you: *Hands up! You're under arrest!* | *The men emerged from the building with their hands up.* **b)** used to tell people to put their arm straight up in the air if they know the answer to a question or want to say something: *Hands up if you agree with what Eric was saying.*
10 **at hand** *formal* **a)** likely to happen soon: *Recent economic performance suggests that a major crisis is at hand.* **b)** close to you and available to be used: *Don't worry,* ***help is at hand!*** **c)** needing to be dealt with now: *Peter turned his attention to the task at hand.*
11 **to hand** *BrE* something that is to hand is close to you, so that you can reach it easily
12 **on hand** close by and ready when needed: *Our staff are always on hand to help.*
13 **by hand a)** done or made by a person rather than a machine: *We had to wash our clothes by hand.* **b)** delivered by someone personally, rather than being sent through the post, emailed etc
14 **(at) first hand** if you know or experience something first hand, you have personal experience of it: *a chance to view at first hand the workings of the court*
15 **(at) second/third/fourth hand** if you know something

H

second, third etc hand, someone tells you about it, but you have no personal experience of it: *Until now, information has been second or third hand, but this news comes from someone who was there.*
16 at the hands of sb caused or done by a particular person - used about something bad or unpleasant that someone does: *Anyone who **suffered at the hands of** care workers will be entitled to compensation.* | *This is their third defeat at the hands of the world champions.*
17 get your hands on sth *informal* to succeed in getting something: *She's only marrying him to get her hands on his money.*
18 lay your hands on sth to find or get something: *I would read any book I could lay my hands on.*
19 come to hand if something comes to hand, it is there for you to use - used especially about something that is there by chance: *They ran, picking up **whatever** weapons **came to hand**.*
20 get your hands on sb *spoken* to catch someone you are angry with: *Just wait till I get my hands on you!*
21 have a hand in sth to influence or be involved in something: *He had a hand in both goals.*
22 hand in hand a) (go) hand in hand if two things go hand in hand, they are closely connected: *Wealth and power go hand in hand in most societies.* | **[+with]** *They say that genius often goes hand in hand with madness.* **b)** if two people walk, stand etc hand in hand, they walk, stand etc while they are holding each other's hand: *They walked hand in hand in silence up the path.*
23 have sth/sb on your hands to have a difficult job, problem, situation etc to deal with: *I'm afraid we have a murder on our hands, Inspector.*
24 be off your hands if something or someone is off your hands, you are not responsible for them anymore: *Once this problem is off our hands we can relax for a while.* | **take sb/sth off sb's hands** *She wants someone to take the kids off her hands occasionally.*
25 try your hand at (doing) sth to try to do something you have not tried before: *John dreamed of being a writer and had tried his hand at poetry.*
26 turn your hand to (doing) sth to do something well, even if it is the first time you have tried: *Larry's one of those men who can turn their hand to anything.*
27 out of hand without even stopping to consider what someone has suggested, asked for etc: **reject/dismiss/refuse etc sth out of hand** *Aromatherapy was dismissed out of hand by traditional doctors.*
28 hands down easily: **win (sth)/beat sb hands down** *Nigel always won hands down in any argument.*
29 have your hands full to be very busy or too busy: *Can't it wait? I already have my hands full.*
30 good with your hands skilful at making things
31 on either/every hand *written* on both sides or in every direction: *Thick forest stood on either hand.*
32 get your hands dirty a) *informal* to do hard or dirty physical work - usually used in questions or negative statements: *It's not that the jobs aren't there, it's just that she doesn't want to get her hands dirty.* **b)** to get involved in the difficult, dishonest, or unpleasant side of something: *He never talked to the media or got his hands dirty in any way.*
33 keep your hand in to do something that you used to do a lot, so you do not forget how to do it: *You should at least work part-time, just to keep your hand in.*
34 hand in glove closely connected with someone, especially in an illegal activity: *Far from being independent, the government and media work hand in glove.*
35 hand over fist *informal* if you gain or lose something hand over fist, you gain or lose it very quickly: *Five years ago, the company was losing money hand over fist.*
36 a big hand *spoken* used to tell the people who are watching a performance to CLAP or CHEER loudly: *Let's all **give** the girls **a big hand**.*
37 all hands on deck (*also* **all hands to the pumps** *BrE*) *informal* used to say that everyone is needed to help in a particular situation: *With only half an hour to get everything ready, it was all hands on deck.*
38 the left hand does not know what the right hand is doing used to say that two parts of an organization that should be doing the same thing are each doing different things without the other knowing
39 WORKER [C] someone who does physical work on a farm, factory, ship etc: *farm hands*
40 CARDS [C] **a)** the playing cards given to one person in a game: *a winning hand* **b)** a single game of cards
41 CLOCK [C] a long thin piece of metal that points at the numbers on a clock: **hour/minute/second hand** → see picture at CLOCK[1]
42 WRITING [singular] *old-fashioned* someone's HANDWRITING
43 sb's hands are tied if someone's hands are tied, they cannot help in a particular situation because of rules, laws etc: *The bank claims its hands are tied by federal regulators.*
44 tie/bind sb hand and foot a) to tie up someone's hands and feet **b)** to make it very difficult or impossible for someone to do what they think is best
45 can do sth with one hand (tied) behind your back *spoken* used to say that you can do something very easily
46 not do a hand's turn *BrE old-fashioned informal* to do no work at all
47 sb's hand (in marriage) *old-fashioned* permission for a man to marry a particular woman: *He asked for her hand in marriage.*
48 HORSE [C] a unit for measuring the height of a horse, equal to about ten centimetres → CASH-IN-HAND, FREEHAND, HANDS-ON, LEFT-HAND, RIGHT-HAND, → **be an old hand (at sth)** at OLD(17), → **bite the hand that feeds you** at BITE[1](15), → **have blood on your hands** at BLOOD[1](2), → **have your hands/fingers in the till** at TILL[2](3), → **force sb's hand** at FORCE[2](7), → **overplay your hand** at OVERPLAY(2), → **shake sb's hand/shake hands with sb** at SHAKE[1](4), → **wash your hands of sth** at WASH[1](5)

COLLOCATIONS

ADJECTIVES

sb's right/left hand *She held the book in her right hand.*

VERBS

wave your hand *Marta waved a hand to attract his attention.*
clap your hands *They were singing and clapping their hands.*
wash your hands *Go wash your hands before dinner.*
hold hands (with sb) *Joanne and Kevin held hands on the sofa.*
shake sb's hand (*also* **shake hands with sb**) *'Nice to meet you,' he said, as they shook hands.*
take sb's hand (=hold someone's hand) | **take sb by the hand** (=hold someone's hand in order to take them somewhere) | **join hands** (=take hold of the hands of people on either side of you) | **clasp your hands** (=hold them together tightly) | **fold your hands** (=put your hands together and rest them on something) | **raise your hand** (*also* **put your hand up**) (=lift your hand, especially when you want to ask or answer a question)

PHRASES

in sb's hand *He had a suitcase in his hand.*
on your hands and knees (=in a crawling position) *They got down on their hands and knees to search.*
the palm of your hand (=the inside surface of your hand) *The phone could fit into the palm of his hand.*
the back of your hand (=the outside surface of your hand) | **with your bare hands** (=without using a tool, weapon, machine etc)

hand[2] ●●○ W2 *v* [T]
1 to give something to someone else with your hand: **hand sb sth** *He handed the teacher a slip of paper.* | **hand sth to sb** *He lit a cigarette and handed it to her.* | *This form must be handed to all employees.*
2 you have to hand it to sb *spoken* used to say that you

admire someone: *You have to hand it to her. She's really made a success of that company.*

hand sth ↔ **around** (*also* **hand sth round** *BrE*) *phr v* to offer something to each person in a group: *Willie helped hand the mugs around.*

hand sth ↔ **back** *phr v*

1 to give something back to the person who gave it to you, with your hand: **[+to]** *Kurt examined the document and handed it back to her.* | **hand sb sth ↔ back** *She handed him his pen back.*

2 to give something back to the person who used to own it: **[+to]** *The land was handed back to its original owner.* | **hand sb sth ↔ back** *The government has promised to hand investors back their money.*

hand sth ↔ **down** *phr v*

1 to give or leave something to people who will live after you: **[+to]** *The ring was handed down to her from her grandmother.* | *stories handed down by word of mouth* → HAND-ME-DOWN

2 hand down a decision/ruling/sentence etc to officially announce a decision, punishment etc

hand sth ↔ **in** *phr v* to give something to someone in authority: *Tom has handed in his resignation.* | *Did you hand your homework in on time?*

hand sth ↔ **on** *phr v* to give something to someone: *He was accused of handing on government secrets.*

hand sth ↔ **out** *phr v* to give something to each person in a group SYN **distribute**: *Could you start handing these books out please?* | **[+to]** *He was handing out leaflets to members of the audience.* → HANDOUT

hand over *phr v*

1 hand sth ↔ over to give something to someone with your hand, especially because they have asked for it or should have it: *The soldiers were ordered to hand over their guns.* | **[+to]** *He handed the phone over to me.*

2 to give someone power or responsibility over something which you used to be in charge of: **hand sth ↔ over (to sb)** *On his retirement, he handed the business over to his son.* | *Political control has been handed over to religious leaders.* | **[+to]** *Now she feels the time has come to hand over to someone else.*

hand·bag /ˈhændbæɡ/ ●●○ S3 *n* [C]

1 a small bag in which a woman carries money and personal things SYN **purse** *AmE* → see picture at BAG[1]

2 handbags *informal* used humorously to describe a situation in which two people are fighting, but in a way that is so weak or lacking in force that the fight is funny to watch: *Dennis looked like he threw a punch, but it was just handbags.*

hand·ball /ˈhændbɔːl $ -bɒːl/ *n* **1** [U] a game in which two teams try to score points by throwing or hitting a ball with their hands **2** [U] a game in which players hit a ball against a wall with their hand **3** [C] a ball that is used to play handball **4** [C,U] the act of touching the ball with your hands in a game of football, which is not allowed: *The referee gave a free kick for handball.*

hand·bill /ˈhændˌbɪl/ *n* [C] a small printed notice or advertisement that is given to people: *Students distributed handbills calling for better funding for schools.*

hand·book /ˈhændbʊk/ ●○○ *n* [C] a short book that gives information or instructions about something SYN **manual**: *the Fiction Writer's Handbook*

hand·brake /ˈhændbreɪk/ *n* [C] *BrE* a BRAKE in a car that you pull up with your hand to stop the car from moving when it is parked SYN **emergency brake** *AmE* → see picture at CAR

hand·car /ˈhændkɑː $ -kɑːr/ *n* [C] *AmE* a small railway vehicle that people move along by pushing large handles up and down

hand·cart /ˈhændkɑːt $ -kɑːrt/ *n* [C] a small vehicle that you push or pull by hand and use for carrying goods

hand·clap /ˈhændklæp/ *n BrE* **slow handclap** if people give someone a slow handclap, they hit their hands together slowly to show that they disapprove of them

hand·craft·ed /ˈhændˌkrɑːftɪd $ -ˌkræft-/ *adj* skilfully made by hand, not by machine SYN **handmade**: *a handcrafted rocking chair*

hand·cuff /ˈhændkʌf/ *v* [T] to put handcuffs on someone

hand·cuffs /ˈhændkʌfs/ *n* [plural] a pair of metal rings joined by a chain. Handcuffs are used for holding a prisoner's wrists together: *They* ***put handcuffs on*** *the two men and led them away.* | **in handcuffs** *He was brought into the court in handcuffs.* | *a* ***pair of handcuffs***

ˌhand-eye co-ordiˈnation *n* [U] the way in which your hands and eyes work together, especially in sport, so that you can throw, hit, and catch a ball

hand·ful /ˈhændfʊl/ ●●○ *n*

1 [C] an amount that you can hold in your hand: **[+of]** *The boy picked up a handful of stones and started throwing them at us.*

2 a handful of sth a very small number of people or things: *There were only a handful of people there.*

3 be a handful *informal* someone, especially a child, who is a handful is difficult to control: *She's a lovely child, but she can be a bit of a handful sometimes.*

ˈhand greˌnade *n* [C] a small bomb that you throw

hand·gun /ˈhændɡʌn/ *n* [C] a small gun that you hold in one hand when you fire it

hand·held /ˈhændheld/ *n* [C] a PDA

ˌhand-ˈheld *adj* a hand-held machine is small enough to hold in your hand when you use it: *a hand-held camera* | *hand-held video games*

hand·hold /ˈhændhəʊld $ -hoʊld/ *n* [C] a part of something that you can hold onto when climbing it

hand·i·cap[1] /ˈhændikæp/ ●○○ *n* [C]

1 *old-fashioned* if someone has a handicap, a part of their body or their mind has been permanently injured or damaged. Many people think that this word is offensive.

2 a situation that makes it difficult for someone to do what they want: *Not speaking the language is a real handicap.*

3 an advantage that is given to a weaker player in a game of GOLF: *He's improved a lot, and his handicap has come down from 18 to 12.*

4 a race for horses in which the best horses carry extra weight so that all the horses have an equal chance of winning

handicap[2] *v* (**handicapped**, **handicapping**) [T] to make it difficult for someone to do something that they want or need to do: *The charity is handicapped by lack of funds.*

hand·i·capped /ˈhændikæpt/ *adj old-fashioned* **1** if someone is handicapped, a part of their body or their mind has been permanently injured or damaged. Many people think that this word is offensive: *a special school for mentally handicapped children* **2 the handicapped** [plural] people who are handicapped. Many people think that this expression is offensive. → DISABLED

hand·i·craft /ˈhændikrɑːft $ -kræft/ (*also* **craft**) *n* [C usually plural] **1** an activity such as sewing or making baskets, in which you use your hands in a skilful way to make things **2** something that someone has made in a skilful way using their hands: *a shop selling handicrafts*

hand·i·ly /ˈhændəli/ *adv* **1** something that is handily placed is in a position where it can easily be reached or used: *She kept the key handily by the back door.* **2** *AmE* if you win something handily, you win easily

hand·i·work /ˈhændiwɜːk $ -wɜːrk/ *n* [U] **sb's handiwork** **a)** something that someone has made or done using their hands in a skilful way: *She stood back and admired her handiwork.* **b)** something that someone has done or caused: *The explosion looks like the handiwork of terrorists.*

ˈhand job *n* [C] *informal* the act of touching or rubbing a man's sex organs to give him sexual pleasure

hand·ker·chief /ˈhæŋkətʃɪf $ -kər-/ ●○○ *n* [C] a piece of cloth that you use for drying your nose or eyes SYN **hankie**, **tissue**

H

han·dle¹ /ˈhændl/ ●●● S1 W2 *v*
1 DO WORK [T] to do the things that are necessary to complete a job: *I handled most of the paperwork. | The case is being handled by a top lawyer. | The finance department handles all the accounts. | Computers can handle huge amounts of data.*
2 DEAL WITH A SITUATION [T] to deal with a situation or problem by behaving in a particular way and making particular decisions: *The headmaster handled the situation very well. | I knew I had handled the matter badly. | Leave it to me. I can handle it. | Most customers were satisfied with the way their complaints were handled. | Opposition leaders will be watching carefully to see how the prime minister handles the crisis.* THESAURUS ▸ DEAL
3 DEAL WITH A PERSON [T] to deal with a person or behave towards them in a particular way, especially in order to keep them happy: *Some customers are quite difficult to handle.*
4 NOT BECOME UPSET [T] to not become upset in a difficult situation: *She can't handle it when people criticize her. | He doesn't handle stress very well.*
5 HOLD [T] to touch something or pick it up and hold it in your hands: *He had never handled a weapon before. | We teach the children to handle the animals gently. | He was roughly handled by the mob.* THESAURUS ▸ TOUCH
6 CONTROL A VEHICLE **a)** [T] to control the movement of a vehicle or an animal: *I didn't know if I'd be able to handle such a large vehicle.* **b)** [I] the way a vehicle handles is how easy it is to control: **handles well/badly** *The car handles well, even on wet roads.*
7 MOVE GOODS [T] to move goods from one place to another: *The Post Office handles nearly 2 billion letters and parcels over the Christmas period.*
8 BUY/SELL GOODS [T] to buy or sell goods: *Bennet was charged with* ***handling stolen goods****.*

HANDLES

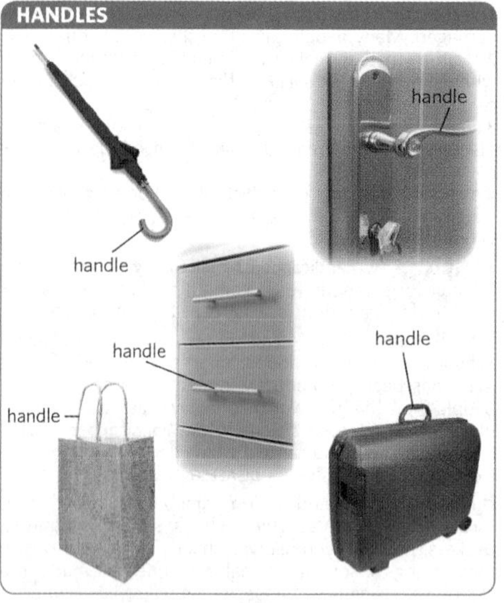

handle² ●●● S1 W3 *n* [C]
1 the part of a door that you use for opening it: *Then he turned the handle and went in.*
2 the part of an object that you use for holding it: *a knife with a carved wooden handle | the handle of his cup | a broom handle*
3 **get a handle on sth** to start to understand a situation, subject etc: *It's difficult to get a handle on how widespread this problem is.* → **fly off the handle** at FLY¹(16)

han·dle·bar mous·tache /ˌhændlbɑː məˈstɑːʃ $ -bɑːr ˈmʌstæʃ/ *n* [C] a long thick MOUSTACHE which curves upwards at both ends

han·dle·bars /ˈhændlbɑːz $ -bɑːrz/ ●○○ *n* [plural] (*also* **handlebar** [C]) the bar above the front wheel of a bicycle or MOTORCYCLE that you turn to control its direction → see picture at BICYCLE

han·dler /ˈhændlə $ -ər/ *n* [C] **1** someone who trains an animal, especially a dog: *a police dog handler* **2** someone who touches, carries, or moves things as their job: *All food handlers should be properly trained. | baggage handlers at the airport* **3** someone who helps and advises an important person: *She is kept well away from the press by her handlers.*

hand·ling /ˈhændlɪŋ/ *n* [U] **1** the way in which someone does a job or deals with a situation, problem, or person: **[+of]** *The president has been much criticized for his handling of the crisis. | Such a situation needs very careful handling.* **2** the act of touching something: *The equipment should be able to withstand a certain amount of rough handling.* **3** the act of buying, selling, or moving goods: *cargo handling | A special licence is required for the manufacture or handling of any dangerous chemical.* **4** the way in which a vehicle can be controlled, especially how easy it is for a driver to control it: *It's a lovely little car – the ride is comfortable and the handling excellent.*

ˈhandling ˌcharge *n* [C] the amount that someone charges for dealing with goods or moving them from one place to another

hand·loom /ˈhændluːm/ *n* [C] a small machine for weaving by hand

ˈhand ˌluggage *n* [U] the small bags that you carry with you when you are travelling on a plane

hand·made /ˌhændˈmeɪd◂/ *adj* made by people using their hands, not by a machine → **man-made**: *a pair of expensive handmade shoes*

hand·maid·en /ˈhændˌmeɪdn/ (*also* **hand·maid** /ˈhændmeɪd/) *n* [C] **1** *old-fashioned* a female servant **2** *formal* something that supports an idea, system, or way of life: **[+of]** *Science must not become the handmaiden of the state.*

ˈhand-me-down *n* [C] a piece of clothing which has been used by someone and then given to another person: *She refused to wear hand-me-downs. | hand-me-down clothes*

hand·out /ˈhændaʊt/ ●●○ *n* [C]
1 money or goods that are given to someone, for example because they are poor: *people who have to live on handouts from the state | a cash handout*
2 a piece of paper with information, which is given to people who are attending a lesson, meeting etc: *Please read the handout.*

hand·o·ver /ˈhændəʊvə $ -oʊvər/ *n* [singular] **1** the act of giving someone else control of a place or business: *The president will remain in office until the official handover in April. |* **[+of]** *a smooth* ***handover of power*** *| the handover of the business |* **[+to]** *The handover to civilian government has been delayed.* **2** the act of giving something to someone: **[+of]** *They demanded the immediate handover of all relevant documents.* → **hand over** at HAND²

hand·picked /ˌhændˈpɪkt◂/ *adj* someone who is handpicked has been carefully chosen for a special purpose: *one of his handpicked advisers*

hand·plant /ˈhændplɑːnt $ -plænt/ *n* [C] a movement in SKATEBOARDING and SNOWBOARDING in which you hold the back part of your board with one hand and put your other hand down on the top edge of a RAMP as you turn to ride back down the ramp

hand·rail /ˈhænd-reɪl/ *n* [C] a long bar that is fixed to a wall for people to hold while they walk up or down stairs → see picture at RAIL¹

hand·saw /ˈhændsɔː $ -sɒː/ *n* [C] a small tool for cutting wood, which has a flat metal blade with a lot of sharp V-shaped teeth → see picture at TOOL¹

hand·set /ˈhændset/ *n* [C] **1** the part of a telephone that you hold near your ear and mouth **2** the part of a MOBILE PHONE that you hold in your hand

hands·free /ˈhændzfriː/ *adj* [only before noun] a handsfree machine is one that you can use without using your hands: *a handsfree phone*

hand·shake /ˈhændʃeɪk/ *n* [C] **1** the act of taking someone's right hand and shaking it, which people do when they meet or leave each other or when they have made an agreement: *He greeted me with a handshake and a glass of wine.* | *Her handshake was warm and firm.* **2** a special signal sent between two computers, FAX machines etc when they begin to exchange information —**handshaking** *n* [U] → GOLDEN HANDSHAKE

ˈhands-off *adj* [only before noun] a hands-off way of organizing something involves letting people do what they want and make their own decisions, without telling them what to do: *a* ***hands-off style*** *of management* | *The government has a* ***hands-off approach*** *to the industry.*

hand·some /ˈhænsəm/ ●●● W3 *adj*
1 a) a man who is handsome looks attractive SYN **good-looking**: *an extremely handsome young man* | *Sam was* ***tall, dark, and handsome***. | *his handsome face* **b)** a woman who is handsome looks attractive in a strong healthy way

> **REGISTER**
> In everyday English, people usually say **good-looking** rather than **handsome**: *Her new boyfriend is really* ***good-looking***.

2 an animal, object, or building that is handsome looks attractive in an impressive way: *a row of handsome Georgian houses*
3 [only before noun] a handsome amount of money is large: *He managed to make a* ***handsome profit*** *out of the deal.* | *a handsome fee*
4 [only before noun] a handsome gift or prize is worth a lot of money: *There are some handsome prizes to be won.*
5 [only before noun] a handsome victory is important and impressive: *They won a handsome victory in the elections.* —**handsomely** *adv*: *He was handsomely rewarded by the king.*

ˈhands-on *adj* [usually before noun] doing something yourself rather than just talking about it or telling other people to do it: *a chance to get some* ***hands-on experience*** *of the job* | *He has a very* ***hands-on approach*** *to management.*

hand·spring /ˈhændsprɪŋ/ *n* [C] a quick movement in which you put your hands on the ground, move your feet over your head, and stand up again

hand·stand /ˈhændstænd/ *n* [C] a movement in which you put your hands on the ground and your legs in the air

HANDSTAND

ˌhand-to-ˈhand *adj* [only before noun] hand-to-hand fighting is a way of fighting in which people use their hands and knives rather than guns: **hand-to-hand fighting/combat etc** *There was fierce hand-to-hand fighting in the streets of the city.* | *They were defeated in hand-to-hand combat.*

ˌhand-to-ˈmouth *adj* if you have a hand-to-mouth existence, you have just enough money and food to live

ˈhand tool *n* [C] a tool that does not use electricity → **power tool**

ˈhand ˌtowel *n* [C] a small piece of cloth that you use for drying your hands → **bath towel**

hand·wash /ˈhændwɒʃ $ -wɒːʃ, -wɑːʃ/ *v* [T] if you handwash a piece of clothing, you wash it by hand, not in a washing machine

hand·writ·ing /ˈhændˌraɪtɪŋ/ *n* [U] the style of someone's writing: *I recognised her handwriting on the envelope.* | *My handwriting has never been very neat.*

hand·writ·ten /ˌhændˈrɪtn◂/ *adj* written by hand, not printed: *a handwritten letter*

hand·y /ˈhændi/ ●●○ S3 *adj* (*comparative* **handier**, *superlative* **handiest**)
1 useful: *It's quite a handy little tool.* | ***It's*** *very* ***handy*** *having a light above your desk.* | *Take your swimming trunks with you – they might* ***come in handy*** (=be useful). THESAURUS USEFUL
2 *informal* near and easy to reach: *I always* ***keep*** *my gun* ***handy*** *just in case.* | *Do you* ***have*** *a piece of paper* ***handy***? | **[+for]** *BrE*: *The house was in Drury Lane, very handy for the theatre.*
3 good at using something, especially a tool: **[+with]** *He's very handy with a screwdriver.*

hand·y·man /ˈhændimæn/ *n* (*plural* **handymen** /-men/) [C] someone who is good at doing repairs and practical jobs in the house

hang[1] /hæŋ/ ●●● S1 W2 *v* (*past tense and past participle* **hung** /hʌŋ/)
1 TOP PART FASTENED **a)** [T always + adv/prep] (*also* **hang up**) to put something in a position so that the top part is fixed or supported, and the bottom part is free to move and does not touch the ground: *Philip hung his coat on a hook behind the door.* | *She hung the sheets on the washing line.* **b)** [I always + adv/prep] to be in a position where the top part is fixed or supported, and the bottom part is free to move and does not touch the ground: *An old-fashioned gas lamp hung from the ceiling.* | *Her long hair hung loose about her shoulders.* | *The shirt hung down almost to his ankles.*
2 PICTURE ETC **a)** [T] to fix a picture, photograph etc to a wall: *I wanted to hang the picture in the hall.* **b)** [I always + adv/prep] if a picture, photograph etc is hanging somewhere, it is fixed to a wall: *There was a family photograph hanging on the wall.* **c) be hung with sth** if the walls of a room are hung with pictures or decorations, the pictures etc are on the walls: *The entrance hall was hung with rich tapestries.*
3 KILL/BE KILLED (*past tense and past participle* **hanged**) [I,T] to kill someone by dropping them with a rope around their neck, or to die in this way, especially as a punishment for a serious crime: **be hanged for sth** *He was hanged for murder.* | **hang yourself** *Corey hanged himself in his prison cell.* | *If he is found guilty, he will almost certainly hang.*
4 PAPER [T] to fasten attractive paper to a wall in order to decorate a room: *We spent the afternoon* ***hanging wallpaper***.
5 DOOR [T] to fasten a door in position: *Hanging a door is quite a tricky job.*
6 MIST/SMOKE/SMELL [I + adv/prep] if something such as smoke hangs in the air, it stays in the air for a long time: *The smoke from the bonfires hung in the air.* | *A thick mist hung over the town.*
7 hang open if a door, someone's mouth etc hangs open, it is open
8 hang in the balance if something hangs in the balance, it is not certain what will happen to it: *The future of the company hangs in the balance.*
9 hang by a thread if something is hanging by a thread, it is in a very dangerous situation and may not continue: *He is still in hospital, his life hanging by a thread.*
10 hang (on) in there (*also* **hang tough** *especially AmE*) *spoken* to remain brave and determined when you are in a difficult situation: *Don't worry. Just hang on in there.*
11 hang your head to look ashamed and embarrassed: *She hung her head, not sure how to reply.* | *Daphne had* ***hung*** *her* ***head in shame***.
12 hang fire to wait for a short while before you do something: *I think we should hang fire for a week.*
13 leave sth hanging in the air to leave something in a situation where it has not been explained, completed, or dealt with: *His resignation has left some important questions hanging in the air.*
14 hang a right/left *AmE spoken* to turn right or left when driving: *Go straight on for two blocks, then hang a left.*
15 [I] *AmE spoken* to spend time somewhere, relaxing and enjoying yourself: **[+with]** *We were just hanging with the dudes at Mike's house.*

H

16 I'll be hanged if *BrE old-fashioned* used to express annoyance or to say that you will not allow something to happen: *I'll be hanged if I'll give them any money!*
17 hang it (all) *BrE old-fashioned* used to say that you are disappointed or annoyed about something
18 hang sth *BrE old-fashioned* used to say that you are not going to do something: *Oh hang the report, let's go for a drink.*
19 I/you might as well be hanged for a sheep as (for) a lamb used to say that, if a small action may have the same bad results for you as a larger one, there is no reason for not doing the larger thing
hang about *phr v BrE*
1 *spoken* to move slowly or take too long doing something: *Come on, we haven't got time to hang about!*
2 hang about (sth) to spend time somewhere without any real purpose: *There were always groups of boys hanging about in the square.* | *He normally hung about the house all day.*
3 hang about! *spoken* **a)** used to ask someone to wait or stop what they are doing **b)** used when you have just noticed or thought of something that is interesting or wrong: *Hang about – that can't be right.*
hang about with sb *phr v BrE informal* to spend a lot of time with someone
hang around/round (sth) *phr v informal* to wait or spend time somewhere, doing nothing: *I hung around the station for an hour but he never came.*
hang around with sb *phr v* to spend a lot of time with someone: *The people I used to hang around with were much older than me.*
hang back *phr v*
1 to stay a short distance away from someone or something, and not go too near them: *Instinctively he hung back in the shelter of a rock.*
2 to not say or do something because you are shy or afraid
hang on *phr v*
1 to hold something tightly: **[+to]** *She hung on to the side of the cart.* | *Hang on tight!*
2 hang on! *BrE spoken* **a)** used to ask or tell someone to wait SYN **hold on**: *Hang on! I'll be back in a minute.* **b)** used when you have just noticed or thought of something that is interesting or wrong
3 hang on sth to depend on something: *Everything hangs on the outcome of this meeting.*
4 hang on sb's words/every word to pay close attention to everything someone is saying: *She was watching his face, hanging on his every word.*
hang on to sth (*also* **hang onto sth**) *phr v* to keep something: *I think I'll hang on to the documents for a bit longer.*
hang out *phr v*
1 *informal* to spend a lot of time in a particular place or with particular people: **[+with]** *I don't really know who she hangs out with.* | *Where do the youngsters hang out?* → HANGOUT
2 hang sth ↔ out to hang clothes outside in order to dry them: *My job was to hang out the washing.* | ***Hang** the wet things **out to dry**.*
3 let it all hang out *informal* to relax and do what you like
4 hang sb out to dry to not give someone support in a difficult situation, for example to let someone else get all the blame for something
hang over sth/sb *phr v* if something bad is hanging over you, you are worried or anxious about it: *The threat of redundancy was still hanging over us.* | *It's not very nice to have huge debts **hanging over** your **head**.*
hang together *phr v*
1 if a plan, story, set of ideas etc hangs together, it is well organized and its different parts go well together: *Her story just doesn't hang together.*
2 if people hang together, they help each other
hang up *phr v*
1 to finish a telephone conversation: *I said goodbye and hung up.* | **[+on]** *Don't hang up on me.*
2 hang sth ↔ up to hang clothes on a hook etc: *She took her coat off and hung it up.*
3 hang up your hat/football boots/briefcase etc *informal* to stop doing a particular kind of work → HANG-UP, HUNG-UP

hang² ●○○ *n* **get the hang of sth** *informal* to learn how to do something or use something: *It seems difficult at first, but you'll soon get the hang of it.*

hang·ar /ˈhæŋə $ -ər/ *n* [C] a very large building in which aircraft are kept

hang·dog /ˈhæŋdɒg $ -dɒːg/ *adj* **hangdog expression/look** an expression that shows you feel sorry or ashamed about something: *I could tell from his hangdog look that things had gone badly.*

hang·er /ˈhæŋə $ -ər/ (*also* **coat hanger**, **clothes hanger**) *n* [C] a curved piece of wood, plastic, or metal with a hook on top, used for hanging clothes on: *She took off her jacket and hung it on a hanger.*

ˌhanger-ˈon *n* (*plural* **hangers-on**) [C] someone who spends a lot of time with a rich or important person, because they hope to get some advantage for themselves: *He was surrounded by a crowd of friends and hangers-on.*

HANG-GLIDER

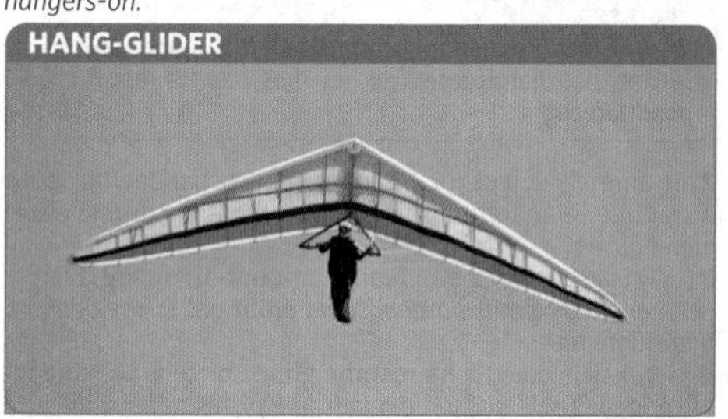

ˈhang-ˌglider *n* [C] **1** a large frame covered with cloth that you hold on to and fly slowly through the air on, without an engine **2** someone who flies using a hang-glider

ˈhang-ˌgliding *n* [U] the sport of flying using a hang-glider

hang·ing /ˈhæŋɪŋ/ *n* **1** [C,U] the act of killing someone by putting a rope around their neck and dropping them, used as a punishment: *public hangings* | *people who believe that bringing back hanging will reduce the amount of crime* **2** [C] a large piece of cloth that is hung on a wall as a decoration: *a colourful wall hanging*

ˌhanging ˈbasket *n* [C] a basket with plants growing in it that is hung on the outside of a building as decoration

hang·man /ˈhæŋmən/ *n* (*plural* **hangmen** /-mən/) [C] someone whose job is to kill criminals by hanging them

hang·nail /ˈhæŋneɪl/ *n* [C] a piece of skin that has become loose near the bottom of your FINGERNAIL

hang·out /ˈhæŋaʊt/ *n* [C] *informal* a place someone likes to go to often: *The bar is a favourite hangout for students.*

hang·o·ver /ˈhæŋəʊvə $ -oʊvər/ ●○○ *n* [C]
1 a pain in your head and a feeling of sickness that you get the day after you have drunk too much alcohol: *I **had a** terrible **hangover** the next day.* THESAURUS HEADACHE
2 a hangover from sth something from the past that still exists or happens but is no longer necessary or useful: *This feeling was a hangover from her schooldays.* | *an institution which is a hangover from Victorian times*

ˈhang-up, **hang·up** /ˈhæŋʌp/ *n* [C] *informal* a feeling of worry or embarrassment about something that you have although there is no real reason to feel this way: *She had cured him of all his hang-ups.* | **[+about]** *She's **got a** real **hang-up** about her body.* → **hang up** at HANG¹

hank /hæŋk/ *n* [C] an amount of wool or thread that has been wound into a loose ball

han·ker /ˈhæŋkə $ -ər/ *v* [I,T] to have a strong desire for something: **hanker after/for** *She hankered for a new life in a different country.* | *holidaymakers who hanker after the sun* | **hanker to do sth** *I've been hankering to visit my father's birthplace for many years.*

han·ker·ing /ˈhæŋkərɪŋ/ *n* [singular] a strong wish to have or do something: **[+for/after]** *his hankering for adventure* | **a hankering to do sth** *I've always had a hankering to be a doctor.*

han·kie, **hanky** /ˈhæŋki/ *n* [C] *informal* a HANDKERCHIEF

hank·y-pank·y /ˌhæŋki ˈpæŋki/ *n* [U] *informal* sexual activity – used humorously

han·som /ˈhænsəm/ (*also* ˈ**hansom** ˌ**cab**) *n* [C] a small vehicle pulled by a horse which was used in the past as a taxi

Ha·nuk·kah, **Chanukah** /ˈhɑːnəkə $ ˈkɑːnəkə, ˈhɑː-/ *n* [C,U] an eight-day Jewish holiday in November or December

ha'penny /ˈheɪpni/ *n* [C] another spelling of HALFPENNY

hap·haz·ard /ˌhæpˈhæzəd◂ $ -ərd◂/ *adj* happening or done in a way that is not planned or organized: **a haphazard way/manner/fashion** *I continued my studies in a rather haphazard way.* | *Educational provision in the country is haphazard.* —**haphazardly** *adv*: *bushes growing haphazardly here and there*

hap·less /ˈhæpləs/ *adj* [only before noun] *literary* unlucky: *The hapless passengers were stranded at the airport for three days.*

hap·pen /ˈhæpən/ ●●● S1 W1 *v* [I]

1 when something happens, there is an event, especially one that is not planned SYN **occur**: *When did the accident happen?* | *It's impossible to predict what will happen next.* | **something/nothing/anything happens** *Something terrible has happened.* | *She carried on as if nothing had happened.* | *This was* **bound to happen** *sooner or later.* | *This kind of thing* **happens all the time**. | *We'll still be friends,* **whatever happens**.

2 something/anything/what happens to sb/sth if something happens to someone or something, they are affected by an event: *He should be here by now – something must have happened to him.* | *The same thing happened to me last year.* | *What's happened to your coat? It's all ripped.*

3 happen to do sth if you happen to do something, you do it by chance: *I happened to see James in town.*

4 sb/sth happens to be sth used when telling someone something in an angry way: *This happens to be my house!*

5 as it happens/it just so happens used to tell someone something that is surprising, interesting, or useful: *As it happens, I know someone who might be able to help.*

6 these things happen used to tell someone not to worry about a mistake they have made, an accident they have caused etc: *It's not your fault – these things happen.*

7 whatever happened to sb/sth? used to ask where a person or thing is now: *Whatever happened to Steve? I haven't seen him for years.* → **accidents (will) happen** at ACCIDENT(5)

THESAURUS

happen used especially when talking about events that have not been planned: *When did the accident happen?* | *Something terrible has happened!*

take place to happen – used especially when talking about events that have been planned or that have already happened: *The conference will take place on the 16th of June.* | *The competition took place on Saturday 30th June.*

occur *formal* to happen – used especially when talking about events that have not been planned: *The incident occurred outside the police station at around 9 pm.*

there is/there are used when saying that a particular event happens: *There was an earthquake about a week ago.* | *There are strikes almost every year.*

come up to happen – used about problems, questions, or opportunities: *There aren't any jobs at the moment, but we'll let you know if* **something comes up**. | *This question often comes up when I'm talking to students.*

arise *formal* to happen unexpectedly – used about problems, arguments, or difficult situations: *A dispute arose about who should receive the money.* | *It is best to deal with the problem as soon as it arises.*

crop up to happen – used about problems or difficult situations, especially ones that are less serious, and can quickly be dealt with: *The banks will contact their customers if a problem crops up.*

strike to happen suddenly and unexpectedly – used about very bad events: *The hurricane struck at around 1 am.* | *Disaster struck, and he lost all movement in his legs.*

turn out to happen in a particular way: *Luckily, everything turned out well.*

happen on/upon sb/sth *phr v literary or old-fashioned* to find something or meet someone by chance SYN **come across**: *I happened on the restaurant by chance.*

hap·pen·ing[1] /ˈhæpənɪŋ/ *n* [C usually plural] something that happens, especially a strange event: **strange/unusual/mysterious etc happenings** *There have been reports of strange happenings in the town.*

happening[2] *adj informal* fashionable and exciting: *Brighton is definitely a happening place.* THESAURUS FASHIONABLE

hap·pen·stance /ˈhæpənstæns/ *n* [C,U] *literary* chance, or something that happens by chance

hap·pi·ly /ˈhæpəli/ ●●○ *adv*

1 in a happy way: *Michelle smiled happily.* | *I'm a* **happily married** *man.* | *So she married the prince, and they* **lived happily ever after** (=used at the end of children's stories to say that someone was happy for the rest of their life).

2 [sentence adverb] fortunately: *Happily, his injuries were not serious.*

3 very willingly: *I'd happily go for you.* | *Most restaurants will happily accept payment by credit card.*

hap·pi·ness /ˈhæpinəs/ ●●● W3 *n* [U] the state of being happy: *Juliet's eyes shone with happiness.* | *We want our children to have the best possible chance of happiness.* THESAURUS PLEASURE

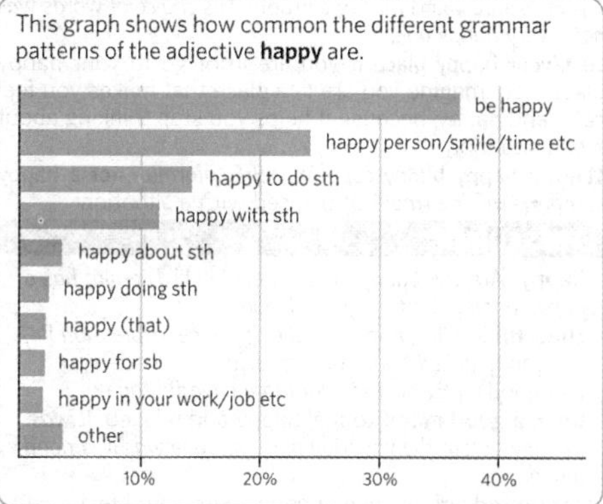

hap·py /ˈhæpi/ ●●● S1 W1 *adj* (*comparative* **happier**, *superlative* **happiest**)

1 having feelings of pleasure, for example because something good has happened to you or you are very satisfied with your life OPP **sad**: *It's a lovely house and we've been very happy here.* | *I've never* **felt happier** *in my life.* | *He was a happy child who rarely cried.* | *the happy faces of the children* | *I loved her and thought I could* **make** *her* **happy**. | **[+about]** *She's very happy about the baby.* | **happy to do sth** *John will be so happy to see you.* | **happy (that)** *I'm happy that everything worked out well in the end.* | **be/feel happy for sb** *What a wonderful opportunity! I'm so happy for you.* | **happy in your work/job etc** | **happy to be doing sth** *We're very happy to be taking part.* | **the happy couple** (=a couple that have just got married or will soon get married)

GRAMMAR: Patterns with happy

• You are **happy to do** something or **happy to be doing** something: *I'm very happy to be here.* ✗ Don't say: *I'm very happy for being here.*

H

• You are **happy that** something has happened or is true: *I'm very happy that I'm here.*
• You are **happy about** something: *I'm so happy about your engagement.* ✗ Don't say: *I'm so happy for your engagement.*
• You are **happy for** someone when something good has happened to them: *Congratulations – I'm happy for you.*

2 [usually before noun] a happy time, relationship, event etc is a good one that makes you feel happy: *This has been the happiest day of my life.* | *They had a very happy marriage.* | *I have lots of happy memories of the place.* | *The story has a **happy ending**, however.* | *When's **the happy event*** (=the birth of your child)?
3 [not before noun] satisfied or not worried: **[+with]** *On the whole, I'm happy with the way I look.* | *People living nearby are not happy with the decision.* | **[+about]** *Mum wasn't happy about Tess going off travelling on her own.* | *I pretended to agree with her, just to **keep** her **happy**.* | **happy doing sth** *I'm quite happy doing what I'm doing.* **THESAURUS** ▸ SATISFIED
4 be happy to do sth to be very willing to do something, especially to help someone: *Our team will be happy to help.* | *I'd be happy to take you in my car.*
5 Happy Birthday/New Year/Christmas etc used to wish someone happiness on a special occasion: *Happy Birthday, Michael!* | *Happy Thanksgiving, everyone!*
6 many happy returns used to wish someone happiness on their BIRTHDAY
7 [only before noun] fortunate or lucky: *By a **happy coincidence**, James was also in town that weekend.* | *I'm in the **happy position** of not having to work.*
8 a happy medium (between sth and sth) a way of doing something that is not extreme but is somewhere between two possible choices: *I always tried to **strike a happy medium** between having a home that looked like a bomb had hit it and becoming obsessively tidy.*
9 [only before noun] *formal* suitable: *His choice of words was not a very happy one.*
10 a/your happy place if you are in or go to your happy place, you imagine you are in a place that makes you feel calm and happy, because it helps you stop thinking about a bad situation
11 not a happy bunny *especially BrE informal*, **not a happy camper** *AmE informal* not pleased with a situation

THESAURUS

happy: *Are you happy in your new job?* | *The film has a happy ending.* | *a happy childhood*
cheerful looking happy: *a cheerful face/expression* | *The room looked bright and cheerful* (=it made you feel good). | *He seems a lot more cheerful today.*
be in a good mood to feel happy and relaxed: *It was the day before the vacation and everyone was in a good mood.*
contented *written* feeling happy with your life, job, situation etc: *He was contented with his job as a cycle mechanic.* | *She sat down with a contented expression on her face.*
pleased/glad [not before noun] happy because something good has happened: *I'm pleased I passed my exam.* | *He was glad to see someone that he knew.*

VERY HAPPY

delighted [not before noun] very happy because something good has happened: *The doctors say they are delighted with her progress.*
thrilled [not before noun] very happy and excited about something: *He's thrilled at the idea of going to Disneyworld.*
overjoyed [not before noun] very happy because you have heard some good news: *She was overjoyed when she found out that her son was safe.*
be on top of the world (*also* **be over the moon** *BrE*) [not before noun] *informal* to be very happy: *I was over the moon when I won the championship.*
ecstatic extremely happy: *The crowd were ecstatic, and cheered wildly.* | *ecstatic fans*
blissful a blissful time is one in which you feel extremely happy: *We stayed on the islands for two blissful weeks.* | *It sounded blissful – sea, sun, and good food.*

happy-clap·py /ˌhæpi ˈklæpi◂/ *adj BrE informal* relating to a Christian church where people sing, shout, show their emotions, and encourage other people to join their church – used to show disapproval: *happy-clappy Christians* —**happy clappy** *n* [C]

ˌhappy-go-ˈlucky *adj* enjoying life and not worrying about things SYN **easy-going**: *a happy-go-lucky person*

ˈhappy hour *n* [C,U] a special time in a bar when alcoholic drinks are sold at lower prices

ˌhappy ˈslapping *n* [C,U] the act of deliberately attacking someone and filming the attack on a MOBILE PHONE

hap·tic /ˈhæptɪk/ *adj technical* relating to the sense of touch or giving the feeling of physically touching something: *Haptic technology can give someone an idea of the 'weight' and 'texture' of a virtual object.*

har·a·kir·i /ˌhærəˈkɪri/ *n* [U] a way of killing yourself by cutting open your stomach, used in the past in Japan to avoid losing honour

ha·rangue /həˈræŋ/ *v* [T] to speak in a loud angry way, often for a long time, in order to criticize someone or to persuade them that you are right: **harangue sb about sth** *He stood on the street corner, haranguing passers-by about the stupidity of the forthcoming war.* —**harangue** *n* [C]

har·ass /ˈhærəs, həˈræs/ ●○○ *v* [T]
1 to make someone's life unpleasant, for example by frequently saying offensive things to them or threatening them: *A number of black youths have complained of being harassed by the police.* | **sexually/racially harass sb** (=harass someone because of their sex or race) *One woman claimed that she had been sexually harassed by a male manager.*
2 to keep attacking an enemy again and again

har·assed /ˈhærəst, həˈræst/ *adj BrE* anxious and tired because you have too many problems or things to do: *He looked pale and harassed.*

har·ass·ment /ˈhærəsmənt, həˈræsmənt/ ●○○ *n* [U] when someone behaves in an unpleasant or threatening way towards you: *African-Americans have been complaining about police harassment for years.* | **[+of]** *Political parties are banned, and harassment of dissidents is commonplace.* | **sexual/racial harassment** (=because of someone's sex or race) *We need effective strategies to combat sexual harassment in the workplace.*

har·bin·ger /ˈhɑːbɪndʒə $ ˈhɑːrbɪndʒər/ *n* [C] *literary or formal* a sign that something is going to happen soon: **[+of]** *These birds are considered to be **harbingers of doom**.*

har·bour[1] *BrE*, **harbor** *AmE* /ˈhɑːbə $ ˈhɑːrbər/ ●●○ *n* [C] an area of water next to the land where the water is calm, so that ships are safe when they are inside it → **bay**: *as they sailed into Portsmouth Harbour*

harbour[2] *BrE*, **harbor** *AmE* *v* [T] **1** to keep bad thoughts, fears, or hopes in your mind for a long time: *I think he's harbouring some sort of grudge against me.* | *She began to harbour doubts over the wisdom of their journey.* **2** to contain something, especially something hidden and dangerous: *Sinks and draining boards can harbour germs.* **3** to protect and hide criminals that the police are searching for **THESAURUS** ▸ PROTECT

ˈharbour ˌmaster *n* [C] the official who is in charge of a harbour

hard[1] /hɑːd $ hɑːrd/ ●●● S1 W1 *adj* (*comparative* **harder**, *superlative* **hardest**)
1 FIRM TO TOUCH firm, stiff, and difficult to press down, break, or cut OPP **soft**: *a hard wooden chair* | *the hardest substance known to man* | *After months without rain, the ground was too hard to plough.*
2 DIFFICULT difficult to do or understand SYN **difficult** OPP **easy**: *This year's exam was much harder than last*

H

year's. | *You'll have to make some hard decisions.* | *They're a hard team to beat.* | **it is hard to believe/imagine/see/know etc** *It was hard to see what else we could have done.* | *It's hard to believe that anyone would say something like that.* | **find it hard to do sth** *I was finding it hard to concentrate.* | *Permanent jobs are* ***hard to come by*** (=difficult to find or get). | **be hard for sb** *It must be hard for her, bringing up three kids on her own.* | *Telling my parents is going to be* ***the hardest thing*** *about it.* | **have a hard time doing sth** (=be difficult for someone to do something) *You'll have a hard time proving that.* | *I had a hard time persuading him to accept the offer.* | *Such criticism was* ***hard to take*** (=difficult to accept). **THESAURUS** DIFFICULT

3 **WORK/EFFORT** [usually before noun] using or involving a lot of mental or physical effort: *To be successful in sport requires* ***hard work*** *and a great deal of determination.* | *After* ***a hard day*** *at work, I just want to come home and put my feet up.* | **a hard day's work/walking/skiing etc** *There's a sauna where you can relax after a hard day's skiing.* | *Becoming a doctor never interested him. It was* ***too much like hard work*** (=it would involve too much work). **THESAURUS** TIRING

4 **FULL OF PROBLEMS** a situation or time that is hard is one in which you have a lot of problems, especially when you do not have enough money: *She's had* ***a hard life.*** | ***Times were hard*** *and they were forced to sell their house.* | *He had clearly* ***fallen on hard times*** (=did not have much money).

5 **be hard on sb a)** to criticize someone in a way that is unfair, or to be too strict with them: *Perhaps I'm too hard on her.* **b)** to have a bad effect on someone: *Divorce can be very hard on children.*

6 **be hard on sth** to have a bad effect on something: *Standing all day is very hard on the feet.*

7 **do sth the hard way** to learn, achieve, or do something after a bad experience or by making mistakes: *He* ***learned the hard way*** *about the harsh reality of the boxing world.* | *Make sure you put the baby's diaper on before you start feeding her. I* ***learned this lesson the hard way.*** | *He earned his promotion the hard way.*

8 **USING FORCE** using a lot of force: *Jane gave the door a* ***good hard*** *push.* | *She gave him a hard slap.*

9 **hard evidence/facts/information etc** facts that are definitely true and can be proved: *There is no hard evidence to support this theory.*

10 **UNKIND** showing no sympathetic or gentle feelings: *a hard face* | *Her voice was hard and cold.* | *You're a hard man, John.*

11 **hard going a)** difficult to do and needing a lot of effort: *A strong wind made the race very hard going.* **b)** boring, or difficult to deal with, talk to etc: *I find some of his friends pretty hard going.*

12 **make hard work of sth** to make something you are doing seem more difficult than it really is: *Juventus were making hard work of what should have been an easy game.*

13 **be hard at it/work** *informal* to be very busy doing something: *Sarah was hard at it on her computer.*

14 **WATER** hard water contains a lot of minerals, and does not mix easily with soap OPP **soft**

15 **hard luck a)** *BrE spoken* used to tell someone that you feel sorry for them because they have not succeeded in what they were trying to do: *'I failed my driving test.' 'Oh, hard luck!'* **b)** when bad things happen to you that are not your fault: *You've had your share of hard luck.* | **[+on]** *It was hard luck on you.* **c)** *spoken* (*also* **hard cheese** *BrE*) used to say that you do not care if someone is having problems, does not like something etc: *If you don't like the idea then hard luck!*

16 **give sb a hard time** *informal* **a)** to treat someone badly or cause problems for them: *Giving you a hard time, is she?* | *They reached the border where officials gave them a hard time.* **b)** to criticize someone a lot: *Hostile critics have given Hartman a hard time.*

17 **have a hard time** to have a lot of problems or bad experiences: *I'm glad she's happy at last – she's had such a hard time.* | *Vegetarians still often* ***have a hard time of it*** *when it comes to eating out.*

18 **drive/strike a hard bargain** to demand a lot or refuse to give too much when you are making an agreement: *The company is believed to have struck a hard bargain.*

19 **hard feelings a)** anger between people because of something that has happened: *We'd known each other too long for hard feelings.* | *I have no hard feelings towards Steve.* **b)** **no hard feelings** *spoken* used to tell someone that you do not want to be angry with them or for them to be angry with you: *I'm sorry it didn't work out, but no hard feelings, eh?*

20 **take a (long) hard look at sth/sb** to think carefully about something, especially with the result that you change your opinions or behaviour: *You should take a long hard look at the issues before committing yourself.*

21 **hard line** a strict way of dealing with someone or something: *The president should abandon his hard line in the region.* | **take/adopt a hard line (on sth)** *The school takes a very hard line on drugs.*

22 **hard news** news stories that are about serious subjects or events: *TV news programs seem to be more interested in gossip than in hard news.*

23 **NOT FRIGHTENED** *BrE spoken* strong, ready to fight, and not afraid of anyone or anything: *He thinks he's really hard.* | *Jones was known as soccer's* ***hard man.***

24 **(as) hard as nails** someone who is hard as nails seems to have no feelings such as fear or sympathy

25 **a hard taskmaster/master** someone who makes people work too hard

26 **a hard winter/frost** a very cold winter or FROST OPP **mild**

27 **the hard left/right** people who have extreme LEFT-WING or RIGHT-WING political aims and ideas SYN **far left/right, extreme**: *concerns about the re-emergence of the hard right in some areas*

28 **LIGHT** *especially literary* hard light is bright and unpleasant SYN **harsh**: *the hard brilliance of the moonlight*

29 **ALCOHOL** [only before noun] *informal* very strong: *hard liquor* | *I never touch* ***the hard stuff*** (=strong alcohol). → HARD DRUGS

30 **a hard left/right** a big turn to the left or right, for example when you are driving SYN **sharp**

31 **PRONUNCIATION** a hard 'c' is pronounced /k/ rather than /s/; a hard 'g' is pronounced /g/ rather than /dʒ/ → **soft** —**hardness** *n* [U]: *a material that would combine the flexibility of rubber with the hardness of glass*

THESAURUS

hard difficult to press down, break, or cut, and not at all soft: *I fell onto the hard stone floor.* | *The clay gets harder as it dries.*

firm not completely hard, but not easy to press or bend – used especially when this seems a good thing: *I like to sleep on a firm mattress.* | *exercises to make your stomach muscles nice and firm*

stiff difficult to bend and not changing shape: *a piece of stiff cardboard* | *The collar of his shirt felt stiff and uncomfortable.*

solid made of a thick hard material and not hollow: *a solid oak door* | *The floor felt strong and solid beneath her feet.*

rigid /ˈrɪdʒəd/ having a structure that is made of a material that is difficult or impossible to bend: *The tent is supported by a rigid frame.* | *Carry sandwiches in a rigid container.*

crisp/crispy used about food that is pleasantly hard, so that it makes a noise when you bite it – often used about things that have been cooked in thin SLICES until they are brown: *Bake the cookies until they are crisp and golden.* | *crispy bacon*

crunchy food that is crunchy makes a noise when you bite on it – often used about things that are fresh, for example fruit, vegetables, and nuts: *a crunchy breakfast cereal* | *The carrots were still nice and crunchy.*

tough meat that is tough is too hard and is difficult to cut or eat: *The meat was tough and flavourless.*

rubbery too hard and bending like rubber rather than breaking – used especially about meat: *The chicken was all rubbery.*

H

COLLOCATIONS CHECK

firm bed/muscles/fruit/vegetables/ground
stiff card/cardboard/collar/material/fingers/body
solid wood/steel/concrete/floor/wall
rigid frame/structure
crisp/crispy apple/bacon/toast/potato/lettuce
crunchy cereal/vegetables/nuts/snack
tough meat
rubbery meat

hard² ●●● S1 W2 *adv* (*comparative* **harder**, *superlative* **hardest**)
1 USING ENERGY/EFFORT using a lot of effort, energy, or attention: *She has **worked hard** all her life.* | *He had **thought long and hard** before getting involved with the project.* | *She **tried her hardest** to ignore what he'd said.* | *Ella was concentrating very hard.* | *I couldn't convince him no matter how hard I tried.*
2 WITH FORCE with a lot of force: *You need to hit the ball hard.* | *He slammed the door hard behind him.* | *It was raining very hard.*
3 BECOME SOLID becoming solid, stiff, or firm: *By now the cement had set hard.*
4 be hard hit/be hit hard to be badly affected by something that has happened: *Sales were hard hit by high interest rates.*
5 be hard put/pressed/pushed to do sth *informal* to have difficulty doing something: *You'd be hard pressed to find anyone better for the job.* → HARD-PRESSED
6 be/feel hard done by *informal* to be or feel unfairly treated: *As a child I felt hard done by, living so far away from my friends.*
7 take sth hard to be very upset about something, especially bad news: *Alan took his mother's death particularly hard.*
8 hard upon/on sth *BrE formal* soon after something: *His second major contract followed hard upon the first.*
9 laugh/cry hard to laugh, cry etc a lot → **HARD BY**, **HARD UP**, → **(hard/hot/close) on sb's heels** at HEEL¹, → **(hard/hot/close) on the heels of sth** at HEEL¹, → **play hard to get** at PLAY¹(23)

ˌhard-and-ˈfast *adj* [only before noun] clear, definite, and always able to be used: *It is impossible to give **hard-and-fast rules**, but here are some points to consider.*

hard·back /ˈhɑːdbæk $ ˈhɑːrd-/ (*also* **hardcover**) *n* [C] a book that has a strong stiff cover: **in hardback** *His first novel sold over 40,000 copies in hardback.* THESAURUS BOOK —**hardback** *adj*: *a **hardback edition** of 'The Joy of Cooking'* → PAPERBACK

hard·ball /ˈhɑːdbɔːl $ ˈhɑːrdbɒːl/ *n* [U] *AmE* **play hardball** *informal* to be very determined to get what you want, especially in business or politics

ˌhard-ˈbitten *adj* not easily shocked or upset, because you have had a lot of experience: *a hard-bitten cop*

hard·board /ˈhɑːdbɔːd $ ˈhɑːrdbɔːrd/ *n* [U] a material made from small pieces of wood pressed together

ˌhard-ˈboiled *adj* **1** a hard-boiled egg has been boiled until it becomes solid → SOFT-BOILED **2** *informal* **a)** not showing your emotions and not influenced by your feelings SYN **tough**: *a hard-boiled marketing executive* **b) hard-boiled film/thriller/fiction etc** a film etc that deals with people who do not show their emotions

ˌhard ˈby *adv, prep BrE old use* very near: *in a house hard by the city gate*

ˌhard ˈcash *n* [U] paper money and coins, not cheques or CREDIT CARDS

ˈhard ˌcopy *n* [C,U] information from a computer that is printed out onto paper, or the printed papers themselves

ˈhard core *n* [singular] *BrE* **a)** the small group of people that are most active within a group or organization: *the hard core of the Communist Party* **b)** a group of people who cannot be persuaded to change their behaviour or beliefs: *There is still a small hard core of football supporters who cause trouble whenever they can.*

ˌhard-core, **hard·core** /ˈhɑːdkɔː $ ˈhɑːrdkɔːr/ *adj* **1** [only before noun] having an extreme way of life or an extreme belief that is very unlikely to change: *a hard-core drug addict* | *hard-core racists* **2 hard-core pornography** magazines, films etc that show the details of sexual behaviour, often in an unpleasant way

ˌhard ˈcourt *n* [C] an area for playing tennis which has a hard surface, not grass

hard·cov·er /ˈhɑːdkʌvə $ ˈhɑːrdkʌvər/ (*also* **hardback**) *n* [C] a book that has a strong stiff cover THESAURUS BOOK —**hardcover** *adj* → PAPERBACK

ˌhard ˈcurrency *n* [C,U] money that is from a country that has a strong ECONOMY and is therefore unlikely to lose its value

ˌhard ˈdisk *n* [C] a stiff DISK inside a computer that is used for storing information

ˈhard-ˌdrinking *adj* [only before noun] a hard-drinking person drinks a lot of alcohol

ˈhard drive *n* [C] the part of a computer where information and programs are stored, consisting of HARD DISKS and the electronic equipment that reads what is stored on them → **disk drive**

ˌhard ˈdrugs *n* [plural] very strong illegal drugs such as HEROIN and COCAINE → **SOFT DRUG**

ˌhard-ˈearned *adj* [only before noun] earned or achieved after a lot of effort: **hard-earned money/cash etc** *Don't be too quick to part with your hard-earned cash.* | *a hard-earned victory*

ˌhard-ˈedged *adj* dealing with difficult subjects or criticizing someone severely in a way that may offend some people: *a hard-edged collection of songs*

hard·en /ˈhɑːdn $ ˈhɑːrdn/ ●○○ *v* [I,T]
1 to become firm or stiff, or to make something firm or stiff OPP **soften**: *It will take about 24 hours for the glue to harden.*
2 if your attitude hardens, or if something hardens it, you become more strict and determined and less sympathetic OPP **soften**: *Attitudes towards the terrorists have hardened even more since the attack.*
3 *written* if your face or voice hardens, or if something hardens it, you look or sound less sympathetic or happy OPP **soften**: *His face hardened momentarily, then he looked away.*
4 harden your heart to make yourself not feel pity or sympathy for someone

hard·ened /ˈhɑːdnd $ ˈhɑːr-/ *adj* **1 hardened criminal/police officer etc** a criminal, police officer etc who has had a lot of experience of things that are shocking and is therefore less affected by them **2 become hardened (to sth)** to become used to something shocking because you have seen it many times

ˌhard-ˈfought *adj* a hard-fought game, competition etc involves two opposing sides who are trying very hard to defeat each other: **a hard-fought battle/contest/game etc** *one of the most hard-fought games this season* | *a hard-fought battle for the presidency*

ˌhard ˈhat *n* [C] a protective hat, worn especially by workers in places where buildings are being built → see picture at **HAT**

ˌhard-ˈheaded *adj* practical and able to make difficult decisions without letting your emotions affect your judgment: *a hard-headed business tycoon*

hard-heart·ed /ˌhɑːd ˈhɑːtɪd $ ˌhɑːrd ˈhɑːr-/ *adj* not caring about other people's feelings OPP **soft-hearted** THESAURUS UNKIND

ˌhard-ˈhitting *adj* criticizing someone or something in a strong and effective way: *a hard-hitting report*

ˌhard ˈlabour *BrE*, **hard labor** *AmE* *n* [U] punishment in prison which consists of hard physical work

ˌhard-ˈline *adj* having extreme political beliefs, and refusing to change them: *a hard-line Marxist* → **hard line** at **HARD¹(21)**

H

hard·lin·er /ˌhɑːdˈlaɪnə◂, ˈhɑːdlaɪnə $ ˌhɑːrdˈlaɪnər◂/ *n* [C] a politician who wants political problems to be dealt with in a strong and extreme way

ˌhard-ˈluck ˌstory *n* (*plural* **hard-luck stories**) [C] a story you tell someone about bad things that have happened to you, in order to get their sympathy or help

hard·ly /ˈhɑːdli $ ˈhɑːrdli/ ●●● S2 W2 *adv*
1 almost not: *My parents divorced when I was six, and I hardly knew my father.* | *The children were so excited they* ***could hardly*** *speak.* | *I* ***can hardly*** *believe it.* | ***Hardly anyone*** (=almost no one) *writes to me these days.* | *Dad ate* ***hardly anything*** (=almost nothing). | *There was* ***hardly any*** (=very little) *traffic.* | *She lives in Spain, so we* ***hardly ever*** (=almost never) *see her.* | **hardly a day/week/month etc goes by without/when** (=used to say that something happens almost every day, week etc) *Hardly a month goes by without another factory closing down.*
2 used to mean 'not', when you are suggesting that the person you are speaking to will agree with you: *It's* ***hardly surprising*** *that she won't answer his calls after the way he's treated her.* | *You* ***can hardly*** *blame Tom for not waiting.* | *My boss* ***could hardly*** *be described as handsome.* | **hardly the time/place/person etc** (=a very unsuitable time, place, person etc) *This is hardly the place to discuss the matter.*
3 used to say that something has only just happened: *The building work has hardly begun.* | **had hardly ... when/before** *She had hardly sat down when the phone rang.*

GRAMMAR

Word order

- **Hardly** usually comes before a main verb: *He hardly said a word.*
- **Hardly** comes after the first auxiliary verb: *I can hardly believe you said that.* | *We could hardly have known what was going to happen next.* ✗ Don't say: *I hardly can believe you said that.*
- **Hardly** usually comes after the verb 'be' when it is used in simple tenses such as 'is' or 'was': *This was hardly surprising.*
- In writing, you can use **hardly** at the beginning of a sentence before an auxiliary to say that one thing happens very soon after another thing: ***Hardly had*** *the rain stopped, when the sun came out.*

Negatives

You say **hardly any**: *There's hardly any milk.*
✗ Don't say: *There's hardly no milk.*
GRAMMAR GUIDE ▸ ADVERBS

USAGE: Hard, hardly

Hardly is not the adverb of **hard**. The adverb of **hard** is **hard**: *I work hard.* ✗ Don't say: *I work hardly.*

ˌhard-ˈnosed *adj* [usually before noun] not affected by emotions, and determined to get what you want: *a hard-nosed businessman*

ˌhard of ˈhearing *adj* [not before noun] **1** unable to hear very well → **deaf 2 the hard of hearing** [plural] people who are unable to hear very well

ˈhard-on *n* [C] *informal not polite* an ERECTION(1)

ˌhard ˈporn *n* [U] magazines, films etc that show sexual behaviour in an unacceptable, sometimes violent way → SOFT PORN

ˌhard-ˈpressed *adj* having a lot of problems and not enough money or time: *The new exams will only add to the workload of already hard-pressed teachers.* → **be hard pressed to do sth** at HARD²(5)

ˌhard ˈrock *n* [U] a type of ROCK MUSIC that is played loudly, has a strong beat, and uses electric instruments

hard·scrab·ble /ˈhɑːdskræbəl $ ˈhɑːrd-/ *adj* [only before noun] **1** hardscrabble land has poor soil and will not produce good crops of food, and sometimes not any food at all: *I remembered it being green and humid, nothing like this hardscrabble land.* **2** poor, and working on land that does not produce enough food to eat or crops to sell: *The town is also home to hardscrabble residents who have to eat at the soup kitchen.*

ˌhard ˈsell *n* [singular] a way of selling something in which there is a lot of pressure on you to buy OPP **soft sell** → SELL¹

hard·ship /ˈhɑːdʃɪp $ ˈhɑːrd-/ ●○○ *n* [C,U] something that makes your life difficult or unpleasant, especially a lack of money, or the condition of having a difficult life: *an economic policy that* ***caused*** *great* ***hardship*** *for many people* | *Many students are* ***suffering*** *severe financial* ***hardship***. | **[+of]** *the hardships of war*

ˌhard ˈshoulder *n* [singular] *BrE* the area at the side of a big road where you are allowed to stop if you have a problem with your car SYN **shoulder** *AmE*

ˈhard site *n* [C] a prison, especially one controlled by the army, where the prisoners are kept in uncomfortable conditions and treated extremely severely

ˌhard ˈup *adj* **1** if you are hard up, you do not have much money: *I'm a bit hard up at the moment.* **2** not having something that you want or need: *'How about a date with Tom?' 'No, thanks, I'm not that hard up.'* | **[+for]** *The media are obviously hard up for stories.*

hard·ware /ˈhɑːdweə $ ˈhɑːrdwer/ ●●○ *n* [U]
1 computer machinery and equipment, as opposed to the programs that make computers work → SOFTWARE
2 equipment and tools for your home and garden
3 the machinery and equipment that is needed to do something: *tanks and other military hardware*

ˌhard-ˈwearing *adj BrE* products that are hard-wearing will remain in good condition for a long time even when they are used a lot SYN **long-wearing** *AmE*

ˌhard-ˈwired *adj* **1** *technical* computer systems that are hard-wired are controlled by HARDWARE rather than SOFTWARE and cannot be easily changed by the user **2** if an attitude, way of behaving etc is hard-wired, it is a natural part of a person's character that they are born with and cannot change: *The desire to communicate seems to be hard-wired into our brains.*

ˌhard-ˈwon *adj* achieved only after a lot of effort and difficulty: *her hard-won independence*

hard·wood /ˈhɑːdwʊd $ ˈhɑːrd-/ *n* [C,U] strong heavy wood from trees such as OAK, used for making furniture → SOFTWOOD

ˌhard-ˈworking ●●○ *adj* working with a lot of effort SYN **industrious**: *a hard-working teacher*

har·dy /ˈhɑːdi $ ˈhɑːrdi/ *adj* **1** strong and healthy and able to bear difficult living conditions: *hardy mountain goats* **2** a hardy plant is able to live through the winter —**hardiness** *n* [U]

ˌhardy peˈrennial *n* [C] **1** a hardy plant that produces flowers for several years **2** *BrE* an idea that is often suggested or discussed

hare¹ /heə $ her/ *n* (*plural* **hare** *or* **hares**) [C] an animal like a rabbit but larger, which can run very quickly

hare² *v* [I always + adv/prep] *BrE informal* to run or go very fast: **[+off]** *He hared off down the road.*

ˈhare-brained *adj* a hare-brained plan or idea is very silly or unlikely to succeed: *his latest* ***hare-brained scheme***

hare·lip /ˌheəˈlɪp $ ˌher-/ *n* [singular] *old-fashioned* an offensive word for the condition of having your top lip divided into two parts because it did not develop correctly before birth

har·em /ˈhɑːriːm, hɑːˈriːm $ ˈhɑːrəm, ˈher-/ *n* [C] **1** the group of wives or women who lived with a rich or powerful man in some Muslim societies in the past **2** part of a Muslim house that is separate from the rest of the house, where only women live

ˈharem ˌpants (*also* **ˈharem ˌtrousers**) *n* [plural] very loose trousers for women, that fit tightly at the ANKLES

har·i·cot /ˈhærɪkəʊ $ -koʊ/ (*also* **ˌharicot ˈbean**) *n* [C] *BrE* a small white bean SYN **navy bean** *AmE*

hark /hɑːk $ hɑːrk/ *v* **1 hark at him/her/you!** *BrE old-fashioned spoken* used when you think someone is saying something stupid or acting as if they are more important

than they really are: *Hark at him! I bet he couldn't do any better.* **2 hark!** *old use* used to tell someone to listen
hark back *phr v* to remember and talk about things that happened in the past: **[+to]** *It's useless to continually hark back to the past.*
hark back to sth *phr v* to be similar to something in the past: *music that harks back to the early age of jazz*

har·ken /ˈhɑːkən $ ˈhɑːr-/ *v* [I] another spelling of HEARKEN

har·le·quin[1] /ˈhɑːlɪkwɪn $ ˈhɑːr-/ *n* [C] a character in some traditional plays who wears brightly coloured clothes and plays tricks

harlequin[2] *adj* [only before noun] a harlequin pattern is made up of DIAMOND shapes in many different colours

Har·ley Street /ˈhɑːli striːt $ ˈhɑːr-/ a street in central London where many well-known and expensive doctors have their offices: *a Harley Street specialist*

har·lot /ˈhɑːlət $ ˈhɑːr-/ *n* [C] *old use* a PROSTITUTE

harm[1] /hɑːm $ hɑːrm/ ●●○ S3 W3 *n* [U]
1 damage, injury, or trouble caused by someone's actions or by an event: *The scandal did his career a lot of harm.* | *Our children deserve protection from harm.* → GRIEVOUS BODILY HARM
2 come to no harm/not come to any harm to not be hurt or damaged: *She was relieved to see the children had come to no harm.*
3 mean no harm/not mean any harm to have no intention of hurting or upsetting anyone: *She's a terrible gossip but she means no harm.*
4 there's no harm in doing sth/it does no harm to do sth *spoken* used to suggest something to someone: *There's no harm in trying.* | *It does no harm to ask.*
5 it wouldn't do sb any harm to do sth *spoken* used to suggest that someone should do something that may be helpful or useful to them: *It wouldn't do you any harm to get some experience first.*
6 out of harm's way a) if someone or something is out of harm's way, they are in a place where they cannot be hurt or damaged: *Copies of your documents should be kept in a safe place, well out of harm's way.* **b)** if something dangerous is out of harm's way, it is in a place where it cannot hurt anyone or damage anything: *If you have small children, make sure that you store all medicines out of harm's way.*

COLLOCATIONS

VERBS

do (sth) harm *Try to choose products that do the least harm to the environment.*
cause (sb/sth) harm *Very small amounts of the chemical cause no lasting harm.*
inflict harm (=cause harm, especially physical harm) *None of us wants to inflict harm on another human being.*
suffer harm | **prevent harm**

ADJECTIVES

great/serious/significant harm *If you drink too much alcohol, you can do yourself serious harm.*
physical harm *They were afraid that he would do them some actual physical harm.*
psychological/emotional harm | **irreparable harm** (=that cannot be made better) | **untold harm** (=so much harm that it cannot be described completely)

PHRASES

do more harm than good (=cause more problems rather than improve a situation) *If you don't warm up properly, exercise may do more harm than good.*
no harm done *spoken* (=used to tell someone not to worry about something they have done) | **where's the harm in that?** *spoken* (=used when you think that something seems reasonable, although other people may not)

COMMON ERRORS

⚠ Don't say 'give harm' or 'make harm'. Say **do harm** or **cause harm**.

harm[2] ●●○ *v* [T]
1 to have a bad effect on something: *chemicals that harm the environment*

REGISTER

In everyday English, people usually say that something **is bad for** something rather than that it **harms** something: *chemicals that* ***are bad for*** *the environment*

2 to physically hurt a person or animal: *The kidnappers didn't harm him, thank God.*
3 harm sb's image/reputation to make people have a worse opinion of a person or group

THESAURUS

harm to have a bad effect on someone or something: *Many working mothers said having children harmed their careers.* | *A little hard work never harmed anyone.*
damage to harm something badly. **Damage** is more serious than **harm**: *His reputation was damaged and his career was in ruins.* | *The affair has damaged people's confidence in the government.*
be bad for sb/sth to be likely to harm someone or something: *Too much fatty food is bad for you.* | *All this rain is bad for business.*
be detrimental to sth *formal* to be bad for something: *The new housing development will be detrimental to the character of this small town.*
impair *formal* to harm something, especially someone's ability to do something or the correct working of a system: *Any amount of alcohol that you drink will impair your ability to drive.*
prejudice /ˈpredʒədɪs/ to have a bad effect on the future success of something: *Don't do anything to prejudice our chances of winning.*

harm·ful /ˈhɑːmfəl $ ˈhɑːrm-/ ●●○ *adj* causing harm: *the harmful effects of smoking* | **[+to]** *chemicals that are harmful to the environment*

THESAURUS

harmful causing physical harm – used especially about things that cause harm to your health, the environment etc: *Smoking is harmful to your health.* | *drugs with harmful side effects*
be bad for sb/sth to have a harmful effect on someone or something. This phrase is very commonly used in everyday English when saying that something is harmful: *Everyone knows that too much alcohol is bad for you.*
damaging used about things that cause permanent physical harm, or that have a bad effect in other ways, for example on people's opinion of someone: *Acid rain has a damaging effect on trees and the soil.* | *The allegations were very damaging to his career.*
detrimental *formal* causing harm or having a bad effect on something: *Employers are worried that the new laws will have a detrimental effect on their business.* | *chemicals that are detrimental to the environment*
negative a negative effect is one that is bad and causes problems: *The car tax had a negative effect on car sales.* | *the negative impact of the recession in the US*
hazardous hazardous substances are likely to be dangerous to people's health and safety: *Hazardous waste needs to be disposed of safely.* | *hazardous chemicals*
toxic toxic substances, smoke etc are poisonous: *toxic waste* | *toxic fumes* | *Toxic chemicals spilled into the river.*

pernicious /pəˈnɪʃəs $ pər-/ *formal* used about something that has a gradual bad effect which is not easy to notice, especially on people's morals, or on their health: *the pernicious effects of violent video games | the pernicious effect of secondhand smoke*

harm·less /ˈhɑːmləs $ ˈhɑːrm-/ ●○○ *adj*
1 unable or unlikely to hurt anyone or cause damage: *Her brother's a bit simple, but he's quite harmless.*
2 not likely to upset or offend anyone: *It was just a bit of* ***harmless fun****.* —**harmlessly** *adv*: *The spear whistled harmlessly over his head.* —**harmlessness** *n* [U]

har·mon·ic /hɑːˈmɒnɪk $ hɑːrˈmɑː-/ *adj technical* relating to the way notes are played or sung together to give a pleasing sound: *harmonic scales*

har·mon·i·ca /hɑːˈmɒnɪkə $ hɑːrˈmɑː-/ *n* [C] a small musical instrument that you play by blowing or sucking and moving it from side to side near your mouth SYN **mouth organ**

har·mo·ni·ous /hɑːˈməʊniəs $ hɑːrˈmoʊ-/ *adj* **1** harmonious relationships are ones in which people are friendly and helpful to one another **2** sounds that are harmonious are very pleasant **3** parts, colours etc that are harmonious look good or work well together: *The decor is a harmonious blend of traditional and modern.* —**harmoniously** *adv*

har·mo·ni·um /hɑːˈməʊniəm $ hɑːrˈmoʊ-/ *n* [C] a musical instrument with a KEYBOARD and metal pipes like a small ORGAN

har·mo·nize (*also* **-ise** *BrE*) /ˈhɑːmənaɪz $ ˈhɑːr-/ *v* **1** [I] if two or more things harmonize, they work well together or look good together: **[+with]** *The new offices harmonize with the other buildings in the area.* **2** [T] to make two or more sets of rules, taxes etc the same: *the proposal to harmonize tax levels throughout the EU* **3** [I] to sing or play music in harmony

har·mo·ny /ˈhɑːməni $ ˈhɑːr-/ ●○○ *n* (*plural* **harmonies**)
1 [C usually plural, U] notes of music combined together in a pleasant way: **in harmony** *a choir singing in perfect harmony | the gorgeous vocal harmonies on 'Mexicali Rose' | three-part harmonies* THESAURUS▸ MUSIC
2 [U] when people live or work together without fighting or disagreeing with each other: *I do believe it is possible for different ethnic groups to live together in harmony.* | **peace and harmony** *an era of peace and harmony* | **live/work etc in harmony**
3 be in harmony with sth *formal* to agree with another idea, feeling etc, or look good with other things: *Your suggestions are not in harmony with the aims of this project.*
4 [U] the pleasant effect made by different things that form an attractive whole: *the harmony of sea and sky* → DISCORD

har·ness¹ /ˈhɑːnəs $ ˈhɑːr-/ *n* [C,U] **1** a set of leather bands used to control a horse or to attach it to a vehicle it is pulling **2** a set of bands used to hold someone in a place or to stop them from falling: *a safety harness* **3 in harness** *BrE* doing your usual work: *I felt glad to be back in harness.* **4 in harness (with sb)** *BrE* working closely with another person or group

harness² *v* [T] **1** to control and use the natural force or power of something: *We can harness the power of the wind to generate electricity.* **2** to fasten two animals together, or to fasten an animal to something using a harness **3** to put a harness on a horse

harp¹ /hɑːp $ hɑːrp/ *n* [C] a large musical instrument with strings that are stretched across a vertical frame with three corners, and that you play with your fingers → see picture at STRINGED INSTRUMENT —**harpist** *n* [C]

harp² *v*
harp on about sth *BrE*, **harp on sth** *AmE phr v informal* to talk about something continuously, especially in a way that is annoying or boring: *My grandfather harps on about the war all the time.*

har·poon /hɑːˈpuːn $ hɑːr-/ *n* [C] a weapon used for hunting WHALES —**harpoon** *v* [T]

harp·si·chord /ˈhɑːpsɪkɔːd $ ˈhɑːrpsɪkɔːrd/ *n* [C] a musical instrument like a PIANO, used especially in the past —**harpsichordist** *n* [C]

har·py /ˈhɑːpi $ ˈhɑːrpi/ *n* (*plural* **harpies**) [C] **1** *literary* a cruel woman **2 Harpy** a cruel creature in ancient Greek stories, with the head and upper body of a woman and the wings and feet of a bird

har·ri·dan /ˈhærɪdən/ *n* [C] *old-fashioned* a bad-tempered unpleasant woman

har·row /ˈhærəʊ $ -roʊ/ *n* [C] a farming machine with sharp metal blades, used to break up the earth before planting crops → **plough** —**harrow** *v* [I,T]

har·row·ing /ˈhærəʊɪŋ $ -roʊ-/ *adj* very frightening or shocking and making you feel very upset: *a* ***harrowing experience*** *| a harrowing story*

har·rumph¹ /həˈrʌmf/ *interjection* used to show that you disapprove of something

harrumph² *v* [I,T] to make noises or say things that show you disapprove of something: *'This is ridiculous!' he harrumphed.*

har·ry /ˈhæri/ *v* (**harried**, **harrying**, **harries**) [T] **1** to keep attacking an enemy **2** to keep asking someone for something in a way that is upsetting or annoying

harsh /hɑːʃ $ hɑːrʃ/ ●●○ *adj*
1 CONDITIONS harsh conditions are difficult to live in and very uncomfortable SYN **severe**: *The hostages are being held in* ***harsh conditions****.* | **harsh winter/weather/climate** *the harsh Canadian winters | a young girl suddenly exposed to the* ***harsh realities*** *of life*
2 TREATMENT/CRITICISM severe, cruel, or unkind: **harsh criticism/treatment/punishment etc** *His theory met with harsh criticism from colleagues. | the harsh measures taken against the protesters | 'She's an idiot!' 'Aren't you being a bit harsh?' | a harsh authoritarian regime | He had* ***harsh words*** (=severe criticism) *for the Government.* THESAURUS▸ STRICT
3 SOUND unpleasantly loud and rough OPP **soft**: **harsh voice/laugh/tone etc** *His voice was harsh and menacing.*
4 LIGHT/COLOUR unpleasantly bright OPP **soft**: *She stood outside, blinking in the harsh sunlight.* THESAURUS▸ BRIGHT
5 LINES/SHAPES ETC ugly and unpleasant to look at: *the harsh outline of the factories against the sky*
6 CLEANING SUBSTANCE too strong and likely to damage the thing you are cleaning: *My skin is quite sensitive and I find some soaps too harsh.* —**harshly** *adv*: *'Shut up,' Boris said harshly.* —**harshness** *n* [U]

hart /hɑːt $ hɑːrt/ *n* [C] *old use* a male DEER

har·vest¹ /ˈhɑːvɪst $ ˈhɑːr-/ ●●○ *n*
1 [C,U] the time when crops are gathered from the fields, or the act of gathering them: **at harvest/at harvest time** *every year at harvest time* | **wheat/rice/grape etc harvest** *It rained for the potato harvest.*
2 [C] the crops that have been gathered, or the amount and quality of the crops gathered: **good/bumper harvest** (=a lot of crops) *Plum growers are expecting a bumper harvest this year.* | **poor/bad harvest** (=few crops)
3 reap a harvest to get good or bad results from your actions: *The company is now reaping the harvest of careful planning.*

harvest² ●○○ *v*
1 [I,T] to gather crops from the fields
2 [T] to take or collect for use, especially to take a part of someone's body to put into someone else's body: *His family has given permission for his organs to be harvested.*

har·vest·er /ˈhɑːvɪstə $ ˈhɑːrvəstər/ *n* [C] someone who gathers crops → **combine harvester** at COMBINE²(1)

ˌharvest ˈfestival *n* [C] *especially BrE* a church service held in the autumn to thank God for the harvest → THANKSGIVING

has /z, əz, həz; *strong* hæz/ the third person singular of the present tense of HAVE

ˈhas-been *n* [C] *informal* someone who was important or popular but who has now been forgotten

hash¹ /hæʃ/ *n* **1 make a hash of sth** *informal* to do something very badly: *I made a real hash of my exams.*

2 [U] *informal* HASHISH **3** [C,U] a dish made with cooked meat and potatoes: ***corned beef hash*** **4** [C,U] *BrE* the symbol #

hash² *v*

hash sth ↔ **out** *phr v AmE informal* to discuss something very thoroughly and carefully, especially until you reach an agreement: *The reorganization plan was hashed out September 16.*

ˌhash ˈbrowns *n* [plural] potatoes that are cut into very small pieces, pressed together, and cooked in oil

hash·ish /ˈhæʃɪʃ, -iːʃ/ *n* [U] the strongest form of the drug CANNABIS

hash·tag¹, **hash tag** /ˈhæʃtæg/ *n* [C] a word in a Twitter message with # in front of it, which indicates what the message is about. People can search for hashtags in order to find messages about a particular subject.

hashtag² *v* [T] to put a hashtag before a word on Twitter

has·n't /ˈhæzənt/ the short form of 'has not': *Hasn't she finished yet?*

hasp /hɑːsp $ hæsp/ *n* [C] a flat piece of metal used to fasten a door, lid etc

has·sle¹ /ˈhæsəl/ *n* **1** [C,U] *spoken* something that is annoying, because it causes problems or is difficult to do: *I don't feel like cooking tonight, it's too much hassle.* | *It's such a hassle not having a washing machine.* THESAURUS PROBLEM **2** [C] *AmE informal* an argument between two people or groups: *hassles with the management*

hassle² *v* (**hassled**, **hassling**) [T] *informal* to annoy someone, especially by asking them many times to do something: *Stop hassling me! I said I'll call them tomorrow.*

has·sock /ˈhæsək/ *n* [C] **1** a small CUSHION for kneeling on in a church **2** *AmE* a soft round piece of furniture used as a seat or for resting your feet on SYN **pouffe** *BrE*

hast /hæst/ **thou hast** *old use* a way of saying 'you have'

haste /heɪst/ ●○○ *n* [U]

1 great speed in doing something, especially because you do not have enough time SYN **hurry**: *I soon regretted my haste.* | **in your haste to do sth** *In his haste to leave, he forgot his briefcase.*

> **REGISTER**
> In everyday English, people usually say **hurry** rather than **haste**: *In my* ***hurry****, I left my coat behind.*

2 in haste *written or formal* quickly or in a hurry: *They left in haste, without even saying goodbye.*

3 make haste *old use* to hurry or do something quickly

4 more haste less speed *BrE*, **haste makes waste** *AmE* used to say that it is better to do something slowly, because if you do it too quickly you will make mistakes

has·ten /ˈheɪsən/ *v formal* **1** [T] to make something happen faster or sooner: *Their departure was hastened by an abnormally cold winter.* **2** [I] to do or say something quickly or without delay SYN **hurry**: **hasten to do sth** *I hastened to assure her that there was no danger.* **3 I hasten to add** used when you realize that what you have said may not have been understood correctly: *an exhausting course, which, I hasten to add, was also great fun* **4** [I always + adv/prep] *literary* to go somewhere quickly

hast·i·ly /ˈheɪstəli/ ●○○ *adv written* quickly, perhaps too quickly SYN **hurriedly**: *a hastily arranged news conference* | *'Don't worry,' Jenny added hastily. 'I checked with Lizzie first.'*

hast·y /ˈheɪsti/ *adj* **1** done in a hurry, especially with bad results SYN **hurried**: *He soon regretted his hasty decision.* | *a hasty breakfast* THESAURUS FAST **2 be hasty** to do something too soon, without careful enough thought: *Let's not be hasty – sit down for a moment.*

hat /hæt/ ●●● S1 W3 *n* [C]

1 a piece of clothing that you wear on your head: *Maria was wearing a beautiful new hat.* | **straw/cowboy/bowler etc hat** | **in a hat** *a man in a fur hat* | **bowler-hatted/top-hatted etc** (=wearing a bowler hat, top hat etc) *a bowler-hatted gentleman*

HATS

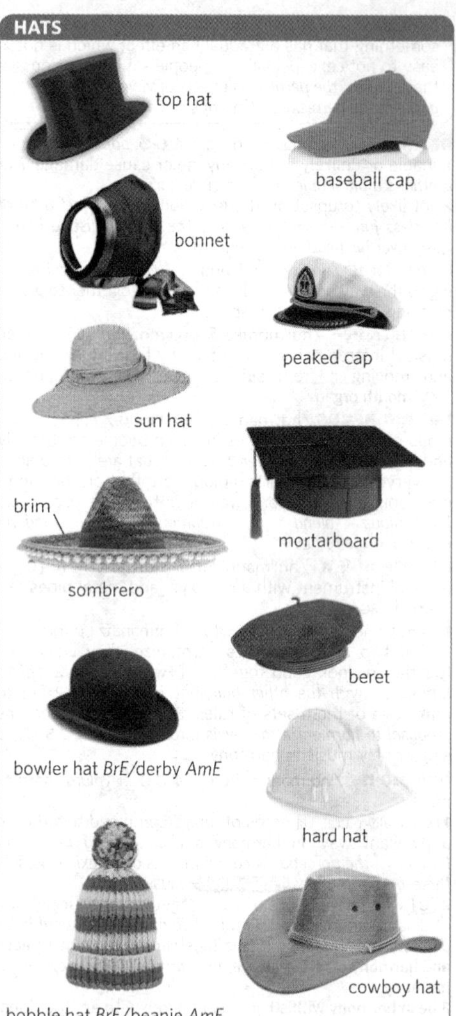

2 keep sth under your hat *informal* to keep something secret

3 be wearing your teacher's/salesman's etc hat (*also* **have your teacher's/salesman's etc hat on**) *informal* to be performing the duties of a teacher etc, which are not your only duties: *I'm a manager now and only put my salesman's hat on when one of our sales reps is having real problems.*

4 I take my hat off to sb (*also* **hats off to sb**) *informal* used to say you admire someone very much because of what they have done: *I take my hat off to Ian – without him we'd have never finished this project on time.*

5 be drawn/pulled/picked out of the/a hat if someone's name is drawn out of a hat, they are chosen, for example as the winner of a competition, because their name is the first one that is taken out of a container containing the names of all the people involved: *The first correct entry out of the hat on September 2nd will win a prize.*

6 pass the hat around to collect money from a group of people, especially in order to buy someone a present

7 throw/toss your hat into the ring to say publicly that you will compete in an election or for a job → HARD HAT, OLD HAT, → **at the drop of a hat** at DROP²(5), → **I'll eat my hat** at EAT(8), → **hang up your hat** at HANG UP, → **be talking through your hat** at TALK¹(29)

hat·band /ˈhætbænd/ *n* [C] a band of cloth or leather fastened around a hat as a decoration

ˈhat box *n* [C] a special box used for carrying a hat in

hatch[1] /hætʃ/ ●○○ *v*
1 (*also* **hatch out**) [I,T] if an egg hatches, or if it is hatched, it breaks, letting the young bird, insect etc come out: *The eggs take three days to hatch.*
2 (*also* **hatch out**) [I,T] if a young bird, insect etc hatches, or if it is hatched, it comes out of its egg: *All the chicks have hatched out.*
3 hatch a plot/plan/deal etc to form a plan etc in secret

hatch[2] *n* [C] **1** a hole in a ship or aircraft, usually used for loading goods, or the door that covers it: **escape hatch** (=a hole in an aircraft etc through which you can escape) **2** (*also* **hatchway**) a small hole in the wall, floor, or ceiling of a room, or the door that covers it **3 down the hatch** *spoken informal* something you say before drinking an alcoholic drink quickly

hatch·back /ˈhætʃbæk/ *n* [C] a car with a door at the back that opens upwards

hatch·er·y /ˈhætʃəri/ *n* (*plural* **hatcheries**) [C] a place for hatching eggs, especially fish eggs

hatch·et /ˈhætʃɪt/ *n* [C] a small AXE with a short handle → **bury the hatchet** at BURY(9)

ˈhatchet-ˌfaced *adj* having an unpleasantly thin face with sharp features

ˈhatchet ˌjob *n* [C] *BrE informal* a newspaper article, television programme etc that criticizes someone severely and unfairly: **[+on]** *They were afraid I was going to* ***do a hatchet job*** *on them.*

ˈhatchet ˌman *n* [C] *informal* someone who is employed to make unpopular changes in an organization

hatch·ing /ˈhætʃɪŋ/ *n* [U] fine lines drawn on or cut into a surface

hatch·way /ˈhætʃweɪ/ *n* [C] a HATCH[2](2)

This graph shows how common the different grammar patterns of the verb **hate** are.

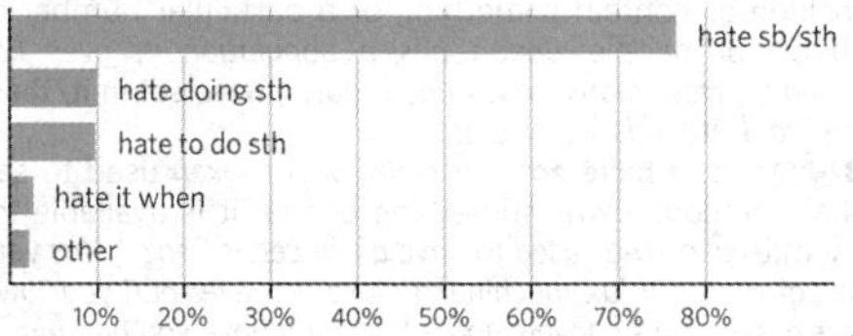

hate sb/sth	~77%
hate doing sth	~10%
hate to do sth	~10%
hate it when	~3%
other	~2%

(Scale: 10% 20% 30% 40% 50% 60% 70% 80%)

hate[1] /heɪt/ ●●● S1 W3 *v* [T]
1 to dislike something very much OPP **love**: *It's the kind of movie you either love or hate.* | *He hates his job.* | **hate doing sth** *Paul hates having his picture taken.* | **hate to do sth** *I hate to see you unhappy.* | **hate it when** *Pam hates it when Lee calls her at work.* | **hate sb doing sth** *Jenny's mother hates her staying out late.*
2 to dislike someone very much and feel angry towards them OPP **love**: *Why do you hate me so much?* | **hate sb for (doing) sth** *She hated him for being so happy.* | **hate yourself** *I hated myself for feeling jealous of her.* | **hate sb's guts** *informal* (=hate someone very much)
3 I'd hate (for) sb/sth to do sth *spoken* used to emphasize that you do not want something to happen: *I'd hate you to go.* | *I'd hate for him to think I wasn't interested.*
4 I hate to think what/how/where etc *spoken* used when you feel sure that something would have a bad result, or when an idea is unpleasant to think about: *I hate to think what would have happened if you hadn't called the police.*
5 I hate to say it, but .../I hate to tell you this, but ... *spoken* used when saying something that you do not want to say, for example because it is embarrassing: *I hate to say it, but I was glad when he went home.*
6 I hate to ask/interrupt/disturb etc *spoken* used to say that you are sorry that you have to ask etc: *I hate to ask you this, but would you mind giving me a lift home?* | *I hate to interrupt, but it's urgent.* —**hated** *adj*: *the hated security police*

GRAMMAR: Using the progressive

- **Hate** is not usually used in the progressive. You say: *I hate that record.* | *He hated her new boyfriend.*

✗ Don't say: *I am hating that record.* | *He was hating her new boyfriend.*

- In spoken English, people sometimes say **I'm hating** to describe their feelings about something that is happening right now: *I'm hating every minute of this film.*

GRAMMAR GUIDE ▶ VERBS

THESAURUS

hate *v* [T] to dislike someone or something very much: *Billy hated his stepfather.* | *He hated the fact that his wife was more successful than he was.*

can't stand/can't bear to hate someone or something. **Can't stand** is less formal than **hate**, and is very common in everyday English: *She's OK, but I can't stand her husband.* | *He couldn't bear the thought of life without Nicole.* | *She can't stand being on her own.*

loathe /ləʊð $ loʊð/, **detest** *v* [T not in progressive] to hate something or someone very much. **Loathe** and **detest** are a little more formal than **hate**: *He loathed housework.* | *Greg had detested his brother for as long as he could remember.*

despise *v* [T not in progressive] to hate someone or something very much and have no respect for them: *He despised the man and could never forgive him for what he had done.* | *They despised the wealth and consumerism of the West.*

abhor /əbˈhɔː $ əbˈhɔːr, æb-/ *v* [T not in progressive] *formal* to hate something because you think it is morally wrong: *He abhorred violence.* | *We abhor racism in any form.*

hate[2] ●●○ *n* [U] an angry unpleasant feeling that someone has when they hate someone and want to harm them SYN **hatred** OPP **love**: *Her eyes were full of hate.* | **[+for]** *Mrs Williams has spoken of her hate for her husband's killers.* → **pet hate** at PET[3](2)

ˈhate camˌpaign *n* [C] a series of things that a person or group does in order to upset or harm someone they hate

ˈhate crime *n* [C,U] a crime that is committed against someone only because they belong to a particular race, religion etc

hate·ful /ˈheɪtfəl/ *adj old-fashioned* very bad, unpleasant, or unkind SYN **odious**: *It was all the fault of that hateful man!*

ˈhate mail *n* [U] letters that express a lot of hatred towards the person to whom they are sent: *She complained to the police after receiving hate mail.*

hat·er /ˈheɪtə $ -ər/ *n* [C] **1** someone who hates a type of person or thing: *I'm not a man hater.* | *He was a hater of injustice.* **2** *informal* someone who expresses their disapproval of a person, often on the Internet or Twitter – used to show disapproval: *We love you – just ignore the haters!*

hath /hæθ/ *old use* has

Hath·a yo·ga /ˌhɑːtə ˈjəʊgə, ˌhɑːθə- $ -ˈjoʊ-/ *n* [U] a type of YOGA in which most of the exercises are done in a standing position, and none are done sitting down. People also breathe in a special way that allows them to relax and MEDITATE while they exercise.

hat·pin /ˈhætˌpɪn/ *n* [C] a long pin that is used to make a woman's hat stay on her head

ha·tred /ˈheɪtrɪd/ ●●○ *n* [C,U] an angry feeling of extreme dislike for someone or something OPP **love**: *A look of pure hatred flashed across her face.* | **[+of/for/towards]** *his intense hatred of all foreigners* | *Abby made no secret of her hatred for her father.* | **passionate/intense/deep etc hatred** *Ellis was a sick young man with a deep hatred of women.* | *the old hatreds and prejudices that simmered below the surface*

ˈhat stand *n* [C] a tall pole with hooks at the top used to hang coats and hats on

hat·ter /ˈhætə $ -ər/ *n* [C] *old-fashioned* someone who makes or sells hats → **as mad as a hatter** at MAD(2)

H

ˈhat tip *n* [C] an expression of thanks, especially for information or an idea: **[+to]** *A hat tip to Fiona Smith, who drew this case to my attention.*

ˈhat trick *n* [C] a series of three successes, especially in sports such as football when the same person scores three times: *Saunders* ***scored a hat trick*** *in the final game of the series.* | **[+of]** *a hat trick of victories*

haugh·ty /ˈhɔːti $ ˈhɒː-/ *adj* behaving in a proud unfriendly way → **stuck up**: *a haughty laugh* —**haughtily** *adv* —**haughtiness** *n* [U]

haul¹ /hɔːl $ hɒːl/ ●●○ *v* [T]

1 to pull something heavy with a continuous steady movement: **haul sth off/onto/out of etc sth** *She hauled her backpack onto her back.* | *the steam locomotive which hauled the train* | *I hauled the door shut behind me.* THESAURUS PULL

2 haul yourself up/out of etc sth a) to move somewhere with a lot of effort, especially because you are injured or tired: *Patrick hauled himself painfully up the stairs.* **b)** to succeed in achieving a higher position in society, in a competition etc: *He is confident that the club can haul themselves further up the league.*

3 haul sb over the coals *BrE* to criticize someone severely because they have done something wrong SYN **rake sb over the coals** *AmE*

4 haul off and hit/punch/kick sb *AmE informal* to try to hit someone very hard

5 haul ass *AmE spoken not polite* to hurry

haul sb **off** *phr v* to force someone to go somewhere that they do not want to go, especially to prison: *Police handcuffed him and hauled him off to jail.*

haul sb **up** *phr v informal* to officially bring someone to a court of law to be judged: **[+before/in front of]** *Campbell was hauled up in front of the magistrate.*

haul² *n* [C] **1** a large amount of illegal or stolen goods: *The gang escaped with a haul worth hundreds of pounds.* | **[+of]** *A haul of stolen cars has been seized by police officers.* **2 long/slow haul** something that takes a lot of time and effort: *At last we've won our freedom but* ***it's been a long*** *bitter* ***haul****.* **3 for the long haul** until something that will take a long time is done or achieved: *I'm* ***in*** *this* ***for the long haul*** (=going to stay involved until the end). **4 over the long haul** over a long period of time: *Over the long haul, these small increases add up.* **5** the amount of fish caught when fishing with a net → LONG-HAUL, SHORT-HAUL

haul·age /ˈhɔːlɪdʒ $ ˈhɒːl-/ *n* [U] the business of carrying goods in trucks or trains for other companies: *the road haulage industry*

haul·i·er /ˈhɔːliə $ ˈhɒːliər/ *BrE*, **haul·er** / $ ˈhɔːlə, ˈhɒːlər/ *AmE n* [C] a company that carries goods in trucks or trains for other companies

haunch /hɔːntʃ $ hɒːntʃ/ *n* [C] **1 haunches** [plural] the part of your body that includes your bottom, your HIPS, and the tops of your legs: **on your haunches** *They squatted on their haunches playing dice.* **2** one of the back legs of a four-legged animal, especially when it is used as meat

haunt¹ /hɔːnt $ hɒːnt/ ●●○ *v* [T]

1 if the soul of a dead person haunts a place, it appears there often: *The pub is said to be haunted by the ghost of a former landlord.*

2 to make someone worry or make them sad: *Clare was haunted by the fear that her husband was having an affair.*

3 to cause problems for someone over a long period of time: *an error that would* ***come back to haunt*** *them for years to come*

haunt² *n* [C] a place that someone likes to go to often: **[+of]** *The Café Vienna was a* ***favourite haunt*** *of journalists and actors.*

haunt·ed /ˈhɔːntɪd $ ˈhɒːn-/ ●●○ *adj*

1 a haunted building is believed to be visited regularly by the soul of a dead person: *a* ***haunted house***

2 haunted expression/look a very worried or frightened expression

haunt·ing /ˈhɔːntɪŋ $ ˈhɒːn-/ *adj* sad but also beautiful and staying in your thoughts for a long time: *a haunting melody* —**hauntingly** *adv*

haute cou·ture /ˌəʊt kuːˈtjʊə $ ˌoʊt kuːˈtʊr/ *n* [U] the business of making and selling expensive and fashionable clothes for women —**haute couturier** *n* [C]

haute cui·sine /ˌəʊt kwɪˈziːn $ ˌoʊt-/ *n* [U] cooking of a very high standard, especially French cooking → **cordon bleu**

hau·teur /əʊˈtɜː $ hɒːˈtɜːr/ *n* [U] *formal* a proud, very unfriendly manner

have¹ /v, əv, həv; *strong* hæv/ ●●● S1 W1 *auxiliary verb* (*past tense and past participle* **had** /d, əd, həd; *strong* hæd/, *third person singular* **has** /z, əz, həz; *strong* hæz/)

1 used with past participles to form PERFECT tenses: *Our guests have arrived.* | *Has anyone phoned?* | *We've been spending too much money.* | *I hadn't seen him for 15 years.* | *'I hope you've read the instructions.' 'Yes, of course I have.'* | *You haven't done much, have you?*

2 sb had better/best do sth used to say that someone should do something: *You'd better phone to say you'll be late.* | *We'd better not tell Jim about our plans just yet.*

3 had sb done sth *formal* if someone had done something: *Had we known about it earlier, we could have warned people of the danger.*

have² /hæv/ ●●● S1 W1 *v* [T]

1 QUALITY/FEATURE (*also* **have got** *especially BrE*) used to say what someone or something looks like, what qualities or features they possess etc: *She has dark hair and brown eyes.* | *Sullivan's music does have a certain charm.* | *You need to have a lot of patience to be a teacher.* | *Wild rice has a very nutty flavour.* | *He didn't even have the courtesy to answer my letter.* | **have it in you** (=have the skill or special quality needed to do something) *You should have seen the way Dad was dancing – I didn't know he had it in him!*

2 INCLUDE/CONTAIN (*also* **have got** *especially BrE*) to include or contain something or a particular number of things or people: *Japan has a population of over 120 million.* | *How many pages has it got?* | **have sth in it/them** *The tank still has water in it.*

3 OWN (*also* **have got** *especially BrE*) *spoken* used to say that someone owns something or that it is available for them to use: *They used to have a Mercedes Benz.* | *Has your secretary got a fax machine?* | *Have you ever had your own business?* | *He's a lovely dog – how long have you had him?* | *Can I have the car tonight, Dad?* THESAURUS OWN

4 CARRY/HOLD (*also* **have got** *especially BrE*) to be holding something or carrying it with you: *Have you got a match?* | *Look out! He's got a gun.* | **have sth on/with you** *Have you got any money on you?* | *I'm afraid I don't have my address book with me.*

> **GRAMMAR: Using the progressive**
> Senses 1-4 of **have** are not used in the progressive.
> ✗ Don't say: *I am having ...* | *It is having ...*

5 DO STH *BrE* to do something: **have a look/walk/sleep/talk/think etc** *We were just having a look around.* | *Are you going to have a swim?*

6 EAT/DRINK/SMOKE to eat, drink, or smoke something: *She sat down and had another drink.* | *Someone had been having a cigarette in the toilet.* | **have lunch/a meal etc** *I usually have breakfast at about seven o'clock.* THESAURUS EAT

7 EXPERIENCE to experience something or be affected by something: *We've been having a lot of difficulties with our new computer system.* | *I'm afraid your son has had a serious accident.* | *He is in hospital having treatment for a knee injury.* | *I hope you have a good holiday.* | **have a good/terrible etc time** *Thanks for everything – we had a great time.* | **have sb doing sth** *He found it quite natural to have people fussing over him.*

8 IDEA/FEELING (*also* **have got** *especially BrE*) to think of something or to experience a particular feeling: *If you have any good ideas for presents, let me know.* | *I have lots of happy memories of my time in Japan.* | *He had an awful feeling of guilt.*

9 DISEASE/INJURY/PAIN (*also* **have got** *especially BrE*) to suffer from a disease, injury, or pain: *Sarah's got a cold.* | *One of the victims had a broken leg.*

10 AMOUNT OF TIME (*also* **have got** *especially BrE*) if you have a particular amount of time, it is available for you to do something: *You have just 30 seconds to answer the question.* | **have time (to do sth)** *I haven't time to stop and talk just now.*

11 RECEIVE (*also* **have got** *especially BrE*) to receive something: *I had lots of phone calls.* | **have sth from sb** *Have you had any news yet from Graham?* | *I expect he had some help from his father.*

12 have your hair cut/your house painted etc to pay a professional person to cut your hair etc for you: *Where do you normally have your hair done?* | *We'd only just had a new engine put in.*

13 have sth stolen/broken/taken etc if you have something stolen, broken etc, someone steals, breaks etc something that belongs to you: *She had all her jewellery stolen.* | *Mullins had his nose broken in a fight.*

14 have sth ready/done/finished etc to have made something ready to be used, or have finished doing something: *I should have the car ready by Monday.*

15 IN A POSITION OR STATE (*also* **have got** *especially BrE*) used to say that your body or something else is in a particular position or state, because you moved or did something: **have sth open/closed/on etc** *I had my eyes half-closed.* | *Janice likes to have the window open.* | *She had her back to the door.* | **have sth doing sth** *He's always got the stereo playing.*

16 FAMILY/FRIENDS (*also* **have got** *especially BrE*) used to say that there is someone who is your relation or friend: *She has an uncle in Wisconsin.* | *It was nice for Alice to have friends of her own age.*

17 JOB/DUTY (*also* **have got** *especially BrE*) to be employed in a particular job or to be responsible for doing something: *Her boyfriend has a well-paid job.* | *The headteacher has responsibility for the management of the school.* | **have sth to do** *I can't stand here talking – I have work to do* (=there is work that I must do).

18 EMPLOY/BE IN CHARGE OF (*also* **have got** *especially BrE*) to employ or be in charge of a group of workers: *Margaret Gillies currently has a team of 20 volunteers working for her.*

19 GOODS/ROOMS AVAILABLE (*also* **have got** *especially BrE*) if a shop or a hotel has goods or rooms, they are available for you to buy or use: *Do you have any single rooms?* | *They didn't have any sweaters in my size.*

20 have (got) sb with you if you have someone with you, they are present with you: *Luckily I had a friend with me who spoke German.*

21 HOLD SB (*also* **have got** *especially BrE*) to hold someone violently by a part of their body: *They had him by the throat.*

22 VISITORS/GUESTS if you have visitors or guests, they have come to your home, office etc: *Sorry, I didn't realize you had visitors.* | *We had friends to stay over the weekend.*

23 EVENT if you have an event such as a meeting, party, or concert, it happens because you have organized it: *We're having a party on Saturday – you're very welcome to come.*

24 EFFECT to cause a particular result: *a mistake that could have disastrous results* | *Cardew was having a bad influence on the other students.*

25 OPPORTUNITY used to say that an opportunity or choice is available for you: *If you have the chance, you should go and see it – it's a really good film.* | *Women managers have a choice as to whether they wear trousers or a skirt.* | *Last year I had the honour of meeting the Prince of Wales.*

26 BABY if a woman has a baby, it is born from her body: *Anna insisted on having the baby at home.*

27 MAKE SB DO STH **a)** to affect someone in a way that makes them start doing something: **have sb laughing/crying etc** *Within minutes he had the whole audience laughing and clapping.* **b)** to persuade or order someone to do something: **have sb doing sth** *She had me doing all kinds of jobs for her.* | **have sb do sth** *especially AmE*: *I'll have Hudson show you to your room.*

28 have done with sth to finish or settle an argument or a difficult situation: *I should throw you out now and have done with it.*

29 rumour/legend/word has it used when you are reporting what people say or what a story says: *Rumour has it that Kim is not his child.*

30 have (got) sth/sb (all) to yourself if you have a place, time, or person all to yourself, you do not have to share them with anyone else: *He couldn't wait to have Beth all to himself.* | *It was the first time I'd had a room to myself.*

31 SEX *informal* to have sex with someone: *I expect she's had lots of men.*

32 have it off/away with sb *BrE informal* to have sex with someone

SPOKEN PHRASES

33 can/could/may I have say this to politely ask someone to give you something: *Can I have the bill, please?* | *Could we have our ball back?*

34 I'll have/we'll have say this to ask for something that you have chosen in a restaurant or shop: *I'll have a T-bone steak and chips, please.*

35 OFFERING SB STH used to offer something to someone: *Have another sandwich.* | *Won't you have a drink before you go?* | *Please have a seat, and the doctor will be right with you.*

36 NOT ALLOW **won't/can't have sth** used to say that someone will not allow something to happen: *They're trying to play tricks on me again, but I won't have it.* | **won't/can't have sb doing sth** *I won't have you walking home all by yourself.* | *We can't have people wandering about on private land.*

37 sb had (got) it coming used to say that you are not sorry that something bad has happened to someone, because they deserved it: *I'm not surprised his wife left him – he's had it coming for years.*

38 I've got it used to say you have suddenly thought of the solution to a problem or that you suddenly understand a situation

39 you have me there (*also* **you've got me there**) used to say that you do not know the answer to a question: *'What makes you think women can't do that kind of work?' He scratched his head. 'Well, now, you've got me there.'*

40 I'll have you know used to start to tell someone something when you are annoyed with them: *I'll have you know you're insulting the woman I love.*

41 have (got) it in for sb to want to make life difficult for someone because you dislike them: *Dean thinks his teachers have it in for him.*

42 sb/sth has had it a) if someone has had it, they are going to fail or die, or be in serious trouble: *Press the wrong button and you've had it.* **b)** if someone has had it, they are very tired or annoyed and cannot continue with something: *I can't believe he's done it again. I've had it with him!* **c)** *BrE* if something has had it, it no longer works and cannot be repaired: *The engine's had it.*

43 be not having any (of that) to refuse to agree to something, listen to someone etc: *I tried to explain to her, but she just wasn't having any of it.*

44 sb has been had used to say that someone has been deceived, for example by being tricked into paying too much: *You paid £200? You've been had!*

USAGE: Have got, have

- In British spoken English, people usually use **have got** instead of **have** for many of its meanings. **Have** sounds more formal and is the usual choice in written English. You say: *He's got a cold.* You write: *He has a cold.*
- In questions in British spoken English, **Have you got ...?** is often used instead of **Do you have ...?** You say: *Have you got his address?* You write: *Do you have his address?*
- In negative sentences in British spoken English, you use **haven't got** or **hasn't got**. You say: *He hasn't got any money.* You write: *He does not have any money.*

H

• **Have got** is mainly used in the present tense. In the past tense you usually use **had**, and in the future you usually use **will have**.
• In American English, **have got** is much less common. It is used when you want to emphasize what you are saying: *He's got a gun!* It is also often used in the phrase **have got to** (=have to): *We've got to go.*
• In negative sentences, British speakers often say **I haven't got ...** where American speakers say **I don't have ...** In questions, British speakers say **Have you got ...?** where American speakers say **Do you have ...?**

have on
1 have (got) sth on to be wearing a piece of clothing or type of clothing: *He had his best suit on. | Jimmy* ***had nothing on*** *but his socks.*
2 have (got) the TV/radio/washing machine etc on if you have your television, radio etc on, you have switched it on and it is working: *Billie has the radio on all day long.*
3 be having sb on *especially BrE* to be trying to make someone believe something that is not true, especially as a joke: *Don't believe a word he says. He's having you on!*
4 have (got) sth on *BrE* to have arranged to do something, go somewhere etc, especially when this means you cannot do something else: *Sorry, I can't help you this weekend – I've got too much on already.*
5 have (got) sth on sb to know about something bad that someone has done: *What do the police have on him?*
6 have (got) nothing on sb/sth *informal* to not be nearly as good as someone or something else: *Rock 'n' roll has got nothing on these African rhythms.*
have (got) sth **against** sb/sth *phr v* to dislike or be opposed to someone or something for a particular reason: *I don't know what it is, but Roger seems to have something against women. | I can't see what you've got against the idea. | I* ***have nothing against*** *foreigners* (=have no reason to dislike them).
have (got) sb **in** *phr v BrE* if you have someone in, they are doing some work in your home, for example building work: *We've had the builders in, so everything's in a mess.*
have sth **out** *phr v*
1 to have a tooth etc removed by a medical operation
2 have it out (with sb) *informal* to settle a disagreement or difficult situation by talking to the person involved, especially when you are angry with them: *I'm going round to his house to have it out with him.*
have sb **over** (*also* **have sb round** *especially BrE*) *phr v* if you have someone over, they come to your house for a meal, drink etc because you have invited them: *We must have you over for dinner before we leave.*
have sb **up** *phr v BrE informal* to make someone go to a court of law because you think they have committed a crime: **be had up for sth** *Last year he was had up for drunken driving.*

have³ ●●● S1 W3 *v*, **have to do sth** (*also* **have got to do sth** *especially BrE*)
1 if you have to do something, you must do it because it is necessary or because someone makes you do it: *We don't have to rush – there's plenty of time. | I hate having to get up early in the morning. | If you earn more than £5,000, you will have to pay tax. | I've got to be at the hospital at 4 o'clock. | It'll have to be on a Sunday. I'll be working every other day.*

REGISTER
In writing, people often prefer to say someone **is forced to do** something or **is obliged to do** something, as these sound more formal than **have to do** something: *They* ***had to*** *pay tax on the full amount.* → *They* ***were obliged to*** *pay tax on the full amount. | Many businesses* ***have had to*** *close.* → *Many businesses have* ***been forced to*** *close.*

2 used to say that it is important that something happens, or that something must happen if something else is to happen: *There has to be an end to the violence. | You've got to believe me! | There will have to be a complete ceasefire before the Government will agree to talks. | You have to be good to succeed in this game.*
3 used to tell someone how to do something: *First of all you have to mix the flour and the butter.*
4 used to say that you are sure that something will happen or something is true: *House prices have to go up sooner or later. | This has to be a mistake. | You have got to be joking! | No one else could have done it – it had to be Neville.*
5 used to suggest that someone should do something because you think it would be enjoyable or useful: *You'll have to come and meet my wife some time.*
6 *spoken* used when something annoying happens in a way that things always seem to happen: *Of course, it had to happen today, when all the shops are shut.*
7 *spoken* used to say that only one thing or person is good enough or right for someone: *For Francesca it has to be the Ritz – nowhere else will do.*
8 do you have to do sth? *spoken* used to ask someone to stop doing something that annoys you: *Lieutenant, do you have to keep repeating everything I've just said?*
9 I have to say/admit/confess *spoken* used to show that you are making an honest statement even though it may be embarrassing for you: *I have to say I don't know the first thing about computers.* → MUST¹

ha·ven /ˈheɪvən/ ●○○ *n* [C] a place where people or animals can live peacefully or go to in order to be safe → **sanctuary**: **[+for]** *The riverbanks are a haven for wildlife. | St Ives is a haven for artists.* | **a haven of peace/tranquillity/calm** *In the middle of the city, this garden is a haven of tranquillity.* → SAFE HAVEN, TAX HAVEN

ˌhave-ˈnots *n* **the have-nots** the poor people in a country or society: *a country where* ***the have-nots*** *far outnumber* ***the haves*** → HAVES

have·n't /ˈhævənt/ the short form of 'have not'

hav·er·sack /ˈhævəsæk $ -ər-/ *n* [C] *BrE old-fashioned* a bag that you carry on your back SYN **backpack, rucksack**

haves /hævz/ *n* **the haves** the rich people in a country or society: *the widening gap between* ***the haves*** *and* ***the have-nots*** → HAVE-NOTS

hav·oc /ˈhævək/ *n* [U] a situation in which there is a lot of damage or a lack of order, especially so that it is difficult for something to continue in the normal way SYN **chaos**: **cause/create havoc** *A strike will cause havoc for commuters. | policies that would* ***wreak havoc on*** *the country's economy | Rain has continued to* ***play havoc with*** *sporting events.*

haw /hɔː $ hɒː/ *v* another spelling of HA(1) → **hum and haw** at HUM¹(4)

Haˌwaiian ˈshirt *n* [C] a shirt with short sleeves, worn by men, with patterns of Hawaiian things such as flowers, PALM TREES, and ocean waves

hawk¹ /hɔːk $ hɒːk/ *n* [C] **1** a large bird that hunts and eats small birds and animals **2** a politician who believes in using military force OPP **dove 3 watch sb like a hawk** to watch someone very carefully **4 have eyes like a hawk** to be quick to notice things, especially small details

hawk² *v* **1** [T] to try to sell goods, usually by going from place to place and trying to persuade people to buy them **2** [I,T] to cough up PHLEGM

hawk·er /ˈhɔːkə $ ˈhɒːkər/ *n* [C] someone who carries goods from place to place and tries to sell them

ˈhawk-eyed *adj* quick to notice small details SYN **observant**

hawk·ish /ˈhɔːkɪʃ $ ˈhɒːk-/ *adj* supporting the use of military force in order to deal with political problems —**hawkishness** *n* [U]

haw·ser /ˈhɔːzə $ ˈhɒːzər/ *n* [C] *technical* a thick rope or steel CABLE used on a ship

haw·thorn /ˈhɔːθɔːn $ ˈhɒːθɔːrn/ *n* [C,U] a small tree with small white flowers, red berries, and sharp points

hay /heɪ/ ●●○ *n* [U]
1 long grass that has been cut and dried, used as food for cattle
2 make hay (while the sun shines) to take the opportunity

to do something now, because you may not be able to do it later

3 hit the hay *informal* to go to bed → **a roll in the hay** at ROLL²(10)

ˈhay ˌfever *n* [U] a medical condition, like a bad COLD that is caused by breathing in POLLEN (=dust from plants)

hay·loft /ˈheɪlɒft $ -lɒːft/ *n* [C] the top part of a farm building where hay is stored

hay·mak·ing /ˈheɪˌmeɪkɪŋ/ *n* [U] the process of cutting and drying long grass to make hay

hay·rick /ˈheɪrɪk/ *n* [C] a HAYSTACK

hay·ride /ˈheɪraɪd/ *n* [C] *AmE* a ride in a CART filled with hay, usually as part of a social event

hay·stack /ˈheɪstæk/ (*also* **hayrick**) *n* [C] a large, firmly built pile of hay → **like looking for a needle in a haystack** at NEEDLE¹(7)

hay·wire /ˈheɪwaɪə $ -waɪr/ *adj* **go haywire** *informal* to start working in completely the wrong way: *My computer's gone haywire.*

haz·ard¹ /ˈhæzəd $ -ərd/ ●●○ *n* [C]

1 something that may be dangerous, or cause accidents or problems: **[+to/for]** *Polluted water sources are a hazard to wildlife.* | *That pile of rubbish is a **fire hazard*** (=something that is likely to cause a fire). | **health/safety hazard** *the health hazard posed by lead in petrol*

2 a risk that cannot be avoided: **the hazards of sth** *the economic hazards of running a small farm* | **occupational hazard** (=a danger that exists in a job) *Divorce seems to be an occupational hazard for politicians.*

hazard² *v* [T] **1** to say something that is only a suggestion or guess and that might not be correct: *$50,000? I don't know. I'm only **hazarding a guess**.* **2** *formal* to risk losing your money, property etc in an attempt to gain something

ˈhazard ˌlights *n* [plural] special lights on a vehicle that flash to warn other drivers of danger

haz·ard·ous /ˈhæzədəs $ -zər-/ ●○○ *adj* dangerous, especially to people's health or safety: **[+to]** *The chemicals in paint can be **hazardous to health**.* | *the disposal of **hazardous waste*** THESAURUS ▸ DANGEROUS, HARMFUL

haze¹ /heɪz/ *n* [singular, U] **1** smoke, dust, or mist in the air which is difficult to see through: **[+of]** *a haze of cigarette smoke* | *The sun was surrounded by a golden haze.* **2** the feeling of being very confused and unable to think clearly: *a drunken haze*

haze² *v* [T] *AmE* to play tricks on a new student or to make them do silly or dangerous things, as part of joining the school or a club at the school —**hazing** *n* [U]: *bizarre hazing rituals*

haze over *phr v* to become HAZY: *The sky hazed over.*

ha·zel¹ /ˈheɪzəl/ *n* **1** [C,U] a small tree that produces nuts **2** [U] the green-brown colour of some people's eyes

hazel² *adj* hazel eyes are a green-brown colour

ha·zel·nut /ˈheɪzəlnʌt/ *n* [C] the nut of the HAZEL¹ tree → see picture at **NUT¹**

haz·mat, **HazMat** /ˈhæzmæt/ *n* [U] (***hazardous materials***) substances that are dangerous to people's health: *Paint and other chemicals can be taken to a HazMat center for disposal.*

haz·y /ˈheɪzi/ *adj* **1** air that is hazy is not clear because there is a lot of smoke, dust, or mist in it: *hazy sunshine* **2** an idea, memory etc that is hazy is not clear or exact SYN **vague**: *My memories of the holiday are rather hazy.* | **[+about]** *She was a little hazy about the details.* —**hazily** *adv* —**haziness** *n* [U]

H-bomb /ˈeɪtʃ bɒm $ -bɑːm/ *n* [C] *informal* HYDROGEN BOMB

HCF /ˌeɪtʃ siː ˈef/ *technical* the abbreviation of ***highest common factor***

HD /ˌeɪtʃ ˈdiː◂/ *adj* (***high-definition***) HD televisions or video equipment produce very clear pictures

he¹ /i, hi; *strong* hiː/ ●●● S1 W1 *pron* [used as the subject of a verb]

1 used to refer to a man, boy, or male animal that has already been mentioned or is already known about: *'Where's Paul?' 'He's gone to the cinema.'* | *It was he who first suggested the idea.*

2 used when talking about someone who may be male or female. Some people think this use is old-fashioned. → **they**: *Everyone should do what he considers best.*

3 He used when writing about God

he² /hiː/ *n* [singular] *informal* a male person or animal: *I discovered that Mel wasn't a he, but a she.*

he- /hiː/ *prefix* a male animal: *a he-goat*

H.E. the written abbreviation of ***His/Her Excellency***, used in the title of an AMBASSADOR

head¹ /hed/ ●●● S1 W1 *n*

1 TOP OF BODY [C] the top part of your body that has your face at the front and is supported by your neck: *He kissed the top of her head.* | *Alan fell asleep as soon as he put his head on the pillow.* | *They dived **head first** into the water.* | *She was dressed in black **from head to toe*** (=over all her body). | *He still **has a full head of hair*** (=has all his hair, even though he is getting rather old).

2 MIND [C] your mind or mental ability: *The problem only exists inside his head.* | **do sth in your head** (=calculate something mentally) *I can't do those figures in my head.* | ***Use your head** to work out the answer.* | **come into/pop into your head** *Jackie said the first thing that came into her head.* | **get sth into your head** (=understand something) *'It's over, Jake,' she said. 'Try and get that into your head.'* | **take/get it into your head (to do sth)** (=decide to do something, especially something stupid) *At about two in the morning, Alan took it into his head to go for a swim.* | **get/put sth out of your head** (=stop thinking or worrying about something) *Try to put it out of your head for the time being.* | **put sth into sb's head** (=make someone think or believe something) *What's put that idea into her head?* | **get your head round sth** *BrE* (=be able to understand something) *I just can't get my head round what's been going on here.*

3 CALM/SENSIBLE **a) keep your head** to remain calm and sensible in a difficult or frightening situation: *We need a candidate who can keep his or her head even when clients get aggressive.* | **keep a clear/cool/calm head** *Get to sleep early tonight – you'll need to keep a clear head tomorrow at the trial.* **b) lose your head** to become unable to behave calmly or sensibly in a difficult or frightening situation: *You'll be OK as long as you don't lose your head and forget he's the real enemy.* **c) have your head screwed on (straight/right)** *informal* to be sensible and able to deal with difficult situations: *He wondered what Gemma thought about it all. She seemed to have her head screwed on.*

4 PERSON IN CHARGE [C] **a)** a leader or person in charge of a group or organization: **[+of]** *You should discuss the matter with your head of department.* | *A meeting of Commonwealth **heads of state** will be held next month.* | **head waiter/chef/gardener etc** (=the person in charge of a group of waiters etc) **b)** (*also* **head teacher**) *BrE* the person in charge of a school SYN **principal** *AmE*: *From now on all violent incidents should be reported directly to the head.* → CROWNED HEAD, HEAD BOY, HEAD GIRL, HEADMASTER, HEADMISTRESS

5 FRONT/LEADING POSITION [singular] the front or the most important position: **(at) the head of sth** *Jenny marched proudly at the head of the procession.* | ***At the head of the table*** (=the place where the most important person sits) *sat the senior partners.* | **at sth's/sb's head** *The band of soldiers marched into the yard, their defeated captain at their head.*

6 CRAZY [C usually singular] used in particular phrases to talk about someone being crazy or very stupid: *People going out in conditions like this **need** their **heads examined**.* | **be off your head** *BrE*: *You must be off your head if you think that.* | *If I walk in looking like that, they'll think I'm **not right in the head**.*

7 a head/per head for each person: *Dinner works out at $30 a head.* | *average incomes per head*

8 RIVER/VALLEY [C usually singular] the place where a river, valley etc begins

9 come to a head (*also* **bring sth to a head**) if a problem or

H

difficult situation comes to a head, or something brings it to a head, it suddenly becomes worse and has to be dealt with quickly: ***Things came to a head** in the summer of 1997.*
10 FLOWER/PLANT [C] the top of a plant where its flowers or leaves grow: *She was outside cutting the **dead heads** off the roses.* | **[+of]** *a head of lettuce*
11 HEIGHT/DISTANCE [singular] the length of a head, used to measure height or distance: *She saw her father, **a head above** the rest of the crowd.* | **by a (short) head** (=used to say that a horse won or lost a race but only by a small amount)
12 COIN **heads** the side of a coin that has a picture of a person's head on it: **heads or tails?** *BrE spoken* (=used to decide something, by asking someone which side of a coin they guess will be showing when you throw it in the air and it lands) → **tails** at TAIL[1]
13 laugh/shout/scream etc your head off *informal* to laugh, shout etc very loudly: *Fans were screaming their heads off.*
14 have a good/fine/thick etc head of hair to have a lot of hair on your head
15 get/put your head down *informal* **a)** to start working in a quiet determined way: *It's time you got your head down and did some revision.* **b)** *BrE* to sleep
16 keep your head down to try to avoid being noticed or getting involved in something: *Do what you're told and keep your head down.*
17 as soon as your head hits the pillow if you fall asleep as soon as your head hits the pillow, you fall asleep as soon as you lie down
18 be out of/off your head *informal* to not know what you are doing because you have taken drugs or drunk too much alcohol: *He was off his head on various drugs.*
19 go to sb's head *informal* **a)** if alcohol goes to your head, it quickly makes you feel drunk **b)** if success goes to someone's head, it makes them feel more important than they really are: *She never let fame go to her head.*
20 TOOL [C usually singular] the wide end of a long narrow tool or piece of equipment
21 put your heads together to discuss a difficult problem together: *The next morning, we all put our heads together to decide what should be done.*
22 go over sb's head a) to be too difficult for someone to understand: *The explanation went completely over my head.* **b)** to do something without discussing it with a particular person or organization first, especially when you should have discussed it with them
23 can't make head or/nor tail of sth *informal* to be completely unable to understand something
24 have your head in the clouds to think about something in a way that is not practical or sensible, especially when you think things are much better than they really are
25 have a (good) head for figures/facts/business etc to be naturally good at doing calculations, remembering facts etc
26 head for heights the ability to look down from high places without feeling ill or nervous
27 a big head *informal* the opinion that you are much better, more important, more skilful etc than you really are: *I suppose I did do OK, but I'd be silly to get a big head about it.*
28 keep your head above water to manage to continue to live on your income or keep your business working when this is difficult because of financial problems: *For years they struggled to keep their heads above water.*
29 be/stand head and shoulders above sb to be much better than other people: *One contestant stood head and shoulders above the rest.*
30 hold up your head (*also* **hold your head high**) to show pride or confidence, especially in a difficult situation: *If you do this, you'll never be able to hold your head up again.*
31 be (like) banging/bashing etc your head against a brick wall *spoken* used to say that you are making no progress at all in what you are trying hard to do: *I've tried to talk some sense into them, but it's like banging my head against a brick wall.*
32 bang/knock sb's heads together *spoken* used to say that two people or groups should be forced to stop arguing and start to behave sensibly
33 bite/snap sb's head off to talk to someone very angrily with no good reason: *I offered to help her, but she just bit my head off.*
34 turn/stand sth on its head to make people think about something in the opposite way to the way it was originally intended: *The attorney quickly turned his main defense argument on its head.*
35 give sb their head to give someone the freedom to do what they want to do
36 be/fall head over heels in love to love or suddenly start to love someone very much: *Sam was head over heels in love with his new bride.*
37 heads will roll *spoken* used to say that someone will be punished severely for something that has happened: *Heads will roll for this!*
38 on your own head be it *spoken* used to tell someone that they will be blamed if the thing they are planning to do goes wrong
39 do your head in *BrE spoken informal* to make you feel confused and annoyed: *Turn that noise down – it's doing my head in!*
40 be/get in over your head to be or get involved in something that is too difficult for you to deal with: *In business, start small and don't get in over your head.*
41 be over your head in debt *AmE* to owe so much money that there is no possibility of paying it all back
42 go head to head with sb to deal with or oppose someone in a very direct and determined way: *Rather than go head to head with their main rivals, they decided to try a more subtle approach.*
43 heads up! *AmE spoken* used to warn people that something is falling from above
44 BEER [C] the layer of small white BUBBLES on the top of a glass of beer
45 ELECTRONICS [C] a piece of equipment that changes information on something MAGNETIC, such as a recording tape or computer HARD DISK, into electrical messages that electronic equipment can use
46 head of cattle/sheep etc [plural] a particular number of cows, sheep etc: *a farm with 20 head of cattle*
47 head of water/steam pressure that is made when water or steam is kept in an enclosed space
48 get/build up a head of steam to become very active after starting something slowly
49 LAND [singular] *BrE* a high area of land that sticks out into the sea – used in names: *Beachy Head*
50 INFECTION [C] the centre of a swollen spot on your skin
51 give (sb) head *informal* to perform ORAL SEX on someone
→ **bury your head in the sand** at BURY(8), → **knock sth on the head** at KNOCK[1](16), → **off the top of your head** at TOP[1](18), → **sb can do sth standing on their head** at STAND[1](40), → **turn sb's head** at TURN[1](18), → **two heads are better than one** at TWO(8)

COLLOCATIONS

VERBS

turn your head *John turned his head to look at the boy.*
shake your head (=move it from side to side, especially to show disagreement) *'It's too much,' he said, shaking his head.*
nod your head (=move it up and down, especially to show agreement) *The audience nodded their heads enthusiastically.*
sb's head hurts/aches/throbs *Her head was throbbing and she needed to lie down.*
raise/lift your head (=look up) | **bow/bend/lower your head** (=look down) | **hang your head** (=look down, especially because you are ashamed) | **scratch your head** (=especially because you do not understand something)

ADJECTIVES

bare *The sun beat down on her bare head.*
bald *His bald head shone with sweat.*

sb's blonde/dark/grey etc head (=with blonde etc hair) *I saw my son's blond head sticking out from the car window.*

head + NOUN

head injury *Wearing a helmet reduces the risk of head injuries.*

head² ●●● S2 W2 *v*
1 GO TOWARDS (*also* **be headed**) [I always + adv/prep] to go or travel towards a particular place, especially in a deliberate way: **[+for/towards/back etc]** *The ship was heading for Cuba.* | *It's about time we were* ***heading home.*** | **head north/south etc** *We headed south towards the capital.* | *Where are you guys headed?*
2 FUTURE **be heading** (*also* **be headed**) [I always + adv/prep] if you are heading for a particular situation, especially a bad one, it seems likely to happen: **[+for]** *Forecasters predict the region's economy is heading for disaster.* | *Where is your life heading?*
3 BE IN CHARGE (*also* **head up**) [T] to be in charge of a team, government, organization etc: *David was asked to head up the technical team.* | *an interim government headed by the former prime minister*
4 AT TOP [T] **a)** to be at the top of a list or group of people or things: *The movie heads the list of Oscar nominations.* **b) be headed** if a page is headed with a particular name, title, image etc, it has it on the top: *The page was headed 'Expenses'.* | *officially-headed writing paper*
5 AT FRONT [T] to be at the front of a line of people: *a procession headed by the Queen*
6 FOOTBALL [I,T always + adv/prep] to hit the ball with your head, especially in football → see picture at FOOTBALL

head off *phr v*
1 to leave to go to another place: *I'm heading off now.*
2 head sth ↔ off to prevent something from happening, especially something bad: *The president intervened to head off the conflict.*
3 head sb ↔ off to stop someone going somewhere by moving in front of them: *Soldiers headed them off at the border.*

-head /hed/ *suffix* [in nouns] **1** the top of something: *the pithead* (=the top of a coal mine) | *a letterhead* (=a name and address printed at the top of a letter) **2** the place where something begins: *a fountainhead*

head·ache /ˈhedeɪk/ ●●● S2 W3 *n* [C]
1 a pain in your head: *If you have a headache, you should take some aspirin.*
2 *informal* a problem that is difficult or annoying to deal with: *Security* ***is a big headache for*** *airline operators.* —**headachy** *adj*: *a headachy feeling*

GRAMMAR: Countable or uncountable?

Headache is a countable noun: *I have* ***a*** *headache.*
✗ Don't say: *I have headache.*

COLLOCATIONS

ADJECTIVES

bad/terrible/severe *I've got a really bad headache.*
a splitting headache (=a very bad headache) *The next day he woke up with a splitting headache.*
a slight headache (*also* **a bit of a headache** *spoken*) (=one that is not very serious)

VERBS

have a headache (*also* **have got a headache** *spoken*) *She's not coming – she says she's got a headache.*
get headaches/suffer from headaches (=regularly have a headache) *He often gets headaches at school.*
give sb a headache *The music was starting to give him a headache.*
cause headaches | **complain of a headache** (=say that you have a headache) | **a headache goes away** (=it stops)

COMMON ERRORS

⚠ Don't say 'a strong/heavy headache'. Say **a bad headache**.
Don't say 'a little headache'. Say **a slight headache** or **a bit of a headache**.

THESAURUS

headache a pain in your head: *Looking at a computer for a long time can give you a headache.*
hangover a headache and feeling of sickness that you get the day after you have drunk too much alcohol: *The next day I had a terrible hangover.*
migraine /ˈmiːɡreɪn, ˈmaɪ- $ ˈmaɪ-/ a very bad headache, which makes you feel sick and have difficulty seeing: *He has suffered from migraines all his life.*

head·band /ˈhedbænd/ *n* [C] a band that you wear around your head to keep your hair off your face or as a decoration

head·bang·er /ˈhedbæŋə $ -ər/ *n* [C] *informal* someone who enjoys HEAVY METAL music and moves their head around violently to the beat of the music —**headbanging** *n* [U] —**headbang** *v* [I]

head·board /ˈhedbɔːd $ -bɔːrd/ *n* [C] the upright board at the end of a bed where your head is

ˌhead ˈboy *n* [C] the boy who is chosen in a British school each year to represent the school

head·butt /ˈhedbʌt/ *v* [T] to deliberately hit someone with your head

head·case /ˈhedkeɪs/ *n* [C] *informal* a crazy person

ˈhead cold *n* [C] a cold that makes it difficult for you to breathe

ˈhead count *n* **1** [C] the act of counting how many people are present in a particular place at one time: *The teachers* ***did a head count*** *to check that none of the kids was missing.* **2** [C,U] *technical* the number of people working for a company

head·dress /ˈhed-dres/ *n* [C] something that someone wears on their head, especially for decoration on a special occasion: *The bride wore white with a pearl headdress.*

HEADDRESS

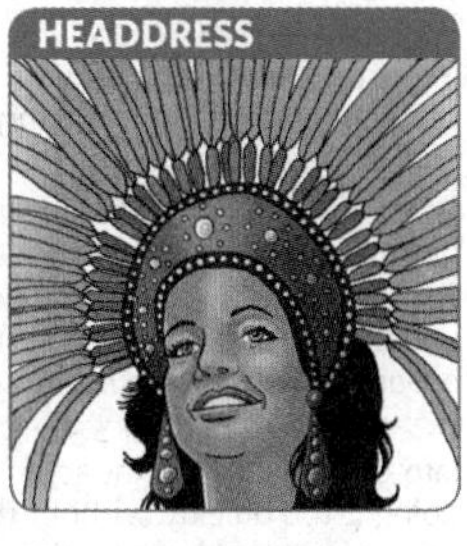

head·ed /ˈhedɪd/ *adj*
1 red-headed/curly-headed etc having red hair, curly hair etc: *a* ***bald-headed man*** (=having no hair) *in a shiny suit* **2 two-headed/three-headed etc** having two heads etc: *a two-headed monster* **3 headed notepaper/paper** *BrE* paper for writing letters that has your name and address printed at the top

head·er /ˈhedə $ -ər/ *n* [C] **1** an action in football in which you hit the ball with your head **2** information at the top of a page, especially things such as numbers that appear on each page of a document **3** information at the beginning of an email message that shows when it was sent, who wrote it etc → DOUBLE-HEADER

head-first, **head·first** /ˌhedˈfɜːst◂ $ -ˈfɜːrst◂/ *adv* **1** if you fall head-first, your head goes down first, and the rest of your body follows afterwards: **dive/fall/jump/plunge head-first** *I fell head-first down the stairs.* **2** if you do something head-first, you become involved in it too quickly, without having time to think about it carefully: *a remark that sent him tumbling head-first into another controversy*

ˈhead game *n* [C usually plural] *AmE informal* if you play head games with someone, especially someone you are in a romantic relationship with, you deceive them or try to get them to behave as you want them to: *He's obviously* ***playing head games*** *with you.*

head·gear /ˈhedɡɪə $ -ɡɪr/ *n* [U] hats and other things that you wear on your head

ˌhead ˈgirl *n* [C] the girl who is chosen in a British school each year to represent the school

head·hunt·er /ˈhedˌhʌntə $ -ər/ *n* [C] someone who finds people with the right skills and experience to do particular jobs, and who tries to persuade them to leave their present jobs —**headhunt** *v* [T]

head·ing /ˈhedɪŋ/ ●●○ *n* [C]
1 the title written at the beginning of a piece of writing, or at the beginning of part of a book: *chapter headings*
2 a name that is given to a group of things or people, that helps to describe them as a group: *writers who might* ***come under the heading of*** *postmodern fiction writers*

head·lamp /ˈhedlæmp/ *n* [C usually plural] a HEADLIGHT

head·land /ˈhedlənd/ *n* [C] an area of land that sticks out from the coast into the sea SYN **promontory**

head·less /ˈhedləs/ *adj* **1** without a head: *a headless corpse* **2 run around like a headless chicken** *informal* to be going from one place to another in a way that is not organized at all

head·light /ˈhedlaɪt/ (*also* **headlamp**) *n* [C usually plural] **1** one of the large lights at the front of a vehicle, or the beam of light produced by this: *Suddenly, a figure appeared* ***in*** *my* ***headlights***. → see picture at CAR **2 like a rabbit/deer caught in headlights** so frightened or confused that you do not know what to do

head·line¹ /ˈhedlaɪn/ ●●○ *n* [C]
1 the title of a newspaper report, which is printed in large letters above the report: *a paper carrying the front-page headline: 'Space Aliens meet with President'*
2 **the headlines** the important points of the main news stories that are read at the beginning of a news programme on radio or television
3 **make/grab (the) headlines** (*also* **be in/hit the headlines**) to be reported in many newspapers and on radio and television: *a scandal that grabbed the headlines for weeks | The former MP found himself back in the headlines again.*

headline² *v* **1** [I,T] to appear as the main performer or band in a show: *Beyoncé is headlining at the festival this year.* **2** [T] to give a headline to an article or story

ˈheadline-ˌgrabbing *adj* headline-grabbing news is important and reported in many newspapers and on radio and television: *The story was headline-grabbing material in the nationals.*

head·lin·er /ˈhedlaɪnə $ -ər/ *n* [C] the main performer or band in a concert

head·lock /ˈhedlɒk $ -lɑːk/ *n* [C] a way of holding someone around their neck so that they cannot move: *His opponent* ***had*** *him* ***in a headlock***.

head·long /ˈhedlɒŋ $ -lɒːŋ/ *adv* **1 rush/plunge headlong into sth** if you rush headlong into something, you start doing it too quickly without thinking carefully **2** with your head first and the rest of your body following SYN **headfirst**: *I* ***fell headlong into*** *a pool of icy water.* **3** very quickly, without looking where you are going: *Mortimer almost* ***ran headlong into*** *a patrol.* —**headlong** *adj*

head·man /ˈhedmæn/ *n* (*plural* **headmen** /-men/) [C] the most important man in a village where a tribe lives SYN **chief**

head·mas·ter /ˌhedˈmɑːstə $ ˈhedˌmæstər/ ●○○ *n* [C] *BrE* a male teacher who is in charge of a school SYN **head teacher**, **principal** *AmE*

head·mis·tress /ˌhedˈmɪstrɪs $ ˈhedˌmɪs-/ *n* [C] *BrE* a female teacher who is in charge of a school SYN **head teacher**, **principal** *AmE*

ˌhead ˈoffice *n* [C] the main office of a company

ˌhead of ˈstate *n* (*plural* **heads of state**) [C] the main representative of a country, such as a queen, king, or president, who may not have duties in the country's government

ˌhead-ˈon *adv* **1 crash/collide/smash etc head-on** if two vehicles crash etc head-on, the front part of one vehicle hits the front part of the other **2** if someone deals with a problem head-on, they do not try to avoid it, but deal with it in a direct and determined way: **face/tackle/meet sth head-on** *The police are trying to tackle car crime head-on.* **3** if two people or teams meet head-on in an argument, competition etc, they compete against each other and try to win in a very determined way —**head-on** *adj*: *a* ***head-on collision***

head·phones /ˈhedfəʊnz $ -foʊnz/ ●●○ *n* [plural] a piece of equipment that you wear over your ears to listen to the radio, music etc without other people hearing it

head·piece /ˈhedpiːs/ *n* [C] something you wear on your head, usually for decoration

head·quar·tered /ˈhedˌkwɔːtəd, hedˈkwɔːtəd $ -ɔːrtərd/ *adj* **be headquartered** to have your headquarters at a particular place: *Many top companies are headquartered in northern California.*

head·quar·ters /ˈhedˌkwɔːtəz, ˌhedˈkwɔːtəz $ -ɔːrtərz/ ●●○ W3 *n* (*plural* **headquarters**) [C] (*abbreviation* **HQ**)
1 the main building or offices used by a large company or organization: *the headquarters of the United Nations*
2 the place from which military operations are controlled

head·rest /ˈhed-rest/ *n* [C] the top part of a chair or of a seat in a car, plane etc that supports the back of your head → see picture at CAR

head·room /ˈhed-rʊm, -ruːm/ *n* [U] **1** the amount of space above your head, especially when you are in a car **2** *BrE* the amount of space above a vehicle when it is under a bridge

head·rush /ˈhedrʌʃ/ *n* [C] a sudden feeling of extreme pleasure and excitement, especially one that you get soon after using an illegal drug such as ECSTASY or COCAINE

head·scarf /ˈhedskɑːf $ -skɑːrf/ *n* (*plural* **headscarves** /-skɑːvz $ -skɑːrvz/) [C] a square piece of cloth that women wear on their heads and tie under their chins

ˈhead-ˌscratcher *n* [C] *informal* something that is hard to understand, explain, or decide about: *John's computer problem was a real head-scratcher.*

head·set /ˈhedset/ *n* [C] a set of HEADPHONES, often with a MICROPHONE attached

HEADSET

microphone

head·ship /ˈhedʃɪp/ *n* [C] **1** the position of being in charge of an organization **2** *BrE* the job of being in charge of a school

head·space /ˈhedspeɪs/ *n* [singular] *informal* your general mental and emotional condition: *Before I start on a painting, I need to be in the right headspace.*

head·stand /ˈhedstænd/ *n* [C] a position in which you turn your body UPSIDE DOWN, with your head and hands on the floor and your legs and feet in the air: *Can you* ***do a headstand***?

ˌhead ˈstart *n* [C] **1** an advantage that helps you to be successful: **give sb/get/have a head start** *Give your children a head start by sending them to nursery school.* **2** a start in a race in which you begin earlier or further ahead than someone else

head·stone /ˈhedstəʊn $ -stoʊn/ *n* [C] a piece of stone on a GRAVE, with the name of the dead person written on it SYN **gravestone**, **tombstone**

head·strong /ˈhedstrɒŋ $ -strɒːŋ/ *adj* very determined to do what you want, even when other people advise you not to do it THESAURUS ▸ DETERMINED

ˌheads-ˈup *n* [singular] *informal* a warning that something may happen: *Here's a heads-up for investors in real-estate stocks.*

ˌhead ˈtable *n* [C] a table at a formal meal where the most important people sit, or the people who are giving speeches sit

ˌhead ˈteacher, **headteacher** ●●○ *n* [C] *BrE* the teacher who is in charge of a school SYN **principal** *AmE*

ˌhead-to-ˈhead *adv* competing directly with another

person or group: *Courier companies are* ***going head-to-head with*** *the Post Office.* —**head-to-head** *adj*: *a head-to-head contest* —**head-to-head** *n* [C]

ˈhead-ˌturner *n* [C] *informal* someone or something that is very attractive or interesting to look at, so they attract attention: *She was a real head-turner, and every man would look around and watch her go past.*

head·wa·ters /ˈhedwɔːtəz $ -wɒːtərz, -wɑː-/ *n* [plural] the streams that form a river

head·way /ˈhedweɪ/ *n* **make headway a)** to make progress towards achieving something – used especially when this is difficult: **[+towards/in/with etc]** *Foreign firms have made little headway in the US market.* **b)** to move forwards – used especially when this is slow or difficult: *Stormy weather stopped the ship from making headway.*

head·wind /ˈhedˌwɪnd/ *n* [C,U] a wind that blows directly towards you when you are moving OPP **tailwind**

head·word /ˈhedwɜːd $ -wɜːrd/ *n* [C] *technical* one of the words whose meaning is explained in a dictionary

head·y /ˈhedi/ *adj* [usually before noun] **1** a heady smell, drink etc is pleasantly strong and seems to affect you strongly: *a heady combination of wine and brandy* **2** very exciting in a way that makes you feel as if you can do anything you want to: *the heady atmosphere of the early sixties*

heal /hiːl/ ●●○ *v* [I,T]

1 (*also* **heal up**) if a wound or a broken bone heals or is healed, the flesh, skin, or bone grows back together and becomes healthy again: *It took three months for my arm to heal properly.*

2 to make someone who is ill become healthy again, especially by using natural powers or prayer → **cure**: *a preacher who claims that he can heal the sick*

3 to become mentally or emotionally strong again after a bad experience, or to help someone to do this: *The trauma of divorce can often be healed by successful remarriage.*

4 if an argument or disagreement between people heals or you heal it, the people stop arguing or disagreeing: **heal the wounds/breach/division/rift** *Our main goal must be to heal the divisions in our society.* | *The rift between the two younger men never healed.*

heal over *phr v* if a wound or an area of broken skin heals over, new skin grows over it and it becomes healthy again

heal·er /ˈhiːlə $ -ər/ *n* [C] **1** someone who is believed to be able to cure people using natural powers, rather than by using medicine → **faith healer** at FAITH HEALING **2** something that makes a bad experience seem less painful: *Time is a great healer.*

heal·ing /ˈhiːlɪŋ/ *n* [U] **1** the treatment of illness using natural powers or prayer rather than medicine: *The medical establishment is taking healing increasingly seriously.* → FAITH HEALING **2** the process of becoming healthy and strong again: *the healing process*

health /helθ/ ●●● S1 W1 *n* [U]

1 the general condition of your body and how healthy you are: *I'm worried about my husband's health.*

2 the work of providing medical services to keep people healthy: *The government has promised to spend more on health and education.* | *health insurance* | *nurses and other health workers* → PUBLIC HEALTH

3 when you have no illness or disease: *Even if you haven't got much money, at least you've got your health.* | *When we last met, he was* ***glowing with health*** (=was clearly very healthy).

4 how successful something such as a business, an organization, or a country's ECONOMY is: *The monthly trade figures are seen as an indicator of the health of the economy.* → **a clean bill of health** at CLEAN[1](13)

COLLOCATIONS

ADJECTIVES

good *Physical exercise is essential to good health.*
excellent *At the age of 70, her health is excellent.*
poor *He wanted to join the army but his health was too poor.*
ill health *He retired early due to ill health.*
failing health (=when someone is becoming more ill) | **mental health** | **physical health**

VERBS

damage your health *There is no doubt that smoking can seriously damage your health.*
endanger your health (=cause danger to your health) *Being overweight endangers your health.*
sb's health improves | **sb's health deteriorates** (=gets worse)

health + NOUN

health care (=care from doctors, nurses etc) *Many Americans cannot afford even basic health care.*
a health problem *He missed a lot of time at work through health problems.*
a health risk/hazard/threat (=something that could damage your health) | **health benefits** | **a health warning** (=a warning printed on a product that could harm you)

PHRASES

be in good/poor health (=be healthy/unhealthy) *Her parents were elderly and in poor health.*
be good/bad for your health *Eating plenty of vegetables is good for your health.*
sb's state of health | **health and well-being**

ˌhealth and ˈsafety *n* [U] an area of government and law concerned with people's health and safety, especially at work: *health and safety regulations*

ˈhealth care, healthcare ●●○ *n* [U] the services that are provided for looking after people's health, or the activity of doing this: *The government has promised better health care for all.* | *An ageing population requires greater expenditure on health care.* —**health-care** *adj*: *health-care professionals*

ˈhealth ˌcentre *BrE*, **health center** *AmE* *n* [C] a building where several doctors work, and where people can go for medical treatment → **clinic**

ˈhealth club *n* [C] a place where people who have paid to become members can go to do physical exercise

ˈhealth farm *n* [C] *BrE* a place where people pay to stay so that they can do physical exercise, eat healthy food, and have beauty treatments SYN **health spa** *AmE*

ˈhealth food *n* [C,U] food that contains only natural substances, and that is good for your health

health·ful /ˈhelθfəl/ *adj formal* likely to make you healthy: *healthful mountain air*

ˈhealth proˌfessional *n* [C] someone such as a doctor, nurse, DENTIST etc, whose job involves people's health

ˈhealth ˌservice *n* [C] a public service that is responsible for providing people with medical care: *reforms to the health service* → NATIONAL HEALTH SERVICE, THE

ˈhealth ˌspa *n* [C] *AmE* a place where people pay to stay so that they can do physical exercise, eat healthy food, and have beauty treatments SYN **health farm** *BrE*

ˈhealth ˌtourism *n* [U] **1** travelling to a foreign country in order to receive cheap or free medical treatment – used to show disapproval **2** having a holiday that involves taking part in sports activities or doing things such as having beauty treatments

ˈhealth ˌvisitor *n* [C] a nurse in Britain who visits people in their homes

health·y /ˈhelθi/ ●●● S3 W3 *adj* (*comparative* **healthier**, *superlative* **healthiest**)

1 PERSON/ANIMAL/PLANT physically strong and not likely to become ill or weak: *a healthy baby boy* | *I've always been perfectly healthy until now.*

2 GOOD FOR YOUR BODY good for your body: *a healthy lifestyle* | *a* ***healthy diet*** | *the importance of* ***healthy eating***

3 SHOWING GOOD HEALTH showing that you are healthy: *Her face had a* ***healthy glow.*** | *All of our kids have* ***healthy appetites*** (=they like to eat a lot).

H

4 BEHAVIOUR/ATTITUDE used to describe an attitude, feeling, or behaviour that is natural, normal, and sensible: *I don't think it's healthy for her to spend so much time alone.* | **healthy respect/disrespect/scepticism etc** *a healthy disrespect for silly regulations*
5 COMPANY/RELATIONSHIP ETC a healthy company, society, relationship, ECONOMY etc is working effectively and successfully: *a healthy economy with a well-trained workforce*
6 AMOUNT large and showing that someone is successful – used about amounts of money: *a healthy profit* | *a healthy bank balance* —**healthily** *adv* —**healthiness** *n* [U]

THESAURUS

healthy having good health: *A good diet keeps you healthy.* | *They tested the drug on healthy volunteers.*
well used especially when describing or asking about how someone feels or looks: *I don't feel well.* | *How was James – did he look well?*
fine *spoken* used in a reply to a question about your health, or when talking about someone else's health. Use **fine** only in replies or statements, not in questions: *'Hi, Tom, how are you?' 'Fine, thanks.'* | *She had a bad cold, but she's fine now.*
all right/OK *spoken* not ill or injured. These expressions are very commonly used in everyday spoken English: *You look pale – are you feeling all right?* | *He's had an accident but he's OK.*
better less ill than you were, or no longer ill: *I'm feeling a lot better now.*
fit healthy, especially because you exercise regularly: *She keeps fit by cycling everywhere.*
in (good) shape healthy and fit: *Jogging keeps me in pretty good shape.*
robust *literary* healthy and strong, and not likely to become ill: *He had a robust constitution* (=a strong and healthy body). | *robust plants*
be/look a picture of health to look very healthy: *She looked a picture of health as she posed for the cameras.*

heap[1] /hiːp/ ●●○ *n* [C]
1 a large untidy pile of things: *a rubbish heap* | **[+of]** *There was a heap of stones where the building used to be.* | **in a heap** *The envelopes for posting lay in a heap on her desk.* | *We piled the branches into heaps for burning.* → see picture at PILE[1]
2 **heaps** *informal* a lot of something: **[+of]** *The children have heaps of energy.* | **heaps better/bigger etc** (=much better, bigger etc)
3 **fall/collapse etc in a heap** to fall down and lie without moving: *They finally collapsed in a heap on the grass.*
4 *humorous* an old car that is in bad condition
5 **at the top/bottom of the heap** high up and successful or low down and unsuccessful in an organization or in society: *The very poor are at the bottom of the heap.*
6 **be struck all of a heap** *BrE old-fashioned informal* to be suddenly very surprised or confused

heap[2] *v* [T] 1 (*also* **heap up**) to put a lot of things on top of each other in an untidy way SYN **pile**: **[+on]** *Jean heaped logs on the fire.* 2 **heap sth with sth** to put a lot of something on a surface SYN **pile**: *She gave him a glass of whisky and heaped his plate with food.* 3 **heap praise/insults etc on sb** to praise, insult etc someone a lot: *He heaped all the blame on his secretary.*

heaped /hiːpt/ *BrE*, **heaping** /hiːpɪŋ/ *AmE adj* **heaped teaspoon/tablespoon etc** an amount of something that is as much as a spoon can hold: *Add three heaped teaspoons of sugar.*

hear /hɪə $ hɪr/ ●●● S1 W1 *v* (*past tense and past participle* **heard** /hɜːd $ hɜːrd/)
1 HEAR SOUNDS/WORDS ETC [I,T] to know that a sound is being made, using your ears: *She heard a sudden loud crash.* | *Did anyone see or hear anything last night?* | **can hear** *I could hear the sound of traffic.* | **hear sb/sth doing sth** *Jenny could hear them arguing outside.* | **hear sb do sth** *She heard Tom go upstairs.* | **hear what/who etc** *I couldn't hear what they were saying most of the time.* | **be heard to do sth** *She didn't want to be heard to criticize him.* | **sb doesn't hear too well/very well** (=they have problems with their hearing) *Old Zeke doesn't hear too well anymore.*
2 LISTEN TO SB/STH [T] to listen to what someone is saying, the music they are playing etc: *Maggie did not wait to hear an answer.* | *Did you hear that programme on whales the other night?* | **hear what** *I want to hear what the doctor has to say.* | **I hear what you say/what you're saying** *spoken* (=used to tell someone that you have listened to their opinion, but do not agree with it) *I hear what you say, but I don't think we should rush this decision.*
3 BE TOLD STH [I,T] to be told or find out a piece of information: *I heard a rumor that he was getting married soon.* | **hear (that)** *I'm so sorry to hear he died.* | *She'll* **be pleased to hear** *that she can leave hospital tomorrow.* | **[+about]** *Teresa heard about the decision later.* | **[+of]** *I've heard of a job which would be just right for you.* | *This was* **the first** *I'd* **heard of** *any trouble in the area* (=I had just heard news of trouble for the first time). | *He was* **last heard of** *in Washington* (=he was in Washington the last time someone had information about him). | **hear anything/much of sb/sth** *We don't hear anything of him these days.* | **so I hear/so I've heard** *spoken* (=used to say that you have been told something or know it already) *There's a nasty infection going round, so I hear.* | **hear what/how/who etc** *Did you hear what happened to Julia?* | *I've* **heard it said** *that they met in Italy.*
4 IN COURT [T] to listen to all the facts in a case in a court of law in order to make a legal decision: *The Supreme Court heard the case on Tuesday.*
5 **have heard of sb/sth** to know that someone or something exists because they have been mentioned to you before: *'Do you know Jill Marshall?' 'No, I've never heard of her.'*
6 **not hear the last of sb** used to say that someone will continue to complain about something or cause problems: *I'll sue him. He hasn't heard the last of me yet.*
7 **you could hear a pin drop** used to emphasize how quiet a place is: *You could have heard a pin drop in there.*
→ UNHEARD OF

SPOKEN PHRASES

8 **won't/wouldn't hear of it** used to say that you refuse to agree with a suggestion or proposal: *I said we should go back, but Dennis wouldn't hear of it.*
9 **I/he etc will never hear the end of it** used to say that someone will continue to talk about something for a long time: *If my Mum finds out, I'll never hear the end of it.*
10 **be hearing things** to imagine you can hear a sound when really there is no sound: *There's no one there. I must be hearing things.*
11 **(do) you hear?** used to emphasize that you are giving someone an order and they must obey you: *I want you to leave right now. Do you hear?*
12 **you can't hear yourself think** used to emphasize how noisy a place is: *Just shut up, Tom. I can't hear myself think.*
13 **now hear this!** *AmE old use* used to introduce an important official announcement
14 **hear! hear!** used in a discussion or meeting to say that you agree with what the speaker is saying
15 **have you heard the one about ...** used when asking someone if they know a joke
16 **I've heard that one before** used when you do not believe someone's excuse or explanation
17 **let's hear it for sb** used to say that someone deserves praise, or to ask people to show their approval of someone by CLAPPING

GRAMMAR: Using the progressive

• In meanings 1, 2, and 3, **hear** is not usually used in the progressive. You say: *I heard a strange sound.*
✗ Don't say: *I was hearing a strange sound.*
• **Hear** is often used with **can**: *I could hear a strange sound.*

• In spoken English, people sometimes say **I'm hearing** to talk about something they have been told recently, especially more than once: *I've been hearing some nice things about you.*
GRAMMAR GUIDE ▸ VERBS

USAGE: Hear or listen?

Don't confuse **hear** (=a sound comes into your ears) with **listen to** (=hear and pay attention to something).
You say: *You should listen to my advice.* ✗ Don't say: *You should hear my advice.*
You say: *I lay in bed listening to music.* ✗ Don't say: *I lay in bed hearing music.*

THESAURUS

hear to know that a sound is being made, using your ears: *There's no need to shout – I can hear you!* | *Voices could be heard in the distance.*
listen to pay attention to something, using your ears: *I was listening to the news on the car radio.* | *He never listens to anything I say.*
make out to hear something with difficulty: *When I got closer, I could make out a human voice.* | *I could just make out what he was saying.*
overhear to accidentally hear another person's conversation: *I overheard her say to her friend that she had lost something.*
catch to hear something that someone says: *Sorry, I didn't catch your name.* | *I caught the last few minutes of the programme.*
tune in to listen to a programme – often used in announcements on the radio: *Tune in for all the latest news and views from around the world.* | *Thousands of people tune in to the show every week.*

hear from sb *phr v*
1 to receive news or information from someone: *Do you ever hear from Jack?* | *Police want to hear from anyone who has any information.* | *I **look forward to hearing from you*** (=hope to receive news from you).
2 to listen to someone giving their opinion in a radio or television discussion programme: *a chance to hear from some of the victims of violent crime*

hear sb **out** *phr v* to listen to all of what someone wants to tell you without interrupting them: *Just hear me out, will you?*

hear·er /ˈhɪərə $ ˈhɪrər/ *n* [C] someone who hears something SYN **listener**

hear·ing /ˈhɪərɪŋ $ ˈhɪr-/ ●●● S3 W2 *n*
1 [U] the sense which you use to hear sounds: **have good/bad etc hearing** *She has remarkable hearing for a lady of her age.* | *a child with a hearing disability* → HARD OF HEARING
2 [C] a meeting of a court or special committee to find out the facts about a case: *a court hearing* | *a disciplinary hearing*
3 [C usually singular] an opportunity for someone to explain their actions, ideas, or opinions: *Let's give both sides **a fair hearing**.*
4 in/within sb's hearing if you say something in someone's hearing, you say it where they can hear you: *There are some words we don't use in the children's hearing.*

ˈhearing aid *n* [C] a small object which fits into or behind your ear to make sounds louder, worn by people who cannot hear well

ˈhearing-imˌpaired *adj* **a)** not able to hear well SYN **hard of hearing** → **deaf b) the hearing-impaired** people who are not able to hear well

hear·ken, **harken** /ˈhɑːkən $ ˈhɑːr-/ *v* [I + to] *literary* to listen

hear·say /ˈhɪəseɪ $ ˈhɪr-/ *n* [U] something that you have heard about from other people but do not know to be definitely true or correct → **rumour**: *I wouldn't take any notice of it – it's just hearsay.*

hearse /hɜːs $ hɜːrs/ *n* [C] a large car used to carry a dead body in a COFFIN at a funeral

heart /hɑːt $ hɑːrt/ ●●● S1 W1 *n*
1 BODY ORGAN [C] the organ in your chest which pumps blood through your body: *Regular exercise is good for the heart.* | *Can you **hear** my **heart beating**?* | *Her cheeks were hot and her **heart was pounding**.* | *My **heart raced**. Were we going to land safely?* | *Daniel had no history of **heart problems**.* | *She suffers from a rare **heart condition**.* | *His breathing and **heart rate** were now normal.* → see picture at HUMAN[1]
2 EMOTIONS/LOVE [C] the part of you that feels strong emotions and feelings: *His heart was full of anger and grief.* | *The plight of the refugees had tugged at the nation's heart.* | *The doctor had an extremely kind heart.* | *She could hardly speak for the **ache** in her **heart**.* | *It would **break** Kate's **heart*** (=make her extremely sad) *to leave the lovely old house.* | *He left the country **with a heavy heart*** (=great sadness). | *Edith loved her boy with all her **heart and soul**.* | *I was still pretty innocent then when it came to **affairs of the heart*** (=matters relating to love and sex). | *a woman with a **heart of gold*** (=very kind character) | *Sometimes I think he's got a **heart of stone*** (=very cruel character). | *I'm glad I **followed** my **heart** rather than my head for once.* | *My father told me never to let my **heart rule** my **head**.* | **kind-hearted/cold-hearted/hard-hearted etc** (=having a kind, unkind, cruel etc character) *He thinks of himself as a warm-hearted and caring human being.*
3 YOUR CHEST [C usually singular] the part of your chest near your heart: *He put his hand on his heart.*
4 SHAPE [C] a shape used to represent a heart
5 from the (bottom of your) heart with great sincerity and strength of feeling: *Leonard spoke from the heart.* | *I want to thank you from the bottom of my heart.* | *She sang the songs **straight from the heart**.*
6 in your heart (of hearts) if you know, feel, or believe something in your heart, you are secretly sure about it although you may not admit it: *In her heart she knew she would never go.* | ***Deep in his heart**, he wanted Laura back.*
7 IMPORTANT PART OF STH [singular] the most important or central part of a problem, question etc: **the heart of sth** *difficult issues **at the heart of** science policy* | *We must **get to the heart of** the problem.*
8 ENCOURAGEMENT [U] confidence and courage: *This inspiring service **gave** us **new heart**.* | *We mustn't **lose heart** when people complain.* | *We've got to **take** a bit of **heart** from the fact that we won.*
9 at heart if you are a particular kind of person at heart, that is the kind of person that you really are even though you may appear or behave differently: *He may be a working class boy at heart, but his lifestyle has been transformed.* | *Let's face it, we're all romantics at heart.*
→ **have sb's (best) interests at heart** at INTEREST[1](5), → **young at heart** at YOUNG[1](5)
10 THE CENTRE OF AN AREA [C] the middle part of an area furthest from the edge: **in the heart of sth** *a house in the heart of London* | **at the heart of sth** *an old house at the heart of an ancient forest*
11 close/dear to sb's heart very important to someone: *The president liked to go to Williamsburg, a place close to his heart.* | *Money is dear to Kathleen's heart.*
12 the hearts and minds of sb the thoughts, emotions, and attitudes a group of people have about a particular subject, which is a combination of their strong emotional feelings and their calm and sensible thoughts: *The president must try to **win the hearts and minds of** the voters.*
13 by heart when you know something by heart, you remember all of it exactly: *After a few days of phoning Stephanie, he knew her number by heart.* | *Actors have to learn their lines by heart.*
14 sb's heart sinks used to say that someone suddenly lost hope and began to feel unhappy: *Her heart sank when she saw the number of books she had to read.*
15 with all your heart with all your strength, energy, or emotion: *He hates Los Angeles with all his heart.* | *We sang the hymn with all our hearts.*
16 take sth to heart to consider what someone says to

you very seriously, often because it upsets you: *Anne took his criticisms very much to heart.* | *We took Stephen's warnings to heart.*

17 sb's heart goes out to sb used to say that someone feels a lot of sympathy towards another person: *My heart goes out to the families of the victims.*

18 CARD GAMES **a)** [C] a heart shape printed in red on a PLAYING CARD **b) hearts** [plural] the SUIT (=set) of playing cards that have these shapes on them: *the ace of hearts* **c)** [C] one of the cards in this set: *Have you got any hearts?*

19 do sth to your heart's content to do something as much as you want: *She had lazed around the pool to her heart's content.* | *The dog can run to its heart's content out there.*

20 sb's heart misses/skips a beat used to say that someone suddenly feels a moment of fear or excitement: *His heart missed a beat as he saw the body of a small child at the water's edge.*

21 set your heart on sth to want something very much: *His father bought him the bike he had set his heart on.* | *She had set her heart on becoming a hairdresser.*

22 a man/woman etc after my own heart someone who likes the same things or behaves in the same way that you do: *Geoff really is a man after my own heart.*

23 cry/sing etc your heart out if you cry, sing etc your heart out, you do it with all your energy or emotion: *He found me crying my heart out and was so kind.* → **eat your heart out** at EAT(4), → **pour your heart out** at POUR

24 your heart's desire/everything your heart could desire the one thing you want most, or everything that you could possibly want: *To have a baby was her heart's desire.*

25 not have the heart to do something to be unable to do something because it will make someone unhappy: *I didn't have the heart to tell her that her beautiful vase was broken.*

26 sb's heart isn't in it used to say that someone does not really want to do something: *She's getting bored with the job and her heart's not in it.*

27 do sth out of the goodness of your heart to do something out of kindness, not because you have been asked or expect a reward: *All these people were helping us out of the goodness of their hearts.*

28 take sb to your heart if people take someone to their hearts, they like them very much: *The fans have taken Hudson to their hearts.*

29 VEGETABLE [C] the firm middle part of some vegetables: *artichoke hearts*

30 give/lose your heart to sb to start to love someone very much

31 my heart was in my mouth used to say that you suddenly felt very afraid

32 sb's heart is in the right place *informal* used to say that someone is really a kind person and has the right feelings about something important: *I don't think his idea will work, though his heart's in the right place.*

33 it does your heart good to see/hear sth used to say that something makes you feel happy

34 sb's heart leaps *literary* used to say that someone suddenly feels happy and full of hope: *'I couldn't live without you,' he said and Jane's heart leapt.*

35 be in good heart *formal* to feel happy and confident: *The team are in good heart and ready for the season's matches.*

36 have a heart! used to tell someone not to be too strict or unkind - used humorously

37 know the way to sb's heart to know the way to please someone - used humorously

38 my heart bleeds (for sb) used to say that you do not really feel any sympathy towards someone → **a broken heart** at BROKEN[2](9), → **cross my heart** at CROSS[1](11), → **have a change of heart** at CHANGE[2](1), → **sick at heart** at SICK[1](9), → **strike at the heart of sth** at STRIKE[1](7), → **wear your heart on your sleeve** at WEAR[1](8), → **win sb's heart** at WIN[1](3)

COLLOCATIONS

VERBS

sb's heart beats *Her heart was beating fast.*
sb's heart pounds/thuds/thumps (=it beats very strongly) *He reached the top, his heart pounding.*
sb's heart races (=it beats very fast)

heart + NOUN

heart trouble/problems *You should not take this medication if you have heart problems.*
heart disease *Smoking increases the risk of heart disease.*
a heart condition (=something wrong with your heart) *The baby was born with a heart condition.*
sb's heart rate (=the number of times someone's heart beats per minute)

ADJECTIVES

healthy *Eating oily fish can help maintain a healthy heart.*
a bad/weak heart (=an unhealthy heart)

heart·ache /ˈhɑːteɪk $ ˈhɑːrt-/ *n* [U] a strong feeling of great sadness and anxiety

ˈheart atˌtack ●●○ *n* [C]
1 a sudden serious medical condition in which someone's heart stops working normally, causing them great pain: **have/suffer a heart attack**
2 give sb/have a heart attack *informal* to make someone suddenly feel frightened, surprised, or shocked, or to suddenly feel this way: *You almost gave me a heart attack there!*

heart·beat /ˈhɑːtbiːt $ ˈhɑːrt-/ *n* [C,U] **1** the action or sound of your heart as it pumps blood through your body **2 be a heartbeat away from sth** to be very close to a situation or position **3 in a heartbeat** *AmE* very quickly, without delay: *Things can change in a heartbeat.* **4 the heartbeat of sth** *AmE* the main origin of activity or excitement in a place or organization

heart·break /ˈhɑːtbreɪk $ ˈhɑːrt-/ *n* [U] great sadness or disappointment

heart·break·ing /ˈhɑːtˌbreɪkɪŋ $ ˈhɑːrt-/ *adj* making you feel extremely sad or disappointed —**heartbreakingly** *adv*

heart·brok·en /ˈhɑːtˌbrəʊkən $ ˈhɑːrtˌbroʊ-/ *adj* extremely sad because of something that has happened THESAURUS ▸ SAD

heart·burn /ˈhɑːtbɜːn $ ˈhɑːrtbɜːrn/ *n* [U] an unpleasant burning feeling in your stomach or chest caused by acid from your stomach → **indigestion**

ˈheart disˌease *n* [C,U] an illness which prevents your heart from working normally

heart·en /ˈhɑːtn $ ˈhɑːr-/ *v* [T] to make someone feel happier and more hopeful OPP **dishearten**: *I was heartened to see her looking so well.* —**heartening** *adj* —**hearteningly** *adv*

ˈheart ˌfailure *n* [U] a serious medical condition in which someone's heart stops working properly, often resulting in death → **heart attack**

heart·felt /ˈhɑːtfelt $ ˈhɑːrt-/ *adj* very strongly felt and sincere: *a heartfelt apology*

hearth /hɑːθ $ hɑːrθ/ *n* [C] **1** the area of floor around a FIREPLACE in a house **2 hearth and home** *literary* your home and family

heart·i·ly /ˈhɑːtəli $ ˈhɑːr-/ *adv* **1** with energy and enjoyment: *'Great to see you,' she said heartily.* | *Hugh* ***laughed heartily*** *at the joke.* **2** completely or very much: *This is a book I* ***heartily recommend*** *to all hill walkers.* | *Madge had become* ***heartily sick of*** *the city.* **3 eat heartily** to eat a large amount

heart·land /ˈhɑːtlənd $ ˈhɑːrt-/ *n* [C] **1 the heartland** the central part of a country or area of land **2** the most important part of a country or area for a particular activity, or the part where a political group has most support: *the Democratic heartlands of the Deep South*

H

heart·less /ˈhɑːtləs $ ˈhɑːrt-/ *adj* cruel and not feeling any pity: *How can you be so heartless?* THESAURUS CRUEL —**heartlessly** *adv* —**heartlessness** *n* [U]

ˌheart-ˈlung maˌchine *n* [C] a machine that pumps blood and oxygen around someone's body during a medical operation

ˌHeart of ˈEngland, the the central area of England, which is very industrial. This expression is used especially to make the area sound more attractive to tourists.

heart·rend·ing /ˈhɑːtˌrendɪŋ $ ˈhɑːrt-/ *adj* making you feel great pity SYN **heartbreaking**: *heartrending stories of children being taken from their parents*

ˈheart-ˌsearching *n* [U] the process of examining very carefully your feelings about something or your reasons for doing something SYN **soul-searching**

ˈheart-ˌstopping *adj* very exciting or frightening

heart·strings /ˈhɑːtˌstrɪŋz $ ˈhɑːrt-/ *n* [plural] **tug/tear/pull at sb's heartstrings** to make someone feel strong love or sympathy

heart·throb /ˈhɑːtθrɒb $ ˈhɑːrtθrɑːb/ *n* [C] a famous actor, singer etc who is very attractive to women

ˌheart-to-ˈheart *n* [C] a conversation in which two people say honestly and sincerely what they really feel about something: *Why don't you* ***have a heart-to-heart with*** *him and sort out your problems?* —**heart-to-heart** *adj*: *a heart-to-heart talk*

heart·warm·ing /ˈhɑːtˌwɔːmɪŋ $ ˈhɑːrtˌwɔːr-/ *adj* making you feel happy because you see other people being happy or kind to each other: *a heartwarming sight* —**heartwarmingly** *adv*

heart·y /ˈhɑːti $ ˈhɑːrti/ *adj* **1** happy and friendly and usually loud: *a hearty laugh* **2** *old-fashioned* strong and healthy → **hale and hearty** at HALE **3** a hearty meal is very large **4** *especially BrE* with a friendly, noisy, and happy manner that is not sincere —**heartiness** *n* [U] → HEARTILY

heat¹ /hiːt/ ●●● S2 W2 *n*

1 WARMTH [U] warmth or the quality of being hot: *Ice needs heat to melt.* | *Insulating the attic is a good way to reduce heat loss.*

2 the heat very hot weather or a high temperature: *The heat was making them tired.* | *Angela liked to rest during* ***the heat of the day*** (=the hottest part of the day). | *Firefighters were beaten back by* ***the intense heat****.*

3 IN COOKING [C usually singular, U] the level of temperature used when cooking or heating something: **low/medium/high heat** *Cook the chicken portions over a high heat.* | **turn off/down/up the heat** *When the milk comes to the boil, turn off the heat.* | *Now* ***reduce*** *the* ***heat*** *and cover the pan.*

4 STRONG FEELINGS [U] strong feelings, especially anger or excitement: *Reconciliation services can* ***take the heat out of*** (=reduce the anger in) *the dispute.* | **in the heat of sth** *Quick decisions had to be made in the heat of the negotiations.* | ***In the heat of the moment*** (=when feelings were very strong), *Nick threatened to resign.*

5 PRESSURE [U] strong pressure on someone: ***The heat is on*** (=there is a lot of pressure) *as schools struggle to finish their entries by the deadline.* | *The team* ***turned up the heat*** (=used more effort against their opponents) *in the last few minutes to score two more goals.* | *There was a lot of heat, and it affected our relationship.*

6 SYSTEM TO HEAT BUILDING [U] *AmE* the system in a house or other building that keeps it warm in the winter, or the warmth from this system SYN **heating** *BrE*: *Can you turn up* ***the heat****?*

7 IN A RACE [C] a part of a race or competition whose winners then compete against each other in the next part: *Bill finished second in his heat.*

8 on heat *BrE*, **in heat** *AmE* if a female animal is on heat, her body is ready to have sex with a male → DEAD HEAT, WHITE HEAT, → **if you can't stand the heat, get out of the kitchen** at STAND¹(16)

heat² ●●● S3 W3 *v* [T] to make something become warm or hot SYN **warm up**: *Heat the milk until it boils.*

heat sth **through** *phr v* to heat food thoroughly

heat up *phr v*

1 to become warm or hot, or to make something become warm or hot: *The stove takes a while to heat up.* | **heat sth ↔ up** *I heated up the remains of last night's supper.*

2 if a situation heats up, it becomes dangerous or full of problems

heat·ed /ˈhiːtɪd/ ●○○ *adj*

1 a heated SWIMMING POOL, room etc is made warm using a heater

2 heated argument/debate/discussion etc an argument etc that is full of angry and excited feelings —**heatedly** *adv*

heat·er /ˈhiːtə $ -ər/ ●●● S3 *n* [C] a machine for making air or water hotter: *Did you turn the heater off?*

ˈheat exˌhaustion *n* [U] weakness and sickness caused by doing too much work, exercise etc in hot weather

heath /hiːθ/ *n* [C] an area of open land where grass, bushes, and other small plants grow, especially in Britain

hea·then¹ /ˈhiːðən/ *adj old-fashioned* not connected with or belonging to the Christian religion or any of the large established religions

heathen² *n* (*plural* **heathen** *or* **heathens**) [C] *old-fashioned* **1** someone who is not connected with the Christian religion or any of the large established religions - used to show disapproval → **pagan** **2** someone who refuses to believe in something - often used humorously

heath·er /ˈheðə $ -ər/ *n* [U] a low plant with small purple, pink, or white flowers which grows on hills

Heath Rob·in·son /ˌhiːθ ˈrɒbənsən $ -ˈrɑː-/ *adj BrE* a Heath Robinson machine, system etc is very complicated in an amusing way but not at all practical

heat·ing /ˈhiːtɪŋ/ ●●○ S3 *n* [U] *especially BrE* a system for making a room or building warm SYN **heat** *AmE* → CENTRAL HEATING

heat·proof /ˈhiːtpruːf/ *adj* heatproof material cannot be damaged by heat

ˈheat pump *n* [C] part of a machine that takes heat from one place to another

ˈheat rash *n* [C,U] painful or ITCHY red spots on someone's skin caused by heat

ˈheat-reˌsistant *adj* not easily damaged by heat

ˈheat-ˌseeking *adj* a heat-seeking weapon is able to find and move towards the hot gases from an aircraft or ROCKET and destroy it

heat·stroke /ˈhiːtstrəʊk $ -stroʊk/ *n* [U] fever and weakness caused by being outside in the heat of the sun for too long → SUNSTROKE

ˈheat wave *n* [C] a period of unusually hot weather, especially one that continues for a long time OPP **cold spell**

heave¹ /hiːv/ ●○○ *v*

1 PULL/LIFT [I,T] to pull or lift something very heavy with one great effort: **heave sb/sth out of/into/onto etc sth** *Alan heaved his suitcase onto his bed.* | *Mary heaved herself out of bed.* | **[+on/at]** *BrE*: *We had to heave on the rope holding the anchor to get it on board.* THESAURUS PULL

2 THROW [T] to throw something heavy using a lot of effort: *John heaved the metal bar over the fence.* THESAURUS THROW

3 heave a sigh to breathe in and then breathe out noisily and slowly once: *Rebecca* ***heaved a sigh of relief****.*

4 MOVE UP AND DOWN [I] to move up and down with very strong movements: *Michael's shoulders heaved with silent laughter.* | *The sea heaved up and down beneath the boat.*

5 VOMIT [I] *informal* to VOMIT

6 (*past tense and past participle* **hove**) **heave in sight/into view** *literary* to appear, especially by getting closer from a distance: *A few moments later a large ship hove into view.* → HEAVING

heave to *phr v* (*past tense and past participle* **hove to** /ˌhəʊv ˈtuː $ ˌhoʊv-/) *technical* if a ship heaves to, it stops moving

heave² *n* **1** [C] a strong pulling, pushing, or lifting movement: *He gave the door a good heave.* **2** [U] *literary* a strong rising or falling movement

ˌheave-ˈho *interjection, n* **1** *old-fashioned* used as an encouragement to a person or group of people who are pulling something, especially on ships **2 give someone the (old) heave-ho** *informal* to end a relationship with someone, or to make someone leave their job

heav·en /ˈhevən/ ●●● S3 W3 *n*

1 PLACE OF GOD (*also* **Heaven**) [singular] the place where God is believed to live and where good people are believed to go when they die → **paradise**: **in heaven** *He believed that he and his wife would one day be together again in heaven.*

2 ENJOYABLE SITUATION [U] *informal* an extremely enjoyable situation or place SYN **paradise**: *Sitting by the pool with a good book is my idea of heaven.* | **in heaven** *Put a baseball in his hand and he's in heaven.* | *Living on the farm for Jim was* **heaven on earth**. | **a match/marriage made in heaven** (=a happy and successful marriage)

SPOKEN PHRASES

3 for heaven's sake a) used to show that you are annoyed or angry: *Oh, for heaven's sake, Mark, do you have to make everything into a joke?* **b)** used to emphasize a question, request, order, or opinion: *For heaven's sake, let's all get to sleep.*

4 heaven (only) knows a) used to emphasize that you do not know something: *He won't tell me what he thinks. Heaven knows why.* **b)** used to emphasize what you are saying: *Sue can't take a holiday yet, though heaven knows she needs a rest.*

5 heaven help sb a) used to express sympathy for someone who is in a dangerous or difficult situation: *'The two boys are going to the dentist on Thursday.' 'Heaven help the dentist.'* **b)** used to say that you will be very angry with someone if they do something: ***Heaven help** him **if** he ever comes back here again!*

6 heaven forbid used to say that you very much hope something will not happen: *What would you do financially if, heaven forbid, your husband died?*

7 what/how/why etc in heaven's name used when asking a surprised and angry question: *Where in heaven's name have you been?*

8 the heavens *literary* the sky: *He looked up towards the heavens.* | *Just then,* **the heavens opened** (=it started to rain heavily).

9 move heaven and earth to try very hard to achieve something: *I would move heaven and earth to help her.* → **be in seventh heaven** at SEVENTH[1](2), → **thank heaven(s)** at THANK(2)

heav·en·ly /ˈhevənli/ ●○○ *adj*

1 *old-fashioned* extremely pleasant, enjoyable, or beautiful: *That smells heavenly.* | *We found a tiny hotel in a heavenly spot with a beautiful bay.*

2 [only before noun] *biblical* existing in or belonging to heaven: *God's heavenly kingdom* | **heavenly Father** (=God) | **the Heavenly Host** (=all the angels)

3 *literary* existing in or relating to the sky or stars: ***heavenly bodies*** (=the Moon, PLANETS, and stars)

Heav·ens! /ˈhevənz/ (*also* **Good Heavens!**, **ˌHeavens aˈbove!**) *interjection* used to express surprise, especially when you are annoyed: *Good Heavens, what a mess!*

ˌheaven-ˈsent / $ ˈ.. ./ *adj literary* happening fortunately at exactly the right time: *a heaven-sent opportunity*

heav·en·ward /ˈhevənwəd $ -wərd/ (*also* **heav·en·wards** /-wədz $ -wərdz/) *adv literary* towards the sky

heav·ily /ˈhevəli/ ●●○ W3 *adv*

1 in large amounts, to a high degree, or with great severity SYN **very**: *I became* ***heavily involved*** *in politics.* | *The report was* ***heavily criticized*** *in the press.* | *a* ***heavily populated*** *area* | *thousands of* ***heavily armed*** *troops* | *His wife was* ***heavily pregnant*** *at the time.* | **it rains/snows heavily** *It's been raining heavily all day.* | **drink/smoke heavily** *Paul was drinking heavily by then.* | **heavily dependent/reliant/influenced** *Britain is heavily dependent on imports for its raw materials.*

2 sleep heavily if you sleep heavily, you cannot be woken easily

3 breathe heavily to breathe slowly and loudly: *Breathing heavily, I stopped and sat down to rest.*

4 heavily built having a large broad body that looks strong

5 if you do or say something heavily, you do it slowly and with a lot of effort, especially because you are sad or bored: *He was walking heavily, his head down.* | *Emily sighed heavily.* | *'I suppose so,' she said heavily.*

6 be heavily into sth *informal* to do something a lot or be very interested in it: *Sid was heavily into drugs by the time he left school.*

heav·ing /ˈhiːvɪŋ/ *adj BrE informal* very busy or full of people: **[+with]** *The city was heaving with shoppers.*

heav·y¹ /ˈhevi/ ●●● S1 W1 *adj* (*comparative* **heavier**, *superlative* **heaviest**)

1 WEIGHT weighing a lot OPP **light**: *The wardrobe was too heavy for me to move on my own.* | *a heavy suitcase* | *The males are seven times heavier than the females.* | ***How heavy is the parcel*** (=how much does it weigh?)?

2 AMOUNT/DEGREE/SEVERITY great in amount, degree, or severity: *The* ***traffic*** *going into London was very* ***heavy***. | ***Heavy rain*** *has caused flooding in many areas.* | ***Heavy fighting*** *was reported near the border.* | ***Heavy drinking*** *during pregnancy can damage your baby.* | *I used to be a* ***heavy smoker***. | *the* ***heavy burden*** *of taxation* | *If found guilty, they face* ***heavy fines*** *or even prison.* | *There were* ***heavy casualties*** *on both sides.* | *England's* ***heavy defeat*** *in yesterday's match* | *She's in bed with a* ***heavy cold***. | *the film's* ***heavy use*** *of special effects*

3 NEEDING PHYSICAL EFFORT needing a lot of physical strength and effort: *My son does most of the* ***heavy*** *outdoor* ***work***. | *She has a bad back and can't do any* ***heavy lifting***.

4 NEEDING MENTAL EFFORT not easy or entertaining and needing a lot of mental effort: *I want something to read on holiday – nothing too heavy.*

5 heavy going difficult to understand or deal with: *I* ***found*** *his latest novel a bit* ***heavy going***.

6 be heavy on sth *informal* to use a lot or too much of something: *The car's rather heavy on oil.*

7 heavy with sth *literary* full of something: *The apple trees were heavy with fruit.* | *The garden was heavy with the scent of summer.* | *'Of course,' she said, her voice heavy with sarcasm.*

8 heavy schedule/timetable/day etc a time in which you have a lot to do: *Let's go to bed. We've got a heavy day tomorrow.*

9 heavy breathing breathing that is slow and loud → HEAVY BREATHER

10 make heavy weather of sth *BrE* to make something that you are doing seem more difficult or complicated than it really is – used to show disapproval: *Why does he need to make such heavy weather of a simple task?*

11 WEAPONS/MACHINES [only before noun] large and powerful: *tanks and other heavy weapons* | ***heavy artillery*** (=large powerful guns) | *a company which manufactures* ***heavy machinery***

12 MATERIALS/CLOTHES ETC heavy materials, clothes, shoes, or objects are thick or solidly made: *a heavy winter coat* | *the sound of heavy boots* | *Melt the butter in a heavy pan over a medium heat.* | *heavy velvet curtains*

13 FOOD solid and making your stomach feel full and uncomfortable OPP **light**: *a heavy meal* | *heavy fruitcake*

14 EYES if your eyes are heavy, it is difficult to keep them open, usually because you are tired: *His eyes felt heavy with fatigue.*

15 BODY/FACE **a)** large, broad, and solid: *his heavy features* | *Kyle is a tall man with a* ***heavy build*** (=a large broad body). **b)** *AmE* used to politely describe someone who is fat SYN **large**

16 WITH FORCE hitting something or falling with a lot of force or weight: *the sound of heavy footsteps in the hall* | *Ali caught him with a heavy blow to the jaw.*

17 GROUND **a)** soil that is heavy is thick and solid **b)** a sports ground or race track that is heavy is muddy: *a very heavy pitch* | ***The going*** *was* ***heavy*** (=it was muddy for the horse races) *at Cheltenham yesterday.*

18 SMELL strong and usually sweet: **heavy scent/perfume etc** *the heavy scent of the lilies*

19 AIR too warm and not at all fresh because there is no wind: *Even at dusk the air was still heavy.*
20 EMOTIONS *informal* a relationship or situation that is heavy involves serious or strong feelings: *She didn't want things to* **get** *too* **heavy** *at such an early stage in their relationship.*
21 get heavy (with sb) *informal* to start behaving in a threatening or strict way: *He came round and started getting heavy about the money I owed him.*
22 heavy silence/atmosphere a situation in which people do not speak and feel sad, anxious, or embarrassed: *A heavy silence fell upon the room.*
23 heavy sky/clouds clouds that look dark and grey as though it will soon rain
24 heavy sleeper someone who does not wake easily
25 heavy irony/sarcasm remarks that very clearly say the opposite of what you really feel
26 heavy seas sea with big waves
27 with a heavy heart *literary* feeling very sad: *It was with a heavy heart that Kate said goodbye.*
28 heavy date *AmE* a very important DATE (=an occasion when you meet someone you like in a romantic way) with a BOYFRIEND or GIRLFRIEND - usually used humorously —**heaviness** *n* [U]

heavy² *adv* **1 time hangs/lies heavy on your hands** if time hangs or lies heavy on your hands, it seems to pass slowly because you are bored or have nothing to do **2 be heavy into sth** *AmE spoken informal* to be very involved in an activity, especially one that is not good for you: *Eric was real heavy into drugs for a while.*

heavy³ *n* (*plural* **heavies**) [C] *informal* a large strong man who is paid to protect someone or to threaten other people

ˌheavy ˈbreather *n* [C] a man who telephones a woman and does not speak, but breathes loudly, in order to get sexual pleasure —**heavy breathing** *n* [U]

ˌheavy ˈcream *n* [U] *AmE* thick cream SYN **double cream** *BrE*

ˌheavy-ˈduty *adj* **1** heavy-duty materials are strong and thick and not easily damaged: *heavy-duty canvas* THESAURUS STRONG **2** heavy-duty machines or equipment are designed to be used for very hard work **3** *especially AmE informal* very complicated, serious, or extreme: *Today, she was going to do some heavy-duty cleaning.*

ˌheavy ˈgoods ˌvehicle *n* [C] an HGV

ˌheavy-ˈhanded *adj* taking too much action or extreme action, especially without thinking about other people's feelings: *a heavy-handed style of management* —**heavy-handedness** *n* [U]

heavy-heart·ed /ˌhevi ˈhɑːtɪd $ -ˈhɑːr-/ *adj literary* very sad

ˌheavy ˈhitter *n* [C] *AmE* **1** a person or company that has a lot of power, especially in business or politics **2** a BASEBALL player who hits the ball very hard

ˌheavy ˈindustry *n* [U] industry that produces large goods such as cars and machines, or materials such as coal, steel, or chemicals → LIGHT INDUSTRY

ˌheavy ˈmetal *n* **1** [U] a type of ROCK music with a strong beat, played very loudly on electric GUITARS **2** [C] *technical* a metal that has a high DENSITY, such as gold, MERCURY, or LEAD. Many heavy metals are poisonous.

ˌheavy ˈpetting *n* [U] *old-fashioned* sexual activities that do not involve actually having sex

ˌheavy-ˈset *adj* someone who is heavy-set is large and looks strong or fat

heav·y·weight /ˈheviweɪt/ *n* [C] **1** someone or something that is very important or has a lot of influence: *one of the heavyweights of the movie industry* **2** a BOXER who weighs more than 91 kilograms, and who belongs to the heaviest weight class of boxers

He·bra·ic /hɪˈbreɪ-ɪk/ *adj formal* connected with the Hebrew language or people: *Hebraic literature*

He·brew /ˈhiːbruː/ *n* **1** [U] the language traditionally used by the Jewish people **2** [C] a member of the Jewish people in ancient times —**Hebrew** *adj*

heck¹ /hek/ *interjection informal* **1** used to show that you are annoyed or to emphasize what you are saying: *Oh heck! I've lost my keys!* | *'Do you believe him?' 'Heck, no.'* **2 did he heck/will it heck etc** *BrE* used to say in a strong way that someone did not do something, something will not happen etc: *'Did he offer to pay for it?' 'Did he heck.'*

heck² *n* [singular, U] *spoken informal* **1** used like 'hell' to emphasize what you are saying: *It cost* **a heck of a** *lot of money.* | **where/how/who etc the heck** *Where the heck are we?* | *He sure as heck didn't tell me.* **2 what the heck** used to say that you will do something even though you really should not do it: *It's rather expensive, but what the heck.* **3 for the heck of it** for fun, or for no particular reason

heck·le /ˈhekəl/ *v* [I,T] to interrupt and try to embarrass someone who is speaking or performing in public —**heckler** *n* [C] —**heckling** *n* [U]

hec·tare /ˈhektɑː, -teə $ -ter/ *n* [C] (*written abbreviation* **ha**) a unit for measuring area, equal to 10,000 square metres → **acre**

hec·tic /ˈhektɪk/ *adj* **1** very busy or full of activity: *I've had a pretty hectic day.* | *a hectic social life* THESAURUS BUSY **2** *written* if your face is a hectic colour, it is very pink: *the hectic flush on her cheeks*

hec·tor /ˈhektə $ -ər/ *v* [I,T] to speak to someone in an angry threatening way: *a hectoring tone of voice*

he'd /id, hid; *strong* hiːd/ **1** the short form of 'he had': *By the time I got there he'd gone.* **2** the short form of 'he would': *I'm sure he'd help if he could.*

hedge¹ /hedʒ/ ●●○ *n* [C]
1 a row of small bushes or trees growing close together, usually dividing one field or garden from another
2 something that protects you against possible problems, especially financial loss: **[+against]** *Buying a house will be a hedge against inflation.* → **look as if you've been dragged through a hedge backwards** at DRAG¹(13)

hedge² *v* (**hedged**, **hedging**) [I,T] **1** to avoid giving a direct answer to a question: *You're hedging again - have you got the money or haven't you?* | *'That depends on my partner,' she hedged.* **2 hedge your bets** to reduce your chances of failure or loss by trying several different possibilities instead of one: *It's a good idea to hedge your bets by applying to more than one college.*

hedge against sth *phr v* to try to protect yourself against possible problems, especially financial loss: *Smart managers will hedge against price increases.*

hedge in *phr v* **be hedged in 1** to be surrounded or enclosed by something: *The building was hedged in by trees.* **2** if you feel hedged in by something, you feel that your freedom is restricted by it

ˈhedge ˌfund *n* [C] an organization that makes INVESTMENTS for people and organizations with large amounts of money, not the general public, in ways that often involve big risks

HEDGEHOG

hedge·hog /ˈhedʒhɒg $ -hɑːg, -hɒːg/ *n* [C] a small brown European animal whose body is round and covered with sharp needle-like SPINES

hedge·row /ˈhedʒrəʊ $ -roʊ/ *n* [C] *BrE* a line of bushes growing along the edge of a field or road

he·don·ist /ˈhiːdən-ɪst/ *n* [C] someone who believes that pleasure is the most important thing in life —**hedonism** *n* [U] —**hedonistic** /ˌhiːdənˈɪstɪk◂/ *adj*

hee·bie-jee·bies /ˌhiː bi ˈdʒiːbiz/ *n* [plural] *informal* a nervous or frightened feeling: *Looking into the dark cave* **gave** *me* **the heebie-jeebies**.

heed¹ /hiːd/ *v* [T] *formal* to pay attention to someone's

H

advice or warning: *If she had only* **heeded** *my* **warnings**, *none of this would have happened.*

heed² *n* **pay heed to sth/take heed of sth** *formal* to pay attention to something, especially something someone says, and seriously consider it: *The government was taking little heed of these threats.* | *Tom paid no heed to her warning.*

heed·less /ˈhiːdləs/ *adj* **heedless of sth** *literary* not paying attention to something: *O'Hara rode on, heedless of danger.* —**heedlessly** *adv*

heel¹ /hiːl/ ●●○ *n* [C]

1 OF YOUR FOOT the curved back part of your foot → **toe**

2 OF A SHOE the raised part on the bottom of a shoe that makes the shoe higher at the back: *black boots with high heels* | **high-heeled/low-heeled/flat-heeled etc** *her low-heeled blue shoes* → see picture at SHOE¹

3 OF A SOCK the part of a sock that covers your heel

4 OF YOUR HAND the part of your hand between the bottom of your thumb and your wrist: *Using the heel of your hand, press the dough firmly into shape.*

5 **heels** [plural] a pair of women's shoes with high heels: *Whenever she* **wore heels** *she was taller than the men she worked with.*

6 **at sb's heels** if a person or animal is at your heels, they are following closely behind you: *He could hear the dog trotting at his heels.*

7 **a) (hard/hot/close) on the heels of sth** very soon after something: *The decision to buy Peters* **came** *hard* **on the heels of** *the club's promotion to Division One.* **b) (hard/hot/close) on sb's heels** following closely behind someone, especially in order to catch or attack them: *With the enemy army hard on his heels, he crossed the Somme at Blanche-Taque.*

8 **bring sb to heel** to force someone to behave in the way that you want them to

9 **come to heel** *BrE* **a)** if a dog comes to heel, it comes back to its owner when the owner calls it **b)** if someone comes to heel, they start to behave in the way that you want them to

10 **take to your heels** *written* to start running away: *As soon as he saw me he took to his heels.*

11 **turn/spin on your heel** *written* to suddenly turn away from someone, especially in an angry or rude way: *Before anyone could say a word, he turned on his heel and walked out of the room.*

12 **under the heel of sb/sth** completely controlled by a government or group: *a people under the heel of an increasingly dictatorial regime*

13 BAD MAN *old-fashioned* a man who behaves badly towards other people → ACHILLES' HEEL, DOWN-AT-HEEL, WELL-HEELED, → **click your heels** at CLICK¹(1), → **cool your heels** at COOL²(4), → **dig your heels in** at DIG¹(4), → **drag your heels** at DRAG¹(8), → **be/fall head over heels in love** at HEAD¹(36), → **kick your heels** at KICK¹(9)

heel² *v* **1 heel!** *spoken* used to tell your dog to walk next to you **2** [T] to put a heel on a shoe

heel over *phr v* if something heels over, it leans to one side as if it is going to fall: *The ship was heeling over in the wind.*

heel·flip /ˈhiːlflɪp/ *n* [C] a movement in SKATEBOARDING in which you push your heel down hard on the SKATEBOARD as you jump upwards off the board. The board turns around sideways in a complete circle and you land on it again when it has finished turning. —**heelflip** *v* [I]

Heel·ys /ˈhiːliz/ *n* [plural] *trademark* shoes with one or more wheels in the heel, so that you can roll along when you want to

heft /heft/ *v* [T] **1** to lift something heavy: **heft sth onto/into etc sth** *He hefted his bag into the car.* **2** to lift or hold something in order to judge how heavy it is: *Quinn hefted the package in his hands.*

hef·ty /ˈhefti/ ●○○ *adj* [usually before noun]

1 big and heavy: *a tall hefty man* | *a* **hefty tome** (=large thick book) | *hefty camera equipment*

2 a hefty amount of something, especially money, is very large: *a hefty fine*

3 *BrE* a hefty blow, kick etc is done using a lot of force: *He aimed a hefty kick at the door.* | *a hefty shove*

he·gem·o·ny /hɪˈgeməni, ˈhedʒəməni $ hɪˈdʒeməni, ˈhedʒəmoʊni/ *n* [U] *formal* a situation in which one state or country controls others

heif·er /ˈhefə $ -ər/ *n* [C] a young cow that has not yet given birth to a CALF → **bullock**, **ox**, **steer**

height /haɪt/ ●●● S2 W3 *n*

1 HOW TALL [C,U] how tall someone or something is: *Sam's about the same height as his sister now.* | *State your age, height, and weight.* | *buildings of different heights* | **six feet/ten metres etc in height** *None of these sculptures was less than three metres in height.* | **a height of six feet/ten metres etc** *Sunflowers can grow to a height of 15 feet.* → see picture at DIMENSION

2 DISTANCE ABOVE THE GROUND [C,U] the distance something is above the ground: *It's a miracle she didn't break her neck falling from that height.* | **a height of 2,500 feet/10,000 metres etc** *The aircraft was flying at a height of 10,000 metres.* | **gain/lose height** (=move higher or lower in the sky) *The plane was rapidly losing height.*

3 HIGH PLACE **a)** [C] a place or position that is a long way above the ground: **from a height** *a bird that opens shellfish by dropping them from a height onto rocks* | *Rachel had always been* **scared of heights**. | **have a head for heights** (=not be afraid of heights) **b) heights** [plural] a particular high place - used especially in place names: *the Golan Heights*

4 **new/great/dizzy etc heights a)** a very high level of achievement or success: **rise to/reach etc ... heights** *He reached the dizzy heights of the national finals.* | *They* **took** *ice dancing* **to new heights**. **b)** a very great level or degree: *War fever had reached new heights.*

5 **the height of sth** the busiest or most extreme part of a period or activity SYN **peak**: *the height of the tourist season*

6 **be at the height of your success/fame/powers etc** to be more successful, famous etc than at any other time: *The Beatles were at the height of their fame.*

7 **be the height of fashion/stupidity/luxury etc** to be extremely fashionable, stupid etc: *Flared trousers were considered to be the height of fashion in those days.*

height·en /ˈhaɪtn/ ●○○ *v* [I,T] if something heightens a feeling, effect etc, or if a feeling etc heightens, it becomes stronger or increases SYN **intensify** → **strengthen**: *There are fears that the march will heighten racial tension.* | *Increased levels of fat in the diet could heighten the risk of cancer.* | **heighten (sb's) awareness (of sth)** (=make people realize something more clearly) *The case has heightened public awareness of the problem of sexual harassment.*

hei·nous /ˈheɪnəs/ *adj formal* **1** very shocking and immoral: *a* **heinous crime** **2** *AmE spoken informal* extremely bad: *The food in the cafeteria is pretty heinous.* —**heinousness** *n* [U]

heir /eə $ er/ ●○○ *n* [C]

1 the person who has the legal right to receive the property or title of another person when they die: **[+to]** *John was the sole heir to a vast estate.* | **heir to the throne** (=the person who will become king or queen)

2 the person who will take over a position or job after you, or who does things or thinks in a similar way to you: *Jonson was his political heir as leader of the Nationalist Party.*

ˌheir apˈparent *n* (*plural* **heirs apparent**) [C] **1** an heir whose right to receive the family property, money, or title cannot be taken away **2** someone who seems very likely to take over a person's job, position etc when that person leaves

heir·ess /ˈeərəs, ˈeəres $ ˈer-/ *n* [C] a woman who will receive or has received a lot of money or property after the death of an older member of her family

heir·loom¹ /ˈeəluːm $ ˈer-/ *n* [C] a valuable object that has been owned by a family for many years and that is passed from the older members to the younger members: *a family heirloom*

heirloom² *adj* [only before noun] an heirloom vegetable

H

or plant is one of a kind that was first grown many years ago, and has now become rare or unusual SYN **heritage**: *They sell many kinds of heirloom seeds.*

Heis·man Tro·phy, the /ˈhaɪsmən ˌtrəʊfi/ (*also* **Heisman Memorial Trophy** *formal*) a prize given each year to the best college football player in the US

heist /haɪst/ *n* [C] *AmE informal* an act of stealing something very valuable from a shop, bank etc SYN **robbery**: *a jewelry heist* —**heist** *v* [T]

held /held/ the past tense and past participle of HOLD

hel·i·cop·ter /ˈheləkɒptə $ -kɑːptər/ ●●● S3 *n* [C] a type of aircraft with large metal blades on top which turn around very quickly to make it fly SYN **chopper**

ˈhelicopter ˌpad (*also* **hel·i·pad** /ˈhelipæd/) *n* [C] an area where helicopters can land

ˈhelicopter ˌparents *n* [plural] parents who try too hard to protect their children and organize their lives, even when their children have left school

he·li·o·trope /ˈhiːliətrəʊp, ˈhe- $ ˈhiːliətroʊp/ *n* [C] a garden plant with nice-smelling pale purple flowers

hel·i·port /ˈhelipɔːt $ -pɔːrt/ *n* [C] a small airport for HELICOPTERS

he·li-ski·ing /ˈheliˌskiːɪŋ/ *n* [U] the sport of flying a HELICOPTER to a place in the mountains where you can SKI on deep snow that no one else has skied on

he·li·um /ˈhiːliəm/ *n* [U] a gas that is lighter than air and is used to make BALLOONS float. It is a chemical ELEMENT: symbol He

he·lix /ˈhiːlɪks/ *n* (*plural* **helices** /-ləsiːz/) [C] *technical* a line that curves and rises around a central line SYN **spiral**
→ **DOUBLE HELIX**

hell¹ /hel/ ●●○ S3 *n*

1 WHEN YOU DIE [U] (*also* **Hell**) the place where the souls of bad people are believed to be punished after death, especially in the Christian and Muslim religions

2 SUFFERING [singular, U] a place or situation in which people suffer very much, either physically or emotionally: *War is hell.* | *My mother* **made** *my* **life hell**. | *These past few days have been a* **living hell**. | *She must have* **gone through hell** *every day, the way we teased her about her weight.* | **pure/absolute/sheer etc hell** *They described the war zone as sheer hell.* | *He says his time in jail was* **hell on earth**.

3 UNPLEASANT SITUATION [singular, U] *informal* a situation, experience, or place that is very unpleasant: *The traffic was hell this morning.* | **pure/absolute/sheer etc hell** *'How was your exam?' 'Sheer hell!'*

4 what/how/why/where etc the hell? *spoken not polite* used to show that you are very surprised or angry: *How the hell are we going to do that?*

5 a/one hell of a sth *spoken not polite* used to emphasize the idea that something is very big, very good, very bad etc: *I've come one hell of a long way to get here.* | *Envy like yours is a hell of a good motive for murder.*

6 go to hell! *spoken not polite* used when you are very angry with someone: *If John doesn't like it, he can go to hell!*

7 feel/look like hell *spoken not polite* to feel or look very ill or tired: *I've been feeling like hell all week.*

8 beat/surprise/scare the hell out of sb *informal not polite* to beat, surprise etc someone very much: *We have only one aim: to beat the hell out of the opposition.*

9 (just) for the hell of it *spoken not polite* for no serious reason, or only for fun: *They shot people just for the hell of it.*

10 what the hell! *spoken not polite* used to say that you will do something and not worry about any problems it causes: *Elaine poured herself a large glass of whisky – what the hell, it was Christmas.*

11 to hell with sb/sth *spoken not polite* used to say that you do not care about someone or something anymore: *I want to live for the present, and to hell with the consequences.*

12 run/hurt/fight etc like hell *informal not polite* to run, fight etc very quickly or very much: *My new shoes hurt like hell.*

13 like hell/the hell *spoken not polite* used to say that you do not agree with what someone has said: *'You keep out of this, Ma.' 'Like hell I will.'*

14 the sth/sb from hell *informal not polite* something or someone that is the worst you can imagine: *She was the flatmate from hell.* | *It was the holiday from hell.*

15 guilty/shy/mad/angry etc as hell *spoken not polite* very guilty, shy etc: *If I had your problems, I'd be mad as hell.*

16 sure as hell *spoken not polite* used to emphasize that something is true: *I don't scare easily, but I was sure as hell scared.*

17 give sb hell *informal not polite* to treat someone in an unpleasant or angry way: *She didn't like him, and gave him hell at the slightest opportunity.*

18 get the hell out (of somewhere) *informal not polite* to leave a place quickly and suddenly: *Let's get the hell out of here!*

19 there'll be hell to pay *spoken not polite* used to say that people will be very angry: *If they find us there'll be hell to pay.*

20 go to hell and back to go through a very difficult situation: *I'd go to hell and back for that boy.*

21 all hell broke loose *informal not polite* used to say that people suddenly become very noisy or angry: *Journalists woke him with the news and all hell broke loose.*

22 come hell or high water *informal not polite* in spite of any problems or difficulties: *I decided I would get the job done by Friday, come hell or high water.*

23 go to hell in a handbasket *AmE informal not polite* if a system or organization has gone to hell in a handbasket, it has stopped working well and is now working very badly: *The education system in this country has gone to hell in a handbasket.*

24 hell's bells (*also* **hell's teeth** *BrE*) *spoken old-fashioned* used to express great annoyance or surprise

25 play (merry) hell with sth *BrE informal* to make something stop working or happening as it should: *The cold weather played hell with the weekend sports schedule.*

26 raise hell *informal not polite* to protest strongly and angrily about a situation

27 run/go hell for leather *informal not polite* to run as fast as possible

28 hell on wheels *AmE informal not polite* someone who does exactly what they want and does not care what happens as a result.

29 when hell freezes over *informal not polite* used to say that something will never happen

30 catch hell *AmE spoken not polite* to be blamed or punished: *You'll catch hell when your Mom comes home!* → **not a hope in hell (of doing sth)** at HOPE²(3)

hell² *interjection not polite* **1** used to express anger or annoyance: *Oh hell! I've left my purse at home.* **2** used to emphasize a statement: *Well, hell, I don't know!*

he'll /il, hil; *strong* hiːl/ the short form of 'he will' or 'he shall': *Don't worry, he'll be there.*

ˌhell-ˈbent *adj* [not before noun] very determined to do something, especially something that other people do not approve of: **hell-bent on (doing) sth** *young people who are hell-bent on having a good time*

Hel·lene /ˈheliːn/ *n* [C] *formal* a Greek, especially an ancient Greek

Hel·len·ic /heˈlenɪk/ *adj* connected with the history, society, or art of the ancient Greeks

ˈhell-hole *n* [C] a very dirty, ugly, and unpleasant place: *The school was a hell-hole.*

hell·ish /ˈhelɪʃ/ *adj informal* extremely bad or difficult: *I've had a hellish day at work.* —**hellishly** *adv*: *a hellishly difficult exam*

hel·lo (*also* **hallo**, **hullo** *BrE*) /həˈləʊ, he- $ -ˈloʊ/ ●●● S1 *interjection, n* [C]

1 used as a greeting when you see or meet someone: *Hello, John! How are you?* | *Stanley, come and* **say hello** *to your nephew.* | *Well,* **hello there**! *I haven't seen you for ages.*

2 used when answering the telephone or starting a telephone conversation: *Hello – may I speak to Anne?*

3 used when calling to get someone's attention: *Hello! Is there anybody home?*

4 used when you think someone is not acting sensibly or

H

has said something stupid: *You didn't remember her birthday? Hello!*
5 *BrE* used to show that you are surprised or confused by something: *Hello! What's happened here?*
6 say hello to have a quick conversation with someone: *Promise you'll look in and say hello when you have time.*

hell·uv·a /ˈheləvə/ *adj, adv spoken* used to emphasize that someone or something is very good, bad, big etc: *He's got a helluva temper.* | *He's a helluva nice guy.*

helm /helm/ *n* **1** [C] the wheel or control which guides a ship or boat **2 at the helm a)** in charge of something: *We have a new prime minister at the helm.* **b)** guiding a ship or boat **3 take the helm a)** to start being in charge of something such as a business or organization: *Wright took the helm at the food retailer in December 2001.* **b)** to start guiding a ship or boat

hel·met /ˈhelmɪt/ ●●● W3 *n* [C] a strong hard hat that soldiers, MOTORCYCLE riders, the police etc wear to protect their heads → **CRASH HELMET**, **PITH HELMET** → see picture at **SPORT**[1]

hel·met·ed /ˈhelmɪtɪd/ *adj* wearing a helmet

helms·man /ˈhelmzmən/ *n* (*plural* **helmsmen** /-mən/) [C] someone who guides a ship or boat

help[1] /help/ ●●● S1 W1 *v*
1 [I,T] to make it possible or easier for someone to do something by doing part of their work or by giving them something they need: *If there's anything I can do to help, just give me a call.* | **help sb (to) do sth** *I helped her to carry her cases up the stairs.* | *She helped him choose some new clothes.* | *herbal products that help you to relax and sleep* | **help (to) do sth** *She was coming to help clean the machines.* | **help sb with sth** *Can I help you with the washing up?* | *My father said he's going to help me with the fees.* | **help sb on/off with sth** (=help someone put on or take off a piece of clothing) *Here, let me help you on with your coat.* | **help sb somewhere** (=help someone get to a particular place, especially because they are old, ill, or hurt) *She helped the old man across the road.*
2 [I,T] to make a situation better, easier, or less painful: *Crying won't help.* | *If you get rid of your car you could be helping the environment.* | ***It helps*** *my concentration* ***if*** *I listen to music while I'm working.* | ***It helped*** *a lot to know that someone understood how I felt.* | *Eight hours of deep sleep* ***helped enormously****.*
3 help yourself (to sth) a) to take some of what you want, without asking permission – used especially when offering food to someone: *Please help yourself to some cake.* **b)** *informal* to steal something: *Obviously he had been helping himself to the money.*
4 help! *spoken* used to call people and ask them to help you when you are in danger
5 sb can't help (doing) sth (*also* **sb can't help but do sth**) used to say that someone is unable to change their behaviour or feelings, or to prevent themselves from doing something: *She* ***couldn't help it if*** *she was being irrational.* | *'Stop biting your nails.' 'I* ***can't help it****.'* | *I can't help the way I feel about you.* | *Lee could not help but agree with her.* | **sb can't help feeling/thinking/wondering etc sth** *I can't help feeling that there has been a mistake.* | *I couldn't help thinking about the past.*
6 I couldn't help myself/she couldn't help herself etc to be unable to stop yourself from doing something you should not do: *She knew she sounded just like her mother but she couldn't help herself.*
7 it can't be helped *spoken* used to say that there is nothing you can do to change a bad situation: *She said she had to leave him for a while; it couldn't be helped.*
8 sb is helping the police with their enquiries *BrE* the police are interviewing someone about a crime, especially because they believe that this person may have committed the crime
9 a helping hand help and support: **give/lend/offer etc sb a helping hand** *She's been giving me a helping hand with the children.*
10 not if I can help it *spoken* used to say that you are not going to do something: *'Are you going to watch the school play?' 'Not if I can help it.'*
11 God help him/them etc *spoken* used to say that something bad may happen to someone: *'Good luck.' 'God help me. I think I'm going to need it.'*
12 so help me (God) used when making a serious promise, especially in a court of law

THESAURUS

help to make it easier for someone to do something, by doing something for them or giving them something they need: *Is there anything I can do to help?* | *Dad, I can't do my homework. Will you help me?*
assist *formal* to help someone: *He was employed to assist the manager in his duties.* | *Some of the guests assisted with the preparation of the food.*
aid *formal* to help someone to do something – used especially when saying that something helps your body to do something: *Coffee can aid concentration.* | *Fennel aids the digestion.* | *There are plenty of materials to aid the teacher.*
help out to help someone, especially because there are not enough people to do all the work, or they need someone to give them something: *Organizing the school trip will be a lot of work, so I need some volunteers to help out.* | *My parents have helped us out on several occasions by sending us money.*
give sb a hand *informal* to help someone to do something, especially by carrying or lifting things: *Can you give me a hand moving these boxes?*
lend a hand *informal* to help someone, especially when there are not enough people to do something: *Scott is moving on Saturday and we promised to lend a hand.*

help sth ↔ **along** *phr v* to make a process or activity happen more quickly or easily: *She asked a few questions to help the conversation along.*
help out *phr v* to help someone because they are busy or have problems: *Do you need anyone to help out in the shop?* | **help sb ↔ out (with sth)** *I helped her out when Stella became ill.* | *She was helping him out with his mortgage repayments.*

help[2] ●●● S1 W1 *n*
1 [U] things you do to make it easier or possible for someone to do something: *Thank you for all your help.* | **help with sth/with doing sth** *Do you want any help with the washing up?* | **help to do sth** *I could do with some help to bring the bags in from the car.* | **help (in) doing sth** *He asked for my help in getting an interview with her.* | **with the help of sb/with sb's help** *We manage, with the help of a nurse who comes daily.*
2 [singular, U] if someone or something is a help to you, they are useful and make it easier for you to do something: *That map isn't much help.* | **with the help of sth** *I managed to make myself understood with the help of a phrase book.* | **be of great/little/no/some etc help (to sb)** *Let me know if I can be of any help to you.* | **be a (great/big/tremendous/real etc) help (to sb)** *Any information would be a great help.* | *You've been a real help to me, Carrie.*
3 [U] advice, treatment, information, or money which is given to people who need it: *A lot of these children need professional help.* | **[+with]** *You may be able to ask for help with the rent.* | *We received no help from the police.*
4 [U] a part of a computer program that helps someone using it by giving additional information
5 the help *AmE* someone's servant or servants

COLLOCATIONS

VERBS

give sb help *Do you want me to give you some help?*
ask (sb) for help *He asked for help with the cleaning.*
need help *Some of the older patients need help with walking.*
get/receive help *She gets no help from her husband.*
offer (your) help *The taxi driver offered his help and we accepted.*

H

provide help *The government should do more to provide help for people who are looking for work.*
appeal for help (=publicly ask for help) *The police are appealing for help to track down the killer.*
enlist sb's help (=persuade someone to help you) *She enlisted the help of a private investigator to find her missing son.*

'help desk *n* [C] a department of a company that people call for help, especially with computer problems

help·er /ˈhelpə $ -ər/ ●○○ *n* [C]
1 someone who helps another person SYN **assistant**: *I was a classroom helper at the local primary school.*
2 *AmE* someone who is employed to do some of the work in someone else's home

help·ful /ˈhelpfəl/ ●●● S2 W3 *adj*
1 providing useful help in making a situation better or easier: *Thank you for your advice; it's been very helpful.* | **it is helpful (for sb) to do sth** *It is helpful to discuss your problems with your friends.* | *It is helpful for family members to gain a basic understanding of the illness.* | ***It is helpful if*** *we address a few key questions here.* | **helpful in doing sth** *We hope this leaflet has been helpful in answering your questions.* | **helpful advice/hints/suggestions etc** *Our sales staff are there to give you helpful advice.* THESAURUS ▸ USEFUL
2 always willing to help people: *She's a helpful child.* | *I'm only trying to be helpful.* —**helpfully** *adv* —**helpfulness** *n* [U]

help·ing /ˈhelpɪŋ/ ●○○ *n* [C] the amount of food that someone gives you or that you take SYN **serving**: *a double helping of pie*

help·less /ˈhelpləs/ ●○○ *adj*
1 unable to look after yourself or to do anything to help yourself: *He began to feel depressed and helpless.* | *a vicious attack on a helpless victim* | *Newman threw out a hand in a helpless gesture.*
2 unable to control a strong feeling that you have: **[+with]** *He was near to death, and I was helpless with fear.* | **helpless laughter/rage/tears etc** *We both collapsed into helpless giggles.* —**helplessly** *adv* —**helplessness** *n* [U]

help·line /ˈhelplaɪn/ *n* [C] a telephone number that you can ring if you need advice or information

help·mate /ˈhelpmeɪt/ (*also* **help·meet** /-miːt/) *n* [C] *literary* a helpful partner, usually a wife

'help screen *n* [C] a screen that appears when you ask for help in using a computer program, showing extra information or advice

hel·ter-skel·ter[1] /ˌheltə ˈskeltə $ ˌheltər ˈskeltər/ *adv* done quickly, in a disorganized way: *He ran helter-skelter down the slope.*

helter-skelter[2] *n* [C] *BrE* a tall structure in a FAIRGROUND which you sit on at the top and slide round and round to the bottom

hem[1] /hem/ *n* [C] the edge of a piece of cloth that is turned under and stitched down, especially the lower edge of a skirt, trousers etc THESAURUS ▸ EDGE

hem[2] *v* (**hemmed**, **hemming**) **1** [T] to turn under the edge of a piece of material or clothing and stitch it in place **2 hem and haw** *AmE* to keep pausing before saying something, and avoid saying it directly SYN **hum and haw** *BrE*
hem *sb/sth* ↔ **in** *phr v* **1** to surround someone or something closely: *They were hemmed in on all sides by the soldiers and the dogs.* | *The market place is hemmed in by shops and banks.* **2** to make someone feel that they are not free to do what they want to do: *They hem in the child with endless rules and restrictions.*

'he-man *n* (*plural* **he-men**) [C] *humorous* a strong man with powerful muscles

hematology /ˌhiːməˈtɒːlədʒi/ *n* [U] the American spelling of HAEMATOLOGY

hem·i·sphere /ˈheməsfɪə $ -fɪr/ ●○○ *n* [C]
1 a half of the Earth, especially one of the halves above and below the EQUATOR: *the Northern hemisphere* → see picture at **EARTH**[1]
2 one of the two halves of your brain
3 half of a SPHERE (=an object which is round like a ball) —**hemispherical** /ˌhemɪˈsferɪkəl/ *adj*

hem·line /ˈhemlaɪn/ *n* [C] the length of a dress, skirt etc: *Short hemlines are in this spring.*

hem·lock /ˈhemlɒk $ -lɑːk/ *n* [C,U] a very poisonous plant, or the poison that is made from it

he·mo·glo·bin /ˌhiːməˈgləʊbɪn $ ˈhiːməˌgloʊbɪn/ *n* [U] the American spelling of HAEMOGLOBIN

he·mo·phil·i·a /ˌhiːməˈfɪliə/ *n* [U] the American spelling of HAEMOPHILIA

he·mo·phil·i·ac /ˌhiːməˈfɪliæk/ *n* [C] the American spelling of HAEMOPHILIAC

hem·or·rhage /ˈhemərɪdʒ/ *n* [C,U] the American spelling of HAEMORRHAGE

hem·or·rhoids /ˈhemərɔɪdz/ *n* [plural] the American spelling of HAEMORRHOIDS

hemp /hemp/ *n* [U] a type of plant that is used to make rope and sometimes to produce the drug CANNABIS

hen /hen/ ●○○ *n* [C]
1 an adult female chicken
2 a fully grown female bird

hence /hens/ ●○○ AWL *adv formal*
1 [sentence adverb] for this reason: *The area was full of black smoke from factories, hence the name "the Black Country."* | *The cost of transport is a major expense for an industry. Hence factory location is an important consideration.* THESAURUS ▸ THEREFORE
2 ten days hence/five months hence etc ten days from now, five months from now etc

hence·forth /ˌhensˈfɔːθ, ˈhensfɔːθ $ -ɔːrθ/ (*also* **hence·for·ward** /ˌhensˈfɔːwəd $ -ˈfɔːrwərd/) *adv formal* from this time on: *multiple sclerosis (henceforth referred to as MS)*

hench·man /ˈhentʃmən/ *n* (*plural* **henchmen** /-mən/) [C] a faithful supporter of a political leader or a criminal, who is willing to do illegal things or use violence

'hen house *n* [C] a small building where chickens are kept

Hen·ley Re·gat·ta /ˌhenli rɪˈgætə/ (*also* **Henley**) a series of boat races for ROWING BOATS, held every year on the River Thames near the town of Henley in the south of England. Henley is also a fashionable social event, especially for rich and UPPER-CLASS people.

hen·na /ˈhenə/ *n* [U] a reddish-brown substance used to change the colour of hair or skin —**henna** *v* [T]

'hen ˌparty *n* [C] *BrE informal* a party for women only, that happens just before one of them gets married → **STAG PARTY**

hen·pecked /ˈhenpekt/ *adj* a man who is henpecked is always being told what to do by his wife, and is afraid to disagree with her: *a henpecked husband*

he·pat·ic /hɪˈpætɪk/ *adj* [only before noun] *medical* relating to your LIVER

hep·a·ti·tis /ˌhepəˈtaɪtɪs◂/ *n* [U] a disease of the LIVER that causes fever and makes your skin yellow. There are several types of hepatitis: hepatitis A, which is less severe, and hepatitis B and C, which are much more serious.

hep·ta·gon /ˈheptəgən $ -gɑːn/ *n* [C] a shape with seven straight sides → **polygon** —**heptagonal** /hepˈtægənəl/ *adj*

hep·tath·lon /hepˈtæθlən/ *n* [singular] a women's sports competition involving seven running, jumping, and throwing events

her[1] /ə, hə; *strong* hɜː $ ər, hər *strong* hɜːr/ ●●● S1 W1 *determiner* [possessive form of 'she']
1 belonging to or connected with a woman, girl, or female animal that has already been mentioned: *She looked at her watch.* | *Her room was pleasant and airy.* | *She makes* ***her own*** *clothes.*
2 *old-fashioned* connected with a country, ship, car etc that has already been mentioned: *Her top speed is about 110 miles an hour.*

H

her² ●●● S1 W1 *pron* [object form of 'she']
1 used to refer to a woman, girl, or female animal that has already been mentioned or is already known about: *Jane? I don't really know her.* | *Margaret wants me to go with her.* | *Give her the keys.* | *I think it was her, but I'm not sure.*
2 *old-fashioned* used to refer to a country, ship, car etc that has already been mentioned: *God bless this ship and all who sail in her.*

her·ald¹ /ˈherəld/ ●○○ *v* [T]
1 to be a sign of something that is going to come or happen soon: *A flash of lightning heralded torrential rain.* | *Flashing blue lights heralded the arrival of the police.*
2 to say publicly that someone or something will be good or important: **be heralded as sth** *When it opened, the hospital was heralded as a new way forward in nursing care.*

herald² *n* **1** [C] someone who carried messages from a ruler in the past **2 herald of sth** a sign that something is soon going to happen: *a bowl of daffodils, the first bright heralds of spring*

her·ald·ry /ˈherəldri/ *n* [U] the study of COATS OF ARMS —**heraldic** /heˈrældɪk/ *adj*

herb /hɜːb $ ɜːrb, hɜːrb/ ●●○ *n* [C] a small plant that is used to improve the taste of food, or to make medicine → **spice**: *Sprinkle the dish with chopped fresh herbs.*

her·ba·ceous /həˈbeɪʃəs $ hɜːrˈbeɪ-, ɜːr-/ *adj technical* plants that are herbaceous have soft stems rather than hard stems made of wood

herˌbaceous ˈborder *n* [C] part of a garden where people grow plants that live for many years and do not need to be replaced

herb·al /ˈhɜːbəl $ ˈɜːr-, ˈhɜːr-/ *adj* [only before noun] made of herbs: *herbal remedies* | *herbal tea*

herb·al·ist /ˈhɜːbəlɪst $ ˈɜːr-, ˈhɜːr-/ *n* [C] someone who grows, sells, or uses HERBS, especially to treat illness

ˌherbal ˈmedicine *n* **1** [U] the practice of treating illness using plants **2** [C,U] medicine made from plants

herb·i·cide /ˈhɜːbɪsaɪd $ ˈhɜːr-,ˈɜːr-/ *n* [C,U] *technical* a substance used to kill unwanted plants

her·bi·vore /ˈhɜːbəvɔː $ ˈhɜːrbəvɔːr, ˈɜːr-/ *n* [C] an animal that only eats plants → **carnivore**, **omnivore** —**herbivorous** /hɜːˈbɪvərəs $ hɜːr-, ɜːr-/ *adj*

her·cu·le·an /ˌhɜːkjʊˈliːən◂, hɜːˈkjuːliən $ -ɜːr-/ *adj* needing great strength or determination: *a herculean task*

herd¹ /hɜːd $ hɜːrd/ ●●○ *n*
1 [C] a group of animals of one kind that live and feed together → **flock**: **[+of]** *a herd of cattle* | *herds of elephants*
THESAURUS ▸ GROUP
2 the herd people generally, especially when thought of as being easily influenced by others: *You have to be an individual; it's no use running with the herd.* | *the* ***herd instinct*** (=the need to behave in the same way as everyone else does)

herd² *v* **1** [T always + adv/prep] to bring people together in a large group, especially roughly: *The prisoners were* ***herded together****.* | *I don't want to be herded around with a lot of tourists.* | **herd sb into sth** *The visitors were herded into two large halls.* **2** [T] to make animals move together in a group: *It was Tom's duty to herd the cows.* **3 sth is like herding cats** used to say that trying to control or organize a group of people is very difficult

herds·man /ˈhɜːdzmən/ *n* (*plural* **herdsmen** /-mən/) [C] a man who looks after a herd of animals

here /hɪə $ hɪr/ ●●● S1 W1 *adv*
1 in this place: *What are you doing here?* | *Shall we eat here?* | *Come here for a minute.* | *This switch here controls the lights.* | *My friend here will show you the way.* | **up/down/in/out here** *What was she doing up here in the woods?* | *Would you close the window? It's cold in here.* | *Come on. I'm* ***over here****.* | *Will you be* ***back here*** *tonight?* | *There are no good pubs* ***round here****.* | *Let's settle the matter* ***here and now****.*
2 at this point in time: *Spring is here at last.* | *Here is your chance to change your life.* | *Here is where the trouble starts.*
3 here and there scattered around or happening in several different places: *The house just needs a bit of paint here and there.*

SPOKEN PHRASES

4 here is/are sth (*also* **here it is/here they are**) **a)** used when you are giving something to someone, or showing something to them: *Here's the money you lent me.* | *Here are some pictures of John when he was little.* **b)** used when you have found something you were looking for: *Have you seen my pen? Oh, here it is.*
5 used when you are giving or offering something to someone: *Here, have my chair. I don't mind standing.*
6 here you are/here you go used when you are giving something to someone: *Here you are, a boxful of tools.* | *'Here you go.' Callum handed her a glass of orange juice.*
7 at this point in a discussion: *Here I'd like to add a note of caution.* | *There is no space to discuss this issue here.* | *I'm not sure what you mean here.*
8 here goes! (*also* **here we go**) used when you are going to try to do something difficult or dangerous, and you do not know what will happen: *I've never ridden a motorbike before, so here goes!*
9 here we go used when you are starting to do something or when something is starting to happen: *Right, here we go, the game's starting.*
10 here's to sb/sth used when you are going to drink something to wish someone good luck, show your respect for them etc: *Here's to the happy couple.* | *Here's to your new job.*
11 here he/she etc is (*also* **sb/sth is here**) used to say that someone or something has arrived: *Here they are, late as usual.* | *Ah, look – here's the postman.* | *Tony's here for his messages.*
12 here we are used when you have finally arrived somewhere you were travelling to: *Here we are – home at last.*
13 here comes sb/sth used when you can see something or someone arriving: *Here comes lunch.*
14 *BrE* used to get someone's attention or to show that you are annoyed: *Here! Just what do you think you're doing?*
15 here we go again *informal* used when something unpleasant is beginning to happen again: *Most of us are peaceful and decent, but here we go again, in our fifth war of this century.*

16 here to stay if something is here to stay, it has become a part of life and will continue to be so: *Mobile phones are definitely here to stay.*
17 here, there, and everywhere *informal* in many different places: *I spent the weekend driving the kids here, there, and everywhere.*
18 neither here nor there not important: *'You never liked him much, did you?' 'What I think about him is neither here nor there. He's your friend.'*
19 the here and now the present time: **in the here and now** *To be able to live fully in the here and now, one must first learn how to honour the past.*
20 sb/sth is here to do sth used to say what someone or something's duty or purpose is: *We're here to serve you.*
21 here he/she etc is (doing sth) used to describe the present situation, especially one you did not expect to happen: *Here I am in Fiji!*

GRAMMAR: Patterns with here

- You use **here** on its own, when you are talking about a place or organization: *The people here are poor.* | *Do you work here?* ✗ Don't say: *The people in here are poor.* | *Do you work in here?*
- You use **in here** when talking about the inside of a building, room, cupboard etc: *It's crowded in here.* | *There aren't enough chairs in here.*
- You say **come here**: *Before I came here, I didn't speak any English.* ✗ Don't say: *come to here*

USAGE: Here is, there is

- Use **here is** when giving or showing something to someone: *Here is the book you wanted.*

H

• Use **there is** or **there are** to say what is in a place: *There are many species of birds here.* ✗ Don't say: *Here are many species of birds.*

here·a·bouts /ˌhɪərəˈbaʊts, ˈhɪərəbaʊts $ ˌhɪr-,ˈhɪr-/ *adv* somewhere near the place where you are: *There must be a pub hereabouts.*

here·af·ter¹ /ˌhɪərˈɑːftə $ ˌhɪrˈæftər/ *adv* **1** [sentence adverb] *formal* from this time **2** *formal* after death: *his belief in God and a life hereafter* **3** *law* in a later part of an official or legal document: *the Ulster Democratic Unionist Party (hereafter UDUP)*

hereafter² *n* **the hereafter** a life after death: *Do you believe in the hereafter?*

here·by /ˌhɪəˈbaɪ, ˈhɪəbaɪ $ ˌhɪr-,ˈhɪr-/ *adv law* as a result of this statement - used in official situations: *I hereby agree to the conditions of this contract.*

he·red·i·ta·ry /həˈredətəri $ -teri/ ●○○ *adj*
1 a quality or illness that is hereditary is passed from a parent to a child before the child is born → **genetic**
2 *BrE* a hereditary position, rank, or title can be passed from an older to a younger person in the same family, usually when the older one dies → **inherit**: *a hereditary peer*

he·red·i·ty /həˈredəti/ *n* [U] the process by which mental and physical qualities are passed from a parent to a child before the child is born → **genetics**

here·in /ˌhɪərˈɪn $ ˌhɪr-/ *adv formal* in this place, situation, document etc: *the conditions stated herein* | *Herein lies a problem.* → THEREIN

here·in·af·ter /ˌhɪərɪnˈɑːftə $ ˌhɪrɪnˈæftər/ *adv law* later in this official statement, document etc: *the Council of the Law Society (hereinafter called the Council)*

here·of /ˌhɪərˈɒv $ hɪrˈʌv, -ˈɑːv/ *adv formal or law* relating to or belonging to this document: *This Agreement commences on the date of signature hereof.* → THEREOF

her·e·sy /ˈherəsi/ *n* (*plural* **heresies**) [C,U] **1** a belief that disagrees with the official principles of a particular religion: *He was executed for heresy.* **2** a belief, statement etc that disagrees with what a group of people believe to be right: *To come to work without a shirt and tie was considered heresy.*

her·e·tic /ˈherətɪk/ *n* [C] someone who is guilty of heresy: *Cranmer was put to death as a heretic.* —**heretical** /həˈretɪkəl/ *adj*

here·to /ˌhɪəˈtuː $ ˌhɪrˈtuː/ *adv formal* to this: *A copy of the document is hereto appended.*

here·to·fore /ˌhɪətʊˈfɔː $ ˈhɪrtʊfɔːr/ *adv formal* before this time: *In recent years, we have seen greater emphasis than heretofore on the voice of the consumer.*

here·up·on /ˌhɪərəˈpɒn $ ˌhɪrəˈpɑːn/ *adv formal* at or after this moment

here·with /ˌhɪəˈwɪð, -ˈwɪθ $ ˌhɪr-/ *adv formal* with this letter or document: *I enclose a copy of this report herewith for your information.*

her·i·ta·ble /ˈherətəbəl/ *adj law* property that is heritable can be passed from the older members of a family to the younger ones

her·i·tage¹ /ˈherətɪdʒ/ ●○○ *n* [singular, U]
1 the traditional beliefs, values, customs etc of a family, country, or society → **inheritance**: *the importance of preserving the national heritage* | *beautiful old buildings which are part of our heritage* | **cultural/architectural/literary etc heritage** *the cultural heritage of Italy*
2 (of) mixed/multiple heritage *formal* having parents of different races: *There are identity issues for mixed heritage children.*

heritage² *adj BrE* [only before noun] a heritage vegetable or plant is one of a kind that was first grown many years ago, and has now become rare or unusual SYN **heirloom**: *We grow heritage varieties of vegetables.*

her·maph·ro·dite /hɜːˈmæfrədaɪt $ hɜːr-/ *n* [C] a living thing that has both male and female sexual organs —**hermaphrodite** *adj*

her·met·ic·ally /həˈmetɪkli $ hər-/ *adv technical* **hermetically sealed** very tightly closed so that air cannot get in or out SYN **airtight** —**hermetic** *adj*

her·mit /ˈhɜːmɪt $ ˈhɜːr-/ *n* [C] someone who lives alone and has a simple way of life, usually for religious reasons → RECLUSE

her·mit·age /ˈhɜːmətɪdʒ $ ˈhɜːr-/ *n* [C] a place where a hermit lives or has lived in the past

ˈhermit ˌcrab *n* [C] a kind of CRAB that lives in the empty shells of other sea creatures

her·ni·a /ˈhɜːniə $ ˈhɜːr-/ *n* [C,U] a medical condition in which an organ pushes through the muscles that are supposed to contain it SYN **rupture**

he·ro /ˈhɪərəʊ $ ˈhɪroʊ/ ●●● W3 *n* (*plural* **heroes**) [C]
1 a man who is admired for doing something extremely brave → **heroine**: *He had dared to speak out against injustice, and overnight he became a* ***national hero***. | *His father was a* ***war hero***, *a former fighter pilot.* | *the* ***unsung heroes*** *who drove convoys of aid to Bosnia* | **[+of]** *a hero of the Great War* | *A man* ***hailed as a hero*** *for 50 years has been unmasked as a traitor.*
2 the man or boy who is the main character in a book, film, play etc → **heroine**: **[+of]** *Phileas Fogg, hero of Jules Verne's 'Around the World in Eighty Days'*
3 a man who is admired very much for a particular skill or quality → **heroine**: **sb's hero** *When I was small, Uncle Fred was my hero.* | **[+of]** *Einstein is the hero of those who explore science at its deepest level.*
4 *AmE* a long thin SANDWICH filled with meat, cheese etc
5 from hero to zero *informal* used to say that someone goes from being very successful or admired to being very unsuccessful or unpopular

he·ro·ic /hɪˈrəʊɪk $ -ˈroʊ-/ ●○○ *adj*
1 extremely brave or determined, and admired by many people SYN **courageous**: *her* ***heroic efforts*** *to save her family* | *Lawrence's* ***heroic struggle*** *against his destiny* | *She portrayed him as a* ***heroic figure***. THESAURUS ▶ BRAVE
2 a heroic story, poem etc has a hero in it, usually from ancient LEGENDS
3 on a heroic scale/of heroic proportions very large or great: *a battle on a heroic scale* —**heroically** /-kli/ *adv*

heˌroic ˈcouplet *n* [C] a pair of lines in poetry which end with the same sound and have five beats in each line

he·ro·ics /hɪˈrəʊɪks $ -ˈroʊ-/ *n* [plural] brave actions or words, often ones that are meant to seem impressive to other people: *America's present need is not heroics, but calm diplomacy.*

her·o·in /ˈherəʊɪn $ -roʊ-/ *n* [U] a powerful and illegal drug made from MORPHINE: **be on/use/take heroin** | *a* **heroin addict**

her·o·ine /ˈherəʊɪn $ -roʊ-/ ●○○ *n* [C]
1 a woman who is admired for doing something extremely brave → **hero**: **[+of]** *a heroine of the French Resistance*
2 the woman or girl who is the main character in a book, film, play etc → **hero**: **[+of]** *Mira, the fictional heroine of 'The Women's Room'*
3 a woman who is admired very much for a particular skill or quality → **hero, idol**: **sb's heroine** *Oprah is my heroine.*

her·o·is·m /ˈherəʊɪzəm $ -roʊ-/ *n* [U] very great courage OPP **cowardice**: *stories of heroism and self-sacrifice*

her·on /ˈherən/ *n* [C] a large bird with very long legs and a long beak, that lives near water

HERON

ˈhero ˌworship *n* [U] great admiration for someone who is thought to be very brave, good, skilful etc - often used to show disapproval → **idolatry** —**hero-worship** *v* [T]

her·pes /ˈhɜːpiːz $ ˈhɜːr-/ *n* [U] a very infectious disease that causes spots on the skin, for example on the sexual organs or face

H

her·ring /ˈherɪŋ/ *n* (*plural* **herrings** *or* **herring**) [C] a long thin silver sea fish that can be eaten → RED HERRING

her·ring·bone /ˈherɪŋbəʊn $ -boʊn/ *n* [U] a pattern consisting of a continuous line of V shapes, used in cloth etc

hers /hɜːz $ hɜːrz/ ●●● S3 W3 *pron* [possessive form of 'she'] used to refer to something that belongs to or is connected with a woman, girl, or female animal that has already been mentioned: *He bent and touched his mouth to hers.* | *These are my gloves. Hers are in the drawer.* | *The idea was hers.* | **of hers** *Paul's a* **friend of hers**.

her·self /əˈself, hə-; *strong* hɜː- $ ər-, hər- *strong* hɜːr-/ ●●● S2 W1 *pron* [reflexive form of 'she']
1 used to show that the woman or girl who does something is affected by her own action: *She cut herself on some broken glass.* | *She made herself a cup of coffee.*
2 a) used to emphasize that you are talking about one particular woman or girl: *It must be true that she's leaving because she told me so herself.* | *The ornate Town Hall was opened by Queen Victoria herself.* **b)** used after 'like', 'as', or 'except' instead of 'her': *She met other mothers in the same situation as herself.*
3 (all) by herself a) alone: *Miss Bennet lives by herself.* **b)** without help from anyone else: *The little girl wrote the letter all by herself.*
4 not be/feel/seem herself *informal* if a woman or girl is not herself, she does not feel or behave as she usually does, for example because she is upset or ill: *You must forgive her – she's not herself at present.*
5 have sth (all) to herself if a woman or girl has something to herself, she does not have to share it with anyone else: *Alice had the house to herself while her parents were away.*

hertz /hɜːts $ hɜːrts/ *n* (*plural* **hertz**) [C] (*written abbreviation* **Hz**) a unit for measuring the FREQUENCY of SOUND WAVES

he's /iz, hiz; *strong* hiːz/ **1** the short form of 'he is': *He's a writer.* | *He's reading.* **2** the short form of 'he has': *He's bought a new car.*

hes·i·tan·cy /ˈhezətənsi/ (*also* **hes·i·tance** /-təns/) *n* [U] when someone is uncertain or slow in doing or saying something

hes·i·tant /ˈhezɪtənt/ *adj* uncertain about what to do or say because you are nervous or unwilling: *Gail gave me a hesitant little smile.* | **hesitant about (doing) sth** *They seemed hesitant about coming in.* | **hesitant to do sth** *She is hesitant to draw conclusions until the study is over.* —**hesitantly** *adv*

H

hes·i·tate /ˈhezɪteɪt/ ●●○ W3 *v*
1 [I] to pause before saying or doing something because you are nervous or not sure: *Kay hesitated for a moment and then said 'yes'.* | **[+about/over]** *He was still hesitating over whether to leave or not.*
2 don't hesitate to do sth used to tell someone that it is correct or right for them to do something and they do not have to worry about offending anyone: *Don't hesitate to contact me if you need any more information.* —**hesitatingly** *adv*

hes·i·ta·tion /ˌhezɪˈteɪʃən/ ●○○ *n* [C,U] when someone hesitates: *After some hesitation one of them began to speak.* | **without hesitation** *He agreed without hesitation.* | **have no hesitation in doing sth** *I would have no hesitation in recommending Philip for the position.* | **a slight/brief/momentary etc hesitation** *There was a slight hesitation in Jamie's voice.*

hes·si·an /ˈhesiən $ ˈheʃən/ *n* [U] *BrE* thick rough cloth sometimes used for making SACKS SYN **burlap** *AmE*

hetero- /hetərəʊ, -rə $ -roʊ, -rə/ *prefix* other, opposite, different: **heterosexual** (=attracted to the opposite sex)

het·e·ro·dox /ˈhetərədɒks $ -dɑːks/ *adj formal* heterodox beliefs, practices etc are not approved of by a particular group, especially a religious one

het·e·ro·ge·ne·ous /ˌhetərəʊˈdʒiːniəs $ -roʊ-/ (*also* **het·e·rog·e·nous** /ˌhetəˈrɒdʒənəs◂ $ -ˈrɑː-/) *adj formal* consisting of parts or members that are very different from each other OPP **homogeneous**: *a heterogeneous collection of buildings* —**heterogeneously** *adv* —**heterogeneity** /ˌhetərəʊdʒəˈniːəti $ -roʊ-/ *n* [U]

het·e·ro·sex·u·al /ˌhetərəˈsekʃuəl◂/ ●○○ *adj* sexually attracted to people of the opposite sex SYN **straight** → **bisexual**, **homosexual**

het up /ˌhet ˈʌp/ *adj* [not before noun] *BrE informal* anxious, upset, or slightly angry: **[+about/over]** *Mike tends to* ***get het up*** *about silly things.*

heu·ris·tic /hjʊˈrɪstɪk/ *adj formal* **1** heuristic education is based on discovering and experiencing things for yourself **2** helping you in the process of learning or discovery —**heuristically** /-kli/ *adv*

heu·ris·tics /hjʊˈrɪstɪks/ *n* [U] *formal* the study of how people use their experience to find answers to questions or to improve performance

hew /hjuː/ *v* (*past tense* **hewed**, *past participle* **hewed** *or* **hewn** /hjuːn/ *literary*) [I,T] to cut something with a cutting tool: *hewn stone* → ROUGH-HEWN

hex /heks/ *n* [C] *AmE* an evil CURSE that brings trouble: *I think he's trying to* ***put a hex on*** *me.* —**hex** *v* [T]

hex·a·dec·i·mal /ˌheksəˈdesəməl◂/ (*also* **hex**) *adj technical* hexadecimal numbers are based on the number 16 and are mainly used on computers

hex·a·gon /ˈheksəgən $ -gɑːn/ *n* [C] a shape with six sides → **polygon** → see picture at SHAPE[1] —**hexagonal** /hekˈsægənəl/ *adj*

hex·am·e·ter /hekˈsæmɪtə $ -ər/ *n* [C] *technical* a line of poetry with six main beats

ˈhex key (*also* **ˈhex wrench**) *n* [C] (***hexagon key***) an ALLEN KEY

hey /heɪ/ ●●○ *interjection*
1 a shout used to get someone's attention or to show surprise, interest, or annoyance: *Hey, wait a minute!*
2 *informal* hello: *Hey, what's up?*
3 but hey *informal* said when you do not think something is important: *I would have liked to go, but hey, it's no big deal.*

hey·day /ˈheɪdeɪ/ *n* [C usually singular] the time when someone or something was most popular, successful, or powerful: **in sb's heyday** *Greta Garbo in her heyday*

hey pres·to /ˌheɪ ˈprestəʊ $ -toʊ/ *interjection BrE* used to say that something happens so easily that it seems to be magic SYN **presto** *AmE*

H5N1 /ˌeɪtʃ faɪv en ˈwʌn/ *n* [U] a type of BIRD FLU that can kill people

HGV /ˌeɪtʃ dʒiː ˈviː/ *n* [C] *BrE* (***heavy goods vehicle***) a large road vehicle used for moving goods SYN **truck**

hi /haɪ/ ●●● S1 *interjection informal* hello: *Hi! How are you?* | ***Hi there!*** *I haven't seen you for ages.*

hi·a·tus /haɪˈeɪtəs/ *n* [C usually singular] **1** *formal* a break in an activity, or a time during which something does not happen or exist: *Talks between the two countries have resumed after a six-year hiatus.* | **[+in]** *a hiatus in research* | **a brief/short/long hiatus** *There was a brief hiatus in the war.* **2** *technical* a space where something is missing, especially in a piece of writing

hi·ber·nate /ˈhaɪbəneɪt $ -ər-/ *v* [I] if an animal hibernates, it sleeps for the whole winter —**hibernation** /ˌhaɪbəˈneɪʃən $ -bər-/ *n* [U]

hi·bis·cus /haɪˈbɪskəs/ *n* [C,U] a tropical plant with large brightly coloured flowers

hic·cup[1], **hiccough** /ˈhɪkʌp, -kəp/ *n* [C] **1** [usually plural] a sudden repeated stopping of the breath, usually caused by eating or drinking too fast: **get/have hiccups** *BrE*, **get/have the hiccups** *AmE*: *Don't drink so fast – you'll get hiccups.* **2** a small problem or delay: **[+in]** *a hiccup in the negotiations*

hiccup[2] *v* (**hiccupped**, **hiccupping**) [I] to have hiccups

hick /hɪk/ *n* [C] *AmE informal* someone who lives in the countryside, and is thought to be uneducated or stupid —**hick** *adj*: *hick towns*

hick·ey /ˈhɪki/ *n* [C] *AmE* a red mark on someone's skin caused by someone else sucking it as a sexual act SYN **love bite** *BrE*

hick·o·ry /ˈhɪkəri/ *n* (*plural* **hickories**) [C,U] a North American tree that produces nuts, or the wood that comes from this tree

hid /hɪd/ *v* the past tense of HIDE

hid·den¹ /ˈhɪdn/ *v* the past participle of HIDE

hidden² ●●○ *adj*
1 difficult to see or find: *the use of hidden cameras | Some areas can hold hidden dangers for dogs. | the hidden meaning behind his words | Be on the lookout for hidden costs in hotel bills.*
2 not easy to notice or realize: *He wants each pupil to have the chance to discover* ***hidden talents****.*
3 hidden agenda the secret purpose behind a plan or activity that you do not tell other people about – used to show disapproval: *Voters suspected a hidden political agenda. | Was there a hidden agenda behind this decision?*

hide¹ /haɪd/ ●●● S2 W2 *v* (*past tense* **hid** /hɪd/, *past participle* **hidden** /ˈhɪdn/)
1 [T] to deliberately put or keep something or someone in a place where they cannot easily be seen or found: **hide sth in/under/behind etc** *Marcia hid the pictures in her desk drawer. | She* ***keeps*** *a bottle of gin* ***hidden*** *behind a stack of books.* | **hide sth/sb from sb** *He was accused of trying to hide evidence from the police.*
2 [T] to cover something so that it cannot be seen clearly: *The church roof was half hidden by trees. | Her tangled hair hid her face.*
3 [I] to go or stay in a place where no one will see or find you: *Quick, he's coming! We'd better hide.* | **[+in/under/behind etc]** *Harry hid under the bed.* | **hide from sb** *Weiss spent two years hiding from the Nazis.*
4 [T] to keep someone in a place where other people will not find them: *The old woman hid him in her cellar for three days.* | **hide sb from sb** *We'll have to hide him from the soldiers.*
5 [T] to keep your real feelings, plans, or the truth secret, so that they cannot be known by other people: **hide your disappointment/embarrassment/confusion etc** *She laughed to hide her nervousness. | He took off his ring to* ***hide the fact*** *that he was married. | He told the jury that he is innocent and has nothing to hide.* | **hide sth from sb** *Don't try to hide anything from me.* → **hide your light under a bushel** at BUSHEL

THESAURUS

hide to make something difficult to see or find, or to not show your true feelings: *He hid the gun in his pocket. | She tried to hide her anger.*
conceal *formal* to hide something, especially by carefully putting it somewhere. Also used when talking about hiding your feelings, especially in negative sentences: *Several kilos of drugs were concealed in the back of the truck. | He could not conceal his feelings any longer.*
cover up to put something over another thing that you do not want people to see, in order to hide it completely: *People cover up cracks with wallpaper or tiles. | I used some make-up to cover up the spots.*
disguise to make someone or something seem like a different person or thing, so that other people cannot recognize them: *She managed to get into the camp by disguising herself as a soldier.*
camouflage to hide something by covering it with materials that make it look like the things around it: *We camouflaged the plane by covering it with leaves. | The troops used charcoal to camouflage their faces.*
obscure *literary* to make it difficult to see something clearly: *The view was obscured by mist.*
mask to make something less noticeable, for example a taste, a smell, a sound, or a feeling: *The lemon helps to mask the taste of the fish. | Helen had turned on the radio to mask the noise of the traffic. | He did little to mask his contempt.*

hide² *n* [C] **1** *BrE* a place from which you can watch animals or birds without being seen by them SYN **blind** *AmE* **2** an animal's skin, especially when it has been removed to be used for leather: *ox hide gloves* **3 have/tan sb's hide** *spoken* to punish someone severely – used humorously **4 sb's hide** *spoken* used to talk about someone when they are in a difficult situation: *He would say anything in court to try and* ***save*** *his own* ***hide*** (=save himself). **5 not see hide nor hair of sb** *spoken* to not see someone anywhere for a fairly long time: *I haven't seen hide nor hair of him for ages.*

ˌhide-and-ˈseek (*also* **ˌhide-and-go-ˈseek** *AmE*) *n* [U] a children's game in which one player shuts their eyes while the others hide, and then goes to look for them

hide·a·way /ˈhaɪdəweɪ/ *n* [C] a place where you can go when you want to be alone

hide·bound /ˈhaɪdbaʊnd/ *adj* having old-fashioned attitudes and ideas – used to show disapproval: *hidebound reactionaries*

hid·e·ous /ˈhɪdiəs/ *adj* extremely unpleasant or ugly: *a hideous dress | hideous crimes | Dinnertime that day was hideous.* —**hideously** *adv*: *Her face was hideously scarred.* —**hideousness** *n* [U]

hide·out /ˈhaɪdaʊt/ *n* [C] a place where someone goes because they do not want anyone to find them

hid·ing /ˈhaɪdɪŋ/ *n* **1** [U] when someone stays somewhere in secret, especially because they have done something illegal or are in danger: **be in/go into/come out of hiding** *He went into hiding in 1973.* **2** [singular] *spoken informal* **a)** a severe physical punishment SYN **beating**: *You'll* ***get a good hiding*** *when you come home! | You're not too big for a hiding, you know.* **b)** an occasion when you defeat someone in a sports game **3 be on a hiding to nothing** *BrE informal* to be completely wasting your time trying to do something

ˈhiding ˌplace *n* [C] a place where you can hide or where you can hide something

hier·ar·chi·cal /haɪˈrɑːkɪkəl $ -ɑːr-/ ●○○ AWL *adj* if a system, organization etc is hierarchical, people or things are divided into levels of importance: **hierarchical structure/organization/system etc** *a hierarchical society* —**hierarchically** /-kli/ *adv*

hier·ar·chy /ˈhaɪrɑːki $ -ɑːr-/ ●○○ AWL *n* (*plural* **hierarchies**)
1 [C,U] a system of organization in which people or things are divided into levels of importance: *a rigid social hierarchy | She worked her way up through the corporate hierarchy to become president.*
2 [C] the most important and powerful members of an organization: *the church hierarchy*

hier·o·glyph /ˈhaɪrəˌɡlɪf/ *n* [C] a picture or symbol used to represent a word or part of a word, especially in the ancient Egyptian writing system

hier·o·glyph·ics /ˌhaɪrəˈɡlɪfɪks/ *n* [plural, U] pictures and symbols used to represent words or parts of words, especially in the ancient Egyptian writing system —**hieroglyphic** *adj*: *hieroglyphic script*

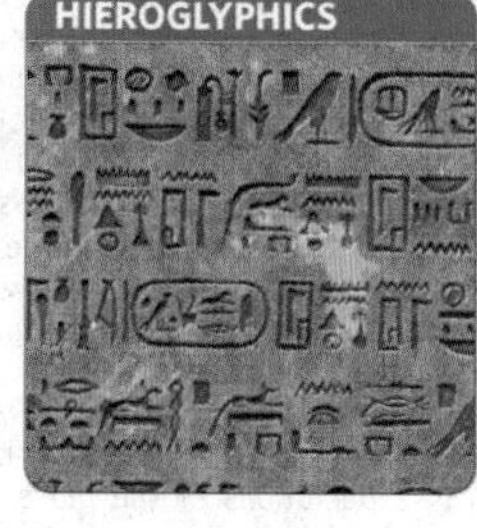
HIEROGLYPHICS

hi-fi /ˈhaɪ faɪ, ˌhaɪ ˈfaɪ/ *n* (*plural* **hi-fis**) [C] *old-fashioned* a piece of high-quality electronic equipment for playing recorded music SYN **stereo** —**hi-fi** *adj*: *hi-fi speakers*

hig·gle·dy-pig·gle·dy /ˌhɪɡəldi ˈpɪɡəldi/ *adj* things that are higgledy-piggledy are mixed together in an untidy way SYN **untidy** —**higgledy-piggledy** *adv*

Higgs bo·son /ˌhɪɡz ˈbəʊsən $ -ˈboʊ-/ (*also* **Higgs particle**) *n* [C usually singular] *technical* a piece of matter smaller than an atom that is thought to give mass to other very small pieces of matter

H

high[1] /haɪ/ ●●● S1 W1 *adj* (*comparative* **higher**, *superlative* **highest**)

1 FROM BOTTOM TO TOP measuring a long distance from the bottom to the top OPP **low**: *This is the highest mountain in Japan.* | *The camp was surrounded by a high fence.* | **100 feet/30 metres etc high** *waves up to 40 metres high* | *a ten-foot high statue* | ***How high** is the Eiffel Tower?* | **chest/waist/knee etc high** (=as high as your chest etc) *The grass was knee-high.* ⚠ Do not use **high** to describe people, animals, trees, and plants. Use **tall**: *You're getting very tall* (*NOT You're getting very high*). | *a tall palm tree* (*NOT a high palm tree*)

2 ABOVE GROUND in a position that is a long way, or a longer way than usual, above the ground, floor etc OPP **low**: *The apartment had spacious rooms with high ceilings.* | *a high shelf* | *high altitudes* | *The sun was already high in the sky.* | ***High up** among the clouds, we saw the summit of Everest.*

3 LARGE NUMBER a high amount, number, or level is large, or larger than usual OPP **low**: *Temperatures remained high for the rest of the week.* | *Lower-paid workers often cannot afford the high cost of living in the capital.* | **high level/degree/rate etc (of sth)** *High levels of car use mean our streets are more congested than ever.* | *high crime rates* | *high interest rates* | **high price/charge/tax etc** *If you want better public services, you'll have to pay higher taxes – it's as simple as that.* | *The train was approaching **at high speed**.* | **high proportion/percentage etc (of sth)** (=a very large part of a number) *A high proportion of women with children under five work full-time.* THESAURUS ▸ EXPENSIVE

4 GOOD STANDARD a high standard, quality etc is very good OPP **low**: *a high-performance computer* | **high quality** *a range of high-quality goods at low prices* | *Our aim is to provide the highest quality service to all our customers.* | **high standard** (=very good levels of work, achievement, behaviour etc) *The general standard of the entries was very high.* | *Our guests expect us to **maintain high standards**.*

5 CONTAINING A LOT containing a lot of a particular substance or quality OPP **low**: **high in sth** *Choose foods that are high in fiber and low in calories.* | **a high sugar/salt/fibre etc content** *Red meat tends to have a high fat content.*

6 RANK/POSITION having an important position in society or within an organization OPP **low**: *a **high rank** in the US Navy* | *the City's highest honour* | **high up** (=in a powerful position) *someone high up in the CIA* | **high office** (=an important position) *Both of them **held high office** in the Anglican Church.* | **high society** (=rich people of the highest social class) → HIGH-CLASS, HIGH-RANKING, HIGH-UP, → **friends in high places** at FRIEND[1](12)

7 ADVANCED [only before noun] advanced and often complicated: *We can offer all the benefits of the latest **high technology**.* | *the world of **high finance*** | **the higher animals/mammals/organisms etc** (=animals etc that are more intelligent or advanced than others)

8 high opinion/regard/praise etc strong approval of someone or something, or an expression of strong approval: *I've always **had a high opinion of** her work.* | **hold sb/sth in high esteem/regard** (=respect them very much) *As an educationalist, he was held in very high esteem.* | *Romsey **earned high praise** from his boss.*

9 high priority (*also* **high on the list/agenda**) important and needing to be done or dealt with quickly: *Most people feel that education needs to be given higher priority.* | *Arms control is high on the agenda.*

10 high hopes/expectations when someone hopes or expects that something will be very good or successful: *My expectations of the place were never very high, but I didn't think it would be this bad.* | **have high hopes/expectations** *Like many young actors, I had high hopes when I first started out.*

11 SOUND near or above the top of the range of sounds that humans can hear OPP **low**: *I always had difficulty reaching the high notes* (=when singing). | *a high squeaky voice* → HIGH-PITCHED

12 high point (*also* **high spot**) *BrE* an especially good part of an activity or event: *The visit to the ancient capital city was one of the high points of the tour.*

13 high ground a) an area of land that is higher than the area surrounding it: *Villagers herded the livestock to high ground to keep them safe during the floods.* **b)** a better, more moral, or more powerful position in an argument or competition: *Neither side in this conflict can claim the **moral high ground**.*

14 high spirits feelings of happiness and energy, especially when you are having fun: *It was a bright sunny day and we set off **in high spirits**.* | *I don't think they intended any harm – it was just high spirits.*

15 HAPPY/EXCITED [not before noun] happy and excited: *I was still high from the applause.*

16 DRUGS [not before noun] behaving in a strange and excited way as the result of taking drugs: **[+on]** *Most people there were high on cocaine.* | **get high** (=take a drug to make yourself high) | *Steve was as **high as a kite*** (=strongly affected by drugs or alcohol).

17 SEA/RIVER having risen to a high level OPP **low**: *The river is at its highest in spring.* → HIGH TIDE

18 it is high time sb did sth used to say that something should be done now: *It's high time you got a job.*

19 TIME the middle or the most important part of a particular period of time: *high summer* | **high noon** (=12 o'clock in the middle of the day) → HIGH SEASON

20 high wind a strong wind

21 high alert a situation in which people are told to be ready because there is a strong possibility of an attack or of something dangerous happening: **put/place sb on high alert** *Troops were put on high alert.*

22 high life/living the enjoyable life that rich and fashionable people have: *We're all stuck here, while he's off living the high life in New York.*

23 high drama/adventure very exciting events or situations: *a life with moments of high drama*

24 end/finish/begin etc (sth) on a high note to end, finish something etc in a successful way: *The team finished their tour on a high note in Barbados.*

25 high principles/ideals ideas about personal behaviour based on the belief that people should always behave in an honest and morally good way: *a man of **high moral principles***

26 high and mighty talking or behaving as if you think you are better or more important than other people: *Don't get high and mighty with me.*

27 be/get on your high horse to give your opinion about something in a way that shows you think you are definitely right and that other people are wrong: *If she'd get down off her high horse for a moment, she might realize there's more than one point of view here.*

28 FOOD *BrE* cheese, meat etc that is high is not fresh and has a strong smell or taste

29 high days and holidays *BrE* special occasions

30 high complexion/colouring *BrE* a naturally pink or red face

31 in high dudgeon *formal* in an angry or offended way – often used humorously

32 LANGUAGE **a) high style/register** *BrE* a very formal style of language, especially used in literature **b) high German/Dutch etc** a form of a language used for formal purposes that is often different from the ordinary form used by most people → HIGHLY, → **stink to high heaven** at STINK[1](1)

THESAURUS

BUILDINGS/MOUNTAINS ETC

high measuring a long distance from the bottom to the top – used about mountains, walls, and buildings: *the highest mountain in the world* | *The castle was surrounded by high walls.* | *a high cliff*

tall high – used about people, trees, plants, and buildings. **Tall** is used especially about things that are high and narrow: *tall marble columns* | *A cat was hiding in the tall grass.* | *a tall modern building*

majestic *especially written* very impressive because of being very big and tall – used about mountains, buildings, trees, and animals: *the majestic mountains of the Himalayas*

soaring [only before noun] *especially written* used about a building or mountain that looks extremely tall and impressive: *a soaring skyscraper*
towering [only before noun] *especially written* extremely high, in a way that seems impressive but also often rather frightening: *The sky was shut out by the towering walls of the prison.* | *towering trees*
lofty [usually before noun] *literary* very high and impressive – used in literature: *the lofty peaks in the far distance*
high-rise [usually before noun] a high-rise building is a tall modern building with a lot of floors containing apartments or offices: *a high-rise apartment block*

COLLOCATIONS CHECK

high mountain/building/wall/fence
tall person/tree/plant/building/tower/statue
majestic mountain/building/tree/animal
soaring building/tower/mountain
towering wall/tree/mountain/building
lofty building/mountain/tree/heights
high-rise building

SOUNDS

high-pitched higher than most sounds or voices: *He has a rather high-pitched voice.* | *Bats make high-pitched squeaks.*
shrill high and unpleasant: *Her voice became more shrill.* | *The bird has rather a shrill cry.*
piercing extremely high and loud, in a way that is unpleasant: *a piercing scream*
squeaky making very high noises that are not loud: *a squeaky gate* | *squeaky floorboards* | *a squeaky little voice*

high² ●●● S2 W3 *adv*
1 ABOVE THE GROUND at or to a level high above the ground, the floor etc OPP **low**: *He kicked the ball high into the air, over the heads of the crowd.* | **[+above/into etc]** *Hotel Miramar is situated high above the bay.* | *A ski lift whisks you high into the mountains.*
2 VALUE/COST/AMOUNT at or to a high value, cost, amount etc OPP **low**: *If prices shoot up any higher, no one will be able to afford to live in the area.* | *Tom scored higher than anyone else in the class.*
3 SOUND with a high sound: *A strange cry* ***rang high*** *into the night.*
4 ACHIEVEMENT at or to a high rank or level of achievement, especially within a company OPP **low**: *It seems that the higher you rise, the less time you have to actually do your job.* | *My parents always encouraged me to* ***aim high***.
5 (leave sb/sth) high and dry a) if someone is left high and dry, they are left without any help or without the things that they need **b)** if a boat, area etc is left high and dry, it is left on land because the water that surrounded it has gone down: *The once-thriving port of Rye was left high and dry as sea levels retreated.*
6 look/search high and low to try to find someone or something by looking everywhere: *We looked high and low for Sandy but couldn't find her.* → **hold your head high** at HOLD¹(16), → **live high on the hog** at LIVE¹(26), → **be riding high** at RIDE¹(6), → **run high** at RUN¹(28)

high³ ●○○ *n* [C]
1 NUMBER/AMOUNT the highest price, number, temperature etc that has ever been recorded, or that has been recorded within a particular period of time: *Highs of 40°C were recorded in the region last summer.* | **a new/record/ten-year etc high** *The price of oil* ***reached a new high*** *this week.*
2 EXCITEMENT *informal* a feeling of great happiness or excitement: *They're bound to* ***be on a high*** *after such an incredible victory.* | *the emotional* ***highs and lows*** *of a new romance*
3 DRUGS a feeling of pleasure or excitement produced by some drugs
4 WEATHER an area of high PRESSURE that affects the weather
5 SCHOOL a short form of HIGH SCHOOL, used in the name of a school: *Benjamin Franklin High*
6 from on high from someone in a position of authority – used humorously: *An order came from on high.*
7 on high *formal* **a)** at a high temperature as measured by an electric OVEN etc: *Microwave on high for eight minutes.* **b)** *formal* in a high place or heaven: *An angel came from on high.*

-high /haɪ/ *suffix* [in adjectives] of a particular height: *The wall was about chest-high* (=as high as your chest). | *a 7,000 metre-high mountain*

high·ball /ˈhaɪbɔːl $ -bɒːl/ *n* [C] *especially AmE* an alcoholic drink, especially WHISKY or BRANDY mixed with water or SODA

ˈhigh ˌbeams *n* [plural] *AmE* lights at the front of a car that are on as brightly as possible

ˌhigh-ˈborn *adj formal* born into the highest social class OPP **low-born**

high·boy /ˈhaɪbɔɪ/ *n* [C] *AmE* a piece of tall wooden furniture with many drawers SYN **tallboy** *BrE*

high·brow /ˈhaɪbraʊ/ *adj* **1** a highbrow book, film etc is very serious and may be difficult to understand **2** someone who is highbrow is interested in serious or complicated ideas and subjects SYN **intellectual** —**highbrow** *n* [C] → **LOWBROW, MIDDLEBROW**

high·chair /ˌhaɪˈtʃeə $ ˈhaɪtʃer/ *n* [C] a special tall chair that a young child sits in to eat → see picture at **CHAIR¹**

ˌHigh ˈChurch *n* [singular] the part of the Church of England that is closest in its beliefs to the Roman Catholic Church —**High Church** *adj* → **LOW CHURCH**

ˌhigh-ˈclass *adj* [usually before noun] of good quality and style, and usually expensive OPP **low-class**: *a high-class restaurant*

ˌhigh comˈmand *n* [singular] the most important leaders of a country's army, navy etc: *the German High Command*

ˌhigh comˈmission *n* [C] **1** a group of people working for a government or an international organization to deal with a specific problem **2** a group of people with official duties concerning the relationship of one Commonwealth country with another —**High Commissioner** *n* [C]

ˌHigh ˈCourt *n* [C usually singular] a court of law that is at a higher level than ordinary courts and that can be asked to change the decisions of a lower court

ˌhigh-defiˈnition *adj* [only before noun] a high-definition television or computer shows images very clearly

ˈhigh-end *adj* [usually before noun] *AmE* relating to products or services that are more expensive and of better quality than other products of the same type: *high-end computer memory chips* → **LOW-END**

ˌhigher eduˈcation *n* [U] college or university education as opposed to school or HIGH SCHOOL → **further education**

ˌhigher matheˈmatics *n* [U] different types of advanced mathematics that are studied and taught at universities

ˌhigher-ˈup *n* [C] *informal* someone who has a high rank in an organization: *Rumour has it that the higher-ups want to push the schedule forward.*

ˌhigh exˈplosive *n* [C,U] a substance that explodes with great power and violence

high·fa·lu·tin /ˌhaɪfəˈluːtɪn◂ $ -tn◂/ *adj informal* highfalutin language or behaviour seems silly although it is intended to be impressive – used to show disapproval

ˌhigh fiˈdelity *adj* [usually before noun] high fidelity recording equipment produces sound that is very clear → **HI-FI**

ˌhigh ˈfive *n* [C] *especially AmE* the action of hitting someone's open hand with your own above your heads to show that you are pleased about something

ˌhigh-ˈflier, high flyer *n* [C] someone who is extremely successful in their job or in school —**high-flying** *adj*

ˌhigh-ˈflown *adj* high-flown language sounds impressive but does not have much real meaning

H

ˌhigh-ˈgrade *adj* [only before noun] of the best quality: *high-grade beef*

ˌhigh-ˈhanded *adj* using your authority in an unreasonable way: *She resented his high-handed manner.* | *high-handed and insensitive management decisions* —**high-handedly** *adv* —**high-handedness** *n* [U]

ˌhigh ˈheels *n* [plural] women's shoes with high heels

ˈhigh jinks (*also* **hi-jinks** *AmE*) /ˈhaɪdʒɪŋks/ *n* [plural] *old-fashioned* noisy or excited behaviour when people are having fun: *youthful high jinks*

ˈhigh jump *n* **1 the high jump** a sports event in which someone runs and jumps over a bar that is raised higher each time they jump **2 be (in) for the high jump** *BrE informal* if someone is for the high jump, they will be punished for something they have done wrong —**high jumper** *n* [C]

high·land /ˈhaɪlənd/ *adj* [only before noun] **1** (*also* **Highland**) relating to the Scottish Highlands or its people: *Highland pipers* **2** in or relating to an area with a lot of mountains → **lowland**: *the highland capital of Quito*

High·land·er /ˈhaɪləndə $ -ər/ *n* [C] someone from the Scottish Highlands

high·lands /ˈhaɪləndz/ *n* [plural] **1 the Highlands** an area in the north of Scotland where there are a lot of mountains **2** an area of a country where there are a lot of mountains: *forested highlands* → LOWLANDS

ˌhigh-ˈlevel ●○○ *adj* [only before noun]
1 in a powerful position or job, or involving people who are in powerful positions or jobs: *high-level executives* | **high-level meetings/talks/negotiations etc** *a high-level conference on arms control*
2 at a high degree or strength: *The virus has shown high-level resistance to penicillin.*
3 involving very technical or complicated ideas
4 a high-level computer language is similar to human language rather than machine language → LOW-LEVEL

high·light[1] /ˈhaɪlaɪt/ ●●○ W3 AWL *v* [T]
1 to make a problem or subject easy to notice so that people pay attention to it: *Your résumé should highlight your skills and achievements.* THESAURUS EMPHASIZE
2 to mark written words with a special coloured pen, or in a different colour on a computer: *Use the cursor to highlight the name of the document you want to print.*
3 to make some parts of your hair a lighter colour than the rest —**highlighting** *n* [U]

highlight[2] ●●○ *n*
1 [C] the most important, interesting, or enjoyable part of something such as a holiday, performance, or sports competition: **[+of]** *That weekend in Venice was definitely the highlight of our trip.* | **[+from]** *At 11.30 we'll be showing highlights from the third round of the FA Cup.*
2 highlights [plural] areas of hair that have been made a lighter colour than the rest
3 [C] *technical* a light bright area on a painting or photograph

high·light·er /ˈhaɪlaɪtə $ -ər/ *n* [C] a special light-coloured pen used for marking words in a book, article etc → see picture at STATIONERY

high·ly /ˈhaɪli/ ●●● S2 W2 *adv*
1 [+ adj, adv] very: **highly successful/effective/efficient** *a highly successful politician* | *Tom's mother was highly critical of the school's approach.* | *highly competitive industries* | *a highly desirable neighborhood* | **highly unlikely/likely/improbable/probable** *It's highly unlikely that the project will be finished on time.* | *T.S. Eliot's highly influential poem, 'The Waste Land'* | *a highly controversial issue*
2 [+adj, adv] to a high level or standard: **highly skilled/trained/educated** *She is a highly educated woman.* | *highly paid experts* | *a highly developed economy*
3 highly placed in an important or powerful position: *a highly placed government official*
4 highly strung *especially BrE*, **high-strung** *AmE* nervous and easily upset or excited: *a highly strung child*
5 if you think highly of someone or something, you think they are very good and you admire them: **think/speak highly of sb** *I've always thought very highly of Michael.* | *a* ***highly regarded*** *author*

ˌhigh-ˈmaintenance *adj* needing a lot of care or attention: *a high-maintenance hairstyle* | *His girlfriend is pretty high-maintenance.*

ˌHigh ˈMass *n* [C,U] a very formal church ceremony in the Roman Catholic Church

ˌhigh-ˈminded *adj* having very high moral standards or principles SYN **high-principled**: *a high-minded sermon on charity* —**high-mindedly** *adv* —**high-mindedness** *n* [U]

High·ness /ˈhaɪnəs/ *n* [C] **Your/Her/His Highness** used to speak to or about a royal person such as a prince or princess

ˌhigh-ˈoctane *adj* **1** high-octane petrol is of a very high quality **2** very exciting or full of energy – used especially in newspapers and magazines: *This movie provides plenty of high-octane entertainment.*

ˌhigh-perˈformance *adj* **high-performance cars/computers/tyres etc** cars, computers etc that are able to go faster, do more work etc than normal ones

ˌhigh-ˈpitched *adj* a high-pitched voice or sound is very high OPP **low-pitched** THESAURUS HIGH

ˌhigh-ˈpowered *adj* [usually before noun] **1** a high-powered machine, vehicle, or piece of equipment is very powerful: *a high-powered automobile* **2** very important or successful: *a high-powered publisher*

ˌhigh-ˈpressure *adj* [only before noun] **1** a high-pressure job or situation is one in which you need to work very hard SYN **stressful 2 high-pressure sales/selling methods etc** very direct and often successful ways of persuading people to buy something: *high-pressure sales techniques* **3** containing or using a very high pressure or force of water, gas, air etc: *high-pressure hoses*

ˌhigh-ˈpriced *adj* costing a lot of money OPP **low-priced, inexpensive**: *high-priced apartments*

ˌhigh ˈpriest *n* [C] **1** *informal* someone who is famous for being the best at a type of art, music etc, and whose ideas or work change the way that other people think about and make art, music etc: **[+of]** *the high priest of modern jazz* **2** the most important PRIEST in some religions

ˌhigh ˈpriestess *n* [C] **1** *informal* a woman who is famous for being the best at a type of art, music etc, and whose ideas or work change the way that other people think about and make art, music etc **2** the most important PRIESTESS in some religions

ˌhigh-ˈprincipled *adj* having high moral standards

ˌhigh-ˈprofile *adj* [only before noun] attracting a lot of public attention, usually deliberately OPP **low profile**: *a high-profile public figure* —**high profile** *n* [singular]

ˌhigh-ˈranking *adj* [only before noun] having a high position in a government or other organization OPP **low-ranking**: *high-ranking officials*

ˌhigh reˈlief *n* [U] **1** a form of art in which figures cut in stone or wood stand out from the surface → BAS-RELIEF **2 throw sth into high relief** to make something very clear and easy to notice

ˈhigh-rise *adj* [only before noun] high-rise buildings are tall buildings with many levels THESAURUS HIGH —**high rise** *n* [C]: *They live in a high rise on the East Side.* → LOW-RISE

ˌhigh-ˈrisk *adj* [only before noun] involving a risk of death, injury, failure etc OPP **low-risk**: *high-risk investments* | **high-risk patients/groups etc** *cancer screening for women over 55 and other high-risk groups* THESAURUS DANGEROUS

ˈhigh road *n* [C] **1** *old-fashioned* a main road **2 take the (moral) high road** *AmE* to do what you believe is right according to your beliefs: *Daley has taken the high road in his campaign.*

ˌhigh ˈroller *n* [C] *AmE informal* someone who spends a lot of money carelessly or risks a lot of money on games, races etc

ˈhigh school ●●● S2 W2 *n*
1 [C,U] a school in the US and Canada for children of 14 or 15 to 18 years old → **junior high school**: **in high school** *We*

were friends in high school. | *high school students* | *high school graduates*
2 [singular] used in the names of some schools in Britain for children from 11 to 18 years old: *Leytonstone High School for Girls* → SECONDARY SCHOOL

ˌhigh ˈseas *n* **the high seas** *literary* the areas of ocean around the world that do not belong to any particular country

ˌhigh ˈseason *n* [singular, U] *especially BrE* the time of year when businesses make a lot of money and prices are high, especially in the tourist industry SYN **peak season** → LOW SEASON

ˌhigh-ˈsounding *adj* [only before noun] high-sounding statements, principles etc seem very impressive but are often insincere

ˈhigh-speed ●○○ *adj* [only before noun]
1 designed to travel or operate very fast: *a high-speed train* | **high-speed computer/network/modem etc** *high-speed Internet access* THESAURUS ▸ FAST
2 high-speed chase a situation when the police drive very fast to try to catch someone in a car

ˌhigh-ˈspirited *adj* **1** someone who is high-spirited has a lot of energy and enjoys fun and adventure **2** a high-spirited horse is nervous and hard to control

ˈhigh street *n BrE* **1** [C] the main street of a town where most of the shops and businesses are: *Camden High Street* | **in/on the high street** *A new bookshop had opened in the high street.* | **high street banks/shops/stores etc**
2 the high street used to talk about shops and the money people spend in them: *This year was exceptionally difficult on the high street.*

ˌhigh ˈtable *n* [singular, U] *BrE* the table where the most important people at a formal occasion sit SYN **head table**

high·tail /ˈhaɪteɪl/ *v* **hightail it** *informal* to leave a place quickly: *kids hightailing it down the street on their bikes*

ˌhigh ˈtea *n* [C,U] *BrE* a meal of cold food, cakes etc eaten in the early evening

high-tech /ˌhaɪ ˈtek◂/ ●○○ *adj* [usually before noun]
1 using high technology: *high-tech industries* | *a £1 million high-tech security system* | *high-tech weapons* → LOW-TECH THESAURUS ▸ ADVANCED, MODERN
2 high-tech furniture, designs etc are made in a very modern style —**high tech** *n* [U]

ˌhigh techˈnology *n* [U] the use of the most modern machines and methods in industry, business etc

ˌhigh-ˈtension *adj* **high-tension wires/cables etc** wires etc that have a powerful electric current going through them

ˌhigh ˈtide *n* **1** [C,U] the point or time at which the sea reaches its highest level OPP **low tide**: *High tide is at seven in the morning.* | **at high tide** *The waves became much more powerful at high tide.* **2** [singular] the time when something is at its best or most successful: *the high tide in the party's fortunes*

ˈhigh-tops, hi-tops *n* [plural] *AmE informal* sports shoes that cover your ANKLES —**high-top** *adj*: *high-top basketball shoes*

ˌhigh ˈtreason *n* [U] the crime of putting your country in great danger, for example by giving military secrets to the enemy

ˈhigh-up *n* [C] *BrE informal* someone who has a high rank in an organization SYN **higher-up**

ˌhigh ˈwater *n* [U] the period of time during which the water in a river or the sea is at its highest level because of the TIDE OPP **low water** → **come hell or high water** at HELL[1](22)

ˌhigh ˈwater mark *n* [singular] **1** the mark that shows the highest level that the sea or a river reaches **2** the time when someone or something is most successful: **[+of]** *the high water mark of Herrera's presidency*

high·way /ˈhaɪweɪ/ ●●● S3 W2 *n* [C]
1 *especially AmE* a wide main road that joins one town to another: *Interstate Highway 75* → FREEWAY, EXPRESSWAY, MOTORWAY
2 the public highway *BrE law* a road or roads that the public has the right to use
3 highway robbery *AmE informal* a situation in which something costs you a lot more than it should: *It's highway robbery, charging that much for gas!*

ˌHighway ˈCode *n* [singular] the set of official rules and laws about driving and using roads in Britain

high·way·man /ˈhaɪweɪmən/ *n* (*plural* **highwaymen** /-mən/) [C] someone who stopped people and carriages on the roads and robbed them, especially in the 17th and 18th centuries

ˈhighway paˌtrol *n* [singular] the police who make sure that people obey the law on main roads in the US

ˈhigh wire *n* [C usually singular] a tightly stretched rope or wire high above the ground that someone walks along as part of a CIRCUS performance SYN **tightrope**

hi·jab /hɪˈdʒɑːb/ *n* [C] a piece of cloth covering the head and neck, which some Muslim women wear

hi·jack[1] /ˈhaɪdʒæk/ ●○○ *v* [T]
1 to use violence or threats to take control of a plane, vehicle, or ship → **carjack**: *The airliner was hijacked by a group of terrorists.*
2 to take control of something and use it for your own purposes: *Some people think the party has been hijacked by right-wing extremists.* —**hijacker** *n* [C]

hijack[2] *n* [C] *BrE* when a plane, vehicle etc is hijacked

hi·jack·ing /ˈhaɪdʒækɪŋ/ *n* **1** [C,U] the use of violence or threats to take control of a plane: *the recent series of airplane hijackings* **2** [U] the act of stealing goods from vehicles

hi·jinks /ˈhaɪdʒɪŋks/ *n* [plural] an American spelling of HIGH JINKS

hike[1] /haɪk/ ●●○ *n* [C]
1 a long walk in the mountains or countryside: *a hike in the woods*
2 *especially AmE informal* a large increase in prices, wages, taxes etc SYN **rise**: **[+in]** *The president has proposed a hike in the minimum wage.* | **price/rate/tax etc hikes** *Several airlines have proposed fare hikes, effective October 1.*
3 take a hike *AmE spoken* used to tell someone rudely to go away

hike[2] ●●○ *v*
1 [I,T] to take a long walk in the mountains or countryside: **hike sth** *AmE*: *His dream is to hike the Appalachian Trail.* THESAURUS ▸ WALK
2 (*also* **hike up**) [T] *especially AmE* to increase a price, tax etc by a large amount SYN **raise**

hike sth ↔ **up** *especially AmE*
1 to lift up a piece of your clothing: *She hiked her skirt up to climb the stairs.*
2 to increase a price, tax etc by a large amount

hik·er /ˈhaɪkə $ -ər/ *n* [C] someone who walks long distances in the mountains or country for pleasure

hik·ing /ˈhaɪkɪŋ/ ●●○ *n* [U] the activity of taking long walks in the mountains or country → **walking**: *We're going to do some hiking this summer.* | *Utah is a great place to* **go hiking**.

hi·lar·i·ous /hɪˈleəriəs $ -ˈler-/ ●○○ *adj* extremely funny: *a hilarious story* THESAURUS ▸ FUNNY —**hilariously** *adv*

GRAMMAR
Hilarious is not used with 'very'. You say: *The film was absolutely hilarious.* ✗ Don't say: *The film was very hilarious.*
GRAMMAR GUIDE ▸ ADJECTIVES

hi·lar·i·ty /hɪˈlærəti/ *n* [U] laughter, or a feeling of fun: *Eva joined in the hilarity as much as anyone.*

hill /hɪl/ ●●● S2 W2 *n* [C]
1 an area of land that is higher than the land around it, like a mountain but smaller → **uphill, downhill**: *Their house is on a hill overlooking the sea.* | *A cart was making its way up the hill.*

H

2 a slope on a road: *There's a* **steep hill** *ahead.* → DOWNHILL[1], UPHILL[1]
3 the Hill *AmE* CAPITOL HILL
4 over the hill no longer young, and therefore no longer attractive or good at doing things: *Kathleen thinks she's over the hill, but she's only 32.*
5 it doesn't amount to a hill of beans *AmE spoken* it is not important

COLLOCATIONS

ADJECTIVES

steep *She pushed her bicycle up the steep hill.*
rolling/gentle hills (=hills with slopes that are not steep) *He loved the green rolling hills of Dorset.*
a long hill *The bus started going up the long hill into town.*

VERBS

climb a hill (=walk or drive up a hill) *She climbed the hill out of the village.*
go down a hill *It's best to use a low gear when you are going down steep hills.*

PHRASES

the top of a hill *The view from the top of the hill was beautiful.*
the brow/crest of a hill (=the top part of a hill) *A tank appeared over the brow of the hill.*
the bottom/foot of a hill

hill + NOUN

a hill town *the hill towns of Tuscany*
hill country (=a rural area where there are a lot of hills)

hill·bil·ly /ˈhɪlbɪli/ *n* (*plural* **hillbillies**) [C] *AmE* an insulting word meaning an uneducated poor person who lives in the mountains

hill·ock /ˈhɪlək/ *n* [C] *especially BrE* a little hill

hill·side /ˈhɪlsaɪd/ ●○○ *n* [C] the sloping side of a hill

ˈhill ˌstation *n* [C] a town in the hills in South Asia

hill·top /ˈhɪltɒp $ -tɑːp/ *n* [C] the top of a hill

hill·walk·ing /ˈhɪlˌwɔːkɪŋ $ -ˌwɒːk-/ *n* [U] *BrE* the activity of walking on hills for pleasure —**hillwalker** *n* [C]

hill·y /ˈhɪli/ ●●○ *adj* (*comparative* **hillier**, *superlative* **hilliest**) having a lot of hills: **hilly region/area/terrain etc**

hilt /hɪlt/ *n* [C] **1** the handle of a sword or knife, where the blade is attached **2 to the hilt** completely: **support/defend/back sb to the hilt** *I'm backing the PM to the hilt on this.*

him /ɪm; *strong* hɪm/ ●●● S1 W1 *pron* [object form of 'he']
1 used to refer to a man, boy, or male animal that has already been mentioned or is already known about: *Are you in love with him? | Why don't you ask him yourself? | He repeated what she had told him. | I knew it was him as soon as I heard his voice.*
2 used when talking about someone who may be male or female. Some people think this use is old-fashioned: *If you can convince a child you love him, you can teach him anything.*

him·self /ɪmˈself; *strong* hɪmˈself/ ●●● S1 W1 *pron* [reflexive form of 'he']
1 a) used to show that the man or boy who does something is affected by his own action: *In despair, the young boy had hanged himself. | His name is James but he calls himself Jim. | He poured himself a glass of orange juice.* **b)** used after words such as 'everyone', 'anyone', and 'someone' to talk about people in general being affected by their own actions: *Everyone should learn to respect himself.*
2 a) used to emphasize that you are talking about one particular man or boy: *It was the president himself who opened the door. | It must be true – he said so himself.* **b)** used after 'like', 'as', or 'except' instead of 'him': *The other passengers were all refugees like himself.*
3 (all) by himself a) alone: *He's lived by himself since his wife died. | Winston was sitting all by himself.* **b)** without help from anyone else: *It was the first time he felt he had achieved something by himself.*
4 not be/feel/seem himself *informal* if a man or boy is not himself, he does not feel or behave as he usually does, for example because he is upset or ill: *Rick hasn't seemed himself lately.*
5 have sth (all) to himself if a man or boy has something to himself, he does not have to share it with anyone else: *John at last had a bedroom all to himself.*

hind[1] /haɪnd/ *adj* [only before noun] relating to the back part of an animal with four legs: **hind legs/feet/quarters/limbs** → **talk the hind legs off a donkey** at TALK[1](10)

hind[2] *n* [C] *BrE* a female DEER

hin·der /ˈhɪndə $ -ər/ ●○○ *v* [T] to make it difficult for something to develop or succeed SYN **hamper**: *His career has been hindered by injury. | policies that will hinder rather than help families* ⚠ Do not confuse with **prevent** (=to make it impossible for someone to do something): *His poor health prevented him from going to work (NOT His poor health hindered him from going to work).*

REGISTER
In everyday English, people often say something **gets in the way of** something rather than **hinders** it: *This could* ***get in the way of*** *rescue attempts. | Poor English* ***got in the way of*** *his progress.*

Hin·di /ˈhɪndi/ *n* [U] an official language in India

hind·most /ˈhaɪndməʊst $ -moʊst/ *adj* → **devil take the hindmost** at DEVIL(13)

hind·quar·ters /ˈhaɪndˌkwɔːtəz $ -ˌkwɔːrtərz/ *n* [plural] the back part of an animal with four legs

hin·drance /ˈhɪndrəns/ *n* **1** [C] something or someone that makes it difficult for you to do something: **[+to]** *The floods have been a major hindrance to relief efforts. | A degree is* **more of a hindrance than a help** *in British industry.* **2** [U] *formal* the act of making it difficult for someone to do something: *Visitors are allowed to wander without hindrance.* → **without let or hindrance** at LET[2](2)

hind·sight /ˈhaɪndsaɪt/ *n* [U] the ability to understand a situation only after it has happened → **foresight**: **with/in hindsight** *With hindsight, I should have seen the warning signs.* | **the benefit/wisdom of hindsight** *With the benefit of hindsight, it's easy to criticize.*

Hin·du /ˈhɪnduː, ˌhɪnˈduː◂/ *n* (*plural* **Hindus**) [C] someone whose religion is Hinduism —**Hindu** *adj*: *a Hindu temple*

Hin·du·is·m /ˈhɪndu-ɪzəm/ *n* [U] the main religion in India, which includes belief in REINCARNATION

hinge[1] /hɪndʒ/ *n* [C] a piece of metal fastened to a door, lid etc that allows it to swing open and shut

HINGE

hinge[2] *v* [T] to attach something using a hinge GRAMMAR **Hinge** is usually passive. —**hinged**: *a hinged lid*

hinge on/upon sth *phr v* if a result hinges on something, it depends on it completely: *His political future hinges on the outcome of this election. | The case against him hinged on Lewis's evidence.*

hint[1] /hɪnt/ ●●○ *n* [C]
1 something that you say or do to suggest something to someone, without telling them directly: *There have been* **hints that** *he may take up coaching. | 'Look, I can't tell you.' 'Oh, come on,* **give** *me* **a hint**.' | **[+about/as to]** *Miles had been* **dropping** *heavy* **hints** *about the cost of petrol. | I made it clear I wasn't interested in him, but he didn't* **take the hint**.
2 a very small amount or sign of something: **[+of]** *'When?' he asked with a hint of impatience. | We shall have to turn back if there's the slightest hint of fog.*

3 a useful piece of advice about how to do something SYN **tip**: **helpful/handy hints** | **[+on/about]** *helpful hints on looking after houseplants*

hint² ●●○ *v* [I,T] to suggest something in an indirect way, but so that someone can guess your meaning SYN **imply**: **[+at]** *What are you hinting at?* | **hint (that)** *He hinted strongly that he might be prepared to send troops in.*

hin·ter·land /ˈhɪntəlænd $ -ər-/ *n* [singular] an area of land that is far from the coast, large rivers, or the places where people live: *the rural hinterland*

hip¹ /hɪp/ ●●● S3 *n* [C]
1 one of the two parts on each side of your body between the top of your leg and your waist: *She stood there with her hands on her hips glaring at him.* | *The old lady had fallen and broken her hip.*
2 the red fruit of some kinds of ROSES SYN **rose hip**

hip² *adj informal* **1** doing things or done according to the latest fashion SYN **cool**: *McMillan's novel gets my vote for hippest book of the year.* **2 be/get hip to sth** to learn about a new product, idea etc: *More and more people are getting hip to e-banking.*

hip³ *interjection* **hip, hip, hooray!** used as a shout of approval

HIP /hɪp/ *n* [C] the abbreviation of HOME INFORMATION PACK

ˈhip flask *n* [C] a small container for alcoholic drinks, that fits into your pocket

ˈhip hop, hip-hop *n* [U] **1** a type of popular dance music with a regular heavy beat and spoken words → **rap** **2** a type of popular CULTURE that began among young African-Americans in big cities, which includes hip hop music, dancing, and GRAFFITI art

hip·pie, hippy /ˈhɪpi/ *n* [C] someone, especially in the 1960s, who opposed violence peacefully and often wore unusual clothes, had long hair, and took drugs for pleasure

hip·po /ˈhɪpəʊ $ -poʊ/ *n* (*plural* **hippos**) [C] *informal* a hippopotamus

ˌhip ˈpocket *n* [C] a back pocket in a pair of trousers or a skirt

Hip·po·crat·ic oath /ˌhɪpəkrætɪk ˈəʊθ $ -ˈoʊθ/ *n* [singular] the promise made by doctors that they will obey the principles of the medical profession

hip·po·pot·a·mus /ˌhɪpəˈpɒtəməs $ -ˈpɑː-/ *n* (*plural* **hippopotamuses** *or* **hippopotami** /-maɪ-/) [C] a large grey African animal with a big head and mouth that lives near water → **rhinoceros**

hip·py /ˈhɪpi/ *n* [C] another spelling of HIPPIE

hip·ster /ˈhɪpstə $ -ər/ *n* **1** [C] *informal* someone who is considered fashionable: *Legendary hipsters Stomp bring street theater to Boston this week.* **2 hipsters** [plural] *BrE* trousers that fit tightly over your HIPS and do not cover your waist

hire¹ /haɪə $ haɪr/ ●●● S2 W3 *v* [T]
1 *BrE* to pay money to borrow something for a short period of time SYN **rent** *AmE*: *The best way to explore the island is to hire a car.* | *What does it cost to hire a boat for a week?*
2 a) to employ someone for a short time to do a particular job: *Employers hire skilled people on fixed-term contracts.* | **hire sb to do sth** *A City lawyer has been hired to handle the case.* **b)** *AmE* to employ someone: *Businesses may only hire foreign workers where an American cannot be found.* | *the power to* ***hire and fire*** (=employ and dismiss people)

hire sth ↔ **out** *phr v BrE*
1 to allow someone to borrow something for a short time in exchange for money: **[+to]** *a little company that hires out boats to tourists*
2 hire yourself out to arrange to work for someone: *They were so poor they had to hire themselves out on the farms.*

hire² *n* [U] *BrE* an arrangement in which you pay a sum of money to borrow something for a short time: *a* ***car hire*** *company* | **for hire** *boats for hire* | **on hire** *The crane is on hire from a local firm.* → **ply for hire** at PLY¹(3)

ˌhired ˈhand *n* [C] someone who is employed to help on a farm

hire·ling /ˈhaɪəlɪŋ $ ˈhaɪr-/ *n* [C] *old-fashioned* someone who will work for anyone who will pay them – used to show disapproval

ˌhire ˈpurchase *n* [U] *BrE* (*abbreviation* **HP**) a way of buying expensive goods by regularly paying small amounts over a period of time SYN **installment plan** *AmE*

hir·sute /ˈhɜːsjuːt, hɜːˈsjuːt $ ˈhɜːrsuːt, hɜːrˈsuːt/ *adj literary humorous* having a lot of hair on your body and face → **hairy**

his /ɪz; *strong* hɪz/ ●●● S1 W1 *determiner, pron* [possessive form of 'he']
1 used to refer to something that belongs to or is connected with a man, boy, or male animal that has already been mentioned: *Leo took off his coat and sat down.* | *I love his sense of humour, don't you?* | *Even* ***his own*** *mother would not have recognized him.* | *My eyesight is better than his.* | *Lewis denies that the child is his.* | *My relatives all live in the States – his are in France.* | **of his** *Garry introduced us to some* ***friends of his.*** | *Perhaps he's ashamed of that car of his.*
2 used to refer to something that belongs to or is connected with someone who may be male or female. Some people think this use is old-fashioned: *Everyone had his own work to do.* | *the obligations of a doctor to his patients*

His·pan·ic¹ /hɪˈspænɪk/ *adj* from or relating to countries where Spanish or Portuguese are spoken, especially ones in Latin America → **Latino**: *Miami's Hispanic community* | *Hispanic Studies*

Hispanic² *n* [C] someone who comes from a country where Spanish or Portuguese is spoken, especially one in Latin America → **Latino, Latina**: *In California, Hispanics make up 19.2 percent of the population.*

hiss /hɪs/ ●○○ *v*
1 [I,T] to say something in a loud whisper: *'Get out!' she hissed furiously.* | **[+at]** *She hissed at me to be quiet.*
2 [I] to make a noise which sounds like 'ssss': *The cat backed away, hissing.* | *Snakes only hiss when they are afraid.*
THESAURUS SOUND
3 [I,T] if a crowd hisses a speaker, they interrupt them with angry sounds to show that they do not like them → **boo**: *He was booed and hissed during a stormy meeting.*
—**hiss** *n* [C]: *She heard a faint hiss as the metal struck the water.*

ˈhissy ˌfit *n* [C] *informal* a sudden moment of unreasonable anger and annoyance SYN **tantrum**: **throw/have a hissy fit** *Williams threw a hissy fit when she decided her hotel room wasn't big enough.*

his·ta·mine /ˈhɪstəmiːn/ *n* [C,U] *medical* a chemical substance produced by your body during an ALLERGIC reaction → **antihistamine**

his·to·gram /ˈhɪstəgræm/ *n* [C] *technical* a BAR CHART

his·to·ri·an /hɪˈstɔːriən/ ●●○ W3 *n* [C] someone who studies history, or the history of a particular thing: **art/literary/military etc historian**

his·tor·ic /hɪˈstɒrɪk $ -ˈstɔː-, -ˈstɑː-/ ●●○ *adj* [usually before noun]
1 a historic place or building is very old: *the restoration of historic buildings* | *ancient historic sites* | *our historic monuments*
2 a historic event or act is very important and will be recorded as part of history: *a historic meeting of world leaders* | *'It is a* ***historic moment,*** *' he told journalists.*
3 *formal* having taken place or existed in the past: *It's unlikely that the share price will exceed historic levels.*
4 historic times are the periods of time whose history has been recorded → **prehistoric**: *Extinct volcanoes are those that have not erupted in historic times.*

his·tor·i·cal /hɪˈstɒrɪkəl $ -ˈstɔː-, -ˈstɑː-/ ●●○ W2 *adj* [usually before noun]
1 relating to the past: *places* ***of historical interest*** | *It is important to look at the novel in its* ***historical context.***

2 connected to the study of history: **historical evidence/research etc**
3 historical events, facts, people etc happened or existed in the past: *Was King Arthur a real historical figure?*
4 describing or based on events in the past: *a historical novel* —**historically** /-kli/ *adv*: *How historically significant is this discovery?*

his,toric 'present *n* [singular] *technical* the present tense, used in some languages to describe events in the past to make them seem more real

his·to·ry /ˈhɪstəri/ ●●● S2 W1 *n* (*plural* **histories**)
1 PAST EVENTS [U] all the things that happened in the past, especially the political, social, or economic development of a nation: ***Throughout history*** *the achievements of women have been largely ignored.* | **[+of]** *the post-war history of Europe* | *No man in* ***recent history*** *has done more to rebuild the Democratic Party.* | *the* ***early history*** *of Scotland* | *Other meteor storms have occurred in* ***recorded history***. | *a museum devoted to* ***local history*** | *one of the darkest episodes in* ***American history*** | *an interesting* ***period in*** *Egyptian* ***history*** | *a decision that* ***changed the course of history*** | *a college* ***steeped in history*** | ***History shows that*** *the usual response to violent protest is repression.*
2 DEVELOPMENT OF STH [singular, U] the events that took place from the beginning and during the development of a particular place, activity, institution etc: **[+of]** *the worst disaster in the history of space travel* | **long/brief/75-year etc history** *The 1970s were the most successful in the theater's long history.*
3 SUBJECT [U] the study of past events as a subject in school or university: **European/art/economic etc history** *a degree in European history* | **ancient/modern history** | *a history lesson*
4 ACCOUNT [C] an account of past events: **[+of]** *a history of World War II* | *a* ***potted history*** (=very short) *of Gielgud's life (BrE)*
5 PAST LIFE [C,U] a record of something that has affected someone or been done by them in the past: **medical/employment/career etc history** *Your doctor will ask for your medical history.* | **[+of]** *Is there any history of heart disease in your family?* | *The defendant* ***had a history of*** *violent assaults on women.*
6 **make history** to do something important that will be recorded and remembered: *Lindbergh made history when he flew across the Atlantic.*
7 **sth will go down in history** used to say that something is important enough to be remembered and recorded: *This day will go down in history as the start of a new era in South Africa.*
8 **history repeats itself** used to say that things often happen in the same way as they did before
9 **the history books** the record of past events: *Mozart's genius earned him a place in the history books.*
10 **... and the rest is history** *informal* used to say that everyone knows the rest of a story you have been telling
11 **that's (past/ancient) history** *spoken informal* used to say that something is not important anymore → NATURAL HISTORY, CASE HISTORY

his·tri·on·ics /ˌhɪstriˈɒnɪks $ -ˈɑːn-/ *n* [plural] very loud and emotional behaviour that is intended to get sympathy and attention – used to show disapproval —**histrionic** *adj*

hit¹ /hɪt/ ●●● S1 W2 *v* (*past tense and past participle* **hit**, *present participle* **hitting**)
1 TOUCH SB/STH HARD [T] to touch someone or something quickly and hard with your hand, a stick etc: *He raised the hammer and hit the bell.* | **hit sb/sth with sth** *The robbers hit him over the head with a baseball bat.*
2 CRASH INTO STH [T] to move into something or someone quickly and with force: *The tanks exploded as the plane hit the ground.* | *He was hit by a car.*
3 HURT YOURSELF [T] to move a part of your body quickly against something accidentally, causing pain SYN **bang**: *The ceiling's low, so be careful you don't hit your head.* | **hit sth on/against sth** *She slipped and hit her head on the sidewalk.*
4 SPORT [T] **a)** if you hit a ball or other object, you make it move forward quickly by hitting it with a BAT, stick etc SYN **strike**: ***Hit*** *the ball as* ***hard*** *as you can.* **b)** to get points by hitting a ball in a game such as BASEBALL or CRICKET: *Last year, Griffey hit 49 home runs.*
5 PRESS [T] *informal* to press a part in a machine, car, etc to make it work: *Maria hit the brakes just in time.*
6 ATTACK [T] to attack something or wound someone with a bomb, bullet etc: *Our ship was* ***badly hit*** *and sank within minutes.* | *A second shot hit her in the back.* | *The bomb failed to* ***hit*** *its* ***target***.
7 AFFECT BADLY [I,T] if something bad hits a place or a person, it suddenly happens and affects people badly: *The village has been hit by a devastating drought.* | *Hurricane Louis is expected to hit at the weekend.* | **be badly/severely/hard hit** *The company has been hard hit by the drop in consumer confidence.* | *The south of the country is* ***the worst hit*** *by the recession.*
8 HAVE PROBLEMS [T] to experience trouble, problems etc: **hit a snag/problems/a bad patch etc** *My father hit a bad patch, and had to sell the house.*
9 REACH A LEVEL/NUMBER [T] to reach a particular level or number: *Sales have* ***hit the*** *1 million* ***mark***. | **hit a peak/an all-time high etc** *Earnings hit a peak in the early 1980s.* | **hit rock-bottom/an all-time low etc** *Oil prices have hit rock-bottom.*
10 REALIZE [T] if a fact hits you, you suddenly realize its importance and feel surprised or shocked: *It's impossible to pinpoint a moment when* ***it hit*** *me* ***that*** *I was 'a success'.* | *He was gone before they* ***knew what*** *had* ***hit*** *them* (=realized what had happened).
11 SMELL/SIGHT ETC [T] if a smell or sight hits you, you suddenly smell or see it: *The smell of stale smoke hit him as he entered.*
12 ARRIVE [T] *informal* to arrive at a place: *They hit the main road two kilometres further on.* | **hit town** *AmE*: *I'll look for work as soon as I hit town.*
13 **hit the road/trail** *informal* to begin a journey
14 **hit the shops/streets** if a product hits the shops, it becomes available to buy: *I managed to get a copy of the book before it hit the shops.*
15 **hit the headlines** to be reported widely on television, in newspapers etc: *The couple hit the headlines last year when their relationship broke down.*
16 **hit the bottle** *informal* to start drinking too much alcohol regularly: *After his marriage failed, he hit the bottle big time.*
17 **hit the dirt/the deck** *informal* to fall to the ground in order to avoid something dangerous: *My first instinct was to hit the dirt.*
18 **hit a (brick) wall** *informal* to suddenly not be able to make any progress: *I felt I'd hit a wall with my playing.*
19 **hit the buffers/skids** *informal* if a plan, project etc hits the buffers, it fails: *Croft's comeback hit the skids yesterday when she lost in the quarter-finals.*
20 **hit sb when they are down** *informal* to upset or harm someone when they are already defeated
21 **hit sb where it hurts** *informal* to do something that you know will upset someone in the most damaging way: *Hit your husband where it hurts – in his wallet!*
22 **hit it off (with sb)** *informal* if two people hit it off, they like each other as soon as they meet: *I knew you'd hit it off with Mike.*
23 **hit the big time** (*also* **hit it big** *AmE*) *informal* to suddenly become very famous, successful, and rich: *The 25-year-old painter hopes to hit it big in New York.*
24 **hit the ground running** to start doing something successfully without any delay: *Law graduates are expected to hit the ground running.*
25 **hit the jackpot a)** to win a lot of money **b)** to have a big success: *Owens hit the jackpot in his first professional game with the Cowboys.*
26 **hit the nail on the head** *informal* used to say that what someone has said is exactly right: *You've hit the nail on the head there, David.*
27 **hit home a)** if a remark, criticism etc about you hits

H

home, you realize that it is true: *Graham didn't reply, but she could see her words had hit home.* **b)** if a blow or kick hits home, it hits the thing it is aimed at

28 hit the spot *informal* to have exactly the good effect that you wanted, especially when you are hungry or thirsty

29 hit the roof/ceiling *informal* to be very angry: *Ranieri returned, saw the mess, and hit the roof.*

30 hit the sack (*also* **hit the hay** *AmE*) *informal* to go to bed → **the shit hits the fan** at SHIT²(17), → **hit/strike paydirt** at PAYDIRT

hit back *phr v* to attack or criticize a person or group that has attacked or criticized you SYN **retaliate**: **[+at]** *The actress hit back at claims that she had threatened a member of staff.* | **[+with]** *United were a goal down, but hit back with an equalizer.* | **hit back by doing sth** *He hit back by calling his critics 'lazy'.*

hit on sb/sth *phr v*

1 (*also* **hit upon sth**) to have an idea or discover something suddenly or unexpectedly SYN **come up with**: *Then we* ***hit on the idea of*** *asking viewers to donate money over the Net.*

2 *AmE informal* to talk to someone in a way that shows you are sexually attracted to them: *Dave has hit on most of the women in the department.*

hit out *phr v* to try to hit someone: *When he felt someone grab him, he hit out wildly.*

hit out at sb/sth *phr v* (*also* **hit out against sb/sth**) to express strong disapproval of someone or something SYN **attack**: *The bishop hit out at the government's policy on the homeless.*

hit sb **up for** sth *phr v AmE spoken* to ask someone for money: *Did he hit you up for cash again?*

hit sb **with** sth *phr v informal*

1 to tell someone something interesting, exciting, or shocking: *The next morning, Steve hit me with the truth.*

2 *AmE* to punish or try to harm someone by doing something that will cause problems for them: *The next day, we found they'd hit us with a lawsuit.*

hit² ●●● S3 W3 *n* [C]

1 SUCCESSFUL something such as a film, play, song etc that is very popular and successful: **a hit single/show/record etc** *the hit musical 'The Phantom of the Opera'* | **a big/smash/number 1 etc hit** *The Beatles' greatest hits.* | *Which band* ***had a hit*** *with 'Bohemian Rhapsody'?* | **be a hit with sb** (=be liked by them) *It's hoped the new museum will be a big hit with families.*

2 HIT STH an occasion when something that is aimed at something else touches it, reaches it, or damages it: *Our ship took a* ***direct hit*** *and sank.*

3 COMPUTER **a)** an occasion when someone visits a website: *The site had 2,000 hits in the first week.* **b)** a result of a computer search, especially on the Internet: *thousands of irrelevant hits*

4 take a hit to be badly affected in some way: *The region's economy will take a hit if the airbase is closed.*

5 *informal* a feeling of pleasure obtained from taking an illegal drug

6 *informal* a murder that has been arranged to happen → HIT MAN

ˌhit-and-ˈmiss (*also* **ˌhit-or-ˈmiss**) *adj* done in a way that is not planned or organized → **random**: *The campaign was rather a hit-and-miss affair.*

ˌhit-and-ˈrun *adj* [only before noun] a hit-and-run accident is one in which a car driver hits someone and does not stop to help: **hit-and-run driver**

THESAURUS: hit

TO HIT SOMEONE

hit to hit someone quickly and hard with your hand, a stick etc: *He hit him hard in the stomach.* | *I don't like to see people hitting a dog.*

beat to hit someone deliberately many times, especially very hard: *The girl had been beaten to death.* | *He was beating the donkey with a stick.*

strike *written* to hit someone with your hand or a weapon. **Strike** is more formal than **hit** and is mainly used in written English: *Her husband struck her twice across the face.* | *Police say that the man had been struck on the head.*

punch to hit someone hard with your closed hand, especially in a fight: *I punched him on the nose.* | *She was screaming and punching him with her fists.*

thump /θʌmp/ *informal* to punch someone very hard: *Sometimes I just want to thump him.*

beat sb up to hurt someone badly in a violent attack, by hitting them many times: *If I tell the police, they'll beat me up.* | *He had been beaten up and tortured with lighted cigarettes.*

slap to hit someone with your open hand, especially because you are angry with them: *They had a big row and she ended up slapping him.*

spank (*also* **smack** *especially BrE*) to hit someone, especially a child, with your open hand in order to punish them: *Should a parent ever smack a child?*

TO HIT SOMETHING

hit: *Jack hit the ball and it flew over the fence.*

knock to hit a door or window with your closed hand in order to attract the attention of the people inside: *Someone was knocking on the door.* | *I knocked loudly but no one came.*

strike *written* to hit a surface. **Strike** is more formal than **hit** and is mainly used in written English: *The ball struck the side of the goal.*

whack /wæk/ *informal* to hit something very hard: *Edmonds whacked the ball into the air.*

bash to hit something hard, especially in a way that causes damage: *The police had to bash the door down to get in.*

tap to gently hit something with your fingers, often in order to attract someone's attention: *I tapped him on the shoulder.* | *I heard someone tapping on the window.*

rap to knock quickly or hit something several times: *He rapped the table with his pen to bring the meeting to order.*

bang to suddenly hit something hard, in a way that makes a loud noise: *Her father banged his fist down on the table angrily.* | *The door suddenly banged shut.*

pound *written* to hit something many times with a lot of force: *I could hear the sea pounding on the rocks.* | *She pounded on the door and shouted wildly.*

hammer *written* to hit something quickly many times making a loud continuous noise: *The rain was hammering on the roof.* | *A crowd of people were outside hammering on the door angrily.*

TO HIT SOMETHING ACCIDENTALLY

hit: *I've got a bad bruise where I hit my leg against the table.* | *The car hit a tree.*

bump to hit a part of your body against something, especially because you do not see or notice it: *Careful you don't bump your head – the ceiling's very low.*

bang/bash to hit something hard, so that you hurt yourself or damage something: *He banged into the car in front.* | *I bashed my knee climbing over a gate.*

stub to hit your toe against something and hurt it: *I stubbed my toe on the piano leg.*

hitch[1] /hɪtʃ/ *v* **1** [I,T] *informal* to get free rides from the drivers of passing cars by standing at the side of the road and putting a hand out with the thumb raised SYN **hitchhike**: **[+across/around/to]** *He plans to hitch right round the coast of Ireland.* | **hitch a ride/lift (with sb)** *We hitched a ride with a trucker.* **2** [T] (*also* **hitch up**) to move a piece of clothing you are wearing so that it is higher than it was before: *She hitched her skirt above her knees and knelt down.* **3 get hitched** *informal* to get married: *They got hitched without telling their parents.* **4** [T] (*also* **hitch up**) to lift yourself into a higher position by pushing with your hands: **hitch yourself (up) onto/on sth** *Gail hitched herself up onto the high stool.* **5 a)** [T always + adv/prep] to fasten something to something else, using a rope, chain etc: **hitch sth to sth** *He hitched our pick-up to his trailer.* | *a goat hitched to a fence* **b)** [T] (*also* **hitch up**) to fasten an animal to something with wheels so that the animal can pull it forwards: *I hitched up the horse and drove out into the fields.*

hitch[2] *n* [C] **1** a small problem that makes something difficult or delays it for a short time: **technical/slight/last-minute hitch** *In spite of some technical hitches, the first program was a success.* | *The whole show* ***went without a hitch***. THESAURUS PROBLEM

> **REGISTER**
> In written English, people usually prefer to use **(small/minor) problem** rather than **hitch**, which sounds slightly informal: *There were some* ***minor technical problems*** *when the product was first released.*

2 a type of knot: *a half hitch*

hitch·hike /ˈhɪtʃhaɪk/ ●○○ (*also* **hitch**) *v* [I] to travel to places by getting free rides from drivers of passing cars: **[+around/to/across etc]** *She spent her gap year hitch-hiking around the world.* —**hitchhiker** *n* [C]: *I picked up a hitchhiker on our way back.*

hi-tech /ˌhaɪˈtek◂/ *adj informal* another spelling of HIGH-TECH

hith·er /ˈhɪðə $ -ər/ *adv old use* here: *Coloured fish darted* ***hither and thither*** (=backwards and forwards).

hith·er·to /ˌhɪðəˈtuː◂ $ -ər-/ ●○○ *adv formal* up to this time: *a species of fish* ***hitherto unknown*** *in the West*

ˈ**hit list** *n* [C] *informal* the names of people, organizations etc that a person or group plans to harm: **on sb's hit list** *He was on a terrorist's hit list.* | **[+of]** *The company drew up a hit list of shops it expects to close.*

ˈ**hit man** *n* [C] a criminal who is employed to kill someone SYN **assassin**

ˈ**hi-tops** *n* [plural] another spelling of HIGH-TOPS

ˈ**hit paˌrade** *n* **the hit parade** *old-fashioned* a list that shows which popular records have sold the most copies

ˈ**hit squad** *n* [C] a group of criminals who are employed to kill someone

HIV /ˌeɪtʃ aɪ ˈviː◂/ *n* [U] a type of VIRUS (=a very small living thing that causes disease) that enters the body through blood or sexual activity, and can develop into AIDS → **AIDS**: **HIV positive/negative** (=having or not having HIV in your body)

hive[1] /haɪv/ *n* **1** [C] (*also* **beehive**) a small box where BEES are kept, or the bees that live in this box → see picture at **HOME**[1] **2 a hive of industry/activity etc** *BrE* a place that is full of people who are very busy: *This marketplace was once a hive of activity.* **3 hives** [U] a skin disease in which a person's skin becomes red and sore

hive[2] *v*

hive sth ↔ **off** *phr v BrE* to sell one part of a business: *the trend for television companies to hive off their advertising departments*

ˈ**hive mind** *n* [singular] a situation in which people all have similar thoughts, and it seems that their minds are working together like one single mind. The idea of a **hive mind** comes from insects such as bees, which work closely together as a group, like a single ORGANISM: *When you're online, it's easy to get caught up in the hive mind of the internet.*

hi·ya /ˈhaɪjə/ *interjection informal* used to say 'hello'

hm, **hmm** /m, hm/ *interjection* a sound that you make to express doubt, a pause, or disagreement

H.M. (*also* **HM** *BrE*) /ˌeɪtʃ ˈem/ the abbreviation of ***His/Her Majesty***: *HM the Queen*

HMS /ˈeɪtʃ em es/ (***His/Her Majesty's Ship***) used before the name of a ship in the British navy: *HMS Belfast*

HNC /ˌeɪtʃ en ˈsiː/ *n* [C] (***Higher National Certificate***) a British college or university examination, usually in a technical or business subject. HNCs are lower in level than HNDs.

HND /ˌeɪtʃ en ˈdiː/ *n* [C] (***Higher National Diploma***) a British college or university examination, usually in a technical or business subject

ho /həʊ $ hoʊ/ *n* (*plural* **hos** *or* **hoes**) [C] *AmE spoken informal* **1** a PROSTITUTE **2** *not polite* an offensive word for a woman or girl who you do not respect because she is too willing to have sex with many different people SYN **slut**

hoard[1] /hɔːd $ hɔːrd/ *n* [C] a collection of things that someone hides somewhere, especially so they can use them later: **[+of]** *the discovery of a hoard of gold coins*

hoard[2] (*also* **hoard up**) *v* [T] to collect and save large amounts of food, money etc, especially when it is not necessary to do so: *families who hoarded food during the strike* —**hoarder** *n* [C]: *I'm a hoarder when it comes to clothes.*

hoard·ing /ˈhɔːdɪŋ $ ˈhɔːr-/ *n* [C] *BrE* **1** a large board fixed high on a wall outside on which large advertisements are shown SYN **billboard** *AmE*: *advertising hoardings* → see picture at **SIGN**[1] **2** a high fence around a piece of land where something is being built

hoar·frost /ˈhɔːfrɒst $ ˈhɔːrfrɒːst/ *n* [U] *formal* a thin layer of ice that forms on objects outside when it is very cold SYN **frost**: *A light hoarfrost covered the fields.*

hoarse /hɔːs $ hɔːrs/ *adj* if you are hoarse, or if your voice is hoarse, you speak in a low rough voice, for example because your throat is sore: *He was hoarse from laughing.* | **hoarse voice/whisper/groan etc** —**hoarsely** *adv* —**hoarseness** *n* [U]

hoar·y /ˈhɔːri/ *adj* **1** [usually before noun] a hoary joke, remark etc is so well known that people no longer find it amusing or interesting: *Not that* ***hoary old chestnut*** (=old idea, joke, remark etc) *again.* **2** *old-fashioned* grey or white in colour, especially through age

hoax /həʊks $ hoʊks/ *n* [C] **1** a false warning about something dangerous: *a* ***bomb hoax*** | ***hoax calls*** (=telephone calls giving false information) *to the police* **2** an attempt to make people believe something that is not true: *an* ***elaborate hoax***

hob /hɒb $ hɑːb/ *n* [C] *BrE* the flat top of a COOKER

hob·ble /ˈhɒbəl $ ˈhɑː-/ *v* **1** [I always + adv/prep] to walk with difficulty, especially because your legs or feet hurt → **limp**: *He hobbled into the room on crutches.* THESAURUS WALK **2** [T] to deliberately make sure that a plan, system etc cannot work successfully: *Many start-ups are hobbled by a lack of sufficient capital.* GRAMMAR **Hobble** is usually passive in this meaning. **3** [T] to loosely fasten two of an animal's legs together, to stop it from running away

hob·by /ˈhɒbi $ ˈhɑː-/ ●●● *n* (*plural* **hobbies**) [C] an activity that you enjoy doing in your free time → **interest**, **pastime**: *What are your hobbies?* | *Susan's hobbies include reading, cooking, and drama.* | *Retirement gave him the time to pursue his hobbies.* —**hobbyist** *n* [C]: *a magazine for aircraft modelling hobbyists*

> **REGISTER**
> In everyday English, people often talk about what they do **in** their **free time** rather than use the word **hobbies**: *What do you do in your free time?* | *In my free time, I like reading and cooking.*

hob·by·horse /ˈhɒbihɔːs $ ˈhɑːbihɔːrs/ *n* [C] **1** a subject that someone has strong opinions about and that they talk about too much: *I'm afraid safe driving isn't Harry's only hobbyhorse.* | **be on your hobbyhorse** *Vicky was on her* *hobbyhorse again.* **2** an old-fashioned toy made of a horse's head on a stick

hob·gob·lin /hɒb'gɒblən, 'hɒbgɒb- $ 'hɑːbgɑːb-/ *n* [C] a GOBLIN

hob·nailed /'hɒbneɪld $ 'hɑːb-/ (*also* **hob·nail** /-neɪl/) *adj* [only before noun] *especially BrE old-fashioned* hobnailed boots have large nails fastened to the bottom to make them last longer

hob·nob /'hɒbnɒb $ 'hɑːbnɑːb/ *v* (**hobnobbed**, **hobnobbing**) [I] *informal* to spend time talking to people who are in a higher social position than you: **[+with]** *He spent the first day hobnobbing with the management.*

ho·bo /'həʊbəʊ $ 'hoʊboʊ/ *n* (*plural* **hobos**) [C] *AmE* someone who travels around and has no home or regular job SYN **tramp** *BrE*

Hob·son's choice /ˌhɒbsənz 'tʃɔɪs $ ˌhɑːb-/ *n* [U] a situation in which there is only one thing you can do, so you do not really have any choice at all

hock¹ /hɒk $ hɑːk/ *n* **1** [U] *BrE* a German white wine: *a glass of hock* **2 in hock** *informal* **a)** in debt: **be in hock to sb** *The fashion chain is still in hock to the banks.* **b)** something that is in hock has been sold temporarily because its owner needs some money: *He's a musician, but his guitar is in hock.* **3** [C] a piece of meat from above the foot of a pig: *pork hocks* **4** [C] the middle joint of an animal's back leg → see picture at HORSE¹

hock² *v* [T] *informal* to sell something temporarily because you need some money SYN **pawn**

hock·ey /'hɒki $ 'hɑːki/ ●●○ *n* [U]
1 *BrE* a game played on grass by two teams of 11 players, with sticks and a ball SYN **field hockey** *AmE*
2 *AmE* a game similar to hockey, but played on ice SYN **ice hockey** *BrE* → see picture at SPORT¹

ho·cus-po·cus /ˌhəʊkəs 'pəʊkəs $ ˌhoʊkəs 'poʊ-/ *n* [U] a method or belief that you think is based on false ideas: *He thinks psychology is a load of hocus-pocus.*

hod /hɒd $ hɑːd/ *n* [C] *BrE* a box with a long handle, used for carrying bricks

hodge-podge /'hɒdʒ pɒdʒ $ 'hɑːdʒ pɑːdʒ/ *n* [singular] *AmE informal* a lot of things mixed up together in no order SYN **jumble**, **hotch-potch** *BrE*

hoe /həʊ $ hoʊ/ *n* [C] a garden tool with a long handle, used for removing WEEDS (=unwanted plants) from the surface of the soil —**hoe** *v* [I,T]

hog¹ /hɒg $ hɑːg, hɒːg/ *n* [C] **1** *especially AmE* a large pig that is kept for its meat → **boar**, **sow** **2 go the whole hog** *informal* to do something thoroughly: *Let's go the whole hog and order champagne.* **3 go hog wild** *AmE informal* to suddenly do an activity in an uncontrolled way **4** *informal* someone who takes too much of something that should be shared SYN **pig**: *You greedy hog!* → ROAD HOG

hog² *v* (**hogged**, **hogging**) [T] *informal* to keep, use, or have all of something that should be shared: *How much longer are you going to hog the bathroom?* | *He's been hogging the limelight* (=having all the attention, praise etc).

Hog·ma·nay /'hɒgmənеɪ $ ˌhɑːgmə'neɪ/ *n* [U] *BrE* New Year's Eve and the parties that take place at that time in Scotland

hogs·head /'hɒgzhed $ 'hɑːgz-, 'hɒːgz-/ *n* [C] *BrE* a large container for holding beer, or the amount that it holds

hog·wash /'hɒgwɒʃ $ 'hɑːgwɑːʃ, 'hɒːg-, -wɒːʃ/ *n* [U] *informal* stupid or untrue talk SYN **nonsense**, **rubbish**: *That's a load of hogwash!*

ˌho 'ho *interjection* used to represent the sound of laughter

ˌho-'hum¹ *interjection informal* used to say that you are bored

ho-hum² *adj informal* not very good or interesting: *The main courses were great, but the desserts were ho-hum.*

hoick /hɔɪk/ (*also* **hoick up**) *v* [T] *BrE informal* to lift or pull something up with a sudden movement: *She hoicked her skirt up and began to dance.*

hoi pol·loi /ˌhɔɪ pə'lɔɪ/ *n* [U] an insulting word for ordinary people

hoist¹ /hɔɪst/ (*also* **hoist up**) *v* [T] **1** to raise, lift, or pull something up, especially using ropes: *The crew hurried to hoist the flag.* **THESAURUS** LIFT **2 be hoist with/by your own petard** *formal* to be harmed or embarrassed by the plans you had made to hurt other people – often used humorously

hoist² *n* **1** [C] a piece of equipment used for lifting heavy objects with ropes → **crane**: *a boat hoist* **2** [usually singular] a movement that lifts something up: *Give me a hoist onto your shoulders.*

ho·key /'həʊki $ 'hoʊ-/ *adj AmE* expressing emotions in an old-fashioned or silly way: *a hokey song*

ho·kum /'həʊkəm $ 'hoʊ-/ *n* [U] *informal* something that seems true or impressive but that is wrong or not sincere: *All that talk is just a bunch of hokum.*

hold¹ /həʊld $ hoʊld/ ●●● S1 W1 *v* (*past tense and past participle* **held** /held/)

1 IN YOUR HAND/ARMS a) [T] to have something in your hand, hands, or arms: *Could you hold my bag for me?* | **hold sth in your hand/arms** *He was holding a knife in one hand.* | *I held the baby in my arms.* | **hold hands** (=hold each other's hands) *They sat holding hands under a tree.* | **hold sb close/tightly** (=with your arms around someone) *Max held her close and wiped away her tears.* **b)** [T always + adv/prep] to move your hand or something in your hand in a particular direction: **hold sth out/up etc** *He **held out** his **hand** to help her to her feet.* | *Hold the picture up so we can see it.*

2 EVENT [T] to have a meeting, party, election etc in a particular place or at a particular time: *This year's conference will be held at the Hilton Hotel.* | *A thanksgiving ceremony was held to mark the occasion.* | *The funeral was held on a grey day in November.* | *In April, the president **held talks with** Chinese leaders.*

3 KEEP STH IN POSITION [T] to make something stay in a particular position: **hold sth open/up etc** *We used rolled-up newspapers to hold the windows open.* | *Remember to hold your head up and keep your back straight.* | **hold sth in place/position** *A couple of screws should hold it in place.* | *Lift your head off the floor and hold this position for five seconds.*

4 JOB/TITLE [T] **a)** to have a particular job or position, especially an important one: *Do you really think he's capable of holding such a responsible position?* | **hold the post/position/office etc (of sth)** *She was the first woman to hold the office of Australian state premier.* | *The governor had held the post since 1989.* | *Whoever is elected will **hold office*** (=have an important political position) *for four years.* **b)** to have a particular title or record, because you have won a competition, are the best at something etc: *The programme still **holds the record for** the longest running TV series.* | *The last Briton to hold the title was Bert Nicholson.*

5 KEEP/STORE [T] to keep something to be used when it is needed: *Further copies of the book are held in the library.* | *Weapons were held at various sites.*

6 KEEP STH AVAILABLE FOR SB [T] to agree not to give something such as a ticket, a place at a restaurant, a job etc to anyone except a particular person: *We can hold the reservation for you until next Friday.* | **hold sth open** *You can't expect them to hold the job open for much longer – you'll have to decide whether you want it or not.*

7 KEEP SB SOMEWHERE [T] to keep someone somewhere, and not allow them to leave: *Police are holding two men in connection with the robbery.* | **hold sb prisoner/hostage/captive** *A senior army officer was held hostage for four months.* | **hold sb incommunicado** (=keep someone somewhere and not allow them to communicate with anyone)

8 OPINION [T not in progressive] to have a particular opinion or belief: *Experts hold varying opinions as to the causes of the disease.* | **be widely/generally/commonly held** (=be the opinion of a lot of people) *This view is not widely held.* | **be held to be sth** *She was held to be one of the most talented actors of her time.* | **hold that** *The judge held that the child's interests in this case must come first.*

H

9 hold sb responsible/accountable/liable (for sth) to say or decide that someone should accept the responsibility for something bad that happens: *If anything happens to her, I'll* ***hold*** *you* ***personally responsible****.* | *He may have had a terrible childhood, but he should still be held accountable for his own actions.*

10 OWN STH [T] to officially own or possess money, a document, a company etc: *He holds shares in ICI.* | *Do you hold a valid passport?* | *a* ***privately-held*** *company*
THESAURUS ▸ OWN

11 CONTAIN A PARTICULAR AMOUNT [T not in progressive] to have the space to contain a particular amount of something: *The movie theater holds 500 people.* | *The tank should hold enough to last us a few days.*

12 SUPPORT [I,T] to be strong enough to support the weight of something or someone: *Careful! I'm not sure that branch will hold you.* | *The bridge didn't look as though it would hold.*

13 STAY AT SAME LEVEL [I,T] to stay at a particular amount, level, or rate, or to make something do this: *The bank is holding interest rates at 4%.* | *Since then, the pound has* ***held steady*** *against the dollar.* | **hold sb's interest/attention** (=make someone stay interested) *Colourful pictures help hold the students' interest.*

14 NOT CHANGE [I] to continue to be true, good, available etc: *What I said yesterday holds.* | *Does your invitation still hold?* | **hold true/good** *Twenty years on, his advice still holds good.* | **weather/luck holds (out)** (=continues to be good) *If our luck holds, we could reach the final.*

15 STOP/DELAY [T] *spoken* used in particular phrases to tell someone to wait or not to do something: *I'll have a tuna fish sandwich please – and hold the mayo* (=do not give me any). | **hold it!** *Hold it! We're not quite ready.* | **hold your horses!** (=used to tell someone to do something more slowly or carefully)

16 hold your head up (*also* **hold your head high**) to behave as if you are proud of yourself or respect yourself: *They may have lost the game, but I still think they've earned the right to hold their heads high today.*

17 hold your breath a) to deliberately not breathe out for a short time: *Hold your breath and count to ten.* **b)** to not breathe out and try not to make a sound because you do not want to be noticed: *Julie shrank back against the wall and held her breath.* **c) not hold your breath** *spoken* used to say that you do not expect something to happen, even though someone has said it will: *He promised he'd phone, but I'm not holding my breath.*

18 hold (your) fire a) to not shoot at someone when you were going to **b)** to not criticize, attack, or oppose someone when you were going to: *The president urged his party to hold fire on the issue a few days longer.*

19 TELEPHONE [I] (*also* **hold the line**) *spoken* to wait until the person you have telephoned is ready to answer: *Mr Stevens is busy at the moment – would you like to hold?* | *Please hold the line while I transfer you.*

20 ARMY [T] if an army holds a place, it controls it or defends it from attack: *The French army held the town for three days.*

21 MUSICAL NOTE [T] to make a musical note continue for a particular length of time

22 FUTURE [T] *formal* if the future holds something, that is what may happen: *Thousands of workers are waiting to see* ***what the future holds****.*

23 HAVE A QUALITY [T] *formal* to have a particular quality: **hold (little) interest/appeal/promise etc** *Many church services hold little appeal for modern tastes.*

24 hold your own (against sb) to successfully defend yourself or succeed in a difficult situation, competition etc: *He was a good enough player to hold his own against the Americans.*

25 not hold a candle to sb/sth to be much worse than someone or something else

26 be left holding the baby *BrE*, **be left holding the bag** *AmE* to be left as the only person responsible for dealing with a difficult situation, especially something someone else started: *He was left holding the financial baby when his musical partner joined another band.*

27 hold sway to have a lot of influence or power: *Among people here, traditional values still hold sway.*

28 hold court to get the attention of everyone while you are talking, especially when you are trying to entertain people: *Joey would walk into the bar and hold court all night.*

29 hold your tongue *spoken* used to tell someone to stop talking or to not tell someone about something: *I reckon you've just got to learn to hold your tongue.*

30 hold all the cards to have all the advantages in a situation in which people are competing or arguing: *'There's not much we can do. They seem to hold all the cards,' said Dan gloomily.*

31 hold fast (to sth) to keep believing strongly in something

32 hold a conversation to have a conversation

33 hold the fort to be responsible for something while the person usually responsible for it is not there: *She's holding the fort while the manager's on holiday.*

34 hold the lead/advantage to be winning in a competition, game etc: *Celtic held the lead in the first half.*

35 there's no holding sb (back) *spoken* used to say that someone is so determined to do something that you cannot prevent them from doing it

36 can hold your drink/liquor/alcohol etc to be able to drink a lot of alcohol without getting drunk or ill

37 not hold water if an excuse, a statement etc does not hold water, it does not seem to be true or reasonable

38 hold sth/sb dear *formal* to care about something or someone a lot: *We were facing the loss of everything we held dear.*

39 hold the road if a car holds the road well, you can drive it quickly around bends without losing control

40 hold that thought *spoken* used to tell someone to remember what has just been said and then continue discussing it or thinking about it later → **hold a course** at COURSE[1](8)

THESAURUS

hold to have something in your hand, hands, or arms: *Maria came in holding a letter.* | *Can I hold the baby?*

grip to hold something very tightly and not let it go: *He gripped her arm so she couldn't walk away.* | *Jenny gripped the side of the boat to steady herself.*

clutch to hold something tightly, especially because you do not want to drop or lose it: *A businessman hurried past, clutching his briefcase.*

clasp *written* to hold someone or something tightly, closing your fingers or arms around them: *She was clasping a bunch of small summer flowers.* | *He clasped her in his arms and kissed her.*

get/take hold of sth to take something in your hand or hands and hold it: *I took hold of the handle and pulled as hard as I could.*

grasp *written* to take hold of something firmly, especially in a determined way: *She grasped the lowest branch and pulled herself up into the tree.*

grab to take hold of something suddenly and often violently: *He grabbed my bag and ran off with it.*

seize /siːz/ *written* to take hold of something suddenly and often violently: *A police officer ran after him and seized the gun.*

hang on (to sth) to hold on to something or someone tightly to support yourself: *He hung on to the rail at the back of the motorbike.*

keep hold of sth to continue to hold something: *Greg was struggling to keep hold of the dog.*

hold sth **against** sb *phr v* to continue to dislike someone or not forgive them because of something bad they have done in the past: *You can't still hold that against him, surely?*

hold back *phr v*

1 hold sb/sth ↔ back to make someone or something stop moving forward: *Police in riot gear held back the demonstrators.*

2 hold sth ↔ back to stop yourself from feeling or showing

a particular emotion: *She struggled to **hold back** her **tears**.* | *Anger flooded through her. She couldn't hold it back.*
3 hold sb/sth ↔ back to prevent someone or something from making progress: *They felt the British economy was being held back by excessive government controls.*
4 hold (sb) back to be unwilling to do something, especially because you are being careful, or to make someone unwilling to do something: *In the current situation many investors are holding back.* | *She wanted to tell him but pride held her back.*
5 hold sth ↔ back to keep something secret: *Tell me all about it – don't hold anything back!*
hold sb/sth **↔ down** *phr v*
1 to make someone or something stay on something, and stop them from moving away or escaping: *We had to hold the tent down with rocks to stop it blowing away.* | *It took three strong men to hold him down.*
2 to prevent the level of something such as prices from rising: *We will aim to hold down prices.*
3 hold down a job to succeed in keeping a job for a period of time: *He's never held down a job for longer than a few weeks.*
4 to keep people under control or limit their freedom: *The people were held down for centuries by their conquerors.*
hold forth *phr v* to give your opinion on a subject, especially for a long time: **[+on]** *The speaker was holding forth on the collapse of modern society.*
hold off *phr v*
1 to delay doing something: *Buyers have been holding off until the price falls.* | **hold off (on) doing sth** *Hold off making your decision until Monday.*
2 hold sb ↔ off a) to prevent someone who is trying to attack or defeat you from succeeding: *Not even a gun could hold him off forever.* **b)** to prevent someone from coming towards you or succeeding in speaking to you: *There's already a crowd of reporters outside – I'll try to hold them off for a while.*
3 if rain or bad weather holds off, it does not start, although it looked as if it would: *The rain held off until after the game.*
hold on *phr v*
1 *spoken* **a)** to wait for a short time: *Hold on, I'll just get my coat.* **b)** used when you have just noticed, heard, or remembered something interesting or wrong: *Hold on a minute! Isn't that your brother's car over there?* **c)** used to ask someone on the telephone to wait until the person they want to talk to is available: *Can you hold on? I'll try to find her.*
2 to have your hands or arms tightly around something: ***Hold on tight!*** | **[+to]** *Hold on to my arm.*
3 to continue doing something that is very difficult to do: *San Francisco held on to win 4–2.*
hold on to sb/sth *phr v* to keep something rather than losing it, selling it, or giving it to someone else: *The soldiers held on to the bridge for three more days.* | *I think I'll hold on to these old records for now.*
hold out *phr v*
1 hold out sth to think or say that something is possible or likely to happen, especially something good: **not hold out much hope/hold out little hope** *Negotiators aren't holding out much hope of a peaceful settlement.* | **hold out the prospect/promise of sth** *alternative methods which hold out the promise of improved health*
2 if a supply of something holds out, there is still some left: *Water supplies won't hold out much longer.*
3 to continue to successfully defend a place that is being attacked: *The rebels held out for another night but then fresh forces arrived.*
4 to try to prevent yourself from doing something that someone is trying to force you to do: **[+against]** *I didn't know how much longer I could hold out against their relentless questioning.*
hold out for sth *phr v* to not accept anything less than you have asked for: *Transport workers are holding out for a 20% pay rise.*
hold out on sb *phr v informal* to not tell someone about something important: *She must have been holding out on him all these years.*

hold sth **over** *phr v*
1 *formal* to do or deal with something at a later time: *The matter was held over for further review.* GRAMMAR **Hold over** is usually passive in this meaning. → HOLDOVER
2 hold sth over sb to use something bad that you know about someone to make them do what you want: *He knows I've been in prison and is holding it over me.*
3 be held over *especially AmE* if a play, film, concert etc is held over, it is shown for longer than planned because it is very popular
hold to sth *phr v*
1 if you hold to a belief, principle, promise etc, you believe it or behave according to it: *He admitted he did not hold to the traditional view of God.*
2 hold sb to sth to make someone do what they have promised: *'I'll ask him tomorrow.' 'OK, but I'm going to hold you to that.'*
3 hold sb to sth *BrE* to prevent your opponent in a sports game from getting more than a particular number of points: *Norway held Holland to a 2–2 draw.*
hold together *phr v*
1 if a group or an organization holds together, or if something holds it together, it stays strong and does not separate into different parts or groups: *Against all expectations, the coalition held together well.* | **hold sth ↔ together** *In those days the church held the community together.*
2 to remain whole and good enough to use, or to make something do this: *Incredibly, the raft held together till we reached the opposite shore.* | **hold sth ↔ together** *I wondered how the structure was held together.*
hold up *phr v*
1 hold sth ↔ up to support something and prevent it from falling down: *The roof is held up by massive stone pillars.*
2 hold sb/sth ↔ up to delay someone or something: *Sorry I'm late – I was held up at work.* GRAMMAR **Hold up** is often passive in this meaning.
3 hold up sth to rob or try to rob a place or person by using violence: *Two armed men held up a downtown liquor store last night.* → HOLD-UP
4 to not become weaker: *His physical condition has held up well.*
hold sb/sth **up as** sth *phr v* to use someone or something as a good example or as proof of something: *The school is **held up as a model** for others.* | *This incident will be held up as proof that tougher controls are needed.*
hold with sth *phr v* **not hold with sth** *BrE* used to say that someone does not approve of something: *He says he doesn't hold with all this politically correct stuff.* | **not hold with doing sth** *I don't hold with hitting children in any circumstances.*

hold² ●●● S2 W3 *n*
1 HOLDING STH [singular] the action of holding something with your hands SYN **grip**: **[+on]** *She released her **tight hold on** the dog.* | *He **tightened** his **hold**, refusing to let her go.* | *Make sure you **keep hold of** my hand when we cross the road.* | *I **took hold of** her hand and gently led her away.* | ***Grab hold of** the rope and pull yourself up.*
2 get hold of sth (*also* **get a hold of sth** *AmE*) to find or borrow something so that you can use it: *I need to get hold of a car.* | *She managed to get a hold of a copy.*
3 get hold of sb (*also* **get a hold of sb** *AmE*) to find and speak to someone about something: *I must get hold of Vanessa to see if she can babysit.*
4 CONTROL/POWER [singular] control, power, or influence over something or someone: **get/keep a hold on/of sth** *He struggled to get a hold of his emotions.* | *I've always kept **a tight hold** on our finances.* | *I realized that the woman **had a hold over** my father.*
5 on hold a) if something is on hold, it is going to be done or dealt with at a later date rather than now: *The plans are on hold until after the election.* | *Since having the kids, my career has been **put on hold**.* **b)** if you are on hold, you are waiting to talk to someone on the telephone: *We try not to keep people on hold for more than a couple of minutes.* | *The agent **put** me **on hold** while she consulted a colleague.*
6 take (a) hold to start to have a definite effect: *The fever was beginning to take hold.*

H

7 get hold of an idea/an impression/a story etc to learn or begin to believe something: *Where on earth did you get hold of that idea?*
8 FIGHT [C] a particular position that you hold an opponent in, in a fight or a sport such as WRESTLING
9 CLIMBING [C] somewhere you can put your hands or feet to help you climb something: *The cliff was steep and it was difficult to find a hold.*
10 SHIP [C] the part of a ship below the DECK[1](1) where goods are stored
11 no holds barred when there are no rules or limits on what you are allowed to do: *It seems there are no holds barred when it comes to making a profit.*

hold·all /ˈhəʊld-ɔːl $ ˈhoʊld-ɒːl/ *n* [C] *BrE* a large bag used for carrying clothes and other things when you are travelling → see picture at **BAG**[1]

hold·er /ˈhəʊldə $ ˈhoʊldər/ ●●○ *n* [C]
1 someone who owns or controls something: *the 800 metres world record holder | Season-ticket holders are furious at the rise in rail fares. | British passport holders |* **[+of]** *holders of ordinary shares*
2 something that is used to hold an object: **candle/cigarette/test-tube etc holder**

hold·ing /ˈhəʊldɪŋ $ ˈhoʊl-/ *n* [C] something which a person owns, especially land or SHARES in a company: **[+in]** *The government has decided to sell its 21% holding in the firm. |* **land/property/currency etc holding** *companies with large property holdings*

ˈholding ˌcompany *n* [C] a company that completely or partly owns other companies, as well as doing business itself

ˈholding ˌpattern *n* [C usually singular] **1** the path that an aircraft flies along while it is waiting for permission to land **2** a situation in which you cannot act because you are waiting for the result of something: **in a holding pattern** *My career is in a holding pattern right now.*

hold·o·ver /ˈhəʊldˌəʊvə $ ˈhoʊldˌoʊvər/ *n* [C] *AmE* an action, feeling, or idea that has continued from the past into the present SYN **hangover**: **[+from]** *Her fear of dogs is a holdover from her childhood.* → **hold over** at **HOLD**[1]

ˈhold-up *n* [C] **1** a situation that stops something from happening or making progress SYN **delay**: *traffic hold-ups on the highway | Despite the odd hold-up, we finished on time.* **2** *informal* an attempt to rob a place or person by threatening them with a weapon SYN **robbery**: *a bank hold-up* → **hold up** at **HOLD**[1]

H

HOLE

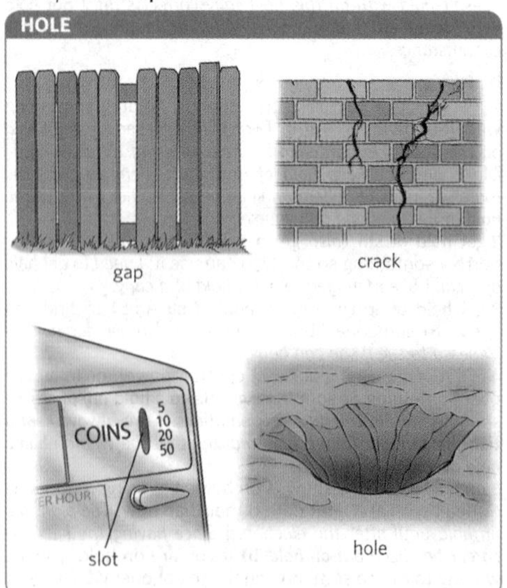

hole[1] /həʊl $ hoʊl/ ●●● S1 W2 *n* [C]
1 SPACE IN STH SOLID an empty space in something solid: **[+in]** *There was a huge hole in the road. | I began* **digging** *a* **hole** *for the plant.* ⚠ Don't say there is a hole 'on' something. Say there is a hole **in** something.
2 SPACE STH CAN GO THROUGH a space in something solid that allows light or things to pass through: **[+in]** *They climbed through a hole in the fence. | These socks are* **full of holes**. | *bullet holes* (=made by bullets)
3 EMPTY PLACE a place where someone or something should be, but is missing: **[+in]** *Their departure will leave a gaping hole in Grand Prix racing.*
4 WEAK PART a weak part or fault in something such as an idea or plan: *The theory is* **full of holes**. | **[+in]** *If you have holes in your game, work on them.*
5 ANIMAL'S HOME the home of a small animal: *a rabbit hole*
6 UNPLEASANT PLACE *informal* an unpleasant place: *I've got to get out of this hole.*
7 GOLF **a)** a hole in the ground that you try to get the ball into in the game of golf **b)** one part of a GOLF COURSE with this kind of hole at one end → see picture at **GOLF**
8 hole in one when someone hits the ball in golf from the starting place into the hole with only one hit
9 make a hole in sth *informal* to use a large part of an amount of money, food etc: *Holidays can make a big hole in your savings.*
10 be in a hole *informal* to be in a difficult situation
11 be in the hole *AmE spoken* to owe money: *I was something like $16,000 in the hole already.*
12 need/want sth like a hole in the head *spoken* used to say that you definitely do not need or want something: *I need this conversation like a hole in the head.* → **ace in the hole** at **ACE**[1](7), → **BLACK HOLE**, → **square peg in a round hole** at **SQUARE**[1](12), → **WATERING HOLE**

THESAURUS

hole an empty space in the surface of something, which sometimes goes all the way through it: *A fox had dug a hole under our fence. | Rain was coming in through a hole in the roof.*
space an empty area between two things, into which you can put something: *Are there any empty spaces on the bookshelf? | a parking space*
gap an empty area between two things or two parts of something, especially one that should not be there: *He has a gap between his two front teeth. | I squeezed through a gap in the hedge.*
opening a hole that something can pass through or that you can see through, especially at the entrance of something: *The train disappeared into the dark opening of the tunnel. | I looked through the narrow opening in the wall.*
leak a small hole where something has been damaged or broken that lets liquid or gas flow in or out: *a leak in the pipe | The plumber's coming to repair the leak.*
puncture *especially BrE* a small hole in a tyre through which air escapes: *My bike's got a puncture.*
crack a very narrow space between two things or two parts of something: *The snake slid into a crack in the rock. | She was peering through the crack in the curtains.*
slot a straight narrow hole that you put a particular type of object into: *You have to put a coin in the slot before you dial the number. | A small disk fits into a slot in the camera.*
crater a round hole in the ground made by an explosion or by a large object hitting it hard: *a volcanic crater*

hole[2] *v* **1** [I,T] to hit the ball into a hole in golf: *He* **holed** *the* **putt** *with ease.* → see picture at **GOLF** **2 be holed** if a ship is holed, something makes a hole in it

hole out *phr v* to hit the ball into a hole in golf

hole up (*also* **be holed up**) *phr v informal* to hide somewhere for a period of time: **[+in/with/at]** *The gunmen are still holed up in the town.*

ˌhole-in-the-ˈwall *n* [C] **1** *BrE informal* a machine in or outside a bank from which you can obtain money using a special card SYN **ATM**, **cash machine** **2** *AmE* a small dark shop or restaurant

hol·ey /ˈhəʊli $ ˈhoʊ-/ *adj* full of holes: *holey sweaters*

hol·i·day[1] /ˈhɒlədi, -deɪ $ ˈhɑːlədeɪ/ ●●● S1 W2 *n*
1 [C,U] *BrE* (*also* **holidays**) a time of rest from work, school etc SYN **vacation** *AmE*: *The school holidays start tomorrow.* | **on holiday** *I'm away on holiday until the 1st of June.* | **in the holidays** *He came to stay with us in the school holidays.* | **[+from]** *a holiday from her usual responsibilities*

> **REGISTER**
> In everyday British English, when someone is temporarily away from their work or studies, people often say they are **off**, rather than **on holiday**. Note, however, that **off** can also mean that someone is away from their work or studies because they are sick: *'Where's Kate?' 'She's **off** this week.'*

2 [C,U] *BrE* (*also* **holidays**) a period of time when you travel to another place for pleasure SYN **vacation** *AmE*: *We're going to Spain for our holidays.* | **on holiday** *He caught malaria while on holiday in Africa.* | *I haven't had a proper holiday for two years.*
3 [C] a day fixed by law on which people do not have to go to work or school: *The 4th of July is a **national holiday** in the US.*
4 the holiday season (*also* **the holidays**) **a)** *AmE* the period between Thanksgiving and New Year **b)** *BrE* the period in the summer when most people take a holiday → BANK HOLIDAY, PUBLIC HOLIDAY

> **COLLOCATIONS – MEANINGS 1 & 2**
>
> **VERBS**
> **go on holiday** *The children were excited about going on holiday.*
> **have/take a holiday** *Teachers cannot take holidays during term time.*
> **book a holiday** *I booked the holiday online.*
>
> **ADJECTIVES/NOUN + holiday**
> **a skiing/camping/walking etc holiday** *They went on a camping holiday in France.*
> **a package holiday** (=a holiday in which you pay a price that includes travel, room, and food) *The company organizes package holidays to Spain and Greece.*
> **a summer holiday** *They were going to a house on the coast for their summer holidays.*
> **a winter holiday** *Why not try a winter holiday for a change?*
> **a family holiday** *I first visited Orkney on a family holiday when I was a boy.*
> **an annual holiday** (=a holiday you take every year) | **your dream holiday** (=the best holiday you can imagine)
>
> **holiday + NOUN**
> **a holiday resort** (=a place with many hotels where a lot of people go on holiday) *a holiday resort in Spain*
> **a holiday destination** (=a town or country where a lot of people go on holiday) *Marmaris is one of Turkey's most popular holiday destinations.*
> **a holiday brochure** (=a magazine that shows what holidays you can take) | **holiday photos** (*also* **holiday snaps** *informal*) (=photographs that you take when you are on holiday) | **a holiday romance** (=a brief romantic relationship with someone you meet on holiday) | **a holiday abroad** (=a holiday in a country other than the one you live in)
>
> **PHRASES**
> **the holiday of a lifetime** (=a very good or expensive holiday that you will only take once)

holiday[2] *v* [I] *BrE* to spend your holiday in a place – used especially in news reports SYN **vacation** *AmE*: **[+in/at]** *They're holidaying in Majorca.*

ˈholiday ˌcamp *n* [C] *BrE* a place where people go for their holidays and where activities are organized for them

ˈholiday ˌhome *n* [C] *BrE* a house that someone owns where they go during their holidays

hol·i·day·mak·er /ˈhɒlədiˌmeɪkə $ ˈhɑːlədeɪˌmeɪkər/ *n* [C] *BrE* someone who has travelled to a place on holiday → **tourist** SYN **vacationer** *AmE*

ˌholier-than-ˈthou *adj* showing that you think you are morally better than other people – used to show disapproval SYN **self-righteous**

hol·i·ness /ˈhəʊlinəs $ ˈhoʊ-/ *n* **1** [U] the quality of being pure and good in a religious way **2 Your/His Holiness** used as a title for talking to or about the Pope

ho·lis·tic /həʊˈlɪstɪk $ hoʊ-/ *adj* **1** considering a person or thing as a whole, rather than as separate parts: *a holistic approach to design* **2 holistic medicine/treatment/healing etc** medical treatment based on the belief that the whole person must be treated, not just the part of their body that has a disease → **alternative medicine** —**holistically** /-kli/ *adv*

ˌhol·lan·daise /ˌhɒlənˈdeɪz $ ˈhɑːləndeɪz/ (*also* **ˌhollandaise ˈsauce**) *n* [U] a creamy sauce made with butter, eggs, and LEMON

hol·ler /ˈhɒlə $ ˈhɑːlər/ *v* [I,T] *especially AmE informal* to shout loudly SYN **yell**: **[+at]** *I heard someone hollering at me.* —**holler** *n* [C]

hol·low[1] /ˈhɒləʊ $ ˈhɑː-/ ●●○ *adj*
1 EMPTY INSIDE having an empty space inside: *a hollow tree* THESAURUS▸ EMPTY
2 hollow eyes/cheeks etc eyes etc where the skin sinks inwards: *He was short and thin, with hollow eyes.*
3 SOUND a hollow sound is low and clear like the sound made when you hit something empty: *There was a hollow thump as the cars collided.*
4 NO VALUE words, events, or people that are hollow have no real worth or value: *They won, but it was a **hollow victory**.* | *Even as he spoke, Ivan was well aware of the **hollow ring** to his words.*
5 hollow laugh/voice etc a hollow laugh or voice makes a weak sound and is without emotion —**hollowly** *adv*: *Sam laughed hollowly.* —**hollowness** *n* [U]

hollow[2] *n* [C] a place in something that is at a slightly lower level than its surface SYN **dip**: *Make a slight hollow in the middle of each cake.*

hollow[3] *v* [T] to make the surface of something curve inwards: *The steps were hollowed by centuries of use.* GRAMMAR **Hollow** is usually passive.
hollow sth ↔ **out** *phr v* to make a hole or empty space by removing the inside part of something

hol·ly /ˈhɒli $ ˈhɑːli/ *n* (*plural* **hollies**) [C,U] a small tree with sharp dark green leaves and red berries (BERRY), or the leaves and berries of this tree, used as a decoration at Christmas → see picture at FLOWER[1]

hol·ly·hock /ˈhɒlihɒk $ ˈhɑːlihɑːk/ *n* [C] a tall thin garden plant with many flowers growing together

Hol·ly·wood /ˈhɒliwʊd $ ˈhɑː-/ a part of Los Angeles in California where films are made, often used to refer to the film industry in general: *She is one of Hollywood's major stars.*

Holmes, Sher·lock /həʊmz, ˈʃɜːlɒk $ ˈʃɜːrlɑːk/ the main character in the stories by Sir Arthur Conan Doyle. He is very clever and he always notices very small details and then uses them to guess what has happened. He is known for wearing a DEERSTALKER (=a type of hat), smoking a PIPE, and playing the VIOLIN. People often think he uses the phrase 'Elementary, my dear Watson' when he is explaining to his friend, Dr Watson, how easy it is to understand something. In fact, this phrase does not appear in any of the stories. Nevertheless, people sometimes use it to emphasize how simple a solution to a problem is.

hol·o·caust /ˈhɒləkɔːst $ ˈhɑːləkɒːst/ *n* [C] **1** a situation in which there is great destruction and a lot of people die: *a nuclear holocaust* **2 the Holocaust** the killing of millions of

H

Jews and other people by the Nazis during the Second World War → **genocide**

hol·o·gram /ˈhɒləɡræm $ ˈhoʊl-,ˈhɑːl-/ *n* [C] a kind of photograph made with a LASER that looks as if it is not flat when you look at it from an angle —**holographic** /ˌhɒləˈɡræfɪk◂ $ ˌhoʊl-, ˌhɑːl-/ *adj* —**holography** /hɒˈlɒɡrəfi $ hoʊ-, hɑː-/ *n* [U]

hols /hɒlz $ hɑːlz/ *n* [plural] *BrE old-fashioned* holidays

Hol·stein /ˈhɒlstaɪn $ ˈhoʊl-/ *n* [C] *AmE* a black and white cow SYN **Friesian** *BrE*

hol·ster /ˈhəʊlstə $ ˈhoʊlstər/ *n* [C] a leather object for carrying a small gun, that is worn on a belt

ho·ly /ˈhəʊli $ ˈhoʊ-/ ●●● W3 *adj* (*comparative* **holier**, *superlative* **holiest**)
1 connected with God and religion → **sacred**: *the holy city of Varanasi* THESAURUS ▶ RELIGIOUS
2 very religious: *a holy man*
3 holy cow/mackerel etc *spoken* used to express feelings such as surprise or fear
4 a holy terror *informal* someone, especially a child, who causes problems for other people → **take (holy) orders** at ORDER[1](18)

ˌHoly ˈBible, the the holy book of the Christian religion SYN **the Bible**

ˌHoly Comˈmunion *n* [U] the Christian ceremony in which people eat bread and drink wine as signs of Christ's body and blood SYN **Communion**

ˌHoly ˈFamily, the Jesus, his mother Mary, and her husband Joseph

ˌHoly ˈFather *n* [singular] used when speaking to or about the Pope

ˌHoly ˈGhost, the God in the form of a SPIRIT according to the Christian religion SYN **Holy Spirit**

ˌHoly ˈGrail *n* **1** [singular] something that people want very much, but which is very difficult or impossible to achieve: **[+of]** *Nuclear fusion is the Holy Grail of energy production.* **2 the Holy Grail** the cup believed to have been used by Christ before his death

ˈHoly Land, the the parts of the Middle East where most of the events mentioned in the Bible happened

ˌholy of ˈholies *n* [singular] **1** *humorous* a special place where only a few people are allowed to go **2 the Holy of Holies** the most holy part of a Jewish temple

ˌHoly ˈSee, the *formal* the authority of the Pope, and everything he is responsible for

ˌHoly ˈSpirit *n* [singular] God in the form of a SPIRIT according to the Christian religion SYN **Holy Ghost**

ˈholy ˌwar *n* [C] a war that is fought to defend the beliefs of a religion → **crusade**, **jihad**

ˌholy ˈwater *n* [U] water that has been BLESSed by a priest

ˈHoly Week *n* [singular] the week before Easter in the Christian church

ˌHoly ˈWrit *n* [U] **1** writing or instructions that people treat as if it were completely true in every detail: *Lenin's word was by no means accepted as holy writ.* **2** *old-fashioned* the Bible

hom·age /ˈhɒmɪdʒ $ ˈhɑː-/ *n* [singular] *formal* something you do to show respect for someone or something you think is important: *The film* ***pays homage to*** *Martin Scorsese's 'Mean Streets'.*

hom·bre /ˈɒmbreɪ $ ˈɑːm-/ *n* [C] *AmE informal* a man, especially one who is strong

hom·burg /ˈhɒmbɜːɡ $ ˈhɑːmbɜːrɡ/ *n* [C] a soft hat for men, with a wide BRIM (=edge)

HOMES (ANIMALS)

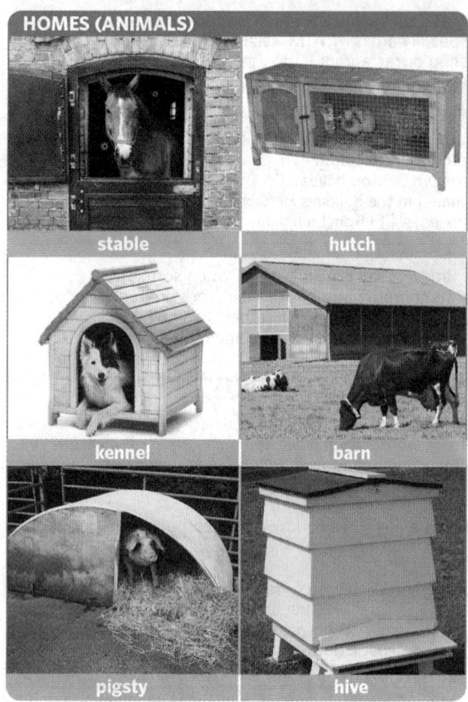

home¹ /həʊm $ hoʊm/ ●●● S1 W1 *n*
1 PLACE WHERE YOU LIVE [C,U] the house, apartment, or place where you live: *They have a beautiful home in California.* | *Good luck in your new home!* | **at home** *Last night we stayed at home and watched TV.* | **away from home** *He was spending more and more time away from home.* | **work from/at home** (=do your work at home instead of at a company office) | *A family of birds* ***made*** *their* ***home*** (=started living) *under the roof.*
2 FAMILY [C,U] the place where a child lived with his or her family: *Jack* ***left home*** *when he was 16.* | *Were you still* ***living at home*** (=with your parents)? | *Carrie moved out of the* ***family home*** *a year ago.*
3 WHERE YOU CAME FROM/BELONG [C,U] the place where you came from or where you usually live, especially when this is the place where you feel happy and comfortable: *She was born in Italy, but she's* ***made*** *Charleston her* ***home***. | **back home** *The folks back home don't really understand what life is like here.*
4 YOUR COUNTRY [U] the country where you live, as opposed to foreign countries: **at home** *auto sales at home and abroad* | **back home** *He's been travelling, but he's kept up with what's going on back home.*
5 be/feel at home a) to feel comfortable in a place or with a person: **[+in/with]** *I'm already feeling at home in the new apartment.* | *After a while we began to feel at home with each other.* **b)** to feel happy or confident about doing or using something: **[+with/in]** *Practise using the camera until you feel quite at home with it.*
6 PROPERTY [C] a house, apartment etc considered as property which you can buy or sell: *Attractive modern homes for sale.*
7 FOR TAKING CARE OF SB [C] a place where people who are very old or sick, or children who have no family, are looked after: *an old people's home* | *I could never* ***put*** *Dad* ***into a home***. → CHILDREN'S HOME, NURSING HOME, REST HOME
8 make yourself at home *spoken* used to tell someone who is visiting you that they should relax: *Sit down and make yourself at home.*
9 make sb feel at home to make someone feel relaxed by being friendly towards them: *We like to make our customers feel at home.*
10 the home of sth a) the place where something was first

discovered, made, or developed: *America is the home of baseball.* **b)** the place where a plant or animal grows or lives: *India is the home of elephants and tigers.*
11 SPORTS TEAM **at home** if a sports team plays at home, they play at their own sports field OPP **away**: **[+to]** *Birmingham Bullets are at home to Kingston.*
12 home from home *BrE*, **home away from home** *AmE* a place that you think is as pleasant and comfortable as your own house
13 home sweet home used to say how nice it is to be in your own home
14 dogs'/cats' home *BrE* a place where animals with no owners are looked after
15 find a home for sth *BrE* to find a place where something can be kept: *Can you find a home for the piano?*
16 what's that when it's at home? *BrE spoken* used humorously to ask what a long or unusual word means
17 GAMES [U] a place in some games or sports which a player must try to reach in order to win a point → HOME PLATE, HOME RUN

THESAURUS

home the house, apartment, or place where you live: *More and more people are working from home. | It was past midnight by the time I got home.*
house a building that someone lives in, especially a building intended for one person, couple, or family: *Shall we meet at your house? | Have you seen Dave's new house – it's huge!*
place *spoken informal* the house, apartment, or room where someone lives: *We went to Sara's place after the movie.*
residence *formal* the house or apartment where someone lives, especially a large or official one: *The prime minister's official residence is 10 Downing Street.*
holiday home *BrE*, **vacation home** *AmE* a house that someone owns by the sea, in the mountains etc, where they go for their holidays: *They bought a luxury holiday home in Spain.*

home² ●●● S1 W1 *adv*
1 to or at the place where you live: *Is Sue home from work yet?* | **bring/take sb/sth home** *They brought the baby home from the hospital on Friday.* | *We* ***stayed home*** *last night.* | *I'm* ***going home*** *now. See you tomorrow.* | **come/get/reach etc home** (=arrive at your home) *It was midnight by the time we got home.* | *What time are you coming home?*
2 take home £120 per week/$600 a month etc to earn a certain amount of money after tax has been taken off: *The average worker takes home around $300 a week.*
3 hit/drive/hammer etc sth home a) to make sure that someone understands what you mean by saying it in an extremely direct and determined way: *We really need to drive this message home.* **b)** to hit or push something firmly into the correct position
4 bring sth home to sb/come home to sb to make you realize how serious, difficult, or dangerous something is: *The episode has brought home to me the pointlessness of this war.*
5 hit/strike home if a remark, situation, or experience hits home, it makes you realize how serious, difficult, or dangerous something is: *She could see that her remark had hit home.*
6 be home and dry *BrE informal* to have succeeded in doing something
7 be home free *AmE informal* to have succeeded in doing the most difficult part of something: *If I last five years with no symptoms, I'll be home free.* → **close to home** at CLOSE²(19)

GRAMMAR: Patterns with home

• You **go home**, **come home**, or **get home**: *We all went home. | I wish he'd come home. | What time did you get home?* ✗ Don't say: *We all went to home. | I wish he'd come to home. | What time did you get to home?*
• You **go back home** or **come back home**: *Why don't you go back home and rest?* ✗ Don't say: *back to home*

home³ ●●● W3 *adj* [only before noun]
1 relating to or belonging to your home or family: **home address/number** (=the address or telephone number of your house) | *These children need a proper* ***home life***.
2 done at home or intended for use in a home: *good old-fashioned* ***home cooking*** | *a home computer*
3 played or playing at a team's own sports field, rather than an opponent's field: **home team/game/crowd/club etc** *The home team took the lead after 25 minutes.*
4 relating to a particular country, as opposed to foreign countries SYN **domestic**: *The meat was destined for the home market.*

home⁴ ●○○ *v*
home in on sth *phr v*
1 to aim exactly at an object or place and move directly to it: *The bat can home in on insects using a kind of 'radar'.*
2 to direct your efforts or attention towards a particular fault or problem: *He homed in on the one weak link in the argument.*

'home base *n* **1** [C, usually singular] the place that someone returns to in order to rest, learn new things, or exchange information: *The band's home base is Seattle.* **2** [C, usually singular] the main office of a company SYN **headquarters** **3** [singular] *AmE* the place where you stand to hit the ball in baseball SYN **home plate**

home·bod·y /ˈhəʊmˌbɒdi $ ˈhoʊmˌbɑːdi/ *n* (*plural* **homebodies**) [C] *informal* someone who enjoys being at home

home·boy /ˈhəʊmbɔɪ $ ˈhoʊm-/ *n* [C] *AmE informal* a friend or someone from the same area or GANG as you – used especially by young people

ˌhome ˈbrew *n* [U] *informal* beer made at home —**home-brewed** *adj*

home·buy·er /ˈhəʊmˌbaɪə $ ˈhoʊmˌbaɪər/ *n* [C] someone who is buying a home

home·com·ing /ˈhəʊmˌkʌmɪŋ $ ˈhoʊm-/ *n* **1** [C] an occasion when someone comes back to their home after a long absence **2** [C,U] *AmE* an occasion when former students return to their high school or college

ˌHome ˈCounties, the the counties (COUNTY) around London

ˌhome ecoˈnomics *n* [U] the study of cooking, sewing, and other skills used at home, taught as a subject at school

ˌhome ˈfront *n* [singular] the people who stay and work in their own country while others go abroad to fight in a war: **on the home front** *The film is set on the home front in 1943.*

home·girl /ˈhəʊmgɜːl $ ˈhoʊmgɜːrl/ *n* [C] a female HOMEY

home·grown /ˌhəʊmˈgrəʊn◂ $ ˌhoʊmˈgroʊn◂/ *adj* **1** made or produced in your own country, town etc: *home-grown rock stars* **2** homegrown vegetables and fruit are grown in your own garden

ˌhome ˈhelp *n* [C] *BrE* someone who helps ill or old people in their homes with cleaning, cooking etc

ˌHome Inforˈmation Pack *n* [C] (*abbreviation* **HIP**) a set of documents that a person in England and Wales must show to people who want to buy their home. These include documents showing who owns the home, and how much energy it uses.

home·land /ˈhəʊmlænd, -lənd $ ˈhoʊm-/ ●○○ *n* [C]
1 the country where someone was born
2 a large area of land where a particular group of people can live

ˌhomeland seˈcurity *n* [U] actions taken by the US government after the TERRORIST attacks of September 11th, 2001 to prevent TERRORISM within the US. These actions include watching people who are thought to be involved in TERRORIST activities, and putting them in prison if necessary. They also include preparations for using the army, police, doctors etc immediately if there is a terrorist attack.

home·less /ˈhəʊmləs $ ˈhoʊm-/ ●●○ *adj*
1 without a home: *Thousands of people have been* ***made*** *homeless.*
2 the homeless [plural] people who have nowhere to live, and who often live on the streets —**homelessness** *n* [U]

ˌhome ˈloan *n* [C] *informal* an amount of money that you borrow in order to buy a home SYN **mortgage**

home·ly /ˈhəʊmli $ ˈhoʊm-/ *adj* **1** *BrE* simple in a way that makes you feel comfortable: *a modern hotel with a homely atmosphere* **2** *BrE* a homely person is warm and friendly and enjoys home life: *Mrs Keane is a comfortable, homely person.* **3** *AmE* not very attractive SYN **plain** *BrE*

home·made /ˌhəʊmˈmeɪd◂ $ ˌhoʊm-/ *adj* made at home and not bought from a shop OPP **shop-bought**: *homemade cake*

home·mak·er /ˈhəʊmˌmeɪkə $ ˈhoʊmˌmeɪkər/ *n* [C] *especially AmE* a woman who works at home cleaning and cooking etc and does not have another job SYN **housewife**

ˌhome ˈmovie *n* [C] a film you make, often of a family occasion, that is intended to be shown at home SYN **home video**

ˌhome ˈoffice *n* [C] a room in someone's home where that person works, which usually has equipment such as a computer, FAX machine etc → **study**

ˈHome ˌOffice, the the British government department that deals with keeping order in the country, controlling who enters the country etc → **Foreign Office**

ho·me·op·a·thy /ˌhəʊmiˈɒpəθi $ ˌhoʊmiˈɑːp-/ *n* [U] a system of medicine in which a disease is treated by giving extremely small amounts of a substance that causes the disease —**homeopathic** /ˌhəʊmiəˈpæθɪk◂ $ ˌhoʊ-/ *adj* —**homeopath** /ˈhəʊmiəˌpæθ $ ˈhoʊ-/ *n* [C]

home·own·er /ˈhəʊmˌəʊnə $ ˈhoʊmˌoʊnər/ ●○○ *n* [C] someone who owns their home

home·page, **home page** /ˈhəʊmpeɪdʒ $ ˈhoʊm-/ ●●● S2 W1 *n* [C] the first page of a website, which often contains LINKS to other pages on that website

ˈhome plate *n* [singular] the place where you stand to hit the ball in baseball, and the last place the player who is running must touch in order to get a point SYN **home base** → see picture at BASEBALL

hom·er /ˈhəʊmə $ ˈhoʊmər/ *n* [C] *AmE informal* a home run in baseball —**homer** *v* [I]

ˈhome room *n* [C] *AmE* a classroom where students have to go at the beginning of every school day

ˌhome ˈrule *n* [U] the right of a country or area to have its own government and laws

ˌhome ˈrun *n* [C] a long hit in BASEBALL which allows the player who hits the ball to run around all the BASES and get a point: *I didn't think I could* ***hit*** *a* ***home run****.*

home·school /ˈhəʊmskuːl $ ˈhoʊm-/ *v* [I,T] to teach children at home instead of sending them to school: *She and her husband homeschool their three kids.* | *Why did you decide to homeschool?* | *homeschooled students* —**homeschooling** *n* [U]: *information about homeschooling* —**homeschool** *adj* [only before noun]: *homeschool programs* | *a group of homeschool families*

ˌHome ˈSecretary *n* [C] the British government minister who is in charge of the Home Office → **Foreign Secretary**

home·sick /ˈhəʊmˌsɪk $ ˈhoʊm-/ ●●○ *adj* feeling unhappy because you are a long way from your home THESAURUS SAD —**homesickness** *n* [U]

ˈhome ˌsourcing *n* [U] *AmE* the practice of providing a service, especially dealing with telephone calls from customers, using people working from their homes

home·spun /ˈhəʊmspʌn $ ˈhoʊm-/ *adj* **1** homespun ideas are simple and ordinary **2** homespun cloth is woven at home

home·stay /ˈhəʊmsteɪ $ ˈhoʊm-/ *n* [U] *AmE* an arrangement in which someone from a foreign country stays with local people while studying or on holiday: *Homestay accommodation is available for students from abroad.*

home·stead¹ /ˈhəʊmsted, -stəd $ ˈhoʊm-/ *n* [C] **1** a farm and the area of land around it **2** *AmE* a piece of land, usually for farming, given to people in the past by the US government

homestead² *v* [I,T] *AmE* to live and work on a homestead —**homesteader** *n* [C]

ˌhome ˈstretch *n* [singular] **1** (*also* **home straight** *BrE*) the last part of a race where there is a straight line to the finish **2** the last part of an activity or journey: **in/into the home stretch** *as the election campaign headed into the home stretch*

ˌhome ˈtown *especially BrE*, **home·town** *especially AmE* /ˌhəʊmˈtaʊn $ ˌhoʊm-/ *n* [C] the place where you were born and spent your childhood: **sb's home town** *He hired a car and drove up to his home town.* | *She's written for her hometown newspaper.*

ˌhome ˈtruth *n* [C usually plural] a true but unpleasant fact that someone tells you about yourself: *It's time someone* ***told*** *him* ***a few home truths****.*

ˌhome ˈvideo *n* [C] *BrE* a film you make, often of a family occasion, that is intended to be shown at home SYN **home movie** *AmE*

home·ward /ˈhəʊmwəd $ ˈhoʊmwərd/ *adv* **1** (*also* **homewards** *BrE*) towards home: *She turned and made her way homeward.* **2 homeward bound** *literary* going towards home —**homeward** *adj*: *his homeward trip*

home·work /ˈhəʊmwɜːk $ ˈhoʊmwɜːrk/ ●●● S2 *n* [U]
1 work that a student at school is asked to do at home → **classwork**: ***For homework****, finish the exercise on page 14.*
2 if you do your homework, you prepare for an important activity by finding out information you need → **research**: *It's worth* ***doing*** *a bit of* ***homework*** *before buying a computer.*

GRAMMAR: Countable or uncountable?

- **Homework** is an uncountable noun and is not used in the plural. You say: *The teacher gave us a lot of homework.* ✗ Don't say: *The teacher gave us a lot of homeworks.*
- **Homework** is always followed by a singular verb. *The homework* ***was*** *really difficult.*
- When talking about one essay or exercise that you have to do, you say a **piece of homework**: *I just have one more piece of homework to do.*

COLLOCATIONS

VERBS

do your homework *Paul, have you done your homework?*
give (sb) homework (*also* **set (sb) homework** *BrE*) *The teacher gave them some homework to do by Monday.*
help sb with their homework *I often have to help her with her homework.*
hand in your homework (=give it to the teacher) *You must hand in your homework by Friday.*

NOUNS + homework

biology/history/French etc homework *The science homework was really hard.*

COMMON ERRORS

⚠ Don't say 'make/write your homework'. Say **do your homework**.

home·work·er /ˈhəʊmˌwɜːkə $ ˈhoʊmˌwɜːrkər/ *n* [C] someone who does their job in their home → **teleworker** —**homeworking** *n* [U]

hom·ey¹ /ˈhəʊmi $ ˈhoʊ-/ *adj especially AmE* pleasant, like home SYN **homely** *BrE*: *The restaurant has a relaxed homey atmosphere.*

homey² *n* [C] *AmE informal* a friend or someone who comes from your area or GANG

hom·i·cid·al /ˌhɒməˈsaɪdl◂ $ ˌhɑː-/ *adj* likely to murder someone: *a homicidal maniac*

hom·i·cide /ˈhɒmɪsaɪd $ ˈhɑː-/ ●○○ *n*
1 [C,U] *especially AmE* the crime of murder → **manslaughter** THESAURUS CRIME
2 [U] *AmE* the police department that deals with murders

hom·i·ly /ˈhɒməli $ ˈhɑː-/ *n* (*plural* **homilies**) [C] **1** *formal* advice about how to behave that is often unwanted **2** *literary* a speech given as part of a Christian church ceremony

hom·ing /ˈhəʊmɪŋ $ ˈhoʊm-/ *adj* a bird or animal that has a homing instinct has a special ability that helps it find its way home over long distances

ˈ**homing deˌvice** *n* [C usually singular] a special part of a weapon that helps it to find its target

ˈ**homing ˌpigeon** *n* [C] a PIGEON that is able to find its way home over long distances

hom·i·nid /ˈhɒmənɪd $ ˈhɑː-/ *n* [C] *technical* a human being, or a member of the group of animals from which human beings have developed

hom·i·ny /ˈhɒmɪni $ ˈhɑː-/ *n* [U] *AmE* a food made from crushed dried CORN(2)

ho·mo /ˈhəʊməʊ $ ˈhoʊmoʊ/ *n* (*plural* **homos**) [C] *taboo informal* a very offensive word for a HOMOSEXUAL. Do not use this word.

homo- /həʊməʊ, -mə, hɒmə $ hoʊmoʊ, -mə, hɑːmə/ *prefix formal or technical* same: **homosexual** (=sexually attracted to people of the same sex) | **homographs** (=words spelled the same way)

ho·moe·o·path /ˈhəʊmiəˌpæθ $ ˈhoʊ-/ *n* [C] a British spelling of HOMEOPATH

ho·moe·op·athy /ˌhəʊmiˈɒpəθi $ ˌhoʊmiˈɑːp-/ *n* [U] a British spelling of HOMEOPATHY

ho·mo·ge·ne·ous /ˌhəʊməˈdʒiːniəs◂ $ ˌhoʊ-/ ●○○ (*also* **ho·mo·ge·nous** /həˈmɒdʒɪnəs $ -ˈmɑː-/) *adj* consisting of people or things that are all of the same type → **heterogeneous**: *a homogeneous society* —**homogeneously** *adv*

ho·mo·ge·nize (*also* **-ise** *BrE*) /həˈmɒdʒənaɪz $ -ˈmɑː-/ *v* [T] to change something so that its parts become similar or the same: *plans to homogenize the various school systems*

ho·mo·ge·nized (*also* **-ised** *BrE*) /həˈmɒdʒənaɪzd $ -ˈmɑː-/ *adj* homogenized milk has had the cream on top mixed with the milk

hom·o·graph /ˈhɒməgrɑːf, ˈhəʊ- $ ˈhɑːməgræf, ˈhoʊ-/ *n* [C] *technical* a word that is spelled the same as another, but is different in meaning, origin, grammar, or pronunciation. For example, the noun 'record' is a homograph of the verb 'record'. → **homonym**, **homophone**

hom·o·nym /ˈhɒmənɪm, ˈhəʊ- $ ˈhɑː-, ˈhoʊ-/ *n* [C] *technical* a word that is spelled the same and sounds the same as another, but is different in meaning or origin. For example, the noun 'bear' and the verb 'bear' are homonyms. → **homograph**, **homophone**

ho·mo·pho·bi·a /ˌhəʊməˈfəʊbiə $ ˌhoʊməˈfoʊ-/ *n* [U] hatred and fear of HOMOSEXUALS THESAURUS PREJUDICE —**homophobic** *adj*

hom·o·phone /ˈhɒməfəʊn, ˈhəʊ- $ ˈhɑːməfoʊn, ˈhoʊ-/ *n* [C] *technical* a word that sounds the same as another but is different in spelling, meaning, or origin. For example, 'knew' and 'new' are homophones. → **homograph**, **homonym**

Ho·mo sa·pi·ens /ˌhəʊməʊ ˈsæpienz $ ˌhoʊmoʊ ˈseɪpiənz/ *n* [U] *technical* the type of human being that exists now

ho·mo·sex·u·al /ˌhəʊməˈsekʃuəl, ˌhɒmə- $ ˌhoʊ-/ ●○○ *adj formal* if someone, especially a man, is homosexual, they are sexually attracted to people of the same sex SYN **gay** → **heterosexual**, **bisexual**: *Ruth's brother was homosexual.* | *homosexual men* | *a homosexual relationship* —**homosexual** *n* [C] —**homosexuality** /ˌhəʊməsekʃuˈæləti, ˌhɒ- $ ˌhoʊ-/ *n* [U]

hon /hʌn/ *pron AmE spoken* a short form of HONEY, used to address someone you love: *I'm sorry, hon.*

Hon. (*also* **Hon** *BrE*) **1** the written abbreviation of ***honourable***: *the Hon George Borwick* **2** *BrE* the written abbreviation of ***honorary***, used in official job titles: *the Hon. Treasurer*

hon·cho /ˈhɒntʃəʊ $ ˈhɑːntʃoʊ/ *n* (*plural* **honchos**) [C] *informal* an important person who controls something, especially a business SYN **boss**: *the **head honcho***

hone /həʊn $ hoʊn/ *v* [T] **1** to improve your skill at doing something, especially when you are already very good at it: *He set about **honing** his **skills** as a draughtsman.* | ***finely honed*** (=extremely well-developed) *intuition*
2 *formal* to make knives, swords etc sharp SYN **sharpen**

hon·est /ˈɒnɪst $ ˈɑːn-/ ●●● S2 W3 *adj*
1 CHARACTER someone who is honest always tells the truth and does not cheat or steal OPP **dishonest**: *He was a hard-working honest man.* | *Ann had an honest face.*
2 STATEMENT/ANSWER ETC not hiding the truth or the facts about something SYN **frank**: *Do you want my honest opinion?* | *an honest answer* | ***Let's be honest**: the only reason she married him was for his money.* | **[+with]** *At least he was honest with you.* | **[+about]** *She was always very honest about her feelings.* → see Thesaurus box on *p. 884*
3 to be honest (with you) *spoken* used when you tell someone what you really think: *To be honest, I don't like him very much.*
4 honest! *spoken* used to try to make someone believe you: *I didn't mean to hurt him, honest!*
5 honest to God *spoken* used to emphasize that something you say is true: *Honest to God, I wasn't there.*
6 WORK honest work is done using your own efforts and without cheating: *I bet he's never **done an honest day's work** in his life!* | *I'm just trying to **earn an honest living**.*
7 ORDINARY GOOD PEOPLE honest people are not famous or special, but behave in a good, socially acceptable way: *She came from a good honest working-class background.*
8 make an honest woman (out) of sb *old-fashioned* to marry a woman because you have had a sexual relationship with her

hon·est·ly /ˈɒnəstli $ ˈɑːn-/ ●●○ S3 *adv*
1 used to emphasize that what you are saying is true, even though it may seem surprising: *I honestly don't know how old my parents are.* | *I can honestly say that I never worry about him now.*
2 *spoken* used when you are shocked or annoyed by something someone has said or done SYN **really**: *Honestly! Do you ever listen?*
3 *spoken* used to try to make someone believe that what you have just said is true: *It wasn't me, honestly!*
4 in an honest way SYN **truthfully**: *Tell me honestly, Kate, what do you think of John?* | *We talked openly and honestly.* | *'No, I don't,' she answered honestly.*

ˌ**honest-to-ˈgoodness** *adj* [only before noun] simple and good: *plain honest-to-goodness home cooking*

hon·es·ty /ˈɒnəsti $ ˈɑːn-/ ●●○ *n* [U]
1 the quality of being honest OPP **dishonesty**: *a politician of rare honesty and courage*
2 in all honesty used when telling someone that what you are saying is what you really think: *It was not, in all honesty, a very good start.*

ˈ**honesty box** *n* [C] *BrE* a box for people to put money in to pay for something, when there is no one there to take the payment

hon·ey /ˈhʌni/ ●●● S2 *n*
1 [U] a sweet sticky substance produced by BEES, used as food
2 *spoken especially AmE* used to address someone you love SYN **love**: *Hi, honey.*
3 [C] *informal* an attractive woman

hon·ey·bee /ˈhʌnibiː/ *n* [C] a BEE that makes honey → **hive**

hon·ey·comb /ˈhʌnikəʊm $ -koʊm/ *n* [C] **1** a structure made by BEES, which consists of many six-sided cells in which honey is stored **2** something that is arranged or shaped in this pattern

H

hon·ey·combed /ˈhʌnikəʊmd $ -koʊmd/ *adj* [+with] filled with many holes, hollow passages etc

hon·ey·dew /ˈhʌnidjuː $ -duː/ *n* **1** [U] a sticky substance that some insects leave on plants **2** [C] (*also* **honeydew melon**) a type of MELON with yellow skin and green flesh

hon·eyed /ˈhʌnid/ *adj* **1** *literary* honeyed words or honeyed voices sound soft and pleasant, but are often insincere **2** tasting like HONEY or covered in honey

hon·ey·moon¹ /ˈhʌnimuːn/ ●○○ *n* [C]
1 a holiday taken by two people who have just got married: **on your honeymoon** *We went to Italy on our honeymoon.*
2 (*also* **honeymoon period**) the period of time when a new government, leader etc has just started and no one criticizes them: *By 1987, the* ***honeymoon was over****.*

honeymoon² *v* [I always + adv/prep] to go somewhere for your honeymoon —**honeymooner** *n* [C]

hon·ey·pot /ˈhʌnipɒt $ -pɑːt/ *n* [C] *BrE* something that is attractive to a lot of people SYN **magnet**

hon·ey·suck·le /ˈhʌniˌsʌkəl/ *n* [C,U] a climbing plant with pleasant-smelling yellow or pink flowers

honk¹ /hɒŋk $ hɑːŋk, hɒːŋk/ *n* [C] **1** a loud noise made by a car horn **2** a loud noise made by a GOOSE

honk² *v* [I,T] if a car horn or a GOOSE honks, it makes a loud noise: *Several drivers honked their horns.*

hon·ky, **honkie** /ˈhɒŋki $ ˈhɑːŋ-, ˈhɒːŋ-/ *n* (*plural* **honkies**) [C] *AmE taboo* a very offensive word for a white person, used by black people. Do not use this word.

honky-tonk¹ /ˈhɒŋki tɒŋk $ ˈhɑːŋki tɑːŋk, ˈhɒːŋki tɒːŋk/ *n* [C] *AmE* a cheap bar where COUNTRY MUSIC is played

honky-tonk² *adj* **honky-tonk music/piano** a type of piano music that is played in a loud cheerful way

hon·or /ˈɒnə $ ˈɑːnər/ *n* [C,U] the American spelling of HONOUR

hon·or·a·ble /ˈɒnərəbəl $ ˈɑːn-/ *adj* the American spelling of HONOURABLE

ˌhonorable ˈdischarge *n* [C] *AmE* if you leave the army with an honorable discharge, your behaviour and work have been very good OPP **dishonorable discharge**

hon·o·rar·i·um /ˌɒnəˈreəriəm $ ˌɑːnəˈrer-/ *n* (*plural* **honoraria** /-riə/) [C] *formal* a sum of money offered to a professional for a piece of advice, a speech etc

hon·or·ar·y /ˈɒnərəri $ ˈɑːnəreri/ ●○○ *adj*
1 an honorary title, rank, or university degree is given to someone as an honour: *Brown received an honorary doctorate from Seoul University.*
2 an honorary position in an organization is held without receiving any payment
3 an honorary member of a group is treated like a member of that group but does not belong to it

hon·o·ree /ˌɒnəˈriː $ ˌɑːn-/ *n* [C] someone who receives an honour or AWARD: *Guests clapped and cheered for the honorees.*

hon·or·if·ic /ˌɒnəˈrɪfɪk◂ $ ˌɑːnə-/ *n* [C] an expression or title that is used to show respect for the person you are speaking to

ˈhonor roll *n* [C] *AmE* a list of the best students in a school or college

ˈhonor ˌsystem *n* [singular] *AmE* an agreement between members of a group to obey rules, although no one checks to make sure that they are being followed

hon·our¹ *BrE*, **honor** *AmE* /ˈɒnə $ ˈɑːnər/ ●●○ W3 *n*
1 STH THAT MAKES YOU PROUD [singular] something that makes you feel very proud: *Over 100 players competed for* ***the honour of*** *representing the county in the National Finals.* | **it is an honour to do sth** *It is an honor to have you here, sir.*
2 RESPECT [U] the respect that you, your family, your country etc receive from other people, which makes you feel proud: **[+of]** *He was prepared even to die in order to* ***defend*** *the* ***honour*** *of his family.* | **national/family/personal etc honour** *For the French team, winning tomorrow's game is a matter of national honour.*
3 in honour of sb/sth a) in order to show how much you admire and respect someone: *The stadium was named in honour of the club's first chairman.* | **in sb's honour** *A special dinner will be held in her honour.* **b)** to celebrate an event: *An oak tree was planted* ***in honour of the occasion****.*
4 GIVEN TO SB [C] something such as a special title or MEDAL given to someone to show how much people respect them for what they have achieved: *Reverend Peters was nominated for the honour by colleagues at Walworth Methodist Church.* | **highest honour** (=most important honour) *The medal is the highest* ***honour*** *the association can* ***bestow*** (=give).
5 MORAL PRINCIPLES [U] strong moral beliefs and standards of behaviour that make people respect and trust you: *My father was a* ***man of honour*** *and great integrity.* | *Her actions were always guided by a deep* ***sense of honour*** (=strong desire to do what is morally right). | **matter/point/question of honour** (=something that you feel you must do because of your moral principles) *It had become a point of honour not to tell him about Lori.*

THESAURUS: honest

NOT CHEATING, STEALING, LYING ETC

honest always saying what is true, and not cheating, stealing etc: *I liked them because they were good honest people.* | *You can trust Noah – he's totally honest.*
reputable known to be honest and good in your business or work – used about people, companies, or organizations: *It's best to buy from a reputable company.*
above board [not before noun] honest and legal – used about the way something is done, organized etc: *The deal was entirely above board.*
upright *written* always behaving in an honest way: *an upright citizen* | *George was an upright man from a military family.*

NOT HIDING THE TRUTH OR THE FACTS

honest saying what you really think and not hiding the truth or the facts: *I'm going to ask you something, and I want you to be honest with me.* | *an honest answer*
straight *informal* honest and saying what you really think: *I can't help you if you're not straight with me.* | *I need a straight answer.*
open willing to talk about what you think, feel etc in an honest way, rather than trying to hide it: *People have become more open about their feelings.* | *She's very easy to talk to because she's so open.*
frank speaking honestly and directly about something, especially something that people find difficult to discuss: *In his book, he's brutally frank about his experience with his illness.* | *a frank discussion about sex*
direct saying exactly what you think in an honest clear way, even when this might annoy or upset people: *Not everyone liked his direct manner.* | *She can be very direct.*
blunt speaking in a completely honest way, even if it upsets people, when it would be better to be more careful or polite: *Sorry if I was a bit blunt with you.* | *His hard tone and blunt words were hurtful.*
upfront [not before noun] *informal* talking and behaving in an honest way, even when it is difficult to do this, in a way that people respect: *It's best to be upfront about your financial problems.*
candid *formal* honest about the facts, or about your opinions and feelings, even if other people disapprove of them: *He'd always been completely candid about his past.*

6 AT UNIVERSITY/SCHOOL **a) with honours** *BrE* if you pass a university degree with honours, you pass it at a level that is higher than the most basic level **b) with honors** *AmE* if you finish high school or college with honors, you get one of the highest grades **c) First Class/Second Class Honours** *BrE* the highest or second highest level of degree at a British university
7 Your/His/Her Honour used when speaking to or about a judge: *No, Your Honour.*
8 place of honour the seat or place which is given to the most important guest or object: *The vase she gave me occupies the place of honor in my living room.*
9 with full military honours if someone is buried with full military honours, there is a military ceremony at their funeral
10 do the honours *spoken* to pour the drinks, serve food etc at a social occasion: *Liz, would you do the honors?*
11 your word of honour a very serious promise that what you are saying is true: *I won't try to see you again. I* ***give*** *you my* ***word of honour****.*
12 be an honour to sb/sth to bring admiration and respect to your country, school, family etc because of your behaviour or achievements: *He's an honour to his family and his country.*
13 be/feel honour bound to do sth *formal* to feel that it is your moral duty to do something: *We felt honor bound to attend their wedding.*
14 on your honour a) if you swear on your honour to do something, you promise very seriously to do it **b)** *old-fashioned* if you are on your honour to do something, you are being trusted to do it
15 the honours are even used to say that the people or teams in a competition, game etc have done as well as each other or have the same score
16 SEX [U] *old use* if a woman loses her honour, she has sex with a man she is not married to → **guest of honour** at GUEST[1](1), MAID OF HONOUR

COLLOCATIONS

ADJECTIVES

a great honour *It was a great honour to meet my hero in person.*
a rare honour (=a very special honour that is not given to many people) *Being asked to paint a portrait for the queen is a rare honour for any artist.*
a dubious honour (=something that you are not sure that you should be proud of)

VERBS

have the honour *formal As a young man, he had the honour of meeting Winston Churchill.*
do sb the honour *formal* (=used when saying that you feel proud that someone has decided to do something) *Will you do me the honour of becoming my wife?*

honour² *BrE*, **honor** *AmE* ●●○ *v* [T]
1 be/feel honoured (to do sth) to feel very proud and pleased: *I felt very honoured to be included in the team.*
2 *formal* to show publicly that someone is respected and admired, especially by praising them or giving them a special title: **honour sb with sth** *He was honored with an award for excellence in teaching.* | **honour sb for sth** *Two firefighters have been honoured for their courage.*
3 honour a promise/contract/agreement etc to do what you have agreed to do: *Once again, the government has failed to honour its promises.* | *We pray that both sides will continue to honour their commitment to the peace agreement.*
4 to treat someone with special respect: *In a marriage, you need to honour one another.* | *I was treated like an* ***honored guest****.*
5 honour a cheque if your bank honours a cheque that you have given someone, it pays the money to that person
6 sb has decided to honour us with their presence used humorously when someone arrives late, or to someone who rarely comes to a meeting, class etc

hon·our·a·ble *BrE*, **honorable** *AmE* /ˈɒnərəbəl $ ˈɑːn-/ ●○○ *adj*
1 an honourable action or activity deserves respect and admiration: *My father didn't think acting was an honorable profession.*
2 behaving in a way that is morally correct and shows you have high moral standards: *a principled and honourable man*
3 an honourable arrangement or agreement is fair to everyone who is involved in it —**honourably** *adv*

Honourable *BrE*, **Honorable** *AmE adj* **1** (*written abbreviation* **Hon.**) used in Britain in the titles of children whose father is a lord and in the titles of judges and Members of Parliament **2** (*written abbreviation* **Hon.**) used in the US when writing to or about a judge or important person in the government **3 the Honourable Gentleman/the Honourable Lady/my Honourable Friend/the Honourable Member** used by British members of parliament when talking to or about each other in the House of Commons → RIGHT HONOURABLE

ˌhonourable ˈmention *BrE*, **honorable mention** *AmE n* [C] a special honour in a competition for work that was of high quality but did not get a prize

ˈhonour ˌkilling *BrE*, **honor killing** *AmE n* [C] when a woman living in a country or society with very strict rules about women's moral behaviour is murdered by her father or brother because she has had sex with someone who she is not married to

ˈhonours deˌgree *n* [C] a British university degree that is above the basic level in one or two particular subjects: **first/second/third class honours degree** | **joint honours degree** (=a degree in two main subjects)

ˈhonours ˌlist *n* [C] a list of people in Britain who are given a special title or MEDAL as a reward for the things they have done

hooch, **hootch** /huːtʃ/ *n* [U] *especially AmE informal* strong alcohol, especially alcohol that has been made illegally SYN **moonshine**

hoo·chie /ˈhuːtʃi/ *n* [C] *AmE informal* an insulting word for a young woman who wears clothes that allow large parts of her body to be seen and uses a lot of MAKE-UP in order to look sexually attractive → **bimbo**

hood /hʊd/ ●●○ *n* [C]
1 a) a part of a coat, jacket etc that you can pull up to cover your head: *Why don't you* ***put*** *your* ***hood up*** *if you're cold?* **b)** a cloth bag that goes over someone's face and head so that they cannot be recognized or cannot see → **balaclava**: *He was abducted by four men wearing hoods.*
2 *AmE* the metal covering over the engine on a car SYN **bonnet** *BrE*: **under the hood** *Check under the hood and see what that noise is.* → see picture at CAR
3 a cover fitted above a COOKER to remove the smell of cooking → **extractor (fan)**
4 *BrE* a folding cover on a car or PRAM, which gives protection from the rain
5 (*also* **'hood**) *AmE informal* a NEIGHBOURHOOD
6 *AmE informal* a HOODLUM

-hood /hʊd/ *suffix* [in nouns] **1** used to refer to a period of time or a state: *during his childhood* (=when he was a child) | *parenthood* (=the state of being a parent)
2 the people who belong to a particular group: *the priesthood* (=all the people who are priests)

hood·ed /ˈhʊdɪd/ *adj* having or wearing a hood: *a hooded cape*

hood·ie, **hoody** /ˈhʊdi/ *n* [C] *informal* **1** a loose jacket or top made of soft material, which has a HOOD
2 *BrE* a young person who wears a hoodie - sometimes used expressing disapproval because some people connect wearing hoodies with bad or criminal behaviour

HOODIE

H

hood·lum /ˈhuːdləm/ *n* [C] a criminal, often a young person, who does violent or illegal things SYN **gangster**

hood·wink /ˈhʊdˌwɪŋk/ *v* [T + into] to trick someone in a clever way so that you can get an advantage for yourself SYN **con**

hood·y /ˈhʊdi/ *n* [C] another spelling of HOODIE

hoo·ey /ˈhuːi/ *n* [U] *AmE informal* stupid talk SYN **nonsense**

hoof¹ /huːf $ hʊf, huːf/ ●●○ *n* (*plural* **hoofs** *or* **hooves** /huːvz $ hʊvz, huːvz/)
1 [C] the hard foot of an animal such as a horse, cow etc → see picture at HORSE
2 on the hoof *BrE* if you do something on the hoof, you do it quickly while doing something else at the same time

hoof² *v* **hoof it** *informal* to run or walk quickly

hoof·er /ˈhuːfə $ ˈhʊfər,ˈhuː-/ *n* [C] *informal* a dancer, especially one who works in the theatre

hoo-ha /ˈhuː hɑː/ *n* [singular, U] *BrE* noisy talk or excitement about something unimportant SYN **fuss**: *What's all the hoo-ha about?*

hook¹ /hʊk/ ●●● S3 *n* [C]
1 HANGING THINGS a curved piece of metal or plastic that you use for hanging things on → **peg**: *Tom hung his coat on the hook behind the door.*
2 CATCHING FISH a curved piece of thin metal with a sharp point for catching fish → see picture at FISHING
3 let/get sb off the hook to allow someone or help someone to get out of a difficult situation: *I wasn't prepared to let her off the hook that easily.*
4 leave/take the phone off the hook to leave or take the telephone RECEIVER (=the part you speak into) off the part where it is usually placed so that no one can call you
5 be ringing off the hook *AmE* if your telephone is ringing off the hook, a lot of people are calling you
6 INTEREST something that is attractive and gets people's interest and attention SYN **draw**: *You always need a bit of a hook to get people to go to the theatre.*
7 by hook or by crook if you are going to do something by hook or by crook, you are determined to do it, whatever methods you have to use: *The police are going to get these guys, by hook or by crook.*
8 HITTING SB a way of hitting your opponent in BOXING, in which your elbow is bent → **punch**, **jab**
9 hook, line, and sinker if someone believes something hook, line, and sinker, they believe a lie completely
→ BOAT HOOK, CURTAIN HOOK, → **sling your hook** at SLING¹(4)

hook² ●○○ *v* [T]
1 FISH to catch a fish with a hook: *I hooked a 20-pound salmon last week.*
2 FASTEN [always + adv/prep] to fasten or hang something onto something else: **hook sth onto/to sth** *Just hook the bucket onto the rope and lower it down.*
3 BEND YOUR FINGER/ARM ETC [always + adv/prep] to bend your finger, arm, or leg, especially so that you can pull or hold something else: *Ruth hooked her arm through Tony's.* | *He tried to hook his leg over the branch.*
4 INTEREST/ATTRACT *informal* to succeed in making someone interested in something or attracted to something: *cigarette ads designed to hook young people*
5 ELECTRONIC EQUIPMENT [always + adv/prep] (*also* **hook up**) to connect a piece of electronic equipment to another piece of equipment or to an electricity supply → **hook-up**: *We've got a CD player, but it's not hooked up yet.* | **hook sth together** *Computers from different manufacturers can often be hooked together.*
6 BALL to throw or kick a ball so that it moves in a curve

hook up with sb/sth *phr v especially AmE informal*
1 a) to start having a sexual relationship with someone **b)** to meet someone and become friendly with them SYN **meet up with**: *Did you ever hook up with Maisy while you were there?* **c)** to agree to work together with another organization for a particular purpose
2 hook sb up with sth to help someone get something that they need or want SYN **fix up with**: *Do you think you can hook me up with some tickets for tonight?*

hook·ah /ˈhʊkə/ *n* [C] a pipe for smoking drugs, that consists of a long tube and a container of water

ˌhook and ˈeye *n* (*plural* **hooks and eyes**) [C] a small metal hook and ring used for fastening clothes

hooked /hʊkt/ *adj* **1** curved outwards or shaped like a hook: *a hooked nose* **2** [not before noun] *informal* if you are hooked on a drug, you feel a strong need for it and you cannot stop taking it SYN **addicted**: **[+on]** *I know a girl who* ***got hooked*** *on cocaine.* **3** [not before noun] *informal* if you are hooked on something, you enjoy it very much and you want to do it as often as possible: **[+on]** *I* ***got hooked*** *on TV when I was sick.* **4** having one or more hooks

hook·er /ˈhʊkə $ -ər/ *n* [C] *informal* a woman who has sex with men for money SYN **prostitute**

ˈhook-up *n* [C] a temporary connection between two pieces of equipment such as computers, or between a piece of equipment and an electricity or water supply

hook·y /ˈhʊki/ *n* **play hooky** *AmE old-fashioned* to stay away from school without permission SYN **truant** *BrE*

hoo·li·gan /ˈhuːləɡən/ *n* [C] a noisy violent person who causes trouble by fighting etc: *football hooligans* —**hooliganism** *n* [U]

hoop /huːp $ hʊp, huːp/ *n* [C] **1** a large ring made of wood, metal, plastic etc **2** a large ring that children used to play with in the past, or that CIRCUS animals are made to jump through **3 a)** the ring that you have to throw the ball through to score points in BASKETBALL **b) hoops** [plural] *AmE informal* the game of BASKETBALL **4 jump/go through hoops** if someone makes you jump through hoops, they make you do lots of difficult or boring things before you are allowed to do what you want to do **5** (*also* **hoop earrings**) an EARRING that is shaped like a ring
→ COCK-A-HOOP, HULA HOOP

hooped /huːpt/ *adj BrE* in the shape of a hoop, or containing something in the shape of a hoop: *hooped earrings*

hoop·la /ˈhuːplɑː $ ˈhuːp-, ˈhʊp-/ *n* [U] **1** *especially AmE* excitement about something which attracts a lot of public attention: *all the hoopla that surrounded the trial* **2** *BrE* a game in which prizes can be won by throwing a ring over an object from a distance

hoo·ray /hʊˈreɪ, ˌhuːˈreɪ◂/ ●○○ *interjection* shouted when you are very glad about something —**hooray** *n* [C]
→ **hip hip hooray** at HIP³

Hooray Henry /ˌhʊreɪ ˈhenri/ *n* [C] *BrE* a young man from the highest social class, who is often loud and noisy in his way of behaving and enjoying himself, and is regarded by most people as very stupid

hoot¹ /huːt/ *n* [C] **1** a shout or laugh that shows you think something is funny or stupid: **hoot of laughter/derision etc** *Hoots of laughter rose from the audience.* **2** a sound that an OWL makes **3** a short clear sound made by a vehicle or ship, as a warning **4 be a hoot** *spoken* to be very funny or amusing **5 don't give a hoot/don't care two hoots** *spoken* to not care at all about someone or something: **[+about]** *It was clear that Owen didn't care two hoots about her.*

hoot² *v* **1** [I,T] if a vehicle or ship hoots, it makes a loud clear noise as a warning: **[+at]** *The car behind was hooting at me.* **2** [I] if an OWL hoots, it makes a long 'oo' sound **3** [I,T] to laugh loudly because you think something is funny or stupid: **hoot with laughter/glee/mirth etc** *He had the audience hooting with laughter.*

hootch /huːtʃ/ *n* [U] *especially AmE* another spelling of HOOCH

hoot·er /ˈhuːtə $ -ər/ *n* [C] **1** *BrE* a piece of equipment that makes a loud noise and is used on cars, ships, or in factories SYN **horn** **2** *BrE informal* a nose **3 hooters** [plural] *AmE informal not polite* an offensive word for a woman's breasts

hoover *v* [I,T] *BrE* to clean a floor, CARPET etc using a VACUUM CLEANER (=a machine that sucks up dirt) SYN **vacuum** → see picture at CLEAN²

Hoo·ver /ˈhuːvə $ -ər/ *n* [C] *trademark BrE* a VACUUM CLEANER

hooves /huːvz $ hʊvz, huːvz/ the plural of HOOF

hop¹ /hɒp $ hɑːp/ ●●○ *v* (**hopped**, **hopping**)
1 JUMP [I] to move by jumping on one foot: *a little girl hopping and skipping* → see picture at JUMP¹ THESAURUS JUMP
2 [I] if a bird, an insect, or a small animal hops, it moves by making quick short jumps
3 [I always + adv/prep] *informal* to move somewhere quickly or suddenly: *Hop in – I'll drive you home.* | *Patrick hopped out of bed and quickly got dressed.*
4 hop a plane/bus/train etc *AmE informal* to get on a plane, bus, train etc, especially after suddenly deciding to do so: *So we hopped a bus to Phoenix that night.*
5 hop it! *BrE old-fashioned* used to rudely tell someone to go away
6 hopping mad *informal* very angry SYN **furious**

hop² *n* [C]
1 catch sb on the hop to do something when someone is not expecting it and is not ready
2 JUMP a short jump
3 PLANT **a) hops** [plural] parts of dried flowers used for making beer, which give the beer a bitter taste **b)** the tall plant on which these flowers grow
4 FLIGHT a single short journey by plane: *It's just a* ***short hop*** *from Cleveland to Detroit.*
5 DANCE *old-fashioned* a social event at which people dance → HIP-HOP

hope¹ /həʊp $ hoʊp/ ●●● S1 W1 *v* [I,T]
1 to want something to happen or be true and to believe that it is possible or likely: **hope (that)** *We hope that more women will decide to join the course.* | *I do hope everything goes well.* | *It was hoped that the job would be filled by a local person.* | ***Let's*** *just* ***hope*** *someone finds her bag.* | ***I hope to God*** *I haven't left the car window open.* | **hope to do sth** *Joan's hoping to study law at Harvard.* | **[+for]** *We were hoping for good weather.* | *Liam decided to ignore the warning and just* ***hope for the best*** (=hope that a situation will end well when there is a risk of things going wrong). | *I rang my parents,* ***hoping against hope*** (=hoping for something that is very unlikely to happen or be true) *that they hadn't left yet.*
2 I hope so *spoken* used to say that you hope something that has been mentioned happens or is true: *'Do we get paid this week?' 'I certainly hope so!'*
3 I hope not *spoken* used to say that you hope something that has been mentioned does not happen or is not true: *I don't think I'm busy that day, or at least I hope not.*
4 I'm hoping *spoken* used to say that you hope something will happen, especially because you are depending on it: **I'm hoping (that)** *I'm hoping the car will be fixed by Friday.* | **I'm hoping to do sth** *We were hoping to see you today.*
5 I hope (that) *spoken* used when you want to be polite and to make sure that you are not interrupting or offending someone: *I hope I'm not interrupting you.* | ***I hope you don't mind*** *me asking, but why are you moving?*
6 I should hope so (too) (*also* **I should hope not** *BrE*) *spoken* used to say that you feel very strongly that something should or should not happen: *'They'll get their money back.' 'I should hope so too, after being treated like that.'*

GRAMMAR: Patterns with hope

- You **hope to** do something: *We're hoping to get tickets to the concert.* | *I hope to see you soon.* ✗ Don't say: *I hope see you soon.*
- You **hope that** something happens: *I hope that the rain stops soon.*
- You **hope that** something **will** happen: *I hope that the weather will be fine.*
- You **hoped that** something **would** happen: *She hoped that the weather would be fine.*
- You **hoped that** something **might** happen: *I was hoping that you might come.*
- You **hope that** someone **can** do something: *I hope that I can pass my exam.*
- You **hoped that** someone **could** do something: *She hoped that she could pass her exam.*
- In more formal English, you say **it is hoped that** something **will** happen: *It is hoped that the study will provide some useful information.*
- In all the above patterns, 'that' is often omitted, especially in spoken English: *I hope the rain stops soon.* | *She hoped the weather would be fine.*
- **Hope** is often used in the progressive: *I'm hoping to meet him some day.*
- **Hope** is used in the phrases **I hope so** and **I hope not**, often to give a short answer: *'Will he be here soon?' 'I hope so.'* | *'Do you think it will rain?' 'I hope not!'* ✗ Don't say: *I hope it.*

GRAMMAR GUIDE VERBS

hope² ●●● S2 W2 *n*
1 FEELING [C,U] a feeling of wanting something to happen or be true and believing that it is possible or likely: *When I first arrived in New York, I was full of hope for the future.* | **the hope that** *The president has expressed the hope that relations will improve.* | **hopes for sth** *hopes for an end to the fighting* | **hopes of doing sth** *Rita has hopes of studying to be a nurse.* | **in the hope that** *Should they hang on in the hope that the shares will go up in value?* | **in the hope of doing sth** (=because you hope that you will do something) *Shoppers flocked to the sales in the hope of finding a bargain.*
2 STH YOU HOPE FOR [C] something that you hope will happen: *She told him all her secret hopes and fears.* | **sb's hope is that** *My hope is that by next summer I'll have saved enough money to go travelling.*
3 CHANCE [C,U] a chance of succeeding or of something good happening: **[+of]** *It was the rush hour, and there was no hope of getting a seat.* | *It was a desperate plan, with little hope of success.* | **hope (that)** *There's still a* ***faint hope*** (=a very small chance) *that the two sides will reach an agreement.* | **not a hope!** *spoken* (=used to say that there is no chance of something happening) | **not a hope in hell (of doing sth)** *spoken* (=not even the smallest chance of success) *They don't have a hope in hell of winning.* | **some hope!** (*also* **what a hope!** *BrE*) *spoken* (=used humorously to say that there is no chance that something will happen) *'Your dad might lend you the car.' 'Some hope!'*
4 be sb's last/only/best hope to be someone's last, only etc chance of getting the result they want: *Please help me. You're my last hope.* | **[+of]** *Joshua's only hope of survival was a heart transplant.*
5 be beyond hope if a situation is beyond hope, it is so bad that there is no chance of any improvement: **[+of]** *Some of the houses were beyond hope of repair.*
6 have high/great hopes for sb/sth to be confident that someone or something will be successful: *The weather looked good, so we had high hopes for today.*
7 I/we live in hope *spoken* used when saying that you keep hoping that something will happen - often used humorously when saying that it seems unlikely: *"Do you think your son will ever get a job?" "We live in hope!"*

COLLOCATIONS - MEANINGS 1 & 2

VERBS

have hope *The situation looked bad, but we still had hope that things would get better soon.*
give/offer hope *The research has given hope to thousands of sufferers of the disease.*
lose/give up/abandon hope (=stop hoping) *After so long without any word from David, Margaret was starting to lose hope.*
raise sb's hopes (*also* **get/build sb's hopes up**) (=make someone feel that what they want is likely to happen) *I don't want to raise your hopes too much.*
hold out hope (=say that you think something is likely) *Negotiators did not hold out much hope of a peaceful solution.*
pin your hopes on sth (=hope for one thing that everything else depends on) *After a difficult year, the company is pinning its hopes on its new range of products.*
cling to the hope that (=keep hoping that something will happen, even though it seems

H

unlikely) *They clung to the hope that one day a cure would be found.*
dash/shatter sb's hopes (=make what someone wants seem impossible) *The ending of the talks has dashed any hopes of peace.*
hopes are fading (=people have much less hope of doing something) *Hopes are fading that rescuers will find any more survivors.*

PHRASES

be full of hope *His voice sounded full of hope.*
a glimmer/ray of hope (=a little hope, or something that gives you a little hope) *The new treatment gives patients a glimmer of hope.*
sb's hopes and dreams (=all the things someone hopes for) *We talked about all our hopes and dreams for the future.*
sb's hopes and fears (=all the things someone hopes for and is afraid of)

ADJECTIVES

false hope *We don't want to give people false hopes.*
a vain/forlorn hope (=hope for something that is impossible) *He traveled south in the vain hope of finding work.*
sb's only/one hope *My only hope is that someone may have handed in the keys to the police.*

ˈhoped-for *adj* [only before noun] *written* used to describe something that you want to happen and think is possible or likely: *I was at home when the desperately hoped-for call came through.*

hope·ful¹ /ˈhəʊpfəl $ ˈhoʊp-/ ●●○ *adj*
1 believing that what you hope for is likely to happen SYN **optimistic**: **[+about]** *Everyone's feeling pretty hopeful about the future.* | **hopeful (that)** *I'm hopeful that we can find a solution.* | **be hopeful of (doing) sth** *BrE*: *He is still hopeful of playing in Saturday's game.*
2 making you feel that what you hope for is likely to happen SYN **promising**: *The vote is a* **hopeful sign** *that attitudes in the church are changing.* | *Things might get better, but it doesn't look very hopeful right now.* —**hopefulness** *n* [U]

hopeful² *n* [C] *written* someone who is hoping to be successful, especially in acting, sports, politics etc: *Thousands of* **young hopefuls** *were auditioned for the role.* | *Republican presidential hopefuls*

hope·ful·ly /ˈhəʊpfəli $ ˈhoʊp-/ ●●● S1 *adv*
1 [sentence adverb] a way of saying what you hope will happen, which some people think is incorrect: *Hopefully, I'll be back home by ten o'clock.* | *By then the problem will hopefully have been solved.*
2 in a way that shows that you are hopeful: *'Will there be any food left over?' he asked hopefully.*

hope·less /ˈhəʊpləs $ ˈhoʊp-/ ●●○ S3 *adj*
1 if something that you try to do is hopeless, there is no possibility of it being successful: *We tried to stop the flames from spreading, but we knew it was hopeless.* | *Getting your work published often seems a* **hopeless task**. | *I kept on struggling forward, even though I knew* **it was hopeless**.
2 a hopeless situation is so bad that there is no chance of success or improvement: *The situation is not as hopeless as it might seem.* | *the millions who live in hopeless poverty*
3 *especially BrE informal* very bad SYN **terrible**: *I'm a hopeless cook.* | **hopeless at (doing) sth** *My brother was always pretty hopeless at ball games.* | **[+with]** *I'm hopeless with machinery.* | *I've got a hopeless memory.* | *The public transport system was absolutely hopeless.*
4 feeling no hope: *I began to feel lonely and hopeless.*
5 used, often humorously, to say that someone's bad behaviour cannot be changed: *Oh, James, you really are a* **hopeless case** (=it seems impossible to change your behaviour)! | **hopeless romantic/materialist/drunk etc** *She was a hopeless romantic, always convinced that one day she would meet the man of her dreams.* —**hopelessness** *n* [U]

hope·less·ly /ˈhəʊpləsli $ ˈhoʊp-/ *adv* **1** used when emphasizing how bad a situation is, and saying that it will not get better: *We found ourselves hopelessly outnumbered by the enemy.* | *She felt hopelessly confused.* | *I was trying to find the museum, but I got hopelessly lost.* **2 be/fall hopelessly in love (with sb)** to have or develop very strong feelings of love for someone **3** feeling that you have no hope: *'When will I see you again?' he asked hopelessly.*

ˌhopped-ˈup *adj AmE informal* **1** happy and excited, especially after taking drugs **2** a hopped-up car, engine etc has been made much more powerful

hop·per /ˈhɒpə $ ˈhɑːpər/ *n* [C] a large FUNNEL¹(1)

hop·scotch /ˈhɒpskɒtʃ $ ˈhɑːpskɑːtʃ/ *n* [U] a children's game in which each child has to jump from one square drawn on the ground to another

horde /hɔːd $ hɔːrd/ *n* [C] a large crowd moving in a noisy uncontrolled way: **[+of]** *There were hordes of people inside the station.* THESAURUS ▸ GROUP

ho·ri·zon /həˈraɪzən/ ●●○ *n*
1 the horizon the line far away where the land or sea seems to meet the sky: **on the horizon** *We could see a ship on the horizon.* ⚠ Don't say 'in the horizon'. Say **on the horizon**.
2 horizons [plural] the limit of your ideas, knowledge, and experience: **broaden/expand sb's horizons** *a course of study that will broaden your horizons*
3 on the horizon to seem likely to happen in the future: *Business is good now, but there are a few problems on the horizon.*

hor·i·zon·tal¹ /ˌhɒrəˈzɒntl◂ $ ˌhɑːrəˈzɑːntl◂/ ●●○ *adj* flat and level: *a horizontal surface* THESAURUS ▸ FLAT —**horizontally** *adv* → **diagonal**, **vertical**

horizontal² *n* **1** [C] a horizontal line or surface **2 the horizontal** a horizontal position: *eleven degrees below the horizontal*

hor·mone /ˈhɔːməʊn $ ˈhɔːrmoʊn/ *n* [C] a chemical substance produced by your body that influences its growth, development, and condition —**hormonal** /hɔːˈməʊnəl $ hɔːrˈmoʊ-/ *adj*: *hormonal changes*

ˌhormone reˈplacement ˌtherapy *n* [U] HRT

horn¹ /hɔːn $ hɔːrn/ ●●○ *n*
1 ANIMAL **a)** [C] the hard pointed thing that grows, usually in pairs, on the heads of animals such as cows and goats → **antlers** **b)** [U] the substance that animals' horns are made of: *a knife with a horn handle* **c)** [C] a part of an animal's head that sticks out like a horn, for example on a SNAIL

HORN

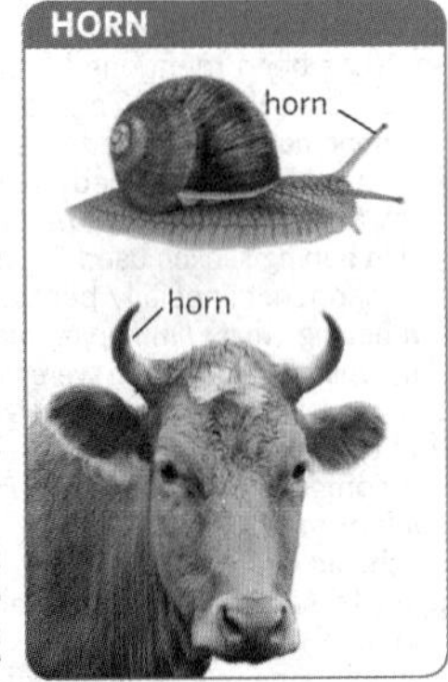

2 ON A CAR [C] the thing in a vehicle that you use to make a loud sound as a signal or warning: **sound/toot/honk/blow your horn** (=make a noise with your horn) → see picture at CAR
3 MUSICAL INSTRUMENT [C] **a)** a musical instrument like a long metal tube that is wide at one end, that you play by blowing **b)** *informal* a TRUMPET **c)** a FRENCH HORN **d)** a musical instrument made from an animal's horn → **ENGLISH HORN**
4 drinking horn/powder horn etc a container in the shape of an animal's horn, used in the past for drinking from, carrying GUNPOWDER etc
5 draw/pull in your horns to reduce the amount of money you spend
6 be on the horns of a dilemma to be in a situation in which you have to choose between two equally unpleasant or difficult situations → **blow your own trumpet/horn** at BLOW¹(21), → **lock horns** at LOCK¹(6), → **take the bull by the horns** at BULL¹(3)

H

horn² *v*
horn in *phr v AmE informal* to interrupt or try to take part in something when you are not wanted SYN **butt in**: **[+on]** *Don't try and horn in on our fun.*

horn·bill /ˈhɔːnˌbɪl $ ˈhɔːrn-/ *n* [C] a tropical bird with a very large beak

horned /hɔːnd $ hɔːrnd/ *adj* [only before noun] having horns or something that looks like horns: *horned cattle* | *a horned toad*

hor·net /ˈhɔːnɪt $ ˈhɔːr-/ *n* [C] **1** a large black and yellow flying insect that can sting → **wasp** **2 hornets' nest** a situation in which there is a lot of trouble and quarrelling: *The new production targets have **stirred up a hornets' nest**.*

horn·pipe /ˈhɔːnpaɪp $ ˈhɔːrn-/ *n* [C] a traditional dance performed by SAILORS, or the music for this dance

horn-rimmed /ˌhɔːn ˈrɪmd◂ $ ˌhɔːrn-/ *adj* **horn-rimmed glasses/spectacles** glasses with frames made of plastic that looks like horn

horn·y /ˈhɔːni $ ˈhɔːrni/ *adj* **1** *informal* sexually excited: *feeling horny* **2** *informal* sexually attractive: *I think he's horny.* **3** skin that is horny is hard and rough **4** made of a hard substance like horn: *the bird's horny beak*

hor·o·scope /ˈhɒrəskəʊp $ ˈhɑːrəskoʊp, ˈhɔː-/ *n* [C] a description of your character and the things that will happen to you, based on the position of the stars and PLANETS at the time of your birth → **zodiac**

hor·ren·dous /hɒˈrendəs, hə- $ hɑː-, hɔː-/ ●○○ *adj*
1 frightening and terrible SYN **horrific**: *a horrendous experience* | *She suffered horrendous injuries.* THESAURUS BAD
2 *informal* extremely unreasonable or unpleasant: *horrendous debts* | *The traffic was horrendous.* —**horrendously** *adv*

hor·ri·ble /ˈhɒrəbəl $ ˈhɔː-, ˈhɑː-/ ●●● S2 *adj*
1 very bad – used, for example, about things you see, taste, or smell, or about the weather: *The weather has been really horrible all week.* | *a horrible smell* | *The food looked horrible, but it tasted OK.* THESAURUS BAD
2 very unpleasant and often frightening, worrying, or upsetting: *a horrible dream* | ***I have a horrible feeling that** we're going to miss the plane.*
3 rude and unfriendly: *She's a horrible person.* | *What a horrible thing to say!* | **be horrible to sb** *Why are you so horrible to me?* THESAURUS UNKIND —**horribly** *adv*: *Her face was horribly scarred.* | *The plan had **gone horribly wrong**.*

THESAURUS

TASTE/SMELL

horrible very bad and unpleasant: *What's that horrible smell?* | *This fish tastes horrible.*
disgusting/revolting horrible, especially in a way that makes you feel slightly sick: *I had to take two spoons of some disgusting medicine.* | *The stench in the room was revolting.*
nasty very unpleasant – often used about a taste that stays in your mouth: *Cheap wine sometimes leaves a nasty taste in your mouth.* | *the nasty smell of bad eggs*
nauseating /ˈnɔːzieɪtɪŋ, -si- $ ˈnɒːzi-, -ʃi-/ horrible and making you feel that you are going to VOMIT – used especially about a smell: *the nauseating smell of stale beer and cigarette smoke*
foul /faʊl/ horrible – used especially when there is decay or waste: *There was a foul smell coming from the water.*

EXPERIENCE, SITUATION, EVENT

horrible/terrible/awful/dreadful very bad and unpleasant: *For one horrible moment, I thought I was going to fall.* | *The refugees were living in dreadful conditions.*
nasty very unpleasant and shocking – used especially about events where people are hurt: *There's been a nasty accident on the motorway.* | *a nasty cut* | *The news came as a nasty shock.*

hor·rid /ˈhɒrɪd $ ˈhɔː-, ˈhɑː-/ *adj especially BrE* **1** *informal* very unpleasant SYN **nasty**: *a horrid smell* **2** *old-fashioned* behaving in a nasty unkind way: *Don't be so horrid!*

hor·rif·ic /hɒˈrɪfɪk, hə- $ hɔː-, hɑː-/ ●○○ *adj* extremely bad, in a way that is frightening or upsetting SYN **horrifying**: **horrific crash/accident/attack etc** *a horrific plane crash* | *His injuries were horrific.* —**horrifically** /-kli/ *adv*

hor·ri·fy /ˈhɒrɪfaɪ $ ˈhɔː-, ˈhɑː-/ ●○○ *v* (**horrified, horrifying, horrifies**) [T] to make someone feel very shocked and upset or afraid: *Henry was horrified by what had happened.* | **horrified to see/hear/find etc** *She was horrified to discover that he loved Rose.*

hor·ri·fy·ing /ˈhɒrəfaɪ-ɪŋ $ ˈhɔː-, ˈhɑː-/ *adj* extremely bad, especially in a way that is frightening or upsetting SYN **horrific**: *murder, rape, and other horrifying crimes* | *It's horrifying to see how much poverty there is here.* —**horrifyingly** *adv*

hor·ror /ˈhɒrə $ ˈhɔːrər, ˈhɑː-/ ●●○ W3 *n*
1 [U] a strong feeling of shock and fear: **in horror** *Staff watched in horror as he set himself alight.* | **with horror** *Many people recoil with horror when they see a big spider like this.* | **to sb's horror** (=making someone shocked or afraid) *To my horror, I realised my shirt was wet with blood.* | *You should have seen the **look of horror** on his face.*
2 [C usually plural] something that is very terrible, shocking, or frightening: **[+of]** *the horrors of war*
3 the horror of something when a situation or event is very unpleasant or shocking: *Dense smoke surrounded them, adding to the horror of the situation.* | *Only when the vehicle was lifted did **the full horror** of the accident become clear.*
4 have a horror of sth to be afraid of something or dislike it very much: *He has a horror of snakes.*
5 little horror *BrE* a young child who behaves badly
6 give sb the horrors to make someone feel unreasonably frightened or nervous
7 horror of horrors *BrE* used to say how bad something is – often used humorously when you think something is not really very bad

ˈhorror ˌmovie *especially AmE*, **ˈhorror ˌfilm** *BrE n* [C] a film in which strange and frightening things happen

ˈhorror ˌstory *n* [C] **1** *informal* a report about bad experiences, bad conditions etc: *horror stories about patients being given the wrong drugs* **2** a story in which strange and frightening things happen

ˈhorror-ˌstruck (*also* **ˈhorror-ˌstricken**) *adj* suddenly very shocked and frightened

hors d'oeu·vre /ɔː ˈdɜːv $ ˌɔːr ˈdɜːrv/ *n* (*plural* **hors d'oeuvres** /-ˈdɜːvz $ -ˈdɜːrvz/) [C] food that is served in small amounts before the main part of the meal → **entrée, main course**

horse¹ /hɔːs $ hɔːrs/ ●●● S1 W1 *n*
1 [C] a large strong animal that people ride and use for pulling heavy things → **pony, equine, equestrian**: *a horse and cart* | *Lee had never ridden a horse before.* → see picture on *p. 890*
2 the horses *BrE informal* horse races: *Jim likes a bet on the horses.*
3 [C] a piece of sports equipment in a GYMNASIUM that people jump over
4 (straight/right) from the horse's mouth if you hear or get information straight from the horse's mouth, you are told it by someone who has direct knowledge of it
5 horses for courses *BrE* the process of matching people with suitable jobs or activities
6 a two/three/four etc horse race a competition or an election that only two etc competitors can win
7 a horse of a different color (*also* **a horse of another color** *AmE*) something that is completely different from another thing
8 horse sense *old-fashioned* sensible judgment gained from experience SYN **common sense**

H

9 [U] *old-fashioned informal* HEROIN → **DARK HORSE**, → **never/don't look a gift horse in the mouth** at **GIFT**[1](7), → **be flogging a dead horse** at **FLOG**(3), → **hold your horses** at **HOLD**[1](15), → **put the cart before the horse** at **CART**[1](5), → **STALKING HORSE**, **WHITE HORSES**

horse[2] *v*

horse around/about *phr v informal* to play roughly → **horseplay**: *Stop horsing around – you'll break something!*

horse·back /ˈhɔːsbæk $ ˈhɔːrs-/ *n* **on horseback** riding a horse —**horseback** *adj* [only before noun]

horse·box /ˈhɔːsbɒks $ ˈhɔːrsbɑːks/ *n* [C] *BrE* a large vehicle for carrying horses, often pulled by another vehicle SYN **horse trailer** *AmE*

ˌhorse ˈchestnut / $ ˈ. ˌ../ *n* [C] **1** a large tree that produces shiny brown nuts and has white or pink flowers **2** a nut from this tree SYN **conker**

ˈhorse-drawn *adj* [only before noun] horse-drawn vehicles are pulled by a horse

horse·fly /ˈhɔːsflaɪ $ ˈhɔːrs-/ *n* (*plural* **horseflies**) [C] a large fly that bites horses and cattle

horse·hair /ˈhɔːsheə $ ˈhɔːrsher/ *n* [U] the hair from a horse's MANE and tail, sometimes used, especially in the past, to fill the inside of furniture

horse·man /ˌhɔːsmən $ ˈhɔːrs-/ *n* (*plural* **horsemen** /-mən/) [C] someone who rides horses

horse·man·ship /ˈhɔːsmənʃɪp $ ˈhɔːrs-/ *n* [U] the skill involved in riding horses

horse·play /ˈhɔːspleɪ $ ˈhɔːrs-/ *n* [U] *old-fashioned* rough noisy play in which people push or hit each other for fun

horse·pow·er /ˈhɔːsˌpaʊə $ ˈhɔːrsˌpaʊr/ *n* (*plural* **horsepower**) [C,U] (*written abbreviation* **hp**) a unit for measuring the power of an engine, or the power of an engine measured like this: *a two-hundred horsepower engine | the superior horsepower of a Volkswagen*

ˈhorse ˌracing *n* [U] a sport in which horses with riders race against each other → **flat racing**, **steeplechase**, **jockey**

horse·rad·ish /ˈhɔːsˌrædɪʃ $ ˈhɔːrs-/ *n* [C,U] a plant whose root has a very strong hot taste

ˈhorse-riding *n* [U] *BrE* the activity of riding horses SYN **riding**

horse·shit /ˈhɔːʃ-ʃɪt $ ˈhɔːrʃ-/ *n* [U] *AmE informal not polite* nonsense SYN **bullshit**

horse·shoe /ˈhɔːʃ-ʃuː, ˈhɔːs- $ ˈhɔːr-/ *n* [C] **1** a U-shaped piece of iron that is fixed onto the bottom of a horse's foot **2** an object in the shape of a horseshoe that is a sign of good luck

ˈhorse show *n* [C] a sports event in which people compete to show their skill in riding horses

ˈhorse-ˌtrading *n* [U] the activity of discussing issues or making deals in which everyone tried hard to gain advantages for their own side, especially in politics or business

ˈhorse ˌtrailer *n* [C] *AmE* a large vehicle for carrying horses, pulled by another vehicle SYN **horsebox** *BrE*

horse·wom·an /ˈhɔːsˌwʊmən $ ˈhɔːrs-/ *n* (*plural* **horsewomen** /-ˌwɪmɪn/) [C] a woman who rides horses

hors·ey, **horsy** /ˈhɔːsi $ ˈhɔːrsi/ *adj* **1** *informal* very interested in horses and riding **2 horsey face/smell etc** a face etc that is like a horse's

hor·ti·cul·ture /ˈhɔːtəˌkʌltʃə $ ˈhɔːrtəˌkʌltʃər/ *n* [U] the practice or science of growing flowers, fruit, and vegetables → **gardening**, **agriculture** —**horticultural** /ˌhɔːtəˈkʌltʃərəl◂ $ ˌhɔːr-/ *adj* —**horticulturalist** *n* [C]

hose[1] /həʊz $ hoʊz/ ●●○ *n*

1 [C] *BrE* a long rubber or plastic tube that can be moved and bent to put water onto fires, gardens etc SYN **hosepipe** *BrE*

2 [U] TIGHTS, STOCKINGS, or socks, used in shops and in the clothing industry SYN **hosiery**

hose[2] *v* [T] **1** to wash or pour water over something or someone, using a hose: **hose sth/sb down** *Would you hose down the car for me?* **2** *AmE informal* to cheat or deceive someone

hose·pipe /ˈhəʊzpaɪp $ ˈhoʊz-/ *n* [C] *BrE* a long hose

ho·sier·y /ˈhəʊzjəri $ ˈhoʊʒəri/ (*also* **hose**) *n* [U] a general word for TIGHTS, STOCKINGS, or socks, used in shops and in the clothing industry

hos·pice /ˈhɒspɪs $ ˈhɑː-/ *n* [C] a special hospital for people who are dying

hos·pi·ta·ble /ˈhɒspɪtəbəl, hɒˈspɪ- $ hɑːˈspɪ-, ˈhɑːspɪ-/ *adj* **1** friendly, welcoming, and generous to visitors OPP **inhospitable**: *The local people were very kind and hospitable.* THESAURUS FRIENDLY **2** used for describing an environment in which things can grow OPP **inhospitable**: *The Sahara is one of the world's least hospitable regions.* —**hospitably** *adv*

hos·pi·tal /ˈhɒspɪtl $ ˈhɑː-/ ●●● S1 W1 *n* [C,U] a large building where sick or injured people receive medical treatment: *They are building a new hospital.* | **in hospital** *BrE*: *She visited him in hospital.* | **in the hospital** *AmE*: *Two people are in the hospital with serious burns.*

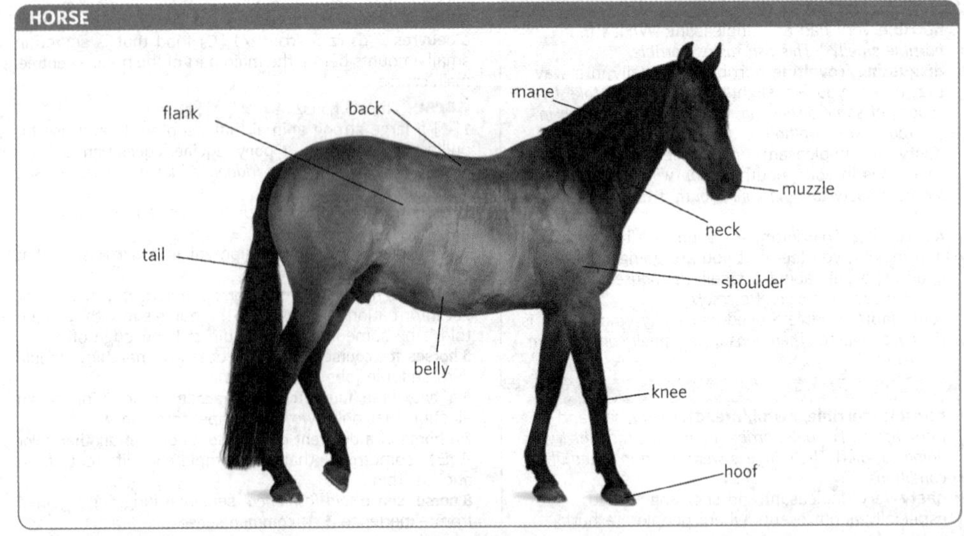

COLLOCATIONS

VERBS

go to hospital *BrE*, **go to the hospital** *AmE The pain got worse and she had to go to the hospital.*
be taken/rushed/airlifted to hospital *BrE*, **be taken/rushed/airlifted to the hospital** *AmE Three people were taken to hospital after a crash on the motorway.*
be admitted to hospital *BrE*, **be admitted to the hospital** *AmE He was admitted to hospital suffering from chest pain.*
leave/come out of hospital *BrE*, **leave/come out of the hospital** *AmE* | **be discharged/released from hospital** *BrE*, **be discharged/released from the hospital** *AmE* (=be allowed to leave a hospital because you are better)

ADJECTIVES/NOUN + hospital

a psychiatric hospital (*also* **a mental hospital** *old-fashioned*) (=for people with mental illnesses) *He was admitted to a secure psychiatric hospital.*
a children's hospital | **a maternity hospital** *BrE* (=for women having babies)

hospital + NOUN

hospital treatment/care *What do older people think of hospital care?*
a hospital stay (=the period someone spends in hospital) *New surgical techniques mean a hospital stay of less than 48 hours.*
a hospital bed | **a hospital ward/room**

hos·pi·tal·i·ty /ˌhɒspəˈtæləti $ ˌhɑː-/ ●○○ *n* [U]
1 friendly behaviour towards visitors: *Thanks for your hospitality over the past few weeks.*

REGISTER
In everyday English, when thanking someone for their hospitality, you usually say **thanks for having me/us**: ***Thanks for having us**. We had a great time.*

2 services such as food and drink that an organization provides for guests at a special event: *the use of a yacht for **corporate hospitality** | There was a reception in the **hospitality suite** before the game.* → **corporate hospitality** at CORPORATE(1)

hos·pi·tal·ize (*also* **-ise** *BrE*) /ˈhɒspɪtl-aɪz $ ˈhɑː-/ *v* [T] if someone is hospitalized, they are taken into a hospital for treatment GRAMMAR **Hospitalize** is usually passive. —**hospitalization** /ˌhɒspɪtl-aɪˈzeɪʃən $ ˌhɑːspɪtl-ə'zeɪ-/ *n* [U]

host¹ /həʊst $ hoʊst/ ●●○ W3 *n* [C]
1 AT A PARTY someone at a party, meal etc who has invited the guests and who provides the food, drink etc → **hostess**: *Our host greeted us at the door.*
2 ON TELEVISION/RADIO someone who introduces and talks to the guests on a television or radio programme SYN **compere** *BrE*: *a game show host*
3 COUNTRY/CITY a country, city, or organization that provides the necessary space, equipment etc for a special event: **host country/government/city etc** *the host city for the next Olympic Games* | **play host (to sth)** (=provide the place, food etc for a special meeting or event) *The gallery is playing host to an exhibition of sculpture.*
4 a (whole) host of people/things a large number of people or things: *A host of show business celebrities have pledged their support.*
5 IN CHURCH **the Host** *technical* the bread that is used in the Christian ceremony of Communion
6 ANIMAL/PLANT *technical* an animal or plant on which a smaller animal or plant is living as a PARASITE

host² ●●○ *v* [T]
1 to provide the place and everything that is needed for an organized event: *Which country is going to host the next World Cup?*
2 to introduce a radio or television programme: *Next week's show will be hosted by Sarah Cox.*

hos·tage /ˈhɒstɪdʒ $ ˈhɑː-/ ●○○ *n* [C]
1 someone who is kept as a prisoner by an enemy so that the other side will do what the enemy demands → **kidnap**: *The group are **holding** two tourists **hostage** (=keeping them as hostages). | a family **taken hostage** at gunpoint*
2 be (a) hostage to sth to be influenced and controlled by something, so that you are not free to do what you want: *Our country must not be **held hostage to** our past.*
3 a hostage to fortune something that you have promised to do that may cause you problems in the future

hos·tel /ˈhɒstl $ ˈhɑː-/ ●○○ *n* [C]
1 a place where people can stay and eat fairly cheaply
2 a YOUTH HOSTEL
3 a place where people who have no homes can stay

hos·tel·ry /ˈhɒstəlri $ ˈhɑː-/ *n* (*plural* **hostelries**) [C] *old use* a PUB or hotel

host·ess /ˈhəʊstɪs $ ˈhoʊ-/ *n* [C] **1** a woman at a party, meal etc who has invited all the guests and provides them with food, drink etc → **host 2** a woman who introduces and talks to the guests on a television or radio show → **host 3** a woman who shows people to seats in a restaurant in the US **4** a woman whose job is to entertain men at a NIGHTCLUB

hos·tile /ˈhɒstaɪl $ ˈhɑːstl, ˈhɑːstaɪl/ ●○○ *adj*
1 angry and deliberately unfriendly towards someone, and ready to argue with them: *Southampton fans gave their former coach a **hostile reception**. | Carr wouldn't meet Feng's stare, which was **openly hostile**. | his **hostile attitude*** | **[+to/towards]** *The boy feels hostile towards his father.* THESAURUS▸ UNFRIENDLY
2 opposing a plan or idea very strongly: **[+to/towards]** *Senator Lydon was hostile to our proposals.*
3 belonging to an enemy: *hostile territory*
4 used to describe conditions that are difficult to live in, or that make it difficult to achieve something: **hostile environment/climate/terrain etc** *a guide to surviving in even the most hostile terrain | Sales increased last year despite the hostile economic environment.*
5 hostile takeover/bid a situation in which a company tries to buy another company that does not want to be bought

hos·til·i·ty /hɒˈstɪləti $ hɑː-/ ●○○ *n*
1 [U] when someone is unfriendly and full of anger towards another person: **[+towards/between]** *hostility towards foreigners* | **[+toward]** *AmE*: *hostility toward religious minorities* | **open/outright hostility** (=hostility that is clearly shown) *They eyed each other with open hostility.*
2 [U] strong or angry opposition to something: *The reform program was greeted with hostility by conservatives.* | **[+to/towards]** *There is a lot of public hostility to the tax. | Pictures of refugees aroused **popular hostility** (=felt by a lot of people) towards the war.* | **[+toward]** *AmE*: *Republican hostility toward slavery*
3 hostilities [plural] *formal* fighting in a war: *a cessation of hostilities*

hos·tler /ˈɒslə $ ˈhɑːstlər, ˈɑːs-/ *n* [C] the usual American spelling of OSTLER

hot¹ /hɒt $ hɑːt/ ●●● S1 W2 *adj* (*comparative* **hotter**, *superlative* **hottest**)
1 HIGH TEMPERATURE **a)** something that is hot has a high temperature – used about weather, places, food, drink, or objects OPP **cold**: *a hot day in July | **It's** so **hot** in here. Can I open the window? | Be careful, the water's very hot. | The bar serves **hot and cold food**.* | *people who live in **hot countries*** (=where the weather is usually hot) | **scorching/baking/roasting hot** (*also* **boiling/broiling hot** *AmE*) (=used about weather that is very hot) *a scorching hot week in August* | **stifling/sweltering/unbearably hot** (=used about weather that is very hot and uncomfortable) *The office gets unbearably hot in summer.* | **boiling/scalding/steaming hot** (=used about liquid that is extremely hot) *The coffee was scalding hot.* | **piping hot** (=used about food that is nice and hot) *Serve the soup piping hot.* | **red hot** (=used to describe an object or surface that is very hot) *The handle was red hot.* | **white hot** (=used to describe metal that is extremely hot) *He held the metal in the flame until it became white hot.* **b)** if

H

you feel hot, your body feels hot in a way that is uncomfortable: *I was hot and tired after the journey.* | *The wine made her feel hot.* **c)** if clothes are hot, they make you feel too hot in a way that is uncomfortable: *This sweater's too hot to wear inside.*

2 SPICY food that tastes hot has a burning taste because it contains strong spices OPP **mild**: *a hot curry* THESAURUS ➤ TASTE

3 VERY POPULAR/FASHIONABLE *informal* something or someone that is hot is very popular or fashionable, and everyone wants to use them, see them, buy them etc: *one of the hottest young directors in Hollywood* | *Gareth Bale is one of soccer's* ***hottest properties*** (=actors or sports players who are very popular). | *The movie is going to be this summer's* ***hot ticket*** (=an event that is very popular or fashionable, and that everyone wants to go and see). | **be the hottest thing since (sliced bread)** (=used about someone or something that is very good and popular, so that everyone wants them)

4 GOOD *informal* very good, especially in a way that is exciting: *a hot young guitar player* | *a hot piece of software* | *His new film is* ***hot stuff*** (=very good). | **be hot at doing sth** *She's pretty hot at swimming, too.* | **not so hot/not very hot** *informal* (=not very good) *Some of the tracks on the record are great, but others are not so hot.* | **be hot shit** *AmE informal not polite* (=used about someone or something that people think is very good)

5 SEXY **a)** *informal* someone who is hot is very attractive sexually: *The girls all think he's* ***hot stuff***. **b)** *informal* a film, book, photograph etc that is hot is sexually exciting: *his hot and steamy first novel* **c) a hot date** *informal* a meeting with someone who you feel very attracted to sexually: *She has a hot date with Michel.* **d) be hot on/for sb** *informal* to be sexually attracted to someone

6 DIFFICULT/DANGEROUS [not before noun] *informal* difficult or dangerous to deal with: *If* ***things get too hot*** (=a situation becomes too difficult or dangerous to deal with), *I can always leave.* | *Wilkinson found his opponent a little* ***too hot to handle*** (=too difficult to deal with or beat). | *The climate was too hot politically to make such radical changes.*

7 a hot issue/topic etc a subject that a lot of people are discussing, especially one that causes a lot of disagreement: *The affair was a hot topic of conversation.* | *one of the hottest issues facing medical science*

8 in the hot seat in an important position and responsible for making difficult decisions

9 in hot water if someone is in hot water, they are in trouble because they have done something wrong: *The finance minister found himself in hot water over his business interests.* | **land/get yourself in hot water** *She got herself in hot water with the authorities.*

10 ANGRY **a) get hot under the collar** *spoken* to become angry – used especially when people get angry in an unreasonable way about something that is not important: *I don't understand why people are getting so hot under the collar about it.* **b) have a hot temper** someone who has a hot temper becomes angry very easily → HOT-TEMPERED

11 hot and bothered *informal* upset and confused because you have too much to think about or because you are in a hurry: *People were struggling with bags and cases, looking hot and bothered.*

12 have/hold sth in your hot little hand *informal* used to emphasize that you have something: *You'll have the report in your hot little hands by Monday.*

13 RECENT/EXCITING NEWS hot news is about very recent events and therefore interesting or exciting: *Do you want to hear about all the latest* ***hot gossip***?

14 be hot off the press if news or a newspaper is hot off the press, it has just recently been printed

15 CHASING SB/STH CLOSELY **a) in hot pursuit** following someone quickly and closely because you want to catch them: *The car sped away, with the police in hot pursuit.* **b) hot on sb's trail/tail** close to and likely to catch someone you have been chasing: *The other car was hot on his tail.* **c) hot on sb's heels** following very close behind someone: *Mrs Bass's dog was already hot on his heels.*

16 come/follow hot on the heels of sth to happen or be done very soon after something else: *The news came hot on the heels of another plane crash.*

17 hot on the trail of sth very close to finding something: *journalists hot on the trail of a news story*

18 blow/go hot and cold to keep changing your mind about whether you like or want to do something: *She keeps blowing hot and cold about the wedding.*

19 go hot and cold to experience a strange feeling in which your body temperature suddenly changes, because you are very frightened, worried, or shocked

20 I don't feel too hot/so hot/very hot *spoken informal* I feel slightly ill: *I'm not feeling too hot today.*

21 be hot on sth *informal* **a)** to know a lot about something: *He's pretty hot on aircraft.* **b)** *BrE* to be very strict about something SYN **tight**: *The company is very hot on security.*

22 be hot for sth *informal* to be ready for something and want it very much: *Europe is hot for a product like this.* | *He was hot for revenge.*

23 be hot to trot *informal* **a)** to be ready to do something or be involved with something **b)** to feel sexually excited and want to have sex with someone

24 hot competition if the competition between people or companies is hot, they are all trying very hard to win or succeed: *Competition for the best jobs is getting hotter all the time.*

25 hot favourite the person, team, horse etc that people think is most likely to win

26 hot tip a good piece of advice about the likely result of a race, business deal etc: *a hot tip on the stock market*

27 STOLEN GOODS *informal* goods that are hot have been stolen

28 MUSIC *informal* music that is hot has a strong exciting RHYTHM

29 more sth than you've had hot dinners *BrE spoken humorous* used to say that someone has had a lot of experience of something and has done it many times: *She's delivered more babies than you've had hot dinners.*

30 hot money money that is frequently moved from one country to another in order to make a profit → HOTLY, HOTS

THESAURUS

PERSON

hot used especially when you feel uncomfortable: *I feel really hot.*
warm a little hot, especially in a way that feels comfortable: *Are you warm enough?*
boiling (hot) *spoken* very hot: *You must be boiling in that sweater!*
feverish feeling very hot because you are ill: *His head ached and he felt feverish.*

WEATHER

hot used especially when you feel uncomfortable: *a hot day* | *It's too hot to do any work.*
warm a little hot, especially in a way that seems pleasant: *a warm summer's evening*
boiling (hot) *spoken* very hot: *The weather was boiling hot.* | *a boiling hot day*
baking (hot) *BrE* very hot and dry: *a baking hot afternoon* | *It's baking out there in the garden – I need a drink.*
scorching (hot) very hot: *It was another scorching hot July day.*
humid/muggy hot and damp: *Hong Kong gets very humid at this time of year.*

ROOM

hot used especially when you feel uncomfortable: *The office was uncomfortably hot.*
warm a little hot, especially in a way that seems pleasant: *It's nice and warm by the fire.*
boiling (hot) *spoken* very hot: *It's boiling in here. Can I open the window?*
like an oven much too hot in a way that is uncomfortable – used about rooms and buildings: *The inside of the shed was like an oven.*

H

FOOD/LIQUID/SOMETHING YOU TOUCH
hot: *a hot drink | hot meals*
warm a little hot, especially in a way that seems pleasant: *The bread was still warm from the oven.*
boiling (hot) *spoken* very hot: *The water's boiling hot.*
lukewarm /ˌluːkˈwɔːm◂ $ -ˈwɔːrm◂ / slightly warm, but not hot enough - used about liquids: *a cup of lukewarm coffee | The bath water was lukewarm.*

hot² *v* (**hotted**, **hotting**)
hot up *phr v BrE informal* **1** if something hots up, there is more activity or excitement: *Things generally hot up a few days before the race.* **2 the pace hots up** used to say that the speed of something increases

ˌhot ˈair *n* [U] things that someone says that are intended to sound impressive but do not really mean anything or are not true: *The theory was dismissed as a lot of hot air.*

hot-ˈair balˌloon *n* [C] a large BALLOON filled with hot air, used for carrying people up into the sky → see picture at **BALLOON¹**

hot·bed /ˈhɒtbed $ ˈhɑːt-/ *n* **a hotbed of sth** a place where a lot of a particular type of activity, especially bad or violent activity, happens: *the university was a hotbed of radical protest*

ˌhot-ˈblooded *adj* having very strong emotions such as anger or love, that are difficult to control SYN **passionate**

ˈhot ˌbutton *n* [C] *AmE* a problem or subject that causes a lot of arguments or strong feelings between people: *Your letter certainly hit a hot button.* —**hot-button** *adj*: *hot-button issues*

ˌhot ˈcake *BrE*, **hot·cake** *AmE* /ˈhɒtkeɪk $ ˈhɑːt-/ *n* [C] **1 be selling/going like hot cakes** if things are selling like hot cakes, they are very popular and a lot of people are buying them very quickly: *Copies of the book are selling like hot cakes.* **2** *AmE* a PANCAKE

ˌhot ˈchocolate *n* [C,U] a hot drink made with chocolate powder and milk or water → **cocoa**

hotch·potch /ˈhɒtʃpɒtʃ $ ˈhɑːtʃpɑːtʃ/ *BrE*, **hodgepodge** *AmE n* [singular] *informal* a number of things mixed up without sensible order or arrangement

ˌhot-cross ˈbun *n* [C] a round sweet bread roll with a mark in the shape of a cross on top, that is traditionally eaten just before Easter

ˌhot ˈdesk *n* [C] *BrE* a desk that is used by different workers on different days, instead of by the same worker every day —**hot-desking** *n* [U]

ˈhot dish *n* [C,U] *AmE* hot food cooked and served in a deep covered dish

ˈhot dog¹ / $ ˈ../ *n* [C] a cooked SAUSAGE in a long piece of bread

ˈhot dog² *v* (**hot dogged**, **hot dogging**) [I] *AmE informal* to do dangerous and exciting tricks or movements in sports such as SKIING or SURFING

ho·tel /həʊˈtel $ hoʊ-/ ●●● S2 W1 *n* [C] a building where people pay to stay and eat meals: *I've booked the flights and the hotel. | We'll be at the Hotel Ibis.*

COLLOCATIONS

VERBS
stay at/in a hotel *We stayed in a hotel near the airport.*
check into a hotel (*also* **book into a hotel** *BrE*) *He checked into the hotel a little after 2 pm.*
check out of a hotel (=leave a hotel) | **run/manage a hotel**

hotel + NOUN
a hotel room *She was watching TV in her hotel room.*
hotel accommodation *BrE*, **hotel accommodations** *AmE* (=rooms in a hotel) *The price includes hotel accommodation.*
a hotel guest *Hotel guests have free use of the gym and pool.*
the hotel restaurant/bar/gym | the hotel reception/lobby

ADJECTIVES
a luxury hotel (=an expensive and comfortable hotel) *a luxury hotel in central London*
a two-star/three-star etc hotel (=a hotel that has been given a particular rating)

THESAURUS
hotel a building where people pay to stay and eat meals: *We're staying at a hotel in Salzburg. | the Plaza Hotel in New York*
motel a hotel for people travelling by car, usually with a place for the car near each room: *the Palm Court Motel on Highway 23*
inn a small hotel, especially an old one in the countryside. Also used in the names of some big modern hotels: *an 18th-century country inn | the Holiday Inn*
bed and breakfast (*also* **B & B**) a private house or small hotel, where you can sleep and have breakfast: *There's a nice bed and breakfast in the village.*
guesthouse a private house where people can pay to stay and have meals: *We stayed in a well-run guesthouse near the sea.*
hostel/youth hostel a very cheap hotel where people can stay for a short time while they are travelling. Hostels are used especially by young people: *New Zealand has a network of small hostels, ideal for backpackers.*

ho·tel·i·er /həʊˈtelieɪ, -liə $ ˌoʊtəlˈjeɪ, ˌhoʊ-/ *n* [C] someone who owns or manages a hotel

ˌhot ˈflush *BrE*, **ˌhot ˈflash** *AmE* / $ ˈ../ *n* [C] a sudden hot feeling, especially one that women have during their MENOPAUSE

hot·foot /ˌhɒtˈfʊt $ ˈhɑːtfʊt/ *v* **hotfoot it** *informal* to walk or run quickly: *I hotfooted it out of there as soon as possible.* —**hotfoot** *adv*: *Karl arrived hotfoot from the airport.*

hot·head /ˈhɒthed $ ˈhɑːt-/ *n* [C] someone who does things too quickly without thinking —**hotheaded** /ˌhɒtˈhedɪd◂ $ ˌhɑːt-/ *adj*

hot·house¹ /ˈhɒthaʊs $ ˈhɑːt-/ *n* [C] **1** a heated building, usually made of glass, where delicate plants can grow → **GREENHOUSE 2 hothouse atmosphere/environment etc** a situation or place where there is a lot of activity and ideas

hothouse² *v* [T] to give a child a lot of education at a young age because you want them to be very good at something - often used to show disapproval: *Some parents hothouse their children by giving them educational toys when they are very young.*

ˈhot key *n* [C] one or more keys that you can press on a computer KEYBOARD to make the computer quickly do a particular set of actions → **macro**

hot·line, **ˈhot line** /ˈhɒtlaɪn $ ˈhɑːt-/ *n* [C] a special telephone line for people to find out about or talk about something: *Call our crime hotline today.*

ˈhot link *n* [C] a HYPERLINK that allows you to move from one place in a computer document to another, or to a particular place in a different document, especially on the Internet

hot·ly /ˈhɒtli $ ˈhɑːtli/ *adv* **1** in an excited or angry way: **hotly debated/disputed/denied etc** *The rumor has been hotly denied.* **2** done with a lot of energy and effort: *one of the most* ***hotly contested*** *congressional elections | The man ran out of the store,* ***hotly pursued*** (=chased closely) *by security guards.*

ˈhot pants *n* [plural] very short tight women's SHORTS

hot·plate /ˈhɒtpleɪt $ ˈhɑːt-/ *n* [C] a metal surface, usually on a COOKER, that can be heated so that you can cook a pan of food on it

hot·pot /ˈhɒtpɒt $ ˈhɑːtpɑːt/ *n* [C,U] **1** *BrE* a mixture of meat, potatoes, and onions, cooked slowly together → **stew 2** *AmE* a piece of electrical equipment with a small container, used to boil water

ˌhot poˈtato *n* [C] a subject or problem that no one wants to deal with, because it is difficult and any decision might make people angry: *The issue has become a **political hot potato**.*

ˈhot rod *n* [C] *AmE informal* an old car that has been fitted with a powerful engine to make it go faster

hots /hɒts $ hɑːts/ *n* **have/get the hots for sb** *informal* to be sexually attracted to someone

hot·shot /ˈhɒtʃɒt $ ˈhɑːtʃɑːt/ *n* [C] *informal* someone who is very successful and confident: *a hotshot lawyer*

hot spot, hot·spot /ˈhɒtspɒt $ ˈhɑːtspɑːt/ *n* [C] **1** a place where there is a lot of heat or RADIATION: *Many microwaves heat unevenly, leading to hot spots in the milk.* | *Hot spots of radioactivity were found near the power station.* **2** a place that is popular for entertainment or a particular activity: *They played regularly at legendary hot spots such as the UFO Club.* **3** a place where there is likely to be fighting or a particular problem: *The report identified eight pollution hot spots.* **4** a part of a computer image on the screen that you can CLICK on to make other pictures, words etc appear **5** a place in a public building where there is a computer system with an ACCESS POINT, which allows people in the building with a WIRELESS computer or BLUETOOTH MOBILE PHONE to connect to a service such as the Internet **6** *especially AmE* a place where a fire can spread from

ˌhot ˈspring *n* [C] a place where hot water comes up naturally from the ground SYN **geyser**

ˌhot-ˈtempered *adj* having a tendency to become angry easily → **hot temper** at HOT[1]

hot·tie /ˈhɒti $ ˈhɑːti/ *n* [C] *informal* someone who is very sexually attractive

ˌhot ˈtub *n* [C] a heated bath that several people can sit in together → JACUZZI

ˌhot-ˈwater ˌbottle *n* [C] a rubber container full of hot water, used to make a bed warm

ˈhot-wire *v* [T] *informal* to start the engine of a vehicle using the wires of the IGNITION system instead of a key

hou·mous, houmus /ˈhuːməs, ˈhʊ-/ *n* [U] other spellings of HUMUS[1]

hound[1] /haʊnd/ *n* [C] **1** a dog that is fast and has a good sense of smell, used for hunting **2** *informal* a dog

hound[2] *v* [T] **1** to keep following someone and asking them questions in an annoying or threatening way → **harass**: *After the court case, Lee was hounded relentlessly by the press.* **2 hound sb out (of/from sth)** to make things so unpleasant for someone that they are forced to leave a place, job etc SYN **drive out**: *The family were hounded out of their home by 18 months of abuse.*

hour /aʊə $ aʊr/ ●●● S1 W1 *n* [C]

1 60 MINUTES (*written abbreviation* **hr**) a unit for measuring time. There are 60 minutes in one hour, and 24 hours in one day: *The interview will last about two hours.* | *I study **for an hour** every night.* | *I'll be back **in three hours**.* | ***Three hours later** he was back.* | *Her bag was stolen **within hours of** her arrival.* | *You weren't interested in my story **a half hour** ago.* | *It takes about **a quarter of an hour** to walk into town.* | **[+of]** *After four hours of talks, an agreement was reached.* | *The hotel is only **an hour's drive** from the airport.* | *a top speed of 120 **miles an hour*** | *This was freelance work, **paid by the hour**.* | *a five-hour delay*

2 BUSINESS/WORK ETC **hours** [plural] a fixed period of time in the day when a particular activity, business etc happens: *hours of business 9.00–5.00* | **office/opening hours** *Please call during office hours.* | **working hours/hours of work** *the advantages of flexible working hours* | **visiting hours** (=the time when you can visit someone in hospital) | **after hours** (=after the time when a business, especially a bar, is supposed to close)

3 long/regular/late etc hours used to say how long someone works or does things every day, or when they work or do things: *the **long hours worked** by hospital doctors* | *Many hospital staff have to work **unsocial hours*** (=work in the evenings and weekends so that they cannot spend time with family or friends). | *She knew that he **kept** late **hours*** (=stayed up late). | **work all the hours God sends** (=work all the time that you can)

4 TIME OF DAY a particular period or point of time during the day or night: **in the early/small hours (of the morning)** (=between around midnight and two or three o'clock in the morning) *There was a knock on the door in the early hours of the morning.* | *Who can be calling **at this** late **hour**?* (=used when you are surprised or annoyed by how late at night or early in the morning something is) | **daylight/daytime hours** *The park is open during daylight hours.* | **the hours of darkness/daylight** *literary*: *Few people dared to venture out during the hours of darkness.* | **unearthly/ungodly hour** (=used when you are complaining about how early or late something is) *We had to get up at some ungodly hour to catch a plane.* | **at all hours/at any hour (of the day or night)** (=at any time) *If you have a problem, you know you can call at any hour of the day or night.* | *She's up studying **till all hours*** (=until unreasonably late at night). → **waking hours/life/day etc** at WAKING

5 LONG TIME [usually plural] *informal* a long time or a time that seems long: *We had to spend hours filling in forms.* | **for hours (on end)** *It'll keep the children amused for hours on end.* | *a really boring lecture that went on **for hours and hours*** | *She lay awake for **hour after hour*** (=for many hours, continuously).

6 O'CLOCK the time of the day when a new hour starts, for example one o'clock, two o'clock etc: **strike/chime the hour** (=if a clock strikes the hour, it rings, to show that it is one o'clock, seven o'clock etc) | **(every hour) on the hour** (=every hour at six o'clock, seven o'clock etc) *There are flights to Boston every hour on the hour.* | **10/20 etc minutes before/after the hour** *AmE* (=used on national radio or television in order to give the time without saying which hour it is, because the broadcast may be coming from a different time zone) *It's twelve minutes before the hour, and you're listening to 'Morning Edition' on NPR.*

7 1300/1530/1805 etc hours used to give the time in official or military reports and orders: *The helicopters lifted off at 0600 hours.*

8 by the hour/from hour to hour if a situation is changing by the hour or from hour to hour, it is changing very quickly and very often: *This financial crisis is growing more serious by the hour.*

9 lunch/dinner hour the period in the middle of the day when people stop work for a meal: *I usually do the crossword in my lunch hour.*

10 IMPORTANT TIME [usually singular] an important moment or period in history or in your life: **sb's finest/greatest/darkest hour** *This was our country's finest hour.* | **sb's hour of need/glory etc** (=a time when someone needs help, is very successful etc)

11 of the hour important at a particular time, especially the present time: *one of the burning questions of the hour* | **the hero/man of the hour** (=someone who does something very brave, is very successful etc at a particular time) → **the eleventh hour** at ELEVENTH[1](2), → HOURLY, HAPPY HOUR, RUSH HOUR, ZERO HOUR

hour·glass /ˈaʊəglɑːs $ ˈaʊrglæs/ *n* [C] **1** a glass container for measuring time in which sand moves slowly from the top half to the bottom in exactly one hour → **egg-timer 2 hourglass figure** a woman who has an hourglass figure has a narrow waist in comparison with her chest and HIPS

ˈhour ˌhand *n* [C] the shorter of the two pieces on a clock or watch that show you the time → **minute hand**

hour·ly /ˈaʊəli $ ˈaʊrli/ *adj* [only before noun] **1** happening or done every hour: *hourly news broadcasts* | *Buses run at hourly intervals.* **2 hourly pay/earnings/fees etc** the amount you earn or charge for every hour you work: *They are paid an hourly rate.* —**hourly** *adv*: *The database is updated hourly.*

motor home/ RV *AmE*
bungalow *BrE*/ ranch house *AmE*
terraced house *BrE*/ row house *AmE*
semi-detatched *BrE*/ duplex *AmE*
apartment block *BrE*/ apartment building *AmE*
cottage
chateau
mansion
castle

house¹ /haʊs/ ●●● S1 W1 *n* (*plural* **houses** /ˈhaʊzɪz/)
1 WHERE SOMEONE LIVES [C] **a)** a building that someone lives in, especially one that has more than one level and is intended to be used by one family: *a four-bedroom house* | **in a house** *every room in the house* | **at sb's house** *We met at Alison's house.* | *Why don't you all come over to our house for coffee?* | **move house** *BrE* (=leave your house and go to live in another one) **b) the house** all the people who live in a house SYN **household**: *He gets up at six and disturbs the whole house.* THESAURUS ▸ HOME
2 BUILDING **a) opera/court/movie etc house** a large public building used for a particular purpose **b) House** *BrE* used in the names of large buildings, especially offices: *the BBC television studios at Broadcasting House* **c) hen house/coach house/storehouse etc** a building used for a particular purpose
3 GOVERNMENT [C] a group of people who make the laws of a country: *The president will address both houses of Congress.* | **the House of Commons/Lords/Representatives/Assembly** | *the Speaker of the House* → LOWER HOUSE, UPPER HOUSE
4 COMPANY [C] a company, especially one involved in a particular area of business: *America's oldest* ***publishing house*** | *a small independent* ***software house*** | *an* ***auction house*** | *a famous Italian* ***fashion house***
5 THEATRE [C] **a)** the part of a theatre, cinema etc where people sit OPP **backstage**: *The show has been playing to* ***full houses.*** | *The house was half empty.* | *The* ***house lights*** *went down and the music started.* **b)** the people who have come to watch a performance SYN **audience**: **full/packed/empty house** (=a large or small audience) *The show has been playing to packed houses since it opened.*
6 in house if you work in house, you work at the offices of a company or organization, not at home → IN-HOUSE
7 put/set/get your (own) house in order used to say that someone should improve the way they behave before criticizing other people
8 bring the house down to make a lot of people laugh, especially when you are acting in a theatre
9 be on the house if drinks or meals are on the house, you do not have to pay for them because they are provided free by the owner of the bar, restaurant etc
10 house wine (*also* **house red/white**) ordinary wine that is provided by a restaurant to be drunk with meals: *A glass of house red, please.*
11 get on/along like a house on fire *BrE informal* to quickly have a very friendly relationship
12 set up house to start to live in a house, especially with another person: *The two of them set up house in Brighton.*
13 keep house to regularly do all the cleaning, cooking etc in a house: *His daughter keeps house for him.*
14 SCHOOL [C] *BrE* in some schools, one of the groups that children of different ages are divided into to compete against each other, for example in sports competitions
15 ROYAL FAMILY [C] an important family, especially a royal family: *the House of Windsor*
16 MUSIC [U] HOUSE MUSIC
17 house of God/worship *literary* a church
18 this house *formal* used to mean the people who are voting in a formal DEBATE when you are stating the proposal that is being discussed → **DOLL'S HOUSE**, → **eat sb out of house and home** at EAT(10), → **OPEN HOUSE, PUBLIC HOUSE**, → **(as) safe as houses** at SAFE¹(4)

house² /haʊz/ *v* [T] **1** to provide someone with a place to live: **[+in]** *The refugees are being housed in temporary accommodation.* **2** if a building, place, or container houses something, it is kept there: **[+in]** *The collection is currently housed in the British Museum.* | *the plastic case that houses the batteries*

ˈhouse arˌrest *n* **be under house arrest** to be kept as a prisoner by a government, staying inside your house rather than in a prison

house·boat /ˈhaʊsbəʊt $ -boʊt/ *n* [C] a river boat that you can live in

house·bound /ˈhaʊsbaʊnd/ *adj* not able to leave your house, especially because you are ill or old

house·boy /ˈhaʊsbɔɪ/ *n* [C] *old-fashioned not polite* a man who is employed to do general work at someone's house

house·break·er /ˈhaʊsˌbreɪkə $ -ər/ *n* [C] a thief who enters someone else's house by breaking locks, windows etc SYN **burglar** —**housebreaking** *n* [U]

house·bro·ken /ˈhaʊsˌbrəʊkən $ -ˌbroʊ-/ *adj AmE* a pet animal that is housebroken has been trained not to make the house dirty with its URINE and FAECES SYN **house-trained** *BrE*

ˈhouse call *n* [C] a visit that someone, especially a doctor, makes to a person in that person's home as part of their job

house·coat /ˈhaʊs-kəʊt $ -koʊt/ *n* [C] a long loose coat worn at home to protect clothes while cleaning etc

house·fly /ˈhaʊsflaɪ/ *n* (*plural* **houseflies**) [C] a common type of fly that lives in people's houses

house·ful /ˈhaʊsfʊl/ *n* **a houseful of sth** a large number of people or things in your house: *He grew up in a houseful of women.*

ˈhouse ˌguest *n* [C] a friend or relative who is staying in your house for a short time

house·hold¹ /ˈhaʊshəʊld $ -hoʊld/ ●●○ *n* [C] all the people who live together in one house SYN **house**: *A growing number of households have at least one computer.* |

H

Families are classified by the occupation of ***the head of the household*** (=the person who earns the most money and is most respected in a house).

household² ●●○ *adj* [only before noun]
1 relating to looking after a house and the people in it SYN **domestic**: **household goods/products/items etc** *washing powder and other household products | household chores* **2 be a household name/word** to be very well known: *Coca-Cola is a household name around the world.*

house·hold·er /ˈhaʊsˌhəʊldə $ -ˌhoʊldər/ *n* [C] *formal* someone who owns or is in charge of a house → **homeowner**

ˈhouse ˌhusband *n* [C] a husband who stays at home and does the cooking, cleaning etc → **housewife**

house·keep·er /ˈhaʊsˌkiːpə $ -ər/ *n* [C] someone who is employed to manage the cleaning, cooking etc in a house or hotel ⚠ Do not confuse with **housewife** (=a woman who looks after her house rather than going out to work).

house·keep·ing /ˈhaʊsˌkiːpɪŋ/ *n* [U] **1** the work and organization of things that need to be done in a house, hotel etc, for example cooking and buying food: *the company in charge of the catering and housekeeping at the college* **2** *BrE* (*also* **housekeeping money**) an amount of money that is kept and used to pay for food and other things needed in the home **3** jobs that need to be done to keep a system working properly

house·maid /ˈhaʊsmeɪd/ *n* [C] *old-fashioned* a female servant who cleans someone's house

house·man /ˈhaʊsmən/ *n* (*plural* **housemen** /-mən/) [C] *BrE* someone who has nearly finished training as a doctor and is working in a hospital SYN **intern** *AmE*

ˈhouse ˌmartin *n* [C] a small black and white European bird of the SWALLOW family

house·mas·ter /ˈhaʊsˌmɑːstə $ -ˌmæstər/ *n* [C] *especially BrE* a male teacher who is in charge of one of the houses (=groups of children of different ages) in a school → **housemistress**

house·mate /ˈhaʊsmeɪt/ *n* [C] *BrE* a person who you share a house with but who is not a member of your family SYN **roommate** *AmE* → **flatmate**

house·mis·tress /ˈhaʊsˌmɪstrɪs/ *n* [C] *especially BrE* a female teacher who is in charge of one of the houses (=groups of children of different ages) in a school → **housemaster**

ˈhouse ˌmusic (*also* **house**) *n* [U] a type of popular dance music

ˌhouse of ˈcards *n* [singular] a plan that is so badly arranged that it is likely to fail

ˌHouse of ˈCommons *n* **the House of Commons** the part of the British or Canadian parliament whose members are elected by the people

ˌHouse of ˈLords *n* **the House of Lords** the part of the British parliament whose members are not elected but have positions because of their rank or title

ˌHouse of Repreˈsentatives *n* **the House of Representatives** the larger of the two parts of the US Congress or of the parliament of Australia or New Zealand → **Senate**

ˈhouse ˌparty *n* [C] a group of people who stay as guests in someone's house and have a party there

house·phone /ˈhaʊsfəʊn $ -foʊn/ *n* [C] a telephone that can only be used to make calls within a building, especially a hotel

house·plant /ˈhaʊsplɑːnt $ -plænt/ *n* [C] a plant that you grow inside your house for decoration SYN **pot plant** *BrE*

house·proud /ˈhaʊspraʊd/ *adj BrE* spending a lot of time on keeping your house clean and tidy

house·room /ˈhaʊsruːm, -rʊm/ *n* [U] *BrE* **1** space in a house for a person or thing **2 not give sth houseroom** *informal* used to emphasize that you do not like something and do not want it

ˈhouse-sit *v* (*past tense and past participle* **house-sat**, *present participle* **house-sitting**) [I] to look after someone's house while they are away —**housesitter** *n* [C]

ˌhouse-to-ˈhouse *adj* **house-to-house inquiries/search/collection etc** inquiries etc that are made by visiting each house in a particular area → **door-to-door**: *The abduction sparked a house-to-house search in the Willenhall area.*

house·top /ˈhaʊstɒp $ -tɑːp/ *n* [C] the top part of a house SYN **rooftop**: *a view over the housetops*

ˈhouse-trained *adj BrE* a pet animal that is house-trained has been trained not to make the house dirty with its URINE and FAECES SYN **housebroken** *AmE* —**housetrain** *v* [T]

house·wares /ˈhaʊsweəz $ -werz/ *n* [U, plural] *AmE* small things used in the home, for example plates, lamps etc, or the department of a large shop that sells these things

ˈhouse-ˌwarming *n* [C usually singular] a party that you give to celebrate moving into a new house: *Are you coming to Jo's house-warming on Friday? | a* ***house-warming party***

house·wife /ˈhaʊswaɪf/ ●●● W3 *n* (*plural* **housewives** /-waɪvz/) [C] a married woman who works at home doing the cooking, cleaning etc, but does not have a job outside the house SYN **homemaker** → **house husband**

house·work /ˈhaʊswɜːk $ -wɜːrk/ ●●○ *n* [U] work that you do to take care of a house, for example washing, cleaning etc → **chore**: **do (the) housework** *I spent all morning doing the housework. | I don't like doing housework.*

> **GRAMMAR: Countable or uncountable?**
>
> • **Housework** is an uncountable noun and is not used in the plural. You say: *I help my mother with the housework.* ✗ Don't say: *I help my mother with the houseworks.*
>
> • **Housework** is followed by a singular verb: *All the housework* ***was*** *done by him.*

hous·ing /ˈhaʊzɪŋ/ ●●○ W2 *n*
1 [U] the houses or conditions that people live in: *health problems caused by bad housing | a scheme to provide affordable housing for local people*
2 [U] the work of providing houses for people to live in: *government housing policy | public services such as education, housing and transport*
3 [C] a protective cover for a machine: *the engine housing*

ˈhousing associˌation *n* [C] an organization in Britain, formed by a group of people working together to build or buy homes for themselves

ˈhousing esˌtate *BrE*, **ˈhousing deˌvelopment** *AmE n* [C] a large number of houses that have been built together in a planned way → **council house**

ˈhousing ˌproject *n* [C] *AmE* a group of houses or apartments, usually built with government money, for poor families

Hous·ton /ˈhjuːstən/ **1** a city and port in the US state of Texas, where NASA, the US government space centre, is based **2 Houston, we have a problem** people say this humorously when something goes wrong. These words were first spoken by one of the ASTRONAUTS on the unsuccessful Apollo 13 space MISSION.

hove /həʊv $ hoʊv/ a past tense and past participle of HEAVE

hov·el /ˈhɒvəl $ ˈhʌ-, ˈhɑː-/ *n* [C] a small dirty place where someone lives, especially a very poor person

hov·er /ˈhɒvə $ ˈhʌvər, ˈhɑː-/ ●○○ *v*
1 [I] if a bird, insect, or HELICOPTER hovers, it stays in one place in the air: **[+over/above]** *flies hovering above the surface of the water*
2 [I] to stay nervously in the same place, especially because you are waiting for something or are not certain what to do: *Her younger brother hovered in the background watching us. |* **[+around/about]** *I noticed several reporters hovering around outside the courtroom.*
3 [I always + adv/prep] if a level, price etc hovers around a

H

certain amount, it stays close to that amount, only changing slightly up or down: **[+around/between etc]** *The dollar has been hovering around the 110 yen level.*
4 [T always + adv/prep] to put the CURSOR on something on a computer screen, using the mouse: **hover sth over sth** *When you hover the cursor over the image, the title of the image appears.*

hov·er·craft /ˈhɒvəkrɑːft $ ˈhʌvərkræft, ˈhɑː-/ *n* (*plural* **hovercraft** *or* **hovercrafts**) [C] a vehicle that travels just above the surface of land or water, travelling on a strong current of air that the engines produce beneath it → **hydrofoil**

HOV lane /ˌeɪtʃ əʊ ˈviː leɪn $ -oʊ-/ *n* [C] (***high-occupancy vehicle lane***) a LANE on main roads that can only be used by vehicles carrying three or more passengers when there is a lot of traffic → **bus lane**

how /haʊ/ ●●● S1 W1 *adv*
1 used to ask or talk about the way in which something happens or is done: *How do you spell your name?* | *How can I help you?* | *I'd like to help in some way, but I'm not sure how.* | *He explained how the system worked.* | *We both used to work at the airport – that's how we met.* | **how to do sth** *I don't know how to get to your house.* | *Alan showed me how to load the gun.* | *advice on **how best*** (=the best way) *to invest your money* | *They had a number of suggestions **as to how** the service could be improved.* | *This still leaves **the question of how** local services should be funded.* | **how on earth/in the world etc** (=used for emphasis when you are surprised, angry etc) *How on earth did you find out?*
2 used to ask or talk about the amount, size, degree etc of something: *How big is the state of Louisiana?* | *How many kids do they have now?* | *How long have you been learning English?* | *Do you know how old it is?* | *They couldn't tell exactly how far away the bridge was.* | *She wondered how much Angela already knew.* | **how much?** (=used to ask the price of something) *How much are the tickets?*
3 *spoken* **a)** used to ask about someone's health, especially when you meet them: *'Hi Laurie, how are you?' 'Fine, thanks. How are you?'* | *Has Ros had the baby yet? How is she?* | *'How's your ankle this morning?' 'Better, thanks.'* **b)** used when you meet someone, to ask for news about their life, work etc: *So **how's it going** at work these days? Still enjoying it?* | *'**How are things** with you?' 'Fine.'* | ***How are you doing**?*
4 used to ask someone about their opinion or experience of something: *How was the film?* | *'How's your steak?' 'Mmm, it's good.'* | *How did your exams go?* | *How do you feel about seeing Peter again?* | *How's that? Does that feel comfortable?*
5 used after certain adjectives or verbs to refer to an event or situation: *It's amazing how they've managed to get everything finished so quickly.* | *I remember how she always used to have fresh flowers in the house.*
6 [+adj/adv] used to emphasize the quality you are mentioning: *How lovely to see you!* | *'John's been in an accident.' 'Oh, how awful!'* | *I didn't realize how difficult it was to get tickets.* | *He was impressed at how well she could read.*
7 *old-fashioned or written* used to say that something happens to a very great degree: *How the crowd loved it!*

SPOKEN PHRASES
8 how about ... ? a) used to make a suggestion about what to do SYN **what about**: *No, I'm busy on Monday. How about Tuesday at seven?* | **how about doing sth?** *How about putting the sofa closer to the window?* | *How about we have that game when we get back?* | *How about if we tell the police where Newley is hiding?* | **how's about ... ?** *AmE*: *How's about going to the beach this afternoon?* **b)** used to ask about another person or thing: *'Mary and Ken are still away.' 'And how about Billy?'* | *I need a long cold drink. How about you?*
9 how do you mean? used to ask someone to explain something they have just said: *'What's your family situation?' 'How do you mean?' 'Are you married?'*
10 how come? *informal* used to ask why something has happened or why a particular situation exists, especially when you are surprised by it: *How come Dave's home? Isn't he feeling well?*
11 how do you do? *formal* used as a polite greeting when you meet someone for the first time
12 how can/could sb do sth? used when you are very surprised by something or disapprove strongly of something: *William! How can you say such a thing?* | *How could anyone be so cruel?*
13 how you like/want *BrE informal* in whatever way you like or want: *Then you can arrange it how you like.*
14 how about that!/how do you like that! used when you think something is surprising, rude, impressive etc: *He scored two goals! How about that!*
15 how's that for sth? used to say that you think something is very impressive: *I've already arranged everything. How's that for efficiency?*
16 how ... is that? *informal* **a)** used to say that an action or event has a particular quality to a great degree: *He sent himself a card for Valentine's Day. How sad is that?* **b)** used to say that an action or event does not have a particular quality: *They say they're not going to leave, but how likely is that?*
17 how so? used to ask someone to explain an opinion they have given: *'Rick's parents are a little strange, I think.' 'How so?'*
18 how about if ... ? *informal* used to mention something that may happen, and ask what should be done if it does happen: *How about if we quit now?*
19 and how! *old-fashioned* used to say 'yes' strongly in reply to a question: *'Was Matt drunk?' 'And how!'*

→ **how dare you** at DARE[1](2)

GRAMMAR: Patterns with how
• You use **how** before an ordinary adjective: *We all know how important exercise is.* ✗ Don't say: *We all know how much important exercise is.*
• You use **how much** before a comparative adjective: *They realize how much better life is.* ✗ Don't say: *They realize how better life is.*

USAGE: How or what?
• You use **what** with **look/feel/be like** to ask for or give a description: *What does she look like?* ✗ Don't say: *How does she look like?*
• You use **what** with **think** to ask or talk about someone's opinion: *What do you think of him?* ✗ Don't say: *How do you think of him?*

how·dah /ˈhaʊdə/ *n* [C] a covered seat used for riding an ELEPHANT

how·dy /ˈhaʊdi/ *interjection AmE informal* hello

how·ev·er[1] /haʊˈevə $ -ər/ ●●● S2 W1 *adv*
1 used when you are adding a fact or piece of information that seems surprising, or seems very different from what you have just said SYN **nevertheless**: *This is a cheap and simple process. However, there are dangers.* | *an extremely unpleasant disease that is, however, easy to treat*
2 used to say that it does not matter how big, good, serious etc something is because it will not change a situation in any way SYN **no matter how**: *You should report any incident, however minor it is.* | *We have to finish, however long it takes.* | **however much/many** *I really want the car, however much it costs.*
3 *especially BrE* used to show surprise when you ask how something happens or how someone does something: *However did he get that job?*

however[2] ●●● S2 W3 *conjunction* in whatever way: *You can do it however you like.* | *If we win the match, we'll be delighted, however it happens.* | *However you look at it, it was a wicked thing to do.* **THESAURUS** ▸ **BUT**

how·it·zer /ˈhaʊɪtsə $ -ər/ *n* [C] a heavy gun that fires SHELLS high into the air

howl[1] /haʊl/ ●○○ *v*
1 [I] if a dog, WOLF, or other animal howls, it makes a long loud sound → **bark**: *The dogs howled all night.*
2 [I] to make a long loud cry because you are unhappy, angry, or in pain, or because you are amused or excited:

H

Upstairs, one of the twins began to howl (=cry). | **[+in/with]** *Somewhere, someone was howling in pain.* | *He makes audiences* ***howl with laughter***.
3 [I,T] to shout or demand something angrily: **[+for]** *Republicans have been howling for military intervention.*
4 [I] if the wind howls, it makes a loud high sound as it blows: *wind howling in the trees*
howl sb/sth ↔ **down** *phr v* to prevent someone or something from being heard by shouting loudly and angrily SYN **shout down**

howl² ●○○ *n* [C]
1 a long loud sound made by a dog, WOLF, or other animal → **bark**
2 a loud cry or shout showing pain, anger, unhappiness etc.: **[+of]** *He let out a howl of anguish.* | *There were howls of protest.* | *This suggestion was greeted with* ***howls of laughter***.
3 a loud high sound made by the wind blowing

howl·er /ˈhaʊlə $ -ər/ *n* [C] *informal* a stupid mistake that makes people laugh SYN **blunder**

howl·ing /ˈhaʊlɪŋ/ *adj* **be a howling success** something that is a howling success is extremely successful

ˈ**how-to** *n* [C] a set of instructions telling you how to do something

hp /ˌeɪtʃ ˈpiː/ the abbreviation of ***horsepower***

HP /ˌeɪtʃ ˈpiː/ *n* [U] *BrE* the abbreviation of ***hire purchase***: *We* ***bought*** *the carpets* ***on HP***.

HQ /ˌeɪtʃ ˈkjuː/ *n* [U] the abbreviation of ***headquarters***

hr *BrE*, **hr.** *AmE* (*plural* **hrs**) the written abbreviation of ***hour*** or ***hours***

HRH the written abbreviation of ***His/Her Royal Highness***

HRT /ˌeɪtʃ ɑː ˈtiː $ -ɑːr-/ *n* [U] (***hormone replacement therapy***) treatment for women during and after the MENOPAUSE, in which they are given HORMONES to replace those which they are lacking

HSE, the /ˌeɪtʃ es ˈiː/ (***the Health and Safety Executive***) a British government organization that gives advice to companies about health and safety, and makes rules to prevent workers from being injured or becoming ill at work

ht. (*also* **ht** *BrE*) the written abbreviation of ***height***

HTML /ˌeɪtʃ tiː em ˈel/ *n* [U] *technical* (***hypertext markup language***) a computer language used for producing pages of writing and pictures that can be put on the Internet: *HTML documents*

http /ˌeɪtʃ tiː tiː ˈpiː/ *technical* (***hypertext transfer protocol***) a set of standards that control how computer documents that are written in HTML connect to each other

H_2O /ˌeɪtʃ tuː ˈəʊ $ -ˈoʊ/ *n* [U] the chemical sign for water

hub /hʌb/ ●○○ *n* [C]
1 the central and most important part of an area, system, activity etc, which all the other parts are connected to SYN **centre**: **[+of]** *Birmingham is at the hub of Britain's motorway network.* | *the* ***commercial hub*** *of the region*
2 the central part of a wheel to which the AXLE is joined → see picture at BICYCLE

hub·bub /ˈhʌbʌb/ *n* [singular, U] **1** a mixture of loud noises, especially the noise of a lot of people talking at the same time **2** a situation in which there is a lot of activity, excitement, or argument → **commotion**

hub·by /ˈhʌbi/ *n* (*plural* **hubbies**) [C] *informal* husband

hub·cap /ˈhʌbkæp/ *n* [C] a round metal cover for the centre of a wheel on a vehicle

hu·bris /ˈhjuːbrɪs/ *n* [U] *literary* too much pride

huck·le·ber·ry /ˈhʌkəlbəri $ -beri/ *n* (*plural* **huckleberries**) [C] a small dark blue North American fruit that grows on a bush

huck·ster /ˈhʌkstə $ -ər/ *n* [C] *AmE* someone who tries to sell things in a way that is too forceful and not honest – used to show disapproval —**hucksterism** *n* [U]

hud·dle¹ /ˈhʌdl/ ●○○ *v*
1 [I,T] (*also* **huddle together/up**) if a group of people huddle together, they stay very close to each other, especially because they are cold or frightened: *We lay huddled together for warmth.* | **[+around]** *People huddled around the radio, waiting for news.*
2 [I always + adv/prep] to lie or sit with your arms and legs close to your body because you are cold or frightened: *She huddled under the blankets.* | *The snow blew against his huddled body.*
3 [I] *AmE* to sit or stand with a small group of people in order to discuss something privately: *The executive board huddled to discuss the issue.*
4 [I] if American football players huddle, they gather around one player who tells them the plan for the next part of the game

huddle² *n* [C] **1** a group of people or things that are close together, but not arranged in any particular order, pattern, or system: **[+of]** *a huddle of straw huts* | *Huddles of men stood around talking.* **2** a group of players in American football who gather around one player who tells them the plan for the next part of the game **3 get/go into a huddle** to form a small group away from other people in order to discuss something

hue /hjuː/ *n* [C] *literary* **1** a colour or type of colour → **tint**, **shade**: *a golden hue* THESAURUS COLOUR **2** a type of opinion, belief etc: **of every hue/of all hues** (=of many kinds) *political opinions of every hue*

ˌ**hue and** ˈ**cry** *n* [singular] *written* angry protests about something, usually from a group of people

huff¹ /hʌf/ *v informal* **1 huff and puff a)** to breathe out in a noisy way, especially when you do something that involves a lot of physical effort: *He was huffing and puffing by the time he got to the top.* **b)** to show clearly that you strongly disagree with or are annoyed about something: *After a lot of huffing and puffing, he eventually gave in to our request.* **2** [T] to say something in a way that shows you are annoyed, often because someone has offended you: *'I haven't got time for that now,' huffed Sam irritably.*

huff² *n* **in a huff** feeling angry or bad-tempered, especially because someone has offended you: **go off/walk off/leave etc in a huff** *She stormed out in a huff.*

huff·y /ˈhʌfi/ *adj informal* in a bad MOOD (=the way that you feel), especially because someone has offended you: *Some customers* ***get huffy*** *when you ask them for their ID.* —**huffily** *adv*

hug¹ /hʌg/ ●●○ *v* (**hugged**, **hugging**) [T]
1 to put your arms around someone and hold them tightly to show love or friendship SYN **embrace**: *We stood there crying and hugging each other.* | *She went to her daughter and* ***hugged*** *her* ***tightly***.
2 to put your arms around yourself: **hug your knees/arms/legs etc** *Sarah sat on the floor, hugging her knees.* | **hug yourself** *She stood hugging herself against the cold.*
3 to move along the side, edge, top etc of something, staying very close to it: *The small boats hugged the coast.*
4 if clothes hug your body, they fit closely → **close-fitting**: **body-/figure-hugging** *a figure-hugging dress*
5 to hold something in your arms close to your chest: *He was hugging a big pile of books.*
6 hug yourself with joy/delight etc *BrE* to feel very pleased with yourself: *Kate hugged herself with pleasure after receiving the award.*

GRAMMAR: Reciprocal verbs

Hug is a reciprocal verb. This type of verb is used when saying that two or more people or things do something that involves both or all of them. It does not need to have an object: *She and her friend hugged.* In this sentence, **hug** is intransitive and does not have an object.
You can also say: *She hugged her friend.* | *She and her friend hugged each other.* In these sentences, **hug** is transitive.
GRAMMAR GUIDE VERBS

THESAURUS

hug (*also* **give sb a hug**) to put your arms around someone and hold them tightly to show love or friendship: *Mother hugged him and tucked him into bed.* | *Come here and give me a big hug.*
embrace to put your arms around someone and hold him or her in a caring way. **Embrace** is more formal than **hug**: *Jason warmly embraced his son.* | *The two leaders embraced each other.*
cuddle to put your arms around someone or something as a sign of love, especially a child or a small animal: *She sat on a chair, cuddling her daughter.* | *He cuddled the puppy.*
put your arms around sb to hold someone closely to your body, especially to comfort them or show that you love them: *The woman put her arms around the sobbing boy.*
cradle *written* to hold someone very gently in your arms, like you would hold a baby: *She held the baby in her arms.* | *She cradled his head in her hands and kissed him on the forehead*

hug² ●●○ *n* [C] the action of putting your arms around someone and holding them tightly to show love or friendship SYN **embrace**: *Paul* ***gave*** *me a big* ***hug***. | *Nesta greeted the visitors with hugs and kisses.* → BEAR HUG

huge /hjuːdʒ/ ●●● S1 W2 *adj*
1 extremely large in size, amount, or degree SYN **enormous**: *a huge dog* | *huge crowds* | *Your room's huge compared to mine.* | *These shoes make my feet look huge.* | **a huge amount/sum/quantity etc** *huge sums of money* | *We are only now realizing the* ***huge scale*** *of the problem.* | **a huge loss/profit/increase etc** *a huge increase in cost* | **a huge range/variety/selection etc** *a huge range of issues* | **a huge success/disappointment etc** *The play was a huge success.* | **a huge difference/gap etc** *The new system has made a huge difference.* THESAURUS ▸ BIG
2 *informal* very popular or famous: *David Hasselhoff is huge in Germany.* —**hugeness** *n* [U]

GRAMMAR

Huge is not used with 'very'. You say: *The house is absolutely huge.* ✗ Don't say: *The house is very huge.*
GRAMMAR GUIDE ▸ ADJECTIVES

huge·ly /hjuːdʒli/ ●○○ *adv* very or very much SYN **enormously**: *Her latest album has been hugely successful.* | *The area has changed hugely in the last few years.*

huh /hʌh, hʌ/ *interjection* **1** used to show that you have not heard or understood a question: *'Carly, are you listening to me?' 'Huh?'* **2** *especially AmE* used at the end of a question, often to ask for agreement: *Not a bad little place, huh?* **3** used to show disagreement or surprise, or to show that you do not find something impressive: *'She looks nice.' 'Huh! Too much make-up, if you ask me.'*

hu·la /ˈhuːlə/ *n* [singular] a Polynesian dance done by women using gentle movements of the HIPS

ˈhula hoop *n* [C] a large plastic ring that you swing around your waist by moving your HIPS

hulk /hʌlk/ *n* [C] **1** a large heavy person or thing: *a hulk of a man* **2** the main part of an old ship, vehicle etc that has decayed or been destroyed

hulk·ing /ˈhʌlkɪŋ/ *adj* [only before noun] very big and often awkward: *Two hulking figures guarded the entrance of the club.*

hull¹ /hʌl/ *n* [C] **1** the main part of a ship that goes in the water: **wooden-hulled/steel-hulled etc** (=having a wood, steel etc hull) **2** the outer covering of seeds, rice, grain etc → **husk**

hull² *v* [T] to take off the outer part of vegetables, rice, grain etc

hul·la·ba·loo /ˌhʌləbəˈluː, ˈhʌləbəluː/ *n* [singular] *informal* **1** excited talk, newspaper stories etc, especially when something surprising or shocking is happening SYN **fuss**: *There was a huge hullabaloo when the book was first published.* **2** a lot of noise, especially made by people shouting SYN **commotion**: *She looked up to see what all the hullabaloo was about.*

hul·lo /həˈləʊ, hʌ- $ -ˈloʊ/ *interjection especially BrE* another spelling of HELLO

hum¹ /hʌm/ ●○○ *v* (**hummed, humming**)
1 [I,T] to sing a tune by making a continuous sound with your lips closed: **hum to yourself** *Tony was humming to himself as he drove along.* | *He began to hum a tune.*
2 [I] to make a low continuous sound: *Machines hummed on the factory floor.*
3 [I] if a place hums, it is full of activity – use this to show approval → **busy**: *By nine o'clock, the restaurant was humming.* | **[+with]** *The streets were humming with life.*
4 hum and haw *BrE* to take a long time deciding what to say or do → **hesitate** SYN **hem and haw** *AmE*

hum² *n* [singular] **1** a low continuous sound: **[+of]** *the distant hum of traffic* THESAURUS ▸ SOUND **2 hum of excitement/approval etc** the sound of people talking because they are excited etc

HUMAN BODY

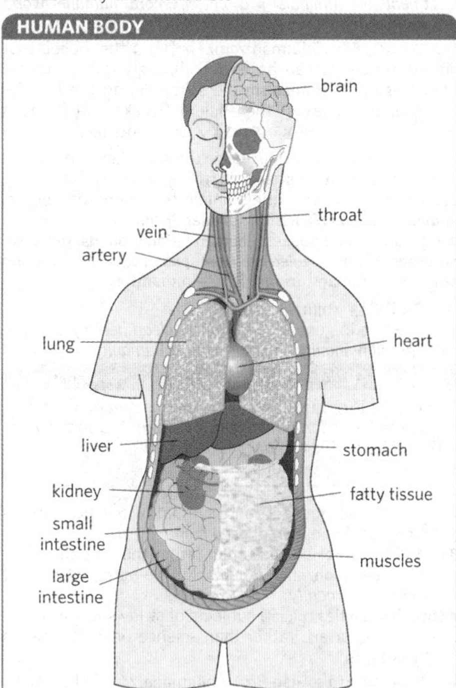

hu·man¹ /ˈhjuːmən/ ●●● S2 W1 *adj*
1 belonging to or relating to people, especially as opposed to machines or animals: *There are many different cell types in* ***the human body***. | *the power of* ***the human mind*** | *The desire for joy lies deep within* ***the human spirit***. | *Infra-red light is invisible to* ***the human eye***. | *theories of* ***human behaviour*** | *different areas of* ***human experience*** | *respect for the absolute value of* ***human life*** | *The accident was the result of* ***human error***. | *The meat was declared unfit* ***for human consumption***.
2 human weaknesses, emotions etc are those that are typical of people: *He was also a person with very obvious human failings.*
3 sb is only human used to say that someone should not be blamed for what they have done
4 having the same feelings and emotions as ordinary people: *He's really not so bad. When you get to know him he seems quite human.*
5 a/the human touch someone, especially someone in authority, who has the human touch deals with people in a kind friendly way and is able to understand their feelings and problems: *The president has been accused of lacking the human touch.*

6 human interest a quality that makes a story interesting because it is about people's feelings, lives, relationships etc
7 the human condition the experiences, emotions, needs etc that all people share, especially considered as a situation from which it is impossible to escape
8 human chain a line of people: *Firefighters **formed** a **human chain** to carry the brothers to safety.*
9 put a human face on sth (*also* **give sth a human face**) to make an important event or principle understandable to ordinary people by directing their attention to the way it affects a particular person: *Anne Frank was the girl whose diary put a human face on the Holocaust.*
10 capitalism/communism/socialism etc with a human face a capitalist etc economic and political system that does not ignore people's needs

human² ●●● W3 (*also* ˌ**human 'being**) *n* [C] a person

hu·mane /hjuːˈmeɪn/ *adj* treating people or animals in a way that is not cruel and causes them as little suffering as possible OPP **inhumane**: *the campaign for the humane treatment of criminals | a better, **more humane** world* —**humanely** *adv*

hu·man·is·m /ˈhjuːmənɪzəm/ *n* [U] **1** the belief that human problems can be solved through science rather than religion **2 Humanism** the study during the Renaissance of the ideas of the ancient Greeks and Romans —**humanist** *n* [C] —**humanistic** /ˌhjuːməˈnɪstɪk◂/ *adj*

hu·man·i·tar·i·an /hjuːˌmænəˈteəriən $ -ˈter-/ ●○○ *adj* [only before noun] concerned with improving bad living conditions and preventing unfair treatment of people: **humanitarian aid/assistance/relief** *Humanitarian aid is being sent to the refugees.* | **humanitarian grounds/reasons/purposes** *He was released from prison on humanitarian grounds.* —**humanitarian** *n* [C] —**humanitarianism** *n* [U]

hu·man·i·ty /hjuːˈmænəti/ ●○○ *n*
1 [U] people in general: *We want a clean healthy environment for **all humanity**. | crimes against humanity*

> **GRAMMAR**
>
> **Humanity** is not used with 'the' in this meaning. You say: *The future for humanity is uncertain.* ✗ Don't say: *The future for the humanity is uncertain.*
> GRAMMAR GUIDE ▸ NOUNS

2 [U] kindness, respect, and sympathy towards others OPP **inhumanity**: *a man of deep humanity*
3 [U] the state of being human rather than an animal or machine: **common/shared humanity** *We must never forget our common humanity.*
4 (the) humanities [plural] subjects of study such as literature, history, or art, rather than science or mathematics SYN **(the) arts**

hu·man·ize (*also* **-ise** *BrE*) /ˈhjuːmənaɪz/ *v* [T] to make a place or system more pleasant or more suitable for people: *an attempt to humanize prison conditions*

hu·man·kind /ˌhjuːmənˈkaɪnd/ *n* [U] people in general SYN **mankind**

hu·man·ly /ˈhjuːmənli/ *adv* **humanly possible a)** used to emphasize that something is possible: *She wanted to put as much distance as was humanly possible between herself and Adrian.* **b)** used to emphasize that someone did all they could: *The doctors did everything humanly possible to save the child's life.*

ˌ**human 'nature** *n* [U] **1** the qualities or ways of behaving that are natural and common to most people **2 it's (only/just) human nature** *spoken* used to say that a particular feeling or way of behaving is normal and natural

hu·man·oid /ˈhjuːmənɔɪd/ *adj* having a human shape and human qualities: *The robot was humanoid in appearance.* —**humanoid** *n* [C]

ˌ**human 'race** *n* **the human race** all people, considered together as a group SYN **mankind**

ˌ**human re'sources** / $ ˌ.. ˈ.../ *n* [U] (*abbreviation* **HR**) in a company, the department that deals with employing, training, and helping people

> **GRAMMAR: Singular or plural verb?**
>
> • **Human resources** is usually followed by a singular verb: ***Human resources deals** with changes to contracts.*
> • In British English, you can also use a plural verb: ***Human resources deal** with changes to contracts.*
> GRAMMAR GUIDE ▸ NOUNS

ˌ**human 'right** ●○○ *n* [C usually plural] one of the basic rights that many societies think every person should have to be treated in a fair equal way without cruelty, for example by their government, or the right to vote: *human rights violations*

ˌ**human 'shield** *n* [C] someone who is taken and kept as a prisoner by a criminal in order to protect the criminal from being killed, injured, or caught

hum·ble¹ /ˈhʌmbəl/ ●○○ *adj*
1 not considering yourself or your ideas to be as important as other people's OPP **proud** → **humility**: *a modest and humble man*
2 having a low social class or position: *He started his career as a humble peanut farmer.* | **humble background/origins etc** *Iacocca rose from humble beginnings to become boss of Ford.*
3 in my humble opinion *spoken* used humorously to give your opinion about something
4 my humble apologies *BrE spoken* used humorously to say you are sorry
5 [only before noun] simple and ordinary, but useful or effective: ***The humble** potato may be the key to feeding the world's population.*
6 eat humble pie to admit that you were wrong about something
7 your humble servant *BrE old use* a formal way of ending a letter
8 sb's humble abode someone's house or apartment – used humorously: *Welcome to our humble abode.* —**humbly** *adv*

humble² *v* **1 be humbled** if you are humbled, you realize that you are not as important, good, kind etc as you thought you were: *You can't help but be humbled when you enter this cathedral.* **2** [T] to easily defeat someone who is much stronger than you are: *The mighty U.S. army was humbled by a small Southeast Asian country.* **3 humble yourself** to show that you are not too proud to ask for something, admit you are wrong etc: *I knew he had humbled himself to ask for my help.* —**humbling** *adj*: ***a humbling experience***

hum·ble·brag·ging /ˈhʌmbəlˌbræɡɪŋ/ *n* [U] the action of telling people how good your life, achievements etc are in a way that makes them seem not very good, because you do not want to seem BOASTFUL – used to show disapproval: *She's always humblebragging by complaining about the number of parties she has to go to.* —**humblebrag** *n* [C]: *I find his humblebrags both annoying and hilarious.*

hum·bug /ˈhʌmbʌɡ/ *n* **1** [U] insincere or dishonest words or behaviour: *He dismissed the prime minister's comments as 'pure humbug'.* **2** [C] *BrE* a hard sweet made from boiled sugar, usually with a PEPPERMINT taste **3** [C] *old-fashioned* someone who behaves in a dishonest or insincere way, for example by pretending to be someone they are not SYN **imposter**

hum·ding·er /hʌmˈdɪŋə $ -ər/ *n* **a humdinger** *informal* a very exciting or impressive game, performance, or event: *a real humdinger of a match*

hum·drum /ˈhʌmdrʌm/ *adj* boring and ordinary, and having no variety or interest SYN **tedious**: **humdrum existence/job/life etc** *the prisoners' humdrum routine*
THESAURUS ▸ BORING

hu·me·rus /ˈhjuːmərəs/ *n* (*plural* **humeri** /-raɪ/) [C] *technical* the bone between your shoulder and elbow

hu·mid /ˈhjuːmɪd/ ●●○ *adj* if the weather is humid, you feel uncomfortable because the air is very wet and usually hot → **humidity**: *Tokyo is extremely humid in midsummer.* | **humid air/climate etc** THESAURUS ▸ DAMP, HOT, WET

hu·mid·i·fi·er /hjuːˈmɪdəfaɪə $ -ər/ *n* [C] a machine that makes the air in a room less dry

hu·mid·i·fy /hjuːˈmɪdɪfaɪ/ *v* (**humidified**, **humidifying**, **humidifies**) [T] to add very small drops of water to the air in a room etc because the air is too dry

hu·mid·i·ty /hjuːˈmɪdəti/ ●○○ *n* [U]
1 the amount of water contained in the air: *The room is kept at 72 degrees and 50% relative humidity.*
2 when the air is very warm and wet: *a day of hot sunshine and humidity*

hu·mil·i·ate /hjuːˈmɪlieɪt/ ●○○ *v* [T] to make someone feel ashamed or stupid, especially when other people are present SYN **embarrass**: *Her boss humiliated her in front of all her colleagues.* —**humiliated** *adj*: *I've never felt so humiliated in all my life.*

hu·mil·i·at·ing /hjuːˈmɪlieɪtɪŋ/ *adj* making you feel ashamed, embarrassed, and angry because you have been made to look weak or stupid SYN **embarrassing**: *a* ***humiliating defeat*** —**humiliatingly** *adv*

hu·mil·i·a·tion /hjuːˌmɪliˈeɪʃən/ ●○○ *n*
1 [U] a feeling of shame and great embarrassment, because you have been made to look stupid or weak: *the humiliation of having to ask her parents for money*
THESAURUS ▸ SHAME
2 [C] a situation that makes you feel humiliated: *The government suffered a series of political humiliations.*

hu·mil·i·ty /hjuːˈmɪləti/ *n* [U] the quality of not being too proud about yourself – use this to show approval: *He spoke with great humility about his role, praising the efforts of his teammates above his own.* SYN **modesty** → **humble**

Hum·mer /ˈhʌmə $ -ər/ *n* [C] *trademark* a large American car made for travelling over rough ground

ˈ**humming bird** *n* [C] a very small brightly coloured tropical bird whose wings move very quickly

hum·mock /ˈhʌmək/ *n* [C] *BrE* a very small hill

hum·mus /ˈhuːməs, ˈhʊ-/ *n* [U] another spelling of HUMUS[1]

hu·mon·gous (*also* **humungous** *BrE*) /hjuːˈmʌŋgəs/ *adj informal* very big SYN **enormous**: *rich people living in humongous houses*

hu·mor·ist /ˈhjuːmərɪst $ ˈhjuː-, ˈjuː-/ *n* [C] someone, especially a writer, who tells funny stories → **comedian**

hu·mor·ous /ˈhjuːmərəs $ ˈhjuː-, ˈjuː-/ ●●○ *adj* funny and enjoyable: *humorous stories* | *The film has some mildly humorous moments.* **THESAURUS** ▸ FUNNY —**humorously** *adv*

> **REGISTER**
> In everyday English, people usually say something is **funny** rather than **humorous**: *He told lots of* ***funny*** *stories.*

hu·mour[1] *BrE*, **humor** *AmE* /ˈhjuːmə $ ˈhjuːmər, ˈjuː-/ ●●○ *n* [U]
1 the ability or tendency to think that things are funny, or funny things you say that show you have this ability: *his humour and charm* | *Greg's feeble attempt at humour* | *English humour* | *It's vital to have a* ***sense of humor*** *in this job.* | *The host puts the contestants at ease with his own* ***brand of humour***. | *He showed* ***flashes of humor*** *that delighted the audience.*
2 the quality in something that makes it funny and makes people laugh: *He failed to see the humour of the situation.*
3 in a good/an ill/a bad humour *formal* in a good or bad mood → GOOD HUMOUR
4 out of humour *BrE old-fashioned* in a bad mood

humour[2] *BrE*, **humor** *AmE* *v* [T] to do what someone wants or to pretend to agree with them so that they do not become upset: *'Of course,' he said, humouring her.*

hu·mour·less *BrE*, **humorless** *AmE* /ˈhjuːmələs $ ˈhjuːmər-,ˈjuː-/ *adj* too serious and not able to laugh at things that other people think are funny —**humourlessly** *adv*

hump[1] /hʌmp/ *n* **1** [C] a large round shape that rises above the surface of something: *the hump of a hill* **2 speed/traffic humps** *BrE* a series of humps in the road, designed to make traffic slow down **3** [C] a raised part on the back of a CAMEL **4** [C] a raised part on someone's back that is caused by an unusually curved SPINE → **hunchback** **5 be over the hump** to have finished the most difficult part of something **6 give sb the hump/get the hump** *BrE spoken* to make someone feel angry or upset, or to feel angry or upset

hump[2] *v informal* **1** [T] *BrE* to carry something heavy from one place to another with difficulty SYN **heave**, **lug** → **drag**: **hump sth down/along/across etc** *I managed to hump the suitcases upstairs.* **2** [I,T] *not polite* to have sex with someone

hump·back /ˈhʌmpbæk/ *n* [C] **1** a HUMPBACK WHALE **2** a HUNCHBACK

ˌ**hump-backed ˈbridge** (*also* ˌ**humpback ˈbridge**) *n* [C] *BrE* a short bridge with a steep slope on each side → see picture at **BRIDGE**[1]

ˌ**humpback ˈwhale** (*also* **humpback**) *n* [C] a large WHALE

humph /hʌmf, hmh, hm/ *interjection* used to show that you do not believe something or do not approve of something

humus[1], **hummus** /ˈhuːməs, ˈhʊ-/ *n* [U] a Greek food made from a soft mixture of CHICKPEAS, oil, and GARLIC

hu·mus[2] /ˈhjuːməs/ *n* [U] soil made of decayed plants, leaves etc that is good for growing plants → **compost**

hunch[1] /hʌntʃ/ *n* [C] if you have a hunch that something is true or will happen, you feel that it is true or will happen → **suspicion**: **have a hunch (that)** *I had a hunch that something like this would happen.* | **sb's hunch** *My hunch is that she's his mother.*

hunch[2] *v* **1** [I always + adv/prep] to bend down and forwards so that your back forms a curve: **[+over]** *He had to hunch over the steering wheel to see anything.* **2 hunch your shoulders** to raise your shoulders into a rounded shape because you are cold, anxious etc —**hunched** *adj*: *a hunched figure sitting by the fire*

hunch·back /ˈhʌntʃbæk/ *n* [C] *not polite* an offensive word for someone who has a large raised part on their back because their SPINE curves in an unusual way

hun·dred /ˈhʌndrɪd/ ●●● S2 W2 *number, n* (*plural* **hundred** *or* **hundreds**)
1 the number 100: *The tree was probably a hundred years old.* | **two/three/four etc hundred** *I make nine hundred dollars a week.* | *a journey of 15 hundred miles* | **hundreds of people/years/pounds etc** *Hundreds of people were reported killed or wounded.*
2 a very large number of things or people: **a hundred** *They've had this argument a hundred times before.* | **hundreds of sth** *He's had hundreds of girlfriends.*
3 a/one hundred percent *spoken* **a)** completely: *I'm not a hundred percent sure where she lives.* **b)** *BrE* completely well: *I'm still not really feeling a hundred percent.*
4 give a hundred percent (*also* **give a hundred and ten percent**) to do everything you can in order to achieve something: *Everyone on the team gave a hundred percent.*
5 [C] a piece of paper money that is worth 100 dollars or 100 pounds —**hundredth** *adj*: *her hundredth birthday* —**hundredth** *n* [C]

hun·dred·weight /ˈhʌndrədweɪt/ *n* (*plural* **hundredweight**) [C] (*written abbreviation* **cwt**) a unit for measuring weight, equal to 112 pounds or 50.8 kilograms in Britain, and 100 pounds or 45.3 kilograms in the US

hung /hʌŋ/ a past tense and past participle of HANG

hun·ger[1] /ˈhʌŋgə $ -ər/ ●●○ *n*
1 [U] lack of food, especially for a long period of time, that can cause illness or death SYN **starvation**: **die of/from hunger** *Thousands of people are dying from hunger every day.*
2 [U] the feeling that you need to eat → **thirst**: *Try to satisfy your hunger by eating some fruit.* | **hunger pangs** (=sudden feelings of being hungry)
3 [singular, U] a strong need or desire for something SYN **desire**: **[+for]** *her hunger for knowledge* | *a hunger for success*

hunger² *v*
hunger for/after sth *phr v literary* to want something very much: *The nation was hungering for change.*

ˈhunger strike *n* [C,U] a situation in which someone refuses to eat for a long time in order to protest about something: *A total of 300 students occupied the building and over 50* ***went on hunger strike****.* —**hunger striker** *n* [C]

ˌhung ˈjury *n* [singular] a JURY that cannot agree whether someone is guilty of a crime

hung·o·ver /hʌŋˈəʊvə $ -ˈoʊvər/ *adj* if someone is hungover, they feel ill because they drank too much alcohol the previous evening → HANGOVER

ˌhung ˈparliament *n* [C] *BrE* a parliament in which no political party has more elected representatives than the others added together

hun·gri·ly /ˈhʌŋgrəli/ *adv* **1** in a way that shows you want to eat something very much → **greedily**: *She hungrily ate a slice of bread.* **2** *literary* in a way that shows you want something very much: *He hungrily kissed her mouth.*

hun·gry /ˈhʌŋgri/ ●●● S2 *adj* (*comparative* **hungrier**, *superlative* **hungriest**)
1 wanting to eat something → **thirsty**: *I was cold, tired, and hungry. | If you* ***get hungry****, there's some cold chicken in the fridge. | Do you still feel hungry?*
2 ill or weak as a result of not having enough to eat for a long time: *We can't justify wasting food when half the world is hungry.*
3 go hungry to not have enough to eat: *Thousands of families go hungry every day.*
4 wanting or needing something very much SYN **eager**: **[+for]** *She is hungry for success. |* **hungry to do sth** *Stan was hungry to learn.*
5 the hungry [plural] people who do not have enough food to eat
6 power-hungry/news-hungry etc wanting power, news etc very much: *a power-hungry politician*

THESAURUS
WANTING TO EAT
hungry wanting to eat something: *We were really hungry after our long walk.*
peckish [not before noun] *BrE informal* a little hungry: *I'm feeling a bit peckish. What's in the fridge?*
starving/ravenous /ˈrævənəs/ (*also* **starved** *AmE*) [not before noun] *spoken* very hungry and wanting to eat as soon as possible: *I missed lunch and I'm absolutely starving. | Sam's always ravenous when he gets home from school.*
I could eat a horse! *spoken* used to say that you are very hungry: *'Are you hungry?' 'Yeah, I could eat a horse.'*
appetite the desire for food that you have when you are hungry: *Exercise usually gives me an appetite.*

ˌhung-ˈup *adj* **be hung-up about/on sth** *informal* to be thinking or worrying too much about someone or something → HANG-UP

hunk /hʌŋk/ *n* [C] **1** a thick piece of something, especially food, that has been taken from a bigger piece: **[+of]** *a hunk of bread* THESAURUS PIECE **2** *informal* a sexually attractive man with a big strong body

hun·ker /ˈhʌŋkə $ -ər/ *v*
hunker down *phr v AmE* **1** to bend your knees so that you are sitting on your heels very close to the ground SYN **squat 2** to make yourself comfortable in a safe place, especially for a long time **3** *informal* to prepare yourself for a difficult situation

hunk·y /ˈhʌŋki/ *adj* a man who is hunky is sexually attractive and has a big strong body → **macho** THESAURUS STRONG

hun·ky-dor·y /ˌhʌŋki ˈdɔːri/ *adj* [not before noun] *informal* if a situation is hunky-dory, everyone feels happy and there are no problems SYN **OK**

hunt¹ /hʌnt/ ●●● W3 *v*
1 [I,T] to chase animals and birds in order to kill or catch them: *the slopes where I hunted deer as a kid | Wolves tend to hunt in packs* (=hunt in groups).
2 [I] to look for someone or something very carefully SYN **search**: **[+for]** *The kids were hunting for shells on the beach. | Detectives are busy hunting for clues.* THESAURUS SEARCH
3 [I,T] to search for and try to catch a criminal or someone who is your enemy: *The police are still hunting the killer. |* **[+for]** *The FBI were called in to hunt for the spy.*
4 [I,T] *BrE* to hunt FOXes as a sport, riding on horses and using dogs
hunt sb/sth ↔ **down** *phr v* to search for a person or animal until you catch them, especially in order to punish or kill them: *The government agency was created to hunt down war criminals.*
hunt sb/sth ↔ **out** *phr v*
1 to search for someone or something in order to catch, kill, or destroy them: *The plane was on a mission to hunt out enemy submarines.*
2 to search for and find something that you need or want, but that is difficult to find: *In the school library, he hunted out books on politics.*

hunt² ●●○ *n* [C]
1 an occasion when people chase animals in order to kill or catch them: **lion/rhino/stag etc hunt**
2 [usually singular] a search for someone or something that is difficult to find: **[+for]** *the hunt for the missing child |* **the hunt is on** (=used to say that people have started looking for someone or something) | **murder hunt** (=a search for a person who has killed someone) | **have a hunt around for sth** *BrE informal* (=look for something) *I'll have a hunt around for it in my desk.* → TREASURE HUNT, WITCH-HUNT
3 a sporting event in Britain in which people ride on horses and hunt FOXes using dogs
4 in Britain, a group of people who regularly hunt FOXes together

hunt·er /ˈhʌntə $ -ər/ ●●○ *n*
1 [C] a person who hunts wild animals, or an animal that hunts other animals for food
2 souvenir/autograph/bargain etc hunter someone who looks for or collects a particular type of thing → BOUNTY HUNTER

ˌhunter-ˈgatherer *n* [C] a member of a group of people that lives by hunting and looking for plants that can be eaten, rather than by keeping animals for food or by growing crops

hunt·ing /ˈhʌntɪŋ/ ●●○ *n* [U]
1 chasing and killing animals for food or sport
2 in Britain, the sport of hunting FOXes SYN **foxhunting**
3 job-hunting/house-hunting/flat-hunting the activity of looking for a job, house, or flat
4 go hunting to hunt for animals, especially as a sport —**hunting** *adj*: *a hunting rifle*

ˈhunting ˌground *n* [C] **1** a place where animals are hunted **2 a happy/good hunting ground (for sth)** a place where people who are interested in a particular thing can easily find what they want: *Madeira used to be a happy hunting ground for antique collectors.*

hunt·ress /ˈhʌntrɪs/ *n* [C] *literary* a female hunter

ˌhunt saboˈteur *n* [C] *BrE* a member of a group that tries to stop people from hunting FOXes

hunts·man /ˈhʌntsmən/ *n* (*plural* **huntsmen** /-mən/) [C] *literary* **1** a man who hunts animals **2** *BrE* someone who hunts FOXes for sport

hur·dle¹ /ˈhɜːdl $ ˈhɜːr-/ ●●○ *n*
1 [C] a problem or difficulty that you must deal with before you can achieve something SYN **obstacle**: *Finding enough money for the project was the first hurdle. |* **overcome/clear/get over etc a hurdle** (=deal successfully with a problem)
2 [C] one of a series of small fences that a person or horse has to jump over during a race: **clear a hurdle** (=successfully jump over a hurdle)
3 the 100-metres/400-metres hurdles a race in which the runners have to jump over hurdles

hurdle² *v* **1** [I,T] to jump over something while you are running: *He hurdled the fence and ran off down the street.* **2** [I] to run in hurdle races —**hurdler** *n* [C] —**hurdling** *n* [U]

ˈhurdle rate *n* [C] a particular amount of profit that someone expects to get before they will decide to INVEST in something

hur·dy-gur·dy /ˈhɜːdi ˌɡɜːdi $ ˌhɜːrdi ˈɡɜːrdi/ *n (plural* **hurdy-gurdies***)* [C] a small musical instrument that you play by turning a handle → **barrel organ**

hurl /hɜːl $ hɜːrl/ ●○○ *v*
1 [T always + adv/prep] to throw something with a lot of force, especially because you are angry: *Demonstrators were hurling bricks through the windows. | He hurled a chair across the set, smashing lamps and vases.* THESAURUS THROW
2 hurl abuse/insults/accusations etc (at sb) to shout at someone in a loud and angry way: *He was accused of hurling abuse at the referee.*
3 hurl yourself at/against etc sb/sth to throw yourself at someone or something with a lot of force: *She wanted to hurl herself into his arms.*
4 [I,T] *AmE informal* to VOMIT

hurl·ing /ˈhɜːlɪŋ $ ˈhɜːr-/ *n* [U] an Irish ball game played with sticks by two teams of 15 players —**hurler** *n* [C]

hur·ly-bur·ly /ˈhɜːli ˌbɜːli $ ˌhɜːrli ˈbɜːrli/ *n* [U] a lot of busy noisy activity: *the hurly-burly of city life*

hur·ray /hʊˈreɪ/ *(also* **hur·rah***)* /hʊˈrɑː/ *interjection* HOORAY → **hip, hip, hurray!** at HIP³

hur·ri·cane /ˈhʌrɪkən $ ˈhɜːrəkeɪn/ ●●○ *n* [C] a storm that has very strong fast winds and that moves over water → **cyclone, typhoon, tornado** THESAURUS STORM, WIND

ˈhurricane ˌlamp *n* [C] a lamp that has a glass cover to protect the flame inside from the wind

hur·ried /ˈhʌrid $ ˈhɜːrid/ *adj* [usually before noun] done more quickly than usual SYN **rushed** OPP **leisurely**: *a hurried meal* THESAURUS FAST —**hurriedly** *adv*

hur·ry¹ /ˈhʌri $ ˈhɜːri/ ●●● S3 W3 *v* (**hurried, hurrying, hurries**)
1 [I,T] to do something or go somewhere more quickly than usual, especially because there is not much time SYN **rush**: *If we hurry, we'll get there in time. | I hate having to hurry a meal. | We'll have to hurry, otherwise we'll miss the start. | There's no need to hurry. We've got plenty of time.* | **hurry to do sth** *They were hurrying to catch their train.* | **[+through/along/down etc]** *She hurried down the corridor as fast as she could.* | **[+after]** *John hurried after his girlfriend.*
2 [T] to make someone do something more quickly SYN **rush**: *Don't hurry me. I'm doing this as fast as I can.* | **hurry sb into (doing) sth** *She doesn't want to be hurried into making a decision.*
3 [T always + adv/prep] to take someone or something quickly to a place SYN **rush**: **hurry sth to/through/across etc sth** *Emergency supplies have been hurried to the areas worst hit by the famine.*

THESAURUS

hurry to go somewhere or do something more quickly than usual, for example because you are late or you must finish something soon: *If you don't hurry, you'll miss the bus. | We have plenty of time. There's no need to hurry.*
rush to go somewhere very quickly, or to do something too quickly and without thinking carefully enough: *Everyone rushed out into the street to see what was happening. | Try to answer the questions calmly, without rushing.*
dash to go somewhere very quickly, especially because there is something important or urgent you must do: *I've got to dash to the shops to get some more milk.*
in a hurry/in a rush doing something quickly because you do not have much time, usually with the result that you make mistakes: *She had left in a hurry, and forgotten her passport. | I had to choose a present for her in a rush.*
get a move on/get moving *informal* to start to do something or go somewhere more quickly than before: *Get a move on – it's already 8 o'clock!*
get cracking *informal* to start working quickly: *It's time you got cracking with your homework.*

hurry up *phr v*
1 hurry up! *spoken* used to tell someone to do something more quickly: *Hurry up! We're late!*
2 hurry sb/sth up to make someone do something more quickly, or to make something happen more quickly: *See if you can hurry things up a little.*

hurry² ●●● S3 *n*
1 in a hurry more quickly than usual SYN **in a rush**: *Sorry, I can't stop, I'm in a hurry. | You'll make mistakes if you do things in too much of a hurry.* | **be in a hurry to do sth** *Why are you in such a hurry to leave?* ⚠ Do not say that you are 'in hurry'. Say that you are **in a hurry**.
2 (there's) no hurry *spoken* used to tell someone that they do not have to do something quickly or soon: *Pay me back whenever you can. There's no great hurry.*
3 sb will not be doing sth (again) in a hurry *spoken* used to say that someone does not want to do something again: *We won't be going back there again in a hurry.*
4 in your hurry to do sth while you are trying to do something too quickly: *In his hurry to leave the room, he tripped over a chair.*
5 be in no hurry/not be in any hurry (to do sth) a) to be able to wait because you have a lot of time in which to do something: *Take your time – I'm not in any hurry.* **b)** to be unwilling to do something or not want to do it soon: *He was clearly in no hurry to reply to our letter.*
6 what's (all) the hurry?/why (all) the hurry? *spoken* used to say that someone is doing something too quickly: *We've got plenty of time – what's all the hurry?*

hurt¹ /hɜːt $ hɜːrt/ ●●● S1 W2 *v (past tense and past participle* **hurt***)*
1 INJURE SB [T] to injure yourself or someone else: *Was anyone hurt in the accident? | Put that thing down – you might hurt someone with it.* | **hurt your arm/leg/nose etc** *He hurt his knee playing football.* | **hurt yourself** *Be careful you don't fall and hurt yourself.* → see Thesaurus box on *p. 903*
2 FEEL PAIN [I] to feel pain in part of your body → **ache**: *My back hurts. | Where does it hurt? | It hurts when I try to move my leg.* | **hurt like hell** *informal* (=hurt very much) *My shoulder hurts like hell.*
3 CAUSE PAIN [T] to cause pain in a part of your body: *The sun's hurting my eyes.*
4 INSULT SB [I,T] to make someone feel very upset, unhappy, sad etc: *I didn't mean to* ***hurt*** *your* ***feelings***. | **it hurts (sb) to do sth** *What hurts is that he never even said goodbye. | It hurt me to think that you hated me.*
5 BAD EFFECT [T] to have a bad effect on someone or something, especially by making them less successful or powerful: *Foreign competition has hurt the company's position in the market.*
6 be hurting *AmE* **a)** *informal* to feel very upset or unhappy about something: *Martha's going through a divorce and really hurting right now.* **b)** if a group, organization etc is hurting, they do not have something important that they need: **[+for]** *The team is hurting for quarterbacks.*
7 sth won't/doesn't hurt *spoken* said when you think someone should do something or that something is a good idea: *The house looks pretty good, but a fresh paint job wouldn't hurt either.* | **it won't/doesn't hurt (sb) to do sth** *It won't hurt Julia to get up early for a change.*

hurt² ●●● S3 *adj*
1 [not usually before noun] suffering pain or injury SYN **injured**: **badly/seriously hurt** *Fortunately, no one was seriously hurt. | Sometimes players* ***get hurt*** *in training.*
2 very upset or unhappy because someone has said or done something unkind, dishonest, or unfair: *Rachel* ***felt hurt*** *and betrayed. | He's no good for you, Jenny. You'll only* ***get hurt*** *again. | his hurt pride | She wore a hurt expression on her face.* | **very/deeply hurt** *Alice was deeply hurt that she hadn't been invited.*

hurt³ ●○○ *n* [C,U] a feeling of great unhappiness because someone, especially someone you trust, has

H

treated you badly or unfairly: *She saw the hurt in his eyes.* | *all the hurts and wrongs of the past* → **harm**

hurt·ful /ˈhɜːtfəl $ ˈhɜːrt-/ ●○○ *adj* making you feel very upset or offended SYN **unkind**: **hurtful remark/comment etc** THESAURUS▶ UNKIND —**hurtfully** *adv* —**hurtfulness** *n* [U]

hur·tle /ˈhɜːtl $ ˈhɜːr-/ *v* [I always + adv/prep] if something, especially something big or heavy, hurtles somewhere, it moves or falls very fast: *All of a sudden, a car came hurtling round the corner.*

hus·band¹ /ˈhʌzbənd/ ●●● S1 W1 *n*
1 [C] the man that a woman is married to → **wife**: *Have you met my husband Roy?* THESAURUS▶ MARRIED
2 ex-husband a man that a woman used to be married to
3 husband and wife a man and woman who are married to each other

husband² *v* [T] *formal* to be very careful in the way you use your money, supplies etc and not waste any

hus·band·ry /ˈhʌzbəndri/ *n* [U] **1** *technical* farming: *animal husbandry* **2** *old-fashioned* careful management of money and supplies

hush¹ /hʌʃ/ *v* **1 hush** *spoken* used to tell people to be quiet, or to comfort a child who is crying or upset: *Hush, now. Try to get to sleep.* **2** [T] *written* to make someone stop shouting, talking, crying etc: *Ella asked them to hush their voices.* **3** [I] *written* to stop shouting, talking etc: *The audience hushed as he stepped onto the stage.*

hush sth ↔ **up** *phr v* to prevent people from knowing about something dishonest or immoral SYN **cover up**: *The whole affair was hushed up by the government.*

hush² *n* **1** [singular] a period of silence, especially when people are expecting something to happen: ***A** sudden **hush fell over** the crowd.* **2 a bit of hush** *BrE spoken* used to ask people, especially noisy children, to be quiet: ***Let's have a bit of hush**, please, gentlemen.*

hushed /hʌʃt/ *adj* [usually before noun] quiet because people are listening, waiting to hear something, or talking quietly: *A hushed courtroom awaited the verdict.* | **hushed tones/voice/whispers etc** (=quiet speech) *They spoke **in hushed tones** at the table.* THESAURUS▶ QUIET

ˌhush-ˈhush / $ ˈ. ./ *adj informal* very secret: *Everything was very hush-hush.* THESAURUS▶ SECRET

ˈhush ˌmoney *n* [U] money that is paid to someone not to tell other people about something embarrassing

husk¹ /hʌsk/ *n* **1** [C,U] the dry outer part of corn, some grains, seeds, nuts etc **2** [C] the useless outer part of something that remains after the important or useful part is gone or has been used: **[+of]** *His drug addiction had turned him into a husk of his former self.*

husk² *v* [T] to remove the husks from grains, seeds etc

hus·ky¹ /ˈhʌski/ *adj* **1** a husky voice is deep, quiet, and attractive: *'Come quickly,' she said in a husky whisper.* **2** *especially AmE* a man or boy who is husky is big and strong —**huskily** *adv*

husky² *n* (*plural* **huskies**) [C] a dog with thick hair used in Canada and Alaska to pull SLEDGES over the snow

hus·sar /hʊˈzɑː $ -ɑːr/ *n* [C] a British CAVALRY soldier

hus·sy /ˈhʌsi, ˈhʌzi/ *n* (*plural* **hussies**) [C] *old-fashioned* a woman who is sexually immoral

hus·tings /ˈhʌstɪŋz/ *n* **the hustings** the process of trying to persuade people to vote for you by making speeches etc: **at/on the hustings** *The senator is usually at his best on the hustings.*

hus·tle¹ /ˈhʌsəl/ *v* (**hustled**, **hustling**) **1** [T] to make someone move quickly, especially by pushing them roughly: **hustle sb into/out of/through etc sth** *I was hustled out of the building by a couple of security men.* | **hustle sb away** *He was hustled away by police officers.* **2** [I] *AmE* to do something with a lot of energy and determination: *Cindy's not a great player, but she really hustles.* **3** [I] *AmE* to hurry in doing something or going somewhere: *We need to hustle if we're going to make this flight.* **4** [I,T] *AmE* to sell or obtain things in an illegal or dishonest way: *thieves hustling stolen goods on the street* **5** [I] *AmE informal* to work as a PROSTITUTE, or to be in charge of prostitutes

hustle² *n* [U] **1** busy and noisy activity: *the **hustle and bustle** of the market place* **2** *AmE* ways of getting money that involve cheating or deceiving people **3** *AmE* when someone does something quickly, with a lot of effort and eagerness: *The team has a lot of talent but no hustle.*

hus·tler /ˈhʌslə $ -ər/ *n* [C] **1** *especially AmE* someone who tries to trick people into giving them money **2** *AmE* a PROSTITUTE

THESAURUS: hurt

TO INJURE YOURSELF OR SOMEONE ELSE

hurt to damage part of your body, or someone else's body: *She slipped on the ice and hurt herself badly.* | *Be careful you don't hurt anyone with that knife.*

injure to hurt yourself quite severely, or to be hurt in an accident or fighting: *One of our players has injured his leg, and will be out of the game for weeks.* | *Four people have been seriously injured on the Arizona highway.*

wound to deliberately hurt someone using a weapon such as a knife or gun: *The gunmen shot and killed twelve people and wounded three others.*

maim /meɪm/ [usually passive] to hurt someone very severely, especially so that they lose an arm, leg etc, often as the result of an explosion: *In countries where there are landmines, people are killed and maimed daily.*

break to hurt a part of your body by breaking a bone in it: *The X-ray showed that I had broken my wrist.*

bruise to hurt a part of your body when you fall on it or hit it, causing a dark mark to appear on your skin: *Cathy fell off her bike and bruised her legs badly.*

sprain/twist to hurt your knee, wrist, shoulder etc by suddenly twisting it while you are moving: *I jumped down from the wall and landed awkwardly, spraining my ankle.*

strain/pull to hurt one of your muscles by stretching it or using it too much: *When you are lifting heavy loads, be careful not to strain a back muscle.*

dislocate to damage a joint in your body in a way that moves the two parts of the joint out of their normal position: *Our best batsman dislocated his shoulder during training.*

WHEN PART OF YOUR BODY FEELS PAINFUL

hurt if part of your body hurts, it feels painful: *My chest hurts when I cough.*

ache to hurt with a continuous pain: *I'd been walking all day and my legs were really aching.*

throb to feel a bad pain that comes and goes again in a regular and continuous way: *Lou had a terrible headache and his whole head seemed to be throbbing.*

sting to feel a sharp pain, or to make someone feel this, especially in your eyes, throat, or skin: *My throat stings every time I swallow.* | *This injection may sting a little.*

smart to hurt with a sudden sharp pain - used especially about your eyes, or your skin where something has hit you: *Her eyes were smarting from the thick smoke.* | *Jackson's face was still smarting from the punch.*

pinch if something you are wearing pinches you, it is too tight and presses painfully on your skin: *The shirt was a bit too small and it was pinching my neck.*

sth is killing me *spoken informal* used when something feels very painful: *My legs are killing me.* | *These shoes are killing me.*

a bad back/leg/arm etc if you have a bad back/leg/arm etc, it feels painful: *He's off work with a bad back.*

H

hut /hʌt/ ●●○ *n* [C] a small simple building with only one or two rooms → **shack**: *a wooden hut*

hutch /hʌtʃ/ *n* [C] **1** a small wooden CAGE that small animals are kept in, especially rabbits → see picture at HOME[1] **2** *AmE* a piece of furniture used for storing and showing dishes

hy·a·cinth /ˈhaɪəsənθ/ *n* [C] a garden plant with blue, pink, or white bell-shaped flowers and a sweet smell

hy·ae·na /haɪˈiːnə/ *n* [C] a British spelling of HYENA

hy·brid /ˈhaɪbrɪd/ ●○○ *n* [C]
1 an animal or plant produced from parents of different breeds or types → **cross-breed**: **[+of]** *a hybrid of wheat and rye* **THESAURUS** MIXTURE
2 something that consists of or comes from a mixture of two or more other things: *hybrid architecture* | **[+of]** *a unique hybrid of blues, country, pop, and gospel music*

ˈ**hybrid car** *n* [C] a car that has both a petrol or DIESEL engine and an electric motor

hy·brid·ize (*also* **-ise** *BrE*) /ˈhaɪbrədaɪz/ *v* [I,T] *technical* to form a new type of plant or animal from two existing types, so that the new type has some qualities from each of the other types SYN **crossbreed** —**hybridization** /ˌhaɪbrədaɪˈzeɪʃən $ -də-/ *n* [U]

hy·dra /ˈhaɪdrə/ *n* **1 Hydra** a snake in ancient Greek stories with many heads that grow again when they are cut off **2** [C] *formal* a problem that is very difficult to get rid of because it keeps returning

hy·drant /ˈhaɪdrənt/ *n* [C] a FIRE HYDRANT

hy·drate[1] /ˈhaɪdreɪt/ *v* [T] to supply someone or something with water to keep them healthy and in good condition OPP **dehydrate**: *After you run, drink plenty of water to stay well hydrated.* —**hydration** /haɪˈdreɪʃən/ *n* [U]

hydrate[2] *n* [C] *technical* a chemical substance that contains water

hy·draul·ic /haɪˈdrɒlɪk, -ˈdrɔː- $ -ˈdrɒː-/ *adj* [usually before noun] moved or operated by the pressure of water or other liquid: *a hydraulic pump* | *hydraulic brakes* —**hydraulically** /-kli/ *adv*

hy·draul·ics /haɪˈdrɒlɪks, -ˈdrɔː- $ -ˈdrɒː-/ *n* **1** [plural] parts of a machine or system that use the pressure of water or other liquids to move or lift things **2** [U] the study of how to use the pressure of water or other liquids to produce power

hydro- /haɪdrəʊ, -drə $ -droʊ, -drə/ *prefix* **1** relating to water, or using water: *hydroelectricity* (=produced by water power) | *hydrotherapy* (=treatment of disease using water) **2** relating to HYDROGEN, or containing it: *hydrocarbons*

hy·dro·car·bon /ˌhaɪdrəˈkɑːbən $ -ˈkɑːr-/ *n* [C] *technical* a chemical compound that consists of HYDROGEN and CARBON, such as coal or gas

hy·dro·chlor·ic ac·id /ˌhaɪdrəklɒrɪk ˈæsɪd $ -klɔː-/ *n* [U] a strong acid used especially in industry

hy·dro·e·lec·tric /ˌhaɪdrəʊ-ɪˈlektrɪk◂ $ -droʊ-/ *adj* using water power to produce electricity: *a huge hydroelectric power station* —**hydroelectricity** /ˌhaɪdrəʊɪlekˈtrɪsəti $ -droʊ-/ *n* [U]

hy·dro·foil /ˈhaɪdrəfɔɪl/ *n* [C] a large boat with wing-shaped parts on the bottom that lift it above the surface of the water when it travels fast → **hovercraft**

hy·dro·gen /ˈhaɪdrədʒən/ ●●○ *n* [U] a colourless gas that is the lightest of all gases, forms water when it combines with oxygen, and is used to produce AMMONIA and other chemicals. It is a chemical ELEMENT: symbol H

hy·dro·gen·at·ed /ˈhaɪdrədʒəˌneɪtɪd, haɪˈdrɒdʒə- $ ˈhaɪdrədʒəˌneɪtɪd, haɪˈdrɑː-/ *adj* hydrogenated oils and fats have been treated with hydrogen to make them solid

ˈ**hydrogen ˌbomb** *n* [C] a very powerful NUCLEAR bomb

ˌ**hydrogen perˈoxide** *n* [U] a chemical liquid used for killing BACTERIA and for making hair and other substances lighter in colour

hy·dro·pho·bi·a /ˌhaɪdrəˈfəʊbiə $ -ˈfoʊ-/ *n* [U] **1** *technical* RABIES **2** fear of water

hy·dro·plane[1] /ˈhaɪdrəpleɪn/ *n* [C] **1** a HYDROFOIL **2** *AmE* a plane that can take off from and land on water

hydroplane[2] *v* [I] **1** *AmE* if a car hydroplanes, it slides on a wet road in a way that is out of control SYN **aquaplane** *BrE* **2** if a boat hydroplanes, it travels very quickly, just touching the surface of the water

hy·drox·ide /haɪˈdrɒksaɪd $ -ˈdrɑːk-/ *n* [C,U] *technical* a chemical COMPOUND that contains an oxygen atom combined with a HYDROGEN atom

hy·e·na (*also* **hyaena** *BrE*) /haɪˈiːnə/ *n* [C] a wild animal like a dog that makes a sound like a laugh

hy·giene /ˈhaɪdʒiːn/ ●○○ *n* [U] the practice of keeping yourself and the things around you clean in order to prevent diseases: *the importance of* **personal hygiene** | **oral/dental hygiene** | *a* **food hygiene** *training course* | **good/poor/proper hygiene** *The Consumers' Association blames poor hygiene standards.*

hy·gien·ic /haɪˈdʒiːnɪk $ -ˈdʒe-, -ˈdʒiː-/ ●○○ *adj* clean and likely to prevent BACTERIA, infections, or disease from spreading: *An inspector ensures that food is prepared in hygienic conditions.* —**hygienically** /-kli/ *adv*

hy·gien·ist /ˈhaɪdʒiːnɪst, haɪˈdʒiːnɪst/ *n* [C] *BrE* someone who helps a DENTIST by cleaning patients' teeth and giving advice about keeping teeth healthy SYN **dental hygienist**

hy·men /ˈhaɪmən/ *n* [C] a piece of skin that partly covers the entrance to the VAGINA of some girls or women who have not had sex

hymn /hɪm/ ●○○ *n* [C]
1 a song of praise to God: *He liked to* **sing hymns** *as he worked.*
2 a hymn to sth a book, film, song etc that strongly praises a person or idea: *Their first single was a hymn to selfishness called 'Looking After Number One'.*
3 be singing from the same hymn book/sheet *BrE* used to say that two or more people understand each other and are thinking about something in the same way

ˈ**hymn book** (*also* **hym·nal** /ˈhɪmnəl/ *technical*) *n* [C] a book of hymns

hype[1] /haɪp/ *n* [U] attempts to make people think something is good or important by talking about it a lot on television, the radio etc – used to show disapproval → **exaggeration**: *Some experts are concerned that the new drug won't live up to all the hype.* | *Despite the* **media hype**, *I found the film very disappointing.*

hype[2] (*also* **hype up**) *v* [T] to try to make people think something is good or important by talking about it a lot on television, the radio etc → **promote**: *The director is just using the controversy to hype his movie.*

hype sb **up** *phr v* to make someone feel excited

ˌ**hyped ˈup** *adj informal* very excited or nervous, and unable to keep still SYN **overexcited**

hy·per /ˈhaɪpə $ -ər/ *adj informal* extremely excited or nervous about something: *No, don't give Luke any candy – it'll make him hyper.*

hyper- /haɪpə $ -pər/ *prefix* **1** more than usual, especially too much: *hypersensitive* (=too sensitive) | *hyper-inflation* | *a hyper-extended knee* **2** beyond the usual size or limits: *a hyperlink* (=from one website to another)

hy·per·ac·tive /ˌhaɪpərˈæktɪv◂/ *adj* someone, especially a child, who is hyperactive is too active, and is not able to keep still or be quiet for very long → **attention deficit disorder** **THESAURUS** ENERGETIC —**hyperactivity** /ˌhaɪpərækˈtɪvəti/ *n* [U]

hy·per·bo·le /haɪˈpɜːbəli $ -ɜːr-/ *n* [C,U] a way of describing something by saying it is much bigger, smaller, worse etc than it actually is SYN **exaggeration**: *It was not hyperbole to call it the worst storm in twenty years.* **THESAURUS** LANGUAGE —**hyperbolic** /ˌhaɪpəˈbɒlɪk◂ $ -pərˈbɑː-/ *adj*

hy·per·crit·i·cal /ˌhaɪpəˈkrɪtɪkəl◂ $ -pər-/ *adj* too eager to criticize other people and things, especially about small details —**hypercritically** /-kli/ *adv*

hy·per·in·fla·tion /ˌhaɪpərɪnˈfleɪʃən/ *n* [U] a very fast rise in prices that seriously damages a country's ECONOMY

hy·per·link /ˈhaɪpəlɪŋk $ -pər-/ *n* [C] a word or picture in a WEBSITE or computer document that will take you to another page or document if you CLICK on it: *We should encourage hyperlinks to each other's webpages.*

hy·per·mar·ket /ˈhaɪpəˌmɑːkɪt $ -pərˌmɑːr-/ *n* [C] *BrE* a very large SUPERMARKET

hy·per·sen·si·tive /ˌhaɪpəˈsensətɪv◂ $ -pər-/ *adj* **1** if someone is hypersensitive to a drug, substance etc, their body reacts very badly to it SYN **allergic**: **[+to]** *I discovered I was hypersensitive to caffeine.* **2** very easily offended or upset: **[+to]** *She's hypersensitive to any form of criticism.* —**hypersensitivity** /ˌhaɪpəsensəˈtɪvəti $ -pər-/ *n* [U]

hy·per·ten·sion /ˌhaɪpəˈtenʃən $ -pər-/ *n* [U] *medical* a medical condition in which your BLOOD PRESSURE is too high

hy·per·text /ˈhaɪpəˌtekst $ -pər-/ *n* [U] *technical* a way of writing computer documents that makes it possible to move from one document to another by CLICKing on words or pictures, especially on the Internet

hy·per·ven·ti·late /ˌhaɪpəˈventəleɪt $ -pərˈventl-eɪt/ *v* [I] to breathe too quickly or too deeply, so that you get too much OXYGEN and feel DIZZY —**hyperventilation** /ˌhaɪpəventəˈleɪʃən $ -parventlˈeɪ-/ *n* [U]

hy·phen /ˈhaɪfən/ ●●○ *n* [C] a short written or printed line (-) that joins words or SYLLABLES → **dash**

hy·phen·ate /ˈhaɪfəneɪt/ *v* [T] to join words or SYLLABLES with a HYPHEN —**hyphenated** *adj* —**hyphenation** /ˌhaɪfəˈneɪʃən/ *n* [U]

hyp·no·sis /hɪpˈnəʊsɪs $ -ˈnoʊ-/ *n* [U] **1** a state similar to sleep, in which someone's thoughts and actions can be influenced by someone else: **under hypnosis** *While under hypnosis, the victim was able to describe her attacker.* **2** the act of producing this state

hyp·no·ther·a·py /ˌhɪpnəʊˈθerəpi $ -noʊ-/ *n* [U] the use of hypnosis to treat emotional or physical problems —**hypnotherapist** *n* [C]

hyp·not·ic[1] /hɪpˈnɒtɪk $ -ˈnɑː-/ *adj* **1** making you feel tired or unable to pay attention to anything else, especially because of a regularly repeated sound or movement: *His voice had a smooth* ***hypnotic effect***. | *the hypnotic beat of the drum* **2** [only before noun] relating to HYPNOSIS: *a hypnotic trance* —**hypnotically** /-kli/ *adv*

hypnotic[2] *n* [C] *technical* a drug that helps you to sleep SYN **sleeping pill**

hyp·no·tise /ˈhɪpnətaɪz/ *v* [T] a British spelling of HYPNOTIZE

H

hyp·no·tis·m /ˈhɪpnətɪzəm/ *n* [U] the practice of hypnotizing people

hyp·no·tist /ˈhɪpnətɪst/ *n* [C] someone who hypnotizes people

hyp·no·tize (*also* **-ise** *BrE*) /ˈhɪpnətaɪz/ *v* [T] **1** to produce a sleep-like state in someone so that you can influence their thoughts and actions **2** to be so interesting or exciting that people cannot think of anything else SYN **mesmerized**: *We were completely hypnotized by her performance of the Haydn.* GRAMMAR **Hypnotize** is usually passive in this meaning.

hy·po /ˈhaɪpəʊ $ -poʊ/ *n* (*plural* **hypos**) [C] *informal* a HYPODERMIC

hypo- /haɪpəʊ, -pə $ -poʊ, -pə/ *prefix technical* less than usual, especially too little: *hypothermia* (=condition in which your body temperature is too low) | *a hypodermic injection* (=given under the skin)

hy·po·al·ler·gen·ic, **hypoallergenic** /ˌhaɪpəʊæləˈdʒenɪk $ ˌhaɪpoʊælər-/ *adj* hypoallergenic substances or materials do not cause a bad reaction when you touch them or eat them

hy·po·chon·dri·a /ˌhaɪpəˈkɒndriə $ -ˈkɑːn-/ *n* [U] when someone continuously worries that there is something wrong with their health, even when they are not ill

hy·po·chon·dri·ac /ˌhaɪpəˈkɒndriæk $ -ˈkɑːn-/ *n* [C] someone who always worries about their health and thinks they may be ill, even when they are really not ill —**hypochondriac** *adj*

hy·poc·ri·sy /hɪˈpɒkrəsi $ -ˈpɑː-/ ●○○ *n* [U] when someone pretends to have certain beliefs or opinions that they do not really have – used to show disapproval OPP **sincerity**: *It would be sheer hypocrisy to pray for success, since I've never believed in God.*

hyp·o·crite /ˈhɪpəkrɪt/ *n* [C] someone who pretends to have certain beliefs or opinions that they do not really have – used to show disapproval

hyp·o·crit·i·cal /ˌhɪpəˈkrɪtɪkəl◂/ ●○○ *adj* behaving in a way that is different from what you claim to believe – used to show disapproval OPP **sincere**: **it's hypocritical (of sb) to do sth** *It's hypocritical of Sue to go to Tom's party when she can't stand him.*

hy·po·der·mic[1] /ˌhaɪpəˈdɜːmɪk◂ $ -ɜːr-/ *n* [C] an instrument with a very thin hollow needle used for putting drugs directly into the body through the skin SYN **syringe**

hypodermic[2] *adj* used to give an INJECTION beneath the skin: *a hypodermic needle*

hy·pot·e·nuse /haɪˈpɒtənjuːz $ -ˈpɑːtənuːs, -nuːz/ *n* [C] *technical* the longest side of a TRIANGLE that has a RIGHT ANGLE

hy·po·ther·mi·a /ˌhaɪpəʊˈθɜːmiə $ -poʊˈθɜːr-/ *n* [U] a serious medical condition caused by extreme cold

hy·poth·e·sis /haɪˈpɒθəsɪs $ -ˈpɑː-/ ●○○ AWL *n* (*plural* **hypotheses** /-siːz/)
1 [C] an idea that is suggested as an explanation for something, but that has not yet been proved to be true SYN **theory**: *One hypothesis is that the victim fell asleep while driving.* | **prove/test/support etc a hypothesis** *We hope that further research will confirm our hypothesis.* | **[+about]** *The authors reject the hypothesis about unemployment contributing to crime.*
2 [U] ideas or guesses, rather than facts SYN **speculation**: *All this is mere hypothesis.*

hy·poth·e·size (*also* **-ise** *BrE*) /haɪˈpɒθəsaɪz $ -ˈpɑː-/ AWL *v* [I,T] to suggest a possible explanation that has not yet been proved to be true: **hypothesize that** *Scientists hypothesize that the dinosaurs were killed by a giant meteor.*

hy·po·thet·i·cal /ˌhaɪpəˈθetɪkəl◂/ ●○○ AWL *adj* based on a situation that is not real, but that might happen: **hypothetical situation/example/question** *Brennan brought up a hypothetical case to make his point.* | *The question is* ***purely hypothetical***. → **imaginary** —**hypothetically** /-kli/ *adv*

hys·ter·ec·to·my /ˌhɪstəˈrektəmi/ *n* (*plural* **hysterectomies**) [C,U] a medical operation to remove a woman's UTERUS

hys·te·ri·a /hɪˈstɪəriə $ -ˈsteriə/ ●○○ *n* [U]
1 extreme excitement that makes people cry, laugh, shout etc in a way that is out of control: *In a fit of hysteria, Silvia blamed me for causing her father's death.*
2 a situation in which a lot of people feel fear, anger, or excitement, which makes them behave in an unreasonable way: *Since the general's death, the population has been gripped by* ***mass hysteria***.
3 *medical* a medical condition that upsets someone's emotions and makes them suddenly feel very nervous, excited, anxious etc

hys·ter·i·cal /hɪˈsterɪkəl/ ●○○ *adj*
1 unable to control your behaviour or emotions because you are very upset, afraid, excited etc: *Janet became hysterical and began screaming.* | *Everyone in the studio burst into* ***hysterical laughter***.
2 *informal* extremely funny SYN **hilarious**: *It was* ***absolutely hysterical***! *I've never laughed so much.* —**hysterically** /-kli/ *adv*

hys·ter·ics /hɪˈsterɪks/ *n* [plural] *spoken* **1** when you are unable to control your behaviour or emotions because you are very upset, afraid, excited etc: *She* ***went into hysterics*** *when she heard about her husband.* | **have hysterics** *BrE* (=be extremely upset or angry) *Mum'd have hysterics if she knew what you'd done.* **2** **in hysterics** if someone is in hysterics, they are laughing and not able to stop: *The audience was in hysterics.*

Hz the written abbreviation of ***hertz***

I i

I¹ /aɪ/ ●●● S1 W1 *pron* [used as the subject of a verb] used by the person speaking or writing to refer to himself or herself: *I moved to this city six years ago.* | *I'm not late again, am I?* | *My husband and I enjoy going to the theatre.*

GRAMMAR: Patterns with I

• You say: *Sarah and I went for coffee.* ✗ Don't say: *I and Sarah*
• In everyday English, you say that someone is older, younger, taller etc **than me**: *They were older than me.*
• You can also say: *They were older than I was.* It sounds very formal to say **than I**.

I², **i** /aɪ/ *n* (*plural* **I's, i's**) **1** [C,U] the ninth letter of the English alphabet **2** [C] the number one in the system of ROMAN NUMERALS **3 I-25, I-40 etc** the name of an INTERSTATE (=important road between states in the US)

i- /aɪ/ *prefix* [in nouns] used in the names of some products or services that involve using the Internet: *iTunes* (=trademark for a service allowing you to buy music over the Internet)

-i /-i/ *suffix* (*plural* **-is**) **1** [in nouns] a person from a particular country or place, or their language: *two Pakistanis* | *speakers of Hindi* **2** [in adjectives] of a particular place or country: *Bengali food* | *the Israeli army*

i·amb /ˈaɪæm $ ˈaɪæm, ˈaɪæmb/ (*also* **i·am·bus** /aɪˈæmbəs/) *n* [C] *technical* a unit of RHYTHM in poetry, that has one short or weak beat followed by a long or strong beat, as in the word 'alive' —**iambic** /aɪˈæmbɪk/ *adj*

iˌambic penˈtameter *n* [C,U] a common pattern of beats in English poetry, in which each line consists of five iambs

-ian /iən/ *suffix* [in adjectives and nouns] another form of the suffix -AN: *Dickensian characters* (=like those in Dickens' books) | *a librarian* (=someone who works in a library)

-iana /iɑːnə $ iænə/ (*also* **-ana**) *suffix* [in nouns] a group or collection of objects, papers etc that are related to someone or something: *Victoriana* | *Shakespeariana*

I·be·ri·an /aɪˈbɪəriən $ -ˈbɪr-/ *adj* relating to Spain or Portugal, or its people → **Spanish**: *the Iberian peninsula*

i·bex /ˈaɪbeks/ *n* (*plural* **ibexes** *or* **ibex**) [C] a wild goat that lives in the mountains of Europe, Asia, and North Africa

ib·id /ˈɪbɪd/ (*also* **ib·i·dem** /ˈɪbɪdem, ɪˈbaɪdem/) *adv* used in formal writing to mean from the same book, writer, or article as the one that has just been mentioned

-ibility /əbɪləti/ *suffix* [in nouns] another form of the suffix -ABILITY: *invincibility* | *flexibility*

i·bis /ˈaɪbɪs/ *n* (*plural* **ibises**) [C] a large bird with a long beak and long legs that is related to the STORK

-ible /əbəl/ *suffix* [in adjectives] another form of the suffix -ABLE: *irresistible* | *visible*

i·bu·pro·fen /ˌaɪbjuːˈprəʊfen $ -ˈproʊfən/ *n* [U] a medicine that reduces pain, INFLAMMATION, and fever

-ic /ɪk/ *suffix* **1** [in adjectives] of, like, or related to a particular thing: *photographic* (=of photography) | *an alcoholic drink* (=containing alcohol) | *polysyllabic* (=containing several SYLLABLES) | *pelvic* (=of the pelvis) | *Byronic* (=like or connected with the poet Byron) **2** [in nouns] someone who is affected by a particular unusual condition, a mental illness for example: *an alcoholic* (=someone who cannot stop drinking alcohol) —**-ically** /ɪkli/ [in adverbs]: *photographically*

-ical /ɪkəl/ *suffix* [in adjectives] another form of the suffix -IC(1): *historical* (=of history) | *satirical* —**-ically** /ɪkli/ [in adverbs]: *historically*

ICBM /ˌaɪ siː biː ˈem/ *n* [C] (***Intercontinental Ballistic Missile***) a MISSILE that can travel very long distances

ICE

ice¹ /aɪs/ ●●● S2 W3 *n*
1 [U] water that has frozen into a solid state → **icy**: *Would you like some ice in your drink?* | *Her hands were as cold as ice.* | *The city spent $7 million to remove snow and ice from the roads.*
2 keep/put something on ice to do nothing about a plan or suggestion for a period of time: *I'm putting my plans for a new car on ice until I finish college.*
3 be (skating) on thin ice to be in a situation in which you are likely to upset someone or cause trouble: *Don't be late again, Hugo – you're skating on thin ice.*
4 the ice a specially prepared surface of ice where you can ICE-SKATE or play ICE HOCKEY: *The two teams are ready to take to the ice.*
5 [C] **a)** a frozen sweet food made with fruit juice SYN **sorbet b)** *especially BrE old-fashioned* an ICE CREAM
6 [U] *AmE* diamonds → **BLACK ICE, DRY ICE,** → **break the ice,** → **cut no ice, BREAK¹**(29), **CUT¹**(39)

COLLOCATIONS

ADJECTIVES

thick *Thick ice was preventing the ship from moving.*
thin *The ice is too thin to skate on.*
black ice (=a layer of thin ice on a road that is very difficult to see) *Black ice on the roads is making driving conditions very dangerous.*
crushed ice (=broken into small pieces, for example to add to a drink) *Serve the cocktail with crushed ice.*

VERBS

be covered in ice *Our driveway was covered in ice.*
ice melts *The ice in my glass had begun to melt.*
ice forms *Ice was forming on the surface of the lake.*
ice cracks *We could feel the ice cracking beneath our feet.*

ice + NOUN

an ice cube (=a small square piece of ice that you add to a drink) *She put a couple of ice cubes in her glass.*
ice crystals (=very small pieces of ice that form naturally)

PHRASES

a block of ice *The fish were packed in blocks of ice, ready for transportation.*
a lump of ice (=a large piece of ice)
a sheet of ice *A thin sheet of ice had formed over the surface of the pond.*
a slab of ice (=a thick flat piece of ice)

ice² *v* [T] *especially BrE* to cover a cake with ICING (=a mixture made of liquid and very fine sugar) SYN **frost** *AmE* → **icing**

ice sth ↔ **down** *phr v AmE* to cover an injured part of the body in ice to stop it from swelling: *Make sure you ice that ankle down as soon as you get inside.*

ice over/up (*also* **be iced over/up**) *phr v* to become covered with ice → **icy**: *Schools were closed when the roads iced over.* | *The plane's engines had iced up.*

ˈIce Age *n* [C] one of the long periods of time, thousands of years ago, when ice covered many northern countries

ice·berg /ˈaɪsbɜːɡ $ -bɜːrɡ/ ●○○ *n* [C] a very large mass of ice floating in the sea, most of which is under the surface of the water → **the tip of the iceberg** at TIP¹(4)

ˌiceberg ˈlettuce *n* [C,U] a firm round pale green LETTUCE

ˌice-ˈblue *adj* very pale blue: *his ice-blue eyes* —**ice-blue** *n* [U]

ice·bound /ˈaɪsbaʊnd/ *adj* surrounded by ice, especially so that it is impossible to move

ice·box /ˈaɪsbɒks $ -bɑːks/ *n* [C] *AmE old-fashioned* **1** a REFRIGERATOR **2** a special cupboard into which people in the past put ice in order to keep food cold

ice·break·er /ˈaɪsˌbreɪkə $ -ər/ *n* [C] **1** something that you say or do to make people less nervous when they first meet: *This game is an effective icebreaker at the beginning of a semester.* → **break the ice** at BREAK¹(29) **2** a ship that cuts a passage through floating ice

ˈice ˌbucket *n* [C] **1** a container filled with ice to keep bottles of wine cold → see picture at ICE¹ **2** a container in which pieces of ice are kept for putting in drinks

ˈice cap *n* [C] an area of thick ice that permanently covers the North and South Poles

ˌice-ˈcold *adj* extremely cold: *ice-cold drinks*

ˌice ˈcream / $ ˈ../ ●●● S2 *n*
1 [U] a frozen sweet food made of milk, cream, and sugar, with fruit, nuts, chocolate etc sometimes added to it: *vanilla ice cream*
2 [C] a small amount of this food for one person: *Mummy, can I have an ice cream?*

ˈice cream ˌcone *n* [C] a hard thin cooked cake shaped like a CONE, that you put ice cream in, or one of these with ice cream in it

ˈice cream ˌparlor *n* [C] *AmE* a restaurant that only sells ice cream

ˌice-cream ˈsoda *n* [C] a mixture of ice cream, sweet SYRUP, and SODA WATER, served in a tall glass

ˈice cube *n* [C] a small block of ice used to make drinks cold

iced /aɪst/ *adj* **1** iced drinks are made very cold or served with ice: *iced water* | *iced tea* | *iced coffee* **2** an iced cake has ICING on the top

ˈice ˌfishing *n* [U] the sport of catching fish through a hole in the ice on a lake or river

ˈice floe *n* [C] an area of ice floating in the sea, that has broken off from a larger mass

ˈice ˌhockey *n* [U] *BrE* a sport played on ice, in which players try to hit a hard flat round object into the other team's GOAL with special sticks SYN **hockey** *AmE*

ˈice ˌlolly *n* (*plural* **ice lollies**) [C] *BrE* a piece of sweet-tasting ice on a stick, that you suck SYN **popsicle** *AmE*

ice·man /ˈaɪsmæn/ *n* (*plural* **icemen** /-men/) [C] *AmE* a man who delivered ice to people's houses in the past, so that they could keep food cold

ICE num·ber /ˌaɪ siː ˈiː ˌnʌmbə $ -ər/ *n* [C] (***In Case of Emergency number***) the telephone number of a relative or friend that you store in your MOBILE PHONE so that people know who to call if you are badly injured

ˈice pack *n* [C] **1** a bag containing ice that is put on injured or painful parts of your body to keep them cold **2** a large area of crushed ice floating in the sea → PACK ICE

ˈice pick *n* [C] a sharp tool used for cutting or breaking ice

ˈice rink *n* [C] a specially prepared surface of ice where you can ICE-SKATE

ˈice sheet *n* [C] an ICE CAP

ˈice skate *n* [C usually plural] a special boot with thin metal blades on the bottom, that allows you to move quickly on ice → see picture at SKATE

ˈice-skate *v* [I] to slide on ice wearing ice skates —**ice-skater** *n* [C] —**ice-skating** *n* [U]

ˈice ˌwater *n* [C,U] very cold water with pieces of ice in it, or a glass of this

-ician /ɪʃən/ *suffix* [in nouns] a skilled worker who deals with a particular thing: *a beautician* (=someone who gives beauty treatments) | *a technician* (=someone with technical or scientific skills)

i·ci·cle /ˈaɪsɪkəl/ *n* [C] a long thin pointed piece of ice hanging from a roof or other surface

-icide /ɪsaɪd/ (*also* **-cide**) *suffix* [in nouns] someone or something that kills a particular person or thing, or the act of killing: *insecticide* (=chemical substance for killing insects) | *suicide* (=the act of killing yourself) —**-icidal** /ɪsaɪdl/ *suffix* [in adjectives] —**-icidally** /ɪsaɪdl-i/ *suffix* [in adverbs]

i·ci·ly /ˈaɪsəli/ *adv* if you say something icily, or look at someone icily, you do it in an angry or very unfriendly way: *'I want you to leave now,' she said icily.*

ic·ing /ˈaɪsɪŋ/ *n* [U] **1** a mixture made from very fine light sugar and liquid, used to cover cakes SYN **frosting** *AmE* **2 the icing on the cake** something that makes a very good experience even better: *It was a great day, but meeting her there was just the icing on the cake!*

ˈicing ˌsugar *n* [U] *BrE* very fine light sugar that is mixed with liquid to make icing SYN **powdered sugar** *AmE*

ick·y /ˈɪki/ *adj spoken* very unpleasant, especially to look at, taste, or feel SYN **yucky**: *There was some icky black stuff between the tiles.*

i·con /ˈaɪkɒn $ -kɑːn/ ●●○ *n* [C]
1 a small sign or picture on a computer screen that is used to start a particular operation: *To open a new file, click on the icon.*
2 someone famous who is admired by many people and is thought to represent an important idea: *a sixties cultural icon*
3 (*also* **ikon**) a picture or figure of a holy person that is used in worship in the Greek or Russian Orthodox Church —**iconic** /aɪˈkɒnɪk $ -ˈkɑː-/ *adj*

ICON

i·con·o·clast /aɪˈkɒnəklæst $ -ˈkɑː-/ *n* [C] *formal* someone who attacks established ideas and customs

i·con·o·clas·tic /aɪˌkɒnəˈklæstɪk◂ $ -ˌkɑːn-/ *adj formal* iconoclastic ideas, opinions, writings etc attack established beliefs and customs: *Wolfe's theories were revolutionary and iconoclastic.* —**iconoclasm** /aɪˈkɒnəklæzəm $ -ˈkɑː-/ *n* [U]

i·co·nog·ra·phy /ˌaɪkəˈnɒɡrəfi $ -ˈnɑː-/ *n* [U] the way that a particular people, religious or political group etc represent ideas in pictures or images: *Native American iconography*

-ics /ɪks/ *suffix* [in nouns] **1** the scientific study or use of something: *linguistics* (=the study of language) | *electronics* (=the study or making of electronic equipment) **2** the actions typically done by someone with particular skills: *athletics* (=running, jumping, throwing etc) | *acrobatics* **3** used to make nouns out of words ending in -ICAL or -IC: *the acoustics* (=sound qualities) *of the hall*

ICT /ˌaɪ siː ˈtiː/ *n* [U] (***Information and Computer Technology***) a school subject in Britain which teaches children how to use computers and other electronic equipment, and how to use the Internet, software etc

ICU /ˌaɪ siː ˈjuː/ *n* [C] (***intensive care unit***) a department in a hospital that gives special attention and treatment to people who are very sick or badly injured

ic·y /ˈaɪsi/ ●○○ *adj*
1 extremely cold SYN **frosty**: *an icy wind* | *The bath water was icy cold.*
2 covered in ice: *an icy mountain road*

3 an icy remark, look etc shows that you feel annoyed with or unfriendly towards someone: *an icy stare* → **ICILY** —**iciness** *n* [U]

id /ɪd/ *n* [U] *technical* according to Freudian PSYCHOLOGY, the part of your mind that is completely unconscious but has hidden needs and desires → **EGO(2), SUPEREGO**

I'd /aɪd/ **1** the short form of 'I had': *I wish I'd said that.* **2** the short form of 'I would': *I'd leave now if I were you.*

ID[1] /ˌaɪ ˈdiː/ *n* [C,U] a document that shows your name and date of birth, usually with a photograph SYN **identification**: *I'll need to see some ID. | a fake ID*

ID[2] *v* [T] *spoken* to IDENTIFY a criminal or dead body: *Police are still looking for someone who can ID the body.*

ID card /aɪ ˈdiː kɑːd $ -kɑːrd/ *n* [C] an IDENTITY CARD

-ide /aɪd/ *suffix* [in nouns] *technical* a chemical substance made up of two or more ELEMENTS: *cyanide | oxide*

i·dea /aɪˈdɪə/ ●●● S1 W1 *n*

1 PLAN/SUGGESTION [C] a plan or suggestion for a possible course of action, especially one that you think of suddenly: *You should talk to Ken - he's always full of good ideas. | I knew it was a bad idea to leave him on his own. | It was my wife's idea to move house.* | **[+for]** *The idea for the book came from an old war movie.* | **the idea of doing sth** *I had the idea of asking Katie for help.* ⚠ Don't say 'the idea to do something'. Say **the idea of doing something**. However, you can say **it is a good idea to do something** and **it was someone's idea to do something**.

2 KNOWLEDGE [C,U] a general understanding of something, based on some knowledge about it: *Could you* ***give me an idea of*** *how bad his injuries are? | You must* ***have some idea*** (=have at least a little knowledge) *of what happened to the money. | Don't worry if you don't understand it right now - you'll* ***get the idea*** (=begin to understand or be able to do something). | **have no idea/not have any idea** *She doesn't have any idea where they've gone.* | **a general/rough idea** (=a not very exact idea) *Can you give me a rough idea of how much the repairs will cost?* | **not have the faintest/slightest/foggiest idea** *spoken*: *I don't have the faintest idea what to get Rachel for her birthday.*

3 AIM/INTENTION [C,U] the aim, intention, or purpose of doing something: *The idea is to teach children to save money.* | **[+of/behind]** *The idea behind the outing is to encourage employees to get to know each other. | They wanted Mike to go to law school, but he* ***had other ideas*** (=had different plans).

4 HOW YOU IMAGINE STH TO BE [C,U] an image in your mind of what something is like or should be like: **[+of]** *Chefs differ in their idea of what makes a good dessert. | I only* ***have a*** *vague* ***idea*** *of the kind of work I'll be doing. | It helps if you have a* ***clear idea*** *of what you want.* | **not my idea of sth** *Chocolate milk and a piece of cake is not my idea of dinner.* | ***The very idea*** *of kissing him made her feel physically sick.*

5 BELIEF/OPINION [C usually plural] someone's opinion or belief about something: **[+about]** *She had some rather unusual ideas about raising children.* | **where did you get that idea?** (=used to say that what someone thinks is completely wrong) *No, I'm not seeing Jane. Where did you get that idea?*

6 PRINCIPLE [C] a principle or belief about how something is or should be: **[+of]** *The whole idea of democracy was something strange and new to most people.* | **idea that** *It's based on the idea that all people are created equal.*

7 have an idea (that) to be fairly sure that something is true, without being completely sure: *I'm not sure where my necklace is, but I* ***have a pretty good idea*** *who took it.*

8 get the wrong idea to think that something is true when it is not: *Don't get the wrong idea about Dan and Helen – they're just friends.*

9 have the right idea to act or think in a way that will probably lead to the correct result: *He still makes a few mistakes but I reckon he's got the right idea.*

10 that's/there's an idea *spoken* used to say that you like what someone has just suggested: *'Why don't you invite Paula to come with us?' 'There's an idea.'*

11 that's the idea *spoken* **a)** used to tell someone who is learning to do something that they are doing it the right way, in order to encourage them: *Keep your knees bent and lean forward slightly. That's the idea!* **b)** used to emphasize what the main point of something is, or to say that someone understands that point: *'You're thinking of getting a new job?' 'Yeah, that's the idea.'*

12 bright idea a very clever idea, often used in a joking way to mean a very stupid idea or action: *Whose bright idea was it to leave the back door wide open?*

13 give sb ideas/put ideas into sb's head to make someone think of doing something that they had not thought of doing before, especially something that they should not do: *Nick tells me he wants a motorbike. Have you been putting ideas into his head?*

14 is it sb's idea of a joke? used when you are surprised and often rather annoyed by what someone has said or done: *'She wants you to do it by tomorrow.' 'Is that your idea of a joke?'*

15 what's the big idea? *spoken* used when you cannot understand why someone has done something

16 you have no idea (how/what etc) *spoken* used when you are telling someone that something is extremely good, bad etc: *You have no idea how worried I was.*

17 the idea! *old-fashioned spoken* used to express surprise or disapproval when someone has said something stupid → **buck your ideas up** at **BUCK UP**

COLLOCATIONS

VERBS

have an idea *I've had an idea. Why don't we walk into town?*
get an idea *She got the idea from an article in a magazine.*
give sb an idea *What gave you the idea for the book?*
come up with an idea (=think of an idea) *He's always coming up with interesting ideas.*
hit on an idea *informal* (=suddenly think of an idea) *Then we hit on the idea of renting a cottage.*
toy with an idea *informal* (=think about using an idea, but not very seriously) *I'm toying with the idea of going back to college.*
brainstorm ideas (=get a group of people to all try and think of ideas) | **share/exchange ideas** (=tell someone else your ideas, and learn their ideas)
an idea comes to sb (=someone suddenly thinks of an idea) *The idea came to me while I was having a bath.*

ADJECTIVES

a good/bad idea *Keeping the drinks cold in the bath was a good idea.*
a great/brilliant/excellent idea *What a great idea!*
a bright idea (=a very good idea - often used ironically) *Whose bright idea was it to leave the washing out in the rain?*
a clever idea *It seemed like a clever idea at the time.*
interesting *The idea sounded interesting, but I didn't think it would work.*
stupid/ridiculous/crazy | **original/innovative** (=no one has thought of it before) | **a half-baked idea** (=an idea that has not been carefully thought out)

PHRASES

be full of ideas (*also* **be bursting with ideas**) (=have a lot of ideas) *The children were enthusiastic and full of ideas.*

THESAURUS

idea something that you think of, especially something that you could do or suggest: *I think that's an excellent idea. | Let me know if you have any good ideas.*
thought something that comes into your mind: *The thought had entered my mind that he might be lying. | It was a worrying thought. | She was lost in her thoughts.*

impression the idea that you have in your mind about what someone or something is like: *What was your impression of him?*
inspiration a good and original idea, which makes you think of doing or creating something: *Where did you get your inspiration from for the book?*
brainwave *BrE*, **brainstorm** *AmE* a sudden new and clever idea, especially one that solves a problem: *I thought I'd have to sell the house, but then I had a brainwave.*
concept an idea of how something is, or how something should be done: *Concepts of beauty are different in different cultures.* | *the traditional concept of marriage*
notion an idea about life or society, especially one that is a little silly or old-fashioned: *There is no evidence to support the notion that poverty is caused by laziness.*

i·deal[1] /ˌaɪˈdɪəl◂/ ●●○ S3 W3 *adj*
1 the best or most suitable that something could possibly be SYN **perfect**: *advice on how to reach your ideal weight* | *The scheme offers an* ***ideal opportunity*** *for youngsters to get training.* | *With so much rain, conditions are far from ideal.* | **[+for]** *An elastic waist makes these jeans ideal for the larger woman.* | *an ideal place for a walk*
2 [only before noun] an ideal world, job, system etc is one that you imagine to be perfect, but that is not likely to really exist SYN **perfect**: ***In an ideal world*** *there would be no need for a police force.*

ideal[2] ●●○ *n* [C]
1 a principle about what is morally right or a perfect standard that you hope to achieve: **[+of]** *the ideal of a free and democratic society* | *the long-vanished ideals of the 1950s*
2 a perfect example of what something should be like: **[+of]** *Are our ideals of beauty changing?*

i·deal·ise /aɪˈdɪəlaɪz/ *v* [T] a British spelling of IDEALIZE

i·deal·is·m /aɪˈdɪəlɪzəm/ *n* [U] **1** the belief that you should live your life according to high standards and principles, even when they are very difficult to achieve → **realism**: *the idealism of the younger generation* | *religious idealism* **2** *technical* a way of using art or literature to show the world as a perfect place, even though it is not → **realism**, **naturalism**

i·deal·ist /aɪˈdɪəlɪst/ *n* [C] someone who tries to live according to high standards or principles, especially in a way that is not practical or possible → **realist**

i·deal·is·tic /ˌaɪdɪəˈlɪstɪk◂/ ●○○ *adj* believing that you should live according to high standards and principles, even if they cannot really be achieved, or showing this belief → **realistic**: *idealistic young doctors* | *the idealistic values of the 1960s* —**idealistically** /-kli/ *adv*

i·deal·ize (*also* **-ise** *BrE*) /aɪˈdɪəlaɪz/ *v* [T] to imagine or represent something or someone as being perfect or better than they really are: *Society continues to idealize the two-parent family.* | *an idealized view of marriage* —**idealization** /aɪˌdɪəlaɪˈzeɪʃən $ -lə-/ *n* [C,U]

i·deal·ly /aɪˈdɪəli/ ●●○ S3 *adv*
1 used to describe the way you would like things to be, even though this may not be possible: [sentence adverb] *Ideally, your car should have high-security locks.* | *Fruit and vegetables should ideally be organically grown.*
2 ideally suited/placed/situated etc having the best qualities, experience, knowledge etc for a particular situation: *He was ideally suited for the job.* | *The hotel is ideally located for enjoying the beauty of Yorkshire.*

id·em /ˈɪdem, ˈaɪdem/ *written* from the same book, writer etc as the one that has just been mentioned

i·dent /ˈaɪdent/ *n* [C] a short statement, often involving a piece of music, that tells you the name of a radio station or television CHANNEL, which is broadcast between programmes: *TV idents*

i·den·ti·cal /aɪˈdentɪkəl/ ●●○ AWL *adj* exactly the same, or very similar: *four identical houses* | **[+to/with]** *Nutritionally, infant formulas are almost identical to breast milk.* | *The ingredients are identical with those of competing products.* | **[+in]** *The sisters were identical in appearance and character.* THESAURUS SAME, SIMILAR —**identically** /-kli/ *adv*

iˌdentical ˈtwin *n* [C usually plural] one of a pair of brothers or sisters born at the same time, who develop from the same egg and look almost exactly alike → **fraternal twin**

i·den·ti·fi·a·ble /aɪˈdentəfaɪəbəl/ ●○○ AWL *adj* able to be recognized: **[+as]** *She looked young, and was immediately identifiable as a trainee.* | **[+by]** *The police were identifiable by their uniform.*

i·den·ti·fi·ca·tion /aɪˌdentɪfɪˈkeɪʃən/ ●●○ AWL *n* [U]
1 (*abbreviation* **ID**) official papers or cards, such as your PASSPORT, that prove who you are: *Do you have any identification?* | **form/proof of identification** *Bring some form of identification, preferably a passport.* | *fingerprinting as a* ***means of identification***
2 when someone says officially that they know who someone else is, especially a criminal or a dead person: *His body was taken to Brighton mortuary for identification.*
3 when you recognize something or discover exactly what it is: **[+of]** *the identification of customer needs* | *the identification of children who need professional help*
4 the act of saying that two things are very closely related: **identification of sth with sth** *the identification of sexism with women's oppression*
5 a strong feeling of sympathy with someone that makes you able to share their feelings: **[+with]** *my identification with the heroine of the book*

iˌdentifiˈcation paˌrade (*also* **identity parade**) *n* [C] *BrE* a process in which someone who has seen a crime take place looks at a group of people to see if they can recognize the criminal SYN **line-up** *AmE*

i·den·ti·fy /aɪˈdentɪfaɪ/ ●●● W1 AWL *v* (**identified, identifying, identifies**) [T]
1 to recognize and correctly name someone or something: *He was too far away to be able to identify faces.* | *The police took fingerprints and* ***identified the body***. | **identify sb/sth as sb/sth** *Eyewitnesses identified the gunman as an army sergeant.* | *The aircraft were identified as American.* THESAURUS RECOGNIZE
2 to recognize something or discover exactly what it is, what its nature or origin is etc: *Scientists have identified the gene that causes abnormal growth.* | *They identified a number of problem areas.*
3 if a particular thing identifies someone or something, it makes them easy to recognize: **identify sb as sb** *His accent identified him as a Frenchman.*

identify with *phr v*
1 identify with sb/sth to feel sympathy with someone or be able to share their feelings: *Humans can easily identify with the emotional expressions of chimpanzees.* | *He identified with our distress.*
2 identify sb with sth to think that someone is very closely related to or involved with something such as a political group: *She has always been identified with the radical left.*
3 identify sth with sb/sth to think that something is the same as, or closely related to, something else: *the attempt to identify crime with poverty and social problems*

i·den·ti·kit /aɪˈdentɪˌkɪt/ *n* [C] *trademark BrE* **1** a method used by the police in which a picture of a criminal is produced from descriptions given by people who have seen the crime take place SYN **composite** *AmE*: *an identikit picture* **2** used to describe things that are all exactly the same, with no interesting or unusual features: *new identikit cities*

i·den·ti·ty /aɪˈdentəti/ ●●○ W2 AWL *n* (*plural* **identities**)
1 [C,U] someone's identity is their name or who they are: ***The identity of*** *the killer is still unknown.*
2 [U] the qualities and attitudes that a person or group of people have, that make them different from other people: *Children need continuity, security, and a* ***sense of identity***. | *Travelling alone can lead to a* ***loss of identity***. | **national/**

cultural/social etc identity (=a strong feeling of belonging to a particular group, race etc) *Our strong sense of national identity has been shaped by our history.* | **identity crisis/crisis of identity** (=a feeling of uncertainty about who you really are and what your purpose is) *My father experienced an identity crisis in middle age.*
3 [U] *formal* exact SIMILARITY between two things

COLLOCATIONS

ADJECTIVES

sb's real/true identity *The true identity of the author was not revealed until 100 years later.*
a new/different identity *He avoided arrest by adopting a new identity.*
a false identity (=when someone pretends to be another person)

VERBS

find out/discover sb's identity *The police have yet to discover the victim's identity.*
know sb's identity *He wanted to know the identity of his real father.*
hide/conceal sb's identity *She used a false name to conceal her identity.*
reveal/disclose sb's identity (=show or say who a person is) *The company did not reveal the identity of the prospective buyer.*
give away sb's identity (=accidentally reveal it) | **protect sb's identity** (=make sure no one finds out who someone is) | **adopt/assume an identity** (=give yourself a new identity)

identity + NOUN

identity card/papers/documents (=documents that show who you are) *Each member of staff is issued with an identity card.*
an identity parade *BrE* (=when someone looks at a line of people to see if they recognize a criminal) | **identity theft/fraud** (=the crime of stealing another person's personal details in order to pretend to be that person)

PHRASES

proof of identity (=something that proves you are who you say you are) *You'll need proof of identity, such as a driving licence.*
a case of mistaken identity (=when people think that someone is a different person, especially with the result that they are accused of something that they did not do)

i'dentity ˌcard *n* [C] a card with your name, date of birth, and photograph on it, that proves who you are SYN **ID card**

i'dentity paˌrade *n* [C] *BrE* an IDENTIFICATION PARADE

i'dentity ˌtheft (*also* **i'dentity ˌfraud**) *n* [U] any crime in which someone steals personal information about and belonging to another person, for example their bank account number or the number of their driving LICENCE, and uses this information to deceive other people and get money or goods

id·e·o·gram /ˈɪdiəgræm/ (*also* **id·e·o·graph** /-grɑːf $ -græf/) *n* [C] a written sign, for example in Chinese, that represents an idea or thing rather than the sound of a word → **hieroglyphics**

i·de·o·lo·gic·al /ˌaɪdiəˈlɒdʒɪkəl◂ $ -ˈlɑː-/ ●○○ AWL *adj* based on strong beliefs or ideas, especially political or economic ideas: *The party is split by ideological differences.* —**ideologically** /-kli/ *adv*

i·de·o·logue /ˈaɪdiəˌlɒg $ -ˌlɒːg, -ˌlɑːg/ (*also* **i·de·ol·o·gist** /ˌaɪdiˈɒlədʒɪst $ -ˈɑːl-/) *n* [C] someone whose actions are very much influenced by an ideology

i·de·ol·o·gy /ˌaɪdiˈɒlədʒi $ -ˈɑːl-/ ●○○ AWL *n* (*plural* **ideologies**) [C,U] a set of beliefs on which a political or economic system is based, or which strongly influence the way people behave → **philosophy**: *the ideologies of fascism and communism* | *a new ideology based on individualism*

ˌIdes of 'March, the March 15th, famous for being the day on which Julius Caesar was killed by a group of his former friends because they thought he had too much power. Caesar is supposed to have been warned by a FORTUNE-TELLER to 'beware the Ides of March'. People sometimes use this expression when giving a warning.

id·i·o·cy /ˈɪdiəsi/ *n* (*plural* **idiocies**) [C,U] something that you think is extremely silly or stupid SYN **stupidity**: *The idiocy of his behaviour appalled her.* | *He smiled calmly at the idiocies of mankind.*

id·i·o·lect /ˈɪdiəlekt/ *n* [C,U] *technical* the way in which a particular person uses language → **DIALECT**

id·i·om /ˈɪdiəm/ ●●○ *n*
1 [C] a group of words that has a special meaning that is different from the ordinary meaning of each separate word. For example, 'under the weather' is an idiom meaning 'ill'. THESAURUS ▸ **PHRASE, WORD**
2 [C,U] *formal or technical* a style of expression in writing, speech, or music that is typical of a particular group of people: *the new musical idiom*

id·i·o·mat·ic /ˌɪdiəˈmætɪk◂/ ●○○ *adj*
1 idiomatic expression/phrase an idiom
2 typical of the natural way in which someone speaks or writes when they are using their own language: *He had the ability to write fluent and idiomatic English.* | *the idiomatic richness of the Spanish language* —**idiomatically** /-kli/ *adv*

id·i·o·syn·cra·sy /ˌɪdiəˈsɪŋkrəsi/ *n* (*plural* **idiosyncrasies**) [C] **1** an unusual habit or way of behaving that someone has: *my uncle's idiosyncrasies* **2** an unusual or unexpected feature that something has: *one of the many idiosyncrasies of English spelling* —**idiosyncratic** /ˌɪdiəsɪnˈkrætɪk◂/ *adj*

id·i·ot /ˈɪdiət/ ●●○ S3 *n* [C]
1 a stupid person or someone who has done something stupid: *It was all your fault, you idiot.*
2 *old use* someone who is mentally ill or has a very low level of intelligence —**idiotic** /ˌɪdiˈɒtɪk◂ $ -ˈɑːt-/ *adj*: *Stop asking such idiotic questions.* —**idiotically** /-kli/ *adv*

'idiot-ˌproof *adj* something that is idiot-proof is so easy to use or do that even stupid people will not break it or make a mistake → **foolproof**: *idiot-proof instructions*

i·dle¹ /ˈaɪdl/ ●○○ *adj*
1 not working or producing anything OPP **busy**: *I cannot afford to leave the land* ***lying idle***. | *The whole team* ***stood idle****, waiting for the mechanic.* | *The workers have been idle for the last six months.*
2 not serious, or not done with any definite intention: *She was not a woman to make* ***idle threats***. | **idle chatter/talk/gossip etc** | *It was only from* ***idle curiosity*** *that she went into the barn.*
3 lazy: *Go and wake up that idle brother of yours.*

REGISTER
Idle sounds rather old-fashioned and literary. In everyday English, people usually say **lazy**: *She's not stupid, just* ***lazy***.

4 it is idle to do sth it is not worth doing something, because nothing will be achieved: *It would be idle to deny that progress was made.*
5 the idle rich rich people who do not have to work —**idleness** *n* [U] —**idly** *adv*: *They sat chatting idly.* | *I cannot* ***stand idly by*** *and let him take the blame.*

idle² *v* **1** [I] if an engine idles, it runs slowly while the vehicle, machine etc is not moving: *He flicked a switch and let the boat idle.* **2** [I] to spend time doing nothing: *Sometimes he went for a walk; sometimes he just idled.* **3** [T] *AmE* to stop using a factory or stop providing work for your workers, especially temporarily SYN **shut down**: *The company has idled a number of its US plants indefinitely.*

idle sth ↔ **away** *phr v* to spend time in a relaxed way, doing nothing: *They idled their time away in the pub.*

I

id·ler /ˈaɪdlə $ -ər/ *n* [C] *old-fashioned* someone who is lazy and does not work

i·dol /ˈaɪdl/ ●○○ *n* [C]
1 someone or something that you love or admire very much SYN **hero**: **[+of]** *She is the idol of countless teenagers.* | *She had made an idol of her husband.* | *a **pop idol***
2 a picture or STATUE that is worshipped as a god → **effigy**

i·dol·a·try /aɪˈdɒlətri $ -ˈdɑː-/ *n* [U] **1** the practice of worshipping idols **2** when you admire someone or something too much —**idolatrous** *adj*

i·dol·ize (*also* **-ise** *BrE*) /ˈaɪdəl-aɪz/ *v* [T] to admire and love someone so much that you think they are perfect: *They had one child, a girl whom they idolized.* THESAURUS ADMIRE

id·yll /ˈɪdəl,ˈɪdɪl $ ˈaɪdl/ *n* [singular] *literary* a place or experience in which everything is peaceful and everyone is perfectly happy: *a **rural idyll***

i·dyl·lic /ɪˈdɪlɪk, aɪ- $ aɪ-/ *adj* an idyllic place or time is very beautiful, happy, and peaceful, with no problems or dangers: **idyllic setting/surroundings/scene etc** *If you want old-world tradition in an idyllic setting, this is the hotel for you.* —**idyllically** /-kli/ *adv*: *idyllically happy*

-ie /i/ *suffix* [in nouns] *informal* another form of the suffix -Y: *dearie*

i.e. /ˌaɪ ˈiː/ ●●○ written before a word or phrase that gives the exact meaning of something you have just written or said: *The film is only open to adults, i.e. people over 18.*

IED /ˌaɪ iː ˈdiː/ *n* [C] (***improvised explosive device***) a bomb that has been made using whatever materials are available. IEDs are used by TERRORISTS or people who are opposed to their government rather than by official military forces.

IELTS /ˈaɪelts/ *n* [U] *trademark* (***International English Language Testing System***) a test for people whose first language is not English that shows how good their English is. The test is taken by people who want to study, work, or live in an English-speaking country. People who take the test do not have to get a certain score in order to pass it. Instead, they are given a grade from 0 to 9.

if[1] /ɪf/ ●●● S1 W1 *conjunction*
1 used when talking about something that might happen or be true, or might have happened: *We'll stay at home if it rains.* | *If you need money, I can lend you some.* | *If I didn't apologize, I'd feel guilty.* | *If you had worked harder, you would have passed your exams.* | *What would happen to your family if you were to die in an accident?* | *If Dad were here, he would know what to do.* | *Taste the soup and add salt and pepper **if necessary**.* | *I want to get back by five o'clock **if possible**.* | *I think I can fix it tomorrow. **If not**, you'll have to wait till Friday.* | *Is the book available, and **if so**, where?* | *The missiles can be fired **only if** the operator types in a six-digit code.* | *We'll face that problem **if and when** it comes along* (=if it happens or when it happens). | ***If by any chance** you can't manage dinner tonight, perhaps we can at least have a drink together.*
2 used to mention a fact, situation, or event that someone asks about, or is not certain about: *He stopped to ask me if I was all right.* | *I don't know if what I am saying makes any sense.* | *I doubt if anyone will remember me.* | *I'm not sure **if** this is the right road **or not**.*
3 used to mention a type of event or situation when talking about what happens on occasions of that type: *If I go to bed late, I feel dreadful in the morning.* | *Plastic will melt if it gets too hot.*
4 used when saying what someone's feelings are about a possible situation: *You don't seem to care if I'm tired.* | *I'm sorry if I upset you.* | *It would be nice if we could spend more time together.*
5 *spoken* used when making a polite request: *I wonder if you could help me.* | *I'd be grateful if you would send me further details.* | *Would you mind if I open a window?* | *If you would just wait for a moment, I'll try to find your papers.*
6 used when you are adding that something may be even more, less, better, worse etc than you have just said: *Brian rarely, if ever, goes to bed before 3 am.* | *Their policies have changed little, if at all, since the last election.* | *Her needs are just as important as yours, if not more so.* | *The snow was now two feet deep, making it difficult, if not impossible, to get the car out.*
7 even if used to emphasize that, although something may happen or may be true, it will not change a situation: *I wouldn't tell you even if I knew.* | *Even if she survives, she'll never fully recover.*
8 if anything used when adding a remark that changes what you have just said or makes it stronger: *It's warm enough here in London. A little too warm, if anything.*
9 *spoken* used during a conversation when you are trying to make a suggestion, change the subject, or interrupt someone else: *If I might just make a suggestion, I think that the matter could be easily settled with a little practical demonstration.* | *If I could just take one example to illustrate this.*
10 if I were you *spoken* used when giving advice and telling someone what you think they should do: *I wouldn't worry about it if I were you.*
11 if only a) used to express a strong wish, especially when you know that what you want cannot happen: *If only he had talked to her sooner!* | *If only I weren't so tired!* **b)** used to give a reason for something, although you think it is not a good one: *Media studies is regarded as a more exciting subject, if only because it's new.*
12 used to say that, although something may be true, it is not important: *If he has a fault at all, it is that he is too generous.* | *Her only problem, if you can call it a problem, is that she expects to be successful all the time.*
13 used when adding one criticism of a person or thing that you generally like: *The eldest son was highly intelligent, if somewhat lazy.* | *Lunch was a grand if rather noisy affair.*
→ **as if** at AS²(9), → **if ever there was one** at EVER(15), → **what if ... ?** at WHAT

GRAMMAR

Choosing the right tense

- You use **if** with the present tense, when talking about possible future events: *If I see him, I'll tell him.* ✗ Don't say: *If I will see him, I'll tell him.*
- You use **if** with the past tense to talk about something that is unlikely or impossible: *If I won the lottery, I would leave my job.* ✗ Don't say: *If I would win the lottery ...*
- In everyday spoken English, you say **if I was**: *If I was younger, I'd do it myself.*
- In more formal English, you say **if I were**: *If I were in your position, I'd ask for help.*
- You use **if** with the past perfect to talk about something that did not happen: *If they had tried to stop the protest, there would have been a riot.* ✗ Don't say: *If they would have tried to stop the protest ...*
- You also use **if** with the present perfect, when talking about whether something has happened or not: *If she hasn't called by tomorrow, I'll call her.*

Comparison

if
- You say: *I'm not sure if I heard him correctly.* | *I don't know if he is guilty.*

whether
- You say: *I'm not sure whether I heard him correctly.* | *I don't know whether he is guilty.*
- You can use **whether** after a preposition: *We discussed the issue of whether to pay.* ✗ Don't say: *the issue of if to pay*
- You can say **whether to do** something: *He doesn't know whether to accept.* ✗ Don't say: *He doesn't know if to accept.*

GRAMMAR GUIDE VERBS

THESAURUS

if used when talking about the possibility that something might happen or be true: *He faces a long*

prison sentence if the court finds him guilty. | *If scientists' predictions are correct, average global temperatures could rise by 6 degrees.*
unless if something does not happen, or if someone does not do something: *The star is difficult to see unless the sky is very clear.* | *Doctors said they could not treat the boy unless his parents gave their permission.*
whether or not used when saying that it does not matter if something happens or not, or if something is true or not: *Most people will get better on their own, whether or not they receive medical treatment.* | *I'm still going, whether she likes it or not.*
otherwise used when saying that there will be a bad result if someone does not do something, or if something does not happen: *Drink plenty of water – otherwise you will become dehydrated.*
in case in order to deal with something that might happen: *She did not think it would rain, but she took her umbrella just in case.* | *It is best to keep a medical kit ready in case of emergency.*
as long as/provided that only if something else happens or is true: *Visitors are welcome, as long as they bring their own tent.* | *Anyone can join the course, provided that there is space available.*
on condition that used when you agree to do something only if someone first agrees to do something else: *He was offered the job on condition that he went on a month-long training course.*

if² *n* [C] *informal* **1 ifs and buts** *BrE*, **ifs, ands, or buts** *AmE* if you do not want any ifs and buts, you want someone to do something quickly without arguing: *No ifs and buts – just make sure the job is done by tomorrow!* **2 and it's a big if** used to say that something is not likely to happen: *The team will go racing next year if – and it's a very big if – they can raise £6 million.* **3** something that may or may not happen: *There are too many ifs in this plan of yours.*

if·fy /ˈɪfi/ *adj informal* **1** *BrE* not very good: *That meat smells a bit iffy to me.* **2** not certain to happen SYN **doubtful**: *The July date is still rather iffy.*

-iform /əfɔːm $ əfɔːrm/ *suffix* [in adjectives] *technical* having a particular shape: *cruciform* (=cross-shaped)

-ify /ɪfaɪ/ (*also* **-fy**) *suffix* [in verbs] **1** to make something be in a particular state or condition: *to purify* (=make or become pure) | *to clarify the situation* (=make it clear) **2** to fill someone with a particular feeling: *Spiders terrify me* (=make me very afraid). **3** *informal* to do something in a silly or annoying way: *to speechify* (=make speeches in a way that shows you are trying to sound important) **4** to make something or someone be like or typical of a person or group: *Frenchified* (=like the French)

ig·loo /ˈɪgluː/ *n* [C] a house made from blocks of hard snow or ice

IGLOO

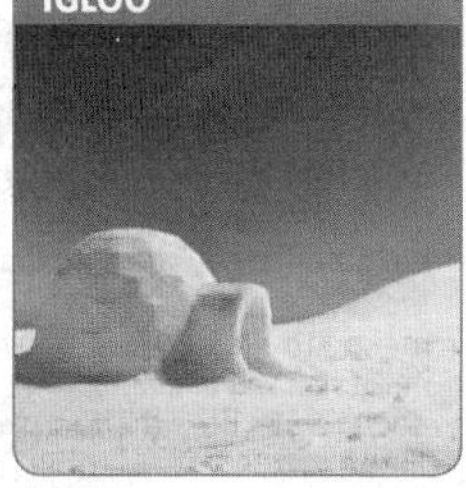

ig·ne·ous /ˈɪgniəs/ *adj technical* igneous rocks are formed from LAVA (=hot liquid rock)

ig·nite /ɪgˈnaɪt/ *v* **1** [I,T] *formal* to start burning, or to make something start burning: *The petrol tank suddenly ignited.* | *The candle ignited the plastic.* THESAURUS ▸ BURN **2** [T] to start a dangerous situation, angry argument etc: *events which ignited the war in Europe*

ig·ni·tion /ɪgˈnɪʃən/ *n* **1** [singular] the electrical part of a vehicle's engine that makes it start working **2** [C usually singular] the place in a car where you put in a key to start the engine → see picture at **CAR** **3** [U] *formal* the act of starting to burn or of making something start to burn

ig·no·ble /ɪgˈnəʊbəl $ -ˈnoʊ-/ *adj formal* ignoble thoughts, feelings, or actions are ones that you should feel ashamed or embarrassed about SYN **base**: *ignoble feelings of intense jealousy*

ig·no·min·i·ous /ˌɪgnəˈmɪniəs/ *adj formal* making you feel ashamed or embarrassed SYN **humiliating**: **ignominious defeat/failure/retreat etc** | *an* ***ignominious end*** *to his career* —**ignominiously** *adv*

ig·no·mi·ny /ˈɪgnəmɪni/ *n* [U] *formal* an event or situation that makes you feel ashamed or embarrassed, especially in public SYN **humiliation**: **[+of]** *He feared the ignominy of being exposed as a spy.* THESAURUS ▸ SHAME

ig·no·ra·mus /ˌɪgnəˈreɪməs/ *n* (*plural* **ignoramuses**) [C] *old-fashioned* someone who does not know about things that most people know about

ig·no·rance /ˈɪgnərəns/ ●●○ AWL *n* [U]
1 lack of knowledge or information about something: *Excuse my ignorance, but how does it actually work?* | **[+of]** *our ignorance of the true situation* | **in ignorance** *I would have remained in ignorance if Shaun hadn't mentioned it.* | **[+about]** *public fear and ignorance about AIDS*
2 ignorance is bliss used to say that if you do not know about a problem, you cannot worry about it

ig·no·rant /ˈɪgnərənt/ ●●○ AWL *adj*
1 not knowing facts or information that you ought to know: *an ignorant and uneducated man* | **[+of]** *Political historians are often rather ignorant of economics.* | **[+about]** *Many people remain* ***blissfully ignorant*** *about the dangers of too much sun* (=happy because they do not know about the dangers).
2 caused by a lack of knowledge and understanding: *an ignorant remark* | *ignorant opinions*
3 *BrE spoken* rude or impolite: *ignorant behaviour* —**ignorantly** *adv*

ig·nore /ɪgˈnɔː $ -ˈnɔːr/ ●●● S2 W2 AWL *v* [T]
1 to deliberately pay no attention to something that you have been told or that you know about: *You can't* ***ignore the fact*** *that many criminals never go to prison.* | *problems which we can't afford to ignore*
2 to behave as if you had not heard or seen someone or something: *The phone rang, but she ignored it.* | *Sam rudely ignored the question.* | **completely/totally ignore sb/sth** *He had completely ignored her remark, preferring his own theory.*

REGISTER
In everyday British English, people often say **take no notice of** something or **not take any notice of** something rather than **ignore** something: *There are signs telling you not to smoke, but people* ***don't take any notice of*** *them.*

i·gua·na /ɪˈgwɑːnə/ *n* [C] a large tropical American LIZARD → see picture at **REPTILE**

i·kon /ˈaɪkɒn $ -kɑːn/ *n* [C] another spelling of ICON

il- /ɪ/ *prefix* the form used for IN- before l: *illogical* (=not logical)

ilk /ɪlk/ *n* [singular] a particular type SYN **kind**: **of that/his/their etc ilk** *Irving Berlin and composers of his ilk* | **sb and that/his/their etc ilk** *Mrs Taylor and her ilk talk absolute rubbish.*

This graph shows how common the adjectives **ill** and **sick** are in British and American English.

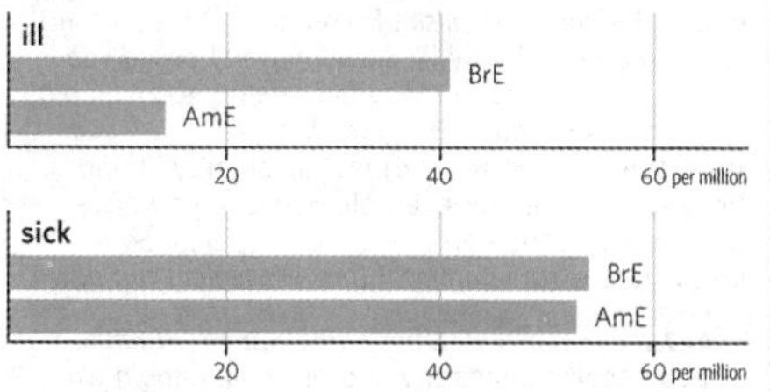

In British English the word **ill** means not healthy. Americans usually use **sick** for this meaning. In British English **sick** can be used in this way, but is more commonly used in expressions such as **be sick** or **feel sick** meaning 'to vomit or feel that you are going to vomit'.

ill¹ /ɪl/ ●●● S3 W2 *adj*
1 *especially BrE* suffering from a disease or not feeling well

SYN **sick** *AmE*: *Bridget can't come – she's ill.* | *I was feeling ill that day and decided to stay at home.* | **[+with]** *Her husband has been ill with bladder trouble.* | *a hospice for the terminally ill*
2 [only before noun] bad or harmful: *Many people consumed the poisoned oil without* ***ill effects***. | *the neglect and* ***ill treatment*** *of children* | *He was unable to join the army because of* ***ill health***.
3 ill at ease nervous, uncomfortable, or embarrassed: *He always felt shy and ill at ease at parties.*
4 it's an ill wind (that blows nobody any good) *spoken* used to say that every problem brings an advantage for someone → ILL FEELING, ILL WILL

COLLOCATIONS

VERBS

be ill *What's wrong? Are you ill?*
feel ill *I've been feeling ill since I woke up this morning.*
look ill *He looked rather ill when I saw him.*
become ill (*also* **get ill** *informal*) *She became ill after eating oysters.*
fall ill *formal* (=become ill) *Louise fell ill while she was on holiday.*
be taken ill (=become ill suddenly) *Henry was suddenly taken ill and had to go to the hospital.*
make sb ill *I think it was the heat that made me ill.*

ADVERBS

seriously ill (=very ill) *Any seriously ill patients are usually sent to a state hospital.*
gravely ill *formal* (=extremely ill) *She went to visit her grandfather, who was gravely ill.*
critically ill (=so ill that you might die) *He got news that his mother was critically ill in hospital.*
terminally ill (=having a very serious illness that you will die from) | **chronically ill** (=having a long-term illness that cannot be cured and will not get better) | **mentally ill** (=having an illness of your mind)

THESAURUS

ill [not before noun] *especially BrE* suffering from a disease or not feeling well: *Her mother is seriously ill in hospital.* | *I woke up feeling really ill.*
sick *especially AmE* ill: *She's been sick with the flu.* | *a sick child* | *Dan got sick on vacation.*
not very well [not before noun] ill, but not seriously ill: *Sarah's not very well – she has a throat infection.*
unwell [not before noun] *formal* ill: *The singer had been unwell for some time.*
poorly [not before noun] *BrE spoken* ill: *Your grandmother's been very poorly lately.*
in a bad way [not before noun] very ill because of a serious injury or disease: *You'd better call an ambulance – she looks like she's in a bad way.*
be off sick *BrE*, **be out sick** *AmE* to be not at work because of an illness: *Two teachers were off sick yesterday.*

SLIGHTLY ILL

under the weather (*also* **off colour** *BrE*) [not before noun] *informal* slightly ill: *Sorry I haven't called you – I've been a bit under the weather lately.* | *You look a bit off colour – are you sure you're OK?*
run down [not before noun] feeling slightly ill and tired all the time, for example because you have been working too hard, or not eating well: *Some people take extra vitamins if they are feeling run down.*

OFTEN ILL

in poor health unhealthy and often ill: *Chopin was already in poor health when he arrived on the island.*
delicate weak and likely to become ill easily: *She was delicate and pale and frequently complained of headaches.* | *He had a* ***delicate constitution*** *and throughout his adult life suffered from various illnesses.*
sickly a sickly child is often ill: *He was a sickly child and spent a lot of time at home on his own.*

ill² *adv* **1 sb can ill afford (to do) sth** to be unable to do or have something without making the situation you are in very difficult: *I was losing weight which I could ill afford to lose.* | *Most gamblers can ill afford their habit.* **2 think/speak ill of sb** *formal* to think or say unpleasant things about someone: *She really believes you should never speak ill of the dead.* **3 bode ill** *formal* to give you a reason to think that something bad will happen: *The look on his face boded ill for somebody.*

ill³ *n* **1 ills** [plural] problems and difficulties: *He wants to cure all the ills of the world.* **2** [U] *formal* harm, evil, or bad luck: *She did not like Matthew but she would never wish him ill.*

ill- /ɪl/ *prefix* badly or not enough: *ill-concealed boredom* | *ill-formed sentences*

I'll /aɪl/ the short form of 'I will' or 'I shall': *I'll see you tomorrow.*

ˌill-adˈvised *adj* not sensible or not wise, and likely to cause problems in the future SYN **unwise**: **ill-advised to do sth** *You would be ill-advised to go out alone at night.* | *ill-advised remarks* —**ill-advisedly** /-ədˈvaɪzdəli/ *adv*

ˌill-asˈsorted *adj* an ill-assorted group of people or things do not seem to belong together in a group

ˌill-ˈbred *adj* rude or behaving badly, especially because your parents did not teach you to behave well

ˌill-conˈceived *adj* not planned well and not having an aim that is likely to be achieved: *The policy was ill-conceived and misguided.*

ˌill-conˈsidered *adj* decisions, actions, ideas etc that are ill-considered have not been carefully thought about: *The tax reforms are ill-considered.*

ˌill-deˈfined *adj* **1** not described clearly enough: *Some jobs in the company are pretty ill-defined.* **2** not clearly marked, or not having a clear shape SYN **indistinct**: *The borders were vague and ill-defined.*

ˌill-disˈposed *adj formal* unfriendly or unsympathetic: *an ill-disposed character*

il·le·gal¹ /ɪˈliːɡəl/ ●●● W3 AWL *adj* not allowed by the law SYN **unlawful** OPP **legal**: *illegal drugs* | *They were involved in illegal activities.* | **it is illegal to do sth** *It is illegal to sell tobacco to someone under 16.* —**illegally** *adv*: *They entered the country illegally.* —**illegality** /ˌɪlɪˈɡæləti/ *n* [U]

COLLOCATIONS

ADVERBS

completely/totally illegal *The deal was completely illegal.*
highly illegal (=completely illegal) *It all sounds highly illegal.*
strictly illegal *formal* (=completely illegal – used for emphasis) *Phone tapping is strictly illegal.*
technically illegal (=according to the exact details of a law)

VERBS

be illegal *It is illegal to sell tobacco products to anyone under the age of 16.*
become illegal *The drug did not become illegal until the 1970s.*
make sth illegal *He was involved in the campaign to make hunting illegal.*
declare sth illegal *The strike was declared illegal on July 7.*

illegal + NOUN

an illegal weapon *He was charged with carrying an illegal weapon.*
illegal drugs *She was found guilty of possession of illegal drugs.*
an illegal substance (=an illegal drug) | **illegal parking/gambling/hunting etc** | **illegal immigrants** | **illegal activities** | **an illegal act** | **illegal use of sth**

illegal² *n* [C] *AmE spoken* an illegal immigrant: *Illegals are still slipping through in unacceptable numbers.*

il,legal 'immigrant (*also* **il,legal 'alien** *AmE*) *n* [C] someone who comes to live in another country without official permission

il·le·gi·ble /ɪ'ledʒəbəl/ *adj* difficult or impossible to read OPP **legible**: *His handwriting is totally illegible.* —**illegibly** *adv* —**illegibility** /ɪ,ledʒə'bɪləti/ *n* [U]

il·le·git·i·mate /,ɪlə'dʒɪtəmət◂/ *adj* **1** born to parents who are not married OPP **legitimate**: *his illegitimate son* **2** not allowed or acceptable according to rules or agreements OPP **legitimate**: *a distinction between legitimate and illegitimate trade* —**illegitimately** *adv* —**illegitimacy** *n* [U]

,ill-e'quipped *adj* not having the necessary equipment or skills for a particular situation or activity: **ill-equipped to do sth** *The rebels were ill-equipped to cope with Western weapons and forces.* | **[+for]** *Their army is ill-equipped for modern warfare.*

,ill-'fated *adj literary* unlucky and leading to serious problems or death: *an ill-fated venture*

,ill 'feeling *n* [U] angry feelings towards someone: *'I'm sorry. No ill feeling?' 'None,' she replied.*

,ill-'fitting *adj* ill-fitting clothes do not fit the person who is wearing them OPP **well-fitting**: *Many children have problems with their feet, caused by ill-fitting shoes.*

,ill-'founded *adj formal* based on something that is untrue: *His fears proved ill-founded.*

,ill-gotten 'gains *n* [plural] money that was obtained in an unfair or dishonest way – used humorously

il·lib·e·ral /ɪ'lɪbərəl/ *adj formal* **1** not supporting people's rights to say or do what they want OPP **liberal**: *illiberal and undemocratic policies* **2** not generous —**illiberally** *adv* —**illiberality** /ɪ,lɪbə'ræləti/ *n* [U]

il·li·cit /ɪ'lɪsɪt/ ●○○ *adj* not allowed by laws or rules, or strongly disapproved of by society → **illegal**: *illicit drugs* | *the* ***illicit trade*** *in stolen cattle* —**illicitly** *adv*

,ill-in'formed *adj* knowing less than you should about a particular subject: **[+about]** *Some employers are ill-informed about education.*

il·lit·e·rate[1] /ɪ'lɪtərət/ *adj* **1** someone who is illiterate has not learned to read or write **2** badly written, in an uneducated way: *It was an illiterate letter, full of mistakes.* **3 economically/politically/scientifically etc illiterate** knowing very little about economics, politics etc —**illiteracy** *n* [U]

illiterate[2] *n* [C] someone who has not learned to read or write

,ill-'judged *adj formal* an action that is ill-judged has not been thought about carefully enough OPP **well-judged**: *an ill-judged choice of words*

,ill-'mannered *adj formal* not polite and behaving badly in social situations OPP **well-mannered** THESAURUS ▸ RUDE

ill·ness /'ɪlnəs/ ●●● S3 W3 *n* [C,U] a disease of the body or mind, or the condition of being ill: *She had all the normal childhood illnesses.* | *Her mother was recovering from a serious illness.* | *I've never missed a day's work through illness.* | *ways to improve your health and reduce the risk of illness* → DISEASE

COLLOCATIONS

VERBS

have an illness *When did you first find out that you had the illness?*
suffer from an illness *She suffers from a rare illness.*
get/develop an illness *She developed the illness when she was in her 50s.*
contract an illness *formal* (=get an illness by catching it from another person) *He contracted the illness while he was working abroad.*
recover from an illness *It took several months for him to recover from his illness.*
be diagnosed with an illness (=be found by doctors to have an illness) | **cause/lead to illness** | **prevent illness**

ADJECTIVES/NOUN + illness

serious/severe *His illness is more severe than the doctors first thought.*
minor (=not serious) *He suffered a succession of minor illnesses.*
fatal (=causing death quite quickly) *She developed a fatal illness.*
life-threatening (=likely to cause death) *Doctors say that his illness isn't life-threatening.*
terminal (=causing death eventually, and not possible to cure) *At that point the illness was thought to be terminal.*
incurable (=not possible to cure) | **acute** (=becoming serious very quickly) | **chronic** (=that lasts a long time, and cannot be cured)
a long/short illness *She nursed him through his long illness.*
a debilitating illness (=that makes you very weak) | **a childhood illness** | **a mental/psychiatric illness**

PHRASES

the symptoms of an illness *Symptoms of the illness include vomiting and severe headaches.*
a period of illness

COMMON ERRORS

⚠ Don't say 'a heavy illness'. Say **a serious illness** or **a severe illness**.

THESAURUS

illness something wrong with your health which makes you feel ill: *Her husband was in hospital for six months with a serious illness.*
disease a particular illness, especially one that spreads to other people easily or that affects one part of your body: *childhood diseases such as measles and chickenpox* | *heart disease*
infection an illness that is caused by BACTERIA or a VIRUS: *His cough got worse and worse and became a chest infection.*
condition a health problem that affects you permanently or for a long time: *a medical condition such as asthma* | *a heart condition*
problem [usually after a noun] something that is wrong with a particular part of your body or your health in general: *a serious back problem* | *health problems*
trouble [singular, only after a noun] illness or pain that affects a particular part of your body: *I've had a bit of stomach trouble.*
disorder *formal* an illness that prevents a particular organ of your body from working properly, or affects the way you behave: *a liver disorder* | *a blood disorder* | *Anorexia nervosa is an eating disorder.*

AN ILLNESS THAT IS NOT VERY SERIOUS

bug *informal* an illness that spreads to other people very easily but that is not very serious: *There's a bug going round at school and a lot of the children are absent.* | *a flu bug*
complaint *medical* an illness that affects a particular part of your body, especially one that is not very serious – used by doctors: *a minor skin complaint* | *Deakin suffers from a back complaint called arachnoiditis.*
ailment /'eɪlmənt/ *formal* an illness that affects a particular part of your body, especially one that is not serious: *People often go to their doctor about relatively minor ailments.* | *The ointment is used to treat ailments such as small wounds and insect bites.*

THE GENERAL STATE OF BEING ILL

illness the general state of being ill: *Stress is emerging today as a major cause of illness.*
sickness the state of being ill, especially when it stops you working: *absence from work due to sickness*

ill health *formal* the state of being ill, usually for a long period of time: *Research shows that there is a link between air pollution and ill health.*

il·lo·gi·cal /ɪˈlɒdʒɪkəl $ ɪˈlɑː-/ AWL *adj* not sensible or reasonable OPP **logical**: *illogical and unreasonable fear* | **it is illogical to do sth** *It is illogical to assume you can do the work of three people.* —**illogically** /-kli/ *adv* —**illogicality** /ɪˌlɒdʒəˈkæləti $ ɪˌlɑː-/ *n* [U]

ˌill-preˈpared *adj* not ready for something: **[+for]** *The country was ill-prepared for war.*

ˌill-ˈserved *adj* [not before noun] not helped by something or not represented well: *The northeast of the country is ill-served by the rail network.*

ˌill-ˈstarred *adj literary* unlucky and likely to cause or experience a lot of problems or unhappiness: *an ill-starred love affair*

ˌill-ˈsuited *adj* not useful for a particular purpose: **[+to]** *a country ill-suited to wheat farming*

ˌill-ˈtempered *adj formal* **1** easily made angry or impatient SYN **bad-tempered** **2** an ill-tempered meeting, argument etc is one in which people are angry and often rude to each other: *Six players were sent off in an ill-tempered game.*

ˌill-ˈtimed *adj* happening, done, or said at the wrong time OPP **well-timed**: *His remarks were ill-timed.*

ˌill-ˈtreat *v* [T] to be cruel to someone, especially to a child or animal: *a rescue centre for ill-treated horses* —**ill-treatment** *n* [U]

il·lu·mi·nate /ɪˈluːməneɪt, ɪˈljuː- $ ɪˈluː-/ ●○○ (*also* **illumine**) *v* [T]
1 to make a light shine on something, or to fill a place with light: *A single candle illuminated his face.* | *At night the canals are beautifully illuminated.*
2 *formal* to make something much clearer and easier to understand: *The report illuminated the difficult issues at the heart of science policy.*

il·lu·mi·nat·ed /ɪˈluːməneɪtəd, -ˈljuː- $ -ˈluː-/ *adj* **1** lit up by lights: *An illuminated sign flashed on and off.* **2 illuminated manuscript/book** a book of a type produced by hand in the Middle Ages, whose pages are decorated with gold paint and bright colours

il·lu·mi·nat·ing /ɪˈluːməneɪtɪŋ, ɪˈljuː- $ ɪˈluː-/ *adj* making things much clearer and easier to understand: *a very illuminating book*

il·lu·mi·na·tion /ɪˌluːməˈneɪʃən, ɪˌljuː- $ ɪˌluː-/ *n formal*
1 [U] lighting provided by a lamp, light etc: *White candles, the only illumination, burned on the table.* | *soft illumination*
2 [C usually plural] a picture or pattern painted on a page of a book, especially in the past: *the illuminations in a medieval manuscript* **3 illuminations** [plural] *BrE* a show of coloured lights used to make a town bright and colourful: *the Blackpool illuminations* **4** [C,U] *formal* a clear explanation or understanding of a particular subject

il·lu·mine /ɪˈluːmən, ɪˈljuː- $ ɪˈluː-/ *v* [T] another word for ILLUMINATE

il·lu·sion /ɪˈluːʒən/ ●○○ *n* [C]
1 an idea or opinion that is wrong, especially about yourself → **delusion**: **illusion that** *They suffer from the illusion that they cannot solve their problems.* | *She* ***was under no illusion that*** *he loved her.* | ***It is an illusion that*** *the Arctic is dark in winter.* | *She* ***had no illusions about*** *her physical attractiveness.* | *'I hate to shatter your illusions,' he said.*
2 something that seems to be different from the way it really is: **[+of]** *He was unlikely to be satisfied with the illusion of power.* | **give/create an illusion** *The mirrors in the room gave an illusion of greater space.* | *Credit creates the illusion that you can own things without paying for them.*
→ OPTICAL ILLUSION

il·lu·sion·ist /ɪˈluːʒənɪst/ *n* [C] someone who does surprising tricks that make things seem to appear or happen SYN **magician**

il·lu·so·ry /ɪˈluːsəri/ (*also* **il·lu·sive** /ɪˈluːsɪv/) *adj formal* false but seeming to be real or true: *First impressions can often prove illusory.*

il·lus·trate /ˈɪləstreɪt/ ●●○ AWL *v* [T]
1 to make the meaning of something clearer by giving examples: *Let me give an example to* ***illustrate*** *the* ***point.*** | *She illustrated her discussion with diagrams.*
2 to be an example which shows that something is true or that a fact exists: **illustrate that** *This dispute illustrates that the regime is deeply divided.* | **illustrate how** *The following examples illustrate how this operates in practice.* | *This illustrates a fundamental weakness in the system.*
3 to put pictures in a book, article etc: *Over a hundred diagrams, tables and pictures illustrate the book.*
THESAURUS ▸ DRAW

il·lus·tra·tion /ˌɪləˈstreɪʃən/ ●●○ AWL *n*
1 [C] a picture in a book, article etc, especially one that helps you to understand it: *The book contains 62 pages of illustrations.*
2 [C,U] a story, event, action etc that shows the truth or existence of something very clearly: **[+of]** *a striking illustration of 19th-century attitudes to women* | *For the purposes of illustration, some of the more important symptoms are listed below.* THESAURUS ▸ EXAMPLE
3 [U] the act or process of illustrating something

il·lus·tra·tive /ˈɪləstreɪtɪv, -strət- $ ɪˈlʌstrətɪv/ AWL *adj*
1 helping to explain the meaning of something: **[+of]** *The case is illustrative of a common pattern.* | ***For illustrative purposes****, only a simple example is given here.* **2** having pictures, especially to help you understand something: *graphics and other illustrative material* → ILLUSTRATE

il·lus·tra·tor /ˈɪləstreɪtə $ -ər/ *n* [C] someone who draws pictures, especially for books

il·lus·tri·ous /ɪˈlʌstriəs/ *adj formal* famous and admired because of what you have achieved: *She has had an illustrious career.* | *Wagner was just one of many illustrious visitors to the town.*

ˌill ˈwill *n* [U] unfriendly or unkind feelings towards someone: *He said the accusation had been made from hatred and ill will.*

im- /ɪm, ɪ/ *prefix* the form used for IN- before b, m, or p: *immobilize* | *impossible*

I'm /aɪm/ the short form of 'I am': *I'm a student.*

IM /ˌaɪ ˈem/ *n* [U] (***instant messaging***) a type of service available on the Internet that allows you to quickly exchange written messages with people that you know

iMac /ˈaɪmæk/ *n* [C] *trademark* a type of computer made by the Apple computer company. iMacs are an unusual design and are produced in a range of bright colours.

im·age /ˈɪmɪdʒ/ ●●● S2 W1 AWL *n* [C]
1 PUBLIC OPINION the opinion people have of a person, organization, product etc, or the way a person, organization etc seems to be to the public → **reputation**: **[+of]** *attempts to improve the image of the police* THESAURUS ▸ REPUTATION
2 IDEA IN MIND a picture that you have in your mind, especially about what someone or something is like or the way they look: **[+of]** *He had no visual image of her, only her name.* | *He had the clearest* ***image in*** *his* ***mind*** *of his mother and father.*
3 PICTURE/WHAT YOU SEE **a)** a picture of an object in a mirror or in the LENS of a camera: *She peered closely at her image in the mirror.* **b)** a picture on the screen of a television, cinema, or computer: *Jill Sharpe was little more than a name, a glossy image on a television screen.* **c)** a picture or shape of a person or thing that is copied onto paper or is cut in wood or stone: *carved images*
4 DESCRIPTION a word, phrase, or picture that describes an idea in a poem, book, film etc: *He paints a very romantic image of working-class communities.*
5 be the (very/living/spitting) image of sb to look exactly like someone or something else: *He's the spitting image of his mother.*
6 in the image of sb/sth *literary* in the same form or shape as someone or something else: *According to the Bible, man was made in the image of God.* → MIRROR IMAGE

I

COLLOCATIONS

ADJECTIVES/NOUN + image

a good/positive image *We want to give people a positive image of the town.*
a bad/negative image *It's difficult to explain why the industry has such a bad image.*
a wholesome/clean-cut image (=morally good and never doing anything bad) *The recent scandal has damaged his clean-cut image.*
an upmarket image *BrE*, **an upscale image** *AmE* (=expensive and good quality) *The company is trying to promote an upmarket image.*
a downmarket image *BrE*, **a downscale image** *AmE* (=cheap and not good quality) *The store has struggled to break away from its downmarket image.*
the traditional image of sth *They want to improve the traditional image of English food.*
the popular image of sth *The popular image of the spy as a glamorous figure of mystery is far from the reality.*
sb's/sth's public image (=the image that many people have of someone or something) | **sb's screen image** (=how someone seems in films or on TV)

VERBS

have an image *The product has a rather downmarket image.*
create an image *The company is trying to create an image of quality and reliability.*
improve your image *The casino industry was keen to improve its image.*
damage your image *Has this scandal damaged the company's image?*
live up to your image (=be like the image you have presented of yourself) *He has certainly lived up to his wild rock-star image.*
present/project/promote an image (=behave in a way that creates a particular image) *He presented an image of himself as an energetic young leader.*
cultivate an image (=try to encourage or develop an image) | **tarnish an image** (=damage it slightly) | **lose/shed an image** (=get rid of it)

image + NOUN

an image problem *Politicians have an image problem as far as many young people are concerned.*

im·ag·e·ry /ˈɪmɪdʒəri/ ●○○ AWL *n* [U] the use of words or pictures to describe ideas or actions in poems, books, films etc: **[+of]** *the imagery of love* | *Their dreams commonly involved complex stories with* ***visual imagery***.
THESAURUS LANGUAGE

i·ma·gi·na·ble /ɪˈmædʒənəbəl/ *adj* **1** used to emphasize that something is the best, worst etc that can be imagined: *The travel brochure is full of the most wonderful resorts imaginable.* **2** used to emphasize that something includes every possible example of something: *He seems to have been influenced by* ***every imaginable*** *musical style.*

i·ma·gi·na·ry /ɪˈmædʒənəri $ -neri/ ●○○ *adj* not real, but produced from pictures or ideas in your mind → **fictional**: *As she listened, she played an imaginary piano on her knees.* | *We must protect older people from harm, whether it is real or imaginary.*

i·ma·gi·na·tion /ɪˌmædʒəˈneɪʃən/ ●●● S3 W3 *n*
1 [C,U] the ability to form pictures or ideas in your mind: *a storyteller with an incredible imagination* | *It does not take much imagination to understand their grief.* | *With a little imagination, you can find great inexpensive gifts.*
2 be (a figment of) sb's imagination to be something that someone imagines, not something that really exists or happens: *Did you hear that noise, or was it my imagination?* | *These people do exist; they're not figments of my imagination.*
3 in sb's imagination only existing or happening in someone's mind, not in real life: *For the refugees, home exists only in their imagination.*
4 capture/catch sb's imagination to make people feel very interested and excited: *American football really captured the imagination of the British public.*
5 leave sth to sb's imagination to deliberately not describe something because you think someone can guess or imagine it: *Mercifully, the writer leaves most of the physical horrors to our imagination.*
6 leave little/nothing to the imagination a) if someone's clothes leave little or nothing to the imagination, the clothes are very thin or are worn in a way that shows the person's body: *Her black satin dress left nothing to the imagination.* **b)** if something sexual or violent is described in a way that leaves nothing to the imagination, it is described in too much detail
7 use your imagination *spoken* used to tell someone that they can easily guess the answer to a question, so you should not need to tell them → **not by any stretch of the imagination** at STRETCH²(4)

COLLOCATIONS

ADJECTIVES

a good imagination *She's a lively child, with a good imagination.*
great imagination *His paintings show great imagination.*
a vivid/fertile imagination (=an ability to think of a lot of ideas and things that could happen) *She had a fertile imagination and a great sense of humour.*
an overactive/fevered imagination (=a mind that imagines strange things that are not real) *These stories are the product of an overactive imagination.*
the public imagination *The story captured the public imagination.*
creative imagination *I don't have the creative imagination to be a writer.*

VERBS

have (an) imagination *Her poems show that she has a lot of imagination.*
use your imagination *Musicians need to use their imagination as well as their technical skills.*
show/display imagination *His latest paintings display a vivid imagination.*
lack imagination | **fire/stimulate sb's imagination** (=make someone use their imagination)

PHRASES

be full of imagination *Her stories are full of imagination.*
a lack of imagination *Their policies show a lack of imagination.*
let your imagination run wild (*also* **let your imagination run riot** *BrE*) (=allow yourself to imagine many strange or wonderful things)

i·ma·gi·na·tive /ɪˈmædʒənətɪv/ ●○○ *adj*
1 containing new and interesting ideas: *an* ***imaginative use*** *of computer technology* | *children's imaginative play* | *an imaginative solution to the litter problem*
2 good at thinking of new and interesting ideas: *an imaginative child* —**imaginatively** *adv*

This graph shows how common the different grammar patterns of the verb **imagine** are.

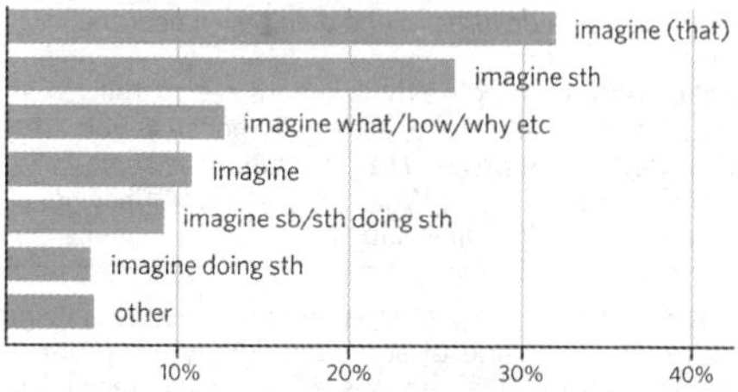

imagine (that)
imagine sth
imagine what/how/why etc
imagine
imagine sb/sth doing sth
imagine doing sth
other
10% 20% 30% 40%

i·ma·gine /ɪˈmædʒɪn/ ●●● S1 W2 *v* [T]
1 to form a picture or idea in your mind about what something could be like: **imagine (that)** *Imagine that you*

have just won a million pounds. | Imagine life without hot water. | **imagine what/how/why etc** *Can you imagine what it's like when it's really hot out here in Delhi?* | **imagine sb doing sth** *She could imagine dark-robed figures moving silently along the stone corridors.* | **(just) imagine doing sth** *Imagine doing a horrible job like that! | Just imagine going all that way for nothing!* | **imagine sb/sth as sth** *He didn't quite dare to imagine himself as a real artist.* | **imagine sb in/with/without etc sth** *Somehow, I can't imagine him without a beard.* | **it's difficult/easy/possible/impossible etc to imagine sth** *After such a dry summer, it's difficult to imagine what rain looks like.*

GRAMMAR

Imagine is followed by an **-ing** form, not an infinitive. You say: *I can't imagine living without music.* ✗ Don't say: *I can't imagine to live without music.*

GRAMMAR GUIDE ▸ VERBS

2 to have a false or wrong idea about something: *Perhaps she'd never really been there at all – perhaps she'd just imagined it.* | *imagined dangers* | **imagine (that)** *She had imagined that the doctor would be male.* | *I was surprised when I saw the farm. I had imagined it would be much bigger.* | **imagine sth/sb to be sth** *There's nobody here. You're just* ***imagining things***.

3 [not in progressive] to think that something is true or may happen, but without being sure or having proof: *'A very complicated subject, I imagine,' said Edwin.* | **imagine (that)** *You are obviously tired and I imagine that nothing would make you admit it.*

4 you can/can't imagine sth *BrE spoken* used to emphasize how good, bad etc something is: **You can/can't imagine how/what/why etc** *You can imagine how angry I was! | You can't imagine what a terrible week we had.*

THESAURUS

imagine to form a picture or idea in your mind about what something might be like: *When I think of Honolulu, I imagine long white beaches and palm trees. | I can't really imagine being a millionaire.*

visualize to form a picture of someone or something in your mind, especially something that is definitely going to happen or exist in the future: *Anna visualized meeting Greg again at the airport. | The finished house may be hard to visualize.*

picture to form a clear picture of something or someone in your mind: *I can still picture my father, even though he died a long time ago. | The town was just how she had pictured it from his description.*

envisage /ɪnˈvɪzɪdʒ/ *especially BrE*, **envision** to imagine something as possible or likely to happen in the future: *How do you envisage your career developing over the next ten years?*

conceive of sth *formal* to imagine a situation, especially one that is difficult to imagine: *For many people, music is so important that they cannot conceive of life without it.*

fantasize to imagine something exciting that you would like to happen, but that is very unlikely to happen: *I used to fantasize about becoming a film star.*

daydream to imagine pleasant things, so that you forget where you are and what you should be doing: *Mark began to daydream, and didn't even hear the teacher's question.*

hallucinate to imagine that you are seeing things that are not really there, especially because you are ill or have taken drugs: *The drug can cause some people to hallucinate. | When I saw the walls moving, I thought I must be hallucinating.*

im·ag·ing /ˈɪmɪdʒɪŋ/ *n* [U] a technical process in which pictures of the inside of someone's body are produced, especially for medical reasons: *New imaging technologies mean that doctors are better able to screen for breast cancer.*

i·ma·gin·ings /ɪˈmædʒənɪŋz/ *n* [plural] *literary* situations or ideas that you imagine, but which are not real or true: *In my* ***wildest imaginings****, I could not have foreseen what a wonderful life lay before me.*

im·am, **Imam** /ˈɪmɑːm, ˈɪmæm/ *n* [C] a Muslim religious leader

im·bal·ance /ɪmˈbæləns/ ●○○ *n* [C,U] a lack of a fair or correct balance between two things, which results in problems or unfairness SYN **inequality**: **[+in]** *The government must* ***redress*** *the* ***imbalance*** (=put it right) *in spending on black and white children.* | **[+between]** *the current imbalance between farming and conservation interests* | *a hormonal imbalance* —**imbalanced** *adj*: *Many pupils follow an imbalanced curriculum.*

im·be·cile /ˈɪmbəsiːl $ -səl/ *n* [C] someone who is very stupid or behaves very stupidly SYN **idiot**: *He looked at me as if I was a total imbecile.* —**imbecilic** /ˌɪmbəˈsɪlɪk◂/ *adj* —**imbecility** /ˌɪmbəˈsɪləti/ *n* [C,U]

im·bed /ɪmˈbed/ *v* [T] (**imbedded, imbedding**) another spelling of EMBED

im·bibe /ɪmˈbaɪb/ *v* [I,T] *formal* **1** to drink something, especially alcohol – sometimes used humorously: *Both men imbibed considerable quantities of gin.* **2** to accept and be influenced by qualities, ideas, values etc: *She had imbibed the traditions of her family.*

im·bro·gli·o /ɪmˈbrəʊliəʊ $ ɪmˈbroʊlioʊ/ *n* (*plural* **imbroglios**) [C] a difficult, embarrassing, or confusing situation, especially in politics or public life: *a political imbroglio*

im·bue /ɪmˈbjuː/ *v*

imbue sb/sth **with** sth *phr v formal* to make someone or something have a quality, idea, or emotion very strongly: *His philosophical writings are imbued with religious belief.*

IMEI /ˌaɪ em iː ˈaɪ/ *n* [C] *technical* (***international mobile equipment identifier***) a number that each MOBILE PHONE has, which it sends whenever someone uses it to make a phone call

IMF, the /ˌaɪ em ˈef/ (***the International Monetary Fund***) an international organization that tries to encourage trade between countries and to help poorer countries develop economically

IMHO (***in my humble opinion***) used in emails or on the Internet when giving your opinion about something: *IMHO you should call him.*

im·i·tate /ˈɪmɪteɪt/ ●●○ *v* [T]

1 to copy the way someone behaves, speaks, moves etc, especially in order to make people laugh: *She was a splendid mimic and loved to imitate Winston Churchill.* ⚠ Do not use **imitate** to mean 'do the same thing as someone else'. Use **copy**: *She worries that Tom will copy his brother (NOT imitate his brother) and leave home.*

2 to copy something because you think it is good: *vegetarian products which imitate meat | The Japanese have no wish to imitate Western social customs and attitudes.* —**imitator** *n* [C]

im·i·ta·tion /ˌɪmɪˈteɪʃən◂/ ●●○ *n*

1 [C,U] when you copy someone else's actions: **by imitation** *Many people think that children learn language by imitation.* | *The remake of 'Casablanca' was a* ***pale imitation*** (=something that is much less good than the thing it imitates) *of the original movie.*

2 [C] when you copy the way someone speaks or behaves, especially in order to be funny SYN **impression**: *She acted, she danced, she* ***did imitations***. | **[+of]** *his imitation of an American accent*

3 [C] a copy of something: **[+of]** *She wore an imitation of a sailor's hat.* | **imitation fur/pearls/silk/leather etc** (=something that looks like an expensive material but is a copy of it) *an imitation fur coat* THESAURUS ▸ ARTIFICIAL, FALSE

im·i·ta·tive /ˈɪmətətɪv $ -teɪtɪv/ *adj formal* copying someone or something, especially in a way that shows you do not have any ideas of your own: *Young people might be provoked into imitative crime by the exploits they see on TV.*

I

im·mac·u·late /ɪˈmækjələt/ ●○○ *adj*
1 very clean and tidy OPP **messy**: *He wore an immaculate dark blue suit.* | *an immaculate kitchen* THESAURUS▸ CLEAN, TIDY
2 exactly correct or perfect in every detail SYN **flawless**: *her immaculate stage performances* —**immaculately** *adv*

im·ma·nent /ˈɪmənənt/ *adj formal* **1** a quality that is immanent seems to be present everywhere: *Love is a force immanent in the world.* **2** God or another spiritual power that is immanent is present everywhere —**immanence** *n* [U]

im·ma·te·ri·al /ˌɪməˈtɪəriəl◂ $ -ˈtɪr-/ *adj* **1** not important in a particular situation SYN **irrelevant**: *If you sign a document, it is wholly immaterial whether you have read it carefully or not.* **2** *formal* not having a physical body or form: *our immaterial soul*

im·ma·ture /ˌɪməˈtʃʊə $ -ˈtʃʊr/ ●○○ AWL *adj*
1 someone who is immature behaves or thinks in a way that is typical of someone much younger – used to show disapproval SYN **childish** OPP **mature**: *He forgave his son's immature behaviour.*
2 not fully formed or developed: *measures to protect immature whales* —**immaturity** *n* [U]

im·mea·su·ra·ble /ɪˈmeʒərəbəl/ *adj* used to emphasize that something is too big or too extreme to be measured: *The refugee problem has now reached immeasurable proportions.* —**immeasurably** *adv*: *Your Spanish has improved immeasurably.*

im·me·di·a·cy /ɪˈmiːdiəsi/ *n* [U] when something is important or urgent because it relates to a situation or event that is happening now: **[+of]** *the immediacy of everyday experience* | *Television brings a new immediacy to world events.*

im·me·di·ate /ɪˈmiːdiət/ ●●● S3 W2 *adj*
1 happening or done at once and without delay: *Our* ***immediate response*** *to the attack was sheer horror.* | *They promise* ***immediate action*** *to help the unemployed.* | *If the eyes are affected, seek immediate medical attention.*
2 [only before noun] existing now, and needing to be dealt with quickly: *Let's try and solve the most* ***immediate problem****.* | *There is an* ***immediate danger*** *of war.*
3 [only before noun] happening just before or just after someone or something else: *The most* ***immediate effect*** *of retirement is a dramatic reduction in living standards.* | *He promised that there would be no tax increases in* ***the immediate future****.*
4 [only before noun] next to, or very near to, a particular place: *It is a thriving shopping centre for the people who live in the* ***immediate area****.*
5 immediate family people who are very closely related to you, such as your parents, children, brothers, and sisters

im·me·di·ate·ly¹ /ɪˈmiːdiətli/ ●●● S2 W1 *adv*
1 without delay SYN **at once**: *Mix in the remaining ingredients and serve immediately.* | *The telephone rang, and he answered it immediately.*
2 very soon before or after something: **immediately after/following sth** *He retired immediately after the end of the war.* | **immediately before/preceding sth** *I can't remember what happened immediately before the crash.*
3 immediately obvious/apparent able to be seen or understood very easily: *The solution to this problem is not immediately obvious.*
4 [+adj/adv] very near to something: **immediately behind/above/below/in front of etc sth** *the seat immediately behind the driver*
5 immediately involved/affected/concerned etc very closely involved etc in a particular situation: *Those most immediately involved in the disaster will be given support.*

THESAURUS

immediately very soon after something else happens, and without any delay: *Sam immediately offered to help.*
at once immediately – used especially for emphasis: *Remove the pie from the oven and serve at once.* | *He came home at once when he heard his wife was ill.*
right away (*also* **straightaway** *BrE*) *especially spoken* immediately, especially because something is urgent. Right away and **straightaway** are less formal than **immediately**, and are very common in everyday spoken English: *If this happens, let us know right away.* | *I apologized straightaway.*
instantly if something happens instantly, it happens immediately after something else, with almost no time between: *The boy was killed instantly.* | *The message is sent instantly from your computer.*
right now/this minute *spoken* if someone orders you to do something right now, they want you to do it immediately, especially because they are annoyed with you: *The head teacher wants to see you right now.*
without delay immediately, because it is important that you do something as soon as possible: *If you lose your passport, you should contact the embassy without delay.*

immediately² *conjunction BrE formal* as soon as: *Immediately you begin to speak, he gives you his full attention.*

im·me·mo·ri·al /ˌɪməˈmɔːriəl◂/ *adj* starting longer ago than people can remember, or than written history shows: **from/since time immemorial** *Markets have been held here since time immemorial.*

im·mense /ɪˈmens/ ●●○ *adj* extremely large SYN **enormous**: *People who travel by rail still read an immense amount.* | *Regular visits from a social worker can be of immense value to old people living alone.*

im·mense·ly /ɪˈmensli/ ●○○ *adv* very much SYN **extremely**: *Champagne wines became* ***immensely popular*** *in the 18th century.* | **immensely powerful/strong/important etc** *Nationalism is an immensely powerful force.* | *We enjoyed the play immensely.*

im·men·si·ty /ɪˈmensəti/ *n* (*plural* **immensities**)
1 [C,U] used to emphasize the great size of something, especially something that cannot be measured: **[+of]** *the immensity of outer space* **2** [U] used to emphasize the great size and seriousness of something such as a problem you have to deal with or a job you have to do: **[+of]** *the immensity of the problem*

im·merse /ɪˈmɜːs $ -ɜːrs/ *v* [T] **1** to put someone or something deep into a liquid so that they are completely covered: **immerse sb/sth in sth** *Immerse your foot in ice-cold water to reduce the swelling.* THESAURUS▸ PUT
2 immerse yourself in sth to become completely involved in an activity: *He left school at 16 and immersed himself in the Labour Party.* —**immersed** *adj*: *She was far too immersed in her studies.*

im·mer·sion /ɪˈmɜːʃən, -ʒən $ ɪˈmɜːrʒən/ *n* **1** [U] the action of immersing something in liquid, or the state of being immersed: **[+in]** *his near-fatal immersion in the icy Atlantic Ocean* **2** [U] the fact of being completely involved in something you are doing: **[+in]** *my immersion in black music and culture* **3** [U] *technical* the language teaching method in which people are put in situations where they have to use the new language **4** [C] *BrE informal* an immersion heater

imˈmersion ˌheater *n* [C] *BrE* an electric water heater that provides hot water for a house

im·mer·sive /ɪˈmɜːsɪv $ -ɜːr-/ *adj* making you feel you are really taking part in the events you are seeing on a screen or hearing about, or are really in a VIRTUAL environment: *immersive video games*

im·mi·grant /ˈɪməgrənt/ ●●○ W3 AWL *n* [C] someone who enters another country to live there permanently → **emigrant**: *an illegal immigrant* | *a new wave of immigrants from the Middle East*

im·mi·grate /ˈɪmɪgreɪt/ ●●○ AWL *v* [I] to come into a country in order to live there permanently → **emigrate**, **migrate**: *His father and mother immigrated when he was two.*

im·mi·gra·tion /ˌɪmɪˈgreɪʃən/ ●●○ W3 AWL *n* [U]
1 the process of entering another country in order to live there permanently → **emigration**: *He called for a common European policy on immigration.*

2 the total number of people who immigrate: *Immigration fell in the 1980s.*
3 (*also* **immigration control**) the place at an airport, sea port etc where officials check the documents of everyone entering the country

im·mi·nent /ˈɪmɪnənt/ ●○○ *adj* an event that is imminent, especially an unpleasant one, will happen very soon: **imminent danger/threat/death/disaster etc** *He was in imminent danger of dying.* | *A new trade agreement is imminent.* —**imminence** *n* [U]: *the imminence of the General Election* —**imminently** *adv*

im·mo·bile /ɪˈməʊbaɪl $ ɪˈmoʊbəl/ *adj* **1** not moving at all SYN **motionless**: *She could see a figure sitting immobile, facing the sea.* **2** unable to move or walk normally: *Kim's illness had rendered her completely immobile.* —**immobility** /ˌɪməˈbɪləti/ *n* [U]

im·mo·bi·lize (*also* **-ise** *BrE*) /ɪˈməʊbəlaɪz $ ɪˈmoʊ-/ *v* [T] **1** to prevent someone or something from moving: *The broken limb must be immobilized immediately.* | *She was immobilized with a broken leg.* **2** to stop something from working: *The car's security device will immobilize the ignition system.* —**immobilization** /ɪˌməʊbəlaɪˈzeɪʃən $ ɪˌmoʊbələ-/ *n* [U]

im·mo·bi·liz·er (*also* **-iser**) /ɪˈməʊbəlaɪzə $ ɪˈmoʊbəlaɪzər/ *n* [C] *BrE* a piece of equipment that is fitted to a car to stop it moving if someone tries to steal it

im·mod·e·rate /ɪˈmɒdərət $ ɪˈmɑː-/ *adj formal* not within reasonable and sensible limits SYN **excessive**: *immoderate drinking* —**immoderately** *adv*

im·mod·est /ɪˈmɒdɪst $ ɪˈmɑː-/ *adj* **1** having a very high opinion of yourself and your abilities, and not embarrassed about telling people how clever you are OPP **modest**: *Webb was an immodest publicist of his own achievements.* **2** clothes that are immodest show too much of someone's body SYN **revealing** OPP **modest** **3** *old-fashioned* behaviour that is immodest shocks or embarrasses people: *They thought it was immodest for both sexes to swim together.* —**immodestly** *adv* —**immodesty** *n* [U]

im·mo·late /ˈɪməleɪt/ *v* [T] *formal* to kill someone or destroy something by burning them —**immolation** /ˌɪməˈleɪʃən/ *n* [U]

im·mor·al /ɪˈmɒrəl $ ɪˈmɔː-/ *adj* **1** morally wrong → **amoral**: *Deliberately making people suffer is immoral.* | ***It's immoral** to be rich while people are starving and homeless.* **2** not following accepted standards of sexual behaviour —**immorally** *adv* —**immorality** /ˌɪməˈræləti/ *n* [U]: *the immorality of bombing civilians*

im·mor·tal /ɪˈmɔːtl $ -ɔːr-/ *adj* **1** living or continuing forever OPP **mortal**: *Plato believed that the soul is immortal.* **2** an immortal line, play, song etc is so famous that it will never be forgotten: *In the immortal words of Henry Ford, 'If it ain't broke, don't fix it.'* —**immortal** *n* [C]

im·mor·tal·i·ty /ˌɪmɔːˈtæləti $ -ɔːr-/ *n* [U] the state of living forever or being remembered forever: *the immortality of the soul*

im·mor·tal·ize (*also* **-ise** *BrE*) /ɪˈmɔːtəlaɪz $ -ɔːr-/ *v* [T] to make someone or something famous for a long time, especially by writing about them, painting a picture of them etc: *Dickens' father was immortalized as Mr Micawber in 'David Copperfield'.* GRAMMAR **Immortalize** is usually passive.

im·mo·va·ble /ɪˈmuːvəbəl/ *adj* **1** impossible to move: *Lock your bike to something immovable like a railing or lamp-post.* **2** impossible to change or persuade: *The president is immovable on this issue.* —**immovably** *adv*

im·mune /ɪˈmjuːn/ ●○○ *adj*
1 [not before noun] someone who is immune to a particular disease cannot catch it: *Once we've had the disease, we're immune for life.*
2 **immune response/reaction** the reaction of the body's immune system to something that is harmful: *HIV is a progressive disease which the immune response ultimately fails to control.*
3 [not before noun] not affected by something that happens or is done: **[+to]** *The Labour Party is not immune to new ideas.*
4 [not before noun] specially protected from something unpleasant: **[+from]** *The senior members of the group appeared to be immune from arrest.*

imˈmune ˌsystem *n* [C] the system by which your body protects itself against disease: *My immune system is not as strong as it ought to be.*

im·mu·nise /ˈɪmjənaɪz/ *v* [T] a British spelling of IMMUNIZE

im·mu·ni·ty /ɪˈmjuːnəti/ ●○○ *n* [U]
1 the state or right of being protected from particular laws or from unpleasant things: **[+from]** *They were **granted immunity** from prosecution.*
2 the state of being immune to a disease: **[+to]** *immunity to infection* | **[+from]** *immunity from smallpox*

im·mu·nize (*also* **-ise** *BrE*) /ˈɪmjənaɪz/ *v* [T] to protect someone from a particular illness by giving them a VACCINE SYN **vaccinate**, **inoculate**: **immunize sb against sth** *There is still no vaccine to immunize people against the virus.* —**immunization** /ˌɪmjənaɪˈzeɪʃən $ -nə-/ *n* [C,U]

im·mu·nol·o·gy /ˌɪmjəˈnɒlədʒi $ -ˈnɑː-/ *n* [U] the scientific study of the prevention of disease and how the body reacts to disease

im·mure /ɪˈmjʊə $ ɪˈmjʊr/ *v* [T] *formal or literary* to shut someone in a place so that they cannot get out

im·mu·ta·ble /ɪˈmjuːtəbəl/ *adj formal* never changing or impossible to change: *This decision should not be seen as immutable.* —**immutably** *adv* —**immutability** /ɪˌmjuːtəˈbɪləti/ *n* [U]

i-mode phone /ˈaɪ məʊd ˌfəʊn $ -moʊd ˌfoʊn/ *n* [C] a MOBILE PHONE that has a small screen which you can use for Internet and email services

imp /ɪmp/ *n* [C] **1** a child who behaves badly, but in a way that is funny **2** a small creature in stories who has magic powers and behaves very badly → IMPISH

im·pact¹ /ˈɪmpækt/ ●●● S3 W2 AWL *n*
1 [C] the effect or influence that an event, situation etc has on someone or something: **[+on/upon]** *We need to assess the impact on climate change.* | **major/significant/profound etc impact** *Higher mortgage rates have already **had** a major **impact** on spending.* | **[+of]** *an international meeting to consider the **environmental impacts** of global warming*
⚠ Don't say 'cause an impact' on something. Say **have an impact** on something. THESAURUS ▸ EFFECT
2 [C,U] the force of one object hitting another: *The force of the impact knocked the breath out of her.*
3 **on impact** at the moment when one thing hits another: *The plane's wing was damaged on impact.*

im·pact² /ɪmˈpækt/ AWL *v* [I,T] *especially AmE* to have an important or noticeable effect on someone or something: **[+on/upon]** *The Food Safety Act will progressively impact on the way food businesses operate.*

im·pact·ed /ɪmˈpæktɪd/ *adj* a tooth that is impacted is growing under another tooth so that it cannot develop properly

im·pair /ɪmˈpeə $ -ˈper/ ●○○ *v* [T] to damage something or make it not as good as it should be: *The illness had impaired his ability to think and concentrate.* THESAURUS ▸ HARM

im·paired /ɪmˈpeəd $ -ˈperd/ *adj* damaged, less strong, or not as good as before: *impaired vision* | **visually/hearing/mentally etc impaired** (=used to describe someone who cannot see, hear etc well)

im·pair·ment /ɪmˈpeəmənt $ ɪmˈper-/ *n* [C,U] **mental/visual/cognitive/hearing etc impairment** a condition in which a part of a person's mind or body is damaged or does not work well

im·pa·la /ɪmˈpɑːlə/ *n* (*plural* **impala**) [C] a large African ANTELOPE

im·pale /ɪmˈpeɪl/ *v* [T] if someone or something is impaled, a sharp pointed object goes through them: **be**

impaled on sth *Their heads were impaled on Charles Bridge as a warning to others.* —**impalement** *n* [C,U]

im·pal·pa·ble /ɪmˈpælpəbəl/ *adj formal* **1** impossible to touch or feel physically OPP **palpable 2** very difficult to understand

im·pan·el /ɪmˈpænl/ *v* [T] another spelling of EMPANEL

im·part /ɪmˈpɑːt $ -ɑːrt/ *v* [T] *formal* **1** to give a particular quality to something: **impart sth to sth** *Use a piece of fresh ginger to impart a Far Eastern flavour to simple ingredients.* **2** to give information, knowledge, wisdom etc to someone: *She had information that she couldn't wait to impart.*

im·par·tial /ɪmˈpɑːʃəl $ -ɑːr-/ ●○○ *adj* not involved in a particular situation, and therefore able to give a fair opinion or piece of advice SYN **fair** OPP **biased**: *We offer* ***impartial advice*** *on tax and insurance. | an* ***impartial inquiry*** *into the deaths | an impartial observer* —**impartially** *adv* —**impartiality** /ɪmˌpɑːʃiˈæləti $ -ɑːr-/ *n* [U]

im·pass·a·ble /ɪmˈpɑːsəbəl $ ɪmˈpæ-/ *adj* a road, path, or area that is impassable is impossible to travel along or through: *The mountains are impassable.*

im·passe /æmˈpɑːs $ ˈɪmpæs/ *n* [singular] a situation in which it is impossible to continue with a discussion or plan because the people involved cannot agree: **at an impasse** *The political process is at an impasse. | Negotiations seemed to have* ***reached*** *an* ***impasse***. **THESAURUS** PROGRESS

im·pas·sioned /ɪmˈpæʃənd/ *adj* full of strong feeling and emotion: *She appeared on television to make an* ***impassioned plea*** *for help. | an impassioned speech*

im·pas·sive /ɪmˈpæsɪv/ *adj* not showing any emotion: *Her* ***impassive face*** *showed no reaction at all.* —**impassively** *adv*: *The children studied him impassively.* —**impassivity** /ˌɪmpæˈsɪvəti/ *n* [U]

im·pa·tience /ɪmˈpeɪʃəns/ *n* [U] **1** annoyance at having to accept delays, other people's weaknesses etc OPP **patience**: **[+with]** *his impatience with the slowness of bureaucratic procedures | A note of impatience had entered his voice.* **2** great eagerness for something to happen, especially something that is going to happen soon: **impatience to do sth** *She was bursting with impatience to tell Natalia what had happened.*

im·pa·tient /ɪmˈpeɪʃənt/ ●○○ *adj*
1 annoyed because of delays, someone else's mistakes etc OPP **patient**: **become/grow impatient (with sb/sth)** *We are growing impatient with the lack of results. | He turned away with an impatient gesture.*
2 [not before noun] very eager for something to happen and not wanting to wait: **impatient to do sth** *Alec strode down the street, impatient to be home.* | **impatient for sb to do sth** *He was eager to talk to Shildon and impatient for him to return from lunch.* —**impatiently** *adv*

im·peach /ɪmˈpiːtʃ/ *v* [T] *law* if a government official is impeached, they are formally charged with a serious crime in a special government court: *The governor was impeached for using state funds improperly.* —**impeachment** *n* [C,U]

im·pec·ca·ble /ɪmˈpekəbəl/ *adj* without any faults and impossible to criticize SYN **perfect**: *She has taught her children* ***impeccable manners***. *| a bar with impeccable service* —**impeccably** *adv*: *impeccably dressed*

im·pe·cu·ni·ous /ˌɪmpɪˈkjuːniəs◂/ *adj formal* having very little money, especially over a long period – sometimes used humorously: *He came from a respectable if impecunious family.* —**impecuniously** *adv* —**impecuniousness** *n* [U]

im·ped·ance /ɪmˈpiːdəns/ *n* [singular, U] *technical* a measure of the power of a piece of electrical equipment to stop the flow of an ALTERNATING CURRENT

im·pede /ɪmˈpiːd/ *v* [T] to make it difficult for someone or something to move forward or make progress: *Storms at sea* ***impeded*** *our* ***progress***.

im·ped·i·ment /ɪmˈpedəmənt/ *n* [C] **1** a physical problem that makes speaking, hearing, or moving difficult: *a* ***speech impediment*** **2** a situation or event that makes it difficult or impossible for someone or something to succeed or make progress: **[+to]** *War is one of the greatest impediments to human progress.*

im·ped·i·men·ta /ɪmˌpedəˈmentə/ *n* [plural] things that you think you need to have or do, but which can slow your progress – often used humorously

im·pel /ɪmˈpel/ *v* (**impelled**, **impelling**) [T] *formal* if something impels you to do something, it makes you feel very strongly that you must do it → **compel**: **impel sb to do sth** *The lack of democracy and equality impelled the oppressed to fight for independence.*

im·pend·ing /ɪmˈpendɪŋ/ *adj* an impending event or situation, especially an unpleasant one, is going to happen very soon: **impending danger/doom/death/disaster etc** *She had a sense of impending disaster. |* ***impending changes*** *in government legislation*

im·pen·e·tra·ble /ɪmˈpenətrəbəl/ *adj* **1** impossible to get through, see through, or get into: *The trees formed a dark and* ***impenetrable barrier***. *| the impenetrable blackness of the night* **2** very difficult or impossible to understand: *impenetrable legal jargon* —**impenetrably** *adv* —**impenetrability** /ɪmˌpenətrəˈbɪləti/ *n* [U]

im·per·a·tive[1] /ɪmˈperətɪv/ *adj* **1** extremely important and needing to be done or dealt with immediately: ***It is imperative that*** *politicians should be good communicators.* | **it is imperative (for sb) to do sth** *It is imperative to meet face to face with the client.* **2** *technical* an imperative verb is one that expresses an order, such as 'stand up' —**imperatively** *adv*

imperative[2] *n* [C] **1** something that must be done urgently: *A broad and balanced education is an imperative for raising standards.* **2** *formal* an idea or belief that has a strong influence on people, making them behave in a particular way: *Sharing food is the most important* ***moral imperative*** *in Semai society.* **3** *technical* the form of a verb that expresses an order. For example, in the order 'Come here', 'come' is in the imperative.

im·per·cep·ti·ble /ˌɪmpəˈseptəbəl $ -pər-/ *adj* almost impossible to see or notice: *Such changes are imperceptible to even the best-trained eye.* —**imperceptibly** *adv*: *The daylight faded almost imperceptibly into night.* —**imperceptibility** /ˌɪmpəseptəˈbɪləti $ -pər-/ *n* [U]

im·per·fect[1] /ɪmˈpɜːfɪkt $ -ɜːr-/ ●○○ *adj* not completely correct or perfect SYN **flawed**: *the imperfect world we live in* —**imperfectly** *adv* —**imperfection** /ˌɪmpəˈfekʃən $ -pər-/ *n* [C,U]

imperfect[2] *n* **the imperfect** *technical* the form of a verb which is used when talking about an action in the past that is not complete. For example, 'I was eating'.

im·pe·ri·al /ɪmˈpɪəriəl $ -ˈpɪr-/ *adj* [only before noun] **1** relating to an EMPIRE or to the person who rules it: *Britain's imperial expansion in the 19th century* **2** relating to the system of weights and measurements based on pounds, INCHes, miles etc

im·pe·ri·al·is·m /ɪmˈpɪəriəlɪzəm $ -ˈpɪr-/ *n* [U] **1** a political system in which one country rules a lot of other countries → **colonialism**: *a book on the history of British imperialism* **2** the way in which a rich or powerful country's way of life, culture, businesses etc influence and change a poorer country's way of life etc: **cultural/economic/social etc imperialism** *Small nations resent Western cultural imperialism.* —**imperialist** *n* [C] —**imperialist**, **imperialistic** *adj*

im·per·il /ɪmˈperəl/ *v* (**imperilled**, **imperilling** *BrE*, **imperiled**, **imperiling** *AmE*) [T] *formal* to put something or someone in danger SYN **endanger**: *Tax increases now might imperil economic recovery.*

im·pe·ri·ous /ɪmˈpɪəriəs $ -ˈpɪr-/ *adj* giving orders and expecting to be obeyed, in a way that seems too proud: *She raised her hand in an imperious gesture.* —**imperiously** *adv* —**imperiousness** *n* [U]

im·per·ish·a·ble /ɪmˈperɪʃəbəl/ *adj formal* existing or continuing for a long time or forever: *a set of imperishable truths*

im·per·ma·nent /ɪmˈpɜːmənənt $ -ɜːr-/ *adj formal* not staying the same forever SYN **temporary** OPP **permanent**: *single-storey structures, built from cheap and impermanent materials* —**impermanence** *n* [U]: *His philosophy stressed the impermanence of the world.*

im·per·me·a·ble /ɪmˈpɜːmiəbəl $ -ɜːr-/ *adj technical* not allowing liquids or gases to pass through OPP **permeable**: *No paint is impermeable to water vapour.*

im·per·mis·si·ble /ˌɪmpɜːˈmɪsəbəl $ -ɜːr-/ *adj formal* something that is impermissible cannot be allowed OPP **permissible**

im·per·son·al /ɪmˈpɜːsənəl $ -ɜːr-/ *adj* **1** not showing any feelings of sympathy, friendliness etc: *Business letters do not have to be impersonal and formal.* | *Sometimes she seems a very impersonal, even unkind, mother.* THESAURUS UNFRIENDLY **2** a place or situation that is impersonal does not make people feel that they are important: *I hate staying in hotels; they're so impersonal.* | *a formal and impersonal style of management* **3** *technical* in grammar, an impersonal sentence or verb is one where the subject is represented by 'it' or 'there', as in the sentence 'It rained all day' —**impersonally** *adv*

im·per·son·ate /ɪmˈpɜːsəneɪt $ -ɜːr-/ *v* [T] **1** to pretend to be someone else by copying their appearance, voice, and behaviour, especially in order to deceive people: *Do you know it is a very serious offence to impersonate a police officer?* **2** to copy someone's voice and behaviour, especially in order to make people laugh: *In the film, he amusingly impersonates a woman.* —**impersonation** /ɪmˌpɜːsəˈneɪʃən $ -ɜːr-/ *n* [C,U]: *He's renowned for his Elvis impersonation.*

im·per·son·a·tor /ɪmˈpɜːsəneɪtə $ -ˈpɜːrsəneɪtər/ *n* [C] someone who copies the way that other people look, speak, and behave, as part of a performance: *a female impersonator*

im·per·ti·nent /ɪmˈpɜːtɪnənt $ -ɜːr-/ *adj* rude and not respectful, especially to someone who is older or more important SYN **cheeky**: *He was always asking impertinent questions.* | *You are an impertinent young woman.* THESAURUS RUDE —**impertinently** *adv* —**impertinence** *n* [U]

im·per·tur·ba·ble /ˌɪmpəˈtɜːbəbəl $ -pərˈtɜːr-/ *adj* remaining calm and unworried in spite of problems or difficulties SYN **unflappable** —**imperturbably** *adv* —**imperturbability** /ˌɪmpətɜːbəˈbɪləti $ -pərtɜːr-/ *n* [U]

im·per·vi·ous /ɪmˈpɜːviəs $ -ɜːr-/ *adj* [not before noun] **1** *formal* not affected or influenced by something and seeming not to notice it: **[+to]** *His ego was impervious to self-doubt.* **2** *technical* not allowing anything to enter or pass through: *impervious volcanic rock* | **[+to]** *materials that are impervious to water*

im·pe·ti·go /ˌɪmpəˈtaɪgəʊ $ -goʊ/ *n* [U] an infectious skin disease

im·pet·u·ous /ɪmˈpetʃuəs/ *adj* tending to do things very quickly, without thinking carefully first, or showing this quality SYN **impulsive**: *He was high-spirited and impetuous.* | *She might live to regret this impetuous decision.* —**impetuously** *adv* —**impetuousness** *n* [U] —**impetuosity** /ɪmˌpetʃuˈɒsəti $ -ˈɑː-/ *n* [U]

im·pe·tus /ˈɪmpɪtəs/ ●○○ *n* [U]
1 an influence that makes something happen or makes it happen more quickly: **[+for]** *The report may* ***provide*** *further* ***impetus*** *for reform.* | *The discovery* ***gave*** *fresh* ***impetus to*** *the research.*
2 *technical* the force that makes an object start moving, or keeps it moving

im·pi·e·ty /ɪmˈpaɪəti/ *n* (*plural* **impieties**) [C,U] *formal* lack of respect for religion or God, or an action that shows this → **impious**

im·pinge /ɪmˈpɪndʒ/ *v*
impinge on/upon sb/sth *phr v formal* to have a harmful effect on someone or something: *Personal problems experienced by students may impinge on their work.* —**impingement** *n* [C,U]

im·pi·ous /ˈɪmpiəs/ *adj formal* lacking respect for religion or God → **impiety**: *an impious crime* —**impiously** *adv* —**impiousness** *n* [U]

imp·ish /ˈɪmpɪʃ/ *adj* showing a lack of respect or seriousness in a way that is amusing rather than bad SYN **mischievous**: *a little girl with dark hair and an impish grin* —**impishly** *adv*

im·plac·a·ble /ɪmˈplækəbəl/ *adj* very determined to continue opposing someone or something: *implacable enemies* | *The government faces* ***implacable opposition*** *on the issue of nuclear waste.* —**implacably** *adv*: *He remained* ***implacably opposed to*** *Stalin's regime.* —**implacability** /ɪmˌplækəˈbɪləti/ *n* [U]

im·plant¹ /ɪmˈplɑːnt $ ɪmˈplænt/ *v* **1** [T] to strongly fix an idea, feeling, attitude etc in someone's mind or character: **implant sth in sth** *A deep sense of patriotism had been implanted in him by his father.* **2** [T] to put something into someone's body by performing a medical operation: *Surgeons successfully implanted an artificial hip.* | **implant sth in/into sth** *A donor egg fertilised by her husband's sperm will be implanted in her womb.* **3** [I] *medical* if an egg or EMBRYO implants, it begins to develop normally: *The fertilized egg implants and becomes a foetus.* —**implantation** /ˌɪmplɑːnˈteɪʃən $ -plæn-/ *n* [U]

im·plant² /ˈɪmplɑːnt $ -plænt/ *n* [C] something artificial that is put into someone's body in a medical operation → **transplant**: *silicone breast implants*

im·plau·si·ble /ɪmˈplɔːzəbəl $ -ˈplɒː-/ *adj* difficult to believe and therefore unlikely to be true OPP **plausible**: **implausible theory/idea/explanation etc** *Margaret found his excuse somewhat implausible.* | *It's not entirely implausible that a galaxy could be identical to our own.* —**implausibly** *adv* —**implausibility** /ɪmˌplɔːzəˈbɪləti $ -ˌplɒː-/ *n* [U]

im·ple·ment¹ /ˈɪmpləment/ ●●○ W3 AWL *v* [T] to take action or make changes that you have officially decided should happen: **implement a policy/plan/decision etc** *We have decided to* ***implement*** *the committee's recommendations* ***in full.*** —**implementation** /ˌɪmpləmenˈteɪʃən/ *n* [U]: *the implementation of the peace plan*

im·ple·ment² /ˈɪmpləmənt/ AWL *n* [C] a tool, especially one used for outdoor physical work

im·pli·cate /ˈɪmplɪkeɪt/ ●○○ AWL *v* [T]
1 to show or suggest that someone is involved in a crime or dishonest act: *The allegations implicated Abe to such an extent he was forced to resign.* | **implicate sb in sth** *Three police officers are implicated in the cover-up.*
2 *formal* if something is implicated in something bad or harmful, it is shown to be its cause: **be implicated in sth** *Viruses are known to be implicated in the development of some cancers.*

im·pli·ca·tion /ˌɪmplɪˈkeɪʃən/ ●●○ W2 AWL *n*
1 [C usually plural] a possible future effect or result of an action, event, decision etc: **[+of]** *What are the implications of these proposals?* | *This election* ***has*** *profound* ***implications for*** *the future of U.S. democracy.* | **consider/discuss/examine the implications** *His talk will examine the* ***wider implications*** *of the Internet revolution.* | **practical/financial/political etc implications**
2 [U] a situation in which it is shown or suggested that someone or something is involved in a crime or a dishonest act → **implicate**: **the implication of sb (in sth)** *the implication of the former Chief of Staff in a major scandal*
3 [C,U] a suggestion that is not made directly but that people are expected to understand or accept → **imply**: *They are called 'Supertrams',* ***the implication being that*** (=which is meant to suggest that) *they are more advanced than earlier models.* | **by implication** *The law bans organized protests and, by implication, any form of opposition.*

im·pli·cit /ɪmˈplɪsɪt/ ●○○ AWL *adj*
1 suggested or understood without being stated directly OPP **explicit**: **implicit criticism/threat/assumption** *Her words contained an implicit threat.* | *His statement is being seen as implicit criticism of the work of research laboratories.*
2 *formal* forming a central part of something, but without

being openly stated: **[+in]** *Confidentiality is implicit in your relationship with a counselor.*
3 complete and containing no doubts: **implicit faith/trust/belief** *They had implicit faith in his powers.* —**implicitly** *adv*: *They believed implicitly in their own superiority.*

im·plode /ɪmˈpləʊd $ -ˈploʊd/ *v* [I] **1** *technical* to explode inwards OPP **explode**: *The windows on both sides of the room had imploded.* **2** *written* if an organization or system implodes, it fails suddenly, often because of faults that it has SYN **collapse**: *Most nations learned their lesson during the 1930s, when trade imploded and incomes plunged.* —**implosion** /ɪmˈpləʊʒən $ -ˈploʊ-/ *n* [C,U]

im·plore /ɪmˈplɔː $ -ɔːr/ *v* [I,T] *formal* to ask for something in an emotional way SYN **beg**: *'Don't go,' I implored her.* | **implore sb to do sth** *She implored the soldiers to save her child.* —**imploring** *adj*: *a ragged child with imploring eyes*

im·ply /ɪmˈplaɪ/ ●●○ W2 AWL *v* (**implied, implying, implies**) [T]
1 to suggest that something is true, without saying this directly → **infer, implication**: **imply (that)** *Cleo blushed. She had not meant to imply that he was lying.* | *an implied threat*
2 if a fact, event etc implies something, it shows that it is likely to be true SYN **suggest**: **imply (that)** *The high level of radiation in the rocks implies that they are volcanic in origin.*
3 if one thing implies another, it proves that the second thing exists: *Democracy implies a respect for individual liberties.* | *High profits do not necessarily imply efficiency.*

im·po·lite /ˌɪmpəˈlaɪt◂/ *adj* not polite SYN **rude**: *an impolite remark* | **it is impolite (of sb) (to do sth)** *Would it be impolite of me to ask exactly where you've been?* —**impolitely** *adv*

im·pol·i·tic /ɪmˈpɒlətɪk $ -ˈpɑː-/ *adj formal* behaving in a way that is not careful and that could make people think you are not sensible SYN **unwise**: *It was considered impolitic of him to spend too much time with the party radicals.*

im·pon·der·a·ble /ɪmˈpɒndərəbəl $ -ˈpɑːn-/ *n* [C usually plural] *formal* something that cannot be exactly measured, judged, or calculated: *There are too many imponderables to make an accurate prediction.* —**imponderable** *adj*: *an imponderable question*

im·port¹ /ˈɪmpɔːt $ -ɔːrt/ ●●○ *n*
1 [C,U] a product that is brought from one country into another so that it can be sold there, or the business of doing this OPP **export**: *a ban on beef imports* | *the abolition of* ***import duties*** (=taxes) | **[+from]** *cheap imports from Asia* | *American demand for Japanese imports* (=goods from Japan) | *the import of electrical goods* THESAURUS ▸ **PRODUCT**
2 [C] something new or different that is brought to a place where it did not previously exist: *The beetle is thought to be a European import.*
3 [U] *formal* importance or meaning → **significance**: *a matter of no great import*

im·port² /ɪmˈpɔːt $ -ɔːrt/ ●●○ *v* [T]
1 to bring a product from one country into another so that it can be sold there OPP **export**: *In 2001, Britain exported more cars than it imported.* | **import sth from sth** *All the meat is imported from France.*
2 to introduce something new or different in a place where it did not previously exist: *The unusual designs were probably imported from Iran.* | **import sth to/into sth** *The US comedy format was gradually imported to UK screens.*
3 to move information from one computer to another OPP **export**: **import sth from/into sth** *You can now import graphics from other applications.* —**imported** *adj*: *imported autos* | *imported data*

im·por·tance /ɪmˈpɔːtəns $ -ɔːr-/ ●●● S3 W1 *n* [singular, U] the quality of being important: **the importance of sth** *the importance of regular exercise* | *I agree about the importance of these proposals* (=the reasons why they are important). | **of importance** *They make decisions about various matters of importance* (=important matters). | *He was* ***full of his own importance*** (=he behaved in an annoying way which showed that he thought he was very important).

COLLOCATIONS

VERBS

have importance *This is an issue that has importance for all of us.*
attach importance to sth (=think it is important) *She attached great importance to loyalty.*
recognize/realize the importance of sth *We all recognize the importance of his work.*
emphasize/stress the importance of sth *I'd like to emphasize the importance of reading exam questions carefully.*
lose its importance *The island lost its importance when trade routes changed.*
exceed sth in importance *formal* (=be more important than something else)

ADJECTIVES

great/considerable/enormous importance *Crime rates have great importance for the government.*
vital/crucial/critical importance (=very great) *This research is of vital importance.*
central/fundamental importance *The central importance of interest rates is widely recognized.*
particular importance *Tourism has particular importance in some regions.*
equal importance *When applying for a job, qualifications and experience are often of equal importance.*
relative importance *We discussed the relative importance of these different sources of revenue.*
growing/increasing importance *the growing importance of the Internet as a source of information*
economic/political importance | **local/national importance** | **practical importance** (=related to things that happen, rather than just ideas)

PHRASES

a sense/feeling of importance (=a feeling that you are an important person) *Sitting behind the big desk gave her a feeling of importance.*
be of little/no importance *Where the money came from is of no importance.*
be of the utmost importance/be of paramount importance (=be extremely important) *It is of the utmost importance that this matter is kept confidential.*
be of primary importance *formal* (=be the most important thing) | **be of secondary importance** *formal* (=be less important than another thing)

im·por·tant /ɪmˈpɔːtənt $ -ɔːr-/ ●●● S1 W1 *adj*
1 an important event, decision, problem etc has a big effect or influence on people's lives or on events in the future: *a very important meeting* | *The accident taught him an important lesson.* | *Happiness is more important than money.* | *'What did you say?' 'Oh, nothing important.'* | **it is important (to do sth)** *It's important to explain the procedure to the patient.* | ***It's*** *vitally* ***important that*** *you understand the danger.* | **[+for]** *It was important for the president to continue his schedule, regardless of the bomb threat.* | **[+to]** *Nothing could be more important to me than my family.*
⚠ When you mean that you care about something a lot, say that it is **important to** you, not that it is 'important for' you.
2 people who are important have a lot of power or influence: *a very important customer* | *They carry guns because it makes them* ***feel important***.

THESAURUS

important having a big effect on people's lives or on events in the future: *an important decision* | *Good qualifications are increasingly important.*
big important or serious: *It's a big decision.* | *a big problem*
significant important enough to be noticeable or have a big effect: *There is no significant difference between the performance of male and female students.* | *The Internet has brought about significant changes in people's lives.*

I

noteworthy *formal* important or interesting enough to deserve your attention: *The castle is the island's most noteworthy feature.* | *The jury's verdict was noteworthy for a number of reasons.*

VERY IMPORTANT

essential very important, especially for the success, health, or safety of someone or something: *It is essential to speak the local language.* | *essential supplies of food and clothing*
vital/crucial extremely important, because without it there could be serious problems: *His evidence was vital to the case.* | *The US plays a crucial role in the region.*
key extremely important and having a big effect: *Wheeler had a key role in the development of the atom bomb.* | *Timing is key.*
of great/considerable importance very important: *In the construction industry, health and safety are of considerable importance.*
momentous very important because it has a very great effect on the future: *Momentous events were taking place in Russia.* | *a momentous decision*

MOST IMPORTANT

main/chief/principal [only before noun] most important: *What was your main aim?* | *the principal reason for their decision*
major [usually before noun] one of the most important or serious things: *Smoking is a major cause of heart disease.* | *Street crime is a major problem.*
central/primary [usually before noun] most important - used especially when talking about the main thing that people are discussing, worried about, or trying to do: *Education will be the central issue in the election.* | *Our primary concern is passenger safety.*
paramount /ˈpærəmaʊnt/ *formal* more important than anything else, so that you must consider it when deciding what to do: *Airport security is of paramount importance.* | *The needs of the students are paramount.*

im·por·tant·ly /ɪmˈpɔːtəntli $ -ɔːr-/ ●●○ *adv*
1 [sentence adverb] used to show that your next statement or question is more, equally etc important than what you said before: **more/most/less/equally importantly** *Most importantly, you must keep a record of everything you do.*
2 in a way that shows you think that what someone is saying or doing is important: *He strode importantly into the room.*

im·por·ta·tion /ˌɪmpɔːˈteɪʃən $ -ɔːr-/ *n* **1** [C,U] *formal* the act of bringing something new or different to a place where it did not previously exist, or something that arrives in this way: **[+of]** *restrictions on the importation of American movies* **2** [U] *technical* the business of bringing things into a country from other countries in order to sell them SYN **import**: **[+of]** *a law prohibiting the importation of tuna*

im·port·er /ɪmˈpɔːtə $ -ˈpɔːrtər/ ●○○ *n* [C] a person, company, or country that buys goods from other countries so they can be sold in their own country OPP **exporter**

im·por·tu·nate /ɪmˈpɔːtʃənət $ -ɔːr-/ *adj formal* continuously asking for things in an annoying or unreasonable way: *importunate demands* —**importunity** /ˌɪmpəˈtjuːnəti $ -pərˈtuː-/ *n* [U]

im·por·tune /ˌɪmpəˈtjuːn $ ˌɪmpərˈtuːn/ *v* [T] *formal* to ask someone for something continuously in an annoying or unreasonable way → **beg**

im·pose /ɪmˈpəʊz $ -ˈpoʊz/ ●●○ W2 AWL *v*
1 [T] if someone in authority imposes a rule, punishment, tax etc, they force people to accept it: *The court can impose a fine.* | **impose sth on sth/sb** *The government imposed a ban on the sale of ivory.*
2 [T] to force someone to have the same ideas, beliefs etc as you: **impose sth on sb** *parents who impose their own moral values on their children*
3 [I] *formal* to expect or ask someone to do something for you when this is not convenient for them: **[+on/upon]** *We could ask to stay the night, but I don't want to impose on them.*
4 [T] to have a bad effect on something or someone and to cause problems for them: **impose a burden/hardship etc (on sb/sth)** *Military spending imposes a huge strain on the economy.*

REGISTER
In everyday English, people usually say **put a ban/tax/burden/strain** on something rather than **impose a ban/tax/burden/strain** on something: *The government **put** a higher **tax on** cigarettes.* | *This **puts** a lot of **strain on** families.*

im·pos·ing /ɪmˈpəʊzɪŋ $ -ˈpoʊ-/ *adj* large, impressive, and appearing important: *an imposing building* | *He's a tall, quietly spoken, but imposing figure.*

im·po·si·tion /ˌɪmpəˈzɪʃən/ ●○○ AWL *n*
1 [U] the introduction of something such as a rule, punishment, tax etc: **[+of]** *the imposition of martial law*
2 [C usually singular] *formal* something that someone expects or asks you to do for them, which is not convenient for you: *I know it's an imposition, but could I use your bathroom?*

im·pos·si·ble¹ /ɪmˈpɒsəbəl $ ɪmˈpɑː-/ ●●● S2 W2 *adj*
1 something that is impossible cannot happen or be done OPP **possible**: *'I want to speak to Mr Franks.' 'I'm afraid that's impossible.'* | ***It's impossible to** be accurate about these things.* | *The noise **made** sleep **impossible**.* | *Members with young children often **found it impossible to** attend evening meetings.* | *It is difficult to find work these days, but for blind people it is **virtually impossible**.* | *He was faced with a **seemingly impossible** task.* | *It was **physically impossible** to get the fridge through the door.* | *Six months ago, peace seemed an **impossible dream**.* | *Such mental attitudes are **difficult, if not impossible**, to change.*
2 a situation that is impossible is one that you cannot deal with: *We were in an impossible situation. Whatever we decided to do would upset someone.* | *Helen's refusal to cooperate **put** me **in an impossible position**.* | *His attitude is **making life impossible** for the rest of the team.* | *He was facing impossible odds.*
3 behaving in a very unreasonable and annoying way: *Oh, you're just impossible!* —**impossibly** *adv*: *Some sales managers think selling abroad is impossibly difficult.* —**impossibility** /ɪmˌpɒsəˈbɪləti $ -ˌpɑː-/ *n* [C,U]: *One hundred percent airline security is a practical impossibility.*

GRAMMAR
Impossible is not used with 'very'. You say: *It was an absolutely impossible task.* ✗ Don't say: *It was a very impossible task.*
GRAMMAR GUIDE ▸ ADJECTIVES

THESAURUS
impossible something that is impossible cannot happen or be done: *It's impossible to get a taxi around here.* | *At times, finding a job felt like an impossible task.*
impractical something that is impractical is too expensive, takes too much time, is too difficult etc and therefore it is not sensible to try to do it: *It's a nice idea, but it's totally impractical.* | *We cannot all just stop using our cars - that would be completely impractical.*
out of the question used when saying that something is completely impossible, especially because it is not allowed: *It's out of the question for you to go alone.*
there's no way *informal* used when saying that you think something is completely impossible: *There's no way we can get to the airport in less than an hour.*
inconceivable impossible to imagine or believe: *It seemed inconceivable that there could be an end to the fighting in Northern Ireland.*

I

unthinkable impossible to imagine or believe - used especially about something that seems very shocking to people: *In those days it was unthinkable for a lady to work outside the home.*
unattainable impossible to achieve: *an unattainable goal | Victory seemed unattainable.*
it can't be done *spoken* used when saying very definitely that something is impossible: *I'm afraid it can't be done.*

impossible² *n* **the impossible** something that cannot be done: **attempt/do/ask etc the impossible** *I just want to be able to buy healthy food at a reasonable price. Is that asking the impossible?*

im·pos·tor, **imposter** /ɪmˈpɒstə $ ɪmˈpɑːstər/ *n* [C] someone who pretends to be someone else in order to trick people: *The nurse was soon discovered to be an impostor.*

im·po·tent /ˈɪmpətənt/ *adj* **1** unable to take effective action because you do not have enough power, strength, or control: *Emergency services seem impotent in the face of such a disaster. | impotent rage* **2** a man who is impotent is unable to have sex because he cannot get an ERECTION —**impotently** *adv* —**impotence** *n* [U]: *political impotence*

im·pound /ɪmˈpaʊnd/ *v* [T] *law* if the police or law courts impound something you have or own, they keep it until it has been decided that you can have it back SYN **confiscate**: *He sued the police after they impounded his car.*

im·pov·e·rish /ɪmˈpɒvərɪʃ $ ɪmˈpɑː-/ *v* [T] **1** to make someone very poor: *Falling coffee prices have impoverished many Third World economies. | families impoverished by debt* **2** to make something worse in quality: *Fast-growing trees remove nutrients and impoverish the soil.* —**impoverished** *adj*: *an impoverished student* —**impoverishment** *n* [U]: *spiritual impoverishment*

im·prac·ti·ca·ble /ɪmˈpræktɪkəbəl/ *adj formal* impossible or very difficult to do for practical reasons: *It was an appealing plan but quite impracticable.* —**impracticably** *adv* —**impracticability** /ɪmˌpræktɪkəˈbɪləti/ *n* [U]

im·prac·ti·cal /ɪmˈpræktɪkəl/ *adj* **1** not sensible or possible for practical reasons: *The road toll scheme was dismissed as impractical. | James was a foolish man, full of impractical plans.* **THESAURUS** ▸ IMPOSSIBLE **2** not good at dealing with ordinary practical matters, such as making or repairing things: *Sandra was hopelessly impractical around the house.* —**impractically** /-kli/ *adv* —**impracticality** /ɪmˌpræktɪˈkæləti/ *n* [U]: *the sheer impracticality of collecting DNA from such a large population*

im·pre·ca·tion /ˌɪmprɪˈkeɪʃən/ *n* [C] *literary* an offensive word or phrase, used when someone is very angry

im·pre·cise /ˌɪmprɪˈsaɪs◂/ AWL *adj* not clear or exact OPP **precise**, **exact**: *vague imprecise estimates | Alcohol affects the brain, making speech slurred and imprecise.* —**imprecisely** *adv* —**imprecision** /-ˈsɪʒən/ *n* [U]: *an imprecision in the terminology*

im·preg·na·ble /ɪmˈpregnəbəl/ *adj formal* **1** a building that is impregnable is so strong that it cannot be entered by force: *an impregnable fortress* **2** strong and impossible to change or influence: *her impregnable obstinacy*

im·preg·nate /ˈɪmpregneɪt $ ɪmˈpreg-/ *v* [T] **1** to make a substance spread completely through something, or to spread completely through something: **impregnate sth with sth** *The mats have to be impregnated with disinfectant.* **2** *technical* to make a woman or female animal PREGNANT

im·pre·sa·ri·o /ˌɪmprəˈsɑːriəʊ $ -rioʊ/ *n* (*plural* **impresarios**) [C] someone who organizes performances in theatres, concert halls etc

im·press /ɪmˈpres/ ●●○ S3 W3 *v* [T]
1 [not in progressive] to make someone feel admiration and respect: *Steve borrowed his dad's sports car to impress his girlfriend.* | **impress sb with/by sth** *We were very impressed by the standard of work. | One candidate in particular impressed us with her knowledge. | I think the chief exec was* ***favourably impressed*** *by your presentation. | 'He's a lawyer?' Mum looked* ***suitably impressed*** (=as impressed as you would expect).
2 to make the importance of something clear to someone: **impress sth on sb** *Father impressed on me the value of hard work.*
3 to press something into a soft surface so that a mark or pattern appears on it: *patterns impressed in the clay*

im·pres·sion /ɪmˈpreʃən/ ●●○ S3 W2 *n*
1 [C,U] the opinion or feeling you have about someone or something because of the way they seem: *When we looked around the school we got a very good impression. | I got the impression that she wasn't very happy with her job.* | **[+of]** *What was your impression of Roger?* **THESAURUS** ▸ IDEA
2 be under the impression (that) to believe that something is true when it is not: *I'm sorry, I was under the impression that you were the manager.*
3 [C] if you do an impression of a famous person, you copy their speech or behaviour in order to make people laugh SYN **imitation**: *Jean* ***does*** *a great* ***impression of*** *Madonna.*
4 [C] a picture or drawing of what someone or something might look like, or what something will look like in the future: **[+of]** *an* ***artist's impression*** *of the new building*
5 [C] a mark left by pressing something into a soft surface: *Some of the fallen trees had* ***left*** *a clear* ***impression*** *in the hardened mud.*
6 [C] all the copies of a book printed at one time → **edition**

COLLOCATIONS

VERBS

make an impression *Think about what sort of impression you want to make.*
give an impression *Her speech definitely gave the impression that she was enthusiastic about the project.*
create an impression (*also* **convey an impression** *formal*) *Arriving late won't create a very good impression.*
get an impression *What sort of impression did you get of the city?*
leave an impression on sb (=make someone remember a person, place, or thing) *Janet certainly left an impression on him.*

ADJECTIVES

a good/positive impression *He was keen to make a good impression on his boss.*
a bad/negative impression *Arriving late for an interview gives a very negative impression.*
sb's first/initial/immediate impression *My first impression was that Terry's version of the events was untrue.*
a clear/vivid impression *He had the clear impression that most people were in favour of the idea.*
a vague impression (=not very clear) *Dave only had a vague impression of the man who had attacked him.*
a strong/deep impression (=one that someone feels very strongly) *She made a strong impression on me the first time I met her.*
a lasting impression (=one that someone remembers for a long time) *Sam's performance had clearly made a lasting impression on the audience.*
a wrong/misleading impression *The advertisement gave a misleading impression of the product.*
a false/mistaken impression *He had the mistaken impression that Julia was married.*
the overall/general impression *The general impression was of a very efficiently run company.*
the distinct impression (=used when something seems very clear to you) *We were left with the impression that the contract was ours if we wanted it.*

PHRASES

first impressions count (=the impression you make when you first meet someone is important)

im·pres·sion·a·ble /ɪmˈpreʃənəbəl/ *adj* someone who is impressionable is easily influenced, especially because they are young: *The kids are at an* ***impressionable age***.

im·pres·sion·is·m, **Impressionism** /ɪmˈpreʃənɪzəm/ *n* [U] **1** a style of painting used especially in France in the 19th century that uses colour instead of details of form to produce effects of light or feeling → **realism 2** a style of music from the late 19th and early 20th centuries that produces feelings and images by the quality of sounds rather than by a pattern of notes

im·pres·sion·ist /ɪmˈpreʃənɪst/ *n* [C] **1** someone who copies the speech or behaviour of famous people in order to entertain other people **2 Impressionist** someone who uses impressionism in the paintings or music that they produce: *impressionist painters*

im·pres·sion·is·tic /ɪmˌpreʃəˈnɪstɪk◂/ *adj* based on a general feeling of what something is like, rather than on specific facts or details: *The officers seemed to make only an impressionistic assessment.* —**impressionistically** /-kli/ *adv*

im·pres·sive /ɪmˈpresɪv/ ●●○ W3 *adj* something that is impressive makes you admire it because it is very good, large, important etc: *The figures certainly look impressive.* | *Among the guests was an* ***impressive array of*** *authors and critics.* **THESAURUS** GOOD —**impressively** *adv*: *Production standards are impressively high.* —**impressiveness** *n* [U]

im·pri·ma·tur /ˌɪmprəˈmeɪtə, -ˈmɑː- $ -ər/ *n* [singular] **1** *formal* approval of something, especially from an important person: *His actions have the imprimatur of the Secretary of State.* **2** *technical* official permission to print a book, given by the Roman Catholic Church

im·print[1] /ˈɪmprɪnt/ *n* [C] **1** the mark left by an object being pressed into or onto something: **[+of]** *the imprint of her hand on the soft sand* **2** *technical* the name of a PUBLISHER as it appears on a book

im·print[2] /ɪmˈprɪnt/ *v* **1** [T] to print or press the mark of an object on something: **imprint sth on/in/onto sth** *One snowy morning, footprints and tyre marks were imprinted in the snow.* **2** *literary* to become fixed in your mind or memory so that you never forget: **imprint sth on your mind/memory/brain etc** *The sight of Joe's dead body was imprinted on his mind forever.*

im·pris·on /ɪmˈprɪzən/ ●○○ *v* [T]
1 to put someone in prison or to keep them somewhere and prevent them from leaving: *The government imprisoned all opposition leaders.* | *She was imprisoned within his strong arms.*
2 if a situation or feeling imprisons people, it restricts what they can do: *Many elderly people feel imprisoned in their own homes.*

im·pris·on·ment /ɪmˈprɪzənmənt/ ●○○ *n* [U] the state of being in prison, or the time someone spends there: *They were sentenced to 6 years' imprisonment.* | ***life imprisonment***

im·prob·a·ble /ɪmˈprɒbəbəl $ -ˈprɑː-/ *adj* **1** not likely to happen or to be true SYN **unlikely** OPP **probable**: *a film with an improbable plot* | *It seems* ***highly improbable*** *that he had no knowledge of the affair.* **2** surprising and slightly strange SYN **unlikely**: *improbable combinations of colours* —**improbably** *adv* —**improbability** /ɪmˌprɒbəˈbɪləti $ -ˌprɑː-/ *n* [C,U]

im·promp·tu /ɪmˈprɒmptjuː $ ɪmˈprɑːmptuː/ *adj* done or said without any preparation or planning: **impromptu speech/party/meeting etc** *The band gave an impromptu concert.* —**impromptu** *adv*

im·prop·er /ɪmˈprɒpə $ -ˈprɑːpər/ *adj* **1** dishonest, illegal, or morally wrong: **it is improper (for sb) to do sth** *He realised that it was improper for a police officer to accept gifts.* | **improper behaviour/conduct/dealings etc** *allegations of improper banking practices* | *improper sexual conduct* **2** not sensible, right, or fair in a particular situation SYN **inappropriate**: **it is improper to do sth** *It would be improper of me to comment before the election outcome is known.* **3** wrong or not correct —**improperly** *adv*: *If you are improperly dressed, you will not be admitted.*

imˌproper ˈfraction *n* [C] *technical* a FRACTION such as 107/8 in which the top number is larger than the bottom number OPP **proper fraction**

im·pro·pri·e·ty /ˌɪmprəˈpraɪəti/ *n* (*plural* **improprieties**) [C,U] *formal* behaviour or an action that is wrong or unacceptable according to moral, social, or professional standards: *Accusations of impropriety were made against the company's directors.*

im·prov /ˈɪmprɒv $ -prɑːv/ *n* [U] *informal* (**improvisation**) acting, singing, performing etc without preparing what you will say first: *comedy improv*

im·prove /ɪmˈpruːv/ ●●● S2 W1 *v* [I,T] to make something better, or to become better: *a course for students wishing to improve their English* | *The doctors say she is improving* (=after being ill). | *You could use the money for improving your home.* | *Many wines* ***improve with age*** (=get better as they get older).

> **REGISTER**
> In everyday English, people often say something **gets better** rather than **improves**: *Her English is definitely* ***getting better***. | *I hope things* ***get better*** *soon.*

improve on/upon sth *phr v* to do something better than before or make something better than before: *Bertorelli has scored 165 points, and I don't think anyone will improve on that.*

im·proved /ɪmˈpruːvd/ ●●○ *adj* [usually before noun] better than before: *improved performance* | *Our washing powder now has a* ***new improved*** *formula.*

im·prove·ment /ɪmˈpruːvmənt/ ●●● S3 W2 *n*
1 [C,U] the act of improving something, or the state of being improved: **[+in/on/to]** *There's been a big improvement in the children's behaviour.* | *an improvement on earlier models* | *We need to carry out some improvements to the system.* | *Our results have shown some improvement this month.*
2 [C] a change or addition that improves something: *Are you making some improvements to your home?*

COLLOCATIONS – MEANINGS 1 & 2

VERBS

be an improvement (on sth) *This version of the software is a clear improvement on its predecessor.*
see/notice an improvement *After taking the tablets, he noticed some improvement in his energy levels.*
show an improvement *The sales figures show a major improvement.*
represent an improvement (=be an improvement) *A pre-tax profit of 4.3 million pounds represents a 5% improvement on last year.*

ADJECTIVES

a big improvement *The situation today is a big improvement on the 1980s.*
a great/vast/major improvement (=very big) *The new computer system was a vast improvement.*
a dramatic improvement (=very big and quick) *With the new treatment we saw a dramatic improvement in his condition.*
a significant/substantial/considerable improvement (=quite big) *There has been a considerable improvement in trading conditions.*
a marked/noticeable improvement (=that people can notice) *Joanna's work showed a marked improvement.*
a slight improvement *Sales figures have shown a slight improvement this month.*
a gradual improvement | **a general improvement** | **a continuous/steady improvement** (=happening slowly and gradually) | **further improvement** (=more improvement)

PHRASES

signs of improvement *The patient is showing signs of improvement.*
room for improvement (=the possibility that something could be done better) *There's room for improvement in the way the tickets are sold.*

I

im·prov·i·dent /ɪmˈprɒvɪdənt $ -ˈprɑː-/ *adj formal* too careless to save any money or to plan for the future → **spendthrift** —**improvidence** *n* [U] —**improvidently** *adv*

im·pro·vise /ˈɪmprəvaɪz/ *v* [I,T] **1** to do something without any preparation, because you are forced to do this by unexpected events: *I forgot to bring my notes, so I had to improvise.* **2** to make something by using whatever you can find because you do not have the equipment or materials that you need: *There were no nappies, so we had to improvise with what we could find.* | *Annie improvised a sandpit for the children.* **3** to invent music, words, a statement etc from your imagination, rather than planning or preparing it first: *I just started playing, and the other guys started improvising around me.* | *an improvised sketch* —**improvisation** /ˌɪmprəvaɪˈzeɪʃən $ ɪmˌprɑːvə-/ *n* [C,U]

im·pru·dent /ɪmˈpruːdənt/ *adj formal* not sensible or wise SYN **unwise**: *The banks made hundreds of imprudent loans in the 1970s.* —**imprudently** *adv* —**imprudence** *n* [C,U]

im·pu·dent /ˈɪmpjədənt/ *adj formal or old-fashioned* rude and showing no respect to other people SYN **cheeky** —**impudence** *n* [U]: *He stared at me with a mixture of impudence and hostility.*

im·pugn /ɪmˈpjuːn/ *v* [T] *formal* to express doubts about someone's honesty, courage, ability etc: *I did not mean to impugn her professional abilities.*

im·pulse /ˈɪmpʌls/ ●○○ *n*
1 [C,U] a sudden strong desire to do something without thinking about whether it is a sensible thing to do SYN **urge**: **impulse to do sth** *a sudden impulse to laugh* | *Marge's first impulse was to run.* | *Gerry couldn't* ***resist the impulse*** *to kiss her.* | **on impulse** *On impulse, I picked up the phone and rang her.* | *Most beginners* ***buy*** *plants* ***on impulse*** *and then hope for the best.* | **impulse buying/shopping** (=when you buy things that you had not planned to buy)
2 [C] *technical* a short electrical signal that travels in one direction along a nerve or wire: *The eye converts light signals to nerve impulses.*
3 [C] a reason or aim that causes a particular kind of activity or behaviour: *It is the passions which provide the main impulse of music.*

im·pul·sion /ɪmˈpʌlʃən/ *n* [singular, U] *formal* a strong force or desire that causes something to happen or exist

im·pul·sive /ɪmˈpʌlsɪv/ ●○○ *adj* someone who is impulsive does things without considering the possible dangers or problems first → **rash**: *Rosa was impulsive and sometimes regretted things she'd done.* | *In a burst of impulsive generosity, I offered to pay.* —**impulsively** *adv*: *'Oh, Anne, I do love you!' he said impulsively.* —**impulsiveness** *n* [U]

im·pu·ni·ty /ɪmˈpjuːnəti/ *n* **do sth with impunity** if someone does something bad with impunity, there is no risk that they will be punished for it: *It's astonishing that these criminals are free to walk the streets with impunity.*

im·pure /ɪmˈpjʊə $ -ˈpjʊr/ *adj* **1** not pure or clean, and often consisting of a mixture of things instead of just one OPP **pure**: *drug dealers selling impure heroin* **2** *old-fashioned* impure thoughts, feelings etc are morally bad because they are about sex – sometimes used humorously: *He tried, without success, to rid his mind of any impure thoughts about Julia.*

im·pu·ri·ty /ɪmˈpjʊərəti $ -ˈpjʊr-/ *n* (*plural* **impurities**) **1** [C usually plural] a substance of a low quality that is contained in or mixed with something else, making it less pure: *All natural minerals contain impurities.* | *Our oatmeal face mask absorbs impurities from your skin.* **2** [U] the state of being impure

im·pute /ɪmˈpjuːt/ *v*
impute sth **to** sb *phr v formal* to say, often unfairly, that someone is responsible for something bad or has bad intentions: *The police were not guilty of the violence imputed to them.* —**imputation** /ˌɪmpjʊˈteɪʃən/ *n* [C,U]

in[1] /ɪn/ ●●● S1 W1 *prep*
1 used with the name of a container, place, or area to say where someone or something is: *There's some sugar in the cupboard.* | *My mother was in the kitchen.* | *He took us for a drive in his new car.* | *I found her sitting up in bed.* | *Manson spent fifteen years in prison.* | *a hole in the ground* | *Mr Fisher is in Boston this week.* | *My parents live in New Zealand now.*
2 into a container, place etc: *I never went in pubs.* | *He almost drowned when he fell in the river.* | *You can put your pyjamas in the bottom drawer.* | *Get in the car.* | *She looked in her handbag, but her keys were not there.*
3 used to say how something is done or happens: *a room furnished in the modern style* | *Her parents always talk to her in German.* | *She shouted my name in a harsh voice.* | *a short note scribbled in pencil* | *The title was printed in capital letters.* | *We waited in silence.*
4 used with the names of months, years, seasons etc to say when something happens: *Shaw first visited Russia in 1927.* | *Bright yellow flowers appear in late summer.* | *He retired in October.*
5 during a period of time: *It was amazing how much we managed to do in a day.* | *the hardest decision I ever made in my life*

> **GRAMMAR**
> • You say: *I got a card from my sister this morning.* | *I hope to go to Europe next summer.* ✗ Don't say: *in this morning* | *in next summer*
> • You say: *The group meets three times a month.* ✗ Don't say: *three times in a month*
> • You can say **in one** week, month etc when emphasizing how often something happens: *He was stopped for speeding three times in one month.*

6 at the end of a period of time: *I'll be with you in a minute.* | *The results will be announced in two weeks' time.*
THESAURUS ▸ AFTER
7 used with negatives or with 'first' to say how much time has passed since the last time something happened: *I haven't enjoyed myself so much in years.* | *It was the team's first win in eighteen months.*
8 used to name the book, document, film etc where something or someone appears: *You shouldn't believe everything you read in the newspapers.* | *Which actress starred in the film 'Cleopatra'?* | *There are a few mistakes in your essay.* | *In his speech, Professor Leary praised the work of the volunteers.*
9 making up the whole of something or included as part of something: *There are twelve programmes in the series.* | *How many minutes are there in an hour?* | *Think of a word with eight letters in it meaning 'cold'.* | *Owen will be playing in the England team tomorrow.*
10 doing or affecting a particular kind of job: *a career in industry* | *He's been in politics for fifteen years.* | *reforms in education*
11 wearing something: *He looked very handsome in his uniform.* | *She was dressed in a blue linen suit.*
12 used to talk about the state or situation of something or someone: *I hear that their marriage is in trouble.* | *The engine appears to be in good condition.* | *His life was in danger.* | *The castle now lies in ruins.*
13 used to say what activity a group of people do: *About 4,000 students took part in the protest.* | *his role in the negotiations*
14 used to talk about the shape, arrangement, or course of something or someone: *I want you all to stand in a circle.* | *She slept curled up in a ball.* | *Can you walk in a straight line?*
15 used between a smaller number and a larger number to say how common or how likely something is: *One in ten homes now has cable TV.* | *Smokers have a one in three chance of dying from their habit.*
16 used before a plural number or amount to say how many people or things are involved, or how many there are in each group: *Eggs are still sold in half dozens.* | *The children work in pairs.* | **in their hundreds/thousands etc** (=in very large numbers) *People flocked in their thousands to greet their new princess.*
17 used between a smaller number or amount and a larger one to say what a rate is: *Income tax stands at 23 pence in the pound.* | *a hill with a gradient of one in six*

I

18 used to say what colour something is or what it is made of: *Do you have the same pattern in blue? | a sculpture in white marble*
19 used to say what specific thing your statement is related to: *Milk is very rich in calcium. | Clark had become more extreme in his opinions. | an increase in fuel prices | The street is about a mile in length.*
20 used to refer to the weather or the physical conditions somewhere: *I've been standing in the rain for over an hour. | Would you prefer to sit in the shade?*
21 used to say what feeling you have when you do something: *She looked at me in horror. | It was all done purely in fun.*
22 used before the name of someone or something when you are saying how they are regarded: *You have a very good friend in Pat. | In Dwight D. Eisenhower the Republicans had found the ideal candidate.*
23 used to say what person or thing has the quality you are mentioning: *There was a hint of spring in the air. | I don't think Freddy had it in him to be a killer. | She's everything I'd want in a wife* (=she has every quality I would want a wife to have).
24 used to name the substance, food, drink etc that contains something: *Vitamin D is found in butter.*
25 used to say how many parts something is divided into: *a radio serial in four parts* | **in two/halves/pieces etc** *I tore the letter in two and threw the pieces in the fire.*
26 while doing something or while something is happening, and as a result of this: *In all the confusion, it is quite possible that some people got tickets without paying. | In my excitement, I forgot all about the message.* | **in doing sth** *In trying to protect the queen, Howard had put his own life in danger.*
27 in that used after a statement to begin to explain in what way it is true: *I've been lucky in that I have never had to worry about money.*
28 be in your 20s/30s/40s etc to be between the ages of 20 and 29, 30 and 39 etc: *Matthews was already in his mid-40s.* → **in all** at ALL[1](11)

in² ●●● S1 W1 *adv*
1 into or inside a container, place, vehicle etc OPP **out**: *Eric held the boat steady while the children got in. | He went to the ticket machine and put a coin in. | She dived in and swam out to the yacht.*
2 inside or into a building, especially your home or the place where you work OPP **out**: *Come in and sit down. | I'm afraid Mr Stewart won't be in until tomorrow morning. | We're staying in this evening.*
3 if a train, boat, or plane is in, it has arrived at a station, airport etc: *Our train's not in yet. | When's her flight due in?*
4 given or sent to a person or organization to be dealt with by them: *All entries must be in by next week. | Letters have been pouring in from all over the country. | Have you handed your essay in yet?*
5 if you write, paint, or draw something in, you add it in the correct place: *Fill in your name and address on the form provided. | The information is typed in by trained keyboarders.*
6 if a player or team is in during a game of CRICKET, they are batting (BAT)
7 if a ball is in during a game, it is inside the area where the game is being played OPP **out**: *Agassi's second serve was just in.*
8 if a politician or a political party is in, they have been elected: *Labour recorded its highest vote ever, but the Tories got in again.*
9 towards the centre SYN **inward(s)**: *The map had started to curl in at the edges.*
10 when the TIDE is in, the sea by the shore is at its highest level OPP **out**: *The tide was in, and the sea lapped against the harbour wall.*
11 be in for sth if someone is in for something unpleasant, it is going to happen to them: *I'm afraid he's in for a bit of a disappointment.*
12 be in for it *informal* if someone is in for it, they are going to be punished: *If they find out what I've done, I'll be in for it, won't I?*
13 be/get in on sth to be or become involved in something that is happening: *I think you ought to be in on this discussion, Ted.*
14 be in with sb *informal* to have a friendly relationship with someone: *She's in with the theatrical crowd. | You have to* **be well in with** *the directors* (=be very friendly with them) *if you want to get promotion here.*
15 be in at the beginning/start (of sth) to be present or involved when something starts → **have (got) it in for sb** at HAVE[2](41)

in³ *adj informal* fashionable OPP **out**: *Red is definitely the in colour this year. | Long skirts are in at the moment. | I joined the club because it seemed the in thing to do.* THESAURUS ▸ FASHIONABLE

in⁴ *n* **1 the ins and outs of sth** all the facts and details of something: *The book guides you through the ins and outs of choosing and growing garden flowers.* **2** [singular] *especially AmE* a way of getting the opportunity to do something or influence someone: *The job is pretty boring, but it's an in to a career in publishing.*

in⁵ *BrE*, **in.** *AmE* (*plural* **in** *or* **ins**) the written abbreviation of ***inch*** or ***inches***

in- /ɪn/ *prefix* the opposite or lack of something SYN **not** → **un-**, **il-**, **im-**, **ir-**: *insensitive* (=not sensitive) | *incautious* (=not cautious) | *inattention* (=lack of attention)

in·a·bil·i·ty /ˌɪnəˈbɪləti/ ●●○ *n* [singular, U] the fact of being unable to do something: **inability to do sth** *Alcoholism can result in an inability to cope. | the government's inability to enforce the ceasefire*

in ab·sen·ti·a /ˌɪn æbˈsentiə $ -ˈsenʃə/ *adv law* without being present: *He was tried in absentia.*

in·ac·ces·si·ble /ˌɪnəkˈsesəbəl◂/ AWL *adj* **1** difficult or impossible to reach OPP **accessible**: *In winter, the villages are inaccessible by road.* | **[+to]** *A long flight of stairs made the center inaccessible to disabled visitors.* **2** difficult or impossible to understand or afford OPP **accessible**: *Stockhausen's music is thought to be difficult and inaccessible.* —**inaccessibly** *adv* —**inaccessibility** /ˌɪnəksesəˈbɪləti/ *n* [U]

in·ac·cu·ra·cy /ɪnˈækjərəsi/ AWL *n* (*plural* **inaccuracies**) **1** [C] a statement that is not completely correct: *Jansen's review contained several inaccuracies.* THESAURUS ▸ MISTAKE **2** [U] a lack of correctness: *As a journalist, you simply cannot tolerate inaccuracy.*

in·ac·cu·rate /ɪnˈækjərət/ ●○○ AWL *adj* not completely correct OPP **accurate**: *A lot of what has been written about him is inaccurate.* | **inaccurate information/data etc** *He was fined $300,000 for making inaccurate statements to Congress.* THESAURUS ▸ WRONG —**inaccurately** *adv*

in·ac·tion /ɪnˈækʃən/ *n* [U] the fact that someone is not doing anything: *Several newspapers have criticized the president for inaction.*

in·ac·tive /ɪnˈæktɪv/ *adj* **1** not doing anything, not working, or not moving OPP **active**: *The brain cells are inactive during sleep. | Young people are becoming politically inactive.* **2** not taking part in something that normally you would take part in: *Graham's knee injury means he will be inactive for Sunday's game.* **3** *technical* an inactive substance does not react chemically with other substances

in·ac·tiv·i·ty /ˌɪnækˈtɪvəti/ *n* [U] the state of not doing anything, not moving, or not working: *Don't suddenly take up violent exercise after years of inactivity. | The time spent between jobs should not be a* ***period of inactivity***.

in·ad·e·qua·cy /ɪnˈædəkwəsi/ AWL *n* (*plural* **inadequacies**) **1** [U] a feeling that you are not as good, clever, skilled etc as other people: *Unemployment can cause* ***feelings of inadequacy*** *and low self-esteem.* **2** [U] the fact of not being good enough in quality, ability, size etc for a particular purpose: **[+of]** *the inadequacy of local health care* **3** [C usually plural] a fault or weakness: *I'm quite aware of my own inadequacies.*

in·ad·e·quate /ɪnˈædəkwət/ ●●○ AWL *adj* **1** not good enough, big enough, skilled enough etc for a particular purpose OPP **adequate**: *inadequate resources* |

[+for] *The parking facilities are inadequate for a busy shopping centre.* | **totally/wholly/woefully/hopelessly etc inadequate** *The building's electrical system was completely inadequate.* | *The new air conditioning system* ***proved inadequate****.*
2 someone who feels inadequate thinks other people are better, more skilful, more intelligent etc than they are: *The teacher made us* ***feel inadequate*** *and stupid if we made mistakes.* —**inadequately** *adv*: *Colleges have been inadequately funded for years.*

in·ad·mis·si·ble /ˌɪnədˈmɪsəbəl◂/ *adj law* inadmissible information is not allowed to be used in a court of law: *The* **evidence** *was ruled* **inadmissible**. —**inadmissibility** /ˌɪnədmɪsəˈbɪləti/ *n* [U]

in·ad·vert·ent·ly /ˌɪnədˈvɜːtəntli $ -ɜːr-/ *adv* without realizing what you are doing SYN **accidentally** OPP **deliberately**: *Viruses can be spread inadvertently by email users.* | *Robinson's name was inadvertently omitted from the list.* —**inadvertent** *adj*: *inadvertent exposure to chemicals* —**inadvertence** *n* [U]

in·ad·vis·a·ble /ˌɪnədˈvaɪzəbəl◂/ *adj* [not before noun] an action that is inadvisable is not sensible SYN **unwise**: *Changes in the patient's condition may make surgery inadvisable.* | **it is inadvisable to do sth** *It is inadvisable to involve more than one contractor on a project.*

in·a·li·en·a·ble /ɪnˈeɪliənəbəl/ *adj* [usually before noun] *formal* an inalienable right, power etc cannot be taken from you: *inalienable human rights*

i·nam·o·ra·ta /ɪˌnæməˈrɑːtə/ *n* [C] *literary* the woman that a man loves – sometimes used humorously SYN **lover**

i·nane /ɪˈneɪn/ *adj* very stupid or without much meaning: *Most pop lyrics are pretty inane.* | *an inane remark* —**inanely** *adv*: *Dave smiled inanely.* —**inanity** /ɪˈnænəti/ *n* [C,U]

in·an·i·mate /ɪnˈænəmət/ *adj* not living: *an* ***inanimate object***

ˈin-app *adj* available from within an APPLICATION on a SMARTPHONE or computer: *in-app purchases*

in·ap·pli·ca·ble /ˌɪnəˈplɪkəbəl, ɪnˈæplɪkəbəl $ ɪnˈæplɪk-/ *adj* rules, statements, questions etc that are inapplicable are not suitable, correct, or able to be used in a particular situation OPP **applicable**: **[+to]** *Most of the new regulations are inapplicable to us.*

in·ap·pro·pri·ate /ˌɪnəˈprəʊpri-ət $ -ˈproʊ-/ ●●○ AWL *adj* not suitable or right for a particular purpose or in a particular situation OPP **appropriate**: **wholly/totally/completely etc inappropriate** *His comments were wholly inappropriate on such a solemn occasion.* | **it is inappropriate (for sb) to do sth** *It would be inappropriate for me to comment until we know more of the facts.* | **[+for]** *an inappropriate gift for a child* | **[+to]** *marketing techniques that are totally inappropriate to education* | **inappropriate behaviour/response/language etc** —**inappropriately** *adv*: *inappropriately dressed* —**inappropriateness** *n* [U] —**inappropriacy** *n* [U]

in·apt /ɪnˈæpt/ *adj formal* an inapt phrase, statement etc is not right for a particular situation → **inept**: *a very inapt comment* —**inaptly** *adv* —**inaptness** *n* [U]

in·ar·tic·u·late /ˌɪnɑːˈtɪkjələt◂ $ -ɑːr-/ *adj* **1** not able to express your feelings clearly or easily OPP **articulate**: *He left me inarticulate with rage.* **2** speech that is inarticulate is not clearly expressed or pronounced OPP **articulate**: *Making an inarticulate sound, he turned away.* —**inarticulately** *adv* —**inarticulateness** *n* [C,U] —**inarticulacy** *n* [C,U]

in·as·much as /ˌɪnəzˈmʌtʃ əz/ *conjunction formal* used to explain the way in which what you are saying is true: *Ann is guilty, inasmuch as she knew what the others were planning.*

in·at·ten·tion /ˌɪnəˈtenʃən/ *n* [U] lack of attention SYN **carelessness**: *a moment of inattention* | **[+to]** *inattention to detail*

in·at·ten·tive /ˌɪnəˈtentɪv◂/ *adj* not giving enough attention to someone or something OPP **attentive**: *accidents caused by inattentive or reckless drivers* —**inattentively** *adv* —**inattentiveness** *n* [U]

in·au·di·ble /ɪnˈɔːdəbəl $ -ˈɒː-/ *adj* too quiet to be heard OPP **audible**: *The noise of the wind made her cries inaudible.* **THESAURUS** ▸ QUIET —**inaudibly** *adv*: *'No,' she whispered, almost inaudibly.* —**inaudibility** /ɪnˌɔːdəˈbɪləti $ -ˌɒː-/ *n* [U]

in·au·gu·ral /ɪˈnɔːgjərəl $ ɪˈnɒː-/ *adj* [only before noun] **1** an inaugural speech is the first given by someone who is starting an important job: *the president's inaugural address* | *the inaugural lecture of the new Professor of American Literature* **2** an inaugural event is the first in a planned series of similar events: *the plane's inaugural flight* | *the inaugural match of Major League Soccer* —**inaugural** *n* [C] *AmE*: *More than 200,000 people attended Carter's inaugural.*

in·au·gu·rate /ɪˈnɔːgjəreɪt $ -ˈnɒː-/ *v* [T] **1** to hold an official ceremony when someone starts doing an important job in government: **inaugurate sb as sth** *On 8 January 1959 de Gaulle was inaugurated as first president of the Fifth Republic.* **2** to open a building or start an organization, event etc for the first time: *The Turner Prize was inaugurated in 1984.* **THESAURUS** ▸ ESTABLISH **3** *formal* if an event inaugurates an important change or period of time, it comes at the beginning of it: *The International Trade Agreement inaugurated a period of high economic growth.* —**inauguration** /ɪˌnɔːgjəˈreɪʃən $ ɪˌnɒː-/ *n* [C,U]: *President Hoover's inauguration*

in·aus·pi·cious /ˌɪnɔːˈspɪʃəs◂ $ ˌɪnɒː-/ *adj formal* seeming to show that success in the future is unlikely OPP **auspicious**: *an* ***inauspicious start*** —**inauspiciously** *adv*

ˌin-ˈbetween *adj* in the middle between two points, sizes, periods of time etc → **midpoint**: *She was at that in-between age, neither a girl nor a woman.*

in·board /ˈɪnbɔːd $ -bɔːrd/ *adj* inside a boat: **inboard motor/engine** → OUTBOARD MOTOR

in·born /ˌɪnˈbɔːn◂ $ -ɔːrn◂/ *adj* an inborn quality or ability is one you have had naturally since birth: *Mammals have an inborn fear of snakes.* | *Good taste is inborn and cannot be learned.*

in·bound /ˈɪnbaʊnd/ *adj AmE* an inbound flight or train is arriving at a place SYN **incoming** *BrE* OPP **outbound**

ˌin-ˈbounds *adv AmE* if the ball is in-bounds in a sport, it is in the playing area

in·box, **in box** /ˈɪnbɒks $ -bɑːks/ ●●○ *n* [C]
1 the place in a computer email program where new messages arrive: *I had 130 emails in my inbox this morning.* **2** *AmE* a container on an office desk that is used to hold letters, documents etc that you must deal with SYN **in tray** *BrE* → OUTBOX

in·bred /ˌɪnˈbred◂/ *adj* **1** produced by inbreeding **2** having developed as a natural part of your character: *inbred ambition*

in·breed·ing /ˈɪnbriːdɪŋ/ *n* [U] when children, animals, or plants are produced from closely related members of the same family: *He was born with a rare bone disease, probably the result of aristocratic inbreeding.*

in·built /ˈɪnbɪlt/ *adj* [only before noun] *BrE* an inbuilt quality, feature etc is part of the nature of someone or something: *plants with inbuilt resistance to disease* | *History has an inbuilt tendency to repeat itself.*

Inc. /ɪŋk/ the written abbreviation of ***Incorporated*** → **Ltd**, **plc**: *General Motors Inc.*

in·cal·cu·la·ble /ɪnˈkælkjələbəl/ *adj formal* too great to be calculated SYN **immeasurable**: *Her contribution to our work is incalculable.* | **incalculable importance/value/worth etc** *treasures of incalculable value* | **incalculable harm/damage/suffering etc** *The outbreak of hostilities will cause incalculable misery.*

in·can·des·cent /ˌɪnkænˈdesənt◂ $ -kən-/ *adj* **1** very angry: *The prince was said to be* ***incandescent with rage****.* **2** *technical* producing a bright light when heated: *the invention of the incandescent lamp* **3** *literary* very bright: *incandescent flowers* —**incandescence** *n* [U]

I

in·can·ta·tion /ˌɪnkænˈteɪʃən/ *n* [C,U] special words that someone uses in magic, or the act of saying these words → **spell**: *a book of spells and incantations*

in·ca·pa·ble /ɪnˈkeɪpəbəl/ ●○○ AWL *adj* [not before noun] not able to do something OPP **capable**: **[+of]** *He seemed incapable of understanding how she felt.* | *Seventy-five percent of the electorate believe his party is incapable of government.* | *The stroke* ***rendered*** *her* ***incapable*** *of speech.* —**incapability** /ɪnˌkeɪpəˈbɪləti/ *n* [U]

GRAMMAR

Someone is **incapable of doing** something: *He is incapable of lying.* ✗ Don't say: *He is incapable to lie.*

GRAMMAR GUIDE ▸ **ADJECTIVES**

in·ca·pa·ci·tate /ˌɪnkəˈpæsɪteɪt/ AWL *v* [T] *formal* **1** to make you too ill or weak to live and work normally: *Her mother has been incapacitated by a fall.* | *an incapacitating injury* **2** to stop a system, piece of equipment etc from working properly: *A successful attack would incapacitate military training camps.* —**incapacitation** /ˌɪnkəpæsɪˈteɪʃən/ *n* [U]

in·ca·pa·ci·ty /ˌɪnkəˈpæsəti/ *n* [singular, U] *formal* lack of the ability to do things or to do something: *temporary incapacity through illness* | **mental/physical/intellectual etc incapacity** *Evidence of his mental incapacity was never produced in court.* | **incapacity to do sth** *The main problem is the author's incapacity to convey his ideas.*

in·car·ce·rate /ɪnˈkɑːsəreɪt $ -ɑːr-/ *v* [T] *formal* to put or keep someone in prison SYN **imprison**: *He spent 10 years incarcerated.* —**incarceration** /ɪnˌkɑːsəˈreɪʃən $ -ˌkɑːr-/ *n* [U]

in·car·nate[1] /ɪnˈkɑːnət $ -ɑːr-/ *adj* **1** **be evil/beauty/greed etc incarnate** to have an extreme amount of a particular quality: *He is now respectability incarnate.* **2** having taken human form: *Jesus, the incarnate Son of God* | *The media cast him as* ***the devil incarnate*** (=someone very evil).

in·car·nate[2] /ˈɪnkɑːneɪt $ -ɑːr-/ *v* [T] *formal* **1** to represent a particular quality in a physical or human form: *The crown incarnates national power.* **2** to make something appear in a human form

in·car·na·tion /ˌɪnkɑːˈneɪʃən $ -ɑːr-/ *n* **1** [C,U] the state of living in the form of a particular person or animal. According to some religions, people have several different incarnations. → **reincarnation**: *She believes she was an Egyptian queen* ***in a previous incarnation***. **2** [C] a period of time when someone or something has a particular job, use etc: *The building has gone through several incarnations: as a station, a café, and, most recently, a club.* **3** **the/an incarnation of sth** someone who has a lot of a particular quality, or represents it: *She was the incarnation of wisdom.* **4** [singular] the act of God coming to Earth in the human form of Christ, according to the Christian religion

in·cau·tious /ɪnˈkɔːʃəs $ -ˈkɒː-/ *adj* if you are incautious, you do not think about the possible bad results of your actions: *incautious remarks* | *The wine had made her incautious.* —**incautiously** *adv*

in·cen·di·a·ry[1] /ɪnˈsendiəri $ -dieri/ *adj* **1** [only before noun] designed to cause a fire: **incendiary bomb/device** *The explosion seems to have been caused by an incendiary device.* **2** an incendiary speech, piece of writing etc is intended to make people angry: *a hip-hop album with incendiary lyrics*

incendiary[2] *n* (*plural* **incendiaries**) [C] a bomb designed to cause a fire

in·cense[1] /ˈɪnsens/ *n* [U] a substance that has a pleasant smell when you burn it: *a church filled with the smell of incense* | *lighted incense sticks*

in·cense[2] /ɪnˈsens/ *v* [T] to make someone very angry: *Spectators were incensed by the referee's decision.*

in·censed /ɪnˈsenst/ *adj* [not before noun] very angry SYN **furious**: **[+at]** *Fans were incensed at the decision to ban the song.* | **incensed that** *Passengers are incensed that rail companies make huge profits while service remains poor.*

in·cen·tive /ɪnˈsentɪv/ ●●○ AWL *n* [C,U] something that encourages you to work harder, start a new activity etc → **motivation**: *As an* ***added incentive***, *there's a bottle of champagne for the best team.* | **create/provide/give sb an incentive** *Awards provide an incentive for young people to improve their skills.* | **incentive to do sth** *Farmers lack any incentive to manage their land organically.* | **economic/financial/tax etc incentives** *a recycling drive backed with financial incentives*

in·cen·ti·vize (*also* **-ise** *BrE*) /ɪnˈsentəvaɪz/ *v* [T] to give someone a reason to do something, especially by offering them a reward: *How should a company incentivize its employees?*

in·cep·tion /ɪnˈsepʃən/ *n* [singular] *formal* the start of an organization or institution: *a CD collection covering the band from its inception in 1994*

in·ces·sant /ɪnˈsesənt/ *adj* [usually before noun] continuing without stopping SYN **constant**: *The child's incessant talking started to irritate her.* | *incessant rain* —**incessantly** *adv*: *They quarreled incessantly.*

in·cest /ˈɪnsest/ *n* [U] sex between people who are closely related in a family: *Abortions would only be allowed in cases of rape or incest.*

in·ces·tu·ous /ɪnˈsestʃuəs/ *adj* **1** involving sexual activity between people who are closely related in a family: *an incestuous relationship* **2** involving a small group of people who only spend time with or help each other, not people outside the group - used to show disapproval: *an incestuous political community*

inch[1] /ɪntʃ/ ●●● S2 W3 *n* [C]

1 (*written abbreviation* **in** *BrE or* **in.** *AmE*) a unit for measuring length, equal to 2.54 centimetres. There are 12 inches in a foot: *The curtains were an inch too short.* | *Rainfall here is under 15 inches a year.* | **a one-/two-/three- etc inch sth** *a six-inch nail*

2 a very small distance: *Derek leaned closer, his face* ***only inches from*** *hers.* | *The bus missed us* ***by inches***. | *On several occasions, they came* ***within inches*** *of death.*

3 **every inch a)** completely or in every way: *With her designer clothes and elegant hair, she* ***looks every inch*** *the celebrity.* **b)** the whole of an area or distance: **[+of]** *Every inch of space in the tiny shop was crammed with goods.* | *Italy deserved to win, though Greece made them fight* ***every inch of the way***.

4 **give sb an inch and they'll take a yard/mile** used to say that, if you allow someone a little freedom or power, they will try to take more

5 **inch by inch** moving very gradually and slowly: *Inch by inch, he lowered himself from the roof.*

6 **not give/budge an inch** to refuse to change your decision or opinion, even though people are trying to persuade you to do this: *Neither side is prepared to give an inch in the negotiations.*

7 **beat/thrash etc sb to within an inch of their life** to beat someone very hard and thoroughly: *Another word out of you and I'll beat you to within an inch of your life.*

inch[2] *v* [I,T always + adv/prep] to move very slowly in a particular direction, or to make something do this: *I inched forward along the ground.*

in·cho·ate /ɪnˈkəʊət $ -ˈkoʊ-/ *adj formal* inchoate ideas, plans, attitudes etc are only just starting to develop

in·ci·dence /ˈɪnsɪdəns/ AWL *n* [C usually singular] *formal* the number of times something happens, especially crime, disease etc → **rate**: **[+of]** *Why did the incidence of heroin use continue to climb?* | **high/low etc incidence** *Smokers had the highest incidence of colds.*

in·ci·dent /ˈɪnsɪdənt/ ●●○ W3 AWL *n* [C]

1 an event, especially one that is unusual, important, or violent: *Am I at risk because of some incident in my sexual past?* | *Roads were sealed off because of a major incident.* | **without incident** *The plane landed without incident.*

THESAURUS ▸ **EVENT**

REGISTER

Incident is used mainly in journalism or in formal contexts. In everyday English, people usually say **something happened** rather than talking about **an incident**: *Am I at risk because of* ***something that happened*** *in my past?*

2 a serious disagreement between two countries: *You could have caused a major* ***diplomatic incident***.

COLLOCATIONS

ADJECTIVES

a serious incident *The road is closed following a serious incident earlier today.*
a major incident (=very serious) *The most recent major incident was an explosion at an oil refinery.*
a small/minor incident *An apparently minor incident sparked off rioting.*
the whole incident *The whole incident was caught on CCTV.*
a separate incident *Young men were killed in two separate incidents on the same day.*
a related incident (=connected to another incident) *The report describes a number of related incidents.*
an isolated incident (=one that happens on its own, not together with others) *Luckily the attack turned out to be an isolated incident.*
the latest incident (=the most recent one) | **a dramatic incident** (=unexpected and exciting) | **a violent incident** | **a tragic incident** (=one that involves someone's death) | **an unfortunate incident** (=involving an accident or argument) | **an embarrassing incident** | **a strange/unusual incident** | **a shooting/stabbing incident** (=when someone is shot or stabbed)

VERBS

an incident happens *The incident happened as Mrs Edwards was walking her dog.*
an incident occurs *formal*: *The tragic incident occurred just after midnight.*
cause an incident *His carelessness caused a major incident.*
provoke/spark off an incident (=cause it to happen suddenly) *It is claimed that the police provoked the incident.*
be involved in an incident *All those involved in the incident were sacked.*
deal with/handle an incident | **describe an incident**

in·ci·den·tal[1] /ˌɪnsəˈdentl◂/ *adj* **1** happening or existing in connection with something else that is more important: *Increased motivation is more than an* ***incidental benefit*** *of reward schemes.* | **[+to]** *companies that carry out investment business that is incidental to their main activity* **2** [not before noun] naturally happening as a result of something: **[+to]** *Drinking too much is almost incidental to bartending.*

incidental[2] *n* [C usually plural] something that you have to do, buy etc which you had not planned to: *Carry extra cash for taxis, tips, and other incidentals.*

in·ci·den·tal·ly /ˌɪnsəˈdentəli/ ●○○ AWL *adv*
1 [sentence adverb] used to add more information to what you have just said, or to introduce a new subject that you have just thought of SYN **by the way**: *Incidentally, where were you born?* | *The wine, incidentally, goes very well with a mature cheese.*
2 in a way that was not planned, but as a result of something else: *Quite incidentally, I got some useful information at the party.*

ˌincidental ˈmusic *n* [U] music played during a play, film etc that helps produce a particular feeling

ˈincident ˌroom *n* [C] *BrE* a room in a police station or other place, where police work on solving a particular serious crime

in·cin·e·rate /ɪnˈsɪnəreɪt/ *v* [T] *formal* to burn something completely in order to destroy it: *All the infected clothing was incinerated.* —**incineration** /ɪnˌsɪnəˈreɪʃən/ *n* [U]: *an incineration plant*

in·cin·e·ra·tor /ɪnˈsɪnəreɪtə $ -ər/ *n* [C] a machine designed to burn things in order to destroy them

in·cip·i·ent /ɪnˈsɪpiənt/ *adj* [only before noun] *formal* starting to happen or exist: *a sign of incipient madness*

in·cise /ɪnˈsaɪz/ *v* [T always + prep] *formal* to cut a pattern, word etc into something, using a sharp instrument: *an inscription incised in stone*

in·ci·sion /ɪnˈsɪʒən/ *n* [C] a neat cut made into something, especially during a medical operation

in·ci·sive /ɪnˈsaɪsɪv/ *adj* showing intelligence and a clear understanding of something: **incisive remarks/criticism etc** *Her questions were well-formulated and incisive.* —**incisively** *adv* —**incisiveness** *n* [U]

in·ci·sor /ɪnˈsaɪzə $ -ər/ *n* [C] one of the eight flat teeth at the front of your mouth → CANINE[2](1), MOLAR

in·cite /ɪnˈsaɪt/ *v* [T] to deliberately encourage people to fight, argue etc → **encourage**: *They were charged with inciting racial hatred.* | **incite sb to do sth** *a person who incites others to commit an offence* | **incite sb to sth** *There was no evidence that he had incited members of the group to violence.* —**incitement** *n* [C,U]: *incitement to murder*

in·ci·vil·i·ty /ˌɪnsəˈvɪləti/ *n* (*plural* **incivilities**) [C,U] *formal* impolite behaviour, remarks etc

in·clem·ent /ɪnˈklemənt/ *adj formal* inclement weather is unpleasantly cold, wet etc

in·cli·na·tion /ˌɪŋkləˈneɪʃən/ ●○○ AWL *n*
1 [C,U] a feeling that makes you want to do something: *My* ***natural inclination*** *was to say no.* | **inclination to do sth** *Neither of my children* ***showed*** *the slightest* ***inclination*** *to follow me into journalism.* | *Teachers simply do not have* ***the time or the inclination*** *to investigate these matters.*
2 [C,U] a tendency to think or behave in a particular way: **inclination to do sth** *an inclination to see everything in political terms* | **[+to/towards]** *She's troubled by her son's inclination toward atheism.* | **by inclination** *Bart was a romantic by inclination.*
3 [C] a movement made down towards the ground: *She greeted Maggie with an inclination of the head.*
4 [C,U] *formal* a slope, or the angle at which something slopes

in·cline[1] /ɪnˈklaɪn/ AWL *v* **1** [T] *formal* if a situation, fact etc inclines you to do or think something, it influences you towards a particular action or opinion: **incline sb to do sth** *The accident inclined him to reconsider his career.* **2** [I] *formal* to think that a particular belief or opinion is most likely to be correct: **incline to do sth** *I incline to accept the official version of events.* | **[+to/towards]** *I incline to the opinion that this principle extends to cases of religious discrimination.* **3** [I,T] to slope at a particular angle, or to make something do this: *The telescope is inclined at an angle of 43 degrees.* **4 incline your head** to bend your neck so that your head is lowered

in·cline[2] /ˈɪnklaɪn/ AWL *n* [C] a slope: *a steep incline*

in·clined /ɪnˈklaɪnd/ ●○○ *adj*
1 be inclined to agree/think/believe etc to hold a particular opinion, but not very strongly: *Arthur has some strange ideas, but on this occasion I'm inclined to agree with him.*
2 be inclined to do sth/inclined to sth to be likely to do something or behave in a particular way: *Commandos are inclined to shoot first and ask questions later.* | *He was inclined to self-pity.*
3 be/feel inclined (to do sth) to want to do something, but without having a strong desire: *It was Sunday morning, and she was not inclined to get up yet.* | *You can visit our chat rooms, if you* ***feel so inclined***.
4 artistically/musically/mathematically etc inclined naturally interested in or good at art, music etc: *For the artistically inclined, the markets are full of interest.*
5 sloping or leaning in a particular direction

in·close /ɪnˈkləʊz $ -ˈkloʊz/ *v* [T] another spelling of ENCLOSE

in·clos·ure /ɪnˈkləʊʒə $ -ˈkloʊʒər/ *n* [C,U] another spelling of ENCLOSURE

in·clude /ɪnˈkluːd/ ●●● S1 W1 *v* [T]
1 if one thing includes another, the second thing is part of the first: *Does the price include postage?* | *His job includes looking after under-21 teams.* | *The curriculum includes courses in computing.*
2 to make someone or something part of a larger group or set OPP **exclude**: *The team is stronger now they've included*

Roscoe. | **include sth in/on sth** *Service is included in the bill.* | *Would you include a mobile phone on your list of essentials?*

GRAMMAR

Prepositions with include

• You **include** someone or something **in** a group, total, statement etc: *Insurance is included in the price.* ✗ Don't say: *Insurance is included on the price.*
• You **include** something or someone **on** a list: *His name was included on the team sheet.*

Using the progressive

• **Include** is not used in the progressive. You say: *The book includes a chapter on Europe.* ✗ Don't say: *The book is including a chapter on Europe.*
• However, the present participle **including** is very commonly used as a preposition: *It costs $150 including tax.*

GRAMMAR GUIDE ▸ **VERBS**

in·clud·ed /ɪnˈkluːdɪd/ *adj* [only after noun] including someone or something: *Everyone has to go to the dentist, you included.*

in·clud·ing /ɪnˈkluːdɪŋ/ ●●● S2 W1 *prep* used to introduce something or someone that is part of a larger group or amount you have just mentioned OPP **excluding**: *The price is £25.50, including postage and packing.* | *You'll need a variety of skills, including leadership and negotiating.*

REGISTER
In written or business English, people often prefer to use **excluding** rather than **not including**, as it sounds more formal: *The cost is $49.95* ***excluding*** *tax.*

in·clu·sion /ɪnˈkluːʒən/ ●○○ *n*
1 [U] the act of including someone or something in a larger group or set, or the fact of being included in one: **[+in]** *His inclusion in the team has caused controversy.* | *photos chosen* ***for inclusion in*** *the magazine* | **[+of]** *the inclusion of early recordings on the CD*
2 [C] someone or something that has been included in a larger group: *With the recent inclusions, there will be 28 delegates in all.*

in·clu·sive /ɪnˈkluːsɪv/ ●○○ *adj*
1 an inclusive price or cost includes everything OPP **exclusive**: **all-inclusive/fully inclusive** *The fully inclusive fare for the trip is £22.* | **[+of]** *The rent is £120 a week, inclusive of heating.*
2 including a wide variety of people, things etc OPP **exclusive**: *Not everyone shares his vision of an inclusive America.*
3 (from) April to June inclusive/15 to 20 inclusive etc used to refer to a range of months, numbers etc, including the ones that start and end the range

REGISTER
In everyday American English, people usually use **through** rather than **inclusive**: *They are open Monday* ***through*** *Friday.*

in·cog·ni·to /ˌɪnkɒɡˈniːtəʊ $ ˌɪnkɑːɡˈniːtoʊ/ *adv* if a famous person does something incognito, they do it without letting people know who they are → **disguise**: *That night, Lenin travelled incognito to the party headquarters.*

in·co·her·ent /ˌɪnkəʊˈhɪərənt◂ $ -koʊˈhɪr-/ AWL *adj* **1** not expressed or organized clearly, and therefore difficult to understand: *an incoherent over-long action movie* | *He called the policy 'incoherent and ill thought-out'.* **2** speaking in a way that cannot be understood, because you are drunk, feeling a strong emotion etc: *Ben, drunk and incoherent, slumped in a chair.* —**incoherently** *adv*: *She began to mutter incoherently.* —**incoherence** *n* [U]

in·come /ˈɪŋkʌm, ˈɪn-/ ●●● S2 W1 *n* [C,U] the money that you earn from your work or that you receive from INVESTMENTS, the government etc → **salary**: **on an income** *People on higher incomes should pay more tax.* | **[+from]** *income from savings and pensions* | ***low-income*** *families*
THESAURUS ▸ SALARY → **PRIVATE INCOME**, **unearned income** at UNEARNED

COLLOCATIONS

VERBS

have an income (*also* **receive an income** *formal*) *We have an income of over $100,000 a year.*
provide an income *The properties he rented out provided him with an income.*
generate an income (=provide one) *He decided to invest the money to generate an income for the future.*
increase your income *She took on extra work to increase her income.*
supplement/add to your income (=increase your income, for example by doing an extra job) *Ted supplemented his income by doing part-time work in the evenings.*
sb's income rises/increases/goes up *They saw their income rise considerably over the next few years.*
sb's income falls/goes down

ADJECTIVES/NOUN + income

a high/large income *He has a relatively high income.*
a low/small income *Rent takes a large chunk of their small income.*
sb's annual income *Brian's annual income is around £43,000.*
the average income *The report compares average incomes across different European countries.*
the national income (=the income of a country) *A large proportion of the national income comes from food exports.*
family/household income *She works in a shop to supplement the family income.*
disposable income (=your income after tax and necessary bills have been paid) *People spend a high proportion of their disposable income running a car.*
gross income (=income before you have paid tax) | **net income** (=income after you have paid tax) | **taxable income** (=the part of your income on which you pay tax) | **a joint income** (=that two or more people have) | **sb's personal income**

income + NOUN

an income level/group *The tax rate rises with the individual's income level.*
an income bracket (=income level) *In general, people in higher income brackets live longer.*
income tax (=tax that you pay on your income) | **incomes policy** *BrE* (=government controls on wages)

PHRASES

a source of income *His pension was his only source of income.*
loss of income *You can buy insurance to protect you against loss of income if you are ill.*

in·com·er /ˈɪnkʌmə $ -ər/ *n* [C] *BrE* someone who comes to live in a place: *We've lived here for 17 years, but they still see us as incomers.*

ˈincome supˌport *n* [U] money that is given by the government in Britain to people who have no income or a very low income → **welfare**

ˈincome tax *n* [U] tax paid on the money that you earn

in·com·ing /ˈɪnkʌmɪŋ/ *adj* [only before noun] **1** arriving at or coming to a place OPP **outgoing**: *incoming flights* | *Incoming calls were monitored.* | *the incoming tide* **2** an incoming president, government etc has just been elected or chosen OPP **outgoing**: *the incoming administration*

in·com·mu·ni·ca·do /ˌɪnkəmjuːnɪˈkɑːdəʊ $ -doʊ/ *adv, adj* if you are incommunicado, you are in a place where other people cannot speak to you: *He is reportedly being* ***held incommunicado*** *at a military prison.*

in·com·pa·ra·ble /ɪnˈkɒmpərəbəl $ -ˈkɑːm-/ *adj* extremely good, beautiful etc, and much better than

I

others: *an incomparable view of San Marco | a wine of incomparable flavour* —**incomparably** *adv*

in·com·pat·i·ble /ˌɪnkəmˈpætəbəl◂/ ●○○ AWL *adj* **1** two people who are incompatible have such different characters, beliefs etc that they cannot have a friendly relationship OPP **compatible**: *I don't know why they ever got married. They're totally incompatible.* **2** two things that are incompatible cannot exist or be accepted together: **[+with]** *Business interests are incompatible with public office.* | *Politeness and truth are often* ***mutually incompatible***. **3** two things that are incompatible are of different types and so cannot be used together OPP **compatible**: **[+with]** *The laser printer is incompatible with the new computer.* | *incompatible blood groups* —**incompatibility** /ˌɪnkəmpætəˈbɪləti/ *n* [U]: *sexual incompatibility*

in·com·pe·tence /ɪnˈkɒmpətəns $ -ˈkɑːm-/ *n* [U] lack of the ability or skill to do a job properly OPP **competence**: **managerial/professional etc incompetence** *allegations of professional incompetence | The report blamed police incompetence for the tragedy.*

in·com·pe·tent /ɪnˈkɒmpɪtənt $ -ˈkɑːm-/ *adj* not having the ability or skill to do a job properly OPP **competent**: *an incompetent manager | weak incompetent leadership* —**incompetent** *n* [C] —**incompetently** *adv*

in·com·plete¹ /ˌɪnkəmˈpliːt◂/ ●○○ *adj* not having everything that should be there, or not completely finished OPP **complete**: *Unfortunately, I do not have the information because our records are incomplete. | an incomplete process | TV ads implied that a woman was* ***incomplete without*** *a man.* —**incompletely** *adv* —**incompleteness** *n* [U]

incomplete² *n* [C] *AmE* a GRADE given to school or college students when they have not completed all the work for a course

in·com·pre·hen·si·ble /ɪnˌkɒmprɪˈhensəbəl $ -ˌkɑːm-/ ●○○ *adj* difficult or impossible to understand: *legal documents full of incomprehensible jargon | I find your attitude quite incomprehensible.* | **[+to]** *His accent made his speech incomprehensible to me.* —**incomprehensibly** *adv* —**incomprehensibility** /ɪnˌkɒmprɪhensəˈbɪləti $ -ˌkɑːm-/ *n* [U]

in·com·pre·hen·sion /ɪnˌkɒmprɪˈhenʃən $ -ˌkɑːm-/ *n* [U] the state of not being able to understand something: *He spread his hands in a gesture of incomprehension.*

in·con·ceiv·a·ble /ˌɪnkənˈsiːvəbəl/ AWL *adj* too strange or unusual to be thought real or possible: *A few years ago a car fuelled by solar energy would have been inconceivable.* | ***It is inconceivable that*** *a man in such a powerful position could act so unwisely.* **THESAURUS** ▸ IMPOSSIBLE —**inconceivably** *adv*

in·con·clu·sive /ˌɪnkənˈkluːsɪv◂/ AWL *adj* not leading to a clear decision or result OPP **conclusive**: *The evidence against the two men was inconclusive. | A coalition government was formed after inconclusive elections.* —**inconclusively** *adv* —**inconclusiveness** *n* [U]

in·con·gru·i·ty /ˌɪnkənˈgruːəti/ *n* (*plural* **incongruities**) [C,U] the fact that something is strange, unusual, or unsuitable in a particular situation: *The incongruity of her situation struck Gina with unpleasant force.* | **[+between]** *He didn't see the slightest incongruity between the idealism of his plays and his own morals.*

in·con·gru·ous /ɪnˈkɒŋgruəs $ -ˈkɑːŋ-/ *adj* strange, unexpected, or unsuitable in a particular situation: *The new theatre looks utterly incongruous in its setting.* —**incongruously** *adv*

in·con·se·quen·tial /ɪnˌkɒnsəˈkwenʃəl◂ $ -ˌkɑːn-/ *adj* not important SYN **insignificant**: *inconsequential but amusing chatter* —**inconsequentially** *adv*

in·con·sid·er·a·ble /ˌɪnkənˈsɪdərəbəl◂/ *adj* **not inconsiderable** *formal* used to emphasize that something is large or important SYN **considerable**: *He has built up a not inconsiderable business empire.*

in·con·sid·er·ate /ˌɪnkənˈsɪdərət◂/ ●○○ *adj* not caring about the feelings, needs, or comfort of other people SYN **thoughtless** OPP **considerate**: *inconsiderate motorists* | **it was inconsiderate (of sb) to do sth** *It was very inconsiderate of you to keep us waiting.* **THESAURUS** ▸ UNKIND —**inconsiderately** *adv*

in·con·sis·ten·cy /ˌɪnkənˈsɪstənsi/ AWL *n* (*plural* **inconsistencies**) **1** [U] when someone keeps changing their behaviour, reactions etc so that other people become confused OPP **consistency 2** [C,U] a situation in which two statements are different and cannot both be true SYN **contradiction**: *There were several* ***glaring inconsistencies*** (=very noticeable differences) *in his report.* | **[+between]** *Defence counsel looks for inconsistency between witness statements.*

in·con·sis·tent /ˌɪnkənˈsɪstənt◂/ ●○○ AWL *adj* **1** two statements that are inconsistent cannot both be true SYN **contradictory** OPP **consistent**: *The accounts of the witnesses are inconsistent.* | **[+with]** *His results are inconsistent with our data.* **2** not right according to a particular set of principles or standards OPP **consistent**: **[+with]** *His conduct was inconsistent with what is expected of a congressman.* **3** inconsistent behaviour, work etc changes too often from good to bad OPP **consistent**: *The team's performance has been highly inconsistent this season.*

in·con·so·la·ble /ˌɪnkənˈsəʊləbəl◂ $ -ˈsoʊ-/ *adj* so sad that it is impossible for anyone to comfort you: *The boy was inconsolable after the death of his dog.* —**inconsolably** *adv*: *She wept inconsolably.*

in·con·spic·u·ous /ˌɪnkənˈspɪkjuəs◂/ *adj* not easily seen or noticed OPP **conspicuous**: *an inconspicuous little restaurant | She stood by the wall, trying to* ***look inconspicuous***. —**inconspicuously** *adv*

in·con·stant /ɪnˈkɒnstənt $ -ˈkɑːn-/ *adj literary* unfaithful in love or friendship —**inconstancy** *n* [U]

in·con·test·a·ble /ˌɪnkənˈtestəbəl◂/ *adj* clearly true and impossible to disagree with SYN **indisputable**: *We had incontestable proof of her innocence.*

in·con·ti·nent /ɪnˈkɒntɪnənt $ -ˈkɑːn-/ *adj* unable to control the passing of liquid or solid waste from your body —**incontinence** *n* [U]

in·con·tro·ver·ti·ble /ɪnˌkɒntrəˈvɜːtəbəl $ ɪnˌkɑːntrəˈvɜːr-/ *adj* definitely true and impossible to be proved false SYN **indisputable**: *CCTV provided incontrovertible evidence that he was at the scene of the crime.* —**incontrovertibly** *adv*

in·con·ve·ni·ence¹ /ˌɪnkənˈviːniəns/ *n* **1** [U] problems caused by something which annoy or affect you: *We apologise for the delay and any inconvenience caused.* | **the inconvenience of (doing) sth** *the inconvenience of having to find another buyer* **2** [C] someone or something that causes problems for you: *a minor inconvenience* | **[+to]** *His early arrival was clearly an inconvenience to his host.*

inconvenience² *v* [T] to cause problems for someone: *I don't want to inconvenience you any further.*

in·con·ve·ni·ent /ˌɪnkənˈviːniənt◂/ ●○○ *adj* causing problems, often in a way that is annoying OPP **convenient**: *Monday's a bit inconvenient for me. How about Wednesday? | Am I calling at an inconvenient time?* —**inconveniently** *adv*

in·cor·po·rate /ɪnˈkɔːpəreɪt $ -ɔːr-/ ●○○ AWL *v* [T] to include something as part of a group, system, plan etc: **incorporate sth into/in sth** *We've incorporated many environmentally friendly features into the design of the building. | Our original proposals were not incorporated in the new legislation.* —**incorporation** /ɪnˌkɔːpəˈreɪʃən $ -ɔːr-/ *n* [U]: *the incorporation of the college into the university*

In·cor·po·rat·ed /ɪnˈkɔːpəreɪtɪd $ -ɔːr-/ AWL *adj* (*written abbreviation* **Inc.**) used after the name of a company in the US to show that it has become a CORPORATION → **limited**

in·cor·po·re·al /ˌɪnkɔːˈpɔːriəl $ -kɔːr-/ *adj formal* not existing in any physical form: *Plato demonstrated the incorporeal nature of the soul.*

I

in·cor·rect /ˌɪnkəˈrekt◂/ ●●○ *adj*
1 not correct or true: *The information you gave us was incorrect.* THESAURUS ▸ WRONG
2 not following the rules of polite or fair behaviour SYN **impolite**: *It would be incorrect of me to comment.* —**incorrectly** *adv*: *Sorry, you answered incorrectly.*

in·cor·ri·gi·ble /ɪnˈkɒrədʒəbəl $ -ˈkɔː-/ *adj* someone who is incorrigible is bad in a way that cannot be changed or improved – often used humorously: **an incorrigible liar/rogue etc** | *Peter, you are an incorrigible flirt!* —**incorrigibly** *adv*

in·cor·rup·ti·ble /ˌɪnkəˈrʌptəbəl◂/ *adj* **1** someone who is incorruptible cannot be persuaded to do wrong or illegal things: *A good judge must be incorruptible.* **2** *formal* material that is incorruptible will never decay and cannot be destroyed —**incorruptibility** /ˌɪnkərʌptəˈbɪləti/ *n* [U]

in·crease¹ /ɪnˈkriːs/ ●●● S2 W1 *v* [I,T] if you increase something, or if it increases, it becomes bigger in amount, number, or degree OPP **decrease, reduce**: *The population* ***increased dramatically*** *in the first half of the century.* | *political tensions that might increase the likelihood of war* | *Visits to the site have increased threefold since May.* | **increase in value/price/importance etc** *Investments are certain to increase in value.* | **increase (sth) by sth** *Food prices increased by 10% in less than a year.* | **increase (sth) from/to sth** *The salary is £18,600 a year, increasing to £23,000.* —**increasing** *adj*: *the increasing difficulty of finding trained staff* | *European leaders watched events unfold with increasing alarm.* —**increased** *adj*: *an increased incidence of childhood leukaemia*

GRAMMAR

Increase belongs to a group of verbs where the same noun can be the subject of the verb or its object.
- You can say: *They increased the price of gas.* In this sentence, 'the price of gas' is the object of **increase**.
- You can say: *The price of gas increased.* In this sentence, 'the price of gas' is the subject of **increase**.

GRAMMAR GUIDE ▸ VERBS

THESAURUS

TO INCREASE

increase to become larger in number, amount, or degree: *Sales increased by 25%.* | *The level of violence has increased.*
go up to increase. **Go up** is less formal than **increase**, and is the usual verb to use in everyday English: *The price of coffee has gone up.*
rise to increase. **Rise** sounds a little formal and is often used when talking about the level of something increasing: *The demand for oil has been rising steadily.* | *Living standards have risen dramatically.*
grow to increase, especially gradually over a period of time – used about numbers or amounts: *Since 1990, US imports of foreign goods have grown at a rate of 7.7% per year.*
escalate to increase to a high level – used about things that you do not want to increase such as costs, crimes, or violence: *Fuel prices are escalating.* | *The fighting has escalated.*
double/triple to become twice as much or three times as much: *Since 1950, the number of people dying from cancer has almost doubled.*
expand to become larger in size, or to include a wider range of activities: *The business has expanded at a rate of 15% per year.* | *We are hoping to expand into mobile phone services.*
soar to increase and reach a very high level – used about numbers and amounts, or about feelings: *The temperature soared to 36.6 degrees Centigrade.* | *His confidence soared.*
shoot up to increase very quickly and suddenly – used about prices, numbers, or temperatures: *Share prices shot up 30% over the last week.*

TO MAKE SOMETHING INCREASE

increase to make something larger in number, amount, or degree: *Being overweight increases the risk of having a heart attack.* | *We need to increase the number of police officers on the streets.*
put sth up to increase prices, taxes etc. **Put sth up** is less formal than **increase**, and is the usual verb to use in everyday English: *The landlord has put the rent up again.* | *They're always putting up gas prices.*
raise to increase something such as prices or taxes, or levels or standards: *The bank has raised interest rates for the third time this year.* | *The school aims to raise students' levels of achievement.*
double/triple to increase the amount of something so that it is twice or three times as large: *The airline plans to double the number of passengers it carries by 2015.* | *High blood pressure triples the risk of strokes.*
boost to increase sales, profits, production etc, especially when they have been lower than you want them to be: *Growing affluence has boosted sales.* | *Oil exports boosted the economy.*
expand to increase something so that it contains a wider range of things, or to increase the size of a business: *The company plans to expand its retail operations.* | *Supermarkets have expanded their ranges to include non-food items.*
extend to increase something such as your power or influence, or the number of things you are involved in: *We are hoping to extend the range of services that we offer.* | *The company plans to extend its dominance of the world car market.*
step up sth to increase your efforts or activities, especially to change a situation: *Security has been stepped up following the bombing.*
heighten to increase a feeling or effect: *The attack has heightened concerns about racism in schools.*
maximize to increase something as much as possible: *Businesses try to maximize efficiency and cut costs.*

in·crease² /ˈɪnkriːs/ ●●● S2 W1 *n* [C,U] a rise in amount, number, or degree OPP **decrease**: **[+in]** *an increase in the crime rate* | *Recent* ***tax increases*** *have affected the poor more than the rich.* | *the* ***dramatic increase*** *in the population aged over 65* | *There has been a* ***marked increase*** *in the use of firearms.* | *Cases of tuberculosis are* ***on the increase***.

in·creas·ing·ly /ɪnˈkriːsɪŋli/ ●●○ W2 *adv* more and more all the time: *Marketing techniques are becoming increasingly sophisticated.* | *Increasingly, young people distrust all forms of government.*

in·cred·i·ble /ɪnˈkredəbəl/ ●●○ S3 *adj*
1 extremely good, large, or great SYN **unbelievable**: *The view is just incredible.* | *There was blood everywhere and the pain was incredible.* THESAURUS ▸ GOOD
2 too strange to be believed, or very difficult to believe SYN **unbelievable**: ***It's incredible that*** *he survived the fall.* | ***It's incredible how much*** *Tom has changed since he met Sally.* | *I* ***find it*** *almost* ***incredible that*** *no one noticed these errors.*

in·cred·i·bly /ɪnˈkredəbli/ ●●○ S3 *adv*
1 [+adj/adv] *informal* extremely: *Nicotine is incredibly addictive.*
2 [sentence adverb] in a way that is hard to believe: *The knife had pierced his heart, but incredibly he was still alive.*

in·cre·du·li·ty /ˌɪnkrəˈdjuːləti $ -ˈduː-/ *n* [U] a feeling that you cannot believe something SYN **disbelief**: *When she told her family she was gay, they reacted with a mixture of shock and incredulity.*

in·cred·u·lous /ɪnˈkredjələs $ -dʒə-/ *adj* unable or unwilling to believe something: *'You sold the car?' she asked, incredulous.* | **incredulous look/expression/voice etc** *She shot him an incredulous look.* —**incredulously** *adv*

in·cre·ment /ˈɪŋkrəmənt/ *n* [C] **1** a regular increase in the amount of money someone is paid: *a salary of*

£18,000, with ***annual increments*** *of 2.5%* **2** *formal* the amount by which a number, value, or amount increases

in·cre·men·tal /ˌɪŋkrəˈmentl◂/ *adj formal* **1** [usually before noun] increasing in amount or value gradually and by a regular amount: *incremental pay scales* **2** happening gradually over time: *Mr Kennedy said that progress on reforms would be incremental.* | *a process of incremental change* —**incrementally** *adv*: *You need to make changes in your diet incrementally.*

ˌincremental ˈbackup *n* [U] a system of making copies of computer FILES and keeping them safe in case the computer becomes damaged. Only new documents or documents that have changed are copied, because this is quicker than copying all the files every time.

in·crim·i·nate /ɪnˈkrɪməneɪt/ *v* [T] to make someone seem guilty of a crime: **incriminate yourself** *He refused to answer questions for fear he might incriminate himself.* —**incriminating** *adj*: *incriminating evidence* —**incrimination** /ɪnˌkrɪməˈneɪʃən/ *n* [U]

ˈin-crowd *n* **the in-crowd** a small group of people in an organization who are fashionable, popular, or powerful, but who do not let many other people join them: *I was never one of the in-crowd at school.*

in·cu·bate /ˈɪŋkjəbeɪt/ *v* [I,T] **1** if a bird incubates its eggs, or if the eggs incubate, they are kept warm until they HATCH (=the birds inside are born) **2** *medical* if a disease incubates, or if you incubate it, it develops in your body until you show physical signs of it —**incubation** /ˌɪŋkjəˈbeɪʃən/ *n* [U]: *Hepatitis has a long incubation period.*

in·cu·ba·tor /ˈɪŋkjəbeɪtə $ -ər/ *n* [C] **1** a piece of hospital equipment into which very small or weak babies are put to keep them alive and warm **2** a heated container for keeping eggs warm until they HATCH (=the young birds are born) **3** an organization which helps new businesses to develop by giving them office space, services, and equipment, and providing them with business and technical advice: *a high-tech incubator on the east coast*

in·cu·bus /ˈɪŋkjəbəs/ *n* (*plural* **incubuses** *or* **incubi** /-baɪ/) [C] **1** someone or something that causes a lot of worries or problems: *Joyce regarded his US citizenship as a moral and political incubus.* **2** a male DEVIL that in the past was believed to have sex with a sleeping woman → **SUCCUBUS**

in·cul·cate /ˈɪŋkʌlkeɪt $ ɪnˈkʌl-/ *v* [T] *formal* to fix ideas, principles etc in someone's mind: **inculcate sth in/into sb** *I try to inculcate a sense of responsibility in my children.* | *Not all schools manage to successfully inculcate a love of learning.* —**inculcation** /ˌɪŋkʌlˈkeɪʃən/ *n* [U]

in·cum·ben·cy /ɪnˈkʌmbənsi/ *n* (*plural* **incumbencies**) [C usually singular, U] *formal* the state of holding an official position, especially in politics, or the time when someone holds an official position

in·cum·bent[1] /ɪnˈkʌmbənt/ *n* [C] *formal* someone who has been elected to an official position, especially in politics, and who is doing that job at the present time: *In the June elections, Morris easily defeated the incumbent, Tom Smith.*

incumbent[2] *adj formal* **1 it is incumbent upon/on sb to do sth** if it is incumbent upon you to do something, it is your duty or responsibility to do it: *It is incumbent upon parents to control what their children watch on TV.* **2 the incumbent president/priest/government etc** the president etc at the present time

in·cur /ɪnˈkɜː $ -ˈkɜːr/ ●○○ *v* (**incurred**, **incurring**) [T] *formal*

1 if you incur a cost, debt, or a fine, you have to pay money because of something you have done: **incur expenses/costs/losses/debts etc** *If the council loses the appeal, it will incur all the legal costs.* | *the heavy losses incurred by airlines since September 11th*

2 if you incur something unpleasant, it happens to you because of something you have done: **incur sb's displeasure/wrath/disapproval etc** *She wondered what she'd done to incur his displeasure this time.*

in·cur·a·ble /ɪnˈkjʊərəbəl $ -ˈkjʊr-/ *adj* **1** impossible to cure OPP **curable**: **incurable disease/illness/condition** *She has a rare, incurable disease.* **2** impossible to change: *an incurable optimist* —**incurably** *adv*: *incurably romantic*

in·cur·sion /ɪnˈkɜːʃən, -ʒən $ ɪnˈkɜːrʒən/ *n* [C] *formal* **1** a sudden attack into an area that belongs to other people: **[+into]** *a combined British and French incursion into China in 1857* **2** the sudden arrival of something or someone into a place or activity where they do not belong or have not been before, used especially to say that they are not welcome: **[+into]** *The media was criticized for its thoughtless incursion into the domestic grief of the family.* | *the Japanese incursion into the U.S. domestic electronics market*

in·debt·ed /ɪnˈdetɪd/ *adj* **1 be (deeply/greatly) indebted to sb** to be very grateful to someone for the help they have given you: *We are deeply indebted to Dr Allen.* **2** owing money to someone: *the 17 most* ***heavily indebted*** *nations* —**indebtedness** *n* [U]

in·de·cen·cy /ɪnˈdiːsənsi/ *n* (*plural* **indecencies**) **1** [U] *law* behaviour that is sexually offensive, especially INDECENT EXPOSURE **2** [C] *formal* an action that is shocking or offensive

in·de·cent /ɪnˈdiːsənt/ *adj* **1** something that is indecent is shocking and offensive, usually because it involves sex or shows parts of the body that are usually covered: *He was found guilty of possessing indecent photographs.* | *You can't go out in that dress – it's positively indecent!* **2** completely unacceptable: *The funeral formalities were performed with almost* ***indecent haste***. —**indecently** *adv*: *an indecently short skirt*

inˌdecent asˈsault *n* [C,U] *law* the crime of making a sexual attack on someone, touching or threatening to touch them, but not RAPING them (=forcing them to have sex)

inˌdecent exˈposure *n* [U] *law* the criminal offence of deliberately showing your sex organs in a place where this is likely to offend people

in·de·ci·pher·a·ble /ˌɪndɪˈsaɪfərəbəl◂/ *adj* impossible to read or understand SYN **illegible**: *an indecipherable signature*

in·de·ci·sion /ˌɪndɪˈsɪʒən/ *n* [U] the state of being unable to decide what to do: *There were weeks of indecision about who would go and when.*

in·de·ci·sive /ˌɪndɪˈsaɪsɪv◂/ ●○○ *adj*

1 unable to make clear decisions or choices OPP **decisive**: *a weak and indecisive leader*

2 not having a clear result SYN **inconclusive**: *a confused, indecisive battle* —**indecisively** *adv* —**indecisiveness** *n* [U]

in·deed /ɪnˈdiːd/ ●●● S1 W1 *adv*

1 [sentence adverb] used to emphasize a statement or answer: *The blood tests prove that Vince is indeed the father.* | *'Would it help if you had an assistant?' 'It would indeed.'*

2 [sentence adverb] *formal* used to introduce an additional statement that emphasizes or supports what you have just said: *I didn't mind at all. Indeed, I was pleased.*

3 *especially BrE* used with 'very' and an adjective or adverb to emphasize a statement or description: *Most of the essays were very good indeed.* | *Thank you very much indeed.*

4 *BrE spoken* used to show that you are surprised or annoyed by something that someone has just told you: *'He said he was too busy to see you.' 'Did he, indeed?'*

5 why/how/who etc indeed? *spoken* used when someone has asked you a question, to show that you do not know the answer and you do not think there can be a satisfactory answer: *'Why would John have left without saying a word?' 'Why indeed?'*

in·de·fat·i·ga·ble /ˌɪndɪˈfætɪgəbəl/ *adj formal* determined and never giving up SYN **tireless**: *an indefatigable campaigner for human rights* —**indefatigably** *adv*

in·de·fen·si·ble /ˌɪndɪˈfensəbəl◂/ *adj* **1** too bad to be excused or defended: *The law is morally indefensible and in* need of reform. **2** impossible or very difficult to defend from military attack —**indefensibly** *adv*

in·de·fi·na·ble /ˌɪndɪˈfaɪnəbəl◂/ *adj* an indefinable feeling, quality etc is difficult to describe or explain: *She felt an indefinable sadness.* —**indefinably** *adv*

in·def·i·nite /ɪnˈdefənət/ ●○○ (AWL) *adj*
1 an indefinite action or period of time has no definite end arranged for it: *The next day the union voted to begin an indefinite strike.* | *The picture has been loaned for an indefinite period to the National Gallery.*
2 not clear or exact (SYN) **vague**: *Teachers find the report's terminology so indefinite that it is confusing.*

inˌdefinite ˈarticle *n* [C] *technical* the word 'a' or 'an' → **definite article**

in·def·i·nit·ely /ɪnˈdefənətli/ ●○○ (AWL) *adv*
1 for a period of time for which no definite end has been arranged: *The project has been postponed indefinitely.*
2 without giving clear or exact details

inˌdefinite ˈpronoun *n* [C] *technical* a word such as 'some', 'any', or 'either' that is used instead of a noun, but does not say exactly which person or thing is meant

in·del·i·ble /ɪnˈdeləbəl/ *adj* **1** impossible to remove or forget (SYN) **permanent**: *Her words left an indelible impression on me for years to come.* **2 indelible ink/pencil/marker etc** ink etc that makes a permanent mark which cannot be removed —**indelibly** *adv*: *a moment indelibly imprinted on my mind*

in·del·i·cate /ɪnˈdelɪkət/ *adj formal* likely to embarrass or shock people (SYN) **rude**: *an indelicate comment* —**indelicacy** *n* [U]

in·dem·ni·fy /ɪnˈdemnɪfaɪ/ *v* (**indemnified**, **indemnifying**, **indemnifies**) [T] *law* **1** [+against/for] to promise to pay someone if something they own is damaged or lost **2** [+for] to pay someone money because of loss, injury, or damage that they have suffered —**indemnification** /ɪnˌdemnɪfɪˈkeɪʃən/ *n* [C,U]

in·dem·ni·ty /ɪnˈdemnəti/ *n* (*plural* **indemnities**) *law*
1 [U] protection against loss or damage, especially in the form of a promise to pay for any losses or damage: *insurance providing indemnity against future liabilities*
2 [C] a payment for the loss of money, goods etc → **compensation**

in·dent¹ /ɪnˈdent/ *v* [T] to start a line of writing further towards the middle of the page than other lines: *Use the Tab key to indent the first line of the paragraph.*

in·dent² /ˈɪndent/ *n* [C] *especially BrE* **1** an official order for goods or equipment: **[+for]** *He cancelled the indent for silk scarves.* **2** an indentation

in·den·ta·tion /ˌɪndenˈteɪʃən/ (*also* **indent**) *n* [C]
1 a space at the beginning of a line of writing **2** a cut into the surface or edge of something: *Make an indentation in the center of each cookie.*

in·dent·ed /ɪnˈdentɪd/ *adj* an indented edge or surface has cuts or marks in it: *our deeply indented coastline*

in·den·ture /ɪnˈdentʃə $ -ər/ *n* [C,U] a formal contract, especially in the past, between an APPRENTICE and his MASTER (=employer), or the act of arranging this —**indentured** *adj*: *indentured servants*

in·de·pen·dence /ˌɪndəˈpendəns/ ●●● (W2) *n* [U]
1 political freedom from control by the government of another country: **[+from]** *Nigeria gained independence from Britain in 1960.*
2 the time when a country becomes politically independent: *The country has made great advances since independence.*
3 the freedom and ability to make your own decisions in life, without having to ask other people for permission, help, or money: *ways of helping old people maintain their independence* | *Having a job gives you* ***financial independence.***

COLLOCATIONS – MEANINGS 1 & 2

ADJECTIVES

full/complete independence *The country gained complete independence from Britain in the 1960s.*
political/economic independence *Zambia achieved political independence without a prolonged conflict.*
national independence *The struggle for national independence lasted over 20 years.*
local independence *The new constitution aims to strengthen local independence.*

VERBS

get independence *The country eventually got its independence in 1960.*
gain/achieve/win independence (=get independence) *Our aim was to achieve full independence.*
declare independence *Estonia declared independence on August 20th.*
grant sth independence (=allow a country to become independent) *It was General de Gaulle who granted Algeria independence.*
move towards independence (=gradually achieve it over a period of time)

independence + NOUN

Independence Day (=a day on which a country's independence is celebrated) | **independence celebrations**

PHRASES

the struggle for independence *The struggle for independence continued for three decades.*

Indeˈpendence ˌDay *n* [C,U] **1** the day every year on which a country celebrates its independence from another country that controlled it in the past **2** this day in the US, celebrated on 4th July

in·de·pen·dent /ˌɪndəˈpendənt◂/ ●●● (S2) (W2) *adj*
1 NOT OWNED/CONTROLLED BY STH [usually before noun] an independent organization is not owned or controlled by, or does not receive money from, another organization or the government: *There are plans to split the corporation into a number of smaller independent companies.* | *an independent charity* | *small independent bookshops* | **[+of]** *We need a central bank that is independent of the government.* | **independent school** *especially BrE* (=one not owned or paid for by the government) | *schools in the independent sector* | **independent television/radio/broadcasting etc** *BrE* (=not owned or paid for by the government) *independent television companies* | **independent film** (=one not made or produced by a large film production company)
2 FAIR [usually before noun] an independent organization or person is not involved in a particular situation, and can therefore be trusted to be fair in judging it: *an independent panel of scientists* | *An* ***independent body*** (=group of people who work together) *has been set up to monitor government spending.* | *There were no independent witnesses to the shooting.* | **independent inquiry/advice/opinion etc** (=carried out by or given by an independent person or organization) *Human rights groups have called for an independent inquiry into the killings.* | *the results of an independent study*
3 COUNTRY an independent country is not governed or controlled by another country: *India* ***became independent*** *in 1947.*
4 PERSON **a)** confident and able to do things by yourself in your own way, without needing help or advice from other people (OPP) **dependent**: *Now that my sons are more independent, I have more time for myself.* | *an independent young woman* | *He's helping other people with spinal injuries to lead an independent life.* | **[+of]** *By this age, the child becomes relatively independent of his mother.* **b)** having enough money to live, without having to ask for help from other people: *It was always very important to me to be* ***financially independent.*** | **[+of]** *Robert aimed to be independent of his parents by the time he was twenty.*
5 independent study/learning when you study on your own, rather than being taught by a teacher: *The tapes can be used in class or for independent study.*
6 woman/man etc of independent means someone who has their own income from property, INVESTMENTS etc, so that they do not have to work or depend on anyone else

7 SEPARATE if one thing is independent of another, the two are not connected, or the second thing does not influence the first: **[+of]** *reports from two separate sources entirely independent of one another* | *Three independent studies all arrived at the same conclusion.*
8 POLITICIAN [usually before noun] an independent politician does not belong to a particular party: ***Independent candidates*** *won three seats.* —**independently** *adv*: *The two departments operate independently of each other.* | *She had elderly parents who could no longer live independently.*

Independent *n* [C] a politician who does not belong to a political party

ˌindependent ˈclause *n* [C] *technical* a CLAUSE which can make a sentence by itself, for example 'she went home' in the sentence 'She went home because she was tired.' SYN **main clause**

ˈin-depth *adj* [only before noun] thorough, complete, and considering all the details: **in-depth study/research/analysis etc** *an in-depth study of patients' needs* | *a series of in-depth interviews*

in·de·scri·ba·ble /ˌɪndɪˈskraɪbəbəl◂/ *adj* something that is indescribable is so terrible, so good, so strange etc that you cannot describe it, or it is too difficult to describe: *a feeling of indescribable joy* —**indescribably** *adv*: *an indescribably awful smell*

in·de·struc·ti·ble /ˌɪndɪˈstrʌktəbəl◂/ *adj* too strong to be destroyed: *her indestructible optimism* | *Gold is virtually indestructible.* THESAURUS STRONG —**indestructibility** /ˌɪndɪstrʌktəˈbɪləti/ *n* [U]

in·de·ter·mi·na·ble /ˌɪndɪˈtɜːmənəbəl◂ $ -ɜːr-/ *adj* impossible to find out or calculate exactly: *water of indeterminable depth* —**indeterminably** *adv*

in·de·ter·mi·nate /ˌɪndɪˈtɜːmənət◂ $ -ɜːr-/ *adj* impossible to know about definitely or exactly: *a girl of indeterminate age* —**indeterminately** *adv* —**indeterminacy** *n* [U]

in·dex[1] /ˈɪndeks/ ●●○ W2 AWL *n* [C]
1 (*plural* **indexes**) an alphabetical list of names, subjects etc at the back of a book, with the numbers of the pages where they can be found
2 (*plural* **indexes**) a set of cards or a DATABASE containing information, usually arranged in alphabetical order and used especially in a library
3 (*plural* **indices** /ˈɪndəsiːz/) a standard by which the level of something can be judged or measured: **[+of]** *The changing size of an infant's head is considered an index of brain growth.*
4 (*plural* **indices** /ˈɪndəsiːz/ *or* **indexes**) *technical* a system by which prices, costs etc can be compared to those of a previous date

index[2] AWL *v* [T] **1** if documents, information etc are indexed, an index is made for them: *The reports are indexed by subject and location.* **2** to arrange for the level of wages, PENSIONS etc to increase or decrease according to the level of prices: **be indexed to sth** *BrE*: *demands that wages be indexed to the rise in prices* | **be indexed for sth** *AmE*: *an amount indexed for inflation* GRAMMAR **Index** is usually passive. —**indexation** /ˌɪndekˈseɪʃən/ *n* [C,U]

ˈindex card *n* [C] a small card for writing on, used especially in an INDEX[1](2)

ˈindex ˌfinger *n* [C] the finger next to your thumb SYN **forefinger** → see picture at HAND[1]

ˌindex-ˈlinked *adj BrE technical* index-linked wages, PENSIONS etc increase or decrease according to the rise or fall in prices

In·di·an[1] /ˈɪndiən/ *n* **1** [C] someone from India **2** [C] a member of one of the races that lived in North, South, and Central America before the Europeans arrived SYN **Native American** **3** [singular] *BrE informal* a meal of Indian food, or a restaurant that sells Indian food: *Do you fancy going out for an Indian?*

Indian[2] *adj* **1** relating to India or its people **2** relating to the Indians of North, South, and Central America

ˌIndian ˈsummer *n* [C] **1** a period of warm weather in autumn **2** a happy or successful time, especially near the end of your life or CAREER

Frequencies of the verbs **indicate** and **show** in spoken and written English.

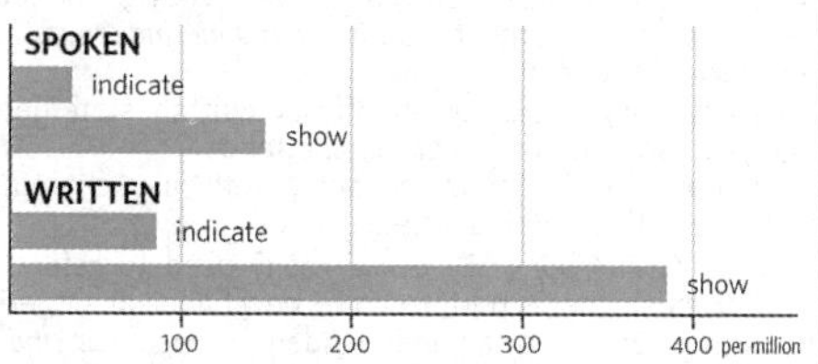

This graph shows that **show** is much more common than **indicate** in both spoken and written English. This is because **show** is much more general in meaning and is more commonly used in informal English than **indicate**.

in·di·cate /ˈɪndɪkeɪt/ ●●● S3 W1 AWL *v*
1 [T] to show that a particular situation exists, or that something is likely to be true: **indicate (that)** *Research indicates that over 81% of teachers are dissatisfied with their salary.* | *Long skid marks on the pavement indicated the driver had attempted to brake.* | *The study indicates a connection between poverty and crime.*
2 [T] to say or do something to make your wishes, intentions etc clear: *The Russians have already indicated their willingness to cooperate.* | *Professor Johnson has indicated his intention to retire at the end of next year.* | **indicate (that)** *Ralph patted the sofa to indicate that she should join him.* | *Please indicate your preference on the booking form.*
3 [T] to direct someone's attention to something or someone, for example by pointing: *'That's her,' said Toby, indicating a girl on the other side of the room.*
4 [T] to represent something: *Sales targets are indicated on the graph by a vertical dotted line.*
5 [I,T] *BrE* to show the direction in which you intend to turn in a vehicle, using lights or your hands SYN **signal**: *Don't forget to indicate before you pull out.*

in·di·ca·tion /ˌɪndɪˈkeɪʃən/ ●●○ S3 W3 AWL *n* [C,U] a sign, remark, event etc that shows what is happening, what someone is thinking or feeling, or what is true: **[+of]** *Dark green leaves are a good indication of healthy roots.* | *He gave no indication at all of his own feelings.* | *Could you* ***give*** *me some* ***indication*** *as to when I am likely to receive a reply?* | **indication (that)** *Taking a career history along with you will be a clear indication that you are well organized.* | *Indications are that the situation hasn't improved much.* | *There is* ***every indication*** (=there are very clear signs) *that it is true.* THESAURUS SIGN

in·dic·a·tive[1] /ɪnˈdɪkətɪv/ ●○○ AWL *adj*
1 **be indicative of sth** to be a clear sign that a particular situation exists or that something is likely to be true: *This behaviour is indicative of her whole attitude, I'm afraid.*
2 *technical* an indicative verb form is used for making statements

indicative[2] AWL *n* [C,U] *technical* the form of a verb that is used to make statements. For example, in the sentences 'Penny passed her test' and 'Michael likes cake', the verbs 'passed' and 'likes' are in the indicative.

in·di·ca·tor /ˈɪndəkeɪtə $ -ər/ ●○○ AWL *n* [C]
1 something that can be regarded as a sign of something else SYN **sign**: *All the main economic indicators suggest that trade is improving.* THESAURUS SIGN
2 *BrE* one of the lights on a car that flash to show which way the car is turning SYN **turn signal** *AmE* → see picture at CAR
3 a POINTER on a machine that shows the temperature, pressure, speed etc

in·di·ces /ˈɪndəsiːz/ a plural of INDEX

in·dict /ɪnˈdaɪt/ ●○○ *v* [I,T] *especially AmE law* to officially charge someone with a criminal offence: **indict sb for sth** *He was indicted for vehicular homicide in 1987.* THESAURUS ACCUSE

in·dict·a·ble /ɪnˈdaɪtəbəl/ *adj especially AmE law* an indictable offence is one for which you can be indicted

I

in·dict·ment /ɪnˈdaɪtmənt/ ●○○ *n*
1 be an indictment of sth to be a very clear sign that a system, method etc is very bad or very wrong: *The fact that these children cannot read is a damning indictment of our education system.*
2 [C] *especially AmE law* an official written statement charging someone with a criminal offence
3 [U] *especially AmE law* the act of officially charging someone with a criminal offence

in·die[1] /ˈɪndi/ *adj* [only before noun] used to refer to popular music that is performed by new bands or singers, and produced by small independent companies: *indie music | an indie band*

indie[2] *n* [C] a small independent company, especially one that produces popular music

in·dif·fer·ence /ɪnˈdɪfərəns/ ●○○ *n* [U] lack of interest or concern: **[+to]** *his apparent indifference to material luxuries | Whether you stay or leave is* ***a matter of*** *total* ***indifference to*** *me* (=I do not care).

in·dif·fer·ent /ɪnˈdɪfərənt/ ●○○ *adj*
1 not at all interested in someone or something: **[+to]** *Sarah was absolutely indifferent to him, and it hurt.*
2 not particularly good SYN **mediocre**: *an indifferent cook*
—**indifferently** *adv*

in·di·ge·nous /ɪnˈdɪdʒənəs/ *adj formal* indigenous people or things have always been in the place where they are, rather than being brought there from somewhere else SYN **native**: **[+to]** *Blueberries are indigenous to America. | the many indigenous cultures which existed in Siberia*

in·di·gent /ˈɪndɪdʒənt/ *adj formal* very poor

in·di·ges·ti·ble /ˌɪndɪˈdʒestəbəl◂/ *adj* **1** food that is indigestible cannot easily be broken down in the stomach into substances that the body can use **2** information that is indigestible is not easy to understand: *indigestible statistics*

in·di·ges·tion /ˌɪndɪˈdʒestʃən/ *n* [U] pain that you get when your stomach cannot break down food that you have eaten → **heartburn**

in·dig·nant /ɪnˈdɪɡnənt/ *adj* angry and surprised because you feel insulted or unfairly treated: **[+at/about]** *Liz was indignant at the way her child had been treated. | an indignant reply* —**indignantly** *adv*: *'Of course I didn't tell her!' Sasha said indignantly.*

in·dig·na·tion /ˌɪndɪɡˈneɪʃən/ *n* [U] feelings of anger and surprise because you feel insulted or unfairly treated: *To his indignation, Charles found that his name was not on the list.* | **with/in indignation** *Lou's voice quivered with indignation.* | **[+at/about/over]** *Her indignation at such rough treatment was understandable. | He stormed into her office, full of* ***righteous indignation***.

in·dig·ni·ty /ɪnˈdɪɡnəti/ *n* (*plural* **indignities**) [C,U] a situation that makes you feel very ashamed and not respected: *The prisoners were subjected to all sorts of indignities.* | **the indignity of (doing) sth** *Two of the diplomats* ***suffered the indignity of*** *being arrested.* | **the final/ultimate/crowning etc indignity**

in·di·go /ˈɪndɪɡəʊ $ -ɡoʊ/ *n* [U] a dark purple-blue colour → **purple** —**indigo** *adj*

in·di·rect /ˌɪndəˈrekt◂/ ●●○ *adj*
1 not directly caused by something OPP **direct**: *Losing weight is an* ***indirect result*** *of smoking cigarettes. | The* ***indirect effects*** *of climate change may be profound.*
2 an indirect way to a place is not the straightest way OPP **direct**: *They took an indirect route, avoiding the town centre.*
3 not saying or showing something in a clear definite way OPP **direct**: *George's comments were an indirect way of blaming me.* —**indirectly** *adv*: *Perhaps I was indirectly responsible for the misunderstanding.*

ˌindirect ˈcost *n* [C usually plural] *technical* money that a business must spend, not directly on its products or services, but on other things such as buildings or wages

ˌindirect ˈdiscourse *n* [U] *AmE technical* INDIRECT SPEECH

ˌindirect ˈobject *n* [C] *technical* an OBJECT of a verb that refers to the person that something is given to, said to, made for etc. For example, in the sentence 'I asked him a question', the indirect object is 'him'. → **direct object**

ˌindirect ˈspeech *BrE*, **indirect discourse** *AmE* (*also* **reported speech**) *n* [U] *technical* a way of reporting what someone said without repeating their exact words. For example, in the sentence 'Julia said that she didn't want to go', the clause 'that she didn't want to go' is indirect speech. Her actual words were 'I don't want to go'. → **direct speech**

ˌindirect ˈtax *n* [C] a tax that is added to the cost of goods and services → **direct tax** —**ˌindirect taxˈation** *n* [U]

in·dis·cer·ni·ble /ˌɪndɪˈsɜːnəbəl◂ $ -ɜːr-/ *adj* very difficult to see, hear, or notice: *The path was almost indiscernible in the mist.*

in·dis·ci·pline /ɪnˈdɪsɪplɪn/ *n* [U] *formal* a lack of control in the behaviour of a group of people, with the result that they behave badly OPP **discipline**: *Indiscipline among the troops eventually led to a riot.*

in·dis·creet /ˌɪndɪˈskriːt◂/ *adj* careless about what you say or do, especially by talking about things which should be kept secret OPP **discreet**: *It was very indiscreet of Colin to tell them about our plan.*

in·dis·cre·tion /ˌɪndɪˈskreʃən/ AWL *n* [C,U] an action or remark that shows a lack of good judgment, especially one that is morally unacceptable: *Earl describes his past links with the racist group as a* ***youthful indiscretion***. *| rumours of the former president's sexual indiscretions*

in·dis·crim·i·nate /ˌɪndɪˈskrɪmənət◂/ *adj* an indiscriminate action is done without thinking about what harm it might cause: **indiscriminate attacks/killing/violence/bombing etc** *terrorists responsible for indiscriminate killing | the* ***indiscriminate use*** *of chemical fertilizers* —**indiscriminately** *adv*: *Soldiers fired indiscriminately into the crowd.*

in·di·spen·sa·ble /ˌɪndɪˈspensəbəl◂/ ●○○ *adj* someone or something that is indispensable is so important or useful that it is impossible to manage without them SYN **essential**: **[+to]** *This book is indispensable to anyone interested in space exploration.* | **indispensable for/in (doing) sth** *Meat is not indispensable for maintaining a healthy diet. | Mobile phones have become an* ***indispensable part*** *of our lives.* THESAURUS ▸ USEFUL

in·dis·posed /ˌɪndɪˈspəʊzd $ -ˈspoʊzd/ *adj* [not before noun] *formal* **1** ill and therefore unable to be present: *Mrs Rawlins is temporarily indisposed.* **2 indisposed to do sth** not willing to do something

in·dis·po·si·tion /ɪnˌdɪspəˈzɪʃən/ *n* [C,U] *formal* a slight illness

in·dis·pu·ta·ble /ˌɪndɪˈspjuːtəbəl/ *adj* an indisputable fact must be accepted because it is definitely true: *The evidence was indisputable.* THESAURUS ▸ TRUE —**indisputably** *adv*

in·dis·so·lu·ble /ˌɪndɪˈsɒljəbəl◂ $ -ˈsɑː-/ *adj formal* an indissoluble relationship cannot be destroyed: *the indissoluble link between language and culture* —**indissolubly** *adv*

in·dis·tinct /ˌɪndɪˈstɪŋkt◂/ AWL *adj* an indistinct sound, image, or memory cannot be seen, heard, or remembered clearly OPP **distinct**: *She muttered something indistinct. | My memory of what happened next is indistinct.* —**indistinctly** *adv*

in·dis·tin·guish·a·ble /ˌɪndɪˈstɪŋɡwɪʃəbəl/ ●○○ *adj* things that are indistinguishable are so similar that you cannot see any difference between them: **[+from]** *an artificial material that is almost indistinguishable from real silk* THESAURUS ▸ SAME

in·di·vid·u·al[1] /ˌɪndəˈvɪdʒuəl◂/ ●●○ S3 W3 AWL *adj*
1 [only before noun] considered separately from other people or things in the same group: ***Each individual*** *leaf on the tree is different. | the needs of the individual customer*
2 [only before noun] belonging to or intended for one person rather than a group: *Children get more individual attention in small classes. | You can have the bathroom designed to suit your* ***individual needs***. *| individual portions of jam*

3 an individual style, way of doing things etc is different from anyone else's – usually used to show approval SYN **distinctive**: *a tennis player with a highly individual style | a very individual way of dressing*

individual² ●●○ S3 W3 AWL *n* [C]
1 a person, considered separately from the rest of the group or society that they live in: *the rights of the individual | Each individual receives two genes, one inherited from each parent. | Most churches were built with donations from* ***private individuals*** (=ordinary people, rather than the government or companies).
2 a person of a particular kind, especially one who is unusual in some way: *a strange-looking individual*

in·di·vid·u·al·is·m /ˌɪndəˈvɪdʒuəlɪzəm/ AWL *n* [U] **1** the belief that the rights and freedom of individual people are the most important rights in a society: *Capitalism encourages competition and individualism.* **2** the behaviour or attitude of someone who does things in their own way without being influenced by other people

in·di·vid·u·al·ist /ˌɪndəˈvɪdʒuəlɪst/ AWL *n* [C] someone who does things in their own way and has different opinions from most other people: *Geoff was too much of an individualist to be team captain.* —**individualistic** /ˌɪndəvɪdʒuəˈlɪstɪk◂/ (*also* **individualist**) *adj*: *She has a highly individualistic approach to painting.*

in·di·vid·u·al·i·ty /ˌɪndəvɪdʒuˈæləti/ ●○○ AWL *n* [U] the qualities that make someone or something different from other things or people: *We like our staff to show their individuality rather than wear a uniform.*

in·di·vid·u·al·ized (*also* **-ised** *BrE*) /ˌɪndəˈvɪdʒuəlaɪzd/ *adj* designed to fit the special needs of a particular person or thing: *an individualized training program* —**individualize** *v* [T]

in·di·vid·u·al·ly /ˌɪndəˈvɪdʒuəli/ ●●○ AWL *adv* separately, not together in a group OPP **collectively**: *The bridegroom thanked them all individually. | individually wrapped portions of cheese*

in·di·vid·u·ate /ˌɪndəˈvɪdʒueɪt/ *v formal* **1** [T] to make someone or something clearly different from others of the same kind: *The characters in the play are beautifully individuated.* **2** [I] *AmE* to have an idea of yourself as an independent person, separate from other people

in·di·vis·i·ble /ˌɪndəˈvɪzəbəl◂/ *adj* something that is indivisible cannot be separated or divided into parts OPP **divisible** —**indivisibly** *adv*

Indo- /ɪndəʊ $ -doʊ/ *prefix* [in nouns and adjectives] Indian and something else: *Indo-European languages*

in·doc·tri·nate /ɪnˈdɒktrəneɪt $ ɪnˈdɑːk-/ *v* [T] to train someone to accept a particular set of beliefs, especially political or religious ones, and not consider any others: *People were indoctrinated not to question their leaders.* —**indoctrination** /ɪnˌdɒktrəˈneɪʃən $ ɪnˌdɑːk-/ *n* [U]: *The military in particular were subjected to intense political indoctrination.*

ˌIndo-ˈEuropean *adj* the Indo-European group of languages includes English, French, Hindi, Russian, and most of the other languages of Europe and northern India

in·do·lent /ˈɪndələnt/ *adj formal* lazy —**indolence** *n* [U]

in·dom·i·ta·ble /ɪnˈdɒmətəbəl $ ɪnˈdɑː-/ *adj formal* having great determination or courage: *an indomitable old lady |* **indomitable spirit/will/courage etc** *Alice was a woman of indomitable spirit.*

in·door /ˈɪndɔː $ -ɔːr/ ●●○ *adj* [only before noun] used or happening inside a building OPP **outdoor**: *an indoor swimming pool | the world indoor athletics championship | Too much central heating can harm indoor plants.*

USAGE: Indoor, indoors

Indoor is an adjective and **indoors** is an adverb.
You say: *indoor sports* ✗ Don't say: *indoors sports*
You say: *I stayed indoors.* ✗ Don't say: *I stayed indoor.*

in·doors /ˌɪnˈdɔːz◂ $ -ɔːrz◂/ ●●○ *adv* into or inside a building OPP **outdoors**: *Let's go indoors and have something to eat. | It rained all day so we had to stay indoors.*

in·dorse /ɪnˈdɔːs $ -ɔːrs/ *v* [T] another spelling of ENDORSE

in·drawn /ˈɪndrɔːn $ -drɒːn/ *adj* **indrawn breath** *written* air that someone breathes in in a way that can be heard, especially because they are shocked: *She heard Mitch's swiftly indrawn breath.*

in·du·bi·ta·bly /ɪnˈdjuːbətəbli $ ɪnˈduː-/ *adv formal* certainly or without doubt: *Mr Sachs is indubitably charming.* —**indubitable** *adj*

in·duce /ɪnˈdjuːs $ ɪnˈduːs/ ●○○ AWL *v* [T]
1 *formal* to persuade someone to do something, especially something that does not seem wise: **induce sb to do sth** *Nothing would induce me to vote for him again.*
2 *medical* to make a woman give birth to her baby, by giving her a special drug: *She had to be induced because the baby was four weeks late. | The doctor decided to* ***induce labour***.
3 *formal* to cause a particular physical condition: *Patients with eating disorders may use drugs to induce vomiting. |* **drug-induced/stress-induced etc** *a drug-induced coma*

in·duce·ment /ɪnˈdjuːsmənt $ ɪnˈduːs-/ *n* [C,U] a reason for doing something, especially something that you will get as a result: **inducement to do sth** *Businesses were offered inducements to move to the area. |* ***financial inducements*** *to attract good job candidates*

in·duct /ɪnˈdʌkt/ *v* [T] *formal* **1** to officially give someone a job or position of authority, especially at a special ceremony: **be inducted to/into sth** *Eighteen new junior ministers were inducted into the government.* **2** to officially introduce someone into an important place of honour at a special ceremony: **be inducted into sth** *Barry was inducted into the Basketball Hall of Fame in 1987.* **3** *AmE* to officially introduce someone into a group or organization, especially the army

in·duc·tee /ˌɪndʌkˈtiː/ *n* [C] *AmE* someone who is joining a special group, especially the army

in·duc·tion /ɪnˈdʌkʃən/ AWL *n* **1** [C,U] the introduction of someone into a new job, company, official position etc, or the ceremony at which this is done: **induction course/programme/period etc** *a two-day induction course | Mrs Simpson is responsible for the induction of new library staff.* **2** [C,U] *medical* the process of making a woman give birth to her baby by giving her a special drug **3** [U] *technical* the production of electricity in one object by another that already has electrical or MAGNETIC power **4** [U] *technical* a process of thought that uses known facts to produce general rules or principles → DEDUCTION

inˈduction ˌcoil *n* [C] *technical* a piece of electrical equipment that changes a low VOLTAGE to a higher one

in·duc·tive /ɪnˈdʌktɪv/ *adj technical* **1** using known facts to produce general principles: *inductive reasoning* **2** connected with electrical or MAGNETIC induction

in·dulge /ɪnˈdʌldʒ/ ●○○ *v*
1 [I,T] to let yourself do or have something that you enjoy, especially something that is considered bad for you: **[+in]** *Most of us were too busy to indulge in heavy lunchtime drinking. | Eva had never been one to indulge in self-pity. |* **indulge yourself** *Even if you're dieting, you can indulge yourself* (=eat what you want) *once in a while. | Ray has enough money to indulge his taste for expensive wines.*
2 [T] to let someone have or do whatever they want, even if it is bad for them: *His mother spoiled him, indulging his every whim.*
3 [I] to take part in an activity, especially an illegal one: **[+in]** *Women do not indulge in crime to the same extent as men.*

in·dul·gence /ɪnˈdʌldʒəns/ *n* **1** [U] the habit of allowing yourself to do or have whatever you want, or allowing someone else to do or have whatever they want → **self-indulgence** at **SELF-INDULGENT** **2** [C] something that you do or have for pleasure, not because you need it: *An occasional glass of wine was his only indulgence.* **3** [U] *formal* willingness to ignore someone's faults or weaknesses: *a spirit of indulgence and forgiveness* **4** [C] a promise of

I

freedom from punishment by God, sold by priests in the Middle Ages

in·dul·gent /ɪnˈdʌldʒənt/ *adj* willing to allow someone, especially a child, to do or have whatever they want, even if this is not good for them: *toys bought by their indulgent grandparents* —**indulgently** *adv*

in·dus·tri·al /ɪnˈdʌstriəl/ ●●● S3 W1 *adj*
1 relating to industry or the people working in it: **industrial production/output** *Industrial production has risen by 0.5% since November.* | **industrial development/growth** *rapid post-war industrial development* | **industrial conflict/dispute/unrest** (=disagreement between workers and their employers) *Last year 1.3 million workers took part in industrial disputes.* | **industrial accident/injury** (=happening at work)
2 having many industries: **industrial countries/nations/states** *a meeting of the world's major industrial nations* | **industrial area/zone** *pollution in industrial areas* | *By 1900, Britain was a mainly* ***industrial society****.*
3 of the type used in industry: *cleaning products that are for* ***industrial use*** *only* (=not to be used at home) —**industrially** *adv*

inˌdustrial ˈaction *n* [U] *BrE* an action such as a STRIKE (=stopping work) taken by workers involved in a disagreement with their employer

inˌdustrial archaeˈology *n* [U] the study of old factories, machines etc

inˌdustrial ˈarts *n* [U] *AmE* a subject taught in school about how to use tools, machinery etc

inˌdustrial ˈespionage *n* [U] stealing secret information from one company in order to help another company

inˌdustrial esˈtate *BrE*, **inˌdustrial ˈpark** *AmE n* [C] a piece of land, often on the edge of a town, where there are factories and businesses

in·dus·tri·al·is·m /ɪnˈdʌstriəlɪzəm/ *n* [U] the system by which a society gets its wealth through industries and machinery

in·dus·tri·al·ist /ɪnˈdʌstriəlɪst/ ●○○ *n* [C] a person who owns or runs a factory or industrial company

in·dus·tri·al·i·za·tion (*also* **-isation** *BrE*) /ɪnˌdʌstriəlaɪˈzeɪʃən $ -ələ-/ *n* [U] when a country or place develops a lot of industry —**industrialize** /ɪnˈdʌstriəlaɪz/ *v* [I,T]

in·dus·tri·al·ized (*also* **-ised** *BrE*) /ɪnˈdʌstriəlaɪzd/ ●○○ *adj* an industrialized country or place has a lot of factories, mines etc

inˌdustrial reˈlations *n* [plural] the relationship between workers and employers

Inˌdustrial Revoˈlution, the the period in the 18th and 19th centuries in Europe and the US when machines were invented and the first factories were established

inˈdustrial-ˌstrength *adj* an industrial-strength substance is very strong – often used humorously: *They served us industrial-strength coffee.*

inˌdustrial triˈbunal *n* [C] *BrE* a court that judges disagreements between workers and their employers

in·dus·tri·ous /ɪnˈdʌstriəs/ *adj* someone who is industrious works hard SYN **hard-working** —**industriously** *adv*

in·dus·try /ˈɪndəstri/ ●●● S2 W1 *n* (*plural* **industries**)
1 [U] **a)** the large-scale production of goods or of substances such as coal and steel: *This type of software is widely used in industry.* | *workers in manufacturing industry* **b)** the people who work in industry: *an agreement that will be welcomed by both sides of industry* (=employers and workers)
2 [C] businesses that produce a particular type of thing or provide a particular service: *I work in the oil industry.* | *Italy's thriving tourist industry*
3 [U] *formal* the fact of working hard: *Gould is a man of great industry.*
4 [singular] an area of work which has grown too large – used to show disapproval: *another book from the Shakespeare industry*

COLLOCATIONS – MEANINGS 1 & 2

ADJECTIVES/NOUN + industry

an important/major industry *Agriculture is still a major industry in Scotland.*
a thriving industry (=one that is doing very well) *Software development soon became a thriving industry in the area.*
a growing industry *Tourism is a growing industry in many parts of the developing world.*
a declining industry (=one that is doing badly) *Coal and steel are declining industries in Britain.*
manufacturing industry (=industries in which goods are produced in factories) *The last twenty years has seen a decline in manufacturing industry.*
a service industry (=businesses that provide a service, such as banking and tourism) *Most of the new jobs are in service industries.*
heavy industry (=industries that involve the production of large goods) *Shipbuilding and other heavy industry developed in the north of Britain.*
light industry (=industries that involve the production of small goods) *Jobs in light industry are increasing.*
modern industry *Modern industry needs to be in places where there are good transport links.*
a traditional industry (=an industry that has been in a particular area for a long time) *The shipyards, the traditional industry in the northeast, had closed.*
the coal/car/textile etc industry *The town was very dependant on the car industry.*
the agricultural/fishing industry | **the tourist/travel industry** | **the leisure/entertainment industry** | **the film/music industry** (=the work of producing films or music)

VERBS

an industry grows/expands *The clothing industry grew rapidly during the 1960s.*
an industry declines (=becomes less successful) *The shipping industry declined after World War II.*
develop an industry *More investment is needed to develop new industries such as tourism.*
damage an industry *Financial scandals have damaged the industry in recent years.*
nationalize an industry (=make it owned by the state) | **privatize an industry** (=make it privately owned, rather than owned by the state) | **regulate an industry** (=control an industry so that it does not make unfair profits)

industry + NOUN

an industry leader (=one of the most successful companies in a particular industry) *We are now a mature company and an industry leader.*
industry experts (=people who know a lot about a particular industry) | **industry analysts** (=people who study a particular industry to see how it is developing)

PHRASES

a captain of industry (=someone who runs a large company and has a lot of influence) *He rose to be a great captain of industry.*
trade and industry (=producing goods, and buying and selling them) *He works for the Department of Trade and Industry.*

ˈin-ear *adj* [only before noun] in-ear HEADPHONES fit inside your ear

i·ne·bri·a·ted /ɪˈniːbrieɪtɪd/ *adj formal* drunk

in·ed·i·ble /ɪnˈedəbəl/ *adj* if something is inedible, you cannot eat it because it tastes bad or is poisonous OPP **edible**: *The meat was so burnt that it was inedible.*

in·ed·u·ca·ble /ɪnˈedjəkəbəl $ -dʒə-/ *adj formal* impossible or very difficult to educate

in·ef·fa·ble /ɪnˈefəbəl/ *adj formal* too great to be described in words SYN **indescribable**: *ineffable joy* —**ineffably** *adv*

in·ef·fec·tive /ˌɪnəˈfektɪv◂/ ●○○ *adj* something that is ineffective does not achieve what it is intended to achieve OPP **effective**: **ineffective in doing sth** *The chemical was almost totally ineffective in killing the weeds.* | **[+against]** *Various drugs have proved ineffective against the virus.* | *an ineffective marketing campaign* —**ineffectively** *adv* —**ineffectiveness** *n* [U]: *the ineffectiveness of most diets*

> **REGISTER**
> In everyday English, people usually say that something **does not work** rather than saying that it **is ineffective**: *These drugs **don't work** against bird flu.*

in·ef·fec·tu·al /ˌɪnəˈfektʃuəl◂/ *adj* not having the ability, confidence, or personal authority to get things done: *an ineffectual leader* | *She remembered her ineffectual efforts to comfort him.* —**ineffectually** *adv*

in·ef·fi·cient /ˌɪnəˈfɪʃənt◂/ ●○○ *adj* not using time, money, energy etc in the best way OPP **efficient**: *an inefficient use of resources* | *Local government was inefficient.* —**inefficiently** *adv* —**inefficiency** *n* [C,U]: *problems due to the inefficiency of management*

in·el·e·gant /ɪnˈelɪgənt/ *adj* not graceful or attractive OPP **elegant**: *an inelegant expression* —**inelegantly** *adv* —**inelegance** *n* [U]

in·el·i·gi·ble /ɪnˈelədʒəbəl/ *adj* not allowed to have or do something because of a law or rule OPP **eligible**: **[+for]** *Temporary workers are ineligible for the pension scheme.* | **ineligible to do sth** *People under 18 are ineligible to vote.* —**ineligibility** /ɪnˌelədʒəˈbɪləti/ *n* [U]

in·e·luc·ta·ble /ˌɪnɪˈlʌktəbəl◂/ *adj formal* impossible to avoid SYN **unavoidable** —**ineluctably** *adv*

in·ept /ɪˈnept/ *adj* not good at doing something OPP **capable**, **skilful**: *inept leadership* | *He was criticized for his inept handling of the problem.* | **politically/socially inept** *Blake was intellectually able but politically inept.* → **inapt** —**ineptly** *adv*

in·ept·i·tude /ɪˈneptɪtjuːd $ -tuːd/ *n* [U] *formal* lack of skill SYN **incompetence**: *the ineptitude of the people in charge*

in·e·qual·i·ty /ˌɪnɪˈkwɒləti $ -ˈkwɑː-/ ●●○ *n* (*plural* **inequalities**) [C,U] an unfair situation, in which some groups in society have more money, opportunities, power etc than others OPP **equality**: **[+in]** *There are inequalities in wealth distribution.* | **[+of]** *inequality of opportunity* | **[+between]** *inequalities between men and women* | **social/gender/racial etc inequality** *a policy that aims to redress racial inequalities*

in·eq·ui·ta·ble /ɪnˈekwətəbəl/ *adj formal* not equally fair to everyone: *an inequitable distribution of wealth* —**inequitably** *adv*

in·eq·ui·ty /ɪnˈekwəti/ *n* (*plural* **inequities**) [C,U] *formal* lack of fairness, or something that is unfair OPP **equity**: **[+of]** *the inequities of the legal system* | **[+in]** *inequities in the distribution of research funding* | **racial/social inequity** *a report on racial inequity in the UK*

in·e·rad·i·ca·ble /ˌɪnɪˈrædɪkəbəl◂/ *adj formal* impossible to change or remove: *ineradicable hostility* —**ineradicably** *adv*

in·ert /ɪˈnɜːt $ -ɜːrt/ *adj* **1** *technical* not producing a chemical reaction when combined with other substances: *inert gases* **2** *literary* not moving, or not having the strength or power to move: *He lay, inert, in his bed.* **3** not willing to do anything: *The government was inert and inefficient.* —**inertness** *n* [U]

in·er·tia /ɪˈnɜːʃə $ -ɜːr-/ *n* [U] **1** when no one wants to do anything to change a situation: *political inertia* **2** *technical* the force that keeps an object in the same position or keeps it moving until it is moved or stopped by another force **3** a lack of energy and a feeling that you do not want to do anything SYN **apathy** —**inertial** *adj*

in·es·ca·pa·ble /ˌɪnɪˈskeɪpəbəl◂/ *adj* an inescapable fact or situation is one that you cannot avoid or ignore: *She didn't want to confront the inescapable fact that she would have to sell the house.* | *The inescapable conclusion is that he was murdered by someone in his own family.* —**inescapably** *adv*

in·es·sen·tial /ˌɪnəˈsenʃəl◂/ *adj formal* not needed SYN **unnecessary** OPP **essential**: *inessential details* —**inessentials** *n* [plural]

in·es·ti·ma·ble /ɪnˈestəməbəl/ *adj formal* too much or too great to be calculated: *a painting of **inestimable value***

in·ev·i·ta·bil·i·ty /ɪˌnevətəˈbɪləti/ AWL *n* [singular, U] the fact that something is certain to happen, or something that is certain to happen: **[+of]** *the inevitability of death*

in·ev·i·ta·ble /ɪˈnevətəbəl/ ●●○ W3 AWL *adj* **1** certain to happen and impossible to avoid: *A further escalation of the crisis now seems inevitable.* | **it is inevitable (that)** *It's inevitable that doctors will make the occasional mistake.* | **inevitable consequence/result** *Disease was an inevitable consequence of poor living conditions.* THESAURUS ▸ CERTAIN **2 the inevitable** a situation that is certain to happen: *One day the inevitable happened and I got a speeding ticket.*

in·ev·i·ta·bly /ɪˈnevətəbli/ ●●○ W3 AWL *adv* used for saying that something is certain to happen and cannot be avoided: *The decision will inevitably lead to political tensions.* | [sentence adverb] *Inevitably, the situation did not please everyone.*

in·ex·act /ˌɪnɪgˈzækt◂/ *adj* not exact: *Earthquake prediction is an **inexact science**.*

in·ex·cu·sa·ble /ˌɪnɪkˈskjuːzəbəl◂/ *adj* inexcusable behaviour is too bad to be excused: *an inexcusable act of aggression* —**inexcusably** *adv*

in·ex·haus·ti·ble /ˌɪnɪgˈzɔːstəbəl◂ $ -ˈzɒːs-/ *adj* something that is inexhaustible exists in such large amounts that it can never be finished or used up: *She has an **inexhaustible supply** of funny stories.* | *a man of inexhaustible energy*

in·ex·o·ra·ble /ɪnˈeksərəbəl/ *adj formal* an inexorable process cannot be stopped SYN **unstoppable**: *the inexorable decline of Britain's manufacturing industry* | *the seemingly inexorable rise in crime* —**inexorably** *adv* —**inexorability** /ɪnˌeksərəˈbɪləti/ *n* [U]

in·ex·pen·sive /ˌɪnɪkˈspensɪv◂/ ●○○ *adj* cheap – use this to show approval OPP **expensive**: *a good selection of inexpensive wines* | *Painting is a relatively inexpensive way to enhance your home.* THESAURUS ▸ CHEAP —**inexpensively** *adv*

in·ex·pe·ri·ence /ˌɪnɪkˈspɪəriəns $ -ˈspɪr-/ *n* [U] lack of experience: *youthful inexperience*

in·ex·pe·ri·enced /ˌɪnɪkˈspɪəriənst◂ $ -ˈspɪr-/ ●○○ *adj* not having had much experience: *inexperienced pilots*

in·ex·pert /ɪnˈekspɜːt $ -ɜːrt/ *adj formal* not having the skill to do something OPP **expert**: *an inexperienced and inexpert teacher* —**inexpertly** *adv*

in·ex·plic·a·ble /ˌɪnɪkˈsplɪkəbəl◂ $ ɪnˈeksplɪkəbəl, ˌɪnɪkˈsplɪk-/ *adj* too unusual or strange to be explained or understood SYN **incomprehensible**, **strange**: *inexplicable behaviour* | ***For some inexplicable reason,*** *he felt depressed.* —**inexplicably** *adv*

in·ex·pres·si·ble /ˌɪnɪkˈspresəbəl◂/ *adj formal* an inexpressible feeling is too strong to be described in words: *inexpressible gratitude* —**inexpressibly** *adv*

in·ex·press·ive /ˌɪnɪkˈspresɪv◂/ *adj* a face that is inexpressive shows no emotion

in ex·tre·mis /ˌɪn ɪkˈstriːmɪs/ *adv formal* **1** in a very difficult situation when you need to do something very extreme **2** at the moment of death

in·ex·tric·a·ble /ˌɪnɪkˈstrɪkəbəl◂, ɪnˈekstrɪk-/ *adj formal* two or more things that are inextricable are closely related and affect each other: *the inextricable connection between language and culture*

in·ex·tric·a·bly /ˌɪnɪkˈstrɪkəbli, ɪnˈekstrɪk-/ *adv* **be inextricably linked/bound up/mixed etc** if two or more things are inextricably linked etc, they are very closely related and affect each other: *Physical health is inextricably linked to mental health.* | *Economic and social history are inextricably bound up with each other.*

in·fal·li·ble /ɪnˈfæləbəl/ *adj* **1** always right and never making mistakes OPP **fallible**: *No expert is infallible.* | *an* *infallible memory* **2** something that is infallible always works or has the intended effect → **fail-safe**: *He had an infallible cure for a hangover.* —**infallibly** *adv* —**infallibility** /ɪnˌfæləˈbɪləti/ *n* [U]

in·fa·mous /ˈɪnfəməs/ ●○○ *adj* well known for being bad or evil: *an infamous killer | Los Angeles' infamous smog |* **[+for]** *This area is infamous for drugs and prostitution.* THESAURUS FAMOUS —**infamously** *adv*

in·fa·my /ˈɪnfəmi/ *n* [U] the state of being evil or well known for evil things

in·fan·cy /ˈɪnfənsi/ *n* [U] **1** the period of a child's life before they can walk or talk: **in infancy** *In the past, many children died in infancy.* **2** the time when something is just starting to be developed: *the infancy of radio broadcasting | Genetic engineering is still* ***in its infancy***.

in·fant¹ /ˈɪnfənt/ ●●○ W3 *n*
1 [C] *formal* a baby or very young child: *An infant's skin is very sensitive.* THESAURUS BABY → SUDDEN INFANT DEATH SYNDROME
2 infants [plural] children in school in Britain between the ages of four and eight

infant² *adj* [only before noun] **1 infant school/teacher/class etc** a school, teacher etc for children aged between four and eight in Britain **2** intended for babies or very young children: *infant formula milk* **3** an infant company, organization etc has just started to exist or be developed: *infant industries*

in·fan·ti·cide /ɪnˈfæntɪsaɪd/ *n* [U] the crime of killing a child

in·fan·tile /ˈɪnfəntaɪl/ *adj* **1** infantile behaviour seems silly in an adult because it is typical of a child SYN **childish**: *infantile jokes* **2** [only before noun] *technical* relating to or affecting babies and very young children: *infantile development*

ˌinfantile paˈralysis *n* [U] *old-fashioned* POLIO

ˌinfant morˈtality rate *n* [C] the number of deaths of babies under one year old, expressed as the number out of every 1,000 babies born alive in a year

in·fan·try /ˈɪnfəntri/ *n* [U] soldiers who fight on foot: *an infantry regiment* → CAVALRY

in·fan·try·man /ˈɪnfəntrimən/ *n* (*plural* **infantrymen** /-mən/) [C] a soldier who fights on foot

in·fat·u·at·ed /ɪnˈfætʃueɪtɪd/ *adj* having strong feelings of love for someone or a strong interest in something that makes you unable to think in a sensible way: **[+with]** *John had become infatuated with the French teacher. | My mother's infatuated with dieting.*

in·fat·u·a·tion /ɪnˌfætʃuˈeɪʃən/ *n* [C,U] a strong feeling of love for someone or interest in something, especially a feeling that is unreasonable and does not continue for a long time → **obsession**: **[+with]** *the current infatuation with seventies style | Shaw's infatuation with the actress is evident in his writing.*

in·fect /ɪnˈfekt/ ●●○ *v* [T]
1 to give someone a disease: *People with the virus may feel perfectly well, but they can still infect others. |* **[+with]** *the number of people infected with HIV*
2 to make something contain something harmful that gives people a disease: **be infected with sth** *Eggs known to be infected with salmonella were allowed to go on sale.* GRAMMAR **Infect** is usually passive in this meaning.
3 if a feeling or interest that you have infects other people, it makes them begin to feel the same way or have the same interest: *Lucy's enthusiasm soon infected the rest of the class.*
4 if a VIRUS infects your computer or DISK, it changes or destroys the information in or on it

in·fect·ed /ɪnˈfektɪd/ *adj* **1** a part of your body or a wound that is infected has harmful BACTERIA in it which prevent it from HEALing → **disinfect**: *an infected finger | Clean the wound so it doesn't* ***get infected***. **2** food, water etc that is infected contains BACTERIA that spread disease **3** if a computer or DISK is infected, the information in or on it has been changed or destroyed by a computer VIRUS

in·fec·tion /ɪnˈfekʃən/ ●●○ W3 *n*
1 [C] a disease that affects a particular part of your body and is caused by BACTERIA or a VIRUS: *The baby had an ear infection. |* **[+of/in]** *an infection of the bladder* THESAURUS ILLNESS
2 [U] when someone is infected by a disease: *Always sterilize the needle to prevent infection.*

COLLOCATIONS

VERBS

have an infection *I think you've got an infection, so you need to rest.*
suffer from an infection *He was suffering from an infection of the lungs.*
get/develop an infection *She got a nasty throat infection which meant she couldn't sing.*
treat an infection *Antibiotics are used to treat the infection.*
fight/combat an infection *A new drug is being developed to combat the infection.*
spread an infection (*also* **transmit an infection** *formal*) *Pregnant women can transmit the infection to their unborn child.*
an infection spreads *The infection spread to her chest.*
an infection clears up (=goes away) | **be exposed to an infection**

ADJECTIVES/NOUN + infection

serious/severe *He was admitted to hospital with a serious infection.*
slight/minor (=not serious) *She's suffering from a slight infection.*
nasty *informal* (=a serious infection) *He's got a really nasty infection.*
acute *medical* (=a serious infection that develops suddenly) *The disease usually occurs as an acute infection of the throat.*
an ear/eye infection *She was given antibiotics for an ear infection.*
a chest infection (=an infection in the lungs) | **a throat/kidney etc infection** | **a bacterial/viral/fungal infection** (=caused by bacteria, a virus, or a fungus) | **a secondary infection** *medical* (=an additional infection that happens as a result of the main illness)

PHRASES

the source of an infection *Doctors are trying to locate the source of the infection.*

in·fec·tious /ɪnˈfekʃəs/ ●○○ *adj*
1 an infectious illness can be passed from one person to another, especially through the air you breathe: *infectious diseases | Flu is* ***highly infectious***.
2 someone who is infectious has an illness and could pass it to other people
3 infectious feelings or laughter spread quickly from one person to another: *an* ***infectious smile*** *|* ***infectious enthusiasm*** —**infectiously** *adv*

in·fer /ɪnˈfɜː $ -ɜːr/ ●○○ AWL *v* (**inferred, inferring**) [T] to form an opinion that something is probably true because of information that you have: **infer sth from sth** *A lot can be inferred from these statistics. |* **infer that** *From the evidence, we can infer that the victim knew her killer.*

in·fer·ence /ˈɪnfərəns/ ●○○ AWL *n*
1 [C] something that you think is true, based on information that you have: **draw/make inferences (about/from sth)** *What inferences have you drawn from this evidence?*
2 [U] when someone infers something: **by inference** *He was portrayed as a hero and, by inference, Thompson as the villain.* —**inferential** /ˌɪnfəˈrenʃəl◂/ *adj*: *inferential evidence* —**inferentially** *adv*

in·fe·ri·or¹ /ɪnˈfɪəriə $ -ˈfɪriər/ ●●○ *adj*
1 not good, or not as good as someone or something else OPP **superior**: *I felt very inferior among all those academics. | wine of inferior quality | inferior goods |* **[+to]** *I*

I

always felt slightly inferior to her. | *Their performance was* ***inferior to that of*** *other teams.*
2 *formal* lower in rank OPP **superior**: *an inferior court of law* | *He refused to accept a job of inferior status.*

inferior² *n* [C] someone who has a lower position or rank than you in an organization OPP **superior**

in·fe·ri·or·i·ty /ɪnˌfɪəriˈɒrəti $ -ˌfɪriˈɔːr-/ *n* [U] when someone or something is not good or not as good as someone or something else OPP **superiority**: *moral inferiority* | **sense/feeling of inferiority** *He had a deep-rooted feeling of inferiority.*

inˌferiˈority ˌcomplex *n* [C usually singular] a continuous feeling that you are much less important, clever etc than other people

in·fer·nal /ɪnˈfɜːnl $ -ɜːr-/ *adj* **1** [only before noun] *old-fashioned* used to express anger or annoyance about something: *I wish the children would stop that infernal noise.* **2** *literary* relating to HELL and evil → **hell** —**infernally** *adv*

in·fer·no /ɪnˈfɜːnəʊ $ -ɜːrnoʊ/ *n* (*plural* **infernos**) [C] **1** an extremely large and dangerous fire - used especially in news reports: **raging/blazing inferno** *Within minutes, the house had become a raging inferno.* THESAURUS ▸ FIRE
2 *literary* when someone has very strong feelings that are difficult to control: *She was desperately trying to calm the inferno raging within her.*

in·fer·tile /ɪnˈfɜːtaɪl $ -ˈfɜːrtl/ *adj* **1** unable to have babies: *infertile couples* **2** infertile land or soil is not good enough to grow plants in

in·fer·til·i·ty /ˌɪnfəˈtɪləti $ -fər-/ *n* [U] when someone is unable to have a baby: *There are many possible causes of infertility in women.* | *infertility treatments*

in·fest /ɪnˈfest/ *v* [T] **1** if insects, rats etc infest a place, there are a lot of them and they usually cause damage: **be infested with sth** *The kitchen was infested with cockroaches.* | **shark-infested/rat-infested etc** *shark-infested waters* **2** if a place is infested with things or people you do not want, there are too many of them there: **be infested with sth** *an area infested with holiday homes* —**infestation** /ˌɪnfeˈsteɪʃən/ *n* [C,U]

in·fi·del /ˈɪnfədəl/ *n* [C] *literary not polite* an offensive word for someone who has a different religion from you

in·fi·del·i·ty /ˌɪnfəˈdeləti/ *n* (*plural* **infidelities**) [C,U] when someone has sex with a person who is not their wife, husband, or partner: *marital infidelity*

in·field /ˈɪnfiːld/ *n* [singular] **1** the part of a CRICKET field nearest to the player who hits the ball OPP **outfield** **2** the part of a baseball field inside the four bases OPP **outfield** → see picture at **BASEBALL** **3** the group of players in this part of the CRICKET or baseball field —**infielder** *n* [C]

in·fight·ing /ˈɪnfaɪtɪŋ/ *n* [U] when members of the same group or organization argue, or compete with each other in an unfriendly way: *political infighting*

in·fill /ˈɪnfɪl/ *n* [U] *especially BrE* **1** something that is used to fill a space: *infill panels* **2** the process of filling a space, especially by building new houses: *infill developments* —**infill** *v* [I,T]

in·fil·trate /ˈɪnfɪltreɪt $ ɪnˈfɪltreɪt, ˈɪnfɪl-/ *v* **1** [I always + adv/prep, T] to secretly join an organization or enter a place in order to find out information about it or harm it: *Police attempts to infiltrate neo-Nazi groups were largely unsuccessful.* | **[+into]** *Rebel forces have been infiltrating into the country.* **2** [T] to secretly put people into an organization or place in order to find out information or to harm it: **infiltrate sb into sth** *They repeatedly tried to infiltrate assassins into the palace.* **3** [T] to become a part of something - used especially to show disapproval: *Commercialism has been infiltrating universities for the past decade.* —**infiltrator** *n* [C] —**infiltration** /ˌɪnfɪlˈtreɪʃən/ *n* [U]

in·fi·nite /ˈɪnfənət/ ●●○ AWL *adj*
1 very great in amount or degree: *a woman of infinite patience* | **an infinite number/variety of sth** *There was an infinite variety of drinks to choose from.*
2 without limits in space or time OPP **finite**: *The universe is infinite.* → **in sb's (infinite) wisdom** at **WISDOM**(4), → **NON-FINITE**

in·fi·nite·ly /ˈɪnfənətli/ ●○○ AWL *adv* [+adj/adv] very much - used especially when comparing things: *This school is infinitely better than the last one I went to.* | *someone with infinitely more experience*

in·fin·i·tes·i·mal /ˌɪnfɪnəˈtesəməl◂/ *adj* extremely small SYN **minuscule**: *infinitesimal changes in temperature* —**infinitesimally** *adv*: *infinitesimally small*

in·fin·i·tive /ɪnˈfɪnətɪv/ ●●○ *n* [C] *technical* in grammar, the basic form of a verb, used with 'to' in English. In the sentence 'I want to watch television', 'to watch' is an infinitive. → **SPLIT INFINITIVE**

in·fin·i·tude /ɪnˈfɪnɪtjuːd $ -tuːd/ *n* [singular, U] *formal* a number or amount without limit: *the vast infinitude of space*

in·fin·i·ty /ɪnˈfɪnəti/ *n* **1** [U] a space or distance without limits or an end: *the infinity of space* **2** [singular, U] a number that is too large to be calculated: *In the equation below, as E goes to zero, n approaches infinity.* | **[+of]** *There is an infinity of possible solutions.*

inˈfinity pool *n* [C] a swimming pool that has been built in a special position so that someone swimming in the pool can see as far as the HORIZON (=the line far away where the land or sea seems to meet the sky)

in·firm /ɪnˈfɜːm $ -ɜːrm/ *adj* **1** weak or ill for a long time, especially because you are old: *Her grandmother is elderly and infirm.* THESAURUS ▸ WEAK **2 the infirm** people who are weak or ill for a long time, especially because they are old: *The hotel is on a hill, which is not ideal for the infirm.*

in·fir·ma·ry /ɪnˈfɜːməri $ -ɜːr-/ *n* (*plural* **infirmaries**) [C] **1** a hospital - often used in the names of hospitals in Britain **2** a room in a school or other institution where people can get medical treatment

in·fir·mi·ty /ɪnˈfɜːməti $ -ɜːr-/ *n* (*plural* **infirmities**) [C,U] *formal* bad health or a particular illness

in fla·gran·te /ˌɪn fləˈgænteɪ, -ti/ *adv formal* during the act of having sex, especially with someone else's husband or wife - sometimes used humorously → **red-handed**: *They were caught in flagrante by Donna's husband.*

in·flame /ɪnˈfleɪm/ *v* [T] to make someone's feelings of anger, excitement etc much stronger: *The shooting inflamed ethnic tensions.*

in·flamed /ɪnˈfleɪmd/ *adj* a part of your body that is inflamed is red and swollen, because it is injured or infected: *an inflamed eye*

in·flam·ma·ble /ɪnˈflæməbəl/ *adj* **1** *formal* inflammable materials or substances will start to burn very easily SYN **flammable** OPP **nonflammable**: *Petrol is* ***highly inflammable***. **2** easily becoming angry or violent, or making people angry or violent: *inflammable language*

in·flam·ma·tion /ˌɪnfləˈmeɪʃən/ *n* [C,U] swelling and pain in part of your body, which is often red and feels hot: **[+of]** *inflammation of the colon*

in·flam·ma·to·ry /ɪnˈflæmətəri $ -tɔːri/ *adj* **1** an inflammatory speech, piece of writing etc is likely to make people feel angry: *inflammatory remarks* **2** *medical* an inflammatory disease or medical condition causes inflammation: *inflammatory bowel disease*

in·fla·ta·ble¹ /ɪnˈfleɪtəbəl/ *adj* an inflatable object has to be filled with air before you can use it: *an inflatable mattress*

inflatable² *n* [C] an object that has to be filled with air before you can use it, especially a boat or toy

in·flate /ɪnˈfleɪt/ *v* **1** [I,T] to fill something with air or gas so it becomes larger, or to become filled with air or gas: *It took us half an hour to inflate the dinghy.* | *Her life jacket failed to inflate.* **2** [T] to make something seem more important or impressive than it really is: *The success further inflated his self-confidence.* | **be grossly/vastly/hugely inflated** *The numbers of people involved have been grossly inflated by the media.* **3** [I,T] *technical* to increase in price, or to make something increase in price: *Hotels often inflate prices at particular times of the year.* | *Costs were inflating.*

I

in·flat·ed /ɪnˈfleɪtɪd/ *adj* **1** inflated prices, amounts etc are high and unreasonable: **grossly/vastly/hugely inflated** *company directors on grossly inflated salaries* **2** inflated ideas, opinions etc about someone or something make them seem better, more important etc than they really are: *He has a very inflated opinion of himself.* **3** filled with air or gas

in·fla·tion /ɪnˈfleɪʃən/ ●●○ W3 *n* [U]
1 a continuing increase in prices, or the rate at which prices increase: *Inflation is now at over 16%.*
2 the process of filling something with air

COLLOCATIONS

ADJECTIVES/NOUN + inflation

low *France had achieved low inflation and steady growth.*
high *Inflation remained high throughout this period.*
annual inflation *Annual inflation in 1990 was 8.1%.*
rising inflation *The country was hit by rising inflation.*
spiralling/soaring inflation (=inflation that is increasing quickly and out of control) | **price/wage inflation** (=increasing prices/wages)

inflation + NOUN

the inflation rate/the rate of inflation *The current inflation rate stands at 4.1%.*
the inflation figures *April's inflation figures are likely to show a further fall.*

VERBS

cause/lead to inflation *Too much government borrowing can lead to inflation.*
fuel inflation/push up inflation (=make inflation worse) *The increase in food prices is fuelling inflation.*
control/curb inflation (=prevent it from increasing more) *These measures are designed to curb inflation.*
fight/combat inflation *An economic plan to combat inflation was drawn up.*
reduce inflation/get inflation down *The government has promised to reduce inflation to 3%.*
inflation rises *Inflation rose steadily from the mid-1960s.*
inflation falls *Inflation fell by 0.5% last month.*
inflation is running at 3%/4% etc (*also* **inflation stands at 3%/4% etc**) (=used to talk about the present rate of inflation) *Inflation currently stands at 3.2%.*
keep pace with inflation (=be at the same level as inflation) *Salaries have not kept pace with inflation.*

in·fla·tion·a·ry /ɪnˈfleɪʃənəri $ -ʃəneri/ *adj* relating to or causing price increases: *inflationary pressures in the economy | A new round of wage increases could trigger an* ***inflationary spiral*** (=a continuing rise in both wages and prices).

in·flect /ɪnˈflekt/ *v* [I] *technical* if a word inflects, its form changes according to its meaning or use

in·flect·ed /ɪnˈflektɪd/ *adj technical* an inflected language contains many words which change their form according to their meaning or use

in·flec·tion, **inflexion** /ɪnˈflekʃən/ *n* **1** [U] *technical* the way in which a word changes its form to show a difference in its meaning or use **2** [C] *technical* one of the forms of a word that changes in this way, or one of the parts that is added to it **3** [C,U] the way the sound of your voice goes up and down when you are speaking —**inflectional** *adj*

in·flex·i·ble /ɪnˈfleksəbəl/ AWL *adj* **1** unwilling to make even the slightest change in your attitudes, plans etc OPP **flexible**: *inflexible attitudes towards change* **2** inflexible rules, arrangements etc are impossible to change OPP **flexible**: *This approach is too inflexible and too costly.* **3** inflexible material is stiff and will not bend OPP **flexible** —**inflexibly** *adv* —**inflexibility** /ɪnˌfleksəˈbɪləti/ *n* [U]

in·fle·xion /ɪnˈflekʃən/ *n* [C,U] another spelling of INFLECTION

in·flict /ɪnˈflɪkt/ ●●○ *v*
1 [T] to make someone suffer something unpleasant: **inflict sth on/upon sb** *The strikes inflicted serious damage on the economy. | Detectives warned that the men could inflict serious injury.*
2 inflict yourself/sb on sb to visit or be with someone when they do not want you – used humorously: *Was it really fair to her friends to inflict her nephew on them?* —**infliction** /ɪnˈflɪkʃən/ *n* [U]: *the deliberate infliction of pain*

ˈin-flight *adj* [only before noun] provided during a plane journey: *in-flight entertainment*

in·flow /ˈɪnfləʊ $ -floʊ/ *n* **1** [C] the movement of people, money, goods etc into a place OPP **outflow**: **[+of]** *an inflow of funds from abroad* **2** [singular, U] the flow of water into a place OPP **outflow**

in·flu·ence¹ /ˈɪnfluəns/ ●●● S3 W1 *n*
1 [C,U] the power to affect the way someone or something develops, behaves, or thinks, without using direct force or orders: *As a scientist, his influence was immense.* | **[+on/over]** *the unions' influence over local politics*
THESAURUS ▶ EFFECT
2 [C] someone or something that has an influence on other people or things: **bad/good/positive etc influence (on sb)** *Gayle's mother said I was a bad influence on her daughter. | For centuries the country remained untouched by* ***outside influences.***
3 under the influence (of alcohol/drink/drugs etc) drunk or feeling the effects of a drug

COLLOCATIONS – MEANINGS 1 & 2

VERBS

have an influence on sb/sth *His works have had an influence on many modern writers.*
exert an influence *formal* (=have an influence) *Technology exerts a powerful influence over our lives.*
use your influence *She wasn't afraid to use her influence to get what she wanted.*
exercise/wield influence *formal* (=use it) *The Federal Reserve exercises influence on the economy by setting short-term interest rates.*
come/fall under the influence of sb/sth (=be influenced by someone or something) *They had come under the influence of a religious sect.*

ADJECTIVES

a good/positive influence *Television can have a positive influence on young people.*
a bad/negative influence *He thought her friends were a bad influence.*
a big/great influence *The goalkeeper's injury had a big influence on the match.*
an important/significant/major influence *Parents have an important influence on children's development.*
considerable influence *Well-organized pressure groups can exert considerable influence on the government.*
a strong/powerful influence *The press can have a powerful influence on the way people vote.*
a deep/profound influence *His writings had a profound influence on the Romantic poets.*
a growing influence *Many people are worried about the growing influence of these websites.*
a lasting influence (=continuing for a long time) *His travels in Africa had a lasting influence on his work.*
a direct/indirect influence *The Cubist painters had a direct influence on his work.*
a calming/soothing influence *The music seemed to have a calming influence.*
sb's personal influence *Frank used his personal influence to get his son a job at the newspaper.*
political/cultural/economic influence *French political influence began to dominate the country.*
outside/external influence (=happening from outside a country or a situation) | **undue influence** (=too much influence)

influence² ●●● S3 W2 *v* [T] to affect the way someone or something develops, behaves, thinks etc without directly forcing or ordering them: *Marx was* ***strongly influenced*** *by the historian Niebuhr.* | **influence a**

decision/outcome/choice etc *Several factors are likely to influence this decision.* | **influence sb to do sth** *What influenced you to take up nursing?* THESAURUS ▸ PERSUADE

in·flu·en·tial /ˌɪnfluˈenʃəl◂/ ●●○ *adj* having a lot of influence and therefore changing the way people think and behave: *He had influential friends.* | **[+in]** *Dewey was influential in shaping economic policy.* | *a* ***highly influential*** *art magazine* THESAURUS ▸ POWERFUL

in·flu·en·za /ˌɪnfluˈenzə/ *n* [U] *medical* an infectious disease that is like a very bad cold SYN **flu**

in·flux /ˈɪnflʌks/ *n* [C] the arrival of large numbers of people or large amounts of money, goods etc, especially suddenly: **[+of]** *a sudden influx of cash* | **massive/great/huge etc influx** *a large influx of tourists in the summer*

in·fo /ˈɪnfəʊ $ -foʊ/ *n* [U] *informal* information

in·fo·com /ˈɪnfəʊkɒm $ -foʊkɑːm/ *n* [C] a company whose business is to provide information or communication technology, for example a telephone company or a company that provides connections to the Internet

in·fo·me·di·a·ry /ˌɪnfəʊˈmiːdiəri $ ˌɪnfoʊˈmiːdieri/ *n* (*plural* **infomediaries**) [C] a company that collects information from people about the type of products they buy, how often they buy a product etc, and pays them for this information. It then sells the information to other companies, but does not pass on private details such as someone's name or address etc.

in·fo·mer·cial /ˈɪnfəʊmɜːʃəl $ -foʊmɜːr-/ *n* [C] a long television advertisement that provides a lot of information and seems like a normal programme

in·form /ɪnˈfɔːm $ -ɔːrm/ ●●○ S3 W3 *v* [T] *formal*
1 to officially tell someone about something or give them information: *They decided to inform the police* | **inform sb about/of sth** *Please inform us of any change of address as soon as possible.* | **inform sb (that)** *We regret to inform you that your application has been rejected.* THESAURUS ▸ TELL
2 *formal* to influence someone's attitude or opinion: *Her experience as a refugee informs the content of her latest novel.*
inform on/against sb *phr v* to tell the police or an enemy information about someone that will harm them: *He denied that he had ever informed on his neighbours.*

in·for·mal /ɪnˈfɔːməl $ -ɔːr-/ ●●● W3 *adj*
1 relaxed and friendly without being restricted by rules of correct behaviour OPP **formal**: *The atmosphere at work is fairly informal.* | *The two groups met for informal talks.*
2 an informal style of writing or speaking is suitable for ordinary conversations or letters to friends OPP **formal**
3 informal clothes are suitable for wearing at home or in ordinary situations SYN **casual** OPP **formal** —**informally** *adv* —**informality** /ˌɪnfɔːˈmæləti $ -fɔːr-/ *n* [U]

in·for·mant /ɪnˈfɔːmənt $ -ɔːr-/ ●○○ *n* [C]
1 someone who secretly gives the police, the army etc information about someone else SYN **informer**: *One of the witnesses was a paid informant for the FBI.*
2 *technical* someone who gives information about their language, social customs etc to someone who is studying them

This graph shows some of the words most commonly used with the noun **information**.

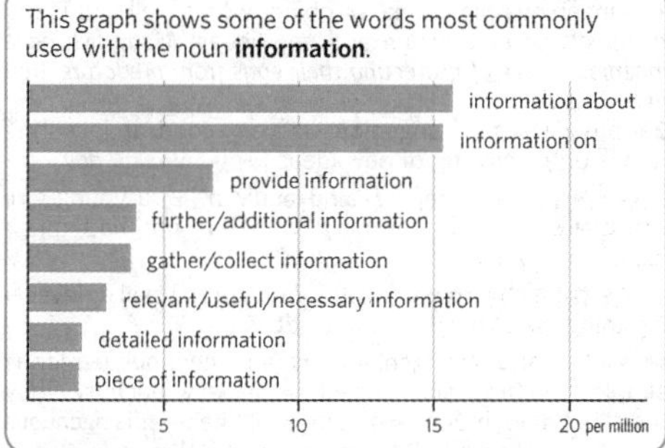

in·for·ma·tion /ˌɪnfəˈmeɪʃən $ -fər-/ ●●● S1 W1 *n* [U]
1 facts or details that tell you something about a situation, person, event etc: *I need more information.* | **[+that]** *We have received information that Grant may have left the country.* | **[+about/on]** *The book contains information about a wide variety of subjects.* | **my/our etc information is** (=used to say what you know about a situation) *My information is that Gary wants to stay with the club.* → **inside information** at INSIDE[3](2)

> **REGISTER**
> In everyday English, in informal contexts, people often use the expression **tell someone something** rather than using the noun **information**: *I wonder if you could* ***give*** *me* ***some information*** *about your childhood.* → *I wonder if you could* ***tell*** *me* ***something*** *about your childhood.*

> **GRAMMAR: Countable or uncountable?**
> • **Information** is an uncountable noun and is not used in the plural. You say: *I need some information about hotels.* ✗ Don't say: *I need some informations about hotels.*
> • **Information** is always followed by a singular verb: *The information* ***is*** *strictly confidential.*
> • When talking about one fact or detail, you say a **piece of information** or a **bit of information**: *He told me an interesting piece of information.*

2 *AmE* the telephone service which provides telephone numbers to people who ask for them SYN **directory enquiries** *BrE*
3 for sb's information used when you provide a document or some information, because you think it may be useful for someone: *I'm attaching a copy of the report for your information.*
4 For your information... *spoken* used when you are telling someone that they are wrong about a particular fact: *For your information, I've worked as a journalist for six years.*
5 for information only written on copies of letters and documents that are sent to someone who needs to know about them but does not have to deal with them
6 too much information! *spoken informal* used when someone has just told you details that you think are embarrassing or unpleasant, and you do not want to hear any more: *'I was really ill at the weekend - I had to stay on the toilet all day.' 'Too much information!'* —**informational** *adj*

> **COLLOCATIONS**
> **ADJECTIVES/NOUN + information**
> **useful/valuable** *The information he gave me was very useful.*
> **correct/accurate** *Are you sure this information is correct?*
> **wrong/false** *He was jailed for providing false information to the police.*
> **relevant** (=about the subject you are interested in) *Some of the information in the article is not particularly relevant.*
> **confidential/secret** *That information was confidential and should not have been passed on.*
> **more/further/additional information** *For more information, visit our website.*
> **new information** *The police have received new information about the case.*
> **the latest information** (=information that has been discovered very recently) *We have access to all the latest information.*
> **the necessary information** *This leaflet should provide you with all the necessary information.*
> **detailed information** | **financial/economic information** | **background information** (=information explaining what happened before the present situation)
> **VERBS**
> **have information** *Do you have any information about coach trips to Oxford?*

I

contain information *The documents contained top secret information.*
get/receive information *It is vital that people receive the information they need.*
give/provide information *a booklet giving information about local education services*
collect/gather information *The job consisted of gathering information about consumer needs.*
look for information (*also* **seek information** *formal*) *Journalists going to the building to seek information were denied entry.*
exchange information (=give information to each other) *The meetings provided an opportunity to exchange information.*
disseminate information *formal* (=give it to a lot of people) *The internet plays a key role in disseminating information.*

PHRASES

a piece/bit of information (*also* **an item of information** *formal*) *He provided me with several useful pieces of information.*
a source of information (=someone or something that can provide information) *Newspapers are valuable sources of information.*

infor'mation ˌcentre *n* [C] a place where you can get information about an area, event etc

ˌinformation 'overload *n* [U] when someone gets too much information at one time, for example on the Internet, and becomes tired and unable to think very carefully about any of it: *The greater the amount of data, the greater the risk of information overload.*

infor'mation reˌtrieval *n* [U] the process of finding stored information, especially on a computer

ˌinforˌmation 'science *n* [U] the science of collecting, arranging, storing, and sending out information

information su·per·high·way /ˌɪnfəmeɪʃən ˌsuːpəˈhaɪweɪ, -sjuː- $ -fərmeɪʃən ˌsuːpər-/ *n* **the information superhighway** the Internet

infor'mation techˌnology *n* [U] (*abbreviation* **IT**) the study or use of electronic processes for gathering and storing information and making it available using computers

infor'mation ˌtheory *n* [U] *technical* the mathematical principles related to sending and storing information

in·for·ma·tive /ɪnˈfɔːmətɪv $ -ɔːr-/ ●○○ *adj* providing many useful facts or ideas: *an informative and entertaining book* —**informatively** *adv*

in·formed /ɪnˈfɔːmd $ -ɔːr-/ ●○○ *adj*
1 having a lot of knowledge or information about a particular subject or situation: *Informed sources said it was likely that the president would make a televised statement.* | **well-informed/ill-informed** *I became reasonably well-informed about the subject.*
2 informed decision/choice/judgment etc a decision etc that is based on knowledge of a subject or situation: *Good information is essential if people are to make informed choices about services.*
3 keep sb informed to give someone the latest news and details about a situation: *Please keep me **fully informed** of any developments.*

in·form·er /ɪnˈfɔːmə $ -ɔːrmər/ *n* [C] someone who secretly tells the police, the army etc about criminal activities, especially for money SYN **informant**

in·fo·tain·ment /ˌɪnfəʊˈteɪnmənt $ -foʊ-/ *n* [U] television programmes that deal with important subjects in a way that people can enjoy

in·fo·war /ˈɪnfəʊwɔː $ -foʊwɔːr/ *n* [U] attacks on computer systems, for example with VIRUSes, that are intended as acts of war against an enemy

infra- /ɪnfrə/ *prefix technical* below something in a range: *the infra-red end of the spectrum* → **ULTRA-(2)**

in·frac·tion /ɪnˈfrækʃən/ *n* [C,U] *formal* an act of breaking a rule or law: **[+of]** *minor infractions of the rules*

inf·ra-red /ˌɪnfrə ˈred◂/ *adj* infra-red light gives out heat but cannot be seen → **ULTRAVIOLET**

in·fra·struc·ture /ˈɪnfrəˌstrʌktʃə $ -ər/ ●○○ AWL *n* [C,U] the basic systems and structures that a country or organization needs in order to work properly, for example roads, railways, banks etc: *Some countries lack a suitable economic infrastructure.* | *a $65 billion investment package in education, health care and infrastructure* —**infrastructural** *adj*

in·fre·quent /ɪnˈfriːkwənt/ *adj* not happening often SYN **rare** OPP **frequent**: *They would make infrequent visits to the house.* —**infrequency** *n* [U]

in·fre·quent·ly /ɪnˈfriːkwəntli/ *adv* **1** not often SYN **rarely** OPP **frequently**: *Jeremy does play cricket, but very infrequently.* **2 not infrequently** *formal* fairly often: *The censors changed some names and dialogue and, not infrequently, banned controversial films.*

in·fringe /ɪnˈfrɪndʒ/ ●○○ *v* [T] to do something that is against a law or someone's legal rights: *A backup copy of a computer program does not infringe copyright.* —**infringement** *n* [C,U]: *the infringement of human rights*
infringe on/upon sth *phr v* to limit someone's freedom in some way: *Some students argued that the rule infringed on their right to free speech.*

in·fu·ri·ate /ɪnˈfjʊərieɪt $ -ˈfjʊr-/ *v* [T] to make someone extremely angry SYN **anger**: *Her actions infuriated her mother.* | ***It infuriated** him **that** Beth was with another man.*

in·fu·ri·a·ting /ɪnˈfjʊərieɪtɪŋ $ -ˈfjʊr-/ *adj* very annoying: *The infuriating thing is that he is always right.* —**infuriatingly** *adv*: *an infuriatingly tricky crossword puzzle*

in·fuse /ɪnˈfjuːz/ *v* **1** [T] *formal* to fill something or someone with a particular feeling or quality: **be infused with sth** *Her books are infused with humour and wisdom.* | **infuse sth into sth** *These new designers are infusing fresh interest into the New York fashion scene.* **2** [I,T] if you infuse tea or HERBS, or if they infuse, you leave them in very hot water while their taste passes into the water

in·fu·sion /ɪnˈfjuːʒən/ *n* **1** [C,U] the act of putting a new feeling or quality into something: **[+of]** *Further education badly needs the infusion of more resources.* **2** [C,U] *medical* the act of putting medicine slowly into someone's body, or the medicine itself: *intravenous infusions of cardiac drugs* **3** [C] a drink made with HERBS in hot water that is usually taken as a medicine

-ing /ɪŋ/ *suffix* **1** forms the present participle of verbs: *They're dancing.* | *to go dancing* | *a dancing bear* **2** [in U nouns] the action or process of doing something: *She hates swimming.* | *No parking.* **3** [in C nouns] **a)** an example of doing something: *to hold a meeting* **b)** a product or result of doing something: *a beautiful painting* **4** [in nouns] something used to do something or used for making something: *a silk lining* | *ten metres of curtaining* (=cloth for curtains)

'in-game *adj* used or happening while playing an electronic game: *in-game advertisements* | *in-game behavior*

in·ge·ni·ous /ɪnˈdʒiːniəs/ ●○○ *adj*
1 an ingenious plan, idea, or object works well and is the result of clever thinking and new ideas: *Many fish have ingenious ways of protecting their eggs from predators.* | *an ingenious device*
2 someone who is ingenious is very good at inventing things or at thinking of new ideas —**ingeniously** *adv*

in·gé·nue /ˈænʒeɪnjuː $ ˈændʒənuː/ *n* [C] a young girl, especially in a film or play, who has not had much experience of life

in·ge·nu·i·ty /ˌɪndʒəˈnjuːəti $ -ˈnuː-/ *n* [U] skill at inventing things and thinking of new ideas

in·gen·u·ous /ɪnˈdʒenjuəs/ *adj* an ingenuous person is simple, trusting, and honest, especially because they have not had much experience of life → **disingenuous** —**ingenuously** *adv* —**ingenuousness** *n* [U]

in·gest /ɪnˈdʒest/ *v* [T] *technical* to take food or other substances into your body → **digest** —**ingestion** /ɪnˈdʒestʃən/ *n* [U]

in·gle·nook /ˈɪŋɡəlnʊk/ *n* [C] *BrE* a seat by the side of a large open FIREPLACE, or the space that it is in

in·glo·ri·ous /ɪnˈɡlɔːriəs/ *adj literary* causing shame and dishonour SYN **humiliating**: *an inglorious defeat* —**ingloriously** *adv*

in·got /ˈɪŋɡət/ *n* [C] a piece of pure metal, especially gold, usually shaped like a brick

in·grained /ɪnˈɡreɪnd/ *adj* **1** ingrained attitudes or behaviour are firmly established and therefore difficult to change: **[+in]** *The idea of doing our duty is* ***deeply ingrained*** *in most people.* **2** ingrained dirt is under the surface of something and very difficult to remove

in·grate /ɪnˈɡreɪt, ˈɪŋɡreɪt $ ˈɪŋɡreɪt/ *n* [C] *formal* an ungrateful person

in·gra·ti·ate /ɪnˈɡreɪʃieɪt/ *v* **ingratiate yourself (with sb)** to try very hard to get someone's approval – used to show disapproval → **flatter**: *His policy is to ingratiate himself with anyone who might be useful to him.*

in·gra·ti·at·ing /ɪnˈɡreɪʃieɪtɪŋ/ *adj* trying too hard to get someone's approval – used to show disapproval: *an ingratiating smile* —**ingratiatingly** *adv*

in·grat·i·tude /ɪnˈɡrætɪtjuːd $ -tuːd/ *n* [U] the quality of not being grateful: *I've never seen such ingratitude!*

in·gre·di·ent /ɪnˈɡriːdiənt/ ●●○ *n* [C]
1 one of the foods that you use to make a particular food or dish: *Combine all the ingredients in a large bowl.* | *The food is home-cooked using fresh ingredients.*
2 a quality you need to achieve something: *John* ***has*** *all* ***the ingredients of*** *a great player.* | *Investment in new product development is an* ***essential ingredient*** *of corporate success.*
3 active ingredient the substance in a product such as a medicine that causes the product's intended result: *Acetic acid is the chief active ingredient in vinegar.*

in·gress /ˈɪnɡres/ *n* [U] *literary* the right to enter a place, or the act of entering it

ˈin-group *n* [C] a small group of people involved in an organization or activity who like the same things and are friendly with each other, but do not want other people to join them SYN **clique**

in·grow·ing /ˌɪnˈɡrəʊɪŋ◂ $ -ˈɡroʊ-/ *BrE*, **in·grown** /-ˈɡrəʊn◂ $ -ˈɡroʊn◂/ *AmE adj* [no comparative] an ingrowing TOENAIL grows inwards, cutting into the surrounding skin

in·hab·it /ɪnˈhæbɪt/ ●●○ *v* [T] if animals or people inhabit an area or place, they live there SYN **live**: *The woods are inhabited by many wild animals.* | *inhabited islands* THESAURUS ▸ LIVE —**inhabitable** *adj*

> **REGISTER**
> **Inhabit** is mainly used in formal or scientific contexts. In everyday English, people usually say someone **lives in** a place: *Millions of people* ***live in*** *these shantytowns.*

in·hab·i·tant /ɪnˈhæbɪtənt/ ●●○ *n* [C] one of the people who live in a particular place: *a city of six million inhabitants*

in·ha·lant /ɪnˈheɪlənt/ *n* [C,U] a medicine or drug that you breathe in, for example when you have a cold

in·hale /ɪnˈheɪl/ *v* [I,T] to breathe in air, smoke, or gas OPP **exhale**: *It is dangerous to inhale ammonia fumes.* | *Myra lit another cigarette and* ***inhaled deeply*** (=breathed in a lot of smoke). —**inhalation** /ˌɪnhəˈleɪʃən/ *n* [U]: *One man was treated for* ***smoke inhalation*** (=when you breathe smoke from a fire).

in·hal·er /ɪnˈheɪlə $ -ər/ *n* [C] a small plastic tube containing medicine that you breathe in, in order to make breathing easier

in·here /ɪnˈhɪə $ -ˈhɪr/ *v*
inhere in sth *phr v technical* to be a natural part of something

in·her·ent /ɪnˈhɪərənt, -ˈher- $ -ˈhɪr-, -ˈher-/ ●○○ AWL *adj formal* a quality that is inherent in something is a natural part of it and cannot be separated from it: **[+in]** *I'm afraid the problems you mention are inherent in the system.* | *Every business has its own inherent risks.* —**inherently** *adv*: *Firefighting is an inherently dangerous occupation.*

in·her·it /ɪnˈherɪt/ ●●○ *v*
1 [I,T] to receive money, property etc from someone after they have died: **inherit sth from sb** *He inherited a fortune from his grandmother.* | *inherited wealth* THESAURUS ▸ GET
2 [T] if you inherit a situation, especially one in which problems have been caused by other people, you have to deal with it: *The present government inherited a closed, state-dominated economy.*
3 [T] to have the same character or appearance as your parents: **inherit sth from sb** *Mr. Grass inherited his work ethic from his father.* | *I inherited my mother's curly hair.*
4 [T] to get something that someone else does not want anymore: **inherit sth from sb** *We inherited the furniture from the previous tenants.*

in·her·i·tance /ɪnˈherətəns/ ●○○ *n*
1 [C,U] money, property etc that you receive from someone who has died: *Lucinda has to fight for her life and her inheritance in this gripping novel.*
2 [U] physical or mental qualities that you inherit from your family: *Our genetic inheritance cannot be changed.*
3 [U] ideas, skills, literature etc from the past that influence people in the present: *ideas that have become part of our cultural inheritance*

inˈheritance ˌtax *n* [U] a tax that you have to pay when you receive money or property from someone who has died

in·he·r·i·tor /ɪnˈherɪtə $ -ər/ *n* [C] **1** someone who receives money, property etc from someone who has just died **2** someone who follows in an established way of life or thinking: **[+of]** *These writers are inheritors of his work.*

in·hib·it /ɪnˈhɪbɪt/ ●○○ AWL *v* [T]
1 to prevent something from growing or developing well: *An unhappy family life may inhibit children's learning.*
2 to make someone feel embarrassed or nervous so that they cannot do or say what they want to: **inhibit sb from doing sth** *Recording the meeting may inhibit people from expressing their real views.*

in·hib·it·ed /ɪnˈhɪbɪtɪd/ *adj* too embarrassed or nervous to do or say what you want SYN **shy**: **[+about]** *Many people are inhibited about discussing sexual matters.*

in·hi·bi·tion /ˌɪnhəˈbɪʃən/ ●○○ AWL *n*
1 [C,U] a feeling of shyness or embarrassment that stops you doing or saying what you really want: *She had no inhibitions about saying what she felt.* | *People tend to* ***lose*** *their* ***inhibitions*** *when they've drunk a lot of alcohol.*
2 [U] *technical* when something is restricted or prevented from happening or developing: *a marked inhibition of cell growth*

in·hos·pi·ta·ble /ˌɪnhɒˈspɪtəbəl $ -hɑː-/ *adj* **1** an inhospitable place is difficult to live or stay in because the weather conditions are unpleasant or there is no shelter: *an inhospitable climate* | *He trekked across some of the most inhospitable terrain in the world.* **2** an inhospitable person does not welcome visitors in a friendly way: **[+to]** *Some governments are inhospitable to aid workers.*

ˌin-ˈhouse *adj, adv* working within a company or organization: *We have an in-house training unit.* | *The keyboarding is done in-house.*

in·hu·man /ɪnˈhjuːmən/ *adj* **1** very cruel or without any normal feelings of pity: *The refugees had suffered degrading and inhuman treatment.* **2** lacking any human qualities in a way that seems strange or frightening: *a strange inhuman sound* —**inhumanly** *adv*

in·hu·mane /ˌɪnhjuːˈmeɪn/ *adj* extremely cruel and causing unacceptable suffering: *the inhumane treatment of political prisoners* | *I was shocked by the inhumane conditions.* THESAURUS ▸ CRUEL —**inhumanely** *adv*

in·hu·man·i·ty /ˌɪnhjuːˈmænəti/ *n* [U] very cruel behaviour or actions: *the inhumanity of some political systems*

in·im·i·cal /ɪˈnɪmɪkəl/ *adj formal* making it difficult for something to exist or happen: *a cold, inimical climate* | **[+to]** *conditions inimical to development*

in·im·i·ta·ble /ɪˈnɪmətəbəl/ *adj* too good or skilful for anyone else to copy with the same high standard SYN **unique**: *the inimitable Billie Holiday* | **your own inimitable way/style etc** *He entertained us in his own inimitable style.* —**inimitably** *adv* → IMITATE

in·iq·ui·tous /ɪˈnɪkwɪtəs/ *adj formal* very unfair and morally wrong: *an iniquitous system of taxation*

in·iq·ui·ty /ɪˈnɪkwəti/ *n (plural* **iniquities***)* [C,U] *formal* the quality of being very unfair or evil, or something that is very unfair: **[+of]** *He went on and on about the iniquities of bourgeois oppression.* | *They were trying to protect their son from iniquity.* → **den of iniquity** at DEN(6)

i·ni·tial¹ /ɪˈnɪʃəl/ ●●○ S3 W2 AWL *adj* [only before noun] happening at the beginning SYN **first**: *an initial investment of £5,000* | **initial stage/phase/period** *the initial stages of the disease* | *The initial response has been encouraging.*

initial² ●●○ *n* [C]

1 the first letter of someone's first name: *'Can I have your initial, Mr Davies?' 'It's G, Mr G Davies.'*

2 initials [plural] the first letters of all your names in order: *His initials are DPH: they stand for David Perry Hallworth.*

initial³ *v* (**initialled**, **initialling** *BrE*, **initialed**, **initialing** *AmE*) [T] to write your initials on a document to make it official or to show that you agree with something → **sign**: *The two countries have initialled a new defence co-operation agreement.*

i·ni·tial·ly /ɪˈnɪʃəli/ ●●○ S3 W3 AWL *adv* at the beginning: *Stan initially wanted to go to medical school.* | *Initially, I thought I would only stay there a year.*

i·ni·ti·ate¹ /ɪˈnɪʃieɪt/ ●○○ AWL *v* [T]

1 *formal* to arrange for something important to start, such as an official process or a new plan: *They have decided to initiate legal proceedings against the newspaper.* | *Intellectuals have initiated a debate on terrorism.*

2 to tell someone about something or show them how to do something: **initiate sb into sth** *Those kids were initiated into heroin use at a young age.*

3 to introduce someone into an organization, club, group etc, usually with a special ceremony: **initiate sb into sth** *At the age of thirteen, the boys in the tribe are initiated into manhood.*

i·ni·ti·ate² /ɪˈnɪʃiət/ *n* [C] someone who has been allowed to join a particular organization, club, or group and has been taught its secrets

i·ni·ti·a·tion /ɪˌnɪʃiˈeɪʃən/ AWL *n* [C,U] **1** the process of officially introducing someone into a club or group, or of introducing a young person to adult life, often with a special ceremony: *The club has an* ***initiation ceremony*** *for new members.* | **initiation rite/ritual** *initiation rituals for young boys at puberty* | **[+into]** *rites of initiation into their religion* **2** the act of starting something such as an official process, a new plan etc: **[+of]** *the initiation of criminal proceedings*

i·ni·tia·tive /ɪˈnɪʃətɪv/ ●●○ W3 AWL *n*

1 DECISIONS [U] the ability to make decisions and take action without waiting for someone to tell you what to do: *I wish my son would* ***show*** *more* ***initiative***. | *Don't keep asking me for advice.* ***Use*** *your* ***initiative***. | *Lt. Carlos was not obeying orders. He* ***acted on*** *his* ***own initiative*** (=he was not told what to do).

2 PLAN [C] an important new plan or process to achieve a particular aim or to solve a particular problem: *a government initiative to help exporters* | *an education initiative* | **[+for]** *a new initiative for peace in the Middle East*
THESAURUS ➤ PLAN

3 CONTROL **the initiative** if you have or take the initiative, you are in a position to control a situation and decide what to do next: *Why don't you* ***take the initiative*** *and ask him out?* | *Politicians need to* ***seize the initiative*** *from the terrorists.* | *The government must not* ***lose the initiative*** *in the fight against terrorism.*

4 LAW [C] *law* a process by which ordinary citizens can officially suggest a change in the law by signing a PETITION

i·ni·ti·a·tor /ɪˈnɪʃieɪtə $ -ər/ AWL *n* [C] someone who thinks of and starts a new plan or process: **[+of]** *the initiator of the proposal*

in·ject /ɪnˈdʒekt/ ●●○ *v* [T]

1 to put liquid, especially a drug, into someone's body by using a special needle: **inject sth into sb/sth** *The drug is injected directly into the base of the spine.* | **inject sb with sth** *I have to inject myself with insulin.*

2 to improve something by adding excitement, interest etc to it: **inject sth into sth** *Traditional handbag makers are injecting more fun into their designs.* | *A market building can inject new life into an area.*

3 to provide more money, equipment etc for something: **inject sth into sth** *They need to inject more money into sports facilities.*

in·jec·tion /ɪnˈdʒekʃən/ ●●○ *n*

1 [C,U] an act of putting a drug into someone's body using a special needle → **shot**: *The nurse* ***gave*** *me a tetanus* ***injection***. | **[+of]** *an injection of insulin* | *The children hate* ***having injections***. | *The only sure treatment is antibiotics, preferably by injection.*

2 [C] an addition of money to something in order to improve it: **[+of]** *a massive injection of public funds* | *Our local football club may fold unless it* ***gets*** *a* ***cash injection***.

3 [C,U] the act of forcing a liquid into something: *a fuel injection system*

inˌjection ˈmoulding *n* [U] a process of making something in which plastic is forced into a particular shape, using a lot of pressure —**injection-moulded** *adj*: *injection-moulded fittings*

ˈin-joke *n* [C] a joke that is only understood by a particular group of people

in·ju·di·cious /ˌɪndʒuːˈdɪʃəs◂/ *adj formal* an injudicious action, remark etc is not sensible and is likely to have bad results: *He has apologized for his injudicious remarks.* —**injudiciously** *adv*

in·junc·tion /ɪnˈdʒʌŋkʃən/ *n* [C] **1** *law* an order given by a court, which tells someone not to do something: **[+against]** *The family is* ***seeking*** *an* ***injunction*** *against the book's publication.* | *The judge refused to* ***grant*** *an* ***injunction***. | *They failed to* ***obtain*** *an* ***injunction***. **2** *formal* a piece of advice or an order from someone in authority

in·jure /ˈɪndʒə $ -ər/ ●●● W3 AWL *v* [T]

1 to hurt yourself or someone else, for example in an accident or an attack → **wound**: *Angus injured his leg playing rugby.* | **be badly/seriously/critically injured** *Two people have been critically injured in an accident.*
THESAURUS ➤ HURT

2 injure sb's pride/feelings etc to say unfair or unpleasant things that hurt someone's pride, feelings etc

> **REGISTER**
> In everyday English, people usually say **hurt** rather than **injure**: *He* ***hurt*** *his leg playing rugby.* | *He really* ***hurt*** *my feelings.*

in·jured /ˈɪndʒəd $ -ərd/ ●●○ AWL *adj*

1 having a wound or damage to part of your body → **wounded**: *an injured bird* | *Chelsea have three injured players.* | *Grandpa was* ***badly injured*** *in the war.* | *The car accident* ***left*** *him seriously* ***injured***.

2 the injured the people who have been hurt → **the wounded**: *Many of the injured are still in a serious condition.*

3 injured look/expression etc a look that shows you feel you have been treated unfairly

4 injured pride/feelings etc a feeling of being upset or offended because you think you have been unfairly treated

5 the injured party *formal* the person who has been unfairly treated in a particular situation

in·ju·ri·ous /ɪnˈdʒʊəriəs $ -ˈdʒʊr-/ *adj formal* causing injury, harm, or damage: **[+to]** *Smoking is injurious to health.*

in·ju·ry /ˈɪndʒəri/ ●●● S3 W2 AWL *n (plural* **injuries***)*

1 [C,U] a wound or damage to part of your body caused by an accident or attack: *She was taken to hospital with*

serious head injuries. | **[+to]** *The driver of the truck suffered injuries to his legs and arms.* | *Beckham has missed several games* ***through injury*** (=because of injury). | *He's a lawyer who specializes in personal injury claims.*
2 [U] *law* damage to someone's REPUTATION, CAREER, or feelings: **[+to]** *He says that the allegations caused serious injury to his reputation.* → **add insult to injury** at ADD(8)

COLLOCATIONS

ADJECTIVES/NOUN + injury

serious *The injury wasn't serious.*
terrible (=very bad) *Some of the victims suffered terrible injuries.*
fatal (=that kills someone) *Fortunately, his injuries weren't fatal.*
minor *A man was treated in hospital for minor injuries.*
permanent *The brain can be affected by permanent injury after a serious accident.*
a nasty injury (=quite bad) *Fairground rides can cause some nasty injuries.*
a head/leg/shoulder etc injury *He suffered a shoulder injury while playing rugby.*
a spinal injury (=an injury to the spine) | **a facial injury** (=an injury to the face) | **a sports injury** (=one you get while doing sport) | **an industrial injury** (=one that happens at work) | **internal injuries** (=injuries inside your body) | **multiple injuries** (=large number of injuries at the same time)

VERBS

have an injury *Tom was OK, and had just a few minor injuries.*
suffer an injury *He suffered a serious leg injury in a motorcycle accident.*
get an injury *informal* (=suffer an injury) *He couldn't take the chance of getting an injury.*
sustain/receive an injury *formal* (=suffer an injury) *She sustained an injury to her hip.*
treat an injury *The injury was treated at the local hospital.*
recover from an injury *It took her six months to recover from the injury.*
escape/avoid injury *Two workmen narrowly escaped injury when a wall collapsed.*
cause an injury *The injury was caused by flying glass from the car windscreen.*
inflict an injury on sb *formal* (=make someone have an injury) *Jenkins was accused of inflicting a head injury on one of his former colleagues.*
do yourself an injury *BrE informal* (=accidentally hurt yourself) *Be careful with that knife or you'll do yourself an injury.*
an injury happens/occurs *The injury occurred five minutes into the game.*

PHRASES

be prone to injury (=often get injuries) *She was rather prone to injury and often missed matches as a result.*

injury + NOUN

injury problems *BrE*: *He suffered injury problems throughout his career as a footballer.*

THESAURUS

injury damage to part of your body caused by an accident or an attack: *The passengers were taken to hospital with minor injuries.*
wound an injury, especially a deep cut in your skin made by a knife, bullet, or bomb: *He died of a gunshot wound to the head.*
cut a small injury made when a sharp object cuts your skin: *Blood was running from a cut on his chin.*
bruise a dark mark on your skin that you get when you fall or get hit: *Jack often comes home from playing rugby covered in bruises.*
graze/scrape a small injury that marks your skin or breaks the surface slightly: *She fell off her bike and got a few grazes on her legs and knees.*
gash a long deep cut: *He had a deep gash across his forehead.*
bump an area of skin that is swollen because you have hit it against something: *How did you get that bump on your head?*
sprain an injury to your ANKLE, WRIST, knee etc, caused by suddenly twisting it: *It's a slight sprain – you should rest your ankle for a week.*
strain an injury to a muscle caused by stretching it or using it too much: *a muscle strain in his neck*
fracture a crack or broken part in a bone: *a hip fracture*

ˈinjury ˌtime *n* [U] *BrE* playing time added on to a game such as football because of time lost when players are injured → **extra time**

in·jus·tice /ɪnˈdʒʌstɪs/ ●○○ *n*
1 [C,U] a situation in which people are treated very unfairly and not given their rights: **[+of]** *the injustice of slavery* | **[+against]** *innumerable injustices against the black population* | *The movie deals with injustices suffered by Native Americans.* | *He had developed a deep* ***sense of*** *social* ***injustice****.*
2 do sb an injustice to judge someone's character or abilities unfairly: *To say that you are a poor cook is to do yourself an injustice.*

ink¹ /ɪŋk/ ●●○ *n*
1 [C,U] a coloured liquid that you use for writing, printing, or drawing: *Please write* ***in*** *black* ***ink****.*
2 [U] the black liquid in sea creatures such as OCTOPUSes and SQUID

ink² *v* [T] **1** to put ink on something **2** to make a document, agreement etc official and legal by writing your SIGNATURE on it: *The two companies have inked a deal.*

ink sth ↔ **in** *phr v* to complete something done in pencil by drawing over it in ink

ink·jet print·er /ˈɪŋkdʒet ˌprɪntə $ -ər/ *n* [C] an electronic PRINTER, usually connected to a small computer → **dot-matrix printer, laser printer**

ink·ling /ˈɪŋklɪŋ/ *n* [C usually singular] a slight idea about something → **suspicion**: *I* ***had an inkling*** *that she was pregnant.* | **[+of]** *She had absolutely no inkling of what was going on.*

ˈink pad *n* [C] a small box containing ink on a thick piece of cloth, used for putting ink onto a STAMP that is then pressed onto paper

ink·well /ˈɪŋk-wel/ *n* [C] a container for ink which fits into a hole in a desk

ink·y /ˈɪŋki/ *adj* **1** *literary* very dark – used especially in poetry: *I stared out into the inky blackness of the night.* **2** marked with ink: *inky fingers*

in·laid /ˌɪnˈleɪd◂/ *adj* **1** an inlaid box, table, floor etc has little pieces of another material set into its surface for decoration: **[+with]** *a wooden jewellery box inlaid with ivory* **2** [+in/into] metal, stone etc that is inlaid into the surface of another material is set into its surface as decoration

in·land¹ /ˈɪnlənd/ *adj* [only before noun] an inland area, city etc is not near the coast: *the largest area of inland water in the southeast*

in·land² /ɪnˈlænd/ *adv* in a direction away from the coast and towards the centre of a country: *The mountains are five miles inland.* | *We set off inland.*

ˈin-laws *n* [plural] *informal* your relatives by marriage, especially the father and mother of your husband or wife → **mother-in-law, father-in-law**: *We have to spend Christmas with the in-laws.*

in·lay /ˈɪnleɪ/ *n* **1** [C,U] a material which has been set into the surface of furniture, floors etc for decoration, or the pattern made by this: *a cedarwood casket with gold inlay* **2** [C] a substance used by a DENTIST to fill a hole in a decayed tooth

in·let /ˈɪnlet, ˈɪnlɪt/ *n* [C] **1** a narrow area of water that reaches from the sea or a lake into the land: *There are*

I

several sheltered inlets along the coast. **2** the part of a machine through which liquid or gas flows in OPP **outlet**: *a fuel inlet*

ˌin-line ˈskate *n* [C] a special boot for ROLLER SKATING, with a single row of wheels attached under it SYN **Rollerblade** → see picture at **SKATE¹**

in lo·co pa·ren·tis /ɪn ˌləʊkəʊ pəˈrentɪs $ -ˌloʊkoʊ-/ *adv formal or law* having the responsibilities of a parent for someone else's child → **guardian**: *As a teacher, you should regard yourself as being in loco parentis.*

in·mate /ˈɪnmeɪt/ ●○○ *n* [C] someone who is being kept in a prison

in me·mo·ri·am /ɪn məˈmɔːriəm/ *prep* an expression meaning 'in memory of', used especially on the stone above the place where a dead person is buried

in·most /ˈɪnməʊst $ -moʊst/ *adj* [only before noun] **1** your inmost feelings, desires etc are your most personal and secret ones: *In his inmost heart, he knew he didn't love me.* **2** *formal* furthest inside a place, and so difficult to see or find: *Apparently there are bats in the inmost caves.*

inn /ɪn/ ●●○ *n* [C]
1 a small hotel or PUB, especially an old one in the countryside **THESAURUS** ▸ **HOTEL**
2 a word used in the names of some PUBS and hotels: *We're staying at the Holiday Inn.*

in·nards /ˈɪnədz $ -ərdz/ *n* [plural] *informal* **1** the parts inside your body, especially your stomach SYN **guts** **2** the parts inside a machine

in·nate /ɪˈneɪt◂/ ●○○ *adj*
1 an innate quality or ability is something you are born with: *Children have an innate ability to learn language.*
2 an innate belief is something you feel strongly about and are unlikely to change: *the innate conservatism of the farming community* —**innately** *adv*: *the army's innately conservative values*

in·ner /ˈɪnə $ -ər/ ●●○ W2 *adj* [only before noun]
1 on the inside or close to the centre of something OPP **outer**: *an inner room | inner London | the inner ear*
2 inner thoughts or feelings are ones that you feel strongly but do not always show to other people: *Yoga gives me a sense of inner calm. | She'll need great inner strength to get over the tragedy. | She never shared her inner thoughts with anyone.*
3 relating to things which happen or exist but are not easy to see: *the inner workings of the film industry | the fascinating inner life of a political party*
4 inner circle the few people in an organization, political party etc who control it or share power with its leader: *members of the president's inner circle*
5 sb's inner voice thoughts or feelings inside your head which seem to warn or advise you: *My inner voice told me to be cautious.*

ˌinner ˈchild *n* [singular] the emotions and feelings you had as a child that still form a part of your character as an adult

ˌinner ˈcity *n* (*plural* **inner cities**) [C] the part near the middle of a city, especially where the buildings are in a bad condition and the people are poor: *the problems of our inner cities* —**inner-city** *adj*: *inner-city schools*

in·ner·most /ˈɪnəməʊst $ -nərmoʊst/ *adj* [only before noun] **1** your innermost feelings, desires etc are your most personal and secret ones: *a man who would never share his innermost thoughts with anyone* **THESAURUS** ▸ **PRIVATE** **2** *formal* furthest inside or nearest to the centre OPP **outermost**: *the innermost depths of the cave*

ˈinner tube *n* [C] a rubber tube filled with air that is inside a tyre

in·ning /ˈɪnɪŋ/ *n* [C] one of the nine playing periods in a game of baseball or SOFTBALL

in·nings /ˈɪnɪŋz/ *n* (*plural* **innings**) **1** [C] the period of time in a game of CRICKET when a team or player BATS **2 he/she had a good innings** *BrE informal* used about someone who has died to say that they had a long life

in·nit /ˈɪnɪt/ *BrE informal* **1** used as a way of saying 'isn't it': *It's cold, innit?* **2** used after a statement for emphasis, instead of any QUESTION TAG. This use is very non-standard and is grammatically incorrect, but has become common in spoken English among some young people: *He's a bad man, innit* (=used instead of 'isn't he').

inn·keep·er /ˈɪnˌkiːpə $ -ər/ *n* [C] *old use* someone who owns or manages an INN

in·no·cence /ˈɪnəsəns/ ●●○ *n* [U]
1 the fact of being not guilty of a crime OPP **guilt**: *Can you **prove** your **innocence**?* | **protest/maintain your innocence** (=say repeatedly that you are not guilty) *The prisoners continued to protest their innocence.*
2 lack of experience of life or of knowledge of the bad things in the world: *In our innocence, we believed everything we were told. | the innocence of childhood*
3 in all innocence if you do or say something in all innocence, you have no intention of doing harm or of offending anyone

in·no·cent¹ /ˈɪnəsənt/ ●●○ W3 *adj*
1 not guilty of a crime OPP **guilty**: *Nobody would believe that I was innocent.* | **[+of]** *He's innocent of murder. | The court **found** him **innocent** and he was released.*
2 innocent victims/bystanders/people etc people who get hurt or killed in a war or crime although they are not directly involved in it: *Many innocent civilians are among the casualties.*
3 done or said without intending to harm or offend anyone: *He was startled by their angry reaction to his innocent remark.*
4 not having much experience of the bad things in the world, so that you are easily deceived SYN **naive**: *I was thirteen years old and very innocent.* —**innocently** *adv*

innocent² *n* [C] someone who does not have much experience of the bad things in life

in·noc·u·ous /ɪˈnɒkjuəs $ ɪˈnɑːk-/ *adj* not offensive, dangerous, or harmful SYN **harmless**: *an innocuous remark | He's a perfectly innocuous young man.* —**innocuously** *adv*

in·no·vate /ˈɪnəveɪt/ AWL *v* [I,T] to start to use new ideas, methods, or inventions: *the need for large businesses to innovate | The company has successfully innovated new products and services.*

in·no·va·tion /ˌɪnəˈveɪʃən/ ●●○ AWL *n*
1 [C] a new idea, method, or invention: **[+in]** *recent innovations in English teaching*
2 [U] the introduction of new ideas or methods: *We must encourage innovation if the company is to remain competitive.* | **[+in]** *We need to encourage innovation in industry. | Many people feel bewildered by the speed of **technological innovation**.*

in·nov·at·ive /ˈɪnəvətɪv $ ˈɪnəˌveɪtɪv/ ●○○ AWL (*also* **innovatory**) *adj*
1 an innovative idea or way of doing something is new, different, and better than those that existed before: *an **innovative approach** to language teaching | innovative schemes for recycling waste materials* **THESAURUS** ▸ **NEW**
2 using clever new ideas and methods: *an innovative design team*

in·no·va·tor /ˈɪnəveɪtə $ -ər/ AWL *n* [C] someone who introduces changes and new ideas

in·no·va·to·ry /ˈɪnəveɪtəri $ ˈɪnəvətɔːri/ *adj* INNOVATIVE

in·nu·en·do /ˌɪnjuˈendəʊ $ -doʊ/ *n* (*plural* **innuendoes** *or* **innuendos**) [C,U] a remark that suggests something sexual or unpleasant without saying it directly, or these remarks in general → **double entendre**: *His writing is full of sexual innuendoes. | a campaign based on rumour, innuendo, and gossip*

in·nu·me·ra·ble /ɪˈnjuːmərəbəl $ ɪˈnuː-/ *adj* very many, or too many to be counted SYN **countless**: *She's served on innumerable committees.* **THESAURUS** ▸ **MANY**

in·nu·mer·ate /ɪˈnjuːmərət $ ɪˈnuː-/ *adj* unable to do simple calculations or understand basic mathematics → **illiterate** —**innumeracy** *n* [U]

i·noc·u·late /ɪˈnɒkjəleɪt $ ɪˈnɑː-/ *v* [T] to protect someone against a disease by putting a weak form of the disease into their body using a needle → **immunize, vaccinate**: **inoculate sb against sth** *All the children had been inoculated against hepatitis.* —**inoculation** /ɪˌnɒkjəˈleɪʃən $ -ˌnɑːk-/ *n* [C,U]

in·of·fen·sive /ˌɪnəˈfensɪv◂/ *adj* unlikely to offend or upset anyone: *Her husband was a small, inoffensive-looking man.*

in·op·e·ra·ble /ɪnˈɒpərəbəl $ ɪnˈɑː-/ *adj* **1** an inoperable illness or medical condition cannot be treated by an operation: *an inoperable brain tumour* **2** something that is inoperable cannot be used: *The bombing rendered the airfield inoperable.*

in·op·e·ra·tive /ɪnˈɒpərətɪv $ ɪnˈɑː-/ *adj formal* **1** a machine that is inoperative is not working, or is not in working condition **2** a system or a law that is inoperative does not work anymore or cannot be made to work

in·op·por·tune /ɪnˈɒpətjuːn $ ˌɪnɑːpərˈtuːn◂/ *adj formal* **1** an inopportune moment or time is not suitable or good for something OPP **opportune**: *I'm afraid you've called at rather an* ***inopportune moment.*** **2** happening at an unsuitable or bad time: *an inopportune visit*

in·or·di·nate /ɪˈnɔːdənət $ -ɔːr-/ *adj* far more than you would reasonably or normally expect SYN **excessive**: *Testing is taking up an* ***inordinate amount*** *of teachers' time.* —**inordinately** *adv*: *She's inordinately fond of her parrot.*

in·or·gan·ic /ˌɪnɔːˈɡænɪk◂ $ -ɔːr-/ *adj* not consisting of anything that is living: *inorganic matter* —**inorganically** /-kli/ *adv*

ˌinorganic ˈchemistry *n* [U] *technical* the part of chemistry concerning the study of substances that do not contain CARBON → **organic chemistry**

in·pa·tient /ˈɪnˌpeɪʃənt/ *n* [C] someone who stays in a hospital while they receive treatment → OUTPATIENT

in·put[1] /ˈɪnpʊt/ ●●○ W3 AWL *n*

1 [U] information that is put into a computer OPP **output**: *If the input data specified it, the file will close and the process terminates.*

2 [C,U] ideas, advice, money, or effort that you put into a job or activity in order to help it succeed: **[+into/to]** *Farmers contributed most of the input into the survey.* | **[+from]** *We'll need input from community nurses.*

3 [C,U] *technical* electrical power that is put into a machine for it to use

input[2] ●○○ AWL *v* (*past tense and past participle* **inputted** *or* **input**, *present participle* **inputting**) [T] to put information into a computer OPP **output**: **be input to sth** *The information is input to our computer system.*

in·quest /ˈɪŋkwest/ *n* [C] **1** a legal process to find out the cause of someone's death: **[+into]** *The coroner will* ***hold*** *an* ***inquest*** *into the deaths.* | *The inquest heard that she died from multiple injuries.* **2** an unofficial discussion about the reasons for someone's defeat or failure to do something: **[+into]** *The Tories will* ***hold*** *a private* ***inquest*** *into why they were defeated.*

in·qui·e·tude /ɪnˈkwaɪətjuːd $ -tuːd/ *n* [U] *literary* a feeling of anxiety

in·quire, **enquire** /ɪnˈkwaɪə $ -ˈkwaɪr/ ●○○ *v* [I,T] *formal* to ask someone for information: *'Why are you doing that?' the boy inquired.* | **[+about]** *I am writing to inquire about your advertisement in 'The Times'.* | **inquire whether/why/how etc** *The waiter inquired whether we would like to sit near the window.* | **inquire sth of sb** *'Where's the station?' she inquired of a passer-by.* | *Toby would have liked to* ***inquire further*** (=ask more questions). THESAURUS ASK —**inquirer** *n* [C]

inquire after sb/sth *phr v* to ask about someone's health, what they are doing etc: *He called me aside to inquire after my daughter.*

inquire into sth *phr v* to ask questions in order to get more information about something: *The investigation will inquire into the company's financial dealings.*

in·quir·ing, **enquiring** /ɪnˈkwaɪərɪŋ $ -ˈkwaɪr-/ *adj* [only before noun] **1** an inquiring look or expression shows that you want to ask about something: *She raised an inquiring eyebrow towards Murray.* **2 an inquiring mind** someone who has an inquiring mind is very interested in finding out more about everything: *As a child, he had a lively inquiring mind.* —**inquiringly** *adv*: *Victor looked at her inquiringly.*

in·quir·y, **enquiry** /ɪnˈkwaɪəri $ ɪnˈkwaɪri, ˈɪŋkwəri/ ●●○ S3 W2 *n* (*plural* **inquiries**)

1 [C] a question you ask in order to get information: **[+about]** *We're getting a lot of inquiries about our new London–Rio service.* | **[+from]** *inquiries from potential applicants* | *I don't know who sent the gift, but I'll* ***make*** *some* ***inquiries.*** | **help the police with their inquiries** *BrE* (=to answer questions about a crime) THESAURUS QUESTION

2 [U] the act or process of asking questions in order to get information: *On further inquiry, it emerged that Malcolm had not been involved in the incident.* | *The local council set up a committee of inquiry to look into policing arrangements.* | **scientific/intellectual inquiry**

3 [C] an official process to find out about something: **[+into]** *a judicial inquiry into the deaths* | **launch/set up/hold an inquiry (into sth)** *The Civil Aviation Authority has agreed to hold an inquiry into the accident.* | *The police have launched a* ***murder inquiry.*** | *Parents have called for an* ***independent inquiry*** *into the accident.* → **line of inquiry** at LINE[1](12)

in·qui·si·tion /ˌɪŋkwəˈzɪʃən/ *n* **1 the Inquisition** a Roman Catholic organization in the past whose aim was to find and punish people who had unacceptable religious beliefs **2** [C usually singular] a series of questions that someone asks you in a threatening or unpleasant way: *I had to face a two-hour inquisition from my parents about where I'd been.*

in·quis·i·tive /ɪnˈkwɪzətɪv/ *adj* **1** asking too many questions and trying to find out too many details about something or someone: *I'd have asked more questions, but I didn't want to seem inquisitive.* **2** interested in a lot of different things and wanting to find out more about them → **curious**: *a cheerful, inquisitive little boy* | *an inquisitive mind* —**inquisitively** *adv*: *He peeped inquisitively into the drawer.* —**inquisitiveness** *n* [U]

in·quis·i·tor /ɪnˈkwɪzɪtə $ -ər/ *n* [C] **1** someone who is asking you a lot of difficult questions and making you feel very uncomfortable **2** an official of the Inquisition —**inquisitorial** /ɪnˌkwɪzəˈtɔːriəl◂/ *adj* —**inquisitorially** *adv*

in·road /ˈɪnrəʊd $ -roʊd/ *n* [usually plural] **make inroads into/on sth a)** to have an important effect or influence on something, especially by taking something away from it: *Video is making huge inroads into attendance figures at movie theaters* (=taking away its customers). | *They have made significant inroads into the European market.* | *The administrative workload is making massive inroads into our working day* (=taking away time). **b)** to make some progress towards achieving something difficult: *We haven't made much of an inroad into the backlog of work.*

in·rush /ˈɪnrʌʃ/ *n* [C usually singular] a sudden flow of something that enters a place: *The inrush of fresh air filled the room.*

ˌins and ˈouts *n* [plural] all the exact details of a complicated situation, problem, system etc: **[+of]** *I don't really know all* ***the ins and outs*** *of the matter.*

in·sane /ɪnˈseɪn/ ●○○ *adj*

1 *informal* completely stupid or crazy, often in a way that is dangerous: *That's an insane risk.* | *The whole idea sounds absolutely insane to me.* | *Why did you do that? Have you* ***gone insane****?*

2 someone who is insane is permanently and seriously mentally ill so that they cannot live in normal society: *The killer was declared criminally insane.*

3 the insane people who are mentally ill: *a hospital for the insane*

4 drive sb insane *informal* to make someone feel more and more annoyed or angry, usually over a long period of time SYN **drive sb mad**: *My little brother's been driving me insane all weekend.* —**insanely** *adv*: *insanely jealous* | *She giggled insanely.*

in·san·i·ta·ry /ɪnˈsænətəri $ -teri/ *adj* insanitary conditions or places are very dirty and likely to cause disease SYN **unsanitary** *AmE* THESAURUS DIRTY

in·san·i·ty /ɪn'sænəti/ *n* [U] **1** the state of being seriously mentally ill, so that you cannot live normally in society SYN **madness**: *The court acquitted Campbell on the grounds of temporary insanity.* **2** very stupid actions that may cause you serious harm SYN **lunacy**: *Can't they see the insanity of dumping radioactive waste in the sea?*

in·sa·tia·ble /ɪn'seɪʃəbəl/ *adj* always wanting more and more of something: **insatiable appetite/desire/demand etc (for sth)** *his insatiable appetite for power* | *our insatiable thirst for knowledge* —**insatiably** *adv*

in·scribe /ɪn'skraɪb/ *v* [T] to carefully cut, print, or write words on something, especially on the surface of a stone or coin → **engrave**: *Inside the cover someone had inscribed the words 'To Thomas, with love'.* | **be inscribed in/on sth** *The team's name is inscribed on the base of the trophy.* | **be inscribed with sth** *The tomb was inscribed with a short poem.*

in·scrip·tion /ɪn'skrɪpʃən/ ●○○ *n* [C] a piece of writing inscribed on a stone, in the front of a book etc: *a Latin inscription on the memorial stone*

in·scru·ta·ble /ɪn'skru:təbəl/ *adj* someone who is inscrutable shows no emotion or reaction in the expression on their face so that it is impossible to know what they are feeling or thinking: *He stood silent and inscrutable.* —**inscrutably** *adv* —**inscrutability** /ɪnˌskru:tə'bɪləti/ *n* [U]

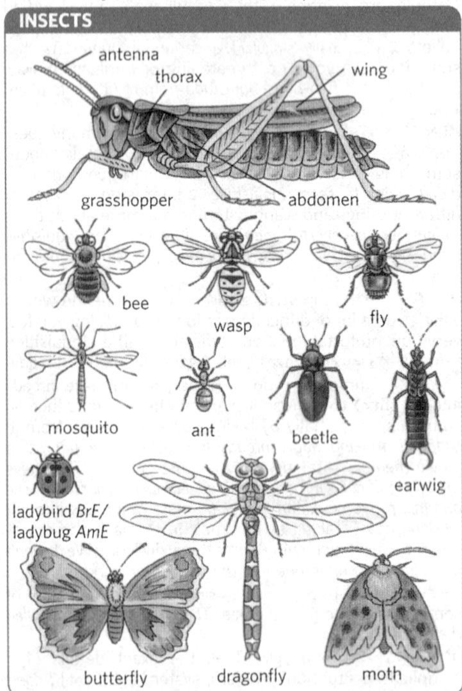

in·sect /'ɪnsekt/ ●●● W3 *n* [C] a small creature such as a fly or ANT, that has six legs, and sometimes wings: *an insect bite* | *flying insects* | *Don't forget to bring* ***insect repellent*** (=a chemical to keep insects away).

in·sec·ti·cide /ɪn'sektɪsaɪd/ *n* [U] a chemical substance used for killing insects → PESTICIDE —**insecticidal** /ɪnˌsektə'saɪdl◂/ *adj*

in·sec·ti·vore /ɪn'sektəvɔ: $ -vɔ:r/ *n* [C] a creature that eats insects for food → **carnivore**, **herbivore**, **omnivore** —**insectivorous** /ˌɪnsek'tɪvərəs◂/ *adj*

in·se·cure /ˌɪnsɪ'kjʊə◂ $ -'kjʊr◂/ ●○○ AWL *adj*
1 not feeling at all confident about yourself, your abilities, or your relationships with people: **[+about]** *She's very insecure about her appearance.* | *She* ***felt*** *lonely and* ***insecure*** *away from her family.* THESAURUS ▶ CONFIDENT
2 a job, INVESTMENT etc that is insecure does not give you a feeling of safety, because it might be taken away or lost at any time: *Many of them work in low-paid insecure jobs.*
3 a building or structure that is insecure is not safe, because it could fall down —**insecurity** *n* [C,U]: *Student teachers often suffer from a great sense of insecurity.* | *her deepest fears and insecurities* —**insecurely** *adv*

in·sem·i·nate /ɪn'seməneɪt/ *v* [T] to put SPERM into a woman or female animal in order to make her have a baby —**insemination** /ɪnˌsemə'neɪʃən/ *n* [U] → ARTIFICIAL INSEMINATION

in·sen·sate /ɪn'senseɪt/ *adj formal* **1** not able to feel things **2** unreasonable and crazy: *an insensate hatred of America*

in·sen·si·bil·i·ty /ɪnˌsensə'bɪləti/ *n* [U] **1** *formal* the state of being unconscious **2** *old-fashioned* inability to experience feelings such as love, sympathy, anger etc

in·sen·si·ble /ɪn'sensəbəl/ *adj formal* **1** not knowing about something that could happen to you SYN **unaware**: **[+of]** *She remained insensible of the dangers that lay ahead.* **2** unable to feel something or be affected by it: **[+to/of]** *insensible to the cold* **3** *literary* not conscious: *He fell to the ground, insensible.* —**insensibly** *adv*

in·sen·si·tive /ɪn'sensətɪv/ *adj* **1** not noticing, or not taking the care to notice, other people's feelings, and not realizing when they are upset or when something that you do will upset them: *One insensitive official insisted on seeing her husband's death certificate.* | *an insensitive remark* | **[+to]** *She's totally insensitive to Jack's feelings.* THESAURUS ▶ UNKIND **2** [not before noun] not paying attention to what is happening or to what people are saying, and therefore not changing your behaviour because of it: **[+to]** *Companies that are insensitive to global changes will lose sales.* | *The service is insensitive to the needs of local people.* **3** [not before noun] not affected by physical effects or changes: **[+to]** *insensitive to pain* —**insensitively** *adv* —**insensitivity** /ɪnˌsensə'tɪvəti/ *n* [U]

in·sep·a·ra·ble /ɪn'sepərəbəl/ *adj* **1** people who are inseparable are always together and are very friendly with each other: *Jane and Sarah soon became inseparable companions.* | **[+from]** *Tom was inseparable from his dog Snowy.* **2** things that are inseparable cannot be separated or cannot be considered separately: **[+from]** *Britain's economic fortunes are inseparable from the world situation.* —**inseparably** *adv* —**inseparability** /ɪnˌsepərə'bɪləti/ *n* [U]

in·sert[1] /ɪn'sɜ:t $ -ɜ:rt/ ●○○ AWL *v* [T]
1 to put something inside or into something else: **insert sth in/into/between sth** *His hand shook slightly as he inserted the key into the lock.*
2 to add something to the middle of a document or piece of writing: **insert sth in/into/between sth** *His manager inserted a new clause into his contract.* | *Insert your comments in the space below.*

in·sert[2] /'ɪnsɜ:t $ -ɜ:rt/ *n* [C] **1** printed pages that are put inside a newspaper or magazine in order to advertise something: *a six-page insert on computer software* **2** something that is designed to be put inside something else: *He wore special inserts in his shoes to make him look taller.*

in·ser·tion /ɪn'sɜ:ʃən $ -ɜ:r-/ AWL *n* **1** [U] the act of putting something inside something else **2** [C] something that is added to the middle of a document or piece of writing

ˌin-'service *adj* **in-service training/courses etc** training etc that you do while you are working in a job

in·set[1] /'ɪnset/ *n* [C] **1** a small picture, map etc in the corner of a page or larger picture etc, which shows more detail or information: *The venture earned Mr Taylor (inset) millions of dollars.* **2** something which is fixed into or onto the surface of something else: *a pendant with a diamond inset*

in·set[2] /ɪn'set/ *v* (*past tense and past participle* **inset**, *present participle* **insetting**) [T] **1** if something is inset with decorations or jewels, they are fixed into or on its surface: **inset sth with sth** *a wooden box inset with ivory* | **inset sth into sth** *spotlights inset into the ceiling* **2** to put a small picture, map etc on a printed page

in·shore /ˌɪnˈʃɔː◂ $ -ˈʃɔːr◂/ *adv* near, towards, or to the shore OPP **offshore**: *The fishing boats usually stay close inshore.* —**inshore** *adj*: *inshore waters*

in·side¹ /ɪnˈsaɪd/ ●●● S2 W2 *adv, prep*
1 CONTAINER in or into a container or other closed space so as to be completely covered or surrounded OPP **outside**: *The jewels were locked away inside the safe.* | *I sent the money inside an envelope addressed to Ann.* | *Carl picked up the book and stuffed it inside his jacket.* | *Her car was locked and the keys were inside.*
2 BUILDING/ROOM in or into a building or room OPP **outside**: *It's raining. We'll have to go inside.* | *She could hear voices inside, but no one came to the door.* | *Mail was piled up just inside the doorway.* | *The sound was coming from inside the house.* | **[+of]** *AmE*: *There were 20 people packed inside of her dorm room.*
3 COUNTRY/AREA in a country or area – used when you want to emphasize that something is happening there and not in other places OPP **outside**: *Very little is known of events inside this mysterious country.* | *The guerrillas were said to be operating from bases inside the war zone.*
4 ORGANIZATION if someone is inside a group or organization, they are part of it OPP **outside**: *women's influence inside the party* | *The information comes from sources inside the company.* | *Discussions should involve local people both inside and outside the school.*
5 HEAD/MIND if something happens inside you, or inside your head or mind, it is part of what you think and feel, especially when you do not express it: *You just don't understand how I feel inside!* | *Steve's a strange guy – you never know what's going on inside his head.* | *Anger bubbled up deep inside her.* | **[+of]** *AmE*: *Something inside of me told me not to trust him.*
6 BODY in your body: *She could feel the baby kicking inside her.* | *You'll feel better once you've got a good meal inside you* (=after you have eaten something).
7 TIME **a)** in less than a particular amount of time: *A full report is expected inside three months.* | **inside the hour/month etc** (=before an hour, month etc has passed) *We'll be back inside the hour.* | **[+of]** *especially AmE*: *Our aim is to get the whole job finished inside of a week.* **b)** less than a particular amount of time OPP **outside**: *Jonson's time of 9.3 seconds was just inside the world record.*
8 PRISON *informal* in prison: *My boyfriend's been inside for a year.*

in·side² /ɪnˈsaɪd, ˈɪnsaɪd/ ●●● S3 *n*
1 the inside the inner part of something, which is surrounded or hidden by the outer part OPP **the outside**: **on the inside** *The apple's rotten on the inside.* | **[+of]** *condensation on the inside of the window* | *The door had been locked from the inside.*
2 inside out with the usual outside parts on the inside: *You've got that jumper inside out.* | *Her umbrella blew inside out.* | *I always* ***turn*** *my jeans* ***inside out*** *to wash them.*
3 turn a room/building etc inside out to search a place very thoroughly by moving everything that is in it: *The drug squad turned the apartment inside out.*
4 know sth inside out *BrE*, **know sth inside and out** *AmE* to know something in great detail: *She knows her subject inside out.*
5 on the inside someone who is on the inside is a member of a group or an organization: *Someone on the inside must have helped with the robbery.*
6 on the inside *BrE* if a car passes another car on the inside, it passes on the side that is away from the driver
7 sb's inside/insides *informal* someone's stomach: *My insides are beginning to complain about the lack of food.*

in·side³ /ˈɪnsaɪd/ ●●● S3 *adj*
1 in or facing the inner part of something: *the inside pages of the newspaper* | *the inside pocket of his jacket*
2 inside information/the inside story etc information that is available only to people who are part of a particular group or organization: *Police believe the robbers may have had inside information.*
3 the inside lane *BrE* the LANE that is furthest away from the middle of the road OPP **outside lane**

in·sid·er /ɪnˈsaɪdə $ -ər/ *n* [C] someone who has a special knowledge of a particular organization because they are part of it OPP **outsider**: *an insider's view of the way that a Japanese company works*

inˌsider ˈtrading (*also* **inˌsider ˈdealing**) *n* [U] the crime of using secret information that you have about a company, or knowledge of a situation, to buy or sell SHARES at a profit

ˌinside ˈtrack *n* [C] **1** the part of a circular track for racing that is nearest to the centre of the circle and is therefore shorter **2** *AmE* a position that gives someone an advantage over the people they are competing against: *the inside track to success in business*

in·sid·i·ous /ɪnˈsɪdiəs/ *adj formal* an insidious change or problem spreads gradually without being noticed, and causes serious harm: *an insidious trend towards censorship of the press* —**insidiously** *adv* —**insidiousness** *n* [U]

in·sight /ˈɪnsaɪt/ ●○○ AWL *n*
1 [C] a sudden clear understanding of something or part of something, especially a complicated situation or idea: **[+into]** *The article* ***gives*** *us a real* ***insight*** *into the causes of the present economic crisis.* | *The research* ***provides*** *new* ***insights*** *into the way we process language.*
2 [U] the ability to understand and realize what people or situations are really like: *a woman of great insight*

in·sight·ful /ˈɪnsaɪtfəl/ AWL *adj* able to understand, or showing that you understand, what a situation or person is really like SYN **perceptive**: *an insightful analysis*

in·sig·ni·a /ɪnˈsɪgniə/ *n* (*plural* **insignia**) [C] a BADGE or sign that shows what official or military rank someone has, or which group or organization they belong to → **emblem**: *the royal insignia* | *military insignia*

in·sig·nif·i·cant /ˌɪnsɪgˈnɪfɪkənt◂/ ●○○ AWL *adj* too small or unimportant to consider or worry about SYN **trivial**: *You realize that your problems are insignificant in comparison.* | **insignificant number/amount** THESAURUS UNIMPORTANT —**insignificantly** *adv* —**insignificance** *n* [U]

in·sin·cere /ˌɪnsɪnˈsɪə◂ $ -ˈsɪr◂/ ●○○ *adj* pretending to be pleased, sympathetic etc, especially by saying nice things, but not really meaning what you say: *an insincere smile* | *an offer which she knew to be impractical and insincere* —**insincerely** *adv* —**insincerity** /ˌɪnsɪnˈserəti/ *n* [U]

in·sin·u·ate /ɪnˈsɪnjueɪt/ *v* [T] **1** to say something which seems to mean something unpleasant without saying it openly, especially suggesting that someone is being dishonest SYN **imply**: **insinuate that** *Are you insinuating that the money was stolen?* | *What are you trying to insinuate?* **2** *formal* to gradually gain someone's love, trust etc by pretending to be friendly and sincere: *He managed to insinuate his way into her affections.* | **insinuate yourself into sth** *He insinuated himself into Mehmet's confidence.* **3** *formal* to move yourself or a part of your body into a place: *a large cat insinuated itself through the gap*

in·sin·u·a·tion /ɪnˌsɪnjuˈeɪʃən/ *n* **1** [C] something that someone says which seems to mean something unpleasant, but does not say this openly: *She rejected the insinuation that she was partly to blame.* **2** [U] when someone says something insinuating

in·sip·id /ɪnˈsɪpɪd/ *adj* **1** food or drink that is insipid does not have much taste SYN **bland**: *an insipid pasta dish* **2** not interesting, exciting, or attractive: *insipid colours* —**insipidly** *adv* —**insipidness, insipidity** /ˌɪnsəˈpɪdəti/ *n* [U]

in·sist /ɪnˈsɪst/ ●●● S3 W2 *v* [I]
1 to say firmly and often that something is true, especially when other people think it may not be true: **insist (that)** *Mike insisted that he was right.* | *His friends insisted he had no connection with drugs.* | **insist on sth** *She kept insisting on her innocence.*
2 to demand that something should happen: *Stay for supper –* ***I insist!*** | **insist (that) sb should do sth** *They insisted that everyone should come to the party.* | *He insisted I should take a taxi.* | **insist on sth** *We insist on the highest standards*

of cleanliness in the hotel. | **insist on/upon doing sth** *He insisted upon checking everything himself.*
3 if you insist *spoken* used when agreeing to do something that you do not really want to do: *'Why don't you call them up today?' 'Oh, if you insist!'*
4 insist on doing sth to keep doing something, especially something that is inconvenient or annoying: *She will insist on washing her hair just when I want to have a bath.*

GRAMMAR: Patterns with insist

- You **insist on** something: *She insists on her own bedroom.*
- You **insist on doing** something: *She insists on having her own bedroom.* ✗ Don't say: *She insists her own bedroom.*
- In everyday English, you **insist that** someone **does** something: *I insist that he waits.*
- In formal English, you **insist that** someone **do** something, using the base form of the verb (=infinitive without 'to'): *I insist that he wait.*
- You use the base form of the verb when talking about the past: *I insisted that he* ***wait***. In everyday English, people also say: *I insisted that he* ***waited***.
- You **insist that** someone **should do** something: *They insisted that I should join them.* This pattern is often used in the past, when reporting what someone has insisted.

GRAMMAR GUIDE ▸ VERBS

THESAURUS

insist to say firmly that someone should do something or that something should happen: *She insisted that it was her turn to drive.*
demand to say very strongly and sometimes angrily that you want something or that something must happen: *I wrote a letter to the company, demanding an apology and a refund.* | *The guards demanded to see her ID.*
require [usually passive] *formal* if you are required to do something, a rule or law says that you must do it: *The successful applicant will be required to sign a two-year contract.*
be adamant to say very firmly that something must happen or is right, and refuse to change your mind when other people try to persuade you: *The actress has always been adamant about keeping her private life private.*
won't take no for an answer *informal* to insist that someone must do what you say or ask: *You're coming home with me – I won't take no for an answer.*
put your foot down to say very firmly that someone must not do something: *Ed was talking about dropping out of school, but Mom and Dad put their foot down.*

in·sis·tence /ɪnˈsɪstəns/ *n* [U] when you demand that something should happen and refuse to let anyone say no: **insistence that** *his insistence that they discuss the problem* | **[+on]** *an insistence on punctuality* | **at sb's insistence** (=because someone insisted) *At her father's insistence, she joined them for a drink.*

in·sis·tent /ɪnˈsɪstənt/ *adj* **1** demanding firmly and repeatedly that something should happen: **insistent that** *She was insistent that they should all meet for dinner.* | **[+on]** *They were insistent on good manners.* **2** making a continuous pattern of sounds that is difficult to ignore: *the music's insistent rhythm* —**insistently** *adv*: *The bell rang again insistently.*

in si·tu /ɪn ˈsɪtjuː $ ɪn ˈsaɪtuː/ *adv* if something remains in situ, it remains in its usual place

in·so·far /ˌɪnsəˈfɑː $ -ˈfɑːr/ *adv* → **in so far as** at FAR[1](20)

in·sole /ˈɪnsəʊl $ -soʊl/ *n* [C] the inside part of a shoe, or a piece of cloth, leather etc which is the same shape as your foot that you put inside your shoe

in·so·lent /ˈɪnsələnt/ *adj* rude and not showing any respect → **cheeky**: *an insolent tone of voice* | *You insolent child!* THESAURUS ▸ RUDE —**insolently** *adv* —**insolence** *n* [U]

in·sol·u·ble /ɪnˈsɒljəbəl $ ɪnˈsɑːl-/ *adj* **1** an insoluble problem is or seems impossible to solve: *insoluble conflicts within the department* **2** an insoluble substance does not become a liquid when you put it into a liquid OPP **soluble** → **dissolve**

in·sol·va·ble /ɪnˈsɒlvəbəl $ ɪnˈsɑːl-/ *adj especially AmE* an insolvable problem is or seems impossible to solve SYN **insoluble** —**insolvably** *adv*

in·sol·vent /ɪnˈsɒlvənt $ ɪnˈsɑːl-/ *adj* not having enough money to pay what you owe SYN **bankrupt**: *The company was later* ***declared insolvent*** (=officially said to be insolvent). —**insolvency** *n* [C,U]

in·som·ni·a /ɪnˈsɒmniə $ ɪnˈsɑːm-/ *n* [U] if you suffer from insomnia, you are not able to sleep

in·som·ni·ac /ɪnˈsɒmniæk $ ɪnˈsɑːm-/ *n* [C] someone who cannot sleep easily —**insomniac** *adj*

in·so·much /ˌɪnsəʊˈmʌtʃ $ -soʊ-/ *adv formal*
1 insomuch that *especially AmE* to such a degree that
2 another form of the word INASMUCH

in·sou·ci·ance /ɪnˈsuːsiəns/ *n* [U] *formal* a cheerful feeling of not caring or worrying about anything SYN **nonchalance**: *an air of insouciance* —**insouciant** *adj* —**insouciantly** *adv*

in·sourc·ing /ˈɪnˌsɔːsɪŋ $ -ˌsɔːr-/ *n* [U] the use of workers inside a company to do a job rather than workers from outside the company

in·spect /ɪnˈspekt/ ●●○ AWL *v* [T]
1 to examine something carefully in order to find out more about it or to find out what is wrong with it: *I got out of the car to* ***inspect the damage***. | *Police inspected the scene and interviewed all the staff.* | **inspect sth for sth** *The police will inspect the venue for safety.* THESAURUS ▸ EXAMINE
2 to make an official visit to a building, organization etc to check that everything is satisfactory and that rules are being obeyed: *The building is regularly inspected by the fire-safety officer.* | *General Allenby arrived to inspect the troops.* THESAURUS ▸ CHECK

REGISTER
In everyday English, people usually say **take a look at** something or someone or, in British English, **have a look at** something or someone rather than **inspect** something or someone: *Can I* ***take a look at*** *your ticket, please?*

in·spec·tion /ɪnˈspekʃən/ ●●○ W3 AWL *n* [C,U]
1 an official visit to a building or organization to check that everything is satisfactory and that rules are being obeyed: **[+of]** *regular inspections of the prison* | *An* ***inspection*** *was* ***carried out*** *at the school.* | **tour of inspection** (=an official visit to inspect something)
2 a careful examination of something to find out more about it or to check for anything wrong: **for inspection** *Copies of the documents are available for inspection* (=people can look at them) *at local libraries.* | **(on) close/closer inspection** (=when looked at in detail) *However, on closer inspection, a number of problems emerged.* | *Close inspection of the plane's engines revealed several small defects.*

in·spec·tor /ɪnˈspektə $ -ər/ ●●○ S3 W3 AWL *n* [C]
1 an official whose job is to check that something is satisfactory and that rules are being obeyed: *ticket inspectors* | *a Health and Safety inspector* | *Standards of discipline at the school were strongly criticized in the inspector's report.*
2 a police officer of middle rank: *Inspector Blake* → CHIEF INSPECTOR

in·spec·tor·ate /ɪnˈspektərət/ *n* [C] *BrE* the group of INSPECTORS who officially inspect schools, factories etc

inˌspector of ˈtaxes *n* [C] *BrE* a government official who calculates what tax each person should pay SYN **tax inspector**

in·spi·ra·tion /ˌɪnspəˈreɪʃən/ ●●○ *n* [C,U]
1 a good idea about what you should do, write, say etc, especially one which you get suddenly: *The Malvern Hills have* ***provided inspiration*** *for many artists and musicians over the decades.* | *He raised his eyes to the altar as if* ***seeking inspiration****.* | *He* ***draws inspiration from*** *ordinary scenes.* | *Mary Quant's* ***inspiration comes from*** *the glam style of the seventies.* | *He had a sudden* ***flash of inspiration****.* | *He has always been a* ***source of inspiration*** *for me.* THESAURUS IDEA
2 a person, experience, place etc that gives you new ideas for something you do: *The seascapes of Cape Cod were her inspiration.* | **[+for/behind]** *He was the inspiration for Wordsworth's poem 'The Old Huntsman'.*
3 be an inspiration to sb to make someone feel encouraged to be as good, successful etc as possible: *People like Tara are an inspiration to us all.*
4 under the inspiration of sb used to say who made a person or group want to do something: *the spread of improved nursing under the inspiration of Florence Nightingale*

in·spi·ra·tion·al /ˌɪnspəˈreɪʃənəl◂/ *adj* providing encouragement or new ideas for what you should do: *Jones proved an inspirational figure in Welsh rugby.*

in·spire /ɪnˈspaɪə $ -ˈspaɪr/ ●●○ *v* [T]
1 to encourage someone by making them feel confident and eager to do something: *We need someone who can inspire the team.* | **inspire sb to do sth** *He inspired many young people to take up the sport.* | **inspire sb to sth** *I hope this success will inspire you to greater efforts.* | *Inspired by the sunny weather, I decided to explore the woods.*
2 to make someone have a particular feeling or react in a particular way: *Gandhi's quiet dignity inspired great respect.* | **inspire confidence** (=make people feel confident because they trust your ability) *His driving hardly inspires confidence.* | *The hospital's record does* ***not inspire confidence****.*
3 to give someone the idea for something, especially a story, painting, poem etc: *The story was inspired by a chance meeting with an old Russian duke.* | *a range of designs inspired by wild flowers*
4 *technical* to breathe in

in·spired /ɪnˈspaɪəd $ -ˈspaɪrd/ *adj* **1** having very exciting special qualities that are better than anyone or anything else: *an inspired leader* | *an inspired performance* **2 inspired guess/choice etc** a good or successful guess, choice etc that is based on inspiration not facts: *In an inspired move, they took on the relatively inexperienced Ray Unwin as director.* **3 politically/religiously etc inspired** started for political, religious etc reasons: *We suspect that the violence was politically inspired.*

in·spir·ing /ɪnˈspaɪərɪŋ $ -ˈspaɪr-/ *adj* giving people a feeling of excitement and a desire to do something great OPP **uninspiring**: *inspiring music* | *King was a great orator and an inspiring leader.*

in·sta·bil·i·ty /ˌɪnstəˈbɪləti/ AWL *n* (*plural* **instabilities**) [C,U] **1** when a situation is not certain because there is the possibility of sudden change OPP **stability**: *the instability of the market* | *political instability in the region* **2** mental problems that are likely to cause sudden changes of behaviour → **unstable**: *nervous instability*

in·stall /ɪnˈstɔːl $ -ˈstɒːl/ ●●○ W3 *v* [T]
1 to put a piece of equipment somewhere and connect it so that it is ready to be used: *They've installed the new computer network at last.* | *Security cameras have been installed in the city centre.*
2 to add new software to a computer so that it is ready to be used OPP **uninstall**: *We've installed new anti-virus software.*
3 *formal* to put someone in an important job or position, especially with a ceremony: *Churchill was installed as Chancellor of the university.*
4 install yourself in/at etc to settle somewhere as if you are going to stay for a long time

in·stal·la·tion /ˌɪnstəˈleɪʃən/ ●●○ *n*
1 [U] when someone fits a piece of equipment somewhere: *the installation and maintenance of alarm systems*
2 [C] a piece of equipment that has been fitted in its place: *The whole computer installation was nearly new.*
3 [C] a place where industrial or military equipment, machinery etc has been put: *nuclear installations*
4 [C] a piece of modern art which can include objects, light, sound etc
5 [U] *formal* the ceremony of putting someone in an important job or position: *the installation of the new bishop*

inˈstallment ˌplan *n* [singular, U] *AmE* a system of paying for goods by a series of small regular payments SYN **hire purchase** *BrE*

in·stal·ment (*also* **installment** *AmE*) /ɪnˈstɔːlmənt $ ɪnˈstɒːl-/ *n* [C] **1** one of a series of regular payments that you make until you have paid all the money you owe: *the second instalment of a loan* | *They're letting me* ***pay*** *for the washing machine* ***by*** *monthly* ***instalments****.* **2** one of the parts of a story that appears as a series of parts, especially in a magazine, newspaper etc: *the first instalment of a science fiction trilogy*

in·stance¹ /ˈɪnstəns/ ●●○ W2 AWL *n*
1 for instance for example: *We need to rethink the way we consume energy. Take, for instance, our approach to transport.*
2 [C] an example of a particular kind of situation: **[+of]** *They came across many instances of discrimination.* | **instance where/when** *instances where safety regulations have been breached* | ***In this instance*** *I think she was mistaken.* THESAURUS EXAMPLE
3 in the first instance at the beginning of a series of actions: *Anyone wishing to join the society should apply in the first instance to the secretary.*
4 at sb's instance *formal* because of someone's wish or request

instance² AWL *v* [T] *formal* to give something as an example: *She instanced the first chapter as proof of his skill in constructing scenes.*

in·stant¹ /ˈɪnstənt/ ●●○ W3 *adj*
1 [usually before noun] happening or produced immediately SYN **immediate**: *an instant success* | *a system that provides instant access to client information* | *The women took an instant dislike to one another.* | *The programme brought an instant response.*
2 [only before noun] instant food, coffee etc is in the form of powder and prepared by adding hot water: *instant coffee* | *instant soup*

instant² ●○○ *n*
1 [C usually singular] a moment: *She caught his eye* ***for an instant****.* | *When the rain started, the crowd vanished* ***in an instant*** (=immediately). | **[+of]** *an instant of panic* | *She stepped towards the door and, in that very same instant, the doorbell rang.*
2 the instant (that) as soon as something happens: *The instant I saw him, I knew he was the man from the restaurant.* | *Jen burst out laughing the instant she walked in.*
3 this instant *spoken* used when telling someone, especially a child, to do something immediately SYN **now**: *Come here this instant!*

in·stan·ta·ne·ous /ˌɪnstənˈteɪniəs◂/ *adj* happening immediately: *modern methods of instantaneous communication* —**instantaneously** *adv*

in·stant·ly /ˈɪnstəntli/ ●●○ *adv* immediately: *All four victims died instantly.* | *The information was instantly available.* THESAURUS IMMEDIATELY

ˌinstant ˈmessaging *n* [U] a type of service available on the Internet that allows you to quickly exchange written messages with people that you know: *instant messaging services* —**instant message** *n* [C]

ˌinstant ˈreplay *n* [C] *AmE* an important moment in a sports game on television that is shown again immediately after it happens SYN **action replay** *BrE*

in·stead /ɪnˈsted/ ●●● S1 W1 *adv*
1 instead of sb/sth used to say what is not used, does not happen etc, when something else is used, happens etc: *You probably picked up my keys instead of yours.* | *Could I*

I

have tuna instead of ham? | Instead of being annoyed, he seemed quite pleased.
2 used to say what is done, when you have just said that a particular thing is not done: *Geoff didn't study law. Instead, he decided to become an actor. | If Jo can't attend the meeting, I could go instead.*

in·step /ˈɪnstep/ *n* [C] **1** the raised part of your foot between your toes and your ANKLE **2** the part of a shoe that covers your instep

in·sti·gate /ˈɪnstɪgeɪt/ *v* [T] **1** to make a process start, especially one relating to law or politics: *Charles instigated a programme of reforms.* **2** to persuade someone to do something bad or violent: *He accused union leaders of instigating the disturbances.* —**instigator** *n* [C]

in·sti·ga·tion /ˌɪnstəˈgeɪʃən/ *n* [U] **1 at sb's instigation** (*also* **at the instigation of sb**) *formal* because of someone's suggestion, request, or demand: *an inquiry set up at the instigation of the White House* **2** the act of starting something

in·stil *BrE*, **instill** *AmE* /ɪnˈstɪl/ *v* (**instilled, instilling**) [T] to teach someone to think, behave, or feel in a particular way over a period of time: **instil confidence/fear/discipline etc into sb** *A manager's job is to instil determination into his players.*

in·stinct /ˈɪnstɪŋkt/ ●●○ *n* [C,U] a natural tendency to behave in a particular way or a natural ability to know something, which is not learned → **intuition**: **[+for]** *Animals have a* ***natural instinct*** *for survival.* | **instinct to do sth** *the human instinct to form relationships* | **by instinct** *Birds build nests by instinct.* | **sexual/maternal/survival instinct** | *Her* ***instinct told*** *her that something was wrong.* | **sb's first instinct** (=what someone feels like doing first when something happens) *His first instinct was to rush back to Isobel.*

in·stinc·tive /ɪnˈstɪŋktɪv/ ●○○ *adj* based on instinct and not involving thought: *a mother's instinctive love* —**instinctively** *adv*

in·stinc·tu·al /ɪnˈstɪŋktʃuəl/ *adj technical* instinctive

in·sti·tute¹ /ˈɪnstɪtjuːt $ -tuːt/ ●●○ W3 AWL *n* [C] an organization that has a particular purpose such as scientific or educational work, or the building where this organization is based → **academy**: *research institutes* | **[+of/for]** *the Institute for Space Studies*

institute² AWL *v* [T] *formal* to introduce or start a system, rule, legal process etc SYN **begin**: *We had no choice but to institute court proceedings against the airline.*

in·sti·tu·tion /ˌɪnstɪˈtjuːʃən $ -ˈtuː-/ ●●○ W3 AWL *n*
1 [C] a large organization that has a particular kind of work or purpose: **financial/educational/research etc institution** *the government and other political institutions | powerful institutions such as world banks | the Institution of Electrical Engineers* THESAURUS ORGANIZATION
2 [C] an important system of organization in society that has existed for a long time: ***social institutions*** *such as the family and religion* | **the institution of marriage/monarchy etc** *The scandal threatened to undermine the institution of the presidency.*
3 [C] a building that people are sent to when they need to be looked after, for example old people or children with no parents - often used to show disapproval: *I was determined not to put my mother in an institution. | a* ***mental institution*** (=for the mentally ill)
4 [U] when something is started or introduced, especially something relating to the law or politics: **[+of]** *the institution of divorce proceedings*
5 be an institution if a person, place, event etc is an institution, they have been an important part of a place for a very long time - often used humorously: *The British pub isn't just somewhere to drink - it's an institution.*

in·sti·tu·tion·al /ˌɪnstəˈtjuːʃənəl $ -ˈtuː-/ ●○○ AWL *adj* [usually before noun]
1 relating to an institution: *children in institutional care*
2 institutional attitudes and behaviour have existed for a long time in an organization and have become accepted as normal even though they are bad: *accusations of* ***institutional racism*** *in the police force*

in·sti·tu·tion·al·ize (*also* **-ise** *BrE*) /ˌɪnstəˈtjuːʃənəlaɪz $ -ˈtuː-/ *v* [T] **1** *old-fashioned* to put someone in an institution for old people, a mental hospital etc **2** to make something a normal accepted part of a social system or organization: *the struggle to institutionalize equality for women*

in·sti·tu·tion·al·ized (*also* **-ised** *BrE*) /ˌɪnstəˈtjuːʃənəlaɪzd $ -ˈtuː-/ AWL *adj* **1** institutionalized attitudes and behaviour have existed for a long time in an organization and have become accepted as normal even though they are bad: **institutionalized racism/sexism etc** *institutionalized corruption within the state* **2** someone who has become institutionalized has lived for a long time in a prison, mental hospital etc and now cannot easily live outside one **3** forming part of a society or system: *institutionalised democracy*

ˌin-ˈstore *adj* [only before noun] happening within a large shop or store: *an in-store bakery*

in·struct /ɪnˈstrʌkt/ ●●○ AWL *v* [T]
1 to officially tell someone what to do → **order**: **instruct sb to do sth** *His secretary was instructed to cancel all his engagements.* | **instruct (sb) that** *The judge immediately instructed that Beattie be released. | Eva went straight to the hotel,* ***as instructed*** (=as she had been told). | **instruct sb what to do** *He had instructed the slaves what to say when questioned.* THESAURUS ORDER
2 *formal* to teach someone something, or show them how to do something: **instruct sb in sth** *Greater effort is needed to instruct children in road safety.* | **instruct sb how to do sth** *Employees are instructed how to make a complaint.* THESAURUS TEACH
3 *BrE formal* to officially tell someone about something: **be instructed that** *I was instructed that £20,000 had been paid into my account.*
4 *BrE law* to employ a lawyer to represent you in court

in·struc·tion /ɪnˈstrʌkʃən/ ●●● S3 W2 AWL *n*
1 instructions [plural] the written information that tells you how to do or use something → **directions**: *Press 'Enter' and follow the on-screen instructions.* | **[+for]** *Both products come with instructions for use.* | **instructions on (how to do) sth** *Are there any instructions on how to plant the trees?*
2 [C usually plural] a statement telling someone what they must do → **orders**: **instructions to do sth** *He had* ***specific instructions*** *to check everyone's identity cards.* | **instructions that** *Mrs Edwards* ***gave instructions*** *that she was not to be disturbed.* | **on sb's instructions** (=having been told by someone to do something) *On the landlord's instructions, the barmaid refused to serve him.* | ***My instructions are*** (=I have been told) *to give the package to him personally. | Make sure you* ***carry out*** *the doctor's* ***instructions****.* | **be under instruction to do sth** (=to have been told to do something) *The police were under instruction to fire if necessary.*
3 [U] *formal* teaching that you are given in a particular skill or subject: *religious instruction | driving instruction* | **[+in]** *The school* ***gives instruction*** *in first aid.* | **under instruction** (=being taught) *This group of trainees is still under instruction.*

COLLOCATIONS

VERBS

follow the instructions (=do what the instructions tell you to do) *You should follow the instructions on the packet.*
read the instructions *Always read the instructions before switching on the machine.*
provide/supply instructions (=give someone instructions) *Detailed instructions are supplied with the software.*
come with instructions *The tent comes with instructions on how to put it up.*
the instructions say/tell you to do sth *The instructions say that you should take the tablets after meals.*

ADJECTIVES/NOUN + instructions

clear *The instructions that I got with the phone weren't very clear.*

I

detailed *There are detailed instructions on the back of the box.*
written instructions *Each member of the team was issued with written instructions.*
full/comprehensive instructions (=very detailed) *There are comprehensive instructions for completing and filing the new tax form.*
step-by-step instructions (=giving details of each thing you should do in order) *This book gives step-by-step instructions for making curtains.*
the manufacturer's instructions (=the instructions given by the company that made something) | **safety instructions** | **operating instructions** | **cooking instructions**

instruction + NOUN

an instruction book/manual *The instruction manual for the camera is over 150 pages long.*
an instruction booklet/leaflet/sheet

COMMON ERRORS

⚠ Don't say 'instructions how to do something' or 'instructions to do something'. Say **instructions on how to do something**.

in·struc·tion·al /ɪnˈstrʌkʃənəl/ *adj formal* providing instruction → **educational**: **instructional programmes/materials/techniques etc** *a free instructional video*

in·struc·tive /ɪnˈstrʌktɪv/ AWL *adj* providing a lot of useful information SYN **informative**: *Thank you, that was very instructive.* | *an instructive comparison*

in·struc·tor /ɪnˈstrʌktə $ -ər/ ●●○ AWL *n* [C]
1 someone who teaches a sport or practical skill: *a driving instructor* | *ski instructors* THESAURUS ▸ TEACHER
2 *AmE* someone who teaches in an American college or university and who has a rank below ASSISTANT PROFESSOR: *a social studies instructor*

in·stru·ment /ˈɪnstrəmənt/ ●●● W2 *n* [C]
1 TOOL a small tool used in work such as science or medicine: *surgical instruments*
2 MUSIC an object used for producing music, such as a piano or VIOLIN SYN **musical instrument** → **instrumental, instrumentalist**: *electronic instruments* | **brass/wind/percussion/stringed etc instrument**
3 FOR MEASURING a piece of equipment for measuring and showing distance, speed, temperature etc: *a failure of the flight instruments* | *sensitive earthquake-detecting instruments*
4 METHOD [usually singular] something or someone that is used to get a particular result: **[+of]** *Interest rates are an important instrument of economic policy.* | **instrument for (doing) sth** *Good management should be an instrument for innovation.*
5 FOR HURTING something that is used to hit or hurt someone: *Death was due to a blow on the head with a* ***blunt instrument***. | **instrument of torture** (=an object used to make people suffer pain until they give information)
6 instrument of fate/God *literary* someone or something that is used by a power beyond our control

in·stru·men·tal[1] /ˌɪnstrəˈmentl◂/ *adj* **1 be instrumental in (doing) sth** *formal* to be important in making something happen: *He was instrumental in developing links with European organizations.* **2** instrumental music is for instruments, not for voices —**instrumentally** *adv*

instrumental[2] *n* [C] a piece of music in which no voices are used, only instruments

in·stru·men·tal·ist /ˌɪnstrəˈmentəlɪst/ *n* [C] someone who plays a musical instrument → VOCALIST

in·stru·men·ta·tion /ˌɪnstrəmenˈteɪʃən/ *n* [U] **1** the way in which a piece of music is arranged to be played by several different instruments **2** the set of instruments used to help in controlling a machine: *aircraft instrumentation*

ˈ**instrument** ˌ**panel** *n* [C] the board in front of the pilot of an aircraft, where all the instruments are → **dashboard**

in·sub·or·di·na·tion /ˌɪnsəbɔːdəˈneɪʃən $ -ˌbɔːrdnˈeɪ-/ *n* [U] *formal* when someone refuses to obey a person who has more authority than them SYN **disobedience**: *Howell was fired for* ***gross insubordination***. —**insubordinate** /ˌɪnsəˈbɔːdənət $ -ɔːr-/ *adj*

in·sub·stan·tial /ˌɪnsəbˈstænʃəl◂/ *adj* **1** *formal* not solid, large, strong, or definite: *The evidence seemed very insubstantial.* | *an insubstantial meal* | *the insubstantial outline of a ship* **2** *literary* not existing as a real object or person: *insubstantial ghosts*

in·suf·fe·ra·ble /ɪnˈsʌfərəbəl/ *adj* extremely annoying or unpleasant SYN **unbearable**: *an insufferable bully* | *The heat was insufferable.* —**insufferably** *adv*

in·suf·fi·cient /ˌɪnsəˈfɪʃənt◂/ ●●○ AWL *adj formal* not enough, or not great enough: *Insufficient resources have been devoted to the health service.* | **[+for]** *His salary was insufficient for their needs.* | **insufficient (sth) to do sth** *The heating is insufficient to kill the bacteria.* | *At the moment, there's insufficient evidence to arrest anyone.* —**insufficiently** *adv* —**insufficiency** *n* [singular, U]

in·su·lar /ˈɪnsjələ $ ˈɪnsələr, ˈɪnʃə-/ *adj* **1** interested in your own group, country, way of life etc and no others - used to show disapproval → **parochial**: *an insular community* | *the insular world of the law* **2** *formal* relating to or like an island —**insularity** /ˌɪnsjəˈlærəti $ -sə-, -ʃə-/ *n* [U]

in·su·late /ˈɪnsjəleɪt $ ˈɪnsə-, ˈɪnʃə-/ *v* [T] **1** to cover or protect something with a material that stops electricity, sound, heat etc from getting in or out: **insulate sth from/against sth** *Pipes may need insulating against the cold.* | *an insulated attic* **2** to keep someone apart from particular experiences or influences, especially unpleasant ones: **insulate sb from sth** *The royal family tried to insulate him from the prying eyes of the media.*

ˈ**insulating** ˌ**tape** *n* [U] a type of sticky tape used for wrapping around electric wires to insulate them

in·su·la·tion /ˌɪnsjəˈleɪʃən $ ˌɪnsə-/ *n* [U] **1** when something is insulated or someone insulates something: *Good insulation can save you money on heating bills.* **2** material used to insulate something, especially a building: *glass-fibre insulation*

in·su·la·tor /ˈɪnsjəleɪtə $ ˈɪnsəleɪtər/ *n* [C] a material or object which does not allow electricity, heat, or sound to pass through it OPP **conductor**: *Wood is an excellent insulator.*

in·su·lin /ˈɪnsjəlɪn $ ˈɪnsə-/ *n* [U] a substance produced naturally by your body which allows sugar to be used for energy: *diabetic patients requiring insulin*

in·sult[1] /ɪnˈsʌlt/ ●●○ *v* [T]
1 to offend someone by saying or doing something they think is rude: *Nobody insults my family and gets away with it!* | *I hope Andy won't be insulted if I don't come.* | **insult sb by doing sth** *They insult us by ignoring our complaints.*
2 insult sb's intelligence to say or do something that suggests you think someone is stupid: *I won't insult your intelligence by lying. Yes, I told him.*

in·sult[2] /ˈɪnsʌlt/ ●●○ *n* [C]
1 a remark or action that is offensive or deliberately rude: *She was shouting insults at her boyfriend.* | *$200 for all that work? It's an insult.* | *Their offer was so low I* ***took*** *it* ***as an insult*** (=thought it was meant to be an insult).
2 be an insult to sb's intelligence to offend someone by being too simple or stupid: *Some advertising is an insult to our intelligence.* → **add insult to injury** at ADD(8)

in·sult·ing /ɪnˈsʌltɪŋ/ ●●○ *adj* very rude and offensive to someone: *insulting remarks* | **[+to]** *Sexist language is insulting to women.* THESAURUS ▸ RUDE —**insultingly** *adv*

in·su·pe·ra·ble /ɪnˈsjuːpərəbəl◂ $ ɪnˈsuː-/ *adj formal* an insuperable difficulty or problem is impossible to deal with: *There were* ***insuperable obstacles***, *and the plan was abandoned.* | *As usual, the hero was facing* ***insuperable odds***.

in·sup·port·a·ble /ˌɪnsəˈpɔːtəbəl $ -ˈpɔːr-/ *adj formal* extremely bad or annoying SYN **unbearable**: *insupportable pain* | *Her behaviour was insupportable.*

in·sur·ance /ɪnˈʃʊərəns $ -ˈʃʊr-/ ●●● S2 W2 *n*
1 [U] an arrangement with a company in which you pay

them money, especially regularly, and they pay the costs if something bad happens, for example if you become ill or your car is damaged → **assurance**, **third party insurance**: *Your father* ***took out insurance*** *to cover the mortgage.* | **health/car/travel etc insurance** | **[+against]** *insurance against loss of income due to unemployment* | **[+on/for]** *Do you have insurance on your house and its contents?* | **claim (for) sth on your insurance** (=get an insurance company to pay for something) *We can probably claim the damage on our insurance.* → LIFE INSURANCE
2 [U] the business of providing insurance: *My brother works in insurance.* | **insurance company/group etc** *the insurance industry*
3 [U] *BrE* the money that you pay regularly to an insurance company SYN **insurance premium**: **[+on]** *How much is the insurance on your car?*
4 [singular, U] protection against something bad happening: **[+against]** *An extra lock on the door is an added insurance against burglars.* → NATIONAL INSURANCE

in'surance ad,juster *n* [C] *AmE* someone who is employed by an insurance company to decide how much to pay people who have had an accident, had something stolen etc SYN **loss adjuster** *BrE*

in'surance ,broker (*also* **in'surance ,agent**) *n* [C] someone who arranges and sells insurance as their job

in'surance ,policy *n* (*plural* **insurance policies**) [C] a written agreement for insurance with an insurance company

in'surance ,premium *n* [C] the money that you pay regularly to an insurance company

in·sure /ɪnˈʃʊə $ -ˈʃʊr/ ●●○ *v*
1 [I,T] to buy insurance so that you will receive money if something bad happens to you, your family, your possessions etc: *Have you insured the contents of your home?* | **insure (sth/sb) against loss/damage/theft/sickness etc** *It is wise to insure your property against storm damage.* | **insure sth for £1,000/$2,000 etc** *You should insure the painting for at least £100,000.*
2 [T] to provide insurance for something or someone: *Many companies won't insure young drivers.*
3 [T] an American spelling of ENSURE

insure (yourself) **against** sth *phr v* to protect yourself against the risk of something bad happening by planning or preparing: *Take advice to insure yourself against being misled.*

in·sured /ɪnˈʃʊəd $ -ˈʃʊrd/ *adj* **1** if someone or something is insured, there is insurance relating to them: *Apparently the jewellery wasn't insured.* | **insured to do sth** *I'm not insured to drive Anne's car.* **2 the insured** *law* the person or people who are insured

in·sur·er /ɪnˈʃʊərə $ -ˈʃʊrər/ *n* [C] a person or company that provides insurance

in·sur·gen·cy /ɪnˈsɜːdʒənsi $ -ɜːr-/ *n* (*plural* **insurgencies**) [C,U] *formal* an attempt by a group of people to take control of their government using force and violence SYN **rebellion** → **counterinsurgency**

in·sur·gent /ɪnˈsɜːdʒənt $ -ɜːr-/ *n* [C usually plural] *formal* one of a group of people fighting against the government of their own country, or against authority SYN **rebel**: *communist insurgents* —**insurgent** *adj*

in·sur·mount·a·ble /ˌɪnsəˈmaʊntəbəl◂ $ -sər-/ *adj formal* an insurmountable difficulty or problem is too large or difficult to deal with: *The language difference proved an* ***insurmountable barrier.***

in·sur·rec·tion /ˌɪnsəˈrekʃən/ *n* [C,U] *formal* an attempt by a large group of people within a country to take control using force and violence SYN **rebellion**: **[+against]** *an* ***armed insurrection*** *against the party in power* —**insurrectionist** *n* [C]

in·tact /ɪnˈtækt/ ●○○ *adj* [not before noun] not broken, damaged, or spoiled: *Only the medieval tower had* ***remained intact.*** | *His reputation* ***survived intact.***

in·ta·gli·o /ɪnˈtɑːliəʊ $ -lioʊ/ *n* (*plural* **intaglios**) [C,U] the art of cutting patterns into a hard substance, or the pattern that you get by doing this → **engraving**

in·take /ˈɪnteɪk/ *n* **1** [singular, U] the amount of food, drink etc that you take into your body: **[+of]** *Try to reduce your intake of fat.* | **a high/low intake** *a high intake of carbohydrates* | **food/alcohol/calorie etc intake** *Sickness may develop from inadequate fluid intake.* **2** [C,U] the number of people who join a school, profession etc at a particular time: **[+of]** *an intake of around 120 students each year* **3** [C] a tube, pipe etc through which air, gas, or liquid enters a machine: *a leak on the air intake to the carburettor* **4 intake of breath** a sudden act of breathing in, especially when you are shocked

in·tan·gi·ble /ɪnˈtændʒəbəl/ *adj* **1** an intangible quality or feeling is difficult to describe exactly: *The island has an intangible quality of holiness.* **2** intangible things have value but do not exist physically – used in business: ***intangible assets*** *such as customer goodwill* —**intangibly** *adv* —**intangible** *n* [C usually plural]: *intangibles like pension schemes and holidays*

in·te·ger /ˈɪntədʒə $ -ər/ *n* [C] *technical* a whole number: *6 is an integer, but 6.4 is not.*

in·te·gral /ˈɪntəgrəl/ ●○○ AWL *adj*
1 forming a necessary part of something: *Vegetables are an* ***integral part*** *of our diet.* | **[+to]** *Statistics are integral to medical research.*
2 [usually before noun] *BrE* provided as part of something, rather than being separate: *a racing car seat with an integral harness* —**integrally** *adv*

in·te·grate /ˈɪntɪgreɪt/ ●○○ AWL *v* [I,T]
1 if two or more things integrate, or if you integrate them, they combine or work together in a way that makes something more effective: **integrate (sth) into/with sth** *Colourful illustrations are integrated into the text.* | *Transport planning should be integrated with energy policy.* | *computers of different makes that integrate with each other*
2 to become part of a group or society and be accepted by them, or to help someone do this: **integrate (sb) into/with sth** *We're looking for people who can integrate with a team.* | *Many children with learning difficulties are integrated into ordinary schools.*
3 *especially AmE* to end the practice of separating people of different races in schools, colleges etc SYN **desegregate** OPP **segregate**

in·te·grat·ed /ˈɪntɪgreɪtɪd/ AWL *adj* an integrated system, institution etc combines many different groups, ideas, or parts in a way that works well: *an integrated public transport system* | *a racially integrated community*

,integrated 'circuit *n* [C] *technical* a very small set of electronic connections printed on a single piece of SEMICONDUCTOR material instead of being made from separate parts

in·te·gra·tion /ˌɪntɪˈgreɪʃən/ ●○○ AWL *n* [U]
1 the combining of two or more things so that they work together effectively: **[+of]** *the integration of data from other surveys*
2 when people become part of a group or society and are accepted by them: **[+into]** *The family unit is supported by its integration into a wider social network.*
3 the process of getting people of different races to live and work together instead of separately → **assimilation**: *problems of* ***racial integration***

in·teg·ri·ty /ɪnˈtegrəti/ ●○○ AWL *n* [U]
1 the quality of being honest and strong about what you believe to be right: **personal/professional/political etc integrity** *a man of great moral integrity*
2 *formal* the state of being united as one complete thing: *the* ***territorial integrity*** *of the country*

in·teg·u·ment /ɪnˈtegjəmənt/ *n* [C] *technical* something such as a shell which covers something else

in·tel·lect /ˈɪntəlekt/ ●○○ *n*
1 [C,U] the ability to understand things and to think intelligently: **superior/considerable/keen etc intellect** *He combined a formidable intellect with a talent for speaking.*
2 [C] someone who is very intelligent

in·tel·lec·tu·al[1] /ˌɪntəˈlektʃuəl◂/ ●●○ W3 *adj*
1 relating to the ability to understand things and think

intelligently → **mental**: **intellectual development/ability/activity etc** *a job that requires considerable intellectual effort*
2 an intellectual person is well-educated and interested in serious ideas and subjects such as science, literature etc → **academic**: *Mark's very intellectual.*
3 needing serious thought in order to be understood: *an intellectual film* —**intellectually** *adv*: *intellectually stimulating* → INTELLIGENT

intellectual² ●○○ *n* [C] an intelligent well-educated person who spends time thinking about complicated ideas and discussing them → **academic**: *a leading British intellectual* —**intellectualism** *n* [U]

in·tel·lec·tu·al·ize (*also* **-ise** *BrE*) /ˌɪntəˈlektʃuəlaɪz/ *v* [I,T] to think or talk about something in a serious complicated way, especially rather than expressing your feelings

ˌintellectual ˈproperty *n* [U] *law* something which someone has invented or has the right to make or sell, especially something that cannot legally be copied by other people

in·tel·li·gence /ɪnˈtelədʒəns/ ●●● S3 W3 AWL *n* [U]
1 a) the ability to learn, understand, and think about things: *To be good at the game, you need a reasonable level of intelligence.* | **high/low intelligence** *John showed high intelligence from an early age.* **b)** a high level of this ability: *a woman who had both beauty and intelligence* → ARTIFICIAL INTELLIGENCE
2 a) information about the secret activities of foreign governments, the military plans of an enemy etc: *According to our intelligence, further attacks were planned.* | **intelligence operations/sources/reports etc** *Intelligence sources denied the reports.* **b)** a group of people or an organization that gathers this information for their government: **intelligence agencies/services etc** *In Britain there are three main intelligence organizations.* | *US Military Intelligence*

inˈtelligence ˌquotient *n* [C] IQ

in·tel·li·gent /ɪnˈtelədʒənt/ ●●● S3 W3 AWL *adj*
1 an intelligent person has a high level of mental ability and is good at understanding ideas and thinking clearly: *a group of **highly intelligent*** (=very intelligent) *students* | *Sontag was once famously described as the most intelligent woman in America.*
2 an intelligent comment, question, conversation etc shows that you have thought about something carefully and understand it well: *an intelligent question* | *You can't have an intelligent conversation with him.*
3 an intelligent creature is able to think and understand: *Are there **intelligent beings** on other planets?* | *forms of **intelligent life***
4 an intelligent machine, system etc is able to learn and use information —**intelligently** *adv*

THESAURUS

intelligent having a high level of mental ability, and good at thinking clearly and understanding ideas: *The top universities aim to select the most intelligent students.*
clever *especially BrE*, **smart** *especially AmE* intelligent, so that you can think and learn quickly and find ways to solve problems: *That was very clever of you. How did you do that?* | *I wasn't smart enough to be a lawyer.*
bright intelligent – used especially about children and young people: *He's a very bright kid.* | *the brightest student in the class*
brilliant extremely intelligent and good at the work you do: *a brilliant scientist*
gifted a gifted child is much more intelligent than most other children: *a special school for gifted children*
wise able to make good decisions and give sensible advice, especially because you have a lot of experience: *a wise old man*
cunning/crafty good at using your intelligence to get what you want, often by making secret plans or tricking people: *She was cunning enough to keep this latest piece of information secret.* | *He's a crafty old devil!*
brainy *informal* intelligent and good at studying: *My sister is the brainy one in our family.*

inˌtelligent deˈsign *n* [U] the belief that living things were designed by an intelligent god, rather than developing by natural processes

in·tel·li·gent·si·a /ɪnˌteləˈdʒentsiə/ *n* **the intelligentsia** the people in a society who are most highly educated and who are most interested in new ideas, especially in art, literature, or politics

in·tel·li·gi·ble /ɪnˈtelədʒəbəl/ *adj* if speech, writing, or an idea is intelligible, it can be easily understood OPP **unintelligible**: *His reply was barely intelligible.* | **[+to]** *The report needs to be intelligible to the client.* —**intelligibly** *adv* —**intelligibility** /ɪnˌtelədʒəˈbɪləti/ *n* [U]

in·tem·per·ate /ɪnˈtempərət/ *adj formal* **1** intemperate language or behaviour shows a lack of control, which other people think is unacceptable: *the judge's intemperate outburst* **2** regularly drinking too much alcohol —**intemperance** *n* [U]

in·tend /ɪnˈtend/ ●●● S2 W1 *v* [T]
1 to have something in your mind as a plan or purpose → **intention**: **intend to do sth** *I intend to spend the night there.* | **intend sb/sth to do sth** *I didn't intend her to see the painting until it was finished.* | *I never intended things to turn out the way they did.* | **intend that** ***It is intended that*** *these meetings will become a regular event.* | **intend doing sth** *We intend looking at the situation again.* | *I **fully intend*** (=definitely intend) *to return home next year.*

REGISTER
In everyday English, people usually say **plan to do** something or **plan on doing** something, rather than **intend to do** something or **intend doing** something:
*I **plan to** spend the night there.* | *I didn't **plan on** things **taking** so long. OR I didn't **plan for** things **to take** so long.*

2 be intended for sb/sth to be provided or designed for a particular person or purpose: *The book is intended for children aged 5–7.*
3 intended target/victim/destination etc the person, thing, result etc that an action is intended to affect or reach: *It seems likely that General Rogers was the killer's intended victim.*

THESAURUS

intend to do sth to have decided that you want to do something at some time in the future: *He intends to appeal against the decision.*
be going to do sth *especially spoken* to intend to do something – used when you have made definite arrangements to do it: *We're going to have a meeting about it next week.* | *I'm going to start karate lessons.*
mean to do sth *especially spoken* to intend to do something – used especially when you forget to do something or when something does not happen in the way you intended: *I've been meaning to call you for ages.* | *Sorry, I didn't mean to scare you.*
plan to do sth to intend to do something – used especially when you have thought carefully about how and when you will do it: *The airline plans to start flights to Thailand in July.* | *Jane and Rob are planning to get married next year.*
set out to do sth to intend to do something – used when someone is very determined and knows clearly what they want to do: *He set out to make a movie that would challenge people's prejudices.*
aim to do sth to intend to do something – used when saying what someone hopes to achieve: *We aim to finish the work by next week.*
propose to do sth *formal* to intend to do something – used when saying what someone suggests doing: *How do you propose to deal with the situation?*
have sb/sth in mind to imagine that something is the kind of thing that you want to happen, or that

someone is the person you want to choose: *'How about going out for a pizza?' 'That wasn't exactly what I had in mind.'* | *Who do you have in mind?*
have no intention of doing sth to have decided that you will definitely not do something: *Tom has no intention of retiring just yet.*

in·tense /ɪn'tens/ ●●○ W3 AWL *adj*
1 having a very strong effect or felt very strongly: *Young people today are under intense pressure to succeed.* | *the intense heat of the desert* | *The pain was so intense I couldn't sleep.* | *He took an intense interest in all religious matters.* | *a look of intense dislike*
2 intense activity is very serious, uses a lot of effort, and often involves doing a great deal in a very short time: *The job demands intense concentration.* | *At least 3,000 people were killed in a week of intense fighting.*
3 someone who is intense is serious and has very strong feelings or opinions – used to show disapproval: *She's a little too intense for me.* —**intensely** *adv*: *He disliked Kate intensely.*

in·ten·si·fi·er /ɪn'tensəfaɪə $ -ər/ *n* [C] *technical* a word, usually an adverb, that is used to emphasize an adjective, adverb, or verb, for example the word 'absolutely' in the phrase 'that's absolutely wonderful'

in·ten·si·fy /ɪn'tensɪfaɪ/ ●○○ AWL *v* (**intensified, intensifying, intensifies**) [I,T] to increase in degree or strength, or to make something do this: *In June the civil war intensified.* | *His mother's death intensified his loneliness.* —**intensification** /ɪnˌtensɪfɪ'keɪʃən/ *n* [singular, U]: *an intensification of fighting in the region*

in·ten·si·ty /ɪn'tensəti/ ●○○ AWL *n* (*plural* **intensities**)
1 [U] the quality of being felt very strongly or having a strong effect: *The intensity of the hurricane was frightening.*
2 [U] the quality of being serious and having very strong feelings or opinions: *He spoke with great intensity.*
3 [C,U] *technical* the strength of something such as light or sound: *an instrument which measures light intensity*

in·ten·sive /ɪn'tensɪv/ ●●○ AWL *adj*
1 involving a lot of activity, effort, or careful attention in a short period of time: *a one-week intensive course in English* | *a day of intensive negotiations*
2 intensive farming/agriculture farming which produces a lot of food from a small area of land
3 energy-intensive/knowledge-intensive etc involving or needing a lot of energy, knowledge etc: *a knowledge-intensive industry* → CAPITAL-INTENSIVE, LABOUR-INTENSIVE —**intensively** *adv*

inˌtensive 'care *n* [U] a department in a hospital that treats people who are very seriously ill or badly injured, or the continuous and thorough treatment given to PATIENTS there: **in intensive care** *He is still in intensive care in Bristol General Hospital.*

in·tent¹ /ɪn'tent/ ●○○ *adj*
1 be intent on/upon (doing) sth to be determined to do something or achieve something: *She was intent on pursuing a career in business.*
2 giving careful attention to something so that you think about nothing else: *his intent gaze* | **[+on/upon]** *Intent upon her work, she didn't notice the cold.* —**intently** *adv*: *Jake listened intently.*

intent² ●○○ *n* [U]
1 *formal* what you intend to do SYN **intention**: *She behaved foolishly but with good intent.*
2 *law* the intention to do something illegal: **with intent (to do sth)** *Jones was found guilty of wounding with intent.* | *He is charged with possession of a gun with intent to commit a robbery.*
3 to all intents and purposes (*also* **for all intents and purposes** *AmE*) used to say that a situation is not exactly as you describe it, but the effect is the same as if it were: *The war was, to all intents and purposes, over.*

in·ten·tion /ɪn'tenʃən/ ●●● S3 W2 *n* [C,U] a plan or desire to do something → **intend**: **have no/every intention of doing sth** *I have no intention of retiring just yet.* | *They went into town* **with the intention of** *visiting the library.* | **intention to do sth** *It is our intention to be the number one distributor of health products.* | **good intentions/the best (of) intentions** (=intentions to do something good or kind, especially when you do not succeed in doing it) *He thinks the minister is full of good intentions that won't be carried out.* ⚠ Do not say that someone 'has no intention to do something'. Say that someone **has no intention of doing something**. THESAURUS PURPOSE → WELL-INTENTIONED

in·ten·tion·al /ɪn'tenʃənəl/ ●●○ *adj* done deliberately and usually intended to cause harm SYN **deliberate** OPP **unintentional**: *I did trip him, but it wasn't intentional.* —**intentionally** *adv*: *intentionally vague promises*

in·ter /ɪn'tɜː $ -'tɜːr/ *v* (**interred, interring**) [T] *formal* to bury a dead person

inter- /ɪntə $ -tər/ *prefix* between or involving two or more different things, places, or people → **intra-, intro-**: *interdepartmental* (=between or involving different departments in a company, government etc) | *an interstate* (=a road that goes between states)

in·ter·act /ˌɪntər'ækt/ ●●○ AWL *v* [I]
1 if people interact with each other, they talk to each other, work together etc: **[+with]** *Lucy interacts well with other children in the class.*
2 if one thing interacts with another, or if they interact, they affect each other: **[+with]** *The immune system interacts with both the nervous system and the hormones.*

in·ter·ac·tion /ˌɪntər'ækʃən/ ●●○ W3 AWL *n* [C,U]
1 a process by which two or more things affect each other: **[+of]** *Price is determined through the interaction of demand and supply.* | **[+with/between]** *the complex interaction between mind and body*
2 the activity of talking to other people, working together with them etc: **[+with/between]** *the degree of interaction between teacher and student*

in·ter·ac·tive /ˌɪntər'æktɪv◂/ ●●○ AWL *adj*
1 an interactive computer program, television system etc allows you to communicate directly with it, and does things in reaction to your actions: *interactive computer systems* | *the museum's interactive exhibits*
2 involving talking and working together: *interactive teaching methods such as role playing* —**interactively** *adv* —**interactivity** /ˌɪntəræk'tɪvəti/ *n* [U]

ˌinteractive 'whiteboard *n* [C] a large board, for example in a classroom, which is connected to a computer so that information from the computer can be shown on it and controlled by touching the board

in·ter·a·gen·cy /ˌɪntər'eɪdʒənsi◂/ *adj* [only before noun] between or involving different organizations or different departments within a government: *interagency co-operation* | *an interagency task force*

in·ter a·li·a /ˌɪntər 'eɪliə, -'ɑːliə/ *adv formal* among other things: *The paper discussed, inter alia, political, economic, and social issues.*

in·ter·breed /ˌɪntə'briːd $ -ər-/ *v* (*past tense and past participle* **interbred** /-'bred/) [I + with, T] to produce young animals from parents of different breeds or groups → **crossbreed, inbreeding**

in·ter·cede /ˌɪntə'siːd $ -ər-/ *v* [I] *formal* to speak in support of someone, especially in order to try to prevent them from being punished → **intercession**: **[+with]** *My good friend, Senator Bowie, interceded with the authorities on my behalf.*

in·ter·cept /ˌɪntə'sept $ -ər-/ ●○○ *v* [T] to stop something or someone that is going from one place to another before they get there: *an attempt to intercept drugs being smuggled over the border* | *His phone calls were intercepted.* —**interception** /-'sepʃən/ *n* [C,U]

in·ter·ces·sion /ˌɪntə'seʃən $ -tər-/ *n formal* **1** [U] when someone talks to a person in authority in order to prevent something bad happening to someone else → **intercede** **2** [C,U] a prayer asking for someone to be helped or cured

in·ter·change¹ /'ɪntətʃeɪndʒ $ -ər-/ *n* **1** [C,U] an

exchange, especially of ideas or thoughts: **[+of]** *the interchange of ideas between students and staff* **2** [C] a point where two or more MOTORWAYS or main roads meet

in·ter·change² /ˌɪntəˈtʃeɪndʒ $ -ər-/ *v* [I,T] to put each of two things in the place of the other, or to be exchanged in this way

in·ter·change·a·ble /ˌɪntəˈtʃeɪndʒəbəl $ -tər-/ *adj* things that are interchangeable can be used instead of each other: *These two words are almost interchangeable.* | *a camera with interchangeable lenses* —**interchangeably** *adv* —**interchangeability** /ˌɪntətʃeɪndʒəˈbɪləti $ -tər-/ *n* [U]

in·ter·cit·y /ˌɪntəˈsɪti◂ $ -tər-/ *adj* [only before noun] happening between two or more cities, or going from one city to another: *intercity rivalry* | *intercity trains*

in·ter·col·le·giate /ˌɪntəkəˈliːdʒət $ -tər-/ *adj* [only before noun] intercollegiate competitions, especially sports competitions, happen between teams from different colleges: **intercollegiate athletics/sports etc**

in·ter·com /ˈɪntəkɒm $ ˈɪntərkɑːm/ *n* [C] a communication system by which people in different parts of a building, aircraft etc can speak to each other: *The pilot's voice came* ***over the intercom***.

in·ter·con·nect /ˌɪntəkəˈnekt $ -tər-/ *v* [I,T] **1** if two systems, places etc are interconnected, or if they interconnect, they are joined together: *a series of interconnected lakes* | *interconnecting rooms* | *Our operating system can now interconnect with other networks.* **2** if two facts, ideas, events etc are interconnected, or if they interconnect, they are related and one is affected by or caused by the other: *In Freud's theory, the two areas of sexuality and violence are interconnected.* | *a number of separate but interconnected issues* —**interconnection** /-ˈnekʃən/ *n* [C,U]: *the interconnection between rich and poor countries*

in·ter·con·ti·nen·tal /ˌɪntəkɒntəˈnentl◂ $ -tərkɑːn-/ *adj* going from one CONTINENT to another, or happening between two continents: *an intercontinental flight* | *intercontinental trade*

in·ter·course /ˈɪntəkɔːs $ ˈɪntərkɔːrs/ *n* [U] *formal* **1** (*also* **sexual intercourse**) the act of having sex **2** an exchange of ideas, feelings etc which make people or groups understand each other better: *social intercourse*

in·ter·cut /ˌɪntəˈkʌt $ -ər-/ *v* (*past tense and past participle* **intercut**, *present participle* **intercutting**) [T] if a film is intercut with particular pictures, sounds, or music, they appear in different places during the film

in·ter·de·nom·i·na·tio·nal /ˌɪntədɪnɒməˈneɪʃənəl $ ˌɪntərdənɑː-/ *adj* between or involving Christians from different groups

in·ter·de·part·men·tal /ˌɪntəˌdiːpɑːtˈmentl $ ˌɪntərdɪˌpɑːrtˈmentl/ *adj* [usually before noun] between or involving different departments of a company, government etc: *intense interdepartmental rivalry*

in·ter·de·pen·dence /ˌɪntədɪˈpendəns $ -tər-/ (*also* **in·ter·de·pen·den·cy** /-dənsi/) *n* [C usually singular, U] a situation in which people or things depend on each other: **[+of]** *the interdependence of our body's immune and nervous systems*

in·ter·de·pen·dent /ˌɪntədɪˈpendənt◂ $ -tər-/ *adj* depending on or necessary to each other: *countries with interdependent economies* **THESAURUS** RELATED —**interdependently** *adv*

in·ter·dict /ˈɪntədɪkt $ -ər-/ *n* [C] **1** *law* an official order from a court telling someone not to do something **2** *technical* a punishment in the Roman Catholic Church, by which someone is not allowed to take part in church ceremonies —**interdict** /ˌɪntəˈdɪkt $ -ər-/ *v* [T] —**interdiction** /-ˈdɪkʃən/ *n* [C,U]

in·ter·dis·ci·plin·ary /ˌɪntəˌdɪsəˈplɪnəri $ ˌɪntərˈdɪsəpləneri/ *adj* involving ideas, information, or people from different subjects or areas of study: *an interdisciplinary research centre*

in·terest¹ /ˈɪntrɪst/ ●●● S2 W1 *n*

1 [singular, U] if you have an interest in something or someone, you want to know or learn more about them: **[+in]** *My parents encouraged my interest in science.* | *I'd recommend this book to anyone who* ***has an interest in*** *jazz.* | *Ben has* ***shown an interest in*** *learning French.* | *My mother had never* ***expressed*** *any* ***interest in*** *the garden.* | *Babies soon begin to* ***take an interest in*** *the world around them.* | *John appeared to* ***have no interest in*** *girls.* | *I watched the first few episodes, but soon* ***lost interest***. | *The last round of bidding* ***aroused*** *considerable* ***interest***. | *Our survey reveals a disturbing* ***lack of interest*** *in teacher training.* | *I read your article* ***with*** *great* ***interest***.

2 [C usually plural] an activity that you enjoy doing or a subject that you enjoy studying: *His interests include walking and golf.* | *As a biologist, my main interest has been human genetics.* | *Her* ***outside interests*** (=interests that are not part of her work) *were numerous.*

3 [U] a quality or feature of something that attracts your attention or makes you want to know more about it: *A Persian rug will* ***add*** *colour and* ***interest*** *to your hallway.* | **be of (no) interest (to sb)** (=be interesting or not interesting to someone) *It's a book that will be of interest to a wide range of readers.* | *What you do in your private life is of no interest to me.* | *art galleries, museums and other* ***places of interest*** | *topics* ***of general interest*** (=that everyone wants to know about)

4 [U] **a)** the extra money that you must pay back when you borrow money: **[+on]** *The interest on the loan is 16% per year.* | *How much are the monthly* ***interest payments***? **b)** money paid to you by a bank or financial institution when you keep money in an account there: *an account that* ***pays*** *higher* ***interest*** | *The more you save, the more* ***interest*** *you'll* ***earn***. → COMPOUND INTEREST, INTEREST RATE, SIMPLE INTEREST

5 [C usually plural, U] the things that bring advantages to someone or something: **protect/look after/safeguard sb's interests** *The regulations were introduced in order to safeguard the interests of local fishing communities.* | **be in sb's (best) interest(s) (to do sth)** (=be the best thing for someone) *The court decided that it was in the girl's best interests to remain with her grandparents.* | **have sb's (best) interests at heart** (=care about someone and want to do what is best for them) *He has your best interests at heart, you know.* | *We've got to balance economic interests and environmental interests.*

6 be in the national/public interest to be good or necessary for the safety or success of a country and its people: *I believe it is in the public interest that these facts are made known.*

7 in the interest(s) of justice/safety/efficiency etc in order to make a situation or system fair, safe etc: *The race was postponed in the interests of safety.*

8 (just) out of interest/as a matter of interest *spoken* used to say that you are asking a question only because you are interested and not because you need to know: *Just out of interest, how much did they offer you?*

9 [C] if you have an interest in a particular company or industry, you own shares in it: *The company is believed to be keen to sell its extensive brewing interests.* | *His business interests are spread throughout Europe.* | **controlling interest** (=enough shares to control what decisions are taken) *In 1986 GM acquired a controlling interest in the sports car maker Lotus.*

10 [C usually plural] a group of people in the same business who share aims or ideas: *Farming interests now dominate many of the National Park committees.* | *The majority of Brazil's huge commercial interests support the measure.* | *the need to reduce the influence of* ***special interests*** (=groups who are concerned about particular subjects)

11 have no interest in doing sth to not want to do something: *I have no interest in continuing this conversation.*

12 declare an interest (in sth) to officially state that you are connected with something or someone, and so cannot be completely fair and independent when making a decision involving them

13 human interest/love interest the part of a story, film, or event which is interesting because it shows things about people's lives or romantic relationships: *As a trainee reporter, she spent most of her time on* ***human interest***

stories. → SELF-INTEREST, → **conflict of interest** at CONFLICT[1](6), → **vested interest** at VESTED(1)

interest² ●●● W2 *v* [T]

1 to make someone want to pay attention to something and find out more about it: *Here's an article which might interest you.* | ***What interests** me **is** all the history of these places.* | **it interests sb that/how/to do** ***It may interest** you **to know that** a number of scholarships are available.*

2 interest yourself in sth *formal* to give something a lot of attention because you want to find out more about it: *He had always interested himself in foreign affairs.*

3 to try to persuade someone to buy, do, or eat something: **interest sb in sth** *The salesman tried to interest me in the higher-priced model.* | **Could I interest you in a drink/dessert etc?** (=used as a polite way of offering someone a drink etc)

in·terest·ed /ˈɪntrɪstɪd/ ●●● S1 W2 *adj*

1 giving a lot of attention to something because you want to find out more about it or because you enjoy it OPP **uninterested, bored**: **[+in]** *I've always been interested in music.* | *All she's interested in is clothes.* | *I wasn't sure if he was really interested or if he was just being polite.* | **interested to hear/know/see etc** *I'd be very interested to hear your opinion.*

2 if you are interested in doing or having something, you want to do it or have it: *I've got a spare ticket for the opera, if you're interested.* | **interested in (doing) sth** *Sheila's interested in starting her own business.* | *Would you be interested in a second-hand car?*

3 interested party/group a person or group that is directly or personally concerned with a situation and is likely to be affected by its results OPP **disinterested**: *All interested parties are invited to attend the meeting.* —**interestedly** *adv*

GRAMMAR: Patterns with interested

- You are **interested in** something: *She is interested in politics.* ✗ Don't say: *She is interested on politics.*
- You are **interested in doing** something: *Are you interested in working abroad?* ✗ Don't say: *Are you interested to work abroad?*
- You say that you **would be interested to hear/know/see/find out** something: *I would be interested to know what she thinks about the idea.* ✗ Don't use *interested to* with other verbs such as 'have' or 'buy'.

GRAMMAR GUIDE ▸ ADJECTIVES

ˌinterest-ˈfree *adj* an interest-free LOAN has no interest charged on it: *interest-free credit*

ˈinterest ˌgroup *n* [C] a group of people who join together to try to influence the government in order to protect their own particular rights, advantages etc SYN **lobby**

in·terest·ing /ˈɪntrəstɪŋ/ ●●● S1 W2 *adj* if something is interesting, you give it your attention because it seems unusual or exciting or provides information that you did not know about OPP **uninteresting, boring**: *That's an interesting question.* | *a really interesting TV programme* | **find sth interesting** *I found his talk very interesting.* | *Did you meet any interesting people?* | **it is interesting to see/know etc** *It will be interesting to see what happens when he gets a bit older.* | ***It's interesting that** no one remembers seeing the car.* ⚠ Do not confuse **interested**, which describes a feeling, and **interesting**, which describes something that interests you: *Are you interested in ballet?* | *an interesting talk on photography*

THESAURUS

interesting keeping your attention and making you want to know more: *There's an interesting article in the newspaper today.* | *The lecture was really interesting.*

fascinating very interesting: *a fascinating subject* | *Everything about ancient Egypt is absolutely fascinating.*

stimulating giving you new ideas or experiences in a way that is interesting and enjoyable: *a stimulating conversation* | *I found him very stimulating to be with and full of ideas.*

intriguing interesting because of being unusual, mysterious, or unexpected, so that you want to find out more: *Their research has produced some intriguing results.*

absorbing/engrossing interesting in a way that keeps your attention completely or for a long time: *Growing your own vegetables can be an absorbing hobby.* | *her engrossing first novel*

gripping/riveting/compelling used about a very interesting story, film etc that you feel you must keep reading or watching: *a gripping story of love and death* | *He gives a riveting performance as a tough street cop.*

enthralling /ɪnˈθrɔːlɪŋ $ -ˈθrɒːl-/ very interesting and exciting – used especially about a performance you are watching or listening to: *Pakistan won an enthralling match by two wickets.*

spellbinding very interesting because of being so strange, unusual, or wonderful: *The book is a spellbinding tale of her life in China.*

I couldn't put it down *spoken* used when saying that a book was so interesting that you could not stop reading it: *It's a great book – I found that I couldn't put it down.*

in·terest·ing·ly /ˈɪntrəstɪŋli/ *adv* **1** [sentence adverb] used to introduce a fact that you think is interesting: *Interestingly, none of their three children ever married.* | ***Interestingly enough**, Pearson made no attempt to deny the rumour.* **2** in an interesting way: *His essay was clearly and interestingly written.*

ˈinterest ˌrate *n* [C] the PERCENTAGE amount charged by a bank etc when you borrow money, or paid to you by a bank when you keep money in an account there

in·ter·face¹ /ˈɪntəfeɪs $ -ər-/ ●○○ *n* [C]

1 the way in which you see the information from a computer program on a screen, or how you type information into the program → **GUI**

2 *technical* the part of a computer system that connects two different machines

3 the way in which two subjects, events etc affect each other: **[+between]** *The book deals with the interface between accountancy and law.*

4 *technical* the surface where two things touch each other

interface² *v* **1** [I,T + with] *technical* if you interface two parts of a computer system, or if they interface, you connect them **2** [I + with] if two people or groups interface with each other, they communicate with each other and work together

in·ter·faith /ˈɪntəfeɪθ $ -ər-/ *adj* [only before noun] between or involving people of different religions: *an interfaith Thanksgiving service*

in·ter·fere /ˌɪntəˈfɪə $ -tərˈfɪr/ ●●○ *v* [I] to deliberately get involved in a situation where you are not wanted or needed SYN **meddle**: *My daughter-in-law said that I was interfering, but I was only trying to help.* | **[+in]** *It's not the church's job to interfere in politics.*

interfere with sth/sb *phr v*

1 to prevent something from succeeding or from happening in the way that was planned: *Anxiety can interfere with children's performance at school.*

2 if something interferes with a radio or television broadcast, it spoils the sound or picture that you receive

3 *BrE* to touch a child sexually: *He was arrested for interfering with young boys.*

in·ter·fer·ence /ˌɪntəˈfɪərəns $ -tərˈfɪr-/ ●●○ *n* [U]

1 an act of interfering: **[+in]** *I resent his interference in my work.* | *Industrial relations should be free from state interference.*

2 unwanted noise on the radio, television, or on the telephone, or faults in the television picture

3 *especially AmE* the act of blocking or touching another player in a sports game, for example by standing in front of them or holding on to them, when you are not supposed to SYN **obstruction** *BrE*

4 run interference *AmE* **a)** to protect a player who has the ball in American football by blocking players from the opposing team **b)** to help someone to achieve something by dealing with people or problems that might cause them trouble

in·ter·fer·on /ˌɪntəˈfɪərɒn $ ˌɪntərˈfɪrɑːn/ *n* [U] a chemical substance that is produced by your body to fight against VIRUSes that cause disease

in·ter·ga·lac·tic /ˌɪntəgəˈlæktɪk◂ $ -tər-/ *adj* between the large groups of stars in space

in·ter·gen·e·ra·tion·al /ˌɪntədʒenəˈreɪʃənəl $ -tər-/ *adj* between or involving people from different age groups: *intergenerational communication*

in·ter·gov·ern·men·tal /ˌɪntəgʌvəˈmentl, -vən- $ -ˈɪntərgʌvərn-/ *adj* [only before noun] between or involving governments of different countries: *an intergovernmental conference*

in·ter·im¹ /ˈɪntərɪm/ ●○○ *adj* [only before noun]
1 intended to be used or accepted for a short time only, until something or someone final can be made or found: *an interim report | He received an interim payment of £10,000. | An interim government was established.*
2 interim period the period of time between two events: *During the interim period, air quality has deteriorated.*

interim² *n* **in the interim** in the period of time between two events SYN **meanwhile**: *The child will be adopted, but a relative is looking after him in the interim.*

in·te·ri·or¹ /ɪnˈtɪəriə $ -ˈtɪriər/ ●●○ *n*
1 [C usually singular] the inner part or inside of something OPP **exterior**: *The interior of the church was dark. | the car's warm interior*
2 the interior the part of a country that is farthest away from the coast: *The interior of the country is mainly desert.*
3 Minister/Department of the Interior the government minister or department that deals with matters within a country rather than abroad

interior² ●○○ *adj* [only before noun] inside or indoors OPP **exterior**: *The interior walls are all painted white.*

inˌterior ˈdecorator *n* [C] an interior designer —**interior decorating** (*also* **interior decoration**) *n* [U]

inˌterior deˈsigner *n* [C] someone whose job is to plan and choose the colours, materials, furniture etc for the inside of buildings, especially people's houses —**interior design** *n* [U]

in·ter·ject /ˌɪntəˈdʒekt $ -ər-/ *v* [I,T] *formal* to interrupt what someone else is saying with a sudden remark: *'That's absolute rubbish!' he interjected.*

in·ter·jec·tion /ˌɪntəˈdʒekʃən $ -ər-/ *n* **1** [C] *technical* a word or phrase used to express a strong feeling such as shock, pain, or pleasure SYN **exclamation** **2** [C,U] *formal* an interruption, or the act of interrupting

in·ter·laced /ˌɪntəˈleɪst◂ $ -ər-/ *adj* things that are interlaced are joined together, with parts of the one thing going over or around parts of the other: *patterns of interlaced squares* —**interlace** *v* [I,T]

in·ter·link /ˌɪntəˈlɪŋk $ -ər-/ *v* [I,T] to connect or be connected with something else: *a chain of interlinking loops*

in·ter·lock /ˌɪntəˈlɒk $ ˌɪntərˈlɑːk/ *v* [I,T] if two or more things interlock, or if they are interlocked, they fit firmly together: *a puzzle with 500 interlocking pieces*

in·ter·loc·u·tor /ˌɪntəˈlɒkjətə $ ˌɪntərˈlɑːkjətər/ *n* [C] *formal* your interlocutor is the person you are speaking to

in·ter·lop·er /ˈɪntələʊpə $ -tərloʊpər/ *n* [C] someone who enters a place or group where they should not be

in·ter·lude /ˈɪntəluːd $ -ər-/ *n* [C] **1** a period of time between two events or situations, during which something different happens: *a brief interlude of peace before a return to the battlefield* **2** a short period of time between the parts of a play, concert etc SYN **intermission** **3** a short piece of music, talk etc used to fill such a period **4** a short romantic or sexual meeting or relationship: *a romantic interlude*

in·ter·mar·ry /ˌɪntəˈmæri $ -ər-/ *v* (**intermarried, intermarrying, intermarries**) [I] **1** if people from two social, racial, or religious groups intermarry, people from one group marry people from the other: **[+with]** *Over the centuries, these Greeks intermarried with the natives.* **2** to marry someone within your own group or family: *It is not unusual for royal cousins to intermarry.* —**intermarriage** /-ˈmærɪdʒ/ *n* [C,U]: ***intermarriage between** ethnic groups*

in·ter·me·di·a·ry /ˌɪntəˈmiːdiəri $ ˌɪntərˈmiːdieri/ *n* (*plural* **intermediaries**) [C] a person or organization that tries to help two other people or groups to agree with each other → **go-between**: *Jackson **acted as** an **intermediary** between the two parties.* —**intermediary** *adj* [only before noun]: *an intermediary role in the talks*

in·ter·me·di·ate¹ /ˌɪntəˈmiːdiət◂ $ -tər-/ ●●● AWL *adj*
1 a) an intermediate class, course etc is at a level of knowledge or skill that is between the basic level and the advanced level: *a book aimed at students at the intermediate level and above* **b)** intermediate students, sports players etc have reached a level of knowledge or skill that is between the basic level and the advanced level: *intermediate learners of English*
2 an intermediate stage in a process of development is between two other stages: *an intermediate stage during which the disease is dormant*

intermediate² *n* [C] a student, sports player etc who has reached a level of knowledge or skill that is between the basic level and the advanced level: *a ski resort suited to beginners and intermediates*

interˈmediate ˌschool *n* [C] *AmE* a JUNIOR HIGH SCHOOL or MIDDLE SCHOOL

in·ter·ment /ɪnˈtɜːmənt $ -ɜːr-/ *n* [C,U] *formal* the act of burying a dead body SYN **burial** → **inter**

in·ter·mi·na·ble /ɪnˈtɜːmənəbəl $ -ɜːr-/ *adj* very long and boring SYN **endless**: *interminable delays* **THESAURUS** LONG —**interminably** *adv*: *an interminably long speech*

in·ter·min·gle /ˌɪntəˈmɪŋgəl $ -tər-/ *v* [I,T] to mix together, or mix something with something else: *The pain and the anger were intermingled.* GRAMMAR **Intermingle** is usually passive when used as a transitive verb.

in·ter·mis·sion /ˌɪntəˈmɪʃən $ -tər-/ *n* [C] *especially AmE* a short period of time between the parts of a play, concert etc SYN **interlude, interval** *BrE*

in·ter·mit·tent /ˌɪntəˈmɪtənt◂ $ -tər-/ *adj* stopping and starting often and for short periods SYN **sporadic**: *The weather forecast is for sun, with intermittent showers.* —**intermittently** *adv*

in·ter·mix /ˌɪntəˈmɪks $ -ər-/ *v* [I,T] to mix together, or mix things together

in·tern¹ /ɪnˈtɜːn $ -ɜːrn/ *v* [T] to put someone in prison without charging them with a crime, for political reasons or during a war → **internee, internment**

in·tern² /ˈɪntɜːn $ -ɜːrn/ *n* [C] *AmE* **1** someone who has nearly finished training as a doctor and is working in a hospital SYN **houseman** *BrE* → **internship** **THESAURUS** DOCTOR **2** someone, especially a student, who works for a short time in a particular job in order to gain experience → **internship**

in·ter·nal /ɪnˈtɜːnl $ -ɜːr-/ ●●○ W2 AWL *adj* [usually before noun]
1 within a particular country SYN **domestic** OPP **external**: *We have no interest in interfering in the **internal affairs** of other countries. | the threat to **internal security** | internal markets*
2 within a company or organization rather than outside it OPP **external**: *There's to be an internal inquiry into the whole affair. | the internal mail*
3 inside your body OPP **external**: **internal organs/injuries**
4 inside something rather than outside OPP **external**: *They've knocked down a couple of internal walls.*
5 existing in your mind SYN **inner**: *internal doubts* —**internally** *adv*: *The matter will be dealt with internally. | This medicine must not be taken internally.*

inˌternal comˈbustion ˌengine *n* [C] an engine that produces power by burning petrol, used in most cars

in·ter·nal·ize (*also* **-ise** *BrE*) /ɪnˈtɜːnəlaɪz $ -ɜːr-/ AWL *v*

I

[T] if you internalize a particular belief, attitude, behaviour etc, it becomes part of your character —**internalization** /ɪnˌtɜːnəlaɪˈzeɪʃən $ ɪnˌtɜːrnələ-/ *n* [U]

inˌternal ˈmedicine *n* [U] *AmE* a type of medical work in which doctors treat illnesses that do not need operations

Inˌternal ˈRevenue ˌService (*also* **Inˌternal ˈRevenue**) (*abbreviation* **the IRS**) the government organization in the US which is responsible for collecting national taxes.

in·ter·na·tion·al¹ /ˌɪntəˈnæʃənəl◂ $ -tər-/ ●●● S2 W1 *adj* relating to or involving more than one nation → **national**: **international trade/market/competition** | *the response of the international community* | *the UN and other international organizations* → INTERNATIONAL RELATIONS, INTERNATIONALLY

international² *n* [C] **1** an international sports game **2** *BrE* someone who plays for one of their country's sports teams → **national**

ˌInternational ˈDate Line *n* [singular] an imaginary line that goes from the NORTH POLE to the SOUTH POLE, to the east of which the date is one day later than it is to the west

in·ter·na·tion·al·is·m /ˌɪntəˈnæʃənəlɪzəm $ -tər-/ *n* [U] the belief that nations should work together and help each other —**internationalist** *n* [C] —**internationalist** *adj*

in·ter·na·tion·al·ize (*also* **-ise** *BrE*) /ˌɪntəˈnæʃənəlaɪz $ -tər-/ *v* [T] to make something international or bring it under international control —**internationalization** /ˌɪntənæʃənəlaɪˈzeɪʃən $ ˌɪntərnæʃənələ-/ *n* [U]

in·ter·na·tion·al·ly /ˌɪntəˈnæʃənəli $ -tər-/ *adv* in many different parts of the world → **international**: *These days businesses have to be able to compete internationally.* | **internationally famous/recognized/known etc** *an internationally famous sculptor*

ˌInternational ˈMonetary ˌFund *n* the IMF

ˌinternational reˈlations *n* [plural] the political relationships between countries, or the study of this

in·ter·ne·cine /ˌɪntəˈniːsaɪn◂ $ ˌɪntərˈniːsən◂, -ˈnesiːn◂/ *adj* [only before noun] *formal* internecine fighting or struggles happen between members of the same group or nation: *internecine warfare*

in·tern·ee /ˌɪntɜːˈniː $ -ɜːr-/ *n* [C] someone who is put into prison during a war or for political reasons, without having had a TRIAL → **intern**

In·ter·net, internet /ˈɪntənet $ -tər-/ ●●● S2 W2 *n* **the Internet** a computer system that allows millions of computer users around the world to exchange information: *Do you have access to the Internet?* | **on the Internet** *You can find all kinds of information on the internet.*

GRAMMAR: Patterns with Internet

• You do something **on the Internet**: *We do most of our shopping on the Internet.* | *They met on the Internet.*
✗ Don't say: *We do most of our shopping by Internet.* | *They met by Internet.*
• You usually say **the Internet**: *I often use the Internet to find out information.* ✗ Don't say: *I often use Internet to find out information.*
GRAMMAR GUIDE ▸ NOUNS

COLLOCATIONS

VERBS

use the Internet *More and more companies are using the Internet to conduct their business.*
go on the Internet *I went on the Internet to find some information for my assignment.*
access the Internet/connect to the Internet *You can access the Internet from your mobile phone.*
surf the Internet (=look at different websites) *She spends hours surfing the Internet every evening.*
download sth from the Internet *I downloaded the file from the Internet.*
buy sth on the Internet *He bought the chairs on the Internet.*

Internet + NOUN

an Internet connection *a high-speed Internet connection*
Internet access *Not everyone has Internet access at home.*
an Internet address (=the address of a website) *The company charges $100 to register a new internet address.*
an Internet service provider (=a company that allows you to connect to the Internet) *Your Internet service provider should be able to solve the problem.*
Internet shopping/banking *The new regulations will increase customer confidence in Internet shopping.*
an Internet user *The number of Internet users is doubling every six months.*
Internet use *The software allows parents to control children's Internet use.*
Internet traffic (=the number of people using the Internet) | **Internet dating** (=using the Internet to meet people for a romantic relationship) | **an Internet café** (=a café with computers, where people can pay to use the Internet)

ˈInternet ˌbanking (*also* **online banking**) *n* [U] a service provided by banks so that people can find out information about their bank account, pay bills etc using the Internet

ˈInternet ˌdating *n* [U] using the Internet to arrange meetings with other people in the hope of finding someone to have a romantic relationship with

In·ter·net·ese /ˌɪntənetˈiːz $ -tər-/ *n* [U] a very informal style of written language, used in emails or CHAT ROOM messages etc, that does not follow the normal rules of grammar and does not, for example, use capital letters, PUNCTUATION etc – used to show disapproval

in·tern·ist /ˈɪntɜːnɪst $ -ɜːr-/ *n* [C] *AmE* a doctor who has a general knowledge about all illnesses and medical conditions of organs inside your body, and who treats illnesses that do not need operations

in·tern·ment /ɪnˈtɜːnmənt $ -ɜːr-/ *n* [U] the practice of keeping people in prison during a war or for political reasons, without charging them with a crime → **intern**: *an internment camp*

in·tern·ship /ˈɪntɜːnʃɪp $ -ɜːrn-/ *n* [C] *AmE* **1** a job that lasts for a short time, that someone, especially a student, does in order to gain experience → **intern** **2** a job that someone who has nearly finished training as a doctor does in a hospital → **intern**

in·ter·pen·e·trate /ˌɪntəˈpenətreɪt $ -tər-/ *v* [I,T] *formal* to spread through something or spread through each other —**interpenetration** /ˌɪntəpenəˈtreɪʃən $ -tər-/ *n* [C,U]

in·ter·per·son·al /ˌɪntəˈpɜːsənəl◂ $ -tərˈpɜːr-/ *adj* relating to relationships between people: *interpersonal skills* | *interpersonal communication*

in·ter·plan·e·ta·ry /ˌɪntəˈplænətəri◂ $ ˌɪntərˈplænəteri◂/ *adj* [only before noun] between the PLANETS: *interplanetary space missions*

in·ter·play /ˈɪntəpleɪ $ -ər-/ *n* [U] the way in which two people or things affect each other: **[+of]** *the interplay of ideas* | **[+between]** *the interplay between military and civilian populations*

In·ter·pol /ˈɪntəpɒl $ -tərpoʊl/ *n* an international police organization that helps national police forces to catch criminals

in·ter·po·late /ɪnˈtɜːpəleɪt $ -ɜːr-/ *v* [T] *formal* **1** to put additional words into a piece of writing SYN **insert** **2** to interrupt someone by saying something —**interpolation** /ɪnˌtɜːpəˈleɪʃən $ -ˌtɜːr-/ *n* [C,U]

in·ter·pose /ˌɪntəˈpəʊz $ -tərˈpoʊz/ *v* [T] *formal* **1** to put yourself or something else between two other things: *She interposed herself between the general and his wife.* **2** to say something when other people are having a conversation or argument, interrupting them: *'That might be difficult,' interposed Regina.*

in·ter·pret /ɪnˈtɜːprɪt $ -ɜːr-/ ●●○ W3 AWL *v*
1 [I,T] to translate spoken words from one language into another: *They spoke good Spanish, and promised to interpret for me.*
2 [T] to believe that something someone does or something that happens has a particular meaning: **interpret sth as sth** *His refusal to work late was interpreted as a lack of commitment to the company.*
3 [T] to explain the meaning of something: *Freud's attempts to interpret the meaning of dreams*
4 [T] to perform a part in a play, a piece of music etc in a way that shows your feelings about it or what you think it means

in·ter·pre·ta·tion /ɪnˌtɜːprɪˈteɪʃən $ -ɜːr-/ ●●○ W3 AWL *n* [C,U]
1 the way in which someone explains or understands an event, information, someone's actions etc: *One possible interpretation is that they want you to resign.* | *It's difficult to* ***put*** *an accurate* ***interpretation on*** (=explain) *the survey results.* | *What exactly the author meant by that statement is* ***open to interpretation*** (=able to be understood or explained in different ways).
2 the way in which someone performs a play, a piece of music etc and shows what they think and feel about it: *Laurence Olivier's brilliant interpretation of Henry V*

in·ter·pre·ta·tive /ɪnˈtɜːprətətɪv $ ɪnˈtɜːrprəteɪtɪv/ AWL (*also* **interpretive**) *adj* **1** relating to, explaining, or understanding the meaning of something: *Reading is an interpretative process.* **2** relating to how feelings are expressed through music, dance, art etc: *interpretive dance*

in·ter·pret·er /ɪnˈtɜːprɪtə $ -ˈtɜːrprɪtər/ ●○○ *n* [C]
1 someone who changes spoken words from one language into another, especially as their job → **translator**: *Speaking* ***through an interpreter*** (=using an interpreter), *Ahmed said, 'I'm very worried about my wife and children.'*
2 a computer program that changes an instruction into a form that can be understood directly by the computer

in·ter·pre·tive /ɪnˈtɜːprətɪv $ -ɜːr-/ AWL *adj* INTERPRETATIVE

in·ter·ra·cial /ˌɪntəˈreɪʃəl◂/ *adj* between different races of people → **multiracial**: *interracial marriage*

InterRail /ˈɪntəreɪl $ -tər-/ *adj, v* [I] *trademark* an InterRail pass allows you to travel around several European countries. People often talk about students 'going interrailing' (=travelling using this pass): *We spent three weeks InterRailing around Europe.*

in·ter·reg·num /ˌɪntəˈregnəm/ *n* (*plural* **interregnums** *or* **interregna** /-nə/) [C] *formal* a period of time when a country or organization has no ruler or leader, and they are waiting for a new one

in·ter·re·late /ˌɪntərɪˈleɪt/ *v* [I] if two things interrelate, they are connected and have an effect on each other: *We will be discussing how the interests of state, parent and child interrelate.* | **[+with]** *Each part of the course interrelates with all the others.*

in·ter·re·lat·ed /ˌɪntərɪˈleɪtɪd◂/ *adj* things that are interrelated are connected and have an effect on each other: *Unemployment and inflation are interrelated.* | *Many interrelated factors are at work here.* THESAURUS RELATED

in·ter·re·la·tion·ship /ˌɪntərɪˈleɪʃənʃɪp/ (*also* **in·ter·re·la·tion** /-rɪˈleɪʃən/) *n* [C,U] a connection between two things that makes them affect each other

in·ter·ro·gate /ɪnˈterəgeɪt/ *v* [T] to ask someone a lot of questions for a long time in order to get information, sometimes using threats SYN **question**: *The police interrogated the suspect for several hours.* THESAURUS ASK —**interrogator** *n* [C]: *He refused to tell his interrogators anything.*

in·ter·ro·ga·tion /ɪnˈterəgeɪʃən/ ●○○ *n* [C,U] the process of interrogating someone: *a long interrogation* | ***Under interrogation****, he admitted that he had taken the money.*

in·ter·rog·a·tive¹ /ˌɪntəˈrɒgətɪv◂ $ -ˈrɑː-/ *adj*
1 *technical* an interrogative sentence, PRONOUN etc asks a question or has the form of a question. For example, 'who' and 'what' are interrogative pronouns. **2** *written* if someone gives you an interrogative look or uses an interrogative voice, they want to know the answer to a question SYN **questioning** —**interrogatively** *adv*

interrogative² *n technical* **1 the interrogative** the form of a sentence or verb that is used for asking questions → **indicative**: *Put this statement into the interrogative.* **2** [C] a word such as 'who' or 'what' that is used in asking questions

in·ter·rupt /ˌɪntəˈrʌpt/ ●●● S3 *v*
1 [I,T] to stop someone from continuing what they are saying or doing by suddenly speaking to them, making a noise etc: *Will you stop interrupting me!* | *Sorry to interrupt, but I need to ask you to come downstairs.*
2 [T] to make a process or activity stop temporarily: *My studies were interrupted by the war.*
3 [T] if something interrupts a line, surface, view etc, it stops it from being continuous —**interruption** /-ˈrʌpʃən/ *n* [C,U]: *We can talk here without interruption.* ⚠ Do not use **interruption** to mean a short period when students or workers can stop working and relax. Use **break**: *Between the two classes there is a 15-minute break.*

in·ter·sect /ˌɪntəˈsekt $ -ər-/ *v* **1** [I,T] if two lines or roads intersect, they meet or go across each other **2** [T] to divide an area with several lines, roads etc: *The plain is intersected by a network of canals.* GRAMMAR **Intersect** is usually passive in this meaning.

in·ter·sec·tion /ˌɪntəˈsekʃən, ˈɪntəsekʃən $ -tər-/ ●●● S3 *n*
1 [C] a place where roads, lines etc cross each other, especially where two roads meet SYN **junction** *BrE*
2 [U] the act of intersecting something

in·ter·sex /ˈɪntəseks $ -tər-/ *adj* an intersex person is not clearly either male or female biologically

in·ter·sperse /ˌɪntəˈspɜːs $ -tərˈspɜːrs/ *v* [T] **1 be interspersed with sth** if something is interspersed with a particular kind of thing, it has a lot of them in it: *sunny periods interspersed with showers* **2 intersperse sth with sth** to put something in between pieces of speech or writing, parts of a film etc

in·ter·state¹ /ˈɪntəsteɪt $ -tər-/ *n* [C] *AmE* a wide road that goes between states, on which cars can travel very fast → **freeway**

interstate² *adj* [only before noun] involving different states, especially in the US: *interstate commerce*

in·ter·stel·lar /ˌɪntəˈstelə◂ $ -tərˈstelər◂/ *adj* [only before noun] happening or existing between the stars

in·ter·stice /ɪnˈtɜːstɪs $ -ɜːr-/ *n* [C usually plural] *formal* a small space or crack in something or between things

in·ter·twine /ˌɪntəˈtwaɪn $ -tər-/ *v* [I,T] **1** if two situations, ideas etc are intertwined, they are closely related to each other: **be closely/inextricably intertwined** *The problems of crime and unemployment are closely intertwined.* **2** if two things intertwine, or if they are intertwined, they are twisted together: **[+with]** *a necklace of rubies intertwined with pearls*

in·ter·val /ˈɪntəvəl $ -tər-/ ●●○ W3 AWL *n* [C]
1 the period of time between two events, activities etc: *He left the room, returning after a short interval with a message.* | **[+between]** *The interval between arrest and trial can be up to six months.*
2 sunny/bright intervals *BrE* short periods of fine weather between cloudy weather, rainy weather etc
3 at weekly/20-minute etc intervals every week, 20 minutes etc: *The trains run at half-hourly intervals.*
4 at regular intervals a) something that happens at regular intervals happens often: *The phone rang at regular intervals all afternoon.* **b)** objects that are placed at regular intervals have all been placed at the same distance from each other: *Trees had been planted at regular intervals.*
5 *BrE* a short period of time between the parts of a play, concert etc SYN **intermission** *AmE*: *We can get some drinks in the interval.*
6 *technical* the amount of difference in PITCH between two musical notes

in·ter·vene /ˌɪntəˈviːn $ -tər-/ ●●○ AWL *v*
1 [I] to become involved in an argument, fight, or other difficult situation in order to change what happens: **[+in]** *The police don't usually like to intervene in disputes between husbands and wives.* | *The army will have to intervene to prevent further fighting.*
2 [I,T] to interrupt someone when they are speaking: *'Stop shouting, Emily,' John intervened.*
3 [I] if an event intervenes, it delays or interrupts something else: *He was just establishing his career when the war intervened.*
4 [I] if a period of time intervenes, it comes between two events: *In the six years that intervened, I saw them once.*

in·ter·ven·ing /ˌɪntəˈviːnɪŋ $ -tər-/ AWL *adj* **the intervening years/months/period etc** time that passes between two events: *I hadn't seen him since 1980, and he had aged a lot in the intervening years.*

in·ter·ven·tion /ˌɪntəˈvenʃən $ -tər-/ ●●○ W3 AWL *n* [C,U] the act of becoming involved in an argument, fight, or other difficult situation in order to change what happens: *government intervention to regulate prices*

in·ter·ven·tion·ist /ˌɪntəˈvenʃənɪst $ -tər-/ *adj* based on the belief of a government or organization that it should take action or spend money to influence the ECONOMY (=financial system) or what happens in other countries: **interventionist approach/role/policy** *The UN adopted a more interventionist approach in the region.* —**interventionism** *n* [U]

in·ter·view¹ /ˈɪntəvjuː $ -ər-/ ●●● S2 W1 *n*
1 [C,U] a formal meeting at which someone is asked questions in order to find out whether they are suitable for a job, course of study etc: **[+for]** *an interview for a job on the 'Los Angeles Times'* | *a portfolio of work presented* ***at interview***
2 [C] an occasion when a famous person is asked questions about their life, experiences, or opinions for a newspaper, magazine, television programme etc: **[+with]** *an interview with the president* | **newspaper/radio/television interview** | *Elton John* ***gave*** *an* ***interview to*** *Barbara Walters* (=he answered her questions). | *an* ***exclusive interview*** (=one that is given to only one newspaper, programme etc)
3 [C] an official meeting with someone who asks you questions: *a police interview*

COLLOCATIONS

VERBS

have an interview *She has an interview next week for a teaching job in Paris.*
go for an interview (*also* **attend an interview** *formal*) *I went for an interview at a software company yesterday.*
get an interview *He was one of only five people to get an interview out of more than 100 people who applied.*
be called/invited for (an) interview *Applicants who are called for interview may be asked to have a medical exam.*
do an interview (*also* **conduct an interview** *formal*) *The interview was conducted in French.*
give sb an interview (=interview someone) *We gave her an interview, but decided not to offer her the job.*

ADJECTIVES/NOUN + interview

a job interview *Try to predict the questions you might get in your job interview.*
an informal/formal interview *Applicants will normally have an informal interview with the manager.*
the first interview (*also* **the preliminary interview** *formal*) *He felt the first interview had gone well.*
a second/follow-up interview (=a more detailed interview after you have been successful in a previous interview) *She was asked back for a second interview.*
a mock interview (=one that you do for practice, rather than a real interview) | **a face-to-face interview** (=in which people meet in person) | **a telephone interview**

interview + NOUN

interview technique *The book gives some useful advice on interview technique.*
an interview question | **the interview panel** (=the group of people interviewing someone)

interview² ●●○ S3 W3 *v* [T] to ask someone questions during an interview: **interview sb for sth** *We're interviewing six candidates for the job.* | **interview sb about sth** *The police want to interview you about the accident.* THESAURUS ASK —**interviewing** *n* [U]: *interviewing skills*

in·ter·view·ee /ˌɪntəvjuˈiː $ -tər-/ *n* [C] the person who answers the questions in an interview

in·ter·view·er /ˈɪntəvjuːə $ -tərvjuːər/ ●○○ *n* [C] the person who asks the questions in an interview

in·ter·war /ˌɪntəˈwɔː◂ $ -tərˈwɔːr◂/ *adj* [only before noun] happening or relating to the period between the First and the Second World Wars: *the interwar years*

in·ter·weave /ˌɪntəˈwiːv $ -ər-/ *v* (*past tense* **interwove** /-ˈwəʊv $ -ˈwoʊv/, *past participle* **interwoven** /-ˈwəʊvən $ -ˈwoʊ-/) [T usually passive] **1** if two things are interwoven, they are closely related or combined in a complicated way: **closely/inextricably/tightly etc interwoven** *The two themes are inextricably interwoven in the book.* | **be interwoven with sth** *practical help for the bereaved interwoven with emotional support* **2** to weave two or more things together: **be interwoven with sth** *silk interwoven with gold and silver threads* GRAMMAR **Interweave** is usually passive.

in·tes·tate /ɪnˈtesteɪt, -stət/ *adj* **die intestate** *law* to die without having made a WILL (=a statement about who you want to have your property after you die)

in·tes·tine /ɪnˈtestɪn/ *n* [C] the long tube in your body through which food passes after it leaves your stomach SYN **gut** —**intestinal** *adj* → LARGE INTESTINE, SMALL INTESTINE

ˌin-ˈthing *n* **be the in-thing** *informal* to be very fashionable at the moment

in·ti·ma·cy /ˈɪntəməsi/ *n* **1** [U] a state of having a close personal relationship with someone: **[+of]** *the intimacy of marriage* | **[+between]** *a close sense of intimacy between parent and child* **2 intimacies** [plural] things you say or do to someone you have a close personal relationship with: *She thought back over the intimacies they'd shared and the plans they'd made.* **3** [U] a situation in which you feel you are in private with someone: *the cosy intimacy of the café* **4** [U] *formal* sex – used especially by lawyers and police when they want to avoid using the word 'sex'

in·ti·mate¹ /ˈɪntəmət/ ●○○ *adj*
1 RESTAURANT/MEAL/PLACE private and friendly so that you feel comfortable: *the intimate atmosphere of a country pub* | *an intimate meal for two* | *The collection has been moved from its* ***intimate setting*** *to the British Museum.*
2 FRIENDS having an extremely close friendship: *an intimate friend of Picasso's* | *an intimate relationship* | *She's* ***on intimate terms with*** *people in government.*
3 intimate knowledge of sth very detailed knowledge of something as a result of careful study or a lot of experience: *his intimate knowledge of the coal industry*
4 PRIVATE relating to very private or personal matters: *the publication of* ***intimate details*** *of their affair* THESAURUS PRIVATE
5 SEX *formal* **a)** relating to sex: *The virus can only be transmitted through intimate contact.* **b) be intimate with sb** to have sex with someone
6 intimate link/connection etc a very close connection between two things: *the intimate connection between physical and mental health* —**intimately** *adv*: *The two aspects are intimately connected.* | *I am intimately acquainted with the state of my bank account.*

in·ti·mate² /ˈɪntɪmeɪt/ *v* [T] *formal* to make people understand what you mean without saying it directly: **intimate that** *He intimated, politely but firmly, that we were not welcome.* | **intimate sth to sb** *She had already intimated to me her wish to leave.*

in·ti·mate³ /ˈɪntəmət/ *n* [C] *formal* a close personal friend

in·ti·ma·tion /ˌɪntəˈmeɪʃən/ *n* [C,U] *formal* **1** an indirect or unclear sign that something may happen: *the first intimations of the approaching conflict* **2** the act of officially telling someone about something: *Without early intimation of the dates of the training sessions, enthusiasm for training could decrease.*

in·tim·i·date /ɪnˈtɪmədeɪt/ ●○○ *v* [T]
1 to frighten or threaten someone into making them do what you want: **intimidate sb into doing sth** *They tried to intimidate the young people into voting for them.* | *Attempts to intimidate her failed.*
2 to make someone feel worried and not confident: *The whole idea of going to Oxford intimidated me.* —**intimidation** /ɪnˌtɪməˈdeɪʃən/ *n* [U]: *She had endured years of intimidation and violence.* | *the intimidation of voters*

in·tim·i·dat·ed /ɪnˈtɪmɪdeɪtɪd/ *adj* [not before noun] feeling worried and lacking confidence because of the situation you are in or the people you are with: *I was shy, and felt intimidated by the older students.*

in·tim·i·dat·ing /ɪˈtɪmədeɪtɪŋ/ *adj* making you feel worried and not confident: *Some people find interview situations very intimidating.* THESAURUS ▸ FRIGHTENING

in·to /ˈɪntə; *before vowels* ˈɪntʊ; *strong* ˈɪntuː/ ●●● S1 W1 *prep*
1 TO THE INSIDE OF STH to the inside or inner part of a container, place, area etc: *Come into the office.* | *He thrust his hand into his coat pocket.* | *There must be another way into the cave.* | *Sue got back into bed and pulled the quilt over her head.* | *I've got to go into town this morning.* | *We dived into the sea.*
2 BECOMING INVOLVED used to say that someone becomes involved in a situation or activity, or becomes part of a group: *At the age of 16, I went into the printing trade as an apprentice.* | *They tried to drag me into their quarrel.* | *a player who deserves to get back into the England team*
3 CHANGING used to say that someone or something starts being in a different state or form: *She fell into a deep sleep.* | *The whole banking system was thrown into confusion.* | *I screwed my wet handkerchief into a ball.* | *Cut the cake into pieces.* | *Neruda's poems have been translated into English.*
4 HITTING STH used to say that a person or vehicle hits someone or something after moving towards them: *He almost bumped into me as he rushed past.* | *The car swerved and crashed into the wall.*
5 DIRECTION in a particular direction: *They rode off into the sunset.* | *Make sure you're speaking directly into the microphone.*
6 TIME at or until a certain time: *Andy and I talked well into the night.* | *John was well into his forties before he got married.*
7 FINDING OUT used to say what someone is trying to find out information about: *an investigation into the events leading up to his death* | *I've been doing some research into this.*
8 DIVIDING NUMBERS *spoken* used when you are dividing one number by another: *Eight into twenty-four is three.*
9 be into sth *spoken* to like and be interested in something: *I'm really into folk music.*
10 be into sb *AmE informal* to owe someone money: *He's into me for $50.*

in·tol·e·ra·ble /ɪnˈtɒlərəbəl $ -ˈtɑː-/ ●○○ *adj* too difficult, bad, annoying etc for you to accept or deal with OPP **tolerable**: *'This is intolerable!' exclaimed Sir Rufus.* | *The pain had become intolerable.* | **intolerable burden/strain/pressure** *Caring for an elderly relative can become an intolerable burden.* —**intolerably** *adv*

in·tol·e·rance /ɪnˈtɒlərəns $ -ˈtɑː-/ ●○○ *n*
1 [U] unwillingness to accept ways of thinking and behaving that are different from your own OPP **tolerance**: **racial/religious intolerance** THESAURUS ▸ PREJUDICE
2 [C,U] an inability to take particular medicines or eat particular foods without suffering bad effects → **allergic**: **[+of]** *an intolerance of alcohol* | **food/glucose/lactose intolerance**

in·tol·e·rant /ɪnˈtɒlərənt $ -ˈtɑː-/ *adj* **1** not willing to accept ways of thinking and behaving that are different from your own OPP **tolerant**: **[+of]** *people who are intolerant of other people's political beliefs* **2** not able to take particular medicines or eat particular foods without suffering bad effects → **allergic**: **[+of]** *A number of patients were intolerant of the diet.* | *She's lactose-intolerant* (=unable to drink particular types of milk).

in·to·na·tion /ˌɪntəˈneɪʃən/ *n* **1** [C,U] the way in which the level of your voice changes in order to add meaning to what you are saying, for example by going up at the end of a question: *intonation patterns* **2** [U] *technical* the playing or singing of correct musical notes

in·tone /ɪnˈtəʊn $ -ˈtoʊn/ *v* [T] *formal* to say something slowly and clearly without making your voice rise and fall much as you speak: *The priest intoned the blessing.*

in to·to /ˌɪn ˈtəʊtəʊ $ -ˈtoʊtoʊ/ *adv* as a whole SYN **totally**: *They accepted the plan in toto.*

in·tox·i·cant /ɪnˈtɒksəkənt $ -ˈtɑːk-/ *n* [C] *technical* something that makes you drunk

in·tox·i·cat·ed /ɪnˈtɒksɪkeɪtɪd $ -ˈtɑːk-/ *adj* **1** *formal* drunk OPP **sober**: *The driver was clearly intoxicated.* **2** happy, excited, and unable to think clearly, especially as a result of love, success, power etc: **[+by/with]** *He rapidly became intoxicated with his own power.* —**intoxicate** *v* [T] —**intoxication** /ɪnˌtɒksɪˈkeɪʃən $ -ˌtɑːk-/ *n* [U]

in·tox·i·cat·ing /ɪnˈtɒksəkeɪtɪŋ $ -ˈtɑːk-/ *adj* **1** *formal* intoxicating drinks can make you drunk **2** making you feel happy, excited, and unable to think clearly: *the intoxicating combination of her beauty and wit*

intra- /ɪntrə/ *prefix formal or technical* **1** inside SYN **within**: *intra-departmental* (=within a department) **2** into: *an intravenous injection* (=into a vein)

in·trac·ta·ble /ɪnˈtræktəbəl/ *adj formal* **1** an intractable problem is very difficult to deal with or solve: *the seemingly intractable problem of human greed* **2** having a strong will and difficult to control —**intractability** /ɪnˌtræktəˈbɪləti/ *n* [U]

in·tra·mu·ral /ˌɪntrəˈmjʊərəl◂ $ -ˈmjʊr-/ *adj AmE* happening within one school, or intended for the students of one school: *an intramural softball competition* → EXTRAMURAL

in·tra·net /ˈɪntrənet/ *n* [C] a computer network used for exchanging or seeing information within a company → **Internet, extranet**

in·tran·si·gent /ɪnˈtrænsədʒənt/ *adj formal* unwilling to change your ideas or behaviour, in a way that seems unreasonable SYN **stubborn**: *an intransigent attitude* —**intransigence** *n* [U]: *He accused the government of intransigence.*

in·tran·si·tive /ɪnˈtrænsətɪv/ *adj technical* an intransitive verb has a subject but no object. For example, in the sentence 'They arrived,' 'arrived' is intransitive. Intransitive verbs are marked [I] in this dictionary. OPP **transitive** —**intransitively** *adv*

in·tra·pre·neur /ˌɪntrəprəˈnɜː $ -ˈnɜːr/ *n* [C] someone who works for a large company and whose job is to develop new ideas or ways of doing business for that company → **entrepreneur** —**intrapreneuring** *n* [U]

in·tra·state /ˈɪntrəsteɪt/ *adj* [only before noun] *AmE* within one US state → **interstate**: *intrastate commerce*

in·tra·ve·nous /ˌɪntrəˈviːnəs◂/ *adj* [only before noun] through or into a VEIN (=tube in the body taking blood back to the heart) → **injection**: *an intravenous injection* | *intravenous drug users* —**intravenously** *adv*

ˈin tray *n* [C] a container on your desk for work and letters that need to be dealt with OPP **out tray** → see picture at TRAY

in·trep·id /ɪnˈtrepɪd/ *adj* willing to do dangerous things or go to dangerous places - often used humorously SYN **brave**: *intrepid explorers* THESAURUS ▸ BRAVE

in·tri·ca·cy /ˈɪntrɪkəsi/ *n* (*plural* **intricacies**) **1 the intricacies of sth** the complicated details of something: *the* *intricacies of private banking* **2** [U] the state of containing a large number of parts or details: *designs of amazing intricacy and sophistication*

in·tri·cate /ˈɪntrɪkət/ ●○○ *adj* containing many small parts or details that all work or fit together → **complex**: *intricate patterns* THESAURUS COMPLICATED —**intricately** *adv*: *intricately woven fabric*

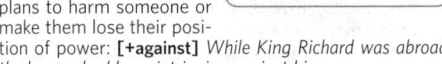

INTRICATE

an intricate pattern

in·trigue¹ /ɪnˈtriːg/ ●○○ *v*

1 [T] if something intrigues you, it interests you a lot because it seems strange or mysterious: *Other people's houses always intrigued her.*

2 [I] *formal* to make secret plans to harm someone or make them lose their position of power: **[+against]** *While King Richard was abroad, the barons had been intriguing against him.*

in·trigue² /ˈɪntriːg/ *n* [C,U] the making of secret plans to harm someone or make them lose their position of power, or a plan of this kind: *It's an exciting story of **political intrigue** and murder.* | *a **web of intrigue*** (=complicated set of secret plans) | **[+of]** *the political intrigues of the capital*

in·trigued /ɪnˈtriːgd/ *adj* very interested in something because it seems strange or mysterious: **[+by/with]** *He was intrigued by her reaction.* | **intrigued to know/learn etc** *She was intrigued to know what he planned to do next.*

in·tri·guing /ɪnˈtriːgɪŋ/ *adj* something that is intriguing is very interesting because it is strange, mysterious, or unexpected SYN **fascinating**: *The magazine carries an intriguing mixture of high fashion, gossip and racing.* THESAURUS INTERESTING —**intriguingly** *adv*

in·trin·sic /ɪnˈtrɪnsɪk, -zɪk/ ●○○ AWL *adj* being part of the nature or character of someone or something OPP **extrinsic**: *the **intrinsic interest** of the subject* | **intrinsic nature/quality/value/property of sth** *There is nothing in the intrinsic nature of the work that makes it more suitable for women.* | **[+to]** *Flexibility is intrinsic to creative management.* —**intrinsically** /-kli/ *adv*: *Science is seen as intrinsically good.*

in·tro /ˈɪntrəʊ $ -troʊ/ *n* (*plural* **intros**) [C] *informal* a short part at the beginning of a song, piece of writing etc → **introduction**

intro- /ɪntrə/ *prefix* into, especially into the inside: *introspection* (=examining your own feelings)

in·tro·duce /ˌɪntrəˈdjuːs $ -ˈduːs/ ●●● S2 W1 *v* [T]

1 WHEN PEOPLE MEET if you introduce someone to another person, you tell them each other's names for the first time: *Have you two been introduced? Tom, this is Greg.* | **introduce sb to sb** *June, let me introduce you to Bob.* | **introduce yourself** (=formally tell someone who you are) *May I introduce myself? My name is Meg Johnson.*

2 NEW SYSTEM/PRODUCT to bring a plan, system, or product into use for the first time: *They want to introduce a system of identity cards.* | *The store have introduced a new range of food for children.*

> REGISTER
> In everyday British English, people often say **bring in** a plan, law, system etc rather than **introduce** it: *They want to **bring in** a system of identity cards.*

3 BRING STH TO A PLACE to bring a type of thing somewhere for the first time: **introduce sth to/into sth** *The grey squirrel was introduced into Britain from North America.*

4 NEW EXPERIENCE to show someone something or tell them about it for the first time: **introduce sb to sth/introduce sth to sb** *Malcolm introduced me to the joys of wine-tasting.*

5 PROGRAMME/PUBLIC EVENT to speak at the beginning of and sometimes during a television or radio programme, or at the beginning of a public event: *Jim Adams will introduce tonight's programme.*

6 START A CHANGE to make something new start to happen or exist in a situation: *The peace agreement has introduced a feeling of optimism here.*

7 LAW to formally present a possible new law to be discussed: *Several senators introduced legislation aimed at sexual harassment.*

8 PUT STH INTO STH *technical* to put something carefully into something else: **introduce sth into sth** *Fuel was introduced into the jet pipe.*

in·tro·duc·tion /ˌɪntrəˈdʌkʃən/ ●●● S3 W2 *n*

1 NEW SYSTEM/PRODUCT [U] the act of bringing something into use for the first time: **[+of]** *the introduction of a range of new products* | *With the introduction of independent taxation, a married woman's position is much clearer.*

2 BRING STH TO A PLACE **a)** [U] the act of bringing something somewhere for the first time: **[+of]** *the introduction of Buddhism to China nearly 2,000 years ago* **b)** [C] a type of thing that is brought somewhere for the first time: *The potato was a 16th-century introduction.*

3 WHEN MEETING SB [C] the act of formally telling two people each other's names when they first meet: *Pete, are you going to **make the introductions**?* | *Our first contestant **needs no introduction*** (=everyone already knows the person).

4 BOOK/SPEECH [C] a written or spoken explanation at the beginning of a book, speech etc: *In the introduction, he explains why he wrote the book.* | *Mr Brown gave a brief introduction to the course.*

5 MUSIC [C] a short part at the beginning of a song or piece of music

6 EXPLANATION [C] something that explains the basic facts of a subject: **[+to]** *The book is a useful introduction to British geology.*

7 NEW EXPERIENCE [C] someone's first experience of something: **[+to]** *an introduction to water sports*

8 LETTER [C] a letter by someone else that explains who you are, which you can give to a person you have not met before

in·tro·duc·to·ry /ˌɪntrəˈdʌktəri◂/ ●○○ *adj* [only before noun]

1 said or written at the beginning of a book, speech etc in order to explain what it is about: **introductory chapter/paragraph** *the objectives described in the introductory chapter* | *as the chairman said in his **introductory remarks***

2 intended for people who have never done a particular activity before: *an **introductory course** in data processing*

3 introductory offer/price etc a special low price that is charged for a new product for a limited period of time: *Don't miss our introductory offer!*

in·tro·spec·tion /ˌɪntrəˈspekʃən/ *n* [U] the process of thinking deeply about your own thoughts, feelings, or behaviour

in·tro·spec·tive /ˌɪntrəˈspektɪv◂/ *adj* tending to think deeply about your own thoughts, feelings, or behaviour: *a shy and introspective person* —**introspectively** *adv*

in·tro·vert /ˈɪntrəvɜːt $ -ɜːrt/ ●○○ *n* [C] someone who is quiet and shy, and does not enjoy being with other people OPP **extrovert**

in·tro·vert·ed /ˈɪntrəvɜːtɪd $ -ɜːr-/ *adj* someone who is introverted is quiet and shy and does not enjoy being with other people OPP **extrovert, extroverted** THESAURUS SHY —**introversion** /ˌɪntrəˈvɜːʃən $ -ˈvɜːrʒən/ *n* [U]

in·trude /ɪnˈtruːd/ ●○○ *v* [I]

1 to interrupt someone or become involved in their private affairs, in an annoying and unwanted way: *Would I be intruding if I came with you?* | **[+into/on/upon]** *Employers should not intrude into the private lives of their employees.*

2 to come into a place or situation, and have an unwanted effect: **[+on]** *It is to be hoped that TV cameras never intrude on this peaceful place.*

in·trud·er /ɪnˈtruːdə $ -ər/ ●○○ *n* [C]
1 someone who illegally enters a building or area, usually in order to steal something: *The police think the intruder got in through an unlocked window.*
2 someone who is in a place where they are not wanted: *At first I felt like an intruder in their family.*

in·tru·sion /ɪnˈtruːʒən/ ●○○ *n* [C,U]
1 when someone does something, or something happens, that affects your private life or activities in an unwanted way: **[+into/on/upon]** *I resented this intrusion into my domestic affairs.* | *the unwelcome intrusion of the press*
2 when something comes into a place or situation and has an unwanted effect: *the intrusion of badly designed new buildings in the historic high street*

in·tru·sive /ɪnˈtruːsɪv/ *adj* affecting someone's private life or interrupting them in an unwanted and annoying way: *They found the television cameras too intrusive.*

in·tu·it /ɪnˈtjuːɪt $ -ˈtuː-, -ˈtjuː-/ *v* [T] *formal* to know or guess something because of a feeling you have, rather than because of facts you know

in·tu·i·tion /ˌɪntjuˈɪʃən $ -tu-, -tju-/ ●○○ *n*
1 [U] the ability to understand or know something because of a feeling rather than by considering the facts SYN **instinct**: *feminine intuition* | *Intuition told her it was unwise to argue.*
2 [C] an idea about what is true in a particular situation based on a feeling rather than facts: **intuition (that)** *He had an intuition there was trouble brewing.* | *We should trust our intuitions.*

in·tu·i·tive /ɪnˈtjuːətɪv $ -ˈtuː-, -ˈtjuː-/ *adj* **1** an intuitive idea is based on a feeling rather than on knowledge or facts SYN **instinctive**: *He seemed to have an intuitive awareness of how I felt.* **2** someone who is intuitive is able to understand situations without being told or having any proof about them —**intuitively** *adv*

In·u·it[1] /ˈɪnjuɪt, ˈɪnuɪt $ ˈɪnuɪt/ *adj* relating to the Inuit → **Eskimo**

Inuit[2] *n* [C] **1** someone who belongs to a race of people who live in the very cold northern areas of North America → **Eskimo 2 the Inuit** [plural] the people who belong to this race

I·nuk /ˈɪnʊk $ ɪˈnʌk/ *n* [C] another word for an Inuit

in·un·date /ˈɪnəndeɪt/ *v* [T] **1 be inundated (with/by sth)** to receive so much of something that you cannot easily deal with it all SYN **swamp**: *After the broadcast, we were inundated with requests for more information.* **2** *formal* to cover an area with a large amount of water SYN **flood**: *The tidal wave inundated vast areas of cropland.* —**inundation** /ˌɪnənˈdeɪʃən/ *n* [C,U]

in·ure /ɪˈnjʊə $ ɪˈnjʊr/ *v*
inure sb **to** sth *phr v* to make someone become used to something unpleasant, so that they are no longer upset by it: **be/become inured to sth** *Nurses soon become inured to the sight of suffering.*

in·vade /ɪnˈveɪd/ ●●○ *v*
1 [I,T] to enter a country, town, or area using military force, in order to take control of it: *The Romans invaded Britain 2,000 years ago.* **THESAURUS** ATTACK
2 [T] to go into a place in large numbers, especially when you are not wanted: *Every summer, the town is invaded by tourists.* | *Fans invaded the pitch at half time.*
3 [T] to get involved in something in an unwanted and annoying way: *What right does he have to invade my privacy?* | *Patients are given the feeling that they mustn't try to invade medical territory* (=try to deal with things that are not their responsibility). → INVASION

in·vad·er /ɪnˈveɪdə $ -ər/ *n* [C] a soldier or a group of soldiers who enter a country or town by force in order to take control of it: *Invaders ransacked the town.*

in·val·id[1] /ɪnˈvælɪd/ ●○○ *adj*
1 a contract, ticket, claim etc that is invalid is not legally or officially acceptable OPP **valid**: *Without the right date stamped on it, your ticket will be invalid.*
2 an argument, reason etc that is invalid is not based on true facts or clear ideas, and lacks good judgment OPP **valid**
3 if something you type into a computer is invalid, the computer does not recognize or accept it: *Filename in invalid format.*

in·va·lid[2] /ˈɪnvəliːd, -lɪd $ -lɪd/ *n* [C] someone who cannot look after themselves because of illness, old age, or injury: *I resented being treated as an invalid.* —**invalid** *adj* [only before noun]

in·va·lid[3] *v*
be invalided out (*also* **be invalided home**) *phr v BrE* to have to leave the army, navy etc because you are ill or injured

in·val·i·date /ɪnˈvælədeɪt/ ●○○ AWL *v* [T]
1 to make a document, ticket, claim etc no longer legally or officially acceptable: *Failure to disclose all relevant changes may invalidate your policy.*
2 to show that something such as a belief or explanation is wrong: *Later findings invalidated the theory.*

in·va·lid·it·y /ˌɪnvəˈlɪdəti/ AWL *n* [U] *formal* **1** the state of being too ill, old, or injured to work: *invalidity benefit* **2** the state of being not legally or officially acceptable

in·val·u·a·ble /ɪnˈvæljuəbəl, -jəbəl $ -ˈvæljəbəl/ ●○○ *adj* extremely useful: **[+to/for]** *Your advice has been invaluable to us.* | **invaluable in/for (doing) sth** *This help was invaluable in focussing my ideas.* | *The internet is an invaluable source of information.* **THESAURUS** USEFUL

in·var·i·a·ble /ɪnˈveəriəbəl $ -ˈver-/ AWL *adj*
1 always happening in the same way, at the same time etc: *His invariable answer was 'Wait and see.'*
2 *technical* never changing OPP **variable**: *Mass, unlike weight, is invariable.*

in·var·i·a·bly /ɪnˈveəriəbli $ -ˈver-/ ●○○ AWL *adv* if something invariably happens or is invariably true, it always happens or is true: *It invariably rains when I go there.* | *The security guards were invariably ex-servicemen.*

in·va·sion /ɪnˈveɪʒən/ ●●○ *n*
1 [C,U] when the army of one country enters another country by force, in order to take control of it: **[+of]** *the invasion of Normandy*
2 [C] the arrival in a place of a lot of people or things, often where they are not wanted: *the annual invasion of teenagers for the Glastonbury Festival*
3 invasion of privacy a situation in which someone tries to find out details about another person's private affairs in a way that is upsetting and often illegal

in·va·sive /ɪnˈveɪsɪv/ *adj* **1** invasive medical treatment involves cutting into someone's body: *invasive surgery* **2** an invasive disease spreads quickly and is difficult to stop: *invasive bladder cancers* **3** an invasive plant spreads quickly in a garden or other area, so that it becomes a problem

in·vec·tive /ɪnˈvektɪv/ *n* [U] *formal* rude and insulting words that someone says when they are very angry → **insult**: *He let out a stream of invective.*

in·veigh /ɪnˈveɪ/ *v*
inveigh against sb/sth *phr v formal* to criticize someone or something strongly

in·vei·gle /ɪnˈveɪgəl, ɪnˈviː- $ ɪnˈveɪ-/ *v*
inveigle sb **into** sth *phr v formal* to persuade someone to do what you want, especially in a dishonest way: **inveigle sb into doing sth** *She had inveigled me into taking messages to her lover.*

in·vent /ɪnˈvent/ ●●● S3 W3 *v* [T]
1 to make, design, or think of a new type of thing: *Alexander Graham Bell invented the telephone in 1876.* ⚠ Do not confuse with **discover** (=to be the first person to find something or to know that it exists): *Scientists have discovered a new type of bacteria.*
2 to think of an idea, story etc that is not true, usually in order to deceive people: *They invented a very convincing alibi.*

THESAURUS

invent to think of an idea for a new product, machine etc, and design it or make it: *The telephone*

I

was invented by Alexander Graham Bell. | Who invented the Internet?
create to make or design something new and original: *We decided to create the software ourselves. | For her latest book, she has created a whole new group of characters.*
think of sth/think up sth to produce a new idea, plan, method, excuse etc by thinking: *I've thought of an idea. | They're always trying to think up new ways to improve efficiency.*
come up with sth to produce a new idea, a way of dealing with something etc, especially a good one: *How did you come up with that idea? | Ellis came up with the solution to the problem immediately.*
make sth up to invent a story, song, game, excuse etc: *My mother used to make up bedtime stories for us. | I didn't want to go to the class, so I decided to make up an excuse.*
dream sth up to think of an idea or plan, especially one that seems unusual or even crazy: *It can't be easy dreaming up new advertisements all the time. | I wonder who dreamt up that idea!*
devise *formal* to invent a way of doing something, especially one that is clever or complicated: *This system was devised as a way of measuring students' progress.*
conceive *formal* to think of a new idea, plan etc and develop it in your mind: *The project was originally conceived by a Dutch businessman two years ago.*

in·ven·tion /ɪnˈvenʃən/ ●●● W3 *n*
1 [C] a useful machine, tool, instrument etc that has been invented: *The dishwasher is a wonderful invention.*
2 [U] the act of inventing something: *The invention of the computer has revolutionized the business world.*
3 [C,U] a story, explanation etc that is not true: *They subsequently admitted that the story was pure invention.*
4 [U] the ability to think of new and clever ideas: *With such powers of invention, he should get a job easily.*

in·ven·tive /ɪnˈventɪv/ *adj* able to think of new, different, or interesting ideas SYN **creative**: *one of the most talented and inventive drummers in modern music* —**inventively** *adv* —**inventiveness** *n* [U]

in·ven·tor /ɪnˈventə $ -ər/ *n* [C] someone who has invented something, or whose job is to invent things

in·ven·tory /ˈɪnvəntri $ -tɔːri/ ●○○ *n* (*plural* **inventories**)
1 [C] a list of all the things in a place: **[+of]** *We made an inventory of everything in the apartment.*
2 [C,U] *AmE* all the goods in a shop SYN **stock**

in·verse[1] /ˌɪnˈvɜːs◂ $ -ɜːrs◂/ *adj* [only before noun]
1 if there is an inverse relationship between two amounts, one gets bigger at the same rate as the other gets smaller: *Clearly, the amount of money people save increases* ***in inverse proportion to*** *the amount they spend. | the inverse relationship between prices and interest rates*
2 *technical* exactly opposite —**inversely** *adv*

inverse[2] *n* [singular] *technical* the complete opposite of something → **reverse**

in·ver·sion /ɪnˈvɜːʃən $ -ˈvɜːrʒən/ *n* [C,U] **1** *formal* the act of changing something so that it is the opposite of what it was before, or of turning something upside down (=the bottom is on the top and the top is on the bottom)
2 *technical* a type of weather condition in which the air nearest the ground is cooler than the air above it

in·vert /ɪnˈvɜːt $ -ɜːrt/ *v* [T] *formal* to put something in the opposite position to the one it was in before, especially by turning it upside down (=the bottom is on the top and the top is on the bottom) → **upside down**

in·ver·te·brate /ɪnˈvɜːtəbrət, -breɪt $ -ɜːr-/ *n* [C] a living creature that does not have a BACKBONE → **vertebrate** THESAURUS ANIMAL —**invertebrate** *adj*

inˌverted ˈcomma ●○○ *n* [C usually plural] *BrE*
1 one of a pair of marks (') or (') that are put at the beginning and end of a written word, sentence etc to show that someone said it or wrote it, or when writing the title of a book, song etc SYN **quotation mark** → PUNCTUATION MARK
2 in inverted commas *spoken* used to show that a word you are using to describe something is only what it is usually called, and not what you think it really is: *Her friends, in inverted commas, all disappeared when she was in trouble.*

inˌverted ˈsnobbery *n* [U] *BrE* the idea that everything that is typical of the upper classes must be bad

in·vest /ɪnˈvest/ ●●○ S3 W3 AWL *v*
1 [I,T] to buy shares, property, or goods because you hope that the value will increase and you can make a profit: *I've got a few thousand dollars I'm looking to invest. |* **invest (sth) in sth** *Oliver made a fortune by investing in antique furniture. | Williams invested a large sum of money in Swiss stocks. | He had* ***invested heavily*** (=invested a lot of money) *in the bond market.*
2 [I,T] if a government, business, or organization invests in something, they spend a large amount of money to improve it or help it succeed: **invest (sth) in sth** *The city has invested millions of dollars in the museum. | The factory plans to invest in new computers.*

> **REGISTER**
> In everyday English, people often say **put money in/into** something rather than **invest in** something: *He* ***put money into*** *his brother's business. | The government* ***put in*** *millions of pounds.*

3 [T] to use a lot of time, effort etc or spend money in order to make something succeed: **invest sth in sth** *It was very difficult to leave a home we had invested so much in.*

invest (sth) **in** sth *phr v* to buy something or spend money or time on something, because it will be useful for you: *It's about time you invested in a new shirt. | Everyone here has a lot invested in their careers.*

invest sb/sth **with** sth *phr v formal*
1 to officially give someone power to do something: *Jody has invested Alan with great power over her career.*
2 to make someone or something seem to have a particular quality or character: *Richard's heavy-rimmed glasses invested him with an air of intelligence.*

in·ves·ti·gate /ɪnˈvestɪgeɪt/ ●●● W2 AWL *v*
1 [I,T] to try to find out the truth about something such as a crime, accident, or scientific problem: *The state police are investigating the incident. | The study investigates the impact of violent TV programming on children. | I heard a noise and went downstairs to investigate.*

> **REGISTER**
> In everyday English, people often say **look into** something rather than **investigate** something: *I'll ask my colleague to* ***look into*** *it.*

2 [T] to try to find out more about someone's character, actions etc, because you think they may have been involved in a crime: *Penney was already being investigated by the police on suspicion of murder.*

in·ves·ti·ga·tion /ɪnˌvestɪˈgeɪʃən/ ●●● W2 AWL *n*
1 [C] an official attempt to find out the truth about or the cause of something such as a crime, accident, or scientific problem: *The investigation continued for nearly three years. |* **[+into]** *The authorities are planning to launch a full-scale investigation into the crash. |* **[+of]** *Baker demanded an investigation of the district attorney's office. | a* ***criminal investigation*** *| A private detective was hired to* ***conduct*** *the* ***investigation***.
2 [U] the act of investigating something: **[+of]** *the investigation of computer fraud |* **under investigation** (=being investigated) *The whole issue is still under investigation.*

in·ves·ti·ga·tive /ɪnˈvestəgətɪv $ -geɪtɪv/ AWL *adj* **investigative journalism/report/work** work or activities that involve investigating something

in·ves·ti·ga·tor /ɪnˈvestəgeɪtə $ -ər/ ●●○ AWL *n* [C] someone who investigates things, especially crimes: *police investigators* → PRIVATE INVESTIGATOR

in·ves·ti·ga·to·ry /ɪnˈvestəɡətəri $ -ɡətɔːri/ *adj* [only before noun] relating to investigating something: *the investigatory powers of the Office of Fair Trading*

in·ves·ti·ture /ɪnˈvestətʃə $ -tʃʊr/ *n* [C] *formal* a ceremony at which someone is given an official title: **[+of]** *the investiture of the Prince of Wales*

in·vest·ment /ɪnˈvestmənt/ ●●○ W3 AWL *n*
1 [C,U] the use of money to get a profit or to make a business activity successful, or the money that is used: *We plan to buy some property as an investment.* | **[+in]** *That year, Japanese investment in American real estate totaled $13.06 billion.* | **[+of]** *Each of us was required to put up a minimum investment of £5,000.*
2 [C] something that you buy or do because it will be useful later: **a good/sound investment** *The lessons cost me over £500, but I consider them a good investment.*
3 [singular, U] when you spend a large amount of time, energy, emotion etc on something: *a huge investment of time and effort*

COLLOCATIONS – MEANING 1

VERBS

make an investment (in sth) *We have made a huge investment in our website.*
attract investment *The company is trying to attract investment from overseas.*
stimulate/encourage investment *The government has cut taxes in order to stimulate investment.*
protect your investment *It's best to invest in several funds, in order to protect your investment.*
recoup your investment (=get back the money that you have invested)

ADJECTIVES

a good investment *Property is usually a good investment.*
a bad/poor investment *The shares turned out to be a poor investment.*
a big/major/massive/huge investment *Developing a new computer system is always a big investment for any organisation.*
a safe investment (=in which you are unlikely to lose money) *Electricity shares are still a safe investment.*
a risky investment (=in which you are likely to lose money) *Risky investments usually have higher yields.*
foreign/overseas investment *The government is eager to attract foreign investment to fund building projects.*
a long-term investment (=one that will give you profit after a long time) *Buying a house is a long-term investment.*
a short-term investment (=one that will give you profit in a short time) | **private investment** (=investment by private individuals) | **public investment** (=investment by the government or state) | **capital investment** (=investment in machines, equipment etc)

investment + NOUN

an investment scheme *BrE*, **an investment program** *AmE*: *Most investment schemes are subject to tax.*
an investment opportunity *She took advantage of a unique investment opportunity.*
an investment adviser | **an investment banker** | **investment income** (=money that you earn from your investments)

PHRASES

the (rate of) return on an investment (=profit from an investment) *We expect a high return on our investment.*

inˈvestment ˌbank *n* [C] a bank that buys and sells SECURITIES, STOCKS, or BONDS —**investment banker** *n* [C] —**investment banking** *n* [U]

inˈvestment ˌclub *n* [C] a group of people who meet regularly to decide which investments to buy and sell together, with money that they all put into the group: *O'Hara belongs to an investment club in Detroit.*

in·vest·or /ɪnˈvestə $ -ər/ ●●○ AWL *n* [C] someone who gives money to a company, business, or bank in order to get a profit

in·vet·e·rate /ɪnˈvetərət/ *adj* [only before noun] *written*
1 inveterate liar/smoker/womanizer etc someone who lies a lot, smokes a lot etc and cannot stop
2 inveterate fondness/distrust/hatred etc an attitude or feeling that you have had for a long time and cannot change

in·vid·i·ous /ɪnˈvɪdiəs/ *adj written* unpleasant, especially because it is likely to offend people or make you unpopular: *By innocently lying to detectives, she'd put herself* ***in an invidious position***.

in·vi·gi·late /ɪnˈvɪdʒəleɪt/ *v* [I,T] *BrE* to watch people who are taking an examination and make sure that they do not cheat SYN **proctor** *AmE* —**invigilator** *n* [C]

in·vig·o·rate /ɪnˈvɪɡəreɪt/ *v* [T] **1** if something invigorates you, it makes you feel healthier, stronger, and have more energy: *At my age, the walk into town is enough to invigorate me.* | *He felt invigorated after a day in the country.*
2 to make the people in an organization or group feel excited again, so that they want to make something successful: *Carey's hope was that the church would be renewed and invigorated.*

in·vig·o·ra·ting /ɪnˈvɪɡəreɪtɪŋ/ *adj* making you feel healthy and giving you a lot of energy: *an invigorating swim before breakfast*

in·vin·ci·ble /ɪnˈvɪnsəbəl/ *adj* **1** too strong to be destroyed or defeated: *an invincible army* | *Young athletes think of themselves as invincible.* **2** an invincible belief, attitude etc is extremely strong and cannot be changed —**invincibility** /ɪnˌvɪnsəˈbɪləti/ *n* [U]

in·vi·o·la·ble /ɪnˈvaɪələbəl/ *adj formal* an inviolable right, law, principle etc is extremely important and should be treated with respect and not broken or removed —**inviolability** /ɪnˌvaɪələˈbɪləti/ *n* [U]: *the inviolability of the country's borders*

in·vi·o·late /ɪnˈvaɪələt/ *adj formal* something that is inviolate cannot be attacked, changed, or destroyed

in·vis·i·ble /ɪnˈvɪzəbəl/ ●●○ AWL *adj*
1 something that is invisible cannot be seen OPP **visible**: *The house was surrounded by trees, and invisible from the road.* | **[+to]** *The plane is meant to be invisible to radar.* | *Using a telescope, Galileo discovered stars that were* ***invisible to the naked eye***. | **virtually/practically/almost etc invisible**
2 not noticed, or not talked about: *There's an invisible barrier that keeps women out of top jobs.*
3 invisible earnings/exports/trade etc money that is made from services and TOURISM rather than from products —**invisibly** *adv* —**invisibility** /ɪnˌvɪzəˈbɪləti/ *n* [U]

inˌvisible ˈink *n* [U] ink that cannot be seen on paper until it is heated, treated with chemicals etc, and is used for writing secret messages

in·vi·ta·tion /ˌɪnvɪˈteɪʃən/ ●●● S2 *n*
1 [C] a written or spoken request to someone, inviting them to go somewhere or do something: **an invitation to do sth** *an invitation to speak at a scientific conference* | **[+to]** *Roger never turns down an invitation to dinner.*
2 [U] the act of being invited or of inviting someone to go somewhere or do something: **by invitation** *Attendance at the seminars is* ***by invitation only*** (=only those people who have been invited can attend). | *They were always dropping by, usually without invitation.* | **at sb's invitation/at the invitation of sb** *Kegl traveled to Nicaragua at the invitation of the Education Minister.*
3 [C] a card inviting someone to attend a party, wedding etc: **party/wedding invitation** *We sent out more than 300 wedding invitations.* | **[+to]** *Did you get an invitation to Jason's party?*
4 [singular, U] encouragement to do something: **take sth as an invitation to do sth** *He seemed to take my silence as an invitation to talk.*
5 be an open invitation for/to sb to make it very easy for

someone to rob you or harm you: *Leaving the car unlocked is just an open invitation to thieves.*

COLLOCATIONS - MEANINGS 1, 2 & 3

VERBS

get/receive an invitation *Did you get an invitation to Janet's party?*
have an invitation *The following week, I had an invitation to give a talk in Cambridge.*
accept an invitation *She accepted his invitation to dinner.*
take up sb's invitation/take sb up on their invitation (=accept someone's invitation) *I decided to take them up on their invitation to dinner.*
refuse/turn down an invitation (*also* **decline an invitation** *formal*) *She turned down an invitation to take part in a televised debate.*
give sb an invitation (*also* **issue/extend an invitation** *formal*) *He has issued an invitation to the Chinese president to come to Washington.*
send (sb) an invitation | **thank sb for an invitation**

ADJECTIVES/NOUN + invitation

a party/wedding invitation *He had a wedding invitation from Rob and Jen.*
a dinner/lunch invitation *Fred's wife has accepted the dinner invitation.*
a formal/official invitation *The president received a formal invitation to visit Nigeria.*
a personal invitation *Each parent was sent a personal invitation for the school's open day.*
sb's kind invitation *It gives me great pleasure to accept your kind invitation.*
an open/standing invitation (=an invitation to do something at any time you like) *Phillip kindly gave me an open invitation to stay at his villa in Tuscany.*
a long-standing invitation (=an invitation which someone has had for a long time)

invitation + NOUN

an invitation card (=a card with an invitation printed on it)

PHRASES

a flood of invitations (=a lot of invitations) *He got a flood of invitations to appear on TV and radio shows.*

in·vite¹ /ɪnˈvaɪt/ ●●● S1 W2 *v* [T]
1 to ask someone to come to a party, wedding, meal etc: **invite sb to sth** *Who should we invite to the party?* | **invite sb to do sth** *Gail invited me to stay with her while her husband was out of town.* | **invite sb for sth** *Why don't you* **invite** *her* **for a drink** *at the club one evening?* | *I'm afraid I wasn't invited.*

GRAMMAR: Prepositions with invite

- You **invite** someone **to** an event or a place: *Did they invite you to the wedding?* | *She invited me to her house.*
- You **invite** someone **for** a meal or a period of time: *He invited us for brunch.* | *I'll invite them for the weekend.*

2 to politely ask someone to do something: **invite sb to do sth** *Anyone interested in contributing articles is invited to contact the editor.*
3 to encourage something bad to happen, especially without intending to: *Any government that sells arms to dictators is inviting trouble.*
invite sb **along** *phr v* to ask someone if they would like to come with you when you are going somewhere: *Why don't you invite Barbara along?*
invite sb **back** *phr v*
1 to ask someone to come to your home, hotel etc after you have been out somewhere together: **[+for]** *Richard often used to invite me back for coffee after the show.*
2 to ask someone to come to your home, your office etc again: *If you keep arguing with Gerry, they won't invite us back.*
invite sb **in** *phr v* to ask someone to come into your home: *After a few seconds, the door opened and Mrs Barnes invited me in.*
invite sb **out** *phr v* to ask someone to go somewhere with you, especially to a restaurant or film: **[+for]** *We invited Clarissa out for ice cream.*
invite sb **over** (*also* **invite sb round** *BrE*) *phr v* to ask someone to come to your home, usually for a drink or a meal: **[+for]** *Max has invited me over for dinner.*

in·vite² /ˈɪnvaɪt/ *n* [C] *informal* an invitation to a party, meal etc

in·vit·ing /ɪnˈvaɪtɪŋ/ *adj* something that is inviting is very attractive and makes you want to be near it, try it, taste it etc: *The log fire looked warm and inviting.* —**invitingly** *adv*: *She smiled invitingly.*

in vi·tro fer·ti·li·za·tion /ɪn ˌviːtrəʊ fɜːtəlaɪˈzeɪʃən $ -troʊ fɜːrtələ-/ *n* [U] *technical* a process in which a human egg is FERTILIZEd outside a woman's body → **test-tube baby**

in vivo /ɪn ˈviːvəʊ $ -voʊ/ *adj technical* taking place in the body —**in vivo** *adv*

in·vo·ca·tion /ˌɪnvəˈkeɪʃən/ *n* **1 the invocation** *AmE* a speech or prayer at the beginning of a ceremony or meeting **2** [C,U] *literary* a request for help, especially from a god

in·voice¹ /ˈɪnvɔɪs/ ●○○ *n* [C] a list of goods that have been supplied or work that has been done, showing how much you owe for them → **bill** THESAURUS BILL

invoice² *v* [T] to send someone an invoice

in·voke /ɪnˈvəʊk $ -ˈvoʊk/ AWL *v* [T] *formal* **1** if you invoke a law, rule etc, you say that you are doing something because the law allows or forces you to: *The UN threatened to invoke economic sanctions if the talks were broken off.* **2** to make a particular idea, image, or feeling appear in people's minds by describing an event or situation, or by talking about a person → **evoke**: *a painting that invokes images of the Rocky Mountains* | *During his speech, he invoked the memory of Harry Truman.* **3** to use a law, principle, or THEORY to support your views **4** to operate a computer program **5** to ask for help from someone more powerful than you, especially a god: *St. Genevieve is often invoked against plagues.* **6** to make spirits appear by using magic: *invoking the spirits of their ancestors*

in·vol·un·ta·ry /ɪnˈvɒləntəri $ ɪnˈvɑːlənteri/ *adj* **1** an involuntary movement, sound, reaction etc is one that you make suddenly and without intending to because you cannot control yourself: *When Willie tapped on the window, Miguel gave an involuntary jump.* **2** happening to you although you do not want it to: *involuntary part-time workers* —**involuntarily** *adv*

in·volve /ɪnˈvɒlv $ ɪnˈvɑːlv/ ●●● S2 W1 AWL *v* [T]
1 if an activity or situation involves something, that thing is part of it or a result of it: *What will the job involve?* | *I didn't realize putting on a play involved so much work.* | **involve doing sth** *Running your own business usually involves working long hours.*
2 to include or affect someone or something: *These changes will involve everyone on the staff.* | *There have been four accidents involving Forest Service planes.*
3 to ask or allow someone to take part in something: **involve sb in (doing) sth** *Try to involve as many children as possible in the game.* | *We want to involve the workforce at all stages of the decision-making process.*
4 involve yourself to take part actively in a particular activity: **[+in]** *Reilly involves himself in every aspect of his company's business.*

in·volved /ɪnˈvɒlvd $ ɪnˈvɑːlvd/ ●●● S2 W3 *adj*
1 be/get involved to take part in an activity or event, or be connected with it in some way: **[+in]** *More than 30 software firms were involved in the project.* | *I don't want to get involved in some lengthy argument about who is to blame.* | *I'm afraid your son's been* **involved in an accident** (=he is one of the people in an accident). | **[+with]** *Landel has been involved with the Hercules project for years.* | **actively/deeply/heavily involved** (=involved very much) *Mrs. Cummings has been actively involved with the church for years.*

GRAMMAR: Prepositions with involved

• Someone is **involved in** something: *He is involved in the family business.* | *Don't get involved in their problems.* ✗ Don't say: *involved into something*
• Someone is **involved with** a project, person, or group: *She got involved with the youth club.*
GRAMMAR GUIDE ▶ ADJECTIVES

2 work/effort etc involved in doing sth the amount of work, effort etc that is needed in order to make something succeed: *Most people don't realize the amount of effort involved in writing a novel.*
3 be involved with sb a) to be having a romantic relationship with someone, especially a sexual one: *The senator denied that he was* ***romantically involved*** *with a member of his staff.* **b)** to spend time with someone that you have a relationship with: *Fathers are encouraged to be more involved with their families.*
4 having so many different parts that it is difficult to understand SYN **complicated**: *The plot was so involved that very few people knew what was going on.* THESAURUS ▶ COMPLICATED

in·volve·ment /ɪnˈvɒlvmənt $ -ˈvɑːlv-/ ●●○ W3 AWL *n*
1 [U] the act of taking part in an activity or event, or the way in which you take part in it SYN **participation**: *School officials say they welcome parental involvement.* | **[+in]** *His new book examines the United States' involvement in World War II.* | **[+with]** *Carey's possible involvement with a series of robberies*
2 [C] something that you take part in or spend time doing: *sporting involvements* | *her political involvements*
3 [U] the feeling of excitement and satisfaction that you get from an activity: **[+in]** *Weaver admitted a strong* ***emotional involvement*** *in her client's case.*
4 [C,U] a romantic relationship between two people, especially when they are not married to each other: **[+with]** *Donna knew nothing of her husband's involvement with another woman.*

in·vul·ne·ra·ble /ɪnˈvʌlnərəbəl/ *adj* someone or something that is invulnerable cannot be harmed or damaged if you attack or criticize them OPP **vulnerable**: *Gerry's confidence made him feel invulnerable.* | **[+to]** *We will not be satisfied until this city is safe and invulnerable to attack.* —**invulnerability** /ɪnˌvʌlnərəˈbɪləti/ *n* [U]

in·ward /ˈɪnwəd $ -wərd/ ●○○ *adj written*
1 [only before noun] felt or experienced in your own mind but not expressed to other people OPP **outward**: *a feeling of inward satisfaction* | *inward panic*
2 towards the inside or centre of something —**inwardly** *adv*: *I managed to smile, but inwardly I was furious.*

ˌinward inˈvestment *n* [U] *technical* INVESTMENT in a country's industry or businesses that comes from foreign countries

ˈinward-ˌlooking *adj* an inward-looking person or group is more interested in themselves than in other people – used to show disapproval

in·wards /ˈɪnwədz $ -wərdz/ *especially BrE*, **inward** *AmE adv* towards the inside of something OPP **outwards**: *A breeze blew the curtains inwards.*

ˈin-word *n* [C] a word that is popular at a particular time, or among a particular group of people, but that does not usually continue to be popular for long: *the latest in-word amongst teenagers*

ˌin-your-ˈface (*also* **in-yer-face**) *adj BrE informal* in-your-face behaviour is intended to be noticed and to shock or upset people

i·o·dine /ˈaɪədiːn $ -daɪn/ *n* [U] a dark blue chemical substance that is used on wounds to prevent infection. It is a chemical ELEMENT: symbol I

i·on /ˈaɪən $ ˈaɪən, ˈaɪɑːn/ *n* [C] *technical* an atom which has been given a positive or negative force by adding or taking away an ELECTRON → **proton**

-ion /ən/ *suffix* [in nouns] the act, state, or result of doing something: *the completion of the task* (=act of finishing it) | *his election* (=he was elected) *to the post* | *Young children demand a lot of attention.*

I·on·ic /aɪˈɒnɪk $ aɪˈɑː-/ *adj* made in the simply decorated style of ancient Greek buildings → **Doric**: *an Ionic column*

i·on·ize (*also* **-ise** *BrE*) /ˈaɪənaɪz/ *v* [I,T] to form ions or make them form —**ionization** /ˌaɪənaɪˈzeɪʃən $ -nə-/ *n* [U]

i·on·i·zer (*also* **-iser** *BrE*) /ˈaɪənaɪzə $ -ər/ *n* [C] a machine used to make the air in a room more healthy by producing negative IONS

i·on·o·sphere /aɪˈɒnəsfɪə $ aɪˈɑːnəsfɪr/ *n* **the ionosphere** the part of the ATMOSPHERE which is used to help send radio waves around the Earth

i·o·ta /aɪˈəʊtə $ -ˈoʊtə/ *n* **not one/an iota** not even a small amount SYN **bit**: *It won't make an iota of difference.*

IOU /ˌaɪ əʊ ˈjuː $ -oʊ-/ *n* [C] *informal* a note that you sign to say that you owe someone some money

IPA /ˌaɪ piː ˈeɪ◂/ *n* [singular] (***International Phonetic Alphabet***) a system of special signs, used to represent the sounds made in speech

IP ad·dress /ˌaɪ ˈpiː əˌdres/ *n* [C] (***Internet Protocol address***) a special number that is used to IDENTIFY a computer, and which the computer needs in order to be able to connect to the Internet

IPC /ˌaɪ piː ˈsiː/ *n* [C,U] *technical* (***intellectual property crime***) the crime of illegally copying and selling something which is another person's work

IPO /ˌaɪ piː ˈəʊ $ -ˈoʊ/ *n* [C] (***initial public offering***) the first time that STOCK in a company is available for the public to buy on the STOCK MARKET

iPod /ˈaɪpɒd $ -pɑːd/ *n* [C] *trademark* a small piece of electronic equipment for playing music, made by the Apple computer company. You can carry an iPod around with you and it can store a very large amount of music which you get from the Internet, from a CD, or from another iPod. iPods can also store videos and games.

ip·so fac·to /ˌɪpsəʊ ˈfæktəʊ $ -soʊ ˈfæktoʊ/ *adv formal* used to show that something is known from or proved by the facts

IQ /ˌaɪ ˈkjuː/ *n* [C] (***intelligence quotient***) your level of intelligence, measured by a special test, with 100 being the average result: *an IQ of 130*

ir- /ɪ/ *prefix* used instead of IN- before the letter r SYN **not**: *irregular* (=not regular)

IRA *n* **1 the IRA** (***the Irish Republican Army***) /ˌaɪ ɑːr ˈeɪ/ an illegal organization that wants to unite Northern Ireland and the Republic of Ireland → **Sinn Fein** **2** [C] (***individual retirement account***) /ˈaɪrə/ a special bank account in which people living in the US can save money for their RETIREMENT without paying tax on it until later

i·ras·ci·ble /ɪˈræsəbəl/ *adj written* easily becoming angry SYN **bad-tempered**: *an irascible old man*

i·rate /ˌaɪˈreɪt◂/ *adj* extremely angry, especially because you think you have been treated unfairly SYN **furious**: *an irate customer*

ire /aɪə $ aɪr/ *n* [U] *written* anger: **raise/arouse/draw sb's ire** (=make someone angry) *The proposal has drawn the ire of local residents.*

ir·i·des·cent /ˌɪrəˈdesənt◂/ *adj formal* showing colours that seem to change in different lights: *small iridescent blue flies* —**iridescence** *n* [U]

i·rid·i·um /ɪˈrɪdiəm/ *n* [U] a hard and very heavy metal that is combined with PLATINUM to make jewellery and is used in scientific instruments. It is a chemical ELEMENT: symbol Ir

i·ris /ˈaɪərɪs $ ˈaɪrɪs/ *n* [C] **1** a tall plant with long thin leaves and large purple, yellow, or white flowers → see picture at **FLOWER**[1] **2** the round coloured part of your eye, that surrounds the black PUPIL → see picture at **EYE**[1]

I·rish[1] /ˈaɪərɪʃ $ ˈaɪrɪʃ/ *adj* relating to Ireland or its people

Irish[2] *n* **the Irish** [plural] people from Ireland

ˌIrish ˈcoffee *n* [C,U] coffee with cream and WHISKY

I·rish·man /ˈaɪərɪʃmən $ ˈaɪr-/ *n* (*plural* **Irishmen** /-mən/) [C] a man from Ireland

I

ˌIrish ˈstew *n* [C,U] a dish of meat, potatoes, and onions boiled together

I·rish·wom·an /ˈaɪərɪʃˌwʊmən $ ˈaɪr-/ *n* (*plural* **Irish-women** /-ˌwɪmɪn/) [C] a woman from Ireland

IRIS print /ˈaɪərəs prɪnt $ ˈaɪrəs-/ *n* [C] *trademark* a very high-quality print that is made using a special PRINTER which is controlled by a computer and which SPRAYS very small drops of coloured ink onto the paper

ˈiris scan *n* [C] an examination of someone's IRIS (=the round coloured part in the centre of the eye) using special computer equipment in order to IDENTIFY them. Iris scans are done by the police and IMMIGRATION officials at some airports to check the information on someone's PASSPORT or ID CARD. SYN **eye scan**

irk /ɜːk $ ɜːrk/ *v* [T] if something irks you, it makes you feel annoyed SYN **annoy**

irk·some /ˈɜːksəm $ ˈɜːrk-/ *adj formal* annoying: *an irk-some journey*

IRL (***in real life***) used in emails, TEXT MESSAGES, SOCIAL NETWORKING SITES etc to show that you are talking about what happens in real life and not in a television programme or on the Internet: *Have you ever met him IRL?*

i·ron[1] /ˈaɪən $ ˈaɪərn/ ●●● S2 W3 *n*

1 METAL [U] a common hard metal that is used to make steel, is MAGNETIC, and is found in very small quantities in food and blood. It is a chemical ELEMENT: symbol Fe: *the **iron and steel** industry | a driveway with large iron gates | **iron ore** (=rock that contains iron) | the absorption of iron from food* → WROUGHT IRON, CAST IRON

2 FOR CLOTHES [C] a thing used for making clothes smooth, which has a heated flat metal base

3 have several irons in the fire to be involved in several different activities or have several plans all happening at the same time: *He has several economic irons in the fire, including gold and diamond mines.*

4 SPORT [C] a GOLF CLUB made of metal rather than wood: *a 5-iron*

5 CHAINS irons [plural] *especially literary* a chain used to prevent a prisoner from moving: *leg irons* → **a will of iron/an iron will** at WILL[2](1), → **pump iron** at PUMP[2](8), → **rule sb/sth with a rod of iron** at RULE[2](5), → **strike while the iron's hot** at STRIKE[1](28)

iron[2] ●●● S3 *v* [T] to make clothes smooth using an iron SYN **press**: *Have you ironed my shirt?* → IRONING

iron sth ↔ **out** *phr v* to solve or get rid of problems or difficulties, especially small ones: *We need to iron out a few problems first.*

iron[3] *adj* [only before noun] very firm and strong or determined: *He runs the company with an **iron fist**.*

ˈIron Age *n* **the Iron Age** the period of time about 3,000 years ago when iron was first used for making tools, weapons etc → BRONZE AGE, STONE AGE

i·ron·clad /ˈaɪənklæd $ -ərn-/ *adj* **1** an ironclad agreement, proof, defence etc is so strong and sure that it cannot be changed or argued against: *an ironclad guarantee* **2** *old-fashioned* covered with iron: *an ironclad battleship*

ˌIron ˈCurtain, the the name that was used for the border between the Communist countries of Eastern Europe and the rest of Europe

ˌiron-ˈgrey *BrE*, **iron-gray** *AmE adj* iron-grey hair is dark grey

i·ron·ic /aɪˈrɒnɪk $ aɪˈrɑː-/ ●○○ (*also* **i·ron·i·cal** /-ɪkəl/) *adj*

1 an ironic situation is one that is unusual or amusing because something strange happens, or the opposite of what is expected happens or is true: *Your car was stolen at the police station! How ironic! | **It's ironic that** her husband smoked for thirty years, and yet she's the one who died of lung cancer. | In **an ironic twist**, the most trustworthy character in the film turned out to be the thief.*

2 using words that are the opposite of what you really mean, often in a joking way: *ironic comments | When I told Lucy I loved her book, she thought I was being ironic.* → SARCASTIC

i·ron·i·cally /aɪˈrɒnɪkli $ aɪˈrɑː-/ ●○○ *adv*

1 [sentence adverb] used when talking about a situation in which the opposite of what you expected happens or is true: *Ironically, his cold got better on the last day of his holiday.*

2 in a way that shows you really mean the opposite of what you are saying: *'Oh, no problem!' said Terry, ironically.*

i·ron·ing /ˈaɪənɪŋ $ -ər-/ *n* [U] **1** the activity of making clothes smooth with an iron: *I hate **doing the ironing**.* **2** clothes that are waiting to be ironed or have just been ironed: *I'm tired and there's still a **pile of ironing** to do.*

ˈironing ˌboard *n* [C] a small narrow table used for ironing clothes

ˌiron ˈlung *n* [C] a large machine with a metal case used to help people to breathe

i·ron·mon·ger /ˈaɪənˌmʌŋɡə $ ˈaɪərnˌmʌŋɡər, -ˌmɑːŋ-/ *n* [C] *BrE old-fashioned* **1** someone who works in or owns a shop that sells tools and equipment for your home and garden **2 ironmonger's** a shop that sells this equipment —**ironmongery** *n* [U]

ˌiron ˈrations *n* [plural] small amounts of high-energy food, carried by soldiers, mountain climbers etc

i·ron·ware /ˈaɪənweə $ ˈaɪərnwer/ *n* [U] articles made of iron

i·ron·work /ˈaɪənwɜːk $ ˈaɪərnwɜːrk/ *n* [U] fences, gates etc made of iron bent into attractive shapes

i·ron·y /ˈaɪərəni $ ˈaɪrə-/ ●○○ *n* (*plural* **ironies**)

1 [C,U] a situation that is unusual or amusing because something strange happens, or the opposite of what is expected happens or is true: *Life is full of little ironies.* | **tragic/cruel/bitter etc irony** *The tragic **irony is that** the drug was supposed to save lives.*

2 [U] when you use words that are the opposite of what you really mean, often in order to be amusing: **trace/hint/touch of irony** *Wagner calls his program 'the worst talk show in America,' without a hint of irony.* | **heavy irony** *BrE* (=a lot of irony) *'Of course Michael won't be late; you know how punctual he always is,' she said with heavy irony.*

THESAURUS LANGUAGE → SARCASM, DRAMATIC IRONY

ir·ra·di·ate /ɪˈreɪdieɪt/ *v* [T] **1** *technical* if someone or something is irradiated, X-RAYS or RADIOACTIVE beams are passed through them **2** *technical* if food is irradiated, it is treated with RADIATION in order to kill BACTERIA and make it last longer **3** *literary* to make something look bright as if a light is shining onto it GRAMMAR **Irradiate** is usually passive. —**irradiation** /ɪˌreɪdiˈeɪʃən/ *n* [U]

ir·ra·tion·al /ɪˈræʃənəl/ ●○○ AWL *adj* not based on clear thought or reason SYN **unreasonable** OPP **rational, reasonable**: *an irrational fear of flying | He's becoming increasingly irrational.* —**irrationally** *adv* —**irrationality** /ɪˌræʃəˈnæləti/ *n* [U]

ir·rec·on·ci·la·ble /ɪˌrekənˈsaɪləbəl◂/ *adj* **1** irreconcilable positions etc are so strongly opposed to each other that it is not possible for them to reach an agreement: **irreconcilable differences/conflicts** *The differences between the landowners and the conservationists were irreconcilable from the start.* **2** if two beliefs or ideas are irreconcilable, it is not possible to believe both of them: **[+with]** *This belief was irreconcilable with the Church's doctrine of salvation.* **3 irreconcilable differences** strong disagreements between two people who are married, given as a legal reason for getting a DIVORCE

ir·re·cov·er·a·ble /ˌɪrɪˈkʌvərəbəl◂/ *adj formal* something that is irrecoverable is lost or has gone and you cannot get it back: *irrecoverable loss of sight | The insurance premium is wholly irrecoverable.*

ir·re·deem·a·ble /ˌɪrɪˈdiːməbəl◂/ *adj* **1** *formal* too bad to be corrected, repaired, or saved: *Very few children are irredeemable.* **2** *technical* irredeemable BONDS pay interest to the person who is lending money but do not have a set date saying when the money being lent must be paid back —**irredeemably** *adv*

ir·re·duc·i·ble /ˌɪrɪˈdjuːsəbəl◂ $ -ˈduː-/ *adj written* an irreducible sum, level etc cannot be made smaller or simpler → **reduce** —**irreducibly** *adv*

I

ir·re·fu·ta·ble /ˌɪrɪˈfjuːtəbəl◂ $ ɪˈrefjətəbəl, ˌɪrɪˈfjuː-/ *adj* an irrefutable statement, argument etc cannot be proved to be wrong, and must be accepted → **refute**: **irrefutable evidence/proof/facts** *irrefutable proof of his innocence* —**irrefutably** *adv*

ir·re·gard·less /ˌɪrɪˈɡɑːdləs $ -ɑːr-/ *adv* without being affected or influenced by something. Some people think that this is not correct English. SYN **regardless**

ir·reg·u·lar[1] /ɪˈreɡjələ $ -ər/ ●○○ *adj*
1 having a shape, surface, pattern etc that is not even, smooth, or balanced SYN **uneven** OPP **regular**: *a jagged, irregular coastline* | *It has a highly irregular shape, covered in bumps and indentations.*
2 not happening at times that are an equal distance from each other OPP **regular**: *He's receiving medication for an irregular heartbeat.* | *Beamish only returned to Britain* ***at irregular intervals***.
3 not happening or done at the normal time for doing something OPP **regular**: *Funeral directors often work long,* ***irregular hours***.
4 *formal* not obeying the usually accepted legal or moral rules: *It would be* ***highly irregular*** (=extremely irregular) *for a minister to accept payments of this kind.*
5 **irregular verb/plural etc** a verb or a form of a word that does not follow the usual pattern of grammar, such as the verb 'catch' or the plural 'fish' OPP **regular**
6 *AmE* a word meaning CONSTIPATED (=unable to easily pass food waste from your body), used in order to be polite —**irregularly** *adv* —**irregularity** /ɪˌreɡjəˈlærəti/ *n* [C,U]: *The club were found guilty of financial irregularities.*

irregular[2] *n* [C] a soldier who is not an official member of a country's army

ir·rel·e·vance /ɪˈreləvəns/ AWL (*also* **ir·rel·e·van·cy** /-vənsi/) *n* 1 [U] a lack of importance in a particular situation 2 [C] someone or something that is not important in a particular situation: **[+of]** *debates on the irrelevance of the education system*

ir·rel·e·vant /ɪˈreləvənt/ ●●○ AWL *adj* not useful or not relating to a particular situation, and therefore not important OPP **relevant**: *We're focussing too much on irrelevant details.* | *Students viewed Latin as boring and irrelevant.* | **largely/totally/completely etc irrelevant** *His age is completely irrelevant if he can do the job.* | **[+to]** *The defendant's lawyer argued that his past offenses were irrelevant to this case.* —**irrelevantly** *adv*

ir·re·li·gious /ˌɪrɪˈlɪdʒəs◂/ *adj formal* opposed to religion, or not having any religious feeling

ir·re·me·di·a·ble /ˌɪrɪˈmiːdiəbəl◂/ *adj formal* so bad that it is impossible to make it better

ir·rep·a·ra·ble /ɪˈrepərəbəl/ *adj written* irreparable damage, harm etc is so bad that it can never be repaired or made better: *Extensive mining will cause irreparable damage to the area.* —**irreparably** *adv*

ir·re·place·a·ble /ˌɪrɪˈpleɪsəbəl◂/ *adj* too special, valuable, or unusual to be replaced by anything else: *Works of art were lost, many of them irreplaceable.* THESAURUS ▸ VALUABLE

ir·re·pres·si·ble /ˌɪrɪˈpresəbəl◂/ *adj written* full of energy, confidence, and happiness so that you never seem unhappy: *an irrepressible optimist* —**irrepressibly** *adv*

ir·re·proach·a·ble /ˌɪrɪˈprəʊtʃəbəl◂ $ -ˈproʊtʃ-/ *adj formal* something, such as someone's behaviour, that is irreproachable is so good that you cannot criticize it

ir·re·sis·ti·ble /ˌɪrɪˈzɪstəbəl◂/ ●○○ *adj*
1 so attractive, desirable etc that you cannot prevent yourself from wanting it: **[+to]** *Tax-cutting proposals could* ***prove irresistible*** *to lawmakers.* | *Men* ***find*** *Natalie* ***irresistible***.
2 too strong or powerful to be stopped or prevented: *I was overcome by an* ***irresistible urge*** *to cry.* —**irresistibly** *adv*

ir·res·o·lute /ɪˈrezəluːt/ *adj formal* unable to decide what to do SYN **uncertain** OPP **resolute** —**irresolution** /ɪˌrezəˈluːʃən/ *n* [U]

ir·re·spec·tive /ˌɪrɪˈspektɪv/ *adv formal* **irrespective of sth** used when saying that a particular fact has no effect on a situation and is not important SYN **regardless**: *The course is open to anyone, irrespective of age.*

ir·re·spon·si·ble /ˌɪrɪˈspɒnsəbəl◂ $ -ˈspɑːn-/ ●○○ *adj* doing careless things without thinking or worrying about the possible bad results OPP **responsible**: **totally/highly/completely etc irresponsible** *When it comes to money, Dan is completely irresponsible.* | **it is irresponsible (for sb) to do sth** *It would be irresponsible not to turn up for work without calling.* | *It was highly irresponsible of him to leave the children on their own in the pool.* THESAURUS ▸ CARELESS —**irresponsibly** *adv*: *He was acting totally irresponsibly.* —**irresponsibility** /ˌɪrɪspɒnsəˈbɪləti $ -spɑːn-/ *n* [U]

ir·re·triev·a·ble /ˌɪrɪˈtriːvəbəl◂/ *adj formal* 1 an irretrievable situation cannot be made right again: *the irretrievable breakdown of their marriage* 2 **irretrievable loss** the loss of something that you can never get back —**irretrievably** *adv*: *irretrievably lost*

ir·rev·e·rent /ɪˈrevərənt/ *adj* someone who is irreverent does not show respect for organizations, customs, beliefs etc that most other people respect – often used to show approval: *his irreverent sense of humour* | *She has an irreverent attitude towards marriage.* —**irreverently** *adv* —**irreverence** *n* [U]

ir·re·ver·si·ble /ˌɪrɪˈvɜːsəbəl◂ $ -ɜːr-/ AWL *adj* 1 irreversible damage, change etc is so serious or so great that you cannot change something back to how it was before OPP **reversible**: *Fossil fuels have caused irreversible damage to the environment* 2 if an illness or bad physical condition is irreversible, it will continue to exist and cannot be cured: *Miller is in an irreversible coma.* | *irreversible blindness* —**irreversibly** *adv*: *His reputation was irreversibly damaged by the affair.*

ir·rev·o·ca·ble /ɪˈrevəkəbəl/ *adj* an irrevocable decision, action etc cannot be changed or stopped: *Think about the situation carefully before you take an irrevocable step.* —**irrevocably** *adv*: *machines that irrevocably changed the pattern of rural life*

ir·ri·gate /ˈɪrɪɡeɪt/ *v* [T] 1 to supply land or crops with water: *The water in Lake Powell is used to irrigate the area.* | **irrigated land/farms/crops** 2 *technical* to wash a wound with a flow of liquid —**irrigation** /ˌɪrəˈɡeɪʃən/ *n* [U]: *major irrigation projects*

ir·ri·ta·ble /ˈɪrətəbəl/ *adj* getting annoyed quickly or easily SYN **crabby**, **bad-tempered**: *Jo was tired, irritable, and depressed.* —**irritably** *adv* —**irritability** /ˌɪrətəˈbɪləti/ *n* [U]

ˌirritable ˈbowel ˌsyndrome *n* [U] *medical* (*abbreviation* **IBS**) a medical condition in which you have problems with your BOWELS, typically including pain, DIARRHOEA, and CONSTIPATION

ir·ri·tant /ˈɪrɪtənt/ *n* [C] 1 *formal* something that keeps annoying you over a period of time: *Low-flying aircraft are a* ***constant irritant*** *in this area.* 2 a substance that can make a part of your body painful and sore: *a skin irritant*

ir·ri·tate /ˈɪrɪteɪt/ ●●○ *v* [T]
1 to make someone feel annoyed or impatient, especially by doing something many times or for a long period of time: ***It*** *really* ***irritates*** *me when he doesn't help around the house.*
2 to make a part of your body painful and sore: *This cream may* ***irritate*** *sensitive* ***skin***.

ir·ri·tat·ed /ˈɪrɪteɪtɪd/ ●●○ *adj*
1 feeling annoyed and impatient about something: **[+about/at/with/by]** *John was getting irritated by all her questions.* THESAURUS ▸ ANGRY
2 painful and sore: *Her throat and eyes were irritated.*

ir·ri·tat·ing /ˈɪrəteɪtɪŋ/ ●●○ *adj* an irritating habit, situation etc keeps annoying you: *He's the most irritating man I've ever met.* | *He was smiling in a way I* ***found*** *very* ***irritating***. | **irritating habit/characteristics/mannerisms** *She has an irritating habit of interrupting.* | *a dry irritating cough* —**irritatingly** *adv*

ir·ri·ta·tion /ˌɪrɪˈteɪʃən/ *n* 1 [U] the feeling of being annoyed about something, especially something that happens repeatedly or for a long time: *The heavy traffic is*

I

a constant **source of irritation**. | **[+at/with]** *The doctor's irritation at being interrupted showed.* **2** [C] something that makes you annoyed: *The children are just an irritation for him when he's trying to work.* **3** [C,U] a painful sore feeling on a part of your body: *The astringent can* ***cause irritation*** *to sensitive skin.* | *a throat irritation*

ir·rup·tion /ɪˈrʌpʃən/ *n* [C] *formal* a sudden rush of people or things into a place

is /s, z, əz; *strong* ɪz/ the third person singular of the present tense of BE

-isation /aɪzeɪʃən $ əzeɪ-/ *suffix* a British spelling of -IZATION

ISBN /ˌaɪ es biː ˈen/ *n* [C] (***International Standard Book Number***) a number that is given to every book that is PUBLISHed

ISDN /ˌaɪ es diː ˈen/ *n* [U] (***Integrated Services Digital Network***) a system that is used to send computer information at very high speed along an electronic wire similar to a telephone line

-ise /aɪz/ *suffix* [in verbs] a British spelling of -IZE

-ish /ɪʃ/ *suffix* **1** [in nouns] the people or language of a particular country or place: *Are the British unfriendly?* | *learning to speak Turkish* | *She's Swedish.* **2** [in adjectives] of a particular place: *Spanish food* (=from Spain) **3** [in adjectives] typical of or like a particular type of person: *foolish behaviour* (=typical of a fool) | *Don't be so childish!* (=do not behave like a child) | *snobbish* **4** [in adjectives] the ending of some adjectives that show disapproval: *selfish* **5** [in adjectives] rather SYN **quite**: *youngish* (=not very young, but not old either) | *tallish* | *reddish hair* **6** [in adjectives] *spoken* APPROXIMATELY: *We'll expect you around eightish* (=at about eight o'clock). | *He's fortyish* (=about 40 years old).

Is·lam /ˈɪslɑːm, ˈɪz-, ɪsˈlɑːm/ *n* [U] **1** the Muslim religion, which was started by Muhammad and whose holy book is the Quran (Koran) **2** the people and countries that follow this religion —**Islamic** /ɪzˈlæmɪk,ɪs-/ *adj*

Is·lam·ist /ˈɪzləməst, -lɑːm-/ *n* [C] someone who strictly follows the teachings of Islam and believes it should have more influence —**Islamism** [U]

Is·lam·o·pho·bi·a /ɪsˌlɑːməˈfəʊbia, ɪz- $ -ˈfoʊ-/ *n* [U] hatred or fear of Muslims **THESAURUS** PREJUDICE —**Islamophobic** *adj*

is·land /ˈaɪlənd/ ●●● S3 W2 *n* [C] a piece of land completely surrounded by water → **insular**: *The Cayman Islands* | *the Greek island of Crete* | **on an island** *No cars are allowed on the island.* → DESERT ISLAND

is·land·er /ˈaɪləndə $ -ər/ *n* [C] someone who lives on an island

isle /aɪl/ *n* [C] a word for an island, used in poetry or in names of islands: *the British Isles*

is·let /ˈaɪlɪt/ *n* [C] *literary* a very small island

is·m /ˈɪzəm/ *n* [C] *informal* used to describe a set of ideas or beliefs whose name ends in 'ism', especially when you think that they are not sensible or practical

-ism /ɪzəm/ *suffix* [in nouns] **1** a political belief or religion based on a particular principle or the ideas and beliefs of a particular person: *socialism* | *Buddhism* **2** the action or process of doing something: *his criticism of my work* **3** an action or remark that has a particular quality: *her witticisms* (=funny remarks) **4** the state of being like something or someone, or having a particular quality: *heroism* (=being a HERO; bravery) | *magnetism* (=being MAGNETIC) **5** illness caused by too much of something: *alcoholism* **6** the practice of treating people unfairly because of something: *sexism* (=making unfair differences between men and women) | *racism*

is·n't /ˈɪzənt/ the short form of 'is not'

iso- /aɪsəʊ, -sə $ -soʊ, -sə/ *prefix technical* the same all through or in every part SYN **equal**: *an isotherm* (=line joining places of equal temperature)

i·so·bar /ˈaɪsəbɑː $ -bɑːr/ *n* [C] *technical* a line on a weather map joining places where the air pressure is the same

ISLAND

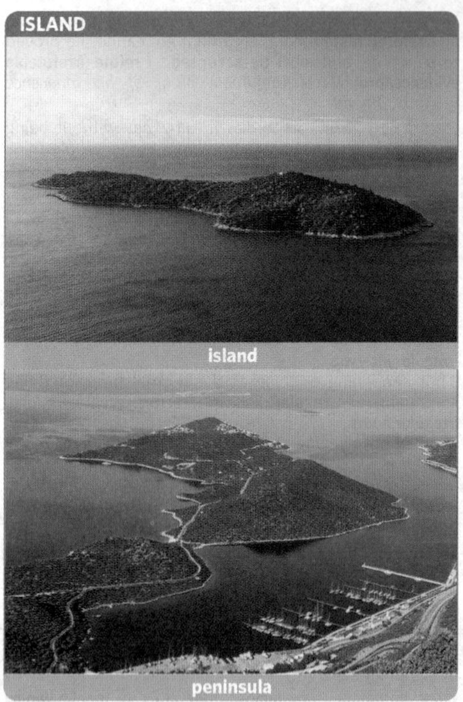

island

peninsula

i·so·late /ˈaɪsəleɪt/ ●○○ AWL *v* [T]
1 to separate one person, group, or thing from other people or things: *The town was isolated by the floods.* | *The US has sought to isolate Cuba both economically and politically.* | **isolate sb from sb** *Presley's phenomenal early success isolated him from his friends.* | **isolate sb from sth** *Newborn babies must be isolated from possible contamination.*
2 if you isolate an idea, problem etc, you consider it separately from other things that are connected with it: **isolate sth from sth** *It is impossible to isolate political responsibility from moral responsibility.*
3 *technical* to separate a substance, disease etc from other substances so that it can be studied: **isolate sth from sth** *The hepatitis B virus has been isolated from breast milk.*

i·so·lat·ed /ˈaɪsəleɪtɪd/ ●○○ AWL *adj*
1 an isolated building, village etc is far away from any others SYN **remote**: *small isolated communities* | *Not many people visit this isolated spot.*
2 feeling alone and unable to meet or speak to other people: *Young mothers often feel isolated.* **THESAURUS** FAR
3 an isolated action, event, example etc happens only once, and is not likely to happen again: **isolated incident/case/event** *Police say that last week's protest was an isolated incident.*

i·so·la·tion /ˌaɪsəˈleɪʃən/ ●○○ AWL *n* [U]
1 when one group, person, or thing is separate from others: *Because of its geographical isolation, the area developed its own unique culture.* | **[+of]** *the isolation of rural areas* | **international/diplomatic/political isolation** *the country's continuing political isolation* | **in isolation** *The political prisoner had been held in* ***complete isolation***. | *The mansion sits in* ***splendid isolation*** *on top of the hill* (=it is far from everything and looks impressive). | **isolation hospital/ward** *BrE*: *Scarlet fever victims had to go to the isolation hospital.* | *a patient's isolation period*
2 when someone feels alone and unable to meet or speak to other people: *Retirement can often cause feelings of isolation.* | *elderly people living in social isolation*
3 in isolation (from sth) if something exists or is considered in isolation, it exists or is considered separately from other things that are connected with it: *The future of*

health care cannot be considered in isolation from economic factors.

i·so·la·tion·is·m /ˌaɪsəˈleɪʃənɪzəm/ AWL *n* [U] beliefs or actions that are based on the political principle that your country should not be involved in the affairs of other countries —**isolationist** *adj*: *isolationist policies* —**isolationist** *n* [C]

i·so·met·rics /ˌaɪsəˈmetrɪks/ *n* [plural] exercises that make your muscles stronger by pushing against each other

i·sos·ce·les tri·an·gle /aɪˌsɒsəliːz ˈtraɪæŋɡəl $ -ˌsɑː-/ *n* [C] *technical* a TRIANGLE in which two of the sides are the same length → **EQUILATERAL TRIANGLE** → see picture at **TRIANGLE**

i·so·therm /ˈaɪsəθɜːm $ -ɜːrm/ *n* [C] *technical* a line on a weather map joining places where the temperature is the same

i·so·ton·ic drink /ˌaɪsətɒnɪk ˈdrɪŋk $ -tɑː-/ *n* [C] a drink made especially for people who are exercising or playing sport, containing ELECTROLYTEs which help your body take in liquid effectively, and CARBOHYDRATEs that give your body extra energy

i·so·tope /ˈaɪsətəʊp $ -toʊp/ *n* [C] *technical* one of the possible different forms of an atom of a particular ELEMENT (=simple chemical substance)

ISP /ˌaɪ es ˈpiː/ *n* [C] (***Internet service provider***) a business that provides a connection to the Internet for people's computers

Is·rae·li[1] /ɪzˈreɪli/ *adj* relating to Israel or its people: *the Israeli government*

Israeli[2] *n* [C] someone from Israel

Is·rael·ite /ˈɪzrəlaɪt $ ˈɪzriə-/ *n, adj biblical* someone who lived in Israel in the past when it was ruled by kings, or relating to this country or its people

is·sue[1] /ˈɪʃuː, ˈɪsjuː $ ˈɪʃuː/ ●●● S1 W1 *n*

1 SUBJECT/PROBLEM [C] a subject or problem that is often discussed or argued about, especially a social or political matter that affects the interests of a lot of people: *Abortion is a highly controversial issue.* | *We should raise the issue of discrimination with the council.* | *The key issue is whether workers should be classified as 'employees'.*

2 MAGAZINE [C] a magazine or newspaper printed for a particular day, week, or month: **[+of]** *The article appeared in the January issue of 'Nature'.* | **the current/latest issue** *Have you seen the latest issue?*

3 take issue with sb/sth to disagree or argue with someone about something: *It is difficult to take issue with his analysis.* | **take issue with sb over sth** *I must take issue with you over what you said yesterday.*

4 make an issue (out) of sth to argue about something, especially in a way that annoys other people because they do not think it is important: *I was upset by Eleanor's remarks, but didn't make an issue of it.*

5 have issues (with sb/sth) *informal* **a)** to have problems dealing with something because of something that happened in the past: *There's a self-help group for people who have issues with money.* **b)** if you have issues with someone or something, you do not agree with or approve of them: *I have a few issues with Marc.*

6 at issue *formal* the problem or subject at issue is the most important part of what you are discussing or considering: *At issue here is the extent to which exam results reflect a student's ability.*

7 ACT OF GIVING STH [singular] the act of officially giving people something to use: *the issue of identity cards to all non-residents*

8 SET OF THINGS FOR SALE [C] a new set of something such as SHARES or stamps, made available for people to buy: *We launched the* ***share issue*** *on March 1.* | *a new issue of bonds*

9 die without issue *old use* to die without having any children

COLLOCATIONS

VERBS

discuss/debate an issue *They met to discuss the issue of working conditions at the factory.*
raise an issue/bring up an issue (=say an issue should be discussed) *Some important issues were raised at the meeting.*
deal with/tackle an issue (*also* **address an issue** *formal*) *The government must deal with the issue of gun crime.*
decide/settle/resolve an issue (=solve it) *The issue was settled after some tough negotiations.*
face an issue (=accept that an issue exists and deal with it) *Politicians seem to be reluctant to face the issue.*
avoid/evade an issue (*also* **dodge/duck an issue** *informal*) (=avoid discussing an issue) *There is no point in evading the issue any longer.*
confuse/cloud/muddy the issue (=make an issue more difficult to understand or deal with than it needs to be) *You must not let your feelings cloud the issue.*
highlight an issue (=bring attention to it) *The minister used his speech to highlight the issue of global warming.*
an issue comes up (*also* **an issue arises** *formal*) (=people started to discuss it) *The issue arose during a meeting of the Budget Committee.*
the issues surrounding sth *This chapter discusses the ethical issues surrounding genetically modified foods.*

ADJECTIVES

a political/social/economic etc issue *They discussed a number of political issues.*
an important issue *The committee met several times to discuss this important issue.*
a key/major/big issue (=very important) *For me, the big issue is cost.*
a difficult/complex issue *He was able to grasp complex issues quickly.*
a controversial/sensitive issue (=an issue that causes strong feelings and arguments) *Abortion is a controversial issue.*
a thorny issue (*also* **a vexed issue** *formal*) (=a difficult one that causes disagreement) *Illegal immigration is always a thorny issue.*
a burning issue (=a very important and urgent issue) *For country-dwellers, transport is a burning issue.*
wider issues (=more general issues, that affect more people or things) *This is a question that raises much wider issues.*
a topical issue (=an issue that is important at the present time) *The magazine discusses topical issues in science.*
the underlying issue (=the cause, or a more important problem that is related to something) | **a fundamental issue** (=a basic and important issue) | **an unresolved issue** (=that has not been dealt with)

PHRASES

a range of issues *A range of issues were debated at the meeting.*
sth is not the issue *spoken* (=something is not the most important problem or part) *Price alone is not the issue.*

issue[2] ●●○ S3 W2 AWL *v* [T]

1 to officially make a statement, give an order, warning etc: *Silva* ***issued*** *a* ***statement*** *denying all knowledge of the affair.* | *a warning issued by the Surgeon General*

2 if an organization or someone in an official position issues something such as documents or equipment, they give these things to people who need them: **issue a passport/permit/visa etc** *The US State Department issues millions of passports each year.* | **issue sb with sth** *All the workers were issued with protective clothing.* | **issue sth to sb** *The policy document will be issued to all employees.*

3 to officially produce something such as new stamps, coins, or SHARES and make them available to buy
issue forth *phr v literary* if something issues forth, it comes out of a place or thing: **[+from]** *A low grunt issued forth from his throat.*
issue from sth *phr v literary* if something issues from a place or thing, it comes out of it: *Smoke issued from the factory chimneys.*
-ist /ɪst/ *suffix* **1** [in nouns] someone who believes in a particular religion or set of principles or ideas: *a Buddhist | an atheist | a Scottish Nationalist* **2** [in adjectives] relating to or showing a particular political or religious belief: *her socialist views | rightist parties* (=political parties with RIGHT-WING opinions) **3** [in nouns] someone who studies a particular subject, plays a particular instrument, or does a particular type of work: *a linguist* (=someone who studies or learns languages) | *a novelist* (=someone who writes NOVELS) | *a guitarist* (=someone who plays the GUITAR) | *a machinist* (=someone who operates a machine) → **-OLOGIST** **4** [in adjectives] treating people unfairly because of something: *a very sexist remark* (=making unfair differences between men and women) **5** [in nouns] someone who treats people unfairly because of something: *They're a bunch of racists.*
isth·mus /ˈɪsməs/ *n* [C] a narrow piece of land with water on both sides, that connects two larger areas of land: *the Isthmus of Panama*
it[1] /ɪt/ ●●● S1 W1 *pron* [used as subject or object]
1 used to refer to a thing, animal, situation, idea etc that has already been mentioned or is already known about: *'Where's your office?' 'It's on the third floor.' | I love the spring – it's a wonderful time of the year. | There were people crying, buildings on fire. It was terrible! | Don't blame me. It wasn't my idea. | This little beast is a lemur and it lives in Madagascar.*
2 used to refer to the situation that someone is in now, or what is happening now: *I can't stand it any longer. I'm resigning. | How's it going, Bob? I haven't seen you for ages. | And the worst of it is the car isn't even paid for yet. | Stop it, you two. You're just being silly.*
3 used as the subject or object of a verb when the real subject or object is later in the sentence: *It worries me the way he keeps changing his mind. | What's it like being a sailor? | Apparently it's cheaper to fly than to go by train. | It's a pity you couldn't come. | It seems that we are not welcome here. | I found it hard to concentrate.*
4 used as the subject of a sentence when you are talking about the weather, the time, a distance etc: *Is it still raining? | It was 4 o'clock and the mail still hadn't come. | It's my birthday today. | It's over 200 miles from London to Manchester. | It gets dark very early in the winter. | It's three years since I last saw her.*
5 used with the verb 'be' to emphasize that you are talking about one particular thing, person, group etc and not any other: *It's Lawrence you should be talking to. | It was malaria that killed him. | It was in New Zealand that Elizabeth first met Mr Cronje.*
6 used to refer to a baby when you do not know what sex the baby is: *What will you call it if it's a boy?*
7 a) used to say who a person is: *'Who's that over there?' 'It's Robert Morley.'* **b)** *spoken* used to say who is speaking, especially on the telephone: *Hello, it's Frank here. | It's all right, it's only me.*
8 *informal* used to refer to sex: *Have you done it with him yet?*
9 if it wasn't/weren't for sb/sth (*also* **if it hadn't been for sb/sth**) used to say who or what prevents or prevented something from happening: *We would have arrived much earlier if it hadn't been for the snow.*
10 *informal* a particular ability or quality that is needed in order to do something: *In a job like advertising, you've either got it or you haven't!*
11 this is it *spoken* used to say that something you expected to happen is actually going to happen: *This is it, boys – the moment we've been waiting for.*
12 that's it *spoken* **a)** used to say that something is completely finished or that a situation cannot be changed: *That's it, then. There's nothing more we can do.* **b)** used to tell someone that they are doing something correctly: *Slowly ... slowly. Yeah, that's it.* **c)** (*also* **that does it**) used when you are angry about a situation and you do not want it to continue: *That's it. I'm leaving.*
13 think you're it *informal* to think you are more important than you are: *Just because he got a higher mark, he really thinks he's it.*
it[2], **It** *adj informal* **it bag/dress/shoes etc** a bag, dress etc that is very fashionable and desirable: *I've managed to get my hands on this season's it bag.*
IT /ˌaɪ ˈtiː/ ●●○ *n* [U] (***information technology***) the study or use of electronic processes and equipment for storing information and making it available
I·tal·i·an[1] /ɪˈtæliən/ *adj* relating to Italy, its people, or its language
Italian[2] *n* **1** [C] someone from Italy **2** [U] the language used in Italy
I·tal·i·a·nate /ɪˈtæliəneɪt/ *adj* with an Italian style or appearance: *an Italianate villa*
i·tal·i·cize (*also* **-ise** *BrE*) /ɪˈtælɪsaɪz/ *v* [T] to put or print something in italics —**italicized** *adj*
i·tal·ics /ɪˈtælɪks/ *n* [plural] a type of printed letters that lean to the right, often used to emphasize particular words: **in italics** *This example is written in italics.* —**italic** *adj*: *italic script* → **ROMAN**, see picture at **FONT**
Italo- /ɪtæləʊ $ -loʊ/ *prefix* [in nouns and adjectives] Italian and something else: *a joint Italo-German proposal*
itch[1] /ɪtʃ/ ●○○ *v*
1 [I,T] if part of your body or your clothes itch, you have an unpleasant feeling on your skin that makes you want to rub it with your nails → **scratch**: *My feet were itching terribly. | The label on this shirt itches me.*
2 be itching to do sth/be itching for sth *informal* to want to do something very much and as soon as possible: *He was itching for a fight.*
itch[2] *n* [singular] **1** an uncomfortable feeling on your skin that makes you want to rub it with your nails: *Scratch my back – I* ***have*** *an* ***itch****.* **2** *informal* a strong desire to do or have something: **[+for]** *an itch for adventure*
itch·y /ˈɪtʃi/ ●○○ *adj* (*comparative* **itchier**, *superlative* **itchiest**)
1 if part of your body is itchy, it feels slightly unpleasant and you want to rub it with your nails: *My eyes sometimes get red and itchy in the summer. | an itchy rash*
2 if clothes are itchy, they make your skin feel slightly unpleasant, so that you want to rub your skin with your nails SYN **scratchy**: *These tights are all itchy.*
3 wanting to go somewhere new or do something different: *He's had that job now for about eight years, and he's starting to* ***get itchy****. | I've only been back home for a few months and I've already got* ***itchy feet*** (=the desire to go somewhere new).
4 itchy fingers *informal* someone with itchy fingers is likely to steal things: *I tucked the bills deep into my pocket, away from itchy fingers.* —**itchiness** *n* [U]
it'd /ˈɪtəd/ *usually spoken* the short form of 'it would' or 'it had': *I'd do it if I thought it'd help.*
-ite /aɪt/ *suffix* **1** [in nouns] a follower or supporter of a particular idea or person – often used to show disapproval: *a group of Trotskyites* (=followers of Trotsky's political ideas) | *the Pre-Raphaelites* **2** [in adjectives] relating to a particular set of religious or political ideas, or to the ideas of a particular person: *his Reaganite opinions* **3** someone who lives in a particular place or belongs to a particular group: *a Brooklynite* (=someone from Brooklyn) | *the Israelites* (=in the Bible)
i·tem /ˈaɪtəm/ ●●● S3 W2 AWL *n*
1 [C] a single thing, especially one thing in a list, group, or set of things: *He opened the cardboard box and took out each item. | The store is having a sale on furniture and household items.* | **item on the agenda/list/menu** *We went on to the next item on the agenda.* | **item of clothing/furniture/jewellery etc** (=a single piece of clothing, furniture, jewellery etc) | ***luxury items*** *such as exotic spices and*

perfumes | *The original 1965 bottle is now a* ***collector's item*** (=one of a set of objects people like to collect because they are interesting or valuable). **THESAURUS** ▸ THING
2 [C] a single, usually short, piece of news in a newspaper or magazine, or on television: *I also saw that* ***news item*** *in the Sunday Times.*
3 be an item *informal* if two people are an item, they are having a romantic or sexual relationship

i·tem·ize (*also* **-ise** *BrE*) /ˈaɪtəmaɪz/ *v* [T] to make a list and give details about each thing on the list: *an itemized bill*

it·e·rate /ˈɪtəreɪt/ *v* [T] **1** if a computer iterates, it goes through a set of instructions before going through them for a second time **2** *formal* to say or do something again SYN **repeat** —**iteration** /ˌɪtəˈreɪʃən/ *n* [C,U] —**iterative** /ˈɪtərətɪv/ *adj* [only before noun]: *iterative processes*

ˈIt girl *n* [C] a fashionable and attractive young woman, especially one from a rich UPPER-CLASS family, who is well-known because she goes to a lot of fashionable events that people read about in newspapers and magazines

i·tin·e·rant /aɪˈtɪnərənt/ *adj* [only before noun] *formal* travelling from place to place, especially to work: *itinerant labourers* —**itinerant** *n* [C]

i·tin·e·ra·ry /aɪˈtɪnərəri $ -nəreri/ *n* (*plural* **itineraries**) [C] a plan or list of the places you will visit on a journey

-itis /aɪtɪs/ *suffix* [in nouns] **1** an illness or infection that affects a particular part of your body: *tonsillitis* (=infection of the TONSILS) **2** *humorous* the condition of having too much of something or liking something too much: *televisionitis* (=watching too much television)

it'll /ˈɪtl/ *usually spoken* the short form of 'it will': *It'll be dark before they get back.*

its /ɪts/ ●●● S1 W1 *determiner* [possessive form of 'it'] used to refer to something that belongs to or is connected with a thing, animal, baby etc that has already been mentioned: *Salzburg is famous for its beautiful buildings.* | *The hotel has* ***its own*** *pool.* ⚠ Do not confuse with **it's** (='it is' or 'it has').

it's /ɪts/ **1** the short form of 'it is': *It's raining.* **2** the short form of 'it has': *It's been cloudy all day.* ⚠ Do not confuse with **its**, which is the possessive form of 'it'.

it·self /ɪtˈself/ ●●● S1 W1 *pron* [reflexive form of 'it']
1 used to show that a thing, organization, animal, or baby that does something is affected by its own action: *The cat lay on the sofa, washing itself.* | *The machine switches itself off when the process is complete.* | *a small local enterprise that has transformed itself into a highly successful company*
2 used to emphasize that you are talking about one particular thing, organization etc: *We've checked the wiring, so the problem may be the television itself.*
3 in/of itself considered separately from any other facts: *There is a slight infection in the lung, which in itself is not serious.*
4 (all) by itself a) alone: *Will the dog be safe left in the car by itself?* **b)** without help or without a person making it work: *The door seemed to open all by itself.*
5 (all) to itself not shared with other things: *This idea deserves a chapter to itself.*
6 be patience/kindness/simplicity etc itself to be very patient, kind, simple etc: *Loading the software is simplicity itself.*

it·sy-bit·sy /ˌɪtsi ˈbɪtsi◂/ (*also* **it·ty-bit·ty** /ˌɪti ˈbɪti◂/) *adj* [only before noun] *spoken* very small – used humorously

iTV /ˌaɪ tiː ˈviː/ *n* [U] (***interactive television***) a type of television programme that allows people who are watching at home to answer questions or find out more information by using a computer or special equipment

ITV /ˌaɪ tiː ˈviː/ (***Independent Television***) a group of British television companies that are paid for by advertising

-ity /əti/ (*also* **-ty**) *suffix* [in nouns] the state of having a particular quality, or something that has that quality: *with great regularity* (=regularly) | *such stupidities* (=stupid actions or remarks)

IUD /ˌaɪ juː ˈdiː/ *n* [C] (***intra-uterine device***) a small plastic or metal object used inside a woman's UTERUS (=place where a baby develops) to prevent a woman from becoming PREGNANT SYN **coil**

IV /ˌaɪ ˈviː/ *n* [C] *AmE* (***intravenous***) medical equipment that is used to put liquid directly into your blood SYN **drip** *BrE*

-ive /ɪv/ *suffix* [in nouns and adjectives] someone or something that does something or can do something: *an explosive* (=substance that can explode) | *a detective* (=someone who tries to discover facts about crimes) | *the adoptive parents* (=who ADOPT a child)

I've /aɪv/ *usually spoken* the short form of 'I have': *I've never been here before.*

IVF /ˌaɪ viː ˈef/ *n* [U] (***in vitro fertilization***) a process in which a human egg is FERTILIZEd outside a woman's body → **test-tube baby**

i·vied /ˈaɪvid/ *adj literary* covered with ivy

i·vo·ry /ˈaɪvəri/ ●○○ *n* (*plural* **ivories**)
1 [U] the hard smooth yellowish-white substance from the TUSKS (=long teeth) of an ELEPHANT: *an ivory chess set*
2 [U] a yellowish-white colour: *an ivory silk wedding gown*
3 [C often plural] something made of ivory, especially a small figure of a person or animal: *a collection of ivories*

ˌivory ˈtower *n* [C] a place or situation where you are separated from the difficulties of ordinary life and so are unable to understand them, used especially to describe a college or university → **academia**: *an academic in an ivory tower*

i·vy /ˈaɪvi/ *n* (*plural* **ivies**) [C,U] a climbing plant with dark green shiny leaves → **POISON IVY**

ˈIvy ˌLeague, the a group of eight old and respected universities in the northeastern US → **Oxbridge** —**Ivy League** *adj*: *an Ivy League college*

-ization (*also* **-isation** *BrE*) /aɪzeɪʃən $ əzeɪ-/ *suffix* makes nouns from verbs ending in -IZE: *civilization* | *crystallization*

-ize (*also* **-ise** *BrE*) /aɪz/ *suffix* [in verbs] **1** to make something have more of a particular quality: *We need to modernize our procedures.* (=make them more modern) | *Americanized spelling* (=spelling made more American) | *privatized transport* (=bus or train services that are owned and operated by private companies) **2** to change something to something else, or be changed to something else: *The liquid crystallized* (=turned into CRYSTALS). **3** to speak or think in the way mentioned: *to soliloquize* (=speak a SOLILOQUY, to yourself) | *I sat and listened to him sermonizing* (=speaking solemnly, as if in a SERMON). **4** to put into a particular place: *She was hospitalized after the accident.*

Jj

J¹, j /dʒeɪ/ *n* (*plural* **J's, j's**) [C,U] the tenth letter of the English alphabet

J² the written abbreviation of ***joule*** or ***joules***

jab¹ /dʒæb/ *v* (**jabbed, jabbing**) [I,T] to push something into or towards something else with short quick movements: **[+at]** *She jabbed at the elevator buttons.* | *When I didn't respond, he* ***jabbed*** *a* ***finger*** *at me.* | **jab sb with sth** *Stop jabbing me with your elbow!* | **jab sth into sth** *The soldier jabbed a rifle into his ribs.*

jab² *n* [C] **1** a sudden hard hit, especially with a pointed object or your FIST (=closed hand): *a boxer with a good* ***left jab*** **2** something you say to criticize someone or something else: *White House officials* ***took a*** *sharp* ***jab*** *at the Democrats' plan.* **3** *BrE informal* an INJECTION given to prevent you from catching a disease SYN **shot**: *a typhoid jab*

jab·ber /ˈdʒæbə $ -ər/ *v* [I,T] to talk quickly in an excited and unclear way – used to show disapproval: *The tourists were jabbering away on the bus.* —**jabber** *n* [singular, U]

jack¹ /dʒæk/ *n* [C] **1** a piece of equipment used to lift a heavy weight off the ground, such as a car, and support it while it is in the air: *a hydraulic jack* **2** a card used in card games that has a man's picture on it and is worth less than a queen and more than a ten: **jack of hearts/clubs etc** | *a pair of jacks* **3** an electronic connection for a telephone or other electric machine: *a phone jack* **4 a) jacks** [plural] a children's game in which the players try to pick up small objects called jacks while BOUNCING and catching a ball **b)** a small metal or plastic object that has six points, used in this game **5** a small white ball at which players aim larger balls in the game of BOWLS **6 jack (shit)** *AmE spoken not polite* a rude expression meaning anything at all: *He doesn't know jack shit about cars.* → **JUMPING JACK, UNION JACK**

jack² *v*

jack sb **around** *phr v AmE spoken* to waste someone's time by deliberately making things difficult for them: *Stop jacking me around and make up your mind!*

jack sth ↔ **in** *phr v BrE informal* to stop doing something: *I'd love to jack in my job and go and live in the Bahamas.*

jack off *phr v AmE informal not polite* to MASTURBATE

jack sth ↔ **up** *phr v* **1** to lift something heavy off the ground using a jack: *Jack the car up higher – I can't get the tire off.* **2** *informal* to increase prices, sales etc by a large amount: *They're just interested in jacking up their profit margins.*

jack·al /ˈdʒækɔːl, -kəl $ -kəl/ *n* [C] a wild animal like a dog that lives in Asia and Africa and eats the remaining parts of dead animals

jack·ass /ˈdʒæk-æs/ *n* [C] *AmE spoken not polite* an offensive word for an annoying stupid person SYN **idiot**

jack·boot /ˈdʒækbuːt/ *n* [C] a boot worn by soldiers that covers their leg up to the knee —**jackbooted** *adj*

jack·daw /ˈdʒækdɔː $ -dɒː/ *n* [C] a black bird like a CROW that sometimes steals small bright objects

jack·et /ˈdʒækɪt/ ●●● S2 W3 *n* [C]
1 a short light coat: **a leather/denim/linen etc jacket** *a suede jacket* → **BOMBER JACKET, DINNER JACKET, LIFE JACKET, STRAITJACKET(1)**
2 the part of a suit that covers the top part of your body: *Gene has to wear a jacket and tie to work.* | *tweed jackets* → **SPORTS JACKET**
3 a stiff piece of folded paper that fits over the cover of a book to protect it SYN **dust jacket**
4 *AmE* a stiff paper cover that protects a record SYN **sleeve** *BrE*
5 a cover that surrounds and protects some types of machines

JACKETS

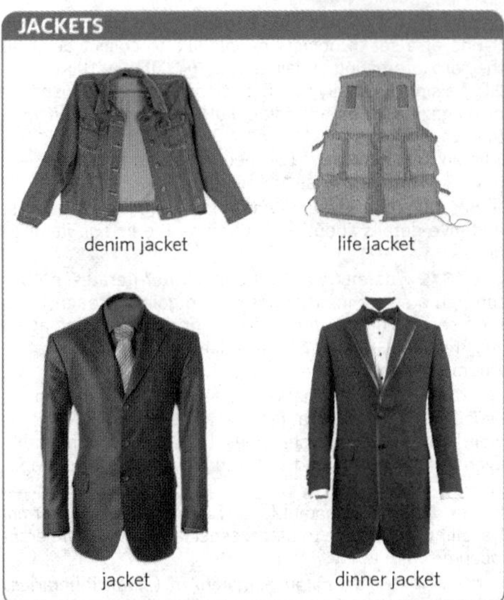

denim jacket | life jacket | jacket | dinner jacket

ˈjacket poˌtato *n* [C] *BrE* a potato baked with its skin on SYN **baked potato**

ˌJack ˈFrost *n* [singular] a way of describing FROST as a person – used especially when talking to children

jack·ham·mer /ˈdʒækˌhæmə $ -ər/ *n* [C] *AmE* a large powerful tool used to break hard materials such as the surface of a road SYN **pneumatic drill** *BrE*

ˈjack-in-the-ˌbox *n* [C] a children's toy shaped like a box, with a figure inside that springs out when the box is opened

ˈjack-knife¹ *n* (*plural* **jack-knives**) [C] **1** a knife with a blade that folds into its handle **2** a DIVE in which you bend at the waist when you are in the air

jack-knife² *v* [I] if a large vehicle with two parts jack-knifes, it slides out of control and the back part swings towards the front part: *The truck skidded on the ice and jack-knifed.*

ˌjack-of-ˈall-trades *n* [singular] someone who can do many different types of work, but who often is not very skilled at any of them

jack-o'-lan·tern /ˌdʒæk ə ˈlæntən $ -ərn/ *n* [C] a PUMPKIN(1) that has a face cut into it and a CANDLE put inside to shine through the holes

JACK-O'-LANTERN

jack·pot /ˈdʒækpɒt $ -pɑːt/ *n* [C] a large amount of money that you can win in a game that is decided by chance: *a £50,000 jackpot* | *jackpot winners* → **hit the jackpot** at **HIT¹(25)**

jack·rab·bit /ˈdʒækˌræbɪt/ *n* [C] a large North American HARE (=animal like a large rabbit) with very long ears

Jack Rob·in·son /ˌdʒæk ˈrɒbənsən $ -ˈrɑː-/ *n* **before you can say Jack Robinson** *old-fashioned* very quickly or suddenly

ˌJack the ˈLad *n* [singular] *BrE spoken* a young man who enjoys drinking alcohol and going out with his male friends, and who thinks he is sexually attractive

Jac·o·be·an /ˌdʒækəˈbiːən◂/ *adj* belonging to or typical of the period between 1603 and 1625 in Britain, when James I was king of England: *Jacobean drama*

Jac·o·bite /ˈdʒækəbaɪt/ *n* [C] someone in the 17th or 18th centuries who supported King James II of England and wanted one of his DESCENDANTS to rule England —**Jacobite** *adj*

J

Ja·cuz·zi /dʒəˈkuːzi/ *n* [C] *trademark* a large indoor bath that makes hot water move in strong currents around your body → **HOT TUB, SPA**(2)

jade /dʒeɪd/ *n* [U] **1** a hard, usually green, stone often used to make jewellery: *a jade necklace* **2** (*also* **jade green**) the light green colour of jade

ja·ded /ˈdʒeɪdɪd/ *adj* someone who is jaded is no longer interested in or excited by something, usually because they have experienced too much of it: *The concert should satisfy even the most jaded critic.*

jag /dʒæg/ *n* [C] *informal* **crying/shopping/talking etc jag** a short period of time when you suddenly cry etc without controlling how much you do it

jag·ged /ˈdʒægɪd/ *adj* having a rough or pointed edge or surface: *the broken bottle's* ***jagged edge*** | *the jagged rocks of St. Saviour's Point* **THESAURUS** **SHARP** —**jaggedly** *adv*

jag·u·ar /ˈdʒægjuə $ ˈdʒægwɑːr/ *n* [C] a large South American wild cat with brown and yellow fur with black spots → see picture at **BIG CAT**

jail[1] (*also* **gaol** *BrE*) /dʒeɪl/ ●●● S3 W2 *n* [C,U] a place where criminals are kept as part of their punishment, or where people who have been charged with a crime are kept before they are judged in a law court SYN **prison**: *He's been* ***in jail*** *for three months already.* **THESAURUS** **PRISON**

COLLOCATIONS

VERBS

go to jail *They're going to jail for a long time.*
send sb to jail *The judge sent Meyer to jail for six years.*
put sb in jail *The government would put him in jail if he stayed in the country.*
throw sb in jail (=put someone in jail) | **spend time/three months/six years etc in jail** | **serve time/five years etc in jail** (=spend time in jail) | **get out of jail** | **release sb from jail** | **escape from jail**

ADJECTIVES/NOUN + jail

the local jail *The suspects were taken to the local jail.*
a town/city/county jail | **a high-/top-/maximum-security jail**

jail + NOUN

a jail sentence *He's serving a 7-year jail sentence.*
a jail term (=period of time in jail) | **a jail cell**

jail[2] (*also* **gaol** *BrE*) ●●○ *v* [T] to put someone in jail SYN **imprison**: **jail sb for sth** *Watson was jailed for tax evasion.* | **jail sb for two months/six years/life etc** *They ought to jail her killer for life.*

jail·bait /ˈdʒeɪlbeɪt/ *n* [U] *informal* someone who is legally too young to have sex with

jail·bird (*also* **gaolbird** *BrE*) /ˈdʒeɪlbɜːd $ -bɜːrd/ *n* [C] *old-fashioned informal* someone who has spent a lot of time in prison

jail·break (*also* **gaolbreak** *BrE*) /ˈdʒeɪlbreɪk/ *n* [C] an escape or an attempt to escape from prison, especially by several people

jail·er (*also* **gaoler** *BrE*) /ˈdʒeɪlə $ -ər/ *n* [C] *old-fashioned* someone who is in charge of guarding a prison or prisoners

jail·house /ˈdʒeɪlhaʊs/ *n* [C] *AmE* a building that has a jail in it → **prison**

jal·a·pe·ño /ˌhæləˈpeɪnjəʊ $ ˌhɑːləˈpeɪnjoʊ/ *n* [C] a small, very hot green PEPPER used especially in Mexican food

ja·lop·y /dʒəˈlɒpi $ -ˈlɑːpi/ *n* (*plural* **jalopies**) [C] *old-fashioned* a very old car in bad condition → **BANGER**(2)

jam[1] /dʒæm/ ●●● S3 *n*

1 FOOD [C,U] a thick sweet substance made from boiled fruit and sugar, eaten especially on bread → **jelly**: *strawberry jam* | *a jam sandwich* | *jam jars*

2 CARS/PEOPLE [C] a situation in which it is difficult or impossible to move because there are so many cars or people: *Sorry we're late. We got stuck in a* ***traffic jam***.

3 MACHINE [C] a situation in which a machine does not work because something is stopping a part from moving: *It caused a jam in the printer.*

4 DIFFICULT SITUATION [C usually singular] *informal* a difficult situation: **(be/get) in/out of/into a jam** *We became friends after he helped me out of a jam.*

5 MUSIC [C] **a)** a JAM SESSION **b)** a song or piece of music, especially one by a RAP or ROCK group

6 kick out the jams *AmE informal* to play ROCK MUSIC loudly and with a lot of energy or emotion: *Make no mistake – these guys know how to kick out the jams.*

7 jam tomorrow *BrE informal* good things someone promises you, which never happen: *There is an element of 'jam tomorrow' about some of the government's policies.*

jam[2] ●●○ *v* (**jammed**, **jamming**)

1 PUSH HARD [T always + adv/prep] to push something somewhere using a lot of force, until it can move no further: *He jammed his foot on the accelerator and the car sped off.* | *A chair had been jammed up against the door.*

2 MACHINE [I,T] (*also* **jam up**) if a moving part of something jams, or if you jam it, it no longer works properly because something is preventing it from moving: *The front roller has jammed on the photocopier.*

3 BLOCK [I,T] (*also* **jam up**) if a lot of people or vehicles jam a place, they fill it so that it is difficult to move SYN **cram**: *Crowds jammed the entrance to the stadium.* | **[+into]** *They all jammed into the car.* → **JAMMED**(2)

4 MUSIC [I] (*also* **jam out**) to play music in an informal way with other people → **JAM SESSION**

5 jam on the brakes to slow down a car suddenly by putting your foot down hard on the BRAKE

6 jam sb's/the switchboard if telephone calls jam the switchboard of an organization, so many people are phoning the organization that it cannot deal with them all: *Viewers jammed the switchboard with complaints.*

7 RADIO [T] to deliberately prevent broadcasts or other electronic signals from being received, by broadcasting signals on the same WAVELENGTH

8 sb is jamming *AmE spoken* used to say that someone is doing something very quickly or well

jam out *phr v* to dance to music

jamb /dʒæm/ *n* [C] a post that forms the side of a door or window

jam·ba·la·ya /ˌdʒæmbəˈlaɪə/ *n* [U] a dish from the southern US, containing rice and SEAFOOD

jam·bo·ree /ˌdʒæmbəˈriː/ *n* [C] a big noisy party or event

jammed /dʒæmd/ *adj* [not before noun] **1** stuck and impossible to move: *Ben had got his finger jammed in the door.* **2** full of people or things SYN **packed**: *The place is jammed. We'll never get in.* | **[+with]** *The town was completely jammed with traffic.* → **JAM-PACKED** **3** if people are jammed in a place, there are a lot of them there, so that there is no space between them: *We were jammed together, shoulder to shoulder, in the narrow corridor.*

jam·mies /ˈdʒæmiz/ *n* [plural] *AmE informal* PYJAMAS

jam·my /ˈdʒæmi/ *adj BrE* **1** [only before noun] *informal* lucky – used especially when someone has got something good without having to use any special effort or skill: *The jammy devil won £1,000.* **2** covered in JAM, or like jam

ˌjam-ˈpacked *adj* [not before noun] *informal* full of people or things SYN **crowded**: **[+with]** *The place was jam-packed with tourists.*

ˈjam ˌsession (*also* **jam**) *n* [C] an occasion when JAZZ or ROCK musicians play music together in an informal way

Jan. (*also* **Jan** *BrE*) the written abbreviation of ***January***

Jane Doe /ˌdʒeɪn ˈdəʊ $ -ˈdoʊ/ *n* [C,U] *AmE* used especially by the police to refer to a woman whose name is not known → **JOHN DOE**

jan·gle /ˈdʒæŋgəl/ *v* [I,T] **1** if metal objects jangle, or if you jangle them, they make a sound when they hit each other: *Her bracelets jangled on her wrist.* | *Dev jangled his car keys.* **2** if your nerves jangle, or if something jangles your nerves, you feel nervous or upset: *The harsh sound jangled his nerves.* —**jangle** *n* [singular]

J

jan·i·tor /ˈdʒænɪtə $ -ər/ *n* [C] *especially AmE* someone whose job is to look after a school or other large building SYN **caretaker** *BrE*

Jan·u·a·ry /ˈdʒænjuəri, -njʊri $ -njueri/ ●●● S2 W2 *n* (*plural* **Januaries**) [C,U] (*written abbreviation* **Jan.**) the first month of the year, between December and February: **next/last January** *I haven't heard from him since last January.* | **in January** *She started working there in January.* | **on January 6th** *Rosie's party was on January 6th.* | **on 6th January** *BrE*: *He took office on 6th January 1999.* | **January 6** *AmE*: *The package arrived January 6.*

Ja·nus /ˈdʒeɪnəs/ in Roman MYTHOLOGY, the god of gates and doorways and of new beginnings. Janus is usually shown in pictures with two faces, one of which looks back at the past while the other looks forward towards the future. The expression 'Janus-faced' is a literary way of describing someone who is TWO-FACED (=they change what they say according to who they are talking to, in an insincere and unpleasant way).

Jap /dʒæp/ *n* [C] *taboo* a very offensive word for someone from Japan. Do not use this word.

Jap·a·nese[1] /ˌdʒæpəˈniːz◂/ *adj* relating to Japan, its people, or its language: *a Japanese car*

Japanese[2] *n* **1 the Japanese** [plural] people from Japan **2** [U] the language used in Japan

jape /dʒeɪp/ *n* [C] *BrE old-fashioned* a trick or joke

jar[1] /dʒɑː $ dʒɑːr/ ●●● S3 *n* [C]
1 a glass container with a wide top and a lid, used for storing food such as JAM or HONEY, or the amount it contains: *a jam jar* | *half a jar of peanut butter* → see picture at **CONTAINER**
2 a container made of clay, stone etc, used especially in the past for keeping food or drink in
3 *BrE informal* a glass of beer: *We'd had a few jars down the pub.*

jar[2] *v* (**jarred**, **jarring**) **1** [I,T] to make someone feel annoyed or shocked: *His enthusiasm jarred.* | *His words jarred Harriet.* | **[+on]** *The screaming was starting to* ***jar on*** *my* ***nerves.*** **2** [I,T] to shake or hit something in a way that damages it or makes it loose: *Alice landed badly, jarring her ankle.* **3** [I] to be different in style or appearance from something else and therefore look strange SYN **clash**: **[+with]** *There was a modern lamp that jarred with the rest of the room.* —**jarring** *adj*

jar·gon /ˈdʒɑːgən $ ˈdʒɑːrgən, -gɑːn/ ●○○ *n* [U] words and expressions used in a particular profession or by a particular group of people, which are difficult for other people to understand - often used to show disapproval → **argot**: *Keep it simple and avoid the use of jargon.* | **technical/scientific/legal/medical etc jargon** *documents full of legal jargon* THESAURUS ▸ **WORD**

jar·head /ˈdʒɑːhed $ ˈdʒɑːr-/ *n* [C] *AmE informal* a US MARINE (=soldier who serves on a ship)

jas·mine /ˈdʒæzmɪn/ *n* [C,U] a plant that grows up a wall, frame etc and has small sweet-smelling white or yellow flowers

jas·per /ˈdʒæspə $ -ər/ *n* [U] a red, yellow, or brown stone that is not very valuable

jaun·dice /ˈdʒɔːndɪs $ ˈdʒɒːn-, ˈdʒɑːn-/ *n* [U] a medical condition in which your skin and the white part of your eyes become yellow

jaun·diced /ˈdʒɔːndɪst $ ˈdʒɒːn-, ˈdʒɑːn-/ *adj* **1** thinking that people or things are bad, especially because you have had bad experiences in the past: *He has a very* ***jaundiced view*** *of the world.* | *She viewed politics and politicians with a* ***jaundiced eye*** (=in a jaundiced way). **2** suffering from jaundice

jaunt /dʒɔːnt $ dʒɒːnt, dʒɑːnt/ *n* [C] a short trip for pleasure: *a weekend jaunt*

jaun·ty /ˈdʒɔːnti $ ˈdʒɒːnti, ˈdʒɑːnti/ *adj* **1** showing that you are confident and happy: *He had a jaunty walk.* | *Her hat was set* ***at a jaunty angle.*** **2** jaunty music is fast and makes you feel happy: *a jaunty tune* —**jauntily** *adv* —**jauntiness** *n* [U]

ja·va /ˈdʒɑːvə $ ˈdʒævə, ˈdʒɑː-/ *n* [U] *AmE informal* coffee

Ja·va /ˈdʒɑːvə/ *n* [U] *trademark* a computer language, used especially to write programs for the Internet

jav·e·lin /ˈdʒævəlɪn/ *n* **1** [C] a long stick with a pointed end, thrown as a sport **2 the javelin** a sports event in which competitors throw a javelin

jaw[1] /dʒɔː $ dʒɒː/ ●●○ *n*
1 [C] one of the two bones that your teeth are in: *a broken jaw* | **lower/upper jaw** *an animal with two rows of teeth in its lower jaw*
2 [C usually singular] the lower part of your face. Its shape is sometimes thought to show your character: *He punched him on the jaw.* | *a rugged physique and a strong square jaw* | *She's got a very determined jaw.*
3 sb's jaw dropped used to say that someone looked surprised or shocked: *'You're not serious, are you?' Ellen's jaw dropped.*
4 jaws [plural] **a)** the mouth of a person or animal, especially a dangerous animal **b)** the two parts of a machine or tool that move together to hold something tightly
5 the jaws of death/defeat/despair etc *literary* a situation in which something unpleasant almost happens: *She had saved him from the jaws of death.*

jaw[2] *v* [I] *informal* to talk: *Stop jawing and let me get on with the work!*

jaw·bone /ˈdʒɔːbəʊn $ ˈdʒɒːboʊn/ *n* [C] one of the bones that your teeth are in, especially the lower bone

jaw·break·er /ˈdʒɔːˌbreɪkə $ ˈdʒɒːˌbreɪkər/ *n* [C] *AmE* a round hard sweet

ˈjaw-ˌdropping *adj informal* very impressive or surprising: *This mountainous region has jaw-dropping scenery.*

jaw·line /ˈdʒɔːlaɪn $ ˈdʒɒː-/ *n* [C] the shape of the lower part of someone's face: *a square jawline*

ˌJaws of ˈLife *n* **the Jaws of Life** *trademark* a tool used to make a hole in a car, truck etc after an accident, so that the people inside can be taken out

jay /dʒeɪ/ *n* [C] a bird of the CROW family that is noisy and brightly coloured

jay·walk·ing /ˈdʒeɪˌwɔːkɪŋ $ -ˌwɒː-/ *n* [U] when someone walks across a road at a place where it is dangerous to cross —**jaywalker** *n* [C] —**jaywalk** *v* [I]

jazz[1] /dʒæz/ ●●○ *n* [U]
1 a type of music that has a strong beat and parts for performers to play alone: *a jazz band* | *a jazz club* | *modern jazz*
2 and all that jazz *spoken* and things like that: *I'm fed up with work, meetings, and all that jazz.*

jazz[2] *v*
jazz sth ↔ **up** *phr v informal* to make something more attractive or exciting: *Jazz up your everyday meals with our new range of seasonings.*

jazzed /dʒæzd/ *adj* [not before noun] *AmE spoken* excited

jazz·y /ˈdʒæzi/ *adj informal* **1** brightly coloured and modern: *a jazzy tie* **2** similar to the style of jazz music

JCB /ˌdʒeɪ siː ˈbiː/ *n* [C] *trademark BrE* a vehicle used for digging and moving earth → **digger**

jeal·ous /ˈdʒeləs/ ●●● S2 *adj*
1 feeling unhappy because someone has something that you wish you had → **envious**: **[+of]** *Why are you so jealous of his success?* | *You're just jealous of her.*
2 feeling angry and unhappy because someone you like or love is showing interest in another person, or another person is showing interest in them: *She gets jealous if I even look at another woman.* | *He was talking to Nina to* ***make*** *me* ***jealous.*** | **jealous husband/wife/lover etc**
3 jealous of sth *formal* wanting to keep or protect something that you have, because you are proud of it: *a country jealous of its heritage*

GRAMMAR

Someone is **jealous of** someone or something: *She was jealous of her sister.* ✗ Don't say: *jealous about*

GRAMMAR GUIDE ▸ **ADJECTIVES**

THESAURUS

jealous feeling unhappy because someone has something that you want and cannot have: *Maybe he's jealous because I got the job and he didn't.* | *Sharon had always been jealous of her sister's long blonde hair.*
envious *especially written* wishing that you had something nice or special that someone else has: *When I saw the garden, I was really envious.* | *She knew she was beautiful and enjoyed the envious looks of other women.*
green with envy very envious: *You'll be green with envy when you see their new house.*

jeal·ous·ly /ˈdʒeləsli/ *adv* **1** if you jealously guard or protect something, you try very hard to keep or protect it: *a* ***jealously guarded*** *secret* **2** if you do something jealously, you are feeling jealous when you do it: *Ludens watched Marcus jealously.*

jeal·ous·y /ˈdʒeləsi/ ●●○ *n* (*plural* **jealousies**) [C,U] a feeling of being jealous → **envy**: **a pang/stab/twinge of jealousy** (=a sudden feeling of jealousy) *Polly felt a sharp pang of jealousy when she saw Paul with Suzanne.* | ***Sexual jealousy*** *is a common motive for murder.* | *feelings of* ***professional jealousy*** | *He quickly discovered the* ***petty jealousies*** *and gossip of village life.*

jeans /dʒiːnz/ ●●● S2 W3 *n* [plural] trousers made of DENIM (=a strong, usually blue, cotton cloth)

Jeep /dʒiːp/ *n* [C] *trademark* a type of car made for travelling over rough ground

jeer /dʒɪə $ dʒɪr/ *v* [I,T] to laugh at someone or shout unkind things at them in a way that shows you do not respect them: *'You know I'm right!' she jeered.* | *The president was booed and jeered by a crowd of protesters.* | **[+at]** *Fans jeered at the referee.* —**jeer** *n* [C]: *There were jeers and booing from the audience.* —**jeering** *n* [U]

jeer·ing /ˈdʒɪərɪŋ $ ˈdʒɪr-/ *adj* [only before noun] a jeering remark or sound is unkind and shows that you do not respect someone: *jeering laughter*

Jeeves /dʒiːvz/ a character in many humorous stories by P. G. Wodehouse. Jeeves is the VALET (=male servant) of an UPPER-CLASS young man called Bertie Wooster, and is a very patient sensible man. Wooster depends on him a lot and he always manages to solve Wooster's problems.

jeez /dʒiːz/ *interjection informal* used to express feelings such as surprise, anger, annoyance etc

jeg·gings /ˈdʒegɪŋz/ *n* [plural] very tight JEANS, or LEGGINGS that are the same colour blue as jeans

Je·ho·vah /dʒɪˈhəʊvə $ -ˈhoʊ-/ a name given to God in the Old Testament (=first part of the Bible)

Je,hovah's 'Witness *n* [C] a member of a religious organization that believes the end of the world will happen soon and sends its members to people's houses to try to persuade them to join

je·june /dʒɪˈdʒuːn/ *adj formal* **1** ideas that are jejune are too simple: *jejune political opinions* **2** boring

Jek·yll and Hyde /ˌdʒekəl ənd ˈhaɪd/ *n* [C] someone who is sometimes nice but at other times is unpleasant

jell /dʒel/ *v* [I] another spelling of GEL

jel·lied /ˈdʒelid/ *adj* [only before noun] *especially BrE* cooked or served in jelly: *jellied eels*

Jell-O, **jello** /ˈdʒeləʊ $ -loʊ/ *n* [U] *trademark AmE* a soft sweet food made from fruit juice and GELATIN SYN **jelly** *BrE*

jel·ly /ˈdʒeli/ ●●● S3 *n* (*plural* **jellies**)
1 [C,U] *BrE* a soft sweet food made from fruit juice and GELATIN SYN **Jell-O** *AmE*: *raspberry jelly*
2 [C,U] a thick sweet substance made from boiled fruit and sugar with no pieces of fruit in it, eaten especially on bread → **jam**: *a peanut butter and jelly sandwich* | *damson jelly*
3 [U] *especially BrE* a soft solid substance made from meat juices and GELATIN
4 [U] a substance that is solid but very soft, and moves easily when you touch it: *frogs' eggs floating in a protective jelly*
5 feel like/turn to jelly if your legs or knees feel like jelly, they start to shake because you are frightened or nervous
6 jellies [plural] *BrE informal* drugs that make you feel relaxed and sleepy, which some people use illegally
7 jellies [plural] shoes made of clear coloured plastic

'jelly ,baby *n* [C] *BrE* a small soft sweet made in the shape of a baby, that comes in a variety of colours

'jelly bean *n* [C] a small soft sweet with different tastes and colours that is shaped like a bean

JELLYFISH

jel·ly·fish /ˈdʒelifɪʃ/ *n* (*plural* **jellyfish**) [C] a sea animal that has a round transparent body and can sting you

'jelly ,roll *n* [C] *AmE* a long thin cake that is rolled up with JAM or cream inside SYN **Swiss roll** *BrE*

jem·my /ˈdʒemi/ *n* (*plural* **jemmies**) *BrE*, **jimmy** (*plural* **jimmies**) *AmE* [C] a short strong metal bar used especially by thieves to break open locked doors, windows etc —**jemmy** *v* [T]

je ne sais quoi /ˌʒə nə seɪ ˈkwɑː/ *n* [singular] a good quality that you cannot easily describe - often humorous: *the je ne sais quoi that makes the village magical*

jeop·ar·dize (*also* **-ise** *BrE*) /ˈdʒepədaɪz $ -ər-/ *v* [T] to risk losing or spoiling something important: *large-scale military offensives which could jeopardize the UN peace process*

jeop·ar·dy /ˈdʒepədi $ -ər-/ *n* **in jeopardy** in danger of being lost or harmed: *Thousands of jobs are in jeopardy.* | **put/place sth in jeopardy** *The killings could put the whole peace process in jeopardy.*

jer·e·mi·ad /ˌdʒerəˈmaɪəd/ *n* [C] *formal* a long speech or piece of writing that complains about a situation, or says that bad things will happen

jerk¹ /dʒɜːk $ dʒɜːrk/ ●○○ *v*
1 [I,T] to move with a quick sudden movement, or to make part of your body move in this way: *Wilcox* ***jerked*** *his* ***head*** *to indicate that they should move on.* | *'Is that the only way out of here?' he asked,* ***jerking*** *a* ***thumb*** *at the door.* | **[+back/up/forwards etc]** *Suddenly, he jerked back in his chair.* | *The sound of the phone* ***jerked*** *me* ***awake***.
2 [I,T] to pull something suddenly and roughly: **[+at]** *Doyle jerked at the girl's hair to make her sit down.* | *She* ***jerked open*** *the car door and got out.*

jerk sb **around** *phr v AmE informal* to waste someone's time or deliberately make things difficult for them

jerk off *phr v especially AmE informal not polite* to MASTURBATE

jerk out sth *phr v written* to say something quickly and nervously: *'Don't lie,' she jerked out.*

jerk² *n* [C] **1** a sudden quick movement: *He gave a sudden* ***jerk of*** *his* ***head***. | **with a jerk** *She started the car with a jerk and hit the bumper of the car in front.* **2** *informal* someone, especially a man, who is stupid or who does things that annoy or hurt other people SYN **idiot**: *I swore at him for being such a jerk.*

jerk³ *adj* **jerk chicken/pork etc** meat that has been left in spices or covered with spices before being cooked

jer·kin /ˈdʒɜːkɪn $ -ɜːr-/ *n* [C] a short jacket that covers your body but not your arms, worn in the past

jerk·y¹ /ˈdʒɜːki $ -ɜːr-/ *adj* jerky movements are rough, with many starts and stops OPP **smooth**: *His skin was dry and hot, his breathing rapid and jerky.* | *The bus came to a jerky halt.* —**jerkily** *adv* —**jerkiness** *n* [U]

jerky² *n* [U] *AmE* meat that has been cut into thin pieces and dried in the sun or with smoke

J

jer·ry-built /ˈdʒeri ˌbɪlt/ *adj* built cheaply, quickly, and badly

jer·sey /ˈdʒɜːzi $ -ɜːr-/ *n* **1** [C] a shirt made of soft material, worn by players of sports such as football and RUGBY **2** [C] *BrE* a piece of clothing made of wool that covers the upper part of your body and your arms SYN **sweater 3** [U] a soft material made of cotton or wool

Jersey *n* [C] a light brown cow that gives high-quality milk

Je·ru·sa·lem ar·ti·choke /dʒəˌruːsələm ˈɑːtətʃəʊk $ -ˈɑːrtətʃoʊk/ *n* [C] a vegetable with roots that you can eat

jest¹ /dʒest/ *n* [C] *formal* something you say that is intended to be funny, not serious SYN **joke**: *I wasn't sure whether to treat her words as a jest.* | **in jest** *His serious face told me that he was not speaking in jest.*

jest² *v* [I] *formal or old use* to say things that you do not really mean in order to amuse people: *'Do I look as if I am jesting?' she asked, her face pale and tense.* —**jestingly** *adv*

jest·er /ˈdʒestə $ -ər/ *n* [C] a man employed in the past by a ruler to entertain people with jokes, stories etc

Je·su·it /ˈdʒezjuɪt $ ˈdʒeʒuɪt, ˈdʒezuɪt/ *n* [C] a man who is a member of the Roman Catholic Society of Jesus

Je·sus¹ /ˈdʒiːzəs/ (*also* ˌ**Jesus** ˈ**Christ**) the man who Christians believe was the son of God, and on whose life and ideas Christianity is based

Jesus² *interjection not polite* used to express anger, surprise, or shock: *Jesus! That was close!* ⚠ Be careful about using **Jesus** in this way, because Christians find it offensive.

jet¹ /dʒet/ ●●○ *n*

1 [C] a fast plane with a jet engine: **jet fighter/aircraft/airliner** *a squadron of F-6 jet fighter aircraft* | *He owns a* ***private jet***. → JUMBO JET

2 [C] a narrow stream of liquid or gas that comes quickly out of a small hole, or the hole itself: **[+of]** *She soaped herself beneath the refreshing jets of water.*

3 [U] a hard black stone that is used for making jewellery

jet² *v* (**jetted**, **jetting**) [I always + adv/prep] **1** *informal* to travel by plane, especially to many different places: **[+off]** *We're jetting off for a sunshine holiday in the Caribbean.* | *business executives jetting around the world* **2** if a liquid or gas jets out from somewhere, it comes quickly out of a small hole

ˌ**jet-ˈblack** *adj* very dark black: *jet-black hair* —**jet black** *n* [U]

ˌ**jet ˈengine** *n* [C] an engine that pushes out a stream of hot air and gases behind it, used in aircraft → **rocket engine** → see picture at PLANE¹

ˈ**jet lag** *n* [U] the tired and confused feeling that you can get after flying a very long distance, especially because of the difference in time between the place you left and the place you arrived at: *I'm* ***suffering from jet lag*** *but I'll feel better after a good night's sleep.* —**jet-lagged** *adj*

jet·lin·er /ˈdʒetlaɪnə $ -ər/ *n* [C] *AmE* a large aircraft, especially one that carries passengers

ˌ**jet-ˈpropelled** *adj* using a jet engine for power

ˌ**jet proˈpulsion** *n* [U] the use of a jet engine for power

jet·sam /ˈdʒetsəm/ *n* [U] things that are thrown from a ship and float on the sea towards the shore → **flotsam and jetsam** at FLOTSAM

ˈ**jet set** *n* **the jet set** *old-fashioned* rich and fashionable people who travel a lot —**jet-setter** *n* [C]

ˈ**Jet Ski** *n* [C] *trademark* a small fast vehicle on which one or two people can ride over water for fun

ˈ**jet stream** *n* [singular] a current of very strong winds high above the Earth's surface

jet·ti·son /ˈdʒetəsən, -zən/ *v* [T] **1** to get rid of something or decide not to do something any longer: *The scheme was jettisoned when the government found it too costly.* **2** to throw things away, especially from a moving plane or ship

jet·ty /ˈdʒeti/ *n* (*plural* **jetties**) [C] a wide wall or flat area built out into the water, used for getting on and off boats → **pier**

Jew /dʒuː/ *n* [C] someone whose religion is Judaism, or who is a member of a group whose traditional religion is Judaism

jew·el /ˈdʒuːəl/ ●●○ *n* [C]

1 a valuable stone, such as a diamond SYN **gem**

2 jewels [plural] jewellery or other objects made with valuable stones and used for decoration: *She loved dressing up and wearing priceless jewels.*

3 a very small stone used in the machinery of a watch

4 something or someone that is very valuable, attractive, or important: *He introduced her to Budapest, a jewel of a city.*

5 the jewel in the crown the best or most valuable part of something: *Puddings are the jewel in the crown of British cookery.* → CROWN JEWEL

ˈ**jewel ˌcase** *n* [C] a plastic box for holding a CD

jew·elled *BrE*, **jeweled** *AmE* /ˈdʒuːəld/ *adj* decorated with jewels: *the famous jewelled eggs of Fabergé*

jew·el·ler *BrE*, **jeweler** *AmE* /ˈdʒuːələ $ -ər/ *n* [C] **1** someone who buys, sells, makes, or repairs jewellery **2 jeweller's** a shop selling jewellery and watches

jew·el·lery *BrE*, **jewelry** *AmE* /ˈdʒuːəlri/ ●●○ *n* [U] small things that you wear for decoration, such as rings or NECKLACES: *She wears a lot of gold jewelry.* → COSTUME JEWELLERY, see picture at BOX¹

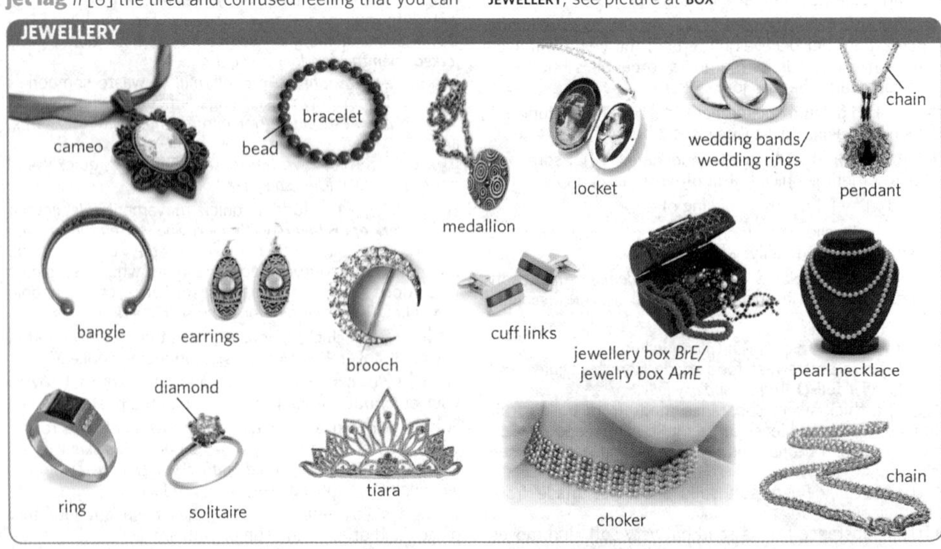

J

GRAMMAR: Countable or uncountable?

• **Jewellery** is an uncountable noun and is not used in the plural. You say: *The thieves stole all my jewellery.*
✗ Don't say: *The thieves stole all my jewelleries.*
• **Jewellery** is always followed by a singular verb: *Their jewellery **is** very fashionable.*
• When talking about one ring, necklace etc, you say a **piece of jewellery** or an **item of jewellery**: *She bought an expensive piece of jewellery.*
GRAMMAR GUIDE ▸ NOUNS

Jew·ish /ˈdʒuːɪʃ/ *adj* relating to Jews or Judaism: *the Jewish religion | My husband is Jewish.*

Jew·ry /ˈdʒuːri/ *n* [U] *old use* the Jewish people

Jez·e·bel /ˈdʒezəbel, -bəl/ *n* [C] *old use* a sexually immoral woman

jib¹ /dʒɪb/ *n* [C] **1** a small sail in front of the large sail on a boat → **mainsail 2** the long part of a CRANE

jib² *v* (**jibbed, jibbing**) [I] *especially BrE* to be unwilling to do or accept something: **[+at]** *He jibbed at the price I asked for.*

jibe¹, **gibe** /dʒaɪb/ *n* [C] an unkind remark intended to make someone seem silly: *She was tired of his cheap jibes.*

jibe² *v* **1** [I] *AmE informal* if two statements, reports etc jibe with each other, the information in them matches: **[+with]** *His report did not jibe with the facts.* **2** [I + at] to say something that is intended to make someone seem silly

jif·fy /ˈdʒɪfi/ (*also* **jiff** /dʒɪf/) *n* **in a jiffy** *spoken* very soon: *I'll be with you in a jiffy.*

ˈJiffy bag *n* [C] *trademark BrE* a thick soft envelope, used for posting things that might break

jig¹ /dʒɪɡ/ *n* [C] **1** a type of quick dance, or a piece of music for this dance **2** a piece of equipment for holding a tool, a piece of wood etc in position

jig² *v* (**jigged, jigging**) [I always + adv/prep] to dance or move up and down with quick short movements

jig·ger /ˈdʒɪɡə $ -ər/ *n* [C] a unit for measuring alcohol, equal to one and a half OUNCES, or the small glass this is measured with

jig·ger·y-po·ker·y /ˌdʒɪɡəri ˈpəʊkəri $ -ˈpoʊ-/ *n* [U] *BrE informal* secret dishonest activity to make something seem what it is not: *There's been some jiggery-pokery with the figures.*

jig·gle /ˈdʒɪɡəl/ *v* [I,T] to make something move from side to side or up and down with short quick movements, or to move like this: *She jiggled the handle of the pram to make the baby stop crying. | 'Wake up,' he said, jiggling up and down on the bed.*

jig·gy /ˈdʒɪɡi/ *adj* **get jiggy** *AmE informal* **a)** to dance with a lot of energy to popular music **b)** to have sex

JIGSAW

jig·saw /ˈdʒɪɡsɔː $ -sɒː/ ●●○ *n* [C]
1 (*also* **ˈjigsaw ˌpuzzle**) a picture cut up into many pieces that you try to fit together
2 [usually singular] a very complicated situation, especially one that you are trying to understand: *As he explained, another **piece of the jigsaw** fell into place.*
3 a tool for cutting out shapes in thin pieces of wood → see picture at TOOL¹

ji·had /dʒɪˈhɑːd, dʒɪˈhæd/ *n* [C] a holy war fought by Muslims, or an occasion when a Muslim has to make some kind of SACRIFICE in his or her life

ji·had·i /dʒɪˈhɑːdi/ (*also* **ji·had·ist** /dʒɪˈhɑːdɪst/) *n* [C] a Muslim who is fighting a holy war

jil·bab /dʒɪlˈbɑːb/ *n* [C] a long piece of clothing with long sleeves that is worn by some Muslim women

jilt /dʒɪlt/ *v* [T] to suddenly end a close romantic relationship with someone: *She jilted her fiancé just before the wedding.*

jim·my /ˈdʒɪmi/ *n* (*plural* **jimmies**) [C] the American form of the word JEMMY —**jimmy** *v* [T]

jin·gle¹ /ˈdʒɪŋɡəl/ *v* [I,T] to shake small metal things together so that they make a sound, or to make this sound: *He jingled his car keys.*

jingle² *n* **1** [C] a short song used in advertisements **2** [singular] the sound of small metal objects being shaken together THESAURUS ▸ SOUND

jin·go·is·m /ˈdʒɪŋɡəʊɪzəm $ -ɡoʊ-/ *n* [U] a strong belief that your own country is better than others – used to show disapproval → **nationalism**: *a mood of warlike jingoism* —**jingoistic** /ˌdʒɪŋɡəʊˈɪstɪk◂ $ -ɡoʊ-/ *adj*

jink /dʒɪŋk/ *v* [I] to change direction suddenly: *He jinked left, then right, throwing the plane into steep and sudden turns.*

jinks /dʒɪŋks/ *n* [U] → HIGH JINKS

jinn /dʒɪn/ *n* [C] a GENIE

jinx /dʒɪŋks/ *n* [singular] someone or something that brings bad luck, or a period of bad luck that results from this: *The company had suffered so many disasters that some employees feared a jinx.*

jinxed /dʒɪŋkst/ *adj* often having bad luck, or making people have bad luck: *They seem to be jinxed when it comes to playing in the UK.*

jit·ter·bug /ˈdʒɪtəbʌɡ $ -ər-/ *n* [singular] a fast JAZZ dance popular in the 1940s

jit·ters /ˈdʒɪtəz $ -ərz/ *n* [plural] *informal* a nervous worried feeling, especially before an important event: *The jitters are worst in the capital, where 61% of people are fearful of a terrorist attack.*

jit·ter·y /ˈdʒɪtəri/ *adj informal* anxious or nervous OPP **relaxed**: *It was probably the tension that made him jittery.* THESAURUS ▸ NERVOUS

jive¹ /dʒaɪv/ *n* **1** [C,U] a very fast dance, popular especially in the 1930s and 1940s, performed to fast JAZZ music **2** [U] *AmE informal* statements that you do not believe are true: *Don't give me any of that jive!*

jive² *v* **1** [I] to dance a jive **2** [T] *AmE informal* to try to make someone believe something that is not true

Jnr *BrE* the written abbreviation of ***junior***, used after the name of a man who has the same name as his father → **Snr**: *Sammy Davis Jnr*

job /dʒɒb $ dʒɑːb/ ●●● S1 W1 AWL *n*
1 WORK [C] the regular paid work that you do for an employer: *Do you enjoy your job? | It was the first paid job I ever had. | He's been in the job for six years. | I'm looking for a new job. | Your pension can be affected if you change jobs.* → JOB DESCRIPTION

REGISTER
In everyday English, people usually ask **What do you do?** or **What does she/he do?** when asking what someone's job is.

2 DUTY [singular] something that you are responsible for doing: *Raising kids can be a difficult job. | **It's my job to** make sure that the work is finished on time. |* **the job of sb/sth** *The job of the jury is to assess the credibility of the witness. |* **the job of doing sth** *I was given the job of making sure that everyone had enough to drink. | All too often councils **fall down on the job*** (=not do what they should) *of keeping the streets clean.*

REGISTER
In written English, people often prefer to use **task** or **duty** rather than **job**, as they sound more formal: *Our first **task** was to prepare the agenda for the meeting.*

3 STH YOU MUST DO [C] a particular thing you have to do, considered as work SYN **task**: *My parents were always*

J

finding little jobs for me to do. | *Filleting fish can be quite a fiddly job.* | *Tiling the bathroom is going to be a* ***big job***. | *Sam does* ***odd jobs*** (=small jobs in the house or garden) *for friends and neighbours.* | **the job of doing sth** *The job of choosing the right computer for you is made easy by this magazine.* | *We need to* ***get on with the job of*** *finding someone to replace him.* | **do a good/great/marvellous etc job** *Whoever did the plastering did a brilliant job.* | **make a good/bad etc job of (doing) sth** *She hates doing the cleaning, but she always makes a good job of it.*

4 on the job a) while you are doing a particular job: *Most clerical training is done on the job.* **b)** doing a particular job: *We've got some of our best people on the job.* **c)** *BrE spoken informal* having sex

5 I'm only/just doing my job *spoken* used to say that it is not your fault if you have to do something in your work that other people do not like

6 it's more than my job's worth *BrE spoken* used to tell someone that you cannot do what they want because you would lose your job if you did – often used humorously

7 do the job *spoken* to have the effect or produce the result that you want: *A little more glue should do the job.*

8 job done *informal* used to say that someone has done something that was necessary, especially quickly and easily: *When we scored three times in the first half, we thought, 'Job done.'*

9 have a job doing sth/have a job to do sth *BrE spoken* to have difficulty doing something: *I think we might have a job parking in town.*

10 do a job on sb/sth *especially AmE informal* to have a damaging effect on someone or something: *The sun does quite a job on people's skin.*

11 COMPUTER [C] an action done by a computer: *a print job*

12 CRIME [C] *informal* a crime in which money is stolen from a bank, company etc: *a bank job* | *Police believe it was an* ***inside job*** (=done by someone who works for the company where the crime happens).

13 a nose/boob job *informal* an operation to improve the appearance of your nose or breasts: *She looks completely different in this photo – she must have had a nose job.*

14 just the job *BrE spoken* exactly what is needed for a particular purpose or situation: *This bag is just the job for carrying your sports gear.*

15 TYPE OF THING [singular] *spoken* used to say that something is of a particular type: *Jack's got a new car – a red two-seater job.*

16 jobs for the boys *BrE* when someone in an important position gives work to their friends, especially when this gives the friends an unfair advantage: *The council chief was suspended over allegations of jobs for the boys.*

17 job of work *BrE* something that you have to do even if you do not enjoy it

18 job lot *BrE* a mixed group of things that are sold together: *a job lot of furniture* → HATCHET JOB, → **(it's a) good job** at GOOD[1](50), → **make the best of a bad job** at BEST[3](9)

J

COLLOCATIONS

VERBS

have a job *Mark doesn't have a job right now.*
apply for a job *I've applied for a job at the university.*
offer sb a job *Well, Miss Taylor, we'd like to offer you the job.*
get/find a job *Eventually, Mary got a job as a waitress.*
land a job (=get a job, especially unexpectedly) *My husband finally landed a job in marketing.*
take a job (=accept a job you are offered) *I was so desperate that I took the first job that came along.*
hold down a job (=keep a job) | **lose your job** | **leave/quit your job** | **be out of a job** (=not have a job)

ADJECTIVES

temporary/permanent *The job is only temporary, but I'm hoping it will be made permanent.*
part-time/full-time *He had a part-time job at the pet shop.*
a steady job (=a job that is likely to continue) *I haven't had a steady job since last March.*
a dead-end job (=a job with low wages and no chance of progress)

job + NOUN

job satisfaction (=the enjoyment you get from your job) *Levels of job satisfaction vary between departments.*
job security (=how permanent your job is likely to be) *As an actor, he has very little job security.*
job losses/cuts *The factory is closing, with 600 job losses.*

THESAURUS

job *n* [C] the regular paid work that you do for an employer: *a full-time job* | *John got a job in a car factory.*
work *n* [U] activities that you are paid for doing – used either when you work for an employer or when you work in your own business: *I started work when I was 18.* | *He graduated from college last year and is still looking for work.*
profession *n* [C] a job for which you need special education and training: *There are now a lot more women in* ***the legal profession***. | *Many teachers are leaving the profession.*
occupation *n* [C] *formal* a job, or a type of job – often used on official documents: *Please give your name, age, and occupation.* | *a traditionally male occupation*
career *n* [C] the work you do or plan to do for most of your life: *I'm interested in a career in journalism.*
position *n* [C] *formal* a particular job within an organization: *I am writing to apply for the position of technical assistant.*
post *n* [C] *formal* a job, especially an important one in a large organization: *She has held the post of managing director for two years.*
vacancy/opening *n* [C] a job that is available for someone to do: *The hospital has been unable to* ***fill*** *the* ***vacancy***. | *There are very few openings in scientific research.*
appointment *n* [C] an important job which someone is asked to do: *He took an appointment as US trade ambassador in Geneva.*
posting *n* [C] a situation in which someone is sent somewhere to do a job for a period of time by the organization they work for: *This was his first posting outside the UK.*
employment *n* [U] the fact of having a job: *The factory will provide employment for local people.*

job·ber /ˈdʒɒbə $ ˈdʒɑːbər/ *n* [C] *especially BrE* someone whose job is buying and selling STOCKS and SHARES → **stockbroker**

job·bing /ˈdʒɒbɪŋ $ ˈdʒɑː-/ *adj BrE* **jobbing builder/gardener/printer etc** someone who does small pieces of work for different people

ˈjob ˌcentre *n* [C] a place run by the British government, where jobs are advertised and training courses are provided for people who are looking for work

ˈjob creˌation *n* [U] the process of making more paid jobs available: *job creation schemes*

ˈjob deˌscription *n* [C] an official list of the work and responsibilities that you have in your job

job·less /ˈdʒɒbləs $ ˈdʒɑːb-/ *adj* **1** without a job SYN **unemployed** THESAURUS UNEMPLOYED **2 the jobless** [plural] people who are jobless

ˈjob ˌseeker *n* [C] *BrE* someone who does not have a job and is looking for one

ˈjob-ˌsharing *n* [U] an arrangement by which two people both work PART-TIME doing the same job —**jobshare** /ˈdʒɒbʃeə $ ˈdʒɑːbʃer/ *n* [C] —**jobshare** *v* [I]

jobs·worth /ˈdʒɒbzwɜːθ $ ˈdʒɑːbzwɜːrθ/ *n* [C] *BrE informal* someone who follows the rules of their job too exactly without using any imagination

jock /dʒɒk $ dʒɑːk/ *n* [C] *informal* **1** *AmE* someone, especially a student, who plays a lot of sport and is often considered to be stupid **2** *BrE* someone from Scotland - sometimes used in an insulting way **3** a DISC JOCKEY

jock·ey¹ /ˈdʒɒki $ ˈdʒɑːki/ *n* [C] someone who rides horses in races

jockey² *v* [I] to compete strongly to get into the best position or situation, or to get the most power: **[+for]** *photographers* ***jockeying for position*** *at the bar | After the war, rival politicians began to jockey for power.*

ˈJockey ˌshorts *n* [plural] *trademark* a type of men's cotton underwear that fits very tightly → **underpants**

jock·strap /ˈdʒɒkstræp $ ˈdʒɑːk-/ *n* [C] a piece of men's underwear that supports their sex organs during sport

joc·u·lar /ˈdʒɒkjələ $ ˈdʒɑːkjələr/ *adj formal* joking or humorous → **jolly**: *He sounded in a jocular mood.* —**jocularly** *adv* —**jocularity** /ˌdʒɒkjəˈlærəti $ ˌdʒɑː-/ *n* [U]

jodh·purs /ˈdʒɒdpəz $ ˈdʒɑːdpərz/ *n* [plural] a special type of trousers that you wear when riding horses

Joe /dʒəʊ $ dʒoʊ/ *n* **1 Joe Public/Bloggs** *BrE*, **Joe Blow/Schmo** *AmE spoken* the ordinary average person **2 Joe College/Citizen etc** *AmE spoken* someone who is a typical example of people in a particular situation or involved in a particular activity

joe·y /ˈdʒəʊi $ ˈdʒoʊi/ *n* [C] a young KANGAROO

jog¹ /dʒɒg $ dʒɑːg/ ●●○ *v* (**jogged**, **jogging**)
1 [I] to run slowly and steadily, especially as a way of exercising: *I* ***go jogging*** *every morning.* THESAURUS ▸ RUN
2 [T] to knock or push something lightly by mistake SYN **bump**: *You jogged my elbow.*
3 jog sb's memory to make someone remember something: *Perhaps this photo will help to jog your memory.*

jog along *phr v informal* to continue in the same way as usual: *We were jogging along comfortably and enjoying our work.*

jog² *n* [singular] **1** a slow steady run, especially done as a way of exercising: *He set off along the riverbank at a jog. | Mike* ***goes for a*** *two-mile* ***jog*** *every morning.* **2** a light knock or push done by accident

jog·ger /ˈdʒɒgə $ ˈdʒɑːgər/ *n* [C] someone who runs slowly and steadily as a way of exercising: *a jogger out for his early morning run*

jog·ging /ˈdʒɒgɪŋ $ ˈdʒɑː-/ ●●○ *n* [U] the activity of running slowly and steadily as a way of exercising

ˈjogging suit *n* [C] loose thick cotton clothes that you wear when you are jogging SYN **sweat suit**

jog·gle /ˈdʒɒgəl $ ˈdʒɑː-/ *v* [I,T] *informal* to shake or move up and down slightly, or to make something move in this way

john /dʒɒn $ dʒɑːn/ *n* [C] *AmE informal* **1** a toilet **2** the customer of a PROSTITUTE

ˌJohn ˈBull *n old-fashioned* **1** [U] England or the English people **2** [C] a typical Englishman, especially one who does not like foreigners

ˌJohn ˈDoe *n* [C,U] *AmE* used especially by the police to refer to a man whose name is not known → JANE DOE

john·ny /ˈdʒɒni $ ˈdʒɑːni/ *n* (*plural* **johnnies**) [C] **1** *BrE informal* a CONDOM **2** *old-fashioned* a man

John o' Groats /ˌdʒɒn ə ˈgrəʊts $ ˌdʒɑːn ə ˈgroʊts/ a place in northeast Scotland that is thought of as the most northern part of the UK, although in fact it is not. It is used especially in the phrase 'from John o' Groats to Land's End', Land's End being thought of as the furthest point in the southwest of the UK.

joie de viv·re /ˌʒwɑː də ˈviːvrə/ *n* [U] a feeling of general pleasure and excitement

join¹ /dʒɔɪn/ ●●● S1 W1 *v*
1 GROUP/ORGANIZATION [T] to become a member of an organization, society, or group: *When did you join the Labour Party? | I decided to join the army. | You can enjoy a sport without joining a club or belonging to a team.*
2 ACTIVITY [T] to begin to take part in an activity that other people are involved in: *Many sacrificed their weekend to join the hunt for the missing girl. | the benefits of joining our pension scheme | Church leaders have joined the campaign to end foxhunting.*
3 GO TO SB [T] to go somewhere in order to be with someone or do something with them: *She joined her aunt in the sitting room. | The immigrants were soon joined by their wives and children.* ⚠ Don't say 'join with' someone. **Join** is always followed by an object in this sense: *I'll join you later.*
4 DO STH TOGETHER [I,T] to do something together with someone else, or as a group: **join sb for sth** *I invited them to join us for a glass of wine.* | **join (with) sb in doing sth** *I'm sure you'll all join me in thanking today's speaker.* | **join (with) sb to do sth** *Parents have joined with health experts to produce a video for bereaved families.* | **join together** *Three police forces have joined together to buy a helicopter.*
5 CONNECT **a)** [T] to connect or fasten things together: *Join the two pieces of wood with strong glue.* | **join sth to sth** *The island is joined to the mainland by a causeway.* **b)** [I,T] if two roads, rivers etc join, they come together and become connected at a particular point: *Finally, we arrived at Dartmouth, where the River Dart joins the sea. | the point where the two roads join*
6 join a queue *BrE*, **join a line** *AmE* to go and stand at the end of a line of people: *He went in and joined the queue for the toilets.*
7 join hands if people join hands, they hold each other's hands: *They joined hands and danced round and round.*
8 join the club *spoken* used to say that you and a lot of other people are in the same situation: *'I'm having difficulty knowing what today's debate is about.' 'Join the club, Geoffrey.'*
9 join battle *formal* to begin fighting
10 be joined in marriage/holy matrimony *formal* to be married
11 be joined at the hip *informal* if two people are joined at the hip, they are always together and are very friendly - often used to show disapproval → **join/combine forces** at FORCE¹(10), → **if you can't beat 'em, join 'em** at BEAT¹(23)

join in (sth) *phr v* to take part in something that a group of people are doing or that someone else does: *In the evening there was a barbecue, with the whole village* ***joining in the fun****. | He stared at them without joining in the conversation. | He laughed loudly, and Mattie joined in.*

join up *phr v*
1 to become a member of the army, navy, or air force
2 *BrE* to connect things, or to become connected: **join sth ↔ up** *The dots are joined up by a line.*

join up with sb/sth *phr v* to combine with or meet other people in order to do something: *Three months ago, they joined up with another big company that sells arms.*

join² *n* [C] a place where two parts of an object are connected or fastened together: *It's been glued back together so well you can hardly see the join.*

joined-ˈup *adj* [only before noun] *BrE* **1** joined-up writing has all the letters in each word connected to each other **2** joined-up systems, institutions etc combine different groups, ideas, or parts in a way that works well: ***joined-up government*** | *the need for* ***joined-up thinking*** *between departments*

join·er /ˈdʒɔɪnə $ -ər/ *n* [C] someone who makes wooden doors, window frames etc → CARPENTER

join·er·y /ˈdʒɔɪnəri/ *n* [U] the trade and work of a joiner → CARPENTRY

joint¹ /dʒɔɪnt/ ●●○ S3 W2 *adj* [only before noun]
1 involving two or more people or groups, or owned or shared by them: *The two ministers have issued a* ***joint statement****. | Both companies are involved in the* ***joint development*** *of a new medium-sized car. | The meal was a* ***joint effort*** (=two or more people worked on it together). | *Manchester United and Arsenal are* ***joint favourites*** *to win the title* (=are thought to have the same chance of winning). | *Both parties must sign the form if the account is to be* ***in joint names*** (=belong to two named people).

2 joint venture a business activity begun by two or more people or companies working together
3 joint resolution *law* a decision or law agreed by both houses of the US Congress and signed by the president —**jointly** *adv*: *tenants who are jointly responsible for their rent*

joint² *n* [C] **1** a part of your body that can bend because two bones meet there: **knee/neck/hip/elbow etc joint** *a permanently damaged knee joint* **2** *BrE* a large piece of meat, usually containing a bone: **[+of]** *a joint of beef* **3** a place where two things or parts of an object are joined together: *What should I use to seal the joint between the carport roof and the house wall?* **4 out of joint a)** if a bone in your body is out of joint, it has been pushed out of its correct position **b)** if a system, group etc is out of joint, it is not working properly: *Something is out of joint in our society.* → **put sb's nose out of joint** at NOSE¹(15) **5** *informal* a cheap bar, club, or restaurant: *a hamburger joint* → CLIP JOINT **6** *informal* a cigarette containing CANNABIS SYN **spliff** → **case the joint** at CASE²(2)

joint³ *v* [T] to cut meat into joints

joint·ed /ˈdʒɔɪntɪd/ *adj* having joints and able to move and bend: *a jointed puppet*

ˌjoint ˈhonours *n* [U] a university degree course in Britain in which two main subjects are studied → **single honours**

ˌjoint-ˈstock ˌcompany *n* [C] *AmE* a company that is owned by all the people with SHARES in it

joist /dʒɔɪst/ *n* [C] one of the beams that support a floor or ceiling

joke¹ /dʒəʊk $ dʒoʊk/ ●●● S2 W3 *n* [C]
1 something that you say or do to make people laugh, especially a funny story or trick: **[+about]** *a joke about absent-minded professors* | *I couldn't go out with someone **for a joke**, could you?*
2 be a joke *informal* to be completely useless, stupid, or unreasonable: *The whole meeting was a joke.*
3 go/get/be beyond a joke a situation that has got beyond a joke has become serious and worrying: *This rain's getting beyond a joke – let's go inside.*
4 sth is no joke used to emphasize that a situation is serious or that someone really means what they say: *The risk he's taking is no joke.* | *It's no joke bringing up a child on your own.*
5 sb can take a joke used to say that someone is able to laugh at jokes about themselves: *Your problem is you just can't take a joke.*
6 make a joke (out) of sth to treat something serious as if it was intended to be funny: *He could not bring himself to apologise. Instead, he tried to make a joke of it.*
7 sb's idea of a joke *spoken* a situation that someone else thinks is funny but you do not: *Look, if this is your idea of a joke, I don't find it at all funny.*
8 the joke's on sb used to say that something has happened to make someone seem stupid, especially when they were trying to make other people seem stupid
→ IN-JOKE, PRACTICAL JOKE, → **standing joke** at STANDING¹(3)

COLLOCATIONS

VERBS

tell a joke (=repeat a funny story) *He was always telling jokes and making people laugh.*
make a joke (*also* **crack a joke**) (=say something intended to be funny) *He was cracking jokes and seemed relaxed and happy.*
get a joke (=understand a joke and find it funny) *She never gets my jokes.*
laugh at sb's jokes | **play a joke on sb** (=trick someone to make people laugh)

ADJECTIVES

a good/funny joke *I heard a really good joke the other day.*
a bad/terrible joke (=not funny) *Dad was known for his bad jokes.*
a cruel/sick joke (=very unkind) | **an old joke** | **a dirty joke** (=about sex) | **a practical joke** (=that involves tricking someone) | **an inside/a private joke** (=that only a few people who are involved in something will understand)

PHRASES

a joke falls flat (=people don't find a joke funny) *His practical jokes usually fell flat.*
be the butt of a joke (=be the person a joke is made about, so that people laugh at you)

COMMON ERRORS

⚠ Don't say 'say a joke'. Say **tell a joke**.

joke² ●●● S3 *v* [I]
1 to say things that are intended to be funny and that you do not really mean: **[+about]** *I never joke about money.* | **[+with]** *As we left the hospital, he joked with the staff.* | **joke that** *His father joked that his son was trying to put him out of business.* | *Calm down, Jo, I was **only joking**.*
2 you're joking/you must be joking (*also* **you've got to be joking**) *spoken* used to tell someone that what they are suggesting is so strange or silly that you cannot believe that they are serious: *'Tell him.' 'You must be joking – he'd never believe me.'*
3 joking apart/aside *BrE* used before you say something serious after you have been joking —**jokingly** *adv*

jok·er /ˈdʒəʊkə $ ˈdʒoʊkər/ *n* [C] **1** *informal* someone who behaves in a way you think is stupid: *Look at that joker – he's doing 25 miles an hour at the most.* **2** a PLAYING CARD that has no fixed value and is only used in some card games **3** someone who makes a lot of jokes **4 the joker in the pack** something or someone whose effect on future events cannot be known

jok·ey, **joky** /ˈdʒəʊki $ ˈdʒoʊ-/ *adj informal* not serious, and tending to make people laugh OPP **serious**: *Dave was a sweet man, very jokey about everything.* —**jokily** *adv* —**jokiness** *n* [U]

jol·lies /ˈdʒɒliz $ ˈdʒɑː-/ *n* **get your jollies** *AmE spoken* to get pleasure from a particular experience or activity, especially a strange activity

jol·li·fi·ca·tion /ˌdʒɒlɪfɪˈkeɪʃən $ ˌdʒɑː-/ *n* [C,U] *old-fashioned* fun and enjoyment

jol·li·ty /ˈdʒɒləti $ ˈdʒɑː-/ (*also* **jollities** [plural]) *n* [U] *formal* when people are happy and enjoying themselves: *a night of riotous jollity*

jol·ly¹ /ˈdʒɒli $ ˈdʒɑːli/ *adj especially BrE* **1** happy and enjoying yourself: *Everybody was in a very relaxed and jolly mood.* **2** *old-fashioned* very pleasant and enjoyable: *We had a jolly time with the family.*

jolly² *adv BrE old-fashioned informal* **1** very: *Sounds like a **jolly good** idea to me.* | *It was all **jolly good fun**.* **2 jolly well** used to emphasize an opinion or to show that you are annoyed: *Right, I'm going to clear up, and you can jolly well help me.* **3 jolly good!** *spoken* used to say that you are pleased by what someone has just said

jolly³ *v* (**jollied**, **jollying**, **jollies**) *BrE*
jolly sb **along** *phr v* to try to make someone do something faster by encouraging them: *He jollied people along and got useful information out of them.*
jolly sb **into** sth *phr v informal* to gently persuade someone to do something: *She jollied the children into going for a walk.*
jolly sth ↔ **up** *phr v* to make an event or place more pleasant or exciting

ˌJolly ˈRoger *n* [singular] a black flag with a picture of bones on it, used in the past by PIRATES SYN **skull and crossbones**

jolt¹ /dʒəʊlt $ dʒoʊlt/ *v* **1** [I,T] to move suddenly and roughly, or to make someone or something move in this way SYN **jerk**: *We jolted along rough wet roads through an endless banana plantation.* **2** [T] to give someone a sudden shock or surprise: *The phone jolted him awake.* | **jolt sb into/out of sth** *It jolted me into making the decision to quit.* | *Her sharp words seemed to jolt him out of his depression.*

jolt² *n* [C usually singular] **1** a sudden shock: **[+of]** *Melanie* *experienced a jolt of surprise.* | **with a jolt** *Henry sat up with a jolt.* | *The oil crisis has* ***given*** *the government quite* ***a jolt.*** **2** a sudden rough shaking movement: *People felt the first jolt of the earthquake at about 8 am.*

Jones·es /ˈdʒəʊnzɪz $ ˈdʒoʊn-/ *n* → **keep up with the Joneses** at KEEP UP

josh /dʒɒʃ $ dʒɑːʃ/ *v* [I,T] *old-fashioned* to talk to someone or laugh at them in a gentle joking way: *The guys josh him and call him an egghead.*

joss stick /ˈdʒɒs ˌstɪk $ ˈdʒɑːs-/ *n* [C] a stick of INCENSE

jos·tle /ˈdʒɒsəl $ ˈdʒɑː-/ *v* **1** [I,T] to push or knock against someone in a crowd, especially so that you can get somewhere or do something before other people: **[+for]** *Followers of the president jostled for position in front of the TV cameras.* **2** [I] to compete for something such as attention or a reward: *A thousand thoughts were jostling around inside my mind.*

jot[1] /dʒɒt $ dʒɑːt/ *v* (**jotted**, **jotting**)

jot sth ↔ **down** *phr v* to write a short piece of information quickly: *Let me jot down your number and I'll call you tomorrow.*

jot[2] *n* **not a jot** *old-fashioned* not at all or none at all: *There was not a jot of humour in the man.*

jot·ter /ˈdʒɒtə $ ˈdʒɑːtər/ *n* [C] *BrE* a small book for writing notes in SYN **notebook**

jot·tings /ˈdʒɒtɪŋz $ ˈdʒɑː-/ *n* [plural] *informal* short notes, usually written to remind yourself about something: *her private jottings*

joule /dʒuːl $ dʒuːl, dʒaʊl/ *n* [C] (*written abbreviation* **J**) a unit for measuring energy or work

jour·nal /ˈdʒɜːnl $ -ɜːr-/ ●●○ AWL *n* [C]

1 a serious magazine produced for professional people or those with a particular interest: *the British Medical Journal*

2 a written record that you make of the things that happen to you each day SYN **diary**: *He decided to* ***keep*** *a* ***journal***.

jour·nal·ese /ˌdʒɜːnəlˈiːz $ -ɜːr-/ *n* [U] language that is typical of newspapers

jour·nal·is·m /ˈdʒɜːnəl-ɪzəm $ -ɜːr-/ ●●○ *n* [U] the job or activity of writing news reports for newspapers, magazines, television, or radio: *a career in journalism* | *The hospital has been the target of* ***investigative journalism*** (=journalism that examines an event or situation in order to find out the truth).

jour·nal·ist /ˈdʒɜːnəl-ɪst $ -ɜːr-/ ●●● W3 *n* [C] someone who writes news reports for newspapers, magazines, television, or radio → **reporter**: *a well-known journalist and broadcaster* —**journalistic** /ˌdʒɜːnəlˈɪstɪk◂ $ -ɜːr-/ *adj* [only before noun]: *journalistic skills*

jour·ney[1] /ˈdʒɜːni $ -ɜːr-/ ●●● S3 W2 *n* [C]

1 *especially BrE* an occasion when you travel from one place to another, especially over a long distance SYN **trip** *AmE*: **[+to/from/between]** *my journey to China* | **[+through/across etc]** *a journey across Europe* | *the friends they made* ***on the journey***

2 *literary* a long and often difficult process by which someone or something changes and develops: *our journey through life* | *The novel is an account of his spiritual journey.*

COLLOCATIONS

VERBS

make a journey *I still use my car, but now I make fewer journeys.*

go on a journey (=make a long journey) *We are going on a journey to a strange country.*

begin/start a journey *He began the journey home across London.*

set off on a journey (*also* **embark on a journey** *formal*) (=start a long journey) | **break your journey** (=make a short stop on a journey) | **continue your journey**

ADJECTIVES/NOUN + journey

a car/plane/bus etc journey *the six-hour train journey to London*

a long journey *They arrived tired from their long journey.*

a difficult journey *It was a difficult journey, especially in the winter months.*

a safe journey (=used especially to wish someone a good journey) *Have a safe journey.*

an epic journey (=a very long and eventful journey) | **a wasted journey** (=one that did not achieve the result you wanted) | **the outward journey** (=the journey to a place) | **the return journey** (=the journey back from a place) | **the homeward journey** (=the journey back home)

PHRASES

a leg/stage of a journey (=one part of a journey) *We set off on the final leg of our journey.*

THESAURUS

journey *especially BrE* an occasion when you travel from one place to another – used especially about travelling a long distance, or travelling somewhere regularly: *The journey took us over three hours.* | *My journey to work normally takes around 30 minutes.*

trip a journey to visit a place: *How about a trip to the seaside on Saturday?* | *a business trip*

tour a journey for pleasure, during which you visit several different towns, areas etc: *Last summer we went on a tour of Europe.*

excursion a short journey by a group of people to visit a place, especially while they are on holiday: *The cost of the holiday includes excursions to nearby places of interest.*

expedition a long and carefully organized journey, especially to a dangerous or unfamiliar place: *Scott's expedition to the Antarctic* | *a military expedition*

commute the journey to and from work that someone does every day: *People are fed up with the daily commute on overcrowded trains.*

pilgrimage /ˈpɪlgrəmɪdʒ/ a journey to a holy place for religious reasons: *the annual pilgrimage to Mecca*

trek a long journey, for example over mountains or through forests, especially one that people do on foot for pleasure: *a two-week trek across the Atlas Mountains*

travel *n* [U] the general activity of moving from one place to another: *Her new job involves a lot of travel.*

sb's travels *n* [plural] someone's journeys to or in places that are far away: *I'm longing to hear all about your travels in China.*

BY PLANE/BOAT/CAR/BICYCLE ETC

flight a journey by air: *You should check in at the airport two hours before your flight.*

voyage /ˈvɔɪ-ɪdʒ/ a long journey over the sea: *MacArthur's epic round-the-world voyage*

crossing a short journey by boat from one piece of land to another: *A 30-minute ferry crossing takes you to the island.*

cruise a journey by boat for pleasure: *a Mediterranean cruise* | *a cruise down the Nile*

drive a journey in a car, often for pleasure: *The drive through the mountains was absolutely beautiful.*

ride a short journey in a car, or on a bicycle or horse: *It's a twenty-minute taxi ride to the station.* | *a bike ride*

journey[2] *v* [I always + adv/prep] *literary* to travel: *They left the town and journeyed south.* THESAURUS ▸ TRAVEL

jour·ney·man /ˈdʒɜːnimən $ -ɜːr-/ *n* (*plural* **journeymen** /-mən/) [C] *old-fashioned* **1** a trained worker who works for someone else **2** an experienced worker whose work is acceptable but not excellent

jour·no /ˈdʒɜːnəʊ $ ˈdʒɜːrnoʊ/ *n* (*plural* **journos**) [C] *BrE informal* a JOURNALIST

joust /dʒaʊst/ *v* [I] **1** to fight with LANCES (=long sticks) while riding horses, as part of a formal competition in the past **2** to compete or argue with someone: **[+with]** *The*

J

minister and I have often jousted with each other. —**joust** *n* [C]

Jove /dʒəʊv $ dʒoʊv/ *n* **by Jove!** *BrE old-fashioned* used to express surprise or to emphasize something: *By Jove, you're right!*

jo·vi·al /ˈdʒəʊviəl $ ˈdʒoʊ-/ *adj* friendly and happy: *He addressed me in a jovial manner.* —**jovially** *adv* —**joviality** /ˌdʒəʊviˈæləti $ ˌdʒoʊ-/ *n* [U]

jowl /dʒaʊl/ *n* [C usually plural] the skin that covers your lower jaw on either side of your face: *a man with* ***heavy jowls*** (=jowls that hang down slightly) → **cheek by jowl** at CHEEK[1](3)

joy[1] /dʒɔɪ/ ●●● W3 *n*

1 [U] great happiness and pleasure: *the look of joy on her face* | **with/for joy** *I leaped into the air with joy.* | *She wept for joy.* | *I didn't exactly* ***jump for joy*** (=I was not very pleased) *when I heard the news.* **THESAURUS** ▸ PLEASURE

> **REGISTER**
> **Joy** is used especially in literature. In everyday English, rather than say they did something **with joy**, people usually say that they were **(really) pleased/happy/glad** to do it: *Thank you for your letter. I was* ***really pleased*** *to get it.*

2 [C] something or someone that gives you happiness and pleasure: **[+of]** *one of the joys of travelling alone* | *The garden was his* ***pride and joy***. | **be a joy to watch/drive/use etc** *The children's singing was a joy to listen to.*

3 no joy *BrE spoken* if you have no joy, you do not succeed in getting something: *I phoned the pub, but no joy. The landlord didn't know where she was.*

> **COLLOCATIONS**
>
> **PHRASES**
>
> **be filled with joy/be full of joy** *I was full of joy at the thought of seeing her again.*
> **tears of joy** *She began to cry again, but they were tears of joy.*
> **a feeling of joy** *A feeling of total joy swept over him.*
> **a sense of joy** | **a look of joy** | **shouts/cries of joy**
>
> **ADJECTIVES**
>
> **great joy** *To her great joy, she became the mother of two beautiful baby girls.*
> **pure/sheer/complete joy** (=a lot of joy, not mixed with other feelings) *It was a moment of pure joy.*
> **overwhelming joy** *formal* (=very great joy) | **true/real joy**
>
> **VERBS**
>
> **bring joy to sb** (=make someone feel joy) *Her children have brought her great joy.*
> **give (sb) joy** *His music has given people a lot of joy over the years.*
> **feel/experience joy** *He had never felt the joy of watching the seasons come and go.*
> **be jumping for joy** (=be very pleased about something) *She tried to stay calm, but she was secretly jumping for joy.*
> **express your joy** (=show it)

joy[2] *v* [I] *literary* to be happy because of something

joy·ful /ˈdʒɔɪfəl/ *adj* very happy, or likely to make people very happy OPP **joyless**: *Christmas is a joyful occasion for children.* | *the joyful news* —**joyfully** *adv* —**joyfulness** *n* [U]

joy·less /ˈdʒɔɪləs/ *adj* without any happiness at all OPP **joyful**: *a joyless marriage* —**joylessly** *adv*

joy·ous /ˈdʒɔɪəs/ *adj literary* very happy, or likely to make people very happy: *a joyous occasion* | *Our music is a joyous celebration of life.* —**joyously** *adv* —**joyousness** *n* [U]

joy·rid·ing /ˈdʒɔɪˌraɪdɪŋ/ *n* [U] the crime of stealing a car and driving it in a fast and dangerous way for fun —**joyride** *v* [I] —**joyrider** *n* [C]

joy·stick /ˈdʒɔɪˌstɪk/ *n* [C] an upright handle that you use to control something such as an aircraft or a computer game

JP /ˌdʒeɪ ˈpiː/ *n* [C] the abbreviation of ***Justice of the Peace*** SYN **magistrate**

JPEG (*also* **JPG**) /ˈdʒeɪ peg/ *n* [C] *technical* (***Joint Photographic Experts Group***) a type of computer FILE used on the Internet that contains pictures, photographs, or other images → **MPEG**

Jr. *AmE* the written abbreviation of ***junior***, used after the name of a man who has the same name as his father → **Sr.**: *Alan Parks, Jr.*

jub·i·lant /ˈdʒuːbələnt/ *adj* extremely happy and pleased because of a success: *Radicals were jubilant at getting rid of him.* | *The fans were in jubilant mood as they left the stadium.* —**jubilantly** *adv*

ju·bi·la·tion /ˌdʒuːbəˈleɪʃən/ *n* [U] *formal* happiness and pleasure because you have been successful: *There was jubilation that a local team had come first.*

ju·bi·lee /ˈdʒuːbəliː, ˌdʒuːbəˈliː/ *n* [C] a date that is celebrated because it is exactly 25 years, 50 years etc after an important event → DIAMOND JUBILEE, GOLDEN JUBILEE, SILVER JUBILEE

Ju·da·is·m /ˈdʒuːdeɪ-ɪzəm, ˈdʒuːdə- $ ˈdʒuːdə-, ˈdʒuːdi-/ *n* [U] the Jewish religion based on the sacred books known as the Hebrew Scriptures. These writings contain many of the books that are also in the Old Testament of the Christian BIBLE. —**Judaic** /dʒuːˈdeɪ-ɪk/ *adj*

Ju·das /ˈdʒuːdəs/ *n* [C] someone who is not loyal to a friend SYN **traitor**

jud·der /ˈdʒʌdə $ -ər/ *v* [I] if a vehicle or machine judders, it shakes violently: *The engine juddered to life.* —**judder** *n* [C]

judge[1] /dʒʌdʒ/ ●●● S2 W2 *n* [C]

1 the official in control of a court, who decides how criminals should be punished: *The trial judge specifies the number of years to be spent in prison.* | **federal judge/high court judge etc** (=a judge in a particular court)

2 someone who decides on the result of a competition: *The panel of judges included several well-known writers.* → see picture at UMPIRE[1]

3 a good/bad judge of sth someone whose opinion on something is usually right or wrong: *Sandra's a very good judge of character.*

4 be the judge (of sth) to be the person whose opinion on something matters or is accepted: *No one else can say what its value to you is – only you can be the judge of that.*

5 let me be the judge of that *spoken* used to tell someone angrily that you do not need their advice

6 be judge and jury (*also* **act as judge and jury**) to make or have the power to make an important decision affecting someone by yourself – used showing disapproval

7 as sober as a judge someone who is as sober as a judge is not drunk at all

judge[2] ●●● S3 W3 *v* (**judged, judging**)

1 OPINION [I,T] to form or give an opinion about someone or something after thinking carefully about all the information you know about them: *You should never judge a person by their looks.* | *Judge us on the improvements we make in the economy.* | *The therapist* ***judged that*** *Margaret had made a serious attempt to kill herself.* | *pollutants that were judged hazardous to human health* | *I am in no position to* ***judge whether*** *what she is doing is right or wrong.* | *The economic results of the reforms are very* ***difficult to judge***. | *The likelihood of future bombs was* ***impossible to judge***. | *We* ***judge the success of*** *a product by the number of sales it brings in.* | *His conduct,* ***judged objectively*** *by what he has done, is dishonest.* | *Robert wanted to go and help him, but* ***judged it best to*** *stay where he was.* | *Do not* ***judge*** *her too* ***harshly***, *as she was very young at the time.*

2 judging by/from sth used to say that you are making a guess based on what you have just seen, heard, or learned: *Judging by his jovial manner, he must have enjoyed his meal.* | *Judging from what you say in your letter, you don't sound well.*

3 COMPETITION [I,T] to decide on the result of a competition: *I had the difficult task of judging the competition.* | **judge sb on sth** *Competitors will be judged on speed and accuracy.*

4 CRITICIZE [I,T] to form an opinion about someone, especially in an unfair or criticizing way: *He just accepts people for what they are and he doesn't judge them.*
5 LAW [T] to decide whether someone is guilty of a crime in court
6 it's not for sb to judge used to say that you do not think someone has the right to give their opinion about something: *Was it the right decision? It's not for us to judge.*
7 as far as I can judge used to say that you think what you are saying is true, but you are not sure
8 don't judge a book by its cover used to say that you should not form an opinion based only on the way something looks

judg·ment (*also* **judgement** *BrE*) /ˈdʒʌdʒmənt/ ●●○ W2 *n*
1 OPINION [C,U] an opinion that you form, especially after thinking carefully about something: *It's too soon to* ***make a judgment*** *about what the outcome will be.* | *In my judgment, we should accept his offer.* | **pass judgment (on sth)** (=give your opinion, especially a negative one) *Our aim is to help him, not to pass judgment on what he has done.* | *I'd advise you to* ***reserve judgment*** (=not decide your opinion before you have all the facts). | **against your better judgment** (=even though you do not think it is a sensible thing to do) *I lent him the money, against my better judgment.*
2 ABILITY TO DECIDE [U] the ability to make sensible decisions about what to do and when to do it: *I've known him for years and I trust his judgment.* | **professional/personal etc judgment** *The minister showed a lack of political judgment.* | *a decision based on* ***sound judgment*** (=good judgment) | *Watch carefully and* ***use*** *your* ***judgment***. → **error of judgment** at ERROR(3)
3 LAW [C,U] an official decision given by a judge or a court of law: *The company were fined £6 million, following a recent* ***court judgment***.
4 a judgment (on sb/sth) *formal* something bad that happens to someone and seems like a punishment for the things they have done wrong
5 judgment call *AmE informal* a decision you have to make yourself because there are no fixed rules in a situation → LAST JUDGMENT, VALUE JUDGMENT, → **sit in judgment** at SIT(10)

judg·ment·al (*also* **judgemental** *BrE*) /dʒʌdʒˈmentl/ *adj* criticizing people very quickly – used to show disapproval

ˌJudgment Day, **Judgement Day** *n* [singular, not with 'the'] (*also* **the day of judgment**) the last day of the world when all people will be judged by God for what they have done, according to Christianity and some other religions

ju·di·ca·ture /ˈdʒuːdəkətʃə $ -ər/ *n* **the judicature** *formal* judges as a group, and the organization, power etc of the law

ju·di·cial /dʒuːˈdɪʃəl/ *adj* relating to the law, judges, or their decisions → **legislative**: *the judicial system* —**judicially** *adv*

ju·di·cia·ry /dʒuːˈdɪʃəri $ -ʃieri, -ʃəri/ *n* **the judiciary** *formal* all the judges in a country who, as a group, form part of the system of government

ju·di·cious /dʒuːˈdɪʃəs/ *adj formal* done in a sensible and careful way SYN **wise**: *a judicious choice* —**judiciously** *adv*

ju·do /ˈdʒuːdəʊ $ -doʊ/ ●●○ *n* [U] a Japanese sport or method of defence, in which you try to throw your opponent onto the ground → **black belt**

jug /dʒʌg/ ●●○ *n* [C]
1 *BrE* a container with a wide curved opening at the top and a handle, used especially at meals for pouring liquids SYN **pitcher** *AmE*: *a milk jug*
2 *AmE* a deep round container with a very narrow opening at the top and a handle, used for holding liquids SYN **pitcher** *BrE*
3 (*also* **jugful** /ˈdʒʌgfʊl/) the amount of liquid that a jug will hold: **[+of]** *a jug of water*
4 jugs [plural] *not polite* a woman's breasts

JUG

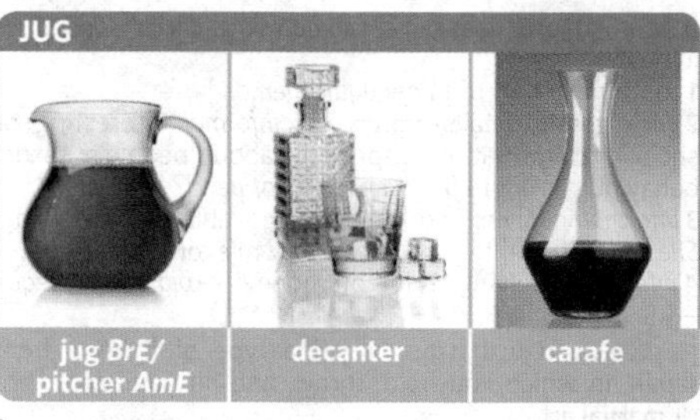
jug *BrE*/ pitcher *AmE* | decanter | carafe

jug·ger·naut /ˈdʒʌgənɔːt $ -ərnɒːt/ *n* [C] **1** *BrE* a very large vehicle that carries goods over long distances SYN **semi** *AmE* **2** a very powerful force, organization etc whose effect or influence cannot be stopped: *the juggernaut of industrialization*

jug·gle /ˈdʒʌgəl/ ●●○ *v*
1 [I,T] to keep three or more objects moving through the air by throwing and catching them very quickly: **[+with]** *One guy was juggling with five balls.*
2 [I,T] to try to fit two or more jobs, activities etc into your life, especially with difficulty: **juggle sth (with sth)** *It's hard trying to juggle a job with kids and the housework.*
3 [T] to change things or arrange them in the way you want, or in a way that makes it possible for you to do something: **juggle sth around** *If I juggle these appointments around, I can fit you in.*
→ **balancing/juggling act** at ACT[1](12)

JUGGLE

jug·gler /ˈdʒʌglə $ -ər/ *n* [C] someone who juggles objects in the air, especially to entertain people

jug·gling /ˈdʒʌgəlɪŋ/ *n* [U] **1** the skill of keeping three or more objects moving through the air by throwing and catching them: *a display of juggling* → see picture at JUGGLE **2** the practice of changing things or arranging them in a way that makes it possible for you to do something: *It took a lot of juggling and rearrangement of figures before the loan was approved.* **3** when someone who has a good job in a profession they have trained for is also secretly involved in an illegal activity

jug·u·lar /ˈdʒʌgjələ $ -ər/ *n* [C usually singular] **1 jugular vein** the large VEIN in your neck that takes blood from your head back to your heart **2 go for the jugular** *informal* to criticize or attack someone very strongly, especially in order to harm them

juice[1] /dʒuːs/ ●●● S2 *n*
1 [C,U] the liquid that comes from fruit and vegetables, or a drink that is made from this: *a* ***carton of*** *orange* ***juice*** | *A Coke and a tomato juice, please.*
2 [C usually plural] the liquid that comes out of meat when it is cooked
3 gastric/digestive juice(s) the liquid inside your stomach that helps you to DIGEST food
4 [U] *informal* something that produces power, such as petrol or electricity: *Okay, turn on the juice.* → **stew in your own juice** at STEW[2](2)

juice[2] *v* [T] to get the juice out of fruit or vegetables
juice sth ↔ **up** *phr v AmE informal* to make something more interesting or exciting

ˈjuice bar *n* [C] a sort of café that serves drinks made from freshly pressed fruit

juiced /dʒuːst/ *adj* [not before noun] *AmE informal* **1** (*also* **juiced up**) excited **2** *old-fashioned* drunk

juic·er /ˈdʒuːsə $ -ər/ *n* [C] a kitchen tool used for getting juice out of fruit

J

juic·y /ˈdʒuːsi/ ●●○ *adj* (*comparative* **juicier**, *superlative* **juiciest**)
1 containing a lot of juice: *a juicy lemon*
2 juicy gossip/details/stories etc *informal* interesting or shocking information, especially about people's sexual behaviour: *Want to hear a juicy bit of news?*
3 *informal* involving work that is enjoyable and satisfying: *She's been trying to get a really juicy role for years.*
4 *informal* involving a lot of money: *a big juicy cheque* —**juiciness** *n* [U]

ju·jit·su /dʒuːˈdʒɪtsuː/ *n* [U] a type of fighting from Japan, in which you hold, throw, and hit your opponent → **martial art**

juke·box /ˈdʒuːkbɒks $ -bɑːks/ *n* [C] a machine in bars, restaurants etc that plays music when you put money in it

ˈjukebox ˌmusical *n* [C] a play that includes the songs of one particular group or singer: *'Mamma Mia!' is a jukebox musical based on the songs of ABBA.*

ju·li·enne /ˌdʒuːliˈen◂/ *adj* julienne vegetables have been cut into narrow pieces: *The lamb is served with julienne carrots.* —**julienne** *v* [T]

Ju·ly /dʒʊˈlaɪ/ ●●● S2 W3 *n* (*plural* **Julies**) [C,U] (*written abbreviation* **Jul.**) the seventh month of the year, between June and August: **next/last July** *Laura came over to England last July.* | **in July** *I plan to graduate in July.* | **on July 6th** *Two months later, on July 6th, he fired Owens.* | **on 6th July** *BrE*: *'When's the concert?' 'On 6th July.'* | **July 6** *AmE*: *The competition ends July 6.*

jum·ble¹ /ˈdʒʌmbəl/ *n* **1** [singular] a lot of different things mixed together in an untidy way, without any order: **[+of]** *a jumble of old toys* | *Inside, she was a jumble of emotions.* **2** [U] *BrE* things to be sold at a jumble sale SYN **rummage** *AmE*

jumble² (*also* **jumble up**) *v* [T] to mix things together in an untidy way, without any order: *The photographs were all jumbled up.* | *Ben's words became jumbled.* GRAMMAR **Jumble** is usually passive. THESAURUS ▶ **MIX**

ˈjumble sale *n* [C] *BrE* a sale of used clothes, books etc in order to get money for a local church, school etc SYN **rummage sale** *AmE*

jum·bo /ˈdʒʌmbəʊ $ -boʊ/ *adj* [only before noun] *informal* larger than other things of the same type: *jumbo-sized hot dogs*

ˈjumbo jet (*also* **jumbo**) *n* [C] a very large plane for carrying passengers

JUMP

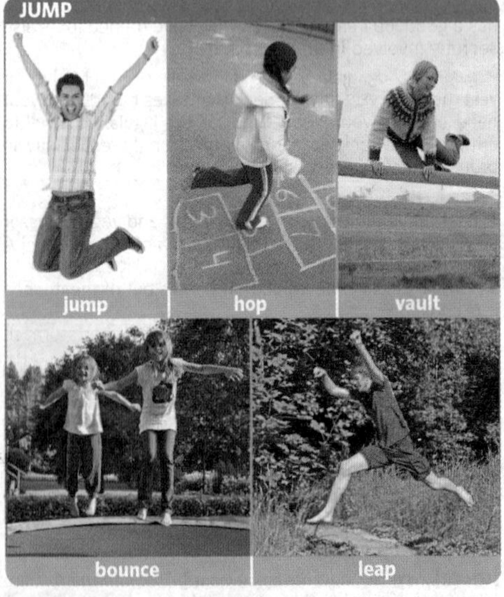

jump¹ /dʒʌmp/ ●●● S2 W3 *v*
1 UPWARDS **a)** [I] to push yourself up into the air, or over or away from something etc, using your legs: *How high can you jump?* | **jump over/across/onto etc sth** *He jumped over the wall and ran off.* | *Fans were* ***jumping up and down*** (=jumping repeatedly) *and cheering.* | **jump clear (of sth)** (=jump out of danger) *We managed to jump clear of the car before it hit the wall.* **b)** [T] to go over or across something by jumping: *He jumped the gate, landing on the concrete.* → see picture at **JUMP¹**
2 DOWNWARDS [I] to let yourself drop from a place that is above the ground: *The cats* ***jumped down*** *and came to meet us.* | **jump from/out of/onto etc sth** *Three people saved themselves by jumping from the window.*
3 MOVE FAST [I always + adv/prep] to move quickly or suddenly in a particular direction SYN **leap**: **[+up/back/in etc]** *Matt jumped up to answer the phone.* | *We all jumped in a taxi.* | *She* ***jumped to*** *her* ***feet*** *and left.*
4 IN FEAR/SURPRISE [I] to make a quick sudden movement because you are surprised or frightened: *Marcia jumped. 'What's that noise?'* | *Sorry, I didn't mean to* ***make*** *you* ***jump*** (=surprise or frighten you). | *Don't shout. I nearly* ***jumped out of*** *my* ***skin*** (=was very shocked or frightened)!
5 INCREASE [I] to increase or improve suddenly and by a large amount: **jump (from …) to sth** *Profits jumped to £2.6 million last year.* | *Norway jumped from ninth to third place.* ⚠ Do not say that an amount, level, price etc 'jumps up'. Say that it **jumps**.
6 KEEP CHANGING [I,T] to change quickly and often from one idea, place, position etc to another – used to show disapproval: **jump from sth to sth** *Cathy kept jumping from one topic to another.* | **jump about/around (sth)** *I've been jumping about the file instead of working straight through it.*
7 MISS A STAGE [I,T] to move suddenly to a further part of a book, discussion etc leaving out the part in between: *I'm afraid I jumped a couple of chapters.* | **[+to]** *The movie suddenly* ***jumped ahead*** *to the future.*
8 MACHINE [I] if a machine or piece of equipment jumps, it moves suddenly because something is wrong with it: *Why does the video keep jumping like this?*
9 ATTACK [T] *informal* to attack someone suddenly: *Somebody jumped him in the park last night.*
10 jump to conclusions to form an opinion about something before you have all the facts: *There may be a simple explanation. Let's not jump to conclusions.*
11 jump the gun to start doing something too soon, especially without thinking about it carefully
12 jump for joy to be extremely happy and pleased
13 jump down sb's throat *informal* to suddenly speak angrily to someone
14 jump the queue *BrE* to go in front of others who are already waiting in a line – used to show disapproval → QUEUE-JUMPING
15 jump through hoops to do a series of things that are difficult or annoying, but that are necessary in order to achieve something: *We had to jump through hoops to get our visas in time.*
16 jump ship a) to leave an organization that you are working for, especially in order to join another: *The best employees jumped ship at the first opportunity.* **b)** to leave a ship on which you are working as a sailor, without permission
17 jump bail to leave a town, city, or country where a court of law has ordered you to stay until your TRIAL¹(1)
18 jump to it! *spoken* used to order someone to do something immediately
19 (go) jump in a lake! *spoken* used to rudely tell someone to go away
20 jump the rails *BrE*, **jump the tracks** *AmE* if a train jumps the rails, it suddenly goes off the metal tracks it is moving along
21 jump a light (*also* **jump the lights**) to drive through red TRAFFIC LIGHTS without stopping
22 jump a train *especially AmE* to travel on a train, especially a FREIGHT TRAIN, without paying
23 jump the shark *informal* if a television series jumps the shark, something silly happens in it and from that time people stop thinking it is good
24 CAR [T] *AmE* to JUMP-START a car
25 SEX [T] *spoken not polite* to have sex with someone

J

THESAURUS

jump *v* [I,T] to push yourself up into the air, over something etc, using your legs: *The cat jumped up onto the table.* | *He jumped over the stream.*
skip *v* [I] to move forwards with little jumps between your steps, especially because you are feeling happy: *The little girl was skipping down the street.*
hop *v* [I] to jump or move around on one leg: *He was hopping around because he'd injured his foot.*
leap *v* [I,T] *especially written* to suddenly jump up high or a long way: *The deer leapt over the fence.* | *Tina leapt onto the boat as it was moving away.*
bounce *v* [I] to jump up and down several times, especially on something that has springs in it: *Children love bouncing on beds.*
dive *v* [I] to jump into water with your head and arms first: *Zoë dived into the swimming pool.*
vault /vɔːlt $ vɒːlt/ *v* [I,T] *especially written* to jump over something in one movement, using your hands or a pole to help you: *He vaulted the ticket barrier and ran for the exit.* | *Ben tried to vault over the bar.*

jump at sth *phr v* to eagerly accept the chance to do something: *I jumped at the chance of a trip to Hong Kong.*
jump in *phr v* to interrupt someone or suddenly join a conversation: *Lena quickly jumped in with a diverting remark.*
jump on sb *phr v informal* to criticize or punish someone, especially unfairly: **[+for]** *He used to jump on me for every little mistake.*
jump out at sb *phr v* if something jumps out at you, it is extremely noticeable, often in a way you do not like: *I don't like jewellery that jumps out at you.*

jump² ●●● S3 *n* [C]
1 UP an act of pushing yourself suddenly up into the air using your legs SYN **leap**: *the best jump of the competition* | *a dancer famous for his impressive jumps*
2 DOWN an act of letting yourself drop from a place that is above the ground: **do/make a jump** *Douglas made his first 10,000-foot parachute jump yesterday.*
3 INCREASE a sudden large increase in an amount or value: **[+in]** *a jump in inflation rates*
4 PROGRESS *especially BrE* a large or sudden change, especially one that improves things: *The new law is a great* ***jump forward*** *for human rights.*
5 with a jump *BrE* if you wake, sit up etc with a jump, you do it very suddenly because you are surprised or shocked: *She woke with a jump, hearing a noise downstairs.*
6 keep/stay etc a jump ahead (of sb) *BrE informal* to keep your advantage over the people you are competing with by always being the first to do or know something new
7 STH YOU JUMP OVER a fence, gate, or wall that a person or horse has to jump over in a race or competition: *Her horse* ***cleared*** *all* ***the jumps*** *in the first round.*
8 get a jump on sb/sth *AmE informal* to gain an advantage, especially by doing something earlier than usual or earlier than someone else: *I want to get a jump on my Christmas shopping.* → HIGH JUMP, LONG JUMP, SKI JUMP, TRIPLE JUMP, → **take a running jump** at RUNNING²(8)

ˈjump ball *n* [C] the act of throwing the ball up in a game of BASKETBALL, so that one player from each team can try to gain control of it → see picture at BASKETBALL

ˌjumped-ˈup *adj* [only before noun] *BrE informal* a jumped-up person thinks they are more important than they really are, because they have improved their social position: *a jumped-up little bureaucrat*

jump·er /ˈdʒʌmpə $ -ər/ ●●○ S3 *n* [C]
1 *BrE* a piece of clothing made of wool that covers the upper part of your body and arms SYN **sweater, pullover**
2 *AmE* a dress without SLEEVES usually worn over a shirt SYN **pinafore** *BrE*
3 a person or animal that jumps

ˈjumper ˌcables *n* [plural] *AmE* thick wires used to connect the batteries (BATTERY) of two cars in order to start the car that has lost power

ˌjumping ˈjack *n* [C] *AmE* a jump that is done from a standing position with your arms and legs pointing out to the side

ˌjumping-ˈoff ˌpoint *n* [C] a place to start from, especially at the beginning of a journey

ˈjump jet *n* [C] an aircraft that can take off and land by going straight up and down

ˈjump leads *n* [plural] *BrE* thick wires used to connect the batteries (BATTERY) of two cars in order to start the car that has lost power

ˈjump rope *n* [C] *AmE* a long piece of rope that children use for jumping over SYN **skipping rope** *BrE* —**jump rope** *v* [I]

ˈjump shot *n* [C] an action in BASKETBALL in which you throw the ball towards the basket as you jump in the air

ˌjump-ˈstart *v* [T] **1** (*also* **jump** *AmE*) to start a car whose BATTERY has lost power by connecting it to the battery of another car **2** to help a process or activity to start or become more successful: *Congress hopes the tax cut will jump-start the economy.* —**jump start** *n* [C]

jump·suit /ˈdʒʌmpsuːt, -sjuːt $ -suːt/ *n* [C] a piece of clothing like a shirt and a pair of trousers joined together, worn especially by women

ˈjump-up *n* [U] a type of popular music from the Caribbean with a strong regular beat, or a party, event etc where this music is played: ***jump-up kids*** (=young people who like this type of music)

jump·y /ˈdʒʌmpi/ *adj* worried or nervous, especially because you are expecting something bad to happen SYN **anxious** THESAURUS▸ NERVOUS

Jun. (*also* **Jun** *BrE*) the written abbreviation of ***June***

junc·tion /ˈdʒʌŋkʃən/ ●●○ *n* [C] a place where one road, track etc joins another SYN **intersection**: *the junction of Abbot Road and Mill Street* | *Junction 5 on the M40*

junc·ture /ˈdʒʌŋktʃə $ -ər/ *n* [C usually singular] *formal* a particular point in an activity or period of time: ***At this juncture****, I suggest we take a short break.* | *The talks are at a* ***critical juncture*** (=very important point).

June /dʒuːn/ ●●● S2 W3 *n* [C,U] (*written abbreviation* **Jun.**) the sixth month of the year, between May and July: **next/last June** *I finished school last June.* | **in June** *My birthday is in June.* | **on June 6th** *We met on June 6th.* | **on 6th June** *BrE*: *He resigned on 6th June.* | **June 6** *AmE*: *The first round will be held June 6.*

jun·gle /ˈdʒʌŋɡəl/ ●●○ *n*
1 [C,U] a thick tropical forest with many large plants growing very close together: *the Amazon jungle* THESAURUS▸ FOREST
2 [singular] a situation in which it is difficult to become successful or get what you want, especially because a lot of people are competing with each other: *the media jungle*
3 [singular] something that is very untidy, complicated, or confusing: **[+of]** *a jungle of freeways and highways*
4 [U] a type of very fast dance music → CONCRETE JUNGLE, → **law of the jungle** at LAW(8)

ˈjungle ˌgym *n* [C] *AmE* a large frame made of metal bars for children to climb on SYN **climbing frame** *BrE*

junior¹ ●●● W3 *adj* [only before noun]
1 having a low rank in an organization or profession OPP **senior**: *a junior doctor* | **[+to]** *There are several people junior to me* (=with a lower rank than me).
2 relating to sport for young people below a particular age: *the junior football club*
3 *BrE* relating to a school for children below the age of 11: *the junior classrooms*
4 *AmE* relating to the year before the final year of HIGH SCHOOL or college: *the second semester of my* ***junior year*** → SENIOR¹

junior² ●○○ *n*
1 be two/five/ten etc years sb's junior (*also* **be sb's junior by two/five/ten etc years**) *written* to be two, five, ten etc years younger than someone: *She married a man seven years her junior.*
2 [C] a young person who takes part in sport for people

J

below a particular age: *The juniors use the courts on Tuesday night.*
3 [C] *especially BrE* someone who has a low rank in an organization or profession: *an office junior*
4 [C] *BrE* a child who goes to a JUNIOR SCHOOL
5 [C] *AmE* a student in the year before the final year of HIGH SCHOOL or college → **FRESHMAN, SENIOR²(1), SOPHOMORE**
6 Junior *AmE spoken* a name used humorously when speaking to or about a boy or a younger man, especially your son: *Where's Junior?*

Ju·ni·or /ˈdʒuːniə $ -ər/ (*written abbreviation* **Jr.** *AmE*, **Jnr** *BrE*) used after the name of a man or boy who has the same name as his father: *John F. Kennedy, Jr.*

ˌjunior ˈcollege *n* [C,U] a college in the US or Canada where students take a course of study that continues for two years SYN **community college**

ˌjunior ˈhigh school (*also* **junior ˈhigh**) *n* [C,U] a school in the US and Canada for children aged between 12 and 14 or 15 → **MIDDLE SCHOOL(2), SENIOR HIGH SCHOOL**

ˈjunior ˌschool *n* [C,U] a school in Britain for children aged 7 to 11

ˌjunior ˈvarsity *n* [C,U] *AmE* (*abbreviation* **JV**) a team of younger or less experienced sports players who represent a school or university → **varsity**

ju·ni·per /ˈdʒuːnəpə $ -ər/ *n* [C,U] a small bush that produces purple BERRIES that can be used in cooking

junk¹ /dʒʌŋk/ ●●● S2 *n*
1 [U] old or unwanted objects that have no use or value: *This cupboard's full of junk.* ⚠ Do not use **junk** when you are talking about things such as empty packets, cans, and bottles that are left in a public place. Use **litter**: *Don't drop litter in the street.*
2 [U] JUNK FOOD
3 [C] a Chinese sailing boat

junk² *v* [T] to get rid of something because it is old or useless

ˈjunk bond *n* [C] a BOND which has a high risk and is often sold to pay for a TAKEOVER

jun·ket /ˈdʒʌŋkɪt/ *n* [C] *especially AmE informal* an expensive trip paid for by government money or by a business for people they employ – used to show disapproval

ˈjunk food (*also* **junk**) *n* [U] *informal* food that is not healthy, for example because it contains a lot of fat, sugar etc → **fast food**

junk·ie, **junky** /ˈdʒʌŋki/ *n* (*plural* **junkies**) [C] *informal* **1** someone who takes dangerous drugs and is dependent on them **2 a TV/sports etc junkie** someone who likes something so much that they seem to be dependent on it – used humorously: *a technology junkie*

ˈjunk mail *n* [U] letters, especially advertisements, that are sent by organizations to large numbers of people – used to show disapproval → **spam**

ˈjunk shop *n* [C] a shop that buys and sells old furniture, clothes etc

junk·y /ˈdʒʌŋki/ *n* [C] another spelling of JUNKIE

ˈjunk yard *n* [C] *AmE* a place where old or broken furniture, cars etc can be left, or bought and sold

jun·ta /ˈdʒʌntə, ˈhʊntə/ *n* [C] a military government that has gained power by using force

Ju·pi·ter /ˈdʒuːpɪtə $ -ər/ *n* the PLANET that is fifth in order from the Sun and is the largest in the SOLAR SYSTEM: *a space probe on its way to Jupiter*

Ju·ras·sic /dʒʊˈræsɪk / *adj* belonging or relating to the period of time from about 210 million years ago to about 140 million years ago, when there were DINOSAURS and the first MAMMALS and birds: *the Jurassic period*

ju·rid·i·cal /dʒʊˈrɪdɪkəl/ *adj formal* relating to judges or the law

jur·is·dic·tion /ˌdʒʊərəsˈdɪkʃən $ ˌdʒʊr-/ *n* [U] the right to use an official power to make legal decisions, or the area where this right exists: **[+over sb/sth]** *The committee **has jurisdiction** over all tax measures.*

ju·ris·pru·dence /ˌdʒʊərəsˈpruːdəns $ ˌdʒʊr-/ *n* [U] *formal* the science or study of law

ju·rist /ˈdʒʊərɪst $ ˈdʒʊr-/ *n* [C] *formal* someone who has a very detailed knowledge of law

ju·ror /ˈdʒʊərə $ ˈdʒʊrər/ *n* [C] a member of a jury

ju·ry /ˈdʒʊəri $ ˈdʒʊri/ ●●○ S3 W3 *n* (*plural* **juries**) [C]
1 a group of often 12 ordinary people who listen to the details of a case in court and decide whether someone is guilty or not: *the **members of the jury** | The jury found him not guilty. | the right to **trial by jury*** | **sit/serve on a jury** (=be part of a jury)
2 a group of people chosen to judge a competition
3 the jury is (still) out on sth used to say that something has not been finally decided: *Is it good value? The jury is still out on that.* → **GRAND JURY**

ˈjury box *n* [C usually singular] the place where the jury sits in a court

ˈjury ˌservice *BrE*, **ˈjury ˌduty** *AmE n* [U] a period of time during which you must be part of a jury

jus /ʒuː/ *n* [singular, U] a thin sauce for meat or fish: *lamb served with a red wine jus*

Frequencies of the adverb **just** in spoken and written English.

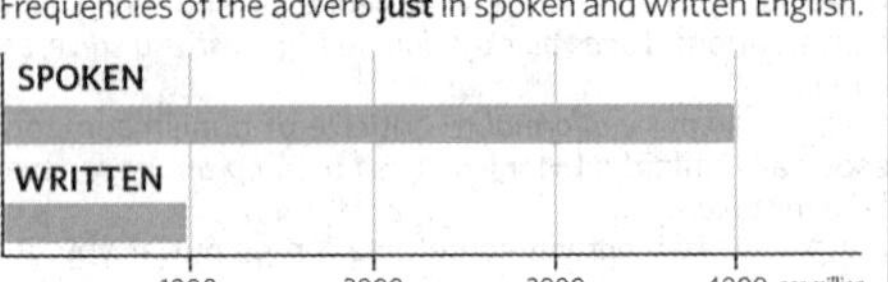

This graph shows that the adverb **just** is much more common in spoken English than in written English. This is because it has special uses in spoken English and is used in a lot of common spoken phrases.

just¹ /dʒəst; *strong* dʒʌst/ ●●● S1 W1 *adv*
1 exactly: *A good strong cup of coffee is just what I need right now. | The house was large and roomy; just right for us. | She looks just like her mother. | Just what do you think you're trying to do?* | **just on** *BrE*: *It's just on three o'clock. | **Just then** (=exactly at that moment), Mrs Robovitch appeared at the bedroom door. | **Just as** (=at the exact moment when) I opened the door, the telephone started to ring. | A nice hot bath – **just the thing** (=exactly the right thing) to relax sore muscles.* THESAURUS EXACTLY
2 nothing more than the thing, amount, action etc that you are mentioning SYN **only**: *It's nothing serious – just a small cut. | Don't be too hard on him – he's just a kid. | Can you wait just a few minutes? | It's not just me – there are other people involved as well.*

REGISTER
In written English, people often prefer to use **simply** rather than **just**, which sounds rather informal: *It's **simply** a question of priorities.*

3 only a short time ago: *John's just told me that he's getting married. | I've just been out shopping.* THESAURUS RECENTLY
4 at this moment or at that moment: *Wait a minute – I'm just coming. | He was just leaving when the phone rang. | I'm just finishing my homework – it won't take long. | The concert was just about to start.*
5 used to emphasize what you are saying: *It just isn't true. | I just love being in the mountains. | It was just wonderful to see Joyce again. | I just wish I could believe you.*
6 only by a small amount, time, distance etc: **just before/after/over etc** *We moved here just after our son was born. | I saw her just before she died. | It's just under three centimetres long.*
7 used to show that something which happens almost does not happen SYN **barely, hardly**: *He just managed to get home before dark. | We could just see the coast of France in the distance. | Those pants **only just** fit you now. | She was earning **just enough** money to live on* (=enough but not more than enough).

8 just about almost: *The plums are just about ripe now.* | *Just about everybody will be affected by the tax increases.*
9 just as good/bad/big etc equally as good, bad, big etc: *Brad is just as good as the others.* | *I love this country just as much as you do.*
10 just have to do sth used to say that someone has to do something because nothing else is possible: *We'll just have to watch and see what happens.* | *You just have to accept things and get on with your life.*
11 not just any used to emphasize that you are talking about a particular thing or person that is especially good or important: *For the best results, use olive oil. Not just any olive oil, mind – only the finest quality will do.*
12 would just as soon if you would just as soon do something, you would prefer to do it: *I'd just as soon stay at home – I don't really enjoy parties.*
13 may just/might just might possibly: *You could try Renee. She might just know where they live now.* | *It may just have been a coincidence.*
14 not just yet not now, but probably soon: *I can't leave just yet. I've still got a couple of letters to write.*
15 just because ... it doesn't mean used to say that, although one thing is true, another thing is not necessarily true: *Just because you're older than me, it doesn't mean you can tell me what to do.*

SPOKEN PHRASES
16 just a minute/second/moment a) used to ask someone to wait for a short time while you do something: *Just a minute, I'll see if I can find it for you.* **b)** used to interrupt someone in order to ask them something, disagree with them etc: *Just a minute! How do I know you're not telling me a pack of lies?*
17 a) used when politely asking something or telling someone to do something: *Could I just say a few words before we start?* | *Would you just explain to us how the system works.* **b)** used when firmly telling someone to do something: *Look, just shut up for a minute!* | *Now, just listen to what I'm telling you.*
18 it's just that used when explaining the reason for something, especially when someone thinks there is a different reason: *No, I do like Chinese food. It's just that I'm not hungry.*
19 just now a) a very short time ago: *Where have my glasses gone? I had them just now.* **b)** *especially BrE* at this moment: *We're busy just now – can you come back later?*
20 just think/imagine/look used to tell someone to imagine or look at the same thing that you are imagining or looking at: *Just think – in a week we'll be lying on a beach in the sun!*
21 it's/that's just as well used to say that it is fortunate that something is true or happened because otherwise there would be problems: *It's just as well we'd prepared everything beforehand.*
22 isn't she just/aren't they just etc *old-fashioned* used to strongly agree with something someone has said about a person or thing: *'He's a selfish, rude, ignorant man!' 'Isn't he just!'*
23 just so a) with everything arranged neatly and tidily: *Her house always has to be just so.* **b)** *old-fashioned* used to say yes or agree with something: *'You should have beaten them, shouldn't you?' 'Just so.'*

→ **just the same** at SAME[2](3), → **just in case** at CASE[1](7), → **just my luck** at LUCK[1](12), → **might just as well** at MIGHT[1](9)

GRAMMAR: Word order
- **Just** comes before a main verb: *I just saw him.*
- **Just** comes after 'be' when it is the main verb: *She is just seventeen.*
- **Just** comes after the first auxiliary verb: *I have just seen him.* ✗ Don't say: *I just have seen him.*

just[2] /dʒʌst/ ●●○ *adj*
1 morally right and fair: *Henry sincerely believed that he was fighting a just war.* | *a just settlement* | *Charlemagne was respected as a just ruler.* **THESAURUS** FAIR
2 deserved by someone: *a just reward for their loyal service* | *What would be a just punishment for such a crime?* | *I hope that he's caught and* ***gets his just deserts*** (=is punished in the way he deserves). —**justly** *adv*: *These men are criminals, but they must be dealt with justly.* | *an achievement of which we can be justly proud*

jus·tice /ˈdʒʌstɪs/ ●●● W2 *n*
1 SYSTEM OF JUDGEMENT [U] the system by which people are judged in courts of law and criminals are punished: *a book on the* ***criminal justice system*** | *The killers will be* ***brought to justice*** (=caught and punished). | *Acts of terrorism must not* ***escape justice***. → MISCARRIAGE OF JUSTICE
2 FAIRNESS [U] fairness in the way people are treated OPP **injustice**: *Children have a strong* ***sense of justice***. | *His people came to him* ***demanding justice***. → POETIC JUSTICE
3 BEING RIGHT [U] the quality of being right and deserving fair treatment: *No one doubts the justice of our cause.*
4 do justice to sb/sth (*also* **do sb/sth justice**) to treat or represent someone or something good, beautiful etc in a way that is as good as they deserve: *The photo doesn't do her justice.* | *No words can do justice to the experience.*
5 do yourself justice to do something such as a test well enough to show your real ability: *Sara panicked in the exam and didn't do herself justice.*
6 justice has been done/served used to say that someone has been treated fairly or has been given a punishment they deserve
7 JUDGE [C] (*also* **Justice**) **a)** *AmE* a judge in a law court **b)** *BrE* the title of a judge in the High Court → **rough justice** at ROUGH[1](16)

ˌJustice of the ˈPeace *n* [C] (*abbreviation* **JP**) someone who judges less serious cases in small law courts and, in the US, can perform marriage ceremonies

jus·ti·fi·a·ble /ˈdʒʌstəfaɪəbəl/ AWL *adj* actions, reactions, decisions etc that are justifiable are acceptable because they are done for good reasons: *justifiable anger* | **economically/commercially justifiable** | *Are these experiments morally justifiable?* —**justifiably** *adv*

ˌjustifiable ˈhomicide *n* [U] *law* a situation in which you are not punished for killing someone, usually because you did it to defend yourself

jus·ti·fi·ca·tion /ˌdʒʌstɪfɪˈkeɪʃən/ ●●○ AWL *n* [C,U]
1 a good and acceptable reason for doing something: **justification for (doing) sth** *There is* ***no justification for*** *holding her in jail.* | *Hoggart felt,* ***with some justification****, that his colleagues had let him down.* **THESAURUS** REASON
2 in justification (of sb/sth) in order to explain why an idea or action is right: *He made a speech in justification of his actions.*

jus·ti·fied /ˈdʒʌstɪfaɪd/ ●●○ AWL *adj*
1 having an acceptable explanation or reason: *In the Chief Constable's view, the use of force was* ***fully justified***. | **justified in doing sth** *Under the circumstances, the principal was justified in expelling this student.*
2 right/left justified *technical* used to describe a page where the words form a straight edge on the right or left side of the page

jus·ti·fy /ˈdʒʌstɪfaɪ/ ●●○ S3 W3 AWL *v* (**justified, justifying, justifies**) [T]
1 to give an acceptable explanation for something that other people think is unreasonable: *Ministers must appear before Parliament and justify their actions.* | **justify doing sth** *How can we justify spending so much money on arms?* | **justify yourself** (=prove that what you are doing is reasonable) *I don't have to justify myself to you or anyone else.*
2 to be a good and acceptable reason for something: *Nothing justifies murdering another human being.*
3 *technical* to arrange lines of words on a page or computer screen so that they form a straight edge on both the right and left sides

ˈjust-in-time *adj* [only before noun] *technical* if goods are produced or bought using a just-in-time system, they are produced or bought just before they are needed so that the company does not have to store things for a long time: *just-in-time manufacturing methods*

jut /dʒʌt/ (*also* **jut out**) *v* (**jutted, jutting**) **1** [I always + adv/prep] something that juts out sticks out further than the other things around it: *Tall jagged rocks jutted out over the beach.* **2** [T] if you jut your chin out, you move it so that it sticks forward: *She jutted her chin out aggressively as she glowered back at him.* —**jutting** *adj*: *jutting cliffs*

jute /dʒuːt/ *n* [U] a natural substance that is used for making rope and rough cloth

ju·ve·nile /ˈdʒuːvənaɪl $ -nəl, -naɪl/ *adj* **1** [only before noun] *law* relating to young people who are not yet adults: *juvenile crime | a juvenile court* **THESAURUS** YOUNG **2** silly and typical of a child rather than an adult - used to show disapproval SYN **childish**: *a very juvenile sense of humour* **3** *technical* juvenile birds or animals are young —**juvenile** *n* [C]

ˌjuvenile deˈlinquent *n* [C] a child or young person who behaves in a criminal way SYN **young offender** —**juvenile delinquency** *n* [U]

jux·ta·pose /ˌdʒʌkstəˈpəʊz $ ˈdʒʌkstəpoʊz/ *v* [T] *formal* to put things together, especially things that are not normally together, in order to compare them or to make something new: **juxtapose sth with sth** *a style of decor that juxtaposes antiques with modern furniture* —**juxtaposition** /ˌdʒʌkstəpəˈzɪʃən/ *n* [C,U]

J

K[1], **k** /keɪ/ *n* (*plural* **K's, k's**) [C,U] the 11th letter of the alphabet

K[2] /keɪ/ **1** (*also* **k**) *informal* an abbreviation of ***one thousand***: *a salary of £30k a year* **2** an abbreviation of ***kilobyte*** or ***kilobytes*** **3** (*also* **k**) a written abbreviation of ***kilometre*** or ***kilometres***: *a 20k international race walker* **4** the abbreviation of ***Kelvin*** or ***Kelvins***

ka·bob /kəˈbɒb $ -ˈbɑːb/ *n* [C] an American spelling of KEBAB

kaf·fee·klatch /ˈkæfeɪklætʃ $ ˈkɑːfi-, ˈkɒːfi-/ *n* [C] *AmE* an informal social situation when people drink coffee and talk

kaf·fir /ˈkæfə $ -ər/ *n* [C] *taboo* a very offensive word for a black person, used by white people in South Africa. Do not use this word.

kaf·tan /ˈkæftæn $ kæfˈtæn/ *n* [C] another spelling of CAFTAN

Ka·lash·ni·kov /kəˈlæʃnɪkɒf $ -kɒːf/ *n* [C] a type of RIFLE (=long gun) that can fire very quickly

kale /keɪl/ *n* [C,U] a dark green vegetable with curled leaves → see picture at **VEGETABLE**[1]

ka·lei·do·scope /kəˈlaɪdəskəʊp $ -skoʊp/ *n* [C] **1** a pattern, situation, or scene that is always changing and has many details or bright colours: **[+of]** *a kaleidoscope of cultures* **2** a tube with mirrors and pieces of coloured glass at one end, which shows coloured patterns when you turn it

ka·lei·do·scop·ic /kəˌlaɪdəˈskɒpɪk◂ $ -ˈskɑː-/ *adj* kaleidoscopic scenes, colours, or patterns change often and quickly

kam·i·ka·ze /ˌkæmɪˈkɑːzi◂/ *adj* [only before noun] **1 kamikaze pilot** a pilot who deliberately crashes his plane on enemy camps, ships etc knowing he will be killed **2** used to describe someone who is willing to take risks, without caring about their safety: *kamikaze lorry drivers*

kan·ga·roo /ˌkæŋgəˈruː◂/ *n* (*plural* **kangaroos**) [C] an Australian animal that moves by jumping and carries its babies in a POUCH (=a special pocket of skin) on its stomach → **marsupial**

ˌkangaroo ˈcourt *n* [C] an unofficial court that punishes people unfairly

ka·o·lin /ˈkeɪəlɪn/ *n* [U] a type of white clay used in medicine

ka·pok /ˈkeɪpɒk $ -pɑːk/ *n* [U] a very light material like cotton, used for filling soft things like CUSHIONS

ka·put /kəˈpʊt/ *adj* [not before noun] *spoken* broken: *The TV's* ***gone kaput***.

kar·a·o·ke /ˌkæriˈəʊki $ ˌkɑːrəˈoʊ-/ *n* [U] an activity that people do for entertainment, in which someone sings a popular song while a karaoke machine plays the music to the song: *a karaoke bar*

kar·at /ˈkærət/ *n* [C] an American spelling of CARAT

ka·ra·te /kəˈrɑːti/ ●●○ *n* [U] a Japanese fighting sport, in which you use your feet and hands to hit and kick → **judo**

kar·ma /ˈkɑːmə $ -ɑːr-/ *n* [U] **1** the belief that all the good and bad things that you do in this life affect how good or bad your future lives will be, according to the Hindu and Buddhist religions **2** *informal* the feeling that you get from a person, place, or action: **good/bad karma** *The house had a lot of bad karma.* —**karmic** *adj*

kart /kɑːt $ kɑːrt/ *n* [C] a small motor vehicle with an open frame and four wheels, used in races SYN **go-kart** —**karting** *n* [U]

kar·zy, **karzi** /ˈkɑːzi $ ˈkɑːr-/ *n* [C] another spelling of KHAZI

ka·ty·did /ˈkeɪtidɪd/ *n* [C] *AmE* a type of large GRASSHOPPER

kay·ak /ˈkaɪæk/ *n* [C] a type of light boat, usually for one person, that is moved using a PADDLE → **canoe** —**kayaking** *n* [U]

ka·zoo /kəˈzuː/ *n* (*plural* **kazoos**) [C] a simple musical instrument that you play by holding it to your lips and making sounds into it

KB, **Kb** a written abbreviation of ***kilobyte*** or ***kilobytes*** → **MB**

KC /ˌkeɪ ˈsiː/ *n* [C] *BrE* (***King's Counsel***) the highest level of BARRISTER (=lawyer who speaks in court) in Britain when the ruler is a king → **QC**

ke·bab /kəˈbæb $ kəˈbɑːb/ (*also* **kabob** *AmE*) *n* [C] small pieces of meat and vegetables cooked on a stick

kedg·e·ree /ˈkedʒəriː $ ˈkedʒəriː, ˌkedʒəˈriː/ *n* [U] a cooked dish of fish, rice, and eggs mixed together

keel[1] /kiːl/ *n* **1 on an even keel** steady, without any sudden changes: **keep sth/get sth back on an even keel** *Now that the crisis is over, we must try to get things back on an even keel.* **2** [C] a bar along the bottom of a boat that keeps it steady in the water

keel[2] *v*

keel over *phr v* to fall over sideways: *Several soldiers keeled over in the hot sun.*

keel·haul /ˈkiːlhɔːl $ -hɒːl/ *v* [T] **1** to punish someone severely – often used humorously **2** to pull someone under the keel of a ship with a rope as a punishment

keen[1] /kiːn/ ●●○ S3 W3 *adj*

1 WANT STH *especially BrE* wanting to do something or wanting something to happen very much SYN **eager**: **keen to do sth** *He told me that he was keen to help.* | **keen on doing sth** *I wasn't keen on going there on my own.* | **keen for sth to happen** *The government is keen for peace talks to start again.* | **keen that** *The chairman is keen that the company should expand its product range.*

2 LIKE **be keen on sb/sth** *BrE spoken* to like someone or something: *I'm not keen on cabbage.* | **not too/not very/not that keen on sth** *She likes Biology, but she's not too keen on Physics.* | *My flatmates want to have a party, but I'm not* ***keen on the idea***.

3 HOBBY/INTEREST *especially BrE* someone who is keen on something is very interested in it or enjoys doing it very much: *a keen photographer* | *keen golfers* | **[+on]** *Daniel's very keen on tennis.* | **mad keen on sth** (=very keen on something) *spoken*: *I was mad keen on dinosaurs when I was little.* | *She takes* ***a keen interest in*** *politics and current affairs.*

4 EAGER TO WORK/LEARN someone who is keen is eager to work or learn, and enjoys doing it: *keen students* | *The kids in my class are all very keen.* | *She was new in the job and* ***keen as mustard*** (=very keen).

5 SIGHT/SMELL/HEARING a keen sense of smell or keen sight or hearing is an extremely good ability to smell etc: *Dogs have a very keen sense of smell.* | *She has* ***a keen eye for*** (=is good at noticing) *talent.*

6 MIND someone with a keen mind is quick to understand things: *a keen understanding of commerce* | *With her keen mind and good business sense, she soon became noticed.*

7 FEELING a keen feeling is one that is strong and deep: *As she walked away, Joe felt* ***a keen sense of*** *loss.*

8 COMPETITION used to describe a situation in which people compete strongly: *We won the contest in the face of* ***keen competition***.

9 ATTRACTED **be keen on sb** *BrE* to be sexually attracted to someone

10 SHARP *literary* a keen knife or blade is extremely sharp

11 WIND *old-fashioned* a keen wind is cold and strong

12 PRICES *BrE* keen prices are low —**keenly** *adv*: *I was keenly aware of the dangers.* —**keenness** *n* [U]

GRAMMAR

You are **keen on** something or **keen on doing** something: *We're all very keen on sports.* ✗ Don't say: *We're all very keen of sports.*

GRAMMAR GUIDE ▶ **ADJECTIVES**

keen² *v* [I] *old use* to sing a loud sad song for someone who has died

keep¹ /kiːp/ ●●● S1 W1 *v* (*past tense and past participle* **kept** /kept/)

1 NOT CHANGE [linking verb, T] to stay in a particular state, condition, or position, or to make someone or something do this: **keep (sb/sth) warm/safe/dry etc** *We huddled around the fire to keep warm.* | **keep calm/awake/sane etc** *I was struggling to keep awake.* | **keep sth clean/tidy** *Keep your room tidy.* | **keep sb busy/amused/occupied** *some toys to keep the kids amused* | *You won't be able to* ***keep*** *it* ***secret*** *forever.* | *Peter cycles to work to* ***keep fit***. | *Don't* ***keep*** *us* ***in suspense*** *any longer!* | **keep (sb/sth) away/back/off/out etc** *The police put up barriers to keep the crowds back.* | *If I were you, I'd keep away from that area at night.* | *a sign saying 'Danger: Keep Out'* | *The little boy kept close to his mother.* | **keep (sb) out of sth** *Keep him out of trouble.* | *You keep out of this, Mother* (=do not get involved). *It's no concern of yours.* | *How can I cut your hair if you won't* ***keep still!*** | **keep left/right** (=stay to the left or right of a path or road as you move) | **keep sb/sth doing sth** *Jane kept the engine running.*

GRAMMAR: Linking verbs

Keep is used as a linking verb in this meaning. It links the subject of the sentence with an adjective: *I try to keep busy.* | *The fruit will keep fresh for several weeks.*

2 CONTINUE DOING STH [I] (*also* **keep on**) to continue doing something or to do the same thing many times: **keep (on) doing sth** *I keep thinking about Joe, all alone in that place.* | *I keep telling you, but you won't listen!* | *She pretended not to hear, and kept on walking.*

3 NOT GIVE BACK [T] to have something and not give it back to the person who had it before: *You can keep it. I don't need it anymore.*

4 NOT LOSE [T] to continue to have something and not lose it or get rid of it: *We decided to keep our old car instead of selling it.* | *I kept his letters for years.* | *In spite of everything, Robyn's managed to keep her sense of humor.*

5 STORE STH [T always + adv/prep] to leave something in one particular place so that you can find it easily: *Where do you keep your teabags?* | *George kept a bottle of whiskey under his bed.*

6 MAKE SB STAY IN A PLACE [T always + adv/prep] to make someone stay in a place, especially a prison or hospital: *He was kept in prison for a week without charge.*

7 DELAY SB [T] to delay someone: *He should be here by now. What's keeping him?*

8 DO WHAT YOU PROMISED [T] to do what you have promised or agreed to do: **keep your word/promise** *How do I know you'll keep your word?* | *patients who fail to* ***keep*** *their* ***appointments***

9 keep a secret to not tell anyone about a secret that you know: *Can I trust you to keep a secret?*

10 keep sth quiet/keep quiet (about sth) to not say anything in order to avoid telling a secret or causing problems

11 keep a record/account/diary etc to regularly record written information somewhere

12 keep going a) keep (sb) going to have or to give someone enough hope and emotional strength to continue living and doing things in a bad situation: *That woman's been through such a lot – I don't know how she keeps going.* | *Her letters were the only thing that kept me going while I was in prison.* **b) keep (sth) going** if you keep a business, institution, regular event etc going, you keep it open or make it continue to happen: *The library costs £5 million a year to run, and the council can't afford to keep it going.* **c) keep going** to continue doing something difficult: *Persevere and keep going until you reach your ideal weight.* **d) keep sb going** if something keeps you going, it is enough to satisfy your need while you are waiting to get something bigger or better: *I'll have a biscuit to keep me going until dinner time.*

13 FOOD [I] if food keeps, it stays fresh enough to be eaten: *Eat the salmon because it won't keep till tomorrow.*

14 ANIMALS [T] to own and look after animals: *We keep chickens and a couple of pigs.*

15 STOP OTHER PEOPLE FROM USING STH [T] to stop other people from using something, so that it is available for someone SYN **save**: *Will you keep a seat for me?*

16 keep sb waiting to make someone wait before you meet them or see them: ***Sorry to keep you waiting*** *– I got stuck in a meeting.*

17 keep guard/watch to guard a place or watch around you all the time

18 SHOP [T] *BrE old-fashioned* to own a small business and work in it

19 PROVIDE SB WITH THINGS [T] to provide someone with money, food etc: *He did not earn enough to keep a wife and children.* | **keep sb in sth** *There's enough money there to keep you in champagne for a year!*

20 PROTECT [T] *formal* to guard or protect someone: *The Lord bless you and keep you.* | *His only thought was to* ***keep*** *the child* ***from harm***.

21 keep goal/wicket to be the player in a team whose job is to protect the GOAL or WICKET → **GOALKEEPER**, **WICKET KEEPER**

SPOKEN PHRASES

22 keep quiet used to tell someone not to say anything or make any noise: *Keep quiet! I'm trying to watch the game.*

23 how are you keeping? used to ask if someone is well: *'Hi, Mark! How are you keeping?' 'Oh, not so bad.'*

24 keep your hair/shirt on! used to tell someone to be more calm, patient etc

25 sb can keep sth used to say that you do not want or are not interested in something: *She can keep her wild parties and posh friends – I like the quiet life.*

26 it'll keep used to say that you can tell someone something or do something later: *'I don't have time to listen now.' 'Don't worry, it'll keep.'*

keep at sth *phr v*

1 keep at it *spoken* to continue to do something, although it is difficult or hard work: *I know it's hard, but keep at it! Don't give up!*

2 keep sb at sth to force someone to continue to work hard and not let them stop

keep back *phr v*

1 keep sth ↔ back to deliberately not tell someone all that you know about something: *I got the feeling he was keeping something back.*

2 keep sth ↔ back to not show your feelings, even though you want to very much: *She was struggling to* ***keep back the tears***.

3 keep sb ↔ back to prevent someone from being as successful as they could be SYN **hold back**: *Fear and stereotypes have kept women back for centuries.*

4 keep sth ↔ back *especially BrE* to not give or pay something that you were going to give: *They kept back some of his wages to pay for the damage.*

keep sb/sth ↔ **down** *phr v*

1 to prevent the size, cost, or quantity of something from increasing or being too great: *We need to keep costs down.*

2 to succeed in keeping food in your stomach, instead of bringing it up again out of your mouth, when you are ill: *I could hardly keep anything down for about three days.*

3 used to ask someone to make less noise: ***Keep your voice down*** *– she'll hear you!* | *Can you* ***keep it down*** *– I'm trying to work.*

4 to prevent a group of people from becoming as successful and powerful as the other people in a society: *Plantation owners kept slaves down by refusing them an education.*

keep from *phr v*

1 keep (sb/sth) from sth to prevent someone from doing something or prevent something from happening: **keep sb from (doing) sth** *His ex-wife had kept him from seeing his children.* | *I hope I haven't kept you from your work.* | **keep sth**

K

from doing sth *Put the pizza in the bottom of the oven to keep the cheese from burning.* | **keep (yourself) from doing sth** *The play was so boring I could hardly keep myself from falling asleep.*
2 keep sth from sb to prevent someone from knowing something, by deliberately not telling them about it SYN **withhold**: *The government had wanted to keep this information from the public.*
keep sb **in** *phr v*
1 to make someone stay in hospital because they are too ill to go home: *They kept her in overnight for observation.*
2 *BrE* to force someone to stay inside, especially as a punishment in school
keep in with sb *phr v BrE* to try to stay friendly with someone, especially because this helps you: *It's a good idea to keep in with the boss.*
keep off *phr v*
1 keep sth ↔ off to prevent something from touching or harming something: *She held an old piece of cloth over them both to keep the rain off.* | **keep sth off sth** *How are we going to keep the flies off this food?*
2 keep your hands off sb/sth used to tell someone not to touch someone or something: *Keep your hands off me!*
3 keep (sb) off sth to not eat, drink, or take something that is bad for you, or to stop someone else from eating, drinking, or taking it: *Keep off fatty foods.* | *a programme aimed at keeping teenagers off drugs*
4 keep off sth *especially BrE* to avoid talking about a particular subject, especially so that you do not upset someone SYN **avoid, stay off**
5 keep sth ↔ off if you keep weight off, you do not get heavier again after you have lost weight
6 *BrE* if rain keeps off, it does not fall
keep on *phr v*
1 to continue doing something, or to do something many times: **keep on doing sth** *You just have to keep on trying.*
2 keep sb ↔ on to continue to employ someone, especially for longer than you had planned: *If you're good, they might keep you on after Christmas.*
3 *BrE informal* to talk continuously about something or repeat something many times, in a way that is annoying SYN **go on**: **[+about]** *There's no need to* ***keep on and on*** *about it!* | **[+at]** *If I didn't keep on at the children, they'd never do their homework.*
keep to sth *phr v*
1 to stay on a particular road, course, piece of ground etc: *It's best to keep to the paths.*
2 to do what has been decided in an agreement or plan, or what is demanded by law: *Keep to the speed limits.*
3 keep to the point/subject etc to talk or write only about the subject you are supposed to be talking about
4 keep sth to sth to prevent an amount, degree, or level from becoming higher than it should: *Costs must* ***be kept to a minimum.***
5 keep sth to yourself to not tell anyone about something: *I'd appreciate it if you kept it to yourself.*
6 keep to yourself (*also* **keep yourself to yourself** *BrE*) to live a very quiet private life and not do many things that involve other people
keep up *phr v*
1 keep sth ↔ up to continue doing something: *I don't think I can keep this up any longer.* | **keep up the good work!** (=continue to work hard and well)
2 if a situation keeps up, it continues without stopping or changing SYN **continue**: *How long can the economic boom keep up?*
3 to go as quickly as someone else: **[+with]** *I had to walk fast to keep up with him.*
4 to manage to do as much or as well as other people OPP **fall behind**: **[+with]** *Jack's having trouble keeping up with the rest of the class.* | **keep up with the Joneses** (=try to have the same new impressive possessions that other people have)
5 to continue to read and learn about a particular subject, so that you always know about the most recent facts, products etc: **[+with]** *Employees need to keep up with the latest technical developments.*
6 keep sth ↔ up to make something continue at its present level or amount, instead of letting it decrease: *NATO kept up the pressure on the Serbs to get out of Kosovo.*
7 if one process keeps up with another, it increases at the same speed and by the same amount: **[+with]** *Food production is not keeping up with population growth.*
8 keep sth ↔ up to continue to practise a skill so that you do not lose it: *I used to speak French, but I haven't kept it up.*
9 keep sb up *informal* to prevent someone from going to bed: *I hope I'm not keeping you up.*
10 keep your spirits/strength/morale etc up to stay happy, strong, confident etc by making an effort: *We sang as we marched, to keep our spirits up.*
11 keep up appearances to pretend that everything in your life is normal and happy even though you are in trouble, especially financial trouble
keep up with sb *phr v* to write to, telephone, or meet a friend regularly, so that you do not forget each other

keep² *n* **1 sb's keep** the cost of providing food and a home for someone: **earn your keep** (=do things in return for the things that are provided for you) *It's time you got a job and started earning your keep.* **2 for keeps** *informal* forever: *Marriage ought to be for keeps.* **3** [C] a large strong tower, usually in the centre of a castle

ˈkeep-away *n* [U] *AmE* a children's game in which you try to catch a ball that is being thrown between two other people SYN **piggy in the middle** *BrE*

keep·er /ˈkiːpə $ -ər/ *n* [C] **1** someone who looks after animals: *a beekeeper* | *Bob is head lion keeper at the zoo.* → GAMEKEEPER, ZOO-KEEPER **2** someone whose job is to look after a particular place or thing: *a lighthouse keeper* | **[+of]** *the keeper of Greek coins in the British Museum* **3** *BrE informal* a GOALKEEPER **4 I am not sb's keeper** *spoken* used to say that you are not responsible for someone else's actions → WICKET KEEPER

ˌkeep ˈfit *n* [U] *BrE old-fashioned* a class in which you do exercises to keep yourself healthy → **aerobics** —**keep-fit** *adj*

keep·ie-up·pie /ˌkiːpi ˈʌpi/ *n* [U] the activity of making a football go up and down in the air many times without touching the ground, using short light kicks to control the ball's movements

keep·ing /ˈkiːpɪŋ/ *n* **1 in keeping (with sth)** matching something, or suitable in a particular situation: *In keeping with tradition, everyone wore black.* **2 out of keeping (with sth)** not matching something or not suitable in a particular situation: *The cheerful cover of the book is out of keeping with the sad story told inside it.* **3 in sb's keeping** being looked after or guarded by someone → SAFEKEEPING

keep·sake /ˈkiːpseɪk/ *n* [C] a small object that you keep to remind you of someone SYN **memento**

kef·fi·yeh /keˈfiːə/ *n* [C] a piece of cloth traditionally worn on the head by Arab men

keg /keg/ *n* [C] a round wooden or metal container with a flat top and bottom, used for storing beer → **barrel**: **keg beer/bitter** *BrE* (=beer served from a keg) → see picture at CONTAINER

keg·ger /ˈkegə $ -ər/ (*also* **ˈkeg ˌparty**) *n* [C] *AmE informal* a big outdoor party where beer is served from kegs

keis·ter /ˈkaɪstə $ ˈkiːstər/ *n* [C] *AmE spoken* your BUTTOCKS (=the part of your body that you sit on)

kelp /kelp/ *n* [U] a type of flat brown SEAWEED (=a plant that grows in the sea)

Kel·vin /ˈkelvɪn/ *n* [U] (*written abbreviation* **K**) a scale of temperature in which water freezes at 273.15 K and boils at 373.15 K —**Kelvin** *adj*

ken /ken/ *n* **beyond your ken** if something is beyond your ken, you have no knowledge or understanding of it: *mysteries beyond our ken*

ken·nel /ˈkenl/ *n* [C] **1** a small building made for a dog to sleep in → see picture at HOME[1] **2** (*also* **kennels** [plural]) *BrE* a place where dogs are kept for BREEDING or are cared for while their owners are away: **boarding/quarantine kennels** *The puppy, which may have rabies, is at a quarantine kennel.*

ke·no /ˈkiːnəʊ $ -oʊ/ *n* [U] a game played in CASINOS, in which you try to win money by guessing which numbers a computer will choose

Ken,tucky 'Derby, the a famous race for three-year-old horses that is held each year on the first Saturday in May in Louisville, Kentucky. It is part of the Triple Crown.

kept /kept/ the past tense and past participle of KEEP

,kept 'woman *n* [C] *old-fashioned* a woman who is given a place to live, money, and clothes by a man who visits her for sex – often used humorously SYN **mistress**

kerb *BrE*, **curb** *AmE* /kɜːb $ kɜːrb/ *n* [C] the edge of the PAVEMENT (=raised path) at the side of a road: *His car mounted the kerb and ploughed into a bus queue.* **THESAURUS** EDGE

'kerb ,crawler *BrE*, **curb crawler** *AmE* *n* [C] a man who drives his car slowly along the road looking for a PROSTITUTE (=a women who has sex for money) —**kerb crawling** *n* [U]: *He was arrested for kerb crawling.*

ker·chief /ˈkɜːtʃɪf $ ˈkɜːr-/ *n* [C] a square piece of cloth, worn on the head or around the neck

ker·ching /kəˈtʃɪŋ $ kər-/ *interjection informal* a sound like that made by a TILL in a shop – used to say that someone or something is getting a lot of money: *There were people lined up around the block on the movie's opening night – kerching!*

ker·fuf·fle /kəˈfʌfəl $ kər-/ *n* [singular] *BrE informal* unnecessary noise and activity SYN **fuss**

ker·nel /ˈkɜːnl $ ˈkɜːr-/ *n* [C] **1** the part of a nut or seed inside the shell, or the part inside the stone of some fruits **2** [usually singular] one of the small yellow pieces on a corn COB **3** [usually singular] the most important part of a statement, idea, plan etc SYN **core**: **[+of]** *This evidence is the kernel of the defendants' case.* **4** [usually singular] a very small part or amount of something: **[+of]** *There may be* ***a kernel of truth*** *in what he says.*

ker·o·sene, **kerosine** /ˈkerəsiːn/ *n* [U] *especially AmE, AusE* a clear oil that is burnt to provide heat or light SYN **paraffin** *BrE*: *a kerosene lamp*

kes·trel /ˈkestrəl/ *n* [C] a type of bird that is like a small FALCON

ke·ta·mine /ˈketəmiːn/ *n* [U] a substance designed as an ANAESTHETIC and PAINKILLER, that some people use as an illegal drug

ketch /ketʃ/ *n* [C] a small sailing ship with two MASTS

ketch·up (*also* **catsup** *AmE*) /ˈketʃəp/ ●●○ *n* [U] a thick cold red sauce made from TOMATOes that you put on food: *a bottle of tomato ketchup*

ket·tle /ˈketl/ ●●● S3 *n* [C]

KETTLE

1 a container with a lid, a handle, and a SPOUT, used for boiling and pouring water SYN **teakettle** *AmE*: *She filled the kettle and switched it on.* | *The kettle's boiling* (=the water in it is boiling). | ***Put the kettle on*** (=start boiling water in a kettle)*, will you?*
2 *AmE* a large pot, used for making soup
3 another/a different kettle of fish *informal* used to say that a situation is very different from one that you have just mentioned: *She enjoys public speaking, but being on TV is a different kettle of fish.*

ket·tle·bells /ˈketlˌbelz/ *n* [plural] round iron weights with handles, used for exercises to strengthen your muscles

ket·tle·drum /ˈketldrʌm/ *n* [C] a large metal drum with a round bottom, used in an ORCHESTRA. A set of kettledrums is called TIMPANI.

ket·tling /ˈketl-ɪŋ/ *n* [U] a way of controlling the movement of protesters, in which the police form lines and do not let people leave an area for some time

kew·pie doll /ˈkjuːpi dɒl $ -dɑːl/ (*also* **kewpie**) *n* [C] a type of plastic DOLL from America with a fat body and a curl of hair on its head

key¹ /kiː/ ●●● S1 W2 *n* [C]
1 LOCK a small specially shaped piece of metal that you put into a lock and turn in order to lock or unlock a door, start a car etc: **house/car keys** *I lost my house keys.* | ***A bunch of keys*** *hung from his belt.* | **[+to]** *I can lend you a* ***spare key*** *to the store until you get one cut* (=made). ⚠ Don't say 'the key of' something. Say **the key to** something. → MASTER KEY, see picture at LOCK²
2 IMPORTANT PART **the key** the part of a plan, action etc that will make it possible for it to succeed: **[+to]** *Working well as a team is* ***the key to success****.* | *a discovery that may* ***hold the key*** *to our understanding of the universe*
3 COMPUTER the buttons that you press on a computer KEYBOARD to operate the computer: *Press the 'Escape' key to exit.* | **hot key/shortcut key** (=a special key on a computer, that does specific things)
4 MUSIC **a)** [usually plural] the wooden or metal parts that you press on a piano and some wind instruments in order to play them: *piano keys* **b)** a scale of notes that begins with one particular note, or the quality of sound this scale has: *a tune in the key of A minor* → see picture at PIANO¹
5 MAP/DRAWING a list of the signs, colours etc used on a map or technical drawing etc that explains what they mean
6 TEST the printed answers to a test or set of questions in a book
7 ISLAND [usually plural] a small flat island, especially one that is part of a group near the coast: *the Florida Keys*

key² ●●○ S3 W2 *adj* [no comparative] very important or necessary: *China's support is key to the success of the coalition.* | **key factor/points/questions etc** | *The president makes all the* ***key decisions*** *on foreign policy.* | **key role/player/figure etc** (=one with a lot of influence on a result) *The show has been hit by the departure of key personnel.* **THESAURUS** IMPORTANT, MAIN → LOW-KEY

key³ ●●○ *v* [T]
1 *AmE informal* if you key a win for your team, you help it win a game because you play very well: *Abdul keyed the game with three touchdowns.*
2 *BrE* to prepare a surface so that a covering such as paint will stick to it
key sth ↔ **in** *phr v* to put information into a computer or other machine, using buttons or a keyboard: *Key in your password and press 'Return'.*
key sth **to** sth *phr v AmE*
1 to make or change a system so that it works well with something else: *The daycare hours are keyed to the needs of working parents.*
2 if the level, price, or value of something is keyed to something else, it is related to it and they rise and fall at the same time: *Pensions are keyed to the rate of inflation.* → KEYED UP

KEYBOARDS

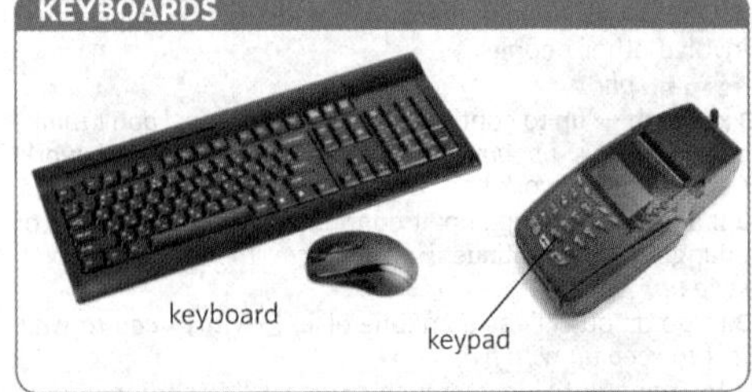

key·board¹ /ˈkiːbɔːd $ -bɔːrd/ ●●● S3 *n* [C]
1 a board with buttons marked with letters or numbers that are pressed to put information into a computer or other machine: *a computer keyboard*
2 the row of keys on some musical instruments that you press in order to play them
3 (*also* **keyboards**) [plural] an electronic musical instrument similar to a piano that can make sounds like many

different instruments → **synthesizer**: *Chris Kelly (guitar) and Benny Hayes (keyboards and vocals)*

keyboard² *v* [I,T] to put information into a computer, using a keyboard —**keyboarding** *n* [U]: *keyboarding errors*

key·board·er /ˈkiːˌbɔːdə $ -ˌbɔːrdər/ *n* [C] someone whose job is to put information into a computer, using a keyboard → **typist**

key·board·ist /ˈkiːbɔːdɪst $ -ɔːr-/ *n* [C] someone who plays the keyboard

ˈkey card *n* [C] a special plastic card that you put in an electronic lock to open a door etc

ˈkey chain *n* [C] a chain with a key ring attached, used for holding keys

ˌkeyed ˈup *adj* [not before noun] worried or excited: **[+with/about/at]** *Travis was keyed up at the thought of seeing Rosie again.*

key·hold·er /ˈkiːˌhəʊldə $ -ˌhoʊldər/ *n* [C] someone who is officially responsible for keeping the key to an office building, factory etc

key·hole /ˈkiːhəʊl $ -hoʊl/ *n* [C] the hole in a lock that you put the key in: *I peeped through the keyhole and watched them.*

ˌkeyhole ˈsurgery *n* [U] *BrE* medical operations done through a very small hole in the body

key·log /ˈkiːlɒg $ -lɒːg, -lɑːg/ *v* [T] to record which computer keys are pressed, often secretly

key·log·ger /ˈkiːˌlɒgə $ -ˌlɒːgər, ˌ-lɑːg-/ *n* [C] a piece of software that records which computer keys are pressed

key·note¹ /ˈkiːnəʊt $ -noʊt/ *n* [C] the main point in a book, system of beliefs, activity etc that influences everything else: **[+of]** *Unprecedented change has been the keynote of the electronic revolution.*

keynote² *adj* [only before noun] relating to the most important part of a formal meeting, report etc: **keynote speech/address/lecture etc** *He is scheduled to deliver the keynote address at an awards ceremony.* | *Bill Gates is booked as the* ***keynote speaker***.

keynote³ *v* [I,T] to give the keynote speech at a formal meeting, ceremony etc: *The event is usually keynoted by the prime minister.*

key·pad /ˈkiːpæd/ *n* [C] a small box with buttons on it, used to put information into a computer, telephone etc

key·pal /ˈkiːpæl/ *n* [C] someone with whom you regularly exchange email → **pen pal**: *If your daughter is interested in having a keypal next year, please have her get in touch.*

ˈkey ring *n* [C] a metal ring that you keep keys on

ˈkey ˌsignature *n* [C] a set of marks at the beginning of a line of written music to show which KEY it is in

key·stone /ˈkiːstəʊn $ -stoʊn/ *n* **1** [C] the large central stone in an ARCH that keeps the other stones in position **2** [singular] *formal* the most important part of an idea, belief, or process that influences how it develops: **[+of]** *The keystone of any personal injury case is medical evidence.*

ˌKeystone ˈCops, the a group of characters in humorous US SILENT FILMS. They are police officers who are very stupid and are always making silly mistakes. A group of people, especially police officers, are sometimes compared to the Keystone Cops if they fail to do something properly because they have made stupid mistakes.

key·stroke /ˈkiːstrəʊk $ -stroʊk/ *n* [C] the action of pressing a key on a computer or other machine

key·word /ˈkiːwɜːd $ -wɜːrd/ *n* [C] a word that you type into a computer so that it will search for that word on the Internet: *You can find the site by entering the keyword 'Quark'.*

ˌkey ˈworker *n* [C] *especially BrE* someone such as a teacher, nurse, or FIREFIGHTER who does a useful and important job and is paid by the state: *We need to provide affordable housing for key workers.*

kg (*plural* **kg** *or* **kgs**) the written abbreviation of ***kilogram*** or ***kilograms*** → **mg**

kha·ki /ˈkɑːki $ ˈkæki, ˈkɑːki/ *n* [U] **1** a dull green-brown or yellow-brown colour **2** cloth of this colour, especially when worn by soldiers —**khaki** *adj*: *a khaki uniform*

kha·kis /ˈkɑːkiz $ ˈkækiz, ˈkɑː-/ *n* [plural] trousers made of khaki cloth

kha·lif /ˈkeɪləf, kɑːˈliːf/ *n* [C] another spelling of CALIPH

khan /kɑːn/ *n* [C] a ruler or official in India or central Asia, or their title

kha·zi /ˈkɑːzi $ ˈkɑːr-/ (*also* **karzy**, **karzi**) *n* [C] *BrE informal* a toilet

kHz the written abbreviation of ***kilohertz*** → **MHz**

kib·ble /ˈkɪbəl/ *n* [U] small round pieces of dried dog or cat food

kib·butz /kɪˈbʊts/ *n* (*plural* **kibbutzim** /-sɪm/) [C] a type of farm in Israel where many people live and work together

kib·itz /ˈkɪbɪts/ *v* [I] *AmE informal* **1** to make unhelpful remarks while someone is doing something **2** to talk about things that everyone already knows in a boring way: *incessant philosophical kibitzing* —**kibitzer** *n* [C]: *the usual crowd of kibitzers*

kib·lah, **qiblah** /ˈkɪblə/ *n* [singular] the direction towards which Muslims turn when they pray

ki·bosh /ˈkaɪbɒʃ $ -bɑːʃ/ *n* **put the kibosh on sth** *old-fashioned informal* to stop a plan, idea etc from developing SYN **ruin**

kick¹ /kɪk/ ●●● S2 W3 *v* [I,T]

1 to hit something with your foot: **kick sth down/over/around etc** *Billy was kicking a ball around the yard.* | *The police kicked the door down.* | **kick sb in the stomach/face/shin etc** *There was a scuffle and he kicked me in the stomach.*

2 to move your legs as if you are kicking something: *He kicked off his shoes and lay back on the bed.* | *a row of dancers kicking their legs in the air* | *A horse trotted past, kicking up dust from the road.*

3 kick yourself *spoken* used to say that you are annoyed with yourself because you have done something silly, made a mistake etc: *You'll kick yourself when I tell you the answer.* | *United will be kicking themselves for missing several chances.*

4 kick the habit to stop doing something that is a harmful habit, such as smoking, taking drugs etc: *The scheme helps smokers to kick the habit.*

5 kick sb when they are down to criticize or attack someone who is already in a weak or difficult position: *The media can't resist kicking a man when he's down.*

6 kick sb in the teeth (*also* **kick sb in the stomach/pants** *AmE*) *informal* to disappoint someone or treat them badly at a time when they need help: *We all have times when life kicks us in the teeth.*

7 kick sb's ass/butt *AmE informal not polite* to punish or defeat someone: *We're gonna kick San Francisco's ass good tonight.*

8 kick ass *AmE informal not polite* used to say that someone or something is very good or impressive: *Tucson pop band Shoebomb kick some serious ass.*

9 kick your heels *BrE* to waste time waiting for something: *We were left kicking our heels for half the day.*

10 kick up your heels to enjoy yourself a lot at a party, event etc: *The charity ball is a chance to kick up your heels and help a good cause.*

11 kick sth into touch *BrE informal* to stop a plan or project before it is completed: *A hitch resulted in the deal being kicked firmly into touch.*

12 kick up a fuss/stink/row *informal* to complain loudly about something: *Won't he kick up a fuss when he discovers they're missing?*

13 kicking and screaming protesting violently or being very unwilling to do something: *The company* ***was dragged kicking and screaming*** *into the 21st century.*

14 kick the shit out of sb *informal not polite* to hurt someone very badly by kicking them many times

15 kick against the pricks *BrE informal* to hurt or damage yourself by trying to change something that cannot be changed

16 kick sb upstairs to move someone to a new job that

K

seems to be more important than their last one, but that actually gives them less influence
17 be kicking (it) *AmE spoken* to be relaxing and having a good time: *I was just kicking with my buddies.*
18 be kicking it *AmE spoken* to be having a romantic or sexual relationship with someone: **[+with]** *My sources say that she was kicking it with Thomas while she was on tour.*
19 kick over the traces *BrE old-fashioned* to start behaving badly by refusing to accept any control or rules
20 kick the bucket *old-fashioned* to die – used humorously
kick (out) against sth *phr v* to react strongly against something: *She has kicked out against authority all her life.*
kick around *phr v*
1 kick sth around to think about or discuss an idea before making a decision: *We kicked that suggestion around and in the end decided to go ahead.*
2 kick sb around to treat someone badly and unfairly: *I have my pride, you know. They can't kick me around.*
3 kick around (sth) to be in a place doing things, but without any firm plans SYN **knock around**: *He kicked around India for a few months.*
4 to be left in a place untidily or forgotten: *There's a copy of the report kicking around somewhere.*
kick back *phr v AmE* to relax: *Your waitress will take your order while you kick back and enjoy the game.*
kick in *phr v*
1 *informal* to start or to begin to have an effect: *The storm is expected to kick in shortly after sunrise.* | *The painkillers kicked in and he became sleepy.*
2 kick in (sth) to join with others in giving money or help SYN **chip in**: *Bill never wants to kick in.* | *We were each asked to kick in 50 cents toward the cost.*
3 kick sb's head/face/teeth in to injure someone badly by kicking them: *He threatened to come round and kick my head in.*
4 kick a door in to kick a locked door so hard that it breaks open: *We had to get the police to kick the door in.*
kick off *phr v*
1 if a meeting, event, or a football game kicks off, it starts: *What time does the laser show kick off?* | *The match kicks off at noon.* | **[+with]** *The series kicked off with an interview with Brando.*
2 *informal* if you kick off a discussion, meeting, event etc, you start it: *OK Marion, would you care to kick off?* | **kick sth ↔ off (with sth)** *I'm going to kick off today's meeting with a few remarks about the budget.*
3 kick sb off sth *informal* to remove someone from a team or group: *Joe was kicked off the committee for stealing funds.*
4 *AmE informal* to die
5 *BrE spoken* if a fight kicks off, people start fighting: *I think it might **kick off** in here with all these football fans around.*
kick sb **↔ out** *phr v* to make someone leave a place, job etc SYN **throw out**: *Bernard's wife kicked him out.* | **[+of]** *He was kicked out of the golf club.*

kick² ●●○ S3 *n* [C]
1 a movement of your foot or leg, usually to hit something with your foot: *Brazil scored with the last kick of the match.* | *Rory **aimed a kick at** her leg and missed.* | *kung fu kicks* | *If the door won't open, just **give it a** good **kick**.*
2 the act of kicking the ball in a sports game such as football, or the ball that is kicked and the direction it goes in: *Benjamin struck a post with an overhead kick.* | **free/penalty kick** (=an opportunity, allowed by the rules, for a player in one team to kick the ball without being stopped by the other team) *Pearce came forward to **take** the free **kick**.*
3 something that you enjoy because it is exciting SYN **thrill**: **get a kick out of/from (doing) sth** *Gerald gets a kick out of dressing as a woman.* | **give sb a kick** *It gives her a kick to get you into trouble.* | **do sth (just) for kicks** *She used to steal from shops for kicks.*
4 a kick up the arse/backside/pants etc *informal* criticism or strong encouragement to make someone do something they should have done: *What Phil **needs** is **a good kick up the arse**.*
5 a kick in the teeth *informal* something that is very disappointing or upsetting that happens when you need support: *This broken promise is a real kick in the teeth for our fans.*
6 a kick *informal* used to talk about the strong effect of a drink or drug or the strong taste that some food has: *The wine had a real kick.*
ˈkick-ass *adj AmE informal* strong, powerful, and sometimes violent: *a kick-ass attitude*
kick·back /ˈkɪkbæk/ *n* [C] *informal* money that someone pays secretly and dishonestly in return for someone's help SYN **bribe**
kick·ball /ˈkɪkbɔːl $ -bɒːl/ *n* [U] an American game for children, similar to baseball, in which you kick the ball
kick·box·ing /ˈkɪkˌbɒksɪŋ $ -ˌbɑːks-/ *n* [U] a form of BOXING in which you kick someone as well as hitting them —**kickboxer** *n* [C]
kick·er /ˈkɪkə $ -ər/ *n* **1** [C] a player in a sports team who kicks the ball to score points **2** [singular] *AmE* a surprising or important ending to something: *The kicker came when the reporter asked the runner whether she was tired.*
kick·flare trou·sers /ˈkɪkfleə ˌtraʊzəz $ -fler ˌtraʊzərz/ (*also* **kickflares**) *n* [plural] *BrE* women's trousers that become wider below the knee → **flares**
kick·flip /ˈkɪkflɪp/ *n* [C] another word for a HEELFLIP
kick·off /ˈkɪk-ɒf $ -ɒːf/ *n* [C usually singular] **1** the time when a football game starts, or the first kick of the game: *Kickoff is at 3.00.* **2** *informal* the beginning of a new activity
kick·stand /ˈkɪkstænd/ *n* [C] a thin piece of metal on the bottom of a bicycle or MOTORCYCLE that supports it in an upright position when it is not moving → see picture at **MOTORBIKE**
ˈkick-start¹ *v* [T] **1** to do something to help a process or activity start or develop more quickly: *He urged further interest rate cuts in a bid to kick-start the economy.* **2** to start a MOTORCYCLE using your foot
kick-start² *n* **1** [C] (*also* **ˈkick-starter**) the part of a MOTORCYCLE that you press with your foot to start it **2** [singular] action taken to make a plan, project etc start or develop more quickly: *Motivation is the kick-start you need to succeed at work.*
kid¹ /kɪd/ ●●● S1 W2 *n*
1 [C] *informal* a child: *She'd always loved animals since she was a **little kid**.* | *He's married with three kids.* | *A neighbor volunteered to keep an eye on **the kids*** (=their children or the children they are responsible for). THESAURUS ▸ CHILD

> **REGISTER**
> **Kid** is informal. For formal or written styles use **child**: *Research suggests that **children** from abusive families are likely to repeat violent behaviour.*

2 [C] *informal* a young person: *college kids*
3 [C usually singular] used by adults to address a person who is younger than them: *Hey kid, come here.*
4 kid's stuff (*also* **kid stuff** *AmE*) something that is too easy or boring: *Pokémon? Oh boy, that is kid stuff!*
5 a) [C] a young goat **b)** [U] very soft leather made from the skin of a young goat: *a pair of white kid boots*
6 kid gloves a way of treating someone kindly and carefully because they easily become upset: **treat/handle sb with kid gloves** *I want you to treat Hayley with kid gloves today. She's still upset about her father.*
kid² ●●○ *v* (**kidded**, **kidding**) *informal*
1 [I,T] to say something that is not true, especially as a joke SYN **joke**: **just/only kidding** *Don't get mad – I was only kidding.*
2 [T] to make jokes or say funny things about someone in a friendly way SYN **tease**: **kid sb about sth** *We were kidding Mom about being a grandmother.* | **kid sb (that)** *My friends kidded me that my gear would fill the car.*
3 no kidding?/are you kidding?/you're kidding *spoken* used when you are so surprised by what someone has told you

that you do not completely believe them: *Carlotta's 39? No kidding?*
4 no kidding *spoken* **a)** used to say that you understand and agree with what someone has just said: *'That girl has some major problems.' 'Yeah, no kidding.'* **b)** used to emphasize a threat or that you are telling the truth: *If you break that thing, you'll be grounded for a week – no kidding. | And then he saw us and – no kidding – he asked us if we wanted a ride.*
5 [T] to let yourself believe something that is untrue or unlikely: **kid yourself (that)** *Don't kid yourself he'll ever change. | We thought we could change the world. Just* ***who were we trying to kid****?*
6 I kid you not *spoken* used to emphasize that you are telling the truth —**kidding** *n* [U]
kid around *phr v* to behave in a silly way: *Stop kidding around and listen.*

kid³ *adj* **kid sister/brother** *especially AmE informal* your kid sister or brother is younger than you are SYN **little sister/brother** *BrE*

kid·die¹, **kiddy** /ˈkɪdi/ *n* [C] *especially BrE informal* a young child: *a sandpit for the kiddies*

kiddie², **kiddy** *adj* [only before noun] made for, involving, or intended for young children: *a kiddie seat*

ˈkiddie-cam *n* [C] a camera that allows parents to see their children when the parents are somewhere else

kid·do /ˈkɪdəʊ $ -doʊ/ *n* (*plural* **kiddos**) [C usually singular] *AmE spoken informal* used by adults to address a young person: *Come on, kiddo, let's go.*

kid·nap /ˈkɪdnæp/ ●●○ *v* (**kidnapped**, **kidnapping** *also* **kidnaped**, **kidnaping** *AmE*) [T] to take someone somewhere illegally by force, often in order to get money for returning them → **ransom**: *Police appealed for witnesses after a woman was kidnapped at gunpoint.* —**kidnapper** *n* [C]: *the hunt for the kidnapper* —**kidnapping** (*also* **kidnap**) *n* [C,U]: *a series of kidnappings*

kid·ney /ˈkɪdni/ ●●○ *n*
1 [C] one of the two organs in your lower back that separate waste products from your blood and make URINE: *a kidney transplant* → see picture at **HUMAN¹**
2 [C,U] one or more of these organs from an animal, used as food: *steak and kidney pie*

ˈkidney bean *n* [C] a dark red bean that is shaped like the letter C

kid·ult /ˈkɪdʌlt/ *n* [C] an adult who likes to play games or buy things that most people consider more suitable for children

kike /kaɪk/ *n* [C] *taboo* a very offensive word for someone who is Jewish. Do not use this word.

kill¹ /kɪl/ ●●● S1 W1 *v*
1 MAKE SB/STH DIE [I,T] to make a person or animal die: *Why did she kill her husband? | Murray held a gun to his head and threatened to kill him. | Four people were killed when a train plunged into a flooded river.* | **be killed instantly/outright** (=immediately) *The driver was killed instantly. | Bleach kills household germs. | Smoking kills.*
2 kill yourself a) to cause your own death: *You're going to kill yourself on that bike. | After her husband died, Mary tried to kill herself.* **b)** to work very hard to achieve something, in a way that makes you ill or tired: *It's not worth killing yourself over it.* | **kill yourself to do sth** *He about killed himself to make the business go.*
3 MAKE STH STOP/FAIL [T] to make something stop operating or fail: *Joe pulled in and killed the engine. | The out-of-town shopping centre will kill local trade.* | **kill your speed** (=drive slowly)
4 BE ANGRY WITH SB [T] *informal* to be very angry with someone: *Mom will kill me if I'm late.*
5 ANNOYED/SAD [T] to make someone feel annoyed, sad, concerned etc: **it kills sb to do sth** *It kills me to see him working so hard. | What happened next?* ***The suspense is killing me.***
6 would/could kill for sth (*also* **would kill to do sth**) to want something so much that you will do almost anything to get it or do it: *I could kill for a smoke right now. | In those days, actors would kill to break into film.*
7 my head/back etc is killing me *spoken* used to say that a part of your body is hurting a lot: *I've walked miles and my feet are killing me.*
8 kill time/an hour etc to spend time doing something which is not important, while you are waiting to do something important or waiting for something else to happen: *With time to kill, he took a cab to the centre.*
9 kill a beer/bottle of wine etc *spoken* to drink or finish drinking a beer etc quickly: *Let's kill these beers and go.*
10 MAKE SB LAUGH [T] to make someone laugh a lot: **kill yourself laughing** *They weren't bothered – in fact, they were killing themselves laughing.*
11 it won't/wouldn't kill sb (to do something) *spoken* used to say that someone could easily do something, and ought to do it: *It wouldn't kill you to help out once in a while.*
12 (even) if it kills me *spoken* used to emphasize that you are determined to do something, even though it is very difficult: *I'm completing this course, even if it kills me.*
13 kill two birds with one stone to achieve two things with one action
14 kill the goose that lays the golden egg to destroy the thing that brings you profit or success
15 kill the fatted calf to welcome someone home with a big meal etc after they have been away for a long time
16 kill sb with kindness to be too kind to someone, in a way that actually harms them
17 kill or cure used to say that something you are going to do will be either successful or fail completely → **dressed to kill** at DRESSED(3)

THESAURUS

kill to make someone die: *The driver and his passenger were killed in the crash. | He was killed by rival gang members.*
murder to deliberately kill someone – used when talking about this as a crime: *He was convicted of murdering his wife.*
commit manslaughter to kill someone without intending to – used when talking about this as a crime: *The court ruled that the guard had committed manslaughter.*
assassinate to deliberately kill an important person, especially a politician: *He was part of a plot to assassinate Hitler.*
slay to kill someone or something in a violent way – used in newspaper reports and also in old stories: *Two teenagers were slain in the shootings. | St. George slew the dragon.*
execute *formal* (*also* **put sb to death**) to kill someone as a punishment for a crime: *McVeigh, who killed 168 people in a bombing attack, was executed by lethal injection.*
eliminate to kill someone in order to prevent them from causing trouble: *a ruthless dictator who eliminated all his rivals*
take sb out *informal* to kill someone in order to get rid of them, especially an enemy or someone who is causing trouble for you: *US forces used air strikes to take out the enemy positions. | One of the other drug dealers may have decided to take him out.*
bump sb off *humorous informal* to kill someone: *He was so irritating I felt like bumping him off myself.*

TO KILL YOURSELF

commit suicide to kill yourself: *He committed suicide after the death of his girlfriend.*
take your own life *formal* to kill yourself: *He had taken his own life while he was severely depressed. | They believe that it is a sin to take your own life.*

TO KILL A LARGE NUMBER OF PEOPLE

massacre to kill a large number of people in a violent way: *Thousands of peaceful demonstrators were massacred by the soldiers.*
slaughter to kill a large number of people in a violent way. Slaughter is also used about killing

animals for food: *The army slaughtered thousands of civilians in an effort to stop the revolt.* | *The pigs were slaughtered on the farm.*
exterminate to kill large numbers of a particular group, so that they no longer exist: *Hitler's goal was to exterminate the Jews.*

kill sth ↔ **off** *phr v*
1 to cause the death of a lot of living things SYN **destroy**: *Pollution is rapidly killing off plant life.*
2 to stop or remove something completely SYN **destroy**: *These figures kill off any hope that the economy is poised for recovery.*

kill² *n* **1** [C usually singular] the act of killing a hunted animal: *He raised his knife for the kill.* **2 move in/close in for the kill** to come closer to something in order to kill, defeat, or destroy it: *Enemy submarines were moving in for the kill.* **3** [singular] an animal that is killed by another animal: *The cubs will share the remains of the kill.*

kill·er¹ /ˈkɪlə $ -ər/ ●●○ *n* [C]
1 a person, animal, or thing that kills: *Heart disease is America's number one killer.* | *the hunt for her killers* | *weed killer* → **serial killer** at SERIAL²(1)
2 *informal* something or someone that is very difficult, tiring, or boring: *The new project is a killer.*
3 *informal* something that is very exciting or impressive: *I'm not saying the film is a killer, but it's cool.*

killer² *adj* [only before noun] **1** very harmful or dangerous: *a killer hurricane* | *a swarm of killer bees* **2** *informal* very attractive, good, impressive etc: *a book called 'How to Build a Killer Website'* | **killer heels** (=women's shoes with very high heels) **3 killer instinct** a very strong desire to succeed in a situation or activity etc that is very competitive: *Young players these days lack the killer instinct.*

killer app /ˈkɪlər æp/ (*also* **killer application**) *n* [C] a piece of computer SOFTWARE that many want to buy, especially one that works so well on a particular machine that people want to buy it

ˈkiller whale *n* [C] a black and white WHALE that eats meat

kill·ing /ˈkɪlɪŋ/ ●●○ *n* [C]
1 the act of killing someone deliberately SYN **murder**: *a series of gangland killings* | *They murdered fifteen boys in a* ***killing spree*** (=an occasion when someone murders many people in a short period of time) *across southern California.*
2 make a killing *informal* to make a lot of money in a short time: *He made a killing on the stock exchange.*

kill·joy /ˈkɪldʒɔɪ/ *n* [C] someone who spoils other people's pleasure

kiln /kɪln/ *n* [C] a special OVEN for baking clay pots, bricks etc

ki·lo /ˈkiːləʊ $ -loʊ/ ●●● S3 *n* (*plural* **kilos**) [C] a kilogram

kilo- /kɪlə/ *prefix* [in nouns] a thousand - used with units of measurement

kil·o·byte /ˈkɪləbaɪt/ *n* [C] (*written abbreviation* **K** *or* **KB**) a unit for measuring computer information, equal to 1,024 BYTES

kil·o·gram (*also* **kilogramme** *BrE*) /ˈkɪləgræm/ ●●● S3 W3 *n* [C] (*written abbreviation* **kg**) a unit for measuring weight, equal to 1,000 grams

kil·o·hertz /ˈkɪləhɜːts $ -ɜːr-/ *n* (*plural* **kilohertz**) [C] (*written abbreviation* **kHz**) a unit for measuring the FREQUENCY of SOUND WAVES, especially radio signals, equal to 1,000 HERTZ

kil·o·me·tre *BrE*, **kilometer** *AmE* /ˈkɪləˌmiːtə, kɪˈlɒmɪtə $ kɪˈlɑːmɪtər/ ●●● S3 W3 *n* [C] (*written abbreviation* **km**) a unit for measuring distance, equal to 1,000 metres

kil·o·watt /ˈkɪləwɒt $ -wɑːt/ *n* [C] (*written abbreviation* **kW**) a unit for measuring electrical power, equal to 1,000 WATTS

ˌkilowatt ˈhour *n* [C] (*written abbreviation* **kWh**) a unit for measuring electrical power, equal to the amount of work produced by one kilowatt in one hour

kilt /kɪlt/ *n* [C] a type of thick skirt made of TARTAN (=material with a pattern of lines and squares) that is traditionally worn by Scottish men —**kilted** *adj*

kil·ter /ˈkɪltə $ -ər/ *n* **out of kilter/off kilter** not working as well as usual: *Pollution has* ***thrown*** *the Earth's chemistry* ***out of kilter***.

kim·chi /ˈkɪmtʃi/ *n* [U] a Korean hot-tasting dish made of PICKLED cabbage and other vegetables

ki·mo·no /kɪˈməʊnəʊ $ -ˈmoʊnoʊ/ *n* (*plural* **kimonos**) [C] a traditional piece of Japanese clothing like a long loose coat, worn at special ceremonies

kin /kɪn/ *n* [plural] **1** *informal* (*also* **kinsfolk**, **kinfolk** *AmE old-fashioned*) your family **2 next of kin** *formal* your most closely related family: *We'll have to notify the next of kin of his death.* → **kindred** → KITH AND KIN

kind¹ /kaɪnd/ ●●● S1 W1 *n*
1 [C,U] one of the different types of a person or thing that belong to the same group SYN **sort, type**: **[+of]** *They sell all kinds of things.* | *The flowers attract several different kinds of insects.* | *Greg was working on some kind of deal in Italy.* | *Get me a sandwich - any kind will do.*
2 the kind used to describe a person with a particular character, feelings, opinions etc: *Ted just isn't the marrying kind.* | *Rob isn't the kind to worry.*
3 sb's kind of person/thing/place etc the type of person, thing, place etc that someone usually likes: *It's not my kind of place - it's too quiet.*
4 kind of (*also* **kinda** *AmE*) *spoken* slightly but not exactly, or in some ways SYN **sort of**: *I'm kind of glad I didn't win.* | *He's kinda dumb, isn't he?*
5 a kind of (a) sth *spoken* used to say that your description of something is not exact: *a kind of reddish-brown color*
6 two/three etc of a kind two, three etc people or things that are very similar: *You and Joe are two of a kind.*
7 one of a kind the only one of a particular type of thing: *Each plate is handpainted and one of a kind.*
8 something of the/that kind *spoken* something similar to what was expected or talked about: *Rosa was shocked by the news, although she had suspected something of the kind might happen.*
9 nothing/anything of the kind *spoken* used to emphasize that what has been said is not true: *I never said anything of the kind!*
10 of a kind used to say that something is not as good as it should be: *Elections of a kind are held, but there is only one party to vote for.*
11 in kind reacting to something someone has done by doing the same thing: *After recent bombings, counter-terrorist forces could retaliate in kind.* → **payment in kind** at PAYMENT(3)

kind² ●●● S3 W3 *adj* (*comparative* **kinder**, *superlative* **kindest**)
1 saying or doing things that show that you care about other people and want to help them or make them happy OPP **unkind** → **kindly**, **kindness**: **[+to]** *They've been very kind to me.* | *It wasn't a very kind thing to say.* | *She's a very kind and generous person.* | **it's kind of sb (to do sth)** *It's kind of you to say that.* | *It's really kind of them to let us use their pool.* | *We thanked the priest for his* ***kind words***. | *Thank you for your help. You've been* ***most kind*** (=said when thanking someone very politely). | **thank you for your kind invitation/offer** (=said when thanking someone very politely for their invitation or offer) | *Ms Jarvis is unable to accept your* ***kind invitation***.

GRAMMAR

You are **kind to** someone: *He was kind to her.* ✗ Don't say: *He was kind with her.*

GRAMMAR GUIDE ▸ ADJECTIVES

2 not causing harm or suffering: **[+to]** *Life has been very kind to me.* | *I need a soap that's kinder to my skin.* | *Let's hope the weather's kind tomorrow.*
3 would you be kind enough to do sth/be so kind as to do sth *formal* used to make a polite request: *Would you be kind enough to close the door, please?*

REGISTER

In everyday English, people usually say **please could you ...?** or **would you mind ...?** because the expressions with **kind** can sound too formal and unfriendly: *Would you mind closing the door?*

4 kind regards *written* used to end a formal but fairly friendly letter

THESAURUS

kind someone who is kind tries to help people and make them happy or comfortable, and shows that they care about them: *They were very kind to us and let us stay in their house as long as we liked.* | *a kind old lady* | *a kind thing to say*
nice *especially spoken* friendly and kind. Nice is very common in everyday spoken English and is often used instead of **kind**: *Everyone has been so nice to me.* | *It's nice of you to invite me here.* | *He seems such a nice man.*
generous kind because you give people money, presents etc: *'I'll pay for the meal.' 'That's very generous of you.'* | *a generous gift*
considerate thinking about other people's feelings, and careful not to do anything that will upset them: *Our neighbours are very considerate and always keep their TV turned down.* | *a considerate driver*
thoughtful thinking of things you can do to make other people happy or feel good – used especially when someone does something such as giving someone a present or helping someone: *It was thoughtful of you to send him a card.* | *Some thoughtful person had taken her bag to the lost property office.*
caring kind and wanting to help and look after people: *She's lucky to have such a loving and caring husband.* | *The British are well-known for their caring attitude toward animals.*
sympathetic saying kind things to someone who has problems and behaving in a way that shows you care about them: *My boss was very sympathetic and said I should take some time off work.* | *She gave him a sympathetic smile.*
good kind and showing that you want to help – used especially in the following phrases: ***It was good of you to*** *come and see me.* | *She's always been very* ***good to*** *us.*
sweet *informal* very kind – used especially when you like someone very much, or you are very pleased because of something they have done: *I was given the flowers by a sweet little old lady who lived next door.* | *It's sweet of you to ask.*
kind-hearted/warm-hearted *especially written* having a kind and friendly character, which makes other people like you: *He was a wonderful father, kind-hearted and always laughing.* | *The town is full of warm-hearted, helpful people.*
benevolent *formal* kind and wanting to help people – often used about someone who is important or who people respect: *a benevolent ruler* | *They believe in the existence of a benevolent God who will save mankind.* | *He listened politely, like some benevolent uncle.*

kin·der·gar·ten /ˈkɪndəɡɑːtn $ -dərɡɑːrtn/ *n* [C,U] **1** *AmE* a school or class for children aged five **2** *BrE* a school for children aged two to five SYN **nursery school**

kind-heart·ed /ˌkaɪnd ˈhɑːtɪd◂ $ -ɑːr-/ *adj* kind and generous: *a kind-hearted gesture* **THESAURUS** ▸ KIND —**kind-heartedly** *adv* —**kind-heartedness** *n* [U]

kin·dle /ˈkɪndl/ *v* [I,T] **1** if you kindle a fire, or if it kindles, it starts to burn **2** to make someone feel interested, excited, hopeful etc: **kindle sth in sb** *A love of poetry was kindled in him by his mother.*

Kindle *n trademark* a special small computer that you can hold in your hands and use to read an E-BOOK (=book that is stored electronically rather being made of paper). Users can DOWNLOAD content for the machine from the Internet. The Kindle was developed by a company called Amazon.com

kin·dling /ˈkɪndlɪŋ/ *n* [U] small sticks, leaves etc that you use to start a fire → **firewood**

kind·ly¹ /ˈkaɪndli/ ●●○ *adv*
1 in a kind way SYN **generously**: **kindly offer/agree/give etc** *Mr Nunn has kindly agreed to let us use his barn for the dance.*
2 not take kindly to sth to be unwilling to accept a situation because it annoys you: *She does not take kindly to criticism.*
3 look kindly on sb/sth to approve of someone or something: *Jimmy would probably not look too kindly on our request.*
4 *spoken formal* a word meaning 'please', which is often used when you are annoyed: *Will you kindly put that book back?*

kindly² *adj old-fashioned* kind and caring for other people: *Mrs Gardiner was a kindly old soul.* —**kindliness** *n* [U]

kind·ness /ˈkaɪndnəs/ ●●○ *n*
1 [U] kind behaviour towards someone: *I can't thank you enough for your kindness.*

REGISTER

In everyday English, when you are thanking people for helping you, the normal phrase to use is **Thanks for (all) your help**. The phrase **Thank you for your kindness** sounds very polite and slightly old-fashioned.

2 [C] a kind action: **do sb a kindness** *It would be doing him a kindness to tell him the truth.* → **kill sb with kindness** at KILL¹(16)

kin·dred¹ /ˈkɪndrɪd/ *n* [U] *old use* your whole family → **kin**

kindred² *adj* [only before noun] **1 a kindred spirit** someone who thinks and feels the way you do **2** *formal* belonging to the same group or family: *The protest included members of Free the Streets and kindred organisations.*

ki·net·ic /kɪˈnetɪk, kaɪ-/ *adj technical* relating to movement: *kinetic energy*

ki·net·ics /kɪˈnetɪks, kaɪ-/ *n* [U] the science that studies movement

kin·folk /ˈkɪnfəʊk $ -foʊk/ *n* [plural] *AmE old-fashioned* KINSFOLK

king /kɪŋ/ ●●● W1 *n* [C]
1 RULER (*also* **King**) a man who rules a country because he is from a royal family → **queen**: **[+of]** *Henry VIII, King of England* | *On 2 December Henry VI was* ***crowned king*** (=made the king at an official ceremony).
2 THE BEST **the king of sth** someone or something that people think is the most important or best of a particular type of person or thing: *the King of Rock 'n' Roll* | *the king of Swiss cheeses* | *The lion is* ***the king of the jungle***.
3 SUCCESSFUL if you live like a king, feel like a king etc, you are very successful, happy, rich etc: *With her at my side, I felt like a king.*
4 CHESS the most important piece in CHESS → see picture at CHESS
5 CARDS a playing card with a picture of a king on it
6 IMPORTANT **be king** if something is king at a particular

K

time, it has a big influence on people: *back in the days when jazz was king*
7 a king's ransom a very large amount of money
king·dom /ˈkɪŋdəm/ ●●○ *n* [C]
1 a country ruled by a king or queen: *the United Kingdom* | **[+of]** *the kingdom of Thailand*
2 the animal/plant/mineral kingdom one of the three parts into which the natural world is divided
3 the kingdom of heaven/God (*also* **God's kingdom**) heaven
4 kingdom come *informal* a phrase used to describe the end of the world, death, or the end of time: *He left the gas on and nearly* ***blew*** *us all* ***to kingdom come***.
king·fish·er /ˈkɪŋˌfɪʃə $ -ər/ *n* [C] a small brightly coloured bird with a blue body that catches fish in rivers
king·ly /ˈkɪŋli/ *adj formal* good enough for a king, or typical of a king: *a kingly feast*
king·mak·er /ˈkɪŋˌmeɪkə $ -ər/ *n* [C] someone who influences the choice of people for important jobs: *Her death thrust Newman into the position of kingmaker.*
king·pin /ˈkɪŋˌpɪn/ *n* [C usually singular] **1** the person or thing in a group that is the most important or that has the most power – used especially in news reports: **crime/drug etc kingpin** *a mafia kingpin* **2** *technical* a thin strong piece of metal used in HINGES
ˌKing's ˈCounsel *n* [C] *BrE* a KC
ˌKing's ˈEnglish (*also* **Queen's English**) *n* **the King's English** *old-fashioned* correct English, as it is spoken in Britain
ˌking's ˈevidence *n* **turn King's evidence** *BrE* to give information about other criminals in order to get a less severe punishment → **Queen's evidence** SYN **state's evidence** *AmE*
king·ship /ˈkɪŋʃɪp/ *n* [U] the official position or condition of being a king: *the responsibilities of kingship*
ˈking-size (*also* **ˈking-sized**) *adj* **1** very large, and usually the largest size of something: *a king-size bed* | *king-sized cigarettes* **2** *informal* very big, strong, or extreme: *a king-size headache*
kink¹ /kɪŋk/ *n* [C] **1** a twist in something that is normally straight: **[+in]** *The water hose had a kink in it.* **2** a small problem in a plan, system etc: *Given the size of the task, a few kinks are inevitable.* **3** something strange or dangerous in someone's character
kink² *v* [I,T] to have, get, or make a kink: *Take care to avoid kinking the wire.*
kink·y /ˈkɪŋki/ *adj* **1** *informal* having or showing unusual ways of getting sexual excitement: *kinky sex videos* **2** kinky hair has a lot of small curves —**kinkiness** *n* [U] —**kinkily** *adv*
kins·folk /ˈkɪnzfəʊk $ -foʊk/ (*also* **kinfolk** *AmE*) *n* [plural] *old-fashioned* your family
kin·ship /ˈkɪnʃɪp/ *n* **1** [U] *literary* a family relationship: *the ties of kinship* **2** [singular, U] a strong connection between people → **rapport**: **[+between]** *The sense of kinship between the two men is surprising.* | *He* ***felt a kinship*** *with the only other American on the base.*
kins·man /ˈkɪnzmən/ *n* (*plural* **kinsmen** /-mən/) [C] *old use* a male relative
kin·swom·an /ˈkɪnzˌwʊmən/ *n* (*plural* **kinswomen** /-ˌwɪmɪn/) [C] *old use* a female relative
ki·osk /ˈkiːɒsk $ -ɑːsk/ *n* [C] **1** a small building in the street, where newspapers, sweets etc are sold **2** *BrE old-fashioned* a public telephone box
kip¹ /kɪp/ *n* [singular, U] *BrE informal* a period of sleep: *I've only* ***had*** *an hour's* ***kip***. | *We ought to* ***get some kip***.
kip² *v* (**kipped**, **kipping**) [I] *BrE informal* to sleep somewhere, especially somewhere that is not your home: **[+down]** *There are rooms for drivers to kip down for the night.* | **[+on]** *Mum says you can kip on the sofa tonight.*
kip·per /ˈkɪpə $ -ər/ *n* [C] a HERRING (=type of fish) that has been preserved using smoke and salt —**kippered** *adj*: *kippered herring*
kirk /kɜːk $ kɜːrk/ *n* **1** [C] a church – used in Scotland and northern England **2 the Kirk** the Church of Scotland
kirsch /kɪəʃ $ kɪrʃ/ *n* [U] a strong alcoholic drink made from CHERRY juice
kis·met /ˈkɪzmet, ˈkɪs-/ *n* [U] *literary* the things that will happen to you in your life SYN **fate**
kiss¹ /kɪs/ ●●● S3 W3 *v*
1 [I,T] to touch someone with your lips as a greeting, to show them love, or as part of a sexual relationship: *Maggie leaned forward and kissed her cheek.* | *Georgina took him in her arms and kissed him on the lips.* | *Jim and Mary kissed* (=they kissed each other). | **kiss sb gently/lightly** *He kissed her gently and stroked her hair.* | **kiss sb goodbye/good night etc** *Kiss Daddy good night.*

GRAMMAR: Reciprocal verbs

Kiss is a reciprocal verb. This type of verb is used when saying that two or more people do something that involves both or all of them. It does not need to have an object: *We kissed.* In this sentence, **kiss** is intransitive and does not have an object.
You can also say: *We kissed each other.* | *I kissed her.* In these sentences, **kiss** is transitive.
GRAMMAR GUIDE ▸ VERBS

2 [T] to touch something with your lips as a sign of respect: *She raised the crucifix to her lips and kissed it.*
3 kiss goodbye to sth/kiss sth goodbye *informal* to accept that you will lose something or lose an opportunity to do something: *She knew if she concentrated on her marriage she could kiss her career goodbye.*
4 kiss sth better *spoken* used, especially to a child, to say that you will take away the pain of something by kissing them: *Here, let Mommy kiss it better.*
5 kiss my ass *AmE informal not polite* an insulting expression used to show that you do not respect someone
6 kiss (sb's) ass *AmE informal not polite* to be too nice to someone who can give you something you want – used to show disapproval
7 [T] *literary* if the wind, sun etc kisses something, it gently moves or touches it
kiss up to sb *phr v AmE informal* to try to please someone in order to get them to do something for you – used to show disapproval SYN **suck up to** *BrE*: *If you say that, it'll look like you're kissing up to me.*
kiss² ●●● S3 *n* [C]
1 an act of kissing: *Do you remember your first kiss?*
2 give sb the kiss of life *especially BrE* to make someone start breathing again by blowing air into their lungs when they have almost DROWNed etc
3 the kiss of death *informal* something that spoils or ruins a plan, activity etc → FRENCH KISS

COLLOCATIONS

VERBS

give sb a kiss *I always give the kids a kiss before they go to school.*
blow sb a kiss (=to kiss your hand and then blow across it towards someone) *Joe blew her a kiss and waved goodbye.*
plant a kiss on sb's cheek/forehead etc (=to kiss someone on their cheek etc)

ADJECTIVES/NOUN + kiss

a big/little kiss *She put her arms around him and gave him a big kiss.*
a quick kiss *He gave her a quick kiss before leaving for work.*
a gentle/tender kiss *She could still feel that last tender kiss.*
a passionate kiss | **a long/lingering kiss** | **a sloppy kiss** (=a kiss with rather wet lips) | **a farewell/goodnight kiss** (=when saying goodbye or goodnight to someone) | **your first kiss**

PHRASES

love and kisses (=used at the end of a letter) *See you soon. Lots of love and kisses from Anna.*

kiss·a·gram /ˈkɪsəɡræm/ *n* [C] another spelling of KISSOGRAM

ˌkiss-and-ˈtell *n* [C usually singular] a story, article, book etc in which someone tells the public the secret details of a romantic relationship that they had with a famous person

kis·ser /ˈkɪsə $ -ər/ *n* [C] *informal* **1** [usually singular] your mouth: *She slapped me right in the kisser.* **2** a person who is kissing: **a good/bad etc kisser**

ˌkissing ˈcousin *n* [C] *AmE old-fashioned* someone you are not closely related to, but whom you know well

kiss·o·gram, **kissagram** /ˈkɪsəɡræm/ *n* [C] a humorous greeting for your BIRTHDAY etc that is delivered by someone in a special COSTUME who kisses you

KISS prin·ci·ple /ˈkɪs ˌprɪnsəpəl/ *n* **the KISS principle** the idea that products or processes should be kept as simple as possible because they will be more effective and easier to use. KISS is an abbreviation of 'keep it simple, stupid'.

kit¹ /kɪt/ ●●○ S3 *n*
1 [C] a set of tools, equipment etc that you use for a particular purpose or activity: *Sally keeps her make-up kit in her bag.* | *a bike repair kit* | *a shaving kit* | *a drum kit*
2 [C] something that you buy in parts and put together yourself: *model kits for making boats* | *kit cars*
3 [U] electronic equipment, especially computers and computer software: *The new kit includes wireless keyboard and gaming headset.*
4 [C,U] *BrE* a set of clothes and equipment that you use for a particular purpose such as playing a sport: *sports kit* | *football kits*
5 [U] a set of clothes and equipment used by soldiers, SAILORS etc: *The soldiers are trained to jump from the planes with full kit on.*
6 get your kit off *BrE informal* to take your clothes off
7 the whole kit and caboodle *old-fashioned* everything
→ **DRUM KIT, FIRST AID KIT, TOOL KIT**

kit² *v* (**kitted**, **kitting**)
kit sb/sth ↔ **out/up** *phr v BrE* if someone or something is kitted out with clothes or equipment, they are provided with the clothes or equipment needed for an activity: **be kitted out with/in** *The studio is lavishly kitted out with camera equipment.* | *Mark was kitted up in skis, boots, and equipment.* GRAMMAR **Kit out** is usually passive.

kit bag, **kit·bag** /ˈkɪtbæɡ/ *n* [C] *especially BrE* a long narrow bag used by soldiers, SAILORS etc for carrying their clothes and other possessions

kitch·en /ˈkɪtʃɪn/ ●●● S1 W2 *n* [C]
1 the room where you prepare and cook food: *Sam went into the kitchen to make a pot of tea.* | *She is in the kitchen making a meal.*
2 everything but the kitchen sink *humorous* used when someone has brought too many things with them

kitch·en·a·li·a /ˌkɪtʃəˈneɪliə/ *n* [U] containers, tools etc used in a kitchen, especially old ones that people collect: *On the shelves is a display of copper kitchenalia.*

ˌkitchen ˈcabinet *n* [C] a group of people who give advice informally to the leader of the government, not officially

kitch·en·ette /ˌkɪtʃəˈnet/ *n* [C] a small room or area where you can prepare and eat food, especially in an office or FLAT

ˌkitchen ˈgarden *n* [C] *BrE* a part of a garden where you grow your own fruit and vegetables SYN **vegetable patch/plot**

ˈkitchen ˌroll (*also* **ˌkitchen ˈtowel**) *n* [U] *BrE* thick paper used for cleaning up small amounts of liquid, food etc

ˌkitchen ˈsink ˌdrama *n* [C] *BrE* a serious play or film about problems that families have at home

kitch·en·ware /ˈkɪtʃənweə $ -wer/ *n* [U] pots, pans, and other things used for cooking

kite¹ /kaɪt/ ●○○ *n* [C]
1 a light frame covered in coloured paper or plastic that you let fly in the air on the end of one or two long strings
2 a type of HAWK (=bird that eats small animals)
3 *AmE informal* an illegal cheque
4 fly a kite to make a suggestion to see what people will think of it → **go fly a kite** at FLY¹(24), → **high as a kite** at HIGH¹(24)

KITE

kite² *v* [I,T] *AmE informal* **1** (*also* **kite up**) to raise the cost of something SYN **hike up**: *Soaring medical costs keep kiting up insurance premiums.* **2** to obtain money using an illegal cheque

kite boarding, **kite·board·ing** /ˈkaɪtˌbɔːdɪŋ $ -ˌbɔːr-/ *n* [U] **1** another word for KITE SURFING **2** the activity of being pulled across land by a large KITE attached to a board with wheels

ˈkite-ˌflying *n* [U] **1** the game or sport of flying a kite **2** *BrE* when you tell people about an idea, plan etc in order to get their opinion

Kite·mark /ˈkaɪtmɑːk $ -mɑːrk/ *n* [C] *trademark* a mark in the shape of a KITE, which is officially put on goods in Britain to show that their quality is of a good standard

ˈkite ˌsurfing, **kitesurfing** *n* [U] the activity of moving across water on a SURFBOARD while holding a large KITE which is attached to strong strings

kith and kin /ˌkɪθ ən ˈkɪn/ *n* [plural] *old-fashioned* family and friends

kitsch /kɪtʃ/ *n* [U] objects, films etc that are cheap and unfashionable, and which often amuse people because of this —**kitsch**, **kitschy** *adj*

kit·ten /ˈkɪtn/ ●●● S3 *n* [C]
1 a young cat
2 have kittens *BrE spoken informal* to be very anxious or upset about something

ˈkitten ˌheels *n* [plural] shoes or boots worn by women, with very thin high heels that curve under the shoes —**kitten-heel** *adj* [only before noun]: *kitten-heel ankle boots* → see picture at **SHOE¹**

kit·ten·ish /ˈkɪtn-ɪʃ/ *adj old-fashioned* a kittenish woman behaves in a silly way in order to attract men

kit·ty /ˈkɪti/ *n* (*plural* **kitties**) [C] **1** [usually singular] the money that people have collected for a particular purpose: *How much money is there left in the kitty?* **2** [usually singular] the money that the winner of a game of cards receives **3** a word for a cat, used especially by children

ˈkitty-ˌcorner *adv AmE informal* on the opposite corner of a street from a particular place: **[+from/to]** *The drugstore is kitty-corner from the bank.*

ki·wi /ˈkiːwiː/ *n* [C] **1** a New Zealand bird that cannot fly **2** *informal* someone from New Zealand

ˈkiwi fruit *n* [C] a small sweet fruit with a brown skin, which is green inside → see picture at **FRUIT¹**

klans·man /ˈklænzmən/ *n* (*plural* **klansmen** /-mən/) [C] *AmE* a member of the Ku Klux Klan

Klax·on /ˈklæksən/ *n* [C] *trademark* a loud horn used on police cars and other official vehicles in the past

Kleen·ex /ˈkliːneks/ *n* (*plural* **Kleenex**) [C,U] *trademark* a TISSUE: *a box of Kleenex*

klep·to·ma·ni·a /ˌkleptəˈmeɪniə/ *n* [U] a mental illness in which you have a desire to steal things

klep·to·ma·ni·ac /ˌkleptəˈmeɪniæk/ (*also* **klep·to** /ˈkleptəʊ $ -toʊ/ *informal*) *n* [C] someone suffering from kleptomania

Klon·dike, the /ˈklɒndaɪk $ ˈklɑːn-/ an area in northwest Canada, in the Yukon. Gold was discovered there in the 1890s, and this caused a GOLD RUSH (=when many people go to an area to look for gold). If a lot of people

K

hurry to a particular place to do an activity, the situation is sometimes said to be 'like the Klondike'.

kludge /klu:dʒ, klʌdʒ/ *n* [C] a computer system or program that is made or written very quickly and not very well —**kludge** *v* [T]

klutz, **clutz** /klʌts/ *n* [C] *AmE* someone who drops things and falls easily —**klutzy** *adj*

km (*plural* **km** *or* **kms**) the written abbreviation of ***kilometre*** or ***kilometres***

knack /næk/ *n informal* **1** [singular] a natural skill or ability → **talent**: **knack for doing sth** *Some people seem to **have a knack** for making money.* | **knack of doing sth** *Thomson's knack of scoring vital goals makes him important to the team.* **2 have a knack of doing sth** *BrE* to have a tendency to do something: *He has a knack of saying the wrong thing.*

knack·er /ˈnækə $ -ər/ *v* [T] *BrE spoken informal* **1** to become extremely tired SYN **exhaust**: **knacker yourself (out)** *Slow down – you'll knacker yourself out!* **2 knacker your elbow/hand etc** to hurt your elbow etc so that you cannot use it

knack·ered /ˈnækəd $ -ərd/ *adj BrE spoken informal* **1** extremely tired SYN **exhausted** **2** too old or broken to use SYN **clapped-out** *BrE*: *a knackered old bike*

ˈknackers' yard (*also* **knacker's**) *n* [C] *BrE* **1** a place where horses are killed **2 ready/fit for the knacker's yard** too old to be useful or to work properly

knap·sack /ˈnæpsæk/ *n* [C] *AmE* a bag that you carry on your shoulders SYN **backpack**, **rucksack**

knave /neɪv/ *n* [C] **1** *BrE* the playing card with a value between the ten and queen SYN **jack**: *the knave of hearts* → CARD[1](7) **2** *old-fashioned* a dishonest boy or man —**knavish** *adj*: *cunning, knavish tricks* —**knavishly** *adv*

knav·e·ry /ˈneɪvəri/ *n* [U] *old use* dishonest behaviour

knead /ni:d/ *v* [T] **1** to press a mixture of flour and water many times with your hands: ***Knead** the **dough** for three minutes.* **2** to press someone's muscles many times to help cure pain or to help them relax

knee[1] /ni:/ ●●● S2 W2 *n* [C]

1 the joint that bends in the middle of your leg: *Lucy had a bandage round her knee.* | **on your knees** *She was on her knees (=kneeling), weeding the garden.* | **sink/fall/drop to your knees** (=move so that you are kneeling) *Tim fell to his knees and started to pray.* | *a knee injury*

2 the part of your clothes that covers your knee: *His jeans had holes in both knees.*

3 on sb's knee on the top part of your legs when you are sitting down: *Daddy, can I sit on your knee?*

4 knees knocking (together) if your knees are knocking, you are feeling very afraid or very cold

5 on your knees in a way that shows you have no power but want or need something very much: *He went on his knees begging for his job back.*

6 bring sb/sth to their knees a) to defeat a country or group of people in a war: *The bombing was supposed to bring the country to its knees.* **b)** to have such a bad effect on an organization, activity etc that it cannot continue SYN **cripple**: *The recession has brought many companies to their knees.*

7 put/take sb over your knee *old-fashioned* to punish a child by hitting them

8 on bended knee(s) *old-fashioned* in a way that shows great respect for someone → **learn/be taught sth at your mother's knee** at MOTHER[1](4), → **the bee's knees** at BEE(5), → **weak at the knees** at WEAK(13)

knee[2] *v* [T + in] to hit someone with your knee: *I kneed him in the groin.*

ˈknee ˌbreeches *n* [plural] tight trousers that end at your knee, worn especially in the past

ˈknee cap *n* [C] the bone at the front of your knee

knee·cap /ˈni:kæp/ *v* (**kneecapped**, **kneecapping**) [T] to shoot someone's knee caps as an unofficial punishment → see picture at SKELETON

ˌknee-ˈdeep *adj* **1** deep enough to reach your knees: **[+in]** *knee-deep in mud* | *knee-deep in snow* **2** [not before noun] *informal* having a lot of something: **[+in]** *knee-deep in work*

ˌknee-ˈhigh *adj* **1** tall enough to reach your knees: *knee-high grass* **2 knee-high to a grasshopper** *old-fashioned* used when talking about the past to say that someone was a young child then

knee-jerk /ˈni:dʒɜ:k $ -dʒɜ:rk/ *v* [I] to react to a situation too quickly, usually by saying or doing something without thinking properly about it

ˈknee-jerk *adj* [only before noun] a knee-jerk reaction, answer etc is what you feel or say about a situation from habit, without thinking about it SYN **automatic**: *A victim's knee-jerk reaction to the crime is often revenge.*

kneel /ni:l/ ●●○ (*also* **kneel down**) *v* (*past tense and past participle* **knelt** /nelt/ *or* **kneeled** *AmE*) [I] to be in or move into a position where your body is resting on your knees: *Tom knelt down and patted the dog.* | **[+on]** *She knelt on the floor and put more wood on the fire.* → see picture at CROUCH

ˈknee-length *adj* long or tall enough to reach your knees: *a knee-length skirt*

ˈknees-up *n* [C] *BrE informal* a noisy party: *After the wedding there was a bit of a knees-up.*

knell /nel/ *n* [C] *literary* the sound of a bell being rung slowly because someone has died → DEATH KNELL

knelt /nelt/ a past tense and past participle of KNEEL

knew /nju: $ nu:/ *v* the past tense of KNOW[1]

knick·er·bock·ers /ˈnɪkəˌbɒkəz $ ˈnɪkərˌbɑ:kərz/ *n* [plural] short loose trousers that fit tightly at your knees, worn especially in the past

knick·ers /ˈnɪkəz $ -ərz/ *n* [plural] **1** *BrE* a piece of women's underwear worn between the waist and the top of the legs SYN **panties**: *a pair of frilly knickers* → see picture at UNDERWEAR **2** *AmE* KNICKERBOCKERS **3 (don't) get your knickers in a twist** *BrE spoken* used to say that someone is upset, or to tell someone not to get upset

knick-knack /ˈnɪk næk/ *n* [C] a small object used as a decoration SYN **ornament**: *They had various knick-knacks on the top of the bookcase.*

KNIVES

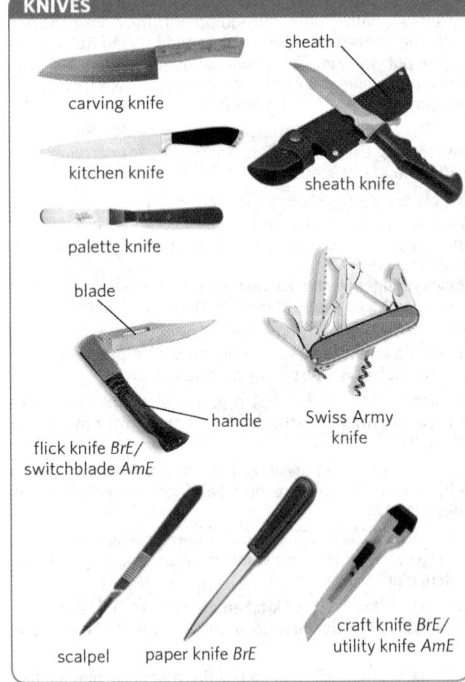

knife[1] /naɪf/ ●●● S3 W3 *n* (*plural* **knives** /naɪvz/) [C]

1 a metal blade fixed into a handle, used for cutting or as

a weapon → **scalpel**: *a knife and fork | Some young people are carrying knives to defend themselves. | a kitchen knife | Use a sharp knife to cut the melon into sections.* → **CARVING KNIFE, FLICK KNIFE, PALETTE KNIFE, PAPER KNIFE, PENKNIFE**
2 the knives are out (for sb) *informal* used to say that people are being extremely unfriendly in criticizing someone: *The knives are out for the vice president.*
3 twist/turn the knife (in the wound) to say something that makes someone more upset about a subject they are already unhappy about
4 stick/put etc the knife in/into someone *BrE informal* to dislike someone and be very unfriendly towards them
5 under the knife *informal* having a medical operation
6 you could cut the atmosphere/air/tension with a knife used to say that you felt the people in a room were angry with each other
7 like a (hot) knife through butter *informal* used to say that something happens or is done very easily, without any problems

knife² *v* [T] to put a knife into someone's body SYN **stab**: *She had been* ***knifed to death***. —**knifing** *n* [C]

ˈknife-edge *n* [singular] **1** a situation in which the result is extremely uncertain: **on a knife-edge** *His future in the job is* ***balanced on a knife-edge***. *| a knife-edge vote* **2** a situation which makes someone very anxious: **on a knife-edge** *Living with him, she is constantly on a knife-edge. | the knife-edge of insecurity* **3** something that is narrow or sharp

knife·point /ˈnaɪfpɔɪnt/ *n* **at knifepoint** using a knife to threaten someone: *An eighty-year-old man was robbed at knifepoint in his home.*

knight¹ /naɪt/ ●○○ *n* [C]
1 a man with a high rank in the past who was trained to fight while riding a horse: *knights in armour* → **WHITE KNIGHT**
2 a man who has received a KNIGHTHOOD and has the title SIR before his name
3 the CHESS piece with a horse's head on it → see picture at **CHESS**
4 a knight in shining armour a brave man who saves someone, especially a woman, from a dangerous situation

knight² *v* [T] to give someone the rank of knight

ˌknight ˈerrant *n* [C] a knight in the past who travelled looking for adventure

knight·hood /ˈnaɪthʊd/ *n* [C,U] a British rank and title that are given to a man as an honour for achievement or for doing good things → **Dame**

knight·ly /ˈnaɪtli/ *adj literary* relating to knights or typical of a knight, especially behaving with courage and honour: *knightly deeds of chivalry*

knit /nɪt/ ●●○ *v* (*present participle* **knitting**) [I,T]
1 (*past tense and past participle* **knitted**) to make clothing out of wool, using two KNITTING NEEDLES → **crochet**: *My grandmother taught me how to knit. | She's knitting a sweater.* | **knit sb sth** *Emily knitted him some socks.*
2 (*past tense and past participle* **knitted**) to use a PLAIN (=basic) knitting stitch: *Knit one, purl one.*
3 (*past tense and past participle* **knit**) to join people, things, or ideas more closely together, or to be joined closely together: **[+together]** *In a good report, individual sentences knit together in a clear way that readers can follow.* | **closely/tightly etc knit** (=with all the members having close relationships) *a closely knit community | Harold is part of a tightly knit team.*
4 (*past tense and past participle* **knit**) a bone that knits after being broken grows into one piece again: **[+together]** *The pin holds the bones in place while they knit together.*
5 knit your brows to show you are worried, thinking hard etc by moving your EYEBROWS together —**knitter** *n* [C]
→ **CLOSE-KNIT, TIGHT-KNIT**

knit·ting /ˈnɪtɪŋ/ ●○○ *n* [U]
1 something that is being knitted
2 the activity or action of knitting clothes

ˈknitting ˌneedle *n* [C] one of the two long sticks with round ends that you use to knit something

knit·wear /ˈnɪt-weə $ -wer/ *n* [U] knitted clothing: *a knitwear shop*

knives /naɪvz/ the plural of KNIFE¹

KNOB

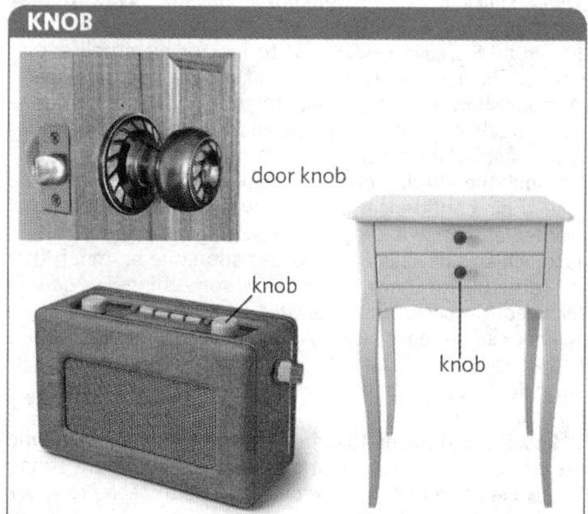

knob /nɒb $ nɑːb/ *n* [C] **1** a round handle or thing that you turn to open a door, turn on a television etc: *He thought the door was locked, but he* ***turned the knob*** *and the door opened. | a brass* ***door knob*** *| I adjusted the volume knob and sat down.* → see picture at **MICROSCOPE 2 a knob of sth** a small piece of something SYN **lump**: *Melt a knob of butter in the pan.* **3** *BrE spoken not polite* a PENIS **4 with (brass) knobs on** *BrE spoken old-fashioned* used especially by children to reply to an insult: *'You're fat and lazy.' 'Fat and lazy to you with brass knobs on!'*

knob·bly /ˈnɒbli $ ˈnɑːbli/ (*also* **knob·by** /ˈnɒbi $ ˈnɑːbi/ *AmE*) *adj* with hard parts that stick out from under the surface of something: *knobbly knees*

knock¹ /nɒk $ nɑːk/ ●●● S1 W3 *v*
1 DOOR [I] to hit a door or window with your closed hand to attract the attention of the people inside: *I knocked and knocked but nobody answered.* | **[+at/on]** *We knocked at the door but there was no one there. | Wilson went up and knocked on the door.* **THESAURUS** ▸ HIT
2 HIT AND MOVE STH [T always + adv/prep] to hit something with a short quick action so that it moves or falls: **knock sth out of/from sth** *As I got up, I knocked a pencil out of its holder. | He knocked the knife from my hand.* | **knock sth over** *At that moment, Sally knocked over her glass of wine.* | **knock sth aside** *She tried to knock the gun aside but she was not fast enough.*
3 HIT SB HARD [T always + adv/prep] to hit someone very hard: *He* ***knocked*** *her* ***to the ground*** *and kicked her.* | **knock sb unconscious/cold/senseless** (=hit someone so hard that they fall unconscious) *Simon could knock a man unconscious with one punch to the jaw. | Garry answered the door only to be* ***knocked flying*** *as two policemen came rushing in.*
4 HIT PART OF YOUR BODY [T] to hit something with part of your body: **knock sth against sth** *Morse knocked his shin against a suitcase that had been left just inside the door.* | **knock sth on sth** *She knocked her head on a stone.*
5 knock on doors to go to every house or apartment in an area asking the people who live there for information or support: *Gathering that information means knocking on doors and asking people questions.*
6 be knocking on the door to be wanting to join a group or team – used in news reports: *Five countries have permanent seats on the UN Security Council, but Germany and Japan, among others, are knocking on the door.*
7 REMOVE WALL [T] to remove a wall or part of a building in order to make a bigger room or space: **knock sth into sth** *We could make a bigger living space by knocking two rooms into one.* | **knock sth through** *The wall between the kitchen and the dining room has been partially knocked through.*
8 knock a hole in/through sth to make a hole in something, especially a wall: *We could knock a hole through the wall into the cupboard.*

9 CRITICIZE [T] to criticize someone or their work, especially in an unfair or annoying way: *The British press always knock British winners at any sport.* | *'Designer fashion is silly.' '**Don't knock it**; it's an important industry.'* THESAURUS CRITICIZE
10 BALL [T always + adv/prep] to kick or hit a ball somewhere: *The aim is to knock the ball into the opposing goal.*
11 knock sb for six *BrE informal* to shock or upset someone very much or make them physically weak: *This flu has really knocked me for six.*
12 knock the stuffing out of sb *informal* to make someone lose their confidence: *Suzanne was very upset when her mother left home. It knocked the stuffing out of her.*
13 knock sb sideways *BrE* to upset someone so much that it is difficult for them to deal with something: *His daughter's death knocked Tom sideways.*
14 knock some sense into sb/into sb's head *informal* to make someone learn to behave in a more sensible way: *The struggle to build up her own business had knocked some sense into her.*
15 knock (sb's) heads together *informal* to tell people who are arguing that they must stop and behave more sensibly: *None of them can agree and it needs someone to knock heads together.*
16 knock sth on the head *BrE informal* to stop something happening: *We wanted to go for a picnic, but the rain's knocked that on the head.*
17 knock sb's socks off (*also* **knock sb dead**) *spoken* to surprise and please someone by being very impressive: *With that dress, you'll knock him dead.*
18 knock sb off their pedestal/perch to stop admiring someone that you previously thought was perfect: *The press were determined to knock the princess off the pedestal that they had put her on.*
19 knock spots off sb/sth *BrE spoken* to be much better than someone or something: *The new computer system knocks spots off the old one.*
20 knock on wood *AmE* used to say that you hope your good luck so far will not change SYN **touch wood** *BrE*
21 knock it off *spoken* used to tell someone to stop doing something, because it is annoying you
22 MAKE A NOISE [I] if an engine or pipes etc are knocking, they make a noise like something hard being hit, usually because something is wrong with them
23 HEART [I] if your heart is knocking, it is beating hard, especially because you are afraid SYN **pound**
24 I'll knock your head/block off *spoken* used when threatening to hit someone very hard: *If you say that again, I'll knock your head off!*
25 knock the bottom out of sth *informal* to make something such as a market or industry fail suddenly: *A sudden drop in supplies of certain chemicals could knock the bottom out of the engineering industry.* → **knock/beat sb/sth into a cocked hat** at COCKED HAT(1), → **knock sb into shape** at SHAPE[1](3), → **knees knocking (together)** at KNEE[1](4)

knock around (*also* **knock about** *BrE*) *phr v informal*
1 HIT SB **knock sb around** to hit someone several times: *My father used to knock me around.*
2 RELAX **knock around (sth)** to spend time somewhere, without doing anything very serious or important SYN **hang around**: *On Saturdays I knock around with my friends.* | *We spent the day just knocking around the house.*
3 TRAVEL **knock around sth** to travel to different places SYN **kick around**: *For a couple of years we knocked around the Mediterranean.*
4 IDEAS **knock sth ↔ around** to discuss and think about an idea, plan etc with other people: *We've been knocking around a few ideas.*
5 BALL **knock sth around** *BrE* to play a game with a ball, but not in a serious way SYN **kick about**
6 BE SOMEWHERE *BrE* if something or someone is knocking around, it is somewhere but you are not sure exactly where: *Is there a screwdriver knocking about anywhere?*

knock sb/sth **back** *phr v informal*
1 knock sth ↔ back to quickly drink large quantities of a drink, especially an alcoholic drink: *Brenda knocked the brandy back quickly.*
2 knock sb back sth to cost you a lot of money: *His new car knocked him back several thousand dollars.*
3 knock sb back *BrE* to make someone feel upset, shocked, or physically weak

knock sb/sth **down** *phr v*
1 HIT/PUSH SB **knock sb ↔ down** to hit or push someone so that they fall to the ground: *Something hit him from behind and knocked him down.* → KNOCKDOWN[2]
2 HIT SB WITH A VEHICLE **knock sb ↔ down** to hit someone with a vehicle while you are driving, so that they are hurt or killed: *A child was in hospital last night after being knocked down by a car.*
3 DESTROY **knock sth ↔ down** to destroy a building or part of a building SYN **demolish**: *They want to knock the house down and rebuild it.*
4 REDUCE PRICE **knock sth ↔ down** *informal* to reduce the price of something by a large amount: *The new stove we bought was knocked down from $800 to $550.* → KNOCKDOWN[1]
5 ASK SB TO REDUCE PRICE **knock sb down to sth** *informal* to persuade someone to reduce the price of something they are selling you: *She's asking for £150 but I'll try to knock her down to £100.*

knock sth **into** sb *phr v* to make someone learn something: *Parsons must knock these lessons into the team before Saturday.*

knock off *phr v informal*
1 STOP WORK **knock off (sth)** to stop working and go somewhere else: *There was no one in the office because they'd all knocked off for lunch.* | *Do you want to **knock off early** today?* | *We usually **knock off work** at about twelve on Saturday.*
2 REDUCE A PRICE **knock sth ↔ off** to reduce the price of something by a particular amount: *I'll knock off £10.* | **knock sth off sth** *Travel agents are knocking £50, and sometimes £100, off the price of holidays.*
3 REDUCE AMOUNT **knock sth ↔ off** to reduce a total by a particular amount: **knock sth off sth** *Moving house will knock an hour off Ray's journey to work.*
4 PRODUCE **knock sth ↔ off** to produce something quickly and easily: *Roland makes a lot of money knocking off copies of famous paintings.*
5 MURDER **knock sb ↔ off** to murder someone
6 STEAL **knock sth ↔ off** *BrE* to steal something

knock out *phr v*
1 UNCONSCIOUS **knock sb ↔ out** to make someone become unconscious or go to sleep: *The champion knocked Biggs out in the seventh round.* | **knock yourself out** *His head hit a table as he fell and he knocked himself out.* | *The nurse gave me some medicine which totally knocked me out.* → KNOCKOUT[1](1)
2 DEFEAT **knock sb/sth ↔ out** to defeat a person or team in a competition so that they can no longer take part: *The German team were knocked out in the first round.* | **knock sb/sth out of sth** *He first hit the headlines when he knocked Becker out of the French Open Tournament.* → KNOCKOUT[1](3)
3 DESTROY **knock sth ↔ out** to damage something so that it does not work: *The air raids were planned to knock out communications on the ground.*
4 ADMIRE **knock sb out** *informal* if something knocks you out, it is very impressive and surprises you because it is so good: *She loved the movie. It knocked her out.* → KNOCKOUT[1](2)
5 PRODUCE **knock sth ↔ out** *informal* to produce something easily and quickly: *Paul has been knocking out new songs for the album.*
6 knock yourself out *informal* to work very hard in order to do something well

knock sb/sth **↔ over** *phr v*
1 to hit someone with a vehicle while you are driving, so that they are hurt or killed: *A woman was knocked over by a bus last year.*
2 *AmE informal* to rob a place such as a shop or bank and threaten or attack the people who work there

knock sth **↔ together** *phr v informal* to make something quickly, using whatever you have available: *We should be*

K

able to knock something together with what's in the fridge (=make a meal from items of food in the fridge).

knock sb/sth ↔ **up** *phr v informal*

1 to make something quickly and without using much effort: *Michael knocked up a shed in the back garden.*

2 *BrE* to wake someone up by knocking on their door: *What time do you want me to knock you up in the morning?*

3 *informal not polite* to make a woman PREGNANT

knock² ●●○ *n*

1 [C] the sound of something hard hitting a hard surface: *a loud knock at the door | a knock in the engine*

2 [C] the action of something hard hitting your body: *He got a knock on the head when he fell.*

3 take a knock *informal* to have some bad luck or trouble: *Clive's taken quite a few hard knocks lately.*

knock·a·bout /ˈnɒkəbaʊt $ ˈnɑːk-/ *adj* [only before noun] *BrE* knockabout humour involves making fun of someone or something in a rough way, or behaving in a silly way

knock·back /ˈnɒkbæk $ ˈnɑːk-/ *n* [C] a refusal or REJECTION that you receive

knock·down¹ /ˈnɒkdaʊn $ ˈnɑːk-/ *adj* [only before noun] *informal* a knockdown price is very cheap

knockdown² *n* [C] when a BOXER falls down when he is hit

ˌknock-down-ˈdrag-out *adj* [only before noun] *AmE informal* a knock-down-drag-out argument or fight is an extremely angry or violent one

knock·er /ˈnɒkə $ ˈnɑːkər/ *n* [C] **1** a piece of metal on an outside door of a house that you hit against the door to attract the attention of the people inside → DOORKNOCKER **2 knockers** [plural] *spoken not polite* an offensive word meaning a woman's breasts

ˌknock-ˈkneed *adj* having knees that point slightly inwards → **bow-legged**

knock·off /ˈnɒkɒf $ ˈnɑːkɒːf/ *n* [C] *AmE informal* a cheap copy of something expensive

ˈknock-on *adj* **have a knock-on effect (on sth)** *BrE* to start a process in which everything that happens causes something else to happen: *These price rises will have a knock-on effect on the economy.*

knock·out¹ /ˈnɒk-aʊt $ ˈnɑːk-/ *n* [C] **1** when a BOXER hits his opponent so hard that he falls down and cannot get up again: *The fight ended in a knockout.* **2** *informal* someone or something that is very attractive or successful: *Her dress was a knockout.* **3** a type of competition in which only the winning players or teams at each stage continue to play until there is only one winner

knockout² *adj informal* **1 knockout punch/blow a)** a hard hit that knocks someone down so that they cannot get up again **b)** an action or event that causes defeat or failure: *High interest rates have been a knockout blow to the business.* **2** relating to a type of competition in which only the winning players or teams at each stage continue to play: *Scotland's failure to get through the knockout stage of the competition* **3 knockout pills/drops etc** PILLS etc that make someone unconscious

ˈknock-up *n* [C] *BrE* the time before a tennis match officially starts when the players hit the ball to each other for practice → **warm-up**

knoll /nəʊl $ noʊl/ *n* [C] a small round hill

KNOT

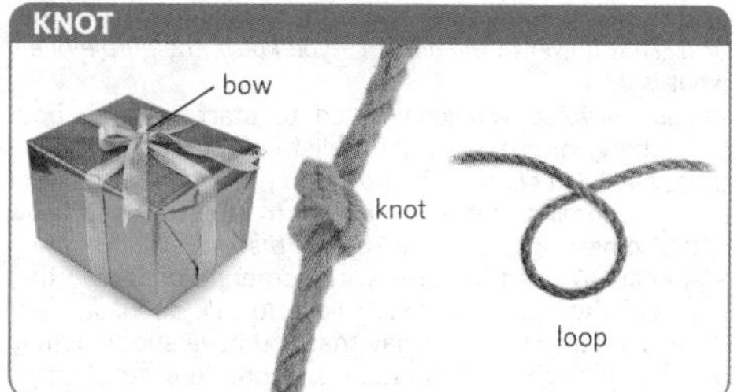

knot¹ /nɒt $ nɑːt/ ●●○ *n* [C]

1 STRING/ROPE ETC **a)** a part where one or more pieces of string, rope, cloth etc have been tied or twisted together: *Are you any good at* ***tying knots****? | Thread the string through the hoop and* ***tie it in a knot****.* **b)** a part where hair, a thread etc has become accidentally twisted together: *I can't get the knots out of my hair.* | **[+in]** *There's a knot in my shoelace.*

2 HAIR STYLE a hair style in which your hair is arranged in a tight round shape on top of your head

3 WOOD a hard round place in a piece of wood where a branch once joined the tree

4 SHIP'S OR AIRCRAFT'S SPEED a unit for measuring the speed of ships and aircraft, equal to about 1,853 metres per hour

5 PEOPLE a small group of people standing close together: **[+of]** *Knots of delegates stood around outside the conference centre.*

6 FEELING a tight uncomfortable feeling caused by a strong emotion such as fear or anger: **[+of]** *a knot of anxiety in her stomach | Her stomach* ***was in knots****.*

7 HARD MASS a tight painful place in a muscle → GORDIAN KNOT, → **at a rate of knots** at RATE¹(7), → **tie the knot** at TIE²(5), → **tie yourself (up) in knots** at TIE¹(6)

knot² *v* (**knotted**, **knotting**) **1** [T] to tie together two ends or pieces of string, rope, cloth etc: *A pretty scarf was loosely knotted around her neck.* **2** [I] if hair, a thread etc knots, it becomes twisted together **3** [I,T] if a muscle or other part of your body knots, or is knotted, it feels tight and uncomfortable: *Fear and anxiety knotted her stomach.*

knot·ted /ˈnɒtɪd $ ˈnɑː-/ *adj*

1 TIED tied in a knot or in several knots: *a knotted handkerchief on his head*

2 MUSCLE if a muscle or other part of your body is knotted, it feels tight and uncomfortable: *knotted shoulder muscles*

3 get knotted! *BrE spoken* used to tell someone rudely to go away or that you do not agree with them

4 HANDS knotted hands or fingers are twisted because of old age or too much work

knot·ty /ˈnɒti $ ˈnɑːti/ *adj* **1** difficult to solve: *a knotty problem* **2** knotty wood contains a lot of hard round places where branches once joined the tree

know¹ /nəʊ $ noʊ/ ●●● S1 W1 *v* (*past tense* **knew** /njuː $ nuː/, *past participle* **known** /nəʊn $ noʊn/)

1 HAVE INFORMATION [I,T] to have information about something: *Who knows the answer? | There are instructions telling you everything you need to know. | Didn't you know that?* | **know what/how/where etc** *Do you know what time it is? | I don't know where to go.* | **know (something/nothing etc) about sth** *I need to know more about the job before I decide whether to apply for it. | Little is known about the author's childhood. | I* ***know all about*** *David and what he's been up to!* | **know (something/nothing etc) of sth** *I wonder if he knew of the plan? | Do you know of any good restaurants in the area? | You know nothing of this business.* | **know (that)** *We know that greenhouse gases can affect the climate.* | ***Let*** *me* ***know*** (=tell me) *what time you're planning to arrive. | I thought you'd* ***want to know*** *immediately.* | ***If you must know****, I was with James last night* (=used when you are angry because someone wants to know something). | **without sb/sb's knowing** *He slipped out of the house without his parents knowing* (=secretly). | ***How did*** *he* ***know*** (=how did he find information about) *our names?* | **as you/we know** *'I'm divorced, as you know,' she said briefly.* | **be known to do sth** *Smoking is known to increase a person's risk of developing lung cancer.*

GRAMMAR

In more formal English, you say **it is known that** or **it is known who/why/what etc**: *It is known that the drug causes infertility. | It is not known how many people were killed.*

2 BE SURE [I,T] to be sure about something: *'Are you seeing Jim tomorrow?' 'I don't know yet.'* | **know (that)** *I know I won't get the job. | Ruth knew that she couldn't continue in the relationship for much longer.* | **know what/why/how etc** *I know exactly what you need!* | **know if/whether** *The boy*

K

stared at him uncertainly, not knowing whether to believe him. | *I don't know if I'll be able to come.* | **knowing (that)** *She forced herself to go out, knowing that she would feel more depressed if she stayed at home.* | ***How do you know*** (=what makes you sure) *he won't do it again?* | **know sb/sth to be sth** *It's a story that I know to be true.* | *I think he's still living in Chicago, but I don't* ***know for sure***. | ***As far as I know****, they're arriving on Saturday* (=used when you think something is true but are not sure). | *I doubt I'll win, but* ***you never know*** (=used when you cannot be sure about something, but something good might happen). **THESAURUS** SURE

3 BE FAMILIAR WITH SB/STH [T] to be familiar with a person, place etc: *I've known her for twenty years.* | *Are you really thinking of leaving Kevin for a guy you barely know?* | *Do you know the nightclub on the corner of Maine Street?* | *I don't* ***know*** *him very* ***well***. | *We're still* ***getting to know*** *each other really.* | **know sb from sth** *I know her from school.* | **know sb as sth** *Many people knew him as a local businessman.* | *Hepburn* ***is best known for*** (=people are most likely to be familiar with) *her roles in classic films such as 'My Fair Lady'.* | *The museum outlines the development of the city* ***as we know it*** *today.* | *Does he* ***know the way*** *to your house* (=know how to get there)? | *I grew up here; I* ***know*** *the place* ***like the back of my hand*** (=I know it very well). | *I only* ***know*** *her* ***by sight*** (=I often see her but have not really spoken to her). | *She didn't* ***know me from Adam*** (=she did not know me at all), *but she was really helpful.* | **knowing sb/if I know sb** (=used to say that you expect someone to behave in a particular way because you know them well) *Knowing Sumi, my note's probably still in her pocket.* | *He'll be chatting up the women, if I know Ron!*

4 REALIZE [I,T] to realize, find out about, or understand something: *She knew the risks involved.* | *Hardly knowing what he was doing, Nick pulled out a cigarette.* | **know (that)** *Suddenly she knew that something was terribly wrong.* | **know how/what/why etc** *I didn't know how difficult it would be.* | **know to do sth** *She knows not to tell anyone.* | **(do you) know what I mean?** (=used to ask if someone understands or has the same feeling as you) *It's nice to have a change sometimes. Know what I mean?* | **if you know what I mean** *Sometimes it's better not to ask too many questions, if you know what I mean.* | *'I just felt so tired.' 'Yeah,* ***I know what you mean****.'* (=I understand, because I have had the same experience) | *I* ***should have known*** *it wouldn't be easy.* | *I* ***might have known*** (=I am annoyed but not surprised) *you would take that attitude.* | **know exactly/precisely** *I know exactly how you feel.* | **know perfectly well/full well/only too well** *He knew full well that what he was doing was dangerous.* | **sb will never know/no one will ever know** *Just take it. No one will ever know.* | *'That's not what I mean,* ***and you know it****,' he protested.* | **if I had known/if I'd have known** *I wouldn't have come if I'd known you were so busy.* | ***Little did*** *she* ***know*** (=she did not know) *that years later she would have her own pool and luxury apartment in Florida.* | *She* ***knew nothing of*** *what had happened earlier that day.*

5 SKILL/EXPERIENCE [T] to have learned a lot about something or be skilful and experienced at doing something: *I don't know enough history to make a comparison.* | *I taught him everything he knows.* | *I know some French.* | **know how to do sth** *Do you know how to change a fuse?* | **[+about]** *I have a friend who knows about antiques.* | *Bessie knew nothing about football.* | *Politicians* ***know all about*** *the power of language.* | *I* ***don't know the first thing about*** (=I know nothing about) *looking after children.* | *I don't really* ***know what*** *I'm* ***doing*** (=I do not have enough skill and experience to deal with something) *when it comes to cars.* | *The staff are dedicated people who clearly* ***know what*** *they* ***are talking about***. | *She* ***knew from experience*** *that exams made her very nervous.* | **know your job/subject/stuff** (=be good at and know all you should about a job or subject) | *a decent manager who* ***knows the ropes*** (=has a lot of experience) | *My cousin* ***knows a thing or two*** (=knows a lot) *about golf.* | **know a song/tune/poem etc** (=be able to sing a song, play a tune, say a poem etc because you have learned it) *Do you know all the words to 'As Time Goes By'?*

K

6 KNOW SB'S QUALITIES [T] to think that someone has particular qualities: **know sb as sth** *I knew him as a hard-working, modest, and honest politician.* | **know sb for sth** *In fact, I knew her for a tough-minded young woman.*

7 know better a) to be wise or experienced enough not to do something: *It's just prejudice from educated people who* ***should know better****.* | *Eva* ***knew better than to*** *interrupt one of Mark's jokes.* **b)** to know or think you know more than someone else: *Everyone thought it was an accident. Only Dan knew better.*

8 not know any better used to say that someone does something bad or stupid because they have not been told or taught that it is wrong: *Drugs are being sold to children who don't know any better.*

9 know sth inside out (*also* **know sth backwards** *BrE*, **know sth backwards and forwards** *AmE*) to be very familiar with something, especially because you have learned about it or because you have a lot of experience: *Erikson knows the game inside out.*

10 know your way around sth a) to be so familiar with something that you are confident and good at using it: *She knows her way around a wine list.* **b)** to be familiar with a place so that you know where things are: *I don't know my way around the city yet.*

11 make yourself known (to sb) *formal* to introduce yourself to someone: *After she had gone, Paul made himself known to Dr Heatherton.*

12 RECOGNIZE [T] to be able to recognize someone or something: *Honestly, it had been so long, I hardly knew her.* | **know sb/sth by sth** *He looked very different, but I knew him by his voice.* **THESAURUS** RECOGNIZE

13 know sb/sth as sth to have a particular name: *The main street between the castle and the palace is known as 'the Royal Mile'.* | *Nitrous oxide is* ***commonly known as*** *laughing gas.*

14 know sth from sth to understand the difference between one thing and another: *Lloyd doesn't even know his right from his left.* | *At what age do children start to know right from wrong?*

15 EXPERIENCE [T] to have experience of a particular feeling or situation: *I don't think he ever knew true happiness.* | **[+about]** *I know all about being poor.* | *I've* ***never known*** (=have never experienced) *this to happen in all the time I've worked here.* | *I've* ***never known*** *him* ***to*** *shout* (=he never shouts).

16 sb/sth is not known to be sth *or* **sb/sth has never been known to do sth** used to say there is no information that someone or something has particular qualities: *This species is not known to be vicious.*

17 I've known sb/sth to do sth *or* **sb/sth has been known to do sth** used to say that someone does something sometimes or that something happens sometimes, even if it is unusual: *People have been known to drive 500 miles just to visit the shop.* | *This type of fish has been known to live for 10 years or more.*

SPOKEN PHRASES

18 you know a) used to emphasize a statement: *There's no excuse, you know.* **b)** used to make sure that someone understands what you are saying: *I felt very upset, you know?* **c)** used when you want to keep someone's attention, but cannot think of what to say next: *Well, you know, we've got a job to do here.* **d)** used when you are explaining or describing something and want to give more information: *That flower in the garden – you know, the purple one – what is it?*

19 you know/do you know used to start talking about something, or make someone listen: *You know, I sometimes feel I don't know him at all.* | *Do you know, when I went out this morning that man was still there.* | **(do) you know what/something?** *You know what? I think he's lonely.*

20 I know a) used to agree with someone or to say that you feel the same way: *'We have to talk about it, Rob.' 'Yeah, I know.'* **b)** used to say that you have suddenly had an idea, thought of a solution to a problem etc: *I know! Let's go out for a meal on your birthday.* **c)** used to stop someone from interrupting because they have an opinion about what you are saying: *It sounds silly, I know, but I will*

explain. | *I know, I know, I should have had the car checked out before now.*
21 I don't know a) used to say that you do not have the answer to a question: *'When did they arrive?' 'I don't know.'* **b)** used when you are not sure about something: *'How old do you think he is?' 'Oh, I don't know – sixty, seventy?'* | **[+what/how/whether etc]** *I don't know whether to call him.* | **I don't know that** *I don't know that you need a passport for travelling within the EU.* **c)** used to show that you disagree slightly with what has just been said: *'I couldn't live there.' 'Oh, I don't know. It might not be so bad.'* **d)** *BrE* used to show that you are slightly annoyed: *Oh, I don't know! You're hopeless!*
22 I don't know how/why etc used to criticize someone: *I don't know how people could keep an animal in those conditions.*
23 I don't know about you, but ... used to give your opinion, decision, or suggestion when you are not sure that the person you are talking to will feel the same way: *I don't know about you, but I'll be glad when Christmas is over.*
24 I don't know how to thank you/repay you used to thank someone
25 wouldn't you know (it) used to say that something is not at all surprising: *I was told in no uncertain terms that Helen, wouldn't you know it, didn't approve.*
26 you don't know used to emphasize how strong your feelings are: *You don't know how much I missed him.*
27 I wouldn't know used to say that you do not know the answer to something and that you are not the person who would know
28 what does sb know? used to say angrily that someone's opinion is wrong or that it is not important: *What does she know about relationships?*
29 how should I know?/how am I to know?/how do I know? used to say that it is not reasonable to expect that you should know something: *'When will they be back?' 'How should I know?'*
30 how was I to know?/how did I know? used as an excuse when something bad has happened: *How was I to know that the file was confidential?*
31 be not to know *BrE* used to say that you do not mind that someone has made a mistake because they could not have avoided it: *'Sorry, I didn't realize you had guests.' 'That's all right – you weren't to know.'*
32 I ought to know used to emphasize that you know about something because you made it, experienced it etc: *'Are you sure there's no sugar in this coffee?' 'Of course. I ought to know – I made it!'*
33 for all I know used to emphasize that you do not know something and say that it is not important to you: *I don't know where she is. She could have been kidnapped for all I know.*
34 not that I know of used to say that you think the answer is 'no' but there may be facts that you do not know about: *'Did he call earlier?' 'Not that I know of.'*
35 Heaven/God/who/goodness knows! a) used to say that you do not know the answer to a question: *'Where do you think he's disappeared to this time?' 'God knows!'* | *Goodness knows why she didn't go herself.* **b)** used to emphasize a statement: *Goodness knows, I've never liked the woman, but I didn't know how bad it would be to work with her.*
36 knowing my luck used to say that you expect something bad will happen because you are usually unlucky: *Knowing my luck, the train will be late.*
37 (well,) what do you know? used to express surprise: *Well, what do you know? Look who's here!*
38 if you know what's good for you used to tell someone that they should do something, or something bad will happen: *You'll keep your mouth shut about this if you know what's good for you!*
39 you know who/what used to talk about someone or something without mentioning their name: *I saw you know who yesterday.*

---

40 there's no knowing it is impossible to know: *There was no knowing who might have read the letter.*
41 let it be known/make it known (that) *formal* to make sure that people know something, especially by getting someone else to tell them: *Farrar let it be known that he saw nothing wrong with the proposed solutions.*
42 not want to know *BrE informal* to not be interested in someone and what they want to say: *She'd approached several model agencies but they just didn't want to know.*
43 know the score *informal* to understand a situation and all the good and bad features about it: *I knew the score before I started the job.*
44 not know what hit you *informal* to feel shocked and confused because something happens when you are not expecting it to: *Poor man – I don't think he knew what hit him.*
45 know your place used to say that someone understands that they are less important than other people – usually used humorously: *I know my place. I'll get back to the kitchen!*
46 know no bounds *formal* if a feeling or quality knows no bounds, it is not limited in any way: *His enthusiasm knew no bounds.*
47 sb knows best used to say that someone should be obeyed or that their way of doing things should be accepted because they are experienced: *She always thinks she knows best.* | *I have always hated the attitude that 'the doctor knows best'.*
48 before you know it used to say that something happens very quickly and when you are not expecting it: *You'll be home before you know it.*
49 know different/otherwise *informal* to know that the opposite of something is true: *He told people he didn't care about her, but deep down he knew different.*
50 know your own mind to be confident and have firm ideas about what you want and like
51 you will be delighted/pleased etc to know (that) *formal* used before you give someone information that they will be pleased to hear: *You will be pleased to know that we have accepted your offer.*
52 it's ..., Jim, but not as we know it *informal humorous* used to say that something is completely different from what we would normally expect something of its type to be: *It's the blues, Jim, but not as we know it.* → **the next thing I/she etc knew** at NEXT[1](6)

GRAMMAR: Using the progressive

- **Know** is not used in the progressive. You say: *I know who that is.* | *Do you know this song?* ✗ Don't say: *I'm knowing who that is.* | *Are you knowing this song?*
- However, the participle **knowing** is sometimes used: *Knowing she would appreciate it, I offered to help.*

GRAMMAR GUIDE ▸ VERBS

know² *n* **in the know** *informal* having more information about something than most people: *People in the know say that interest rates will have to rise again soon.*

ˈknow-all *n* [C] *BrE informal* someone who behaves as if they know everything – used to show disapproval SYN **know-it-all** *AmE*

ˈknow-how *n* [U] *informal* knowledge, practical ability, or skill to do something: *those who* ***have the know-how*** *to exploit the technology to the fullest* | ***the know-how needed*** *by today's practising lawyer* | *No other company had the* ***technical know-how*** *to deal with the disaster.* THESAURUS ▸ KNOWLEDGE

know·ing /ˈnəʊɪŋ $ ˈnoʊ-/ *adj* [only before noun] showing that you know all about something, even if it has not been discussed directly: *He gave us a* ***knowing look.*** | *She exchanged a* ***knowing smile*** *with her mother.*

know·ing·ly /ˈnəʊɪŋli $ ˈnoʊ-/ *adv* **1** in a way that shows you know about something secret or embarrassing: *She smiled knowingly at us.* **2** deliberately OPP **accidentally**: *He would never knowingly upset people.* THESAURUS ▸ DELIBERATELY

ˈknow-it-all *n* [C] *especially AmE informal* someone who behaves as if they know everything – used to show disapproval SYN **know-all** *BrE*

K

knowl·edge /ˈnɒlɪdʒ $ ˈnɑː-/ ●●● S2 W1 *n* [U]
1 the information, skills, and understanding that you have gained through learning or experience: **[+of]** *He did not have much knowledge of American history.* | **[+about]** *the need to increase knowledge about birth control*

REGISTER
In everyday English, people usually say that someone **knows about** something rather than **has knowledge of/about** something: *He didn't* ***know much about*** *American history.*

2 when you know about a particular situation or event, or the information you have about it: *Evans* ***denied all knowledge of*** *the robbery.* | *I* ***had no knowledge of*** *this whatsoever until 'The Times' contacted me.* | **(secure/safe) in the knowledge that** *Kay smiled, secure in the knowledge that she was right.* | **be common/public knowledge** (=be known about by everyone) *Their affair is public knowledge.* | **to (the best of) sb's knowledge** (=used to say that someone may not know the true facts) *To the best of my knowledge, the new project will be starting in June.* | *To our knowledge, this is the first time it's happened.* | *'Is it true that she's leaving the company?'* ***'Not to my knowledge*** (=I do not think so).' | **without sb's knowledge** *He was annoyed to find the contract had been signed without his knowledge.* | *She acted* ***with the full knowledge of*** *her boss* (=her boss knew about her action). | *Ministers publicly denied that they had* ***prior knowledge*** *of the attack* (=they denied that they knew that it was going to happen). → GENERAL KNOWLEDGE, → **working knowledge** at WORKING[1](9)

GRAMMAR: Countable or uncountable?
• **Knowledge** is an uncountable noun and is not used in the plural. You say: *He has a lot of technical knowledge.* ✗ Don't say: *He has a lot of technical knowledges.*
• **Knowledge** is always followed by a singular verb: *Expert knowledge* ***is*** *necessary.*
• When talking about something that you know or learn, you say a **piece of knowledge**: *This is a useful piece of knowledge.*

COLLOCATIONS
VERBS
have some knowledge of sth *The book assumes that you already have some knowledge of physics.*
get knowledge (*also* **gain/acquire knowledge** *formal*) *He gets all his knowledge about politics from watching the television.*
increase/improve your knowledge *If you want to improve your knowledge of the language, you should go and live in France.*
broaden/expand your knowledge (=increase your knowledge) *The course is designed to help students broaden their knowledge of modern American literature.*
show/demonstrate your knowledge *The test should be an opportunity for students to demonstrate their knowledge.*
ADJECTIVES/NOUN + knowledge
general knowledge (=knowledge about a lot of different subjects) *The questions are intended to test your general knowledge.*
scientific/technical knowledge *the practical application of scientific knowledge*
specialist/expert knowledge *Making profitable investments requires specialist knowledge.*
detailed knowledge *You need to have a detailed knowledge of criminal law.*
first-hand/personal knowledge (=knowledge from experiencing something yourself) *writers who had no first-hand knowledge of war*
basic knowledge (=knowledge of the basic aspects of something) *These things are obvious to anyone with even a basic knowledge of computers.*
in-depth/thorough knowledge (=detailed knowledge about all of a particular subject) | **intimate knowledge** (=knowledge about something because you are involved in it) | **inside knowledge** (=knowledge that you have because you are part of a group) | **background knowledge** (=knowledge that you need before you can understand or do something)
PHRASES
a thirst for knowledge (=a desire to learn more) *She arrived at college with a thirst for knowledge.*
sb's breadth of knowledge (=when you know a lot about all the different parts of something) *They lack his breadth of knowledge about the industry.*
COMMON ERRORS
⚠ Don't say 'learn knowledge'. Say **gain knowledge** or **acquire knowledge**.

THESAURUS
knowledge the facts and information that you have learned, and the understanding you have gained: *Our knowledge of other cultures and societies has improved.* | *scientific knowledge*
expertise special knowledge about how to do something, that you get through experience, training, or study: *The technical expertise was provided by a Japanese company.* | *They need people with medical expertise.*
know-how practical knowledge about how to do something: *Business leaders often lack the local know-how to tackle problems in specific countries.* | *financial know-how*
wisdom good sense and judgment, based on knowledge and experience: *the wisdom of the older family members* | *It's a matter of common wisdom that newspapers cannot be trusted.*
grasp how much you know about a situation or subject, and how well you understand it: *He's been praised for his grasp of the country's economic problems.* | *She has a good grasp of the language.*

knowl·edge·a·ble /ˈnɒlɪdʒəbəl $ ˈnɑː-/ *adj* knowing a lot: **[+about]** *Graham's very knowledgeable about wines.* —**knowledgeably** *adv*

known[1] /nəʊn $ noʊn/ *v* the past participle of KNOW[1]

known[2] ●●○ W3 *adj*
1 [only before noun] used about something that people know about or have discovered: *a study of all the known facts* | *her last known address* | *Apart from vaccines, there is no known way to protect against meningitis.*
2 [only before noun] a known criminal, drug dealer etc is someone who people know to be regularly involved in criminal activities or to do other things that are disapproved of: *He was found with several other known sex offenders.* | *a known liar*
3 be known for sth to be famous or known about by a lot of people because of something: *He's known for his good looks.* | *The region is known for its fine wines.*
4 well-known/little-known/lesser-known used when saying how famous someone is: *works by lesser-known French artists*

knuck·le[1] /ˈnʌkəl/ *n* [C] **1** your knuckles are the joints in your fingers, including the ones where your fingers join your hands: *Her knuckles whitened as she gripped the gun.* **2** a piece of meat around the lowest leg joint of a pig: *a knuckle of pork* **3 near the knuckle** *BrE informal* rude, or likely to give offence: *Some of his jokes are a bit near the knuckle.* → **a rap on/over the knuckles** at RAP[1](6), → **rap sb on/over the knuckles** at RAP[2](5)

knuckle[2] *v*
knuckle down *phr v informal* to suddenly start working or studying hard SYN **get down to**: *If he doesn't knuckle down soon, he'll never get through those exams.* | **[+to]** *He is clearly ready to knuckle down to the task.*
knuckle under *phr v informal* to accept someone's authority or orders although you do not want to

ˈknuckle-ˌdragger *n* [C] *informal* a man who is stupid

ˈknuckle-ˌduster *n* [C] a piece of metal that covers all the knuckles of the hand, used as a weapon

knuck·le·head /ˈnʌkəlhed/ *n* [C] *AmE spoken* someone stupid - used when you are not very angry with them SYN **blockhead** *BrE*

KO¹ /ˌkeɪ ˈəʊ $ -ˈoʊ/ the abbreviation of ***knockout***

KO² *v* (*past tense and past participle* **KO'd**, *third person singular* **KO's**, *present participle* **KO'ing**) [T] *informal* to hit someone so hard that they become unconscious

ko·a·la /kəʊˈɑːlə $ koʊ-/ (*also* **koˌala ˈbear** / $.ˈ.. ˌ./) *n* [C] an Australian animal like a small grey bear with no tail that climbs trees and eats leaves

kohl /kəʊl $ koʊl/ *n* [U] a black pencil used around women's eyes to make them more attractive

kohl·ra·bi /kəʊlˈrɑːbi $ koʊl-/ *n* [U] a vegetable of the CABBAGE family

kook /kuːk/ *n* [C] *AmE informal* someone who is silly or crazy —**kooky** *adj*

kook·a·bur·ra /ˈkʊkəbʌrə/ *n* [C] an Australian bird whose song sounds like laughter

ko·ra /ˈkɔːrə/ *n* [C] a West African HARP which has 21 strings and a SOUND BOX made from a GOURD

Ko·ran, the (*also* **the Quran, the Qur'an**) /kɔːˈrɑːn, kə- $ kəˈræn, -ˈrɑːn/ the holy book of the Muslims —**Koranic** /kəˈrænɪk/ *adj*

kor·ma /ˈkɔːmə $ ˈkɔːr-/ *n* [C,U] an Indian dish made with meat and cream: *chicken korma*

ko·sher /ˈkəʊʃə $ ˈkoʊʃər/ *adj* **1 a)** kosher food is prepared according to Jewish law **b)** kosher restaurants or shops sell food prepared in this way **2** *informal* something that is kosher is honest, legal, or really what it is claimed to be: *Are you sure this offer is kosher?*

kow·tow /ˌkaʊˈtaʊ/ *v* [I] *informal* to be too eager to obey or be polite to someone in authority: **[+to]** *We will not kowtow to the government.*

KP /ˌkeɪ ˈpiː/ *n* [U] *AmE* work that soldiers or children at a camp have to do in a kitchen

kph /ˌkeɪ piː ˈeɪtʃ/ (***kilometres per hour***) used to describe the speed of something, especially a vehicle or the wind → **mph**

kraal /krɑːl/ *n* [C] a village in South Africa with a fence around it

kraut /kraʊt/ *n* [C] *taboo* a very offensive word for someone from Germany. Do not use this word.

Krem·lin, the /ˈkremlɪn/ the government of Russia and the former USSR, or its buildings in Moscow

krill /krɪl/ *n* [U] small SHELLFISH

Kriss Krin·gle /ˌkrɪs ˈkrɪŋgəl/ *n AmE* another name for SANTA CLAUS

kro·na /ˈkrəʊnə $ ˈkroʊ-/ *n* (*plural* **kronor** /-nɔː $ -nɔːr/) [C] the standard unit of money in Sweden and Iceland

kro·ne /ˈkrəʊnə $ ˈkroʊ-/ *n* (*plural* **kroner** /-nə $ -nər/) [C] the standard unit of money in Denmark and Norway

Kru·ger·rand /ˈkruːgəˌrænd/ *n* [C] a South African gold coin

kryp·ton /ˈkrɪptɒn $ -tɑːn/ *n* [U] a colourless gas that is found in very small quantities in the air and is used in FLUORESCENT lights and LASERS. It is a chemical ELEMENT: symbol Kr

kt the written abbreviation of ***knot***

Kt the written abbreviation of ***knight***

ku·dos /ˈkjuːdɒs $ ˈkuːdɑːs/ *n* [U] the state of being admired and respected for being important or for doing something important SYN **prestige**: *He acquired kudos just by appearing on television.*

Ku Klux Klan, the /ˌkuː klʌks ˈklæn/ a secret American political organization of Protestant white men who oppose people of other races or religions

kum·quat /ˈkʌmkwɒt $ -kwɑːt/ *n* [C] a fruit that looks like a very small orange

kung fu /ˌkʌŋ ˈfuː/ *n* [U] an ancient Chinese fighting art in which you attack people with your hands and feet → **martial art**

Kurd /kɜːd $ kɜːrd/ *n* [C] a member of a people living in Iran, Iraq, and Turkey

kvetch /kvetʃ/ *v* [I] *AmE informal* to keep complaining —**kvetch** *n* [C]

kW the written abbreviation of ***kilowatt*** or ***kilowatts***

kWh the written abbreviation of ***kilowatt hour*** or ***kilowatt hours***

K

L[1], **l** /el/ (*plural* **L's, l's**) *n* **1** [C,U] the 12th letter of the English alphabet **2** [C] the number 50 in the system of ROMAN NUMERALS

L[2] **1** the written abbreviation of ***large***, used on clothes to show the size **2** the written abbreviation of ***lake***, used on maps **3** the written abbreviation of ***learner***, used on cars to show that the driver is a learner → **L-PLATE**

l **1** the written abbreviation of ***litre*** or ***litres*** **2** the written abbreviation of ***line***

la /lɑː/ *n* [U] the sixth note in a musical SCALE, according to the SOL-FA system

lab /læb/ ●●● S3 *n* [C] *informal* a LABORATORY: *the school science lab*

Lab the written abbreviation of ***Labour***, in British politics

LABELS

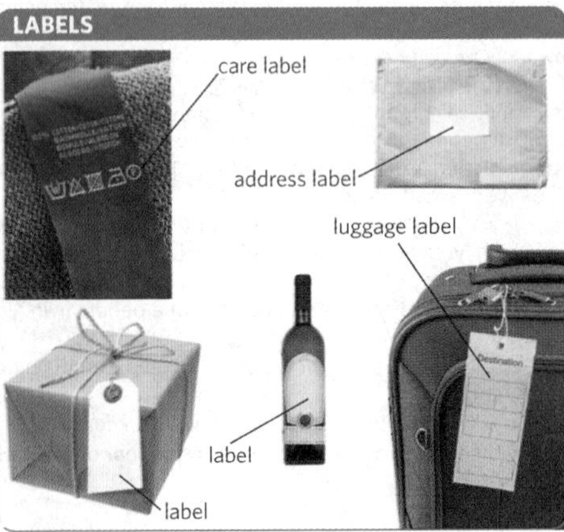

la·bel[1] /ˈleɪbəl/ ●●● S3 W3 AWL *n* [C]
1 a piece of paper or another material that is attached to something and gives information about it → **care label**: *a luggage label* | **on the label** *It says 'Dry clean' on the label.*
2 a word or phrase which is used to describe a person, group, or thing, but which is unfair or not correct: *Men these days have to avoid attracting the 'sexist' label.*
3 a record company: *their new release on the Ace Sounds label*
4 designer label clothes made by fashionable companies: *Fancy designer labels tend to come with fancy price tags to match.* → **OWN LABEL**

label[2] ●○○ AWL *v* (**labelled**, **labelling** *BrE*, **labeled**, **labeling** *AmE*) [T]
1 to attach a label onto something or write information on something: *Label the diagram clearly.* | **label sth sth** *The file was labelled 'Top Secret'.* | **label sth with sth** *Each bag of seeds is labelled with the grower's name.*
2 to use a word or phrase to describe someone or something, but often unfairly or incorrectly: **label sb/sth (as) sth** *The newspapers had unjustly labelled him a troublemaker.* | *The regime was inevitably labelled as 'communist'.*

la·bi·a /ˈleɪbiə/ *n* [plural] *technical* the outer parts of the female sex organ

la·bi·al /ˈleɪbiəl/ *n* [C] *technical* a speech sound made using one or both lips → **bilabial** —**labial** *adj*

la·bor /ˈleɪbə $ -ər/ *n, v* AWL the American spelling of LABOUR

la·bor·a·tory /ləˈbɒrətri $ ˈlæbrətɔːri/ ●●● W3 *n* (*plural* **laboratories**) [C] a special room or building in which a scientist does tests or prepares substances: *a* ***research laboratory*** | **laboratory tests/experiments/studies** | *tests on laboratory animals* → **LANGUAGE LABORATORY**

ˈ**Labor Day** *n* [U] *AmE* a public holiday in the US on the first Monday in September

la·bored /ˈleɪbəd $ -bərd/ AWL *adj* the American spelling of LABOURED

la·bor·er /ˈleɪbərə $ -bərər/ *n* [C] the American spelling of LABOURER

la·bo·ri·ous /ləˈbɔːriəs/ *adj* taking a lot of time and effort: **laborious process/task/business etc** *Collecting the raw materials proved a long and laborious task.* | *the laborious business of drying the crops* —**laboriously** *adv*: *A beetle began to crawl laboriously up his leg.*

ˈ**labor** ˌ**union** *n* [C] *AmE* an organization that represents the ordinary workers in a particular trade or profession, especially in meetings with employers SYN **trade union** *BrE*

labour[1] *BrE*, **labor** *AmE* ●●○ S3 W3 AWL *n*
1 WORK [U] work, especially physical work: *The garage charges £30 an hour for labour.* | *Many women do hard* ***manual labour*** (=work with their hands). | *Workers* ***withdrew*** *their* ***labour*** (=protested by stopping work) *for twenty-four hours.* → **HARD LABOUR**
2 WORKERS [U] all the people who work for a company or in a country: *a shortage of skilled labor* | *We need to reduce our labour costs.*
3 BABY [singular, U] the process of giving birth to a baby: **in labour** *Meg was in labour for ten hours.* | *Diane* ***went into labour*** *at 2 o'clock.* | **a long/short/difficult labour** | *The* ***labour pains*** *were unbearable.* | **labour ward/room** (=a room in a hospital where women give birth)
4 a labour of love something that is hard work but that you do because you want to
5 sb's labours *formal* a period of hard work: *After several hours' gardening, we sat down to admire the results of our labours.*

COLLOCATIONS – MEANING 2

ADJECTIVES/NOUN + labour

skilled/unskilled labour *Employers want to keep skilled labour because of the cost of training.*
cheap labour (=workers who have low wages) *Women and children were used as cheap labour.*
casual labour (=workers who do jobs that are not permanent) *The industry makes use of a large supply of casual labour.*
child labour | **slave labour**

labour + NOUN

the labour force (=all the people who work in a country or for a company) *We need an educated labour force.*
the labour supply (=all the people available to work) *What was the effect of the war on the labour supply?*
the labour market (=the people looking for work and the jobs available) *the percentage of women in the labour market*
a labour shortage | **labour costs**

labour[2] *BrE*, **labor** *AmE* ●○○ AWL *v* [I]
1 to work hard: *They laboured all day in the mills.* | **[+over]** *I've been labouring over this report all morning.* | **labour to do sth** *Ray had little talent but labored to acquire the skills of a writer.*
2 labour under a delusion/misconception/misapprehension etc to believe something that is not true: *She had laboured under the misconception that Bella liked her.*
3 labour the point to describe or explain something in too much detail or when people have already understood it
4 [always + adv/prep] to move slowly and with difficulty: *I could see the bus labouring up the steep, windy road.*

La·bour /ˈleɪbə $ -ər/ *n* the British LABOUR PARTY → **Liberal Democrat**: **under Labour** *Most people will pay higher taxes under Labour.* | *They always* ***vote Labour***. | **Labour MP/candidate** —**Labour** *adj*: *a Labour policy*

ˈlabour camp *BrE*, **ˈlabor camp** *AmE n* [C] a prison camp where prisoners have to do hard physical work

la·boured *BrE*, **labored** *AmE* /ˈleɪbəd $ -bərd/ (AWL) *adj* **1** if someone's breathing is laboured, it is difficult for them to breathe **2** if writing or speaking is laboured, it takes a lot of effort and is not good: *Some of the episodes are very laboured.*

la·bour·er *BrE*, **laborer** *AmE* /ˈleɪbərə $ -ər/ ●○○ *n* [C] someone whose work needs physical strength, for example building work → **worker**: *a farm labourer*

ˈlabour exˌchange *n* [C] *old-fashioned* a British government office where people went to find jobs in the past → **job centre**

ˈlabour force *BrE*, **labor force** *AmE n* [C usually singular] all the people who work for a company or in a country

la·bour·ing *BrE*, **laboring** *AmE* /ˈleɪbərɪŋ/ *adj* [only before noun] **1 labouring class/family etc** *old-fashioned* people who do hard physical work and who do not have a lot of money or power, considered as a group: *They wanted to provide education for the labouring classes.* **2** involving hard physical work: *a labouring job*

ˌlabour-ˈintensive *BrE*, **labor-intensive** *AmE adj* an industry or type of work that is labour-intensive needs a lot of workers → **capital-intensive**: *labour-intensive farming methods*

ˈlabour ˌmarket *BrE*, **labor market** *AmE n* [C] the people looking for work and the jobs that are available at that time: *married women re-entering the labour market*

ˈlabour ˌmovement *BrE*, **labor movement** *AmE n* **the labour movement** the organizations, political parties etc that represent working people

ˈlabour ˌrelations *BrE*, **labor relations** *AmE n* [plural] the relationship between employers and workers: *a company with good labour relations*

ˈlabour-ˌsaving *BrE*, **labor-saving** *AmE adj* [only before noun] making it easier for you to do a particular job: **labour-saving device/gadget/equipment etc**

Lab·ra·dor /ˈlæbrədɔː $ -ɔːr/ *n* [C] a large dog with fairly short yellow or black hair

la·bur·num /ləˈbɜːnəm $ -ɜːr-/ *n* [C,U] a small tree with long hanging stems of yellow flowers and poisonous seeds

lab·y·rinth /ˈlæbərɪnθ/ *n* [C] **1** a large network of paths or passages which cross each other, making it very difficult to find your way (SYN) **maze**: **[+of]** *a labyrinth of underground tunnels* **2** something that is very complicated and difficult to understand: **[+of]** *Decisions are frequently delayed in the labyrinth of Whitehall committees.* —**labyrinthine** /ˌlæbəˈrɪnθaɪn◂/ *adj*: *labyrinthine corridors*

lace[1] /leɪs/ ●○○ *n*
1 [U] a fine cloth made with patterns of many very small holes: *a handkerchief trimmed with lace | lace curtains*
2 [C usually plural] a string that is pulled through special holes in shoes or clothing to pull the edges together and fasten them (SYN) **shoelace**

LACE

lace[2] *v* [T] **1** (*also* **lace up**) to fasten something by tying a lace (SYN) **tie**: *Lace up your shoes or you'll trip over.* | **lace sth to sth** *The canvas was laced to a steel frame.* **2** to add a small amount of alcohol or a drug to a drink: **lace sth with sth** *coffee laced with Irish whiskey* **3** to weave or twist several things together: **lace sth together** *Hannah laced her fingers together.*

lace sth **with** sth *phr v* **1** to include something all through something you write or say: *He laces his narrative with a great deal of irrelevant information.* **2 be laced with sth** *written* to have some of a quality: *Iris's voice was heavily laced with irony.*

la·ce·rate /ˈlæsəreɪt/ *v* [T] **1** to cut skin deeply with something sharp: *His fingers were badly lacerated by the broken glass.* **2** to criticize someone very strongly

la·ce·ra·tion /ˌlæsəˈreɪʃən/ *n* [C,U] *technical* a cut in your skin: **[+to]** *multiple lacerations to the upper arms*

ˈlace-up *n* [C usually plural] *especially BrE* a shoe that is fastened with a lace → **slip-ons** —**lace-up** *adj*: *shiny black lace-up shoes*

lace·work /ˈleɪswɜːk $ -wɜːrk/ *n* [U] lace, or something that looks like lace

lach·ry·mose /ˈlækrəməʊs $ -moʊs/ *adj formal* often crying (SYN) **tearful**

lack[1] /læk/ ●●● (S3) (W2) *n* [singular, U] when there is not enough of something, or none of it (SYN) **shortage** (OPP) **surplus**: **[+of]** *new parents suffering from lack of sleep | Too many teachers are treated with a lack of respect. | comments based on a* ***total lack of*** *information | Does their* ***apparent lack of*** *progress mean they are not doing their job properly? | tours that are cancelled* ***for lack of*** *bookings | There was* ***no lack of*** *willing helpers. | health problems linked to poor diet and a* ***relative lack of*** *exercise*

lack[2] ●●○ (W3) *v*
1 [T] to not have something that you need, or not have enough of it: *Alex's real problem is that he lacks confidence.*
⚠ Do not use 'in' or 'of' after the verb **lack**: *We lack ideas (NOT We lack in/of ideas).* However, you can use these prepositions after **be lacking in** and **a lack**: *We are lacking in ideas. | There is a lack of ideas.*
2 not lack for sth *formal* to have a lot of something: *He does not lack for critics.*

lack·a·dai·si·cal /ˌlækəˈdeɪzɪkəl◂/ *adj* not showing enough interest in something or not putting enough effort into it: *David has a rather lackadaisical approach to his work.*

lack·ey /ˈlæki/ *n* [C] someone who always does what a particular person tells them to do – used to show disapproval

lack·ing /ˈlækɪŋ/ ●●○ *adj* [not before noun]
1 not having enough of something or any of it: **[+in]** *He was* ***lacking in confidence****. | She seems to be entirely lacking in intelligence. | The new designs have all been* ***found lacking*** *in some important way.*
2 if something that you need or want is lacking, it does not exist: *Financial backing for the project is still lacking. | These qualities are* ***sadly lacking*** *today.*

lack·lus·tre *BrE*, **lackluster** *AmE* /ˈlækˌlʌstə $ -ər/ *adj* **1** not exciting, impressive etc (SYN) **dull**: *a lacklustre performance* **2** not shining (SYN) **dull**: *lacklustre hair*

la·con·ic /ləˈkɒnɪk $ -ˈkɑː-/ *adj* using only a few words to say something (OPP) **verbose** —**laconically** /-kli/ *adv*: *'She left,' said Pascoe laconically.*

lac·quer[1] /ˈlækə $ -ər/ *n* [U] **1** a liquid painted onto metal or wood to form a hard shiny surface → **varnish** **2** *old-fashioned* HAIRSPRAY

lacquer[2] *v* [T] **1** to cover something with lacquer: *a black lacquered box* **2** *old-fashioned* to use lacquer on your hair

la·crosse /ləˈkrɒs $ ləˈkrɒːs/ *n* [U] a game played on a field by two teams of ten players, in which each player has a long stick with a net on the end of it and uses this to throw, catch, and carry a small ball

lac·tate /lækˈteɪt $ ˈlækteɪt/ *v* [I] if a woman or female animal lactates, she produces milk to feed her baby or babies with

lac·ta·tion /lækˈteɪʃən/ *n* [U] *technical* the production of milk by a woman or female animal

lac·tic ac·id /ˌlæktɪk ˈæsɪd/ *n* [U] an acid produced by muscles after exercising and found in sour milk

lac·tose /ˈlæktəʊs $ -toʊs/ *n* [U] a type of sugar found in milk, sometimes used as a food for babies and sick people

la·cu·na /ləˈkuːnə/ *n* (*plural* **lacunae** /-niː/ *or* **lacunas**) [C] *formal* a place where something is missing in a piece of writing (SYN) **gap**

lac·y /ˈleɪsi/ *adj* made of LACE or looking like lace: *lacy underwear | a plant with delicate, lacy leaves*

lad /læd/ ●●○ S3 *n* [C] *BrE*
1 *old-fashioned or informal* a boy or young man → **lass**: *a* ***young lad*** | *Things were different when I was a lad.* THESAURUS▸ MAN
2 the lads *spoken* a group of male friends that a man works with or spends his free time with: *a night out with the lads* | **one of the lads** (=a member of your group of friends)
3 a bit of a lad *spoken* a man that people like even though he behaves rather badly: *That Chris is a bit of a lad, isn't he?*
4 lad culture *informal* the way in which some young men behave, involving typically male activities such as drinking a lot of alcohol, driving fast cars, and watching football – used to show disapproval
5 (*also* **stable lad**) a boy or man who works with horses SYN **stable boy** → JACK THE LAD

lad·der¹ /ˈlædə $ -ər/ ●●● S3 *n* [C]
1 a piece of equipment used for climbing up to or down from high places. A ladder has two bars that are connected by RUNGS (=short bars that you use as steps): *She* ***climbed up*** *the* ***ladder***. | *He hurt himself* ***falling off*** *a* ***ladder***. → ROPE LADDER, STEPLADDER
2 a series of levels which someone moves up and down within an organization, profession, or society: **career/corporate ladder** *Stevens slowly worked his way up the corporate ladder.* | *Becoming a doctor would be a step up the* ***social ladder***. | *the first step on the ladder of success*

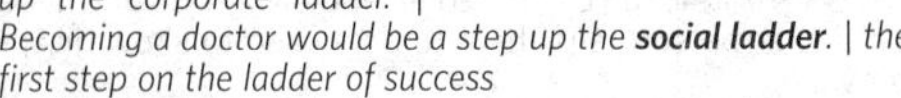

LADDER
ladder
stepladder

3 *BrE* a long thin hole in STOCKINGS or TIGHTS where some stitches have broken SYN **run** *AmE*: *Yes, I know I've got a ladder in my tights.*

ladder² *v* [I,T] *BrE* if STOCKINGS or TIGHTS ladder, or if you ladder them, a long thin hole is made in them because some stitches have broken SYN **run** *AmE* THESAURUS▸ TEAR

lad·die, **laddy** /ˈlædi/ *n* [C] *BrE informal* a boy

lad·dish /ˈlædɪʃ/ *adj BrE* a young man who is laddish likes spending time with other men, drinking alcohol, and enjoying things like sport, sex, and music → **lad**

lad·dis·m /ˈlædɪzəm/ *n* [U] *BrE* the attitudes and behaviour of some young men in Britain, who drink a lot of alcohol, and are mainly interested in sport, sex, and music → **lad**: *the culture of laddism*

la·den /ˈleɪdn/ *adj* **1** *literary* heavily loaded with something, or containing a lot of something: **[+with]** *The tables were laden with food.* | **fully/heavily laden** *The lorry was fully laden.* | ***snow-laden*** *branches* **2** having a lot of a particular quality, thing etc: **[+with]** *She was laden with doubts about the affair.* | *trucks laden with equipment* | *a* ***debt-laden*** *company*

lad·ette /læˈdet/ *n* [C] *BrE* a young woman who likes to do some things that young men typically do, such as drinking a lot of alcohol and talking about sex and sports → **lad**

la-di-da, **lah-di-dah** /ˌlɑː diː ˈdɑː/ *adj informal* used to describe someone's behaviour when you think they are talking and behaving as if they consider themselves better than other people SYN **snobbish**: *a la-di-da attitude*

ˈladies' man (*also* **lady's man**) *n* [singular] *old-fashioned* a man who likes to spend time with women, and thinks they enjoy being with him

ˈladies' room *n* [C] *AmE* a women's toilet SYN **the ladies** *BrE* → **men's room**

lad·ing /ˈleɪdɪŋ/ *n* [U] BILL OF LADING

la·dle¹ /ˈleɪdl/ *n* [C] a large deep spoon with a long handle, used for lifting liquid food, especially soup, out of a container

ladle² (*also* **ladle out**) *v* [T] to put soup or other liquid food onto plates or into bowls, especially using a ladle

ˈlad mag *n* [C] a type of magazine that is intended for young men. It typically contains a lot of pictures of young women wearing very little clothing, and most of the writing in it is about clothes, cars, drinking, sport etc.

la·dy /ˈleɪdi/ ●●● S1 W2 *n* (*plural* **ladies**) [C]
1 a) a woman of a particular type or age: **young/old/elderly etc lady b)** a word meaning woman, used especially to describe women's sports or products made for women: **ladies' team/champion/championship etc** *the ladies' darts team* | **ladies' fashion/clothing/shoes etc** *ladies' underwear* **c)** a word meaning woman, used in order to be polite → **gentleman**: *The young lady at reception sent me up here.* | *Give your coat to the lady over there.* | **lady doctor/lawyer etc** (=a doctor, lawyer etc who is a woman. Some women think this use is offensive) THESAURUS▸ WOMAN

> **REGISTER**
> **Lady** often sounds old-fashioned, especially when it is used about younger women. In everyday English, people usually say **woman**: *His cousin is a 26-year-old woman who works in a kindergarten.*

2 a woman who is polite and behaves very well → **gentleman**: *She knows how to behave like a lady.*
3 Lady used as the title of the wife or daughter of a British NOBLEMAN or the wife of a KNIGHT: *Lady Spencer*
4 the ladies a) *BrE* a women's toilet SYN **ladies' room** *AmE* → **the gents' b)** a word meaning women, often used humorously: *His boyish good looks made him a favourite with the ladies.* → LADIES' MAN
5 ladies *spoken formal* used to speak to a group of women: *Ladies and gentlemen, may I have your attention please?*
6 a woman, especially one with a strong character – used to show approval: *She can be a tough lady to negotiate with.*
7 lady friend a woman that a man is having a romantic relationship with – often used humorously SYN **girlfriend**: *I saw Chris with his new lady friend.*
8 lady of leisure a woman who does not work and has a lot of free time – used humorously: *So you're a lady of leisure now that the kids are at school?*
9 *AmE spoken* used when talking directly to a woman you do not know, when you are angry with her: *Hey, lady, would you mind getting out of my way?*

> **REGISTER**
> Addressing a woman directly as **lady** sounds rude. In polite American English, people use **Miss** or **Ma'am** instead: *Can I help you,* ***Miss***?

10 Our Lady an expression used to mean Mary, the mother of Jesus Christ
11 the lady of the house *old-fashioned* the most important woman in a house, usually the mother of a family
12 *old-fashioned* a woman born into a high social class in Britain: *I could see the Queen, surrounded by her lords and ladies.*
13 *old-fashioned* a man's wife: *the captain and his lady* → BAG LADY, → **cleaning lady** at CLEANING, FIRST LADY, → **leading lady** at LEADING¹, LOLLIPOP LADY, OLD LADY, → **young lady** at YOUNG¹(3)

la·dy·bird /ˈleɪdibɜːd $ -bɜːrd/ *BrE*, **la·dy·bug** /ˈleɪdibʌg/ *AmE n* [C] a small round BEETLE (=a type of insect) that is usually red with black spots → see picture at INSECT

ˌlady-in-ˈwaiting *n* (*plural* **ladies-in-waiting**) [C] a woman who looks after and serves a queen or PRINCESS

la·dy·like /ˈleɪdilaɪk/ *adj old-fashioned* if a woman or girl is ladylike, she behaves in a polite and quiet way that was once believed to be typical of or suitable for women: *ladylike behaviour*

la·dy·ship /ˈleɪdiʃɪp/ *n* **your/her ladyship a)** used as a way of speaking to or talking about a woman with the title of Lady → **lordship b)** *BrE spoken humorous* used to talk about a woman who thinks she is very important: *Do you think her ladyship will be joining us?*

ˈlady's man *n* [singular] *old-fashioned* another spelling of LADIES' MAN

lag¹ /læg/ ●○○ *v* (**lagged, lagging**)
1 [I,T] to move or develop more slowly than others: **[+behind]** *She stopped to wait for Ian who was lagging behind.* | *Britain is lagging behind the rest of Europe.*
2 [T] *BrE* to cover water pipes etc with a special material to prevent the water inside them from freezing or the heat from being lost: *We've had the hot-water tank lagged.*

lag² *n* [C] a delay or period of waiting between one event and a second event: *a* ***time lag*** → JET LAG, OLD LAG

la·ger /ˈlɑːɡə $ -ər/ *n* [C,U] *BrE* a light-coloured beer, or a glass of this type of beer: **can/bottle/glass etc of lager** *a pint of lager*

ˈlager lout *n* [C] *BrE informal* a young man who drinks too much and then behaves violently or rudely

lag·gard /ˈlæɡəd $ -ərd/ *n* [C] *old-fashioned* someone or something that is very slow or late —**laggardly** *adj*

lag·ging /ˈlæɡɪŋ/ *n* [U] *BrE* special material used to protect a water pipe or container from heat or cold

la·goon /ləˈɡuːn/ *n* [C] **1** a lake of sea water that is partly separated from the sea by rocks, sand, or CORAL: *a coastal lagoon* **2** *AmE* a small lake which is not very deep, near a larger lake or river

lah-di-dah /ˌlɑː diː ˈdɑː/ *adj* another spelling of LA-DI-DA

laid /leɪd/ the past tense and past participle of LAY

ˌlaid-ˈback *adj* relaxed and seeming not to be worried about anything OPP **uptight**: *I don't know how you can be so laid-back about your exams.* | **laid-back attitude/manner/approach etc** *He is famed for his laid-back attitude.* THESAURUS ▶ CALM

lain /leɪn/ *v* the past participle of LIE¹

lair /leə $ ler/ *n* [C] **1** the place where a wild animal hides and sleeps SYN **den 2** a place where you go to hide or to be alone SYN **den**: *a smuggler's lair*

laird /leəd $ lerd/ *n* [C] *BrE* a person who owns a very large area of land in Scotland

lai·ry /ˈleəri $ ˈleri/ *adj BrE informal* behaving in a way that is very loud, or with too much confidence: *He's a bit lairy, your friend Mick.*

lais·sez-faire, **laisser-faire** /ˌleseɪ ˈfeə, ˌleɪ- $ -ˈfer/ *n* [U]
1 the principle that the government should allow the ECONOMY or private businesses to develop without any state control or influence: *the policy of laissez-faire* | **laissez-faire economics/capitalism 2 laissez-faire attitude/approach etc** when you do not become involved in other people's personal affairs

la·i·ty /ˈleɪəti/ *n* **the laity** all the members of a religious group apart from the priests → **layman**

lake /leɪk/ ●●● S3 W3 *n*
1 [C] a large area of water surrounded by land: *Lake Michigan*
2 wine/milk etc lake *BrE* a very large amount of wine, milk etc that has been produced but is not needed or used → **mountain**

GRAMMAR: Patterns with lake

in the lake
• You use **in the lake** to talk about things that happen in the water: *You can swim in the lake.* | *Are there any fish in the lake?*

on the lake
• You use **on the lake** to talk about things that happen on the surface of a lake or are very close to the edge of a lake: *We go sailing on the lake.* | *They have a cottage on the lake.*

at the lake
• You use **at the lake** when thinking of a lake as a place where you can go: *We spend summers at the lake.* | *There's a café at the lake.*

THESAURUS

lake a large area of water surrounded by land: *Lake Michigan* | *We went for a swim in the lake.*
lagoon an area of water that is separated from the sea by rocks, sand, or CORAL: *a tropical lagoon* | *coastal lagoons*
reservoir a lake, especially an artificial one, where water is stored before it is supplied to people's houses: *The reservoirs supply water to Greater Manchester.*
pond a small area of fresh water that is smaller than a lake, which is either natural or artificially made: *There were several ducks on the village pond.*
pool a small area of still water in a hollow place: *a pool of water near the summit of the mountain* | *a* ***rockpool*** (=a pool in some rocks near the sea)
puddle a very small area of water on the ground, especially after it has been raining: *She turned quickly to avoid stepping in a puddle.*
waterhole a small area of water in a dry country, where wild animals go to drink: *The waterhole is used by elephants.*

lake·side /ˈleɪksaɪd/ *adj* [only before noun] beside a lake: *a lakeside restaurant* —**lakeside** *n* [singular]

lam /læm/ *n* **on the lam** *AmE informal* escaping or hiding from someone, especially the police: *Brenner was recaptured after three weeks on the lam.*

la·ma /ˈlɑːmə/ *n* [C] a Buddhist priest in Tibet or Mongolia

lamb¹ /læm/ ●●○ S3 *n*
1 [C] a young sheep
2 [U] the meat of a young sheep → **mutton**: *roast lamb* | *a* ***leg of lamb*** | **lamb chop/cutlet/stew etc**
3 [C] *spoken* used to talk to or talk about someone who is gentle and lovable, especially a child: *Ben's asleep now, the little lamb.*
4 like a lamb to the slaughter used when someone is going to do something dangerous, but they do not realize it or have no choice
5 like a lamb quietly and without any argument: *Suzie went off to school like a lamb today.* → **mutton dressed as lamb** at MUTTON(2)

lamb² *v* [I] to give birth to lambs: *The ewes are lambing this week.* —**lambing** *n* [U]: *the* ***lambing season***

lam·ba·da /læmˈbɑːdə $ lɑːm-, ləm-/ *n* [singular, U] a sexy modern dance from Brazil in which two people hold each other closely and move their bodies at the same time

lam·bast, **lambaste** /ˈlæmbæst/ *v* [T] *formal* to criticize someone or something very strongly, usually in public SYN **slate**: *Democrats lambasted the president's budget plan for being 'inadequate'.*

lambs·wool /ˈlæmzwʊl/ *n* [U] soft wool from LAMBS, used for making clothes: **lambswool jumper/sweater/blanket etc**

la·mé /ˈlɑːmeɪ $ lɑːˈmeɪ/ *n* [U] cloth containing gold or silver threads: *a gold lamé dress*

lame¹ /leɪm/ *adj* **1 a)** unable to walk properly because your leg or foot is injured or weak: *a lame dog* | **go lame** (=become lame) **b) the lame** [plural] people who are lame
2 a lame excuse or explanation is weak and difficult to believe: **lame excuse/explanation** *She gave some lame excuse about missing the bus.* | *a* ***lame attempt*** *to deflect criticism* → LAMELY **3** *informal* boring or not very good SYN **poor**: *A lot of the songs on this album are a bit lame.* | *the company's lame performance* —**lameness** *n* [U]

lame² *v* [T] to make a person or animal unable to walk properly SYN **cripple**: *He was lamed in the accident.* GRAMMAR **Lame** is usually passive.

ˌlame ˈduck *n* [C] **1** a person, business etc that is having problems and needs help **2 lame duck president/governor/legislature etc** *informal* a president, GOVERNOR etc with no real power because his or her period in office will soon end

lame·ly /ˈleɪmli/ *adv written* if you say something lamely, you do not sound confident and other people find it difficult to believe you SYN **weakly**: *'It wasn't my responsibility,' he lamely explained.*

la·ment¹ /lə'ment/ *v written* **1** [I,T] to express feelings of great sadness about something: *The nation lamented the death of its great war leader.* **2** [T] to express annoyance or disappointment about something you think is unsatisfactory or unfair: **lament that** *He lamented that people had expected too much of him too soon.* | *She* ***lamented the fact that*** *manufacturers did not produce small packs for single-person households.* | **lament the lack/absence/decline etc of sth** *Steiner lamented the lack of public interest in the issue.*

lament² *n* [C] a song, piece of music, or something that you say, that expresses a feeling of sadness: *A lone piper played a lament.* | **[+for]** *a lament for the dead*

lam·ent·a·ble /'læməntəbəl, lə'mentəbəl/ *adj formal* very unsatisfactory or disappointing SYN **terrible**: *a* ***lamentable state of affairs*** | *a* ***lamentable lack*** *of support for the idea* | ***It is lamentable that*** *the officer failed to deal with the situation.* —**lamentably** *adv*

lam·en·ta·tion /ˌlæmən'teɪʃən/ *n* [C,U] *formal* deep sadness or something that expresses it: *There was lamentation throughout the land at news of the defeat.*

lam·i·nate /'læmənət/ *n* [C,U] laminated material

lam·i·nated /'læmɪneɪtɪd/ *adj* **1** laminated material is made by joining several thin layers on top of each other: *laminated glass* **2** covered with a thin layer of plastic for protection: *a laminated ID card* —**laminate** *v* [T]

LAMPS

lamp /læmp/ ●●● S3 *n* [C]
1 an object that produces light by using electricity, oil, or gas: **table/desk/bedside lamp** | **oil/electric/fluorescent lamp** → FOG LAMP, HEADLAMP, HURRICANE LAMP, SAFETY LAMP, STANDARD LAMP
2 a piece of electrical equipment used to provide a special kind of heat, especially as a medical treatment: **infra-red/ultraviolet lamp** → SUNLAMP, BLOWLAMP

lamp·light /'læmp-laɪt/ *n* [U] the soft light produced by a lamp: *Her eyes shone in the lamplight.*

lamp·light·er /'læmpˌlaɪtə $ -ər/ *n* [C] someone whose job was to light lamps in the street in the past

lam·poon /læm'puːn/ *v* [T] to criticize someone or something in a humorous way that makes them seem stupid SYN **parody**: *The prime minister was frequently lampooned in political cartoons.* —**lampoon** *n* [C]

'lamp-post, **lamp post**, **lamp·post** /'læmp-pəʊst $ -poʊst/ *n* [C] a tall pole that supports a light over a street or public area → see picture at LAMP

lamp·shade /'læmpʃeɪd/ *n* [C] a cover fixed over a LIGHT BULB for decoration and in order to reduce or direct its light

LAN /læn/ *n* [C] *technical* (***local area network***) a system that connects computers to each other within a building or organization so that people can use and work on the same information → **WAN**

lance¹ /lɑːns $ læns/ *n* [C] a long thin pointed weapon that was used in the past by soldiers riding on horses

lance² *v* [T] to cut a small hole in someone's flesh with a sharp instrument to let out PUS (=yellow liquid produced by infection)

ˌlance 'corporal *n* [C] a low level rank in the Marines or the British army, or someone who has this rank

lan·cet /'lɑːnsɪt $ 'læn-/ *n* [C] **1** a small very sharp pointed knife with two cutting edges, used by doctors to cut skin and flesh SYN **scalpel** **2 lancet window/arch** *technical* a tall narrow window or ARCH that is pointed at the top

land¹ /lænd/ ●●● S1 W1 *n*
1 GROUND [U] an area of ground, especially when used for farming or building: *They own a lot of land.* | *He bought a piece of land.* THESAURUS COUNTRY → DOCKLAND, FARMLAND
2 NOT SEA [U] the solid dry part of the Earth's surface: *After 21 days at sea, we sighted land.* | **by land** *Troops began an assault on the city by land and sea.* | **on land** *The crocodile lays its eggs on land.* | **land bird/animal** *The white stork is one of the biggest land birds of the region.* → DRY LAND
3 COUNTRY [C] *literary* a country or area: *Their journey took them to many* ***foreign lands***. | **native land** (=the land where you were born) *He's fiercely proud of his native land.* | *Australia represented a real* ***land of opportunity*** *for thousands of people.* THESAURUS GROUND
4 NOT CITY **the land** the countryside thought of as a place where people grow food: **live off the land** (=grow or catch all the food you need) *A third of the region's population still lives off the land.* | **work/farm the land** (=grow crops) *Many people were forced to give up working the land.*
5 PROPERTY [U] the area of land that someone owns: *He ordered us to get off his land.* | **private/public/common land**
6 see/find out how the land lies *spoken* to try to discover what the situation really is before you make a decision
7 in the land of the living *spoken* awake – used humorously
8 the land of milk and honey an imaginary place where life is easy and pleasant
9 (in) the land of nod *old-fashioned* asleep → **be/live in cloud-cuckoo-land** at CLOUD¹(7), → DRY LAND, DREAMLAND, FAIRYLAND, → **the lie of the land** at LIE³(3), → NEVER-NEVER LAND, PROMISED LAND, WASTELAND, WONDERLAND

COLLOCATIONS

PHRASES

an acre/hectare of land *The family owned hundreds of acres of land.*
a piece of land (=an area of land) *He built a house on a piece of land near the river.*
a plot/parcel of land (=a piece of land) | **a strip of land** (=a narrow piece of land) | **a tract of land** (=a large area of land)

ADJECTIVES

fertile/rich (=good for growing crops) *The land near the river is very fertile.*
poor (=not good for growing crops) *It is poor land that should never have been farmed.*
vacant/derelict *BrE* (=unused) *The houses could be built on derelict land.*
open land (=land on which there are no buildings) *In the middle of the city are several hundred acres of open land.*
agricultural land | **arable land** (=land that crops are grown on) | **industrial land** (=land where factories

L

can be built and industry take place) | **housing/building land** *BrE* (=land where houses can be built)

COMMON ERRORS

⚠ Don't say 'a large land' or 'a small land'. Say **a large piece of land** or **a small piece of land**.

THESAURUS

land an area that is owned by someone or that can be used for farming or building houses: *This is private land.* | *They moved to the country and bought some land.*
farmland land that is used for farming: *The area is one of gently rolling hills and farmland.*
territory land that belongs to a country or that is controlled by a country during a war: *His plane was forced to make an emergency landing in Chinese territory.* | *The army was advancing into enemy territory.*
the grounds the gardens and land around a big building such as a castle, school, or hospital: *The grounds of the castle are open to visitors every weekend.* | *the school grounds*
estate a large area of land in the country, usually with one large house on it and one owner: *The film is set on an English country estate.*

land² ●●● S2 W3 *v*
1 PLANE/BIRD/INSECT **a)** [I] if a plane, bird, or insect lands, it moves safely down onto the ground OPP **take off**: *Flight 846 landed five minutes ago.* | *The bird landed gracefully on the water.* **b)** [T] to make a plane move safely down onto the ground at the end of a journey: *The pilot managed to land the aircraft safely.*
2 ARRIVE BY BOAT/PLANE [I] to arrive somewhere in a plane, boat etc: **[+on/in/at etc]** *We expect to be landing in Oslo in about fifty minutes.* | *In 1969, the first men landed on the Moon.* THESAURUS▸ ARRIVE
3 FALL/COME DOWN [I always + adv/prep] to come down through the air onto something SYN **drop**: **[+in/on/under etc]** *A large branch landed on the hood of my car.* | *Louis fell out of the tree and landed in a holly bush.* | *She fell and **landed heavily** on the floor.* | *A couple of bombs landed quite near to the village.*
4 GOODS/PEOPLE [T] if a boat or aircraft lands people or goods, it brings them to a place, and the people get out or the goods are carried out: *The troops were landed by helicopter.*
5 JOB/CONTRACT ETC [T] *informal* to succeed in getting a job, contract etc that was difficult to get: *He landed a job with a law firm.* | **land yourself sth** *Bill's just landed himself a part in a Broadway show.*
6 land sb in trouble/hospital/court etc to cause someone to have serious problems or be in a difficult situation: *Connie's going to land herself in big trouble if she keeps arriving late for work.* | *She developed pneumonia which landed her in hospital.*
7 land sb in it *BrE spoken informal* to get someone into trouble by telling other people that they did something wrong SYN **drop sb in it**: *Geoff landed me in it by saying I should have checked that the door was locked.*
8 PROBLEMS [I always + adv/prep] to arrive unexpectedly, and cause problems: **[+in/on/under etc]** *Just when I thought my problems were over, this letter landed on my desk.*
9 land a punch/blow etc to succeed in hitting someone
10 land on your feet to get into a good situation again, after having problems: *She certainly landed on her feet when she got that job.*
11 CATCH FISH [T] to catch a fish

GRAMMAR

Land belongs to a group of verbs where the same noun can be the subject of the verb or its object.
• You can say: *He landed the plane in a field.* In this sentence, 'the plane' is the object of **land**.
• You can say: *The plane landed in a field.* In this sentence, 'the plane' is the subject of **land**.
GRAMMAR GUIDE▸ VERBS

land up *phr v BrE informal* to be in a particular place, situation, or position after a lot of things have happened to you SYN **end up**: **[+in]** *We landed up in a bar at 3 am.* | *Be careful that you don't land up in serious debt.* | **[+with]** *I landed up with five broken ribs.*
land sb **with** sth *phr v informal* to give someone something unpleasant to do, because no one else wants to do it: *Maria's been landed with all the tidying up as usual.* GRAMMAR **Land with** is usually passive.

ˈland ˌagent *n* [C] *BrE* someone whose job is to look after land, cattle, farms etc that belong to someone else

lan·dau /ˈlændɔː $ -daʊ/ *n* [C] a four-wheeled carriage that is pulled by horses and has a top that folds back

ˈland-based *adj* placed on or living on the land: *land-based missiles* | *land-based animals*

ˈland bridge *n* [C] a narrow piece of land connecting two large areas of land, especially long ago in the past: *Thousands of years ago, people crossed the land bridge between Asia and North America.*

land·ed /ˈlændɪd/ *adj* [only before noun] **1 landed gentry/family/nobility** a family or group that has owned a lot of land for a long time **2** including a lot of land: *landed estates*

land·fall /ˈlændfɔːl $ -fɒːl/ *n* **1** [C] a LANDSLIDE(2) **2** [C,U] *literary* the land that you see or arrive at after a long journey by sea or air, or the act of arriving there

land·fill /ˈlændfɪl/ *n* **1** [U] the practice of burying waste under the ground, or the waste buried in this way **2** [C] a place where waste is buried under the ground

land·hold·ing, land-holding /ˈlændˌhəʊldɪŋ $ -ˌhoʊl-/ *n* [C,U] the land that is owned by someone

land·ing /ˈlændɪŋ/ ●●○ *n*
1 [C,U] the action of bringing an aircraft down to the ground after being in the air OPP **take-off**: *take-off and landing procedures* | **crash/emergency landing** (=a sudden landing caused by a problem with the engine etc) | *the Apollo **Moon landings*** → SOFT LANDING
2 [C] the floor at the top of a set of stairs or between two sets of stairs: *the first-floor landing*
3 [C] the action of bringing soldiers onto land that is controlled by the enemy: *the first landings of American Marines at Da Nang*
4 [C] a LANDING STAGE

ˈlanding ˌcraft *n* (*plural* **landing craft**) [C] a flat-bottomed boat that opens at one end so that soldiers and equipment can be moved directly onto the shore

ˈlanding gear *n* [U] an aircraft's wheels and other parts that support them SYN **undercarriage** → see picture at PLANE¹

ˈlanding net *n* [C] *BrE* a net on a long handle used for lifting a fish out of the water after you have caught it

ˈlanding stage *n* [C] *BrE* a wooden structure for moving passengers and goods to and from boats → **jetty**

ˈlanding strip *n* [C] a flat piece of ground that has been prepared for aircraft to use SYN **airstrip**

land·la·dy /ˈlændˌleɪdi/ *n* (*plural* **landladies**) [C] **1** a woman who rents a room, building, or piece of land to someone → **landlord 2** *BrE* a woman who owns or manages a PUB → **landlord**

land·less /ˈlændləs/ *adj* owning no land

land·line /ˈlændˌlaɪn/ *n* [C] a telephone connection that uses wires, as opposed to a MOBILE PHONE: *I'll be at home, so you can call me on the landline.*

land·locked /ˈlændlɒkt $ -lɑːkt/ *adj* a landlocked country, state etc is surrounded by other countries, states etc and has no coast

land·lord /ˈlændlɔːd $ -lɔːrd/ ●●○ W3 *n* [C]
1 a man who rents a room, building, or piece of land to someone → **landlady**
2 *BrE* a man who owns or manages a PUB → **landlady**

land·lub·ber /ˈlændˌlʌbə $ -ər/ *n* [C] *old-fashioned* someone who does not have much experience of the sea or ships

land·mark /ˈlændmɑːk $ -mɑːrk/ ●○○ *n* [C]
1 something that is easy to recognize, such as a tall tree or building, and that helps you know where you are: *One of Belfast's most famous landmarks, the Grosvenor Hall, has been demolished.*
2 one of the most important events, changes, or discoveries that influences someone or something: *The discovery of penicillin was a landmark in the history of medicine.* | **landmark decision/case/ruling** *The Supreme Court issued a landmark decision in January 2001.*

land·mass /ˈlændmæs/ *n* [C] *technical* a large area of land such as a CONTINENT

land·mine /ˈlændmaɪn/ *n* [C] a bomb hidden in the ground that explodes when someone walks or drives over it

ˈland ˌoffice *n* [C] a government office in the US that keeps records about the sale of land and who buys and sells it SYN **land registry** *BrE*

land·own·er /ˈlændˌəʊnə $ -ˌoʊnər/ ●○○ *n* [C] someone who owns land, especially a large amount of it: *wealthy landowners* —**landowning** *adj*: *Britain's landowning aristocracy* —**landownership** *n* [U]

ˈland reˌform *n* [C,U] the political principle of sharing farmland so that more people own some of it

ˈland ˌregistry *n* (*plural* **land registries**) [C] a government office in Britain that keeps records about the sale of land and who owns it SYN **land office** *AmE*

land·scape¹ /ˈlændskeɪp/ ●●● W3 *n*
1 [C] an area of countryside or land of a particular type, used especially when talking about its appearance: *the beauty of the New England landscape* | **rural/industrial/urban etc landscape** THESAURUS ▸ COUNTRY
2 [C] a picture showing an area of countryside or land: *English landscape artists* → see picture at PAINTING
3 **the political/social landscape** the general situation in which a particular activity takes place: *Recent electoral shocks have shaken the European political landscape.*
4 [U] a way of printing a document in which the long sides are horizontal and the short sides are vertical → **portrait** → **a blot on the landscape** at BLOT²(2)

landscape² *v* [T] to make a park, garden etc look attractive and interesting by changing its design, and by planting trees and bushes etc: *The area around the mill pond has also been landscaped.* —**landscaping** *n* [U]

ˌlandscape ˈarchitect *n* [C] someone whose job is to plan the way an area of land looks, including roads, buildings, and planted areas —**landscape architecture** *n* [U]

ˌlandscape ˈgardening *n* [U] the profession or art of arranging gardens and parks so that they look attractive and interesting —**landscape gardener** *n* [C]

ˌLand's ˈEnd *n* a place on the southwest coast of England, which is generally thought of as the furthest point in the southwest of the UK. It is used especially in the phrase 'from John o' Groats to Land's End', because John o' Groats is thought of as the furthest point in the northeast of the UK.

land·slide /ˈlændslaɪd/ *n* [C] **1** [usually singular] a victory in an election in which one person or party gets a lot more votes than all the others: *a **landslide** election **victory*** | **by a landslide** *The SNP candidate **won by a landslide**.* THESAURUS ▸ VICTORY **2** a sudden fall of a lot of earth or rocks down a hill, cliff etc

land·slip /ˈlændslɪp/ *n* [C] *BrE* a small fall of earth or rocks down a hill, cliff etc, that is smaller than a landslide

land·ward /ˈlændwəd $ -wərd/ *adj* facing towards the land and away from the sea → **seaward**: *the landward side of the hill* —**landwards** *adv*

lane /leɪn/ ●●● S3 W3 *n* [C]
1 a narrow road in the countryside → **path**: *a quiet **country lane***
2 a road in a city, often used in road names: *the Hilton Hotel in Park Lane* | *a network of alleys and **back lanes*** (=narrow unimportant roads, often behind a row of houses)
3 one of the two or three parallel areas on a road which are divided by painted lines to keep traffic apart: *That idiot **changed lanes** without signalling.* | **the inside/middle/outside lane** *Use the outside lane for overtaking only.* | **the fast/slow lane** *Cars in the fast lane were travelling at over 80 miles an hour.* | **three-lane motorway/highway/road** → BUS LANE, CYCLE LANE
4 one of the narrow parallel areas marked for each competitor in a running or swimming race
5 a line or course along which ships or aircraft regularly travel between ports or airports: *busy **shipping lanes*** → **life in the fast lane** at FAST LANE(1), → **walk/trip down memory lane** at MEMORY(7)

lan·guage /ˈlæŋgwɪdʒ/ ●●● S1 W1 *n*
1 ENGLISH/FRENCH/ARABIC ETC [C,U] a system of communication by written or spoken words, which is used by the people of a particular country or area: *How many languages do you speak?* | *one of the best-known poems in the English language*
2 COMMUNICATION [U] the use of written or spoken words to communicate: *the origins of language*
3 STYLE/TYPE OF WORDS [U] a particular style or type of words: **legal/medical/technical etc language** *The letter was written in complicated legal language.* | **spoken/written language** *The expression is mainly used in written language.* | **ordinary/everyday language** *He is able to explain complicated ideas in simple everyday language.* | **literary/poetic language** *The plays are full of old-fashioned poetic language.* | **[+of]** *the language of science*
4 SWEARING [U] *informal* words that most people think are offensive: **mind/watch your language** *spoken* (=stop swearing) | **bad/foul/abusive language**
5 **strong language a)** angry words used to tell people exactly what you mean **b)** words that most people think are offensive SYN **swearing**
6 COMPUTERS [C,U] *technical* a system of instructions for operating a computer: *a **programming language** for the Web*
7 SIGNS/ACTIONS/SOUNDS [C,U] signs, movements, or sounds that express ideas or feelings: **[+of]** *the language of bees* | *the language of dolphins* → BODY LANGUAGE, SIGN LANGUAGE, → **speak the same language** at SPEAK(11)

COLLOCATIONS

VERBS

speak a language *Can you speak a foreign language?*
use a language *The children use their native language at home.*
learn a language *Immigrants are expected to learn the language of their new country.*
master a language (=succeed in learning a language well) | **know a language**

ADJECTIVES/NOUN + language

a foreign language *He found learning a foreign language extremely difficult.*
the English/Japanese/Spanish etc language *She had some knowledge of the Spanish language.*
sb's first/native language (=the language someone first learned as a child) *His first language was Polish.*
a second language (=a language you speak that is not your first language) | **modern languages** (=languages that are spoken now) | **a dead language** (=a language that is no longer spoken) | **an official language** (=the language used for official business in a country) | **a common language** (=a language that more than one person or group speaks, so that they can understand each other)

language + NOUN

the language barrier (=the problem of communicating with someone when you do not speak the same language) *Because of the language barrier, it was hard for doctors to give good advice to patients.*
a language student/learner *Language learners often have problems with tenses.*
a language teacher | **language teaching**

PHRASES

sb's command of a language (=someone's ability to speak a language)

THESAURUS

TECHNIQUES USED IN LANGUAGE

metaphor a way of describing something by referring to it as something different and suggesting that it has similar qualities to that thing: *The beehive is a metaphor for human society.*

simile an expression that describes something by comparing it with something else, using the words as or like, for example 'as white as snow': *The poet uses the simile 'soft like clay'.*

irony the use of words that are the opposite of what you really mean, often in order to be amusing: *'I'm so happy to hear that,' he said, with more than a trace of irony in his voice.*

bathos a sudden change from a subject that is beautiful, moral, or serious to something that is ordinary, silly, or not important: *The play is too sentimental and full of bathos.*

hyperbole a way of describing something by saying that it is much bigger, smaller, worse etc than it actually is – used especially to excite people's feelings: *In his speeches, he used a lot of hyperbole. | journalistic hyperbole*

alliteration the use of several words together that all begin with the same sound, in order to make a special effect, especially in poetry: *the alliteration of the 's' sound in 'sweet birds sang softly'*

imagery the use of words to describe ideas or actions in a way that makes the reader connect the ideas with pictures in their mind: *the use of water imagery in Fitzgerald's novel 'The Great Gatsby' | She uses the imagery of a bird's song to represent eternal hope.*

rhetorical question a question that you ask as a way of making a statement, without expecting an answer: *When he said 'how can these attitudes still exist in a civilized society?', he was asking a rhetorical question.*

ˈlanguage laˌboratory / $ ˈ.. ˌ..../ *n* (*plural* **language laboratories**) [C] a room in a school or college where you can learn to speak a foreign language by listening to tapes and recording your own voice

lan·guid /ˈlæŋɡwɪd/ *adj literary* **1** moving slowly and involving very little energy: *He greeted Charles with a languid wave of his hand.* **THESAURUS** ➤ **SLOW 2** slow and not involving any activity: *We spent a languid afternoon by the pool.* —**languidly** *adv*

lan·guish /ˈlæŋɡwɪʃ/ *v* [I] **1** if someone languishes somewhere, they are forced to remain in a place where they are unhappy: **[+in]** *Shaw languished in jail for fifteen years.* **2** if something languishes, it fails to improve and develop or become successful → **founder** (OPP) **flourish**: *The housing market continues to languish. | The shares are languishing at just 46p after yesterday's fall. | West Ham United are currently languishing at the bottom of the league.*

lan·guor /ˈlæŋɡə $ -ər/ *n* [U] *literary* **1** a pleasant feeling of laziness: *Lying there beside her, he was filled with an agreeable languor.* **2** when the air is heavy and there is no wind: *the languor of a hot afternoon* —**languorous** *adj* —**languorously** *adv*

lank /læŋk/ *adj* lank hair is thin, straight, and unattractive

lank·y /ˈlæŋki/ *adj* someone who is lanky is tall and thin, and moves awkwardly (SYN) **gangling**: *a lanky young man* —**lankiness** *n* [U]

lan·o·lin /ˈlænəl-ɪn/ *n* [U] an oil that is obtained from sheep's wool, and is used in skin creams

lan·tern /ˈlæntən $ -ərn/ *n* [C] a lamp that you can carry, consisting of a metal container with glass sides that surrounds a flame or light → CHINESE LANTERN, MAGIC LANTERN

lan·yard /ˈlænjəd $ -jərd/ *n* [C] **1** a thin rope or RIBBON worn around your neck to carry something such as a WHISTLE or IDENTITY CARD **2** a rope or string, especially on a ship

lap¹ /læp/ ●●○ *n* [C]

1 the upper part of your legs when you are sitting down (SYN) **knee**: **on sb's lap** *Shannon sat on her mother's lap.* | **in sb's lap** *His hands were folded in his lap.*

2 a single journey around a race track: *Rubens Barrichello finished a lap ahead of his team-mate.* | **lap of honour** *BrE*, **victory lap** *AmE* (=a lap to celebrate winning) *The entire team **took a victory lap** in front of their cheering fans.*

3 *AmE* a single journey from one end of a swimming pool to another: **do/run/swim a lap** *Every morning she swims 50 laps in the pool.*

4 a part of a long journey (SYN) **leg**: **[+of]** *The **last lap** of their **journey** was by ship.*

5 in the lap of luxury having an easy and comfortable life with a lot of money, possessions etc: *She wasn't used to **living in the lap of luxury**.*

6 in the lap of the gods *BrE* if the result of something is in the lap of the gods, you do not know what will happen because it depends on things you cannot control

LAP

Shannon is sitting on her mother's lap.

lap² *v* (**lapped, lapping**) **1** [I,T] if water laps something or laps against something such as the shore or a boat, it moves against it or hits it in small waves: **[+against/over etc]** *The waves lapped gently against the rocks. | The tide was lapping the harbour wall.* **2** (*also* **lap up**) [T] if an animal laps water, milk etc, it drinks it by putting its tongue into it **3** [T] to pass a competitor in a race who is one complete lap behind you: *Erik Gomas spun off the track when trying to lap Andrew Scott.* —**lapping** *n* [U]: *She could hear the soft lapping of the sea.*

lap sth ↔ **up** *phr v* **1** to enjoy something without worrying about whether it is good, true etc: *She's lapping up all the attention she's getting. | The humour was lapped up by an appreciative crowd.* **2** if an animal laps up water, milk etc, it drinks it by putting its tongue into it: *The cat began to lap up the milk.*

lap·a·ros·cop·y /ˌlæpəˈrɒskəpi $ -ˈrɑːs-/ *n* (*plural* **laparoscopies**) [C,U] *medical* a medical examination or operation in which a special tube is put into someone's body through a small cut so that the organs inside can be seen —**laparoscopic** /ˌlæpərəˈskɒpɪk/ *adj*

ˈlap ˌdancing *n* [U] a type of dancing in which a young woman uses sexy movements and removes her clothes while sitting on a customer's LAP in a NIGHTCLUB —**lap dancer** *n* [C]

ˈlap dog, **lap·dog** /ˈlæpdɒɡ $ -dɒːɡ/ *n* [C] **1** a small pet dog **2** someone who is completely under the control of someone else and will do anything they say – used to show disapproval

la·pel /ləˈpel/ *n* [C] the part of the front of a coat or JACKET that is joined to the collar and folded back on each side

LAPEL

lap·i·da·ry /ˈlæpədəri $ -deri/ *adj* [only before noun] **1** *formal* well-written and accurate: *the **lapidary** style of the poem* **2** *technical* relating to the cutting or polishing of valuable stones or jewels

lap·is laz·u·li /ˌlæpəs ˈlæzjʊli $ -ˈlæzəli/ *n* [C,U] a valuable bright blue stone, used especially in jewellery

lap·py /ˈlæpi/ *n* [C] *informal* a LAPTOP

lapse¹ /læps/ *n* [C] **1** a short period of time during which you fail to do something well or properly, often caused by not being careful: **momentary/temporary/occasional etc lapse** *Despite the occasional lapse, this was a fine performance by the young saxophonist.* | *A defensive lapse by Keown allowed Tottenham to score.* | **[+in]** *lapses in security* | **[+of]** *A single* ***lapse of concentration*** *cost Sampras the game.* | *a lapse of judgement* | *After taking the drug, several patients suffered* ***memory lapses*** (=when you cannot remember something for a short time). **2** a failure to do something you should do, especially to behave correctly: *He forgot to offer Darren a drink, but Marie did not appear to notice the lapse.* **3** [usually singular] a period of time between two events: *The usual* ***time lapse*** *between request and delivery is two days.* | **[+of]** *a lapse of about ten seconds*

lapse² *v* [I] **1** to gradually come to an end or to stop for a period of time: *The conversation lapsed.* **2** *especially BrE* if a contract, agreement etc lapses, it comes to an end, usually because an agreed time limit has passed: *Your booking will automatically lapse unless you confirm it.*

> **REGISTER**
> In everyday English, people usually say that a contract or agreement **runs out** rather than **lapses**:
> *His club membership had* ***run out***.

3 to stop believing in or following a religion: *those people who have lapsed from the practice of their religion* **4** *formal* if a period of time lapses, it passes: *Many years had lapsed since her first visit to Wexford.*

lapse into sth *phr v* **1 lapse into unconsciousness/silence/sleep etc** to go into a quiet or less active state: *He lapsed into a coma and died two days later.* | *Alison lapsed into puzzled silence.* **2** to begin to behave or speak in a way that you did before: *She lapsed back into her old ways.* | *Occasionally he lapsed into his native German.* **3** to get into a worse state or become worse: *Following his death, the Empire lapsed into chaos.* | *His poetry often lapses into sentimentality.*

lapsed /læpst/ *adj* [only before noun] no longer having the beliefs you used to have, especially religious beliefs OPP **practising**: *a* ***lapsed Catholic***

lap·top /ˈlæptɒp $ -tɑːp/ ●●● S2 W2 (*also* **ˌlaptop ˈcomputer**) *n* [C] a small computer that you can carry with you → **desktop**

lap·wing /ˈlæpˌwɪŋ/ *n* [C] a small black and white European bird with raised feathers on its head SYN **peewit**

lar·ce·ny /ˈlɑːsəni $ ˈlɑːr-/ *n* (*plural* **larcenies**) [C,U] *law* the act or crime of stealing SYN **theft** → PETTY LARCENY

larch /lɑːtʃ $ lɑːrtʃ/ *n* [C,U] a tree that looks like a PINE tree but drops its leaves in winter

lard¹ /lɑːd $ lɑːrd/ *n* [U] white fat from pigs that is used in cooking

lard² *v* [T] to put small pieces of BACON onto meat before cooking it

lard sth **with** sth *phr v* to include a lot of something, especially something that is not necessary, in a speech, piece of writing, plan etc: *a speech larded with Biblical quotations*

ˈlard-ass *n* [C] *AmE spoken not polite* an offensive word for someone who is fat

lar·der /ˈlɑːdə $ ˈlɑːrdər/ *n* [C] a small room or large cupboard for storing food in a house → **pantry**

large¹ /lɑːdʒ $ lɑːrdʒ/ ●●● S1 W1 *adj* (*comparative* **larger**, *superlative* **largest**)
1 big in size, amount, or number OPP **small**: *Los Angeles is the second largest city in the US.* | *The T-shirt comes in Small, Medium and Large.* | *a large ovenproof pan* | *large sums of money* | *those who drink* ***large amounts*** *of coffee* | *A* ***large number*** *of students have signed up for the course.*
THESAURUS ▶ BIG
2 a large person is tall and often fat OPP **small**
THESAURUS ▶ FAT
3 be at large if a dangerous person or animal is at large, they have escaped from somewhere or have not been caught: *The escaped prisoners are still at large.*
4 the population/public/society/world etc at large people in general: *The chemical pollution poses a threat to the population at large.*
5 the larger issues/question/problem/picture more general facts, situations, or questions related to something: *The book helps to explain the larger picture in the Middle East.*
6 in large part/measure *formal* mostly: *Their success was due in large part to their ability to speak Spanish.*
7 (as) large as life *BrE spoken* used when someone has appeared or is present in a place where you did not expect to see them: *I turned a corner and there was Joe, as large as life.*
8 larger than life someone who is larger than life is very amusing or exciting in an attractive way
9 by and large used when talking generally about someone or something: *Charities, by and large, do not pay tax.*
→ **loom large** at LOOM¹(3), → **writ large** at WRIT²

large² *v* **large it (up)** *BrE informal* to enjoy yourself, especially in a way that involves drinking alcohol, dancing etc: *Here's a picture of us larging it up in Brighton last summer.*

ˌlarge inˈtestine *n* [C] the lower part of your BOWELS, where food is changed into solid waste matter → **small intestine** → see picture at **HUMAN¹**

large·ly /ˈlɑːdʒli $ ˈlɑːr-/ ●●○ W2 *adv* mostly or mainly: *The state of Nevada is largely desert.* | *It had been a tiring day, largely because of all the tedious waiting.*

ˌlarge-ˈscale ●○○ *adj* [only before noun]
1 using or involving a lot of effort, people, supplies etc OPP **small-scale**: *a large-scale rescue operation*
2 a large-scale map, model etc is drawn or made bigger than usual, so that more details can be shown

lar·gesse, largess /lɑːˈʒes $ lɑːrˈdʒes/ *n* [U] *formal* when someone gives money or gifts to people who have less than they do, or the money or gifts that they give SYN **generosity**

larg·ish /ˈlɑːdʒɪʃ $ ˈlɑːr-/ *adj informal* fairly big

lar·go /ˈlɑːgəʊ $ ˈlɑːrgoʊ/ *adj, adv technical* played or sung slowly and seriously —**largo** *n* [C]

lar·i·at /ˈlæriət/ *n* [C] *AmE* a LASSO

lark¹ /lɑːk $ lɑːrk/ *n* [C] **1** a small brown singing bird with long pointed wings SYN **skylark** **2** *informal* something that you do to amuse yourself or as a joke: **as/for a lark** *I only went along for a lark.* **3 blow/sod/bugger etc that for a lark** *BrE spoken not polite* used when you stop doing something or refuse to do something because it needs too much effort: *Paint the whole room? Sod that for a lark!* **4** *BrE spoken* used to describe an activity that you think is silly or difficult: *Salad again? How long are you going to keep up this healthy eating lark?* **5 be up with the lark** to get up very early

lark² *v*
lark about/around *phr v BrE informal* to have fun by behaving in a silly way SYN **mess about**: *A couple of boys were larking about in the pool.*

lar·va /ˈlɑːvə $ ˈlɑːrvə/ *n* (*plural* **larvae** /-viː/) [C] a young insect with a soft tube-shaped body, which will later become an insect with wings SYN **grub** → **pupa** —**larval** *adj*

lar·yn·gi·tis /ˌlærɪnˈdʒaɪtɪs/ *n* [U] an illness which makes talking difficult because your larynx and throat are swollen

lar·ynx /ˈlærɪŋks/ *n* (*plural* **larynges** /ləˈrɪndʒiːz/ *or* **larynxes**) [C] the part in your throat where your voice is produced → **vocal cords**

la·sa·gne *BrE*, **lasagna** *AmE* /ləˈsænjə, -ˈzæn- $ -ˈzɑːn-/ *n* [C,U] a type of Italian food made with flat pieces of PASTA, meat, or vegetables, and cheese

L

las·civ·i·ous /ləˈsɪviəs/ *adj* showing strong sexual desire, or making someone feel this way: *a lascivious wink* —**lasciviously** *adv* —**lasciviousness** *n* [U]

la·ser /ˈleɪzə $ -ər/ ●●○ *n* [C]
1 a piece of equipment that produces a powerful narrow beam of light that can be used in medical operations, to cut metals, or to make patterns of light for entertainment: *laser surgery*
2 a beam of light produced by a laser

ˈlaser ˌdisk *n* [C] a DISK like a CD which can be read by laser light and used in computers or to watch films

ˈlaser ˌpointer *n* [C] a small piece of equipment that produces a laser beam, used by teachers and people who are giving talks in order to point at things on a map, board etc

ˈlaser ˌprinter *n* [C] a machine connected to a computer system which prints by using laser light

lash[1] /læʃ/ *v*
1 TIE [T always + adv/prep] to tie something tightly to something else with a rope SYN **bind**: **lash sth to sth** *The oars were lashed to the sides of the boat.*
2 WIND/RAIN/SEA [I always + adv/prep, T] if the wind, sea etc lashes something, it hits it with violent force: *Giant waves lashed the sea wall.* | **[+against/down/across]** *The wind lashed violently against the door.*
3 HIT [T] to hit a person or animal very hard with a whip, stick etc: *Oliver lashed the horses to go faster.*
4 TAIL [I,T] if an animal lashes its tail, or if its tail lashes, it moves it from side to side quickly and strongly, especially because it is angry
5 CRITICIZE [I,T] to criticize someone angrily – used especially in newspapers: *Democrats lashed Republican plans, calling them extreme.* | **[+back]** *Gallins lashed back at those who accused him of corruption.*

lash out *phr v*
1 to suddenly speak angrily to someone or criticize someone angrily: **[+at]** *Olson lashed out at the media.*
2 to try to hit someone with a series of violent uncontrolled movements: **[+at]** *She would suddenly lash out at other children.*

lash[2] *n* [C] **1** a hit with a whip, especially as a punishment: *They were each given fifty lashes.* **2** [usually plural] one of the hairs that grow around the edges of your eyes SYN **eyelash** **3** a sudden or violent movement like that of a whip: *With a lash of its tail, the lion sprang at its prey.* **4** the thin piece of leather at the end of a whip **5 on the lash** *BrE informal* drinking a lot of alcohol in PUBs or bars: *We went out on the lash last night.*

lash·ing /ˈlæʃɪŋ/ *n* [C] **1** a punishment in which someone is hit with a whip SYN **whipping** **2** a rope that fastens something tightly to something else **3 lashings of sth** *BrE old-fashioned* a large amount of food or drink: *apple pie with lashings of cream*

lass /læs/ (*also* **las·sie** /ˈlæsi/) *n* [C] a girl or young woman – used especially in Scotland and the north of England → **lad**

las·si·tude /ˈlæsɪtjuːd $ ˈlæsətjuːd, -tuːd/ *n* [U] *formal* tiredness and lack of energy or interest SYN **weariness**

las·so[1] /ləˈsuː, ˈlæsəʊ $ -soʊ/ *n* (*plural* **lassos** *or* **lassoes**) [C] a rope with one end tied in a circle, used to catch cattle and horses, especially in the western US

lasso[2] *v* [T] to catch an animal using a lasso

last[1] /lɑːst $ læst/ ●●● S1 W1 *determiner, adj*
1 most recent or nearest to the present time → **next(12)**: *I hadn't seen him since the last meeting.* | **last night/week/year etc** *Did you see the game on TV last night?* | *The law was passed last August.* | *Interest in golf has grown rapidly in the last ten years.* | *Things have changed since* ***the last time*** (=the most recent occasion) *you were here.*
2 happening or existing at the end, with no others after OPP **first**: *I didn't read the last chapter of the book.* | *The next meeting will be held in the last week in June.* | **the last person/thing etc to do sth** *Anna was the last person to see him alive.* | **last but one/two etc** (=last except for one other, two others etc) *on the last but one day of his trial* | **second/next to last** (=last except for one other) *the second to last paragraph*
3 remaining after all others have gone, been used etc: *Can I have the last piece of cake?* | **every last** (=used to emphasize that you mean all of something) *All the money was gone; every last penny of it.*
4 the last minute/moment the latest possible time before something happens: *Travelers will find it hard to get a hotel room at the last minute.* | *He never makes a decision until almost the last moment.*
5 the last person/thing used to make a strong negative statement about someone or something: *She's the last person I'd expect to meet in a disco* (=I would not expect to meet her in a disco at all). | *Money was the last thing I cared about right now.* | **the last thing sb needs/wants** *The last thing she needed was for me to start crying too.*
6 be the last straw to be the final thing in a series of annoying things that makes someone very angry: *He'd broken his promise again, and it was the last straw.*
7 last thing (at night) at the very end of the day: *Take a couple of these pills last thing at night to help you sleep.*
8 on your last legs *informal* **a)** very tired: *Sarah looks as if she's on her last legs.* **b)** very ill and likely to die soon
9 on its last legs *informal* old or in bad condition, and likely to stop working soon: *The car's on its last legs.*
10 be the last word in sth to be the best, most modern, or most comfortable example of something: *It's the last word in luxury holidays.* → **last resort** at RESORT[1](2), → **with your last/dying breath** at BREATH(9), → LAST HURRAH, → **have the last laugh** at LAUGH[2](6), → **the last/final word** at WORD[1](15)

THESAURUS

THE ONE BEFORE THIS ONE

last most recent or nearest to the present time: *His last film was much better.* | *It rained all day last Saturday.* | *The last time I saw her was two years ago.*
previous [only before noun] before this one, or before the one that you are talking about: *See the diagram in the previous chapter.* | *His previous records had all been jazz records.* | *How much were you earning in your previous job?*
former [only before noun] *formal* existing or having a particular position in the past, but not now: *the former Soviet Union* | *the former US president* | *Interest rates are unlikely to return to their former level.*
old [only before noun] used about a person or thing that existed in the past, but has been replaced by a newer one: *an old boyfriend* | *The old model was much slower.*

THE ONE THAT COMES AT THE END

last [only before noun] happening or existing at the end, with no others after: *What time does the last train leave?* | *Our house is the last one on the right.*
final [only before noun] last in a series of actions, events, parts of a story etc: *It's the final game of the championship tomorrow.* | *the final scene of the film*
closing [only before noun] used about the last part of a long period of time, or of an event, book etc that has been exciting or interesting: *the closing years of the twentieth century* | *Barnes scored the winning goal in the closing minutes of the game.*
concluding [only before noun] used about the last part of a piece of writing, a speech, or an organized event, that ends it in a definite way: *the concluding section of the report* | *the judge's concluding remarks*
penultimate /peˈnʌltəmət, pə-/ [only before noun] the one before the last one: *the penultimate chapter*

last[2] ●●● S1 W1 *adv*
1 most recently before now → **next**: *When I last saw her, she was working in New York.*

GRAMMAR

Choosing the right tense

Last is used with the simple past: *I last saw her in 2008.* ✗ Don't say: *I have last seen her in 2008.*

Word order

• **Last** usually comes before a main verb: *I last went to London in June.*
• **Last** comes after 'be' when it is the main verb: *I was last in London in June.*
• **Last** comes after the first auxiliary: *When did you last hear from Tara?*

2 after everything or everyone else OPP **first**: *Who is speaking last?* | *Add the flour last.* | **last of all** (=used when giving a final point or piece of information) *Last of all, I'd like to thank everyone for coming.*
3 last but not least used when mentioning the last person or thing in a list, to emphasize that they are still important: *Last but not least, let me introduce Jane, our new secretary.*

last³ ●●● S1 W1 *n, pron*
1 the last the person or thing that comes after all the others OPP **first**: *I think this box is the last.* | **the last to do sth** *He was the first to arrive and the last to leave.*
2 at (long) last if something happens at last, it happens after you have been hoping, waiting, or working for it a long time: *At last it was time to leave.* | *We reached the summit at last.*
3 the day/week/year etc before last the day, week etc before the one that has just finished: *I sent the letter off the week before last.*
4 the last of sth the remaining parts of something: *John ate the last of the bread at lunchtime.*
5 sb hasn't heard the last of sb/sth if you have not heard the last of someone or something, they may return and cause problems for you in the future: *We haven't heard the last of football violence.*
6 sb will never hear the last of sth if you will never hear the last of something, someone will be angry with you about it for a long time: *If my mother sees me, I'll never hear the last of this.*
7 the last I heard *spoken* used to tell someone the most recent news that you know about a person or situation: *The last I heard, she was at college studying law.*
8 to the last *formal* until the end of an event or the end of someone's life: *He died in 1987, insisting to the last he was innocent.*

last⁴ ●●● S1 W2 *v*
1 [I always + adv/prep, T] to continue for a particular length of time: **[+for/until/through etc]** *The hot weather lasted for the whole month of June.* | **last an hour/ten minutes etc** *Each lesson lasts an hour.* | *The ceasefire didn't last long.*
THESAURUS CONTINUE
2 [I,T] to continue to exist, be effective, or remain in good condition for a long time: *This good weather won't last.* | **last (sb) two days/three weeks etc** *A good coat will last you ten years.* | *Cut flowers will last longer if you put flower food in the water.*
3 [I always + adv/prep] (*also* **last out (sth)** *BrE*) to manage to remain in the same situation, even when this is difficult: *They won't be able to last much longer without fresh supplies.* | *If you go into the job with that attitude, you won't last long.* | *She feared she might not be able to last out the afternoon in court without fainting.*
4 [I,T always + adv/prep] to be enough for someone for a period of time SYN **do**: **last (sb) for/until/to etc** *The batteries should last for 20 hours playing time.* | *We only had $50 to last us the rest of the month.*

last⁵ *n* [C] a piece of wood or metal shaped like a human foot, used by someone who makes and repairs shoes

ˌlast ˈcall *n* [U] *AmE* the time when customers in a bar can order one more drink before the bar closes SYN **last orders** *BrE*

ˌlast-ˈditch *adj* **a last-ditch attempt/effort etc** a final attempt to achieve something before it is too late: *The negotiators made a last-ditch effort to reach an agreement.*

ˌlast hurˈrah *n* [C usually singular] *AmE* a final effort, event etc at the end of a long period of work, a life etc: *He's made it clear that this Olympics, his third, will be his last hurrah.*

last·ing /ˈlɑːstɪŋ $ ˈlæs-/ ●○○ *adj* [usually before noun] strong enough, well enough planned etc to continue for a very long time SYN **long-lasting**: *The reforms will bring* ***lasting benefits.*** | *Their generosity made a* ***lasting impression*** *on me.* | *a solution that would bring* ***lasting peace***
THESAURUS LONG, PERMANENT

ˌlast ˈjudgment *n* **the last judgment** the time after death when everyone is judged by God for what they have done in life, according to Christianity and some other religions SYN **judgment day**

last·ly /ˈlɑːstli $ ˈlæst-/ ●●○ *adv* [sentence adverb] used when telling someone the last thing at the end of a list or a series of statements OPP **firstly**: *Lastly, could I ask all of you to keep this information secret.*

ˌlast-ˈminute ●○○ *adj* [only before noun] happening or done as late as possible before something else happens: *a few last-minute changes to the script*

ˈlast name ●●● S2 *n* [C] *especially AmE* a SURNAME

ˌLast ˌNight of the ˈProms, the the last concert of the Proms, a series of concerts held each summer in the Royal Albert Hall in London. The second part of the concert always consists of the same tunes and songs, and the people who go to the concert join in with the singing. Some of them wear silly hats and have their faces painted. The concert ends with the PATRIOTIC song *Land of Hope and Glory*, and many people sing it while waving UNION JACKS (=British national flags).

ˌlast ˈorders *n* [plural] *BrE* the time when customers in a bar or PUB can order one more drink before the bar closes SYN **last call** *AmE*

ˌlast ˈpost *n* **the last post** the tune played on a BUGLE at British military funerals, or to call soldiers back to camp for the night

ˌlast ˈrites *n* [plural] **the last rites** the ceremony performed in some religions, especially the Catholic religion, for people who are dying

lat. (*also* **lat** *BrE*) the written abbreviation of ***latitude***

latch¹ /lætʃ/ *n* [C] **1** a small metal or plastic object used to keep a door, gate, or window closed: *Gwen lifted the latch and opened the gate.* → see picture at LOCK
2 *especially BrE* a type of lock for a door that you can open from the inside by turning a handle, but that you need a key to open from the outside: **on the latch** (=shut but not locked) *Ray went out, leaving the door on the latch.*

latch² *v* [T] to fasten a door, gate, or window with a latch

latch on *phr v BrE informal* to understand: *He's so thick it took him ages to latch on.*

latch onto sb/sth (*also* **latch on to sb/sth**) *phr v informal* **1** to become very interested in something: *Don't just latch on to the latest management fads.* **2** to follow someone and keep trying to talk to them, get their attention etc, especially when they would prefer to be left alone: *He latched onto Sandy at the party and wouldn't go away.* **3** to hold tightly to something with your hand, mouth etc: *a baby latching on to its mother's breast*

latch·key /ˈlætʃkiː/ *n* [C] **1** a key that opens a lock on an outside door of a house or an apartment **2 latchkey kid** *old-fashioned* a child whose parents both work and who spends time alone in the house after school

late¹ /leɪt/ ●●● S1 W1 *adj* (*comparative* **later**, *superlative* **latest**)
1 AFTER EXPECTED TIME arriving, happening, or done after the time that was expected, agreed, or arranged OPP **early**: *Sorry I'm late – I overslept.* | **ten minutes/two hours etc late** *You're half an hour late.* | *The train was even later than usual.* | *We apologize for the late departure of flight AZ709.* | *There are penalties if loan repayments are late.* | **[+for]** *Cheryl was late for school.* | **[+with]** *We've never been late with the rent.*
2 NEAR THE END [only before noun] used to refer to the part near the end of a period of time OPP **early**: *Paul's in his*

L

late forties. | *a late eighteenth-century building* | *in the late 1980s* | *By late afternoon, she had done 10 drawings.*

3 be too late to arrive or do something after the time when something could or should have been done: *He shouted a warning but **it was too late**.* | **too late to do sth** *Are we too late to get tickets?* | *It was too late to turn back.*

4 AFTER USUAL TIME happening or done after the usual or normal time: *a late breakfast* | *The harvest was late this year because of the rain.* | *She looked tired – too many **late nights*** (=nights when she went to bed after the normal time).

5 EVENING near the end of a day: *the late movie* | ***It's late*** *– I'd better go home.*

6 DEAD [only before noun] dead: **late husband/wife** *Mrs. Moore's late husband*

7 late developer/bloomer a) a child who develops socially, emotionally, or physically at a later age than other children **b)** someone who does not become successful until they are older

8 it's (a little/bit) late in the day (to do sth) used to show disapproval because someone has done something too late: *It's a bit late in the day to start having objections.*

9 late of sth *formal* used about someone who has died fairly recently: *Billy Hicks, late of this parish* —**lateness** *n* [U]: *penalties for lateness at work* | *despite the lateness of the hour*

GRAMMAR: Patterns with late

- You are **late for** work, school, a meeting etc: *I was late for my appointment.*
- You are **late for** your train, bus, plane etc: *Hurry up or you'll be late for your train!*
- You are **late with** something that you have to produce, for example your work or the rent: *He was always late with his homework.*
- You are **late doing** something: *They were late paying the rent.*
- You can also say that someone is **late in doing** something: *They were late in paying the rent.*

THESAURUS

late arriving or happening after the time that was expected or arranged: *Sorry I'm late.* | *The bus was late.* | *Spring seems to be very late this year.*

not on time not arriving or doing something at the time that was expected or arranged: *He never hands his homework in on time.* | *If we don't leave on time, we'll miss the flight.*

overdue not done or happening by the expected time – used especially about payments that are late or library books that should have been returned: *Your rent is three weeks overdue.* | *I had to pay a £3 fine on some overdue library books.*

be behind with sth *BrE*, **be behind on sth** *AmE* to be late in doing something that you have to do: *I can't come out because I'm behind with my English essay.*

be held up to be made late for a meeting, appointment etc by something that happens, especially by bad traffic: *I was held up by a traffic jam.*

be delayed to be prevented from arriving, leaving, or happening at the expected time – often used about public transport: *The flight was delayed by bad weather.*

belated /bɪˈleɪtəd/ given or done late – used especially about something that someone has forgotten or failed to do: *a belated birthday card* | *I'm still hoping for a belated apology from him.*

tardy *especially AmE formal* arriving or happening late: *a habitually tardy person* | *a tardy decision*

be in arrears /əˈrɪəz $ əˈrɪrz/ *formal* to have not made one or more regular payments at the time when you should: *One in eight mortgage payers are in arrears.*

late² ●●● S2 W3 *adv* (*comparative* **later**, *superlative* **no superlative**)

1 after the usual time: *The stores are open later on Thursdays.* | *Ellen has to **work late** tonight.* | *Can you stay late?*

2 after the arranged or expected time OPP **early**: **ten minutes/two hours etc late** *The bus came ten minutes late.*

3 too late after the time when something could or should have been done: *The advice came too late.*

4 near to the end of a period of time or an event: **[+in]** *The wedding took place late in May.* | *It was not a place to walk in **late at night**.*

5 as late as sth used to express surprise that something considered old-fashioned was still happening so recently: *Capital punishment was still used in Britain as late as the 1950s.*

6 of late *formal* recently: *Birth rates have gone down of late.*

7 late in life if you do something late in life, you do it at an older age than most people do it

8 better late than never used to say that you are glad someone has done something, or to say that they should do something even though they are late → **run late** at RUN¹(39)

ˈlate-ˌbreaking *adj* late-breaking news concerns events that happen just before a news broadcast or just before a newspaper is printed

late·com·er /ˈleɪtˌkʌmə $ -ər/ *n* [C] someone who arrives late

late·ly /ˈleɪtli/ ●●● S2 *adv* recently: *What have you been doing lately?* | *Lately, I've had trouble sleeping.* THESAURUS RECENTLY

GRAMMAR: Choosing the right tense

Lately is usually used with perfect tenses (for example 'I have been'), not with the simple past (for example 'I was'). You say: *I've been very busy lately.*
✗ Don't say: *I was very busy lately.*

ˈlate-night *adj* [only before noun] happening late at night: *late-night television* | *late-night shopping*

la·tent /ˈleɪtənt/ *adj* something that is latent is present but hidden, and may develop or become more noticeable in the future → **dormant**: **[+in]** *The virus remains latent in the body for many years.* | *latent aggression* —**latency** *n* [U]

lat·er¹ /ˈleɪtə $ -ər/ ●●● S1 W1 *adv*

1 after the time you are talking about or after the present time: *I'm going out for a bit – I'll see you later.* | **two years/three weeks etc later** *He became Senator two years later.* | **later that day/morning/week etc** *The baby died later that night.* | **later in the day/week/year** *The dentist could fit you in later in the week.* THESAURUS AFTER

2 later on at some time after the present time: *I can't eat all of this – I'll finish it later on.*

3 not later than sth used to say that something must be done by a particular time in the future: *Completed entry forms should arrive not later than 31st July.*

later² *adj* [only before noun] **1** coming in the future or after something else OPP **earlier**: *The role of marketing is dealt with in a later chapter.* | *The launch was postponed to a later date.* **2** more recent OPP **earlier**: *The engine has been greatly improved in later models.* **3 in later years/life** when someone is older: *Using a sunscreen when you are young helps you to have healthy skin in later years.*

lat·e·ral /ˈlætərəl/ *adj formal* **1** relating to the sides of something, or movement to the side: *The wall is weak and requires lateral support.* **2** relating to positions, jobs, relationships etc that are at the same level or rank: *Employees can expect lateral moves to different departments, to gain experience.* —**laterally** *adv*

ˌlateral ˈthinking *n* [U] a way of thinking in which you use your imagination to see relationships between things that are not normally thought of together

lat·ers /ˈleɪtəz $ -ərz/ *interjection informal* goodbye

lat·est¹ /ˈleɪtɪst/ ●●● S2 W2 *adj* [only before noun] the most recent or the newest: *all the latest gossip* | *His latest film is one of the funniest he's ever made.*

latest² *n* **1 the latest** *informal* the most recent or newest thing: **[+in]** *Wednesday's session was the latest in a series of planning meetings.* | **the latest in ... technology/equipment**

L

(=the most modern equipment) *using the latest in medical technology* **2 at the latest** no later than the time mentioned: *I should be back by 11 o'clock at the latest.*

la·tex /ˈleɪteks/ *n* [U] **1** a thick white liquid produced by some plants, especially the rubber tree, and used in making rubber, paint, glue etc: *a doctor's latex gloves* **2** an artificial substance similar to latex

lath /lɑːθ, læθ $ læθ/ *n* [C] a long flat narrow piece of wood used in building to support PLASTER (=material used to cover walls)

lathe /leɪð/ *n* [C] a machine that shapes wood or metal, by turning it around and around against a sharp tool

la·ther¹ /ˈlɑːðə $ ˈlæðər/ *n* [singular, U] **1** a white mass of bubbles produced by mixing soap in water **2** a white mass that forms on a horse's skin when it has been SWEATing SYN **foam 3 get in a lather** (*also* **work yourself into a lather**) *informal* to get very anxious or upset about something: *By the time Alan called, Jody had worked herself into a lather.* **4 in a lather** very worried, upset, or excited: *He was in a lather of anticipation.*

lather² *v* **1** [I] to produce a lather: *This soap lathers really well.* **2** [T] to cover something with lather

Lat·in¹ /ˈlætɪn $ ˈlætn/ *n* **1** [U] the language used in ancient Rome **2** [C] someone from Latin America **3** [C] someone from a southern European country whose language developed from Latin, for example Spain, Portugal, or Italy

Latin² *adj* **1** relating to the Latin language: *a Latin inscription* **2** from or relating to South America: *Latin music* **3** from or relating to southern European countries whose languages developed from Latin, for example Spain, Portugal, or Italy

La·ti·na /læˈtiːnə/ *n* [C] *AmE* a woman in the US whose family comes from Latin America → **Hispanic**

ˌLatin Aˈmerican *adj* relating to South or Central America, or its people

La·ti·no /læˈtiːnəʊ $ -noʊ/ *n* (*plural* **Latinos**) [C] *AmE* a man in the US whose family comes from Latin America. The plural 'Latinos' can mean a group of men and women, or just men. → **Hispanic** —**Latino** *adj*: *Latino culture*

lat·i·tude /ˈlætɪtjuːd $ -tuːd/ *n* **1** [C,U] the distance north or south of the EQUATOR (=the imaginary line around the middle of the world), measured in degrees → **longitude** → see picture at **EARTH¹** **2 latitudes** [plural] an area at a particular latitude: *The birds breed in northern latitudes.* | *the planet's southernmost latitudes* **3** [U] *formal* freedom to choose what you do or say: **considerable/greater latitude** (=a lot of freedom to choose) *Pupils enjoy considerable latitude in deciding what they want to study.* | **[+in/for]** *Employees should have some latitude in organizing their work.* —**latitudinal** /ˌlætɪˈtjuːdɪnəl $ -ˈtuːdn-əl/ *adj*

la·trine /ləˈtriːn/ *n* [C] a toilet that is outdoors in a camp or military area

lat·te /ˈlæteɪ $ ˈlɑː-/ *n* [C,U] very strong coffee with a lot of STEAMed milk in it, or a cup of this type of coffee

lat·ter¹ /ˈlætə $ -ər/ ●●○ W2 *n* **the latter** *formal* the second of two people or things just mentioned OPP **former**: *Where unemployment and crime are high, it can be assumed that the latter is due to the former.*

latter² ●○○ *adj* [only before noun] *formal*
1 being the second of two people or things, or the last in a list just mentioned OPP **former**: *In the latter case, buyers pay a 15% commission.*
2 the latter part of a period of time is nearest to the end of it: *Celebrations are planned for the latter part of November.*

ˈlatter-day *adj* [only before noun] **1 a latter-day Versailles/Tsar/Robin Hood etc** something or someone that exists now but is like a famous thing or person that existed in the past: *He ruled his business empire like a latter-day Tsar.* **2** relating to a recent period of time, rather than an earlier one: *Latter-day students could never meet the college entrance standards required in the 1940s.*

lat·ter·ly /ˈlætəli $ -ər-/ *adv BrE formal* **1** recently: *Scientists have studied the Moon through telescopes, and, latterly, from satellites.* **2** towards the end of a period of time → **formerly**: *O'Rourke retired after a 15-year career with the company, latterly as chief executive.*

lat·tice /ˈlætɪs/ *n* [C] **1** (*also* **lat·tice·work** /ˈlætəswɜːk $ -wɜːrk/) a pattern or structure made of long pieces of wood, plastic etc that cross each other so that the spaces between them are shaped like DIAMONDS **2** *technical* a regular arrangement of objects

ˌlattice ˈwindow (*also* **ˌlatticed ˈwindow**) *n* [C] *BrE* a type of window made of many small pieces of glass shaped like DIAMONDS

laud /lɔːd $ lɒːd/ *v* [T] *formal* to praise someone or something

laud·a·ble /ˈlɔːdəbəl $ ˈlɒːd-/ *adj formal* deserving praise, even if not completely successful SYN **praiseworthy**: *a laudable attempt* —**laudably** *adv*

lau·da·num /ˈlɔːdənəm $ ˈlɒː-/ *n* [U] a substance containing the drug OPIUM, used in the past to control pain and help people to sleep

laud·a·to·ry /ˈlɔːdətəri $ ˈlɒːdətɔːri/ *adj formal* expressing praise: *a laudatory biography*

laugh¹ /lɑːf $ læf/ ●●● S2 W2 *v*
1 [I] to make sounds with your voice, usually while you are smiling, because you think something is funny: *Maria looked at him and laughed.* | **[+at/about]** *'I didn't know what I was doing,' she said, laughing at the memory.* | *Tony was* ***laughing so hard*** *he had to steady himself on the table.* | *Nora* ***laughed so much*** *that she nearly cried.* | **laugh heartily/uproariously/hysterically etc** (=laugh a lot) *The kids tumbled around on the floor, laughing hysterically.* | *He couldn't help it; he* ***burst out laughing*** (=suddenly started laughing). | **laugh your head off** | *He's one of the few writers who can make me* ***laugh out loud.***
2 [T] to say something in a voice that shows you are amused: *'You look ridiculous!' Nick laughed.*
3 not know whether to laugh or cry to feel upset or annoyed about something bad that has happened, but also able to see that there is something funny about it: *And when I couldn't find the passports – honestly, I didn't know whether to laugh or cry!*
4 don't make me laugh *spoken* used when someone has just told you something that is completely untrue, asked for something impossible etc: *'Can you finish this by tomorrow?' 'Don't make me laugh.'*
5 no laughing matter *informal* something serious that should not be joked about: *It's no laughing matter having to walk by a group of rowdy drunks every night just to get home.*
6 be laughed out of court (*also* **be laughed out of town/business etc** *AmE*) if a person or idea is laughed out of court etc, the idea is not accepted because people think it is completely stupid: *We can't propose that! We'd be laughed out of court!*
7 you have to laugh *spoken* used to say that, even though a situation is annoying or disappointing, you can also see that there is something funny about it
8 be laughing all the way to the bank *informal* to make a lot of money without making much effort
9 sb will be laughing on the other side of their face *spoken* used to say that although someone is happy or confident now, they will be in trouble later
10 be laughing *BrE spoken informal* to be happy or in a good situation, for example because something has had a successful result for you: *Well they paid me, didn't they, so I'm laughing.*
11 laugh in sb's face to behave towards someone in a way that shows that you do not respect them: *I told my sister what I thought, and she just laughed in my face.*
12 laugh up your sleeve to be secretly happy, especially because you have played a trick on someone or criticized them without them knowing

THESAURUS

laugh to make sounds with your voice and move your face, because you think that something is funny: *He looked so funny that we couldn't stop laughing.*

L

giggle to laugh quickly in a high voice, especially in a slightly silly way, or because you are nervous or embarrassed: *A group of teenage girls were giggling in a corner.* | *She tends to giggle when she meets new people.*
chuckle to laugh quietly, especially because you are thinking about or reading something funny: *He was chuckling to himself over an article in the paper.*
snigger *BrE*, **snicker** *AmE* to laugh quietly in an unkind or unpleasant way, for example when someone is hurt or embarrassed: *Billy stood up and started to sing, and one or two people sniggered.*
roar with laughter to laugh very loudly, especially with a deep voice: *I could hear my father roaring with laughter at something on TV.*
shriek with laughter to laugh very loudly, especially with a high voice: *Patsy chased him down the stairs, shrieking with laughter.*
howl with laughter to laugh very loudly – used especially about a group of people laughing together: *His plays have made audiences howl with laughter.*
in stitches laughing so much that you cannot stop: *It was such a funny film – it had us all in stitches.*
guffaw /gəˈfɔː $ -ˈfɒː/ to laugh very loudly and without trying to stop yourself: *The audience guffawed at his nonstop jokes.*
cackle to laugh loudly in an unpleasant way: *The old woman cackled at the trouble she was causing.*

laugh at sb/sth *phr v*
1 to make unkind or funny remarks about someone, because they have done or said something you think is stupid SYN **tease**: *I'm afraid the other kids will laugh at me because I don't understand.*
2 to seem not to care about something that most people would worry about: *Young offenders just laugh at this sort of sentence.*

laugh sth ↔ **off** *phr v* to pretend that something is less serious than it really is by laughing or joking about it: *Knox laughed off rumors that he would be running for mayor.*

laugh² ●●● S3 *n*
1 [C] the act of laughing or the sound you make when you laugh: *He gave a short laugh.* | **with a laugh** *'What a mess!' she said, with a laugh.*
2 [C] if something is a laugh, you have fun and enjoy yourself when you are doing it: *We all went to the beach last night – **it was a really good laugh**.* | *The other campers were nice, and **we had a great laugh** together.* | *It was a great holiday with **lots of laughs**.*
3 sb is a (good) laugh *BrE* used to say that someone is amusing and fun to be with: *I like Peter – he's a good laugh.*
4 for laughs (*also* **for a laugh** *BrE*) for fun: *We took the hot-air balloon ride, just for laughs.*
5 that's a laugh *spoken* used to say that something is silly or unlikely: *Me? Star in a film? That's a laugh.*
6 have the last laugh to finally be successful, win an argument etc, after other people have earlier criticized you, defeated you etc: *Men make jokes about women drivers, but women have the last laugh – their insurance rates are cheaper.*
7 be a laugh a minute *informal* to be very funny – sometimes used humorously to mean that someone or something is not at all funny

COLLOCATIONS

VERBS

give/let out a laugh *She gave a loud laugh.*
get a laugh (*also* **draw a laugh** *BrE written*) (=be laughed at) *Most of his jokes didn't even get a laugh.*
get a laugh out of sb (=make someone laugh) *I always managed to get a laugh out of my audience.*
have a laugh about/at/over sth (=laugh about something) *The farmer had a good laugh at our attempts to catch the horse.*
I could use a laugh (=I want to hear something funny to cheer me up) *Tell me what she said - I could use a laugh.*

ADJECTIVES/NOUN + laugh

a good laugh *We all got a good laugh out of it later.*
a big laugh *There was a big laugh from the crowd.*
a short/little/small laugh *He let out a nervous little laugh.*
a loud/soft laugh | **a belly laugh** (=a deep loud laugh)

laugh·a·ble /ˈlɑːfəbəl $ ˈlæ-/ *adj* something that is laughable is impossible to believe or be serious about, because it is so silly or bad SYN **ridiculous**: *The promises are so far from reality that they are laughable.* THESAURUS▸ STUPID —**laughably** *adv*

ˈlaughing gas *n* [U] *informal* a gas that is sometimes used to stop you feeling pain during an operation

laugh·ing·ly /ˈlɑːfɪŋli $ ˈlæ-/ *adv* **1** if something is laughingly called something, the name is a joke, or is not suitable: *The news network was laughingly referred to as the 'Disaster Channel'.* **2** if you do something laughingly, you are laughing while you do it

ˈlaughing stock (*also* **laugh·ing·stock** *AmE*) /ˈlɑːfɪŋstɒk $ ˈlæfɪŋstɑːk/ *n* [C] someone who is a laughing stock has done something so silly that people have no respect for them: *The programme has **made** the U.S. **a laughing stock**.*

ˈlaugh lines *n* [plural] the American form of LAUGHTER LINES

laugh·ter /ˈlɑːftə $ ˈlæftər/ ●●● W3 *n* [U] when people laugh, or the sound of people laughing: *Foster joined in the laughter.* | *He looked shocked, then **burst into laughter*** (=started laughing). | **roar/scream/shriek with laughter** (=laugh very loudly) *Audiences roared with laughter.* | *He **shook with laughter**.* | **peals/gales/howls etc of laughter** (=loud laughs) *The comment brought peals of laughter from her classmates.*

ˈlaughter lines *n* [plural] *BrE* lines on your skin around your eyes, which can be seen when you laugh → **wrinkle** SYN **laugh lines** *AmE*

ˈlaugh track *n* [C] recorded laughter that is used during a television show to make it sound as if people are laughing during the performance SYN **canned laughter**

launch¹ /lɔːntʃ $ lɒːntʃ/ ●●○ W2 *v* [T]
1 START STH to start something, usually something big or important: *The organization has launched a campaign to raise $150,000.* | *The Canadian police plan to launch an investigation into the deal.* | **launch an attack/assault/offensive** *The press launched a vicious attack on the president.* | *The book launched his career as a novelist.*
2 PRODUCT to make a new product, book etc available for sale for the first time: *The company hopes to launch the new drug by next October.*
3 BOAT to put a boat or ship into the water
4 SKY/SPACE to send a weapon or spacecraft into the sky or into space: *A test satellite was launched from Cape Canaveral.* THESAURUS▸ SHOOT
5 COMPUTER to make a computer program start SYN **open**: *Double-click on an icon to launch an application.*
6 launch yourself forwards/up/from etc to jump up and forwards into the air with a lot of energy

launch into sth *phr v*
1 to suddenly start a description or story, or suddenly start criticizing something: *Nelson launched into a blistering criticism of greedy lawyers.*
2 to suddenly start doing something: *Don't just launch into exercise without warming up first.*

launch out *phr v BrE* to start something new, especially something that involves risk

launch² ●●○ *n* [C]
1 when a new product, book etc is made available or made known: **[+of]** *the launch of a new women's magazine* | *a new **product launch***
2 a large boat with a motor
3 when a weapon or spacecraft is sent into the sky or into space

launch·er /ˈlɔːntʃə $ ˈlɒːntʃər/ *n* [C] an object that is used to send a weapon or spacecraft into the sky: *a rocket launcher*

ˈlaunch pad (*also* **ˈlaunching pad**) *n* [C] **1** a base from which a weapon or spacecraft is sent up into the sky **2** an event, group, or activity that helps someone start something: **[+for]** *Ellington's band was a launching pad for many gifted jazz musicians.*

launch·pad /ˈlɔːntʃpæd $ ˈlɒːntʃ-/ *n* [C] a place on the Internet that helps you start to find information about a particular subject: *Their website is a good launchpad to other sites.*

laun·der /ˈlɔːndə $ ˈlɒːndər/ *v* [T] **1** to put money which has been obtained illegally into legal businesses and bank accounts, so that you can hide it or use it: *He was jailed for* ***laundering*** *drug* ***money***. **2** *formal* to wash and IRON clothes, sheets etc

laun·der·ette /ˌlɔːndəˈret $ ˌlɒːn-/ (*also* **laundrette** /lɔːnˈdret $ lɒːn-/ *BrE*, **Laun·dro·mat** /ˈlɔːndrəmæt $ ˈlɒːn-/ *trademark AmE*) *n* [C] a place where you can go to wash your clothes in machines that work when you put coins in them

laun·dry /ˈlɔːndri $ ˈlɒːn-/ ●●● S3 *n* (*plural* **laundries**)
1 [U] clothes, sheets etc that need to be washed or have just been washed: *She* ***did the laundry*** (=washed the clothes etc) *and hung it out to dry.* | *Ben was folding laundry.* | **clean/dirty laundry** *a pile of dirty laundry*
2 [C] a place or business where clothes etc are washed and IRONed → **air/wash your dirty laundry** at DIRTY¹(7)

ˈlaundry ˌbasket *n* [C] **1** *BrE* a large basket that you put dirty clothes in until you wash them SYN **hamper** *AmE* **2** a basket used for carrying clothes that have been or need to be washed

ˈlaundry list *n* [C] *informal* a list of a lot of different things: *a laundry list of criticisms*

lau·re·ate /ˈlɔːriət/ *n* [C] someone who has been given an important prize or honour, especially the NOBEL PRIZE: *Nigeria's Nobel laureate, Wole Soyinka* → POET LAUREATE

laur·el /ˈlɒrəl $ ˈlɔː-, ˈlɑː-/ *n* **1** [C,U] a small tree with smooth shiny dark green leaves that do not fall in winter **2 rest/sit on your laurels** to be satisfied with what you have achieved and therefore stop trying to achieve anything new **3 look to your laurels** to work hard in order not to lose the success that you have achieved **4 laurels** [plural] honours that you receive for something you have achieved: *academic laurels*

lav /læv/ *n* [C] *BrE spoken* a LAVATORY

la·va /ˈlɑːvə/ *n* [U] hot liquid rock that flows from a VOLCANO, or this rock when it has become solid → see picture at VOLCANO

ˈlava ˌlamp *n* [C] a lamp that has a coloured liquid substance inside it that moves up and down → see picture at LAMP

lav·a·to·ri·al /ˌlævəˈtɔːriəl◂/ *adj BrE* lavatorial jokes are about going to the toilet

lav·a·to·ry /ˈlævətəri $ -tɔːri/ ●○○ *n* (*plural* **lavatories**) [C] *formal* a toilet or the room a toilet is in

lav·en·der /ˈlævəndə $ -ər/ *n* **1** [C,U] a plant that has grey-green leaves and purple flowers with a strong pleasant smell **2** [U] a pale purple colour

lav·ish¹ /ˈlævɪʃ/ ●○○ *adj*
1 large, impressive, or expensive: *a royal palace on a* ***lavish*** *scale* | *a* ***lavish lifestyle*** | *The food was lavish.*
2 very generous: **[+with/in]** *We were always lavish with financial aid in times of crisis.* | *He was always lavish in his praise of my efforts.* —**lavishly** *adv*: *their lavishly illustrated catalogue* —**lavishness** *n* [U]

lavish² ●○○ *v* [T] to give someone or something a lot of love, praise, money etc: **lavish sth on/upon sb** *He lavished attention on her.* | **lavish sb with sth** *Hug your children and lavish them with love.*

law /lɔː $ lɒː/ ●●● S1 W1 *n*
1 SYSTEM OF RULES [U] (*also* **the law**) the whole system of rules that people in a particular country or area must obey: *Elected officials ought to obey the law.* | **by law** *By law, seat belts must be worn by all passengers.* | **under English/international etc law** *This is illegal under English law.*
2 A RULE [C] a rule that people in a particular country or area must obey: *laws passed by Parliament* | **under a law** *Five people arrested under anti-terrorism laws were released without charge.* | **[+on]** *European laws on equal opportunities* | **[+against]** *The laws against drug use were very strict.* THESAURUS ▸ RULE
3 law and order a situation in which people respect the law, and crime is controlled by the police, the prison system etc: *We are concerned about the* ***breakdown of law and order*** *in the country.*
4 POLICE **the law** the police: *I think she may be in trouble with the law.*
5 WHAT ALWAYS HAPPENS [C] something that always happens in nature or society, or a statement that describes this: **[+of]** *the law of supply and demand* | *the laws of nature* | *the law of gravity*
6 STUDY/PROFESSION [U] (*also* **the law**) law as a subject of study, or the profession of being a lawyer: *She's studying law in London.*
7 SPORT/ACTIVITY [C] one of the rules which controls a sport or activity: *the laws of football*
8 the law of the jungle a) the idea that people should only look after themselves and not care about other people if they want to succeed **b)** the principle that only the strongest creatures will stay alive
9 the law of averages the PROBABILITY that one result will happen as often as another if you try something often enough: *The law of averages says we'll win at least once.*
10 be a law unto himself/herself etc to behave in an independent way and not worry about the usual rules of behaviour or what other people do or think: *Boys his age are a law unto themselves.*
11 take the law into your own hands to do something illegal in order to put right something that you think is not fair, for example by violently punishing someone instead of telling the police: *vigilantes who take the law into their own hands*
12 go to law to go to court in order to settle a problem: *the right of consumers to go to law if they need to*
13 be above the law someone who is above the law does not have to obey the law: *Many ministers seem to regard themselves as being above the law.*
14 there's no law against sth *spoken* used to tell someone who is criticizing you that you are not doing anything wrong
15 there ought to be a law against sth *spoken* used to say that you do not think something should be accepted or allowed: *There ought to be a law against cutting off power supplies in the middle of February.*
16 sb's word is law used to say that someone is always obeyed without argument → SOD'S LAW, → **lay down the law** at LAY, → **unwritten law** at UNWRITTEN

COLLOCATIONS – MEANINGS 1 & 2

VERBS

obey the law *Citizens have a duty to obey the law.*
break the law (=do something illegal) *Is the company breaking the law?*
pass a law *New Jersey passed a law requiring helmets for scooter riders.*
become law (=officially be made a law) *For a bill to become law, it must be approved by both Houses of Parliament.*
make laws | **introduce a law** | **enforce a law** (=make people obey a law) | **flout a law** (=deliberately disobey a law) | **repeal a law** (=officially end a law) | **a law prohibits sth** (=says that it is not allowed)

PHRASES

sth is against the law (=it is illegal) *The children knew that shoplifting was against the law.*

L

stay/act within the law (=not do illegal things) *The security forces must act within the law.*

ADJECTIVES/NOUN + law

strict/tough *the country's strict anti-tobacco laws*
tax/copyright/divorce etc law(s) *an accountant who knows about tax law*
criminal law (=laws concerning crimes) | **civil law** (=laws concerning disagreements between people, rather than crimes) | **international law** (=laws that all countries agree to obey) | **English/German etc law** | **federal law** (=the law of the US, not a particular state) | **state law** (=the law in a US state) | **common law** (=laws that have come from customs and the decisions of judges) | **case law** (=law based on previous court cases)

ˈlaw-aˌbiding *adj* respectful of the law and obeying it: *a **law-abiding citizen***

ˈlaw-ˌbreaker *n* [C] someone who does something illegal SYN **criminal** —**law-breaking** *n* [U]

ˈlaw court *n* [C] a room or building where legal cases are judged

ˈlaw enˌforcement *n* [U] the job of making sure that the law is obeyed: *law enforcement agencies*

ˈlaw enforcement ˌagent *n* [C] *AmE* a police officer

ˈlaw firm *n* [C] a company that provides legal services and employs many lawyers

law·ful /ˈlɔːfəl $ ˈlɒː-/ ●○○ *adj formal or law* allowed or recognized by law SYN **legal**: ***It is** not **lawful** to kill or injure a pet animal.* | *a lawful arrest* | *his lawful wife* —**lawfully** *adv* —**lawfulness** *n* [U]

law·less /ˈlɔːləs $ ˈlɒː-/ *adj* not obeying the law, or not controlled by the law OPP **law-abiding**: *this increasingly lawless society* | *These border areas are among the most lawless regions in the world.* —**lawlessness** *n* [U]

law·mak·er /ˈlɔːmeɪkə $ ˈlɒːmeɪkər/ ●○○ *n* [C] *especially AmE* any elected official responsible for making laws SYN **legislator**

law·man /ˈlɔːmæn $ ˈlɒː-/ *n* (*plural* **lawmen** /-men/) [C] *AmE informal* any officer who is responsible for making sure that the law is obeyed

lawn /lɔːn $ lɒːn/ ●●● S2 *n*
1 [C,U] an area of ground in a garden or park that is covered with short grass: *I spent all morning **mowing** the **lawn*** (=cutting the grass). | *a carefully tended lawn*
2 [U] a fine cloth made from cotton or LINEN

ˈlawn ˌbowling *n* [U] *AmE* a game played on grass in which you try to roll a big ball as near as possible to a smaller ball SYN **bowls** *BrE*

ˈlawn chair *n* [C] *AmE* a light chair that you use outside, especially one that folds up

ˈlawn ˌmower *n* [C] a machine that you use to cut grass → see picture at **GARDEN**

ˈlawn ˌparty *n* [C] *AmE* a formal party held outside in the afternoon, especially in a large garden SYN **garden party** *BrE*

ˌlawn ˈtennis *n* [U] *formal* TENNIS

ˈlaw school *n* [C,U] a part of a university or a special school in the US where you study to become a lawyer after you get your BACHELOR'S DEGREE

law·suit /ˈlɔːsuːt, -sjuːt $ ˈlɒːsuːt/ ●○○ *n* [C] a problem or complaint that a person or organization brings to a court of law to be settled SYN **suit**: **[+against]** *His lawyer **filed** a **lawsuit** against the city.*

law·yer /ˈlɔːjə $ ˈlɒːjər/ ●●● S3 W2 *n* [C] someone whose job is to advise people about laws, write formal agreements, or represent people in court

lax /læks/ *adj* not strict or careful enough about standards of behaviour, work, safety etc SYN **slack**: **lax in (doing) sth** *The company has been lax in carrying out its duties.* | ***lax security*** —**laxity** (*also* **laxness**) *n* [U]

lax·a·tive /ˈlæksətɪv/ *n* [C] a medicine or something that you eat which makes your BOWELS empty easily —**laxative** *adj*

lay[1] /leɪ/ *v* the past tense of LIE[1]

lay[2] ●●● S1 W2 *v* (*past tense and past participle* **laid** /leɪd/)
1 PUT SB/STH DOWN [T always + adv/prep] to put someone or something down carefully into a flat position SYN **place**: *He laid his hand on my shoulder.* | *They laid a wreath at the place where so many people died.* | ***Lay** the material **flat** on the table.* **THESAURUS** PUT
2 lay bricks/carpet/concrete/cables etc to put or fasten bricks, a CARPET etc in the correct place, especially on the ground or floor: *The carpet was laid last week.* | *The project involved laying an oil pipeline across the desert.*
3 BIRD/INSECT ETC [I,T] if a bird, insect etc lays eggs, it produces them from its body: *The flies **lay** their **eggs** on decaying meat.* | *A cuckoo is able to lay in a range of different nests.*
4 TABLE [T] *BrE* to put the cloth, plates, knives, forks etc on a table, ready for a meal SYN **set**: *John was **laying the table**.* | *As she spoke, she was laying him a place at the table.*
5 lay the foundations/groundwork/base to provide the conditions that will make it possible for something to happen or be successful: **[+for]** *Mandela helped lay the foundations for a new democratic South Africa.* | *It was an invention which **laid the foundations of** modern radio technology.*
6 GIVE INFORMATION [T] *formal* to make a statement, give information etc in an official or public way SYN **put**: *Several proposals have been laid before the committee.*
7 lay emphasis/stress on sth *formal* to emphasize something because you believe it is very important: *a political philosophy that lays great stress on individual responsibility*
8 lay a hand/finger on sb [usually in negatives] to touch someone with the intention of hurting them: *I swear I didn't lay a finger on him.* | *If you lay one hand on me, I'll scream.*
9 lay sth bare/open a) to show what something is really like, or stop hiding facts, feelings etc: *Every aspect of their private life has been laid bare.* **b)** to remove the thing that is covering or hiding something else: *When the tide goes out, vast stretches of sand are laid bare.*
10 lay sb/sth open to sth to do something that makes it possible for other people to blame you, criticize you etc: **lay yourself open to sth** *By doing that, he laid himself open to ridicule.* | *Not to have taken action would have **laid** the department **open to charges of** negligence.*
11 lay waste sth (*also* **lay waste to sth**) *formal* to destroy or damage something, especially in a war: *The island was laid waste and abandoned.* | *an attack which laid waste to hundreds of villages*
12 lay plans/a trap etc to carefully prepare all the details of something: *We are laying plans now in order to be successful in the future.* | **the best-laid plans** (=plans that have been made carefully) *Bad weather can upset even the best-laid travel plans.*
13 lay claim to (doing) sth to say that something belongs to you or say that you deserve something: *The town can lay claim to having the oldest theatre in Britain.* | *No one has laid claim to the property.*
14 lay siege to sb/sth a) if a group of people lay siege to a place, they try to get control by surrounding it: *The armies laid siege to Vienna in 1529.* **b)** to do everything you can to get someone to talk to you or notice you: *A group of young men were always at the stage door, trying to lay siege to the girls.*
15 HAVE SEX get laid *informal* to have sex with someone: *All he wants to do is go out and **get laid**.*
16 LIE [I] *spoken* to be in a position in which you are flat – some people consider this use to be incorrect SYN **lie**
17 RISK MONEY [T] *especially BrE* to risk an amount of money on the result of a race, sports game etc SYN **bet**: **lay sth on sth** *She laid £50 on the favourite, Golden Boy.* | **lay money (that)** *I'd lay money that he will go on to play for England.*
18 lay sb/sth on the line a) to state something, especially a threat, demand, or criticism, in a very clear way: ***Lay it on***

L

the line and tell them what's really been happening. **b)** (*also* **put sb/sth on the line**) to risk losing your life, your job etc, especially in order to help someone: *I've laid myself on the line for him once already.*
19 lay sth at the door of sb/sth (*also* **lay sth at sb's door**) to blame something or someone for something: *The continued divisions within the party cannot be laid entirely at his door.* | *Many illnesses are being laid at the door of stress.*
20 lay sb low a) if an illness lays someone low, they are unable to do their normal activities for a period of time: **be laid low with sth** *She's been laid low with flu for a week.* GRAMMAR **Lay low** is usually passive in this meaning. **b)** *literary* to make someone fall down, or injure them seriously
21 lay sb to rest *formal* to bury someone after they have died: *She was laid to rest beside her husband.* → **lay/put sth to rest** at REST[1](10)
22 lay the ghost (of sth) to finally stop being worried or upset by something from the past → **lay your hands on sth** at HAND[1](18), → **lay the blame on sb/sth** at BLAME[2], → **put/lay your cards on the table** at CARD[1](13)

GRAMMAR: Comparison

lay
- You **lay** something somewhere: *She lays a lace cloth over the table.* ✗ Don't say: *She lies a lace cloth over the table.*
- You **lay** someone somewhere: *Lay him down gently.*
- **Lay** is also the past tense of **lie**: *I lay on the bed.* ✗ Don't say: *I laid on the bed.*

lie
- Someone **lies** somewhere: *She was lying on her back.* | *Let's just lie here for a while.* ✗ Don't say: *She was laying on her back.* | *Let's just lay here for a while.*
- The past tense of **lie** is **laid**: *She laid the baby in its cot.* ✗ Don't say: *She lay the baby in its cot.*

lay about sb *phr v literary or old-fashioned* to attack someone violently SYN **set about**: **[+with]** *He laid about his attackers with a stick.*
lay sth ↔ **aside** *phr v*
1 to stop using something and put it down, especially so you can do something else SYN **put aside**: *Richard had laid aside his book to watch what was happening.*
2 to stop behaving in a particular way, or stop having particular feelings, especially so you can achieve something SYN **put aside**: *On the day of the wedding, all arguments between the families were laid aside.* | *As a doctor, you often need to lay aside your personal feelings.*
3 (*also* **lay sth ↔ by**) to keep something, especially money, so you can use it in the future SYN **put by**: *She'd laid aside a few pounds each week from her wages.*
lay sth ↔ **down** *phr v*
1 OFFICIALLY STATE to officially state something or say that rules, principles etc must be obeyed: *He had already clearly laid down his view in his opening speech.* | **lay down that** *The contract laid down that the work must be completed before 2025.*
2 WEAPONS if people lay down their weapons, they stop fighting: *The terrorists were urged to* ***lay down*** *their* ***arms***.
3 lay down the law to tell other people what to do, how they should think etc, in a very strong or impolite way: *I could hear him laying down the law.*
4 lay down your life *formal* to die in order to help other people: **[+for]** *He was even prepared to lay down his life for his friends.*
5 KEEP to store something, especially wine, to use in the future
6 RECORD to record your music, for example in a recording STUDIO: *They are just about to start* ***laying down tracks*** *for their second album.*
lay sth ↔ **in** *phr v especially BrE formal* to get and store a supply of something to use in the future: *He likes to lay in a few special drinks for the festive season.*
lay into sb/sth *phr v* to attack or criticize someone or something: *Outside the club, two men were laying into each other.*

lay off *phr v*
1 lay sb ↔ off to stop employing someone because there is no work for them to do → **lay-off**: *The company laid off 250 workers in December.* | *Millions of people have been laid off in the steel industry.*
2 lay off (sth) *informal* to stop using or doing something: *I think you'd better lay off alcohol for a while.* | **lay off doing sth** *I had to lay off running for several months.*
3 lay off (sb) *informal* to stop annoying someone or hurting them: *Just lay off, will you!* | *I wish he'd lay off me!*
4 lay sth ↔ off to pass the ball to someone in your team in a game such as football – used in sports reports: **lay sth off to sb** *Murphy has the ball and then lays it off to Owen.*
lay sth **on** *phr v*
1 lay sth ↔ on *especially BrE* to provide something such as food, entertainment, or transport for a group of people: *They laid on a buffet for his farewell party.* | *A bus has been laid on to take you home.*
2 lay sth on sb to ask someone to do something, especially something that is difficult or something they will not want to do: *Sorry to lay this on you, but we need someone to give a talk at the conference next week.*
3 lay it on (thick) *informal* **a)** to praise someone or something too much, especially in order to get what you want **b)** to talk about something in a way that makes it seem more important, serious etc than it really is SYN **exaggerate**
lay sb/sth ↔ **out** *phr v*
1 SPREAD to spread something out: *Lay out the map on the table and let's have a look.*
2 ARRANGE to arrange or plan a building, town, garden etc SYN **set out**: *The garden is laid out in a formal pattern.*
3 EXPLAIN to describe or explain something clearly SYN **set out**: *The financial considerations are laid out in a booklet called 'How to Borrow Money'.*
4 SPEND *informal* to spend money, especially a lot of money → **outlay**: **lay out sth on sth** *What's the point in laying out money on something you'll only wear once?*
5 HIT *informal* to hit someone so hard that they fall down and become unconscious: *One of the guards had been laid out and the other was missing.*
6 BODY to prepare a dead body so that it can be buried
lay over *phr v AmE* to stay somewhere for a short time before continuing your trip → **layover**
lay up *phr v*
1 be laid up (with sth) to have to stay in bed because you are ill or injured: *I was laid up for a week with flu.*
2 to stop using a boat or vehicle, especially while it is being repaired: **lay sth ↔ up** *Most of the yachts were laid up for the winter.*
3 lay sth ↔ up *old-fashioned* to collect and store something to use in the future: *We started laying up firewood for the winter.*

lay³ ●○○ *adj* [only before noun] **a)** not trained or not knowing much about a particular profession or subject → **layman**: *lay witnesses* **b)** not in an official position in the church: *a lay preacher*

lay⁴ *n* [C] **1 the lay of the land a)** the situation that exists at a particular time: *Get the lay of the land before you make any decisions.* **b)** the appearance of an area of land, for example the way it slopes **2 the lay of sth** the appearance of something and where each part of it is: *Mr. Lowe will give you the lay of the camp and tell you what we're going to be doing.* **3 be a good/quick/easy etc lay** *informal* to be a good, quick etc person to have sex with **4** *literary* a poem or song

lay·a·bout /ˈleɪəbaʊt/ *n* [C] *BrE informal* a lazy person who avoids work

lay·a·way /ˈleɪəweɪ/ *n* [U] *AmE* a method of buying goods in which you give the seller of the goods a small amount of money to keep the goods until you can pay the full price: *I put the dress on layaway.* —**layaway** *adj*

ˈlay-by *n* (*plural* **lay-bys**) [C] *BrE* a space next to a road where vehicles can stop

L

lay·er¹ /ˈleɪə $ -ər/ ●●● S3 W3 AWL *n* [C]
1 an amount or piece of a material or substance that covers a surface or that is between two other things: **[+of]** *A* ***thick layer*** *of dust lay on the furniture.* | *The moon was shining through a* ***thin layer*** *of cloud.* | *He pulled off* ***layer upon layer of*** *clothing* (=many layers of clothing). | **in layers** *Arrange the peppers, garlic and tomatoes in layers.*
→ OZONE LAYER
2 one of several different levels in a complicated organization, system, set of ideas etc: **[+of]** *We are operating with fewer layers of management.* | *There are multiple layers of meaning in the story.* | *the* ***multi-layered*** *nature of organizations* (=they have many layers)

LAYER
layer
tier

layer² AWL *v* [T] **1** to make a layer of something or put something down in layers: *Layer the raw sliced vegetables in a shallow baking dish.* **2** to cut someone's hair so that the hair on top is in shorter lengths than the lower hair: *I have layered, shoulder-length brown hair.*

lay·ette /leɪˈet/ *n* [C] a complete set of clothing and other things that a new baby needs

lay·man /ˈleɪmən/ *n* (*plural* **laymen** /-mən/) [C]
1 someone who is not trained in a particular subject or type of work, especially when they are being compared with someone who is → **laywoman** OPP **expert**: *To* ***the layman*** (=laymen in general) *all these plants look pretty similar.* | *If you don't understand what the doctor says, ask to have it explained* ***in layman's terms*** (=in simple language).
2 someone who is not a priest but is a member of a church → **laywoman**

ˈlay-off *n* [C] an occasion when an employer ends a worker's employment for a temporary period of time because there is not enough work: *more lay-offs in the car industry* → LAY OFF

lay·out /ˈleɪaʊt/ ●●○ *n* [C]
1 the way in which something such as a town, garden, or building is arranged: **[+of]** *the layout of the park* | *All the flats in the building had the same layout.*
2 the way in which writing and pictures are arranged on a page: **[+of]** *the layout of a business letter* | *page layout software* → LAY

lay·o·ver /ˈleɪəʊvə $ -oʊvər/ *n* [C] *AmE* a short stay between parts of a journey, especially a long plane journey SYN **stopover** *BrE*

lay·per·son /ˈleɪˌpɜːsən $ -pɜːr-/ *n* (*plural* **laypersons** *or* **laypeople** /-ˌpiːpəl/) [C] a LAYMAN or LAYWOMAN

ˌlay ˈreader *n* [C] someone in Christian churches who is not a priest but who has been given authority to lead a religious service

ˈlay-up *n* [C] a throw in BASKETBALL made from very close to the basket or from under it

lay·wom·an /ˈleɪˌwʊmən/ *n* (*plural* **laywomen** /-ˌwɪmɪn/) [C] **1** a woman not trained in a particular subject or type of work, especially when she is being compared with someone who is → **layman** OPP **expert**
2 a woman who is not a priest but is a member of a church → **layman**

Laz·a·rus /ˈlæzərəs/ if someone rises like Lazarus, they get better after a serious illness or other hopeless situation. This expression comes from the Bible story about Lazarus, a friend of Jesus. When he died, Jesus brought him back to life: *From three-nil down at half-time, Manchester United made the biggest comeback since Lazarus, eventually winning 5–3.*

laze /leɪz/ *v* [I always + adv/prep] to relax and enjoy yourself in a lazy way: **[+in]** *We spent the afternoon lazing in the sun.* | **[+about/around]** *We lazed around, gazing at the views.* —**laze** *n* [singular]

la·zy /ˈleɪzi/ ●●● S3 *adj* (*comparative* **lazier**, *superlative* **laziest**)
1 not liking work and physical activity, or not making any effort to do anything: *the laziest boy in the class* | *He felt too lazy to get out of bed.*
2 a lazy period of time is spent doing nothing except relaxing OPP **busy**: *We spent lazy days relaxing on the beach.* —**lazily** *adv* —**laziness** *n* [U]

la·zy·bones /ˈleɪzibəʊnz $ -boʊnz/ *n* (*plural* **lazybones**) [C] *informal* a lazy person - often used in a friendly way to someone you like: *Come on, lazybones! Get out of bed.*

lb *BrE*, **lb.** *AmE* (*plural* **lb** *or* **lbs**) the written abbreviation of ***pound*** or ***pounds*** in weight

lbw /ˌel biː ˈdʌbəljuː/ *adv* (***leg before wicket***) a way in which your INNINGS can end in CRICKET, when the ball hits your leg if it is in front of the WICKET

LCD /ˌel siː ˈdiː/ *n* [C] (***liquid crystal display***) the part of a watch, CALCULATOR, or small computer where numbers or letters are shown by means of an electric current that is passed through a special liquid

leach /liːtʃ/ (*also* **leach out**) *v* [I,T] *technical* if a substance leaches or is leached from a larger mass such as the soil, it is removed from it by water passing through the larger mass: *The manufacturers say that there is no danger of the aluminium leaching into the water.*

lead¹ /liːd/ ●●● S1 W1 *v* (*past tense and past participle* **led** /led/)
1 TAKE SB SOMEWHERE [I,T usually + adv/prep] to take someone somewhere by going in front of them while they follow, or by pulling them gently: **lead sb to/into etc sth** *A nurse took her arm and led her to a chair.* | *The horses were* ***led to safety***. | **lead sb away/down etc** *She was led away from the courtroom in tears.* | *The manager* ***led the way*** *through the office.* THESAURUS TAKE
2 GO IN FRONT [I,T] to go in front of a line of people or vehicles: *A firetruck was leading the parade.*
3 BE IN CHARGE [I,T] to be in charge of an organization, country, or team, or a group of people who are trying to do something: *He has led the party for over twenty years.* | *Some people say she is too old to* ***lead the country*** (=be in charge of its government). | *Beckham* ***led*** *his team* ***to victory***. | **lead an investigation/inquiry/campaign** *The investigation will be led by Inspector Scarfe.* | *They are leading a campaign to warn teenagers about the dangers of drug abuse.* | **lead a revolt/rebellion/coup etc** *The rebellion was led by the King's brother.* | **lead an attack/assault** *Nelson preferred to lead the attack himself from the front.* | *a man who was* ***born to lead*** | *a communist-led strike*
4 CAUSE STH TO HAPPEN [I,T] to cause something to happen or cause someone to do something: **[+to]** *the events that led to the start of the First World War* | *A degree in English could lead to a career in journalism.* | **lead sb into sth** *Her trusting nature often* ***led*** *her* ***into trouble***. | **lead sb to do sth** *What led him to kill his wife?* | **lead to sb doing sth** *His actions could lead to him losing his job.*
5 CAUSE SB TO BELIEVE STH [T] to make someone believe something, especially something that is not true: **lead sb to believe/expect/understand sth** *He had led everyone to believe that his family was very wealthy.* | *The hotel was terrible, and not at all what we had been led to expect.* | *Our research* ***led*** *us* ***to the conclusion*** *that the present system is unfair.*
6 INFLUENCE [T] to influence someone to make them do something that is wrong: **lead sb into sth** *His brother led him into a life of crime.* | *He's not a bad boy. He's just* ***easily led*** (=it is easy for other people to persuade him to do things that he should not do).
7 BE MORE SUCCESSFUL [T] to be more successful than other people, companies, or countries in a particular activity: **lead the world/market/pack/field** *US companies lead the world in biotechnology.* | **lead the way** (=be the first to do something, and show other people how to do it) *The Swedes have led the way in data protection.*
→ LEADING¹(1)

8 BE WINNING [I,T] to be winning a game, competition etc OPP **lose**: *At half-time, Brazil led 1-0.* | *With 15 laps to go, Schumacher led the race.* | *The polls showed Obama leading Romney by 3 percent.* | **lead by ten points/two goals etc** *Nadal was leading by two sets.*

9 PATH/DOOR ETC [I,T always + adv/prep] used to say where a path, wire etc goes or what place is on the other side of a door: **[+to/towards]** *The path led down to a small lake.* | **[+from/out of]** *the major artery leading from the heart* | **[+into]** *the door leading into the hallway* | **lead sb to/into sth** *The riverside path leads visitors to a small chapel.*

10 LIFE [T] if you lead a particular kind of life, that is what your life is like: **lead a normal/quiet/busy etc life** *If the operation succeeds, Carly will be able to lead a normal life.* | *He has* ***led a charmed life*** (=been very fortunate). | **lead a life of luxury/poverty etc** | **lead the life of a ...** *She now leads the life of a recluse.* | **lead a double life** (=deceive people by keeping different parts of your life separate and not letting anyone know the whole truth) *Joe had been leading a double life, seeing an ex-model while his wife believed he was on business.* | *They* ***lead*** *a nomadic* ***existence***.

11 DISCUSSION ETC [T always + adv/prep] to control the way a discussion, conversation etc develops: *I tried to lead the conversation back to the subject of money.*

12 lead sb up the garden path *informal* to deliberately deceive someone

13 lead sb astray a) to encourage someone to do bad or immoral things which they would not normally do **b)** to make someone believe something that is not true

14 lead nowhere/not lead anywhere to not produce any useful result: *So far police investigations seem to have led nowhere.*

15 lead by example to show the people you are in charge of what you want them to do by doing it yourself: *The best managers lead by example.*

16 lead sb by the nose to influence someone so much that you can completely control everything that they do: *Politicians think they can easily lead people by the nose.*

17 this/that leads (me) to sth used to introduce a new subject that is connected to the previous one: *That leads me to my final point. Where are we going to get the money?*

18 sb has their own life to lead used to say that someone wants to be able to live their life independently, without having to do things that other people want them to do

19 lead sb a merry old dance/a right old dance *BrE* to cause a lot of problems or worries for someone

20 market-led/export-led etc most influenced by the market, by EXPORTS etc: *an export-led economic recovery*

21 lead the eye if a picture, view etc leads the eye in a particular direction, it makes you look in that direction: *marble columns that lead the eye upward*

22 CARD GAME [I,T] to play a particular card as your first card in one part of a card game

THESAURUS

lead to take a person or animal somewhere by going in front of them while they follow, or by pulling them gently: *Rachel led Jo into the kitchen.* | *She was leading a horse, which seemed to have a bad leg.*

take to take someone somewhere with you when you have the transport, know the way, are paying etc: *I took her to see a film.* | *Matt's taking me in his car.*

guide to take someone through or to a place you know, showing them the way: *Ali guided us through the streets to his house on the edge of the town.*

show to take someone to a place such as a table in a restaurant or a hotel room and leave them there: *A waitress showed us to our table.* | *We were shown to our seats near the front of the theatre.*

point to show someone which direction to go using your hand or a sign: *The sign back there pointed this way.*

escort to take someone somewhere, protecting them, guarding them, or showing them the way: *He was escorted from the court by police.* | *The president's car will be escorted by a military convoy.*

usher to show someone the way to a room or building nearby, usually as part of your job: *His housekeeper ushered us into the living room.*

shepherd to carefully take someone somewhere – used especially about a group of people: *The police shepherded thousands of people to safety in the cathedral.*

direct *formal* to tell someone where to go or how to get somewhere: *He directed us to a café a few blocks away.* | *Can you direct me to the station?*

lead off *phr v*

1 to start a meeting, discussion, performance etc by saying or doing something: *I'd like to lead off by thanking Rick for coming.* | **[+with]** *The French team led off with two quick goals in the first five minutes.* | **lead sth ↔ off** *Hal led the evening off with some folk songs.*

2 lead off (sth) if a road, room etc leads off a place, you can go directly from that place along that road, into that room etc: **lead off from sth** *He pointed down a street leading off from the square.* | *a large room, with doors leading off it in all directions*

3 to be the first player to try to hit the ball in an INNING (=period of play) in a game of baseball

lead sb **on** *phr v* to deceive someone, especially to make them think you love them: *He thought she loved him, but in fact she was just leading him on.*

lead on to sth (*also* **lead onto sth**) *phr v especially BrE* to cause something to develop or become possible at a later time: *Alan Turing's work led onto the development of modern computers.*

lead with sth *phr v*

1 if a newspaper or television programme leads with a particular story, that story is the main one: *The 'Washington Post' leads with the latest news from Israel.*

2 to use a particular hand to begin an attack in BOXING, or a particular foot to begin a dance: *Adam led with his left and punched his opponent on the jaw.*

lead up to sth *phr v*

1 if a series of events or a period of time leads up to an event, it comes before it or causes it: *the weeks that led up to her death* | *the events leading up to his dismissal*

2 to gradually introduce an embarrassing, upsetting, or surprising subject into a conversation: *She had already guessed what he was leading up to.*

lead[2] ●●○ S3 W2 *n*

1 the lead the first position in a race or competition: *She* ***was in the lead*** *from start to finish.* | *The Canadians* ***went into the lead*** *after only 30 seconds.* | *The goal* ***put*** *Holland* ***into the lead***. | *The Bears* ***took the lead*** *for the first time this season.*

2 [singular] the amount or distance by which one competitor is ahead of another: *The Chicago Bulls* ***had a narrow lead*** (=were winning by a small number of points). | **[+over]** *The Socialists now have a commanding lead over their opponents.*

3 [singular] if someone follows someone else's lead, they do the same as the other person has done: *Other countries are likely to* ***follow*** *the U.S.'s* ***lead***. | *The Government should* ***give*** *industry a* ***lead*** *in tackling racism* (=show what other people should do). | *The black population in the 1960s* ***looked to*** *Ali* ***for a lead*** (=looked to him to show them what they should do).

4 take the lead (in doing sth) to be the first to start doing something or be most active in doing something: *The U.S. took the lead in declaring war on terrorism.*

5 [C] a piece of information that may help you to solve a crime or mystery SYN **clue**: *The police have checked out dozens of leads, but have yet to find the killer.*

6 [C] the main acting part in a play, film etc, or the main actor: **play the lead/the lead role** *He will play the lead role in 'Hamlet'.* | *Powers was* ***cast in*** *the* ***lead role*** (=he was chosen to play it). | **the male/female lead** *They were having trouble casting the female lead.* | *the film's* ***romantic lead***

7 lead singer/guitarist etc the main singer, GUITARIST etc in a group: **[+of/with]** *the lead singer of Nirvana*

8 [C] *BrE* a piece of rope, leather, or chain for holding or controlling a dog SYN **leash**: **on a lead** *All dogs must be kept on a lead.*

L

9 [C] *BrE* a wire used to connect a piece of electrical equipment to the power supply SYN **cord** *AmE* → JUMP LEADS

lead[3] /led/ *n* **1** [U] a soft heavy grey metal that melts easily and is poisonous, used on roofs, or in the past for water pipes. It is a chemical ELEMENT: symbol Pb **2** [C,U] the central part of a pencil that makes the marks when you write **3 go down like a lead balloon** *informal* if a suggestion or joke goes down like a lead balloon, people do not like it at all **4** [U] *AmE old-fashioned* bullets: *They filled him full of lead.* **5 leads** [plural] **a)** sheets of lead used for covering a roof **b)** narrow pieces of lead used for holding small pieces of glass together to form a window

lead·ed /ˈledɪd/ *adj* **1** leaded petrol contains lead OPP **unleaded** **2** leaded windows have narrow pieces of lead separating small square or DIAMOND-shaped pieces of glass

leaded lights /ˌledəd ˈlaɪts/ *n* [plural] *BrE* leaded windows

lead·en /ˈledn/ *adj* **1** *literary* a leaden sky or sea is dark grey **2** *literary* if your body feels leaden, you move slowly, because you are tired, unhappy etc SYN **heavy**: *She stumbled forward, her legs leaden.* **3** dull: *a leaden joke* **4** a leaden feeling is a feeling of great unhappiness or anxiety **5** made of lead

lead·er /ˈliːdə $ -ər/ ●●● S2 W1 *n* [C]
1 IN CONTROL the person who directs or controls a group, organization, country etc → **ruler**: **[+of]** *the leader of the local black community* | **party/union/government/opposition etc leader** | **political/military/religious leader** | *the largest ever gathering of* ***world leaders*** (=people who are in charge of countries) | **natural/born leader** (=someone who naturally has all the qualities needed to be a leader) *His air of confidence makes him a natural leader.*
2 COMPETITION the person or group that is in front of all the others in a race or competition: *County Championship leaders of Hampshire*
3 PRODUCT/COMPANY the product or company that is the best or most successful: **[+in]** *a world leader in defence and space electronics* | *These products are firmly established as the* ***market leaders***.
4 NEWSPAPER *BrE* a piece of writing in a newspaper giving the paper's opinion on a subject SYN **editorial**: *'The Times' leader column*
5 MUSICIAN *BrE* the main VIOLIN player in an ORCHESTRA SYN **concertmaster** *AmE*
6 MUSICAL DIRECTOR *AmE* someone who directs the playing of a musical group SYN **conductor** *BrE*
7 TAPE *technical* the part at the beginning of a film or recording tape which has nothing on it
8 BRANCH *technical* a long thin branch that grows from the stem of a bush or tree beyond other branches

THESAURUS

leader the person who directs or controls a group, organization, country etc: *Party members will vote next week to elect a new leader.* | *leaders of developing nations from around the world*
ruler someone, such as a king or queen or a military leader, who has official power over a country or area: *Sheik Mohammed, ruler of Dubai* | *Argentina's former military rulers*
head of state someone who leads a country or state: *Twenty-one heads of state will meet at the annual World Trade summit.*
figurehead someone who is seen as the leader of a country or organization, although he or she does not have any real power: *the Queen's role as a national figurehead* | *There are advantages in having a respected personality as a figurehead for the organisation.*
ringleader someone who leads a group that is doing something illegal or wrong: *The alleged ringleaders of the gang have been arrested.* | *the ringleaders of the airplane bomb plot*

lead·er·ship /ˈliːdəʃɪp $ -ər-/ ●●○ S3 W3 *n*
1 [C,U] the position of being the leader of a group, organization, country etc: **[+of]** *the leadership of the Labour party* | **under sb's leadership** *Our prospects of winning an election will be better under his leadership.* | *The US must now take a firm* ***leadership role***. | *the Conservative* ***leadership contest*** | *The next* ***leadership election*** *is due in November.*
2 [U] the quality of being good at leading a group, organization, country etc: *She has great faith in her own* ***leadership qualities***. | *someone with vision and leadership*
3 [C] *BrE* all the people who lead a group, organization, country etc: *the country's military leadership* | *The party leadership is in agreement.*
4 [U] the position of being in front of others in an activity or competition: *Leadership in science is important to our nation.*

lead-free /ˌled ˈfriː◂/ *adj* lead-free petrol or paint contains no LEAD SYN **unleaded**

lead-in /ˈliːd ɪn/ *n* [C] remarks made by someone to introduce a radio or television show

lead·ing[1] /ˈliːdɪŋ/ ●●○ W3 *adj* [only before noun]
1 best, most important, or most successful: *The army* ***played a leading role*** *in organizing the attempted coup.* | *the leading industrial nations* | *a leading heart specialist* | ***leading members*** *of the government*
2 leading edge a) *technical* the part of something that is at the front of it when it moves **b)** the part of an activity where the most modern and advanced equipment and methods are used: **[+of]** *This is the leading edge of medical technology.* → LEADING-EDGE
3 leading light a respected person who leads a group or organization, or is important in a particular area of knowledge or activity: *The two women were leading lights of the women's union.*
4 leading question a question that deliberately tricks someone into giving the answer you want: *Don't ask leading questions.*
5 leading lady/man the woman or man who acts the most important female or male part in a film, play etc → LEADING ARTICLE

lead·ing[2] /ˈledɪŋ/ *n* [U] *technical* LEAD used for covering roofs, for window frames etc

leading ar·ti·cle /ˌliːdɪŋ ˈɑːtɪkəl $ -ˈɑːr-/ *n* [C] *BrE* a piece of writing in a newspaper giving the paper's opinion on a subject SYN **editorial**

leading-edge /ˌliːdɪŋ ˈedʒ/ *adj* [only before noun] leading-edge machines, systems etc are the most modern and advanced ones available: *leading-edge technologies for military and computer applications*

lead-off /ˈliːd ɒf $ -ɒːf/ *adj* [only before noun] *AmE* happening or going first or before others

lead story /ˈliːd ˌstɔːri/ *n* [C] the most important report in a newspaper or news programme, which is put first

lead time /ˈliːd taɪm/ *n* [U] the time that it takes to make or produce something

lead-up /ˈliːd ʌp/ *n* [singular] the things that are done in the time before an important event SYN **run-up**: *the lead-up to the election*

leaf[1] /liːf/ ●●● S2 W2 *n* (*plural* **leaves** /liːvz/)
1 PLANT [C] one of the flat green parts of a plant that are joined to its stem or branches: *a flowering bush with large shiny leaves* | **[+of]** *Add a few leaves of fresh basil to the salad.* | **be in leaf/come into leaf** (=have or start growing leaves, at a particular time of year) *The forest was just coming into leaf.* → see picture at TREE
2 take a leaf out of sb's book to copy the way someone else behaves because you want to be like them or be as successful as they are: *They are committing $3m to research. We could take a leaf out of their book.*
3 turn over a new leaf to change the way you behave and become a better person: *I see fatherhood as a chance to turn over a new leaf.*
4 PAGE [C] *formal* a page of a book: *He slipped the letter between the leaves of his notebook.* → LOOSE-LEAF, OVERLEAF
5 PART OF TABLE [C] a part of the top of a table that can

L

be taken out to make the table smaller → **shake like a leaf** at SHAKE[1](2)

leaf[2] *v*

leaf through sth *phr v* to turn the pages of a book quickly, without reading it properly SYN **skim through**: *She picked up the magazine and leafed through it.*

leaf·less /ˈliːfləs/ *adj* a leafless tree or bush has no leaves on it

leaf·let[1] /ˈliːflɪt/ ●●○ *n* [C] a small book or piece of paper advertising something or giving information on a particular subject: **[+on]** *a leaflet on skin cancer* | **hand/pass/give/send out a leaflet** *Students were handing out election leaflets at the station.*

leaflet[2] *v* [I,T] to give leaflets to people: *He's leafleting the neighbourhood.*

ˈ**leaf mould** *BrE*, **leaf mold** *AmE n* [U] dead decaying leaves that improve soil

leaf·y /ˈliːfi/ *adj* **1** having a lot of leaves: *leafy green vegetables such as spinach* **2** having a lot of trees and plants: *a leafy suburb*

league /liːg/ ●●● W2 *n* [C]
1 a group of sports teams or players who play games against each other to see who is best: *He makes his football league debut tomorrow.* | *the Rugby* ***League Championship*** | **be (at the) top/bottom of the league** (=be the best or the worst team in a group)
2 a group of people or countries who have joined together because they have similar aims, political beliefs etc: *the National Socialist League*
3 not be in the same league (as sb/sth) to be not nearly as good or important as someone or something else: *They're not in the same league as the French at making wine.*
4 be in a different league to be much better than someone or something else: *For most of the match, Brazil were in a different league, and won 4-0.*
5 be out of your league to not be skilled or experienced enough to do or deal with something
6 be in league (with sb) to be working with someone secretly, especially for a bad purpose: *Vernon was accused by his enemies of being in league with the devil.*
7 an ancient unit for measuring distance, equal to three miles or about 4,828 metres on land, and three NAUTICAL MILES or 5,556 metres at sea

ˈ**league** ˌ**table** *n* [C] *especially BrE* a list in which people, teams, or organizations are shown in order of their success or quality: *The government's school league tables are published today.*

leak[1] /liːk/ ●●○ *v*
1 [I,T] if a container, pipe, roof etc leaks, or if it leaks gas, liquid etc, there is a small hole or crack in it that lets gas or liquid flow through: *The roof is leaking.* | *A tanker is leaking oil off the coast of Scotland.* → see picture at DRIP[1]
2 [I always + adv/prep] if a gas or liquid leaks somewhere, it gets through a hole in something SYN **seep**: **[+into/from/out]** *Sea water was leaking into the batteries which powered the electric motors.*
3 [T] to deliberately give secret information to a newspaper, television company etc: *The report's findings had been leaked.* | **leak sth to sb** *civil servants who leak information to the press* THESAURUS▸ REVEAL

leak out *phr v* if secret information leaks out, a lot of people find out about it: *No sooner had the news leaked out than my telephone started ringing.*

leak[2] ●●○ *n* [C]
1 a small hole that lets liquid or gas flow into or out of something: *There is a leak in the ceiling.* | *The boat had* ***sprung a leak*** (=a hole had appeared in it). THESAURUS▸ HOLE
2 a gas/oil/water etc leak an escape of gas or liquid through a hole in something: *A gas leak caused the explosion.*
3 a situation in which secret information is deliberately given to a newspaper, television company etc: *It became evident from the leaks that something important was going on.*
4 take/have a leak *informal* to get rid of waste liquid from your body SYN **urinate**

leak·age /ˈliːkɪdʒ/ *n* [C,U] **1** when gas, water etc leaks in or out, or the amount of it that has leaked **2** the deliberate spreading of secret information: *leakages of confidential information*

leak·y /ˈliːki/ *adj* a container, roof etc that is leaky has a hole or crack in it so that liquid or gas passes through it: *The house had a leaky roof.*

lean[1] /liːn/ ●●○ S3 *v* (*past tense and past participle* **leaned** *or* **leant** /lent/ *especially BrE*)

LEAN

1 [I always + adv/prep] to move or bend your body in a particular direction: **[+forward/back/over etc]** *They were leaning forward, facing each other.* | *Lean back and enjoy the ride.* | *She leant towards him and listened.*
2 [I always + adv/prep] to support yourself in a sloping position against a wall or other surface: **[+against/on]** *He was leaning on the bridge, watching the boats go by.*
3 [I,T always + adv/prep] to put something in a sloping position where it is supported, or to be in that position: **lean (sth) against/on sth** *A huge mirror was leaning against the wall.* | *He leant his bicycle against the fence.*
4 [I] to slope or bend from an upright position: *trees leaning in the wind*

lean on sb *phr v*
1 to depend on someone for support and encouragement, especially at a difficult time: *The couple lean on each other for support.*
2 *informal* to try to influence someone, especially by threatening them: *He won't pay unless you lean on him.*

lean towards sth *phr v* to tend to support, or begin to support, a particular set of opinions, beliefs etc: *Canada, the UK and Japan leant towards the US view.*

lean[2] *adj* **1** thin in a healthy and attractive way: *He was lean, tall, and muscular.* THESAURUS▸ THIN **2** lean meat does not have much fat on it OPP **fatty 3** a lean organization, company etc uses only as much money and as many people as it needs, so that nothing is wasted **4** a lean period is a very difficult time because there is not enough money, business etc: *His wife was a source of constant support during the* ***lean years***. —**leanness** *n* [U]

lean·ing /ˈliːnɪŋ/ *n* [C] a tendency to prefer or agree with a particular set of beliefs, opinions etc SYN **inclination**: *his radical* ***political leanings*** | **[+towards]** *a leaning towards the Right*

leant /lent/ a past tense and past participle of LEAN

ˈ**lean-to** *n* [C] a small roughly-made building that is built against the side of a larger building → **shed**

leap[1] /liːp/ ●●○ *v* (*past tense and past participle* **leapt** /lept/ *especially BrE*, **leaped** *especially AmE*)
1 JUMP **a)** [I always + adv/prep] to jump high into the air or to jump in order to land in a different place: *She leapt over the fence.* | *The smaller animals can easily leap from tree to tree.* **b)** [T] *literary* to jump over something: *Brenda leaped the gate and ran across the field.* THESAURUS▸ JUMP
2 MOVE FAST [I always + adv/prep] to move very quickly and with a lot of energy: *I leapt up the stairs three at a time.* | *He leapt out of bed.* | *She* ***leapt to*** *her* ***feet*** (=stood up quickly) *and started shouting.*
3 INCREASE [I] to increase quickly and by a large amount OPP **tumble**: **[+to]** *Profits leapt to £376m.* | *He leapt 27 places to second spot.*
4 leap at the chance/opportunity to accept an opportunity very eagerly: *I leapt at the chance of studying abroad.*
5 leap to sb's defence *BrE*, **leap to sb's defense** *AmE* to

quickly defend someone: *When her younger brother was being bullied she leapt to his defence.*
6 HEART [I] *literary* if your heart leaps, you feel a sudden surprise, happiness, or excitement: *My heart leaped when I saw Paul at the airport.* → **look before you leap** at LOOK[1](12)

leap out at sb *phr v* if a word or phrase in a piece of writing leaps out at you, you notice it particularly, because it is interesting, important etc SYN **jump out at**

leap[2] ●●○ *n* [C]
1 a big jump SYN **bound**: *He threw a stick into the river and the dog went after it in a* ***flying leap****.*
2 a large increase or change: **quantum/great/huge etc leap** *a quantum leap* (=very great increase or change) *in population levels* | **[+in]** *a 16% leap in pre-tax profits* | **[+forward]** *the huge leap forward that took place in the 1980s*
3 by/in leaps and bounds if something increases, develops, grows etc by leaps and bounds, it does it very quickly: *Lifeboat technology has advanced by leaps and bounds.*
4 a leap of (the) imagination (*also* **an imaginative leap**) a mental process that is needed to understand something difficult or see the connection between two very different ideas
5 leap in the dark something you do without knowing what will happen as a result
6 leap of faith something you do even though it involves a risk, hoping that it will have a good result

leap·frog[1] /ˈliːpfrɒg $ -frɔːg, -frɑːg/ *n* [U] a children's game in which someone bends over and someone else jumps over them

LEAPFROG

leapfrog[2] *v* (**leapfrogged**, **leapfrogging**) [I,T] to suddenly become better, more advanced etc than people or organizations that were previously better than you: *The company leapfrogged its rivals into a leading position.*

leapt /lept/ a past tense and past participle of LEAP

ˈleap year *n* [C] a year, which happens every fourth year, when February has 29 days instead of 28

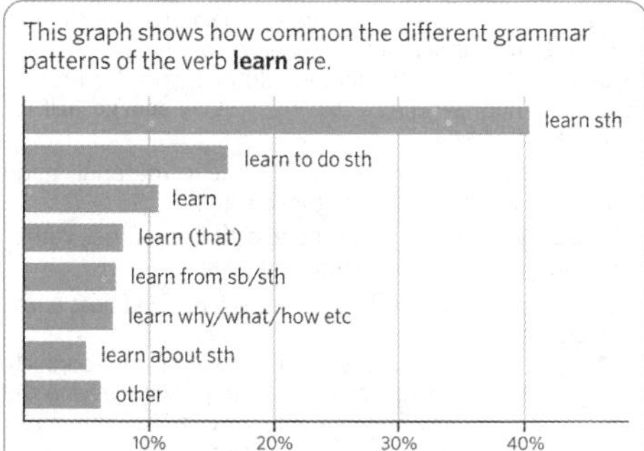

learn /lɜːn $ lɜːrn/ ●●● S1 W1 *v* (*past tense and past participle* **learned** *or* **learnt** /lɜːnt $ lɜːrnt/ *especially BrE*)
1 SUBJECT/SKILL [I,T] to gain knowledge of a subject or skill, by experience, by studying it, or by being taught → **teach**: *What's the best way to learn a language?* | **learn (how) to do sth** *I learnt to drive when I was 17.* | *Hector spent the winter learning how to cope with his blindness.* | *The teacher's task is to help the pupil learn.* | **learn (sth) from sb** *I learned a lot from my father.* | **[+about]** *Kids can have fun and learn about music at the same time.* | **learn what** *Youngsters must learn what is dangerous and what is not to be feared.* | *The student will* ***learn from experience*** *about the importance of planning.*

GRAMMAR: Patterns with learn
- You **learn to do** something: *She's learning to play the piano.*
- You **learn how to do** something: *She is learning how to play the piano.* ✗ Don't say: *She is learning playing the piano.*

GRAMMAR GUIDE ▸ VERBS

2 FIND OUT [I,T] *formal* to find out information or news by hearing it from someone else or reading it SYN **discover**: *I didn't tell her the truth. She would learn it for herself soon enough.* | **[+of/about]** *He learned about his appointment by telephone yesterday.* | **learn (that)** *Last week I learned that I was pregnant.* | *She was* ***surprised to learn*** *that he was a lot older than she had thought.* | **learn whether/who/why** *I waited to learn whether I'd secured a college place.* | *We have yet to learn who will be the new manager.*
3 REMEMBER [T] to get to know something so well that you can easily remember it SYN **memorize**: *The actors hardly had time to* ***learn*** *their* ***lines*** *before filming started.*
4 CHANGE YOUR BEHAVIOUR [I,T] to gradually understand a situation and start behaving in the way that you should: **learn (that)** *They have to learn that they can't just do whatever they like.* | **learn to do sth** *Young hairdressers must learn to treat the client as a person, not a head of hair.* | *I've told him a hundred times not to bully people, but he* ***never learns****.* | **[+from]** *You have to* ***learn from*** *your* ***mistakes*** (=understand why what you did was wrong). | *the* ***lessons learned*** *in the Gulf War*
5 sb has learned their lesson used to say that someone will not do something wrong or stupid again, because they suffered as a result: *I've learned my lesson; I've now got a burglar alarm and a guard dog.*
6 learn (sth) the hard way to understand a situation or develop a skill by learning from your mistakes and bad experiences
7 that'll learn sb! *spoken* used when something bad has just happened to someone as a result of their actions, especially when they ignored a warning → **live and learn** at LIVE[1](20)

THESAURUS

learn to gain knowledge of a subject or skill, especially by being taught or trained: *How long have you been learning Italian?* | *At what age can you learn to drive in America?*

study to learn about a subject by reading books, going to classes etc, especially at school or university: *She's studying music at Berkeley College in California.*

train to learn the skills and get the experience that you need in order to do a particular job: *Julie's training to be a nurse.*

pick sth up to learn something without much effort, by watching or listening to other people: *It's easy to pick up a language when you're living in a country.* | *The rules of the game are easy – you'll soon pick them up.*

get the hang of sth *informal* to learn how to do or use something that is fairly complicated, especially with practice: *It took me a while to get the hang of all the features on my new camera.*

revise *BrE*, **review** *AmE* to study facts again, especially on your own, in order to learn them before an examination: *Jenny's upstairs revising for her Maths exam tomorrow.*

master to learn something so well that you have no difficulty with it, especially a skill or a language: *She gave me a book called 'Mastering the Art of French Cooking'.* | *I learnt Spanish for years but I never really mastered it.*

learn·ed /ˈlɜːnɪd $ ˈlɜːr-/ *adj formal* **1** a learned person has a lot of knowledge because they have read and studied a lot: *a learned professor* **2 learned books/works etc** books etc that are written by people who have a lot of knowledge: *learned works on natural history* —**learnedly** *adv*

learn·er /ˈlɜːnə $ ˈlɜːrnər/ ●●○ *n* [C]
1 someone who is learning to do something: **[+of]** *a new dictionary for learners of business English* | *the needs of* ***slow learners*** | *attractive grammar books for* ***adult learners*** THESAURUS ▸ STUDENT
2 (*also* **learner driver**) *BrE* someone who is learning to drive a car

ˈlearner's ˌpermit *n* [C] *AmE* an official document that gives you permission to learn to drive SYN **provisional licence** *BrE*

learn·ing /ˈlɜːnɪŋ $ ˈlɜːr-/ ●●○ *n* [U] knowledge gained through reading and study: *a man of great learning*

ˈlearning curve *n* [C] the rate at which you learn a new skill: *Everyone in the centre has been through a very* ***steep learning curve*** (=they had to learn very quickly).

ˈlearning ˌdifficulties *n* [plural] a mental problem that affects someone's ability to learn: *a school for children with learning difficulties*

ˈlearning disaˌbility *n* [C,U] a mental problem that affects someone's ability to learn

learnt /lɜːnt $ lɜːrnt/ a past tense and past participle of LEARN

lease¹ /liːs/ ●○○ *n* [C]
1 a legal agreement which allows you to use a building, car etc for a period of time, in return for rent: **[+on]** *They* ***took out a lease*** *on a seven-acre field.* | *The landlord refused to* ***renew*** *his* ***lease***. | *The 99-year* ***lease expired*** *in 1999.* | *Do you understand all* ***the terms of*** *the* ***lease***?
2 a new lease of life *especially BrE*, **a new lease on life** *AmE* **a)** if something has a new lease of life, it is changed or repaired so that it can continue: *Historic buildings can have a new lease of life through conversion.* **b)** if someone has a new lease of life, they become healthy, active, or happy again after being weak, ill, or tired: *an operation to give her a new lease of life*

lease² ●○○ *v* [T]
1 to use a building, car etc under a lease: *I'm interested in leasing your cottage.* | **lease sth from sb** *They lease the site from the council.*
2 (*also* **lease out**) to let someone use a building, car etc under a lease: **lease sth to sb** *The building was leased to a health club.*

lease·back /ˈliːsbæk/ *n* [C,U] *technical* an arrangement in which you sell or give something to someone, but continue to use it by paying them rent

lease·hold /ˈliːshəʊld $ -hoʊld/ *adj especially BrE* leasehold property is property that you will own only for the period of time stated in a lease → **freehold** —**leasehold** *adv*

lease·hold·er /ˈliːshəʊldə $ -hoʊldər/ *n* [C] someone who lives in a leasehold house, apartment etc → **freeholder**

leash¹ /liːʃ/ ●○○ *n* [C] *especially AmE*
1 a piece of rope, leather etc fastened to a dog's collar in order to control it SYN **lead** *BrE*: **on/off a leash** *At her side on a leash trotted a small grey dog.* | *Never leave your dog off the leash outside a store.*
2 keep/have sb on a leash to control someone – used humorously: *Marcus keeps you on a short leash, does he?*

leash² *v* [T] *AmE* to put a leash on a dog

least¹ /liːst/ ●●● S1 W1 *determiner, pron*
1 at least a) not less than a particular number or amount: *It will take you at least 20 minutes to get there.* | *He had at least £100,000 in savings.* | **at the (very) least** (=not less than and probably much more than) *It would cost $1 million at the very least.* **b)** even if something better is not true or is not done: *At least he didn't lie to me.* | *I don't expect you to pay me, but you could at least cover my expenses.* | *The house still needed a lot of work, but at least the kitchen was finished.* **c)** used when you are correcting or changing something that you have just said: *They all knew I was on their side. At least, that's what they said.* | *I made everything perfectly clear – or at least I thought I did.*
2 at the (very) least used when mentioning the least extreme thing that happens, is needed etc: *Computer viruses are at the very least annoying and often actually destructive.*
3 the least a) the smallest amount: *Women work in those sectors of the job market which pay the least.* | *Which method causes the least damage to the environment?* **b)** used to emphasize how small something is, especially when it hardly exists at all: *I haven't the least idea what you are talking about.* | *He used to wake at the least noise.* **c)** used when you are saying what someone should do in a situation, and suggesting that they should really do more: *The least you could do is give me her phone number.* | *The least they could have given her is some money towards the rent.*
4 not the least/not in the least/not the least bit none at all, or not at all: *I tried to convince them, but they weren't the least interested.* | *I'm not in the least afraid of you anymore.* | *His voice was alert, not the least bit sleepy.*
5 to say the least used to show that something is worse or more serious than you are actually saying: *His teaching methods were strange, to say the least.*
6 the least of sb's worries/problems/troubles/concerns something that someone is not worried about because there are other more important problems: *What I looked like was the least of my problems.*
7 it's the least I can do *spoken* used to say that you are very willing to do something or to reply to someone's thanks: *I'll look after them – it's the least I can do.* → **last but not least** at LAST²(3)

least² ●●○ *adv*
1 less than anything or anyone else OPP **most**: *The journey would impose extra expense on those least able to afford it.* | *It is quite amazing what turns up when you are least expecting it.* | *He's my least favourite member of staff.*
2 least of all especially not a particular person or thing: *She hardly ever lost her temper – least of all with Anne.*
3 not least *formal* used to emphasize that something is important: *My mother was upset about his appearance here, not least because she felt it was invading her privacy.*

least·ways /ˈliːstweɪz/ (*also* **least·wise** /-waɪz/) *adv informal* at least SYN **anyway**: *There's no way to cross the mountains, leastways at this time of the year.*

ˌleast ˈworst *adj* [only before noun] the least worst choice is the best choice from a list of choices that you think are all bad: *Often it's a question of choosing the least worst option.*

leath·er /ˈleðə $ -ər/ ●●● W3 *n*
1 [U] animal skin that has been treated to preserve it, and is used for making shoes, bags etc: *The inside of the bag was lined with soft leather.* | *elegant leather boots*
2 leathers [plural] special leather clothes worn for protection by someone riding a MOTORCYCLE → **run/go hell for leather** at HELL¹(27)

leath·er·ette /ˌleðəˈret/ *n* [U] a cheap material made to look like leather SYN **Naugahyde** *AmE*

leath·er·y /ˈleðəri/ *adj* hard and stiff like leather, rather than soft or smooth: *her leathery brown skin*

leave¹ /liːv/ ●●● S1 W1 *v* (*past tense and past participle* **left** /left/)
1 GO AWAY [I,T] to go away from a place or a person: *My baby gets upset when I leave the room.* | *Before leaving the train, make sure you have all your belongings with you.* | *Leave the motorway at Junction 7.* | **[+at]** *The plane leaves at 12.30.* | **[+for]** *I tried calling him, but he'd already left for work.* | **leave (sth/sb) soon/now/later etc** *If he left immediately, he'd catch the 7.30 train.* | **leave (sth/sb) to do sth** *Frances left work early to meet her mother.* | **leave sb doing sth** *Never leave children playing near water unattended.* | **leave sb to sth** *I'll* ***leave*** *you* ***to it*** (=go away and let you continue with what you are doing). | *My youngest boy has* ***not left*** *my* ***side*** (=has stayed near me) *since his daddy was killed.* | **leave sb in peace** (=go away from someone so that they can think, work etc alone) *Just a few more questions, then we'll leave you in peace.*
2 STOP [I,T] if you leave your job, home, school etc, you permanently stop doing that job, living at home etc: *Over the past two years, 20 staffers have left.* | **leave home/**

L

school/college etc *How old were you when you left home* (=your parents' home)? | *My daughter got a job after she left school.* | *The lawsuit will be postponed until the president **leaves office**.* | **leave a job/country/Spain etc** *Many missionaries were forced to leave the country.* | *It seems that Tony has **left** the band **for good*** (=permanently). | **leave (sb/sth) to do sth** *Laura left her native England to live in France.*

3 leave sb/sth alone a) to stop annoying or upsetting someone: *Oh, just leave me alone, will you?* | *Leave the boy alone, he can make up his own mind.* **b)** to go away from someone so that they are on their own: *Six-year-old Gemma had been left alone in the house.* **c)** to stop touching something: *Leave that alone. You'll break it.* **d)** (*also* **leave well (enough) alone**) to stop being involved in or trying to change a situation: *Why can't they just leave well alone and let us concentrate on teaching?*

4 LET STH/SB STAY [T always + adv/prep] to make or allow something or someone to stay in a place when you go away: **leave sth/sb in/with/behind etc** *Are you leaving the kids with Grandma on Saturday?* | *As soon as I'd shut the door, I realized I'd left the keys inside.* | *Did anybody leave a jacket behind last night?* | *She **left** her son **in the care of** a friend.* | **leave sb to do sth** *He left Ruth to find her own way home.* | *Students were **left to** their **own devices*** (=left alone and allowed to do whatever they wanted) *for long periods.* | **leave sb for dead** *The girl had been attacked and left for dead.*

5 NOT CHANGE/MOVE STH [T] to let something remain in a particular state, position, or condition: **leave sth on/off/out etc** *You've left your lights on.* | *She must have left the phone off the hook.* | **leave sth open/empty/untidy etc** *I wish you'd stop leaving the door open.* | *The trial left many questions unanswered.* | **leave a space/gap etc** *Leave the next two lines blank for the tutor's comments.* | *Drivers should always **leave room** for cyclists.* | **leave sth doing sth** *I'll just leave the engine running while I go in.* | *Don't **leave** tools **lying about**.* | **leave sth to do sth** *Leave the pots to soak overnight.*

6 RESULT OF ACCIDENT/ILLNESS/EVENT [T] if an event, accident, illness etc leaves you in a particular condition, you are in that condition because of it: *An explosion at a chemical plant has left one worker dead and four injured.* | **leave sb with sth** *Although the infection cleared up, he was left with a persistent cough.* | **leave sb doing sth** *The incident left her feeling confused and hurt.* | *The announcement has left shareholders nursing huge losses.*

7 be left (*also* **have sth left**) if something is left, it remains after everything else has gone, been taken away, or used: *I've only got a few dollars left.* | *There were a couple of seats left at the back.* | *We don't have much time left.* | *He pointed to **what was left of** the house* (=used when very little is left). | ***All that** was **left** was a pile of bones.* | **[+over]** *After we've paid the bills, there's never much left over.* | *They ate some bread rolls left over from the night before.*

8 LETTER/MESSAGE/THING [T] to deliver a message, note, package etc for someone or put it somewhere so that they will get it later: *She left a message on his answerphone.* | **leave sb sth** *Can you leave me some money for the bus?* | **leave sth with sb** *Ian left this note with me.* | **leave sth for sb** *A guy left these flowers for you.*

9 DELAY [T] to not do something or to do it later than you intended: *Leave the dishes. I'll do them later.* | *So much had been **left undone**.* | **leave sth until the last minute/until last** *If you **leave** your preparation **until the last minute**, you'll reduce your chances of passing.* | *I left the best bit until last.* | *I want to think about it. Can I **leave** it **for now**?* | *I'm afraid you've **left it too late** to change your ticket.* | **leave it at that** (=used to say that you will not do any more of something, because you have done enough) *Let's leave it at that for today.*

10 LET SB DECIDE/BE RESPONSIBLE [T] to let someone else decide something or be responsible for something: **leave sth to sb** ***Leave it to** me. I'll make sure it gets posted.* | *The choice of specialist subject is left entirely to the students.* | **leave it (up) to sb to do sth** *I'll leave it up to you to decide.* | *She leaves it to the reader to draw their own conclusions.* | **leave doing sth to sb** *Is it okay if I leave writing the results to you?* | **leave sth with sb** *Leave it with me, I'll fix it for you.* | *He's not the sort to **leave** things **to chance*** (=take no action and just wait to see what happens). | **leave sb with no choice/option** (=force someone to take a particular action) *You leave me with no choice but to fire you.* | **leave sb to do sth** *BrE: Clive moved to London, leaving Edward to run the Manchester office.*

11 HUSBAND/WIFE ETC [I,T] to stop living with or having a relationship with your husband, partner etc: *Martha was always threatening to leave, but I never believed her.* | **leave sb for sb** *Mr Rushworth left his partner of 10 years for a younger woman.*

12 WHEN YOU DIE [T] **a)** to arrange for someone to receive your money, property etc after you die SYN **bequeath**: *Aunt Alice died, leaving almost $5 million.* | **leave sb sth** *Hugo left me his mother's ring.* | *In his will, he had left all his children a small sum of money.* | **leave sth to sb/sth** *Have you thought of **leaving** a gift **to charity** after you die?* **b) leave a wife/children etc** used when someone dies before their wife, children etc: *PC Davis leaves a wife and three small children.* THESAURUS GIVE

13 MARK [T] to make a mark that remains afterwards: **leave a mark/stain/scar etc** *The wine had left a permanent mark on the tablecloth.* | *He staggered to the door, **leaving a trail** of blood.* | *Make sure that you don't leave any footprints.*

14 NOT EAT/DRINK [T] if you leave food or drink that you have been given, you do not eat or drink it: *'I'm really hungry now.' 'That's because you left half your lunch.'* | *He rose from the table, **leaving** his brandy **untouched**.*

15 leave sb/sth standing (*also* **leave sb/sth in the dust** *AmE*) *informal* to be much better, quicker, more successful etc than someone or something else: *In terms of fitness, he discovered that Kate left him standing.*

16 leave a lot/sth/much to be desired to be very unsatisfactory: *Inspectors say health and safety procedures at the factory leave a lot to be desired.*

17 MATHEMATICS [T] in a sum, to have a particular amount remaining: *Three from seven leaves four.*

18 leave sth aside/to one side to not think about or consider one part of something for a time, so that you can consider another part of it: ***Leaving aside** for a moment the question of expense, what would your view be of the suggested changes?*

19 leave sb/sth be *old-fashioned* to not upset, speak to, or annoy someone or to not touch something

20 leave go/hold of sth *BrE spoken informal* to stop holding something

21 leave it to sb (to do sth) *AmE spoken informal* used to say that no one should be surprised that someone does something, because it is typical or expected of them: *Leave it to you to have the whole day planned out!*

22 Elvis/sb/sth has left the building *especially AmE informal* used humorously to emphasize that something is definitely over or that someone has gone and will not return → **sb can take it or leave it** at TAKE[1](21), → **be left holding the baby/bag** at HOLD[1](26)

leave sb/sth ↔ **behind** *phr v*

1 to not take someone or something with you when you leave a place: *I think I might have left my wallet behind.* | *He departed for Washington, leaving the children behind with their mother.*

2 if a person, country, or organization is left behind, they do not develop as quickly or make as much progress as other people, countries etc: *In class, a child with poor eyesight can soon get left behind.* | *a fear of being left behind by better-organized rivals*

3 (*also* **leave sb/sth behind you**) to permanently stop being involved with a person, place, or situation: *It's time to **leave the past behind**.* | *Although Armstrong overcame the circumstances of his birth, he never really left New Orleans behind.*

4 (*also* **leave sb/sth behind you**) to move away from someone or something: *They had left the city behind and were heading into open country.* | *Sarah, with her long legs, soon **left** the rest of us **far behind**.*

5 (*also* **leave sth behind you**) to produce a thing or situation that remains after you have gone: *He drove off,* *leaving behind him a trail of blue smoke.* | *the mess the previous government left behind*

leave off *phr v*

1 to stop doing something: **take up/pick up/continue (sth) etc where sb left off** (=continue something that has stopped for a short time) *Barry took up the story where Justine had left off.* | **leave off doing sth** *BrE informal*: *'Will you leave off nagging?' he snarled.*

2 leave sb/sth off (sth) to not include something such as someone's name in a list or other document: *Why was her name left off the list?*

leave sb/sth ↔ **out** *phr v*

1 to not include someone or something: *She outlined the case to him, being careful not to leave anything out.* | **leave sb/sth out of sth** *Kidd has been left out of the team.*

2 be/feel left out to feel that you are not accepted or welcome in a situation: *New fathers often feel left out when baby arrives.*

3 leave it out! *BrE spoken* used to tell someone to stop lying, pretending, or being annoying

leave² ●●○ S3 W3 *n*

1 HOLIDAY [U] time that you are allowed to spend away from your work, especially in the armed forces: *I've applied for three days' leave.* | **on leave** *navy officers home on leave* | *Your basic* ***annual leave*** *is 20 days.*

2 maternity/sick/compassionate leave time that you are allowed to spend away from work because you have had a baby, because you are ill, or because of a personal problem such as the death of a relative

3 leave of absence a period of time that you are allowed to spend away from work for a particular purpose: *She's been given leave of absence to attend a computer course.*

4 PERMISSION [U] *formal* permission to do something: *All this was done entirely without my leave.* | **leave to do sth** *a petition for leave to appeal to the European court* | **grant/obtain/ask/seek etc leave (to do sth)** *He asked leave to speak to her in private.*

5 without so much as a by your leave *old-fashioned* without asking permission, in a way that seems very rude: *He marched into my office without so much as a by your leave.*

6 take leave of your senses to suddenly start behaving in a strange way: *You want to marry him? Have you taken leave of your senses?*

7 take leave of sb/take your leave *formal* to say goodbye to someone

leav·en¹ /ˈlevən/ (*also* **leav·en·ing** /ˈlevənɪŋ/) *n* **1** [U] *technical* a substance, especially YEAST, that is added to a mixture of flour and water so that it will swell and can be baked into bread → **unleavened** **2** [singular, U] *literary* something that makes an event or situation less boring, serious, or sad

leaven² *v* [T] *formal* to make something less boring, serious, or sad

leaves /liːvz/ the plural of LEAF

ˈleave-ˌtaking *n* [C] *literary* an act of saying goodbye when you go away

leav·ings /ˈliːvɪŋz/ *n* [plural] *old-fashioned* things that are left because people do not want them

lech¹, **letch** /letʃ/ *v*

lech after/over sb *phr v BrE informal* to show sexual desire for someone in a way that is unpleasant or annoying: *a middle-aged man leching after young girls*

lech², **letch** (*also* **letch·er** /ˈletʃə $ -ər/) *n* [C] a man who shows his sexual desire for women in a way that is unpleasant or annoying

lech·er·ous /ˈletʃərəs/ *adj* a lecherous man shows his sexual desire for women in a way that is unpleasant or annoying: *a lecherous old man* —**lecherously** *adv*

lech·er·y /ˈletʃəri/ *n* [U] *old-fashioned* sexual desire or pleasure that is considered bad because it is not part of a romantic relationship: *There was a hint of lechery in his eyes.*

lec·tern /ˈlektən $ -ərn/ *n* [C] an object with a sloping surface that you put an open book or notes on while you are speaking to people in public

lec·ture¹ /ˈlektʃə $ -ər/ ●●● S2 W3 *n* [C]

1 a long talk on a particular subject that someone gives to a group of people, especially to students in a university → **speech**: **[+on]** *He regularly gives lectures on modern French literature.* THESAURUS ▸ SPEECH

2 an act of criticizing someone or warning them about something in a long serious talk, in a way that they think is unfair or unnecessary: **[+on/about]** *My father caught me and* ***gave*** *me a long* ***lecture*** *about the dangers of drink.*

COLLOCATIONS

VERBS

give a lecture (*also* **deliver a lecture** *formal*) *She gave a fascinating lecture on crime in the 1800s.*

do a lecture *informal*: *He's doing a lecture on modern poetry.*

go to a lecture (*also* **attend a lecture** *formal*) *Have you been to any of Professor MacPherson's lectures?*

listen to a lecture *Most students spend about a quarter of their time listening to lectures.*

lecture + NOUN

a lecture hall/room (*also* **a lecture theatre** *BrE*) *The lecture hall was packed.*

lecture notes *Can I borrow your lecture notes?*

a lecture tour (=a trip that someone takes to many different places to give a lecture) *He's on a lecture tour of the US.*

PHRASES

a series of lectures (*also* **a course of lectures** *BrE*) *a series of lectures on the history of art*

lecture² ●●○ AWL *v*

1 [T] to talk angrily or seriously to someone in order to criticize or warn them, in a way that they think is unfair or unnecessary: *I wish you'd stop lecturing me!* | **lecture sb about/on sth** *He began to lecture us about making too much noise.*

2 [I] to talk to a group of people on a particular subject, especially to students in a university: **[+on]** *He lectures on European art at Manchester University.* THESAURUS ▸ TEACH

lec·tur·er /ˈlektʃərə $ -ər/ ●●○ AWL *n* [C] **a)** someone who gives lectures, especially in a university: *She's a brilliant lecturer.* **b)** a teacher in a British university or college: **[+in]** *a lecturer in medieval studies at Edinburgh University* THESAURUS ▸ TEACHER

lec·ture·ship /ˈlektʃəʃɪp $ -ər-/ *n* [C] a teaching job at a university or college in Britain, in which someone gives lectures to students: **[+in]** *He was offered a lectureship in mathematics at Bristol University.*

led /led/ the past tense and past participle of LEAD¹

-led /led/ *suffix* [in adjectives] having a particular thing as the most important cause or influence: *an export-led economic recovery*

LED /ˌel iː ˈdiː/ *n* [C] *technical* (***light-emitting diode***) a small electronic object that produces light when an electrical current is sent through it. LEDs are used, for example, as lights on electrical equipment, and to make words and pictures on large screens.

ledge /ledʒ/ ●○○ *n* [C]

1 a narrow flat piece of rock that sticks out on the side of a mountain or cliff: *We crept carefully along the narrow ledge.* | *He leapt onto a ledge of rock.*

2 a narrow shelf: *There's some money on the* ***window ledge*** (=narrow shelf below the window).

led·ger /ˈledʒə $ -ər/ *n* [C] a book in which a business, bank etc records how much money it receives and spends

ˈledger line *n* [C] a line on which you write musical notes that are too high or too low to be shown on a STAVE

lee /liː/ *n* **1 in/under the lee of sth** next to something, and protected from the wind by that thing: *We sat in the lee of a tall hedge.* **2 the lees** *technical* the thick substance that collects at the bottom of a bottle of wine

leech /liːtʃ/ *n* [C] **1** a small soft creature that fixes itself to the skin of animals in order to drink their blood

2 someone who takes advantage of other people by taking their money, food etc → **parasite**: *The family began to see him as a leech.*

leek /liːk/ *n* [C] a vegetable with a long white stem and long flat green leaves, which tastes like an onion → see picture at VEGETABLE[1]

leer /lɪə $ lɪr/ *v* [I] to look at someone in an unpleasant way that shows that you think they are sexually attractive: **[+at]** *She was sick of old men leering at her.* —**leer** *n* [C]

leer·y /ˈlɪəri $ ˈlɪri/ *adj informal* careful in the way that you deal with something or someone because you do not trust them SYN **wary**: **[+of]** *I was very leery of him after I found out he had lied to Jennifer.*

lee·ward /ˈliːwəd, ˈluːəd $ -ərd/ *adj, adv* **1** the leeward side of something is the side that is sheltered from the wind OPP **windward**: *We camped on the* ***leeward side*** *of the mountain.* **2** *technical* a leeward direction is the same direction as the wind is blowing OPP **windward**: **to leeward** (=in a leeward direction) *The ship cruised slowly to leeward.*

lee·way /ˈliːweɪ/ *n* [U] **1** freedom to do things in the way you want to: **[+in]** *The government does not* ***have*** *much* ***leeway*** *in foreign policy.* | **leeway to do sth** *Try to* ***give*** *teenagers more* ***leeway*** *to make their own decisions.* **2 make up leeway** *BrE* if you have to make up leeway, you have to do extra work because you have not done as much work as you should have done: *We've got quite a lot of leeway to make up.*

left[1] /left/ ●●● S1 W1 *adj* [only before noun]
1 your left side is the side of your body that contains your heart OPP **right**: *She held out her left hand.* | *a scar on the left side of his face*
2 on the same side of something as your left side OPP **right**: *Take the next left turn.* | *the left bank of the river* | *a pile of papers on the left side of the desk*
3 have two left feet *informal* to move in an awkward way when you are running or doing a sport: *a tall, clumsy-looking boy with two left feet*
4 the left hand doesn't know what the right hand is doing used to say that one part of a group or organization does not know what the other parts are doing

left[2] ●●● S3 W3 *adv* towards the direction or side that is on the left OPP **right**: *Turn left just after the school.*

left[3] ●●● S3 W3 *n*
1 the left/sb's left the side of your body that contains your heart OPP **right**: **on/to the left (of sth)** *Take the next road on the left.* | *Our house is just to the left of the school.* | **on/to sb's left** *On your left you can see the Houses of Parliament.*
2 (from) left to right from the left side to the right side of something: *The photo shows, from left to right, his daughters Molly, Fiona, and Anne.*
3 the left/the Left political parties and groups that support the ideas and beliefs of SOCIALISM. They usually want large industries to be owned by the state, and to use taxes to help solve social problems OPP **right**: *He has support from the Left.* | *politicians on the left of the party* | *The party is moving further to the left.*
4 [C] a hit made with your left hand OPP **right**
5 take a left (*also* **hang a left** *AmE*) to turn left: *Take the next left* (=turn left at the next road).

left[4] the past tense and past participle of LEAVE[1]

ˈleft-click *v* [I] to press the left button of a computer mouse

ˈleft field *n* [U] **1** a position in baseball in the left side of the OUTFIELD → **right field 2 out of/from left field** *informal* something that comes out of left field is unexpected: *People don't know how to react when a question like that comes at them out of left field.*

ˌleft-ˈhand ●●○ *adj* [only before noun] on the left side of something OPP **right-hand**: *We live about halfway down the street on the* ***left-hand side***.

ˌleft-hand ˈdrive *adj* a left-hand drive vehicle is one in which the driver sits on the left → **right-hand drive**

ˌleft-ˈhanded ●●○ *adj*
1 a left-handed person uses their left hand for writing, throwing etc OPP **right-handed**
2 [only before noun] left-handed tools have been made for left-handed people to use: *left-handed scissors*
3 left-handed compliment *AmE* a statement that seems to express admiration or praise, but at the same time is insulting SYN **backhanded compliment** *BrE*

ˌleft-ˈhander *n* [C] someone who uses their left hand for writing, throwing etc OPP **right-hander**

left·ie /ˈlefti/ *n* [C] another spelling of LEFTY

left·ist /ˈleftɪst/ *adj* supporting LEFT-WING ideas or groups OPP **rightist**: *a coalition of leftist parties* —**leftist** *n* [C]: *a group of radical leftists*

ˌleft ˈluggage ˌoffice *n* [C] *BrE* a place in a station, airport etc where you can pay to leave your bags and collect them later

ˌleft-of-cen·tre *BrE*, **left-of-center** *AmE adj* supporting ideas and aims that are between the centre and the left in politics OPP **right-of-centre**: *a modern left-of-centre party with wide appeal*

left·o·ver[1] /ˈleftəʊvə $ -oʊvər/ *adj* [only before noun] remaining after all the rest has been used, taken, or eaten: *leftover vegetables* | *a few pieces of leftover carpet*

leftover[2] *n* **1 leftovers** [plural] food that has not been eaten at the end of a meal: *Give the leftovers to the dog.* **2** [singular] something from an earlier time that still remains, even though it is not really useful or important anymore SYN **hangover**: **[+from]** *The headmaster was a leftover from the Victorian era.*

left·wards /ˈleftwədz $ -wərdz/ *especially BrE*, **leftward** /-wəd $ -wərd/ *AmE adv* on or towards the left OPP **rightwards**: *Follow the path leftwards.* —**leftward** *adj*

ˌleft-ˈwing ●○○ *adj* a left-wing person or group supports the political aims of groups such as SOCIALISTS and COMMUNISTS OPP **right-wing**: *a left-wing newspaper* | *a left-wing political organization* | *She's got very left-wing views.* —**left wing** *n* [singular]: *the left wing of the Labour party* —**left-winger** *n* [C]: *She is supported by left-wingers in the party.*

left·y, leftie /ˈlefti/ *n* (*plural* **lefties**) [C] **1** *especially BrE informal* someone who has left-wing political ideas - used to show disapproval: *a group of liberals and lefties* **2** *especially AmE informal* someone who uses their left hand for writing, throwing etc —**lefty** *adj*: *I don't get on with his lefty friends.*

leg[1] /leg/ ●●● S1 W1 *n*
1 BODY PART [C] one of the long parts of your body that your feet are joined to, or a similar part on an animal or insect: *a young boy with skinny legs* | *She fell and broke her leg.* | **four-legged/long-legged etc** *four-legged animals*
2 MEAT [C,U] the leg of an animal when it is cooked and eaten as food: *roast leg of lamb*
3 FURNITURE [C] one of the upright parts that support a piece of furniture: *One of the legs on the table was a bit wobbly.* | *a chair leg* | *a three-legged stool*
4 CLOTHING [C] the part of your trousers that covers your leg: *The legs of my jeans were covered in mud.* | *He rolled up his* ***trouser legs*** *and waded out into the stream.*
5 JOURNEY/RACE [C] one part of a long journey or race: **[+of]** *the final leg of the Tour de France*
6 SPORT [C] *BrE* one of the series of games in a football competition played between two teams: *Leeds will have to win the second leg if they are to go forward to the finals.*
7 not have a leg to stand on *informal* to be in a situation where you cannot prove or legally support what you say: *If you didn't sign a contract, you won't have a leg to stand on.*
8 get your leg over *BrE informal not polite* to have sex with someone
9 have legs *AmE informal* if a piece of news has legs, people continue to be interested in it and talk about it
→ **on its last legs** at LAST[1](9), → **on your last legs** at LAST[1](8), → **pull sb's leg** at PULL[1](11), → LEG-PULL, LEG-UP, PEG LEG, SEA LEGS, → **shake a leg** at SHAKE[1](9), → **show a leg** at SHOW[1](24), → **stretch your legs** at STRETCH[1](7)

leg² *v* (**legged**, **legging**) **leg it** *BrE informal* to run in order to escape from someone or something: *We saw him coming, and legged it out of the house.*

leg·a·cy¹ /ˈlegəsi/ ●○○ *n* (*plural* **legacies**) [C]
1 something that happens or exists as a result of things that happened at an earlier time: **[+of]** *The invasion **left a legacy** of hatred and fear.* | **[+from]** *a legacy from the colonial period*
2 money or property that you receive from someone after they die SYN **inheritance**: *She received a small legacy from her aunt.*

legacy² *adj* [only before noun] **1** a legacy system, piece of software etc is one that people continue to use, although more modern ones are available **2 legacy data** old information that an organization has, especially information stored in an old-fashioned way

le·gal /ˈliːɡəl/ ●●● S2 W1 AWL *adj*
1 if something is legal, you are allowed to do it or have to do it by law OPP **illegal**: *What the company has done is perfectly legal.* | *plans to make the carrying of identity cards a legal requirement* | *He had twice the **legal limit** of alcohol in his bloodstream.* | *a pressure group that is campaigning to **make** cannabis **legal***
2 [only before noun] concerned with or relating to the law: *free **legal advice*** | *a costly legal dispute* | *the Scottish **legal system*** | **the legal profession** (=lawyers)
3 legal action/proceedings the use of the legal system to settle an argument, put right an unfair situation etc: *She threatened to take legal action against the hospital.*

ˌlegal ˈaid *n* [U] a system in which a government gives money to people who need a lawyer but cannot afford to pay for one: *They have been granted legal aid and now intend to take their case to court.*

le·gal·ese /ˌliːɡəlˈiːz/ *n* [U] *informal* language used by lawyers that is difficult for most people to understand

ˌlegal ˈhigh *n* [C] a drug taken for pleasure that can be bought legally

ˌlegal ˈholiday *n* [C] *AmE* an official holiday on which most government offices and banks are closed SYN **bank holiday** *BrE*

le·gal·ise /ˈliːɡəlaɪz/ *v* [T] a British spelling of LEGALIZE

le·gal·ist·ic /ˌliːɡəˈlɪstɪk◂/ *adj* too concerned about small legal details: *a legalistic interpretation of the agreement*

le·gal·i·ty /lɪˈɡæləti/ AWL *n* **1** [U] the fact of being allowed by law: **[+of]** *Several ministers have questioned the legality of the ban.* **2 legalities** [plural] the legal parts of an agreement: *We've sold the house and are just waiting to complete all the legalities.*

le·gal·ize (*also* **-ise** *BrE*) /ˈliːɡəlaɪz/ ●●○ *v* [T] to make something legal so that people are allowed to do it OPP **criminalize**: *Abortion was legalized in the 1960s.* —**legalization** /ˌliːɡəlaɪˈzeɪʃən $ -lə-/ *n* [U]: *a campaign calling for the legalization of certain drugs*

le·gal·ly /ˈliːɡəli/ ●●○ AWL *adv*
1 according to the law: *They are still legally married.* | *Which of them is **legally responsible** for the accident?* | *a **legally binding** agreement*
2 if you can do something legally, you are allowed to do it by law OPP **illegally**: *The station can now broadcast legally.*

ˈlegal pad *n* [C] a book containing sheets of yellow writing paper with lines on it, of a type sold in the US

ˈlegal ˌsystem *n* [C] the laws and the way they work in a particular country: *the British legal system*

ˌlegal ˈtender *n* [U] coins or bank notes that people can officially use as money in a particular country

leg·ate /ˈleɡət/ *n* [C] an important official representative, especially an official representative of the POPE

leg·a·tee /ˌleɡəˈtiː/ *n* [C] *law* someone who receives money or property from a person who has died

le·ga·tion /lɪˈɡeɪʃən/ *n* [C] **1** a group of government officials who work in a foreign country and represent their own government in that country: *a member of the British legation in Beijing* **2** the building or office where a legation works

le·ga·to /lɪˈɡɑːtəʊ $ -toʊ/ *adj, adv technical* music that is played legato is played very smoothly, so that each note connects to the next one without a pause

le·gend /ˈledʒənd/ ●●○ *n*
1 [C,U] an old well-known story, often about brave people, adventures, or magical events → **myth**: *a book of ancient Greek legends* | **[+of]** *the legend of St George and the dragon* | **according to legend** *According to legend, he escaped by leaping from the cliffs into the sea.* | *Local **legend has it that*** (=says that) *the island was the original Garden of Eden.* THESAURUS STORY
2 [C] someone who is famous and admired for being extremely good at doing something: **tennis/footballing/music etc legend** *We must put more money into the sport if we want to create the tennis legends of the future.* | *a marvellous player who was **a legend in** his **own lifetime*** THESAURUS STAR → **living legend** at LIVING¹(6)
3 be a legend *BrE informal* to be a person that you admire a lot – used especially by young people: *My stepfather is an absolute legend.*
4 [C] *literary* words that have been written somewhere, for example on a sign: *A sign above the door bore the legend 'Patience is a Virtue'.*
5 [C] *technical* the words that explain a picture or map → **key**

le·gen·da·ry /ˈledʒəndəri $ -deri/ ●●○ *adj*
1 very famous and admired: *Lonnie Johnson, the legendary blues guitarist* | *Her singing was legendary.* THESAURUS FAMOUS
2 [only before noun] talked about in a legend → **mythical**: *The cave is the home of a legendary giant.*

le·ger·de·main /ˌledʒədəˈmeɪn $ -dʒər-/ *n* [U] *formal* when you deceive people cleverly: *economic legerdemain*

leg·gings /ˈleɡɪŋz/ *n* [plural] **1** tight trousers for women, which stretch to fit the shape of your body **2** a pair of trousers that you wear over other clothes to protect your legs

leg·gy /ˈleɡi/ *adj* **1** a woman or child who is leggy has long legs: *a leggy blonde* **2** a leggy plant has grown too tall very quickly and its stem cannot support its weight very well

le·gi·ble /ˈledʒəbəl/ *adj* written or printed clearly enough for you to read OPP **illegible**: *Her handwriting was so tiny it was barely legible.* —**legibly** *adv* —**legibility** /ˌledʒəˈbɪləti/ *n* [U]

le·gion¹ /ˈliːdʒən/ *n* [C] **1** a large group of soldiers, especially in ancient Rome **2** *literary* a large number of people

legion² *adj* [not before noun] *literary* very many SYN **numerous**: *The stories of her adventures were legion.*

le·gion·a·ry /ˈliːdʒənəri $ -neri/ *n* (*plural* **legionaries**) [C] a member of a legion

le·gion·naire /ˌliːdʒəˈneə $ -ˈner/ *n* [C] a member of a legion, especially the French Foreign Legion

ˌlegionˈnaires' disˌease *n* [U] a serious disease that affects your lungs

ˈleg irons *n* [plural] metal chains that are put around a prisoner's legs → **manacle**

le·gis·late /ˈledʒəsleɪt/ AWL *v* [I] **1** to make a law about something: **[+on]** *Only Parliament has the power to legislate on constitutional matters.* | **[+for/against]** *The government has promised to legislate against discrimination.* | *We must legislate for equal pay.* | **legislate to do sth** *We must legislate to control these drugs.* **2 legislate for sth** to think about how something may affect what you are doing, and do something to prepare for it: *You can't legislate for bad luck.*

le·gis·la·tion /ˌledʒəˈsleɪʃən/ ●●○ W3 *n* [U] a law or set of laws: *This is a very important **piece of legislation*** (=law). | **[+on]** *the legislation on abortion* | **legislation to do sth** *new legislation to protect children* | **introduce/bring in legislation** *The government has promised to bring in new legislation to combat this problem.* | **under new/existing/current etc legislation** *Both individuals and companies can be prosecuted under the new legislation.*

L

Formality in spoken and written English

What does it mean to 'know' a word? The basic meaning is obviously important, but you also need to know how it is spelt, how it is pronounced, how it behaves grammatically in a sentence, and how it is used with other words (its collocations). You also need to know the types of context and situations in which the word can be used appropriately.

Many words and phrases have similar meanings; they are, on the surface, synonymous. However, not all synonyms are appropriate for use in different contexts. Throughout this dictionary, we have included a number of Register notes to highlight the differences between synonymous words or phrases that are more typical of spoken or written English, or of formal or informal contexts. Look, for example, at the entry for **proceed**. There you will find a note that explains that *proceed* is typical of formal contexts, and in informal contexts, a native speaker is more likely to say *go ahead*. Look out for these notes to ensure that you choose the most appropriate vocabulary for spoken and written contexts.

Thesaurus notes also highlight differences between closely related synonyms. Look, for example, at the Thesaurus box at **allow**. There you will find that *let* is used much more in everyday English than *allow*, while *permit* is used especially in more formal contexts, for example in written notices and announcements.

The following pages focus on functional language – language that you use to do something, such as agreeing with someone or asking someone to do something for you – contrasting synonymous words and phrases to explain which ones are more appropriate for formal written contexts and which are more suited to informal spoken contexts.

Contents

Agreeing

in everyday English

you're right/that's right etc
used when you agree with what someone says:
'It's too far to walk.' 'You're right. Let's get a taxi.' | *'This food was grown without any artificial fertilizers.' 'That's right, it's completely organic.'* | *He is right when he says that the world economy is facing its most serious challenge in half a century.*

I agree
this sounds a little more serious and more formal than saying **you're right**:
'All this packaging is unnecessary. It's bad for the environment.' 'I agree.' | *I agree that there is no such thing as a bad dog, only a bad owner.* | *I agree with Professor Murphy's analysis of the situation.*

⚠ Don't say 'agree someone's opinion' or 'agree to someone's opinion'. Say **agree with** someone's opinion.

I know
used in spoken English when you have the same feeling or have had the same experience as someone:
'It's really hot today.' 'I know – I wish I hadn't worn my sweater.'

⚠ This phrase is very commonly used in everyday conversation, when sympathizing and agreeing with the other person.

in formal English

share sb's view/concern/fear etc
to have the same opinion, concern, fear etc as someone else:
I share her concerns about the lack of women in high academic positions. | *There are many people who would share this view.*

be of the same opinion/view
to agree with someone:
Oppenheimer and many of the world's leading scientists were of the same view. | *Are we all of the same opinion* (=said in a formal meeting)?

⚠ This phrase is used especially when saying that a group of people agree about something.

subscribe to a view/theory etc
to agree with an opinion, idea etc and believe that it is right:
Some people think that we should abandon farm subsidies, but I, for one, do not subscribe to this view. | *Today, the majority of scientists subscribe to the so-called 'big bang' theory of the origins of the universe.*

concur with sb/sth
to agree with someone. This is a very formal use.
I concur with the previous speaker on both points. | *There are many educators who would concur with her opinion.*

sb makes a good/valid point
used in formal situations when you agree with a particular thing that someone has said:
The author makes a good point when he argues that we should look at the wider social causes of crime.

sb's point is well made
used when you think that someone has clearly shown that they are right, and that what they say is

important, especially when you want to add something else as well:
Weber's point is well made, but is obviously not the whole story.

⚠ This phrase is used especially in formal arguments and discussions.

it is generally/widely accepted that *also* **there is a widely held view/belief that**
used when saying that most people agree that something is true:
It is now generally accepted among scientists that global warming is occurring as a result of human activities.

strongly agreeing

I totally agree!/I couldn't agree more!/My feelings exactly!
used in spoken English when you completely agree with someone:
'He's such a nice man.' 'I couldn't agree more!' | 'What a waste of time!' 'My feelings exactly!'

I agree entirely/wholeheartedly *also* **I am entirely in agreement with sb**
used in more formal English when you completely agree with someone:
I agree entirely with the Chief Judge's conclusion. | I wholeheartedly agree with the previous writer regarding this company. | He found himself entirely in agreement with Churchill.

Absolutely!/Definitely!/Exactly!
used in spoken English when answering someone quickly and saying that you completely agree:
'I think gas prices are much too high.' 'Absolutely!' | 'We should ask them for more money.' 'Definitely!'

Totally! *AmE informal*
used in spoken English when answering someone quickly and saying that you completely agree:
'The guy is an idiot!' 'Totally!'

You're telling me! *informal*
used in spoken English, especially when you have had the same experience:
'The trains are so unreliable these days.' 'You're telling me – mine was half an hour late this morning.'

partly agreeing

I agree up to a point/to some extent
used when you partly agree with someone:
'The economic situation doesn't look too good at the moment.' 'I agree with you up to a point, but I don't think it's nearly as bad as people are saying.' | I agree to some extent with this statement.

I have some sympathy with sb/sth
used when saying that you understand the reasons why someone thinks something, although you do not necessarily agree with them completely:
I have some sympathy with the argument that the monarchy seems out of place in our modern world.

there is some/a lot of truth in sth
used when you think that some or a lot of what someone says is right:
Although these warnings may sound very dramatic, there is some truth in them. | His ideas about love are a bit strange, but there's a lot of truth in what he says.

I suppose so/I guess so
used in spoken English when you have some doubts about something that someone has said:
'I think it's an excellent idea.' 'I suppose so, but we don't know how much it will all cost.'

Disagreeing

in everyday English

I don't agree/I disagree
used when you do not agree with someone or something:
'I think art should be about creating beautiful objects.' 'I don't agree. That's a very old-fashioned way of looking at art.' | I disagree with the idea that boys and girls should attend separate schools.

no it isn't/no she doesn't etc
used when saying that something is not true, in a very direct way:
'The hotel's right next to the airport.' 'No it isn't! It's miles away!' | 'You get much more money than I do.' 'No I don't! Whatever gave you that idea?'

that's not true/that is not the case
used when saying that something is not true, in a very direct way:
'You were on the phone for hours.' 'That's not true – it was only about 10 minutes!' | Although some people have tried to suggest that global warming is a myth, unfortunately that is not the case.

in formal English

I/sb would dispute sth
used when saying that you disagree with something:
I would dispute the idea that violent images on television cause people to commit acts of violence. | He is regarded as the US's finest ever golfer, although there are those who would dispute that.

I/sb would take issue with sb/sth
used when saying that you disagree with someone or something:
I would take issue with some of the report's findings. | There are many people who would take issue with him on this.

I (would) beg to differ
used when saying that you have a different opinion about something, especially in formal discussions:
That's your opinion. I beg to differ. I think the situation is far more complicated than you suggest. | It has been said that rising oil prices will not really affect economic growth. Well, I would beg to differ on this.

I don't/can't accept sth
used when saying firmly that you do not believe that something is true:
You're implying that he was being deliberately dishonest, and I really can't accept that. | I'm sorry, but I just do not accept that argument. | I simply cannot accept that it is justified to use torture.

⚠ When disagreeing, people sometimes begin by saying **I'm afraid** or **I'm sorry**. This is not an apology, but a way of making their disagreement sound more polite: *I'm afraid I don't agree with you. | I'm sorry but that really isn't the case.*

politely disagreeing

I'm not so sure/Are you sure?
used when expressing doubt about what someone has just said:
'I think the government's doing a good job.' 'I'm not so sure – look what's happened to the economy.' | 'The next meeting's on July 26th.' 'Are you sure? I thought it was on the 25th.'

⚠ Expressing doubt or uncertainty is a much more polite way of disagreeing than saying directly that you think the other person is wrong.

I wouldn't say that
used when disagreeing with someone in a polite way, especially when you think someone is exaggerating:
'She's much better looking than I am.' 'I wouldn't say that!' | 'It will cost a fortune to get another one.' 'I wouldn't say that!'

I take/see your point, but .../you may have a point, but ...
used when saying that something else is more important:
'I think that people who carry knives should be severely punished.' 'I take your point, but what if they feel that they have to carry them for their own protection?'

Yes, but .../I know, but ...
used when adding a different opinion instead of directly disagreeing:
'I think we should go by plane – it's much quicker.' 'Yes, but it's also more expensive.' | 'He's always taking time off work.' 'I know, but there are reasons for that.'

sb is mistaken
used when saying that you think that someone has the wrong idea about something, without saying directly that they are 'wrong':
He is mistaken if he believes that the United States can win the war on terror by military means. | I think you're mistaken about her. She's just doing her job.

sb is entitled to their opinion/everyone is entitled to their opinion
used when saying politely that you think that someone is wrong, especially when you think most people would disagree with them:
Everyone is entitled to their opinion, but the facts just don't support what you're saying. | Of course he's entitled to his opinion, but I think he is in a minority on this issue.

with all (due) respect/with the greatest of respect
used when you are about to disagree with someone in a polite way in a formal discussion:
With all due respect to Mr Jessell, I doubt whether Einstein's theories are relevant to this question. | With the greatest of respect, I disagree with your analysis.

strongly disagreeing

I completely/totally disagree *also* **I don't agree at all**
used when disagreeing strongly with someone or something:
I completely disagree with Professor Leigh's comments. | 'It's one of her best books!' 'I don't agree at all. I thought it was very dull.'

How can you say that?/I can't believe that you've just said that
used when you are very surprised by what someone has just said, especially when you think they are completely wrong:
'I think they should all be taken out and shot.' 'I can't believe you've just said that!'

Don't be ridiculous!/You've got to be kidding!/Rubbish! *BrE*/**No way!** *AmE*
used in informal spoken English when disagreeing with someone very strongly, and saying that you think they are completely wrong:
'I'm too tired to do the washing up!' 'Rubbish! You haven't done anything all day!' | 'I think she likes you.' 'Don't be ridiculous!' | 'He's the best player they've ever had.' 'No way! Johnson was.'

Apologizing

in everyday English

sorry/I'm sorry
the usual word to use when apologizing to someone:
Sorry I'm late – the traffic was really bad. | *I'm really sorry about all the things I said.* | *We're deeply sorry* (=very sorry) *for what happened.* | *Sorry to bother you – can I ask you about something?*

> ⚠ When saying that you are very sorry, you often say that you are **so sorry**: *I'm so sorry about the delay.* | *We're so sorry we couldn't be at the meeting.*

excuse me/pardon me
used when you have accidentally touched or pushed someone, or made a noise such as sneezing or yawning. Also used when interrupting someone, when you want someone to repeat something, or when you have made a small embarrassing mistake:
Excuse me! I didn't mean to stand on your foot. | *He yawned and said 'Pardon me! It's been a long day!'* | *Excuse me – may we come in?* | *Pardon me, I didn't catch your name.* | *Excuse me, I meant to say 50, not 15.*

> ⚠ **Excuse me** and **pardon me** are more common in American English than in British English. When British people accidentally touch or push someone, or make a small embarrassing mistake, they usually say **sorry**.

I beg your pardon
used when you have made a small mistake. Also used when you have not heard what someone said, and you want them to repeat it:
'That's my chair.' 'Oh, I do beg your pardon.' | *'Her name is Fumie.' 'I beg your pardon?' 'F-U-M-I-E.'*

> ⚠ **I beg your pardon** sounds a little more formal than **I'm sorry** or **excuse me**.

forgive me
used when saying that you feel sorry about something, especially when you have said or done something that might upset, annoy, or offend someone:
Forgive me. I didn't mean to hurt your feelings. | *Forgive me for saying this, but you don't look very well.*

> ⚠ **Forgive me** sounds very polite.

I owe you an apology
used when you have done something that you later find out to be wrong or unfair – a slightly formal expression:
I owe you an apology for not believing you. | *I think you owe him some kind of apology – you shouldn't have spoken to him in the way that you did.*

I feel bad/terrible/awful about sth
used when telling someone that you regret something and feel sorry about it:
I feel terrible now about what I said. | *I feel bad that I lied to my parents.*

in formal English

I apologize/we would like to apologize
used when apologizing in a formal way when you have done something that you regret, for example when you have offended someone. Also used in formal announcements, notices, and letters from companies and organizations:
I apologize for my behaviour yesterday. | *The airline would like to apologize for any inconvenience caused by the cancellation of the flight.* | *Do you find that suggestion offensive? If so, I apologize.*

⚠ You **apologize to** someone **for** something you have done.

please accept my/our apologies for sth
used when apologizing for something, especially in formal written English:
Please accept our apologies for the delay in responding to your email. | *First of all, please accept my apologies for any confusion about the dates of the conference.*

I/we regret sth
used when telling someone about something that you apologize for, or that the other person may feel disappointed about, especially in formal written English:
I regret that I will be unable to join you at the meeting. | *We regret that on this occasion your application has been unsuccessful.* | *The 'Evening Post' has since removed the story from its website, and we regret the error.*

replying to an apology

don't worry/that's OK/that's all right
used when accepting someone's apology in everyday spoken English:
'Sorry, I didn't realize that you were having dinner.' 'That's perfectly OK – do join us.' | *'I feel really bad about all the mess.' 'Don't worry. I can always clear it up later.'*

it doesn't matter/it's not a problem/no problem *also* **no worries** *BrE informal*
used when telling someone that something is not important:
'Sorry we're late.' 'It doesn't matter – we've only just started.' | *'I've forgotten to bring any money with me – I'm really sorry.' 'It's not a problem. I can lend you some.'*

it's no big deal/it's not the end of the world/these things happen
used when telling someone that something is not serious and they should not feel worried about it:
'I'm so sorry about the vase.' 'It's not the end of the world – we can always get another one.' | *'I wish we hadn't argued.' 'That's all right. These things happen.'*

forget it
used when accepting someone's apology and quickly telling them not to worry, in a friendly way. Also used when you still feel annoyed and do not want to talk to the other person, or accept their apology:
'Sorry I was so angry with you the other day.' 'Forget it – you had every right to be annoyed.' | *'Sorry if I made you look stupid.' 'Just forget it, will you!'*

apology accepted
used when accepting someone's apology. This phrase sounds rather formal and not very friendly, and is often used when you still feel a little annoyed:
'I'm sorry I'm late for class.' 'Apology accepted – but make sure that it doesn't happen again.'

Opinions

in everyday English

I think (that)
this is the usual way of talking about your opinions in everyday English:
I think that the law should be changed. | *We always thought he was so cool.* | *Do you think that people should be able to work as many hours as they like?*

⚠ Don't use this phrase in essays and formal writing. See next page for written alternatives.

I believe (that)
used when talking about strongly held beliefs, especially about moral issues:
I believe that the death penalty should be abolished. | *I believe it is wrong to kill animals.* | *We firmly believe that the value of life is not measured by wealth.*

⚠ **I believe (that)** sounds rather serious, and is used about things that you believe in very strongly.

I feel (that)
used when talking about your opinions, especially when they are based on your general feelings:
I feel he is too old for the job. | *I feel that appearances are very important.* | *I can't help feeling that our main priority should be dealing with climate change.*

personally/as far as I'm concerned
used when you want to emphasize your own personal opinion:
Personally, I don't care how much it costs. | *As far as I'm concerned, they should stop complaining and get on with their work.* | *He can say what he likes, as far as I'm concerned.*

it seems to me (that) *also* **the way I see it** *spoken*/**if you ask me** *spoken*
used when giving your opinion about something, especially when there is a lot that you want to say about a situation:
It seems to me that the world would be a much better place if we didn't rely so much on our cars. |
The way I see it, there are only two real choices. | *If you ask me, they should give kids fewer tests, not more.*

⚠ Using these phrases will give you time to think about what you want to say. In addition, it is a good idea to vary your language and use them instead of always saying 'I think that ...'

in my opinion/view
used when talking about your opinions, especially about serious subjects:
In my opinion, he's mistaken. | *It is, in my view, one of the finest buildings in London.* | *Learning Chinese characters is, in my opinion, the most time-consuming and difficult part of the language.*

⚠ Don't use **in my opinion** in formal essay writing. See next page for written alternatives.
⚠ Don't say 'according to my opinion'. **Say in my opinion/in my view.**

speaking as
used when introducing your opinion by mentioning something important about yourself, which makes you able to talk about it from personal experience, or affects your feelings about it:
Speaking as a regular user of the railway, I can only say that the service has gone down in recent months. |
Speaking as a mother of two young children, I feel really concerned about the future of our planet.

in formal written English

> ⚠ In formal written English, you usually avoid using phrases that begin with 'I', and 'in my opinion' when writing about your opinions. In essays, it is often better to quote other people's opinions to support your argument, rather than saying 'I think that ...' This will give your argument more authority.

in this writer's view/opinion *also* **it is this writer's view/opinion that**
used in formal writing instead of **in my opinion**:
This is the most important section of the book, in this writer's opinion. | It is this writer's view that the new city centre is a great improvement on the old one.

---

as sb points out/notes/remarks
used when referring to another writer's opinions, and what they have said:
As Lowry points out in her article, teaching does not have the same status as research. | As Dawkins notes in his discussion of the evolution of the eye, 'eyes have evolved between 40 and 60 times, in many different invertebrate groups.'

---

express the view/opinion that
used when referring to another writer's opinions, and what they have said:
Freud himself expressed the view that some dreams may be forgotten because they are too upsetting. | Thomas Jefferson expressed the opinion that for a state to be healthy, it needed to have a revolution every 20 years.

---

according to sb
used when saying what other people, organizations, reports etc have said:
According to the researchers, 'some patients tended to see their illness as a punishment'. | Locally grown food can be better for the environment than organic food, according to a report published yesterday.

> ⚠ Don't say 'according to me' or 'according to my opinion'. You can only use **according to** when saying what other people, reports etc have said.

---

be of the opinion that/take the view that
used when saying what someone's opinion is:
Six out of ten EU citizens were of the opinion that the European Union should have a single currency. | The Court took the view that he had acted legally.

---

it is sb's belief that
used when saying what someone believes to be true:
It is our belief that children should enjoy their time at school. | It was their belief that certain individuals were born with criminal tendencies.

---

for sb
used when saying what someone's opinion is, especially when this is a general opinion that affects their other ideas about a subject:
For Dawkins, genes are everything, or at least they can account for everything. | For Ruskin, art was something that could not be produced using machines.

---

from sb's point of view/standpoint
used when saying how someone's situation affects their opinion:
From the farmers' point of view, it is better to have too much rain than none at all. | From a business standpoint, it made perfect sense to combine the two operations together.

Requests

asking someone to do something in everyday English

can you
this is the usual way of asking someone to do something:
Can you open the window? | Can you tell him I'll call him later?

will you
this sounds rather direct and is used especially when telling someone you know well to do simple things for you:
Please will you pass the salt? | Will you get me another drink from the fridge?

could you/would you/do you think you could
these phrases sound more polite than **can you** or **will you**. You use them especially when talking to people you do not know well, or when asking someone to do something difficult or important:
Could you put this case up on the rack for me? | Do you think you could give her a message?

would you mind/I wonder if you would mind
these phrases sound more polite than **could you**. You use them especially when talking to people you do not know well:
Would you mind closing the door? | I wonder if you would mind coming into my office for a minute?

⚠ If someone asks you **Would you mind doing sth?**, you can say **(No) of course not** if you agree to do what they ask. For example: *'Would you mind looking after the children for me?' 'Of course not. That would be fine.'*
If you don't want to do what someone asks, you usually say **I'm afraid/I'm sorry** and then give a reason. For example: *'Would you mind looking after the children for me?' 'I'm afraid I've arranged to go out this evening.'*

could you possibly/is there any way you could
used when asking someone to do something that is likely to be difficult or inconvenient for them, when you think the answer could easily be 'no':
Is there any way you could change the date of the meeting? | Do you think you could possibly lend me some money until next Friday?

more formal ways of asking someone to do something

I was wondering if you could/would it be possible for you to
used when asking someone to do something in a very formal and polite way, especially when you are not sure that they will be able to do what you ask:
I was wondering if you could help me? I'm trying to find the principal's office. | Would it be possible for you to come in for an interview some time next week?

I would be grateful if you could/I would appreciate it if you could
used in formal letters and in other official contexts:
I would be grateful if you could send me an application form. | I would appreciate it if you could answer a few questions for me, Mrs Atkins.

would you be so kind as to
an extremely polite phrase, used when speaking very carefully to someone you have never met before:
Would you be so kind as to fill out this form? | Would you be so kind as to excuse me for a moment (=used when telling someone that you need to leave them for a few minutes)?

we request that .../you are requested not to do sth
used in official requests and instructions, especially on notices and in announcements:
We request that you turn off your cell phone while you are in the building. | Library users are kindly requested not to bring in food or drink.

asking for permission in everyday English

can I
this is the usual way of asking for permission to do something:
Can I come with you? | Can I watch the news? | Can we go now?

is it all right if I/is it OK if I
these are other ways of asking for permission to do something which are also commonly used in everyday English:
Is it all right if I open the window? | Is it OK if I take some time off work?

may I/could I/do you think I could
these phrases sound more polite than **can I**. You use them especially when talking to people that you do not know well:
May I come in? | Could I use your phone? | Do you think we could take a five minute break?

do/would you mind if I
these phrases sound more polite than **can I**. You use them especially when talking to people that you do not know well:
Do you mind if I call you Chris? | Would you mind if I took your picture?

⚠ If someone asks you **do/would you mind if I?**, you can say **(No) of course not** when giving them permission. For example: *'Would you mind if I asked you a question?' 'Of course not. Go ahead!'* If you don't want to give permission, you usually say **I'm afraid** or **I'm sorry but** and then give a reason. For example: *'Do you mind if I stay a few more minutes?' 'I'm sorry but I have another appointment.'*

more formal ways of asking for permission

I was wondering if I could/I was wondering if it might be possible for me to
used when asking someone for permission in a very formal and polite way. Used in spoken English, and also in formal letters:
I was wondering if I could have a few more days to finish my assignment. | I was wondering if it might be possible for me to come and look around the department.

would it bother you if I
used when asking permission to do something in a very polite way, when you want to be careful not to cause problems for someone:
Would it bother you if I put you on our mailing list?

⚠ If someone asks you **would it bother you if I ... ?** and you say **yes**, it means that you do not want them to do it. If you say **no**, that means that you are happy for them to do it.

with your permission, I'd like to
used when checking with someone if you can do something, especially in official contexts:
With your permission, I'd like to forward your email to our accounts department.

Suggestions

in everyday English

why don't you/we
this is the usual way of making a suggestion in spoken English:
Why don't you talk to her about it? | *Why don't we go out for a meal some time?*

let's
used when suggesting that you should do something together soon:
Let's meet in front of Shibuya station. | *Let's see what's in the movie guide.*

if I were you, I would *or* **I'd**
used when suggesting what you think is the best thing for someone to do, based on your personal experience and knowledge:
If I were you, I would be very careful about giving your address on any public websites. | *If I were you, I'd take it easy for the next few days.*

how about/what about
used when someone has asked you to suggest a time, place, idea etc:
'When's a good day for you?' 'How about Monday?' | *'Where do you think we should go?' 'What about Barcelona? It's supposed to be very beautiful.'*

what do you think about
used when suggesting something, and asking someone what they think about it:
What do you think about a holiday in Greece? | *What do you think about a party at my place on Saturday?*

you could always/we could always/there's always
used when suggesting ideas to someone, when they are not sure about what to do:
You could always ask someone to record the programme for you. | *We could always go for a walk.* | *There's always the pub on the corner.*

less direct ways of making suggestions

what if/suppose
used when suggesting something as a possible idea:
'What if we painted the room yellow?' 'That sounds a bit too bright to me.' | *Suppose you asked the same question in a different way?*

⚠ People often make suggestions in a less direct way by using **maybe** or **perhaps**, or by using **may/might**. See the examples below.

maybe we could/perhaps you could
used when making a suggestion in a less direct way:
Maybe we could ask people if they'd be interested in having a concert? | *Perhaps you could change the settings on your computer?*

you might like to/you may want to
used when suggesting what someone should do in a less direct way:
You might like to ask them for their advice. | *You might like to try giving your lawyer a call.* | *If you're thinking of buying a holiday home in the sun, you might like to consider Croatia.*

Hello

in spoken English

hi
used as a friendly greeting when you meet someone, or start a telephone conversation with someone:
Hi, everybody. Welcome to our new home! | Hi, Gwen – did you have a nice weekend?

hello
used when you meet someone, or when you start a telephone conversation with someone:
Hello. Could I speak to someone in customer service, please? | Hello, Mrs Jones. How are you?

⚠ In everyday English, most people usually say **hi** because it sounds more friendly. **Hello** is used especially when talking to people you do not know well.

hey *informal especially AmE*
used as a friendly greeting when you see someone you know well and you want to start talking to them:
Hey, Scott! Good to see you!

good morning/afternoon/evening
used when meeting someone at a particular time of day:
Morning everyone. Sorry I'm late. | Good morning, class! | Good afternoon, Mr Smith.

⚠ **Good morning** etc sounds rather formal. In everyday English, people usually just say **Morning!** etc, without saying 'good'.

How are you?
used when you are greeting someone, especially when starting a conversation with them:
'Hi Helen. How are you?' 'I'm fine. And you?'

How are you doing?/How's it going?/How are things? *informal*
used when you are greeting someone, especially when starting a conversation with them:
'Hi, Helen. How are you doing?' 'I'm good, thanks. How about you?' | How's it going, Tom? I haven't seen you for a long time!

What's up?/What's happening? *informal*
used when you are greeting someone, especially when starting a conversation with them:
Hey Joey. What's up, buddy? | Hi, Ray. What's happening? How are they treating you these days?

⚠ These phrases sound very informal.

How do you do? *formal*
used when you meet someone for the first time, especially after you have just been told their name:
'John, I'd like you to meet our new project manager, Nisha Patel.' 'How do you do?'

⚠ **How do you do** sounds very formal. These days people often just say **hi** when meeting someone for the first time.

pleased/good/nice to meet you
used when you meet someone for the first time and have just been told their name:
'Richard, this is my brother Ronnie.' 'Nice to meet you, Ronnie.' | 'My name is Lena Curtis.' 'Pleased to meet you. I'm David Bennet.'

Goodbye

in spoken English

bye/goodbye
used when you are leaving or when someone is leaving you:
'Bye, Annie.' 'Bye, Mom.' | *'Goodbye, Mrs Moore.' 'Goodbye, Dr Aziz.'* | *Thank you for calling. Goodbye.* | *Bye for now* (used especially on the phone when you will speak to someone again soon). *Call me if you need anything.*

> ⚠ **Goodbye** sounds rather formal and is used especially when talking to people you do not know well. In everyday English, people usually just say **bye**.

night/good night
used when leaving someone in the evening, or before they go to bed:
Night everyone. | *Good night. Sleep well.*

> ⚠ **Good night** sounds rather formal, especially in British English. In everyday English, people usually just say **night**.

bye bye/night night
used especially when talking to children:
'Say bye bye to Daddy!' 'Bye bye!'

see you
used when saying goodbye to a friend who you will see again soon:
'See you, Darren.' 'See you on Monday!' | *'I'm going now.' 'Okay. See you tomorrow.'* | *Safe trip back guys, and we'll see you soon.* | *See you later, Michelle.*

later/catch you later *informal*
used when saying goodbye to a friend who you will see or talk to them again soon:
'Later, John.' 'Later, Steve.' | *'See you, Keith.' 'Catch you later!'*

> ⚠ **Later** sounds very informal and is used especially by young people.

see you around *informal*
used when saying goodbye to someone, when you are not sure when you will see them again:
He spent the holiday with me and then just said 'See you around' and left.

so long *AmE informal*
used when saying goodbye to someone, when you will not see them again very soon:
'So long,' he said. 'Don't forget to write.' | *She grabbed him by the shoulders and hugged him affectionately. 'So long, Nick.'*

have a good weekend/a great trip/a nice time etc
used when saying goodbye to someone to wish them a good weekend, an enjoyable trip etc:
Have a nice weekend. | *Have a great time at the concert, guys!*

have a good one *informal especially AmE*
used when saying goodbye to someone in a friendly informal way:
I'll talk to you later. Have a good one!

> ⚠ The 'one' in **have a good one** does not really mean anything. It is just part of the phrase.

have a nice day
used especially by people working in shops when saying goodbye to customers:
Here's your change. Have a nice day.

take care *also* **look after yourself** *BrE*
used when saying goodbye to someone, especially someone you like, to show that you care about them:
'Bye love! Take care.' 'You too! Bye!'

cheerio *BrE*
goodbye:
'Right ... we're going now. Cheerio then!' 'Bye!'

⚠ **Cheerio** sounds rather old-fashioned and is used especially by older people.

in emails and informal letters

all the best/best
used at the end of informal emails:
Hope to see you soon. All the best, Joanne

⚠ You usually end informal emails with your first name. You can also end with the first letter of your first name, for example *All the best, J.* If you have just exchanged several emails with someone, you can leave out your name at the end, because it is understood.

regards/best wishes
used at the end of emails to people you often write to, or people you work with, especially people who are not close friends. **Regards** sounds a little formal:
Speak to you soon. Regards, David. | *Thanks for all your hard work. Best wishes, Michael*

love/love from *informal*
used at the end of emails to close friends and family:
Take care. Love, Katie | *Look forward to seeing you. Love from Mum*

in formal letters and emails

yours sincerely *BrE*/**sincerely** *AmE*/**yours truly** *AmE*
used at the end of formal letters and emails:
We will contact you directly, as soon as your order is ready. Yours sincerely, Paula Jordan (Ms), Customer Sales Manager | *Thank you for your interest in our products. Yours truly, Stephen Merill*

⚠ In British English, **yours sincerely** is used only if you have used the person's name at the start of the letter or email. In American English, **sincerely** and **yours truly** can be used to end any formal letter or email.

yours faithfully *BrE*/**sincerely** *AmE*/**yours truly** *AmE*
used at the end of formal letters and emails:
I await your reply. Yours faithfully, Lisa Johnson (Mrs)

⚠ In British English, **yours faithfully** is used when you do not know the name of the person you are writing to. In American English, **sincerely** and **yours truly** can be used to end any formal letter or email.

Thank you

in everyday English

thank you

Thank you for all your help. | I'm writing to say thank you on behalf of everyone at Rockford Productions Inc. for your support and encouragement during the past year. | I just wanted to send a big thank-you from all of us for making last weekend so enjoyable.

⚠ Be careful about spelling. **Thank you** is usually spelt as two words, but the noun **thank-you** is spelt with a hyphen.
⚠ Don't say 'I thank you'. Just say **thank you**, or **I just wanted to say thank you**.

thanks

in everyday spoken English, people usually say **thanks** rather than **thank you**:
Thanks again for a lovely evening. | Many thanks for all your hard work. | You did a great job. Thanks a lot!

I can't thank you enough

used when you are very pleased because someone has been very helpful or generous:
I can't thank you enough for everything you did on my wedding day!

it is good/nice/kind of you *also* **that's kind of you**

used when thanking someone for doing or saying something:
It was good of you to come all this way. | It's nice of you to say those things. | 'I've brought you some more coffee.' 'That's very kind of you.'

in more formal English

I appreciate

used when thanking someone, especially when they have been very helpful to you:
I really appreciate all your comments and suggestions. | We appreciate everything you've done for us.

I am most grateful/deeply grateful

used when thanking someone in a formal way:
I am deeply grateful to my colleague, Helen Jones, for her guidance and encouragement. | We are most grateful to all those who have lent works to the exhibition.

I would like to express my appreciation/gratitude

used when thanking someone in a very formal way, especially in a formal speech:
I would like to express my appreciation to the French government for hosting this meeting and for their kind hospitality.

replying when someone says thank you

don't mention it/you're welcome/my pleasure

used when replying to someone who has just thanked you:
'Thanks for letting us use your office.' 'Don't mention it!' | 'Thank you for all your advice.' 'You're welcome!' | 'Thank you for showing us around the college.' 'My pleasure.'

anytime/no problem/that's all right

these sound more informal than **don't mention it etc** and are very common in everyday spoken English:
'You've been really helpful!' 'Anytime!' | 'Thanks for showing me around the city.' 'That's all right!'

Contents

1 Adjectives

1.1 Position of adjectives in a sentence

Most adjectives go in two main places in a sentence: before a noun or after linking verbs like ***be***, ***look***, ***feel***, ***seem*** etc.

When you use an adjective before a noun, the adjective is in the **attributive** position.

*We had a **delicious** meal.* | *She gave a **wonderful** speech.*

When you use an adjective after the verb ***be*** or a linking verb (e.g. ***look***, ***feel***, ***taste***, ***seem***), the adjective is in the predicative position.

*Her speech was **wonderful**.* | *The meal tasted **delicious**.*

Some adjectives are only attributive - you can only use them before nouns.

*her **late** husband* | *an **atomic** bomb* | *the **entire** evening* | *an **indoor** swimming pool*

Some adjectives are only predicative - you can only use them after verbs.

*The baby is **asleep**.* | *I'm **afraid**.* | *He felt very **ashamed**.*

Adjectives can also go after the object of a sentence, in the structure: verb + object + adjective.

*We've **painted the bedroom yellow**.* | *The news **made her sad**.* | *I'll **get the room ready** for our guests.*

Sometimes, adjectives with similar meanings behave in different ways grammatically:

- *Her husband is **sick**.*
- *She is looking after her **sick** husband.*

but:

- *Her husband **is ill**.*

✗ *She is looking after her ill husband.*

1.2 Order of adjectives

When you use more than one adjective before a noun to describe something, the adjectives are usually in this order:

Type of adjective	Examples
Opinion	*good, nice, beautiful, bad, interesting*
Size	*big, small, tiny, huge, long*
Other qualities	*hot, cold, well-behaved*
Age	*old, young, new*
Shape	*round, square*
Colour	*red, blue, black*
Origin	*English, American, African*
Material	*cotton, wool, gold*
Purpose/type	*electric, manual, tropical*

a wise old man | *tiny red spots* | *a cool cotton shirt* | *a young American singing star*

1.3 Using *and* with adjectives

When you use two or more adjectives in a predicative position, ***and*** is necessary before the last one.

The room was ***small and dirty****.*
She was ***tall, slim and beautiful****.*

When you use two or more adjectives in an attributive position, ***and*** is necessary:

- with colour adjectives;

  a ***blue and yellow*** *jersey* ✗ Don't say: *a blue yellow jersey*
- when the adjectives describe different parts of the same thing;

  a ***diamond and sapphire*** *ring* ✗ Don't say: *a diamond sapphire ring*
- when the adjectives describe similar aspects of something, to say that it belongs in two or more different classes;

  political and social *philosophy* ✗ Don't say: *political social philosophy*

1.4 Using *very* with adjectives

Do not use **very** with adjectives that already have **very** as part of their meaning.

hilarious = very funny	*delighted* = very pleased	
terrible = very bad	*great* = very good	
enormous = very big	*critical* = very important	
▪ *a very funny story*	▪ *a hilarious story*	✗ *a very hilarious story*
▪ *a very good idea*	▪ *a great idea*	✗ *a very great idea*

To emphasize these adjectives, you can use adverbs like ***really*** or ***absolutely***.

an ***absolutely hilarious*** *film | We were* ***really delighted*** *to hear your news. | The children think he's* ***absolutely amazing****.*

Some adjectives are ungradable because they describe something that is either true or it is not. Do not use **very** with these adjectives.

free (something either costs money or it does not)
impossible (something is either possible or it is not)
unconscious (someone is either conscious or they are not)
unique (something is either unique or it is not)
an impossible goal ✗ Don't say: *a very impossible goal*
a unique talent ✗ Don't say: *a very unique talent*

To emphasize these adjectives, you can use adverbs like ***absolutely***, ***completely*** or ***totally***.

It was clear that the man was ***completely unconscious****.*
We're trying to come up with something ***totally unique****.*
Tickets are ***absolutely free****.*

1.5 Using adjectives as nouns

You can use ***the*** + adjective to refer to a group of people. In this case, the adjective is used as a plural noun and is followed by a plural verb.

*She devoted her life to helping **the poor**.*
***The injured** are being airlifted to hospital.*

You often use this structure with adjectives of nationality.

***The French** are very proud of their cuisine.*
*Jade is prized by **the Chinese** as the most precious of gems.*

1.6 Adjectives with prepositions

Some adjectives have to be used with particular prepositions. Here are some examples.

angry with	*I am very **angry with** you!*
capable of	*A force 10 wind is **capable of** blowing the roofs off houses.*
engaged to	*Sue has been **engaged to** Tom for a year.*
interested in	*I've always been **interested in** modern art.*
keen on	*I'm not **keen on** skinny jeans.*
late for	*You'll be **late for** school.*

Sometimes adjectives with similar meanings are used with different prepositions.

*They were **ashamed of** their children's behaviour.*
*They were **embarrassed by** their children's behaviour.*

Some adjectives can be used with more than one preposition, with different meanings.

*Her parents are **concerned about** her progress at school.* (= worried about)
*The paper is **concerned with** the effects of computer games on development.* (= related to, about)
*Your mother was very **good to** me* (= kind to).
*Fish is **good for** you* (= healthy for).
*She's very **good at** painting* (= able to do it well).
*She felt **guilty about** lying to her husband* (= sorry for).
*He was found **guilty of** murder* (= responsible for).

ⓘ To find out which preposition to use with an adjective, look up the adjective in the dictionary.

1.7 Comparative and superlative of adjectives

-er/-est

Use -***er*** and -***est*** to form the comparative and superlative of one-syllable adjectives and some two-syllable adjectives.

*The cream claims to make your skin **softer**.*
*Mount Everest is the **highest** mountain in the world.*
*She's the **prettiest** girl in the class!*

more/most

Use **more** and **most** to form the comparative and superlative of adjectives with three or more syllables, and some two-syllable adjectives.

*How can I make my talk **more interesting**?*
*She's the **most beautiful** woman I've ever seen!*
*You should be **more careful** in the future.*
*He's the **most thoughtful** person I've ever met.*

-er/-est or more/most?

For two-syllable adjectives ending in **-y**, use **-er/-est**.

*heav**y** – heavi**er** – heavi**est***
*eas**y** – easi**er** – easi**est***
*happ**y** – happi**er** – happi**est***
*bus**y** – busi**er** – busi**est***

With some two-syllable adjectives, you can use both **-er/-est** and ***more/most***. In general, the ***more/most*** form is becoming more common with these adjectives.

clever – cleverer/more clever – cleverest/most clever

For adjectives ending in **-ed** and **-ing**, use **more/most**, not **-er/-est**.

*The film was even **more boring** than the book!*
*It was the **most tired** I had ever felt.*

For the adjectives ***real***, ***right*** and ***wrong***, use ***more/most***, not **-er/-est**.

*Sometimes, dreams feel **more real** than reality.*

Irregular forms

Some adjectives have irregular comparative and superlative forms.

Adjective	Comparative	Superlative
good	*better*	*best*
bad	*worse*	*worst*
ill	*worse*	–
far	*farther/further*	*farthest/furthest*
old	*older/elder*	*oldest/eldest*

*The situation is getting **worse**.*
*Sally is my **best** friend.*
*Victor was his **eldest** son.*

ⓘ If you are not sure how to form the **comparative** and **superlative** of an **adjective**, look up the **adjective** in the dictionary.

2 Adverbs

2.1 Adverbs of frequency

You use adverbs of frequency to describe how often something happens. Here are some common adverbs of frequency: ***always***, ***frequently***, ***never***, ***normally***, ***occasionally***, ***often***, ***rarely***, ***sometimes***, ***usually***.

Adverbs of frequency usually go before the verb in a sentence, after the subject.

*Some people **never listen**.*
*She **rarely goes out** these days.*

With the verb be, the adverb usually goes after the verb.

*Karen **was always** happy.*
*He **is often** late for work.*

With modal or auxiliary verbs, the order is: subject + modal/auxiliary verb + adverb + verb.

***I've never been** to Greece.*
*You **can sometimes see** the sea from here.*

Some adverbs of frequency can go at the beginning of a sentence.

***Sometimes** you can see the sea from here.*
***Usually**, I start work at eight.*

In formal written English, the adverbs ***never***, ***rarely*** and ***seldom*** can go at the beginning of a sentence, for emphasis. In this case, the word order changes to: adverb + auxiliary verb + subject + verb.

***Seldom had I experienced** such sadness.*
***Rarely do you see** talent like hers.*

Adverbs that refer to a definite frequency, for example ***monthly***, ***daily*** or ***weekly***, go after the verb.

*Most people get paid **monthly**.*

2.2 Adverbs of manner

You use adverbs of manner to describe how something happens. They usually go after the verb, or after the object, if there is one.

*He **works hard**.*
*She **smiled sweetly**.*
*She **speaks English well**.*
*He **finished his meal quickly**.*

Adverbs of manner ending in ***-ly*** can also go between the subject and verb, or at the beginning of a sentence, for emphasis.

***She slowly walked** across the room.*
***Slowly, she walked** across the room.*

2.3 Adverbs of place

Here are some common adverbs of place: ***here***, ***there***, ***home***, ***abroad***, ***inside***, ***upstairs***, ***around***. Adverbs of place usually go at the end of a sentence.

*I'll see you **there**.*
*Have you ever been **abroad**?*

They can also go at the beginning of the sentence, for emphasis.

***Here**, we do things a little differently.*

2.4 Adverbs of time

Here are some common adverbs of time: ***today***, ***tomorrow***, ***yesterday***, ***before***, ***soon***. Adverbs of time usually go at the end of a sentence.

I haven't seen Mick **today**.
We're leaving **tomorrow**.

They can also go at the beginning of the sentence, for emphasis.

Today, *we're staying at home.*
Soon, *things will be different.*

2.5 Adverbs of certainty

Adverbs of certainty show how confident the writer or speaker is about the truth of something. Here are some common adverbs of certainty: ***definitely***, ***probably***, ***certainly***, ***obviously***, ***clearly***, ***perhaps***, ***maybe***.

Adverbs of certainty usually go before the verb in a sentence, or after an auxiliary or modal verb.

He ***probably thinks*** *you are wrong.*
*They****'ll definitely win*** *on Saturday.*
She **is probably** *still at the shops.*
He **is definitely** *in favour of the idea.*

Perhaps and ***maybe*** usually go at the beginning of the sentence.

Maybe *she didn't get your message.*
Perhaps *he missed his bus.*

Some adverbs of certainty (e.g. ***clearly***, ***presumably***, ***apparently***) can behave as sentence adverbs – they relate to the whole of a sentence. They can express the speaker's attitude on what is being said or written. In this case, they usually go at the beginning or end of the sentence.

Clearly, *something has gone wrong.*
He's retired now, **presumably**.

2.6 Adverbs of degree

You use adverbs of degree to make adjectives and adverbs stronger or weaker. Here are some common adverbs of degree: ***fairly***, ***extremely***, ***absolutely***, ***utterly***, ***highly***, ***totally***, ***completely***, ***entirely***, ***really***, ***very***, ***quite***, ***rather***.

The information was **really** *helpful.*
She works **fairly** *quickly.*

You often use adverbs of degree with ungradable adjectives/adverbs, to refer to extreme qualities that we don't usually grade or compare.

Her performance was **absolutely amazing**.
Keith's plan worked **really brilliantly**!

3 Nouns

3.1 Countable and uncountable nouns

Countable nouns have a singular and plural form. You can use them with ***a/an*** and with numbers.

*There's **a man** here to see you.*
*I've just bought **two T-shirts**.*

Uncountable nouns do not have a plural form. You cannot use them with ***a/an*** and they are followed by a singular verb.

▪ *The book contains a lot of useful **information**.*
✗ *The book contains a lot of useful informations.*
▪ *The **information** in this book **is** very useful.*
✗ *The informations in this book are very useful.*

To refer to quantity with uncountable nouns, you can use a phrase with a countable noun + ***of***.

a piece of advice
an item of clothing
a sheet of paper
a bar of soap
a slice of cake
a cup of coffee
a packet of sugar
a tube of toothpaste
a litre of milk
a kilo of sugar
a gram of flour
a metre of cable

Some nouns can be countable or uncountable, but with a change in meaning.

*Do you like **coffee**?* (uncountable = the drink)
*I'll have **a coffee**, please.* (countable = a cup of the drink)
*She's very good at **painting**.* (uncountable = the activity)
*It's one of the artist's best **paintings**.* (countable = work of art)
*I need some writing **paper**.* (uncountable = the material)
*He's gone out to buy **a paper**.* (countable = newspaper)

ⓘ **Nouns** like these usually have more than one definition in the dictionary, one labelled **[U]** and the other labelled **[C]**.

Sometimes, you can use an uncountable noun as countable (usually in the plural form), to talk about a particular type of something.

*Fatty **foods** are bad for your health.*
*There are many different skin **creams**.*

ⓘ **Nouns** like these are labelled **[C,U]** in the dictionary.

3.2 Singular and plural nouns

Some nouns look like plural nouns because they end in **-s**, but they are, in fact, uncountable. You use a singular verb with these nouns.

Many of these are subjects that you can study (e.g. ***business studies***, ***electronics***, ***genetics***, ***home economics***, ***linguistics***).

__Physics__ is my favourite subject at school.

Others are types of physical activity (e.g. ***aerobics***, ***athletics***, ***gymnastics***).

I realized that __athletics__ was great fun.

There are also some names of diseases that are uncountable but end in **-s** (e.g. ***diabetes***, ***measles***, ***mumps***, ***rabies***, ***shingles***).

__Shingles__ is most common in older adults.

You can use some nouns with a singular or plural verb, depending on the meaning (e.g. ***acoustics***, ***economics***, ***logistics***, ***semantics***, ***statistics***).

- You use a singular verb when talking about the subject of study.

  __Economics is__ the study of how people choose to use resources. | *__Aerodynamics is__ a branch of dynamics.*

- You use a plural verb when talking about a particular feature or aspect of something.

  The __economics are__ simple (= the economic aspects, the way in which money influences something). | *The __aerodynamics__ of a racing car __are__ very important* (= the aerodynamic qualities).

Some nouns end in **-s** in both the singular and plural form (e.g. ***means***, ***series***, ***crossroads***, ***species***).

This __is__ my favourite comedy __series__. | *Both __series are__ available on DVD.*

Some nouns are only plural and are followed by a plural verb. These are usually nouns that refer to things with two parts (e.g. ***binoculars***, ***jeans***, ***pyjamas***, ***scissors***, ***shorts***, ***trousers***) and other nouns ending in **-s** (e.g. ***belongings***, ***clothes***, ***congratulations***, ***earnings***, ***outskirts***, ***surroundings***).

The __scissors are__ in that drawer. | *I believe __congratulations are__ in order.*

To count nouns that refer to things with two parts, you can use **a pair of**.

I've just bought __two pairs of jeans__.

3.3 Collective nouns

Collective nouns (also called group nouns) are nouns that refer to a group of people.

audience, ***band***, ***committee***, ***company***, ***congregation***, ***family***, ***government***, ***jury***, ***team***

These nouns are usually followed by a singular verb.

The __government has to__ do something. | *The __team plays__ in red and white.*

In British English, these nouns can take a singular or plural verb. Singular verb forms are common when we think of the group of people as a whole, as a single unit. Plural verb forms are common when the noun refers to the members of the group considered as individuals.

Mario's __family is__ Italian (= the group as a whole). | *Mario's __family have decided__ to move to Florence* (= each individual in the group).

3.4 Nouns and prepositions

Preposition + noun

Many nouns are used with particular prepositions in fixed phrases. Here are some common preposition + noun combinations.

at breakfast/lunch/dinner/supper
at the cinema/theatre
at university
by accident
by bike/bus/car/boat/train/plane/sea/air
for breakfast/lunch/dinner/supper
in conclusion
in my opinion
in the morning/afternoon/evening
in the world
on fire
on foot

Sometimes you can use more than one preposition with a noun, but the meaning is different.

Make sure you arrive for your interview ***on time***. (= at the right time, not late)
I hope my passport arrives ***in time***. (= with enough time to be able to do something, before something happens)
She got up three times ***in the night***. (= during the night)
Never go out alone ***at night***. (= when it is night and not day)
He's ***on television*** *tonight*. (= appearing on a programme)
She works ***in television***. (= in the business of television)

Noun + preposition

Many nouns are followed by particular prepositions. Here are some common noun + preposition combinations.

advice on/about
answer to
argument about (something)/with (someone)
beginning of
cause of
comment on
decrease in
difference between
difficulty with/in
discussion about (something)/with (someone)
example of
increase in
information about/on
interest in
lack of
need for
permission for
problem with
proof of
reaction to
reason for
reply to
search for

ⓘ To find the right **preposition(s)** to use with a **noun**, look up the **noun** in the dictionary.

3.5 Using articles with nouns

When to use *a/an*

You use the indefinite article ***a/an*** with singular countable nouns. Use it:

- to talk about any one of a group, kind or class, without saying which particular thing, person, place etc you mean;

  *There's **a** car parked outside their house.* | *She was talking to **an** old man.*
- with jobs, nationalities and religions/beliefs;

  He's a plumber.
  *My father is **an** Italian.*
  *I'm **an** atheist.*
- to define something or say what it is used for;

  ***A** zebra is **a** wild animal that looks like **a** horse.*
  *She uses this room as **a** studio.*
- with large numbers and fractions, to mean 'one';

  ***a** thousand* | *one and **a** half* | ***a** quarter* | *half **a** mile*
- with expressions of quantity and frequency, to mean 'each' or 'per';

  *six euros **a** kilo* | *two dollars **a** bag* | *twice **a** day* | *80 miles **an** hour*

When to use *the*

You use the definite article ***the***:

- when you are talking about something unique or specific, or something the reader or listener already knows about;

  ***the** moon* | ***the** sun* | ***the** world* | ***the** sky*
  *I didn't like **the** music in **the** film.*
  *All **the** computers in **the** building were down.*
  *No one knows who committed **the** crime.*
  *They go to the school in **the** village.*
- with the names of some countries, oceans/seas, rivers, deserts, mountain ranges and regions;

  ***the** UK*
  ***the** Atlantic*
  ***the** Black Sea*
  ***the** Mississippi*
  ***the** Sahara*
  ***the** Andes*
- with the names of hotels, cinemas, theatres, museums and newspapers;

  ***the** Hilton*
  ***the** Odeon*
  ***the** National Theatre*
  ***the** New York Times*

- with surnames, adjectives of nationality and other adjectives, when they are used as nouns to refer to a group of people;

  the Johnsons (= the Johnson family)
  the Italians (= people from Italy)
  the poor (= poor people)

When not to use an article

You do not use an article:

- with uncountable or plural nouns, when you are talking about something in general;

  I like music.
  Crime is increasing in this area.

- with the names of people, most countries, continents, cities, towns and states, streets, squares and parks;

  Emma Jones
  Japan
  Europe
  Paris
  Washington
  Downing Street
  Trafalgar Square
  Hyde Park

- with meals, games, sports, school subjects and languages;

  Have you had breakfast?
  I love chess.
  Do you play basketball?
  She's always hated Maths.
  Do you speak English?

- with times, months or days.

  We went to bed at midnight.
  I'll see you on Tuesday.
  They're getting married in May.

- with institutions and places (e.g. ***school***, ***prison***, ***hospital***, ***college***, ***university***, ***church***), when you are talking about the purpose they are used for;

  *When did you start **school**?* (as a student)
  *She is in **hospital**.* (as a patient)

  but:

  *There was a fire in **the school** four years ago.* (the building itself)
  *She went to **the hospital** to see her friend.* (as a visitor)

4 Verbs

4.1 Transitive and intransitive verbs

Transitive or intransitive?

A transitive verb normally takes an object. The object can be a noun, a noun phrase or a pronoun.

*Did you **enjoy the film**?*
*We **need more printer paper**.*
*It's OK, I've **found it**.*

A verb followed by a ***that*** clause is also considered to be transitive. You can omit ***that*** from the clause.

*I **know** that you're busy.*
*He **said** he was coming later.*

An intransitive verb does not normally take an object.

*She **cried**.*
*The sun **is setting**.*
*Did you **sleep** well?*

To link an intransitive verb with a noun, you need a preposition.

- *I **agree with** your comment.* (✗ Don't say: *I agree your comment.*)
- *We **apologize for** the delay.* (✗ Don't say: *We apologize the delay.*)
- *She **waited for** him.* (✗ Don't say: *She waited him.*)

ⓘ **Transitive verbs** are labelled **[T]** in the dictionary. **Intransitive verbs** are labelled **[I]**.

Transitive and intransitive

Some verbs can be both transitive and intransitive.

Have you eaten anything? (transitive) | *Have you eaten?* (intransitive)

Sometimes the meaning is different.

*They managed to **recover** some of the money.* (= to get it back; transitive)
*She is **recovering** from an operation.* (= starting to feel well again; intransitive)

There is a group of verbs where the same noun can be the subject of the verb or its object;

- Many of these verbs are to do with cooking (e.g. ***boil***, ***bake***, ***cook***, ***fry***, ***roast***);

  *I'm **cooking** some **pasta**.* (transitive; *pasta* = object)
  *Some **pasta** is **cooking**.* (intransitive; *pasta* = subject)

- other verbs that behave like this are: ***begin***, ***blow***, ***break***, ***change***, ***dry***, ***fasten***, ***fill***, ***open***, ***ring***, ***start***, ***vary***;

  *Someone **rang** the **bell**.* (transitive; *bell* = object)
  *The **bell rang**.* (intransitive; *bell* = subject)

4.2 Verb patterns

Verb + -*ing* form

Some verbs are followed by an **-ing** form. Some of these verbs are: ***admit***, ***avoid***, ***consider***, ***delay***, ***deny***, ***finish***, ***imagine***, ***keep***, ***mention***, ***mind***, ***miss***, ***practise***, ***recall***, ***recommend***, ***risk***.

*They managed to **avoid being** seen.*
*I **considered applying** for a new job.*
*Can you **imagine living** in a house like that?*

These verbs can also be followed by a noun.

*We try to **avoid trouble**.*
*She **considered** their **offer**.*
*I can't **imagine a situation** in which I'd lie to my parents.*

If a verb is followed by a preposition, you use an **-ing** form after the preposition. Some of these verbs are: ***accuse sb of***, ***apologize for***, ***complain about***, ***concentrate on***, ***discourage sb from***, ***dream of***, ***forgive sb for***, ***insist on***, ***object to***, ***persist in***, ***prevent sb from***, ***succeed in***, ***thank sb for***, ***think about/of***.

*She **dreamed of being** a dancer.*
*They **insist on having** 24 hours' notice.*

These verbs can also be followed by a preposition + a noun.

*She **dreamed of** a **career** as a dancer.*
*They **insist on** 24 hours' **notice**.*

Verb + to-infinitive

Some verbs are followed by a **to**-infinitive. Some of these verbs are: ***agree***, ***arrange***, ***ask***, ***choose***, ***decide***, ***expect***, ***fail***, ***help***, ***hope***, ***intend***, ***learn***, ***manage***, ***offer***, ***plan***, ***prepare***, ***pretend***, ***promise***, ***refuse***, ***want***.

*She **agreed to help** us.*
*I **expect to see** him this weekend.*
*They **failed to notice** that the money was missing.*

Verb + -*ing* form or to-infinitive

Some verbs can be followed by either an **-ing** form or a **to**-infinitive. The meaning may be the same, slightly different or completely different. Some of these verbs are: ***begin***, ***bother***, ***continue***, ***forget like***, ***love***, ***mean***, ***prefer***, ***regret***, ***remember***, ***start***, ***stop***, ***try***.

*The little girl **started crying/to cry**.* (same meaning)
*He's **stopped buying** CDs.* (= He does not buy CDs any more.)
*He **stopped to buy** some CDs.* (= He stopped what he was doing in order to buy some CDs.)
*I **tried to explain**.* (= I made an effort to explain, when this was difficult.)
*I **tried using** less sugar.* (= I did this to discover whether it would be successful.)

ⓘ For more information about particular **verbs**, their patterns and their uses, look up the **verb entries** in the dictionary.

4.3 Modal verbs

The verbs ***can***, ***could***, ***may***, ***might***, ***must***, ***ought to***, ***shall***, ***should***, ***will*** and ***would*** are modal verbs.

You use the base form of a verb (infinitive without *to*) after modal verbs. They have the same form in all persons (*I, you, he, she, it, you, they*).

*I **can ride** a bike.*
*We **must go** home.*
*He **might be** at work.*

You can use modal verbs to talk about the present, past or future. Sometimes, when you talk about the past, you use the perfect form: modal verb + *have* + past participle.

*He **could have done** it.*
*You **must have been** very worried.*

The verbs ***have to***, ***need (to)***, ***be able to*** and ***be allowed to*** are often used in similar ways to modal verbs.

*We **have to go** home.*

You use modal verbs when you want to talk about the following: ***ability***, ***certainty***, ***intention***, ***obligation***, ***necessity***, ***offers***, ***permission***, ***possibility***, ***predictions***, ***probability***, ***requests***, and ***suggestions, advice and criticism***.

Ability

You use ***can*** to talk about ability in the present or future.

*I **can** ride a bike.*
*He **can't** come with us tomorrow.*

To talk about ability in the past, you use ***could*** or ***was/were able to***.

*I **could** ride a bike when I was five.*
*I **was able to** ride a bike when I was five.*
*We **couldn't** hear you.*
*We **weren't able to** hear you.*

When talking about the past, you normally use ***was/were able to*** to talk about ability in a particular instance:

*Thankfully, they **were able to** get everybody out of the burning building.*

Certainty

You use ***must*** when you are making a guess which you are fairly certain is correct.

*He **must** be hungry.*
*They **must** have arrived by now.*

You can use ***will*** when you are completely certain that your guess is correct.

*It **will** rain this evening.*
*He **will** have left by now.*

You use ***can't*** when you are fairly certain that something is not true.

*That **can't** be Nick – he's in China.*
*She **can't** have been there – she was with me.*

Intention

You use ***will*** when saying that someone intends to do something, or asking whether someone intends to do something.

*I **will** spend a few days at my sister's.*
*They **won't** stay long.*
***Will** you be there on Saturday?*

In British English, people sometimes also say ***I shall*** or ***we shall***.

*I **shall** spend a few days at my sister's.*

The negative of ***shall*** is ***shan't***.

*We **shan't** stay long.*

When talking about the past or reporting someone's intentions, you use **would**.

*She said she **would** come with me.*

Obligation

You use ***must*** or ***have to*** when you are saying that someone has a duty to do something, for example because of a law or rule.

*Passengers **must** wear seat belts.*
*You **have to** answer two questions in the exam.*

In spoken English, you can also use ***have got to***.

*You**'ve got to** get permission from your parents.*

When talking about the past, you use ***had to***.

*Passengers **had to** wear seat belts.*
*We **had to** answer two questions in the exam.*

You use ***must not*** to express prohibition, to say that something is not allowed.

*Visitors **must not** walk across the grass.*
*You **mustn't** use your phone in here.*

Necessity

You use ***must***, ***have to*** or ***need to*** when you are saying that something is necessary.

*I **must** get some milk.*
*You **have to** enter a password.*
*We **need to** buy a ticket first.*

In spoken English, you can also use ***have got to***.

*You**'ve got to** enter a password.*

When talking about the past, you use ***had to***.

*We **had to** take the stairs because the lift wasn't working.*

When talking about the future, you use ***will have to*** or ***will need to***.

*We **will have to** leave at six.*
*You **will need to** buy a ticket first.*

To say that something is not necessary, you use ***needn't***, ***don't need to*** or ***don't have to***.

*You **needn't** finish the report today.*
*We **didn't need to** buy a ticket.*
*I **don't have to** wear a uniform at work.*

Compare ***didn't need to*** and ***needn't have***.

*He **didn't need to go** to work yesterday.* (= He didn't go to work because it wasn't necessary.)
*He **needn't have gone** to work yesterday.* (= He went to work but it wasn't necessary.)

Offers

You use ***I'll ...***, ***Can I ...?***, ***Could I ...?*** or ***May I ...?*** when you are offering to do something for someone. ***May I ...?*** sounds more formal and polite.

***I'll** carry this bag for you.*
***Can I** get you some water?*
***Could I** help you with that suitcase?*
***May I** open the door for you, Madam?*

In British English, people sometimes also use ***Shall I ...?***

***Shall I** carry bag this for you?*

Permission

You use ***can***, ***could*** or ***may*** when asking for permission. ***Could*** is more polite than ***can***. ***May*** is more polite and more formal.

***Can** I sit here with you?*
***Could** I use your phone?*
***May** I be excused?*

You use ***can*** or ***may*** when giving or refusing permission. ***May*** is more formal.

*You **can** use my phone, if you like.*
*You **can't** sit here.*
*Thank you. You **may** go now.*

You can also use ***be allowed to*** to talk about permission.

***Are** students **allowed to** use the equipment?*
*We **weren't allowed to** leave the classroom.*

Possibility

You use ***may*** or ***could*** when saying that it is possible that something is true but you are not certain.

*He **may** be at home.*
*They **could** have already left.*

You can also use ***might*** in this way, especially when talking about something that is possible but unlikely.

*He **might** be in his office but I think he's probably gone home.*

In questions, you use ***might*** or ***could***.

***Might** he be in his office?*
***Could** they have already left?*

You use ***may not*** or ***might not*** (but not ***could not***) in negative sentences to say that something is possible.

*She **may not** be at work.* (= It is possible that she is not at work.)
*They **might not** have left yet.* (= It is possible that they haven't left yet.)

To say that something is not possible, you use ***can't***.

*She **can't** be at work.* (= It is not possible that she is at work.)
*They **can't** have left yet.* (= It is not possible that they have left.)

Predictions

You use ***will*** to make predictions, to talk about what you think or guess will happen.

*I think James **will** win the competition.*

You use ***would*** when reporting what someone predicted.

*He said the bus **would** be there in a minute.*

Probability

You use ***should*** or ***ought to*** when saying that something will probably happen, although you are not certain.

*It **should** be a nice day tomorrow.*
*We **ought to** be there by six.*

You use ***must have*** + past participle when saying what you think has probably happened.

*She's late. She **must have been** held up.*

Requests

You use ***can***, ***could***, ***will*** or ***would*** when asking someone to do something. ***Could*** and ***would*** are more polite than ***can*** and ***will***.

***Can** you turn that music down?*
***Could** you help me with something?*
***Will** you phone me later?*
***Would** you bring us some coffee, please?*

Suggestions, advice and criticism

You use ***should*** and ***ought to*** when you think it is good idea for someone to do something.

*You **should** get there early.*
*You **ought to** see a doctor as soon as possible.*

You can also use these verbs in the negative, when you think something is a bad idea.

*You **shouldn't** say things like that.*
*You **oughtn't to** put that there.*

You use ***should*** (***not***) ***have*** + past participle, ***ought*** (***not***) ***to have*** + past participle or ***could have*** + past participle when criticizing someone's past actions.

*You **should have said** something.*
*You **oughtn't to have left** the engine running.*
*You **could have told** me that you were running late.*

You use ***can***, ***could*** and ***shall*** to make suggestions.

***Shall** we say six o'clock, then?*
*We **can** stay in and watch a DVD.*
*We **could** go to the cinema.*

You often use ***should*** after verbs connected with advice, such as ***advise***, ***demand***, ***propose***, ***recommend***, ***suggest***, ***think***, ***tell***, ***warn***.

*His lawyer **advised him that he should** plead guilty.*
*Someone **suggested that she should** write a book about her experiences.*
*I **think you should** train as a teacher.*

4.4 Phrasal verbs

What is a phrasal verb?

A phrasal verb is a verb that is made up of two or three words. The first word is a verb and the second word is a particle (either an adverb or a preposition such as ***in***, ***on*** or ***up***).

get up | turn off | deal with | catch up with | look forward to

You cannot guess the meaning of a phrasal verb from the meaning of each of its parts. For example, in the sentence below, the meaning of the phrasal verb ***carry out*** (= do) is not related to the normal meaning of ***carry*** or the normal meaning of ***out***.

*The scientists **carried out** an experiment.*

Phrasal verbs are very common in both spoken and written English. Your English will often sound more natural if you use a phrasal verb instead of a single verb.

*It was too hard, so I **gave up**.* (= more natural than 'It was too hard, so I *abandoned* it.')
*The teacher **told** us **off**.* (= less formal than 'The teacher *scolded* us.')
*She **found out** the truth.* (= less formal than 'She *discovered* the truth.')

> ⓘ For the meanings and uses of particular phrasal verbs, look up the verb (***come***, ***get***, ***take*** etc) in the dictionary.

Different types of phrasal verb

Intransitive phrasal verbs

Some phrasal verbs are intransitive – they do not take an object.

What time do we need to get up?
Look out – there's a car coming!
The plane took off on time.

Transitive phrasal verbs

Some phrasal verbs are transitive – they take an object. The object can come before or after the particle. These are called separable phrasal verbs.

*She **brought up** her sister's children.*	*She **brought** her sister's children **up**.*
*We **called off** the meeting.*	*We **called** the meeting **off**.*
***Look up** the word in the dictionary.*	***Look** the word **up** in the dictionary.*

If the object is a long noun phrase, it usually comes after the particle.

- *I **turned off** the lights in the front room.* ✗ *I turned the lights in the front room off.*
- *He **took out** a high-interest short-term loan.* ✗ *He took a high-interest short-term loan out.*

If the object is a pronoun (***it***, ***him***, ***them*** etc), it must come before the particle.

- *She **brought** them **up**.* ✗ *She brought up them.*
- *We **called** it **off**.* ✗ *We called off it.*

> ⓘ The dictionary uses a special symbol (↔) between the verb and a particle, to show you that a phrasal verb is separable.
> ***bring sb ↔ up** | **call sth ↔ off***

Some verbs must have the object between the verb and the particle.

- *Doing the same thing every day was beginning to **get** Jo **down**.*

✗ *Doing the same thing every day was beginning to get down Jo.*

ⓘ The dictionary shows this type of **verb** as follows:
get sb down

Some verbs must have the object after the particle. These verbs are called inseparable phrasal verbs.

- *We'll **look after** the children.* ✗ *We'll look the children after.*
- *He didn't **take to** the work at first.* ✗ *He didn't take the work to at first.*

ⓘ The dictionary shows inseparable **phrasal verbs** as follows:
look after sb/sth

Phrasal verbs with two particles

Some phrasal verbs have two particles: an adverb and a preposition.

*cut **down on** | get **on with** | keep **up with***

Some of these verbs can also be used without the preposition.

*I'm trying **to cut down on** salt. I'm trying to **cut down**.*
*She doesn't **get on with** Pete. She and Pete don't **get on**.*
*He couldn't **keep up with** the others. He couldn't **keep up**.*

Others cannot be used without the preposition, for example:

- *Let's see what she **comes up with**.* ✗ *Let's see what she comes up.*
- *I'm **looking forward to** the end of term.* ✗ *I'm looking forward.*

The parts of these verbs are never separated. The object always comes after both the adverb and the preposition.

- *He couldn't **keep up with** the others.* ✗ *He couldn't keep with the others up.*

4.5 Short responses

so, not

When you answer a question or respond to what someone has said, you can use **so** or **not** with the following verbs to avoid repeating the same words: ***appear***, ***believe***, ***expect***, ***guess***, ***hope***, ***imagine***, ***seem***, ***suppose***, ***think***.

You use **so** for a positive response.

*'Will you finish today?' 'Yes, I **expect so**.*
*'Are they coming on Saturday?' 'Yes, I **believe so**.'*

For a negative response, you can use **not** with some of these verbs.

'Didn't she like it?' ▪ *'I **guess not**.'* ✗ Don't say: *'I don't guess so.'*
'Will this happen again?' ▪ *'I **hope not**.'* ✗ Don't say: *'I don't hope so.'*

With other verbs, it can sound formal or unnatural to use **not**. It is more usual to say ***I don't ... so***.

'Is she leaving?' ▪ *'I don't think so.'* ✗ Don't say: *'I think not.'*
'Are they coming?' ▪ *'I don't imagine so.'* ✗ Don't say: *'I imagine not.'*

Subject + auxiliary/modal verb

To avoid repetition, you can also use an auxiliary or modal verb instead of a complete clause.

'You're not listening to me!' 'I am!' (= I am listening to you.)
'Who won the race?' 'I did.' (= I won the race.)
'Have you finished your essay?' 'No, I haven't.' (= No, I haven't finished my essay.)
'They were all really worried.' 'We were, too.' (= We were really worried, too.)

so, neither/nor

You can also use the following structures to avoid repeating the same words when you respond to a statement.

so + auxiliary/modal verb + subject, to respond to a positive statement.

*'I'm having great time.' '**So am I**.'*
*'Emma failed her driving test.' '**So did Sophia**.'*

neither/nor + auxiliary/modal verb + subject, to respond to a negative statement.

*'I didn't like the film.' '**Neither/Nor did I**.'*
*'We weren't at all pleased with the results.' '**Neither/Nor were we**.'*

4.6 Using the continuous (progressive) form of verbs

How to form the continuous form of verbs

You form the continuous form (also known as the progressive form) of a verb using **be** + **-ing**.

*I**'m doing** my homework.* (present continuous)
*He **wasn't joking**.* (past continuous)
*We**'ve been waiting** for three hours!* (present perfect continuous)
*He **had been working** since eight o'clock.* (past perfect continuous)
*We **will be staying** with some friends.* (future continuous)
*By noon, she **will have been working** for twelve hours.* (future perfect continuous)

When to use continuous forms

In general, you use continuous forms when talking about something that is, was or will be temporary, ongoing or incomplete at the time referred to (as opposed to something permanent or something that has been completed).

*I**'m staying** with a friend at the moment.* (a temporary situation)
*They **were living** in Spain at the time.* (a temporary situation)
*She**'s been studying** since four.* (ongoing; she is still studying now)
*At four o'clock, he **had been waiting** for two hours.* (ongoing; he was still waiting at four o'clock)
*I**'ll** still **be working** at midnight.* (ongoing/incomplete; I will finish work after midnight)

When not to use continuous forms

You do not usually use continuous forms:

- with state verbs (verbs that express states of being, feeling, thinking, possessing etc rather than actions) for example: ***admire***, ***be***, ***believe***, ***exist***, ***hate***, ***have***, ***know***, ***like***, ***love***, ***need***, ***prefer***, ***remember***, ***think***, ***understand***, ***want***;

- *The house* ***consists of*** *two floors.* ✗ *The house is consisting of two floors.*
- *I* ***like*** *it here very much.* ✗ *I am liking it here very much.*
- *I* ***didn't believe*** *what I had just heard.* ✗ *I wasn't believing what I had just heard.*
- *I* ***don't need*** *any help right now, thanks.* ✗ *I'm not needing any help right now, thanks.*

• with sense verbs (***feel***, ***hear***, ***see***, ***smell***, ***sound***, ***taste***);

- ***Did*** *you* ***hear*** *that sound?* ✗ *Were you hearing that sound?*
- *We* ***saw*** *some interesting birds.* ✗ *We were seeing some interesting birds.*
- *Mm! Something* ***smells*** *good!* ✗ *Mm! Something's smelling good!*

• with some other verbs, e.g. ***agree***, ***appear***, ***be***, ***concern***, ***contain***, ***depend***, ***disagree***, ***include***, ***look*** (= seem), ***involve***, ***matter***, ***mean***, ***owe***, ***seem***;

- *I totally* ***agree*** *with you.* ✗ *I am totally agreeing with you.*
- *She* ***promised*** *to write every week.* ✗ *She was promising to write every week.*
- *The final decision* ***will depend*** *on a number of factors.* ✗ *The final decision will be depending on a number of factors.*

You can use some of the verbs above in the continuous form, when they describe actions, not states.

I ***admire*** *her for her bravery.* (= like and respect)
*I'****m*** *just* ***admiring*** *the view.* (= looking at)
He acts as though I don't ***exist***. (= be alive)
*They'****re existing*** *on just a few pounds a week.* (= staying alive, surviving)
The soup ***tastes*** *delicious.* (= have a particular taste)
*Should I spit when I'****m tasting*** *wine?* (= try something to see how it tastes)

Some verbs that are not used in the continuous can still be used as present participles.

Hardly ***knowing*** *why, she started to cry.*
He published a book ***consisting of*** *four short stories.*
She even earned the respect of her ***doubting*** *colleagues.*

4.7 Using the passive

How to form the passive

You usually form the passive with the correct form of **be** + a past participle.

This soup ***is made*** *from potatoes.* (present simple passive)
A new hospital ***is being built*** *in the town.* (present continuous passive)
Her new book ***has*** *just* ***been published***. (present perfect passive)
We ***were told*** *we had to take a test.* (past simple passive)
The suspects ***were being interviewed***. (past continuous passive)
The room ***had been cleaned*** *before we arrived.* (past perfect passive)
Their first album ***will be released*** *next month.* (future simple passive)

When to use the passive

You use the passive when you want to focus on the action itself, not the doer of the action (the agent). You also use it when the agent action is not known, not important or obvious.

The problem ***has been sorted out***. (It is not important who did this.)
Their car ***has been stolen***. (You do not know who stole it.)
The two men ***have been arrested***. (Obviously, the police arrested them.)

Important points about the passive

You cannot use intransitive verbs in the passive.

- *Her father died in 2001.* ✗ *Her father was died in 2001.*

Some verbs can be used in the passive in restricted ways.

- *An idea* ***was suggested*** *to me.* ✗ *I was suggested an idea.*
- *The rules* ***were explained*** *to them.* ✗ *They were explained the rules.*

Some verbs are often or usually used in the passive.

I ***was born*** *in Germany.*
The thieves ***have been arrested.*** ('They have arrested the thieves' is possible but less common.)

You often use some verbs in the structure: ***it*** + passive + ***that*** clause. Some of these verbs are: ***agree***, ***believe***, ***claim***, ***discover***, ***expect***, ***fear***, ***know***, ***report***, ***suggest***, ***think***.

It is believed that *the men are dead.*
It was expected that *the whole school would attend.*
It has been reported that *there has been an explosion.*

This structure is often used in academic writing.

It was discovered that *the disease was carried in drinking water.*
It is thought that *birds learn the positions of the stars and use them to navigate.*

You can also use some of the verbs above in the structure: subject + passive + ***to***-infinitive.

The men are believed to be *dead.*
The whole school was expected to attend.

When you want to mention the agent in a passive sentence, you use ***by***.

I was attacked ***by a dog.***
The Statue of Liberty was designed ***by Frédéric Auguste Bartholdi.***

In everyday English, people often use ***get*** instead of ***be***.

Kevin ***got arrested*** *for dangerous driving.* (= was arrested)

---

have/get something done

You can use ***have/get*** + object + past participle when you arrange for someone else to do something for you.

*She****'s going to have her car cleaned.***
*We****'re getting the house repainted.***
I ***had my hair cut.*** ('I cut my hair' means that you cut it yourself. Don't say 'I cut my hair' to mean that someone else cut it for you.)

You can also use ***have*** + object + past participle to talk about something happening to someone that they did not choose or want.

We ***had our tickets checked.***
I ***had my bag stolen*** *last night.*

You can use ***get*** + object + past participle about something that you do yourself, when you want to emphasize that you have to make an effort in order to complete it, or that there is a lot to be done.

ⓘ For more information on particular **reporting verbs** and their patterns, look up the **verb entries** in the dictionary.

4.8 Using the subjunctive

What is the subjunctive?

The subjunctive is a verb form that you use to talk about unreal situations or things that are not certain to happen. In the subjunctive, the verb form does not change according to person (***I***, ***he***, ***she***, ***it etc***). For all verbs except **were**, the subjunctive is the same as the infinitive without ***to***. In the example below, the verbs ***be*** and ***contact*** are in the subjunctive.

The manager requests that you all ***be*** *present at next week's meeting.*
It is important that she **contact** *Mr Dawson as soon as possible.*

Subjunctive in *that* clauses

Some verbs are often followed by a subjunctive in a ***that*** clause, especially in more formal English. Some of these verbs are: ***advise***, ***ask***, ***command***, ***demand***, ***insist***, ***propose***, ***recommend***, ***request***, ***suggest***, ***wish***.

We ***demand that they be*** *punished!*
I ***recommend that she get*** *professional help.*

In clauses like this, ***should*** is also often used.

We ***demand that they should be*** *punished.*
I ***recommend that she should get*** *professional help.*

Some adjectives can also be followed by a subjunctive, especially in more formal English. They are used in the phrase ***It is ... that ...*** . Some of these adjectives are: ***best***, ***crucial***, ***desirable***, ***essential***, ***imperative***, ***important***, ***necessary***, ***recommended***, ***urgent***, ***vital***.

It is essential that *he* ***pay*** *attention.*
It is important that *everyone* ***understand***.

In everyday English, people often use the present simple instead of the subjunctive.

I ***recommend that she gets*** *professional help.*
It is important that *everyone* ***understands***.

Subjunctive *were*

Were, the past subjunctive of ***be*** is often used when talking about something impossible or unreal, with ***if*** and ***I wish***.

If *I* ***were*** *you, I'd leave.*
If *he* ***were*** *here now, he would be proud.*
I wish *he* ***were*** *here.*
I wish *I* ***were*** *taller.*

In everyday English, people often use **was**.

If *he* ***was*** *here now, he would be proud.*
I wish *he* ***was*** *here.*

4.9 Conditionals

You usually form conditional sentences with two clauses: an ***if*** clause and a main clause. The ***if*** clause states the condition and the main clause states the result. The ***if*** clause can come at the beginning or end of the sentence. When it is at the beginning, you use a comma after it.

Zero conditional

You use the zero conditional to talk about something that is always or generally true. You use the present simple in both clauses.

> ***If*** *plants* ***don't get*** *enough water, they* ***die****.*

You can use ***when*** instead of ***if*** in zero conditional sentences.

> ***When*** *plants don't get enough water, they die.*

First conditional

You use the first conditional to talk about something that is possible in the future. You use the present simple in the ***if*** clause and a future tense in the main clause.

> ***If*** *the government* ***doesn't change*** *course, things* ***will get*** *worse.*

You can also use a modal verb or the imperative in the main clause.

> ***If*** *I* ***see*** *her, I* ***can give*** *her your message.*
> ***If*** *you* ***have*** *any problems,* ***give*** *me a call.*

You can use ***unless*** instead of ***if not*** in the ***if*** clause.

> *You can't park here* ***if you don't have*** *a permit.*
> *You can't park here* ***unless you have*** *a permit.*

Second conditional

You use the second conditional to talk about something that is impossible in the present or something that is possible but unlikely in the future. You use the past simple in the ***if*** clause and ***would*** in the main clause.

> ***If*** *you* ***had*** *a sister,* ***would*** *you* ***feel*** *differently?*
> ***If*** *we* ***won*** *the lottery, we* ***would*** *never* ***work*** *again.*

Third conditional

You use the third conditional to talk about something that was possible in the past but didn't happen. You use the past perfect in the ***if*** clause and ***would have*** + past participle in the main clause.

> ***If*** *I* ***had known*** *about the party, I* ***would have come****.*

Mixed conditionals

You can use the second and third conditionals in the same sentence to talk about a past event that has an effect on the present. The ***if*** clause refers to the past (third conditional) and the main clause refers to the present (second conditional).

> ***If*** *you* ***had remembered*** *to phone her, she* ***would be*** *here now.*
> ***If*** *he* ***had got*** *on that plane, he****'d be*** *dead now!*

4.10 Talking about the future

Future forms

You can use the forms below to talk about the future.

Form	Use	Example
Future simple (*will*)	for decisions you make at the time of speaking	*Oh, you're going out? Wait, I'**ll come** with you.*
	for general predictions about the future (often with ***I think***, ***I hope***, ***I expect***, ***I'm sure*** etc)	*I'm sure you'**ll have** a great time at the party.*
	for offers, promises, requests and threats	*I'**ll carry** that bag for you.* *I **won't tell** anyone, don't worry.*
shall	for offers and suggestions	***Shall** I **drive** you to the station?* ***Shall** we **go** out?*
be going to	for intentions	*I'**m going** to visit my grandparents this weekend.*
	for predictions, when they are based on something you see in the present	*Look at those clouds – it'**s going to rain**.*
Present continuous	for arrangements	*We'**re travelling** by train.*
Present simple	for events that are part of a timetable or schedule	*His flight **gets** in at 10.00.* *My German exchange partner **arrives** tomorrow.*
Future continuous (*will + -ing*)	for actions that will be in progress at a particular time in the future	*I'**ll be working** at noon.*
	for events that are expected to happen or will happen if things go as planned	*We'**ll be arriving** around lunchtime.*
Future perfect simple (*will have* + past participle)	for events that will be completed before a particular time in the future	*The game **will have finished** by the time we get back.*
Future perfect continuous (*will have been + -ing*)	to emphasize the duration of a state or action that you expect will continue after the time mentioned	*We **will have been living** here for ten years this summer.*

Future time clauses

You often use these time words and phrases to talk about the future: ***after***, ***as soon as***, ***before***, ***by the time***, ***once***, ***when***, ***whenever***, ***while***, ***until***. You use the present simple after these time expressions, **not *will***.

*He plans to travel **after** he **finishes** college.* ✗ Don't say: *after he will finish college*
*It will be dark **by the time** we **get** there.* ✗ Don't say: *by the time we will get there*
*Come and see us **whenever** you **feel** like it.*
*Will you do a lot of walking **while** you **are** in Scotland?*
*I'll call you **when** the plane **lands**.*

Conditional clauses

You also use the following expressions to talk about possible future events as the result of an action: ***as long as***, ***if***, ***in case***, ***on condition that***, ***provided/providing*** **(*that*)**, ***unless***, ***whether***. You use the present simple, after these expressions, **don't use *will***.

*We'll be in time for the flight **as long as** we **leave** by eight.* ✗ Don't say: *as long as we will leave*
***If** you **see** Tom, give him my regards.* ✗ Don't say: *If you will see*
*I won't do it **unless** I **get** some help.*

Future in the past

When you talk about the past, sometimes you need to refer to things that were in the future at that time. To do this, you use the same forms that you use to refer to the future, but you make the verbs past.

*I **was going to phone** her last night but I forgot. (am/is/are going to → was/were going to)*
*I **was meeting** a friend in five minutes, so I had to hurry.* (present continuous → past continuous)
*We all thought she **would win**, but she didn't. (will → would)*

Other ways to talk about the future

You can also use the following structures to talk about the future:

- ***be*** + ***to***-infinitive, to talk about official plans and arrangements or an obligation to do something at a later time than now;

  *The president **is to arrive** at 10.30 on Monday morning.*
  *You **are to be** here by 10.30.*
  *You **are not to enter** this room.*

- ***be due*** + ***to***-infinitive, to talk about something you expect will happen at a particular time in the future;

  *The team **is due to fly** to Italy next month.*
  *His new book **is due to be published** next year.*

- ***be about*** + ***to***-infinitive, to talk about something you expect will happen very soon. You often use ***just*** with this structure;

  *She **is about to leave**.*
  *We**'re just about to have** lunch.*

4.11 Reported speech

Tense changes in reported speech

When reporting what someone said without quoting them directly, tenses usually change as follows:

- present simple → past simple

  *'I **want** to go home.' → He said that he **wanted** to go home.*

- present continuous → past continuous

  *'You**'re going** too fast.' → She warned me that I **was going** too fast.*

- past simple → past perfect

  *'They **won**.' → He announced that they **had won**.*

- present perfect → past perfect

  *'I**'ve** just **seen** him.' → She said that she **had** just **seen** him.*

- ***will** → **would***

  *'I **will** be there at eight.' → Maria promised that she **would** be there at eight.*

- ***can** → **could***

  *'We **can** help you.' → I said that we **could** help them.*

- ***must** → **had to***

  *'I **must** go.' → She said that she **had to** go.*

- The tense does not change when the reporting verb is in a present tense.

  *'I **like** them all.' → She **says** that she **likes** them all.*

- Past perfect tenses do not change.

  *'I **had** already **seen** it.' → He said that he **had** already **seen** it.*
  *'I**'d been waiting** for hours.' → She claimed that she**'d been waiting** for hours.*

- ***Could***, ***would***, ***might***, ***should*** and ***ought to*** do not change.

  *'They **could** come too.' → He pointed out that they **could** come too.*

Reported questions

When reporting a question, you use the same word order as for a statement.

*'**Does she like** jazz?' → He asked if **she liked** jazz.*
*'**Do you have** a pen?' → She asked if **I had** a pen.*
*'**Is he** married?' → I asked whether **he was** married.*
*'How **are you feeling**?' → She asked how **I was feeling**.*

When the question begins with a question word, you use the question word in the reported question.

*'**Where** are you going?' → She asked **where** I was going.*
***What** do you think?' → They asked **what** we thought.*

When the question can be answered by 'yes' or 'no', you use ***if*** or ***whether*** in the reported question.

*'Can I go home?' → She asked **if/whether** she could go home.*
*'Do you want any more?' → I asked **if/whether** they wanted any more.*

Reported requests, commands and advice

When reporting what someone has told another person to do, you often use the pattern reporting verb + object + ***to***-infinitive.

'You should see a doctor.' → She ***told me to see*** *a doctor. | She* ***advised me to see*** *a doctor.*
'Get out!' → She ***told me to get*** *out. | She* ***ordered me to get*** *out.*

With many reporting verbs, you can also use a ***that*** clause, often with ***should***.

She ***told me that I should see*** *a doctor. | She* ***advised that I should see*** *a doctor.*

Some reporting verbs are usually or always used with a ***that*** clause rather than an infinitive.

She ***suggested that I should see*** *a doctor. → ~~She suggested me to see a doctor.~~*

Reporting verbs

There are many reporting verbs that you can use instead of ***say*** or ***tell***. Here are some examples: ***advise***, ***announce***, ***claim***, ***complain***, ***explain***, ***invite***, ***point out***, ***promise***, ***suggest***, ***warn***.

He ***advised*** *me to talk to my boss. | She* ***explained*** *that she had missed her bus.*
He ***promised*** *to phone me after the meeting. | I* ***warned*** *them not to go near the dog.*

ⓘ For more information on particular reporting verbs and their patterns, look up the verb entries in the dictionary.

5 Prepositions

5.1 Prepositions of place

You can use the prepositions below to talk about where somebody or something is.

Preposition	Example
at	*What time did you arrive* ***at*** *the station?*
on	*I left the letter* ***on*** *your desk this morning.*
over	*There was a lamp hanging* ***over*** *the table.*
above	*There was a sign* ***above*** *the entrance.*
in, inside	*OK, let's see what's* ***in/inside*** *that box.*
outside	*The red car parked* ***outside*** *our house is my brother's.*
under	*The cat was hiding* ***under*** *the bed.*
below	*Mr Gower's office is directly* ***below*** *mine.*
near	*We'd like to sit* ***near*** *the window, please.*
next to	*The little girl sitting* ***next to*** *Jane is her daughter.*
beside	*Who's that standing* ***beside*** *Keith?*
by	*She's just bought a beautiful house* ***by*** *the river.*
in front of	*The bus stops right* ***in front of*** *my school.*
behind	*She turned around to look at Eve, who was standing* ***behind*** *her.*
opposite	*There's a supermarket* ***opposite*** *our house.*
among	*The teacher was standing* ***among*** *a crowd of children.*
between	*Ella sat down* ***between*** *Jo and Kevin.*

5.2 Prepositions of movement

You can use the prepositions below to talk about the direction in which somebody or something is moving.

Preposition	Example
up	*Come on, let's walk* ***up*** *that hill.*
down	*Anna ran* ***down*** *the stairs.*
onto	*The musicians walked* ***onto*** *the stage.*
into	*He got* ***into*** *his car and drove away.*
out of	*I got* ***out of*** *bed and ran downstairs.*
from	*What time did you get home* ***from*** *work?*
to	*Could you drive me* ***to*** *the airport tomorrow?*
towards	*She stood up and walked* ***towards*** *me.*
over	*The dog jumped* ***over*** *the fence.*

round	*The earth moves **round** the sun.*
along	*They went for a walk **along** the river.*
across	*He swam **across** the river.*
off	*She fell **off** her bike and hurt her knee.*
past	*Tim walked right **past** me and didn't even say hello.*
through	*You'll have to drive **through** the tunnel to get there.*

5.3 Prepositions of time

You can use the prepositions below to talk about when something happens or to refer to the length of time that something lasts.

Preposition	Use/meaning	Examples
at	with clock times and points or periods of time	***at*** *nine o'clock,* ***at*** *midnight,* ***at*** *the beginning/end,* ***at*** *the weekend,* ***at*** *night*
in	with parts of the day, months, years, seasons, centuries	***in*** *the morning,* ***in*** *July,* ***in*** *2014,* ***in*** *the winter,* ***in*** *the last century*
on	with days or dates	***on*** *Monday,* ***on*** *my birthday,* ***on*** *5 January,* ***on*** *Christmas Day*
by	to mean 'no later than'	*We'll need the report **by** the end of the week.*
before	to mean 'earlier than something'	*I always have a shower **before** breakfast.*
after	to mean 'later than something'	*Let's meet here **after** the show.*
since	to mean 'from a time in the past until a later time or until now'	*I've known Kat **since** 2010.*
for	to show how long an action continues for	*We've been waiting here **for** three hours!*
during	to mean 'all through a period of time' or 'at some point in a period of time'	*I worked in a hotel **during** the summer. Her husband died **during** the war.*
until/till	to mean 'up to' (the time mentioned)	*Let's wait here **until** she comes back.*
past	to mean 'later than a particular time'	*It was **past** midnight when she phoned me.*
through	to mean 'later than a particular time'	*She had to work **through** the night to finish her project.*

5.4 Prepositions before particular words

Some prepositions are often used before particular words to form fixed expressions. There are a lot of preposition + noun combinations in English, and they are very common in both written and formal English. Here are some examples:

at	*at first, at last, at least, at once, at present, at the moment, at times*
by	*by accident, by chance, by far, by heart, by mistake*
for	*for a while, for ages, for a change*
from	*from memory, from time to time, from bad to worse, from now on*
in	*in a hurry, in advance, in cash, in general, in other words, in time, in stock*
on	*on average, on business, on duty, on foot, on purpose, on the whole, on time*
out of	*out of breath, out of control, out of fashion, out of order, out of stock, out of the way*
under	*under control, under discussion, under pressure, under way*

Mr Fox is in a meeting ***at the moment****.* | *You need to be more careful* ***from now on****.* | *I'm sorry, I didn't do it* ***on purpose****.* | *Don't worry, everything is* ***under control****.*

5.5 Prepositions after particular words

You have to use particular prepositions after some adjectives, verbs and nouns. For adjectives and nouns, see 1.6 and 3.4 above. Here are some examples of verb + preposition combinations:

apologize to	*I really think you should* ***apologize*** *to your father.*
listen to	***Listen*** *carefully to the instructions or you won't know what to do.*
reply to	*She hasn't* ***replied*** *to my email yet.*
stare at	*You shouldn't* ***stare at*** *people. It's rude.*
worry about	*Don't* ***worry about*** *me. I'm fine.*

The Grammar guide and interactive grammar practice are available online at **www.longmandictionaries.com**

le·gis·la·tive /ˈledʒəslətɪv $ -leɪtɪv/ ●○○ AWL *adj* [only before noun] concerned with making laws: *The new assemblies will have no **legislative power**.* | **legislative assembly/council/body etc** (=one with the power to make laws) *the main legislative body of the EU* | *new legislative measures to stem the flow of drugs into the US* | ***legislative elections***

le·gis·la·tor /ˈledʒəsleɪtə $ -ər/ ●○○ AWL *n* [C] someone who has the power to make laws or belongs to an institution that makes laws

le·gis·la·ture /ˈledʒəsleɪtʃə, -lətʃə $ -ər/ ●○○ AWL *n* [C] an institution that has the power to make or change laws: **state/national/federal etc legislature** *the state legislature of Virginia*

le·git /ləˈdʒɪt/ *adj* [not before noun] *spoken informal* **1** legal or allowed by official rules: *Don't worry, the deal's strictly legit.* **2** honest and not trying to deceive people: *Are you sure he's legit?*

le·git·i·mate[1] /ləˈdʒɪtəmət/ ●●○ *adj*
1 fair or reasonable: *That's a **perfectly legitimate** question.* | *Most scientists believe **it is legitimate** to use animals in medical research.*
2 acceptable or allowed by law: *Their business operations are perfectly legitimate.*
3 a legitimate child is born to parents who are legally married to each other OPP **illegitimate** —**legitimately** *adv*: *a legitimately elected government* | *He complained quite legitimately about his treatment.* —**legitimacy** *n* [U]: *Opponents have questioned the legitimacy of the ruling.*

le·git·i·mate[2] /lɪˈdʒɪtɪmeɪt/ *v* [T] the usual American form of LEGITIMIZE

le·git·i·mize (*also* **-ise** *BrE*) /lɪˈdʒɪtəmaɪz/ *v* [T] **1** to make something that is unfair or morally wrong seem acceptable and right: *There is a danger that these films legitimize violence.* **2** to make something official or legal: *Acceptance by the UN would effectively legitimize the regime.* **3** when parents legitimize a child, they get married so that the child becomes LEGITIMATE[1](3)

leg·less /ˈlegləs/ *adj* **1** [not before noun] *BrE informal* very drunk **2** without legs

LEG·O /ˈlegəʊ $ -oʊ/ *n* [U] *trademark* a toy made by the LEGO group, consisting of small plastic bricks that fit together to build things

ˈleg-pull *n* [C usually singular] *BrE* a joke in which you make someone believe something that is not true: *My first reaction was that this must be a leg-pull.* → **pull sb's leg** at PULL[1](11)

ˈleg room *n* [U] space for your legs in front of the seats in a car, theatre etc: *There wasn't enough leg room.*

leg·ume /ˈlegjuːm, lɪˈgjuːm/ *n* [C] *technical* a plant such as a bean plant that has seeds in a POD (=a long thin case) —**leguminous** /lɪˈgjuːmɪnəs/ *adj*

ˈleg-up *n* **give sb a leg-up** *informal* **a)** to help someone to get up to a high place by joining your hands together so they can use them as a step **b)** *BrE* to help someone succeed in their job

leg·work /ˈlegwɜːk $ -wɜːrk/ *n* [U] *informal* the hard boring work that has to be done in order to achieve something: *He has a team of volunteers who do most of the legwork for him.*

lei·sure /ˈleʒə $ ˈliːʒər/ ●●○ W3 *n* [U]
1 time when you are not working or studying and can relax and do things you enjoy: *Most people now enjoy shorter working hours and more **leisure time**.* | *Watching television is now the nation's most popular **leisure activity**.* | *The hotel offers various **leisure facilities** such as a swimming pool and sauna.* | *The **leisure industry*** (=the business of providing leisure activities) *is now an important part of the economy.* THESAURUS ▸ FUN
2 at (your) leisure if you do something at your leisure, you do it slowly and without hurrying: *Come round for lunch and then we can discuss it at leisure.* | *Take the leaflets home and read them at your leisure.*
3 gentleman/lady of leisure someone who does not have to work – used humorously

ˈleisure ˌcentre ●●○ *n* [C] *BrE* a place where people can do many different sports activities, exercise classes etc

lei·sured /ˈleʒəd $ ˈliːʒərd/ *adj* [only before noun] **1** leisured people do not have to work because they are rich: *the leisured aristocracy* **2** doing things slowly because you feel relaxed and are enjoying yourself: *They seemed to live a very leisured life.*

lei·sure·ly /ˈleʒəli $ ˈliːʒərli/ *adj* if you do something in a leisurely way, you do it in a slow relaxed way, without hurrying: *After lunch we went for a leisurely stroll.* | *working at a leisurely pace* THESAURUS ▸ SLOW —**leisurely** *adv*: *He sipped leisurely at his drink.*

lei·sure·wear /ˈleʒəweə $ ˈliːʒərwer/ *n* [U] clothes that are made to be worn when you are relaxing or playing sport

leit·mo·tif, **leitmotiv** /ˈlaɪtməʊˌtiːf $ -moʊ-/ *n* [C] **1** *technical* a musical phrase that is repeated several times during a long musical work and represents a particular character or idea **2** something that is seen or heard very many times and so becomes a typical feature of a place, time, or person: *Her designs in clothing became a leitmotif of the 1970s.*

lem·ming /ˈlemɪŋ/ *n* [C] a small animal that looks like a rat. Lemmings are known for following each other in large numbers and killing themselves by jumping off cliffs into the sea.

lem·on[1] /ˈlemən/ ●●● S3 *n*
1 [C,U] a fruit with a hard yellow skin and sour juice: *a slice of lemon* | *Add a few drops of lemon juice.* → see picture at FRUIT[1]
2 [U] *BrE* a drink that tastes of lemons: *a glass of fizzy lemon*
3 [U] (*also* **lemon yellow**) a pale yellow colour
4 [C] *especially AmE informal* something that is useless because it fails to work or to work properly: *I soon realized the van was a lemon.*
5 [C] *BrE informal* a silly person: *He just stood there looking like a real lemon.*

lemon[2] (*also* **ˌlemon ˈyellow**) *adj* pale yellow in colour

lem·on·ade /ˌleməˈneɪd◂/ ●●○ *n* [C,U]
1 *BrE* a sweet FIZZY drink that tastes of lemons: *a glass of lemonade* | *Would you like a lemonade?*
2 a drink made from lemons, sugar, and water

ˌlemon ˈcurd *n* [U] *BrE* a sweet food made from eggs, butter, and lemon juice that is eaten on bread

ˈlemon ˌgrass *n* [U] a type of grass that grows in warm countries and is used in cooking

ˌlemon ˈsole *n* [C] a type of flat fish that is cooked and eaten

ˈlemon ˌsqueezer *n* [C] a small kitchen tool that you use for getting the juice out of a lemon

lem·on·y /ˈleməni/ *adj* smelling or tasting of lemons: *a lovely lemony flavour*

le·mur /ˈliːmə $ -ər/ *n* [C] an animal that looks like a monkey and has a long thick tail

lend /lend/ ●●● S3 W3 *v* (*past tense and past participle* **lent** /lent/)
1 a) [T] to let someone borrow money or something that belongs to you for a short time → **borrow**: **lend sth to sb** *I lent my CD player to Dave and I haven't got it back yet.* | **lend sb sth** *The hospital agreed to lend us a wheelchair.* | *Can you lend me £10 until tomorrow?* **b)** [I,T] if a bank or financial institution lends money, it lets someone have it on condition that they pay it back later, often gradually, with an additional amount as INTEREST: *The government is trying to encourage the banks to lend more.* | **lend sth to sb** *A lot of banks are unwilling to lend money to new businesses.* | **lend sb sth** *The building society agreed to lend us £60,000.*

L

2 lend (sb) a hand to help someone do something, especially something that needs physical effort: *Can you lend me a hand with this?*
3 [T] *formal* to give a situation, event etc a particular quality: **lend sth to sth** *The presence of members of the royal family lent a certain dignity to the ceremony.*
4 lend an ear to listen to someone, especially in a sympathetic way: *He's always prepared to lend a sympathetic ear.*
5 lend itself to sth to be suitable for being used in a particular way: *None of her books really lends itself to being made into a film.*
6 lend (your) support (to sth) to support or help someone: *The government has now lent its support to the campaign.*
7 lend weight/support to sth to make an opinion or belief seem more likely to be correct: *The police have new evidence which lends weight to their theory.*
8 lend your name to sth to announce publicly that you support something that someone is trying to do: *The French prime minister has now lent his name to the protest.*

THESAURUS

lend (*also* **loan** *especially AmE*) to let someone borrow money or something that belongs to you for a short time: *Can you lend me $20? | Did you lend that book to Mike? | The documents were loaned by the local library.*
let sb use sth/let sb have sth to let someone use something that belongs to you for a short time, especially a room, a house, or something big and expensive: *Some friends are letting us use their house while they are on vacation. | Dad said he'd let me have his car for the weekend.*
be on loan if something is on loan, it has been lent to a person or organization in an official way – often used about a library book or a work of art: *The museum has an exhibition of paintings on loan from the Louvre. | According to the computer, this book is still out on loan.*

lender /ˈlendə $ -ər/ ●○○ *n* [C] a person or organization that lends money to people on condition that they pay it back: *Several lenders are offering very attractive rates of interest at the moment.*

ˈlending ˌlibrary *n* [C] a library that lends books, records etc for people to use at home → **reference library**

ˈlending rate *n* [C] the rate of INTEREST[1](4) that you have to pay to a bank or other financial institution when you borrow money from them SYN **interest rate**

length /leŋθ/ ●●● S2 W2 *n*
1 SIZE [C,U] the measurement of how long something is from one end to the other → **breadth**, **width**: *We measured the length and width of the living room.* | **a length of 1 metre/2 feet etc** *Some fish can grow to a length of four feet.* | **2 feet/10 metres etc in length** *The hotel pool is 15 metres in length. | You'll need several pieces of string of different lengths.* → see picture at DIMENSION
2 TIME [C,U] the amount of time that you spend doing something or that something continues → **duration**: **[+of]** *Your pension will depend on your length of employment. | What's the average length of stay in hospital?* | **(not) for any length of time** (=not for very long) *He wasn't left alone for any length of time.*

REGISTER
In everyday English, people usually talk about **how long** something is in space or time, rather than using the noun **length**: *We need to know the **length** of the table.* → *We need to know **how long** the table is.* | *He was annoyed by the **length** of time he had to wait.* → *He was annoyed by **how long** he had to wait.*

3 BOOKS/FILMS ETC [C,U] the amount of writing in a book, or the amount of time that a film, play etc continues: **[+of]** *We had to cut the length of the book by one third.* | **of this length** *Films of this length* (=as long as this) *are pretty unusual.*
4 run/stretch/walk etc the (full) length of sth to go or move from one end to the other of something: *The wall ran the full length of the garden. | They walked the length of the pier.*
5 shoulder-length/knee-length etc reaching down as far as your shoulders etc: *shoulder-length hair | an ankle-length dress*
6 go to some/great/any lengths (to do sth) to try very hard or to do whatever is necessary to achieve something that is important to you: *He went to great lengths to keep their name out of the papers. | Bella would go to any lengths to fulfil her ambition.*
7 at (some/great etc) length a) if you talk at length about something, you talk about it for a long time: **speak/talk etc at length** *The young people spoke at length about their experiences. | We've already discussed the subject at great length.* **b)** *literary* after a long time: *'I don't agree,' she said at length.*
8 the length and breadth of the area/country/land etc in or through every part of a large area: *The police searched the length and breadth of the country.*
9 PIECE [C] a piece of something long and thin: **a length of rope/pipe/wire etc**
10 IN RACES [C] the measurement of a horse, boat etc from one end to the other – used when saying how far the horse, boat etc is ahead of another: *The horse **won by** three lengths.*
11 SWIMMING [C] the distance from one end of a swimming pool to the other: **do/swim a length** *She does at least 20 lengths a day.* → **hold sth at arm's length** at ARM[1](8), → **keep/hold sb at arm's length** at ARM[1](9), → FULL-LENGTH[1]

length·en /ˈleŋθən/ *v* [I,T] to make something longer or to become longer OPP **shorten**: *Can you lengthen this skirt for me? | The days lengthened as summer approached.*

REGISTER
In everyday English, people usually say that something **gets longer** rather than **lengthens**: *The days began to **get longer**.*

length·wise /ˈleŋθwaɪz/ (*also* **length·ways** /-weɪz/ *BrE*) *adv* in the direction or position of the longest side: *Lay the bricks lengthwise.*

length·y /ˈleŋθi/ ●●○ (*comparative* **lengthier**, *superlative* **lengthiest**) *adj* [usually before noun]
1 continuing for a long time, often too long OPP **brief**: *A lengthy period of training is required. | An accident is causing some lengthy delays.* THESAURUS▸ LONG
2 a speech, piece of writing etc that is lengthy is long and often contains too many details: *a lengthy report*

le·ni·ent /ˈliːniənt/ *adj* not strict in the way you punish someone or in the standard you expect: *the lenient sentences handed down by some judges | School examiners say that marking has become more lenient in recent years.* —**leniently** *adv* —**leniency, lenience** *n* [U]: *the trend towards greater leniency for most offenders*

lens /lenz/ ●●○ *n* [C]
1 the part of a camera through which light travels onto the surface where the image is recorded: *a standard 50 mm lens* → TELEPHOTO LENS, WIDE-ANGLE LENS, ZOOM LENS
2 a piece of curved glass or plastic which makes things look bigger, smaller, or clearer when you look through it: *glasses with powerful lenses | the lens of the microscope* → see picture at MICROSCOPE
3 the clear part inside your eye that FOCUSes so you can see things clearly
4 a CONTACT LENS

lent /lent/ the past tense and past participle of LEND

Lent *n* [U] the 40 days before Easter when some Christians eat less food or stop doing something that they enjoy —**Lenten** *adj*

len·til /ˈlentl, -təl/ *n* [C] a small round seed like a bean, dried and used for food

len·to /ˈlentəʊ $ -toʊ/ *adj, adv technical* music that is played lento is played slowly

Le·o /ˈliːəʊ $ ˈliːoʊ/ *n* (*plural* **Leos**) **1** [U] the fifth sign of the ZODIAC, represented by a lion, which some people believe affects the character and life of people born

L

between July 24 and August 23 **2** [C] someone who was born between July 24 and August 23

le·o·nine /ˈliːənaɪn/ *adj literary* like a lion in character or appearance

leop·ard /ˈlepəd $ -ərd/ *n* [C] **1** a large animal of the cat family, with yellow fur and black spots, which lives in Africa and South Asia → see picture at BIG CAT **2 a leopard can't change its spots** used to say that people cannot change their character

le·o·tard /ˈliːətɑːd $ -ɑːrd/ *n* [C] a tight piece of clothing that looks a little like a woman's SWIMSUIT and is worn for exercise or dancing, especially by women

LEP /ˌel iː ˈpiː/ *adj* [only before noun] *AmE technical* (***limited English proficient***) relating to someone whose first language is not English and who cannot communicate very well in English: *The number of* ***LEP students*** *has risen since 1993.*

lep·er /ˈlepə $ -ər/ *n* [C] **1** someone who has leprosy **2** someone that people avoid because they have done something that people disapprove of: *They treated me as if I was a leper.*

lep·re·chaun /ˈleprəkɔːn $ -kɑːn, -kɔːn/ *n* [C] an imaginary creature in the form of a little old man, in old Irish stories

lep·ro·sy /ˈleprəsi/ *n* [U] a very serious infectious disease in which the flesh and nerves are gradually destroyed → **leper** —**leprous** *adj*

les·bi·an /ˈlezbiən/ *n* [C] a woman who is sexually attracted to other women → **gay** —**lesbian** *adj* —**lesbianism** *n* [U]

le·sion /ˈliːʒən/ *n* [C] *technical* damage to someone's skin or part of their body such as their stomach or brain, caused by injury or illness: *acute gastric lesions*

less¹ /les/ ●●● S1 W1 *adv*

1 not so much or to a smaller degree OPP **more**: *Maybe he would worry less if he understood the situation.* | *In recent years she has appeared in public less frequently.* | **less (...) than** *Tickets were less expensive than I had expected.* | **much/a lot/far less** *Social class matters a lot less than it used to.* | **not ... any the less/no less** (=not less) *Your second point is no less important.* | *It's a common problem but this doesn't make it any the less disturbing.* | *I know he's done a dreadful thing, but I don't love him any the less.* | **be less a ... than a ...** (=be not so much like one thing as another) *'Will you please come with me?' It was less a request than a command.*

2 less than helpful/honest/enthusiastic etc not at all helpful, honest etc: *He was less than enthusiastic about the idea.*

3 less and less used to say that a quality, situation etc gradually decreases OPP **more and more**: *As the years went by, he seemed to care less and less about his reputation.* | *Smoking is becoming less and less acceptable.*

4 much/still less used to say that a greater thing is even less true, likely, or possible than the thing you have just mentioned: *These people can scarcely afford to buy food, still less luxury goods like perfume.* | *I didn't think Dave would ever read a book, much less write one himself.*

less² ●●● S1 W1 *determiner, pron*

1 a smaller amount or not as much OPP **more**: *Doctors recommend eating less salt.* | *People today seem to have less time for each other.* | *Most of us got £4 an hour, but some received even less.* | **[+of]** *The map covered less of the area than I'd thought.* | *Flying is less of a risk than driving.* | **less (...) than** *She knows less than I do about it.* | **less than 10/100 etc** *a distance of less than 100 metres* | **much/a lot less** *It costs much less to go by bus.*

USAGE: Less, fewer

- You use **less** before an uncountable noun: *These light bulbs use less electricity.*
- You use **fewer** before a plural noun: *There were fewer cars in those days.* ✗ Don't say: *There were less cars in those days.* Although you will hear people say this in everyday spoken English, it is considered to be incorrect.

2 no less a) used to emphasize that an amount or number is large: **no less than** *By 1977, the USA was importing no less than 45% of its oil.* **b)** used to emphasize that the person or thing you are talking about is important or impressive: *Our awards were presented by the mayor, no less.* | *The message came from* ***no less a person than*** *the prime minister.*

3 nothing less than sth used to emphasize how important, serious, or impressive something is: *His appearance in the show was nothing less than a sensation.*

4 less and less a decreasing amount of something OPP **more and more**: *They began spending less and less time together.* | **[+of]** *The band was doing less and less of that kind of music.*

5 in less than no time very quickly or very soon: *In less than no time they found that they owed over $10,000.*

6 less of sth *BrE spoken* used to tell a child to stop doing something: *Less of that noise, please!*

less³ *prep formal* taking away or not including a particular amount SYN **minus**: *What is 121 less 36?* | *He gave us our money back, less the $2 service charge.*

-less /ləs/ *suffix* [in adjectives] **1** without something: *I felt powerless.* | *a childless couple* | *tasteless food* **2** not doing or using something: *You're too careless.* | *It's perfectly harmless.* **3** not possible to treat or affect in a particular way: *on countless occasions* | *She's tireless.*

les·see /leˈsiː/ *n* [C] *law* someone who is allowed to use a house, building, land etc for a period of time in return for payment to the owner → **lessor**

less·en /ˈlesən/ ●○○ *v* [I,T] to become smaller in size, importance, or value, or make something do this SYN **reduce**: **lessen the risk/chance/possibility etc (of sth)** *Exercise lessens the risk of heart disease.* | **lessen the impact/effect/importance (of sth)** *The new project will lessen the effects of car pollution.* | *Gradually her anxiety lessened.*

less·er /ˈlesə $ -ər/ ●●○ *adj* [only before noun]

1 *formal* not as large, as important, or as much as something else OPP **greater**: *They originally asked for $5 million, but finally settled for a lesser sum.* | **to a lesser extent/degree** *This was true in Madrid and, to a lesser extent, Valencia and Seville.* → **lesser mortals** at MORTAL², → **to a greater or lesser extent** at EXTENT(1)

2 the lesser of two evils (*also* **the lesser evil**) the less unpleasant or harmful of two unpleasant choices

3 *technical* used in the names of some types of animal, bird, or plant that are slightly smaller than the main type —**lesser** *adv*: *the lesser-known artists of the period* | *one of Glasgow's lesser-used venues*

les·son /ˈlesən/ ●●● S2 W3 *n* [C]

1 LEARNING A SKILL a period of time in which someone is taught a particular skill, for example how to play a musical instrument or drive a car: *piano lessons* | **have/take lessons** *She's started taking driving lessons.* | **[+in/on]** *lessons in First Aid* | *lessons in road safety*

2 IN SCHOOL *BrE* a period of time in which school students are taught a particular subject SYN **class** *AmE*: *Lessons start at 9 o'clock.* | **French/physics/art etc lesson** *I've got a double maths lesson next.* | **[+in/on]** *Andrew* ***gives*** *private* ***lessons*** *in Spanish.*

3 EXPERIENCE something that provides experience or information that you can learn from and use: **learn a lesson** (=gain useful experience or information) *There were important lessons to be learned from these discoveries.* | *The government has failed to learn* ***the lessons of history.*** | **[+to]** *The men's courage and faith is a lesson to us all.* | *Now* ***let that be a lesson to you*** *all* (=be careful to avoid having the same bad experience again). | *Her fate should be a* ***salutary lesson*** (=one that teaches or warns you about something).

4 BOOK a part of a book that is used for learning a particular subject, especially in school: *Turn to lesson 25.*

5 CHURCH a short piece that is read from the Bible during a religious ceremony → **sb has learned their lesson** at LEARN(5), → **teach sb a lesson** at TEACH(6)

les·sor /le'sɔː $ -'sɔːr/ *n* [C] *law* someone who allows someone else to use their house, building, land etc for a period of time for payment → **lessee**

lest /lest/ ●○○ *conjunction literary*
1 in order to make sure that something will not happen: *She turned away from the window lest anyone see them.*
2 used to show that someone is afraid or worried that a particular thing might happen: **worried/concerned/anxious etc lest ...** *He paused, afraid lest he say too much.* | *She worried lest he should tell someone what had happened.*

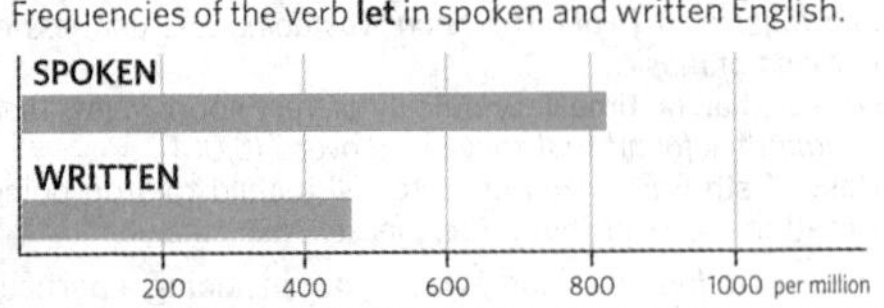

let¹ /let/ ●●● S1 W1 *v* (*past tense and past participle* **let**, *present participle* **letting**)
1 ALLOW [T not in passive] to allow someone to do something → **allow**, **permit**: *I can't come out tonight – my dad won't let me.* | **let sb do sth** *Let Johnny have a go on the computer now.* | *Some people seem to let their kids do whatever they like.* | *Let me have a look at that letter.* | **let sb have sth** (=give something to someone) *I can let you have another £10, but no more.* THESAURUS ALLOW

REGISTER
In written English, people often prefer to use **allow sb to do sth** rather than **let sb do sth**, as it is slightly more formal: *We must **allow** young people **to** develop independence.*

2 NOT STOP STH HAPPENING [T] to not stop something happening, or to make it possible for it to happen: **let sb/sth do sth** *Jenny let the note fall to the ground.* | *Don't let anyone know it was me who told you.* | *Max let the door swing open.* | *Let the cookies cool down before you try them.* | **let yourself be beaten/persuaded/fooled etc** *I stupidly let myself be persuaded to take part in a live debate.*
3 let go a) to stop holding something or someone: *Let go! You're hurting me.* | **[+of]** *The guard let go of the lead, and the dog lunged forward.* **b)** to accept that you cannot change something and stop thinking or worrying about it: *Sometimes you just have to learn to let go.*
4 let sb go a) to allow someone to leave a place where they have been kept SYN **release**: *The police had to let him go through lack of evidence.* | *The hijackers were persuaded to let some hostages go.* **b)** to make someone leave their job – used in order to avoid saying this directly: *I'm afraid we had to let several of our staff go.*

SPOKEN PHRASES
5 SUGGEST/OFFER [T] used to make a suggestion or to offer help: **let's do sth** *Let's make a start, shall we?* | *Let's all get together over Christmas.* | ***Let's not** jump to conclusions – he might have been delayed.* | **let sb do sth** *Let me help you with those bags.* | *Let me give you a piece of advice.* | **let's hope (that)** *Let's hope he got your message in time.* | **don't let's do sth** *BrE informal*: *Don't let's argue like this.*
6 let's see (*also* **let me see**) used when you are thinking about or trying to remember something: *Today's date is – let me see, March 20th.* | *Now, let's see, where did I put your application form?*
7 let me think used to say that you need time to think about or remember something: *What was his name, now? Let me think.*
8 let him/her/them etc used to say that you do not care if someone does something they are threatening to do: *'She says she's going to sell her story to the newspapers!' 'Well, let her!'*
9 let's face it/let's be honest used to say that someone must accept an unpleasant fact or situation: *Let's face it, no one's going to lend us any money.*
10 let's just say (that) used to say that you are not going to give someone all the details about something: *'So who did it?' 'Let's just say it wasn't anyone in this family.'*

11 let yourself go a) to relax completely and enjoy yourself: *For goodness sake, Peter, why don't you just let yourself go for once?* **b)** to stop looking after yourself properly, for example by not caring about your appearance: *Poor Dad. He's really let himself go since Mum died.*
12 let sth go a) to not punish or criticize someone for something they have done wrong: *OK, I'll let it go this time.* **b)** to stop worrying or thinking too much about something: *It's time to let the past go.* **c)** *informal* to sell something for a particular amount: **let sth go for £20/$200 etc** *I couldn't let it go for less than £300.*
13 WISH [T not in passive] used to say that you wish or hope that something happens, or does not happen: **(not) let sb/sth do sth** *Don't let him be the one who died, she prayed.*
14 let alone used after a negative statement to say that the next thing you mention is even more unlikely: *The baby can't even sit up yet, let alone walk!*
15 let sth drop/rest/lie to stop talking about or trying to deal with something: *It seems the press are not going to let the matter rest.*
16 let slip to accidentally tell someone something that should have been kept secret: **[+that]** *Liz let slip that she'd seen him quite recently.*
17 RENT [T] *especially BrE* to charge someone an amount of money for the use of a room or building SYN **lease** → **hire**, **rent**: *Interhome has over 20,000 houses to let across Europe.* | **let sth to sb** *I've let my spare room to a student.* | **let sb sth** *Would you consider letting me the garage for a few months?* | **let sth out to sb** *We let the smaller studios out to local artists.* | **To Let** *written* (=written on a sign outside a building to show that it is available for renting)
18 MATHEMATICS **let sth be/equal/represent sth** *technical* used in mathematics to mean that you give something a particular measurement or value in order to make a calculation: *Let angle A equal the sum of the two opposite sides.*
19 let yourself in for sth *informal* to do something that will cause you a lot of trouble: *I don't think Carol realizes what she's letting herself in for.*
20 never let a day/week/year etc go by without doing sth used to say that someone does a particular thing very regularly: *They never seem to let a year go by without introducing a new version of their software.*
21 let the good times roll *informal* used to say that it is time for people to start having fun
22 let sb have it *informal* to attack someone → **let fly (sth)** at FLY¹(17), → **let it all hang out** at HANG OUT, → **live and let live** at LIVE¹(21), → **let it/her rip** at RIP¹(6), → **let rip** at RIP¹(5)

let sb/sth ↔ **down** *phr v*
1 to not do something that someone trusts or expects you to do: *She had been **let down badly** in the past.* | *The worst feeling is having let our fans down.* | **let the side down** *BrE* (=disappoint a group of people that you belong to)
2 to make someone or something less successful or effective: *McKenzie's judgement rarely lets him down.*
3 to move something or someone to a lower position: *Let down a rope so that I can climb up.* | *Carefully, she let herself down into the water.*
4 let your hair down *informal* to relax and enjoy yourself, especially after working hard: *Visitors young and old let their hair down and enjoyed the show.*
5 let your guard/defences down to relax and stop worrying about what might happen or what someone might find out about you: *Maggie never really lets her guard down, does she?*
6 let sb down lightly/gently to give someone bad news in a way that will not upset them too much: *I get asked out on dates quite often, but I always try to let the guy down gently.*
7 *BrE* to allow the air to escape from something so that it loses its shape and becomes flat: *Someone's let my tyres down!*
8 to make a piece of clothing longer by unfolding a folded edge OPP **take up**

GRAMMAR: Comparison

let

• You **let** someone **do** something: *Her boss lets her work from home.* ✗ Don't say: *let someone to do something*

Let is not used in the passive.

allow

• You **allow** someone **to do** something: *Her boss allows her to work from home.*

• Something **is allowed**: *Working from home is allowed.*

Allow is often used in the passive.

permit

• Something **is permitted**: *Working from home is permitted.*

• Someone **is permitted to do** something: *Employees are permitted to work from home.*

Permit is usually used in the passive.

let sb **in on** sth *phr v* to tell something that is secret or only known by a few people: *TV chef Raymond Blanc lets us in on the secrets of his kitchen.* | *Would someone mind letting me in on the joke?*

let sb/sth **into** sth *phr v*

1 to tell someone something that is secret or private: *It was time to let the rest of the family into the secret.*

2 *technical* to put something such as a window or a decoration into a wall: *Two large windows were let into the wall each side of the door.* GRAMMAR **Let into** is usually passive in this meaning.

let sb/sth **off** *phr v*

1 to not punish someone: *I'll let you off this time, but don't do it again.* | **[+with]** *After checking our identities, the customs men let us off with a warning.* | **let sb off the hook** (=allow someone to escape punishment or criticism) *He'd decided to make Sandra wait before letting her off the hook.* | **let sb off lightly/easily** (=give someone a less serious punishment than they deserve) *I think young criminals are let off far too lightly.*

2 let sb off (sth) if someone in authority lets you off something you should do, they give you permission not to do it: *You've worked hard all week, so I'll let you off today.*

3 let sth ↔ off to make something explode: *One boy had let off a firework in class.* → **let/blow off steam** at STEAM[1](4)

let on *phr v informal* to tell someone something, especially something you have been keeping secret: **let on (that)** *Don't let on that I told you.* | **let on who/why/how etc** *We never did let on how we found out.* | *I'm sure he knows more than he's letting on.*

let out *phr v*

1 let out sth to suddenly make a loud sound such as a shout or cry: **let out a scream/cry/roar etc** *He let out a cry of disbelief.*

2 let sth ↔ out to make a piece of clothing wider or looser, especially because it is too tight

3 let sth ↔ out *BrE* to charge someone an amount of money for the use of a room or building: *We're letting out our son's old room to a student.*

4 *AmE* if a school, college, film etc lets out, it ends and the people attending it can leave: *What time does the movie let out?* → **let the cat out of the bag** at CAT(2)

let up *phr v*

1 to become less severe or harmful: *The wind had dropped and the rain gradually let up.*

2 to be less severe, unkind, or violent towards someone: *Even when the crowd had scattered, the police didn't let up.*

3 to stop working as hard as you were: *You're doing really well, but you can't afford to let up now.*

let² *n* **1** [C] *BrE* an arrangement in which a house or flat is rented to someone: *An agency is managing the let.* | *a long-term let* **2 without let or hindrance** *law* happening freely without being prevented in any way

-let /lɪt/ *suffix* [in nouns] a small kind of something: *a booklet* | *a piglet*

letch /letʃ/ *v* another spelling of LECH

let·down /ˈletdaʊn/ ●○○ *n* [singular] *informal* an event, performance etc that is not as good as you expected it to be SYN **disappointment**: *The end of the book was a real letdown.* → **let down** at LET[1]

le·thal /ˈliːθəl/ ●●○ *adj*

1 causing death, or able to cause death → **fatal**: *a* ***lethal dose*** *of heroin* | *a* ***lethal weapon*** | *death by* ***lethal injection*** | *a* ***lethal cocktail*** *of drink and pills* | **[+to]** *These chemicals are lethal to fish.*

2 *informal* likely to be powerful or dangerous – often used humorously: *They were all drinking lethal amounts of tequila!* | *Higher taxes and higher inflation were* ***a lethal combination***.

le·thar·gic /ləˈθɑːdʒɪk $ -ˈθɑːr-/ *adj* feeling as if you have no energy and no interest in doing anything SYN **lazy** OPP **energetic**: *The hot weather was making us all lethargic.* **THESAURUS** SLOW —**lethargically** /-kli/ *adv*

leth·ar·gy /ˈleθədʒi $ -ər-/ *n* [U] the feeling of being lethargic: *New mothers often complain of lethargy and mild depression.*

let's /lets/ ●●● S1 the short form of 'let us', used especially to make suggestions: *Let's go!*

USAGE: Let's, let's not

• You say: *Let's not argue.* In British English, you can also say: *Don't let's argue.* ✗ Don't say: *Let's don't argue.*

• Don't confuse **let's** and **lets**. You write: *Let's introduce ourselves.* ✗ Don't write: *Lets introduce ourselves.*

let·ter¹ /ˈletə $ -ər/ ●●● S1 W1 *n* [C]

1 a written or printed message that is usually put in an envelope and sent by mail: **[+from/to]** *I got a letter from Melanie today.* | *Bart's writing a letter to his parents.* → CHAIN LETTER, LETTER OF CREDIT, OPEN LETTER

2 a sign in writing or printing that represents a speech sound: *There are 26 letters in the English alphabet.* | *Fill in the form in* ***capital letters*** (=written in their large form). → BLOCK LETTERS

3 to the letter paying exact attention to the details of something: *I followed the instructions to the letter, but it still wouldn't work.*

4 the letter of the law the exact words of a law or agreement rather than the intended or general meaning: *employees who stick to the letter of the law in their contracts* → **the spirit of the law** at SPIRIT[1](11)

5 *AmE* a large cloth letter that you sew onto a jacket, given as a reward for playing in a school or college sports team: *Mark got a letter in soccer.*

6 English/American/German etc letters [plural] *formal* the study of the literature of a particular country or language: *a major figure in English letters* → DEAD LETTER, MAN OF LETTERS

COLLOCATIONS

VERBS

get a letter (*also* **receive a letter** *formal*) *I got a letter from my mother.*

write a letter *He wrote a letter inviting her to visit.*

send a letter *The school sent a letter to all the children's parents.*

post a letter *BrE*, **mail a letter** *AmE* | **answer a letter/reply to a letter** | **open a letter** | **read a letter** | **a letter comes/arrives** | **a letter is addressed to sb** (=has their name and address on the envelope)

ADJECTIVES/NOUN + letter

long/short *She was thrilled to get a long letter from her son.*

formal/informal *The letter sounded very formal.*

a personal letter *I don't want him reading my personal letters.*

a business letter | **an official letter** | **a love letter** | **a thank-you letter** | **a covering letter** *BrE*, **a cover letter** *AmE* (=that you send with your CV to an employer)

PHRASES

a letter of thanks/introduction/complaint etc
I finally got a letter of apology from the company.

COMMON ERRORS

⚠ Don't say 'invitation letter' or 'complaint letter'. Say **letter of invitation** or **letter of complaint**.

letter² *v* **1** [T] to write, draw, paint etc letters or words on something: *The card was neatly lettered P. A. DUFFY.* | **be lettered in sth** *Several pages are lettered in gold.* GRAMMAR **Letter** is usually passive in this meaning. **2** [I] *AmE* to earn a LETTER¹(5) in a sport: **[+in]** *He lettered in basketball at Brandeis.*

'letter ˌbomb *n* [C] a small bomb hidden in a package and sent to someone in order to kill or harm them

let·ter·box /ˈletəbɒks $ ˈletərbɑːks/ *n* [C] **1** *BrE* a narrow hole in a door, or a special box outside a house where letters, packages etc are delivered SYN **mailbox** *AmE* **2** *BrE* a box in a post office or street, in which letters are posted SYN **postbox** *BrE*, **mailbox** *AmE*

let·ter·box·ing /ˈletəˌbɒksɪŋ $ -terˌbɑːks-/ *n* [U] when a film from the cinema is broadcast on television with black bands at the top and bottom of the television screen so that the film will have the same DIMENSIONS as it did on a cinema screen

let·tered /ˈletəd $ -ərd/ *adj formal* well educated

let·ter·head /ˈletəhed $ -ər-/ *n* **1** [C] the name and address that is printed at the top of a sheet of writing paper **2** [U] *AmE* paper that has the name and address of a person or business printed at the top of it: *The letter had been written on university letterhead.*

let·ter·ing /ˈletərɪŋ/ *n* [U] **1** written or drawn letters, especially of a particular type, size, colour etc: *Chinese lettering* **2** the art of writing or drawing letters or words

ˌletter of 'credit *n* [C] an official letter from a bank allowing a particular person to take money from another bank

ˌletter-'perfect *adj AmE* correct in every detail: *a letter-perfect product*

'letter-size *adj AmE* letter-size paper is 8½ INCHes wide and 11 inches long

let·ting /ˈletɪŋ/ *n* [C] *BrE* a house or apartment that can be rented: *short-term holiday lettings* | **a letting agent/agency** (=one that arranges lettings)

let·tuce /ˈletɪs/ ●●● S3 *n* [C,U] a round vegetable with thin green leaves eaten raw in SALADS → see picture at **VEGETABLE¹**

'let-up (*also* **let·up** *AmE*) /ˈletʌp/ *n* [singular, U] when something unpleasant stops or becomes less difficult, severe etc: **no let-up/not any let-up** *The pressure at work continued without any let-up.* | **[+in]** *Streets were flooded, but still there was no let-up in the rain.* → **let up** at **LET¹**

leu·ke·mi·a (*also* **leukaemia** *BrE*) /luːˈkiːmiə/ *n* [U] a type of CANCER of the blood, that causes weakness and sometimes death

lev·ee /ˈlevi/ *n* [C] a special wall built to stop a river flooding

lev·el¹ /ˈlevəl/ ●●● S1 W1 *n* [C]

1 AMOUNT the amount or degree of something, compared to another amount or degree: *Inflation fell to its lowest level in 30 years.* | **[+of]** *Increased supplies are needed to meet the level of demand.* | *Dolphins show a high level of intelligence.* THESAURUS ▸ **AMOUNT**

2 STANDARD a particular standard of skill or ability, for example in education or sport: **at ... level** *Students at this level may have problems with basic grammar.* | *What level do you think you're at?* | **beginner/advanced/national etc level** *Few athletes can compete at international level.* | *an advanced-level coursebook* → **A LEVEL**

3 HEIGHT the height of something in relation to the ground or to another object: **at ... level** *Your arms should be at the same level as your desk.* | **eye/knee/shoulder etc level** (=the same height as your eyes etc) *Skirts this year are just above knee level.* | **water/oil etc level** (=the height of the water etc from the ground or the bottom of a container) *Check the water level in the car radiator.* → **GROUND LEVEL, SEA LEVEL**

4 FLOOR/GROUND a floor or area of ground that is at a particular height, especially when you can go up or down to other floors or areas: **on ... level** *Didn't we park the car on Level 2?* | *The town is built on different levels.* | *The medical center is on one level* (=so that you do not have to go up or down). → **SPLIT-LEVEL**

5 RANK OF JOB a particular position in a system that has different ranks of importance: **at ... level** *Training is offered at each level in the department.* | **at board/management/senior etc level** *Further talks at ministerial level were held.* → **HIGH-LEVEL, LOW-LEVEL**

6 WAY OF UNDERSTANDING a way of considering or understanding something: **on ... level** *The story can be understood on many different levels.* | **on a personal/practical/superficial etc level** *I agree with you, but only on a theoretical level.*

7 at local/state/national etc level happening within a small area or the whole area of a state, country etc: *These changes are taking place at regional level.*

8 be on the level *informal* to be honest and legal: *This is all on the level, right?*

9 descend/sink to sb's level to behave as badly as someone: *If you hit him back, you'll only be descending to his level.*

10 TOOL a tool used for checking that a surface is flat SYN **spirit-level**

COLLOCATIONS

ADJECTIVES/NOUN + level

high *The level of salt in his diet was too high.*
low *The level of violent crime is lower than ten years ago.*
a record level (=the highest ever level) *Sales have reached record levels.*
noise/pollution levels *Noise levels are unacceptably high.*
price/income/wage levels *Wage levels had failed to keep up with inflation.*
stress level *I find exercise helps with my stress levels.*
energy/fitness level

VERBS

a level rises/goes up/increases *The level of unemployment has increased.*
a level falls/goes down/decreases *Pollution levels have fallen slightly.*
achieve/reach a level *China's imports of wheat reached record levels.*
remain/stay at a level *The fees are likely to remain at current levels.*
maintain a level *It's difficult to maintain the same level of physical fitness.*
increase a level | **reduce a level**

level² ●●○ *adj*

1 flat and not sloping in any direction: *The floors in the old house were not completely level.* | *a level surface suitable for wheelchairs* THESAURUS ▸ **FLAT**

2 a) two things that are level are at the same height as each other: **[+with]** *Your eyes should be level with the top of the screen.* | *The curtains aren't quite level.* **b)** *BrE* two sports teams, competitors etc that are level have the same number of points: **[+with]** *Before the weekend, Madrid was level with Barcelona.* | *They* **finished level**, *with ten points each.* → **LEVEL-PEGGING c)** having the same value or position as something or someone else: **[+with]** *Borrowing rates rose to over 8%, roughly level with those in America.* | *He cycled along beside her, keeping level.*

3 a level playing field a situation in which different people, companies, countries etc can all compete fairly because no one has special advantages: *Small businesses want to compete on a level playing field with larger ones.*

4 do your level best (to do sth) to try as hard as possible to do something: *I'll do my level best to help you.*

5 level voice/look/gaze a steady voice, look etc that shows you are calm or determined

6 level teaspoon/cup etc (of sth) an amount of a substance that fills a spoon, cup etc to the top but no more, used as a measure in cooking → **heaped**: *Add one level teaspoon of salt.* → **draw level** at DRAW[1](11)

level[3] ●○○ *v* (**levelled**, **levelling** *BrE*, **leveled**, **leveling** *AmE*)
1 [T] (*also* **level sth ↔ off/out**) to make something flat and smooth: *Workers leveled the wet concrete with a piece of wood. | Cover with a layer of sand and level it off.*
2 [T] to knock down or destroy a building or area completely: *Bombs levelled a large part of the town.*
3 [I,T] *BrE* to make the score in a game or competition equal: *He slipped the ball into the net to* ***level the score*** *at 1-1. | United went ahead but the visitors levelled in the 73rd minute.*
4 level the playing field to make a situation in which people are competing fair, with no one having special advantages
5 level criticism/charges/accusations etc at/against sb to aim criticism etc at a particular person, country etc, especially publicly: *the criticism levelled at the United States | Serious allegations were levelled against the minister.*
level sth **at** sb/sth *phr v* to aim something such as a weapon at someone or something: *Slowly he levelled his gun at the tiger.*
level off/out *phr v*
1 to stop going up or down and continue at the same height: *After climbing steeply, the path levelled off. | The plane levelled out at 30,000 feet.*
2 to stop rising or falling and become steady: *Inflation has begun to level off.*
3 level sth ↔ off/out to make something flat and smooth
level with sb *phr v informal* to speak honestly to someone, after hiding some unpleasant facts from them: *She decided to level with him and tell him how she felt.* → **be on the level** at LEVEL[1](8)

ˌlevel ˈcrossing *n* [C] *BrE* a place where a railway crosses a road, usually protected by gates SYN **railroad crossing** *AmE*

ˌlevel-ˈheaded *adj* calm and sensible in making judgments or decisions OPP **hot-headed**

lev·el·ler *BrE*, **leveler** *AmE* /ˈlevələ $ -ər/ *n* [C] something, especially death or illness, that makes people of all classes and ranks seem equal

ˌlevel-ˈpegging *n* **be level-pegging** *BrE* if competitors in a race, election etc are level-pegging, they are equal and it is difficult to know who will win

le·ver[1] /ˈliːvə $ ˈlevər/ ●○○ *n* [C]
1 a stick or handle on a machine or piece of equipment, that you move to operate it: ***Pull*** *this* ***lever*** *to open the gate.* → GEAR LEVER
2 a long thin piece of metal that you use to lift something heavy by putting one end under the object and pushing the other end down
3 something you use to influence a situation to get the result that you want: *Rich countries use foreign aid as a lever to achieve political aims.*

lever[2] *v* [T] **1** to move something with a lever: **lever sth off/up/out etc** *He levered the stone into place.* **2 lever yourself up** (*also* **lever yourself onto/out of etc sth**) to move your body by pushing on something with your arms to help you: *He slowly levered himself up.* **3** to make someone leave a particular job, situation etc: **lever sb out** *They're trying to lever him out of his job.*

le·ver·age[1] /ˈliːvərɪdʒ $ ˈle-, ˈliː-/ *n* [U] **1** influence that you can use to make people do what you want: *diplomatic leverage by the US* **2** the action, power, or use of a lever

leverage[2] *v* [T] *AmE technical* **1** to make money available to someone in order to INVEST or to buy something such as a company: *the use of public funds to leverage private investment* **2** to spread or use RESOURCES (=money, skills, buildings etc that an organization has available), ideas etc again in several different ways or in different parts of a company, system etc: **leverage sth across sth** *Reusable software is leveraged across many applications.*

ˌleveraged ˈbuyout *n* [C] *technical* when someone borrows money to buy all or most of the STOCK of a company by promising to pay the bank back by selling the company's ASSETS if they cannot pay back the money they borrowed

le·vi·a·than /lɪˈvaɪəθən/ *n* [C] *literary* **1** something very large and strong: *a leviathan of a ship* **2** a very large and frightening sea animal

lev·i·tate /ˈlevɪteɪt/ *v* [I,T] to rise and float in the air by magic, or to make someone or something do this —**levitation** /ˌlevɪˈteɪʃən/ *n* [U]

lev·i·ty /ˈlevəti/ *n* [U] *formal* lack of respect or seriousness when you are dealing with something serious OPP **gravity**

lev·y[1] /ˈlevi/ AWL *v* (**levied**, **levying**, **levies**) [T] to officially say that people must pay a tax or charge: **levy a tax/charge/fine etc (on sth)** *a new tax levied on all electrical goods*

levy[2] AWL *n* (*plural* **levies**) [C] an additional sum of money, usually paid as a tax: **[+on]** *He wants to impose a levy on landfill waste.*

lewd /luːd/ *adj* using rude words or movements that make you think of sex: *lewd comments* —**lewdly** *adv* —**lewdness** *n* [U]

lex·i·cal /ˈleksɪkəl/ *adj technical* dealing with words, or related to words

lex·i·cog·ra·phy /ˌleksɪˈkɒɡrəfi $ -ˈkɑː-/ *n* [U] the skill, practice, or profession of writing dictionaries —**lexicographer** *n* [C] —**lexicographical** /ˌleksɪkəˈɡræfɪkəl◂/ *adj*

lex·i·con /ˈleksɪkən $ -kɑːn, -kən/ *n* **1 the lexicon** *technical* all the words and phrases used in a language or that a particular person knows **2** [C] an alphabetical list of words with their meanings, especially on a particular subject or in a particular language: *a lexicon of geographical terms*

lex·is /ˈleksɪs/ *n* [U] *technical* all the words in a language SYN **vocabulary**

ley /leɪ, liː/ (*also* **ˈley line**) *n* [C] an imaginary line connecting buildings, places etc that is believed to follow an ancient track that has special power

LGBT /ˌel dʒiː biː ˈtiː/ the abbreviation of ***lesbian, gay, bisexual, transgender***

li·a·bil·i·ty /ˌlaɪəˈbɪləti/ ●○○ *n*
1 [U] legal responsibility for something, especially for paying money that is owed, or for damage or injury: **[+for]** *Tenants have legal liability for any damage they cause.* | **[+to]** *your liability to capital gains tax* | **liability to do sth** *The court ruled there was no liability to pay any refund.*
2 liabilities [plural] *technical* the amount of debt that must be paid OPP **assets**
3 [singular] someone or something that is likely to cause problems for someone: *A kid like Tom would be a liability in any classroom.* | **[+to]** *The outspoken minister has become a liability to the government.*
4 liability to sth *law* the amount by which something is likely to be affected by a particular kind of problem, illness etc → LIMITED LIABILITY

li·a·ble /ˈlaɪəbəl/ ●○○ *adj* [not before noun]
1 liable to do sth likely to do or say something or to behave in a particular way, especially because of a fault or natural tendency SYN **likely**: *The car is liable to overheat on long trips. | He was liable to just show up without warning.*
2 legally responsible for the cost of something: **[+for]** *people who are liable for income tax at a higher rate*
3 likely to be affected by a particular kind of problem, illness etc SYN **prone**: **[+to]** *You're more liable to injury when you don't get regular exercise.*
4 *law* likely to be legally punished or forced to do something by law: **[+to/for]** *Anyone found trespassing is liable to a maximum fine of $100.*

li·aise /liˈeɪz/ *v* [I] to exchange information with someone who works in another organization or department so that you can both be more effective: **[+with]** *Council officers are liaising closely with local groups.* | **[+between]** *The education officer liaises between students, schools and colleges.*

li·ai·son /li'eɪzən $ 'liːəzɑːn, li'eɪ-/ ●○○ *n*
1 [singular, U] the regular exchange of information between groups of people, especially at work, so that each group knows what the other is doing: **[+between]** *close liaison between the army and police* | **[+with]** *better liaison with other agencies* | **in liaison with sth** *The project has been set up in liaison with the art department.*
2 [C] (*also* **liaison officer**) someone whose job is to talk to different departments or groups and to tell each of them about what the others are doing: **[+to]** *Renee Ball, liaison to the State Parks Authority*
3 [C] a secret sexual relationship between a man and a woman, especially a man and a woman who are married but not to each other → **affair**

li·ar /'laɪə $ -ər/ ●●○ *n* [C] someone who deliberately says things which are not true: *Are you calling me a liar?*

lib /lɪb/ *n* → AD-LIB, WOMEN'S LIB

li·ba·tion /laɪ'beɪʃən/ *n* [C] *formal* a gift of wine to a god

lib·ber /'lɪbə $ -ər/ *n* **women's libber** → WOMEN'S LIB

Lib Dem /ˌlɪb 'dem◂/ *n* [C] *BrE* the abbreviation of *Liberal Democrat* —**Lib Dem** *adj*

li·bel¹ /'laɪbəl/ ●○○ *n* [C,U] when someone writes or prints untrue statements about someone so that other people could have a bad opinion of them → **slander**: **for libel** *Holt* ***sued*** *the newspaper* ***for libel.*** | **a libel action/case/trial** (=a court case against someone for libel) | *restrictions on press freedom, such as* ***libel laws***

libel² *v* (**libelled, libelling** *BrE*, **libeled, libeling** *AmE*) [T] to write or print a libel against someone → **slander**

li·bel·lous *BrE*, **libelous** *AmE* /'laɪbələs/ *adj* containing untrue written statements about someone which could make other people have a bad opinion of them → **slanderous**: *libellous gossip*

lib·e·ral¹ /'lɪbərəl/ ●○○ AWL *adj*
1 willing to understand and respect other people's ideas, opinions, and feelings: *a more liberal attitude towards sexuality* | *I had quite liberal parents.*
2 supporting or allowing gradual political and social changes OPP **conservative**: *a more liberal policy on issues of crime and punishment*
3 allowing people or organizations a lot of political or economic freedom: **liberal state/society/democracy etc**
4 generous or given in large amounts: *a liberal supply of drinks* | **[+with]** *If only they were as liberal with their cash.*
→ LIBERALLY
5 not exact: *a* ***liberal interpretation*** *of the original play*
6 liberal education a kind of education which encourages you to develop a large range of interests and knowledge and respect for other people's opinions

liberal² ●○○ AWL *n* [C] someone with liberal opinions or principles OPP **conservative**

Liberal *n* [C] someone who supports or belongs to the former Liberal Party in Britain or the Liberal Party in Canada —**Liberal** *adj*

ˌliberal 'arts *n* [plural] *especially AmE* the areas of learning which develop someone's ability to think and increase their general knowledge, rather than developing technical skills

ˌLiberal 'Democrats *n* [plural] a British political party → **Labour Party** —**Liberal Democrat** *adj*

lib·e·ral·is·m /'lɪbərəlɪzəm/ AWL *n* [U] liberal opinions and principles, especially on social and political subjects OPP **conservatism**

lib·e·ral·i·ty /ˌlɪbə'ræləti/ *n* [U] *formal* **1** understanding of, and respect for, other people's opinions **2** the quality of being generous

lib·e·ral·ize (*also* **-ise** *BrE*) /'lɪbərəlaɪz/ AWL *v* [T] to make a system, laws, or moral attitudes less strict —**liberalization** /ˌlɪbərəlaɪ'zeɪʃən $ -rələ-/ *n* [U]

lib·e·ral·ly /'lɪbərəli/ AWL *adv* **1** using or including plenty of something, especially in a generous way: *Apply the glue liberally to both surfaces.* | *dark hair liberally sprinkled with grey* **2** with liberal ideas or opinions: *The people around here are more liberally inclined than back home.*

'liberal ˌstudies *n* [plural] *especially BrE* subjects that are taught in order to increase someone's general knowledge and their ability to write, speak, and study more effectively → **liberal arts**

lib·e·rate /'lɪbəreɪt/ ●○○ AWL *v* [T]
1 to free someone from feelings or conditions that make their life unhappy or difficult: **liberate sb from sth** *women's freedom to pursue careers liberated from childcare* | *the liberating power of education*
2 to free prisoners, a city, a country etc from someone's control: *A few days later, our armies liberated the city.* —**liberation** /ˌlɪbə'reɪʃən/ *n* [U]: *liberation from oppression* | *the liberation of Paris in August 1944* —**liberator** /'lɪbəreɪtə $ -ər/ *n* [C]

lib·e·rat·ed /'lɪbəreɪtɪd/ AWL *adj* free to behave in the way you want, and not restricted by traditional rules of social and sexual behaviour: *a liberated woman*

libe'ration theˌology *n* [U] a modern form of Christian teaching and activity, mainly in the Roman Catholic Church, that is based on the idea that the Church should work to change bad social, political, and economic conditions

lib·er·tar·i·an /ˌlɪbə'teəriən $ -bər'ter-/ *n* [C] someone who believes strongly that people should be free to do and think what they want to, without any government control —**libertarian** *adj*

lib·er·tine /'lɪbətiːn $ -ər-/ *n* [C] *literary* someone who leads an immoral life and always looks for pleasure, especially sexual pleasure —**libertine** *adj*

lib·er·ty /'lɪbəti $ -ər-/ ●●○ *n* (*plural* **liberties**)
1 FREEDOM [U] the freedom and the right to do whatever you want without asking permission or being afraid of authority: *the fight for liberty and equality* | **individual/personal liberty** *threats to individual liberty* | **religious/political/economic liberty** *struggles for political liberty*
2 LEGAL RIGHT [C usually plural] a particular legal right: *liberties such as freedom of speech* → CIVIL LIBERTY
3 WITHOUT PERMISSION [singular] something you do without asking permission, especially which may offend or upset someone else: **take the liberty of doing sth** *I took the liberty of cancelling your reservation.*
4 be at liberty to do sth *formal* to have the right or permission to do something: *I am not at liberty to discuss these matters.*
5 take liberties with sb/sth a) to make unreasonable changes in something such as a piece of writing: *The film-makers took too many liberties with the original novel.* **b)** *old-fashioned* to treat someone without respect by being too friendly too quickly, especially in a sexual way: *He's been taking liberties with our female staff.*
6 at liberty *formal* if a prisoner or an animal is at liberty, they are no longer in prison or enclosed in a small place SYN **free**

li·bi·do /lɪ'biːdəʊ $ -doʊ/ *n* (*plural* **libidos**) [C,U] *technical* someone's desire to have sex SYN **sex drive** —**libidinous** /lɪ'bɪdɪnəs/ *adj*

Li·bra /'liːbrə/ *n* **1** [U] the seventh sign of the ZODIAC, represented by a pair of SCALES, which some people believe affects the character and life of people born between September 24 and October 23 **2** (*also* **Libran**) [C] someone who was born between September 24 and October 23 —**Libran** *adj*

li·brar·i·an /laɪ'breəriən $ -'brer-/ ●●○ *n* [C] someone who works in a library —**librarianship** *n* [U]

li·bra·ry /'laɪbrəri, -bri $ -breri/ ●●● S2 W1 *n* (*plural* **libraries**) [C]
1 a room or building containing books that can be looked at or borrowed → **bookshop**: *a public library* | **school/college/university library** | *a* ***library book*** | ***library staff***
2 a group of books, CDs etc, collected by one person
3 a room in a large house where books are kept
4 a set of books, CDs, videos etc that are produced by the same company and have the same general appearance: *a library of modern classics*

L

5 library pictures/footage *BrE* film or pictures used in a television programme which are not recent

li·bret·tist /lɪˈbretɪst/ *n* [C] someone who writes librettos

li·bret·to /lɪˈbretəʊ $ -toʊ/ *n* (*plural* **librettos**) [C] the words of an OPERA or musical play

lice /laɪs/ the plural of LOUSE[1]

li·cence *BrE*, **license** *AmE* /ˈlaɪsəns/ ●●● S3 W2 *n*

1 DOCUMENT [C] an official document giving you permission to own or do something for a period of time → **permit**: *The dealers applied for an export licence.* | *He was arrested for **driving without a license**.* | *The Tennessee Valley Authority **applied for a license** to operate the facility.* | *The owner of land could **grant a licence** to cut and remove timber.* | *I forgot to **renew** my **licence**.* | *Persistent offenders face **losing** their **licence**.* → DRIVING LICENCE

2 AGREEMENT [C,U] an agreement with a company or organization giving permission to make, sell, or use their product: **under licence** *Guinness is brewed under licence in South Africa.* | **single-user/10-user/site licence** (=permission for computer software to be used by a certain number of people or in a certain place only) | *a **licence agreement***

3 FREEDOM [U] freedom to do or say what you think is best: *Headteachers should be allowed greater licence in the exercise of their power.*

4 artistic/poetic licence the way in which a painter or writer changes the facts of the real world to make their story, description, or picture of events more interesting or more beautiful

5 EXCUSE [C,U] the freedom or opportunity to behave in a way that is wrong or immoral: **licence to do sth** *Police say it gives youngsters licence to break the law.*

6 licence to print money an opportunity to make a lot of money without much work or effort – especially used to show disapproval

li·cense (*also* **licence** *BrE*) /ˈlaɪsəns/ AWL *v* [T] to give official permission for someone to do or produce something, or for an activity to take place: **be licensed to do sth** *a restaurant which is licensed to sell alcohol* | *The vaccine has been licensed by the US Food and Drug Administration.* GRAMMAR **License** is usually passive.

li·censed (*also* **licenced** *BrE*) /ˈlaɪsənst/ ●○○ AWL *adj*

1 *BrE* having a licence to sell alcoholic drinks: *a licensed restaurant*

2 a car, gun etc that is licensed is one that someone has official permission to own or use

3 having been given official permission to do a particular job: *a licensed private investigator*

li·cen·see /ˌlaɪsənˈsiː/ *n* [C] someone who has official permission to do something

ˈlicense plate *n* [C] *AmE* one of the signs with numbers on it at the front and back of a car SYN **number plate** *BrE* → see picture at CAR

ˈlicensing ˌlaws *n* [plural] the British laws that say when and where you can sell alcohol

li·cen·ti·ate /laɪˈsenʃiət/ *n* [C] *formal* someone who has been given official permission to practise a particular art or profession

li·cen·tious /laɪˈsenʃəs/ *adj formal* behaving in a sexually immoral or uncontrolled way —**licentiously** *adv* —**licentiousness** *n* [U]

li·chee /ˈlaɪtʃiː/ *n* [C] another spelling of LYCHEE

li·chen /ˈlaɪkən, ˈlɪtʃən/ *n* [U] a grey, green, or yellow plant that spreads over the surface of stones and trees → **moss**

lick[1] /lɪk/ ●●● S3 *v*

1 TONGUE [T] to move your tongue across the surface of something in order to eat it, wet it, clean it etc: *The dog jumped up and licked her face.* | **lick sth ↔ up** *A cat licked up the drops spilt on the floor.* | **lick sth off sth** *He licked the drops off his upper lip.*

2 SPORT [T] *informal* to defeat an opponent: *I bet we could lick the best teams in Georgia.*

3 FLAMES/WAVES [I,T] *literary* if flames or waves lick something, they touch it again and again with quick movements: **[+at/against]** *Soon the flames were licking at the curtains.*

4 have (got) sth licked *informal* to have succeeded in dealing with a difficult problem: *Just when you think you've got it licked, it comes back.*

5 lick your lips (*also* **lick your chops** *AmE*) to feel eager and excited because you are expecting to get something good: *Scottish rugby fans are licking their lips in anticipation.*

6 lick your wounds to quietly think about the defeat or disappointment you have just suffered

7 lick sb's boots to obey someone completely because you are afraid of them or want to please them → **knock/lick sb/sth into shape** at SHAPE[1](3)

lick[2] *n* **1** [C usually singular] when you move your tongue across the surface of something: *Can I have a lick of your ice cream?* **2 a lick of paint/colour etc** a small amount of paint etc put onto the surface of something to improve its appearance: *It'll be okay after a lick of paint.* **3 not a lick of sth** *AmE old-fashioned* not even a small amount of something: *Ann won't do a lick of work around the house.* **4** [C] *informal* part of a song played on a GUITAR: *a bluesy guitar lick* **5 at a great/fair lick** *BrE informal* very fast **6 give sth a lick and a promise a)** *BrE* to wash or clean something quickly and carelessly **b)** *AmE* to do a job quickly and carelessly **7** [C] *informal* an act of hitting someone

lick·e·ty-split /ˌlɪkəti ˈsplɪt/ *adv AmE old-fashioned* very quickly

lick·ing /ˈlɪkɪŋ/ *n* [singular] *informal* **1** a defeat in a sports competition or match SYN **hammering**: *We got a real licking in the final.* **2** a severe beating as a punishment

lic·o·rice /ˈlɪkərɪs, -rɪʃ/ *n* [U] the American spelling of LIQUORICE

lid /lɪd/ ●●● S3 *n*

1 COVER [C] a cover for the open part of a pot, box, or other container: **dustbin/saucepan etc lid** *the name on the coffin lid* | **[+of]** *He carefully lifted the lid of the box.* → TOP[1](4), see picture at PAN[1]

2 EYE [C] an EYELID

3 keep a/the lid on sth to control a situation very carefully, especially so that it does not cause problems: *keeping the lid on inflation* | *Kline keeps a very tight lid on his private life.*

4 put a/the lid on sth *informal* to do something that finally stops something or ruins or ends someone's plans or hopes: *Let's put a lid on all these rumours.*

5 take the lid off sth (*also* **lift the lid on sth**) to let people know the true facts about a bad or shocking situation: *a documentary that takes the lid off the world of organized crime*

lid·ded /ˈlɪdɪd/ *adj* **1 heavy-lidded eyes** eyes with large EYELIDS **2** a lidded container, pot etc has a lid

li·do /ˈliːdəʊ, ˈlaɪ- $ ˈliːdoʊ/ *n* (*plural* **lidos**) [C] *BrE* an outdoor public area, often at a beach, lake etc, for swimming and lying in the sun

lie[1] /laɪ/ ●●● S2 W1 *v* (*past tense* **lay** /leɪ/, *past participle* **lain** /leɪn/, *present participle* **lying**, *third person singular* **lies**)

1 FLAT POSITION **a)** [I] to be in a position in which your body is flat on the floor, on a bed etc: **[+on/in etc]** *He was lying on the bed smoking a cigarette.* | *Don't lie in the sun for too long.* | **lie there** *For a few minutes he just lay there.* | **lie still/awake etc** *She would lie awake worrying.* | *The dog was lying dead on the floor.* **b)** (*also* **lie down**) [I always + adv/prep] to put yourself in a position in which your body is flat on the floor or on a bed: **[+on]** *Lie flat on the floor.* | **[+back]** *She lay back against the pillows.* **c)** [I always + adv/prep] to be in a flat position on a surface: **[+on/in etc]** *The papers were lying neatly on his desk.*

2 EXIST [I always + adv/prep] if a problem, an answer, blame etc lies somewhere, it is caused by, exists, or can be found in that thing, person, or situation: **fault/blame/responsibility lies with sb** *Part of the blame must lie with social services.* | **the problem/answer etc lies with/in sth** *The difficulty lies in providing sufficient evidence.* | *The strength of the book **lies in the fact that** the material is from classroom*

L

experience. | **herein/therein lies the problem/dilemma etc** *And herein lies the key to their achievements.*
3 PLACE [I always + adv/prep] if a town, village, etc lies in a particular place, it is in that place: *The town lies in a small wooded valley.* | *The Tasman Sea lies between Tasmania and Australia.*
4 FUTURE [I always + adv/prep] if something lies ahead of you, lies in the future etc, it is going to happen to you in the future: **[+ahead]** *How will we cope with the difficulties that lie ahead?* | **[+before]** *A blank and empty future lay before me.* | *I was wondering what **lay in store** for us.*
5 CONDITION [linking verb] to be in a particular state or condition: **lie empty/open/hidden etc** *The book lay open on the table.* | *The town now **lay in ruins**.*
6 lie at the heart/centre/root of sth to be the most important part of something, especially the main cause of it: *the issue that lies at the heart of the present conflict*
7 lie low a) to remain hidden because someone is trying to find you or catch you: *We'll have to lie low until tonight.* **b)** to wait and try not to be noticed by anyone: *He decided to lie low for a while after the report came out.*
8 lie in wait (for sb) a) to remain hidden in a place and wait for someone so that you can attack them: *a giant crocodile lying in wait for its prey* **b)** if something bad lies in wait for you, it is going to happen to you
9 lie (in) second/third/fourth etc (place) *BrE* to be in second, third etc position in a competition: *Liverpool are lying third in the football championship.*
10 lie heavy on sb *formal* if something lies heavy on you, it makes you feel unhappy: *The feelings of guilt lay heavy on him.*
11 DEAD PERSON [I always + adv/prep] if someone lies in a particular place, they are buried there: ***Here lies** Percival Smythe* (=written on a gravestone).
12 lie in state if an important person who has died lies in state, their body is put in a public place so that people can go and look at the body in order to show their respect for that person → **let sleeping dogs lie** at SLEEP[1](7)
lie around (*also* **lie about** *BrE*) *phr v*
1 lie around (sth) if something is lying around, it has been left somewhere in an untidy way, rather than being in its proper place: *If you **leave** your shoes **lying around** like that, you'll trip over them.* | *Papers and books lay around the room in complete chaos.*
2 if you lie around, you spend time lying down and not doing anything: *I felt so lazy just lying around on the beach all day.*
lie behind sth *phr v* if something lies behind an action, it is the real reason for the action even though it may be hidden: *She soon guessed what lay behind his question.* | *Two basic assumptions lay behind the policy.*
lie down *phr v*
1 to put yourself in a position in which your body is flat on the floor or on a bed: *Just lie down on the bed.*
2 take sth lying down *informal* to accept bad treatment without complaining: *I'm not going to take this lying down!*
lie in *phr v BrE* to remain in bed in the morning for longer than usual → LIE-IN
lie up *phr v BrE* to hide or rest somewhere for a period of time: *The next day they lay up in a cave.*

lie[2] ●●● S3 W3 *v* (**lied, lying, lies**) [I]
1 to deliberately tell someone something that is not true: *I could tell from her face that she was lying.* | **[+to]** *I would never lie to you.* | **[+about]** *She lied about her age.* | **lie through your teeth** (=say something that is completely untrue)
2 if a picture, account etc lies, it does not show the true facts or the true situation: *Statistics can often lie.* | *The camera never lies.*

lie[3] ●●● S3 *n*
1 [C] something that you say or write that you know is untrue: *I always know when he's telling lies.* | **[+about]** *I knew that soon she would hear the lies about me.*
2 give the lie to sth *formal* to show that something is untrue: *This report gives the lie to the company's claims.*
3 the lie of the land a) the way that a situation is developing at a particular time: *I'll talk to him and get the lie of the land before we go over.* **b)** the way an area of land has been formed and the physical features it has
4 (I) tell a lie *BrE spoken* used when you realize that something you have just said is not correct: *It was £25, no, tell a lie, £35.* → **live a lie** at LIVE[1](16)

COLLOCATIONS
VERBS
tell (sb) a lie *He got into trouble for telling a lie.*
believe a lie *How could you believe his lies?*
spread lies (=tell them to a lot of people) *How dare you spread such vicious lies?*

ADJECTIVES
a complete/total/outright lie (=something that is completely untrue) *Of course the whole thing was a complete lie.*
a white lie (=a small lie that you tell someone for good reasons, for example to avoid hurting their feelings) *We all have to tell white lies sometimes.*
a downright lie (=used when something is clearly a lie, especially when you feel annoyed) *That's a downright lie. I never said any such thing!*
a vicious lie (=one that is very unkind and very untrue) | **a blatant lie** (=an obvious lie) | **a barefaced lie** *BrE*, **a bald-faced lie** *AmE* (=an obvious lie that is told with no sense of shame) | **an elaborate lie** | **a big lie**

PHRASES
a pack of lies *informal* (*also* **a tissue of lies** *BrE formal*) (=a lot of lies) *Everything he had told me was a pack of lies.*

COMMON ERRORS
⚠ Don't say 'say a lie'. Say **tell a lie**.

'lie de,tector *n* [C] a piece of equipment used especially by the police to check whether someone is lying, by measuring sudden changes in their heart rate SYN **polygraph**: *He was asked to take a **lie detector test**.*

'lie down *n* [singular] *BrE* a short rest, usually on a bed: *I'm going upstairs to **have a lie down**.*

liege /liːdʒ/ *n* [C] **1** (*also* **liege lord**) a lord who was served and obeyed in the Middle Ages **2** (*also* **liegeman**) someone who had to serve and obey a lord in the Middle Ages

'lie-in *n* [singular] *BrE* an occasion when you stay in bed longer than usual in the morning: *I always **have a lie-in** on a Sunday.*

li·en /ˈliːən, liːn/ *n* [C + on] *law* the legal right to keep something that belongs to someone who owes you money, until the debt has been paid

lieu /ljuː, luː $ luː/ *n* **in lieu (of sth)** *formal* instead of: *extra time off in lieu of payment*

Lieut *BrE*, **Lieut.** *AmE* a written abbreviation of ***lieutenant***

lieu·ten·ant /lefˈtenənt $ luːˈten-/ *n* [C] **1 a)** a fairly low rank in the armed forces, or an officer of this rank **b)** a fairly high rank in the US police force, or an officer of this rank **2 lieutenant colonel/general/governor etc** an officer or official with the rank just below COLONEL, GENERAL[2], GOVERNOR etc **3** someone who does work for, or in place of, someone in a higher position SYN **deputy**

life /laɪf/ ●●● S1 W1 *n* (*plural* **lives** /laɪvz/)
1 TIME SB IS ALIVE [C,U] the period of time when someone is alive: *Learning goes on throughout life.* | *You have your whole life ahead of you.* | **in sb's life** *For the first time in my life I was happy.* | *I've never been so embarrassed in my life!* | *I've known John **all my life*** (=since I was born). | *His main aim **in life** was to have fun.* | *It was one of the best days **of my life**.* | *The accident scarred him **for life*** (=for the rest of his life). | *She knew she'd feel guilty **for the rest of** her **life**.* | *Raj **spent** his **life** caring for others.* | *Bonington spent his entire **adult life** in France.* | *We don't know much about the poet's **early life*** (=when he was young). | *Poor diet can lead to a whole range of diseases **in later life*** (=when you are older). |

L

She married ***late in life*** (=when she was fairly old). | *He's a* ***life member*** (=continuing until he dies) *of the club.*

2 **STATE OF BEING ALIVE** [C,U] the state of being alive: *The right to life is the most basic of human rights.* | *Danny was a cheerful little boy who loved life.* | *Two firefighters risked their lives to save the children.*

3 **WAY SB LIVES** [C usually singular] the way you live your life, and what you do and experience during it: **lead/live/have a ... life** *The operation should enable Bobby to lead a normal life.* | *She just wanted to live a quiet life.* | *Having a baby* ***changes*** *your* ***life*** *completely.* | *The family moved to Australia to* ***start a new life.*** | *Ken's whole* ***life revolved around*** *surfing* (=that was the main interest and purpose of his life). | *You shouldn't let your boyfriend* ***rule your life*** (=control and affect everything you do). | *My grandmother had* ***a hard life*** (=a life full of problems). | *She's led a very* ***sheltered life*** (=a life in which you have been protected from unpleasant things). | **a life of crime/poverty/misery etc** *He had been drawn into a life of crime.*

4 **PARTICULAR SITUATION/JOB** [C,U] **a)** the experiences, activities, and ways of living that are typical of being in a particular job, situation, society etc: *Why do so few women enter political life?* | *the British* ***way of life*** | **city/country/village etc life** *Noise has become one of the main pollutants of modern city life.* | **army/student/college etc life** *He missed the routine of army life.* | *Are you enjoying* ***married life****?* **b)** the time in your life when you are doing a particular job, are in a particular situation etc: **sb's life as sth** *Now a celebrity chef, he rarely talks about his life as an army cook.* | *Sara admits to having affairs throughout her* ***married life.*** | *Most of his* ***working life*** *was spent in the shipyards.*

5 social/personal/sex etc life the activities in your life relating to your friends, your family, sex etc: *I don't need advice about my love life.* | *traditional views of family life* | *Children need a caring and happy home life.*

6 **HUMAN EXISTENCE** [U] human existence, considered as a variety of experiences and activities: *My Aunt Julia had very little experience of life.* | *Life has a way of changing the best of plans.* | *For some people, religion gives life a meaning.* | **daily/everyday life** *the frustrations and disappointments of everyday life* | *I try to see the funny* ***side of life.***

7 **TIME WHEN STH EXISTS/WORKS** [C usually singular] **a)** the period of time during which something happens or exists: **[+of]** *The issues will not be resolved during the life of the present parliament.* | **start/begin/come to life as sth** *The building began life as a monastery.* **b)** the period of time during which something is still good enough to use: **[+of]** *What's the average life of a passenger aircraft?* | *Careful use can* ***extend the life*** *of your washing machine.* → SHELF LIFE

8 **LIVING THINGS** [U] **a)** the quality of being alive that people, animals, plants etc have and that objects and dead things do not have: *Ben felt her neck for a pulse or any other* ***sign of life.*** | *In the springtime, everything* ***comes to life*** *again.* **b)** living things, such as people, animals, or plants: *Is there life on other planets?* | **human/animal/plant/bird etc life** *The island is rich in bird life.* → WILDLIFE

9 be sb's (whole) life to be the most important thing or person to someone: *Music is Laura's whole life.*

10 life and death (*also* **life or death**) used for emphasizing that a situation, decision etc is extremely urgent and important, especially because someone is at risk of dying: *Don't call me unless it's* ***a matter of life and death.*** | *a life or death decision* | *A doctor's job involves life and death situations.*

11 **GAME** [C] a chance in a game, especially a computer game, in which you can be defeated or do something wrong and can still continue playing: *He's up to level five and still has three lives left.*

12 **ACTIVITY** [U] activity or movement: *The house was quiet and there was no* ***sign of life.*** | *She was always so cheerful and* ***full of life.***

13 **INTEREST/EXCITEMENT** [U] a quality of being interesting or exciting: *Try to* ***put some life*** *into your writing.* | *The game really* ***came to life*** *after a magnificent goal from Rooney.* | *A gifted teacher can really* ***bring*** *literature* ***to life*** *for his or her students.*

14 come to life/roar into life/splutter into life etc to suddenly start working: *Finally the car spluttered into life.*

15 make life difficult/easier etc to make it difficult, easier etc to do something: *Surely computers are supposed to make life easier, not more complicated!* | **[+for]** *Why make life difficult for yourself?*

16 the life and soul of the party *BrE*, **the life of the party** *AmE* someone who enjoys social occasions and is fun and exciting to be with

17 life and limb *formal* your life and physical health – used especially when this is threatened in some way: *She* ***risks life and limb*** *every day in her job as an undercover investigator.*

18 get a life! *spoken* used to tell someone that you think they are boring and should find more exciting things to do: *You guys should just stop moaning and get a life!*

19 that's life (*also* **such is life**) *spoken* used to say that something is disappointing but you have to accept it: *Oh well, that's life!*

20 life's a bitch *spoken not polite* used to say that bad things happen in life

21 this is the life *spoken* used when you are relaxing and doing something you enjoy: *Ah, this is the life! Lying on the beach, sipping cool drinks.*

22 the shock/surprise/game etc of sb's life the biggest shock or surprise, the best game etc that someone has ever had: *I had the surprise of my life when I saw John standing there.* → **have the time of your life** at TIME[1](41)

23 how's life? *spoken* used to ask someone if they are well, what they have been doing etc: *Hi Bob! How's life?* | *How's life been with you?*

24 life goes on *spoken* used to say that you must continue to live a normal life even when something sad or disappointing has happened: *We both miss him, but life goes on.*

25 a life of its own a) if something has a life of its own, it seems to move or work by itself: *The ball seemed to have acquired a life of its own.* **b)** if something has a life of its own, it exists and develops without depending on other things: *Slowly but surely, the project is* ***taking on a life of its own.***

26 cannot for the life of me *spoken* used to say that you cannot remember or understand something even when you try hard: *I couldn't for the life of me remember his name.*

27 life's too short *spoken* used to say that you should not waste time doing something or worrying about something: *Forget about it. Life's too short.* | **[+for]** *Life's too short for moping about.* | **life's too short to do sth** *Life's too short to bear grudges.*

28 not on your life *spoken* used as a reply to a question or suggestion to say that you definitely will not do something: *'Are you going to go and work for him then?' 'Not on your life!'*

29 the woman/man/girl etc in your life the woman or man you are married to or are having a relationship with – used especially in advertisements: *This is the ideal gift for the man in your life.*

30 **PRISON** [U] (*also* **life imprisonment**) the punishment of being put in prison for the rest of your life: **be sentenced to/get/be given life** *He was sentenced to life for the murder.* | *I think she should get life.* → LIFE SENTENCE, LIFER

31 **ART** [U] when you paint, draw etc something you are looking at, especially a person or animal: *She's taking classes in* ***life drawing.*** → STILL LIFE

32 frighten/scare the life out of sb *informal* to make someone feel very frightened: *Don't do that! You scared the life out of me!*

33 there's life in the old dog yet *spoken* used to say that although someone or something is old, they are still able to do something – used humorously

34 live/lead/have the life of Riley *informal* to have a very easy and comfortable life and not have to work hard: *He spends all day lounging by the pool and living the life of Riley.*

35 **BOOK/FILM** [U] the story of someone's life SYN **biography**: *Boswell's 'Life of Johnson'*

36 the next life (*also* **the life to come, life after death**) the time after death, in which some people believe life continues in another form: *She expects to meet her dead*

husband in the next life. → **as large as life** at LARGE¹(7), → CHANGE OF LIFE, → **for dear life** at DEAR²(6), → DOUBLE LIFE, → **high life** at HIGH¹(22), → **a new lease of life** at LEASE¹(2), → **quality of life** at QUALITY¹(5), → **real life** at REAL¹(3), REAL-LIFE, → **true to life** at TRUE¹(9), → WALK OF LIFE

COLLOCATIONS - MEANING 2

VERBS

save sb's life *The money you give will save the life of a child.*
risk your life *He risked his life to help Jews during the Second World War.*
lose your life (=die) *Hundreds of people lost their lives on the first day of the fighting.*
take a/sb's life (=kill someone) *All cultures consider it wrong to take a life for no reason.*
take your own life (=kill yourself) *He was depressed and decided to take his own life.*
claim the life of sb (=kill someone - used of a thing) *The disease claimed the lives of up to a quarter of the population.*
cost lives/cost sb their life (=result in deaths/in someone's death) | **give your life/lay down your life** (=die in order to save other people, or because of a strong belief) | **endanger the life of sb** | **spare sb's life** (=not kill someone, when you could kill them) | **be fighting for your life** (=be so ill or injured that you might die) | **cling to life** (=try to stay alive, even though you are very ill or injured)

PHRASES

owe your life to sb (=be still alive because of someone's actions) *The victim said he owed his life to the stranger who helped him.*
take your life in your hands (=put yourself in a dangerous situation)

COMMON ERRORS

⚠ Don't say 'the cost of life'. Say **the cost of living**.

ˈlife-afˌfirming *adj* making you feel good about life and the world generally: *a life-affirming account of her recovery from serious illness*

ˈlife asˌsurance *n* [U] *BrE* LIFE INSURANCE

ˈlife belt *n* [C] **1** *BrE* a LIFE BUOY **2** *AmE* a special belt you wear in the water to prevent you from sinking

life·blood /ˈlaɪfblʌd/ *n* [U] **1** the most important thing needed by an organization, relationship etc to continue to exist or develop successfully: **[+of]** *Communication is the lifeblood of a good marriage.* **2** *literary* your blood

life·boat /ˈlaɪfbəʊt $ -boʊt/ *n* [C] **1** a boat that is sent out to help people who are in danger at sea: **lifeboat crew/station/service 2** a small boat carried by ships in order to save people if the ship sinks

ˈlife ˌbuoy *n* [C] a large ring made out of material that floats, which you throw to someone who has fallen in the water, to prevent them from drowning

ˈlife choice *n* [C] an important decision which you make about your life, for example where you choose to live, what kind of job you do, whether you get married etc

ˈlife coach *n* [C] someone whose job is to help other people be successful in their lives. A life coach helps his or her CLIENT to be clear about what they want to do in the future and helps them to make a plan that will allow them to achieve their aims.

ˈlife ˌcycle *n* [C] all the different levels of development that an animal or plant goes through during its life

ˌlife exˈpectancy *n* [C] **1** the length of time that a person or animal is expected to live **2** the length of time that something is expected to continue to work, be useful etc

ˈlife form *n* [C] a living thing such as a plant or animal: *life forms on other planets*

life·guard /ˈlaɪfgɑːd $ -gɑːrd/ *n* [C] someone whose job at a beach or swimming pool is to help swimmers who are in danger

ˌlife ˈhistory *n* [C] all the events and changes that happen during the life of a living thing

ˈlife inˌsurance *n* [U] a type of insurance that someone makes regular payments into so that when they die their family will receive money SYN **life assurance**

ˈlife ˌjacket *n* [C] *BrE* a piece of clothing that can be filled with air and worn around your upper body to stop you from sinking in the water SYN **life vest** *AmE*

LIFE JACKET

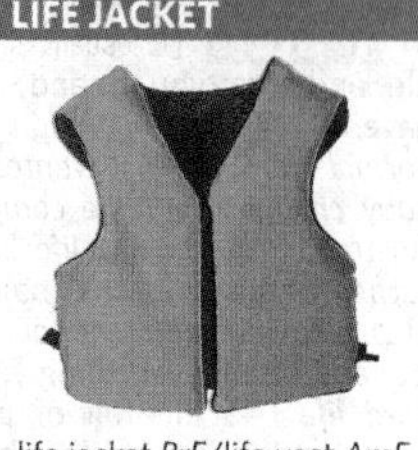

life jacket *BrE*/life vest *AmE*

life·less /ˈlaɪfləs/ *adj* **1** *literary* dead or appearing to be dead: *Anton's* ***lifeless body*** *was found floating in the lake.* **2** lacking the positive qualities that make something or someone interesting, exciting, or active OPP **lively**: *The actors' performances were lifeless.* **3** not living, or not having living things on it: *The surface of the Moon is arid and lifeless.* **4** lifeless hair or skin is in bad condition and does not look healthy SYN **dull** —**lifelessly** *adv* —**lifelessness** *n* [U]

life·like /ˈlaɪflaɪk/ *adj* a lifelike picture, model etc looks exactly like a real person or thing: *a very lifelike statue*

life·line /ˈlaɪflaɪn/ *n* [C] **1** something which someone depends on completely: **[+to]** *The telephone is her lifeline to the rest of the world.* | **[+for]** *The organization has proved to be a lifeline for thousands of needy families.* **2** a rope used for saving people in danger, especially at sea

life·long /ˈlaɪflɒŋ $ -lɔːŋ/ ●○○ *adj* [only before noun] continuing or existing all through your life: *She became a* ***lifelong friend*** *of ours.* | *David finally realized his* ***lifelong ambition.***

ˌlife ˈpeer *n* [C] someone who has the rank of a British PEER (=lord or lady) but who cannot pass it on to their children

ˈlife preˌserver *n* [C] *AmE* something such as a LIFE BELT or LIFE JACKET that can be worn in the water to prevent you from sinking

lif·er /ˈlaɪfə $ -ər/ *n* [C] *informal* someone who has been sent to prison for the rest of their life

ˈlife raft *n* [C] a small rubber boat that can be filled with air and used by passengers on a sinking ship

life·sav·er /ˈlaɪfseɪvə $ -ər/ *n* [C] **1** someone or something that helps you avoid a difficult or unpleasant situation: *A microwave oven can be a real lifesaver when you're pressed for time.* **2** someone or something that prevents you from dying: *The seat belt is the biggest single lifesaver in cars.* **3** a LIFEGUARD

ˈlife-ˌsaving¹, **life·sav·ing** /ˈlaɪfˌseɪvɪŋ/ *adj* [only before noun] life-saving medical treatments or equipment are used to help save people's lives: **life-saving surgery/treatment/drugs etc** *The boy needs a life-saving transplant operation.*

life-saving², **life·sav·ing** /ˈlaɪfˌseɪvɪŋ/ *n* [U] the skills necessary to save a person from drowning: *All of the staff have been trained in lifesaving.*

ˈlife ˌscience *n* [C usually plural] subjects such as BIOLOGY that are concerned with the study of humans, plants, and animals → EARTH SCIENCE, PHYSICAL SCIENCE

ˌlife ˈsentence *n* [C] the punishment of sending someone to prison for the rest of their life or for a very long time: *Miller is* ***serving*** *a* ***life sentence*** *for murder.*

ˈlife-size (*also* **ˈlife-sized**) *adj* a picture or model of something or someone that is life-size is the same size as they really are: *a life-sized statue of the president*

life·span /ˈlaɪfspæn/ ●○○ *n* [C] the average length of time that someone will live or that something will continue to work → **lifetime**: *Men have a shorter lifespan than women.* | **a lifespan of 5 days/10 years etc** *A TV set has an average lifespan of 11 years.*

L

ˈlife ˌstory *n* [C] the story of someone's whole life: *She insisted on* ***telling*** *me her whole* ***life story****.*

life·style /ˈlaɪfstaɪl/ ●●○ *n* [C] the way a person or group of people live, including the place they live in, the things they own, the kind of job they do, and the activities they enjoy: *Regular exercise is part of a* ***healthy lifestyle****.* | **lavish/comfortable/simple etc lifestyle** *They lead an extremely lavish lifestyle.*

ˈlife supportˌsystem *n* [C] **1** (*also* **life support machine**) a piece of equipment that keeps someone alive when they are extremely ill **2** a piece of equipment that keeps people alive in conditions where they would not normally be able to live, such as in space

ˈlife-ˌthreatening *adj* a life-threatening situation, illness, or injury could cause a person to die → **fatal**
THESAURUS SERIOUS

life·time /ˈlaɪftaɪm/ ●●○ *n* [C usually singular]
1 the period of time during which someone is alive or something exists → **lifespan**: **during/in sb's lifetime** *During her lifetime she had witnessed two world wars.* | *It's the sort of opportunity you see only* ***once in a lifetime****.*
2 the chance/experience etc of a lifetime the best opportunity, experience etc that you will ever have: *It was the holiday of a lifetime.*
3 not in this lifetime *spoken* not at all SYN **never**: *'Would you go out with him after he dropped you?' 'Not in this lifetime.'*

ˈlife vest *n* [C] *AmE* a LIFE JACKET

lift¹ /lɪft/ ●●● S2 W2 *v*
1 MOVE STH UPWARDS [T] (*also* **lift up**) to move something or someone upwards into the air: *Sophie lifted the phone before the second ring.* | *He lifted the lid on the pot of soup.* | *The lumber was lifted by crane and dropped into the truck.* | **lift sb/sth onto/into/out of etc sth** *They lifted Andrew onto the bed.* | **lift sb from sth** *The driver was lifted from the wreck.*
2 PART OF THE BODY [I,T] (*also* **lift up**) to move part of your body up to a higher position SYN **raise**: **lift your hand/arm/leg etc** *She lifted her hand to knock on the door once again.* | *Pam lifted her shoulders in a little shrug.* | **lift your head/eyes** (=move your head or eyes up so that you can look at something) *She lifted her head to gaze at him.* | *He heard a scream and the hairs on the back of his neck began to lift.*
3 CONTROLS/LAWS [T] to remove a rule or a law that says that something is not allowed: **lift a restriction/an embargo/sanctions etc** *The government plans to lift its ban on cigar imports.*
4 BY PLANE [T always + adv/prep] to take people or things to or from a place by aircraft: *More troops are being lifted into the area as the fighting spreads.*
5 not lift a finger (to do sth) *informal* to do nothing to help: *He never lifted a finger to help me with the kids.*
6 lift sb's spirits to make someone feel more cheerful and hopeful
7 CLOUDS/MIST [I] if cloud or mist lifts, it disappears
8 SAD FEELINGS [I] if feelings of sadness lift, they disappear: *Jan's depression seemed to be lifting at last.*
9 USE SB'S IDEAS/WORDS [T] to take words, ideas etc from someone else's work and use them in your work, without stating where they came from and as if they were your own words etc: **lift sth from sb/sth** *The words were lifted from an article in a medical journal.*
10 STEAL [T] *informal* to steal something: **lift sth from sb/sth** *They had lifted dozens of CDs from the store.*
11 VOICE [T] (*also* **lift up**) *literary* if you lift your voice, you speak, shout, or sing more loudly SYN **raise**
12 INCREASE [T] to make prices, profit etc increase: *The U.S. may use tax cuts to lift the economy.*
13 VEGETABLES [T] to dig up vegetables that grow under the ground: *She was lifting potatoes.*

THESAURUS

lift (up) to move something or someone upwards to a higher position, especially something heavy, either by using your hands or a machine: *You shouldn't lift anything heavy if you have a bad back.* | *He lifted the girl up onto his knee.* | *They used a crane to lift the carriages back onto the rails.*
raise to lift something to a higher position for a short time before lowering it again. **Raise** is more formal than **lift**: *The bridge can be raised to allow ships to pass under it.* | *'Cheers, everyone!' said Larry, raising his glass.*
pick up to lift something up from the ground, from a table etc, especially something small or light: *She picked up her bag and left the room.* | *Tom picked the papers up off the floor.* | *Why don't you just pick up the phone and call him?*
scoop up to lift someone or something quickly from the ground, from a table etc, using your hand or arm: *She bent down and scooped up the little dog.*
hoist to lift up something which is heavy and difficult to carry: *Joe picked up the sack and hoisted it onto the truck.*
elevate *technical* to lift something to a higher position and keep it there: *The doctor advised me to rest and elevate my ankle.*
put your hand up to lift your arm into the air, for example because you want to speak in a class or when voting: *Put your hand up if you know the answer.*

lift off *phr v* if an aircraft or spacecraft lifts off, it leaves the ground and rises into the air

lift² ●●● S3 W3 *n*
1 IN A BUILDING [C] *BrE* a machine that you can ride in, that moves up and down between the floors in a tall building SYN **elevator** *AmE*: *They* ***took the lift*** *down to the bar.* | *It's on the 3rd floor. Let's* ***use the lift****.*
2 IN A CAR [C] if you give someone a lift, you take them somewhere in your car SYN **ride**: *Do you want a lift into town?* | *John* ***gave*** *me* ***a lift*** *home.* | *He very kindly* ***offered*** *me* ***a lift****.*
3 give sb/sth a lift a) to make someone feel more cheerful and more hopeful: *The new park has given everyone in the neighbourhood a lift.* **b)** to make something such as a business, the economy etc operate better: *The Bank of England's announcement gave the stock market a lift today.*
4 LIFTING MOVEMENT [C] a movement in which something is lifted or raised up: *She does sit-ups and leg lifts every morning.*
5 WIND/AIRCRAFT [U] the pressure of air that keeps something such as an aircraft up in the air or lifts it higher
→ CHAIRLIFT, SKI LIFT

ˈlift-off *n* [C,U] the moment when a vehicle that is about to travel in space leaves the ground → **take-off**

lig·a·ment /ˈlɪɡəmənt/ *n* [C] a band of strong material in your body, similar to muscle, that joins bones or holds an organ in its place → **tendon**: *He* ***tore*** *a* ***ligament*** *in his left knee.* | ***damaged*** *ankle* ***ligaments***

light¹ /laɪt/ ●●● S1 W1 *n*
1 NATURAL/ARTIFICIAL LIGHT a) [U] the energy from the Sun, a flame, a lamp etc that allows you to see things: *We saw a flash of light.* | **in/by the light of sth** *Everything looked grey in the dim light of the oil lamp.* | *I read by the light of the fire.* | **in/into the light** *The man moved forward into the light.* **b)** [C] a particular type of light, with its own particular colour, level of brightness etc: *The colours look different in different lights.*
2 LAMP/ELECTRIC LIGHT ETC [C] **a)** something that produces light, especially electric light, to help you to see: *Ahead of us we could see the lights of the city.* | *We're having a mixture of wall lights and ceiling lights in different parts of the house.* | **turn/switch/put on a light** *I switched on the light in the bedroom.* | **turn/switch/put off a light** *Don't forget to switch the lights off when you go out.* | **turn/switch/put out a light** *Can you turn the light out downstairs?* | **a light is/comes/goes on** *The lights in the office were still on.* | *The street lights were just beginning to come on.* | *He left a light on in the kitchen.* | **a light is off/out** *Make sure all the lights are off when you leave.* | *Suddenly all the* ***lights*** *in the house* ***went out****.* | *Can you* ***turn the light down*** (=make it less bright) *a bit?* → **the bright lights** at BRIGHT(14) **b)** something

L

such as a lamp that you can carry to give you light: *Shine a light over here, will you?*

3 TRAFFIC CONTROL [C usually plural] one of a set of red, green, and yellow lights used for controlling traffic SYN **traffic lights**: *We waited for the lights to change.* | *Eventually the lights turned green.* | *The driver had failed to stop at a red light.* → GREEN LIGHT

4 ON A VEHICLE [C usually plural] one of the lights on a car, bicycle etc that help you to see at night: *He was dazzled by the lights of oncoming traffic.* | *You've left your lights on.* → BRAKE LIGHT, HEADLIGHT, PARKING LIGHT

5 first light *literary* the time when light first appears in the morning sky: *We set out at first light the next day.*

6 be/stand in sb's light to prevent someone from getting all the light they need to see or do something: *Could you move to the left a little – you're standing in my light.*

7 FOR A CIGARETTE **a light** a match or something else to light a cigarette: *Have you got a light, please?*

8 IN SB'S EYES [singular] *literary* an expression in someone's eyes that shows an emotion or intention SYN **gleam**: *There was a murderous light in his eyes.*

9 set light to sth to make something start burning: *The candle fell over and set light to the barn.*

10 come to light/be brought to light if new information comes to light, it becomes known: *This evidence did not come to light until after the trial.* | *The mistake was only brought to light some years later.*

11 throw/shed/cast light on sth to provide new information that makes a difficult subject or problem easier to understand: *Melanie was able to shed some light on the situation.* | *These discoveries may throw new light on the origins of the universe.*

12 in the light of sth *BrE*, **in light of sth** *AmE* if you do or decide something in the light of something else, you do it after considering that thing: *In light of this tragic event, we have canceled the 4th of July celebrations.*

13 in a new/different/bad etc light if someone or something is seen or shown in a particular light, people can see that particular part of their character: *I suddenly saw my father in a new light.* | *This incident will put the company in a very bad light.*

14 see the light a) to suddenly understand something: *At last doctors have seen the light!* **b)** to begin to believe in a religion very strongly

15 see the light (of day) a) if an object sees the light of day, it is taken from the place where it has been hidden, and becomes publicly known: *Some of these documents will probably never see the light of day.* **b)** if a law, decision etc sees the light of day, it comes into existence for the first time

16 light at the end of the tunnel something that gives you hope for the future after a long and difficult period: *It's been a hard few months, but we're finally beginning to see the light at the end of the tunnel.*

17 have your name in lights *informal* to be successful and famous in theatre or films

18 go/be out like a light *informal* to go to sleep very quickly because you are very tired: *I went straight to bed and went out like a light.*

19 a leading light in/of sth *informal* someone who is important in a particular organization: *She's one of the leading lights of the local dramatic society.*

20 the light of sb's life the person that someone loves more than anyone else: *Her son was the light of her life.*

21 WINDOW [C] a window in a roof or wall that allows light into a room → **hide your light under a bushel** at BUSHEL, RED-LIGHT DISTRICT, → **be all sweetness and light** at SWEETNESS(3), → **in the cold light of day** at COLD¹(9)

COLLOCATIONS

ADJECTIVES/NOUN + light

bright/strong *The light was so bright he had to shut his eyes.*
blinding/dazzling (=extremely bright) *The white buildings reflected a blinding light.*
dim (=not bright) *Gradually her eyes became accustomed to the dim light.*
good (=bright enough) *Stand over here where the light is good.*
poor/bad (=not bright enough) *The light was too poor for me to read.*
soft/warm (=light that seems slightly yellow or orange) | **cold/harsh** (=light that seems slightly blue) | **the morning/dawn light** | **natural light** (=light produced by the sun) | **artificial light** (=light produced by lamps)

VERBS

light shines *The light from the streetlamp shone through the curtains.*
light comes from somewhere *The only light came from the fire.*
light streams/floods in (=a large amount of light comes in) *Light streamed in through the window.*
light falls on/across etc sth *The light fell on her book.*
light illuminates sth *formal* (=makes it bright or able to be seen) | **the light is fading** (=it is getting darker as the sun is going down) | **produce light** (*also* **emit light** *technical*) | **cast light** (=send light onto something) | **reflect light** | **sth is bathed in light** *literary* (=something has a lot of light shining on it)

PHRASES

a beam/ray/shaft of light (=a thin line of light) *There was a shaft of light from the doorway.*
a flash of light (=a bright light that appears suddenly for a very short time) *A flash of light caught his attention.*
a pool/circle of light (=an area of light)

light² ●●● S1 W1 *adj* (*comparative* **lighter**, *superlative* **lightest**)

1 COLOUR a light colour is pale and not dark: *You look nice in light colours.* | **light blue/green/grey etc** *She had blue eyes and light brown hair.* | *I wanted a lighter yellow paint for the walls.* THESAURUS COLOUR

2 DAYLIGHT **it is/gets light** if it is light, there is the natural light of day OPP **dark**: *We'll keep on looking while it's still light.* | *It was seven o'clock and just starting to* ***get light***.

3 ROOMS a room that is light has plenty of light in it, especially from the sun OPP **dark**: *The kitchen was light and spacious.* | *The office was a big light room at the back of the house.* THESAURUS BRIGHT

4 NOT HEAVY not very heavy: *You can carry this bag – it's fairly light.* | *You should wear light, comfortable shoes.* | *The truck was quite light and easy to drive.* | *She was* ***as light as a feather*** (=very light) *to carry.* → LIGHTEN, LIGHTWEIGHT²

5 NOT GREAT if something is light, there is not very much of it or it is not very great OPP **heavy**: *Traffic is lighter before 8 a.m.* | *A light rain began to fall.* | *She was wearing only light make-up.* | *people who have suffered only light exposure to radiation*

6 CLOTHES light clothes are thin and not very warm: *She took a light sweater in case the evening was cool.* | *a light summer coat*

7 WIND a light wind is blowing without much force OPP **strong**: *Leaves were blowing about in the light wind.* | *There was a light easterly breeze.*

8 SOUND a light sound is very quiet OPP **loud**: *There was a light tap at the door.* | *Her voice was light and pleasant.*

9 TOUCH a light touch is gentle and soft: *She gave him a light kiss on the cheek.* | *He felt a light tap on his shoulder.*

10 WORK/EXERCISE light work is not hard or tiring: *I found him some light work to do.* | *She only has a few light duties around the house.* | *The doctor has advised me to take regular light exercise.*

11 FOOD **a)** food or drink that is light either does not have a strong taste or does not make you feel full very quickly, for example because it does not contain very much fat, sugar, or alcohol OPP **rich**: *We had a light white wine with the fish.* | *a light, refreshing dessert* | *a new light cheese spread with virtually no fat* **b)** a light meal is a small meal OPP **big**: *I had a light lunch in town.* | *a delicious light snack* **c)** food that is light contains a lot of air: *a type of light, sweet bread* | *Beat the mixture until it is light and fluffy.*

L

12 PUNISHMENT a light punishment is not very severe OPP **harsh**: *a fairly light sentence*
13 a light smoker/drinker/eater etc someone who does not smoke etc very much
14 light sleep/doze a sleep from which you wake up easily: *I fell into a light sleep.*
15 a light sleeper someone who wakes up easily if there is any noise etc: *She's quite a light sleeper.*
16 NOT SERIOUS not serious in meaning, style, or manner, and only intended to entertain people: *His speech gradually became lighter in tone. | an evening of light music | It's a really good book if you want a bit of* ***light reading****. | The show looks at some of the lighter moments from the world of politics.*
17 light relief something that is pleasant and amusing after something sad or serious: *I'm glad you've arrived – we could all do with a little light relief!*
18 make light of sth to joke about something or treat it as not being very serious, especially when it is important: *She tried to make light of the situation, but I could tell that she was worried.*
19 on a lighter note/in a lighter vein used when you are going to say something less sad or serious: *On a lighter note, the concert raised over £300 for school funds.*
20 make light work of sth to do something or deal with something quickly and easily: *A freezer and microwave oven can make light work of cooking.*
21 be light on your feet to be able to move quickly and gracefully: *She's very agile and light on her feet.*
22 a light heart *literary* someone who has a light heart feels happy and not worried: *I set off for work with a light heart.* → LIGHT-HEARTED
23 SOIL light soil is easy to break into small pieces OPP **heavy**: *Carrots grow well in light soils.* —**lightness** *n* [U]: *a lightness of touch*

light³ ●●● S2 W3 *v* (*past tense and past participle* **lit** *or* **lighted**)
1 [I,T] to start to burn, or to make something start to burn: *He stopped to light a cigarette. | I lit the fire and poured a drink. | I couldn't get the candles to light.*
2 [T] to provide light for a place: **be lit by/with sth** *The room was lit by one large, central light. | The porch is always* ***well lit*** *at night. | The kitchen was warm and* ***brightly lit****. | a* ***poorly lit*** *car park* GRAMMAR **Light** is usually passive in this meaning.
3 light the/sb's way to provide light for someone while they are going somewhere: *We had only a few torches between us to light the way.*
light on/upon sth *phr v literary*
1 to notice or find something by chance: *His eye lit on a ruby ring. | I thought I might have lit upon an ancient manuscript.*
2 if a bird or insect lights on something, it stops flying and stands on it
light out *phr v AmE informal* to run away, especially because you are afraid
light up *phr v*
1 light sth ↔ up to give light to a place or to shine light on something: *The flames lit up the sky. | The fountain is lit up at night.*
2 to become bright with light or colour: *At night the harbour lights up. | As the screen lit up, he typed in his password.*
3 a) if someone's face or eyes light up, they show pleasure, excitement etc: **[+with]** *His eyes lit up with laughter. | Her face lit up with pleasure.* **b) light sth ↔ up** to make someone's face or eyes show pleasure or excitement: *Suddenly a smile lit up her face. | A mischievous gleam lit up her eyes.*
4 *informal* to light a cigarette: *I watched Paul light up again.*

light⁴ *adv* → **travel light** at TRAVEL¹(1)

ˌlight ˈaircraft *n* [C] a small plane

ˌlight ˈale *n* [U] a type of fairly weak pale beer

ˈlight bulb *n* [C] the glass object inside a lamp that produces light and has to be replaced regularly SYN **bulb**

light·ed /ˈlaɪtɪd/ *adj* **1** a lighted window, room etc is bright because there is a light on inside **2** a lighted CANDLE, match etc is burning at one end OPP **unlit**

ˌlight-emitting ˈdiode *n* [C] *technical* (*abbreviation* **LED**) a small electronic object that produces light when an electrical current is sent through it. Light-emitting diodes are used, for example, as lights on electrical equipment, and to make words and pictures on large screens.

light·en /ˈlaɪtn/ *v* **1** [T] to reduce the amount of work, worry, debt etc that someone has OPP **increase**: **lighten the load/burden/workload** *We should hire another secretary to lighten Barbara's workload.* **2** [I,T] to become brighter or less dark, or to make something brighter etc OPP **darken**: *As the* ***sky lightened****, we were able to see where we were.* **3** [I,T] if you lighten something such as a mood or ATMOSPHERE, or if it lightens, it becomes less sad or serious: **lighten the atmosphere/mood/conversation** *Nora didn't respond to my attempts to lighten the conversation.* **4** [I] if someone's face or expression lightens, they begin to look more cheerful: *His whole face would lighten when anyone mentioned Nancy.* **5** [I,T] to reduce the weight of something, or to become less heavy **6 lighten up** *spoken* used to tell someone not to be so serious about something: *You need to lighten up a bit.*

light·er /ˈlaɪtə $ -ər/ *n* [C] **1** a small object that produces a flame for lighting cigarettes etc **2** a large open low boat used for loading and unloading ships

ˌlight-ˈfingered *adj informal* likely to steal things

ˌlight ˈgreen *adj especially BrE* avoiding some companies whose products or activities are thought to be morally unacceptable, but based on less strict principles than DARK GREEN: *light green consumers | light green investments*

ˌlight-ˈheaded *adj* unable to think clearly or move steadily, for example during a fever or after drinking alcohol SYN **dizzy**: *The sun and the wine had made him a little light-headed.* —**light-headedness** *n* [U]

light-heart·ed /ˌlaɪt ˈhɑːtɪd $ -ɑːr-/ *adj* **1** not intended to be serious: *a light-hearted comedy* THESAURUS▸ FUNNY **2** cheerful and not worried about anything: *I found her in a light-hearted mood.* —**light-heartedly** *adv* —**light-heartedness** *n* [U]

ˌlight ˈheavyweight *n* [C] a BOXER who weighs less than 79.38 kilograms, and who is heavier than a MIDDLEWEIGHT but lighter than a CRUISERWEIGHT

light·house /ˈlaɪthaʊs/ *n* [C] a tower with a powerful flashing light that guides ships away from danger

ˌlight ˈindustry *n* [C,U] industry that produces small goods, for example computers, in small factories using light machinery → **heavy industry**

light·ing /ˈlaɪtɪŋ/ ●●○ S3 *n* [U] the lights that light a room, building, or street, or the quality of the light produced: *Better* ***street lighting*** *might help to reduce crime. |* **fluorescent/electric lighting** *Fluorescent lighting is much cheaper to use than light bulbs. |* **subdued/dim/soft lighting** (=lighting that is not very bright) | **artificial/natural lighting**

ˈlighting rig *n* [C] a structure that holds the lights for a stage in a theatre, at an outdoor concert etc

light·ly /ˈlaɪtli/ ●●○ *adv*
1 with only a small amount of weight or force SYN **gently**: *I knocked lightly on the door.*
2 using or having only a small amount of something: *a lightly greased pan | lightly armed soldiers*
3 take/treat/approach sth lightly to do something without serious thought: *Divorce is not a matter you can afford to take lightly.*
4 get off lightly (*also* **be let off lightly**) to be punished in a way that is less severe than you deserve: *He got off lightly because his father was a lawyer.*
5 without worrying, or without appearing to be worried: *'Things will be fine,' he said lightly.*

ˈlight ˌmeter *n* [C] an instrument used by a photographer to measure how much light there is

light·ning[1] /ˈlaɪtnɪŋ/ ●●○ *n* [U]
1 a powerful flash of light in the sky caused by electricity and usually followed by THUNDER: *Two farmworkers were* ***struck by lightning*** (=hit by lightning). | ***Lightning flashed*** *overhead.* → see picture at **FORK[1]**
2 like lightning extremely quickly: *Mitch moved like lightning and caught the little girl before she fell.*
3 lightning never strikes twice something bad or unpleasant is not likely to happen to the same people or in the same place twice

lightning[2] *adj* [only before noun] very fast, and often without warning: *a lightning attack* | **at/with lightning speed** (=extremely quickly)

ˈlightning bug *n* [C] *AmE* an insect with a tail that shines in the dark SYN **firefly**

ˈlightning conˌductor *n* [C] *BrE* a metal wire or bar that is attached to the side of a building and goes from the top to the ground, used to protect the building from lightning

ˈlightning ˌrod *n* [C] *AmE* **1** a LIGHTNING CONDUCTOR **2** someone or something who gets most of the criticism, blame, or public attention when there is a problem, although they may not be responsible for it: **be a lightning rod for sth** *The senator has become a lightning rod for criticism.*

ˌlightning ˈstrike *n* [C] *BrE* a STRIKE (=act of stopping work) without any warning

ˈlight pen *n* [C] a piece of equipment like a pen, used to draw or write on a computer screen

ˈlight polˌlution *n* [U] artificial light from towns etc that makes the sky less dark at night, so that the stars cannot be seen clearly

ˌlight ˈrailway *BrE*, **ˌlight ˈrail** *AmE n* [C] an electric railway system that uses light trains and usually carries only passengers, not goods

light·ship /ˈlaɪtʃɪp/ *n* [C] a small ship that stays near a dangerous place at sea and guides other ships using a powerful flashing light

ˈlight show *n* [C] a type of entertainment that uses a series of moving coloured lights, at a POP concert

ˈlights-out *n* [U] the time at night when a group of people who are in a school, the army etc must put the lights out and go to sleep

light·stick /ˈlaɪtstɪk/ *n* [C] a GLOWSTICK

light·weight[1] /ˈlaɪt-weɪt/ *n* [C] **1** someone who has no importance or influence, or who does not have the ability to think deeply – used to show disapproval OPP **heavyweight**: *an intellectual lightweight* **2** a BOXER who weighs less than 61.24 kilograms, and who is heavier than a FEATHERWEIGHT but lighter than a WELTERWEIGHT **3** someone or something of less than average weight

lightweight[2] *adj* **1** weighing less than average SYN **light**: *a torch made from lightweight plastic* **2** lightweight clothing or material is thin, so you can wear it in warm weather: *a lightweight jacket* **3** showing a lack of serious thought – used to show disapproval: *a lightweight novel*

ˈlight year *n* [C] **1** the distance that light travels in one year, about 9,460,000,000,000 kilometres, used for measuring distances between stars: *a star 3,000 light years from Earth* **2 light years ahead/better etc than sth** *informal* much more advanced, much better etc than someone or something else: *The Japanese company is light years ahead of its European competitors.* **3 light years ago** *informal* a very long time ago: *It all seems light years ago now.*

lig·nite /ˈlɪgnaɪt/ *n* [U] a soft substance like coal, used as FUEL

lik·a·ble, likeable /ˈlaɪkəbəl/ *adj* likable people are nice and easy to like: *a friendly likeable little boy* **THESAURUS** NICE

like[1] /laɪk/ ●●● S1 W1 *prep*
1 SIMILAR similar to something else, or happening in the same way: *Her hair is dark brown like mine.* | *A club should be like a big family.* | *He eats like a pig!* | **look/sound/feel/taste/seem like** *The garden looked like a jungle.* | *At last he felt like a real soldier.* | *My experience is* **very much like** *that described in the book.* | *He's* **very like** *his brother.* | *Sometimes you sound* **just like** (=exactly like) *my mum!* | *He's growing* **more like** *his father every day.* | *He looked* **nothing like** (=not at all like) *the man in the police photograph.*
2 what is sb/sth like? *spoken* used when asking someone to describe or give their opinion of a person or thing: *What's their house like inside?* | *What are Dan's parents like?*
3 EXAMPLE for example: ***Things like*** *glass, paper, and plastic can all be recycled.* | *Try to avoid fatty foods like cakes and biscuits.*

> **REGISTER**
> In written English, people usually use **for example, for instance**, or **such as** rather than **like**: *packaging materials,* ***for instance*** *paper, glass, and plastic* | *Try to avoid fatty foods* ***such as*** *cakes and biscuits.*

4 TYPICAL typical of a particular person: **be like sb to do sth** *It's not like Steven to be late.* | *It's* **just like** *her to run away from her responsibilities!*
5 like this/that/so *spoken* used when you are showing someone how to do something: *You have to fold the corners back, like so.*
6 just like that *informal* if you do something just like that, you do it without thinking about it or planning it carefully: *You can't give up your job just like that!*
7 something like not much more or less than a particular amount SYN **about**: *The machinery alone will cost something like thirty thousand pounds.* | *He's scored something like 60 goals this season.*
8 nothing like *BrE* not at all: *Twenty years ago travel was nothing like as easy as it is now.* | *This will be* ***nothing like enough*** *money.*
9 there's nothing like used to say that a particular thing is very enjoyable: *There's nothing like a nice cup of tea!*
10 more like used when giving an amount or number that you think is closer to being right than one that has been mentioned: *The builders say they'll be finished in three months, but I think it'll be more like six.*
11 that's more like it/this is more like it *spoken* used to say that something is better, more correct, or more enjoyable than something else: *That gives us a total of 52 – that's more like it.* | *She sat down by the pool and took a sip of her wine. 'This is more like it,' she said.*
12 more like it *BrE spoken* used when you want to change something that has been said, to make it more true: *'Poor David,' she said. 'Poor Harriet, more like it!'*
13 what are you like! *BrE spoken informal* used in a joking, friendly way, when you are surprised by what someone has just said or done: *'I think she's a lovely lady.' 'What are you like!'*

like[2] ●●● S1 W1 *v* [T]
1 THINK STH IS NICE to enjoy something or think that it is nice or good → **love** OPP **dislike**: *I like your jacket.* | *I don't really like classical music.* | *Do you like this colour?* | *I like my coffee quite weak.* | *I don't* **like it** *when you get angry.* | **How** *do you* **like** *living in London* (=how much do you like it)? | **like doing sth** *I don't like talking in public.* | **like to do sth** *I like to see people enjoying themselves.* | *I* **quite like** *their new album.* | *We* **really liked** *the film.* | *The time I* **like best** (=like most of all) *is the evening when it's cool.* | **like sth about sb/sth** *One of the things I like about John is his sense of humour.* | *I didn't* **like the idea** *of being a single parent.*
2 LIKE A PERSON to think that someone is nice or enjoy being with them: *Jessica's really nice, but I don't like her boyfriend.* | *You'll like my brother.* | *I* **really like** *Sam.* | *She's a lovely girl and I* **like** *her* **very much**. | *In time, I* **got to like** *her* (=began to like her).
3 APPROVE OF STH to approve of something and think that it is good or right: *I don't like dishonesty.* | *I don't* **like the way** *he shouts at the children.* | **like doing sth** *He's never liked talking about people behind their backs.* | **like sb doing sth** *I don't like him taking all the credit when he didn't do any of the work.* | **like to do sth** *She doesn't like to swear in front of the children.*

4 DO STH REGULARLY to try to do something regularly or make something happen regularly: **like to do sth** *I like to get up early and get a bit of work done before breakfast.* | **like sb to do sth** *We like our students to take part in college sports activities.*

5 WANT **would like a)** used to say that you want something or want to do something → **love**: *I'd like a cheeseburger, please.* | **would like to do sth** *I'd like to see that film.* | *There's something I'd like to tell you.* | *I'd like to apologize for my behaviour yesterday.* | *I'd **just like** to say how grateful we are for your help.* | **would like sb to do sth** *He would like us all to be at the meeting.* **b)** used to ask someone if they want something or want to do something: *Would you like a drink?* | *What would you like to eat?* | *Contact our office if you would like more information.* | **would sb like to do sth** *Would you like to come with us?* | ***How would you like*** (=would you like) *to spend the summer in Italy?* | **would sb like sb to do sth** *Would you like me to pick you up in the morning?*

6 whatever/wherever/anything etc you like whatever thing you want, in whatever place you want etc: *You can sit wherever you like.* | *You can choose anything you like from the menu.*

7 as long as you like/as much as you like etc as long, as much etc as you want: *You know you're welcome to stay with us as long as you like.* | *Take as many as you like.*

8 (whether you) like it or not used to emphasize that something unpleasant is true or will happen and cannot be changed: *Like it or not, people are often judged by their appearance.*

9 I'd like to think/believe (that) used to say that you wish or hope something is true, when you are not sure that it is: *I'd like to think that we offer an excellent service.* | *I would like to believe that the company can be successful in the future.*

10 FACEBOOK to CLICK a Facebook 'like' button on a WEBPAGE to show that you like or agree with something

SPOKEN PHRASES

11 if you like *BrE* **a)** used to suggest or offer something to someone: *I can give you her phone number, if you like.* | *If you like, I could go with you.* **b)** used to agree to something, even if it is not really what you want yourself: *'Shall we get a takeaway on the way home?' 'If you like.'* **c)** used to suggest one possible way of describing something or someone: *We don't have a proper agreement, but we have an informal understanding, if you like.*

12 ROMANTIC to think someone is sexually attractive → **love**: *Do you think Alex likes me?*

13 I'd like to see you/him do sth used to say that you do not believe someone can do something: *I'd like to see you organize a conference!*

14 how would you like sth? used to ask someone to imagine how they would feel if something bad happened to them instead of to you or someone else: *How would you like being left alone for hours in a strange place?* | *How would you like it if someone treated you in that way?*

15 I like that! *BrE* used to say that what someone has said or done is rude and unfair: *I like that! She didn't even say thank you!*

16 like it or lump it used to say that someone must accept a situation or decision they do not like because it cannot be changed

GRAMMAR

Patterns with like

- You **like** someone or something: *I like my teacher.* | *She likes tennis.*
- You **like doing** something: *She likes playing tennis.*
- You **like to do** something: *She likes to play tennis at weekends.* ✗ Don't say: *She likes play tennis.*
- **Like doing** something and **like to do** something both mean the same thing. You use **like to do** especially when saying that someone does something regularly or often.

Using the progressive

- **Like** is not usually used in the progressive. You say: *I like animals.* | *She liked to make cakes.* ✗ Don't say: *I am liking animals.* | *She was liking to make cakes.*
- In spoken English, people sometimes say **I'm liking** to describe their present feelings about something that is happening right now or that they have just seen or heard about: *I'm liking this music – what is it?*

GRAMMAR GUIDE ▸ VERBS

THESAURUS

like to think that someone or something is nice: *I like your dress – it's a beautiful colour.* | *I like travelling by train.* | *Everybody liked Mr Schofield.*

be fond of sb/sth *especially BrE* to like someone or something, especially something that you have liked for a long time or someone who you have known for a long time: *Connie had always been fond of animals.* | *Over the years, I've become quite fond of him.*

be keen on sb/sth *spoken* to like someone or something – often used in negative sentences: *I like Maria but I'm not keen on her husband.* | *Our English teacher was very keen on Shakespeare, but I couldn't stand him.*

be into sth *informal* to like doing a particular activity or be interested in a particular subject – used especially by young people: *She's really into music at the moment.* | *What kind of films are you into?*

have a thing about sb/sth *informal* to like someone or something, especially something surprising or unusual: *I've always had a thing about wolves.* | *He has this thing about tall women.*

be partial to sth *formal* to like to have something – often used humorously: *He's partial to the occasional glass of wine.*

sth grows on you used when saying that you begin to like something, especially something that you did not like before: *I didn't like the colour of the room at first, but it's growing on me.*

TO LIKE SOMETHING VERY MUCH

love/adore to like something very much. **Adore** is stronger than **love** but is less common: *I love the smell of coffee.* | *The children absolutely adore her books.*

be crazy about sth (*also* **be mad about sth** *BrE informal*) to be extremely interested in an activity and spend a lot of time doing it or watching it: *Jonah's crazy about basketball.* | *She's always been mad about horses.*

have a passion for sth to like an activity very much, because it gives you a lot of pleasure or excitement: *From a very early age he had a passion for fast cars.*

be addicted to sth to like doing something so much that you spend all your free time doing it: *My son's addicted to computer games – he hardly ever comes out of his room.*

like[3] ●●● W3 *n*

1 sb's likes and dislikes the things that someone likes and does not like: *We all have our own likes and dislikes when it comes to food.*

2 and the like/and such like and similar things: *Soldiers, policemen, and the like were all called in to help with the emergency.* | *They believe that the government does not spend enough money on health, education, and such like.*

3 the likes of sb/sth *spoken* **a)** used to talk about someone you do not like or do not approve of: *I don't want you spending time with the likes of him.* **b)** used to talk about people of a particular type: *Information is collected through the likes of the FBI, CIA, and Scotland Yard.*

4 the like of sb/sth (*also* **sb's/sth's like**) *formal* something similar to someone or a particular person or thing, or of equal importance or value: *This will be a show the like of*

L

which has never been seen before. | The man was a genius. We shall not see his like again.

like⁴ ●●● S1 *conjunction*
1 in the same way as. Some people consider this use to be incorrect: *No one else can score goals like he can!* | *Don't talk to me like you talk to a child.*
2 like I say/said *spoken* used when you are repeating something that you have already said: *Like I said, I don't mind helping out on the day.* | *I'm sorry, but, like I say, she's not here at the moment.*
3 *informal* as if. Some people think that this use is not correct English: *He looked at me like I was mad.* | *It looks like it's going to rain.* | *This meat smells like it's gone bad.*

like⁵ ●●○ S3 *adv spoken*
1 used in speech to fill a pause while you are thinking what to say next: *The water was, like, really cold.* | *I was just, like, standing there.*
2 I'm/he's/she's like ... a) used to tell the exact words someone used: *I asked Dave if he wanted to go, and he's like, no way!* **b)** used to describe an event, feeling, or person, when it is difficult to describe or when you use a noise instead of words: *She was like, huh?* (=she did not understand)
3 as like as not/like enough *BrE* probably: *The ambulance will be too late, as like as not.*

like⁶ *adj formal* **1** [only before noun] similar in some way: *The second dispute was sorted out in a like manner.* | *They get on well together because they are* ***of like mind.*** | *Try to buy two fish* ***of like size.*** THESAURUS ▸ SIMILAR **2 be like to do sth** *old use* to be likely to do something

-like /laɪk/ *suffix* [in adjectives] used after a noun to say that something is similar to or typical of the noun: *a jelly-like substance* | *childlike simplicity* | *ladylike behaviour*

like·a·ble /ˈlaɪkəbəl/ *adj* another spelling of LIKABLE

like·li·hood /ˈlaɪklihʊd/ ●●○ *n* [singular, U]
1 the degree to which something can reasonably be expected to happen SYN **probability**: **[+of]** *Using a seat-belt will reduce the likelihood of serious injury in a car accident.* | **little/lower/high/greater etc likelihood** *There was very little likelihood of her getting the job.* | **likelihood (that)** *They must face the likelihood that the newspaper might go bankrupt.*
2 in all likelihood almost certainly: *If I refused, it would in all likelihood mean I'd lose my job.*

like·ly¹ /ˈlaɪkli/ ●●● S1 W1 *adj* (*comparative* **likelier**, *superlative* **likeliest**)
1 something that is likely will probably happen or is probably true OPP **unlikely**: *Snow showers are likely tomorrow.* | **likely outcome/effects/consequences etc** *What are the likely effects of the law going to be?* | *the most* ***likely cause*** *of the problem* | **likely to do/be sth** *Children who live in the country's rural areas are* ***very likely*** *to be poor.* | **more/less/most/least likely** *Young drivers are far more likely to have accidents than older drivers.* | *It is* ***more than likely*** (=almost certain) *the votes will have to be counted again.* | *It could have been an accident, but that was* ***hardly likely*** (=not very likely). | *He could offer no* ***likely explanation*** *when I asked him.*
2 [only before noun] suitable for a particular purpose: *the three most* ***likely candidates*** *for president* | *One likely source of energy is wind power.*
3 a likely story *spoken* used to tell someone you do not believe what they have just said

likely² ●●○ *adv*
1 probably: **most/very likely** *I'd very likely have done the same thing in your situation.* | **(as) likely as not** *spoken* (=very probably) *As likely as not, the meeting will take place in the village pub.*
2 not likely! *spoken especially BrE* used to disagree strongly, or to say that something will not happen: *'He said you'd be giving them a lift.' 'Not likely!'*

ˌlike-ˈminded *adj* [usually before noun] having similar interests and opinions: *a chance to meet* ***like-minded people*** —**like-mindedness** *n* [U]

lik·en /ˈlaɪkən/ *v*
liken sb/sth **to** sb/sth *phr v formal* to say that someone or something is similar to another person or thing SYN **compare**: *Critics have likened the new theater to a supermarket.*

like·ness /ˈlaɪknəs/ *n* **1** [C,U] the quality of being similar in appearance to someone or something SYN **resemblance**: **[+to]** *Hugh's uncanny likeness to his father* | *I can see the* ***family likeness.*** **2** [C] a painting or photograph of a person, especially one that looks very like the person: **good/perfect/true etc likeness** | **[+of]** *That's a remarkable likeness of Julia.*

like·wise /ˈlaɪk-waɪz/ ●○○ AWL *adv*
1 *formal* in the same way SYN **similarly**: *Nanny put on a shawl and told the girls to* ***do likewise.*** | [sentence adverb] *The clams were delicious. Likewise, the eggplant was excellent.*
2 likewise *spoken* used to return someone's greeting or polite statement: *'You're always welcome at our house.' 'Likewise.'*

lik·ing /ˈlaɪkɪŋ/ *n* **1 liking for sb/sth** *formal* when you like someone or something: *Jim and Keith* ***had a liking*** *and respect for each other.* | *She's developed a liking for theatre.* **2 take a liking to sb/sth** to begin to like someone or something: *He immediately took a liking to Steve.* **3 be to sb's liking** *formal* if something is to someone's liking, they like it or think it is satisfactory: *I hope everything was to your liking, sir.* **4 for sb's liking** if something is too crowded, serious, long etc for someone's liking, they think it is too crowded, serious, long etc

li·lac /ˈlaɪlək/ *n* **1** [C] a small tree with pale purple or white flowers **2** [U] a pale purple colour SYN **mauve** —**lilac** *adj*: *a lilac dress*

Lil·li·put /ˈlɪlɪpʌt, -pʊt/ an imaginary country in the book *Gulliver's Travels* by Jonathan Swift, where all the people, animals, and buildings are very small. Places where everything is small are sometimes said to be like Lilliput. —**Lilliputian** /ˌlɪləˈpjuːʃən/ *n* [C]

lil·li·pu·tian /ˌlɪləˈpjuːʃən◂/ *adj formal* extremely small compared to the normal size of things

Li·lo /ˈlaɪləʊ $ -loʊ/ *n* (*plural* **Lilos**) [C] *trademark BrE* a rubber MATTRESS filled with air and used as a bed or for floating on water

lilt /lɪlt/ *n* [singular] a pleasant pattern of rising and falling sound in someone's voice or in music: *the lilt of a Scottish accent* —**lilting** *adj*: *a lilting melody*

lil·y /ˈlɪli/ *n* (*plural* **lilies**) [C] one of several types of plant with large bell-shaped flowers of various colours, especially white → **gild the lily** at GILD(3), → WATER LILY → see picture at FLOWER¹

lily-liv·ered /ˌlɪli ˈlɪvəd◂ $ -ərd◂/ *adj old-fashioned* lacking courage SYN **cowardly**

ˌlily of the ˈvalley *n* [C] a plant with several small white bell-shaped flowers

ˌlily-ˈwhite *adj* **1** pure white: *lily-white skin* **2** *informal* morally perfect: *You're not so lily-white yourself!*

li·ma bean /ˈliːmə biːn $ ˈlaɪ-/ *n* [C] a round flat light green bean that grows in America

limb /lɪm/ ●●○ *n* [C]
1 out on a limb alone and without help or support: *All the other countries signed the agreement, leaving Britain out on a limb.* | *He'd* ***gone out on a limb*** (=taken a risk) *to help us.*
2 an arm or leg
3 strong-limbed/long-limbed etc having strong, long etc arms and legs
4 a large branch of a tree → **risk life and limb** at RISK²(1), → **tear sb limb from limb** at TEAR²(9)

lim·ber¹ /ˈlɪmbə $ -ər/ *v*
limber up *phr v* to do gentle exercises in order to prepare your muscles for a race, competition etc

limber² *adj* able to move and bend easily

lim·bo /ˈlɪmbəʊ $ -boʊ/ *n* **1** [singular, U] a situation in which nothing happens or changes for a long period of time, and it is difficult to make decisions or know what to do, often because you are waiting for something else to happen first: **be in limbo** *I'm in limbo now until I know whether I've got the job.* | **[+of]** *the limbo of his eight years in jail* **2 the limbo** a West Indian dance in which the dancer leans backwards and goes under a stick that is lowered gradually

lime¹ /laɪm/ ●○○ *n*
1 [C] a small juicy green fruit with a sour taste, or the tree this grows on → see picture at FRUIT¹
2 [C] a tree with pleasant-smelling yellow flowers SYN **linden**
3 [U] a white substance obtained by burning LIMESTONE, used for making cement, marking sports fields etc SYN **quicklime**
4 [U] a light yellowish green colour

lime² *v* [T] *technical* to add lime to soil to control acid

lime·ade /ˌlaɪmˈeɪd/ *n* [U] a drink made from the juice of limes

ˌlime ˈgreen *n* [U] a light yellowish green colour —**lime-green** *adj*

lime·light /ˈlaɪmlaɪt/ *n* [singular, U] a situation in which someone receives a lot of attention, especially from newspapers, television etc: **in/out of the limelight** *Tad loves being in the limelight.* | *The president's wife wanted to stay out of the limelight.* | *She's afraid this new actor will* ***steal the limelight*** *from her.* | *his few moments of limelight in front of the cameras*

lim·e·rick /ˈlɪmərɪk/ *n* [C] a humorous short poem that has five lines that RHYME

lime·scale /ˈlaɪmskeɪl/ *n* [U] *BrE* a hard white or grey substance that forms on the inside of pipes, TAPS, and water containers

lime·stone /ˈlaɪmstəʊn $ -stoʊn/ *n* [U] a type of rock that contains CALCIUM

li·mey /ˈlaɪmi/ *n* [C] *AmE old-fashioned* a slightly insulting word for someone from Britain

lim·it¹ /ˈlɪmɪt/ ●●● S2 W2 *n* [C]
1 GREATEST/LEAST ALLOWED the greatest or least amount, number, speed etc that is allowed: *a 55 mph speed limit* | **[+for]** *There's no age limit for applicants.* | **[+to/on]** *My wife and I set a limit on how much we spend on clothes.* | **above/over/below a limit** *Pesticide levels in drinking water are already above legal limits in many areas.*
2 GREATEST AMOUNT POSSIBLE (*also* **limits**) the greatest possible amount of something that can exist or be obtained: **[+of]** *the limits of human knowledge* | *He'd* ***reached the limit*** *of his patience.* | *Our finances are already* ***stretched to the limit*** (=we do not have any extra money). | ***There's no limit to*** *what you can do if you try.*
3 PLACE (*also* **limits**) the furthest point or edge of a place, often one that must not be passed: *He had not been outside the limits of the prison walls for 20 years.* | *The public is not allowed within a 2-mile limit of the missile site.* | *Los Angeles* ***city limits***
4 off limits a) beyond the area where someone is allowed to go: *That area of beach was off limits to us 'city kids'.* **b)** beyond what you are allowed to do or have: *His private life is off limits to the press.*
5 within limits within the time, level, amount etc considered acceptable: *You can come and go when you want - within limits.*
6 be over the limit to have drunk more alcohol than is legal or safe for driving
7 know your limits *informal* to know what you are good at doing and what you are not good at: *I know my limits. I'm not an administrator.*
8 have your limits *spoken* to have a set of rules about what is reasonable behaviour, and to not accept behaviour that does not follow these rules: *I have my limits. You will not use that kind of nasty language in class.*

COLLOCATIONS

VERBS

set a limit (*also* **impose a limit** *formal*) *Set a time limit for the completion of the task.*
put a limit on sth *We have to put a limit on the number of participants.*
exceed a limit (=go beyond a limit) *He reported a driver for exceeding the speed limit.*
go over a limit (=go beyond a limit) *Borrowers who go over the spending limit set by the credit card company are penalised.*

ADJECTIVES/NOUN + limit

an upper/lower limit (=the highest/lowest amount allowed) *There is no upper limit on the amount you can borrow.*
a strict limit *There are strict limits on spending.*
a legal limit (=a limit set by law) *The alcohol in his blood was four times more than the legal limit.*
the speed limit *Too many people go over the speed limit in residential areas.*
a time limit | **an age limit** | **a weight/height limit** | **spending limits** | **term limits** *AmE* (=limits on how much time a politician can spend in office)

THESAURUS

limit the highest number, speed, temperature etc that is allowed by a law or rule: *The speed limit is 65 m.p.h.* | *There's no limit on the amount of money that may be brought into the US.* | *Pollution levels are over the official limit.*
restrictions rules or laws that strictly control what you are allowed to do: *Travel restrictions might reduce the spread of the disease.* | *New restrictions have been imposed on immigration.*
limitations limits on what a person or thing is able to do - used especially when you would like to be able to do more: *The president was unwilling to accept limitations on his power.* | *the limitations of the computer system* | *Hikers should know their physical limitations and not take unnecessary risks.*
constraints facts or conditions that limit what you can do, for example not having enough time, money etc: *Financial constraints are forcing many people in their twenties to live with their parents.* | *The last part of the show had to be cut because of time constraints.*

limit² ●●● S3 W2 *v*
1 [T] to stop an amount or number from increasing beyond a particular point: *a decision to limit imports of foreign cars* | **limit sth to sth** *Seating is limited to 500.*
2 [T] to stop someone from doing what they want or from developing and improving beyond a particular point: *A lack of formal education will limit your job opportunities.* | **limit yourself to sth** *I limit myself to two cups of coffee a day.*
3 be limited to sth to exist or happen only in a particular place, group, or area of activity: *The damage was limited to the roof.*

lim·i·ta·tion /ˌlɪmɪˈteɪʃən/ ●●○ W3 *n*
1 [U] the act or process of controlling or reducing something: **[+to]** *Any limitation to the king's power could be permanent.* | *a nuclear limitation treaty* → **damage limitation** at DAMAGE¹(3)
2 [C usually plural] qualities that stop someone or something from being as good or as effective as you wish they could be SYN **weakness**: **[+of]** *Despite the limitations of the survey, it did suggest some general trends.* | *It's a good little car, but it* ***has*** *its* ***limitations***.
3 [C,U] a rule or condition that stops something from increasing beyond a particular point: **[+on/upon]** *a limitation on the number of hours children can work* | **put/place/impose limitations** *The new law imposes limitations on campaign contributions.*

lim·it·ed /ˈlɪmɪtɪd/ ●●● W2 *adj*
1 not very great in amount, number, ability etc: **limited number/amount/time etc** *There are only a limited number of tickets available.* | *My knowledge of the business is limited.* | *The organization has very* ***limited resources***. | *So far, the education reforms have had only* ***limited success***. | **(be of) limited use/value** *Unfortunately, the drug is of limited value in treating cancer.*
2 Limited (*written abbreviation* **Ltd**) used after the name of British business companies that have LIMITED LIABILITY

L

ˌlimited ˈcompany (*also* **ˌlimited liaˈbility ˌcompany**) *n* [C] a company in Britain whose owners only have to pay a limited amount if the company gets into debt → **public limited company**

ˌlimited eˈdition *n* [C] a small number of special copies of a book, picture etc which are produced at one time only

ˌlimited liaˈbility *n* [U] *technical* the legal position of being responsible for paying only a limited amount of debt if something bad happens to yourself or your company

lim·it·ing /ˈlɪmətɪŋ/ *adj* **1** preventing any improvement or increase in something: *A* ***limiting factor*** *in health care is the way resources are distributed.* **2** *informal* preventing someone from developing and doing what they are interested in: *The job's OK, but it's sort of limiting.*

lim·it·less /ˈlɪmətləs/ *adj* without a limit or end SYN **infinite**: *limitless possibilities*

lim·o /ˈlɪməʊ $ -moʊ/ *n* [C] *informal* a limousine

lim·ou·sine /ˈlɪməziːn, ˌlɪməˈziːn/ *n* [C] **1** a very large, expensive, and comfortable car, driven by someone who is paid to drive **2** a small bus that people take to and from airports in the US

limp¹ /lɪmp/ *adj* not firm or strong: *a limp handshake* | *His body suddenly* ***went limp*** *and he fell down on the floor.* —**limply** *adv*: *His arms were* ***hanging limply***. —**limpness** *n* [U]

limp² *v* [I] **1** to walk slowly and with difficulty because one leg is hurt or injured: *Moreno limped off the field with a foot injury.* THESAURUS▸ WALK **2** [always + adv/prep] if a ship or aircraft limps somewhere, it goes there slowly, because it has been damaged: **[+into]** *The damaged liner limped into New York.*

limp along *phr v* if a company, project etc limps along, it is not successful: *The team is limping along in fifth place.*

limp³ *n* [C] the way someone walks when they are limping: *Young walked with* ***a slight limp***.

lim·pet /ˈlɪmpɪt/ *n* [C] a small sea animal with a shell, which holds tightly onto the rock where it lives

lim·pid /ˈlɪmpɪd/ *adj literary* clear or transparent: *limpid blue eyes* —**limpidly** *adv* —**limpidity** /lɪmˈpɪdəti/ *n* [U]

limp-wrist·ed /ˌlɪmp ˈrɪstɪd◂/ *adj* a limp-wristed man is considered to lack male qualities such as strength; sometimes used to say that a man is HOMOSEXUAL

linch·pin, **lynchpin** /ˈlɪntʃˌpɪn/ *n* **the linchpin of sth** the person or thing in a group, system etc that is most important, because everything depends on them

linc·tus /ˈlɪŋktəs/ *n* [U] *BrE* a liquid medicine used for curing coughs

lin·den /ˈlɪndən/ *n* [C] a LIME tree

line¹ /laɪn/ ●●● S1 W1 *n*

1 ON PAPER/ON THE GROUND [C] a long thin mark on a piece of paper, the ground, or another surface: *Draw a* ***straight line*** *across the top of the page.* | *Sign your name on the* ***dotted line*** (=line made up of a series of dots). | *The edges of the pitch are marked by white lines.* | *The goalkeeper just managed to stop the ball going over the line.* | *He raced towards the finishing line.*

2 BETWEEN TWO AREAS [C] an imaginary line on the surface of the Earth, for example showing where one country or area of land stops and another begins: **county/state line** *AmE*: *He was born in a small town just across the state line.* | **line of latitude/longitude** *They were still travelling along the same line of longitude.* THESAURUS▸ BORDER → INTERNATIONAL DATE LINE

3 OF PEOPLE/THINGS [C] **a)** a row of people or things next to each other: **[+of]** *There was a line of fir trees on either side of the road.* | *The four men were* ***standing in a line*** *on the other side of the table.* | *A couple of the posts were* ***out of line*** (=not in a straight row). **b)** especially *AmE* a row of people, cars etc that are waiting one behind the other SYN **queue** *BrE*: *I looked in despair at the long line in front of the ticket office.* | **[+of]** *I joined the line of vehicles waiting to get into the car park.* | **stand/wait in line** *Customers stood in line for 20 minutes at the cash register.* | *He tried to* ***cut in line*** (=go in front of other people who are waiting). | *The woman* ***next in line*** *began to mutter to herself.*

4 DIRECTION [C] the direction or imaginary line along which something travels between two places: *Light travels* ***in a straight line***. | *A boat came into my* ***line of vision*** (=the direction I was looking in). | **line of fire/attack/movement etc** (=the direction in which someone shoots, attacks, moves etc) *I was directly in the animal's line of attack.* | *They knew they needed to block their enemy's* ***supply lines*** (=the direction used for carrying supplies of food etc).

5 ON YOUR FACE [C] a line on the skin of someone's face → **wrinkle**: *She frowned, and* ***deep lines*** *appeared between her eyebrows.* | *There were* ***fine lines*** *around her eyes.* | *No one can avoid lines and wrinkles as they get older.*

6 PHONE [C] a telephone wire or connection: *I'm sorry,* ***the line is busy*** (=someone is already using it). | *There seems to be a fault* ***on the line***. | *There was a click, then* ***the line went dead*** (=suddenly stopped working completely). | *Henry is* ***on the line*** (=on the phone) *from New York.* | *I* ***got on the line to*** (=phoned) *the hospital as soon as I heard about the accident.* | *I wished he would just* ***get off the line***. | *I'm sorry, it's a* ***bad line*** *and I can't hear you.* | ***Hold the line*** (=wait on the phone), *please, and I'll put you through to our sales department.* | *Do you have a separate line for your modem?*

7 FOR TRAINS [C] a track that a train travels along: *We were delayed because of a problem further along the line.* | *When you get to central London, take the Victoria Line to Finsbury Park.* | **railway line** *BrE*, **railroad line** *AmE*: *The trail follows a disused railroad line along the edge of the valley.*

8 BETWEEN TWO TYPES OF THING [C usually singular] the point at which one type of thing can be considered to be something else or at which it becomes a particular thing: **[+between]** *There is a* ***fine line*** *between superstition and religion.* | *The* ***dividing line*** *between luxuries and necessities is constantly changing.* | *Sometimes he found it hard to* ***draw the line*** *between work and pleasure.* | *Her remarks did not quite* ***cross the line*** *into rudeness.* | *Large numbers of families are living on or near the* ***poverty line*** (=the point at which people are considered to be very poor).

9 SHAPE/EDGE [C usually plural] the outer shape of something long or tall: *She was wearing a loose dress which softened the lines of her body.* | *a modern building with clean, elegant lines.*

10 WORDS [C] **a)** a line of written words, for example in a poem or a document: *He quoted a few lines from Shakespeare.* | *Scroll down to line 29.* **b)** a remark: *He liked to introduce himself with a witty opening line.* | *This was one of his favourite* ***chat-up lines*** (=remark for impressing someone you want to attract). **c)** [usually plural] words that someone has to learn and say as part of a play or performance: *Paul often messed up his lines.* | *It always took me ages to* ***learn*** *my* ***lines***.

11 OPINION/ATTITUDE [singular] an opinion or attitude, especially one that someone states publicly and that influences their actions: **[+on]** *I can't agree with the government's line on immigration.* | *Journalists are often too willing to accept* ***the official line*** (=the opinion that a government states officially). | *He found it hard to accept* ***the party line*** (=the official opinion of a political party) *on every issue.* | **take a tough/firm/hard line on sth** *The school takes a very tough line on drugs.* → **toe the line** at TOE²

12 WAY OF DOING STH [C] a particular way of doing something or of thinking about something: **line of argument/reasoning/inquiry etc** *It seemed useless to pursue this line of questioning.* | *Opposition parties soon realized they would have to try a different line of attack.* | *The police are* ***following*** *several different* ***lines*** *of enquiry.* | *We were both thinking* ***along the same lines*** (=in the same way). | *In South Africa, the press developed* ***along*** *very different* ***lines*** (=in a very different way). | *More groups will now be set up* ***on these lines*** (=this way). | *The company's rapid success means it's definitely* ***on the right lines*** (=doing something the right way).

13 SERIES OF EVENTS [C usually singular] a series of events that follow each other: **[+of]** *This is the latest in a* ***long line*** *of political scandals.*

14 IN A WAR [C] the edge of an area that is controlled by

an army, where soldiers stay and try to prevent their enemy from moving forward: *They finally broke through the German line.* | *young soldiers who were sent to the* ***front line*** *to fight* | *One regiment was trapped behind* ***enemy lines***. | *Reinforcements were available just* ***behind the lines***.
15 IN A COMPANY/ORGANIZATION [C] a series of levels of authority within an organization: *Decisions are taken by senior officers and fed down through the* ***line of command*** *to the ordinary soldiers.* | *There should be more direct discussion between managers and workers* ***lower down the line***. → LINE MANAGER
16 OF ROPE/WIRE [C] a piece of strong string, rope, or wire used for a particular purpose: *She hung the clothes out on the* ***washing line*** (=line for hanging wet clothes on to dry). | *The* ***fishing line*** (=line for catching fish) *snapped and the fish got away.*
17 PRODUCT [C] a type of goods for sale in a shop: *The company has just launched a new line of small, low-priced computers.*
18 along these/those lines (*also* **along the lines of sth**) similar to something else: *We usually start with general questions* ***along the lines of***, *'How do you feel?'* | *They're trying to organize a trip to the beach or* ***something along those lines***.
19 along religious/ethnic/party etc lines if people divide along religious, party etc lines, they divide according to the religion, political party, or other group they belong to: *The committee was* ***split along*** *party* ***lines***. | *The community remains* ***divided along*** *religious* ***lines***.
20 on line a) using a computer to get information or to communicate with people: *You can book tickets on line.* | *Most of our sales staff now work on line.* → ONLINE **b)** working properly as planned: *a new nuclear reactor which should be on line by 2005* | *If there is a power failure, the emergency generators should come on line within 15 minutes.*
21 drop sb a line *informal* to write a short letter or email to someone: *Drop me a line and let me know how you're getting on.*
22 don't give me that line *spoken* used to say that you do not believe someone's excuse: *I know for a fact you weren't sick yesterday, so don't give me that line.*
23 fall into line/bring sb into line *informal* to start to do what someone else wants you to do, or to make someone do this: *Now that France and Germany have signed up, other countries will soon fall into line.* | *The few party rebels were soon brought into line.*
24 in line with sth if something changes in line with something else, it changes in the same way and at the same rate as it: *Pensions will be increased in line with inflation.*
25 bring sth into line with sth to change a system so that it works according to a particular set of rules, laws etc: *UK immigration procedures will have to be changed to bring them into line with the latest European ruling.*
26 be out of line *informal* **a)** to say or do something that is not acceptable in a particular situation: *You just keep quiet! You're way out of line.* **b)** to not obey someone, or to do something that you should not do: **get/step out of line** *Anybody who steps out of line will be in deep trouble.*
27 be in line for sth/be in line to do sth to be very likely to get or be given something: *I should be in line for promotion soon.* | **first/second/next etc in line for** *He must be first in line for the editor's job.*
28 be first/second/next etc in line to the throne to be the person who has a right to become a future king or queen: *As the eldest son, he was next in line to the throne.*
29 be on the line if something important is on the line, there is a risk that you might lose it or something bad could happen to it: *From now on, all our jobs are on the line.* | *She knew that her whole future was on the line.* | **put yourself/your neck on the line (for sb)** (=risk something bad happening to you) *I've already put myself on the line for you once, and I'm not going to do it again.*
30 be in sb's line *informal* to be the type of thing that someone is interested in or good at: *Acting's not really in my line, I'm afraid.*
31 get a line on sb/sth *especially AmE informal* to get information about someone or something: *We need to get some kind of a line on these guys.*
32 somewhere along the line *informal* at some time during an activity or period of time: *Somewhere along the line, Errol seemed to have lost interest in her.*
33 down the line *informal* later, after an activity or situation has been continuing for a period of time: *There may be more costs further down the line.* | *Now, three years down the line, we're beginning to see the problems with the treatment.*
34 in the line of duty happening or done as part of your job: *firefighters dying in the line of duty*
35 be in the firing line/in the line of fire a) to be one of the people who could be criticized or blamed for something: *As one of the president's chief advisers, he's bound to be in the firing line.* **b)** to be in a place where a bullet etc might hit you: *A couple of civilians were caught in the firing line.*
36 PUNISHMENT **lines** [plural] *BrE* a punishment given to school children that consists of writing the same thing a lot of times: *He got 50 lines for being cheeky to a teacher.*
37 FAMILY [singular] your family, considered as the people you are related to who lived before you and the people who will live after you: *She comes from a long line of actors.* | *It looks as if Joe might be the last of the line* (=the last in his family). | **the male/female line** *This particular gene is passed down through the male line.* | **line of succession** (=the system by which an important position or property is passed from a parent to their children, and then to their children etc) *Henry the Eighth wanted a male heir to ensure the Tudor line of succession.*
38 JOB [C usually singular] the type of work someone does: **line of work/business** *What line of business is he in?* | **in the building/retail etc line** *She's keen to do something in the fashion line.*
39 TRANSPORT [C] a company that provides transport for moving goods by sea, air, road etc: *He runs a transatlantic shipping line.*
40 DRUG [C] *informal* an amount of an illegal drug in powder form, arranged in a line so it can be breathed in through the nose → **draw the line at** at DRAW[1](16), → **draw a line (between sth)** at DRAW[1](15), → **where do you draw the line?** at DRAW[1](17), → **draw a line under sth** at DRAW[1](18), → **hard line** at HARD[1](21), → **hook, line and sinker** at HOOK[1](9), → **lay sth on the line** at LAY[2](18), → PICKET LINE, → **the poverty line/level** at POVERTY(2), → **read between the lines** at READ[1](14)

line² ●●○ *v* [T]
1 to sew a piece of material onto the inside or back of another piece to make it stronger or warmer: *Are those curtains lined?* | **line sth with sth** *a leather coat lined with silk*
2 to form a layer over the inner surface of something: *The birds use small leaves for lining their nests.* | **line sth with sth** *The cage should be lined with straw.*
3 to form rows along the sides of something: *Crowds lined the route to the palace.* | **be lined with sth** *The street was lined with small shops.* | *a tree-lined avenue*
4 line your own pockets to make yourself richer, especially by doing something dishonest – used to show disapproval

line up *phr v*
1 if people line up, or if you line them up, they stand in a row or line, or you make them do this: *Line up, everybody!* | **line sb ↔ up** *He lined us all up in the corridor.*
2 line sth ↔ up to arrange things in a row: *I lined the bottles up on the sideboard.*
3 line sth ↔ up to move one thing so that it is in the correct position in relation to something else: **[+with]** *The windows should be lined up with the door frame.*
4 line sb/sth ↔ up to arrange for something to happen or for someone to be available for an event: *We've lined up some excellent speakers for tonight.* | *He's already* ***got*** *a new job* ***lined up***. → LINE-UP

lin·e·age /ˈlɪni-ɪdʒ/ *n* [C,U] *formal* the way in which members of a family are DESCENDed from other members → **line, ancestry**: *a family of ancient lineage*

lin·e·al /ˈlɪniəl/ *adj formal* related directly to someone who lived a long time before you: *lineal descendants*

lin·e·a·ment /ˈlɪniəmənt/ *n* [C usually plural] *formal*
1 a feature of your face **2** a typical quality

L

lin·e·ar /ˈlɪniə $ -ər/ *adj* **1** consisting of lines, or in the form of a straight line: *a linear diagram* **2** [only before noun] relating to length: *linear measurements* **3** involving a series of connected events, ideas etc, that move or progress from one stage to the next: *linear thinking* —**linearly** *adv* —**linearity** /ˌlɪniˈærəti/ *n* [U] → LATERAL THINKING

line·back·er /ˈlaɪnˌbækə $ -ər/ *n* [C] a player in American football who tries to TACKLE members of the other team

ˈline-caught *adj* line-caught fish have been caught using hooks on a long string, which causes less harm to other sea creatures than using a net

lined /laɪnd/ *adj* **1** a coat, skirt etc that is lined has a piece of thin material covering the inside → **lining**: *a fleece-lined jacket* **2** paper that is lined has straight lines printed or drawn across it **3** skin that is lined has WRINKLES on it

ˈline ˌdancing *n* [U] a type of dancing in which people dance in lines, all following the same series of steps

ˈline ˌdrawing *n* [C] a DRAWING consisting only of lines

line·man /ˈlaɪnmən/ *n* (*plural* **linemen** /-mən/) [C] *AmE* **1** a player in American football who plays in the front line of a team: **offensive/defensive lineman** **2** someone whose job is to take care of railway lines or telephone wires

ˈline ˌmanagement *n* [U] *BrE* a system of management in which information and instructions are passed from one person to someone immediately higher or lower than them in rank

ˈline ˌmanager *n* [C] *BrE* **1** a manager in a company who is responsible for the main activities of production, sales etc **2 sb's line manager** someone who is one level higher in rank than you in a company and is in charge of your work

lin·en /ˈlɪnɪn/ ●○○ *n* [U]
1 sheets, TABLECLOTHS etc: *bed linen* | *table linen*
2 cloth made from the FLAX plant, used to make high quality clothes, home decorations etc: *a linen jacket*
3 *old use* underwear → **wash your dirty laundry/linen** at DIRTY[1](7)

ˈlinen ˌcupboard *n* [C] *BrE* a cupboard in which sheets, TOWELS etc are kept SYN **linen closet** *AmE*

ˌline of ˈscrimmage *n* [C] a line in American football where the ball is placed at the beginning of a period of play

ˈline-out *n* [C] the way of starting play again in a RUGBY UNION game, when the ball has gone off the field

ˈline ˌprinter *n* [C] a machine that prints information from a computer at a very high speed —**line printing** *n* [U]

lin·er /ˈlaɪnə $ -ər/ ●○○ *n*
1 [C] a piece of material used inside something, especially in order to keep it clean: *a dustbin liner* | *nappy liners*
2 [C] a large ship for passengers: *an* ***ocean liner*** → CRUISE LINER
3 [C,U] *informal* EYELINER

ˈliner ˌnote *n* [usually plural] printed information about the music or musicians that comes with a CD or record

lines·man /ˈlaɪnzmən/ *n* (*plural* **linesmen** /-mən/) [C] an official in a sport who decides when a ball has gone out of the playing area → see picture at TENNIS

ˈline-up *n* [C usually singular] **1** the players in a sports team who play in a particular game: *This was his first match in the* ***starting line-up*** (=the players who begin the game). **2** a group of people, especially performers, who have agreed to be involved in an event: *The line-up included top bands Prodigy and Radiohead.* **3** a number of events or programmes arranged to follow each other: *a wonderful line-up of programmes for Christmas and the New Year* **4** *especially AmE* a row of people who stand in front of a WITNESS to a crime, who is then asked if he or she recognizes any of them as the criminal SYN **identification parade** *BrE*

-ling /lɪŋ/ *suffix* [in nouns] a small, young, or less important type of something: *a duckling* | *princelings*

lin·ger /ˈlɪŋgə $ -ər/ ●○○ *v* [I]
1 (*also* **linger on**) to continue to exist, be noticeable etc for longer than is usual or desirable: *a taste that lingers in your mouth* | *Unfortunately the tax will linger on until April.*
2 (*also* **linger on**) to stay somewhere a little longer, especially because you do not want to leave: **[+over]** *They lingered over coffee and missed the last bus.* | *I spent a week at Kandersteg and could happily have lingered on.*
THESAURUS STAY
3 [always + adv/prep] to continue looking at or dealing with something for longer than is usual or desirable: **[+on/over]** *Mike let his eyes linger on her face.* | *There's no need to linger over this stage of the interview.*
4 (*also* **linger on**) to continue to live although you are slowly dying: *He surprised all the doctors by lingering on for several weeks.*

lin·ge·rie /ˈlænʒəri $ ˌlɑːnʒəˈreɪ, ˈlænʒəri/ *n* [U] women's underwear

lin·ger·ing /ˈlɪŋgərɪŋ/ *adj* [usually before noun] continuing to exist for longer than is usual or desirable: **lingering doubts/suspicions etc** *Any lingering hopes of winning the title soon disappeared.* | *Mr Wilkins suffered a* ***lingering death***. | **lingering smell/aroma/odour** *the lingering aroma of chocolate* —**lingeringly** *adv*

lin·go /ˈlɪŋgəʊ $ -goʊ/ *n* [C usually singular] *informal* **1** a language, especially a foreign one: *I'd like to go to Greece, but I don't* ***speak the lingo***. **2** words or expressions used only by a particular group of people, or at a particular period of time: *academic lingo*

lin·gua fran·ca /ˌlɪŋgwə ˈfræŋkə/ *n* [C usually singular] a language used between people whose main languages are different: *English is the lingua franca in many countries.*

lin·gui·ni /lɪŋˈgwiːni/ *n* [plural] long thin flat pieces of PASTA

lin·guist /ˈlɪŋgwɪst/ ●○○ *n* [C]
1 someone who is good at foreign languages, especially someone who speaks several
2 someone who studies or teaches linguistics

lin·guis·tic /lɪŋˈgwɪstɪk/ ●●○ *adj* related to language, words, or linguistics: *a child's linguistic development* —**linguistically** /-kli/ *adv*

lin·guis·tics /lɪŋˈgwɪstɪks/ ●○○ *n* [U] the study of language in general and of particular languages, their structure, grammar, and history → PHILOLOGY

GRAMMAR: Singular or plural verb?
Linguistics is followed by a singular verb: ***Linguistics is*** *the scientific study of language.*
GRAMMAR GUIDE NOUNS

lin·i·ment /ˈlɪnəmənt/ *n* [U] a liquid containing oil that you rub on your skin when you feel sore or stiff

lin·ing /ˈlaɪnɪŋ/ ●○○ *n* [C,U]
1 a piece of material that covers the inside of something, especially a piece of clothing → **lined**: *a jacket with a silk lining* → **every cloud has a silver lining** at CLOUD[1](6)
2 a substance or material that covers the inside of part of the body: *the lining of the womb*

link[1] /lɪŋk/ ●●● S3 W2 AWL *v*
1 be linked if two things are linked, they are related in some way: *Police think the murders are linked.* | **be linked to/with sth** *Some birth defects are linked to smoking during pregnancy.* | **be closely/directly/strongly etc linked** *Our economy is inextricably linked with America's.*
2 MAKE CONNECTION [T] to make a connection between two or more things or people: *A love of nature links the two poets.* | **link sth/sb to/with sth** *Exactly how do we link words to objects?* | **link sb/sth together** *Strong family ties still linked them together.*
3 JOIN [T] to physically join two or more things, people, or places SYN **connect**: **link sth/sb to/with sth** *The pipe must be linked to the cold water supply.* | **link sb/sth together** *The climbers were linked together by ropes.* | **link sth and sth** *A long bridge links Venice and the mainland.* | *He walked with her,* ***linking arms*** (=putting his arm around her arm).
4 SHOW CONNECTION [T] to show or say that there is a

L

connection between two people, situations, or things: **link sth/sb to/with sth** *He denied reports linking him to Colombian drug dealers.*
5 MAKE STH DEPEND ON STH [T] to make one thing or situation depend on another thing or situation: **link sth to sth** *Pay increases will now be linked to performance.* → INDEX-LINKED
6 CONNECT EQUIPMENT [T] (*also* **link up**) to connect computers, broadcast systems etc, so that electronic messages can be sent between them: **link sth to/with sth** *Local terminals are linked to the central computer.*
7 INTERNET [I] to set up a link to a website or WEBPAGE: *How can I find out who has linked to my blog?*

link in *phr v BrE*
1 to connect with another idea, statement, type of work etc, especially in a way that is useful SYN **tie in**: **[+with]** *This point links in with our earlier discussion.*
2 to happen at the same time as something else SYN **tie in**: **[+with]** *The Minister's visit was scheduled to link in with the meeting in Harare.*

link up *phr v*
1 to connect with something or to make a connection between things, especially so that they can work together: **[+with]** *The train links up with the ferry at Dover.* | **link sth ↔ up (with sth)** *The next stage is to link the film up with the soundtrack.*
2 to connect computers, broadcast systems etc so that electronic messages can be sent between them: **link sth ↔ up (to/with sth)** *All these PCs are linked up to the network.* | *The Internet allows people from all over the world to link up for chat sessions.*
3 to join with someone so that you can do something together: **[+with]** *We linked up with the 'Daily Express' to help run the campaign.* → LINKUP

link² ●●● S3 W2 AWL *n* [C]
1 a way in which two things or ideas are related to each other: **link between sth (and sth)** *the link between drug use and crime* | *There are a number of links between the two theories.*
2 a relationship or connection between two or more people, countries, organizations etc: **[+between]** *the **close link** between teacher and student* | **[+with]** *The company has **strong links** with big investors.* | **forge/establish links** *Organizers of the project hope that international links will be forged.*
3 a person or thing that makes possible a relationship or connection with someone or something else: **[+with]** *For elderly people, TV is a vital link with the outside world.*
4 rail/road/telephone etc link something that makes communication or travel between two places possible: *The office has **direct** computer **links** to over 100 firms.*
5 one of the rings in a chain
6 link in the chain one of the stages involved in a process
7 the links a piece of ground near the sea where golf is played SYN **golf links**
8 a special word or picture in an Internet document that you CLICK on to move quickly to another part of the same document or to another document → **hyperlink**: *Send an email to the above address to report a broken link* (=a link that is not working properly). → CUFF LINK, MISSING LINK, → **weak/weakest link** at WEAK(15)

link·age /ˈlɪŋkɪdʒ/ AWL *n* **1** [C,U] *formal* a LINK²(1): **[+between]** *the linkage between wages and prices* **2** [C,U] a system of links or connections **3** [singular, U] a condition in a political or business agreement by which one country or company agrees to do something, only if the other promises to do something in return

ˈlinking ˌverb (*also* **ˈlink verb**) *n* [C] a verb that connects the subject of a sentence with its COMPLEMENT, for example 'seem' in the sentence 'The house seems big' SYN **copula**

ˈlinking ˌword *n* [C] a word that is used to connect one part of a sentence with another, or to show how one sentence is related to another. For example, 'and', 'although', and 'however' are linking words.

link-up /ˈlɪŋk-ʌp/ *n* [C] a connection between two things, especially organizations or communication systems

lin·net /ˈlɪnɪt/ *n* [C] a small brown singing bird

li·no /ˈlaɪnəʊ $ -noʊ/ *n* [U] *BrE informal* LINOLEUM

li·no·cut /ˈlaɪnəʊkʌt $ -noʊ-/ *n* **1** [U] the art of cutting a pattern on a block of linoleum **2** [C] a picture printed from such a block

li·no·le·um /ləˈnəʊliəm $ -ˈnoʊ-/ *n* [U] a floor covering made from strong shiny material

Li·no·type /ˈlaɪnəʊtaɪp $ -noʊ-/ *n* [U] *trademark* a system for arranging TYPE¹(3) in the form of solid metal lines

lin·seed /ˈlɪnsiːd/ *n* [U] the seed of the FLAX plant

ˌlinseed ˈoil *n* [U] the oil from linseed, used in paints, for protecting wood surfaces etc

lint /lɪnt/ *n* [U] **1** *especially AmE* soft light pieces of thread or wool that come off cotton, wool, or other material SYN **fluff** *BrE* **2** *BrE* soft cotton material used for protecting wounds

lin·tel /ˈlɪntl/ *n* [C] a piece of stone or wood across the top of a window or door, forming part of the frame

Li·nux /ˈlaɪnʌks/ *n* [singular] *trademark* a computer OPERATING SYSTEM that was invented by Linus Torvalds, a Finnish university student. You can get Linux for free, or you can buy it from companies who provide information and instructions on how to operate it.

li·on /ˈlaɪən/ ●●● S3 W3 *n* [C]
1 a large animal of the cat family that lives in Africa and parts of southern Asia. Lions have gold-coloured fur and the male has a MANE (=long hair around its neck). → **lioness** → see picture at **BIG CAT**
2 the lion's share (of sth) the largest part of something: *The firm has captured the lion's share of the UK market.*
3 the lion's den if you go into the lion's den, you go among people who are your enemies

li·on·ess /ˈlaɪənes, -nəs/ *n* [C] a female lion

lion-heart·ed /ˌlaɪən ˈhɑːtɪd◂ $ ˈhɑːr-/ *adj written* very brave SYN **courageous** OPP **cowardly**

li·on·ize (*also* **-ise** *BrE*) /ˈlaɪənaɪz/ *v* [T] *written* to treat someone as being very important or famous

lip /lɪp/ ●●● S3 W2 *n*
1 [C] one of the two soft parts around your mouth where your skin is redder or darker: **upper/lower/top/bottom lip** *His bottom lip was swollen.* | *She had big eyes and **full lips*** (=large and round lips). | *Matt opened the door with a **smile on his lips**.* | *Marty **kissed** me right **on the lips**!* | **thin-lipped/thick-lipped/full-lipped** (=having lips that are thin, or large and round) | *Stephen **pursed** his **lips** with distaste* (=brought them together tightly into a small circle). → TIGHT-LIPPED
2 [C] the edge of a hollow or deep place in the land: **[+of]** *the old road that ran along the lip of the gorge*
3 [C usually singular] the edge of something you use to hold or pour liquid SYN **rim**
4 [U] *informal* talk that is not polite or respectful – used especially by adults to children SYN **cheek**: *Don't **give** me any of your **lip**!*
5 my lips are sealed *spoken* used to say that you will not tell anyone about a secret
6 on everyone's lips being talked about by everyone: *an actress whose name is on everyone's lips* → **bite your lip** at BITE¹(1), → **lick your lips** at LICK¹(5), → **not pass sb's lips** at PASS¹(24), → **read sb's lips** at READ¹(18), → **smack your lips** at SMACK¹(3), → **a stiff upper lip** at STIFF¹(11)

ˈlip balm *n* [C,U] a substance used to protect dry lips

ˈlip gloss *n* [C,U] a substance used to make lips look very shiny

lip·id /ˈlɪpɪd/ *n* [C] *technical* one of several types of FATTY substances in living things, such as fat, oil, or WAX

lip·o·suc·tion /ˈlɪpəʊˌsʌkʃən $ -poʊ-/ *n* [U] a way of removing fat from someone's body, using SUCTION

lip·py¹ /ˈlɪpi/ *n* [C,U] *BrE informal* LIPSTICK: *Wait a minute, I'll just put a bit of lippy on.*

lippy² *adj BrE informal* not showing respect in the way that you speak to someone

lip-read /ˈlɪp riːd/ *v* (*past tense and past participle* **lip-read**) [I,T] to understand what someone is saying by watching the way their lips move, because you cannot hear them —**lip-reading** *n* [U]

lip·ring /ˈlɪprɪŋ/ *n* [C] a small ring that someone puts through their lip, as jewellery

ˈlip salve *n* [C,U] *BrE* a substance used to make sore lips feel better

ˈlip ˌservice *n* **pay lip service to sb/sth** to say that you support or agree with something without doing anything to prove it: *organizations that pay lip service to career development*

ˈlip-ˌsmacking *adj informal* lip-smacking food tastes very good. This word is often used in advertisements. SYN **delicious**: *lip-smacking recipes*

lip·stick /ˈlɪpˌstɪk/ ●●○ *n* [C,U] something used for adding colour to your lips, in the shape of a small stick → see picture at **MAKE-UP**

ˌlipstick ˈlesbian *n* [C] *informal* a LESBIAN (=woman who is sexually attracted to other women) who behaves and dresses in a very FEMININE way

ˈlip-synch *v* [I] to move your lips at the same time as a recording is being played, in order to pretend that you are singing or saying the words —**lip synch** *n* [U]

liq·ue·fac·tion /ˌlɪkwəˈfækʃən/ *n* [U] *technical* the act of making something a liquid or of becoming a liquid

liq·ue·fy /ˈlɪkwəfaɪ/ *v* (**liquefied, liquefying, liquefies**) [I,T] *formal* to become liquid, or make something become liquid

li·queur /lɪˈkjʊə $ lɪˈkɜːr/ *n* [C,U] a sweet very strong alcoholic drink, drunk in small quantities after a meal → **liquor**

liq·uid¹ /ˈlɪkwɪd/ ●●● W3 *n* [C,U] a substance that is not a solid or a gas, for example water or milk: *Add a little more liquid to the sauce.* → **WASHING-UP LIQUID**

liquid² ●●○ *adj*
1 in the form of a liquid instead of a gas or solid: *Children take antibiotics* ***in liquid form***. | *liquid soap*
2 *technical* easily changed into money by being sold or exchanged: *Their shares are more liquid than those of many smaller companies.* → **LIQUID ASSETS**
3 liquid refreshment drink, especially alcoholic drink – used humorously
4 *literary* clear and shiny, like water: *liquid green eyes*
5 *literary* liquid sounds are clear and pure

ˌliquid ˈassets *n* [plural] *technical* the money that a company or person has, and the property they can exchange for money

liq·ui·date /ˈlɪkwədeɪt/ *v* **1** [I,T] to close a business or company and sell the things that belong to it, in order to pay its debts **2** [T] *technical* to pay a debt: *The stock was sold to liquidate the loan.* **3** [T] *informal* to kill someone or destroy something that is causing a problem

liq·ui·da·tion /ˌlɪkwəˈdeɪʃən/ *n* [C,U] **1** the act of closing a company by selling the things that belong to it, in order to pay its debts: *Hundreds of small businesses* ***went into liquidation*** (=were closed). **2** the act of paying a debt

liq·ui·da·tor /ˈlɪkwədeɪtə $ -ər/ *n* [C] an official whose job is to close a company and use any money obtained to pay its debts

li·quid·i·ty /lɪˈkwɪdəti/ *n* [U] *technical* **1** when a business or a person has money or goods that can be sold to pay debts **2** the state of being LIQUID

liq·uid·ize (*also* **-ise** *BrE*) /ˈlɪkwədaɪz/ *v* [T] to crush fruit, vegetables etc into a thick liquid

liq·uid·iz·er (*also* **-iser** *BrE*) /ˈlɪkwədaɪzə $ -ər/ *n* [C] *BrE* a small electric machine that makes solid foods into liquids SYN **blender**

liq·ui·tab /ˈlɪkwɪtæb/ *n* [C] a small bag filled with liquid soap, used in a washing machine

liq·uor /ˈlɪkə $ -ər/ ●○○ *n* [U]
1 *especially AmE* a strong alcoholic drink such as WHISKY SYN **spirit** → **LIQUEUR**
2 *BrE technical* any alcoholic drink

liq·uo·rice *BrE*, **licorice** *AmE* /ˈlɪkərɪs, -rɪʃ/ *n* [U] **1** a black substance produced from the root of a plant, used in medicine and sweets **2** sweets made from this substance

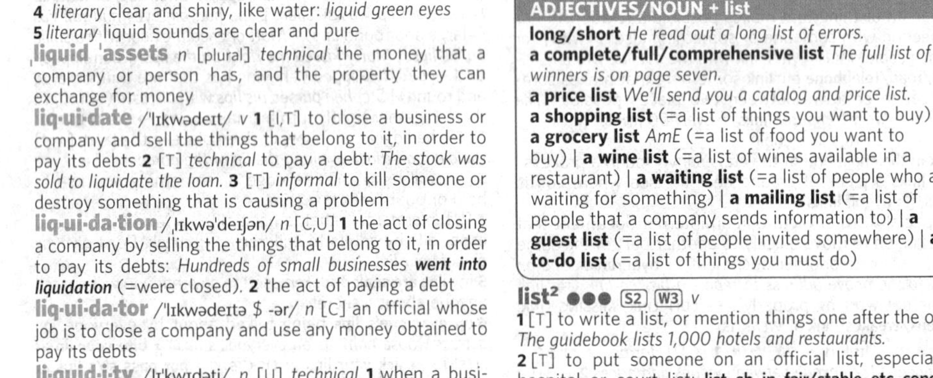
LIQUORICE

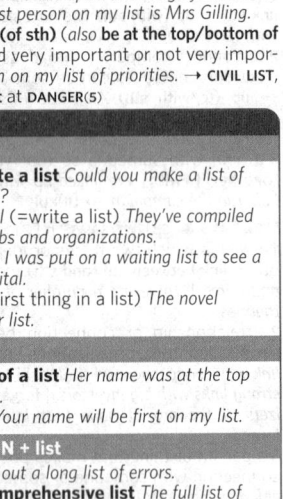

ˈliquor store *n* [C] *AmE* a shop where alcohol is sold SYN **off-licence** *BrE*

lir·a /ˈlɪərə $ ˈlɪrə/ *n* (*plural* **lire** /-reɪ/ *or* **liras**) [C] the standard unit of money in Turkey, and used in Italy and Malta before the EURO

lisp /lɪsp/ *n* [singular] a fault in the way someone speaks which makes them pronounce 's' sounds as 'th': *She speaks with a slight lisp.* —**lisp** *v* [I,T]

lis·som, **lissome** /ˈlɪsəm/ *adj literary* a body that is lissom is thin and graceful SYN **lithe**

list¹ /lɪst/ ●●● S1 W1 *n* [C]
1 a set of names, numbers etc, usually written one below the other, for example so that you can remember or check them: **[+of]** *Make a list of all the things you have to do.* | **on/in a list** *The first person on my list is Mrs Gilling.*
2 be high/low on a list (of sth) (*also* **be at the top/bottom of a list**) to be considered very important or not very important: *A good car is high on my list of priorities.* → **CIVIL LIST**, → **be on the danger list** at **DANGER**(5)

COLLOCATIONS

VERBS

make/draw up/write a list *Could you make a list of any supplies we need?*
compile a list *formal* (=write a list) *They've compiled a list of children's clubs and organizations.*
put sb/sth on a list *I was put on a waiting list to see a specialist at the hospital.*
top a list (=be the first thing in a list) *The novel topped the best-seller list.*

PHRASES

at the top/bottom of a list *Her name was at the top of the list of students.*
first/last on a list *Your name will be first on my list.*

ADJECTIVES/NOUN + list

long/short *He read out a long list of errors.*
a complete/full/comprehensive list *The full list of winners is on page seven.*
a price list *We'll send you a catalog and price list.*
a shopping list (=a list of things you want to buy) | **a grocery list** *AmE* (=a list of food you want to buy) | **a wine list** (=a list of wines available in a restaurant) | **a waiting list** (=a list of people who are waiting for something) | **a mailing list** (=a list of people that a company sends information to) | **a guest list** (=a list of people invited somewhere) | **a to-do list** (=a list of things you must do)

list² ●●● S2 W3 *v*
1 [T] to write a list, or mention things one after the other: *The guidebook lists 1,000 hotels and restaurants.*
2 [T] to put someone on an official list, especially a hospital or court list: **list sb in fair/stable etc condition** *Several passengers were listed in critical condition.* | *The case was listed for trial in the Crown Court.*
3 [I] if a ship lists, it leans to one side

list·ed /ˈlɪstɪd/ *adj BrE* **1** a listed building is one of historical interest in Britain, and is protected by a government order **2** a listed company is one which offers its SHARES for sale on the STOCK EXCHANGE SYN **public company, public corporation** *AmE*

lis·ten¹ /ˈlɪsən/ ●●● S1 W1 *v* [I]
1 to pay attention to what someone is saying or to a sound that you can hear: *Listen! There's a strange noise in the engine.* | **[+to]** *We sat around listening to music.* | **listen carefully/intently/hard etc** *The whole class was listening*

L

attentively. | *Liz stood still and listened hard* (=very carefully). **THESAURUS** ▸ **HEAR**
2 *spoken* used to tell someone to pay attention to what you are going to say: *Listen, I want you to come with me.*
3 to consider what someone says and accept their advice: *I told him not to go, but he just wouldn't listen.* | **[+to]** *I wish I'd listened to Dad.* | *She refused to* ***listen to reason*** (=accept sensible advice).

GRAMMAR: Comparison

listen
• You **listen to** someone or something: *I love listening to classical music.* ✗ Don't say: *I love listening classical music.*
• You **listen to** someone or something **doing** something: *I listened to the rain falling on the roof.*

hear
• You **hear** someone or something: *I heard a sudden shout.*
• You **hear** someone or something **do** something: *I heard something fall into the water.*
• You **hear** someone or something **doing** something: *I heard someone shouting.*

listen for sth *phr v* to listen carefully so that you will notice a particular sound: *Listen for the moment when the music changes.*

listen in *phr v*
1 to listen to a broadcast on the radio: **[+to]** *I must remember to listen in to the news.* → **TUNE IN**
2 to listen to someone's conversation when they do not want you to: **[+on]** *It sounded like someone was listening in on us.*

listen out *phr v BrE informal* to listen carefully so that you will notice a particular sound: **[+for]** *Listen out for the baby in case she wakes up.*

listen up *phr v spoken* used to get people's attention so they can hear what you are going to say: *Hey everybody, listen up!*

listen² *n* **a listen** *BrE informal* an act of listening: ***Have a listen*** *to this new album!*

lis·ten·a·ble /ˈlɪsənəbəl/ *adj informal* pleasant to listen to → **watchable**

lis·ten·er /ˈlɪsənə $ -ər/ ●○○ *n* [C]
1 someone who listens to the radio → **viewer**: *a new programme for younger listeners*
2 a good/sympathetic listener someone who listens carefully and sympathetically to other people

ˈlistening deˌvice *n* [C] a piece of equipment that allows you to listen secretly to other people's conversations SYN **bug**

lis·te·ri·a /lɪˈstɪəriə $ -ˈstɪr-/ *n* [U] a type of BACTERIA that makes you sick

list·ing /ˈlɪstɪŋ/ ●○○ *n*
1 [C] an official or public list: **[+of]** *a listing of all households in the district*
2 listings [plural] lists of films, plays, and other events, with the times and places at which they will happen
3 [C] if a company has a listing on the STOCK EXCHANGE, it can offer its SHARES for sale

list·less /ˈlɪstləs/ *adj* feeling tired and not interested in things: *The heat was making me listless.* —**listlessly** *adv* —**listlessness** *n* [U]

ˈlist price *n* [C] a price that is suggested for a product by the people who make it

list·serv /ˈlɪstˌsɜːv $ -ˌsɜːrv/ *n* [C] a computer program that allows a group of people to send and receive email from each other about a particular subject

lit /lɪt/ a past tense and past participle of LIGHT

lit. (*also* **lit** *BrE*) the abbreviation of ***literature*** or ***literary***: *French lit*

lit·a·ny /ˈlɪtəni/ *n* (*plural* **litanies**) [C] **1** a long list of problems, excuses etc – used to show disapproval: **[+of]** *an endless litany of complaints* **2** a long prayer in the Christian Church in which the priest says a sentence and the people reply

lite /laɪt/ *adj* **1** [usually before noun] *especially AmE* used in the names of some food or drink products to mean that they have fewer CALORIES or less fat than other similar products: *lite beer* **2** [only after noun] *informal* not as serious as the real thing, or less extreme: *Some people see cohabiting as marriage lite.* | *Socialism is communism lite.*

li·ter /ˈliːtə $ -ər/ *n* [C] the American spelling of LITRE

lit·e·ra·cy /ˈlɪtərəsi/ ●○○ *n* [U] the state of being able to read and write OPP **illiteracy** → **numeracy**: *a new adult literacy campaign* → **COMPUTER-LITERATE**

lit·e·ral /ˈlɪtərəl/ ●○○ *adj*
1 the literal meaning of a word or expression is its basic or original meaning → **figurative**: **literal meaning/sense/interpretation etc** *A trade war is not a war in the literal sense.*
2 literal translation a translation that translates each word exactly instead of giving the general meaning in a more natural way OPP **free**
3 literal-minded not showing much imagination —**literalness** *n* [U]

lit·e·ral·ly /ˈlɪtərəli/ ●●○ S3 *adv*
1 according to the most basic or original meaning of a word or expression: *The name of the cheese is Dolcelatte, literally meaning 'sweet milk'.* | *I said I felt like quitting, but I didn't* ***mean*** *it* ***literally*** (=I did not mean exactly what I said)!
2 take sb/sth literally to believe exactly what someone or something says rather than trying to understand their general meaning: *She takes the Bible literally.*
3 used to emphasize that something, especially a large number, is actually true: *The Olympic Games were watched by literally billions of people.*
4 *spoken* used to emphasize a strong expression or word that is not being used in its real or original meaning. Some people consider this use to be incorrect: *Dad was literally blazing with anger.*

lit·e·ra·ry /ˈlɪtərəri $ ˈlɪtəreri/ ●●○ W2 *adj* [only before noun]
1 relating to literature: *a literary prize* | ***literary criticism*** (=the study of the methods used in writing literature)
2 typical of the style of writing used in literature rather than in ordinary writing and talking: *a literary style of writing*
3 liking literature very much, and studying or producing it: *a literary woman*

lit·e·rate /ˈlɪtərət/ *adj* **1** able to read and write OPP **illiterate** → **numerate 2 computer literate/musically literate etc** able to use computers, understand and play music etc **3** well educated

lit·e·ra·ti /ˌlɪtəˈrɑːti/ *n* **the literati** *formal* a small group of people in a society who know a lot about literature

lit·e·ra·ture /ˈlɪtərətʃə $ -tʃʊr/ ●●● S3 W2 *n* [U]
1 books, plays, poems etc that people think are important and good: *He has read many of the major* ***works of literature***. | *Italian literature* **THESAURUS** ▸ **BOOK**
2 all the books, articles etc on a particular subject: **[+on]** *literature on the history of science* | **in the literature** *Several cases of mercury poisoning have been recorded in the literature.*
3 printed information produced by people who want to sell you something or tell you about something: *sales literature*

lithe /laɪð/ *adj* having a body that moves easily and gracefully: *the strong lithe bodies of gymnasts* —**lithely** *adv*

lith·i·um /ˈlɪθiəm/ *n* [U] a soft silver-white metal that is the lightest known metal, is used in BATTERIES, and is often combined with other metals. It is a chemical ELEMENT: symbol Li

lith·o·graph /ˈlɪθəgrɑːf $ -græf/ *n* [C] a printed picture produced by lithography

li·thog·ra·phy /lɪˈθɒgrəfi $ lɪˈθɑː-/ *n* [U] a method of printing in which a pattern is cut into stone or metal so that ink sticks to some parts of it and not others —**lithographic** /ˌlɪθəˈgræfɪk◂/ *adj*

lit·i·gant /ˈlɪtəgənt/ *n* [C] *law* someone who is making a claim against someone or defending themselves against a claim in a court of law

lit·i·gate /ˈlɪtɪgeɪt/ *v* [I,T] *law* to take a claim or complaint against someone to a court of law

lit·i·ga·tion /ˌlɪtəˈgeɪʃən/ *n* [U] *law* the process of taking claims to a court of law: *The threat of litigation can be a deciding factor in some business decisions.*

li·ti·gious /lɪˈtɪdʒəs/ *adj formal* very willing to take disagreements to a court of law – often used to show disapproval: *a litigious society* —**litigiousness** *n* [U]

lit·mus /ˈlɪtməs/ *n* [U] a chemical that turns red when it touches acid, and blue when it touches an ALKALI

ˈlitmus ˌpaper *n* [U] paper containing litmus, used to test whether a chemical is an acid or an ALKALI

ˈlitmus ˌtest *n* [singular] **1** one detail that is examined in order to help you make a decision about how suitable or acceptable someone or something is: **[+of/for]** *The mayoral election is regarded as the litmus test for the integrity of the electoral process.* **2** a test using litmus paper

li·tre *BrE*, **liter** *AmE* /ˈliːtə $ -ər/ ●●● S3 W3 *n*
1 [C] (*written abbreviation* **l**) the basic unit for measuring liquid in the METRIC SYSTEM: **[+of]** *a litre of water* | **litre bottle/drum/container etc** *a litre bottle of wine*
2 2.6/3.5 etc litre engine a measurement that shows the size and power of a vehicle's engine → **cc**: *the Ford's 2.8 litre engine*

lit·ter¹ /ˈlɪtə $ -ər/ ●●● S3 W3 *n*
1 WASTE [U] waste paper, cans etc that people have thrown away and left on the ground in a public place SYN **rubbish**, **trash**, **garbage**: *People who* ***drop litter*** *can be fined in some cities.* | *a town with a litter problem*

GRAMMAR: Countable or uncountable?

• **Litter** is an uncountable noun and is not used in the plural. You say: *The ground is covered in litter.* ✗ Don't say: *The ground is covered in litters.*
• **Litter** is always followed by a singular verb: *Litter* ***was*** *left all over the field.*
• When talking about one piece of paper, can etc, you say a **piece of litter**: *I didn't see a single piece of litter.*

2 BABY ANIMALS [C] a group of baby animals that a mother gives birth to at the same time: **[+of]** *a litter of kittens* THESAURUS ▸ BABY, GROUP
3 FOR CAT'S TOILET [U] small grains of a dry substance that is put in a container that a cat uses as a toilet indoors: *cat litter* | *a litter tray*
4 FOREST [U] (*also* **leaf litter**) dead leaves and other decaying plants on the ground in a forest
5 a litter of sth *literary* a group of things that look very untidy: *A litter of notes, papers, and textbooks were strewn on the desk.*
6 FOR ANIMAL'S BED [U] a substance such as STRAW that a farm animal sleeps on
7 BED [C] a chair or bed for carrying important people, used in past times

litter² *v* **1** [T] (*also* **litter up**) if things litter an area, there are a lot of them in that place, scattered in an untidy way: *Clothes littered the floor.* | **litter sth with sth** *The desk was littered with papers.* **2 be littered with sth** if something is littered with things, there are a lot of those things in it SYN **be full of sth**: *Recent business news has been littered with stories of companies failing.* **3** [I,T] to leave waste paper, cans etc on the ground in a public place **4** [I] *technical* if an animal such as a dog or cat litters, it gives birth to babies

ˈlitter bin (*also* **ˈlitter ˌbasket** *BrE*) *n* [C] a container in a public place, for things people throw away, such as papers or cans SYN **rubbish bin**, **waste bin**, **trash can/garbage can** *AmE* → see picture at **BIN¹**

lit·ter·bug /ˈlɪtəbʌg $ -ər-/ (*also* **ˈlitter lout** *BrE*) *n* [C] *informal* someone who drops paper, cans etc on the ground in public places

L

Frequencies of **a little** and **a bit** in spoken and written British English.

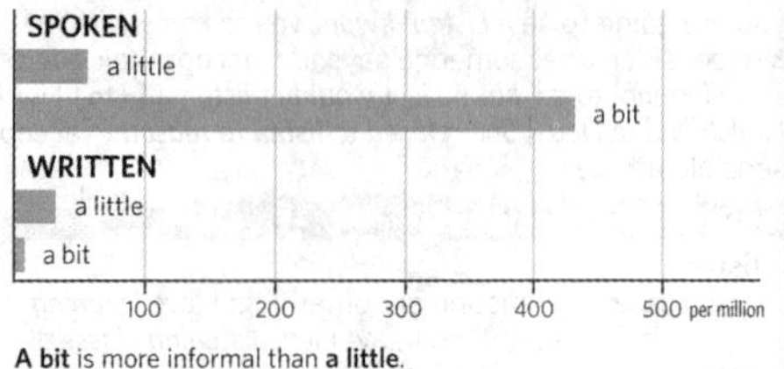

A bit is more informal than **a little**.

lit·tle¹ /ˈlɪtl/ ●●● S1 W1 *adj*
1 SIZE [usually before noun] small in size: *a little house* | *a cake decorated with little flowers* | *She was cutting the meat up into little bits.* | **little tiny/tiny little** *spoken* (=extremely small) *a little tiny puppy* | **little bitty** *AmE spoken* (=extremely small) | **a little something** *informal* (=a small present, or a small amount of food) *I'd like to buy him a little something to thank him.* THESAURUS ▸ SMALL
2 STH YOU LIKE OR DISLIKE [only before noun] used between an adjective and a noun to emphasize that you like or dislike something or someone, although they are not important, impressive etc: *It could be a* ***nice little*** *business.* | *a useful little gadget* | *It was another of her* ***silly little*** *jokes.* | *a boring little man* | **poor little thing** (=used to show sympathy) *The poor little thing had hurt its wing.*
3 a little bit a) a small amount of something: **[+of]** *With a little bit of luck we should finish by five o'clock.* | *I'm going to give you a little bit of advice.* | *Let me tell you a little bit about myself.* **b)** slightly or to a small degree: *I was a little bit disappointed.*
4 TIME/DISTANCE [only before noun] short in time or distance: *You could have a little sleep in the car.* | *We walked a little way along this path.* | *He arrived* ***a little while*** *ago.*
5 YOUNG little children are young: *We didn't have toys like this when I was little.* | **little boy/girl** *two little boys playing in the street* | **sb's little boy/girl** (=someone's son or daughter who is still a child) *Mum, I'm 17 – I'm not your little girl any longer.* | **sb's little brother/sister** (=a younger brother or sister who is still a child) *Her little brother and sister were fighting again.* THESAURUS ▸ YOUNG
6 SLIGHT [only before noun] done in a way that is not very noticeable: *a little smile* | *Nicolo gave a little nod of his head.*
7 UNIMPORTANT [only before noun] **a)** not important: *She gets very angry over little things.* | *There isn't time to discuss every little detail.* **b)** not important – used when you really think that something is important: *There's just that little matter of the £5,000 you owe me.*
8 (just) that little bit better/easier etc better, easier etc by a small amount that will have an important effect: *Working fewer hours will make life just that little bit easier for me.*
9 the little woman *old-fashioned* someone's wife – often used humorously but now considered offensive by many women → **a little bird told me** at **BIRD(4)**

GRAMMAR

Order of adjectives

If there is more than one adjective, the adjectives are usually used in a fixed order.
You say: *What a pretty little cottage!* ✗ Don't say: *What a little pretty cottage!*
You say: *I bought a little black bag.* ✗ Don't say: *I bought a black little bag.*

Comparatives

You can say **smaller** or **smallest**, but 'littler' and 'littlest' are not often used. You say: *Her feet are even smaller than mine.* ✗ Don't say: *Her feet are even littler than mine.* | *Her feet are more little than mine.*

GRAMMAR GUIDE ▸ ADJECTIVES

little² ●●● S1 W1 *determiner, pron*
1 only a small amount or hardly any of something: *There's*

little doubt in my mind that he's guilty. | *I paid little attention to what the others were saying.* | *Little is known about the causes of the problem.* | *Changes in the law have done little to improve the situation.* | **[+of]** *Little of their wealth now remains.* | *There's* **very little** *money left.* | *Many of the students speak* **little or no** *English.* | *He knew* **little or nothing** (=almost nothing) *about fixing cars.* | *My lawyer advised me to say* **as little as possible**. | *He did* **precious little** (=very little) *to help.* | *The laboratory tests are of* **little real** *value.*

2 a little a small amount: *Fortunately I had a little time to spare.* | *Susan speaks a little French.* | *A little over half the class can swim.* | *He walked on a little* (=a short distance) *and then turned back.* | **a little more/less** *Would you like a little more milk in your coffee?* | **[+of]** *The city is regaining a little of its former splendour.*

3 as little as £5/3 months/10 feet etc used to emphasize how surprisingly small an amount is: *Prices for his paintings start from as little as £100.* | *The weather can change completely in as little as half an hour.*

4 what little (*also* **the little (that)**) used to emphasize how small an amount there is, how small an amount is possible etc: *We did what little we could to help.* | *I handed over what little money I had left.*

5 a little (of sth) goes a long way *spoken* used to say that only a small amount of something is needed or has a great effect: *A little kindness goes a long way.*

GRAMMAR: Comparison

a little

- **A little** means 'some, but not a lot'.
- You use **a little** before uncountable nouns: *We still have a little time left.*
- You can say **a little of the**: *A little of the milk got spilled.* ✗ Don't say: *A little of milk got spilled.*

little

- **Little** is mainly used in more formal English. It means 'not much' and emphasizes how small an amount is.
- You use **little** before uncountable nouns: *There is little chance of success.*
- You can say **very little**: *He has very little money.*
- In everyday English, people usually say **not much** instead: *There is not much chance of success.* | *He does not have much money.*

little³ ●●● S1 W1 *adv*

1 a little slightly or to a small degree SYN **a bit**: *She trembled a little as she spoke.* | *He was a little surprised at her request.* | **a little more/better/further etc** *We'll have to wait a little longer to see what happens.*

2 not much or only slightly: *The town has changed little over the years.* | *The situation has improved* **very little**. | **little known/understood etc** (=not known about by many people) *a little known corner of the world* | **little more/better etc (than sth)** *His voice was little more than a whisper.*

3 little did sb know/realize/think etc used to say that someone did not know or think that something would happen or was true: *Little did I know that the course of my life was about to change.*

4 little by little gradually: *Little by little he became accepted by the family.*

5 more than a little/not a little *literary* extremely: *Graham was more than a little frightened by what he had seen.*

GRAMMAR: Word order

You use **a little** before an adjective: *I was a little worried about her.* ✗ Don't say: *I was worried a little about her.*

Little Eng·land·er /ˌlɪtl ˈɪŋgləndə $ -ər/ *n* [C] *disapproving* an English person who thinks that everything English is best, and does not like or trust people from other countries

ˌlittle ˈfinger *n* [C] the smallest finger on your hand → **pinkie** → see picture at HAND¹

ˈlittle ˌpeople *n* [plural] **1** all the people in a country or organization who have no power: *It's the little people who bear the brunt of taxation.* **2 the little people** imaginary people with magic powers, especially Irish LEPRECHAUNS

lit·to·ral /ˈlɪtərəl/ *n* [C] *technical* an area near the coast —**littoral** *adj*

li·tur·gi·cal /lɪˈtɜːdʒɪkəl $ -ɜːr-/ *adj* [only before noun] relating to church services and ceremonies —**liturgically** /-kli/ *adv*

lit·ur·gy /ˈlɪtədʒi $ -ər-/ *n* (*plural* **liturgies**) **1** [C,U] a way of praying in a religious service using a fixed order of words, prayers etc **2 the Liturgy** the written form of these services

liv·a·ble /ˈlɪvəbəl/ *adj especially AmE* another spelling of LIVEABLE

live¹ /lɪv/ ●●● S1 W1 *v*

1 IN A PLACE/HOME [I always + adv/prep] if you live in a place, you have your home there: **[+in/at/near etc]** *They lived in Holland for ten years.* | *He lives just across the street from me.* | *We live only a few miles from the coast.* | *A rather odd family came to* **live next door to** *us.* | *As soon as I saw the place, I knew I didn't want to* **live there**. | *Does Paul still* **live here**? | *We're still looking for* **somewhere to live**. | *They've finally found* **a place to live**. | **[+with]** *My grandmother came to live with us when I was ten.* | *Most seventeen-year-olds still* **live at home** (=live with their parents). | *I'm quite happy* **living alone**. | *The house has 3,600 square feet of* **living space** (=the areas of a house you live in). | **live rough** *BrE* (=live outside because of having no home) *I ran away from home and lived rough for nine months.*

2 PLANT/ANIMAL [I always + adv/prep] a plant or animal that lives in a particular place grows there or has its home there: **[+in/on etc]** *These particular birds live on only one island in the Pacific.*

3 AT A PARTICULAR TIME [I always + adv/prep] if you live at a particular time, you are alive then: **[+before/in/at]** *He lived in the eighteenth century.* | *She lived at a time when women were not expected to work.* | *Gladstone lived during a period of great social change.* | **the best/greatest etc that/who ever lived** (=the best, greatest etc who has been alive at any time) *He's probably the best journalist who ever lived.*

4 BE/STAY ALIVE [I] to be alive or be able to stay alive: *Without light, plants couldn't live.* | *He is extremely ill and not expected to live.* | *The baby only lived a few hours.* | *People on average are* **living** *much* **longer** *than before.* | *I'll never forget this* **for as long as I live**. | **live to (be) 80/90 etc/live to the age of 80/90 etc** *My grandmother lived to 85.* | *She lived to the age of 79.* | **have two weeks/six months etc to live** *He knows he's only got a few months to live.* | *He did not* **live to see** (=live long enough to see) *the realization of his dream.*

5 WAY OF LIFE [I always + adv/prep, T] to have a particular type of life, or live in a particular way: **live in peace/poverty etc** *The people in this country just want to live in peace.* | *People should not live in fear of crime.* | *We live in hope that a cure will be found.* | **live peacefully/quietly/happily etc** *The two communities live peacefully alongside each other.* | *She thought that she would get married and* **live happily ever after** (=like in a children's story). | *Some people like to live dangerously.* | *Most elderly people prefer to live independently if they can.* | *They earn enough money to* **live well** (=have plenty of food, clothes etc). | *I just want to* **live** *my* **life** *in my own way.* | *He's not well enough to* **live a normal life**. | **live a quiet/active/healthy etc life** *She lives a very busy life.* | *He had chosen to* **live the life of** *a monk.* | *She's now in Hollywood* **living a life of luxury**. | **[+by]** *I have always tried to live by my faith* (=according to my religion). | *We struggle on,* **living from day to day** (=trying to find enough money each day to buy food etc). | *He was tired of* **living out of a suitcase** (=spending a lot of time travelling).

6 EARN A LIVING [I] the way that someone lives is the way that they earn money to buy food etc: *Fishing is the way their families have lived for generations.* | **live by doing sth** *They live by hunting and killing deer.*

7 EXCITING LIFE [I] to have an exciting life: *She wanted to get out and live a little.* | *We're beginning to live at last!*

8 IMAGINE STH [I always + adv/prep] to imagine that things are happening to you: **[+in]** *He lives in a fantasy world.* |

[+through] *She lived through her children's lives.* | *You must stop* ***living in the past*** (=imagining that things from the past are still happening).

9 BE KEPT SOMEWHERE [I always + adv/prep] *BrE informal* the place where something lives is the place where it is kept: *Where do these cups live?* | *Those big dishes live in the cupboard next to the fridge.*

10 STILL EXIST/HAVE INFLUENCE [I] if an idea lives, it continues to exist and influence people: *Democracy still lives!* | *His name will* ***live forever***. | *That day will always* ***live in*** *my* ***memory***.

11 living quarters the part of a building where people live, especially a building that is used by many people or is used for several different purposes: *the White House living quarters*

12 living expenses the money you need to spend in order to live, for example on food or a house: *His tuition is paid, but he'll work to cover his living expenses.*

13 living arrangements the way someone organizes how and where they will live: *Her mother disapproved of the living arrangements, saying that two girls living with four boys was bound to cause problems.*

14 live it up *informal* to do things that you enjoy and spend a lot of money: *Sam was living it up in London.*

15 live by your wits to get money by being clever or dishonest, and not by doing an ordinary job

16 live a lie to pretend all the time that you feel or believe something when actually you do not feel that way: *I knew that I could not continue to live a lie.*

17 be living on borrowed time to be still alive after the time that you were expected to die: *She's been living on borrowed time for the last year.*

18 live in sin *old-fashioned* if people live in sin, they live together and have a sexual relationship without being married → **live together**

19 live and breathe sth to enjoy doing something so much that you spend most of your time on it: *Politics is the stuff I live and breathe.*

20 you live and learn *spoken* used to say that you have just learned something that you did not know before

21 live and let live used to say that you should accept other people's behaviour, even if it seems strange

22 you haven't lived (if/until ...) *spoken* used to say that someone's life will be boring if they do not do a particular exciting thing: *You haven't lived until you've tasted champagne.*

23 sb will live to regret it used to say that someone will wish that they had not done something: *If you marry him, you'll live to regret it.*

24 live to see/fight another day to continue to live or work after a failure or after you have dealt with a difficult situation: *Hopefully, the company will live to fight another day.*

25 live life to the full to enjoy doing a lot of different things: *She believes in living life to the full.*

26 live high on the hog used to say that someone has a nice life because they have a lot of money and buy expensive things – often used to show disapproval

27 live from hand to mouth to have only just enough money to buy food: *We lived from hand to mouth, never knowing where the next meal was coming from.*

28 live the dream to have the kind of life that you always wanted to have, especially after becoming very successful or rich: *I always wanted to be a famous singer, and now I'm living the dream.*

29 long live the King/Queen! etc *spoken* used as an expression of loyal support for a person

30 long live democracy/freedom etc used to say that you hope something continues to exist for a long time: *Long live free education!*

THESAURUS

live to have your home somewhere: *He lives with his parents.* | *Do you like living in Tokyo?* | *Jo lives next to a busy road.*

be from/come from use this when talking about the country, city, or area where you usually live: *'Where are you from?' 'I'm from Japan.'* | *The winner came from Australia.*

inhabit if a group of people or animals inhabit an area, they live there – used especially in written descriptions: *The island is mainly inhabited by sheep.*

reside *formal* to live in a particular country, city etc: *She now resides in the US.*

grow up to live somewhere when you are a child or teenager: *I grew up on a farm in South Africa.*

live sth ↔ **down** *phr v* if someone does not live something down, people never forget about it and never stop laughing at them for it: *She'll never live that down!*

live for sth *phr v* if you live for something, it is the thing that you enjoy or hope for most in your life: *He lived for his art.* | *She had nothing left to live for.* | *She* ***lives for the day when*** *she can have a house of her own.*

live in *phr v BrE* if someone lives in, they live in the place where they work → **live-in**: *Sometimes it can be easier if you have a nanny who lives in.*

live off sb/sth *phr v* to get your income or food from a supply of money or from another person: *Mom used to live off the interest from her savings.* | *Dad lost his job and we had to live off welfare.* | *Most people in the countryside* ***live off the land*** (=live by growing or finding their own food).

live on *phr v*

1 if something lives on, it continues to exist: *Alice's memory will live on.*

2 live on sth to have a particular amount of money to buy food and other necessary things: *I don't know how they manage to live on £55 a week.* | *the number of families who live on benefits*

3 live on sth to eat a lot of a particular type of food: *They live on bread and potatoes.* | *He practically lives on fish and chips!*

live out *phr v*

1 *BrE* if someone lives out, they do not live in the place where they work: *Most home helps prefer to live out.*

2 live out sth to experience or do something that you have planned or hoped for SYN **fulfil**, **realize**: *The money enabled them to live out their dreams.*

3 live out your life to continue to live in a particular way or place until you die: *He lived out his life in solitude.*

live through sth *phr v* to experience difficult or dangerous conditions SYN **endure**: *the generation that lived through the Second World War* | *It was hard to describe the nightmare she had lived through.*

live together *phr v* if people live together, they live in the same house and have a sexual relationship but are not married → **live with**: *They lived together for two years before they got married.*

live up to sth *phr v* if something or someone lives up to a particular standard or promise, they do as well as they were expected to, do what they promised etc: *The bank is insolvent and will be unable to live up to its obligations.* | *The film has certainly* ***lived up to*** *my* ***expectations***.

live with sb/sth *phr v*

1 to accept a difficult situation that is likely to continue for a long time SYN **put up with**, **tolerate**: *You have to learn to live with stress.* | *He has lived with his illness for most of his life.*

2 to live in the same house as someone and have a sexual relationship with them without being married → **live together**: *She's living with her boyfriend now.*

3 if something lives with you, it stays in your mind: *That episode has lived with me all my life.*

live² /laɪv/ ●●○ S3 W3 *adj*

1 LIVING [only before noun] not dead or artificial SYN **living** OPP **dead**: *experiments on live animals* | *Protesters want to stop the export of live sheep and cattle.* | *the number of live births per 1,000 population* | *We were so excited to see* ***real live*** *elephants.*

2 TV/RADIO a live television or radio programme is seen or heard on television or radio at the same time as it is actually happening OPP **prerecorded**: *a live radio phone-in show* | *There will be live TV coverage of tonight's big match.*

3 MUSIC/THEATRE a live performance is one in which the

L

entertainer performs for people who are watching, rather than for a film, record etc: *A lot of the bars have **live music**. | The band will be giving a **live** concert **performance** next week. | We'll be playing you a track from his new **live album*** (=ALBUM that was recorded from a live performance). | *It's always different when you perform in front of a **live audience*** (=an audience watching a live performance).
4 ELECTRICITY a wire or piece of equipment that is live has electricity flowing through it: *Be careful – those wires are live.*
5 BOMBS a live bomb still has the power to explode because it has not been used: *They came across a field of live, unexploded mines.*
6 BULLETS live bullets are real ones that are made of metal and can kill people OPP **blank**: *Troops fired **live ammunition** to disperse the crowd.*
7 ISSUE a live subject or problem is one that still interests or worries people: *Drink-driving is still very much a **live issue**.*
8 live coals pieces of coal that are burning: *She threw the paper onto the live coals.*
9 YOGHURT live YOGHURT contains BACTERIA that are still alive

live[3] /laɪv/ ●●○ *adv*
1 if something is broadcast live, it is broadcast on television or radio as it is actually happening → **prerecorded**: *The ceremony will be **broadcast live** on television. | The match will be **shown live** by the BBC.*
2 if people perform live, they perform in front of people who have come to watch, rather than for a film, record etc: *I love their music, but I've never seen them **perform live**. | The band is **playing live** in Birmingham tonight. | Their latest CD was **recorded live*** (=recorded at a live performance) *in New York.*
3 go live when a system or project goes live, people start to use it after it has been planned and discussed for a long time: *Their new information retrieval system went live last month. | a new security project which will go live in October*

live·a·ble *especially BrE*, **livable** *especially AmE* /ˈlɪvəbəl/ *adj* **1** a situation that is liveable is satisfactory but not good SYN **bearable**: *Having the children had made his life more liveable.* **2 a)** (*also* **liveable in** *BrE*) good enough to live in SYN **habitable**: *We need to do more to make the neighborhood more livable.* **b)** nice to live in: *It's one of the most liveable cities in the US.* **3 a livable wage/salary** *AmE* a salary that is enough for you to buy the things you need, such as food, a house etc

live·blog, **live blog** /ˈlaɪvblɒg $ -blɑːg/ *v* [I,T] to write a BLOG about something as it is happening: *I'm going to liveblog the award ceremony.* —**liveblog** *n* [C]: *a liveblog of the conference* —**liveblogging** *n* [U]

ˈ**lived-in** *adj* **1** lived-in places or clothes look as though they have been used or worn a lot – use this to show approval: **a lived-in look/feel** *The most fashionable jeans this winter have a lived-in look.* **2** someone who has a lived-in face looks fairly old and as though they have had a lot of interesting experiences

live-in /ˈlɪv ɪn/ *adj* [only before noun] **1** a live-in job is one in which you live with the family you work for: *a live-in nanny* **2 live-in lover/boyfriend etc** someone who lives with their sexual partner but is not married to them

live·li·hood /ˈlaɪvlihʊd/ *n* [C,U] the way you earn money in order to live: **a means/source of livelihood** *Fishing is the main source of livelihood for many people in the area. | It's difficult to **earn a livelihood** as an artist. | Bates says he will **lose** his **livelihood** if his driving licence is taken away.*

live·long /ˈlɪvlɒŋ $ -lɒːŋ/ *adj* **all the livelong day** *old-fashioned* a phrase meaning 'all day', used when this seems like a long time to you

live·ly /ˈlaɪvli/ ●●○ S3 *adj* (*comparative* **livelier**, *superlative* **liveliest**)
1 PEOPLE someone who is lively has a lot of energy and is very active: *a lively child*
2 PLACE/SITUATION a place or situation that is lively is exciting because a lot of things are happening: *The hotel is situated next to the lively bustling port. | the city's lively nightlife*
3 MOVEMENTS/MUSIC lively movements or music are very quick and exciting: *a lively Spanish dance*
4 DISCUSSION/DESCRIPTION ETC a lively discussion, description etc is very interesting and involves a lot of ideas: *The book offers a lively account of her travels. | a **lively debate** on environmental issues*
5 MIND/THOUGHTS someone who has a lively mind is intelligent and interested in a lot of things: *Even Paula has shown a **lively interest** in politics. | Charlie has a very **lively imagination*** (=he often invents stories, descriptions etc that are not true).
6 COLOUR very bright: *a lively combination of colours*
7 TASTE something that has a lively taste has a strong but pleasant taste: *The wine has a lively fruity flavour.*
8 look lively! *BrE spoken*, **step lively!** *AmE spoken* used to tell someone to hurry —**liveliness** *n* [U]

liv·en /ˈlaɪvən/ *v*
liven up *phr v* **1** to become more exciting, or to make an event become more exciting: *The party really livened up when Mattie arrived.* | **liven sth ↔ up** *Why don't we invite Jane? That'll liven things up!* **2 liven sth ↔ up** to make something look, taste etc more interesting SYN **brighten up**: *Why not liven up the room with some flowers?* **3** to become more interested or excited, or to make someone feel like this: *After a few drinks she livened up a little.*

liv·er /ˈlɪvə $ -ər/ ●●○ *n*
1 [C] a large organ in your body that produces BILE and cleans your blood → see picture at **HUMAN**[1]
2 [C,U] the liver of an animal, used as food

liv·e·ried /ˈlɪvərid/ *adj* **1** wearing LIVERY: *a liveried servant* **2** *BrE* painted with the colours and designs that represent a company: *liveried aircraft*

liv·er·ish /ˈlɪvərɪʃ/ *adj BrE old-fashioned* slightly ill, especially after eating or drinking too much

Liv·er·pud·li·an /ˌlɪvəˈpʌdliən $ -vər-/ *n* [C] someone from the city of Liverpool in England —**Liverpudlian** *adj*

ˈ**liver** ˌ**sausage** *BrE*, **liv·er·wurst** *AmE* /ˈlɪvəwɜːst $ -vərwɜːrst/ *n* [U] a cooked soft SAUSAGE made from LIVER

liv·e·ry /ˈlɪvəri/ *n* (*plural* **liveries**) **1** [C,U] *BrE* the colours and designs used by a company on its property and vehicles **2** [C,U] a special uniform worn by servants in past times **3** [U] the business of keeping and taking care of horses, especially in past times: *a livery stable* → **LIVERIED**

lives /laɪvz/ the plural of LIFE

live·stock /ˈlaɪvstɒk $ -stɑːk/ ●○○ *n* [plural, U] animals such as cows and sheep that are kept on a farm → **cattle**

live wire /ˌlaɪv ˈwaɪə $ -ˈwaɪr/ *n* [C] **1** *informal* someone who is very active and has a lot of energy **2** a wire that has electricity passing through it

liv·id /ˈlɪvɪd/ *adj* **1** extremely angry SYN **furious**: *She was absolutely livid that he had lied.* THESAURUS ANGRY
2 *formal* a mark on your skin that is livid is dark blue and grey: *livid bruises* **3** *literary* a face that is livid is very pale

liv·ing[1] /ˈlɪvɪŋ/ ●●○ *adj*
1 alive now OPP **dead**: *He's one of the greatest living composers. | The sun affects all **living things*** (=people, animals, and plants). | *a **living language*** (=one that people still use)
2 living proof if someone is living proof of a particular fact, they are a good example of how true it is: **living proof (that)** *I'm living proof that you don't need a college degree to be successful.* | **[+of]** *the living proof of government economic incompetence*
3 in/within living memory during the time that anyone can remember: *It was the worst storm in living memory.*
4 a living death a life that is so unpleasant that it seems better to be dead
5 a living hell a very unpleasant situation that makes you suffer for a long time: *These past few days have been a living hell.*
6 living legend someone who is famous for being

L

extremely good at something, and who still does that activity: *His music has made him a living legend.* → **scare/frighten the (living) daylights out of sb** at DAYLIGHT(3), → **beat/knock the (living) daylights out of sb/sth** at DAYLIGHT(4)

living² ●○○ *n*
1 [C usually singular] the way that you earn money or the money that you earn: *It's not a great job, but it's a living.* | *What do you* ***do for a living****?* (=what do you do as a job?) | **earn/make a living** *It's hard to make a decent living as a musician.* | **scrape/scratch a living** (=get just enough to eat or live)
2 the living all the people who are alive as opposed to dead people OPP **the dead**
3 [U] the way in which someone lives their life: *the stresses of city living*
4 [C] the position or income of a PARISH priest → **COST OF LIVING, STANDARD OF LIVING,** → **in the land of the living** at LAND¹(7)

ˌliving ˈbandage *n* [C] a BANDAGE made from skin cells, especially cells that have been taken and grown from the PATIENT's own skin

ˌliving ˈfossil *n* [C] an ancient animal or plant that still exists and has not changed

ˈliving room ●●● S3 *n* [C] the main room in a house where people relax, watch television etc SYN **lounge**

ˈliving ˌstandard *n* [C usually plural] the level of comfort and the amount of money that people have SYN **standard of living**: *Living standards have improved over the last century.* | *rising living standards* | *There's been a decline in the living standards of old people.*

ˌliving ˈwage *n* [singular] a salary that is high enough to allow you to buy the things that you need to live: *jobs that don't even pay a living wage*

ˌliving ˈwill *n* [C] a document explaining what medical or legal decisions someone should make if you become so ill that you cannot make those decisions yourself

liz·ard /ˈlɪzəd $ -ərd/ ●●○ *n* [C] a type of REPTILE that has four legs and a long tail → see picture at **REPTILE**

ll., ll the abbreviation of *lines*, used in writing to refer to specific lines of a poem etc: *ll. 24-35*

lla·ma /ˈlɑːmə/ *n* [C] a South American animal with thick hair like wool, and a long neck

LLB *BrE*, **LL.B.** *AmE n* [C] (***Bachelor of Laws***) a first university DEGREE in law

LLD *BrE*, **LL.D.** *AmE n* [C] (***Doctor of Laws***) a DOCTORATE in law

LLM *BrE*, **LL.M.** *AmE n* [C] (***Master of Laws***) a university DEGREE in law that you can get after your first degree

lo /ləʊ $ loʊ/ *interjection* **1** *old use* used to tell someone to look at something that is surprising **2 lo and behold** *spoken* used before mentioning something surprising that happened - used humorously: *We had just been talking about John when, lo and behold, he walked into the room.*

load¹ /ləʊd $ loʊd/ ●●● S1 W3 *n* [C]
1 AMOUNT OF STH a large quantity of something that is carried by a vehicle, person etc: **[+of]** *a load of wood* | *The lorry had* ***shed its load*** (=the load had fallen off). | *The plane was carrying a* ***full load*** *of fuel.*
2 a load (of sth) (*also* **loads (of sth)** *BrE*) *informal* a lot of something: *We got a load of complaints about the loud music.* | *Don't worry, there's loads of time* | **loads to do/see/eat etc** *There's loads to see in Paris.*
3 a bus load/car load/truck load etc the largest amount of something that a vehicle can carry: *a bus load of tourists*
4 a load of crap/bull etc (*also* **a load of rubbish** *BrE*) *spoken not polite* used to say that something is bad, untrue, or stupid: *I thought the game was a load of crap.*
5 WORK the amount of work that a person or machine has to do: *The computer couldn't handle the load and crashed.* | **a light/heavy load** (=not much or a lot of work) *Hans has a heavy teaching load this semester.* | *My* ***work load*** *has doubled since Henry left.* | *They hired more staff in order to* ***spread the load****.*
6 WORRY a problem or worry that is difficult to deal with: *When someone is depressed, the extra load of having financial problems can make the situation worse.* | *Knowing he was safe was* ***a load off*** *my* ***mind*** (=I felt less worried). | *Coping with ill health was a heavy load to bear.*
7 WASHING a quantity of clothes that are washed together in a washing machine: *I've already done three* ***loads of laundry*** *this morning.*
8 get a load of sb/sth *spoken* used to tell someone to look at or listen to something that is surprising or funny: *Get a load of this! Your stars say you are going to meet someone who's rich.*
9 WEIGHT the amount of weight that something is supporting: *a load-bearing wall* | *It increased the load on the wheels.*
10 ELECTRICITY *technical* an amount of electrical power that is being produced

load² ●●● S2 W3 *v*
1 [I,T] (*also* **load up**) to put a large quantity of something into a vehicle or container OPP **unload**: *Have you finished loading up?* | *It took an hour to load the van.* | *Will you help me load the dishwasher?* | **load sth into/onto sth** *Emma loaded all the groceries into the car.* | *He loaded the cups onto a tray.* | **load sth with sth** *She loaded up the car with camping gear.* THESAURUS▸ FILL → see picture at **FILL**
2 [T] to put a necessary part into something in order to make it work, for example bullets into a gun or film into a camera: **load sth with sth** *Did you load it with 200 or 400 film?* | **load sth into sth** *Can you load the CD into the player, please?*
3 [I,T] to put a program into a computer: *The program takes a while to load.* | *To load the file, press the 'return' key.*
4 [I] (*also* **load up**) if a ship, aircraft etc loads, goods are put onto it: *The first ship to load at the new port was the 'Secil Angola'.* | **[+with]** *The boat called at Lerwick to load up with fresh vegetables.*

load sb/sth **down** *phr v*
1 to give someone more work or problems than they can deal with SYN **weigh down**: **be/feel loaded down with sth** *Jane felt loaded down with money worries.*
2 to make someone carry too many things SYN **weigh down**: **be loaded down with sth** *I was loaded down with bags so I took a taxi.* GRAMMAR **Load down** is often used in the passive.

load up on sth *phr v AmE* to get a lot of something so that you are sure you will have enough SYN **stock up (on)**: *People were loading up on bottled water.*

load sb **(up) with** sth *phr v* to give someone a lot of things, especially things they have to carry

load·ed /ˈləʊdɪd $ ˈloʊ-/ *adj*
1 GUN/CAMERA containing bullets, film etc: *a loaded pistol*
2 FULL a loaded vehicle or container is full of things: *a loaded trailer* | *She came back carrying a loaded tray.* | **[+with]** *a truck loaded with bananas*
3 RICH [not before noun] *informal* very rich: *Giles can afford it - he's loaded.*
4 loaded with sth *informal* full of a particular quality, or containing a lot of something: *snacks loaded with fat* | *a collection of paintings loaded with cultural significance*
5 WORD/STATEMENT a loaded word, statement etc has more meanings than you first realize and is intended to influence the way you think: *He 'deserved' it? That's a loaded word.* | *There was a loaded silence.*
6 a loaded question a question that is unfair because it is intended to affect your opinions and make you answer in a particular way → **leading question** at LEADING¹(4)
7 DRUNK [not before noun] *AmE informal* very drunk: *Greg used to come home loaded almost every night.*
8 the dice/odds are loaded against sb/sth used to say that someone or something is unlikely to succeed or win
9 sth is loaded against sb/sth used to say that a system, situation, or organization is unfair and some people have a disadvantage SYN **biased**: *The justice system is loaded against people from ethnic minorities.*
10 loaded dice DICE that have weights in them so that they always fall with the same side on top, used to cheat in games

ˈloading ˌbay *BrE*, **ˈloading dock** *AmE n* [C] an area at the side of a large shop or WAREHOUSE from which goods are taken off or put onto trucks

loaf[1] /ləʊf $ loʊf/ ●●● S3 *n* (*plural* **loaves** /ləʊvz $ loʊvz/)
1 [C] bread that is shaped and baked in one piece and can be cut into SLICES: *a* ***loaf of bread*** | **white/wholemeal/granary etc loaf** *BrE* | **a sliced loaf** *BrE* → see picture at **BREAD**
2 [C,U] food that has been cut into very small pieces, pressed together, and baked: *a meat loaf*
3 use your loaf *BrE old-fashioned* used to tell someone to think more carefully about what they are doing

loaf[2] *v* [I] *written* to spend time somewhere and not do very much SYN **hang around/round**: **[+around/about]** *They spend all day loafing around on street corners.*

loaf·er /ˈləʊfə $ ˈloʊfər/ *n* [C] **1 Loafer** *trademark* a flat leather shoe that does not need to be fastened onto your foot → see picture at **SHOE**[1] **2** someone who is lazy and does nothing when they should be working

loam /ləʊm $ loʊm/ *n* [U] good quality soil consisting of sand, clay, and decayed plants —**loamy** *adj*

loan[1] /ləʊn $ loʊn/ ●●● S2 W2 *n*
1 [C] an amount of money that you borrow from a bank etc: **[+of]** *a loan of £60,000* | *I had to take out a loan to buy my car.* | *It'll be years before we've paid off the loan.*
2 [singular] when you lend something to someone: **[+of]** *Thanks for the loan of your camera.*
3 on loan (from sb/sth) if something or someone is on loan, they have been borrowed: *The book I wanted was out on loan.* | *paintings on loan from the Louvre* | *Cantona initially went on loan to Leeds United.*

COLLOCATIONS

VERBS

take out a loan (=borrow money) *Most home buyers take out a loan.*
repay/pay off/pay back a loan (=give back the money you borrowed, usually over a period of time) *You can repay the loan early without a penalty.*
give sb a loan *I hoped to persuade my bank manager to give us a loan.*
make a loan (=give someone a loan) *Banks are cautious about making new loans.*
ask for/apply for a loan | **get a loan** | **secure a loan (on sth)** (=agree to give the lender something if you do not pay back the loan on time)

ADJECTIVES/NOUN + loan

a £20,000/$5,000 etc loan *The company asked for a £100,000 loan.*
a bank loan (=money lent by a bank) *What is the interest you will pay on a bank loan?*
a home/car loan (=a loan to buy a home or a car) | **a personal loan** (=money lent to a person, rather than a company) | **a business loan** (=money lent to a business) | **a student loan** (=money lent to a student to pay for university) | **a long-term/short-term loan** (=to be paid back after a long/short time) | **an interest-free loan** (=on which you pay no interest) | **a low-interest loan**

loan + NOUN

a loan repayment | **a loan agreement** (=that says how much the loan will be, how much you will pay back each month etc)

loan[2] ●●○ *v* [T]
1 *AmE* to lend someone something, especially money: **loan sb sth** *Can you loan me $5?* | *Jeff's loaned us his car for the weekend.*
2 (*also* **loan out** *BrE*) to lend something valuable to someone: *The National Library has loaned several manuscripts.* | **loan sth to sb/sth** *Two of the steam trains have been loaned to other railways.*

ˈloan shark *n* [C] someone who lends money at very high rates of INTEREST and will often use threats or violence to get the money back

loan·word /ˈləʊnwɜːd $ ˈloʊnwɜːrd/ *n* [C] a word taken into one language from another SYN **borrowing**

loath, **loth** /ləʊθ $ loʊθ/ *adj* **be loath to do sth** *formal* to be unwilling to do something SYN **reluctant** OPP **willing**: *Sarah was loath to tell her mother what had happened.*

loathe /ləʊð $ loʊð/ *v* [T] to hate someone or something very much SYN **detest**: *He loathes their politics.* | **loathe doing sth** *I absolutely loathe shopping.* **THESAURUS** ▸ **HATE**

GRAMMAR: Using the progressive

Loathe is not used in the progressive. You say: *She loathes housework.* ✗ Don't say: *She is loathing housework.*
GRAMMAR GUIDE ▸ **VERBS**

loath·ing /ˈləʊðɪŋ $ ˈloʊð-/ *n* [singular, U] a very strong feeling of hatred: **[+for]** *her loathing for her first husband* | **[+of]** *a loathing of war* | *The nightmare left her with a sense of* ***fear and loathing***.

loath·some /ˈləʊðsəm $ ˈloʊθ-/ *adj* very unpleasant or cruel SYN **repulsive**: *that loathsome little man*

loaves /ləʊvz $ loʊvz/ the plural of LOAF

lob /lɒb $ lɑːb/ *v* (**lobbed**, **lobbing**) [T always + adv/prep]
1 *informal* to throw something somewhere, especially over a wall, fence etc: *The kids were lobbing pine cones into the neighbor's yard.* **THESAURUS** ▸ **THROW** **2** to kick or hit a ball in a slow high curve, especially in a game of tennis or football: *Nadal lobbed the ball high over Murray's head.* → see picture at **TENNIS** —**lob** *n* [C]

lob·by[1] /ˈlɒbi $ ˈlɑːbi/ ●○○ *n* (*plural* **lobbies**) [C]
1 a wide passage or large hall just inside the entrance to a public building SYN **foyer**: *a hotel lobby* | *I'll meet you in the entrance lobby.*
2 a) a hall in the British parliament where members of parliament and the public meet **b)** one of the two passages in the British parliament where members go to vote for or against a BILL
3 a group of people who try to persuade a government that a particular law or situation should be changed: *the anti-foxhunting lobby* | *a powerful environmental lobby group*

GRAMMAR: Singular or plural verb?

• In this meaning, **lobby** is usually followed by a singular verb: *The business lobby* ***has*** *warned the government against raising taxes.*
• In British English, you can also use a plural verb: *The business lobby* ***have*** *warned the government against raising taxes.*
GRAMMAR GUIDE ▸ **NOUNS**

4 an attempt to persuade a government to change a law, make a new law etc: *a mass lobby of Parliament by women's organizations*

lobby[2] ●○○ *v* (**lobbied**, **lobbying**, **lobbies**) [I,T] to try to persuade the government or someone with political power that a law or situation should be changed: **[+for/against]** *The group is lobbying for a reduction in defence spending.* | **lobby sb to do sth** *We've been lobbying our state representative to support the new health plan.* —**lobbyist** *n* [C]

lobe /ləʊb $ loʊb/ *n* [C] **1** the soft piece of flesh at the bottom of your ear SYN **earlobe** **2** *technical* a round part of an organ in your body, especially in your brain or lungs

lo·bot·o·my /ləˈbɒtəmi $ ləˈbɑː-/ *n* (*plural* **lobotomies**) [C] a medical operation to remove part of someone's brain in order to treat their mental problems —**lobotomize** *v* [T]

lob·ster /ˈlɒbstə $ ˈlɑːbstər/ ●●○ *n*
1 [C] a sea animal with eight legs, a shell, and two large CLAWS → see picture at **SHELLFISH**
2 [U] the flesh of a lobster, which is eaten

lob·ster·pot /ˈlɒbstəpɒt $ ˈlɑːbstərpɑːt/ *n* [C] a trap shaped like a basket in which lobsters are caught

lo·cal¹ /ˈləʊkəl $ ˈloʊ-/ ●●● S1 W1 *adj* [usually before noun]
1 relating to the particular area you live in, or the area you are talking about: *local hospital | local residents*
2 *technical* affecting or limited to one part of your body: *a local infection*

local² *n* [C] **1** [usually plural] someone who lives in the place where you are or the place that you are talking about: *We asked one of the locals to recommend a restaurant.* **2** *BrE* a PUB near where you live, especially one where you often drink: *I usually have a pint or two at my local on Friday nights.* **3** *AmE* a bus, train etc that stops at all regular stopping places → **express 4** *AmE* a branch of a TRADE UNION

lo-cal /ˌləʊ ˈkæl◂ $ ˌloʊ-/ *adj* lo-cal food or drink does not contain many CALORIES

ˌlocal ˌarea ˈnetwork *n* [C] *technical* LAN

ˌlocal auˈthority *n* [C] the group of people responsible for the government of a particular area, town, or city in the UK SYN **local government** *AmE*: *Central government is trying to stop local authorities overspending.*

ˈlocal ˌcall *n* [C] a telephone call to a place near you that does not cost much money OPP **long-distance**

ˌlocal ˈcolour *BrE*, **local color** *AmE* *n* [U] additional details in a story or picture that give you a better idea of what a place is really like: *His description of the smells from the market added a touch of local color.*

ˌlocal ˈcouncil *n* [C] the group of people responsible for providing houses, schools, parks etc in a small area such as a town

lo·cale /ləʊˈkɑːl $ loʊ-/ *n* [C] *formal* the place where something happens or where the action takes place in a book or a film SYN **setting**: *people who see the countryside as a locale for recreation*

ˌlocal ˈgovernment *n* [C,U] the government of cities, towns etc rather than of a whole country: *They want to give more power to local government. | Many local governments are against the idea.* → **state, national, federal**

ˌlocal ˈhistory *n* [U] the history of a particular area

lo·cal·is·m /ˈləʊkəlɪzəm $ ˈloʊ-/ *n* [U] the belief that the people in a small area should govern themselves, eat and use things produced locally, deal with local problems etc

lo·cal·i·ty /ləʊˈkæləti $ loʊ-/ *n* (*plural* **localities**) [C] *formal* a small area of a country, city etc SYN **area**: *weather reports from several different localities* | **in the locality** *Both sea fishing and freshwater angling are available in the locality.*

lo·cal·ize (*also* **-ise** *BrE*) /ˈləʊkəlaɪz $ ˈloʊ-/ *v* [T] *formal* **1** to find out exactly where something is: *A mechanic is trying to localize the fault.* **2** to limit the effect that something has, or the size of area it covers: *They hoped to localize the fighting.* —**localization** /ˌləʊkəlaɪˈzeɪʃən $ ˌloʊkələ-/ *n* [U]

lo·cal·ized (*also* **-ised** *BrE*) /ˈləʊkəlaɪzd $ ˈloʊ-/ *adj formal* happening within a small area: *localized flooding | a localized infection*

lo·cal·ly /ˈləʊkəli $ ˈloʊ-/ ●●○ *adv*
1 in or near the area where you are, or the area you are talking about: *I live locally, so it's easy to get to the office.*
2 in particular small areas: *Most of the country will be dry, but there will be some rain locally.* THESAURUS ▸ NEAR

ˌlocal ˈpaper *n* [C] **1** a newspaper that contains mainly local news → **national 2** *AmE* a newspaper that contains local, national, and international news

ˌlocal ˈradio *n* [U] a radio service that broadcasts programmes for a particular area of the country → **national**

ˌlocal ˈrag *n* [C] *BrE informal* a local newspaper

ˈlocal time *n* [U] the time of day in a particular part of the world: *We'll arrive in Boston at 4 o'clock local time.*

lo-carb /ˌləʊ ˈkɑːb $ ˌloʊ ˈkɑːrb/ *adj* lo-carb food does not have a lot of CARBOHYDRATE in it

L

lo·cate /ləʊˈkeɪt $ ˈloʊkeɪt/ ●●○ W3 AWL *v*
1 **be located in/near etc sth** to be in a particular position or place SYN **be situated**: *The business is located right in the center of town.*
2 [T] to find the exact position of something: *We couldn't locate the source of the radio signal.* THESAURUS ▸ FIND
3 [T] to put or build something in a particular place: *Large retail chains are usually only prepared to locate stores in areas of high population density.*
4 [I always + adv/prep] *AmE* to come to a place and start a business, company etc there: **[+in/at etc]** *We are offering incentives for companies to locate in our city.*

Frequencies of the nouns **location**, **place** and **spot** in spoken and written English.

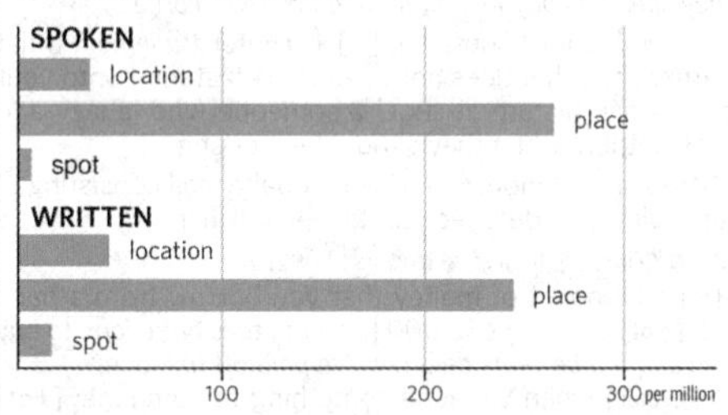

This graph shows that **place** is much more common than **location** or **spot** in both spoken and written English. This is because **place** is the most general of the three words. **Location** is used to mean a particular place or position, especially in relation to other buildings, areas etc. **Spot** is used especially to mean a pleasant place where you spend time.

lo·ca·tion /ləʊˈkeɪʃən $ loʊ-/ ●●● S3 W2 AWL *n*
1 [C] a particular place, especially in relation to other areas, buildings etc: *His apartment is in a really good location. | its isolated **geographical location*** THESAURUS ▸ PLACE

REGISTER
Location is often used when talking about buying or selling property. In everyday English in other contexts, people usually say **place**: *It can be stressful moving to a new **place**.*

2 [C] the position of something: **[+of]** *The map shows the **precise location** of the crash.*
3 [C,U] a place away from a film STUDIO where scenes are filmed: *It was hard to find a suitable location for the desert scenes.* | **on location** *Most of the movie was shot on location in Africa.*
4 [U] the act of finding the position of something: *The main problem for engineers was the location of underground rivers in the area.*

loˈcation ˌsharing *n* [U] the process of letting people know where you are by using APPs on your computer or MOBILE PHONE

lo·ca·vore /ˈləʊkəvɔː $ ˈloʊkəvɔːr/ *n* [C] *especially AmE* someone who eats only food that has been produced near to where they live

loch /lɒx, lɒk $ lɑːk, lɑːx/ *n* [C] a lake or a part of the sea partly enclosed by land in Scotland: *Loch Ness*

lo·ci /ˈləʊsaɪ $ ˈloʊsaɪ, -ki/ the plural of LOCUS

lock¹ /lɒk $ lɑːk/ ●●● S2 W3 *v*
1 FASTEN STH [I,T] to fasten something, usually with a key, so that other people cannot open it, or to be fastened like this: *Did you lock the car? | I can't get this drawer to lock.*
2 KEEP IN A SAFE PLACE [T always + adv/prep] to put something in a place and fasten the door, lid etc with a key: **lock sth in sth** *Lock the cat in the kitchen.*
3 FIXED POSITION [I,T] to become fixed in one position and impossible to move, or to make something become fixed: *The wheels suddenly locked.* | **lock sth around/round sth** *He locked his hands around the younger man's throat. | A moment later they were **locked in an embrace*** (=holding

each other very tightly in a loving or friendly way). | *Their* **eyes locked together** (=they could not look away from each other) *for an instant.*
4 FIXED SITUATION [T] if you are locked in a situation, you cannot get out of it: **be locked in/into sth** *The two groups are locked in a vicious cycle of killing.* | *The company is locked into a five-year contract.* GRAMMAR **Lock** is usually passive in this meaning.
5 be locked in battle/combat/dispute etc to be involved in a long, serious argument or fight with someone: *They are now locked in a bitter custody battle over the three children.*
6 lock arms if people lock arms, they join their arms tightly with the arms of the people on each side: *The police locked arms to form a barrier against the protesters.*
7 lock horns (with sb) to argue or fight with someone: *The band have now locked horns with their record company over the album.* —**lockable** *adj*

lock sb/sth ↔ **away** *phr v*
1 to put something in a safe place and lock the door, lid etc SYN **lock up**: *He locked his money away in the safe.*
2 to put someone in prison SYN **lock up**: *I hope they lock him away for years.*
3 lock yourself away to keep yourself separate from other people by staying in your room, office etc

lock in *phr v*
1 lock sb in (sth) to prevent someone from leaving a room or building by locking the door: *She locked herself in.* | *They locked the director in his office.*
2 lock sth ↔ in to do something so that a price, offer, agreement etc cannot be changed: *Sell your stocks now to lock in some of the gains of recent months.*
3 lock sth ↔ in to make the taste, liquid etc remain in something: *This method of cooking locks in the flavour of the meat.*

lock onto sth *phr v* if a MISSILE or SATELLITE locks onto a TARGET or signal, it finds it and follows it closely

lock sb ↔ **out** *phr v*
1 to keep someone out of a place by locking the door: **[+of]** *I locked myself out of the house!*
2 if employers lock workers out, they do not let them enter their place of work until they accept the employers' conditions for settling a disagreement → **LOCKOUT**

lock up *phr v*
1 to make a building safe by locking the doors, especially at night: *I'll leave you to lock up.* | **lock sth ↔ up** *Don't forget to lock up the warehouse.*
2 lock sth ↔ up to put something in a safe place and lock the door, lid etc SYN **lock away**
3 lock sb ↔ up to put someone in prison SYN **lock away**: *Rapists should be locked up.*
4 be locked up (in sth) if your money is locked up, you have put it into a business, INVESTMENT etc and cannot easily move it or use it

lock² ●●● S2 *n*
1 FASTENING [C] a thing that keeps a door, drawer etc fastened and is usually opened with a key or by moving a small metal bar: *I'm sorry, there isn't a lock on the bathroom door.* | *The key turned stiffly in the lock.* | *a bike lock* → **pick a lock** at PICK¹(10)
2 under lock and key a) kept safely in a box, cupboard etc that is locked: *Dad keeps all his liquor under lock and key.* **b)** kept in a place such as a prison
3 lock, stock, and barrel including every part of something: *He moved the whole company, lock, stock, and barrel, to Mexico.*
4 HAIR a) [C] a small number of hairs on your head that grow and hang together: **[+of]** *He gently pushed a lock of hair from her eyes.* **b) locks** [plural] *literary* someone's hair: *long flowing locks*
5 ON A RIVER ETC [C] a part of a CANAL or river that is closed off by gates so that the water level can be raised or lowered to move boats up or down a slope
6 IN A FIGHT [C] a HOLD which WRESTLERs use to prevent their opponent from moving: *a head lock*
7 VEHICLE [C,U] *BrE* the degree to which a vehicle's front wheels can be turned in order to turn the vehicle
8 RUGBY [C] a playing position in the game of RUGBY

LOCKS

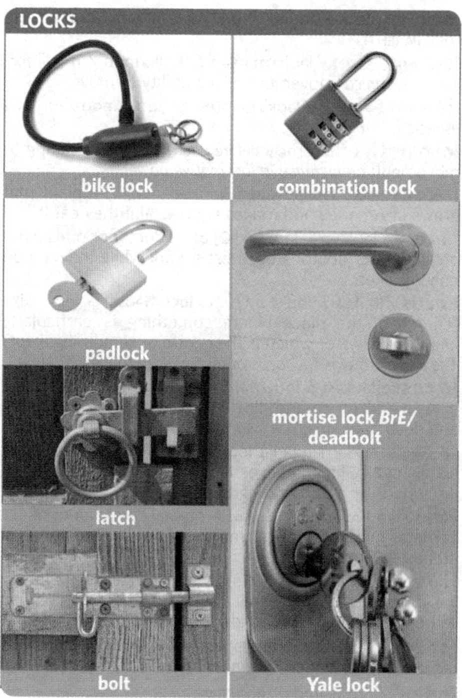

9 a lock on sth *AmE* complete control of something: *Pro football still has a lock on male viewers aged 18 to 34.* → **AIR LOCK, COMBINATION LOCK**

lock·down /ˈlɒkdaʊn $ ˈlɑːk-/ *n* [C,U] **1** a time when prisoners are not allowed out of their rooms, usually after there has been violence in the prison **2** a time when all the doors in a building are locked in order to protect the people inside from danger: *The school went into lockdown after the shooting.*

locked-ˈin ˌsyndrome *n* [U] a medical condition in which someone is conscious and knows what is happening around them but is unable to move their body or speak

lock·er /ˈlɒkə $ ˈlɑːkər/ ●○○ *n* [C]
1 a small cupboard with a lock in a school, sports building, office etc, where you can leave clothes or possessions while you do something
2 *AmE* a very cold room used for storing food in a restaurant or factory: *a meat locker*

ˈlocker room *n* [C] a room in a school, sports building etc where people change their clothes and leave them in lockers

lock·et /ˈlɒkɪt $ ˈlɑː-/ *n* [C] a piece of jewellery that you wear around your neck on a chain, with a small metal case in which you can put a picture, a piece of hair etc → see picture at **JEWELLERY**

lock·jaw /ˈlɒkdʒɔː $ ˈlɑːkdʒɒː/ *n* [U] *informal* TETANUS

ˈlock ˌkeeper *n* [C] someone whose job is to open and close the gates of a LOCK on a CANAL

lock·out /ˈlɒkaʊt $ ˈlɑːk-/ *n* [C] a situation when a company does not allow workers to go back to work, especially in a factory, until they accept the employers' conditions → **lock out** at **LOCK¹**

lock·smith /ˈlɒkˌsmɪθ $ ˈlɑːk-/ *n* [C] someone who makes and repairs locks

lock·step /ˈlɒkstep $ ˈlɑːk-/ *n* **in lockstep** *AmE* in exactly the same way or at the same rate

ˈlock-up *n* [C] **1** a small prison where a criminal can be kept for a short time **2** (*also* **lock-up garage**) *BrE* a garage that you can rent to keep cars, goods etc in

lo·co /ˈləʊkəʊ $ ˈloʊkoʊ/ *adj AmE informal* crazy → **IN LOCO PARENTIS**

lo·co·mo·tion /ˌləʊkəˈməʊʃən $ ˌloʊkəˈmoʊ-/ *n* [U] *formal or technical* movement or the ability to move

lo·co·mo·tive¹ /ˌləʊkəˈməʊtɪv $ ˌloʊkəˈmoʊ-/ *n* [C] *especially AmE* a railway engine

locomotive² *adj* [only before noun] *technical* relating to movement: *an increase in locomotive power*

lo·co·weed /ˈləʊkəʊwiːd $ ˈloʊkoʊ-/ *n* [C] a plant that grows in America and makes animals ill if they eat it

lo·cum /ˈləʊkəm $ ˈloʊ-/ *n* [C] *BrE* a doctor or priest who does another doctor's or priest's work while they are on holiday, ill etc

lo·cus /ˈləʊkəs $ ˈloʊ-/ *n* (*plural* **loci** /ˈləʊsaɪ $ ˈloʊ-, -ki/) [C] *formal* the place where something is particularly known to exist, or which is the centre of something: **[+of]** *The Politburo was the locus of all power in the Soviet Union.*

lo·cust /ˈləʊkəst $ ˈloʊ-/ *n* [C] an insect that lives mainly in Asia and Africa and flies in a very large group, eating and destroying crops: *a swarm of locusts*

lo·cu·tion /ləʊˈkjuːʃən $ loʊ-/ *n technical* **1** [U] a style of speaking **2** [C] a phrase, especially one used in a particular area or by a particular group of people

lode /ləʊd $ loʊd/ *n* [C usually singular] an amount of ORE (=metal in its natural form) found in a layer between stones → **MOTHER LODE**

lode·star /ˈləʊdstɑː $ ˈloʊdstɑːr/ *n* [singular] *literary* **1** a principle or fact that guides someone's actions **2** the POLE STAR, used to guide ships at sea

lode·stone, **loadstone** /ˈləʊdstəʊn $ ˈloʊdstoʊn/ *n* [C,U] *old use* a piece of iron that acts as a MAGNET

lodge¹ /lɒdʒ $ lɑːdʒ/ ●○○ *v*

1 lodge a complaint/protest/appeal etc *BrE* to make a formal or official complaint, protest etc: **[+with]** *He lodged an appeal with the High Court.* | **[+against]** *They lodged a complaint against the doctor for negligence.*

2 BECOME STUCK [I,T always + adv/prep] to become firmly stuck somewhere, or to make something become stuck OPP **dislodge**: **[+in]** *The fishbone lodged in her throat.* | **be lodged in/between/behind etc sth** *The bullet was lodged in his spine.*

3 PUT SB SOMEWHERE [T] to provide someone with a place to stay for a short time: *a building used to lodge prisoners of war* | **lodge sb in/at sth** *The refugees were lodged in old army barracks.*

4 PUT STH SOMEWHERE [T] *BrE formal* to put something important in an official place so that it is safe: **lodge sth with sb** *Be sure to lodge a copy of the contract with your solicitor.* | **lodge sth in sth** *The money was lodged in a Swiss bank account.*

5 STAY SOMEWHERE [I always + adv/prep] *old-fashioned* to pay to live in a room in someone's house: **[+at/with etc]** *John lodged with a family in Bristol when he first started work.*

lodge² ●○○ *n* [C]

1 a small house on the land of a large country house, usually at the main entrance gate

2 a room or small building at the entrance to a college, institution etc for someone whose job is to watch who enters and leaves: *the porter's lodge*

3 a house or hotel in the country or mountains where people can stay when they want to go hunting, shooting etc

4 a local meeting place for some organizations, or the group of people who belong to one of these organizations: *He was a member of a Masonic lodge.*

5 a BEAVER's home

6 *AmE* a traditional home of Native Americans, or the group of people that live in it

lodg·er /ˈlɒdʒə $ ˈlɑːdʒər/ *n* [C] someone who pays rent for a room in someone's house SYN **boarder** *AmE*: *We have decided to* ***take in lodgers*** *to help pay the mortgage.*

lodg·ing /ˈlɒdʒɪŋ $ ˈlɑː-/ *n* **1** [U] a place to stay: *It's £90 a week for* ***board and lodging*** (=meals and a room). **2** [C usually plural] *old-fashioned* a room in someone's house which you live in and pay rent for: *Paul found lodgings in the Marylebone Road.*

ˈlodging house *n* [C] *BrE old-fashioned* a building where people can rent rooms to live or stay in SYN **boarding house**

lo-fi /ˈləʊ faɪ $ ˈloʊ-/ *adj* (**low fidelity**) lo-fi recordings have unclear sound or extra noises

loft¹ /lɒft $ lɒːft/ ●○○ *n* [C]

1 UNDER A ROOF *BrE* a room or space under the roof of a building, usually used for storing things in SYN **attic**: *Our neighbours have just done a* ***loft conversion*** (=changed the loft into bedrooms).

2 ON A FARM a raised area in a BARN used for keeping HAY or other crops in: *a hayloft*

3 PART OF A ROOM *AmE* a raised area above the main part of a room, usually used for sleeping

4 TYPE OF APARTMENT a space above a business, factory etc that was once used for storing goods, but has been changed into living space: *She's just bought a loft in Manhattan.*

5 FOR BIRDS a set of CAGES used to keep PIGEONS in

6 IN A CHURCH the raised place in a church where the ORGAN or CHOIR is

loft² *v* [T] to hit a ball very high in GOLF or CRICKET

loft·y /ˈlɒfti $ ˈlɒː-/ *adj* **1** *literary* lofty mountains, buildings etc are very high and impressive: *He stayed at the Four Seasons Hotel, from whose* ***lofty heights*** *he could see across New York.* THESAURUS **HIGH** **2** lofty ideas, beliefs, attitudes etc show high standards or high moral qualities – use this to show approval: *lofty ideals of equality and social justice* | *He had set himself the lofty goal of reaching the world's top five.* **3** seeming to think you are better than other people – used to show disapproval: *She has such a lofty manner.* —**loftily** *adv* —**loftiness** *n* [U]

log¹ /lɒg $ lɒːg, lɑːg/ ●●○ S3 *n* [C]

1 a thick piece of wood from a tree: *a roaring log fire*

2 an official record of events, especially on a journey in a ship or plane: *The captain always* ***keeps a log***.

3 a LOGARITHM → **it's as easy as falling off a log** at **FALL¹**(31), → **sleep like a log/top** at **SLEEP¹**(1)

log² ●●○ *v* (**logged**, **logging**)

1 [T] to make an official record of events, facts etc: *All phone calls are logged.*

2 [T] to travel a particular distance or for a particular length of time, especially in a plane or ship: *The pilot has logged 1,200 flying hours.*

3 [I,T] to cut down trees

log in/on *phr v* to do the necessary actions on a computer system that will allow you to begin using it: **[+to]** *You need to log on to your home page.*

log off/out *phr v* to stop using a computer system by giving it particular instructions

lo·gan·ber·ry /ˈləʊgənbəri $ ˈloʊgənberi/ *n* (*plural* **loganberries**) [C] a soft dark red fruit like a large RASPBERRY

log·a·rith·m /ˈlɒgərɪðəm $ ˈlɒː-, ˈlɑː-/ *n* [C] *technical* a number representing another number in a mathematical system so that complicated calculations can be done as simple addition

ˈlog book *n* [C] **1** *BrE* an official document containing details about a vehicle and the name of its owner **2** an official record of events, especially on a journey in a ship or plane

ˌlog ˈcabin *n* [C] a small house made of LOGS

LOG CABIN

log·ger /ˈlɒgə $ ˈlɒːgər, ˈlɑː-/ *n* [C] someone whose job is to cut down trees SYN **lumberjack**

log·ger·heads /ˈlɒgəhedz $ ˈlɒːgər-, ˈlɑː-/ *n* **be at loggerheads (with sb)** if two people are at loggerheads, they disagree very strongly: **[+over]** *He is at* *loggerheads with many of his own party over the issue of taxation.*

log·gi·a /ˈlɒdʒiə $ ˈloʊdʒə/ *n* [C] an open area with a floor and a roof that is built on the side of a house on the ground floor

log·ging /ˈlɒgɪŋ $ ˈlɔː-, ˈlɑː-/ *n* [U] the work of cutting down trees in a forest

lo·gic /ˈlɒdʒɪk $ ˈlɑː-/ ●●○ *n*

1 [singular, U] a way of thinking about something that seems correct and reasonable, or a set of sensible reasons for doing something: **[+behind]** *The logic behind this statement is faulty.* | **[+of]** *What's the logic of your argument?* | **accept/follow/see sb's logic** *It's easy to understand his logic.* | *There is **a certain logic** in their choice of architect.* | **commercial/industrial/economic logic** *Commercial logic has forced the two parts of the company closer together.*

2 [U] a formal method of reasoning, in which ideas are based on previous ideas

3 [U] *technical* a set of choices that a computer uses to solve a problem

lo·gic·al /ˈlɒdʒɪkəl $ ˈlɑː-/ ●●○ S3 AWL *adj*

1 seeming reasonable and sensible OPP **illogical**: *It's a logical site for a new supermarket, with the housing development nearby.* | *a logical conclusion*

2 using a thinking process in which facts and ideas are connected in a correct way: *The detective has to discover the murderer by logical deduction.* —**logically** /-kli/ *adv*: *He tried to think logically.*

lo·gi·cian /ləˈdʒɪʃən $ loʊ-/ AWL *n* [C] someone who studies or is skilled in logic

-logist /lədʒɪst/ *suffix* [in nouns] another form of the suffix -OLOGIST

lo·gis·tic /ləˈdʒɪstɪk $ loʊ-/ (*also* **lo·gis·tic·al** /-tɪkəl/) *adj* relating to the logistics of doing something: *the logistical problems of implementing the proposals* —**logistically** /-kli/ *adv*

lo·gis·tics /ləˈdʒɪstɪks $ loʊ-/ *n* **1** [plural] the practical arrangements that are needed in order to make a plan that involves a lot of people and equipment successful: *the day-to-day logistics involved with mining* | **[+of]** *the logistics of travelling with small children* **2** [U] the business of transporting things such as goods to the place where they are needed

GRAMMAR: Singular or plural verb?

- In meaning 1, **logistics** is followed by a plural verb: *The **logistics** of the camping trip **were** really complicated.*
- In meaning 2, **logistics** is followed by a singular verb: ***Logistics is** our speciality.*

GRAMMAR GUIDE ▶ NOUNS

log·jam /ˈlɒgdʒæm $ ˈlɔːg-, ˈlɑːg-/ *n* [C] **1** a situation in which a lot of problems are preventing progress from being made **2** a tightly packed mass of floating LOGS on a river

lo·go /ˈləʊgəʊ $ ˈloʊgoʊ/ ●○○ *n* [C] a small design that is the official sign of a company or organization

log·roll·ing /ˈlɒgˌrəʊlɪŋ $ ˈlɔːgˌroʊ-, ˈlɑːg-/ *n* [U] *AmE informal* **1** the practice in the US Congress of helping a member to pass a BILL, so that they will do the same for you later **2** the practice of praising or helping someone, so that they will do the same for you later

-logue (*also* **-log** *AmE*) /lɒg $ lɔːg, lɑːg/ *suffix* [in nouns] something that is written or spoken: *a monologue* (=a speech by one person)

-logy /lədʒi/ *suffix* [in nouns] another form of the suffix -OLOGY: *mineralogy* (=the study of minerals)

loin /lɔɪn/ *n* **1 loins** [plural] *literary* the part of your body below your waist and above your legs, which includes your sexual organs **2** [C,U] a piece of meat from the lower part of an animal's back: *roast loin of pork* → **gird (up) your loins** at GIRD(1)

loin·cloth /ˈlɔɪnklɒθ $ -klɔːθ/ *n* [C] a piece of cloth that men in some hot countries wear around their waist to cover their sexual organs

loi·ter /ˈlɔɪtə $ -ər/ *v* [I] **1** to stand or wait somewhere, especially in a public place, without any clear reason SYN **hang about**, **hang around**: *Five or six teenagers were loitering in front of the newsagent's.* THESAURUS ▶ STAY **2** to move or do something slowly, or to keep stopping when you should keep moving

LOL **1** (***laughing out loud***) used in emails, TEXT MESSAGES etc to show that you think something is funny **2** (***lots of love***) used at the end of a friendly email, TEXT MESSAGE, or letter to someone you know well

Lo·li·ta /ləˈliːtə/ *n* [C] a girl who is too young to have sex legally, but who behaves in a sexually attractive way. This name comes from a character in the novel *Lolita* (1955) by Vladimir Nabokov. It is the story of a MIDDLE-AGED man who has very strong sexual feelings for a young girl.

loll /lɒl $ lɑːl/ *v* **1** [I always + adv/prep] to sit or lie in a very lazy and relaxed way SYN **lounge**: **[+around/about/beside etc]** *He lolled back in his chair.* **2** [I,T] if your head or tongue lolls or if you loll your head, you allow it to hang in a relaxed uncontrolled way

lol·li·pop /ˈlɒlipɒp $ ˈlɑːlipɑːp/ *n* [C] a hard sweet made of boiled sugar on a stick SYN **lolly** *BrE*

ˈlollipop ˌlady, **ˈlollipop ˌman** *n* [C] *BrE* someone whose job is to help children cross a road safely on their way to school

lol·lop /ˈlɒləp $ ˈlɑː-/ *v* [I always +adv/prep] *written* to run with long awkward steps: **[+down/up/along etc]** *The dog came lolloping up the path.*

lol·ly /ˈlɒli $ ˈlɑːli/ *n* (*plural* **lollies**) *BrE informal* **1** [C] frozen juice or ice cream on a stick SYN **ice lolly** **2** [C] a hard sweet made of boiled sugar on a stick SYN **lollipop** **3** [U] *old-fashioned* money – used humorously

lone /ləʊn $ loʊn/ *adj* [only before noun] **1** used to talk about the only person or thing in a place, or the only person or thing that does something SYN **solitary**: *A **lone figure** was standing at the bus stop.* | *He was by no means a **lone voice** criticizing the government.* | *a **lone gunman*** | *the **lone survivor** of a shipwreck* **2 lone mother/father/parent etc** *BrE* someone who looks after their children on their own SYN **single**: *a **lone-parent family*** **3 lone wolf** someone who prefers to be alone

lone·ly /ˈləʊnli $ ˈloʊn-/ ●●● S3 *adj* (*comparative* **lonelier**, *superlative* **loneliest**)

1 unhappy because you are alone or do not have anyone to talk to SYN **lonesome** *AmE*: *a lonely old man* | *Don't you get lonely being on your own all day?* ⚠ Do not use **lonely** to mean 'without anyone else'. Use **alone**: *She is afraid to travel alone (NOT travel lonely).*

2 a lonely experience or situation makes you unhappy because you are alone or do not have anyone to talk to: *a lonely journey* | **lonely life/existence** *He led a lonely life with few friends.*

3 the lonely [plural] people who are lonely

4 a lonely place is a long way from where people live and very few people go there SYN **lonesome** *AmE*, **remote**, **desolate**: **lonely place/road/spot etc** —**loneliness** *n* [U]

THESAURUS

lonely (*also* **lonesome** *AmE*) unhappy because you are alone or do not have any friends: *Tammy felt very lonely when she first arrived in New York.* | *I get so lonesome here with no one to talk to.*

isolated lonely because your situation makes it difficult for you to meet people: *People caring for sick relatives often feel very isolated.*

alienated feeling that you do not belong in a particular place or group: *In high school she felt somehow different and alienated from other students.*

homesick unhappy because you are a long way from your home and the people who live there: *When I first went to Germany, I was very homesick.*

L

miss sb used when saying that you feel unhappy because someone is not there with you: *I miss you.* | *She misses her friends.*

ˌlonely ˈhearts *n* **lonely hearts club/column/ad** *BrE* a club or an advertisement page of a newspaper that is used by people who want to meet someone that they can have a romantic relationship with

lon·er /ˈləʊnə $ ˈloʊnər/ *n* [C] someone who prefers to be alone or who has no friends: *Ken's always been a bit of a loner.*

lone·some /ˈləʊnsəm $ ˈloʊn-/ ●○○ *adj AmE*
1 very unhappy because you are alone or have no friends SYN **lonely**: *Beth is lonesome without the children.*
2 a lonesome place is a long way from where people live and very few people go there SYN **lonely**, **remote**: *a lonesome spot near the canyon*
3 on/by your lonesome *informal* alone

long[1] /lɒŋ $ lɒːŋ/ ●●● S1 W1 *adj* (*comparative* **longer**, *superlative* **longest**)
1 GREAT LENGTH measuring a great length from one end to the other OPP **short**: *a long table* | ***long hair*** | *the longest tunnel in the world* | *He stretched out his **long legs**.* | *a **long line** of people*
2 GREAT DISTANCE continuing or travelling a great distance from one place to another OPP **short**: *a long distance* | *Springfield is **a long way** from Chicago.* | *Liz lives in Cheltenham, which is **a long way away**.* | **long journey/walk/flight/drive etc** (=a journey etc over a large distance that takes a lot of time) *It's a long walk to the shops from here.*
3 LARGE AMOUNT OF TIME continuing for a large amount of time, or for a larger amount of time than usual OPP **short**: *a **long period of time*** | *a **long history** of success* | *He has a **long memory**.* | **(for) a long time/while** *He's been gone a long time.* | *I haven't been there for a long while.* | *It **took** a **long time** to get everything ready.* | *She died **a long time ago**.* | **long silence/pause/delay etc** *There was a long silence before anybody spoke.* | *She's recovering from a **long illness**.* | *Doctors often **work long hours*** (=work for more time than is usual). | **the longest time** *AmE spoken* (=a very long time) *It took me the longest time to figure out how to open the windows.*
4 PARTICULAR LENGTH/DISTANCE/TIME used to talk or ask about a particular length, distance, or time: ***How long** is your garden?* | *How long is the film?* | *The cable is not quite **long enough**.* | **two metres/three miles etc long** *The bridge is 140 feet long.* | **two hours/three days etc long** *The speech was twenty minutes long.*
5 WRITING containing a lot of words, letters, names, or pages OPP **short**: *a long novel* | *a **long list*** | *He has a very **long name**.* | *He owes money to a list of people **as long as your arm*** (=a very long list).
6 CLOTHING covering all of your arms or legs OPP **short**: *a long dress* | *a **long-sleeved** shirt*
7 TIRING/BORING *spoken* making you feel tired or bored: *It's been a **long day**.*
8 VOWEL *technical* a long vowel in a word is pronounced for a longer time than a short vowel with the same sound OPP **short**
9 how long is a piece of string? *BrE spoken* used when there is no definite answer to a question: *'How long will it take to finish the project?' 'How long is a piece of string?'*
10 the long and (the) short of it *spoken* used when you are telling someone the most important facts about something rather than all the details: *The long and the short of it is that we missed the train.*
11 the long arm of sb/sth *written* the power of someone or something that has authority, especially to catch and punish someone: *He won't escape **the long arm of the law**.*
12 long face a sad or disappointed expression on someone's face
13 long in the tooth *informal* too old – used humorously: *I'm getting a bit long in the tooth for this sort of thing.*
14 not long for this world *literary* likely to die or stop existing soon
15 long on sth having a lot of a quality: *He was **short on** patience, **but long on** a sense of his own worth.*
16 long odds if there are long odds against something happening, it is very unlikely that it will happen
17 in the long run/term used when talking about what will happen at a later time or when something is finished: *All our hard work will **be worth it in the long run**.*
18 long shot someone or something with very little chance of success: *Chelsea are a 20–1 long shot to win the championship.*
19 long time no see *spoken* used humorously to say hello when you have not seen someone for a long time
20 take the long view (of sth) to think about the effect that something will have in the future rather than what happens now
21 a long way very much, far, or a great amount or degree: *We're still **a long way from** achieving our sales targets.* | *Psychiatry has **come a long way** (*=developed a lot*) since the 1920s.* | *Your contributions will **go a long way towards** helping children in need* (=will help to reach a goal). | **by a long way/shot** *informal* (*also* **by a long chalk** *BrE*) (=used when something is much better, quicker, cheaper etc) *It was his best performance this year, by a long way.* | **not by a long way/shot** *informal* (*also* **not by a long chalk** *BrE*) (=not at all or not nearly) *He had not told Rory everything, not by a long shot.*
22 long weekend three or more days, including Saturday and Sunday, when you do not have to go to work or school → **at (long) last** at LAST[3](2), → **it's a long story** at STORY(10), → **cut/make a long story short** at STORY(11), → **a little (of sth) goes a long way** at LITTLE[2](5), → **have a long way to go** at WAY[1](19)

GRAMMAR: Order of adjectives

If there is more than one adjective, the adjectives are usually used in a fixed order.
You say: *I had a nice long bath.* ✗ Don't say: *I had a long nice bath.*
You say: *She wore a long black coat.* ✗ Don't say: *She wore a black long coat.*
GRAMMAR GUIDE ▸ ADJECTIVES

long[2] ●●● S1 W1 *adv*
1 for a long time: *Have you been **waiting long**?* | *Reform of the law is **long overdue**.* | ***long established** traditions*
2 used to ask and talk about particular amounts of time: ***How long** will it take to get there?* | *Try to keep going for **as long as possible**.* | *It **took** me **longer** than I thought it would.*
3 at a time that is a long time before or after a particular time: **long before/after sth** *This all happened long before you were born.* | **long ago/since** *He should have left her long ago.* | ***It wasn't long before*** (=soon) *Lisa arrived.*
4 for long [usually in questions and negatives] for a long time: *Have you known them for long?* | *I haven't seen her **for so long** that I've forgotten what she looks like.*
5 as/so long as a) used to say that one thing can happen or be true only if another thing happens or is true: *You can go out to play as long as you stay in the back yard.* **b)** used to say that one thing will continue to happen or be true if another thing happens or is true at the same time: *As long as we keep playing well, we'll keep winning games.*
6 (for) as long as used to talk about something continuing for the amount of time that you want, need, or is possible: *You can stay for **as long as** you **want**.* | *She tried to stay awake for **as long as** she **could**.* | *The fruit should be left on the tree **as long as possible**.*
7 no longer/not any longer used when something used to happen or be true in the past but does not happen or is not true now: *The extra workers won't be needed any longer.* | *It's no longer a secret.*

REGISTER
In everyday English, people usually say **not any longer** or **not anymore** (especially AmE)**/not any more** (BrE), rather than **no longer**, which sounds slightly formal or literary: *He **no longer** lives here.* → *He doesn't live here **any longer** OR **anymore**.*

8 before long soon or in a short time: *Before long a large*

L

crowd had gathered outside the building. | *It's likely that the law will be abolished before long.*
9 sb/sth/it won't be long *spoken* used to say that someone or something will be ready, will be back, will happen etc soon: *Wait here – I won't be long.* | *Dinner won't be long.*
10 all day/year/summer etc long during all of the day etc
11 so long *spoken especially AmE* goodbye
12 long live sb/sth used to show support for a person, idea, principle, or nation: *Long live the King!*

long³ ●●○ *v* [I] to want something very much, especially when it seems unlikely to happen soon: **long to do sth** *He longed to see her again.* | **[+for]** *She longed for the chance to speak to him in private.* | **long for sb to do sth** *She longed for him to return.* → LONGED-FOR, LONGING

long. the written abbreviation of ***longitude***

ˌlong-aˈwaited, **long awaited** *adj* [only before noun] a long-awaited event, moment etc is one that you have been waiting a long time for: *the long-awaited news of his release from prison*

long·bow /ˈlɒŋbəʊ $ ˈlɒːŋboʊ/ *n* [C] a large BOW made from a long thin curved piece of wood, used in the past for hunting or fighting

ˌlong-ˈdistance ●○○ *adj* [only before noun]
1 travelling over a long distance: **long-distance runner** | **long-distance lorry driver** | **long-distance travel/journey/flight/commuting etc**
2 long-distance call a telephone call to a place that is far away OPP **local** —**long-distance** *adv*

ˌlong diˈvision *n* [U] a method of dividing one large number by another

ˌlong-drawn-ˈout (*also* **ˈlong-drawn**) *adj* [only before noun] continuing for a longer time than is wanted or necessary SYN **protracted**: *The official enquiry was a long-drawn-out process.* THESAURUS ▸ LONG

ˈlonged-for *adj* [only before noun] a longed-for thing or event is one that you want very much: *the birth of her first longed-for child*

lon·gev·i·ty /lɒnˈdʒevəti $ lɑːn-, lɒːn-/ *n* [U]
1 the amount of time that someone or something lives: **[+of]** *the greater longevity of women compared with men* | *The worms have a longevity of about two years.* **2** long life or the long time that something lasts: *The ancient Chinese claimed that garlic promoted longevity.* **3** the amount of time that something lasts: **[+of]** *the longevity of an athlete's career*

long·hand /ˈlɒŋhænd $ ˈlɒːŋ-/ *n* [U] if you write something in longhand, you write it by hand using complete words, rather than TYPING it or using special short forms of words → **shorthand**

ˈlong-haul *adj* **long-haul flight/route/destination etc** a long-haul flight etc is over a very long distance OPP **short-haul**

long·horn /ˈlɒŋhɔːn $ ˈlɒːŋhɔːrn/ *n* [C] a cow with long horns

long·ing /ˈlɒŋɪŋ $ ˈlɒːŋɪŋ/ *n* [singular, U] a strong feeling of wanting something or someone: *She looked back with longing on the good old days.* | **[+for]** *His heart was filled with longing for Cynthia.* | **[+to]** *She felt a longing to throw herself into his arms.*

long·ing·ly /ˈlɒŋɪŋli $ ˈlɒːŋ-/ *adv* in a way that shows that you want someone or something very much: *She **thought longingly** of returning to Paris.* | **look/gaze longingly at sb/sth** *He looked longingly at the tray of cakes.* —**longing** *adj*

long·ish /ˈlɒŋɪʃ $ ˈlɒːŋɪʃ/ *adj informal* fairly long OPP **shortish**

lon·gi·tude /ˈlɒndʒɪtjuːd $ ˈlɑːndʒɪtuːd/ *n* [C,U] the distance east or west of a particular MERIDIAN (=imaginary line along the Earth's surface from the North Pole to the South Pole), measured in degrees → **latitude**: *The town lies at longitude 12° east.* → see picture at EARTH¹

lon·gi·tu·di·nal /ˌlɒndʒɪˈtjuːdɪnəl◂ $ ˌlɑːndʒɪˈtuː-/ *adj technical* **1** relating to the development of something over a period of time: **longitudinal study/survey/research etc** *a longitudinal study of unemployed workers* **2** going from top to bottom, not across: *longitudinal stripes* **3** measured according to longitude —**longitudinally** *adv*

THESAURUS: long

long continuing for a long time: *The film was very long.* | *There has been a long period without rain.*
lengthy continuing for a long time, especially longer than you want or expect: *Drivers face lengthy delays on all roads out of the city.* | *Police are going through the lengthy process of re-examining all the evidence.* | *He faces a lengthy prison sentence.*
long-running [only before noun] continuing for a long time – used especially about disputes, campaigns, or shows: *He has been involved in a long-running dispute with his neighbour.* | *The programme is one of the longest-running series on television.* | *a long-running campaign to prevent the airport from being built*
long-lasting continuing for a long time – used especially about effects or relationships: *Stress can have long-lasting effects.* | *While at the school, she made many long-lasting friendships.*
protracted *formal* continuing for a long time, especially an unusually long time: *Despite protracted negotiations, they were unable to reach an agreement.* | *The couple have been involved in a protracted battle for custody of their children.*
prolonged continuing for a long time, especially longer than expected, or longer in a way that makes a situation worse: *He returned to work after a prolonged absence.* | *Studies have linked prolonged use of the drug to cancer.* | *a prolonged period of economic decline*
extended [only before noun] continuing for a long time – used especially about visits, trips, breaks etc that last longer than was planned: *an extended stay in hospital* | *He took an extended break from work after his father died.* | *She didn't like being away from home for extended periods.*
lasting [only before noun] strong enough or great enough to continue for a long time: *The negotiations were aimed at achieving a lasting peace.* | *This affair has done lasting damage to the president's credibility.* | *The book left a lasting impression on me.*
enduring continuing for a long time – used especially about memories, influences, or feelings of liking someone or something: *One of my most enduring memories is of going on holiday to France with my parents.* | *the enduring appeal of Conan Doyle's stories* | *his enduring love for Ireland*
marathon [only before noun] continuing for a very long time and needing a lot of energy, patience, or determination: *It was a marathon session of talks which continued until 3 am.* | *He arrived after a marathon journey across Europe.*

TOO LONG

long-winded continuing for too long – used about speeches, answers, explanations etc: *a very long-winded answer to a simple question* | *He gave a long-winded speech about the company's vision for the future.*
interminable very long and boring: *They faced an interminable wait in the departure lounge of the airport.* | *The journey seemed interminable.*
long-drawn-out [only before noun] used about a process that continues for much too long: *The news heightened expectations that the long-drawn-out investigation might be coming to a close.*

long johns /ˈlɒŋ dʒɒnz $ ˈlɒːŋ dʒɑːnz/ *n* [plural] warm underwear with long legs

ˈ**long jump** *n* **the long jump** a sport in which each competitor tries to jump further than anyone else → **high jump** —**long jumper** *n* [C]

ˌ**long-ˈlasting** *adj* continuing for a long time OPP **short-lived**: *The impact of divorce on children can be long-lasting.* | **long-lasting effect/result** THESAURUS LONG

ˌ**long-ˈlife** *adj* **1** long-life products continue working longer than ordinary ones: *long-life batteries* **2** *BrE* long-life foods stay fresh longer than ordinary ones: *long-life milk*

long-lived /ˌlɒŋ ˈlɪvd◂ $ ˌlɒːŋ ˈlaɪvd/ *adj* living or existing for a long time OPP **short-lived**: *Ostriches are long-lived birds.* | *the band's long-lived appeal*

ˌ**long-ˈlost** *adj* [only before noun] lost or not seen for a long time: *long-lost treasures* | **long-lost brother/cousin/friend etc**

ˌ**long-playing ˈrecord** *n* [C] an LP SYN **album** → **single**

ˌ**long-ˈrange** *adj* [only before noun] **1** able to hit something that is a long way away OPP **short-range**: ***long-range** nuclear **missiles*** | *He scored with a long-range shot.* **2** relating to a time that continues far into the future OPP **short-range**: **long-range planning/plan/forecast etc** *a long-range weather forecast* | *the long-range goal of the project*

ˌ**long-ˈrunning** *adj* [only before noun] used to talk about something that has been continuing for a long time: *a **long-running saga*** | **long-running dispute/battle/debate/feud etc** *She was involved in a long-running legal battle.* | **long-running show/musical/soap opera etc** THESAURUS LONG

ˌ**long-ˈserving** *adj* [only before noun] having a particular job or position for a long time: *a **long-serving member** of the committee*

long·shore·man /ˈlɒŋʃɔːmən $ ˈlɒːŋʃɔːr-/ *n* (*plural* **longshoremen**) [C] *AmE* someone whose job is to load and unload ships at a DOCK SYN **docker** *BrE*

ˌ**long-ˈsighted** *adj BrE* able to see objects or read things clearly only when they are far from your eyes OPP **short-sighted** SYN **far-sighted** *AmE*

ˌ**long-ˈstanding**, **long·stand·ing** /ˌlɒŋˈstændɪŋ◂ $ ˌlɒːŋ-/ *adj* having continued or existed for a long time: *a **long-standing member** of the committee* | **long-standing debate/dispute etc** *a long-standing feud between the two families* | *the **long-standing problem** of keeping costs down* | *I have a long-standing arrangement with the bank.*

ˌ**long-ˈstay** *adj* [only before noun] *BrE* **1** relating to care or treatment over a long period of time: **long-stay hospital/ward/bed etc** | **long-stay patient/resident 2** a long-stay car park is a place where people can leave their cars for a long period of time OPP **short-stay**

ˌ**long-ˈsuffering** *adj* [usually before noun] patient in spite of problems or other people's annoying behaviour: *his long-suffering wife*

ˌ**long-ˈterm** ●●○ W3 *adj* [usually before noun] continuing for a long period of time, or relating to what will happen in the distant future OPP **short-term**: *the **long-term future** of the fishing industry* | *the **long-term interests** of the company* | **the long-term unemployed** (=people who have not had a job for a long time) | *the **long-term effects** of alcohol on the body* | **long-term plan/strategy/solution** | **long-term loan/investment** → **in the long term** at TERM[1](4)

ˈ**long-time**, **long·time** /ˈlɒŋtaɪm $ ˈlɒːŋ-/ *adj* [only before noun] having existed or continued to be a particular thing for a long time: *a long-time supporter of civil rights* | **long-time friend/lover etc**

ˈ**long ˌwave** *n* [U] (*written abbreviation* **LW**) radio broadcasting or receiving on waves of 1,000 metres or more in length → **medium wave**, **short wave**, **FM**

long-wind·ed /ˌlɒŋ ˈwɪndɪd◂ $ ˌlɒːŋ-/ *adj* **1** continuing to talk for too long or using too many words in a way that is boring: *His speeches tend to be rather long-winded.* THESAURUS LONG **2** if a way of doing something is long-winded, it is very complicated: *The whole process is incredibly long-winded.*

loo /luː/ *n* (*plural* **loos**) [C] *BrE informal* a toilet: *I need to **go to the loo*** (=use the toilet).

loo·fah /ˈluːfə/ *n* [C] a rough bath SPONGE, made from the dried inner part of a tropical fruit

look[1] /lʊk/ ●●● S1 W1 *v*

1 SEE [I] to turn your eyes towards something, so that you can see it: *We sneaked out while Jessie's mom wasn't looking.* | *If you look carefully you can see that the painting represents a human figure.* | *Gina covered her eyes, afraid to look.* | **[+at]** *'It's time we left,' Ian said, looking at his watch.* | *The men all turned to look at her as she entered the room.* | **[+away/over/down etc]** *Dad looked up from his paper and smiled.* | *'We can't go out in this weather,' said Bob, looking out of the window.*

GRAMMAR: Prepositions with look

- You **look at** someone or something: *She was looking at the baby.* | *I looked at the screen.* ✗ Don't say: *She was looking to the baby.* | *I looked to the screen.*
- If you **look to** someone, you depend on them: *He always looked to his father for advice.*

2 SEARCH [I] to try to find something: *I looked everywhere but Jimmy was nowhere to be found.* | **[+for]** *Could you help me look for my contact lens?* | *If you're looking for a bargain, try the local market.* | **[+in/under/between etc]** *Try looking under the bed.*

3 SEEM [linking verb] to seem: *From the way things look at the moment, the Republicans are unlikely to win this election.* | **look good/bad etc** *The future's looking good.* | **it looks as if/as though/like** (=it seems likely that) *It looks as if it might rain later.* | *It looks like they won't be needing us anymore.* | *You **made** me **look** really stupid in front of all my friends!*

4 APPEARANCE [linking verb] to have a particular appearance: *How do I look?* | **look tired/happy/sad etc** *You look tired. You should go to bed.* | **look as if/as though/like** *He looked as if he hadn't washed for a week.* | *What did the man **look like**?* | *My sister doesn't **look** anything **like** me.* → **look like a million dollars** at MILLION(4)

GRAMMAR: Linking verbs

Look is a linking verb in meanings 3 and 4. This type of verb links the subject of the sentence with an adjective or noun: *It looks windy outside.* | *You look beautiful.* | *She made him look a fool.*

5 look daggers at sb *informal* to look at someone with a very angry expression on your face

6 look sb up and down to look at someone carefully from their head to their feet, as if you are forming an opinion about them

7 look sb in the eye to look directly at someone when you are speaking to them, especially to show that you are not afraid of them or that you are telling the truth: *Owen didn't dare look his father in the eye.*

8 look down your nose at sb/sth to behave as if you think that someone or something is not good enough for you: *He looks down his nose at anyone foreign.*

9 look the other way to ignore something bad that is happening and not try to stop it: *Prison guards looked the other way as the man was attacked by fellow prisoners.*

10 look no further used to say that something you are offering is exactly what someone has been trying to find: *Want a quiet country retreat for your weekend break? Then look no further!*

11 FACE A DIRECTION [I always + adv/prep] if a building looks in a particular direction, it faces that direction: *The cabin looks east, so we get the morning sun.*

12 look before you leap used to say that it is sensible to think about the possible dangers or difficulties of something before doing it

13 be looking to do sth *informal* to be planning or expecting

L

to do something: *We're looking to buy a new car early next year.*
14 look under the bonnet *BrE*, **look under the hood** *AmE* to look at or find out about the less noticeable features of something: *Look under the bonnet of the company before investing in it.*

SPOKEN PHRASES
15 look a) used to tell someone to look at something that you think is interesting, surprising etc: *Look! There's a fox!* **b)** used to get someone's attention so that you can suggest something or tell them something: *Look. Why don't you think about it and give me your answer tomorrow? | Look, I've had enough of this. I'm going home.*
16 look out! used to warn someone that they are in danger SYN **watch out**: *Look out! There's a car coming.*
17 look at that! used to tell someone to look at something that you think is interesting, bad etc: *Look at that! What a horrible mess!*
18 look who's here! used when someone arrives unexpectedly: *Well, look who's here! It's Jill and Paul!*
19 don't look now used to say that you have seen someone but do not want them to know you have noticed them: *Oh no! Don't look now but here comes Tony.*
20 look what you're doing/look where you're going etc used to tell someone to be careful: *Look where you're putting your feet! There's mud all over the carpet!*
21 look what you've done! used to angrily tell someone to look at the result of a mistake they have made or something bad they have done: *Look what you've done – my jacket's ruined!*
22 look here *old-fashioned* used to get someone's attention in order to tell them something, especially when you are annoyed with them: *Look here, you can't say things like that to me!*
23 (I'm) just looking used when you are in a shop, to say that you are only looking at things, but do not intend to buy anything now: *'Can I help you?' 'No, thanks. I'm just looking.'* → **look kindly on sb/sth** at KINDLY[1](3)

THESAURUS
look to turn your eyes towards someone or something, so that you can see them: *You should never look directly at the sun. | After a while, he turned and looked at me.*
have/take a look *especially spoken* to look at something quickly, especially in order to find or check something: *I'll have a look in my desk. | Take a look at this!*
glance to look at someone or something for a short time and then look quickly away: *Damien glanced nervously at his watch.*
peek/peep (*also* **take a peek/peep**) to look quickly at something – used especially when you are not supposed to look, or when you are looking through a small gap: *The door was open so he peeked inside. | Katy peeped at her birthday present on the table.*
peer to look very carefully, especially because you cannot see well: *Kenji was peering at the screen.*
glare to look at someone in an angry way: *She glared at me as I got up to leave.*
stare to look at someone or something for a long time without moving your eyes: *It's rude to stare. | She stared straight into the camera.*
gaze to look at someone or something for a long time, often without realizing that you are doing it: *She gazed out of the window. | He lay on his bed gazing at the ceiling.*
gape to look at someone or something for a long time, usually with your mouth open, because you are very shocked or surprised: *People gaped at him with wide-open mouths.*
regard *formal* to look at someone or something, especially in a particular way: *He regarded her steadily.*

look after sb/sth *phr v especially BrE*
1 to take care of someone by helping them, giving them what they need, or keeping them safe SYN **take care of**: *Don't worry, I'll look after the kids tomorrow. | Susan looked after us very well. She's an excellent cook. | You could tell that the horse had been* ***well looked after***.
2 to be responsible for dealing with something SYN **take care of**: *I'm leaving you here to look after the business until I get back.*
3 look after yourself *spoken* used when you are saying goodbye to someone in a friendly way
4 can look after yourself to not need anyone else to take care of you: *Don't worry about Maisie – she can look after herself.*
look ahead *phr v* to think about and plan for what might happen in the future: *Looking ahead, we must expect radical changes to be made in our system of government.*
look around (*also* **look round** *BrE*) *phr v*
1 to try to find something: **[+for]** *Jason's going to start looking around for a new job.*
2 look around/round (sth) to look at what is in a place such as a building, shop, town etc, especially when you are walking: *Do we have to pay to look around the castle? | Let's look round the shops.*
look at sb/sth *phr v*
1 to turn your eyes towards someone or something, so that you can see them: *The twins looked at each other and smiled.*
2 to read something quickly in order to form an opinion of it: *I really can't comment on the report – I haven't had time to look at it yet.*
3 to examine something and try to find out what is wrong with it: *You should get the doctor to look at that cut. | Can you look at my car? There's a strange noise coming from the front wheel.*
4 to study and think about something, especially in order to decide what to do: *We need to look very carefully at ways of improving our efficiency.*
5 look at sb/sth *spoken* used to mention someone or something as an example: *You don't have to be smart to be good at music – look at Gary.*
6 to think about something in a particular way SYN **see**: *I'd like to be friends again, but Richard doesn't look at it that way.*
7 not much to look at *informal* if someone or something is not much to look at, they are not attractive
look back *phr v*
1 to think about something that happened in the past: **[+on/to]** *When I look back on those days I realize I was desperately unhappy. |* ***Looking back on it***, *I still can't figure out what went wrong.*
2 never look back to become more and more successful, especially after a particular success: *After winning the scholarship he never looked back.*
look down on sth/sb *phr v* to think that you are better than someone else, for example because you are more successful, or of a higher social class than they are: *Mr Garcia looks down on anyone who hasn't had a college education.*
look for sb/sth *phr v*
1 to try to find something that you have lost, or someone who is not where they should be SYN **search for**: *I'm looking for Steve – have you seen him? | Detectives are still looking for the escaped prisoner.* → SEARCH[2](1)
2 be looking for sb/sth to be trying to find a particular kind of thing or person: *I'm sorry, we're really looking for someone with no family commitments. |* **be (just) what/who you are looking for** *'Salubrious'! That's just the word I was looking for.*
3 be looking for trouble *informal* to be behaving in a way that makes it likely that problems or violence will happen: *They walked into a bar looking for trouble.*
look forward to sth *phr v* to be excited and pleased about something that is going to happen: *I'm really looking forward to our vacation. |* **look forward to doing sth** *My mother says she's looking forward to meeting you.*
look in *phr v informal* to make a short visit to someone, while you are going somewhere else, especially if they are ill or need help SYN **drop in, call in**: **[+on]** *I promised to look in on Dad and see if he's feeling any better.*

L

look into sth *phr v* to try to find out the truth about a problem, crime etc in order to solve it SYN **investigate**: *Police are looking into the disappearance of two children.*

look on *phr v*

1 to watch something happening, without being involved in it or trying to stop it → **onlooker**: *Only one man tried to help us, the rest just looked on in silence.*

2 look on sb/sth (*also* **look upon sb/sth**) to consider someone or something in a particular way, or as a particular thing: **[+as]** *I look on him as a good friend.* | **[+with]** *Strangers to the village are looked upon with a mixture of fear and suspicion.*

look sth ↔ **out** *phr v* to search for and find a particular thing among your possessions: *I'll look out some of my old books for you.*

look out for sb/sth *phr v*

1 to pay attention to what is happening around you, so that you will notice a particular person or thing if you see them → **lookout**: *Look out for your Aunt while you're at the station.* | *He's looking out for a nice apartment downtown.*

2 to try to make sure that someone is treated well: *My older brother always looked out for me when we were kids.* | **look out for yourself/number one** (=think only of the advantages you can get for yourself)

look sth/sb ↔ **over** *phr v* to examine something or someone quickly, without paying much attention to detail: *Do you have a few minutes to look these samples over?*

look round *phr v BrE* to LOOK AROUND

look through sb/sth *phr v*

1 to look for something among a pile of papers, in a drawer, in someone's pockets etc SYN **go through**: *I've looked through all my papers but I still can't find the contract.*

2 to not notice or pretend to not notice someone you know, even though you see them: **look straight/right through sb** *I saw Fiona in the street yesterday and she looked straight through me.*

look to sb/sth *phr v*

1 to depend on someone to provide help, advice etc: **[+for]** *We look to you for support.* | **look to sb to do sth** *They're looking to the new manager to make the company profitable.*

2 to pay attention to something, especially in order to improve it: *We must look to our defences.*

look up *phr v*

1 if a situation is looking up, it is improving SYN **improve, get better**: *Now the summer's here **things are looking up**!*

2 look sth ↔ up if you look up information in a book, on a computer etc, you try to find it there: *Look the word up in your dictionary.* | *I'll just look up the train times.*

3 look sb ↔ up to visit someone you know, especially when you are in the place where they live for a different reason: *Don't forget to look me up when you come to Atlanta.*

look up to sb *phr v* to admire or respect someone: *I've always looked up to Bill for his courage and determination.*

look² ●●● S1 W1 *n*

1 LOOK AT [C usually singular] an act of looking at something: **have/take a look (at sb/sth)** *Let me have a look at that – I think it's mine.* | *Take a **good look** at the photo and see if you recognize anyone in it.* | *I **took one look** at the coat and decided it wasn't worth £50.* | **have/take a look around** (*also* **have/take a look round** *BrE*) (=look at all the things in a particular place) *I have a special interest in old houses. Do you mind if I take a look around?*

2 EXPRESSION [C] an expression that you make with your eyes or face: **give sb a look** *Mike gave him such a severe look he didn't dare argue.* | *Why has Jake been giving me **dirty looks*** (=unfriendly looks) *all morning?*

3 CONSIDER [singular] an act of examining something and thinking about it: **have/take a look (at sb/sth)** *Have you had a chance to take a look at my proposal yet?* | *I asked the vet to have a **quick look** at the puppies as well.* | *It's time to take a **fresh look** at the old problem of low pay.* | *This month, take a **long hard look*** (=examine very carefully) *at where your money is going.*

4 SEARCH [singular] an attempt to find something: *I can't find them anywhere. **Have a look** yourself.* | *She had a **good look*** (=searched carefully) *through the files.*

5 APPEARANCE [C usually singular] the appearance that someone or something has: *The area has a very seedy look to it.* | *Mr Flynn had a tired, ill look in his eyes.* | **not like the look of sb/sth** (=think that something bad has happened or will happen because of something's appearance) *We should turn back now. It's getting dark and I don't like the look of those rain clouds.*

6 WAY STH SEEMS [C] the way something seems to be: *The neighbours are back from holiday **by the looks of it*** (=that is how it seems). | *I don't like **the look of** this new policy* (=I do not like the way it seems).

7 BEAUTY **looks** [plural] physical attractiveness: *Fiona's got everything – looks, money and youth.* | *You get your **good looks** from your mother.* | *When she **lost her looks*** (=became less attractive) *she found it difficult to get work.*

8 FASHION [singular] a particular style in clothes, hair, furniture etc: *The hippy look is back again.*

9 if looks could kill used to say that someone is looking at someone else in a very angry or unfriendly way

look·a·like, **look-alike** /ˈlʊkəlaɪk/ *n* [C] *informal* someone who looks very similar to someone who is famous: *a Madonna lookalike*

look·er /ˈlʊkə $ -ər/ *n* [C] *informal* someone who is attractive, usually a woman

ˈlook-in *n* **get/have a look-in** [usually in negatives] *BrE informal* to have a chance to take part in or succeed in something: *Arsenal barely got a look-in* (=were very unsuccessful) *during the second half of the match.*

ˈlooking glass *n* [C] *old-fashioned* a MIRROR

look·out /ˈlʊk-aʊt/ *n*

1 be on the lookout for sb/sth to continuously watch a place or pay attention in order to find something you want or to be ready for problems or opportunities → **look out for**: *We're always on the lookout for new business opportunities.* | *Police were on the lookout for anyone behaving suspiciously.*

2 keep a lookout to keep watching carefully for something or someone, especially for danger: **[+for]** *We were instructed to keep a lookout for enemy aircraft.* | *When you're driving, **keep a sharp lookout*** (=watch extra carefully) *for cyclists.*

3 PERSON [C] someone whose duty is to watch carefully for something, especially for danger

4 PLACE [C] a place for a lookout to watch from

5 that's/it's sb's lookout *BrE informal* used to say that someone is responsible for deciding what they will do, and will have to suffer any bad results: *If he wants to keep seeing her, that's his lookout.*

ˌlook-ˈsee *n* [singular] *informal* a quick look at something SYN **glance**

loom¹ /luːm/ ●○○ *v* [I]

1 [always + adv/prep] to appear as a large unclear shape, especially in a threatening way: **[+up/out/ahead etc]** *Suddenly a mountain loomed up in front of them.*

2 if a problem or difficulty looms, it is likely to happen very soon: *An economic crisis is **looming on the horizon**.*

3 loom large to seem important, worrying, and difficult to avoid: *Fear of failure loomed large in his mind.*

loom² *n* [C] a frame or machine on which thread is woven into cloth

loon /luːn/ *n* [C] **1** a large North American bird that eats fish and that makes a long high sound **2** *informal* a silly or strange person – used humorously

loon·y¹ /ˈluːni/ *n* (*plural* **loonies**) [C] *informal* someone who is crazy or strange: *Her brother's a complete loony.*

loony² *adj informal* silly, crazy, or strange: *a loony idea*

ˈloony bin *n* [C] *informal* an expression meaning a hospital for people who are mentally ill, usually considered offensive SYN **psychiatric hospital**

loop¹ /luːp/ ●●○ *n* [C]

1 SHAPE OR LINE a shape like a curve or a circle made by a line curving back towards itself, or a piece of wire, string etc that has this shape: **loop of wire/rope/string etc** *A loop*

of wire held the gate shut. | **belt loop** (=a loop of material for holding a belt on trousers etc) → see picture at KNOT[1]
2 COMPUTER a set of operations in a computer program that are continuously repeated
3 FILM/MUSIC a film or music loop contains images or sounds that are continuously repeated
4 be in the loop/be out of the loop *informal* to be or not be part of a group of people who make important decisions
5 knock/throw sb for a loop *AmE informal* to surprise and upset someone
6 ROAD/RAILWAY *BrE* a road or railway line that leaves the main road or track and then joins it again further on

loop² *v* **1** [I,T] to make a loop or make something into a loop: **loop sth over/around etc sth** *He looped the rope over the post.* **2** [I] to move in a circular direction that forms the shape of a loop: *The ball looped over the goalkeeper into the back of the net.* **3 loop the loop** to fly a plane up and around in a circle so that the plane is UPSIDE DOWN for a time **4** (*also* **loop in**) [T] *informal* to give someone the latest news or information about a situation: **[+on]** *Keep me looped in on any further developments.*

loop·hole /ˈluːphəʊl $ -hoʊl/ *n* [C] a small mistake in a law that makes it possible to avoid doing something that the law is supposed to make you do: **legal/tax loophole** | **[+in]** *a loophole in the law*

loop·y /ˈluːpi/ *adj informal* **1** crazy or strange **2 go loopy** *BrE* **a)** to become extremely angry **b)** to become mentally ill

LOOSE

tight clothing baggy/loose clothing

loose¹ /luːs/ ●●● S3 W3 *adj*
1 NOT FIRMLY ATTACHED not firmly fastened in place: *a loose floorboard* | *This tooth feels very loose.* | *The screw has* **come loose** (=became loose). ⚠ Do not confuse the adjective **loose** /luːs/ with the verb **lose** /luːz/ (=stop having something, become unable to find something etc): *They thought they might lose their jobs.*
2 NOT ATTACHED not attached to anything else: *loose papers* | *His rear wheel spun on the* **loose stones**. | *The potatoes are sold loose* (=not packed in a container). | *The driver had forgotten to fasten the safety chain and the trailer* **came loose** (=became unattached).
3 NOT TIED TIGHTLY not tied or fastened very tightly: *a loose knot*
4 HAIR if your hair is loose, it hangs freely rather than being tied back: *Her hair fell loose around her shoulders.*
5 CLOTHES loose clothes are big and do not fit your body tightly SYN **loose-fitting**, **baggy** OPP **tight**: *a loose sweat-shirt*
6 FREE free from being controlled or held in a cage, prison, or institution: **break/get loose** (=escape) *A 34-year-old inmate broke loose from the sheriff's office yesterday.* | **turn/let/set sth loose** (=let something go free) *Don't let your dog loose on the beach.*
7 NOT EXACT [usually before noun] not exact or thoroughly done: *a loose translation* | *a* **loose interpretation** *of the law*
8 NOT VERY CONTROLLED not strictly controlled or organized: **loose federation/alliance/group etc** *a loose federation of political groups* | *loose arrangement* (=an arrangement that can easily be changed)
9 NOT SOLID not pressed tightly together in a solid mass: **loose soil/earth**
10 SPORT not under the control of either team in a game of football, RUGBY etc: *Sheringham was the first player to reach the* **loose ball**.
11 cut loose a) to free yourself from someone or something, or their influence: **cut yourself loose (from sth)** *He cut himself loose from the constraints of family life.* **b)** *AmE informal* to start enjoying yourself in a happy noisy way after a period of controlled behaviour: *I'm ready to cut loose and enjoy the weekend.*
12 let (sth ↔) loose to speak or behave in an uncontrolled way: *She let loose a string of four-letter words.*
13 let sb loose on sth to allow someone to deal with something in the way they want to, when you think they will make mistakes or do something wrong: *Whatever you do, don't let Derek loose on the garden.*
14 be at a loose end (*also* **be at loose ends** *AmE*) to have nothing to do: *I was at a loose end so I decided to go see an old movie.*
15 loose ends parts of something that have not been completed or correctly done: *We've nearly finished, but there are still a few* **loose ends** *to be* **tied up** (=dealt with or completed).
16 loose change coins that you have in your bag or pocket
17 loose cannon someone who cannot be trusted because they say or do things you do not want them to
18 hang/stay loose *AmE spoken* used to tell someone to stay calm, or not to worry about something
19 BODY WASTE having a problem in which the waste from your BOWELS has too much liquid in it: *loose bowels*
20 IMMORAL *old-fashioned* behaving in a way that is considered to be sexually immoral: *a* **loose woman** | *loose morals*
21 TALK *old-fashioned* not careful about what you say or who is listening: *There's been a bit of* **loose talk** *about it.*
—**looseness** *n* [U]

loose² *v* [T] *literary* **1** to make something unpleasant begin: *And now the anger Maggie had feared was loosed.* **2** to make something loose or to untie someone or something, especially an animal **3** to fire an ARROW, a bullet from a gun etc

loose sth **on/upon** sb/sth *phr v* to allow something dangerous or harmful to begin to affect a situation or other people: *the evils loosed upon humanity in World War II*

loose³ *n* **be on the loose** if a criminal or dangerous animal is on the loose, they have escaped from prison or from their cage

ˌloose-ˈfitting *adj* loose-fitting clothes are big and do not fit your body closely, so that they are comfortable SYN **baggy** OPP **tight-fitting**, **tight**: *a loose-fitting jacket*

ˌloose-ˈleaf *adj* [only before noun] having pages that can be put in and removed easily: **loose-leaf file/binder/format**

loose·ly /ˈluːsli/ ●○○ *adv*
1 in a way that is not firm or tight: *A towel was loosely wrapped around his neck.*
2 in a way that is not exact: *The film is* **loosely based on** *the novel.* | *'El Libre' was loosely translated as 'the free one'.*
3 in a way that is not strictly controlled or organized: *a loosely structured organization*

loos·en /ˈluːsən/ ●○○ *v*
1 [I,T] to make something less tight or less firmly fastened, or to become less tight or less firmly fastened OPP **tighten**: *You'll need a spanner to loosen that bolt.* | *The screws have loosened.* | *Harry loosened his tie.* → see picture at UNDO
2 [T] to make laws, rules etc less strict SYN **relax** OPP **tighten**: *Congress has loosened the restrictions on immigration.*
3 loosen your grip/hold a) to reduce the control or power you have over someone or something: **[+on]** *The government has loosened its hold on the media considerably.* **b)** to

start holding someone or something less tightly than you were before OPP **tighten**: **[+on]** *He loosened his grip on David's arm.*
4 loosen sb's tongue to make someone talk more than usual, especially about things they should not talk about
loosen up *phr v*
1 to stop worrying and become more relaxed, or to make someone do this: *She loosened up after she'd had a drink.* | **loosen sb ↔ up** *His welcoming smile helped loosen her up.*
2 if your muscles loosen up, or if something loosens them up, they stop feeling stiff: **loosen sth ↔ up** *A massage will loosen up your joints.*

loot¹ /luːt/ *v* [I,T] to steal things, especially from shops or homes that have been damaged in a war or RIOT: *Shops were looted and burned.* —**looter** *n* [C] —**looting** *n* [U]

loot² *n* [U] **1** goods taken by soldiers from a place where they have won a battle SYN **plunder 2** *informal* goods or money that have been stolen SYN **spoils 3** *informal* things that you have bought or been given in large amounts - used humorously: *Jodie came home from the mall with bags of loot.*

lop /lɒp $ lɑːp/ (*also* **lop off**) *v* (**lopped**, **lopping**) [T] **1** to cut something, especially branches from a tree, usually with a single strong movement SYN **chop**, **chop off**: *Workmen have lopped off more branches in an effort to save the tree.* **2** to reduce an amount, especially of money, by a particular amount: *They lopped £16 off the price.* | **lop sth from sth** *Citicorp plans to lop $1.5 billion a year from its operating costs.*

lope /ləʊp $ loʊp/ (*also* **lope off**) *v* [I always + adv/prep] to run easily with long steps: **[+along/across/up etc]** *He loped off down the corridor.* —**lope** *n* [singular]

lop·sid·ed /ˌlɒpˈsaɪdɪd $ ˌlɑːp-/ *adj* **1** having one side that is lower or heavier than the other: *a lopsided grin* **2** unequal or uneven, especially in an unfair way: *a lopsided 8-0 victory*

lo·qua·cious /ləʊˈkweɪʃəs $ loʊ-/ *adj formal* a loquacious person likes to talk a lot SYN **talkative** —**loquacity** /ləʊˈkwæsəti $ loʊ-/ —**loquaciousness** *n* [U]

lord¹ /lɔːd $ lɔːrd/ *n* **1** [C] (*also* **Lord**) a man who has a rank in the ARISTOCRACY, especially in Britain, or his title → **lady**: *Lord Salisbury* **2** [C] a man in MEDIEVAL Europe who was very powerful and owned a lot of land: *the feudal lords* **3 my lord** *BrE spoken* used to address a judge or BISHOP, and in the past to address a lord **4 sb's lord and master** someone who must be obeyed because they have power over you - used humorously

lord² *v* **lord it over sb** to behave in a way that shows you think you are better or more powerful than someone else: *He didn't use his position on the council to lord it over people.*

Lord *n* [singular] **1 a)** a title of God or Jesus Christ, used when praying: *Thank you, Lord, for your blessings.* **b) the Lord** God or Jesus Christ, used when talking about God: *The Lord helps and guides us.* **2 Lord (only) knows** *spoken* **a)** used when you do not know the answer to something: **Lord knows how/who/where etc** *Lord knows how old she is now.* **b)** used to emphasize that something is true: *Lord only knows I tried my best to get this right.* **3 (Good) Lord!/Oh Lord!** *spoken* said when you are suddenly surprised, annoyed, or worried about something SYN **heavens**: *Good Lord! Is that the time?* **4** the title of someone who has a particular type of official job in Britain: *Lord Mayor of London* **5 the Lords** *BrE* the House of Lords → **the Commons 6 Our Lord** a phrase meaning Jesus Christ

lord·ly /ˈlɔːdli $ -ɔːr-/ *adj* **1** behaving in a way that shows you think you are better or more important than other people: *a lordly disdain for the common man* **2** very big and impressive: *a lordly feast* —**lordliness** *n* [U]

Lord's /lɔːrz $ lɔːrdz/ the most famous CRICKET ground in the UK, in northwest London. Many important cricket games are played there, and it is the HEADQUARTERS of the MCC, the club which makes the rules for the game of cricket.

lord·ship /ˈlɔːdʃɪp $ -ɔːr-/ *n* [C] **1 your/his lordship** used when talking to or talking about a LORD, or when talking to a British judge or BISHOP(1) → **ladyship 2 his lordship** *BrE spoken* a man who thinks he is very important - used humorously: *So when will his lordship be back?*

ˌLord's ˈPrayer *n* **the Lord's Prayer** the most important prayer of the Christian religion

lore /lɔː $ lɔːr/ *n* [U] knowledge or information about a subject, for example nature or magic, that is not written down but is passed from person to person: *According to local lore, a ghost still haunts the castle.*

lor·ry /ˈlɒri $ ˈlɔːri, ˈlɑːri/ ●●● S3 *n* (*plural* **lorries**) [C] *BrE*
1 a large vehicle for carrying heavy goods SYN **truck** → see picture at TRUCK¹
2 it fell off the back of a lorry *spoken* used humorously to say that something was probably stolen

lose /luːz/ ●●● S1 W1 *v* (*past tense and past participle* **lost** /lɒst $ lɔːst/)
1 STOP HAVING ATTITUDE/QUALITY ETC [T] to stop having a particular attitude, quality, ability etc, or to gradually have less of it → **loss**: *I've lost my appetite.* | **lose confidence/interest/hope etc** *The business community has lost confidence in the government.* | *Carol lost interest in ballet in her teens.* | *Try not to* ***lose heart*** (=become sad and hopeless) - *there are plenty of other jobs.* | **lose face** (=stop having as much respect from other people) *A settlement was reached in which neither side lost face.* | **lose weight/height/speed etc** *You're looking slim. Have you lost weight?* | *The plane emptied its fuel tanks as it started losing altitude.* | **lose your sight/hearing/voice/balance etc** *Mr Eyer may lose the sight in one eye.* | *The tour was postponed when the lead singer lost his voice.* | *Julian lost his balance and fell.* | **lose your touch** (=become less skilled at doing something you used to do well) *This latest movie proves Altman is by no means losing his touch.* | *By the time the ambulance arrived, Douglas had* ***lost consciousness***. | **lose all sense of time/direction/proportion etc** *When he was writing, he lost all sense of time.* | **lose sight of sth** (=forget an important fact about a situation) *We must never* ***lose sight of the fact that*** *man must work in harmony with nature.*
2 NOT WIN [I,T] to not win a game, argument, election, war etc OPP **win** → **defeat**: *They played so badly they deserved to lose.* | *Klinger lost his seat in the election.* | *Arkansas just lost three games in a row.* | *He just can't bear to lose an argument.* | **[+to]** *The Beavers have dropped only one game since losing to Oregon in January.* | **lose (sth) by 1 goal/10 votes/20 points etc** *The government lost by one vote.* | *The Communist candidate* ***lost by a whisker*** (=a very small amount). | *Freddie died in 1982 after* ***losing*** *his* ***battle*** *against AIDS.* | **lose sb sth** *It was a rash decision, and it lost him the race* (=caused him to lose the race).
3 CANNOT FIND STH [T] to become unable to find someone or something: *I've lost the tickets for tonight's show.* | *I followed her on foot, but lost her in the crowd.* | *It was thought the manuscript had been* ***lost forever***. | **be/get lost in the post** *BrE*, **be/get lost in the mail** *AmE*: *The parcel must have got lost in the post.* | **lose track of sth/sb** (=stop knowing where someone or something is) *He lost track of her after her family moved away.* | **lose sight of sth/sb** (=stop being able to see someone or something) *Don't try to walk in a heavy snowstorm as you may lose sight of your vehicle.* → LOST PROPERTY
4 STOP HAVING STH [T] if you lose something that is important or necessary, you then no longer have it, especially because it has been taken from you or destroyed → **loss**: *David's very upset about* ***losing*** *his* ***job***. | *Hundreds of people* ***lost*** *their* ***homes*** *in the floods.* | *My family* ***lost everything*** *in the war.* | *He was over the limit and will* ***lose*** *his* ***licence***. | *Ninety naval aircraft were lost and thirty damaged.* | **lose a chance/opportunity** *If you hesitate, you may lose the opportunity to compete altogether.* | **lose sth to sb/sth** *We were losing customers to cheaper rivals.* | *She was about to lose her husband to a younger woman.* | *California has lost 90% of its wetlands to development.* | **lose an arm/leg/eye etc** *He lost his leg in a motorcycle accident.* | *He's* ***lost a lot of blood*** *but his life is not in danger.* | **lose sb sth** *the mistakes*

which lost him his kingdom (=caused him to lose his kingdom)

5 DEATH [T] **a) lose your life** to die: *a memorial to honor those who lost their lives in the war* **b)** if you lose a relative or friend, they die – use this when you want to avoid saying the word 'die' → **loss**: *One woman in Brooklyn lost a husband and two sons in the gang wars.* | *Sadly, Anna* ***lost the baby*** (=her baby died before it was born). | **lose sb to cancer/AIDS etc** *He lost his father to cancer* (=his father died of cancer) *last year.* | *Peter was* ***lost at sea*** *when his ship sank.*

6 MONEY [I,T] if you lose money, you then have less money than you had before → **loss**: **[+on]** *The company is in debt after losing an estimated $30 million on its dotcom enterprise.* | *Creditors and investors* ***stand to lose*** (=risk losing) *vast sums after the company's collapse.* | *A lot of people* ***lost*** *their* ***shirts*** (=lost a lot of money) *on Ferraris in the eighties.* | *It's a great deal – we can't lose!* | **lose sb sth** *The stock market crash lost the banks £70 million* (=caused them to lose £70 million).

7 have nothing to lose *spoken* if you have nothing to lose, it is worth taking a risk because you cannot make your situation any worse: *You might as well apply for the job – you've got nothing to lose.* | **have nothing to lose but your pride/reputation etc** *The working class has nothing to lose but its chains* (=disadvantages, restrictions etc). | **have a lot/too much to lose** (=used to say that you could make your situation much worse) *These youngsters know they have too much to lose by protesting against the system.*

8 TIME [T] **a)** if you lose time, you do not make progress as quickly as you want to or should: **lose time/2 days/3 hours etc** *Vital minutes were lost because the ambulance took half an hour to arrive.* | *In 1978, 29 million days were lost in industrial action.* | *Come on,* ***there's no time to lose*** (=do not waste time). | **lose no time in doing sth** (=do something immediately) *Murdock lost no time in taking out a patent for his invention.* **b)** if a watch, clock etc loses time, it runs too slowly and shows an earlier time than it should OPP **gain**

9 lose your way/bearings a) to stop knowing where you are or which direction you should go in: *I lost my way in the network of tiny alleys.* **b)** to become uncertain about your beliefs or what you should do: *The company seems to have lost its way of late.*

10 lose touch (with sb/sth) a) if two people lose touch, they gradually stop communicating, for example by no longer phoning or writing to each other: *I've lost touch with all my old school friends.* | *They lost touch when Di got married and moved away.* **b)** if you lose touch with a situation or group, you are then no longer involved in it and so do not know about it or understand it: *They claim the prime minister has lost touch with the party.* | *It sometimes appears that the planners have lost touch with reality.*

11 lose your temper/cool/rag to become angry: **[+with]** *Diana was determined not to lose her temper with him.*

12 lose your head to become unable to behave calmly or sensibly: *You've all heard that Nadal lost his head over a girl?*

13 lose your mind to become crazy SYN **go crazy, go mad**: *Nicholas looked at her as if she'd lost her mind.*

14 lose it *spoken informal* **a)** to become very angry and upset: *She completely lost it with one of the kids in class.* **b)** (*also* **lose the plot**) to become crazy or confused: *I could see people thinking I'd totally lost the plot.*

15 lose yourself in sth to be paying so much attention to something that you do not notice anything else: *She listened intently to the music, losing herself in its beauty.*

16 ESCAPE [T] if you lose someone who is chasing you, you manage to escape from them: *There's a better chance of losing him if we take the back route.*

17 CONFUSE SB [T] *spoken informal* to confuse someone when you are trying to explain something to them: *Explain it again – you've lost me already.*

18 REMOVE STH [T] to remove a part or feature of something that is not necessary or wanted: *You could lose the last paragraph to make it fit on one page.*

19 lose something in the translation/telling to be less good than the original form: *The joke loses something in the translation.* → LOST², → **lose count** at COUNT²(3), → **lose sleep over sth** at SLEEP²(4)

lose out *phr v* to not get something good, valuable etc because someone else gets it instead: *The deal will ensure that shareholders do not lose out financially.* | **[+to]** *He lost out to Roy Scheider for the lead role.* | **[+on]** *Workers who don't take up training may lose out on promotion.*

los·er /ˈluːzə $ -ər/ ●●○ *n* [C]

1 someone who is in a worse situation than they were, because of something that has happened OPP **winner**: *If the strike continues, the people of Galway will be the real losers.*

2 someone who is never successful in life, work, or relationships: *What a loser!* | *The guy's a* ***born loser***.

3 someone who has lost a competition, game, election etc OPP **winner**: **good/bad loser** (=someone who behaves well or badly after losing)

loss /lɒs $ lɔːs/ ●●● S2 W1 *n*

1 [C,U] the fact of no longer having something, or of having less of it than you used to have, or the process by which this happens: **[+of]** *The court awarded Ms Dixon £7,000 for damages and* ***loss of earnings***. | *a disease which causes fever and a* ***loss of appetite*** | *This did not explain his apparent* ***loss of interest*** *in his wife.* | *her* ***loss of confidence*** *in herself* | *a certain feeling of* ***loss of control*** | *a temporary* ***loss of memory*** | *The animal was weak through* ***loss of blood***. | *The company is closing down two of its factories, leading to 430* ***job losses***. | ***Weight loss*** *should be gradual.* | *a type of* ***hearing loss*** *that affects language development*

2 [C,U] if a business makes a loss, it spends more than it earns: *The company* ***made a loss*** *of $250,000 last year.* | *The magazine's losses totaled almost $5 million.* | *profit and loss* | **run/operate etc at a loss** (=to earn less money from something you sell than it costs you to produce it) *Two of the mines are running at a loss.* | *a loss-making rural railway*

3 [C,U] the death of someone: **[+of]** *She must be feeling very lonely after the loss of her husband.* | *I'm sorry to hear of your family's* ***sad loss*** (=the death of someone you love). | *US forces withdrew after suffering* ***heavy losses*** (=many deaths). | *The war has led to a tragic* ***loss of life***.

4 be at a loss to be confused and uncertain about what to do or say: *When her son finally left home, Emily felt completely at a loss.* | **be at a loss to do sth** *Detectives are so far at a loss to explain the reason for his death.* | *He seemed, for once,* ***at a loss for words*** (=unable to think what to say).

5 [U] a feeling of being sad or lonely because someone or something is not there anymore: *the deep* ***sense of loss*** *I felt after my divorce*

6 [singular] a disadvantage caused by someone or something leaving or being removed: **[+to]** *We see your going as a* ***great loss*** *to the company.*

7 that's/it's sb's loss *spoken* said when you think someone is being stupid for not taking a good opportunity: *Well, if he doesn't want to come, it's his loss.* → **cut your losses** at CUT¹(29), → **a dead loss** at DEAD¹(10)

ˈloss adˌjuster *n* [C] *BrE* someone who is employed by an insurance company to decide how much should be paid to people who make a CLAIM SYN **insurance adjuster** *AmE*

ˈloss ˌleader *n* [C] a product that is sold at a very low price in order to attract customers into a shop

ˈloss-ˌmaking *adj* [only before noun] *especially BrE* a loss-making product or business does not make any money OPP **profit-making**, **profitable**: *The company has sold many of its loss-making businesses to cut debts.*

loss·y /ˈlɒsi $ ˈlɔːsi/ *n* [U] **lossy compression** a way of making a computer file smaller, but which involves losing some of the information in it

lost¹ /lɒst $ lɔːst/ the past tense and past participle of LOSE

lost² ●●● S2 W3 *adj*

1 CANNOT FIND YOUR WAY if you are lost, you do not know where you are and are unable to find your way somewhere: *'Are you lost?' the driver asked.* | *I* ***got*** *thoroughly* ***lost*** *on the way here.* | *a lost child*

L

2 CANNOT BE FOUND if something is lost, you had it but cannot now find it SYN **missing**: *two boys searching for a lost ball*
3 WASTED **a)** lost time or opportunities have not been used in the way that would have given you the greatest advantage: *It'll be impossible to make up the lost time.* **b) lost sales/business/earnings etc** sales, business etc that you could have had but did not: *The strike has cost the company £2 million in lost revenue.*
4 feel/be lost to not feel confident about what to do or how to behave: *It's not unusual to feel rather lost when you first start college. | She's a great friend and I'd* ***be lost without*** *her.*
5 Get lost! *spoken* used to rudely tell someone to go away or to stop annoying you
6 NOT NOTICING [not before noun] thinking so hard about something, or being so interested in something, that you do not notice what is happening around you: **[+in]** *Harry just stood there,* ***lost in thought****. | Amy lay on her bed, totally lost in her book.*
7 get lost (in sth) to be forgotten or not noticed in a complicated process or in a busy time: *It's easy for your main points to get lost in a long speech.*
8 NOT UNDERSTAND **be lost** to be completely confused by a complicated explanation: *'Do you understand what I mean?' 'Not really. I'm a bit lost.'*
9 be lost on sb if something is lost on someone, they do not understand or want to accept it: *The joke was completely lost on Chris.*
10 be lost for words to be unable to say anything because you are very surprised, upset etc: *For once in her life, she was lost for words.*
11 NOT EXISTING [only before noun] that no longer exists or that you no longer have: *the relics of a lost civilization | She wept for her broken dreams and lost youth.*
12 lost cause something that has no chance of succeeding: *Trying to interest my son in classical music is a lost cause.*
13 lost soul someone who does not seem to know where they are or what to do - often used humorously
14 all is not lost used to say that success is still possible, even though there have been problems or failures → **give sb up for dead/lost etc** at GIVE UP, LONG-LOST, → **make up for lost time** at MAKE UP FOR, → **there is no love lost between sb and sb** at LOVE²(10)

ˌlost-and-ˈfound *n* **the lost-and-found** *AmE* a place where things that are lost are kept until someone comes to claim them SYN **lost property** *BrE*

ˌlost ˈproperty *n* [U] *BrE* **1** things that people have lost or accidentally left in a public place, which are kept until someone collects them **2** (*also* **Lost Property**) a place where these things are kept until someone comes to claim them SYN **lost-and-found** *AmE*: *Thankfully, someone had handed my bag into Lost Property.*

lot¹ /lɒt $ lɑːt/ ●●● S1 W1 *pron, adv*
1 a lot (*also* **lots** *informal*) a large amount or number: *We've spent a lot on the children's education. | 'How many CDs have you got?' 'Lots.'* | **[+of]** *They paid a lot of money for that house. | I eat a lot of vegetables. | There were lots of people at the party.* | **an awful lot** (*also* **a whole lot** *informal*) (=a very large amount or number) *He spends an awful lot of time on the computer.* | **a lot to do/learn/say etc** *I still have a lot to learn. | It's a great city, with lots to see and do.*

GRAMMAR: Comparison

a lot of
• **A lot of** is fairly informal and is mainly used in spoken English or informal written English.
• You can use **a lot of** with a plural noun and a plural verb: *A lot of people* ***were*** *hurt.*
• You can use **a lot of** with an uncountable noun and a singular verb: *A lot of money* ***was*** *spent on it.*

lots of
• **Lots of** is more informal than **a lot of**, but is used in exactly the same way.
• You say: *Lots of people* ***were*** *hurt. | Lots of money* ***was*** *spent on it.*

many, a large amount of
• In written English, you usually use **many** or **a large amount of**.
• You use **many** with a plural noun and a plural verb: *Many people were hurt.*
• You use **a large amount of** with an uncountable noun and a singular verb: *A large amount of money was spent on it.*
• When talking about years, days, weeks etc, you usually use **many** instead of **a lot of**: *The book took many years to write.* ✗ Don't say: *The book took a lot of years to write.*

2 a lot (*also* **lots** *informal*) if someone or something is a lot better, faster, easier etc, they are much better, faster etc SYN **much**: *My headache is lots better, thanks. | She has a lot more contact with clients these days. | You'll get there a lot quicker if you take the motorway. | The house is a lot tidier now Chris has left home.*
3 a lot used to say that something happens to a great degree or often: *Things have changed a lot since I was a child. | Paul travels a lot on business. | I've been worrying a lot about my health. | She likes you a lot.*
4 have a lot on your plate *informal* to have a large number of problems to deal with or a large amount of work to do
5 have a lot on your mind to have a lot of problems that you are worried about: *'You're quiet today.' 'I've got a lot on my mind.'*
6 have a lot on *BrE* to be very busy, with a large number of things to do in a short time: *I can't help you now - I've got rather a lot on.* → **thanks a lot** at THANKS¹(1), → **a fat lot of good/use** at FAT¹(5), → **have a lot to answer for** at ANSWER FOR

lot² ●●● S2 *n*
1 GROUP OF PEOPLE/THINGS [C] a group of people or things considered together: *Could you help me carry this lot upstairs?* | **[+of]** *The last lot of people offered £70,000. | I did three lots of exams last summer. | Come on, you lot, hurry up! | His friends are a strange lot.*
2 the lot *especially BrE* the whole of an amount or number of things, people etc: *We'll do everything - cooking, washing, ironing - the lot. | I can't believe you ate* ***the whole lot****. | I think that's the lot* (=everything is included). | **the lot of you/them/us** (=all of you, them, or us) *Shut up, the lot of you!*
3 SB'S SITUATION [singular] your lot is your work, duties, social position etc, especially when they could be better: *She seems happy enough with her lot. | The unions have always tried to improve the lot of their members.*
4 LAND [C] *especially AmE* an area of land used for building on or for another purpose: *the* ***vacant lot*** (=empty land) *behind the Commercial Hotel | a used-car lot* → PARKING LOT
5 FILM [C] a building and the land surrounding it where films are made SYN **studio**: *the Universal Studios lot*
6 THING TO BE SOLD [C] something, or a group of things, that is sold at an AUCTION: *Lot 54 is a Victorian lamp.*
7 CHOOSING **a) by lot** if someone is chosen by lot, several people each take a piece of paper or an object from a container, and the person who is chosen is the one who gets a particular marked paper or object: *In Athens at that time, judges were* ***chosen by lot****.* **b) draw/cast lots** to choose something or someone by lot: *We drew lots to decide who should go first.*
8 throw in/cast your lot with sb/sth to join or support someone or something, and accept that what happens to them will affect what happens to you: *In 1915 Italy threw in her lot with the Allies.* → **bad lot** at BAD¹(21), → **a job lot** at JOB(18)

loth /ləʊθ $ loʊθ/ *adj* [not before noun] another spelling of LOATH

Lo·tha·ri·o /ləˈθɑːriəʊ $ ləʊˈθeəə-/ *n* [C] a man whose main interest is in having sex with as many women as possible without having a serious relationship with any of them. Lothario is a character in Nicholas Rowe's play *The Fair Penitent* (1703) who persuades a woman to have sex with him, but is later disloyal to her: *the office Lothario*

L

lo·tion /ˈləʊʃən $ ˈloʊ-/ *n* [C,U] a liquid mixture that you put on your skin or hair to clean, SOFTEN, or protect it: *suntan lotion*

lot·sa /ˈlɒtsə $ ˈlɑːt-/ a way of writing 'lots of' to show how it sounds when it is spoken

lot·te·ry /ˈlɒtəri $ ˈlɑː-/ ●○○ *n* (*plural* **lotteries**)
1 [C] a game used to make money for a state or a CHARITY in which people buy tickets with a series of numbers on them. If their number is picked by chance, they win money or a prize → **raffle, draw**: *a lottery ticket | Do you really think* ***winning the lottery*** *would make you happy?* | **national/state lottery**
2 [C,U] *AmE* a system of deciding who will get something by choosing people's names by chance: **by lottery** *The State Department issues 55,000 visas each year by lottery.*
3 a lottery a situation in which what happens depends on chance and is not certain to be successful: *That's the trouble with capitalism. It's a lottery.*

lot·to /ˈlɒtəʊ $ ˈlɑːtoʊ/ *n* [C] a game used to make money, in which people buy tickets with a series of numbers on them. If their number is picked by chance, they win money or a prize.

lo·tus /ˈləʊtəs $ ˈloʊ-/ *n* [C] **1** a white or pink flower that grows on the surface of lakes in Asia and Africa, or the shape of this flower used in decorations **2** a fruit that gives you a pleasant dreamy feeling after you eat it, according to ancient Greek stories

ˈlotus poˌsition *n* [singular] a way of sitting, used especially in YOGA, in which you sit with your legs crossed and with each foot resting on the top of the opposite leg: *monks sitting in the lotus position*

loud¹ /laʊd/ ●●● S2 W3 *adj* (*comparative* **louder**, *superlative* **loudest**)
1 making a lot of noise OPP **quiet**: *The book fell to the floor with a loud bang. | The music was so loud that I had to shout. | 'Who's there?' asked David in a loud voice.*
2 someone who is loud talks too loudly and confidently: *The more Tom drank, the louder he became.*
3 loud clothes are too bright or have too many bright patterns SYN **garish, gaudy**: *a loud checked suit*
4 be loud in your praise/opposition/support etc to express your approval or disapproval very strongly: *The local business community was loud in its support for the scheme.*
—**loudly** *adv*: *Ben laughed loudly. | She spoke more loudly than she intended.* —**loudness** *n* [U]

THESAURUS

loud making a lot of noise – used about sounds, voices, or music: *a loud explosion | He was talking in a very loud voice. | The music was too loud.*
noisy making a lot of noise – used about people, machines, and places that are too loud: *The traffic was so noisy. | noisy neighbours | a noisy bar*
rowdy rowdy people behave in a noisy and uncontrolled way. A rowdy place such as a bar is full of noisy people, often behaving badly: *rowdy football fans | a rowdy bar*
raucous /ˈrɔːkəs $ ˈrɒː-/ *especially written* unpleasantly loud – used about the excited sound of groups of people: *raucous laughter | raucous crowds*
resounding [only before noun] used to describe a loud noise when something hits another thing, that seems to continue for a few seconds. Also used about people cheering or shouting loudly: *The door hit the wall with a resounding crash. | a resounding cheer*

VERY LOUD

thunderous extremely loud and deep in sound: *His remarks received* ***thunderous applause*** *from the audience.*
deafening /ˈdefənɪŋ/ so loud that you cannot hear anything else: *The noise was deafening – like a thousand fireworks going off at one time.*
ear-splitting so loud that your ears feel uncomfortable: *He played the music at ear-splitting volume.*
piercing extremely loud, high, and unpleasant to hear: *a piercing scream*

COLLOCATIONS CHECK

loud sound/voice/music
noisy person/place/machine/traffic
rowdy crowd/fans/bar
raucous laughter/crowd/atmosphere
resounding thud/crash/cheer/applause
thunderous applause
deafening sound/noise
piercing voice/scream/whistle/sound

loud² ●●● S3 *adv* (*comparative* **louder**, *superlative* **loudest**)
1 spoken in a way that makes a lot of noise SYN **loudly**: *Could you speak a little louder? | You've got the telly on too loud.*
2 loud and clear in a way that is very easy to understand: *The message came through loud and clear.*
3 out loud in such a way that people can hear you SYN **aloud**: *Read it out loud, so we can all hear. | Harriet laughed out loud in astonishment.* → **actions speak louder than words** at ACTION¹(13), → **for crying out loud** at CRY¹(4)

loud·hail·er /ˌlaʊdˈheɪlə $ -ər/ *n* [C] *BrE* a piece of equipment with a MICROPHONE, that you can hold in your hand and speak through to make your voice louder SYN **megaphone, bullhorn** *AmE*

loud·mouth /ˈlaʊdmaʊθ/ *n* [C] someone who talks too much and says offensive or stupid things —**loudmouthed** /ˈlaʊdmaʊθt/ *adj*: *loudmouthed sports fans*

loud·speak·er /ˌlaʊdˈspiːkə, ˈlaʊdˌspiːkə $ -ər/ *n* [C]
1 a piece of equipment used to make sounds louder: **from/over/through a loudspeaker** *The voice over the loudspeaker* (=using the loudspeaker) *said the flight was delayed.* **2** a SPEAKER(3)

lough /lɒx, lɒk $ lɑːk, lɑːx/ *n* [C] in Ireland, a lake or a part of the sea almost surrounded by land: *Lough Neagh*

lounge¹ /laʊndʒ/ ●●○ S3 *n* [C]
1 a WAITING ROOM at an airport: *the* ***departure lounge***
2 a public room in a hotel or other building, that is used by many people as a place to relax: *the television lounge*
3 *BrE* the main room in a house where people relax, watch television etc SYN **living room**
4 *BrE* a lounge bar
5 *AmE* a COCKTAIL BAR → **COCKTAIL LOUNGE, SUN LOUNGE**

lounge² ●○○ *v* [I]
1 [always + adv/prep] to stand, sit, or lie in a lazy or relaxed way: *Nathan was lounging on the grass bank outside the cottage.* THESAURUS▸ SIT
2 lounge around (*also* **lounge about** *BrE*) to spend time relaxing and doing nothing, often when you should be doing something SYN **laze around**: *James does nothing but lounge around the apartment.*

ˈlounge bar *n* [C] *BrE* a comfortable bar in a PUB or hotel SYN **saloon bar** → **public bar**

loung·er /ˈlaʊndʒə $ -ər/ *n* [C] *BrE* a SUN LOUNGER

ˈlounge suit *n* [C] *BrE old-fashioned* a suit that a man wears during the day, especially to work in an office

lounge·wear /ˈlaʊndʒweə $ -wer/ *n* [U] comfortable clothes that people wear when relaxing at home

louse¹ /laʊs/ *n* [C] **1** (*plural* **lice** /laɪs/) a small insect that lives on the hair or skin of people or animals
2 (*plural* **louses**) *informal* someone who is nasty and unpleasant

louse² *v*

louse sth ↔ **up** *phr v informal* to make something worse rather than better, or to spoil something SYN **mess up**: *That idiot loused up my chance of promotion.*

lou·sy /ˈlaʊzi/ *adj* (*comparative* **lousier**, *superlative* **lousiest**) **1** *especially spoken* of very bad quality SYN **awful, terrible**: *What lousy weather! | The food was lousy. | a lousy film* THESAURUS▸ BAD **2 feel lousy** *spoken* if you feel lousy, you feel ill **3** *spoken* not very good at doing something SYN **hopeless, terrible**: **[+at/with]** *I'm lousy at tennis. | Brenda's lousy with kids. | a lousy teacher* **4** *spoken* small,

L

useless, or unimportant: *He left me a lousy fifty cent tip.* **5 be lousy with sth** *AmE old-fashioned* **a)** a place that is lousy with people of a particular kind is too full of them: *The town was lousy with tourists.* **b)** someone who is lousy with money has a lot more of it than they need

lout /laʊt/ *n* [C] a rude violent man SYN **yob** —**loutish** *adj*: *loutish behaviour* —**loutishly** *adv* —**loutishness** *n* [U] → LAGER LOUT

lou·vre *BrE*, **louver** *AmE* /ˈluːvə $ -ər/ *n* [C] **1** a narrow piece of wood, glass etc in a door or window, that slopes towards the outside to let some light in and keep rain or strong sun out **2 louvre window/door** *BrE* a door or window made of these pieces of wood, glass etc —**louvred** *adj*: *louvred shutters*

lov·a·ble, **loveable** /ˈlʌvəbəl/ *adj* friendly and attractive: *a sweet lovable child*

love[1] /lʌv/ ●●● S1 W1 *v*

1 ROMANTIC ATTRACTION [T not in progressive] to have a strong feeling of AFFECTION for someone, combined with sexual attraction: *I love you, Tracy.* | *He was the only man she had ever loved.*

2 CARE ABOUT [T not in progressive] to care very much about someone, especially a member of your family or a close friend: *I love my grandad so much.* | *I've always loved children.* | **much-loved/well-loved** *In 1941, her much-loved sister was killed in an accident.* | *Many people feel guilty after the death of a* ***loved one****.*

3 LIKE/ENJOY [T] to like something very much or enjoy doing something very much: *I love carrots.* | *Jeff loves his work.* | *I love the way she sings that song.* | *Amy had always loved New York.* | **love doing sth** *I love going out to restaurants.* | **love to do sth** *We all love to talk about ourselves.* | **I'd love to (do sth)** *spoken* (=used to say that you would really like to do something) *'Would you like to come swimming with us?' 'I'd love to.'* | *I'd have loved to have stayed till the end.* | *I'd love to know just why they did that.* THESAURUS ▸ LIKE

4 LOYALTY [T not in progressive] to have a strong feeling of loyalty to your country, an institution etc: *Dad's always loved the navy.*

5 I love it! *spoken* used when you are amused by something, especially by someone else's mistake or bad luck: *'And then her boyfriend walked in and saw her kissing Ray.' 'I love it!'*

6 sb's going to love sth *spoken* **a)** used to say that someone will enjoy something: *Listen guys, you're going to love this.* **b)** used to say that someone will not be pleased about something: *I'm going to love telling him we've changed our minds again.* → LOVER

GRAMMAR

Patterns with love

- You **love** someone or something: *I love my children.* | *She loves jazz.*
- You **love doing** something: *She loves listening to jazz.*
- You **love to do** something: *She loves to listen to jazz in her spare time.* ✗ Don't say: *She loves listen to jazz.*
- **Love doing** something and **love to do** something both mean the same thing. You use **love to do** especially when saying that someone does something regularly or often.

Using the progressive

- The usual rule is that **love** is not used in the progressive. ✗ Don't say: *I am loving my children.* | *She is loving jazz.*
- In spoken English, people sometimes say **I'm loving** something they have just seen or heard: *I'm loving his new show* (=I like it a lot).

GRAMMAR GUIDE ▸ VERBS

THESAURUS

love to like someone very much and care a lot about them - used especially about people in your family or someone who you are sexually attracted to: *I love my wife and children very much.* | *Have you ever said 'I love you' and not really meant it?*

adore to love and admire someone very much: *When she was a child she adored her father.*

be in love (with sb) to feel that you love someone and want to have a romantic relationship with them: *We were both young and very much in love.* | *Karen was in love with a man who was much older than her.*

be infatuated with sb to love someone a lot and keep thinking about them, in a way that seems silly because you do not know them very well: *He became infatuated with a woman he met at a conference.*

have a crush on sb to love and be sexually attracted to someone you are not having a relationship with, usually someone older: *Jane had a crush on the German teacher.*

be crazy about sb *informal* to love someone very much - used for emphasis: *She's crazy about you.*

be devoted to sb to love someone very much and give them a lot of attention: *He was devoted to his wife and his children.*

dote on sb *written* to love someone very much, especially a much younger family member, and behave very kindly to them: *He dotes on his grandchildren.*

love[2] ●●● S1 W1 *n*

1 FOR FAMILY/FRIENDS [U] a strong feeling of caring about someone, especially a member of your family or a close friend OPP **hate, hatred**: *What these kids need is love and support.* | **[+for]** *a mother's love for her child*

2 ROMANTIC [U] a strong feeling of liking someone a lot combined with sexual attraction: **[+for]** *Their love for each other grew deeper every day.* | *Tara is madly in love with you.*

3 PERSON YOU LOVE [C] someone that you feel a strong romantic and sexual attraction to: *He was her* ***first love****.* | **the love of your life** (=the person that you feel or felt the most love for)

4 PLEASURE/ENJOYMENT **a)** [singular, U] a strong feeling of pleasure and enjoyment that something gives you: **[+of/for]** *my love of nature* | *He* ***had a*** *great* ***love*** *of music.* | *I* ***fell in love with*** *Amsterdam the very first time I visited the city.* **b)** [C] something that gives you a lot of pleasure and enjoyment: *Sailing was her great love.*

5 make love (to/with sb) a) to have sex with someone that you love **b)** *old use* to say LOVING things to someone, to kiss them etc

6 send/give your love (to sb), send/give sb your love to ask someone to give your LOVING greetings to someone else when they see them, write to them etc: *Aunt Mary sends her love.*

7 love (from sb)/lots of love/all my love *written* used at the end of a letter to a friend, a member of your family, or someone you love: *See you soon. Lots of love, Clare.*

8 (my) love *BrE spoken informal* **a)** a word used when you are talking to someone you love SYN **darling**: *'Hello, love,' said her father.* **b)** a friendly way of talking to someone who you do not know, especially to a woman or child. Many women consider this to be impolite or offensive: *What's your name, love?*

9 be a love and .../... there's a love *BrE spoken* used when you are asking someone, especially children and members of your family, to do something: *Give these to your sisters, there's a love.*

10 there is no love lost between sb and sb if there is no love lost between two people, they dislike each other

11 TENNIS [U] an expression meaning 'no points', used in the game of tennis

12 not for love or/nor money *informal* if you cannot get something or do something for love or money, it is impossible to obtain or to do: *I can't get hold of that book for love nor money.*

13 love triangle a situation in which someone is having a sexual relationship with the partner of a close friend - used especially in newspapers

L

14 for the love of God (*also* **for the love of Mike/Pete**) *old-fashioned spoken* used to show that you are extremely angry, disappointed etc → **a labour of love** at LABOUR[1](4)

COLLOCATIONS - MEANING 2

VERBS

be in love *Are you in love with her?*
fall in love (=start being in love) *I fell in love with her the minute I saw her.*
find love (=meet someone to love) *I never thought I would find love.*
return sb's love (=love someone who loves you)

PHRASES

love at first sight (=when you love someone as soon as you meet them) *For Marion and Ron it was love at first sight.*
very much in love *They were obviously very much in love.*
madly/deeply in love (=very much in love) *I married Dan because I was madly in love.*
head over heels in love (=very much in love)

ADJECTIVES

true love (=real love) *She felt that she had finally found true love.*
romantic love *Romantic love was not always the reason for marriage.*
sexual love | **unrequited love** (=love for someone who does not love you) | **undying love** (=love that does not stop)

love + NOUN

a love song/story *a tragic love story*
a love letter

ˈlove afˌfair *n* [C] **1** a romantic sexual relationship, usually between two people who are not married to each other → AFFAIR(3) **2** a strong enjoyment of something: **[+with]** *America's love affair with the automobile*

love·bird /ˈlʌvbɜːd $ -bɜːrd/ *n* [C] **1 lovebirds** [plural] two people who show by their behaviour that they love each other very much – used humorously **2** a small brightly coloured PARROT

ˈlove bite *n* [C] *BrE* a red mark on someone's skin caused by someone else sucking it as a sexual act SYN **hickey** *AmE*

ˈlove child *n* [C] a child whose parents are not married – used especially in newspapers

ˌloved-ˈup *adj informal* **1** feeling full of romantic love for someone **2** feeling full of love towards everyone, especially as a result of using the illegal drug ECSTASY: *loved-up clubbers having a ball*

ˌlove-ˈhate reˌlationship *n* [C usually singular] if you have a love-hate relationship with someone or something, sometimes you really like or love them, and sometimes you really dislike or hate them: **[+with]** *her love-hate relationship with professional golf*

ˈlove-in *n* [C] *informal* an occasion when people say or show that they like or admire each other a lot; used to show disapproval: *The interview turned out to be a love-in, with the interviewer and the star heaping compliments on each other.*

ˈlove ˌinterest *n* [C] the character in a movie, book, or play that the main character loves

love·less /ˈlʌvləs/ *adj* without love: **loveless marriage/childhood/relationship etc**

ˈlove letter *n* [C] a letter that someone writes to tell someone else how much they love them

ˈlove life *n* [C,U] the part of your life that involves your romantic and sexual relationships

love·lorn /ˈlʌvlɔːn $ -lɔːrn/ *adj literary* sad because the person you love does not love you SYN **lovesick**

love·ly /ˈlʌvli/ ●●● S1 W3 *adj* (*comparative* **lovelier**, *superlative* **loveliest**)
1 *especially BrE* beautiful or attractive: *She had a lovely face.* | *What a lovely house!* | *You* **look lovely** *in that dress.* | *He was a* **lovely little** *boy.* | *What a lovely day!* THESAURUS BEAUTIFUL
2 *spoken especially BrE* very pleasant, enjoyable, or good: *Thank you for a lovely evening.* | *That was a lovely cup of tea.* THESAURUS NICE
3 *informal especially BrE* friendly and pleasant: *Richard's a lovely person.*
4 *BrE spoken* used to say that something is not at all enjoyable or good: *'The cat threw up all over the carpet!' 'Lovely!'* | *You've made a lovely mess in here.*
5 lovely and warm/fresh/clean etc *BrE spoken* used to emphasize how good something is: *This bread's lovely and fresh.*
6 *BrE spoken* used to show that you are pleased with something: *Push it right across. That's it, lovely.*
—**loveliness** *n* [U]

GRAMMAR: Order of adjectives

If there is more than one adjective, the adjectives are usually used in a fixed order.
You say: *We had lovely warm weather.* ✗ Don't say: *We had warm lovely weather.*
You say: *That's a lovely red dress.* ✗ Don't say: *That's a red lovely dress.*
GRAMMAR GUIDE ADJECTIVES

love·mak·ing /ˈlʌvˌmeɪkɪŋ/ *n* [U] sexual activity, especially the act of having sex

ˈlove nest *n* [C usually singular] a place where two people who are having a romantic relationship live or meet each other – used humorously

lov·er /ˈlʌvə $ -ər/ ●●○ W3 *n* [C]
1 someone's lover is the person they are having a sexual relationship with but who they are not married to → **mistress**: *He killed his wife's lover.* | *Nicola and I were lovers.* | *a pair of* ***young lovers***
2 someone who likes something very much: ***music lovers*** | ***animal lovers*** | **[+of]** *lovers of the outdoors*

ˈlove rat *n* [C] *BrE informal* a man who has a wife or girlfriend but has sex with someone else – used in newspapers

ˈlove seat *n* [C] **1** *AmE* a small SOFA for two people **2** a seat in the shape of an S for two people, designed so that they can face each other

love·sick /ˈlʌvˌsɪk/ *adj* spending all your time thinking about someone you love, especially someone who does not love you: *a lovesick teenager*

lov·ey /ˈlʌvi/ *n* [C] *BrE spoken informal* a word used to address a woman or child, that many women think is offensive → LUVVIE

lovey-dov·ey /ˌlʌvi ˈdʌvi◂/ *adj informal* behaviour that is lovey-dovey is too romantic: *a lovey-dovey phone call*

lov·ing /ˈlʌvɪŋ/ ●●○ *adj*
1 [only before noun] behaving in a way that shows you love someone: **loving wife/family/parents etc** *the confidence he had gained from having a warm and loving family* | *What that child needs is plenty of* ***loving care***. | *He's* ***very loving*** *and affectionate with his sister.*
2 peace-loving/fun-loving/home-loving etc thinking that peace, having fun etc is very important: *a peace-loving nation*
3 done with a lot of care and attention: *the* ***loving care*** *with which the house has been restored* —**lovingly** *adv*: *She smiled at him lovingly.* | *the plane he had lovingly built*

low¹ /ləʊ $ loʊ/ ●●● S1 W1 *adj* (*comparative* **lower**, *superlative* **lowest**)
1 SMALL AMOUNT/LEVEL/VALUE **a)** small, or smaller than usual, in amount, level, or value OPP **high**: **low income/pay/wages** *families existing on very low incomes* | *In May, the price of cocoa fell to its lowest level since 1975–76.* | *Morale has been low since the latest round of job cuts.* | *In this sort of investment, the risks are fairly low.* | *low temperatures* | *the need for low-cost housing* | *a low-security prison* **b) low in sth** having less than the usual amount of a substance or chemical OPP **high**: *food that is low in*

calories | **low-fat/low-salt etc** *low-alcohol beer* **c) in the low 20s/30s etc** if a number, temperature, or level is in the low 20s, 30s etc, it is between 21 and 23, 31 and 33 etc: *Tonight, temperatures in most areas will be in the low 50s.* **THESAURUS** ▸ CHEAP, SMALL

2 HEIGHT a) having a top that is not far above the ground OPP **high**: *a low wall | a long low building* **b)** at a point that is not far above the ground or near the bottom of something OPP **high**: *low clouds | The sun was low in the sky now. | Store raw meat on the lowest shelf.* **c)** below the usual height OPP **high**: *a low bridge | a low ceiling | The river is very low today.*

3 STANDARDS/QUALITY bad, or below an acceptable or usual level or quality SYN **poor** OPP **high**: *Their safety standards seem to be pretty low. | Cost-cutting has led to a lower quality of service. | the children's low achievement in school*

4 SUPPLY if you are low on something, or if your supply of something is low, there is not much of it left: **be/get/run low (on sth)** *We're running low on gas. | Stocks are getting low.*

5 VOICE/SOUND a) not loud: *I heard a low moaning noise. | The volume is too low – turn it up. | a low whisper* **b)** not high: *a low note* **THESAURUS** ▸ QUIET

6 LIGHT a light that is low is not bright SYN **dim**: *Use low lighting to give the room a romantic atmosphere.*

7 HEAT if you cook something over a low heat or in a low OVEN, you cook it using only a small amount of heat OPP **high**

8 BATTERY a BATTERY that is low does not have much power left in it

9 CLOTHES a low dress, BLOUSE etc does not cover your neck and the top of your chest → **low-cut**

10 UNHAPPY [not before noun] unhappy and without much hope for the future SYN **depressed**: *He was feeling a bit low, so I did my best to cheer him up. | Terry seems to be* ***in rather low spirits*** *today.* —**lowness** *n* [U] → **be at a low ebb** at EBB[1](2)

low² ●●● W1 *adv* (*comparative* **lower**, *superlative* **lowest**)

1 in or to a low position or level: *He bent low over the engine. | She pulled her hat* ***low down*** *over her eyes. | I had the radio on low.*

2 near the ground or the bottom of something: *That plane's flying too low! | There was a hole* ***low down*** *in the hedge.*

3 if you play or sing musical notes low, you play or sing them with deep notes: *Sing those bars an octave lower.*

4 be brought low *old-fashioned* to become much less rich or important → **search/look high and low** at HIGH[2](6), → **lay sb low** at LAY[2](20), → **lie low** at LIE[1](7)

low³ ●○○ *n* [C]

1 a low price, level, or value OPP **high**: **fall to/hit/reach etc a new low** (=be worth less than ever before) *The euro has fallen to a new low against the dollar. | Public confidence in the legal system is at an* ***all-time low*** (=much lower or worse than ever before).

2 a very difficult time in someone's personal or working life: **highs and lows (of sth)** (=good times and bad times) *the highs and lows of an actor's life*

3 a) the lowest point that the temperature reaches during a particular time OPP **high**: *The overnight low will be 8°C.* **b)** an area of low pressure in the air OPP **high**: *a low moving in over the Pacific*

4 the lowest of the low a) *informal* someone you think is completely unfair, cruel, immoral etc **b)** someone from a low social class – often used humorously

low⁴ *v* [I] *literary* if cattle low, they make a deep sound

low·brow /ˈləʊbraʊ $ ˈloʊ-/ *adj* lowbrow entertainment, newspapers, books etc are easy to understand and are not concerned with serious ideas about art, CULTURE etc – used to show disapproval OPP **highbrow** → **middlebrow**

ˌLow ˈChurch *n* [U] the part of the Church of England that believes in the importance of faith and studying the BIBLE rather than in religious ceremonies → HIGH CHURCH

ˌlow-ˈclass *adj* **1** *old-fashioned* WORKING CLASS OPP **high-class**: *a low-class bar* **2** not good quality OPP **high-class**

ˌlow-ˈcut *adj* a low-cut dress is shaped so that it shows a woman's neck and the top of her chest

low·down /ˈləʊdaʊn $ ˈloʊ-/ *n* **the lowdown (on sth/sb)** *informal* the most important facts about something: *Ryan* ***gave*** *me* ***the lowdown*** *on the meeting.*

ˈlow-down *adj* [only before noun] *informal* dishonest and unkind: *What a low-down, dirty trick.*

ˈlow-end *adj* [usually before noun] *especially AmE* relating to products or services that are less expensive and of lower quality than other products of the same type OPP **high-end**: *low-end desktop computers*

low·er¹ /ˈləʊə $ ˈloʊər/ ●●● W3 *adj*

1 [only before noun] below something else, especially below something of the same type OPP **upper**: *Nina chewed her lower lip anxiously. | Ruth went down to the lower deck* (=lower level on a ship). | **your lower limbs** (=your legs)

2 [only before noun] at or near the bottom of something OPP **upper**: *the lower slopes of the mountain | She suffers with pain in her lower back.*

3 smaller in number or amount OPP **higher**: *Temperatures will be lower over the weekend.*

4 [only before noun] less important than something else of the same type OPP **higher**: *the lower levels of management*

lower² ●●○ S3 W3 *v*

1 REDUCE [I,T] to reduce something in amount, degree, strength etc, or to become less: *Do you think we should lower the price? | After 20 minutes lower the temperature to 325°. | drugs to lower blood pressure | Helen* ***lowered*** *her* ***voice*** (=made it quieter) *as they approached. | His* ***voice lowered*** (=became quieter). **THESAURUS** ▸ REDUCE

> **REGISTER**
> In everyday English, people usually say that someone **turns down** the temperature or volume rather than **lowers** it: *Can you* ***turn*** *the heating* ***down****?*

2 MOVE DOWN [T] to move something down from higher up OPP **raise**: *Very gently, he lowered the dog onto the rug by the fire. | The flags were lowered to half-mast. | Greg watched as the coffin was lowered.* | **lower yourself** *He lowered himself carefully down from the top of the wall.*

3 lower your eyes/head to look down OPP **raise**: *Christina blushed and lowered her eyes.*

4 lower yourself [usually in negatives] to behave in a way that makes people respect you less: *I wouldn't lower myself to speak to her after what she's done.*

5 lower the tone (of sth) to make something not as nice as it was: *They thought an influx of students would lower the tone of the neighborhood. | Trust you to lower the tone of the conversation* (=include rude jokes etc in what you say)*!* —**lowered** *adj*: *He leaned forward and spoke in a lowered voice.*

low·er³ (*also* **lour** *BrE*) /ˈlaʊə $ -ər/ *v* [I] *literary* **1** when the sky or the weather lowers, it becomes dark because there is going to be a storm SYN **darken**: *lowering clouds* **2** to look threatening or annoyed SYN **frown**: *The other driver lowered at us as we passed him.*

ˌlower ˈcase *n* [U] letters in their small forms, such as a, b, c etc OPP **upper case** → **capital** —**lower case** *adj*: *lower case letters*

ˌlower ˈclass *n* [C] (*also* **lower classes** [plural]) *old-fashioned* the social class that has less money, power, or education than anyone else. This is now considered offensive. → **working class**, **middle class**, **upper class** —**lower-class** *adj*

ˌLower ˈHouse (*also* **ˌLower ˈChamber**) *n* [singular] a group of elected representatives who make laws in a country, for example the HOUSE OF COMMONS in Britain or the HOUSE OF REPRESENTATIVES in the US → **upper house**

ˌlower ˈorders *n* **the lower orders** *old-fashioned* an offensive expression for WORKING CLASS people considered as a group

ˈlower school *n* [C] the classes of a school in Britain that are for younger students, usually aged 11–13

ˌlowest ˌcommon deˈnominator *n* [U] **1** the biggest possible number of people, including people who are very easily influenced or are willing to accept low standards: *Television quiz shows often seem to target the lowest common denominator.* **2** *technical* the smallest number that the bottom numbers of a group of FRACTIONS can be divided into exactly → **DENOMINATOR**

ˌlow-ˈfat *adj* containing or using only a small amount of fat → **full-fat**: *low-fat yoghurt | a low-fat diet*

ˌlow-ˈflying *adj* flying close to the ground: *a low-flying aircraft*

ˌlow ˈgear *n* [C,U] one of a vehicle's GEARS that you use when you are driving at a slow speed

ˈlow-grade *adj* [only before noun] **1** not very good in quality: *inexpensive low-grade paper* **2** a low-grade medical condition is not very serious: *a low-grade fever*

ˌlow-ˈkey *adj* not intended to attract a lot of attention to an event, subject, or thing: *They want the funeral to be as low-key as possible. | a low-key military operation*

low·lands /ˈləʊləndz $ ˈloʊ-/ *n* [plural] an area of land that is lower than the land around it → **highlands**: *the Scottish lowlands* —**lowland** *adj* [only before noun]: *a wild lowland landscape | lowland farmers* —**lowlander** *n* [C]

ˌlow-ˈlevel *adj* **1** close to the ground: *low-level bombing attacks on military targets* **2** relating to people who are not in powerful positions or jobs OPP **high-level**: *routine, low-level, clerical tasks* **3** at a low degree or strength OPP **high-level**: *a low-level tension headache* **4** a low-level computer language is used to give instructions to a computer and is similar to the language that the computer operates in OPP **high-level**

ˈlow life *n* **1** [U] the life and behaviour of people who are involved in criminal or immoral activities: *a novel about low life in Chicago in the 1930s* **2** [C] (*also* **lowlife**) *AmE informal* someone who is involved in crime or who is bad: *Pete turned out to be a real lowlife.* —**lowlife** /ˈləʊlaif $ ˈloʊ-/ *adj AmE informal*: *Charlie may be lowlife, but he isn't stupid.*

low·lights /ˈləʊlaɪts $ ˈloʊ-/ *n* [plural] a dark colour that can be used to change the natural colour of some of your hair → **highlights**

low·ly /ˈləʊli $ ˈloʊ-/ *adj* low in rank, importance, or social class – sometimes used humorously SYN **humble**: *He was a lowly assistant gardener.* ⚠ **Lowly** is never an adverb. **Low** is used as an adverb as well as an adjective: *A helicopter flew low over their heads.*

ˌlow-ˈlying *adj* low-lying land is not far above the level of the sea: *Vast areas of low-lying land have been flooded.*

ˌlow-ˈmaintenance *adj* not needing a lot of care or attention: *a low-maintenance garden*

ˌlow-ˈpaid *adj* providing or earning only a small amount of money: *As part-time, low-paid workers, the women earned very little.*

ˌlow-ˈpitched *adj* **1** a low-pitched musical note or sound is deep OPP **high-pitched**: *the low-pitched hum of the generator* **2** **low-pitched roof** a roof that is not steep

ˈlow point *n* [C] the worst moment of a situation or activity OPP **high point**: *The low point in my life was when I was hit by a drunk driver.*

ˌlow-ˈpressure *n* [U] a condition of the air over a large area that affects the weather OPP **high-pressure**

ˌlow ˈprofile *n* **keep a low profile** to not go to places or be careful not to do anything that will attract attention to yourself or your actions OPP **high profile**: *He's not the sort of politician to keep a low profile for long.*

ˌlow-ˈprofile *adj* **1** [usually before noun] not receiving or wanting any attention OPP **high-profile**: *The US took a very low-profile role in the talks.* **2** [only before noun] *BrE* designed to be lower than other things of the same type: *low-profile tyres*

ˈlow-rent *adj* not expensive or not good quality – used to show disapproval

ˈlow-rise *adj* [only before noun] **1** a low-rise building does not have many STOREYS → **high-rise** **2** low-rise trousers have a low top and do not come up to your waist

ˌlow-ˈrisk *adj* [usually before noun] likely to be safe or without problems OPP **high-risk**: *low-risk investments*

ˈlow ˌseason *n* [U] *BrE* the time of year when fewer people are on holiday and there is less business for hotels etc, and prices are usually lower than normal SYN **off-season** OPP **high season**

ˌlow-ˈslung *adj* [only before noun] low and closer to the ground than usual: *a low-slung sports car*

ˌlow-ˈspirited *adj* unhappy or DEPRESSED

low-tech /ˌləʊ ˈtek◂ $ ˌloʊ-/ *adj* not using the most modern machines or methods in business or industry OPP **high-tech**: *He made low-tech, budget space movies.*

ˌlow ˈtide *n* [C,U] the time when sea water is at its lowest level OPP **high tide**: *You can walk across to the island at low tide.*

ˌlow ˈwater *n* [U] the time when the water in a river or the sea is at its lowest level → **high water**

ˌlow ˈwater ˌmark *n* [C] a mark showing the lowest level reached by a river or other area of water → **high water mark**

lox /lɒks $ lɑːks/ *n* [U] *especially AmE* SALMON that has been treated with smoke in order to preserve it

loy·al /ˈlɔɪəl/ ●●○ *adj* always supporting your friends, principles, country etc OPP **disloyal**: **[+to]** *The army has* ***remained loyal*** *to the government. | a* ***loyal supporter*** *of the team | her many years of* ***loyal service*** *to the company | loyal customers* —**loyally** *adv*: *He has always loyally defended the president.*

loy·al·ist /ˈlɔɪəlɪst/ *n* [C] **1** someone who continues to support a government or country, especially during a period of change **2** **Loyalist** someone from Northern Ireland who believes that Northern Ireland should remain part of the United Kingdom, and not become part of the Republic of Ireland → **Republican** —**loyalist** *adj*

loy·al·ty /ˈlɔɪəlti/ ●●○ *n* (*plural* **loyalties**)
1 [U] the quality of remaining faithful to your friends, principles, country etc: **[+to/towards]** *Elizabeth understood her husband's loyalty to his sister.*
2 [C usually plural] a feeling of support for someone or something: **local/regional/tribal/family etc loyalty/loyalties** *In the rural areas, family and tribal loyalties continue to be important. | the agony of* ***divided loyalties*** (=loyalty to two different or opposing people) *for the children in a divorce*

ˈloyalty card *n* [C] a card given by a shop, SUPERMARKET, etc to its regular customers allowing them to have advantages such as lower prices, money back on goods etc

loz·enge /ˈlɒzəndʒ $ ˈlɑː-/ *n* [C] **1** a small flat sweet, especially one that contains medicine: *a cough lozenge* **2** a shape similar to a square, with two angles of less than 90° opposite each other and two angles of more than 90° opposite each other

LP /ˌel ˈpiː/ *n* [C] (***long-playing record***) a record that turns 33 times per minute, and usually plays for between 20 and 25 minutes on each side SYN **album** → **single, CD**

LPG /ˌel piː ˈdʒiː/ (*also* **ˌLP ˈgas**) *n* [U] (***liquefied petroleum gas***) a type of liquid FUEL that is burned to produce heat or power

L-plate /ˈel pleɪt/ *n* [C] a flat white square with a red letter L on it, that must be attached to the car of someone who is learning to drive in Britain → **P-plate**

LRP /ˌel ɑː ˈpiː $ -ɑːr-/ *n* [U] *BrE* (***lead replacement petrol***) a special type of PETROL that does not contain LEAD and is meant to be used in older cars

LSD /ˌel es ˈdiː/ *n* [U] an illegal drug that makes you see things as more beautiful, strange, frightening etc than usual, or makes you see things that do not exist SYN **acid**

Lt. (*also* **Lt** *BrE*) a written abbreviation of ***lieutenant***

Ltd the written abbreviation of ***Limited***, used in the names of companies or businesses → **Inc., plc**: *M. Dixon & Son Ltd*

lu·bri·cant /ˈluːbrɪkənt/ *n* [C,U] a substance such as oil that you put on surfaces that rub together, especially parts of a machine, in order to make them move smoothly and easily

lu·bri·cate /ˈluːbrɪkeɪt/ *v* [T] **1** to put a lubricant on something in order to make it move more smoothly: *Lubricate all moving parts with grease.* **2** *informal* to help things to happen without any problems: *Vic's working day is lubricated by endless cups of coffee.* —**lubrication** /ˌluːbrɪˈkeɪʃən/ *n* [U]

lu·bri·cious /luːˈbrɪʃəs/ *adj formal* too interested in sex, in a way that seems unpleasant or unacceptable —**lubriciously** *adv*

lu·cid /ˈluːsɪd/ *adj* **1** expressed in a way that is clear and easy to understand: *You must write in a clear and lucid style.* **2** able to understand and think clearly, used especially about someone who is not always able to do this: *In her more lucid moments the old lady would talk about her past.* —**lucidly** *adv*: *He was lucidly aware of political realities.* —**lucidity** /luːˈsɪdəti/ *n* [U]

Lu·ci·fer /ˈluːsəfə $ -ər/ *n* the Devil

luck[1] /lʌk/ ●●● S2 W3 *n* [U]

1 SUCCESS (*also* **good luck**) good things that happen to you by chance: *You're not having much luck today, are you? | He's had good luck with his roses this year. | It was an incredible piece of luck.* | **by luck** *It was only by luck that they managed to avoid hitting the rocks near the shore.*

2 bad luck the bad things that happen to someone by chance, not because of something they did: *I've had nothing but bad luck since I moved to this town.*

3 CHANCE when good or bad things happen to people by chance: *Roulette is a game of luck.*

4 with (any) luck/with a bit of luck *spoken* if things happen in the way that you want SYN **hopefully**: *With a bit of luck, you might get a flight tomorrow.*

5 wish sb (the best of) luck to tell someone that you hope they will be successful in something they are going to do: *She wished me luck in the exam, then left.*

6 good luck/best of luck *spoken* used to tell someone that you hope they will be successful in something they are going to do: *Good luck in this enormous project you are undertaking.*

7 good luck to sb *spoken* used to say that you do not mind what someone does because it does not affect you: *I say, good luck to him.*

8 any luck?/no luck? *spoken* used to ask someone if they have succeeded in doing something: *'Oh, there you are. Any luck?' 'No, I didn't catch a single fish.'*

9 be in luck to be able to do or get something, especially when you did not expect to: *You're in luck – it's stopped snowing.*

10 be out of luck to be prevented from getting or doing something by bad luck: *The team were out of luck again at Scarborough on Saturday.*

11 do sth for luck to do something because you think it might bring you good luck: *She crossed her fingers for luck.*

12 just my luck *spoken* used to say that you are not surprised something bad has happened to you, because you are usually unlucky: *I didn't get to the phone in time. Just my luck!*

13 no such luck *spoken* used to say you are disappointed because something good that you hoped would happen did not happen: *'Have you got Sunday off?' 'No such luck.'*

14 better luck next time used to say that you hope someone will be more successful the next time they try to do something

15 as luck would have it used to say that something happened by chance: *As luck would have it, my best friend is the most wonderful cook in the world.*

16 try/chance your luck to do something because you hope you will be successful, even though you know you may not be: *After the war my father went to Canada to try his luck at farming there.*

17 be down on your luck to have no money because you have had a lot of bad luck over a long period of time: *When someone is down on their luck, friends are very difficult to find.*

18 the luck of the draw the result of chance rather than something you can control

19 some people have all the luck *spoken* used to say that you wish you had what someone else has

20 bad/hard/tough luck *BrE spoken* used to express sympathy when something unpleasant has happened to someone → **tough luck** at TOUGH[1](7)

21 with/knowing sb's luck *spoken* used to say that you expect something bad to happen to someone because bad things often do happen to them: *With my luck, I'd lose if I backed the only horse in a one horse race.*

22 worse luck *BrE spoken* unfortunately: *'Would your boyfriend like a drink?' 'He's not my boyfriend, worse luck!'*

23 luck is on sb's side if luck is on someone's side, things go well for them: *Luck was on my side; all the traffic lights were green.*

24 (one) for luck *spoken* used when you take, add, or do something for no particular reason, or in order to say that you hope good things happen → HARD-LUCK STORY, → **push your luck** at PUSH[1](12)

COLLOCATIONS – MEANINGS 1, 2, & 3

ADJECTIVES

good luck *These birds are said to bring good luck.*
bad luck *His bad luck continued.*
sheer/pure luck (=chance, and not skill or effort) *She managed to catch hold of the rope by sheer luck.*
dumb luck *AmE* (=sheer good luck, not influenced by anything you did) | **beginner's luck** (=good luck that happens when you first try something)

VERBS

have good/bad luck *I've had a bit of bad luck.*
have more/less luck *I hope you have more luck in the next competition.*
have no luck (*also* **not have much/any luck**) (=not be lucky or successful) *I'd been looking for a job for weeks, but had had no luck.*
can't believe your luck *I couldn't believe my luck as my number was called out!*
sb's luck holds (=they continue having good luck) | **sb's luck runs out** (=they stop having good luck) | **bring sb (good/bad) luck**

PHRASES

a piece/stroke of luck (=something good that happens by chance) *What a piece of luck that he arrived when he did!*
a run of good/bad luck (=a series of good or bad things) *The team has had a run of bad luck lately, losing their last five games.*
a matter of luck (=something that depends on chance) *Winning is a matter of luck.*
an element of luck (=an amount of luck that is involved in something) *There is always an element of luck when hiring someone for a job.*

luck[2] *v*

luck out *phr v AmE informal* to be lucky: *Yeah, we really lucked out and got a parking space right in front.*

luck·i·ly /ˈlʌkəli/ ●●○ S3 *adv* [sentence adverb] used to say that it is good that something happened or was done because if it had not, the situation would be unpleasant or difficult SYN **fortunately**: *Luckily the museum was not damaged by the earthquake.* | **luckily for sb** *Luckily for them, he braked in time.*

luck·less /ˈlʌkləs/ *adj literary* having no luck in something you are trying to do SYN **unfortunate**: *He died in the desert like so many other luckless explorers.*

luck·y /ˈlʌki/ ●●● S2 W3 *adj* (*comparative* **luckier**, *superlative* **luckiest**)

1 having good luck SYN **fortunate** OPP **unlucky**: **be lucky to do/be sth** *The children were lucky to survive the fire which destroyed their home.* | **lucky enough to do sth** *those of us lucky enough to own our own homes* | **lucky if** *I'll be lucky if I get any of my money back.* | **lucky (that)** *I was tremendously lucky that I didn't die in the accident.* | **[+with]** *We've been*

L

very lucky with the weather. | **count/consider/think yourself lucky** *Count yourself lucky you've got a husband like Jack.* | **get lucky** (=be lucky on a particular occasion) *You might get lucky and find a bargain.*
2 resulting from good luck: *I didn't really know your name – it was just a* ***lucky guess.*** | *A middle-aged woman had a* ***lucky escape*** *when a tree crashed down onto her car.* | **it is lucky (that)** *It's lucky that no-one was hurt.*
3 bringing good luck: *a lucky charm*
4 lucky you/me etc *spoken* used to say that someone is fortunate to be able to do something: *'My husband's a rich man, and devoted to me.' 'Lucky you.'*
5 be sb's lucky day *spoken* used to say that something good and often unexpected will happen to someone: *We're going to win. I just know it's our lucky day*
6 you'll/you'd be lucky! *spoken* used to tell someone that what they want probably will not happen: *'Fifty pounds should be enough.' 'You'll be lucky!'*
7 I/you should be so lucky! *spoken* used to tell someone that what they want is not likely to happen, especially because it is unreasonable: *You want three weeks holiday? You should be so lucky!* → **strike it lucky** at STRIKE[1](20), → **thank your lucky stars** at THANK(3), → **third time lucky** at THIRD[1](2)

THESAURUS

lucky happening because of good luck, or bringing you good luck: *a lucky guess* | *Seven is considered a lucky number.*
fortunate happening because of good luck.
Fortunate is more formal than **lucky**: *It was extremely fortunate that there was no one in the building when the bomb went off.* | *I'm in the fortunate position of doing a job I love.*
it's a good thing (that) (*also* **it's a good job (that)** *BrE*) *spoken* used when saying that there would have been problems if something had not happened: *It's a good thing that you brought an umbrella with you.* | *It's a good job I'm here to help.*
miraculous extremely lucky in a way that is almost unbelievable: *The doctor gave her a month to live but she made a miraculous recovery.* | *It was miraculous that no one was seriously injured in the accident.*
fortuitous /fɔːˈtjuːɪtəs/ *formal* happening because of good luck: *a fortuitous decision* | *a fortuitous coincidence* | *It was fortuitous that no one else was hurt.*
a fluke /fluːk/ *informal* something that happens by chance, not because of skill or good judgment: *The goal was a fluke.* | ***By a fluke,*** *he managed to get the question right.*

ˌlucky ˈdip *n BrE* **1** [C] a game in which you put your hand into a container filled with small objects, and choose one without looking SYN **grab bag** *AmE* **2** [singular] a situation in which what happens depends on chance SYN **lottery**

lu·cra·tive /ˈluːkrətɪv/ ●○○ *adj* a job or activity that is lucrative lets you earn a lot of money SYN **profitable**: **lucrative business/market/contract etc** *He inherited a lucrative business from his father.*

lu·cre /ˈluːkə $ -ər/ *n* **filthy lucre** *informal* money or wealth – used to show disapproval

Lud·dite /ˈlʌdaɪt/ *n* [C] someone who is opposed to using modern machines and methods SYN **technophobe**

lu·di·crous /ˈluːdəkrəs/ *adj* completely unreasonable, stupid, or wrong SYN **ridiculous**: *It is ludicrous to suggest that I was driving under the influence of alcohol.* | *The court granted him the ludicrous sum of £100 in damages.* | *That's a ludicrous idea.* THESAURUS STUPID —**ludicrously** *adv*: *a ludicrously inadequate army* —**ludicrousness** *n* [U]

lu·do /ˈluːdəʊ $ -doʊ/ *n* [U] *trademark BrE* a game played with COUNTERS (=small flat round objects) on a board

lug[1] /lʌg/ *v* (**lugged, lugging**) [T] *informal* to pull or carry something heavy with difficulty: **lug sth around** *It's a huge book, not something you'd like to lug around.* | **lug sth up/into/onto etc sth** *She began to lug her suitcase up the stairs.*

lug[2] *n* [C] **1** [usually plural] a part of something that sticks out and can be used as a handle or a support **2** *BrE humorous* an ear SYN **lughole 3** *AmE* a rough, stupid, or awkward person: *You big lug!*

luge /luːʒ/ *n* [C] a vehicle with blades instead of wheels on which you slide down a track made of ice as a sport → **bobsleigh**

lug·gage /ˈlʌgɪdʒ/ ●●○ *n* [U] the cases, bags etc that you carry when you are travelling SYN **baggage** *AmE*: *They searched his luggage for illegal drugs.* → HAND LUGGAGE

GRAMMAR: Countable or uncountable?

- **Luggage** is an uncountable noun and is not used in the plural. You say: *He carried our luggage to our room.* ✗ Don't say: *He carried our luggages to our room.*
- **Luggage** is always followed by a singular verb: *What happens if my luggage* ***gets*** *lost?*
- When talking about one suitcase or bag, you say a **piece of luggage** or an **item of luggage**: *Each piece of luggage can weigh up to 20 kilos.*

GRAMMAR GUIDE NOUNS

ˈluggage rack *n* [C] **1** a shelf in a train, bus etc for putting luggage on **2** *AmE* a special frame on top of a car that you tie luggage on SYN **roof rack** *BrE*

lug·ger /ˈlʌgə $ -ər/ *n* [C] a small boat with one or more sails

lug·hole /ˈlʌghəʊl, ˈlʌgəʊl $ -oʊl/ *n* [C] *BrE humorous* an ear

lu·gu·bri·ous /luːˈguːbriəs/ *adj literary* very sad and serious – sometimes used humorously SYN **melancholy, morose**: *his lugubrious tear-stained face* —**lugubriously** *adv*

lug·worm /ˈlʌgwɜːm $ -wɜːrm/ *n* [C] *BrE* a small WORM that lives in sand by the sea, often used to catch fish

luke·warm /ˌluːkˈwɔːm◂ $ -ˈwɔːrm◂/ *adj* **1** food, liquid etc that is lukewarm is slightly warm and often not as hot or cold as it should be SYN **tepid**: *She sipped some lukewarm coffee from her mug.* THESAURUS HOT **2** not showing much interest or excitement: *His idea got only a* ***lukewarm response*** *from the committee.*

lull[1] /lʌl/ *v* [T] **1** to make someone feel calm or as if they want to sleep: *The hum of the tyres on the road lulled her to sleep.* **2** to make someone feel safe and confident so that they are completely surprised when something bad happens: **lull sb into (doing) sth** *The police lulled me into believing that they did not suspect us.* | *Earthquakes here are rare and this has* ***lulled*** *people* ***into a false sense of security*** (=made people think they were safe when they were not).

lull[2] *n* [C] **1** a short period of time when there is less activity or less noise than usual: **[+in]** *a brief lull in the conversation* | *a lull in the fighting* **2 the lull before the storm** a short period of time when things are calm, that is followed by a lot of activity, noise, or trouble

lul·la·by /ˈlʌləbaɪ/ *n* (*plural* **lullabies**) [C] a slow quiet song sung to children to make them go to sleep

lum·ba·go /lʌmˈbeɪgəʊ $ -goʊ/ *n* [U] pain in the lower part of the back

lum·bar /ˈlʌmbə $ -ər/ *adj technical* relating to the lower part of the back: *pain in the lumbar region*

lum·ber[1] /ˈlʌmbə $ -ər/ *v* **1** [I always + adv/prep] to move in a slow awkward way: **[+up/towards/into/along etc]** *They lumbered along slowly.* | *A blue bus lumbered past.* **2** [T] *informal* to give someone a job or responsibility that they do not want: **get/be lumbered with sth** *A career was less easy once I was lumbered with a husband and children.* **3** [I] *AmE* to cut down trees in a large area and prepare them to be sold

lumber[2] *n* [U] **1** pieces of wood used for building, that have been cut to specific lengths and widths SYN **timber** **2** *BrE informal* large objects that are no longer useful or wanted

lum·ber·jack /ˈlʌmbədʒæk $ -ər-/ *n* [C] *old-fashioned* someone whose job is cutting down trees for wood SYN **logger**

L

lum·ber·man /ˈlʌmbəmən $ -bər-/ *n* (*plural* **lumbermen** /-mən/) [C] someone in the business of cutting down large areas of trees in order to sell them for wood

lum·ber·mill /ˈlʌmbəmɪl $ -bər-/ *n* [C] *AmE* a building where trees are cut up to make wood SYN **sawmill** *BrE*

ˈlumber room *n* [C] *BrE* a room where old furniture, broken machines etc are kept

lum·ber·yard /ˈlʌmbəjɑːd $ -bərjɑːrd/ *n* [C] *AmE* a place where wood is kept before it is sold

lu·mi·na·ry /ˈluːmənəri $ -neri/ *n* (*plural* **luminaries**) [C] someone who is very famous or highly respected for their skill at doing something or their knowledge of a particular subject: *luminaries of Parisian society*

lu·mi·nes·cence /ˌluːməˈnesəns/ *n* [U] *technical or literary* a soft shining light: *The moonlight gave everything a strange luminescence.* —**luminescent** *adj*

lu·mi·nous /ˈluːmɪnəs/ *adj* **1** shining in the dark: *luminous paint | Her large dark eyes were almost luminous.* **2** very brightly coloured, especially in green, pink, or yellow SYN **Day-Glo**: *luminous green socks* —**luminously** *adv* —**luminosity** /ˌluːməˈnɒsəti $ -ˈnɑː-/ *n* [U] *technical*: *the sun's luminosity*

lump¹ /lʌmp/ ●●○ *n* [C]
1 a small piece of something solid, without a particular shape: *Strain the custard to remove lumps.* | **[+of]** *Melt a lump of butter in your frying-pan.* THESAURUS PIECE → see picture at PIECE¹
2 a small hard swollen area that sticks out from someone's skin or grows in their body, usually because of an illness: *You should never ignore a breast lump.*
3 a small square block of sugar: *One lump or two?*
4 a lump in/to sb's throat a feeling that you want to cry: *There was a lump in her throat as she gazed at the child.*
5 take your lumps *AmE informal* to accept the bad things that happen and not let them affect you: *According to experts, the company took its lumps but is on the road to profitability.*
6 *BrE spoken* someone who is stupid or CLUMSY: *He's a big fat lump.*

lump² *v* [T] **1 lump it** *informal* to accept a situation or decision you do not like because you cannot change it: *They've been told: take the lower interest rate, or lump it. | It's the law so you can **like it or lump it**.* **2** to put two or more different people or things together and consider them as a single group, sometimes wrongly: **lump sth together** *You can't lump the symptoms together and blame them all on stress.* | **lump sb/sth in with sb/sth** *The danger is that people who pay their bills on time will be lumped in with those that don't.*

lump·ec·to·my /lʌmpˈektəmi/ *n* (*plural* **lumpectomies**) [C] an operation in which a TUMOUR is removed from someone's body, especially from a woman's breast

lum·pen /ˈlʌmpən, ˈlʊm-/ *adj* **1** relating to the poorest and least educated people from the WORKING CLASS **2** large, heavy, and lumpy: *Her body felt lumpen and awkward.*

lump·ish /ˈlʌmpɪʃ/ *adj* heavy and awkward

ˌlump ˈsum *n* [C] an amount of money given in a single payment: *When you retire you'll get a lump sum of £80,000.*

lump·y /ˈlʌmpi/ *adj* covered with or containing small solid pieces: *a lumpy mattress*

lu·na·cy /ˈluːnəsi/ *n* [U] **1** a situation or behaviour that is completely crazy SYN **madness**: *It would be **sheer lunacy** to turn down a job offer like that.* **2** *old-fashioned* mental illness

lu·nar /ˈluːnə $ -ər/ *adj* relating to the Moon or to travel to the Moon: *studies of the lunar surface | a lunar eclipse*

ˌlunar ˈmonth *n* [C] a period of 28 or 29 days between one NEW MOON and the next

lu·na·tic /ˈluːnətɪk/ *n* [C] **1** someone who behaves in a crazy or very stupid way – often used humorously: *This hotel is run by a lunatic!* **2** *old-fashioned* a very offensive word for someone who is mentally ill: *a dangerous lunatic* **3 the lunatic fringe** *BrE* the small group of people in a political group or organization who have the most extreme opinions or ideas —**lunatic** *adj* [only before noun]: *lunatic behaviour*

ˈlunatic aˌsylum *n* [C] *old-fashioned* a hospital where people who are mentally ill are cared for. This word is now considered to be offensive.

lunch¹ /lʌntʃ/ ●●● S1 W2 *n* [C,U]
1 a meal eaten in the middle of the day: *What's for lunch? | I've just had lunch with John.* | **at lunch** *I'm afraid he's at lunch until two.* | **over lunch** *A dozen senators met over lunch with the Chinese ambassador.*

GRAMMAR: Patterns with lunch

for lunch
- You eat something **for lunch**: *I had chicken for lunch.*

✗ Don't say: *I had chicken on lunch. | I had chicken at lunch.*

at lunch
- You use **at lunch** to talk about something that happens while you are eating lunch: *We can talk about it at lunch.*
- You also use **at lunch** to say that someone has gone somewhere else to eat lunch: *I went to see her, but she was at lunch.*

2 there's no (such thing as a) free lunch used to say that you cannot get anything without working for it or paying for it
3 out to lunch *informal* behaving or talking in a strange or crazy way

COLLOCATIONS

VERBS

have lunch *Have you had lunch?*
eat lunch *What time do you usually eat lunch?*
have sth for lunch *I usually have sandwiches for lunch.*
take sb (out) to lunch (=pay for someone else's lunch when you go to a restaurant) | **go out for/to lunch** (=have lunch at a restaurant) | **come for/to lunch** (=come to someone's house for lunch) | **break for lunch** (=stop doing something in order to eat lunch) | **make lunch**

ADJECTIVES/NOUN + lunch

a light lunch (=a small lunch) *After a light lunch, he would take a nap each afternoon.*
a packed lunch *BrE*, **a bag/sack lunch** *AmE* (=food such as sandwiches that you take to school etc) *Most of the children had brought packed lunches.*
a business/working lunch (=a lunch during which you also do business) | **a school lunch** (=a lunch provided by a school) | **Sunday lunch** *BrE* (=a hot lunch eaten on Sunday)

lunch + NOUN

a lunch break (=a time when you stop working to eat lunch) *We took a half hour lunch break.*
the lunch hour (=the time when people stop working to eat lunch) *I try to go out for a walk during my lunch hour.*
a lunch date (=when you meet someone for lunch)

lunch² *v* [I] *formal* to eat lunch: **[+with]** *I will be lunching with a client.* | **[+on]** *I lunched on bread and olives.* | **[+at/in]** *We lunched at Maxim's.*

lunch·box /ˈlʌntʃbɒks $ -bɑːks/ *n* [C] a box in which food is carried to school, work etc → see picture at BOX¹

ˈlunch break *n* [C] the time in the middle of the day when people at work or at school stop working to eat lunch

ˈlunch ˌcounter *n* [C] *old-fashioned* a place that serves simple meals for lunch, or a small restaurant that is only open at lunchtime

lunch·eon /ˈlʌntʃən/ *n* [C,U] *formal* lunch

ˈluncheon meat *n* [U] meat that has been cooked, then pressed down, and is often sold in a can

ˈluncheon ˌvoucher *n* [C] in Britain, a special ticket that can be used to pay for meals usually given to you by your employer

ˈlunch hour *n* [C] the period of time in the middle of the day when people stop working in order to eat: *I did the shopping during my lunch hour.*

lunch·room /ˈlʌntʃruːm, -rʊm/ *n* [C] *AmE* a large room in a school or office where people can eat

lunch·time /ˈlʌntʃtaɪm/ ●●○ S3 *n* [C,U] the time in the middle of the day when people usually eat their LUNCH: **at lunchtime** *Some people prefer to eat their main meal at lunchtime.* | *a lunchtime drink*

lung /lʌŋ/ ●●○ *n* [C] one of the two organs in your body that you breathe with: *Smoking can cause lung cancer.* → **IRON LUNG** → see picture at **HUMAN**[1]

lunge /lʌndʒ/ *v* [I] to make a sudden strong movement towards someone or something, especially to attack them: **[+at/forward/towards/out etc]** *The goats lunged at each other with their horns.* | *John lunged forward and grabbed him by the throat.* —**lunge** *n* [C]: *Brad made a lunge towards his opponent, but missed.*

lung·ful /ˈlʌŋfʊl/ *n* [C] the amount of air, smoke etc that you breathe in at one time: **[+of]** *Polly took in a lungful of crisp cool air.*

lu·pus /ˈluːpəs/ *n* [U] one of several diseases that affect the skin and joints

lurch[1] /lɜːtʃ $ lɜːrtʃ/ *v* [I] **1** to walk or move suddenly in an uncontrolled or unsteady way: **[+forward/to/towards/into etc]** *Sam hit the gas and the car lurched forward.* | *He lurched to his feet.* **2 your heart/stomach lurches** used to say that your heart or stomach seems to move suddenly because you feel shocked, frightened etc: *Virginia's heart lurched painfully in her chest.* **3 lurch from one crisis/extreme etc to another** (*also* **lurch from crisis to crisis**) to seem to have no plan and no control over what you are doing: *The industry lurches from crisis to crisis.*

lurch[2] *n* [C] **1** a sudden movement: *The train gave a violent lurch.* **2 leave sb in the lurch** to leave someone at a time when you should stay and help them

lure[1] /lʊə, ljʊə $ lʊr/ ●○○ *v* [T]
1 to persuade someone to do something, especially something wrong or dangerous, by making it seem attractive or exciting: **lure sb into (doing) sth** *People may be lured into buying tickets by clever advertising.* | **lure sb away** *Computer games are luring youngsters away from their lessons.*
2 to attract customers, workers, money etc from another company or place: **lure sb back/away** *The bank launched an advertising campaign to lure back its traditional customers.* | *It's very difficult to lure talent away from Silicon Valley.*

lure[2] ●○○ *n* [C]
1 [usually singular] something that attracts people, or the quality of being able to do this: **[+of]** *the lure of easy money* | *Malc wasn't mature enough to resist the lure of drink and drugs.*
2 an object used to attract animals or fish so that they can be caught SYN **decoy**

lu·rid /ˈlʊərɪd, ˈljʊərɪd $ ˈlʊrɪd/ *adj* **1** a description, story etc that is lurid is deliberately shocking and involves sex or violence SYN **explicit**: *lurid headlines* | *He told me in lurid detail what would happen to me.* **2** too brightly coloured SYN **gaudy**: *a lurid orange dress* —**luridly** *adv*

lurk /lɜːk $ lɜːrk/ ●○○ *v* [I]
1 to wait somewhere quietly and secretly, usually because you are going to do something wrong: **[+in/behind/beneath/around etc]** *She didn't see the figure lurking behind the bushes.*
2 if something such as danger, a feeling etc lurks somewhere, it exists, but you may not see it or know about it: *a dark formless danger, lurking in the shadows*
3 if you lurk in a CHAT ROOM on the Internet, you read what other people are writing to each other, but you do not write any messages yourself: **[+in]** *I think it's sort of creepy how people lurk in chat rooms.* —**lurker** *n* [C]

lus·cious /ˈlʌʃəs/ *adj* **1** extremely good to eat or drink: *a luscious and fragrant dessert wine* **2** *informal* very sexually attractive: *her luscious body*

lush[1] /lʌʃ/ *adj* **1** plants that are lush grow many leaves and look healthy and strong: *a lush green mountainous island* | *The fields were lush with grass and flowers.* **2** very beautiful, comfortable, and expensive SYN **luxurious**: *lush carpets* **3** lush music has a lot of pleasant-sounding instruments or voices together: *lush vocal harmonies* **4** *informal* very attractive or nice – used especially by young people: *He looks so lush in this pic!*

lush[2] *n* [C] *informal* an ALCOHOLIC

lust[1] /lʌst/ *n* **1** [C,U] very strong sexual desire, especially when it does not include love: *My feelings for Lauren were pure lust.* **2** [singular, U] a very strong desire to have something, usually power or money – used to show disapproval: **[+for]** *Hitler's* ***lust for power*** **3 (a) lust for life** a strong determination to enjoy life as much as possible – used to show approval: *the happy-go-lucky lust for life so typical of southern Italy*

lust[2] *v*

lust after/for sb/sth *phr v* **1** to be strongly sexually attracted to someone, and think about having sex with them: *She had secretly lusted after him for years.* **2** to want something very much, especially something that you do not really need: *This is a car to lust after.*

lus·ter /ˈlʌstə $ -ər/ *n* [singular, U] the American spelling of LUSTRE

lust·ful /ˈlʌstfəl/ *adj* feeling or showing strong sexual desire: *She ignored his lustful glances.* —**lustfully** *adv*

lus·tre *BrE*, **luster** *AmE* /ˈlʌstə $ -ər/ *n* [singular, U] **1** an attractive shiny appearance: *Her thick, black hair shone with lustre.* **2** the quality that makes something interesting or exciting: *There'll be a celebrity guest to* ***add lustre to*** *the occasion.*

lus·trous /ˈlʌstrəs/ *adj* shining in a soft gentle way: *Her hair was beautifully dark and lustrous.*

lust·y /ˈlʌsti/ *adj* strong and healthy SYN **powerful**: *the lusty cry of a new-born baby* | *her strong, lusty young husband* —**lustily** *adv*: *Her mother was singing lustily.*

lute /luːt/ *n* [C] a musical instrument like a GUITAR with a round body, played with the fingers or a PLECTRUM (=small piece of plastic, metal etc), especially in the past → see picture at **STRINGED INSTRUMENT** —**lutenist** /ˈluːtənɪst/ *n* [C]

luv /lʌv/ *n BrE informal* an informal way of spelling LOVE: *Come on, luv, don't cry.*

luv·vie /ˈlʌvi/ *n BrE* **1** another spelling of LOVEY **2** [C] *informal* an actor who behaves to other people in a very friendly way that is not sincere

luxe /lʌks/ *adj* expensive and of good quality – used especially in magazines: *Her new collection features skirts in luxe fabrics like velvet and silk brocade.*

lux·u·ri·ant /lʌgˈzjʊəriənt, ləgˈʒʊəriənt $ ləgˈʒʊriənt/ *adj* **1** growing strongly and thickly: *luxuriant black hair* | *luxuriant vegetation* **2** beautiful and pleasant to watch or listen to: *the film's luxuriant visuals* —**luxuriantly** *adv*: *She yawned luxuriantly.* —**luxuriance** *n* [U]

lux·u·ri·ate /lʌgˈzjʊərieɪt, ləgˈʒʊəri- $ ləgˈʒʊri-/ *v* [I usually + adv/prep] to relax and enjoy something: **[+in]** *He ran a hot bath and luxuriated in it for half an hour.*

lux·u·ri·ous /lʌgˈzjʊəriəs, ləgˈʒʊəriəs $ ləgˈʒʊriəs/ ●○○ *adj* very expensive, beautiful, and comfortable: *a luxurious 30-room villa* —**luxuriously** *adv*: *The cabin was luxuriously furnished.*

lux·u·ry /ˈlʌkʃəri/ ●●○ *n* (*plural* **luxuries**)
1 [U] very great comfort and pleasure, such as you get from expensive food, beautiful houses, cars etc: **in luxury** *She stole to keep her boyfriend in luxury.* | *He was leading* ***a life of luxury*** *in Australia.* | **luxury hotel/car/home etc** (=expensive and large) *We stayed in a five-star luxury hotel.* | *The dress is lambswool – pure luxury.*
2 [C] something expensive that you do not need, but you buy for pleasure and enjoyment OPP **necessity**: *luxuries like chocolate and perfume*
3 afford/have/enjoy the luxury of sth to have something

that is very pleasant or convenient, that you are not always able to have: *For the first time in three years, they actually had the luxury of a whole day together.* → **in the lap of luxury** at LAP[1](5)

LW the written abbreviation of ***long wave***

-ly /li/ *suffix* **1** [in adverbs] in a particular way: *She smiled happily.* | *He was walking slowly.* **2** [in adverbs] considered in a particular way: *Politically speaking it was a rather unwise remark.* | *a financially sound proposal* **3** [in adjectives and adverbs] happening at regular periods of time: *an hourly check* (=done every hour) | *They visit monthly* (=once every month). **4** [in adjectives] like a particular thing in manner, nature, or appearance: *with queenly grace* | *a motherly woman* (=showing the love, kindness etc of a mother)

ly·ce·um /laɪˈsiːəm/ *n* [C] *AmE old-fashioned* a building used for public meetings, concerts, speeches etc

ly·chee, **litchi** /ˈlaɪtʃi/ *n* [C] a small round fruit with a rough pink-brown shell outside and sweet white flesh inside → see picture at **FRUIT[1]**

lych·gate, **lichgate** /ˈlɪtʃgeɪt/ *n* [C] a gate with a roof leading into the area surrounding a church

Ly·cra /ˈlaɪkrə/ *n* [U] *trademark* a material that stretches, used especially for making sports clothes that fit tightly

ly·ing /ˈlaɪ-ɪŋ/ the present participle of LIE

Lyme dis·ease /ˈlaɪm dɪˌziːz/ *n* [U] a serious illness that is caused by a bite from a TICK[1](2)

lymph /lɪmf/ *n* [U] a clear liquid that is formed in your body and passes into your blood system to fight against infection —**lymphatic** /lɪmˈfætɪk/ *adj*

ˈlymph node (*also* **ˈlymph gland**) *n* [C] a small rounded SWELLING in your body through which lymph passes before entering your blood system

lynch /lɪntʃ/ *v* [T] if a crowd of people lynches someone, they kill them, especially by HANGing them, without a TRIAL —**lynching** *n* [C]

ˈlynch mob *n* [singular] a group of people that kills someone by HANGing them, without a legal TRIAL

lynch·pin /ˈlɪnʃ pɪn/ *n* [C] another spelling of LINCHPIN

lynx /lɪŋks/ *n* (*plural* **lynx** *or* **lynxes**) [C] a large wild cat that has no tail and lives in forests SYN **bobcat** *AmE* → see picture at **BIG CAT**

lyre /laɪə $ laɪr/ *n* [C] a musical instrument with strings across a U-shaped frame, played with the fingers, especially in ancient Greece

lyr·ic[1] /ˈlɪrɪk/ ●○○ *n*

1 lyrics [plural] the words of a song: *He wrote some great music, but the lyrics weren't that good.*

2 [C] (*also* **ˌlyric ˈpoem**) *technical* a poem, usually a short one, written in a lyric style

lyric[2] *adj* [only before noun] expressing strong personal emotions such as love, in a way that is similar to music in its sounds and RHYTHM: *Wordsworth was one of the greatest lyric poets of his time.*

lyr·i·cal /ˈlɪrɪkəl/ *adj* **1** beautifully expressed in words, poetry, or music: *lyrical love poetry* **2 wax lyrical** to talk about and praise something in a very eager way: *One fisherman waxed lyrical about the variety of fish in the river.*

lyr·i·cally /ˈlɪrɪkli/ *adv* **1** in relation to the words of a song: *The album is musically unexciting but lyrically superb.* **2** with beautiful language or music: *He lyrically described the countryside around his home.*

lyr·i·cis·m /ˈlɪrɪsɪzəm/ *n* [U] gentle or romantic emotion, expressed in writing or music: *The lyricism of Tennyson's poetry is magnificent.*

lyr·i·cist /ˈlɪrɪsɪst/ *n* [C] someone who writes the words for songs

Mm

M, m /em/ (*plural* **M's, m's**) *n* **1** [C,U] the 13th letter of the English alphabet **2** [C] the number 1,000 in the system of ROMAN NUMERALS **3 M6, M25 etc** the name of a MOTORWAY in Britain

m (*also* **m.**) **1** the written abbreviation of ***metre*** or ***metres*** **2** the written abbreviation of ***mile*** or ***miles*** **3** the written abbreviation of ***million*** **4** the written abbreviation of ***male*** **5** the written abbreviation of ***married*** **6** the written abbreviation of ***medium***, used on clothes to mean an average size

Ma /mɑː/, **ma** *n* [C] *informal* **1** mother: *What's for dinner, Ma?* **2** *old-fashioned* used to mean 'Mrs' in some country areas of the US: *old Ma Harris*

MA *BrE*, **M.A.** *AmE* /ˌem ˈeɪ/ *n* [C] (***Master of Arts***) a university degree in a subject such as history, languages, or English literature that you can get after your first degree: **[+in]** *He* ***did*** *an* ***MA*** *in graphic design at Manchester.* | *Vanessa Clark, MA*

ma'am /mæm, mɑːm, məm $ mæm/ *n* **1** *AmE spoken* used to address a woman in a polite and respectful way: *May I help you, ma'am?* **2** *BrE spoken* used to address the Queen or another woman in authority

mac, **mack** /mæk/ *n* [C] *BrE* a coat which you wear to keep out the rain SYN **mackintosh**

Mac /mæk/ *n* **1** [C] *trademark informal* (**(Apple) Macintosh**) a type of personal computer → **PC**: *Can you run this software on a Mac?* **2** *AmE spoken old-fashioned* used to address a man whose name you do not know

ma·ca·bre /məˈkɑːbrə, -bə $ -brə, -bər/ *adj* very strange and unpleasant and connected with death or with people being seriously hurt: *a macabre tale* | *a macabre sense of humour*

ma·cad·am /məˈkædəm/ *n* [U] a road surface made of a mixture of broken stones and TAR or ASPHALT SYN **tarmac** *BrE*

mac·a·da·mi·a /ˌmækəˈdeɪmiə/ *n* [C] a sweet white nut that grows on a tropical tree, or the tree that produces this nut

mac·a·ro·ni /ˌmækəˈrəʊni $ -ˈroʊ-/ *n* [U] a type of PASTA in the shape of small tubes: **macaroni cheese** *BrE* **/macaroni and cheese** *AmE* (=macaroni cooked with a cheese sauce)

mac·a·roon /ˌmækəˈruːn/ *n* [C] a small round cake made of sugar, eggs, and crushed ALMONDS or COCONUT

ma·caw /məˈkɔː $ -ˈkɒː/ *n* [C] a large brightly coloured bird like a PARROT, with a long tail

MACAW

mac·chi·a·to /ˌmækiˈɑːtəʊ $ ˌmɑːkiˈɑːtoʊ/ *n* [C] an ESPRESSO (=strong black Italian coffee) with a small amount of milk added

mace /meɪs/ *n* **1** [U] a spice made from the dried shell of a NUTMEG **2** [C] a heavy ball with sharp points on a short metal stick, used in the past as a weapon **3** [C] a decorated stick that is carried by an official in some ceremonies as a sign of power → **sceptre**

Mace *n* [U] *trademark* a chemical which makes your eyes and skin sting painfully. Police officers sometimes carry Mace in cans to defend themselves.

ma·cer·ate /ˈmæsəreɪt/ *v* [I,T] *technical* to make something soft by leaving it in water, or to become soft in this way

Mach /mæk $ mɑːk/ *n* [U] a unit for measuring speed, especially of an aircraft, in relation to the speed of sound. Mach 1 is the speed of sound, Mach 2 is twice the speed of sound etc: *a plane with a maximum speed of Mach 3*

ma·chet·e /məˈʃeti, məˈtʃeti/ *n* [C] a large knife with a broad heavy blade, used as a weapon or a tool: *a machete attack*

Mach·i·a·vel·li·an /ˌmækiəˈveliən◂/ *adj* using clever but immoral methods to get what you want SYN **devious**

mach·i·na·tions /ˌmækəˈneɪʃənz, ˌmæʃə-/ *n* [plural] *formal* secret, clever, and often unfair methods used to achieve something – used to show disapproval: **[+of]** *the* ***political machinations*** *of far right groups*

ma·chine¹ /məˈʃiːn/ ●●● S1 W1 *n* [C]

1 a piece of equipment with moving parts that uses power such as electricity to do a particular job: **washing/sewing etc machine** *Is the washing machine working now?* | *Could you get me a coffee from the* ***drinks machine****?* | *The* ***fax machine*** *is broken.* | **switch/turn a machine on/off** *Turn the machine off before removing the cover.* | **by machine** *The letters are sorted by machine.* | *Did you put my dirty shirts in the machine* (=washing machine)*?* | *I left a message for you on your machine* (=telephone answering machine). | *The machine wouldn't let me have any money* (=cash machine).

→ **ANSWERING MACHINE, CASH MACHINE, VENDING MACHINE**

2 a computer: *My machine's just crashed.*

3 a group of people who control and organize something – often used to show disapproval: *the bureaucrats of* ***the party machine*** | *the government's* ***propaganda machine*** | *the powerful American* ***war machine***

4 *informal* a vehicle, especially a MOTORBIKE: *Riders have to learn to handle their machines in all conditions.* | *That's a* ***mean machine*** (=very fast and attractive vehicle) *you have there.*

5 a person or animal that does something very well or without having to think about it: *In the tiger, nature has produced the perfect hunting machine.* | *I'm not a golfing machine. I make mistakes just like anyone else.*

6 someone who seems to behave like a machine and to have no feelings or thoughts SYN **automaton**

7 a well-oiled machine something that works very smoothly and effectively: *The office runs like a well-oiled machine.*

machine² *v* [T] **1** to fasten pieces of cloth together using a sewing machine **2** to make or shape something using a machine

maˈchine ˌcode (*also* **maˈchine ˌlanguage**) *n* [C,U] *technical* instructions in the form of numbers that are put into a computer

maˈchine gun *n* [C] a gun that fires a lot of bullets very quickly: *There came the sound of men shouting and a burst of machine gun fire.*

maˈchine-gun *v* (**machine-gunned, machine-gunning**) [T] to shoot at someone or something with a machine gun: *He was machine-gunned in an ambush.*

maˈchine-head *n* [C] a small button attached to the strings on an instrument such as a GUITAR that you turn in order to make the instrument play in tune

maˈchine-made *adj* made using a machine OPP **handmade**

maˌchine-ˈreadable *adj* in a form that can be understood and used by a computer: *information stored in machine-readable form*

ma·chin·e·ry /məˈʃiːnəri/ ●●○ W3 *n* [U]

1 machines, especially large ones: **agricultural/industrial/factory etc machinery** | *The use of* ***heavy machinery*** *has damaged the site.* | *a* ***piece of machinery***

2 a system or set of processes for doing something: **[+of]** *the machinery of government* | **machinery for (doing) sth** *The company has no effective machinery for resolving disputes.*

3 the parts inside a machine that make it work: *Be careful not to get anything caught in the machinery.*

ma'chine ˌshop *n* [C] a place where people make products, especially out of metal, using machines to cut and shape them

ma'chine ˌtool *n* [C] a tool for cutting and shaping metal, wood etc, usually one that uses electricity

ma'chine ˌwashable *adj* if clothes are machine washable, it is possible to wash them in a washing machine safely

ma·chin·ist /mə'ʃiːnɪst/ *n* [C] someone who operates a machine, especially in a factory: *All the women are highly skilled machinists.*

ma·chis·mo /mə'tʃɪzməʊ, -'kɪz- $ mɑː'tʃɪzmoʊ, mə-/ *n* [U] traditional male behaviour that emphasizes how brave, strong, and sexually attractive a man is

mach·o /'mætʃəʊ $ 'mɑːtʃoʊ/ *adj informal* behaving in a way that is traditionally typical of men, for example being strong or brave, or not showing your feelings – used humorously or in order to show disapproval: *He's sick of being cast as the hard* ***macho man*** *in films.* | *a car with a macho image* **THESAURUS** ▸ MAN

Mac·in·tosh /'mækɪntɒʃ $ -tɑːʃ/ (*also* **Apple Macintosh**) (*also* **Mac** *informal*) *n* [C] *trademark* a type of personal computer

mack /mæk/ *n* [C] *BrE* another spelling of MAC

mack·e·rel /'mækərəl/ *n* (*plural* **mackerel**) [C,U] a sea fish that has oily flesh and a strong taste: *smoked mackerel* → see picture at FISH[1]

mack·in·tosh /'mækɪntɒʃ $ -tɑːʃ/ *n* [C] *BrE old-fashioned* a coat which you wear to keep out the rain SYN **mac**, **raincoat**

ma·cra·mé /mə'krɑːmi $ ˌmækrə'meɪ/ *n* [U] the art of tying string in patterns to make things

mac·ro /'mækrəʊ $ -roʊ/ *n* (*plural* **macros**) [C] a set of instructions for a computer, stored and used as a unit: *You can* ***run*** *a* ***macro*** *to change to US spelling.*

macro- /mækrəʊ $ -roʊ/ *prefix technical* large and concerning a whole system rather than particular parts of it OPP **micro**: *macroeconomics* | *macromolecular structures*

mac·ro·bi·ot·ic /ˌmækrəʊbaɪ'ɒtɪk◂ $ -kroʊbaɪ'ɑːtɪk/ *adj* macrobiotic food consists mainly of grains and vegetables, with no added chemicals: *a healthy macrobiotic diet*

mac·ro·cos·m /'mækrəʊˌkɒzəm $ -kroʊˌkɑː-/ *n* [C] a large complicated system such as the whole universe or a society, considered as a single unit OPP **microcosm**

mac·ro·ec·o·nom·ics /ˌmækrəʊekə'nɒmɪks,-iːkə- $ -kroʊekə'nɑː-, -iːkə-/ *n* [U] the study of large economic systems such as those of a whole country or area of the world → **microeconomics** —**macroeconomic** *adj*

mad /mæd/ ●●● S2 W3 *adj* (*comparative* **madder**, *superlative* **maddest**)

1 ANGRY [not before noun] *informal especially AmE* angry: **[+at]** *Are you still mad at me?* | *We* ***get mad*** *at each other sometimes, like any family.* | **[+about]** *There's no need to* ***get mad*** *about it!* | *You* ***make*** *me so* ***mad****!* | **[+with]** *BrE*: *His wife will be really mad with him.* | **go mad** *BrE* (=become very angry) *Look at this mess! Mum will go mad!* | **hopping mad** (=very angry) | **(as) mad as hell** (=a rude way of saying very angry) **THESAURUS** ▸ ANGRY

2 CRAZY *especially BrE* crazy or very silly: *He can't possibly get that finished in time. He* ***must be mad****!* | *I'd* ***go mad*** (=start to feel crazy) *if I was stuck at home all day.* | *He's been* ***driving*** *me* ***mad****!* | *You've agreed to marry him! Are you mad?* | *Surely no one would be mad enough to fly in this weather?* | *My friends all think I'm* ***stark raving mad*** (=completely crazy). | *It's enough to send you* ***barking mad*** (=completely crazy). | **as mad as a hatter/March hare** (=completely crazy)

> **GRAMMAR**
>
> In this meaning, **mad** is not used with 'very'. You say: *It's an absolutely mad idea.* ✗ Don't say: *It's a very mad idea.*
>
> **GRAMMAR GUIDE** ▸ ADJECTIVES

3 UNCONTROLLED *especially BrE* behaving in a wild uncontrolled way, without thinking about what you are doing: **mad dash/rush/panic etc** *We all made a mad dash for the door.* | **mad with grief/fear/jealousy etc** *When she heard of her son's death, she was mad with grief.* | *When Italy scored, the crowd* ***went mad*** (=became very excited). | *We* ***went a bit mad*** (=spent a lot of money) *and ordered champagne.*

4 be mad about/for/on sb/sth *informal especially BrE* to like someone or something very much SYN **crazy**: *My nine-year-old is mad about Robbie Williams.* | *He's mad about computer games.* | *All the girls at school are mad for him.* | **be mad keen (on sth)** *'Did you enjoy the film?' 'I wasn't mad keen.'* | **be mad for it** (=want to do something very much)

5 MENTALLY ILL *especially BrE old-fashioned informal* mentally ill SYN **insane**: *Mr Rochester's mad wife* | *He turned towards me with a mad look in his eyes.* | *the cartoon figure of the* ***mad scientist***

6 like mad *informal* very much, very quickly, or with a lot of energy: *I caught my thumb in the door and it hurt like mad.* | *She ran like mad to catch the bus.*

7 don't go mad *BrE spoken* used to tell someone not to work too hard, get too excited, or spend too much money: *I know you've got a lot to do but don't go mad.*

8 power-mad/money-mad/sex-mad etc only interested in having power, money etc and doing everything possible to get it: *a power-mad dictator*

mad·am /'mædəm/ ●○○ *n*

1 *formal* used to address a woman in a polite way, especially a customer in a shop SYN **ma'am** *AmE*: *Are you being served, Madam?*

2 Dear Madam *formal* used at the beginning of a business letter to a woman, when you do not know her name

3 Madam President/Ambassador etc used to address a woman who has an important official position

4 [C] a woman who is in charge of a BROTHEL

5 a (proper) little madam *BrE informal* a young girl who is very confident and who expects other people to do everything she wants

Mad·ame /'mædəm, mə'dɑːm/ *n* (*plural* **Mesdames** /meɪ'dæm $ -'dɑːm/) used to address or refer to a French-speaking woman, especially one who is married → **Mademoiselle**, **Monsieur**: *Madame Lefèvre*

mad·cap /'mædkæp/ *adj* [only before noun] *old-fashioned* **1** a madcap idea seems crazy and unlikely to succeed: *a madcap scheme* **2** a madcap person behaves in a crazy and often funny way: *He plays a madcap game show host.*

ˌmad 'cow disˌease *n* [U] *informal* BSE

mad·den /'mædn/ *v* [T] *literary* to make someone very angry or annoyed: *The unfortunate animal was maddened with pain.*

mad·den·ing /'mædənɪŋ/ *adj* very annoying SYN **infuriating**: *maddening delays* —**maddeningly** *adv*: *He moved carefully and maddeningly slowly.*

made /meɪd/ *v* **1** the past tense and past participle of MAKE **2 factory-made/German-made/homemade etc** made in a factory, in Germany, at home etc: *sales of Japanese-made cars* **3 have (got) it made** *informal* to have everything that you need for success or for a happy life: *Nice house, good job, lovely family – you've got it made!* **4 see/find out what sb is (really) made of** *informal* to find out how strong, brave etc someone is or how skilful they are at doing something: *Come on then! Let's see what you're made of.* **5 I'm not made of money** *spoken* used when someone has asked you to pay for something in order to say that you cannot afford it and that you think they are being unreasonable: *I can't buy you shoes as well – I'm not made of money!* **6 be made for each other** *informal* to be completely suitable for each other, especially as husband and wife: *Sue and Joe were made for each other.* **7 be made (for life)** *informal* to be so rich that you will never have to work again: *If the deal is successful, I'll be made for life.* **8 be made up** *spoken informal* to feel very pleased and satisfied about something that has happened: *When I heard she was pregnant, I was really made up for her.*

Ma·dei·ra /mə'dɪərə $ -'dɪrə/ *n* [U] a strong sweet wine

Ma'deira cake *n* [C,U] a kind of plain yellow cake

Mad·e·moi·selle /ˌmædəmwəˈzel/ *n* (*plural* **Mesdemoiselles** /ˌmeɪdəmwəˈzel/) used to address or refer to a young French-speaking woman who is not married → **Madame, Monsieur**: *Mademoiselle Dubois*

ˌmade-to-ˈmeasure *adj* made-to-measure clothes, curtains etc are specially made to fit OPP **off-the-peg**

ˌmade-to-ˈorder *adj* made-to-order clothing, furniture etc is made for one particular customer: *made-to-order curtains*

ˈmade-up *adj* **1** a story, name, word etc that is made-up is not true or real: *She used a made-up name.* **2** wearing MAKE-UP on your face: *She was **heavily made-up*** (=wearing a lot of make-up).

mad·house /ˈmædhaʊs/ *n* [C usually singular] **1** a place with a lot of people, noise, and activity: *It's like a madhouse in here.* **2** *old use* a PSYCHIATRIC hospital

ˌMadison ˈAvenue a street in New York City that is famous as the centre of the advertising business. Its name is sometimes used to mean the US advertising business in general: *Madison Avenue marketing techniques*

mad·ly /ˈmædli/ *adv* **1** extremely and in a very strong way SYN **wildly**: *She fell **madly in love** with him.* | *Suddenly, I felt madly jealous.* **2** in a wild uncontrolled way SYN **wildly**: *The sign swung madly in the wind.*

mad·man /ˈmædmən/ *n* (*plural* **madmen** /-mən/) [C] **1** someone who behaves in a wild uncontrolled way: *He drives **like a madman**.* **2** *old-fashioned* a man who is mentally ill

ˈmad ˌmoney *n* [U] *AmE informal* money that you have saved so that you can spend it when you see something you want

mad·ness /ˈmædnəs/ ●●○ *n* [U]

1 *especially BrE* very stupid behaviour that could be dangerous or have a very bad effect: **it is madness (for sb) to do sth** *It would be madness to drive all that way on your own.* | *Cutting down the forest is **sheer madness*** (=completely crazy).

2 serious mental illness SYN **insanity**: *His family has a history of madness.*

3 moment/fit of madness when someone does something without thinking clearly: *In a moment of madness, I agreed to have the party at my house.* → **there's method in/to sb's madness** at METHOD(3)

Ma·don·na /məˈdɒnə $ məˈdɑː-/ *n* **1 the Madonna** Mary, the mother of Jesus, in the Christian religion **2** [C] a picture or figure of Mary

ma·dra·sa, **madrassa** /məˈdræsə/ *n* [C] an Islamic school or college

mad·ri·gal /ˈmædrɪɡəl/ *n* [C] a song for several singers without musical instruments, popular in the 16th century

mad·wom·an /ˈmædwʊmən/ *n* (*plural* **madwomen** /-ˌwɪmɪn/) [C] *old-fashioned* a woman who is mentally ill

mael·strom /ˈmeɪlstrəm/ *n* [C] **1** a confusing situation full of events or strong emotions that is difficult to understand or deal with SYN **whirlpool**: **[+of]** *a maelstrom of conflicting emotions* **2** dust or water that moves very quickly in circles: *A spinning maelstrom of rain swept around the mountain.* **3** a violent storm

maes·tro /ˈmaɪstrəʊ $ -roʊ/ *n* (*plural* **maestros**) [C] someone who can do something very well, especially a musician

maf·i·a /ˈmæfiə $ ˈmɑː-, ˈmæ-/ *n* **1 the Mafia** a large organized group of criminals who control many illegal activities, especially in Italy and the US **2** [singular] a powerful group of people within an organization or profession who support and protect each other: *the medical mafia*

maf·i·o·so /ˌmæfiˈəʊsəʊ $ ˌmɑːfiˈoʊsoʊ, ˌmæ-/ *n* (*plural* **mafiosi** /-siː/) [C] a member of the Mafia

mag /mæɡ/ *n* [C] *informal* a magazine: *music mags*

mag·a·zine /ˌmæɡəˈziːn $ ˈmæɡəziːn/ ●●● S2 W2 *n* [C]

1 a large thin book with a paper cover that contains news stories, articles, photographs etc, and is sold weekly or monthly: **fashion/computer/women's etc magazine** *a glossy fashion magazine* | *She's the editor of a popular women's magazine.* | *a magazine article* | *She glanced over the magazine racks.*

2 a television or radio programme which is made up of a number of reports: *a local news magazine programme*

3 the part of a gun that holds the bullets

4 the part that holds the film in a camera or PROJECTOR

5 a room or building for storing weapons, explosives etc

GRAMMAR

You read or see something **in a magazine**: *He read an interview with her in a magazine.* ✗ Don't say: *He read an interview with her on a magazine.*

GRAMMAR GUIDE ▸ NOUNS

ma·gen·ta /məˈdʒentə/ *n* [U] a dark reddish purple colour —**magenta** *adj*

mag·got /ˈmæɡət/ *n* [C] a small creature like a WORM that is the young form of a FLY and lives in decaying food, flesh etc

Ma·gi /ˈmeɪdʒaɪ/ *n* **the Magi** [plural] the three wise men who brought gifts to the baby Jesus, according to the Christian religion

ma·gic¹ /ˈmædʒɪk/ ●●● S3 W3 *n* [U]

1 the power to make impossible things happen by saying special words or doing special actions: *Do you believe in magic?* → **BLACK MAGIC, WHITE MAGIC**

2 a special, attractive, or exciting quality: *Paris has **lost** some of its **magic** for me over the years.* | **[+of]** *the magic of Christmas*

3 the skill of doing tricks that look like magic in order to entertain people, or the tricks that are done SYN **conjuring**

4 like magic/as if by magic in a surprising way that seems impossible to explain: *As if by magic, the waiter suddenly appeared with a tray of drinks.*

5 work/weave your magic if something or someone works or weaves their magic, they produce a good change or effect in a way that they are often able to do: *The warm weather and the beautiful scenery began to work their magic and she started to relax.*

6 work like magic to be very effective

magic² ●●● S3 W3 *adj*

1 [only before noun] in stories, a magic word or object has special powers that make the person using it able to do impossible things: *a book of **magic spells*** | *a magic sword*

2 relating to the skill of doing tricks to entertain people: *His best **magic trick** is sawing a lady in half.*

3 magic number/word a number or word that is particularly important or desired in a particular situation: *The magic words 'a million pounds' will get everyone's attention.*

4 the magic word the word 'please' – used when speaking to children: *What's the magic word then, Katie?*

5 magic touch a special ability to make things work well or to make people happy: *She's got a magic touch with babies.*

6 magic moment a short time which seems beautiful and special: *She didn't want to spoil this magic moment.*

7 magic circle a group of powerful people who are friendly with each other and help each other: *His outspokenness denied him access to the magic circle and he was never given high office.*

8 *BrE spoken* very good or very enjoyable SYN **great**: *'Did you have a good time?' 'Yeah, it was magic!'*

magic³ *v* (**magicked, magicking**) *BrE*

magic sb/sth **away** *phr v* to make someone or something disappear or go somewhere by using magic: *I wish I could magic us away to a warm beach.*

magic sth ↔ **up** *phr v* to make something appear suddenly and unexpectedly

ma·gic·al /ˈmædʒɪkəl/ ●●○ *adj*

1 very enjoyable, exciting, or romantic, in a strange or special way: *that magical evening we spent together*

2 relating to magic or able to do magic: *magical powers* —**magically** /-kli/ *adv*

ˌmagic ˈbullet *n* [C] **1** a drug or treatment that can cure a disease or illness quickly and easily **2** *informal* something that solves a difficult problem in an easy way: *There's no magic bullet for school reform.*

ˌmagic ˈcarpet *n* [C] in stories, a CARPET that can fly through the air and carry people from one place to another

ˌmagic ˈeye *n* [C] a PHOTOELECTRIC CELL

ma·gi·cian /məˈdʒɪʃən/ *n* [C] **1** a man in stories who can use magic SYN **sorcerer**, **wizard 2** an entertainer who performs magic tricks SYN **conjurer**

ˌmagic ˈlantern *n* [C] a piece of equipment used in the past to make pictures shine onto a wall or screen

ˌMagic ˈMarker *n* [C,U] *trademark* a large pen with a thick soft point

ˌmagic ˈmushroom *n* [C] a type of MUSHROOM that has an effect like some drugs, and makes you see things that are not really there

ˌmagic ˈwand *n* [C] **1** a stick used by a MAGICIAN **2** a way to solve problems or difficulties immediately - used humorously: *I wish I could just* **wave a magic wand** *and make everything all right.*

ma·gis·te·ri·al /ˌmædʒəˈstɪəriəl◂ $ -ˈstɪr-/ *adj* **1** a magisterial way of behaving or speaking shows that you think you have authority: *his magisterial voice* **2** a magisterial book is written by someone who has very great knowledge about a subject: *his magisterial study of the First World War* **3** [only before noun] connected with or done by a magistrate —**magisterially** *adv*

ma·gis·tra·cy /ˈmædʒəstrəsi/ *n* [U] **1** the official position of a magistrate, or the time during which someone has this position **2 the magistracy** magistrates considered together as a group

ma·gis·trate /ˈmædʒəstreɪt, -strət/ ●○○ *n* [C] someone, not usually a lawyer, who works as a judge in a local court of law, dealing with less serious crimes SYN **Justice of the Peace**

ˈMagistrates' ˌCourt *n* [C] one of the courts of law in each area of England and Wales which deal with less serious crimes

mag·ma /ˈmæɡmə/ *n* [U] *technical* hot melted rock below the surface of the Earth → see picture at **VOLCANO**

mag·na cum lau·de /ˌmæɡnə kʊm ˈlaʊdeɪ, -kʌm ˈlɔːdi $ -kʊm ˈlaʊdi/ *adj, adv* with high honour - used to show that someone has finished American high school or college at the second of the three highest levels of achievement that students can reach → **cum laude**, **summa cum laude**

mag·nan·i·mous /mæɡˈnænɪməs/ *adj* kind and generous, especially to someone that you have defeated: *a magnanimous gesture* —**magnanimously** *adv* —**magnanimity** /ˌmæɡnəˈnɪməti/ *n* [U]

mag·nate /ˈmæɡneɪt, -nət/ *n* [C] a rich and powerful person in industry or business SYN **tycoon**: **steel/oil/shipping etc magnate** *a powerful media magnate*

mag·ne·sia /mæɡˈniːʃə, -ʒə/ *n* [U] → **MILK OF MAGNESIA**

mag·ne·si·um /mæɡˈniːziəm/ *n* [U] a common silver-white metal that burns with a bright white flame. It is a chemical ELEMENT: symbol Mg

mag·net /ˈmæɡnɪt/ ●●○ *n* [C]
1 a piece of iron or steel that can stick to metal or make other metal objects move towards itself → **magnetism**
2 something or someone that attracts many people or things → **magnetism**: **[+for]** *The region has become a magnet for small businesses.* | **attract/draw sb/sth like a magnet** *She drew men to her like a magnet.* | **babe/chick magnet** *informal* (=a man who is attractive to women)

MAGNET

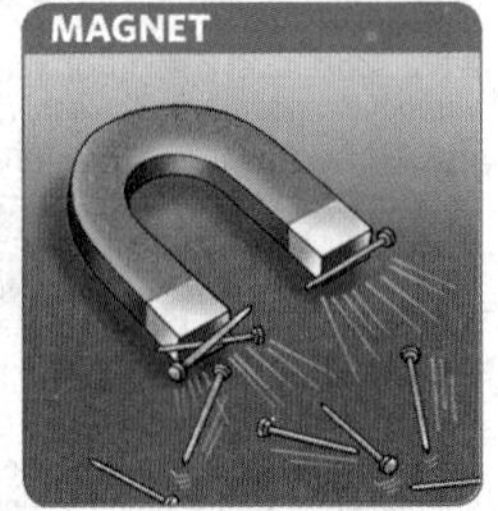

mag·net·ic /mæɡˈnetɪk/ ●●○ *adj*
1 concerning or produced by MAGNETISM: *magnetic forces*
2 having the power of a magnet or behaving like a magnet: *a magnetic bulletin board*
3 magnetic personality/charm etc qualities that make other people feel strongly attracted to you —**magnetically** /-kli/ *adv*

magˌnetic ˈdisk *n* [C] a DISK containing MAGNETIC TAPE that stores information to be used by a computer

magˌnetic ˈfield *n* [C] an area around an object that has magnetic power: *the Earth's magnetic field*

magˌnetic ˈmedia *n* [plural, U] magnetic methods of storing information for computers, for example a HARD DISK or MAGNETIC TAPE

magˌnetic ˈnorth *n* [U] the northern direction shown by the needle on a COMPASS → **TRUE NORTH**

magˌnetic ˈpole *n* [C] **1** one of the two points that are not firmly fixed but are near the North and South Poles of the Earth, towards which the needle on a COMPASS points **2** one of two points at the ends of a MAGNET where its power is strongest

magˌnetic ˈresonance ˌimaging *n* [U] *medical* (*written abbreviation* **MRI**) the process of using strong MAGNETIC FIELDS to make an image of the inside of someone's body for medical reasons

magˌnetic ˈtape *n* [U] tape on which sound, pictures, or computer information can be recorded

mag·net·is·m /ˈmæɡnətɪzəm/ *n* [U] **1** the physical force that makes two metal objects pull towards each other or push each other apart **2** if someone has magnetism, they have powerful exciting qualities that attract people to them: *his personal magnetism*

mag·net·ize (*also* **-ise** *BrE*) /ˈmæɡnətaɪz/ *v* [T] **1** to make iron or steel able to pull other pieces of metal towards itself **2** to have a powerful effect on people so that they feel strongly attracted to you: *His dark flashing eyes seemed to magnetize her.* —**magnetization** /ˌmæɡnətaɪˈzeɪʃən $ -tə-/ *n* [U]

mag·ne·to /mæɡˈniːtəʊ $ -toʊ/ *n* (*plural* **magnetos**) [C] a piece of equipment containing one or more MAGNETS that is used for producing electricity, especially in the engine of a car

ˈmagnet ˌschool *n* [C] *AmE* a school that has more classes in a particular subject than usual, and so attracts students from a wide area

mag·ni·fi·ca·tion /ˌmæɡnɪfɪˈkeɪʃən/ *n* **1** [U] the process of making something look bigger than it is: **at high/low etc magnification** *When viewed at high magnification, it is clear that the crystals are quite different.* | *greater levels of magnification* | **under magnification** *The colour is evident even under low magnification.* **2** [C] the degree to which something is able to make things look bigger: *binoculars with a magnification of x12* (=which make things look 12 times as big)

mag·nif·i·cent /mæɡˈnɪfəsənt/ ●●○ *adj* very good or beautiful, and very impressive: *a magnificent performance* | *The twelve-mile coastline has magnificent scenery.* | *She looked magnificent in a long red dress.* **THESAURUS** **BEAUTIFUL** —**magnificently** *adv* —**magnificence** *n* [U]

mag·ni·fi·er /ˈmæɡnɪfaɪə $ -ər/ *n* [C] an object which makes things look bigger

mag·ni·fy /ˈmæɡnɪfaɪ/ *v* (**magnified**, **magnifying**, **magnifies**) [T] **1** to make something seem bigger or louder, especially using special equipment: *At the Sheffield arena, the speakers were magnified ten times on a giant screen.* | *A public address system magnifies all the little noises and coughs.* **2** to make something seem more important than it really is SYN **exaggerate**: *The report tends to magnify the risks involved.* **3** *formal* to make something much worse or more serious: *The results of economic mismanagement were magnified by a series of natural disasters.*

ˈmagnifying ˌglass *n* [C] a round piece of glass with a handle, used to make objects or print look bigger → **MAGNIFY** → see picture at **OPTICAL**

mag·ni·tude /ˈmæɡnɪtjuːd $ -tuːd/ ●○○ *n*
1 [U] the great size or importance of something: **[+of]** *They didn't seem to appreciate the magnitude of the problem.* | **of such/this/similar etc magnitude** *We did not think the cuts would be of this magnitude.* | *an increase of this* ***order of magnitude*** (=size)
2 [C] *technical* the degree of brightness of a star
3 [C] *technical* the force of an EARTHQUAKE

mag·no·li·a /mæɡˈnəʊliə $ -ˈnoʊ-/ *n* **1** [C] a tree with large white, pink, yellow, or purple flowers **2** [U] a very pale cream colour —**magnolia** *adj*

mag·num /ˈmæɡnəm/ *n* [C] **1** a large bottle containing about 1.5 litres of wine, CHAMPAGNE etc **2** a powerful type of gun that you can use with one hand: *a .44 magnum*

ˌmagnum ˈopus *n* [singular] the most important piece of work by a writer, COMPOSER or artist

mag·pie /ˈmæɡpaɪ/ *n* [C] **1** a bird with black and white feathers and a long tail **2** *informal* someone who likes collecting things

mag·stripe /ˈmæɡstraɪp/ *n* [C] a MAGNETIC STRIP inside a plastic card such as a CREDIT CARD, on which information is stored electronically. The information can be read when the card is pushed through a special machine.

ma·ha·ra·jah, **maharaja** /ˌmɑːhəˈrɑːdʒə/ *n* [C] an Indian prince or king

ma·ha·ra·ni, **maharanee** /ˌmɑːhəˈrɑːniː/ *n* [C] an Indian PRINCESS or queen

ma·ha·rish·i /ˌmɑːhəˈriːʃi/ *n* [C] a Hindu holy teacher

ma·hat·ma /məˈhætmə $ məˈhɑːt-/ *n* a title used for a wise and holy man in India

mah·jong, **mahjongg** /ˌmɑː ˈdʒɒŋ $ -ˈʒɑːŋ/ *n* [U] a Chinese game played with small pieces of wood or bone

ma·hog·a·ny /məˈhɒɡəni $ məˈhɑː-/ *n* (*plural* **mahoganies**) **1** [C,U] a type of hard reddish brown wood used for making furniture, or the tree that produces this wood **2** [U] a dark, reddish brown colour —**mahogany** *adj*

ma·hout /mɑːˈhuːt, məˈhaʊt $ məˈhaʊt/ *n* [C] someone who rides and trains ELEPHANTS

maid /meɪd/ ●●○ *n* [C]
1 a female servant, especially in a large house or hotel: *a kitchen maid*
2 *old use* a woman or girl who is not married → **OLD MAID**

maid·en[1] /ˈmeɪdn/ *n* [C] **1** *literary* a young girl, or a woman who is not married SYN **damsel** **2** (*also* **maiden over**) in CRICKET, an OVER in which no runs are scored

maiden[2] *adj* **1 maiden flight/voyage** the first journey that a plane or ship makes **2 maiden speech** *BrE* the first speech that someone makes in parliament

ˌmaiden ˈaunt *n* [C] *old-fashioned* an AUNT who has never married

maid·en·head /ˈmeɪdnhed/ *n old use* **1** [U] the state of being a female VIRGIN SYN **virginity** **2** [C] a HYMEN

maid·en·ly /ˈmeɪdnli/ *adj literary old-fashioned* used to describe the behaviour of a girl or young woman who is shy about showing her body, talking about sex etc, especially in the past: *maidenly modesty*

ˈmaiden name ●○○ *n* [C] a woman's family name before she got married and started using her husband's family name → **married name**

ˌmaid of ˈhonour *BrE*, **maid of honor** *AmE n* (*plural* **maids of honour**) [C] **1** the most important BRIDESMAID at a wedding **2** an unmarried woman who works for a queen or a PRINCESS

maid·ser·vant /ˈmeɪdˌsɜːvənt $ -ɜːr-/ *n* [C] *old-fashioned* a female servant

mail[1] /meɪl/ ●●● S3 W3 *n* [U]
1 the letters and packages that are delivered to you: *You shouldn't read other people's mail.* | *He found a mountain of mail waiting for him.* | *She promised to* ***forward my mail*** *to my new address* (=send it from your old home or office to your new one). | *He gets sacks of* ***fan mail*** (=letters from people who admire him). | ***hate mail*** (=letters from people who hate you)
2 *especially AmE* the system of collecting and delivering letters and packages SYN **post** *BrE*: *The mail here's really slow and unreliable.* | *The product will be sold mainly through the mail.* | **in the mail** *I'll put the check in the mail tomorrow.* | **by mail** *Did you send the document by mail?* | **registered/express/first-class etc mail** *I sent my application by registered mail.* | *Most reports are sent via* ***internal mail*** (=a system of sending documents to people inside the same organization).
3 messages that are sent and received on a computer SYN **email**: *I* ***check my mail*** *a couple of times a day.* | *She's just received another* ***mail message*** *from them.*
4 ARMOUR made of small pieces of metal, worn by soldiers in the Middle Ages → **VOICEMAIL**

mail[2] ●●● S3 *v* [T] *especially AmE*
1 to send a letter or package to someone SYN **post** *BrE*: **mail sth to sb** *The weekly newsletter is mailed to women all over the country.*
2 to send a document to someone using a computer SYN **email**: **mail sth to sb** *Can you mail it to me as an attachment?*

mail sth ↔ **out** *phr v* to send letters, packages etc to a lot of people at the same time SYN **send out**: *The department has just mailed out 300,000 notices.*

mail·bag /ˈmeɪlbæɡ/ *n* [C] **1** a large strong bag used for carrying mail on trains etc **2** *AmE* a bag used to deliver letters to people's houses SYN **postbag** *BrE*

mail·bomb /ˈmeɪlbɒm $ -bɑːm/ *n* [C] a large number of email messages sent to the same computer, with the result that the computer has too much email and cannot work properly anymore

mail·box /ˈmeɪlbɒks $ -bɑːks/ ●●○ *n* [C] *AmE*
1 a box, usually outside a house, where someone's letters are delivered or collected → see picture at **POSTBOX**
2 a container where you post letters SYN **postbox** *BrE*
3 the part of a computer's memory where email messages are stored

ˈmail ˌcarrier *n* [C] *AmE old-fashioned* someone whose job is to deliver mail SYN **mailman**

ˈmail drop *n* [C] *AmE* **1** an address where someone's mail is delivered, which is not where they live **2** a box in a post office where your mail can be left

mail·er /ˈmeɪlə $ -ər/ *n* [C] *especially AmE* a container or envelope used for sending something small by post

mail·ing /ˈmeɪlɪŋ/ *n* **1** [C] something that is sent to people by post, especially to advertise something: *A catalogue and order form are included with this mailing.* | *A mailing had gone out to every school in the country.*
2 [C,U] the process of sending something to people by post: *A very effective mailing of product samples was carried out last year.* | *mailing costs*

ˈmailing list *n* [C] **1** a list of names and addresses kept by an organization, so that it can send information or advertising material by post: **on a mailing list** *I have included you on my mailing list for new EFL software.* **2** a list of names and email addresses kept on a computer so that you can send the same message to a group of people at the same time

mail·man /ˈmeɪlmæn/ *n* (*plural* **mailmen** /-men/) [C] *AmE* someone who delivers letters and packages to people's houses SYN **postman** *BrE*

ˌmail ˈorder *n* [U] a method of buying and selling in which the buyer chooses goods at home and orders them from a company which sends them by post: **by mail order** *It is available by mail order from Green Life Products.* | *a mail order catalogue*

mail·shot /ˈmeɪlʃɒt $ -ʃɑːt/ *n* [C] advertisements or information that a company sends to many people at one time by post: *We're sending out a mailshot telling our customers about our new products.*

ˈmail slot *n* [C] *AmE* a LETTERBOX

ˈmail train *n* [C] a train that carries letters and packages

maim /meɪm/ *v* [T] to wound or injure someone very seriously and often permanently: *Landmines still kill or maim about 300 people every month.* **THESAURUS** ▸ **HURT**

main¹ /meɪn/ ●●● S1 W1 *adj* [only before noun] **1** larger or more important than all other things, ideas etc of the same kind: *The main reason for living in Spain is the weather.* | *What do you consider to be the main problem?* | *Our main concern is that the children are safe.* | *a summary of the main points of the agreement* | *the main aim of the meeting* | *I'll meet you outside the main entrance.* | *the main bedroom* THESAURUS▸ IMPORTANT **2 the main thing** *spoken* used to say what is the most important thing in a situation: *As long as you're not hurt, that's the main thing.* | *The main thing is not to panic.* → **an eye for/on/to the main chance** at EYE¹(22)

main² *n* **1** [C] a large pipe or wire carrying the public supply of water, electricity, or gas: *The report found that many of Yorkshire's water mains needed replacing.* | *a burst gas main* **2** *BrE* **a) the mains** the place on a wall where you can connect something to a supply of electricity: *You can run the torch off batteries or plug it into the mains.* | **at the mains** *Make sure that the television is turned off at the mains.* **b) mains gas/water/electricity** gas, water, or electricity supplied to a building through a pipe or wire: *The heater will run off mains gas or bottled gas.* **3 in the main** mostly: *Their job in the main consisted of cleaning and maintaining the building.*

ˌmain ˈclause ●●○ *n* [C] *technical* a CLAUSE that can stand alone as a complete sentence → **subordinate clause**

ˌmain ˈcourse *n* [C] the main part of a meal: *What are you going to have for your main course?* | *starter, main course and dessert*

ˌmain ˈdrag *n* **the main drag** *AmE informal* the main street in a town or city where big shops and businesses are: *the restaurants that line the main drag*

main·frame /ˈmeɪnfreɪm/ *n* [C] a large powerful computer that can work very fast and that a lot of people can use at the same time: *If a problem does occur, a signal is automatically sent to the mainframe.*

main·land /ˈmeɪnlənd, -lænd/ ●○○ *n* **the mainland** the main area of land that forms a country, as compared to islands near it that are also part of that country: *flights between a Greek island and the mainland* | **on the mainland** *terrorist attacks both in Northern Ireland and on the mainland* —**mainland** *adj* [only before noun]: *mainland Britain*

ˌmain ˈline *n* [C] an important railway that connects two cities: *the main line to Moscow* —**main-line** *adj* [only before noun]: *a main-line station*

main·line¹ /ˈmeɪnlaɪn/ *adj* [only before noun] accepted by or involving most people in a society SYN **mainstream**: *mainline politics*

mainline² *v* [I,T] *informal* to INJECT an illegal drug directly into your blood: *He was mainlining heroin.*

main·ly /ˈmeɪnli/ ●●● S2 W2 *adv* used to mention the main part or cause of something, the main reason for something etc SYN **primarily**: *Her illness was caused mainly by stress.* | *The workforce is mainly made up of women.* | *I don't go out much, mainly because I have to look after the kids.* | *Increased sales during the summer were mainly due to tourism.* | *We talked about various things – work, mainly.*

> **REGISTER**
> In written English, people often prefer to use **chiefly** or **primarily**, which sound more formal than **mainly**:
> *The disease is caused **chiefly** by poor sanitation.*

main·mast /ˈmeɪnmɑːst, -məst $ -mæst, -məst/ *n* [C] the largest or most important of the MASTS on a ship

ˌmain ˈroad *n* [C] a large and important road: *We live just off the main road.* | **[+to/from/between]** *the main road from Bern to Lausanne*

main·sail /ˈmeɪnsəl $ -seɪl/ *n* [C] the largest and most important sail on a ship

main·spring /ˈmeɪnsprɪŋ/ *n* [C] **1 the mainspring of sth** the most important reason or influence that makes something happen: *Christian faith was the mainspring of Peter's life.* | *Small companies are the mainspring of the British economy.* **2** the most important spring in a watch or clock

main·stay /ˈmeɪnsteɪ/ *n* **the mainstay of sth a)** an important part of something that makes it possible for it to work properly or continue to exist: *Agriculture is still the mainstay of the country's economy.* **b)** someone who does most of the important work for a group or organization: *She was the mainstay of the team.*

main·stream¹ /ˈmeɪnstriːm/ ●○○ *n* **the mainstream** the most usual ideas or methods, or the people who have these ideas or methods: **[+of]** *Environmental ideas have been absorbed into the mainstream of European politics.* | *Genet started as a rebel, but soon became part of the literary mainstream.*

mainstream² *adj* [only before noun] accepted by or involving most people in a society: *Deaf children can often be included in mainstream education.* | *the mainstream political parties*

mainstream³ *v* [T] *AmE* to include a child with physical or mental problems in an ordinary class —**mainstreaming** *n* [U]

ˈMain Street *n* **1** the most important street, with many shops and businesses on it, in many small towns in the US SYN **high street** *BrE* **2** [U] *AmE* ordinary people who believe in traditional American values: *The president's new proposals won't go down too well on Main Street.*

> **THESAURUS: main**
>
> **main** larger or more important than all the others: *the main entrance of the building* | *the main reason for his decision*
> **chief/principal** most important. **Chief** and **principal** are more formal than **main**, and are often used in written English: *Coffee is the country's principal export.* | *What is the company's chief objective?*
> **major** very important or serious: *Smoking is a major cause of heart disease.* | *Street crime is becoming a major problem.*
> **key** most important, or the one that everything or everyone else depends on: *Education is likely to be a key issue in the election campaign.* | *Hooper was a key member of the team.* | *Diet is key.*
> **number one** *especially spoken* most important or best – this phrase sounds a little informal and it is used especially in spoken English: *Reliability is the number one priority.* | *the number one cause of death* | *He is still in the number one position.*
> **primary** most important – used especially about the most important aim, role, cause, or concern. **Primary** is more formal than **main**: *The primary aim of the project was to help students develop their communication skills.* | *Security is our primary concern.*
> **prime** very important or most important – used especially about the most important reason, cause, or aim, or about the most likely TARGET or SUSPECT. **Prime** is more formal than **main**: *Their prime objective is to increase profits for their shareholders.* | *Tourists are prime targets for theft and robbery.*
> **core** most important – used especially about the things that people should pay most attention to: *the core skills of reading and writing* | *He wants the company to focus on its core business – advertising.*
> **central** most important and having more influence than anything else: *The U.S. played a central role in the peace negotiations.* | *a central theme of the book*
> **predominant** most common, typical, or important: *Yellow was the predominant colour everywhere.* | *High arched windows are a predominant feature in English churches.* | *New York still has a predominant role in the contemporary art world.*

M

main·tain /meɪnˈteɪn, mən-/ ●●● S2 W1 AWL *v* [T]
1 MAKE STH CONTINUE to make something continue in the same way or at the same standard as before: *Careers Officers maintain contact with young people when they have left school.* | *Britain wants to maintain its position as a world power.* | *A lot depends on building and maintaining a good relationship with your customers.* | *The hotel prides itself on maintaining high standards.* | *How can we maintain control of spending?*
2 LEVEL/RATE to make a level or rate of activity, movement etc stay the same: *It is important to maintain a constant temperature inside the greenhouse.* | *This is the most efficient way to build up and maintain a reasonable level of physical fitness.*
3 SAY to strongly express your belief that something is true SYN **claim**: **maintain (that)** *Critics maintain that these reforms will lead to a decline in educational standards.* | **maintain your innocence** (=say that you did not commit a crime) *He maintained his innocence and said the allegations were 'ridiculous'.*
4 LOOK AFTER STH to keep a machine, building etc in good condition by checking and repairing it regularly: *The report found that safety equipment had been very poorly maintained.* | *The company is responsible for maintaining public telephone boxes.*
5 PROVIDE MONEY/FOOD to provide someone with the things they need, such as money or food SYN **provide for**: *How can you maintain a family on $900 a month?*

main·te·nance /ˈmeɪntənəns/ ●●○ W3 AWL *n* [U]
1 the repairs, painting etc that are necessary to keep something in good condition: *the cost of repairs and maintenance* | **[+of]** *The caretaker is responsible for the maintenance of the school buildings.* | *The theatres were closed on Saturday and Sunday for* ***routine maintenance***. | *Engineers are* ***carrying out essential maintenance work*** *on the main line to Cambridge.* | *an evening class in* ***car maintenance*** | **maintenance crew/man/staff** (=someone who looks after buildings and equipment for a school or organization)
2 the act of making a state or situation continue: **[+of]** *The purpose of the UN is the maintenance of international peace and security.* | *The maintenance of a firm currency plays an important part in the battle against inflation.*
3 *BrE* money paid by someone who is DIVORCED to their former wife or husband SYN **alimony**: *They have to find the fathers who abandon their children and make them pay maintenance.*

mai·son·ette /ˌmeɪzəˈnet/ *n* [C] *BrE* an apartment on two floors that has its own front door and is part of a larger building

mai·tre d' /ˌmetrə ˈdiː $ ˌmeɪ-/ (*also* **maître d'hôtel** /ˌmetrə dəʊˈtel $ ˌmeɪtrə doʊ-/) *n* [singular] someone who is in charge of a restaurant, and who welcomes guests, gives orders to the waiters etc

maize /meɪz/ *n* [U] *BrE* a tall plant with large yellow seeds that grow together on a COB (=long hard part), and that are cooked and eaten as a vegetable SYN **corn** *AmE* → see picture at **VEGETABLE**[1]

Maj. (*also* **Maj** *BrE*) the written abbreviation of ***major***: *Maj. John Wright*

ma·jes·tic /məˈdʒestɪk/ *adj* very big, impressive, or beautiful: *This lovely village is surrounded by majestic mountain scenery.* THESAURUS HIGH —**majestically** /-kli/ *adv*

ma·jes·ty /ˈmædʒəsti/ *n* (*plural* **majesties**) **1 Your/Her/His Majesty** used when talking to or about a king or queen → **Your/Her/His Highness**: *The prime minister is here to see you, Your Majesty.* | *His Majesty the King* **2** [U] the quality that something big has of being impressive, powerful, or beautiful SYN **grandeur**: **[+of]** *the pure majesty of the Alps*

ma·jor[1] /ˈmeɪdʒə $ -ər/ ●●● S1 W1 AWL *adj*
1 [usually before noun] having very serious or worrying results OPP **minor**: *There is a major problem with parking in London.* | *The loss of their goalkeeper through injury was a major setback for the team.* | *He underwent major heart surgery recently.* | *It could have sparked a major confrontation.* THESAURUS IMPORTANT, MAIN
2 [usually before noun] very large or important, when compared to other things or people of a similar kind OPP **minor**: **major role/part/factor etc** *Britain played a major role in the negotiations.* | *There are two major political parties in the US.* | *The government's major concern is with preventing road accidents.* | *Smoking is one of the major causes of cancer.* | *the major developments in computer technology* | *a major road* THESAURUS BIG
3 [not before noun] *AmE spoken* very important: *This is major? You got me out of bed for this?*
4 a major KEY is based on a musical SCALE in which there are SEMITONES between the third and fourth and the seventh and eighth notes → **minor**: *a symphony in D major*

major[2] ●○○ *n* [C]
1 an officer of middle rank in the British or US army or MARINES, or in the US air force → **DRUM MAJOR**
2 *especially AmE* the main subject that a student studies at college or university: *Her major is history.*
3 *AmE* someone studying a particular subject as their main subject at college or university: *She's a history major.*
4 the majors [plural] the MAJOR LEAGUES

major[3] ●○○ *v*
major in sth *phr v especially AmE* to study something as your main subject at college or university: *He's majoring in Political Science.*
major on sth *phr v especially BrE* to pay particular attention to one subject or thing: *The company is planning to major on offering the machines we need.*

ma·jor·do·mo /ˌmeɪdʒəˈdəʊməʊ $ -dʒərˈdoʊmoʊ/ *n* (*plural* **majordomos**) [C] *old-fashioned* someone in charge of the servants in a large house

ma·jor·ette /ˌmeɪdʒəˈret/ (*also* **drum majorette**) *n* [C] a girl who spins a BATON while marching with a band

ˌmajor ˈgeneral *n* [C] an officer of high rank in the British or US army, or the US air force

ma·jor·i·ty /məˈdʒɒrəti $ məˈdʒɔː-, məˈdʒɑː-/ ●●● S2 W1 AWL *n* (*plural* **majorities**)
1 MOST PEOPLE OR THINGS [singular] most of the people or things in a group OPP **minority**: **[+of]** *The majority of workers find it quite hard to live on the amount of money they earn.* | **great/vast/overwhelming majority of sth** (=almost all of a group) *In the vast majority of cases the disease is fatal.* | **be in the majority** (=form the largest group) *In this city, Muslims are in the majority.* → **SILENT MAJORITY**

GRAMMAR: Singular or plural verb?

- You use a plural verb with **the majority of**, when it is followed by a plural noun: *The* ***majority of*** *patients* ***are*** *women.*
- You use a plural verb with **the majority** on its own, when you are considering members of a group as individual people: *He sees several patients a day. The* ***majority are*** *women.*
- You usually use a singular verb with **majority**, when considering people as a single group: *The majority* ***is*** *unwilling to listen to the views of the minority.* In British English, you can also use a plural verb in this meaning.

GRAMMAR GUIDE NOUNS

2 MOST VOTES [C] if one person or group wins a majority in an election, they win more votes than other people or groups: **majority of 50/100 etc** *He won by a majority of 500.* | *The Labour Party* ***won*** *a huge* ***majority*** *at the last general election.* | **clear/overall/absolute majority** (=a situation in which one party wins more votes in an election than all the other parties) *The party won an absolute majority in Portugal in 1987.* | **small/narrow majority** *The government gained only a narrow majority, with 151 votes against 144.* | **Labour/Conservative etc majority** *The Labour majority was reduced to just 15 seats at the last election.*
3 majority vote/decision/verdict etc a vote or decision in which more people vote for something than vote against it: *The committee takes decisions by majority vote.* | *The jury found him guilty by a majority verdict.*
4 majority stake/shareholding etc when one person or group owns a bigger share of a company than other

people or groups and so is able to control what happens to the company: *Alex Golding held a majority shareholding in Golding plc.*

5 BECOMING AN ADULT [U] *BrE law* the age when someone legally becomes an adult OPP **minority**: **reach majority/the age of majority** *He became a partner in the family firm on reaching his majority.*

ma'jority ˌleader *n* [C] the person who organizes the members of the political party that has the most people elected, in the US House of Representatives or Senate → **minority leader**

maˌjority 'rule *n* [U] a system of government in which every person in a country has the right to vote and the group which wins the most votes has power: *It took many years of struggle to establish majority rule in South Africa.*

ˌmajor-'league *adj* [only before noun] **1** connected with the Major Leagues: *a major league pitcher* **2** important, large, or having a lot of influence: *a major-league player in California politics*

ˌMajor 'Leagues *n* **the Major Leagues** the group of teams that make up the highest level of American professional baseball → **Minor Leagues**

ma·jor·ly /ˈmeɪdʒəli $ -ər-/ *adv* [+adj/adv] *informal* extremely: *I was majorly upset, as you can imagine.*

make[1] /meɪk/ ●●● S1 W1 *v* (*past tense and past participle* **made** /meɪd/)

1 PRODUCE [T] to produce something, for example by putting the different parts of it together: *I'm going to show you how to make a box for your tools.* | *A family of mice had made their nest in the roof.* | *She made her own wedding dress.* | *The company has been making quality furniture for over 200 years.* | *They met while they were making a film.* | *Make a list of all the things you need.* | **make sb sth** *He made her a toy horse, using just some straw and bamboo twigs.* | **be made from sth** *Paper is made from wood.* | **be made (out) of sth** *a shirt made of silk* | **make sth from/out of sth** *She's very good at making things from old scraps of material.* | **Japanese-made/English-made etc** (=produced in Japan etc) → **make the bed** at BED[1](1), → see picture at ASSEMBLE

2 DO [T] used with some nouns to say that someone does something: *Anyone can make a mistake.* | *I can't make a decision just yet.* | *I need to make a quick phone call.* | *You could have made more effort to talk to him.* | *He made no attempt to apologize.* | *Could I make a suggestion?* | *There are a few points I'd like to make.* | *The police were called but no arrests were made.* | *I suppose we should make a start on cleaning this room.* | *Stop making such a fuss!*

3 COOK [T] to cook or prepare food or drink: *When was the last time you made a cake?* | *John was making breakfast in the kitchen.* | *Who's going to make the tea?* | **make sb sth** *I'll make you some sandwiches.* THESAURUS COOK

4 CAUSE [T] to cause something to happen, or cause a particular state or condition: *Its beautiful beaches make this a highly popular area with tourists.* | *It was this movie which made him a star.* | *His attitude made him very unpopular with colleagues.* | *The photo makes her look much older than she really is.* | **make sb/sth do sth** *I like him because he makes me laugh.* | **make sth difficult/easy/possible etc** *The use of computers has made it possible for more people to work from home.* | **make sth the best/worst/most expensive etc** *Over 80,000 people attended, making it the biggest sporting event in the area.* | *The president has* ***made it clear*** *that he is not going to change his mind.*

> **REGISTER**
> In written English, people often use **cause sb to do sth** rather than **make sb do sth**, as it sounds more formal: *His attitude* ***caused*** *him* ***to*** *be unpopular with colleagues.*

5 FORCE [T] to force someone to do something: **make sb do sth** *My parents always make me do my homework before I go out.* | **be made to do sth** *I was made to wait four hours before I was examined by a doctor.* THESAURUS FORCE

6 MARK/HOLE ETC [T] to cause a mark, hole etc to appear: **make a hole/dent/mark etc** *Make a hole in the paper.* | *The cup has made a mark on the table.*

7 **make it a)** to succeed in getting somewhere in time for something or when this is difficult: *If we run, we should make it.* | **[+to]** *With blood pouring from his leg, he made it to a nearby house.* **b)** to be successful at something, for example in your job: *He came to the US and not only made it but* ***made it big*** (=was extremely successful). | *So far, relatively few women have* ***made it to the top*** *in the business world.* | **[+as]** *He was told he had no talent and would never make it as a professional singer.* | **[+to]** *England look less likely to make it to the finals.* | **make it to manager/director etc** *How did anyone so stupid make it to manager?* **c)** *spoken* to be able to go to an event, meeting etc that has been arranged: *I'm really sorry, but I won't be able to make it on Sunday after all.* | *Nice to see you. I'm glad you could make it.* **d)** *informal* to continue to live after you have been seriously ill or badly injured: *Frank was very ill, and the doctors didn't think he'd make it.* **e)** to manage to deal with a difficult experience: **[+through]** *I couldn't have made it through those times without the support of my boyfriend.* **f)** used to say or ask what time it is according to your own or someone else's watch: *What time do you make it?* | *I make it ten past three.*

8 **make the meeting/the party/Tuesday etc** *spoken* to be able to go to something that has been arranged for a particular date or time: *I'm sorry, I can't make Friday after all.* | *Will you be able to make the next meeting?*

9 ACHIEVE STH [T] to succeed in achieving a particular position, rate etc: *He was never good enough to make the team.* | *I don't think we'll make the deadline.*

10 GET MONEY [T] to earn or get money: *The plan could cost you more than you would make.* | *They* ***made a profit*** *of £140 million.* | *His one aim in life was to* ***make money***. | *She hopes to* ***make a living*** (=earn the money she needs to live) *from writing children's books.* | *He's* ***made a fortune*** (=earned a lot of money) *selling computers on the Internet.* | **make sth out of sth** *How easy is it to make money out of gardening?* THESAURUS EARN

11 HAVE A QUALITY [linking verb] to have the qualities that are necessary for a particular job, use, or purpose: **[+noun]** *I'm sure you will make a very good teacher.* | *The hall would make an ideal venue for a wedding reception.* | *An old cardboard box makes a comfortable bed for a kitten.*

> **GRAMMAR: Linking verbs**
> **Make** is a linking verb in this meaning. It links the subject of the sentence with an adjective and noun: *You'll make a wonderful father.* | *The leaves make a pretty table decoration.*

12 **make it/that sth** *spoken* used to correct what you have just said: *Can we have two cups of coffee, please? No, make that three.*

13 **make do** to manage with the things that you have, even though this is not really enough: *I hardly had any food in the house so I just had to make do.* | **[+with/without]** *I usually make do with a cup of coffee for breakfast.* | *For many people,* ***make do and mend*** (=when someone manages with the things they have and does not buy anything new) *was a harsh reality.*

14 **make yourself heard/understood/known etc** to succeed in getting someone to hear you, understand you, or know that you are there: *I had to shout to make myself heard above the music.*

15 BE A TOTAL [linking verb] to be a particular amount when added together: *Two and two make four.* | *There are nine people coming, plus me, which makes ten.*

16 CALCULATE [T] used to say what you have calculated a number to be: *I make that $150 altogether.*

17 SPORTS SCORE [T] to achieve a particular score in a sports game: *Surrey had made 92 by lunchtime.*

18 **make sb captain/leader etc** to give someone a new job or position in a group, organization etc: *She's now been made a full partner.* | *He was made mayor in 1998.*

19 **make believe** to pretend or imagine that something is true when it is not: *I tried to make believe she was happy, but knew deep down it wasn't true.* → MAKE-BELIEVE

20 **make like** *informal* to behave as if something is true when it is not: *He makes like he never met me before.*

21 **make as if to do sth** *literary* to seem as if you are going to do something but then not do it: *She made as if to speak but then stopped.*

22 ARRIVE [T] *old-fashioned* to arrive at or get to a particular place, especially when it is difficult: *I don't think we're going to make the town before nightfall.*

23 make the papers/headlines/front page etc to be interesting or important enough to be printed in a newspaper, reported on television etc: *News of their divorce made the headlines.*

24 make or break to cause something or someone either to be very successful or to fail completely: *Critics can make or break a young performer.* → MAKE-OR-BREAK

25 that makes two of us *spoken* used to say that you agree with someone or that something that is true of them is true of you too: *'I haven't a clue what's going on.' 'That makes two of us.'*

26 MAKE STH PERFECT [T] *informal* to make something complete or successful: *The hat makes the outfit.*

27 make it with sb *old-fashioned informal* to have sex with someone → MADE, → **make sb's day** at DAY(19), → **make friends** at FRIEND[1](3), → **make good** at GOOD[1](35), → **make sense** at SENSE[1](5)

GRAMMAR: Comparison

be made of

• You use this when saying which material is used to make something. The material has not been changed and can still be recognized: *The table is made of wood. | The ring was made of solid gold.*

be made from

• You use this especially when the materials used to make something have been completely changed and cannot be recognized: *The drink is made from cherries. | Cheese is made from milk.* ✗ Don't say: *made by cherries | made by milk*

be made by

• You use this when saying who makes something: *The pots are made by local craftsmen.*

• You also use this when saying how something is made: *Tar is made by heating coal to a high temperature.*

THESAURUS

make used about things you make yourself, or things that are made in a factory: *Diane makes all her own clothes. | My camera was made in China.*

produce to make something in large quantities to be sold, or to make something as the result of a natural process: *The factory produces high-quality steel. | The pancreas is a gland in your body which produces hormones.*

create to make something new and original: *Tarantino created a whole new style of films. | Many companies invest a lot of money in creating new products.*

manufacture to make machines, cars, equipment etc in factories: *The company manufactures aircraft parts.*

mass-produce to make very large quantities of something in a factory: *They developed a way to mass-produce the drug.*

develop to design and make something new over a period of time: *In 1962, Enders developed an effective vaccine against measles. | The company is developing new anti-virus software.*

form to make something as the result of a natural process or chemical reaction: *Hydrogen and oxygen combine to form water. | The research will help us understand how planets are formed.*

generate to make something such as heat, electricity, or power: *Wind can be used to generate electricity.*

make away with sb/sth *phr v*

1 *informal* to steal something and take it away with you: *Thieves made away with the contents of the safe.*

2 *old-fashioned* to kill someone

make for sth *phr v*

1 to go in the direction of a particular place SYN **head for**: *I think it's time we made for home.*

2 to cause a particular result or situation: *Both teams are on good form, which should make for a great game.* → **made for each other** at MADE(6)

make sb/sth **into** sth *phr v*

1 to change something so that it has a different form or purpose SYN **convert**: *We can make your room into a study.*

2 to change someone's character, job, position in society etc: *The movie made her into a star overnight.*

make sth **of** sb/sth *phr v*

1 to have a particular opinion about or understanding of something or someone: *I didn't know what to make of her. | What do you make of the idea?*

2 to use the opportunities that you have in order to become successful: *I want to make something of my life.* | **make sth of yourself** *She has the ambition and talent to make something of herself.*

3 make the most of sth to get as much advantage as you can from a situation while you are able to: *We've only got one day in Paris, so we'd better make the most of it.*

4 make too much of sth to treat something as if it is more important than it really is: *It would be a mistake to make too much of these findings.* → **make much of sb/sth** at MUCH[2](17)

5 make a day/night/evening of it *informal* to spend a whole day, night etc doing something, because you have chosen to: *We decided to take a picnic and make a day of it.* → **make a go of sth** at GO[2](3), → **make the best of sth** at BEST[3](9), → **see what sb is made of** at MADE(4)

make off *phr v* to leave quickly, especially in order to escape: *The men made off as the police arrived.* | **[+along/across/through etc]** *The getaway car made off towards Horrocks Avenue.*

make off with sth *phr v informal* to steal something and take it away with you: *Thieves broke into the school and made off with computer equipment worth £40,000.*

make out *phr v*

1 SEE/HEAR **make sth ↔ out** to be just able to see or hear something: *He could just make out a dark shape moving towards him.* | **make out who/what etc** *I couldn't make out what he was saying.*

2 UNDERSTAND STH **make sth ↔ out** to understand something, especially the reason why something has happened: **make out what/how/why etc** *I couldn't make out what I had done to annoy her.* | ***As far as I can make out**, he has never been married.*

3 UNDERSTAND SB **make sb ↔ out** [usually in questions and negatives] to understand someone's character and the way they behave: *Stuart's a strange guy – I can't make him out at all.*

4 WRITE CHEQUE ETC **make sth ↔ out** to write something such as a bill or cheque: *She was making out a list of people to invite. | The book gives advice on making out a will.* | **[+to]** *Make the cheque out to 'Grays Ltd'.*

5 SAY/PRETEND **make sb/sth ↔ out** to say that something is true when it is not: *The situation was never as bad as the media made out.* | **make out (that)** *She always tried to make out that I was wrong and she was right.* | **make sb/sth out to be sth** *He makes me out to be some sort of idiot.*

6 make out a case (for sth) to find good reasons that prove something or show why you need something: *We made out a case for hiring another assistant.*

7 SUCCEED *especially AmE* to succeed or progress in a particular way SYN **get on**: *How did you make out this morning?*

8 SEX *informal especially AmE* to kiss and touch someone in a sexual way

9 make out like a bandit *AmE informal* to get or win a lot of money: *The lawyers made out like bandits.*

make sth **out of** sb/sth *phr v* to change a person or thing into something else: *The Olympics can make sporting heroes out of previously little-known athletes.*

make sth/sb **↔ over** *phr v*

1 *especially BrE* to officially and legally give money or property to someone else SYN **transfer**: **[+to]** *He made over the whole estate to his son.*

2 to change someone or something so that they look

different or have a different use: *Redgrave has made herself over completely for her movie role.* → MAKEOVER
make towards sth *phr v BrE formal* to start moving towards something: *She made towards the door.*
make up *phr v*
1 FORM/BE make up sth to combine together to form something SYN **constitute**: *Women make up only a small proportion of the prison population.* | **be made up of sth** *The committee is made up of representatives from every state.*

GRAMMAR: Using the progressive

• **Make up** is not used in the progressive in this meaning. You say: *Oxygen makes up roughly 20% of the atmosphere.* ✗ Don't say: *Oxygen is making up roughly 20% of the atmosphere.*
• However, the participle form **making up** is often used: *Customers under 25 are important, making up a quarter of the total.*

2 PRETEND STH IS TRUE make sth ↔ up to pretend that something is true in order to deceive someone: *I think they're making the whole thing up.* → MADE-UP(1)
3 INVENT make sth ↔ up to produce a new story, song, game etc by thinking: *Nick made up a song about them.* | *When you're the boss you can make up your own rules.* | *I've given talks so many times that now I just* ***make*** *them* ***up as I go along*** (=think of things to say as I am speaking).
4 PREPARE make sth ↔ up to prepare something by mixing things or putting things together: *I could make up a bed for you on the sofa.* | *Can you make up a bottle of milk for the baby?*
5 SB'S FACE make sb ↔ up to put MAKE-UP (=special coloured substances) on someone's face in order to make them look better or different: *They made him up as an old man for the last act of the play.* | *One lucky winner will have the chance to be made up and photographed.* ⚠ Do not use the verb 'make up' when you are talking about putting make-up on your own face. Say that you **put on (your) make-up.** → MADE-UP(2)
6 NUMBER/AMOUNT make sth ↔ up *especially BrE* to add to an amount in order to bring it up to the level that is needed: *I saved as much as I could, and my parents made up the rest.* | *The company will be forced to pay $6 million to* ***make up the difference****.*
7 TIME/WORK make sth ↔ up to work at times when you do not usually work, because you have not done as much work as you should: *I'm trying to make up the time I lost while I was sick.* | *Is it OK if I make the work up next week?*
8 FRIENDS (*also* **make it up**) *informal* to become friendly with someone again after you have had an argument: **[+with]** *Have you made up with Patty yet?* | *Oh come on! Why don't you just* ***kiss and make up****?*
9 FROM CLOTH make sth ↔ up to produce something from cloth by cutting and sewing: *The dress had been made up to her exact requirements.* | **[+into]** *I plan on making that material up into a dress.* → **make up your mind** at MIND[1](3)
make up for sth *phr v*
1 to make a bad situation better, or replace something that has been lost SYN **compensate**: *The team will be anxious to make up for a disappointing start to the season.* | *I don't eat breakfast but I make up for it at lunch.* | *The good days* ***more than make up for*** *the bad ones.*
2 to have so much of one quality that it is not important that you do not have much of another one: **[+in/with]** *What Jay lacked in experience, he made up for in enthusiasm.* | *Caroline doesn't have a natural talent for music but she makes up for it with hard work.*
3 to do something to show that you are sorry for doing something that upset or annoyed someone: *I'm sorry I was late. To make up for it, let me treat you to a meal.*
4 make up for lost time a) to work more quickly, or at times when you do not usually work, because something has prevented you from doing the work before: *We rehearsed all day Saturday, to make up for lost time.* **b)** to do a lot of something in an eager way because you have not had a chance to do it before: *Palin didn't travel much as a young man but he's certainly made up for lost time now.*
make up to sb *phr v*
1 make (it) up to sb to do something to show that you are sorry about the problems you have caused someone: *I'll make it up to you somehow.* | *He was looking for a way to make up to her for what he had done.*
2 *BrE informal* to say nice things to someone or be very friendly to them in order to get an advantage for yourself – used to show disapproval
3 be made up to captain/manager etc to be given a higher position in an organization SYN **promote**: *He was a security guard before he was made up to reception manager.*

make² ●●○ *n*
1 [C] the name of a particular product or of the company that makes it: *What make is your car?* | **[+of]** *It's one of the most popular makes of satellite phone on the market.*
2 be on the make *informal* to be trying to get money or power – used to show disapproval: *He was just a salesman on the make.*

ˈmake-beˌlieve *n* [U] when you imagine or pretend that something is real or true: *He seems to be living in a* ***world of make-believe****.* | *children in the middle of a make-believe adventure*

ˌmake-or-ˈbreak *adj* something that is make-or-break will lead to either success or failure: *This could be a make-or-break speech for the prime minister.*

make·o·ver /ˈmeɪkəʊvə $ -oʊvər/ *n* [C] **1** if you give someone a makeover, you make them look more attractive by giving them new clothes, a new hairstyle etc **2** if you give a place a makeover, you make it look more attractive by painting the walls, putting in new furniture etc: *It's time we* ***gave*** *the kitchen* ***a makeover****.*

mak·er /ˈmeɪkə $ -ər/ ●●○ *n* [C]
1 a person or company that makes a particular type of goods: **car/film/shoe etc maker** *a quality furniture maker* | *a leading Japanese computer maker* | **[+of]** *The makers of the car claim that it uses up to 50% less fuel than other similar cars.*
2 a machine or piece of equipment that makes something: **coffee/pasta etc maker** *Grind the beans to suit your coffee maker.*
3 decision-maker/policymaker/peacemaker etc someone who does something or makes something happen: *Who's the decision-maker in this department?* | *health care administrators and policymakers* → TROUBLEMAKER, HOLIDAYMAKER
4 meet your maker *informal* to die – used humorously

make·shift /ˈmeɪkʃɪft/ *adj* made to be used for a short time only when nothing better is available: *The refugees slept in makeshift tents at the side of the road.*

MAKE-UP

ˈmake-up, make·up /ˈmeɪkʌp/ ●●○ *n*
1 FOR YOUR FACE [U] coloured substances that are put on

your face to improve or change your appearance: *I don't usually wear much make-up.* → **make up** at MAKE[1]
2 PEOPLE IN A GROUP [singular] the make-up of a group or team is the combination of people that are in it: **[+of]** *We should change the make-up of the team.*
3 CHARACTER **sb's make-up** the qualities that a person has, which form their character: *Pride has always been an important part of his make-up.* | **sb's genetic/psychological make-up** *a possible link between genetic make-up and criminal behaviour*
4 TEST [C] (*also* **make-up test**) *AmE* a test that you take in school when you were not able to take a previous test

COLLOCATIONS

VERBS

wear make-up *They're not allowed to wear make-up to school.*
have make-up on (=be wearing make-up) *She had no make-up on.*
use make-up *She rarely uses make-up.*
put on make-up (*also* **apply make-up** *formal*) *Gloria watched her mother put on her make-up.*
do your make-up (=put on make-up) | **take off make-up** (*also* **remove make-up** *formal*) | **touch up/fix your make-up** (=put a little more make-up on after some has come off)

ADJECTIVES/NOUN + make-up

heavy make-up (=a lot of make-up) *a girl in high heels and heavy make-up*
eye make-up *She was wearing far too much eye make-up.*
stage make-up (=make-up that actors wear in plays)

make-up + NOUN

a make-up artist (=someone whose job is to put make-up on actors, people appearing on television etc)

ˈmake-weight /ˈmeɪkˌweɪt/ *n* [C] a person or thing that is not very important but is included so there is the right number of people or the right amount of something

ˈmake-work *n* [U] *AmE* work that is not important but is given to people to keep them busy

mak·ing /ˈmeɪkɪŋ/ *n* [U] **1** the process of making something: **[+of]** *companies involved in the making of nuclear weapons* | **cheese making/cider making etc** *a region famous for its cheese making* **2 decision-making/policymaking** the process of deciding something: *people involved in decision-making at the highest level* **3 be the making of sb** to make someone a much better or more successful person: *You'll see - a couple of years abroad will be the making of him.* **4 have the makings of sth** to have the qualities or skills necessary to do a particular job: *He has the makings of a world-class footballer.* **5 be a long time/ten years etc in the making** to take a long time, ten years etc to make: *a book that was ten years in the making* **6 be of your own making** problems that are of your own making have been caused by you and no one else: *He admits that a lot of his troubles are entirely of his own making.*

mal- /mæl/ *prefix* bad or badly: *a malformed limb* (=wrongly shaped) | *The children had been maltreated* (=treated cruelly).

mal·ad·just·ed /ˌmæləˈdʒʌstɪd◂/ *adj* a maladjusted child behaves badly and is unable to form good relationships with people because he or she has emotional problems OPP **well-adjusted**

mal·ad·min·i·stra·tion /ˌmælədmɪnəˈstreɪʃən/ *n* [U] *formal* careless or dishonest management: *He accused the local authority of maladministration.*

mal·a·droit /ˌmæləˈdrɔɪt◂/ *adj formal* not clever or sensitive in the way you deal with people

mal·a·dy /ˈmælədi/ *n* (*plural* **maladies**) [C] **1** *formal* a serious problem in society **2** *old use* an illness

ma·laise /məˈleɪz, mæ-/ *n* [singular, U] *formal* **1** a general problem that is difficult to describe in an exact way: *a general malaise within society* **2** a general feeling that you are slightly ill or not happy in your life

mal·a·prop·is·m /ˈmæləprɒpɪzəm $ -prɑː-/ *n* [C] *literary* an amusing mistake that you make when you use a word that sounds similar to the word you intended to say but means something completely different

ma·lar·i·a /məˈleəriə $ -ˈler-/ *n* [U] a disease that is common in hot countries and that you get when a type of MOSQUITO bites you —**malarial** *adj*: *malarial fever*

ma·lar·key /məˈlɑːki $ -ˈlɑːr-/ *n* [U] *informal* things which you think are silly or untrue SYN **nonsense**: *I'm not interested in all this scientific malarkey.* | *You don't believe in ghosts* ***and all that malarkey****, do you?*

mal·con·tent /ˈmælkəntent $ ˌmælkənˈtent/ *n* [C] *formal* someone who is likely to cause trouble because they are not happy with the way things are organized - used to show disapproval

male[1] /meɪl/ ●●● S3 W2 *adj*
1 typical of or relating to men or boys OPP **female** → **masculine**: *a deep male voice* | *traditional male values* | *Motor-racing has largely been* ***a male preserve*** (=something that only men have been involved with).
2 a male person or animal cannot have babies or lay eggs OPP **female**: *adult male bears* | *Many women earn less than their male colleagues.*
3 a male plant or flower cannot produce fruit OPP **female**
4 *technical* a male PLUG has parts that stick out and that fit into a hole or SOCKET OPP **female**

male[2] ●●● W3 *n* [C]
1 a male animal OPP **female**: *The male is usually bigger and more brightly coloured than the female.* THESAURUS MAN
2 a man OPP **female**: *Police described her attacker as a white male aged about 25.*

ˌmale ˈchauvinist *n* [C] a man who believes that men are better than women and has fixed traditional ideas about the way men and women should behave - used to show disapproval: *I'm afraid Bill's a bit of a male chauvinist.* | **male chauvinist pig** (=an insulting name for a male chauvinist) —**male chauvinism** *n* [U]

mal·e·dic·tion /ˌmæləˈdɪkʃən/ *n* [C] *old-fashioned formal* a wish that something bad will happen to someone SYN **curse**

ˌmale-ˈdominated *adj* involving mostly men or controlled mostly by men: *a male-dominated profession*

mal·e·fac·tor /ˈmæləfæktə $ -ər/ *n* [C] *old-fashioned formal* someone who does bad or illegal things

ˌmale ˈmenopause *n* [singular] a period in the middle of a man's life when he sometimes feels anxious and unhappy because he is getting older - often used humorously

ˌmale-voice ˈchoir *n* [C] a large group of men who sing together

ma·lev·o·lent /məˈlevələnt/ *adj formal* a malevolent person wants to harm other people SYN **evil** OPP **benevolent**: **malevolent look/stare/smile etc** *He gave her a dark, malevolent look.* —**malevolence** *n* [U] —**malevolently** *adv*

mal·feas·ance /mælˈfiːzəns/ *n* [U] *law* illegal or dishonest activity

mal·for·ma·tion /ˌmælfɔːˈmeɪʃən $ -fɔːr-/ *n* [C,U] *technical* when a part of someone's body is badly formed SYN **deformity**: *children suffering from malformations of the legs and arms*

mal·formed /ˌmælˈfɔːmd◂ $ -ˈfɔːrmd◂/ *adj technical* if a part of someone's body is malformed, it is badly formed SYN **deformed**: *malformed limbs*

mal·func·tion /mælˈfʌŋkʃən/ *n* [C] a fault in the way a machine or part of someone's body works: *a malfunction in one of the engines* | **[+of]** *a malfunction of the immune system* | *an equipment malfunction* —**malfunction** *v* [I]: *A warning light seems to have malfunctioned.*

mal·ice /ˈmælɪs/ *n* [U] **1** the desire to harm someone because you hate them: **with malice** *His eyes gleamed with malice.* | **sheer/pure malice** *She did it out of sheer malice.* |

M

James ***bore*** *her no* ***malice*** (=did not feel any malice towards her). **2 with malice aforethought** *law* with the deliberate intention of doing something that is against the law

ma·li·cious /məˈlɪʃəs/ *adj* very unkind and cruel, and deliberately behaving in a way that is likely to upset or hurt someone: *a malicious girl* | **malicious gossip/rumour** *Who is responsible for these malicious rumours?* THESAURUS UNKIND —**maliciously** *adv* —**maliciousness** *n* [U]

ma·lign¹ /məˈlaɪn/ *v* [T] to say unpleasant things about someone that are untrue SYN **slander**: *She had seen herself repeatedly maligned in the newspapers.* | *a* ***much maligned*** *politician* GRAMMAR **Malign** is usually passive.

malign² *adj formal* harmful OPP **benign**: *a malign influence*

ma·lig·nan·cy /məˈlɪgnənsi/ *n* (*plural* **malignancies**) **1** [C] *medical* a TUMOUR **2** [U] *formal* a feeling of great hatred

ma·lig·nant /məˈlɪgnənt/ *adj* **1** *medical* a malignant disease is one such as CANCER, which can develop in an uncontrolled way and is likely to cause someone's death OPP **benign**: *She developed a malignant tumour in her breast.* **2** *formal* showing that you hate someone: *a malignant look*

ma·lin·ger /məˈlɪŋgə $ -ər/ *v* [I usually in progressive] to avoid work by pretending to be ill: *He accused Frank of malingering.* —**malingerer** *n* [C]

mall /mɔːl, mæl $ mɒːl/ ●●● S3 W3 *n* [C] *especially AmE* a large area where there are a lot of shops, usually a covered area where cars are not allowed SYN **shopping centre**: *Let's meet at the mall and go see a movie.* | *a huge new* ***shopping mall*** → STRIP MALL

mal·lard /ˈmælɑːd $ -ərd/ *n* [C] a type of wild duck

mal·le·a·ble /ˈmæliəbəl/ *adj* **1** *technical* something that is malleable is easy to press or pull into a new shape: *malleable steel* **2** *formal* someone who is malleable can be easily influenced or changed by other people: *a malleable child* —**malleability** /ˌmæliəˈbɪləti/ *n* [U]

mal·let /ˈmælɪt/ *n* [C] **1** a wooden hammer with a large end **2** a wooden hammer with a long handle that you use for playing CROQUET or POLO → see picture at CROQUET

MALLET

mal·low /ˈmæləʊ $ -oʊ/ *n* [C,U] a plant with pink or purple flowers → MARSHMALLOW

mall·rat /ˈmɔːlræt $ ˈmɒːl-/ *n* [C usually plural] *AmE informal* a young person who goes to SHOPPING MALLS a lot in order to be with their friends, not to buy things

mal·nour·ished /ˌmælˈnʌrɪʃt◂ $ -ˈnɜː-, -ˈnʌ-/ *adj* someone who is malnourished is ill or weak because they have not had enough good food to eat: *malnourished children*

mal·nu·tri·tion /ˌmælnjʊˈtrɪʃən $ -nʊ-/ *n* [U] when someone becomes ill or weak because they have not eaten enough good food → **nutrition**: *refugees suffering from malnutrition*

mal·o·dor·ous /mælˈəʊdərəs $ -ˈoʊ-/ *adj literary* smelling unpleasant SYN **smelly**

mal·prac·tice /mælˈpræktɪs/ *n* [C,U] *law* when a professional person makes a mistake or does not do their job properly and can be punished by a court: *Her doctor was found guilty of malpractice.*

malt /mɔːlt $ mɒːlt/ *n* **1** [U] grain, usually BARLEY, that has been kept in water for a time and then dried. It is used for making beer, WHISKY etc. **2** [C] *AmE* a drink made from milk, malt, and ICE CREAM that usually has something else such as chocolate added: *a cheeseburger and a chocolate malt* **3** [C,U] (*also* **malt whisky**) a type of high-quality WHISKY from Scotland

malt·ed /ˈmɔːltɪd $ ˈmɒːl-/ (*also* **ˌmalted ˈmilk**) *n* [C] *AmE* a MALT(2)

Mal·tese Cross /ˌmɔːltiːz ˈkrɒs $ ˌmɒːltiːz ˈkrɒːs/ *n* [C] a cross with four pieces that become wider as they go out from the centre

ˌmalt ˈliquor *n* [U] *AmE* a type of beer

mal·treat /mælˈtriːt/ *v* [T] to treat a person or animal cruelly SYN **mistreat**: *The hostages said they were hungry but had not been maltreated.* —**maltreatment** *n* [U]: *evidence of animal maltreatment*

mal·ware /ˈmælweə $ -wer-/ *n* [U] software that is designed to get onto a computer and cause harm to the information there or problems with the way it works

mam /mæm/ *n* [C] mother – used in Scotland and northern England SYN **mum**

ma·ma¹, **mamma**, **momma** /ˈmɑːmə/ ●●○ *n* [C] *AmE* a mother – used by or to children SYN **mummy**: *I want my mama!*

ma·ma² /məˈmɑː/ *n* [C] *BrE old-fashioned* mother

mama's boy /ˈmɑːməz ˌbɔɪ/ *n* [C] *AmE* a boy or man who lets his mother look after him and protect him too much, so that people think he is weak SYN **mummy's boy** *BrE*: *You've got to stand up for yourself – stop being such a mama's boy.*

mam·ba /ˈmæmbə $ ˈmɑːmbə, ˈmæmbə/ *n* [C] a poisonous African snake that is black or green

mam·bo /ˈmæmbəʊ $ ˈmɑːmboʊ/ *n* (*plural* **mambos**) [C,U] a dance, originally from Cuba, or the music for this dance

mam·ma /ˈmɑːmə/ *n* [C] *AmE* another spelling of MAMA¹

mam·mal /ˈmæməl/ ●●○ *n* [C] a type of animal that drinks milk from its mother's body when it is young. Humans, dogs, and whales are mammals. THESAURUS ANIMAL —**mammalian** /mæˈmeɪliən/ *adj*

mam·ma·ry /ˈmæməri/ *adj* [only before noun] *technical* connected with or relating to the breasts: *normal mammary tissue* | *mammary cancer*

ˈmammary ˌgland *n* [C] *technical* the part of a woman's breast that produces milk, or a similar part of a female animal

mam·mo·gram /ˈmæməgræm/ *n* [C] an X-RAY picture of a woman's breasts used to check for signs of CANCER

mam·mo·gra·phy /mæˈmɒgrəfi $ -ˈmɑː-/ *n* [U] examination of a woman's breasts using X-RAYS to check for signs of CANCER

mam·mon /ˈmæmən/ *n* [U] *formal* money, wealth, and profit, regarded as something bad because people want or think about them too much

mam·moth¹ /ˈmæməθ/ *adj* [only before noun] extremely large SYN **enormous**, **gigantic**: *Reforming the prison system would be a mammoth task.* | *a mammoth corporation*

mammoth² *n* [C] an animal like a large hairy ELEPHANT that lived on Earth thousands of years ago

mam·my /ˈmæmi/ *n* (*plural* **mammies**) [C] mother – used especially in Ireland

man¹ /mæn/ ●●● S1 W1 *n* (*plural* **men** /men/)

1 MALE PERSON [C] an adult male human → **woman**: *There were two men and a woman in the car.* | *He's a very kind man.* | *a man's watch* | *Don't keep Hansen waiting – he's a busy man.*

2 STRONG/BRAVE [C usually singular] a man who has the qualities that people think a man should have, such as being brave, strong etc: *Come on,* ***be a man*** *now. No more crying.* | *He wasn't* ***man enough*** (=strong or brave enough) *to face up to his responsibilities.* | **make a man (out) of sb** (=make a boy or young man start behaving in a confident way) *Running his own business has really made a man out of Terry.*

3 PERSON [C] a person, either male or female – used especially in formal situations or in the past: *All men are equal in the eyes of the law.* | *a man's right to work*

4 PEOPLE [U] people as a group: *This is one of the worst diseases* ***known to man***. | *the evolution of man* | **prehistoric/**

Stone Age/modern man (=people who lived at a particular stage of human development)
5 WORKER a) [C usually plural] a man who works for an employer: *Why were there no protests from the men at the factory?* **b)** [C] a man who does a job for you, especially repairing something: *Has the man been to fix the TV?* | **gas man/rent man etc** *I waited all day for the gas man.* **c) the man from sth** a man who works for a particular company or organization: *Was that the man from the PR agency?*
6 PARTICULAR KIND OF MAN [C] **a)** a man who comes from a particular place, does a particular kind of work, or is connected with a particular organization, especially a university or company: *I think she married a Belfast man.* | *I've been a military man all my life.* | *Even a Harvard man has a lot to learn about politics.* **b)** a man who likes, or likes doing, a particular thing: *I'm more of a jazz man myself.* | *Are you a betting man?*
7 man! *spoken* **a)** used when speaking to an adult male, especially when you are excited, angry etc: *Stop talking nonsense, man!* **b)** used when speaking to someone, especially an adult male: *You look great, man!*
8 SOLDIER [C usually plural] a soldier or SAILOR who is under the authority of an officer: *The captain ordered his men to fire.*
9 HUSBAND [C] *informal* a woman's husband or boyfriend: **sb's man** *She spent five years waiting for her man to come out of prison.*
10 the man *spoken* **a)** used to talk about a man you dislike, a man who has done something stupid etc: *Don't listen to him – the man's a complete idiot.* **b) The Man** *AmE old-fashioned* someone who has authority over you, especially a police officer
11 sb's your man *spoken* used to say that a particular man is the best person for a job, situation etc: *If you need repairs done in the house, Brian's your man.*
12 you da man! you're the man! *AmE spoken* used to praise someone for having done something well
13 our man *spoken* used by the police to refer to a man that they are watching or trying to find, especially because they think he is responsible for a crime: *Gareth couldn't possibly be our man. He couldn't possibly be a murderer.* | *Perhaps our man parked his car at the station and took the train.*
14 our man in/at sth a man who is the representative of a country or organization in a particular place: *our man in Rome* | *a report on the accident from our man at the scene*
15 men in (grey) suits *informal* the men who control businesses, organizations etc, considered as a group, especially when you think they are boring
16 a man of his word a man you can trust, who will do what he has promised to do: *He had promised to help, and Sally knew that Dr Neil was a man of his word.*
17 a man of few words a man who does not talk very much: *Being a man of few words, his message was short and to the point.*
18 be your own man to behave and think independently without worrying about what other people think: *I'm my own man. I say what I believe.*
19 the man of the moment/hour/year a man who has recently done something important: *Olson was the man of the hour when the team beat the Tigers.*
20 it's every man for himself *spoken* used to say that people will not help each other: *In journalism it's every man for himself.*
21 the man in the street (*also* **the man on the Clapham omnibus** *BrE old-fashioned*) the average man or the average person SYN **Joe Bloggs/Schmo**: *This kind of music doesn't appeal to the man in the street.*
22 a man of the people a man who understands and expresses the views and opinions of ordinary people: *The prime minister is a man of the people.*
23 a man's man a man who enjoys being with other men and doing sports and activities with them, and is popular with men rather than women: *He enjoyed his reputation as a man's man, but was careful never to neglect his family.*
24 a ladies' man a man who is popular with women and who likes to go out with a lot of different women: *Paul likes to think he's a bit of a ladies' man.*
25 man and boy *BrE* if a man has done something man and boy, he has done it all his life: *I've worked on that farm man and boy.*
26 man and wife if a man and a woman are man and wife, they are married: *I now pronounce you man and wife* (=you are now officially married).
27 live as man and wife if a man and a woman live as man and wife, they live together as if they are married, although they are not
28 as one man *written* if a group of people do something as one man, they do it together: *The audience rose as one man to applaud the singers.*
29 to a man/to the last man *written* used to say that all the men in a group do something or have a particular quality: *They were socialists to a man.*
30 man-about-town a rich man who goes out a lot to parties, clubs, theatres etc: *In his designer suit and shiny shoes he looked quite the man about town.*
31 man of God/man of the cloth a priest: *You'd believe a man of the cloth, wouldn't you?*
32 my (good) man *BrE old-fashioned spoken* used when talking to someone of a lower social class – do not use this phrase: *My good man, I really don't think you should be here.*
33 my man *spoken* used by some men to greet a friend: *Jason, my man! How's it going?*
34 your/yer man *spoken* used to talk about a particular man – used mainly in Ireland: *I've got to go and see yer man this afternoon.*
35 SERVANT [C] *old-fashioned* a male servant: *My man will drive you to the station.*
36 GAME [C] one of the pieces you use in a game such as CHESS
37 every man jack *old-fashioned* each person in a group: *Spies, every man jack of them, I'd bet.*
38 kick/hit a man when he's down to treat someone badly when you know that they already have problems: *Most of his rivals couldn't resist kicking a man when he was down.*
39 man's best friend a dog
40 the man of the house the most important male member of a family, who is responsible for doing things such as paying bills, making important decisions etc: *Since my father's death, my eldest brother has been the man of the house.* → **BEST MAN, MAN-TO-MAN, NEW MAN, OLD MAN,** → **be a man/woman of the world** at **WORLD**[1](21)

THESAURUS

man an adult male human: *a young man* | *Sir Edmund Hillary was the first man to climb Mount Everest.*
guy (*also* **bloke/chap** *BrE*) *informal* a man: *She'd arranged to meet a guy in the bar.* | *Alex is a really nice bloke.*
gentleman *formal* a man – used as a very polite way of talking about a man: *an elderly gentleman* | *Please could you serve this gentleman?*
boy a young male person, usually a child or a teenager: *a teenage boy*
lad *old-fashioned informal* a boy or young man: *When I was a young lad, I wanted to join the army.*
youth a teenage boy or young man – used especially in news reports to show disapproval: *Gangs of youths roam the streets.*
male *formal* a man – used especially by the police or in science and research contexts. The adjective **male** is much more common than the noun: *We are investigating the death of an unidentified male.* | *The condition is usually found only in males.*

RELATING TO MEN

male *adj* a male teacher, singer etc is a man. Male jobs are the kind of jobs that men typically do: *Most science teachers are male.* | *a male nurse* | *We are trying to recruit more women to do traditionally male jobs such as engineering.*

masculine considered to be more typical of a man than of a woman: *He had a very masculine face.* | *masculine aggression*
manly having the qualities that people expect and admire in a man, such as being brave and strong: *He took off his shirt, revealing his manly chest.* | *It isn't considered manly to cry.*
macho behaving in a way that is traditionally typical of men, for example by being strong and tough and not showing your feelings – used especially either humorously or to show disapproval: *Stallone always plays macho men.* | *He's far too macho to drink mineral water.*

man² ●○○ *v* (**manned, manning**) [T] to work at, use, or operate a system, piece of equipment etc: *A team of volunteers are manning the phones.* | *the first manned spacecraft*
man up *phr v informal* if a man mans up, he makes an effort to behave bravely: *You need to man up and tell her to leave!*

man³ *interjection especially AmE* used to emphasize what you are saying, especially when you are angry, surprised, disappointed etc: *Man, that was a lucky escape!* | ***Oh, man!*** *I can hear the bullets.*

man·a·cle /ˈmænəkəl/ *n* [C usually plural] an iron ring on a chain that is put around the wrist or ANKLE of a prisoner —**manacle** *v* [T] —**manacled** *adj*

man·age /ˈmænɪdʒ/ ●●● S1 W1 *v*
1 BUSINESS [T] to direct or control a business or department and the people, equipment, and money involved in it: *He was asked to manage a new department.* | *Managing a football team is harder than you think.* | *The company had been very badly managed.* | *a brewery which has been owned and managed by the same family for over 100 years*
THESAURUS ▶ CONTROL
2 DO STH DIFFICULT [I,T] to succeed in doing something difficult, especially after trying very hard: **manage to do sth** *I finally managed to push the huge animal away.* | *How do you manage to stay so slim?* | *We* ***somehow managed*** *to persuade him.* | *Juventus managed two goals in the last ten minutes.* | *I don't know how I'll* ***manage it****, but I'll be there.*
THESAURUS ▶ SUCCEED

REGISTER
In written English, people often use **succeed in doing** something rather than **manage to do** something, as it sounds more formal: *At a time of depression, Roosevelt* ***succeeded in*** *restoring hope.*

3 DEAL WITH PROBLEMS [I] to succeed in dealing with problems, living in a difficult situation etc: *I don't know how she manages with seven children.* | *We didn't have the proper equipment, but we managed somehow.* | **[+without]** *How do you manage without a washing machine?* | **[+with]** *I can't afford to get you a new coat – you'll have to manage with the one you've got.*
4 TIME/MONEY ETC [T] to use your time, money etc sensibly, without wasting it: *Paying a little each month can help you manage your money.* | *You need to learn to manage your time more effectively.* | *Consultants can help academic institutions to manage their resources more efficiently.*
5 LIVE WITHOUT MUCH MONEY [I] to succeed in buying the things that you need in order to live even though you do not have very much money SYN **get by**: *I honestly don't know how we'll manage now Keith's lost his job.* | *It'll be tight, but I guess I'll just about manage.* | **[+on]** *People like Jim have to manage on as little as $75 a week.*
6 NOT NEED HELP [I,T] *spoken* to be able to do something or carry something without help: *Can you manage all right, Mum?* | *You'll never manage that suitcase; let me take it.* | *Thank you, but I think I can manage perfectly well on my own.*
7 KEEP TIDY [T] *especially BrE* to succeed in keeping something neat and tidy: *He'll never manage such a big garden on his own.*
8 CONTROL [T] to control the behaviour of a person or animal, so that they do what you want: *It's hard to manage your children and do the shopping.* | *The horse was huge and vicious. Giles was the only one who could manage her.*
9 BE STRONG ENOUGH [T] to be able to do something because you are strong enough or healthy enough: *He tried to walk, but managed only a few shaky steps.*
10 EAT/DRINK [T] to be able to eat or drink something: *Could you manage another drink?*
11 CAUSE PROBLEMS [T] to do something that causes problems – used humorously: **manage to do sth** *Andrews has managed to get himself sacked.* | *I don't know how I managed to arrive so late.*
12 manage a few words/a smile etc to make yourself say or do something when you do not really want to: *Tom looked tired but still managed a smile.* | **manage to smile/speak/laugh etc** *'Through here,' he managed to say, almost out of breath.*
13 HAVE TIME FOR [T] to be able to meet someone or do something, even though you are busy: ***Can you manage*** *dinner tonight?* | *'Is there any chance you could work late?' 'I think I* ***could manage*** *an hour.'*

GRAMMAR: Comparison
manage
• You **manage to do** something: *She managed to persuade him.* ✗ Don't say: *She managed persuading him.*
• You can say that you **manage** something or just that you **manage**: *Did you manage it?* | *Somehow I managed.*
succeed
• You **succeed in doing** something: *She succeeded in persuading him.* ✗ Don't say: *She succeeded to persuade him.*
• You can also use **succeed** on its own: *I hope you succeed.* ✗ Don't say: *I hope you succeed it.*
GRAMMAR GUIDE ▶ VERBS

man·age·a·ble /ˈmænɪdʒəbəl/ *adj* easy to control or deal with OPP **unmanageable**: *Divide the task into manageable sections.* —**manageability** /ˌmænɪdʒəˈbɪləti/ *n* [U]

man·age·ment /ˈmænɪdʒmənt/ ●●● S1 W1 *n*
1 [U] the activity of controlling and organizing the work that a company or organization does: **good/bad management** *good management and co-operation with staff* | *a lack of management skills* | *a management consultant* | *management training courses*
2 [singular, U] the people who are in charge of a company or organization: *The management has agreed to the policy.* | *The shareholders demanded a change in management.* | *management decisions* | *The factory* ***is under new management****.* | **senior/top management** *It is difficult to retain top management.* | *a member of the senior management team* | **middle management** (=the people in charge of small groups within an organization)

GRAMMAR: Singular or plural verb?
• In this meaning, **management** is usually followed by a singular verb: *The management* ***is*** *bringing in a new IT system.*
• In British English, you can also use a plural verb: *The management* ***are*** *bringing in a new IT system.*
GRAMMAR GUIDE ▶ NOUNS

3 [U] the way that people control and organize different situations that happen in their lives or their work: **[+of]** *careful management of the economy* | *traffic management* | *The successful applicant will have experience in project management.* | *courses in time management* | **crisis management** (=when you deal with an unusually difficult or dangerous situation)

ˌmanagement ˈbuyout *n* [C] when a company's managers buy the company they work for

ˈmanagement conˌsultant *n* [C] someone who is paid to advise the management of a company how to improve their organization and working methods

man·ag·er /ˈmænɪdʒə $ -ər/ ●●● S1 W1 *n* [C] **1** someone whose job is to manage part or all of a company or other organization: **bank/sales/project etc manager** *She's now assistant marketing manager for the southeast area.* | *one of our regional managers* | **[+of]** *the* ***general manager*** *of Chevrolet* | *a* ***middle manager*** *in a computer company* (=someone who manages a small part of a company) → LINE MANAGER **2** someone who is in charge of training and organizing a sports team: *the new England manager* | **[+of]** *the manager of Lazio* **3** someone who is in charge of the business affairs of a singer, an actor etc

man·ag·er·ess /ˌmænɪdʒəˈres $ ˈmænɪdʒərɪs/ *n* [C] *old-fashioned* a woman who is in charge of a business, especially a shop or restaurant

man·a·ge·ri·al /ˌmænəˈdʒɪəriəl $ -ˈdʒɪr-/ ●○○ *adj* relating to the job of a manager: *managerial skills*

ˌmanaging diˈrector *n* [C] *BrE* someone who is in charge of a large company or organization SYN **chief executive officer**

ma·ña·na /məˈnjɑːnə/ *adj, adv* a word meaning 'tomorrow', used to talk about someone who seems too relaxed and always delays doing things: *a mañana attitude* —**mañana** *n* [U]

ˌman-at-ˈarms *n* (*plural* **men-at-arms**) [C] *old use* a soldier

man·a·tee /ˈmænətiː/ *n* [C] a large sea animal with FLIPPERS and a large flat tail, which eats plants

ˈman bag *n* [C] a fashionable bag for a man to carry with him

ˈman boobs *n* [plural] *informal* areas of fat or muscle on a man's chest that look like breasts

Man Book·er Prize, the /mæn ˈbʊkə ˌpraɪz $ -kər-/ an important prize given every year in the UK for the best full-length novel written by a citizen of the British Commonwealth or the Republic of Ireland during the previous 12 months. It is also often called simply the Booker Prize: *Man Booker Prize-winning author Yann Martel*

Man·cu·ni·an /mænˈkjuːniən/ *n* [C] someone from the city of Manchester in England —**Mancunian** *adj*

man·da·la /ˈmændələ, mænˈdɑːlə/ *n* [C] a picture of a circle around a square, that represents the universe in the Hindu and Buddhist religions

man·da·rin /ˈmændərɪn/ *n* [C] **1** (*also* **ˌmandarin ˈorange**) a kind of small orange with skin that is easy to remove **2** *BrE* an important government official who people think has too much power: *Civil Service mandarins* **3** an important government official in the former Chinese EMPIRE

Mandarin *n* [U] the official language of China, spoken by most educated Chinese people

ˌmandarin ˈorange *n* [C] a MANDARIN

man·date¹ /ˈmændeɪt/ ●○○ *n* **1** [C] if a government or official has a mandate to make important decisions, they have the authority to make the decisions because they have been elected by the people to do so: **mandate to do sth** *The president was elected with a* ***clear mandate*** *to tackle violent crime.* | **[+for]** *a* ***popular mandate*** *for election reform* | **[+from]** *I* ***sought a mandate*** *from my constituents to oppose this tax.* | **have/be given a mandate** *Sometimes a president thinks he has more of a mandate than he really does.* **2** [C] an official instruction given to a person or organization, allowing them to do something: *Matters debated in meetings do not become a mandate automatically.* **3** [C,U] the power given to one country to govern another country

man·date² /mænˈdeɪt/ *v* [T] **1** *formal* to tell someone that they must do a particular thing: *These measures were mandated by the IMF.* | **mandate that** *Justice mandates that we should treat all candidates equally.* **2** to give someone the right or power to do something: **be mandated to do sth** *The committee was mandated to co-ordinate measures to help Poland.*

man·dat·ed /mænˈdeɪtɪd/ *adj* [only before noun] a mandated country has been placed under the control of another country: *mandated territories*

man·da·to·ry /ˈmændətəri $ -tɔːri/ ●○○ *adj* if something is mandatory, the law says it must be done SYN **compulsory, obligatory** → **discretionary**: **[+for]** *Crash helmets are mandatory for motorcyclists.* | *Murder carries a* ***mandatory*** *life* ***sentence.*** | *The Council has* ***made*** *it* ***mandatory*** *for all nurses to attend a refresher course every three years.*
THESAURUS NECESSARY

man·di·ble /ˈmændəbəl/ *n* [C] *technical* **1** the jaw bone of an animal or fish, especially the lower jaw **2** the outside part of a bird's beak **3** the part of an insect's mouth that it uses for eating

man·do·lin, **mandoline** /ˌmændəˈlɪn/ *n* [C] a musical instrument with eight metal strings and a round back, played with a PLECTRUM (=small piece of plastic, metal etc) → see picture at **STRINGED INSTRUMENT**

man·drake /ˈmændreɪk/ *n* [C] a poisonous plant that was once thought to have magic powers

man·drill /ˈmændrɪl/ *n* [C] a large monkey that lives in West Africa and that has a red and blue face

mane /meɪn/ *n* [C] **1** the long hair on the back of a horse's neck, or around the face and neck of a lion → see pictures at **BIG CAT**, **HORSE¹** **2** *literary* a person's long thick hair: *her mane of hair*

ˈman-eater *n* [C] **1** a wild animal that kills and eats people **2** a woman who people think is frightening because she has many sexual partners – used humorously —**man-eating** *adj*: *a man-eating shark*

ma·neu·ver /məˈnuːvə $ -ər/ *n, v* the American spelling of MANOEUVRE

ma·neu·ve·ra·ble /məˈnuːvərəbəl/ *adj* the American spelling of MANOEUVRABLE

ma·neu·ve·ring /məˈnuːvərɪŋ/ *n* [C,U] the American spelling of MANOEUVRING

ˈman flu *n* [U] a cold that a man has, which he calls FLU to make it sound more serious – used humorously: *If your husband's got man flu, try and be patient with him as he complains about how awful he's feeling.*

ˌMan ˈFriday *n* a loyal and trusted servant or helper. This name comes from a character in the book *Robinson Crusoe* by Daniel Defoe. He is a black man who becomes Crusoe's servant and friend after Crusoe saves him from being killed by CANNIBALS (=people who eat other people). Crusoe calls him Man Friday because he met him on a Friday.

man·ful·ly /ˈmænfəli/ *adv old-fashioned* in a brave determined way: *Ed struggled manfully with his case.*

man·ga /ˈmæŋgə/ *n* [U] Japanese COMIC books. The pictures in the stories usually go from right to left in the same way as Japanese writing, and the characters often have very large eyes. → **ANIME**

man·ga·nese /ˈmæŋgəniːz/ *n* [U] a grey-white metal that breaks easily and is used to make steel and glass. It is a chemical ELEMENT: symbol Mn

mange /meɪndʒ/ *n* [U] a skin disease of animals that makes them lose their fur

man·ger /ˈmeɪndʒə $ -ər/ *n* [C] a long open container that horses, cattle etc eat from

mange·tout /ˌmɒnʒˈtuː $ ˌmɑːnʒ-/ *n* [C] *BrE* a long flat green vegetable whose outer part is eaten as well as the seeds SYN **snow pea** *AmE* → see picture at **VEGETABLE¹**

man·gle¹ /ˈmæŋgəl/ *v* [T] **1** to damage or injure something badly by crushing or twisting it: *The trap closed round her leg, badly mangling her ankle.* **2** to spoil something such as a speech or piece of music, by saying or playing it badly: *The orchestra had mangled Bach's music.* —**mangled** *adj* [only before noun]: *the mangled remains of the aircraft*

mangle² *n* [C] a machine used in former times to remove water from washed clothes by pressing them between two ROLLERS

man·go /ˈmæŋgəʊ $ -goʊ/ *n* (*plural* **mangoes**) [C] a tropical fruit with a thin skin and sweet yellow flesh → see picture at FRUIT[1]

man·grove /ˈmæŋgrəʊv $ -groʊv/ *n* [C] a tropical tree that grows in or near water and grows new roots from its branches: *a mangrove swamp*

mang·y /ˈmeɪndʒi/ *adj* **1** suffering from MANGE: *thin mangy dogs* **2** *informal* dirty and in bad condition: *a mangy-looking rug*

man·han·dle /ˈmænhændl/ *v* [T] **1** to push or handle someone roughly: **manhandle sb into/through etc sth** *It had ended with Tony physically manhandling her out of the house.* **2** to move a heavy object using force: **manhandle sth into/onto/across etc sth** *We lifted it off the truck and manhandled it into the workshop.*

man·hole /ˈmænhəʊl $ -hoʊl/ *n* [C] a hole in the surface of a road covered by a lid. It is used to examine underground pipes, wires etc.

man·hood /ˈmænhʊd/ *n* **1** [U] qualities such as strength, courage, and sexual power, that people think a man should have: *Why did he feel he had to **prove** his **manhood** in the company of women?* **2** [U] the state of being a man and no longer a boy → **womanhood**: **reach/attain manhood** *He had barely reached manhood when he married.* **3** [U] *literary* all the men of a particular nation: *America's manhood* **4** [singular] *especially literary* a PENIS

ˈman-hour *n* [C] the amount of work done by one person in one hour: *The main structure takes only about 40 man-hours to erect.*

man·hunt /ˈmænhʌnt/ *n* [C] an organized search for someone who might have committed a crime or a prisoner who has escaped: *Police have **launched** a nationwide **manhunt**.*

ma·ni·a /ˈmeɪniə/ *n* [C,U] **1** a strong desire for something or interest in something, especially one that affects a lot of people at the same time SYN **craze**: **[+for]** *the Victorian mania for butterfly collecting* | **religious/football/disco etc mania** *Keep-fit mania has hit some of the girls in the office.* **2** *medical* a serious mental illness → **manic**

ma·ni·ac /ˈmeɪniæk/ ●○○ *n* [C]
1 *informal* someone who behaves in a stupid or dangerous way SYN **lunatic**: *He drove **like a maniac** to the hospital.* | *Suddenly this maniac ran out into the middle of the road.*
2 religious/sex maniac *informal* someone who you think is too involved or interested in religion or sex SYN **freak**: *The woman's a sex maniac if you ask me.*
3 someone who is mentally ill: **homicidal maniac** (=someone who kills people)

ma·ni·a·cal /məˈnaɪəkəl/ *adj* behaving as if you are crazy —**maniacally** /-kli/ *adv*

man·ic /ˈmænɪk/ *adj* **1** *informal* behaving in a very anxious or excited way: *She seemed slightly manic.* | *Mortimer continued to shoot, a manic grin on his face.* **2** *medical* relating to a feeling of great happiness or excitement that is part of a mental illness

ˌmanic deˈpression *n* [U] a mental illness that causes someone to feel very strong emotions of happiness and sadness in a short period of time

ˌmanic deˈpressive *n* [C] someone with manic depression

man·i·cure /ˈmænəkjʊə $ -kjʊr/ *n* [C,U] a treatment for the hands that includes cutting and polishing the nails → **pedicure** → see picture at NAIL[1] —**manicure** *v* [T]

man·i·cured /ˈmænəkjʊəd $ -kjʊrd/ *adj* **1** manicured hands or fingers have nails that are neatly cut and polished: *slim, **perfectly manicured** fingers* **2** manicured gardens or LAWNS are very neat and tidy: *The ball rolled across the immaculately manicured lawn.*

man·i·cur·ist /ˈmænɪkjʊərɪst $ -kjʊr-/ *n* [C] someone whose job is to cut and polish people's nails

man·i·fest[1] /ˈmænəfest/ ●○○ *v* [T] *formal*
1 to show a feeling, attitude etc: *The shareholders have manifested their intention to sell the shares.* | **manifest sth in/as/through sth** *A dog's protective instincts are manifested in increased alertness.*
2 manifest itself to appear or to become easy to see: *His illness began to manifest itself at around this time.*

manifest[2] *adj formal* plain and easy to see SYN **obvious**, **patent**: *a manifest error of judgment* | **be made/become manifest** (=be clearly shown) *Their devotion to God is made manifest in ritual prayer.* —**manifestly** *adv*: *a manifestly unfair system*

manifest[3] *n* [C] a list of passengers or goods carried on a ship, plane, or train: *the ship's cargo manifest*

man·i·fes·ta·tion /ˌmænəfeˈsteɪʃən $ -fə-/ *n formal* **1** [C] a very clear sign that a particular situation or feeling exists: **[+of]** *These latest riots are a clear manifestation of growing discontent.* **2** [C,U] the act of appearing or becoming clear: **[+of]** *Manifestation of the disease often doesn't occur until middle age.*

man·i·fes·to /ˌmænəˈfestəʊ $ -toʊ/ *n* (*plural* **manifestos**) [C] a written statement by a political party, saying what they believe in and what they intend to do: *the Labour Party's election manifesto* | *The Tories are due to publish their manifesto tomorrow.*

man·i·fold[1] /ˈmænəfəʊld $ -foʊld/ *adj formal* many and of different kinds: *The reasons for this situation are manifold.*

manifold[2] *n* [C] *technical* an arrangement of pipes through which gases enter or leave a car engine

man·i·kin, **mannikin** /ˈmænɪkɪn/ *n* [C] **1** a model of the human body, used for teaching art or medicine **2** *literary* a very small man

ma·nil·a, **manilla** /məˈnɪlə/ *n* [U] strong brown paper used for making envelopes: *a large manila envelope*

man·i·ped·i /ˌmæni ˈpedi/ *n* [C] a MANICURE and PEDICURE done on the same occasion

ma·nip·u·late /məˈnɪpjəleɪt/ ●○○ AWL *v* [T]
1 to make someone think and behave exactly as you want them to, by skilfully deceiving or influencing them: *He was one of those men who manipulated people.* | *You have the constant feeling you are being manipulated.* | **manipulate sb into (doing) sth** *The thought that any parent would manipulate their child into seeking fame just appalled me.*
2 to work skilfully with information, systems etc to achieve the result that you want: *software designed to store and manipulate data* | *You can integrate text with graphics and manipulate graphic images.*
3 *medical* to move and press bones or muscles to remove pain in them
4 to use skill in moving or handling something: *The workmen manipulated some knobs and levers.* —**manipulation** /məˌnɪpjəˈleɪʃən/ *n* [U]: *allegations of political manipulation* | *manipulation of photographic images*

ma·nip·u·la·tive /məˈnɪpjələtɪv $ -leɪ-/ AWL *adj* **1** clever at controlling or deceiving people to get what you want – used to show disapproval: *She was sly, selfish, and manipulative.* **2** *technical* relating to the ability to handle objects in a skilful way: *Before a child can learn a musical instrument, he or she first needs to acquire the necessary manipulative skills.* **3** [only before noun] *technical* relating to the skill of moving bones and joints into the correct position

ma·nip·u·la·tor /məˈnɪpjəleɪtə $ -ər/ *n* [C] someone who is skilful at getting what they want by cleverly controlling or deceiving other people

man·kind /ˌmænˈkaɪnd/ ●●○ *n* [U] all humans considered as a group SYN **humankind**, **man** → **womankind**: *Since earliest times, mankind has been fascinated by fire.* | *one of the most important events in **the history of mankind***

man·ky /ˈmæŋki/ *adj BrE informal* looking dirty and unattractive SYN **mangy**: *a manky old sweater*

man·ly /ˈmænli/ *adj* having qualities that people expect and admire in a man, such as being brave and strong SYN **masculine**: *a deep manly voice* THESAURUS MAN —**manliness** *n* [U]

ˌman-ˈmade ●○○ *adj*
1 man-made materials and substances are not natural SYN **artificial** OPP **natural**: *fabrics made using a combination of natural and man-made fibres* THESAURUS ARTIFICIAL

M

2 made by people, rather than by natural processes: *Europe's largest man-made lake*

man·na /ˈmænə/ *n* [U] **1 manna from heaven** something very good that you get when you did not expect to, just when you really need it **2** the food which, according to the Bible, was provided by God for the Israelites in the desert after their escape from Egypt

man·ne·quin /ˈmænəkɪn/ *n* [C] **1** a model of the human body, used for showing clothes in shop windows **2** *old-fashioned* a woman whose job is to wear fashionable clothes and show them to people SYN **model**

MANNEQUIN

man·ner /ˈmænə $ -ər/ ●●● S3 W2 *n*
1 [singular] *formal* the way in which something is done or happens: **manner of (doing) sth** *It seemed rather an odd manner of deciding things.* | *He felt some guilt over the manner of her death.* | **in a ... manner** *I had hoped you would behave in a more responsible manner.* | *The issue will be resolved in a manner that is fair to both sides.* | *criticism of* **the manner in which** *the bishop was appointed* | **in the usual/normal etc manner** *The matter should be submitted to the accounts committee in the usual manner.*

REGISTER
In everyday English, people usually say **in a ... way** rather than **in a ... manner**, or they use an adverb instead: *They behaved* ***in a*** *very reasonable* ***way***. | *They behaved very* ***reasonably***.

2 [singular] the way in which someone behaves towards or talks to other people: *She has a calm relaxed manner.* | **[+towards]** *Something in Beth's manner towards him had changed.* | *Sophie resented his high-handed manner.*
THESAURUS ▸ BEHAVIOUR
3 manners [plural] polite ways of behaving in social situations: *Her children all had such* ***good manners***. | ***It's bad manners*** *to talk with your mouth full* (=talk and eat at the same time). | *His* ***manners*** *were* ***impeccable***. | *Dad gave us a lecture about our* ***table manners***. | *You* ***mind your manners***, *young man!* | *'Lesley just got up and left.' 'Some people* ***have no manners***.' | *Good heavens, child,* ***where are your manners***?
4 manners [plural] *formal* the customs of a particular group of people: *a book about the life and manners of Victorian London*
5 in a manner of speaking in some ways, though not exactly: *'Are you his girlfriend?' Nicola asked. 'In a manner of speaking.'*
6 all manner of sth *formal* many different kinds of things or people: *We would discuss all manner of subjects.* | *The British Isles have been conquered by all manner of people.*
7 in the manner of sb/sth *formal* in the style that is typical of a particular person or thing: *a painting in the manner of the early Impressionists*
8 what manner of ...? *literary* what kind of: *What manner of son would treat his mother in such a way?*
9 not by any manner of means *BrE spoken formal* not at all: *I haven't lost my interest in politics by any manner of means.*
10 (as) to the manner born if you do something new as to the manner born, you do it in a natural confident way, as if you have done it many times before → BEDSIDE MANNER

man·nered /ˈmænəd $ -ərd/ *adj* **1 well-mannered/bad-mannered etc** polite, impolite etc in the way you behave in social situations: *He is the most well-mannered, well-behaved boy I know.* **2** behaviour, speech, or writing that is mannered is not natural and is intended to make people admire you – used to show disapproval: *Hickstone gave a very mannered performance in the lead role.*

man·ner·is·m /ˈmænərɪzəm/ *n* [C] a way of speaking or moving that is typical of a particular person: *He has the same mannerisms as his father.*

man·ni·kin /ˈmænɪkɪn/ *n* [C] another spelling of MANIKIN

man·nish /ˈmænɪʃ/ *adj* a woman who is mannish, or who wears mannish clothes, looks or behaves like a man – used especially when this is considered unattractive: *She had strong, almost mannish features.* | *a mannish jacket* —**mannishly** *adv*

man·o a man·o /ˌmænəʊ ɑː ˈmænəʊ $ ˌmɑːnoʊ ɑː ˈmɑːnoʊ/ *adv* with only two people involved SYN **one-to-one**: *He finally faced up to his father, mano a mano, telling him he was going to leave college.*

ma·noeu·vra·ble *BrE*, **maneuverable** *AmE* /məˈnuːvərəbəl/ *adj* if something, especially a vehicle, is manoeuvrable, it can be moved or turned easily: *a ship which was surprisingly fast and manoeuvrable* —**manoeuvrability** /məˌnuːvərəˈbɪləti/ *n* [U]

ma·noeu·vre¹ *BrE*, **maneuver** *AmE* /məˈnuːvə $ -ər/ ●○○ *n*
1 [C] a skilful or careful movement that you make, for example in order to avoid something or go through a narrow space: *A careful driver will often stop talking before carrying out a complex manoeuvre.*
2 [C,U] a skilful or carefully planned action intended to gain an advantage for yourself: *They tried by diplomatic maneuvers to obtain an agreement.*
3 manoeuvres [plural] military activities, such as pretending to fight a battle, which are done as practice or training SYN **exercises**: *Large-scale* ***military manoeuvres*** *are being carried out near the border.* | **on manoeuvres** *troops on night manoeuvres*
4 room for manoeuvre/freedom of manoeuvre the possibility of changing your plans or decisions in order to achieve what you want: *As I see it, Lisa, you don't really have a great deal of room for manoeuvre.*

manoeuvre² *BrE*, **maneuver** *AmE* *v* **1** [I,T always + adv/prep] to move or turn skilfully or to move or turn something skilfully, especially something large and heavy: *She managed to manoeuvre expertly into the parking space.* | **manoeuvre yourself into/out of sth** *Josh manoeuvred himself out of bed and hobbled to the door.* | *We manoeuvred the TV in front of the sofa.* **2** [I,T] to use cleverly planned and often dishonest methods to get the result that you want: **manoeuvre sb into/out of sth** *It was a well-organized plan to maneuver company president John Woolford out of office.* | *Businesses manoeuvred to have their industry organized to their own advantage.*

ma·noeu·vring *BrE*, **maneuvering** *AmE* /məˈnuːvərɪŋ/ *n* [C,U] the use of clever and sometimes dishonest methods to get what you want: *diplomatic manoeuvrings* | *months of political manoeuvring*

ˌman of ˈletters *n* (*plural* **men of letters**) [C] a male writer, especially one who writes NOVELS or writes about literature

ˌman-of-ˈwar (*also* **man-o'-war**) /ˌmæn ə ˈwɔː $ -ˈwɔːr/ *n* (*plural* **men-of-war**) [C] a ship with guns that was used in the past in sea battles

man·or /ˈmænə $ -ər/ *n* [C] **1** (*also* **manor house**) a big old house with a large area of land around it **2** the land that belonged to an important man, under the FEUDAL system **3** *BrE informal* the area that a group of police officers are responsible for SYN **patch, turf**

ma·no·ri·al /məˈnɔːriəl/ *adj* [only before noun] relating to a manor: *a study based on manorial records*

man·pow·er /ˈmænˌpaʊə $ -paʊr/ *n* [U] all the workers available for a particular kind of work: *trained manpower* | *a scheme to increase police manpower*

man·qué /ˈmɒŋkeɪ $ mɑːŋˈkeɪ/ *adj* **artist/actor/teacher etc manqué** someone who could have been successful as an artist etc, but never became one

man·sard /ˈmænsɑːd $ -ɑːrd/ (*also* **ˈmansard roof**) *n* [C] *technical* a roof whose lower part slopes more steeply than its upper part

man·scap·ing /ˈmæn,skeɪpɪŋ/ *n* [U] the removal or shaping of the hair on a man's face or body – used especially in newspapers and magazines

manse /mæns/ *n* [C] the house of a Christian minister, especially in Scotland

man·ser·vant /ˈmæn,sɜːvənt $ -ɜːr-/ *n* [C] *old-fashioned* a male servant, especially a man's personal servant SYN **valet**

-manship /mənʃɪp/ *suffix* [in U nouns] a particular art or skill: *seamanship* (=sailing skill) | *statesmanship* (=skill at being a political or government leader)

man·sion /ˈmænʃən/ ●●○ *n* [C]
1 a very large house: *a beautiful country mansion* → see picture at HOUSE[1]
2 Mansions used in Britain in the names of some apartment buildings: *19 Carlyle Mansions*

ˈman-sized (*also* **ˈman-size**) *adj* [only before noun] **1** large and considered suitable for a man: *a man-sized breakfast* | *man-size tissues* **2** about the same size as a man: *man-sized plants*

man·slaugh·ter /ˈmæn,slɔːtə $ -,slɒːtər/ ●○○ *n* [U] *law* the crime of killing someone illegally but not deliberately → **homicide**, **murder**: *She was cleared of murder but found guilty of manslaughter.*

man·tel·piece /ˈmæntlpiːs/ (*also* **man·tel** /ˈmæntl/ *especially AmE*, **man·tel·shelf** /ˈmæntlʃelf/ *BrE*) *n* [C] a wooden or stone shelf which is the top part of a frame surrounding a FIREPLACE: *The clock on the mantelpiece struck 10.*

man·tis /ˈmæntɪs/ *n* (*plural* **mantises** *or* **mantids** /-tɪdz/) [C] a PRAYING MANTIS

man·tle¹ /ˈmæntl/ *n* **1 take on/assume/wear the mantle of sth** *formal* to accept or have an important duty or job: *It is up to Europe to take on the mantle of leadership in environmental issues.* **2 a mantle of snow/darkness etc** *literary* something such as snow or darkness that covers a surface or area: *A mantle of snow lay on the trees.* **3** [C] a loose piece of outer clothing without sleeves, worn especially in former times **4** [C] a cover that is put over the flame of a gas or oil lamp to make it shine more brightly **5** [singular] *technical* the part of the Earth around the central CORE → see picture at EARTH[1]

mantle² *v* [T] *literary* to cover the surface of something

,man-to-ˈman *adj* [only before noun] *informal* **1** if two men have a man-to-man talk, they discuss something in an honest direct way **2** playing a sport in such a way that one person on your team tries to stay close to one person on the other team —**man-to-man** *adv*: *You two need to discuss this man-to-man.*

man·tra /ˈmæntrə/ *n* [C] **1** a word or sound that is repeated as a prayer or to help people MEDITATE: **recite/repeat a mantra** *He closed his eyes and began to recite a Buddhist mantra.* **2** a word or phrase representing a rule or principle which someone often uses, but which other people often find annoying or boring: *The Treasury Secretary has stuck to his mantra that 'a strong dollar is in America's interest'.* **3** a piece of holy writing in the Hindu religion

man·u·al¹ /ˈmænjuəl/ ●●○ AWL *adj*
1 manual work involves using your hands or your physical strength rather than your mind SYN **blue-collar**: **manual job/labour/worker etc** *low-paid manual jobs* | *People in manual occupations have a lower life expectancy.*
2 operated or done by hand or without the help of electricity, computers etc OPP **automatic**: *a manual typewriter* | *a five-speed manual gearbox* | *It would take too long to do a manual search of all the data.*
3 relating to how well you use your hands to make or do things: *No great* ***manual dexterity*** (=skill in using your hands) *is required to perform the technique.* —**manually** *adv*

manual² ●●○ AWL *n* [C]
1 a book that gives instructions about how to do something, especially how to use a machine: **instruction/training/reference etc manual** *Consult the* ***computer manual*** *if you have a problem.* | *a* ***user manual***
2 on manual if a machine is on manual, it can only be operated by hand and not AUTOMATICALLY

man·u·fac·ture¹ /,mænjəˈfæktʃə $ -ər/ ●●○ *v* [T]
1 to use machines to make goods or materials, usually in large numbers or amounts: *the company that manufactured the drug* | *manufactured goods* THESAURUS▸ MAKE
2 to invent an untrue story, excuse etc SYN **fabricate**: *If the media can manufacture stories like this, who are we supposed to believe?*
3 *technical* if your body manufactures a particular useful substance, it produces it

manufacture² *n* **1** [U] the process of making goods or materials using machines, usually in large numbers or amounts: *Cost will determine the methods of manufacture.* **2 manufactures** [plural] *technical* goods that are produced in large quantities using machinery

man·u·fac·tur·er /,mænjəˈfæktʃərə $ -ər/ ●●○ W2 *n* [C] (*also* **manufacturers** [plural]) a company that makes large quantities of goods: *Read the manufacturer's instructions before using your new dishwasher.* | *The fridge was sent back to the manufacturers.*

man·u·fac·tur·ing /,mænjəˈfæktʃərɪŋ/ ●●○ W3 *n* [U] the process or business of producing goods in factories → **production**: *Thousands of jobs had been lost in manufacturing.* | *the manufacturing industry*

ma·nure /məˈnjʊə $ məˈnʊr/ *n* [U] waste matter from animals that is mixed with soil to improve the soil and help plants grow —**manure** *v* [T]

man·u·script /ˈmænjəskrɪpt/ ●○○ *n* [C]
1 a book or piece of writing before it is printed: **in manuscript** *I read his novel in manuscript.* | *Unfortunately, parts of the* ***original manuscript*** *have been lost.*
2 a book or document written by hand before printing was invented: *a fine collection of medieval manuscripts*

Manx /mæŋks/ *adj* from or relating to the Isle of Man or its people: *the Manx government*

,Manx ˈcat *n* [C] a breed of cat that has no tail or only a very short tail

man·y /ˈmeni/ ●●● S1 W1 *determiner, pron, adj*
1 a large number of people or things OPP **few** → **more**, **most**, **much**: *Many people have to use a car to travel to work.* | *I don't have many friends.* | *She has lived in Spain for many years.* | *Do you get many visitors?* | *Some of the houses have bathrooms but many do not.* | *His third novel is regarded by many* (=a lot of people) *as his best.* | **[+of]** *Many of our staff work part-time.* | *There are plenty of bars, many of them serving excellent food.* | *There are* ***so many*** *things we disagree about.* | ***Not many*** (=only a few) *people can afford my services.* | *You've been reading* ***too many*** *romantic novels* (=more than you should). | *One job loss is* ***one too many*** (=one more than is acceptable, needed etc). | **the many people/things etc** *We should like to thank the many people who have written to us offering their support.* | **many hundreds/thousands/millions** *military equipment worth many millions of dollars* | **a great many/a good many/very many** (=a very large number) *Most of the young men went off to the war, and a great many never came back.* | *It all happened a good many years ago.*
2 how many used to ask or talk about how large a number or quantity is: *How many sisters do you have?* | *I didn't know how many tickets to buy.*
3 as many a number that is equal to another number: *They say the people of Los Angeles speak 12 languages and teach* ***just as many*** *in the schools.* | **as many (...) as** *Grandfather claimed to have as many medals as the general.* | *There weren't as many people at the meeting as we had hoped.* | **in as many days/weeks/games etc** *A great trip! We visited five countries in as many days* (=in five days). | **twice/three times etc as many** *The company now employs four times as many women as men.*
4 as many as 50/1,000 etc used to emphasize how surprisingly large a number is: *As many as 10,000 civilians are thought to have fled the area.*
5 many a sth *formal or old-fashioned* a large number of people or things: *Many a parent has had to go through this*

same painful process. | *I've sat here* **many a time** (=often) *and wondered what happened to her.*

6 many's the time/day etc (that/when) *old-fashioned* used to say that a particular thing has happened often: *Many's the time we've had to borrow money in order to get through the month.*

7 have had one too many *informal* to be drunk: *Don't pay any attention to him – he's had one too many.*

8 many thanks *written* used especially in letters to thank someone for something: **[+for]** *Many thanks for your letter of 17 March.*

9 the many *formal* a very large group of people, especially the public in general: *This war is another example of the few sacrificing their lives for the many.* → **in as many words** at WORD[1]

GRAMMAR: Patterns with many

- You use **many** before plural nouns to talk about people or things in general: *Many people were against the decision.*
- You say **many of the**: *Many of the houses are empty.* ✗ Don't say: *many of houses*
- You say **many of my/her/his etc** or **many of them/us/you**: *Many of her friends have already left home.* | *Many of them are excellent.*
- You use **many** directly before an adjective: *We saw many interesting things.* ✗ Don't say: *We saw many and interesting things.*

THESAURUS

many a large number of people or things – used in everyday English in questions and negative sentences, and after 'too' and 'so'. In formal or written English, you can also use it in other sentences: *There weren't many people at the meeting.* | *Did you get many birthday presents?* | *Many people voted against the proposal.*

a lot many. **A lot** is less formal than **many** and is the usual phrase to use in everyday English: *A lot of tourists visit Venice in the summer.* | *The club has a lot more members now.*

dozens/hundreds/thousands/millions many – used when you cannot be exact but the number is two dozen or more, two hundred or more etc: *At least five people died and dozens more were injured in a gas explosion.* | *They've wasted thousands of pounds on the project.*

a large number of *written* a lot of a particular type of person or thing: *China plans to build a large number of nuclear power plants.*

numerous *formal* many – used especially when saying that something has happened many times: *We've contacted him on numerous occasions.* | *Numerous studies have shown a link between smoking and lung cancer.*

countless/innumerable /ɪˈnjuːmərəbəl $ ɪˈnuː-/ [only before noun] many – used when it is impossible to count or imagine how many. **Innumerable** is more formal than **countless**: *He spent countless hours in the gym.* | *They had been given innumerable warnings.*

a host of many – used especially when something seems surprising or impressive: *Age is the biggest risk factor in a host of diseases.* | *People leave jobs for* ***a whole host of*** *reasons.*

a raft of many – used especially when talking about ideas, suggestions, changes in business or politics: *The report made a raft of recommendations.* | *The new government is planning* ***a whole raft of*** *changes.*

quite a few *especially spoken* a fairly large number of people or things: *We've had quite a few problems with the software.* | *I've met quite a few of his friends.*

lots *informal* many: *I've invited lots of people.* | *'How many cats has she got?' 'Lots!'*

tons/loads *informal* many – a very informal use: *I've got tons of books.* | *Have a strawberry – there are loads here.*

ˈman-year *n* [C] *technical* the amount of work done by one person in a year, used as a measurement: *The project will take five man-years to complete.*

ˌmany-ˈsided *adj* consisting of many different qualities or features: *a complex many-sided personality*

Mao·ri /ˈmaʊri/ *n* **1** [C] someone who belongs to the race of people that first lived in New Zealand and now forms only a small part of the population **2** [U] the language used by the Maori people —**Maori** *adj*: *Maori children*

map[1] /mæp/ ●●● S2 W2 *n* [C]

1 a drawing of a particular area, for example a city or country, which shows its main features, such as its roads, rivers, mountains etc: **[+of]** *a map of Mexico City* | *According to the map we should turn left.* | **on a map** *I'm just trying to find Vancouver on the map.*

2 a drawing of an area showing some kind of special feature, for example the type of rocks, weather, population etc SYN **chart**: *an archaeological map of the area* | *the colour* ***weather map*** *in the newspaper* | **political map** (=one showing where political parties have power, or where countries are)

3 put sth on the map to make a place famous: *It was the Olympic Games that really put Seoul on the map.*

4 off the map *informal* a long way from any large town: *It's a small place in Nebraska. Right off the map.* → **wipe sth off the map** at WIPE[1](8)

COLLOCATIONS

VERBS

look at a map *She stopped the car to look at the map.*
read a map (=look at and understand the information on a map) *He drove while I read the map.*
study a map (=look carefully at a map) *They studied the map before setting out.*
draw a map *He drew me a map of the route.*
check a map (*also* **consult a map** *formal*) (=look at a map to get information) *I don't know how to get to Berlin without consulting a map.*
be marked on a map (=put a mark or symbol on a map to show where something is) *The path is clearly marked on the map.*
find sth on a map | **spread out/unfold a map**

ADJECTIVES/NOUN + map

detailed | **accurate** | **large-scale** (=showing a small area in a lot of detail)
a road map *a road map of Texas*
a street map *There's a street map outside the town hall.*
a tourist map *The museum is marked on most tourist maps.*
an Ordnance Survey map *BrE* (=a map showing the roads, paths, hills etc of an area in detail)

PHRASES

the contours on a map (=the lines on a map showing the height of mountains and valleys) *Contours on the map are given in feet.*

map[2] ●○○ *v* (**mapped**, **mapping**) [T]

1 to make a map of a particular area: *He spent the next fifteen years mapping the Isle of Anglesey.*

2 to discover or show information about something, especially about its shape or arrangement, or how it moves or works: *The points at which stress and anxiety emerge can be mapped.*

map onto sth *phr v* to match something or have a direct relationship with something

map sth ↔ **out** *phr v* to plan carefully how something will happen: *Her own future had been mapped out for her by wealthy and adoring parents.*

ma·ple /ˈmeɪpəl/ ●○○ *n*

1 (*also* **maple tree**) [C] a tree which grows mainly in northern countries such as Canada. Its leaves have five points and turn red or gold in autumn.

2 [U] the wood from a maple

ˌmaple ˈsyrup *n* [U] a sweet sticky liquid obtained from some kinds of maple tree, which is eaten especially on PANCAKES

ˈmap-ˌreading *n* [U] the practice of using a map to find which way you should go —**map-reader** *n* [C]

mar /mɑː $ mɑːr/ ●○○ *v* (**marred**, **marring**) [T] to make something less attractive or enjoyable SYN **spoil**: *Their wedding was marred by the death of Jenny's mother a week earlier.* | *A frown marred his handsome features.* **THESAURUS** SPOIL

Mar. (*also* **Mar** *BrE*) the written abbreviation of ***March***

mar·a·bou, **marabout** /ˈmærəbuː/ *n* [C] a large African STORK (=a long-legged bird)

ma·ra·cas /məˈrækəz $ -ˈrɑː-, -ˈræ-/ *n* [plural] a pair of hollow balls with handles, filled with small objects, that you shake and use as a musical instrument

mar·a·schi·no /ˌmærəˈskiːnəʊ◂, -ˈʃiː- $ -noʊ◂/ *n* [U] a sweet alcoholic drink made from a type of black CHERRY

ˌmaraschino ˈcherry *n* [C] a CHERRY that has been kept in maraschino. Maraschino cherries are used to decorate alcoholic drinks or cakes.

mar·a·thon¹ /ˈmærəθən $ -θɑːn/ ●●○ *n* [C]
1 a long race of about 26 miles or 42 kilometres: *the Boston Marathon* | *Garcia* ***ran*** *the* ***marathon*** *in just under three hours.*
2 an activity that continues for a long time and needs a lot of energy, patience, or determination: *We finished the job but it was quite a marathon.*

marathon² *adj* [only before noun] a marathon event continues for a long time and needs a lot of energy, patience, or determination: *a marathon round of negotiations* **THESAURUS** LONG

mar·a·thon·er /ˈmærəθɒnə $ -θɑːnər/ (*also* **ˈmarathon ˌrunner**) *n* [C] someone who runs in a marathon: *an Olympic marathoner*

ma·raud·ing /məˈrɔːdɪŋ $ -ˈrɒː-/ *adj* [only before noun] *written* a marauding person or animal moves around looking for something to destroy or kill: *marauding street gangs* —**marauder** *n* [C]

mar·ble /ˈmɑːbəl $ ˈmɑːr-/ ●●○ *n*
1 [U] a type of hard rock that becomes smooth when it is polished, and is used for making buildings, STATUES etc: *The columns were of white marble.* | *a marble statue*
2 [C] a small coloured glass ball that children roll along the ground as part of a game
3 marbles [U] a game played by children using marbles
4 lose your marbles *informal* to start behaving in a crazy way SYN **go mad**
5 [C] a STATUE or SCULPTURE made of marble

mar·bled /ˈmɑːbəld $ ˈmɑːr-/ *adj* **1** having an irregular pattern of lines and colours: *a marbled book cover* | *marbled meat* (=with lines of fat in it) **2** made of marble: *the marbled hallway*

march¹ /mɑːtʃ $ mɑːrtʃ/ ●●○ *v*
1 [I] if soldiers or other people march somewhere, they walk there quickly with firm regular steps: **[+across/along/past etc]** *On 29 August the royal army marched into Inverness.* | *We marched 50 km across the foothills.* | **[+on]** *He gathered his troops and prepared to march on the capital* (=march to the capital in order to attack it). | **Quick march!** (=an order to tell people to start marching) **THESAURUS** WALK
2 [I always + adv/prep] if a large group of people march somewhere, they walk there together to express their ideas or protest about something: *An estimated 5,000 people marched through the city to demonstrate against the factory closures.* | **[+on]** *Outraged citizens marched on City Hall* (=marched to City Hall), *demanding the police chief's resignation.*
3 [I always + adv/prep] to walk somewhere quickly and with determination, often because you are angry: **[+off/out etc]** *Brett marched out of the office, slamming the door behind him.*
4 [T always + adv/prep] to force someone to walk somewhere with you, often pushing or pulling them roughly: **march sb to/into etc sth** *Mr Carter marched us to the principal's office.*
5 be given/get your marching orders *BrE informal* to be ordered to leave, especially because someone no longer wants you to work for them or no longer wants a relationship with you
6 time marches on used to say that as time goes by, situations change and things do not remain the same

march² ●●○ *n* [C]
1 an organized event in which many people walk together to express their ideas or protest about something: *The police decided not to ban the march.* | **protest/civil rights/peace etc march** I ***went on*** *a lot of peace* ***marches*** *when I was a student.*
2 when soldiers walk with firm regular steps from one place to another: *The general led his forces on a long march southwards.*
3 on the march a) an army that is on the march is marching somewhere **b)** a belief, idea etc that is on the march is becoming stronger and more popular: *Fascism is on the march again in some parts of Europe.*
4 a day's march/two weeks' march etc the distance a group of soldiers can march in a particular period of time: *Lake Van was still three days' march away.*
5 the march of time/history/progress etc *formal* the way that things happen or change over time and cannot be stopped: *You can't control the march of science.* | *She was desperate to* ***halt the march of time*** *upon her face and figure.*
6 a piece of music for people to march to: *military marches* | *a funeral march*
7 marches [plural] the area around the border between England and Wales or between England and Scotland
→ **steal a march on** at STEAL¹(8)

March ●●● S2 W2 *n* [C,U] (*written abbreviation* **Mar.**) the third month of the year, between February and April: **next/last March** *She started work here last March.* | **in March** *The theatre opened in March 2001.* | **on March 6th** *There's a meeting on March 6th.* | **on 6th March** *BrE*: *I wrote to my bank on 6th March.* | **March 6** *AmE*: *The hospital is scheduled to open March 6.*

march·er /ˈmɑːtʃə $ ˈmɑːrtʃər/ *n* [C] a member of a group of people that are walking somewhere in order to express their ideas or protest about something → **demonstrator**, **protester**: *civil rights marchers*

ˈmarching ˌband *n* [C] a group of musicians who march as they play musical instruments

mar·chio·ness /ˌmɑːʃəˈnes $ ˈmɑːrʃənəs/ *n* [C] **1** the wife of a MARQUIS **2** a woman who has the rank of MARQUIS

ˈmarch-past *n* [singular] when soldiers march past an important person during a ceremony: *300 war veterans took part in the parade and march-past.*

Mar·di Gras /ˌmɑːdi ˈgrɑː $ ˈmɑːrdi grɑː/ *n* [U] the day before LENT begins, or the music, dancing etc that happen on this day in some countries

mare /meə $ mer/ *n* [C] **1** a female horse or DONKEY → **stallion**, **filly** **2 mare's nest a)** a discovery that seems important but is actually of no value **b)** a confused situation or a very untidy place **3** *BrE spoken informal* if someone is having a mare, things are going very badly for them at the moment. It is short for NIGHTMARE: *The Arsenal goalkeeper had a mare in the first half.*

mar·ga·rine /ˌmɑːdʒəˈriːn, ˌmɑːgə- $ ˈmɑːrdʒərɪn/ ●●○ *n* [U] a yellow substance similar to butter but made from vegetable or animal fats, which you eat with bread or use for cooking

mar·ga·ri·ta /ˌmɑːgəˈriːtə $ ˌmɑːr-/ *n* [C] an alcoholic drink made with TEQUILA and LEMON or LIME juice

marge /mɑːdʒ $ mɑːrdʒ/ *n* [U] *BrE spoken informal* margarine

mar·gin /ˈmɑːdʒɪn $ ˈmɑːr-/ ●●○ AWL *n* [C]
1 the empty space at the side of a page: *Someone had scribbled a note* ***in the margin***. | *Use double spacing and wide margins to leave room for comments.* → see picture at EDGE¹ **THESAURUS** EDGE

2 the difference in the number of votes, points etc that exists between the winners and the losers of a competition or election: **by a wide/narrow/significant etc margin** *They're a world-class team and it was no surprise that they won by such a wide margin.* | **by a margin of 10 points/100 votes etc** *The bill was approved by a margin of 55 votes.*
3 the difference between what it costs a business to buy or produce something and what they sell it for: *Margins are low and many companies are struggling.* | *Within 10 years they had a gross* ***profit margin*** *of 50%.*
4 [usually singular] an additional amount of something such as time, money, or space that you include in order to make sure that you are successful in achieving something: *It'll take about 30 minutes to dry but I'd allow a* ***safety margin*** *of, say, another 10 minutes.*
5 margin of error the degree to which a calculation might or can be wrong: *The survey has a margin of error of 2.1%.*
6 margin for error how many mistakes you can make and still be able to achieve something: *At this late stage in the competition there is no margin for error.*
7 *technical or literary* the edge of something, especially an area of land or water: *the western margin of southern Africa*
8 on the margin(s) a person on the margins of a situation or group has very little power, importance, or influence SYN **on the fringes**: *unemployed youths living* ***on the margins*** *of society*

COLLOCATIONS – MEANING 2

ADJECTIVES

a large/big margin *By a large margin, the book sold more copies than any other this year.*
a huge margin (=a very big one) *They won the championship by a huge margin.*
a small margin *Visitors from other parts of Scotland exceeded foreign visitors by only a small margin.*
a narrow margin (=a very small one) *The proposal passed, but only by a narrow margin.*

VERBS

win by a large/small etc margin *The party won by a huge margin.*
lose by a large/small etc margin *He lost by only a narrow margin.*

mar·gin·al /ˈmɑːdʒɪnəl $ ˈmɑːr-/ ●○○ AWL *adj*
1 a marginal change or difference is too small to be important OPP **significant**: *a marginal increase in the unemployment figures* | *a marginal improvement in profits*
2 *technical* relating to a change in cost, value etc when one more thing is produced, one more dollar is earned etc: *marginal revenue*
3 marginal seat/constituency *BrE* a SEAT in a parliament or similar institution, which can be won or lost by a small number of votes
4 marginal people or groups are not considered powerful or important OPP **mainstream**: *The album contains too many songs by marginal bands.*
5 [only before noun] written in a margin: *marginal notes*

mar·gin·al·ize (*also* **-ise** *BrE*) /ˈmɑːdʒənəlaɪz $ ˈmɑːr-/ *v* [T] to make a person or a group of people unimportant and powerless in an unfair way: *Female employees complained of being marginalized by management.* —**marginalized** *adj* —**marginalization** /ˌmɑːdʒənəlaɪˈzeɪʃən $ ˌmɑːrdʒənələ-/ *n* [U]

mar·gin·al·ly /ˈmɑːdʒənəl-i $ ˈmɑːr-/ AWL *adv* not enough to make an important difference SYN **slightly** OPP **significantly**: *Gina's grades have improved marginally since last term.* | *The new system is only marginally more efficient than the old one.*

ma·ri·a·chi /ˌmæriˈɑːtʃi $ ˌmɑː-/ *n* [U] a kind of Mexican dance music

Marie Ce·leste, the /ˌmæri sɪˈlest, ˌmɑːri- $ məˌriː-/ a sailing ship that was found in the Atlantic Ocean in 1872, with no one on it. The ship was undamaged, and a table was prepared for a meal. No one knows why the sailors left the ship, or what happened to them. People sometimes describe a place that is DESERTED (=nobody is there) as being like the Marie Celeste.

mar·i·gold /ˈmærəgəʊld $ -goʊld/ *n* [C] a plant with yellow or orange flowers

mar·i·jua·na /ˌmærəˈwɑːnə, -ˈhwɑːnə/ *n* [U] an illegal drug smoked like a cigarette, made from the dried leaves of the HEMP plant SYN **cannabis**

ma·rim·ba /məˈrɪmbə/ *n* [C] a musical instrument like a XYLOPHONE

ma·ri·na /məˈriːnə/ *n* [C] a small port or area of water where people keep boats that are used for pleasure

mar·i·nade /ˌmærəˈneɪd/ *n* [C,U] a mixture of oil and spices in which meat or fish is put for a time before being cooked

mar·i·nate /ˈmærəneɪt/ (*also* **mar·i·nade** /ˈmærəneɪd/) *v* [I,T] to put meat or fish in a marinade, or to be left in a marinade for some time: **marinate (sth) in sth** *fish marinated in olive oil, garlic and vinegar*

ma·rine /məˈriːn/ ●●○ *adj* [only before noun]
1 relating to the sea and the creatures that live there: *the enormous variety of* ***marine life*** | *the effects of oil pollution on* ***marine mammals*** | *marine biology*
2 relating to ships or the navy SYN **maritime**

Marine *n* [C] a soldier who serves on a ship, especially a member of the Royal Marines or the US Marine Corps

Maˈrine Corps *n* **the Marine Corps** one of the main parts of the US armed forces, consisting of soldiers who serve on ships

mar·i·ner /ˈmærənə $ -ər/ *n* [C] *literary* a SAILOR

MARIONETTE

marionette
finger puppets
glove puppet *BrE*/ hand puppet *AmE*

mar·i·o·nette /ˌmæriəˈnet/ *n* [C] a PUPPET whose arms and legs are moved by pulling strings

mar·i·tal /ˈmærətl/ ●○○ *adj* [only before noun] relating to marriage: *marital problems* | *the increase in marital breakdown* | **marital bliss** (=the state of being very happily married – used humorously)

ˌmarital ˈstatus *n* [U] whether someone is married – used especially on official forms: *Marital status: married/single/divorced* | *They asked questions about the age, sex and marital status of all the people in the house.*

mar·i·time /ˈmærətaɪm/ ●○○ *adj* [only before noun]
1 relating to the sea or ships SYN **marine**: *San Francisco has lost nearly all of its maritime industry.*
2 near the sea: *the Canadian maritime provinces*

mar·jo·ram /ˈmɑːdʒərəm $ ˈmɑːr-/ *n* [U] a herb that smells sweet and is used in cooking

mark¹ /mɑːk $ mɑːrk/ ●●● S2 W2 *v*
1 WRITE ON STH [T] to write or draw on something, so that someone will notice what you have written: *I've marked the pages you need to look at.* | **mark sth with sth** *When you're done, put your sheet in the envelope marked with your name.* | **mark sth on sth** *Peter marked his name on the first page.* | **mark sth personal/fragile/urgent etc** *a document marked 'confidential'* | **mark sb present/absent** (=write on an official list that someone is there or not there, especially in school) *Any student who is more than 20 minutes late for class will be marked absent.* | *All school uniform should be* ***clearly marked*** *with the child's name.*
2 DAMAGE [I,T] to make a mark on something in a way

that spoils its appearance or damages it, or to become spoiled in this way: *Take off your shoes so you don't mark the floor.* | *The disease had marked her face for life.* | *The table marks easily, so please be careful.*

3 **CELEBRATE** [T] to celebrate an important event: *celebrations to mark Australia Day* | **mark sth with sth** *Carter's 90th birthday will be marked with a large party at the Savoy Hotel.* | *Mrs Lawson was presented with a gold watch to* ***mark*** *the* ***occasion***.

4 **SHOW POSITION** [T] to show where something is: *A simple wooden cross marked her grave.* | *He had marked the route on the map in red.* | **mark sth with sth** *Troop positions were marked with colored pins.* | *She placed a bookmark between the pages to* ***mark*** *her* ***place***.

5 **YEAR/MONTH/WEEK** [T] if a particular year, month, or week marks an important event, the event happened on that date during a previous year: *This week marks the 250th anniversary of the birth of Joseph Priestley.*

6 **SHOW A CHANGE** [T] to be a sign of an important change or an important stage in the development of something: *Her latest novel marks a turning point in her development as a writer.* | *The move seemed to mark a major change in government policy.* | *These elections* ***mark the end of*** *an era.*

7 **QUALITY/FEATURE** [T] if something is marked by a particular quality or feature, it is a typical or important part of that thing SYN **characterize**: *The villages of East Anglia are marked by beautiful churches with fine towers.* GRAMMAR **Mark** is usually passive in this meaning.

8 **STUDENT'S WORK** [T] *especially BrE* to read a piece of written work and put a number or letter on it to show how good it is SYN **grade** *AmE*: *I've got a pile of exam papers to mark.*

9 **SPORT** [T] *especially BrE* to stay close to a player of the opposite team during a game SYN **guard** *AmE*

10 be marking time to spend time not doing very much except waiting for something else to happen: *I was just marking time until a better job came up.*

11 mark time if soldiers mark time, they move their legs as if they were marching, but remain in the same place

12 (you) mark my words! *spoken* used to tell someone that they should pay attention to what you are saying: *They're going to regret firing me, you mark my words!*

13 mark you *BrE old-fashioned* used to emphasize something you say SYN **mind you**: *Her uncle's just given her a car – given, mark you, not lent.* → MARKED

mark sb/sth ↔ **down** *phr v*

1 to write something down, especially in order to keep a record: *Mark down everything you eat on your daily chart.* | **mark sb/sth down as sth** *The teacher marked him down as absent.*

2 to reduce the price of something OPP **mark up** → **markdown**: *Winter coats have been marked down from $80 to $50.*

3 *especially BrE* to give a student a lower result in a test, paper etc because they have made mistakes: *Students will be marked down for failing to follow directions.*

mark sb/sth **down as** sth *phr v BrE* to consider someone or something to be a particular type of person or thing: *When I first saw Gilbert play I marked him down as a future England player.*

mark sb/sth ↔ **off** *phr v*

1 to make an area separate by drawing a line around it, putting a rope around it etc: *The competitors' arena had been marked off with cones.*

2 to make a mark on a list to show that something has been done or completed SYN **tick off**, **check off**: *Mark off each of the names on the list as I call them out.*

3 *BrE* to make something or someone different from other things or people of a similar type SYN **distinguish**: **[+from]** *Sara's natural flair for languages marked her off from the other students.*

mark sb/sth ↔ **out** *phr v*

1 to show the shape or position of something by drawing lines around it: *A volleyball court had been marked out on the grass.*

2 *BrE* to make someone or something seem very different from or better than other similar people or things: **mark sb/sth out as sth** *His stunning victory marked him out as the very best horse of his era.* | **mark sb out for sth** *She seemed marked out for success.*

mark sth ↔ **up** *phr v*

1 to increase the price of something, so that you sell it for more than you paid for it OPP **mark down**: *Compact discs may be marked up as much as 80%.* → MARK-UP

2 to write notes or instructions for changes on a piece of writing, music etc: *I have to mark up the pages and send them back to the printer.*

mark² ●●● S3 W2 *n* [C]

1 **DIRT** a spot or dirty area on something that spoils its appearance: *I can't get these marks out of my T-shirt.* | *His feet* ***left*** *dirty* ***marks*** *all over the floor.* | *The* ***skid marks*** (=marks left by a car's tyres) *were over 30 feet long.*

2 **DAMAGED AREA** a cut, hole, or other small sign of damage: **burn/scratch/bite etc mark** *a burn mark on the kitchen table* | *There were scratch marks all over the victim's body.*

3 **COLOURED AREA** a small area of darker or lighter colour on a plain surface such as a person's skin or an animal's fur: *The kitten is mainly white with black marks on her back.* → BIRTHMARK

4 **WRITING** a shape or sign that is written or printed: *What do those strange marks at the top mean?* | ***Make*** *a* ***mark*** *at the bottom of the page.*

5 **LEVEL/NUMBER** a particular level, number, amount etc: **pass/reach/approach etc the ... mark** *The temperature is not expected to reach the 20 degree mark in the next few days.* | *In 1976 unemployment in Britain passed the one million mark.*

6 **STUDENT'S WORK** *especially BrE* a letter or number given by a teacher to show how good a student's work is SYN **grade** *AmE*: **good/high mark** *The highest mark was a B+.* | *Her* ***marks*** *have been a lot* ***lower*** *this term.* | *She always* ***gets*** *good* ***marks***. | **pass mark** (=the mark you need in order to pass an exam) *The pass mark was 75%.* | **full/top marks** (=the highest possible mark)

7 full/top marks for effort/trying/persistence etc *BrE spoken* used to praise someone for trying hard to do something, even though they did not succeed: *I have to* ***give*** *you* ***top marks*** *for determination.*

8 high/low mark approval or disapproval of something or of the way someone has done something: *Parents* ***gave*** *the kit* ***high marks***. | *his low marks as transportation chief*

9 make/leave your mark to become successful or famous: *It took him only two games to make his mark.* | **[+as]** *He made his mark as a pianist in the 1920s.* | **[+on/in]** *He has left his mark on baseball history.*

10 leave/make its mark on sb/sth to affect someone or something so that they change in a permanent or very noticeable way: *Singers like Franklin and Redding helped gospel music make its mark on popular culture.* | *Growing up during the war had left its mark on her.*

11 off the mark/wide of the mark not correct SYN **inaccurate**: *Our cost estimate was* ***way off the mark***.

12 close to the mark correct: *His next guess was closer to the mark.*

13 be a mark of sth to show that someone or something is a particular thing, has a particular quality etc SYN **be a sign of sth**: *The ability to perform well under pressure is the mark of a true champion.*

14 a mark of respect/honour/affection etc something that happens or is done to show respect, honour etc: **[+for]** *The plaque awarded to Grant is a mark of recognition for his years of service.* | *There was a two-minute silence* ***as a mark of respect*** *for the dead.* **THESAURUS** ▸ SIGN

15 Mark 2/6 etc (*also* **mark 2/6 etc**) **a)** *especially BrE* a particular type or model of a car, machine etc: *an old Mark 2 Ford Cortina* **b)** a measurement used in Britain for the temperature of a gas OVEN: *Cook for 40 minutes at* ***gas mark*** *6.*

16 hit/miss the mark a) to hit or miss the thing that you were shooting at **b)** to succeed or fail to have the effect you wanted: *Although it contains a certain amount of truth, this theory ultimately misses the mark.*

17 be quick/slow/first etc off the mark *informal* to be quick, slow, first etc to understand things or react to situations:

You'll have to be quick off the mark if you want to find a job around here.
18 not up to the mark *BrE* **a)** not good enough: *Her work just isn't up to the mark.* **b)** *old-fashioned* not well and healthy: *I'm not feeling quite up to the mark today.*
19 the halfway mark the point in a race, journey, or event that is halfway between the start and the finish
20 bear the mark of sth a) to show the physical signs of something which happened in the past: *His face bore the marks of many missions.* **b)** if something bears the mark of something or someone, it has signs that show who or what made it or influenced it: *His speech bore all the marks of his military background.*
21 on your mark(s), get set, go! *spoken* said in order to start a race
22 MONEY the standard unit of money used in Germany before the EURO
23 SIGNATURE *old use* a sign in the form of a cross, used by someone who is not able to write their name ⚠ Do not use **mark** to mean 'a product made by a particular company'. Use **make** or **brand**: *an expensive make of camera | a well-known brand of toothpaste* → EXCLAMATION MARK, → **overstep the mark** at OVERSTEP(2), → PUNCTUATION MARK, QUESTION MARK, SPEECH MARKS

THESAURUS
A DIRTY MARK
mark a dirty area on something that spoils its appearance: *The bark of the tree had made black marks on her trousers.*
spot a small mark on something: *a grease spot on my shirt*
stain a mark that is difficult to remove, especially one made by a dark liquid: *a wine stain on the tablecloth | blood stains*
smudge a mark that is made when something touches against a surface: *There was a smudge of lipstick on his cheek. | He had a smudge of chalk on his jacket.*
smear a mark that is made by a small amount of something spread across a surface: *The table had a smear of paint on the top.*
fingerprint (*also* **fingermark** *BrE*) a mark on the surface of something that is made by someone's fingers: *The glass was covered with greasy fingerprints.*

mark·down /ˈmɑːkdaʊn $ ˈmɑːrk-/ *n* [C] a reduction in the price of something → **mark down**: **[+of]** *a markdown of 15%*

marked /mɑːkt $ mɑːrkt/ ●●○ *adj*
1 [only before noun] very easy to notice SYN **noticeable**: *a marked lack of enthusiasm | The patient showed a marked improvement in her condition after changing medication. | Miller's organized desk stood* ***in marked contrast to*** *the rest of the office.*
2 marked man/woman a person who is in danger because someone wants to harm them

mark·ed·ly /ˈmɑːkɪdli $ ˈmɑːr-/ ●○○ *adv* in a way that is very easy to notice: *Johnson and Rivera have* ***markedly different*** *leadership styles. | Trade has increased markedly.*

mark·er /ˈmɑːkə $ ˈmɑːrkər/ ●●○ *n* [C]
1 an object, sign etc that shows the position of something: *He buried the bodies in a single grave with a wooden cross as a marker.*
2 something which shows that a quality or feature exists or is present SYN **mark**: **[+of/for]** *antibodies which are a marker of hepatitis | the use of slang as a marker of social identity*
3 (*also* **marker pen** *BrE*) a large pen with a thick point made of FELT, used for marking or drawing things → MAGIC MARKER, see picture at STATIONERY
4 put/lay/set down a marker *BrE* to say or do something that clearly shows what you will do in the future

ˈmarker pen *n* [C] *BrE* a MARKER(3)

mar·ket¹ /ˈmɑːkɪt $ ˈmɑːr-/ ●●● S1 W1 *n*
1 PLACE TO BUY THINGS [C] **a)** a time when people buy and sell goods, food etc, or the place, usually outside or in a large building, where this happens: *I usually buy all my vegetables at the market.* | **fish/fruit and vegetable/flower etc market** *There's a good antiques market here on Sundays.* | **street market** (=with a lot of different people selling things from tables, STALLS etc in the street) **b)** *AmE* a shop that sells food and things for the home SYN **grocery store**
2 the market a) the STOCK MARKET: *Most analysts are forecasting a further downturn in the market. | As soon as she graduated from college, she started to* ***play the market*** (=risk money on the stock market). | ***The markets*** (=all the stock markets in the world) *are better prepared for a weakening economy than they were ten years ago.* **b)** the total amount of trade in a particular kind of goods: *Honda is trying to increase its* ***market share****. | the state of the art market* | **the housing/property etc market** *Investors in the* ***property market*** *are worried about rising inflation.* | **[+in]** *the world market in aluminum* → BEAR MARKET, BULL MARKET **c)** the system in which all prices and wages depend on what goods people want to buy, how many they buy etc: *The president believes prices should be determined by the market, not the government.* → FREE MARKET
3 on the market available for people to buy: *The manufacturers say the device will be on the market by May. | Handguns are freely available* ***on the open market*** (=for anyone to buy). | *They knew it wasn't a good time to sell their house, but they still* ***put*** *it* ***on the market*** (=offered it for sale). | *a revolutionary new drug that has just* ***come onto the market*** ⚠ Don't say 'in the market'. Say **on the market**.
4 COUNTRY/AREA [C] a particular country or area where a company sells its goods or where a particular type of goods is sold: *Our main overseas market is Japan.* | **international/home/UK etc market** *The domestic market makes up about 75% of their sales.* | **[+for]** *The world's largest market for illegal drugs is the US.*
5 PEOPLE WHO BUY [singular] the number of people who want to buy something, or the type of people who want to buy it: **[+for]** *The market for specialist academic books is pretty small. |* ***Is there a market*** *for his invention?* | **niche/specialist market** THESAURUS▸ CUSTOMER
6 be in the market for sth to be interested in buying something: *This is a bad time to be in the market for a new car.*
7 the job/labour market the people looking for work, and the number of jobs that are available: *The job market has been badly hit by the recession.*
8 a buyer's/seller's market a time that is better for buyers because prices are low, or better for sellers because prices are high: *I'll look for a house next year when it's more of a buyer's market.* → **corner the market** at CORNER²(3), → **price yourself out of the market** at PRICE²(4)

market² *v* [T] **1** to try to persuade people to buy a product by advertising it in a particular way, using attractive packages etc: *If you could ever figure out how to market this, you'd make a fortune.* | **market sth for sb** *They plan to market the toy for children aged 2 to 6.* | **market sth as sth** *Electric cars are being marketed as safe for the environment.*
2 to make a product available in shops: *The turkeys are marketed ready-to-cook.*

mar·ket·a·ble /ˈmɑːkətəbəl $ ˈmɑːr/ *adj* marketable goods, skills etc can be sold easily because people want them: *The program is designed to provide students with real, marketable skills.* —**marketability** /ˌmɑːkətəˈbɪləti $ ˌmɑːr-/ *n* [U]

ˈmarket ˌday *n* [C,U] *BrE* the day in the week when there is a market in a particular town

ˈmarket-ˌdriven *adj* market-driven activities, products, developments etc are a result of public demand for a particular product, service, or skill: *a market-driven economy*

ˌmarket eˈconomy *n* [C] an economic system in which companies are not controlled by the government but decide what they want to produce or sell, based on what they believe they can make a profit from

mar·ket·eer /ˌmɑːkəˈtɪə $ ˌmɑːrkəˈtɪr/ (*also* **mar·ket·er** /ˈmɑːkɪtə $ ˈmɑːrkɪtər/) *n* [C] someone who sells goods or services —**marketeering** *n* [U]

ˌmarket ˈforces *n* [plural] the way that the behaviour of buyers and sellers affects the levels of prices and wages, without any influence from the government

ˌmarket ˈgarden *n* [C] *BrE* an area of land where vegetables and fruit are grown so that they can be sold SYN **truck farm** *AmE* —**market gardener** *n* [C]

mar·ket·ing /ˈmɑːkətɪŋ $ ˈmɑːr-/ ●●○ S3 W3 *n* [U] the activity of deciding how to advertise a product, what price to charge for it etc, or the type of job in which you do this: *a clever marketing ploy | Company sales improved dramatically following a $2 million marketing campaign. | a career in* ***sales and marketing*** *| Cushman is director of marketing for a chain of Italian restaurants. | the UK marketing manager*

ˌmarket ˈleader *n* [C] the company that sells the most of a particular type of product, or the product that is the most successful one of its type: *the UK market leader in sports shoes*

ˈmarket-led *adj BrE* MARKET-DRIVEN

mar·ket·mak·er /ˈmɑːkətˌmeɪkə $ ˈmɑːrkətˌmeɪkər/ *n* [C] *BrE technical* an organization such as a bank or a BROKER that keeps a supply of STOCKS and SHARES available for people who want to buy them

mar·ket·place /ˈmɑːkətpleɪs $ ˈmɑːr-/ ●○○ *n* [C] **1 the marketplace** the part of business activity that is concerned with buying and selling goods in competition with other companies: *Some retailers worry that new regulations will hurt their ability to compete in the marketplace.* **2** an open area in a town where a market is held

ˌmarket ˈprice *n* [C] the price of something on a MARKET at a particular time

ˌmarket reˈsearch *n* [U] a business activity which involves collecting information about what goods people buy and why they buy them: *They had to conduct market research, then advertise the product.*

ˈmarket share *n* [C,U] the PERCENTAGE of sales in a MARKET that a company or product has

ˈmarket town *n* [C] *BrE* a town where there is an outdoor market, usually once or twice a week

ˌmarket ˈvalue *n* [C,U] **1** the value of a product, building etc based on the price that people are willing to pay for it, rather than the cost of producing it or building it **2** the total value of all the SHARES on a STOCK MARKET, or the value of a particular company's shares

mark·ing /ˈmɑːkɪŋ $ ˈmɑːr-/ *n* **1** [C usually plural, U] things painted or written on something, especially something such as an aircraft, road, vehicle etc: *The marking on the road is unclear. | strange markings on the walls of the cave* **2** [C usually plural, U] the coloured patterns and shapes on an animal's fur, on leaves etc: *This dolphin is noted for its distinctive black and white markings. | the vivid markings of the angelfish* **3** [U] *especially BrE* the activity of checking students' written work SYN **grading** *AmE*: *I have to do a lot of marking tonight. | the setting and marking of exams*

mark·ka /ˈmɑːkə $ ˈmɑːr-/ *n* (*plural* **markkaa** /-kɑː/) [C] the standard unit of money used in Finland before the Euro

marks·man /ˈmɑːksmən $ ˈmɑːrks-/ *n* (*plural* **marksmen** /-mən/) [C] someone who can shoot a gun very well

marks·man·ship /ˈmɑːksmənʃɪp $ ˈmɑːrks-/ *n* [U] the ability to shoot a gun very well

ˈmark-up *BrE*, **mark·up** *AmE* /ˈmɑːkʌp $ ˈmɑːrk-/ *n* [C] an increase in the price of something, especially from the price a shop pays for something to the price it sells it for → **mark up**: *The retailer's mark-up is 50%.*

marl /mɑːl $ mɑːrl/ *n* [U] **1** soil consisting of LIME and CLAY **2** cloth which has pale threads running through another colour: *a jacket available in black or grey marl*

mar·lin /ˈmɑːlɪn $ ˈmɑːr-/ *n* (*plural* **marlin**) [C] a large sea fish with a long sharp nose, which people hunt for sport

mar·ma·lade /ˈmɑːməleɪd $ ˈmɑːr-/ *n* [U] a JAM made from fruit such as oranges, LEMONS, or GRAPEFRUIT, usually eaten at breakfast

mar·mo·set /ˈmɑːməzet $ ˈmɑːrməset, -zet/ *n* [C] a type of small monkey with long hair and large eyes that lives in Central and South America

mar·mot /ˈmɑːmət $ ˈmɑːr-/ *n* [C] a small European or American animal with fur and short front legs which lives under the ground

ma·roon¹ /məˈruːn/ *n* [U] a dark brownish red colour —**maroon** *adj*

maroon² *v* [T] if you are marooned somewhere, you are left in a place where there are no other people and where you cannot escape → **stranded**: *The car broke down and left us marooned in the middle of nowhere.*

marque /mɑːk $ mɑːrk/ *n* [C] *BrE* the well-known name of a type of car or other product, especially an expensive one: *the prestigious Ferrari marque*

mar·quee /mɑːˈkiː $ mɑːr-/ *n* [C] **1** *BrE* a large tent at an outdoor event or large party, used especially for eating or drinking in **2** *AmE* a large sign above the door of a theatre or cinema which covers the entrance and gives the name of the play or film **3** *AmE* **marquee player, actor etc** someone who people want to see because they are good or famous

mar·quess /ˈmɑːkwɪs $ ˈmɑːr-/ *n* [C] *BrE* a MARQUIS

mar·quet·ry /ˈmɑːkətri $ ˈmɑːr-/ *n* [U] a pattern made of coloured pieces of wood laid together, or the art of making these patterns

mar·quis /ˈmɑːkwɪs $ ˈmɑːr-/ *n* [C] a man who, in the British system of NOBLE titles, has a rank between DUKE and EARL: *the Marquis of Bath*

mar·riage /ˈmærɪdʒ/ ●●● S2 W2 *n*
1 [C,U] the relationship between two people who are married, or the state of being married: *She has three daughters from a previous marriage. |* **[+to]** *his marriage to Marilyn Monroe |* **[+between]** *In Denmark they have legalized marriage between gay couples.*

> **REGISTER**
> In everyday English, when talking about the action of marrying, people usually use the expression **get married** rather than **marriage**: *I think they're too young for* ***marriage***. → *I think they're too young to* ***get married***.

2 [C] the ceremony in which two people get married SYN **wedding**: *The marriage took place at St Bartholomew's Church.*
3 by marriage if you are related to someone by marriage, they are married to someone in your family, or you are married to someone in theirs: *her cousin by marriage*

COLLOCATIONS

ADJECTIVES

a happy/unhappy marriage *Ours was a very happy marriage.*
a successful marriage *The key to a successful marriage is friendship.*
a failed/broken marriage *After two failed marriages, she was not willing to risk marrying again.*
sb's first/second etc marriage *She had two children from her first marriage.*
a previous marriage | **an arranged marriage** (=when your parents choose the person you will marry) | **a same-sex/gay marriage** (=a marriage between two homosexual people, which is not legal in many places)

VERBS

have a long/happy etc marriage *They have a happy marriage.*
a marriage ends *Her three marriages all ended in divorce.*
a marriage breaks down/up (=ends because of disagreements) *Liz's marriage broke up after only eight months.*

save your marriage (=do things to try to stay together as a married couple) | **consummate a marriage** *formal* (=make your marriage complete by having sex)

PHRASES

the breakdown/breakup of sb's marriage (=the end of it) *The breakup of her marriage had a devastating effect on her.*
a proposal of marriage *formal* (=when someone asks you to marry them) *She rejected his proposal of marriage.*
be born outside marriage (=be born when your parents are not married) | **sex before/outside marriage** | **ask for sb's hand in marriage** *old-fashioned* (=ask someone to marry you, or ask their parents for permission to marry)

COMMON ERRORS

⚠ Don't say 'marriage life'. Say **married life**.

mar·riage·a·ble /ˈmærɪdʒəbəl/ *adj old-fashioned* suitable for marriage: *a girl of marriageable age*

ˈmarriage ˌbureau *n* [C] *BrE old-fashioned* an organization that helps people find partners to marry

ˈmarriage cerˌtificate *n* [C] an official document that proves that two people are married

ˌmarriage ˈguidance *BrE*, **ˌmarriage ˈcounseling** *AmE n* [U] advice given to people who are having difficulties in their marriage

ˈmarriage ˌlicence *BrE*, **marriage license** *AmE n* [C] an official written document saying that two people are allowed to get married

ˈmarriage lines *n* [plural] *BrE old-fashioned* a MARRIAGE CERTIFICATE

ˌmarriage of conˈvenience *n* [C] **1** an agreement between two or more countries, businesses, or people that is only made for political or economic reasons **2** a marriage for political or economic reasons, not for love

ˈmarriage ˌvow *n* [C usually plural] a promise that you make during the marriage ceremony

mar·ried /ˈmærid/ ●●● S2 W2 *adj*
1 having a husband or a wife: *Are you married or single? | They've been married for eight years. | Married men earn 70 percent more than single men.* | **[+to]** *Nicole is married to my brother. | We're* ***getting married*** (=marrying) *next month.* | **married couple/man/woman** *a* ***happily married*** *man | When she first came to London, she was* ***newly married*** *and out of work. | So, how do you like* ***married life****?*
2 be married to sth to give most of your time and attention to a job or activity: *I was married to my job.*

GRAMMAR: Prepositions with married

• You are **married to** someone: *He is married to an American. | Last year I got married to Tom.* ✗ Don't say: *He is married with an American. | Last year I got married with Tom.*
• You use **married with** when talking about how many children someone has: *Richard is now happily married with two young children.*

THESAURUS

married having a husband or wife: *How long have you been married? | a married couple*
single not married: *Chris is 45 and still single. | single mothers*
engaged having formally agreed to marry someone in the future: *Jane and Pete have just* ***got engaged****. | engaged couples*
live together to share a home and have a sexual relationship, but not be married: *More and more couples are choosing to live together rather than get married.*
separated no longer living with your husband or wife because of problems in your marriage: *I think Joan and Brian are separated now.*
divorced no longer married because you have legally ended your marriage: *My parents* ***got divorced*** *when I was 10. | divorced men*
widowed no longer married because your husband or wife has died: *He's a widowed father of two.*

HUSBAND/WIFE ETC

husband/wife the man/woman you are married to: *My wife's a teacher.*
partner the person you live with and have a sexual relationship with. **Partner** is often used when people are not married, or when you do not know if they are married. It is also used when talking about same-sex couples: *He lives with his partner Ruth and their eight-month-old son.*
fiancé/fiancée the man/woman you are engaged to: *He and fiancée Wendy Hodgson will marry in July.*
divorcee a woman who is divorced: *The prince announced his intention to marry Mrs Wallis Simpson, an American divorcee.*
widow/widower a woman or man whose husband or wife has died: *Imelda Marcos, the widow of the former president*
spouse *formal* your spouse is your husband or wife: *The rule applies to spouses and children of military personnel.*

SOMEONE WHO IS NOT MARRIED

bachelor a man who has never been married: *He's a* ***confirmed bachelor*** (=a man who has decided he will never marry).
spinster *old-fashioned* a woman who has never been married and is no longer young: *The house was owned by an elderly spinster.*

mar·row /ˈmærəʊ $ -roʊ/ *n* **1** [U] the soft fatty substance in the hollow centre of bones SYN **bone marrow**: *a bone marrow transplant* **2** [C,U] *BrE* a large long dark green vegetable that grows on the ground → see picture at VEGETABLE[1] **3 chilled/frozen/shocked etc to the marrow** *BrE literary* very cold, shocked etc

ˈmarrow bone *n* [C,U] *BrE* a large bone that contains a lot of marrow

mar·ry /ˈmæri/ ●●● S1 W2 *v* (**married**, **marrying**, **marries**)
1 [I,T] if you marry someone, you become their husband or wife → **married**: *He married Bea in 1925. | I'm going to ask her to marry me on St Valentine's Day. | She* ***married young*** (=at a young age). | *People in higher social classes are more likely to* ***marry late*** (=when they are older than is usual). | *Sophia had, in a sense,* ***married beneath her*** (=married someone of a lower social class than her).

REGISTER

In everyday English, rather than saying that two people **marry**, people usually say that they **get married**. *My parents* ***got married*** *in 1986.*

GRAMMAR: Reciprocal verbs

Marry is a reciprocal verb. This type of verb is used when saying that two or more people do something that involves both or all of them. It does not need to have an object: *Their parents did not want them to marry.* In this sentence, **marry** is intransitive and does not have an object.
You can also say: *His parents did not want them to marry each other. | His parents did not want him to marry her.* In these sentences, **marry** is transitive.
GRAMMAR GUIDE ▸ VERBS

2 [T] to perform the ceremony at which two people get married: *The priest who married us was really nice.*
3 [T] to find a husband or wife for one of your children: **marry sb to sb** *She was determined to marry all of her daughters to rich men.*

4 [T] (*also* **marry up**) *formal* to combine two different ideas, designs, tastes etc together: **marry sth with/to sth** *The building's design marries a traditional style with modern materials.* | **marry sth and sth** *He writes fiction that marries up realism and the supernatural.*
5 not the marrying kind not the type of person who wants to get married: *I'm just not the marrying kind.*

marry into sth *phr v* to join a family or social group by marrying someone who belongs to it: *She married into a very wealthy family.*

marry sb ↔ **off** *phr v* to find a husband or wife for someone - used to show disapproval: **[+to]** *They married her off to the first young man who came along.*

Mars /mɑːz $ mɑːrz/ *n* the small red PLANET that is fourth in order from the Sun and is nearest the Earth → **Martian**: *the enormous volcanoes known to exist on Mars*

Mar·seil·laise /ˌmɑːseɪˈez $ ˌmɑːr-/ *n* **the Marseillaise** the national song of France

marsh /mɑːʃ $ mɑːrʃ/ *n* [C,U] an area of low flat ground that is always wet and soft → **bog**, **swamp** —**marshy** *adj*: *The crane lives in marshy habitats.*

mar·shal¹ /ˈmɑːʃəl $ ˈmɑːr-/ *n* [C] **1** an officer of the highest rank in the army or air force of some countries: *Marshal Zhukov* | *the Marshal of the Royal Air Force* **2** an official in charge of an important public event or ceremony: *Heston has been named* ***grand marshal*** *of the parade.* **3** a person who controls crowds, traffic etc at a sports event or other public event: *I could see a marshal on the finish line waving a yellow flag.* **4 federal/US marshal** *AmE* a police officer employed by the national government to make sure people do what a COURT ORDER says they must do **5** *AmE* the officer in charge of a fire department

marshal² *v* (**marshalled**, **marshalling** *BrE*, **marshaled**, **marshaling** *AmE*) [T] **1** to organize your thoughts, ideas etc so that they are clear, effective, or easy to understand: **marshal your thoughts/arguments etc** *He paused for a moment as if to marshal his thoughts.* **2** to organize all the people or things that you need in order to be ready for a battle, election etc: *The general* ***marshalled*** *his* ***forces*** *for a major offensive.* | *Senator Bryant attempted to* ***marshal support*** *for the measure.* **3** to control or organize a large group: *The teacher marshalled the children into one group.*

ˈmarshalling ˌyard *n* [C] *BrE* a place where railway WAGONS are brought together to form trains

ˈmarsh gas *n* [U] gas formed from decaying plants under water in a MARSH SYN **methane**

marsh·land /ˈmɑːʃlænd $ ˈmɑːrʃ-/ *n* [U] an area of low wet ground that is always soft → **fen**

marsh·mal·low /ˌmɑːʃˈmæləʊ $ ˈmɑːrʃmeloʊ/ *n* [C,U] a very soft light white or pink sweet, made of sugar and egg WHITE

mar·su·pi·al /mɑːˈsuːpiəl $ mɑːr-/ *n* [C] an animal such as a KANGAROO which carries its babies in a pocket of skin on its body —**marsupial** *adj*

mart /mɑːt $ mɑːrt/ *n* [C] **1** *AmE* a place where goods are sold - used especially in the names of shops: *the largest furniture mart in the region* | *K-Mart* **2** *BrE* a market, especially one where animals are sold

mar·ten /ˈmɑːtən, -tn $ ˈmɑːrtn/ *n* [C] a small animal with a long body and a tail that lives mainly in trees and that eats smaller animals: *a pine marten*

mar·tial /ˈmɑːʃəl $ ˈmɑːr-/ *adj* [only before noun] connected with war and fighting: *martial music* → COURT-MARTIAL¹

ˌmartial ˈart *n* [C usually plural] a sport such as JUDO or KARATE, in which you fight with your hands and feet. Martial arts were developed in Eastern Asia: *a martial arts expert*

ˌmartial ˈlaw *n* [U] a situation in which the army controls an area instead of the police, especially because of fighting against the government: **impose/declare martial law** *The government may declare martial law in response to the latest violence in the region.* | *In May,* ***martial law*** *was* ***lifted*** (=ended) *in most areas.* | **under martial law** *According to press reports, the country is now under martial law.*

Mar·tian /ˈmɑːʃən $ ˈmɑːr-/ *n* [C] an imaginary creature from the PLANET Mars —**Martian** *adj*

mar·tin /ˈmɑːtɪn $ ˈmɑːrtn/ *n* [C] a small bird like a SWALLOW

mar·ti·net /ˌmɑːtəˈnet $ ˌmɑːr-/ *n* [C] *formal* someone who is very strict and makes people obey rules exactly SYN **disciplinarian**: *The woman in charge was a martinet who treated us like children.*

Mar·ti·ni /mɑːˈtiːni $ mɑːr-/ *n* [C,U] *trademark* **1** a popular BRAND of VERMOUTH **2** an alcoholic drink made by mixing GIN or VODKA with VERMOUTH: *a* ***dry*** (=not sweet) ***Martini***

mar·tyr¹ /ˈmɑːtə $ ˈmɑːrtər/ ●○○ *n* [C]
1 someone who dies for their religious or political beliefs and is admired by people for this: *St Stephen, the first Christian martyr* | **[+to]** *He was a martyr to the cause of racial harmony.* | *The army has been held back because the government is reluctant to* ***make martyrs of*** *the protesters.*
2 someone who tries hard to get other people's sympathy by complaining about how hard their life is - used to show disapproval: *I think she rather relishes the role of martyr.*
3 be a martyr to sth *BrE spoken* to suffer a lot because of an illness, problem, or bad situation: *She's a martyr to her arthritis.*

martyr² *v* [T] if someone is martyred, they are killed because of their religious beliefs: *Becket was martyred in 1170.* | **be martyred for sth** *Catherine was martyred for her faith.*

mar·tyr·dom /ˈmɑːtədəm $ ˈmɑːrtər-/ *n* [U] death as a martyr: *In that year, thousands of Christians suffered martyrdom for their faith.*

mar·tyred /ˈmɑːtəd $ ˈmɑːrtərd/ *adj* **a martyred look/expression/air etc** *especially BrE* an unhappy look or expression that is intended to make other people feel sorry for you: *He did not reply, but got into the car glumly, with a martyred expression.*

mar·vel¹ /ˈmɑːvəl $ ˈmɑːr-/ *v* (**marvelled**, **marvelling** *BrE*, **marveled**, **marveling** *AmE*) [I,T] to feel or express great surprise or admiration at something, especially someone's behaviour: *'The man is a genius,' marvelled Claire.* | **[+at/over]** *I marvelled at my mother's ability to remain calm in a crisis.* | *Visitors to Rome marvel over the beauty of the city.* | **marvel that** *I marvelled that anyone could be so stupid.*

marvel² *n* [C] something or someone that is extremely useful or skilful SYN **miracle**, **wonder**: *an engineering marvel* | *I don't know how he did it - he's an absolute marvel!* | **[+of]** *the marvels of modern science*

mar·vel·lous *BrE*, **marvelous** *AmE* /ˈmɑːvələs $ ˈmɑːr-/ ●●○ S3 *adj* extremely good, enjoyable, impressive etc SYN **wonderful**: *'How was your holiday?' 'Marvellous!'* | *We had a marvellous time.* | *I can't stand him, but my wife thinks he's marvellous.* | ***It's marvellous*** *what they can do these days.* —**marvellously** *adv*

Marx·is·m /ˈmɑːksɪzəm $ ˈmɑːr-/ *n* [U] the system of political thinking invented by Karl Marx, which explains changes in history as the result of a struggle between social classes

Marx·ist¹ /ˈmɑːksɪst $ ˈmɑːr-/ *adj* relating to or based on Marxism: *a Marxist perspective*

Marxist² *n* [C] someone who agrees with Marxism

Mary Pop·pins /ˌmeəri ˈpɒpənz $ -ˈpɑː-/ someone whose behaviour is almost too good to be true is sometimes compared to Mary Poppins, the main character of a 1964 US film in which Julie Andrews appears as a NANNY (=a woman who is employed to take care of the children in a family) called Mary Poppins, who has magical powers and can fly

mar·zi·pan /ˈmɑːzəpæn $ ˈmɑːrtsə-, ˈmɑːrzə-/ *n* [U] a sweet food made from ALMONDS, sugar, and eggs, used to make sweets and for covering cakes

masc. (*also* **masc** *BrE*) the written abbreviation of ***masculine***

mas·ca·ra /mæˈskɑːrə $ mæˈskærə/ *n* [U] a dark substance used to colour your EYELASHes and make them look thicker → see picture at **MAKE-UP**

mas·cot /ˈmæskət, -kɒt $ -kɑːt/ *n* [C] an animal or toy, or a person dressed as an animal, that represents a team or organization, and is thought to bring them good luck: *the **official mascot** of the 2002 World Cup* | *Rocky the Raccoon, the **team mascot***

mas·cu·line /ˈmæskjəlɪn/ ●●○ *adj*
1 having qualities considered to be typical of men or of what men do OPP **feminine**: *They're nice curtains, but I'd prefer something a little more masculine.* | *She has a very masculine voice.* | *Hunting was a typically masculine occupation.* THESAURUS MAN
2 in some languages, a masculine noun, PRONOUN etc belongs to a class of words that have different INFLECTIONS from FEMININE or NEUTER words: *The word for 'book' is masculine in French.*

mas·cu·lin·i·ty /ˌmæskjəˈlɪnəti/ *n* [U] the features and qualities considered to be typical of men OPP **femininity**: *Children's ideas of masculinity tend to come from their fathers.* | *boys trying to **prove** their **masculinity***

ma·ser /ˈmeɪzə $ -ər/ *n* [C] *technical* a piece of equipment that produces a very powerful electric force → **laser**

mash¹ /mæʃ/ (*also* **mash up**) *v* [T] to crush something, especially a food that has been cooked, until it is soft and smooth: *Mash the bananas.* —**masher** *n* [C]: *a potato masher*

mash² *n* [U] **1** *BrE informal* potatoes that have been boiled and then crushed and mixed with milk until they are smooth: *bangers (=sausages) and mash* **2** a mixture of MALT or crushed grain and hot water, used to make beer or WHISKY **3** a mixture of grain cooked with water to make a food for animals

mashed /mæʃt/ *adj* **1** been pressed until is smooth: *mashed potatoes* **2** [not before noun] *BrE informal* very drunk or strongly affected by drugs: *We **got** completely **mashed** last night.*

ˈmash-up *n* [C] a piece of music, a video, a website etc that uses parts of two or more pieces of music, videos, etc: *a mash-up of two dance tracks*

MASKS

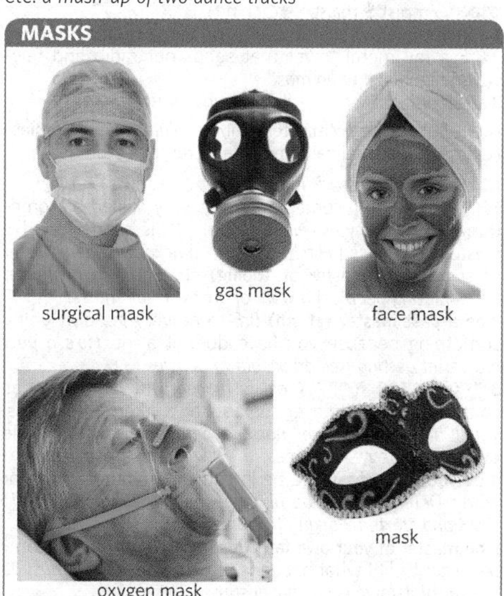
surgical mask
gas mask
face mask
oxygen mask
mask

mask¹ /mɑːsk $ mæsk/ ●●○ *n* [C]
1 something that covers all or part of your face, to protect or to hide it: *a surgical face mask* | *He was attacked and robbed by two people **wearing masks**.*
2 something that covers your face, and has another face painted on it, which is used for ceremonies or special occasions: *a Halloween mask*
3 [usually singular] an expression or way of behaving that hides your real emotions or character SYN **front**: *Her sarcasm is a mask for her insecurity.*
4 a substance that you put on your face and leave there for a short time to clean the skin or make it softer SYN **face pack**: *a facial mask* → **DEATH MASK, GAS MASK**

mask² *v* [T] **1** if a smell, taste, sound etc is masked by a stronger one, it cannot be noticed because of the stronger one: *Liz turned on a radio to mask the noise.* | *Air-fresheners mask bad smells instead of removing them.* THESAURUS HIDE **2** to hide your feelings or the truth about a situation: *Men often mask their true feelings with humour.* **3** to cover or hide something so that it cannot be clearly seen: *The new accommodation block has all but masked the original building.*

masked /mɑːskt $ mæskt/ *adj* wearing a mask: *Masked gunmen opened fire on the bus.*

ˌmasked ˈball *n* [C] a formal dance at which everyone wears masks

ˈmasking tape *n* [U] long narrow paper that is sticky on one side, used especially to protect the edge of an area which you are painting

mas·o·chis·m /ˈmæsəkɪzəm/ *n* [U] **1** sexual behaviour in which someone gains pleasure from being hurt or punished → **sadism**, **sado-masochism** **2** behaviour that makes it seem that someone wants to suffer or have problems: *Unconscious masochism seemed to drive her from one disaster to the next.* —**masochist** *n* [C] —**masochistic** /ˌmæsəˈkɪstɪk◂/ *adj*: *masochistic behavior* —**masochistically** /-kli/ *adv*

ma·son /ˈmeɪsən/ *n* [C] a STONEMASON

Mason *n* [C] a FREEMASON

Mason-Dix·on Line, the /ˌmeɪsən ˈdɪksən laɪn/ the border between the states of Maryland and Pennsylvania in the US. It is known for dividing the states of the South where it was legal to own SLAVES from the states of the North where it was illegal, until the end of the American Civil War. Some people still consider it to be a dividing line between the North and South of the US.

Ma·son·ic /məˈsɒnɪk $ -ˈsɑː-/ *adj* involved or connected with FREEMASONRY: *a Masonic lodge*

ˈMason jar *n* [C] *trademark AmE* a glass pot with a tight lid, used for preserving fruit and vegetables SYN **Kilner jar** *BrE*

ma·son·ry /ˈmeɪsənri/ *n* [U] **1** the bricks or stone from which a building, wall etc has been made: *Several people were buried under falling masonry.* **2** the skill of building with stone

Masonry *n* [U] FREEMASONRY

masque /mɑːsk $ mæsk/ *n* [C] a type of play popular in England in the 16th and 17th centuries that included music, dancing, and songs: *a Court masque*

mas·que·rade¹ /ˌmæskəˈreɪd/ *n* **1** [C] a formal dance or party where people wear MASKS and unusual clothes **2** [C,U] a way of behaving or speaking that hides your true thoughts or feelings SYN **pretence**: *She didn't really love him, but she kept up the masquerade for the children's sake.*

masquerade² *v* [I] to pretend to be something or someone different: **[+as]** *A number of police officers masqueraded as demonstrators.* | *Some of these breakfast foods are just candy masquerading as cereals.* | **[+under]** *He was masquerading under a false name.*

mass¹ /mæs/ ●●○ S3 W3 *n*
1 LARGE AMOUNT **a)** [C] a large amount of a substance which does not have a definite or regular shape: *The food had congealed into a sticky mass.* | **[+of]** *a high mass of rock* **b)** [C usually singular] a large amount or quantity of something: **[+of]** *a huge mass of data* **c) masses of sth** *BrE informal* a large amount of something, or a lot of people or things: *Masses of books covered every surface in the room.*
2 CROWD [singular] a large crowd: **[+of]** *There was a mass of people around the club entrance.* | *The road was blocked by a **solid mass** of protesters.* THESAURUS GROUP

3 the masses all the ordinary people in society who do not have power or influence: *The trains provided cheap travel for the masses.*
4 the mass of people/the population/workers etc most of the people in a group or society SYN **the majority**: *The war is strongly supported by the mass of the population.*
5 CHURCH CEREMONY (*also* **Mass**) **a)** [C,U] the main ceremony in some Christian churches, especially the Roman Catholic Church, which celebrates the last meal that Jesus Christ ate: *What time do you* ***go to mass****?* | **morning/evening/midnight etc Mass** *Will I see you at morning Mass?* | **say/celebrate Mass** (=perform this ceremony as a priest) → HIGH MASS **b)** [C] a piece of music written to be performed at the ceremony of mass: *Mozart's Mass in C minor*
6 SCIENCE [U] *technical* the amount of material in something: *The Sun makes up 99.9% of the mass of our solar system.* → CRITICAL MASS

mass² ●●○ W3 *adj* [only before noun] involving or intended for a very large number of people: *a mass protest* | *weapons of mass destruction* | *the problem of mass unemployment* | **mass marketing/entertainment etc** *a mass marketing campaign* | *Email has made mass mailings possible at the touch of a button.*

mass³ *v* [I,T] to come together, or to make people or things come together, in a large group SYN **gather**: **mass (sth) behind/along/in etc sth** *Western reports say that troops have been massing in the region since December.* | *grey clouds massing behind the mountains* | *Both countries have massed troops along the border.*

mas·sa·cre¹ /ˈmæsəkə $ -ər/ ●○○ *n*
1 [C,U] when a lot of people are killed violently, especially people who cannot defend themselves: *the only survivor of the massacre* | **[+of]** *the massacre of several hundred pro-democracy demonstrators* | **the Boston/Peterloo/Harperville etc massacre** *the infamous Peterloo massacre of 1819*
2 [C] *informal* a very bad defeat in a game or competition: *United lost in a 9–0 massacre.*

massacre² ●○○ *v* [T]
1 to kill a lot of people or animals in a violent way, especially when they cannot defend themselves: *The army massacred more than 150 unarmed civilians.* | *Tens of thousands of dolphins and small whales are brutally massacred every year.* THESAURUS ▸ KILL
2 *informal* to defeat someone very badly in a game, competition etc: *The Cougars massacred the Bucs last night, 38–7.*
3 *informal* to spoil part of a play, a song etc by performing it very badly: *Unfortunately, Jones absolutely massacres the role of Ophelia.*

mas·sage¹ /ˈmæsɑːʒ $ məˈsɑːʒ/ ●○○ *n* [C,U] the action of pressing and rubbing someone's body with your hands, to help them relax or to reduce pain in their muscles or joints: *Massage helps ease the pain.* | *Why don't you* ***have*** *a* ***massage****?* | *Joan* ***gave*** *me a gentle neck* ***massage****.* | **body/shoulder/foot etc massage** *A full-body massage lasts around one hour.*

massage² *v* [T] **1** to press and rub someone's body with your hands, to help them relax or to reduce pain in their muscles: *Alex massaged Helena's aching back.* | **massage sth into sth** *Gently massage the lotion into your skin.*
2 to change official numbers or information in order to make them seem better than they are – used to show disapproval SYN **cook the books**: *Myers accused the government of deliberately* ***massaging*** *the unemployment* ***figures****.*
3 massage sb's ego to try to make someone feel that they are important, attractive, intelligent etc: *The portrait painter had the power to massage the king's ego or to expose his flaws.*

ˈmassage ˌparlour *BrE*, **massage parlor** *AmE* / $ ˌ. ˌ../ *n* [C] **1** a BROTHEL (=place where people pay to have sex) – used to pretend that it is not a brothel **2** a place where you pay to have a massage

masse → EN MASSE

massed /mæst/ *adj* [only before noun] in a large group: **massed ranks/forces** *I look around me at the massed ranks of reporters.* | **massed choir/band** *BrE* (=several choirs or bands singing or playing together as one large group)

mas·seur /mæˈsɜː $ -ˈsɜːr/ *n* [C] someone who gives MASSAGES

mas·seuse /mæˈsɜːz $ mæˈsuːz/ *n* [C] **1** a woman who gives MASSAGES **2** a PROSTITUTE

mas·sif /ˈmæsiːf $ mæˈsiːf/ *n* [C] a group of mountains forming one large solid shape

mas·sive /ˈmæsɪv/ ●●● S2 W3 *adj*
1 very large, solid, and heavy: *The bell is massive, weighing over 40 tons.* | *the castle's massive walls* THESAURUS ▸ BIG
2 unusually large, powerful, or damaging: *My phone bill was massive last month.* | *massive increases in the number of homeless* | *Club members can get a massive discount of £50.* | **massive stroke/heart attack etc** *He suffered a massive stroke.* | **massive argument/row etc** *BrE*: *I had a massive argument with her.*
3 *BrE informal* extremely good: *Listen to this. It's a massive song.* —**massively** *adv*: *The president was massively popular.*

ˈmass-ˌmarket *adj* [only before noun] designed for sale to as wide a range of people as possible: **mass-market paperback/novel/film etc** *a mass-market paperback priced at $8.99* —**mass market** *n* [C]

ˌmass ˈmedia *n* **the mass media** all the people and organizations that provide information and news for the public, including television, radio, and newspapers: *The crime received heavy coverage in the mass media.*

ˌmass ˈmurderer *n* [C] someone who has murdered a lot of people

ˌmass-proˈduced *adj* produced in large numbers using machinery, so that each object is the same and can be sold cheaply → **mass production**: *mass-produced furniture* —**mass-produce** *v* [T]

ˌmass proˈduction *n* [U] when products are made in large numbers by machines so that they can be sold cheaply → **mass-produced**

ˌmass ˈtransit *n* [U] *technical* methods of transport by which large numbers of people can travel around a city: *The city has virtually no mass transit.*

mast /mɑːst $ mæst/ ●○○ *n* [C]
1 a tall pole on which the sails or flags on a ship are hung
2 *BrE* a tall metal tower that sends out radio and television signals: *a radio mast*
3 a tall pole on which a flag is hung → HALF-MAST

mas·tec·to·my /mæˈstektəmi/ *n* (*plural* **mastectomies**) [C] *medical* a medical operation to remove a breast

mas·ter¹ /ˈmɑːstə $ ˈmæstər/ ●●○ S3 W3 *n* [C]
1 SKILLED PERSON someone who is very skilled at something: **[+of]** *Runyon was a master of the short story.* | *a master of disguise* | *Hitchcock was an acknowledged master of suspense.* | **master at (doing) sth** *She's a master at manipulating people.* | *a work of art by a true master*
2 be a past master (at sth) *BrE* to be very good at doing something because you have done it a lot: *He's a past master at getting free drinks out of people.*
3 MAN WITH AUTHORITY *old-fashioned* **a)** a man who has control or authority over servants or workers → **mistress**: *You'll have to ask the master's permission.* **b)** the male owner of a dog → **mistress**
4 be your own master to be in control of your own life or work: *Determined to be his own master, Simmons quit in 1998 and started working freelance.*
5 be master of your own fate/destiny *literary* to be in complete control of what happens to you: *Our country must be master of its own economic destiny.*
6 ORIGINAL a document, record etc from which copies are made: *I gave him the master to copy.*
7 Master of Arts/Science/Education etc a university DEGREE in an ARTS subject, a science subject etc that you can get after your first degree → MA, M.SC., MED, MPHIL, → **Bachelor of Arts/Science/Education etc** at BACHELOR(2)
8 TEACHER **a)** *BrE old-fashioned* a male teacher → **headmaster**, **headmistress** **b)** (*also* **Master**) a wise person

whose ideas and words other people accept and follow: *a Zen master*

9 YOUNG BOY (*also* **Master**) *old-fashioned* used when speaking or referring to a young boy: *How's young Master Toby today?*

10 UNIVERSITY OFFICIAL (*also* **Master**) the person who is in charge of some university colleges in the UK: *the Master of Trinity College, Cambridge*

11 CAPTAIN *old-fashioned* someone who is in charge of a ship → GRAND MASTER, OLD MASTER, QUIZMASTER

master² ●●○ *v* [T]

1 to learn a skill or a language so well that you have no difficulty with it: *the skills needed to master a new language | I never quite **mastered the art of** walking in high heels.* THESAURUS ▸ LEARN

2 to manage to control a strong emotion SYN **overcome**: *He had learned to master his fear of heights.*

master³ *adj* [only before noun] **1** a master copy of a document, recording etc is the one from which copies are made: **master list/copy/recording etc** *We've lost the master disk.* **2** most important or main: *the master control center at NASA* **3 master craftsman/chef/plumber etc** someone who is very skilled at a particular job, especially a job that involves working with your hands: *a society of master chefs*

ˌmaster-at-ˈarms *n* [C] an officer with police duties on a ship

ˈmaster ˌbedroom *n* [C] the largest bedroom in a house or apartment, often with its own bathroom

mas·ter·class, master class /ˈmɑːstəˌklɑːs $ ˈmæstərˌklæs/ *n* [C] a lesson, especially in music, given to very skilful students by someone famous

mas·ter·ful /ˈmɑːstəfəl $ ˈmæstər-/ *adj* **1** controlling people or situations in a skilful and confident way: *Klein handled the situation in a masterful way.* **2** done with great skill and understanding SYN **masterly**: *a masterful analysis of the text* —**masterfully** *adv*: *Jack strode masterfully into the room.*

ˈmaster key *n* [C] a key that will open all the door locks in a building

mas·ter·ly /ˈmɑːstəli $ ˈmæstərli/ *adj* done or made very skilfully SYN **masterful**: *He gave a masterly display in round one of the World Chess Championship.*

mas·ter·mind¹ /ˈmɑːstəmaɪnd $ ˈmæstər-/ *n* [singular] someone who plans and organizes a complicated operation, especially a criminal operation: *a criminal mastermind* | **[+of/behind]** *He is suspected of being the mastermind behind the bombings.*

mastermind² *v* [T] to think of, plan, and organize a large, important, and difficult operation: *The project was masterminded by Morris, then aged 29. | Ridley, as commerce secretary, masterminded the privatisation.*

ˌMaster of ˈArts *n* [C] an MA

ˌmaster of ˈceremonies *n* [C] someone who introduces guests or performers at a social or public occasion SYN **emcee**: *the master of ceremonies for the Miss World Pageant*

ˌMaster of ˈScience *n* [C] an MS or an M.SC.

mas·ter·piece /ˈmɑːstəpiːs $ ˈmæstər-/ ●●○ *n* [C]

1 a work of art, a piece of writing or music etc that is of very high quality or that is the best that a particular artist, writer etc has produced SYN **masterwork**: *Mary Shelley was just 18 when she wrote the horror masterpiece 'Frankenstein'.*

2 a very good example of something: **[+of]** *The shark is a masterpiece of evolution.*

ˈmaster plan *n* [C usually singular] a detailed plan for controlling everything that happens in a complicated situation: *The job losses were part of a master plan aimed at transforming the structure of the company. | a master plan to modernize the health care system*

ˈmaster ˌrace *n* [C] a race of people who consider themselves better than other races, and who believe that they should rule over them

mas·ter's /ˈmɑːstəz $ ˈmæstərz/ *n* [C] *informal* a MASTER'S DEGREE

ˈmaster's deˌgree (*also* **master's** *informal*) *n* [C] a university DEGREE such as an MA, M.SC., or M.S., that you can get by studying for one or two years after your first degree

ˈMasters ˌTournament, the (*also* **US Masters Tournament, US Masters**) a golf competition held once each year in the US

mas·ter·stroke /ˈmɑːstəstrəʊk $ ˈmæstərstroʊk/ *n* [C] a very clever, skilful, and often unexpected action that is completely successful: *That ad campaign was an absolute masterstroke.* | **[+of]** *a masterstroke of diplomacy*

ˈmaster ˌswitch *n* [C] the switch that controls the supply of electricity to the whole of a building or area

mas·ter·work /ˈmɑːstəwɜːk $ ˈmæstərwɜːrk/ *n* [C] a painting, SCULPTURE, piece of music etc that is the best that someone has done SYN **masterpiece**: *'Otello' is Verdi's riveting masterwork.*

mas·ter·y /ˈmɑːstəri $ ˈmæ-/ *n* [U] **1** thorough understanding or great skill: **[+of]** *She possesses complete technical mastery of her instrument.* **2** complete control or power over someone or something → **master**: **[+of/over]** *humankind's mastery over the environment*

mast·head /ˈmɑːsthed $ ˈmæst-/ *n* [C] **1** the name of a newspaper, magazine etc printed in a special design at the top of the first page **2** the top of a MAST on a ship

mas·tic /ˈmæstɪk/ *n* [U] a type of glue that does not crack or break when it is bent

mas·ti·cate /ˈmæstɪkeɪt/ *v* [I,T] *formal* to chew food —**mastication** /ˌmæstɪˈkeɪʃən/ *n* [U]

mas·tiff /ˈmæstɪf/ (*also* **bull mastiff**) *n* [C] a large strong dog, often used to guard houses

mas·ti·tis /mæˈstaɪtɪs/ *n* [U] a painful swelling of the breast or UDDER (=the part of some animals that gives milk)

mas·tur·bate /ˈmæstəbeɪt $ -tər-/ *v* [I,T] to give yourself or another person sexual pleasure by touching or rubbing the sexual organs —**masturbation** /ˌmæstəˈbeɪʃən $ -tər-/ *n* [U]

mat¹ /mæt/ ●●○ *n* [C]

1 a small piece of thick rough material which covers part of a floor: *Wipe your feet on the mat.*

2 a small flat piece of wood, cloth etc which protects a surface, especially on a table: *a **beer mat*** (=a mat for putting a glass of beer on) | *a mouse mat* (=for a computer mouse) → PLACE MAT

3 a piece of thick soft material used in some activities for people to sit on, fall onto etc: *a yoga mat | a prayer mat*

4 go to the mat (for sb/sth) *informal* to do everything you can to solve a difficult problem, win an argument, support someone etc: *The mayor is willing to go to the mat on this issue.*

5 a thick mass of something such as hairs or leaves → **matted**: **[+of]** *a floating mat of vegetation* → MATTING

mat² *adj* another spelling of MATT

mat·a·dor /ˈmætədɔː $ -ɔːr/ *n* [C] a man who fights and kills BULLS during a BULLFIGHT SYN **bullfighter**

match¹ /mætʃ/ ●●● S2 W2 *n*

1 GAME [C] *especially BrE* an organized sports event between two teams or people: *It's our last match of the season.* | **cricket/football/tennis etc match** | *They're preparing for a **big*** (=important) ***match** tomorrow.* | **[+against/between/with]** *the match between Nigeria and Ireland* | **home/away match** (=a match played at a team's own sports ground, or at a different ground) *Good teams win their home matches. | McClaire's goal earned him the title of **man of the match*** (=the person in a team who plays best).

2 FIRE [C] a small wooden or paper stick with a special substance at the top, that you use to light a fire, cigarette etc: *a box of matches | Don't let your children play with matches.* | **strike/light a match** (=rub a match against a surface to produce a flame) *Peg struck a match and lit the candle. | I tore up the letter and **put a match to** it* (=made it burn, using a match).

3 COLOURS/PATTERNS [singular] something that is the same colour or pattern as something else, or looks

M

attractive with it: **[+for]** *That shirt's a perfect match for your blue skirt.*
4 GOOD OPPONENT [singular] someone who is much stronger, cleverer etc than their opponent: *Carlos was* ***no match for*** *the champion.* | *This time you've* ***met*** *your* ***match****, Adam Burns! I'm not giving up without a fight!* | *Guerrilla tactics proved* ***more than a match for*** *the Soviet military machine.*
5 shouting match (*also* **slanging match** *BrE*) a loud angry argument in which two people insult each other: *The meeting degenerated into a shouting match.*
6 MARRIAGE [singular] a marriage or two people who are married: *They're* ***a perfect match****.* | **a match made in heaven** (=a marriage of two people who are exactly right for each other) | *Claire* ***made a good match*** (=married someone suitable).
7 SUITABILITY [singular] a situation in which something is suitable for something else, so that the two things work together successfully: **[+between]** *We need to establish a match between students' needs and teaching methods.* → **mix and match** at MIX[1](6)

match² ●●● S3 W2 *v*
1 LOOK GOOD TOGETHER [I,T] if one thing matches another, or if two things match, they look attractive together because they are a similar colour, pattern etc → **matching**: *We painted the cabinets green to match the rug.* | *Do you think this outfit matches?* | *a beech dining table with four chairs to match* (=chairs that match it)

GRAMMAR
You say: *Her bag matched her shoes.* ✗ Don't say: *Her bag matched with her shoes.* | *Her bag matched to her shoes.*

2 LOOK THE SAME [I,T] two things that match look the same because they are a pair: *Your socks don't match.*
3 SEEM THE SAME [I,T] if two things match, or if one matches the other, there is no important difference between them: *The suspect matched the descriptions provided by witnesses.* | *Their actions do not match their words.* | **match exactly/closely/perfectly** *The copy closely matches the original.*
4 SUITABLE [T] to be suitable for a particular person, thing, or situation SYN **suit**: *Teaching materials should match individual students' needs.* | *We'll help you find a home that will match your requirements.* | **well-matched/ill-matched** *a well-matched pair*
5 CONNECT [T] to put two people or things together that are similar to or somehow connected with each other: **match sth to/with sb/sth** *Can you name the animals and match them to the correct countries?* | *All checked-in baggage must be matched with a passenger travelling on the aircraft.*
6 BE EQUAL [T] to be equal to something in value, size, or quality: *His strength is matched by his intelligence.* | *Few cities in Europe can match the cultural richness of Berlin.* | *Fancy designer labels tend to come with fancy price tags to match.* | **evenly/equally matched** *The two candidates are fairly evenly matched.*
7 MAKE EQUAL [T] to make something equal to something else: **match sth to sth** *Lindsey matched her steps to those of the other girl as they walked.* | *an attempt to match financial resources to need*
8 GIVE MONEY [T] to give a sum of money that is equal to a sum given by someone else: *The government has promised to match any private donations to the earthquake fund.*
9 COMPETITION [T] if you are matched against someone else in a game or competition, you are competing against them: **be matched against/with sb** *Federer was matched against Nadal in the final.*

match up *phr v*
1 match sb/sth ↔ up to put two people or things together that are related to or suitable for each other: *The employment agency exists to match up graduates and IT companies.* | **[+with]** *My mother spent her life trying to match me up with various women.*
2 if two things match up, they seem the same or are connected in some way: *Their accounts just don't match up.* | **[+with]** *The DNA samples found on her body did not match up with a sample taken from the accused.*
3 match up to sb's hopes/expectations/ideals etc to be as good as you hoped, expected etc SYN **measure up to**: *Unfortunately, the product's performance did not match up to the manufacturer's promise.*

match·book /ˈmætʃbʊk/ *n* [C] a small folded piece of thick paper containing paper matches

match·box /ˈmætʃbɒks $ -bɑːks/ *n* [C] a small box containing matches → see picture at CONTAINER

ˈmatch-fit *adj* [not before noun] *BrE* a sports player who is match-fit is well and fit enough to play —**match-fitness** *n* [U]: *A question mark still hangs over Rooney's match-fitness.*

match·ing /ˈmætʃɪŋ/ ●○○ *adj* [only before noun] having the same colour, style, or pattern as something else → **match**: *a necklace with matching earrings* THESAURUS▸ SIMILAR

match·less /ˈmætʃləs/ *adj literary* more intelligent, beautiful etc than anyone or anything else SYN **unparalleled**: *the matchless beauty of the Parthenon*

match·mak·er /ˈmætʃˌmeɪkə $ -ər/ *n* [C] someone who tries to find a suitable partner for someone else to marry —**matchmaking** *n* [U]: *Perhaps we should do a little bit of matchmaking and introduce them.*

ˈmatch-play *n* [singular] a method of scoring in golf based on the number of holes that are won, rather than the number of STROKES needed to reach each hole

ˌmatch ˈpoint *n* **1** [U] a situation in tennis when the person who wins the next point will win the match **2** [C] the point that a player must win in order to win a tennis match → **game point**

match·stick /ˈmætʃˌstɪk/ *n* [C] **1** a wooden match **2 matchstick men/figures** *BrE* people in pictures who have been drawn with thin lines to represent their arms, legs, and bodies, as if by a child SYN **stick person** *AmE*

match·wood /ˈmætʃwʊd/ *n* [U] very small pieces of wood: *Their boat was shattered into matchwood against the rocks and sank instantly.*

mate¹ /meɪt/ ●●○ S3 *n*
1 SB YOU DO STH WITH [C] someone you work with, do an activity with, or share something with: **class/team/work etc mate** *Dad's office mates are throwing a party for him.* | **house/flat/room mate** (=someone you share a house, room etc with)
2 FRIEND [C] *BrE informal* **a)** a friend: *I'm going out with my mates tonight.* | **good/best mate** *He's good mates with John.* | *Most of my* ***school mates*** *are black.* **b)** used as a friendly way to address a man: *What's the time, mate?* THESAURUS▸ FRIEND
3 ANIMAL [C] the sexual partner of an animal
4 HUSBAND/WIFE [C] *AmE* a husband or wife – used especially in magazines SYN **partner**: *How do women choose their mates?*
5 SAILOR [C] a ship's officer who is one rank below the captain
6 NAVY OFFICER [C] a US Navy PETTY OFFICER
7 builder's/plumber's/electrician's etc mate *BrE* someone who works with and helps a skilled worker
8 GAME [U] CHECKMATE in the game of CHESS

mate² ●○○ *v*
1 [I] if animals mate, they have sex to produce babies: **[+with]** *It's quite common for male birds to mate with several females.*
2 [T] to put animals together so that they will have sex and produce babies: *Rabbits can be mated as early as six months old.*
3 [T] to achieve the CHECKMATE of your opponent in CHESS

ma·ter /ˈmeɪtə, ˈmɑː- $ ˈmeɪtər/ *n* [C] *BrE old-fashioned* mother – now used humorously → **pater** → ALMA MATER

ma·te·ri·al¹ /məˈtɪəriəl $ -ˈtɪr-/ ●●● S1 W1 *n*
1 [C,U] cloth used for making clothes, curtains etc SYN **fabric**: *curtain material* | *scraps of material* | *a cape made of a soft material*
2 [C,U] a solid substance such as wood, plastic, or metal:

materials like wood or stone | **organic/plant material** *Animals depend on plant material for food.* | *harmful* ***radioactive material*** | *a paper company which imports* ***raw materials*** (=substances which have not been treated) *from North America.* | *recycled material*

3 [U] (*also* **materials** [plural]) the things that are used for making or doing something: **reading/writing etc material(s)** *Videos often make good teaching material.* | *a supply of* ***building materials*** | *artists' materials*

4 [U] information or ideas used in books, films etc: *His act contains a lot of new material.* | **[+for]** *Anita is collecting material for a novel.* | *the* ***raw material*** (=information that has not been carefully examined) *for an article*

5 officer/executive etc material someone who is good enough for a particular job or position: *He's a good soldier, but not really officer material.*

material² ●○○ *adj* [usually before noun]

1 relating to your money, possessions, living conditions etc, rather than the needs of your mind or soul OPP **spiritual**: **material goods/possessions/wealth etc** *The spiritual life is more important than material possessions.* | *a society that places high importance on* ***material rewards***

2 relating to the real world and physical objects, rather than religious or SPIRITUAL things OPP **spiritual**: *According to some,* ***the material world*** *is all that exists.*

3 *law* important and needing to be considered when making a decision OPP **irrelevant**: *material evidence* | **[+to]** *facts material to the investigation*

4 *formal* important and having a noticeable effect OPP **immaterial**: *material changes to the schedule* → MATERIALLY

ma·te·ri·al·is·m /məˈtɪəriəlɪzəm $ -ˈtɪr-/ *n* [U]

1 the belief that money and possessions are more important than art, religion, moral beliefs etc – used to show disapproval: *a reaction to a world full of shallow materialism*

2 the belief that only physical things really exist —**materialist** *adj*: *materialist philosophy* —**materialist** *n* [C]: *We confess to being hopeless materialists, surrounded by our own cool stuff.*

ma·te·ri·a·lis·tic /məˌtɪəriəˈlɪstɪk◂ $ -ˌtɪr-/ *adj* concerned only with money and possessions rather than things of the mind such as art, religion, or moral beliefs – used to show disapproval: *He's so materialistic.* | *the materialistic values of American society* —**materialistically** /-kli/ *adv*

ma·te·ri·al·ize (*also* **-ise** *BrE*) /məˈtɪəriəlaɪz $ -ˈtɪr-/ *v* [I]

1 to happen or appear in the way that you expected: *Problems were expected, but they never materialized.* | *The money we had been promised* ***failed to materialize***.

2 to appear in an unexpected and strange way: *The figure of a man suddenly materialized in the shadows.* —**materialization** /məˌtɪəriəlaɪˈzeɪʃən $ -lə-/ *n* [U]

ma·te·ri·al·ly /məˈtɪəriəli $ -ˈtɪr-/ *adv* **1** *formal* in a big enough or strong enough way to change a situation: *This would materially affect US security.* **2** [sentence adverb] in relation to possessions and money, rather than the needs of a person's mind or soul OPP **spiritually**: *Materially, we are better off than ever before.*

ma·té·ri·el /məˌtɪəriˈel $ -ˌtɪr-/ *n* [U] *formal* supplies of weapons used by an army

ma·ter·nal /məˈtɜːnl $ -ɜːr-/ ●○○ *adj*

1 typical of the way a good mother behaves or feels → **paternal**: *Annie was wonderfully warm and maternal.* | *She seems to have a strong* ***maternal instinct*** (=desire to have babies and take care of them).

2 [only before noun] relating to a mother or to being a mother → **paternal**: *the relationship between maternal age and infant mortality*

3 maternal grandfather/aunt etc your mother's father, sister etc —**maternally** *adv*

ma·ter·ni·ty¹ /məˈtɜːnəti $ -ɜːr-/ ●○○ *adj* [only before noun] relating to a woman who is PREGNANT or who has

just had a baby → **paternity**: *a maternity dress* | **maternity benefits/pay etc** (=money that the government or employers give to a woman after she has had a baby)

maternity² *n* [U] the state of being a mother

ma'ternity ˌleave *n* [U] time that a mother is allowed to spend away from work when she has a baby → **paternity leave**: **on maternity leave** *Karen will be on maternity leave next month.*

mat·ey¹ /'meɪti/ *adj BrE informal* behaving as if you were someone's friend: **[+with]** *She's been very matey with the boss lately.*

matey² *n BrE informal* used by men as a very informal or disrespectful way of speaking to another man

math /mæθ/ ●●● S2 *n* [U] *AmE* mathematics SYN **maths** *BrE*: *Tim's good at math and science.* | *a set of simple* ***math problems*** (=questions that are related to math) | *She's learning calculus in math class.* | *a math test*

math·e·mat·i·cal /ˌmæθə'mætɪkəl◂/ ●●○ *adj*
1 relating to or using mathematics: **mathematical equation/calculation/formula etc** | *mathematical analysis* | *the development of mathematical skills* | *a mathematical genius*
2 [only before noun] calculating things in a careful exact way: *The whole trip was planned with mathematical precision.*
3 mathematical certainty something that is completely certain to happen
4 a mathematical chance (of sth) a very small chance that something will happen —**mathematically** /-kli/ *adv*

math·e·ma·ti·cian /ˌmæθəmə'tɪʃən/ *n* [C] someone who studies or teaches mathematics, or is a specialist in mathematics

MATHEMATICAL INSTRUMENTS

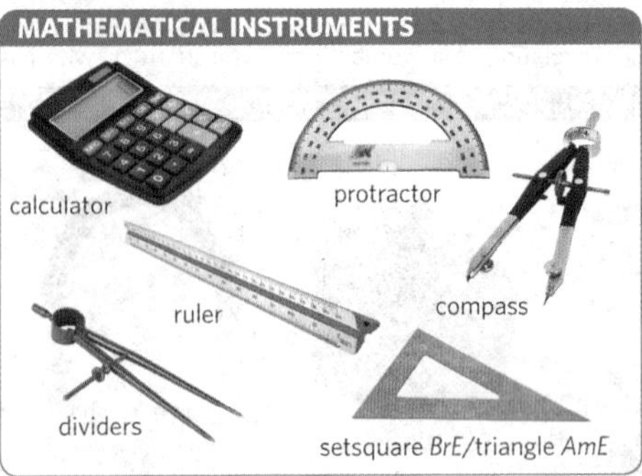

math·e·mat·ics /ˌmæθə'mætɪks/ ●●● W3 *n* [U]
1 the science of numbers and of shapes, including ALGEBRA, GEOMETRY, and ARITHMETIC
2 the calculations that are involved in a particular situation or plan

GRAMMAR: Singular or plural verb?

- In meaning 1, **mathematics** is followed by a singular verb: ***Mathematics is*** *her best subject at school.*
- In meaning 2, **mathematics** can be followed by a singular or plural verb: *The* ***mathematics*** *of the project* ***is/are*** *very complicated.*

GRAMMAR GUIDE ▸ NOUNS

maths /mæθs/ ●●● S2 *n* [U] *BrE informal* mathematics SYN **math** *AmE*: *the new maths teacher* | *maths lessons* | *She got top marks in maths and chemistry.*

mat·i·née /'mætəneɪ $ ˌmætn'eɪ/ *n* [C] a performance of a play or film in the afternoon

'matinée ˌidol / $ ..'. ˌ../ *n* [C] *old-fashioned* an actor who is very popular with women

'matinée ˌjacket / $ ..'. ˌ../ *n* [C] *BrE old-fashioned* a short coat for a baby

mat·ing /'meɪtɪŋ/ *n* [U] sex between animals: *the mating season*

mat·ins, **mattins** /'mætənz $ 'mætnz/ *n* [U] the first prayers of the day in the Christian religion SYN **morning prayer**

ma·tri·arch /'meɪtriɑːk $ -ɑːrk/ *n* [C] a woman, especially an older woman, who controls a family or a social group → **patriarch**

ma·tri·ar·chal /ˌmeɪtri'ɑːkl◂ $ -'ɑːr-/ *adj* **1** ruled or controlled by women: *a matriarchal society* **2** relating to or typical of a matriarch → **patriarchal**

ma·tri·ar·chy /'meɪtriɑːki $ -ɑːr-/ *n* (*plural* **matriarchies**) [C,U] **1** a social system in which the oldest woman controls a family and its possessions → **patriarchy** **2** a society in which women hold all the power → **patriarchy**

mat·ri·cide /'mætrɪsaɪd/ *n* [U] *formal* the crime of murdering your mother → **parricide**, **patricide**

ma·tric·u·late /mə'trɪkjəleɪt/ *v* [I] *formal* to officially begin studying at a university or, in the US, at a school or college: **[+at]** *Aged only 15, he matriculated at the University of Leipzig.* | ***matriculated students*** —**matriculation** /məˌtrɪkjə'leɪʃən/ *n* [U]

mat·ri·mo·ny /'mætrəməni $ -moʊni/ *n* [U] *formal* the state of being married SYN **marriage**: *They were joined together in* ***holy matrimony***. —**matrimonial** /ˌmætrə'məʊniəl $ -'moʊ-/ *adj*

ma·trix /'meɪtrɪks/ *n* (*plural* **matrices** /-trəsiːz/ *or* **matrixes**) [C] *technical* **1** an arrangement of numbers, letters, or signs in rows and COLUMNs that you consider to be one amount, and that you use in solving mathematical problems: *a matrix table* **2** a situation from which a person or society can grow and develop: *the cultural matrix* **3** a living part in which something is formed or develops, such as the substance from which your FINGERNAILs grow **4** a MOULD (=hollow container) into which melted metal, plastic etc is poured to form a shape **5** the rock in which hard stones or jewels have formed → DOT-MATRIX PRINTER

ma·tron /'meɪtrən/ *n* [C] **1** *literary* an older married woman **2** *BrE old-fashioned* a nurse who is in charge of the other nurses in a hospital **3** *BrE* a woman who works as a nurse in a private school **4** *AmE* a woman who is in charge of women and children in a school or prison

ma·tron·ly /'meɪtrənli/ *adj* used to describe a woman who is fairly fat and no longer young - to avoid saying this directly: *a matronly woman of 50*

ˌmatron of 'honour *BrE*, **matron of honor** *AmE n* (*plural* **matrons of honour**) [C] a married woman who helps the BRIDE on her wedding day → **bridesmaid**

matt *BrE*, **matte** /mæt/ *adj* matt paint, colour, or photographs have a dull surface, not shiny OPP **gloss**: *matt black*

mat·ted /'mætɪd/ *adj* matted hair or fur is twisted or stuck together in a thick mass: *a cat with a dirty matted coat* | **[+with]** *Her hair was matted with blood.*

mat·ter¹ /'mætə $ -ər/ ●●● S1 W1 *n*
1 SUBJECT/SITUATION [C] a subject or situation that you have to think about or deal with: *There are important matters we need to discuss.* | **[+for]** *The legal arrangements for the sale are a matter for negotiation.*

REGISTER
Matter is used especially in formal or official contexts. In everyday English, people usually use **subject**, or just say **it**: *I've talked to him about* ***the matter***. → *I've talked to him about* ***it***.

2 matters [plural] a situation that you are in or have been describing: *Maybe some of these suggestions will help to improve matters.* | *Matters can be more easily sorted out once you get to the resort.* | *His long absences* ***didn't help matters*** (=made the situation worse). | **to make matters worse** (=used to say that something makes a bad situation worse) *The team has lost the last two games and, to make matters worse, two of its best players are injured.* | **to complicate matters further** (=used to say that something makes a complicated situation more complicated) *To* *complicate matters further, the law on this issue has been changed.*

3 MATERIAL [U] **a)** the material that everything in the universe is made of, including solids, liquids, and gases: *particles of matter* **b) waste/solid/organic/vegetable etc matter** a substance that consists of waste material, solid material etc **c)** a yellow or white substance in wounds or next to your eye

4 as a matter of fact *spoken* used when adding more details about what you have just said: *'Have you had many visitors yet?' 'No, as a matter of fact you're the first.'* | *I knew him when we were in college – as a matter of fact we were on the same course.* → MATTER-OF-FACT

5 what's the matter?/something's the matter/nothing's the matter etc *spoken* used to ask or talk about why someone seems worried, unhappy, or ill, why something about a situation seems wrong, or why a machine seems not to be working properly: *What's the matter? You look as though you've been crying.* | *'Is something the matter?' 'Just a headache – I'll be fine in a minute.'* | *You look worried. Is there anything the matter?* | *What's the matter with Bill?* | *What's the matter with your eye? It looks red.* | *I know something's the matter. You're frightened of something.* | *Nothing's the matter, honestly, I'm fine.* | *There was nothing the matter with it* (=it was all right) *when I lent it to him.* | *She had something the matter with her back.*

6 the truth/fact of the matter is (that) *spoken* used when saying what you think is really true concerning a situation: *The truth of the matter is that we don't know exactly how the disease is spread.*

7 for that matter used to say that what you are saying about one thing is also true about something else: *Ben never touched beer, or any kind of alcohol for that matter.* | *He's an artist who has never been as well-known here, or for that matter as well-respected, as he has been in the USA.*

8 be (quite) a different matter (*also* **be (quite) another matter**) *especially BrE* used to say that a situation or action is very different from the one you have just mentioned, and may not be as easy, pleasant etc: *She didn't mind seeing him in a group but an intimate dinner in a restaurant was another matter altogether.*

9 take matters into your own hands to deal with a problem yourself because other people have failed to deal with it: *Local people took matters into their own hands and hired their own security guards.*

10 it's only/just a matter of time used to say that something will definitely happen in the future: *It can only be a matter of time before someone is seriously injured.*

11 a matter of life and/or death a situation that is extremely serious or important, especially one in which someone could die: *The delay in the arrival of the ambulance could be a matter of life and death.* | *Can't it wait? It's hardly a matter of life or death, is it?*

12 be a matter of opinion used to say that people have different opinions about something, especially when you yourself have a negative opinion: *Whether or not he is any good as a manager is a matter of opinion.*

13 be a matter of (personal) taste/choice/preference used to say that different people like different things: *I can't say which wine is best – it's a matter of personal taste.*

14 be a matter of principle to be something that you feel you must or must not do, because of your moral principles: *She couldn't take the money. It was a matter of principle.*

15 be a matter of doing sth used to say that an action involves doing something: **be simply/largely/merely etc a matter of doing sth** *Reducing the number of road deaths is not simply a matter of improving roads.*

16 a matter of seconds/weeks/hours etc only a few seconds, weeks etc: *The ambulance arrived in a matter of minutes.* | *The bullet missed his head* ***by a matter of*** *inches.*

17 as a matter of sth because of a particular belief or quality: *He invited her as a matter of courtesy.* | *As a matter of fairness, he should be allowed to give his version of events.*

18 as a matter of interest *BrE spoken* used when you ask or tell someone something that interests you but is not important: *Just as a matter of interest, which school did you go to?*

19 as a matter of urgency if something is done or should be done as a matter of urgency, it is done or should be done very soon: *That procedure should be streamlined as a matter of urgency.*

20 as a matter of course/routine if something is done as a matter of course or routine, it is the correct and usual thing to do in a particular situation: *We will contact your former employer as a matter of course.*

21 no matter how/whether/what etc (*also* **no matter the ...**) used to say that something is true or that something happens whatever the situation is: *Feeding a baby is a messy job no matter how careful you are.* | *I'm determined to visit Japan no matter what it costs.* | *He visited her every day no matter the weather.*

22 no matter what *spoken* used to say that you will definitely do something: *I'll call you tonight, no matter what.*

23 no matter *spoken formal or old-fashioned* used to say that something is not important and will not affect a situation: *'I'm afraid I forgot to bring a towel.' 'No matter, I've got one you can borrow.'*

24 it's a matter of fact (that) used to say that something is a fact: *It's a matter of fact that the team have not performed as well this season.*

25 the little/small matter of sth *spoken* something that is not important or not difficult – used when you really think something is important or difficult: *He seemed unworried by the small matter of the war that was in progress.* | *There's the small matter of tonight's game if we are to reach the finals.*

26 no matter that used to say that something is not important and will not affect a situation: *I would always be an outsider here – no matter that I spoke fluent Spanish.*

27 reading/printed etc matter things that are written for people to read: *As well as textbooks and other printed matter, courses may include video and audio cassettes.* → GREY MATTER, SUBJECT MATTER, → **not mince matters** at MINCE[1](3), → **mind over matter** at MIND[1](43)

COLLOCATIONS

ADJECTIVES

a serious/important matter *It is a very serious matter to mislead the police.*
an urgent matter (=something that needs to be dealt with quickly)
a weighty matter (=an important matter) *I was surprised that this weighty matter was decided so quickly.*
a small/trivial matter (=a matter that is not important) *Walking out over such a small matter may seem ridiculous.*
a simple/easy matter (=something that is easy to do) *Putting together the bookcases is a fairly simple matter.*
a personal/private matter *We never spoke about personal matters.*
a financial/legal/religious etc matter | **a practical matter**

VERBS

discuss the matter *She refused to discuss the matter.*
raise the matter (with sb) (=discuss something with someone) *If you need further training, raise the matter with your manager.*
consider the matter (=think about something)
settle/resolve the matter (=decide something) | **pursue the matter** (=keep discussing or asking about something)
investigate the matter (=try to find out the truth about something) *The police said they were investigating the matter.*
let the matter rest/drop (=stop discussing or worrying about something) *I was too curious to let the matter drop.*

PHRASES

a matter of importance (=something important) *He consulted her on all matters of importance.*
a matter of concern (=something that concerns people) *Safety standards in the industry have become a matter of concern.*
a matter for debate/negotiation/discussion (=something to be debated/negotiated etc) *How to solve the housing crisis is a matter for debate.*
be a matter for sb (to decide) (=be something that a particular person should decide) *This is a matter for the judge.*
the matter at hand (*also* **the matter in hand** *BrE*) (=the thing you are dealing with now) *Do not let yourself be distracted from the matter in hand.*
be no laughing matter (=be something serious and important, though it might seem funny) | **the heart/crux of the matter** (=the most important part of something) | **matters arising from/out of sth** (=things connected with or caused by a particular event)

matter² ●●● S1 W3 *v*
1 [I not in progressive] to be important, especially to be important to you, or to have an effect on what happens: **it doesn't etc matter if** *Will it matter if I'm a little late?* | *If I have to stay late at work tonight, it won't matter because we can go out another night.* | **it doesn't etc matter who/why/what etc** *It doesn't matter what you wear, as long as you look neat and tidy.* | *Does it matter what I think?* | **it doesn't etc matter that** *It does not matter that the gun was in fact unloaded.* | *Do you think it matters that the cups and saucers don't match?* | **it doesn't matter about sth** *Just give me $5 – it doesn't matter about the rest.* | **[+to]** *He had lost many of the people who mattered to him.* | **matter a lot/a great deal** *It mattered a great deal to her what other people thought of her.* | **not matter much/matter little** *I don't think it matters much what you study.* | *campaigning on issues that* ***really matter*** | **all that matters/the only thing that matters** *All that matters is that you are safe.* | *Money was the only thing which mattered to him.* | *I don't care what it looks like –* ***what matters is*** *that it works.* | *At last she was with the man she loved and* ***nothing else mattered****.* | *She said very little during the meal.* ***Not that it mattered*** (=it was not important).
2 it doesn't matter *spoken* **a)** used to tell someone that you are not angry or upset about something, especially something that they have done: *'I've spilled some coffee on the carpet.' 'It doesn't matter.'* **b)** used to say that you do not mind which one of two things you have: *'Red or white wine?' 'Oh, either. It doesn't matter.'*
3 what does it matter? *spoken* used to say that something is not important: *It all happened so long ago now, what does it matter?* | *What does it matter how old I am?*

ˌmatter-of-ˈfact *adj* showing no emotion when you are talking about something exciting, frightening, upsetting etc: **[+about]** *Jan was surprisingly matter-of-fact about her divorce.* | **matter-of-fact voice/tone** *Use a matter-of-fact tone when disciplining your children.* —**matter-of-factly** *adv*

mat·ting /ˈmætɪŋ/ *n* [U] strong rough material, used for making MATS: *straw matting*

mat·tins /ˈmætənz $ ˈmætnz/ *n* [U] another spelling of MATINS

mat·tock /ˈmætək/ *n* [C] a tool used for digging, with a long handle and a metal blade

mat·tress /ˈmætrɪs/ ●●○ *n* [C] the soft part of a bed that you lie on: **firm/soft/hard etc mattress** *an old, lumpy mattress*

ma·tu·ra·tion /ˌmætʃəˈreɪʃən/ AWL *n* [U] *formal* the period during which something grows and develops → **mature**: *cell maturation*

ma·ture¹ /məˈtʃʊə $ -ˈtʃʊr/ ●●○ AWL *adj*
1 SENSIBLE someone, especially a child or young person, who is mature behaves in a sensible and reasonable way, as you would expect an adult to behave OPP **immature**: *Laura is very* ***mature for*** *her* ***age****.* | *We're* ***mature enough*** *to disagree on this issue but still respect each other.*
2 FULLY GROWN fully grown and developed OPP **immature**: *Mature apple trees are typically 20 feet tall.* | *The new leader wants his country to be seen as a mature democracy.* | *The human brain isn't* ***fully mature*** *until about age 25.* | **physically/emotionally/sexually mature** *Most girls are sexually mature by about 14 years of age.*
3 WINE/CHEESE ETC *BrE* mature cheese, wine etc has a good strong taste which has developed during a long period of time OPP **mild**: *mature cheddar*
4 OLDER a polite or humorous way of describing someone who is no longer young SYN **middle-aged**: *wedding fashions for mature brides* | *a respectable gentleman* ***of mature years***
5 NOVEL/PAINTING ETC a mature piece of work by a writer or an artist is done late in their life and shows a high level of understanding or skill: *His mature work reveals a deep sense of enjoyment of nature.*
6 on mature reflection/consideration *formal* after thinking carefully and sensibly about something for a long time: *On mature reflection we have decided to decline their offer.*
7 FINANCIAL a mature BOND or POLICY is ready to be paid
8 mature market/industry *technical* a mature industry or market is one where growth is quite low and there are fewer competitors than before —**maturely** *adv*: *If you want us to treat you as an adult, you have to act maturely.*

mature² ●○○ AWL *v*
1 [I] to become fully grown or developed: *As the fish matures, its colours and patternings change.* | **[+into]** *She has matured into a fine writer.*
2 [I] to become sensible and start to behave sensibly and reasonably, like an adult: *He has matured a lot since he left home.* | *He wants to prove just how much he has matured both as a player and as a man.*
3 [I] if a financial arrangement such as a BOND or an insurance POLICY matures, it becomes ready to be paid
4 [I,T] if cheese, wine etc matures, or if it is matured, it develops a good strong taste over a period of time: *Few beers brewed in Britain are matured in the bottle.* | *The olives are pulped, then left to mature.*

maˌture ˈstudent *n* [C] *BrE* a student at a university or college who is over 25 years old

ma·tu·ri·ty /məˈtʃʊərəti $ -ˈtʃʊr-/ ●○○ AWL *n* [U]
1 the quality of behaving in a sensible way like an adult OPP **immaturity**: *Beth shows a maturity way beyond her 16 years.* | *One day you'll have the maturity to understand.*
2 the time or state when someone or something is fully grown or developed: **at maturity** *The tree will reach only 5 feet at maturity.* | **reach/come to/grow to maturity** *These insects reach* ***full maturity*** *after a few weeks.* | *the era when the Republic came to* ***political maturity*** | **sexual/emotional/physical maturity** *He lacks the emotional maturity to appreciate poetry.*
3 the time when a financial arrangement such as a BOND or an insurance POLICY becomes ready to be paid

mat·zo, **matzoh** /ˈmɒtsə $ ˈmɑː-/ *n* (*plural* **matzos**) [C,U] **1** a large thin piece of flat bread, eaten by Jewish people during PASSOVER **2** a type of flour used to make bread, cakes etc especially by Jewish people during PASSOVER: *herrings dipped in matzo and fried*

maud·lin /ˈmɔːdlɪn $ ˈmɒː-/ *adj* **1** talking or behaving in a sad, silly, and emotional way, especially when drunk: **get/grow/become maudlin** *Sir Ralph was becoming maudlin after his third glass of claret.* **2** a maudlin song, story, film etc tries too hard to make people feel emotions such as love or sadness and seems silly: *a song that is tender without being maudlin*

maul /mɔːl $ mɒːl/ *v* [T] **1** if an animal mauls someone, it injures them badly by tearing their flesh: *A mentally ill man was mauled after climbing into the lions' enclosure at London Zoo.* **2** to strongly criticize something, especially a new book, play etc: *Her latest book was absolutely mauled by the critics.* **3** to touch someone in a rough sexual way which they think is unpleasant: *What makes you think you've got the right to maul me like that?* **4** *informal* to defeat someone very easily – used especially in sports reports: *Stanford have looked quite good lately. They absolutely mauled Notre Dame last weekend.* —**mauling** *n* [singular]: *Brown got a mauling over the government's failure to fulfil its promises.*

maun·der /ˈmɔːndə $ ˈmɒːndər/ *v* [I] *especially BrE* to talk or complain about something for a long time in a boring way: **[+on/about]** *What are you maundering on about, George?*

Maun·dy Thurs·day /ˌmɔːndi ˈθɜːzdi, -deɪ $ ˌmɒːndi ˈθɜːrz-/ *n* [U] the Thursday before Easter

mau·so·le·um /ˌmɔːsəˈliːəm $ ˌmɒː-/ *n* [C] a large stone building made specially to contain the body of a dead person, or the dead bodies of an important family → **tomb**: *the Lenin Mausoleum*

mauve /məʊv $ moʊv/ *n* [U] a pale purple colour —**mauve** *adj*: *mauve flowers*

ma·ven /ˈmeɪvən/ *n* [C] *AmE* someone who knows a lot about a particular subject: **food/fashion/sports etc maven** *A food maven could also be called a gourmet.*

mav·e·rick /ˈmævərɪk/ *n* [C] an unusual person who has different ideas and ways of behaving from other people, and is often very successful: *He's always been a bit of a maverick.* —**maverick** *adj* [only before noun]: *a maverick detective*

maw /mɔː $ mɒː/ *n* [C] **1** *formal* something which seems to swallow or use up things completely: **[+of]** *Millions of dollars were poured into the maw of defense spending.* **2** *literary* an animal's mouth or throat

mawk·ish /ˈmɔːkɪʃ $ ˈmɒː-/ *adj* showing too much emotion in a way that is embarrassing SYN **sentimental**: *a mawkish love story* —**mawkishly** *adv* —**mawkishness** *n* [U]

max¹ /mæks/ *n* [C] *informal* **1** the abbreviation of ***maximum***: *Five people will fit, but that's the max.* **2 to the max** to the greatest degree possible: *We had the air conditioner turned up to the max.* —**max** *adj, adv*: *Let's say two hours to get there, max.*

max² *v*

max out *phr v AmE informal* **1 max sth ↔ out** to use something such as money or supplies so that there is none left: *I maxed out my Visa.* **2** to do too much, eat too much etc: **[+on]** *'Want a beer?' 'Nah, I maxed out on booze this weekend.'*

max·i /ˈmæksi/ *adj* **maxi dress/skirt/coat** a long dress, skirt, or coat that reaches to the ANKLES —**maxi** *n* [C]

max·il·lo·fa·cial /mækˌsɪləʊˈfeɪʃəl $ -sɪloʊ-/ *adj* [only before noun] *medical* relating to the upper jaw and face: *maxillofacial surgery*

max·im /ˈmæksɪm/ *n* [C] a well-known phrase or saying, especially one that gives a rule for sensible behaviour → **saying**

max·i·mal /ˈmæksəməl/ *adj technical* as much or as large as possible OPP **minimal**: *the right conditions for a maximal increase in employment* —**maximally** *adv*

max·i·mize (*also* **-ise** *BrE*) /ˈmæksəmaɪz/ ●○○ AWL *v* [T]

1 to increase something such as profit or income as much as possible OPP **minimize**: **maximize profit/revenue etc** *The company's main function is to maximize profit.* THESAURUS ▸ INCREASE

2 to CLICK on a special part on a window on a computer screen so that it becomes as big as the screen OPP **minimize**

3 to use something in a way that gives you the greatest practical value or the best results: *We need to maximize the space.* | **maximize opportunities/chances etc** *The career center will help you maximize your opportunities.* —**maximization** /ˌmæksəmaɪˈzeɪʃən $ -səmə-/ *n* [U]

max·i·mum¹ /ˈmæksəməm/ ●●● S3 W2 AWL *adj* [only before noun] the maximum amount, quantity, speed etc is the largest that is possible or allowed OPP **minimum**: *The car has a maximum speed of 120 mph.* | *They made maximum use of the resources available.* | *To get the maximum benefit, do the exercises slowly.* | *Display the hologram under a strong light for maximum effect.* | *The plant is operating* ***at maximum capacity***. | **maximum amount/number etc** *Work out the maximum amount you can afford to spend.* | *The award will consist of a lump sum to a* ***maximum value*** *of $5,000.* | **maximum sentence/penalty/fine etc** *She faces a maximum penalty of life in prison.*

maximum² ●●● S3 W3 AWL *n* [C] the largest number or amount that is possible or is allowed SYN **minimum**: **[+of]** *He faces a maximum of seven years in prison.* | *The company will reimburse you* ***up to a maximum of*** *$1,000.* | *We might have a third child, but that's* ***the absolute maximum***.

may¹ /meɪ/ ●●● S1 W1 *modal verb*

1 POSSIBILITY if something may happen or may be true, there is a possibility that it will happen or be true but this is not certain SYN **might**: *I may be late, so don't wait for me.* | *Some chemicals may cause environmental damage.* | *There may not be enough money to pay for the repairs.* | *Well, I may have been wrong.* | *They may have called while you were out.* | ***It may be that*** *Minoan ships were built and repaired here.* | *Your job* ***may well*** *involve some travelling* (=it is fairly likely).

2 POSSIBLE TO DO STH if something may be done, completed etc in a particular way, that is how it is possible to do it SYN **can**: *The problem may be solved in a number of different ways.*

3 ALLOWED **a)** used to say that someone is allowed to do something SYN **can**: *Thank you. You may go now.* | *There is a set of rules to show what members may and may not do.* | *You may sit down or stand, just as you wish.* | *No one may own more than 10% of the shares.* **b) may I/we ...?** *spoken formal* used to ask politely for permission to do something: *May I come in and wait?* | *May we use your office for a few minutes?*

4 IN POLITE EXPRESSIONS *spoken formal* used to say, ask, or suggest something in a polite way: *All these things, if I may say so, are entirely irrelevant.* | *Who, may I ask, is Wotherspoon?* | *May I suggest that you consider the matter further before taking any action.*

5 ALTHOUGH used to say that even though one thing is true, something else which seems very different is also true: *I may be slow, but at least I don't make stupid mistakes.* | *Although this may sound like a simple process, great care is needed.* | *Strange as it may seem, I always felt I belonged here.*

6 may as well *spoken* used to suggest that someone should do something, because there is no good reason to do anything else SYN **might as well**: *If there's nothing more to do, we may as well go to bed.* | *You may as well tell us now – we'll find out sooner or later.*

7 may sb/sth do sth *formal* used to express a wish or hope: *We pray for those who died – may they rest in peace.* | *It is a fine tradition and long may it continue!*

8 PURPOSE *formal* used after 'so that' or 'in order that' to say that someone does something in order to make something else possible: *The hero sacrifices his life so that his friend may live.*

9 be that as it may *formal* in spite of what you have just mentioned: *Perhaps there isn't one single system that will work for everyone. Be that as it may, we all need order in our lives.*

10 may well used to say that there is a good reason for a reaction, question, or feeling: *'What's all the noise?' 'You* ***may well ask***.*'*

GRAMMAR: Comparison

may

- You say **May I?** when asking for permission: *May I ask you a question?*
- You say **you may** when giving someone permission: *You may go now.*
- You say that something **may** happen or be true: *I may be late.* | *He may be in his office.*
- You say that something **may have** happened: *They may have already gone home.*
- You use **may not** in negative sentences: *I may not be here much longer.* | *He may not have understood what you said.*

might
• In everyday English, you can use **might** in the same way as **may** to say that something is possible.
• You can say that something **might** happen or be true: *I might be late.* | *He might be in his office.*
• You can say that something **might have** happened: *They might have already gone home.*
• In everyday English, you can also use **might not** or **mightn't**: *I might not be here much longer.* | *He mightn't have understood.*
GRAMMAR GUIDE ▸ VERBS

may² *n* [U] *BrE* the white or pink flowers of the HAWTHORN

May ●●● S2 W3 *n* [C,U] the fifth month of the year, between April and June: **next/last May** *She started work here last May.* | **in May** *The theatre opened in May.* | **on May 6th** *We don't have any meetings on May 6th, do we?* | **on 6th May** *BrE*: *An agreement was signed on 6th May 1977.* | **May 6** *AmE*: *Michael's getting married May 6.*

ˌMay ˈBall *n* [C] a formal dance held by colleges at the universities of Oxford and Cambridge every year in June. Students dress formally for a May Ball, and it is expensive to go to one.

may·be /ˈmeɪbi/ ●●● S1 W1 *adv* [sentence adverb]
1 used to say that something may happen or may be true but you are not certain SYN **perhaps**: *Maybe it's all just a big misunderstanding.* | *'Do you think he'll come back?' 'Maybe.'* | *Maybe they're right, but* ***maybe not***. | *You have talent,* ***maybe even*** *genius.* | *He said he'd finish the work soon - maybe tomorrow.*

REGISTER
In written English, people often prefer to use **perhaps**, because it is slightly more formal than **maybe**: ***Perhaps*** *this explains why the figure is so high.*

2 *spoken* used to reply to a suggestion or idea when either you are not sure if you agree with it, or you do not want to say 'yes' or 'no': *'I think Sheila would be an excellent manager.' 'Maybe.'*
3 used to show that you are not sure of an amount or number: *The problems really started maybe two or three years ago.* | *He looked like he was thirty, maybe thirty-five years old.*
4 *spoken* used to make a suggestion you are not quite sure about: *If the bill doesn't seem right, maybe you should give them a call.* | *Maybe I can ride the bicycle and follow you.*

ˈMay Day *n* [C,U] the first day of May, when LEFT-WING political parties in some countries celebrate, and when people traditionally celebrate the arrival of spring

may·day /ˈmeɪdeɪ/ *n* [singular] a radio signal used to ask for help when a ship or plane is in serious danger → SOS

may·est /ˈmeɪəst/ *v* **thou mayest** *old use* you may

May·flow·er, the /ˈmeɪflaʊəʳ/ the ship that took the Pilgrim Fathers to Plymouth, Massachusetts in the US in 1620. They were Puritans who left England because they wanted to start a new society where they would be free to practise their religion. In the US, people sometimes say that someone's family 'came over on the Mayflower' when they mean that they originally arrived in the US a very long time ago.

may·fly /ˈmeɪflaɪ/ *n* (*plural* **mayflies**) [C] a small insect that lives near water, and only lives for a short time

may·hem /ˈmeɪhem/ *n* [U] an extremely confused situation in which people are very frightened or excited SYN **chaos**: *There was* ***complete mayhem*** *after the explosion.* | **cause/create/wreak mayhem** *For some children, the first fall of snow is an opportunity to create mayhem.*

may·n't /ˈmeɪənt/ *BrE old-fashioned* the short form of 'may not'

may·o /ˈmeɪəʊ $ -oʊ/ *n* [U] *informal* mayonnaise

may·on·naise /ˌmeɪəˈneɪz $ ˈmeɪəneɪz/ *n* [U] a thick white sauce, made of raw egg YOLKS and oil, often eaten on sandwiches or SALAD

mayor /meə $ ˈmeɪər/ ●●● W2 *n* [C]
1 the person who has been elected to lead the government of a town or city: *the election of the London mayor*
2 someone who is chosen or elected each year in Britain to represent a town or city at official public ceremonies —**mayoral** *adj*: *mayoral duties*

mayor·al·ty /ˈmeərəlti $ ˈmeɪərəlti/ *n* [U] *formal* the position of mayor, or the period when someone is mayor

mayor·ess /ˈmeərɪs $ ˈmeɪərɪs/ *n* [C] *BrE* the wife of a mayor, or a woman who shares the work of a mayor

may·pole /ˈmeɪpəʊl $ -poʊl/ *n* [C] a tall pole around which people danced on May Day in the past

mayst /meɪst/ *v* **thou mayst** *old use* you may

may've /ˈmeɪəv/ *spoken* the short form of 'may have': *You may've heard this story before.*

MAZE

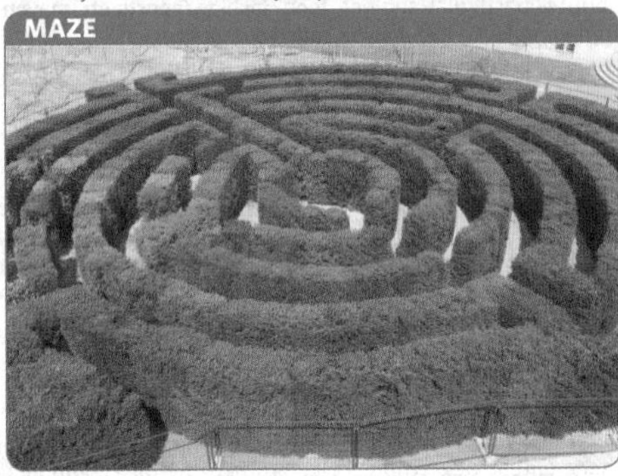

maze /meɪz/ ●○○ *n* [C]
1 a complicated and confusing arrangement of streets, roads etc: **maze of streets/paths/tunnels etc** *the maze of narrow streets* | *I was led through a maze of corridors.*
2 a large number of rules, instructions etc which are complicated and difficult to understand: **maze of rules/regulations etc** *a maze of new laws*
3 a specially designed system of paths, often in a park or public garden, which is difficult to find your way through: *We got completely lost in the maze.* | *the famous Hampton Court maze*
4 a children's game, played on paper, in which you try to draw a line through a complicated group of lines without crossing any of them

ma·zur·ka /məˈzɜːkə $ -ɜːr-/ *n* [C] a fast traditional Polish dance, or the music for this dance

MB /ˌem ˈbiː/ (*also* **Mb**) the written abbreviation of ***megabyte*** or megabytes

MBA (*also* **M.B.A.** *AmE*) /ˌem biː ˈeɪ/ *n* [C] (***Master of Business Administration***) a university degree in the skills needed to be in charge of a business that you can get after your first degree. A person who has this degree is also called an MBA: *Rick is a 32-year-old MBA from Harvard.* | **do/have an MBA**

MBE /ˌem biː ˈiː/ *n* [C] (***Member of the Order of the British Empire***) a special honour given to some British people for things they have done for their country

MC /ˌem ˈsiː/ *n* [C] **1** (***Master of Ceremonies***) someone who introduces guests or performers at a social or public occasion SYN **emcee 2** the person in a RAP group who holds the MICROPHONE and says the words to the songs **3** (***Military Cross***) a MEDAL given to British army officers for being brave

MCC, the /ˌem siː ˈsiː/ (***the Marylebone Cricket Club***) a famous CRICKET club that was established in 1787 and is based at Lord's cricket ground in North London

McCoy /məˈkɔɪ/ *n* **the real McCoy** *informal* something that is real and is not a copy, especially something valuable: *In the movie, the two thieves try to discover whether the banknotes are fakes or the real McCoy.*

m-com·merce /ˈem ˌkɒmɜːs $ -ˌkɑːmɜːrs/ *n* [U] (***mobile***

commerce) the buying or selling of goods and services using a radio connection to the Internet, for example using a LAPTOP or MOBILE PHONE → **e-commerce**

MD *BrE*, **M.D.** *AmE* /ˌem ˈdiː/ *n* **1** [C] (***Doctor of Medicine***) a university DEGREE in medicine that you can get after your first degree **2** [C] *BrE* the abbreviation of ***managing director*** → **CEO 3** [U] the abbreviation of ***muscular dystrophy***

MDF /ˌem diː ˈef/ *n* [U] a type of heavy wooden board that can be used for making cheap furniture, cupboards etc. It is made by gluing wood FIBRES together under heat and pressure.

me /mi; *strong* miː/ ●●● S1 W1 *pron* [object form of 'I'] **1** used by the person speaking or writing to refer to himself or herself: *Stop, you're hurting me.* | *He bought me a drink.* | *Give that book to me.* | *She's two years older than me.* | *That's me, standing on the left.*
2 me too *spoken* used to tell someone that you feel the same way as they do, that you are in a similar situation etc: *'I'm hungry!' 'Me too.'*
3 me neither (*also* **nor me**) *spoken* used to say that you agree with a negative statement that someone has just made: *'I can't believe he's fifty.' 'Me neither.'*
4 me time *informal* time when you can relax or do things that you enjoy doing, usually on your own: *Recognize that your partner needs some me time.*

ME /ˌem ˈiː/ *n* **1** [U] *BrE* (***myalgic encephalomyelitis***) an illness that makes you feel very tired and weak and can last for a long time: *ME sufferers* **2** [C] *AmE* the abbreviation of ***medical examiner***

me·a cul·pa /ˌmeɪə ˈkʊlpə/ *interjection* used humorously to admit that something is your fault

mead /miːd/ *n* **1** [U] an alcoholic drink made from HONEY: *a glass of mead* **2** [C] *literary* a meadow: *the flowery mead*

mead·ow /ˈmedəʊ $ -doʊ/ ●○○ *n* [C] a field with wild grass and flowers

mead·ow·lark /ˈmedəʊlɑːk $ -doʊlɑːrk/ *n* [C] a brown North American bird with a yellow breast

mea·gre *BrE*, **meager** *AmE* /ˈmiːgə $ -ər/ *adj* a meagre amount of food, money etc is too small and is much less than you need → **substantial**: *a meagre diet of bread and beans* | **meagre income/earnings/wages etc** *He supplements his meager income by working on Saturdays.* | *a school with* **meagre resources** —**meagrely** *adv* —**meagreness** *n* [U]

meal /miːl/ ●●● S2 W2 *n*
1 [C] an occasion when you eat food, for example breakfast or dinner, or the food that you eat on that occasion: *We must have a meal together some time.* | *Dinner is the main meal of the day for most people.*
2 [U] grain that has been crushed into a powder, for making flour or animal food → **BONEMEAL**
3 make a meal (out) of sth *BrE informal* to spend too much time or effort doing something: *He made a real meal out of parking the car.*

COLLOCATIONS

VERBS

have a meal (=eat a meal) *We usually have our evening meal fairly early.*
eat a meal *When they had eaten their meal, they went out for a walk.*
cook/make a meal (*also* **prepare a meal** *formal*) *Who cooks most of the meals?*
serve a meal *The bar serves snacks and meals.*
go (out) for a meal | **take sb (out) for a meal**

ADJECTIVES/NOUN + meal

an evening/midday meal *The evening meal is served at 7.30.*
the main meal *They had their main meal at lunchtime.*
a three-course/five-course etc meal (=a meal with several separate parts) *a three-course meal, including appetizer and dessert*
a good meal (=a meal that is large enough and tastes good) *We'll get a good meal there.*
a decent meal/a square meal (*also* **a proper meal** *BrE*) (=with enough good food to satisfy you) | **a big/large meal** | **a hot meal** | **a delicious meal** | **a heavy meal** (=with a lot of rich food) | **a light meal** (=with not a lot of food) | **a simple meal** | **a balanced meal** (=with some of each type of food, to keep you healthy) | **a school meal** (=provided by a school)

COMMON ERRORS

⚠ Don't say 'take a meal'. Say **have a meal**.

mea·lie /ˈmiːli/ *n* [C,U] *informal* MAIZE, or a piece of maize

ˌmeals-on-ˈwheels *n* a service in Britain in which hot meals are taken to old or sick people in their homes

ˈmeal ˌticket *n* [C] **1** *informal* something or someone that you depend on to give you money or food: *There were times when he suspected he was just a meal ticket to her.* **2** a card that you buy and then use to get meals at school or work, or at a special event: *The meal ticket is $15 and includes three meals with beverages.*

meal·time /ˈmiːltaɪm/ *n* [C,U] a time during the day when you have a meal: **at mealtimes** *The only time I see the boys is at mealtimes.*

meal·y /ˈmiːli/ *adj* **1** fruit or vegetables that are mealy are dry and do not taste good: *These apples are kind of mealy.* **2** containing MEAL

ˌmealy-ˈmouthed *adj* not brave enough or honest enough to say clearly and directly what you really think – used to show disapproval: *Most people felt Mr Major fought a pretty mealy-mouthed campaign in which radical ideas were either dropped or blunted.*

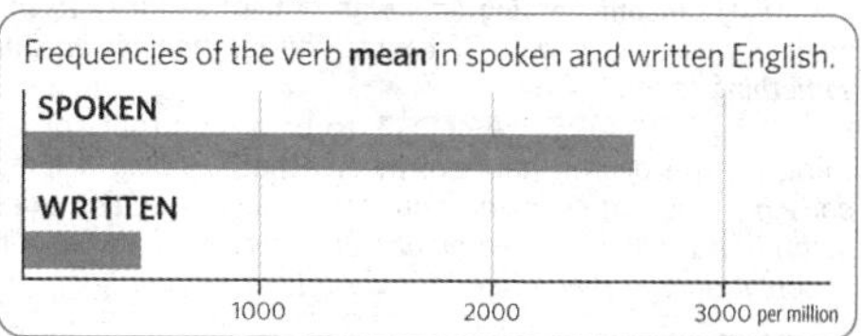

mean¹ /miːn/ ●●● S1 W1 *v* [T] (*past tense and past participle* **meant** /ment/)
1 HAVE A PARTICULAR MEANING to have or represent a particular meaning: ***What does*** *'patronizing'* ***mean?*** | *The red light means 'Stop'.* | *The report fails to define* ***what is meant by*** *the term 'key issues'.* | **mean (that)** *This light means you're running low on fuel.*

REGISTER

In written English, people often prefer to say that something **indicates** something is the case, rather than using **mean**: *The light* ***indicates*** *that fuel supplies are low.*

2 INTEND TO SAY STH to intend a particular meaning when you say something: **mean (that)** *I meant we'd have to leave early – that's all.* | *It's pretty obvious* ***what*** *she* ***means.*** | **(do) you mean** *spoken* (=used to check you have understood what someone intended to say) *Do you mean you've changed or Chris has changed?* | **do/if you know/see what I mean?** *spoken* (=used to check that someone understands you) *I want to buy her something really special, if you know what I mean.* | *We're still married but living apart in the same house, if you see what I mean.* | *Oh yeah!* ***I see what you mean*** (=I understand what you are trying to say). | ***What I mean is,*** *I don't feel alone anymore* (=used to explain more about what you have said). | *'I didn't really like him.'* ***'I know what you mean,*** *I didn't get on with him either* (=used to say you understand and have had the same experience). | *'In three hours' time, I'll be a free man.'* ***'How do you mean*** (=used to ask someone to explain what they have just said)?'
3 INTEND TO DO STH to intend to do something or intend that someone else should do something: **mean to do sth** *I've been meaning to ask you if you want to come for a meal*

next week. | *I didn't mean to upset you.* | **mean sb/sth to do sth** *I didn't mean this to happen at all.* | *I never meant you to find out.* | **mean for sb to do sth** *especially AmE*: *I didn't mean for her to get hurt.* | *I'm sure she* ***didn't mean it*** (=she did not intend to upset or hurt someone). | **mean no harm/offence/disrespect** (=not intend to harm, offend etc someone) *I'm sure he didn't mean any harm.* | *He may sound a bit rude at times, but he* ***means well*** (=intends to be helpful or kind, even if it does not seem like that). | *I wasn't criticizing you, I really* ***meant it for the best*** (=wanted to be helpful, although my actions had the wrong effect).

4 RESULT IN STH to have a particular result or involve something: *The merger will mean the closure of the company's Sydney office.* | *Don't let him see you. It will only mean trouble.* | **mean (that)** *The high cost of housing means that many young people can't afford to buy a house.* | **mean doing sth** *My new job will mean travelling all over the world.* | *Dieting also means being careful about which foods you buy.*

5 BE FAMILIAR if a name, word etc means something to you, you are familiar with it or you understand it: *He said his name was 'Randall' but it* ***meant nothing to*** *me* (=I was not familiar with it). | ***Does*** *the name Bryce* ***mean anything to*** *you?* | *You need to use analogies which will* ***mean something to*** *the reader.*

6 SAY STH SERIOUSLY to be serious about what you are saying or writing: *With children, if you say 'no', you have to* ***mean it***. | *I* ***meant what I said*** *earlier.* | *You don't* ***really mean*** *that, do you?*

7 HOW IMPORTANT SB/STH IS used for saying how important someone or something is to you: **mean sth to sb** *I know how much your work means to you.* | *The medal* ***meant a lot to*** *him.* | **mean the world to sb/mean everything to sb** (=be very important to someone) *He meant the world to her.* | *Time* ***meant nothing*** (=it was not important) *to me while I was travelling.* | *Of course the relationship* ***meant something*** *to me.*

8 SHOW STH IS TRUE/WILL HAPPEN to be a sign that something is true or will happen: **mean (that)** *Finding a lump does not necessarily mean you have cancer.* | *Clear skies mean that it will be a cold night.* | *Just because he's been in prison, it doesn't mean that he's violent.*

SPOKEN PHRASES

9 what do you mean ...? a) used when you do not understand what someone is trying to say: *'You'll be careful won't you?' 'What do you mean?'* **b)** used when you are very surprised or annoyed by what someone has just said: *What do you mean, you've cancelled the trip?* | *What do you mean by that?* **c)** used when you are very annoyed by what someone has just done: *What do you mean by calling me at this time of night?*

10 SAY WHICH PERSON/THING used to say that a particular person or thing is the one that you are talking about, pointing to etc: *'Hey you!' 'Do you mean me?'* | *I meant the pink dress, not the red one.*

11 I mean a) used when explaining or giving an example of something, or when pausing to think about what you are going to say next: *You're more of an expert than me. I mean, you've got all that experience.* | *It's just not right. I mean, it's unfair isn't it?* **b)** used to quickly correct something you have just said: *She plays the violin, I mean the viola, really well.*

12 see what I mean? used when something that happens proves what you said before: *See what I mean? Every time she calls me up she wants me to do something for her.*

13 that's what I mean used when someone is saying the same thing that you were trying to say earlier: *'We might not have enough money.' 'That's what I mean, so we'd better find out the price first.'*

14 I mean to say used when adding a reason or explanation for something you have just said, especially something you feel strongly about: *Of course she wants to see the children – I mean to say, it's only natural isn't it?*

15 mean business to be determined to do something: *This decision shows the public that we mean business.*

16 be meant to do sth a) if you are meant to do something, you should do it, especially because someone has told you to or because you are responsible for it: *Come on, Ellen, you're meant to be helping me.* | *I thought the police were meant to protect people.* **b)** to be intended to do something: *The diagram is meant to show the different stages of the process.*

17 be meant to be good/excellent/bad etc used to say that you have heard or read that something is good, bad etc: *The play is meant to be really good.*

18 be meant for sb/sth to be intended for a particular person or purpose: *a book meant for children*

19 be meant for sb if two people are meant for each other, they are very suitable as partners for each other: *They were meant for each other.* | *She's meant for him.*

20 sb was never meant for sth/to be sth used to say that someone is not at all suitable for a particular job or activity: *I was never meant for the army.*

21 sth was meant to be/happen used to say that you think a situation was certain to happen and that no one could have prevented it: *Dan left me after a month so I guess it just wasn't meant to be.*

22 know/understand what it means to be sth to have experienced a particular situation, so that you know what it is like: *I know what it means to be alone in a foreign country.*

GRAMMAR: Using the progressive

Mean is not used in the progressive in any of its senses, except for sense 3. You say: *What does this word mean?* | *This means trouble.* ✗ Don't say: *What is this word meaning?* | *This is meaning trouble.*
GRAMMAR GUIDE ▸ VERBS

mean² ●●● S3 *adj* (*comparative* **meaner**, *superlative* **meanest**)

1 CRUEL cruel or not kind: *That was a mean thing to do.* | *I felt a bit mean asking him to help.* | *It's a mean trick to play on someone.* | ***It was mean of*** *him not to invite her.* | **[+to]** *Don't be so mean to her!* THESAURUS ▸ UNKIND

2 NOT GENEROUS *BrE* not wanting to spend money, or not wanting to use much of something SYN **stingy, cheap** *AmE*: *He's too mean to buy a present for his wife.* | **[+with]** *He's always been mean with his money.* | *It was supposed to be garlic bread, but they'd been a bit mean with the garlic.*

3 no mean feat/achievement/task etc something that is very difficult to do, so that someone who does it deserves to be admired: *They sold 1 million cards in the first year of business – no mean feat, given the problems many businesses are facing.*

4 be no mean performer/player etc to be very good at doing something: *Kinnock is no mean performer on the rugby field.*

5 a mean sth *informal* used to say that something is very good or that someone is very good at doing something: *He plays a mean game of poker.* | *They serve a mean Sunday brunch at the restaurant on Fourth Street.*

6 AVERAGE [only before noun] *technical* average: *The study involved 60 patients with a mean age of 58.2 years.* | *The mean annual rainfall was 852 mm.*

7 POOR [only before noun] *literary* poor or looking poor: *She walked briskly through the mean and dirty streets.* —**meanly** *adv* —**meanness** *n* [U]

mean³ *n* **1 the mean** *technical* the average amount, figure, or value: *The mean of 7, 9 and 14 is 10.* **2 the/a mean between sth and sth** a method of doing something which is between two very different methods, and better than either of them: *It's a case of finding the mean between firmness and compassion.* → MEANS

me·an·der /miˈændə $ -ər/ *v* [I] **1** if a river, stream, road etc meanders, it has a lot of bends rather than going in a straight line: **[+along/across/down etc]** *The river meandered gently along the valley floor.* **2** [always + adv/prep] to walk somewhere in a slow relaxed way rather than take the most direct way possible: **[+along/through etc]** *Cows still meander through these villages.* **3** (*also* **meander on**) if a conversation or piece of writing meanders on, it is too long and has no purpose or structure —**meanderings** *n* [plural]: *his aimless meanderings through Europe* —**meander** *n* [C]

mean·ie, **meany** /ˈmiːni/ *n* [C] *spoken* an unkind person used especially by children: *Don't be such a meanie!*

mean·ing /ˈmiːnɪŋ/ ●●● S2 W1 *n*
1 OF A WORD/SIGN ETC [C,U] the thing or idea that a word, expression, or sign represents: **[+of]** *I don't know the precise meaning of the word 'gleaned'.*
2 IDEAS IN SPEECH/BOOK ETC [C,U] the thoughts or ideas that someone wants you to understand from what they say, do, write etc: **[+of]** *The meaning of her words was clear. We'd lost our jobs.* | **[+behind]** *She hardly dared to understand the meaning behind his statement.*
3 what's the meaning of this? *spoken* used to demand an explanation: *What's the meaning of this? I asked you to be here an hour ago!*
4 PURPOSE/SPECIAL QUALITY [U] the quality that makes life, work etc seem to have a purpose or value: *Life seemed to have* ***lost*** *its* ***meaning*** *since Janet's death.* | *Her studies no longer seemed to* ***have*** *any* ***meaning***. | *For many people it is religion that* ***gives meaning to*** *their existence.*
5 TRUE NATURE [U] the true nature and importance of something: **[+of]** *We seem to have forgotten the* ***true meaning*** *of Christmas.*
6 (not) know the meaning of sth to have, or not have, experience and understanding of a particular situation or feeling: *Living in a war zone, the children knew the meaning of fear.* | *Guilty! She doesn't know the meaning of the word!*

COLLOCATIONS – MEANINGS 1 & 2

VERBS

have a meaning *The same word may have several different meanings.*
take on a meaning (=begin to have a new meaning) *The word 'chaos' has taken on a special scientific meaning.*
understand the meaning *The pictures help the children understand the meanings of the words.*
know the meaning *Do you know the meaning of the word 'paraphrase'?*
get sb's meaning (*also* **take sb's meaning** *BrE*) (=understand what someone is saying in an indirect way) *He's not like other people, if you get my meaning.*
grasp the meaning (=begin to understand the meaning) | **carry meaning** (*also* **bear a meaning** *formal*) (=have a meaning) | **convey meaning** (=express a meaning)

ADJECTIVES

precise/specific/exact *The term 'stress' has a precise meaning to an engineer.*
a hidden meaning *She felt there was a hidden meaning behind his words.*
a double meaning (=two meanings at the same time) *Everything he said had a double meaning.*
the literal meaning *The literal meaning of 'telephone' is 'far-away sound'.*
the figurative/metaphorical meaning (=different from its usual or basic meaning) | **sb's/sth's true meaning**

mean·ing·ful /ˈmiːnɪŋfəl/ ●●○ *adj*
1 having a meaning that is easy to understand and makes sense: *Without more data we cannot make a meaningful comparison of the two systems.* | *Teaching history to five-year-olds in a* ***meaningful way*** *can be very difficult.* | **[+to]** *Rules must be put in a context that is meaningful to the children.*
2 meaningful look/glance/smile etc a look that clearly expresses the way someone feels, even though nothing is said: *Sam and Barbara exchanged meaningful glances.*
3 serious, important, or useful: *They want a chance to do* ***meaningful work***. | *I want a mature and meaningful relationship.* | *a meaningful conversation* —**meaningfully** *adv*

mean·ing·less /ˈmiːnɪŋləs/ ●○○ *adj*
1 having no purpose or importance and therefore not worth doing or having: *He said a few meaningless words to his hostess and looked around the room.* | *a repetitive and meaningless task* | **absolutely/utterly/completely meaningless** *a statistic that is absolutely meaningless* | **virtually/fairly/largely meaningless**
2 not having a meaning that you can understand or explain: *Chinese characters are just meaningless symbols to me.* —**meaninglessness** *n* [U]

means /miːnz/ ●●○ S3 W2 *n* (*plural* **means**)
1 METHOD [C] a way of doing or achieving something: **[+of]** *For most people, the car is still their main* ***means of transport***. | *The only* ***means of communication*** *was sign language.* | *The window was our only* ***means of escape***. | *Do you have any* ***means of identification***? | *art as a* ***means of expression*** | *Homework should not be used as* ***a means of*** *controlling children.* | *I* ***had no means of*** *telling him I would be late.* | *Brian was prepared to* ***use any means*** *to get what he wanted.* | *They had entered the country* ***by unlawful means***. | *the means by which performance is assessed* THESAURUS ▸ METHOD
2 MONEY [plural] the money or income that you have: **have the means to do sth** *I don't have the means to support a family.* | *Paying for your children to go to a private school is* ***beyond the means of*** *most people* (=too expensive for most people). | *Try to live* ***within*** *your* ***means*** (=only spending what you can afford). | *His father was a* ***man of means*** (=a rich man).
3 by all means! *spoken* used to mean 'of course' when politely allowing someone to do something or agreeing with a suggestion: *'Can I bring Alan?' 'By all means!'*
4 by no means/not by any means not at all: *It is by no means certain that the game will take place.* | *She's not a bad kid, by any means.*
5 by means of sth *formal* using a particular method or system: *The blocks are raised by means of pulleys.*
6 a means to an end something that you do only to achieve a result, not because you want to do it or because it is important: *For Geoff, the job was simply a means to an end.*
7 the means of production the material, tools, and equipment that are used in the production of goods → **ways and means** at WAY[1](1)

ˌmean-ˈspirited *adj* not generous or sympathetic

ˈmeans test *n* [C] an official check in order to find out whether someone is poor enough to need money from the government —**means-tested** *adj*: *means-tested benefits*

meant /ment/ the past tense and past participle of MEAN

mean·time /ˈmiːntaɪm/ ●●○ *adv*
1 (*also* **in the meantime**) in the period of time between now and a future event, or between two events in the past SYN **meanwhile**: *The doctor will be here soon. In the meantime, try and relax.* | *I didn't see her for another five years, and in the meantime she had got married and had a couple of kids.*
2 for the meantime for the present time, until something happens: *The power supply should be back soon – for the meantime we'll have to use candles.*

mean·while /ˈmiːnwaɪl/ ●●● W2 *adv* [sentence adverb]
1 while something else is happening: *Cook the sauce over a medium heat until it thickens. Meanwhile start boiling the water for the pasta.* THESAURUS ▸ WHILE
2 (*also* **in the meanwhile**) in the period of time between two events: *The flight will be announced soon. Meanwhile, please remain seated.* | *I knew I wouldn't get my exam results for several weeks, and I wasn't sure what to do in the meanwhile.*
3 used to compare two things, especially if they are completely different and are happening at the same time: *The incomes of male professionals went up by almost 80%. Meanwhile, part-time women workers saw their earnings fall.*

mean·y /ˈmiːni/ *n* [C] another spelling of MEANIE

mea·sles /ˈmiːzəlz/ (*also* **the measles**) *n* [U] an infectious illness in which you have a fever and small red spots on your face and body. People often have measles when they are children. → **GERMAN MEASLES**

GRAMMAR: Singular or plural verb?

Measles is followed by a singular verb: ***Measles is*** *potentially a very serious illness.*

GRAMMAR GUIDE ▸ NOUNS

meas·ly /ˈmiːzli/ *adj informal* very small and disappointing in size, quantity, or value – used to show disapproval: *All I got was a measly £5.*

mea·su·ra·ble /ˈmeʒərəbəl/ *adj* **1** large or important enough to have an effect that can be seen or felt SYN **noticeable**: *The law has had little measurable effect since it was introduced two years ago.* **2** able to be measured OPP **immeasurable**: *measurable results* —**measurably** *adv*: *The company is working to make its environmental performance measurably better.*

MEASURE

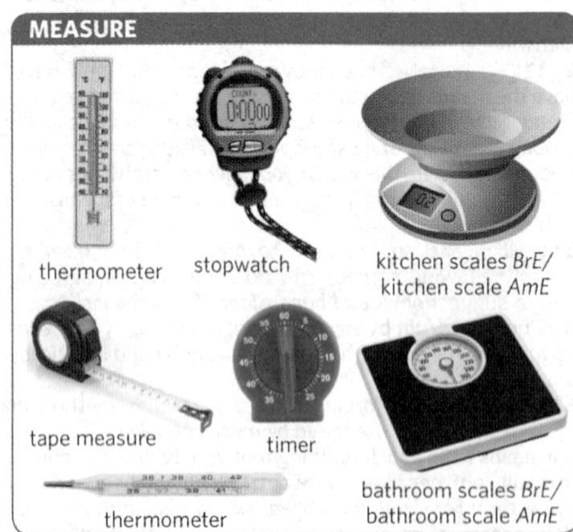

mea·sure¹ /ˈmeʒə $ -ər/ ●●● S2 W2 *v*

1 [T] to find the size, length, or amount of something, using standard units such as INCHes, metres etc: *The rainfall was measured over a three-month period.* | **measure sb for sth** (=measure someone in order to make clothes for them) *She was being measured for her wedding dress.* | **measure sth in sth** *We can measure the energy that food provides in calories.* | **measuring jug/cup/tape** (=one used for measuring)

2 [T] to judge the importance, value, or true nature of something SYN **assess**: *Doctors say it is too early to measure the effectiveness of the drug.* | **measure sth by sth** *Education shouldn't be measured purely by examination results.*

3 [linking verb] to be a particular size, length, or amount: *The room measures 6 x 6 metres.* | *The earthquake measured 6.5 on the Richter scale.*

4 [T] if a piece of equipment measures something, it shows or records a particular kind of measurement: *An odometer measures the number of miles your car travels.*

measure sb/sth **against** sb/sth *phr v* to judge someone or something by comparing them with another person or thing: *Bridget did not think she had to measure herself against some ideal standard.* | *Measured against our budget last year, $2.7 million seems small.*

measure sth ↔ **off** *phr v* to measure a particular length or distance, and make a mark so that you can see the beginning and end: *He measured off three yards of rope.*

measure sth ↔ **out** *phr v* to take a specific amount of liquid, powder etc from a larger amount: *Measure out 100 grams of flour.*

measure up *phr v*

1 to be good enough to do a particular job or to reach a particular standard: *We'll give you a week's trial in the job to see how you measure up.* | **[+to]** *How will the Secretary General measure up to his new responsibilities?*

2 to measure something before you do something, for example before you put in new furniture, cupboards etc: *I'd better measure up before I start laying the carpet.* | **measure sth ↔ up** *Measure up any items that you want to keep in the kitchen.*

measure² ●●○ W2 *n* [C]

1 ACTION an action, especially an official one, that is intended to deal with a particular problem SYN **step**: ***Measures*** *are being* ***taken*** *to reduce crime in the city.* | **drastic/tough/extreme etc measures** *drastic measures to reduce traffic problems* | *New* ***safety measures*** *were being demanded after last night's horrific train crash.* | *The new bridge was erected as a* ***temporary measure*** *to replace the one which was destroyed by floods.* | **precautionary/preventative measure** (=something done to stop something bad from happening) *He was kept in hospital overnight as a precautionary measure.*

2 half measures things done to deal with a difficult situation that are not effective or firm enough: *This was no time for half measures and compromises.*

3 SIGN/PROOF **be a measure of sth** *formal* be a sign of the importance, strength etc of something, or a way of testing or judging something: *The flowers and tears at the funeral were a measure of the people's love for her.* | *Exam results are not necessarily* ***a true measure of*** *a student's abilities.*

4 AMOUNT **a measure of sth** an amount of something good or something that you want, for example success or freedom: *The new law gives local governments a significant measure of control over their own finances.* | *I met a number of sportsmen who had achieved a measure of success* (=some success).

5 UNIT OF MEASUREMENT **a)** an amount or unit in a measuring system: *a table of* ***weights and measures*** **b)** a standard amount of an alcoholic drink

6 in large measure/in some measure a lot or quite a lot – used when talking about the reason or cause of something: *The improvements* ***are due in large measure to*** *his leadership.*

7 in equal measure used when the amount of one thing is the same as the amount of another thing: *I was angry and embarrassed in equal measure.*

8 for good measure in addition to what you have already done, given, or included: *Why don't you try phoning them one more time, for good measure?*

9 beyond measure very much or very great – used when you want to emphasize what you are saying: *Her work has* ***improved beyond measure****.*

10 the full measure of sth *formal* the whole of something: *Ralph received the full measure of his mother's devotion.*

11 in full measure *formal* if someone gives something back in full measure, they give back as much as they received: *They returned our hospitality in full measure.*

12 have/get the measure of sth to become familiar with something, so that you can control or deal with it

13 have/get the measure of sb *BrE* to know what someone's strengths and weaknesses are, so that you are able to deal with them or defeat them: *She soon got the measure of her opponent.*

14 THING USED FOR MEASURING something used for measuring, for example a piece of wood or a container → TAPE MEASURE

15 MUSIC a group of notes and RESTS, separated from other groups by vertical lines, into which a piece of music is divided SYN **bar** *BrE* → MADE-TO-MEASURE, → **give sb short measure** at SHORT¹(23)

mea·sured /ˈmeʒəd $ -ərd/ *adj* if you do something in a measured way, you do it in a careful and controlled way, not in an excited or sudden way: *a measured response to the problem* | *She spoke* ***in measured tones****.*

mea·sure·less /ˈmeʒələs $ -ʒər-/ *adj literary* too great to be measured SYN **immeasurable**: *Otto had measureless charm.*

mea·sure·ment /ˈmeʒəmənt $ -ʒər-/ ●●● W3 *n*

1 [C] the length, height etc of something: **waist/chest/leg etc measurement** *What's your waist measurement?* | **take/make measurements** (=measure something) *Take measurements of the room before you buy any new furniture.* | **take sb's measurements** (=measure someone in order to make or get clothes for them) *The assistant took my measurements and showed me what was available in my size.*

M

2 [U] the act of measuring something: **[+of]** *the measurement of performance* | ***accurate measurement*** *of body temperature*

ˈmeasuring ˌjug *BrE*, **ˈmeasuring ˌcup** *AmE* *n* [C] a container used for measuring liquids in cooking

ˈmeasuring ˌtape *n* [C] a TAPE MEASURE

meat /miːt/ ●●● S2 W3 *n*
1 [C,U] the flesh of animals and birds eaten as food: *I gave up eating meat a few months ago.* | *raw meat* | *a meat pie* | *a selection of cold meats* | **red meat** (=a dark-coloured meat, for example BEEF) | **white meat** (=meat that is pale in colour, for example CHICKEN)
2 [U] something interesting or important in a talk, book, film etc: *There's* ***no meat to*** *their arguments.* | *We then got down to* ***the*** *real* ***meat of*** *the debate* (=the main and most interesting part of it).
3 sb doesn't have much meat on him/her *BrE*, **need some (more) meat on your bones** *AmE informal* used to say that someone looks very thin
4 one man's meat is another man's poison used to say that something that one person likes may not be liked by someone else
5 be easy meat *BrE informal* if someone is easy meat, they are easy to defeat, deceive, or hurt: **[+for]** *San Marino should be easy meat for England in next week's match.*
6 the meat and potatoes *AmE informal* the most important or basic parts of a discussion, decision, piece of work etc: *Let's get down to the meat and potatoes. How much are you going to pay me for this?*
7 be meat and drink to sb *BrE* to be something that someone enjoys doing or finds very easy to do because they have done it many times before: *The first five questions in the quiz were about football, which was meat and drink to Brian.*

meat·ball /ˈmiːtbɔːl $ -bɒːl/ *n* [C] a small round ball made from small pieces of meat, herbs, and egg or BREADCRUMBS pressed together. Meatballs are often served with a sauce.

ˈmeat ˌgrinder *n* [C] *AmE* a machine that cuts meat into very small pieces by forcing it through small holes SYN **mincer** *BrE*

meat·loaf /ˈmiːtləʊf $ -loʊf/ *n* (*plural* **meatloaves** /-ləʊvz $ -loʊvz/) [C,U] meat, herbs, and other foods mixed and baked together in the shape of a LOAF

ˈmeat-ˌpacking *n* [U] *AmE* the preparation of animals that have been killed so that they can be sold as meat: *the meat-packing industry* —**meat-packer** *n* [C]

meat·y /ˈmiːti/ *adj* **1** containing a lot of meat, or tasting strongly of meat: *a delicious meaty gravy* **2** *informal* big and fat, with a lot of flesh: *meaty forearms* **3** *informal* containing a lot of interesting ideas or information: *a meaty article* | *The lecture wasn't very meaty.* **4 meaty role** an interesting or important character that an actor is playing in a play or film: *her first meaty role as an actress*

mec·ca /ˈmekə/ *n* [singular] a place that many people want to visit for a particular reason SYN **magnet**: **[+for]** *Florence is a mecca for students of art history.*

me·chan·ic /mɪˈkænɪk/ ●●○ *n*
1 [C] someone who is skilled at repairing motor vehicles and machinery: *a garage mechanic*
2 the mechanics of (doing) sth the way in which something works or is done: *The mechanics of the process are quite complex.*
3 mechanics [U] **a)** the science that deals with the effects of forces on objects: *fluid mechanics* → QUANTUM MECHANICS **b)** the study of machines: *He is studying mechanics at college.*

me·chan·i·cal /mɪˈkænɪkəl/ ●●○ *adj*
1 affecting or involving a machine: *The flight has been cancelled due to* ***mechanical failure****.* | *The plane had to make an emergency landing because of mechanical problems.*
2 using power from an engine or machine to do a particular kind of work: *a mechanical digger* | *a mechanical device*
3 a mechanical action, reply etc is one you do without thinking, and has been done many times before: *He was asked the same question so many times that the answer became mechanical.*
4 someone who is mechanical understands how machines work
5 *technical* relating to or produced by physical forces: *the mechanical properties of solids* —**mechanically** /-kli/ *adv*: *The actors spoke their lines mechanically, hardly caring about the meaning.* | *I'm not very mechanically minded* (=not good at understanding how machines work and repairing them).

meˌchanical engiˈneering *n* [U] the study of the design and production of machines and tools —**mechanical engineer** *n* [C]

meˌchanical ˈpencil *n* [C] *AmE* a pencil made of metal or plastic, with a thin piece of LEAD (=the part that you write with) inside SYN **propelling pencil** *BrE*

mech·a·nis·m /ˈmekənɪzəm/ ●●○ AWL *n* [C]
1 part of a machine or a set of parts that does a particular job: *the brake mechanism* | *a clock mechanism*
2 a system that is intended to achieve something or deal with a problem: **mechanism for (doing) sth** *existing mechanisms for decision-making* | **mechanism to do sth** *The Army has set up mechanisms to help jobless ex-soldiers get work.*
→ EXCHANGE RATE MECHANISM
3 a system or a way of behaving that helps a living thing to avoid or protect itself from something difficult or dangerous: **defence/control/survival mechanism** *When a person is ill, the body's natural defence mechanisms come into operation.*
4 the way that something works: **[+of]** *the mechanism of the brain*

mech·a·nis·tic /ˌmekəˈnɪstɪk◂/ *adj* tending to explain the behaviour of things in the natural world as if they were machines: *a* ***mechanistic view*** *of the universe* —**mechanistically** /-kli/ *adv*

mech·a·nized (*also* **-ised** *BrE*) /ˈmekənaɪzd/ *adj*
1 a mechanized system or process now uses machines instead of people or animals SYN **automated**: *Car production is now* ***highly mechanized****.* **2** a mechanized army unit uses TANKS and other ARMOURED military vehicles —**mechanize** *v* [T] —**mechanization** /ˌmekənaɪˈzeɪʃən $ -nə-/ *n* [U]: *increasing mechanization of agriculture*

med /med/ *adj* [only before noun] *informal* an abbreviation of MEDICAL: *med school* | *a med student*

Med *n* **the Med** *BrE informal* the Mediterranean Sea or the area surrounding it

MEd *BrE*, **M.Ed.** *AmE* /ˌem ˈed/ *n* [C] (***Master of Education***) a university DEGREE in teaching that you can get after your first degree → **BEd**

med·al¹ /ˈmedl/ ●●● W3 *n* [C] a flat piece of metal, usually shaped like a coin, that is given to someone who has won a competition or who has done something brave: *She won a gold medal at the last Olympics.* | *The two boys were awarded medals for bravery.* → **deserve a medal** at DESERVE(3)

COLLOCATIONS

VERBS

win a medal *They won a medal at the Chelsea Flower Show.*
take a medal (=win a medal) *German runner Stephan Freigang took the bronze medal.*
get a medal (*also* **receive a medal** *formal*) *She received a medal from the Society of Arts.*
give sb a medal | **be awarded a medal**

ADJECTIVES

a gold medal (=for first place) *He won the gold medal in Athens in 2004.*
a silver medal (=for second place) | **a bronze medal** (=for third place)

medal + NOUN

a medal winner *Johnson was a silver medal winner at the Olympic Games.*

medal² *v* (**medalled**, **medalling** *BrE*, **medaled**, **medaling** *AmE*) [I] to win a medal at a competition, especially at the Olympic Games: **[+in]** *Germany has the potential to medal in gymnastics this year.*

me·dal·li·on /mə'dæliən/ *n* [C] a piece of metal shaped like a large coin, worn as jewellery on a chain around the neck: *a silver medallion* → see picture at JEWELLERY

med·al·list *BrE*, **medalist** *AmE* /'medl-ɪst/ *n* [C] someone who has won a medal in a competition: *the Olympic gold medallist*

ˌMedal of 'Honor *n* [C] the most important medal given by the US to a soldier, sailor etc who has done something extremely brave

med·dle /'medl/ *v* [I] **1** to deliberately try to influence or change a situation that does not concern you, or that you do not understand SYN **interfere**: **[+in]** *I don't like other people meddling in the way I run this prison.* | *He accused the US of* ***meddling*** *in China's internal* ***affairs***. | **[+with]** *I'm not the sort of newspaper owner who meddles with editorial policy.* **2** *BrE* to touch something which you should not touch, especially in a careless way that might break it: **[+with]** *You have no right to come in here meddling with my things.* —**meddler** *n* [C] —**meddling** *n* [U] —**meddling** *adj* [only before noun]: *meddling politicians*

med·dle·some /'medlsəm/ *adj* a meddlesome person becomes involved in situations that do not concern them, in a way that annoys people SYN **interfering**: *a meddlesome old woman*

me·di·a /'mi:diə/ ●●● S2 W2 AWL *n*
1 the media all the organizations, such as television, radio, and newspapers, that provide news and information for the public, or the people who do this work: *The scandal was widely reported in* ***the national media***. | *The role of* ***the news media*** *in forming public opinion is very important.* | *The 11-day trial generated intense* ***media interest***. | *A great deal of* ***media hype*** *surrounded the release of the group's latest CD.* | *There will be another war somewhere else and the whole international* ***media circus*** *will move on.*

GRAMMAR: Singular or plural verb?

The media can be followed by a singular or a plural verb: *The media* ***is*** *controlled by the government.* | *The media* ***are*** *controlled by the government.*

GRAMMAR GUIDE ▸ NOUNS

2 the plural of MEDIUM → **MASS MEDIA**, **MULTIMEDIA**

med·i·ae·val /ˌmedi'i:vəl◂ $ ˌmi:-/ *adj* another spelling of MEDIEVAL

me·di·an¹ /'mi:diən/ *n* [C] **1** *AmE* (*also* **'median strip**) a narrow area of land that separates the two sides of a big road in order to keep traffic travelling in different directions apart SYN **central reservation** *BrE* **2** *technical* the middle number or measurement in a set of numbers or measurements that have been arranged in order **3** *technical* a line passing from one of the points of a TRIANGLE to the centre of the opposite side

median² *adj* **1** being the middle number or measurement in a set of numbers or measurements that have been arranged in order → **average**: *The median age of the group is 42.* **2** in or passing through the middle of something

'media ˌstudies *n* [U] the study of how newspapers, radio, television etc work and how they affect society

me·di·ate /'mi:dieɪt/ ●○○ AWL *v*
1 [I,T] to try to end a quarrel between two people, groups, countries etc: **[+between]** *UN officials mediated between the rebel fighters and the government.* | *The former president has agreed to mediate the peace talks.* | **[+in]** *The court was set up to* ***mediate*** *in civil* ***disputes***.
2 [T] *formal or technical* to change the effect or influence of something, especially to make the effect less bad: *Exercise may mediate the effects of a bad diet.* —**mediation** /ˌmi:di'eɪʃən/ *n* [U]

me·di·a·tor /'mi:dieɪtə $ -ər/ *n* [C] a person or organization that tries to end a quarrel between two people, groups, countries etc by discussion → **intermediary**

med·ic /'medɪk/ *n* [C] **1** *BrE informal* a medical doctor **2** *BrE informal* a medical student **3** *AmE* someone in the army who is trained to give medical treatment → **paramedic**

Med·i·caid /'medɪkeɪd/ *n* [U] a system in the US by which the government helps to pay the cost of medical treatment for poor people → **Medicare**

med·i·cal¹ /'medɪkəl/ ●●● S2 W2 AWL *adj* relating to medicine and the treatment of disease or injury: *medical research* | *medical staff* | *a medical student* | *a patient's* ***medical history*** (=the illnesses they have had) | **medical records** (=which show what illnesses and treatment someone has had) | **medical attention/treatment/care** *The injury required urgent medical attention.* | **the medical profession** (=doctors, nurses, and other people who treat people who are ill) —**medically** /-kli/ *adv*: *medically qualified personnel* | *medically fit*

medical² (*also* **ˌmedical exami'nation**) *n* [C] *BrE* an examination of your body by a doctor to see if you are healthy SYN **physical** *AmE*

'medical cerˌtificate *n* [C] an official piece of paper signed by a doctor saying that you are too ill to work or that you are completely healthy → **sick note**

ˌmedical ex'aminer *n* [C] *AmE* a doctor who examines dead people's bodies in order to find out how they died, especially if they died in a sudden or unusual way

'medical ˌofficer *n* [C] a doctor working in the armed forces

ˌmedical prac'titioner *n* [C] *BrE formal* a doctor

'medical school *n* [C,U] a college or university where people study to become doctors

me·dic·a·ment /mɪ'dɪkəmənt, 'medɪ-/ *n* [C] *formal* a substance used to treat a disease

Med·i·care /'medɪkeə $ -ker/ *n* [U] a system by which the US government helps to pay for the medical treatment of old people → **Medicaid**

med·i·cat·ed /'medɪkeɪtɪd/ *adj* medicated soap or SHAMPOO contains a substance to help small medical problems of your skin or hair

med·i·ca·tion /ˌmedɪ'keɪʃən/ ●○○ *n* [C,U] medicine or drugs given to people who are ill: **be on medication (for sth)** *He's on medication for high blood pressure.*

me·di·ci·nal /mə'dɪsənəl/ *adj* **1** used for treating medical problems → **medical**: *Garlic is believed to have* ***medicinal properties*** (=contain things that can cure medical problems). **2 for medicinal purposes a)** used in a humorous way to say that you drink alcohol because it is good for your health: *I keep a bottle of brandy handy – purely for medicinal purposes.* **b)** for use as a medicine: *herbs used in medieval times for medicinal purposes* —**medicinally** *adv*

medi·cine /'medsən $ 'medəsən/ ●●● S2 W3 *n*
1 [C,U] a substance used for treating illness, especially a liquid you drink: *Medicines should be kept out of the reach of children.* | *Have you been* ***taking*** *your* ***medicine***? | *a medicine bottle* | **medicine chest/cabinet** (=for keeping medicine in) ⚠ Do not say that you 'drink medicine'. Say that you **take medicine**.
2 [U] the treatment and study of illnesses and injuries: *She studied medicine at Johns Hopkins University.* | *the remarkable achievements of modern medicine*
3 the best medicine the best way of making you feel better when you are sad: *Laughter is the best medicine.*
4 give sb a dose/taste of their own medicine to treat someone as badly as they have treated you
5 take your medicine (like a man) to accept an unpleasant situation or a punishment that you deserve, without complaining

COLLOCATIONS – MEANING 2

ADJECTIVES

modern medicine (=medicine based on science)
Thanks to modern medicine, these babies will survive.

conventional/orthodox medicine (=ordinary modern medicine) *Some sufferers reject conventional medicine.*
Western medicine (=conventional medicine as developed in Western countries) | **traditional medicine** (=medical treatments that were used before modern medicine) | **alternative/complementary medicine** (=medical treatments that are not part of modern medicine) | **herbal medicine** (=medical treatments that use herbs)

ˈmedicine man (*also* **ˈmedicine ˌwoman**) *n* [C] a person in a Native American tribe who is considered to have the ability to cure illness and disease → **shaman**, **witch-doctor**

med·i·co /ˈmedɪkəʊ $ -koʊ/ *n* (*plural* **medicos**) [C] *informal* a MEDIC

med·i·e·val, **mediaeval** /ˌmediˈiːvəl◂ $ ˌmiː-/ ●●○ W3 *adj*
1 connected with the Middle Ages (=the period between about 1100 and 1500 AD): *These spices were first brought to Italy from the East in medieval times. | a medieval castle*
2 very old or old-fashioned – used in a humorous or disapproving way: *The plumbing in this house is positively medieval!*

me·di·o·cre /ˌmiːdiˈəʊkə◂ $ -ˈoʊkər◂/ *adj* not very good SYN **second rate**: *I thought the book was pretty mediocre. | a mediocre student* —**mediocrity** /ˌmiːdiˈɒkrəti $ -ˈɑːk-/ *n* [U]

med·i·tate /ˈmedɪteɪt/ *v* **1** [I] to think seriously and deeply about something: **[+on/upon]** *She sat quietly, meditating on the day's events.* **2** [I] to spend time sitting in a silent calm state, in order to relax completely or for religious purposes: *I try to meditate for half an hour every evening.* **3** [T] *formal* to plan to do something, usually something unpleasant: *Silently she meditated revenge.*

med·i·ta·tion /ˌmedɪˈteɪʃən/ ●○○ *n*
1 [U] the practice of emptying your mind of thoughts and feelings, in order to relax completely or for religious reasons: *Yoga involves breathing exercises, stretching, and meditation.* → TRANSCENDENTAL MEDITATION
2 [C usually plural, U] the act of thinking deeply and seriously about something: *She found him sitting alone, deep in meditation. | Rob interrupted his father's meditations.*
3 [C usually plural] serious thoughts about a particular subject: **[+on]** *meditations on death and loss*

med·i·ta·tive /ˈmedətətɪv $ -teɪtɪv/ *adj* **1** thinking deeply and seriously about something: *She was in a meditative mood.* **2** relating to the practice of emptying your mind of thoughts and feelings, in order to relax completely or for religious reasons: *meditative techniques* —**meditatively** *adv*

Med·i·ter·ra·ne·an[1] /ˌmedətəˈreɪniən◂/ *n* **a) the Mediterranean** the Mediterranean Sea **b)** the area of southern Europe that surrounds the Mediterranean Sea

Mediterranean[2] *adj* relating to the Mediterranean Sea, or typical of the area of southern Europe around it: *a Mediterranean country | a plant normally only found in a* ***Mediterranean climate***

me·di·um[1] /ˈmiːdiəm/ ●●● S3 AWL *adj*
1 of middle size, level, or amount: *What size shirt does he wear – small, medium or large? |* **(of) medium height/length/build** *She's of medium height. | hair of medium length | Fry the onions over a* ***medium heat*** *until they are golden. |* ***medium to large*** *companies* ⚠ Use **average**, not 'medium', when you want to say that someone's level of skill or ability is neither high nor low: *students of average ability (NOT students of medium ability)*
2 (*also* **medium rare**) meat that is medium or medium rare is partly cooked but still slightly pink inside → **rare**, **well-done**
3 medium dry medium dry wine is slightly sweeter than dry wine
4 medium brown/blue etc a colour which is neither light nor dark: *His jacket's a medium brown colour.*

medium[2] ●○○ AWL *n* (*plural* **media** /-diə/ *or* **mediums**) [C]
1 a way of communicating information and news to people, such as newspapers, television etc → **media**: *Advertising is a powerful medium.*
2 a way of expressing your ideas, especially as a writer or an artist: **[+for]** *the novel as a medium for satire | the visual media* (=painting and films)
3 medium of instruction a language that is used for teaching: *English is still the main medium of instruction in Nigeria.*
4 medium of exchange money or other ways of paying for things
5 *technical* a substance or material in which things grow or exist: *a good* ***growing medium*** *for tomatoes*
6 *technical* a substance through which a force travels → MAGNETIC MEDIA, → **a happy medium** at HAPPY(8)

medium[3] *n* (*plural* **mediums**) [C] someone who claims to have the power to receive messages from dead people

ˈmedium-sized (*also* **ˈmedium-size**) *adj* not small but not large either: *a medium-sized business*

ˈmedium ˌterm *n* [singular] the period of time a few weeks or months ahead of the present → **short-term**, **long-term**: **in the medium term** *The company's prospects look good in the medium term. | medium-term investments*

ˈmedium ˌwave *n* [U] (*written abbreviation* **MW**) a system of radio broadcasting using radio waves between 100 and 1,000 metres in length → **long wave**, **FM**

med·ley /ˈmedli/ *n* [C] **1** a group of songs or tunes sung or played one after the other as a single piece of music: **[+of]** *He played a medley of Beatles songs.* **2** [usually singular] a mixture of different types of the same thing which produces an interesting or unusual effect: **[+of]** *an exotic medley of smells | a medley of architectural styles* **3** a swimming race in which the competitors swim using four different STROKES: *the 400 metres individual medley*

meek /miːk/ *adj* very quiet and gentle and unwilling to argue with people: *He was always so* ***meek and mild****.* —**meekly** *adv*: *'All right,' said Neil meekly.* —**meekness** *n* [U]

meet[1] /miːt/ ●●● S1 W1 *v* (*past tense and past participle* **met** /met/)
1 SEE SB AT AN ARRANGED PLACE [I,T] to go to a place where someone will be at a particular time, according to an arrangement, so that you can talk or do something together: *Meet me at 8.00. | I'll meet you by the main reception desk.* | **meet (sb) for sth** *Why don't we meet for lunch on Friday? | We arranged to meet outside the theatre.* GRAMMAR **Meet** is never passive in this meaning.
2 SEE SB BY CHANCE [I,T] to see someone by chance and talk to them SYN **bump into**: *You'll never guess who I met in town. | I was worried I might meet Henry on the bus.* GRAMMAR **Meet** is never passive in this meaning.
3 SEE SB FOR THE FIRST TIME [I,T] to see and talk to someone for the first time, or be introduced to them: *We first met in Florence. | I met my husband at university. | Jane, come and meet my brother.* | **nice/pleased to meet you** (=used to greet someone politely when you have just met them for the first time) *'This is my niece, Sarah.' 'Pleased to meet you.'* | **(it was) nice meeting you** (=used to say goodbye politely to someone you have just met for the first time) GRAMMAR **Meet** is never passive in this meaning.
4 SEE SB AT AN AIRPORT/STATION ETC [T] to be waiting for someone at an airport, station etc when they arrive in a plane or train: *My dad met us at the station. | She got off the plane to be met by reporters.*
5 COME TOGETHER TO DISCUSS STH [I] to come together in the same place in order to discuss something: *The committee meets once a month. | The two groups will meet next week to discuss the project.*
6 COMPETE AGAINST SB [I,T] to play against another person or team in a competition, or to fight another army in a war: *Manchester United will meet Blackburn Rovers in the sixth round of the Cup. | The two armies finally met on the battlefield at Stamford Bridge.*
7 JOIN OR TOUCH [I,T] if two things meet, they touch or join at a particular place: *The two roads meet just north of Flagstaff. | My hand met his under the table.* GRAMMAR **Meet** is never passive in this meaning.

8 EXPERIENCE A PROBLEM OR SITUATION [T] to experience a problem, attitude, or situation SYN **encounter**, **come across**: *Wherever she went she met hostility and prejudice.*
9 meet a problem/challenge to deal with a problem or something difficult that you have to do: *The new building will mean that we can meet the challenge of increasing student numbers.*
10 meet a need/demand/requirement/condition etc to do something that someone wants, needs, or expects you to do or be as good as they need, expect etc: *The company says it is unable to meet the workers' demands for higher wages.* | *The service is tailored to meet your needs.* | *beaches which* ***meet*** *European* ***standards*** *of cleanliness*
11 meet a deadline to finish something at the time it is meant to be finished: *We are still hoping to meet the November deadline.*
12 meet a goal/target etc to achieve something that you are trying to achieve: *It's impossible to meet the sales targets.* | *The scheme does not* ***meet*** *its* ***objectives****.*
13 meet a debt/cost/expense etc to make a payment that needs to be made: *The government has promised to meet the cost of clearing up after the floods.*
14 there's more to sb/sth than meets the eye used to say that someone or something is more interesting, intelligent etc than they seem to be
15 our/their eyes meet if two people's eyes meet, they look at each other: *Our eyes met momentarily, then he looked away.* | *His eyes met Nina's and she smiled.*
16 meet sb's eye(s)/gaze/glance etc to look directly at someone who is looking at you: *Ruth looked down, unable to meet his eye.* | *She turned to meet his gaze.*
17 meet your eyes if something meets your eyes, you see it: *An extraordinary scene met our eyes as we entered the room.*
18 meet your match to compete against an opponent who is stronger or more skilful than you are: *I think he might have met his match in Simon.*
19 meet sb halfway to do some of the things that someone wants, in order to reach an agreement with them
20 meet (sth) head-on a) if two moving vehicles meet head-on, they are facing each other and hit each other suddenly and violently **b)** if you meet a problem head-on, you deal with it directly without trying to avoid it
21 meet your death/end to die in a particular way: *He met his death at the hands of enemy soldiers.*
22 meet your maker to die – used humorously
23 meet your Waterloo to finally be defeated after you have been successful for a long time → **make ends meet** at END[1](17)

GRAMMAR: Reciprocal verbs

Meet is a reciprocal verb. This type of verb is used when saying that two or more people do something that involves both or all of them. It does not need to have an object: *We met when we were at college.*In this sentence, **meet** is intransitive and does not have an object.
You can also say: *We met each other when we were at college.* | *I met him when we were at college.* In these sentences, **meet** is transitive.
GRAMMAR GUIDE ▸ VERBS

THESAURUS

meet to be in the same place as someone else because you have arranged to see them: *I'll meet you at the restaurant, OK?* | *The two leaders are scheduled to meet again next month.*
get together *informal* to meet with a group of people, in order to do something together: *Why don't we all get together and go out for a drink?* | *Have the students get together in groups of four to work on the problem.*
come together if people come together, they meet in order to discuss things, exchange ideas etc: *Goldman persuaded the heads of the groups to come together for an informal conference.*
meet up *informal* if friends meet up, they meet in order to do something together: *We must meet up some time.* | *Why don't I meet up with you after lunch?*
gather if people gather somewhere, they come together in the same place in order to do something or see something: *Fans have started to gather outside the stadium.* | *Angry crowds gathered in front of the US embassy.*
assemble *formal* if people assemble somewhere, they all come and stand together in the same place, especially as part of an officially arranged plan: *If the fire alarm rings, please assemble in the parking lot.* | *The students began to assemble in the main hall.*

meet up *phr v*
1 to meet someone in order to do something together: *We often meet up after work and go for a drink.* | **[+with]** *I've got to go now, but I'll meet up with you later.*
2 if roads, paths etc meet up, they join together at a particular place: **[+with]** *The path eventually meets up with the main road.*

meet with sb/sth *phr v*
1 to have a meeting with someone: *Representatives of EU countries will meet with senior American politicians to discuss the trade crisis.*
2 (*also* **be met with sth**) to get a particular reaction or result: **meet with opposition/disapproval etc** *His comments have met with widespread opposition.* | **meet with support/approval etc** *Her ideas have met with support from doctors and health professionals.* | **meet with success/failure** (=succeed or fail) *Our attempts at negotiation finally met with some success.*
3 meet with an accident *formal* to be injured or killed in an accident

meet² ●○○ *n* [C]
1 track meet *especially AmE* a sports competition between people running races, jumping over bars etc
2 *BrE* an occasion when a group of people riding horses go out to hunt FOXES

ˌmeet-and-ˈgreet *n* [C]
1 an event that is organized for famous musicians, writers, artists etc to meet and talk to their FANS: *There will be a meet-and-greet after the show.* **2** a service that sends people to greet and help a person or group when they arrive at an airport **3** an event in which parents go to their child's school and meet the teachers and other people who work there

meet·ing /ˈmiːtɪŋ/ ●●● S1 W1 *n* [C]
1 an event at which people meet to discuss and decide things: *We're having a meeting next week to discuss the matter.* | **at a meeting** *I'll raise the matter at the next meeting.* | **in a meeting** *She said that Mr Coleby was in a meeting.* | **[+about/on]** *There was a public meeting about the future of the gallery.* | **[+with]** *I've got a meeting with Mr Edwards this afternoon.* | **[+of]** *a meeting of senior politicians* | **[+between]** *a meeting between unions and management*
2 the meeting *formal* all the people who are at a meeting: *I'd like to put a few ideas before the meeting.*
3 [usually singular] when people meet each other by chance or because they have arranged to do this: *I had felt drawn to Alice ever since our first meeting.*
4 a sports competition or a set of races for horses
5 meeting of minds a situation in which two people have very similar ideas and understand each other very well: *There was a real meeting of minds between the two leaders.*
6 an event at which a group of Quakers (=a Christian religious group) pray together

COLLOCATIONS

VERBS

have a meeting *I had a long meeting with my manager.*
hold a meeting *formal* (=have a meeting) *The meetings are usually held on a Friday.*
go to a meeting (*also* **attend a meeting** *formal*) *All staff members are expected to attend the meeting.*

call a meeting (*also* **convene a meeting** *formal*) (=arrange a meeting) *The board has the power to convene a general meeting if necessary.*
chair a meeting (*also* **preside over a meeting** *formal*) (=lead it) | **address a meeting** (=speak to the people at a meeting) | **adjourn a meeting** (=make it stop for a period of time)

ADJECTIVES/NOUN + meeting

a committee/staff/board etc meeting *A staff meeting will be held at 3 p.m.*
an annual meeting (=an important meeting held once a year) *the annual meeting of the British Medical Association*
a monthly/weekly meeting | **a public/open meeting** (=that anyone can go to) | **a general meeting** *especially BrE* (=that anyone, or anyone in a particular organization, can go to) | **a private/closed meeting** (=that only a few people are allowed to go to) | **a summit meeting** (=between leaders of governments) | **a business meeting** | **a protest meeting** | **an emergency/urgent meeting**

ˈmeeting-house *n* [C] a building where Quakers (=a Christian religious group) pray together

ˈmeeting place *n* [C] a building or place where people meet: *The pub is a popular meeting place for local teenagers.*

meg /meg/ *n* [C] *informal* a MEGABYTE

meg·a /ˈmegə/ *adj informal* very big and impressive or enjoyable: *Their first record was a mega hit.* —**mega** *adv*

mega- /megə/ *prefix* **1** [in nouns] a million - used with units of measurement: *1,000 megawatts of electricity* **2** *informal* extremely: *Her family is megarich!* **3** very big: *a megastore*

meg·a·bit /ˈmegəbɪt/ *n* [C] *technical* a million BITS

meg·a·bucks /ˈmegəbʌks/ *n* [plural] *informal* a very large amount of money: *She's earning megabucks now.*

meg·a·byte /ˈmegəbaɪt/ ●○○ *n* [C] (*written abbreviation* **MB** *or* **Mb**) a unit for measuring computer information, equal to 1,024 KILOBYTEs, and used less exactly to mean one million BYTES

meg·a·hertz /ˈmegəhɜːts $ -ɜːr-/ *n* (*plural* **megahertz**) [C] (*written abbreviation* **MHz**) a unit for measuring FREQUENCY, especially of radio signals, equal to one million HERTZ

meg·a·lith /ˈmegəlɪθ/ *n* [C] a large tall stone put in an open place by people in ancient times, possibly as a religious sign —**megalithic** /ˌmegəˈlɪθɪk◂/ *adj*

meg·a·lo·ma·ni·a /ˌmegələʊˈmeɪniə $ -loʊ-/ *n* [U] when someone wants to have a lot of power for themselves and enjoys having control over other people's lives, sometimes as part of a mental illness

meg·a·lo·ma·ni·ac /ˌmegələʊˈmeɪniæk $ -loʊ-/ *n* [C] someone who wants to have a lot of power for themselves and enjoys having control over other people's lives —**megalomaniac** *adj*

meg·a·phone /ˈmegəfəʊn $ -foʊn/ *n* **1** [C] a piece of equipment like a large horn which you talk through to make your voice sound louder, when you are speaking to a crowd → see picture at **MICROPHONE** **2** **megaphone diplomacy** the practice of making strong or threatening statements in order to make another country do what you want

meg·a·pix·el /ˈmegəˌpɪksəl/ *n* [C] a million PIXELS - used for measuring the quality of a digital picture, especially when talking about DIGITAL cameras: *a three megapixel camera*

meg·a·star /ˈmegəstɑː $ -stɑːr/ *n* [C] *informal* a very famous singer or actor

meg·a·ton /ˈmegətʌn/ *n* [C] a unit for measuring the power of an explosive, equal to the power of one million TONS of TNT (=a powerful explosive): *a five* ***megaton*** *atomic* ***bomb***

meg·a·watt /ˈmegəwɒt $ -wɑːt/ *n* [C] (*written abbreviation* **MW**) a million WATTS

meh¹ /me/ *interjection informal* used to show that you do not care about something or are not impressed by something: *'Do you like the food?' 'Meh.'*

meh² *adj* [not before noun] *informal* **1** not very good: *I thought the album was just kind of meh.* **2** not caring or feeling excited about something: *I just feel so meh about everything.*

mel·a·mine /ˈmeləmiːn/ *n* [U] a material like plastic that is used to make a hard smooth surface on tables

mel·an·cho·li·a /ˌmelənˈkəʊliə $ -ˈkoʊ-/ *n* [U] *old-fashioned* a feeling of great sadness and lack of energy

mel·an·chol·ic /ˌmelənˈkɒlɪk◂ $ -ˈkɑː-/ *adj literary* feeling very sad

mel·an·chol·y¹ /ˈmelənkəli $ -kɑːli/ *adj* very sad: *The music suited her melancholy mood.*

melancholy² *n* [U] *formal* a feeling of sadness for no particular reason → **depression**: *He sank into deep melancholy.*

me·lange /meɪˈlɑːnʒ/ *n* [singular] *formal* a mixture of different things: **[+of]** *The population is a melange of different cultures.*

mel·a·nin /ˈmelənɪn/ *n* [U] a natural dark brown colour in human skin, hair, and eyes

mel·a·no·ma /ˌmeləˈnəʊmə $ -ˈnoʊ-/ *n* [C] *technical* a TUMOUR on a person's skin which causes CANCER

mel·a·to·nin /ˌmeləˈtəʊnɪn $ -ˈtoʊ-/ *n* [U] a HORMONE that is sometimes used as a drug to help you sleep

Mel·ba toast /ˌmelbə ˈtəʊst $ -ˈtoʊst/ *n* [U] a type of thin dry TOAST that breaks easily

meld /meld/ *v* [I,T] if two things meld, or if you meld them, they combine into one thing: **meld (sth) with sth** *He melded country music with blues to create rock and roll.* | **[+into]** *The raindrops melded into a sheet of water.*

mel·ée /ˈmeleɪ $ ˈmeɪleɪ, meɪˈleɪ/ *n* [C usually singular] a situation in which a lot of people rush around in a confused way: *Luckily no one was hurt in the melée.*

mel·li·flu·ous /məˈlɪfluəs/ *adj formal* a mellifluous voice or piece of music sounds pleasantly smooth

mel·low¹ /ˈmeləʊ $ -loʊ/ *adj*
1 NOT BRIGHT a mellow colour or light looks soft, warm, and not too bright: *the mellow golden light of early evening*
2 NOT LOUD OR HARSH a mellow sound is pleasant and smooth: *a warm, mellow voice*
3 NOT STRONG IN FLAVOUR mellow wine or fruit has a smooth pleasant taste: *its smooth, mellow flavour*
4 NOT STRICT someone who is mellow is gentle and calm and does not criticize other people, because they have a lot of experience of life
5 RELAXED if you feel mellow, you feel calm and relaxed, especially after drinking alcohol THESAURUS ▸ CALM
—**mellowness** *n* [U]

mellow² *v* [I,T] **1** if someone mellows or is mellowed, they become gentler and more sympathetic: *Paul's certainly mellowed over the years.* | *Two pints of beer had mellowed my father.* **2** if colours mellow or are mellowed, they begin to look warm and soft: *The bricks had mellowed to a soft red.* **3** if wine mellows or is mellowed, its taste becomes smoother

mellow (sb) out *phr v AmE informal* to become relaxed and calm, or to make someone like this

me·lod·ic /məˈlɒdɪk $ -ˈlɑː-/ *adj* **1** *formal* something that sounds melodic sounds like music or has a pleasant tune: *Their music is loud and not very melodic.* | *a deep melodic voice* **2** *technical* concerned with the main tune in a piece of music: *There is very little melodic variation in the piece.*

me·lo·di·ous /məˈləʊdiəs $ -ˈloʊ-/ *adj formal* something that sounds melodious sounds like music or has a pleasant tune: *He spoke in a quiet melodious voice.* —**melodiously** *adv*

mel·o·dra·ma /ˈmelədrɑːmə $ -drɑːmə, -dræmə/ *n* [C,U] **1** a story or play in which very exciting or terrible things happen, and in which the characters and the emotions they show seem too strong to be real: *He was behaving like a character in a Victorian melodrama.* **2** a situation in which people become more angry or upset than

M

is really necessary: *Come on, there's no need for all this melodrama.*

mel·o·dra·mat·ic /ˌmelədrəˈmætɪk◂/ *adj* if you behave in a melodramatic way, you become more angry or upset than is really necessary: *Stop being so melodramatic!* —**melodramatically** /-kli/ *adv*

mel·o·dy /ˈmelədi/ ●○○ *n* (*plural* **melodies**)
1 [C] a song or tune: *They played some lovely melodies.* | *a haunting melody* **THESAURUS** ▸ MUSIC
2 [U] the arrangement of musical notes in a way that is pleasant

mel·on /ˈmelən/ ●●○ *n* [C,U] a large round fruit with sweet juicy flesh → see picture at FRUIT[1]

melt /melt/ ●●○ *v*
1 BECOME LIQUID [I,T] if something solid melts or if heat melts it, it becomes liquid → **freeze**, **thaw**: *It was warmer now, and the snow was beginning to melt.* | *Melt the butter in a saucepan.*
2 DISAPPEAR [I] (*also* **melt away**) to gradually disappear: *Opposition to the government melted away.* | *His anger slowly melted.*
3 BECOME LESS ANGRY [I] to become less angry and begin to feel more gentle and sympathetic: *She melted under his gaze.* | *My* **heart** *just* **melted** *when I saw her crying.*
4 melt in your mouth if food melts in your mouth, it is soft and tastes very nice
5 melt into sb's arms/embrace *literary* to allow someone to hold you in their arms and feel that you love them: *Closing her eyes, she melted into his embrace.* → **butter wouldn't melt in sb's mouth** at BUTTER[1](2)

melt away *phr v*
1 if a crowd of people melts away, the people gradually leave: *The demonstrators melted away at the first sign of trouble.*
2 to gradually disappear: *Her determination to take revenge slowly melted away.*

melt sth ↔ **down** *phr v* to heat a metal object until it becomes a liquid, especially so that you can use the metal again: *A lot of the gold was melted down and used for making jewellery.*

melt into sth *phr v*
1 to gradually change into something else: *Her irritation melted into pity.*
2 to gradually become hidden by something: *He is trying to melt into the background.*

melt·down /ˈmeltdaʊn/ *n* [C,U] **1** a very dangerous situation in which the material inside a NUCLEAR REACTOR melts and burns through its container, allowing RADIOACTIVITY to escape **2** a situation in which prices fall by a very large amount or an industry or economic situation becomes much weaker: *The stock market crash might lead to financial meltdown.*

melt·ing /ˈmeltɪŋ/ *adj* [usually before noun] *written* if someone gives you a melting look or speaks to you in a melting voice, it makes you feel pity or love for them —**meltingly** *adv*

ˈmelting point *n* [C,U] the temperature at which a solid substance becomes a liquid

ˈmelting pot *n* [singular] **1** a place where people from different races, countries, or social classes come to live together: *New York has always been a great melting pot.* **2** a situation or place in which many different ideas are discussed **3 in the melting pot** *BrE* an idea or situation that is still in the melting pot is likely to change

mem·ber /ˈmembə $ -ər/ ●●● S1 W1 *n* [C]
1 a person or country that belongs to a group or organization: *The majority of union members voted in favour of a strike.* | **[+of]** *You can also invite members of your family.* | *He is a member of the local tennis club.*

> **REGISTER**
> In everyday English, people usually say there are 3/4/5 etc **people** in their family rather than saying that their family has 3/4/5 etc **members**: *My family has* **eight members**. → *There are* **eight people in my family**.

2 one of a particular group of animals or plants: **[+of]** *The plant is a* **member of** *the lily* **family**. | *Wolves and domestic dogs are* **members of** *the same* **species**.
3 *BrE* a Member of Parliament: **[+for]** *the member for Truro*
4 *formal* a man's sex organ SYN **penis**

> **COLLOCATIONS**
>
> **ADJECTIVES/NOUN + member**
> **a committee/staff/family etc member** *Close friendships developed between crew members on the ship.*
> **a leading member** (=an important member) *a discussion between leading members of the profession*
> **a senior/junior member** (=with a higher or lower rank) *A senior member of the government has resigned.*
> **an active member** (=one who takes part in many activities of an organization) *She was an active member of the church.*
> **a founder member** (=one who helped start an organization) *He was a founder member of the African National Congress.*
> **a staff member** *He became a staff member of the Institute in 2002.*
> **a full member** (=one who has all the possible rights of a member) | **an associate member** (=one who has fewer rights than a full member) | **a life member** (=one who has paid to be a member for their whole life) | **an honorary member** (=one who has been given membership as an honour)
>
> **PHRASES**
> **a member of a committee/of staff etc** *All members of staff attend regular training sessions.*
> **a member of the public** *Members of the public were invited to put forward suggestions.*
> **a member of society** (=a citizen)
>
> **member + NOUN**
> **a member state/country/nation** (=a country that belongs to an international organization) *the member states of the European Union*

ˌMember of ˈParliament *n* (*plural* **Members of Parliament**) [C] (*abbreviation* **MP**) someone who has been elected to represent people in a parliament

mem·ber·ship /ˈmembəʃɪp $ -ər-/ ●●● S3 W2 *n*
1 [U] when someone is a member of a club, group, or organization: **[+of]** *Greece first* **applied for membership** *of the EU in 1975.* | **[+in]** *AmE: I forgot to* **renew** *my* **membership** *in the sailing club.* | *You should carry your* **membership card** *with you at all times.* | **Membership fees** *are being increased this year.*
2 [C,U] all the members of a club, group, or organization: *The membership voted to change the rules about women members.*

> **GRAMMAR: Singular or plural verb?**
> • In this meaning, **membership** is usually followed by a singular verb: *The membership* **supports** *the club's decision.*
> • In British English, you can also use a plural verb: *The membership* **support** *the club's decision.*
> **GRAMMAR GUIDE** ▸ NOUNS

3 [C,U] the number of people who belong to a club, group, or organization: *We're trying to increase our membership.* | *The club has a membership of 200.*

mem·brane /ˈmembreɪn/ *n* [C,U] **1** a very thin piece of skin that covers or connects parts of your body: *Loud noise can damage the delicate membrane in the ear.* **2** a very thin layer of material that covers something —**membranous** /ˈmembrənəs/ *adj*

meme /miːm/ *n* [C] **1** *technical* a type of behaviour or an idea that spreads to other members of a group: *Some people regard religions as cultural memes.* **2** a piece of video, a joke, or something else that spreads quickly on the Internet

me·men·to /məˈmentəʊ $ -toʊ/ *n* (*plural* **mementos**)

M

[C] a small thing that you keep to remind you of someone or something: **[+of]** *I kept the bottle as a memento of my time in Spain.*

mem·o /ˈmeməʊ $ -moʊ/ *n* (*plural* **memos**) [C] a short official note to another person in the same company or organization: *I sent him a memo reminding him about the meeting.* | **[+to/from]** *a memo from the managing director to all heads of department*

mem·oir /ˈmemwɑː $ -wɑːr/ ●○○ *n* [C]
1 memoirs [plural] a book by someone important and famous in which they write about their life and experiences: *Lady Thatcher had just published her memoirs.*
2 *formal* a short piece of writing about a person or place that you knew well, or an event that you experienced

mem·o·ra·bil·i·a /ˌmemərəˈbɪliə/ *n* [plural] things that you keep or collect because they are connected with a famous person, event, or time: *a collection of war memorabilia*

mem·o·ra·ble /ˈmemərəbəl/ ●●○ *adj* very good, enjoyable, or unusual, and worth remembering: *We want to make this a truly memorable day for the children.* —**memorably** *adv*

mem·o·ran·dum /ˌmeməˈrændəm/ *n* (*plural* **memoranda** /-də/ *or* **memorandums**) [C] **1** *formal* a MEMO **2** *law* a short legal document that contains the important details of an agreement

me·mo·ri·al¹ /məˈmɔːriəl/ ●●○ *n*
1 [C] something, especially a stone with writing on it, that reminds people of someone who has died: **[+to]** *The hospital was built as a memorial to King Edward VII.* | **permanent/lasting memorial** *An appeal has been launched to build a lasting memorial to the composer.*
2 [singular] an achievement that reminds people of someone who has died: **[+to]** *The garden is a memorial to one of the finest Victorian gardeners.* → WAR MEMORIAL

memorial² *adj* [only before noun] done or made in order to remind people of someone who has died: **memorial service/ceremony** *A memorial service will be held at 7 pm on Saturday.*

Meˈmorial ˌDay *n* [U] a national holiday in the US on the last Monday in May to remember soldiers who have died in wars

me·mo·ri·a·lize (*also* **-ise** *BrE*) /məˈmɔːriəlaɪz/ *v* [T] to do something so that a person or event will be remembered by people

memoriam → IN MEMORIAM

mem·o·rize (*also* **-ise** *BrE*) /ˈmeməraɪz/ ●●○ *v* [T] to learn words, music etc so that you know them perfectly
THESAURUS ▶ REMEMBER

mem·o·ry /ˈmeməri/ ●●● S2 W1 *n* (*plural* **memories**)
1 ABILITY TO REMEMBER [C,U] someone's ability to remember things, places, experiences etc: **[+for]** *She has a terrible memory for names.* | **from memory** *The pianist played the whole piece from memory.* | **in your memory** *The image has remained in my memory ever since.*
2 STH YOU REMEMBER [C usually plural] something that you remember from the past about a person, place, or experience: **[+of]** *She talked about her memories of the war.* | *He has lots of happy memories of his stay in Japan.* | *When I saw the pictures,* ***the memories came flooding back*** (=I suddenly had many memories about something).
3 COMPUTER **a)** [C] the part of a computer where information can be stored: *The data is stored in the computer's memory.* **b)** [U] the amount of space that can be used for storing information on a computer: *128 Mb of memory* | *Personal computers now have much increased memory capacity.*
4 in/within memory during the time that people can remember: *the worst floods* ***in living memory*** (=since the earliest time that people now alive can remember) | *It's certainly the best England team* ***in recent memory.*** | *The disaster was* ***within the memory of*** *many men still working at the station.*
5 in memory of sb if something is done or made in memory of someone, it is done to remember them and remind other people of them after they have died: *a statue in memory of those who died in the war* | *She set up a charitable fund in her father's memory.*
6 sb's memory the way you remember someone who has died: *She died over 40 years ago but her* ***memory lives on*** (=people still remember her). | **to sb's memory** *There's a bench to his memory in the local park.*
7 a walk/trip down memory lane when you spend some time remembering the past: *She returned to her old school yesterday for a trip down memory lane.*
8 sb's memory is playing tricks on them *spoken* used to say that someone is remembering things wrongly: *My memory must be playing tricks on me; I'm sure I put that book on the desk.*

COLLOCATIONS

ADJECTIVES

good/excellent *I wish my memory was as good as yours.*
bad/poor/terrible *A student with a poor memory may struggle in school.*
short-term memory (=your ability to remember things that you have just seen, heard, or done) *The drug can damage your short-term memory.*
long-term memory (=your ability to remember things that happened a long time ago) | **visual memory** (=your ability to remember things you have seen) | **a photographic memory** (=the ability to remember every detail of things that you have seen)

VERBS

remain/stay/stick in your memory (=be remembered for a long time) *That day will remain in my memory forever.*
refresh/jog your memory (=help someone to remember something) *Perhaps this photograph will refresh your memory?*
lose your memory (=become unable to remember things that happened in the past) | **commit sth to memory** *formal* (=make yourself remember something)

PHRASES

have a short memory (=if you have a short memory, you soon forget things) *Voters have short memories.*
have a long memory (=if you have a long memory, you remember things for a long time) *He has a long memory for people who have let him down.*
have a memory like a sieve (=forget things very easily) | **loss of memory/memory loss** (=when you cannot remember things) | **a lapse of memory/a memory lapse** (=when you cannot remember something for a short time) | **if my memory serves (me correctly/right)** (=used to say that you are almost certain you have remembered something correctly) | **sth is etched in your memory** (=it is impossible to forget)

ˈmemory bank *n* [C] the part of a big computer system that stores information

ˈmemory card *n* [C] a piece of electronic equipment for storing DATA (=information), used in computers, DIGITAL cameras, MOBILE PHONES etc

ˈmemory hog *n* [C] *informal* **1** a computer program that uses a lot of memory **2** someone who uses computer programs that use a lot of the power available, so that other people on the network have trouble using their programs —**memory-hogging** *adj* [only before noun]

ˈMemory Stick *n* [C] *trademark* a small flat card that is used to store information electronically and which fits into PORTABLE electronic machines such as computers, DIGITAL CAMERAS, and WIRELESS telephones

mem·sahib /ˈmemˌsɑːb $ -ˌsɑːhɪb, -ˌsɑːb/ *n* [C] *old-fashioned* a European woman – used in India

men /men/ *n* the plural of MAN

men·ace[1] /ˈmenɪs/ ●○○ *n*
1 [C] something or someone that is dangerous SYN **threat**: **[+of]** *It's the only way to deal with the menace of drug dealing.* | **[+to]** *That man's a* ***menace to society****. He should be locked away.* | *the* ***growing menace*** *of oil pollution at sea*
2 [U] a threatening quality, feeling, or way of behaving: *There was menace in his voice.* | **air/sense of menace** *There was a sense of menace as the sky grew darker.*
3 [C] a person, especially a child, who is annoying or causes trouble SYN **nuisance**: *My little brother's a real menace.*
4 with menaces *BrE law* if someone asks another person for something with menaces, they use threats of violence to get what they want: *He was charged with* ***demanding money with menaces****.*

menace[2] *v* [T] *formal* to threaten: *The elephants are still menaced by poachers.*

men·ac·ing /ˈmenəsɪŋ/ *adj* making you expect something unpleasant SYN **threatening**: *dark menacing clouds* | *a low menacing laugh* | *His tone grew more menacing.* **THESAURUS** FRIGHTENING —**menacingly** *adv*: *He moved towards her menacingly.*

mé·nage /ˈmeɪnɑːʒ $ məˈnɑːʒ/ *n* [C] *formal* all the people who live in a particular house SYN **household**

mé·nage à trois /ˌmeɪnɑːʒ ɑː ˈtrwɑː $ məˌnɑːʒ-/ *n* [singular] a sexual relationship involving three people who live together

me·na·ge·rie /məˈnædʒəri/ *n* [C] a group of wild animals kept privately or for the public to see

mend[1] /mend/ ●●○ *v*
1 REPAIR [T] **a)** to repair a tear or hole in a piece of clothing: *My father used to mend our shoes.* **b)** *BrE* to repair something that is broken or not working SYN **fix**: *When are you going to mend that light in the hall?* | *Tim can mend any broken toy.* **THESAURUS** REPAIR
2 BECOME HEALTHY [I] *informal* if a broken bone mends, it becomes whole again SYN **heal**: *His leg isn't mending as quickly as he'd expected.*
3 mend your ways to improve the way you behave after behaving badly for a long time: *If he doesn't mend his ways, he'll be asked to leave.*
4 mend (your) fences to try to become friendly with someone again after you have offended them or argued with them: *Is it too late to mend fences with your ex-wife?*
5 END A QUARREL [T] to end a quarrel or difficult situation by dealing with the problem that is causing it SYN **repair**: *I've tried to mend matters between us, but she's still very angry.*

mend[2] *n* [C] **1 be on the mend** to be getting better after an illness or after a difficult period SYN **be recovering**: *He's had flu, but he's on the mend.* | *signs that the economy is on the mend* **2** a place in something where it has been repaired

men·da·cious /menˈdeɪʃəs/ *adj formal* not truthful: *mendacious propaganda* —**mendaciously** *adv*

men·da·ci·ty /menˈdæsəti/ *n* [U] *formal* the quality of not being truthful

mend·er /ˈmendə $ -ər/ *n* [C] someone who repairs something

men·di·cant /ˈmendəkənt/ *n* [C] *formal* someone who asks people for money in order to live, usually for religious reasons —**mendicant** *adj*

mend·ing /ˈmendɪŋ/ *n* [U] clothes that need to be repaired

men·folk /ˈmenfəʊk $ -foʊk/ *n* [plural] *old-fashioned* the men in a particular society, family etc → **womenfolk**: *Many women took in washing to supplement the income of their menfolk.*

me·ni·al[1] /ˈmiːniəl/ *adj* menial work is boring, needs no skill, and is not important: *a menial job* | *She did menial tasks about the house.*

menial[2] *n* [C] someone who does menial work, especially a servant in a house

men·in·gi·tis /ˌmenɪnˈdʒaɪtɪs/ *n* [U] a serious illness in which the outer part of the brain becomes swollen

me·nis·cus /məˈnɪskəs/ *n* [C] *technical* the curved surface of a liquid in a tube, caused by SURFACE TENSION

men·o·pause /ˈmenəpɔːz $ -pɒːz/ *n* [singular, U] the time when a woman stops MENSTRUATing, which usually happens around the age of 50 → **male menopause**: *After the menopause a woman cannot bear a child.* —**menopausal** /ˌmenəˈpɔːzəl◂ $ -ˈpɒː-/ *adj*

me·no·rah /məˈnɔːrə/ *n* [C] a Jewish CANDLESTICK that holds seven or nine CANDLES

mensch /menʃ/ *n* [C] *AmE spoken* someone that you like and admire, especially because they have done something good for you

men·ses /ˈmensiːz/ *n* [plural] *medical* the blood that flows out of a woman's body each month

ˈmen's room *n* [C] *especially AmE* the men's toilet SYN **gents** *BrE* → **ladies' room**

men·stru·al /ˈmenstruəl/ *adj* relating to the time each month when a woman loses blood, or the blood that she loses: *the* ***menstrual cycle***

ˌmenstrual ˈperiod *n* [C] *formal* the time each month when a woman menstruates SYN **period**

men·stru·ate /ˈmenstrueɪt/ *v* [I] when a woman menstruates, usually every month, blood flows from her body —**menstruation** /ˌmenstruˈeɪʃən/ *n* [U]

mens·wear /ˈmenzweə $ -wer/ *n* [U] clothing for men – used especially in shops: *the menswear department*

-ment /mənt/ *suffix* [in nouns] used to form a noun from a verb to show actions, the people who do them, or their results: *the government* (=the people who govern a country) | *the replacement of something* (=the action of replacing something) | *some interesting new developments* —**-mental** /mentl/ *suffix* [in adjectives]: *governmental*

men·tal /ˈmentl/ ●●● S2 W2 AWL *adj*
1 [only before noun] relating to the health or state of someone's mind → **psychiatric**: *The centre provides help for people suffering from* ***mental illness****.* | *Stress has an effect on both your physical and* ***mental health****.*
2 [only before noun] relating to the mind and thinking, or happening only in the mind: *a child's mental development* | *You need to develop a positive* ***mental attitude****.* | **mental picture/image** (=a picture that you form in your mind) *I tried to get a mental picture of him from her description.*
3 make a mental note to make a special effort to remember something: *Sarah made a mental note to ask Janine about it later.*
4 mental block a difficulty in remembering something or in understanding something: *I got a complete mental block as soon as the interviewer asked me a question.*
5 go mental *BrE spoken informal* **a)** to get very angry **b)** to start behaving in an uncontrolled or excited way
6 [not before noun] *BrE informal* thinking or behaving in a way that seems crazy or strange: *He must be mental!*
7 *BrE informal* very confused, busy, or exciting: *I had a mental time at the festival – there was all sorts of crazy stuff going on!* —**mentally** *adv*: *I was exhausted, both physically and mentally.*

ˌmental ˈage *n* [C] a measure of someone's ability to think, understand etc, expressed as the average age of a child with that level of ability: *a 25-year-old man with a mental age of seven*

ˌmental aˈrithmetic *n* [U] the act of adding numbers together, multiplying them etc in your mind, without writing them down: *I did a quick bit of mental arithmetic.*

ˈmental ˌhospital *n* [C] *old-fashioned* a hospital where people with mental illnesses are treated SYN **psychiatric hospital**

men·tal·i·ty /menˈtæləti/ ●○○ AWL *n* (*plural* **mentalities**) [C] a particular attitude or way of thinking, especially one that you think is wrong or stupid: *a get-rich-quick mentality* | *I can't understand the mentality of the people who are behind this kind of violence.*

ˌmentally ˈhandicapped *adj old-fashioned* a mentally handicapped person has a problem with their brain, often from the time they are born, that affects their ability to think or control their body movements

ˌmentally ˈill *adj* having an illness that affects your mind and your behaviour

men·tee /ˌmenˈtiː/ *n* [C] someone who is advised and helped by a MENTOR (=more experienced person), for example at work

men·thol /ˈmenθɒl $ -θɒːl, -θɑːl/ *n* [U] a substance that smells and tastes of MINT, used to give cigarettes and sweets a special taste

men·tho·la·ted /ˈmenθəleɪtɪd/ *adj* containing menthol

men·tion¹ /ˈmenʃən/ ●●● S1 W1 *v* [T]

1 to talk or write about something or someone, usually quickly and without saying very much or giving details: *Was my name mentioned at all?* | *Some of the problems were mentioned in his report.* | **mention sth to sb** *I mentioned the idea to Joan, and she seemed to like it.* | **mention (that)** *He mentioned that he was having problems, but he didn't explain.* | ***It's worth mentioning*** (=it is important enough to mention) *that they only studied a very small number of cases.* | ***As I mentioned earlier**, there have been a lot of changes recently.* | *She **mentioned in passing*** (=mentioned in a quick unimportant way) *that you had just been to Rome.* | **now you mention it** (=used to say that you had not thought about something until the speaker mentioned it) *Now you mention it, I haven't seen her around lately.* | **fail/omit/neglect to mention sth** (=not mention something you should mention) *The report failed to mention that most of the landowners do not live on their properties.* THESAURUS SAY

GRAMMAR: Patterns with mention

Mention is a transitive verb and must be followed by an object.
You say: *He mentioned a book he'd read.* ✗ Don't say: *He mentioned about a book.*
You say: *She mentioned that she might be late.* ✗ Don't say: *She mentioned about she might be late.*
GRAMMAR GUIDE VERBS

2 don't mention it *spoken* used to say politely that there is no need for someone to thank you for helping them: *'Thanks for the ride home!' 'Don't mention it.'*

3 not to mention sth used to introduce an additional thing that makes a situation even more difficult, surprising, interesting etc: *Pollution has a negative effect on the health of everyone living in the city, not to mention the damage to the environment.* | *It's too far to walk, **not to mention the fact that** it'll probably be closed by now anyway.*

4 be mentioned in dispatches *BrE* to have your name on an official list of people who have been brave in battle, as an honour

THESAURUS

mention to talk or write about something or someone, usually quickly and without saying very much or giving details: *Kate had mentioned his name a few times, but I had not met him before.* | *Jack mentioned that you might be looking for a new job.*

refer to sb/sth to say something about someone or something in a conversation, speech, or piece of writing: *He had earlier referred to difficulties in gathering evidence.* | *It was not clear which case he was referring to.*

touch on sth to briefly mention a subject during a speech, lesson, piece of writing etc: *This problem has already been touched on in Chapter 4.*

bring sth up to start to talk about a particular subject during a conversation or meeting: *I didn't want to bring up the subject of money.* | *I knew you'd bring that up!*

raise to mention a subject that people should start to discuss or think about. **Raise** is more formal than **bring sth up**: *He promised to raise the issue with the prime minister.* | *They raised a number of points.*

broach to mention a subject that may be embarrassing or upsetting, or that may cause an argument: *I was reluctant to broach the subject of payment.*

cite *formal* to mention something as an example or proof of something else, or as a reason for something: *Hong Kong is often cited as an example of this kind of economic system.*

allude to sth *formal* to mention something in a way that is deliberately not direct: *Many of the ancient Greek poets allude to this myth.*

mention² ●●○ *n* [C usually singular, U] when someone mentions something or someone in a conversation, piece of writing etc: **[+of]** *He **made no mention** of his wife's illness.* | **at the mention of sth** *At the mention of a trip to the seaside, the children got very excited.* | *They all **get a mention*** (=they are all mentioned) *in the book.* | **deserve/merit (a) mention** *There is one other person who deserves **special mention*** (=is especially worth mentioning for something they have done). → HONOURABLE MENTION

men·tor¹ /ˈmentɔː $ -tɔːr/ ●●○ *n* [C] an experienced person who advises and helps a less experienced person

mentor² *v* [T] to be someone's mentor: *Now she mentors undergraduates who are training to be teachers.*

men·tor·ing /ˈmentɔːrɪŋ/ *n* [U] a system where people with a lot of experience, knowledge etc advise and help other people at work or young people preparing for work

men·u /ˈmenjuː/ ●●● S3 *n* [C]

1 a list of all the kinds of food that are available for a meal, especially in a restaurant: *Could we have the menu, please?* | **on the menu** *Is there any fish on the menu?* | *a three-course **set menu*** (=dishes which you do not choose for yourself)

2 a list of things on a computer screen which you can ask the computer to do: *Select PRINT from the main menu.* | **pull-down/drop-down menu** (=a list of choices which appears when you CLICK ON a place on the screen) | **menu-driven** (=operated by using a menu)

ˈmenu-ˌdriven *adj* a menu-driven way of using a computer is one in which the user makes choices from menus

me·ow /miˈaʊ/ *v, n* the usual American spelling of MIAOW

MEP /ˌem iː ˈpiː/ *n* [C] (***Member of the European Parliament***) someone who has been elected as a member of the Parliament of the European Union

meph·e·drone /ˈmefədrəʊn $ -droʊn/ *n* [U] an illegal drug that is similar to AMPHETAMINE

mer·can·tile /ˈmɜːkəntaɪl $ ˈmɜːrkəntiːl, -taɪl/ *adj* [only before noun] *formal* concerned with trade SYN **commercial**: *mercantile law*

Mer·ca·tor pro·jec·tion /məˌkeɪtə prəˈdʒekʃən $ mərˌkeɪtər-/ (*also* **Mercator's projection**) *n* [singular] the usual way a map of the world is drawn

mer·ce·na·ry¹ /ˈmɜːsənəri $ ˈmɜːrsəneri/ *n* (*plural* **mercenaries**) [C] a soldier who fights for any country or group that will pay him: *an army of foreign mercenaries* | *a mercenary soldier*

mercenary² *adj* only interested in the money you may be able to get from a person, job etc: *She did it for purely mercenary reasons.* | *a mercenary attitude*

mer·cer·ized cot·ton (*also* **-ised** *BrE*) /ˌmɜːsəraɪzd ˈkɒtn $ ˌmɜːrsəraɪzd ˈkɑːtn/ *n* [U] cotton that has been treated with chemicals to make it shiny and strong

mer·chan·dise¹ /ˈmɜːtʃəndaɪz, -daɪs $ ˈmɜːr-/ ●○○ *n* [U] *formal* goods that are being sold: *A range of official Disney merchandise was on sale.* | *They inspected the merchandise carefully.* THESAURUS PRODUCT

merchandise² *v* [T] to try to sell goods or services using methods such as advertising SYN **market**: *If the product is properly merchandised, it should sell very well.*

mer·chan·dis·ing /ˈmɜːtʃəndaɪzɪŋ $ ˈmɜːr-/ *n* [U] **1** toys, clothes, and other products relating to a popular film, sports team, singer etc: *The concerts generated £3 million in ticket and merchandising sales.* **2** the way in which shops and businesses try to sell their products: *the director of merchandising*

M

mer·chant /ˈmɜːtʃənt $ ˈmɜːr-/ ●○○ *n* [C]
1 wine/coal/timber etc merchant someone whose job is to buy and sell wine, coal etc, or a small company that does this: *He had a job with an Edinburgh wine merchant.*
2 *old-fashioned* someone who buys and sells goods in large quantities: *the son of a wealthy merchant*
3 con merchant/speed merchant etc *BrE informal* someone who is involved in a particular activity, such as tricking people or driving very fast

mer·chant·a·ble /ˈmɜːtʃəntəbəl $ ˈmɜːr-/ *adj* **of merchantable quality** *law* in a suitable condition to be sold

ˌmerchant ˈbank *n* [C] a bank that provides services for businesses —**merchant banker** *n* [C]

mer·chant·man /ˈmɜːtʃəntmən $ ˈmɜːr-/ *n* (*plural* **merchantmen** /-mən/) [C] *old-fashioned* a ship used for carrying goods

ˌmerchant ˈnavy *BrE*, **ˌmerchant maˈrine** *AmE* *n* [singular] all of a country's ships that are used for trade, not war, and the people who work on these ships: *John worked as a chef in the merchant navy.*

ˌmerchant ˈseaman *n* [C] a sailor in the merchant navy

mer·ci·ful /ˈmɜːsɪfəl $ ˈmɜːr-/ *adj* **1 merciful death/end/release** a death or end to something that seems fortunate because it ends someone's suffering SYN **welcome**: *I think my uncle's death was a merciful release for my poor aunt.* **2** being kind to people and forgiving them rather than punishing them or being cruel OPP **cruel**: *Merciful God, save us.*

mer·ci·ful·ly /ˈmɜːsɪfəli $ ˈmɜːr-/ *adv* fortunately or luckily, because a situation could have been much worse: *Mercifully, I managed to stop the car just in time.* | *The journey was mercifully brief.*

mer·ci·less /ˈmɜːsɪləs $ ˈmɜːr-/ *adj* **1** cruel and showing no kindness or forgiveness: *a merciless attack* | *a merciless killer* **2 merciless heat/cold/wind etc** heat, cold etc that is very great or strong and unpleasant, and does not stop: *It brings some relief from the merciless summer heat.* —**mercilessly** *adv*: *He teased his sister mercilessly.*

mer·cu·ri·al /mɜːˈkjʊəriəl $ mɜːrˈkjʊr-/ *adj* **1** *literary* having feelings that change suddenly and without warning: *an actor noted for his mercurial temperament* **2** *literary* quick and clever: *her mercurial wit* **3** *technical* containing mercury

mer·cu·ry /ˈmɜːkjəri $ ˈmɜːr-/ *n* [U] a heavy silver-white poisonous metal that is liquid at ordinary temperatures, and is used in THERMOMETERS. It is a chemical ELEMENT: symbol Hg

Mercury *n* the PLANET that is nearest the Sun: *Temperatures on Mercury reach as high as 700 K.*

mer·cy /ˈmɜːsi $ ˈmɜːrsi/ ●●○ *n*
1 [U] if someone shows mercy, they choose to forgive or to be kind to someone who they have the power to hurt or punish: *He* ***showed no mercy to*** *his enemies.* | *God* ***have mercy on*** *his soul.* | **beg/cry/plead for mercy** *The boy was screaming and begging for mercy.*
2 at the mercy of sb/sth unable to do anything to protect yourself from someone or something: *After the boat's motor failed, they were at the mercy of the weather.* | *She was completely at his mercy.*
3 mercy flight/mission etc a journey taken to bring help to people: *a mercy mission to help homeless refugees*
4 leave sb to sb's (tender) mercies to let someone be dealt with by another person, who may treat them very badly or strictly – used humorously
5 throw yourself on sb's mercy to ask someone to help you or forgive you when you are in a very bad situation
6 it's a mercy (that) *spoken* used to say that it is lucky that a worse situation was avoided: *It's a mercy the accident happened so near the hospital.* → **be thankful/grateful for small mercies** at SMALL[1](13)

ˈmercy ˌkilling *n* [C,U] the act of killing someone who is very ill or old so that they do not have to suffer anymore SYN **euthanasia**

mere[1] /mɪə $ mɪr/ ●○○ *adj* (*superlative* **merest**) [only before noun, no comparative]
1 used to emphasize how small or unimportant something or someone is: *She lost the election by a mere 20 votes.* | *He's a mere child.* | *It can't be a* ***mere coincidence*** *that they left at the same time.*
2 used to emphasize that something which is small or not extreme has a big effect or is important: *The merest little noise makes him nervous.* | *The mere thought of food made her feel sick.* | ***The mere fact*** *that the talks are continuing is a positive sign.*

mere[2] *n* [C] *literary* a lake

mere·ly /ˈmɪəli $ ˈmɪrli/ ●●○ W2 *adv*
1 used to emphasize how small or unimportant something or someone is SYN **only**: *He's merely a boy – you can't expect him to understand.*
2 used to emphasize that nothing more than what you say is involved SYN **just**: *We're merely good friends.* | *He merely shrugged and walked away.*
3 not merely/rather than merely used before the less important of two ideas in a sentence to emphasize the more important idea: *It's not merely a matter of cost, but whether she's old enough to go on holiday alone.* | *It's important to write these goals down, rather than merely think about them.*

mer·e·tri·cious /ˌmerəˈtrɪʃəs◂/ *adj formal* something that is meretricious seems attractive but has no real value or is not based on the truth: *meretricious research* —**meretriciousness** *n* [U]

merge /mɜːdʒ $ mɜːrdʒ/ ●○○ *v*
1 [I,T] to combine, or to join things together to form one thing: **[+with]** *The bank announced that it was to merge with another of the high street banks.* | *The company plans to merge its subsidiaries in the US.* | **merge sth into sth** *proposals to merge the three existing health authorities into one* | **[+together]** *The villages have grown and merged together over the years.*
2 [I] if two things merge, or if one thing merges into another, you cannot clearly see them, hear them etc as separate things: **[+into]** *She avoided reporters at the airport by merging into the crowds.* | **[+with]** *Memories seemed to merge with reality.*

merg·er /ˈmɜːdʒə $ ˈmɜːrdʒər/ ●○○ *n* [C] the joining together of two or more companies or organizations to form one larger one: **[+of/between]** *a proposed merger between two of the largest software companies* | **[+with]** *There has been a lot of talk about a merger with another leading bank.* | *merger negotiations*

me·rid·i·an /məˈrɪdiən/ *n* **1** [C] one of the imaginary lines from the North Pole to the South Pole, drawn on a map of the Earth **2 the meridian** *technical* the highest point reached by the Sun or another star, when seen from a point on the Earth's surface

me·ringue /məˈræŋ/ *n* [C,U] a light sweet food made by mixing sugar and the white part of eggs together very quickly and then baking it

me·ri·no /məˈriːnəʊ $ -noʊ/ *n* (*plural* **merinos**) [C,U] a type of sheep with long wool, or cloth made from this wool

mer·it[1] /ˈmerɪt/ ●●○ *n*
1 [C] an advantage or good feature of something: **[+of]** *The film* ***has the merit*** *of being short.* | *The merit of the report is its realistic assessment of the changes required.* | *The* ***great merit*** *of the project is its flexibility and low cost.* | *Each of these approaches to teaching* ***has its merits***. | *Tonight's meeting will weigh up the* ***relative merits*** *of the two candidates.*
THESAURUS ADVANTAGE

> **REGISTER**
> **Merit** is used especially in formal contexts. In everyday English, people usually talk about the **good points** of something: *The book does have its* ***good points***.

2 [U] *formal* a good quality that makes someone or something deserve praise: ***There is*** *never any* ***merit in*** *being second best.* | **have (some) merit/be of merit** (=be good) *The suggestion has some merit.* | **on merit** *Students are*

selected solely on merit (=because they are good). | **artistic/literary merit** *a film lacking any artistic merit*
3 judge/consider etc sth on its (own) merits to judge something only on what you see when you look at it rather than on what you know from other people or things: *It's important to judge each case on its merits.*

merit² ●○○ *v* [T] *formal* to be good, important, or serious enough for praise or attention SYN **deserve**: *The results have been encouraging enough to merit further investigation.* | *It's a fascinating book which merits attention.*

mer·i·toc·ra·cy /ˌmerəˈtɒkrəsi $ -ˈtɑː-/ *n* (*plural* **meritocracies**) **1** [C] a social system that gives the greatest power and highest social positions to people with the most ability **2 the meritocracy** the people who have power in a meritocracy → **aristocracy** —**meritocratic** /ˌmerətəˈkrætɪk◂/ *adj*

mer·i·to·ri·ous /ˌmerəˈtɔːriəs◂/ *adj formal* very good and deserving praise

mer·maid /ˈmɜːmeɪd $ ˈmɜːr-/ *n* [C] in stories, a woman who has a fish's tail instead of legs and who lives in the sea

mer·ri·ly /ˈmerəli/ *adv* **1** *written* in a happy way, or in a way that makes you feel happy: *Sylvia laughed merrily.* **2** *literary* quickly and in a pleasant way: *The fire soon began to burn merrily.* | *The clock ticked merrily in the corner.* **3** not thinking about possible problems that might happen as a result of what you are doing – used to show disapproval SYN **blithely**: *Meanwhile, the company is merrily pushing ahead with its plans.*

mer·ri·ment /ˈmerɪmənt/ *n* [U] *literary* laughter, fun, and enjoyment: *Her eyes sparkled with merriment.* | *the sounds of merriment*

mer·ry /ˈmeri/ ●●○ *adj*
1 Merry Christmas! used to say that you hope someone will have a happy time at Christmas SYN **Happy Christmas**
2 *literary* happy SYN **cheerful, jolly**: *He marched off, whistling a merry tune.* | *He's a lovely man with merry eyes and a wide smile.*
3 the more the merrier *spoken* used to say that you are happy for other people to join you in what you are doing: *'Do you mind if I bring Tony?' 'No, of course not. The more the merrier.'*
4 [not before noun] *BrE informal* slightly drunk SYN **tipsy**
5 make merry *old-fashioned* to enjoy yourself by drinking, singing, laughing etc: *Christmas is a time to eat, drink and make merry.*
6 *old use* pleasant: *the merry month of June* —**merriness** *n* [U] → **play (merry) hell with sth** at HELL¹(25), → **lead sb a merry old dance** at LEAD¹(19)

ˈmerry-go-ˌround *n* **1** [C] a machine that turns around and around, and has model animals or cars for children to sit on SYN **carousel** *AmE*, **roundabout** *BrE* **2** [singular] a series of similar events that happen very quickly one after another: **[+of]** *the endless Washington merry-go-round of parties and socializing*

mer·ry·mak·ing /ˈmeriˌmeɪkɪŋ/ *n* [U] *literary* fun and enjoyment, especially drinking, dancing, and singing

me·sa /ˈmeɪsə/ *n* [C] a hill with a flat top and steep sides, in the southwestern US

mes·ca·line, mescalin /ˈmeskəliːn/ *n* [U] a drug made from a CACTUS plant that makes people imagine that they can see things that do not really exist

mesh¹ /meʃ/ *n* **1** [C,U] material made from threads or wires that have been woven together like a net, or a piece of this material: *The windows were covered in wire mesh to keep out flies.* | *a mesh fence* **2** [C usually singular] *literary* a complicated or difficult situation or system: **[+of]** *She had felt trapped by the old mesh of loyalty and shame.*

mesh² *v* [I] **1** if two ideas or things mesh, they fit together very well: **[+with]** *His own ideas did not mesh with the views of the party.* **2** if two parts of an engine or machine mesh, they fit closely together and connect with each other

mes·mer·ic /mezˈmerɪk/ *adj* very attractive or having a very powerful effect, so that people cannot think of anything else SYN **hypnotic**: *a mesmeric performance* | *the mesmeric hum of the bees*

mes·mer·ize (*also* **-ise** *BrE*) /ˈmezməraɪz/ *v* [T] if you are mesmerized by someone or something, you cannot stop watching them or listening to them because they are so attractive or have such a powerful effect SYN **captivate**: *The first time I saw Diana I was mesmerized by her beauty.* GRAMMAR **Mesmerize** is usually passive. —**mesmerizing** *adj*

Mes·o·zo·ic /ˌmezəˈzəʊɪk, ˌmes- $ -ˈzoʊ-/ *adj* belonging or relating to the period of time in the Earth's history, from about 250 million years ago to about 65 million years ago, when DINOSAURS, birds, and plants with flowers first started to exist: *the Mesozoic era*

mes·quite /meˈskiːt/ *n* [C,U] an American tree or bush, or the wood from it that is used to give food a special taste when it is being cooked on a BARBECUE

mess¹ /mes/ ●●● S2 *n*
1 DIRTY/UNTIDY [singular, U] if there is a mess somewhere or a place is a mess, things there are dirty or not neatly arranged: *What a mess!* | *Sorry – the place* ***is a bit of a mess.*** | *When I got home, the house* ***was a complete mess.*** | **in a mess** *BrE*: *The burglars left the house in an awful mess.* | *You can make cookies if you promise not to* ***make a mess*** *in the kitchen.* | **clear/clean up the mess** *Whoever is responsible for this mess can clear it up immediately!* | *She hates mess.*
2 PROBLEMS/DIFFICULTIES [singular, U] a situation in which there are a lot of problems and difficulties, especially as a result of mistakes or carelessness: *My life's* ***such a mess.*** | **in a mess** *The economy is in a terrible mess.* | *You* ***got*** *us* ***into*** *this* ***mess****, Terry. You can get us out of it.* | *All she could do was pray that, somehow, she might be able to* ***sort out*** *the* ***mess*** *she had got herself into.*
3 make a mess of (doing) sth to do something badly: *I feel I've made a real mess of my marriage.* | *Many people make a mess of handling money.*
4 PERSON **be a mess** *informal* if someone is a mess, they look dirty and untidy, or are in a bad emotional state
5 a mess of sth *AmE informal* a lot of something: *a mess of fresh fish*
6 ARMY/NAVY [C] a room in which members of the army, navy etc eat and drink together: *We had lunch in* ***the officers' mess.***
7 WASTE SUBSTANCE [C,U] *BrE informal* solid waste from an animal: *The dog's* ***made a mess*** *on the carpet.*

mess² ●●○ S3 *v*
1 [T] to make something look untidy or dirty: *He scratched his head and messed his hair even more.*
2 [I,T] *BrE* if an animal or person messes something, they use the wrong place as a toilet: *He was so drunk that he messed the bed.*
3 no messing *spoken informal* used to say that something was done very easily: *Williams won very comfortably, no messing.*
4 [I] to have meals in a room where members of the army, navy etc eat together

mess around (*also* **mess about** *BrE*) *phr v informal*
1 to spend time lazily, doing things slowly and in a way that is not planned: *He spent his vacation messing around on the farm.*
2 to behave in a silly way when you should be paying attention or doing something sensible SYN **fool around**: *Stop messing around and get ready for school.*
3 mess sb around to cause a lot of problems for someone, especially by changing your mind often and not being completely honest: *Don't mess me around – I want the money you promised me.*

mess around with sb/sth (*also* **mess about with sb/sth** *BrE*) *phr v informal*
1 to have a sexual relationship with someone that you should not have a sexual relationship with: *She'd been messing around with another man.*
2 to spend time playing with something, repairing it etc: *Dave likes messing around with old cars.*
3 to use something and make annoying changes to it: *Who's been messing around with my camera?*

mess up *phr v informal*
1 mess sth ↔ up to spoil or ruin something, especially

something important or something that has been carefully planned: *It took me ages to get this right – I don't want some idiot to mess it up.* | *She felt she'd messed up her whole life.*
2 mess sth ↔ up to make something dirty or untidy: *Who messed up the kitchen?*
3 to make a mistake and do something badly: *I think I messed up on the last question.* | **mess sth ↔ up** *It doesn't matter if you mess it up, you can always try again.*
4 mess sb ↔ up to make someone have emotional or mental problems: *I messed up my kids.*
5 mess sb ↔ up *AmE informal* to hurt someone especially by hitting them

mess with sb/sth *phr v informal*
1 to get involved with someone or something that may cause problems or be dangerous: *Don't mess with drugs.*
2 to deceive someone or cause trouble for them: *You mess with me, and I'll rip your head off.*
3 to try changing something, especially in a way that damages or spoils it

mes·sage¹ /ˈmesɪdʒ/ ●●● S1 W2 *n* [C]
1 a spoken or written piece of information that you send to another person or leave for them: **[+from]** *There's a message from Karen on the answerphone.* | **[+for]** *I have an urgent message for you.* | *He left a message saying he would probably be a little late.*
2 [usually singular] the main or most important idea that someone is trying to tell people about in a film, book, speech etc: *The message of the film is that good always triumphs over evil.* | *The result of this legal battle* **sends** *an important* **message to** *people in similar situations.* | *It's perfectly possible to* **get** *your* **message across** (=communicate what you want to say) *without being so angry.* | *They use illustrations to* **convey** *their* **message**.
3 get the message *informal* to understand what someone means or what they want you to do: *OK, I get the message – I'm going!*
4 a piece of written information which appears on a computer screen to tell the user about something, especially a problem: **error/warning message** *I keep getting an error message when I try to log on.*
5 on/off message stating or not stating the official opinion of the political party you belong to
6 keep/stick to the message to always emphasize your political party's most important ideas when you are trying to gain people's support: *Don't confuse the voters. Keep to the message.*

COLLOCATIONS

VERBS

get a message (*also* **receive a message** *formal*) *Didn't you get my message?*
send a message *My mum just sent me a text message.*
leave a message (=write or say something that the person will receive later) *Please leave a message after the beep.*
take a message (=write down a message from someone for someone else) *Ellen isn't here. Can I take a message?*
give sb a message (=from someone else) | **pass on/relay/deliver a message** (=give someone a message from someone else)

ADJECTIVES/NOUN + message

an urgent/important message *an urgent message for the commanding officer*
a brief/short message *She left a short message on his answering machine.*
a telephone/phone message (=a message that someone has written down for you from a phone call) | **a text message** (=a written message that you receive on your mobile phone) | **an email/mail message** (=a message that you receive by email)

PHRASES

a message of support/sympathy/congratulations etc *Other celebrities sent messages of support.*

message² *v* [I,T] to send a TEXT MESSAGE or another electronic message, for example a message on a SOCIAL NETWORKING SITE: *You can message several people at once.*

ˈmessage board *n* [C] a place on a website where you can read or leave messages SYN **electronic bulletin board**

mes·sag·ing /ˈmesɪdʒɪŋ/ *n* [U] the system or process of sending messages using electronic equipment: *an electronic messaging system*

ˌmessed ˈup *adj informal* someone who is messed up has emotional or mental problems because of something that has happened to them

mes·sen·ger¹ /ˈmesɪndʒə, -sən- $ -ər/ ●○○ *n* [C]
1 someone whose job is to deliver messages or documents, or someone who takes a message to someone else
2 blame/shoot the messenger to be angry with the person who tells you about something bad, instead of the person who caused it to happen

messenger² *v* [T] to send a letter, package etc somewhere using a messenger

ˈmessenger ˌboy *n* [C] someone who delivered messages to other people as a job in the past

ˈmess hall *n* [C] a large room where soldiers eat

mes·si·ah /məˈsaɪə/ *n* [singular] **1 the Messiah a)** Jesus Christ, who Christians believe has been sent by God to save the world from evil **b)** a great religious leader who, according to Jewish belief, will be sent by God to save the world **2** someone who people believe will solve all their problems: *The club was in desperate need of a new footballing messiah.*

mes·si·an·ic /ˌmesiˈænɪk◂/ *adj formal* **1** someone who has messianic beliefs wants to make very big social or political changes: *Many young people have an admirable messianic zeal about them.* **2** relating to or involving the Messiah

Mes·srs *BrE*, **Messrs.** *AmE* /ˈmesəz $ -ərz/ the plural of MR, used especially in the names of companies: *Messrs Ford and Dobson*

mess·y /ˈmesi/ ●●● S3 *adj* (*comparative* **messier**, *superlative* **messiest**)
1 dirty or untidy: *a messy room* | *Sorry the place is so messy, I haven't had time to clear up.*
2 *informal* a messy situation is complicated and unpleasant to deal with: *He's just been through a particularly messy divorce.*
3 making someone or something dirty or untidy: *messy jobs like plumbing, plastering, and tiling* —**messily** *adv* —**messiness** *n* [U]

mes·ti·zo /meˈstiːzəʊ $ -zoʊ/ *n* (*plural* **mestizos**) [C] someone who has one Hispanic parent and one Native American parent

met /met/ the past tense and past participle of MEET

meta- /metə/ *prefix* **1** beyond or at a higher level: *metaphysical* (=beyond ordinary physical things) **2** relating to a change of state or position: *metabolism* (=the process of changing food into energy)

met·a·bol·ic /ˌmetəˈbɒlɪk◂ $ -ˈbɑː-/ *adj* [only before noun] relating to your body's metabolism: **(high/low) metabolic rate** *Fish normally have a high metabolic rate.* | *Exercise can increase your metabolic rate.* | *the metabolic activity of the brain*

ˌmetabolic ˈsyndrome *n* [U] a combination of medical conditions, including high blood pressure and high levels of CHOLESTEROL in the body, that increase someone's risk of getting heart disease or having a heart attack

me·tab·o·lis·m /məˈtæbəlɪzəm/ *n* [C,U] the chemical processes by which food is changed into energy in your body: *This drug speeds up your metabolism.* | **protein/carbohydrate/alcohol etc metabolism** *The vast majority of alcohol metabolism occurs in the liver.* | **[+of]** *the metabolism of fat by the liver*

me·ta·bol·ize (*also* **-ise** *BrE*) /məˈtæbəlaɪz/ *v* [T] to change food in your body into energy and new cells, using chemical processes

met·a·da·ta /ˈmetədeɪtə/ *n* [plural, U] information that describes what is contained in large computer DATABASES, for example who wrote the information, what it is for, and in what form it is stored

met·al /ˈmetl/ ●●● S2 W2 *n* [C,U] a hard, usually shiny substance such as iron, gold, or steel → **metallic**: *The gate is made of metal.* | *a small black metal box* | *They traded in gold and other* ***precious metals*** (=valuable metals used especially for making jewellery). | *The old trucks were sold as* ***scrap metal*** (=old metal that is melted and used again). → HEAVY METAL

met·a·lan·guage /ˈmetəˌlæŋgwɪdʒ/ *n* [C,U] words that are used for talking about or describing language

ˈmetal deˌtector *n* [C] **1** a machine used to find pieces of metal that are buried under the ground **2** a special frame that you walk through at an airport, used to check for weapons made of metal

ˈmetal faˌtigue *n* [U] weakness in metal that makes it likely to break, caused for example by frequent shaking over a long period

me·tal·lic /məˈtælɪk/ *adj* **1** a metallic noise sounds like pieces of metal hitting each other: *The key turned in the lock with a loud metallic click.* | *The pans made a metallic clatter as they crashed to the floor.* **2** a metallic voice is rough, hard, and unpleasant: *He spoke in a thin, metallic voice.* **3** a metallic colour shines like metal: *He drives a metallic red van.* **4** a metallic taste is bitter and unpleasant, like metal: *The gum left a horrible metallic taste in my mouth.* **5** made of metal or containing metal: *metallic particles*

met·al·lur·gy /məˈtælədʒi $ ˈmetəlɜːrdʒi/ *n* [U] the scientific study of metals and their uses —**metallurgist** *n* [C] —**metallurgical** /ˌmetəˈlɜːdʒɪkəl◂ $ -ˈlɜːr-/ *adj*

met·al·work /ˈmetlwɜːk $ -wɜːrk/ *n* [U] **1** objects made by shaping metal: *a huge collection of antique metalwork* **2** the activity or skill of making metal objects: *Students can study woodwork or metalwork.* —**metalworker** *n* [C]

met·a·ma·te·ri·al /ˈmetəməˌtɪəriəl $ -ˌtɪr-/ *n* [C] *technical* an artificial material that has qualities that natural materials do not have

met·a·mor·phic /ˌmetəˈmɔːfɪk $ -ˈmɔːr-/ *adj technical* metamorphic rock is formed by the continuous effects of pressure, heat, or water: *This metamorphic rock has been compressed for millions of years.*

met·a·mor·phose /ˌmetəˈmɔːfəʊz $ -ˈmɔːrfoʊz/ *v* [I,T] *formal* to change completely and become something different, or to make something change in this way → **transform**: **[+into]** *From an easy-going young girl, she had metamorphosed into a neurotic middle-aged woman.*

METAMORPHOSIS

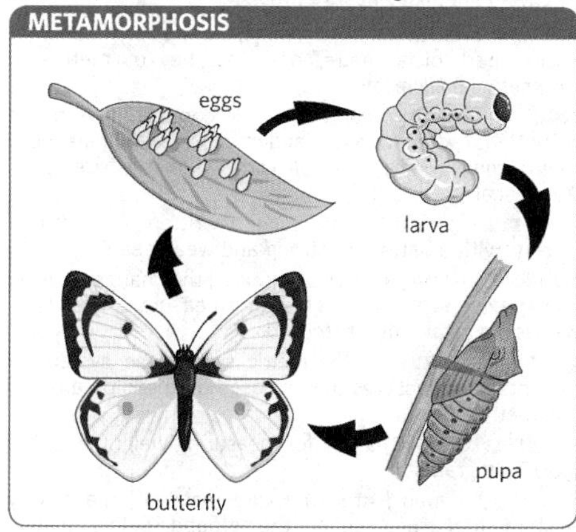

met·a·mor·pho·sis /ˌmetəˈmɔːfəsɪs $ -ˈmɔːr-/ *n* (*plural* **metamorphoses** /-siːz/) [C,U] **1** *formal* a process in which something changes completely into something very different SYN **transformation**: *It took me some time to undergo the metamorphosis from teacher to lecturer.* | *the metamorphosis of China under Deng's economic reforms* **2** a process in which a young insect, FROG etc changes into another stage in its development: *Beetles undergo a complete metamorphosis in their life cycle.*

met·a·phor /ˈmetəfə, -fɔː $ -fɔːr/ ●●○ *n* [C,U]
1 a way of describing something by referring to it as something different and suggesting that it has similar qualities to that thing → **simile**: *She uses some wonderful images and metaphors in her writing.* | *a very creative use of metaphor* THESAURUS LANGUAGE
2 mixed metaphor the use of two different metaphors at the same time to describe something, especially in a way that seems silly or funny
3 something that represents a general idea or quality: **[+for]** *Their relationship is a metaphor for the failure of communication in the modern world.*

met·a·phor·i·cal /ˌmetəˈfɒrɪkəl◂ $ -ˈfɔː-, -ˈfɑː-/ ●○○ *adj*
1 a metaphorical use of a word is not concerned with real objects or physical events, but with ideas or events of a non-physical kind: *The word has a metaphorical as well as a literal meaning.*
2 used to show that you are using a metaphor: *his need to escape from the metaphorical chains that held him* —**metaphorically** /-kli/ *adv*: *She was, literally and metaphorically, in perfect shape.*

met·a·phys·i·cal /ˌmetəˈfɪzɪkəl◂/ *adj* concerned with the study of metaphysics: *A lot of scientists don't like discussing metaphysical matters.*

met·a·phys·ics /ˌmetəˈfɪzɪks/ *n* [U] the part of PHILOSOPHY that is concerned with trying to understand and describe the nature of truth, life, and REALITY

met·a·tar·sal /ˌmetəˈtɑːsəl $ -ɑːr-/ *n* [C] *technical* one of the five bones that stretch from the heel to the toes

mete /miːt/ *v*
mete sth ↔ **out** *phr v formal* if you mete out a punishment, you give it to someone: **[+to]** *He felt he had a right to mete out physical punishment to the children.* | *Judges are meting out harsh sentences for car theft.*

me·te·or /ˈmiːtiə $ -ər/ *n* [C] a piece of rock or metal that travels through space, and makes a bright line in the night sky when it falls down towards the Earth: *Astronomers track large meteors using radar.* | *a* ***meteor shower*** (=a lot of meteors that fall down towards the Earth at the same time)

me·te·or·ic /ˌmiːtiˈɒrɪk◂ $ -ˈɔːrɪk, -ˈɑːrɪk/ *adj* **1** happening very suddenly and quickly: *her* ***meteoric rise*** *from dancer to professional actress* | *The company has experienced meteoric growth.* | *The scandal ended his* ***meteoric*** *political* ***career***. **2** *technical* from a METEOR: *meteoric iron* —**meteorically** /-kli/ *adv*: *His career faded as meteorically as it grew.*

me·te·o·rite /ˈmiːtiəraɪt/ *n* [C] a piece of rock or metal from space that has landed on Earth

me·te·o·rol·o·gy /ˌmiːtiəˈrɒlədʒi $ -ˈrɑː-/ *n* [U] the scientific study of weather conditions —**meteorologist** *n* [C]: *The storms have baffled meteorologists in the United States.* —**meteorological** /ˌmiːtiərəˈlɒdʒɪkəl◂ $ -ˈlɑː-/ *adj*: *satellites that provide meteorological data to the National Weather Service*

me·ter¹ /ˈmiːtə $ -ər/ ●○○ *n* [C]
1 a machine that measures and shows the amount of something you have used or the amount of money that you must pay: **water/gas/electricity meter** *A man came to* ***read*** *the electricity* ***meter***. | *The taxi driver left the meter running while I ran in to pick up my bags.*
2 a machine that measures the level of something: **sound-level/light etc meter**
3 (*also* **parking meter**) a machine which you put money into when you park your car next to it
4 the American spelling of METRE

meter² *v* [T] to measure how much of something is used, and how much you must pay for it, by using a meter: *All our water is metered now.*

-meter /miːtə, mɪtə $ -tər/ *suffix* [in nouns] an instrument for measuring something: *a thermometer* (=an instrument for measuring heat)

ˈmeter maid *n* [C] *AmE old-fashioned* a woman whose job is to make sure that cars are not parked illegally SYN **traffic warden** *BrE*

meth·a·done /ˈmeθədəʊn $ -doʊn/ *n* [U] a drug that is often given to people who are trying to stop taking HEROIN

meth·am·phet·a·mine /ˌmeθæmˈfetəmiːn, -mɪn/ *n* [U] an illegal drug that gives a feeling of energy

me·thane /ˈmiːθeɪn $ ˈme-/ *n* [U] a gas that you cannot see or smell, which can be burned to give heat: *Methane is one of the principal gases contributing to the greenhouse effect.*

meth·a·nol /ˈmeθənɒl $ -nɒːl, -nɑːl/ *n* [U] a type of poisonous alcohol that can be made from wood

me·thinks /mɪˈθɪŋks/ *v* (*past tense* **methought** /-ˈθɔːt $ -ˈθɒːt/) [T] *old use* I think: *Methinks he is not mistaken.*

meth·od /ˈmeθəd/ ●●● S1 W1 AWL *n*
1 [C] a planned way of doing something, especially one that a lot of people know about and use: *traditional teaching methods* | *I think we should try again using a different method.* | **method of/for (doing) sth** *Today's methods of birth control make it possible for a couple to choose whether or not to have a child.* | *effective methods for the storage and retrieval of information* THESAURUS▸ WAY
2 [U] *formal* a well-organized and well-planned way of doing something: *There's no method in the way they do their accounts.*
3 there's method in/to sb's madness used to say that even though someone seems to be behaving strangely, there is a sensible reason for what they are doing

THESAURUS

method a way of doing something, especially one that is well known and often used: *You can choose whichever method of payment you prefer.* | *an environmentally friendly method for treating household waste*
way a set of actions that you use in order to do something. **Way** is more informal than **method** and is used more often in everyday English: *What's the best way to remove wine stains?* | *a new way of treating the disease*
means something that you use to do something or achieve something: *Their main* ***means of transport*** *is their car.* | *E-mail is often the most convenient* ***means of communication.***
approach a way of dealing with a particular problem or situation, especially a way that has been carefully thought about or planned: *Today's approach to raising children is very different from 40 years ago.*
technique a particular way of doing something, for which you need a skill that has to be learned and practised: *tips on how to improve your exam technique* | *More patients are surviving thanks to improved surgical techniques.*
tactics methods that you use in order to achieve what you want, especially in a game or competition: *There were complaints about police tactics used to clear demonstrators.* | *The team was discussing tactics for the game.*
strategy a set of carefully planned methods for achieving something that is difficult and may take a long time: *our sales strategy* | *a strategy to reduce the level of teenage smoking*
mode *formal* a particular way of doing something: *For him, painting is just another* ***mode of expression.*** | *You can choose between several different* ***modes of operation.***

me·thod·i·cal /məˈθɒdɪkəl $ -ˈθɑː-/ AWL *adj*
1 a methodical way of doing something is careful and uses an ordered system: *He always checked every detail in a methodical way.* | *a methodical approach to answering questions* THESAURUS▸ CAREFUL **2** a methodical person always does things carefully, using an ordered system: *She's a very methodical person.* | *He had a neat, methodical mind.* —**methodically** /-kli/ *adv*: *He went through the papers methodically, one by one.*

Meth·o·dist /ˈmeθədɪst/ *n* [C] someone who belongs to a Christian religious group that follows the ideas of John Wesley —**Methodist** *adj*: *a Methodist chapel* —**Methodism** *n* [U]

meth·o·dol·o·gy /ˌmeθəˈdɒlədʒi $ -ˈdɑː-/ ●○○ AWL *n* (*plural* **methodologies**) [C,U] the set of methods and principles that you use when studying a particular subject or doing a particular kind of work: **methodology for (doing) sth** *We've been developing a new methodology for assessing new products.* | *There are some differences in methodology between the two studies.* —**methodological** /ˌmeθədəˈlɒdʒɪkəl◂ $ -ˈlɑː-/ *adj*: *There are a few methodological issues we need to discuss.* —**methodologically** /-kli/ *adv*: *The study was methodologically flawed.*

me·thought /mɪˈθɔːt $ -ˈθɒːt/ *v* the past tense of METHINKS

meths /meθs/ *n* [U] *BrE informal* METHYLATED SPIRITS

Me·thu·se·lah /məˈθjuːzələ $ -ˈθuː-/ *n* **as old as Methuselah** very old

meth·yl al·co·hol /ˌmeθəl ˈælkəhɒl, ˌmiːθaɪl- $ -hɒːl/ *n* [U] *technical* a poisonous alcohol that can be made from wood SYN **methanol**

meth·yl·at·ed spir·its /ˌmeθəleɪtəd ˈspɪrəts/ *n* [U] a type of alcohol that is burned in lamps, heaters etc

me·tic·u·lous /məˈtɪkjələs/ *adj* very careful about small details, and always making sure that everything is done correctly: *He kept meticulous accounts.* | *Their planning and preparation were meticulous.* | *He cleaned the tools with meticulous care.* | *The book describes his journey in meticulous detail.* | **[+in]** *He was meticulous in his use of words.* | **[+about]** *He has always been so meticulous about his appearance.* THESAURUS▸ CAREFUL —**meticulously** *adv*: *The attack was meticulously planned and executed.*

met·i·er /ˈmetieɪ, ˈmeɪ- $ meˈtjeɪ, ˈmetjeɪ/ *n* [C usually singular] *formal* someone's metier is the type of work or activity that they enjoy doing because they have a natural ability to do it well: *Acting is not my metier.*

ˌme-ˈtoo *adj* [only before noun] *informal* a me-too product is one that a company begins to sell after it has seen that other companies are successful with the same type of product – used to show disapproval

me·tre *BrE*, **meter** *AmE* /ˈmiːtə $ -ər/ ●●● S2 W3 *n*
1 [C] (*written abbreviation* **m**) the basic unit for measuring length in the METRIC SYSTEM
2 [C,U] the arrangement of sounds in poetry into patterns of strong and weak beats → **rhythm**

-metre *BrE*, **-meter** *AmE* /miːtə, mɪtə $ -tər/ *suffix* [in nouns] part of a metre, or a number of metres: *a millimetre* | *a kilometer*

met·ric /ˈmetrɪk/ *adj* **1** using or connected with the METRIC SYSTEM of weights and measures → **imperial**: *a metric tonne* | *The parts all come in metric sizes now.* **2** metrical

met·ri·cal /ˈmetrɪkəl/ *adj technical* written in the form of poetry, with a pattern of strong and weak beats

met·ri·ca·tion /ˌmetrɪˈkeɪʃən/ *n* [U] the change to using the METRIC SYSTEM of weights and measures: *Most businesses are in favour of metrication.*

ˈmetric ˌsystem *n* **the metric system** the system of weights and measures that is based on the kilogram and the metre

ˌmetric ˈton *n* [C] a unit for measuring weight, equal to 1,000 kilograms

met·ro /ˈmetrəʊ $ -troʊ/ *n* (*plural* **metros**) [C] a railway system that runs under the ground below a city SYN **subway** *AmE*, **underground** *BrE*: *the Paris Metro* | *It'll be quicker to go on the metro.* | *a* ***metro station***

met·ro·nome /ˈmetrənəʊm $ -noʊm/ *n* [C] a piece of equipment that makes a regular repeated sound like a clock, showing the speed at which music should be played

me·trop·o·lis /mɪˈtrɒpəlɪs $ -ˈtrɑː-/ *n* [C] a very large city that is the most important city in a country or area: *The city has become a huge, bustling metropolis.*
THESAURUS ▸ CITY

met·ro·pol·i·tan /ˌmetrəˈpɒlətən◂ $ -ˈpɑː-/ *adj* [only before noun] **1** relating or belonging to a very large city: *a metropolitan area of South Australia* **2** *technical* relating to France, rather than its COLONIES: *metropolitan France*

ˌMetropolitan Poˈlice, the the police force that is responsible for the London area

met·ro·sex·u·al /ˌmetrəʊˈsekʃuəl $ -troʊ-/ *n* [C] *informal* a man who lives in a city and who spends a lot of time and money on his clothes and appearance. Although a metrosexual may not be GAY (=homosexual), his behaviour is similar to the way gay men are typically thought to behave.

met·tle /ˈmetl/ *n* [U] **1** courage and determination to do something even when it is very difficult: **test/show/prove your mettle** *a crisis which will test the minister's mettle* **2 on your mettle** *BrE* if you are on your mettle, you are ready to try as hard as possible because your abilities are being tested: *We'll have to be on our mettle from the start.* | **keep/put sb on their mettle** *This was just his way of keeping me on my mettle.*

met·tle·some /ˈmetlsəm/ *adj literary* full of energy and determination

mew /mjuː/ *v* [I] if a cat mews, it makes a soft high crying sound: *The cat mewed at me.* —**mew** *n* [C]

mews /mjuːz/ *n* [plural] *BrE* a small street or area surrounded by buildings in a city, where horses used to be kept, but where people now live

Mex·i·can¹ /ˈmeksɪkən/ *adj* relating to Mexico or its people: *the Mexican government* | *the Mexican border* | *Mexican food*

Mexican² *n* [C] someone from Mexico

ˌMexican ˈwave *n* [singular] *BrE* the effect that is made when all the people watching a sport stand up, move their arms up and down, and sit down again one after the other in a continuous movement that looks like a wave moving on the sea

mez·za·nine /ˈmezəniːn, ˈmetsə- $ ˈmezə-/ *n* [C] **1** a small floor that is built between two other floors in a building: *the mezzanine floor* **2** *AmE* the lowest BALCONY in a theatre, or the first few rows of seats in that balcony

mez·zo /ˈmetsəʊ $ -oʊ/ *adv* **mezzo forte/piano etc** *technical* not too loudly, softly etc – used in instructions for performing music

ˌmezzo-soˈprano (*also* **mezzo**) *n* [C] a female singing voice that is lower than a SOPRANO but higher than an ALTO, or a woman with a voice like this

mez·zo·tint /ˈmetsəʊˌtɪnt, ˈmedzəʊ- $ -oʊ-/ *n* [C,U] a picture printed from a metal plate that is polished in places to produce areas of light and shade

MFA /ˌem ef ˈeɪ/ *n* [C] *AmE* (***Master of Fine Arts***) a university DEGREE in a subject such as painting or drawing

mg (*plural* **mg** *or* **mgs**) the written abbreviation of ***milligram*** or ***milligrams***

MHz the written abbreviation of ***megahertz***

mi /miː/ *n* [U] the third note in a musical SCALE according to the SOL-FA system

MI5 /ˌem aɪ ˈfaɪv/ *n* a secret British government organization whose job is to keep Britain safe from attack by enemies inside the country, such as foreign SPIES or TERRORISTS: *a government agent working for MI5*

MI6 /ˌem aɪ ˈsɪks/ *n* a secret British government organization that sends people to foreign countries to try and find out secret political and military information: *He used to work for MI6.* | *the head of MI6*

MIA /ˌem aɪ ˈeɪ/ *n* [C] *AmE* (***missing in action***) a soldier who has disappeared in a battle and who may still be alive: *There are still more than 500 MIAs.*

mi·aow *BrE*, **meow** *AmE* /miˈaʊ/ *v* [I] if a cat miaows, it makes a crying sound —**miaow** *n* [C]: *The cat jumped away with a loud miaow.*

mi·as·ma /miˈæzmə, maɪ-/ *n* [singular] *literary* **1** dirty air or a thick unpleasant mist that smells bad: *He looked up at me through a miasma of cigarette smoke.* | *A foul miasma lay over the town.* **2** an evil influence or feeling that seems to surround a person or place: **[+of]** *The miasma of defeat hung over them.*

mi·ca /ˈmaɪkə/ *n* [U] a mineral that separates easily into small flat transparent pieces of rock, often used to make electrical instruments

mice /maɪs/ *n* the plural of MOUSE

Mich·ael·mas /ˈmɪkəlməs/ *n* [C,U] 29th September, a Christian holy day in honour of Saint Michael

Mick /mɪk/ *n* [C] *taboo* an offensive word for someone from Ireland. Do not use this word.

mick·ey /ˈmɪki/ *n* **take the mickey (out of sb)** *BrE informal* to make someone look silly, often in a friendly way, for example by copying them or by pretending something is true when it is not: *He's always taking the mickey out of me.*

ˌMickey ˈMouse *adj informal* small and not at all important: *The charity has been described as a Mickey Mouse operation.* | *a Mickey Mouse job*

mi·cro /ˈmaɪkrəʊ $ -kroʊ/ *n* (*plural* **micros**) [C] a small computer

micro- /maɪkrəʊ, -krə $ -kroʊ, -krə/ *prefix* [in nouns, adjectives, and adverbs] extremely small → **macro-**, **mini-**: *microelectronics* | *a micro-organism*

mi·crobe /ˈmaɪkrəʊb $ -kroʊb/ *n* [C] an extremely small living thing which you can only see if you use a MICROSCOPE. Some microbes can cause diseases.

mi·cro·bi·ol·o·gy /ˌmaɪkrəʊbaɪˈɒlədʒi $ -kroʊbaɪˈɑːl-/ *n* [U] the scientific study of very small living things such as BACTERIA —**microbiologist** *n* [C] —**microbiological** /ˌmaɪkrəʊbaɪəˈlɒdʒɪkəl $ -kroʊbaɪəˈlɑː-/ *adj*: *a microbiological examination of the fibres found near the body*

mi·cro·blog·ging /ˈmaɪkrəʊˌblɒɡɪŋ $ -kroʊˌblɑː-/ *n* [U] the activity of sending short messages about what you are doing using a SOCIAL NETWORKING service SYN **miniblogging**

mi·cro·brew /ˈmaɪkrəʊˌbruː $ -kroʊ-/ *n* [C] a type of beer that is only produced in small quantities

mi·cro·brew·e·ry /ˈmaɪkrəʊˌbruːəri $ -kroʊ-/ *n* (*plural* **microbreweries**) [C] a small company that makes only a small amount of beer to sell, and often has a restaurant where the beer is served

mi·cro·chip¹ /ˈmaɪkrəʊˌtʃɪp $ -kroʊ-/ (*also* **chip**) *n* [C] a very small piece of SILICON containing a set of electronic parts, which is used in computers and other machines: *Japan's largest producer of microchips* | *the microchip industry*

microchip² *v* (**microchipped**, **microchipping**) [T] to put a microchip in an animal, person, or thing to give information about them SYN **chip**

mi·cro·cli·mate /ˈmaɪkrəʊˌklaɪmət $ -kroʊ-/ *n* [C] the weather patterns in one small area, which are different from the weather patterns in the surrounding area: *The valley has its own unique microclimate.*

mi·cro·com·put·er /ˈmaɪkrəʊkəmˌpjuːtə $ -kroʊkəmˌpjuːtər/ *n* [C] a small computer

mi·cro·cos·m /ˈmaɪkrəʊkɒzəm $ -kroʊkɑː-/ *n* [C] a small group, society, or place that has the same qualities as a much larger one → **macrocosm**: **[+of]** *New York's mix of people is a microcosm of America.* | **in microcosm** *All the problems of society can be seen here in microcosm.* —**microcosmic** /ˌmaɪkrəʊˈkɒzmɪk $ -kroʊˈkɑːz-/ *adj*: *the forces which we see at work on a microcosmic scale*

mi·cro·cred·it /ˈmaɪkrəʊˌkredɪt $ ˈmaɪkroʊ-/ *n* [U] small amounts of money that are lent to people in poor countries to help them start a small business

mi·cro·der·ma·bra·sion /ˌmaɪkrəʊˌdɜːməˈbreɪʒən $ -kroʊˌdɜːr-/ *n* [U] a treatment that makes the skin on your face smoother and more attractive, in which a substance that removes dead skin cells is forced out of a container onto your face → **dermabrasion**

mi·cro·dot /ˈmaɪkrəʊdɒt $ -kroʊdɑːt/ *n* [C] a secret

M

photograph of something such as a document which is reduced to a very small size so that it can easily be hidden

mi·cro·ec·o·nom·ics /ˌmaɪkrəʊekəˈnɒmɪks, -iːkə- $ -kroʊekəˈnɑː-, -iːkə-/ *n* [U] the study of small economic systems that are part of national or international systems → **macroeconomics** —**microeconomic** *adj*

mi·cro·e·lec·tron·ics /ˌmaɪkrəʊɪlekˈtrɒnɪks $ -kroʊɪlekˈtrɑː-/ *n* [U] the practice or study of designing very small electrical CIRCUITS that are used in computers: *the latest developments in microelectronics* —**microelectronic** *adj*: *a new system that has been developed using microelectronic technology*

mi·cro·en·gi·neer·ing /ˌmaɪkrəʊendʒəˈnɪərɪŋ $ -kroʊendʒəˈnɪr-/ *n* [U] the activity of designing structures and machines that are extremely small —**microengineer** *n* [C]

mi·cro·fiche /ˈmaɪkrəʊfiːʃ $ -kroʊ-/ *n* [C,U] a sheet of microfilm which can only be read using a special machine, especially in a library: **on microfiche** *Details of all members are now available on microfiche.*

mi·cro·film /ˈmaɪkrəʊfɪlm $ -kroʊ-/ *n* [C,U] a type of film on which pictures and writing can be made very small, so that large amounts can be stored easily: **on microfilm** *Most of the daily newspapers are available on microfilm.*

mi·cro·fi·nance /ˈmaɪkrəʊˌfaɪnæns $ -kroʊfəˌnæns/ *n* [U] a system that allows people in poor countries to borrow small amounts of money to help them start a small business

mi·cro·gen·e·ra·tion /ˌmaɪkrəʊdʒenəˈreɪʃən $ -kroʊ-/ *n* [U] a process in which a person, group, or small organization produces heat or energy for their own use

mi·cro·light /ˈmaɪkrəʊlaɪt $ -kroʊ-/ *n* [C] a very light small plane for one or two people

mi·cro·man·age /ˈmaɪkrəʊˌmænɪdʒ $ -kroʊ-/ *v* [T] to organize and control all the details of another person's work in a way that they think is annoying —**micromanagement** *n* [U]

mi·crom·e·ter /maɪˈkrɒmɪtə $ -ˈkrɑːmɪtər/ *n* [C] an instrument for measuring very small distances

mi·crom·e·tre *BrE*, **micrometer** *AmE* /ˈmaɪkrəʊˌmiːtə $ -kroʊˌmiːtər/ (*also* **mi·cron** /ˈmaɪkrɒn $ -krɑːn/) *n* [C] a unit for measuring length. There are one million micrometres in one metre.

mi·cro·or·gan·is·m /ˌmaɪkrəʊˈɔːgənɪzəm $ -kroʊˈɔːr-/ *n* [C] a living thing that is so small that it cannot be seen without a MICROSCOPE

mic·ro·pay·ment /ˈmaɪkrəʊˌpeɪmənt $ -kroʊ-/ *n* [C] a small amount of money that you have to pay in order to look at the pages on some websites

MICROPHONE

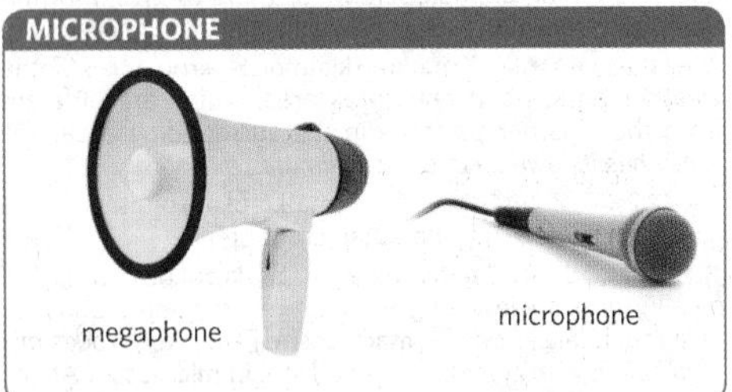

mi·cro·phone /ˈmaɪkrəfəʊn $ -foʊn/ ●●○ *n* [C] a piece of equipment that you speak into to record your voice or make it louder when you are speaking or performing in public: *She spoke confidently into the microphone.* | *They searched the room for hidden microphones.*

mi·cro·pow·er /ˈmaɪkrəʊˌpaʊə $ -paʊr/ *n* [U] electricity that is produced close to the place where it is needed

mi·cro·pro·ces·sor /ˈmaɪkrəʊˌprəʊsesə $ -kroʊˌprɑːsesər/ *n* [C] the central CHIP in a computer, which controls most of its operations

ˈmicro ˌscooter *n* [C] a vehicle like a child's SCOOTER, but smaller and lighter. It is used as a toy, and also by adults, especially as a way of travelling short distances.

MICROSCOPE

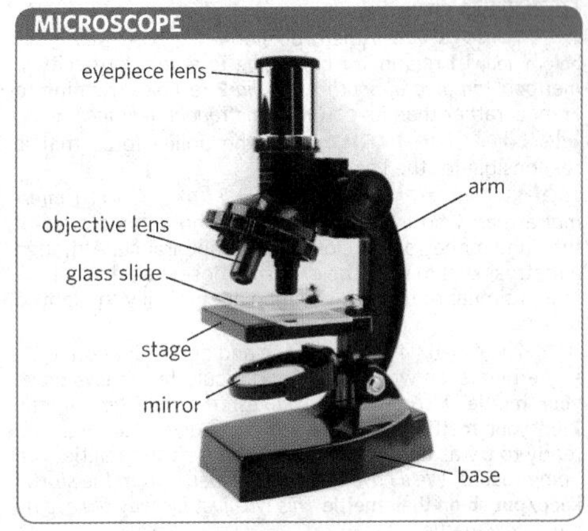

mi·cro·scope /ˈmaɪkrəskəʊp $ -skoʊp/ ●○○ *n* [C]
1 a scientific instrument that makes extremely small things look larger: **under/through a microscope** *Abnormalities in the cells can be seen quite clearly under a microscope.* | *Each sample was examined through a microscope.*
2 put sth under the microscope to examine a situation very closely and carefully: *Our prison system is being put under the microscope after an alarming number of suicides.*

mi·cro·scop·ic /ˌmaɪkrəˈskɒpɪk◂ $ -ˈskɑː-/ *adj*
1 extremely small and therefore very difficult to see: *a microscopic speck of dust* | *Inspectors discovered microscopic cracks in the hull of the submarine.* THESAURUS SMALL
2 [only before noun] using a microscope: *The cells were identified through microscopic analysis.* —**microscopically** /-kli/ *adv*: *The seeds are microscopically small.*

mi·cro·sec·ond /ˈmaɪkrəʊˌsekənd $ -kroʊ-/ *n* [C] one millionth of a second

mi·cro·site /ˈmaɪkrəʊsaɪt $ -kroʊ-/ (*also* **minisite**) *n* [C] a WEBPAGE that is separate from but connected to a website's home page, with a completely different Internet address. It typically gives extra information about the website or advertises a product or service related to the website.

mi·cro·sur·ge·ry /ˈmaɪkrəʊˌsɜːdʒəri $ -kroʊˌsɜːr-/ *n* [U] medical treatment in which a part of someone's body is repaired or removed using very small instruments or LASERS

mi·cro·wave¹ /ˈmaɪkrəweɪv/ ●●● S2 *n* [C]
1 (*also* **ˌmicrowave ˈoven**) a type of OVEN that cooks food very quickly using very short electric waves instead of heat: *I'll heat it up in the microwave.*
2 a very short electric wave that is used in cooking food and sending messages by radio, and in RADAR

microwave² *v* [T] to cook something in a microwave oven: *You can heat it up under the grill or microwave it.* THESAURUS COOK —**microwaveable**, **microwavable** *adj*: *a new range of microwavable snacks*

mid /mɪd/ *prep literary* among or in the middle of

mid- /mɪd/ *prefix* middle: *a young woman in her mid-twenties* | *The mid-sixties were a turning point in sports car design.* | *in mid-July* | *He stopped mid-sentence.* | **mid-morning/afternoon/week etc**

MID the abbreviation of ***mobile Internet device***

mid·air /ˌmɪdˈeə◂ $ -ˈer◂/ *n* **in midair** in the air or the sky, away from the ground: *The planes collided in midair.* —**midair** *adj* [only before noun]: *a midair collision*

Mi·das touch /ˈmaɪdəs ˌtʌtʃ/ *n* **the Midas touch** if someone has the Midas touch, everything they do is successful and makes money for them: *a talented young businessman with the Midas touch*

ˌmid-Atˈlantic *adj* **1 mid-Atlantic accent** a way of speaking that uses a mixture of American and British English sounds and words: *She spoke in a soft mid-Atlantic accent.*
2 mid-Atlantic states/region the US states that are on the Atlantic coast, approximately between New Jersey and Maryland

mid·day /ˌmɪdˈdeɪ◂ $ ˈmɪd-deɪ/ ●●○ *n* [U] the middle of the day, at or around 12 o'clock → **midnight**: **at/around/by etc midday** *I'm meeting him at midday.* | *I got there around midday.* | *By midday it had begun to warm up.* | *We stopped off in Colchester for our* ***midday meal.*** | *the full heat of the* ***midday sun***

mid·den /ˈmɪdn/ *n* [C] *old use* a pile of animal waste or things such as food that have been thrown away

mid·dle[1] /ˈmɪdl/ ●●● (S1) (W2) *n*
1 CENTRE PART **the middle** the part that is nearest the centre of something, and furthest from the sides, edges, top, bottom etc: **[+of]** *We rowed out towards the middle of the lake.* | **in the middle (of sth)** *Jo was standing in the middle of the room.* | *Those are my two brothers, and that's me in the middle.* | *The meat was burnt on the outside and raw in the middle.* | *a huge hole* ***right in the middle*** *of the lawn* | **through the middle (of sth)** *The new road will go* ***right through the middle*** *of the wood.* | **down the middle (of sth)** *Draw a line down the middle of the page.*
2 TIME/EVENT **the middle** the part of an event or period of time that is between the beginning and the end: **[+of]** *events which took place around the middle of the last century* | **in the middle (of sth)** *I'm going to stay with some friends in the middle of May.* | *He gets killed in the middle of the film.* | **the middle of the night/day** *I got a phone call from her in the middle of the night!* | **the middle of the week/month/year etc** *Everything should be sorted out by the middle of next year.*
3 SCALE/RANGE **the middle** the level or position that is between two extreme positions, for example between the best and the worst: *There are plenty of small houses for sale, and quite a lot of very large ones, but very little in the middle.* | **[+of]** *In tests, I always seem to finish around the middle of the class.*
4 BODY [C usually singular] the part of your body around your waist and stomach: **sb's middle** *He was holding a towel around his middle.*
5 be in the middle of (doing) sth to be busy doing something: *Can I call you back – I'm in the middle of a meeting.* | *I was in the middle of sorting some papers when the phone rang.*
6 in the middle of sth if you are in the middle of something, it is happening to you or around you: *At that time Britain was in the middle of a recession.* | *The company is in the middle of a takeover battle.*
7 in the middle of nowhere a long way from the nearest big town: *They live miles away, in the middle of nowhere.*
8 divide/split sth down the middle to divide something into equal halves or groups: *We put all the money together and then split it down the middle.* | *The voters are split down the middle on this issue.* → **piggy in the middle** at PIGGY[1](2)

middle[2] ●●● (S1) (W2) *adj* [only before noun]
1 CENTRE nearest the centre and furthest from the edge, top, end etc: *driving in the middle lane of the motorway* | *the middle drawer of the filing cabinet*
2 TIME/EVENT half of the way through an event or period of time: *They spent the middle part of their vacation in Florida.* | *the middle part of the day*
3 SCALE/RANGE between two extreme levels or positions, for example between the best and worst, the biggest and smallest etc: *a car in the middle price range* | *the middle ranks of the army* | *a middle-income family*
4 in your middle twenties/thirties etc about 25, 35 etc years old
5 middle brother/child/daughter etc the brother etc who is between the oldest and the youngest
6 middle course/way etc a way of dealing with something that is between two opposite and often extreme ways: **[+between]** *The party is seeking to find a middle way between extreme right-wing and left-wing policies.* | *I try to* ***steer a middle course*** *between keeping control of the project and giving responsibility to others.*
7 Middle English/French etc an old form of English, French etc, used in the Middle Ages (=between 1100 and 1500 AD)

ˌmiddle ˈage ●●○ *n* [U] the period of your life between the ages of about 40 and 60, when you are no longer young but are not yet old: *Men who smoke are more likely to have heart attacks in middle age.*

ˌmiddle-ˈaged ●●○ *adj*
1 between the ages of about 40 and 60: *a middle-aged businessman*
2 someone who seems middle-aged seems rather dull and does not do exciting or dangerous things: *Living with Henry had made her feel middle-aged.*
3 middle-aged spread fat that many people develop around their waist as they grow older

ˌMiddle ˈAges *n* **the Middle Ages** the period in European history between about 1100 and 1500 AD

ˌMiddle Aˈmerica *n* [U] **1** the middle part of the United States, which is not on the east or west coasts **2** Americans who are neither very rich nor very poor and who have traditional ideas and beliefs

mid·dle·brow /ˈmɪdlbraʊ/ *adj* middlebrow books, television programmes etc are of fairly good quality but are not very difficult to understand → **highbrow**, **lowbrow**

ˌmiddle ˈC *n* [U] the musical note C, which is the middle note on a piano

ˌmiddle ˈclass ●●○ *n* [singular] (*also* **middle classes**) the social class that includes people who are educated and work in professional jobs, for example teachers or managers → **lower class**, **upper class**, **working class**: *This led to the creation of a new, affluent middle class.* | *Home ownership was once a privilege of the middle classes.*

GRAMMAR: Singular or plural verb?

- **Middle class** is usually followed by a singular verb: *Brazil's middle class* ***has*** *grown in number.*
- In British English, you can also use a plural verb: *Brazil's middle class* ***have*** *grown in number.*

GRAMMAR GUIDE ▸ NOUNS

ˌmiddle-ˈclass ●●○ *adj*
1 typical of people who are educated and work in professional jobs: *a middle-class family* | *They lived a comfortable middle-class life.*
2 middle-class attitudes and ideas are typical of middle-class people and are often concerned with the idea that people should work hard, have a good education, and try to earn enough money to live a comfortable life

ˌmiddle ˈdistance *n* **the middle distance** the part of a picture or view that is between the nearest part and the part that is furthest away: *She just stood there gazing into the middle distance.*

ˈmiddle-ˌdistance *adj* [only before noun] a middle-distance race is neither very short nor very long, for example 800 or 1,500 metres

ˌmiddle ˈear *n* [singular] the part just inside your ear → **inner ear**

ˌMiddle ˈEast *n* **the Middle East** the area that includes Iran and Egypt and the countries which are between them → **Far East** —**Middle Eastern** *adj*

ˌMiddle ˈEngland *n* [U] ordinary English people, who are neither very poor nor very rich, who are usually fairly CONSERVATIVE (=traditional and perhaps rather old-fashioned) in their way of life and opinions, and who usually live outside London

ˌmiddle ˈfinger *n* [C] the longest finger on your hand → see picture at HAND[1]

ˌmiddle ˈground *n* [U] ideas that are not extreme, and that people who oppose each other can agree about: *The negotiators could find no middle ground.*

mid·dle·man /ˈmɪdlmæn/ *n* (*plural* **middlemen** /-men/) [C] someone who buys things in order to sell them to someone else, or who helps to arrange business deals for

M

other people: *He acts as a middleman for British companies seeking contracts in the Gulf.* | *Buy direct from the manufacturer and* **cut out the middleman** (=avoid using a middleman).

ˌmiddle ˈmanagement *n* [U] managers who are in charge of small groups of people, but do not take important decisions that affect the whole organization —**middle manager** *n* [C]

ˌmiddle ˈname ●●○ *n* [C]
1 the name that is between your first name and your family name
2 sth is sb's middle name *informal* used to say that someone has a personal quality very strongly: *Don't worry – discretion is my middle name.*

ˌmiddle-of-the-ˈroad *adj* **1** middle-of-the-road ideas or opinions are not extreme, and so most people are likely to agree with them: *a party offering safe, middle-of-the-road policies* **2** middle-of-the-road voters or politicians have ideas that are not extreme **3** *informal* ordinary and not new, different, or exciting: *Their first album was quite good, but the second was very middle-of-the-road stuff.*

ˌmiddle-ˈranking *adj* having a responsible job or position, but not among the most important people in a company: *middle-ranking officers and bureaucrats*

ˈmiddle school *n* [C,U] **1** a school in Britain for children between the ages of 8 and 12 **2** a school in the US for children between the ages of 11 and 14

ˌmiddle-ˈsized *adj* neither very large nor very small: *a middle-sized company*

mid·dle·ware /ˈmɪdl-weə $ -wer/ *n* [U] software that makes it possible for different programs to work together

mid·dle·weight /ˈmɪdlweɪt/ *n* [C] a BOXER who weighs less than 72.58 kilograms, and who is heavier than a WELTERWEIGHT but lighter than a LIGHT HEAVYWEIGHT

ˌMiddle ˈWest *n* **the Middle West** another form of the MIDWEST

mid·dling /ˈmɪdlɪŋ/ *adj informal* of average size, quality, ability etc: *a tennis player of middling talent*

mid·field /ˈmɪdfiːld/ *n* [U] **1** the middle part of the area where a game such as football is played: *He plays in midfield.* | *an excellent midfield player* **2** the members of a football team who play in the midfield: *The midfield did very well in the first half.*

mid·field·er /ˈmɪdfiːldə $ -ər/ *n* [C] a player in a game of football who usually plays in midfield

midge /mɪdʒ/ *n* [C] a small flying insect that can bite people

midg·et¹ /ˈmɪdʒɪt/ *n* [C] **1** *taboo* a very offensive word for someone who is very short because their body has not grown normally. Do not use this word. → **dwarf** **2** *BrE informal* someone who is not very tall

midget² *adj* [only before noun] very small: *a midget submarine*

mid·i /ˈmɪdi/ *adj* **midi skirt/dress/coat** a skirt, dress etc that comes to the middle of the lower leg → **mini** —**midi** *n* [C]

MIDI /ˈmɪdi/ *n* [U] *technical* (***musical instrument digital interface***) a system that allows computers to communicate with electronic musical instruments

Mid·lands /ˈmɪdləndz/ *n* **the Midlands** the central part of England —**Midland** *adj* —**Midlander** *n* [C]

mid·life cri·sis (*also* **mid-life crisis**) /ˌmɪdlaɪf ˈkraɪsɪs/ *n* [C] a period of worry and lack of confidence that some people experience when they are about 40 or 50 years old and begin to feel that they are getting old

mid·night /ˈmɪdnaɪt/ ●●● S3 *n* [U] 12 o'clock at night → **midday**: **at midnight** *The train is due in at midnight.* | **after/before midnight** *We stayed there until way after midnight.* | *You can't phone her now – it's* **gone midnight** (=after midnight)! | *By the time he arrived, it was well* **past midnight** (=after midnight). | **at/on the stroke of midnight** (=at exactly midnight) *The treaty will come into force on the stroke of midnight tonight.* | *He's gone for a midnight swim.* ⚠ Don't say 'in the midnight'. If you mean 'at 12 o'clock at night' say **at midnight** and if you mean 'very late at night' say **in the middle of the night**. → **burn the midnight oil** at BURN¹(20)

ˌmidnight ˈblue *n* [U] a very dark blue colour —**midnight blue** *adj*

ˌmidnight ˈsun *n* **the midnight sun** the sun that you can see in the middle of the night in summer in the far north or south of the world

mid·point /ˈmɪdpɔɪnt/ *n* [C usually singular] a point that is half of the way through or along something: **[+of]** *At the midpoint of the study, all those taking part were interviewed again.*

ˈmid-range *adj* [only before noun] mid-range products and services are not the most expensive or the cheapest → **top-of-the-range**

mid·riff /ˈmɪdrɪf/ *n* [C] the part of the body between your chest and your waist

mid·sec·tion /ˈmɪdˌsekʃən/ *n* [C usually singular] the middle part of something or of someone's body: *There are 24 missiles in the submarine's midsection.*

mid·ship·man /ˈmɪdʃɪpmən/ *n* (*plural* **midshipmen** /-mən/) [C] someone who is training to become an officer in the British navy

midst¹ /mɪdst/ ●○○ *n*
1 in the midst of sth a) if you are in the midst of an event or situation, it is happening around you: *The government is in the midst of a major crisis.* **b)** in the middle of a place or a group of things or people: *We were sitting in the midst of an elegant and well-dressed audience.*
2 in our/their midst *formal* in a particular group: *I fear we have an enemy in our midst.*

midst² *prep old use* surrounded by people or things

mid·stream /ˌmɪdˈstriːm◂/ *n* [U] **1 in midstream** when something has started and is still happening: *They had to drop the experiment in midstream.* | *He interrupted the official in midstream* (=while the official was still speaking). **2** the middle part of a river: **in midstream** *The boat had anchored in midstream.* —**midstream** *adv*

mid·sum·mer /ˌmɪdˈsʌmə◂ $ -ər◂/ *n* [U] the middle of summer: *a perfect midsummer afternoon*

ˌMidsummer ˈDay (*also* **ˌMidsummer's ˈDay**) *n* [C,U] *BrE* the 24th of June

mid·term¹ /ˌmɪdˈtɜːm $ -ˈtɜːrm/ *n* **1** [U] the middle period of an elected government's time in power **2** [C] *AmE* a test that students take in the middle of a SEMESTER or QUARTER **THESAURUS** ▸ **TEST**

mid·term² /ˈmɪdtɜːm $ -tɜːrm/ *adj* [only before noun] **1** in the middle of an elected government's time in power: *midterm elections* **2** *AmE* in the middle of a SEMESTER or QUARTER → **half-term**: *midterm tests*

mid·town /ˌmɪdˈtaʊn◂/ *adj, adv AmE* in the area of a city that is quite near the centre but is not the main business area → **downtown**, **uptown** —**midtown** *n* [U]

mid·way /ˌmɪdˈweɪ◂ $ ˈmɪdweɪ/ ●○○ *adj, adv*
1 between two places, and the same distance from each of them SYN **halfway**: **[+between]** *The city is midway between Edinburgh and London.*
2 when half a period of time has passed SYN **halfway**: **[+through]** *Leeds scored midway through the first half.*

mid·week /ˌmɪdˈwiːk◂ $ ˈmɪdwiːk/ *adj, adv* on one of the middle days of the week: *There are often discounts available for midweek travel.* —**midweek** *n* [U]: *The match will be played in midweek.*

Mid·west /ˌmɪdˈwest/ *n* **the Midwest** the central area of the United States —**Midwestern** *adj*

mid·wife /ˈmɪdwaɪf/ ●○○ *n* (*plural* **midwives** /-waɪvz/) [C] a specially trained nurse whose job is to help women when they are having a baby

mid·wif·e·ry /ˈmɪdˌwɪfəri $ -ˌwaɪfəri/ *n* [U] the skill or work of a midwife

mid·win·ter /ˌmɪdˈwɪntə◂ $ -ər/ *n* [U] the middle of winter: *The mountains look beautiful in midwinter.*

mid·year /ˈmɪdjɪə $ -jɪr/ *n* [U] the middle of the year:

Sales had improved by midyear. —**midyear** *adj* [only before noun]: *a midyear review*

mien /miːn/ *n* [singular] *literary* a person's typical expression or appearance: *her sorrowful mien*

miffed /mɪft/ *adj spoken* slightly annoyed or upset: *I felt a bit miffed that no one had told me about the trip.*

might¹ /maɪt/ ●●● S1 W1 *modal verb* (*negative short form* **mightn't**)

1 POSSIBILITY a) if something might happen or might be true, there is a possibility that it may happen or may be true, but you are not at all certain: *I might be a few minutes late.* | *She might not want to come with us.* | *He might have missed the train.* | *This* **might well** *be her last public performance* (=it is fairly likely). | *One of the guards* **might easily** *panic and shoot someone* (=it is likely). **b)** used as the past tense of 'may' when reporting that someone talked or thought about the possibility of something: *He might be able to help you.* | *I thought they might have gone home.* | *She was worried that we might get hurt.* **c)** used to say that something was a possibility in the past but did not actually happen: *It was terrifying. We might have been killed.*

2 SUGGESTING used to suggest politely what someone should do: *If you need more information, you might try the Internet.* | *I thought we might go to the new Chinese restaurant on the High Street.* | *It might be a good idea to put those plants in the shade.* | *We're going to a concert. You might like to come with us.*

3 ASKING PERMISSION a) *spoken especially BrE* used to politely ask for permission to do something: *Might I borrow your pen?* | *I wonder if I might speak to your son.* **b)** used when reporting that someone asked for permission to do something: *He asked if he might come in and look around.*

4 SB SHOULD HAVE DONE STH used when you are annoyed because someone has not done something that you think they should do: *You might at least say thank you.* | *They might have cleaned up before they left.*

5 PAST PURPOSE used after 'so that' or 'in order that' to say that someone did something in order to make something else happen or be possible: *I asked for names and addresses so that I might pass on details to the police.*

6 might I say/ask/add etc *spoken especially BrE* used to politely give more information, ask a question, interrupt etc: *Might I ask how old you are?* | *Might I just say how lovely it is to see everyone here today.*

7 I might say/add *spoken* used to emphasize what you are saying: *I was, I might say, not surprised.*

8 I might have known/guessed etc *spoken* used to say that you are not surprised at a situation: *I might have known it was you!* | *I might have guessed I'd get no sympathy from my family.*

9 might (just) as well a) used to suggest that someone should do something, because there is no good reason to do anything else: *I suppose we might as well go home.* **b)** used to say that the effect of an action or situation is the same as if it was another one: *They might as well have a badge on them saying 'Steal me'.* | *He might as well have been a million miles away.*

10 ALTHOUGH used to say that even though something is perhaps true, something different or opposite is also true: *He might be nearly seventeen but he's still very immature.* | *Surprising as it might seem, some tourists actually enjoy the British weather.* | *Although she might understand his beliefs, she could not accept them.* | *Try as I might* (=although I tried hard), *I couldn't work out the answer.*

11 FORMAL QUESTION used to ask a question in a formal and rather unfriendly way: *And who might you be, young man?*

12 might well used to say that there is a good reason for a reaction, question, or feeling: *'What do they hope to achieve?' 'You* **might well ask**.' | *a system of which we in Britain might well be envious* | *This caused a few gasps,* **as well it might**.

might² ●○○ *n* [U]

1 great strength and power: *two individuals who took on the might of the English legal system* | *He swung the axe again* **with all** *his* **might**.

2 might is right *BrE*, **might makes right** *AmE* used to say that powerful people and countries are able to do whatever they want, especially when you disapprove of this

ˈmight-have-ˌbeens *n* [plural] things that you wish had happened in the past but which never did

might·i·ly /ˈmaɪtəli/ *adv* **1** very: *a mightily impressive piece of work* | *I was mightily relieved when we landed at Manchester airport.* **2** *literary* using great strength: *We laboured mightily to rebuild the walls.*

might·n't /ˈmaɪtənt/ *informal especially BrE* the short form of 'might not'

might·y¹ /ˈmaɪti/ ●●○ *adj* (*comparative* **mightier**, *superlative* **mightiest**) *literary* very strong and powerful, or very big and impressive: *the mighty Mississippi river* | *a mighty army* → **high and mighty** at HIGH¹(26)

mighty² *adv AmE informal* very: *You seem mighty sure of your facts.* | *They got out of there mighty fast, I can tell you.*

mi·graine /ˈmiːɡreɪn, ˈmaɪ- $ ˈmaɪ-/ *n* [C,U] an extremely bad headache, during which you feel sick and have pain behind your eyes: **have/get a migraine** *I won't be coming this evening – I've got a migraine.* | **bad/severe migraine** *He suffers from severe migraine.* **THESAURUS▸ HEADACHE**

mi·grant /ˈmaɪɡrənt/ ●○○ AWL *n* [C]

1 someone who goes to live in another area or country, especially in order to find work → **emigrant**, **immigrant**: **migrant worker/labourer** *A lot of factory work is done by migrant workers.* | **economic migrant** (=someone who goes to live in another country because they are likely to find a better job there)

2 a bird or animal that travels regularly from one part of the world to another

mi·grate /maɪˈɡreɪt $ ˈmaɪɡreɪt/ ●○○ AWL *v*

1 [I + from/to] if birds or animals migrate, they travel regularly from one part of the world to another → **migratory**

2 [I + from/to] if people migrate, they go to live in another area or country, especially in order to find work → **emigrate**

3 a) [I,T + from/to] to start using a different computer system, or to arrange for people to start using a different computer system **b)** [T + from/to] to move information or software from one computer system to another

mi·gra·tion /maɪˈɡreɪʃən/ ●○○ AWL *n* [C,U]

1 when large numbers of people go to live in another area or country, especially in order to find work

2 when birds or animals travel regularly from one part of the world to another

3 when people start using a different computer system, or information is moved to a different computer system

mi·gra·to·ry /maɪˈɡreɪtəri, ˈmaɪɡrətəri $ ˈmaɪɡrətɔːri/ AWL *adj* involved in or relating to migration: *migratory birds*

mike¹ /maɪk/ *n* [C] *informal* a MICROPHONE → **OPEN MIKE**

mike² *v*

mike sb ↔ **up** *phr v informal* to fix a MICROPHONE to someone so that their voice can be recorded or made louder

mi·la·dy /mɪˈleɪdi/ *n* another spelling of M'LADY

milch cow /ˈmɪltʃ kaʊ/ *n* [C] **1** something that provides a lot of money for something else: *Farmers in western Canada see themselves as a milch cow for the Eastern establishment.* **2** a cow that is used to provide milk

mild¹ /maɪld/ ●●○ *adj* (*comparative* **milder**, *superlative* **mildest**)

1 WEATHER fairly warm OPP **cold**: *We had an exceptionally mild winter last year.* | *a mild climate*

2 ILLNESS a mild illness or health problem is not serious: *He suffered a mild heart attack.* | *Sometimes the symptoms can be quite mild.* | *a* **mild case** *of food poisoning* | *a* **mild form** *of diabetes*

3 FEELINGS a mild feeling is not very strong: *Both men looked at her in mild surprise.* | *a feeling of mild irritation*
4 FOOD/TASTE not very strong or hot-tasting: *a mild curry* | *a cheese with a pleasant* ***mild flavour*** THESAURUS TASTE
5 CRITICISM a mild criticism does not criticize strongly
6 PROBLEMS/SITUATIONS not serious enough to cause much suffering: *The recession in Germany has been comparatively mild.* | *a mild setback*
7 PEOPLE a mild person has a gentle character and does not easily get angry: *a mild, well-mannered man* | *His voice was soft and mild.*
8 DRUGS/CHEMICALS a mild drug or chemical does not have a very strong effect: *a mild painkiller* | *a mild herbicide*
9 SOAP ETC soft and gentle to your skin: *a mild shampoo*
10 LANGUAGE mild words or language are not very rude or offensive: *I heard him mutter a mild swear word.* → MILDLY —**mildness** *n* [U]

mild² *n* [U] *BrE* dark beer with a slightly sweet taste → **bitter**

mil·dew /ˈmɪldjuː $ -duː/ *n* [U] a white or grey substance that grows on walls or other surfaces in wet, slightly warm conditions —**mildewed** *adj*

mild·ly /ˈmaɪldli/ ●○○ *adv*
1 slightly: *The drug is only mildly addictive.* | *I felt mildly depressed.*
2 to put it mildly *spoken* used to say that you could use much stronger words to describe something: *Losing two members of staff was unfortunate, to put it mildly.*
3 in a gentle way without being angry: *'Of course I don't mind,' she answered mildly.*

ˌmild-ˈmannered *adj* gentle and polite

mile /maɪl/ ●●● S1 W1 *n* [C]
1 (*written abbreviation* **m**) a unit for measuring distance, equal to 1,760 YARDS or about 1,609 metres: *It's forty miles from here to the Polish border.* | *an area 50 miles wide and 150 miles long* | *We walked about* ***half a mile****.* | *He was driving at 70* ***miles per hour****.*
2 the mile a race that is a mile in length: *the first man to run the mile in under four minutes*
3 miles *informal* a very long distance: **[+from]** *We were miles from home, and very tired.* | **[+away]** *You can't go to Portsmouth, it's miles away.* | **for miles** *You can* ***see for miles*** *from here.* | *They lived in a little cottage* ***miles from anywhere*** (=a long way from the nearest town).
4 go the extra mile to try a little harder in order to achieve something, after you have already used a lot of effort: *The president expressed his determination to go the extra mile for peace.*
5 stick out/stand out a mile *informal* to be very easy to see or notice: *It sticks out a mile that you're new here.*
6 can see/spot/tell sth a mile off *informal* if you can see something a mile off, it is very easy to notice: *You can tell a mile off that he likes you.*
7 be miles away *spoken* to not be paying attention to anything that is happening around you: *'Kate!' 'Sorry, I was miles away!'*
8 miles older/better/too difficult etc *BrE informal* very much older, better, too difficult etc SYN **loads**: *The second film's miles better.*
9 by a mile *informal* by a very large amount: *He was the best player on the pitch by a mile.*
10 miles out *BrE informal* a measurement, guess, or calculation that is miles out is completely wrong
11 join the mile high club *informal* to have sex in a plane → NAUTICAL MILE, → **run a mile** at RUN¹(38)

mile·age /ˈmaɪlɪdʒ/ *n* **1** [C usually singular, U] the number of miles a vehicle has travelled since it was made: *Always check the mileage before you buy a secondhand car.* **2** [C usually singular, U] the number of miles someone travels in a vehicle in a particular period of time: *Look for a car hire agreement that offers unlimited mileage.* **3** [C usually singular, U] the number of miles a vehicle can travel using a particular amount of FUEL: *The car's average mileage is 22.73 miles per gallon.* **4** [U] the amount of use or advantage you get from something: *The newspapers wanted to get as much mileage from the story as they could.* **5** [C usually singular, U] (*also* **mileage allowance**) an amount of money that is paid to someone for each mile that they travel when they use their own car for work: *Community nurses are paid a mileage allowance.* **6** [U] the number of miles covered by a country's roads or railways: *plans to treble the country's railway mileage*

mile·om·e·ter, **milometer** /maɪˈlɒmɪtə $ -ˈlɑːmɪtər/ *n* [C] *BrE* an instrument in a car that shows how many miles it has travelled SYN **odometer** *AmE* → see picture at CAR

mile·post /ˈmaɪlpəʊst $ -poʊst/ *n* [C] *AmE* **1** a post next to a road or railway that shows the distance in miles to the next town **2** a MILESTONE(1)

mil·er /ˈmaɪlə $ -ər/ *n* [C] a person or horse that competes in races one mile long

mile·stone /ˈmaɪlstəʊn $ -stoʊn/ ●○○ *n* [C]
1 a very important event in the development of something SYN **milepost** *AmE*: **[+in]** *an important milestone in South African history* | *The treatment of diabetes* ***reached*** *a significant* ***milestone*** *in the 1970s.*
2 a stone next to a road that shows the distance in miles to the next town

mi·lieu /ˈmiːljɜː $ miːˈljɜː, -ˈljuː/ *n* (*plural* **milieux** /-ljɜːz, -ljɜː $ -ˈljɜːz, -ˈljuːz, -ˈljɜː, -ˈljuː/ *or* **milieus**) [C] *formal* the things and people that surround you and influence the way you live and think: *Proust's work reflected his own social and cultural milieu.* | *She never felt happy in a student milieu.*

mil·i·tant /ˈmɪlɪtənt/ ●○○ *adj* a militant organization or person is willing to use strong or violent action in order to achieve political or social change: *militant political activists* | *a militant animal rights group* | *After the assassination of Martin Luther King, black leaders became more militant.* —**militant** *n* [C]: *right-wing militants* —**militancy** *n* [U]: *an increase in trade union militancy* —**militantly** *adv*: *a militantly anti-communist group*

mil·i·ta·ris·m /ˈmɪlətərɪzəm/ *n* [U] the belief that a country should build up its military forces and use them to protect itself and get what it wants: *a country emerging from 20 years of militarism and political repression* —**militarist** *n* [C] —**militaristic** /ˌmɪlətəˈrɪstɪk◂/ *adj*: *a militaristic regime*

mil·i·ta·rized (*also* **-ised** *BrE*) /ˈmɪlətəraɪzd/ *adj* **1** a militarized area is one that has a lot of soldiers and weapons in it: *Kaliningrad is a highly militarized zone.* **2** organized like an army: *the militarized police force*

mil·i·ta·ry¹ /ˈmɪlətəri $ -teri/ ●●● S2 W1 AWL *adj*
1 used by, involving, or relating to the army, navy, or air force: *a military helicopter* | *military equipment* | *The government has threatened to take* ***military action*** *if the rebels do not withdraw from the area.* | *The United States is prepared to use* ***military force*** *to achieve its aims.* | *a raid by European* ***military forces*** (=the army, navy, or air force)
2 with military precision if you do something with military precision, you do it in a very organized and exact way: *The trips are planned with military precision.* —**militarily** *adv*: *Europe may have to intervene militarily if the crisis worsens.*

military² ●●○ AWL *n* **the military** the military forces of a country SYN **the forces**: *He was never tempted to join the military.* | **in the military** *My brother is in the military.* | *The military was sent in to break up the demonstration.*

> **GRAMMAR: Singular or plural verb?**
> • **The military** is usually followed by a singular verb: *The military* ***is*** *helping with the relief effort.*
> • In British English, you can also use a plural verb: *The military* ***are*** *helping with the relief effort.*
> GRAMMAR GUIDE NOUNS

ˌMilitary Aˈcademy *n* [C] **1** a national college where people are trained to be officers in the military forces **2** a private school in the US that gives students military training

ˌMilitary ˈCross *n* [C] a MEDAL given to British army officers for being brave in battle

ˌmilitary poˈlice *n* **the military police** a special police force whose job is to deal with members of the army etc who break the rules

ˌmilitary ˈservice *n* [U] the system in which every adult, or every male adult, in a country has to spend a period of time in the army, navy, or air force → **draft**: *More and more men are refusing to* ***do military service****.*

mil·i·tate /ˈmɪlɪteɪt/ *v*

militate against sth *phr v formal* to prevent something or make it less likely to happen: *Environmental factors militate against building the power station in this area.*

mi·li·tia /məˈlɪʃə/ ●○○ *n* [C] a group of people trained as soldiers, who are not part of the permanent army: *He joined the local militia as soon as he was 16.* | *a militia leader* | *a left-wing militia group*

mi·li·tia·man /məˈlɪʃəmən/ *n* (*plural* **militiamen** /-mən/) [C] a member of a militia

milk¹ /mɪlk/ ●●● S2 W3 *n*

1 [U] a white liquid produced by cows or goats that is drunk by people: *a bottle of milk* | *Would you like some milk in your tea?* | *a pint of semi-skimmed milk*

2 [U] a white liquid produced by female animals and women for feeding their babies: *mothers who believe that* ***breast milk*** *is best for their babies* | *The tiny fox cubs drink nothing but their* ***mother's milk****.*

3 [U] a liquid or juice produced by particular plants, especially the COCONUT

4 [C,U] a thin white liquid used to clean or protect skin SYN **lotion**: *a mild facial cleansing milk*

5 the milk of human kindness *literary* the kind and sympathetic behaviour of most ordinary people → EVAPORATED MILK, → **cry over spilt milk** at CRY¹(3), → **land of milk and honey** at LAND¹(8)

milk² *v* [T] **1** *informal* to get as much money or as many advantages as you can from a situation, in a very determined and sometimes dishonest way: **milk sb/sth for sth** *Their landlord regularly milks them for extra money by claiming for damage to his property.* | *He seems to be* ***milking*** *the incident* ***for all it's worth*** (=getting as much from it as possible). **2** to take milk from a cow or goat: *I helped to milk the cows.* —**milking** *n* [U]: *They had risen at 5.30 to do the milking.*

ˌmilk ˈchocolate *n* [U] chocolate that has milk added to it → **plain chocolate**

ˈmilk churn *n* [C] *BrE* a tall round metal container with a lid, used to carry milk from farms

ˈmilk float *n* [C] *BrE* an electric vehicle that is used for delivering milk to people's houses

ˈmilking maˌchine *n* [C] a machine used for taking milk from cows

ˈmilking ˌparlour *BrE*, **milking parlor** *AmE* *n* [C] a building on a farm where milk is taken from cows

milk·maid /ˈmɪlkmeɪd/ *n* [C] a woman in the past whose job was to get milk from cows on a farm

milk·man /ˈmɪlkmən/ *n* (*plural* **milkmen** /-mən/) [C] someone in Britain whose job is to deliver milk to people's houses each morning

ˌmilk of magˈnesia *n* [U] a thick white liquid medicine used for stomach problems

ˈmilk ˌproduct *n* [C usually plural] a food such as cheese or cream that is made from milk: *I've tried to cut down on milk products.*

ˌmilk ˈpudding *n* [C] *BrE* a sweet food made of rice or other grains baked with milk and sugar

ˈmilk round *n* [C] *BrE* **1** the regular journey a milkman makes every day to deliver milk **2 the milk round** a series of visits to universities in Britain that large companies make each year in order to find students they may want to employ

ˈmilk run *n* [C] *informal* **1** *BrE* a familiar easy journey that you do regularly **2** *AmE* a train journey or regular plane flight with stops in many places

ˈmilk ˌshake *n* [C] **1** *BrE* a sweet drink made of milk with fruit or chocolate added **2** *AmE* a sweet drink made of milk, ICE CREAM, and fruit or chocolate

milk·sop /ˈmɪlksɒp $ -sɑːp/ *n* [C] *old-fashioned* a boy or man who is too gentle and weak, and who is afraid to do anything difficult or dangerous

ˈmilk tooth *n* (*plural* **milk teeth**) [C] *BrE* one of the first set of teeth that babies and young children have SYN **baby tooth**

milk·weed /ˈmɪlkwiːd/ *n* [U] a common North American plant that produces a bitter white substance when its stem is broken

milk·y /ˈmɪlki/ *adj* **1** containing a lot of milk: *a cup of milky coffee* **2** looking, smelling, or tasting like milk: *a sweet, milky flavour* **3** milky skin is white and smooth: *her beautiful milky complexion* **4** *literary* white or pale: *His eyes were a pale milky blue.*

ˌMilky ˈWay, the the pale white band of stars that can be seen across the sky at night → **galaxy**

mill¹ /mɪl/ ●●○ *n* [C]

1 GRAIN a building containing a large machine for crushing grain into flour

2 COTTON/CLOTH/STEEL a factory that produces materials such as cotton, cloth, or steel: **cotton/steel/paper etc mill** *an old Victorian cotton mill*

3 coffee/pepper mill a small machine for crushing coffee or pepper

4 go through the mill to go through a time when you experience a lot of difficulties and problems: *He's really been through the mill recently.*

5 put sb through the mill to make someone answer a lot of difficult questions or do a lot of difficult things in order to test them: *It was a three-day course and they really put us through the mill.*

6 MONEY *AmE* a unit of money equal to 1/10 of a cent, used in setting taxes and for other financial purposes

7 MILLION *spoken* a million: *Are you saying they paid a quarter of a mill for that house?* → RUN-OF-THE-MILL, → **(all) grist to the mill** at GRIST

mill² *v* [T] **1** to crush grain, pepper etc in a mill: *All our flours are milled using traditional methods.* | *Add some freshly milled black pepper.* **2** to press, roll, or shape metal in a machine

mill around/about (sth) *phr v informal* if a lot of people mill around, they move around a place in different directions without any particular purpose: *Crowds of students were milling around in the street.* | *There were a lot of people milling around the entrance.*

mil·len·ni·um /mɪˈleniəm/ ●○○ *n* (*plural* **millennia** /-niə/) [C]

1 a period of 1,000 years: *people who have inhabited this land for millennia*

2 [usually singular] the time when a new 1,000-year period begins: *the beginning of a new millennium* | *events which took place at* ***the turn of*** *the last* ***millennium*** —**millennial** *adj*

mill·er /ˈmɪlə $ -ər/ *n* [C] someone who owns or works in a mill which makes flour

mil·let /ˈmɪlɪt/ *n* [U] the small seeds of a plant similar to grass, used as food

milli- /mɪlə, mɪlɪ/ *prefix* [in nouns] a 1,000th part of a unit: *a millilitre* (=0.001 litres)

mil·li·bar /ˈmɪləbɑː $ -bɑːr/ *n* [C] a unit for measuring the pressure of the ATMOSPHERE (=the mixture of gases surrounding the Earth)

mil·li·gram (*also* **milligramme** *BrE*) /ˈmɪləgræm/ *n* [C] (*written abbreviation* **mg**) a unit for measuring weight. There are 1,000 milligrams in one gram.

mil·li·li·tre *BrE*, **milliliter** *AmE* /ˈmɪləˌliːtə $ -ər/ *n* [C] (*written abbreviation* **ml**) a unit for measuring an amount of liquid. There are 1,000 millilitres in one litre.

mil·li·me·tre *BrE*, **millimeter** *AmE* /ˈmɪləˌmiːtə $ -ər/ ●●○ S3 *n* [C] (*written abbreviation* **mm**) a unit for measuring length. There are 1,000 millimetres in one metre.

mil·li·ner /ˈmɪlənə $ -ər/ *n* [C] someone who makes and sells women's hats

mil·li·ne·ry /ˈmɪlənəri $ -neri/ *n* [U] *formal* **1** the making and selling of women's hats **2** hats

mil·lion /ˈmɪljən/ ●●● S3 W1 *number* (*plural* **million** *or* **millions**)
1 the number 1,000,000: *The book sold more than a million copies.* | **two/three/four etc million** *seven million dollars* | *£37 million of new investment* | **millions of pounds/dollars etc** *Millions of pounds were lost in Western aid.*
2 an extremely large number of people or things: **a million** *I've got a million ideas.* | **millions of sth** *She has millions of friends.*
3 not/never in a million years *spoken* used to emphasize that something is impossible or very unlikely to happen: *She'll never believe me. Not in a million years.*
4 look/feel like a million dollars/bucks *informal especially AmE* to look very attractive or feel very happy and healthy
5 in a million *informal* **a)** the best of all possible people or things: *She's a wife in a million.* | *He's so generous. He's* ***one in a million.*** **b)** used to show how unlikely something is: *It was* ***a chance in a million*** *that we'd find a fossil.* —**millionth** *adj*: *The park has just received its millionth visitor.* —**millionth** *n* [C]

mil·lion·aire /ˌmɪljəˈneə $ -ˈner/ ●●○ *n* [C] someone who is very rich and has at least a million pounds or dollars: *an American millionaire* | *a millionaire businessman*

mil·lion·air·ess /ˌmɪljəˈneərɪs $ -ˈner-/ *n* [C] *old-fashioned* a woman who is very rich and has at least a million pounds or dollars

mil·li·pede /ˈmɪləpiːd/ *n* [C] a long thin small creature with a very large number of legs → **centipede**

mil·li·sec·ond /ˈmɪlɪˌsekənd/ *n* [C] a unit for measuring time. There are 1,000 milliseconds in one second.

mill·pond /ˈmɪlpɒnd $ -pɑːnd/ *n* [C] a very small lake that supplies water to turn the wheel of a WATERMILL

ˌMills and ˈBoon *trademark* a British PUBLISHing company that produces very popular romantic novels, bought especially by women: *Tall, rich, and handsome, Garth was just like the hero of a Mills and Boon book.*

mill·stone /ˈmɪlstəʊn $ -stoʊn/ *n* [C] **1** one of the two large circular stones that crush grain into flour in a MILL **2 a millstone round/around sb's neck** something that causes a lot of problems for someone, and that they cannot get rid of: *Inflation is still a millstone round the neck of British businesses.*

mill·wheel /ˈmɪlwiːl/ *n* [C] *especially BrE* a large wheel that is turned by water flowing past it to provide power to the machinery in a WATERMILL

mil·om·e·ter /maɪˈlɒmɪtə $ -ˈlɑːmɪtər/ *n* [C] another spelling of MILEOMETER

mime[1] /maɪm/ *n* [C,U] the use of movements to express what you want to say without using words, or a play where the actors use only movements: *The children learn through role-play, dance and mime.* | *They will* ***perform*** *a short* ***mime*** *later.* | *a professional* ***mime artist***

mime[2] *v* [I,T] **1** to describe or express something, using movements not words: *Stan put a finger to his mouth, miming 'shush'.* | **mime doing sth** *Soundlessly, she mimed picking up a phone and speaking into it.* **2** to pretend to play or sing a piece of music, without making any sound: **[+to]** *Singers on television often mime to pre-recorded tapes.*

mi·met·ic /məˈmetɪk/ *adj technical* copying the movements or appearance of someone or something else

mim·ic[1] /ˈmɪmɪk/ *v* (**mimicked, mimicking**) [T] **1** to copy the way someone speaks or behaves, especially in order to make people laugh SYN **imitate, take off**: *He could mimic all the teachers' accents.* | *'I'm so sorry,' she mimicked.* **2** to behave or operate in exactly the same way as something or someone else: *Europe should not try to mimic Japan: we have to find our own path to successful modernisation.* | *The drug mimics the action of the body's own chemicals.* **3** if an animal mimics something, it looks or sounds very like it: *a fly whose size and colour exactly mimics that of the wasp* —**mimicry** *n* [U]: *He has a gift for mimicry.*

mimic[2] *n* [C] a person or animal that is good at copying the movements, sound, or appearance of someone or something else → **impressionist, impersonator**

mi·mo·sa /mɪˈməʊzə $ -ˈmoʊsə/ *n* [C,U] **1** a tree with small yellow flowers that grows in hot countries **2** *AmE* a mixture of CHAMPAGNE and orange juice, or a glass of this SYN **Buck's Fizz** *BrE*

min. **1** the written abbreviation of ***minimum*** **2** the written abbreviation of ***minute*** or minutes

min·a·ret /ˌmɪnəˈret, ˈmɪnəret/ *n* [C] a tall thin tower on a MOSQUE, from which Muslims are called to prayer

min·a·to·ry /ˈmɪnətəri $ -tɔːri/ *adj formal* threatening to hurt someone or something

mince[1] /mɪns/ *v* **1** [T] (*also* **mince sth ↔ up**) to cut food, especially meat, into very small pieces, usually using a machine: *minced lamb* | *Mince the meat up with some onion and garlic.* **2** [I always + adv/prep] to walk with very quick, short steps in a way that looks unnatural or silly: *She was mincing about in her high-heeled shoes.* **3 not mince (your) words** to say exactly what you think, even if this might offend people: *Tom didn't mince words and told me straight away that I had failed.*

mince[2] *n* [U] *BrE* meat, especially BEEF, that has been cut into very small pieces using a special machine SYN **ground beef** *AmE*

mince·meat /ˈmɪns-miːt/ *n* [U] **1** a mixture of dried fruits that you use to make sweet dishes **2 make mincemeat of sb/sth** *informal* to completely defeat someone in an argument, fight, or game: *I knew that a good lawyer would make mincemeat of him if I allowed him to give evidence.*

ˌmince ˈpie *n* [C] a PIE filled with mincemeat, especially one that people eat at Christmas

minc·er /ˈmɪnsə $ -ər/ *n* [C] *BrE* a machine that cuts meat into very small pieces by forcing it through small holes SYN **meat grinder** *AmE*

mind[1] /maɪnd/ ●●● S1 W1 *n*
1 ABILITY TO THINK AND IMAGINE [C,U] your thoughts or your ability to think, feel, and imagine things → **mental**: *It is impossible to understand the complex nature of* ***the human mind.*** | *Mind and body are closely related.* | *Meditation involves focussing the mind on a single object or word.* | **in sb's mind** *There was no doubt in my mind that it was the right decision to make.* | *Do you have a clear picture in your mind of what you want?* | *A plan began to form in his mind.* | *The event is still fresh in most people's minds.* | **independence/strength/flexibility of mind** *men who were chosen for their independence of mind*
2 change your mind to change your decision, plan, or opinion about something: *I was afraid that Liz would change her mind and take me back home.* | **[+about]** *If you change your mind about the colour scheme, it's easy to just paint over it.*
3 make up your mind/make your mind up a) to decide which of two or more choices you want, especially after thinking for a long time: *I wish he'd hurry up and make his mind up.* | **[+about]** *He couldn't make up his mind about what to do with the money.* | **make up your mind whether** *Karen couldn't make up her mind whether to apply for membership or not.* **b)** to become very determined to do something, so that you will not change your decision: *No more argument. My* ***mind is made up.*** | **make up your mind to do sth** *He had clearly made up his mind to end the affair.* | **make up your mind that** *I made up my mind there and then that I would never get married.* **c)** to decide what your opinion is about someone or something: **[+about]** *I could never really make my mind up about him.* | *You're old enough to* ***make*** *your* ***own mind up*** *about smoking.*
4 have sb/sth in mind (for sth) to have an idea about who or what you want for a particular purpose: *It was a nice house, but it wasn't quite* ***what*** *we* ***had in mind.*** | *Did you have anyone in mind for the job?* | *Have you any particular colour in mind for the bedroom?*
5 bear/keep sb/sth in mind to remember or think about someone or something when you are doing something: *It's a good idea – I'll keep it in mind.* | *You must always keep the reader in mind when writing a report.* | *Floor tiles can be*

difficult to clean – **worth keeping in mind** *when you choose a new floor.* | **bear/keep in mind that** *Bear in mind that the price does not include flights.* | *More money should be given to housing,* **bearing in mind** (=because of) *the problem of homelessness.*

6 with sb/sth in mind considering someone or something when doing something, and taking suitable action: *Most gardens designed with children in mind are safe but dull.* | *With these aims in mind, the school operates a broad-based curriculum.*

7 on your/sb's mind a) if something is on your mind, you keep thinking or worrying about it: *He looked as though he* **had something on** *his* **mind**. | *Sorry I forgot. I've* **got a lot on** *my* **mind** (=a lot of problems to worry about) *at the moment.* **b)** if something is on your mind, that is what you are thinking about: *She's the type of person who just says what's on her mind.*

8 get/put sb/sth out of your mind (*also* **put sb/sth to the back of your mind**) to stop yourself thinking about someone or something: *I just can't seem to get her out of my mind.* | *You've got to try and put him out of your mind.* | *She put her disappointment to the back of her mind and concentrated on Dana.*

9 cross/enter sb's mind (*also* **come into sb's mind**) [not in progressive] if something crosses your mind, you have a thought or idea: ***It** never **crossed** my **mind that** Lisa might be lying.* | *Suddenly a horrible thought came into my mind.*

10 go/run/flash etc through sb's mind if something goes through your mind, you have a thought, especially for a short time: *She knew what was going through his mind.* | *All kinds of questions ran through my mind.* | *After the accident, one of the things that went through my mind was whether I would be able to drive again.*

11 come/spring to mind [not in progressive] if something comes or springs to mind, you suddenly or immediately think of it: *I just used the first excuse which sprang to mind.* | *A memory of last night came to mind, and he smiled.* | *Fatherhood doesn't immediately spring to mind when you think of James.* ⚠ Do not say that something 'comes to your mind' or 'springs to your mind'. Say that it **comes to mind** or **springs to mind**.

12 CHARACTER [C] used to talk about the way that someone thinks and the type of thoughts they have: *He has a very devious mind.* | *My naturally suspicious mind thought he might be lying.*

13 INTELLIGENCE [C usually singular] your intelligence and ability to think, rather than your emotions: *a mind trained to react with split-second accuracy* | **a brilliant/enquiring/logical etc mind** *a bright child with an enquiring mind*

14 INTELLIGENT PERSON [C] someone who is very intelligent, especially in a particular subject or activity SYN **brain**: *This is one of the issues that has most interested military minds.* | *Some of the finest minds in the country are working on the project.*

15 state/frame of mind the way someone is thinking and feeling at a particular time: *What happened had a lot to do with my state of mind at the time.* | **in a good/positive/relaxed etc frame of mind** *She returned from lunch in a happier frame of mind.* | **in the right/wrong frame of mind** *You have to be in the right frame of mind to play well.*

16 to/in my mind used to show you are giving your opinion about something SYN **in my opinion**: *The Internet, to my mind, represents information exchange at its best.*

17 go/turn over sth in your mind to keep thinking about something because you are trying to understand it or solve a problem: *Corbett rode along, turning over in his mind what Bruce had said.*

18 be the last thing on sb's mind (*also* **be the furthest thing from sb's mind**) to be the thing that someone is least likely to be thinking about: *Insurance was the last thing on my mind when we set off that day.*

19 take/keep/get sb's mind off sth to make someone stop thinking and worrying about something: *Going back to work helped take my mind off Ian's death.* | *Want a game? It might* **take** *your* **mind off things**.

20 set/put sb's mind at rest (*also* **set/put sb's mind at ease**) to make someone feel less worried or anxious: *If you're worried, see a doctor to set your mind at rest.*

21 it/that is a load/weight off sb's mind *informal* used to say that someone does not have to worry about something anymore

22 prey on sb's mind (*also* **play on sb's mind**) if a problem preys on your mind, you cannot stop thinking about it: *Finally, she broached the subject that had been playing on her mind for days.*

23 no one in their right mind ... (*also* **who in their right mind ...?**) *informal* used to say that someone must be stupid or crazy to do something: *Who in their right mind would want to do that job?* | *No woman in her right mind would go out with a man like him.*

24 be out of your mind *informal* to be stupid or crazy: *He must have been out of his mind to employ her.*

25 be out of your mind with worry/grief etc (*also* **be worried/bored etc out of your mind**) to be extremely worried, bored etc: *It was getting late and I was out of my mind with worry.*

26 go out of your mind (*also* **lose your mind**) *informal* to become mentally ill or very worried, bored etc SYN **go crazy**: *Nicole looked at him as if he'd gone out of his mind.*

27 sb's mind goes blank (*also* **sb's mind is a blank**) *informal* if your mind goes blank, you suddenly cannot remember something: *For some inexplicable reason, her mind went completely blank.* | *His heart was thumping and his mind was a complete blank.*

28 go (right/clean) out of sb's mind (*also* **slip sb's mind**) if something goes out of your mind, you forget it, especially because you are very busy: *I'm sorry. So much has been happening, it went clean out of my mind.* | ***It had** completely **slipped** her **mind that** Dave still had a key to the house.*

29 bring/call sth to mind a) to make you think of someone or something SYN **remind sb of sth**: *The wine's sweet nutty taste calls to mind roasted chestnuts.* **b)** *formal* to remember something: *The only thing I could call to mind was something my mother once said.*

30 put sb in mind of sb/sth [not in progressive] *formal* to remind someone of someone or something: *The girl put me in mind of my own daughter.*

31 stick/stay in sb's mind if a name, fact etc sticks in your mind, you remember it for a long time: *For some reason, the name really stuck in Joe's mind.* | *One line from the poem had stayed in her mind.*

32 be of one mind/of the same mind/of like mind *formal* to have the same opinions as someone else: *It can be difficult to meet others of like mind.* | **[+on/about]** *The council and the government are of one mind on the long-term objective.*

33 have a mind of your own a) to have strong opinions about things, and make your own decisions without being influenced by other people: *She's a woman without fear, with a mind of her own, who says what she thinks.* **b)** if an object has a mind of its own, it seems to control itself and does not work or move in the way you want it to: *The bicycle seemed to have a mind of its own and I couldn't steer it straight.*

34 put/set/turn your mind to sth to decide that you want to achieve something and try very hard to do it: *I think anyone can lose weight if they set their mind to it.*

35 sb's mind is not on sth if your mind is not on what you are doing, you are not thinking much about it because you are thinking or worrying about something else: *His mind didn't seem to be on the game at all.*

36 keep your mind on sth to keep paying attention to something, even though it is difficult: *He could hardly keep his mind on what she was saying.* | **keep your mind on the job/task in/at hand** *Making notes is the best way of keeping your mind on the task at hand.*

37 sb's mind wanders if your mind wanders, you no longer pay attention to something, especially because you are bored: *Her mind was beginning to wander.*

38 sb's mind is racing if your mind is racing, you are thinking very quickly and hard about something because you are excited, frightened etc: *He tried to reassure her, but Carrie's mind was racing.*

39 it's all in the mind used to tell someone that they have imagined something and it does not really exist: *He's one*

of those doctors who say you're not really sick and it's all in the mind.

40 in your mind's eye if you see something in your mind's eye, you imagine or remember clearly what it looks like: *She paused, imagining the scene in her mind's eye.*

41 have it in mind *formal* to intend to do something: **have it in mind to do sth** *For a long time I had it in mind to write a book about my experiences.* | **have it in mind that** *I had it in mind that one day I might move to Spain.*

42 have half a mind to do sth *spoken* **a)** (*also* **have a good mind to do sth**) used to say that you might do something to show that you disapprove of something someone has done: *I've a good mind to tell him exactly what I think.* | *I've half a mind to stop him seeing her altogether.* **b)** used to say that you may decide to do something: *I've half a mind to come with you tomorrow.*

43 mind over matter used to say that you can use your thoughts to control physical feelings or an unpleasant situation: *I'm scared, yes, but it's a case of mind over matter.*
→ **in/at the back of your mind** at BACK²(6), → **blow sb's mind** at BLOW¹(15), → **cast your mind back** at CAST¹(9), → **a closed mind** at CLOSED(4), → **be in/at/to the forefront of sb's mind/attention** at FOREFRONT(2), → **give sb a piece of your mind** at PIECE¹(13), → **great minds think alike** at GREAT¹(15), → **know your own mind** at KNOW¹(50), → **the mind boggles** at BOGGLE, → **meeting of minds** at MEETING(5), → ONE-TRACK MIND, → **an open mind** at OPEN¹(16), → **out of sight, out of mind** at SIGHT¹(8), → **peace of mind** at PEACE(3), PRESENCE OF MIND, → **read sb's mind** at READ¹(15), → **set your heart/mind/sights on (doing) sth** at SET¹(13), → **be of sound mind** at SOUND³(5), → **speak your mind** at SPEAK(7), → **be in two minds** at TWO(9)

mind² ●●● S1 W2 *v*

1 FEEL ANNOYED [I,T usually in questions and negatives] to feel annoyed or upset about something → **object**: *I don't mind the heat, in fact I quite like it.* | *The expression on Dan's face showed that he did mind, very much.* | *I wouldn't have minded if she'd asked me first.* | **mind doing sth** *Did you mind being away from home for so long?* | **mind sb doing sth** *Don't your parents mind you staying out so late?* | **mind that** *He didn't mind that other people in the village thought him odd.*

> **REGISTER**
> The expression **mind/not mind (sth)** is used especially in spoken English. In written English, people often use **object/not object (to sth)** instead: *Many people **do not object to** paying higher taxes for better services.* | ***Would you object** if we changed a few details?*

2 not mind doing sth to be willing to do something: *I don't mind waiting a little longer.* GRAMMAR ✗ Don't say: *I don't mind to wait a little longer.*

3 NOT CARE WHICH ONE **not mind** [I,T] *especially BrE* if you do not mind what someone does or what happens, you do not have a strong opinion about it: *'Do you want to go out now or later?' 'I don't really mind.'* | **not mind what/who/where etc** *I don't mind where we go.*

4 mind your own business *informal* to not ask questions about a situation that does not involve you: *Why don't you just mind your own business and leave me in peace?* | *I wish he'd mind his own business.*

5 be minding your own business to be doing something ordinary on your own when something unexpected happens to you: *My father was just driving along, minding his own business, when suddenly a brick came through the window.*

SPOKEN PHRASES

6 never mind a) used to tell someone not to worry or be upset about something: *'We haven't done very well, have we?' 'Never mind. At least we tried.'* | **[+about]** *Never mind about the car. You're safe, and that's the main thing.* **b)** used to say that something is not possible or likely, because even a less extreme thing is not possible or likely: *Well, you would have hardly got a bed in that room, never mind anything else.* | *I don't think I could walk that far, never mind run that far.* **c)** used to tell someone that it is not important to do or consider something now, often because something else is more important: *Never mind me – what about you? What have you been doing?* | *Never mind the dishes – I'll do them later.* | **never mind doing sth** *Never mind looking at the boys, we're supposed to be playing tennis.* | **never mind why/how etc** *Never mind how I got here. Tell me what happened.*

7 I wouldn't mind (doing) sth used to say that you would like something: *'Can I get you anything to drink?' 'I wouldn't mind a coffee.'* | *She's gorgeous! I wouldn't mind looking like that!*

8 would/do you mind ...? a) used to politely ask someone's permission: **would you mind if** *Would you mind if I opened the window?* | *Would you mind if I came with you?* | *I'll have to leave early, do you mind?* **b)** used to politely ask someone to do something: **would you mind doing sth?** *Would you mind waiting outside?* | *'Do you want me to carry this bag for you?' 'Would you mind?'* **c)** used to angrily ask or tell someone to do something: **would you mind doing sth?** *Would you mind telling me what you're doing in here?* | *Would you mind shutting up for a minute?*

9 mind you (*also* **mind**) *BrE* used when saying something that is almost the opposite of what you have just said, or that explains or emphasizes it: *He looks very young in this photo. Mind you, it was taken years ago.* | *I love hot weather, but not too hot, mind.*

10 WARNING **mind!** *BrE* used to warn someone to be careful because they might hurt themselves or someone else, or damage something: *Mind that bike, James!* | ***Mind you don't** fall!* | **mind your head/fingers etc** *Mind your head – the ceiling's a bit low.* | **mind how/where/who etc** *It's slippery, so mind where you're walking!*

11 mind how you go *BrE* used when saying goodbye to someone, to tell them to take care

12 mind you do sth *BrE* used to tell someone to do something: *Mind you behave yourself.*

13 never you mind *especially BrE* used to tell someone that you are not going to tell them something because it is private or secret: *'What's that you were saying to Dad?' 'Never you mind.'*

14 do you mind! used to say to someone that you are annoyed with them because of something they have just done or said: *Do you mind! I just washed that floor!*

15 if you don't mind (*also* **if you wouldn't mind**) **a)** used to check that someone is willing to do something or let you do something: *If you don't mind, I think I'll go to bed now.* | *I'd like to stay a while longer, if you don't mind.* | *We'll go there together – **that's if you don't mind**.* **b)** used when you are annoyed to tell someone what to do or what you are going to do: *Now, if you don't mind, I'd like to get back to bed.* **c)** used humorously or rudely to correct something someone has said: *The name's John, not Jonathan, if you don't mind.* **d)** used to refuse someone's offer politely: *'Do you want to come for a drink?' 'I won't, if you don't mind. I've got a lot of work to do.'*

16 if you don't mind my saying so/if you don't mind me asking used when you are saying or asking something that you think might offend someone: *You're looking tired, if you don't mind my saying so.* | *How old are you, if you don't mind me asking?*

17 I don't mind admitting/telling you/saying etc used to emphasize what you are saying, especially when it could make you seem silly: *I don't mind admitting that I was really scared.*

18 don't mind me a) used to tell someone not to pay any attention to you: *If you want to get on and do something, please don't mind me.* **b)** used when you are annoyed because someone is not paying any attention to you: *Don't mind me! I only live here!*

19 don't mind her/him etc used to say sorry for someone else's behaviour: *Don't mind her. She doesn't mean to be hurtful.*

20 (I) don't mind if I do *old-fashioned* used humorously to accept something such as food or drink that has been offered to you

21 TAKE CARE OF STH/SB [T] *BrE* **a)** to be responsible for something for a short time SYN **watch**: *Will you mind my*

M

bag while I buy my ticket? **b)** to take care of a child while their parents are not there SYN **look after**: *My sister minds the baby while I'm at yoga.*
22 mind the shop *BrE*, **mind the store** *AmE informal* to be in charge of something, while the person who is usually in charge is not there
23 mind your manners/language/p's and q's to be careful about what you say or how you behave so that you do not offend anyone: *She gave him a frown and told him to mind his manners.*
24 OBEY [T] *AmE* to obey someone's instructions or advice: *Some dogs will mind instructions better than others.*

GRAMMAR

Using the progressive

- In most of its meanings, **mind** is not used in the progressive.
- One common exception is the expression **be minding your own business** (sense 5).
- **Mind** can also be used in the progressive when it means 'take care of' (senses 21 and 22): *I'm just minding the shop while she's having lunch.*

Using the passive

- In most of its meanings, **mind** is not used in the passive.
- **Mind** can only be used in the passive when it means 'take care of' (senses 21 and 22): *The children are being minded by a neighbour.*

mind out *phr v* [always in imperative or infinitive] *BrE* used to warn someone to be careful SYN **be careful**: *Mind out. The plates are hot.*

ˈmind-ˌbending *adj* [usually before noun] *informal* **1** mind-bending drugs have a strong effect on your mind and make you have very strange feelings and experiences **2** difficult to understand: *Infinity in space is a mind-bending concept.*

ˈmind-ˌblowing *adj informal* very exciting, shocking, or strange: *a mind-blowing experience*

ˈmind-ˌboggling *adj informal* difficult to imagine and very big, strange, or complicated: *a problem of mind-boggling complexity*

mind·ed /ˈmaɪndɪd/ *adj* **1 serious-minded/evil-minded etc** having a particular attitude or way of thinking: *a very serious-minded girl who studies hard | a tough-minded businessman* **2 be minded to do sth** *formal* to want or intend to do something

mind·er /ˈmaɪndə $ -ər/ *n* [C] *BrE* someone who is employed to protect another person SYN **bodyguard** → CHILDMINDER

mind·ful /ˈmaɪndfəl/ *adj* **mindful of sth** *formal* remembering a particular rule or fact and thinking about it when you are making decisions about what to do SYN **conscious of**: *The school is mindful of its responsibilities towards all the children.*

mind·ful·ness /ˈmaɪndfəlnəs/ *n* [U] a way of improving your mental state that involves paying close attention to everything that you are experiencing, especially during quiet MEDITATION

ˈmind game *n* [C usually plural] *BrE informal* if you play mind games with someone, especially someone you are in a romantic relationship with, you deceive them or try to get them to behave as you want them to: *He's obviously **playing mind games** with you.*

mind·less /ˈmaɪndləs/ *adj* **1** completely stupid and without any purpose SYN **senseless**: *His drinking bouts often ended in acts of mindless violence.* **2** if something is mindless, you can do it or watch it without thinking or using your mind: *Doug was watching something mindless on television. | the mindless routine of military discipline* THESAURUS ▸ EASY **3 mindless of sth** not paying attention to something, especially something dangerous or unpleasant: *After lunch we explored the city, mindless of the rain.* —**mindlessly** *adv*

ˈmind ˌreader *n* [C] someone who knows what someone else is thinking without being told

mind·set /ˈmaɪndset/ *n* [C] someone's general attitude, and the way in which they think about things and make decisions SYN **outlook**: *The company seems to have a very old-fashioned mindset.*

mine¹ /maɪn/ ●●● S1 *pron* [possessive form of 'I'] used by the person speaking or writing to refer to something that belongs to or is connected with himself or herself → **my**: *It was Glen's idea, not mine. | 'Is that your car?' 'No, mine is parked over the road.' | You've got good legs – mine are too thin. | His English is better than mine.* | **of mine** *I want you to meet an old **friend of mine**.*

mine² ●●○ W3 *n* [C]
1 a deep hole or holes in the ground that people dig so that they can remove coal, gold, TIN etc → **mining**: **coal/gold/copper etc mine** *one of the largest coal mines in the country* | **in/down a mine** *the time when children used to work down the mines*
2 a type of bomb that is hidden just below the ground or under water and that explodes when it is touched: *They learnt how to **lay mines*** (=put them in place). | *The ship **struck** a **mine** and sank.* → LANDMINE
3 a mine of information (about/on sth) someone or something that can give you a lot of information about a particular subject and that is therefore very useful or helpful: *The website is a mine of information about all forms of cancer.*

mine³ ●○○ *v* (**mined, mining**)
1 [I,T] to dig large holes in the ground in order to remove coal, gold etc: *Copper has been mined here since the sixteenth century. | This area has been mined for over 300 years.* | **[+for]** *The company first started mining for salt in 1851.*
2 [T] to hide bombs in the sea or under the ground: *All the roads leading to the village had been mined.*

mine·field /ˈmaɪnfiːld/ *n* **1** [C] an area where a lot of bombs have been hidden just below the ground or under water: *They realized they had wandered into a minefield.* **2** [singular] a situation in which there are a lot of dangers and difficulties, and it is difficult to make the right decision: *Choosing the right school can be a bit of a minefield.* | **[+of]** *The new Administration has to pick its way through the minefield of legislation.* | **legal/financial/political etc minefield** *The legalisation of cannabis is a political minefield.*

min·er /ˈmaɪnə $ -ər/ ●●○ *n* [C] someone who works under the ground in a mine to remove coal, gold etc: **coal/gold etc miner** *a strike by coal miners*

min·e·ral /ˈmɪnərəl/ ●●○ W3 *n* [C]
1 a substance that is formed naturally in the earth, such as coal, salt, stone, or gold. Minerals can be dug out of the ground and used: *The area is very **rich in minerals**. | a country with few **mineral resources***
2 a natural substance such as iron that is present in some foods and is important for good health: *Fish is a rich source of vitamins and minerals.*

min·e·ral·o·gy /ˌmɪnəˈrælədʒi $ -ˈrɑː-, -ˈræ-/ *n* [U] the scientific study of minerals —**mineralogist** *n* [C]

ˈmineral ˌwater *n* [C,U] water that comes from under the ground and contains a lot of minerals: *a glass of mineral water*

mine·shaft /ˈmaɪnʃɑːft $ -ʃæft/ *n* [C] a deep narrow hole that goes into the ground to a mine

min·e·stro·ne /ˌmɪnəˈstrəʊni◂ $ -ˈstroʊ-/ (*also* **ˌminestrone ˈsoup**) *n* [U] a type of soup containing vegetables and small pieces of PASTA

mine·sweep·er /ˈmaɪnˌswiːpə $ -ər/ *n* [C] a ship with special equipment for removing bombs from under water —**minesweeping** *n* [U]

mine·work·er /ˈmaɪnˌwɜːkə $ -ˌwɜːrkər/ *n* [C] someone who works in a mine

ming·er /ˈmɪŋə $ -ər/ *n* [C] *BrE informal* an offensive word for someone who is ugly, used especially by young men to describe women they do not think are sexually attractive: *His sister's a complete minger.*

ming·ing /ˈmɪŋɪŋ/ *adj BrE informal humorous* very bad, unpleasant, or ugly: *Those trainers are minging.*

min·gle /ˈmɪŋgəl/ ●○○ *v* (**mingled, mingling**)
1 [I,T] if two feelings, sounds, smells etc mingle, they mix together with each other: *Add the mint and allow the flavours to mingle.* | **[+with]** *Her perfume mingled with the smell of wood smoke from the fire.* | **be mingled with sth** *Her excitement was mingled with a slight feeling of fear.*
2 [I] if you mingle at a party, you move around the room and talk to lots of different people: **[+with]** *She was eager to mingle with the other guests.*

min·gy /ˈmɪndʒi/ *adj BrE informal* not at all generous

min·i /ˈmɪni/ *n* [C] a MINISKIRT

mini- /mɪni, mɪnə/ *prefix* very small or short, compared with others of the same kind: *All the hotel's bedrooms have a mini-bar, telephone and radio.* | *a mini-screen TV*

min·ia·ture¹ /ˈmɪnətʃə $ ˈmɪniətʃər/ ●○○ *adj* [only before noun] much smaller than normal: *miniature roses* | *a miniature railway* | *He looked like a* ***miniature version*** *of his father.* **THESAURUS** ➤ SMALL

miniature² *n* **1 in miniature** exactly like something or someone but much smaller: *She's her mother in miniature.* **2** [C] a very small painting, usually of a person **3** [C] a very small bottle containing an alcoholic drink: *a miniature of whiskey*

ˌminiature ˈgolf *n* [U] *AmE* a type of GOLF game, played for fun, in which you hit a small ball through passages, over bridges and small hills etc SYN **crazy golf** *BrE*

min·ia·tur·ist /ˈmɪnɪtʃərɪst $ ˈmɪniətʃʊr-/ *n* [C] someone who paints very small pictures for money

min·ia·tur·ize (*also* **-ise** *BrE*) /ˈmɪnətʃəraɪz $ ˈmɪniə-/ *v* [T] to make something in a very small size —**miniaturized** *adj*: *a miniaturized listening device*

ˈmini-bar (*also* **min·i·bar**) /ˈmɪnibɑː $ -bɑːr/ *n* [C] a small FRIDGE in a hotel bedroom, in which drinks are kept

min·i·bus /ˈmɪnibʌs/ *n* [C] *especially BrE* a small bus with seats for six to twelve people

min·i·cab /ˈmɪnikæb/ *n* [C] *BrE* a taxi that you have to order by telephone, not one that you can stop in the street

min·i·com·put·er /ˈmɪnikəmˌpjuːtə $ -ər/ *n* [C] a computer that is larger than a PERSONAL COMPUTER and smaller than a MAINFRAME, used by businesses and other large organizations

ˈMini ˌDisc *n* [C] *trademark* a very small round DISK that is used for recording music

min·im /ˈmɪnɪm/ *n* [C] *BrE* a musical note that continues for the length of two CROTCHETS SYN **half note** *AmE*

min·i·mal /ˈmɪnəməl/ ●●○ AWL *adj* very small in degree or amount, especially the smallest degree or amount possible: *The storm caused only minimal damage* | *The cost to taxpayers would be minimal.* | *This is a practical course, with only a minimal amount of theory.* —**minimally** *adv*: *Rates of truancy from school have only increased minimally.*

min·i·mal·is·m /ˈmɪnəməlɪzəm/ *n* [U] a style of art, design, music etc that uses only a very few simple ideas or patterns —**minimalist** *adj*: *minimalist Christmas decorations* —**minimalist** *n* [C]

min·i·mart /ˈmɪnimɑːt $ -mɑːrt/ *n* [C] *AmE* a small shop that stays open very late, selling food, cigarettes etc

ˌmini-ˈme *n* [C usually singular] *informal* someone who looks exactly like you except that they are younger or smaller than you are

min·i·mize (*also* **-ise** *BrE*) /ˈmɪnəmaɪz/ ●●○ AWL *v* [T]
1 to reduce something that is difficult, dangerous, or unpleasant to the smallest possible amount or degree OPP **maximize**: *Every effort is being made to minimize civilian casualties.* | *The rail company is bringing in more trains in an effort to minimize disruption to travellers.*
2 to make something seem less serious or important than it really is SYN **play down**: *We must not minimize the problem of racial discrimination.*
3 to make a document or program on your computer very small when you are not using it but still want to keep it open OPP **maximize**: *Click on the top of the window to minimize it.*

min·i·mum¹ /ˈmɪnəməm/ ●●● S3 W2 AWL *adj* [only before noun] the minimum number, degree, or amount of something is the smallest or least that is possible, allowed, or needed OPP **maximum**: *The minimum number of students we need to run the course is fifteen.* | *The minimum age for retirement is 55.* —**minimum** *adv*: *You'll need two tons of cement, minimum.*

minimum² ●●● S3 W2 AWL *n* [singular]
1 the smallest amount of something or number of things that is possible or necessary OPP **maximum**: **a minimum of two hours/£1,000 etc** *The judge recommended that he should serve a minimum of 12 years.* | **[+of]** *He achieved enviable results with the minimum of effort.* | **absolute/bare minimum** (=the very least amount or number) *Prison inmates are kept in tiny cells, with the bare minimum of furniture.* | **keep/reduce sth to a minimum** *She had reduced her consumption of fat and sugar to an absolute minimum.*
2 at a/the minimum used to say that if nothing else is done, this one thing should be done: *At a minimum, we must recruit two new teachers.*

ˌminimum seˈcurity ˌprison *n* [C] *AmE* a prison that does not restrict prisoners' freedom as much as ordinary prisons SYN **open prison** *BrE*

ˌminimum ˈwage *n* [singular] the lowest amount of money that an employer can legally pay to a worker: *Most of the junior office staff are on the minimum wage* (=being paid the lowest legal amount).

min·ing /ˈmaɪnɪŋ/ ●●○ *n* [U] the work or industry of getting gold, coal etc out of the earth → **mine**: **coal/gold etc mining** *the coal mining industry*

min·ion /ˈmɪnjən/ *n* [C usually plural] someone's minions are the people who just obey their orders and do unskilled work – used humorously: *I was shown into the office by one of her minions.*

ˌmini-ˈroundabout *n* [C] *BrE* a white circle painted on the ground where several roads meet. Vehicles must drive round the circle in one direction only.

min·i·se·ries /ˈmɪniˌsɪəriz $ -ˌsɪr-/ *n* [C] a television film that is divided into several parts. Each part is shown on a different evening.

min·i·site /ˈmɪnisaɪt/ → MICROSITE

min·i·skirt /ˈmɪniskɜːt $ -skɜːrt/ *n* [C] a very short skirt SYN **mini**

min·is·ter¹ /ˈmɪnɪstə $ -ər/ ●●○ *n* [C]
1 a politician who is in charge of a government department, in Britain and some other countries: **[+of]** *the Minister of Agriculture* | **[+for]** *the Minister for Foreign Affairs* | **foreign/defence/finance etc minister** *a meeting of EU foreign ministers* | *a senior* ***Cabinet minister*** → PRIME MINISTER
2 a priest in some Christian churches → **pastor**, **vicar**: *a Baptist minister*
3 someone whose job is to represent their country in another country, but who is lower in rank than an AMBASSADOR

minister² *v* [I] to work as a priest: *Rev Wilson spent 20 years ministering in some of New York's poorest areas.*

minister to sb/sth *phr v formal* to give help to someone who needs it, especially someone who is sick or old: *She spent much time ministering to the sick.* | *ministering to the needs of other people*

min·is·ter·i·al /ˌmɪnəˈstɪəriəl◂ $ -ˈstɪr-/ AWL *adj* [only before noun] connected with or relating to government ministers: *a ministerial meeting* | *The project was approved at ministerial level.*

ˌminister of ˈstate *n* [C] a member of the government in Britain who has an important job in a government department but is not in charge of it

min·i·stra·tions /ˌmɪnəˈstreɪʃənz/ *n* [plural] *formal* the giving of help to people who are ill or who need the help of a priest: *Despite the ministrations of the surgeon, poor Lucy died on the 22 July.*

min·is·try /ˈmɪnəstri/ ●○○ AWL *n* (*plural* **ministries**)
1 [C] a government department that is responsible for one of the areas of government work, such as education or health: **[+of]** *the Ministry of Agriculture* | **foreign/justice/finance etc ministry** *a Defence Ministry spokesman*
2 the ministry the profession of being a church leader, especially in the Protestant Church: *Converted in his early teens, he **entered the ministry*** (=started working as a church leader) *in 1855.*
3 [C usually singular] the work done by a priest or other religious person as a result of their religious beliefs: *the ministry of Jesus*

min·i·van /ˈmɪnivæn/ *n* [C] *AmE* a large car with seats for six to eight people SYN **people carrier** *BrE*

mink /mɪŋk/ *n* (*plural* **mink** *or* **minks**) **1** [C,U] a small animal with soft brown fur, or the very valuable fur of this animal which is used to make coats, hats etc: *a mink coat*
2 [C] a coat or jacket made of mink

min·now /ˈmɪnəʊ $ -noʊ/ *n* [C] **1** a very small fish that lives in rivers and lakes **2** an organization or company that is small and unimportant: *one of the minnows of the computer industry*

mi·nor[1] /ˈmaɪnə $ -ər/ ●●● S2 W2 AWL *adj*
1 small and not very important or serious, especially when compared with other things OPP **major**: *We have made some minor changes to the program.* | *a relatively minor error* | *a minor road* | *They played only a minor role in local government.* | **minor injury/illness/operation etc** (=one that is not very serious or dangerous) *He escaped with only minor injuries.* THESAURUS ▸ SMALL, UNIMPORTANT
2 based on a particular type of musical SCALE: *Mahler's Symphony No. 3 in D minor* | *a minor key*

minor[2] ●○○ *n* [C]
1 *law* someone who is below the age at which they become legally responsible for their actions: *This film contains material unsuitable for minors.* THESAURUS ▸ CHILD
2 *AmE* the second main subject that you study at university for your degree OPP **major**: *I'm taking history as my minor.*
3 the minors the MINOR LEAGUES

minor[3] *v*
minor in sth *phr v AmE* to study a second main subject as part of your university degree OPP **major**: *Sid majored in sociology and minored in political science.*

mi·nor·i·ty /maɪˈnɒrəti $ məˈnɔː-, məˈnɑː-/ ●●● S3 W2 AWL *n* (*plural* **minorities**)
1 [singular] a small group of people or things within a much larger group OPP **majority**: *Gaelic is still spoken in Ireland by a minority.* | **[+of]** *Only a minority of people supported these new laws.* | **small/tiny/substantial/significant minority** *Gay men are a small but significant minority.* | **minority report** (=a report by a minority of a group who do not agree with the others)

> **GRAMMAR: Singular or plural verb?**
> • In this meaning, **minority** is usually followed by a singular verb: *A small minority **refuses** to cooperate.*
> • In British English, you can also use a plural verb: *A small minority **refuse** to cooperate.*
> GRAMMAR GUIDE ▸ NOUNS

2 [C usually plural] **a)** a group of people of a different race, religion etc from most other people in that country: *People from **ethnic minorities** often face prejudice.* | *the very large Russian minorities in Ukraine and Moldova* | *children from **minority groups*** | *the teaching of **minority languages** in schools* | **minority leader/businessman/student etc** *AmE*: *a school with a high proportion of minority students* **b)** *AmE* someone who belongs to a group like this: *Businesses are under pressure to hire minorities and women.*
3 be in the/a minority to form less than half of a group: *Boys are very much in the minority at the dance class.*
4 be in a minority of one to be the only person in a group who has a particular opinion
5 [U] *law* the period of time when someone is below the age at which they become legally responsible for their actions

miˌnority ˈgovernment *n* [C] a government that does not have enough politicians in a parliament to control parliament and take decisions without the support of other parties

miˈnority ˌleader *n* [C] *AmE* the leader of the political party that has fewer politicians in CONGRESS than the leading party → **majority leader**

ˌminor-ˈleague *adj* [only before noun] **1** connected with the Minor Leagues: *a minor-league team* **2** not as important, powerful, or successful as others of the same kind: *Collins was just a minor-league crook.*

ˌMinor ˈLeagues *n* **the Minor Leagues** the groups of teams that form the lower levels of American professional BASEBALL → **Major Leagues**

min·ster /ˈmɪnstə $ -ər/ *n* [C] *BrE* a large or important church: *a carol service at the minster* | *York Minster*

min·strel /ˈmɪnstrəl/ *n* [C] **1** a singer or musician in the Middle Ages **2** one of a group of white singers and dancers who pretended to be black while performing in popular shows in the 1920s

mint[1] /mɪnt/ ●●○ *n*
1 [U] a small plant with green leaves that have a fresh smell and taste and are used in cooking: *new potatoes sprinkled with chopped mint* | *roast lamb with **mint sauce*** | *Decorate with a **sprig of mint**.*
2 [C] a sweet that tastes of PEPPERMINT (=a type of mint with a strong fresh taste): *We sat in the back row, sucking mints.* | *Would you like a mint?*
3 a mint *informal* a large amount of money: *She **made a mint** on the stock exchange last year.*
4 [C] a place where coins are officially made: *coins issued by the Royal Mint*

mint[2] *v* [T] to make a coin: *Only 2,000 of the special commemorative coins are being minted.*

mint[3] *adj* **1 in mint condition** looking new and in perfect condition: *A copy in mint condition would fetch about £2,000.* **2** *BrE informal* very good

mint·ed /ˈmɪntɪd/ *adj* **1 newly/freshly minted** a newly minted word, phrase, idea etc has been invented or produced very recently: *some newly minted theatrical stories* **2** minted food and drinks have mint added to them: *Serve with minted peas.* **3** very rich – used especially by young people

ˌmint ˈjulep *n* [C] *AmE* a drink in which alcohol and sugar are mixed with ice and mint leaves are added

mint·y /ˈmɪnti/ *adj* tasting or smelling of mint: *a fresh, minty flavour*

min·u·et /ˌmɪnjuˈet/ *n* [C] a slow dance of the 17th and 18th centuries, or a piece of music for this dance

mi·nus[1] /ˈmaɪnəs/ ●●● S3 *prep*
1 used to show that one number or quantity is being SUBTRACTED from another OPP **plus**: *17 minus 5 is 12 (17 – 5 = 12).* | *The payment will be refunded to you minus a small service charge.*
2 *informal* without something that would normally be there, or that used to be there: *He came back minus a couple of front teeth.*

minus[2] ●○○ *n* [C]
1 something that is a disadvantage because it makes a situation unpleasant SYN **drawback** OPP **plus**: *There are both **pluses and minuses** to living in a big city.*
2 a MINUS SIGN

minus[3] *adj* **1** [only before noun] *BrE* used to talk about a disadvantage of a thing or situation OPP **plus**: *'Any **minus points**?' 'Well, the engine is rather noisy.'* | ***On the minus side**, there is no free back-up service if things go wrong.*
2 less than zero – used especially when talking about temperatures: *At night temperatures sometimes fall to minus 30°.* | *a minus quantity* **3 A minus/B minus etc** a mark used in a system of judging students' work. An 'A minus' is slightly lower than an 'A', but higher than a 'B'. OPP **plus**

min·us·cule /ˈmɪnəskjuːl/ *adj* extremely small SYN **minute**: *a minuscule amount of food | Her office is minuscule.* THESAURUS ➤ SMALL

ˈ**minus ˌsign** (*also* **minus**) *n* [C] a sign (−) showing that a number is less than zero, or that the second of two numbers is to be SUBTRACTed from the first → **plus sign**

min·ute¹ /ˈmɪnət/ ●●● S1 W1 *n* [C]
1 TIME a unit for measuring time. There are 60 minutes in one hour: *It takes me ten minutes to walk to work. | The train arrived at four minutes past eight. | He returned a few minutes later. | I'll meet you at the car in five minutes.* | **a one/two/three etc minute sth** *a ten-minute bus ride*
2 the last minute the last possible time, just before it is too late: **at the last minute** *He cancelled his trip to England at the last minute.* | **until the last minute** *If you leave your essay until the last minute, you'll almost certainly panic.* → LAST-MINUTE
3 by the minute (*also* **every minute, minute by minute**) used to say that something continues quickly becoming greater, stronger etc: *She was getting angrier by the minute. | His voice was getting stronger every minute.*
4 love/enjoy/hate etc every minute (of sth) *informal* if you love, enjoy etc every minute of an activity or experience, you love, enjoy etc all of it: *I went camping for a week and enjoyed every minute of it.*
5 within minutes very soon after something has happened: *The ambulance was there within minutes.* | **within minutes of doing sth** *He had his car stolen within minutes of arriving at the office.*
6 a minute a very short period of time SYN **moment**: *Sam thought for a minute, then smiled at his brother. | Can I have a word? It will only take a minute.*

SPOKEN PHRASES
7 in a minute very soon: *Wait here. I'll be back in a minute. | Mr Gregson will be with you in a minute.*
8 wait a minute/just a minute/hold on a minute/hang on a minute a) used to tell someone you want them to wait for a short time while you do or say something else: *Just a minute, Margaret, I want to introduce you to Betty. | Wait a minute, let me see if I understand this correctly.* **b)** used to tell someone to stop speaking or doing something for a short time because they have said or done something wrong: *Hold on a minute! That can't be right.*
9 (at) any minute (now) used to say that something will or may happen extremely soon: *We're expecting them any minute now.*
10 have you got a minute? *BrE*, **do you have a minute?** *AmE* used to ask someone if you may talk to them for a short time: *Have you got a minute? I need to ask you some questions.*
11 the minute (that) sb does sth as soon as someone does something: *Tell him I need to see him the minute he arrives.*
12 not think/believe etc for one minute used to say that you certainly do not think something, believe something etc: *I don't think for one minute that he'll do it but I have to ask.*
13 this minute immediately: *Johnny! Get inside, this minute! | You don't have to tell me* ***right this minute***.

14 the next minute immediately afterwards: *I put down the phone and the next minute it rang again.*
15 one minute ... the next (minute) ... used to say that a situation suddenly changes: *One minute they're madly in love and the next they've split up again.*
16 MEETING **minutes** [plural] an official written record of what is said and decided at a meeting: *Will you* ***take*** *the* ***minutes*** (=write them down)? | **[+of]** *Has everyone seen the minutes of last month's meeting?*
17 MATHEMATICS *technical* one of the 60 parts into which a degree of an angle is divided. It can be shown as a symbol after a number. For example, 78° 52' means 78 degrees 52 minutes. → UP-TO-THE-MINUTE

mi·nute² /maɪˈnjuːt $ -ˈnuːt/ ●○○ *adj*
1 extremely small: *You only need a minute amount. | Her handwriting is minute.* THESAURUS ➤ SMALL
2 paying careful attention to the smallest details SYN **meticulous**: *a minute examination of the rock | He explained the plan* ***in minute detail***. —**minutely** *adv*: *She studied the letter minutely.*

min·ute³ /ˈmɪnət/ *v* [T] *especially BrE* to make an official note of something in the record of a meeting: *This discussion is off the record and should not be minuted.*

minute hand /ˈmɪnət hænd/ *n* [C] the long thin piece of metal that points to the minutes on a clock or watch → **hour hand**

min·ute·man /ˈmɪnətmæn/ *n* (*plural* **minutemen** /-men/) [C] *AmE* one of a group of men in the past who were not official soldiers but who were ready to fight at any time

mi·nu·ti·ae /maɪˈnjuːʃiaɪ, mə- $ məˈnuː-/ *n* [plural] very small and exact details: **[+of]** *I'm not interested in the minutiae of the research, just its conclusions.*

minx /mɪŋks/ *n* [C] *old-fashioned* an attractive young woman who does not show respect and who is good at getting what she wants in a clever way

mips /mɪps/ *technical* (***millions of instructions per second***) used to say how fast a computer works

mir·a·cle /ˈmɪrəkəl/ ●●○ *n* [C]
1 something very lucky or very good that happens which you did not expect to happen or did not think was possible: ***It's a miracle*** *you weren't killed! | By some miracle, we managed to catch the plane. | the* ***economic miracle*** *of the 1950s. | She's our miracle baby.* | **small/minor miracle** (=something lucky but not very important) *The fence's survival in these winds seems like a minor miracle.*
2 an action or event believed to be caused by God, which is impossible according to the ordinary laws of nature: *Do you believe in miracles?*
3 miracle cure/drug a very effective medical treatment that cures even serious diseases: *There is no miracle cure for diabetes.*
4 work/perform miracles to have a very good effect or achieve a very good result: *Maybe you should try yoga – it worked miracles for me.*
5 a miracle of sth a very good example of something: *The concert tour was an absolute miracle of organization. | a miracle of modern engineering*

mi·rac·u·lous /mɪˈrækjələs/ *adj* **1** very good, completely unexpected, and often very lucky: *She made a miraculous recovery from her injuries. | They had a miraculous escape when their car plunged into a river.* THESAURUS ➤ LUCKY **2** a miraculous action or event is believed to be caused by God, and is impossible according to the ordinary laws of nature: *miraculous powers of healing* —**miraculously** *adv*: *Miraculously, no one was killed.*

mi·rage /ˈmɪrɑːʒ $ məˈrɑːʒ/ *n* [C] **1** an effect caused by hot air in a desert, which makes you think that you can see objects when they are not actually there **2** a dream, hope, or wish that cannot come true SYN **illusion**: *Perhaps we are just chasing a mirage.*

mire /maɪə $ maɪr/ *n* [U] *literary* **1** deep mud: *The wheels got stuck in the mire.* **2 the mire** a bad or difficult situation that you cannot seem to escape from SYN **quagmire**: *The Party sank deeper into the mire of conflict.* **3 drag sb's name through the mire** to say bad things about someone in public, so that other people have a bad opinion of them

mired /maɪəd $ maɪrd/ *adj* [not before noun] *literary* **1** stuck in a bad situation and unable to get out or make progress: **[+in]** *a government mired in scandal and controversy* **2** stuck in mud or covered in mud

mir·ror¹ /ˈmɪrə $ -ər/ ●●● S3 W3 *n* [C]
1 a piece of special glass that you can look at and see yourself in: **in a mirror** *She was studying her reflection in the mirror. | He spends hours* ***in front of*** *the* ***mirror***! | *When I* ***looked in*** *the* ***mirror*** *I couldn't believe it. I looked fantastic!*
2 a mirror on the inside or side of a vehicle, which the driver uses to see what is behind: *Check your* ***rear-view mirror*** *before you drive away. | a* ***wing mirror***
3 a mirror of sth something that gives a clear idea of what something else is like SYN **reflection**: *We believe the polls are an accurate mirror of public opinion.*

mirror² ●○○ *v* [T] if one thing mirrors another, it is

very similar to it and may seem to copy or represent it SYN **reflect**: *Henry's sad smile mirrored that of his son.* | *The economic recovery in Britain was mirrored in the US.*

ˈmirror ˌimage *n* [C] **1** an image of something in which the right side appears on the left, and the left side appears on the right **2** something that is either very similar to something else or is the complete opposite of it: **[+of]** *The situation is a mirror image of the one Republicans faced 25 years ago.*

ˈmirror site *n* [C] a website that is an exact copy of another one, but which is in a different place on the Internet

mirth /mɜːθ $ mɜːrθ/ *n* [U] *literary* happiness and laughter: *Her body began to shake with mirth.* —**mirthful** *adj*

mirth·less /ˈmɜːθləs $ ˈmɜːrθ-/ *adj literary* mirthless laughter or a mirthless smile does not seem to be caused by real amusement or happiness: *'Now it's your turn,' he said with a mirthless grin.* —**mirthlessly** *adv*: *He smiled mirthlessly.*

mis- /mɪs/ *prefix* **1** bad or badly: *misfortune* (=bad luck) | *He's been misbehaving.* **2** wrong or wrongly: *a miscalculation* | *I misunderstood you.* **3** used to refer to an opposite or the lack of something: *What caused this anger and mistrust* (=lack of trust)?

mis·ad·ven·ture /ˌmɪsədˈventʃə $ -ər/ *n* **1 death by misadventure** *BrE law* the official name for a death caused by an accident: *A verdict of death by misadventure was recorded.* **2** [C,U] *literary* bad luck or an accident

mis·al·li·ance /ˌmɪsəˈlaɪəns/ *n* [C] *formal* a situation in which two people or organizations have agreed to work together, marry each other etc, but are not suitable for each other: *It was a hopeless misalliance.*

mis·an·thro·pist /mɪsˈænθrəpɪst/ (*also* **mis·an·thrope** /ˈmɪsənθrəʊp $ -θroʊp/) *n* [C] *formal* someone who does not like other people and prefers to be alone —**misanthropic** /ˌmɪsənˈθrɒpɪk◂ $ -ˈθrɑː-/ *adj* —**misanthropy** /mɪsˈænθrəpi/ *n* [U]

mis·ap·ply /ˌmɪsəˈplaɪ/ *v* (**misapplied**, **misapplying**, **misapplies**) [T] to use something incorrectly or for a wrong purpose: *In your case the rules have been misapplied.* —**misapplication** /ˌmɪsæplɪˈkeɪʃən/ *n* [U]: *a misapplication of the law*

mis·ap·pre·hen·sion /ˌmɪsæprɪˈhenʃən/ *n* [C] *formal* a mistaken belief or a wrong understanding of something SYN **misunderstanding**: **under a misapprehension** *You seem to be under a misapprehension.* | *I think we should clear up this misapprehension.*

mis·ap·pro·pri·ate /ˌmɪsəˈprəʊprieɪt $ -ˈproʊ-/ *v* [T] *formal* to dishonestly take something that someone has trusted you with, especially money or goods that belong to your employer SYN **embezzle** → **appropriate**: *He claimed the finance manager had misappropriated company funds.* —**misappropriation** /ˌmɪsəprəʊpriˈeɪʃən $ -proʊ-/ *n* [U]: *the misappropriation of public funds*

mis·be·got·ten /ˌmɪsbɪˈɡɒtn◂ $ -ˈɡɑː-/ *adj* [only before noun] *old-fashioned* **1** a misbegotten plan, idea etc is not likely to succeed because it is badly planned or not sensible **2** a misbegotten person is completely stupid or useless: *You misbegotten fool!*

mis·be·have /ˌmɪsbɪˈheɪv/ *v* [I] (*also* **misbehave yourself**) to behave badly, and cause trouble or annoy people OPP **behave**: *George has been misbehaving at school.* | *Students have a tendency to misbehave themselves at exam time.*

mis·be·ha·viour *BrE*, **misbehavior** *AmE* /ˌmɪsbɪˈheɪvjə $ -ər/ *n* [U] bad behaviour that is not acceptable to other people SYN **misconduct**: *Even the most minor forms of misbehaviour were punished.*

mis·cal·cu·late /mɪsˈkælkjəleɪt/ *v* [I,T] **1** to make a mistake when deciding how long something will take to do, how much money you will need etc: *We miscalculated how long it would take to get there.* **2** to make a wrong judgment about a situation: *Tim had miscalculated: Laura would never disobey her father.*

mis·cal·cu·la·tion /mɪsˌkælkjəˈleɪʃən/ *n* [C] **1** a mistake made in deciding how long something will take to do, how much money you will need etc **2** a wrong judgment about a situation

mis·car·riage /ˌmɪsˈkærɪdʒ, ˈmɪskærɪdʒ/ *n* [C,U] if a woman who is going to have a baby has a miscarriage, she gives birth before the baby is properly formed and it dies → **abortion**, **stillbirth**: *She **had** two **miscarriages** before she had her first child.* | *One in five pregnancies **ends in miscarriage**.*

misˌcarriage of ˈjustice *n* (*plural* **miscarriages of justice**) [C,U] a situation in which someone is wrongly punished by a court of law for something they did not do: *the victim of a serious miscarriage of justice*

mis·car·ry /mɪsˈkæri/ *v* (**miscarried**, **miscarrying**, **miscarries**) **1** [I,T] to give birth to a baby before it is properly formed and able to live → **abort**: *She miscarried when she was 10 weeks pregnant.* | *Many babies with serious disabilities are miscarried.* **2** [I] *formal* if a plan miscarries, it is not successful

mis·cast /ˌmɪsˈkɑːst $ -ˈkæst/ *v* (*past tense and past participle* **miscast**) [T] to choose an unsuitable actor to play a particular character in a play or film → **cast**: *She was hopelessly miscast in her last film.* GRAMMAR **Miscast** is usually passive.

mis·ce·ge·na·tion /ˌmɪsədʒəˈneɪʃən $ -sedʒ-/ *n* [U] *formal* when people of different races have a sexual relationship or have children together

mis·cel·la·ne·ous /ˌmɪsəˈleɪniəs◂/ *adj* [only before noun] a miscellaneous set of things or people includes many different things or people that do not seem to be connected with each other: *a miscellaneous assortment of books* | *They receive a grant of £1,094 to cover the cost of miscellaneous expenses.*

mis·cel·la·ny /mɪˈseləni $ ˈmɪsəleɪni/ *n* (*plural* **miscellanies**) [C] a group of different things SYN **variety**: **[+of]** *He earned his living from a miscellany of jobs.*

mis·chance /ˌmɪsˈtʃɑːns $ -ˈtʃæns/ *n* [C,U] *formal* bad luck, or a situation that results from bad luck SYN **misfortune**: *If by some mischance the government get elected again, I think taxes will rise.*

mis·chief /ˈmɪstʃɪf/ ●○○ *n*

1 [U] bad behaviour, especially by children, that causes trouble or damage, but no serious harm: *Now run along, and don't **get into mischief**.* | *They've got enough toys to **keep** them **out of mischief** for a while.* | *If you can't see Nick, you can be sure he's **up to** some **mischief*** (=behaving badly and causing trouble or damage).

2 [U] the pleasure or enjoyment of playing tricks on people or embarrassing them: *Kiki's eyes were bright with mischief.*

3 make mischief *informal* to deliberately cause quarrels or unfriendly feelings between people: **[+between]** *I didn't want to make mischief between them.*

4 do yourself a mischief *BrE informal* to injure yourself slightly: *If you try to lift that box, you'll do yourself a mischief.*

5 [U] *formal* damage or harm that is done to someone or to their property: *The jury cleared him of the charge of criminal mischief.*

ˈmischief-ˌmaker *n* [C] someone who deliberately causes trouble or quarrels SYN **stirrer**

mis·chie·vous /ˈmɪstʃəvəs/ *adj* **1** someone who is mischievous likes to have fun, especially by playing tricks on people or doing things to annoy or embarrass them: *Their sons are noisy and mischievous.* | **mischievous smile/look etc** *Gabby looked at him with a mischievous grin.* | *There was a mischievous gleam in her eyes.* **2** causing trouble or quarrels deliberately: *a mischievous remark* —**mischievously** *adv*: *He grinned mischievously.* —**mischievousness** *n* [U]

mis·con·ceived /ˌmɪskənˈsiːvd◂/ *adj* a misconceived idea, plan, method etc is not a good one because it is based on a wrong understanding of something: *His arguments are totally misconceived.* | *His criticisms are misconceived and misplaced.*

mis·con·cep·tion /ˌmɪskənˈsepʃən/ *n* [C,U] an idea

M

which is wrong or untrue, but which people believe because they do not understand the subject properly SYN **fallacy** → **preconception**: **popular/common misconception** *There is a popular misconception that too much exercise is bad for you.* | **misconception that** *Refugees have the misconception that life is great over here.* | **[+about]** *many people's misconceptions about the blind and deaf*

mis·con·duct /ˌmɪsˈkɒndʌkt $ -ˈkɑːn-/ *n* [U] *formal* bad or dishonest behaviour by someone in a position of authority or trust: *a doctor who has been accused of* ***professional misconduct*** | *He was fired for* ***serious misconduct***. | *She was found guilty of* ***gross misconduct*** (=very serious misconduct).

mis·con·struc·tion /ˌmɪskənˈstrʌkʃən/ *n* [C,U] *formal* an incorrect or mistaken understanding of something SYN **misunderstanding**: *Your ideas are open to misconstruction.*

mis·con·strue /ˌmɪskənˈstruː/ *v* [T] *formal* to MISUNDERSTAND something that someone has said or done SYN **misinterpret**: *His behaviour could easily be misconstrued.*

mis·count /ˌmɪsˈkaʊnt/ *v* [I,T] to count wrongly: *Sorry, I miscounted – we need ten copies, not nine.* | *The votes were deliberately miscounted.*

mis·cre·ant /ˈmɪskriənt/ *n* [C] *formal* a bad person who causes trouble, hurts people etc

mis·deed /ˌmɪsˈdiːd/ *n* [C] *formal* a wrong or illegal action: *He now repents of his past misdeeds.*

mis·de·mea·nour *BrE*, **misdemeanor** *AmE* /ˌmɪsdɪˈmiːnə $ -ər/ *n* [C] **1** *formal* a bad or unacceptable action that is not very serious: *Alfred beat his children for even the smallest misdemeanour.* **2** *law* a crime that is not very serious → **felony**

mis·di·ag·nose /ˌmɪsdaɪəɡˈnəʊz $ -ˈnoʊs/ *v* [T] to give an incorrect explanation of an illness, a problem in a machine etc: **misdiagnose sth as sth** *Her condition was misdiagnosed as arthritis.*

mis·di·rect /ˌmɪsdəˈrekt, -daɪ-/ *v* [T] **1** *formal* to use your effort, energy, abilities etc on doing the wrong thing: *Without well-defined goals, it is likely that efforts will be misdirected.* | *Their criticism is misdirected.* **2** if a judge misdirects a JURY (=the group of people who decide a legal case), he or she gives them incorrect information about the law **3** *formal* to send someone or something to the wrong place: **be misdirected to sth** *Our mail was misdirected to the wrong street.* GRAMMAR **Misdirect** is usually passive. —**misdirection** /-ˈrekʃən/ *n* [U]

mi·ser /ˈmaɪzə $ -ər/ *n* [C] someone who is not generous and does not like spending money → **miserly**

mis·e·ra·bil·ist /ˈmɪzərəbəlɪst/ *n* [C] *BrE* someone who always seems unhappy about things, especially a singer or writer —**miserabilist** *adj*

mis·e·ra·ble /ˈmɪzərəbəl/ ●●● S3 W3 *adj*
1 extremely unhappy, for example because you feel lonely, cold, or badly treated: *I've been so miserable since Pat left me.* | *I spent the weekend* ***feeling miserable***. | *Jan* ***looks*** *really* ***miserable***. | *Why do you* ***make yourself miserable*** *by taking on too much work?* | **as miserable as sin** *BrE* (=very miserable) THESAURUS SAD
2 *especially BrE* always bad-tempered, DISSATISFIED, or complaining: *He's a miserable old devil.*
3 [usually before noun] making you feel very unhappy, uncomfortable etc: *They endured hours of backbreaking work in miserable conditions.* | *Mosquito bites can* ***make life miserable***.
4 miserable weather is cold and dull, with no sun shining: *It was a miserable grey day.* | *two weeks of miserable weather*
5 [only before noun] very small in amount, or very bad in quality: *I can hardly afford the rent on my miserable income.* | *The team gave a miserable performance.*
6 miserable failure *BrE* a complete failure: *Her attempts to learn to drive had been a miserable failure.* —**miserably** *adv*: *I failed miserably in my duty to protect her.*

mi·ser·ly /ˈmaɪzəli $ -zər-/ *adj* **1** a miserly amount or quantity is one that is much too small SYN **measly**, **paltry**: *We were offered a miserly 4% pay rise.* **2** a miserly person is not generous and does not like spending money SYN **mean** —**miserliness** *n* [U]

mis·e·ry /ˈmɪzəri/ ●●○ S3 *n* (*plural* **miseries**)
1 [C,U] great suffering that is caused for example by being very poor or very sick: *What we are witnessing here is human misery on a vast scale.* | *the misery of unemployment* | *the miseries of war*
2 [C,U] great unhappiness: *She looked away so that Tom wouldn't see her misery.* | *His face was a picture of* ***sheer misery*** (=great unhappiness, with no other emotion). | *The news plunged him into* ***abject misery*** (=extreme unhappiness).
3 make sb's life a misery *BrE* to cause so much trouble for someone that they cannot enjoy their life: *Competitive mothers can make their daughters' lives a misery.*
4 put sth/sb out of their misery a) *informal* to make someone stop feeling worried, especially by telling them something they are waiting to hear: *Go on, put them out of their misery and announce the winner.* **b)** to kill a sick or injured animal in order to end its suffering SYN **put down**: *I think you should put the poor creature out of its misery.*
5 [C] *BrE spoken* someone who is always complaining and never enjoys anything: *Don't be such a misery.* | *What's the matter with you,* ***misery guts*** (=a name for someone like this)?

ˈmisery ˌmemoir *n* [C] a book that someone has written about bad things that happened to them when they were a child

mis·field /ˌmɪsˈfiːld/ *v* [I,T] to make a mistake in catching or throwing the ball in some ball games, such as CRICKET —**misfield** /ˈmɪsfiːld/ *n* [C]

mis·fire /ˌmɪsˈfaɪə $ -ˈfaɪr/ *v* [I] **1** if a plan or joke misfires, it goes wrong and does not have the result that you intended → **backfire**: *His attempt at a joke misfired.* | *I was worried that the plan might misfire.* **2** if an engine misfires, the petrol mixture does not burn at the right time **3** if a gun misfires, the bullet does not come out

mis·fit /ˈmɪsˌfɪt/ *n* [C] someone who does not seem to belong in a particular group of people, and who is not accepted by that group, because they are very different from the other group members SYN **outsider**: *I was very conscious of being a misfit at school.* | *a social misfit*

mis·for·tune /mɪsˈfɔːtʃən $ -ɔːr-/ ●○○ *n* [C,U] very bad luck, or something that happens to you as a result of bad luck: *It seems the banks always profit from farmers' misfortunes.* | **have the misfortune to do/of doing sth** *The French soldiers had the misfortune to be caught in the crossfire.*

mis·giv·ing /mɪsˈɡɪvɪŋ/ *n* [C,U] a feeling of doubt or fear about what might happen or about whether something is right SYN **doubt**: **[+about]** *Despite her misgivings about leaving the baby, she decided to accompany her husband.* | **grave/serious/deep misgivings** *Some politicians have expressed grave misgivings about the scheme.* | *Opponents of nuclear energy* ***have*** *deep* ***misgivings*** *about its safety.* | *She eyed the distant shoreline with misgiving.*

mis·guid·ed /mɪsˈɡaɪdɪd/ *adj* **1** intended to be helpful but in fact making a situation worse: *He described the government's economic policy as misguided.* | *a misguided attempt to bring her parents back together* **2** a misguided idea or opinion is wrong because it is based on a wrong understanding of a situation: *His parents still clung to the misguided belief that his common sense would keep him out of serious trouble.* THESAURUS WRONG —**misguidedly** *adv*: *The company misguidedly thought that expansion was the best way to survive.*

mis·han·dle /ˌmɪsˈhændl/ *v* [T] **1** to deal with a situation badly, because of a lack of skill or care: *The prime minister admitted that the crisis had been mishandled.* **2** to treat something roughly, often causing damage: *Some of the goods had been mishandled and damaged.*

mis·hap /ˈmɪshæp/ ●○○ *n* [C,U] a small accident or

mistake that does not have very serious results: *I had a **slight mishap** with one of the glasses.* | *a series of mishaps* | **without mishap** *Only one horse finished the course without mishap.*

mis·hear /ˌmɪsˈhɪə $ -ˈhɪr/ *v* (*past tense and past participle* **misheard** /-ˈhɜːd $ -ˈhɜːrd/) [I,T] to not hear properly what someone says, so that you think they said something different: *It seemed a strange question; I wondered if I had misheard.* | *You must have misheard him.*

mis·hit /ˌmɪsˈhɪt/ *v* (*past tense and past participle* **mishit**, *present participle* **mishitting**) [T] to hit a ball badly in a game or sport: *He completely mishit his shot.* —**mishit** /ˈmɪshɪt/ *n* [C]

mish·mash /ˈmɪʃmæʃ/ *n* [singular] *informal* a mixture of a lot of very different things that are put together in a way that is not organized SYN **hodge-podge**: **[+of]** *The magazine is a jumbled mishmash of jokes, stories, and serious news.*

mis·in·form /ˌmɪsɪnˈfɔːm $ -ɔːrm/ *v* [T] to give someone information that is incorrect: *I am afraid you've been misinformed.* GRAMMAR **Misinform** is usually passive.

mis·in·for·ma·tion /ˌmɪsɪnfəˈmeɪʃən $ -fər-/ *n* [U] incorrect information, especially when deliberately intended to deceive people → **disinformation**

mis·in·ter·pret /ˌmɪsɪnˈtɜːprɪt $ -ɜːr-/ AWL *v* [T] to not understand the correct meaning of something that someone says or does, or of facts that you are considering SYN **misread**, **misconstrue**: *Some parts of the report could be misinterpreted.* | **misinterpret sth as sth** *She had misinterpreted his silence as anger.* —**misinterpretation** /ˌmɪsɪntɜːprɪˈteɪʃən $ -tɜːr-/ *n* [C,U]: *a misinterpretation of the test results*

mis·judge /ˌmɪsˈdʒʌdʒ/ ●○○ *v* [T]
1 to form a wrong or unfair opinion about a person or a situation: *The government misjudged the mood of the electorate.* | *I think you've misjudged her.*
2 to guess an amount or distance wrongly SYN **miscalculate**: *I misjudged the speed of the car coming towards me.* —**misjudgment** (*also* **misjudgement** *BrE*) *n* [C,U]: *He accused the government of a serious foreign policy misjudgement.*

mis·lay /ˌmɪsˈleɪ/ *v* (*past tense and past participle* **mislaid** /-ˈleɪd/) [T] to put something somewhere, then forget where you put it SYN **lose**, **misplace**: *I've mislaid my glasses again.* | *Sometimes students' work does get lost or mislaid.*

mis·lead /ˌmɪsˈliːd/ ●●○ *v* (*past tense and past participle* **misled** /-ˈled/) [T] to make someone believe something that is not true by giving them information that is false or not complete: **mislead sb about/over sth** *Politicians have misled the public over the dangers of these chemicals.* | *Don't be misled by appearances, he's a good worker.* | **mislead sb into believing/thinking etc sth** *Don't be misled into thinking that scientific research is easy.*

mis·lead·ing /ˌmɪsˈliːdɪŋ/ ●●○ *adj* likely to make someone believe something that is not true: *The article was misleading, and the newspaper has apologized.* | **seriously/highly/grossly etc misleading** *These figures are highly misleading.* THESAURUS ▸ WRONG —**misleadingly** *adv*: *The diagrams are misleadingly simple.*

mis·man·age /ˌmɪsˈmænɪdʒ/ *v* [T] if someone mismanages something they are in charge of, they deal with or manage it badly: *The nation's finances had been badly mismanaged.* —**mismanagement** *n* [U]: *the government's mismanagement of the crisis*

mis·match /ˈmɪsmætʃ/ *n* [C] a combination of things or people that do not work well together or are not suitable for each other: **[+between]** *the mismatch between the demand for health care and the supply* —**mismatched** /ˌmɪsˈmætʃt◂/ *adj*: *a mismatched couple*

mis·name /ˌmɪsˈneɪm/ *v* [T] to give something a name that is wrong or not suitable: *a dreary little place that was misnamed the Grand Hotel*

mis·no·mer /mɪsˈnəʊmə $ -ˈnoʊmər/ *n* [C] a wrong or unsuitable name: *'Silent movie' is a misnomer since the movies usually had a musical accompaniment.*

mi·so·gy·nist /mɪˈsɒdʒɪnɪst $ məˈsɑː-/ *n* [C] *formal* a man who hates women —**misogynist**, **misogynistic** *adj*: *deeply misogynist attitudes* —**misogyny** *n* [U]

mis·place /ˌmɪsˈpleɪs/ *v* [T] to lose something for a short time by putting it in the wrong place SYN **mislay**: *Oh dear, I seem to have misplaced the letter.*

mis·placed /ˌmɪsˈpleɪst◂/ *adj* misplaced feelings of trust, love etc are wrong and unsuitable, because the person that you have these feelings for does not deserve them: *I realized that my trust in him was misplaced.* | *She stuck with him through a misplaced sense of loyalty.*

mis·print /ˈmɪs-prɪnt/ *n* [C] a small mistake, especially a spelling mistake, in a book, magazine etc THESAURUS ▸ MISTAKE

mis·pro·nounce /ˌmɪsprəˈnaʊns/ *v* [T] to pronounce a word or name wrongly —**mispronunciation** /ˌmɪsprənʌnsiˈeɪʃən/ *n* [C,U]

mis·quote /ˌmɪsˈkwəʊt/ *v* [T] to make a mistake in reporting what someone else has said: *Dr Hall said he had been misquoted in the press.* —**misquotation** /ˌmɪskwəʊˈteɪʃən $ -kwoʊ-/ *n* [C,U]

mis·read /ˌmɪsˈriːd/ *v* (*past tense and past participle* **misread** /-ˈred/) [T] **1** to make a wrong judgment about a person or situation SYN **misinterpret**: *I think she misread the situation.* | *He may be misreading her intentions.* **2** to read something incorrectly: *The doctor must have misread the notes.* —**misreading** *n* [C,U]: *a misreading of the situation*

mis·re·port /ˌmɪsrɪˈpɔːt $ -ˈpɔːrt/ *v* [T usually passive] to give an incorrect or untrue account of an event or situation: *The facts of the story have been misreported.*

mis·rep·re·sent /ˌmɪsreprɪˈzent/ *v* [T] to deliberately give a wrong description of someone's opinions or of a situation: *These statistics grossly misrepresent the reality.* —**misrepresentation** /ˌmɪsreprɪzenˈteɪʃən/ *n* [C,U]: *a misrepresentation of the truth*

mis·rule /ˌmɪsˈruːl/ *n* [U] *formal* bad government: *The country has suffered years of misrule by a weak and corrupt government.*

miss¹ /mɪs/ ●●● S1 W2 *v*
1 NOT DO STH [T] to not go somewhere or do something, especially when you want to but cannot: *I'm absolutely starving – I missed lunch.* | *He missed 20 games after breaking a bone in his wrist.* | *She was upset at missing all the excitement.* | **miss doing sth** *He had missed being elected by a single vote.*
2 NOT HIT/CATCH [I,T] to fail to hit or catch an object that is close to you, or to fail to hit a distant object that you are aiming at: *Every time she missed the ball she became more angry.* | *He fired, missed and loaded again.* | *The bullet **narrowly missed** her heart.*
3 FEEL SAD ABOUT SB [T] to feel sad because someone you love is not with you: *She missed her family badly.* | *Will you miss me?* | *John will be **sorely missed** by his family and friends.*
4 FEEL SAD ABOUT STH [T] to feel sad because you do not have something or cannot do something you had or did before: *I miss the car, but the bus system is good.* | **miss doing sth** *Ben knew he would miss working with Sabrina.*

> **GRAMMAR**
> **Miss** is followed by an **-ing** form, not an infinitive. You say: *I miss seeing you every day.* ✗ Don't say: *I miss to see you every day.*
> GRAMMAR GUIDE ▸ VERBS

5 TOO LATE [T] to be too late for something: *We got there late and missed the beginning of the movie.* | **miss the train/bus etc** *I overslept and missed the train.*
6 miss a chance/opportunity to fail to use an opportunity to do something: *He certainly wasn't going to miss the chance of making some extra money.* | *Don't miss the chance to see the breathtaking Dolomite Mountains.* | *The **opportunity** was **too good to miss** so we left immediately.*
7 NOT SEE/HEAR [T] to not see, hear, or notice something, especially when it is difficult to notice: *Maeve's sharp eyes*

missed nothing. | *Perhaps there's something the police have missed.* | *It's a huge hotel on the corner.* ***You can't miss it*** (=it is very easy to notice or recognize). | ***You don't miss much**, do you* (=you are good at noticing things)? | *John* ***didn't miss a trick*** (=noticed every opportunity to get an advantage) *when it came to cutting costs.*
8 miss the point to not understand the main point of what someone is saying
9 sth is not to be missed used to say that someone should do something while they have the opportunity: *A journey on one of the steam trains is certainly not to be missed!*
10 AVOID STH [T] to avoid something bad or unpleasant: *If we leave now we should miss the traffic.* | **miss doing sth** *As he crossed the street, a bus just missed hitting him.* | *They* ***narrowly missed*** *being killed in the fire.*
11 I wouldn't miss it for the world *spoken* used to say that you really want to go to an event, see something etc: *'Come to the party.' 'I will. I wouldn't miss it for the world.'*
12 NOTICE STH ISN'T THERE [T] to notice that something or someone is not in the place you expect them to be: *I didn't miss my wallet till it came to paying the bill.*
13 miss the mark to not achieve something you were trying to do: *Their efforts to improve quality have somewhat missed the mark.*
14 miss the boat *informal* to fail to take an opportunity that will give you an advantage: *You'll miss the boat if you don't buy shares now.*
15 without missing a beat if you do something without missing a beat, you do it without showing that you are surprised or shocked: *She handled all of their questions without missing a beat.*
16 sb's heart misses a beat used to say that someone is very excited, surprised, or frightened: *Glancing up at Rick's face, she felt her heart miss a beat.*
17 ENGINE [I] if an engine misses, it stops working for a very short time and then starts again

miss out *phr v*
1 to not have the chance to do something that you enjoy and that would be good for you: *Some children miss out because their parents can't afford to pay for school trips.* | **[+on]** *Prepare food in advance to ensure you don't miss out on the fun!*
2 miss sb/sth ↔ out *BrE* to not include someone or something: *Make sure you don't miss any details out.*

USAGE: Miss, fail to

You use **fail to** when talking about not doing something that you should have done: *Some students failed to pay attention in class.* Don't use **miss** in this meaning.

miss² ●●● S2 W2 *n*
1 Miss used in front of the family name of a woman who is not married to address her politely, to write to her, or to talk about her → **Mrs**, **Mr**: *I'd like to make an appointment with Miss Taylor.* ⚠ Some unmarried women prefer to be addressed as **Ms** because it does not draw attention to whether or not they are married.
2 Miss Italy/Ohio/World etc used to refer to a woman who represents a country, city etc in a beauty competition
3 YOUNG WOMAN *spoken* used as a polite way of speaking to a young woman when you do not know her name → **madam**, **sir**: *Excuse me, miss, you've dropped your umbrella.*
4 TEACHER *BrE spoken* used by children when speaking to a female teacher, whether she is married or not → **sir**: *I know the answer, Miss.*
5 give sth a miss *BrE informal* to decide not to do something: *I'd better give the coffee a miss. I'm due at a meeting in half an hour.*
6 NOT HIT/CATCH [C] an occasion when you fail to hit, catch, or hold something: *Will he score a goal this time? No, no it's a miss.*
7 YOUNG GIRL [C] *BrE spoken* a young girl, especially one who has been bad or rude: *She's a cheeky little miss.* → HIT-AND-MISS, → **near miss** at NEAR²(6)

mis·sal /ˈmɪsəl/ *n* [C] a book containing all the prayers said during each Mass for a whole year in the Roman Catholic Church

mis·shap·en /ˌmɪsˈʃeɪpən, mɪˈʃeɪ-/ *adj* not the normal or natural shape: *an old woman struggling to walk on misshapen feet* | *misshapen carrots*

mis·sile /ˈmɪsaɪl $ ˈmɪsəl/ ●○○ *n* [C]
1 a weapon that can fly over long distances and that explodes when it hits the thing it has been aimed at: *a* ***nuclear missile*** | *a missile attack*
2 an object that is thrown at someone in order to hurt them: *Demonstrators threw missiles at the police.* → BALLISTIC MISSILE, CRUISE MISSILE, GUIDED MISSILE

miss·ing /ˈmɪsɪŋ/ ●●○ *adj*
1 something that is missing is not in its usual place, so that you cannot find it: *We found the missing piece of the jigsaw under the chair.* | *The keys have been missing for ages.* | **[+from]** *Two bottles were missing from the drugs cupboard.* | **go missing** *BrE: The scissors have gone missing again.*
2 if part of something is missing, it is no longer attached or has been destroyed: *Two of her front teeth were missing.* | *The last page of the diary was missing.* | **[+from]** *There's a button missing from your shirt.*
3 someone who is missing has disappeared, and no one knows if they are alive or dead: *Two crew members survived, but two are still missing.* | **go missing** *BrE: Nearly 100,000 young people go missing in Britain each year.* | *When Lily did not come home, her parents called the police to* ***report*** *her* ***missing***.
4 not present or not included in something: **[+from]** *Why is my name missing from the list?* | *Something was missing from her life.*
5 missing in action a soldier who is missing in action has not returned after a battle and their body has not been found

ˌmissing ˈlink *n* [C] **1** a piece of information that you need in order to solve a problem: *Could this be the missing link in the search for a cure for cancer?* **2 the missing link** an animal which was a stage in the development of humans from APES, whose bones have not yet been found

ˌmissing ˈperson *n* (*plural* **missing persons**) [C] someone who has disappeared and whose family has asked the police to try to find them

mis·sion /ˈmɪʃən/ ●●○ W2 *n* [C]
1 AIR FORCE/ARMY ETC an important job that involves travelling somewhere, done by a member of the air force, army etc, or by a spacecraft: *He was sent on over 200 missions before being killed in action.* | **[+to]** *the first manned space mission to Mars* | *US troops taking part in the* ***peacekeeping mission***
2 JOB an important job that someone has been given to do, especially when they are sent to another place: *Her mission was to improve staff morale.* | **on a mission** *scientists on a mission to the rainforest, to study possible medicinal uses of plants* | **rescue/diplomatic/fact-finding etc mission** *a group of US congressmen on a fact-finding mission to Northern Ireland*
3 DUTY something that you feel you must do because it is your duty SYN **calling**, **vocation**: *Tom's mission was to help young people in his local community.* | *His main* ***mission in life*** *is to earn as much money as possible.*
4 PURPOSE the purpose or the most important aim of an organization: *The mission of International House is to enable students of different cultures to live together and build lifelong friendships.* → MISSION STATEMENT
5 GOVERNMENT a group of important people who are sent by their government to another country to discuss something or collect information SYN **delegation**: *a British trade mission to Moscow*
6 RELIGION **a)** religious work that involves going to a foreign country in order to teach people about Christianity or help poor people **b)** a building where this kind of work is done, or the people who work there
7 mission accomplished used when you have successfully achieved something that you were trying to do

8 woman/man with a mission someone who is very determined to achieve what they are trying to do - often used humorously

mis·sion·a·ry¹ /ˈmɪʃənəri $ -neri/ ●○○ *n* (*plural* **missionaries**) [C] someone who has been sent to a foreign country to teach people about Christianity and persuade them to become Christians

missionary² *adj* [only before noun] **1** relating to the work of missionaries: *missionary work | a missionary hospital* **2 missionary zeal** if you do something with missionary zeal, you do it with great eagerness, because you believe strongly that it is a good thing to do: *a young English teacher who taught poetry with missionary zeal*

ˈmissionary poˌsition *n* **the missionary position** the sexual position in which the woman lies on her back with the man on top of her and facing her

ˈmission ˌcontrol *n* [U] the people on Earth who communicate with and guide a spacecraft

ˈmission ˌcreep *n* [U] *AmE* a series of gradual changes in the aim of a group of people, with the result that they do something different from what they planned to do at the beginning

ˈmission ˌstatement *n* [C] **1** an official statement about the aims of a company or organization **2 personal mission statement** a clear statement about what you want to achieve with your life: *Use a personal mission statement to chart your career course.*

mis·sis /ˈmɪsɪz/ *n* [singular] another spelling of MISSUS

mis·sive /ˈmɪsɪv/ *n* [C] *literary* a letter - often used humorously: *An anonymous missive had been pushed under her door.*

mis·spell /ˌmɪsˈspel/ *v* (*past tense and past participle* **misspelt** /-ˈspelt/ *or* **misspelled**) [T] to spell a word wrongly —**misspelling** *n* [C,U]

mis·spend /ˌmɪsˈspend/ *v* (*past tense and past participle* **misspent** /-ˈspent/) [T] **1 misspent youth** someone who had a misspent youth wasted their time or behaved badly when they were young - often used humorously **2** to use time or money badly or wrongly: *Carey admitted misspending company funds.*

mis·step /ˈmɪs-step/ *n* [C] *AmE* a mistake, especially one that is caused by not understanding a situation correctly: *A misstep here could cost millions of dollars.*

mis·sus, missis /ˈmɪsɪz/ *n* [singular] *spoken informal* **1** a man's wife, or girlfriend who lives with him: *How's the missus?* **2** *BrE* used when speaking to a woman whose name you do not know: *Hey, missus, are these your kids?*

mist¹ /mɪst/ ●●○ *n*

1 [C,U] a light cloud low over the ground that makes it difficult for you to see very far → **fog**: *We could just see the outline of the house through the mist. | He vanished into the mist. | The hills were* ***shrouded in mist*** (=covered in mist, so that you could not see them). *| The* ***mist came down*** *off the mountains. | The* ***mists rolled in*** *off the sea* (=came on to the land from the sea)

2 lost in the mists of time if something such as a fact or secret is lost in the mists of time, no one remembers it because it happened so long ago: *The real reasons for the war are now lost in the mists of time.*

3 see sth through a mist of tears *literary* to see something while you are crying

mist² *v* [T] to cover something with very small drops of liquid in order to keep it wet: *The plant has to be misted every day.*

mist over *phr v* **1** if someone's eyes mist over, they become filled with tears: *His eyes misted over at the memory of his wife.* **2** to mist up

mist up *phr v* if a piece of glass mists up, or if something mists it up, it becomes covered with very small drops of water so that you cannot see through it: **mist sth ↔ up** *I can't see where I'm going with the windows all misted up like this.*

mis·take¹ /məˈsteɪk/ ●●● S2 W2 *n*

1 [C] something that has been done in the wrong way, or an opinion or statement that is incorrect → **error**: **[+in]** *We may have made a mistake in our calculations. | The most common mistake is to plant them too deep.* **THESAURUS** FAULT

2 [C] something you do that is not sensible or has a bad result: *Buying the house seemed a great idea at the time, but now I can see it was a* ***terrible mistake****. | Marrying him was* ***the biggest mistake*** *she ever* ***made****.* | **make the mistake of doing sth** *I stupidly made the mistake of giving them my phone number.*

3 by mistake if you do something by mistake, you do it without intending to SYN **accidentally** OPP **deliberately, on purpose**: *Someone must have left the door open by mistake. | I'm sorry, this letter is addressed to you - I opened it by mistake.*

4 in mistake for sb/sth as a result of a mistake in which someone or something is wrongly thought to be someone or something else: *The boy was shot dead in mistake for a burglar.*

5 we all make mistakes *spoken* used to tell someone not to be worried because they have made a mistake

6 make no mistake (about it) *spoken* used to emphasize that what you are saying is true, especially when you are warning about something serious or dangerous: *Make no mistake, this is the most serious threat our industry has ever seen.*

7 and no mistake *BrE spoken informal* used to emphasize the description you have just given: *Miles was a heartbreaker, and no mistake!*

COLLOCATIONS

VERBS

make a mistake *The lab must have made a mistake - this can't be right.*
correct a mistake *Luckily I was able to correct the mistake before my boss saw it.*
realize your mistake *As soon as he realized his mistake he turned in the right direction.*
admit your mistake | **mistakes happen**

ADJECTIVES/NOUN + mistake

a common mistake *A common mistake is to imagine that dogs think like humans.*
a little/minor mistake *The essay was full of little mistakes.*
a serious/grave mistake *There was a serious mistake in the instructions.*
an honest mistake (=a mistake, and not a deliberate action) | **a silly/stupid mistake** | **an easy mistake (to make)** | **a spelling mistake**

PHRASES

be full of mistakes *The article was full of mistakes.*
it is a mistake to think/assume etc sth *It would be a mistake to assume that all snakes are dangerous.*
there must be some mistake (=used when you think someone has made a mistake)

COMMON ERRORS

⚠ Don't say 'do a mistake'. Say **make a mistake**.

THESAURUS

mistake something incorrect that you accidentally do, say, or write: *a spelling mistake | I made a mistake - it should say £230, not £320.*
error *formal* a mistake: *an error in the report | grammatical errors | He had made a serious error on his tax form.*
misprint a small mistake in something that is printed: *There was a misprint in the article, and instead of 'pleasant' it said 'pheasant'.*
typo *informal* a mistake in something that has been typed or printed: *I spotted a couple of typos in the letter.*
inaccuracy *formal* a piece of information that is not completely correct: *The report contained several inaccuracies.*
mix-up a careless mistake in which one name, time, address etc has been confused with another, so that

M

the details of something are wrong: *There was a mix-up over the train times and I missed my train.*
slip-up a careless mistake when you are doing something: *The other team took advantage of the goalie's slip-up.*
oversight a mistake in which you forget something or do not notice something: *Through some oversight, the brochures were not ready by the right date.*
a slip of the tongue a mistake in which you accidentally say a similar sounding word: *When I said Thursday, I meant Tuesday. It was a slip of the tongue.*
faux pas /ˌfəʊ ˈpɑː, ˈfəʊ pɑː $ ˌfoʊ ˈpɑː/ *formal* an embarrassing mistake in a social situation, when you do or say something that you shouldn't: *Harris, trying to be funny, addressed the waiter as 'boy'. A deathly silence followed this faux pas.*

A STUPID MISTAKE

blunder a stupid mistake caused by not thinking carefully enough about what you are saying or doing, which could have serious results: *In a serious blunder by the hospital, two babies were sent home with the wrong parents.*
gaffe /gæf/ an embarrassing and stupid mistake made in a social situation or in public: *a serious gaffe in her speech about immigration*

mistake² ●●○ *v* (*past tense* **mistook** /-ˈstʊk/, *past participle* **mistaken** /-ˈsteɪkən/) [T]
1 to understand something wrongly: *She mistook my meaning entirely.* | *Ken mistook her concern, thinking she was interested in him for another reason.*
2 you can't mistake sb/sth used to say that someone or something is very easy to recognize: *You can't mistake her. She's the one with the long red hair.*
3 there is no mistaking sb/sth used to say that you are certain about something: *There's no mistaking whose children they are – they all look just like Joe.*
mistake sb/sth **for** sb/sth *phr v* to wrongly think that one person or thing is someone or something else: *A woman mistook him for a well-known actor, and asked him for his autograph.* | *The doctor mistook the symptoms for blood poisoning.*

mis·tak·en /məˈsteɪkən/ ●○○ *adj*
1 be mistaken if you are mistaken, you are wrong about something that you thought you knew or saw: *It can't have been my car. You must be mistaken.* | *I thought he said 12 o'clock, but I might have been mistaken.* | *We bought the rug in Turkey, **if I'm not mistaken**.* THESAURUS ▸ WRONG
2 mistaken belief/idea/impression/view etc a mistaken belief etc is not correct: *Marijuana has few withdrawal effects, and this has given rise to the mistaken belief that it is not addictive.* —**mistakenly** *adv*

misˌtaken iˈdentity *n* [U] a situation in which someone believes that they have seen a particular person when in fact it was someone else – used especially in relation to crimes: *The police arrested someone, but it turned out to be a **case of mistaken identity**.*

mis·ter /ˈmɪstə $ -ər/ ●○○ *n*
1 Mister the full form of MR ⚠ In people's names, Mister is always written **Mr**.
2 *spoken especially AmE* used to address a man whose name you do not know: *Thanks, mister.*

mis·time /ˌmɪsˈtaɪm/ *v* [T] to do something at not quite the right time: *He mistimed his kick and missed the ball.*

mis·tle·toe /ˈmɪsəltəʊ $ -toʊ/ *n* [U] a plant with small white berries, which grows on trees. It is traditional to kiss people under a piece of mistletoe at Christmas.

mis·took /məˈstʊk/ *v* the past tense of MISTAKE

mis·treat /ˌmɪsˈtriːt/ *v* [T] to treat a person or animal badly, especially in a cruel way SYN **ill-treat**, **maltreat**: *Security forces are accused of mistreating prisoners.* —**mistreatment** *n* [U]

mis·tress /ˈmɪstrɪs/ *n* [C] **1** a woman that a man has a sexual relationship with, even though he is married to someone else: *The prince had shocked society by living openly with his mistress.* **2** *BrE old-fashioned* a female teacher → **master**: *the new English mistress* **3** the female owner of a dog, horse etc → **master** **4** *old-fashioned* the female employer of a servant → **master**: *The maid looked nervously at her mistress.* **5 be (a/the) mistress of sth** if a woman is a mistress of something, she is in control of it, highly skilled at it etc → **master**: *She appeared to be very much the mistress of the situation.* **6 Mistress** *old use* used with a woman's family name as a polite way of speaking to her → **master**

mis·tri·al /ˌmɪsˈtraɪəl/ *n* [C] a TRIAL in a court of law which is unfair, so that a new trial has to be held: *The judge **declared a mistrial**.*

mis·trust¹ /mɪsˈtrʌst/ *n* [U] the feeling that you cannot trust someone, especially because you think they may treat you unfairly or dishonestly SYN **suspicion**, **distrust**: **[+of]** *He had a deep mistrust of the legal profession.*

mistrust² *v* [T] to not trust someone, especially because you think they may treat you unfairly or dishonestly SYN **distrust**: *As a very small child she had learned to mistrust adults.* —**mistrustful** *adj*: *Some people are very mistrustful of computerised banking.*

mist·y /ˈmɪsti/ ●●○ *adj*
1 misty weather is weather with a lot of mist: *a cold, misty morning*
2 *literary* if your eyes are misty, they are full of tears, especially because you are remembering a time in the past: *He paused, his eyes growing misty.* | *Whenever Maria sees a picture of her mother, she gets **misty-eyed**.*
3 not clear or bright SYN **vague**: *Without my glasses everything is just a misty blur.*

mis·un·der·stand /ˌmɪsʌndəˈstænd $ -ər-/ ●●○ *v* (*past tense and past participle* **misunderstood**) [I,T] to fail to understand someone or something correctly: *Rachel, you must have misunderstood her! Ellie would never say something like that.* | *Don't misunderstand me. She's a very nice person when you get to know her.*

mis·un·der·stand·ing /ˌmɪsʌndəˈstændɪŋ $ -ər-/ ●●○ *n*
1 [C,U] a problem caused by someone not understanding a question, situation, or instruction correctly: *There must have been some misunderstanding. I didn't order all these books.*
2 [C] an argument or disagreement that is not very serious – often used humorously: *Terry had a little misunderstanding with the police last night.* THESAURUS ▸ ARGUMENT

mis·un·der·stood /ˌmɪsʌndəˈstʊd $ -ər-/ *adj* used to describe someone who is not liked by other people in a way that is unfair, because they do not understand him or her: *Rodman claims that he is misunderstood, and that the media have always portrayed him unfairly.*

mis·use¹ /ˌmɪsˈjuːz/ ●○○ *v* [T]
1 to use something for the wrong purpose, or in the wrong way, often with harmful results SYN **abuse**: *Even harmless drugs can be misused.* | *The term 'schizophrenia' is often misused.* | *There is concern that the judges might misuse their power.*
2 to treat someone badly or unfairly → **abuse**

mis·use² /mɪsˈjuːs/ *n* [C,U] the use of something in the wrong way or for the wrong purpose SYN **abuse**: *a system designed to prevent credit card misuse* | **drug/alcohol misuse** *Children who begin smoking when young are at greater risk from drugs misuse.* | **[+of]** *a scandalous misuse of public funds*

mite /maɪt/ *n* [C] **1** a very small creature that lives in plants, CARPETS etc **2** *spoken* a small child, especially one that you feel sorry for: *Poor mite! You must be starving!* **3 a mite** slightly SYN **a bit**: *She's a mite shy.* | *It's a mite too big for the box.* **4 a mite of sth** *old-fashioned* a small amount of something

mi·ter /ˈmaɪtə $ -ər/ *n* [C] the American spelling of MITRE

mit·i·gate /ˈmɪtɪgeɪt/ *v* [T] *formal* to make a situation or the effects of something less unpleasant, harmful, or serious SYN **alleviate**: *Measures need to be taken to mitigate the environmental effects of burning more coal.*

mit·i·gat·ing /ˈmɪtəgeɪtɪŋ/ *adj* **mitigating circumstances/factors** facts about a situation that make a crime or bad mistake seem less serious: *Judges often give reduced sentences where there are mitigating circumstances.*

mit·i·ga·tion /ˌmɪtəˈgeɪʃən/ *n* [U] **1 in mitigation** *law* if you say something in mitigation, you try to make someone's crime or mistake seem less serious or show that they were not completely responsible: *The captain added, in mitigation, that the engines may have been faulty.* **2** *formal* a reduction in how unpleasant, harmful, or serious a situation is: *His marriage had brought a slight mitigation of the monotony of his existence.*

mi·tre *BrE*, **miter** *AmE* /ˈmaɪtə $ -ər/ *n* [C] **1** a tall pointed hat worn by BISHOPS and ARCHBISHOPS **2** (*also* **mitre joint**) a joint between two pieces of wood, in which each piece is cut at an angle

mitt /mɪt/ *n* [C] **1** a type of GLOVE that does not have separate parts for each finger SYN **mitten**: *ski mitts* | *an oven mitt* (=a thick glove used to protect your hand when you hold hot pans) **2** a type of leather GLOVE used to catch a ball in BASEBALL **3** *informal especially BrE* someone's hand: *Robert's put his sticky mitts all over it.*

mit·ten /ˈmɪtn/ *n* [C] a type of GLOVE that does not have separate parts for each finger → see pictures at **SPORT**[1], **GLOVE**

Mit·ty, Wal·ter /ˈmɪti, ˈwɔːltər/ someone who seems very ordinary but who either imagines they have an exciting secret life or who actually does have one. This name, used especially in newspapers, comes from the main character in a story by James Thurber called *The Secret Life of Walter Mitty* (1932). He has a very ordinary life, but spends a lot of time imagining that he is a brave and important person living a dangerous and exciting life: *Their quiet neighbour turned out to be a Walter Mitty character, running a huge drug-smuggling business from his garage.*

mix[1] /mɪks/ ●●● S2 W3 *v*

1 [I,T] if you mix two or more substances or if they mix, they combine to become a single substance, and they cannot be easily separated: *Oil and water don't mix.* | **mix (sth) with sth** *Shake the bottle well so that the oil mixes with the vinegar.* | *The powder is mixed with cold water to form a paste.* | *Mix the soured cream with ketchup.* | **mix sth together** *First mix the butter and sugar together, then add the milk.* | **mix sth in** *Mix in 75 g of butter.* | **mix sth into sth** *Mix the herbs into the sauce.*

2 [T] to combine two or more different activities, ideas, groups of things etc: *Their musical style mixes elements of Eastern culture and Western pop.* | **mix sth with sth** *His books mix historical fact with fantasy.* | *I don't like to* **mix business with pleasure** (=combine business and social activities at the same time).

3 [I] to meet, talk, and spend time with other people, especially people you do not know very well SYN **socialize**: **[+with]** *Charlie doesn't mix well with the other children.*

4 not mix if two different ideas, activities etc do not mix, there are problems when they are combined: *Smoking and babies don't mix.*

5 [T] (*also* **mix up**) to prepare something, especially food or drink, by mixing things together: *Will you mix us some martinis, Bill?*

6 mix and match to choose to put different things together from a range of possibilities: *They can mix and match their uniform, wearing either a sweatshirt or blouse with trousers or a skirt.*

7 [T] *technical* to control the balance of sounds in a record or film

8 mix it (up) *informal* to get involved in a fight with someone: *You don't want to mix it with him. He's been drinking since noon.*

mix sb/sth ↔ **up** *phr v*

1 to make the mistake of thinking that someone or something is another person or thing SYN **confuse, muddle up**: **[+with]** *I always mix him up with his brother. They look so much alike.* | *I think you might be mixing up Wetherall and Newton.* | *I must have* **got** *the times* **mixed up**.

2 to change the way things have been arranged, often by mistake, so that they are no longer in the same order: *My papers* **got** *all* **mixed up**. | *Books on Scottish history were mixed up with books on volcanoes.*

3 to make someone feel confused: *They kept trying to mix me up.*

4 to prepare something by mixing things together: *It was hard work mixing up four tonnes of cement.* → **MIXED UP**, **MIX-UP**

THESAURUS

TO MIX FOODS, LIQUIDS ETC

mix to put different substances or liquids together so that they can no longer be separated: *Mix yellow and blue paint to make green.* | *This cake is really easy – you just mix everything together in the bowl.* | *Concrete is made by mixing gravel with sand, cement, and water.*

combine to mix things together so that they form a single substance. **Combine** is more formal than **mix**: *Combine the flour and the eggs.* | *Steel is produced by combining iron with carbon.*

stir to move a spoon or stick around in a liquid, a pan etc, especially when you are mixing things together: *Keep stirring until the sauce becomes thicker.* | *Stir the sugar into the warm milk.*

blend to mix together soft or liquid substances to form a single smooth substance: *Blend the yogurt with fresh fruit for a great drink.*

beat to mix food together quickly and thoroughly using a fork or kitchen tool – used especially about eggs: *Beat the eggs and add them to the milk and flour.*

whisk to mix foods that are soft or liquid very quickly so that air is mixed in, using a fork or special tool: *Whisk the egg whites until they form soft peaks.*

dilute to mix a liquid with water in order to make it weaker: *Dilute the bleach with two parts water to one part bleach.*

TO MIX STYLES, IDEAS, OR OTHER THINGS

mix to put different styles, ideas, or other things together: *His music mixes jazz and classical styles.* | *The different categories of books were all mixed together.*

combine to mix different styles, ideas, or other things, so that they work together or become a single thing: *Diets are most effective when they are combined with exercise.* | *He combines Greek philosophy with Christian teachings.*

blend to combine parts of different things together, especially in a successful and effective way: *The teaching course blends theory and practice in the classroom.*

fuse to combine different styles in order to form a new style: *The band fuses African rhythms with traditional Celtic music.*

jumble to mix things together in an untidy way, so that they are not in any order: *The jigsaw pieces were all jumbled together in the box.*

mix[2] ●●○ *n*

1 [singular] the particular combination of things or people in a group or thing: **[+of]** *a good mix of people* | *We felt that between us we had the right mix of skills.* | *a complicated mix of colours and textures* | *the region's rich ethnic mix* (=people of different races)

2 [C,U] a combination of substances that you mix together to make something such as a cake SYN **mixture**: **cake/soup etc mix** *Add water to the cake mix and bake at 375°F.*

3 [C] a particular arrangement of sounds, voices, or different pieces of music used on a POP record: *the dance mix*

mixed /mɪkst/ ●●○ *adj*
1 [only before noun] consisting of several different types of things or people: *a very mixed group of women | a mixed salad*
2 mixed feelings/emotions if you have mixed feelings or emotions about something, you are not sure whether you like, agree with, or feel happy about it: **[+about]** *I had mixed feelings about meeting Laura again. | He watched with mixed emotions.*
3 mixed reaction/response/reviews etc if something gets a mixed reaction etc, some people say they like it or agree with it, but others dislike it or disagree with it: *The film has had mixed reviews from the critics. | Media coverage of the event was mixed.*
4 *especially BrE* for both males and females: *a mixed school*
5 a mixed blessing something that is good in some ways but bad in others: *Having your parents living nearby is a mixed blessing.*
6 a mixed bag a) a group of things or people that are all very different from each other: **[+of]** *The concert was a mixed bag of classical and modern music. | Club-goers are a mixed bag these days, and so are the places they go clubbing.* **b)** something that includes both good and bad parts: *The meat was very good, but the vegetables were rather a mixed bag.*
7 (of) mixed race having parents of different races: *children of mixed race*
8 in mixed company when you are with people of both sexes: *It's not the sort of joke you tell in mixed company.*
→ **mixed metaphor** at METAPHOR(2)

ˌmixed aˈbility *adj* [only before noun] a mixed ability school or class teaches all children of the same age together, even if they have different levels of ability: *a mixed ability group | mixed ability teaching*

ˌmixed ˈdoubles *n* [U] a game in a sport such as tennis in which a man and a woman play against another man and woman

ˌmixed eˈconomy *n* [C] an economic system in which some industries are owned by the government and some are owned by private companies

ˌmixed ˈfarming *n* [U] a system of farming in which you grow crops and keep animals

ˌmixed ˈgrill *n* [C] *BrE* a dish consisting of meats such as SAUSAGE, BACON, LIVER etc which have all been GRILLed

ˌmixed ˈmarriage *n* [C,U] a marriage between two people from different races or religions

ˌmixed ˈmedia *n* [U] a combination of substances or materials that are used in a painting, SCULPTURE etc

ˌmixed ˈup *adj* **1 be/get mixed up in sth** to be involved in an illegal or dishonest activity: *He's the last person I'd expect to be mixed up in something like this. | I'd have to be crazy to get mixed up in that kind of thing.* **2 be/get mixed up with sb** to be involved with someone who has a bad influence on you: *When he left college he got mixed up with the wrong people.* **3** [not before noun] confused, for example because you have too many different details to remember or think about: *I get all mixed up over the money whenever I travel abroad.* **4** (*also* **mixed-up**) *informal* confused and suffering from emotional problems SYN **screwed up**: *She's just a crazy mixed-up kid.* → **mix up** at MIX[1], MIX-UP

mix·er /ˈmɪksə $ -ər/ *n* [C] **1** a piece of equipment used to mix things together: *an electric food mixer | a cement mixer | a shower mixer* **2** a piece of equipment or computer software which is used to control the sound levels or picture quality of a recording or film, or a person whose job is to use this equipment: *an audio mixer* **3** a drink that can be mixed with alcohol, especially to make a COCKTAIL: *We can use tonic water or orange juice as mixers.* **4 good mixer** someone who finds it easy to talk to people they do not know: *Media people need to be good mixers and good talkers.* **5** *AmE old-fashioned* a party held so that people who have just met can get to know each other better: *Are you going to the freshman mixer?*

ˈmixer tap *n* [C] *BrE* a TAP which both hot and cold water come through together

ˈmixing bowl *n* [C] a large bowl used for mixing things such as flour and sugar for making cakes

mix·ol·o·gist /mɪkˈsɒlədʒɪst $ -ˈsɑː-/ *n* [C] *informal* someone who makes COCKTAILs in a bar

mix·tape /ˈmɪksteɪp/ *n* [C] a piece of music that is produced by mixing different voices or musical instruments that have already been recorded: *'All types of electronic dance music mixtapes for sale.' | mixtape CDs*

mix·ture /ˈmɪkstʃə $ -ər/ ●●● S3 W3 *n*
1 [C] a combination of two or more different things, feelings, or types of people: **[+of]** *The town is a mixture of the old and the new. | the mixture of different people living in the city | She felt a strange mixture of excitement and fear. | a mixture of emotions*
2 [C,U] a liquid or other substance made by mixing several substances together, especially in cooking → **compound**: **[+of]** *Fill the bread with a mixture of lettuce, tomatoes, and cucumbers. | Pour the mixture into four small dishes.*
3 [C] *technical* a combination of substances that are put together but do not mix with each other

THESAURUS

mixture several different substances, ideas, qualities etc that have been put together, especially so that they form one thing: *Pour the mixture into the cake pan and bake for 50 minutes. | He looked at her with a mixture of admiration and curiosity.*
combination two or more different things, substances etc that are used together or work together: *Doctors use a combination of drugs to combat the disease. | The business failed due to a combination of bad management and a lack of experience.*
blend a mixture of two or more things, qualities, or characteristics, especially ones that combine successfully or in a pleasant way: *The England team is a good side, with a nice blend of experience and youthful energy. | The sauce uses a blend of different ingredients.*
a cross between sth and sth a mixture of very different things – used when you are describing what something looks or sounds like: *The building looked like a cross between a museum and a spaceship.*
hybrid /ˈhaɪbrəd/ something that is produced by combining two or more things, especially using advanced scientific methods: *Scientists are combining human and animal embryos to create genetic hybrids. | These industries use a hybrid of different technologies.*
amalgam /əˈmælgəm/ *formal* a mixture of different things, in which you can still recognize the original features: *The record is an amalgam of hard rock, jazz, and blues.*
synthesis *formal* something that has been made by combining different things, especially information or ideas: *The essay should be a synthesis of the information from various sources.*

ˈmix-up *n* [C] *informal* a mistake that causes confusion about details or arrangements: **[+in]** *Geoffrey rushed in late pleading a mix-up in his diary.* | **[+between]** *A council official blamed a mix-up between departments.* | **[+over]** *There was a mix-up over the hotel booking.* THESAURUS MISTAKE

miz·zen /ˈmɪzən/ *n* [C] **1** (*also* **mizzen mast**) the MAST behind the main mast on a sailing ship **2** (*also* **mizzen sail**) the main sail on a mizzen on a sailing ship

Mk the written abbreviation of ***mark***

ml (*plural* **ml** *or* **mls**) the written abbreviation of ***millilitre*** or millilitres

M'la·dy, **Milady** /mɪˈleɪdi/ *n old use* used by a servant to address a woman who belongs to a NOBLE family: *Will that be all, M'lady?*

m-learn·ing /ˈem ˌlɜːnɪŋ $ -ɜːr-/ *n* [U] (***mobile learning***) learning that involves using SMARTPHONEs and small computers that you carry with you

MLitt, **M.Litt.** /ˌem ˈlɪt/ *n* [C] *BrE* (***Master of Letters***) a university degree that you can get at some British universities by studying for two years after your first degree

M'lord /mə'lɔːd $ -'lɔːrd/ *n* **1** (*also* **M'lud**) used to address a judge **2** *old use* used by a servant to address a man who belongs to a NOBLE family

M'lud /mə'lʌd/ *n* used to address a judge in a British court of law (=short for 'my lord')

mm[1] the written abbreviation of ***millimetre*** or millimetres

mm[2] /m/ used when someone else is speaking and you want to show that you are listening, that you agree with them, or that you are thinking about what they have said: *'That's okay, isn't it?' 'Mm, yeah.' | Mm, I see what you mean.*

MMOG /ˌem em əʊ 'dʒiː $ -oʊ-/ (*also* **MMO**) *n* [C] (***Massively Multiplayer Online Game***) a game on the Internet which continues for many hours or days and which many people are involved in

MMR /ˌem em 'ɑː $ -'ɑːr/ *n* [U] a VACCINE against the diseases MEASLES, MUMPS, and RUBELLA, given to babies at around thirteen months old, and again when children are around four or five years old

MMS /ˌem em 'es/ *n* [U] (***multimedia messaging system***) a way of sending MULTIMEDIA messages to and from MOBILE PHONES

mne·mon·ic /nɪ'mɒnɪk $ nɪ'mɑː-/ *n* [C] something such as a poem or a sentence that you use to help you remember a rule, a name etc —**mnemonic** *adj*

mo /məʊ $ moʊ/ *n* [singular] *BrE spoken* a very short period of time SYN **moment**: *Wait a mo! | I'll be back in a mo.*

mo. *AmE* the written abbreviation of ***month***

M.O. (*also* **MO** *BrE*) /ˌem 'əʊ $ -'oʊ/ *n* **1** [singular] (***modus operandi***) a way of doing something that is typical of a particular person or group **2** [C] *especially BrE* (***medical officer***) an army doctor

moan[1] /məʊn $ moʊn/ ●●○ *v*
1 [I,T] *informal* to complain in an annoying way, especially in an unhappy voice and without good reason: *'I feel seasick already,' she moaned.* | **[+about]** *A lot of people moaned about the parking problems.* | **[+at]** *BrE*: *My mum never stops moaning at me.* | **moan that** *He's always moaning that we use too much electricity.* | *He **moaned and groaned** all the way there.* **THESAURUS▸** COMPLAIN
2 [I] to make a long low sound expressing pain, unhappiness, or sexual pleasure SYN **groan**: *She moaned and cried out in pain.*
3 [I] *literary* if the wind moans, it makes a long low sound: *They could hear the wind moaning in the trees.* —**moaner** *n* [C] *BrE*: *Dad's a gloomy old moaner.*

moan[2] *n* [C] **1** a long low sound expressing pain, unhappiness, or sexual pleasure: **[+of]** *There was a moan of pain from the injured man. | She **gave** a little **moan** of pleasure. | a **low moan*** **2 have a moan (about sth)** *BrE informal* to complain about something: *We were just having a moan about work.* **3** *literary* a low sound made by the wind

moat /məʊt $ moʊt/ *n* [C] **1** a deep wide hole, usually filled with water, dug around a castle as a defence **2** a deep wide hole dug around an area in a ZOO, used to stop animals from escaping —**moated** *adj*

mob[1] /mɒb $ mɑːb/ ●●○ *n* [C]
1 a large noisy crowd, especially one that is angry and violent: **[+of]** *a mob of a few hundred demonstrators | They were immediately surrounded by the mob. | The leadership had been criticized for giving in to **mob rule*** (=when a mob controls the situation rather than the government or the law). **THESAURUS▸** GROUP
2 *informal* a group of people of the same type SYN **gang**: **[+of]** *The usual mob of teenagers were standing on the corner.* | **the heavy mob** *BrE* (=group of strong violent men) *What happens if they send the heavy mob round to find him?*
3 the Mob the MAFIA (=a powerful organization of criminals)
4 the mob *old use* an insulting expression meaning all the poorest and least educated people in society
5 mob of sheep/cattle *AusE* a large group of sheep or cattle

mob[2] *v* (**mobbed, mobbing**) [T] **1** if people mob a famous person, they rush to get close to them and form a crowd around them: *Fans ran onto the pitch and mobbed the batsman.* **2** if a group of birds or animals mob another bird or animal, they all attack it

'mob cap *n* [C] a light cotton hat with a decorative edge, worn by women in the 18th and 19th centuries

ˌmob-'handed *adv BrE informal* together, in a large group: *The police turned up mob-handed after someone complained about the noise.*

mo·bile[1] /'məʊbaɪl $ 'moʊbiːl/ ●●● S1 W2 *n* [C]
1 *BrE* a MOBILE PHONE SYN **cellphone** *AmE*: *Give me a call on my mobile. | Have you got my mobile number?*
2 a decoration made of small objects tied to wires or string which is hung up so that the objects move when air blows around them

mo·bile[2] /'məʊbaɪl $ 'moʊbəl, -biːl/ ●●○ *adj*
1 not fixed in one position, and easy to move and use in different places: *mobile air-conditioners*
2 moving or able to move from one job, area, or social class to another: *a more mobile workforce | People these days are much more **socially mobile**. | an **upwardly mobile*** (=moving to a higher social scale) *professional*
3 able to move or travel easily OPP **immobile**: *She's more mobile now that she has her own car.*
4 mobile library/shop/clinic etc *BrE* a shop etc that is kept in a vehicle and driven from place to place: *Two mobile units provide health care in rural villages.*
5 mobile mouth/face/features *written* features that can change their expression quickly: *His mobile features registered amusement.*

ˌmobile 'home *n* [C] **1** *AmE* a type of house made of metal, that can be pulled by a vehicle and moved to another place **2** *BrE* a large CARAVAN which always stays in the same place and is used as a house SYN **trailer** *AmE*

ˌmobile 'Internet deˌvice *n* [C] (*abbreviation* **MID**) a small computer you can carry with you, with which you can use the Internet

ˌmobile 'phone ●●● S2 W2 *n* [C] a telephone that you can carry with you and use in any place SYN **cellular phone** *AmE*: *mobile phone users*

mo·bil·i·ty /məʊ'bɪləti $ moʊ-/ ●○○ *n* [U]
1 the ability to move easily from one job, area, or social class to another OPP **immobility**: ***social mobility*** | **[+of]** *There is greater **mobility of labour*** (=movement of workers) *between jobs and areas.* | **upward/downward mobility** *jobs and opportunities for upward mobility*
2 the ability to move easily OPP **immobility**: *It improves the strength and mobility of joints. | The key to the army's effectiveness is its increased mobility.* | **mobility allowance** *BrE* (=money paid to sick or disabled people to help pay for transport)

mo'bility ˌscooter *n* [C] a small electric vehicle that you sit on, used by people who have difficulty walking

mo·bil·ize (*also* **-ise** *BrE*) /'məʊbəlaɪz $ 'moʊ-/ ●○○ *v*
1 [T] to encourage people to support something in an active way: *an attempt to mobilize popular opinion | a campaign to **mobilize support** for the strike*
2 [T] to start to use the things or people you have available in order to achieve something: *They failed to mobilize their resources effectively.*
3 [I,T] if a country mobilizes or mobilizes its army, it prepares to fight a war → **demobilize**
4 [T] to help something to move more easily → **immobilize**: *The physiotherapist mobilizes the patient's shoulder.* —**mobilization** /ˌməʊbəlaɪ'zeɪʃən $ ˌmoʊbələ-/ *n* [C,U]: *the mobilization of public opinion*

mob·log·ging /ˈməʊˌblɒɡɪŋ $ ˈmoʊˌblɑː-/ *n* [U] *BrE* the action of adding information to a BLOG (=type of web page) using a MOBILE PHONE or a PDA

MO·BO awards, the /ˈməʊˌbəʊ/ awards which are given each year in the UK to the best musicians producing music of black origin

mob·ster /ˈmɒbstə $ ˈmɑːbstər/ *n* [C] *especially AmE* a member of an organized criminal group SYN **gangster**

moc·ca·sin /ˈmɒkəsɪn $ ˈmɑː-/ *n* [C] a flat comfortable shoe made of soft leather → see picture at SHOE[1]

moch·a /ˈmɒkə $ ˈmoʊkə/ *n* [U] **1** a type of coffee **2** a combination of coffee and chocolate

moch·ac·ci·no /ˌmɒkəˈtʃiːnəʊ $ ˌmoʊkəˈtʃiːnoʊ/ *n* (*plural* **mochaccinos**) [C,U] a drink made of strong coffee, chocolate, and hot milk

mock[1] /mɒk $ mɑːk/ ●○○ *v*
1 [I,T] *formal* to laugh at someone or something and try to make them look stupid by saying unkind things about them or by copying them SYN **make fun of**: *Opposition MPs mocked the government's decision.* | *'Running away?' he mocked.* | *It's easy for you to mock, but we put a lot of work into this play.*

> **REGISTER**
> **Mock** something or someone is used especially in literature. In everyday English, people usually say **make fun of** something or someone: *Stop making fun of the way he talks!*

2 [T] *formal* to make something seem completely useless: *Violent attacks like this mock the peace process.* —**mocking** *adj*: *Her tone was mocking.* —**mockingly** *adv*: *His lips twisted mockingly.* —**mocker** *n* [C]

mock sth ↔ **up** *phr v* to make a FULL-SIZE model of something so that it looks real → MOCK-UP

mock[2] *adj* [only before noun] **1** not real, but intended to be very similar to a real situation, substance etc: *war games with mock battles* | *a mock interview* | *mock marble floors* **2 mock surprise/horror/indignation etc** surprise etc that you pretend to feel, especially as a joke: *She threw her hands up in mock horror.*

mock[3] *n* **1 mocks** [plural] *BrE* school examinations taken as practice before official examinations: *I'm revising for my mocks.* **2 make mock of sb** *literary* to mock someone

mock- /mɒk $ mɑːk/ *prefix* **1** used to show that an attitude or feeling is pretended, not real: *a mock-serious expression* | *His frown was mock-severe.* **2** copying a particular style, especially a style of building: *a mock-Tudor house*

mock·ers /ˈmɒkəz $ ˈmɑːkərz/ *n* **put the mockers on sth** *BrE informal* to spoil an event or someone's plans, or to bring someone bad luck: *Without wishing to put the mockers on things, I'd like to know where the money is going to come from.*

mock·e·ry /ˈmɒkəri $ ˈmɑː-/ *n* **1 make a mockery of sth** to make something such as a plan or system seem completely useless or ineffective: *This building plan makes a mockery of the government's environmental policy.* **2** [U] when someone laughs at someone or something or shows that they think they are stupid: *There was a hint of mockery in his voice.* **3** [singular] something that is completely useless or ineffective: *She said that the trial had been a mockery.*

mock·ing·bird /ˈmɒkɪŋbɜːd $ ˈmɑːkɪŋbɜːrd/ *n* [C] an American bird that copies the songs of other birds

mock·ney /ˈmɒkni $ ˈmɑːk-/ *adj BrE* relating to someone who tries to talk or behave in the same way as Cockneys do, but who is not working class and does not come from the East End of London —**mockney** *n* [C]

mock·tail /ˈmɒkteɪl $ ˈmɑːk-/ *n* [C] a drink that is a mixture of different drinks which does not contain alcohol → **cocktail**

ˌmock ˈturtleneck *n* [C] *AmE* a type of TURTLENECK-SWEATER

mock·u·men·ta·ry /ˌmɒkjʊˈmentəri $ ˌmɑːk-/ *n* (*plural* **mockumentaries**) [C] a funny film or television programme that pretends to show real people and events, although in fact they are not real: *a mockumentary about a fictional rock band*

ˈmock-up *n* [C] a full-size model of something, made before the real thing is built, or made for a film, show etc: **[+of]** *a mock-up of the system* | *a mock-up of a submarine* → **mock up** at MOCK[1]

mod, Mod /mɒd $ mɑːd/ *n* [C] *BrE* a member of a group of young people in Britain in the 1960s who wore a particular type of neat clothes, listened to SOUL MUSIC, and rode MOTOR SCOOTERS → **rocker**

mo·dal[1] /ˈməʊdl $ ˈmoʊdl/ *n* [C] a modal verb

modal[2] *adj technical* **1** [only before noun] modal meanings are concerned with the attitude of the speaker to the hearer or to what is being said **2** related to or written in a musical MODE(5) —**modality** /məʊˈdæləti $ moʊ-/ *n* [U]

ˌmodal auxˈiliary *n* [C] a modal verb

ˌmodal ˈverb (*also* **modal**) *n* [C] *technical* one of these verb forms: can, could, may, might, shall, should, will, would, must, ought to, used to, need, had better, and DARE. They are all used with other verbs to express ideas such as possibility, permission, or intention → **auxiliary verb**

mod cons /ˌmɒd ˈkɒnz $ ˌmɑːd ˈkɑːnz/ *n* **all mod cons** *BrE informal* all the things that are fitted in modern houses to make life easy and comfortable: *a property with all mod cons*

mode /məʊd $ moʊd/ ●○○ AWL *n* [C]
1 *formal* a particular way or style of behaving, living, or doing something: **[+of]** *the most efficient* ***mode of transport*** | *They have a relaxed mode of life that suits them well.* | *Western modes of thought* THESAURUS METHOD
2 *technical* a particular way in which a machine or piece of equipment can operate: *Set the monitor to 256 colour mode.* | *To get out of the 'auto' mode on the camera, turn the knob to 'M'.*
3 be in work mode/holiday mode etc *informal* to have a particular feeling or way of thinking or behaving, because of the situation you are in: *With only minutes to go, we were now in panic mode.*
4 be the mode *formal* to be fashionable at a particular time: *Long skirts were then the mode.*
5 *technical* one of various systems of arranging notes in music, such as MAJOR and MINOR in Western music → **À LA MODE, MODISH**

mod·el[1] /ˈmɒdl $ ˈmɑːdl/ ●●● S2 W1 *n* [C]
1 SMALL COPY a small copy of a building, vehicle, machine etc, especially one that can be put together from separate parts: **[+of]** *They showed us a model of the building.* | *a* ***working model*** (=one with parts which move) *of a steam engine*
2 FASHION someone whose job is to show clothes, hairstyles etc by wearing them at fashion shows or for photographs: *a top fashion model* | *a male model*
3 TYPE OF CAR ETC a particular type or design of a vehicle or machine: *Renault are introducing three new models at the show.* | *Our dishwasher is the* ***latest model*** (=newest design). | *the 2.8 litre V6 model*
4 DESCRIPTION a computer representation or scientific description of something: **[+of]** *Scientists are building computer models of the ocean currents.*
5 SB/STH TO COPY someone or something which people want to copy because they are successful or have good qualities: **[+for]** *It served as a model for other cities.* | *He used English medieval architecture as his model.* | **role model** (=someone that you try to copy because they have qualities you would like to have) *Good teachers can act as* ***positive role models.***
6 model of efficiency/virtue etc someone or something that has a lot of a good quality: *She was a model of honesty and decency.*
7 ART someone who is employed by an artist or photographer to be painted or photographed

model² ●●○ *adj*
1 model aircraft/train/car etc a small copy of an aircraft, train etc, especially one that a child can play with or put together from separate parts: *He is playing with his model railway.* | *She builds model aeroplanes in her spare time.*

MODEL

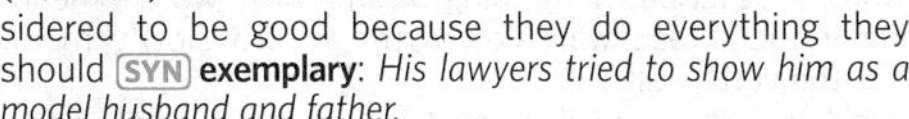

model boat

2 model wife/employee/student etc a wife, EMPLOYEE (=worker) etc who is considered to be good because they do everything they should SYN **exemplary**: *His lawyers tried to show him as a model husband and father.*
3 model prison/farm/school etc a prison etc that has been specially designed or organized to be as good as possible

model³ *v* (**modelled**, **modelling** *BrE*, **modeled**, **modeling** *AmE*) **1** [I,T] to wear clothes at a fashion show or in magazine photographs in order to show them to people: *She's modeling Donna Karan's fall collection.* | *Claire modelled for a few years when she was in her twenties.* **2 model yourself on sb** *BrE*, **model yourself after sb** *AmE* to try to be like someone else because you admire them: *Jim had always modelled himself on his great hero, Martin Luther King.* **3 be modelled on sth** to be designed in a way that copies another system or way of doing something: *Their education system is modelled on the French one.* **4** [T] to do a computer representation or scientific description of a situation or event: *They used a computer to model the possible effects of global warming.* **5** [T] to make something by shaping clay, wood etc —**modeller** *n* [C]

mod·el·ling *BrE*, **modeling** *AmE* /ˈmɒdl-ɪŋ $ ˈmɑː-/ *n* [U]
1 the work of a fashion model: *a career in modelling*
2 the process of making a scientific or computer model of something to show how it works or to understand it better: **[+of]** ***computer modelling*** *of the system* | *economic modelling* **3** the activity of making models of objects

mo·dem /ˈməʊdəm, -dem $ ˈmoʊ-/ *n* [C] a piece of electronic equipment that allows information from one computer to be sent along telephone wires to another computer

mod·e·rate¹ /ˈmɒdərət $ ˈmɑː-/ ●●○ *adj*
1 not very large or very small, very hot or very cold, very fast or very slow etc: *Even moderate amounts of alcohol can be dangerous.* | *a moderate degree of success* | *a student of moderate ability* | *Moderate exercise, such as walking, is recommended.* | *Bake the pie for 30 minutes in a moderate oven.* | *moderate to strong winds*
2 having opinions or beliefs, especially about politics, that are not extreme and that most people consider reasonable OPP **extreme**: *the more moderate members of the party* | *a moderate politician*
3 staying within reasonable or sensible limits OPP **immoderate**: *a moderate smoker* | *moderate wage demands* → MODERATELY

mod·e·rate² /ˈmɒdəreɪt $ ˈmɑː-/ *v* [I,T] **1** *formal* to make something less extreme or violent, or to become less extreme or violent: *The students moderated their demands.* | *He learnt to moderate his anger.* **2** *BrE* to do the work of a MODERATOR

mod·e·rate³ /ˈmɒdərət $ ˈmɑː-/ *n* [C] someone whose opinions or beliefs, especially about politics, are not extreme and are considered reasonable by most people OPP **extremist**, **hardliner**: *He's coming under pressure from moderates in the party.*

mod·e·rate·ly /ˈmɒdərətli $ ˈmɑː-/ ●○○ *adv*
1 fairly, but not very SYN **reasonably**: *a moderately successful film* | *He did moderately well in the exams.*
2 in a way which is not extreme or stays within reasonable limits: *He drinks moderately.*
3 moderately priced neither cheap nor expensive: *Both hotels are moderately priced.*

mod·e·ra·tion /ˌmɒdəˈreɪʃən $ ˌmɑː-/ *n* [U]
1 in moderation if you do something in moderation, such as drinking alcohol or eating certain foods, you do not do it too much OPP **to excess**: *Some people think drinking in moderation can prevent heart disease.* **2** *formal* control of your behaviour, so that you keep your actions, feelings, habits etc within reasonable limits: **[+in]** *Moderation in diet is the way to good health.* | *He encouraged moderation and toleration on religious issues.* **3** *formal* reduction in force, degree, speed etc

mod·e·ra·to /ˌmɒdəˈrɑːtəʊ $ ˌmɑːdəˈrɑːtoʊ/ *adj, adv* at an average speed – used as an instruction on how fast to play a piece of music

mod·e·ra·tor /ˈmɒdəreɪtə $ ˈmɑːdəreɪtər/ *n* [C] **1** someone whose job is to control a discussion or an argument between people **2** *BrE* someone who makes sure that an examination is fair, and that the marks given are fair and correct **3** a religious leader who is in charge of the council of the Presbyterian and United Reformed Churches

mod·ern /ˈmɒdn $ ˈmɑːdərn/ ●●● S1 W1 *adj*
1 [only before noun] belonging to the present time or most recent time SYN **contemporary**: *Such companies must change if they are to compete* ***in the modern world***. | *They are the youngest children* ***in modern times*** *to face murder charges.* | *Smaller families are a feature of* ***modern society***. | *Computers are an essential part of* ***modern life***. | *a book about* ***modern history*** | *The original supermarkets were small by modern standards.* | **Modern Greek/Hebrew etc** (=the form of the language used today)
2 made or done using the most recent designs or methods SYN **up-to-date**: *A lot of progress has been made with the use of* ***modern technology***. | *advances in* ***modern medicine*** | *modern surgical techniques* THESAURUS ▸ NEW
3 [only before noun] modern art, music, literature etc uses styles that have been recently developed and are very different from traditional styles SYN **contemporary**: *an exhibition of modern art* | *modern dance*
4 having very recent attitudes or ways of behaving SYN **progressive** OPP **traditional**: *The school is very modern in its approach to sex education.* → SECONDARY MODERN

THESAURUS

modern something that is modern uses the most recent designs or methods: *The house looks very modern.* | *the city's modern public transportation system*
the latest [only before noun] the newest that is available: *The camera uses the latest digital technology.* | *the very latest mobile phones* | *the latest news*
up-to-date using the most modern technology, ideas, information etc: *The hospital has the most up-to-date equipment in the country.*
newfangled [only before noun] *informal* modern – used when you disapprove of something and do not think it as good as the things that existed before: *He doesn't believe in these new-fangled gadgets.*
high-tech, hi-tech using very advanced technology, especially electronic equipment and computers: *Modern tractors are full of high-tech equipment, including GPS.* | *It's all very hi-tech.*
state-of-the-art using the newest and most advanced features, ideas, and materials that are available: *state-of-the-art technology* | *a state-of-the-art home entertainment system*

COLLOCATIONS CHECK

the latest technology/equipment/news
up-to-date equipment/information/book/map
new-fangled device/contraption/gadget
high-tech industry/company/equipment
state-of-the-art technology/equipment

ˈmodern-day *adj* [only before noun] existing in the present time – used when comparing someone or something to a person or thing in the past SYN **present-day**, **contemporary**: *She's a modern-day Joan of Arc.* | *The modern-day diet has too little fiber in it.*

mod·ern·is·m /ˈmɒdənɪzəm $ ˈmɑːdər-/ *n* [U] a style of art, building etc that was popular especially from the

1940s to the 1960s, in which artists used simple shapes and modern artificial materials → **post-modernism**: *the rise of modernism in Paris* —**modernist** *adj, n* [C]: *the modernist school*

mod·ern·ist·ic /ˌmɒdəˈnɪstɪk◂ $ ˌmɑːdər-/ *adj* designed in a way that looks very modern and very different from previous styles OPP **traditional**: *a modernistic office building*

mo·der·ni·ty /mɒˈdɜːnəti $ məˈdɜːr-/ *n* [U] *formal* the quality of being modern: *a conflict between tradition and modernity*

mod·ern·ize (*also* **-ise** *BrE*) /ˈmɒdənaɪz $ ˈmɑːdər-/ ●○○ *v*
1 [T] to make something such as a system or building more modern: *They need more funds to modernize the country's telephone system.* | *a tastefully modernized old farmhouse*
2 [I] to start using more modern methods and equipment: *The business will lose money if it doesn't modernize.* —**modernizer** *n* [C]: *the conflict between the modernizers and the conservatives* —**modernization** /ˌmɒdənaɪˈzeɪʃən $ ˌmɑːdərnə-/ *n* [U]: *the modernization of the railway system*

ˌmodern ˈlanguage *n* [C] *BrE* a language which is used now, especially a European language such as French or Italian, studied as a subject at school or university: *a degree in modern languages*

ˌmodern penˈtathlon *n* [singular] a sports competition that involves running, swimming, riding horses, FENCING, and shooting guns

mod·est /ˈmɒdɪst $ ˈmɑː-/ ●●○ *adj*
1 NOT PROUD someone who is modest does not want to talk about their abilities or achievements OPP **immodest**, **boastful**: **[+about]** *He was always modest about his role in the Everest expedition.* | *You're too modest! You've been a huge help to us.*
2 NOT BIG not very great, big, or expensive: *a* ***modest increase*** *in costs* | *She had saved a* ***modest amount*** *of money.* | *The new service proved a* ***modest success.*** | *a modest house with a small garden* | *his modest ambitions*
3 SHY shy about showing your body or attracting sexual interest, because you are easily embarrassed OPP **immodest**: *She was a modest girl, always keeping covered, even in summer.*
4 CLOTHES *old-fashioned* modest clothing covers the body in a way that does not attract sexual interest: *a modest knee-length dress* —**modestly** *adv*: *'I was just lucky,' he said modestly.* | *modestly priced meals*

mod·es·ty /ˈmɒdəsti $ ˈmɑː-/ *n* [U] **1** a modest way of behaving or talking: *'Anyone else would have done the same thing,' he said with typical modesty.* **2** unwillingness to show your body or do anything that may attract sexual interest **3 in all modesty** *spoken* used when you want to talk about something good you have done, but you do not want to seem too proud: *I think in all modesty that I can take some small credit for the team's success.* **4 modesty forbids** *spoken* used when saying jokingly that you do not want to talk about your achievements → **false modesty** at FALSE(4)

mod·i·cum /ˈmɒdɪkəm $ ˈmɑː-/ *n* **a modicum of sth** *formal* a small amount of something, especially a good quality: *a modicum of common sense*

mod·i·fi·ca·tion /ˌmɒdɪfɪˈkeɪʃən $ ˌmɑː-/ ●○○ AWL *n*
1 [C] a small change made in something such as a design, plan, or system SYN **alteration**: **[+to]** *We've* ***made*** *one or two* ***modifications*** *to the original design.* | *They have used the same process for almost 50 years with only* ***minor modifications.***
2 [C,U] the act of modifying something, or the process of being modified SYN **alteration**: **[+of]** *The review resulted in the modification of our security procedures.* | **[+in]** *Knowledge of the ill effects of tobacco has led to a modification in smoking behaviour.*

mod·i·fi·er /ˈmɒdəfaɪə $ ˈmɑːdɪfaɪər/ *n* [C] *technical* a word or group of words that gives additional information about another word. Modifiers can be adjectives (such as 'fierce' in 'the fierce dog'), adverbs (such as 'loudly' in 'the dog barked loudly'), or phrases (such as 'with a short tail' in 'the dog with a short tail').

mod·i·fy /ˈmɒdɪfaɪ $ ˈmɑː-/ ●●○ AWL *v* (**modified, modifying, modifies**) [T]
1 to make small changes to something in order to improve it and make it more suitable or effective SYN **adapt**: *The feedback will be used to modify the course for next year.* | *The regulations can only be modified by a special committee.* | **modify sth to do sth** *The seats can be modified to fit other types of vehicle.*
2 *technical* if an adjective, adverb etc modifies another word, it describes something or limits the word's meaning. In the phrase 'walk slowly', the adverb 'slowly' modifies the verb 'walk'.

mod·ish /ˈməʊdɪʃ $ ˈmoʊ-/ *adj old-fashioned* modish ideas, designs etc are modern and fashionable —**modishly** *adv*

mod·u·lar /ˈmɒdjələ $ ˈmɑːdʒələr/ *adj* consisting of separate parts or units which can be put together to form something, often in different combinations: *a modular course in business studies* | *Most colleges now use the modular system of teaching.* | *modular furniture*

mod·u·late /ˈmɒdjəleɪt $ ˈmɑːdʒə-/ *v* **1** [T] *formal* to change the sound of your voice **2** [T] to change a process or activity to make it more controlled, slower, less strong etc: *These drugs modulate the disease process.* **3** [I + from/to] *technical* to move from one KEY to another in a piece of music using a series of related CHORDS **4** [T] *technical* to change the form of a radio signal so that it can be broadcast more effectively —**modulation** /ˌmɒdjəˈleɪʃən $ ˌmɑːdʒə-/ *n* [C,U]

mod·ule /ˈmɒdjuːl $ ˈmɑːdʒuːl/ ●○○ *n* [C]
1 *especially BrE* one of the separate units that a course of study has been divided into. Usually students choose a number of modules to study: *a module in mathematics* | *You choose five modules in the first year.*
2 *technical* one of several parts of a piece of computer software that does a particular job
3 a part of a spacecraft that can be separated from the main part and used for a particular purpose
4 one of several separate parts that can be combined to form a larger object, such as a machine or building

mo·dus op·e·ran·di /ˌməʊdəs ˌɒpəˈrændi $ ˌmoʊdəs ˌɑːpə-/ *n* [singular] *formal* (*abbreviation* **M.O.**) a way of doing something that is typical of a particular person or group

modus vi·ven·di /ˌməʊdəs vɪˈvendi $ ˌmoʊ-/ *n* [singular] *formal* an arrangement between people with very different opinions or habits that allows them to live or work together without quarrelling

mog·gy, **moggie** /ˈmɒgi $ ˈmɑːgi, ˈmɒːgi/ *n* (*plural* **moggies**) [C] *BrE informal* a cat

mo·gul /ˈməʊgəl $ ˈmoʊ-/ *n* [C] **movie/media/gambling etc mogul** a BUSINESSMAN or BUSINESSWOMAN who has great power and influence in a particular industry

mo·hair /ˈməʊheə $ ˈmoʊher/ *n* [U] expensive wool made from the hair of the ANGORA goat: *a mohair sweater*

Mo·ham·med /məʊˈhæməd, mə- $ moʊ-/ the Arab PROPHET who founded the religion of Islam

Mo·hi·can /məʊˈhiːkən $ moʊ-/ *BrE*, **Mo·hawk** /ˈməʊhɔːk $ ˈmoʊhɒːk/ *AmE n* [C] a hairstyle in which the hair is cut off the sides of the head, and the hair on top of the head is made to stick up and is sometimes brightly coloured —**Mohican** *adj*: *a Mohican haircut*

moi /mwɑː/ *pron spoken* me – used humorously to disagree with a negative description of yourself: *Difficult, moi?*

moi·e·ty /ˈmɔɪəti/ *n* (*plural* **moieties**) [C] *law or literary* a half share

moire /mwɑː $ mwɑːr, mwɑːˈreɪ/ *n* [U] a type of silk with a pattern that looks like waves

moist /mɔɪst/ ●○○ *adj* slightly wet, especially in a way that is pleasant or suitable: *Make sure the soil is moist before planting the seeds.* | *a rich, moist chocolate cake* |

warm moist air | *Her eyes were moist* (=she was almost crying). **THESAURUS** DAMP, WET —**moistness** *n* [U]

moist·en /ˈmɔɪsən/ *v* [T] to make something slightly wet: *Moisten the clay if it seems too dry.* | *She* ***moistened*** *her* ***lips*** (=made her lips wet with her tongue).

mois·ture /ˈmɔɪstʃə $ -ər/ ●●○ *n* [U] small amounts of water that are present in the air, in a substance, or on a surface: *Plants use their roots to absorb moisture from the soil.* | *Your skin's moisture content varies according to weather conditions.*

mois·tur·ize (*also* **-ise** *BrE*) /ˈmɔɪstʃəraɪz/ *v* [I,T] **1** to make your skin less dry by using special cream: *You should cleanse, tone and moisturize every day for healthy looking skin.* **2 moisturizing cream/lotion/oil etc** cream, oil etc that you put on your skin or hair to make it less dry

mois·tur·iz·er (*also* **-iser** *BrE*) /ˈmɔɪstʃəraɪzə $ -ər/ *n* [C,U] cream that you put on your skin to make it less dry

mo·jo /ˈməʊdʒəʊ $ ˈmoʊdʒoʊ/ *n* (*plural* **mojos**) [C] *especially AmE informal* **1** your power to attract people or be successful: *Has he lost his mojo?* **2** a bag containing magical things that someone wears

mo·lar /ˈməʊlə $ ˈmoʊlər/ *n* [C] one of the large teeth at the back of the mouth that are used for breaking up food → **incisor** —**molar** *adj*

mo·las·ses /məˈlæsɪz/ *n* [U] *AmE* a thick dark sweet liquid that is obtained from raw sugar plants when they are being made into sugar SYN **treacle** *BrE*

mold /məʊld $ moʊld/ *n, v* the American spelling of MOULD

mol·der /ˈməʊldə $ ˈmoʊldər/ *v* [I] the American spelling of MOULDER

mold·ing /məʊldɪŋ $ ˈmoʊl-/ *n* the American spelling of MOULDING

mold·y /ˈməʊldi $ ˈmoʊl-/ *adj* the American spelling of MOULDY

mole /məʊl $ moʊl/ ●○○ *n* [C]
1 a small dark furry animal which is almost blind. Moles usually live under the ground.
2 a small dark brown mark on the skin that is slightly higher than the skin around it
3 someone who works for an organization while secretly giving information to its enemies

mol·e·cule /ˈmɒlɪkjuːl $ ˈmɑː-/ ●●○ *n* [C] the smallest unit into which any substance can be divided without losing its own chemical nature, usually consisting of two or more atoms: *The molecules of oxygen gas contain just two atoms.* —**molecular** /məˈlekjələ $ -ər/ *adj*: *molecular structure*

mole·hill /ˈməʊlˌhɪl $ ˈmoʊl-/ *n* [C] a small pile of earth made by a MOLE → **make a mountain out of a molehill** at MOUNTAIN(4)

mole·skin /ˈməʊlˌskɪn $ ˈmoʊl-/ *n* [U] **1** thick cotton cloth with a soft surface: *moleskin trousers* **2** the skin of a MOLE

mo·lest /məˈlest/ *v* [T] **1** to attack or harm someone, especially a child, by touching them in a sexual way or by trying to have sex with them SYN **abuse**: *men who molest young boys* **2** *old-fashioned* to attack and physically harm someone: *a dog that was molesting sheep* —**molester** *n* [C] —**molestation** /ˌməʊleˈsteɪʃən $ ˌmoʊ-/ *n* [U]: *sexual molestation* → CHILD MOLESTER

moll /mɒl $ mɑːl/ *n* [C] *especially AmE old-fashioned informal* a criminal's girlfriend: *a gangster's moll*

mol·li·fy /ˈmɒlɪfaɪ $ ˈmɑː-/ *v* (**mollified**, **mollifying**, **mollifies**) [T] *formal* to make someone feel less angry and upset about something SYN **placate**: *He attempted to mollify her.* | *Nature reserves were set up around new power stations to mollify local conservationists.*

mol·lusc *BrE*, **mollusk** *AmE* /ˈmɒləsk $ ˈmɑː-/ *n* [C] a type of sea or land animal that has a soft body covered by a hard shell: *snails and other molluscs* —**molluscan** /məˈlʌskən/ *adj*: *molluscan prey*

mol·ly·cod·dle /ˈmɒliˌkɒdl $ ˈmɑːliˌkɑːdl/ *v* [T] to treat someone too kindly and to protect them too much from anything unpleasant: *He had been mollycoddled as a young boy.*

Mol·o·tov cock·tail /ˌmɒlətɒf ˈkɒkteɪl $ ˌmɑːlətɔːf ˈkɑːk-, ˌmɒːl-/ *n* [C] a simple bomb consisting of a bottle filled with petrol and a lighted cloth SYN **petrol bomb** *BrE*

molt /məʊlt $ moʊlt/ *v* [I] the American spelling of MOULT

mol·ten /ˈməʊltən $ ˈmoʊl-/ *adj* [usually before noun] molten metal or rock has been made into a liquid by being heated to a very high temperature: *molten iron* | **molten lava** (=liquid rock from a VOLCANO)

mol·to /ˈmɒltəʊ $ ˈmoʊltoʊ, ˈmɒːl-/ *adv* very – used in musical instructions: **molto allegro** (=very fast)

mo·lyb·de·num /məˈlɪbdənəm/ *n* [U] a hard silver-white metal that is used to make steel stronger. It is a chemical ELEMENT: symbol Mo

mom /mɒm $ mɑːm/ ●●● S1 *n* [C] *AmE informal* mother SYN **mum** *BrE*: *Mom, can I go over to Lisa's house?* | *My mom says I have to stay home tonight.*

ˌmom-and-ˈpop *adj* [only before noun] *AmE* a mom-and-pop business is owned and managed by a family or a husband and wife: *a real mom-and-pop restaurant*

mo·ment /ˈməʊmənt $ ˈmoʊ-/ ●●● S1 W1 *n* [C]
1 POINT IN TIME a particular point in time: *It was one of the most exciting moments in his life.* | **at this/that moment** (=used for emphasis) *Just at that moment there was a knock on the door.* | *She may be in trouble* ***at this very moment*** *and trying to call you.* | *I remember* ***the moment when*** *I first saw him after the operation.* | *Quinn always seems to be in the right place at the crucial moment.* | *I* ***just this moment*** (=only a very short time ago) *arrived and already Dan wants to know when I'm leaving.* | ***At this moment in time*** *it would be inappropriate to comment on the situation.* | ***From that moment on*** (=after that time) *we were the best of friends.* ⚠ Don't say 'in that moment' when you mean 'at that particular time'. Say **at that moment**: *At that moment, everything stopped.*
2 SHORT TIME a very short period of time: *He was here* ***a moment ago.*** | *Can you spare* ***a few moments*** *to answer some questions?* | **in a moment** (=very soon) *I'll come back to that point in a moment.* | **for a moment** *It was quiet for a moment, then Rae spoke.* | **after a moment** *'I don't understand,' said Louise after a moment.* | *A moment later we heard a splash.* | **wait/just a moment** (=used when you want someone to wait a short time while you do or say something) *Just a moment; let me put these away first.* | *We have to be ready to leave* ***at a moment's notice*** (=very quickly). **THESAURUS** TIME
3 at the moment *BrE especially spoken, AmE formal* now: *Julia's on holiday in Spain at the moment.* | *At the moment, the situation in Haiti is very tense.*
4 for the moment used to say that something is happening or is true now but will probably change in the future: *Well, for the moment we're just friends.* | *For the moment the rain had stopped.*
5 the moment (that) sb does sth as soon as someone does something: *He said he'd phone you the moment he got home.*
6 the last moment if you do something at the last moment or if something happens at the last moment, it happens at the last possible time: **at the last moment** *The operation was cancelled at the last moment.* | *She always* ***leaves*** *everything* ***to the last moment.***
7 (at) any moment extremely soon: *The plumber should be here* ***any moment now.*** | *The roof could collapse at any moment.*
8 OPPORTUNITY [usually singular] a particular time when you have a chance to do something: *His wife Denise was there to share his* ***big moment*** (=opportunity to do something great). | **choose/pick your moment** (=try to choose the best time to do something) *He picked his moment carefully to tell them the news.* | *This was her moment and she knew she had to take it.*
9 moment of madness/weakness/panic etc a short period of time when you do not feel or behave as normal and often do or say something which you later wish you had

not done or said: **in a moment of sth** *In a moment of madness I agreed to go with him.* | *He experienced a brief moment of panic.*
10 one moment ... the next/from one moment to the next used to say that a situation changes very suddenly, often in a way which you do not expect or cannot explain: *One moment she's kissing me, the next she doesn't want to see me again.* | *You never know what's going to happen from one moment to the next.*
11 not believe/think/do sth for a/one moment *especially spoken* used to say that you did not believe, expect etc something at all: *He didn't fool me for a moment.* | *She had never for one moment imagined that it could happen to her.*
12 of the moment the person, idea, word etc of the moment is the one that is most important or popular at the present time: *They interview personalities on a topic of the moment.* | *the mood of the moment*
13 have its/your moments to have periods of being good or interesting: *a movie that had its moments*
14 be having a moment *informal* to be having a time of success or popularity – used especially in magazines: *Short hairstyles are having a moment.*
15 not a moment too soon almost too late: *The ambulance finally arrived, and not a moment too soon.*
16 the moment of truth the time when you will find out if something will work properly, be successful etc
17 be/live in the moment to give your full attention to the situation you are in, and not think about the past or the future
18 of great moment *old-fashioned* important

mo·men·tar·i·ly /ˈməʊməntərəli $ ˌmoʊmənˈterəli/ ●○○ *adv*
1 for a very short time SYN **briefly**: *She was momentarily lost for words.* | *Jimmy paused momentarily.*
2 *AmE* very soon: *Mr Johnson will be with you momentarily.*

mo·men·ta·ry /ˈməʊməntəri $ ˈmoʊmənteri/ ●○○ *adj* continuing for a very short time SYN **brief**: *There was a momentary pause.* THESAURUS ▸ SHORT

mo·men·tous /məʊˈmentəs, mə- $ moʊ-, mə-/ *adj* a momentous event, change, or decision is very important because it will have a great influence on the future: *a **momentous decision*** | ***Momentous events** are taking place in the US.* | *His colleagues all recognized that this was a **momentous occasion**.* | *one of the most momentous days in British sport* THESAURUS ▸ IMPORTANT

mo·men·tum /məʊˈmentəm, mə- $ moʊ-, mə-/ ●○○ *n* [U]
1 the ability to keep increasing, developing, or being more successful: **gain/gather momentum** *The campaign for reform should start to gather momentum in the new year.* | *incentives to **maintain** the **momentum** of European integration* | *Governments often **lose momentum** in their second term of office.* | **[+of]** *the momentum of increasing immigration* | **[+towards]** *the momentum towards economic union*
2 the force that makes a moving object keep moving: **gain/gather momentum** (=move faster) *The wheel was allowed to roll down the slope, gathering momentum as it went.* | *Pratt, without **losing** any **momentum** at all, passed them both and won the race.*
3 *technical* the force or power that is contained in a moving object and is calculated by multiplying its weight by its speed: **[+of]** *the momentum of a particle*

mom·ma /ˈmɒmə $ ˈmɑːmə/ *n* [C] *AmE* another spelling of MAMA[1]

mom·my /ˈmɒmi $ ˈmɑːmi/ ●●● S3 *n* (*plural* **mommies**) [C] *AmE* mother – used by or to young children SYN **mummy** *BrE*

ˈmommy ˌtrack *n* [C] *AmE informal* a situation in which women with children have less opportunity to make large amounts of money or become very successful at their jobs, for example because they are not able to work as many hours as other people

Mon. (*also* **Mon** *BrE*) the written abbreviation of ***Monday***

mon·arch /ˈmɒnək $ ˈmɑːnərk, -ɑːrk/ ●○○ *n* [C] a king or queen —**monarchic** /məˈnɑːkɪk $ -ɑːr-/ **monarchical** *adj*: *the old monarchical system*

mon·arch·ist /ˈmɒnəkɪst $ ˈmɑːnər-/ *n* [C] someone who supports the idea that their country should be ruled by a king or queen

mon·ar·chy /ˈmɒnəki $ ˈmɑːnərki/ ●○○ *n* (*plural* **monarchies**)
1 [U] the system in which a country is ruled by a king or queen: *the abolition of the monarchy* THESAURUS ▸ GOVERNMENT
2 [C] a country that is ruled by a king or queen → **republic**
3 the monarchy the king or queen of a country, and his or her family: *People are going to be questioning the role of the monarchy more and more.*

mon·as·tery /ˈmɒnəstri $ ˈmɑːnəsteri/ *n* (*plural* **monasteries**) [C] a place where MONKS live → **convent**, **nunnery**

mo·nas·tic /məˈnæstɪk/ *adj* **1** relating to MONKS or life in a monastery: *the monastic life* | *a monastic community* | *Roman Catholic **monastic orders*** (=groups of monks) **2** similar to a MONK's way of living, for example quiet, simple, or not having sex: *He led a rather monastic lifestyle.* —**monasticism** /-tɪsɪzəm/ *n* [U]: *early medieval monasticism*

Mon·day /ˈmʌndi, -deɪ/ ●●● S2 W2 *n* [C,U] (*written abbreviation* **Mon.**) the day between Sunday and Tuesday: **on Monday** *It was raining on Monday.* | *The president announced Monday that he would cancel the debt. AmE* | **Monday morning/afternoon etc** *Let's go out for a meal on Monday night.* | **last Monday** *Kelly arrived last Monday.* | **this Monday** *The UK office will open for business this Monday.* | **next Monday** (=Monday of next week) *Shall we meet next Monday?* | **a Monday** (=one of the Mondays in the year) *My birthday's on a Monday this year.*

mon·e·ta·ris·m /ˈmʌnətərɪzəm $ ˈmɑː-/ *n* [U] the belief that the best way to manage a country's ECONOMY is for the government to control and limit the amount of money that is available and being used: *the monetarism of the 1980s* —**monetarist** *adj, n* [C]: *a monetarist view of the economy*

mon·e·ta·ry /ˈmʌnətəri $ ˈmɑːnəteri/ *adj* [only before noun] relating to money, especially all the money in a particular country: *the government's tight monetary policy* | *objects of little monetary value* THESAURUS ▸ FINANCIAL

mon·e·tize (*also* **-ise** *BrE*) /ˈmʌnətaɪz $ ˈmɑː-/ *v* [T] *technical* **1** to change government BONDS and debts into money **2** to make money from people who visit a website, for example by encouraging them to buy things

mon·ey /ˈmʌni/ ●●● S1 W1 *n* [U]
1 what you earn by working and can use to buy things. Money can be in the form of notes and coins or cheques, and can be kept in a bank: *Don't spend all your money on the first day of your holiday!* | *The repairs will cost quite a lot of money.*
2 money in the form of coins or notes that you can carry around with you SYN **cash**: *You'll find some money in my purse.* | *I didn't **have** any **money on me*** (=I was not carrying any money). | **Swiss/Japanese/Turkish etc money** *Don't forget to get some Swiss money before you leave.* | *We can **change** some **money** at the airport* (=change it into the money of another country).
3 someone's wealth, including all the property and other things they own: *The family **made** their **money** in the woollen trade.* | *He had **lost** all his **money** gambling.*
4 the money *informal* the amount of money that you earn for doing a job: *It sounds quite an interesting job, but I don't know what the money's like yet.* | *You have to work long hours and the money's terrible!*
5 pay good money for sth *spoken* to spend a lot of money on something: *Don't let the children jump around on the sofa. I paid good money for that.*
6 put/pump/pour money into sth to give money to a company or business so that it will become successful and you will earn money from it in the future: *No one's going to put money into the company while the market is so unstable.*
7 there's money (to be made) in sth *spoken* used to say that you can earn a lot of money from doing a particular job or

type of business: *There's a lot of money in sport these days.* | *Teaching can be very rewarding, but there's no money in it.*
8 I'm not made of money *spoken* used to say that you cannot afford something when someone asks you to pay for it.
9 have money to burn to have more money than you need, so that you spend it on unnecessary things: *Unless you've got money to burn, these expensive guitars are probably not for you.*
10 get your money's worth to get something worth the price that you paid: *At that price, you want to make sure you get your money's worth.*
11 be in the money *informal* to have a lot of money suddenly, or when you did not expect to
12 money is no object *informal* used to say that someone can spend as much money as they want to on something
13 for my money *spoken* used when giving your opinion about something to emphasize that you believe it strongly: *For my money, he's one of the best TV comedians ever.*
14 put (your) money on sth to risk money on the result of a race or competition
15 I'd put (my) money on sth *spoken* used to say that you feel sure that something will happen
16 my money's on sb/sth (*also* **the smart money's on sb/sth**) *spoken* used to say that you feel sure someone will win a race or competition, or that something will happen
17 money for old rope *BrE spoken* money that you earn very easily by doing a job that is not difficult
18 put your money where your mouth is *informal* to show by your actions that you really believe what you say
19 money talks *spoken* used to say that people with money have power and can get what they want
20 be (right) on the money *AmE spoken* to be completely correct or right: *You were right on the money when you said that he would have to resign.*
21 marry (into) money to marry someone whose family is rich → MONIES, BLOOD MONEY, HUSH MONEY, → **give sb a (good) run for their money** at RUN²(11), → **have a (good) run for your money** at RUN²(12), → **throw money at sth** at THROW¹(19)

COLLOCATIONS

VERBS

have money *I didn't have enough money to pay for it.*
make/earn money *She makes a little money by babysitting.*
spend money (on sth) *More money should be spent on training.*
cost money/cost a lot of money *Good food doesn't have to cost a lot of money.*
save money (=use less money) *Companies fired workers to save money.*
make money (=make a profit) *The farm was beginning to make money at last.*
lose money (=not make a profit, so that you then have less money) | **pay money (for sth)** | **lend sb money** | **borrow money** | **owe sb money** | **waste money (on sth)** | **raise money** (=do something to get money for a charity, school etc) | **give sb their money back** (*also* **refund sb's money**) (=give money back to a customer) | **money goes on sth** (=is spent on something) | **money comes in** (=is earned and received)

ADJECTIVES/NOUN + money

good money (=a lot of money) *Preston earns good money as a lawyer.*
big money *informal* (=a very large amount of money) *Basketball players make big money.*
easy money (=money that you earn easily) *For many, selling drugs seems like easy money.*
spending money (=an amount of money that you can spend on anything you want) | **pocket money/spending money** *BrE* (=a small amount of money that parents regularly give their children) | **government/taxpayers'/public money**

PHRASES

a sum of money (*also* **an amount of money**) *£10,000 seemed a huge sum of money to me.*
be a waste of money *Fancy clothes for a baby are a waste of money.*
be value for money *BrE* (=used when saying that something is worth the amount of money you pay for it) *The holiday was excellent value for money.*

COMMON ERRORS

⚠ Don't say 'gain money'. Say **make money**.

THESAURUS

money what you use to buy things, in the form of notes or coins: *He spent all his money on computer equipment.*
cash money in the form of coins and notes: *I didn't have any cash with me.*
currency the money used in a particular country: *The dollar gained in value against other currencies.* | *a single European currency*
change money in the form of coins of low value: *Do you have any small change?* | *a pocketful of loose change*
note *BrE*, **bill** *AmE* a piece of paper money: *a £20 note* | *a $5 bill*
coin a flat round piece of metal used as money: *She put some coins in the parking meter.* | *He took a coin out of his pocket.*
a ten-pence/50-cent etc piece a coin worth a particular amount

mon·ey·bags /ˈmʌnibægz/ *n* [singular] *informal* someone who has a lot of money – used humorously

ˈmoney ˌbelt *n* [C] a special belt that you can carry money in while you are travelling → see picture at BAG¹

mon·ey·box /ˈmʌnibɒks $ -bɑːks/ *n* [C] *especially BrE* a box in which children put their money to save it

mon·eyed, **monied** /ˈmʌnid/ *adj* [only before noun] *old-fashioned formal* rich: *the monied classes*

mon·ey·grab·bing /ˈmʌnigræbɪŋ/ (*also* **mon·ey·grub·bing** /ˈmʌnigrʌbɪŋ/) *adj* [only before noun] *informal* determined to get a lot of money, even by unfair or dishonest methods: *people who are exploited by moneygrabbing employers* —**moneygrabber, moneygrubber** *n* [C]

ˈmoney ˌlaundering *n* [U] when money that has been obtained illegally is put into legal businesses or bank accounts in different countries, so that it is difficult for people to discover where it came from: *The country is a major centre for money laundering.* | *He will now face trial on money laundering charges.*

mon·ey·lend·er /ˈmʌniˌlendə $ -ər/ *n* [C] someone whose business is to lend money to people, especially someone who makes people pay back a lot more money than they have borrowed —**moneylending** *n* [U]: *Most of his fortune came from moneylending.*

mon·ey·mak·er /ˈmʌniˌmeɪkə $ -ər/ *n* [C] a product or business that earns a lot of money SYN **money-spinner** *BrE* —**money-making** *adj* [only before noun]: *money-making schemes*

ˈmoney ˌmarket *n* [C] all the banks and other institutions that buy, sell, lend, or borrow money, especially foreign money, for profit

ˈmoney ˌorder *n* [C] an official document that you buy in a post office or a bank and send to someone so that they can exchange it for money in a bank → **postal order**

ˈmoney-ˌspinner *n* [C] *BrE* a MONEYMAKER: *We're hoping the show will be a real money-spinner.*

ˈmoney supˌply *n* [singular] *technical* all the money that exists in a country's economic system at a particular time: *his policy of controlling the money supply and cutting public spending*

-monger /mʌŋgə $ mɑːŋgər, mʌŋ-/ *suffix* [in nouns] **1** someone who sells a particular thing: *a fishmonger*

2 rumourmonger/gloom-monger/doom-monger etc someone who says unpleasant things: *The rumourmongers have been busy again.* | *the economic gloom-mongers* → WARMONGER

mon·gol /ˈmɒŋɡəl $ ˈmɑːŋ-/ *n* [C] *taboo old-fashioned* a very offensive word for someone with DOWN'S SYNDROME. Do not use this word. —**mongolism** *n* [U]

mon·goose /ˈmɒŋɡuːs $ ˈmɑːŋ-/ *n* (*plural* **mongooses**) [C] a small furry tropical animal that kills snakes and rats

mon·grel /ˈmʌŋɡrəl $ ˈmɑːŋ-, ˈmʌŋ-/ *n* [C] a dog that is a mix of several different breeds

mon·ied /ˈmʌnid/ *adj* another spelling of MONEYED

mon·ies, moneys /ˈmʌniz/ *n* [plural] *law* money: *If we are no longer able to provide the holiday you booked, we will return to you all monies paid.*

mon·i·ker /ˈmɒnɪkə $ ˈmɑːnɪkər/ *n* [C] *informal* a name, especially one that you choose for yourself or give something – used humorously

mon·i·tor¹ /ˈmɒnɪtə $ ˈmɑːnɪtər/ ●●○ S3 W3 AWL *v* [T]
1 to carefully watch and check a situation in order to see how it changes over a period of time: *Patients who are given the new drug will be asked to monitor their progress.* | *The government is* **monitoring** *the situation* **closely**. | *The temperature is* **carefully monitored**. | **monitor what/how etc** *We need a better system for monitoring what is going on.*
THESAURUS CHECK, WATCH
2 to secretly listen to other people's telephone calls, foreign radio broadcasts etc: *He suspected that his phone calls were being monitored.*

monitor² ●●○ *n* [C]
1 SCREEN a television or part of a computer with a screen, on which you can see pictures or information: **television/TV/computer monitor** *She was staring at her computer monitor.* | **on a monitor** *We could watch what was happening on the TV monitor.*
2 PIECE OF EQUIPMENT FOR MEASURING a piece of equipment that measures and shows the level, speed, temperature etc of something: *a heart monitor* | *The noise monitor recorded 98 decibels.*
3 SB WHO WATCHES AN ACTIVITY someone whose job is to watch an activity or a situation to see how it changes or develops, or to make sure that it is fair and legal: *UN monitors will remain in the country to supervise the elections.* | **peace/human rights etc monitors** *The UN is sending peace monitors to the area.*
4 CHILD a child who has been chosen to help a teacher in some way in class
5 SB WHO LISTENS TO RADIO someone whose job is to listen to news or messages on a radio and report on them

monk /mʌŋk/ *n* [C] a member of an all-male religious group that lives apart from other people in a MONASTERY → **nun** —**monkish** *adj*

mon·key¹ /ˈmʌŋki/ ●●● S3 *n* [C]
1 a small brown animal with a long tail, which uses its hands to climb trees and lives in hot countries
2 *informal* a small child who is very active and likes to play tricks: *Stop that, you little monkey!*
3 monkey business *informal* bad or dishonest behaviour
4 not give a monkey's *BrE spoken informal* to not care at all about something: *To be honest I don't give a monkey's what they do.*
5 make a monkey (out) of sb to make someone seem stupid
6 a monkey on your back *AmE informal* a serious problem that makes your life very difficult, especially being dependent on drugs

monkey² *v*
monkey around (*also* **monkey about** *BrE*) *phr v informal* to behave in a stupid or careless way: *Stop monkeying around and listen to me!*

ˈmonkey bars *n* [plural] *AmE* a structure of bars for children to climb and play on SYN **climbing frame** *BrE*

ˈmonkey nut *n* [C] *BrE informal* a PEANUT in its shell

mon·key·shines /ˈmʌŋkiʃaɪnz/ *n* [plural] *AmE old-fashioned informal* silly tricks or jokes

ˈmonkey wrench *n* [C] *especially AmE* a tool that is used to hold or turn things of different widths SYN **adjustable spanner** *BrE* → **throw a (monkey) wrench in sth** at WRENCH¹, → see picture at TOOL¹

mon·o¹ /ˈmɒnəʊ $ ˈmɑːnoʊ/ *n* [U] *informal* **1** *AmE* an infectious illness that makes your LYMPH NODEs swell and makes you feel weak and tired for a long time afterwards SYN **glandular fever** *BrE* **2** a system of recording or broadcasting sound, in which all the sound comes from only one direction → **stereo**

mono² *adj* using a system of recording or broadcasting sound, in which all the sound comes from only one direction → **stereo**: *an old mono recording*

mono- /mɒnəʊ, -nə $ -noʊ, -nə/ *prefix* one: *a monoplane* (=a plane with only one wing on each side) | *a monolingual dictionary* (=dealing with only one language)

mon·o·chrome /ˈmɒnəkrəʊm $ ˈmɑːnəkroʊm/ *adj* **1** in shades of only one colour, especially shades of grey: *We looked out over the grey, monochrome landscape.* **2** a monochrome picture or screen uses only the colours black, white, and grey OPP **colour**: *a monochrome computer monitor* —**monochromatic** /ˌmɒnəkrəˈmætɪk◂ $ ˌmɑː-/ *adj*

mon·o·cle /ˈmɒnəkəl $ ˈmɑː-/ *n* [C] a round piece of glass that you put in front of one eye to help you see better

mo·nog·a·my /məˈnɒɡəmi $ məˈnɑː-/ *n* [U] **1** the custom of being married to only one husband or wife → **bigamy, polygamy** **2** when a person or animal has a sexual relationship with only one partner: *Monogamy is rare in most animal groups, but is common among birds.* —**monogamous** *adj*: *We live in a monogamous society.* —**monogamously** *adv*

mon·o·gram /ˈmɒnəɡræm $ ˈmɑː-/ *n* [C] a design that is made using the first letters of someone's names and is put on pieces of clothing or other possessions —**monogrammed** *adj*

mon·o·graph /ˈmɒnəɡrɑːf $ ˈmɑːnəɡræf/ *n* [C] an article or short book that discusses a subject in detail

mon·o·ling·ual /ˌmɒnəʊˈlɪŋɡwəl◂ $ ˌmɑːnə-/ *adj* speaking or using only one language → **bilingual, multilingual**: *a monolingual dictionary*

mon·o·lith /ˈmɒnəlɪθ $ ˈmɑː-/ *n* [C] **1** a large powerful organization that cannot change quickly and does not consider the ideas or feelings of the people it affects: *It is misleading to see the legal system as a monolith.* **2** a large tall block of stone, especially one that was put in place in ancient times, possibly for religious reasons

mon·o·lith·ic /ˌmɒnəˈlɪθɪk◂ $ ˌmɑː-/ *adj* **1** a monolithic building is very large, solid, and impressive **2** a monolithic organization, political system etc is very large and powerful and difficult to change: *a monolithic movie company*

mon·o·logue (*also* **monolog** *AmE*) /ˈmɒnəlɒɡ $ ˈmɑːnl-ɒːɡ, -ɑːɡ/ *n* [C] a long speech by one person → **soliloquy, dialogue**: *Henry looked up, then continued his monologue.*

mon·o·ma·ni·a /ˌmɒnəʊˈmeɪniə $ ˌmɑːnoʊ-/ *n* [U] *formal* a very strong interest in one particular idea or subject which prevents you from thinking about anything else: *an obsession with food that verged on monomania* —**monomaniac** /-niæk/ *n* [C]

mon·o·nu·cle·o·sis /ˌmɒnəʊnjuːkliˈəʊsɪs $ ˌmɑːnoʊnuːkliˈoʊ-/ *n* [U] *medical* MONO¹(1)

mon·o·plane /ˈmɒnəʊpleɪn $ ˈmɑːnoʊ-/ *n* [C] a plane with only one wing on each side → **biplane**

mo·nop·ol·is·tic /məˌnɒpəˈlɪstɪk◂ $ -ˌnɑː-/ *adj* controlling or trying to control an industry or business activity completely: *The company wants to maintain its monopolistic position.*

mo·nop·o·lize (*also* **-ise** *BrE*) /məˈnɒpəlaɪz $ -ˈnɑː-/ *v* [T] **1** to have complete control over something so that other people cannot share it or take part in it: *The company has monopolized the soft drinks market.* | *He monopolized the conversation all evening.* **2** to use a lot of

M

someone's time or attention: *Virtually all her time and energy is now monopolized by the children.* —**monopolist** *n* [C]

mo·nop·o·ly /məˈnɒpəli $ məˈnɑː-/ ●●○ *n* (*plural* **monopolies**)
1 [C] if a company or government has a monopoly of a business or political activity, it has complete control of it so that other organizations cannot compete with it: **[+of]** *They are demanding an end to the Communist Party's* ***monopoly of power****.* | *the* ***state monopoly*** *of television* | **[+on/in]** *For years Bell Telephone* ***had*** *a* ***monopoly*** *on telephone services in the US.* | *a monopoly in copper trading*
2 [C] a large company that controls all or most of a business activity: *The company is a state-owned monopoly.*
3 [singular] if someone has a monopoly on something, that thing belongs to them, and no one else can share it: *Teachers do not* ***have*** *a* ***monopoly on*** *educational debate.*

mon·o·rail /ˈmɒnəʊreɪl $ ˈmɑːnə-/ *n* **1** [C,U] a railway system that uses a single RAIL, usually high above the ground **2** [C] a train on a monorail system

mon·o·sod·i·um glu·tam·ate /ˌmɒnəʊˌsəʊdiəm ˈɡluːtəmeɪt $ ˌmɑːnəsoʊ-/ *n* [U] MSG

mon·o·syl·lab·ic /ˌmɒnəsɪˈlæbɪk◂ $ ˌmɑː-/ *adj* **1** someone who speaks in a monosyllabic way does not say very much and does not try to be friendly: *He made monosyllabic replies to my questions.* **2** *technical* a monosyllabic word has only one SYLLABLE

mon·o·syl·la·ble /ˈmɒnəˌsɪləbəl $ ˈmɑː-/ *n* [C] *technical* a word with one SYLLABLE

mon·o·the·is·m /ˈmɒnəʊθiːɪzəm $ ˈmɑːnə-/ *n* [U] the belief that there is only one God → **polytheism** —**monotheist** *n* [C] —**monotheistic** /ˌmɒnəʊθiˈɪstɪk◂ $ ˌmɑːnə-/ *adj*: *monotheistic religions*

mon·o·tone /ˈmɒnətəʊn $ ˈmɑːnətoʊn/ *n* [singular] a sound or way of speaking or singing that continues on the same note without getting any louder or softer, and therefore sounds very boring: *He answered all the lawyer's questions in a dull monotone.*

mo·not·o·nous /məˈnɒtənəs $ məˈnɑː-/ *adj* boring because of always being the same: *a monotonous diet* | *a little boy who wet his bed* ***with monotonous regularity*** **THESAURUS▸** BORING —**monotonously** *adv*: *The rain poured monotonously out of the grey sky.*

mo·not·o·ny /məˈnɒtəni $ məˈnɑː-/ *n* [U] the quality of being always the same, which makes something boring, especially someone's life or work: **[+of]** *She wanted to escape the monotony of her everyday life.* | **relieve/break the monotony** *He suggested a card game to relieve the monotony of the journey.*

mo·nox·ide /məˈnɒksaɪd $ məˈnɑːk-/ *n* → CARBON MONOXIDE

Mon·sieur /məˈsjɜː $ -ˈsjɜːr/ *n* (*plural* **Messieurs** /meɪˈsjɜːz $ -ˈsjɜːrz/) used when speaking to or about a French-speaking man → **Madame**, **Mademoiselle**: *Monsieur Lacombe*

Mon·si·gnor /mɒnˈsiːnjə $ mɑːnˈsiːnjər/ *n* used when speaking to or about a priest of high rank in the Roman Catholic Church: *Monsignor Delgard*

mon·soon /mɒnˈsuːn $ mɑːn-/ *n* [C] **1** [usually singular] the season, from about April to October, when it rains a lot in India and other southern Asian countries **2** the heavy rain that falls during the monsoon, or the wind that brings the rain **THESAURUS▸** RAIN

mon·ster¹ /ˈmɒnstə $ ˈmɑːnstər/ ●●○ *n* [C]
1 IN STORIES an imaginary or ancient creature that is large, ugly, and frightening: *the remains of a prehistoric monster* | *the search for the Loch Ness Monster*
2 CRUEL PERSON someone who is very cruel and evil: *Only a monster could kill all those women.*
3 CHILD a small child, especially one who is behaving badly – used humorously: *I've got to get home and feed this little monster.*
4 STH LARGE *informal* an object, animal etc that is unusually large: *Did you see the fish Dad caught? It was a monster!* | *There's a* ***monster of a*** *spider in the bath!*
5 DANGEROUS PROBLEM a dangerous or threatening problem, especially one that develops gradually and is difficult to manage

monster² *adj* [only before noun] *informal* unusually large SYN **giant**: *a monster cat* | *The song was a monster hit.*

mon·ster·ing /ˈmɒnstərɪŋ $ ˈmɑːn-/ *n informal* **1** [C] if you get a monstering, someone criticizes you severely: *The player* ***got a monstering*** *from his manager.* **2** [U] the activity of behaving in a threatening way towards someone for a period of time —**monster** *v* [T]

mon·stros·i·ty /mɒnˈstrɒsəti $ mɑːnˈstrɑː-/ *n* (*plural* **monstrosities**) [C] something large and ugly, especially a building: *a concrete monstrosity*

mon·strous /ˈmɒnstrəs $ ˈmɑːn-/ *adj* **1** very wrong, immoral, or unfair: ***It's monstrous*** *to charge that much for a hotel room.* | *Such monstrous injustice is hard to understand.* **2** unusually large: *a monstrous nose* **3** unnatural or ugly and frightening SYN **hideous**: *a monstrous shadow on the stairs* —**monstrously** *adv*: *He was ugly and monstrously fat.* | *It was monstrously unfair.*

mon·tage /ˈmɒntɑːʒ $ mɑːnˈtɑːʒ/ *n* **1** [U] the process of making a whole picture, film, or piece of music or writing by combining parts of different pictures, films etc in an interesting and unusual way **2** [C] something made by combining parts of different pictures, films etc in an interesting and unusual way: **[+of]** *a montage of flowers* | *a photo montage*

month /mʌnθ/ ●●● S1 W1 *n* [C]
1 one of the 12 named periods of time that a year is divided into: **this/last/next month** *Phil is coming home for a visit next month.* | *She'll be thirteen this month.* | *I hope I'll have finished the work by* ***the end of the month****.* | *She earns about £350* ***a month*** (=each month). | *We update the schedule at least once a month.* | **the month of May/June etc** *It snowed heavily during the month of January.*
2 a period of about four weeks: *She has an eight-month-old daughter.* | *He'll be away for two months.* | *The symptoms she suffered varied* ***from month to month*** (=every few weeks she had different medical problems). | *a* ***month-long*** *transport strike*
3 months a long time, especially several months: *Redecorating the kitchen took months.* | **for/in months** *I haven't seen him for months.*
4 month after month used to emphasize that something happens regularly or continuously for a period of time: *I felt I was doing the same old thing week after week, month after month.*
5 month by month used when you are talking about a situation that develops slowly and steadily over a period of time: *Unemployment figures are rising month by month.*
6 never/not in a month of Sundays *spoken especially BrE* used to emphasize that something will definitely never happen: *You won't find anyone to do that job in a month of Sundays.*

GRAMMAR: Patterns with month

last month/this month etc
Don't use **in** with these words:
• You say **last month**: *Sales fell sharply last month.*
✗ Don't say: *Sales fell sharply in last month.*
• You say **this month**: *We've been very busy this month.*
✗ Don't say: *We've been very busy in this month.*
• You say **next month**: *It's my birthday next month.*
✗ Don't say: *It's my birthday in next month.*
• You say **that month**: *That month I started a new job.*
✗ Don't say: *In that month I started a new job.*

a month
• You use **a month** when saying how many times in a month something happens: *We eat in restaurants several times a month.* ✗ Don't say: *We eat in restaurants several times in a month.*

in the month of
• You use **in the month of** when saying the month when something happens: *The trees usually flower in the month of May.*

all month
• You use **all month** when talking about something that happens during every part of a month: *It's been raining all month.* ✗ Don't say: *It's been raining all the month.*

month·ly¹ /ˈmʌnθli/ ●●○ *adj* [only before noun]
1 happening once a month: *The mortgage is payable in monthly instalments.* | *a monthly publication*
2 used to talk about the total amount of something that is received, paid, measured, or calculated in a month: *a monthly salary of $850* | *a monthly rainfall of four inches*
3 a monthly ticket, PASS etc can be used for a period of one month —**monthly** *adv*: *They meet monthly to discuss progress.*

monthly² *n* (*plural* **monthlies**) [C] a magazine that appears once a month: *a leading women's monthly*

mon·ty /ˈmɒnti $ ˈmɑːn-/ *n* **the full monty** *informal* something that includes everything possible

mon·u·ment /ˈmɒnjəmənt $ ˈmɑː-/ ●●○ *n* [C]
1 a building, STATUE, or other large structure that is built to remind people of an important event or famous person → **memorial**: *He erected a monument on the spot where his daughter was killed.* | **[+to]** *a fitting monument to the men who died in the battle*
2 a very old building or place that is important historically: ***Ancient monuments** are protected by law.*
3 **be a monument to sb/sth** to show clearly the result of someone's qualities, beliefs, or actions: *The company is a monument to Sir Peter's energy and vision.* → NATIONAL MONUMENT

mon·u·ment·al /ˌmɒnjəˈmentl◂ $ ˌmɑː-/ *adj*
1 [usually before noun] a monumental achievement, piece of work etc is very important and is usually based on many years of work: *a monumental contribution to the field of medicine* | *Charles Darwin's monumental study, 'The Origin of Species'* **2** [only before noun] extremely large, bad, good, impressive etc: *Banks and building societies were yesterday accused of monumental incompetence.* | *a monumental task* | *There was a monumental traffic jam on the freeway.* **3** [only before noun] relating to a monument or built as a monument: *a monumental arch*

mon·u·ment·al·ly /ˌmɒnjəˈmentəli $ ˌmɑː-/ *adv* extremely – usually used of negative qualities: *It was a monumentally stupid thing to do.*

moo /muː/ *v* [I] if a cow moos, it makes a long low sound —**moo** *n* [C]

moobs /muːbz/ *n* [plural] *informal* areas of fat or muscle on a man's chest that look like breasts SYN **man boobs**

MOOC /muːk/ *n* [C] (***massive open online course***) a course available on the Internet that very large numbers of people can take

mooch /muːtʃ/ *v* [T] *AmE informal* to get something by asking someone to give you it, instead of paying for it SYN **scrounge** *BrE*: **mooch sth off sb** *He tried to mooch a drink off me.*

mooch around/about *phr v BrE informal* to move around slowly without any purpose and doing very little: *Beth was happy to mooch around for hours in her nightdress.*

mood /muːd/ ●●● S3 W3 *n*
1 WAY YOU FEEL [C] the way you feel at a particular time: *You're in a good mood this morning!* | *the general mood of depression in the office*
2 **be in a mood** to feel unhappy, impatient, or angry and to refuse to speak normally to other people: *He's been in a real mood all day.* | *Don't talk to her. She's **in one of** her **moods*** (=used about someone who is often unhappy, angry etc).
3 **be/feel in the mood (for sth)** to feel that you would like to do something: *We really felt in the mood for a party.* | *I don't want to talk about it now. I'm not in the mood.*
4 **be in no mood for sth/to do sth** to not want to do something, or be determined not to do something: *I was in no mood for a joke.* | *George was in no mood to be sociable.*
5 **when the mood takes you** at times that are not regular or planned, when you feel that you want to do something: *He used to visit them when the mood took him.*
6 WAY A PLACE OR EVENT FEELS [singular] the way that a place, event, book, film etc seems or makes you feel: *The opening shot of dark, rainy streets sets the mood for the whole film.*
7 GRAMMAR [C] *technical* one of the sets of verb forms in grammar: the INDICATIVE (=expressing a fact or action), the IMPERATIVE (=expressing a command), the INTERROGATIVE (=expressing a question), or the SUBJUNCTIVE (=expressing a doubt or wish)

COLLOCATIONS

ADJECTIVES

a good mood *He was in a good mood when he got home from work.*
a bad mood *The news had put her in a bad mood.*
a confident/optimistic/relaxed etc mood *At the beginning of the negotiations, he was in a confident mood.*
a holiday/party/festive mood (=a happy mood in which you want to enjoy a holiday or party) | **a foul mood** (=very bad and angry) | **a black mood** *BrE* (=very angry or sad) | **a sombre mood** *BrE*, **a somber mood** *AmE* (=serious and slightly sad) | **the general mood** (=the mood of a group of people) | **the public/national mood** (=the mood of the people in a country)

PHRASES

a mood of optimism/despair/excitement etc *There is a new mood of optimism.*
a change of mood *Michael underwent one of his sudden changes of mood.*
the mood of the time/moment (=the way people in general feel at a particular time)

mood + NOUN

mood swings (=changes of mood) *Sudden mood swings can be a sign of mental illness.*

VERBS

reflect/capture sb's mood (=show what someone is feeling) *His comments reflected the national mood.*
match/suit sb's mood *The terrible weather matched her mood.*
lighten sb's mood (=make someone feel happier) | **sb's mood changes**

ˈmood-ˌaltering *adj* [only before noun] mood-altering drugs or substances affect your mind and change the way you think or feel

ˈmood ˌmusic *n* [U] music that is supposed to make you have particular feelings, especially romantic ones

mood·y /ˈmuːdi/ *adj* **1** annoyed or unhappy: *Keith had seemed moody all morning.* **2** often changing quickly from being in a good temper to being in a bad temper SYN **temperamental**: *a moody teenager* | *Lewis was moody and brilliantly clever.* **3** moody places, films, pictures, and music make you feel slightly sad, lonely, or perhaps frightened: *the moody grey sea in the dawn light* —**moodily** *adv*: *She was staring moodily into the fire.* —**moodiness** *n* [U]

moo·la, **moolah** /ˈmuːlə/ *n* [U] *AmE informal* money

moon¹ /muːn/ ●●● S3 W3 *n*
1 **the moon/the Moon** the round object that you can see shining in the sky at night, and that moves around the Earth every 28 days: *the craters on the surface of the Moon* | *The Americans landed on the Moon in 1969.* | *The moon appeared from behind a cloud.* | *The **moon rose** into the sky.* | *The **moon** was **shining** in the sky.*
2 [C usually singular] the appearance or shape of the moon at a particular time: *It was the night of the **full moon**.* | *a clear night with a bright moon* | *a thin crescent moon*
3 [C] a round object that moves around a PLANET other than Earth: *the moons of Saturn*
4 **ask for the moon** (*also* **cry for the moon** *BrE*) *informal* to

ask for something that is difficult or impossible to obtain: *There's no point in crying for the moon.*
5 over the moon *BrE informal* very happy: *She's over the moon about her new job.*
6 many moons ago *literary* a long time ago: *It all happened many moons ago.* → **once in a blue moon** at ONCE[1](15), → **promise sb the moon** at PROMISE[1](3)

COLLOCATIONS – MEANING 2

ADJECTIVES/NOUN + moon

bright *The moon was very bright.*
a full moon (=with a completely round shape) *A full moon hung low in the sky.*
a half moon (=looking like half a circle) | **a crescent moon** (=with a thin curved shape) | **a new moon** (=a very thin moon which is just starting to get bigger) | **a silver/yellow moon** | **a pale moon** | **a harvest moon** (=the full moon that appears in late September or early October)

VERBS

the moon shines *The moon shone through the window.*
the moon rises (*also* **the moon comes up**) *He watched the full moon come up over the trees.*
the moon appears | **the moon comes out** (=appears as it gets dark or a cloud moves) | **the moon hangs somewhere** *literary* (=stays there for a long time) | **the moon sets** (=goes down so that you cannot see it) | **the moon waxes** (=gets bigger each night) | **the moon wanes** (=gets smaller each night)

moon² *v* [I,T] *informal* to bend over and show your BUTTOCKS as a joke or a way of insulting someone
moon about/around *phr v BrE informal* to spend your time lazily, moving around with no real purpose: *I wish you'd stop mooning about and do something useful!*
moon over sb/sth *phr v old-fashioned* to spend your time thinking about someone that you are in love with: *She sits mooning over his photograph for hours.*
moon·beam /ˈmuːnbiːm/ *n* [C] a shining line of light from the moon
ˈMoon Boot *n* [C] *trademark* a thick warm boot made of cloth or plastic, worn in snow and cold weather
moon·less /ˈmuːnləs/ *adj* a moonless sky or night is dark because the moon cannot be seen: *a cloudy, moonless night*
moon·light¹ /ˈmuːnlaɪt/ *n* [U] **1** the light of the moon: **in the moonlight** *The water looked silver in the moonlight.* | **pale/silver moonlight** *The hills were bathed in pale moonlight.* | **by moonlight** *We dined by moonlight.* **2 do a moonlight (flit)** *BrE* to leave a place secretly in the middle of the night in order to avoid paying money that you owe: *They did moonlight flits from one awful apartment to another.*
moonlight² *v* [I] *informal* **1** to have a second job in addition to your main job, especially without the knowledge of the government tax department: *She's been moonlighting as a waitress in the evenings.* **2** *BrE* to do paid work although you are getting money from the government because you do not officially have a job —**moonlighter** *n* [C] —**moonlighting** *n* [U]: *He's been doing some moonlighting for another company.*
moon·lit /ˈmuːnˌlɪt/ *adj* [only before noun] lit by the moon: *a moonlit garden*
moon·scape /ˈmuːnskeɪp/ *n* [singular] an area of land with no plants that looks like the surface of the Moon
moon·shine /ˈmuːnʃaɪn/ *n* [U] *informal* **1** *especially AmE* strong alcoholic drink that is produced illegally **2** *BrE* an idea or statement that is silly or wrong and does not deserve serious attention SYN **nonsense**: *He regarded her plans as romantic moonshine.*
moon·stone /ˈmuːnstəʊn $ -stoʊn/ *n* [C,U] a milky-white stone used in making jewellery: *a moonstone necklace*
moon·struck /ˈmuːnstrʌk/ *adj informal* slightly crazy, especially because you are in love
moor¹ /mʊə $ mʊr/ *n* [C usually plural] *especially BrE* a wild open area of high land, covered with rough grass or low bushes and HEATHER, that is not farmed because the soil is not good enough: *They went grouse shooting up on the moors.* | *the Yorkshire moors*
moor² *v* [I,T] to fasten a ship or boat to the land or to the bottom of the sea using ropes or an ANCHOR: *Two or three fishing boats were moored alongside the pier.*
Moor *n* [C] one of the Muslim people from North Africa who entered Spain in the 8th century and ruled the southern part of the country until 1492
moor·hen /ˈmʊəhen $ ˈmʊr-/ *n* [C] *BrE* a black bird that lives beside streams and lakes
moor·ing /ˈmʊərɪŋ $ ˈmʊr-/ *n* **1 moorings** [plural] the ropes, chains, ANCHORS etc used to fasten a ship or boat to the land or the bottom of the sea: **break free of/slip its moorings** *The great ship slipped her moorings and slid out into the Atlantic.* **2** [C] the place where a ship or boat is moored: *a temporary mooring*
Moor·ish /ˈmʊərɪʃ $ ˈmʊr-/ *adj* relating to the Moors: *Moorish architecture*
moor·land /ˈmʊələnd $ ˈmʊr-/ *n* [U] (*also* **moorlands** [plural]) *especially BrE* wild open countryside covered with rough grass and low bushes: *large areas of* **open moorland** —**moorland** *adj*: *a bleak moorland road*
moose /muːs/ *n* (*plural* **moose**) [C] a large brown animal like a DEER that has very large flat ANTLERS (=horns that grow like branches) and lives in North America, northern Europe, and parts of Asia
moot¹ /muːt/ *adj* **1 a moot point/question** something that has not yet been decided or agreed, and about which people have different opinions: *Whether these controls will really reduce violent crime is a moot point.* **2** *AmE* a situation or possible action that is moot is no longer likely to happen or exist: *The fear that airstrikes could endanger troops is moot now that the army is withdrawing.*
moot² *v* **be mooted** to be suggested for people to consider SYN **put forward**: *The question of changing the membership rules was mooted at the last meeting.*
ˈmoot court *n* [C] *AmE* a court in which law students practise holding TRIALS
mop¹ /mɒp $ mɑːp/ *n* [C] **1** a thing used for washing floors, consisting of a long stick with threads of thick string or a piece of SPONGE fastened to one end: *a mop and bucket* **2** a thing used for cleaning dishes, consisting of a short stick with a piece of SPONGE fastened to one end **3** [usually singular] *informal* a large amount of thick, often untidy hair: **[+of]** *He ran a hand through his mop of fair hair.*
mop² *v* (**mopped**, **mopping**) **1** [I,T] to wash a floor with a wet mop: *She carried on mopping the floor.* → see picture at CLEAN² **2** [T] to dry your face by rubbing it with a cloth or something soft SYN **wipe**: *It was so hot he had to keep stopping to mop his face.* | *The doctor* **mopped** *his* **brow** (=removed sweat from his forehead) *with a handkerchief.* **3** [T] to remove liquid from a surface by rubbing it with a cloth or something soft: **mop sth from sth** *She gently mopped the blood from the wound.* | *He mopped the sweat from his face.* | **mop sth away** *She mopped the tears away with a lacy handkerchief.* **4 mop the floor with sb** *AmE* to completely defeat someone, for example in a game or argument SYN **wipe the floor with sb** *BrE*: *We mopped the floor with the team from Pomona High.*
mop sth/sb ↔ **up** *phr v* **1** to remove liquid with a mop, a cloth, or something soft, especially in order to clean a surface SYN **wipe up**: *Mop the sauce up with your bread.* | *He mopped up the spilt milk.* **2** to remove or deal with something which you think is undesirable or dangerous, so that it is no longer a problem: *The usual solution is to send in infantry to mop up any remaining opposition.* | *The rebellion has been crushed, but mopping-up operations may take several weeks.*
mope /məʊp $ moʊp/ *v* [I] to feel sorry for yourself, without making any effort to do anything or be more

happy: *Don't lie there moping on a lovely morning like this!* | *The week he died, we all sat around and moped.*

mope around/about (sth) *phr v BrE* to move around a place in a sad slow way, especially because you feel unhappy about the situation you are in: *She spends her days moping around the house.* | *Stephen didn't expect her to mope about while he was away on business.*

mo·ped /ˈməʊped $ ˈmoʊ-/ *n* [C] a small two-wheeled vehicle with an engine → **motorcycle**

mop·pet /ˈmɒpɪt $ ˈmɑː-/ *n* [C] *informal* a small child

mo·quette /mɒˈket $ moʊ-/ *n* [U] a thick soft material used for covering furniture: *a moquette armchair*

MOR /ˌem əʊ ˈɑː $ -oʊ ˈɑːr/ *n* [U] (***middle of the road***) music that is relaxing to listen to, but is not very exciting

mo·raine /məˈreɪn/ *n* [C] *technical* a mass of earth or pieces of rock moved along by a GLACIER and left in a line at the bottom of it

mor·al¹ /ˈmɒrəl $ ˈmɔː-/ ●●○ W2 *adj*

1 [only before noun] relating to the principles of what is right and wrong behaviour, and with the difference between good and evil → **morally**, **ethical**: *It is easy to have an opinion on a moral issue like the death penalty for murder.* | **moral philosophy** | **moral standards/values/principles** *I think you can run a business to the highest moral standards.* | *If we accept that certain babies should be allowed to die, we place doctors in a **moral dilemma**.* | *Man is gifted with a **moral sense** by which he distinguishes good from evil.*

2 [only before noun] based on your ideas about what is right, rather than on what is legal or practical: *The book places a high **moral value** on marriage and the family unit.* | *The UN feels that it has the **moral authority*** (=influence because people accept that its beliefs are right) *to send troops to the area.* | **moral duty/obligation/responsibility** *A man has a moral duty to obey the law.* | *It isn't just **lack of moral fibre*** (=lack of the emotional strength to do what you believe is right) *which leads to a rising divorce rate.*

3 moral support encouragement that you give by expressing approval or interest, rather than by giving practical help: *Dad came along to give me some moral support.*

4 moral victory a situation in which you show that your beliefs are right and fair, even if you do not win: *Through Joan of Arc, France won a great moral victory.*

5 always behaving in a way that is based on strong principles about what is right and wrong OPP **immoral**, **amoral**: *a moral man of high integrity*

6 take/claim/seize the moral high ground to claim that you are the only person who does what is morally right in a situation, with the intention of being noticed and considered to be good by the public

7 moral compass a way of recognizing what kind of behaviour is right or wrong: *Has the government lost its moral compass?*

moral² ●○○ *n*

1 morals [plural] principles or standards of good behaviour, especially in matters of sex → **ethics**: *the morals and customs of the Victorian period* | *Values and morals are independent of religious faith.* | *the corruption of **public morals*** (=the standards of behaviour, especially sexual behaviour, expected by society) | *a young woman of **loose morals*** (=low standards of sexual behaviour – often used humorously)

2 [C] a practical lesson about what to do or how to behave, which you learn from a story or from something that happens to you → **message**: **[+of]** *The moral of the film was that crime does not pay.*

mo·rale /məˈrɑːl $ məˈræl/ ●○○ *n* [U] the level of confidence and positive feelings that people have, especially people who work together, who belong to the same team etc: *A win is always good for morale.* | **low/high morale** *low staff morale* | *The failed coup caused a loss of morale within the army.* | **boost/raise/improve/build morale** *There is a need to raise morale in the teaching profession.* | *the prince's **morale-boosting*** (=intended to raise morale) *mission to the war-torn country* | **maintain/keep up/restore morale** *The media feels pressure to keep the morale of the country up in war time.*

mor·al·ist /ˈmɒrəlɪst $ ˈmɔː-/ *n* [C] **1** someone who has very strong beliefs about what is right and wrong and how people should behave – used to show disapproval: *a narrow-minded moralist* **2** a teacher of moral principles

mor·al·ist·ic /ˌmɒrəˈlɪstɪk◂ $ ˌmɔː-/ *adj* with very strong beliefs about what is right and wrong, especially when this makes you judge other people's behaviour: *It's difficult to talk to teenagers about drugs without sounding too moralistic.*

mo·ral·i·ty /məˈræləti/ ●○○ *n* [U]

1 beliefs or ideas about what is right and wrong and about how people should behave: ***sexual morality*** | **public/private/personal morality** *the decline in standards of personal morality* | *The authorities are protectors of public morality.* | **conventional/traditional morality** *a lack of concern for conventional morality*

2 the degree to which something is right or acceptable OPP **immorality**: **[+of]** *a discussion on the morality of abortion*

mor·al·ize (*also* **-ise** *BrE*) /ˈmɒrəlaɪz $ ˈmɔː-/ *v* [I] to tell other people your ideas about right and wrong behaviour, especially when they have not asked for your opinion SYN **preach**: *politicians moralizing about people's sexual behaviour*

mor·al·ly /ˈmɒrəli $ ˈmɔː-/ ●○○ *adv*

1 according to moral principles about what is right and wrong: *What you did wasn't illegal, but it was **morally wrong**.* | *There is a belief that village life is somehow morally superior to city life.* | *Such hypocrisy is morally indefensible.* | *The Constitution is not morally neutral but is based on certain central values.*

2 morally certain *old-fashioned* certain about something that cannot be proved: *I am morally certain that he is incapable of deliberately harming anyone.*

ˌmoral maˈjority *n* **the moral majority** the group of people in a society who have strong moral beliefs and think they are always right. In the US there is an organized group called the Moral Majority, who have strong Christian principles: *Smokers today are often made to feel like social outcasts by the moral majority.*

mo·rass /məˈræs/ *n* **1** [singular] a complicated and confusing situation that is very difficult to get out of: *We're trying to drag the country out of its economic morass.* | **[+of]** *They were **stuck** in a **morass** of paperwork.* **2** [C] *literary* a dangerous area of soft wet ground SYN **marsh**

mor·a·to·ri·um /ˌmɒrəˈtɔːriəm $ ˌmɔː-/ *n* (*plural* **moratoriums** *or* **moratoria**) [C usually singular] **1** an official stopping of an activity for a period of time: **[+on]** *a moratorium on nuclear testing* **2** a law or an agreement that gives people more time to pay their debts: *a two-year moratorium on interest payments*

mor·bid /ˈmɔːbɪd $ ˈmɔːr-/ *adj* **1** with a strong and unhealthy interest in unpleasant subjects, especially death: **morbid fascination/curiosity** *a morbid fascination with instruments of torture* | *The trip was made all the worse by Frankie's **morbid fear** of flying.* | *His head was full of morbid thoughts.* **2** *medical* relating to or caused by a disease: *a morbid gene* —**morbidly** *adv* —**morbidity** /mɔːˈbɪdəti $ mɔːr-/ *n* [U]

mor·dant /ˈmɔːdənt $ ˈmɔːr-/ *adj* **mordant wit/satire/humour** *formal* unkind and insulting humour etc that is also funny SYN **biting**: *The play's mordant comedy makes for compelling viewing.*

more¹ /mɔː $ mɔːr/ ●●● S1 W1 *adv*

1 [used before an adjective or adverb to form the comparative] having a particular quality to a greater degree OPP **less**: *You'll have to be more careful next time.* | *Can't it be done more quickly?* | **much/a lot/far more** *Children generally feel much more confident working in groups.* | **more ... than** *It was a lot more expensive than I had expected.* | *Your health is more important than anything else.* | *Children can often do these puzzles more easily than adults.* | *Selling goods abroad* is **no more** *difficult* (=not more difficult) *than selling to the home market.*

GRAMMAR: Comparatives

More is not used before the **-er** form of an adjective or adverb. You say: *The train is quicker than the bus.*
✗ Don't say: *The train is more quicker.*
GRAMMAR GUIDE ▶ ADJECTIVES

2 used to say that something happens a greater number of times or for longer OPP **less**: *I promised Mum that I'd help more with the housework.* | *You need to get out of the house more.* | **more than** *Children are using the library more than they used to.* | *He travels around* ***a lot more*** *now that he has a car.*
3 used to say that something happens to a greater degree OPP **less**: *She cares* ***a lot more*** *for her dogs than she does for me.* | **more than** *It's his manner I dislike, more than anything else.*
4 more and more used to say that a quality, situation etc gradually increases SYN **increasingly**: *More and more, we are finding that people want to continue working beyond 60.* | *As the disease worsened, he found walking more and more difficult.*
5 more or less almost: *a place where the ground was more or less flat* | *They've settled here more or less permanently.* | *He more or less accused me of lying.*
6 once more a) again, and often for the last time: *May I thank you all once more for making this occasion such a big success.* | *Once more the soldiers attacked and once more they were defeated.* **b)** used to say that someone or something returns to the situation they were in before: *England was once more at war with France.*
7 not anymore (*also* **no more** *literary*) if something does not happen anymore, it used to happen but does not happen now: *Sarah doesn't live here anymore.*
8 more than happy/welcome/likely etc very happy, welcome, likely etc – used to emphasize what you are saying: *The store is more than happy to deliver goods to your home.* | *The police are more than likely to ban the match.*
9 the more ..., the more/the less ... used to say that if a particular activity increases, another change happens as a result: *The more I thought about it, the less I liked the idea.*
10 be more sth than sth to be one thing rather than another: *It was more a worry than a pleasure.*
11 more than a little *formal* fairly: *The lectures were more than a little disappointing.*
12 no more does/has/will etc sb *spoken old-fashioned* used to say that a negative statement is also true about someone else SYN **nor, neither**: *'She didn't know the reason for his leaving.' 'No more do I* (=neither do I).*'*
13 no more ... than used to emphasize that someone or something does not have a particular quality or would not do something: *He's no more fit to be a priest than I am!*
→ **more often than not** at OFTEN(5), → **more fool you/him etc** at FOOL[1](7), → **that's more like it/this is more like it** at LIKE[1](11)

more[2] ●●● S1 W1 *determiner, pron* [comparative of 'many' and 'much']
1 a greater amount or number OPP **less, fewer**: *We should spend more on health and education.* | **more (...) than** *More people are buying new cars than ever before.* | **much/a lot/far more** *Diane earns a lot more than I do.* | **more than 10/100 etc** *Our plane took off more than two hours late.* | *More than a quarter of the students never finished their courses.* | **[+of]** *Viewers want better television, and more of it.* | *Perhaps next year more of us will be able to afford holidays abroad.*
2 an additional number or amount OPP **less**: *I really am interested. Tell me more.* | *We need five more chairs.* | **a little/many/some/any more** *Can I have a little more time to finish?* | *Are there any more sandwiches?* | *I have* ***no more*** *questions.* | **[+of]** *You'd better take some more of your medicine.* | *Don't waste any more of my time.*
3 more and more an increasing number or amount OPP **less and less**: *More and more people are moving to the cities.*
4 not/no more than sth used to emphasize that a particular number, amount, distance etc is not large: *It's a beautiful cottage not more than five minutes from the nearest beach.* | *Opinion polls show that no more than 30% of people trust the government.*
5 the more ..., the more/the less ... used to say that if an amount of something increases, another change happens as a result: *It always seems like the more I earn, the more I spend.*
6 be more of sth than sth to be one thing rather than another: *It was more of a holiday than a training exercise.*
7 no more than a) used to say that something is not too much, but exactly right or suitable: *It's no more than you deserve.* | *Eline felt it was no more than her duty to look after her husband.* **b)** (*also* **little more than**) used to say that someone or something is not very great or important: *He's no more than a glorified accountant.* | *He left school with little more than a basic education.*
8 (and) what's more used to add more information that emphasizes what you are saying: *I've been fortunate to find a career that I love and, what's more, I get well paid for it.*
9 no more sth used to say that something will or should no longer happen: *No more dreary winters – we're moving to Florida.* → **more's the pity** at PITY[1](4)

THESAURUS

more in addition to an amount or number: *Can I have some more coffee?* | *I have one more question.* | *It only costs a few dollars more.*
further [only before noun] *formal* as well as the ones that you have already mentioned: *She will remain in hospital for further tests.* | *They waited for a further two hours.*
supplementary *formal* in addition to the main part of something: *Supplementary information is available on request.* | *a supplementary question* | *supplementary income*
extra in addition to the usual or standard cost, time, amount etc: *They let the kids stay up an extra hour.* | *Some stores charge extra for delivery.* | *Postage is extra.*
additional [only before noun] more than the basic amount or the amount that you expected or agreed. Additional is more formal than **extra**: *An evening job would provide additional income.* | *There may be an additional charge for paying bills by credit card.*

more·ish /ˈmɔːrɪʃ/ *adj BrE spoken* food or drink that is moreish tastes very good, and makes you want to have more of it

more·o·ver /mɔːrˈəʊvə $ -ˈoʊvər/ ●●○ W2 *adv* [sentence adverb] *formal* in addition – used to introduce information that adds to or supports what has previously been said: *The rent is reasonable and, moreover, the location is perfect.* | *The source of the information is irrelevant. Moreover, the information need not be confidential.*

REGISTER

Moreover is very formal. In everyday English, people use **what's more** or **also** instead: *The rent is reasonable and,* ***what's more,*** *the location is perfect.*

mo·res /ˈmɔːreɪz/ *n* [plural] *formal* the customs, social behaviour, and moral values of a particular group: *contemporary social and sexual mores*

morgue /mɔːg $ mɔːrg/ *n* [C] **1** a building or room, usually in a hospital, where dead bodies are kept until they are buried or CREMATED SYN **mortuary 2 be (like) a morgue** to be a place that is very quiet or dull – used humorously

mor·i·bund /ˈmɒrəbʌnd $ ˈmɔː-, ˈmɑː-/ *adj* **1** a moribund organization, industry etc is no longer active or effective and may be coming to an end: *The region's heavy industry is still inefficient and moribund.* | *A cut in interest rates will help the country's moribund housing market.*
2 *literary* slowly dying: *The patient was moribund by the time the doctor arrived.*

Mor·mon /ˈmɔːmən $ ˈmɔːr-/ *n* [C] a member of a religious organization formed in 1830 in the US, officially called The Church of Jesus Christ of Latterday Saints —**Mormon** *adj* —**Mormonism** *n* [U]

morn /mɔːn $ mɔːrn/ *n* [C usually singular] *literary* morning

morn·ing¹ /ˈmɔːnɪŋ $ ˈmɔːr-/ ●●● S1 W1 *n* [C,U]
1 the early part of the day, from when the sun rises until 12 o'clock in the middle of the day: *I hated those cold winter mornings. | I'm not feeling very well this morning. | He stayed in bed late on Sunday morning. | She took the early morning train.*
2 the part of the day from 12 o'clock at night until 12 o'clock in the middle of the day: **two/four o'clock in the morning** *The phone rang at three in the morning. | It's four o'clock in the morning.*
3 in the morning if something will happen in the morning, it will happen during the morning of the following day: *I'll deal with that in the morning.*
4 mornings during the morning of each day: *She works mornings at the local school.*
5 morning, noon, and night used to emphasize that something happens a lot or continuously: *I was on duty morning, noon, and night.* → COFFEE MORNING

GRAMMAR: Patterns with morning

in the morning
• You do something **in the morning**: *What time do you get up in the morning?* ✗ Don't say: *What time do you get up on the morning?*

on Monday/Tuesday etc morning
• You do something **on Monday/Tuesday etc morning**: *I was late for work on Thursday morning.*

on the morning of sth
• Something happens **on the morning of** a particular date or event: *On the morning of March 15, 2008, he was involved in a car accident. | Make sure you arrive in plenty of time on the morning of the exam.*

all morning
• You use **all morning** to say that something happens during a whole morning, from beginning to end: *I've been working hard all morning.* ✗ Don't say: *I've been working hard all the morning.*

COLLOCATIONS

ADJECTIVES/NOUN + morning

Friday/Monday/Saturday etc morning *I'll see you on Monday morning.*
tomorrow morning *Can you have the report ready by tomorrow morning?*
yesterday morning *I haven't seen her since yesterday morning.*
this morning (=today in the morning) *What did you do this morning?*
the next morning/the following morning *His meeting was not until the next morning.*
late morning *By the time he woke, it was late morning.*
the early morning *A light frost covered the fields in the early morning.*
a beautiful/fine/sunny morning *Outside it was a beautiful morning.*
a cold/frosty morning | a summer/winter etc morning

morning + NOUN

the morning sun/light/mist *the warmth of the morning sun*
a morning coffee/run/swim (=that someone does, drinks etc in the morning) *She read the paper while drinking her morning coffee.*
the morning paper/news (=that is published or broadcast in the morning) | **the morning train/flight** (=that leaves in the morning)

PHRASES

early in the morning *He has to get up very early in the morning.*
first thing in the morning (=at the beginning of the morning) *She set off first thing in the morning.*
from morning till night (=all day - used for emphasis) *He works from morning till night.*
in the small hours of the morning (=very early, before dawn)

morning² ●●● S2 *interjection* used to greet someone in the morning: *Morning, everybody!*

ˌmorning-ˈafter pill *n* [C] a drug that a woman can take a few hours after having sex to prevent her from becoming PREGNANT

ˈmorning coat *n* [C] a formal black coat with a long back that is worn as part of morning dress

ˈmorning dress *n* [U] *especially BrE* men's formal clothes that include a morning coat, trousers, and a TOP HAT, worn at daytime ceremonies such as weddings

ˌmorning ˈglory / $ ˈ.. ˌ../ *n* [C,U] a plant that has white, blue, or pink flowers that open in the morning and close in late afternoon

ˌMorning ˈPrayer *n* [U] a morning church service in the Church of England and the Episcopal Church in the US SYN **matins**

ˈmorning room *n* [C] *old-fashioned* a comfortable room that is used in the morning, usually in a large house

ˈmorning ˌsickness *n* [U] a feeling of sickness that some women have during the morning when they are PREGNANT, usually in the early months

ˌmorning ˈstar *n* [singular] a bright PLANET, usually Venus, that you can see in the eastern sky when the sun rises

ˈmorning suit *n* [C] a man's suit that is worn at formal ceremonies during the day, especially weddings

mo·roc·co /məˈrɒkəʊ $ məˈrɑːkoʊ/ *n* [U] fine soft leather used especially for covering books

mo·ron /ˈmɔːrɒn $ -rɑːn/ *n* [C] **1** *informal not polite* a very offensive word for someone who you think is very stupid SYN **idiot**: *Don't leave it there, you moron!* **2** *technical old-fashioned* someone whose intelligence has not developed to the normal level —**moronic** /məˈrɒnɪk $ -ˈrɑː-/ *adj*: *a moronic grin*

mo·rose /məˈrəʊs $ -ˈroʊs/ *adj* bad-tempered, unhappy, and silent: *Daniel seems very morose and gloomy.* —**morosely** *adv*: *He stared morosely at the floor.* —**moroseness** *n* [U]

morph /mɔːf $ mɔːrf/ *v* [I,T] to develop a new appearance or change into something else, or to make something do this: **[+into]** *The river flooded its banks and morphed into a giant sea that swamped the town.*

mor·pheme /ˈmɔːfiːm $ ˈmɔːr-/ *n* [C] *technical* the smallest unit of meaning in a language. The words 'so', 'the', and 'boy' consist of one morpheme. 'Boys' consists of two morphemes, 'boy' and 's': *the past tense morpheme | the plural morpheme*

Mor·phe·us /ˈmɔːfiəs, -fjuːs $ ˈmɔːr-/ **in the arms of Morpheus** *literary* asleep. The word comes from Morpheus, the ancient Greek god of dreams.

mor·phi·a /ˈmɔːfiə $ ˈmɔːr-/ *n* [U] *old-fashioned* morphine

mor·phine /ˈmɔːfiːn $ ˈmɔːr-/ *n* [U] a powerful and ADDICTIVE drug used for stopping pain and making people calmer

morph·ing /ˈmɔːfɪŋ $ ˈmɔːr-/ *n* [U] a computer method that is used to make one image gradually change into a different one

mor·phol·o·gy /mɔːˈfɒlədʒi $ mɔːrˈfɑː-/ *n* (*plural* **morphologies**) *technical* **1** [U] the study of the MORPHEMES of a language and of the way in which they are joined together to make words → **syntax** **2** [U] the scientific study of the form and structure of animals and plants **3** [C,U] the structure of an object or system or the way it was formed —**morphological** /ˌmɔːfəˈlɒdʒɪkəl◂ $ ˌmɔːrfəˈlɑː-/ *adj*: *the morphological features of cells* —**morphologically** /-kli/ *adv*

mor·ris danc·ing /ˈmɒrəs ˌdɑːnsɪŋ $ ˈmɔːrəs ˌdænsɪŋ,

'mɑː-/ *n* [U] traditional English country dancing performed usually by men wearing white clothes decorated with small bells —**morris dancer** *n* [C]

mor·row /ˈmɒrəʊ $ ˈmɔːroʊ, ˈmɑː-/ *n* **1 the morrow** *old use* **a)** the next day SYN **tomorrow**: **on the morrow** *They were to arrive on the morrow.* **b)** the future: ***Take no thought for the morrow*** (=do not worry about the future). **2 on the morrow of sth** *literary* immediately after a particular event: *on the morrow of victory* **3 good morrow** *old use* GOOD MORNING

Morse code /ˌmɔːs ˈkəʊd $ ˌmɔːrs ˈkoʊd/ *n* [U] a system of sending messages in which the alphabet is represented by signals made of DOTs (=short signals) and DASHes (=long signals) in sound or light: **in Morse code** *a message in Morse code*

mor·sel /ˈmɔːsəl $ ˈmɔːr-/ *n* [C] a very small amount of something, especially a small piece of food SYN **scrap**: **[+of]** *a morsel of bread | a morsel of scandal | birds searching for* ***tasty morsels***

mor·tal¹ /ˈmɔːtl $ ˈmɔːrtl/ *adj* **1** not able to live for ever OPP **immortal**: *Her father's death reminded her that she was mortal.* **2 mortal blow/danger/wound etc a)** something very serious that may cause the end of something: *The computer has dealt a mortal blow to traditional printing methods. | Our health service is in mortal danger.* **b)** something that causes death or may cause death → **lethal**: *Near the end of the battle, he received a mortal wound. | the screams of men in* ***mortal combat*** (=fighting until one person kills the other) **3 mortal enemy/foe** an enemy that you hate very much and will always hate: *He glared at Claudia as if she were his mortal enemy.* **4 mortal fear/dread/terror** extreme fear: *She lives in mortal fear of her husband's anger.* **5 sb's mortal remains** *formal* someone's body, after they have died: *the churchyard where his mortal remains lie* (=where his body is buried) **6** *literary* human – used especially when comparing humans with gods, SPIRITs etc: *Both gods and mortal men found her captivating.* **7 mortal coil** *literary* life or the state of being alive: *when Hubbard* ***shuffled off this mortal coil*** (=died)

mortal² *n* [C] **1 lesser/ordinary/mere mortals** ordinary people, as compared with people who are more important, more powerful, or more skilled – used humorously: *She dines in the executive suite, while we lesser mortals use the staff cafeteria.* **2** *literary* a human – used especially when comparing humans with gods, SPIRITs etc → **immortal**

mor·tal·i·ty /mɔːˈtæləti $ mɔːr-/ ●○○ *n* (*plural* **mortalities**)

1 [U] (*also* **morˈtality ˌrate** / $.ˈ.../) the number of deaths during a particular period of time among a particular type or group of people: *Mortality from heart disease varies widely across the world.* | **infant/child/maternal/adult mortality** *an appallingly high* ***infant mortality rate*** (=number of babies who die)

2 [U] the condition of being human and having to die OPP **immortality**: *My mother's death forced me to face the fact of my* ***own mortality***.

3 [C] *technical* a death: *mortalities from cancer*

mor·tal·ly /ˈmɔːtəl-i $ ˈmɔːr-/ *adv* **1** in a way that will cause death SYN **fatally**: *He regarded the* ***mortally wounded*** *man with no pity in his heart.* **2** extremely or greatly: *He was mortally afraid of upsetting her. | I tried to be tactful, but he seemed to be mortally offended.*

ˌmortal ˈsin *n* [C,U] something that you do that is so bad, according to the Roman Catholic Church, that your soul will be punished for ever after death unless you ask to be forgiven

mor·tar /ˈmɔːtə $ ˈmɔːrtər/ *n* **1** [U] a mixture of CEMENT or LIME, and sand and water, used in building for holding bricks or stones together **2** [C] a heavy gun that fires bombs or SHELLS in a high curve: *A cameraman was killed when his vehicle came under* ***mortar fire***. *| a* ***mortar attack*** **3** [C] a stone bowl in which substances are crushed with a PESTLE (=tool with a heavy round end): *You'll need a pestle and mortar to grind the spices.* → **bricks and mortar** at **BRICK¹(2)**

mor·tar·board /ˈmɔːtəbɔːd $ ˈmɔːrtərbɔːrd/ *n* [C] a black cap with a flat square top worn by members of some universities on formal occasions → see picture at **HAT**

mort·gage¹ /ˈmɔːgɪdʒ $ ˈmɔːr-/ ●●○ W3 *n* [C]

1 a legal arrangement by which you borrow money from a bank or similar organization in order to buy a house, and pay back the money over a period of years: *Your building society or bank will help arrange a mortgage. | They've* ***taken out*** *a 30-year* ***mortgage*** (=they will pay for their house over a period of 30 years). *| We decided to use Fred's redundancy money to* ***pay off*** *the* ***mortgage*** (=pay back all the money we borrowed for a mortgage). *|* ***Mortgage rates*** *are set to rise again in the spring. | She was having trouble meeting her* ***mortgage payments***.

2 the amount of money you borrow in the form of a mortgage: *If you earn £20,000 per year, then you may be able to get a mortgage of £60,000.*

mortgage² *v* [T] **1** if you mortgage your home, land, or property, you borrow money, usually from a bank, and if you cannot pay back the money within a particular period of time, the bank has the right to sell your property in order to get the money you owe it: *We mortgaged our house to start Paul's business.* **2 mortgage the/sb's future** to borrow money or do something that is likely to cause problems in the future, that other people will have to deal with: *The report explains how governments are mortgaging their nations' futures.*

mort·ga·gee /ˌmɔːgəˈdʒiː $ ˌmɔːr-/ *n* [C] a person or organization that lends money to people to buy property

mort·ga·gor /ˈmɔːgɪdʒə $ ˈmɔːrgɪdʒər/ *n* [C] a person who borrows money from a bank or other organization in order to buy property

mor·ti·cian /mɔːˈtɪʃən $ mɔːr-/ *n* [C] *AmE* someone whose job is to arrange funerals and prepare bodies to be buried SYN **undertaker** *BrE*

mor·ti·fied /ˈmɔːtɪfaɪd $ ˈmɔːr-/ *adj* extremely offended, ashamed, or embarrassed: **mortified to hear/find etc** *Nora was mortified to discover that her daughter had been out drinking.* **THESAURUS** ASHAMED, EMBARRASSED —**mortification** /ˌmɔːtɪfɪˈkeɪʃən $ ˌmɔːr-/ *n* [U]

mor·ti·fy /ˈmɔːtɪfaɪ $ ˈmɔːr-/ *v* (**mortified**, **mortifying**, **mortifies**) [T] **1** to cause someone to feel extremely embarrassed or ashamed **2 mortify the flesh/yourself** *formal* to try to control your natural physical desires and needs by making your body suffer pain —**mortifying** *adj*

mor·tise, **mortice** /ˈmɔːtɪs $ ˈmɔːr-/ *n* [C] *technical* a hole cut in a piece of wood or stone so that the shaped end of another piece will fit there firmly → **tenon**

ˈmortise lock *n* [C] *BrE* a strong lock that fits into a hole cut in the edge of a door SYN **dead bolt** *AmE* → see picture at **LOCK²**

mor·tu·a·ry¹ /ˈmɔːtʃuəri $ ˈmɔːrtʃueri/ *n* (*plural* **mortuaries**) [C] **1** *BrE* a building or room, for example in a hospital, where dead bodies are kept before they are buried or CREMATED SYN **morgue** **2** *AmE* the place where a body is kept before a funeral and where the funeral is sometimes held

mortuary² *adj* [only before noun] *formal* connected with death or funerals: *a mortuary urn*

mo·sa·ic /məʊˈzeɪ-ɪk $ moʊ-/ ●○○ *n*

1 [C,U] a pattern or picture made by fitting together small pieces of coloured stone, glass etc: *rooms decorated with wall paintings and mosaics | a 3rd-century Roman mosaic floor*

2 [C usually singular] a group of different things that exist next to each other or together: **[+of]** *The forest floor was a mosaic of autumn colours. | the complex mosaic of world cultures*

Mosaic *adj* relating to Moses, the great leader of the Jewish people in ancient times: *the Mosaic law*

Mo·ses bas·ket /ˈməʊzɪz ˌbɑːskɪt $ ˈmoʊzəz ˌbæ-/ *n* [C] *BrE* a large basket with handles, in which a baby can sleep and be carried

mo·sey /ˈməʊzi $ ˈmoʊ-/ *v* [I always + adv/prep] *AmE*

informal **1** to walk somewhere in a slow relaxed way – used humorously: *I guess I'll* ***mosey on down*** *to the store now.* **2 I'd better mosey along/be moseying along** I should leave now: *I'd better mosey along – it's getting late.* —**mosey** *n* [singular]

mosh /mɒʃ $ mɑːʃ/ *v* [I] *informal* to dance very violently at a concert with loud ROCK or PUNK music

'mosh pit *n* [C] *informal* an area in front of the stage at a ROCK or PUNK concert where people dance with a lot of energy, often hitting their bodies against other people

Mos·lem /ˈmɒzlɪm $ ˈmɑːz-/ *n old-fashioned* another spelling of MUSLIM

mosque /mɒsk $ mɑːsk/ ●●○ *n* [C] a building in which Muslims worship

mos·qui·to /məˈskiːtəʊ $ -toʊ/ ●○○ *n* (*plural* **mosquitoes** *or* **mosquitos**) [C] a small flying insect that sucks the blood of people and animals, sometimes spreading the disease MALARIA → see picture at **INSECT**

mos'quito net *n* [C] a net placed over a bed as a protection against mosquitoes → see picture at **NET**[1]

moss /mɒs $ mɒːs/ ●○○ *n* [C,U] a very small green plant that grows in a thick soft furry mass on wet soil, trees, or rocks —**mossy** *adj*: *a high, mossy wall*

mos·sie /ˈmɒzi $ ˈmɑː-/ *n* [C] another spelling of MOZZIE

most[1] /məʊst $ moʊst/ ●●● S1 W1 *adv*

1 [used before an adjective or adverb to form the superlative] having the greatest amount of a particular quality OPP **least**: *She's one of the most experienced teachers in the district.* | *The most important thing is to stay calm.* | *A recent study showed that gardening is* ***easily the most*** *popular activity among the over 50s.* | *We shall find out which system works most effectively.* | *It is the kind of tea most often served in Chinese restaurants.*

GRAMMAR: Comparatives

Most is not used before the **-est** form of an adjective or adverb. You say: *This exercise is one of the hardest.*
✗ Don't say: *This exercise is one of the most hardest.*
GRAMMAR GUIDE ▸ ADJECTIVES

2 to a greater degree or more times than anything else: *What annoyed him most was the way she wouldn't even listen.* | *I guess the food I eat most is pasta.* | ***Most of all****, I just felt sad that it was over.*
3 [+adj/adv] *formal* very: *Thank you for a most interesting evening.* | *I was most surprised to hear of your engagement.*
4 *AmE informal* almost: *He plays poker* ***most every*** *evening.*

USAGE: The most, the more

• You use **the most** when you are comparing one person or thing with all others: *It was the most terrifying experience of my life.*
• In spoken English, you can also use **the most** when comparing just two people or things: *Which is the most enjoyable – tennis or squash?* However, some people think that this is incorrect and use **(the) more** to compare two people or things: *Which is the more enjoyable – tennis or squash?*

most[2] ●●● S1 W1 *determiner, pron* [the superlative of 'many' and 'much']

1 nearly all of the people or things in a group, or nearly all of something SYN **the majority**: *Like most people, I try to take a vacation every year.* | *Most research in this field has been carried out by the Russians.* | **[+of]** *It was Sunday and most of the shops were shut.* | *Most of what Hannah told me wasn't true.* | *Some were barefoot, most were in rags.* | **most of the time/most days etc** (=usually) *Most of the time it's very quiet here.* | *Most evenings we just stay in and watch TV.*
2 a larger amount or number than anyone or anything else: **the most** *The team that scores the most points wins.* | *Which class has the most children in it?* | *It's unfair that you should have to pay the most when you earn so little.* | *The animal that caused most trouble was a little black puppy.*
3 the largest number or amount possible: *The aim is to help patients to obtain most benefit from their treatment.* | **the most** *The most you can hope to achieve is just to get him to listen to your ideas.*
4 at (the) most used to say that you think an amount cannot be larger than the amount you are mentioning: *It'll take 20 minutes at the most.* | *There were at most 50 people in the audience.* | *The boy looked nine* ***at the very most*** (=he was probably younger).
5 for the most part used to say that something is generally true but not completely true: *For the most part, people seemed pretty friendly.*
6 make the most of sth/get the most out of sth to gain the greatest possible advantage from something: *Charming and friendly, she will help you make the most of your visit.* | *advice on how to get the most out of your computer*

GRAMMAR: Patterns with most

• You use **most** before plural nouns to talk about people or things in general: *Most people disagree.*
✗ Don't say: *The most people disagree.*
• You say **most of the**: *Most of the shops are closed.*
✗ Don't say: *most of shops*
• You say **most of my/her/his etc** or **many of them/us/you**: *Most of my friends are at university.* | *Most of them are women.*

-most /məʊst $ moʊst/ *suffix* [in adjectives] nearest to something: *the northernmost town in Sweden* (=the town that is furthest to the north) | *the topmost branches of the tree*

most·ly /ˈməʊstli $ ˈmoʊst-/ ●●● S2 W3 *adv* used to talk about most members of a group, most occasions, most parts of something etc SYN **mainly**: *Green teas are mostly from China or Japan.* | *There were about fifteen people in the lounge, mostly women.* | *He blamed his parents. Mostly he blamed his dad.*

REGISTER

In written English, people often prefer to use **generally** or **for the most part** rather than **mostly**, because they sound more formal: *Many tourists visit the region,* ***generally*** *for skiing.* | *The inhabitants of the village are* ***for the most part*** *elderly.*

MOT /ˌem əʊ ˈtiː $ -oʊ-/ (*also* **ˌMO'T test**) *n* [C] a test in Britain that all cars more than three years old must pass every year in order to show that they are still safe to be driven: *My car's just failed its MOT.* | *an* ***MOT certificate***

mote /məʊt $ moʊt/ *n* [C] *old-fashioned* a very small piece of dust

mo·tel /məʊˈtel $ moʊ-/ ●●○ *n* [C] a hotel for people who are travelling by car, where you can park your car outside your room THESAURUS ▸ HOTEL

mo·tet /məʊˈtet $ moʊ-/ *n* [C] a piece of music on a religious subject

moth /mɒθ $ mɒːθ/ ●○○ *n* [C] an insect related to the BUTTERFLY that flies mainly at night and is attracted to lights. Some moths eat holes in cloth. → see picture at **INSECT**

moth·ball[1] /ˈmɒθbɔːl $ ˈmɒːθbɒːl/ *n* **1** [C usually plural] a small ball made of a strong-smelling chemical, used for keeping moths away from clothes **2 in/into mothballs** kept but not used for a long time: *With the end of the Cold War, several warships were put into mothballs.*

mothball[2] *v* [T] to stop using a factory, equipment etc or to not continue with a plan, temporarily but possibly for a long time: *The hospital manager said the project would be mothballed until funding became available.*

ˈmoth-ˌeaten *adj* **1** cloth that is moth-eaten has had holes eaten in it by moths: *a moth-eaten sweater* **2** old and in bad condition: *a moth-eaten old sofa*

moth·er[1] /ˈmʌðə $ -ər/ ●●● S1 W1 *n* [C]

1 a female parent of a child or animal: *His mother and father are both doctors.* | **mother of two/three etc** (=mother of two/three etc children) *Janet is a full-time teacher and a mother of two.* | *the relationship between* ***mother and child*** | *Goodnight, Mother.* | *Mother said they'd met at university.* | *If*

food is scarce, the mother will feed the smaller, weaker chicks. | **mother cat/bird/hen etc** (=an animal that is a mother)
2 be (like) a mother to sb to care for someone as if you were their mother: *She's like a mother to them. If they need anything she always helps out.*
3 like a mother hen if someone behaves like a mother hen, they try to protect their children too much and worry about them all the time
4 learn/be taught sth at your mother's knee to learn something when you are a very young child: *the prayers which he had been taught at his mother's knee*
5 the mother of sth a) the origin or cause of something: *Westminster is known as 'the mother of parliaments'.* | *Necessity is the mother of invention* (=people have good ideas when the situation makes it necessary). **b)** *informal* a very severe or extreme type of something, usually something bad: *I woke up with **the mother of all** hangovers.*
6 *spoken especially AmE* something very large and usually very good: *a real mother of a car*
7 *AmE taboo spoken* MOTHERFUCKER
8 Mother used to address the woman who is in charge of a CONVENT

mother² *v* [T] to look after and protect someone as if you were their mother, especially by being too kind and doing everything for them: *I don't like being mothered!*

moth·er·board /ˈmʌðəbɔːd $ -ərbɔːrd/ *n* [C] *technical* a board where all the CIRCUITS of a computer are placed

ˈmother ˌcountry *n* [C usually singular] **1** someone's mother country is the country where they or their family were born and to which they feel a very strong emotional connection, even if they are no longer living there SYN **motherland 2** a powerful country that controls or used to control a less powerful country: *The bond between the mother country and her former colonies grew stronger.*

ˌMother ˈEarth *n* the world, considered as the place or thing from which all life comes

moth·er·fuck·er /ˈmʌðəˌfʌkə $ -ðərˌfʌkər/ *n* [C] *AmE taboo spoken* a very offensive word for someone that you dislike very much or that you are very angry with. Do not use this word. —**motherfucking** *adj*

moth·er·hood /ˈmʌðəhʊd $ -ðər-/ *n* [U] the state of being a mother → **fatherhood**: *the challenge of combining a career with motherhood* | *teenagers who are unprepared for motherhood*

moth·er·ing /ˈmʌðərɪŋ/ *n* [U] the process of caring for children in the way that a mother does → **fathering**: *mothering skills* | *Babies and young children need mothering.*

ˈMothering ˌSunday *n* [C,U] *BrE old-fashioned* MOTHER'S DAY

ˈmother-in-ˌlaw ●●○ *n* (*plural* **mothers-in-law**) [C] the mother of your wife or husband

moth·er·land /ˈmʌðəlænd $ -ðər-/ *n* [C usually singular] someone's motherland is the country where they were born and to which they feel a strong emotional connection SYN **mother country**, **fatherland**: *They are willing to die for the motherland.*

moth·er·less /ˈmʌðələs $ -ðər-/ *adj* a motherless child is one whose mother has died → **fatherless**: *homes for children who had been left motherless*

ˈmother lode, **moth·er·lode** /ˈmʌðələʊd $ -ðərloʊd/ *n* [C usually singular] *AmE* **1** a mine that is full of gold, silver etc **2** a place where you can find a lot of a particular type of object: **[+of]** *The Sharper Image catalog is a mother lode of men's gadgets and toys.* **3 hit the mother lode** *informal* to produce or find something that will make you very rich, happy, or successful: *They hit the mother lode with their second album.*

moth·er·ly /ˈmʌðəli $ -ðər-/ *adj* a motherly woman is loving and kind, like a good mother → **maternal**: *her motherly instincts* | *She was a plump, motherly woman in her fifties.* —**motherliness** *n* [U]

ˌMother ˈNature *n* used to talk about nature, especially when it is thought of as a force that affects people and the world: *How could Mother Nature have dealt such a savage blow?*

ˌMother of ˈGod *n* a title for Mary, the mother of Jesus Christ, used in the Roman Catholic Church

ˌmother-of-ˈpearl *n* [U] a pale-coloured hard smooth shiny substance that forms the inside of some SHELLFISH, and is used for making buttons, jewellery etc

ˈmother's boy *n* [singular] *BrE* a man or boy who allows his mother to protect him too much and is considered weak SYN **mama's boy** *AmE*

ˈMother's Day *n* [C,U] a day on which people give cards and presents to their mothers

ˈmother ship *n* [C] a large ship or spacecraft from which smaller boats or spacecraft are sent out

ˌMother Suˈperior *n* [C usually singular] the woman who is in charge of a CONVENT

ˌmother-to-ˈbe *n* (*plural* **mothers-to-be**) [C] a woman who is going to have a baby

ˌmother ˈtongue *n* [C] *especially BrE* your mother tongue is the first and main language that you learnt when you were a child SYN **native language/tongue**: *children for whom English is not their mother tongue*

mo·tif /məʊˈtiːf $ moʊ-/ ●○○ *n* [C]
1 an idea, subject, or image that is regularly repeated and developed in a book, film, work of art etc: *The theme of creation is a recurrent motif in Celtic mythology.*
2 a small picture or pattern used to decorate something plain: *a white T-shirt with a blue fish motif*
3 an arrangement of notes that is often repeated in a musical work

mo·tion¹ /ˈməʊʃən $ ˈmoʊ-/ ●●○ W3 *n*
1 MOVEMENT [U] the process of moving or the way that someone or something moves: **[+of]** *the motion of the planets* | *The rocking motion of the boat made Sylvia feel sick.* | *Newton's first law of motion*
2 MOVING YOUR HEAD OR HAND [C] a single movement of your head or hand, especially one made in order to communicate something SYN **gesture**: **[+of]** *He summoned the waiter with a motion of his hand.* | *Doyle glanced back at Bodie, and **made** a slight **motion with** his head.*
3 SUGGESTION AT A MEETING [C] a proposal that is made formally at a meeting, and then is usually decided on by voting: *The **motion** was **defeated** by 201 votes to 159.* | **motion to do sth/motion that** *We will now vote on the motion that membership charges should rise by 15%.* | **pass/carry/approve a motion** (=accept it by voting) *The motion was carried unanimously.* | *I urge you to **support** this **motion**.* | **propose/put forward/table a motion** (=make a proposal) *I'd like to propose a motion to move the weekly meetings to Thursdays.* | *The **motion** was **seconded*** (=formally supported) *by Mr Levin.* | *The attorneys **filed a motion*** (=made a proposal in a court) *for a temporary restraining order.*
4 in motion *formal* moving from one place or position to another: *The end doors are not to be used when the train is in motion.*
5 set/put sth in motion to start a process or series of events that will continue for some time: *The Church voted to set in motion the process allowing women to be priests.* | *Once the house had been sold, Jane **set the wheels in motion*** (=started the process) *to find somewhere smaller to live.*
6 go through the motions (of doing sth) to do something because you have to do it, without being very interested in it: *I feel so bored at work, like I'm just going through the motions.*
7 BODY WASTE [C] solid waste material that comes out when you empty your BOWELS – used especially by doctors and nurses → SLOW MOTION, TIME AND MOTION STUDY

motion² *v* [I,T] to give someone directions or instructions by moving your hand or head SYN **signal**: **motion (for) sb to do sth** *The police officer motioned for me to pull over.* | **motion to sb to do sth** *He motioned to the barman to refill their glasses.* | **motion sb forward/away etc** *His father motioned him forward.* | **motion sb into/to sth** *I saw her motioning me into the room.*

ˈmotion conˌtrol *n* [U] a way of controlling a computer game, by using movements of your body

ˈmotion conˌtroller *n* [C] a piece of equipment that allows you to control computer games with movements of your body

mo·tion·less /ˈməʊʃənləs $ ˈmoʊ-/ *adj* not moving at all SYN **still**: **stand/sit/lie motionless** *The men stood motionless as Weir held his finger to his lips.* | *Graham remained motionless.* —**motionlessly** *adv*

ˌmotion ˈpicture *n* [C] *especially AmE formal* a film made for the cinema SYN **movie**: *the motion picture industry*

ˈmotion ˌsickness *n* [U] *especially AmE* a feeling of illness that some people get when travelling by car, boat, plane etc SYN **travel sickness**, **carsickness**, **seasickness** *BrE*

mo·ti·vate /ˈməʊtɪveɪt $ ˈmoʊ-/ ●●○ *v* [T]
1 to be the reason why someone does something SYN **drive**: *Was he motivated solely by a desire for power?* | **motivate sb to do sth** *We may never know what motivated him to kill his wife.*
2 to make someone want to achieve something and make them willing to work hard in order to do this: *A good teacher has to be able to motivate her students.* | **motivate sb to do sth** *The profit-sharing plan is designed to motivate the staff to work hard.*

mo·ti·va·ted /ˈməʊtɪveɪtɪd $ ˈmoʊ-/ AWL *adj*
1 very keen to do something or achieve something, especially because you find it interesting or exciting: *The students are all* ***highly motivated****.* | *The key to a successful modern economy is a well-educated and motivated workforce.* **2 politically/economically/financially etc motivated** done for political, economic etc reasons: *a politically motivated decision* | *Police believe the attack was racially motivated.*

mo·ti·va·tion /ˌməʊtəˈveɪʃən $ ˌmoʊ-/ ●●○ AWL *n*
1 [U] eagerness and willingness to do something without needing to be told or forced to do it: **sb's motivation** *efforts to improve employees' motivation* | *Jack is an intelligent pupil, but he lacks motivation.* | *a high level of motivation*
2 [C] the reason why you want to do something: **motivation for (doing) sth** *What was your motivation for becoming a teacher?* | *Escape can be a strong motivation for travel.* | **[+behind]** *There is suspicion about the motivation behind the changes we are debating.* —**motivational** *adj*: *motivational speeches*

mo·ti·va·tor /ˈməʊtəveɪtə $ ˈmoʊtəveɪtər/ *n* [C] something or someone that makes you want to do or achieve something → **incentive**: *Money is a good motivator.*

mo·tive¹ /ˈməʊtɪv $ ˈmoʊ-/ ●●○ AWL *n* [C]
1 the reason that makes someone do something, especially when this reason is kept hidden: *What do you suppose the killer's motive was?* | **motive for (doing) sth** *The police believe the motive for this murder was jealousy.* | **[+behind]** *The motives behind the decision remain obscure.* | *The violence was clearly prompted by political motives.* | *It's not the kind of thing he'd do unless he had an* ***ulterior motive*** (=a reason he kept hidden). THESAURUS ▸ REASON
2 a MOTIF —**motiveless** *adj*: *an apparently motiveless killing*

motive² AWL *adj* [only before noun] *technical* the motive power or force for a machine, vehicle etc makes it move: *Water provided the motive power for the mill.*

mot juste /ˌməʊ ˈʒuːst $ ˌmoʊ-/ *n* (*plural* **mots justes** (*same pronunciation*)) [C] *formal* **the/le mot juste** exactly the right word or phrase: *She paused, searching for the mot juste.*

mot·ley /ˈmɒtli $ ˈmɑːtli/ *adj* [only before noun] **a motley collection/crew/assortment etc** a group of people or things that are very different from each other and do not seem to belong together: *I looked at the motley bunch we were sailing with and began to feel uneasy about the trip.* | *His pockets contained a motley collection of coins, movie ticket stubs, and old candies.*

mo·to·cross /ˈməʊtəʊkrɒs $ ˈmoʊtoʊkrɒːs/ *n* [U] the sport of racing MOTORCYCLES over rough land, up hills, through streams etc

mo·tor¹ /ˈməʊtə $ ˈmoʊtər/ ●●○ S3 W3 *n* [C]
1 the part of a machine that makes it work or move, by changing power, especially electrical power, into movement: *an electric motor* ⚠ **Motor** is not generally used to refer to the part of a vehicle which produces the power for it to move. Use **engine**: *My car needs a new engine.*
2 *BrE old-fashioned or informal* a car: *That's a nice motor you've got, Dave.* → OUTBOARD MOTOR

motor² *adj* [only before noun] **1** *especially BrE* relating to cars or other vehicles with engines: *the motor industry* | *a motor accident* | *motor insurance* **2** having an engine: *a motor scooter* **3** *technical* relating to nerves that make muscles move: *impaired motor function*

motor³ *v* [I always + adv/prep] *BrE old-fashioned* to travel by car: *Bertie is motoring down from London.*

MOTORBIKE

mo·tor·bike /ˈməʊtəbaɪk $ ˈmoʊtər-/ *n* [C] *especially BrE* a small fast two-wheeled vehicle with an engine SYN **motorcycle**

mo·tor·boat /ˈməʊtəbəʊt $ ˈmoʊtərboʊt/ *n* [C] a small fast boat with an engine

mo·tor·cade /ˈməʊtəkeɪd $ ˈmoʊtər-/ *n* [C] a line of official cars, including a car carrying an important person, that is travelling somewhere: *the president's motorcade*

ˈmotor car *n* [C] *BrE formal or old-fashioned* a car

mo·tor·cy·cle /ˈməʊtəˌsaɪkəl $ -tər-/ ●●○ *n* [C] a fast two-wheeled vehicle with an engine SYN **motorbike** —**motorcycling** *n* [U] —**motorcyclist** *n* [C]

ˈmotor home *n* [C] a large vehicle with beds, a kitchen, a toilet etc, used for travelling and holidays → see picture at HOUSE¹

mo·tor·ing /ˈməʊtərɪŋ $ ˈmoʊ-/ *n* [U] *BrE* the activity of driving a car: *These magazines cover all kinds of popular subjects such as motoring, gardening, and sports.* | *He was found guilty of 14* ***motoring offences****.* | *Police and motoring organizations urged drivers to keep their speed down.* | *the sharp rise in motoring costs*

mo·tor·ist /ˈməʊtərɪst $ ˈmoʊtər-/ ●○○ *n* [C] someone who drives a car SYN **driver** → **pedestrian**: *12,000 motorists were stopped for speeding in the police crackdown.*

mo·tor·ized (*also* **-ised** *BrE*) /ˈməʊtəraɪzd $ ˈmoʊ-/ *adj* [only before noun] **1** having an engine – used especially when something does not usually have an engine: *a motorized wheelchair* **2** *BrE* a motorized group of soldiers is one that uses motor vehicles: **motorized division/unit/battalion**

mo·tor·mouth /ˈməʊtəmaʊθ $ ˈmoʊtər-/ *n* [C] *informal* someone who talks too much and too loudly

motor neu·rone dis·ease /ˌməʊtə ˈnjʊərəʊn dɪˌziːz $ ˌmoʊtər ˈnʊroʊn-/ *n* [U] a serious disease that causes a gradual loss of control over the muscles and nerves of the body, resulting in death

ˈmotor pool *n* [C] *AmE* a group of cars, trucks, and other vehicles that are available for people in a particular part of the government or army to use

ˈmotor ˌracing *n* [U] the sport of racing fast cars on a special track

ˈmotor ˌscooter *n* [C] a SCOOTER

ˈmotor ˌvehicle *n* [C] *formal* any vehicle which has an engine, such as a car, bus, or truck: *This road is closed to motor vehicles.*

mo·tor·way /ˈməʊtəweɪ $ ˈmoʊtər-/ ●●● S2 *n* [C] *BrE* a very wide road for travelling fast over long distances, especially between cities → **expressway**, **freeway**, **highway**, **interstate**

mot·tled /ˈmɒtld $ ˈmɑː-/ *adj* covered with spots or coloured areas: **[+with]** *The book's pages were mottled with brown stains.* | *His red, mottled face showed the effect of too much whisky.*

mot·to /ˈmɒtəʊ $ ˈmɑːtoʊ/ *n* (*plural* **mottos** *or* **mottoes**) [C] a short sentence or phrase giving a rule on how to behave, which expresses the aims or beliefs of a person, school, or institution: *'Be prepared' is the motto of the Boy Scouts.* **THESAURUS▸ PHRASE**

mould¹ *BrE*, **mold** *AmE* /məʊld $ moʊld/ ●○○ *n*
1 SHAPED CONTAINER [C] a hollow container that you pour a liquid or soft substance into, so that when it becomes solid, it takes the shape of the container: *Another method, used especially for figures, was to pour the clay into a mould.* | *lime jello in a mould*
2 TYPE OF PERSON [singular] if someone is in a particular mould, or fits into a particular mould, they have all the attitudes and qualities typical of a type of person: **fit (into) a mould** *She didn't quite fit into the standard 'high-flying businesswoman' mould.* | **in the same mould (as sb/sth)/in the mould of sb/sth** *a socialist intellectual in the mould of Anthony Crosland*
3 break the mould to change a situation completely, by doing something that has not been done before: *an attempt to break the mould of British politics*
4 GROWING SUBSTANCE [U] a soft green, grey, or black substance that grows on food which has been kept too long, and on objects that are in warm wet air → **mouldy**: *The chemical was used to kill a mold that grows on peanuts.* | *The walls were black with mould.* → LEAF MOULD

mould² *BrE*, **mold** *AmE* *v* **1** [T] to shape a soft substance by pressing or rolling it or by putting it into a mould: **mould sth into sth** *Mould the sausage meat into little balls.* | *moulded plastic chairs* **2** [T] to influence the way someone's character or attitudes develop: **mould sth/sb into sth** *I try to take young athletes and mold them into team players.* | *an attempt to mold public opinion* **3** [I,T] to fit closely to the shape of something, or to make something fit closely: **mould (sth) to sth** *The lining of the boot molds itself to the shape of your foot.* | *Her wet dress was moulded to her body.*

moul·der *BrE*, **molder** *AmE* /ˈməʊldə $ ˈmoʊldər/ (*also* **moulder away**) *v* [I] to decay gradually: *old papers mouldering away in the attic*

mould·ing *BrE*, **molding** *AmE* /ˈməʊldɪŋ $ ˈmoʊl-/ *n*
1 [C,U] a thin decorative line of PLASTER, wood etc around the edge of a wall, a piece of furniture, a picture frame etc
2 [C] an object produced from a mould

mould·y *BrE*, **moldy** *AmE* /ˈməʊldi $ ˈmoʊl-/ *adj* covered with MOULD: *mouldy cheese* | **go mouldy** *BrE* (=become mouldy) *The bread's gone mouldy.*

moult *BrE*, **molt** *AmE* /məʊlt $ moʊlt/ *v* [I] when a bird or animal moults, it loses feathers or hair so that new ones can grow —**moult** *n* [C,U]

mound /maʊnd/ ●○○ *n* [C]
1 a pile of earth or stones that looks like a small hill: *an ancient burial mound* | **[+of]** *a small mound of dirt*
2 a large pile of something: **[+of]** *There's a mound of papers on my desk.* | *The waiter appeared with a huge mound of spaghetti.* → see picture at **PILE**
3 (*also* **pitcher's mound**) the small hill that the PITCHER stands on in the game of baseball → see picture at **BASEBALL**

mount¹ /maʊnt/ ●●○ *v*
1 ORGANIZE [T] to plan, organize, and begin an event or a course of action: *The National Gallery* **mounted** *an* **exhibition** *of Danish painting.* | **mount a campaign/challenge/search etc** *Friends of the Earth are mounting a campaign to monitor the illegal logging of trees.* | **mount an assault/attack** *Guerrillas have mounted an attack on the capital.*
2 INCREASE [I usually in progressive] to increase gradually in amount or degree: ***Tension** here is **mounting**, as we await the final result.* | *Casualties on both sides of the battle have continued to mount.*
3 HORSE/BICYCLE [I,T] *formal* to get on a horse or bicycle OPP **dismount**: *He mounted his horse and rode on.*
4 GO UP [T] *formal* to go up a step or stairs: *He mounted the stairs and looked around him slowly.* | *A car suddenly mounted the pavement to avoid a vehicle coming in the opposite direction.*
5 PICTURE [T] to fix a picture to a larger piece of stiff paper so that it looks more attractive: **mount sth on/onto sth** *Entries to the photography competition should be mounted on white paper.*
6 SEX [T] *technical* if a male animal mounts a female animal, he gets up onto her back to have sex → MOUNTED

mount up *phr v* to gradually increase in amount: *At £6 a ticket, the cost quickly mounts up.*

mount² ●●○ *n* [C]
1 Mount (*written abbreviation* **Mt**) used as part of the name of a mountain: *Mount Everest*
2 *formal* a horse that you ride on
3 stiff paper that is put behind or around a picture or photograph so that it looks more attractive
4 *literary* a mountain

moun·tain /ˈmaʊntɪn $ ˈmaʊntən/ ●●● S3 W3 *n* [C]
1 a very high hill: *the highest mountain in Austria* | *the Rocky Mountains* | *a steep mountain road* | *magnificent* ***mountain ranges*** (=lines of mountains) | *snow-capped* ***mountain peaks*** (=tops of mountains) | *a mountain rescue team* (=a group of experienced climbers who help people to safety from a mountain) | *She was the first British woman to* ***climb the mountain***.
2 a mountain of sth/mountains of sth a very large pile or amount of something: *I've got mountains of paperwork to deal with.* | *Her husband went off with another woman and left her facing* ***a mountain of debt***.
3 food/butter etc mountain a very large amount of food, butter etc that has been produced but is not needed or used → **lake**
4 make a mountain out of a molehill to treat a problem as if it was very serious when in fact it is not
5 (have) a mountain to climb *BrE* used to say that someone has a lot of work to do to achieve their aim, especially when you believe it will be difficult
6 move mountains to do things that seem impossible: *I have great faith in the power of love to move mountains.*

GRAMMAR: Patterns with mountain

in the mountains
• You use **in the mountains** to refer to an area with several mountains: *They went climbing in the mountains.* | *We stayed in a little village in the mountains.* ✗ Don't say: *on the mountains* | *in the mountain*

on the mountain
• You use **on the mountain** when referring to one particular mountain: *They lost their way and had to spend a night on the mountain.* ✗ Don't say: *in the mountain*

ˌmountain ˈash *n* [C] a type of tree with red or orange-red berries

ˈmountain ˌbike *n* [C] a strong bicycle with a lot of GEARS and wide tyres, specially designed for riding up hills and on rough ground

ˈmountain ˌboard (*also* **all-terrain board**) *n* [C] a long wide board made of plastic or wood, with four rubber wheels, which people use to travel down the sides of mountains for sport —**mountain boarding** *n* [U] —**mountain boarder** *n* [C]

moun·tain·eer /ˌmaʊntəˈnɪə $ ˌmaʊntənˈɪr/ *n* [C] someone who climbs mountains as a sport

moun·tain·eer·ing /ˌmaʊntəˈnɪərɪŋ $ ˌmaʊntənˈɪrɪŋ/ *n* [U] the sport of climbing mountains

ˈmountain goat *n* [C] an animal with thick white fur which looks like a goat and lives in the western mountains of North America

ˈmountain ˌlion *n* [C] a COUGAR

moun·tain·ous /ˈmaʊntɪnəs $ ˈmaʊntənəs/ ●○○ *adj*
1 a mountainous area has a lot of mountains: *the mountainous coast of Wales | a mountainous region*
2 very large in amount or size SYN **massive**: *They were struggling with mountainous debts.*

moun·tain·side /ˈmaʊntənsaɪd $ ˈmaʊntən-/ *n* [C] the side of a mountain: *Great rocks rolled down the mountainside.*

moun·tain·top /ˈmaʊntəntɒp $ ˈmaʊntəntɑːp/ *n* [C] the top part of a mountain

moun·te·bank /ˈmaʊntɪbæŋk/ *n* [C] *literary* a dishonest person who tricks and deceives people

moun·ted /ˈmaʊntɪd/ *adj* **1** riding on a horse: *the mounted police | Jean was mounted on a grey mare.* **2** fixed firmly to a larger thing: *The statue was mounted on a marble base. | music blasting from wall-mounted speakers*

Mount·ie /ˈmaʊnti/ *n* [C] *informal* a member of the Royal Canadian Mounted Police

mount·ing¹ *adj* /ˈmaʊntɪŋ/ [only before noun] gradually increasing – often used about things that cause problems or trouble: *There was **mounting pressure** on him to resign. | The government has come under **mounting criticism** in the press. | They faced **mounting debts**. | There's **mounting evidence** of a link between obesity and some forms of cancer.*

mounting² *n* [C] an object to which other things, especially parts of a machine, are fastened to keep them in place: *The engine is supported by four rubberized mountings.*

mourn /mɔːn $ mɔːrn/ ●○○ *v* [I,T]
1 to feel very sad and to miss someone after they have died SYN **grieve for**: *Hundreds of people gathered to mourn the slain president. |* **[+for]** *They mourned for their children, killed in the war. |* **mourn sb's death/loss/passing** *She still mourns the death of her husband.*
2 to feel very sad because something no longer exists or is no longer as good as it used to be: *The old steam trains were much loved, and we all **mourn** their **passing**.*

mourn·er /ˈmɔːnə $ ˈmɔːrnər/ *n* [C] someone who attends a funeral

mourn·ful /ˈmɔːnfəl $ ˈmɔːrn-/ *adj* very sad: *Durant was thin, mournful and silent. | the slow, mournful music of the bagpipes* **THESAURUS** ▸ SAD —**mournfully** *adv*

mourn·ing /ˈmɔːnɪŋ $ ˈmɔːr-/ *n* [U] **1** great sadness because someone has died: *The Armenian authorities declared May 29 a national day of mourning. |* **in mourning** (=feeling great sadness) *It was the custom to visit those in mourning and sit quietly with them.* **2** black clothes worn to show that you are very sad that someone has died: *She was recently widowed and wearing mourning.*

mouse¹ /maʊs/ ●●● S2 W3 *n* [C]
1 (*plural* **mice** /maɪs/) a small furry animal with a pointed nose and a long tail that lives in people's houses or in fields: *The cat laid a dead mouse at my feet. | a field mouse*
2 (*plural* **mouses**) a small object that you move with your hand to give instructions to a computer: *Select the printer icon and then click the left mouse button.*
3 (*plural* **mice**) *informal* a quiet nervous person → **play cat and mouse** at CAT(4), → **quiet as a mouse** at QUIET¹(1)

mouse² *v*
mouse over sth *phr v* to use a computer mouse to move the CURSOR over a particular thing on the screen: *When you mouse over the menu, the different options appear.*

ˈmouse mat (*also* **ˈmouse pad** *AmE*) *n* [C] a small piece of flat material with a special surface which you move a computer mouse on

ˈmouse miles *n* [plural] *humorous* the amount of time that you spend using a computer

mouse·trap /ˈmaʊs-træp/ *n* [C] a trap for catching mice

mous·sa·ka /muːˈsɑːkə/ *n* [C,U] a Greek dish made from meat, cheese, and AUBERGINES

mousse /muːs/ *n* [C,U] **1 a)** a sweet food made from a mixture of cream, eggs, and fruit or chocolate, which is eaten when it is cold: *chocolate mousse | raspberry mousse* **b)** a food that is mixed and cooked with cream or eggs so that it is very light: *salmon mousse* **2** a substance full of small bubbles that you put in your hair to make it look thicker or to hold its style in place

mous·tache (*also* **mustache** *AmE*) /məˈstɑːʃ $ ˈmʌstæʃ/ ●●● S3 *n* [C] hair that grows on a man's upper lip → **beard**: *He's shaved off his moustache.*

mous·tached (*also* **mustached** *AmE*) /məˈstɑːʃt $ ˈmʌstæʃt/ *adj* [usually before noun] having a moustache: *a young, moustached British officer*

mous·tach·i·oed /məˈstɑːʃiəʊd, -ˈstæ- $ -oʊd/ *adj* another spelling of MUSTACHIOED

mous·y, **mousey** /ˈmaʊsi/ *adj* **1** mousy hair is a dull brown colour **2** a mousy woman is quiet and unattractive

mouth¹ /maʊθ/ ●●● S2 W1 *n* (*plural* **mouths** /maʊðz/) [C]
1 FACE the part of your face which you put food into, or which you use for speaking: *He lifted his glass to his mouth. | Liam was fast asleep with his mouth wide open.*
2 keep your mouth shut *informal* **a)** to not tell other people about a secret: *He demanded £2,000 to keep his mouth shut.* **b)** to not say something even if you think it: *I wished that I'd kept my mouth shut.*
3 open your mouth to prepare to speak: *'I'll go,' Travis said quickly before she could open her mouth. |* **open your mouth to say/speak/protest etc** *Julia opened her mouth to reply, but they were interrupted.*
4 (you) watch your mouth *spoken informal* used to tell someone not to speak in such a rude way
5 ENTRANCE the entrance to a large hole or CAVE: *As the train entered the mouth of the tunnel, the lights came on.*
6 RIVER the part of a river where it joins the sea: *the mouth of the River Tees*
7 BOTTLE/CONTAINER the open part at the top of a bottle or container
8 big mouth *informal* if someone has a big mouth, they say too much or tell another person's secrets
9 me and my big mouth/you and your big mouth etc *spoken* used to criticize yourself or another person for saying something that should not have been said: *Oops, I shouldn't have said that. Me and my big mouth.*
10 mouth to feed/hungry mouth someone who you must provide food for, especially one of your children: *To these parents, a new baby is just another hungry mouth.*
11 make your mouth water if food makes your mouth water, it smells or looks so good you want to eat it immediately: *The smell of the cooked fish made her mouth water.* → MOUTH-WATERING
12 down in the mouth *informal* unhappy: *Tim's looking very down in the mouth.*
13 out of the mouths of babes (and sucklings) used humorously when a small child has just said something clever or interesting
14 be all mouth *BrE spoken* if someone is all mouth, they talk a lot about what they will do but are not brave enough to actually do it → **be born with a silver spoon in your mouth** at BORN¹(8), → **by word of mouth** at WORD¹(14), → **be foaming at the mouth** at FOAM²(2), → **put your foot in your mouth** at FOOT¹(15), → **put your money where your mouth is** at MONEY(18), → **put words into sb's mouth** at WORD¹(22), → **shut your mouth** at SHUT¹(2), → **shoot your mouth off** at SHOOT¹(12), → FOUL-MOUTHED, MEALY-MOUTHED

COLLOCATIONS

VERBS

open/shut/close your mouth *He opened his mouth wide so the doctor could examine his throat.*

M

cover your mouth *She laughed, covering her mouth with her hand.*
wipe your mouth | kiss sb on the mouth | sb's mouth falls/drops open (=in surprise)

ADJECTIVES

dry (=especially because someone is nervous or ill) *My mouth was dry and my hands were shaking.*
a big/large/wide/small mouth *He had a big nose and a big mouth.*
a full mouth (=with large attractive lips) | **a thin mouth** (=with thin lips)

PHRASES

the corner/side of your mouth *A smile lifted the corners of her mouth.*
the roof of your mouth (=the top inside part) *He made a clicking sound with his tongue on the roof of his mouth.*
with your mouth full (=with food in your mouth) *Don't talk with your mouth full.*
with your mouth open | (with your) mouth agape *written* (=with your mouth open in surprise)

mouth² /maʊð/ *v* [T] **1** to move your lips in the same way you do when you are saying words, but without making any sound: *She silently mouthed the words 'Good luck'. | Philip mouthed something through the glass which she did not hear.* **2** to say things that you do not really believe or that you do not understand: *The players mouthed clichés about what they hoped to do at the World Cup. | They mouthed the usual platitudes.*

mouth off *phr v informal* to complain angrily and noisily about something, or talk as if you know more than anyone else: **[+at/to]** *You should have heard Pete mouthing off at Joe.* | **[+about]** *Morris was mouthing off about his former team.*

mouth·ful /ˈmaʊθfʊl/ *n* [C] **1** an amount of food or drink that you put into your mouth at one time: *Michael told his story between mouthfuls.* | **[+of]** *Betty drank a mouthful of beer. | He* **took a mouthful** *of his pudding.* **2 (a bit of) a mouthful** *informal* a long word or phrase that is difficult to say: *Her real name is a bit of a mouthful, so we just call her Dee.* **3 give sb a mouthful** *informal especially BrE* to speak angrily to someone, often swearing at them **4 say a mouthful** *AmE informal* to say a lot of true and important things about something in a few words

ˈmouth ˌorgan *n* [C] a small musical instrument that you play by blowing or sucking and moving it from side to side near your mouth SYN **harmonica**

mouth·piece /ˈmaʊθpiːs/ *n* [C] **1** the part of a musical instrument, telephone etc that you put in your mouth or next to your mouth: *Ben put his hand over the mouthpiece and shouted to me.* **2** [usually singular] a person, newspaper etc that expresses the opinions of a government or a political organization: **[+of]** *The newspaper was the mouthpiece of the National Democratic Party.*

ˌmouth-to-mouth resusciˈtation (*also* **ˌmouth-to-ˈmouth**) *n* [U] a method used to make someone start breathing again by blowing air into their mouth → **CPR**

ˈmouth ˌulcer *BrE*, **canker sore** *AmE n* [C] a sore area in the mouth of people or animals, caused by illness or a disease

mouth·wash /ˈmaʊθwɒʃ $ -wɒːʃ, -wɑːʃ/ *n* [C,U] a liquid used to make your mouth smell fresh or to get rid of infection in your mouth

ˈmouth-ˌwatering *adj* food that is mouth-watering looks or smells extremely good: *a mouth-watering aroma coming from the kitchen*

mouth·y /ˈmaʊθi/ *adj informal* someone who is mouthy talks a lot and says what they think even if it is rude

mov·a·ble¹, **moveable** /ˈmuːvəbəl/ *adj* able to be moved and not fixed in one place or position OPP **immovable**: *a teddy bear with movable arms and legs*

movable², **moveable** *n* [C usually plural] *law* a personal possession such as a piece of furniture

ˌmovable ˈfeast *n* [C] *BrE* **1** *informal* something that happens at different times, so that you are not sure exactly when it will happen **2** a special religious day, such as Easter, the date of which changes each year

move¹ /muːv/ ●●● S1 W1 *v*

1 CHANGE PLACE [I,T] to change from one place or position to another, or to make something do this: *Please keep the doors closed while the train is moving. | 'Come on,' Sue said. No one moved. | Could you move your car, please? It's blocking the road.* | **move quickly/slowly/steadily etc** *The plane moved slowly along the runway, then stopped.* | **[+away/out/to/towards etc]** *He moved closer to her. | Becca moved down the steps and into the yard.* | **[+about/around]** *I could hear someone moving around upstairs. | The bar was so crowded you* **could hardly move**. *| At Christmas, you* **couldn't move for** *toys in this house* (=there were a lot of toys). *| Paul* **couldn't move a muscle** (=could not move at all) *he was so scared.*

2 NEW HOUSE/OFFICE [I,T] if a person or company moves, or if you move them, they go to live or work in a different place: *We've moved seven or eight times in the last five years.* | **[+to/into/from]** *When are you moving to Memphis? | They've moved into bigger offices in London.* | **move sb to/into/from etc sth** *He had to move his mother into a nursing home. | The company is moving its sales center downtown.* | **move house/home** *BrE* (=go to live in a different house) *My parents kept moving house because of my dad's job.*

3 CHANGE OPINION ETC **a)** [I] to change from one opinion or way of thinking to another SYN **shift**: *Neither side is willing to move on the issue of territory.* | **[+towards/away from]** *The two political parties have moved closer towards each other in recent months. | At this stage, children move further away from the influence of their parents, and depend more on their friends.* **b)** [T] to persuade someone to change their opinion: *She won't be moved – it doesn't matter what you say to her.*

4 PROGRESS [I] to make progress in a particular way or at a particular rate: *Things moved quickly once the contract was signed. | The negotiations seem to be moving in the right direction.* | **get/keep things moving** *The plan should boost employment and get things moving in the economy.*

5 TAKE ACTION [I] to start taking action, especially in order to achieve something or deal with a problem: **[+on/against]** *The governor has yet to move on any of the recommendations in the report.* | **move fast/quickly/swiftly** *You'll have to move fast if you want to get a place on the course.*

6 CHANGE JOB/CLASS ETC [I,T] to change to a different job, class etc, or to make someone change to a different job, class etc SYN **transfer**: **move sb to/into/from sth** *Several students were moved from the beginners' class into the intermediate one. | He spent five years at KLP, before moving to IMed as a manager.*

7 EMOTION [T] to make someone feel strong emotions, especially of sadness or sympathy: **be deeply/genuinely/profoundly moved** *Russell was deeply moved by what he heard.* | *His speech* **moved** *the audience* **to tears**. → MOVING(1)

8 CAUSE SB TO DO STH [T] to cause someone to do something: **move sb to do sth** *Seeing her there had moved him to think about the time they had together.* | **be/feel moved to do sth** *I have never before felt moved to write, but I feel I must protest.*

9 TIME/ORDER [T] to change the time or order of something: **move sth to/from sth** *Could we move the meeting to Thursday?*

10 CHANGE SUBJECT [I] to start talking or writing about a different subject: **[+away from/off/to etc]** *We seem to be moving away from the main point of the discussion.* → MOVE ON

11 get moving (*also* **move it**) *spoken* used to tell someone to hurry: *Come on, get moving or you'll be late for school.*

12 it's time I was moving/we ought to get moving etc *spoken* used to say that you need to leave or go somewhere: *I think it's time we were moving. | I ought to get moving – I have to be up early tomorrow.*

13 GAMES [I,T] to change the position of one of the objects used to play a game such as CHESS
14 AT A MEETING [I,T] *formal* to officially make a proposal at a meeting: **move that** *The chairman moves that the meeting be adjourned.* | **move to do sth** *I move to approve the minutes as read.* | **move an amendment** *BrE* (=suggest a change) *They want to move an amendment to the bill.*
15 GO FAST [I] *informal* to travel very fast: *This car can really move!*
16 BE BOUGHT [I] if things of a particular kind are moving, they are being bought, especially at a particular rate: *The highest-priced homes are still moving slowly.*
17 move with the times to change the way you think and behave, as society changes: *If the resorts want to keep attracting tourists, they need to move with the times.*
18 move in ... circles/society/world to spend a lot of time with a particular type of people and know them well: *She spent time in England, where she moved in high society.*
→ **move the goalposts** at GOALPOST(2), → **move in for the kill** at KILL²(2), → **move heaven and earth** at HEAVEN(9), → **when the spirit moves you** at SPIRIT¹(15)

GRAMMAR

Move belongs to a group of verbs where the same noun can be the subject of the verb or its object.
• You can say: *They moved the store to bigger premises.* In this sentence, 'the store' is the object of **move**.
• You can say: *The store moved to bigger premises.* In this sentence, 'the store' is the subject of **move**.
GRAMMAR GUIDE ▸ **VERBS**

THESAURUS

move to go to a different place, or change the position of your body: *Sarah moved away from the window.* | *Every time I move I get a pain in my left shoulder.*
sway to move slowly from one side to the other: *The branches swayed in the wind.* | *Donny swayed drunkenly as he walked back to his car.*
rock to move repeatedly from one side to another, with small gentle movements: *He rocked backward and forward in his chair.* | *The boat rocked from side to side with the waves.*
wobble to move unsteadily from side to side: *The bike wobbled a bit, but she soon got it under control.*
fidget to keep moving or playing with your fingers, hands, feet etc, because you are bored or nervous: *Diana fidgeted nervously with her pencil.*
squirm to make very small movements from side to side with your body, especially because you feel uncomfortable: *By the end of the hour, most of the children were squirming in their seats.*
wriggle to make small movements from side to side, especially in order to get into or out of something: *The dog wriggled under the fence and escaped into the street.* | *She managed to wriggle into the dress, but it was much too tight.*
twitch if part of your body twitches, it makes small movements that you cannot control: *A muscle on Yang's face twitched.*
stir *written* to make a movement – used especially when describing a situation in which no one moves, or someone wakes up: *In the village a dog barked but **no one stirred**.* | *The sleeping child stirred and opened her eyes.*
budge to move – used when you are trying hard to make something move, often without success: *The piano wouldn't budge.*

move along *phr v*
1 if a process or situation is moving along, or if you move it along, it continues and makes progress: *Construction of the bridge is moving along.* | **move sth along** *I hope we can move things along and get the negotiations going again.*
2 move sb ↔ along to officially order someone to leave a public place: *A queue formed by the gates, and a policeman tried to move people along.*

move around *phr v* to change where you live very frequently, especially so that you live in many different parts of a country: *My dad was in the army, so we moved around a lot.*
move away *phr v* to go to live in a different area: *My best friend moved away when I was ten.*
move down (sth) *phr v* to change to a lower group, rank, or level: *Interest rates have moved down.* | *A drop in wages has meant that these families have moved down the economic scale.*
move in *phr v*
1 (*also* **move into sth**) to start living in a new home OPP **move out**: *When are you moving in?* | *Mom and Dad had always planned to move into a smaller house when we grew up.*
2 to start living with someone in the same home: **[+with]** *Steve's going to move in with her.*
3 to start being involved in and controlling a situation that someone else controlled previously: *The big multinationals moved in and started pushing up prices.* | **[+on]** *Investors moved in on a group of car enthusiasts and took over the market.*
4 to go towards a place or group of people, in order to attack them or take control of them: **[+on]** *Police moved in on the demonstrators in the square.*
move off *phr v especially BrE* if a vehicle or group of people moves off, it starts to leave: *Always check behind the car before you move off.*
move on *phr v*
1 CHANGE JOB/CLASS to leave your present job, class, or activity and start doing another one: *I enjoyed my job, but it was time to move on.* | **[+to]** *When you finish, move on to the next exercise.* | **move on to higher/better things** (=get a better job or social position – used humorously) *Jeremy's leaving the company to move on to higher things.*
2 CHANGE/DEVELOP **a)** to develop in your life, and change your relationships, interests, activities etc: *I've moved on since high school, and now I don't have much in common with some of my old friends.* | **[+from]** *She has long since moved on from the roles of her youth.* **b)** to change, progress, improve, or become more modern as time passes: *By the time the software was ready, the market had moved on.*
3 move sb on *BrE* to order someone to leave a particular place – used especially about police: *The police arrived on the scene and began moving the protesters on.*
4 CHANGE SUBJECT to start talking about a new subject in a discussion, book etc: *Before we move on, does anyone have any questions?*
5 CONTINUE JOURNEY to leave the place where you have been staying and continue to another place: *After three days we decided it was time to move on.* | **[+to]** *The exhibition has now moved on to Edinburgh.*
6 TIME if time, the year etc moves on, the time passes: *As time moves on, I'd like the children to play more challenging music.*
7 time is moving on *BrE spoken* used to say that you must leave soon or do something soon, because it is getting late: *Time's moving on – we'd better get back to the car.*
move out *phr v*
1 to leave the house where you are living now in order to go and live somewhere else OPP **move in**: *He moved out, and a year later they were divorced.* | **[+of]** *They moved out of London when he was little.*
2 if a group of soldiers moves out, they leave a place
3 *AmE spoken* to leave: *Are you ready to move out?*
move over *phr v*
1 to change position so that there is more space for someone else: *Move over a little, so I can get in.*
2 to start using a different system, doing a different type of work etc: **[+to]** *Most companies have moved over to computer-aided design systems.*
3 to change jobs, especially within the same organization or industry: **[+from]** *The company's new publisher just moved over from Villard Books.*
4 move over Madonna/Walt Disney/CD-ROMs etc used when saying that something new is becoming more

popular than something older – used humorously: *Move over, Armani, there's a new designer taking the fashion scene by storm.*

move up *phr v*

1 to get a better job in a company, or change to a more advanced group, higher rank, or higher level: *To move up, you'll need the right training.* | *Share prices moved up this month.* | **[+to]** *The kids learn fast, and can't wait to move up to the junior team.* | *He was* **moving up the ladder** (=getting higher and higher positions), *and getting management experience.* | *He's* **moved up in the world** (=got a better job or social position) *in the last few years, and his new flat shows it.*

2 *especially BrE* to change position in order to make more space for other people or things or be near someone else: *There's room for one more if everyone moves up a bit.*

move² ●●● S2 W1 *n* [C]

1 DECISION/ACTION something that you decide to do in order to achieve something: *She's still thinking about her* **next move**. | **move to do sth** *the Board's recent moves to cut interest rates* | *Most of the council members are reluctant to* **make** *such a drastic* **move**. | *The authorities have* **made no move** *to resolve the conflict.* | **a good/wise/smart etc move** *She decided to learn as much about it as she could, which seemed like a wise move.* | *Taking the position was a good* **career move** (=a decision that will improve the type of jobs you can do). | **there are moves afoot (to do sth)** *BrE* (=there are plans, especially secret ones) *It seems there could be moves afoot to close the centre.*

2 MOVEMENT [usually singular] when someone moves for a short time in a particular direction: *Good gymnasts rehearse their moves mentally before a competition.* | *He* **made no move** *to come any nearer.* | *Martin* **made a move** *towards the door.* | **watch/follow sb's every move** *His green eyes followed Cissy's every move.* | *One* **false move** (=move in the wrong direction) *and I'll shoot.*

3 PROGRESS/CHANGE a change, especially one which improves a situation: **[+towards/from/against/to]** *the country's move towards democracy* | *a move away from traditional industries such as coal mining* | *Much more research is being done, which is* **a move in the right direction**.

4 be on the move a) to be travelling from one place to another: *The rebel army is on the move.* **b)** to be busy and active: *Roy is constantly on the move.* **c)** to be changing and developing a lot, especially in a way that improves things: *Museums are on the move, adding exhibits that entertain and educate.*

5 get a move on *spoken* used to tell someone to hurry

6 make the first move to do something first, especially in order to end a quarrel or start a relationship: *Men say they like it when women make the first move.*

7 GAMES when you change the position of one of the objects in a game such as CHESS: *Several moves later, Ron took his king.* | *It's your move, Janet* (=it is your turn to move an object).

8 make a move *BrE informal* to leave a place: *It's getting late – we ought to make a move.*

9 GOING TO A NEW PLACE [usually singular] when you leave one house, office etc, and go to live or work in a different one: *The move to a larger office building is long overdue.*

10 put/make a move on sb *informal* to try to start sexual activity or a sexual relationship with someone

move·a·ble /ˈmuːvəbəl/ *adj* another spelling of MOVABLE

move·ment /ˈmuːvmənt/ ●●● S1 W1 *n*

1 PEOPLE WORKING TOGETHER [C] a group of people who share the same ideas or beliefs and who work together to achieve a particular aim: **civil rights/feminist/peace etc movement** *the civil rights movement of the 1960s* | **movement to do sth** *Mendes led a movement to stop destruction of the rain forest.* | **[+for]** *the movement for independence*

2 POSITION/PLACE [C,U] **a)** when someone or something changes position or moves from one place to another: *the dancer's graceful movements* | **[+of]** *A slight movement of the curtains showed where she was hiding.* | *the movement of goods across the border* | *He motioned to the door with a movement of his head.* **b)** a planned change in the position of a group of soldiers: *reports of* **troop movements** *in the area*

3 CHANGE/DEVELOPMENT [U] a gradual change or development in a situation or in people's attitudes or opinions: *There's been no movement in the peace talks since Thursday.* | **[+towards/away from]** *a movement towards equality with men in the workplace*

4 sb's movements the places where someone goes and the things they do during a certain period: *Police are trying to trace Carter's movements since Tuesday.*

5 MUSIC [C] one of the main parts into which a piece of music is divided, especially a SYMPHONY

6 CLOCK/WATCH [C usually singular] the moving parts of a piece of machinery, especially a clock or watch

7 BODY WASTE [C] *formal* when you get rid of waste matter from your BOWELS

mov·er /ˈmuːvə $ -ər/ *n* [C] **1 mover and shaker** *informal* an important person who has power and influence over what happens in a situation: *He's one of the movers and shakers in Florida politics.* **2** someone or something that moves in a particular way: *Hummingbirds are quick movers.* **3** *especially AmE* someone whose job is to move furniture, boxes etc from one house to another when someone changes where they live **4** something that moves things from one place to another: *an earth mover* **5** a STOCK or SHARE that people are buying and selling a lot of **6** someone who makes a formal proposal at a meeting: *the mover of the motion* → PRIME MOVER

mov·ie /ˈmuːvi/ ●●● S2 W2 *n* [C] *especially AmE*

1 a film made to be shown at the cinema or on television: *It was like one of those old John Wayne movies.* | **in a movie** *She once played the innocent victim in a horror movie.* | **[+about]** *a movie about two gay teenagers who fall in love*

2 the movies a) the cinema: *We* **took** *the kids* **to the movies**. | *In those days, we* **went to the movies** *every week.* | **at the movies** *Why were you at the movies all by yourself?* **b)** films in general, and the events in them: **in (the) movies** *He couldn't believe his luck. It was the sort of thing that only happened in the movies.* **c)** the business of producing films: *a career in the movies* → see Thesaurus box on *p. 1196*

COLLOCATIONS

VERBS

watch/see a movie *We watched the movie and ate popcorn.*

go to a movie *How about going to a movie?*

take in a movie *AmE* (=go to see a movie)

appear in/be in a movie *She's also appeared in ten movies.*

star in a movie (=play one of the main characters) | **a movie stars/features sb** | **make/shoot a movie** | **direct a movie** | **show/screen a movie** | **a movie is released** (=becomes available for the public to see)

ADJECTIVES/NOUN + movie

a classic movie (=an old movie that is very good) *a scene from the classic movie 'Casablanca'*

a hit movie (=a successful movie) *He has directed a string of hit movies.*

a cult movie (=one that a small group of people like very much and watch often) | **a big-budget/low-budget movie** (=one that cost a lot of money to make, or very little money to make)

movie + NOUN

the movie industry *How did you get started in the movie industry?*

a movie star *She looked like a movie star.*

a movie director | **a movie producer** | **a movie premiere** (=the first showing of a movie)

mov·ie·go·er /ˈmuːviˌɡəʊə $ -ˌɡoʊər/ *n* [C] *especially AmE* someone who goes to see films at the cinema, especially regularly SYN **cinemagoer** *BrE*

mov·ie·mak·er /ˈmuːviˌmeɪkə $ -ər/ *n* [C] *especially AmE* a FILM-MAKER

'movie star ●●○ *n* [C] *especially AmE* a famous film actor or actress SYN **film star**

'movie ˌtheater ●●● S3 *n* [C] *AmE* a building where you go in order to watch films SYN **cinema** *BrE*

mov·ing /ˈmuːvɪŋ/ ●●○ *adj*
1 making you feel strong emotions, especially sadness or sympathy: **deeply/very/profoundly moving** *Bayman's book about his illness is deeply moving.* | **moving account/story etc** *a moving account of his childhood in Ireland* | *Attending the memorial service was a* ***moving experience***.
2 [only before noun] changing from one position to another: *a moving stage* | **fast/slow moving etc** *Be careful when changing lanes in fast-moving traffic.* | *an archer learning to hit a* ***moving target***
3 a moving target something that is changing continuously, so that it is very difficult to criticize it or compete against it: *The company is constantly improving the system, making it a moving target.*
4 the moving spirit *formal* someone who makes something start to happen: *He was the moving spirit behind the founding of the union.* —**movingly** *adv*: *She spoke movingly about her father's last days.*

ˌmoving 'picture *n* [C] *old-fashioned especially AmE* a film made to be shown at the cinema

ˌmoving 'staircase *n* [C] *old-fashioned* an ESCALATOR

'moving ˌvan *n* [C] *AmE* a large vehicle used for moving furniture from one house to another SYN **removal van** *BrE*

mow /məʊ $ moʊ/ *v* (*past tense* **mowed**, *past participle* **mown** *or* **mowed** /məʊn $ moʊn/) [I,T] **1** to cut grass using a machine: *It's time to* ***mow*** *the* ***lawn*** *again.* THESAURUS ▸ CUT **2 new-mown hay/grass etc** recently cut grass etc

mow sb ↔ **down** *phr v informal* **1** to kill large numbers of people at the same time, especially by shooting them: *The soldiers were mown down by machine-gun fire.* **2** to kill someone by driving into them fast: *He was sentenced to two years in prison for mowing down a nine-year old girl.*

mow·er /ˈməʊə $ ˈmoʊər/ *n* [C] **1** a machine used for cutting grass SYN **lawnmower** **2** *old use* someone who mows

mox·ie /ˈmɒksi $ ˈmɑː-/ *n* [U] *AmE informal* courage and determination: *He's a small kid, but he has plenty of moxie.*

moz·za·rel·la /ˌmɒtsəˈrelə $ ˌmɑː-/ *n* [U] a white Italian cheese that is often used on PIZZA

mozzie, **mossie** /ˈmɒzi $ ˈmɑː-/ *n* [C] *AusE, BrE informal* a MOSQUITO

MP /ˌem ˈpiː/ ●●○ *n* [C]
1 (***Member of Parliament***) someone who has been elected to a parliament to represent people from a particular area of the country: *Ken Newton, MP* | *a Labour MP* | **[+for]** *She's one of the MPs for Liverpool.*
2 *informal* a member of the MILITARY POLICE

MP3 /ˌem piː ˈθriː/ *n* [C] *trademark* a recording of music that can be DOWNLOADed from the Internet

ˌMP'3 ˌplayer *n* [C] a machine or computer program that plays music which has been DOWNLOADed from the Internet

MP4 play·er /ˌem piː ˈfɔː ˌpleɪə $ -ˈfɔːr ˌpleɪər/ *n* [C] a machine or computer program that plays music or videos that have been DOWNLOADed from the Internet

MPEG /ˈem peg/ *n* [C] *technical* (***Moving Picture Experts Group***) a type of computer FILE used on the Internet that contains sound and video material → **JPEG**

mpg /ˌem piː ˈdʒiː/ (***miles per gallon***) used to describe the amount of petrol used by a car: **do 30/40 etc mpg** *BrE*, **get 30/40 etc mpg** *AmE*: *a car that does 35 mpg*

mph /ˌem piː ˈeɪtʃ/ (***miles per hour***) used to describe the speed of something, especially a vehicle or the wind: *high winds of up to 140 mph*

MPhil, **M.Phil.** /ˌem ˈfɪl/ *n* [C] *BrE* (***Master of Philosophy***) a university degree in a subject such as history, languages, or English literature, that you can get after your first degree → **PhD**

MPV /ˌem piː ˈviː/ *n* [C] *BrE* (***multi-purpose vehicle***) a large car for up to eight people SYN **minivan** *AmE*

Mr *BrE*, **Mr.** *AmE* /ˈmɪstə $ -ər/ ●●● W2
1 used before a man's family name to be polite when you are speaking to him, writing to him, or talking about him: *Mr Smith is the headteacher.* | *Mr. John Smith* | *Mr and Mrs Smith*
2 used when speaking to a man in an official position: *Mr Chairman* | *Mr. President* → MADAM(3)
3 Mr Right a man who would be the perfect husband for a particular woman: *She's finally found Mr Right.*
4 Mr Big *informal* the leader or most important person in a group, especially a criminal group
5 Mr Clean *informal* someone who is honest and always obeys the law
6 Mr Sarcasm/Mr Messy/Mr Forgetful etc *spoken* used

THESAURUS: movie

film *especially BrE*, **movie** *especially AmE* a series of images that tell a story and are shown in a cinema or on television: *What's your favourite movie?* | *It won the award for best foreign film.* | *a made-for-TV movie*
motion picture *formal* (*also* **picture**) a film – used especially by people who make films or by critics: *a major Hollywood motion picture* | *Tell us about your latest picture.*
blockbuster *informal* a very successful film: *Steven Spielberg's latest Hollywood blockbuster*
documentary a film that gives detailed information and facts about a particular subject: *a documentary on the rain forest*
feature film a film made to be shown in cinemas: *The book was later made into a full-length feature film starring Sean Penn.*
comedy a film intended to make people laugh: *Monroe appeared in a number of comedies.*
romantic comedy (*also* **romcom** *BrE informal*) a film about two people who are in love, which is intended to make the people who watch it feel happy: *'Notting Hill' is a romantic comedy starring Julia Roberts and Hugh Grant.*
thriller an exciting film, especially about murder or serious crimes: *'The Birds' is a classic Hitchcock thriller.*
film noir a film that shows strong feelings of fear or evil and whose characters are often immoral, or these films in general: *'The Big Sleep' is a classic Hollywood film noir.*
action film/movie a film that has lots of fighting, explosions etc: *Stallone's latest action movie*
horror film/movie a frightening film about ghosts, murders etc: *She loves watching old horror movies.*
western a film with cowboys in it: *John Wayne is famous for making westerns.*
science fiction film/movie (*also* **sci-fi film/movie** *informal*) a film about imaginary events in the future or in outer space: *'2001: A Space Odyssey' is probably the most famous sci-fi movie ever made.*
silent film/movie an old film without any sound: *The 1920s were the golden age of silent movies.*
animated film/movie/cartoon a film with characters that are drawn or made using a computer: *One of his first animated films was 'Snow White and the Seven Dwarfs'.*
anime /ˈænɪmeɪ, -mə/ a type of Japanese animated film, which often has a science fiction story: *Miyazaki's anime film 'Spirited Away' became an international success.*
CGI the use of computers to create characters and images in a film: *The film uses CGI.* | *Disney's latest CGI movie*
short a short film, usually shown before a longer movie in the cinema: *an animated short*
trailer a series of short scenes from a film or programme, shown in order to advertise it in a cinema, on television etc: *We had to sit through all the trailers.*

humorously to say that someone has a particular quality or behaves in a particular way: *I don't think we need any comments from Mr Sarcasm here.* → **no more Mr Nice Guy!** at GUY(5)

MRI /ˌem ɑːr ˈaɪ/ *n medical* **1** [U] (***magnetic resonance imaging***) the process of using strong MAGNETIC FIELDS to make a picture of the inside of someone's body for medical reasons → **CT scan, X-ray 2** [C] a picture of the inside of someone's body produced with MRI equipment: *Brian had an MRI taken Sunday.*

Mrs *BrE*, **Mrs.** *AmE* /ˈmɪsɪz/ ●●● W2
1 used before a married woman's family name to be polite when you are speaking to her, writing to her, or talking about her → **miss, Mr**: *Mrs. Smith | Mrs Meddeman heads the fundraising committee. | Mr and Mrs David Smith* ⚠ Some women prefer to be addressed as **Ms** because it does not draw attention to whether or not they are married.
2 Mrs Tidy/Mrs Efficient/Mrs Nosy etc *spoken* used humorously to say that a woman has a particular quality or behaves in a particular way: *Mrs Superefficient has already taken care of it.*

MRSA /ˌem ɑːr es ˈeɪ/ *n* [U] *medical* the name for a group of BACTERIA that cannot be treated with normal ANTIBIOTIC drugs. These bacteria are also called SUPERBUGS, and are found in many hospitals.

ms *n* (*plural* **mss**) [C] the written abbreviation of ***manuscript***

Ms *BrE*, **Ms.** *AmE* /mɪz, məz/ ●●● W2 used before a woman's family name when she does not want to be called 'Mrs' or 'Miss', or when you do not know whether she is married or not → **miss, Mrs**: *Dear Ms Johnson, ...*

MS /ˌem ˈes/ *n* [U] (***multiple sclerosis***) a serious illness that gradually destroys the nerves, causing weakness and inability to move

M.S. /ˌem ˈes/ *n* [C] *AmE* (***Master of Science***) a university degree in a science subject that you can get after your first degree

M.Sc. (*also* **MSc** *BrE*) /ˌem es ˈsiː/ *n* [C] (***Master of Science***) a university degree in a science subject that you can get after your first degree

MSG /ˌem es ˈdʒiː/ *n* **1** [U] (***monosodium glutamate***) a chemical that is added to food to make it taste better **2** (*also* **msg**) [C] (***message***) used especially in TEXT MESSAGES sent or received on a MOBILE PHONE

MSSA /ˌem es es ˈeɪ/ *n* [U] *medical* the name for a group of BACTERIA that attack the NERVOUS SYSTEM and that cannot be treated by normal ANTIBIOTIC drugs. These bacteria are also called SUPERBUGS, and are found in hospitals.

Mt. (*also* **Mt** *BrE*) the written abbreviation of ***mount***: *Mt. Everest*

MTF /ˌem tiː ˈef/ *n* [C] (***male-to-female***) someone who has had an operation to change their sex from male to female → **FTM**

MTV /ˌem tiː ˈviː/ *n trademark* (***music television***) a television company that broadcasts popular music and videos of the songs

M25, the /ˌem twenti ˈfaɪv◂/ a British MOTORWAY (=large fast road) that goes all around London, which is also called the London Orbital on some road signs. It is well known for its TRAFFIC JAMS (=when the vehicles stop moving for a long time).

much¹ /mʌtʃ/ ●●● S1 W1 *adv*
1 by a great amount: **much better/greater/easier etc** *Henry's room is much bigger than mine. | These shoes are much more comfortable. | I'm feeling **very much** better, thank you.* | **much too big/old etc** *He was driving much too fast.* | **much the best/most interesting etc** *BrE*: *It's much the best way to do it.*

USAGE: Much

- The adverb **much** is mainly used before comparative adjectives or adjectives with 'too': *He's much older than she is. | The soup was much too salty.*
- It is not usually used before other adjectives, but **much** can be used before **different**, especially in negatives and questions: *It's not much different from when I was young.*

2 a) used to ask or talk about the degree of a difference: **how much older/smaller etc** *She kept weighing herself to see how much heavier she was getting.* **b)** used to ask or talk about how big an additional amount of something is: **how much more/longer/further** *How much longer do we have to wait? | How much further is it?* **c)** used to emphasize the difference you are mentioning: **how much better/nicer/easier etc** *I was surprised to see how much better she was looking. | How much better life would be if we returned to the values of the past!*
3 used to talk about a strong feeling or something that is done often: **how/however much** *You know how much I care about you. | I think you have to accept the pain, however much it hurts. | He talks **too much**. | We're looking forward to your visit **so much**. | Thank you **very much**!* | **much loved/admired/discussed etc** *The money will buy much needed books for the school.*
4 not ... much a) only a little or hardly at all: *'Did you enjoy it?' 'No, not much.' | She isn't much younger than me. | Tony hasn't changed much in the last ten years.* **b)** used to say that something does not often happen: *We don't go to the theatre much anymore. | Kids don't play outside as much as they used to.* → LITTLE³(2)
5 much like sth/much as (*also* **much the same (as sth)**) used to say that something is very similar to something else: *The house was **very much** as I'd remembered it. | The taste is much like butter. | Plants are classified in much the same way as animals.*
6 much to sb's surprise/embarrassment etc *formal* used to say that someone feels very surprised, embarrassed etc when something happens: *Much to my relief, the conversation turned to another topic.*
7 much less used to say that a greater thing is even less true, likely, or possible than the thing you have just mentioned: *The shelves were lined with books which neither Hugo nor Sally would ever open, much less read.*
8 much as although: *Much as I like Bob, I wouldn't want to live with him.*
9 not so much ... as ... used to say that one description of someone or something is less suitable or correct than another: *She was not so much nervous as impatient for the journey to be over.* → **so much the better** at BETTER³(2)

much² ●●● S1 W1 *determiner, pron*
1 a large amount of something: *I don't have much money with me. | Was there much traffic? | He didn't say much about his trip. | Do you get much chance to travel in your job? | After much consideration we have finally arrived at a decision.* | **[+of]** *Much of the city was destroyed in the attack.* | **(far/rather/a little) too much** *There was too much work for one person. | It would cost far too much to have the thing repaired. | It was such a small thing to have caused **so much** trouble.*
2 how much used to ask or talk about the amount or cost of something: *How much is that dress? | How much flour should I use in the sauce? | I know how much hard work goes into looking after a baby.*
3 as much an amount that is equal and not less: **as much (...) as** *I hope you have as much fun as I did. | Just do as much as you can.*
4 as much as 10/100 etc used to emphasize how surprisingly large an amount is: *Some machines cost as much as £20,000.*
5 used in negative expressions to say that something is not important, interesting, good etc: **not/nothing much** *'What are you doing?' 'Oh, not much, really.' | There's nothing much we can do to help. | I **don't think much** of that idea* (=I do not think it is good). | *The car may **not be much to look at*** (=it does not look good) *but it's very reliable. | It's the best book he's written, but **that's not saying much*** (=none of his books is very good).
6 not be much of a sth to not be a good example of something or not be very good at something: *I'm not*

much of a dancer, I'm afraid. | *It wasn't really much of a storm.*
7 be too much for sb to be too difficult for someone to do or bear: *The effort of climbing the stairs had been too much for the old man.* | *The shock had been too much for her – she never recovered.*
8 not be up to much *BrE spoken* to be fairly bad: *The restaurant's very grand but the food isn't up to much.*
9 there is not much in it *informal* used to say that there is little difference between two things or amounts: *'Isn't the woollen carpet more expensive?' 'A little, perhaps, but there's not much in it.'*
10 think/say etc as much to think or say the thing that has just been mentioned: *Carson strongly disapproved of the plan and said as much at the meeting.* | *'Max was lying all the time.' 'I thought as much.'*
11 it was as much as sb could do to do sth used to say that someone only succeeded in doing something with great difficulty: *He looked so stupid, it was as much as I could do to stop myself from laughing.*
12 not/without so much as sth used when you are surprised or annoyed that someone did not do something: *They left without so much as saying goodbye.* | *He'd received not so much as a thank you from Tiffany.*
13 so much for sth used to say that a particular action, idea, statement etc was not useful or did not produce the result that was hoped for: *He's late again. So much for good intentions.*
14 I'll say this/that much for sb/sth used when saying one good thing about someone or something when they are being criticized a lot: *Well, he does admit it when he's wrong, I'll say that much for him.*
15 as much again an additional amount that is equal: *The car only cost me £1,500 but it cost as much again to get it insured.*
16 be a bit much/be too much *BrE spoken* used to say that someone's behaviour is unacceptable or impolite: *It's a bit much expecting you to pay for it all.*
17 make much of sb/sth *formal* to treat a person or thing as though you think they are very important or special: *The press made much of the discovery.* | *They've always made much of their nephews and nieces.*

GRAMMAR

- **Much** is mainly used in questions and negative sentences, or after **too** or **so**: *Was there much snow?* | *There's not much time left.* | *You've used too much soap.*
- **Much** sounds very formal in positive statements. It is usually better to say **a lot of**: *There was a lot of food left.* ✗ Don't say: *There was much food left.*
- You use **much** before uncountable nouns: *I don't have much money.*
- You use **many** before plural nouns: *There are too many advertisements on TV.* ✗ Don't say: *There are too much advertisements on TV.*

ˌmuch-ˈheralded *adj* [only before noun] a much-heralded event, product etc has been talked about a lot before it happens or becomes available: *Ford's much-heralded new sports car*

much·ness /ˈmʌtʃnəs/ *n* **be much of a muchness** *BrE informal* to be very similar in standard, quality etc: *It was hard to choose between the candidates – they were all much of a muchness.*

ˌmuch-ˈvaunted *adj* [only before noun] a much-vaunted plan, achievement etc is one that people say is very good or important, especially when this may not be true: *the president's much-vaunted health-care plan*

muck¹ /mʌk/ *n* [U] *informal* **1** dirt, mud, or another sticky substance that makes something dirty: *Come on, let's wipe that muck off your face.* **2** *BrE* waste matter from animals, sometimes put on land to make plants grow better SYN **manure**: *special machinery for* ***spreading muck*** *onto the fields* | *dog muck* **3** *BrE* something that is unpleasant or of very bad quality: *How can you eat that muck? It looks disgusting.* | *I'm not surprised she left. He* ***treated*** *her* ***like muck*** (=very badly). **4 make a muck of sth** *BrE informal* to do something very badly and make a lot of mistakes SYN **muck up**: *I really made a muck of the exam.* **5 as common as muck** *BrE informal* very common or of a low social class

muck² *v*
muck about/around *phr v BrE informal* **1** to behave in a silly way, especially when you should be working or paying attention to something SYN **mess around**: *Stop mucking about and listen!* | *Some of the boys were mucking around on bikes.* **2 muck sb about/around** to cause trouble for someone, especially by changing your mind a lot or not doing what you promised to do SYN **mess sb around**: *The company kept mucking us around and changing the price.*
muck in *phr v BrE informal* **1** to do your share of the work that is necessary in order to get a job done: *If we all muck in, we could get the whole house painted by the end of the week.* **2** to share space with other people: **[+with]** *There are only three bedrooms. Do you mind mucking in with the other boys?*
muck sth ↔ **out** *phr v BrE* to clean the place where a farm animal lives: *You have to muck out the stables every day in the winter.*
muck sth ↔ **up** *phr v informal* **1** *BrE* to do something badly, so that you fail to achieve something SYN **mess up**: *I really mucked up my driving test first time.* **2** to spoil something, especially an arrangement or plan SYN **mess up**: *The bad weather mucked up our plans for a picnic.* **3** *BrE* to make something dirty SYN **mess up**: *Who's mucked up the carpet in here?*

muck·heap /ˈmʌkhiːp/ *n* [C] *BrE* a pile of MANURE (=animal waste matter) on farmland

muck·rak·ing /ˈmʌk-reɪkɪŋ/ *n* [U] the practice of telling or writing unpleasant and perhaps untrue stories about people's private lives, especially famous people: *Two of the candidates complained of unfair muckraking during the election campaign.* —**muckraking** *adj* —**muckraker** *n* [C]

muck·y /ˈmʌki/ *adj informal* **1** dirty: *Your hands are all mucky.* | *Don't come in here with those mucky boots on.* **2** *BrE* a mucky joke or story etc is slightly rude and about sex SYN **dirty**

mu·cous mem·brane /ˌmjuːkəs ˈmembreɪn/ *n* [C] the thin layer of skin that covers some inner parts of the body, such as the inside of the nose, and produces mucus

mu·cus /ˈmjuːkəs/ *n* [U] a thick liquid produced in parts of your body such as your nose —**mucous** *adj* [only before noun]

mud /mʌd/ ●●○ S3 *n* [U]
1 wet earth that has become soft and sticky: *By the end of the game, all the kids were covered in mud.* | *The path beside the river was slippery with mud.* | *Many villages in Mali consist of mud huts.* | *boots* ***caked with mud*** (=covered in mud) | *It was impossible to move the car – its wheels had got stuck in the mud.* THESAURUS ▸ GROUND
2 here's mud in your eye *spoken old-fashioned* used for expressing good wishes when having an alcoholic drink with someone SYN **cheers** *BrE* → **as clear as mud** at CLEAR¹(18), → **drag sb's name through the mud** at DRAG¹(10), → **sb's name is mud** at NAME¹(15)

mud·bath /ˈmʌdbɑːθ $ -bæθ/ *n* **1** [singular] a large area of mud: *Thousands of young people arriving for the festival soon turned the fields into a mudbath.* **2** [C] a health treatment in which heated mud is put onto your body, especially to reduce pain

mud·dle¹ /ˈmʌdl/ *n* **1 be in a muddle/get into a muddle** *BrE* **a)** to be confused: *I'm in such a muddle, I'd completely forgotten you were coming today.* | **[+over/about]** *My grandmother tends to get into a muddle over names.* **b)** to be untidy or in a disorganized state: *Sorry about the mess – we're in a bit of a muddle at the moment.* | *All my files have got into a muddle somehow.* **2** [C usually singular, U] when there is confusion about something, and things are done wrong as a result: *Our accountant finally managed to sort out the muddle.* | **[+over/about]** *There was a bit of a muddle over our hotel reservations.*

muddle² (*also* **muddle up**) *v* [T] *especially BrE* **1** to put

M

things in the wrong order: *Someone's muddled up all the papers on my desk.* | *The government seems to have lost its way and muddled its priorities.* **2** to confuse one person or thing with another, and make a mistake SYN **mix up**: *The twins are so alike that it's easy to muddle them up.* | *Spanish and Italian are very similar and I sometimes* ***get*** *them* ***muddled up***. | **muddle sth with sth** *Be careful not to muddle the files you've already worked on with the others.* **3** to confuse someone, especially so that they make a mistake: *Don't muddle her with all the extra details at the moment.* | *Could you just repeat those figures – I've* ***got*** *a bit* ***muddled up***.

muddle along/on *phr v* to continue doing something without having any clear plan or purpose, or without having enough help or support: *There's no point in muddling on in the same old job forever.* | *Many of the students complained that they were left to muddle along on their own.*

muddle through (sth) *phr v especially BrE* to succeed in doing something with difficulty, or not in a very satisfactory way: *There were some difficult questions but I managed to muddle through.* | *The team managed to muddle through another season.*

mud·dled /ˈmʌdld/ *adj* confused: *muddled thinking* | *The situation today is very muddled.*

ˌmuddle-ˈheaded *adj BrE* confused or not able to think clearly: *I like her but she's a bit muddle-headed.*

mud·dy¹ /ˈmʌdi/ ●●○ *adj*
1 covered with mud or containing mud: *Take your boots off outside if they're muddy.* | *the muddy waters of the lake* THESAURUS ▸ DIRTY
2 confused and not clear: *On the issue of education, the difference between the two parties is muddy.*
3 colours that are muddy are dull: *The carpet was an unpleasant muddy brown.*
4 sounds that are muddy are not clear

muddy² *v* (**muddied**, **muddying**, **muddies**) [T] **1** to make something dirty with mud: *Lizzy walked around the edge of the field, taking care not to muddy her new shoes.* **2 muddy the waters/the issue** to make a situation more complicated or confusing than it was before – used to show disapproval

mud·flap /ˈmʌdflæp/ *n* [C] a piece of rubber that hangs behind the wheel of a vehicle to prevent mud from getting on the vehicle → see picture at CAR

mud·flat /ˈmʌdflæt/ *n* [C usually plural] **1** an area of muddy land that is covered by the sea when it comes up at HIGH TIDE and uncovered when it goes down at LOW TIDE **2** *AmE* the muddy bottom of a dry lake

mud·guard /ˈmʌdgɑːd $ -gɑːrd/ *n* [C] *BrE* a curved piece of metal or plastic that covers the wheel of a bicycle and prevents mud from getting on the bicycle and rider SYN **fender** *AmE* → see pictures at BICYCLE, MOTORBIKE

mud·pack /ˈmʌdpæk/ *n* [C] a soft mixture containing clay that you spread over your face and leave there for a short time to improve your skin

ˌmud ˈpie *n* [C] **1** a little ball of wet mud made by children as a game **2** *AmE* a DESSERT made of ice cream and chocolate

mud·slide /ˈmʌdslaɪd/ *n* [C] when a lot of wet earth suddenly falls down the side of a hill: *Torrential rains caused a massive mudslide.*

mud·sling·ing /ˈmʌdslɪŋɪŋ/ *n* [U] when someone says bad and often untrue things about someone in order to make other people have a low opinion of them: *There has been a lot of political mudslinging in the battle for votes.* —**mudslinger** *n* [C]

mues·li /ˈmjuːzli/ *n* [U] a mixture of grains, nuts, and dried fruit that is eaten with milk for breakfast SYN **granola** *AmE*

mu·ez·zin /muːˈezɪn, ˈmwezɪn/ *n* [C] a man who calls Muslims to prayer from a MOSQUE

muff¹ /mʌf/ *n* [C] a short tube of thick cloth or fur that you can put your hands into to keep them warm in cold weather → **earmuffs**

muff² *v* [T] *informal* **1** (*also* **muff sth ↔ up**) to spoil a chance to do something well or achieve something: *You'll probably only get one chance to take a photo, so don't muff it!* **2** to fail to catch a ball or kick it properly in a game or sport: *With only the goalkeeper to beat, he completely muffed his shot.* **3 muff your lines** *BrE* if you muff your lines in a play you are acting in, you forget them or say them wrongly

MUFFIN

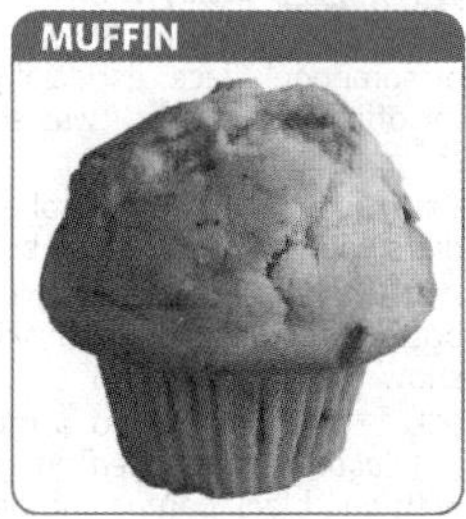

muf·fin /ˈmʌfɪn/ *n* [C] **1** a small, usually sweet cake that sometimes has small pieces of fruit in it: *blueberry muffins* **2** *BrE* a small thick round kind of bread, usually eaten hot with butter SYN **English muffin** *AmE*

ˈmuffin top *n* [C,U] *informal* flesh around someone's waist that sticks out above their trousers: *This exercise will help get rid of muffin top.*

muf·fle /ˈmʌfəl/ *v* [T] **1** to make a sound less loud and clear, especially by covering something: *The falling snow* ***muffled the sound*** *of our footsteps.* | *Her* ***voice*** *was* ***muffled*** *by the pillow in which she had hidden her face.* **2** (*also* **muffle up**) to cover yourself or another person with something thick and warm SYN **wrap up**: **be muffled (up) in sth** *Penelope arrived, muffled up in a thick coat.* GRAMMAR **Muffle** is usually passive in this meaning.

muf·fled /ˈmʌfəld/ *adj* muffled sounds cannot be heard clearly, for example because they come from behind a door or wall SYN **indistinct**: *I could hear muffled voices in the next room.* | *There was the muffled sound of organ practice coming from the chapel.* THESAURUS ▸ QUIET

muf·fler /ˈmʌflə $ -ər/ *n* [C] **1** a long piece of thick cloth that you wear to keep your neck warm SYN **scarf 2** *AmE* a piece of equipment on a vehicle that makes the noise from the engine quieter SYN **silencer** *BrE*

muf·ti /ˈmʌfti/ *n* **1** [C] a Muslim who officially explains Islamic law **2 in mufti** *BrE old-fashioned* wearing ordinary clothes instead of a uniform: *soldiers in mufti*

mug¹ /mʌg/ ●●○ *n* [C]
1 a tall cup used for drinking tea, coffee etc: *a coffee mug* → see picture at CUP¹
2 a large glass with a handle, used especially for drinking beer: *a beer mug*
3 mug/mugful of sth a mug and the liquid inside it: *Two mugs of tea, please.*
4 *BrE spoken informal* someone who is stupid and easy to deceive: *Only a mug would pay that much for a meal.*
5 be a mug's game *BrE spoken* to be something that only stupid people do because it is not likely to be successful or to bring you money: *Gambling is a mug's game.*
6 *spoken informal* a face: *Something scared him. Probably your* ***ugly mug****!*

mug² ●○○ *v* (**mugged**, **mugging**)
1 [T] to attack someone and rob them in a public place: *A lot of people won't go out alone at night because they're afraid of being mugged.* THESAURUS ▸ ATTACK, STEAL
2 [I] *AmE informal* to make silly expressions with your face or behave in a silly way, especially for a photograph or in a play: **[+for]** *All the kids were mugging for the camera.*

mug up *phr v BrE informal* to try to learn something in a short time, especially for an examination SYN **swot up**: **[+on]** *Jeannie can't come. She's busy mugging up on science for her exam.* | **mug sth ↔ up** *Mug up as much as you can about the country before your trip.*

mug·ger /ˈmʌgə $ -ər/ *n* [C] someone who attacks people in a public place and robs them THESAURUS ▸ THIEF

mug·ging /ˈmʌgɪŋ/ *n* [C,U] an attack on someone in which they are robbed in a public place: *Crime is on the increase, especially mugging and burglary.* | *Dudley was the victim of a violent mugging.* THESAURUS ▸ CRIME

mug·gins /ˈmʌgɪnz/ *n* [U] *BrE spoken informal* used

humorously to mean yourself, when you feel stupid because you have let other people treat you unfairly: *Everyone disappeared after supper, leaving muggins here to do the washing-up.*

mug·gy /ˈmʌgi/ *adj informal* muggy weather is unpleasantly warm and the air seems wet SYN **humid** THESAURUS DAMP, HOT, WET

mug·shot /ˈmʌgʃɒt $ -ʃɑːt/ *n* [C] *informal* a photograph of someone's face, especially a criminal's, or one taken for official purposes: *I was shocked to see his mugshot on the front page of the paper.*

mu·ja·hed·din /ˌmuːdʒəheˈdiːn/ *n* [plural] Muslim soldiers with strong religious beliefs

muk·luks /ˈmʌklʌks/ *n* [plural] *AmE* boots with a thick bottom, made of animal skin and used for walking in snow

mu·lat·to /mjuːˈlætəʊ $ mʊˈlætoʊ/ *n* (*plural* **mulattos**) [C] *taboo old-fashioned* an offensive word for someone with one black parent and one white parent. Do not use this word. → **mixed race** at MIXED(7)

mul·ber·ry /ˈmʌlbəri $ -beri/ *n* (*plural* **mulberries**) **1** [C] a dark purple fruit that can be eaten, or the tree on which this fruit grows **2** [U] a dark purple colour

mulch[1] /mʌltʃ/ *n* [C usually singular, U] a substance such as decaying leaves that you put on the soil to improve its quality, to protect the roots of plants, or to stop WEEDS growing

mulch[2] *v* [I,T] to cover the ground with mulch

mule /mjuːl/ *n* [C] **1** an animal that has a DONKEY and a horse as parents → **stubborn as a mule** at STUBBORN(1) **2** *informal* someone who brings illegal drugs into a country by hiding them on or in their body **3** [usually plural] a woman's shoe or SLIPPER that covers the front part of the foot but has no material around the heel → see picture at SHOE[1]

mul·ish /ˈmjuːlɪʃ/ *adj written* refusing to do something or agree to something, in an unreasonable way SYN **stubborn**: *a mulish look*

mull[1] /mʌl/ *v* [T] *usually* **mull sth ↔ over** to think about a problem, plan etc for a long time before making a decision SYN **consider**: *He's mulling over the proposals before making any changes.* | *The company is mulling over a share offer.*

mull[2] *n* [C] an area of land that sticks out into the sea – used in Scotland: *the Mull of Kintyre*

mul·lah /ˈmʌlə, ˈmʊlə/ *n* [C] a Muslim teacher of law and religion

ˌmulled ˈwine *n* [U] wine that has been heated with sugar and spices

mul·let /ˈmʌlɪt/ *n* [C] **1** (*plural* **mullet**) a fairly small sea fish that can be eaten **2** a hairstyle for men in which the hair on the sides and top of the head is short and the hair on the back of the head is long **3 the mullet strategy** a way of designing a website so that the pages a visitor sees first look good and professional, and comments and information from ordinary people are somewhere else on the website

mul·li·ga·taw·ny /ˌmʌlɪgəˈtɔːni $ -ˈtɒːni, -ˈtɑːni/ *n* [U] a type of spicy soup

mul·lion /ˈmʌljən/ *n* [C] *technical* a vertical piece of stone, metal, or wood between two pieces of glass in a window —**mullioned** *adj*

multi- /mʌlti, mʌltə/ *prefix* more than one SYN **many**: *multicoloured* | *a multistorey office block*

mul·ti·cel·lu·lar /ˌmʌltiˈseljələ $ -ər/ (*also* **multicelled**) *adj* [usually before noun] *technical* consisting of many cells: *a multicellular organism*

mul·ti·col·oured *BrE*, **multicolored** *AmE* /ˈmʌltiˌkʌləd $ -ərd/ *adj* having many different colours: *a multicoloured sweatshirt* THESAURUS COLOUR

mul·ti·cul·tur·al /ˌmʌltiˈkʌltʃərəl◂/ ●○○ *adj* involving or including people or ideas from many different countries, races, or religions → **multi-ethnic**: *a multicultural society*

mul·ti·cul·tu·ral·is·m /ˌmʌltiˈkʌltʃərəlɪzəm/ *n* [U] the belief that it is important and good to include people or ideas from many different countries, races, or religions —**multiculturalist** *n* [C]

mul·ti·dis·ci·plin·a·ry /ˌmʌltiˈdɪsəplɪnəri, -dɪsəˈplɪnəri $ -ˈdɪsəpləneri/ *adj* involving people with different jobs or from different areas of study: *a multidisciplinary team of nurses, social workers, and GPs*

ˌmulti-ˈethnic *adj* **1** involving or including people of several different ETHNIC groups → **multicultural**: *multi-ethnic Britain* **2** *AmE* a multi-ethnic person has parents who come from different ETHNIC groups

mul·ti·fa·cet·ed /ˌmʌltiˈfæsɪtɪd◂/ *adj* having many parts or sides: *a multifaceted campaign to reduce teen pregnancy*

ˈmulti-faith *adj* [only before noun] including or involving people from several different religious groups: *a multi-faith gathering*

mul·ti·far·i·ous /ˌmʌltəˈfeəriəs◂ $ -ˈfer-/ *adj formal* of many different kinds: *multifarious business activities*

mul·ti·fo·cals /ˈmʌltiˌfəʊkəlz $ -ˌfoʊ-/ *n* [plural] CONTACT LENSes or glasses that help you to see things that are near and things that are far away —**multifocal** *adj*

mul·ti·func·tion /ˌmʌltiˈfʌŋkʃən◂/ (*also* **mul·ti·func·tion·al** /ˌmʌltiˈfʌŋkʃənəl◂/) *adj* [only before noun] a multifunction machine, piece of equipment, building etc is designed to have several different uses

mul·ti·lat·e·ral /ˌmʌltɪˈlætərəl◂/ *adj* involving several different countries or groups → **bilateral**, **unilateral**: *a multilateral arms treaty*

mul·ti·lin·gual /ˌmʌltɪˈlɪŋgwəl◂/ *adj* using, speaking, or written in several different languages → **bilingual**, **monolingual**: *the problems of a multilingual classroom* | *a multilingual phrasebook* —**multilingualism** *n* [U]

mul·ti·me·di·a /ˌmʌltiˈmiːdiə◂/ *adj* [only before noun] **1** involving computers and computer programs that use a mixture of sound, pictures, video, and writing to give information: *multimedia game programs* | *multimedia equipment* **2** using several different methods of giving information, for example using television, newspapers, books, and computers: *a multimedia exhibition on nuclear power* —**multimedia** *n* [U]

ˌmultimedia ˈmessaging *n* [U] a form of sending and receiving written messages to and from MOBILE PHONES that makes it possible to combine the written message with pictures, video, and sound

mul·ti·mil·lion /ˌmʌltiˈmɪljən◂/ *adj* **multimillion-pound/multimillion-dollar etc** worth or costing many millions of pounds, dollars etc: *a multimillion-dollar lawsuit*

mul·ti·mil·lio·naire /ˌmʌltɪˌmɪljəˈneə $ -ˈner/ *n* [C] someone who has many millions of pounds or dollars

mul·ti·na·tion·al[1] /ˌmʌltɪˈnæʃənəl◂/ ●○○ *adj* **1** a multinational company has factories, offices, and business activities in many different countries: *a multinational media corporation* **2** involving people from several countries: *the UN's multinational peace-keeping force*

multinational[2] ●○○ *n* [C] a large company that has offices, factories etc in many different countries: *Multinationals have made large investments in Thailand.* THESAURUS COMPANY

mul·ti·par·ty /ˌmʌltɪˈpɑːti◂ $ -ˈpɑːr-/ *adj* [only before noun] involving or including more than one political party: *a multiparty democracy*

ˈmulti-ˌplatform *adj* **1** multi-platform software can run on many different types of computer **2** multi-platform information, entertainment etc is delivered through several different MEDIA, for example television and the Internet

ˌmulti-player ˈgaming *n* [U] the playing of computer games on the Internet by more than one person at the same time, using different computers

mul·ti·ple[1] /ˈmʌltəpəl/ ●●○ *adj* [only before noun] many, or involving many things, people, events etc: *Baxter* *was rushed to the hospital with multiple stab wounds. | Having multiple partners increases your risk of sexual diseases. | His new album includes multiple versions of the same songs.*

multiple² *n* [C] **1** a number that contains a smaller number an exact number of times: **[+of]** *20 is a multiple of 5.* **2** *BrE technical* a MULTIPLE STORE

ˌmultiple ˈbirth *n* [C] when more than one baby is born to the same mother at the same time: *The number of multiple births has risen sharply.*

ˌmultiple ˈchoice *adj* a multiple choice examination or question shows several possible answers, and you have to choose the correct one

ˌmultiple personˈality *n* [C] if someone has a multiple personality, they are mentally ill because they have two or more completely separate PERSONALITIES that each behave differently → **split personality**: *multiple personality disorder*

ˌmultiple scleˈrosis *n* [U] *medical* (*abbreviation* **MS**) a serious illness that gradually destroys your nerves, making you weak and unable to walk

ˌmultiple ˈstore *n* [C] *BrE technical* a CHAIN STORE

mul·ti·plex¹ /ˈmʌltəpleks/ (*also* **ˌmultiplex ˈcinema** *BrE*) *n* [C] a cinema that has several different rooms in which it can show films

multiplex² *adj technical* having many different parts

mul·ti·plex·er /ˈmʌltəpleksə $ -ər/ *n* [C] *technical* a piece of computer equipment that is used to send several electrical signals using only one connection, especially with a MODEM —**multiplexing** *n* [U]

mul·ti·pli·ca·tion /ˌmʌltɪplɪˈkeɪʃən/ *n* [U] **1** a method of calculating in which you add a number to itself a particular number of times → **division 2** *formal* a large increase in the size, amount, or number of something: *a multiplication of the number of forms to fill out*

ˌmultipliˈcation sign *n* [C] a sign (×) showing that one number is multiplied by another

ˌmultipliˈcation ˌtable *n* [C] a list, used especially by children in school, that shows the results when each number between one and twelve is multiplied by each number between one and twelve

mul·ti·pli·ci·ty /ˌmʌltəˈplɪsəti/ *n* [singular, U] *formal* a large number or great variety of things: **[+of]** *the multiplicity of courses available to language students*

mul·ti·ply /ˈmʌltəplaɪ/ ●●○ *v* (**multiplied**, **multiplying**, **multiplies**)
1 [I,T] to do a calculation in which you add a number to itself a particular number of times → **divide**: *Children will learn to multiply in the second grade.* | **multiply sth by sth** *Multiply the total by 12.*
2 [I,T] to increase by a large amount or number, or to make something do this: *The amount of information available has multiplied. | Smoking multiplies the risk of heart attacks and other health problems.*
3 [I] to breed: *Bacteria multiply quickly in warm food.*

mul·ti·pur·pose /ˌmʌltiˈpɜːpəs◂ $ -ˈpɜːr-/ *adj* [usually before noun] able to be used for many different purposes: *a multipurpose building | a multipurpose tool*

mul·ti·ra·cial /ˌmʌltɪˈreɪʃəl◂/ *adj* including or involving several different races of people → **multicultural**: *a multiracial society*

mul·ti·skill·ing /ˈmʌltɪˌskɪlɪŋ/ *n* [U] when someone is trained to do several different jobs within the same company

ˌmulti-ˈstorey¹ *adj* [only before noun] *BrE* a multi-storey building has many levels or floors

multi-storey² *n* [C] *BrE spoken* a multi-storey CAR PARK

mul·ti·task /ˈmʌltɪˌtɑːsk $ -ˌtæsk/ *v* [I] to do several things at the same time: *The successful applicant for this job must be able to multitask.* —**multitasker** *n* [C]

mul·ti·task·ing /ˈmʌltiˌtɑːskɪŋ $ -ˌtæs-/ *n* [U] **1** a computer's ability to do more than one job at a time **2** when a person does more than one thing at a time: *Women are traditionally supposed to be good at multitasking.*

mul·ti·tude /ˈmʌltɪtjuːd $ -tuːd/ ●○○ *n*
1 a multitude of sb/sth *formal or literary* a very large number of people or things: *I had never seen such a multitude of stars before. | a multitude of possible interpretations*
2 the multitude(s) ordinary people, especially when they are thought of as not being very well educated: *Political power has been placed in the hands of the multitude.*
3 [C] *literary or biblical* a large crowd of people: *Clamoring multitudes demanded a view of the pope.*
4 cover/hide a multitude of sins to make faults or problems seem less clear or noticeable – used humorously: *Patterned carpet can hide a multitude of sins* (=the carpet is dirty, but the pattern hides it).

mul·ti·tu·di·nous /ˌmʌltɪˈtjuːdɪnəs◂ $ -ˈtuː-/ *adj formal* very many: *language in all its multitudinous forms*

ˈmulti-ˌuser *adj* multi-user computer systems or software can be used by more than one person at the same time

mul·ti·verse /ˈmʌltiˌvɜːs $ -ˌvɜːrs/ *n* [singular] all the universes that might exist: *Everything that can happen does happen somewhere in the multiverse.*

mul·ti·vit·a·min /ˈmʌltɪˌvɪtəmən, -ˌvaɪ- $ -ˌvaɪ-/ *n* [C] a PILL or liquid containing many different VITAMINS

mum¹ /mʌm/ ●●● S1 W2 *n* [C]
1 *BrE* mother SYN **mom** *AmE*
2 mum's the word *spoken* used to tell someone that they must not tell other people about a secret

mum² *adj* **keep mum** *informal* to not tell anyone about a secret

mum·ble /ˈmʌmbəl/ ●●○ *v* [I,T] to say something too quietly or not clearly enough, so that other people cannot understand you → **mutter**: *He bumped into someone and mumbled an apology. | Stop mumbling!* | **mumble to yourself** *A woman on the corner was mumbling to herself.*
THESAURUS SAY —**mumble** *n* [C]

mum·bo-jum·bo /ˌmʌmbəʊ ˈdʒʌmbəʊ $ -boʊ ˈdʒʌmboʊ/ *n* [U] *informal* technical language that is difficult to understand and seems to have no sense: *a bunch of legal mumbo-jumbo*

mum·mer /ˈmʌmə $ -ər/ *n* [C] an actor in a simple traditional play that does not have words —**mumming** *n* [U]

mum·mi·fy /ˈmʌmɪfaɪ/ *v* (**mummified**, **mummifying**, **mummifies**) [T] to preserve a dead body by putting special oils on it and wrapping it with cloth —**mummification** /ˌmʌmɪfɪˈkeɪʃən/ *n* [U]

mum·my /ˈmʌmi/ ●●● S1 *n* (*plural* **mummies**) [C]
1 *BrE* mother – used especially by young children or when you are talking to young children SYN **mommy** *AmE*: *Mummy, can I play outside?*
2 a dead body that has been preserved by wrapping it in cloth, especially in ancient Egypt → **mummify**

ˈmummy's boy *n* [singular] *BrE informal* a MOTHER'S BOY

mumps /mʌmps/ *n* [U] (*also* **the mumps**) an infectious illness which makes your neck swell and become painful

GRAMMAR: Singular or plural verb?

Mumps is followed by a singular verb: ***Mumps is*** *quite serious if you get it as an adult.*

GRAMMAR GUIDE NOUNS

ˌmum-to-ˈbe *n* (*plural* **mums-to-be**) [C] *BrE informal* a MOTHER-TO-BE

munch /mʌntʃ/ *v* [I,T] to eat something noisily: **[+on/at]** *Barry sat munching on an apple. | They'd* ***munched*** *their* ***way through*** (=eaten all of) *three packets of biscuits.*

munch·ies /ˈmʌntʃiz/ *n* [plural] *informal* **1 the munchies** a feeling of wanting to eat something, especially food that is not healthy for you: **have/get the munchies** *Get me a packet of crisps – I have the munchies.* **2** *AmE* foods that are easy to pick up and eat, especially foods served at a party

mun·dane /mʌnˈdeɪn/ ●○○ *adj*
1 ordinary and not interesting or exciting SYN **boring**: *Initially, the work was pretty mundane.* | *The mundane task of setting the table can be fun on holidays.* THESAURUS BORING
2 *literary* concerned with ordinary daily life rather than religious matters SYN **worldly**

mung bean /ˌmʌŋ ˈbiːn/ *n* [C usually plural] a small green bean, usually eaten as a BEANSPROUT

mung·ing /ˈmʌŋɪŋ/ *n* [U] the process of changing part of your email address when you send an email to some websites, so that companies cannot easily copy your address and send you unwanted emails → **spamblocking** —**mung** *v* [T] —**mung** *n* [C]

mu·ni·ci·pal /mjuːˈnɪsəpəl $ mjʊ-/ ●○○ *adj* relating to or belonging to the government of a town or city: *the municipal waste dump* | *municipal elections* —**municipally** *adv*

mu·ni·ci·pal·i·ty /mjuːˌnɪsəˈpæləti $ mjʊ-/ *n* (*plural* **municipalities**) [C] a town, city, or other small area, which has its own government to make decisions about local affairs, or the officials in that government: *the municipality of Berkeley* | *an elected municipality*

mu·nif·i·cent /mjuːˈnɪfəsənt $ mjʊ-/ *adj formal* very generous: *a munificent gift* —**munificence** *n* [U]: *the munificence of the museum's benefactors*

mu·ni·tions /mjuːˈnɪʃənz $ mjʊ-/ *n* [plural] military supplies such as bombs and guns → **ammunition**: *a munitions factory* —**munition** *adj* [only before noun]

mun·ter /ˈmʌntə $ -ər/ *n* [C] *BrE spoken informal* an ugly person, especially a woman: *Who'd want to go out with a munter like her?*

mup·pet /ˈmʌpɪt/ *n* [C] *BrE spoken informal* an insulting word for someone who is stupid or who has done or said something stupid

mu·ral /ˈmjʊərəl $ ˈmjʊrəl/ *n* [C] a painting that is painted on a wall, either inside or outside a building → **fresco** —**mural** *adj* [only before noun]

mur·der¹ /ˈmɜːdə $ ˈmɜːrdər/ ●●● S3 W2 *n*
1 [C,U] the crime of deliberately killing someone → **manslaughter**: *On the night the* ***murder*** *was* ***committed****, he was out of the country.* | *The man* ***accused of*** *her* ***murder*** *will appear in court today.* | **[+of]** *the* ***brutal murder*** *of a child* | *He was found guilty of* ***attempted murder****.* | *She was charged with two counts of* ***first degree murder****.* | *The mother of the* ***murder victim*** *wept in court.* | *Police are searching for the* ***murder weapon****.* | *Detectives have launched a* ***murder investigation****.* THESAURUS CRIME
2 get away with murder *informal* to do anything you want, even things that are wrong, without being punished: *She lets those kids get away with murder.*
3 be murder *spoken* to be very difficult or unpleasant: *It's murder doing the shopping on Saturdays.* | *The traffic was murder this morning.*
4 be murder on sth *spoken* to harm or damage something else: *These new shoes are murder on my feet.* → **scream blue murder** at SCREAM¹(1)

murder² ●●● W3 *v* [T]
1 to kill someone deliberately and illegally: *He was convicted of murdering a policeman.* | *Thousands of civilians were brutally murdered during the civil war.* | *the murdered man* THESAURUS KILL
2 *informal* to spoil a song, play etc by performing it very badly: *It's a good song, but they murdered it.*
3 sb will murder you *spoken* used to tell someone that another person will be very angry with them: *Your dad'll murder you when he hears about it.*
4 I could murder a beer/pizza etc *BrE spoken* used to say that you are very hungry or thirsty and want a particular food or drink
5 *informal* to defeat someone completely: *They murdered us in the final.*

mur·der·er /ˈmɜːdərə $ ˈmɜːrdərər/ ●●○ *n* [C] someone who murders another person: *a convicted murderer* | *his brother's murderer*

M

mur·der·ess /ˈmɜːdərɪs $ ˈmɜːr-/ *n* [C] *old-fashioned* a woman who murders another person

mur·der·ous /ˈmɜːdərəs $ ˈmɜːr-/ *adj* **1** very dangerous and likely to kill people: *a murderous attack* | *murderous drug dealers* **2 murderous look/expression/glare etc** an expression or look which shows that someone is very angry —**murderously** *adv*

murk /mɜːk $ mɜːrk/ *n* [U] *literary* darkness caused by smoke, dirt, or clouds SYN **gloom**

murk·y /ˈmɜːki $ ˈmɜːr-/ *adj* **1** dark and difficult to see through: *murky water* THESAURUS DARK **2** complicated and difficult to understand SYN **obscure**: *The laws on intellectual property are murky.* | *the* ***murky waters*** (=complicated subject) *of sexuality and jealousy* **3** involving dishonest or illegal activities that are kept secret SYN **shady**: *a murky world of fraud and secret deals* | *a politician with a murky past* —**murkiness** *n* [U]

mur·mur¹ /ˈmɜːmə $ ˈmɜːrmər/ ●○○ *v*
1 [I,T] to say something in a soft quiet voice that is difficult to hear clearly: *'Well done,' murmured George.* | *The girl murmured something polite, and smiled.* | *Julie turned over and murmured in her sleep.* THESAURUS SAY
2 [I] to make a soft low sound: *The wind murmured through the trees.*
3 [I + against] *literary especially BrE* to complain to friends and people you work with, but not officially —**murmuring** *n* [C,U]: *murmurings of discontent*

murmur² *n* [C] **1** a soft low sound made by people speaking quietly or a long way away: **[+of]** *the murmur of voices in the other room* | *She replied in a low murmur.* | **murmur of agreement/surprise/regret etc** (=one that expresses a particular feeling) *There was a murmur of agreement from the crowd.* THESAURUS SOUND **2** a complaint, but not a strong or official complaint: **[+of]** *There have been murmurs of discontent over the new rules.* **3 do sth without a murmur** to do something without complaining, especially when this is surprising: *They signed the form without a murmur.* **4** the soft low sound made by water, the wind etc: *the murmur of the little brook* **5 heart murmur** an unusual sound made by the heart, which shows that there may be something wrong with it

Mur·phy's law /ˌmɜːfiz ˈlɔː $ ˌmɜːrfiz ˈlɒː/ *n* [U] *informal especially AmE* a tendency for bad things to happen whenever it is possible for them to do so – used humorously SYN **sod's law** *BrE*

mus·cle¹ /ˈmʌsəl/ ●●● S2 W3 *n*
1 [C,U] one of the pieces of flesh inside your body that you use in order to move, and that connect your bones together: *Relax your* ***stomach muscles****, then stretch again.* | *Regular exercise will help to* ***strengthen your muscles****.* | *Rooney has* ***pulled*** *a* ***muscle*** *in his thigh and won't play tomorrow.*
2 not move a muscle to stay completely still: *The soldier stood without moving a muscle.*
3 [U] power or influence: **military/economic/political etc muscle** *The unions have a lot of political muscle.* | *The agreement will give the UN some muscle to enforce human rights.*
4 [U] physical strength and power: *It* ***took muscle*** *to work in an old-fashioned kitchen.* | **put some muscle into it** (=used to tell someone to work harder) → **flex your muscles** at FLEX¹(2)

muscle² *v* **muscle your way into/through etc sth** to use your strength to go somewhere: *Joe and Tony muscled their way through the crowd.*

muscle in *phr v* to use your power to get involved in or take control of something that someone else was doing, especially in business – used to show disapproval: **[+on]** *Banks are muscling in on the insurance business.*

mus·cle-bound /ˈmʌsəlbaʊnd/ *adj* having large stiff muscles because of too much physical exercise: *muscle-bound weight-lifters*

mus·cled /ˈmʌsəld/ *adj* having large muscles SYN **muscular**: *He had a good body, tanned and well muscled.*

mus·cle·man /ˈmʌsəlmæn/ *n* (*plural* **musclemen** /-men/) [C] **1** a man who has developed big strong muscles by doing exercises **2** a strong man who is employed to protect someone, usually a criminal

Mus·co·vite /ˈmʌskəvaɪt/ *n* [C] someone from the city of Moscow in Russia —**Muscovite** *adj*

mus·cu·lar /ˈmʌskjələ $ -ər/ ●●○ *adj*
1 having large strong muscles: *She was fast and strong, with a slender, muscular body.* | *He's very muscular.* THESAURUS ▸ STRONG
2 concerning or affecting the muscles: *muscular injuries* —**muscularity** /ˌmʌskjəˈlærəti/ *n* [U]

muscular dys·tro·phy /ˌmʌskjələ ˈdɪstrəfi $ -lər-/ *n* [U] a serious illness in which the muscles become weaker over a period of time

mus·cu·la·ture /ˈmʌskjələtʃə $ -tʃʊr/ *n* [singular, U] *medical* all the muscles in the body, considered as a group

muse[1] /mjuːz/ *v* **1** [T] to say something in a way that shows you are thinking about it carefully: *'Somewhere,' he mused, 'I've heard your name before.'* **2** [I] to think about something for a long time SYN **ponder**: **[+on/over/about/upon]** *He mused on how different his life would have been, had he not met Louisa.* —**musing** *n* [C,U]: *her gloomy musings* —**musingly** *adv*

muse[2] *n* [C] **1** someone's muse is the force or person that makes them want to write, paint, or make music, and helps them to have good ideas SYN **inspiration**: *Rossetti's wife and creative muse* **2** (*also* **Muse**) one of the nine ancient Greek goddesses who each represented a particular art or science: *the Muse of History*

mu·se·um /mjuːˈziəm $ mjʊ-/ ●●● S3 W2 *n* [C] a building where important CULTURAL, historical, or scientific objects are kept and shown to the public: *the Museum of Modern Art* | *The museum has an extensive collection of early photographs.*

muˈseum ˌpiece *n* [C] **1** something or someone that is very old-fashioned – often used humorously: *Some of the weapons used by the rebels are museum pieces.* **2** an object that is so valuable or interesting that it should be in a museum

mush[1] /mʌʃ/ *n* **1** [singular, U] an unpleasant soft substance, especially food, which is partly liquid and partly solid: *The boiled vegetables had* ***turned to mush***. | *She trudged through the mush of fallen leaves.* **2** **turn/go to mush** if your brains, heart etc turn to mush, you cannot think clearly or sensibly: *If you watch too much TV, your brains will turn to mush.* **3** [U] *AmE* a thick PORRIDGE made from CORNMEAL **4** [U] a book, film etc that is about love and is SENTIMENTAL: *poetry and mush like that*

mush[2] /mʊʃ/ *n BrE* **1** *spoken informal* used to speak to someone in an angry way: *Oi, mush! Get your hands off my car!* **2** [C] *BrE informal* someone's face or mouth: *I didn't want to see his ugly mush ever again.*

mush[3] /mʌʃ/ *interjection* used to tell a team of dogs that pull a SLEDGE over snow to start moving

mush·room[1] /ˈmʌʃruːm, -rʊm/ ●●● S3 *n* [C] one of several kinds of FUNGUS with stems and round tops, some of which can be eaten → **toadstool**: *mushroom soup* → MAGIC MUSHROOM → see picture at VEGETABLE[1]

mushroom[2] *v* [I] to grow and develop very quickly: *New housing developments mushroomed on the edge of town.*

ˈmushroom ˌcloud *n* [C usually singular] a large cloud shaped like a mushroom, which is caused by a NUCLEAR explosion

mush·y /ˈmʌʃi/ *adj* **1** soft, wet, and unpleasant: *Cook for two minutes until soft but not mushy.* THESAURUS ▸ SOFT **2** expressing or describing love in a silly way: *mushy romance novels*

ˌmushy ˈpeas *n* [plural] *BrE* soft cooked PEAS, eaten especially in the north of England

mu·sic /ˈmjuːzɪk/ ●●● S1 W1 *n* [U]
1 a series of sounds made by instruments or voices in a way that is pleasant or exciting: *I often listen to classical music when I'm in the car.* | *A new piece of music was specially written for the occasion.*
2 the art of writing or playing music: *Peter's studying music at college.* | *music lessons* | **music business/industry etc** *a career in the music business*
3 a set of written marks representing music, or paper with the written marks on it: *I left my music at home.* | *McCartney never learned to* ***read music***. → SHEET MUSIC
4 **be music to your ears** if someone's words are music to your ears, they make you very happy or pleased
5 **set/put sth to music** to write music so that the words of a poem, play etc can be sung → **face the music** at FACE[2](7)

COLLOCATIONS

VERBS

listen to music *Ella was listening to music on her iPod.*
play music *A small band was playing jazz music.*
write/compose music *He composed the music for the 'Lord of the Rings' films.*
make music (=play or compose music) *We began making music together about five years ago.*

ADJECTIVES/NOUN + music

loud/soft/quiet *They were kept awake by loud music from next door.*
pop/rock/classical etc music *Johnny Cash was one of country music's greatest stars.*
live music (=played by musicians on stage) *Most of the bars have live music.*
background music (=that you hear but do not listen to) *the soft background music in the restaurant*
choral music (=sung by choirs) | **instrumental music** (=with no singing) | **chamber music** (=classical music played by a small group of musicians) | **orchestral music** (=classical music played by a large group of musicians) | **piano/organ music**

music + NOUN

a music lover *For music lovers, the city has two world-famous orchestras.*

PHRASES

a piece of music *It's a beautiful piece of music.*

COMMON ERRORS

⚠ Don't say 'classic music'. Say **classical music**.

THESAURUS

music the sounds made by musical instruments or people singing: *The music was really loud.*
tune the main series of musical notes in a piece of music: *a folk song with a pretty tune*
melody the main series of notes in a piece of music that has many notes being played at the same time, especially in classical music: *The soprano sang the melody.*
harmony the chords or notes in a piece of music that support the melody: *the rich harmonies in the symphony*
piece (*also* **piece of music**) an arrangement of musical notes – use this about music without words: *It's a difficult piece to play.*
composition *formal* a piece of music that someone has written: *This is one of his own compositions.*
work a piece of music, especially classical music: *one of Mozart's best-known works*
track one of the songs or pieces of music on a CD: *the album's title track*
number a piece of popular music that forms part of a concert or show: *the show's first number*

mu·sic·al[1] /ˈmjuːzɪkəl/ ●●● S3 W3 *adj*
1 [only before noun] relating to music or consisting of music: *a musical version of the fairy tale 'Cinderella'* | *When he began his musical career, King played only for black audiences.*

2 good at or interested in playing or singing music: *She's very musical and loves to sing.*
3 having a pleasant sound like music: *a sweet musical voice* → MUSICALLY

musical² ●●○ *n* [C] a play or film that includes singing and dancing: *Webber had three musicals playing in London at one time.* | **Broadway/West End musical** (=one that is performed in New York's or London's important theatres) *Carroll appeared in a number of Broadway musicals.*

ˌmusical ˈchairs *n* [U] **1** a children's game in which all the players must sit down on a chair when the music stops, but there is always one chair less than the number of people playing **2** a situation in which people change jobs for no good reason or with no useful result: *Scott is now the finance director, after a long game of musical chairs among top management.*

ˌmusical ˈcomedy *n* [C] *old-fashioned* a musical, especially one from the early 20th century

ˌmusical ˈinstrument *n* [C] something that you use for playing music, such as a piano or GUITAR SYN **instrument**

mu·sic·ally /ˈmjuːzɪkli/ *adv* **1** in a way that is related to music: *It's not as good a show, musically, as 'The Most Happy Fella'.* **2** in a way that sounds like music: *A small fountain splashed musically in the courtyard.*

ˈmusic ˌbox *n* [C] a box that plays a musical tune when you open it

ˈmusic hall *n BrE* **1** [U] a type of entertainment in the theatre in the 19th and early 20th centuries consisting of performances by singers, dancers, and people telling jokes SYN **vaudeville** **2** [C] a theatre used for music hall shows

mu·si·cian /mjuːˈzɪʃən $ mjʊ-/ ●●● W3 *n* [C] someone who plays a musical instrument, especially very well or as a job: *a talented young musician*

mu·si·cian·ship /mjuːˈzɪʃənʃɪp $ mjʊ-/ *n* [U] skill in playing music

mu·si·col·o·gy /ˌmjuːzɪˈkɒlədʒi $ -ˈkɑː-/ *n* [U] the study of music, especially the history of different types of music —**musicologist** *n* [C]

ˈmusic stand *n* [C] a metal frame for holding written music, so that you can read it while playing an instrument or singing

musk /mʌsk/ *n* [U] **1** a substance with a strong smell that is used to make PERFUME **2** *written* a strong smell, especially the way a person smells: *the musk of sweat and muscle* —**musky** *adj*

mus·ket /ˈmʌskɪt/ *n* [C] a type of gun used in the past

mus·ket·eer /ˌmʌskəˈtɪə $ -ˈtɪr/ *n* [C] a soldier in the past who used a musket

musk·mel·on /ˈmʌskˌmelən/ *n* [C] a type of sweet MELON SYN **cantaloupe**

ˈmusk ox *n* (*plural* **musk oxen**) [C] a large animal with long brown or black hair and curved horns, which lives in northern Canada and Greenland

musk·rat /ˈmʌskræt/ *n* [C] an animal which lives in water in North America

Mus·lim /ˈmʊzləm, ˈmʌz-, ˈmʊs-/ *n* [C] someone whose religion is Islam —**Muslim** *adj*

mus·lin /ˈmʌzlɪn/ *n* [U] a very thin cotton cloth used for making dresses and curtains, especially in the past

mu·so /ˈmjuːzəʊ $ -zoʊ/ *n* (*plural* **musos**) [C] *BrE informal* someone who plays popular music or knows a lot about it

muss¹ /mʌs/ (*also* **muss up**) *v* [T] *informal especially AmE* to make something untidy, especially someone's hair: *Briscoe reached down and mussed the boy's hair.*

muss² *n* **no muss, no fuss** used to say that something can be done easily and without problems - used humorously: *It works every time, no muss, no fuss.*

mus·sel /ˈmʌsəl/ *n* [C] a small sea animal with a soft body that can be eaten and a black shell that is divided into two parts → see picture at SHELLFISH

M

must¹ /məst; *strong* mʌst/ ●●● S1 W1 *modal verb* (*negative short form* **mustn't**)
1 (*past tense* **had to**) to have to do something because it is necessary or important, or because of a law or order → **have to**, **oblige**: *All passengers must wear seat belts.* | *It's getting late. I really must go.* | *You must work hard.* | *We must all be patient.* | *Must I pay now?* | *For the engine to work, the green lever must be in the 'up' position.* | *Accidents must be reported to the safety officer.*
2 used in negative sentences to say that something should not happen, because of a rule or law or because of the situation: *You mustn't talk to your mother like that.* | *This book must not be removed from the library.* | *We must never forget how much we owe to these brave men.* | *No one must disturb him while he's sleeping.*
3 used to say you think something is very likely to be true or very likely to have happened: *Sam must be nearly 90 years old now.* | *His new car must have cost around £20,000.* | *You must have been really upset.* | *There must be something wrong with the engine.* | *Karl must've seen 'Star Wars' six or seven times.*
4 *spoken* used to suggest that someone should do something, especially because you think they will enjoy it or you think it is a good idea: *You must come and stay with us in London sometime.* | *'We must do this again,' he said. 'I've enjoyed it thoroughly.'*
5 *especially BrE spoken* used to say that you intend or want to do something: *I must call her tonight.*
6 I must admit/say/confess *spoken* used to emphasize what you are saying: *I must say, it gave me quite a shock.*
7 (why) must you ...? *spoken* used to tell someone that their behaviour upsets or annoys you: *Must you spoil everything?* | *Why must you always be so suspicious?*
8 a must-have/must-see/must-read etc *informal* something that is so good, exciting, or interesting that you think people should have it, see it etc: *The exhibit is a must-see for anyone interested in Japanese art.* | *a must-read novel*
9 if you must (do sth) *spoken* used to tell someone that they are allowed to do something, but that you do not approve of it or agree with it: *All right, come along, if you must.* | *If you must smoke, please go outside.*
10 if you must know *spoken* used when you answer a question that you think someone should not have asked, because it is slightly impolite: *Well, if you must know, I'm thirty-six.* → **you must be joking** at JOKE²(2)

GRAMMAR: Comparison

must
- You say that you **must** do something: *I must get a new key.*
- Don't use 'to' after **must**. ✗ Don't say: *I must to get a new key.*
- You use **must not** when saying someone should not do something, for example because it is dangerous or wrong: *You must not leave without telling me where you're going.*
- You say that something **must have** happened, or that someone **must have** done something, when you are fairly sure that this is true, based on what you know: *They must have caught an earlier train.*

have to
- You say that you **have to** do something: *She has to do some shopping.*
- You use **don't have to** when it is not necessary for someone to do something: *You don't have to leave yet.*
- You use **had to** instead of 'must' when talking about the past: *He had to get up early the next day.*

GRAMMAR GUIDE ▸ VERBS

THESAURUS

must do sth used when saying that it is very important that someone does something, because someone in authority or a rule says this, or because of the situation: *You must be home by midnight.* | *He must not smoke in here.* | *I must remember to call her.*

have to do sth to need to do something because it is necessary or important: *I have to go home early.* | *She has to talk to him first.*
be obliged to do sth to have to do something, because of a rule or law, or because of the situation you are in: *Members of parliament are obliged to declare all their financial interests.* | *He was obliged to admit defeat.*
be required to do sth *formal* to have to do something because of a rule or law – used especially in written notices and official documents: *New students are required to register with a doctor.*
have an obligation to do sth (*also* **be under an obligation to do sth**) to have to do something because it is the duty of someone in your position to do it, or because you have officially agreed to do it: *The landlord is under an obligation to keep the building in good repair.*
be forced/compelled to do sth to have to do something that you do not want to do, because you are in a situation that makes it impossible to avoid: *She was forced to retire early due to ill health.*

must[2] /mʌst/ *n* [C usually singular] something that you must do or must have: *Warm clothes are a must in the mountains.*

mus·tache /məˈstɑːʃ $ ˈmʌstæʃ/ *n* [C] the usual American spelling of MOUSTACHE

mus·ta·chi·oed, **moustachioed** /məˈstæʃiəʊd, -ˈstɑː- $ -ʃioʊd/ *adj* having a MOUSTACHE, especially a large one

mus·tang /ˈmʌstæŋ/ *n* [C] a small wild horse in North America

mus·tard /ˈmʌstəd $ -ərd/ ●●○ *n* [U]
1 a yellow sauce with a strong taste, eaten especially with meat
2 a plant with yellow flowers and seeds that are used to make mustard sauce
3 a yellow-brown colour
4 cut the mustard *informal* to be good enough to do something: *Other magazines have tried to copy ZAPP, but have never quite cut the mustard.* → **keen as mustard** at KEEN[1](4)

ˈmustard gas *n* [U] a poisonous gas that burns the skin, first used during the First World War

mus·ter[1] /ˈmʌstə $ -ər/ ●○○ *v*
1 [T] (*also* **muster up sth**) to get enough courage, confidence, support etc to do something, especially with difficulty SYN **summon (up)**: **muster (up) the courage/confidence/energy etc to do sth** *Finally I mustered up the courage to ask her out.* | *Senator Newbolt has been trying to muster support for his proposals.* | *'It's going to be fine,' replied David,* ***with as much*** *confidence* ***as he could muster***.
2 [I,T] if soldiers muster, or if someone musters them, they come together in a group SYN **gather**: *In April 1185, he began to* ***muster*** *an* ***army***.

muster[2] *n* **1 pass muster (as sth)** to be accepted as good enough for something: *I wasn't sure that our clothing would pass muster at the club door.* **2** [C] *literary* a gathering together of soldiers so that they can be counted, checked etc

must·n't /ˈmʌsənt/ the short form of 'must not': *You mustn't tell Jerry what I've bought.*

must·y /ˈmʌsti/ *adj* a musty room, house, or object has an unpleasant smell, because it is old and has not had any fresh air for a long time: *the musty smell of old books*

mu·ta·ble /ˈmjuːtəbəl/ *adj formal* able or likely to change OPP **immutable** —**mutability** /ˌmjuːtəˈbɪləti/ *n* [U]

mu·tant /ˈmjuːtənt/ *n* [C] **1** an animal or plant that is different in some way from others of the same kind, because of a change in its GENETIC structure **2** something that is very different from others of the same type, in a way that is strange or bad – often used humorously —**mutant** *adj* [only before noun]

mu·tate /mjuːˈteɪt $ ˈmjuːteɪt/ ●○○ *v* [I]
1 if an animal or plant mutates, it becomes different from others of the same kind, because of a change in its GENETIC structure: *Simple organisms like bacteria mutate rapidly.*
2 to change and develop a new form: *Technology continues to mutate at an alarming rate.*

mu·ta·tion /mjuːˈteɪʃən/ ●○○ *n* [C,U]
1 a change in the GENETIC structure of an animal or plant that makes it different from others of the same kind
2 *technical* a change in a speech sound, especially a vowel, because of the sound of the one next to it

mute[1] /mjuːt/ *adj* **1** *written* someone who is mute does not speak, or refuses to speak SYN **silent**: *Billy continued to stand there, mute and defiant.* **2** *old-fashioned* someone who is mute is unable to speak —**mutely** *adv*

mute[2] *v* [T] **1** *formal* to make the sound of something quieter, or make it disappear completely: *Excess noise can be reduced by muting alarms and telephones.* **2** to make a musical instrument sound softer **3** *formal* to reduce the level of criticism, protest, discussion etc that is happening: *The incident so shocked all the students that it muted further protest.*

mute[3] *n* [C] **1** a small piece of metal, rubber etc that you place over or into a musical instrument to make it sound softer **2** *old-fashioned* someone who cannot speak → DEAF MUTE

mut·ed /ˈmjuːtɪd/ *adj* [usually before noun]
1 muted sounds, voices etc are quieter than usual SYN **subdued**: *Everyone was sitting round discussing the accident in muted voices.* **2** a muted reaction to something is not expressed strongly: *There was muted agreement from most of the people in the room.* | *The speech received only a muted response from the unions.* **3** a muted colour or light is soft and gentle, not bright: *muted pinks and blues* **4** a muted musical instrument has been made to sound softer

mu·ti·late /ˈmjuːtəleɪt/ *v* [T] **1** to severely and violently damage someone's body, especially by cutting or removing part of it: *The prisoners had been tortured and mutilated.* | *extra protection for mental patients who might mutilate themselves* **2** to damage or change something so much that it is completely spoiled: *The sculpture was badly mutilated in the late eighteenth century.* —**mutilation** /ˌmjuːtəˈleɪʃən/ *n* [C,U]

mu·ti·neer /ˌmjuːtəˈnɪə $ ˌmjuːtnˈɪr/ *n* [C] someone who is involved in a mutiny

mu·ti·nous /ˈmjuːtɪnəs $ -tn-əs/ *adj* **1** *written* showing by your behaviour or appearance that you do not want to obey someone SYN **rebellious**: *There was a mutinous look in Rosie's eyes.* **2** involved in a mutiny —**mutinously** *adv*

mu·ti·ny /ˈmjuːtɪni $ -tn-i/ *n* (*plural* **mutinies**) [C,U] when soldiers, SAILORS etc refuse to obey the person who is in charge of them, and try to take control for themselves: **[+against]** *He led a mutiny against the captain.* —**mutiny** *v* [I]: *The soldiers had mutinied over the non-payment of wages.*

mutt /mʌt/ *n* [C] *informal* a dog that does not belong to any particular breed SYN **mongrel**

mut·ter /ˈmʌtə $ -ər/ ●●○ *v*
1 [I,T] to speak in a low voice, especially because you are annoyed about something, or you do not want people to hear you: **mutter to yourself** *'I never want to come here again,' he muttered to himself.* | *Elsie muttered something I couldn't catch and walked off.* | *'He's such an unpleasant man,' Alyssia* ***muttered under*** *her* ***breath***. | **[+about]** *What are you two muttering about?* **THESAURUS** SAY
2 [I] to complain about something or express doubts about it, but without saying clearly and openly what you think: **[+about]** *Some senators muttered darkly about the threat to national security.* —**mutter** *n* [singular]: *His voice subsided to a mutter.* —**muttering** *n* [C,U]: *The mutterings about his leadership continued to grow.*

mut·ton /ˈmʌtn/ *n* **1** [U] the meat from a sheep → **lamb**
2 mutton dressed as lamb *BrE* used to describe, in a disapproving way, someone who is wearing clothes that are usually worn by younger people

ˌ**mutton chop ˈwhiskers** *n* [plural] hair that a man allows to grow on the sides of his cheeks

mu·tu·al /ˈmjuːtʃuəl/ ●○○ AWL *adj*
1 mutual feelings such as respect, trust, or hatred are feelings that two or more people have for each other → **reciprocal**: **mutual respect/trust/understanding etc** *Mutual respect is necessary for any partnership to work.* | *European nations can live together in a spirit of mutual trust.* | *I didn't like Dev, and the feeling seemed to be mutual.* | *The two men were a* ***mutual admiration society****, gushing about how much they were learning from each other.*
2 [only before noun] mutual support, help etc is support that two or more people give each other: *MAMA puts new mothers in touch with each other, for* ***mutual support*** *and friendship.*
3 mutual agreement/consent when two or more people both agree to something: *The relationship was ended by mutual agreement.*
4 mutual friend/interest a friend or interest that two people both have: *We discovered a mutual interest in drama.*

ˈ**mutual fund** *n* [C] *AmE* an arrangement managed by a company, in which you can buy SHARES in many different businesses SYN **unit trust** *BrE*

mu·tu·al·ly /ˈmjuːtʃuəli/ ●○○ AWL *adv*
1 mutually acceptable/beneficial/convenient etc something that is mutually acceptable etc is acceptable etc to both or all the people involved: *We eventually arrived at a figure that was mutually acceptable.*
2 mutually exclusive two ideas or beliefs that are mutually exclusive cannot both exist or be true at the same time

muu-muu /ˈmuː muː/ *n* [C] *AmE* a long loose dress

Mu·zak /ˈmjuːzæk/ *n* [U] *trademark* recorded music that is played continuously in airports, shops etc

muz·zle¹ /ˈmʌzəl/ *n* [C] **1** the nose and mouth of an animal, especially a dog or horse → see picture at HORSE¹ **2** a cover that you put over a dog's mouth to stop it from biting people **3** the open end of a gun, where the bullets come out

muzzle² *v* [T] **1** to prevent someone from saying what they think in public SYN **gag**: *an attempt by the government to muzzle the country's media* **2** to put a muzzle over a dog's mouth so that it cannot bite people

muz·zy /ˈmʌzi/ *adj BrE* unable to think clearly, especially because you are ill, sleepy, or drunk: *Juliet's head* ***felt muzzy****, and she hoped she hadn't a cold coming on.*

MW **1** the written abbreviation of ***medium wave*** **2** the written abbreviation of ***megawatt*** or megawatts

mwah /mwɑː/ *interjection informal* the sound of a quick kiss, especially an AIR KISS (=when your lips do not touch the other person) – often used humorously to suggest that someone is not sincere: *Everybody was going 'mwah' and 'darling!'*

my¹ /maɪ/ ●●● S1 W1 *determiner* [possessive form of 'I']
1 used by the person who is speaking to show that something belongs to or is connected with himself or herself: *Have you seen my car keys?* | *My mother phoned last night.* | *I'm sure you don't want to listen to all my problems.* | *Even* ***my own*** *family wouldn't believe me.* | *an apartment* ***of my own***
2 my goodness/my God etc used when you are surprised or shocked about something: *Oh my God! I've missed the train.*
3 my dear/darling/love etc used when talking or writing to someone that you love or like a lot: *Happy Birthday, my love.*

my² *interjection* used when you are surprised, IMPRESSed, or upset: *My! Look at the size of that tree!* | *'It's 3.30.'* ***'Oh my****, I'm going to be late!'*

my·col·o·gy /maɪˈkɒlədʒi $ -ˈkɑː-/ *n* [U] the study of different types of FUNGUS

my·nah bird /ˈmaɪnə bɜːd $ -bɜːrd/ (*also* **mynah**) *n* [C] a large dark Asian bird that can copy human speech

my·o·pi·a /maɪˈəʊpiə $ -ˈoʊ-/ *n* [U] **1** when someone does not think about the future, especially about the possible results of a particular action – used to show disapproval SYN **short-sightedness** **2** *medical* the inability to see clearly things that are far away SYN **short-sightedness** *BrE*, **nearsightedness** *AmE*

my·o·pic /maɪˈɒpɪk $ -ˈɑːpɪk/ *adj* **1** unwilling or unable to think about the future, especially about the possible results of a particular action – used to show disapproval SYN **short-sighted**: *the government's myopic attitude to environmental issues* **2** *medical* unable to see things clearly that are far away SYN **short-sighted** *BrE*, **near-sighted** *AmE* —**myopically** /-kli/ *adv*

myr·i·ad¹ /ˈmɪriəd/ *adj* [usually before noun] *written* very many: *the myriad causes of homelessness* | **a myriad** *We were plagued by a myriad tiny flies.*

myriad² *n* **a myriad of sth/myriads of sth** a very large number of things: *We're still studying a myriad of options.*

myrrh /mɜː $ mɜːr/ *n* [U] a substance that comes from trees and is used for making PERFUME and INCENSE

myr·tle /ˈmɜːtl $ ˈmɜːr-/ *n* [C] a small tree with shiny green leaves and white flowers that smell nice

my·self /maɪˈself/ ●●● S1 W1 *pron* [reflexive form of 'I']
1 used by the person speaking or writing to show that they are affected by their own action: *I blame myself for what has happened.* | *I can look after myself.* | *I'm making myself a sandwich.*
2 a) used to emphasize 'I' or 'me': *Why do I always have to do everything myself?* | *They say it's a beautiful place, but I myself have never been there.* **b)** used after 'like', 'as', or 'except' instead of 'me': *No one is to blame except myself.*
3 (all) by myself a) alone: *I'd like to be by myself for a while.* **b)** without help from anyone else: *I painted the house all by myself.*
4 not feel/be myself *informal* used when the person speaking does not feel well, or is not able to behave normally, for example because he or she is upset or ill: *I haven't been feeling myself lately.* | *Sorry, I'm not myself today. I've had some bad news.*
5 have sth (all) to myself to not have to share something with anyone else: *Everyone else had gone out and I had the apartment all to myself.*

mys·te·ri·ous /mɪˈstɪəriəs $ -ˈstɪr-/ ●●○ *adj*
1 mysterious events or situations are difficult to explain or understand: *The police are investigating the mysterious deaths of children at the hospital.* | *Benson later disappeared* ***in mysterious circumstances****.* | *There's something mysterious going on.* **THESAURUS** ▸ STRANGE
2 a mysterious person is someone who you know very little about and who seems strange or interesting SYN **enigmatic**: *I decided to find out more about my mysterious new neighbour.* | *a mysterious stranger*
3 someone who behaves in a mysterious way says very little about what they are doing SYN **secretive**: **[+about]** *Helen's being very mysterious about her plans.* | *She hid her thoughts behind a mysterious smile.* —**mysteriously** *adv*: *Jackson had mysteriously disappeared.*

mys·te·ry¹ /ˈmɪstəri/ ●●● W3 *n* (*plural* **mysteries**)
1 [C usually singular] an event, situation etc that people do not understand or cannot explain because they do not know enough about it: *Twenty years after the event, his death* ***remains a mystery****.* | *The way her mind worked* ***was*** *always* ***a mystery to*** *him.* | *'Why did he do it?' 'I don't know.* ***It's a complete mystery****.'* | *The police never* ***solved*** *the* ***mystery*** *of Gray's disappearance.* | *But why would anyone want to kill Jack?* ***The mystery deepened****.* | *What happened to the paintings after that is an* ***unsolved mystery****.* | *I don't know how he got the job – it's* ***one of life's little mysteries****.* | *How life began on Earth is one of the great mysteries of science.*
2 [U] the quality that something or someone has when they seem strange, secret, or difficult to understand or explain: *Her dark glasses gave her an* ***air of mystery****.* | *Annie knew that there was some* ***mystery surrounding*** *her birth.* | **be shrouded/veiled in mystery** *The circumstances of his death were veiled in mystery.*
3 [C usually plural] a subject, activity etc that is very

complicated, secret, or difficult to understand, and that people want to learn about: **the mysteries of sth** *his introduction to the mysteries of the perfume business*
4 [C] (*also* **murder mystery**) a story, film, or play about a murder, in which you are not told who the murderer is until the end: *an Agatha Christie mystery*

mystery² *adj* [only before noun] used to describe someone or something that people do not recognize or know anything about, especially when this causes great interest: **mystery man/woman** *Who was the mystery woman spotted on board the yacht with the prince?* | *a* ***mystery virus***

'mystery play *n* [C] a religious play from the Middle Ages, based on a story from the Bible

ˌmystery 'shopper *n* [C] someone whose job is to visit different shops, pretending to be someone who is buying something, but who is really collecting information about what goods people buy and why they buy them. The information is used when planning how to sell a particular product.

'mystery tour *n* [C] *BrE* a trip, usually by bus, in which people do not know exactly where they will be taken

mys·tic¹ /ˈmɪstɪk/ *n* [C] someone who practises MYSTICISM

mystic² *adj* another word for MYSTICAL

mys·tic·al /ˈmɪstɪkəl/ ●○○ (*also* **mystic**) *adj* [usually before noun]
1 involving religious, SPIRITUAL, or magical powers that people cannot understand: *music's spiritual and mystical powers*
2 relating to mysticism: *a mystic ritual* —**mystically** /-kli/ *adv*

mys·ti·cis·m /ˈmɪstɪsɪzəm/ *n* [U] a religious practice in which people try to get knowledge of truth and to become united with God through prayer and MEDITATION

mys·ti·fy /ˈmɪstɪfaɪ/ *v* (**mystified, mystifying, mystifies**) [T] if something mystifies you, it is so strange or confusing that you cannot understand or explain it SYN **baffle**: *Her disappearance has mystified her friends and neighbors.* —**mystifying** *adj*: *Snake charming is always fascinating and at times mystifying.*

mys·tique /mɪˈstiːk/ *n* [U] a quality that makes someone or something seem mysterious, exciting, or special: *Some of the mystique surrounding the presidency has gone forever.*

myth /mɪθ/ ●●● S3 W3 *n* [C,U]
1 an idea or story that many people believe, but which is not true SYN **fallacy**: **[+of]** *the myth of male superiority* | **myth that** *It was important to dispel the myth that AIDS was a gay disease.*
2 an ancient story, especially one invented in order to explain natural or historical events → **mythology**: *a book of Greek myths* | **[+of]** *the myth of Orpheus* | *the giants of myth and fairytale* → URBAN MYTH **THESAURUS** ▸ STORY

COLLOCATIONS

VERBS

create a myth *Stalin created a lot of myths about himself.*
believe a myth *People still believe the myth that money will bring them happiness.*
explode/dispel/debunk a myth (=show that it is not true) *Our goal is to debunk the myth that science is boring.*
perpetuate a myth (=make it continue) | **a myth grows up** (=starts)

ADJECTIVES

a common/popular myth (=that many people believe) *Contrary to popular myth, most road accidents are not the result of speeding.*
a modern myth | **a powerful myth** (=that has a lot of influence on people) | **an enduring myth** (=that has continued for a long time)

PHRASES

be a complete/total myth *It's a complete myth that eating carrots helps you to see in the dark.*
be a bit of a myth (=be not really true) | **the myths surrounding sth** (=relating to something)

myth·ic /ˈmɪθɪk/ (*also* **mythical**) *adj* [usually before noun]
1 very great or famous: *He became a mythic figure in publishing.* **2** **mythic proportions** very great size or importance: *a feat of mythic proportions*

myth·i·cal /ˈmɪθɪkəl/ (*also* **mythic**) *adj* [usually before noun] **1** existing only in an ancient story: *a mythical creature like the Minotaur* **2** imagined or invented: *all these mythical job prospects he keeps talking about*

my·thol·o·gy /mɪˈθɒlədʒi $ -ˈθɑː-/ ●○○ *n* (*plural* **mythologies**) [C,U]
1 set of ancient myths: *characters from classical mythology* | **[+of]** *the mythology of the Persians*
2 ideas or opinions that many people have, but that are wrong or not true: *According to* ***popular mythology****, school days are the best days of your life.* —**mythological** /ˌmɪθəˈlɒdʒɪkəl◂ $ -ˈlɑː-/ *adj*: *The walls are painted with mythological scenes.*

myx·o·ma·to·sis /ˌmɪksəməˈtəʊsɪs $ -ˈtoʊ-/ *n* [U] a disease that kills rabbits

M

N n

N¹, **n** /en/ (*plural* **N's**, **n's**) *n* [C,U] **1** the 14th letter of the English alphabet **2** used in mathematics to represent a number whose value is not known: *The value of n is less than 10.*

N² the written abbreviation of ***north*** or ***northern***

n. (*also* **n** *BrE*) the written abbreviation of ***noun***

'n' /n, ən/ *written informal* a short form of 'and': *rock 'n' roll | fish 'n' chips*

N/A (***not applicable***) written on a form to show that you do not need to answer a question

naan /nɑːn/ *n* [U] another spelling of NAN²

nab /næb/ *v* (**nabbed**, **nabbing**) [T] *informal* **1** to catch or ARREST someone who is doing something wrong: *The police nabbed him for speeding.* **2** to get something or someone quickly, especially before anyone else can get them: *See if you can nab a seat.*

nach·os /ˈnætʃəʊz $ ˈnɑːtʃoʊz/ *n* [plural] Mexican food consisting of small pieces of TORTILLAS covered with cheese, beans etc

na·cre /ˈneɪkə $ -ər/ *n* [U] MOTHER-OF-PEARL

na·dir /ˈneɪdɪə $ -dər/ *n* [singular] *written* the time when a situation is at its worst OPP **zenith**: *By 1932, the depression had* ***reached*** *its* ***nadir***.

nads /nædz/ *n* [plural] *AmE spoken informal* TESTICLES

naff¹ /næf/ *adj BrE informal* something that is naff seems silly, especially because it is unfashionable or shows a lack of good taste → **tacky**: *a really naff film | Babur says the uniform makes him look naff.*

naff² *v*

naff off *phr v BrE spoken informal* used to tell someone rudely to go away

nag¹ /næg/ *v* (**nagged**, **nagging**) [I,T] **1** to keep asking someone to do something, or to keep complaining to someone about their behaviour, in an annoying way → **pester**: *I wish you'd stop nagging!* | **nag sb to do sth** *Nadia's been nagging me to fix the lamp.* | **nag sb about sth** *She keeps nagging me about my weight.* | **[+at]** *He's always nagging at Paula for wearing too much makeup.* **THESAURUS** ASK **2** to make someone feel continuously worried or uncomfortable: **[+at]** *a problem that had been nagging at him for days | One question still nagged me.*

nag² *n* [C] *informal* **1** a person who keeps complaining or asking someone to do something, in an annoying way: *Don't be such a nag!* **2** *old-fashioned* a horse, especially one that is old or in bad condition

nag·ging /ˈnægɪŋ/ *adj* [only before noun] **1** making you worry or feel pain slightly all the time: **nagging feeling/doubt/suspicion etc** *There was still a nagging doubt in the back of her mind. | Lee had a* ***nagging pain*** *in her back.* **2** always complaining: *a nagging wife*

nah /nɑː/ *adv informal* no

nail¹ /neɪl/ ●●● S3 *n* [C]

1 a thin pointed piece of metal with a flat top, which you hit into a surface with a hammer, for example to join things together or to hang something on: *The key was hanging on a nail by the door.* | **hammer/bang/hit a nail into sth** *She hammered a nail into the wall.* → see picture at SCREW

2 your nails are the hard smooth layers on the ends of your fingers and toes: *I've* ***broken*** *my* ***nail***. *| Stop* ***biting*** *your* ***nails***! *| She sat* ***painting*** *her* ***nails*** (=putting a coloured substance on them). *| He still had dirt under his nails.* → FINGERNAIL, TOENAIL

3 nail in sb's/sth's coffin one of several bad things which help to destroy someone's success or hopes: *Observers fear that this strike will be* ***another nail in the coffin*** *of the industry. | the* ***final nail in*** *his* ***coffin***

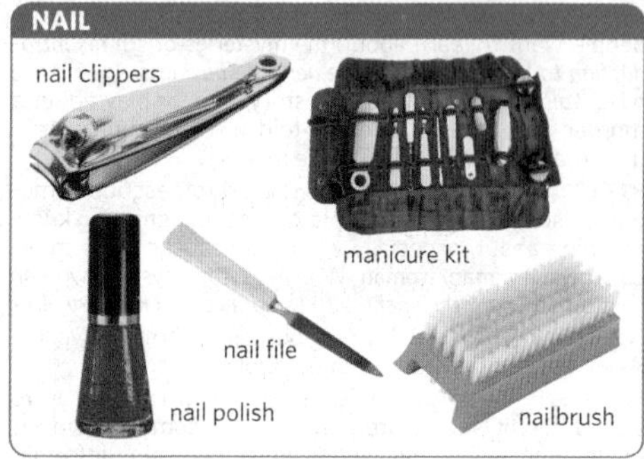

4 as hard/tough as nails very TOUGH and not easily frightened, or not caring about the effects of your actions on other people

5 on the nail a) *BrE* if you pay money on the nail, you pay it immediately **b)** *especially AmE* completely correct: *They* ***got it*** *absolutely* ***on the nail***. → **hit the nail on the head** at HIT¹(26)

nail² *v* [T] **1** [always + adv/prep] to fasten something to something else with nails: **nail sth to sth** *A sign saying 'No Fishing' had been nailed to the tree.* | **nail sth down** *The lid was firmly nailed down.* | **nail sth up** (=permanently close a window or door by fixing something across it using nails) *The windows had been nailed up.* **2** *informal* to catch someone and prove that they are guilty of a crime or something bad: *It took us 10 years to nail the guy who killed our daughter.* | **nail sb for sth** *The state police finally nailed him for fraud.* **3** *informal* if you nail something, you succeed in getting it, after a lot of time or effort: *She finally nailed her dream job.* **4** *informal* to do something perfectly, especially when singing or performing: *I thought that song might be too big for you, but you absolutely* ***nailed it***! **5 nail a lie/myth** *BrE informal* to prove that what someone has said is completely untrue **6 nail your colours to the mast** *BrE* to say clearly and publicly which ideas or which people you support **7 nail sb to the wall/cross** *especially AmE* to punish someone severely

nail sb/sth ↔ **down** *phr v informal* **1** to reach a final and definite agreement or decision about something: *Two days isn't enough time to nail down the details of an agreement.* **2 nail sb down** to force someone to say clearly what they want or what they intend to do: **[+to]** *Before they repair the car, nail them down to a price.*

ˈnail bar *n* [C] a shop where you can have your nails made more attractive SYN **nail salon**

ˈnail-ˌbiter *n* [C] *informal* a very exciting story, film etc

ˈnail-ˌbiting *adj* [only before noun] extremely exciting because you do not know what is going to happen next: *The match went all the way to a nail-biting finish. | some nail-biting moments near the end of the movie* **THESAURUS** EXCITING

nail·brush /ˈneɪlbrʌʃ/ *n* [C] a small stiff brush for cleaning your fingernails

ˈnail ˌclippers *n* [plural] a special tool for cutting your nails neatly

ˈnail file *n* [C] a thin piece of metal with a rough surface used for making your nails a nice shape

nail·gun /ˈneɪlgʌn/ *n* [C] a tool that uses air to shoot nails into wood

ˈnail ˌpolish (*also* **ˈnail ˌvarnish** *BrE*) *n* [U] coloured or transparent liquid which you paint on your nails to make them look attractive: *pink nail polish*

ˈnail ˌsalon / $ ˈ. ˌ./ (*also* **ˈnail bar**) *n* [C] a shop where you can have your nails made more attractive

ˈnail ˌscissors *n* [plural] a small pair of scissors for cutting your nails

na·ive /naɪˈiːv/ ●○○ *adj* not having much experience of how complicated life is, so that you trust people too much and believe that good things will always happen → **innocent**: *a naive young girl | Jim can be so naive sometimes.* | **it is naive to think/suppose/assume etc** *It would be naive to think that this could solve all the area's problems straight away.* —**naively** *adv*: *I had naively imagined that he was in love with me.* —**naivety** /naɪˈiːvəti/ (*also* **naiveté** /naɪˈiːvəteɪ/) *n* [U]: *dangerous political naivety*

na·ked /ˈneɪkɪd/ ●●● S3 *adj*
1 not wearing any clothes or not covered by clothes SYN **nude** → **bare**: *The children ran naked through the yard. | a picture of a naked man | They found the body lying **half naked** in the grass. | The governor ordered the prisoner to be **stripped naked** and whipped.* | **stark naked** (*also* **buck naked/naked as a jaybird** *AmE*) (=completely naked)

> **REGISTER**
> In everyday English, people often say that someone **has nothing on** or **doesn't have anything on** rather than say they **are naked**: *They ran through the yard **with nothing on**.*

2 the naked eye if you can see something with the naked eye, you can see it without using anything to help you, such as a TELESCOPE: **visible to/with the naked eye** *The mite is just visible to the naked eye. | Through his telescope he could see millions of stars that were **invisible to the naked eye**.*
3 weak and unable to protect yourself: *Standing in front on his first day of teaching, Brad **felt** completely **naked**.*
4 naked truth/self-interest/aggression etc truth, SELF-INTEREST, AGGRESSION etc that is not hidden and is shocking: *The president condemned the invasion as an act of naked aggression.*
5 naked light/flame/sword etc a light, flame etc that is not enclosed by a cover: *A naked light bulb dangled from the ceiling.* —**nakedly** *adv* —**nakedness** *n* [U]

nam·by-pam·by /ˌnæmbi ˈpæmbi◂/ *adj informal* too weak and gentle and not strict or TOUGH enough: *For some people soccer has a reputation as a rather namby-pamby sport.* —**namby-pamby** *n* [C]

name[1] /neɪm/ ●●● S1 W1 *n*
1 OF A PERSON [C] what someone is called: *Her name is Mandy Wilson. | What's your last name?* | **by the name of sth** (=called something) *He married a young lady by the name of Sarah Hunt.* | **under the name (of) sth** (=using a different name from your real name) *HH Munro wrote under the name Saki.*
2 OF A THING OR PLACE [C] what a thing, organization, or place is called: **[+of]** *What's the name of the street? | The name of the company has changed.* | **[+for]** *Edo was the ancient name for Tokyo. | The flower's **common name** (=name that is used by ordinary people, not its scientific name) is forget-me-not.* THESAURUS▸ WORD
3 REPUTATION [singular] the opinion that people have about a person or organization SYN **reputation**: *He didn't want to do anything to damage the **good name** of the company. | The restaurant got a **bad name** for slow service. | They **give** the rest of the fans **a bad name**. | The company **has a name for** reliability.* | **make your name/make a name for yourself** (=become famous for something) *He quickly made a name for himself in the Parisian art world.* | **clear your name** (=prove that you did not do something bad or illegal) THESAURUS▸ REPUTATION
4 FAMOUS PERSON/COMPANY/PRODUCT [C] *informal* a person, company, or product that is very famous or is known by many people: **big/famous/household name** *some of the biggest names in show business | It made the company into a household name* (=a very well-known person or thing). THESAURUS▸ STAR
5 call sb names to use unpleasant words to describe someone in order to insult or upset them: *The other kids used to call me names.* | **call sb all the names under the sun** (=use many unpleasant words)
6 in sb's name/in the name of sb a) if something is in someone's name, it officially belongs to them or is for them to use: *The house is in my husband's name. | I've booked a table in the name of Steinmann.* **b)** *formal* as someone else's official representative: *I claim this land in the name of the King!*
7 sth has sb's name on it something seems to be appropriate for or deserved by a particular person: *The match has England's name on it* (=they will win it).
8 in the name of religion/freedom/science etc using religion, freedom etc as the reason why something is done - used especially when you disapprove of what someone is doing: *cruel experiments on animals carried out in the name of science | the things people do in the name of love*
9 have sth to your name *informal* to have or own something - used to emphasize that someone has very little or a lot of something: *He died **without a penny to his name*** (=very poor). | *He didn't have a qualification to his name.*
10 the name of the game *informal* the most important thing in a particular activity or situation: *Quality, that's the name of the game.*
11 cannot put a name to sth *spoken* used to say that someone is not able to say what something is called: *I know the tune but I can't put a name to it.*
12 take sb's name in vain to talk about someone without showing respect for them: *How dare you **take the Lord's name in vain*** (=swear using a word such as 'God' or 'Jesus')?
13 in name only/alone if a situation exists in name only, it does not really exist even though officially people say it does: *a democracy in name only | He was president in name only.*
14 in all/everything but name if something is true in all but name, it is really true, even though people do not officially say that it is true: *She was his wife in all but name.*
15 sb's name is mud *informal* used to say that people are angry with someone because of something he or she has done - used especially humorously: *If anything goes wrong, your name will be mud.* → **drag sb's name through the mud** at DRAG[1](10), → PEN NAME

> **COLLOCATIONS**
> **VERBS**
> **have a name** *All their children have French names.*
> **give sb a name** *They gave their children unusual names.*
> **use a name** (=tell people that you have a particular name) *She may be using a false name.*
> **take a name** (=choose to have a new name) *Are you going to take your husband's name when you get married?*
> **change your name** *Many immigrants changed their names to seem more American.*
> **give (sb) your name** (=tell someone your name, especially someone in an official position) *I gave my name to the receptionist.*
> **know sb's name** *His first name is Tom, but I don't know his last name.*
> **use sb's name** (=say their name when speaking to them) *I didn't know him well enough to use his first name.*
> **call sb's name** (=say someone's name loudly, to get their attention) *He called Jean's name, but there was no answer.*
> **sign your name** *Sign your name here, please.*
> **PHRASES**
> **call sb by their first/full etc name** (=use that name when you speak to them) *Everyone called him by his first name.*
> **go by the name of ...** (=be called something by people, often when that is not your real name) *As he had long red hair, he went by the name of Red.*
> **know sb by name** (=know their name) *The headteacher knew all the children by name.*
> **greet sb by name** (=use someone's name when you see them) *The waiter greeted him by name.*

> **THESAURUS**
> **first name** (*also* **given name** *especially AmE formal*) the name chosen for you by your parents: *People*

N

usually call each other by their first name. | Please write your given name and your date of birth.
Christian name *old-fashioned* first name: *His Christian name was Joseph.*
last name/family name/surname the name that you share with your family or husband. Most English speakers would say **last name. Surname** sounds slightly formal: *Can I have your last name? | Johnson is a common English family name.*
middle name the name between your first and last names: *Harry Potter's middle name is James.*
full name your first name, middle name, and last name: *I need your full name and address.*
maiden name a woman's family name before she married and began using her husband's name: *My mother's maiden name was Higgins.*
married name a woman's family name after she gets married, if she uses her husband's name: *I don't know what her married name is.*
nickname a name that people call you because of your appearance, personality etc, which is not your real name: *At school he was given the nickname 'Shorty'.*
alias /ˈeɪliəs/ a false name, especially one used by a criminal: *He uses a number of aliases.*

name² ●●● S2 W2 *v* [T]
1 GIVE SB A NAME to give someone or something a particular name → **call**: **name sb John/Ann etc** *We named our daughter Sarah.* | **name sb/sth after sb/sth** (=give someone or something the same name as another person or thing) *He was named after his father. | The street is named after the famous South African leader, Nelson Mandela.* | **name sth for sb/sth** *AmE* (=give something the same name as a person or thing) *The college is named for George Washington.* | **a man/woman etc named sth** (=someone with a particular name) *some guy named Bob Dylan*

REGISTER
In everyday English, people usually say someone or something is **called** something rather than **named** something: *He had a friend* ***called*** *Mick.*

2 SAY SB'S OR STH'S NAME to say what the name of someone or something is, especially officially: *The two murder victims have yet to be named.* | **name sb as sth** *The woman who was shot has been named as Mary Radcliff. | She has secret information and is threatening to* ***name names*** (=name the people who were involved in something, especially something bad or illegal). | *They're a lot better than some airlines I* ***could name***. | **name and shame** *BrE* (=say publicly who is responsible for something illegal that has happened, or who has not achieved a particular standard)
3 CHOOSE SB to officially choose someone or something, especially for an important job or prize: **name sb/sth (as) sth** *The film was named best foreign film. | Quinn has been named as the new team manager.* | **name sb to sth** *AmE*: *Fitzgerald was named to the committee by the chairman.*
4 to name but a few/a handful/three etc used after a short list of things or people to say that there are many more you could mention
5 you name it (they've got it)! *spoken* used after a list of things to mean that there are many more you could mention: *Clothes, books – you name it, they've got it!*
6 name the day/date to decide on a date for your wedding
7 name your price *spoken* to say how much you are willing to pay for something or sell something for

ˈname brand *n* [C] *AmE* a popular and well-known product name —**name-brand** *adj* [only before noun]: *name-brand climbing gear* → BRAND NAME

ˈname-ˌcalling *n* [U] when people use unpleasant words to describe someone in order to insult or upset them: *playground teasing including name-calling*

ˈname-check *v* [T] to mention a particular product, person, business etc in something such as an advertisement or speech, or to mention them in order to thank them —**namechecking** *n* [U]

ˈname day *n* [C] the day each year when people of some Christian religions celebrate the particular SAINT (=holy person) whose name they have been given

ˈname-ˌdropping *n* [U] when someone mentions the name of a famous person they have met or have some connection with, in order to seem impressive to other people – used humorously or to show disapproval: *I didn't want to be accused of name-dropping.* —**name-drop** *v* [I] —**name-dropper** *n* [C]

name·less /ˈneɪmləs/ *adj* **1 who shall remain nameless** *spoken* used when you want to say that someone has done something wrong but without mentioning their name, especially to criticize them in a friendly way: *A certain person, who shall remain nameless, forgot to lock the front door.* **2** [only before noun] a nameless person is someone whose name is not known: *the work of some nameless 13th-century writer* **3** [only before noun] a nameless thing does not have a name: *He lay in a nameless grave.* **4** [only before noun] *literary* nameless emotions are very strong and difficult to describe in words: *He managed to calm her nameless fears.* **5** [only before noun] *literary* too terrible to name or describe: *nameless horrors*

name·ly /ˈneɪmli/ ●●○ *adv formal or written* used when saying the names of the people or things you are referring to: *Three students were mentioned, namely John, Sarah and Sylvia.*

name·plate /ˈneɪmpleɪt/ *n* [C] a small sign fastened to something, showing the name of the owner or maker, or the person who lives or works in a place

name·sake /ˈneɪmseɪk/ *n* **sb's namesake** another person, especially a more famous person, who has the same name as someone: *Like his famous namesake, young Washington had a brave, adventurous spirit.*

ˈname tag *n* [C] a small sign with your name on it that you wear

ˈname-tape *n* [C] *BrE* a small piece of cloth with your name on it that is sewn onto clothes, especially schoolchildren's clothes SYN **label** *AmE*

nan¹ /næn/ (*also* **nan·na**) /ˈnænə/ *n* [C] *BrE informal* grandmother – used by children SYN **nanny**

nan², **naan** /nɑːn/ (*also* **ˈnan bread**) *n* [U] a type of bread made without YEAST and eaten with Indian food

nan·ny /ˈnæni/ *n* (*plural* **nannies**) [C] **1** a woman whose job is to take care of the children in a family, usually in the family's own home: *She found a job as a nanny with a wealthy Italian family.* **2** *BrE informal* grandmother – used by children SYN **nan 3 the nanny state** *especially BrE* a government which tries to control the lives of its citizens too much

ˈnanny goat *n* [C] a female goat → **billy goat**

nano- /nænəʊ $ -oʊ/ *prefix* [in nouns] one BILLIONTH part of a unit: *nanometre* (=a billionth of a metre)

nan·o·bot /ˈnænəʊbɒt $ -noʊbɑːt/ *n* [C] in stories and films about the future, a machine that can move and perform jobs, but which is so small that it cannot be seen unless you use special equipment such as a MICROSCOPE

nan·o·ma·chine /ˈnænəʊməʃiːn $ -noʊ-/ (*also* **nan·ite** /ˈnænaɪt/) *n* [C] a machine so small that its parts are made of single MOLECULES. Scientists are trying to make nanomachines for use in medicine.

nan·o·pub·lish·ing, **nano-publishing** /ˌnænəʊˈpʌblɪʃɪŋ $ -noʊ-/ *n* [U] the activity of putting information about a particular subject on a website, usually information sent by people who use the website regularly and are interested in the subject —**nanopublisher** *n* [C]

nan·o·sec·ond /ˈnænəʊˌsekənd $ -noʊ-/ *n* [C] a unit for measuring time. There are a BILLION nanoseconds in a second.

nan·o·tech·nol·o·gy /ˌnænəʊtekˈnɒlədʒi $ -noʊtekˈnɑː-/ *n* [U] *technical* a science which involves developing and making extremely small but very powerful machines

nap¹ /næp/ ●●○ *n*
1 [C] a short sleep, especially during the day: **have/take a nap** *I usually take a nap after lunch.* | *an* ***afternoon nap***
2 [singular] the soft surface on some cloth and leather, made by brushing the short fine threads or hairs in one direction → PILE¹(7)

nap² *v* (**napped**, **napping**) [I] **1 be caught napping** *informal* to not be ready to deal with something when it happens, although you should be ready for it: *The German team were caught napping and Lampard scored the winning goal.* **2** to sleep for a short time during the day

na·palm /ˈneɪpɑːm $ -pɑːm, -pɑːlm/ *n* [U] a substance made from petrol that was used in bombs by US forces to burn fields and villages during the Vietnam war

nape /neɪp/ *n* [singular] *literary* the bottom part of the back of your neck, where the hair ends: ***the*** *soft warm* ***nape of*** *her* ***neck***

naph·tha·lene /ˈnæfθəliːn/ (*also* **naph·tha** /ˈnæfθə/) *n* [U] a type of oil used for FUEL or for making chemicals

nap·kin /ˈnæpkɪn/ *n* [C] **1** a square piece of cloth or paper used for protecting your clothes and for cleaning your hands and lips during a meal SYN **serviette 2** a SANITARY PAD

ˈnapkin ˌring *n* [C] a small ring which a napkin can be kept in

nap·py /ˈnæpi/ *n* (*plural* **nappies**) [C] *BrE* a piece of soft cloth or paper worn by a baby between its legs and fastened around its waist to hold its liquid and solid waste SYN **diaper** *AmE*: *Excuse me while I* ***change*** *the baby's* ***nappy***. | *a* ***dirty nappy*** | **disposable nappies** (=nappies which are made to be used once and thrown away) | **nappy rash** (=sore skin caused by wet nappies)

Nap·ster /ˈnæpstə $ -ər/ *trademark* a former Internet service which allowed people to DOWNLOAD songs for free. It was the first service of its kind. It was shut down by a COURT ORDER in 1999.

narc¹ /nɑːk $ nɑːrk/ *n* [C] *AmE informal* a police officer who deals with the problem of illegal drugs

narc² *v* [I + on] *AmE informal* to secretly tell the police about someone else's criminal activities, especially activities involving illegal drugs

nar·cis·sis·m /ˈnɑːsɪsɪzəm $ ˈnɑːr-/ *n* [U] when someone is too concerned about their appearance or abilities or spends too much time admiring them – used to show disapproval: *He went to the gym every day, driven purely by narcissism.* —**narcissist** *n* [C] —**narcissistic** /ˌnɑːsəˈsɪstɪk◂ $ ˌnɑːr-/ *adj*

nar·cis·sus /nɑːˈsɪsəs $ nɑːr-/ *n* (*plural* **narcissi** /-saɪ/) [C] a yellow or white spring flower, such as the DAFFODIL → see picture at **FLOWER**

nar·co·lep·sy /ˈnɑːkəˌlepsi $ ˈnɑːr-/ *n* [U] *medical* a medical condition which causes someone to keep falling asleep suddenly, without being able to prevent this

nar·cot·ic¹ /nɑːˈkɒtɪk $ nɑːrˈkɑː-/ *n* [C] **1 narcotics** [plural] *especially AmE* strong illegal drugs such as HEROIN or COCAINE: *the narcotics trade* | **narcotics agent** (=a police officer who deals with the problems of narcotics) **2** a type of drug which makes you sleep and reduces pain

narcotic² *adj* **1** [only before noun] *especially AmE* relating to illegal drugs: *narcotic addiction* **2** a narcotic drug takes away pain or makes you sleep

nark /nɑːk $ nɑːrk/ *n* [C] *informal especially BrE* someone who is friendly with criminals and who secretly tells the police about their activities SYN **informer**

narked /nɑːkt $ nɑːrkt/ (*also* **nark·y** /ˈnɑːki $ ˈnɑːr-/) *adj* [not before noun] *BrE informal* angry about something: *There's no need to* ***get narked*** *about it!*

nar·rate /nəˈreɪt $ ˈnæreɪt, næˈreɪt, nə-/ ●○○ *v* [T] *formal*
1 to explain what is happening in a film or television programme as part of the film or programme: *a wildlife film narrated by David Attenborough*
2 to tell a story by describing all the events in order, for example in a book → **narrator**: *The main character narrates the story.*

nar·ra·tion /nəˈreɪʃən $ næ-, nə-/ *n* [C,U] **1** a spoken description or explanation which is given during a film, play etc **2** *formal* the act of telling a story

nar·ra·tive /ˈnærətɪv/ ●○○ *n formal*
1 [C] a description of events in a story, especially in a NOVEL: *At several points in the narrative the two stories cross.*
2 [U] the process or skill of telling a story —**narrative** *adj*: *a narrative poem* | *narrative structure*

nar·ra·tor /nəˈreɪtə $ ˈnæreɪtər, næˈreɪtər, nə-/ ●○○ *n* [C]
1 the person who tells the story in a book or a play
2 the person who describes or explains what is happening in a film or television programme but who is not seen

nar·row¹ /ˈnærəʊ $ -roʊ/ ●●● S3 W2 *adj*
1 NOT WIDE measuring only a small distance from one side to the other, especially in relation to the length OPP **wide** → **broad**: **narrow street/road/path etc** *a long narrow road* | *the narrow passage between the cottage and the house* | *his narrow bed* | *The stairs were very narrow.* | *a long, narrow band of cloud* → see picture at **THIN**
2 narrow escape a situation in which you only just avoid danger, difficulties, or trouble: *A woman* ***had a narrow escape*** *yesterday when her car left the road.* | *He was shaken by his narrow escape from death.*
3 narrow victory/defeat/majority/margin etc a victory etc that is only just achieved or happens by only a small amount → **slim**: *The president won a narrow victory in the election.* | *He persuaded a narrow majority of the party to support the government.* | *Scotland eventually won the match by the narrow margin of 5–4.*

> **REGISTER**
> The expression **a narrow victory/defeat** is used mostly in writing. In everyday British English, people often say that someone **only just won/lost** or, in everyday American English, **barely won/lost**.

4 IDEAS/ATTITUDES a narrow attitude or way of looking at a situation is too limited and does not consider enough possibilities OPP **broad**: *You've got a very* ***narrow view*** *of life.* | *Some teachers have a narrow vision of what art is.* → NARROW-MINDED
5 narrow sense/definition a meaning of a word that is exact or limited OPP **broad**: *I use the word 'neighbour' in its more precise or narrower sense.*
6 LIMITED limited in range or number of things OPP **broad**: *The company offered only a narrow range of financial services.* —**narrowness** *n* [U] → **NARROWLY**, **NARROWS**, → **the straight and narrow** at **STRAIGHT³**(2)

narrow² ●○○ *v* [I,T]
1 to make something narrower, or to become narrower OPP **widen**: *He* ***narrowed*** *his* ***eyes*** *and gazed at the horizon.* | *The track divided into two and narrowed.*
2 if a range, difference etc narrows, or if something narrows it, it becomes less OPP **widen**: *The choice of goods available is narrowing.* | *The economic gap between the two halves of the country was beginning to narrow.*
narrow sth ↔ **down** *phr v* to reduce the number of things included in a range: *The police have narrowed down their list of suspects.* | **[+to]** *I've narrowed it down to one of two people.*

ˈnarrow ˌboat *n* [C] *BrE* a long narrow boat for use on CANALS

ˈnarrow ˌgauge *n* [C,U] a size of railway track of less than standard width: *a narrow gauge railway*

nar·row·ly /ˈnærəʊli $ -roʊ-/ ●○○ *adv*
1 by only a small amount: *He was narrowly defeated in the election.* | *One bullet struck his car, narrowly missing him.* | *A man narrowly escaped death when a fire broke out in his home on Sunday morning.*
2 in a limited way OPP **broadly**: *The law is being interpreted too narrowly.* | *These big general issues should be broken down into more narrowly focused questions.*

N

ˌnarrow-ˈminded / $ ˈ.. ˌ../ *adj* unwilling to accept or understand new or different ideas, opinions, or customs SYN **prejudiced** OPP **broadminded**: *His attitude is narrow-minded and insensitive.* | *narrow-minded nationalism* —**narrow-mindedness** *n* [U]

nar·rows /ˈnærəʊz $ -roʊz/ *n* [plural] **1** a narrow area of water between two pieces of land which connects two larger areas of water: *There are really three lakes, joined by narrows.* **2** *AmE* a narrow part of a river, lake etc

na·ry /ˈneəri $ ˈneri/ *adv old-fashioned* **nary a sth** not one: *They said nary a word.*

NASA /ˈnæsə/ *n* (***National Aeronautics and Space Administration***) a US government organization that controls space travel and the scientific study of space

na·sal¹ /ˈneɪzəl/ *adj* **1** [only before noun] related to the nose: *the nasal passage* **2** a sound or voice that is nasal comes mainly through your nose: *He spoke in a high nasal voice.* **3** [only before noun] *technical* a nasal CONSONANT or vowel such as /n/ or /m/ is one that is produced completely or partly through your nose —**nasally** *adv*

nasal² *n* [C] *technical* a particular speech sound such as /m/, /n/, or /ŋ/ that is made through your nose

nas·cent /ˈnæsənt/ *adj* [usually before noun] *formal* coming into existence or starting to develop: *the country's nascent democracy* | *their nascent industries*

Nash·ville /ˈnæʃvɪl/ the capital city of the state of Tennessee, US, famous as the centre of the COUNTRY AND WESTERN music industry → **GRAND OLE OPRY, THE**

nas·tur·tium /nəˈstɜːʃəm $ -ɜːr-/ *n* [C] a garden plant with orange, yellow, or red flowers and circular leaves

nas·ty /ˈnɑːsti $ ˈnæsti/ ●●● S2 *adj* (*comparative* **nastier**, *superlative* **nastiest**)

1 BEHAVIOUR nasty behaviour or remarks are extremely unkind and unpleasant: *a nasty temper* | *the nasty things that were being written about her* | *There's a nasty streak in her character.* | *Drivers often have a* ***nasty habit*** *of driving too close to cyclists.* | **[+to]** *Don't be so nasty to your mum* (=do not treat her unkindly). | **get/turn nasty** *especially BrE* (=suddenly start behaving in a threatening way) *When Harry refused, Don turned nasty and went for him with both fists.* **THESAURUS▸** UNKIND

2 PERSON someone who is nasty behaves in an unkind and unpleasant way: *I went to school with him – he was nasty then and he's nasty now.* | *You're a* ***nasty little*** *brute!*

3 EXPERIENCE/SITUATION a nasty experience, feeling, or situation is unpleasant: **nasty shock/surprise** *It gave me a nasty shock.* | **nasty feeling/suspicion** *I had a nasty feeling that a tragedy was going to happen.* | *Life has a* ***nasty habit*** *of repeating itself.* | *He had a* ***nasty accident*** *while riding in the forest.* | *When you feel you've been cheated, it always* ***leaves a nasty taste in*** *the* ***mouth*** (=makes you feel upset or angry afterwards). | *The weather* ***turned nasty*** *towards the evening.*

4 SIGHT/SMELL ETC having a bad appearance, smell, taste etc: *What's that nasty smell?* | *a market stall selling* ***cheap and nasty*** *watches* **THESAURUS▸** HORRIBLE

5 INJURY/ILLNESS severe or very painful: *a nasty cut* | *He was carried off the field with a nasty injury.*

6 SUBSTANCE a nasty substance is dangerous: *nasty chemicals*

7 **a nasty piece of work** *BrE* someone who is dishonest, violent, or likely to cause trouble —**nastily** *adv* —**nastiness** *n* [U] → **VIDEO NASTY**

na·tal /ˈneɪtl/ *adj technical* relating to birth: *Green turtles return to their natal island to breed.*

natch /nætʃ/ *adv spoken informal* used to say that something is exactly as you would expect SYN **naturally**: *'What does he drive?' 'A BMW, natch.'*

na·tion /ˈneɪʃən/ ●●● S3 W2 *n* [C]

1 a country, considered especially in relation to its people and its social or economic structure: *the president's radio broadcast to the nation* | *an independent nation* | *the world's leading industrial nations* **THESAURUS▸** COUNTRY

2 a large group of people of the same race and language: *the Cherokee nation*

na·tion·al¹ /ˈnæʃənəl/ ●●● S1 W1 *adj*

1 related to a whole nation as opposed to any of its parts → **local**: *Religion matters very much at a national level.* | *Between 1929 and 1933 America's national income fell by more than half.* | *There are strong indications that the prime minister will call national elections in May.*

2 relating to one particular nation as opposed to other nations → **international**: *We refuse to sign any treaty that is against our national interests.*

3 [only before noun] owned or controlled by the central government of a country: *the National Institute for Space Research* | *the national airline* → **NATIONALLY**

national² *n* [C] someone who is a citizen of a particular country but is living in another country → **alien**, **citizen**, **subject**: ***Foreign nationals*** *were advised to leave the country.* | **French/EU/Japanese etc national** *Turkish nationals who are living in the UK*

ˌnational ˈanthem *n* [C] the official song of a nation that is sung or played on public occasions

ˌnational ˈcostume *n* [C,U] special clothing traditionally worn by the people of a particular country: *folk dancers in national costume*

ˌNational Curˈriculum *n* **the National Curriculum** the course of study that most students follow in England and Wales between the ages of five and 16

ˌnational ˈdebt *n* [C usually singular] the total amount of money owed by the government of a country: *The government taxed fuel highly in order to finance the national debt.*

ˌnational ˈdress *n* [U] NATIONAL COSTUME

ˌNational Enˈquirer, The *trademark* a US weekly TABLOID newspaper known especially for its articles about the relationships of famous people and the things that they do

ˌNational ˈGrid *n* **the National Grid** the system of electricity lines across Britain

ˌNational ˈGuard *n* **the National Guard** a military force in each state of the US which can be used when it is needed by the state or the US government

ˌNational ˈHealth ˌService, the (*abbreviation* **the NHS**) the state system for providing health care in Britain, paid for by taxes

ˌNational Inˈsurance *n* [U] a system organized by the British government in which workers and employers make regular payments, and which provides money for people who are unemployed, old, or ill

na·tion·al·ise /ˈnæʃənəlaɪz/ *v* [T] a British spelling of NATIONALIZE

na·tion·al·is·m /ˈnæʃənəlɪzəm/ ●○○ *n* [U]

1 the desire by a group of people of the same race, origin, language etc to form an independent country: *Scottish nationalism*

2 love for your own country and the belief that it is better than any other country → **patriotism**: *Under his leadership, a strong sense of nationalism emerged.*

na·tion·al·ist¹ /ˈnæʃənəlɪst/ *adj* [only before noun] **1** a nationalist organization, party etc wants to gain or keep political independence for their country and people: *the Scottish Nationalist Party* | *the rise of the nationalist movement* **2** a nationalist organization or party believes that their country is the most important or the best

nationalist² *n* [C] **1** someone who is involved in trying to gain or keep political independence for their country and people: *Welsh nationalists* **2** someone who believes their country is best → **patriot**

na·tion·al·is·tic /ˌnæʃənəˈlɪstɪk◂/ *adj* someone who is nationalistic believes that their country is better than other countries → **patriotic**: *They were encouraging nationalistic sentiment among the students.*

na·tion·al·i·ty /ˌnæʃəˈnæləti/ ●●○ *n* (*plural* **nationalities**)

1 [C,U] the state of being legally a citizen of a particular country → **citizenship**: *people of the same nationality* | **French/Brazilian etc nationality** *He has British nationality.* | **dual nationality** (=the state of being a citizen of two countries)

2 [C] a large group of people with the same race, origin, language etc: *the different nationalities within the former USSR*

na·tion·al·ize (*also* **-ise** *BrE*) /ˈnæʃənəlaɪz/ *v* [T] if a government nationalizes a very large industry such as water, gas, or the railways, it buys it or takes control of it → **privatize**: *The British government nationalized the railways in 1948.* | *a* ***nationalised industry*** —**nationalization** /ˌnæʃənəlaɪˈzeɪʃən $ -nələ-/ *n* [C,U]

na·tion·al·ly /ˈnæʃənəli/ ●●○ *adv* by or to everyone in the nation → **internationally**: *a nationally recognised qualification* | *The programme will be broadcast nationally.*

ˌnational ˈmonument *n* [C] a building, special feature of the land etc that is kept and protected by a government for people to visit

ˌnational ˈpark ●○○ *n* [C] land which is protected by a government because of its natural beauty or historical or scientific interest, and which people can visit: *Yosemite National Park*

ˌnational seˈcurity *n* [U] the idea that a country must keep its secrets safe and its army strong in order to protect its citizens: *The number of people who join the army is so low that it is beginning to threaten national security.*

ˌnational ˈservice *n* [U] the system of making all adults spend a period of time in the army, navy, or air force

ˌnational ˈtreasure *n* [C] a well-known person who is liked by most people in their country

na·tion·hood /ˈneɪʃənhʊd/ *n* [U] the state of being a nation

ˌnation ˈstate *n* [C] a nation that is a politically independent country: *European union is seen as a threat to the sovereignty of the nation state.*

na·tion·wide /ˌneɪʃənˈwaɪd◂, ˈneɪʃənwaɪd/ ●●○ *adj* [usually before noun] happening or existing in every part of the country SYN **countrywide**: *a nationwide search for a missing British tourist* | *nationwide television* —**nationwide** *adv*: *We have 350 sales outlets nationwide.*

na·tive[1] /ˈneɪtɪv/ ●●○ S3 W3 *adj*

1 COUNTRY [only before noun] your native country, town etc is the place where you were born → **home**: *They never saw their native land again.* | *He spent most of his professional life outside his native Poland.*

2 native New Yorker/population/inhabitants etc a person or people who come from or have always lived in a particular place

3 native language/tongue the language you spoke when you first learned to speak SYN **first language**: *English is not the native language for almost half of our overseas visitors.*

4 PLANT/ANIMAL growing, living, produced etc in one particular place SYN **indigenous**: *Singapore has many* ***native species*** *of palm.* | **[+to]** *These fish are native to North America.*

5 ART/CUSTOM [only before noun] native customs, traditions etc are related to people who lived in a particular country before European people arrived there: *the native traditions of Peru* | *stalls selling native jewelry* | *native folklore*

6 NATURAL [only before noun] a native ability is one that you have naturally from birth: *her native wit*

7 go native to behave, dress, or speak like the people who live in the country where you have come to stay or work – used humorously: *Austen has been living in New Guinea so long he's gone native.*

native[2] ●○○ *n* [C]

1 a person who was born in a particular place: **[+of]** *a native of Switzerland*

2 someone who lives in a place all the time or has lived there a long time: **[+of]** *He has become a native of Glasgow.*

3 [usually plural] *not polite* a word used by white people in the past to refer to the people who lived in America, Africa, southern Asia etc before European people arrived, now considered offensive: *He was not certain whether the natives were friendly.*

4 a plant or animal that grows or lives naturally in a place: **[+of]** *The bear was once a native of Britain.*

ˌNative Aˈmerican *n* [C] someone who belongs to one of the races that lived in North America before Europeans arrived

ˌnative ˈspeaker ●●○ *n* [C] someone who has learned a particular language as their first language, rather than as a foreign language → **non-native speaker**: *For the spoken language, students are taught by native speakers.* | **[+of]** *a native speaker of English*

Na·tiv·i·ty /nəˈtɪvəti/ *n* (*plural* **Nativities**) **1 the Nativity** the birth of Jesus Christ **2** [C] a picture or model of the baby Jesus Christ and his parents in the place where he was born: *a Nativity scene*

Naˈtivity ˌplay *n* [C] a play telling the story of the birth of Jesus Christ, performed by children at Christmas: *the school's Nativity play*

NATO /ˈneɪtəʊ $ -toʊ/ *n* (***North Atlantic Treaty Organization***) a group of countries including the US and several European countries, which give military help to each other: *our allies in NATO* | *a NATO country*

nat·ter[1] /ˈnætə $ -ər/ *v* [I] *BrE informal* to talk for a long time about unimportant things SYN **chat**: **[+to/with]** *Sometimes she would pick up the telephone and natter to Charles.* | **[+about]** *Lynne's been nattering on about the wedding for weeks.*

natter[2] *n* [singular] *BrE informal* the act of talking about unimportant things SYN **chat**: *We sat down and* ***had a natter*** *and a cup of tea.*

nat·ty /ˈnæti/ *adj informal* neat and fashionable in appearance: *a natty suit* | *He was a natty dresser.* —**nattily** *adv*

nat·u·ral[1] /ˈnætʃərəl/ ●●● S2 W1 *adj*

1 NATURE existing in nature and not caused, made, or controlled by people → **artificial, man-made**: *the study of* ***the natural world*** (=trees, rivers, animals, plants etc) | *an area of spectacular natural beauty* | ***natural disasters*** (=things such as floods or EARTHQUAKES) | *death from* ***natural causes*** | *the need for natural light in offices*

2 NORMAL normal and as you would expect OPP **unnatural, abnormal**: *At the time, accepting his offer had seemed* ***the most natural thing in the world.*** | **it is natural (for sb) to do sth** *It's not natural for a child of his age to be so quiet.* | ***It's*** *only* ***natural that*** *he should be interested in what happens.* | *It was a* ***perfectly natural*** (=not surprising) *mistake to make.*

3 BEHAVIOUR a natural tendency or type of behaviour is part of your character when you are born, rather than one that you learn later: *Babies have a natural fear of falling.*

4 ABILITY having a particular quality or skill without needing to be taught and without needing to try hard: *a natural musician* | *Cheryl has a natural elegance about her.* | *his natural ability with figures*

5 RELAXED behaving in a way that is normal and shows you are relaxed and not trying to pretend: *Be cool, be natural.*

6 PARENT/CHILD [only before noun] **a)** someone's natural parent or child is their real parent or child, who is BIOLOGICALLY related to them: *An adopted young person has the right to trace his natural parents.* **b)** *old-fashioned* if someone is the natural child of someone, their parents were not married to each other: *He was rumoured to be the natural son of a duke.*

7 REAL not connected with gods, magic, or SPIRITS OPP **supernatural**: *I'm sure there's a perfectly natural explanation.*

8 natural justice/law justice that is based on human reason alone

9 FOOD with nothing added to change the taste: *natural yoghurt*

10 MUSIC *technical* a musical note that is natural has been raised from a FLAT by one SEMITONE or lowered from a SHARP by one semitone → **sharp, flat** —**naturalness** *n* [U]: *Manufacturers now choose to emphasize the naturalness of the ingredients used in their products.*

N

natural² *n* [C] **1 be a natural** to be good at doing something without having to try hard or practise: *People think I am a natural, but I've had to work at it.* **2** *technical* **a)** a musical note that has been changed from a FLAT to be a SEMITONE higher, or from a SHARP to be a semitone lower **b)** the sign in written music that shows this kind of musical note

ˈnatural-born *adj* **natural-born singer/story-teller etc** someone who has always had a particular quality or skill without having had to learn it

ˌnatural ˈchildbirth *n* [U] a method of giving birth to a baby in which a woman chooses not to be given drugs to reduce the pain

ˌnatural ˈgas *n* [U] gas used for heating and lighting, taken from under the earth or under the sea

ˌnatural ˈhistory *n* [U] the study of plants, animals, and minerals: *the Natural History Museum*

nat·u·ral·is·m /ˈnætʃərəlɪzəm/ *n* [U] a style of art or literature which tries to show the world and people exactly as they are → **realism**

nat·u·ral·ist /ˈnætʃərəlɪst/ *n* [C] someone who studies plants or animals

nat·u·ral·is·tic /ˌnætʃərəˈlɪstɪk◂/ (*also* **naturalist**) *adj* painted, written etc according to the ideas of naturalism —**naturalistically** /-kli/ *adv*

nat·u·ral·ize (*also* **-ise** *BrE*) /ˈnætʃərəlaɪz/ *v* **be naturalized** if someone born outside a particular country is naturalized, they become a citizen of that country —**naturalization** /ˌnætʃərəlaɪˈzeɪʃən $ -lə-/ *n* [U]

nat·u·ral·ly /ˈnætʃərəli $ -tʃərəli, -tʃərli/ ●●○ S3 W3 *adv*

1 [sentence adverb] use this to say that something is normal and not surprising: *Naturally, you'll want to discuss this with your wife.* | ***Naturally enough****, she wanted her child to grow up fit and strong.*

2 *spoken* use this to say 'yes' when you agree with someone or when you think the person who asked the question should know that your reply will be 'yes': *'Am I allowed in?' 'Naturally.'*

3 in a way that is the result of nature, not of someone's actions: *My hair is naturally curly.* | **come naturally (to sb)** (=be easy for you to do because you have a natural ability) *Speaking in public seems to come quite naturally to her.*

4 in a relaxed manner without trying to look or sound different from usual: *Just speak naturally and pretend the microphone isn't there.*

ˌnatural phiˈlosophy *n* [U] *old use* science

ˌnatural reˈsource / $ ˌ... ˈ../ *n* [C usually plural] things that exist in nature and can be used by people, for example oil, trees etc: *a country with abundant natural resources*

ˌnatural ˈscience *n* [C,U] chemistry, biology, and physics, considered together as subjects for study, or one of these subjects

ˌnatural seˈlection *n* [U] *technical* the process by which only plants and animals that are naturally suitable for life in their environment will continue to live and breed, while all others will die out → **evolution** → **survival of the fittest** at SURVIVAL(2)

ˌnatural ˈwastage *n* [U] a reduction in the number of people employed by an organization, which happens when people leave their jobs and the jobs are not given to anyone else

na·ture /ˈneɪtʃə $ -tʃər/ ●●● S1 W1 *n*

1 PLANTS/ANIMALS ETC [U] (*also* **Nature**) everything in the physical world that is not controlled by humans, such as wild plants and animals, earth and rocks, and the weather: *We grew up in the countryside, surrounded by the beauties of nature.* | *nature conservation* | **the laws/forces of nature** *The inhabitants of the island fight a constant battle against the forces of nature.* | **in nature** *All these materials are found in nature.* | *Disease is* ***nature's way*** *of keeping the population down.*

> **GRAMMAR**
>
> Don't say 'the nature' in this meaning. You say: *the power of nature* ✗ Don't say: *the power of the nature*
>
> GRAMMAR GUIDE ▸ NOUNS

2 SB'S CHARACTER [C,U] someone's character: *a child with a happy, easy-going nature* | **sb's nature** ***It's*** *just not* ***in*** *Jane's* ***nature*** *to lie.* | **by nature** *She was by nature a very affectionate person.* | *I tried appealing to his* ***better nature*** (=his feelings of kindness) *but he wouldn't agree to help us.* | *Of course she's jealous – it's only* ***human nature*** (=the feelings and ways of behaving that all people have).

3 QUALITIES OF STH [singular, U] the qualities or features that something has: **[+of]** *They asked a lot of questions about the nature of our democracy.* | *He examined the nature of the relationship between the two communities.* | **exact/precise/true nature** *The exact nature of the problem is not well understood.* | **different/political/temporary etc in nature** *Any government funding would be temporary in nature.* | *Capitalist society is* ***by its very nature*** *unstable.*

4 TYPE [singular] a particular kind of thing: **of a personal/political/difficult etc nature** *The support being given is of a practical nature.* | **of this/that nature** *I never trouble myself with questions of that nature.*

5 in the nature of things according to the natural way things happen: *In the nature of things, there is bound to be the occasional accident.*

6 be in the nature of sth *formal* to be similar to a type of thing: *The enquiry will be more in the nature of a public meeting than a formal hearing.*

7 against nature not natural, and morally wrong: *They believe that suicide is against nature.*

8 let nature take its course to allow events to happen without doing anything to change the results: *The best cure for a cold is to let nature take its course.*

9 back to nature a style of living in which people try to live simply and not use modern machines: *city workers who want to* ***get back to nature*** *in their holidays* → **be/become second nature (to sb)** at SECOND¹(10), → **the call of nature** at CALL²(12)

ˈnature reˌserve *n* [C] an area of land in which animals and plants are protected

ˈnature ˌtrail *n* [C] a path through the countryside that is designed so that you can see interesting plants, animals etc along the way

na·tur·ist /ˈneɪtʃərɪst/ *n* [C] someone who enjoys not wearing any clothes because they believe it is natural and healthy to do this SYN **nudist** —**naturism** *n* [U]

na·tur·o·path /ˈneɪtʃərəpæθ/ *n* [C] someone who tries to cure illness using natural things such as plants, rather than drugs —**naturopathy** /ˌneɪtʃəˈrɒpəθi $ -ˈrɑː-/ *n* [U] —**naturopathic** /ˌneɪtʃərəˈpæθɪk◂/ *adj*

naught /nɔːt $ nɒːt/ *pron old use* nothing: *All their plans* ***came to naught*** (=failed).

naugh·ty /ˈnɔːti $ ˈnɒːti, ˈnɑːti/ ●●○ S3 *adj*

1 a naughty child does not obey adults and behaves badly OPP **good**: *You're a very naughty boy! Look what you've done!*

2 *BrE* if an adult does something naughty, they do something that is not right or good, but is not very serious: *I felt a bit naughty going off on my own, leaving the children behind.*

3 naughty jokes/magazines/films etc *BrE old-fashioned* naughty jokes, magazines, films etc deal with sex, especially in a humorous way → **rude**, **blue**

4 the naughty step *BrE* a stair where a child is told to sit for a period of time as a punishment when they have been naughty —**naughtily** *adv* —**naughtiness** *n* [U]

nau·se·a /ˈnɔːziə, -siə $ ˈnɒːziə, -ʃə/ *n* [U] *formal* the feeling that you have when you think you are going to VOMIT (=bring food up from your stomach through your mouth) SYN **sickness**: **feeling/wave of nausea** *A feeling of nausea suddenly came over me.* → **AD NAUSEAM**

nau·se·ate /ˈnɔːzieɪt, -si- $ ˈnɒːzi-, -ʃi-/ *v* [T] to make someone feel that they are going to VOMIT: *The thought of food nauseated me.* | *She felt dizzy and nauseated.*

nau·se·a·ting /ˈnɔːzieɪtɪŋ, -si- $ ˈnɒːzi-, -ʃi-/ *adj* **1** making you feel that you are going to VOMIT SYN **sickening**: *the nauseating smell of rotting fish* THESAURUS HORRIBLE **2** making you feel annoyed or offended SYN **disgusting**: *his nauseating remarks* —**nauseatingly** *adv*

nau·se·ous /ˈnɔːziəs, -siəs $ -ˈnɒːziəs, -ʃəs/ *adj* **1** *especially AmE* feeling that you are going to VOMIT SYN **sick**: *I **felt** slightly **nauseous**.* | *The taste **made** me **nauseous**.* **2** *formal* making you feel that you are going to VOMIT: *a nauseous smell*

nau·ti·cal /ˈnɔːtɪkəl $ ˈnɒː-/ *adj* relating to ships, boats, or sailing: *nautical equipment*

ˌnautical ˈmile *n* [C] a unit for measuring distance at sea, equal to about 1.15 miles or 1,852 metres

na·val /ˈneɪvəl/ ●○○ *adj* [only before noun] relating to the navy or used by the navy: *a naval officer* | *naval battles*

nave /neɪv/ *n* [C] the long central part of a church

na·vel /ˈneɪvəl/ *n* [C] **1** the small hollow or raised place in the middle of your stomach SYN **belly button**, **tummy button** **2 gaze at/contemplate your navel** to spend too much time thinking about your own problems – used humorously

nav·i·ga·ble /ˈnævəgəbəl/ *adj* a river, lake etc that is navigable is deep and wide enough for ships to travel on —**navigability** /ˌnævəgəˈbɪləti/ *n* [U]

nav·i·gate /ˈnævɪgeɪt/ *v* **1** [I,T] to find which way you need to go when you are travelling from one place to another: *I'll drive, you take the map and navigate.* | *Early explorers used to **navigate by the stars**.* | **navigate your way through/to/around sth** *We managed to navigate our way through the forest.* **2** [I,T] to understand or deal with something complicated: *A solicitor will help you navigate the complex legal system.* | **[+through]** *I am currently trying to navigate through a whole stack of information on the subject.* **3** [T] to sail along a river or other area of water: *The river is too dangerous to navigate.* **4** [I,T] to find your way around on a particular website, or to move from one website to another: *The magazine's website is easy to navigate.*

nav·i·ga·tion /ˌnævəˈgeɪʃən/ ●○○ *n* [U]
1 the science or job of planning which way you need to go when you are travelling from one place to another: *compasses and other instruments of navigation*
2 when someone sails a ship along a river or other area of water: *Navigation becomes more difficult further up the river.*
3 when you CLICK on words, pictures etc in order to move between documents that are connected on the Internet —**navigational** *adj* [only before noun]

nav·i·ga·tor /ˈnævəgeɪtə $ -tər/ *n* [C] an officer on a ship or aircraft who plans which way it should go when it is travelling from one place to another

nav·vy /ˈnævi/ *n* (*plural* **navvies**) [C] *BrE* an unskilled worker who does physical work, such as building roads

na·vy /ˈneɪvi/ ●●○ *n* (*plural* **navies**)
1 [C] the part of a country's military forces that fights at sea: *the British Navy* | **in the navy** *Is your brother still in the navy?* | *He **joined the navy** during the war.*
2 [U] a very dark blue colour: *The jacket is available in navy, green, or brown.* —**navy** *adj*

ˈnavy ˌbean *n* [C] *AmE* a small white bean which is cooked and eaten, especially in BAKED BEANS

ˌnavy ˈblue (*also* **navy**) *adj* very dark blue: *a navy blue sweater* —**navy blue** *n* [U]

nay[1] /neɪ/ *adv* **1** [sentence adverb] *literary* used when you are adding something to emphasize what you have just said: *a bright – nay, a blinding light* **2** *old use* used to say no: *Nay, lad. It's not that bad.*

nay[2] *n* [C] a 'no' – used when voting

Na·zi /ˈnɑːtsi/ *n* [C] **1** a member of the National Socialist Party of Adolf Hitler which controlled Germany from 1933 to 1945 **2** someone who uses their authority over others in a very strict or cruel way: *Some of the supervisors are real Nazis.* —**Nazi** *adj* —**Nazism** *n* [U]

N.B. (*also* **NB** *BrE*) *written* (***nota bene***) used to make a reader pay attention to a piece of information

NBA, the /ˌen biː ˈeɪ/ *n* (***the National Basketball Association***) the American organization which arranges professional BASKETBALL games

NBC /ˌen biː ˈsiː/ *n* (***National Broadcasting Company***) one of the main American television companies

NBF /ˌen biː ˈef/ *n* [C] *informal* (***new best friend***) a person who has recently become someone's good friend, especially soon after meeting them – used especially by young people and in magazines: *She has been giving her NBF fashion tips.*

NCO /ˌen siː ˈəʊ $ -ˈoʊ/ *n* [C] (***non-commissioned officer***) an officer of low rank in the British army

-nd /nd/ *suffix* used for forming written ORDINAL numbers with 2: *the 2nd (=second) of March* | *her 22nd birthday*

NE the written abbreviation of ***northeast*** or ***northeastern***

ne·an·der·thal /niˈændəˌtɑːl $ -dərˌθɒːl, -ˌtɑːl/ *n* [C] **1** (*also* **Neanderthal**) an early type of human being **2** a man who is big, ugly, and stupid **3** someone who has old-fashioned ideas and opposes change —**neanderthal** *adj*: *his neanderthal attitude towards women*

Neˈanderthal ˌman *n* [U] an early type of human being who lived in Europe during the STONE AGE

ne·a·pol·i·tan /ˌnɪːəˈpɒlətən◂ $ -ˈpɑː-/ *adj* neapolitan ICE CREAM has layers of different colours and tastes

neap tide /ˈniːp taɪd/ *n* [C] a very small rise and fall of the level of the sea at the times of the first and third quarters of the moon → **spring tide**

near[1] /nɪə $ nɪr/ ●●● S1 W1 *adv, prep*
1 SHORT DISTANCE AWAY only a short distance from a person or thing → **close**, **nearby**: *They live near London.* | *I'm sure they live **somewhere near here**.* | *They moved house to be nearer the school.* | **[+to]** *especially BrE*: *a hotel near to the beach* | *She told the children not to **go near** the canal.* | *I'm warning you – don't **come any nearer**!* | *We heard voices as we **drew near** the village.*
2 SHORT TIME BEFORE soon before a particular time or event: *I didn't remember to phone until near the end of the week.* | **[+to]** *especially BrE*: *I'll give you a ring a bit nearer to Christmas.* | *They should send us more details **nearer the time** of the concert.*
3 ALMOST DOING STH almost doing something or almost in a particular state: *The work is now near completion.* | *A lot of the women were **near tears**.* | *We are **no nearer** an agreement than we were six months ago.* | **[+to]** *He was near to panic as he scrambled out of the building.* | *She was near to crying.* | *He seemed to know that he was near to death.*
4 AMOUNT OR LEVEL almost at a particular amount or level: *Inflation is now near 10%.* | *He looked nearer fifty than forty.* | **[+to]** *Unemployment is now near to its all-time low.* | *Strawberries are near the top of the list.*
5 SIMILAR if something is near something else, it is similar to it: *His story was **near enough** the truth for people to believe it.* | **[+to]** *They say that love is very near to hate.* | *It may not be an exact replica but it's pretty damn near.*
6 near perfect/impossible etc almost perfect, impossible etc: *a near impossible task*
7 draw near if an event is drawing near, it is nearly time for it to happen: *The day of his interview was drawing near.*
8 (as) near as damn it *BrE spoken* used to say that something is very nearly true or correct: *The repairs will cost us £1,000, as near as damn it.*
9 near enough *BrE* used to say that something is nearly true or correct: *It's eleven o'clock, near enough.* | *All three car parks were full, near enough.*
10 nowhere near/not anywhere near used before an adjective or adverb to say that something is definitely not true: *That's nowhere near enough money!* | *The job wasn't anywhere near finished.*
11 not come near sb/sth if one person or thing does not come near another one, it is not at all as good as the other one: *None of the other word processing programs comes near this one.*

N

12 sb will not go near sb/sth if someone will not go near a person or thing, they dislike or are frightened of them and will not speak to the person or use the thing: *He refused to go near a doctor.* | *He made up his mind never to go near a motorcycle again.*
13 so near and yet so far used to emphasize that someone very nearly achieved or got something

THESAURUS

near only a short distance from something or someone: *I live near Salzburg in Austria.* | *If we moved to Dallas, we'd be near my parents.*
close very near something or someone, or almost touching them: *The hotel is* **close to** *the beach.* | *Nancy came and sat close beside me on the bed.*
not far (away) not a long distance away – used when saying that a place is near enough to be easy to get to: *The station's not far away from here.*
nearby near here or near a particular place: *Is there a post office nearby?* | *A group of reporters were waiting nearby.*
within walking distance (of sth) easy to walk to from somewhere, or near enough to something for you to walk there: *There's a good school within walking distance.* | *The house is within walking distance of shopping facilities.*
locally in or near the area where you are or the area you are talking about: *I prefer to buy fruit and vegetables that are grown locally.*
around here (*also* **round here** *BrE*) *spoken* in the general area near here: *Parking is impossible around here.* | *Is there a garage round here?*
in the neighbourhood *BrE*, **in the neighborhood** *AmE* living or existing in the area where you are or the area you are talking about: *We grew up knowing all the other kids in the neighbourhood.* | *There's very little crime in the neighborhood.*
in the vicinity *formal* in the area around and near a particular place – used especially in news reports: *A white van was seen in the vicinity at the time the murder took place.*

near² ●●● S2 W3 *adj*
1 only a short distance away from someone or something → **close, nearby**: *It's a beautiful house but it's 20 miles away from the nearest town.* | *We can meet at the pub or in the restaurant, whichever's nearer for you.*

GRAMMAR: Patterns with near

• You usually use **near** as a preposition. You say: *The hotel is near the airport.*
• You can also say: *The hotel is* **near to** *the airport.*
✗ Don't say: *near from the airport*
• **Near** is not usually used on its own as an adjective. You don't usually say 'The village is near.' You usually say: *The village is* **not far away**.
• You use **nearby** before a noun: *We went to a nearby park.* ✗ Don't say: *We went to a near park.*
• You can use the forms **nearer** and **nearest** as adjectives: *My house is nearer.*
• You can use **nearest** before a noun: *They headed for the nearest beach.*
GRAMMAR GUIDE ▶ ADJECTIVES

2 a near disaster/collapse etc almost a DISASTER, COLLAPSE etc: *The election was a near disaster for the Conservative party.*
3 the nearest thing/equivalent to sth the thing you have that is most like a particular type of thing: *He's the nearest thing to a father I've got.*
4 in the near future soon: *They promised to contact us again in the near future.*
5 be a near thing *BrE* **a)** if something you succeed in doing is a near thing, you manage to succeed but you nearly failed: *They won the championship, but it was a near thing.* **b)** used to say that you just managed to avoid a dangerous or unpleasant situation: *That was a near thing – that truck was heading straight for us.*
6 near miss a) when a bomb, plane, car etc nearly hits something but does not: *a near miss between two passenger aircraft over the airport* **b)** a situation in which something almost happens, or someone almost achieves something
7 to the nearest £10/hundred etc an amount to the nearest £10, hundred etc is the number nearest to it that can be divided by £10, a hundred etc: *Give me the car mileage to the nearest thousand.*
8 a) near relative/relation a relative who is very closely related to you such as a parent: *The death of a near relative is a terrible trauma for a child.* **b) sb's nearest and dearest** someone's family – used humorously
9 [only before noun, no comparative] **a)** used to describe the side of something that is closest to where you are: *the near bank of the river* **b)** *BrE* used when talking about the parts of a vehicle to mean the one that is closest to the side of the road when you drive OPP **off**: *The headlight on the near side isn't working.* → NEARLY —**nearness** *n* [U]

near³ ●●○ *v written*
1 [T] to come closer to a place SYN **approach**: *She began to feel nervous as she neared the house.* | *The ship was nearing the harbour.*
2 [T] to come closer to being in a particular state: *The work is nearing completion.* | *He's 55 now, and nearing retirement.*
3 [T] to come closer to a particular time: *He was nearing the end of his stay in India.*
4 [I] if a time nears, it gets closer and will come soon: *He got more and more nervous as the day of his departure neared.*

near·by /ˈnɪəbaɪ $ ˈnɪr-/ ●●● W3 *adj* [only before noun] not far away: *Lucy was staying in the nearby town of Hamilton.* THESAURUS ▶ NEAR —**nearby** /nɪəˈbaɪ $ ˈnɪr-/ *adv*: *Dan found work on one of the farms nearby.* | *Do you live nearby?*

ˌNear ˈEast *n* **the Near East** the Middle East —**Near Eastern** *adj*: *ancient Near Eastern literature*

near·ly /ˈnɪəli $ ˈnɪrli/ ●●● S1 W1 *adv*
1 *especially BrE* almost, but not quite or not completely SYN **almost**: *It took nearly two hours to get here.* | *Michelle's nearly twenty.* | *Is the job nearly finished?* | *Louise is nearly as tall as her mother.* | *I* **nearly always** *go home for lunch.* | *He* **very nearly** *died.* THESAURUS ▶ ALMOST
2 not nearly not at all: *He's not nearly as good-looking as his brother.* | *We've saved some money, but it's* **not nearly enough**.

GRAMMAR: Comparison

nearly
• Don't use **nearly** before negative words such as 'no' or 'nothing'. ✗ Don't say: *I know nearly nothing about it.* | *There was nearly no traffic.*
almost
• You can use **almost** with negative words such as 'no' or 'nothing': *I know* **almost nothing** *about it.* | *There was* **almost no** *traffic.*
hardly
• You can also form negative sentences using **hardly** with 'any', 'anything' etc: *I know* **hardly anything** *about it.* | *There was* **hardly any** *traffic.*

near·side /ˈnɪəsaɪd $ ˈnɪr-/ *adj* [only before noun] *BrE* on the side of a vehicle that is closest to the side of the road when you drive OPP **offside**: *a scratch on the nearside front wing of the car* —**nearside** *n* [singular]

near·sight·ed /ˌnɪəˈsaɪtɪd◂ $ ˈnɪrsaɪtɪd/ *adj especially AmE* unable to see things clearly unless they are close to you → **far-sighted** SYN **short-sighted** *BrE* —**nearsightedness** *n* [U]

neat /niːt/ ●●● S2 *adj*
1 TIDY tidy and carefully arranged: *neat handwriting* | *His clothes were always* **neat and clean**. | *Everything in the house was* **neat and tidy**. | *She arranged the books in a* **nice neat** *pile.* THESAURUS ▶ TIDY

N

2 LIKING THINGS TIDY someone who is neat likes to keep things tidy: *I've always been quite neat.*
3 GOOD *AmE spoken* very good, pleasant, or enjoyable: *That's a really neat idea. | I liked working for him – he was a neat guy.* THESAURUS ▸ GOOD
4 SMALL something that is neat is small and attractive: *her small, neat features*
5 CLEVER *formal* a neat way of doing or saying something is simple but clever and effective: *In the end we found a very neat solution to the problem. | a neat summary of the main issues*
6 DRINKS *especially BrE* a neat alcoholic drink has no ice or water or any other liquid added SYN **straight**: *I can't drink brandy neat. | drinking neat whisky* —**neatly** *adv*: *He wrote his name neatly at the bottom of the page. | The problem was neatly summed up by one of the teachers.* —**neatness** *n* [U]

neat·en /'ni:tən/ *v* [T] to make something neater: *Put a row of zig-zag stitching along the cut edge to neaten it.*

'neat freak *n* [C] *AmE informal* someone who is very concerned that things should be tidy

neath /ni:θ/ *prep literary* beneath: *neath the stars*

neb·u·la /'nebjələ/ *n* (*plural* **nebulae** /-li:/) [C] **1** a mass of gas and dust among the stars, which often appears as a bright cloud in the sky at night **2** a GALAXY (=mass of stars) which appears as a bright cloud in the sky at night —**nebular** *adj*

neb·u·lous /'nebjələs/ *adj formal* **1** an idea that is nebulous is not at all clear or exact SYN **vague**: *'Normality' is a rather nebulous concept.* **2** a shape that is nebulous is unclear and has no definite edges: *a nebulous ghostly figure*

ne·ces·sar·i·ly /'nesəsərəli, ˌnesə'serəli $ ˌnesə'serəli/ ●●● S2 W2 *adv*
1 not necessarily possibly, but not certainly: *That is not necessarily true. | Expensive restaurants aren't necessarily the best. | Having this disease does not necessarily mean that you will die young. | 'So the school will have to close down, then?' 'Not necessarily.'*
2 *formal* in a way that cannot be different or be avoided SYN **inevitably**: *The care of old people necessarily involves quite a lot of heavy lifting.*

ne·ces·sa·ry¹ /'nesəsəri $ -seri/ ●●● S2 W1 *adj*
1 something that is necessary is what you need to have or need to do → **essential**: *The booklet provides all the necessary information about the college. | No further changes were considered necessary.* | **absolutely/really necessary** *The police are advising motorists to travel only if their journey is absolutely necessary.* | **it is necessary (for sb) to do sth** *It's not necessary to wear a tie. | The doctor says it may be necessary for me to have an operation.* | **make it necessary (for sb) to do sth** *Falling profits made it necessary to restructure the business.* | **necessary for (doing) sth** *A good diet is necessary for maintaining a healthy body.* | **if/when/where necessary** *I'll stay up all night, if necessary, to get it finished.*

REGISTER
In everyday English, instead of saying **it is necessary for sb to do sth**, people usually say that someone **has to do sth**: *The doctor says it might* ***be necessary for me to have*** *an operation.* → *The doctor says I might* ***have to have*** *an operation.*

2 necessary connection/consequence etc a connection, result etc that must exist and cannot be avoided: *The closure of the factory was a necessary consequence of increased competition from abroad.*
3 a necessary evil something bad or unpleasant that you have to accept in order to achieve what you want: *Mr Hurst regarded work as a necessary evil.*

THESAURUS
necessary used to describe something that you need to have or do: *Make sure you bring the necessary documents with you. | It may be necessary for you to have a small operation.*
essential very important and necessary, especially in order to be healthy, successful etc: *Vitamins are essential for healthy growth. | The tourist industry is an essential part of the Spanish economy.*
vital extremely important and necessary, especially in order to avoid serious problems: *A vital piece of equipment on the spacecraft had stopped operating. | It is vital that the aid is sent immediately.*
compulsory if something is compulsory, you must do it because of a rule or law: *Maths and Science are compulsory subjects. | All new staff undergo a compulsory training course.*
obligatory if something is obligatory, you must do it because of a rule or law. **Obligatory** is more formal than **compulsory**: *The use of seatbelts is obligatory. | Safety regulations have made it obligatory for all competitors to wear fist protectors.*
mandatory if something is mandatory, you must do it because it is the law. **Mandatory** is more formal than **compulsory** and sounds stronger: *School attendance is mandatory. | a prisoner serving a mandatory life sentence*
requisite /'rekwəzət/ *formal* [usually before noun] the requisite things are the ones that you need to have in order to do something: *The other candidates lacked the requisite skills.*

necessary² *n* **1 necessaries** [plural] things such as food or basic clothes that you need in order to live **2 do the necessary** *BrE spoken* to do what is necessary: *Leave it to me – I'll do the necessary.*

ne·ces·si·tate /nɪ'sesɪteɪt/ ●○○ *v* [T] *formal* to make it necessary for you to do something: *Lack of money necessitated a change of plan.* | **necessitate doing sth** *This would necessitate interviewing all the staff.*

ne·ces·si·ty /nə'sesəti/ ●●○ *n* (*plural* **necessities**)
1 [C] something that you need to have in order to live OPP **luxury**: *She saw books as a necessity, not a luxury. | A car is an* ***absolute necessity*** *if you live in the country.* | **the basic/bare necessities** *A lot of families cannot even afford to buy the basic necessities of life.*
2 [U] when something is necessary: **[+for]** *He emphasized the necessity for good planning and management.* | **the necessity of (doing) sth** *This illustrates the necessity of keeping accurate records of your work. | Many teachers are now questioning the necessity of formal exams.* | **through/out of necessity** *He only remained with the group out of necessity.* | **economic/practical/political etc necessity** *I'm afraid it's become* ***a matter of*** *economic* ***necessity****.*
3 [C] something that must happen, even if it is unpleasant: *Taxes are a regrettable necessity.*
4 of necessity *formal* used when something happens in a particular way because that is the only possible way it can happen: *Many of the jobs are, of necessity, temporary.*
5 necessity is the mother of invention used to say that if someone really needs to do something, they will find a way of doing it

neck¹ /nek/ ●●● S2 W2 *n*
1 PART OF THE BODY [C] the part of your body that joins your head to your shoulders, or the same part of an animal or bird: **around sb's neck** *Jean wore a string of pearls around her neck. | Mike rubbed the back of his neck. | You have a lot of tension in your neck muscles. | He patted his horse's neck. | She had a mass of golden hair, which she wore in a coil at the* ***nape*** *(=back)* ***of*** *her* ***neck****. | The dog picked up the puppy and carried it by* ***the scruff*** *(=back)* ***of*** *the* ***neck*** *into the house.*
2 CLOTHING [C] the part of a piece of clothing that goes around your neck: **[+of]** *The neck of his shirt was open. | The sweater has a round neck and long sleeves.* | **V-necked/open-necked etc** *a navy V-necked sweater* → CREW NECK, POLO NECK, SCOOP NECK, TURTLENECK, V-NECK → see picture on *p. 1218*
3 NARROW PART [C] the narrow part of something, usually at the top: **[+of]** *Lara put the cork back in the neck of the bottle. | a crack in the neck of the violin*

N

4 be up to your neck in sth a) to be very busy with something: *She's up to her neck in work.* **b)** to be in a difficult situation that is hard to escape from: *Jim's up to his neck in debt.*

5 neck and neck (with sb) *informal* if two competitors or groups are neck and neck in a competition or race, they are level with each other: *Opinion polls show the two main parties are running neck and neck.*

6 in this/sb's neck of the woods *informal* in a particular area or part of the country: *I haven't been in this neck of the woods for years.*

7 get it in the neck *BrE spoken* to be punished or criticized: *If we don't make some changes we'll all get it in the neck.*

8 by a neck *informal* if a race, especially a horse race, is won by a neck, the winner is only a very short distance in front: *Our horse won by a neck.*

9 ATTITUDE [U] (*also* **brass neck**) *BrE informal* a confident attitude that makes you able to do unreasonable or shocking things without feeling embarrassed SYN **nerve, cheek**: *I don't know how they have the neck to charge that much!*

10 LAND [C] a narrow piece of land that comes out of a wider part: *a neck of land between a lake and the sea*

11 (hang) around your neck if something hangs around your neck, it keeps causing you problems → **be breathing down sb's neck** at BREATHE(5), → **I'll wring sb's neck** at WRING(6), → **pain in the neck** at PAIN[1](3), → **risk your neck** at RISK[2](1), → **save sb's neck** at SAVE[1](11), → **stick your neck out** at STICK OUT

neck[2] *v* [I usually in progressive] *informal* if two people are necking, they kiss for a long time in a sexual way —**necking** *n* [U]

neck·band /ˈnekbænd/ *n* [C] a narrow piece of material around the neck of a piece of clothing

neck·er·chief /ˈnekətʃiːf $ -ər-/ *n* [C] a square piece of cloth that is folded and worn tied around the neck

neck·lace /ˈnek-lɪs/ ●●● S3 *n* [C] a string of jewels, BEADS etc or a thin gold or silver chain to wear around the neck: **pearl/gold/diamond etc necklace** *She was wearing a coral necklace.*

neck·let /ˈnek-lɪt/ *n* [C] a short necklace

neck·line /ˈnek-laɪn/ *n* [C usually singular] the shape made by the upper edge of a piece of woman's clothing around or below the neck: *a square neckline* | **low/plunging neckline** (=leaving part of the chest uncovered) *Her evening gown had a plunging neckline.*

neck·tie /ˈnektaɪ/ ●●○ *n* [C] *AmE formal* a man's tie

nec·ro·man·cy /ˈnekrəmænsi/ *n* [U] **1** magic, especially evil magic **2** *literary* the practice of claiming to talk with the dead —**necromancer** *n* [C]

nec·ro·phil·i·a /ˌnekrəʊˈfɪliə, -krə $ -kroʊ-, -krə-/ *n* [U] sexual interest in dead bodies

ne·crop·o·lis /nɪˈkrɒpəlɪs $ -ˈkrɑː-/ *n* [C] an area of land where dead people are buried, especially a large ancient one SYN **cemetery**: *the extensive necropolis which served the Etruscan city of Caere*

nec·tar /ˈnektə $ -ər/ *n* [U] **1** the sweet liquid that BEES collect from flowers **2** thick juice made from particular fruit: *mango nectar* **3** the drink of the gods, in the stories of ancient Greece

nec·ta·rine /ˈnektəriːn $ ˌnektəˈriːn/ *n* [C] a type of fruit like a PEACH that has a smooth skin, or the tree that produces this fruit → see picture at **FRUIT**

née /neɪ/ used to say what a married woman's family name was when she was born. 'Née' is put after her married name and before her old name → **maiden name**: *Mrs Elizabeth Davis, née Williams*

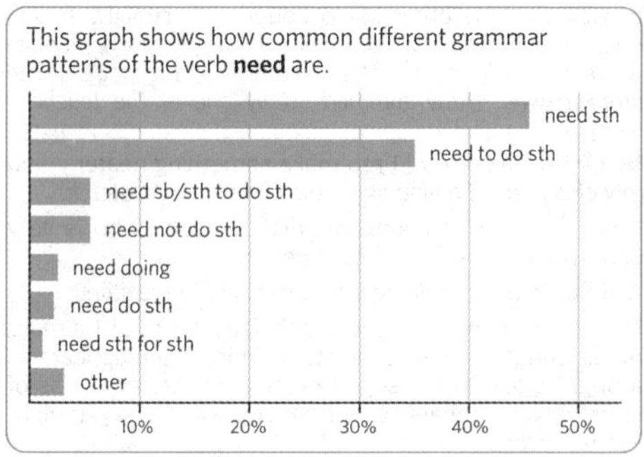

need[1] /niːd/ ●●● S1 W1 *v*

1 [T] to have to have something or someone, because you cannot do something without them, or because you cannot continue or cannot exist without them SYN **require**: *You don't really need a car.* | *Plants need light in order to survive.* | *The camcorder needs a new battery.* | *Are you sure that you have* ***everything you need****?* | **need sth for sth** *I need glasses for reading.* | **need sb to do sth** *I need you to help me with the cooking.* | **need sth desperately/badly/urgently** *More blood donors are urgently needed.* | **much needed/badly needed** *a much needed boost to the local economy*

2 [T] to feel that you want something very much: *I need a drink.* | *If you need anything, just say.* | **need to do sth** *She needed to go out for a walk.*

3 need to do sth used when saying that someone should do something or has to do something: *He needs to see a doctor straightaway.* | *I need to catch up on my office work.* | *You need to let me know by Monday if you want to take part.*

4 [modal] *BrE* used in negative sentences when saying that something is not necessary or not always true → **have to**: **need not/needn't** *You needn't stay long.* | *Going to the dentist need not necessarily be a painful experience.* | **need not have done sth/need not do sth** *You needn't have spent all that money.* | *I needn't have worried.* | **need I/we etc do sth?** *BrE old-fashioned*: *Need we leave so soon?* | **sb need never do sth** *Jim need never find out what I said.*

5 [T] used when saying that something should have something done to it, or has to have something done to it: **sth needs doing** *The house needed painting.* | *Does this shirt need ironing?* | **sth needs to be checked/cleaned/done etc** *The engine will need to be completely checked.* | *The pie doesn't need to be refrigerated.* | **need a (good) wash/clean/cut etc** (=ought to be washed, cleaned etc) *His hair needs a wash.*

6 [T] if a job needs a quality or skill, you must have that quality or skill in order to do it well: *The job needs a lot of patience.* | *Being a teacher needs a high level of motivation.*

7 I need hardly say/tell/remind etc *BrE* used when you think people should already know what you are going to say: *I need hardly remind you that this information is confidential.*

8 you need only do sth/all you need do is ... *BrE* used when saying that you only have to do something in order to do something else: *We need only look at the building to see how much money it will take to repair.* | *All we need do is threaten them.*

9 need I ask/need I say more/need I go on etc? *BrE* used to say that it is not necessary to ask or say more about something, because the rest is clear: *She's lazy, slow, and stubborn. Need I say more?*

N

10 that's all I need/that's just what I didn't need *spoken* used when saying that you did not want something to happen, especially when it seems annoying: *'There's a customer for you on the phone.' 'That's all I need!'*
11 need sth like a hole in the head *informal* used when saying that you definitely do not need something
12 who needs it/them? *spoken* **a)** used to say you are not interested in something: *Make-up, who needs it?* **b)** used to say that someone or something is actually very important to you: *Kids? Who needs them!*

GRAMMAR

Patterns with need

- You say that you **need** something: *You'll need some warm clothes.*
- You say that you **need to do** something: *I need to clean the house.*
- You say that something **needs cutting/cleaning etc** (=it needs to be cut, cleaned etc): *My hair needs cutting.*
- You say that you **need** something **done** (=you want someone to do it for you): *I need my car fixed urgently.*

Negatives

- You say that you **do not need** something: *You don't need a jacket.*
- You say that you **don't need to do** something or you **need not/needn't do** something (=it is not necessary): *I don't need to leave until 10.* | *You needn't apologize.* ✗ Don't say: *I don't need leave.* | *You needn't to apologize.*
- You say that someone **didn't need to do** something (=it was not necessary): *I didn't need to tell him who I was – he already knew.*
- You say that someone **needn't have done** something (=although they have done it, it was not necessary): *We needn't have ordered so much food.*

Using the progressive

Need is not used in the progressive. You say: *I need a break.* ✗ Don't say: *I'm needing a break.*
GRAMMAR GUIDE ▸ VERBS

need² ●●● S1 W1 *n*
1 [singular] a situation in which something is necessary, especially something that is not happening yet or is not yet available: **[+for]** *There's a growing need for new housing in many rural areas.* | **a need to do sth** *We fully recognize the need to improve communications.*
2 [singular, U] a strong feeling that you want something, want to do something, or that you must have something: **[+for]** *the need for job satisfaction* | **feel the need (to do sth)** *Jack did not feel the need to boast about his success.* | *You're welcome to come back and talk any time, if ever you feel the need.*
3 [C usually plural] what someone needs to have in order to live a normal healthy comfortable life: *She works to provide for her family's* ***basic needs.*** | **sb's needs** *Environmentalists argue that the organization fails to address the needs of third world farmers.* | **meet/satisfy a need** (=provide something that people want or need) *The charity exists to meet the needs of elderly people.* | *Schools must satisfy the needs of their pupils.* | *We have loans to meet your* ***every need.***
4 there's no need (for sb) to do sth a) used to say that someone does not have to do something: *There's no need for you to come if you don't want to.* | *There's no need to feel sorry for him.* **b)** *spoken* used to tell someone to stop doing something: *There's no need to shout!*
5 be in need of sth a) to need help, advice, money etc, because you are in a difficult situation: *This project is* ***in urgent need of*** *funding.* | *He is homeless and* ***in desperate need of*** *help.* **b)** to need to be cleaned, repaired, or given attention in some way: *The church was* ***in dire*** (=very great) ***need of*** *repair.*
6 have no need of sth to not need something: *She believes him and has no need of further proof.*
7 [U] when you do not have enough food or money: *cases of severe need in the inner cities* | **in need** *We must care for those in need.*
8 in your hour of need when you are in trouble and need someone to help you: *How could she abandon her father now, in his hour of need?*
9 needs must (when the devil drives) *BrE* used to say that you must sometimes do things that you do not like doing: *It's not the most comfortable way to travel, but needs must.*
→ SPECIAL NEEDS

COLLOCATIONS

ADJECTIVES

a real/clear need (=one that really exists) *There is a real need for after-school care in our area.*
an urgent need (=one that must be dealt with quickly) *The most urgent need was for more teachers.*
a pressing/crying need (=a very urgent need) *There's a crying need for more doctors and nurses.*
a desperate need (=an extremely urgent need) *There is a desperate need to build more housing.*
a growing/increasing need *She emphasized the growing need to deal with environmental problems.*

VERBS

stress/emphasize/underline the need for sth (=say how important it is) *He stressed the need for better training courses.*
eliminate the need for sth (*also* **obviate the need for sth** *formal*) (=make something unnecessary) *The new drug treatment eliminates the need for surgery.*
a need exists *New teaching materials must be created if a need exists for them.*

PHRASES

there is a need for sth *Clearly there is a need for more research.*
there is no need for sth *They felt that there was no need for a formal contract.*
as/if/when the need arises (=if or when something becomes necessary) *Team members move from job to job as the need arises.*
if need be (=if it is necessary) *I can work during my lunch break if need be.*

need·ful /ˈniːdfəl/ *adj old use* necessary: *needful expenditure*

NEEDLES

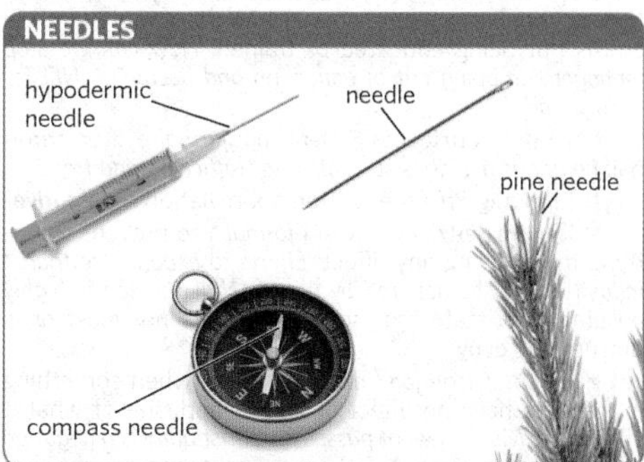

nee·dle¹ /ˈniːdl/ ●●○ *n* [C]
1 SEWING **a)** a small thin piece of steel, with a point at one end and a hole in the other, used for sewing → **pin**: *a needle and thread* | *a tapestry needle* **b)** a KNITTING NEEDLE
2 DRUGS a very thin, pointed steel tube at the end of a SYRINGE, which is pushed into your skin to put a drug or medicine into your body or to take out blood: *She carried hypodermic needles and syringes in her bag.* | *Drug users are at risk when they share needles.*
3 POINTER a long thin piece of metal on a scientific instrument that moves backwards and forwards and points to numbers or directions: *a compass needle*
4 MEDICAL TREATMENT a long, very thin piece of metal

used in ACUPUNCTURE (=a kind of medical treatment originally used in China)
5 LEAF a small needle-shaped leaf, especially from a PINE tree: *pine needles*
6 RECORDS the very small, pointed part in a RECORD PLAYER that touches the record in order to play it
7 like looking for a needle in a haystack *informal* used to say that something is almost impossible to find: *Finding out which file you want can be like looking for a needle in a haystack.* → PINS AND NEEDLES

needle² *v* [T] *informal* to deliberately annoy someone by making unkind remarks or jokes about them SYN **rib**, **tease**: *I just said that to Charlie to needle him.*

nee·dle·point /ˈniːdlpɔɪnt/ *n* [U] pictures made by covering a piece of material with small stitches → **embroidery**

need·less /ˈniːdləs/ ●○○ *adj*
1 needless to say used when you are telling someone something that they probably know or expect: *Needless to say, any contributions of money will be gratefully received.*
2 needless troubles, suffering, loss etc are unnecessary because they could easily have been avoided SYN **unnecessary**: *The report caused needless anxiety to women who have attended the clinic.* | *We need to bring to an end these needless deaths.* | *Charles hates needless waste.*
—**needlessly** *adv*: *People are dying needlessly every year of heart attacks.*

nee·dle·wom·an /ˈniːdlˌwʊmən/ *n* (*plural* **needlewomen** /-ˌwɪmɪn/) [C] a woman who is good at sewing

nee·dle·work /ˈniːdlwɜːk $ -wɜːrk/ *n* [U] the activity or art of sewing, or things made by sewing

need·n't /ˈniːdnt/ *especially BrE* the short form of 'need not': *I needn't have put on this thick coat.*

ˌneed-to-ˈknow *adj* **on a need-to-know basis** if information is given to people on a need-to-know basis, they are given only the details that they need at the time when they need them: *Access to the manufacturing process is on a strictly need-to-know basis.*

need·y /ˈniːdi/ ●○○ *adj*
1 a) having very little food or money: *a needy family* **b) the needy** needy people: *money to help the needy* THESAURUS POOR
2 needing and wanting a lot of love and attention

ne'er /neə $ ner/ *adv literary* never

ˈne'er-do-ˌwell *n* [C] *old use* a lazy useless person

NEET, **Neet** /niːt/ *n* [C] *BrE* (***Not in Employment, Education, or Training***) a young person who does not have a job and is not being educated or trained: *How can we stop teenagers dropping out of education and becoming NEETs?*
—**NEET** *adj*

ne·far·i·ous /nɪˈfeəriəs $ -ˈfer-/ *adj formal* evil or criminal: *nefarious activities such as drug trafficking and fraud*

neg. (*also* **neg** *BrE*) the written abbreviation of ***negative***

ne·gate /nɪˈɡeɪt/ AWL *v* [T] *formal* **1** to prevent something from having any effect: *Efforts to expand the tourist industry could be negated by reports that the sea is highly polluted.* **2** to state that something does not exist or is untrue SYN **deny**

ne·ga·tion /nɪˈɡeɪʃən/ *n* **1** [singular, U] when something is made to have no effect or be the opposite of what it should be: *Much of what passes for Christianity is a negation of Christ's teachings.* **2** [U] when someone says no or disagrees: *He shook his head in silent negation.*

neg·a·tive¹ /ˈneɡətɪv/ ●●● S2 W2 AWL *adj*
1 BAD harmful, unpleasant, or not wanted OPP **positive**: *My drinking was starting to have a negative effect on my work.* | *the negative aspects of ageing* | ***On the negative side**, it will cost a lot.* THESAURUS BAD, HARMFUL
2 NOT LIKING SB/STH considering only the bad qualities of a situation, person etc and not the good ones OPP **positive**: *students with a negative attitude to school* | *They have a uniformly negative image of the police.* | *Jean rarely sounded so negative about her mother.*
3 NO/NOT **a)** saying or meaning 'no': **negative answer/reply/response** *He gave a negative answer without any explanation.* **b)** containing one of the words 'no', 'not', 'nothing', 'never' etc OPP **affirmative**
4 SCIENTIFIC TEST not showing any sign of the chemical or medical condition that was being looked for OPP **positive**: *The pregnancy test was negative.* | *A person can be recently infected by HIV and have a negative result.*
5 ELECTRICITY *technical* a negative CHARGE is carried by ELECTRONS OPP **positive**
6 NUMBER/QUANTITY less than zero SYN **minus** OPP **positive**: *negative numbers* | *a negative return on our investment* (=a loss)
7 BLOOD *technical* used in the names of blood types, meaning not having the RHESUS FACTOR OPP **positive**
—**negatively** *adv*

negative² AWL *n* [C] **1** an image on a photographic film that shows dark areas as light and light areas as dark, from which the final picture is printed: *black and white photographic negatives* **2** a statement or expression that means 'no' OPP **affirmative**: **answer/reply in the negative** *formal* (=say 'no') *The majority of people, when asked whether or not they are creative, will **reply in the negative**.* **3** something bad or harmful OPP **positive**: *The negatives outweigh the positives on this issue.* **4** a negative result from a chemical or scientific test OPP **positive**: *The test will give a proportion of false negatives.*

negative³ *v* [T] *formal* **1** to refuse to accept a proposal or request **2** to prove something to be untrue

ˌnegative ˈequity *n* [U] *BrE* a situation in which someone owes more money on a MORTGAGE (=arrangement to borrow money to pay for a house) than they would receive if they sold their house

neg·a·tiv·i·ty /ˌneɡəˈtɪvəti/ *n* [U] an attitude in which someone considers only the bad qualities of a situation, person etc, not the good ones

ne·glect¹ /nɪˈɡlekt/ ●●○ *v* [T]
1 to fail to look after someone or something properly: *She smoked and drank, neglected the children, and left the clothes unmended.* | *a neglected garden* | *The building has been badly neglected.*
2 to pay too little attention to something: *Many of these ideas have been neglected by modern historians.* | *The police officer was accused of neglecting his duty* (=not doing everything he should).
3 neglect to do sth *formal* to not do something: *You neglected to mention that they had a second album released during 1991.*

neglect² ●●○ *n* [U]
1 failure to look after something or someone, or the condition of not being looked after: **[+of]** *Tenants are complaining about the landlord's neglect of the property.* | **years/decades/centuries etc of neglect** *After years of neglect, the roads were full of potholes.* | *The whole district had an air of abandonment and neglect.*
2 failure to pay proper attention to something: **[+of]** *Five officers were court-martialled for cowardice or neglect of duty.*

ne·glect·ful /nɪˈɡlektfəl/ *adj formal* not looking after something properly, or not giving it enough attention: **[+of]** *She became more and more neglectful of her responsibilities.* —**neglectfully** *adv*

neg·li·gee /ˈneɡləʒeɪ $ ˌneɡləˈʒeɪ/ *n* [C] a very thin, pretty coat, worn over a NIGHTDRESS

neg·li·gence /ˈneɡlɪdʒəns/ *n* [U] failure to take enough care over something that you are responsible for: *negligence in carrying out safety procedures* | *The bridge's architect was sued for criminal negligence.*

neg·li·gent /ˈneɡlɪdʒənt/ *adj* **1** not taking enough care over something that you are responsible for, with the result that serious mistakes are made SYN **irresponsible** OPP **responsible**: **negligent in (doing) sth** *The report stated that Dr Brady had been negligent in not giving the patient a full examination.* | *Mr Brown was found guilty of negligent driving.* THESAURUS CARELESS, GUILTY **2** *literary* a negligent manner or way of dressing is careless, but in a pleasantly relaxed way: *He gave a negligent shrug.* —**negligently** *adv*

neg·li·gi·ble /ˈneglɪdʒəbəl/ *adj* too slight or unimportant to have any effect SYN **insignificant**: *The damage done to his property was negligible.* THESAURUS ▸ UNIMPORTANT

ne·go·ti·a·ble /nɪˈgəʊʃiəbəl, -ʃə- $ -ˈgoʊ-/ *adj* **1** an offer, price, contract etc that is negotiable can be discussed and changed before being agreed on OPP **non-negotiable**: *Part-time barman required. Hours and salary negotiable.* | *The price is not negotiable.* **2** a road, path etc that is negotiable can be travelled along: *The road is only negotiable in the dry season.* **3** *technical* a cheque that is negotiable can be exchanged for money

ne·go·ti·ate /nɪˈgəʊʃieɪt $ -ˈgoʊ-/ ●●○ S3 W3 *v*
1 [I,T] to discuss something in order to reach an agreement, especially in business or politics: **[+with]** *The government refuses to negotiate with terrorists.* | **negotiate an agreement/contract etc** *Union leaders have negotiated an agreement for a shorter working week.* | *His first aim is to get the warring parties back to* ***the negotiating table*** (=discussing something).

GRAMMAR: Reciprocal verbs

Negotiate is a reciprocal verb. This type of verb is used when saying that two or more people or things do something that involves both or all of them: *The two sides have to negotiate.* You can also say: *The two sides have to negotiate with each other.* | *One side has to negotiate with the other.*
GRAMMAR GUIDE ▸ VERBS

2 [T] to succeed in getting past or over a difficult place on a path, road etc: *Guido swung the steering-wheel round to negotiate a corner.*

ne·go·ti·a·tion /nɪˌgəʊʃiˈeɪʃən $ -ˌgoʊ-/ ●●○ W3 *n* [C usually plural, U] official discussions between the representatives of opposing groups who are trying to reach an agreement, especially in business or politics: **[+with]** *The negotiations with the company had reached a crucial stage.* | **[+between]** *This follows private negotiations between the landowner and the leisure centre.* | **[+on/over]** *He is trying to involve community leaders in negotiations on reform.*

COLLOCATIONS

ADJECTIVES/NOUN + negotiation

long/lengthy *After lengthy negotiations, a compromise was finally reached.*
prolonged/protracted (=very long) *Despite protracted negotiations, the two sides have failed to reach agreement.*
difficult *The agreement is the result of two years of long and difficult negotiations.*
delicate (=in which it would be very easy to upset people and cause the negotiations to fail) *The company is about to start delicate negotiations with the union about next year's pay agreement.*
intense (=done with a lot of effort) *The agreement came after months of intense negotiations.*
peace/trade etc negotiations *A new round of global trade negotiations is due to start next week.*

VERBS

enter into/open negotiations (=start negotiations) *They have entered into negotiations to acquire another company.*
conduct negotiations *The country should conduct direct negotiations with its neighbours.*
break off negotiations (=stop them) *The two companies have broken off negotiations on the deal.*
resume negotiations (=start them again) *The pressure is on Israel and the Palestinians to resume peace negotiations.*
negotiations start *Peace negotiations started last week.*
negotiations stall (=stop making progress) | **negotiations break down** (=stop because of disagreement)

PHRASES

be under negotiation (=be being discussed) *The contract is currently under negotiation.*
be open to negotiation (=be able to be discussed) *The price is usually open to negotiation.*
be open to negotiation (=be willing to discuss something) *The president signalled that he is open to negotiation on the budget.*
be subject to negotiation (=be something that must be discussed) *The pay is subject to negotiation.*
a round of negotiations (=one part of a series of negotiations) *the next round of negotiations on trade barriers*
the initial/early/final stages of negotiation | **a breakdown in negotiations** (=an occasion when negotiations cannot continue because of a disagreement)

ne·go·ti·a·tor /nɪˈgəʊʃieɪtə $ -ˈgoʊʃieɪtər/ ●○○ *n* [C] someone who takes part in official discussions, especially in business or politics, in order to try and reach an agreement: *the chief union negotiator*

Ne·gress /ˈniːgrɪs/ *n* [C] *old-fashioned* a word for a black woman, usually considered offensive

Ne·gro /ˈniːgrəʊ $ -groʊ/ *n* (*plural* **Negroes**) [C] *old-fashioned* a word for a black person, usually considered offensive —**Negro** *adj*

ˌNegro ˈspiritual *n* [C] a SPIRITUAL[2]

neigh /neɪ/ *v* [I] if a horse neighs, it makes a long loud noise —**neigh** *n* [C]

neigh·bour *BrE*, **neighbor** *AmE* /ˈneɪbə $ -bər/ ●●● S2 W2 *n* [C]
1 someone who lives next to you or near you: *One of the neighbors complained about the noise from the party.* | *FBI agents were interviewing all their friends and neighbors.* | *Our* ***next-door neighbours*** (=the people who live in the house next to us) *say they'll look after our cat for us while we're away.*
2 a country that is next to another one → **bordering**: *Israel and its Arab neighbours*
3 someone or something that is next to another person or thing of the same type: *The teacher saw Phil passing a note to his neighbour.* | *The garden was divided from its neighbour by a high wall.*

neigh·bour·hood *BrE*, **neighborhood** *AmE* /ˈneɪbəhʊd $ -ər-/ ●●○ S3 W3 *n* [C]
1 an area of a town or city: *She grew up in a quiet neighborhood of Boston.* | *The hotel is situated in a peaceful residential neighbourhood* (=area where there are houses rather than factories or shops). | *a neighbourhood school* THESAURUS ▸ AREA

REGISTER
In everyday British English, instead of saying **in my neighbourhood**, people often say **where I live**: *There aren't many bookshops* ***where I live.***

2 the neighbourhood the area around you or around a particular place, or the people who live there: *Be quiet! You'll wake up* ***the whole neighbourhood!*** | **in the neighbourhood** *Is there a good Chinese restaurant in the neighbourhood?*
3 (something) in the neighbourhood of £500/30% etc a little more or a little less than a particular number or amount SYN **approximately**: *The painting is worth something in the neighborhood of $3,000.*

ˌneighbourhood ˈwatch *BrE*, **neighborhood watch** *AmE* *n* [U] a system, organized by a group of neighbours, in which members of the group regularly watch each other's houses in order to prevent crime

neigh·bour·ing *BrE*, **neighboring** *AmE* /ˈneɪbərɪŋ/ ●○○ *adj* [only before noun] near the place where you are or the place you are talking about SYN **nearby** → **bordering**: *The fair attracted hundreds of people from the neighbouring towns and villages.*

neigh·bour·ly *BrE*, **neighborly** *AmE* /ˈneɪbəli $ -ər-/ *adj* behaving in a friendly and helpful way towards the people who live next to you or towards the countries that are next to you: *the importance of good neighbourly relations between the two countries* —**neighbourliness** *n* [U]

nei·ther¹ /ˈnaɪðə $ ˈniːðər/ ●●● S3 W2 *determiner, pron* not one or the other of two people or things → **either**: *'Would you like tea or coffee?' 'Neither, thanks.' | It was a game in which neither team deserved to win.* | **[+of]** *Neither of them can cook. | Thompson had two strategies,* **neither of which** *seems to have worked very well. | We asked both John and Jerry, but* **neither one** *could offer a satisfactory explanation.*

GRAMMAR: Singular or plural verb?

- You use **neither** before a singular noun, with a singular verb: *Neither answer* ***is*** *right.*
- You use **neither of** before a plural noun or pronoun. In formal speech and in writing, you use a singular verb: *Neither of the answers* ***is*** *right.*
- In speech and informal writing, people sometimes use a plural verb: *Neither of the answers* ***are*** *right.*

neither² ●●● S3 *adv* used to show that a negative statement is also true about another person or thing → **either**: **neither does/can/will etc sb** *'I don't have any money.' 'Neither do I.' | Tom didn't believe a word she said, and neither did the police. | 'I don't like horror movies.'* ***'Me neither.'***

neither³ ●●● W2 *conjunction*
1 neither ... nor ... used when mentioning two things that are not true or possible: *Neither Oleg's mother nor his father spoke English. | The equipment is neither accurate nor safe.*

GRAMMAR: Negatives

After **neither**, use **nor**: ***Neither*** *he* ***nor*** *his wife enjoyed the vacation. | Most of them* ***neither*** *know* ***nor*** *care how it works.* ✗ Don't say: *Neither he or his wife ... | Most of them neither know or care ...*

2 be neither here nor there *spoken* used to say that something is not important because it does not affect a fact or situation SYN **irrelevant**: *The fact that she needed the money for her children is neither here nor there – it's still stealing.*
3 be neither one thing nor the other *spoken* used to say that something or someone cannot be described as either one of two types of thing or person, but is somewhere in the middle of the two: *The New York Times is neither one thing nor the other. It's not really a city newspaper and it's not really a national newspaper either.*
4 *formal* used to add another negative statement about someone or something SYN **nor**: *The authorities were not sympathetic to the students' demands, neither would they tolerate any disruption.*

nel·ly, nellie /ˈneli/ *n* **not on your nelly** *BrE spoken old-fashioned* used to tell someone that you are definitely not going to do something

nem·e·sis /ˈneməsɪs/ *n* [singular] **1** an opponent or enemy that is likely to be impossible for you to defeat, or a situation that is likely to be impossible for you to deal with: **meet/face your nemesis** *In the final he will meet his old nemesis, Roger Federer.* **2** *literary* a punishment that is deserved and cannot be avoided

neo- /niːəʊ, niːə $ niːoʊ, niːə/ *prefix* [in nouns and adjectives] based on a style, set of ideas, or political system that existed in the past SYN **new**: *neo-Georgian architecture | neo-fascists*

ne·o·clas·sic·al /ˌniːəʊˈklæsɪkəl◂ $ ˌniːoʊ-/ *adj* neoclassical art or ARCHITECTURE copies the style of ancient Greece or Rome: *a palace built in a neoclassical style*

ne·o·co·lo·ni·al·is·m /ˌniːəʊkəˈləʊniəlɪzəm $ ˌniːoʊkəˈloʊ-/ *n* [U] when a powerful country uses its economic and political influence to control another country —**neocolonialist** *adj*

ne·o·con·serv·a·tive /ˌniːəʊkənˈsɜːvətɪv $ ˌniːoʊkənˈsɜːr-/ (*also* **ne·o·con**) /ˈniːəʊkɒn $ -oʊkɑːn/ *n* [C] a member of a RIGHT-WING movement that has developed in the US since the 1960s and believes that the US should protect its national interests by using its power to influence other countries —**neoconservative** *adj*

Ne·o·lith·ic, neolithic /ˌniːəˈlɪθɪk◂/ *adj* relating to the last period of the STONE AGE, about 10,000 years ago, when people began to live together in small groups and make stone tools and weapons: *a Neolithic burial ground*

ne·ol·o·gis·m /niːˈɒlədʒɪzəm $ -ˈɑːl-/ *n* [C] *formal* a new word or expression, or a word used with a new meaning SYN **coinage**

ne·on /ˈniːɒn $ -ɑːn/ *n* [U] a colourless gas that is found in small quantities in the air and is used in glass tubes to produce a bright light in electric advertising signs. It is a chemical ELEMENT: symbol Ne: **neon lights/signs** (=ones that use neon) *the neon lights of Las Vegas | A neon sign flashed on and off above the door.*

ne·o·na·tal /ˌniːəʊˈneɪtl◂ $ -oʊ-/ *adj* [only before noun] *technical* relating to babies that have just been born → **antenatal**, **postnatal**: *neonatal care | nurses working in neonatal units*

ne·o·phyte /ˈniːəfaɪt/ *n* [C] *formal* **1** someone who has just started to learn a particular skill, art, job etc **2** a new member of a religious group

neph·ew /ˈnefjuː, ˈnev- $ ˈnef-/ ●●● S3 *n* [C] the son of your brother or sister, or the son of your husband's or wife's brother or sister → **niece**, **uncle**, **aunt**

nep·o·tis·m /ˈnepətɪzəm/ *n* [U] the practice of unfairly giving the best jobs to members of your family when you are in a position of power: *allegations of nepotism and corruption* —**nepotistic** /ˌnepəˈtɪstɪk◂/ *adj* → CRONYISM, → **jobs for the boys** at JOB(16)

Nep·tune /ˈneptjuːn $ -tuːn/ *n* the PLANET that is eighth in order from the Sun: *the discovery of Neptune in 1846*

nerd /nɜːd $ nɜːrd/ *n* [C] *informal* **1** someone who seems only interested in computers and other technical things – used to show disapproval SYN **geek**: *a* ***computer nerd*** **2** someone who seems very boring and unfashionable, and is not good in social situations —**nerdy** *adj*: *nerdy glasses*

Ne·ro /ˈnɪərəʊ/ (37–68 AD) a Roman EMPEROR, said to have killed his mother, wives, and many others. He blamed the Christians for causing the great fire of Rome in AD 64 and many were killed. He is also known for his performances as an actor and musician, and is usually shown in pictures fiddling (=playing the VIOLIN) while Rome is on fire behind him. The expression 'Nero fiddled while Rome burned' is sometimes used to describe a situation in which immediate action is needed, but time is being wasted doing nothing.

nerve¹ /nɜːv $ nɜːrv/ ●●○ S3 W3 *n*
1 WORRIED FEELINGS **nerves** [plural] **a)** used to talk about someone being worried or frightened: **sb's nerves are on edge/in tatters/frayed** (=someone feels very worried or frightened) | **calm/steady your nerves** (=stop yourself feeling worried or frightened) *Sean drank a large glass of brandy to calm his nerves.* | **be a bundle/bag of nerves** (=be extremely worried or frightened) *I remember you were a bundle of nerves on your wedding day.* **b)** the feeling of being worried or a little frightened: *A lot of people* ***suffer from nerves*** *before they go on stage. | 'What's wrong with Rachel?' 'It's just nerves. She's got her driving test tomorrow.'* | **exam/first-night etc nerves**
2 BODY PART [C] nerves are parts inside your body which look like threads and carry messages between the brain and other parts of the body: *a condition which affects the nerves in the back* | **trapped nerve** *BrE*, **pinched nerve** *AmE* (=a nerve that has been crushed between two muscles etc, causing pain)
3 COURAGE [U] courage and confidence in a dangerous, difficult, or frightening situation: **the nerve to do sth** *Not many people* ***have the nerve*** *to stand up and speak in front of a large audience. | She finally* ***found the nerve*** *to tell him she wanted a divorce.* | ***It takes a lot of nerve*** *to report a colleague for sexual harassment.* | **lose your nerve** (=suddenly become very nervous so that you cannot do what you

N

intended to do) *Jensen would've won if he hadn't lost his nerve.* | **hold/keep your nerve** (=remain calm in a difficult situation) *It's hard to keep your nerve when people keep interrupting you.*
4 get on sb's nerves *informal* if someone gets on your nerves, they annoy you, especially by doing something all the time: *She's always moaning. It really gets on my nerves.*
5 LACK OF RESPECT [singular] *spoken* if you say someone has a nerve, you mean that they have done something unsuitable or impolite, without seeming to be embarrassed about behaving in this way SYN **cheek**: *He's **got a nerve** asking for more money.* | *'She didn't say sorry or anything.' '**What a nerve!**'* | **have the nerve to do sth** *She lets me do all the work, and then she has the nerve to criticize my cooking.*
6 touch/hit a (raw) nerve to mention something that makes someone upset, angry, or embarrassed, especially accidentally: *Without realizing, he had touched a raw nerve.*
7 nerves of steel the ability to be brave and calm in a dangerous or difficult situation: *The job requires nerves of steel.* → **strain every nerve** at STRAIN²(6)

nerve² *v* **nerve yourself to do sth/for sth** to force yourself to be brave enough to do something: *The parachutist nerved himself for the jump.*

'nerve cell *n* [C] a NEURON

'nerve ˌcentre *BrE*, **nerve center** *AmE n* [C] the place from which a system, activity, organization etc is controlled: *the ship's nerve center*

'nerve gas *n* [U] a poisonous gas that is used in war to kill or PARALYSE people

nerve·less /ˈnɜːvləs $ ˈnɜːrv-/ *adj written* used to describe someone's fingers when they cannot hold something firmly, especially because they have had a shock: *The key fell from her suddenly nerveless fingers.*

'nerve-ˌracking, **nerve-wracking** *adj* a nerve-racking situation makes you feel very nervous or worried: *Speaking in public can be a nerve-wracking experience.* | *Fran faced a nerve-racking wait for her test results.*

ner·vous /ˈnɜːvəs $ ˈnɜːr-/ ●●● S3 W3 *adj*
1 worried or frightened about something, and unable to relax → **anxious**: **nervous about sth** *She was so nervous about her exams that she couldn't sleep.* | *I wish you'd stop looking at me like that. You're **making** me **nervous**.* | **feel/get nervous** *Paul always gets nervous whenever he has to give a presentation.* | **nervous smile/laugh/look/glance** *'Don't be silly,' she said with a nervous laugh. 'There's no such thing as ghosts.'* | *By the time I got into the interview I **was a nervous wreck*** (=was extremely nervous). | **nervous of sb** *We were all a bit nervous of him at first* (=frightened of him). THESAURUS▸ WORRIED
2 often becoming worried or frightened, and easily upset: *She's a nervous, sensitive child.* | *The film is unsuitable for people **of a nervous disposition*** (=who are easily frightened).
3 [only before noun] relating to the nerves in your body: **nervous condition/illness/disorder** *She was suffering from a nervous condition.* | *He had a **nervous twitch*** (=his body made small uncontrolled movements).
4 nervous exhaustion/strain a mental condition in which you feel very tired, usually caused by working too hard or by a difficult emotional problem —**nervously** *adv*: *She smiled nervously.* —**nervousness** *n* [U]: *Mike's nervousness showed in his voice.*

THESAURUS

nervous worried or a little frightened about something and unable to relax: *Kelly was so nervous about her exam that she couldn't sleep.* | *It makes me nervous when you drive that fast.*
tense worried and unable to relax in a way that makes you get angry or upset easily: *Mary's problems at work were making her tense and irritable.*
uneasy nervous because you feel that something bad might happen, so that you are unable to relax until the danger has passed: *I began to feel uneasy when he still hadn't phoned by 11 o'clock.*
on edge if you are on edge or your nerves are on edge, you feel nervous because you are worried about what might happen: *My nerves were on edge, waiting for the results of the test.* | *Redundancies and other work upheavals have put employees on edge.*
neurotic nervous and anxious in a way that is not normal or reasonable: *She's completely neurotic about food hygiene.* | *a neurotic mother*
edgy/jumpy/jittery nervous because you are worried about what might happen: *Investors are a little edgy about the financial markets these days.*
highly-strung *BrE*, **high-strung** *AmE* becoming nervous or upset easily because that is your character: *Like many musicians, he's very sensitive and highly-strung.*
be a nervous wreck to feel extremely nervous and unable to relax: *After 10 months of teaching, I was a total nervous wreck.*
have butterflies (in your stomach) *informal* to feel nervous about something that you are going to do very soon because it is important and you want to do it well: *Actors often have butterflies before going on stage.*

ˌnervous 'breakdown *n* [C] a mental illness in which someone becomes extremely anxious and tired and cannot deal with the things they usually do: *Colin came close to **having** a **nervous breakdown** last year.*

'nervous ˌsystem *n* [C] your nerves, brain, and SPINAL CORD, with which your body feels pain, heat etc and your movements are controlled

nerv·y /ˈnɜːvi $ ˈnɜːr-/ *adj informal* **1** nervous and easily frightened: *She was all tired and nervy.* **2** *AmE* brave and confident

-ness /nəs/ *suffix* [in nouns] used to form nouns from adjectives: *loudness* | *sadness*

nest¹ /nest/ ●●○ *n* [C]
1 BIRDS a place made or chosen by a bird to lay its eggs in and to live in: *a **bird's nest*** | *In May the females **build** a **nest** and lay their eggs.* | *Young eagles leave the nest after only two months.*
2 INSECTS/ANIMALS a place where insects or small animals live: *a field mouse's nest*
3 leave/fly the nest to leave your parents' home and start living somewhere else when you are an adult: *Both daughters were ready to fly the nest.*
4 nest of spies/thieves/intrigue etc a place where people are secretly doing a lot of illegal or dishonest things
5 nest of tables/boxes etc a set of tables etc that fit inside each other → **feather your nest** at FEATHER²(1), → **mare's nest** at MARE(2), → LOVE NEST

nest² *v* **1** [I] to build or use a nest: *They say eagles used to nest in those rocks.* **2** [T] to organize information, especially in a computer program, so that some of the information is recognized as separate but is included or contained in a larger part of the information: *Phrases are nested in the dictionary entry for the first major word.*

'nest egg *n* [C] an amount of money that you have saved so that you can use it for something special in the future: *They had to use part of their retirement nest egg to pay for their son's college fees.*

nes·tle /ˈnesəl/ *v* **1** [I,T always + adv/prep] to move into a comfortable position, pressing your head or body against someone or against something soft: *Sarah lay there peacefully, the child nestling by her side.* | *He nestled his head against her shoulder.* **2** [I always + adv/prep] *literary* to be surrounded by something, especially hills or countryside: *a tiny village nestling among the foothills of the French Alps*

nest·ling /ˈnestlɪŋ, ˈneslɪŋ/ *n* [C] a very young bird that cannot leave its nest because it is not yet able to fly

net¹ /net/ ●●● S2 W2 *n*
1 INTERNET **the Net** (*also* **the net**) the system that allows millions of computer users around the world to exchange information SYN **the web**: *Bruce spends most evenings **surfing the Net*** (=looking at information in different places on

NETS

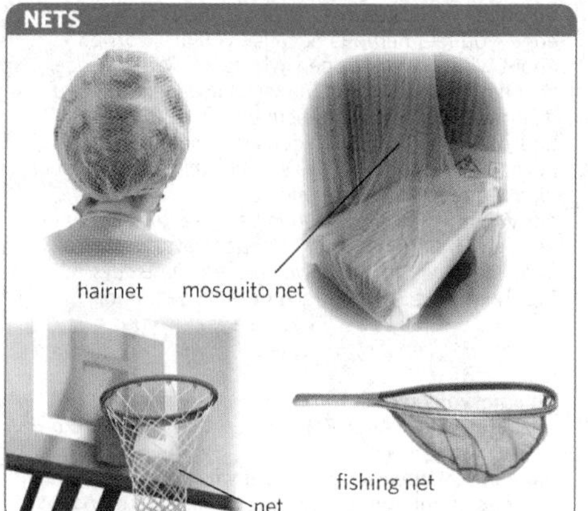

the Internet). | **on the Net** *You might find something on the Net.*

2 FOR FISHING/CATCHING THINGS [C] something used for catching fish, insects, or animals which is made of threads or wires woven across each other with regular spaces between them: *a **fishing net** | a butterfly net*

3 FOR SPORTS [C] **a)** the thing that players must hit the ball over in games such as tennis **b)** the thing behind the posts that players try to kick or hit the ball into in games such as football or HOCKEY → **goal**: *Henry kicked the ball into **the back of the net**.* → see picture at **TENNIS**

4 FOR KEEPING THINGS OUT [C] something used for keeping things out, for example insects or birds, which is made of threads woven across each other with regular spaces between them: *a **mosquito net***

5 MATERIAL [U] very thin material made from fine threads woven together, with small spaces between: ***net curtains***

6 slip through the net if criminals slip through the net, they avoid attempts by the police etc to catch them

7 fall/slip through the net if someone or something falls or slips through the net, a system which was designed to help or check them has not succeeded in doing this: *In a class of 30 children it is easy for some to slip through the net and learn nothing.*

8 cast/spread your net wide to consider or try as many things as possible in order to find what you want: *Record companies are casting their nets wide in search of new talent.*
→ **FISHNET STOCKINGS, HAIRNET, SAFETY NET, NETTING**

net² ●○○ (*also* **nett** *BrE*) *adj* [only before noun]
1 the net amount is the final amount that remains after all the other amounts have been taken away → **gross**: *The **net profit** (=after taxes, costs etc) was up 16.3% last month. | The company reported a **net loss** of $56 million last year. | Vernon estimates the company's **net worth** at over $8 billion. | The United States is a net importer of beef* (=it imports more than it exports).
2 net result/effect the final result or effect of something: *The net result will be higher costs to the consumer.*
3 net weight the weight of something without its container —**net** *adv*: *He earns $40,000 net. | jars of coffee weighing 450 grams net*

net³ *v* (**netted, netting**) **1** [T] *informal* to earn a particular amount of money as a profit after tax has been paid: *I was netting around $64,000 a year.* **2** [T] to succeed in getting something, especially by using your skill: *The company has recently netted several large contracts. | An undercover sweep netted 22 suspects in one evening.* **3** [I,T] *informal* to hit or kick the ball into the net in sport → **score**: *Rooney has netted nine goals for United so far this season.* **4** [T] to catch a fish in a net: *We netted three fish in under an hour.*

net·ball /ˈnetbɔːl $ -bɒːl/ *n* [U] a game similar to BASKETBALL played in Britain, especially by girls

net·book /ˈnetbʊk/ *n* [C] a small light computer that you can carry with you

neth·er /ˈneðə $ -ər/ *adj* [only before noun] *literary* lower down – often used humorously: *exploring the **nether regions** of East Sussex*

net·i·quette /ˈnetɪket/ *n* [U] *informal* the commonly accepted rules for polite behaviour when communicating with other people on the Internet

net·i·zen /ˈnetɪzən/ *n* [C] *informal* someone who uses the Internet, especially someone who uses it in a responsible way: *China and India will soon have far larger numbers of netizens than any Western nation.*

net·pre·neur /ˈnetprənɜː $ -nɜːr/ (*also* **net·re·pre·neur** /ˈnetrəprənɜː $ -nɜːr/) *n* [C] *informal* someone who has started an Internet business

net·speak /ˈnetspiːk/ *n* [U] the expressions, technical words, SLANG etc commonly used on the Internet: *a glossary of netspeak terms*

nett /net/ *adj* a British spelling of NET²

net·ting /ˈnetɪŋ/ *n* [U] material consisting of string, wire etc that has been woven into a net → **mesh**: *a fence of wire netting*

net·tle¹ /ˈnetl/ (*also* **stinging nettle**) *n* [C] a wild plant with rough leaves that sting you → **grasp the nettle** at GRASP¹(4), → **STINGING NETTLE**

nettle² *v* **be nettled (by sth)** *informal* to be annoyed by what someone says or does: *She was nettled by Holman's remark.*

ˈnettle rash *n* [C,U] *BrE* a medical condition that causes areas of red spots on your skin

net·work¹ /ˈnetwɜːk $ -wɜːrk/ ●●● S3 W2 AWL *n* [C]
1 a system of lines, tubes, wires, roads etc that cross each other and are connected to each other: *Hungary's **telephone network** | a high-speed European **rail network** | **[+of]** an elaborate network of canals | the network of blood vessels in the body*
2 a group of radio or television stations, which broadcast many of the same programmes, but in different parts of the same country: *the four biggest **TV networks** | You're listening to the American Armed Forces Network.*
3 a set of computers that are connected to each other so that they can share information
4 a group of people, organizations etc that are connected or that work together: **[+of]** *It's important to build up a network of professional contacts.* → **the old-boy network** at OLD BOY(2)

network² AWL *v* **1** [I,T] to connect several computers together so that they can share information **2** [I] to meet and talk with people who have similar jobs to yours, especially because they may be useful for your work **3** [I,T] to broadcast a radio or television programme on several different CHANNELs at the same time

ˈnetwork aˌdapter, **network adaptor** *n* [C] a piece of equipment in a PC that allows the PC to be connected to a NETWORK

net·work·ing /ˈnetwɜːkɪŋ $ -wɜːr-/ AWL *n* [U] the practice of meeting other people involved in the same kind of work, to share information, support each other etc: *I'm hoping to **do** some **networking** at the conference next week in London.*

neu·ral /ˈnjʊərəl $ ˈnʊr-/ *adj technical* relating to a nerve or the NERVOUS SYSTEM: *signs of **neural activity***

ˌneural comˈputer *n* [C] a computer that is designed to operate in a way similar to the human brain —**neural computing** *n* [U]

neu·ral·gia /njʊˈrældʒə $ nʊ-/ *n* [U] *medical* a sharp pain along the length of a nerve —**neuralgic** *adj*

ˌneural ˈnetwork (*also* **ˌneural ˈnet**) *n* [C] a set of computers that are connected to each other, which share information and operate in a way that is supposed to be similar to the human brain: *By 1989, they were using neural networks to assess credit risks.*

neuro- /njʊərəʊ, -rə $ nʊroʊ, -rə/ *prefix* (*also* **neur-** /njʊər $ nʊr/) *technical* relating to the nerves: *a neurosurgeon*

neu·ro·in·for·mat·ics /ˌnjʊərəʊɪnfəˈmætɪks $ ˌnʊroʊɪnfər-/ *n* [U] a scientific study which combines NEUROSCIENCE (=the study of the brain) and INFORMATION SCIENCE (=the collecting, storing, and arranging of information, especially using powerful computers)

neu·rol·o·gy /njʊˈrɒlədʒi $ nʊˈrɑː-/ *n* [U] *medical* the scientific study of the NERVOUS SYSTEM and its diseases —**neurologist** *n* [C] —**neurological** /ˌnjʊərəˈlɒdʒɪkəl◂ $ ˌnʊrəˈlɑː-/ *adj*: *a neurological disease*

neu·ron /ˈnjʊərɒn $ ˈnʊrɑːn/ (*also* **neu·rone** /-rəʊn $ -roʊn/) *n* [C] a type of cell that makes up the NERVOUS SYSTEM and sends messages to other parts of the body or the brain SYN **nerve cell**

neu·ro·science /ˈnjʊərəʊˌsaɪəns $ ˈnʊroʊ-/ *n* [U] the scientific study of the brain

neu·ro·sis /njʊˈrəʊsɪs $ nʊˈroʊ-/ *n* (*plural* **neuroses** /-siːz/) [C,U] *medical* a mental illness that makes someone unreasonably worried or frightened

neu·ro·the·ol·o·gy /ˌnjʊərəʊθiˈɒlədʒi $ ˌnʊroʊθiˈɑːl-/ *n* [U] the study of how brain chemistry and structure affect religious beliefs and feelings

neu·rot·ic /njʊˈrɒtɪk $ nʊˈrɑː-/ *adj* **1** unreasonably anxious or afraid: *He seemed a neurotic, self-obsessed man.* **THESAURUS▸** NERVOUS **2** *technical* relating to or affected by neurosis: *neurotic disorders* —**neurotic** *n* [C]: *She accused him of being a neurotic.* —**neurotically** /-kli/ *adv*

neu·ro·typ·i·cal /ˌnjʊərəʊˈtɪpɪkəl◂ $ ˌnʊroʊ-/ *adj formal* without AUTISM or ASPERGER'S SYNDROME

neu·ter[1] /ˈnjuːtə $ ˈnuːtər/ *adj technical* a neuter noun, PRONOUN etc belongs to a class of words that have different INFLECTIONS from MASCULINE or FEMININE words → **gender**

neuter[2] *v* [T] **1** to remove part of the sex organs of an animal so that it cannot produce babies → **spay**: *a neutered tomcat* **2** to remove power from something or to stop something from being effective - used to show disapproval: *Plans to reform local government are designed to neuter local democracy.*

neu·tral[1] /ˈnjuːtrəl $ ˈnuː-/ ●●○ AWL *adj*

1 IN AN ARGUMENT ETC not supporting any of the people or groups involved in an argument or disagreement → **partisan**: *I always tried to remain neutral when they started arguing.* | *Clive decided to adopt a neutral position.* | *The British government acted as a neutral observer during the talks.*

2 IN A WAR a country that is neutral does not support any of the countries involved in a war: *During World War II, Sweden was neutral.* | **neutral territory/waters** (=land or sea that is not controlled by any of the countries involved in a war)

3 on neutral ground/territory in a place that is not connected with either of the people, groups, or countries that are involved in a discussion, argument, war, or competition: *The talks will be held on neutral ground.*

4 LANGUAGE language, words etc that are neutral are deliberately chosen to avoid expressing any strong opinion or feeling: *the neutral language of an official news report*

5 VOICE/EXPRESSION if someone says something in a neutral voice, or if they have a neutral expression on their face, they do not show how they are feeling: *Bragg said in a neutral voice, 'The investigation has been closed down.'*

6 COLOUR a neutral colour is a colour such as grey, light brown, or cream: *Neutral tones give the room a feeling of space.*

7 WIRE a neutral wire, for example in a PLUG, has no electrical CHARGE[1](7)

8 CHEMICAL a neutral substance is neither acid nor ALKALINE: *The plant prefers a neutral or slightly acidic soil.* | *a neutral pH of 7.0* —**neutrally** *adv*

neutral[2] *n* **1** [U] the position of the GEARS of a car or machine when no power is being sent from the engine to the wheels or other moving parts: **in/into neutral** *When you start the engine, make sure the car's in neutral.* | *Put the car into neutral.* **2** [C] a country, person, or group that is not involved in an argument or disagreement **3** [C usually plural] a neutral colour

neu·tral·i·ty /njuːˈtræləti $ nuː-/ AWL *n* [U] the state of not supporting either side in an argument or war —**neutralist** /ˈnjuːtrəlɪst $ ˈnuː-/ *adj, n* [C]

neu·tral·ize (*also* **-ise** *BrE*) /ˈnjuːtrəlaɪz $ ˈnuː-/ AWL *v* [T] **1** to prevent something from having any effect SYN **balance out**: *Rising prices neutralize increased wages.* **2** *technical* to make a substance chemically NEUTRAL: *a medicine that neutralizes the acid in the stomach* **3** to make an area NEUTRAL in a war **4** to destroy something that is dangerous to you during a war —**neutralization** /ˌnjuːtrəlaɪˈzeɪʃən $ ˌnuːtrələ-/ *n* [U]

neu·tri·no /njuːˈtriːnəʊ $ nuːˈtriːnoʊ/ *n* (*plural* **neutrinos**) [C] *technical* something that is smaller than an atom and has no electrical charge

neu·tron /ˈnjuːtrɒn $ ˈnuːtrɑːn/ *n* [C] *technical* a part of an atom that has no electrical charge

ˈneutron ˌbomb *n* [C] a type of NUCLEAR bomb that kills people but is not intended to cause much damage to buildings, roads etc

nev·er /ˈnevə $ -ər/ ●●● S1 W1 *adv*

1 not at any time, or not once: *He's never been to Australia.* | *I'm never going back there again, not as long as I live.* | ***It is never too late*** *to give up smoking.* | **never had/did/was etc** *Never had she been so confused.* | **never ever** (=used to emphasize what you are saying) *I'll never ever forgive him for leaving me.* | ***Never again*** (=never after a particular time) *would he return to Naples.* | **never in all my life** (=used to emphasize how bad something was) *Never in all my life have I felt so humiliated.* | **never for one moment** (=used to emphasize that you never thought something) *She had never for one moment imagined that it could happen to her.* | **sb/sth has never been known to do sth** (=used to say that something is strange because it has never happened before) *Max had never been known to leave home without telling anyone.*

2 you never know *spoken* used to say that something which seems unlikely may happen: *Try it! You never know, you might be lucky.*

3 I never knew (that) *spoken* used to mean that you did not know something until now: *I never knew you played the guitar!*

4 never so much as used to emphasize that someone did not do something, especially when this seems surprising: *I do everything for him, and he's never so much as made me a cup of coffee.*

5 that would/will never do *spoken* used to say that you would not want something to happen: *Someone might discover our secret and that would never do.*

6 never! *BrE spoken* used when you are very surprised by something: *'They're getting married next month.' 'Never!'* | *He's never going to cycle all the way to Manchester!* | ***Well I never!*** *I wouldn't have thought she was that old!*

7 (no) I never! *BrE spoken* used to say that you did not do something bad that someone has said you did. Many teachers think this is not correct English: *'You cheated, didn't you?' 'No, I never.'*

8 never say never *informal* used to say that you should not say that you will never do something, because there is always a small possibility that you might do it

9 never say die used to encourage someone not to give up

10 never fear *spoken old-fashioned* used to tell someone not to worry: *She'll be back, never fear.* → **never the twain shall meet** at TWAIN(2)

GRAMMAR: Word order

- **Never** usually comes before a verb: *I **never get** to bed before 11.* ✗ Don't say: *Never I get to bed before 11.*
- **Never** usually comes after the verb 'be': *She **was never** on time.*
- You sometimes use **never** before 'be' to emphasize that two statements are connected: *'Sarah was late that day.' 'I'm not surprised. She **never was** on time!'*
- **Never** usually comes after the auxiliary: *I **have never** liked sports.*
- You sometimes use **never** before an auxiliary to emphasize that two statements are connected: *I don't enjoy football. I **never have** liked sports.*

• In writing, you can use **never** at the beginning of a sentence before an auxiliary to emphasize something: ***Never had** she been so confused.*
GRAMMAR GUIDE ▶ ADVERBS

THESAURUS

never not at any time, or not once: *Ali had never seen snow before. | I'll never forget that day.*
never ever *spoken* used to emphasize that you mean never: *Do you promise never ever to tell anyone else about this?*
not once used to emphasize that you are surprised or annoyed because someone never did something: *She's never said thank you – not once. | Jo hasn't emailed me once in six months.*
not/never for a moment used to emphasize that you never had a particular thought or idea: *'Did you ever suspect he was cheating on you?' 'No, not for a moment.'*
not/never in a million years *spoken* used to say that it is completely impossible that something could ever happen: *Dad will never agree to that – not in a million years!*
at no time *formal* used to emphasize that something never happened: *At no time did anyone suggest that the drug was dangerous. | At no time were the prisoners mistreated.*

ˌnever-ˈending *adj* seeming to continue for a very long time SYN **endless**: *Keeping the house neat and clean is a never-ending battle.* THESAURUS ▶ PERMANENT

nev·er·more /ˌnevəˈmɔː $ -vərˈmɔːr/ *adv literary* never again

ˌnever-ˈnever *n* **on the never-never** *BrE old-fashioned informal* if you buy something on the never-never, you buy it by making small regular payments over a long period SYN **on hire purchase**

ˌnever-ˈnever land *n* [U] an imaginary place where everything is perfect

nev·er·the·less /ˌnevəðəˈles $ -vər-/ ●●○ W2 AWL *adv formal* in spite of a fact that you have just mentioned SYN **nonetheless**: *What you said was true. It was, nevertheless, a little unkind.* THESAURUS ▶ BUT

new /njuː $ nuː/ ●●● S1 W1 *adj*
1 RECENTLY MADE recently made, built, invented, written, designed etc OPP **old**: *the city's new hospital | the new issue of 'Time' magazine | new products on the market | The hardest part of this job is understanding the new technology. | a new range of drugs*
2 RECENTLY BOUGHT recently bought: *Do you like my new dress? | They've just moved into their new home.*
3 NOT THERE BEFORE having just developed: *new leaves on the trees | a young man with new ideas | a new generation of women writers* | **new hope/confidence/optimism etc** (=hope etc that you have only just started to feel) *a medical breakthrough that offers new hope to cancer patients*
4 NOT USED BEFORE not used or owned by anyone before OPP **used**, **second hand**: *New and second-hand books for sale. | I got a used video camera for £300 – it would have cost £1,000 if I'd **bought** it **new**. | Jake arrived in his **brand new*** (=completely new) *car.* | *a **spanking new*** (=completely new) *conference centre*
5 like new/as good as new in excellent condition: *Your watch just needs cleaning and it'll be as good as new.*
6 UNFAMILIAR not experienced before: *Learning a new language is always a challenge. | Living in the city was a new experience for Philip.* | **[+to]** *This idea was new to him.* | **that's a new one on me** *spoken* (=used to say that you have never heard something before) *'The office is going to be closed for six weeks this summer.' 'Really? That's a new one on me.'*
7 RECENTLY ARRIVED having recently arrived in a place, joined an organization, or started a new job: *You're new here, aren't you?* | **[+to/at]** *Don't worry if you make mistakes. You're still new to the job.* | **new member/employee/student etc** *training for new employees* | **new kid on the block** *informal* (=the newest person in a job, school etc) *It's not always easy being the new kid on the block.* | **the new boy/girl** *BrE* (=the newest person in an organization etc – used humorously)
8 RECENTLY CHANGED recently replaced or different from the previous one OPP **old**: *Have you met Keith's new girlfriend? | I'll let you have my new phone number. | the new regime in Beijing*
9 RECENTLY DISCOVERED recently discovered: *the discovery of a new planet | new oilfields in Alaska | important new evidence that may prove her innocence*
10 MODERN modern: *the new breed of politicians*
11 VEGETABLES [only before noun] new potatoes, CARROTS etc are grown early in the season and eaten when young
12 new life/day/era a period that is just beginning, especially one that seems to offer better opportunities: *They went to Australia to start a new life there.*
13 be/feel like a new man/woman to feel much healthier and have a lot more energy than before, or to have a different attitude: *I lost 19 pounds and felt like a new man.*
14 new arrival a) someone who has recently arrived or started work somewhere **b)** a new baby: *The children are thrilled with the new arrival.*
15 new blood new members of a group or organization who will bring new ideas and be full of energy: *What we need in this company is some new blood.*
16 new broom someone who has just started work in a high position in an organization and who is expected to make a lot of changes: *The company seems set to make a fresh start under a new broom.*
17 what's new? *spoken especially AmE* used as a friendly greeting to mean 'how are you?'
18 the new new ideas, styles etc: *This charming hotel is a delightful blend of the old and the new.*
19 sth is the new ... *BrE* used to say that something is thought to be the new fashion that will replace an existing thing: *Brown is the new black* (=brown clothes are very fashionable now).
20 new-made/new-formed/new-laid etc recently made, formed etc → **a new lease of life** at LEASE[1](2), → **turn over a new leaf** at LEAF[1](3) —**newness** *n* [U]

GRAMMAR: Order of adjectives

If there is more than one adjective, the adjectives are usually used in a fixed order.
You say: *We've got a lovely new car.* ✗ Don't say: *We've got a new lovely car.*
You say: *He wore his new blue shirt.* ✗ Don't say: *He wore his blue new shirt.*
GRAMMAR GUIDE ▶ ADJECTIVES

ˌNew ˈAge[1] *adj* relating to SPIRITUAL beliefs, types of medicine, and ways of living that are not traditional Western ones: *the New Age movement*

New Age[2] *n* **(the) New Age** New Age beliefs and ways of living

ˌNew Age ˈtraveller *n* [C usually plural] a member of a group of people in Britain who refuse to live the way other people live in ordinary society, and go from place to place living in vehicles

new·bie /ˈnjuːbi $ ˈnuː-/ *n* [C] *informal* someone who has just started doing something, especially using the Internet or computers

new·born /ˈnjuːbɔːn $ ˈnuːbɔːrn/ *adj* **newborn child/baby/son etc** a child that has just been born —**newborn** *n* [C]

new-build, **new-build** /ˈnjuːbɪld $ ˈnuː-/ *n* [singular] a house or houses that are being built, or that have been built very recently

new·com·er /ˈnjuːkʌmə $ ˈnuːkʌmər/ ●○○ *n* [C]
1 someone who has only recently arrived somewhere or only recently started a particular activity → **novice**: **[+to]** *I'm a relative newcomer to the retail business. | a special award for the most promising newcomer*
2 something that did not exist before: **[+to]** *The most glamorous newcomer to the Volkswagen Golf range is the revamped GTi 16 valve.*

ˌnew eˈconomy *n* [singular] an economic system that is based on computers and modern technology, and is therefore dependent on educated workers: *As we move into a new economy, trade unions will have to reinvent themselves to stay relevant.* —**new economy** *adj*: *new economy methods*

new·fan·gled /ˌnjuːˈfæŋɡəld◂ $ ˌnuː-/ *adj* [only before noun] recently designed or produced – usually used to show disapproval or distrust: *newfangled ideas about children's education* **THESAURUS** MODERN

ˈnew-found *adj* [only before noun] recently obtained, found, or achieved: *He enjoyed his new-found freedom.* | *the children's new-found friends*

ˈnew-look *adj* [only before noun] different from before, especially more modern or more attractive: *the new-look Labour party* | *the new-look football team*

new·ly /ˈnjuːli $ ˈnuːli/ ●●○ W3 *adv* **newly elected/formed/arrived etc** elected etc very recently: *the newly appointed director* | *newly fallen snow* **THESAURUS** RECENTLY

new·ly·weds /ˈnjuːliwedz $ ˈnuː-/ *n* [plural] a man and a woman who have recently married —**newlywed** *adj*

ˌNew ˈMan *n* (*plural* **New Men**) [C] a man who is considered to be very modern because he shares the work of looking after his children, cooking, cleaning the home etc

ˌnew ˈmedia *n* [U] things such as the Internet, DVDs etc that use very modern technology

ˌnew ˈmoney *n* [U] **1** people who have become rich by working, rather than by getting money from their families **2** money that makes someone rich and that is recently earned, rather than from their families

ˌnew ˈmoon *n* **1** [C usually singular] the moon when it first appears in the sky as a thin CRESCENT **2** [U] the time of the month at which the moon is first seen → **full moon**, **half moon**

ˌnew poˈtato *n* (*plural* **new potatoes**) [C] a small potato that is taken from the ground early, and that has a very good taste

ˌnew ˈrich *n* **the new rich** [plural] *AmE* people who have recently become very rich, as opposed to people whose families have always been rich —**new rich** *adj*

news /njuːz $ nuːz/ ●●● S1 W1 *n* [U]

1 information about something that has happened recently: *I hope to have some good news for you soon.* | **news that** *We are delighted at the news that our daughter is expecting a baby.* | **[+on]** *What's the latest news on your university application?* | **[+of/about]** *Everyone is shocked by the news of the arrests.*

2 reports of recent events in the newspapers or on the radio or television: *a late evening news broadcast* | *We've got the* ***news headlines*** *coming up at half past twelve.* | *a news and current affairs programme* | *Here's the sports news from Jane Murray.* | *the* ***latest news*** *from the Olympic stadium* | **[+about/on/of]** *news on the latest developments in the talks* | **news that** *Several evening papers carried the news that a cabinet minister was about to resign.* | **local/regional/national/international news** | *Twenty years ago environmental issues rarely* ***made the news*** (=were rarely considered important enough to be in the news). | **be in the news** *Hong Kong is in the news this morning.* | *His resignation* ***was front page news*** (=was important news). | **news story/report/item** *Never before has a news story triggered such sensational sales of the newspaper.*

3 the news a regular television or radio programme that gives you reports of recent events: *the ten o'clock news* | *Let's* ***watch the news***. | *Be quiet. I want to* ***listen to the news***. | **on the news** *It must be true – I heard it on the news last night.* | **switch/turn/put on the news** (=turn the television or radio on for the news)

4 be good/bad news for sb if the facts about something are good or bad news for someone, they are likely to make life better or worse for them: *There is no legal market for African ivory, which is good news for the elephants.*

5 he's/she's bad news *informal* used to say that someone is likely to cause trouble: *Stay away from that guy, he's bad news.*

6 be news if someone or something is news, people are interested in them at the moment and want to know about them: *European fashions* ***are big news*** *right now in the States.*

7 that's news to me! *spoken* used when you are surprised or annoyed because you have not been told something earlier: *'The meeting's been cancelled.' 'That's news to me!'*

8 I've got news for you *spoken* used to say that you are going to tell someone the facts about something, which they will probably not like to hear: *You may think I'm finished, but I've got news for you – I'll be back.*

9 no news is good news *spoken* used when you have not received any news about someone and you hope this means that nothing bad has happened

GRAMMAR

Countable or uncountable?

- **News** is an uncountable noun and is followed by a singular verb: *The news* ***was*** *not very good.*
- **News** is used with the singular form of words such as **this** and **that**: *He was shocked when he heard this news.* ✗ Don't say: *these news*

Prepositions with the news

- If someone or something is **on the news**, they appear or there is a report about them on a television or radio news programme: *The minister was on the 10 o'clock news.* | *I saw the pictures of the crash on the news.*
- If someone or something is **in the news**, they are being discussed in newspapers and on news programmes: *Education has been in the news a lot this week.*

THESAURUS: new

new: *a new sports centre* | *a new edition of the book*
brand new completely new: *a brand new car*
recent made, produced etc a short time ago: *recent research into brain chemistry*
the latest [only before noun] the most recent: *Have you seen his latest film?* | *the latest fashions from Paris*
modern different from earlier things of the same kind because of using new methods, equipment, or designs: *modern technology* | *modern farming methods* | *a modern kitchen*
original new and completely different from what other people have done or thought of before, especially in a way that seems interesting: *The play is highly original.*
fresh fresh ideas, evidence, or ways of doing things are new and different, and are used instead of previous ones: *We need a fresh approach to the problem.* | *Police think they may have found some fresh evidence that links him to the murder.*
novel new and different in a surprising and unusual way – used especially about a suggestion, experience, or way of doing something: *The club have come up with a novel way of raising cash.*
innovative completely new and showing a lot of imagination – used especially about a design or way of doing something: *an attractive website with an innovative design*
revolutionary completely new in a way that has a very big effect – used especially about an idea, method, or invention: *a revolutionary treatment for breast cancer* | *His theories were considered to be revolutionary at the time.*
newfangled [only before noun] used about something that is new and modern but which you disapprove of: *My grandfather hated all this newfangled technology.*

N

COLLOCATIONS

ADJECTIVES

good news *He's feeling much better, so that's good news.*
great/wonderful news *They're getting married? That's wonderful news!*
welcome news (=good news that makes you happy)
bad/terrible news *'I'm afraid I have bad news,' said Jackson.* | *Have you heard the terrible news about Simon?*
the latest news *Mom sent a letter with all the latest news.*
old news (=news that you have already heard) *She wasn't surprised; it was old news to her.*
important news *I've got some important news to tell you.*
the big news *informal* (=an important piece of news) *The big news is that Polly and Richard are going to get married.*

VERBS

have some news (for sb) *I could tell by his face that he had some news.*
tell sb the news *Jack called him to tell him the good news.*
break the news (to sb) (=tell someone some bad news) *Two policemen came to the door to break the news about her husband.*
spread the news (=tell a lot of people the news) *After she had the baby, her husband made phone calls to spread the happy news.*
hear the news (=hear about something that has happened) *She was really upset when she heard the news.*
welcome the news *formal* (=say that you are pleased about some news) *Environmental groups welcomed the news that the area would be protected.*
greet the news with surprise/delight etc *formal* (=react to the news in a particular way) *Fans greeted the news of the victory with a loud cheer.*
news spreads (=a lot of people find out the news from other people) *News spreads fast in a small town.*

PHRASES

a piece of news (*also* **a bit of news** *BrE*) *Leo thought about this piece of news carefully.*
the good news is .../the bad news is ... (=used to introduce a piece of good and bad news) *The good news is that most stores have the game in stock; the bad news is that it's not cheap.*

ˈnews ˌagency *n* [C] an organization that collects news stories and supplies them to newspapers, radio, and television

news·a·gent /ˈnjuːzˌeɪdʒənt $ ˈnuːz-/ *n* [C] *BrE* **1** someone who owns or works in a shop that sells newspapers, magazines, sweets, and cigarettes **2 newsagent's** a shop which sells newspapers, magazines, sweets, and cigarettes

ˈnews ˌblackout *n* [C] a period of time when news about a particular event is not allowed to be reported: *The Indian government has* ***imposed*** *a* ***news blackout***.

ˈnews ˌbulletin *n* [C] **1** *BrE* a short news programme on radio or television, reporting only the most important information **2** *AmE* a very short news programme on radio or television, broadcast suddenly in the middle of another programme when something very important has happened SYN **newsflash** *BrE*

news·cast /ˈnjuːzkɑːst $ ˈnuːzkæst/ *n* [C] *AmE* a news programme on radio or television

news·cast·er /ˈnjuːzˌkɑːstə $ ˈnuːzˌkæstər/ *n* [C] *especially AmE* someone who reads the news on radio or television SYN **newsreader** *BrE*

ˈnew school, **new-school** *adj* [only before noun] *informal* using new ideas in a type of music or art: *new school hip hop artists*

ˈnews ˌconference *n* [C] a meeting at which someone, especially someone famous or important, speaks to people who work for newspapers or news programmes SYN **press conference**: *The chairman told a news conference that some members of staff would lose their jobs.* | **at/in a news conference** *At a news conference yesterday, the two men described their ordeal.*

news·flash /ˈnjuːzflæʃ $ ˈnuːz-/ *n* [C] *especially BrE* a very short news programme on radio or television, broadcast suddenly in the middle of another programme when something very important has happened SYN **news bulletin** *AmE*: *We interrupt this programme to bring you a newsflash.*

news·group /ˈnjuːzgruːp $ ˈnuːz-/ *n* [C] a discussion group on the Internet, with a place where people with a shared interest can exchange messages

news·hound /ˈnjuːzhaʊnd $ ˈnuːz-/ *n* [C] *informal* someone who collects information for a newspaper or news programme → **journalist**

news·let·ter /ˈnjuːzˌletə $ ˈnuːzˌletər/ ●●○ *n* [C] a short written report of news about a club, organization etc that is sent regularly to people who are interested: *The society publishes a newsletter twice a year.*

news·man /ˈnjuːzmæn $ ˈnuːz-/ *n* (*plural* **newsmen** /-men/) [C] someone who writes or reports news for a newspaper, radio, or television

news·pa·per /ˈnjuːsˌpeɪpə $ ˈnuːzˌpeɪpər/ ●●● S2 W2 *n*
1 [C] a set of large folded sheets of printed paper containing news, articles, pictures, advertisements etc which is sold daily or weekly SYN **paper**: *She had read about it in the newspaper.* | *a series of newspaper articles about life in Cuba*
2 [U] sheets of paper from old newspapers: *Wrap the plates in newspaper to stop them from breaking.* | *Bella laid the flowers out carefully on a* ***sheet of newspaper***.
3 [C] a company that produces a newspaper: *He works for a local newspaper.*

GRAMMAR: Patterns with newspaper

• You read something **in a newspaper**: *She saw an ad in the newspaper.* ✗ Don't say: *on the newspaper*
• You often talk about **the newspaper**: *I read something about it in the newspaper.* ✗ Don't say: *in newspaper*

COLLOCATIONS

VERBS

read a newspaper *Which newspaper do you read?*
get a newspaper (=buy one regularly) *We don't get a newspaper; we tend to watch the news on TV.*
see/read sth in the newspaper *I saw in the newspaper that he had died.*
appear in a newspaper *Her photo appeared in all the newspapers.*
a newspaper reports sth (=has an article on something) *The newspapers reported that the police were treating the death as a suicide.*

ADJECTIVES/NOUN + newspaper

a national newspaper *The story was in all the national newspapers.*
a local newspaper *The store advertises in the local newspaper.*
a daily/weekly/Sunday newspaper (=one that is published every day/week/Sunday) | **a tabloid newspaper** (=a small-sized newspaper, especially one with not much serious news) | **a quality newspaper** *BrE* (=a newspaper with a lot of serious news and good writing)

newspaper + NOUN

a newspaper article/report/story *I read quite an interesting newspaper report on the war.*
a newspaper headline *'Wine is good for you' announced a recent newspaper headline.*

a newspaper column (=a regular article in a newspaper written by a particular journalist) *She writes a regular newspaper column about gardening.* **a newspaper clipping/cutting** (=a story cut out of a newspaper) | **a newspaper reporter** | **a newspaper editor** | **a newspaper proprietor** *BrE* (=owner)

THESAURUS

newspaper: *The New York Times is a popular daily newspaper.*
paper a newspaper. Paper is more common than newspaper in everyday English: *There was an interesting article in the local paper today.* | *the Sunday papers*
the press newspapers and news magazines in general, and the people who write for them: *the freedom of the press*
the media newspapers, magazines, television, radio, and the Internet, considered as a group that provides news and information: *This issue has received a lot of attention in the media.*
tabloid a newspaper that has small pages, a lot of photographs, short stories, and not much serious news: *The tabloids are full of stories about her and her boyfriend.*
broadsheet *BrE* a serious newspaper printed on large sheets of paper, with news about politics, finance, and foreign affairs: *the quality broadsheets*

news·pa·per·man /ˈnjuːspeɪpəˌmæn $ ˈnuːzpeɪpər-/ *n* (*plural* **newspapermen** /-men/) [C] someone who writes or reports news for a newspaper SYN **journalist**

ˈnewspaper ˌstand *n* [C] a NEWSSTAND

news·print /ˈnjuːzˌprɪnt $ ˈnuːz-/ *n* [U] cheap paper used mostly for printing newspapers on

news·read·er /ˈnjuːzˌriːdə $ ˈnuːzˌriːdər/ *n* [C] *BrE* someone who reads the news on television or radio SYN **newscaster**

news·reel /ˈnjuːzriːl $ ˈnuːz-/ *n* [C] a short film of news that was shown in cinemas in the past

ˈnews reˌlease *n* [C] an official statement giving information to the newspapers, radio, and television SYN **press release**: *The University has* **issued** *a* **news release** *announcing the results of their experiments.*

news·room /ˈnjuːzrʊm, -ruːm $ ˈnuːz-/ *n* [C] the office in a newspaper or broadcasting company where news is received and news reports are written

ˈnews-sheet *n* [C] a small newspaper with only a few pages

news·stand /ˈnjuːzstænd $ ˈnuːz-/ *n* [C] a place on a street where newspapers and magazines are sold

news·wom·an /ˈnjuːzˌwʊmən $ ˈnuːz-/ *n* (*plural* **newswomen** /-ˌwɪmɪn/) [C] a woman who writes or reports for a newspaper, radio, or television

news·wor·thy /ˈnjuːzˌwɜːði $ ˈnuːzˌwɜːrði/ *adj* important or interesting enough to be reported in newspapers, on the radio, or on television: *newsworthy events*

news·y /ˈnjuːzi $ ˈnuːzi/ *adj informal* a newsy letter is from a friend or relative and contains a lot of interesting news

newt /njuːt $ nuːt/ *n* [C] a small animal with a long body, short legs, and a tail, which lives partly in water and partly on land

NEWT

ˌNew ˈTestament *n* **the New Testament** the part of the Bible which describes the life of Jesus Christ and what he taught, and the life of the first Christians → **Gospel**, **Old Testament**

New·toni·an /njuːˈtəʊniən $ nuːˈtoʊ-/ *adj* relating to the laws of physics that were discovered by the scientist Isaac Newton: *Newtonian mechanics*

ˈnew town *n* [C] one of several complete towns built in Britain since 1946

ˌnew variant CJˈD *n* [U] a brain disease that kills people, which may be caused by eating BEEF that is affected by BSE → **mad cow disease**

ˌnew ˈwave *n* **1** [C] a group of people who try to introduce new ideas in music, films, art, politics etc: **[+of]** *a new wave of feminism in the sixties and early seventies* **2** [U] (*also* **New Wave**) a type of music that was popular in the 1970s and early 1980s, which uses SYNTHESIZERS and a strong beat, and in which the words are sung without much emotion

ˌNew ˈWorld *n* **the New World a)** North, Central, and South America → **Old World**: *Christopher Columbus's voyage of discovery to the New World* **b)** wines from the New World are from non-European countries such as South Africa, New Zealand, and the United States —**New World** *adj*

ˌNew ˈYear, **new year** ●●○ *n* [U]
1 (*also* **the New Year**) the time when people celebrate the beginning of a new year: *We're going to spend Christmas and the New Year with my parents.* | *The business will be closed over New Year.* | **Happy New Year** (=used as a greeting) | *Our neighbours invited us round to* **see in the new year** (=celebrate the beginning of the year).
2 the new year the first few weeks of the year: *Prices are expected to go up in the new year.*

New Year resoˈlution, **ˌNew Year's resoˈlution** *n* [C] a decision to do something better or to stop doing something bad in the new year: *I haven't* **made** *any* **New Year resolutions** *– I never stick to them anyway.*

ˌNew Year's ˈDay ●●○ *n* [singular, U] 1st January, the first day of the year

ˌNew Year's ˈEve ●●○ *n* [singular, U] 31st December, the last day of the year

New Zea·land·er /njuː ˈziːləndə $ nuː ˈziːləndər/ *n* [C] someone from New Zealand

next[1] /nekst/ ●●● S1 W1 *determiner, adj*
1 the next event, day, time etc is the one that happens after the present one, or the previous one: *I just missed my flight to Chicago. When's the next one?* | *We'll look at the proposals at the next meeting.* | *Over the next couple of months, try to relax more and get more exercise.* | **next week/year/Monday etc** *We're hoping to open the factory sometime next year.* | **the next day/week etc** (=on or during the following day, week etc) *She called me and we arranged to meet the next day.* | **(the) next time** *Next time I go skiing, I'll wear warmer clothes.*
2 the next house, room, place etc is the one that is nearest to where you are now: *Turn left at the next corner.* | *We could hear them arguing in the next room.* → NEXT TO
3 the next person or thing in a list, series etc comes after the one that you are dealing with now: *Read the next two chapters before Friday.* | *Do they have the* **next size up** (=a slightly bigger size)?
4 next biggest/most common etc almost as big, more common etc than the one you are talking about: *Cancer-related diseases are the next biggest killers.*
5 the next best thing the thing or situation that is almost as good as the one you really want: *If I can't be home for Christmas, phoning you on the day is the next best thing.*
6 the next thing I/she etc knew *informal* used when something surprising happens very suddenly: *The next thing I knew, I was lying face down on the pavement.*
7 as the next man/person as any other man or person: *I am as keen to do well as the next man.*

next[2] ●●● S1 W1 *adv*
1 immediately afterwards: *With John here, you never know what will happen next.* | *Next, put it in the oven for 20 minutes.*
2 the next time: *When I next saw her she completely ignored me.*

N

next³ ●●● S3 W3 *pron*
1 the person or thing in a list, series etc that comes after the person or thing you are dealing with now: *What's next on the shopping list?* | **the next to do sth** *Who will be the next to go?*
2 the day/week etc after next the day, week etc that follows the next one: *Have you remembered it's Susie's birthday the week after next?*
3 the next to last the one before the last one: *the next to last day of their visit*
4 next (please) used to tell someone that it is now their turn to speak or their turn to do something
5 be next in line to be the next person, especially to have a job or position

ˌnext ˈdoor¹ ●●● S2 *adv*
1 in the house, room etc next to yours or someone else's: *the boy next door* | *Her office is just next door.*
2 next door to sth next to another building, room etc: *They live next door to the shop.*

next door² *n* [U] *BrE informal* the people living in the house or apartment next to yours SYN **neighbour**: *Have you seen next door's new car?*

ˈnext-door *adj* [only before noun] **1 next-door neighbour** the person who lives in the house or apartment next to yours **2 next-door apartment/office etc** the apartment etc that is next to yours

ˌnext of ˈkin ●○○ *n* [plural, U] your closest living relative or relatives: *May I have your name, address and next of kin, please?*

ˈnext to ●●● S3 W3 *prep*
1 very close to someone or something, with no other person, building, place etc in between: *There was a little girl sitting next to him.*
2 next to nothing very little: *He knows next to nothing about antiques.*
3 used to give a list of things you like, hate etc in order to say what is first on the list: *Next to soccer, I like playing tennis best.*
4 in comparison with someone or something: *Next to her, I'm a very poor cook.*
5 next to impossible/useless etc almost impossible, useless etc: *This crossword puzzle is next to impossible.*

nex·us /ˈneksəs/ *n* [singular] *formal* a connection or network of connections between a number of people, things, or ideas: **[+of]** *a nexus of social relationships*

NFL, the /ˌen ef ˈel/ (***the National Football League***) the organization in charge of the highest level of professional American football in the US. The NFL consists of two LEAGUES (=groups of teams who play against each other), the National Football Conference (NFC) and the American Football Conference (AFC). Every year, the teams that win these leagues play each other in the Super Bowl.

NGO /ˌen dʒiː ˈəʊ $ -ˈoʊ/ *n* [C] (***non-governmental organization***) an organization which helps people, protects the environment etc and which is not run by a government

NHL, the /ˌen eɪtʃ ˈel/ (***the National Hockey League***) the organization in charge of the highest level of professional ICE HOCKEY in the US and Canada. The NHL consists of two LEAGUES (=groups of teams who play against each other), the Eastern Conference and the Western Conference. Every year, the teams that win these leagues play each other in the Stanley Cup.

NHS, the /ˌen eɪtʃ ˈes/ (***the National Health Service***) the British system that provides free medical treatment for everyone, and is paid for by taxes: *NHS hospitals* | **on the NHS** (=free from the NHS) *Can I get my glasses on the NHS?*

ni·a·cin /ˈnaɪəsɪn/ *n* [U] a type of VITAMIN that is good for your skin and your NERVOUS SYSTEM

nib /nɪb/ *n* [C] **1** the pointed metal part at the end of a pen **2 his/her nibs** *old-fashioned informal* someone in authority or someone who thinks they are important: *And how's his nibs this morning?*

nib·ble¹ /ˈnɪbəl/ *v* **1** [I,T] to eat small amounts of food by taking very small bites: *He nibbled the biscuit cautiously.* | **[+at]** *There's a fish nibbling at my bait.* | **[+on]** *He nibbled on a piece of raw carrot.* THESAURUS BITE
2 [T] to gently bite someone in a loving way: *He began to nibble her ear affectionately.*

nibble away at sth *phr v* to take away small amounts of something so that the total amount is gradually reduced: *All these expenses are nibbling away at our savings.* | *The Scottish National Party is beginning to nibble away at Labour's majority.*

nibble² *n* **1** [C] a small bite of something: **[+of]** *She* ***took a nibble*** *of her cookie.* **2 nibbles** [plural] *informal* small things to eat, like CRISPS and PEANUTS, especially at a party **3** [singular] a small amount of interest in something: *We've had the house on the market for a month and not even* ***had a nibble*** *yet.*

NiCad /ˈnaɪkæd/ *n* [C] *trademark* (**nickel-cadmium**) a type of BATTERY that can be RECHARGED, and that is used in cameras and small electronic equipment

nice /naɪs/ ●●● S1 W2 *adj*
1 GOOD pleasant, attractive, or enjoyable: *They've got a very nice house.* | *Did you have a* ***nice time****?* | *It's such a* ***nice day*** (=good weather), *why not go for a swim?* | *What a* ***nice surprise****!* | **look/taste/smell nice** *You look nice in that suit.* | *Mm, something smells nice!* | **nice big/new/long etc** *a nice long holiday* | *a nice new car* | **nice and warm/clean/easy/quiet etc** *The house seemed nice and tidy.* | ***One of the nice things about*** *Christmas is having all the family together.* THESAURUS GOOD
2 FRIENDLY friendly, kind, or polite: *Dave's a really nice guy.* | *That's not a very nice thing to say about your sister!* | **[+about]** *Tim spilt wine all over the sofa, but Martha was very nice about it.* | **[+to]** *They were very nice to me while I was ill.* | **it is nice of sb (to do sth)** *It was nice of you to help.* | *He told me,* ***in the nicest possible way****, that I was interfering too much.* THESAURUS FRIENDLY, KIND
3 STH YOU WANT used to say what you like or what you think would be good or useful: *It's quite nice to live so close to work.* | **it is nice to do sth** *It would be nice to have a break.* | **that'd be nice** (=used to accept an offer or agree with a suggestion) *'Would you like a cup of coffee?' 'Yes, that'd be nice.'* | *I thought it would be a* ***nice idea*** *to send them some flowers.* | ***It would be nice if*** *you could let us know in advance.*

SPOKEN PHRASES
4 it's nice to know (that) used to mean that you feel happier when you know something: *I still haven't heard any news – it would be nice to know what's happening.* | *It's nice to know that there's someone nearby if she needs help.*
5 have a nice day! *AmE* used to say goodbye to someone, especially to customers in shops and restaurants when they are leaving
6 nice to meet you used as a friendly greeting when you meet someone for the first time: *Hello. It's nice to meet you at last.*
7 (it's been) nice meeting/talking to you used when you say goodbye to someone you have met for the first time
8 NOT NICE *BrE* used in a humorous or angry way when you really think that something or someone is not at all good or pleasant: *That's a nice way to treat a friend, I must say!* | *Well, we're in a nice mess now.*
9 nice try used when someone has made a guess or suggestion, or has attempted to do something, to say that it is good, but not quite correct or successful: *'We could phone Mark to come and pick us up.' 'Nice try, Clive, but we haven't got his number.'*
10 nice one! *BrE* used when someone has just said or done something clever, amusing, or helpful: *'Dad said he'd help pay for it.' 'Nice one!'*

11 be (as) nice as pie *BrE* if someone is as nice as pie, they are not angry with you when you were expecting them to be
12 nice work if you can get it *BrE* used humorously to say that someone has a very easy or enjoyable job, especially one which you would like to do
13 DETAIL *formal* involving a very small difference or detail: *a nice point of law*

14 RESPECTABLE *old-fashioned* having high standards of moral and social behaviour: *What's a* ***nice girl*** *like you doing in a place like this?*
15 nice ... shame about the ... *BrE* used when saying that part of something is good or well done, but a more important part is bad or badly done: *Nice video, shame about the song.*
16 make nice (with/to sb) *especially AmE informal* to make an effort to be nice to someone, especially so that they will like you: *It's a good idea to make nice with your girlfriend's parents.* —**niceness** *n* [U]: *The first thing you noticed about him was his niceness.* → **no more Mr Nice Guy!** at GUY(5)

GRAMMAR: Order of adjectives

- If there is more than one adjective, the adjectives are usually used in a fixed order.
You say: *There are some nice old houses.* ✗ Don't say: *There are some old nice houses.*
You say: *I had a nice long sleep.* ✗ Don't say: *I had a long nice sleep.*
- You can use **nice and** followed by another adjective after **be**: *The weather was nice and warm.*
- Before a noun you must leave out **and**: *a nice warm bath* ✗ Don't say: *a nice and warm bath*

GRAMMAR GUIDE ADJECTIVES

THESAURUS

PERSON

nice *especially spoken* friendly, kind, or polite. In written and formal English, it is better to use a more specific and interesting adjective than **nice**: *I like Clare – she's really nice.* | *It was nice of them to offer to help.*
pleasant friendly, polite, and easy to talk to – used especially about someone that you do not know very well: *I only met her once or twice but she seemed pleasant.*
sweet very kind and gentle: *Kylie's a very caring, sweet person.* | *It was sweet of you to send me a card.*
charming behaving in a polite and friendly way, which makes people like you and want to do things for you: *The salesman was very charming.* | *a charming hostess*
engaging interesting or amusing in a way that makes people like you – a rather formal word: *She can be very engaging.* | *an engaging smile*
likeable easy to like and seeming nice and friendly: *Bobby was a likeable kid with an angelic face.*
good-natured having a nice kind character and not getting angry easily: *Everyone likes Mike because he's always so good-natured.*
great *informal* used about someone who you like and admire a lot: *He's a great guy!*
lovely *especially BrE informal* very nice, kind, and friendly: *All the people I met on the course were lovely.* | *a lovely man*

DESCRIBING SOMETHING YOU LIKE OR ENJOY

nice *especially spoken* pleasant or enjoyable: *Did you have a nice day?* | *It was nice to be back home again.*
lovely *especially BrE informal* very nice: *We had a lovely time at the beach.* | *The hotel was lovely.*
fun *informal* if something is fun, you enjoy it: *The holiday was great fun.*
enjoyable giving you pleasure: *We had a very enjoyable evening.*
wonderful very enjoyable: *It was a wonderful concert.*
great (*also* **brilliant** *BrE*) *informal* very enjoyable: *'How was the party?' 'It was great!'* | *We all had a brilliant time.*
charming used about something that seems pleasant and has a lot of qualities that make you like it: *a charming little village in the Italian countryside* | *I thought the restaurant was rather charming.*
delightful *formal* very pleasant or enjoyable: *There are many delightful walks in the area.* | *a delightful evening*
pleasurable *formal* a pleasurable experience or feeling is one that you enjoy: *Shopping in the old city can be a pleasurable experience.*

ˌnice-ˈlooking *adj* attractive → **good-looking**: *a nice-looking young man* | *a nice-looking car*

nice·ly /ˈnaɪsli/ ●●○ S3 *adv*
1 WELL in a satisfactory, pleasant, or attractive way: *He was handsome and nicely dressed.* | *The table fits in nicely with the rest of the furniture.* | *The wound healed up nicely.* | *The garden's* ***coming along*** *very* ***nicely*** *now* (=it is growing well).
2 IN A PLEASANT/FRIENDLY WAY in a pleasant, polite, or friendly way: *I'm sure he'll help if you ask him nicely.*
3 be doing nicely *BrE* to be successful and be earning a lot of money: *The business is doing quite nicely.* | *Ed's* ***doing*** *very* ***nicely for himself*** *out in Japan.*
4 that will do nicely *BrE spoken* used when saying that something is very suitable and is just what you want: *'Will cheese sandwiches be okay?' 'Yes, that'll do nicely.'*
5 EXACTLY *formal* exactly or carefully: *a nicely calculated distance*

ni·ce·ty /ˈnaɪsəti/ *n* (*plural* **niceties**) **1** [C usually plural] a small detail or point of difference, especially one that is usually considered to be part of the correct way of doing something: *social niceties* | *legal niceties* | **[+of]** *the niceties of political diplomacy* **2 to a nicety** *formal* exactly

niche[1] /niːʃ, nɪtʃ $ nɪtʃ, niːʃ/ ●○○ *n*
1 [C] if you find your niche, you find a job or activity that is very suitable for you: *Amanda soon* ***found*** *her* ***niche*** *at the club.* | *He's managed to create a niche for himself in local politics.*
2 [singular] an opportunity to sell a product or service to a particular group of people who have similar needs, interests etc: **[+in]** *He spotted* ***a niche in the market.***
3 [C] a hollow place in a wall, often made to hold a STATUE

niche[2] *adj* [only before noun] relating to selling goods to a particular small group of people who have similar needs, interests etc: *niche marketing* | *a niche market* | *a niche product*

nick[1] /nɪk/ *n* **1 in the nick of time** just before it is too late, or just before something bad happens: *Luckily, help arrived in the nick of time.* **2 in good nick/in bad nick etc** *BrE informal* in good condition or in bad condition: *It's an old car but it's still in good nick.* **3** [C] a very small cut made on the edge or surface of something **4 the nick** *BrE informal* a POLICE STATION

nick[2] *v* [T] **1** *BrE informal* to steal something SYN **pinch**, **steal**: *Someone's nicked my wallet.* | **nick sth from sb/sth** *You nicked those pens from my desk.* THESAURUS STEAL **2** to make a small cut in the surface or edge of something, usually by accident: *He nicked his hand on some broken glass.* **3** *BrE informal* if the police nick you, they catch you and charge you with a crime SYN **arrest**: *You're nicked!*

nick·el /ˈnɪkəl/ *n* **1** [U] a hard silver-white metal that is often combined with other metals, for example to make steel. It is a chemical ELEMENT: symbol Ni **2** [C] a coin in the US or Canada that is worth five cents

ˌnickel-and-ˈdime[1] *v* [T] *AmE informal* to not give enough attention or money to something, with the result that it is not dealt with effectively

nickel-and-dime[2] *adj* [only before noun] *AmE* unimportant or involving little money

nick·name /ˈnɪkneɪm/ ●○○ *n* [C] a name given to someone, especially by their friends or family, that is not their real name and is often connected with what they look like or something they have done: **[+for]** *We had nicknames for all the teachers.* | *Stephen earned himself the nickname Hawkeye.* THESAURUS NAME —**nickname** *v* [T]: *She was nicknamed Sunny because of her happy nature.*

nic·o·tine /ˈnɪkətiːn/ *n* [U] a substance in tobacco which makes it difficult for people to stop smoking

N

ˈnicotine ˌpatch *n* [C] a small piece of material containing nicotine which you stick on your skin to help you stop smoking

ˌnicotine reˈplacement ˌtherapy *n* [C,U] (*written abbreviation* **NRT**) the use of products that contain a small amount of NICOTINE, for example NICOTINE PATCHes, to help people stop smoking

niece /niːs/ ●●● S3 *n* [C] the daughter of your brother or sister, or the daughter of your wife's or husband's brother or sister → **nephew**, **aunt**, **uncle**

nif·ty /ˈnɪfti/ *adj informal* something that is nifty is good because it is clever, skilful, or effective: *a nifty little gadget for squeezing oranges*

nig·gard·ly /ˈnɪgədli $ -ər-/ *adj old-fashioned* **1** a niggardly gift, amount, salary etc is much too small and is given unwillingly: *niggardly wages | a niggardly 2% increase* **2** unwilling to spend money or be generous SYN **stingy**: *a niggardly person*

nig·ger /ˈnɪgə $ -ər/ *n* [C] *taboo* a very offensive word for a black person. Do not use this word.

nig·gle¹ /ˈnɪgəl/ *v* **1** [T] if something niggles you, you keep worrying about it or feeling annoyed about it and you cannot forget it → **bug**: *Something's been niggling her all day. | **It niggles** me **that** we can't go home yet and get warm.* **2** [I] to argue or make criticisms about small unimportant details: *She niggled over every detail of the bill.*

niggle² *n* [C] **1** a slight feeling: *a niggle of doubt* **2** a slight criticism or complaint **3** a slight physical pain: *a niggle in his knee*

nig·gling /ˈnɪgəlɪŋ/ *adj* **1 niggling doubt/worry/suspicion etc** a slight doubt etc that you cannot stop thinking about SYN **nagging 2** a niggling injury or problem is a slight one that does not go away

nigh /naɪ/ *adv* **1 nigh on** *old-fashioned* almost: *There were nigh on 40 people there.* **2** *literary* near or soon: *Winter **draws nigh*** (=will start soon). → WELL-NIGH

night /naɪt/ ●●● S1 W1 *n* [C,U]

1 WHEN IT IS DARK the dark part of each 24-hour period when the sun cannot be seen and when most people sleep OPP **day**: *It was a cold moonlit night. | I didn't sleep too well last night.* | **at night** *At night the temperature drops below zero.* | **in/during the night** *He woke up twice during the night.* | **by night** *Many animals hunt by night.* | **(on) Friday night/that night etc** *There was a storm on Friday night.*

2 EVENING the time during the evening until you go to bed: *We had a really good meal **last night**. | They stay in and watch television **every night**. | She recognised him from **the night before*** (=the previous evening). | *My parents are coming for dinner **tomorrow night**.* | **Friday/Saturday etc night** *There's a party at Ben's place on Saturday night. | We were on our way back from a **night out*** (=an evening when you go to a party, restaurant, theatre etc) *at the theatre. | Anna doesn't like him walking home **late at night**.* | **quiz night/student night etc** (=an evening when a particular event happens, especially at a bar, club etc)

3 nights if you do something nights, you do it regularly or often at night: *I **work nights,** so I'm usually asleep during the day.*

4 night! *spoken* used to say goodbye to someone when it is late in the evening or when they are going to bed SYN **good night**: *Night! See you tomorrow!*

5 night night! *spoken* used to say goodbye to someone, especially a child, when they are going to bed

6 night and day/day and night all the time: *The store is guarded day and night. | We had to work night and day to get it finished.*

7 night or day/day or night at any time: *You can call me any time, night or day.*

8 night after night every night for a long period: *He's out drinking night after night.*

9 first night/opening night the first performance of a play or show → **premiere**: *We saw 'Riverdance' on its opening night.*

10 spend the night with sb/spend the night together to sleep with someone and have sex with them: *And you thought we spent the night together?*

11 a good night's sleep a night when you sleep well: *You'll feel better after a good night's sleep.*

12 (have a) late/early night to go to bed later or earlier than usual: *I think I'll have an early night.* → LATE-NIGHT

13 last thing at night at the end of the day, just before you go to bed: *You should water plants either first thing in the morning or last thing at night.* → NIGHTLY

GRAMMAR: Patterns with night

on ... night

• You say that something happens **on** a particular **night**: *The children stayed at their grandmother's on Friday night. | There will be a full moon on the night of October 21. | They asked him where he was on the night of the fire.*

in the night

• You use **in the night** when saying that something happens at some time during a particular night: *The baby kept crying in the night.* ✗ Don't say: *The baby kept crying on the night.*

at night

• You use **at night** when saying that something often happens during the night: *The noise of the traffic keeps me awake at night.*

by night

• You use **by night** when saying that a person or animal does something at night instead of during the day: *Owls hunt by night. | They travelled by night to avoid being seen by the police.*

COLLOCATIONS

ADJECTIVES/NOUN + night

last night *It rained last night.*

tomorrow night *I should be back by tomorrow night.*

Friday/Saturday etc night *I haven't seen him since Thursday night.*

an early night (=when you go to bed early) *I'm really tired - I need an early night.*

a late night (=when you go to bed late) *We had a late night last night.*

a long night (=a night when you do not sleep or you work hard) *Everyone was tired and grumpy. It had been a long night.*

a sleepless night *She had spent a sleepless night wondering what to do.*

VERBS

spend a night somewhere (=sleep somewhere) *We spent two nights at the Grand Hotel.*

stay the night (=sleep at someone's house) *You're welcome to stay the night if you like.*

have a bad night (=not sleep well, especially when you are ill) *I had a bad night last night.*

night falls *written* (=it starts to become dark) *It grew colder as night fell.*

the night wears on (=continues)

night + NOUN

the night sky *We looked up at the stars in the night sky.*

the night air *The night air was scented with jasmine.*

a night train/bus/flight

PHRASES

all night *He looked as if he'd been up all night.*

all night long (=used to emphasize that something continues for the whole night) *The noise continued all night long!*

late at night *We often get to bed very late at night.*

at this time of night (=used when something happens very late at night, and you are surprised) *Why are you calling me at this time of night?*

late/far into the night (=until very late at night) *Staff worked late into the night to make necessary repairs.*

in the middle of the night *She woke up suddenly in the middle of the night.*

in/at the dead of night *literary* (=in the middle of the night when it is quiet) *He drove through the countryside in the dead of night.*
day and night/night and day (=all the time) *The phones rang day and night.*
morning, noon, and night (=all the time) *She nagged at him morning, noon, and night.*

USAGE: At night or in the morning?
• You use **at night** when talking about a time before midnight: *We didn't get back till 11 o'clock at night.*
• You use **in the morning** when talking about a time after midnight: *We had to get up at four in the morning.*

night·cap /ˈnaɪtkæp/ *n* [C] **1** an alcoholic drink that you have at the end of the evening, just before you go to bed **2** a soft hat that people used to wear in bed

ˈ**night class** *n* [C] a class which takes place during the evening for people who work during the day

night·clothes /ˈnaɪtkləʊðz, -kləʊz $ -kloʊ-/ *n* [plural] clothes that you wear in bed

night·club /ˈnaɪtklʌb/ ●○○ *n* [C] a place where people go to dance and drink, which is open late at night

REGISTER
In everyday English, people often say **club** rather than **nightclub**: *Do want to go out to a* ***club*** *afterwards?*

ˈ**night deˌpository** *n* [C] *AmE* a special hole in the outside wall of a bank into which a customer can put money or documents safely when the bank is closed SYN **night safe** *BrE*

night·dress /ˈnaɪtdres/ *n* [C] a piece of clothing, like a thin dress, that a woman wears in bed

ˈ**night ˌduty** *n* [U] work that is done during the night: **on night duty** *She is on night duty at the hospital.*

night·fall /ˈnaɪtfɔːl $ -fɒːl/ *n* [U] *old-fashioned* the time when it begins to get dark in the evening SYN **dusk**: *Don't worry, we'll be back by nightfall.*

night·gown /ˈnaɪtgaʊn/ *n* [C] *old-fashioned* a night-dress

night·hawk /ˈnaɪthɔːk $ -hɒːk/ *n* [C] *AmE informal* someone who enjoys staying awake all night SYN **night owl**

night·ie /ˈnaɪti/ *n* [C] *informal* a NIGHTDRESS

nigh·tin·gale /ˈnaɪtɪŋgeɪl/ *n* [C] a small bird that sings very beautifully, especially at night

night·life /ˈnaɪtlaɪf/ *n* [U] entertainment in the evening: *The hotel is only a five minute walk from both the beach and the nightlife.*

night·light /ˈnaɪtlaɪt/ *n* [C] a small electric light that you put in a child's room at night

night·ly /ˈnaɪtli/ *adj* happening every night → **daily**: *the nightly talk show* —**nightly** *adv*: *The band plays twice nightly in the bar.*

night·mare /ˈnaɪtmeə $ -mer/ ●●○ *n* [C]
1 a very frightening dream: **[+about]** *Years after the accident I still* ***have nightmares*** *about it.* | *a* ***recurring nightmare*** (=one which you have again and again)
2 [usually singular] a very difficult, unpleasant, or frightening experience or situation: *Traffic was a nightmare.* | **[+for]** *This has been an absolute nightmare for me and my family.* | **nightmare of (doing) sth** *the nightmare of going through divorce* | *It was every teacher's* ***worst nightmare*** (=the worst thing which could have happened). | *a nightmare journey*
3 something terrible that you fear may happen in the future: **[+of]** *the nightmare of a nuclear war* | **nightmare scenario** (=the worst or most frightening situation that you can imagine) —**nightmarish** *adj*

ˈ**night owl** *n* [C] *informal* someone who enjoys staying awake all night

ˈ**night ˌporter** *n* [C] *BrE* someone who works at the main entrance of a hotel during the night

ˈ**night safe** *n* [C] *BrE* a special hole in the outside wall of a bank into which a customer can put money or documents safely when the bank is closed SYN **night depository** *AmE*

ˈ**night school** *n* [U] classes that take place in the evening for people who work during the day

ˈ**night shift** *n* [C] **1** a period of time at night when people regularly work, especially in a factory: **on the night shift** *She's on the night shift this week.* **2** the group of people who work on the night shift: *The night shift was just arriving.*

night·shirt /ˈnaɪt-ʃɜːt $ -ʃɜːrt/ *n* [C] a long loose shirt that someone, especially a man, wears in bed

ˈ**night spot** *n* [C] a place people go to at night for entertainment: *my favourite New York night spot*

night·stand /ˈnaɪtstænd/ *n* [C] *AmE* a small table beside a bed SYN **bedside table** *BrE*

night·stick /ˈnaɪtˌstɪk/ *n* [C] *AmE* a short thick stick carried as a weapon by police officers SYN **truncheon** *BrE*

night·time /ˈnaɪt-taɪm/ *n* [U] the time during the night OPP **daytime**: **at nighttime** *animals that hunt at nighttime*

ˌ**night ˈwatchman** *n* [C] someone whose job is to guard a building at night —**night watch** *n* [U]

night·wear /ˈnaɪtweə $ -wer/ *n* [U] clothes that you wear in bed at night

nig·nog /ˈnɪg nɒg $ -nɑːg/ *n* [C] *BrE taboo old-fashioned* a very offensive word for a black person. Do not use this word.

ni·hil·is·m /ˈnaɪəlɪzəm/ *n* [U] **1** the belief that nothing has any meaning or value **2** the idea that all social and political institutions should be destroyed —**nihilist** *n* [C] —**nihilistic** /ˌnaɪəˈlɪstɪk◂/ *adj*

-nik /nɪk/ *suffix* [in nouns] someone who is connected with a particular activity or set of beliefs: *a peacenik* (=someone who supports peace)

nil /nɪl/ *n* [U] **1** nothing SYN **zero**: *The new machine reduced labour costs to almost nil.* **2** *BrE* the number zero, used in sports results: *Our team won by two goals to nil.*

nim·ble /ˈnɪmbəl/ *adj* **1** able to move quickly and easily with light neat movements SYN **agile**: *nimble fingers* | *a nimble climber* **2 a nimble mind/brain/wit** an ability to think quickly or understand things easily —**nimbly** *adv* —**nimbleness** *n* [U]

nim·bus /ˈnɪmbəs/ *n* (*plural* **nimbuses** *or* **nimbi** /-baɪ/) **1** [C,U] *technical* a dark cloud that may bring rain or snow **2** [C] a HALO

nim·by /ˈnɪmbi/ *n* (*plural* **nimbies**) [C] (***not in my backyard***) someone who does not want a particular activity or building near their home - used to show disapproval —**nimby** *adj*

NiMH /nɪm/ *n* [C] (***nickel-metal hydride***) a type of BATTERY that can be RECHARGEd and that is used in cameras and small electronic equipment

nim·rod /ˈnɪmrɒd $ -rɑːd/ *n* [C] *AmE informal* an insulting word for someone who is stupid or not good at doing something

nin·com·poop /ˈnɪŋkəmpuːp/ *n* [C] *old-fashioned* a stupid person

nine /naɪn/ ●●● S2 W2 *number*
1 the number 9: *He's only been in this job for nine months.* | *We open at nine* (=nine o'clock). | *Kay was taught by her mother till she was nine* (=nine years old).
2 nine times out of ten almost always: *Nine times out of ten we can solve the problem over the phone.*
3 a nine days' wonder a thing or event that makes people very excited for a short time
4 have nine lives to make lucky escapes from dangerous situations → **dressed up to the nines** at DRESSED(4), → **be on cloud nine** at CLOUD[1](5)

nine·pins /ˈnaɪnˌpɪnz/ *n* [U] **1** a game in which you roll a ball at nine bottle-shaped objects to try to hit them so that they fall **2 drop/go down like ninepins** if people or things drop like ninepins, many of them fall down or become ill or injured suddenly all at the same time: *It's*

N

just three weeks into the season and players are dropping like ninepins.

nine·teen /ˌnaɪnˈtiːn◂/ ●●● S3 W3 *number*
1 the number 19: *It was nineteen minutes past seven.* | *I was only nineteen* (=19 years old).
2 nineteen to the dozen if you talk nineteen to the dozen, you talk very quickly and without stopping —**nineteenth** *adj, pron*: *in the nineteenth century* | *her nineteenth birthday* | *I'm planning to leave on* ***the nineteenth*** (=the 19th day of the month).

ˌNineteen ˌEighty-ˈFour (1949) a novel by George Orwell which describes an imaginary society of the future, where the government has complete control of everyone's lives, thoughts, and behaviour, and watches everything they do. The leader of this government is known as Big Brother, and there are pictures of him everywhere, showing the words 'Big Brother is watching you'. The book has had a great influence on the way that people think about and talk about politics, and people sometimes use the phrase 'Nineteen Eighty-Four' to describe a society that is too strictly controlled.

ˌnineteenth ˈhole *n* **the nineteenth hole** an expression used humorously by GOLF players meaning the bar where they drink after playing

ˌnine to ˈfive *adv* between nine o'clock and five o'clock, the normal working hours of an office worker: *She didn't like* ***working nine to five***. —**nine-to-five** *adj*: *a nine-to-five job*

nine·ty /ˈnaɪnti/ ●●● S3 W3 *number*
1 the number 90
2 the nineties [plural] (*also* **the '90s, the 1990s**) the years from 1990 to 1999: *America was far richer in the nineties.* | **the early/mid/late nineties** *The industry received a lot of bad publicity in the early nineties.*
3 be in your nineties to be aged between 90 and 99: **early/mid/late nineties** *My grandfather was in his early nineties when he died.*
4 in the nineties if the temperature is in the nineties, it is between 90 degrees and 99 degrees: **in the low/mid/high nineties** *Temperatures were still in the high nineties.* —**ninetieth** *adj*: *her ninetieth birthday*

nin·ja /ˈnɪndʒə/ *n* [C] in the past, a Japanese fighter with special skills

nin·ny /ˈnɪni/ *n* (*plural* **ninnies**) [C] *old-fashioned* a silly person

ninth¹ /naɪnθ/ ●●● S3 W3 *adj* coming after eight other things in a series: *in the ninth century* | *her ninth birthday* —**ninth** *pron*: *I'm planning to leave* ***on the ninth*** (=ninth day of the month).

ninth² *n* [C] one of nine equal parts of something

nip¹ /nɪp/ *v* (**nipped**, **nipping**) **1** [I always + adv/prep] *BrE informal* to go somewhere quickly or for a short time SYN **pop**: *Have we time to nip down the pub for a quick drink?* | *Another car nipped in* (=moved quickly into a space) *in front of me.* | *I've got to nip home and change my clothes.* **2** [I,T] to bite someone or something lightly: *She gently nipped the lobe of his ear.* | **[+at]** *The fish swam all around her and nipped at her legs.* **3 nip sth in the bud** to prevent something from becoming a problem by stopping it as soon as it starts: *Try to nip this kind of bad behaviour in the bud.* **4** [T] *BrE* to suddenly and quickly press something tightly between two fingers, edges, or surfaces → **pinch**: *Sally nipped her cheeks to make them look less pale.* | *He nipped his finger in the door.* **5** [I,T] *written* if cold weather or the wind nips at part of your body or at a plant, it hurts or damages it: **[+at]** *The frost nipped at our fingers.*

nip sth ↔ **off** *phr v* to remove a small part of something, especially a plant, by pressing it tightly between your finger and thumb: *She nipped off a dead flower.*

nip² *n* [C] **1** the act or result of biting something lightly or pressing something between two fingers, edges, or surfaces: *His dog* ***gave*** *me a painful* ***nip*** *on the leg.* **2** a small amount of strong alcoholic drink: **[+of]** *a nip of brandy* **3 a nip in the air** coldness in the air **4 nip and tuck** *informal* **a)** *AmE* equally likely to happen or not happen: *We made it to the airport, but* ***it was nip and tuck***. **b)** *AmE* if two competitors are nip and tuck in a race or competition, they are doing equally well SYN **neck and neck**: *The fourth quarter was nip and tuck, but the Bulls won 92-90.* **c)** a medical operation on your face or stomach that is done to make you look younger or thinner: *I might consider getting a nip and tuck in a few years' time.*

nipp·er /ˈnɪpə $ -ər/ *n* [C] *BrE informal* a child

nip·ple /ˈnɪpəl/ *n* [C] **1** the small dark circular part of a woman's breast. Babies suck milk through their mother's nipples. **2** one of the two small dark circular parts on a man's chest **3** *AmE* the rubber part on a baby's bottle that a baby sucks milk through SYN **teat** *BrE* **4** a part in an engine or machine made of rubber or plastic and shaped like a nipple. It has a hole in it which liquid can flow or be poured through.

nip·py /ˈnɪpi/ *adj informal* **1** weather that is nippy is slightly cold SYN **chilly**: *It's a bit nippy out there.* **2** *BrE* able to move quickly: *a nippy little car*

ni·qab /nɪˈkɑːb/ *n* [C] a piece of cloth covering the face below the eyes, which some Muslim women wear

nir·va·na /nɪəˈvɑːnə, nɜː- $ nɪr-, nɜːr-/ *n* [U] **1** the final state of complete knowledge and understanding that is the aim of believers in Buddhism **2** a condition of great happiness and a feeling of peace

ni·si /ˈnaɪsaɪ/ → **DECREE NISI**

nit /nɪt/ *n* [C] **1** an egg of a LOUSE (=a small insect that sucks blood), that is sometimes found in people's hair **2** *BrE informal* a silly person

ˈnit-ˌpicking *n* [U] *informal* when someone argues about small unimportant details or tries to find small mistakes in something: *Soames was getting impatient with his daughter's constant nitpicking.* —**nitpicking** *adj* —**nitpicker** *n* [C]

ni·trate /ˈnaɪtreɪt, -trət/ *n* [C,U] used in the name of substances containing NITROGEN and OXYGEN. Nitrates are often used to improve soil: *potassium nitrate* | *high levels of nitrates in drinking water*

ni·tric ac·id /ˌnaɪtrɪk ˈæsɪd/ *n* [U] a powerful acid that is used in explosives and other chemical products

ni·tro·gen /ˈnaɪtrədʒən/ ●●○ *n* [U] a gas that has no colour or smell, and that forms most of the Earth's air. It is a chemical ELEMENT: symbol N

ni·tro·gly·ce·rine, nitroglycerin /ˌnaɪtrəʊˈglɪsərən, -riːn $ -troʊˈglɪsərɪn/ *n* [U] a chemical used to make a powerful liquid explosive and also in some medicines

ni·trous ox·ide /ˌnaɪtrəs ˈɒksaɪd $ -ˈɑːk-/ *n* [U] a gas used by DENTISTS to reduce pain SYN **laughing gas**

nit·ty-grit·ty /ˌnɪti ˈgrɪti/ *n informal* **the nitty-gritty** the basic and practical facts of a subject or activity: *Let's* ***get down to the nitty-gritty*** *and work out the costs.*

nit·wit /ˈnɪt-wɪt/ *n* [C] *informal* a silly person

nix¹ /nɪks/ *v* [T] *AmE informal* to answer no to something or say that you will not allow something: *They nixed the idea of filming in Ireland.*

nix² *adv AmE old-fashioned* no

no¹ /nəʊ $ noʊ/ ●●● S1 W1 *adv*
1 used to give a negative reply to a question, offer, or request OPP **yes**: *'Are you Italian?' 'No, I'm Spanish.'* | *'Do you want any more?'* ***'No thanks.'*** | *'Could you help me write this?' 'No, sorry, I haven't got time at the moment.'* | *He wanted to take me to a disco but I* ***said no***. | *Sixty percent of people voted no.* | *If you're asking whether I feel the same way about her,* ***the answer is no***.

SPOKEN PHRASES

2 used to say that you disagree with a statement: *'You're always complaining about work.' 'No, I'm not!'*
3 used to say that you agree with a negative statement: *'They shouldn't drive so fast.' 'No, it's really dangerous.'*
4 used to tell someone not to do something: *No, Jimmy, don't touch that switch.*
5 used to show that you are shocked, surprised, annoyed, or disappointed by what someone has just told you, or by

what has just happened: *'She's nearly fifty.' 'No, you're kidding!'* | ***Oh no**, I've lost my wallet!*
6 used to correct what you have just said: *He's the director, no, the assistant director, of the company.*

7 won't take no for an answer if someone won't take no for an answer, they are determined that you should agree to do something: *He insists on taking us all out to dinner and he won't take no for an answer.*
8 used before COMPARATIVES to mean 'not even a small amount': *I'll pay you $75 and no more.* | *You're no better than the rest of them.* → **no longer** at LONG²(7)

no² ●●● S1 W1 *determiner*
1 not one or not any: *There's no food left in the fridge.* | *No trains will be affected by this incident.* | *a house with no central heating* | *There's no excuse for that kind of behaviour.*
2 used on signs to say that something is not allowed: *No parking* | *No smoking*
3 in no time *informal* very soon or very quickly: *We'll be home in no time.*
4 there's no doing sth *spoken* used to emphasize that it is not possible to do something: ***There's no knowing** what this lunatic will do next.* | ***There is no denying** the suffering of these families* (=they are definitely suffering).
5 used to emphasize that the opposite of a particular description is true: *That girl's no fool* (=she is intelligent). | *Larry's no friend of mine.* | *If he has to do it all himself, it will be no bad thing* (=a good thing). | *a question of no great importance*

no³ *n* (*plural* **noes**) **1** [singular] a negative answer or decision: *The answer was a definite no.* **2** [C] a vote against a proposal in parliament

No. (*also* **no.**) (*plural* **Nos., nos.**) the written abbreviation of ***number***: *Mozart's piano concerto no. 27*

No. 10 /ˌnʌmbə ˈten $ -bər-/ (***No. 10 Downing Street***) the address of the official home of the British PRIME MINISTER

ˈno-acˌcount (*also* **ˈno-count**) *adj* [only before noun] *AmE old-fashioned informal* a no-account person does not achieve very much because they are so lazy: *a no-account drifter who died of drink*

No·ah's ark /ˌnəʊəz ˈɑːk $ ˌnoʊəz ˈɑːrk/ *n* in the Bible, the large boat built by Noah to save his family and the animals from a flood that covered the earth

nob /nɒb $ nɑːb/ *n* [C] *BrE old-fashioned* a rich person with a high social position

ˈno ball *n* [C] an act of BOWLing the ball in the game of CRICKET in a way that is not allowed by the rules

nob·ble /ˈnɒbəl $ ˈnɑː-/ *v* [T] *BrE informal* **1** to make someone do what you want by illegally offering them money or threatening them → **bribe**: *The jury had been nobbled and the case had to be reheard.* **2** to prevent a horse from winning a race, especially by giving it drugs **3** to get someone's attention, especially in order to persuade them to do something: *I was nobbled by my deaf old aunt and couldn't get away.*

Noˈbel ˌprize *n* [C] one of the prizes given each year to people who have done important work in various types of activity. There are prizes for special achievements in PHYSICS, chemistry, economics, literature, and peace. The Nobel prizes were established by Alfred Nobel and are given in Sweden.

no·bil·i·ty /nəʊˈbɪləti, nə- $ noʊ-, nə-/ *n* **1 the nobility** the group of people in some countries who belong to the highest social class and have titles such as 'Duke' or 'Countess' SYN **the aristocracy 2** [U] the quality of being noble: *the nobility of his intentions*

no·ble¹ /ˈnəʊbəl $ ˈnoʊ-/ ●○○ *adj*
1 morally good or generous in a way that is admired: *It's very noble of you to spend all your weekends helping the old folk.* | *noble ideals*
2 [only before noun] belonging to the nobility: **noble family/blood/birth etc** *a member of an ancient noble family* | *The Marquis would have to marry a woman of noble blood.*
3 something that is noble is very impressive and beautiful: *the old church with its noble tower*
4 noble gas/metal *technical* a noble gas or metal is not affected chemically by other substances → **BASE METAL**
5 noble savage *literary* someone who comes from a society that is less developed or interested in money than western countries, making them morally better than people who live in western countries

noble² *n* [C] a member of the highest social class with a title such as 'Duke' or 'Countess' → **COMMONER**

no·ble·man /ˈnəʊbəlmən $ ˈnoʊ-/ *n* (*plural* **noblemen** /-mən/) [C] a man who is a member of the highest social class and has a title such as 'Duke'

no·blesse o·blige /nəʊˌbles əˈbliːʒ $ noʊ-/ *n* [U] the idea that people who belong to a high social class should behave in a kind and generous way towards people of a lower social class

no·ble·wom·an /ˈnəʊbəlˌwʊmən $ ˈnoʊ-/ *n* (*plural* **noblewomen** /-ˌwɪmɪn/) [C] a woman who is a member of the highest social class and has a title such as 'Duchess'

no·bly /ˈnəʊbli $ ˈnoʊ-/ *adv* **1** in a morally good or generous way that should be admired: *They chose to die nobly rather than to betray their king.* **2 nobly born** *literary* having parents who are members of the NOBILITY

no·bod·y¹ /ˈnəʊbədi $ ˈnoʊbɑːdi, -bədi/ ●●● S1 W2 *pron*
1 no one: *I knocked on the door but nobody answered.*
2 like nobody's business very much, very well, or very fast: *We get along like nobody's business.* → **be nobody's fool** at FOOL¹(5)

GRAMMAR: Negatives

- Don't use another negative word such as 'not' or 'nothing' after **nobody**. You say: *Nobody came.* | ***Nobody** said **anything**.* ✗ Don't say: *Nobody didn't come.* | *Nobody said nothing.*
- Don't use 'of' after **nobody**. ✗ Don't say: *nobody of them* | *nobody of his parents*
- You use **none of** when talking about a group of people: *None of them saw him.*
- You use **neither of** when talking about two people: *Neither of his parents went to the wedding.*
- **Nobody** is written as one word. ✗ Don't write: *no body*

nobody² *n* (*plural* **nobodies**) [C] someone who is not important and has no influence: *I was a nothing and a nobody with everything to prove.*

ˌno-ˈbrainer *n* [singular] *informal* a decision that is easy, and that you do not need to think about, used when you want to emphasize that it is really very easy: *Joining the savings plan is a no-brainer. Just do it.*

ˌno-ˈclaims ˌbonus *n* [C] in Britain, a reduction in the amount that you have to pay for car insurance, because you have not claimed any money during a particular period

ˌno-ˈconfidence *n* [U] **vote of no-confidence/no-confidence vote/motion of no-confidence etc** an official vote where people can say if they no longer think someone or something is good enough: *fears that he may lose a vote of no-confidence in parliament* | *The chairman has survived four no-confidence motions.*

ˈno-count *adj* another form of NO-ACCOUNT

noc·tur·nal /nɒkˈtɜːnl $ nɑːkˈtɜːr-/ *adj* **1** an animal that is nocturnal is active at night: *Hamsters are nocturnal creatures.* **2** *formal* happening at night: *Rebecca paid a nocturnal visit to the flat.*

noc·turne /ˈnɒktɜːn $ ˈnɑːktɜːrn/ *n* [C] a piece of music, especially a soft beautiful piece of piano music

nod¹ /nɒd $ nɑːd/ ●●○ W2 *v* (**nodded, nodding**) [I,T]
1 to move your head up and down, especially in order to show agreement or understanding → **shake**: *I asked her if she was ready to go, and she nodded.* | *Mom **nodded** her **head** sympathetically.* | **nod your approval/agreement etc** (=show your approval etc by nodding) *Corbett nodded his acceptance.*
2 to move your head down and up again once in order to

N

greet someone or give someone a sign to do something: **[+at]** *The judge nodded at the foreman to proceed.* | **[+to]** *She nodded to us as she walked by.*
3 have a nodding acquaintance (with sth) to know a little about a subject but not a lot: *Students will need to have a nodding acquaintance with Spanish.*
4 have a nodding acquaintance (with sb) (*also* **be on nodding terms (with sb)** *BrE*) to know someone but not very well
nod off *phr v* to begin to sleep, usually when you do not intend to and are sitting somewhere: *I missed the movie because I kept nodding off.*

nod² ●●○ *n*
1 [C] an act of nodding: *The woman greeted us with a nod of the head.* | *I showed the doorman my card and he* ***gave*** *a friendly* ***nod***.
2 give sb the nod/get the nod from sb *informal* to give or be given permission to do something: *We're waiting for the boss to give us the nod on this one.*
3 on the nod *BrE informal* by general agreement and without people discussing it: *The chairman's proposals are usually passed on the nod.*
4 a nod's as good as a wink *BrE* used to tell someone that you have understood something, although it was said in an indirect way → **the land of nod** at **LAND¹(9)**

no·dal /ˈnəʊdl $ ˈnoʊ-/ *adj* [only before noun] *technical* being or connected with a node: *the nodal point of the transport system*

nod·dle /ˈnɒdl $ ˈnɑːdl/ *n* [C] *BrE old-fashioned informal* your head or brain: *It's easy enough to do if you just* ***use*** *your* ***noddle*** (=think).

node /nəʊd $ noʊd/ *n* [C] *technical* **1** the place on the stem of a plant from which a leaf or branch grows **2** a place where lines in a network cross or join **3** a part of a computer network where messages can be received or sent **4** a LYMPH NODE

nod·ule /ˈnɒdjuːl $ ˈnɑːdʒuːl/ *n* [C] a small round raised part, especially a small swelling on a plant or someone's body —**nodular** *adj*

No·el /nəʊˈel $ noʊ-/ *n* [U] CHRISTMAS - used especially in songs and on cards

noes /nəʊz $ noʊz/ *n* the plural of NO³

ˌno-ˈfault *adj* [only before noun] *law* **1** a no-fault DIVORCE is one in which both people agree not to be married any longer and do not have to say whose fault this is **2** no-fault car insurance will pay for the damage done in an accident, even if you caused the accident

no-ˈfly ˌzone *n* [C] an area that only particular aircraft are allowed to enter, and in which other aircraft could be attacked

ˌno-ˈfrills *adj* [only before noun] a no-frills product or service includes only basic features and is not of the highest possible quality: *no-frills accommodation*

nog·gin /ˈnɒɡɪn $ ˈnɑː-/ *n* [C] *old-fashioned* **1** a small amount of an alcoholic drink **2** *informal* your head or brain: ***Use*** *your* ***noggin*** (=think).

ˌno-ˈgo ˌarea *n* [C] **1** an area that people should not go to because it is very dangerous: *This part of the city was a no-go area for the police.* **2** a subject that cannot be discussed because it is private or because it may offend people: *She made it clear that her private life was a no-go area.*

ˌno-holds-ˈbarred *adj* [only before noun] a no-holds-barred discussion, situation etc is one in which there are no rules or limits: *Viewers had been promised a no-holds-barred interview with the former mayor.*

ˌno-ˈhoper *n* [C] *BrE* a person or animal who you think has no chance of winning something or of being successful: *a bunch of complete no-hopers*

no·how /ˈnəʊhaʊ $ ˈnoʊ-/ *adv AmE informal* not in any way or in any situation - usually used humorously: *I never liked her nohow.*

noir → **FILM NOIR**

noise¹ /nɔɪz/ ●●● S2 W2 *n*
1 [C,U] a sound, especially one that is loud, unpleasant, or frightening SYN **sound**: *What's that noise?* | **[+of]** *the noise of the traffic* | *Try not to* ***make*** *a* ***noise*** *when you go upstairs.* | **gurgling/banging/crackling etc noise** *There was a strange whistling noise in his ears.* | *There was* ***a lot of noise*** *outside.* | ***Noise levels*** *have been reduced by 20%.* | **traffic/engine/background etc noise** *the problem of aircraft noise near airports*
2 (make) encouraging/optimistic etc noises (about sth) *BrE* to say things which suggest what your opinion or attitude is, without saying it directly: *Both sides were making hopeful noises about the hostages.*
3 make (all) the right noises (about sth) to say the things that other people want or expect to hear: *The health minister seems to be making all the right noises.*
4 make noises about doing sth to say that you are considering doing something: *He is now making noises about starting his own business.*
5 make a (lot of) noise about sth *BrE* to talk about something a lot, so that people will notice it - used to show disapproval: *modern men who make a noise about the fact that they know how to look good*
6 [U] *technical* unwanted signals produced by an electrical CIRCUIT
7 [U] *technical* pieces of unwanted information that can prevent a computer from working effectively
8 noises off the sounds, voices etc that come from actors who are not on the stage at the time → **BIG NOISE**

noise² *v* **be noised abroad/about/around** *old-fashioned especially BrE* if news or information is noised abroad, people are talking about it: *Rumours of an election are being noised abroad.*

noise·less·ly /ˈnɔɪzləsli/ *adv written* without making any sound SYN **silently**: *We crept noiselessly down the hall.* —**noiseless** *adj*: *his noiseless footsteps*

ˈnoise polˌlution *n* [U] very loud or continuous noise which is considered unpleasant and harmful to people

noi·some /ˈnɔɪsəm/ *adj literary* very unpleasant: *noisome smells*

nois·y /ˈnɔɪzi/ ●●● S3 *adj* (*comparative* **noisier**, *superlative* **noisiest**)
1 someone or something that is noisy makes a lot of noise OPP **quiet**: *The kids have been really noisy today.* | *a noisy engine* **THESAURUS** **LOUD**
2 a place that is noisy is full of noise: *The bar was very noisy.* —**noisily** *adv*: *He blew his nose noisily.*

no·mad /ˈnəʊmæd $ ˈnoʊ-/ *n* [C] a member of a tribe that travels from place to place instead of living in one place all the time, usually in order to find grass for their animals

no·mad·ic /nəʊˈmædɪk $ noʊ-/ *adj* **1** nomadic people are nomads: *nomadic herdsmen* **2** if someone leads a nomadic life, they travel from place to place and do not live in any one place for very long: *The son of an air force pilot, he had a somewhat nomadic childhood.*

ˈno-man's-ˌland *n* [singular, U] **1** an area of land that no one owns or controls, especially an area between two borders or opposing armies **2** a situation or type of activity that is not either of two things or is a combination of two things: **[+between]** *the no-man's land between art and science*

ˈno-mark, **no mark** *n* [C] *BrE informal* someone who is not successful and who you have no respect for: *I'm not going to listen to that no-mark.* —**no-mark** *adj*

nom de guerre /ˌnɒm də ˈɡeə $ ˌnɑːm də ˈɡer/ *n* (*plural* **noms de guerre** (*same pronunciation*)) [C] *formal* a name that someone uses instead of their real name, especially someone who is fighting in a war

nom de plume /ˌnɒm də ˈpluːm $ ˌnɑːm-/ *n* (*plural* **noms de plume** (*same pronunciation*)) [C] *formal* a name used by a writer instead of their real name SYN **pen name**

no·men·cla·ture /nəʊˈmeŋklətʃə $ ˈnoʊmənkleɪtʃər/ *n* [U] *formal* a system of naming things, especially in science: **[+of]** *the nomenclature of science* | *zoological nomenclature*

nom·i·nal /ˈnɒmɪnəl $ ˈnɑː-/ ●○○ *adj*
1 nominal sum/charge/fee etc a very small sum of money,

especially when compared with what something would usually cost or what it is worth: *A nominal charge is made for use of the tennis courts.*
2 officially described as being something, when this is not really true: *the* ***nominal head*** *of the rebellion | Their conversion to Christianity was only nominal.*
3 nominal value/rate/income etc *technical* a nominal value etc does not show what something is really worth or really costs, because it does not take into account changes in the price of other goods and services OPP **real**: *If prices rise and the* ***nominal wage*** *remains constant, the real wage falls.*
4 *technical* relating to nouns or used as a noun: *the nominal use of the present participle*

nom·i·nal·ly /ˈnɒmɪnəli $ ˈnɑː-/ *adv* officially described as being something, when this is not really true: *a nominally Christian country | He was nominally in charge of his father's printing company.*

nom·i·nate /ˈnɒməneɪt $ ˈnɑː-/ ●○○ *v* [T]
1 to officially suggest someone or something for an important position, duty, or prize: **nominate sb/sth for sth** *Ferraro was the first woman to be nominated for the job of vice president.* | **nominate sb/sth as sth** *She has been nominated as Best Actress for her part in the film 'Forever Together'.* | **nominate sb to do sth** *I nominate John to represent us at the meeting.* **THESAURUS** SUGGEST
2 to give someone a particular job: **nominate sb as sth** *Next year Mr Jenks will retire and Mr Broadbent will be nominated as his replacement.* | **nominate sb to sth** *She was nominated to the legislative council.*

nom·i·na·tion /ˌnɒməˈneɪʃən $ ˌnɑː-/ ●○○ *n*
1 [C,U] the act of officially suggesting someone or something for a position, duty, or prize, or the fact of being suggested for it: **[+for]** *Who will get the Republican nomination for president? | All the committee's nominations were approved.*
2 [C] the name of a book, film, actor etc that has been suggested to receive an honour or prize: *The nominations for the Academy Awards were announced Tuesday.*
3 [C,U] the act of giving someone a particular job, or the fact of being given that job: **[+as]** *O'Neil's nomination as chief executive*

nom·i·na·tive /ˈnɒmənətɪv, ˈnɒmnə- $ ˈnɑː-/ *n* [C] *technical* a particular form of a noun in some languages, such as Latin and German, which shows that the noun is the SUBJECT of a verb —**nominative** *adj*

nom·i·nee /ˌnɒməˈniː $ ˌnɑː-/ *n* [C] someone who has been officially suggested for an important position, duty, or prize: *the Democratic Party presidential nominee* | **[+for]** *a nominee for the post of vice president*

non- /nɒn $ nɑːn/ *prefix* **1** [in adjectives, nouns, and adverbs] used to say that someone or something is not a particular thing, or does not do a particular thing: *non-British visitors | a non-smoker* (=someone who does not smoke) | *a nonstop flight* (=one in which a plane flies from one place to another without stopping on the way)
2 [in nouns] used to refer to a situation where a particular action did not happen or will not happen: *non-payment of taxes | They were very disappointed at his non-appearance* (=the fact that he did not go to an event where he was expected).

non·a·ge·nar·i·an /ˌnɒnədʒəˈneəriən, ˌnəʊn- $ ˌnoʊnədʒəˈner-, ˌnɑːn-/ *n* [C] someone between 90 and 99 years old

ˌnon-agˈgression *n* [U] a situation in which two countries do not attack or fight each other: *Both sides are now committed to non-aggression.* | **non-aggression pact/treaty/agreement etc** *The countries will come together next week to sign a new non-aggression treaty.*

ˌnon-alcoˈholic *adj* non-alcoholic drinks do not contain alcohol: *non-alcoholic wine | Do you have anything non-alcoholic?*

ˌnon-aˈligned *adj* a non-aligned country does not support, or is not dependent on, any of the powerful countries in the world: *the non-aligned countries of Europe* —**non-alignment** *n* [U]

ˈno-name *adj* [only before noun] no-name products are not made by a well-known company and so do not have a well-known name: *a no-name personal computer*

ˌnon-atˈtendance *n* [U] *formal* failure to go to a place or event where you are supposed to go: *He was taken into care because of his non-attendance at school.*

ˌnon-ˈbinding *adj* a non-binding agreement or decision does not have to be obeyed: *The industry has signed a non-binding agreement to reduce pollution.*

nonce /nɒns $ nɑːns/ *adj* [only before noun] *technical* a nonce word or phrase has been invented for a particular occasion and is only used once

non·cha·lant /ˈnɒnʃələnt $ ˌnɑːnʃəˈlɑːnt/ *adj* behaving calmly and not seeming interested in anything or worried about anything: *'Has he got a girlfriend?' Jill asked, trying to sound nonchalant.* —**nonchalance** *n* [U] —**nonchalantly** *adv*: *He smiled nonchalantly.*

ˌnon-ˈcombatant / $ ˌ..ˈ../ *n* [C] **1** someone who is in the army, navy etc during a war but who does not actually fight, for example an army doctor **2** someone who is not in the army, navy etc during a war SYN **civilian** —**non-combatant** *adj*: *non-combatant military advisers*

ˌnon-commissioned ˈofficer *n* [C] an NCO

ˌnon-comˈmittal *adj* deliberately not expressing your opinion or intentions clearly: **[+about]** *The doctor was non-committal about my mother's chances of recovery. | The driver mumbled a non-committal reply.*

ˌnon-comˈpliance *n* [U] *formal* failure or refusal to do something that you are officially supposed to do: **[+with]** *Companies can be prosecuted for non-compliance with the law.*

non·con·form·ist /ˌnɒnkənˈfɔːmɪst◂ $ ˌnɑːnkənˈfɔːr-/ AWL *n* [C] someone who does not accept the ways of thinking or behaving accepted by most other people in their society or group —**nonconformist** *adj* —**nonconformity** *n* [U]

Nonconformist *adj* relating to one of the Protestant Christian churches that have separated from the Church of England —**Nonconformist** *n* [C] —**Nonconformism** *n* [U]

non·con·trib·u·to·ry /ˌnɒnkənˈtrɪbjətəri $ ˌnɑːnkənˈtrɪbjətɔːri/ *adj* a noncontributory PENSION or insurance plan is paid for by your employer only, and not by you

ˌnon-controˈversial *adj* not likely to cause any arguments or disagreements: *Most of the proposals are fairly non-controversial.*

ˌnon-coopeˈration *n* [U] the refusal to do something that someone in authority tells you to do, especially as a protest

non·count /ˈnɒnkaʊnt $ ˈnɑːn-/ *adj* a noncount noun is UNCOUNTABLE

non·cus·to·di·al /ˌnɒnkʌˈstəʊdiəl◂ $ ˌnɑːnkʌˈstoʊ-/ *adj law* **1 noncustodial sentence/punishment etc** *BrE* a form of punishment which does not involve being sent to prison **2 noncustodial parent/father/mother** a parent who does not have their child living with them after a DIVORCE or SEPARATION, because of a court's decision

ˌnon-ˈdairy *adj* non-dairy foods are not made with milk, butter, cream etc: *non-dairy ice cream*

ˌnon-denomiˈnational *adj* not relating to one particular religion or religious group: *a non-denominational school*

non·de·script /ˈnɒndəˌskrɪpt $ ˌnɑːndəˈskrɪpt/ *adj* someone or something that is nondescript looks very ordinary and is not at all interesting or unusual: *a rather nondescript suburban house*

non-dom /ˌnɒn ˈdɒm $ ˌnɑːn ˈdɑːm/ (*also* **ˌnon-ˈdomicile** *formal*) *n* [C] a foreigner working in Britain who does not pay tax in Britain on the money they make in other countries

none[1] /nʌn/ ●●● S1 W2 *pron*
1 not any amount of something or not one of a group of people or things: *I wish I could offer you some cake but*

N

there's none left. | *Although these were good students, none had a score above 60.* | *She waited for a reply, but none came.* | *Even an old car is better than none.* | **[+of]** *Despite her illness, she had lost none of her enthusiasm for life.* | *I know what people are saying – but none of it is true.* | *None of my friends phones me anymore.* | **none at all/none whatsoever** *'Was there any mail?' 'No, none at all.'*

2 will/would have none of sth (*also* **be having none of sth**) used to say that someone refuses to allow someone to do something or to behave in a particular way: *We offered to pay our half of the cost but Charles* ***would have none of it****.*

3 none but sb *literary* only a particular person or type of person: *a task that none but a man of genius could accomplish*

4 none other than sb used to emphasize that the person involved in something is famous, impressive, or surprising: *The mystery guest turned out to be none other than Cher herself.* → NONETHELESS, → **second to none** at SECOND¹(5), → **bar none** at BAR³(2)

GRAMMAR

Negatives

• Don't use another negative word such as 'not' with **none**. You say: *We got 3 points and they got none.* ✗ Don't say: *We got 3 points and they didn't get none.*

• You can say **not ... any** instead of **none**: *We got 3 points and they did****n't*** *get* ***any****.*

Singular or plural verb?

• You use **none of** before a plural noun or pronoun and a singular verb: *None of us* ***is*** *able to escape the consequences of our actions.*

• In informal English, people often use a plural verb after **none of**: *None of us* ***care*** *what happens to him.*

none² *adv* **1 none the worse/better etc (for sth)** not any worse, better etc than before: *She seems none the worse for her experience.* **2 none the wiser** not having any more understanding or knowledge about something than you had before: *I was none the wiser after his explanation.* **3 none too** not at all: *I was none too pleased to have to take the exam again.*

non·en·ti·ty /nɒˈnentəti $ nɑː-/ *n* (*plural* **nonentities**) [C] someone who has no importance or power and who is not special in any way SYN **nobody**

ˌnon-esˈsential *adj* not completely necessary: *All non-essential travel was cancelled.*

none·the·less /ˌnʌnðəˈles/ ●●○ AWL *adv* [sentence adverb] *formal* in spite of the fact that has just been mentioned SYN **nevertheless**: *The region was extremely beautiful. Nonetheless Gerard could not imagine spending the rest of his life there.* | *The paintings are complex, but have plenty of appeal nonetheless.*

ˌnon-eˈvent *n* [C usually singular] an event that is disappointing because it is much less interesting, exciting, or important than you expected: *In the end, the match turned out to be a non-event.*

ˌnon-executive diˈrector *n* [C] one of the DIRECTORS of a company who gives advice, but who does not make decisions about how the company is run

non·ex·ist·ent /ˌnɒnɪgˈzɪstənt◂ $ ˌnɑːn-/ *adj* something that is nonexistent does not exist at all, or is not present in a particular place: **almost/virtually/practically etc nonexistent** *On a Sunday morning traffic was almost nonexistent.* —**non-existence** *n* [U]

non·fat, non-fat /ˌnɒn ˈfæt◂ $ ˌnɑːn-/ *adj* having all the fat removed: *nonfat milk*

ˌnon-ˈfiction ●●○ *n* [U] books about real facts or events, not imagined ones OPP **fiction** THESAURUS ▸ BOOK —**non-fiction** *adj*

ˌnon-ˈfinite *adj technical* a non-finite verb does not show a particular tense or subject, and is either the INFINITIVE or the PARTICIPLE form of the verb, for example 'go' in the sentence 'Do you want to go home?' OPP **finite**

non·flam·ma·ble /ˌnɒnˈflæməbəl $ ˌnɑːn-/ *adj* non-flammable materials or substances do not burn easily or do not burn at all OPP **flammable** → **inflammable**

ˌnon-governˈmental *adj* [only before noun] a non-governmental organization is independent and not controlled by a government: *Emergency aid is being provided by non-governmental relief organizations.*

ˌnon-interˈvention *n* [U] the practice by a government of not getting involved in the affairs of other countries: *The British government may have to abandon its* ***policy of non-intervention****.* —**non-interventionist** *adj*: *a non-interventionist policy*

ˌnon-ˈiron *adj BrE* non-iron material does not need to be IRONed after it has been washed

ˌnon-judgˈmental (*also* **non-judgemental** *BrE*) *adj* not criticizing people: *A counsellor should always be sympathetic and non-judgmental.*

ˌnon-ˈmember *n* [C] someone who is not a member of a particular club or organization: *The price will be £30 for members, £33 for non-members.* | **[+of]** *non-members of the Labour Party* | **non-member state/country** *imports from non-member countries*

ˌnon-neˈgotiable *adj* **1** a non-negotiable principle or belief is one that you refuse to discuss or change: *He emphasized that the government's anti-nuclear position was non-negotiable.* **2** a cheque, BOND etc that is non-negotiable can only be exchanged for money by the person whose name is on it

ˈno-no *n* [singular] *informal* something that you must not do because it is considered to be unacceptable behaviour: *Colouring your hair was a no-no at that time.*

ˌno-ˈnonsense *adj* [only before noun] very practical and direct, without wasting time on unnecessary things SYN **down-to-earth**: *his no-nonsense attitude to business*

non·pa·reil /ˌnɒnpəˈreɪl $ ˌnɑːnpəˈrel/ *n* **1 nonpareils** [plural] *AmE* very small pieces of coloured sugar used to decorate cakes **2** [C] *AmE* a piece of chocolate covered with nonpareils **3** [singular] *literary* someone or something that is much better than all the others: *reviews by film critic nonpareil Pauline Kael*

ˌnon-partiˈsan / $ ˌ. ˈ.../ *adj* not supporting the ideas of any political party or group: *a non-partisan research group*

ˌnon-ˈpayment *n* [U] when you do not pay the money that you owe in tax, rent etc: **[+of]** *She was finally evicted in April for* ***non-payment of rent****.*

non·plussed (*also* **nonplused** *AmE*) /nɒnˈplʌst $ nɑːn-/ *adj* [not before noun] so surprised by something that you do not know what to say or do SYN **dumbstruck**: **[+by/at]** *Billy was completely nonplussed by Elliot's refusal.* THESAURUS ▸ SURPRISED

ˌnon-preˈscription *adj* [only before noun] a non-prescription drug is one that you can buy in a shop without a written order from a doctor SYN **over-the-counter**

ˌnon-ˈprofit (*also* **ˌnon-ˈprofitmaking** *BrE*, **ˌnot-for-ˈprofit** *especially AmE*) *adj* a non-profit organization uses the money it earns to help people instead of making a profit: *a non-profit educational institution*

ˌnon-prolifeˈration *n* [U] the limiting of the number of NUCLEAR or chemical weapons in the world, especially by stopping countries that do not yet have them from developing them: *Over 20 countries have now signed the Nuclear Non-proliferation Treaty.*

ˌnon-reˈfundable *adj* a non-refundable amount of money cannot be paid back to you: *There is a £40 deposit, which is non-refundable.*

ˌnon-reˈnewable *adj* non-renewable types of energy such as coal or gas cannot be replaced after they have been used: *All countries are being asked to cut down on their use of* ***non-renewable resources****.*

ˌnon-ˈresident *n* [C] **1** someone who does not live permanently in a particular country or area: *A lot of houses in the area are being bought by non-residents.* **2** *BrE* someone who is not staying in a particular hotel: *The hotel restaurant is open to non-residents.* —**non-resident** *adj*

ˌnon-resiˈdential *adj* **1** *BrE* if a course, activity etc is non-residential, you are not provided with a place to stay while you are doing it **2** non-residential areas or buildings are not places where people live

ˌnon-reˈstrictive *adj technical* a non-restrictive RELATIVE CLAUSE gives additional information about a particular person or thing rather than saying which person or thing is being mentioned. For example, in the sentence 'Perry, who is 22, was arrested yesterday', the phrase 'who is 22' is a non-restrictive clause.

ˌnon-reˈturnable *adj* **1** a non-returnable amount of money cannot be paid back to you: *Please send this form back with a non-returnable deposit of £60.* **2** things that are non-returnable cannot be taken back to a shop and used again: *non-returnable bottles*

ˌnon-scienˈtific *adj* not using scientific methods to collect information and form opinions: *The report is based on non-scientific data.*

non·sense /ˈnɒnsəns $ ˈnɑːnsens/ ●●○ S3 *n*
1 UNTRUE/STUPID [singular, U] ideas, opinions, statements etc that are not true or that seem very stupid SYN **rubbish** *BrE*: *'I'm a prisoner in my own home.' 'Nonsense!'* | **absolute/utter/complete nonsense** *'Nobody cares about me.' 'That's absolute nonsense, Mary!'* | **[+about]** *all this nonsense about health foods* | *If you ask me, these modern teaching methods are* ***a load of nonsense*** (=a lot of nonsense). | *He was* ***talking*** *utter* ***nonsense*** *as usual.* | **be a nonsense** *BrE*: *The government's housing policy is a nonsense.* | *By 1832 the idea had become an economic nonsense.* | **it is (a) nonsense to do sth** *It is nonsense to say that mistakes are never made.*
2 ANNOYING BEHAVIOUR [U] behaviour that is stupid and annoying: *You're to* ***stop*** *that* ***nonsense****, do you hear me?* | **not stand/put up with/take any nonsense** (=not accept such behaviour) *She won't stand any nonsense from the kids in her class.*
3 WITHOUT MEANING [U] speech or writing that has no meaning or cannot be understood: *Computer programs look like complete nonsense to me.*
4 make (a) nonsense of sth *BrE* to make an action, system, or plan useless or ineffective: *Having the army still in power makes a nonsense of last year's elections.*
5 nonsense poems/verse/rhymes poetry that is humorous because it does not have a sensible meaning

non·sen·si·cal /nɒnˈsensɪkəl $ nɑːn-/ *adj* ideas, actions, or statements that are nonsensical are not reasonable or sensible: *This is a nonsensical argument.*

non seq·ui·tur /ˌnɒn ˈsekwɪtə $ ˌnɑːn ˈsekwɪtər/ *n* [C] a statement which does not seem to be connected in a reasonable or sensible way with what was said before

ˌnon-ˈslip *adj* a non-slip surface prevents you from slipping and falling: *a non-slip bath mat*

ˌnon-ˈsmoker *n* [C] someone who does not smoke: *an area reserved for non-smokers*

ˌnon-ˈsmoking *adj* **1** a non-smoking area is one where you are not allowed to smoke: *a non-smoking restaurant* **2** [only before noun] used to describe someone who does not smoke: *a non-drinking, non-smoking fitness fanatic*

ˌnon-speˈcific *adj* **1** [only before noun] a non-specific medical condition could have one of several causes: *children with non-specific abdominal pain* **2** not exact or detailed, or not relating to one particular thing → **vague**: *The description was deliberately non-specific.*

ˌnon-ˈstandard *adj* **1** non-standard ways of speaking are not usually considered to be correct by educated speakers of a language: *Non-standard dialects of English are regional dialects.* **2** not the usual size or type: *a non-standard disk size*

non·start·er /ˌnɒnˈstɑːtə $ ˌnɑːnˈstɑːrtər/ *n* [C usually singular] *informal* an idea, a plan, or a person that has no chance of success: *In its present form the scheme is a non-starter.*

ˌnon-ˈstick *adj* a non-stick cooking pan has a special inside surface which prevents food from sticking to it

non·stop /ˌnɒnˈstɒp◂ $ ˌnɑːnˈstɑːp◂/ ●○○ *adj* [usually before noun] without any stops or pauses → **continuous**: *a* ***nonstop flight*** *to Los Angeles* —**nonstop** *adv*: *She talked nonstop for over an hour.*

ˌnon-ˈthreatening *adj* not making someone feel afraid or worried: *It is important to create a safe, non-threatening environment for children.*

ˌnon-ˈtoxic *adj* not poisonous or harmful to your health: *non-toxic paint*

ˌnon-traˈditional *adj* [only before noun] different from the way something happened or from what was considered typical in the past: *older, non-traditional university students* | *non-traditional workdays*

ˌnon-ˈunion (*also* **ˌnon-ˈunionized**) *adj* **1** [usually before noun] non-union workers do not belong to a TRADE UNION (=official organization for workers) **2** businesses or organizations that are non-union do not officially accept TRADE UNIONS, or do not employ their members

non·ver·bal /ˌnɒnˈvɜːbəl◂ $ ˌnɑːnˈvɜːr-/ *adj* not using words: *nonverbal forms of communication* —**nonverbally** *adv*

ˌnon-ˈviolence *n* [U] the practice of opposing a government without using violence, for example by not obeying laws → **passivity**: *She was committed to non-violence.* | *a policy of non-violence*

ˌnon-ˈviolent *adj* not using or not involving violence → **peaceful**: *a non-violent protest against the government* | *an increase in the amount of violent and non-violent crime*

ˌnon-ˈwhite *n* [C] someone who does not belong to a white race → **Caucasian** —**non-white** *adj*

noo·dle /ˈnuːdl/ *n* [usually plural] a long thin piece of food made from a mixture of flour, water, and eggs, usually cooked in soup or boiling water: *Serve the meat with rice or noodles.*

nook /nʊk/ *n* [C] **1** *literary* a small quiet place which is sheltered by a rock, a big tree etc: *a shady nook* **2** a small space in a corner of a room: *the table in the breakfast nook* **3 every nook and cranny** every part of a place: *We searched every nook and cranny.*

nook·ie, nooky /ˈnʊki/ *n* [U] *informal* the activity of having sex – used humorously

noon /nuːn/ ●●● W3 *n* [U] 12 o'clock in the daytime SYN **midday**: **at/before/by noon** *We left home at noon.* | *He rarely gets up before noon.* | *We met at* ***12 noon****.* → **morning, noon, and night** at MORNING[1](5)

noon·day /ˈnuːndeɪ/ *adj* [only before noun] *literary* happening or appearing at noon SYN **midday**: *It was impossible to work in the heat of the* ***noonday sun****.*

ˈno one, no-one ●●● S1 W2 *pron* not anyone SYN **nobody**: *No one likes being criticized.* | *There's no one else I really want to invite apart from you.* | *Has no one phoned about the car?* | *No one can say I didn't warn you.*

GRAMMAR: Negatives

Don't use another negative word such as 'not' or 'nothing' after **no one**. You say: *No one did anything to help.* ✗ Don't say: *No one did nothing to help.*

USAGE: No one, none of, neither of

- Don't use 'of' after **no one.** ✗ Don't say: *no one of us* | *no one of his parents*
- You use **none of** when talking about a group of three or more people: *None of us saw him.*
- You use **neither of** when talking about two people: *Neither of his parents went to the wedding.*

noose /nuːs/ *n* [C] a ring formed by the end of a piece of rope, which closes more tightly as it is pulled, used especially for killing someone by hanging them

nope /nəʊp $ noʊp/ *adv spoken informal* used to say 'no' when you answer someone: *'Hungry?' 'Nope, I just ate.'*

ˈno place *adv especially AmE informal* nowhere: *There's no place left to hide.*

nor /nɔː $ nɔːr/ ●●● S2 W1 *conjunction, adv*
1 neither ... nor ... used when mentioning two things that

N

are not true or do not happen: *He can neither read nor write* (=he cannot read or write). | *Hilary was neither shocked nor surprised by the news.* | *Neither Matt nor Julie said anything.*
2 *formal* used after a negative statement in order to introduce another negative statement containing a similar kind of information: *I don't expect children to be rude, nor do I expect to be disobeyed.* | *It was not my fault, nor his.*
3 *BrE* used after a negative statement to say that the negative statement is also true for someone or something else: *'I don't want to go.' 'Nor do I.'* | *They couldn't understand it at the time, and nor could we.* → NEITHER[3]

nor'- /nɔː $ nɔːr/ *prefix* a PREFIX meaning 'north', used especially by sailors: *nor'east* | *nor'west*

Nor·dic /ˈnɔːdɪk $ ˈnɔːr-/ *adj* relating to the northern European countries of Denmark, Norway, Sweden, Iceland, and Finland, or to their people → **Scandinavian**: *the Nordic countries*

norm /nɔːm $ nɔːrm/ ●○○ AWL *n* [C]
1 the usual or normal situation, way of doing something etc: **be/become the norm** *Short term contracts are now the norm with some big companies.* | *Joyce's style of writing was a striking departure from* ***the*** *literary* ***norm***.
2 norms [plural] generally accepted standards of social behaviour: *terrorists who violate the norms of civilized society* | **social/cultural etc norms**
3 the norm the normal or average standard: **above/below the norm** *28% of children tested below the norm.*

nor·mal[1] /ˈnɔːməl $ ˈnɔːr-/ ●●● S1 W1 AWL *adj*
1 usual, typical, or expected: *A normal working week is 40 hours.* | **it is normal (for sb) to do sth** *It's normal to feel nervous before an exam.* | **quite/perfectly etc normal** *Her room was untidy, but that was quite normal.* | *She was assessed* ***in the normal way***, *and placed on the waiting list.* | *All I want is to lead a* ***normal life***.
2 someone who is normal is mentally and physically healthy and does not behave strangely OPP **abnormal**: *He seems a* ***perfectly normal*** *little boy.* | *They can't be normal to do something like that.*

THESAURUS

normal usual, typical, and as you would expect it to be: *Is this cold weather normal for the time of year?* | *It had been another normal working day in the office.*
ordinary (*also* **regular** *especially AmE*) not special, unusual, or different from normal: *They lived in an ordinary three-bedroomed house.* | *Would you like a regular salad or a Caesar salad?*
average [only before noun] around the usual level or amount: *She is* ***of average height***. | *He is* ***of*** *above* ***average intelligence***.
standard normal – used about methods of doing something, or about the size, shape, features etc of products: *It's standard practice to X-ray hand-baggage at most airports.* | *We stock shoes in all the standard sizes.*
routine used about things that are done regularly as part of a series of things: *The fault was discovered during a routine check of the plane.* | *routine tasks such as shopping and cooking*
everyday [only before noun] used about things that happen or that you use as part of normal life: *He painted scenes of everyday life in France.* | *Sally was still dressed in her everyday clothes.*
common used about birds and plants that are of the most usual type, and in the phrase **the common people** (=people who are not rich and powerful): *the common goldfish* | *an alliance between the aristocracy and the common people*
conventional [only before noun] of the kind that is usually used – used when comparing this with a different or special type: *The engine is more efficient than a conventional diesel engine.* | *the drugs used in conventional medicine* | *conventional weapons* (=not nuclear, chemical, or biological)

normal[2] AWL *n* [U] the usual state, level, or amount: *Thankfully, train services are now* ***back to normal***. | *Slowly her heartbeat* ***returned to normal***. | **above/below normal** *Car sales are still below normal for the time of year.* | **higher/larger/less etc than normal** *The journey took longer than normal.*

nor·mal·i·ty /nɔːˈmæləti $ nɔːr-/ ●○○ AWL (*also* **nor·mal·cy** /ˈnɔːməlsi $ ˈnɔːr-/ *AmE*) *n* [U] a situation in which things happen in the usual or expected way: *We're hoping for a* ***return to normality*** *as soon as possible.* | *We'll soon get back to* ***some semblance of normality***.

nor·mal·ize (*also* **-ise** *BrE*) /ˈnɔːməlaɪz $ ˈnɔːr-/ AWL *v* [I,T] **1** if you normalize a situation, or if it normalizes, it becomes normal again: *Journalists are reporting that the situation has now normalized.* **2** if two countries normalize relations, or if relations normalize, the two countries behave in a normal way towards each other again: ***Relations*** *between the countries were formally* ***normalized*** *in 1997.* —**normalization** /ˌnɔːməlaɪˈzeɪʃən $ ˌnɔːrmələ-/ *n* [U]

nor·mal·ly /ˈnɔːməli $ ˈnɔːr-/ ●●● S1 W2 AWL *adv*
1 usually: *The journey normally takes about two hours.* | [sentence adverb] *Normally, I park behind the theatre.*
2 in a normal way OPP **abnormally**: *The system seems to be working normally now.*

Nor·man /ˈnɔːmən $ ˈnɔːr-/ *adj* **1** built in the style that was popular during the 11th and 12th centuries in Europe: *a Norman church* **2** relating to the Normans, the northern French people who took control of England in the 11th century

nor·ma·tive /ˈnɔːmətɪv $ ˈnɔːr-/ *adj formal* describing or establishing a set of rules or standards of behaviour: *normative guidelines for senators*

no·ro·vi·rus /ˈnɔːrəʊˌvaɪərəs $ -roʊˌvaɪrəs/ *n* [singular] a VIRUS that makes people VOMIT a lot and have DIARRHOEA

Norse[1] /nɔːs $ nɔːrs/ *adj* [only before noun] relating to the people of ancient Scandinavia or their language: *Norse legends*

Norse[2] *n* [U] the language that was spoken by the people of ancient Scandinavia

Norse·man /ˈnɔːsmən $ ˈnɔːrs-/ *n* (*plural* **Norsemen** /-mən/) [C] *literary* a VIKING

north[1], **North** /nɔːθ $ nɔːrθ/ ●●● S2 W1 *n* [singular, U] (*written abbreviation* **N**)
1 the direction that is at the top of a map of the world, above the Equator. It is on the left if you are facing the rising sun: *Which way is north?* | **from/towards the north** *winds blowing from the north* | **to the north (of sth)** *Cheshunt is a few miles to the north of London.*
2 the north the northern part of a country or area: *There's a chance of snow showers in the north.* | **[+of]** *the north of England*

north[2], **North** ●●● S3 W3 *adj* [only before noun] (*written abbreviation* **N**)
1 in the north or facing the north: *The north side of the building doesn't get much sun.* | *He lives in North Wales.*
2 a north wind comes from the north

north[3] ●●● S3 W1 *adv* (*written abbreviation* **N**)
1 towards the north: *The birds fly north in summer.* | **[+of]** *Chicago is four hours north of Indianapolis.* | *a north-facing window*
2 up north *informal* to or in the north of the country: *They've moved up north.*

North, the **1** the northeastern states of the US, especially during the Civil War (1861–65) when they fought against the South **2** the northern part of England, which includes the area north of the Midlands and south of the Scottish border, and contains several large cities, including Manchester, Leeds, Liverpool, and Newcastle **3** the richer countries of the northern parts of the world, especially Europe and North America

north·bound /ˈnɔːθbaʊnd $ ˈnɔːrθ-/ *adj* travelling or leading towards the north: *a northbound bus* | *the northbound lane of the A1*

ˌnorth-ˈcountry *adj* in or from the north of England: *a low north-country voice*

north·east¹, **Northeast** /ˌnɔːθˈiːst◂ $ ˌnɔːrθ-/ ●●○ *n* [U] (*written abbreviation* **NE**) the direction that is exactly between north and east —**northeast** *adv*: *He headed northeast across the open sea.*

northeast², **Northeast** ●●○ *adj* (*written abbreviation* **NE**)
1 a northeast wind comes from the northeast
2 in the northeast of a place: *the northeast outskirts of Las Vegas*

north·east·er /ˌnɔːθˈiːstə $ ˌnɔːrθˈiːstər/ *n* [C] a strong wind or storm coming from the northeast

north·east·er·ly /ˌnɔːθˈiːstəli $ ˌnɔːrθˈiːstərli/ *adj* **1** towards or in the northeast: *They set off in a northeasterly direction.* **2** a northeasterly wind comes from the northeast

north·east·ern /ˌnɔːθˈiːstən $ ˌnɔːrθˈiːstərn/ *adj* (*written abbreviation* **NE**) in or from the northeast part of a country or area: *the northeastern states of the US*

north·east·wards /ˌnɔːθˈiːstwədz $ ˌnɔːrθˈiːstwərdz/ (*also* **northeastward**) *adv* towards the northeast —**northeastward** *adj*

nor·ther·ly /ˈnɔːðəli $ ˈnɔːrðərli/ *adj* **1** towards or in the north: *We set off* ***in a northerly direction.*** **2** a northerly wind comes from the north

nor·thern, **Northern** /ˈnɔːðən $ ˈnɔːrðərn/ ●●● S2 W2 *adj* (*written abbreviation* **N**) in or from the north of a country or area: *a man with a northern accent | Northern Europe*

nor·thern·er, **Northerner** /ˈnɔːðənə $ ˈnɔːrðərnər/ *n* [C] someone from the northern part of a country

ˌnorthern ˈhemisphere, **Northern Hemisphere** *n* **the northern hemisphere** the half of the world that is north of the Equator

nor·thern·most /ˈnɔːðənməʊst $ ˈnɔːrðərnmoʊst/ *adj* furthest north: *the northernmost tip of the island*

ˌNorth ˈPole *n* **the North Pole** the most northern point on the surface of the Earth → MAGNETIC POLE, SOUTH POLE

north·wards /ˈnɔːθwədz $ ˈnɔːrθwərdz/ (*also* **northward**) *adv* towards the north: *We sailed northwards.* —**northward** *adj*: *the northward journey*

north·west¹, **Northwest** /ˌnɔːθˈwest◂ $ ˌnɔːrθ-/ ●●○ *n* [U] (*written abbreviation* **NW**)
1 the direction that is exactly between north and west
2 the northwest the northwestern part of a country —**northwest** *adv*: *She rode northwest toward Boulder.*

northwest², **Northwest** ●●○ *adj* (*written abbreviation* **NW**)
1 a northwest wind comes from the northwest
2 in the northwest of a place: *the northwest suburbs of the city*

north·west·er /ˌnɔːθˈwestə $ ˌnɔːrθˈwestər/ *n* [C] a strong wind or storm coming from the northwest

north·west·er·ly /ˌnɔːθˈwestəli $ ˌnɔːrθˈwestərli/ *adj* **1** towards or in the northwest: *We headed off in a northwesterly direction.* **2** a northwesterly wind comes from the northwest

north·west·ern /ˌnɔːθˈwestən $ ˌnɔːrθˈwestərn/ *adj* (*written abbreviation* **NW**) in or from the northwest part of a country or area: *a town in northwestern Canada*

north·west·wards /ˌnɔːθˈwestwədz $ ˌnɔːrθˈwestwərdz/ (*also* **northwestward**) *adv* towards the northwest —**northwestward** *adj*

nos. (*also* **Nos.**) the written abbreviation of ***numbers***: *nos. 17-33*

nose¹ /nəʊz $ noʊz/ ●●● S2 W2 *n*
1 ON YOUR FACE [C] the part of a person's or animal's face used for smelling or breathing → **nasal**, **nostril**: *Someone punched him on the nose.*
2 (right) under sb's nose a) if something bad or illegal happens under someone's nose, they do not notice it even though it is happening very close to them and they should have noticed it: *The drugs were smuggled in right under the noses of the security guards.* **b)** if something is right under someone's nose, they cannot see it even though it is very close to them: *The key was right under my nose all the time.*
3 stick/poke your nose into sth to become involved in something that does not concern you, in a way that annoys people → **nosy**: *She always has to stick her nose into matters that do not concern her.*
4 keep your nose out (of sth) *spoken* to avoid becoming involved in something that does not concern you: *I wish he'd keep his nose out of my business!*
5 turn your nose up (at sth) *informal* to refuse to accept something because you do not think it is good enough for you: *My children turn their noses up at home cooking.*
6 with your nose in the air behaving as if you are more important than other people and not talking to them: *She just walked past with her nose in the air.*
7 have a (good) nose for sth to be naturally good at finding and recognizing something: *a reporter with a good nose for a story*
8 get (right) up sb's nose *BrE spoken* to annoy someone very much: *I wish he wouldn't keep interrupting. It really gets up my nose.*
9 keep your nose clean *spoken* to make sure you do not get into trouble, or do anything wrong or illegal: *Sid's got to keep his nose clean or he'll end up back in prison.*
10 on the nose *AmE spoken* exactly: *He gets up at 6 a.m. on the nose every morning.*
11 keep your nose to the grindstone *informal* to work very hard, without stopping to rest: *Jim had decided he was going to keep his nose to the grindstone.*
12 have your nose in a book/magazine/newspaper to be reading a book etc, especially with a lot of interest: *She always had her nose in a book.*
13 by a nose if a horse wins a race by a nose, it only just wins
14 have a nose around *BrE spoken* to look around a place in order to try to find something, when there is no one else there
15 put sb's nose out of joint *informal* to annoy someone, especially by attracting everyone's attention away from them: *His nose has been put a bit out of joint ever since Marion got here.*
16 nose to tail *especially BrE* cars, buses etc that are nose to tail are in a line without much space between them: *Traffic was nose to tail for three miles.*
17 PLANE [C] the pointed front end of a plane, ROCKET etc
18 SMELL [singular] the smell of a wine or tobacco SYN **bouquet** → HARD-NOSED, BROWN-NOSE, → **cut off your nose to spite your face** at CUT (10), → NOSE JOB, → **lead sb by the nose** at LEAD¹(16), → **look down your nose at sb/sth** at LOOK¹(8), → **pay through the nose** at PAY¹(16), → **as plain as the nose on your face** at PLAIN¹(1), → **poke your nose into sth** at POKE¹(7), → **powder your nose** at POWDER²(2), → **rub sb's nose in it/in the dirt** at RUB¹(9), → **thumb your nose at sb/sth** at THUMB²(2)

COLLOCATIONS

ADJECTIVES

big *See that guy over there, the one with the big nose?*
small *She had high cheekbones and a small nose.*
long *His nose was long and his chin square.*
straight *Her nose was long, straight and elegant.*
runny (=with liquid coming out) *A runny nose may be the result of an allergic reaction.*
blocked (=so that you cannot breathe easily) *My nose is really blocked and I can't smell anything.*
red (=because you are cold or drunk, or have a cold) *His nose was red from the cold.*
a snub/turned-up nose (=one that curves up at the end) | **a hooked nose** (=one that curves down at the end) | **a Roman/aquiline nose** *formal* (=one that curves out near the top) | **a broken nose** (=one that is not straight because the bone has been broken by a hit or fall)

VERBS

blow your nose (=clear your nose by blowing strongly into a piece of soft paper or cloth) *She blew her nose on a large white handkerchief.*

N

wipe your nose (=wipe liquid away from your nose) *The boy wiped his nose on his sleeve.*
pick your nose (=remove substances from inside your nose with your finger) *Stop picking your nose, Freddy.*
wrinkle your nose (=move the muscles near your nose when you do not like something) *Susan looked at the meal and wrinkled her nose.*
hold your nose (=so that you cannot smell a bad smell) *The smell was so revolting that I had to hold my nose.*
breathe through your nose *Close your eyes and breathe through your nose.*
sb's nose is running (=liquid is coming out) *She was crying hard and her nose was running.*

PHRASES

the bridge of your nose (=the upper part, between your eyes) *Sam pushed his glasses up on the bridge of his nose.*

nose² *v* [I,T always + adv/prep] if a vehicle, boat etc noses forward, or if you nose it forward, it moves forward slowly SYN **edge**: **nose its way along/through etc sth** *The bus nosed its way along the street.* | *She carefully nosed the car forward through the traffic.*

nose around (sth) (*also* **nose about (sth)** *BrE*) *phr v informal* to look around a place in order to try to find something, when there is no one else there: *What were you doing nosing around in my office?*

nose into sth *phr v informal* to try to find out private information about someone or something, especially in a way that is annoying

nose sth ↔ **out** *phr v informal* **1** to discover some information that someone else does not want you to discover: *The media always manage to nose out some interesting facts about a politician's past life.* **2** to defeat someone by a very small amount in a race, competition etc

nose·bag /ˈnəʊzbæg $ ˈnoʊz-/ *n* [C] *BrE* a bag that holds food and is hung around a horse's head

nose·bleed /ˈnəʊzbliːd $ ˈnoʊz-/ *n* [C] if you have a nosebleed, blood starts flowing from your nose

nose·cone /ˈnəʊzkəʊn $ ˈnoʊzkoʊn/ *n* [C] the pointed front part of an aircraft, MISSILE, or ROCKET

nose·dive¹ /ˈnəʊzdaɪv $ ˈnoʊz-/ *n* [C] **1** a sudden very large fall in the price, value, or condition of something: *The pound* ***took a nosedive*** *on the foreign exchange market today.* | *The economy* ***went into a nosedive****.* **2** a sudden steep drop made by a plane with its front end pointing towards the ground: *Everyone screamed as the plane suddenly* ***went into a nosedive****.*

nosedive² *v* [I] **1** if a price, value, or condition of something nosedives, it suddenly goes down or gets much worse SYN **plummet**: *Sales have nosedived since January.* **2** if a plane nosedives, it drops suddenly and steeply with its front end pointing towards the ground

nose·gay /ˈnəʊzgeɪ $ ˈnoʊz-/ *n* [C] *old-fashioned* a small arrangement of flowers

ˈnose job *n* [C] *informal* a medical operation on someone's nose to improve its appearance → **plastic surgery**, **cosmetic surgery**

nos·ey /ˈnəʊzi $ ˈnoʊ-/ *adj* another spelling of NOSY

nosh¹ /nɒʃ $ nɑːʃ/ *n* [U] *informal* **1** *BrE* food **2** *AmE* a small amount of food eaten between meals SYN **snack**

nosh² *v* [I] *informal* to eat

ˌno-ˈshow *n* [C] someone who does not arrive or appear somewhere they were expected to be, for example at a restaurant or a meeting: *The bad weather meant there were a lot of no-shows at the game.*

ˈnosh-up *n* [singular] *BrE informal* a big meal

ˌno-ˈsmoking *adj* NON-SMOKING

nos·tal·gia /nɒˈstældʒə $ nɑː-/ ●○○ *n* [U] a feeling that a time in the past was good, or the activity of remembering a good time in the past and wishing that things had not changed: **[+for]** *nostalgia for the good old days* | *He looked back on his university days with a certain amount of nostalgia.* | *a* ***wave of nostalgia*** *for how great life was in the 1960s*

nos·tal·gic /nɒˈstældʒɪk $ nɑː-/ ●○○ *adj* if you feel nostalgic about a time in the past, you feel happy when you remember it, and in some ways you wish that things had not changed: *Seeing those old school photographs has made me* ***feel*** *quite* ***nostalgic****.* | *a* ***nostalgic look*** *back at the 1950s* | **[+about]** *He remained nostalgic about his days as a young actor.* —**nostalgically** /-kli/ *adv*: *Tim spoke nostalgically of his first visit to Peru.*

nos·tril /ˈnɒstrəl $ ˈnɑː-/ *n* [C] one of the two holes at the end of your nose, through which you breathe and smell things: *The smell of gunpowder filled his nostrils.* | *the horse's* ***flaring nostrils*** (=widened nostrils)

nos·trum /ˈnɒstrəm $ ˈnɑː-/ *n* [C] *formal* an idea that someone thinks will solve a problem easily, but will probably not help at all: *an economic nostrum*

nos·y¹, **nosey** /ˈnəʊzi $ ˈnoʊ-/ ●○○ *adj* (*comparative* **nosier**, *superlative* **nosiest**) always wanting to find out things that do not concern you, especially other people's private affairs: *Don't be so nosy!* | *a nosy neighbor* —**nosiness** *n* [U] —**nosily** *adv*

nosy² *n BrE informal* **a nosy** a thorough look around a place, especially somewhere that belongs to someone else and is private: *I'd love to have a good old nosy in Josey's room!*

ˌnosy ˈparker *n* [C] *BrE informal* someone who is too interested in finding out about other people's affairs – used to show disapproval

not /nɒt $ nɑːt/ ●●● S1 W1 *adv*

1 used to make a word, statement, or question negative: *Most of the stores do not open until 10 am.* | *She's not a very nice person.* | *You were wrong not to inform the police.* | *'Can we go to the park?' 'No, not today, dear.'* | **not at all/not ... at all** (=used to emphasize what you are saying) *The changes were not at all surprising.* | *I do not like his attitude at all.* → **NO¹**, **N'T**

2 used in order to make a word or expression have the opposite meaning: *Edinburgh isn't far now.* | *The food is* ***not very*** *good there.* | **not a lot/much/many etc** (=only a few, only a little etc) *Not much is known about the disease.* | *Not many people have read the report.* | *Most of the hotels are* ***not that*** *cheap* (=they are fairly expensive).

3 used instead of a whole phrase to mean the opposite of what has been mentioned before it: *No one knows if the story is true* ***or not****.* | *I hope to see you tomorrow, but* ***if not****, leave me a message.* | *'Is Mark still sick?' 'I* ***hope not****.'* → **SO¹**(4)

4 not only in addition to being or doing something: **not only ... (but) also ...** *Shakespeare was not only a writer but also an actor.* | **not only do/will/can etc** *Not only do the nurses want a pay increase, they want reduced hours as well.*

5 not a/not one not any person or thing: *Not one of the students knew the answer.* | *There wasn't a cloud in the sky.* | ***Not a single*** *person said thank you.*

6 not that ... used before a sentence or phrase to mean the opposite of what follows it, and to make the previous sentence seem less important: *Sarah has a new boyfriend –* ***not that I care*** (=I do not care). | *Janice had lost some weight,* ***not that it mattered*** (=it did not matter).

7 not at all *BrE spoken* used to be polite when someone has thanked you or asked you to do something: *'Would you mind helping me with my suitcase?' 'Not at all.'*

8 not the sharpest tool in the box/shed (*also* **not the brightest crayon in the box**), **not the brightest bulb on the Christmas tree** *informal* used to say that someone is not very intelligent or is not able to learn things quickly or easily – used humorously

9 – not! *spoken* used, especially by young people, to say that you really mean the opposite of what you have just said: *I really enjoy spending my day working here – not!* → **not half** at HALF³(6), → **not to say** at SAY¹(43)

GRAMMAR: Negatives

• Don't use another negative word such as 'no', 'nothing', or 'nobody' after **not**. Use **any**, **anything**,

anybody etc. You say: *They do **not** have **any** money.* | *I did**n't** know **anybody**.* ✗ Don't say: *They do not have no money.* | *I didn't know nobody.*
• **Not** goes before 'to' in an infinitive verb. You say: *I try **not to** make mistakes.* ✗ Don't say: *I try to not make mistakes.*

no·ta·ble /ˈnəʊtəbəl $ ˈnoʊ-/ ●●○ *adj* [usually before noun] important, interesting, excellent, or unusual enough to be noticed or mentioned: **notable feature/example** *A notable feature of the church is its unusual bell tower.* | **notable achievement/success/victory** | *Every country in the world signed the treaty, with one **notable exception** – the United States.* | **[+for]** *The town is notable for its busy open-air market.*

no·ta·bles /ˈnəʊtəbəlz $ ˈnoʊ-/ *n* [plural] important or famous people: *local notables*

no·ta·bly /ˈnəʊtəbli/ ●●○ W3 *adv*
1 used to say that a person or thing is a typical example or the most important example of something SYN **especially**, **in particular**: *Some early doctors, notably Hippocrates, thought that diet was important.*
2 *formal* in a way that is clearly different, important, or unusual SYN **significantly**: *Emigration has notably increased over the past five years.* | *Notably absent from his statement was any hint of an apology.*

no·ta·rized (*also* **-ised** *BrE*) /ˈnəʊtəraɪzd $ -ˈnoʊ-/ *adj law* signed by a NOTARY

no·ta·ry /ˈnəʊtəri $ ˈnoʊ-/ (*also* ˌ**notary** ˈ**public**) *n* (*plural* **notaries**) [C] someone, especially a lawyer, who has the legal power to make a signed statement or document official

no·ta·tion /nəʊˈteɪʃən $ noʊ-/ *n* [C,U] a system of written marks or signs used to represent something such as music, mathematics, or scientific ideas

notch¹ /nɒtʃ $ nɑːtʃ/ *n* [C] **1** a level on a scale that measures something, for example quality or achievement: *Her new book is several notches above anything else she has written.* | *Jackson raised his voice by a notch.* | *The Spartans turned it up a notch in the second half.* **2** a V-shaped cut or hole in a surface or edge: *Cut a notch near one end of the stick.* **3** *AmE* a passage between two mountains or hills → TOP-NOTCH

notch² *v* [T] **1** to cut a V-shaped mark into something, especially as a way of showing the number of times something has been done **2** *AmE* to notch something up
notch sth ↔ **up** *phr v* to achieve something, especially a victory or a particular total or score: *The Houston Astros have **notched up** another **win**.*

note¹ /nəʊt $ noʊt/ ●●● S1 W2 *n*
1 TO REMIND YOU **a)** [C] something that you write down to remind you of something: *Dave **made a note of** her address and phone number.* | ***Keep a** careful **note of** any problems you have with the software.* **b) make a (mental) note to do sth** to decide that you must remember to do something later: *He made a mental note to arrange a time to meet her.*
2 FOR STUDYING **notes** [plural] information that a student writes down during a lesson, from a book etc: *Can I borrow your **lecture notes**?* | **take/make notes** (=write notes) *I read the first chapter and took notes.*
3 SHORT LETTER [C] a short informal letter: *I was going to **write** Kathy **a note**, but I decided to call her instead.* | *This is just a **quick note** to let you know that I won't be in the office tomorrow.* | *a **suicide note*** (=a note telling someone that you are going to kill yourself) | *a **thank you note*** (=a note to say thank you for something)
4 OFFICIAL LETTER [C] an official letter or document: **sick note** *BrE* (=a note saying that you are too ill to go to work or school) | **delivery note** (=a document showing that goods have been delivered) | **diplomatic note** (=a formal letter from one government to another) → CREDIT NOTE, PROMISSORY NOTE
5 ADDITIONAL INFORMATION [C] a short piece of writing at the bottom of a page or at the end of a book or document which gives more information about something written in the main part: *The notes are at the back of the book.* | **explanatory/guidance notes** *A set of guidance notes is provided to assist applicants in completing the form.* → FOOTNOTE(1)
6 MUSIC [C] a particular musical sound, or a symbol representing this sound: **high/low note** *She has a good voice but has trouble hitting the high notes.*
7 MONEY [C] *BrE* (*also* **bank note**) a piece of paper money worth a particular amount of money SYN **bill** *AmE* → **coin**: *a ten-pound note* THESAURUS MONEY
8 FEELING OR QUALITY [singular] a type of feeling or quality when someone speaks or does something: **[+of]** *There was a note of doubt in her voice.* | *He brought a note of realism into the debate.* | **on a ... note** (=speaking in a particular way) *She ended her speech on a personal note.* | *On a more serious note, I'd like to thank everyone for all their support.*
9 hit/strike the right/wrong note to succeed or not succeed in being right and suitable for a particular occasion: *Bush is hoping to hit the right note again with voters.*
10 take note (of sth) to pay attention to something SYN **notice**: *People were beginning to take note of her talents as a writer.* | *His first album made the music world **stand up and take note**.*
11 sb/sth of note *formal* someone or something important, interesting, or famous: *The college has produced several architects of note.* | *The village has a number of buildings of note.*
12 worthy/deserving of note important or interesting and deserving particular attention → **noteworthy**: *three recent novels that are especially worthy of note* → **compare notes** at COMPARE¹(5)

note² ●●○ *v* [T] *formal*
1 to notice or pay careful attention to something: *He carefully noted the time when they left the building.* | **note (that)** *Please note that the bill must be paid within ten days.* | *It should be noted that parking without a permit attracts a charge of £5.* | **note how** *Note how she is holding her racket.*
2 to mention something because it is important or interesting: **note that** *The judge noted that Miller had no previous criminal record.* THESAURUS SAY
note sth ↔ **down** *phr v* to write something down so that you will remember it: *Note down the main points you want to include in your essay.*

note·book /ˈnəʊtbʊk $ ˈnoʊt-/ ●●● S3 *n* [C]
1 a book made of plain paper on which you can write notes → see picture at STATIONERY
2 (*also* **notebook computer**) a small computer that you can carry with you → **laptop**

ˈ**note card** *n* [C] *AmE* a small folded piece of paper with a picture on it, for writing a short letter SYN **notelet** *BrE*

not·ed /ˈnəʊtɪd $ ˈnoʊ-/ *adj* well known or famous, especially because of some special quality or ability → **renowned**: *a noted author* | **[+for]** *The city is noted for its 18th-century architecture.* THESAURUS FAMOUS

note·let /ˈnəʊtlɪt $ ˈnoʊt-/ *n* [C] *BrE* a small folded piece of paper with a picture on it, for writing a short letter SYN **note card** *AmE*

note·pad /ˈnəʊtpæd $ ˈnoʊt-/ *n* [C] a group of sheets of paper fastened together, used for writing notes

note·pa·per /ˈnəʊtˌpeɪpə $ ˈnoʊtˌpeɪpər/ *n* [U] paper used for writing letters or notes → **writing paper**: **headed notepaper** (=with the sender's address printed on it)

note·wor·thy /ˈnəʊtˌwɜːði $ ˈnoʊtˌwɜːr-/ *adj* important or interesting enough to deserve your attention: *a noteworthy achievement* THESAURUS IMPORTANT

ˌ**not-for-**ˈ**profit** *adj* [only before noun] *especially AmE* NON-PROFIT

noth·er, **'nother** /ˈnʌðə $ -ər/ *determiner informal* **a whole nother ...** used humorously when emphasizing that something is completely different from what you have been talking about. It is a changed form of 'another whole': *Texas is a whole nother country.* | *That's a whole 'nother ball game.*

N

noth·ing¹ /ˈnʌθɪŋ/ ●●● S1 W1 *pron*
1 not anything or no thing: *Nothing ever happens in this town.* | *There's nothing in this box.* | *There was* **nothing else** *the doctors could do.* | *He had* **nothing more** *to say.* | *We* **know nothing about** *her family.* | *I couldn't just stand by and* **do nothing**. | *I promised to* **say nothing** *about it to anyone.* | *We've* **heard nothing** *from her for weeks.* | *There's* **absolutely nothing** *to be ashamed of.* | *'Do you know much about business?'* **'Nothing at all**.' | *She had eaten* **virtually nothing** *at supper.* | *There's* **nothing wrong** *with the data.* | *There's* **nothing new** *about this.* | *A brief search was made but they found* **nothing untoward**.
2 nothing but only: *She'd had nothing but bad luck.*
3 have nothing against sb/sth if you have nothing against someone or something, they do not annoy or offend you: *I have nothing against him personally.*
4 something which is considered unimportant, not interesting, or not worth worrying about: *'What have you been doing?' 'Nothing. Just sitting here.'* | *There's nothing on television tonight.* | *'What did you do last weekend?' 'Oh,* **nothing much**.' | *Politics* **meant nothing** (=was not important) *to me for years.* | *The meal was* **nothing special** (=it was not unusual or interesting) *– just fish with a cheese sauce.*
5 *especially AmE* zero SYN **nil** *BrE*: *We beat them ten to nothing.*
6 have/be nothing to do with sb/sth if you have nothing to do with someone or something, or if someone or something has nothing to do with you, you are not involved or connected with it: *He said that he had nothing to do with the decision.* | *As I said, it's nothing to do with me.* | *That's got nothing to do with you.* | *I* **want nothing to do with** (=do not want to be involved) *the whole thing.* | *My staff had* **nothing whatsoever** *to do with this.*
7 for nothing a) without paying for something or being paid for something: *Why pay a plumber when my brother will do it for nothing?* **b)** if you do something for nothing, you make an effort but do not get the result you want: *We went all that way for nothing.*
8 no money or payment at all: *This service will cost you nothing.* | *When a car has done that many miles, it's worth nothing.*
9 there's nothing like sth used to say that something is very good: *There's nothing like a hot bath after a day's climbing.*
10 there's nothing in/to sth used to say that what people are saying about someone or something is not true: *It seems there's nothing in the rumours that she's pregnant.*
11 if nothing else used to emphasize one good quality or feature that someone or something has, while suggesting that it might be the only good one: *If nothing else, the report points out the need for better math education.*
12 come to nothing if a plan or action comes to nothing, it does not continue or does not achieve anything
13 be nothing if not sth used to emphasize a particular quality that someone or something has: *You've got to admit – he's nothing if not persistent.*
14 nothing doing *spoken* used to refuse to do something
15 (there's) nothing to it *spoken* used to say that something is easy to do: *Anyone can use a computer. There's nothing to it!*
16 it was nothing/think nothing of it *spoken* used when someone has thanked you a lot for something you have done for them: *'Thank you so much.' 'Oh, it was nothing.'*
17 nothing of the sort/kind *spoken* used to say strongly or angrily that something is not true or will not happen: *'I'll pay.' 'You'll do nothing of the sort!'*
18 have nothing on sb *informal* if someone has nothing on you, they are not better than you at something: *She's got nothing on you when it comes to writing.*
19 there's nothing for it but to do sth *BrE* used when there is only one thing you can do in a particular situation: *There was nothing for it but to go back the way we came.* → **sweet nothings** at SWEET¹(13), → **to say nothing of** at SAY¹(45), → **nothing on earth** at EARTH¹(9)

GRAMMAR: Negatives

Don't use **nothing** with another negative word such as 'not'. Use **anything**. You say: *I could* **not** *find* **anything** *suitable.* ✗ Don't say: *I could not find nothing suitable.*

nothing² *adv* **1 be/seem/look nothing like sb/sth** to have no qualities or features that are similar to someone or something else: *She's nothing like her brother.* | *She looked nothing like her photograph.* **2 be nothing less than sth** (*also* **be nothing short of sth**) used to emphasize that something or someone has a particular quality or seems to be something: *His behaviour was nothing short of rudeness.*

noth·ing·ness /ˈnʌθɪŋnəs/ *n* [U] **1** empty space or the complete absence of everything: *Natalie found him looking into nothingness.* **2** the state of not existing: *Is there only nothingness after death?*

This graph shows how common the different grammar patterns of the verb **notice** are.

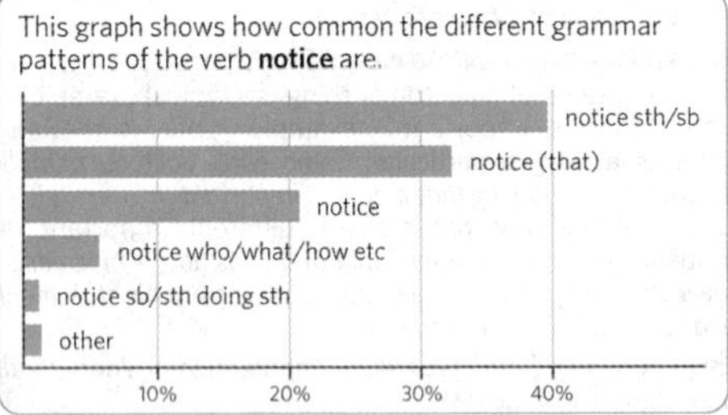

no·tice¹ /ˈnəʊtɪs $ ˈnoʊ-/ ●●● S1 W2 *v* [I,T not in progressive]
1 if you notice something or someone, you realize that they exist, especially because you can see, hear, or feel them: *He noticed a woman in a black dress sitting across from him.* | *I didn't notice any smoke.* | *Have you noticed any change in him?* | **notice (that)** *I noticed that her hands were shaking.* | *He never seems to notice when people take advantage of him.* | **notice who/what/how etc** *She hadn't noticed before quite how grey his hair was.* | **notice sb/sth doing sth** *Did you notice him leaving the party early?* THESAURUS ▸ SEE

GRAMMAR: Using the progressive

Notice is not used in the progressive. You say: *I notice you're wearing glasses.* ✗ Don't say: *I'm noticing you're wearing glasses.*
GRAMMAR GUIDE ▸ VERBS

2 be noticed/get (sb) noticed to get attention, or to make someone get attention: *These clothes will get you noticed and enhance your image.*
3 sb can't help noticing sth (*also* **sb can't help but notice sth**) if someone can't help noticing something, they realize that it exists or is happening even though they are not deliberately trying to pay attention to it: *I couldn't help noticing the bruises on her arm.*

THESAURUS

notice to realize that something is there or that something is happening, because you can see, hear, or feel it: *I noticed that he was rather quiet during dinner.* | *Children don't seem to notice the cold.*
detect to notice something that is difficult to see, hear etc because it is very small, faint, or unclear. Detect is used about people and machines, and is more formal than **notice**: *X-ray telescopes can now detect virtually every type of astronomical object.* | *He thought he detected a flicker of interest in her eyes.*
spot to notice something, especially something that is difficult to see or that you see for a short time only. Spot is more informal than **notice**: *Can you spot the difference between these two pictures?* | *I'm glad you spotted the mistake before it was too late.*
become aware/conscious to gradually begin to notice that something is happening or is true: *I became aware that Mum was getting a lot older.* | *Tessa became conscious of a feeling of guilt.*
can tell to be able to notice something because you

can see, smell, hear it etc: *I could tell that she had been drinking. | Can you tell I've lost weight?*
sth/sb catches your eye used to say that you suddenly notice something or someone because they are interesting, attractive, or good at something: *I saw this shirt in the shop window and it just caught my eye. | Clarke caught the eye of boss Bryan Robson when he scored for Newry last week.*
observe *formal* to notice something as a result of watching or studying it closely: *Psychologists observed that the mice became more aggressive in smaller cages.*
perceive *formal* to notice something, especially that something is happening, or is true, or needs to be done: *The company quickly perceived the need for change. | Doctors perceive that they do not have adequate time to spend with their patients.*
witness to see something happen because you are there at the time: *People have witnessed some great economic changes during the last ten years.*

notice² ●●● S2 W2 *n*
1 ATTENTION [U] when you notice or pay attention to someone or something: *I waved but they* ***took no notice****.* | **not take any/much notice (of sth)** *I did not take much notice of her suggestions. | I hope you'll* ***take notice*** *of what I'm going to tell you. | This problem may have* ***escaped*** *your* ***notice*** *so far* (=you may not have noticed it). | *This never* ***came to*** *my* ***notice*** (=I never knew about this). | *There are several important matters that I'd like to* ***bring to*** *your* ***notice*** (=that I would like you to know about).
2 ON PAPER [C] a written or printed statement that gives information or a warning to people → **sign**: *The notice on the wall said 'No smoking'. | I'll put up a notice about the meeting. |* ***obituary notices*** (=about people who have just died) *in the newspaper* → see picture at SIGN
3 TIME TO PREPARE [U] information or a warning about something that is going to happen → **warning**: **without notice** *These rules are subject to change without notice.* | **sufficient/reasonable notice** *They didn't* ***give*** *me sufficient* ***notice****.* | **advance/prior notice** *When you're on the mailing list, you'll receive advance notice of upcoming events.* | **ten days'/three months' etc notice** (=a warning ten days etc before) *They closed the factory, giving the workers only a week's notice. | Firefighters were prepared to rush out* ***at a moment's notice****.* | **[+of]** *his failure to* ***give notice*** *of his intention to alter the property* | **notice to do sth** *I've been given* ***notice to quit*** *my flat* (=I have been told that I must leave by a certain date). | *Union members* ***served*** *strike* ***notice*** (=warned that they would go on strike) *late last night.*
4 until further notice from now until another change is announced: *The office is closed until further notice.*
5 hand in your notice/give (your) notice to tell your employer that you will be leaving your job soon SYN **resign**: *Jim gave notice on Thursday.*
6 at short notice *BrE*, **on short notice** *AmE* if you do something at short notice, you do not have very much time to prepare for it: *The trip was planned on short notice. | Thanks for agreeing to see me at such short notice. | a cancellation* ***at very short notice***
7 BOOK/PLAY ETC [C usually plural] a statement of opinion, especially one written for a newspaper or magazine, about a new play, book, film etc SYN **review**: *The new play got* ***mixed notices*** (=some good, some bad) *in the newspapers.* → **sit up (and take notice)** at SIT UP

no·tice·a·ble /ˈnəʊtəsəbəl $ ˈnoʊ-/ ●●○ *adj* easy to notice: *Alcohol has a noticeable effect on the body. |* ***It was noticeable that*** *many of them avoided answering the question.* | **noticeable difference/change/increase etc** *a noticeable improvement in air quality* THESAURUS OBVIOUS —**noticeably** *adv*: *She has become noticeably more confident. | The children were noticeably affected by the divorce.*

no·tice·board /ˈnəʊtəsˌbɔːd $ ˈnoʊtəsˌbɔːrd/ ●●○ *n* [C] *BrE* a special board on a wall which notices can be fastened to SYN **bulletin board** *AmE*

no·ti·fi·a·ble /ˈnəʊtəfaɪəbəl $ ˈnoʊ-/ *adj BrE technical* a notifiable disease or crime is one that by law must be reported to the government or to the police

no·ti·fi·ca·tion /ˌnəʊtɪfɪˈkeɪʃən $ ˌnoʊ-/ *n* [C,U] *formal* official information about something: **prior/advance notification** *I was given no prior notification.* | **[+of]** *You should* ***receive notification*** *of the results within a week.* | **official/written/formal notification** *We received official notification that Harry was missing.*

no·ti·fy /ˈnəʊtɪfaɪ $ ˈnoʊ-/ ●○○ *v* (**notified**, **notifying**, **notifies**) [T] to formally or officially tell someone about something SYN **inform**: **notify sb of sth** *You will be notified of any changes in the system.* | **notify sb that** *In August we were notified that our article had been rejected.* THESAURUS TELL

no·tion /ˈnəʊʃən $ ˈnoʊ-/ ●●○ W3 AWL *n* [C]
1 an idea, belief, or opinion: **[+of]** *misguided notions of male superiority | The traditional notion of marriage goes back thousands of years. | She had only a* ***vague notion*** *of what she wanted to do.* | **notion that** *the notion that human beings are basically good | She* ***had no notion*** *what he meant.* | **accept/challenge/reject etc a notion** *They reject the notion of group guilt.* THESAURUS IDEA
2 notions [plural] *AmE* small things such as thread and buttons that are used for sewing

no·tion·al /ˈnəʊʃənəl $ ˈnoʊ-/ *adj* [usually before noun] existing only as an idea or plan, and not existing in reality: *Their calculations were based on a notional minimum wage.*

no·to·ri·e·ty /ˌnəʊtəˈraɪəti $ ˌnoʊ-/ *n* [U] the state of being famous or well known for something that is bad or that people do not approve of: **of notoriety** *John is already a writer of some notoriety.* | **gain/win/achieve notoriety (for sth)** *The local church has gained notoriety for being different.*

no·to·ri·ous /nəʊˈtɔːriəs, nə- $ noʊ-, nə-/ ●○○ *adj* famous or well known for something bad SYN **infamous**: *a notorious computer hacker | notorious cases of human rights abuses* | **[+for]** *a judge notorious for his cruelty and corruption* THESAURUS FAMOUS —**notoriously** *adv*: *Statistics can be notoriously unreliable. | The program is notoriously difficult to learn.*

not·with·stand·ing /ˌnɒtwɪθˈstændɪŋ, -wɪð- $ ˌnɑːt-/ ●○○ AWL *prep, adv formal* in spite of something SYN **despite**: *Notwithstanding differences, there are clear similarities in all of the world's religions. | Fame and fortune notwithstanding, Donna never forgot her hometown.*

nou·gat /ˈnuːgɑː $ -gət/ *n* [U] a type of sticky soft sweet with nuts and sometimes fruit

nought /nɔːt $ nɒːt/ *number* **1** *BrE* the number 0 SYN **zero**: *A billion is 1 with 9 noughts after it.* | **nought point one/two/three etc** (=0.1, 0.2 etc) **2** *old use* used in some expressions to mean nothing: *Peace negotiations* ***came to nought*** (=were not successful).

nough·ties /ˈnɔːtiz $ ˈnɒː-/ *n* **the noughties** the years 2000 to 2009: *The company did well in the late nineties and early noughties.*

ˌnoughts and ˈcrosses *n* [U] *BrE* a game in which two players write 0 or X in a pattern of nine squares, trying to win with a row of three 0's or three X's SYN **tick-tack-toe** *AmE*

noun /naʊn/ ●●● *n* [C] a word or group of words that represent a person (such as 'Michael', 'teacher', or 'police officer'), a place (such as 'France' or 'school'), a thing or activity (such as 'coffee' or 'football'), or a quality or idea (such as 'danger' or 'happiness'). Nouns can be used as the subject or object of a verb (as in 'The teacher arrived' or 'We like the teacher') or as the object of a PREPOSITION (as in 'good at football'). → COMMON NOUN, COUNT NOUN, PROPER NOUN

nour·ish /ˈnʌrɪʃ $ ˈnɜːrɪʃ, ˈnʌ-/ *v* [T] **1** to give a person or other living thing the food and other substances they need in order to live, grow, and stay healthy: *The cream contains vitamin A to nourish the skin. | a* ***well-nourished*** *baby*
2 *formal* to keep a feeling, idea, or belief strong or help it to grow stronger: *We need to nourish our hopes and dreams.*

nour·ish·ing /ˈnʌrɪʃɪŋ $ ˈnɜː-, ˈnʌ-/ *adj* food that is nourishing makes you strong and healthy SYN **nutritious**

N

nour·ish·ment /ˈnʌrɪʃmənt $ ˈnɜː-, ˈnʌ-/ *n* [U] *formal* **1** the food and other substances that people and other living things need to live, grow, and stay healthy: *lack of proper nourishment | The soil provides nourishment for plant roots.* THESAURUS ▶ FOOD **2** something that helps a feeling, idea, or belief to grow stronger: **emotional/intellectual/spiritual nourishment** *a child starved of emotional nourishment*

nous /naʊs $ nuːs, naʊs/ *n* [U] *BrE informal* intelligence and the ability to make good practical decisions SYN **common sense**: *At least she* ***had the nous*** *to ring.*

nou·veau riche /ˌnuːvəʊ ˈriːʃ $ -voʊ-/ *adj* having only recently become rich and spending a lot of money – used to show disapproval SYN **new rich** —**nouveaux riches** *n* [plural]

nou·velle cui·sine /ˌnuːvel kwɪˈziːn/ *n* [U] a style of cooking from France where simple and healthy food is served in an attractive way, usually in small amounts on a big plate

Nov. (*also* **Nov** *BrE*) the written abbreviation of ***November***

no·va /ˈnəʊvə $ ˈnoʊ-/ *n* (*plural* **novas** *or* **novae** /-viː/) [C] a star which explodes and suddenly becomes much brighter for a short time → SUPERNOVA

nov·el¹ /ˈnɒvəl $ ˈnɑː-/ ●●● W3 *n* [C] a long written story in which the characters and events are usually imaginary → **fiction**: *a novel by Jane Austen | It took Vikram Seth three years to write his 1,349-page novel 'A Suitable Boy'.* | **detective/romantic/historical etc novel** *a newly published science fiction novel* THESAURUS ▶ BOOK

novel² ●●○ *adj* [usually before noun] not like anything known before, and unusual or interesting: **novel idea/approach/method etc** *What a novel idea!* THESAURUS ▶ NEW

nov·el·ist /ˈnɒvəlɪst $ ˈnɑː-/ ●●○ *n* [C] someone who writes novels → **author**

nov·el·i·za·tion (*also* **-isation** *BrE*) /ˌnɒvəlaɪˈzeɪʃən $ ˌnɑːvələ-/ *n* [C] the story that was told in a film or television series, written afterwards as a book: *the novelization of Terminator 2*

no·vel·la /nəʊˈvelə $ noʊ-/ *n* [C] a story that is shorter than a novel, but longer than a SHORT STORY

nov·el·ty /ˈnɒvəlti $ ˈnɑː-/ ●○○ *n* (*plural* **novelties**)
1 [U] the quality of being new, unusual, and interesting: **[+of]** *the novelty of the ideas | Many toys have no attraction beyond their* ***novelty value****. | It was fun for a while, but* ***the novelty wore off*** (=it became boring).
2 [C] something new and unusual which attracts people's attention and interest: *Then the Internet was still something of a novelty.*
3 [C] an unusual small cheap object, often given as a present: *a selection of novelties and t-shirts | a novelty key-ring*

No·vem·ber /nəʊˈvembə, nə- $ noʊˈvembər, nə-/ ●●● S2 W2 *n* [C,U] (*written abbreviation* **Nov.**) the 11th month of the year, between October and December: **next/last November** *He started work here last November.* | **in November** *It snowed in early November.* | **on November 6th** *The final will be played on Sunday November 6th.* | **on 6th November** *BrE*: *Five weeks later, on 6th November, they were secretly married.* | **November 6** *AmE*: *There will be no performance November 6.*

nov·ice /ˈnɒvɪs $ ˈnɑː-/ *n* [C] **1** someone who has no experience in a skill, subject, or activity SYN **beginner**: *The computer course is ideal for novices.* | **[+at]** *I'm still a* ***complete novice*** *at the sport. | This trail is not recommended for novice bikers.* **2** someone who has recently joined a religious group to become a MONK or NUN

no·vi·ti·ate, **noviciate** /nəʊˈvɪʃiət, nə-, -ʃieɪt $ noʊˈvɪʃət/ *n* [C] the period of being a novice

now¹ /naʊ/ ●●● S1 W1 *adv*
1 AT THE PRESENT TIME at this time: *They now live in the city centre.* | *There's nothing I can do about this* ***right now*** (=exactly now). | **by now** *Sonia should have been home by now. Do you think she's OK?* | **up to now/until now** *Until now, doctors have been able to do very little to treat this disease.* | *Please try to be more careful* ***from now on*** (=starting from now). | **for now** (=for a short time) *Just leave your shoes on the back porch for now.* | **just now** *especially BrE* (=at the present time) *There are a lot of bargains in the shops just now.*
2 IMMEDIATELY immediately: *The bell has rung – stop writing now. | If we leave now, we'll be there before dark.*
3 REALIZING used when you know or understand something because of something you have just seen, just been told etc: *Having met the rest of the family, she now saw where he got his temper from.*
4 three weeks/two years etc now used to say how long ago something started: *They've been going out together for a long time now. | It's been over five years now since I started working here. | It's now a month since we bought the car and it's broken down three times already.*
5 (every) now and then/now and again sometimes: *I hear from him every now and then.*

SPOKEN PHRASES

6 a) used when getting someone's attention before continuing what you are saying or changing the subject: *Now, let's move on to the question of payment.* **b)** used at the beginning of a sentence when asking for information: *Now, what did you say your name was?* **c)** used when pausing when you are thinking what to say next: *Now, let's see, oh yes – they wanted to know what time you'll be back on Friday.* **d)** used to say that if the situation was different, something different would happen: *Now if I'd been in charge there's no way I'd have let them use the van.* **e)** used to make someone calm, or comfort them when they are angry, upset etc: *Come on now, don't cry.* **f)** used when telling or reminding someone to do something: *Now hurry up! I haven't got all day. | Don't forget now, you have a dental appointment Thursday afternoon.*
7 any day/minute etc now very soon: *The guests will arrive any minute now.*
8 just now a moment ago: *Was that you singing just now?*
9 now then used to get someone's attention before telling them to do something or asking them a question: *Now then, what seems to be the problem here? | Now then, try to sit up and have some of this soup.*
10 well now used when giving an opinion or asking someone to tell you something: *Well now, what's all this I hear about you getting married?*
11 now for sth used when saying what you are going to do next: *Thanks, Norma, and now for a look at tomorrow's weather.*
12 and now used when introducing the next activity, performer etc: *And now, live from New York, it's David Letterman!*
13 now now a) used to make someone calm or comfort them when they are angry, upset etc: *Now now, don't worry. Everything will be okay.* **b)** *especially BrE* used when telling someone not to behave badly: *Now now, leave your sister alone.*
14 not now used to tell someone that you do not want to talk to them or do something now, because you are busy, tired etc: *'Tell me a story.' 'Not now, Daddy's working.'*
15 now what? used when an attempt to do something has failed and you do not know what to do next: *Kate tried each of the keys, but none of them fit. 'Now what?' she thought.*
16 now you're talking used to tell someone that you agree very much with what they are saying: *'Feel like going out for a beer?' 'Now you're talking.'*
17 it's now or never used to say that if someone does not do something now, they will not get another chance to do it: *Quite suddenly, her mind was made up. It was now or never.*
18 now's the time (for sb) to do sth used to say that someone should do something now, because it is the right time to do it: *Now's the time to buy a car, while the interest rates are low.*
19 what is it now?/now what? used when you are annoyed because someone keeps interrupting you or asking you things: *'Mom, can you come here for a minute?' 'What is it now?'*
20 now you tell me! used when you are annoyed or amused because someone has just told you something they should have told you before: *'You didn't need to make anything for dinner – Dad's bringing home pizza.' 'Oh, now you tell me!'*

21 now ... now ... *literary* used to say that at one moment someone or something does one thing and immediately after, they do something else: *The eagle glided through the sky, now rising, now falling.*

THESAURUS

now at this time: *Where are you living now? | The population is much larger now than it used to be.*
currently *formal* now – used when describing what a situation is like: *The firm currently employs 113 people. | Currently, the starting salary is around £20,000.*
at the moment now – used when talking about a short period of time, after which the situation is likely to change: *I think she's at lunch at the moment – can I ask her to call you back? | At the moment I'm working in a restaurant, but I'm hoping to go to college.*
at present/at the present time *formal* (*also* **presently** *AmE*) now – used when you do not expect something that is true now to be permanent: *Many areas are inaccessible at present due to heavy snow. | The official currency is the crown, presently about 30 to the dollar.*
for the time being now – used when a situation is likely to change, especially because an arrangement is only temporary: *You can stay here for the time being, until you find a flat.*

now² ●●● S1 W3 (*also* ˈ**now that**) *conjunction* because of something or as a result of something: *Now that we know each other a little better, we get along fine. | I'm going to relax now the school year is over. | Now that I think of it, I acted the same way when I was his age.*

now·a·days /ˈnaʊədeɪz/ ●●○ S3 *adv* now, compared with what happened in the past SYN **today**: *Nowadays people are rarely shocked by the sex they see on television. | Most people nowadays are aware of the importance of a healthy diet.*

ˌno ˈway *adv spoken* used to emphasize that you will not agree or be able to do something: *'Are you going to offer to work over the weekend?' 'No way!' | No way will we be finished by five o'clock. |* ***There's no way*** *I'm going to pay £500 just for a weekend in Paris.*

no·where /ˈnəʊweə $ ˈnoʊwer/ ●●● S2 *adv*
1 not in any place or to any place: **nowhere to go/live/sit etc** *I have no job and nowhere to live. | Nowhere is drug abuse more of a problem than in the US.*
2 get/go nowhere to have no success or make no progress: *The proposal went nowhere in the Senate.* | **get nowhere with sb/sth** *He was getting nowhere with the Bentley case.* | **get sb nowhere** *A negative attitude will get you nowhere. | I soon realized that being tough was* ***getting*** *me* ***nowhere fast*** (=was not helping me achieve anything).
3 be nowhere to be seen/found (*also* **be nowhere in sight**) to not be in a place, or not be seen or found there: *Typical – another street crime and the police are nowhere to be seen.*
4 nowhere near a) a long way from a particular place: *He swore he was nowhere near her house on the night she died.* **b)** not at all: **nowhere near ready/full/finished etc** *The building's nowhere near finished. | She's* ***nowhere near as*** *pretty* ***as*** *you are.*
5 out of/from nowhere happening or appearing suddenly and without warning: *In the last few seconds, Gunnell came from nowhere to win another gold medal. | From out of nowhere he asks me to marry him!*

GRAMMAR: Negatives

Don't use **nowhere** with another negative word such as 'not'. Use **anywhere**. You say: *You must* ***not*** *smoke* ***anywhere*** *in the building.* ✗ Don't say: *You must not smoke nowhere in the building.*

ˌno-ˈwin *adj* [only before noun] relating to a situation in which whatever you choose to do it will have a bad result: *If my child is sick and I leave work, I'm a bad employee. If I don't, I'm a bad mother. It's a* ***no-win situation***. → WIN-WIN

nowt /naʊt/ *pron BrE informal* nothing – used especially in the north of England: *I've had nowt to eat since yesterday.*

nox·ious /ˈnɒkʃəs $ ˈnɑːk-/ *adj formal* harmful or poisonous SYN **toxic** → **innocuous**: *noxious fumes*

noz·zle /ˈnɒzəl $ ˈnɑː-/ *n* [C] a part that is fitted to the end of a HOSE, pipe etc to direct and control the stream of liquid or gas pouring out

NOZZLE

nr *BrE* the written abbreviation of ***near***, used in addresses: *Sheffield Park Garden, nr Uckfield*

NRA, the /ˌen ɑːr ˈeɪ/ (***the National Rifle Association***) a US organization that supports people's rights to buy and keep guns, and opposes attempts to change the laws and introduce more strict controls on guns

NSU /ˌen es ˈjuː/ *n* [U] *medical* (***non-specific urethritis***) an infection of the URETHRA

n't /ənt/ the short form of 'not': *hadn't | didn't | wouldn't | isn't*

nth /enθ/ *adj informal* **1 to the nth degree** extremely, or as much as possible: *It was boring to the nth degree.* **2** [only before noun] the most recent of a long series of similar things that have happened: *Even after I'd reminded him for the nth time, he forgot.*

nu /njuː $ nuː/ *adj informal* new: *cool nu stuff*

nu·ance /ˈnjuːɑːns $ ˈnuː-/ *n* [C] a very slight, hardly noticeable difference in manner, colour, meaning etc → **subtlety**: *He was aware of every nuance in her voice.* | [+of] *the painting's delicate nuances of color, tone, and texture |* ***subtle nuances*** *of meaning* —**nuanced** *adj*: *a skilful and nuanced performance*

nub /nʌb/ *n* **1 the nub of the problem/matter/argument etc** the main point of a problem etc: *The real nub of the matter is money.* **2** [C] a small rounded piece of something, especially a piece that is left after the rest has been eaten, used etc

nu·bile /ˈnjuːbaɪl $ ˈnuːbəl/ *adj formal* a woman who is nubile is young and sexually attractive – sometimes used humorously

nu·cle·ar /ˈnjuːkliə $ ˈnuːkliər/ ●●○ W2 AWL *adj* [usually before noun]
1 relating to or involving the NUCLEUS (=central part) of an atom, or the energy produced when the nucleus of an atom is either split or joined with the nucleus of another atom: *France's reliance on* ***nuclear energy*** *| a nuclear power station | a nuclear-powered submarine*
2 relating to or involving the use of weapons that use nuclear energy → **anti-nuclear**, **conventional**: **nuclear bomb/weapon/missile etc** *the threat of nuclear attack | concern about the country's nuclear weapons program | With the collapse of the former Soviet Union, the possibility of a* ***nuclear holocaust*** (=a nuclear war that destroys much of the Earth) *was greatly reduced. | a* ***nuclear testing*** *area*

ˌnuclear ˈbomb *n* [C] a very powerful bomb that uses NUCLEAR energy to kill a lot of people and destroy large areas → **atomic bomb**

ˌnuclear deˈterrence *n* [U] the threat of using NUCLEAR weapons to stop an enemy from attacking

ˌnuclear disˈarmament *n* [U] the process or activity of getting rid of NUCLEAR weapons

ˌnuclear ˈfamily *n* [C] a family unit that consists only of a husband, wife, and children → **extended family**

ˌnuclear ˈfission *n* [U] the splitting of the NUCLEUS (=central part) of an atom which results in a lot of power being produced

ˌnuclear-ˈfree *adj* [usually before noun] places that are nuclear-free do not allow NUCLEAR materials to be carried, stored, or used in that area: *a* ***nuclear-free zone***

ˌnuclear ˈfusion *n* [U] a NUCLEAR reaction in which the NUCLEI (=central parts) of atoms join together, which produces power without producing any waste

ˌnuclear ˈphysics *n* [U] the area of physics which is concerned with the structure and features of the NUCLEUS (=central part) of atoms

N

ˌnuclear reˈactor *n* [C] a large machine that produces NUCLEAR energy, especially as a means of generating (GENERATE) electricity

ˌnuclear ˈwaste *n* [U] waste material from NUCLEAR REACTORS, which is RADIOACTIVE: *the problems of nuclear waste disposal*

nu·cle·ic ac·id /njuːˌkliːɪk ˈæsəd, -ˌkleɪ- $ nuː-/ *n* [C,U] one of the two acids, DNA and RNA, that exist in the cells of all living things

nu·cle·us /ˈnjuːkliəs $ ˈnuː-/ *n* (*plural* **nuclei** /-kliaɪ/) [C] **1** the central part of an atom, made up of NEUTRONS, PROTONS, and other ELEMENTARY PARTICLES **2** the central part of almost all the cells of living things **3** a small important group at the centre of a larger group or organization: **[+of]** *the nucleus of an effective team* | *Marantz and Grohl* ***form the nucleus*** *of the Atlanta operation.*

nude¹ /njuːd $ nuːd/ ●●○ *adj*
1 not wearing any clothes SYN **naked**: *I did some work as a* ***nude model*** *when I was in college.* | *Have you ever* ***posed nude*** (=been photographed or painted while nude)?
2 done by or involving people who are not wearing any clothes: *There are several* ***nude scenes*** *in the film.* | *I have no desire to go to a* ***nude beach*** (=a beach where people wear no clothes).
3 a pale pink-brown colour – used in fashion: *nude tights*

nude² *n* **1** [C] a painting, STATUE etc of someone not wearing clothes **2 in the nude** not wearing any clothes SYN **naked**: *He was standing there in the nude.*

NUDGE

nudge /nʌdʒ/ *v* **1** [T] to push someone gently, usually with your elbow, in order to get their attention: *Jill nudged him in the ribs.* THESAURUS▸ PUSH **2** [T always + adv/prep] to move something or someone a short distance by gently pushing: *She nudged the glass towards me.* | *David nudged me out of the way.* **3** [I,T always + adv/prep] to move forward slowly by pushing gently: **nudge your way to/through etc (sth)** *I started to nudge my way to the front of the crowd.* **4** [T always + adv/prep] to gently persuade or encourage someone to take a particular decision or action: **nudge sb into/towards sth** *We're trying to nudge them towards a practical solution.* **5** [T] to almost reach a particular level or amount: *Outside the temperature was nudging 30 degrees Celsius.* —**nudge** *n* [C]: *Hannah* ***gave*** *me a gentle* ***nudge***.

nud·ist /ˈnjuːdɪst $ ˈnuː-/ *n* [C] someone who enjoys not wearing any clothes because they believe it is natural and healthy SYN **naturist** —**nudism** *n* [U]

nu·di·ty /ˈnjuːdəti $ ˈnuː-/ *n* [U] the state of not wearing any clothes: *The play contains scenes of nudity.*

nu·ga·to·ry /ˈnjuːgətəri $ ˈnuːgətɔːri/ *adj formal* having no value

nug·get /ˈnʌgɪt/ *n* [C] **1** a small rough piece of a valuable metal found in the earth: *a* ***gold nugget*** **2** a small round piece of food: *chicken nuggets* **3 nugget of information/wisdom etc** a piece of valuable information, advice etc: *It took months to extract that nugget of information from them.*

nui·sance /ˈnjuːsəns $ ˈnuː-/ ●●○ S3 *n*
1 [C usually singular] a person, thing, or situation that annoys you or causes problems: **a real/awful/terrible etc nuisance** *The dogs next door are a real nuisance.* | **What a nuisance!** *BrE*: *What a nuisance! I've forgotten my ticket.* | **I hate to be a nuisance .../Sorry to be a nuisance ...** *I hate to be a nuisance, but could you move your car to the other side of the street?* | *Stop* ***making a nuisance of yourself*** (=annoying other people with your behaviour)! | ***It's a nuisance*** *having to get up that early on a Sunday morning.*
2 [C,U] *law* the use of a place or property in a way that causes public annoyance: *The nightclub has been declared a* ***public nuisance***.

nuke¹ /njuːk $ nuːk/ *v* [T] *informal* **1** to attack a place using NUCLEAR weapons **2** to cook food in a MICROWAVE OVEN: *Nuke it for two minutes.*

nuke² *n* [C] *informal* a NUCLEAR weapon

null /nʌl/ *adj* **null and void** *law* an agreement, contract etc that is null and void has no legal force SYN **invalid**: *The contract was* ***declared null and void***.

nul·li·fy /ˈnʌlɪfaɪ/ *v* (**nullified**, **nullifying**, **nullifies**) [T] **1** *law* to officially state that something has no legal force: *The election results were nullified because of voter fraud.* **2** *formal* to make something lose its effect or value SYN **cancel out**: *Recent inflation could nullify the economic growth of the last several years.* —**nullification** /ˌnʌlɪfɪˈkeɪʃən/ *n* [U]

nul·li·ty /ˈnʌləti/ *n* [U] *law* the fact that a marriage or contract no longer has any legal force: *a decree of nullity*

numb¹ /nʌm/ ●●○ *adj*
1 a part of your body that is numb is unable to feel anything, for example because you are very cold: *My fingers were so numb I could hardly write.* | *The anaesthetic made his whole face* ***go numb***.
2 unable to think, feel, or react in a normal way SYN **paralysed**: **numb with shock/fear/terror etc** *I just sat there, numb with fear.* —**numbly** *adv*: *She watched numbly as Matt walked away.* —**numbness** *n* [U]: *It caused some numbness in my hand.*

numb² *v* [T] **1** to make someone unable to feel pain or feel things they are touching: *The cold had numbed her fingers.* | *the numbing effect of the drug* **2** to make someone unable to think, feel, or react in a normal way: *He was numbed by the shock of his wife's death.*

num·ber¹ /ˈnʌmbə $ -bər/ ●●● S1 W1 *n*
1 NUMBER [C] a word or sign that represents an exact amount or quantity → **numeral**, **figure**: *They wrote various numbers on a large sheet of paper.* | *Add all the numbers together.* | **an even number** (=2, 4, 6, 8 etc) | **an odd number** (=1, 3, 5, 7 etc) | **a round number** (=one ending in 0) *A hundred pounds is a good round number.* | *I'm no good with numbers.*
2 PHONE [C] a phone number: *My new number is 502-6155.* | **sb's home/office/work number** *I gave him my home number.* | **mobile/fax number** *What's your mobile number?* | *Sorry, you have* ***the wrong number***.
3 IN A SET/LIST [C] a number used to show the position of something in an ordered set or list: *Answer question number 4.* | *a number 17 bus* → **E NUMBER, NO. 10, NUMBER ONE¹**
4 FOR RECOGNIZING SB/STH [C] a set of numbers used to name or recognize someone or something: **model/account etc number** *What is your account number, please?* | *Press 1 to change the printer number.* | *Did you get the number* (=REGISTRATION number) *of the car?* → **BOX NUMBER, PIN, SERIAL NUMBER**
5 AMOUNT [C,U] an amount of something that can be counted SYN **quantity**: **the number of sth** *The number of cars on our roads rose dramatically last year.* | **a number of sth** *We have been friends for a number of years.* | **in number** *The condors have dwindled to an estimated sixty in number.*

GRAMMAR: Singular or plural verb?

- You use a singular verb after **the number of**: ***The number of*** *people* ***is*** *increasing.*
- You use a plural verb after **a number of** (=several): ***A number of*** *issues* ***were*** *discussed.*

6 numbers [plural] how many people there are, especially people attending an event or doing an activity together: *Can you give me some idea of numbers?* | **student/client etc numbers** *Visitor numbers increase in the summer.* | *The* ***sheer weight of numbers*** (=large number of people) *on stage made the performance more impressive.*
7 MUSIC [C] a piece of popular music that forms part of a

longer performance: *Madonna sang several numbers from her latest album.* → PRODUCTION NUMBER **THESAURUS** MUSIC
8 MAGAZINE [C] *BrE* a copy of a magazine or newspaper printed on a particular date SYN **issue**: **[+of]** *I was reading the latest number of 'Surfing'.* | **back numbers** (=old copies) *of 'The Times'*
9 have sb's number *informal* to understand something about someone that helps you deal with them: *Judy had always had his number.*
10 black/elegant etc (little) number *informal* a black, ELEGANT etc dress or suit, especially a woman's: *She was wearing a chic little number.*
11 sb's number comes up someone has the winning number in a competition
12 sb's number is up (*also* **sb's number has come up**) *informal* **a)** used to say that someone will stop being lucky or successful **b)** used to say that someone will die – used humorously: *She told her husband she didn't mind going when her number was up.*
13 the numbers a) information about something that is shown using numbers: *Chris, have you got the numbers yet?* **b)** an illegal game in the US in which people risk money on the appearance of a combination of numbers in a newspaper: ***playing the numbers***
14 by numbers if you do something by numbers, you do it in a basic way by following a set of simple instructions – used to show disapproval: *The last thing we want is teaching by numbers.*
15 do a number on sb/sth *informal* to hurt or damage someone or something badly: *Tod really did a number on the old house. I don't envy the new tenants.*
16 beyond/without number *literary* if things are beyond number, there are so many of them that no one could count them all
17 GROUP OF PEOPLE [U] *formal* a group of people: **one/two/several etc of our/their number** *Only three of our number could speak Italian.* | *They wanted to choose a leader from* ***among their*** *own* ***number***.
18 GRAMMAR [U] *technical* the form of a word, depending on whether one thing or more than one thing is being talked about: *'Horses' is plural in number, while 'horse' is singular.*

COLLOCATIONS – MEANING 5

ADJECTIVES

a large/great number *A large number of children were running around in the playground.*
a vast/huge number (=very large) *We've had a huge number of complaints.*
a high number *There seems to be no reason for the high number of suicides.*
a considerable/substantial/significant number (=quite a large number) *He received a substantial number of votes.*
a good number (=quite a lot) *He has written a good number of books for children.*
a small number *The class had only a small number of students.*
a low number *the low numbers of women involved in sports coaching*
a limited number (=quite small) *A limited number of copies were printed.*
a tiny number (=very small) *Only a tiny number of these animals remain in the wild.*
a growing/increasing number *An increasing number of women are entering the profession.*

VERBS

increase the number of sth *As you improve, increase the number of times you do each exercise.*
reduce the number of sth *We need to reduce the number of cars on the road.*
a number increases/goes up/grows/rises *The number of mobile phones has increased dramatically.*
a number doubles (=becomes twice as big) *The number of road accidents has doubled in the last ten years.*
a number falls/drops/goes down/decreases/declines *The number of new houses being built is falling steadily.*
a number halves (=becomes twice as small)

PHRASES

in large/increasing/limited etc numbers *Birds nest here in large numbers.*
any number of sth (=a very large number of them) *There have been any number of magazine articles about the celebrity couple.*
bring the number to 25, 120 etc *This will bring the number of jobs lost at the company to 85.*

COMMON ERRORS

⚠ Don't say 'a big number of people/things'. Say **a large number of people/things**.

number² ●○○ *v*
1 [T] to give a number to something that is part of an ordered set or list: *They haven't numbered the pages of the report.* | *All the seats in the theatre are numbered.* | *Each check is* ***numbered consecutively***. | *a numbering system* | **number sth (from) 1 to 10/100 etc** *Number the questions 1 to 25.*
2 [linking verb] if people or things number a particular amount, that is how many there are: *The population of the town numbered about 5,000.* | *The men on strike now number 5% of the workforce.*
3 sb's/sth's days are numbered used to say that someone or something cannot live or continue for much longer: *I knew my days were numbered at that firm.*
4 number among sth/be numbered among sth *formal* to be included as one of a particular group: *He was a successful corporate lawyer who numbered among his clients JP Morgan and Standard Oil.*
5 [T] *literary* to count something: *Who can number the stars?*
number off *phr v BrE* if soldiers number off, each one calls out their number when their turn comes SYN **count off** *AmE*

ˈnumber ˌcruncher *n* [C] *informal* someone whose job involves working with numbers, such as an ACCOUNTANT

ˈnumber ˌcrunching *n* [U] *informal* the process of working with a lot of numbers and calculating results —**number-crunching** *adj*

num·ber·less /ˈnʌmbələs $ -bər-/ *adj literary* too many to be counted SYN **countless**: *numberless fish*

ˌnumber ˈone¹ *n* **1** [U] the best, most important, or most successful person or thing in a group: *Until his marriage, his job was number one in his life.* | *Shearson is number one in the market this year.* **2** [C,U] the musical record that is the most popular at a particular time: *number one in the charts* | *They've had three number ones.* **3 look out for number one** (*also* **look after number one**) *spoken* to look after yourself and not worry about other people, in a way that may seem SELFISH **4** [singular, U] *spoken informal* a word meaning URINE, used especially with children to avoid saying this

ˌnumber ˈone² *adj* **1** most important or successful in a particular situation: *The University of Maine has the number one hockey team in the country.* | *Sweden's number one model* **2** first on a list of several things to be considered, done etc: *item number one on the agenda* | *This has got to be our number one task.*

ˈnumber ˌplate *n* [C] *BrE* one of the signs with numbers and letters on it at the front and back of a car → **registration number** SYN **license plate** *AmE*

ˌNumber ˈTen (***Number Ten Downing Street***) the address of the official home of the British prime minister

ˌnumber ˈtwo *n* [singular, U] *spoken informal* a word meaning solid waste from your BOWELS, used especially with children to avoid saying this → **number one**

numb·skull, **numskull** /ˈnʌmskʌl/ *n* [C] *informal* a very stupid person SYN **idiot**: *Look what you've done now, you numbskull!*

nu·me·ra·cy /ˈnjuːmərəsi $ ˈnuː-/ *n* [U] the ability to do calculations and understand simple mathematics

N

→ **literacy**: *The report suggests that students need to improve their numeracy skills.*

nu·me·ral /ˈnjuːmərəl $ ˈnuː-/ *n* [C] a written sign such as 1, 2, or 3 that represents a number → **figure** —**numeral** *adj*

nu·me·rate /ˈnjuːmərət $ ˈnuː-/ *adj* able to do calculations and understand simple mathematics → **literate**

nu·me·ra·tion /ˌnjuːməˈreɪʃən $ ˌnuː-/ *n* [C,U] *technical* a system of counting or the process of counting

nu·me·ra·tor /ˈnjuːməreɪtə $ ˈnuːməreɪtər/ *n* [C] *technical* the number above the line in a FRACTION, for example 5 is the numerator in 5/6 → **denominator**

nu·mer·i·cal /njuːˈmerɪkəl $ nuː-/ ●○○ *adj* expressed or considered in numbers: *a numerical code* | *The home team tried to utilize their numerical advantage* (=the fact that they had more players than the other team). | *Make sure the files are organized* ***in numerical order***. —**numerically** /-kli/ *adv*

nu·me·rous /ˈnjuːmərəs $ ˈnuː-/ ●●○ W3 *adj* many: *Numerous attempts have been made to hide the truth.* | *The two leaders have worked together on* ***numerous occasions***. | **too numerous to mention/list** *The individuals who have contributed to this book are far too numerous to mention.*

THESAURUS ▸ MANY

> **REGISTER**
> In everyday English, people usually say **a lot of** rather than **numerous**: *There were* ***a lot of*** *mistakes in his essay.*

nu·mi·nous /ˈnjuːmɪnəs $ ˈnuː-/ *adj literary* having a mysterious and holy quality, which makes you feel that God is present

nu·mis·mat·ics /ˌnjuːməzˈmætɪks $ ˌnuː-/ *n* [U] the activity of collecting and studying coins and MEDALS

nu·mis·ma·tist /njuːˈmɪzmətɪst $ nuː-/ *n* [C] someone who collects and studies coins and MEDALS

nump·ty, **numptie** /ˈnʌmpti/ *n* (*plural* **numpties**) [C] *BrE informal* an insulting word for someone who is stupid or not good at doing something

nun /nʌn/ *n* [C] someone who is a member of a group of religious women that live together in a CONVENT → **monk**

nun·ci·o /ˈnʌnsiəʊ $ -sioʊ/ *n* (*plural* **nuncios**) [C] a representative of the Pope in a foreign country

nun·ne·ry /ˈnʌnəri/ *n* (*plural* **nunneries**) [C] *old use* a CONVENT

nup·tial /ˈnʌpʃəl/ *adj* [only before noun] *formal* relating to marriage or the marriage ceremony → **wedding**: *a nuptial mass* | *nuptial bliss*

nup·tials /ˈnʌpʃəlz/ *n* [plural] *formal* a wedding

nurse¹ /nɜːs $ nɜːrs/ ●●● S2 W3 *n* [C]
1 someone whose job is to look after people who are ill or injured, usually in a hospital: *The nurse is coming to give you an injection.* | *The school nurse sent Sara home.* | *a male nurse* | *a senior nurse* | *a student nurse* (=someone who is learning to be a nurse) | *a psychiatric nurse* (=a nurse for people who are mentally ill) | *a community nurse* → DISTRICT NURSE, STAFF NURSE
2 *old-fashioned* a woman employed to look after a young child SYN **nanny** → NURSERY NURSE, WET NURSE

nurse² ●○○ *v*
1 SICK PEOPLE **a)** [T] to look after someone who is ill or injured: *He's been nursing an elderly relative.* | *After Ray's operation, Mrs Stallard* ***nursed*** *him* ***back to health***. **b)** [I usually in progressive] to work as a nurse: *She spent several years nursing in a military hospital.*
2 REST [T] to rest when you have an illness or injury so that it will get better: *Shaw has been nursing an injury, and will not play on Sunday.*
3 FEED A BABY **a)** [I,T] *old-fashioned* if a woman nurses a baby, she feeds it with milk from her breasts SYN **breast-feed**: *information on nutrition for nursing mothers* **b)** [I] if a baby nurses, it sucks milk from its mother's breast
4 YOUR FEELINGS [T] to keep a feeling or idea in your mind for a long time, especially an angry feeling: **nurse a grudge/grievance/ambition etc** *For years he had nursed a grievance against his former employer.*
5 TAKE CARE OF STH [T] to take special care of something, especially during a difficult situation: **nurse sth through/along etc** *He bought the hotel in 1927 and managed to nurse it through the Depression.*
6 DRINK [T] *informal* if you nurse a drink, especially an alcoholic one, you drink it very slowly: *Oliver sat at the bar, nursing a bottle of beer.*
7 HOLD [T] *literary* to hold something carefully in your hands or arms close to your body: *a child nursing a kitten*

nurse·maid /ˈnɜːsmeɪd $ ˈnɜːrs-/ *n* [C] *old-fashioned* a woman employed to look after young children

ˌnurse pracˈtitioner *n* [C] a nurse who is trained to do some of the work that is usually done by a doctor

nur·se·ry /ˈnɜːsəri $ ˈnɜːr-/ ●●○ *n* (*plural* **nurseries**) [C]
1 a place where young children are taken care of during the day while their parents are at work
2 a place where plants and trees are grown and sold
3 **nursery education/unit/teacher etc** *BrE* education etc for young children from three to five years old → NURSERY SCHOOL
4 a room in a hospital where babies that have just been born are looked after
5 *old-fashioned* a baby's BEDROOM or a room in a house where young children play

nur·se·ry·man /ˈnɜːsərimən $ ˈnɜːr-/ *n* (*plural* **nurserymen** /-mən/) [C] *BrE* someone who grows plants and trees in a nursery

ˈnursery ˌnurse *n* [C] *BrE* someone who has been trained to look after young children

ˈnursery rhyme ●○○ *n* [C] a short traditional poem or song for children

ˈnursery ˌschool *n* [C] a school for children who are between three and five years old SYN **kindergarten**

ˈnursery ˌslope *n* [C] *BrE* a slope that is not very steep, where people are taught to SKI

nurs·ing /ˈnɜːsɪŋ $ ˈnɜːr-/ ●●○ *n* [U] the job or skill of looking after people who are ill, injured, or old → **nurse**: *I'd love to go into nursing.* | *the nursing profession* | *psychiatric nursing*

ˈnursing home *n* [C] a place where people who are old and ill can live and be looked after SYN **old people's home**

nur·tur·ance /ˈnɜːtʃərəns $ ˈnɜːr-/ *n* [U] *formal* loving care and attention that you give to someone

nur·ture¹ /ˈnɜːtʃə $ ˈnɜːrtʃər/ *v* [T] *formal* **1** to help a plan, idea, feeling etc to develop: *European union is an ideal that has been nurtured since the post-war years.* | *a hatred of foreigners nurtured by the media* **2** to feed and take care of a child or a plant while it is growing: *plants nurtured in the greenhouse* GRAMMAR **Nurture** is usually passive.

nurture² *n* [U] *formal* the education and care that you are given as a child, and the way it affects your later development and attitudes

nut¹ /nʌt/ ●●● S3 *n* [C]
1 FOOD a dry brown fruit inside a hard shell, that grows on a tree: *a pine nut* | *roasted nuts* | *We were sitting round the fire* ***cracking nuts*** (=opening them).
2 TOOL a small piece of metal with a hole through the middle which is screwed onto a BOLT to fasten things together: *Use a wrench to loosen the nut.*
3 CRAZY PERSON *informal* someone who is crazy or behaves strangely: *My dad is such a nut.* | *What are you, some kind of nut?*
4 **golf/opera etc nut** *informal* someone who is very interested in golf etc → **fanatic**: *You don't have to be a sports nut to enjoy skiing.*
5 SEX ORGAN **nuts** [plural] *informal* a man's TESTICLES
6 **the nuts and bolts of sth** *informal* the practical details of a subject or job: *the nuts and bolts of government*
7 **tough/hard nut** *informal* someone who is difficult to deal with: *He may have softened a bit in his old age but he's still a tough nut.*
8 **a hard/tough nut to crack** a difficult problem or situation:

NUTS

Celtic have lost only once this season and will be a tough nut to crack.
9 be off your nut *BrE spoken informal* to be crazy: *You must be off your nut!*
10 do your nut *BrE spoken* to become very angry or worried: *I didn't get home till three – my mum did her nut!*
11 HEAD *BrE spoken old-fashioned* your head or brain: **sb's nut** *Oh come on,* **use your nut***!*

nut² *v* (**nutted**, **nutting**) [T] *BrE spoken* to hit someone with your head SYN **headbutt**: *He just turned round and nutted me!*

ˌnut-ˈbrown *adj* dark brown in colour

nut·case /ˈnʌtkeɪs/ *n* [C] *informal* someone who behaves in a crazy way SYN **idiot**: *He's a complete nutcase.*

nut·crack·er /ˈnʌtˌkrækə $ -ər/ *n* [C] (*also* **nutcrackers** *BrE*) a tool for cracking the shells of nuts

nut·house /ˈnʌthaʊs/ *n* [C] **1** *informal* a place that is loud, unpleasant, and not organized: *I don't want to spend another night in this nuthouse.* **2** *old-fashioned informal* a PSYCHIATRIC hospital

nut job, **nut·job** /ˈnʌtdʒɒb $ -dʒɑːb/ *n* [C] *BrE informal* a crazy person SYN **nutter**

nut·meg /ˈnʌtmeg/ *n* [U] a brown powder made from the seed of a tropical tree, which is used as a spice

nu·tra·ceu·ti·cals /ˌnjuːtrəˈsjuːtɪkəlz $ ˌnuːtrəˈsuː-/ *n* [plural] foods that are designed to improve health and lower the risk of disease, for example by increasing the amount of VITAMINS in them, or removing some of the FAT SYN **functional foods**

nu·tri·ent /ˈnjuːtriənt $ ˈnuː-/ ●○○ *n* [C] a chemical or food that provides what is needed for plants or animals to live and grow: *The plant absorbs nutrients from the soil.* —**nutrient** *adj*

nu·tri·ge·no·mics /ˌnjuːtrɪdʒiːˈnəʊmɪks $ ˌnuːtrɪdʒiːˈnɑː-/ *n* [U] the study of how different foods affect someone's health by the way they react with that person's GENES, for example by making them more or less likely to get heart disease or other illnesses

nu·tri·ment /ˈnjuːtrəmənt $ ˈnuː-/ *n* [U] *formal* a substance that gives plants and animals what they need in order to live and grow SYN **nourishment**

nu·tri·tion /njuːˈtrɪʃən $ nuː-/ ●○○ *n* [U]
1 the process of giving or getting the right type of food for good health and growth → **malnutrition**: *Nutrition and exercise are essential to fitness and health.* | *a nutrition expert* | **poor/good nutrition** *Poor nutrition can cause heart disease in later life.* THESAURUS FOOD
2 the science that deals with the effects of food, VITAMINS etc on people's health

nu·tri·tion·al /njuːˈtrɪʃənəl $ nuː-/ ●○○ *adj* relating to the substances in food that help you to stay healthy: *Cooking vegetables for too long lessens their* ***nutritional value****.* | *the nutritional requirements of pregnant women* | *nutritional deficiencies* —**nutritionally** *adv*

nu·tri·tion·ist /njuːˈtrɪʃənɪst $ nuː-/ *n* [C] someone who has a special knowledge of nutrition

nu·tri·tious /njuːˈtrɪʃəs $ nuː-/ *adj* food that is nutritious is full of the natural substances that your body needs to stay healthy or to grow properly: *Wholemeal bread is more nutritious than white bread.* | *Nuts and fruit make nutritious snacks.* | *The cookbook contains many simple yet* ***highly nutritious*** *meals.*

nu·tri·tive /ˈnjuːtrətɪv $ ˈnuː-/ *adj* **1** relating to nutrition **2** *formal* nutritious

nuts¹ /nʌts/ *adj* [not before noun] *informal* **1** crazy: *Are you nuts?* | *I'm going to* ***go nuts*** (=become crazy) *if I don't find a new job soon.* | *Turn that radio off. It's* ***driving*** *me* ***nuts*** (=annoying me very much). **2 go nuts** *spoken* **a)** to become very excited because something good has just happened: *The crowd went nuts after the third touchdown.* **b)** to become very angry about something: *Mom's going to go nuts if you don't clean this mess up.* **3 be nuts about/over sb/sth** to like someone or something very much: *My wife is nuts about kids.*

nuts² *interjection AmE old-fashioned* **1** used to emphasize that something bad or annoying has happened: *Nuts! Now we're going to be late for the movie.* **2 nuts to sb/sth** used when you are angrily refusing to listen to someone or do something: *'Nuts to that,' he sneered, and left.*

nut·shell /ˈnʌt-ʃel/ *n* [C] **1 in a nutshell** used when you are stating the main facts about something in a short clear way: *Okay, that's our proposal in a nutshell. Any questions?* **2** the hard outer part of a nut

nut·ter /ˈnʌtə $ -ər/ *n* [C] *BrE informal* a crazy person SYN **idiot**: *an absolute nutter*

nut·ty /ˈnʌti/ *adj* **1** *informal* crazy: *It's another of his nutty ideas.* | *She's* ***nutty as a fruitcake*** (=completely crazy). **2** tasting like, or containing, nuts: *This coffee has a rich nutty flavour.* | *a nutty cake*

nuz·zle /ˈnʌzəl/ (*also* **nuzzle up**) *v* [I always + adv/prep, T] to gently rub or press your nose or head against someone to show you like them: *Evan leaned forward and began nuzzling her shoulder.* | **[+against]** *The horses were nuzzling up against each other.*

NVQ /ˌen viː ˈkjuː/ *n* [C] (***National Vocational Qualification***) an examination relating to the skills and knowledge involved in a particular type of work. NVQs are taken in Britain, usually by people who are already working.

NW the written abbreviation of ***northwest*** or ***northwestern***

N-word, **N word** /ˈen wɜːd $ -wɜːrd/ *n* **the N-word** used when you are talking about the word NIGGER but do not want to say it because it is offensive → **f-word**

ny·lon /ˈnaɪlɒn $ -lɑːn/ ●●○ *n*
1 [U] a strong artificial material that is used to make plastics, clothes, rope etc: *nylon fabric* | *The tent was made of nylon.*
2 nylons [plural] *old-fashioned* women's STOCKINGs that are made of nylon

nymph /nɪmf/ *n* [C] **1** one of the SPIRITs of nature who, according to ancient Greek and Roman stories, appeared as young girls living in trees, mountains, streams etc **2** *literary* a beautiful girl or young woman

nym·phet /nɪmˈfet, ˈnɪmfɪt $ nɪmˈfet/ *n* [C] a young girl who is very sexually attractive

nym·pho·ma·ni·ac /ˌnɪmfəˈmeɪniæk/ (*also* **nym·pho** /ˈnɪmfəʊ $ -foʊ/ *informal*) *n* [C] a woman who wants to have sex often, usually with a lot of different men SYN **sex maniac** —**nymphomania** /-niə/ *n* [U]

NZ the written abbreviation of ***New Zealand***

Oo

O

O[1], **o** /əʊ $ oʊ/ *n* (*plural* **O's, o's**) **1** [C,U] the 15th letter of the English alphabet **2** [U] *spoken* zero: *My phone number is six o four double two* (=60422). **3** [U] a common type of blood

O[2] /əʊ $ oʊ/ *interjection* **1** used when praying to a god or, in the past, when speaking to someone in great authority: *O Lord, in you I put my trust.* **2** another form of OH

o' /ə/ *prep* 'of' written as people sometimes say it informally: *a drop o' whisky* → **O'CLOCK**

oaf /əʊf $ oʊf/ *n* [C] someone who is stupid or awkward, especially a man —**oafish** *adj*

oak /əʊk $ oʊk/ ●●○ *n* [C,U] a large tree that is common in northern countries, or the hard wood of this tree: *an oak door* → see picture at **TREE**

oak·en /ˈəʊkən $ ˈoʊ-/ *adj* [only before noun] *literary* made of oak: *an oaken chest*

oa·kum /ˈəʊkəm $ ˈoʊ-/ *n* [U] small pieces of old rope used for filling up small holes in the sides of wooden ships

OAP /ˌəʊ eɪ ˈpiː $ ˌoʊ-/ *n* [C] *BrE* (***old age pensioner***) a person who is old enough to receive a PENSION from the state: *special rates for OAPs*

oar /ɔː $ ɔːr/ *n* [C] **1** a long pole with a wide flat blade at one end, used for rowing a boat → **paddle 2 put/stick/get your oar in** *BrE informal* to get involved in a conversation or situation when the other people do not want you to: *We were getting along fine until you stuck your oar in.*

oar·lock /ˈɔːlɒk $ ˈɔːrlɑːk/ *n* [C] *AmE* one of the small pieces of metal on a rowing boat that holds the oars

oars·man /ˈɔːzmən $ ˈɔːrz-/ *n* (*plural* **oarsmen** /-mən/) [C] someone who rows a boat, especially in races → **rower**

oars·wom·an /ˈɔːzˌwʊmən $ ˈɔːrz-/ *n* (*plural* **oarswomen** /-ˈwɪmɪn/) [C] a woman who rows a boat, especially in races

o·a·sis /əʊˈeɪsɪs $ oʊ-/ *n* (*plural* **oases** /siːz/) [C] **1** a place with water and trees in a desert **2** a peaceful or pleasant place that is very different from everything around it SYN **haven**: **an oasis of calm/serenity/tranquillity etc** *The park was an oasis of peace.*

oast house /ˈəʊst haʊs $ ˈoʊst-/ *n* [C] *BrE* a round building with a pointed top, built for drying HOPS

oat /əʊt $ oʊt/ *adj* [only before noun] made of OATS: *oat biscuits*

ˈ**oat cake** *n* [C] *BrE* a BISCUIT made of oatmeal

oath /əʊθ $ oʊθ/ ●○○ *n* (*plural* **oaths** /əʊðz $ oʊðz/) [C]
1 a formal and very serious promise: **oath of loyalty/allegiance/obedience etc** *an oath of allegiance to the Queen* | **swear/take an oath** *Servicemen have to swear an oath of loyalty to their country.* | *The president took the* ***oath of office*** (=made the official public promises that every president makes when starting their job). | *She could not* ***break her oath.***
2 *law* a formal promise to tell the truth in a court of law: **on/under oath** *The evidence was given under oath.* | *Witnesses are required to* ***take the oath*** (=make this promise).
3 *written* an offensive word or phrase that expresses anger, surprise, shock etc: *He was shouting out oaths as they led him away.*

oat·meal /ˈəʊtmiːl $ ˈoʊt-/ *n* [U] **1** *BrE* crushed OATS used in cooking, especially for making BISCUITS or PORRIDGE **2** *AmE* a soft breakfast food made by boiling crushed OATS SYN **porridge** *BrE* **3** a light brown colour

oats /əʊts $ oʊts/ *n* [plural] the grain from which flour or oatmeal is made and that is used in cooking, or in food for animals → **sow your wild oats** at **SOW**[1](3)

ob·du·rate /ˈɒbdjərət $ ˈɑːbdə-/ *adj formal* very determined not to change your beliefs, actions, or feelings, in a way that seems unreasonable SYN **stubborn**: *They argued, but he remained obdurate.* —**obduracy** *n* [U] —**obdurately** *adv*

o·be·di·ence /əˈbiːdiəns/ ●○○ *n* [U] when someone does what they are told to do, or what a law, rule etc says they must do OPP **disobedience**: **[+to]** *obedience to God* | **in obedience to sth** *He lived in obedience to the church's teachings.* | **blind/unquestioning/complete obedience** (=complete obedience without any thought) *With blind obedience, I allowed my father to organize my life.* | *obedience classes for dogs and their owners*

o·be·di·ent /əˈbiːdiənt/ ●○○ *adj*
1 always doing what you are told to do, or what the law, a rule etc says you must do OPP **disobedient**: *an obedient child* | **[+to]** *citizens who are obedient to the law*

> **REGISTER**
> In everyday English, people usually say that a child is **good** rather than **obedient**: *The children were all very* ***good.***

2 your obedient servant *old use* a phrase used to end a very formal letter —**obediently** *adv*

o·bei·sance /əʊˈbeɪsəns $ oʊ-/ *n* [C,U] *literary* respect and obedience to someone or something, often shown by bending your head or the upper part of your body: **make/pay obeisance (to sb/sth)** *They made obeisance to the sultan.*

ob·e·lisk /ˈɒbəlɪsk $ ˈɑː-, ˈoʊ-/ *n* [C] a tall pointed stone PILLAR, built to remind people of an event or of someone who has died

OBELISK

o·bese /əʊˈbiːs $ oʊ-/ ●○○ *adj* very fat in a way that is unhealthy **THESAURUS** ▸ FAT

o·be·si·ty /əʊˈbiːsəti $ oʊ-/ ●○○ *n* [U] when someone is very fat in a way that is unhealthy

o·bey /əʊˈbeɪ, ə- $ oʊ-, ə-/ ●●● W3 *v* [I,T] to do what someone in authority tells you to do, or what a law or rule says you must do OPP **disobey**: *The little boy made no effort to obey.* | *'Sit!' he said, and the dog obeyed him instantly.* | **obey an order/command** *Soldiers are expected to obey orders without questioning them.* | **obey the law/rules** *Failure to obey the law can lead to a large fine.*
⚠ Don't say 'obey to someone/something'. Say **obey someone/something**: *He refused to obey their orders (NOT obey to their orders).*

> **THESAURUS**
> **obey** to do what someone in authority tells you to do, or what a law or rule says you must do: *You must obey a senior officer at all times.* | *If everyone obeys the rules of the road, safety is much improved.*
> **do what sb says** *especially spoken* to do what someone has advised or ordered you to do. In informal and everyday situations, people usually say **do what sb says** rather than **obey**: *I did what you said but the car still hasn't started.* | *My husband never does what I say.*
> **do what you are told/do as you are told** to do what your parent or teacher says you must do – used especially about children: *At school, we expect the pupils to do what they are told.* | *Do as you're told and sit down.*

follow sb's orders/instructions/advice to do what someone says you should do, or advises you to do: *You must follow your doctor's orders. | I followed the manufacturer's instructions.*
abide by sth *formal* to accept and obey a rule, law, agreement etc: *Players have to abide by the rules of the game.*
respect *formal* to obey the law or customs of a place, even when you do not agree with them, because this is a necessary part of living in a society: *Smokers should respect the law, and only smoke in the privacy of their own homes.*

ob·fus·cate /ˈɒbfəskeɪt $ ˈɑːb-/ *v* [T] *formal* to deliberately make something unclear or difficult to understand SYN **confuse** —**obfuscation** /ˌɒbfəˈskeɪʃən $ ˌɑːb-/ *n* [U]

ob/gyn /ˌəʊbiː ˈgaɪn $ ˌoʊ-/ *n especially AmE informal* **1** [U] the part of medical science that deals with OBSTETRICS and GYNAECOLOGY **2** [C] a doctor who works in this part of medical science

o·bit /ˈəʊbɪt $ ˈoʊ-/ *n* [C] *informal* an obituary

o·bit·u·a·ry /əˈbɪtʃuəri $ -tʃueri/ *n* (*plural* **obituaries**) [C] an article in a newspaper about the life of someone who has just died

ob·ject¹ /ˈɒbdʒɪkt $ ˈɑːb-/ ●●● S2 W2 *n*
1 THING [C] a solid thing that you can hold, touch, or see but that is not alive: *an everyday object such as a spoon | a small metal object | scientists studying plants, animals, or **inanimate objects*** (=things that are not alive) → UFO THESAURUS THING
2 AIM [singular] the purpose of a plan, action, or activity → **goal**, **aim**: **[+of]** *The object of the game is to improve children's math skills. | My object was to explain the decision simply. | The customer will benefit most, and that is **the object of the exercise*** (=the purpose of what you are doing).
3 an object of pity/desire/ridicule etc someone or something that is pitied, wanted etc: *She feared becoming an object of ridicule. | sports cars and other objects of desire | an **object of study*** → SEX OBJECT
4 money/expense is no object used to say that you are willing to spend a lot of money to get something: *Money's no object; I want the best.*
5 object lesson an event or story that shows you the right or wrong way of doing something: **[+in]** *The way ants work is an object lesson in order and organization.*
6 GRAMMAR [C] **a)** a noun or pronoun representing the person or thing that something is done to, for example 'the house' in 'We built the house.' SYN **direct object b)** a noun or pronoun representing the person or thing that is joined by a PREPOSITION to another word or phrase, for example 'the table' in 'He sat on the table.' **c)** the person who is involved in the result of an action, for example 'her' in 'I gave her the book.' SYN **indirect object** → **subject**
7 COMPUTER [C] a combination of written information on a computer and instructions that act on the information, for example in the form of a document or a picture: *multimedia data objects*

ob·ject² /əbˈdʒekt/ ●●○ W3 *v*
1 [I] to feel or say that you oppose or disapprove of something: *If no one objects, I would like Mrs Harrison to be present.* | **object to (doing) sth** *Robson **strongly objected** to the terms of the contract. | I objected to having to rewrite the article.* | **I object** (=used in formal arguments, for example in a court of law) *Mr Chairman, I object. That is an unfair allegation.* THESAURUS COMPLAIN
2 [T] to state a fact or opinion as a reason for opposing or disapproving of something: **object that** *The group objected that the policy would prevent patients from receiving the best treatment. | 'My name's not Sonny,' the child objected.* → OBJECTOR

ˈobject ˌcode *n* [U] MACHINE CODE

ob·jec·ti·fy /əbˈdʒektɪfaɪ/ *v* (**objectified**, **objectifying**, **objectifies**) [T] *formal* to treat a person or idea as a physical object: *a culture that objectifies women* —**objectification** /əbˌdʒektɪfɪˈkeɪʃən/ *n* [U]

ob·jec·tion /əbˈdʒekʃən/ ●●○ W3 *n*
1 [C,U] a reason that you have for opposing or disapproving of something, or something you say that expresses this: *Her objection was that he was too young.* | **[+to]** *He had moral objections to killing animals for food.* | **over the objections of sb** (=in spite of their objections) *The bill was passed over the objections of many Democrats.*
2 objection! *spoken formal* said by lawyers to a judge in a court when they think that what another lawyer has just said should not be allowed

COLLOCATIONS

VERBS
have an objection *Does anyone have any objections to the proposal?*
make an objection (=say what your objection is) *The Parish Council made several objections to the changes.*
raise/voice an objection (=make an objection) *His father raised no objections when John told him that he wanted to become a dancer.*
meet sb's objections (=change something so that someone will no longer object) | **withdraw an objection** (=stop objecting to something) | **lodge an objection** (=formally make an objection)

ADJECTIVES
a strong objection *Parents at the school have voiced strong objections to the closure.*
a serious/major objection *There were serious objections to using the videotaped evidence at the trial.*
the main objection *One of the main objections was that classes were being taught by untrained staff.*
a fundamental objection | **a moral objection** | **a religious objection**

COMMON ERRORS
⚠ Don't say 'say an objection'. Say **make an objection**.

ob·jec·tion·a·ble /əbˈdʒekʃənəbəl/ *adj formal* unpleasant and likely to offend people SYN **offensive**: *objectionable odours | This programme contains scenes some viewers may **find objectionable**.* —**objectionably** *adv*

ob·jec·tive¹ /əbˈdʒektɪv/ ●●○ S3 W3 AWL *n* [C]
1 something that you are trying hard to achieve, especially in business or politics SYN **goal**: *He vowed to **achieve** certain **objectives** before the end of his presidency. | the best way to **accomplish** your **objectives** | The degree program **has** two main **objectives**. | Managers should **set** specific performance **objectives** for their teams. | The **main objective** was to improve children's knowledge of geography. | A **clear objective** was set and adhered to. | One of your first **business objectives** should be to get your own office.* THESAURUS AIM, PURPOSE
2 a place that you are trying to reach, especially in a military attack: *The 4th Division's objective was a town 20 miles to the east.*

objective² ●○○ AWL *adj*
1 based on facts, or making a decision that is based on facts rather than on your feelings or beliefs OPP **subjective**: **objective assessment/measurement/description etc** *It's hard to give an objective opinion about your own children. | Scientists need to be objective when doing research.* | **purely/totally/completely objective** *the importance of a completely objective, independent press*
2 *formal* existing outside the mind as something real, not only as an idea: *The world has an objective reality.* —**objectivity** /ˌɒbdʒekˈtɪvəti $ ˌɑːb-/ *n* [U]

ob·jec·tive·ly /əbˈdʒektɪvli/ AWL *adv* if you consider something objectively, you try to think about the facts, and not be influenced by your own feelings or opinions: *Look at your skills objectively when deciding on a career change.*

ob·jec·tor /əbˈdʒektə $ -tər/ *n* [C] someone who states or shows that they oppose something: **[+to]** *objectors to the new motorway* → CONSCIENTIOUS OBJECTOR

ˈobject-ˌoriented *adj* object-oriented computer programming languages are based on objects that are arranged in a HIERARCHY: *object-oriented programming* | *object-oriented languages*

ob·jet d'art /ˌɒbʒeɪ ˈdɑː $ ˌɑːbʒeɪ ˈdɑːr/ *n* (*plural* **objets d'art** *(same pronunciation)*) [C] a small object used for decoration, with some value as art

ob·la·tion /əˈbleɪʃən/ *n* [C,U] *formal* a gift that is offered to God or a god, or the act of offering the gift

ob·li·gat·e /ˈɒblɪgeɪt $ ˈɑːb-/ *v* [T] *especially AmE* **1** to make someone have to do something, because it is the law, their duty, or the right thing to do SYN **oblige**: **be obligated to do sth** *Tenants are obligated to pay their rent on time.* **2 be/feel obligated** to feel that you must do something because it is right or because someone has done something for you SYN **be/feel obliged**: **be/feel obligated to do sth** *Ava felt obligated to help her mother, even if it meant leaving college.* | **be/feel obligated to sb** *Watson felt obligated to him for the loan.* → OBLIGE

ob·li·ga·tion /ˌɒbləˈgeɪʃən $ ˌɑːb-/ ●●○ W3 *n* [C,U] a moral or legal duty to do something: **[+to]** *America's obligation to its allies* | *Employers* ***have an obligation*** *to treat all employees equally.* | *Parents* ***are under a*** *legal* ***obligation to*** *educate their children.* | *You* ***are under no obligation to*** *buy any more books.* | *Greater resources are needed to* ***meet*** *these* ***obligations***. | *the rights and* ***obligations imposed on*** *them by treaties* | *The government must pay for health care for war veterans – it is an* ***obligation*** *we* ***owe*** *to them.* | *a* ***moral obligation*** *to help the poor* | *He stayed with the team out of a* ***sense of obligation***.

ob·lig·a·to·ry /əˈblɪgətəri $ -tɔːri/ ●○○ *adj*
1 *formal* something that is obligatory must be done because of a law, rule etc SYN **compulsory**, **mandatory**: **it is obligatory for sb (to do sth)** *It is obligatory for companies to provide details of their industrial processes.* THESAURUS NECESSARY
2 [only before noun] used humorously to describe something that is always done or included in a particular situation: *She offered him the obligatory cup of tea.*

Frequencies of **be obliged to**, **must**, and **have to/have got to** in spoken and written English.

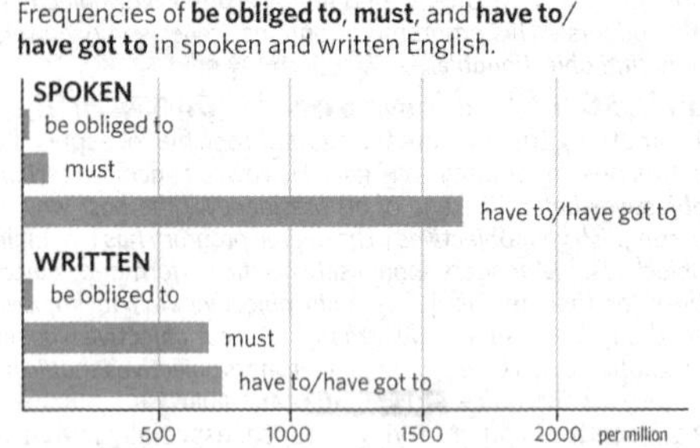

This graph shows that the expressions **have to** and **have got to** are much more common in spoken English than **must** or **be obliged to**. **Have got to** is only used in British English. **Must** is more common in written English. **Be obliged to** is much less common than the others and is only used to say that someone must do something because of a rule or law, or because the situation forces them to do it.

o·blige /əˈblaɪdʒ/ ●○○ *v formal*
1 [T] if you are obliged to do something, you have to do it because the situation, the law, a duty etc makes it necessary: **oblige sb to do sth** *The minister was obliged to report at least once every six months.* | *Circumstances had obliged him to sell the business.* | **feel obliged to do sth** (=feel that you have a duty to do something) *Many parents feel obliged to pay for at least part of the wedding.* ⚠ Do not use **oblige** when you are talking about a person making someone do something they do not want to do. Use **force** or **make**: *They made me (NOT obliged me to) stay behind after school.*

REGISTER
In everyday English, people usually say that you **have to do sth** rather than **are obliged to do sth**: *He* ***had to*** *sell the business.*

2 [I,T] to do something that someone has asked you to do: *It's always a good idea to oblige important clients.* | **happy/glad/ready etc to oblige** *If you need a ride home, I'd be happy to oblige.*
3 I'd be obliged if *spoken formal* used to make a polite request: *I'd be obliged if you'd treat this matter as strictly confidential.*
4 (I'm) much obliged (to you) *spoken old-fashioned* used to thank someone very politely

o·blig·ing /əˈblaɪdʒɪŋ/ *adj* willing and eager to help: *The shop assistant was very obliging.* —**obligingly** *adv*

o·blique[1] /əˈbliːk/ *adj* **1** not expressed in a direct way SYN **indirect**: *an* ***oblique reference*** *to his drinking problem* **2** not looking, pointing etc directly at something: *an oblique glance* **3 oblique line/stroke etc** a sloping line etc **4 oblique angle** *technical* an angle that is not 90 degrees —**obliquely** *adv*

oblique[2] *n* [C] *BrE* a mark (/) used for writing FRACTIONS or for separating numbers, letters, words etc SYN **slash**

o·blit·er·ate /əˈblɪtəreɪt/ *v* [T] **1** to destroy something completely so that nothing remains: *Hiroshima was nearly obliterated by the atomic bomb.* THESAURUS DESTROY
2 to remove a thought, feeling, or memory from someone's mind: *Nothing could obliterate the memory of those tragic events.* **3** to cover something completely so that it cannot be seen: *Then the fog came down, obliterating everything.* —**obliteration** /əˌblɪtəˈreɪʃən/ *n* [U]

o·bliv·i·on /əˈblɪviən/ *n* [U] **1** when something is completely forgotten or no longer important: **sink/slip/pass etc into oblivion** *Wind power presents too many advantages to be allowed to sink into oblivion.* | *The loser's name has been* ***consigned to oblivion*** (=completely forgotten). **2** the state of being unconscious or of not noticing what is happening: *the oblivion of sleep* | *He had drunk himself into oblivion.*

o·bliv·i·ous /əˈblɪviəs/ *adj* [not before noun] not knowing about or not noticing something that is happening around you SYN **unaware**: **[+of/to]** *He seemed oblivious to the fact that he had hurt her.* | **seemingly/apparently oblivious** *Congress was seemingly oblivious to these events.* —**obliviousness** *n* [U]

ob·long /ˈɒblɒŋ $ ˈɑːblɒːŋ/ *adj* **1** *BrE* an oblong shape has four straight sides at 90 degrees to each other, two of which are longer than the other two SYN **rectangular**: *an oblong table* **2** *AmE* an oblong shape is much longer than it is wide: *an oblong leaf* —**oblong** *n* [C]

ob·lo·quy /ˈɒbləkwi $ ˈɑːb-/ *n* [U] *formal* **1** very strong offensive criticism **2** loss of respect and honour

ob·nox·ious /əbˈnɒkʃəs $ -ˈnɑːk-/ *adj* very offensive, unpleasant, or rude: *She's really obnoxious.* | *an obnoxious idea* | *obnoxious odours* —**obnoxiously** *adv* —**obnoxiousness** *n* [U]

o·boe /ˈəʊbəʊ $ ˈoʊboʊ/ *n* [C] a wooden musical instrument like a narrow tube, which you play by blowing air through a REED → see picture at WOODWIND —**oboist** *n* [C]

ob·scene /əbˈsiːn/ ●○○ *adj*
1 relating to sex in a way that is shocking and offensive → **rude**: *Bradford made an* ***obscene gesture***. | ***obscene phone calls*** (=calls from an unknown person saying obscene things) | *obscene photographs*
2 extremely unfair, immoral, or unpleasant, especially in a way that makes you angry: *Some players earn obscene amounts of money.* | *an obscene act of cruelty* —**obscenely** *adv*

ob·scen·i·ty /əbˈsenəti/ *n* (*plural* **obscenities**) **1** [U] sexually offensive language or behaviour, especially in a book, play, film etc: *laws against obscenity* **2** [C usually plural] a sexually offensive word or action → **swear**: *drunken youths screaming obscenities*

ob·scu·ran·tis·m /ˌɒbskjəˈræntɪzəm $ ˌɑːb-/ *n* [U] *formal* the practice of deliberately stopping ideas and facts from being known —**obscurantist** *adj*

ob·scure[1] /əbˈskjʊə $ -ˈskjʊr/ ●○○ *adj*
1 not well known and usually not very important: *an obscure poet* | *The details of his life* ***remain obscure***.
2 difficult to understand: *obscure legal phrases* | ***For some obscure reason***, *the group is very popular.* —**obscurely** *adv*

obscure² ●○○ *v* [T]
1 to make something difficult to know or understand: *Recent successes have* ***obscured the fact*** *that the company is still in trouble.*
2 to prevent something from being seen or heard clearly: *The view was obscured by mist.* THESAURUS ▸ HIDE

ob·scu·ri·ty /əbˈskjʊərəti $ -ˈskjʊr-/ *n* (*plural* **obscurities**)
1 [U] the state of not being known or remembered: **fade/slide/sink etc into obscurity** *The group produced two albums before disappearing into obscurity.* | **live/work/remain etc in obscurity** *O'Brien died in obscurity.* | **from obscurity to sth** *She rose from obscurity to stardom.* **2** [C,U] something that is difficult to understand, or the quality of being difficult to understand: *obscurities in the text*

ob·se·quies /ˈɒbsəkwiz $ ˈɑːb-/ *n* [plural] *formal* a funeral ceremony

ob·se·qui·ous /əbˈsiːkwiəs/ *adj* very eager to please or agree with people who are powerful – used to show disapproval SYN **servile**: *an obsequious smile* —**obsequiously** *adv* —**obsequiousness** *n* [U]

ob·ser·va·ble /əbˈzɜːvəbəl $ -ɜːr-/ *adj* something that is observable can be seen or noticed → **noticeable**: *an observable change in behaviour* —**observably** *adv*

ob·ser·vance /əbˈzɜːvəns $ -ɜːr-/ *n* **1** [U] when someone obeys a law or does something because it is part of a religion, custom, or ceremony: **[+of]** *the observance of a peace agreement* | *the strict observance of Islam* | *the Memorial Day observance* **2** [C] something you do as part of a ceremony, especially a religious ceremony: *religious observances*

ob·ser·vant /əbˈzɜːvənt $ -ɜːr-/ *adj* **1** good or quick at noticing things: *a quiet and observant person* | *Supervisors are trained to be observant.* | *the writer's* ***observant eye*** *for detail* **2** obeying laws, religious rules etc: *observant Jews*

ob·ser·va·tion /ˌɒbzəˈveɪʃən $ ˌɑːbzər-/ ●●○ W3 *n*
1 [C,U] the process of watching something or someone carefully for a period of time: **[+of]** *Bloomfield's approach to linguistics was based on observation of the language.* | *He spent two nights* ***under close observation*** *in hospital.* | *His orders were to* ***keep*** *the men* ***under observation****.* | *Art classes help develop children's* ***powers of observation****.* | ***Careful observation*** *suggests that this is not the case.* | ***Detailed observations*** *were carried out on the behaviour of the students.* | *From their* ***direct observations****, children absorb a model of marriage.*
2 [C] something that you notice when watching something or someone: *Some interesting observations emerged from this research.*
3 [C] a spoken or written remark about something you have noticed: **[+on]** *Darwin's observations on the habits of certain birds* | **[+about]** *Paz* ***makes*** *some* ***observations*** *about the role of the critic.* THESAURUS ▸ COMMENT
4 [U] the act of obeying a law etc SYN **observance** —**observational** *adj*

ˌobserˈvation ˌpost *n* [C] a position from which an enemy can be watched

ˌobserˈvation ˌtower *n* [C] a tall structure built so that you can see a long way, used to watch prisoners, look for forest fires etc

ob·ser·va·to·ry /əbˈzɜːvətəri $ əbˈzɜːrvətɔːri/ *n* (*plural* **observatories**) [C] a special building from which scientists watch the moon, stars, weather etc

ob·serve /əbˈzɜːv $ -ɜːrv/ ●●○ W2 *v*
1 [T not in progressive] *formal* to see and notice something → **observation**: *Scientists have observed a drop in ozone levels over the Antarctic.* | **observe that** *It was observed that 40 percent of patients had high blood pressure.* | **observe sb doing sth** *Officers observed him driving at 90 miles per hour.* | *Predators have been observed to avoid attacking brightly coloured species.* THESAURUS ▸ NOTICE, SEE

> **REGISTER**
> In everyday English, people say that someone **sees**, **notices**, or **spots** something or someone: *She was* ***spotted*** *going into a restaurant with a well-known footballer.*

2 [I,T] to watch something or someone carefully: *The police have been observing his movements.* | *One student performs the experiment, while his partner observes.* | **observe what/how/where** *Observe how the people in the group interact.* THESAURUS ▸ WATCH
3 [T] *formal* to say or write what you have noticed about a situation: *'Sid looks ill,' Doherty observed.* | **observe that** *Keynes observed that humans fall into two classes.*
4 [T] to do what you are supposed to do according to a law or agreement SYN **obey**, **adhere to**: *So far the ceasefire has been observed by both sides.*
5 [T] to do things and obey laws that are part of a religion or custom SYN **follow**

O

ob·serv·er /əbˈzɜːvə $ -ɜːrvər/ ●●○ *n* [C]
1 someone who regularly watches or pays attention to particular things, events, situations etc: **[+of]** *an observer of nature* | *political observers* | *Observers are predicting a fall in interest rates.*
2 someone who attends meetings, classes, events etc to check what is happening: *The UN sent observers to the peace talks.* | *Independent observers monitored the elections.*
3 someone who sees or looks at something: *reports from observers at sea and on dry land* | **casual observer** (=someone looking at something but not very carefully) *A casual observer would have guessed his age at 70.*

ob·sess /əbˈses/ ●○○ *v*
1 [T] if something or someone obsesses you, you think or worry about them all the time and you cannot think about anything else – used to show disapproval: **be obsessed by/with sth/sb** *A lot of young girls are obsessed by their weight.* | *Jody's been obsessed with some lifeguard for months.* GRAMMAR **Obsess** is usually passive in this meaning.
2 be obsessing about/over sth/sb *informal* to think about something or someone much more than is necessary or sensible: *Stop obsessing about your hair. It's fine.*

ob·ses·sion /əbˈseʃən/ ●○○ *n* [C,U] an extreme unhealthy interest in something or worry about something, which stops you from thinking about anything else: *Gambling* ***became an obsession****, and he eventually lost everything.* | **[+with]** *an* ***unhealthy obsession*** *with being thin* | *The current obsession with exam results is actually harming children's education.* | *The game pachinko became a* ***national obsession****.* | *He has an enthusiasm for art,* ***to the point of obsession*** *in my opinion.* | *She looked after him with a devotion* ***bordering on obsession****.* —**obsessional** *adj*

ob·ses·sive¹ /əbˈsesɪv/ *adj* thinking or worrying about something all the time, so that you do not think about other things enough – used to show disapproval: *an obsessive concern with cleanliness and order* | **obsessive about (doing) sth** *I try to stay fit, but I'm not obsessive about it.* —**obsessively** *adv*

obsessive² *n* [C] *BrE technical* someone whose behaviour is obsessive

obˌsessive-comˈpulsive *adj technical* someone who is obsessive-compulsive tends to repeat particular actions in a way that is not necessary, because they have strong anxious feelings: *obsessive-compulsive behaviour*

ob·sid·i·an /əbˈsɪdiən/ *n* [U] a type of rock that looks like black glass

ob·so·les·cence /ˌɒbsəˈlesəns $ ˌɑːb-/ *n* [U]
1 when something becomes old-fashioned and no longer useful, because something newer and better has been invented **2 planned/built-in obsolescence** when a product is designed so that it will soon become unfashionable or impossible to use and will need replacing: *the planned obsolescence of some software*

ob·so·les·cent /ˌɒbsəˈlesənt◂ $ ˌɑːb-/ *adj formal* becoming obsolete

ob·so·lete /ˈɒbsəliːt $ ˌɑːbsəˈliːt/ ●●○ *adj* no longer useful, because something newer and better has been invented → **out-of-date**: *obsolete weapons* | *computer hardware that quickly* ***became obsolete*** | *Will computers* ***render*** *(=make) books* ***obsolete****?* THESAURUS ▸ OLD-FASHIONED

ob·sta·cle /ˈɒbstəkəl $ ˈɑːb-/ ●●○ *n* [C]
1 something that makes it difficult to achieve something:

[+to] *Fear of change is an obstacle to progress.* | *The tax* ***puts obstacles in the way of*** *companies trying to develop trade overseas.* | *Women still have to* ***overcome*** *many* ***obstacles*** *to gain equality.* | *We want to* ***remove*** *all* ***obstacles*** *to travel between the two countries.* | *the single* ***biggest obstacle*** *to a Conservative victory in the next election* | *There are* ***formidable obstacles*** *on the road to peace.*
2 an object which blocks your way, so that you must try to go around it

O

ˈobstacle course *n* [C] **1** a line of objects which people have to jump over, climb through etc in a race **2** a series of difficulties which must be dealt with to achieve a particular aim **3** an area of land with special equipment that soldiers must run through, climb over etc, as part of their training SYN **assault course** *BrE*

ˈobstacle race *n* [C] *BrE* a type of race in which runners have to jump over or climb through various objects

ob·ste·tri·cian /ˌɒbstəˈtrɪʃən $ ˌɑːb-/ *n* [C] a doctor who has special training in obstetrics

ob·stet·rics /əbˈstetrɪks/ *n* [U] the part of medical science that deals with the birth of children —**obstetric** *adj*

ob·sti·nate /ˈɒbstənət $ ˈɑːb-/ *adj* **1** determined not to change your ideas, behaviour, opinions etc, even when other people think you are being unreasonable SYN **stubborn**: *He was the most obstinate man I've ever met.* | *Don't be so obstinate!* | *an* ***obstinate refusal*** *to obey*
2 [only before noun] *BrE* difficult to deal with or get rid of: *obstinate stains* | *a complex and obstinate issue* —**obstinately** *adv* —**obstinacy** *n* [U]

ob·strep·e·rous /əbˈstrepərəs/ *adj formal* noisy and refusing to do what someone asks → **awkward** —**obstreperously** *adv*

ob·struct /əbˈstrʌkt/ *v* [T] **1** to block a road, passage etc SYN **block**: *A small aircraft was obstructing the runway.* | *The column obstructed our view of the stage.* **2** to prevent someone from doing something or something from happening, by making it difficult SYN **block**: *The group is trying to obstruct the peace process.* | *He was fined for obstructing the work of the police.*

ob·struc·tion /əbˈstrʌkʃən/ ●○○ *n*
1 [C,U] when something blocks a road, passage, tube etc, or the thing that blocks it SYN **blockage**: *an operation to remove an obstruction from her throat* | *Police can remove a vehicle that is* ***causing an obstruction.*** | **[+of]** *an unlawful obstruction of the highway*
2 [U] when someone or something prevents or delays a legal or political process: **[+of]** *the obstruction of vital legislation* | *He was found guilty of* ***obstruction of justice.***
3 [U] an offence in football, HOCKEY etc in which a player gets between an opponent and the ball

ob·struc·tion·is·m /əbˈstrʌkʃənɪzəm/ *n* [U] *formal* when someone tries to prevent or delay a legal or political process —**obstructionist** *n* [C]

ob·struc·tive /əbˈstrʌktɪv/ *adj* **1** trying to prevent someone from doing something, by deliberately making it difficult for them: *an obstructive official* | *obstructive tactics*
2 *medical* relating to a blocked tube, passage etc in the body: *obstructive symptoms*

ob·tain /əbˈteɪn/ ●●● S3 W2 AWL *v formal*
1 [T] to get something that you want, especially through your own effort, skill, or work SYN **get**: **obtain sth from sb/sth** *Further information can be obtained from head office.* | *You will need to obtain permission from the principal.* | **obtain sth through sth** *the results obtained through these surveys*
THESAURUS ▸ GET

> **REGISTER**
> In everyday English, people say that they **get** a result, a ticket, some information etc rather than **obtain** it: *You have to* ***get*** *permission from your parents.*

2 [not in progressive] if a situation, system, or rule obtains, it continues to exist: *These conditions no longer obtain.*

ob·tain·a·ble /əbˈteɪnəbəl/ AWL *adj formal* able to be obtained SYN **available**: *The form is obtainable at your local post office.*

ob·trude /əbˈtruːd/ *v* [I,T] *formal* if something obtrudes, or you obtrude something, it becomes noticeable where it is not wanted → INTRUDE

ob·tru·sive /əbˈtruːsɪv/ *adj* noticeable in an unpleasant or annoying way OPP **unobtrusive**: *obtrusive TV antennas* | *The waiters were friendly and not obtrusive.*

ob·tuse /əbˈtjuːs $ -ˈtuːs/ *adj formal* slow to understand things, in a way that is annoying: *'But why?' said Charles, being deliberately obtuse.* —**obtuseness** *n* [U]

obˌtuse ˈangle *n* [C] *technical* an angle between 90 and 180 degrees → **acute angle**

ob·verse /ˈɒbvɜːs $ ˈɑːbvɜːrs/ *n* [singular] **1** *formal* the opposite of a particular situation or feeling SYN **opposite**: **[+of]** *The obverse of victory is defeat.* **2 the obverse** *technical* the front side of a coin or MEDAL OPP **reverse**

ob·vi·ate /ˈɒbvieɪt $ ˈɑːb-/ *v* [T] *formal* to prevent or avoid a problem or the need to do something SYN **eliminate**: *The new treatment* ***obviates the need*** *for surgery.*

ob·vi·ous /ˈɒbviəs $ ˈɑːb-/ ●●● S2 W2 AWL *adj*
1 easy to notice or understand: *The obvious way of reducing pollution is to use cars less.* | **it is obvious (that)** *It was obvious that Gina was lying.* | **[+to]** *It might be obvious to you, but it isn't to me.*
2 behaving in a way that shows you want something very badly, when other people think this behaviour is not suitable: *I know you really like him, but you don't have to be so obvious about it.* → see Thesaurus box on *p. 1257*
3 the/an obvious choice the person or thing that you would expect everyone to choose: *Teaching is an obvious choice of career if you like working with children.*
4 the obvious thing (to do) what clearly seems the best thing to do: *The obvious thing is to speak to her before you make a decision.*
5 state the obvious to say something that is already obvious so it is not necessary to say it: *It is stating the obvious, but regular measurement of blood pressure is essential in older people.* —**obviousness** *n* [U]

> **COLLOCATIONS**
>
> **VERBS**
> **seem/appear obvious** *It seems obvious to me that he is guilty.*
> **sound obvious** *This may sound obvious, but don't forget to put your name on your paper.*
> **become obvious** *It soon became obvious that the boy was not really interested.*
>
> **NOUNS**
> **an obvious reason** *The plan, for obvious reasons, was being kept secret.*
> **an obvious example** *This case is an obvious example of what can go wrong.*
> **an obvious question** *The obvious question is: why?*
> **the obvious answer**
>
> **ADVERBS**
> **glaringly/blindingly obvious** (=extremely obvious) *The cause of her problems is glaringly obvious.*
> **transparently/patently/blatantly obvious** (=clearly obvious) *His interest in her was blatantly obvious.*
> **painfully obvious** (=very obvious, and embarrassing or upsetting) *It became painfully obvious that she and Edward had nothing in common.*
> **immediately obvious** *The cause of the pain was not immediately obvious.*
> **fairly/quite obvious** (*also* **pretty obvious** *spoken*)

ob·vi·ous·ly /ˈɒbviəsli $ ˈɑːb-/ ●●● S1 W2 AWL *adv* used to mean that a fact can easily be noticed or understood SYN **clearly**: *We're obviously going to need more help.* | *Your research has obviously been very thorough.* | *Obviously, this is going to take some time.* | *Cost is obviously important.* | *She frowned and was obviously puzzled.*

oc·a·ri·na /ˌɒkəˈriːnə $ ˌɑːk-/ *n* [C] a WIND INSTRUMENT that has an egg-shaped body, holes which you block with your fingers, and a tube which you blow down

oc·ca·sion[1] /əˈkeɪʒən/ ●●● S1 W2 *n*
1 TIME a) [C] a time when something happens: **on ... occasions** *I've seen Jana with them on several occasions. | On this occasion we were sitting in a park in Madrid. | She had met Zahid on two separate occasions.* **b)** [singular] a suitable or favourable time: **[+for]** *This was the occasion for expressions of friendship by the two presidents.* ⚠ Do not use **occasion** to mean 'a time when it is possible for you to do what you want to do'. Use **opportunity** or **chance**: *Do not waste this opportunity (NOT this occasion).* **THESAURUS** TIME
2 SPECIAL EVENT [C] an important social event or ceremony: *I'm saving this bottle of champagne for a special occasion.* **THESAURUS** EVENT
3 CAUSE/REASON [U] *formal* a cause or reason: *His remark* ***was the occasion of*** *a bitter quarrel. | I* ***had occasion to*** *call on him last year.*
4 if (the) occasion arises *formal* if a particular action ever becomes necessary: *If ever the occasion arises when I want advice, you're the first person I'll come to.*
5 on occasion sometimes but not often: *On occasion, prisoners were allowed visits from their families.*
6 on the occasion of sth *formal* at the time of an important event: *on the occasion of his second wedding* → **rise to the occasion** at RISE[1](9)

COLLOCATIONS - MEANING 2

ADJECTIVES
a special occasion *She used her best china on special occasions.*
a big/great/splendid occasion *The big occasion for country people was the Agricultural Fair.*
a formal occasion *He wore the suit on formal occasions.*
a social occasion *I prefer not to discuss business at social occasions.*
a ceremonial occasion (=a very formal official occasion) | **a happy/joyful occasion** | **a sad/solemn occasion** | **a festive occasion** (=when you celebrate something) | **a historic occasion** (=important as part of history)

VERBS
celebrate an occasion *To celebrate the occasion, a small party was held at his home.*
mark an occasion (=do something special to celebrate an event) *The bells were rung to mark the occasion.*

PHRASES
a sense of occasion (=a feeling that an event is very special or important) *The music gave the event a real sense of occasion.*
enter into the spirit of the occasion (=join in a social occasion in an eager way)

occasion[2] *v* [T] *formal* to cause something: *She had a long career break occasioned by her husband's job being moved to Paris.* | **occasion sb sth** *Your behaviour has occasioned us a great deal of anxiety.*

oc·ca·sion·al /əˈkeɪʒənəl/ ●●○ S3 W3 *adj* [only before noun] happening sometimes but not often or regularly: *He made occasional visits to London. | They had an occasional coffee together after shopping. | He only has occasional use of a car. | We should have enough money left for* ***the occasional*** *trip.*

oc·ca·sion·al·ly /əˈkeɪʒənəli/ ●●● S2 W3 *adv* sometimes, but not regularly and not often: *Occasionally Alice would look up from her books. | We only see each other* ***very occasionally*** (=rarely). **THESAURUS** SOMETIMES

REGISTER
In everyday English, people often say **once in a while** rather than **occasionally**: *We still see her* ***once in a while.***

ocˈcasional ˌtable *n* [C] a small light table that can be easily moved

Oc·ci·dent /ˈɒksɪdənt $ ˈɑːksədənt, -dent/ *n* **the Occident** *literary* the western part of the world, especially Europe and the Americas → **Orient**

oc·ci·den·tal /ˌɒksəˈdentəl◂ $ ˌɑːk-/ *n* [C] *old-fashioned* someone from the western part of the world —**occidental** *adj*

oc·cult[1] /ˈɒkʌlt, əˈkʌlt $ əˈkʌlt, ˈɑːkʌlt/ *n* **the occult** mysterious practices and powers involving magic and SPIRITS: *He was a strange man who dabbled in the occult.* —**occultist** *n* [C]

occult[2] *adj* [only before noun] magical and mysterious: *occult practices | the occult powers*

oc·cu·pan·cy /ˈɒkjəpənsi $ ˈɑːk-/ AWL *n* [U] *formal*
1 the number of people who stay, work, or live in a room or building at the same time: **single/multiple occupancy** *single occupancy room rates | Hotels in Tokyo enjoy over 90% occupancy.* **2** someone's use of a building, hotel, or other space, for living or working in, or the period during which they live or work there: *The day for changing from one occupancy to the next was on a Saturday.*

oc·cu·pant /ˈɒkjəpənt $ ˈɑːk-/ ●○○ AWL *n* [C]
1 someone who lives in a house, room etc → **resident**: *The furniture had been left by the previous occupants.* | **[+of]** *Police are still trying to trace the occupants of the house which was destroyed by fire.*
2 someone who is in a room, vehicle etc at a particular time: *Neither of the car's two occupants was injured.*

oc·cu·pa·tion /ˌɒkjəˈpeɪʃən $ ˌɑːk-/ ●●● S3 W3 AWL *n*
1 [C] a job or profession: *Please state your name, address and occupation. | professional and managerial occupations | manual occupations* **THESAURUS** JOB
2 [U] when a large group of people enter a place and take control of it, especially by military force: **[+of]** *the German occupation of France* | **under occupation** *The area is under occupation* (=controlled by a foreign army).
3 [C] a way of spending your time SYN **pastime**: *One of my childhood occupations was collecting stamps.*
4 [U] when someone lives or stays in a building or place:

THESAURUS: obvious

obvious something that is obvious is very easy to notice or understand - used especially when you are surprised that other people cannot notice it: *There is an obvious connection between the two murders. | It was obvious that something was wrong.*
clear easy to notice that something is true, so that you feel sure about it and have no doubts: *It was clear to me that my father was dying. | There are clear signs of an economic recovery.*
noticeable very easy to notice, especially because you can see, hear, smell, or feel something: *Steroid drugs cause a noticeable change in someone's behaviour. | Road noise tends to be more noticeable in certain weather conditions.*
conspicuous very easy to notice, because of being different from things around them: *a conspicuous white spot on the bird's wings | She tried to make herself look less conspicuous.*
unmistakable extremely obvious, so that you cannot possibly confuse something with something else: *the unmistakable sound of gunfire | The flower's scent is unmistakable.*
self-evident *formal* facts, ideas etc that are self-evident are obvious and true, although some people may not accept them or know about them: *The facts in this case are self-evident and cannot be denied. | We hold these truths to be self-evident* (=we believe that they are obvious and true - from the American Declaration of Independence).
blatant use this about something that someone does which is clearly bad, but which they do not seem to be ashamed of: *a blatant lie | The bill is a blatant attempt to limit our right to free speech.*
can tell to know that something must be true because you can see signs that show this: *Even though it was dark, she could tell it was him. | How can you tell if you've broken your arm?*

When the first scientists came to the region they found little evidence of human occupation.

oc·cu·pa·tion·al /ˌɒkjəˈpeɪʃənəl◂ $ ˌɑːk-/ ●○○ AWL *adj* [only before noun] relating to or caused by your job: *occupational pension schemes | an occupational health centre | occupational disease | Getting injured is* ***an occupational hazard*** (=a risk that always exists in a particular job or activity) *of the sport.* —**occupationally** *adv*

ˌoccupational ˈtherapist *n* [C] someone whose job is to help people get better after an illness by giving them activities to do

O

ˌoccupational ˈtherapy *n* [U] the job of an occupational therapist

oc·cu·pied /ˈɒkjəpaɪd $ ˈɑːk-/ *adj* **1** [not before noun] busy doing something: **[+with]** *His time was occupied with the children. | She's* ***fully occupied*** *with work. | The museum has enough exhibits to* ***keep*** *anyone* ***occupied*** *for an hour or two. | I* ***kept myself occupied*** *by watching television.* **2** [not before noun] a bed, chair, room etc that is occupied is being used: *Sorry, this seat is occupied.* **3** an occupied place is controlled by an army from another country: *occupied territories*

oc·cu·pi·er /ˈɒkjəpaɪə $ ˈɑːkjəpaɪər/ AWL *n* [C] *especially BrE* **1** someone who lives in or uses a particular house, piece of land etc → **resident**: *A large proportion of occupiers now own their homes.* **2** a member of an army that has occupied a city or country by force → **owner-occupier** at OWNER-OCCUPIED

oc·cu·py /ˈɒkjəpaɪ $ ˈɑːk-/ ●●○ W2 AWL *v* (**occupied**, **occupying**, **occupies**) [T]

1 STAY IN A PLACE to live or stay in a place: *He occupies the house without paying any rent. | The building was purchased and occupied by its new owners last year.*

2 FILL TIME if something occupies you or your time, you are busy doing it: *Football occupies most of my leisure time. |* **occupy sb with (doing) sth** *Only six percent of police time is occupied with criminal incidents.*

3 FILL SPACE to fill a particular amount of space SYN **take up**: *Family photos occupied almost the entire wall.*

> **REGISTER**
> In everyday English, people usually say that something **takes up** time or space rather than **occupies** it: *Work* ***takes up*** *most of her time. | That bed* ***takes up*** *almost the whole room.*

4 CONTROL BY FORCE to enter a place in a large group and keep control of it, especially by military force → **invade**: *an occupying army | Students occupied Sofia University on Monday.*

5 occupy sb's mind/thoughts/attention if something occupies your mind etc, you think about that thing more than anything else → **preoccupy**: *Work will occupy your mind and help you forget about him.*

6 USE to use something such as a room, seat, or bed: *Many patients who are occupying hospital beds could be transferred to other places.*

7 OFFICIAL POSITION to have an official position or job SYN **hold**: *Before becoming prime minister, he had already occupied several cabinet posts.* → OCCUPIED

oc·cur /əˈkɜː $ əˈkɜːr/ ●●● S3 W1 AWL *v* (**occurred**, **occurring**) [I] *formal*

1 to happen: *A third of accidental deaths occur in the home. | The explosion occurred at 5.30 a.m.* THESAURUS▸ HAPPEN

> **REGISTER**
> In everyday English, people usually say **happen** rather than **occur**: *The accident* ***happened*** *while she was at school.*

2 [always + adv/prep] to happen or exist in a particular place or situation: **[+in/among etc]** *Whooping cough occurs mainly in young children. | The highest rates of unemployment occur in the inner urban areas.*

occur to sb *phr v* if an idea or a thought occurs to you, it suddenly comes into your mind: **it occurs to sb to do sth** *I suppose it didn't occur to you to phone the police? | It never seems to occur to my children to contact me. |* **it occurs to sb (that)** *It had never occurred to him that he might be falling in love with her.*

oc·cur·rence /əˈkʌrəns $ əˈkɜː- / ●○○ AWL *n*

1 [C] something that happens → **occur**: **frequent/rare/common occurrence** *Laughter was a rare occurrence in his classroom. | Flooding in the area is a common occurrence.* THESAURUS▸ EVENT

2 [singular] the fact of something happening: **[+of]** *The frequent occurrence of earthquakes in the area means that the buildings must be specifically designed to withstand the force.*

OCD /ˌəʊ siː ˈdiː $ ˌoʊ-/ *n* [U] *medical* (***obsessive-compulsive disorder***) a form of mental illness in which a person does the same thing again and again and cannot stop doing it, for example washing their hands many times a day

o·cean /ˈəʊʃən $ ˈoʊ-/ ●●● S3 W2 *n*

1 the ocean *especially AmE* the great mass of salt water that covers most of the Earth's surface SYN **the sea**: *She stood on the beach, gazing at the ocean. | I like to swim in the ocean when it's warm enough.*

2 [C] one of the very large areas of sea on the Earth's surface: *the Pacific Ocean*

3 oceans of sth *informal* a lot of something, especially a liquid: *oceans of champagne* → **a drop in the ocean** at DROP²(8)

> **GRAMMAR: Patterns with ocean**
>
> **in the ocean**
> • You use **in the ocean** to talk about things that happen in the water: *We swam in the ocean. | There are thousands of species of fish in the ocean.*
>
> **on the ocean**
> • You use **on the ocean** to talk about things that happen on the surface of the water: *He dreamed of buying a yacht and sailing on the ocean.*
>
> **by the ocean**
> • You use **by the ocean** to talk about the area near the ocean: *I'd love to live by the ocean.*
>
> GRAMMAR GUIDE▸ NOUNS

o·cean·front /ˈəʊʃənˌfrʌnt $ ˈoʊ-/ *adj* [only before noun] *AmE* on the land along the edge of an ocean SYN **seafront** *BrE*: *oceanfront houses*

o·cean·go·ing /ˈəʊʃənˌgəʊɪŋ $ ˈoʊʃənˌgoʊ-/ *adj* [only before noun] an oceangoing ship is designed to sail across the sea rather than a river or lake SYN **seagoing**: *an oceangoing tanker*

o·ce·an·ic /ˌəʊʃiˈænɪk◂ $ ˌoʊ-/ *adj* [usually before noun] relating to the ocean: *an oceanic island | oceanic waters*

o·cean·og·ra·phy /ˌəʊʃənˈɒgrəfi $ ˌoʊʃənˈɑːg-/ *n* [U] the scientific study of the ocean —**oceanographer** *n* [C]

oc·e·lot /ˈɒsəlɒt $ ˈɑːsəlɑːt, ˈoʊ-/ *n* [C] a large American wild cat that has a pattern of spots on its back

och /ɒx $ ɒːx/ *interjection* used in Scotland and parts of Ireland to express surprise or to emphasize a remark

o·chre *BrE*, **ocher** *AmE* /ˈəʊkə $ ˈoʊkər/ *n* [U] **1** a type of reddish-yellow earth used in paints **2** the reddish-yellow colour of ochre —**ochre** *adj*

ock·er /ˈɒkə $ ˈɑːkər/ *n* [C] an Australian man – used in Australia and New Zealand: *G'day Ocker!*

o'clock /əˈklɒk $ əˈklɑːk/ ●●● S1 W3 *adv* **one o'clock/two o'clock etc** one of the times when the clock shows the exact hour as a number from 1 to 12: *It's already 9 o'clock. | The meeting is at 10 o'clock.* ⚠ Do not use **o'clock** when mentioning minutes or parts of an hour: *ten past nine (NOT ten past nine o'clock) | half past one (NOT half past one o'clock).* Do not use **o'clock** when writing the time in the form 1.00, 2.00 etc.

OCR /ˌəʊ siː ˈɑː $ ˌoʊ siː ˈɑːr/ *n* [U] *technical* (***optical character recognition***) computer software that recognizes numbers and letters of the alphabet which are written on paper, so that information from paper documents can be scanned (SCAN) into a computer

-ocracy /ɒkrəsi $ ɑːk-/ (*also* **-cracy**) *suffix* [in nouns] government by a particular sort of people or according to a particular principle: *democracy* (=government by the people) | *meritocracy* (=government by people with the most ability)

-ocrat /əkræt/ (*also* **-crat**) *suffix* [in nouns] **1** someone who believes in a particular principle of government: *a democrat* (=someone who believes in government by the people) **2** a member of a powerful or governing social class or group: *a technocrat* (=a scientist who controls an organization or country) —**-ocratic** /əkrætɪk/ *suffix* —**-ocratically** /əkrætɪkli/ *suffix*

Oct. (*also* **Oct** *BrE*) the written abbreviation of ***October***

oc·ta·gon /ˈɒktəgən $ ˈɑːktəgɑːn/ *n* [C] a flat shape with eight sides and eight angles → see picture at SHAPE[1] —**octagonal** /ɒkˈtægənəl $ ɑːk-/ *adj*: *an octagonal tower*

oc·tane /ˈɒkteɪn $ ˈɑːk-/ *n* [U] a type of HYDROCARBON that is in FUEL and is used as a measure of its quality: *low octane petrol* | *high octane fuel*

oc·tave /ˈɒktəv, -teɪv $ ˈɑːk-/ *n* [C] **a)** the range of musical notes between the first note of a SCALE and the last one **b)** the first and last notes of a musical SCALE played together

oc·tet /ɒkˈtet $ ɑːk-/ *n* [C] **1** eight singers or musicians performing together **2** a piece of music for an octet

octo-, **oct-** /ɒktəʊ $ ɑːktoʊ/ *prefix* eight, or having eight: *octagon* (=a shape with eight sides) | *octopus* (=a sea creature with eight arms)

Oc·to·ber /ɒkˈtəʊbə $ ɑːkˈtoʊbər/ ●●● S2 W2 *n* [C,U] (*written abbreviation* **Oct.**) the tenth month of the year, between September and November: **next/last October** *We moved in last October.* | **in October** *You're going to be busy in October.* | **on October 6th** *We begin on October 6th.* | **on 6th October** *BrE*: *They were arrested on 6th October.* | **October 6** *AmE*: *The baby was baptized Monday, October 6.*

oc·to·ge·nar·i·an /ˌɒktəʊdʒəˈneəriən, -tə- $ ˌɑːktoʊ-/ *n* [C] someone who is between 80 and 89 years old

oc·to·pus /ˈɒktəpəs $ ˈɑːk-/ *n* (*plural* **octopuses** *or* **octopi** /-paɪ/) [C] a sea creature with eight TENTACLES (=arms)

oc·u·lar /ˈɒkjələ $ ˈɑːkjələr/ *adj medical* relating to your eyes or your ability to see: *ocular muscles*

oc·u·list /ˈɒkjəlɪst $ ˈɑːk-/ *n* [C] *old-fashioned* a doctor who examines and treats people's eyes

OD /ˌəʊ ˈdiː $ ˌoʊ-/ *v* (**OD'd**, **OD'ing**, **OD's**) [I] *informal* **1** (**overdose**) to take too much of a drug so that it is dangerous: **[+on]** *He OD'd on sleeping tablets.* **2** to see, hear, eat etc too much of something: **[+on]** *children who OD on video games* —**OD** *n* [C]

o·da·lisque /ˈəʊdəlɪsk $ ˈoʊ-/ *n* [C] *literary* a beautiful female slave in former times

odd /ɒd $ ɑːd/ ●●● S1 W3 AWL *adj* (*comparative* **odder**, *superlative* **oddest**)

1 STRANGE different from what is normal or expected, especially in a way that you disapprove of or cannot understand: *It was an odd thing to say.* | *an odd way to behave* | *They're an odd couple.* | *There was something odd about him.* | *What she did was unforgivable, but* ***the odd thing was*** *he didn't seem to mind.* | *She was holding an extremely* ***odd-looking*** *weapon.* | **it is/seems odd (that)** *It seemed odd that he wanted a picture of me.* THESAURUS STRANGE

2 the odd occasion/day/moment/drink etc *especially BrE* a few occasions, days etc that happen at various times but not often and not regularly SYN **occasional**: *Lack of sleep doesn't matter on the odd occasion.* | *I take the odd day off work.* | *I like the odd glass of wine with my dinner.* | *Jo smokes the odd cigarette.*

3 VARIOUS [only before noun] not specially chosen or collected: *Any odd scrap of paper will do.*

4 NOT IN A PAIR/SET [only before noun] separated from a pair or set: *an odd shoe* | **odd socks/gloves etc** (=not a matching pair of socks etc) *He was wearing odd socks.*

5 odd number a number that cannot be divided exactly by two, for example 1, 3, 5, 7 etc OPP **even number**

6 20-odd/30-odd etc *spoken* a little more than 20 etc: *I have another 20-odd years to work before I retire.*

7 the odd man/one out *BrE* someone or something that is different from the rest of the group or not included in it: *Which shape is the odd one out?* | *I was always the odd one out at school.* —**oddness** *n* [U] → ODDLY

odd·ball /ˈɒdbɔːl $ ˈɑːdbɒːl/ *n* [C] *informal* someone who behaves in a strange or unusual way SYN **eccentric** —**oddball** *adj*: *a rather oddball sense of humour*

odd·i·ty /ˈɒdəti $ ˈɑː-/ *n* (*plural* **oddities**) **1** [C] a strange or unusual person or thing: *In a class of 120 students there were four women including myself, and I still felt rather an oddity.* **2** [C,U] a strange quality in someone or something: *60s fashions that are remembered for their oddity*

ˌodd-ˈjob man *n* [C] *BrE* a man who does various jobs in people's houses or gardens

ˌodd ˈjobs *n* [plural] small jobs of different types: *I've got a few odd jobs to do this weekend.*

odd·ly /ˈɒdli $ ˈɑːdli/ ●○○ *adv*

1 in a strange or unusual way SYN **strangely**: *She's been behaving oddly this week.*

2 (*also* **oddly enough**) [sentence adverb] used to say that something seems strange or surprising SYN **funnily enough**: *Oddly enough, someone asked me the same question only yesterday.*

odd·ments /ˈɒdmənts $ ˈɑːd-/ *n* [plural] small things of no value, or pieces of a material that were not used when something was made SYN **odds and ends**: *You can make a patchwork quilt from oddments of silk and cotton.*

odds /ɒdz $ ɑːdz/ ●●○ S3 AWL *n* [plural]

1 PROBABILITY **the odds** how likely it is that something will or will not happen: ***The odds are*** (=it is likely) *that he will commit the same crime again.* | **[+of]** *You can narrow the odds of a nasty accident happening in your home by being more safety-conscious.* | **[+against]** *The odds against a plane crash are around a million to one.* | *I'm afraid that* ***the odds are*** *heavily* ***against*** *her winning* (=it is not likely). | ***What are the odds*** (=how likely is it) *that they will mess up?* | *a new company that has* ***beaten the odds*** *and succeeded* (=it was not likely to succeed, but it did)

2 DIFFICULTIES difficulties which make a good result seem very unlikely: *The hospital's director has been battling against the odds to improve patient care.* | *The soldiers' job was to hold on despite impossible odds.*

3 be at odds a) to disagree: **[+with]** | *Briggs found himself at odds with his colleagues.* | **[+over/on]** *The two politicians were at odds over what was the truth.* **b)** if two statements, descriptions, actions etc are at odds with each other, they are different although they should be the same: **[+with]** *Mark's account of what happened is at odds with Dan's.* | *She gave him a sweet smile, totally at odds with the look of dislike in her eyes.*

4 HORSE RACING ETC the numbers that show how much money you will win if you BET on the winner of a horse race or other competition: *The odds are 6-1.* | **[+of]** *At odds of 10-1 he bet a hundred pounds.* | **(at) long/short odds** (=high or low numbers, that show a high or low risk of losing) *Everyone was surprised when Desert Zone won the race, at very long odds.* | **lay/offer (sb) odds** *BrE*: *They are laying odds of 8-1 that the Conservatives will win the next election.*

5 it makes no odds *BrE spoken* used to say that what someone does or what happens is not important: *Pay me now or later – it makes no odds.*

6 pay over the odds *BrE informal* to pay a higher price than is usual or reasonable: *Most residents live in tiny apartments and pay over the odds for them too.*

COLLOCATIONS – MEANING 2

ADJECTIVES

enormous/considerable/incredible odds *He survived a night in the cold water against incredible odds.*

great odds (=a lot of difficulties) *We must hope that, despite great odds, we can achieve a peaceful settlement.*
impossible/overwhelming odds (=making success seem extremely unlikely) *They face impossible odds simply trying to get an education.*

VERBS

beat/overcome/defy the odds (=succeed despite great difficulties) *The baby, born sixteen weeks too early, defied the odds and is celebrating her first birthday.*
battle/struggle against the odds (=work hard despite great difficulties)

PHRASES

against all odds (=despite something seeming very unlikely) *Against all odds, he recovered from his illness.*
the odds are stacked against sb (=there are a lot of difficulties that may prevent someone's success)

ˌodds and ˈends (*also* **ˌodds and ˈsods** *BrE informal*) *n* [plural] small things of various kinds without much value: *He didn't keep much in his desk – just a few odds and ends.*

ˌodds-ˈon *adj* **1 odds-on favourite** the person, horse etc that is most likely to win a race or other competition **2** *BrE informal* very likely: **it's odds on (that)** *It's odds on that she won't come.* | **be odds-on to do sth** *They must have felt they were odds-on to win.*

ode /əʊd $ oʊd/ *n* [C] a poem or song written in order to praise a person or thing: **[+to]** *Keats' 'Ode to a Nightingale'*

o·di·ous /ˈəʊdiəs $ ˈoʊ-/ *adj formal* extremely unpleasant SYN **horrible**: *an odious little man* —**odiously** *adv*

o·di·um /ˈəʊdiəm $ ˈoʊ-/ *n* [U] *formal* a strong feeling of hatred that a lot of people have for someone because of something they have done SYN **opprobrium**: *Internationally Reagan attracted odium for his militarism.*

o·dom·e·ter /əʊˈdɒmɪtə $ oʊˈdɑːmɪtər/ *n* [C] an instrument in a vehicle that shows how many miles or kilometres the vehicle has travelled SYN **milometer** *BrE* → see picture at CAR

o·dor /ˈəʊdə $ ˈoʊdər/ *n* [C] the American spelling of ODOUR

o·do·rif·er·ous /ˌəʊdərˈɪfərəs◂ $ ˌoʊ-/ *adj old-fashioned* ODOROUS

o·dor·less /ˈəʊdələs $ ˈoʊdər-/ *adj* the American spelling of ODOURLESS

o·do·rous /ˈəʊdərəs $ ˈoʊ-/ *adj literary or technical* having a smell: *odorous gases*

o·dour *BrE*, **odor** *AmE* /ˈəʊdə $ ˈoʊdər/ ●○○ *n* [C,U] a smell, especially an unpleasant one: **[+of]** | *the faint odour of damp* | **strong/unpleasant/pungent/offensive etc odour** *obnoxious odours from a factory* THESAURUS▸ SMELL → BODY ODOUR

o·dour·less *BrE*, **odorless** *AmE* /ˈəʊdələs $ ˈoʊdər-/ *adj* having no smell: *a colorless, odorless liquid*

od·ys·sey /ˈɒdəsi $ ˈɑː-/ *n* [C] *literary* **1** a series of experiences that teach you something about yourself or about life: *a spiritual odyssey* **2** a long journey with a lot of adventures or difficulties: **on an odyssey** *They departed Texas on a three-year odyssey that took them as far as Japan.*

OECD /ˌəʊ iː siː ˈdiː $ ˌoʊ-/ *n* **the OECD** (***the Organization for Economic Cooperation and Development***) a group of rich countries who work together to develop trade and economic growth

oe·di·pal /ˈiːdəpəl $ ˈe-/ *adj* [usually before noun] related to an Oedipus complex

Oe·di·pus com·plex /ˈiːdəpəs ˌkɒmpleks $ ˈedəpəs ˌkɑːm-/ *n* according to Freudian PSYCHOLOGY, when a son unconsciously feels sexual desire for his mother, combined with a hatred for his father

o'er /əʊə $ ɔːr/ *adv, prep literary* over – used especially in poetry

oe·soph·a·gus *BrE*, **esophagus** *AmE* /ɪˈsɒfəgəs $ ɪˈsɑː-/ *n* (*plural* **oesophaguses** *or* **oesophagi** /-gaɪ/) [C] the tube which food passes down from your mouth to your stomach → **digestive system** at DIGESTIVE

oes·tro·gen *BrE*, **estrogen** *AmE* /ˈiːstrədʒən $ ˈes-/ *n* [U] a substance that is produced in a woman's OVARIES that causes changes in her body and prepares it for having babies

oeu·vre /ˈɜːvrə $ ˈʊvrə/ *n* [C usually singular] *formal* all the works of an artist or writer SYN **works**: *the oeuvre of Van Gogh*

of /əv, ə; *strong* ɒv $ əv, ə *strong* $ ɑːv/ ●●● S1 W1 *prep*
1 used to show what a part belongs to or comes from: *the back of the house* | *the last scene of the movie* | *the end of the day*
2 used to show who something or someone belongs to or has a connection with: *a friend of Mark's* | *Avocado salad is a favourite of mine.* | *Product inspection is the responsibility of the employees themselves.*
3 used when talking about a feature or quality that something has: *the cost of the meal* | *the beauty of the scenery* | *the length of the swimming pool*
4 used to show what group one or more things or people belong to: *some of the students* | *'Sunflowers' is one of his best-known paintings.* | *Two of the guests are vegetarian.* | *a member of the baseball team*
5 used to show what type of substance or thing you are referring to, when talking about an amount: *two kilos of sugar* | *millions of dollars* | *a bar of chocolate*
6 used to say what something contains: *a cup of coffee* | *several packets of cigarettes* | *truckloads of refugees*
7 used to say what type of things or people are in a group: *a herd of elephants* | *his circle of friends* | *a bunch of bananas*
8 a) used to state specifically which thing of the general type mentioned you are referring to: *the city of New York* | *the art of painting* | *the problem of unemployment* **b)** used to state specifically what a particular number, amount, age etc is: *at the age of 52* | *an increase of 3%*
9 used to talk about things produced by a famous or skilled writer, artist etc: *the plays of Shakespeare* | *the paintings of Picasso* | *the work of a great architect*
10 used to say what a story, some news etc is about, or what a picture, map etc shows: *a story of love and loss* | *news of his arrest* | *a photo of Elizabeth* | *a map of Indonesia*
11 a) used after nouns that refer to actions, or to people who do something, in order to show who or what the action is done to: *the cancellation of the meeting* | *the killing of innocent children* | *supporters of the project* **b)** used after nouns that refer to actions in order to show who or what does the action: *the ringing of the phone* | *the arrival of a visitor*
12 used after some adjectives that describe feelings, to show who or what the feeling is directed towards: *He's always been frightened of spiders.* | *Most children want their parents to feel proud of them.*
13 used when referring to the day, moment etc when something happened: *the day of the accident* | *the week of the festival* | *I was at home* ***at the time of*** *the murder.*
14 used to say where something is in relation to a place or thing: **north/south etc of sth** *a historic seaside town 99 km south of London* | **to the left/right of sth** *To the left of the sofa is a table.* | *I live within a mile of here.*
15 used to describe a person or thing by saying what their main qualities or features are: *Albright was seen as a woman of great determination.* | *It's an area of considerable historical interest.*
16 used to say what someone's age is: *He has two children, a boy of 12 and a girl of 15.*
17 it is kind/stupid/careless etc of sb (to do sth) used to say that someone's action shows a particular quality: *It was kind of you to remember my birthday.*
18 used to say where someone comes from: *the people of China* | *Jesus of Nazareth*
19 used to show the country, organization, or group in which someone has a particular position: *King Philip II of Spain* | *the secretary of the tennis club*

20 used in dates before the name of the month: *the 27th of July*
21 used to say when something happened: *the presidential election of 1825 | one of the biggest upsets of recent years*
22 *AmE spoken* used in giving the time, to mean 'before' SYN **to** *BrE*: *It's **a quarter of seven*** (=6.45).
23 used to show the cause of someone's death: *He died of cancer.*
24 *literary* used to say what material has been used to make something: *a dress of pure silk*
25 of an evening/of a weekend etc *BrE* in the evenings, at WEEKENDS etc: *We often used to walk by the river of an evening.*

GRAMMAR: Possessives

• The usual way to say that something belongs to someone, or that someone is connected with someone, is by using **-'s**. You say: *Tom's car | a child's bike | my sister's boyfriend* ✗ Don't say: *the car of Tom | the bike of a child | the boyfriend of my sister*
• You use **-s'** after a plural noun ending in 's': *a teachers' meeting*
• You use **of mine/yours/his/hers/ours/theirs** when talking about one of several people or things belonging to or connected with someone: *a friend of ours | a habit of mine*
• You use **by** when saying who sang, wrote, or painted something: *a song by Jay-Z* ✗ Don't say: *a song of Jay-Z*

of 'course ●●● S1 W1 *adv*
1 used to show that other people probably already know what you are saying is true, or expect to hear it: *Well, she won, of course. | You should of course keep copies of all your correspondence. | Of course there will be some difficult times ahead.*
2 *spoken* (*also* **course** *informal*) used to emphasize that you are saying 'yes' when someone asks your permission to do something: *'Can I ring you back in a minute?' 'Yes, of course.' | 'Is it OK if I have another cup of coffee?' 'Course, help yourself.'*
3 *spoken* (*also* **course** *informal*) used to emphasize that what you are saying to someone is true or correct: *'Do you really believe her?' 'Of course I do!' | 'I hope this idea of yours works.' 'Course it'll work.'*
4 *spoken* used to show that you accept or agree with what someone has just said: *'Don't get angry. She's only 13.' 'Of course.' | 'The correct answer is 83.' 'Oh, yes, of course.'*
5 of course not/course not *spoken* used to emphasize that you are saying 'no' to something: *'Have you been reading my email?' 'Of course not!' | 'Do you mind if I bring a friend?' 'No, of course not.'*

off[1] /ɒf $ ɔːf/ ●●● S1 W1 *adv, prep, adj*
1 away from a place: *He got into his car and drove off. | Suddenly they turned off and parked in a side road. | Once we were off the main freeway, the trip felt more like a vacation. | Her husband was off on a business trip somewhere. | Are you ready? Off we go. | I must be off now* (=I must leave). *| They were off to Italy* (=leaving to go to Italy) *and wanted to make an early start.*
2 not on something, or removed from something: *Keep off the grass. | As he leaned forward, his hat fell off. | Someone had taken the mirror off the wall. | Take your coat off. | I was trying to scrape the mud off my boots.* ⚠ Don't say 'off of' something. Say **off** something: *She fell off her chair* (NOT *off of her chair*).
3 out of a bus, train, plane etc OPP **on**: *I'll get off at the next stop. | Everyone got off the train at Winnipeg.*
4 a machine, piece of equipment etc that is off is not working or operating OPP **on**: *Will someone switch the radio off? | Make sure all the lights are off.*
5 not at work, school etc because you are ill or on holiday → **absent**: *My secretary's been off with flu for the past week. | Clare had to stay off school because her mother was ill. | You look tired. Why don't you take tomorrow off? | He needs more time off duty for relaxation and rest. | 'Going to work today, mum?' 'No. It's my **day off** today.'*
6 *informal* from someone: *My brother once borrowed some money off him. | I got this necklace off a woman outside the market.*
7 a) used to say how far away something is: *We could see the cliffs of Shetland about two miles off. | Kara's home was a long way off across the sea.* **b)** used to say how much time there is between now and a future event: *With the exams now only a week off, I had to study hard. | Christmas seemed a long way off.* **c)** used to say how likely or unlikely something is: *Any kind of peace agreement still seems a long way off.*
8 a) only a short distance away from a place: *Our hotel was just off the main street. | an island off the coast of France* **b)** connected to a particular room, area, road etc: *There's a small bathroom off the main bedroom. | a narrow street leading off the corner of the square*
9 used to say that a price is reduced by a particular amount: *If you buy more than ten, they knock 10% off.*
10 if an event which has been arranged is off, it will not now take place → **cancelled, postponed**: *The wedding's off. | The race may have to be called off if the bad weather continues.*
11 *BrE informal* behaviour that is off is rude or is not acceptable: *She walked out before the end of your lecture, which I thought was a bit off. | Look, I know when someone's being off with me.*
12 used to say how much of something someone has: **be well/badly off for sth** *The school's fairly well off for books these days. | **How are you off for** sports equipment* (=do you have enough?)? → WELL-OFF, BADLY OFF, BETTER OFF
13 off and on (*also* **on and off**) for short periods but not regularly, over a long period of time: *We've been going out together for five years, off and on.*
14 no longer wanting or liking something: *Toby's been off his food for a few days.* | **go off sth/sb** *BrE*: *I used to enjoy tennis, but I've gone off it a bit now. | She seems to have gone off Mark since he's grown a beard.*
15 no longer taking something such as a drug or medicine OPP **on**: *The operation was a success, and she's off the morphine.*
16 a) food that is off is no longer fresh enough to eat → **rotten, sour**: *Ugh! The milk's off. | Do you think the meat's **gone off**?* **b)** used to say that a particular kind of food is not available in a restaurant although it is on the MENU: *I'm sorry, the fish pie is off today, sir.*
17 *AmE* not as good as usual: *Sales figures for last year were a little off compared with those of the previous year.*
18 *AmE* not correct or not right: *Our calculations were off. | Guess again. You're **way off*** (=very far from being correct).
→ **right off** at RIGHT[2](2), → **straight off** at STRAIGHT[1](7), → **off the top of your head** at TOP[1](18), → **noises off** at NOISE[1](8)

off[2] *adj* [only before noun] **1 off day/week etc** a day, week etc when you are not doing something as well as you usually do: *Brian never usually loses his temper – he must be **having an off day**.* **2 off period/season etc** a period or season which is not as busy as other times of the year: *In the off season, there's hardly anyone staying at the hotel.* **3** *BrE* used to talk about a pair of things such as wheels on a car, to mean the one on the right OPP **near**

off[3] *n BrE* **1 the off** the start of a race or a journey: *The horses were in line, ready for the off.* **2 from the off** from the beginning of something: *She was doubtful about the interview from the off.*

off[4] *v* [T] *AmE informal* to kill someone: *The guy who did this ought to be offed.*

ˌoff-'air *adj* [only before noun] not being broadcast on the radio or television at the present moment OPP **on air, on-air**: *off-air television recordings*

of·fal /ˈɒfəl $ ˈɔː-, ˈɑː-/ *n* [U] *BrE* the inside parts of an animal, for example the heart, LIVER, and KIDNEYs used as food

ˌoff-'balance, off balance *adj* [not before noun] **1** in an unsteady position and likely to fall: **throw/knock/push etc sb off-balance** *The sudden movement of the ship knocked*

them both off balance. **2 catch/throw sb off-balance** to surprise or shock someone because they are not prepared for something that happens: *I was thrown off-balance by some of the more difficult questions I was asked.*

off·beat /ˌɒfˈbiːt◂ $ ˌɒːf-/ *adj informal* unusual and not what people normally expect, especially in an interesting way: *offbeat humour | She's a little offbeat, but she's a wonderful actress.*

ˌoff-ˈcentre *BrE*, **off-center** *AmE adj* [not before noun] not exactly in the centre of something: *Place the photo slightly off-centre, so that there is more space on the page.*

ˈoff-chance, **off chance** *n* **on the off-chance** if you do something on the off-chance that something will happen, you do it hoping that it will happen although it is unlikely: *I just came to see you on the off-chance that Pippa might be here.*

ˌoff-ˈcolour *BrE*, **off-color** *AmE adj* **1** sexually offensive: *off-color jokes* **2** [not before noun] *BrE* slightly ill: *She's been feeling a bit off-colour lately.*

ˈoff-cut *n* [C] *especially BrE* a piece of wood, paper etc that is left after the main piece has been cut and removed

ˌoff-ˈduty *adj* if someone such as a policeman, nurse, or soldier is off-duty, they are not working: *an off-duty guard | I shall be off-duty on Thursday.*

of·fence *BrE*, **offense** *AmE* /əˈfens/ ●●● S3 W2 *n*
1 [C] an illegal action or a crime: *His solicitor said he committed the offence because he was heavily in debt.* | **[+against]** *sexual offences against children* THESAURUS CRIME
2 [U] when you offend or upset someone by something you do or say: **cause/give offence** *The problem was how to say 'no' to her without causing offence.* | *Don't be upset by what he said; he* ***meant no offence*** (=did not intend to offend anyone).
3 no offence *spoken* used to tell someone that you hope that what you are going to say or do will not offend them: *No offense, but this cheese tastes like rubber.*
4 take offence (at sth) to feel offended because of something someone says or does: *I think he took offence at my lack of enthusiasm.*
5 [U] *formal* the act of attacking: *the weapon of offence used during the attack*

COLLOCATIONS

VERBS

commit an offence (=do something that is against the law) *He had committed the offence of dangerous driving.*
charge sb with an offence *In that year, 367 people were charged with terrorist offences.*
convict sb of an offence (=say officially that they are guilty) | **admit an offence**

PHRASES

it is an offence to do sth *It is an offence to carry a weapon in a public place.*
an offence punishable by/with sth *Possession of the drug is an offence punishable by up to one year's imprisonment.*
make sth an offence/make it an offence to do sth

ADJECTIVES/NOUN + offence

a criminal offence *It is a criminal offence to sell alcohol to someone under the age of 18.*
a serious offence *serious offences such as murder or armed robbery*
a minor offence *The police cautioned him for a minor offence.*
a first offence *Because it was a first offence, she was not sent to prison.*
a lesser offence (=one that is not as serious as another offence) | **a federal offense** *AmE* (=a very serious offence against the law of the US, rather than against a state's law) | **a driving/parking/traffic offence** | **a sex/drug/terrorist etc offence**

of·fend /əˈfend/ ●●○ *v*
1 [I,T] to make someone angry or upset by doing or saying something that they think is rude, unkind etc: *His remarks deeply offended many Scottish people.* | **be offended by/at sth** *Liddy was offended by such a personal question.* | *The careful language is designed not to offend.*
2 [T] to seem bad or unacceptable to someone: *A solution must be found that doesn't offend too many people.* | *Some of these new buildings really offend the eye* (=look very ugly).
3 [I] *formal* to commit a crime or crimes: *Many of the young men here are likely to offend again.*
4 [I,T] *formal* to be against people's feelings of what is morally acceptable: **[+against]** *Broadcasters have a responsibility not to offend against good taste and decency.*

of·fend·ed /əˈfendɪd/ *adj* someone who is offended is angry and upset by someone's behaviour or remarks: **feel/look/sound offended** *Stella was beginning to feel a little offended.* | *I knew that Piers would be* ***deeply offended***. | *I* ***get*** *very* ***offended*** *when he talks to me like that.* | *radio listeners who are* ***easily offended***

of·fend·er /əˈfendə $ -ər/ ●●○ *n* [C]
1 someone who is guilty of a crime: *Community punishment is used for less serious offenders.* | *At 16, Scott was already a* ***persistent offender*** (=someone who has been caught several times for committing crimes). → FIRST OFFENDER, SEX OFFENDER, YOUNG OFFENDER
2 someone or something that is the cause of something bad: *Among causes of air pollution, car exhaust fumes may be* ***the worst offender***.

of·fend·ing /əˈfendɪŋ/ *adj* [only before noun]
1 the offending ... the thing that is causing a problem – often used humorously: *I decided to have the offending tooth removed.* **2** relating to or guilty of an illegal offence: *offending behaviour | the offending vehicle* **3** making people feel angry or insulted SYN **offensive**: *his offending remarks*

of·fense¹ /əˈfens/ *n* [C,U] the usual American spelling of OFFENCE

of·fense² /ˈɒfens $ ˈɒːfens, ˈɑː-/ *n* [U] *AmE* the part of a game such as American football, which is concerned with getting points and winning, or the group of players who do this OPP **defense**: *The Bears are going to have to work on their offense this season.*

of·fen·sive¹ /əˈfensɪv/ ●●○ *adj*
1 very rude or insulting and likely to upset people OPP **inoffensive**: *I found her remarks* ***deeply offensive***. | **[+to]** *crude jokes that are offensive to women | offensive behaviour* THESAURUS RUDE
2 *formal* very unpleasant: *an offensive smell*
3 [only before noun] for attacking → DEFENSIVE¹(1): *Jan was convicted of possessing an* ***offensive weapon***. | *The troops took up offensive positions.*
4 *AmE* relating to getting points and winning a game, rather than stopping the other team from getting points OPP **defensive**: *the Jets' offensive strategy* —**offensively** *adv*: *Rick's remarks were offensively racist.* —**offensiveness** *n* [U]

offensive² *n* [C] **1** a planned military attack involving large forces over a long period: *a* ***military offensive*** | *A major* ***offensive*** *was* ***launched*** *on August 22.* **2 go on the offensive** (*also* **take the offensive**) to start attacking or criticizing someone before they start attacking or criticizing you: *Republicans went on the offensive over soaring gasoline prices.* | *The international coalition was ready to take the offensive.* **3 charm/diplomatic offensive** a planned set of actions intended to influence a lot of people

of·fer¹ /ˈɒfə $ ˈɒːfər, ˈɑː-/ ●●● S1 W1 *v*
1 [T] to ask someone if they would like to have something, or to hold something out to them so that they can take it: **offer sb sth** ***Can I offer you*** *something to drink?* | *They offered him a very good job, but he turned it down.* | **offer sth to sb** *Maureen lit a cigarette and offered one to Lucy.* | *The drama school offers places to students who can show talent.*
2 [I,T] to say that you are willing to do something: *I don't need any help, but it was nice of you to offer.* | **offer to do sth** *My dad has offered to pick us up.* | *The newspaper offered to apologise for the article.*

Office

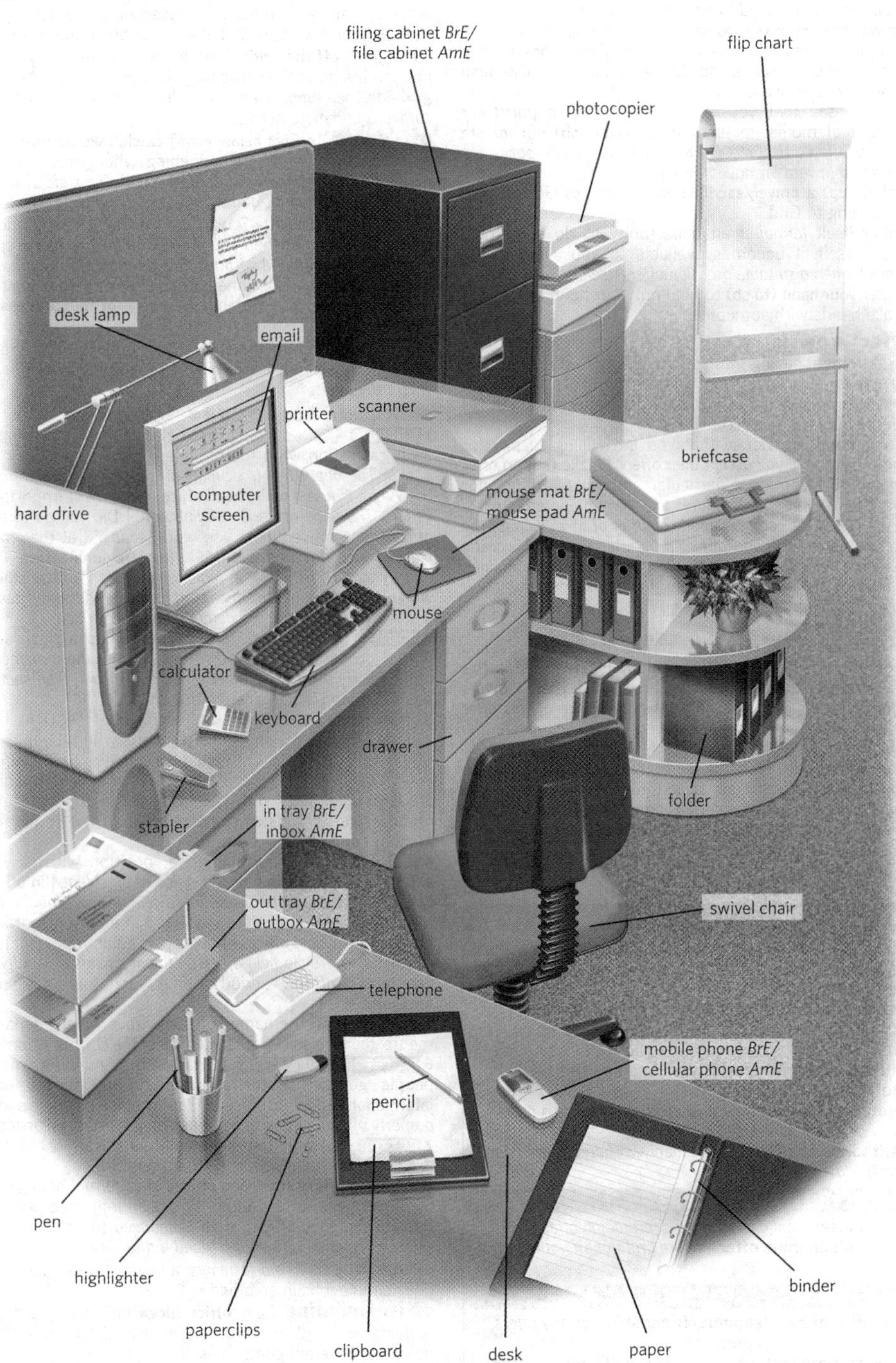
filing cabinet *BrE*/
file cabinet *AmE*
flip chart
photocopier
desk lamp
email
printer
scanner
briefcase
computer screen
hard drive
mouse mat *BrE*/
mouse pad *AmE*
mouse
calculator
keyboard
drawer
folder
stapler
in tray *BrE*/
inbox *AmE*
out tray *BrE*/
outbox *AmE*
swivel chair
telephone
mobile phone *BrE*/
cellular phone *AmE*
pencil
pen
highlighter
paperclips
clipboard
desk
paper
binder

O

3 [T] to provide something that people need or want: **offer advice/help/support etc** *Your doctor should be able to offer advice on diet.* | **offer an opportunity/chance/possibility** *The course offers the opportunity to specialize in the final year.* | *A number of groups* **offer** *their* **services** *free of charge.* | *The Centre offers a wide range of sports facilities.* | **offer sth to sb** *I did what I could to offer comfort to the family.*
4 have sth to offer (sb) to have qualities, opportunities etc that people are likely to want or enjoy: *Canada* **has much to offer** *in terms of location and climate.* | *He felt he* **had nothing to offer** *her that she wanted.*
5 [T] to say that you are willing to pay a particular amount of money for something: **offer (sb) sth for sth** *They've offered us £75,000 for the house.* | *The police are offering a reward for any information.*
6 offer (up) a prayer/sacrifice etc to pray to God or give something to God
7 offer itself *formal* if an opportunity to do something offers itself, it becomes available to you: *I'll raise the subject when a suitable occasion offers itself.*
8 offer your hand (to sb) to hold out your hand in order to shake hands with someone

offer² ●●● S2 W1 *n* [C]
1 a statement saying that you are willing to do something for someone or give them something: **[+of]** *I can't turn down the offer of a free trip to Milan!* | **offer to do sth** *His offer to resign will be accepted.*
2 an amount of money that you are willing to pay for something: *Will you* **accept** *their* **offer**? | **make (sb) an offer (for/on sth)** (=offer a particular amount of money for something) *Within 20 minutes they were prepared to make us an offer.* | *The company* **made an offer of** *$5 million for the site.* | **a generous/good offer** *'I'll be interested if Newcastle make me a good offer,' said the 25-year-old striker.* | **be open to offers** (=be ready to consider people's offers and lower your original price) *We're asking £2,500, but we're open to offers.* → O.N.O.
3 a reduction of the price of something in a shop for a short time → **discount**: *All* **special offers** *advertised in this brochure are subject to availability.* | **[+on]** *There's a* **free offer** *on orders over £45.* | *To* **take advantage** *of this* **offer** (=buy something at the reduced price), *complete the attached forms.*
4 on offer a) available to be bought, chosen, or used: *Activities on offer include sailing, rowing, and canoeing.* | *I was impressed with the designs on offer.* **b)** *BrE* for sale for a short time at a cheaper price than usual: *Lean minced beef is on offer this week.*
5 under offer *BrE* if a house that is for sale is under offer, someone has offered to buy it for a particular price

COLLOCATIONS

VERBS

accept an offer (=say yes to it) *Are you going to accept their offer?*
take up an offer/take sb up on their offer *BrE* (=accept someone's offer) *I might take him up on his offer.*
turn down/refuse/reject/decline an offer (=say no to it) *She declined the offer of a lift.*
get/receive an offer *He received the offer of a place at Cambridge University.*
withdraw an offer *They suddenly withdrew their offer at the last minute.*

ADJECTIVES/NOUN + offer

a job offer *I still did not have a formal job offer.*
a kind/generous offer *We are grateful for your kind offer.*

PHRASES

an offer of help/support/friendship etc *Any offers of help would be appreciated.*
I appreciate your offer (=I am grateful for it – used especially when politely refusing someone's offer) *I appreciate your offer, but I don't need any help.*

of·fer·ing /ˈɒfərɪŋ $ ˈɔː-, ˈɑː-/ *n* [C] **1** a book, play, piece of music etc that someone has written recently: *the latest offering from Nanci Griffith* **2** something that is given to God **3** something that is given as a present to please someone → **burnt offering** at BURNT²(2), → PEACE OFFERING

of·fer·to·ry /ˈɒfətəri $ ˈɔːfətɔːri, ˈɑː-/ *n* (*plural* **offertories**) [C] *formal* **1** the money people give during a religious ceremony in church SYN **collection 2** the offering of the bread and wine to God at a Christian church service

off-ˈgrid, **off the grid** *adverb* if you live off-grid, you do not use the normal electricity, gas, or water supply —**off-grid** *adj*: *They supply all types of off-grid energy products for caravans and motorhomes.*

ˌoff-ˈguard *adj* [not before noun] **catch/take sb off-guard** to surprise someone by happening when they are not expecting something or prepared for it: *The sudden snow storm caught us all off-guard.*

off·hand¹ /ˌɒfˈhænd◂ $ ˌɔːf-/ *adj* **1** *BrE* not very friendly towards someone when you are talking to them: *She said you were a bit offhand with her this afternoon.* | *an offhand tone of voice* **2** said or done without thinking or planning: *an offhand remark* —**offhandedly** *adv* —**offhandedness** *n* [U]

offhand² *adv* immediately, without time to think about it or find out about something: *I can't remember offhand where the file is.*

of·fice /ˈɒfɪs $ ˈɔː-, ˈɑː-/ ●●● S1 W1 *n*
1 BUILDING [C] a building that belongs to a company or an organization, with rooms where people can work at desks: *The department occupies an office just a mile from the White House.* | **main/head office** (=the most important office) *The head office is in Edinburgh.* | *Did you go to* **the office** (=the office where you work) *today?* | **at the office** *Have a nice day at the office.* | **local/regional office** *The agency has a network of regional offices.* | **office staff/workers/equipment etc** *Office staff need well-designed desks and chairs.* | *the increased demand for office space*
2 ROOM [C] a room where someone has a desk and works, on their own or with other people: *the manager's office* | *Sorry, Ann's not in her office right now.* | *Dan shares an office with Lisa.* → see picture on *p. 1263*
3 office hours a) the time between about 9:00 in the morning and 5:00 in the afternoon, when people in offices are working: *Can you phone again during office hours?* **b)** *AmE* the time during the day or week when students can meet with their teacher in the teacher's office: *Professor Lee's office hours are from two to four on Mondays and Thursdays.*
4 JOB [C,U] an important job or position with power, especially in government: *the office of president* | **in office** *She was celebrating ten years in office.* | *A provisional military government* **took office** (=started in an important job or position). | **hold office** (=have a particular important job or position) *Trujillo held office as finance minister.* | *a five-year* **term of office** (=period of time working in an important job)
5 Office used in the names of some government departments: *the Foreign Office* | *the Office of the District Attorney*
6 PLACE FOR INFORMATION [C] a room or building where people go to ask for information, buy tickets etc: **information/ticket etc office** *the tourist office* | *Is there a lost property office?* → BOX OFFICE, POST OFFICE, REGISTRY OFFICE
7 DOCTOR [C] *AmE* the place where a doctor or DENTIST examines or treats people SYN **surgery** *BrE*
8 sb's good offices/the good offices of sb *formal* help given by someone who has authority or can influence people: **through the good offices of sb** *I managed to obtain a visa through the good offices of a friend in the Service.*

ˈoffice ˌboy *n* [C] *old-fashioned* a boy or young man who does simple jobs in an office

ˈoffice ˌbuilding (*also* **ˈoffice block** *BrE*) *n* [C] a large building with many offices in it, especially ones that belong to different companies

ˈoffice ˌholder *n* [C] someone who has an official position, especially in the government

ˌOffice Of ˌPublic ˌSector Inforˈmation, the (*abbreviation* **OPSI**) the organization that is responsible for running Her Majesty's Stationery Office (HMSO) and other public information services in the UK. It is part of The National Archives.

ˌoffice ˈparty *n* [C] a party, especially one held before Christmas, in the office of a company, government department etc for the people who work there

of·fi·cer /ˈɒfəsə $ ˈɒːfəsər, ˈɑː-/ ●●● S1 W1 *n* [C]
1 someone who is in a position of authority in the army, navy etc: **an army/naval/military etc officer** | *a* ***commanding officer*** *of the SAS*
2 someone who is in a position in an organization or the government: *a prison officer* | *the chief medical officer* | *the organization's public information officer* | *The document must be certified by the proper officer of the state.* → CHIEF EXECUTIVE OFFICER, → **press officer** at PRESS OFFICE, PROBATION OFFICER, RETURNING OFFICER
3 a member of the police SYN **police officer**, **policeman**, **policewoman**: *a request for 400 more officers*
4 Officer *AmE* a title for a policeman or policewoman: *Officer Murdoch*

of·fi·cial¹ /əˈfɪʃəl/ ●●● S3 W1 *n* [C] someone who is in a position of authority in an organization: *a government official* | *senior administration officials*

official² ●●● S3 W2 *adj*
1 approved of or done by someone in authority, especially the government: *an official investigation into the causes of the explosion* | *the official policy on education* | *official statistics about illegal drug use* | *You will have to get official permission first.* | *Finally the letter of appointment came, making it all official.*
2 relating to or done as part of an important job or position: **an official visit/engagement etc** *The president was leaving for a four-day official tour of Mexico.* | *the Queen's performance of* ***official duties*** | *They dined in an official capacity with other European leaders.* | *the Lord Mayor's official residence*
3 an official explanation, account etc is one that is given formally and publicly, but may not be true: *Many doubted the official version of events.* | *The* ***official line*** (=what is said publicly by people in authority) *was that the troops were there to protect the King.*
4 chosen to represent someone or an organization, or do something for them: *the company's official logo* | *the official representative from the American administration*
5 an official event is a formal public event: *The official opening of the institute was in May.*

of·fi·cial·dom /əˈfɪʃəldəm/ *n* [U] government departments or the people who work in them – used when you think they are not helpful → **bureaucracy**

of·fi·cial·ese /əˌfɪʃəlˈiːz/ *n* [U] *informal* a way of talking or writing used by government officials, that is unnecessarily difficult to understand

of·fi·cial·ly /əˈfɪʃəli/ ●●○ *adv*
1 publicly or formally: *The new church was* ***officially opened*** *on July 5th.* | *Nothing has yet been* ***officially announced***. | *The scheme was* ***officially launched*** *in May.* | *Has the company officially confirmed the appointment?* | *the number of officially recognized political parties*
2 [sentence adverb] according to what someone says publicly, even though this may not be true: *Officially, the talks never took place.*

ofˌficial reˈceiver *n* [C] *BrE* someone whose job is to take care of the financial affairs of a company or a person that is BANKRUPT

of·fi·ci·ate /əˈfɪʃieɪt/ *v* [I] to perform official duties, especially at a religious ceremony

of·fi·cious /əˈfɪʃəs/ *adj* too eager to tell people what to do – used to show disapproval: *an officious traffic warden* —**officiously** *adv* —**officiousness** *n* [U]

off·ing /ˈɒfɪŋ $ ˈɒː-, ˈɑː-/ *n* **be in the offing** to be likely to happen soon: *Big changes were in the offing.*

ˌoff-ˈkey *adj* **1** music that is off-key sounds unpleasant because it is played slightly above or below the correct PITCH → **in tune**: *The band sounded slightly off-key.* **2** wrong or not suitable for the situation: *The jokes during the violent action scenes seemed off-key.* —**off-key** *adv*: *Someone upstairs was singing off-key.*

ˌoff-ˈkilter *adj* **1** not completely straight or correctly balanced: *The paintings were slightly off-kilter.* **2** unusual in a strange or interesting way: *her off-kilter sense of humour*

ˈoff-ˌlicence *n* [C] *BrE* a shop that sells wine, beer, and other alcoholic drinks, in bottles or cans SYN **liquor store** *AmE*

ˌoff ˈlimits *adj* **be off limits a)** if a place is off limits, you are not allowed to go there SYN **out of bounds**: **[+to/for]** *Footpaths are, of course, off limits to bikers.* **b)** if a subject is off limits, you are not allowed to talk about it: *Unlike most group discussions, nothing was off limits.*

off·line /ˌɒfˈlaɪn◂ $ ˌɒːf-/ *adv* **1** with your computer not connected to the Internet OPP **online**: *I work offline most of the day.* **2** if computer equipment is offline, it is not directly connected to the computer OPP **online**: *The printer was offline all morning.* —**offline** *adj*: *offline storage*

off·load /ˌɒfˈləʊd $ ˌɒːfˈloʊd/ *v* **1** [T] to get rid of something that you do not want by giving it or selling it to someone else: **offload sth onto sb** *The dealer had offloaded some of the shares onto a willing client.* **2 offload your worries/emotions/problems etc** *BrE* to tell someone about your worries etc in order to make yourself feel better **3** [T] to take something off a truck or ship: *The men offloaded their cargo.*

ˌoff-ˈmessage *adj, adv* a politician who is off-message says things that are different from the ideas of the political party they belong to OPP **on-message**

ˌoff-ˈpeak *adj especially BrE* **1** off-peak hours or periods are times that are less busy because fewer people want to do or use something OPP **peak**: *Telephone charges are lower during* ***off-peak periods***. **2** off-peak travel, electricity etc is cheaper because it is done or used at less busy times OPP **peak** —**off-peak** *adv*

ˌoff-ˈpiste *adj* not on the usual SKI slopes: *off-piste skiing* —**off-piste** *adv*

off·print /ˈɒfprɪnt $ ˈɒːf-/ *n* [C] *technical* an article from a magazine that is printed and sold separately

ˈoff-ˌputting *adj BrE* if someone's behaviour or the appearance of something is off-putting, you do not like it or you think it is unattractive: *Some women found the competitive style of the discussions off-putting.* —**off-puttingly** *adv* → **put sb/sth off** at PUT

ˈoff-ramp *n* [C] *AmE* a road for driving off a FREEWAY SYN **slip road** *BrE*

ˌoff-ˈroad *adj* [usually before noun] **1** designed to be used on rough ground as well as on roads: *an* ***off-road vehicle*** **2** going over rough ground: *off-road cycling* | *off-road tracks* —**off-road** *adv*

ˌoff-ˈscreen *adv* when a film actor is not acting OPP **on-screen**: *What's he like off-screen?* —**off-screen** *adj*: *off-screen romances*

ˈoff-seaˌson *n* **the off-season a)** the time of year when not many people are taking holidays SYN **low season** → **high season**: **in the off-season** *Most hotels are closed in the off-season.* **b)** *AmE* the time of year when a sport is not usually played SYN **close season** *BrE* —**ˌoff-ˈseason** *adj, adv*: *Take advantage of our special off-season fares.*

off·set¹ /ˈɒfset, ˌɒfˈset $ ˈɒːfset, ˌɒːfˈset/ ●○○ AWL *v* (*past tense and past participle* **offset**, *present participle* **offsetting**) [T]
1 if the cost or amount of something offsets another cost or amount, the two things have an opposite effect so that the situation remains the same: *Cuts in prices for milk, butter, and cheese will be offset by direct payments to farmers.* | **offset sth against sth** *He was able to offset his travel expenses against tax.*
2 to make something look better by being close to it and different: *His blonde hair offset a deep tan.*
3 to do something that will make an action or activity CARBON NEUTRAL: *If you have to travel by air, offset your carbon emissions by supporting renewable energy projects.*

off·set² /ˈɒfset $ ˈɒːf-/ *adj* relating to a method of

printing in which ink is put onto ROLLERS and the paper then passes between the rollers —**offset** *n* [U]

ˈoffset ˌmortgage *n* [C] a type of MORTGAGE given by banks, in which the money someone has in their bank account is taken away from the amount they owe, reducing the total amount of interest they have to pay

off·shoot /ˈɒfʃuːt $ ˈɒːf-/ *n* [C] **1** something such as an organization which has developed from a larger or earlier one: **[+of]** *The company was originally an offshoot of Bell Telephones.* | *the Mafia and its offshoots* **2** a new stem or branch on a plant

O

off·shore /ˌɒfˈʃɔː◂ $ ˌɒːfˈʃɔːr◂/ *adj* **1** in or under the sea and not far from the coast → **inshore, onshore**: *offshore oil fields* | *an offshore island* **2** **offshore banks/companies/investments etc** banks etc that are based abroad in a country where you pay less tax than in your home country: *offshore financial centres* **3** **offshore wind/current etc** a wind etc that is blowing or moving away from the land OPP **onshore** —**offshore** *adv*: *a boat anchored offshore*

off·shor·ing /ˈɒfʃɔːrɪŋ $ ˈɒːf-/ *n* [U] the business practice of getting work done in another country in order to save money —**offshore** *v* [T]: *Many IT jobs have been offshored.*

off·side¹ /ˌɒfˈsaɪd◂ $ ˌɒːf-/ *adj, adv* in a position, usually ahead of the ball, where you are not allowed to play the ball in sports such as SOCCER and HOCKEY OPP **onside**

off·side² /ˈɒfsaɪd $ ˈɒːf-/ *n* **the offside** *BrE* the side of a car that is nearest to the middle of the road when you are driving it → **nearside** —**offside** *adj*: *the offside headlight*

ˌoff-ˈsite *adj, adv* happening away from a particular place, especially a place of work OPP **on-site**: *the off-site disposal of harmful waste* | *A small team worked off-site on the project.*

off·spring /ˈɒfˌsprɪŋ $ ˈɒːf-/ ●○○ *n* (*plural* **offspring**) [C]
1 someone's child or children - often used humorously: *a young mother trying to control her offspring*
2 an animal's baby or babies SYN **young**: *a lion and its offspring*

off·stage /ˌɒfˈsteɪdʒ◂ $ ˌɒːf-/ *adv* **1** just behind or to the side of a stage in a theatre, where the people watching a play cannot see OPP **onstage**: *There was a loud crash offstage.* **2** when an actor is not acting: *Offstage, Peter seemed a shy sort of person.* —**offstage** *adj*: *offstage noises*

ˈoff-street *adj* **off-street parking** places for parking that are not on public streets

ˌoff-the-ˈcuff *adj* [usually before noun] an off-the-cuff remark, reply etc is one that you make without thinking about it first SYN **spontaneous** —**off-the-cuff** *adv*

ˌoff-the-ˈpeg *BrE*, **ˌoff the ˈrack** *AmE adj* off-the-peg clothes are made in standard sizes, not made especially to fit one person → **made-to-measure** —**off-the-peg, off the rack** *adv*: *It was only a cheap suit, bought off-the-peg.*

ˌoff-the-ˈrecord, **off the record** *adj* an off-the-record remark is unofficial and is not supposed to be made public: *The prime minister's remarks were strictly off the record.* —**off the record** *adv*

ˌoff-the-ˈshelf *adj, adv* already made and available in shops rather than being designed especially for a customer: *off-the-shelf database software*

ˌoff-the-ˈwall *adj informal* very strange or unusual, often in an amusing way: *an off-the-wall concept*

off·track /ˈɒftræk $ ˈɒːf-/ *adj AmE* away from a place where horses race: *Few states allow* ***offtrack betting***.

ˌoff-ˈwhite *n* [U] a white colour that has some yellow or grey in it —**off-white** *adj*: *an off-white blouse*

ˈoff-year *n* [C usually singular] **1** a year when something is not as successful as usual: **[+for]** *an off-year for car sales* **2** *AmE* a year in which no national political elections happen

oft /ɒft $ ɒːft/ *adv literary* often: **oft-repeated/quoted etc** *oft-repeated advice*

of·ten /ˈɒfən, ˈɒftən $ ˈɒːf-/ ●●● S1 W1 *adv*
1 if something happens often, it happens regularly or many times SYN **frequently**: *She often works at the weekend.* | *If you wash your hair too often, it can get too dry.* | ***How often*** *do you see your parents?* | **quite/very often** *I quite often go to Paris on business.* | *Robin is a difficult child; you've said so yourself* ***often enough*** (=a lot of times). | **it is not often (that)** *It's not often that a government minister will admit to being wrong.*
2 if something happens often, it happens in many situations or cases: *It's often difficult to translate poetry.* | **very/quite often** *Very often children who behave badly at school have problems at home.*
3 **all too often** (*also* **only too often**) used to say that something sad, disappointing, or annoying happens too much: *All too often doctors are too busy to explain the treatment to their patients.* | *This type of accident happens only too often.*
4 **every so often** sometimes: *An inspector comes round every so often to check the safety equipment.*
5 **as often as not** (*also* **more often than not**) *spoken* usually: *More often than not the train is late.*

GRAMMAR: Word order

- **Often** usually comes before a verb: *I often go to bed late.*
- **Often** usually comes after the verb 'be': *She is often late.*
- **Often** usually comes after an auxiliary verb such as 'do' or 'have': *I have often wondered what happened to him.*
- **Often** is used at the beginning of a sentence, especially when something seems surprising: *Often I don't go to bed until 2 a.m.*
- **Often** is also used at the end of a sentence: *Do you go to bed late often?*

GRAMMAR GUIDE ▸ ADVERBS

of·ten·times /ˈɒfəntaɪmz $ ˈɒːf-/ *adv AmE informal* often: *Oftentimes I have to wait more than 20 minutes for a bus.*

o·gle /ˈəʊgəl $ ˈoʊ-/ *v* [I,T] to look at someone in a way that shows you think they are sexually attractive - used to show disapproval SYN **leer**: *I didn't like the way he was ogling me.*

OGM /ˌəʊ dʒiː ˈem $ ˌoʊ-/ *n* [C] (***outgoing message***) the message that you record on your telephone and that people will hear if they telephone you and you do not answer the call

O grade /ˈəʊ greɪd $ ˈoʊ-/ *n* [C,U] an examination in a particular subject which children take in schools in Scotland, usually at the age of 16 → **higher** → O LEVEL

o·gre /ˈəʊgə $ ˈoʊgər/ *n* [C] **1** a large imaginary person in children's stories who eats people **2** someone who seems cruel and frightening: *Her father sounded like a real ogre.*

oh /əʊ $ oʊ/ *interjection* **1** used when you want to get someone's attention or continue what you are saying: *Oh, look, I think that's Harry over there.* | *Milk, cereal, juice - oh, and put lettuce on the list too.* **2** used when you are giving an answer to a question: *'Have you met his wife?'* '***Oh, yes****, I know her quite well.'* | *'I hope Jenny won't be angry.'* '***Oh, no****, don't worry about that.'* | **oh, okay/all right** *'Can you lend me ten pounds?' 'Oh, all right, but only until tomorrow.'* **3** used to make a slight pause when you are speaking: *I met your friend in town, oh, what's her name?* **4** used to show that you are very happy, angry, disappointed etc about something: *Oh, aren't those flowers gorgeous!* | *Oh, how awful!* | ***Oh, no****! I've left my keys in the car!* | **oh, good/great** *Oh, good, you're still here.* | **oh, God/oh, dear etc** *Oh, God, I forgot all about it!* | ***Oh, well****, never mind.* **5** used to show that you are surprised about something: *'Frances has left her husband, you know.' 'Oh, has she?'* | *Oh, I didn't know that.*

ohm /əʊm $ oʊm/ *n* [C] a unit for measuring electrical RESISTANCE

o·ho /əʊˈhəʊ $ oʊˈhoʊ/ *interjection old-fashioned* used to show that you are surprised or happy about something

OHP /ˌəʊ eɪtʃ ˈpiː $ ˌoʊ-/ *n* [C] *BrE* the abbreviation of ***overhead projector***

oi /ɔɪ/ *interjection BrE spoken* used to call someone or attract their attention in a way that is not very polite: *Oi, you, come over here a minute!*

oik /ɔɪk/ *n* [C] *BrE informal not polite* an offensive word for someone who you think is not intelligent or well educated, and who speaks or behaves in a rough way —**oikish** *adj*

oil[1] /ɔɪl/ ●●● S2 W1 *n*

1 NATURAL SUBSTANCE UNDER THE GROUND [U] the thick dark liquid from under the ground from which petrol is produced → **crude**: *a rise in the price of oil* | *the importance of protecting our oil supplies* | *an* ***oil refinery*** (=factory where oil is made purer)

2 FUEL [U] a smooth thick liquid that is used to make machines run easily or is burned to produce heat: *Check the oil level in your car every week.* | *The heating system runs on oil.*

3 LIQUID FROM PLANTS [C,U] a smooth thick liquid made from plants or some animals, used especially in cooking or for making beauty products: *cooking oil* | **olive/vegetable/sunflower etc oil** *coconut oil shampoo* | *Fish oils are supposed to help relieve arthritis.* → CASTOR OIL, COD-LIVER OIL, LINSEED OIL

4 PAINT **oils** [plural] paints that contain oil SYN **oil paints**: **in oils** *I usually paint in oils* (=using oils). → **burn the midnight oil** at BURN[1](20), → **pour oil on troubled waters** at POUR(8)

oil[2] *v* [T] **1** to put oil onto part of a machine or part of something that moves, to help it to move or work more smoothly: *The bicycle chain needs oiling.* **2** to put oil or cream onto your skin, for example to protect you from the sun: *I asked Simon to oil my back for me.* **3 oil the wheels** *BrE* to help something to be done in business or politics successfully and easily

ˈoil-based *adj* made with oil as the main substance: *oil-based paints*

ˈoil-ˌbearing *adj* oil-bearing rock contains oil

oil·can /ˈɔɪlkæn/ *n* [C] *BrE* a metal container for oil with a long thin tube for pouring the oil out

oil·cloth /ˈɔɪlklɒθ $ -klɒːθ/ *n* [U] special cloth that has had oil put on it so that it has a smooth surface and water cannot go through it → OILSKIN

oiled /ɔɪld/ *adj* covered with a layer of oil: *Place the sausages on an oiled baking tray.* → WELL-OILED

oil·field /ˈɔɪlfiːld/ *n* [C] an area of land or sea under which there is oil

ˈoil-fired *adj* an oil-fired heating system burns oil to produce heat

ˌoil-ˈfree *adj* an oil-free liquid, skin treatment etc contains no oil: *an oil-free sun lotion*

ˈoil lamp *n* [C] a lamp that works by burning oil → see picture at LAMP

oil·man /ˈɔɪlmæn/ *n* (*plural* **oilmen** /-men/) [C] someone who owns an oil company or works in the oil industry

ˈoil paint *n* [C,U] paint that contains oil

ˈoil ˌpainting *n* **1** [C] a picture painted with oil paint **2** [U] the art of painting with oil paint **3 he's/she's no oil painting** *BrE* used humorously to say that someone is not very attractive

ˈoil pan *n* [C] *AmE* a part of an engine that contains the supply of oil SYN **sump** *BrE*

ˌoil-ˈrich *adj* [only before noun] *BrE* an oil-rich country has plenty of natural oil under the ground from which it is able to make a lot of money: *the oil-rich Gulf States*

ˈoil rig (*also* **ˈoil ˌplatform**) *n* [C] a large structure on the land or in the sea, which has equipment for getting oil from under the ground

oil·seed rape /ˌɔɪlsiːd ˈreɪp/ *n* [U] RAPE[2](3)

oil·skin /ˈɔɪl-skɪn/ *n* **1** [U] special cloth that has had oil put on it so that it has a smooth surface and water cannot go through it: **oilskin coat/jacket/trousers etc** **2 oilskins** [plural] a coat and trousers made of oilskin and worn together **3** [C] a coat made of oilskin → OILCLOTH

ˈoil slick *n* [C] a large area of oil floating on the surface of the sea or a river SYN **slick**

ˈoil ˌtanker *n* [C] a large ship that carries oil

ˈoil well *n* [C] a hole that is dug in the ground so that oil can be taken out

oil·y /ˈɔɪli/ *adj* **1** covered with oil: *He wiped his hands on an oily rag.* **2** similar to oil: *an oily liquid* **3** oily hair or skin contains more natural oil than is usual or desirable SYN **greasy**: *a shampoo for oily hair* **4** oily food contains a lot of oil or fat: *oily fish* **5** someone who is oily is very polite, in a way that other people think is unpleasant and not sincere —**oiliness** *n* [U]

oink /ɔɪŋk/ *interjection* used to represent the sound that a pig makes —**oink** *n* [C]

oint·ment /ˈɔɪntmənt/ *n* [C,U] a soft cream that you rub into your skin, especially as a medical treatment → **fly in the ointment** at FLY[2](5)

OJ /ˈəʊ dʒeɪ $ ˈoʊ-/ *n* [C,U] *AmE spoken* orange juice

Frequencies of the word **okay** in spoken and written English.

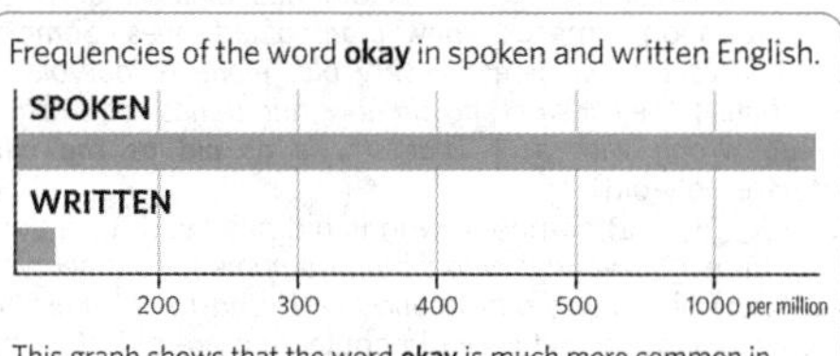

This graph shows that the word **okay** is much more common in spoken English than in written English.

OK[1], **okay** /ˌəʊ ˈkeɪ $ ˌoʊ-/ ●●● S1 *interjection*

1 used to show that you agree with something or give permission for someone to do something: *'Can I take the car today?' 'Okay.'* | *OK, if that's what you prefer.*

2 used to ask someone if they agree with you or will give permission for you to do something: *I'll see you at seven, OK?*

3 used when you start talking about something new, or when you pause before continuing: *OK, let's move on to the next point.* | *Okay, any questions so far?*

4 used to tell someone to stop arguing with you or criticizing you: *OK, OK, so I made a mistake.* | *Look, I'm doing my best, okay?*

OK[2], **okay** ●●● S1 *adj, adv spoken*

1 [not before noun] if you are OK, you are not ill, injured, or unhappy SYN **all right**: *Are you OK?* | *Do you* ***feel OK*** *now?* | *Mum's* ***doing OK*** *now.*

2 [not before noun] something that is OK is acceptable and will not cause any problems SYN **all right**: *Will half past eight be OK?* | *Does my hair look OK?* | **that's/it's OK** *'Sorry I'm late.' 'That's OK.'* | ***Is it OK if*** *I leave my bags here?* | *Yeah, the TV's working OK.* | **it is okay (for sb) to do sth** *It's okay for you to go home now.* | **it is okay with/by sb** *I'll pay you the rest tomorrow, if that's OK with you.*

> **REGISTER**
> People usually avoid **OK** or **okay** in writing, and use more formal words such as **acceptable** or **satisfactory**: *We have to make sure that the quality is* ***acceptable***.

3 [not before noun] satisfactory but not extremely good: *'How was the film?' 'It was okay, but not brilliant.'* | *I think I* ***did okay*** *in the exam.*

4 someone who is OK is nice, pleasant etc: *I've met Jim once, and he seems OK.* | *He's an OK guy.*

OK[3], **okay** *v* (*past tense and past participle* **OK'd**, *present participle* **OK'ing**, *third person singular* **OK's** *or* **okayed, okaying, okays**) [T] *informal* to say officially that you will agree to something or allow it to happen: *The plans have been okayed, so let's get started as soon as possible.*

OK[4], **okay** *n* **give (sb) the OK/get the OK** *informal* to give or get permission to do something: *Did you get the OK from head office?*

o·ka·pi /əʊˈkɑːpi $ oʊ-/ *n* (*plural* **okapi** *or* **okapis**) [C] an African animal like a GIRAFFE, but with a shorter neck

OK Cor·ral, the /ˌəʊ keɪ kəˈrɑːl $ -ˈræl/ a CORRAL (=an area surrounded by fences where animals can be kept) in the town of Tombstone, Arizona. In 1881 it was the scene of a famous gunfight in which Wyatt Earp, his brothers, and Doc Holliday fought against a group of criminals called the Clanton gang. The story was made into a well-known film *Gunfight at the OK Corral* (1957), and this phrase is sometimes used humorously when talking about a fight involving several people: *It was more like the gunfight at the OK Corral than a football game.*

O

o·key-doke /ˌəʊki ˈdəʊk $ ˌoʊki ˈdoʊk/ (*also* **okey-do·key** /-ˈdəʊki $ -ˈdoʊki/) *interjection* used to show that you agree with someone or give permission for someone to do something

o·kra /ˈɒkrə, ˈəʊ- $ ˈoʊ-/ *n* [U] a green vegetable used in cooking, especially in Asia and the southern US → see picture at VEGETABLE[1]

old /əʊld $ oʊld/ ●●● S1 W1 *adj* (*comparative* **older**, *superlative* **oldest**)

1 NOT NEW something that is old has existed or been used for a long time OPP **new**: *a pair of old shoes | Some of the houses around here are very old.* | *one of our oldest traditions | The car's* ***getting old*** *now, and things are starting to go wrong with it.* | *That story's* ***as old as the hills*** (=extremely old).

2 NOT YOUNG **a)** someone who is old has lived for a very long time OPP **young**: *an old man | a home for old people |* **get/grow old** *I can't run around like I used to – I must be getting old.* **b) the old** [plural] people who are old: *the care of the old and sick*

3 AGE used to talk about how long a person or thing has lived or existed: **five/ten/fifty etc years old** *I can't believe you're nearly forty years old! | a house that's 300 years old |* ***How old*** *are you? | Are you* ***older than*** *Sally? | You're* ***old enough*** *to get your own breakfast now.* | *I'm not coming skating. I'm* ***too old for*** *that now.* | **five-year-old/ten-year-old etc sb/sth** *a six-week-old baby | a 500-year-old sword* | **sb is old enough to know better** (=used to say that you think someone should behave more sensibly) | **sb is old enough to be his/her/your mother/father** (=used to say that someone is too old to be having a sexual relationship with someone else)

4 THAT YOU USED TO HAVE [only before noun] your old house, job, girlfriend etc is one that you used to have SYN **former**: *I met up with one of my old girlfriends at the weekend.* | *My old car was always breaking down.* | *That happened when we were still in the old house. | My old boss was awful!* | **old flame** (=someone with whom you used to have a romantic relationship) THESAURUS ▸ LAST

5 FAMILIAR [only before noun] old things are things that are familiar to you because you have seen them or experienced them many times before: *It's good to get back into the old routine.* | *I enjoyed seeing all the old familiar faces. | He comes out with* ***the same old*** *excuses every time!* → **it's the same old story** at STORY(9)

6 VERY WELL KNOWN [only before noun] an old friend, enemy etc is someone you have known for a long time: *Bob's an* ***old friend*** *of mine.* | *an old colleague | They're old rivals.*

7 the old days times in the past: **in the old days** *In the old days people used to fetch water from the pump.*

8 the good old days/the bad old days an earlier time in your life, or in history, when things seemed better or worse than now: *We like to chat about the good old days.*

9 be/feel/look like your old self to feel or look better again after you have been ill or very unhappy: *It's good to see you looking more like your old self again.*

10 any old thing/place/time etc *spoken* used to say that it does not matter which thing, place etc you choose: *Oh, just wear any old thing.* | *Phone any old time – I'm always here.*

11 any old how/way *spoken* in an untidy or careless way: *The papers had been dumped on my desk any old how.*

12 good/poor/silly old etc sb *spoken* used to talk about someone you like: *Good old Keith! | You poor old thing!*

13 a good old sth (*also* **a right old sth** *BrE*) *spoken* used to talk about something you enjoy: *We had a good old talk.*

14 old devil/rascal etc *spoken* used to talk about someone you like and admire: *You old devil! You were planning this all along!*

15 old fool/bastard/bat etc *spoken not polite* used to talk very rudely about someone you do not like: *the stupid old cow*

16 the old guard a group of people within an organization or club who do not like changes or new ideas: *He'll never manage to persuade the old guard.*

17 be an old hand (at sth) to have a lot of experience of something: *I'm an old hand at this game.*

18 be old before your time to look or behave like someone much older than you, especially because of difficulties in your life

19 for old times' sake if you do something for old times' sake, you do it to remind yourself of a happy time in the past

20 the old country *especially AmE* the country that you were born in, but that you no longer live in, used especially to mean Europe

21 an old head on young shoulders *BrE* a young person who seems to think and behave like an older person

22 pay/settle an old score to punish someone for something wrong that they did to you in the past

23 of/from the old school old-fashioned and believing in old ideas and customs: *a doctor of the old school*

24 old wives' tale a belief based on old ideas that are now considered to be untrue

25 of old *literary* from a long time ago in the past: *the knights of old*

26 Old English/Old Icelandic etc an early form of English, Icelandic etc

GRAMMAR: Order of adjectives

If there is more than one adjective, the adjectives are usually used in a fixed order.
You say: *There are some nice old houses.* ✗ Don't say: *There are some old nice houses.*
You say: *She was dressed in old black clothes.* ✗ Don't say: *She was dressed in black old clothes.*
GRAMMAR GUIDE ▸ ADJECTIVES

THESAURUS

PERSON

old having lived for a long time: *an old man | I'm too old to learn a new language.*
elderly a polite word for old: *an elderly lady | a home for* ***the elderly*** (=elderly people)
aging (*also* **ageing** *BrE*) [only before noun] becoming old: *an ageing rock star | the problems of an ageing population*
aged /ˈeɪdʒəd/ [only before noun] *written* aged relatives are very old: *aged parents | She had to look after her aged aunt.*
elder brother/sister *especially BrE* [only before noun] an older brother or sister. **Elder** sounds more formal than **older**: *I have two elder brothers.*
ancient [not usually before noun] *informal* very old – used humorously: *I'll be 30 next year – it sounds really ancient!*
be getting on (in years) *informal* to be fairly old: *He's 60 now, so he's getting on a bit.*
be over the hill (*also* **be past it** *BrE*) *informal* to be too old to do something: *Everyone thinks you're past it when you get to 40.*
geriatric [only before noun] relating to medical care and treatment for old people: *a geriatric hospital | geriatric patients*

THING

old: *an old car | an old Chinese saying*
ancient very old – used about things that existed thousands of years ago, or things that look very old: *ancient civilisations | an ancient Rolls Royce*
antique antique furniture, clocks, jewellery etc are old and often valuable: *an antique writing desk*

age-old used about traditions, problems, or situations that have existed for a very long time: *the age-old tradition of morris dancing | the age-old prejudice against women in positions of power*

ˌold ˈage ●●○ *n* [U] the part of your life when you are old → **middle age**: *You need to start putting money away for your old age.* | **in (sb's) old age** *My mother had a very lively mind, even in her old age.*

ˌold age ˈpension *n* [C,U] *BrE* money that is paid regularly by the state to old people who do not work anymore SYN **social security** *AmE*

ˌold age ˈpensioner *n* [C] *BrE* (*abbreviation* **OAP**) someone who does not work anymore and who receives an old age pension

Old Bai·ley, the /ˌəʊld ˈbeɪli/ the most famous law court in the UK, officially called the Central Criminal Court. It is a CROWN COURT (=a court that deals with very serious crimes) in London, named after the street it is on. Many famous criminals have been judged there, including murderers and TRAITORS (=someone who helps an enemy country).

ˈold ˈboy *n* [C] **1** *BrE* a man who used to be a student at a school: *an old boys' reunion* **2 the old-boy network** the system by which men who went to the same school, belong to the same club etc use their influence to help each other **3** *BrE spoken* an old man: *He's a nice old boy.* **4** *BrE old-fashioned* used when speaking to a male friend: *How are you, old boy?* → OLD GIRL

old·e /ˈəʊldi $ ˈoʊldi/ *adj* an old-fashioned spelling of 'old', used in the names of shops, products etc to make them seem traditional and attractive: ***ye olde** tea shop*

ˌold eˈconomy (*also* **the Old Economy**) *n* [singular] an economic system that is based on older types of industry such as steel, energy, and machinery: *Is the Old Economy really dead?* —**old economy** *adj* [only before noun]: *old economy practices*

old·en /ˈəʊldən $ ˈoʊld-/ *adj* **in (the) olden days** (*also* **in olden times**) a long time ago: *People didn't travel so much in the olden days.*

ˌOld English ˈsheepdog *n* [C] a large dog with long thick grey and white hair

ˌold-esˈtablished *adj* [only before noun] having existed, been in business etc for a long time: *old-established merchant banks*

Old E·to·ni·an /ˌəʊld iːˈtəʊniən/ *n* [C] *BrE* a man who attended Eton College (=a famous and expensive private school in England), usually someone from the highest class in British society

olde-world·e /ˌəʊldi ˈwɜːldi◂ $ ˌoʊldi ˈwɜːr-/ *adj BrE informal* a place that is olde-worlde has been decorated so that it looks old-fashioned: *an olde-worlde pub*

ˌold-ˈfashioned ●●● W2 *adj*
1 not considered to be modern or fashionable anymore OPP **fashionable**: *She wears really old-fashioned clothes! | old-fashioned farming methods | The idea seems rather old-fashioned now.*
2 someone who is old-fashioned has ideas, attitudes etc that were more usual in the past than now SYN **conservative**: *He's very old-fashioned when it comes to music.*

THESAURUS

old-fashioned not considered modern or fashionable – used about styles of clothes, furniture etc, or about words and ideas: *The room was full of big old-fashioned furniture.* | *I can't wear that dress – it's too old-fashioned.*
out-of-date not containing the most recent information and therefore not useful: *This guidebook is completely out-of-date.*
outdated used about machines, equipment, or methods that are old-fashioned and have been replaced by better, more recent ones: *In today's world, technology rapidly becomes outdated.*
dated used about styles etc that were fashionable until recently but now look old-fashioned: *The pictures in this book already look a bit dated.*
unfashionable not fashionable and not popular with people anymore: *They lived in an unfashionable part of London.* | *The word 'patriotic' has become rather unfashionable these days.*
obsolete old-fashioned – used about machines and equipment that are no longer being produced because better ones have been invented: *These days, you buy a computer and it's almost immediately obsolete.*
antiquated *formal* old and not suitable for modern needs and conditions: *antiquated ideas about the constitution* | *an antiquated central heating system*

old fo·gey /ˌəʊld ˈfəʊgi $ ˌoʊld ˈfoʊ-/ *n* [C] *informal* someone who is boring and has old-fashioned ideas about things, especially someone old

ˈold ˌfolk *BrE*, **ˈold ˌfolks** *especially AmE n* [plural] old people – an expression used when talking about old people in a kind way

ˌold ˈfolks' ˌhome *n* [C] *informal* a place where old people live and are looked after when they are unable to look after themselves SYN **old people's home**, **nursing home**

ˈold girl *n* [C] *BrE* **1** a woman who is a former student of a school: *an old girls' reunion* **2** *spoken* an old woman: *She's a nice old girl!* → OLD BOY

ˌOld ˈGlory *n* [U] *AmE informal* the flag of the US

ˈold-growth *adj* [only before noun] **old-growth forests/rainforest/timber etc** forests etc that have been growing in a place for a long time, rather than ones planted more recently

ˌold ˈhat *adj* [not before noun] if something is old hat, a lot of people have said or done the same thing before and it is therefore not new or interesting: *Most of this is probably old hat to you, isn't it?*

old·ie /ˈəʊldi $ ˈoʊldi/ *n* [C] *informal* someone or something that is old, especially an old film or song → GOLDEN OLDIE

old·ish /ˈəʊldɪʃ $ ˈoʊld-/ *adj* fairly old: *an oldish woman*

ˌold ˈlady *n* **sb's old lady** *old-fashioned informal* someone's wife, mother, or girlfriend: *Where's your old lady?*

ˌold ˈlag *n* [C] *BrE old-fashioned* someone who has been in prison many times

ˌold ˈmaid *n* [C] *old-fashioned not polite* an offensive word for a woman who has never married and is not young anymore SYN **spinster**

ˌold ˈman *n* [C] **1** *old-fashioned informal* someone's husband, father, or boyfriend: *I heard her old man beats her.* **2** *BrE old-fashioned* used when speaking to a male friend: *Could I have a word with you, old man?*

ˌold ˈmaster, **Old Master** *n* [C] a famous painter, especially from the 15th to 18th century, or a painting by one of these painters: *a priceless collection of old masters*

ˌold ˈmedia *n* [U] MEDIA such as newspapers, radio, and television that existed before the Internet

ˈold ˌmoney *n* [U] people who come from families that have had a lot of money for a long time, which gives them a high social position: *He invited both the smart set and Perth's old money.*

ˌOld ˈNick *n BrE old-fashioned* the Devil

ˌold ˈpeople's ˌhome *n* [C] *BrE* a place where old people live and are cared for when they are too old to live by themselves SYN **nursing home**

ˌold ˈsalt *n* [C] *old-fashioned* a SAILOR who has had a lot of experience of sailing

ˈold-school *adj* [only before noun] old-fashioned, or relating to ideas from the past: *He was one of the last old-school comics.*

ˌold school ˈtie *n* **the old school tie** *BrE* the situation that exists when people who went to the same private school use their influence to help each other get work or other advantages: *a system based on social class and the old school tie*

old·ster /ˈəʊldstə $ ˈoʊldstər/ *n* [C] *informal* an old person

ˈold-style *adj* [only before noun] similar to the type of something that existed in the past: *old-style communism*

ˌOld ˈTestament *n* **the Old Testament** the first part of the Christian Bible containing ancient Hebrew writings about the time before the birth of Christ → **New Testament**

ˈold-time *adj* [only before noun] typical of what used to exist, be done etc in the past: *old-time remedies*

ˌold ˈtimer *n* [C] **1** someone who has been doing a job or living in a place for a long time and knows a lot about it **2** *especially AmE* an old man

ˌold ˈwoman *n* [C] *BrE old-fashioned informal* **1 sb's old woman** someone's wife or mother **2** a man who pays too much attention to small unimportant details —**old womanish** *adj*

ˌOld ˈWorld *n* **the Old World** the eastern HEMISPHERE, especially Europe, Asia, and Africa → **New World**: *the civilizations of the Old World*

ˈold-world *adj* [only before noun] an old-world place or quality is attractive because it is old or reminds you of the past: *The town has retained much of its* ***old-world charm.***

ole /əʊl $ oʊl/ *adj* [only before noun] *written* used to represent the way some people say 'old': *my ole man*

o·le·ag·i·nous /ˌəʊliˈædʒɪnəs $ ˌoʊ-/ *adj technical* containing, producing, or like oil

o·le·an·der /ˌəʊliˈændə $ ˌoʊliˈændər/ *n* [C,U] a green bush with white, pink, or purple flowers

O lev·el /ˈəʊ ˌlevəl $ ˈoʊ-/ *n* [C,U] (***Ordinary level***) an examination in a range of subjects, formerly done by students in schools in England and Wales, usually at the age of 15 or 16. In 1988, O levels were replaced by GCSEs. → **GCSE, A Level**

ol·fac·to·ry /ɒlˈfæktəri $ ɑːl-, oʊl-/ *adj* [only before noun] *technical* connected with the sense of smell: *the olfactory cells in the nose*

ol·i·garch /ˈɒləgɑːk $ ˈɑːləgɑːrk/ *n* [C] a member of a small group of people who run a country or organization —**oligarchic** /ˌɒləˈgɑːkɪk◂ $ ˌɑːləˈgɑːr-/ *adj*

ol·i·gar·chy /ˈɒləgɑːki $ ˈɑːləgɑːrki/ *n* (*plural* **oligarchies**) **1** [C usually singular] a small group of people who run a country or organization, or a country that is run by a small group of people **2** [U] when a country or organization is run by a small group of people: *Eventually oligarchy took over from democracy.*

ol·i·gop·o·ly /ˌɒləˈgɒpəli $ ˌɑːləˈgɑː-/ *n* (*plural* **oligopolies**) [C] *technical* the control of all or most of a business activity by very few companies, so that other organizations cannot easily compete with them

ol·ive /ˈɒləv $ ˈɑː-/ ●●○ *n*
1 [C] a small bitter egg-shaped black or green fruit, used as food and for making oil
2 [C] (*also* **olive tree**) a tree that produces olives, grown especially in Mediterranean countries: *an* ***olive grove***
3 [U] (*also* **olive green**) a deep yellowish green colour
4 olive skin/complexion skin colour that is typical of people from countries such as Greece, Italy, or Turkey
5 extend/offer/hold out etc an olive branch (to sb) to do or say something in order to show that you want to end an argument with someone —**olive** *adj*: *an olive sweatshirt*

ˌolive ˈoil ●●○ *n* [C,U] a pale yellow or green oil obtained from olives and used in cooking

ol·lie /ˈɒli $ ˈɑː-/ *n* [C] a movement in SKATEBOARDING or SNOWBOARDING in which you push down hard on the back of the board with your foot as you jump upwards and forwards, making the board rise and travel forwards through the air with you —**ollie** *v* [I]

-ologist /ɒlədʒɪst $ ɑːl-/ (*also* **-logist**) *suffix* [in nouns] a person who studies or has knowledge of a particular kind of science: *a biologist*

-ology /ɒlədʒi $ ɑːl-/ (*also* **-logy**) *suffix* [in nouns] **1** the study of something, especially something scientific: *geology* (=the study of rocks and the Earth) | *climatology* (=the study of climate) | *Egyptology* (=the study of ancient Egypt) **2** the things studied by a particular science: *The geology* (=structure of the rocks etc) *of north Devon is particularly interesting.* —**-ological** /əlɒdʒɪkəl $ -lɑː-/ *suffix* [in adjectives] —**-ologically** /əlɒdʒɪkli $ əlɑː-/ *suffix* [in adverbs]: *geologically interesting*

O·lym·pi·ad /əˈlɪmpi-æd/ *n* [C] *formal* a particular occasion of the modern Olympic Games: *the 25th Olympiad*

O·lym·pi·an¹ /əˈlɪmpiən/ *adj* [only before noun] **1** like a god, especially by being calm and not concerned about ordinary things: *He viewed the world with Olympian detachment.* **2** relating to the ancient Greek gods: *Olympian mythology*

Olympian² *n* [C] someone who is taking part in, or who has taken part in, the Olympic Games – used especially in news reports: *the American Olympians*

O·lym·pic /əˈlɪmpɪk/ *adj* [only before noun] relating to the Olympic Games: *an Olympic gold medal*

OˌIympic ˈGames, the (*also* **Olympics, the** [plural]) an international sports event held every four years in different countries: *the 1976 Olympic Games*

OM /ˌəʊ ˈem $ ˌoʊ-/ *n* [C] (***Order of Merit***) a special HONOUR given to someone by the Queen of England

om·bré /ˈɒmbreɪ $ ˈɑːm-/ *adj* ombré clothing or hair has the top part a different colour from the bottom part, with a gradual change between the colours

om·buds·man /ˈɒmbʊdzmən $ ˈɑːm-/ *n* (*plural* **ombudsmen** /-mən/) [C] someone who deals with complaints made by ordinary people against the government, banks, insurance companies etc

o·me·ga /ˈəʊməgə $ oʊˈmegə, -ˈmiː-, -ˈmeɪ-/ *n* the last letter of the Greek alphabet

ome·lette (*also* **omelet** *AmE*) /ˈɒmlət $ ˈɑːm-/ *n* [C] **1** eggs mixed together and cooked in hot fat, sometimes with other foods added: *a cheese omelette* **2 you can't make an omelette without breaking eggs** used to say that it is impossible to achieve anything important without causing a few problems

o·men /ˈəʊmən $ ˈoʊ-/ *n* [C] a sign of what will happen in the future: *The car won't start. Do you think it's an omen?* | **a good/bad/ill omen** *The mist seemed like a bad omen and Sara's heart sank a little.* | **[+of]** *He will regard your presence as an omen of good fortune.* | **[+for]** *It's a good omen for the future.*

-ometer /ɒmɪtə $ ɑːmɪtər/ *suffix* [in nouns] an instrument for measuring something: *a speedometer*

OMG the written abbreviation of ***Oh my God*** – used especially in emails and on the Internet to express admiration, surprise, or shock

om·i·nous /ˈɒmɪnəs $ ˈɑː-/ *adj* making you feel that something bad is going to happen: *'How long will she be ill?' he asked. There was an* ***ominous silence.*** | *The car is making an ominous rattling sound.* —**ominously** *adv*: *The sky looked ominously dark.*

o·mis·sion /əʊˈmɪʃən, ə- $ oʊ-, ə-/ ●○○ *n*
1 [U] when you do not include or do not do something: **[+of]** *The omission of her name was not a deliberate act.* | **[+from]** *his omission from the team*
2 [C] something that has been omitted: *Copies of the lists were posted so that omissions could be corrected.* | **serious/notable/major omission** *Your failing to note her mistakes is a serious omission.* | **a glaring omission** (=one that is very bad and easily noticed)

o·mit /əʊˈmɪt, ə- $ oʊ-, ə-/ ●●○ *v* (**omitted, omitting**) [T]
1 to not include someone or something, either deliberately or because you forget to do it SYN **leave out**: *Please*

don't omit any details, no matter how trivial they may seem. | **omit sth from sth** *Lisa's name had been omitted from the list of honor students.*

REGISTER
In everyday English, people usually say **leave out** rather than **omit**: *Please don't **leave out** any details, no matter how trivial they may seem.*

2 omit to do sth *formal* to not do something, either because you forgot or because you deliberately didn't do it: **omit to mention/say/tell etc** *Oliver omitted to mention that he was married.*

omni- /ɒmnɪ $ ɑːm-/ *prefix* [in nouns and adjectives] everything or everywhere → **all**: *an omnivore* (=an animal that eats all kinds of food)

om·ni·bus¹ /ˈɒmnɪbəs, -bʌs $ ˈɑːm-/ *n* [C] **1** *BrE* a radio or television programme consisting of several programmes that have previously been broadcast separately: *the Saturday **omnibus edition** of 'Brookside'* **2** a book containing several stories, especially by one writer, that have already been printed separately: ***Omnibus editions** of novels tend to be too heavy to be read with comfort.* **3** *BrE old-fashioned* a bus

omnibus² *adj* [only before noun] *AmE* an omnibus law contains several different laws collected together: *an omnibus civil rights bill*

om·nip·o·tent /ɒmˈnɪpətənt $ ɑːm-/ *adj formal* able to do everything SYN **all-powerful** —**omnipotence** *n* [U]

om·ni·pres·ent /ˌɒmnɪˈprezənt◂ $ ˌɑːm-/ *adj formal* present everywhere at all times —**omnipresence** *n* [U]: *the omnipresence of God*

om·nis·cient /ɒmˈnɪsiənt, -ˈnɪʃənt $ ɑːmˈnɪʃənt/ *adj formal* knowing everything: *the book's omniscient narrator* —**omniscience** *n* [U]

om·ni·sham·bles /ˈɒmniʃæmbəlz $ ˈɑːm-/ *n* [singular] *BrE informal* a situation that is bad in every way, or a number of bad situations, which is the result of someone's inability to do their job well, especially in government

om·ni·vore /ˈɒmnəvɔː $ ˈɑːmnəvɔːr/ *n* [C] an animal that eats both meat and plants → **carnivore**, **herbivore**

om·niv·o·rous /ɒmˈnɪvərəs $ ɑːm-/ *adj* **1** an animal that is omnivorous eats both meat and plants → **carnivorous**, **herbivorous** **2** *formal* interested in everything, especially in all books: *an **omnivorous reader***

on¹ /ɒn $ ɑːn, ɒːn/ ●●● S1 W1 *prep*

1 ON A SURFACE a) touching a surface or being supported by a surface: *Leave your things on the table over there.* | *People were sunbathing on the grass.* | *The little girl was sitting on her father's shoulders.* **b)** used to say that someone or something moves so that they are then touching or supported by a surface: *snow falling on the mountainsides* | *He threw himself on the bed.*

2 SUPPORTING YOUR BODY used to say what part of someone's body is touching the ground or another surface and supporting their weight: *She was on her feet in no time.* | *He was on his hands and knees searching for something.* | *Can you stand on your head?*

3 PART HIT/TOUCHED used to say what part of someone or something is hit or touched: *I wanted to punch him on the nose.* | *Matt kissed her on the cheek.*

4 WRITTEN/SHOWN used to say where something is written or shown: *There's a diagram on page 25.* | *He wrote his phone number on a piece of paper.*

5 ATTACHED attached to or hanging from something: *She hung her coat on a hook.* | *Dogs must be kept on a lead at all times.*

6 PLACE in a particular place: *The town is right on the border.* | *Is there a water supply on the island?* | *He grew up on a ranch in California.* | *a store on Fifth Avenue*

7 POSITION in a particular position in relation to something else: *You'll see the school on your left.* | *They live on the opposite side of the town.*

8 LOOKING/POINTING looking or pointing towards something or someone: *His eyes were on the stranger standing in the doorway.* | *She trained her binoculars on the house.*

9 DAY/DATE during a particular day: *They'll be here on Tuesday.* | *I was born on July 1st.* | *We'll see you on Christmas Eve.*

GRAMMAR
Don't use **on** before 'this', 'last', or 'next' and a day of the week. You say: *Term starts this Monday.*| *It was my birthday last Friday.* ✗ Don't say: *on this Monday* | *on last Friday*

10 AFFECTING/RELATING TO affecting or relating to someone or something: *a tax on cigarettes* | *his influence on young people* | *There will be new restrictions on the sale of weapons.* | *What effect will these changes have on the tourist industry?*

11 ABOUT about a particular subject: *Do you have any books on India?* | *You can get information on local services by calling this number.* | *an international conference on global warming* **THESAURUS** ▶ **ABOUT**

12 ORDERS/ADVICE as a result of someone's order, request, or advice: *He was killed on the King's orders.* | *I accepted the offer on the advice of my lawyer.*

13 EAT/DRINK used to talk about what someone usually eats or drinks: *They live mainly on beans, lentils, and rice.* | *Is your baby on solid food yet?*

14 TRANSPORT a) in or into a bus, train, plane etc OPP **off**: *Did you manage to sleep on the plane?* | *Tommy should be on the six o'clock train.* | *She got on the first bus that came along.* **b)** riding something: *a statue of the King on horseback* | *I'll probably come on my bike.*

15 MONEY receiving money for a job or as a regular payment: *He's on quite a good salary now.* | *She must be on at least £50,000 a year.* | *the difficulties faced by families on low incomes*

16 FUEL using a particular type of FUEL or power: *Most buses run on diesel.* | *Does it work on mains electricity?*

17 MEDICINE/DRUGS taking a particular drug or medicine regularly OPP **off**: *Are you still on antibiotics?* | *The doctor put her on Prozac.* | *A lot of these kids are on heroin by the age of 12.*

18 what's sb on? *spoken* used to say that someone is behaving in a very strange way, as if they are taking an illegal drug

19 USING EQUIPMENT using a machine or piece of equipment: *He's been on the computer all afternoon.* | *Is Rachel still on the phone?*

20 MUSICAL INSTRUMENTS playing a musical instrument: *He played a short piece on the piano.* | *The album features Rick Wakeman on keyboards.*

21 RADIO/TELEVISION being broadcast by radio or television: *What's on TV tonight?* | *Did you hear that programme on the radio last night?*

22 RECORDED used to say in what form information is stored or music, films etc are recorded: *The movie is now available on video and DVD.* | *I always keep a backup copy on disk.*

23 ACTIVITY/JOURNEY taking part in an activity or travelling somewhere: *She's on a course all this week.* | *I met him on vacation in Canada.* | *My girlfriend is often away on business trips.*

24 INCLUDED included in a group or team of people or in a list: *Are you still on the management committee?* | *Mr Edwards is no longer on the staff here.* | *Whose team are you on?* | *There was no steak on the menu.* | *What's the next item on the agenda?*

25 WHEN STH HAPPENS *formal* as soon as someone has done something or as soon as something has happened: *Couples are presented with a bottle of wine on their arrival at the hotel.* | *All patients are examined on admission to the hospital.* | **on doing sth** *What was your reaction on seeing him?*

26 COMPARED WITH STH compared with another person or thing: *This essay is a definite improvement on your last one.* | *Sales are 10% up on last year.*

27 CARRYING STH *informal* if you have something on you,

you have it in your pocket, your bag etc: *I don't have any money on me.*
28 PAY **be on sb** *spoken* used to say who is going to pay for something: *The drinks are on me!* | *Each table will get a bottle of champagne* ***on the house*** (=paid for by the restaurant, hotel etc).
29 TELEPHONE NUMBER used to say what number you should use in order to telephone someone SYN **at** *AmE*: *You can contact me on this number.*
30 CAUSING SB PROBLEMS used when something bad happens to you, for example when something you are using suddenly stops working, or someone you have a relationship with suddenly leaves you: *Suddenly the telephone went dead on me.* | *Dorothy's first husband walked out on her.*

O

on² ●●● S1 W1 *adj, adv* [not before noun]
1 CONTINUING used to say that someone continues to do something or something continues to happen, without stopping: *We decided to play on even though it was snowing.* | *He went* ***on and on*** (=talked for a very long time) *about his job all evening.*
2 FURTHER if you move, walk etc on, you move forward or further towards something: *If you walk on a little, you can see the coast.* | *We drove on towards Manchester.*
3 LATER later than or after a particular time: *Now, 40 years on, this is one of the most successful theatres in the country.* | *From that moment on I never believed a word she said.*
4 WEARING STH if you have something on, you are wearing it: *All he* ***had on*** *was a pair of tattered shorts.* | ***Put*** *your coat* ***on****. It's freezing outside.*
5 ATTACHED used to say that something is attached to something else, especially when it is in the correct position OPP **off**: *Is the cover on properly?* | *Remember to put the lid back on.*
6 WRITTEN used to say that something is written somewhere: *He was wearing a badge with his name on.*
7 TRANSPORT in or into a bus, train etc OPP **off**: *The train stopped and two people got on.*
8 LIGHT/MACHINE if a machine, light etc is on, it is operating OPP **off**: *Who left all the lights on?* | *The TV's on, but nobody seems to be watching it.* | *He sat down at the desk and switched on the computer.*
9 BEING BROADCAST if a radio or television programme etc is on, it is being broadcast: *What time is 'Star Trek' on?*
10 EVENTS if an event is on, it has been arranged and is happening or will happen OPP **off**: *The transport union has confirmed that the strike is definitely on.* | *I'd avoid the city centre – there's some kind of procession on.* | *Is the party still on tonight or have they cancelled it?*
11 PERFORMING/SPEAKING performing or speaking in public: *You're on in two minutes.*
12 WORKING if you are on at a particular time, you are doing your job at that time: *I'm not on again until two o'clock tomorrow.*
13 have sth on *informal* if you have something on, there is something that you must do: *I haven't got anything on tomorrow, so I could see you then.* | *We've got a lot on at the moment.*
14 on and off (*also* **off and on**) for short periods but not regularly over a long period of time: *He's been smoking for ten years now, on and off.*
15 be/go/keep on at sb *informal* to keep complaining to someone or asking someone to do something, especially when this annoys them: *I've been on at him to fix that cupboard for weeks now.* | *I wish you wouldn't go on at me the whole time!*
16 be/go/keep on about sth *BrE informal* to keep talking about something, in a way that is boring or annoying: *He's always going on about money.* | *I don't know what you're on about!*
17 be not on *BrE spoken* if something is not on, it is not acceptable or reasonable: *I'm sorry, what you're suggesting is just not on!*
18 be on for sth *spoken* to be ready or willing to do something that someone has suggested: *Right, how many of you are on for a drink after work?*
19 you're on *spoken* used to tell someone that you accept a BET or an invitation to compete against them: *'I bet you £20 he won't turn up.' 'You're on!'* → ONTO

ˈon-air *adj* [only before noun] broadcast while actually happening OPP **off-air**: *an on-air interview*

ˈon-board *adj* [only before noun] carried on a ship, plane, car etc: *an on-board computer*

once¹ /wʌns/ ●●● S1 W1 *adv*
1 on one occasion only: *I've only met her once.* | *Paul's been to Wexford* ***once before****.* | **(just) the once** *BrE spoken*: *Mrs Peterson came in to see Ruth just the once.*
2 once a week/once every three months etc one time every week etc, as a regular activity or event: *Staff meetings take place once a week.* | *They took separate holidays at least once every two years.*
3 at some time in the past, but not now: *Sonya and Ida had once been close friends.* | *She and her husband had once owned a house like this.* | **once-great/proud etc** *It was sad to see the once-great man looking so frail.* | *the once-mighty steel industry*
4 in the past, at a time that is not stated: *I once ran 21 miles.* | *Marx once described religion as the 'opium of the people'.*
5 at once a) immediately or without delay: *Now, go upstairs at once and clean your room!* | *When I saw him I recognized him at once.* **b)** together, at the same time: *I can't do two things at once!* | *Don't all talk at once.*

> **REGISTER**
> In everyday English, when people mean 'immediately', they usually say **right away** or, in British English, **straight away** rather than **at once**: *I recognized him* ***right away****.*

6 once more/once again a) again, after happening several times before: *I looked at myself in the mirror once more.* | *Once again she's refusing to help.* **b)** used to say that a situation changes back to its previous state: *The crowds had all gone home and the street was quiet once more.* **c)** *formal* used before you repeat something that you said before: *Once again, it must be stressed that the pilot was not to blame.*
7 all at once a) if something happens all at once, it happens suddenly when you are not expecting it: *All at once there was a loud banging on the door.* **b)** together, at the same time: *A lot of practical details needed to be attended to all at once.*
8 (every) once in a while sometimes, although not often: *I do get a little anxious once in a while.* | *I saw her in the shop every once in a while.*
9 never once/not once used to emphasize that something has never happened: *I never once saw him get angry or upset.* | *Not once did they finish a job properly.*
10 (just) for once used to say that something unusual happens, especially when you wish it would happen more often: *Be honest for once.* | *Just for once, let me make my own decision.* | *For once Colin was speechless.*
11 once and for all a) if you deal with something once and for all, you deal with it completely and finally: *Let's settle this matter once and for all.* **b)** *BrE spoken* used to emphasize your impatience when you ask or say something that you have asked or said many times before: *Once and for all, will you switch off that television!*
12 once or twice a few times: *I wrote to him once or twice, but he didn't answer.*
13 (just) this once *spoken* used to emphasize that this is the only time you are allowing something, asking for something etc, and it will not happen again: *Go on, lend me the car, just this once.* | *I'll make an exception this once.*
14 once upon a time a) *spoken* at a time in the past that you think was much better than now: *Once upon a time you used to be able to leave your front door unlocked.* **b)** a long time ago – used at the beginning of children's stories
15 once in a blue moon *informal* very rarely: *It only happens like this once in a blue moon.*
16 do sth once too often to repeat a bad, stupid, or dangerous action with the result that you get punished or cause

trouble for yourself: *He tried that trick once too often and in the end they caught him.*
17 once a ..., always a ... *spoken* used to say that people stay the same and cannot change the way they behave and think: *Once a thief, always a thief.*
18 once is/was enough *spoken* used to say that after you have done something one time you do not need or want to do it again
19 once bitten, twice shy used to say that people will not do something again if it has been a bad experience

once² ●●● S1 W1 *conjunction* from the time when something happens: *Once I get him a job, he'll be fine.* | *Once in bed, the children usually stay there.*

ˈonce-over *n* **give sth the/a once-over a)** to look at someone or something quickly to check what they are like **b)** to clean or tidy something quickly

on·col·o·gy /ɒŋˈkɒlədʒi $ ɑːŋˈkɑː-/ *n* [U] the part of medical science that deals with CANCER and TUMOURS —**oncologist** *n* [C]

on·com·ing /ˈɒnˌkʌmɪŋ $ ˈɑːn-, ˈɒːn-/ *adj* **oncoming car/traffic etc** a car etc that is coming towards you: *He crashed into an oncoming car.*

one¹ /wʌn/ ●●● S1 W1 *number*
1 the number 1: *They had one daughter.* | *one hundred and twenty-one pounds* | *Come back at one* (=one o'clock). | *Katie's almost one* (=one year old).
2 one or two a small number of people or things SYN **a few**: *There are one or two things to sort out before I leave.* | **[+of]** *One or two of us knew him quite well.*
3 in ones and twos *BrE* alone or in pairs, rather than in large numbers or groups: *Guests arrived in ones and twos.*

one² ●●● S1 W1 *pron* (*plural* **ones**)
1 used to mean someone or something of a type that has already been mentioned or is known about: *'Have you got a camera?' 'No.' 'You should buy one* (=buy a camera).*'* | *The train was crowded so we decided to catch a later one* (=catch a later train). | **the one(s) (that/who/which)** *The only jokes I tell are the ones that I hear from you.* | **this one/that one/these ones/those ones** *I like all the pictures except this one.*
2 used to refer to a member of a group or pair of people or things: *The children seemed upset. One was crying.* | *She has two daughters. One is a primary school teacher, the other is a musician.* | **[+of]** *One of the girls I work with is getting married.* | *This is one of my favourite books.*

GRAMMAR: Singular or plural verb?
Although **one of** is followed by a plural noun, you use a singular verb: ***One of*** *the windows* ***was*** *open.* | ***One of*** *them* ***has*** *gone.*

3 the one(s) who/that the person or people who: *I was the one who had been attacked, not Richard.* | ***The only ones*** *who will benefit are the shareholders.*
4 one by one used when one person or thing in a group does something, then the next, then the next, especially in a regular way: *One by one each soldier approached the coffin and gave a final salute.*
5 one after another/one after the other if events happen one after the other, they happen without much time between them: *One after another, tropical storms battered the Pacific coastline.*
6 (all) in one if someone or something is many different things all in one, they are all those things: *It's a TV, radio, and VCR all in one.*
7 *formal* used to mean people in general, including yourself: *One can never be too careful.* | *Great pictures make one think.*

REGISTER
In everyday English, people usually use **you** rather than **one**: ***You*** *can never be too careful.*

8 I, for one, ... used to emphasize that you believe something, will do something etc and hope others will do the same: *I, for one, am proud of the team's effort.*
9 ... for one used to give an example of someone or something: *There were several other people absent that afternoon, weren't there? Mr Ashton for one.*
10 be one up (on sb)/get one up on sb to have or get an advantage over someone → ONE-UPMANSHIP
11 put one over on sb *informal* to trick someone: *No one's going to put one over on me!*
12 be at one with sb/sth a) to feel very calm or relaxed in the situation or environment you are in: *She felt as she always did in these mountains: peaceful, without care,* ***at one with nature.*** **b)** *formal* to agree with someone about something: *He was at one with Wheatley on the need to abandon free trade.*
13 *informal* used in particular phrases to mean 'an alcoholic drink': *How about a* ***quick one*** *at the pub?* | **have had one too many** (=have drunk too much alcohol) | **(have) one for the road** (=have one last alcoholic drink before you leave a place)
14 the one about ... *spoken* a joke or humorous story: ***Have you heard the one about*** *the chicken who tried to cross the road?*
15 as one *written* if many people do something as one, they all do it at the same time: *The whole team stood up as one.*
16 a difficult/hard/good etc one a particular kind of problem, question, story etc: *'What do you attribute your long life to?' 'Oh that's a difficult one.'*
17 one and the same the same person or thing: *Muhammad Ali and Cassius Clay are one and the same.*
18 not/never be one to do sth *informal* to never do a particular thing, because it is not part of your character to do it: *Tom is not one to show his emotions.*
19 not/never be (a great) one for (doing) sth *informal* to not enjoy a particular activity, subject etc: *I've never been a great one for watersports.*
20 one of us *spoken* used to say that someone belongs to the same group as you, or has the same ideas, beliefs etc: *You can talk in front of Terry - he's one of us.*
21 one and all *old-fashioned or formal* everyone: *Apologies to one and all.*
22 got it in one! *BrE spoken* used to say that someone has correctly guessed or understood something immediately: *'You're not painting the house again are you?' 'Got it in one!'*
23 little/young ones *spoken* used by some people to mean 'children', especially young children: *She's got four little ones.*
24 you are/he is a one *BrE old-fashioned* used to say that someone's behaviour is amusing, strange, or surprising: *You are a one!* → ONE-TO-ONE

one³ ●●● S1 W1 *determiner*
1 used to emphasize a particular person or thing: *One person I find very difficult is Bob.* | *If there's one thing I can't stand, it's people who bite their nails.*
2 one day/morning/year etc a) on a particular day, morning etc in the past: *One morning I was sitting at my desk when a policeman knocked at my door.* **b)** used to talk about a day, morning etc in the future which is not yet exactly known or decided: *We should go out for a drink one evening.* | *One day she hopes to move to the South Coast.*
3 used to talk about a particular person or thing in comparison with other similar people or things: *Why does my card work in* ***one*** *cash machine and not in* ***another****?*
4 it's one thing to ... it's (quite) another to used to say that the second thing mentioned is very different from the first, and is often much more difficult to do: *It's one thing to say we have a goal; it's another to actually act on it.*
5 for one thing used to introduce a reason for what you have just said: *He couldn't bring himself to say what he thought.* ***For one thing,*** *she seldom stopped to listen.* ***For another,*** *he doubted that he could make himself clear.*
6 be one crazy woman/be one interesting job etc *AmE spoken* to be a very crazy woman, be a very interesting job etc: *You're one lucky guy.*
7 *formal* used before the name of someone you do not know or have not heard of before SYN **a certain**: *He was accused of stealing a horse from one Peter Wright.*

O

one[4] ●●● S3 W3 *adj* [only before noun]
1 only: *Her one concern was to get to the door without being seen.* | *Claire is the one person I can trust.*
2 one and only a) used to emphasize that someone is very famous: ***the one and only*** *Frank Sinatra* **b)** used to emphasize that something is the only one of its kind: *I even tried my one and only French joke on them.*

one[5] *n* [C usually plural] *AmE* a piece of paper money worth one dollar: *I don't have any ones.*

ˌone anˈother ●●○ S3 W3 *pron* each other: *Liz and I have known one another for years.* | *They often stay at one another's houses.*

ˌone-armed ˈbandit *n* [C] a machine with a long handle, into which you put money in order to try to win more money SYN **slot machine**, **fruit machine** *BrE*

ˌone-diˈmensional *adj* simple and not considering or showing all the parts of something – used to show disapproval: *the novel's one-dimensional characters*

ˈone-horse *adj* **1 one-horse town** *informal* a small and boring town **2 one-horse race** a race, competition etc which a particular person or thing looks likely to win easily

ˌone-ˈliner *n* [C] a very short joke or humorous remark

ˈone-man *adj* [only before noun] performed, operated, controlled etc by one person: *He does a* ***one-man show*** *in Las Vegas.* | *a one-man business*

ˌone-man ˈband *n* [C] **1** *informal* an organization or activity in which one person does everything: *The company is really a one-man band.* **2** a street musician who plays several instruments at the same time

one·ness /ˈwʌnnəs/ *n* [U] a peaceful feeling of being part of a whole: **[+with]** *a sense of oneness with nature*

ˌone-night ˈstand *n* [C] **1** *informal* **a)** an occasion when two people have sex, but do not meet each other again: *I'm not into one-night stands.* **b)** a person that you have sex with once and do not see again **2** a performance of music or a play that is given only once in a particular place

ˈone-off[1] *adj* [only before noun] *BrE* happening or done only once, not as part of a regular series SYN **one-shot** *AmE*: *It's yours for a* ***one-off payment*** *of only £200.*

ˌone-ˈoff[2] *n* [C] *BrE* **1** something that is done or made only once: *The deal was a one-off.* **2** *informal* someone who is completely different from anyone else

ˌone-on-ˈone *adj* between only two people: *Virtually all instruction is in small groups or one-on-one.* —**one-on-one** *adv*: *Often, the employer just called in the drivers and bargained with them directly, one-on-one.*

ˌone-parent ˈfamily *n* [C] a family in which there is only one parent who lives with the children SYN **single parent family**, **single-parent family**

ˈone-piece *adj* [only before noun] consisting of only one piece, not separate parts: *a one-piece bathing suit*

on·er·ous /ˈɒnərəs, ˈəʊ- $ ˈɑː-, ˈoʊ-/ *adj formal* work or a responsibility that is onerous is difficult and worrying or makes you tired → **burdensome**: *an* ***onerous task***

one·self /wʌnˈself/ ●○○ *pron formal* the REFLEXIVE form of ONE[3](2): *It is only through study that one really begins to know oneself.*

ˈone-shot *adj* [only before noun] *AmE* happening or done only once SYN **one-off** *BrE*: *This is a one-shot deal. If it doesn't work, it's over.*

ˌone-ˈsided *adj* **1** considering or showing only one side of a question, subject etc in a way that is unfair → **biased**, **balanced**: *The newspapers give a very one-sided account of the war.* **2** an activity or competition that is one-sided is one in which one person or side is much stronger or does much more than the other: *a very boring, one-sided game* | *The conversation was very one-sided.* —**one-sidedly** *adv* —**one-sidedness** *n* [U]

one·sie /ˈwʌnzi/ *n* [C] a comfortable piece of clothing that covers your body, arms, and legs

ˌone-size-fits-ˈall *adj* [only before noun] **1** a one-size-fits-all attitude, method, plan etc is designed to please everyone or be suitable for every situation, often with the result that it is not successful: *a one-size-fits-all public education program* **2** one-size-fits-all clothes are designed so that people of any size can wear them

ˈone-star *adj* [only before noun] a one-star hotel, restaurant etc has been judged to be not of a very high standard

ˈone-stop *adj* **one-stop shop/store etc** a shop where you can buy many different things

ˈone-time *adj* [only before noun] former: *Neil McMurtry, a one-time bus driver, is the lead singer.*

ˌone-to-ˈone *adj* **1** between only two people: *tuition on a one-to-one basis* **2** matching each other exactly: *a one-to-one correspondence between letters and sounds* —**one-to-one** *adv*: *I need to discuss it with him one-to-one.*

ˌone-track ˈmind *n* **have a one-track mind** to be continuously thinking about one particular thing, especially sex

ˌone-ˈtwo *n* [C] a movement in which a BOXER hits his opponent with one hand and then quickly with the other: *Ali* ***gives*** *his opponent* ***the old one-two****, and it's all over.*

one-up·man·ship /wʌnˈʌpmənʃɪp/ *n* [U] attempts to make yourself seem better than other people, no matter what they do

ˌone-ˈway *adj* [usually before noun] **1** a one-way street is one in which vehicles are only allowed to travel in one direction: *the town's* ***one-way system*** **2** *especially AmE* a one-way ticket is for travelling from one place to another but not back again OPP **round-trip** SYN **single** *BrE* **3** a one-way process, relationship etc is one in which only one person makes any effort or provides anything

ˌone-way ˈmirror *n* [C] a mirror which can be used as a window by people secretly watching from the other side of it

ˈone-woman *adj* [only before noun] performed, operated, controlled etc by only one woman: *a* ***one-woman show***

on·go·ing /ˈɒnˌɡəʊɪŋ $ ˈɑːnˌɡoʊɪŋ, ˈɒːn-/ ●●○ AWL *adj* continuing, or continuing to develop: *their ongoing search for a new director* | *ongoing negotiations* | *The discussions are still ongoing.* → **go on** at GO[1]

on·ion /ˈʌnjən/ ●●● S3 *n* [C,U] a round white vegetable with a brown, red, or white skin and many layers. Onions have a strong taste and smell: *Chop the onions finely.* | *red onions* | *home-made onion soup*

on·ion·skin /ˈʌnjənskɪn/ *n* [U] *AmE* very thin light paper, used in the past especially for writing letters

on·line /ˈɒnlaɪn $ ˈɑːn-, ˈɒːn-/ ●●● S2 W2 *adj*
1 connected to other computers through the Internet, or available through the Internet OPP **offline**: *All the city's schools will be online by the end of the year.*
2 directly connected to or controlled by a computer OPP **offline**: *an online printer* —**online** *adv*: *The reports are not available online yet.*

ˌonline ˈauction *n* [C] a type of website in which you can sell things to the person who offers you the highest price

ˌonline ˈbanking (*also* **Internet banking**) *n* [U] a service provided by banks so that people can find out information about their bank account, pay bills etc using the Internet

on·look·er /ˈɒnˌlʊkə $ ˈɑːn-, ˈɒːn-/ *n* [C] someone who watches something happening without being involved in it: *A crowd of onlookers had gathered at the scene of the accident.* → **look on** at LOOK[1]

on·ly[1] /ˈəʊnli $ ˈoʊn-/ ●●● S1 W1 *adv*
1 not more than a particular number, age etc: *Naomi was only 17 when she got married.* | *There are only a few cars on the island.* | *It's only eight o'clock.*
2 used to say that something or someone is not very important, serious etc: *It was only a joke.* | *It's an interesting job, but it's only temporary.* | *They're only small cuts, nothing life-threatening.*
3 nothing or no one except a particular person or thing: *Only the president can authorize a nuclear attack.* | *We use only the best ingredients.* | **women/men/residents etc only** *The car park is for staff only.*

4 used to say that something happens or is possible in one particular situation or place and no others, or for one particular reason: *I'll tell you, but **only if** you don't tell anyone else.* | *I ate the food, but **only because** I was starving.* | *The transfer takes place **only when** the data is complete.*

GRAMMAR: Word order

- **Only** usually comes between the subject and the main verb: *I **only** saw two people.*
- **Only** usually comes between an auxiliary verb and a main verb: *I can **only** see two people.*
- When you want to emphasize what you are saying, you sometimes use **only** at the beginning of a sentence, and put the auxiliary verb before the subject: ***Only** later **did** I understand what she meant.* | ***Only** by improving social and economic conditions **can** good health be achieved.*

5 no earlier than a particular time: **only yesterday/last week/recently** *'When did you email her?' 'Only yesterday.'* | **only then did/would/could etc sb do sth** (=at that moment and not before) *Only then did she tell him about the attack.*
6 only just *BrE* **a)** a very short time ago: *She's only just got up.* **b)** almost not SYN **barely**: *I only just finished my essay in time.*
7 can only hope/wait etc used to say that it is not possible to do more than hope etc: *We can only hope it won't rain on the day.*
8 I can only think/suppose/assume (that) *spoken* used when you are giving a reason for something, to say that you do not know something for certain but think that this is the only possible reason: *I can only assume that it was a mistake.*
9 I only wish/hope *spoken* used to express a strong wish or hope: *'What's happening?' 'I only wish I knew.'*
10 if only *spoken* used to express a strong wish: *If only he'd call!*
11 you'll only *spoken* used to tell someone that what they want to do will have a bad effect: *Don't interfere – you'll only make things worse.*
12 you only have to read/look at/listen to etc sth *spoken* used to say that it is easy to know that something is true because you can see or hear things that prove it: *You only have to look at the statistics to see that things are getting worse.*
13 only to used to say that someone did something, with a disappointing or surprising result: *I arrived only to find that the others had already left.*
14 only too very: *Prices have risen sharply, as we know only too well.* | *Mark was only too happy to agree with her.* → **not only ... but (also)** at NOT(4), → **only have eyes for sb** at EYE[1](32), → **for sb's eyes only** at EYE[1](25)

only² ●●● S1 W1 *adj* [only before noun]
1 used to say that there is one person, thing, or group in a particular situation and no others: *I was the only woman there.* | *He is our only child.* | *I was **the only one** who disagreed.* | *Cutting costs is the only solution.* | *She's the only person for this job.*
2 the only thing/problem is ... *spoken* used when you are going to mention a problem or disadvantage: *I could take you. The only thing is Dan might need the car.*
3 an only child a child who has no brothers or sisters → **the one and only** at ONE[4](2), → **(only) time will tell** at TIME[1](36)

only³ ●○○ *conjunction spoken* used like 'but' to give the reason why something is not possible SYN **except (that)**: *I'd offer to help, only I'm really busy just now.*

ˌon-ˈmessage *adj* [not before noun], *adv* a politician who is on-message says things that are in agreement with the ideas of his or her political party, especially when it appears that he or she is not thinking enough about these ideas OPP **off-message**

o.n.o. *BrE* (***or near/nearest offer***) used in advertisements to show that you are willing to sell something for slightly less money than you have said in the advertisement: *Bicycle for sale: £60 o.n.o.*

ˌon-ˈoff *adj* [only before noun] **1** happening sometimes and not at other times: *an on-off relationship* | *She had an on-off obsession with Mikey.* **2** an on-off switch is the thing you press to make a piece of electrical equipment start and stop working

on·o·mat·o·poe·ia /ˌɒnəmætəˈpiːə $ ˌɑːn-/ *n* [U] *technical* the use of words that sound like the thing that they are describing, for example 'hiss' or 'boom' —**onomatopoeic** *adj*

ˈon-ramp *n* [C] *AmE* a road for driving onto a FREEWAY SYN **slip road** *BrE*

on·rush /ˈɒnrʌʃ $ ˈɑːn-, ˈɒːn-/ *n* [singular] a strong fast movement forward, or the sudden development of something: **[+of]** *the first onrush of the epidemic* —**onrushing** *adj*: *the onrushing tide*

on-screen, **on·screen** /ˈɒnskriːn $ ˈɑːn-, ˈɒːn-/ *adj, adv* appearing on a computer screen, or on a television or cinema screen: *An on-screen tutorial is included in the price of the software.* | *onscreen violence*

on·set /ˈɒnset $ ˈɑːn-, ˈɒːn-/ ●○○ *n* **the onset of sth** the beginning of something, especially something bad: *the onset of winter*

on·shore /ˌɒnˈʃɔː◂ $ ˌɑːnˈʃɔːr◂, ˌɒːn-/ *adj* [only before noun], *adv* **1** on the land, not in the sea → **offshore**, **inshore**: *onshore oil production* **2** onshore winds are moving from the sea towards the land → **offshore**

on·side /ˌɒnˈsaɪd◂ $ ˌɑːn-, ˌɒːn-/ *adj, adv* in a position where you are allowed to play the ball in sports such as football OPP **offside**

ˈon-ˌsite *adj* [only before noun], *adv* at the place or on the area of land that you are talking about OPP **off-site**: *on-site car parking* | *Accommodation is provided on-site.*

on·slaught /ˈɒnslɔːt $ ˈɑːnslɒːt, ˈɒːn-/ *n* [C] **1** a large violent attack by an army: **[+on/against]** *In December they launched a full-scale onslaught on the capital.* **2** strong criticism of someone: **[+on/against]** *his public onslaught on the Conservatives* | **under the onslaught of sth** *He praised his wife for her dignity under the onslaught of the tabloid press.* **3 the onslaught of sth** the effect of something that is unpleasant and could cause damage: *plants that will survive the onslaught of winter*

on·stage /ˌɒnˈsteɪdʒ◂ $ ˌɑːn-. ˌɒːn-/ *adj, adv* on the stage in a theatre OPP **offstage**: *Even today I get nervous before I **go onstage**.*

ˌon ˈstream, **on-stream** *adj, adv* **come/be on stream** if something new comes on stream, it starts to be used or done: *Costs should fall as new technology comes on-stream.*

ˈon-the-job *adj, adv* [only before noun] while working, or at work → **in-service**, **in-house**: *on-the-job training*

ˈon-the-spot *adj* [only before noun] done immediately while you are at a particular place: *Doctors can often give on-the-spot treatment.* → **on the spot** at SPOT[1](5)

on·to, **on to** /ˈɒntə; *before vowels* ˈɒntʊ; *strong* ˈɒntuː $ ˈɑːn-, ˈɒːn-/ ●●● S1 W2 *prep*
1 used to say that someone or something moves to a position on a surface, area, or object: *She watched him walk onto the platform.* | *Don't jump onto (=into) the bus while it's moving.* | *Pour the syrup on to the egg mixture.* | *The car rolled over onto its side.* | **down/out/up etc onto sth** *Let's get back onto the highway.*
2 used to say that a room, door, or window faces towards something or allows movement into another place: *The dining room looks out onto a pretty garden.* | *a gate leading on to a broad track*
3 be onto sb *informal* **a)** (*also* **get onto sb** *especially BrE*) to speak to someone in order to tell them or ask them something: *A number of people have been onto me complaining about the noise.* | *Get onto the Press Office and find out what's happening.* **b)** to know that a particular person did something wrong or committed a crime: *The police are onto him.*
4 be onto sth *informal* **a)** to have discovered or produced something new and interesting: *With the new show, we were onto something big.* | **be onto a good thing/a winner** *I think she's onto a real winner with this song.* **b)** (*also* **get**

onto sth) to be dealing with something or start dealing with something: *I'll get onto it right away.*

on·tol·o·gy /ɒnˈtɒlədʒi $ ɑːnˈtɑː-/ *n* [U] a subject of study in PHILOSOPHY that is concerned with the nature of existence —**ontological** /ˌɒntəˈlɒdʒɪkəl◂ $ ˌɑːntəˈlɑː-/ *adj*

o·nus /ˈəʊnəs $ ˈoʊ-/ *n* [singular] *formal* the responsibility for something: **the onus is on sb to do sth** *The onus is on the prosecution to provide proof of guilt.*

on·ward /ˈɒnwəd $ ˈɑːnwərd, ˈɔːn-/ *adj* [only before noun] moving forward or continuing: *The company offers flights to Amsterdam with onward travel to The Hague.* | *the* ***onward march*** *of science*

O

on·wards /ˈɒnwədz $ ˈɑːnwərdz, ˈɔːn-/ ●○○ (*also* **onward** *AmE*) *adv*
1 from ... onwards beginning at a particular time or age and continuing after that: *from the 1980s onwards*
2 *literary* forwards: *He walked onwards to the head of the lake.*
3 onwards and upwards used to say that the development, increase, or progress of something continues: *With exports strong, the business is moving* ***onwards and upwards****.*

on·yx /ˈɒnɪks $ ˈɑː-/ *n* [U] a stone with lines of different colours in it, often used in jewellery

oo·dles /ˈuːdlz/ *n* **oodles of sth** *informal* a large amount of something: *They've got oodles of money.*

oof /uːf/ *interjection* a sound that you make when you have been hit, especially in the stomach

ooh /uː/ *interjection* said when you think something is very beautiful, unpleasant, surprising etc: *Ooh, that's nice!*

ooh la la /ˌuː lɑː ˈlɑː/ *interjection* said when you think that something or someone is surprising, unusual, or sexually attractive – used humorously

oomph /ʊmf/ *n* [U] *informal* a quality that makes something attractive and exciting and that shows energy: *It's not a bad song, but it needs more oomph.*

oops /ʊps/ *interjection* said when someone falls or makes a small mistake: *Oops, I've spelt that wrong.*

ˈoops-a-ˌdaisy *interjection* said when a child falls

ooze[1] /uːz/ *v* [I always + adv/prep, T] **1** if a thick liquid oozes from something or if something oozes a thick liquid, that liquid flows from it very slowly: **[+from/out of/through]** *The ice cream was melting and oozing out of its wrapper.* | *A cut on his cheek was still oozing blood.*
2 to show a lot of a particular quality or feeling: *Andrew laughed gently,* ***oozing charm****.*

ooze[2] *n* **1** [U] very soft mud, especially at the bottom of a lake or sea **2** [singular] a very slow flow of liquid

ooz·y /ˈuːzi/ *adj informal* soft and wet like mud: *a black, oozy mess*

op /ɒp $ ɑːp/ *n* [C] *BrE informal* a medical operation SYN **operation**: *He's had a minor heart op.*

o·pac·i·ty /əʊˈpæsəti $ oʊ-/ *n* [U] **1** the quality that something has when it is difficult to see through → **opaque 2** the quality that something has when it is difficult to understand SYN **obscurity**

o·pal /ˈəʊpəl $ ˈoʊ-/ *n* [C,U] a type of white stone with changing colours in it, often used in jewellery

o·pa·les·cent /ˌəʊpəˈlesənt◂ $ ˌoʊ-/ *adj literary* having colours that shine and seem to change: *an opalescent sky*

o·paque /əʊˈpeɪk $ oʊ-/ ●○○ *adj* [usually before noun]
1 opaque glass or liquid is difficult to see through and often thick OPP **transparent**: *a shower with an opaque glass door*
2 *formal* difficult to understand SYN **obscure**: *an opaque style of writing* —**opaqueness** *n* [U]

ˈop art *n* [U] art that uses patterns which seem to move or to produce other shapes as you look at them

op. cit. /ˌɒp ˈsɪt $ ˌɑːp-/ an abbreviation used in formal writing to refer to a book that has been mentioned before

OPEC /ˈəʊpek $ ˈoʊ-/ *n* (***Organization of Petroleum Exporting Countries***) an organization of countries that produce and sell oil

ˌop-ˈed *adj AmE* **op-ed page/article** a page in a newspaper that has articles containing opinions on various subjects, or one of these articles

o·pen[1] /ˈəʊpən $ ˈoʊ-/ ●●● S1 W1 *adj*
1 DOOR/CONTAINER ETC not closed, so that things, people, air etc can go in and out or be put in and out OPP **closed, shut**: *He* ***threw*** *the door* ***open*** *and ran down the stairs.* | *an open window* | *The gates* ***swung*** *silently* ***open****.* | *The bar door* ***flew open*** *and a noisy group burst in.* | *All the windows were* ***wide open*** (=completely open). | *She looked at the open suitcase with surprise.* | *There was an open bottle of wine on the table.*
2 EYES/MOUTH not closed, so that your EYELIDS or your lips are apart: *I was so sleepy, I couldn't* ***keep*** *my eyes* ***open****.* | *He was fast asleep with his mouth* ***wide open****.*
3 NOT ENCLOSED [only before noun] not enclosed, or with no buildings, walls, trees etc: *There was open ground at the end of the lane.* | ***open spaces*** *such as parks and gardens* | **open countryside/country** *At weekends people want to leave the town for open countryside.* | *A shoal of fish swam past heading for* ***the open sea*** (=part of the sea away from land). | *The car's performance is good, especially going fast on the* ***open road*** (=a road without traffic where you can drive fast).
4 NOT COVERED without a roof or cover: *The president was riding with his wife in an open car.* | *Martin was struggling with the sails on the open deck.* | *an open drain* | **open to the sky/air/elements** *Many of the tombs had been robbed and left open to the sky.*
5 the open air outdoors: **in the open air** *The dancing was outside, in the open air.* | *Jane wanted to rush to the door and get out into the open air.* → **OPEN-AIR**
6 BUSINESS/BUILDING ETC [not before noun] ready for business and allowing customers, visitors etc to enter OPP **closed, shut**: *The museum is open daily in the summer months.* | *The offices are also open at weekends.* | *After the security alert, most of the firms affected were* ***open for business*** *on Monday morning.* | *The villagers are anxious that their local school is kept open.* | *I declare this exhibition open* (=officially say that it is now open).
7 NOT RESTRICTED allowing everyone, or everyone in a group, to take part in something, know about something, or have a chance to win something: **[+to]** *The competition is open to all readers in the UK.* | *In many schools, governors' meetings are not* ***open to the public****.* | *The discussion was then* ***thrown open*** *for the audience's questions.* | *an open meeting* | *The men's race appears* ***wide open*** (=anyone could win it). | *The painting would fetch several hundred dollars on* ***the open market*** (=a market in which anyone can buy or sell).
8 OPPORTUNITY [not before noun] if an opportunity, a possible action, a job etc is open to you, you have the chance to do it: *The job is being kept open for her.* | **[+to]** *The 1960s was a period when greater opportunities were open to women.* | *So what other* ***options*** *are* ***open*** *to us?* | *There is only one course of action open to the local authority.*
9 NOT SECRET [only before noun] actions, feelings, intentions etc that are open are not hidden or secret: *Her father watched her with open admiration.* | *open hostility between the two nations* | *The party was calling for more* ***open government*** (=when the government makes information freely available). | *The case will be tried* ***in open court*** (=in a court where everything is public). | *It is* ***an open secret*** (=it is supposed to be secret, but most people know about it) *that she is having an affair with another man.*
10 HONEST honest and not wanting to hide any facts from other people: **[+with]** *The couple are quite open with each other about their feelings.* | **[+about]** *She was quite open about her ambitions.* | *his friendly, open manner*
THESAURUS ▸ HONEST
11 CLOTHES not fastened: *the open neck of his shirt* | *She was wearing an open jacket.*
12 NOT YET DECIDED needing more discussion or thought before a decision can be made: *The matter remains* ***an open question****.* | **[+to]** *The new rates of pay are open to negotiation.* | *The test results are open to interpretation.* | **keep/leave your options open** *Officers investigating her death are keeping their options open.*
13 open to sth a) likely to suffer from something or be

affected by something: *The magazine's editor is* ***open to criticism*** *in allowing the article to be printed.* | *The regulations are open to abuse by companies.* | *He has* ***left*** *himself* ***open to*** *accusations of dishonesty.* **b)** willing to consider something new or to accept something new: *Teachers need to be open to children's ideas.* | *The committee is open to suggestions.* | *The owners of the building want to sell and are open to offers.*
14 NOT BLOCKED if a road or line of communication is open, it is not blocked and can be used: *We try to* ***keep*** *the mountain roads* ***open*** *all through the winter.*
15 SPREAD APART spread apart instead of closed, curled over etc: *At night the flowers were open.* | *Johnson raised an open hand.* | *He was sitting in bed with a book lying open* (=with its pages apart so it can be read) *on his knees.*
16 an open mind if you have an open mind, you deliberately do not make a decision or form a definite opinion about something: *It's important to* ***keep an open mind*** *as you study the topic.*
17 be open to question/doubt if something is open to question, there are doubts about it: *Whether the new situation is an improvement is open to question.*
18 welcome/greet sb/sth with open arms to be very pleased to see someone or something: *Mike will be welcomed back into the team with open arms.*
19 an open invitation a) an invitation to visit someone whenever you like **b)** something that makes it easier for criminals to steal, cheat etc: **[+to]** *The lack of security measures provides an open invitation to crime.*
20 be an open book to be something that you know and understand very well: *The natural world was an open book to him.*
21 the door is open there is an opportunity for someone to do something: **[+to]** *Schoolgirls are being told that the door is open to them to pursue careers in science.*
22 keep your eyes/ears open to keep looking or listening so that you will notice anything that is important, dangerous etc
23 open weave/texture cloth with an open weave or texture has wide spaces between the threads → **keep an eye open (for sth)** at EYE[1](14), → **with your eyes open** at EYE[1](19), → OPEN-EYED

open[2] ●●● S1 W1 *v*

1 DOOR/WINDOW ETC [I,T] to move a door, window etc so that people, things, air etc can pass through, or to be moved in this way: *Jack opened the window.* | *He opened the drawer of the desk.* | *She heard a door open and then close.*
2 CONTAINER/PACKAGE [T] to unfasten or remove the lid, top, or cover of a container, package etc: *Louise opened a bottle of wine.* | *He opened the letter and began to read it.* | *The children were opening their presents.* | *Mark was about to open a beer when the doorbell rang.*
3 EYES [I,T] to raise your EYELIDS so that you can see, or to be raised in this way: *Barry was awake long before he opened his eyes.* | *Carrie smelled coffee and her eyes opened reluctantly.*
4 MOUTH [I,T] to move your lips apart, or to be moved in this way: *He opened his mouth but couldn't think what to say.*
5 START OPERATING [I,T] (*also* **open up**) if a place such as an office, shop, restaurant etc opens or is opened, it starts operating or providing a service: *Sarah had recently opened an office in Genoa.* | *French and Scandinavian offices are due to open in the autumn.* | *The Forestry Commission has opened a plant centre selling rare plants.* | *The centre has been a great success since it* ***opened its doors*** *a year ago.*
THESAURUS ESTABLISH
6 SHOP/RESTAURANT ETC [I] (*also* **open up**) to start business, letting in customers or visitors, at a particular time: *What time do the banks open?* | *The bakery opens early.*
7 START AN ACTIVITY [T] to start an activity, event, or set of actions: *The US attorney's office has opened an investigation into the matter.* | *An inquest into the deaths will be opened next week.*
8 COMPUTER [T] to make a document or computer program ready to use: *Click on this icon to open the File Manager.*
9 MEETING/EVENT [I,T] if a meeting etc opens or is opened in a particular way, it starts in that way: *Hughes, opening the Conference, made a dramatic plea for peace.* | **[+with]** *The concert opens with Beethoven's Egmont Overture.*
10 OFFICIAL CEREMONY [T] to perform a ceremony in which you officially state that a building is ready to be used: *The new County Hall building was officially opened by the King.*
11 SPREAD/UNFOLD [I,T] to spread something out or unfold something, or to become spread out or unfolded: *She opened her umbrella.* | *John opened his hand to show her he wasn't holding anything.* | *The flowers only open during bright weather.* | *I sat down and opened my book.* | *She opened the curtains* (=pulled the two curtains apart). | *Dave opened his arms* (=stretched his arms wide apart) *to give her a hug.*
12 MAKE A WAY THROUGH [T] to make it possible for cars, goods etc to pass through a place: *They were clearing away snow to open the tunnel.* | *The peace treaty promises an end to war and* ***opens*** *the* ***borders*** *between the two countries.*
13 FILM/PLAY ETC [I] to start being shown to the public: *Paula and Rachael star as mother and daughter in the play, which opens tonight.* | *The film opened yesterday to excellent reviews.* THESAURUS START
14 open an account to start an account at a bank or other financial organization by putting money into it: *Mary was in the bank to ask about opening a current account.*
15 open fire (on sth) to start shooting at someone or something: *Troops opened fire on the rioters.*
16 open the door/way to sth (*also* **open doors**) to make an opportunity for something to happen: *Research on genes should open the door to exciting new medical treatments.* | *If the record is successful, it could open doors for my career.*
17 open sb's eyes (to sth) to make someone realize something that they had not realized before: *The purpose of the training is to open managers' eyes to the consequences of their own behaviour.*
18 open your mind (to sth) to be ready to consider or accept new ideas
19 open your heart (to sb) to tell someone your real thoughts and feelings because you trust them
20 the heavens opened *literary* it started to rain heavily → **open the floodgates** at FLOODGATE

GRAMMAR

Open belongs to a group of verbs where the same noun can be the subject of the verb or its object.
- You can say: *She opened the door.* In this sentence, 'the door' is the object of **open**.
- You can say: *The door opened.* In this sentence, 'the door' is the subject of **open**.

GRAMMAR GUIDE VERBS

THESAURUS

open used about a door, window, container, package, letter, your eyes, or your mouth: *I opened the door quietly.* | *She was nervous about opening the letter.* | *Open your mouth wide.*
unlock to open a door, drawer, box etc with a key: *You need a key to unlock the safe.*
unscrew to open a lid on a bottle, container etc by turning it: *I carefully unscrewed the lid of the jar.*
force open to open a drawer, window, cupboard etc using force: *The door was locked so we had to force it open.*
unwrap to open a package by removing the paper that covers it: *The children were busy unwrapping their Christmas presents.*
unfasten/undo to make something no longer fastened or tied, for example a seat belt or a piece of clothing: *He unfastened the top button of his shirt.* | *I was so full I had to undo my belt.*

open onto/into sth *phr v* if a room, door etc opens onto or into another place, you can enter that other place directly through it: *The door opens onto a long balcony.*

open out *phr v*
1 if a road, path, or passage opens out, it becomes wider: **[+into]** *Beyond the forest the path opened out into a track.*
2 *BrE* if someone opens out, they become less shy

open up *phr v*
1 OPPORTUNITY if opportunities open up, or a new situation opens them up, they become available or possible: *With a microscope, a whole new world of investigation opens up.* | **open sth ↔ up** *The new international agreement opens up the possibility of much greater co-operation against terrorism.*
2 LAND **open sth ↔ up** if someone opens up an area of land, they make it easier to reach and ready for development: *The new road will open up 300 acres of prime development land.*
3 DOOR/CONTAINER ETC to open something that is closed, locked, or covered: *Open up, this is the police!* | **open sth ↔ up** *He opened up his case and took out a clean sweater.*
4 SHOP/OFFICE ETC **a)** if a shop, office etc opens up or is opened up, someone starts it **b)** if a shop, office etc opens up at a particular time, it starts business at that time
5 DISAGREEMENT/DISCUSSION **open sth ↔ up** to start a discussion or argument: *The article was written with the intention of opening up a public debate.*
6 COMPETITION/RACE if someone opens up a lead in a competition or race, they increase the distance or number of points by which they are winning
7 TALK to stop being shy and say what you really think: *Last night was the first time that Ken had opened up about his feelings.*
8 WITH A GUN to start shooting
9 HOLE/CRACK ETC if a hole, crack etc opens up or is opened up, it appears and becomes wider

open[3] *n* **1 in the open** outdoors: *In the summer, we camped **in the open**.* **2 (out) in the open** information that is out in the open is not hidden or secret: *By now the whole affair was in the open.* | *She never let her dislike for him **come out into the open**.* | *All these concerns need to be **brought out into the open**.*

Open, the one of the important international sports competitions, especially for golf, such as the British Open Championship and the US Open Championship, or for tennis, such as the French, US and Australian Open competitions

ˌopen ˌaccess TˈV *n* [U] television programmes which are PRESENTed by members of the public

ˌopen-ˈair *adj* [usually before noun] happening or existing outdoors SYN **outdoor**: *open-air concerts* | *an open-air swimming pool*

ˌopen-and-shut ˈcase *n* [C usually singular] a legal case or other matter that is easy to prove or decide because the facts are very clear

ˌopen ˈbar *n* [C] *AmE* a bar at an occasion such as a wedding, where drinks are served free

o·pen·cast /ˈəʊpənkɑːst $ ˈoʊpənkæst/ *adj* [usually before noun] *BrE* an opencast mine is one where coal is taken out of holes in the ground near the surface, not from deep under the ground: *opencast mining*

ˈopen day *n* [C] *BrE* a day when a school or an organization invites the public to come in and see the work that is done there

ˌopen-ˈdoor ˌpolicy *n* [C] **1** the principle of allowing people and goods to move into a country freely: *They're pushing forward economic reform and an open-door policy.* **2** the principle of allowing anyone to come to a place at any time, for example in order to discuss something

ˌopen-ˈended *adj* **1** something that is open-ended does not have a definite answer or definite rules about how it must be done: *an open-ended question* | *These interviews are fairly open-ended.* **2** without a particular ending time: *an open-ended agreement*

o·pen·er /ˈəʊpənə $ ˈoʊpənər/ *n* [C] **1** a tool that is used to open cans, bottles etc: *a **can opener*** | *a **bottle opener*** **2** the first of a series of games in a sports competition: *They are hoping to win tomorrow's opener against New Zealand.* **3 for openers a)** *BrE* as a beginning or first stage SYN **to begin with**: *For openers, the band played a couple of old Beatles songs.* **b)** *AmE* used to give one reason, explanation etc for something, although there are others you might mention later too: *It's tough being a reporter. For openers, there are the long hours.*

ˌopen-ˈeyed *adj, adv* awake, or with your eyes open: *She lay there open-eyed.*

ˌopen-faced ˈsandwich, **ˌopen-face ˈsandwich** *n* [C] *AmE* a single piece of bread with meat, cheese etc on top SYN **open sandwich** *BrE*

ˌopen-ˈhanded *adj* **1** generous and friendly: *an open-handed offer of help* **2** done with your hand open: *an open-handed slap*

open-heart·ed /ˌəʊpən ˈhɑːtɪd $ ˌoʊpən ˈhɑːr-/ *adj* kind, sympathetic, and friendly: *They gave us an open-hearted welcome.*

ˌopen-heart ˈsurgery *n* [U] a medical operation in which doctors operate on someone's heart, while a machine keeps the PATIENT's blood flowing

ˌopen ˈhouse *n* **1** [C] *AmE* a day when a school or organization invites the public to come in and see the work that is done there: *Parents are invited to attend the open house next Thursday.* **2** [U] *BrE* if it is open house at someone's home, people are always welcome to visit at any time: *He **kept open house** for a wide range of artists and writers.* **3** [C] a party at someone's house that you can come to at any time during a particular period: *We're **having an open house** Sunday, noon to 5 pm.* **4** [C] *AmE* an occasion when someone who is selling their house lets everyone who is interested in buying it come to see it

o·pen·ing[1] /ˈəʊpənɪŋ $ ˈoʊ-/ ●●○ S3 *n*
1 [C] the time when a new building, road etc is used for the first time, or when a public event begins, especially when it involves a special ceremony: **[+of]** *the official opening of the new theatre* | *the opening of the Cannes film festival*
2 [C] a hole or space in something: **[+in]** *a narrow opening in the fence* THESAURUS ▸ HOLE
3 [C usually singular] the beginning or first part of something: **[+of]** *at the opening of the trial*
4 [C] a job that is available: *There are very few openings in scientific research.* THESAURUS ▸ JOB
5 [C] a chance for someone to do or say something: **[+for]** *His question left an opening for me to say exactly what I thought.*
6 [U] when something opens, or is opened: **[+of]** *I was startled by the sudden opening of the door.*

opening[2] ●○○ *adj* [only before noun] first or beginning: *the opening match of the season* | *the opening chapter of the book* | *the chairman's opening remarks*

ˈopening ˌhours *n* [plural] *BrE* the hours when a shop, bank, bar etc is open to the public

ˌopening ˈnight *n* [C,U] the first night that a new play, film etc is shown to the public SYN **first night**

ˈopening time *n* [C,U] the time that a business opens to the public OPP **closing time**: *We arrived at the pub just before opening time.*

ˌopening ˈup *n* **the opening up of sth** when something is made less restricted and more available to people: *the opening up of opportunities for women* | *the opening up of new areas to cultivation*

ˌopen-jaw ˈfare *n* [C] the price you pay to travel on a plane, train etc when this includes travel to a place and travel back from a different place

ˌopen ˈletter *n* [C] a letter to an important person, which is printed in a newspaper or magazine, usually in order to protest about something

o·pen·ly /ˈəʊpənli $ ˈoʊ-/ ●●○ *adv* in a way that does not hide your feelings, opinions, or the facts: *Sarah* ***talked openly*** *about her problems.* | *He was* ***openly critical*** *of his colleagues.*

ˌopen ˈmarket *n* **1 on the open market** goods that are bought and sold on the open market are sold publicly rather than privately: *The painting would fetch millions of dollars if it was* ***sold on the open market****.* **2** [C usually singular] a system which makes it easy to buy and sell goods with other countries, because there are few restrictions: *There is now an open market within the European Community.*

ˌopen ˈmarriage *n* [C] a marriage in which both partners accept that they will have sex with other people

ˌopen ˈmike *n* [U] *AmE* a time when anyone is allowed to tell jokes, sing etc in a bar or club

ˌopen-ˈminded *adj* willing to consider and accept other people's ideas and opinions OPP **narrow-minded**: **[+about/towards]** *She's quite open-minded about sex.* —**open-mindedness** *n* [U]

ˌopen-ˈmouthed *adj, adv* with your mouth wide open, because you are very surprised or shocked: *We stared open-mouthed as the plane came down.*

ˌopen-ˈnecked *adj* an open-necked shirt is worn with the top button undone

o·pen·ness /ˈəʊpənnəs $ ˈoʊ-/ *n* [U] **1** the quality of being honest and willing to talk about things: **[+of]** *the openness of American society* | **[+about]** *her openness about her problems* **2** the quality of being willing to accept new ideas or people: **[+to/towards]** *the importance of openness to change* **3** the quality of not being enclosed: **[+of]** *the vast openness of the African plains*

ˌopen-ˈplan *adj BrE* an open-plan office, school etc does not have walls dividing it into separate rooms

ˌopen ˈprimary *n* [C] a PRIMARY ELECTION in the US in which any voter may vote for someone from any party

ˌopen ˈprison *n* [C] *BrE* a prison that does not restrict the freedom of prisoners as much as ordinary prisons

ˌopen ˈsandwich *n* [C] *BrE* a single piece of bread with meat, cheese etc on top SYN **open-faced sandwich** *AmE*

ˈopen ˌseason *n* [singular, U] **1** *BrE* the time each year when it is legal to kill particular animals, birds, or fish as a sport OPP **close season**: **[+for]** *the open season for deer* **2 open season (on sb)** a time when a lot of people criticize someone, or a group of people: *It seems to be open season on politicians just now.*

ˌopen ˈsesame *n* [singular] *BrE* an easy way to achieve something that is usually very difficult: **[+to]** *A university degree isn't always an open sesame to a good job.*

ˌopen ˈsource *adj* open source software is provided free, and includes the language the program is written in, so that the people who use it can make changes to the software: *open source software such as Linux* —**open source** *n* [U]

ˈopen ˌsystem *n* [C] *technical* a computer system that can be connected with similar computer systems made by other companies

ˌopen-ˈtoed *adj* **open-toed sandals/shoes** shoes that do not cover the end of your toes

ˌOpen ˌUniˈversity, the (*abbreviation* **the OU**) a British university that teaches adult students mainly in their own homes by means of the Internet. It also runs RESIDENTIAL COURSES.

ˌopen ˈverdict *n* [C] an official decision in a British court saying that the exact cause of someone's death is not known: *The jury* ***returned an open verdict****.* | *He said there was some doubt over the way Grant had died, and* ***recorded an open verdict****.*

ˌopen ˈvowel *n* [C] *technical* a vowel such as /a/ that is pronounced with your tongue flat on the bottom of your mouth

o·pen·work /ˈəʊpənˌwɜːk $ ˈoʊpənˌwɜːrk/ *adj* [only before noun] an openwork object has a pattern of open spaces between the material that it is made from: *an openwork stone screen*

op·e·ra /ˈɒpərə $ ˈɑː-/ ●●○ *n*
1 [C] a musical play in which all of the words are sung → **operetta**: *We* ***go to the opera*** (=go to a performance of opera) *regularly.* | *an* ***opera singer***
2 [U] these plays considered as a form of art —**operatic** /ˌɒpəˈrætɪk◂ $ ˌɑː-/ *adj*: *operatic performances* —**operatically** /-kli/ *adv* → GRAND OPERA, SOAP OPERA

op·e·ra·ble /ˈɒpərəbəl $ ˈɑː-/ *adj* **1** a system which is operable is working OPP **inoperable**: *Less than half the rail network was operable.* **2** a medical condition that is operable can be treated by an operation OPP **inoperable**

ˈopera house *n* [C] a theatre where operas are performed: *the Sydney Opera House*

op·e·rate /ˈɒpəreɪt $ ˈɑːp-/ ●●● S3 W2 *v*
1 MACHINE **a)** [T] to use and control a machine or equipment: *The Lewis family operated a number of boats on the canal.* | *Clive was experienced in operating the computers.* **b)** [I always + adv/prep] if a machine operates in a particular way, it works in that way: **[+in/at]** *Check that the equipment is operating in a safe manner.* | *The bus is designed to operate in all weather conditions.* | *Most freezers operate at below -18°C.*
2 BUSINESS/ORGANIZATION **a)** [I] if a business or organization operates in a particular place or way, it works in that place or way: **[+in/within/from]** *a design company operating from offices in Seattle* | *A playgroup operates on the campus.* | *They were trying to reduce* ***operating costs****.* **b)** [T] to control a business or organization: *Nuns are operating an emergency hospital.*
3 SYSTEM/PROCESS/SERVICE [I,T] if a system, process, or service operates, or if you operate it, it works: *The whole tax system is now operating more efficiently.* | *The new law doesn't operate in our favour.* | *The car parks operate a pay-as-you-leave system.* | *The bus company operates a Monday to Saturday service.*
4 MEDICAL [I] to cut into someone's body in order to repair or remove a part that is damaged: *Doctors had to operate to remove the bullet.* | **[+on]** *the surgeon who operated on Taylor's knee* ⚠ A doctor does not 'operate' a part of a person's body. He or she **operates on** it: *They need to operate on her stomach (NOT operate her stomach).*
5 WORK [I] to do your job or try to achieve things in a particular way: *Most people just can't operate in noisy crowded conditions.* | *Older children often like to operate independently.*
6 SOLDIERS/POLICE [I] if soldiers or police officers are operating in an area, they are working in that area: **[+in]** *Security patrols now operate in some of the most dangerous parts of the city.* | *enemy submarines operating in the Mediterranean*
7 operate as sth to have a particular purpose: *The foam operates as a very effective filter.* | *The car's service manual is designed to operate as a guide for owners.*
8 LAWS/PRINCIPLES [I] to have an effect on something: *the laws of evolution operating on each species*

ˈoperating room *n* [C] *AmE* an OPERATING THEATRE

ˈoperating ˌsystem *n* [C] a system in a computer that helps all the programs in it to work together

ˈoperating ˌtable *n* [C] a special table in an operating theatre which a person lies on when they are having an operation

ˈoperating ˌtheatre *n* [C] *BrE* a room in a hospital where operations are done SYN **operating room** *AmE*

op·e·ra·tion /ˌɒpəˈreɪʃən $ ˌɑːp-/ ●●● S1 W1 *n*
1 MEDICAL [C] the process of cutting into someone's body to repair or remove a part that is damaged: **[+on]** *She's going to need an operation on her ankle.* | **[+for]** *an operation for cancer* | **operation to do sth** *He had an operation to reduce the swelling in his brain.*
2 BUSINESS/ORGANIZATION [C] a business, company, or organization: *The firm set up its own property development*

operation. | *a microchip manufacturing operation* | *Nolan and Barnes were both involved in the operation.*
3 WORK/ACTIVITIES [C,U] the work or activities done by a business or organization, or the process of doing this work: *Many small businesses fail in the first year of operation.* | *The Education Business Partnership has **been in operation** since 1989.*
4 ACTIONS [C] a set of planned actions or activities for a particular purpose: *The UN rescue operation started shortly after dawn.*
5 MACHINE/SYSTEM [U] the way the parts of a machine or system work together, or the process of making a machine or system work: *The aircraft's engine operation was normal.* | **in operation** *Protective clothing must be worn when the machine is in operation.* | *The device has a single button, allowing for easy operation.* | *Careful checks must be made before the factory commences operation.* | *The new investment system **came into operation** in 1999.*
6 PRINCIPLE/LAW/PLAN ETC [U] the way something such as a principle or law works or has an effect: **in operation** *a clear example of the law of gravity in operation* | **come/go into operation** (=begin to have an effect) *The new rule comes into operation on February 1.* | **put/bring sth into operation** (=make something start to work) *A scheme is being brought into operation to see how these changes would work.*
7 MILITARY/POLICE ACTION [C] a planned military or police action, especially one that involves a lot of people: *Britain will carry out a joint **military operation** with the US.*
8 COMPUTERS [C] an action done by a computer

COLLOCATIONS

VERBS

have an operation (*also* **undergo an operation** *formal*) *Harris had a hip operation in October.*
do/carry out an operation (*also* **perform an operation** *formal*) *The operation was carried out by a team of surgeons at Papworth Hospital.*
recover from an operation | **survive an operation**

ADJECTIVES/NOUN + operation

a knee/heart/stomach etc operation *He is almost back to full fitness after a knee operation.*
a major/minor operation *The unit cares for patients recovering from major operations.*
an emergency operation *He had to have his spleen removed in an emergency operation.*
a routine operation (=an operation that is often performed) | **a life-saving operation** | **a transplant operation**

COMMON ERRORS

⚠ Don't say 'take an operation'. Say **have an operation**.
Don't say 'make an operation'. Say **do an operation** or **perform an operation**.

op·e·ra·tion·al /ˌɒpəˈreɪʃənəl◂ $ ˌɑːp-/ ●○○ *adj*
1 [not before noun] working and ready to be used: *The boat should be operational by this afternoon.* | *The new system **became operational** in March.* | *Our main offices are now **fully operational**.* → OPERATIVE[1](1)
2 [only before noun] relating to the operation of a business, government etc: *Patco accepted full responsibility for operational management.* —**operationally** *adv*

ˌoperational reˈsearch, **ˌoperations reˈsearch** *n* [U] the study of the best ways to build and use machines or plan organizations

op·e·ra·tive[1] /ˈɒpərətɪv $ ˈɑːpərə-, ˈɑːpəreɪ-/ *adj* **1** working and able to be used OPP **inoperative**: *Only one runway is operative.* | *the steps to be taken before the scheme can **become operative*** → OPERATIONAL(1) **2 the operative word** used when you repeat a word from a previous sentence to draw attention to its importance: *The new system offers fast solutions. Fast being the operative word.* **3** relating to a medical operation: *patients undergoing **operative procedures***

operative[2] *n* [C] **1** a worker, especially a factory worker – used in business: *the company's overseas operatives* **2** someone who does work that is secret in some way, especially for a government organization: **CIA/FBI/intelligence etc operatives**

op·e·ra·tor /ˈɒpəreɪtə $ ˈɑːpəreɪtər/ ●●○ W3 *n* [C]
1 someone who works on a telephone SWITCHBOARD, who you can call for help: *Hello, operator? Could you put me through to Room 31?*
2 someone who operates a machine or piece of equipment: **machine/computer/radio etc operator** *computers which can be used by untrained operators*
3 a person or company that operates a particular business: *new regulations affecting taxi operators* | *Julian travelled with Caribbean Connection, the UK's leading Caribbean **tour operator*** (=company that arranges holidays). | *a **private operator** running regular passenger services*
4 someone who is good at achieving things by persuading people to help or agree with them: *Monsieur Valentin was a formidable political operator.* | *He may not look it, but Newman is a **smooth operator*** (=someone who is good at persuading people but who you feel you cannot trust).

op·e·ret·ta /ˌɒpəˈretə $ ˌɑːp-/ *n* [C] a funny or romantic musical play in which some of the words are spoken and some are sung → **opera**

oph·thal·mic /ɒfˈθælmɪk $ ɑːf-/ *adj* [only before noun] *medical* relating to the eyes and the illnesses that affect them: *an ophthalmic surgeon*

oph·thal·mol·o·gy /ˌɒfθælˈmɒlədʒi $ ˌɑːfθælˈmɑː-/ *n* [U] *medical* the study of the eyes and diseases that affect them —**ophthalmologist** *n* [C]

o·pi·ate /ˈəʊpiət, -eɪt $ ˈoʊ-/ *n* [C] **1** a drug that contains OPIUM. Opiates can be used to reduce severe pain and help people to sleep. **2** something that makes people stop thinking about the problems in their lives so that they stop trying to make their lives better – used to show disapproval: *Hollywood movies were seen as an opiate for the people.*

o·pine /əʊˈpaɪn $ oʊ-/ *v* [T] *formal* to say what your opinion is about something: **opine that** *The headmistress opined that the trip would make a nice change.*

o·pin·ion /əˈpɪnjən/ ●●● S1 W2 *n*
1 [C,U] your ideas or beliefs about a particular subject: **[+of]** *What's your opinion of Cathy?* | **[+on]** *He asked his wife's opinion on every important decision.* | **[+about]** *The two women had very different opinions about drugs.* | **in my opinion** (=used when giving your opinion) *In my opinion, the law should be changed.* GRAMMAR ✗ Don't say: *on my opinion* | *according to my opinion* → VIEW[1](1)

REGISTER

In everyday English, people usually say **I think ...** rather than **my opinion is ...** or **in my opinion ...**. In questions, people usually ask **what do you think?** rather than **what is your opinion?** ***What do you think** of Cathy?*

2 [C] judgment or advice from a professional person about something: *When choosing an insurance policy it's best to **get** an independent **opinion**.* | *My doctor says I need an operation, but I've asked for a **second opinion*** (=advice from a second doctor to make sure that the first advice is right). | *They took the painting to get an **expert opinion*** (=an opinion from someone who knows a lot).
3 have a high/low/good/bad etc opinion of sb/sth to think that someone or something is very good or very bad: *They have a very high opinion of Paula's work.*
4 be of the opinion (that) to think that something is true: *I was firmly of the opinion that we should not give Jackson any more money.*

COLLOCATIONS

VERBS

have/hold an opinion *Everyone seemed to have a different opinion.*
ask sb (for) their opinion (*also* **ask for sb's**

opinion) *We asked people for their opinions about the Olympics.*
give/express an opinion (=say what your opinion is) *He gave his opinion only when asked.*
voice/state an opinion *written* (=give your opinion, especially in a formal situation) | **form an opinion** (=gradually decide what your opinion is)

ADJECTIVES

the general opinion (=the opinion that most people have about something) *The general opinion seems to be that the government has made a mess of the war.*
popular/public opinion (=what ordinary people think about something) *How much do newspapers influence popular opinion?*
sb's personal opinion *My personal opinion is that his first film was better.*
strong opinions *People have strong opinions about this subject.*

PHRASES

have a difference of opinion (= two people disagree) *He and Luke had a difference of opinion.*
sth is a matter of opinion (=used to say that you disagree, or that people disagree about something) *'He's a very nice man.' 'That's a matter of opinion,' thought Sam.*
contrary to popular opinion (=in spite of what most people think) *Contrary to popular opinion, many cats dislike milk.*
in my humble opinion (=used when giving your opinion, especially when you want to emphasize what you are about to say) *In my humble opinion, he is the greatest sportsman Britain has produced.*
keep your opinions to yourself (=not say what you really think) | **opinion is divided as to/on/over sth** (=people have different opinions about it) | **everyone is entitled to their opinion** (=used especially when politely disagreeing with what someone says)

COMMON ERRORS

⚠ Don't say 'say your opinion'. Say **give your opinion** or **express your opinion**.

o·pin·ion·at·ed /əˈpɪnjəneɪtɪd/ *adj* expressing very strong opinions about things: *I found him very arrogant and opinionated.*

oˈpinion-ˌmakers *n* [plural] people such as politicians or JOURNALISTS who have a lot of influence on the way other people think

oˈpinion poll *n* [C] the process of asking a large group of people the same questions in order to find out what most people think about something: *An opinion poll showed that 70% of adults were against legalizing drugs.*

o·pi·um /ˈəʊpiəm $ ˈoʊ-/ *n* [U] a powerful illegal drug made from POPPY seeds. Drugs made from opium are used to reduce severe pain. → **heroin**

o·pos·sum /əˈpɒsəm $ -ˈpɑː-, ˈpɑːsəm/ (*also* **possum**) *n* [C] one of various small animals from America and Australia that have fur and climb trees

opp. the written abbreviation of ***opposite***

op·po·nent /əˈpəʊnənt $ əˈpoʊ-/ ●●● W3 *n* [C]
1 someone who you try to defeat in a competition, game, fight, or argument: *Graf's opponent in today's final will be Sukova.* | **leading/main/chief opponent** *During the primary elections, McCain was Bush's leading opponent.* | **formidable/worthy opponent** *In debate he was a formidable opponent.* | *He is admired even by his* ***political opponents****.*
2 someone who disagrees with a plan, idea, or system and wants to try to stop or change it OPP **proponent**: **[+of]** *Rodgers was not an opponent of the new airport.* | **bitter/vocal/outspoken opponent** *an outspoken opponent of gun control*

op·por·tune /ˈɒpətjuːn $ ˌɑːpərˈtuːn/ *adj formal* **1 an opportune moment/time** a time that is suitable for doing something: *I waited, hoping for an opportune moment to discuss the possibility of a raise.* **2** done at a very suitable time OPP **inopportune**: *an opportune remark* | *The law reforms were opportune and important.* —**opportunely** *adv*

op·por·tun·is·m /ˌɒpəˈtjuːnɪzəm $ ˌɑːpərˈtuː-/ *n* [U] using every opportunity to gain power, money, or unfair advantages - used to show disapproval: *He accused the diary's publishers of blatant opportunism.*

op·por·tun·ist /ˌɒpəˈtjuːnɪst $ ˌɑːpərˈtuː-/ *n* [C] **1** someone who uses every opportunity to gain power, money, or unfair advantages - used to show disapproval: *Voters dislike opportunists - politicians who change their policies according to opinion polls.* **2** someone who commits a crime because they have a chance to, and not because they planned to: *Most burglars are opportunists.* | *an opportunist crime* —**opportunist** *adj*: *the opportunist policies of wartime leaders* —**opportunistic** /ˌɒpətjuːˈnɪstɪk◂ $ ˌɑːpərtuː-/ *adj*: *opportunistic thefts from cars*

op·por·tu·ni·ty /ˌɒpəˈtjuːnəti $ ˌɑːpərˈtuː-/ ●●● S1 W1 *n* (*plural* **opportunities**)
1 [C,U] a chance to do something or an occasion when it is easy for you to do something: **opportunity to do sth** *a rare opportunity to see inside this historic building* | *I'd like to take this opportunity to thank you all.* | **[+for]** *Games and songs provide an opportunity for classroom interaction.*
2 [C] a chance to get a job or improve your situation at work: *There are fewer opportunities for new graduates this year.* → **equal opportunities** at EQUAL[1](2)

COLLOCATIONS

VERBS

have opportunity *I was lucky enough to have the opportunity to travel.*
take/use opportunity (=do something you have a chance to do) *Several employees took the opportunity to retire early.*
seize/grasp an opportunity (=do something very eagerly when you have the chance) *She saw an opportunity to speak to him, and seized it.*
miss/lose an opportunity (=not do something you have a chance to do) *Dwyer never missed an opportunity to criticize her.*
give sb opportunity *The children should be given the opportunity to make their own choices.*
get an opportunity | **provide/present/open up an opportunity** | **an opportunity comes (along/up)** | **an opportunity arises**

ADJECTIVES

a good/great/wonderful etc opportunity *It's a great opportunity to try new things.*
the ideal/perfect opportunity *I'd been wanting to try sailing, and this seemed like the ideal opportunity.*
a golden opportunity (=a very good opportunity) | **a rare/unique opportunity** | **a once-in-a-lifetime opportunity** (=a very good opportunity that you will only get once) | **a wasted/lost/missed opportunity** (=one you do not use) | **ample opportunity/plenty of opportunity** (=a number of chances to do something)

PHRASES

at the first/earliest opportunity (=as soon as possible) *He decided to leave school at the earliest opportunity.*
at every (possible) opportunity (=whenever possible) *She went to the museum at every opportunity.*
a window of opportunity (=a time when you can do something) | **a land of opportunity** (=a country where people have a lot of good opportunities) | **the opportunity of a lifetime** (=a very good opportunity that you will only get once)

O

Frequencies of **oppose**, **be opposed to**, and **be against** in spoken and written English

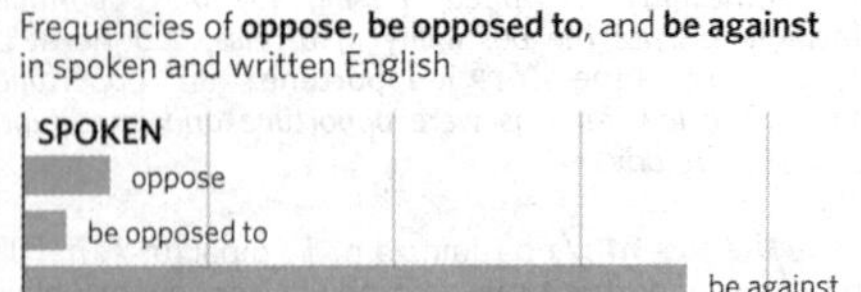
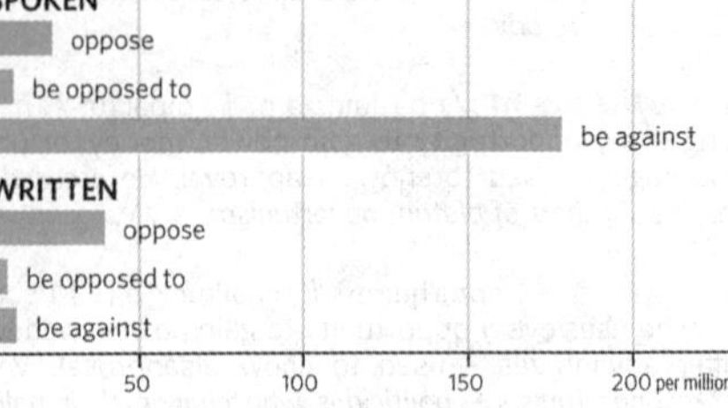

This graph shows that it is much more usual in spoken English to say that you **are against** something, rather than to say that you **oppose** it or **are opposed to** it. This is because **be against** is more informal and more general than **oppose** and **be opposed to**, which often suggest not only disagreeing with and disapproving of something, but also taking action to prevent it.

op·pose /əˈpəʊz $ əˈpoʊz/ ●●○ S3 W3 *v* [T]
1 to disagree with something such as a plan or idea and try to prevent it from happening or succeeding: *Congress is continuing to oppose the president's health care budget.*
2 to fight or compete against another person or group in a battle, competition, or election: *He is opposed by two other candidates.*

op·posed /əˈpəʊzd $ əˈpoʊzd/ ●●○ *adj* [not before noun]
1 be opposed to sth to disagree with something such as a plan or system: *Most of us are opposed to the death penalty.*
2 two ideas that are opposed to each other are completely different from each other: *The principles of capitalism and socialism are **diametrically opposed*** (=completely opposite).
3 as opposed to sth used to compare two things and show that they are different from each other: *Students discuss ideas, as opposed to just copying from books.*

op·pos·ing /əˈpəʊzɪŋ $ əˈpoʊ-/ *adj* [only before noun]
1 opposing teams, groups, or forces are competing, arguing, or fighting against each other: *The opposing armies were preparing for war.* | *The Socialist Party has split into two opposing camps.* **2** opposing ideas, opinions etc are completely different from each other: *Throughout the negotiations Hurst and Jevons took opposing views.*

op·po·site¹ /ˈɒpəzət $ ˈɑːp-/ ●●● S2 W2 *prep*
1 *especially BrE* if one thing or person is opposite another, they are facing each other: *The people sitting opposite us looked very familiar.* | *on the wall opposite the door* ⚠ Do not say that one thing is 'opposite to' or 'opposite of' another. Say that one thing is **opposite** another: *There's a car park opposite the hotel.*
2 play/star/appear etc opposite sb to act with someone in a film, especially as the two main characters: *a comedy in which he stars opposite Julia Roberts*

opposite² ●●● S3 W2 *adj* [only before noun]
1 as different as possible from something else: *I thought the medicine would make him sleep, but it **had the opposite effect**.* | **at the opposite end of the scale/spectrum** *two parties at opposite ends of the political spectrum* | ***At the opposite extreme,** Ashworth's style is very simple and modern.* | *Bob was quicker than Ed? It's usually **the opposite way round**.* | **[+to]** *a political philosophy that was opposite to everything she believed in*
2 the opposite direction, way etc is directly away from someone or something: *She turned and walked off **in the opposite direction**.* | *But the sign was pointing **the opposite way**.*
3 the opposite side, corner, edge etc of something is on the other side of the same area, often facing it: *The store was **on the opposite side of** the street.* | *the drawing on the opposite page* | *They work **at opposite ends of the country*** (=a long distance apart), *so only see each other at weekends.*
4 the opposite sex the other sex. If you are a man, women are the opposite sex: *members of the opposite sex*
5 sb's opposite number someone who has the same job in another similar organization: *a meeting with her opposite number at the Department of Health*

opposite³ ●●○ *n* [C]
1 a person or thing that is as different as possible from someone or something else: **[+of]** *What's the opposite of 'optimistic'?* | *She's quite shy, **the exact opposite of** Becky.* | *The two men were **complete opposites** – Simon tall and fair, Clive short and dark.* | *If anything, **the opposite** was true.* | *Is it sensible to think of masculine/feminine as **polar opposites*** (=exactly or completely opposite)?
2 not ... just/quite the opposite used to say that something is completely different from what has just been said: *I didn't feel sleepy at all – just the opposite, in fact.*
3 opposites attract used to say that often people who have completely different characters become friends or are attracted to each other

opposite⁴ *adv especially BrE* in a position on the other side of the same area: *Hannah lives just opposite.*

op·po·si·tion /ˌɒpəˈzɪʃən $ ˌɑːp-/ ●●○ W3 *n*
1 [U] strong disagreement with, or protest against, something such as a plan, law, or system: **[+to]** *There was a great deal of opposition to the war.* | **[+from]** *They **face opposition** from local residents as well as from environmentalists.* | *He is confident in his ability to **overcome** all **opposition** with his personal charm.* | *The proposals have **aroused the opposition of** teachers.* | ***Strong opposition** resulted in rejection of the bill.* | *Plans to turn the site into a £600 million leisure complex have met with **stiff opposition**.* | *Much **public opposition** to the new law remained.* | *Workers found themselves **in opposition to** local interests.*
2 the opposition in some countries such as Britain, the main political party in Parliament that is not part of the government: *the leader of the Opposition* | *the three main **opposition parties***
3 in opposition in some countries such as Britain, a political party that is in opposition is in Parliament, but is not part of the government: *The Socialists were elected to power after ten years in opposition.*
4 [C,U] the people who you are competing against: *They played well against good opposition.*

GRAMMAR: Singular or plural verb?

- In this meaning, **opposition** is usually followed by a singular verb: *The opposition **was** too strong for us.*
- In British English, you can also use a plural verb: *The opposition **were** too strong for us.*

GRAMMAR GUIDE ▸ NOUNS

5 [C,U] *formal* when two things are completely opposite: **[+between]** *the opposition between capitalism and socialism*

op·press /əˈpres/ *v* [T] **1** to treat a group of people unfairly or cruelly, and prevent them from having the same rights that other people in society have: *native tribes oppressed by the authorities* **2** to make someone feel unhappy, worried, or uncomfortable: *The gloom in the chapel oppressed her.*

op·pressed /əˈprest/ *adj* **1** a group of people who are oppressed are treated unfairly or cruelly and are prevented from having the same rights as other people have: *oppressed minorities* | **the oppressed** (=people who are oppressed) **2** someone who is oppressed feels unhappy, worried, or uncomfortable

op·pres·sion /əˈpreʃən/ ●○○ *n* [U] when someone treats a group of people unfairly or cruelly and prevents them from having the same rights as other people have → **discrimination**: **political/racial/sexual etc oppression** *They suffered years of political oppression.* | *the struggle against oppression*

op·pres·sive /əˈpresɪv/ ●○○ *adj*
1 powerful, cruel, and unfair: *an oppressive military regime*
2 weather that is oppressive is unpleasantly hot with no movement of air: *the **oppressive heat** of the afternoon*

3 a situation that is oppressive makes you unhappy, worried, or uncomfortable: *an oppressive silence | an oppressive atmosphere* —**oppressively** *adv*

op·pres·sor /əˈpresə $ -ər/ *n* [C] a person or group that treats people unfairly or cruelly, and prevents them from having the same rights that other people in society have

op·pro·bri·um /əˈprəʊbriəm $ əˈproʊ-/ *n* [U] *formal* strong criticism or disapproval, especially expressed publicly

opt /ɒpt $ ɑːpt/ ●●○ *v* [I] to choose one thing or do one thing instead of another: **[+for]** *We finally opted for the wood finish.* | **opt to do sth** *Many young people are opting to go on to college.*

opt in *phr v* to decide to join a group or system: **[+to]** *Employees have the choice to opt in to the scheme.*

opt out *phr v*

1 to avoid doing a duty: **[+of]** *You can't just opt out of all responsibility for the child!*

2 to decide not to be part of a group or system: **[+of]** *Britain wants to opt out of the new European regulations.*

3 if a school or hospital in Britain opts out, it decides to control the money that it is given by the government, instead of being controlled by local government

op·tic /ˈɒptɪk $ ˈɑːp-/ *adj* [only before noun] relating to the eyes: *the optic nerve*

OPTICAL INSTRUMENTS

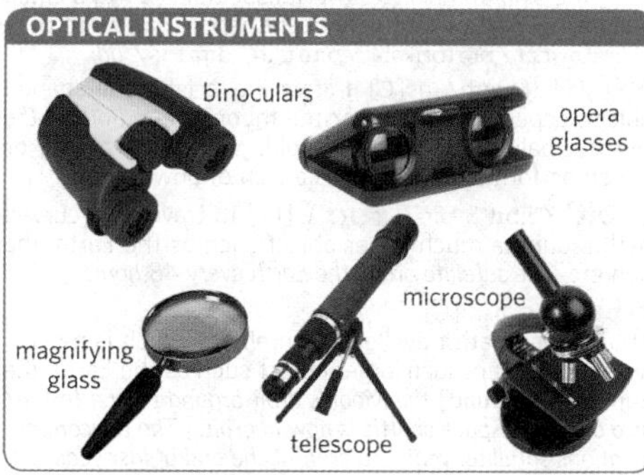

op·ti·cal /ˈɒptɪkəl $ ˈɑːp-/ ●○○ *adj* relating to machines or processes which are concerned with light, images, or the way we see things: *microscopes and other* ***optical instruments*** —**optically** /-kli/ *adv*

ˌoptical ˈcharacter recogˌnition *n* [U] *technical* computer software that recognizes numbers and letters of the alphabet which are written on paper, so that information from paper documents can be scanned (SCAN) into a computer

ˌoptical ˈfibre *BrE*, **optical fiber** *AmE n* [C,U] a long thin thread of glass or plastic along which information can be sent through a phone or computer system, using light

ˌoptical ilˈlusion *n* [C] a picture or image that tricks your eyes and makes you see something that is not actually there

op·ti·cian /ɒpˈtɪʃən $ ɑːp-/ *n* [C] **1** *BrE* someone who tests people's eyes and sells GLASSes in a shop SYN **optometrist** *AmE* **2** *AmE* someone who makes LENSes for GLASSes

op·tics /ˈɒptɪks $ ˈɑːp-/ *n* [U] the scientific study of light and the way we see

op·ti·mal /ˈɒptəməl $ ˈɑːp-/ ●○○ *adj formal* the best or most suitable SYN **optimum**

op·ti·mis·m /ˈɒptəmɪzəm $ ˈɑːp-/ ●●○ *n* [U] a tendency to believe that good things will always happen OPP **pessimism**: **grounds/cause/reason for optimism** *Recent results must give some cause for optimism.* | *There are grounds for* ***cautious optimism****.* | **mood/sense of optimism** *a new sense of optimism in the country* | **optimism (that)** *There was optimism that an agreement could be reached.* | **[+about]** *I don't share his optimism about our chances of success.*

op·ti·mist /ˈɒptəmɪst $ ˈɑːp-/ *n* [C] someone who believes that good things will happen OPP **pessimist**: *He's an* ***eternal optimist*** (=he always believes that good things will happen).

op·ti·mis·tic /ˌɒptəˈmɪstɪk◂ $ ˌɑːp-/ ●●○ *adj*

1 believing that good things will happen in the future OPP **pessimistic**: **[+about]** *Bankers are* ***cautiously optimistic*** *about the country's economic future.* | **optimistic (that)** *We are still relatively optimistic that the factory can be saved.* | *Andrew took a more optimistic view.*

2 thinking that things will be better, easier, or more successful than is actually possible: *an optimistic estimate* | **over-optimistic** *BrE*: *somewhat over-optimistic expectations*

op·ti·mize (*also* **-ise** *BrE*) /ˈɒptəmaɪz $ ˈɑːp-/ *v* [T] to improve the way that something is done or used so that it is as effective as possible: *They need to optimize the use of available resources.*

op·ti·mum /ˈɒptəməm $ ˈɑːp-/ ●○○ *adj* [only before noun] the best or most suitable for a particular purpose or in a particular situation: *optimum conditions for growth* | *This design makes the optimum use of the available space.* —**optimum** *n* [singular]

op·tion /ˈɒpʃən $ ˈɑːp-/ ●●● S1 W2 AWL *n*

1 CHOICE [C] a choice you can make in a particular situation → **optional**: *There are a number of options available.* | *He* ***had*** *two* ***options****.* | *This was not the only* ***option open*** *to him.* | **[+for]** *a range of options for cutting costs* | **one/another option is to do sth** *Another option is to rent somewhere for six months.* | **option of doing sth** *She* ***had the option of*** *staying for an extra year.* | *Teenage mothers often* ***have no option but to*** (=have no other choice except to) *live with their parents.*

2 keep/leave your options open to wait before making a decision: *I'm keeping all my options open for the moment.*

3 COMPUTERS [C] one of the possible choices you can make when using computer software: *Select an option from the main menu.* | *a list of options*

4 easy option (*also* **soft option** *BrE*) the choice which will be the least difficult, least strict, or need the least effort, which someone might choose because they are lazy: *Is community service just a soft option for criminals?*

5 RIGHT TO BUY/SELL [C] *formal* the right to buy or sell something in the future: **[+on]** *The government has agreed to buy 20 planes, with an option on a further 10.* | *Connor now owns 302,000 shares and options.*

6 AT SCHOOL/UNIVERSITY [C] *BrE* one of the subjects that you can choose to study at school for an examination, or as part of a course at a college or university: *advice on choosing your options*

7 STH ADDITIONAL [C] something that is offered in addition to the standard equipment when you buy something new, especially a car

8 first option the chance to buy or get something before anyone else: **[+on]** *They've agreed to give us the first option on their apartment.*

op·tion·al /ˈɒpʃənəl $ ˈɑːp-/ ●●○ AWL *adj* if something is optional, you do not have to do it or use it, but you can choose to if you want to OPP **compulsory**: *three optional courses* | *The other excursions are optional.* | **optional extra** *BrE*: *Leather seats are an optional extra.*

> **REGISTER**
> In everyday English, people often say that you **don't have to do sth** rather than say it is **optional**: *Ties are* ***optional****.* → *You* ***don't have to*** *wear a tie.*

op·tom·e·trist /ɒpˈtɒmɪtrɪst $ ɑːpˈtɑː-/ *n* [C] *AmE* someone who tests people's eyes and orders GLASSes for them SYN **optician** *BrE*

ˈopt-out *n* [C] *BrE* **1** when a person or group chooses not to join a system or accept an agreement: *an* ***opt-out clause*** | **[+on/from]** *the government's opt-out on the euro* **2** when a school or hospital in Britain chooses to control its own money, instead of being controlled by local government: *an opt-out school*

op·u·lent /ˈɒpjələnt $ ˈɑːp-/ *adj formal* **1** very beautiful, with a lot of decoration, and made from expensive materials SYN **luxurious**: *evening dresses in opulent fabrics* **2** very rich and spending a lot of money: *Europe's opulent elite* —**opulence** *n* [U]: *the size and opulence of the rooms*

o·pus /ˈəʊpəs $ ˈoʊ-/ *n* (*plural* **opuses** *or* **opera** /ˈɒpərə $ ˈɑː-/) [usually singular] **1** a piece of music by a great musician, numbered according to when it was written: *Beethoven's Opus 95* **2** *formal* an important work of art by a famous writer, painter etc → MAGNUM OPUS

O

or /ə; *strong* ɔː $ ər *strong* ɔːr/ ●●● S1 W1 *conjunction*
1 POSSIBILITIES/CHOICES used between two words or phrases to show that either of two things is possible, or used before the last in a list of possibilities or choices: *Shall we go out to the cinema or stay at home?* | *You can have ham, cheese, or tuna.* | **... or anything/something** *spoken* (=or something of the same kind) *Would you like a coffee or something?* | *She wasn't involved in drugs* ***or anything like that***. | *Grapes are usually* ***either*** *green* ***or*** *red.* | *He's going to do it* ***whether*** *we like it* ***or not***. | *You must do the job yourself* ***or else*** *employ someone else to do it.* → EITHER[1]
2 AND NOT used after a negative verb when you mean not one thing and also not another thing: *He doesn't have a television or a video.* | *Sonia never cleans or even offers to wash the dishes.*
3 AVOIDING BAD RESULT used to say that something bad could happen if someone does not do a particular thing: *Wear your coat or you'll catch cold.* | *Hurry up or we'll be late.* | *I had to defend myself* ***or else*** *he'd have killed me.* | *You'd better hand over the money,* ***or else*** (=used to threaten someone).
4 CORRECTION used to correct something that you have said or to give more specific information: *It's going to snow tomorrow, or that's what the forecast says.* | *John picked us up in his car,* ***or rather*** *his dad's car which he'd borrowed.* | *We've cleaned it all up,* ***or at least*** *most of it.*
5 PROOF used to prove that something must be true, by saying that the situation would be different if it was not true: *He must be at home, or his car wouldn't be here.* | *It's obviously not urgent* ***or else*** *they would have called us straight away.*
6 UNCERTAIN AMOUNTS used to show that you are guessing at an amount or number because you cannot be exact: *The boy was three or four years of age.* | *I saw Donald leaving a minute or two ago.* | *There's a motel* ***a mile or so*** *down the road* (=about a mile or possibly a little more).

-or /ə $ ər/ *suffix* [in nouns] **1** someone who does something or is doing something: *an actor* (=someone who acts) | *an inventor* | *a translator* **2** something that does something: *a calculator* (=a machine which calculates) | *a word processor* → -ER[2], -AR

or·a·cle /ˈɒrəkəl $ ˈɔː-, ˈɑː-/ *n* [C] **1** someone who the ancient Greeks believed could communicate with the gods, who gave advice to people or told them what would happen **2** a message given by an oracle **3** a person or book that gives advice and information – used humorously

o·rac·u·lar /ɒˈrækjələ, ə- $ ɔːˈrækjələr, ə-/ *adj formal* from or like an oracle

o·ral[1] /ˈɔːrəl/ ●●○ *adj*
1 spoken, not written: *oral history* | *an oral agreement*
2 relating to or involving the mouth: *oral hygiene* —**orally** *adv*: *The drug should be taken orally.* | *The statement may be given orally or in writing.*

oral[2] (*also* **ˈoral exˌam**) *n* [C] **1** *especially BrE* a spoken test, especially in a foreign language: *I've got my French oral tomorrow.* **2** *AmE* a spoken test for a university degree

ˌoral contraˈceptive *n* [C] a drug that a woman takes by mouth, so that she can have sex without having a baby SYN **pill**

ˌoral ˈsex *n* [U] the activity of touching someone's sex organs with the lips and tongue, to give sexual pleasure

ˈoral ˌsurgeon *n* [C] a DENTIST who performs operations in the mouth

or·ange[1] /ˈɒrəndʒ $ ˈɔː-, ˈɑː-/ ●●● S1 W2 *n*
1 [C] a round fruit that has a thick orange skin and is divided into parts inside: ***Peel*** *the* ***oranges*** *and divide them into segments.* | *orange juice* | *orange peel* | *orange groves* (=areas of orange trees)
2 [U] a colour that is between red and yellow: *a bright shade of orange*

orange[2] ●●● S2 W2 *adj* between red and yellow in colour: *an orange shirt*

or·ange·ade /ˌɒrəndʒˈeɪd $ ˌɔː-, ˌɑː-/ *n* [C,U] a drink that tastes like oranges

ˈOrange Bowl, the an important college football game, held every year in Miami, Florida

or·an·ge·ry /ˈɒrəndʒəri $ ˈɔː-,ˈɑː-/ *n* (*plural* **orangeries**) [C] *old-fashioned* a place, usually next to a large expensive house, where orange trees are grown

o·rang·u·tang /ɔːˌræŋuːˈtæŋ $ əˈræŋətæŋ/ (*also* **orangutan** /-tæn/) *n* [C] a large APE with long arms and long orange-brown hair

o·ra·tion /əˈreɪʃən, ɔː-/ *n* [C] a formal public speech

or·a·tor /ˈɒrətə $ ˈɔːrətər, ˈɑː-/ *n* [C] *formal* someone who is good at making speeches and persuading people

or·a·to·ri·o /ˌɒrəˈtɔːriəʊ $ ˌɔːrəˈtɔːrioʊ, ˌɑː-/ *n* (*plural* **oratorios**) [C] a long piece of music in which a large group of people sing

or·a·tory /ˈɒrətri $ ˈɔːrətɔːri, ˈɑː-/ *n* (*plural* **oratories**) **1** [U] the skill of making powerful speeches **2** [C] a small building or part of a church where people can go to pray —**oratorical** /ˌɒrəˈtɒrɪkəl◂ $ ˌɔːrəˈtɔːr-, ˌɑːrəˈtɑː-/ *adj*

orb /ɔːb $ ɔːrb/ *n* [C] **1** *literary* a bright ball-shaped object, especially the sun or the moon: *the red orb of the sun* **2** a ball decorated with gold, carried by a king or queen on formal occasions as a sign of power

or·bit[1] /ˈɔːbɪt $ ˈɔːr-/ ●○○ *v* [I,T] to travel in a curved path around a much larger object such as the Earth, the Sun etc: *The satellite orbits the Earth every 48 hours.*

orbit[2] ●○○ *n* [C]
1 the curved path travelled by an object which is moving around another much larger object such as the Earth, the Sun etc: **[+around]** *the Moon's orbit around the Earth* | **in/into orbit** *The space shuttle is now in orbit.* | *The telecommunications satellite went into orbit at the end of last year.*
2 *formal* the area of power and influence of a person, an organization etc: **within the orbit of sth** *countries within the orbit of the British Commonwealth*

or·bit·al[1] /ˈɔːbɪtl $ ˈɔːr-/ *adj* **1** relating to the orbit of one object around another: *the Earth's orbital path* **2** *BrE* an orbital road goes around a large city: *the M25, London's orbital motorway*

orbital[2] *n* [C] *BrE* a road that goes around a large city to keep the traffic away from the centre SYN **ring road**

or·bit·er /ˈɔːbɪtə $ ˈɔːrbɪtər/ *n* [C] *technical* a spacecraft that is sent into space to travel around the moon or a PLANET without ever landing on it. It carries equipment but not people and is designed to gather information: *a lunar orbiter*

or·chard /ˈɔːtʃəd $ ˈɔːrtʃərd/ ●○○ *n* [C] a place where fruit trees are grown: *a cherry orchard*

or·ches·tra /ˈɔːkəstrə $ ˈɔːr-/ ●●○ *n*
1 [C] a large group of musicians playing many different kinds of instruments and led by a CONDUCTOR: *the Berlin Symphony Orchestra* | *the school orchestra*
2 orchestra section/seats *AmE* the area of seats in a theatre close to and on the same level as the stage

GRAMMAR: Singular or plural verb?

- **Orchestra** is usually followed by a singular verb: *The orchestra* ***was*** *rehearsing for a concert.*
- In British English, you can also use a plural verb: *The orchestra* ***were*** *rehearsing for a concert.*

GRAMMAR GUIDE ▸ NOUNS

or·ches·tral /ɔːˈkestrəl $ ɔːr-/ *adj* relating to or written for an orchestra: *orchestral music*

ˈorchestra pit *n* [C] the space below the stage in a theatre where the musicians sit → see picture at THEATRE

or·ches·trate /ˈɔːkəstreɪt $ ˈɔːr-/ *v* [T] **1** *written* to organize an important event or a complicated plan, especially secretly: *The riots were orchestrated by anti-government forces.* | *a* ***carefully orchestrated*** *promotional campaign* **2** to arrange a piece of music so that it can be played by an orchestra —**orchestration** /ˌɔːkəˈstreɪʃən $ ˌɔːr-/ *n* [C,U]

or·chid /ˈɔːkɪd $ ˈɔːr-/ *n* [C] a plant that has flowers which are brightly coloured and unusually shaped → see picture at FLOWER[1]

or·dain /ɔːˈdeɪn $ ɔːr-/ *v* [T] **1** to officially make someone a priest or religious leader → **ordination**: *Desmond Tutu was ordained in 1960.* | **ordain sb (as) sth** *The church voted to allow women to be ordained as priests.* **2** *formal* to order that something should happen: **ordain that** *The King ordained that deer should not be hunted without a royal licence.*

or·deal /ɔːˈdiːl, ˈɔːdiːl $ ɔːrˈdiːl, ˈɔːrdiːl/ ●○○ *n* [C] a terrible or painful experience that continues for a period of time: **[+of]** *She then had to* ***go through the ordeal*** *of giving evidence.* | *She was forced to* ***face the ordeal of*** *withdrawal symptoms.* | *He was beginning to wonder if he would* ***survive the ordeal.*** | *Teresa had a transplant in 1989 and was just* ***recovering from*** *that* ***ordeal*** *when she suffered a brain hemorrhage.* | *Soon the whole* ***terrifying ordeal*** *would be over.*

or·der[1] /ˈɔːdə $ ˈɔːrdər/ ●●● S1 W1 *n*

1 FOR A PURPOSE **a) in order to do sth** for the purpose of doing something: *Samuel trained every day in order to improve his performance.* | *In order to understand how the human body works, you need to have some knowledge of chemistry.* **b) in order for/that** *formal* so that something can happen or so that someone can do something: *Sunlight is needed in order for the process of photosynthesis to take place in plants.*

2 ARRANGEMENT [C,U] the way that things or events are arranged in relation to each other, so that one thing is first, another thing is second etc SYN **sequence**: **in the right/correct order** *Make sure that you* ***put*** *the books back in the right* ***order.*** | **out of order/in the wrong order** *The files are all out of order.* | **in order** (=one after another, according to a plan) *Then they call out our names in order and we answer yes or no.* | **in alphabetical order** *Their names are* ***arranged*** *in alphabetical* ***order.*** | **in order of importance/difficulty etc** *The cities are listed in order of importance.* | *Students learn the verbs in order of difficulty.* | **in ascending/descending order** (=starting with the lowest or highest number) *The prices are given in ascending order.* | **in reverse order** *She read out the names in reverse order.* | *There seemed to be no* ***logical order*** *to the sections.*

3 INSTRUCTION [C usually plural] an instruction to do something that is given by someone in authority: **order to do sth** *The captain had to give the order to abandon ship.* | **under orders (from sb) (to do sth)** *She is under orders to have a complete rest.* | **on sb's orders** *He was thrown into the river on the emperor's orders.* | **by order of sb** *The company cannot be identified by order of the court.*

4 CONTROLLED SITUATION [U] a situation in which rules are obeyed and authority is respected: *the breakdown of* ***law and order*** | *The riots are a threat to* ***public order.*** | **keep order/keep sb in order** (=stop people from behaving badly) *The physics teacher couldn't keep order in any class.* | *She had trouble keeping her teenage sons in order.* | *The army was called in to* ***restore order.***

5 WELL-ORGANIZED STATE [U] a situation in which everything is controlled, well organized, and correctly arranged: *Let's have some order in here.* | *You need to* ***put*** *your financial affairs* ***in order.*** | *She keeps her room* ***in good order.***

6 FOR FOOD OR DRINK [C] **a)** a request for food or drink in a restaurant or bar: *The waiter* ***took*** *our* ***orders.*** | **last orders** *BrE* (=the last time you can order a drink before a bar closes) *Last orders now please!* **b)** the food or drink you have asked for in a restaurant or bar: *When our order finally arrived we were very hungry indeed.* → SIDE ORDER

7 FOR GOODS [C] **a)** a request by a customer for a company to supply goods: *Goods will be sent within 24 hours of* ***receiving*** *your* ***order.*** | *You can always* ***cancel*** *your* ***order*** *if you change your mind.* | *The government has* ***placed an order for*** (=asked a company to supply) *new weapons.* | *Please complete the enclosed* ***order form.*** | **on order** (=asked for, but not yet received) *My bicycle is on order.* | **make/supply sth to order** (=produce something especially for a particular customer) *They make hand-made shoes to order.* **b)** goods that you have ordered from a company: *Your order has arrived – you can collect it from the store any time.* → MAIL ORDER

8 be out of order a) if a machine or piece of equipment is out of order, it is not working: *The phone is out of order again.* **b)** *BrE informal* if someone's behaviour is out of order, it is unacceptable SYN **out of line** *AmE* **c)** to be breaking the rules in a committee, court, parliament etc: *The MP's remarks were ruled out of order.*

> **REGISTER**
> In everyday English, people usually say that a machine or piece of equipment is **not working** or is **broken** rather than **out of order**: *The phone's* ***not working.***

9 be in order a) if something is in order, it is correct or right: *Everything is in order.* **b)** to be a suitable thing to do or say on a particular occasion: *I hear congratulations are in order.* **c)** if an official document is in order, it is legal and correct: *Is your passport in order?* **d)** if something that you do is in order, it is allowed by the rules in a committee, court, parliament etc

10 be in (good) working/running order in good condition or working well: *She keeps her bicycle in good working order.*

11 SOCIAL/ECONOMIC SITUATION [singular] the political, social, or economic situation at a particular time: **social/political order** *He called the rioters a threat to the social order.* | *The people of South Africa wanted a* ***new order.*** | *He dared to challenge the* ***established*** (=traditional) ***order.***

12 be the order of the day a) to be suitable for a particular occasion or situation: *Casual clothes are the order of the day.* **b)** to be very common at a particular time – used especially when you disapprove of something: *Sexual explicitness is the order of the day.*

13 the order of things the way that life and the world are organized and intended to be: *People accepted the class system as part of the* ***natural order of things.***

14 of a high order/of the highest order (*also* **of the first order**) of a very good kind or of the best kind: *an achievement of the highest order*

15 withdraw/retreat in good order to move away from the enemy in war in an organized way

16 in the order of sth/of the order of sth (*also* **on the order of sth** *AmE*) a little more or a little less than a particular amount, especially a high amount SYN **approximately**: *a figure in the order of $7 million*

17 RELIGIOUS GROUP [C] a society of MONKS or NUNS (=people who live a holy life according to religious rules): *the Benedictine Order* | **[+of]** *the order of Jesuits*

18 take (holy) orders to become a priest

19 SECRET SOCIETY [C] an organization or a society whose members meet for secret ceremonies

20 OFFICIAL HONOUR [C] a group of people who have received a special official reward from a king, president etc for their services or achievements: *the Order of the Garter*

21 MONEY [C] an official piece of paper that can be exchanged for money → MONEY ORDER, POSTAL ORDER

22 the lower orders *BrE old-fashioned* people who belong to the lowest social class

23 ANIMALS/PLANTS [C] *technical* a group of animals or plants that are considered together because they EVOLVED from the same plant or animal → CLASS[1](5), SPECIES

24 COMPUTER [C] *AmE* a list of jobs that a computer has to do in a particular order SYN **queue** *BrE*

25 Order! Order! *spoken* used to ask people to stop talking in a meeting or parliament → PECKING ORDER, POINT OF ORDER, STANDING ORDER, → **call sb/sth to order** at CALL[1](16), → **set/put your own house in order** at HOUSE[1](7), → **be**

given/get your marching orders at MARCH[1](5), → **in short order** at SHORT[1](22), → **under starter's orders** at STARTER, → **tall order** at TALL

COLLOCATIONS – MEANING 3

VERBS

give/issue an order *Do not fire until I give the order.*
obey an order *He refused to obey this order.*
follow orders/carry out orders (=obey them) *The men argued that they had only been following orders.*
take orders from sb (=be given orders by them and obey them) *I don't take orders from you!*
disobey/ignore an order *Anyone who disobeys these orders will be severely punished.*
have orders to do sth *The soldiers had orders to shoot anyone on the streets after 10 o'clock.*
receive an order

ADJECTIVES/NOUN + order

a direct order (=a clear order) *What happens to a soldier who disobeys a direct order?*
strict orders *They had strict orders not to allow anyone through.*
a court order (=when a judge in a court says you must do something) | **an executive order** (=an order from a president) | **doctor's orders** (=when the doctor says you must do something)

order² ●●● S2 W2 *v*
1 ASK FOR FOOD/DRINK [I,T] to ask for food or a drink in a restaurant, bar etc: *Anne ordered another glass of wine.* | *Are you ready to order?* | *He sat down and* ***ordered a meal****.* THESAURUS ▸ ASK
2 ASK FOR GOODS [I,T] to ask for goods or services to be supplied: *I've ordered a new computer from the supplier.* | **order sb sth** *I'll order you a taxi.*
3 TELL SB TO DO STH [T] to tell someone that they must do something, especially using your official power or authority: *The court ordered his release from prison.* | *'Stay right there,' she ordered.* | **order sb to do sth** *Tom was ordered to pay £300 as compensation.* | *Her doctor had ordered her to rest for a week.* | **be ordered back to sth** *The soldiers were ordered back to their units.* | **order that** *He ordered that the house be sold.*
4 ARRANGE [T] to arrange something in an order: *The list is ordered alphabetically.*

THESAURUS – MEANING 3

TO TELL SOMEONE THEY MUST DO SOMETHING

order to tell someone that they must do something, using your official power or authority: *A policeman ordered him to stop.* | *He ordered his men to put down their weapons.*
tell to say to someone that they must do something: *Stop telling me what to do!* | *The headmaster told me to wait outside his office.*
give orders/instructions to tell someone exactly what they must do: *The police chief gave orders to shoot.* | *The doctor gave instructions that she should rest as much as possible.*
command used about a high-ranking person such as a general, captain, or king ordering someone to do something: *The general commanded the troops to fall back.*
instruct *formal* to tell someone to do something, especially when you tell them exactly how it should be done: *The architect was instructed to keep the plans simple.* | *She took three tablets every day,* ***as instructed*** *by her doctor.*
direct to give someone an official or legal order to do something: *The judge directed the jury to find her not guilty.*
subpoena /səˈpiːnə, səb-/ to officially order someone to appear in a court of law in order to answer questions: *Another three of the president's advisors were subpoenaed.*

order sb **around** (*also* **order sb about** *BrE*) *phr v* to give someone orders in an annoying or threatening way: *How dare he order her about like that?*

order sb ↔ **out** *phr v* to order soldiers or police to go somewhere to stop violent behaviour by a crowd: *The governor decided to order out the National Guard.*

ˈorder ˌbook *n* [C usually plural] *especially BrE* a record of how many goods or services a company has been asked to provide, which shows how successful it is financially: *Our order books are full at the moment.*

or·dered /ˈɔːdəd $ ˈɔːrdərd/ (*also* **well-ordered**) *adj* well arranged or controlled: *an ordered existence* | *a well-ordered household* → DISORDERED

or·der·ing /ˈɔːdərɪŋ $ ˈɔːr-/ *n* [C,U] the way in which something is arranged, or the act of arranging something: *a different ordering*

or·der·ly¹ /ˈɔːdəli $ ˈɔːrdərli/ ●○○ *adj*
1 arranged or organized in a sensible or neat way OPP **disorderly**: **in (an) orderly sth** *The tools were arranged in orderly rows.* | *She needs to organize her ideas in a more orderly way.* THESAURUS ▸ TIDY
2 peaceful or well behaved OPP **disorderly**: **in (an) orderly sth** *The elections were conducted* ***in an orderly fashion****.* | *They waited in a dignified and orderly manner outside the church.* —**orderliness** *n* [U]

orderly² *n* (*plural* **orderlies**) [C] **1** someone who does unskilled jobs in a hospital **2** a soldier who does unskilled jobs

ˌorder of ˈmagnitude *n* (*plural* **orders of magnitude**) [C] **1** if something is an order of magnitude greater or smaller than something else, it is ten times greater or smaller in size or amount **2** the scale of the size of something: *That was a problem but this crisis is of a different order of magnitude.*

ˈorder ˌpaper *n* [C] a list of subjects to be discussed in the British Parliament

ˈor·di·nal ˌnumber (*also* **ordinal**) /ˈɔːdɪnəl $ ˈɔːrdənəl/ *n* [C] one of the numbers such as first, second, third etc which show the order of things → CARDINAL NUMBER

or·di·nance /ˈɔːdənəns $ ˈɔːrdənəns/ *n* [C] **1** *AmE* a law, usually of a city or town, that forbids or restricts an activity: *a city ordinance that says parks must be closed at 11 p.m.* **2** an order given by a ruler or governing organization: *a Royal ordinance*

or·di·nand /ˈɔːdənænd $ ˈɔːrdn-/ *n* [C] a person who is preparing to become a priest

or·di·na·ri·ly /ˈɔːdənərəli, ˌɔːdənˈeərəli $ ˌɔːrdənˈerəli/ *adv*
1 [sentence adverb] usually: *Ordinarily, he didn't like to go to the movies.* | *This is not the price at which the CD is ordinarily sold.* **2** in an ordinary or normal way

or·di·na·ry /ˈɔːdənəri $ ˈɔːrdəneri/ ●●● S1 W2 *adj*
1 average, common, or usual, not different or special: *It's just an ordinary camera.* | *The book is about* ***ordinary people****.* | *Art should be part of* ***ordinary life****.* | *It is good because it is written in friendly, ordinary language.* | **out of the ordinary** (=unusual or unexpected) *Anything out of the ordinary made her nervous.* | **in the ordinary way** *BrE* (=as normal) *The money is taxed as income in the ordinary way.* | **sb/sth is no ordinary ...** (=used to say someone or something is very special) *This is no ordinary car.* | *Ruiz is no ordinary prisoner.* THESAURUS ▸ NORMAL
2 not particularly good or impressive: *I thought the paintings were pretty ordinary.* —**ordinariness** *n* [U]

ˈOrdinary ˌlevel *n* [C,U] O LEVEL

ˌordinary ˈseaman *n* [C] a low rank in the British navy

ˌordinary ˈshares *n* [plural] *technical* the largest part of a company's CAPITAL, which is owned by people who have the right to vote at meetings and to receive part of the company's profits

or·di·na·tion /ˌɔːdəˈneɪʃən $ ˌɔːr-/ *n* [C,U] the act or ceremony in which someone is made a priest → **ordain**: *the ordination of women*

ord·nance /ˈɔːdnəns $ ˈɔːr-/ *n* [U] **1** large guns with wheels SYN **artillery** **2** weapons, explosives, and vehicles used in fighting

ˌ**Ordnance ˈSurvey ˌmap** *n* [C] *BrE* a map which shows all the roads, paths, hills etc of an area in detail

or·dure /ˈɔːdjʊə $ ˈɔːrdʒər/ *n* [U] *formal* dirt, especially waste matter from the body

ore /ɔː $ ɔːr/ *n* [C,U] rock or earth from which metal can be obtained: *iron ore | veins of rich ore*

or·e·ga·no /ˌɒrɪˈɡɑːnəʊ $ əˈreɡənoʊ/ *n* [U] a plant used in cooking, especially in Italian cooking

or·gan /ˈɔːɡən $ ˈɔːr-/ ●●○ W3 *n* [C]

1 BODY PART **a)** a part of the body, such as the heart or lungs, that has a particular purpose: *the liver, heart, and other* ***internal organs*** *| loss of blood flow to his* ***vital organs*** *| Extra doses of the hormone caused the animals'* ***reproductive organs*** *to develop sooner than usual. | In Arizona, 480 people are waiting for* ***organ transplants****. | dying people who have agreed to be* ***organ donors*** **b)** a PENIS - used because you want to avoid saying this directly

ORGAN

2 MUSICAL INSTRUMENT **a)** (*also* **pipe organ**) a large musical instrument used especially in churches, with KEYs like a piano and large pipes that air passes through to produce the sound **b)** an electronic musical instrument that produces music similar to a pipe organ, but that does not have pipes: *an electronic organ*

3 ORGANIZATION *formal* an organization that is part of, or works for, a larger organization or group: **[+of]** *The courts are organs of government. | the decision-making organs*

4 NEWSPAPER/MAGAZINE *formal* a newspaper or magazine which gives information, news etc for an organization or group: **[+of]** *the* ***official organ*** *of the Communist Party*

or·gan·die (*also* **organdy** *AmE*) /ˈɔːɡəndi $ ˈɔːr-/ *n* [U] very thin stiff cotton cloth, used as dress material

ˈ**organ ˌgrinder** *n* [C] a musician who plays a BARREL ORGAN in the street

or·gan·ic /ɔːˈɡænɪk $ ɔːr-/ ●●○ W3 *adj*

1 FARMING relating to farming or gardening methods of growing food without using artificial chemicals, or produced or grown by these methods: ***Organic farming*** *is better for the environment. | organic gardening |* **organic food/vegetables/milk etc** *The shop sells organic food. | organic wine*

2 DEVELOPMENT change or development which is organic happens in a natural way, without anyone planning it or forcing it to happen: *The company's path to success was by means of organic growth.*

3 LIVING THINGS living, or produced by or from living things OPP **inorganic**: *Adding* ***organic matter*** *such as manure can improve the soil. | Bacteria act on* ***organic waste****.*

4 PART OF STH an organic system or relationship is one in which the parts or people fit well and in a comfortable way with each other: *an* ***organic relationship*** *between the individual and his community | They believe in the* ***organic unity*** *of the universe.*

5 BODY ORGANS relating to the organs of the body: *organic diseases* —**organically** /-kli/ *adv*: *organically produced cheese | A writer's style must develop organically.*

orˌganic ˈchemistry *n* [U] the study of substances containing CARBON → **inorganic chemistry**

or·gan·is·m /ˈɔːɡənɪzəm $ ˈɔːr-/ ●○○ *n* [C]

1 an animal, plant, human, or any other living thing: *All* ***living organisms*** *have to adapt to changes in environmental conditions. | Genes operate together in determining the characteristics of an* ***individual organism****.*

2 a system made up of parts that are dependent on each other: *A society is essentially an organism.*

or·gan·ist /ˈɔːɡənɪst $ ˈɔːr-/ *n* [C] someone who plays the ORGAN: *a church organist*

or·gan·i·za·tion (*also* **-isation** *BrE*) /ˌɔːɡənaɪˈzeɪʃən $ ˌɔːrɡənə-/ ●●● S2 W1 *n*

1 [C] a group such as a club or business that has formed for a particular purpose: *The public expect high standards from any large organization. | the World Trade Organization | a voluntary organization which helps disabled people with their transport needs | an illegal terrorist organization |* ***international organizations*** *such as the UN*

2 [U] planning and arranging something so that it is successful or effective: *Putting on a show of this kind involves considerable organisation. |* **[+of]** *The college has helped Anne with the organization of the event.*

3 [U] the way in which the different parts of a system are arranged and work together: **[+of]** *There needs to be a change in the organization of the health service.* —**organizational** *adj*: *organizational skills*

THESAURUS

organization a group of people, companies, or countries, which is set up for a particular purpose: *Greenpeace is an international organization that protects the environment. | the World Health Organization*

institution a large important organization such as a bank, church, or university: *The University is an important academic institution. | financial institutions such as banks*

association an organization for people in a particular profession, sport, or activity, which officially represents its members - often used in names: *I met a representative of the National Association of Teachers. | the Football Association*

party an organization of people with the same political aims which you can vote for in elections: *Which political party do you support? | He voted for the Republican Party's candidate.*

body an important group of people who make the rules and advise people about what should be allowed: *the sport's* ***governing body*** *| The government has set up an* ***advisory body****.*

club/society an organization for people who share an interest, for example a sport: *We belong to a tennis club. | I joined the university film society.*

union an organization formed by workers in order to protect their rights: *The union ordered its members out on strike.*

charity an organization which collects money to help people who are poor, sick etc and does not make any profit for itself: *She has raised a lot of money for local charities.*

quango *BrE disapproving* an organization set up by the government, which has official power but whose members have not been elected: *the amount of money that is wasted on government quangos*

or·gan·ize (*also* **-ise** *BrE*) /ˈɔːɡənaɪz $ ˈɔːr-/ ●●● S1 W2 *v*

1 [T] to make the necessary arrangements so that an activity can happen effectively: *The course was organized by a training company. | Students need to learn how to organize their work.*

2 [T] to manage a group of people who are doing something: *The lawyer helped to organize a group of parents who took action for their children. |* **organize yourself** *The scientists need to organize themselves and work as a team.*

3 [T] to arrange something so that it is more ordered or happens in a more sensible way: *He doesn't need you to organize his life for him. | Organize yourself to arrive at places on time.*

4 [T] to arrange things in a particular order or pattern: *We are learning about how genes are organized.*

5 [I,T] to form a TRADE UNION or persuade people to join one: *The law gives workers the right to organize and bargain collectively.*

O

or·gan·ized (*also* **-ised** *BrE*) /ˈɔːɡənaɪzd $ ˈɔːr-/ ●●○ S3 *adj*
1 involving people working together in an effective and well-planned way OPP **disorganized**: *Organized groups of citizens are more successful at changing the government's mind.* | *Organized networks of thieves are stealing cattle.* | **organized religion** (=a religion that has lasted for a long time with leaders and many followers)
2 well/badly/carefully etc organized arranged or ordered well, badly, carefully etc: *a carefully organized campaign* | *I want to work with a well-organized team.* | *a* ***highly organized*** (=well-organized) *social system*
3 achieving your aims in a way that is effective, ordered, and sensible: *It will take me a few days to* ***get organized***.

ˌorganized ˈcrime *n* [U] a large and powerful organization of criminals: *Organized crime is involved in drug trafficking.*

or·gan·iz·er (*also* **-iser** *BrE*) /ˈɔːɡənaɪzə $ ˈɔːrɡənaɪzər/ *n* [C] someone who makes the arrangements for something that is planned to happen: *The organizers had expected about 50,000 people to attend the concert.*

or·gan·o·gram /ɔːˈɡænəɡræm $ ɔːr-/ *n* [C] a drawing that shows the different ranks of the people working in an organization

or·gas·m /ˈɔːɡæzəm $ ˈɔːr-/ *n* [C,U] the greatest point of sexual pleasure: *women who have never* ***had an orgasm*** —**orgasm** *v* [I]

or·gas·mic /ɔːˈɡæzmɪk $ ɔːr-/ *adj* **1** *informal* extremely exciting or enjoyable: *an orgasmic experience* **2** relating to orgasm

or·gy /ˈɔːdʒi $ ˈɔːr-/ *n* (*plural* **orgies**) [C] **1** a wild party with a lot of eating, drinking, and sexual activity: *the* ***drunken orgies*** *of their youth* **2** sexual activity in a group **3 an orgy of sth** used to emphasize that people suddenly do a lot of a particular activity, especially far too much of it: *an orgy of spending* | *an orgy of violence* —**orgiastic** /ˌɔːdʒiˈæstɪk◂ $ ˌɔːr-/ *adj*

o·ri·ent[1] /ˈɔːrient, ˈɒri- $ ˈɔː-/ ●○○ AWL (*also* **orientate** *BrE*) *v*
1 be oriented to/towards/around sth/sb to give a lot of attention to one type of activity or one type of person: *a course that is oriented towards the needs of businessmen* | *A lot of the training is orientated around communications skills.* | *The organization is strongly oriented towards research.*
2 orient yourself a) to find exactly where you are by looking around you or using a map → **disorient**, **disorientated**: *She looked at the street names, trying to orient herself.* **b)** to become familiar with a new situation: **[+to]** *It takes new students a while to orientate themselves to college life.*

o·ri·ent[2] /ˈɔːriənt, ˈɒri- $ ˈɔː-/ *n* **the Orient** *old-fashioned* the eastern part of the world, especially China and Japan → **the East** at EAST[1], OCCIDENT

o·ri·en·tal[1] /ˌɔːriˈentl◂, ˌɒri- $ ˌɔː-/ *adj* relating to or from the eastern part of the world, especially China and Japan: *a beautiful oriental rug* | *oriental art*

oriental[2], Oriental *n* [C] *old-fashioned not polite* a word for someone from the eastern part of the world, especially China or Japan, now considered offensive → OCCIDENTAL

o·ri·en·tal·ist /ˌɔːriˈentələst, ˌɒri- $ ˌɔː-/ *n* [C] someone who studies the languages and culture of oriental countries

o·ri·en·tate /ˈɔːriənteɪt, ˈɒri- $ ˈɔː-/ AWL *v* a British word for ORIENT[1] OPP **disorientate**

o·ri·en·tat·ed /ˈɔːriənteɪtəd, ˈɒ- $ ˈɔː-/ AWL *adj* a British word for ORIENTED

o·ri·en·ta·tion /ˌɔːriənˈteɪʃən, ˌɒri- $ ˌɔː-/ ●○○ AWL *n formal*
1 [C,U] the type of activity or subject that a person or organization seems most interested in and gives most attention to: **[+towards/to]** *The company needs to develop a stronger orientation towards marketing its products.* | *How can we get students to adopt a serious orientation to learning?* | **[+of]** *He was unhappy with the commercial orientation of the organization.*
2 [C,U] the political opinions or religious beliefs that someone has: **political/religious orientation** *The meeting is open to everyone, whatever their political or religious orientation.* | *The party has a broadly socialist orientation.*
3 sexual orientation the fact that someone is HETEROSEXUAL or HOMOSEXUAL: *Discrimination on the grounds of sexual orientation is still far too widespread.*
4 [U] a period of time during which people are trained and prepared for a new job or course of study: *This is orientation week for all the new students.*
5 [C] the angle or position of an object, or the direction in which it is facing

o·ri·ent·ed /ˈɔːrientəd, ˈɒri- $ ˈɔː-/ AWL (*also* **orientated** *BrE*) *adj* giving a lot of time, effort, or attention to one particular thing: *A lot of the younger students don't seem to be politically oriented at all.* | *She's very career orientated.* | *The country's economy is export oriented.*

o·ri·en·teer·ing /ˌɔːriənˈtɪərɪŋ, ˌɒri- $ ˌɔːriənˈtɪr-/ *n* [U] a sport in which people have to find their way quickly across an area in the countryside that they do not know, using a map and a COMPASS

or·i·fice /ˈɒrɪfɪs $ ˈɔː-, ˈɑː-/ *n* [C] *formal* **1** one of the holes in your body, such as your mouth, nose etc: *various bodily orifices* **2** a hole or entrance

o·ri·ga·mi /ˌɒrɪˈɡɑːmi $ ˌɔː-/ *n* [U] the Japanese art of folding paper to make attractive objects

or·i·gin /ˈɒrɪdʒɪn $ ˈɔː-, ˈɑː-/ ●●● W2 *n* [C,U]
1 (*also* **origins** [plural]) the place or situation in which something begins to exist: **[+of]** *a new theory to explain the origins of the universe* | **in origin** *Most coughs are viral in origin.* | *The word is French in origin.* | *The tradition* ***has*** *its* ***origins in*** *the Middle Ages.* | *old folk tales* ***of unknown origin*** | **country/place of origin** (=where something came from) *All meat should be clearly labelled with its country of origin.*
THESAURUS ▸ BEGINNING
2 (*also* **origins**) [plural] the country, race, or type of family which someone comes from → **extraction**: **of French/German/Asian etc origin** *Two thirds of the pupils are of Asian origin.* | *The form asks for information about the person's* ***ethnic origin***. | *Immigrants rarely return to their* ***country of origin***. | *She never forgot her* ***humble origins***.

o·rig·i·nal[1] /əˈrɪdʒɪnəl, -dʒənəl/ ●●● S1 W1 *adj*
1 [only before noun] existing or happening first, before other people or things: *The land was returned to its original owner.* | *The kitchen still has many* ***original features*** (=parts that were there when the house was first built). | *the original meaning of the word* | *The original plan was to fly out to New York.*
2 completely new and different from anything that anyone has thought of before: *I don't think George is capable of having* ***original ideas***! | *That's not a very original suggestion.* | *a* ***highly original*** *design* | *His work is truly original.*
THESAURUS ▸ NEW
3 [only before noun] an original work of art is the one that was made by the artist and is not a copy: *The original painting is now in the National Gallery in London.* | *an original Holbein drawing*

original[2] ●●○ *n* [C]
1 a work of art or a document that is not a copy, but is the one produced by the writer or artist: *The colours are much more striking in the original.* | *I'll keep a copy of the contract, and give you the original.*
2 in the original in the language that a book, play etc was first written in, before it was translated: *I'd prefer to read it in the original.*
3 *informal* someone whose behaviour, clothing etc is unusual and amusing

o·rig·i·nal·i·ty /əˌrɪdʒəˈnæləti/ *n* [U] when something is completely new and different from anything that anyone has thought of before: **[+of]** *I was impressed by the originality of the plan.* | *Her earlier work* ***shows*** *a lot of* ***originality***. | *A lot of his designs lack originality.* | *a young writer of* ***great originality***

o·rig·i·nal·ly /əˈrɪdʒɪnəli, -dʒənəli/ ●●● S2 W2 *adv* in the beginning, before other things happened or before things changed: *The family originally came from France.* | *The building was originally used as a prison.* | *We originally intended to stay for just a few days.* | [sentence adverb] *Originally, we had planned a tour of Scotland but we didn't go in the end.*

oˌriginal ˈsin *n* [U] the tendency to behave in bad or evil ways, which is in all people according to the Christian religion

o·rig·i·nate /əˈrɪdʒəneɪt/ ●●○ *v*
1 [I always + adv/prep, not in progressive] *formal* to come from a particular place or start in a particular situation: *How did the plan originate?* | **[+from]** *A lot of our medicines originate from tropical plants.* | **[+in]** *Many Christmas traditions originated in Germany.* | **[+with]** *The idea originated with the ancient Greek philosophers.* | **[+as]** *The town originated as a small fishing port.*
2 [T] to have the idea for something and start it: *The technique was originated by an Italian artist.*

o·rig·i·na·tor /əˈrɪdʒəneɪtə $ -ər/ *n* [C] the person who first has the idea for something and starts it SYN **initiator**: **[+of]** *Professor Adams was the originator of the project.*

or·i·ole /ˈɔːriəʊl $ -oʊl/ *n* [C] **1** a North American bird that is black with a red and yellow STRIPE on its wing **2** a European bird with black wings and a yellow body

or·mo·lu /ˈɔːməluː $ ˈɔːr-/ *n* [U] a gold-coloured mixture of metals that does not contain real gold: *an ormolu clock*

or·na·ment¹ /ˈɔːnəmənt $ ˈɔːr-/ ●○○ *n*
1 [C] a small object that you keep in your house because it is beautiful rather than useful: *a shelf covered with books and ornaments* | *china ornaments*
2 [U] decoration that is added to something: *The building style is plain, with very little ornament.* | **for ornament** *The coins were only ever used for ornament, not as currency.*

or·na·ment² /ˈɔːnəment $ ˈɔːr-/ *v* **be ornamented with sth** to be decorated with something: *a silver goblet ornamented with pearls* | **richly/exquisitely/lavishly etc ornamented** *a table richly ornamented with carvings*

or·na·men·tal /ˌɔːnəˈmentl◂ $ ˌɔːr-/ *adj* designed to make something look attractive rather than to be used for a particular purpose: *ornamental gardens* | *The pillars in the centre are purely ornamental.*

or·na·men·ta·tion /ˌɔːnəmenˈteɪʃən $ ˌɔːr-/ *n* [U] decoration on an object that makes it look attractive: *a bronze plate with gold ornamentation*

or·nate /ɔːˈneɪt $ ɔːr-/ *adj* covered with a lot of decoration: *an ornate gold mirror* —**ornately** *adv*: *an ornately carved chair*

ORNATE

an ornate mirror

or·ne·ry /ˈɔːnəri $ ˈɔːr-/ *adj AmE* behaving in an unreasonable and often angry way, especially by doing the opposite of what people want you to do: *an ornery kid*

or·ni·thol·o·gist /ˌɔːnɪˈθɒlədʒɪst $ ˌɔːrnəˈθɑː-/ *n* [C] someone who studies birds

or·ni·thol·o·gy /ˌɔːnəˈθɒlədʒi $ ˌɔːrnəˈθɑː-/ *n* [U] the scientific study of birds —**ornithological** /ˌɔːnəθəˈlɒdʒɪkəl◂ $ ˌɔːrnəθəˈlɑː-/ *adj*

or·phan¹ /ˈɔːfən $ ˈɔːr-/ ●○○ *n* [C] a child whose parents are both dead: *The war has left thousands of children as orphans.* | **orphan girl/boy/child** *a poor little orphan girl*

orphan² *v* **be orphaned** to become an orphan: *She was orphaned when her parents died in a plane crash.*

or·phan·age /ˈɔːfənɪdʒ $ ˈɔːr-/ *n* [C] a large house where children who are orphans live and are taken care of: *He was raised in an orphanage.*

or·tho·don·tics /ˌɔːθəˈdɒntɪks $ ˌɔːrθəˈdɑːn-/ *n* [U] the skill or job of helping teeth to grow straight when they have not been growing correctly —**orthodontic** *adj*: *orthodontic treatment*

or·tho·don·tist /ˌɔːθəˈdɒntɪst $ ˌɔːrθəˈdɑːn-/ *n* [C] a DENTIST whose job is to help teeth to grow straight when they have not been growing correctly

or·tho·dox /ˈɔːθədɒks $ ˈɔːrθədɑːks/ ●○○ *adj*
1 orthodox ideas, methods, or behaviour are accepted by most people to be correct and right SYN **conventional**: *orthodox medical treatments* | *He challenged the orthodox views on education.*
2 someone who is orthodox has the opinions and beliefs that are generally accepted as being right, and does not have new or different ideas: *Orthodox economists believe that a recession is now inevitable.* | *an orthodox Marxist*
3 believing in all the traditional beliefs, laws, and practices of a religion: *an orthodox Jew* **THESAURUS** ▸ **RELIGIOUS**

or·tho·dox·y /ˈɔːθədɒksi $ ˈɔːrθədɑː-/ *n* (*plural* **orthodoxies**) [C,U] an idea or set of ideas that is accepted by most people to be correct and right: *He challenged the political orthodoxy of his time.* | *These ideas have now become part of educational orthodoxy.*

or·thog·ra·phy /ɔːˈθɒɡrəfi $ ɔːrˈθɑː-/ *n* [U] *technical* the way in which words are spelled —**orthographic** /ˌɔːθəˈɡræfɪk◂ $ ˌɔːr-/ *adj* —**orthographically** /-kli/ *adv*

or·tho·pe·dic (*also* **orthopaedic** *BrE*) /ˌɔːθəˈpiːdɪk◂ $ ˌɔːr-/ *adj* **1** relating to the medical treatment of problems that affect people's bones or muscles: *an orthopaedic surgeon* | *the orthopedic ward in the hospital* **2 orthopedic bed/chair/shoe etc** one that is designed to help treat medical problems that affect people's bones or muscles —**orthopedically** /-kli/ *adv*

or·tho·pe·dics (*also* **orthopaedics** *BrE*) /ˌɔːθəˈpiːdɪks $ ˌɔːr-/ *n* [U] the part of medicine that treats illnesses or injuries that affect people's bones or muscles

or·tho·pe·dist (*also* **orthopaedist** *BrE*) /ˌɔːθəˈpiːdɪst $ ˌɔːr-/ *n* [C] a doctor with special training in orthopedics

-ory¹ /əri $ ɔːri, əri/ *suffix* [in nouns] a place or thing that is used for doing something: *an observatory* (=a place from where people watch something, especially the stars)

-ory² *suffix* [in adjectives] describes something that does a particular thing: *an explanatory note* (=that gives an explanation) | *a congratulatory telegram* (=that congratulates someone)

Os·car /ˈɒskə $ ˈɑːskər/ *n* [C] *trademark* a prize that is given each year in the US for the best film, actor etc in the film industry. It is officially called an Academy Award: **[+for]** *Who* **got** *the* **Oscar** (=won it) *for best actress?* | *The film* **won** *five* **Oscars**.

os·cil·late /ˈɒsəleɪt $ ˈɑː-/ *v* [I] **1** *formal* to keep changing between two extreme amounts or limits: *The stock market is oscillating wildly at the moment.* | **[+between]** *His income oscillated between £1,500 and £2,000 a month.* **2** *formal* to keep changing between one feeling or attitude and another: **[+between]** *Her attitude towards me oscillated between friendship and hostility.* **3** to move backwards and forwards in a regular way: *The needle on the dial began to oscillate.* **4** *technical* if an electric current oscillates, it changes direction very regularly and very frequently

os·cil·la·tion /ˌɒsəˈleɪʃən $ ˌɑː-/ *n* [C,U]
1 *formal* oscillations are frequent changes between two extreme amounts or limits: **[+in/of]** *oscillations in the value of the dollar* | **[+between]** *oscillating between growth and decline* **2** *formal* oscillations are frequent changes between one feeling or attitude and another: *The drug causes oscillations of mood in some people.* **3** *technical* a regular movement of something from side to side: *the oscillations of a pendulum* **4** *technical* a regular change in direction of an electrical current

os·cil·la·tor /ˈɒsəleɪtə $ ˈɑːsəleɪtər/ *n* [C] *technical* a machine that produces electrical oscillations

os·cil·lo·scope /əˈsɪləskəʊp $ -skoʊp/ *n* [C] *technical* a piece of equipment that shows changes in electrical VOLTAGE as a line on a screen

-oses /əʊsiːz $ oʊ-/ *suffix* the plural form of the suffix -OSIS

o·si·er /ˈəʊziə, ˈəʊʒə $ ˈoʊziər, ˈoʊʒər/ *n* [C] a WILLOW tree whose branches are used for making baskets

-osis /əʊsɪs $ oʊ-/ *suffix* (*plural* **-oses** /əʊsiːz $ oʊ-/) [in nouns] **1** a diseased condition: *silicosis* (=a lung disease) | *neuroses* (=medical conditions that affect the mind) **2** a condition or process: *a metamorphosis* (=change from one state to another) —**-otic** /ɒtɪk $ ɑːtɪk/ *suffix* [in adjectives]: *neurotic* | *hypnotic* —**-otically** /ɒtɪkli $ ɑːt-/ *suffix* [in adverbs]

os·mo·sis /ɒzˈməʊsɪs $ ɑːzˈmoʊ-/ *n* [U] **1** if you learn facts or understand ideas by osmosis, you gradually learn them by hearing them often: **by osmosis** *Children learn new languages by osmosis.* | *He seems to absorb information through a* ***process of osmosis.*** **2** *technical* the gradual process of liquid passing through a MEMBRANE —**osmotic** /ɒzˈmɒtɪk $ ɑːzˈmɑː-/ *adj*

os·prey /ˈɒspreɪ $ ˈɑːspri, -preɪ/ *n* [C] a type of large bird that kills and eats fish

os·si·fy /ˈɒsɪfaɪ $ ˈɑː-/ *v* (**ossified**, **ossifying**, **ossifies**) **1** [I] *formal* to become unwilling to consider new ideas or change your behaviour **2** [I,T] *technical* to change into bone or to make something change into bone —**ossification** /ˌɒsɪfɪˈkeɪʃən $ ˌɑːs-/ *n* [U]

os·ten·si·ble /ɒˈstensəbəl $ ɑː-/ *adj* seeming to be the reason for or the purpose of something, but usually hiding the real reason or purpose: **ostensible reason/purpose/aim** *The ostensible reason for his resignation was ill health.*

os·ten·si·bly /ɒˈstensəbli $ ɑː-/ *adv* if something is ostensibly true, people say that it is true but it is not really true SYN **supposedly**: *She stayed behind at the office, ostensibly to work.*

os·ten·ta·tion /ˌɒstənˈteɪʃən, -ten- $ ˌɑː-/ *n* [U] *formal* when you deliberately try to show people how rich or clever you are, in order to make them admire you: *Her lifestyle was remarkably free from ostentation.*

os·ten·ta·tious /ˌɒstənˈteɪʃəs◂, -ten- $ ˌɑː-/ *adj* **1** something that is ostentatious looks very expensive and is designed to make people think that its owner must be very rich: *She carried her car keys on an ostentatious gold key ring.* | *an ostentatious display of wealth* **2** someone who is ostentatious likes to show everyone how rich they are: *He was vain and ostentatious.* —**ostentatiously** *adv*

osteo- /ɒstiəʊ, -tiə $ ɑːstioʊ, -tiə/ *prefix technical* relating to bones

os·te·o·ar·thri·tis /ˌɒstiəʊɑːˈθraɪtɪs $ ˌɑːstioʊɑːr-/ *n* [U] a medical condition which makes your knees and other joints stiff and painful

os·te·o·path /ˈɒstiəpæθ $ ˈɑː-/ *n* [C] someone who is trained to treat people using osteopathy → **CHIROPRACTOR**

os·te·op·a·thy /ˌɒstiˈɒpəθi $ ˌɑːstiˈɑː-/ *n* [U] a way of treating medical problems such as back pain by moving and pressing the muscles and bones

os·te·o·po·ro·sis /ˌɒstiəʊpəˈrəʊsɪs $ ˌɑːstioʊpəˈroʊ-/ *n* [U] a medical condition in which your bones become weak and break easily: *the risk of developing osteoporosis*

os·tler /ˈɒslə $ ˈɑːslər/ (*also* **hostler** *AmE*) *n* [C] a man who took care of guests' horses at a hotel in the past

os·tra·cize (*also* **-ise** *BrE*) /ˈɒstrəsaɪz $ ˈɑː-/ *v* [T] if a group of people ostracize someone, they refuse to accept them as a member of the group: *She was afraid that if she spoke up her colleagues would ostracize her.* | *He was ostracized by the other students.* —**ostracism** /-sɪzəm/ *n* [U]: *He suffered years of ostracism.*

OSTRICH

os·trich /ˈɒstrɪtʃ $ ˈɒː-, ˈɑː-/ *n* [C] **1** a large African bird with long legs, that runs very quickly but cannot fly **2** *informal* someone who does not deal with difficult problems but tries to pretend that they do not exist

OTC /ˌəʊ tiː ˈsiː◂ $ ˌəʊ-/ the abbreviation of ***over-the-counter***

OTE /ˌəʊ tiː ˈiː $ ˌoʊ-/ *BrE* (***on target earnings***) used in advertisements for jobs to say that the EMPLOYEE will receive the complete pay only if they succeed in doing as much work or selling as many things as the employer wants them to, and will get less pay if they do not succeed

oth·er /ˈʌðə $ ˈʌðər/ ●●● S1 W1 *determiner, adj, pron*

1 THE SECOND OF TWO used to refer to the second of two people or things, which is not the one you already have or the one you have already mentioned: **the/your other** *I can't find my other shoe.* | *One man was arrested, but* ***the other one*** *got away.* | *He kept shifting awkwardly from one foot to the other.* | *She took it for granted that each knew who the other was.*

2 THE REST used to refer to all the people or things in a group apart from the one you have already mentioned or the one that is already known about: **the/your other** *The other hotels are all full.* | *She's much brighter than all the other children in her class.* | *I chose this coat in the end because* ***the other ones*** *were all too expensive.* | **the/your others** *I can see Julie, but where have all the others gone?*

3 ADDITIONAL used to refer to additional people or things of the same kind: *There are one or two other problems I'd like to discuss.* | *I've got some other friends I'd like to invite.* | *Have you* ***any other*** *questions?* | **among others** (=used when mentioning one or more examples) *The guests included, among others, Elizabeth Taylor and Michael Jackson.*

4 DIFFERENT used to refer to a different person or thing from the one you have already mentioned or the one that is already known about: *David and Jessica were playing with two other children.* | *You'd better change into some other clothes.* | *Do you envy other women who seem to manage their lives better?* | *Can we discuss this* ***some other*** *time?* | *There is* ***no other*** *job I would rather do.* | *Saudi Arabia produces more oil than* ***any other*** *country.* | *I hope you will learn to show more respect for others* (=other people). | **some ... others** *Some people are at greater risk than others.*

5 OPPOSITE used to refer to the thing that is opposite you, furthest from you, or moving away from you: **the other side/end/direction etc** *You can park on the other side of the street.* | *He lives at the other end of the road.* | *She drove off in the other direction.*

6 other than apart from a particular person or thing SYN **except**: *The truth was known to no one other than herself.* | *He doesn't eat pork, but other than that he'll eat just about anything.*

7 none other than sb used to emphasize that the person involved in something is famous, impressive, or surprising: *Johnson's defence lawyer was none other than Joe Beltrami.*

8 the other way around/round the opposite of what you have just mentioned: *I always thought that rugby was a rougher game than football, but in fact it's the other way round.* | *Students practise translating from French to English and the other way around.*

9 the other day/morning/week etc used to say that something happened recently, without saying exactly when: *I saw Rufus the other day.*

10 something/someone/somewhere etc or other used when you are not being specific about which thing, person, place etc you mean: *It'll be here somewhere or other.* | *We'll get the money somehow or other.*

11 in other words used when you are expressing an idea or opinion again in a different and usually simpler way: *The tax only affects people on incomes of over $200,000 – in* *other words, the very rich.* | *So he is a fraud, a common thief in other words.*

12 the other woman used to refer to a woman with whom a man is having a sexual relationship, even though he already has a wife or partner: *He left his wife and child and moved in with the other woman.* → ANOTHER, EACH OTHER, → **every other** at EVERY(5), → **on the one hand ... on the other hand** at HAND[1](5)

GRAMMAR: Comparison

other

- You use **other** before a plural noun: *children from other countries* ✗ Don't say: *others countries*

others

- **Others** is a plural pronoun meaning 'other people or things': *We try to help others.*

another

- **Another** is written as one word: *There must be another way of doing it.* ✗ Don't write: *an other*

oth·er·ness /ˈʌðənəs $ ˈʌðər-/ *n* [U] when something is strange and different

oth·er·wise /ˈʌðəwaɪz $ ˈʌðər-/ ●●● S1 W2 *adv*

1 [sentence adverb] used when saying what bad thing will happen if something is not done: *You'll have to go now, otherwise you'll miss your bus.* | *Put your coat on, otherwise you'll get cold.* THESAURUS IF

2 [sentence adverb] used when saying what would have happened or might have happened if something else had not happened: *We were delayed at the airport. Otherwise we would have been here by lunch time.* | *They got two free tickets to Canada, otherwise they'd never have been able to afford to go.*

3 say/think/decide etc otherwise to say, think, or decide something different: *The government claims that the economy is improving, but this survey suggests otherwise.* | *A lot of people think otherwise.*

4 except for what has just been mentioned: *He was tired but otherwise in good health.* | [sentence adverb] *I could hear the distant noise of traffic. Otherwise all was still.* | [+adj/adv] *This spoiled an otherwise excellent piece of work.* | *Their arrival livened up an otherwise dull afternoon.*

5 or otherwise *especially BrE* used to refer to the opposite of what has just been mentioned: *We welcome any comments from viewers, favourable or otherwise.* | *The truth or otherwise of this diagnosis would be revealed in the future.*

6 otherwise engaged *formal* busy doing something else: *I'm afraid I will be otherwise engaged that day.*

7 otherwise known as also called: *Albert DeSalvo, otherwise known as the Boston Strangler*

8 *formal* in a different way: *people who smoke or otherwise abuse their bodies*

9 it cannot be otherwise/how can it be otherwise? *formal* used to say that it is impossible for something to be different from the way it is: *Life in the military is hard – how can it be otherwise?*

oth·er·world·ly /ˌʌðəˈwɜːldli◂ $ ˌʌðərˈwɜːr-/ *adj* relating to religious thoughts and ideas rather than with normal daily life

o·ti·ose /ˈəʊtiəʊs, ˈəʊʃəs $ ˈoʊʃioʊs, ˈoʊti-/ *adj formal* unnecessary

OTT /ˌəʊ tiː ˈtiː $ ˌoʊ-/ *adj BrE informal* (**over-the-top**) remarks, behaviour etc that are OTT are so extreme or unreasonable that they seem stupid or offensive

ot·ter /ˈɒtə $ ˈɑːtər/ *n* [C] an animal with smooth brown fur that swims in rivers and eats fish

ot·to·man /ˈɒtəmən $ ˈɑː-/ *n* [C] a piece of furniture like a large box with a soft top, used as a seat, for resting your feet on when you are sitting, or for storing things

ou·bli·ette /ˌuːbliˈet/ *n* [C] a small room in an old castle where prisoners were kept for a long time

ouch /aʊtʃ/ *interjection* a sound that you make when you feel sudden pain: *Ouch! That hurt!*

ought·a /ˈɔːtə $ ˈɒːtə/ *modal verb informal* a way of saying 'ought to' – used especially in writing to show how it is pronounced by some people: *You oughta tell your mom.*

oughtn't /ˈɔːtnt $ ˈɒː-/ the short form of 'ought not': *You oughtn't to drive if you're tired.*

ought to /ˈɔːt tuː $ ˈɒːt-/ ●●● S1 W1 *modal verb*

1 used to say that someone should do something because it is the best or most sensible thing to do SYN **should**: *You really ought to quit smoking.* | *The company ought to be making changes in its marketing strategy.* | *What sort of crimes ought the police to concentrate on?* | *You were out enjoying yourself when you ought to have been studying.*

2 used to make a suggestion about something you think is a good idea, especially in a social situation SYN **should**: *We ought to get together some time soon.* | *You ought to meet him; he's really nice.* | *We ought to get her some flowers for her birthday.* | *I ought to call Brian.*

3 used to say that someone should do something or something should happen, because it is morally right or fair SYN **should**: *You ought to be ashamed of yourself.* | *The courts ought to treat black and white defendants in exactly the same way.* | *Many people felt that America ought not to take part in the war.*

4 used to say that you think something will probably happen, is probably true etc SYN **should**: *He left two hours ago, so he ought to be there by now.* | *They ought to win – they've trained hard enough.* | *That ought to be enough potatoes for eight people.* | *New technology ought to make this easier.*

GRAMMAR: Patterns with ought to

- You say that someone **ought to do** something: *You ought to explain.*
- You say that someone **ought to have done** something: *You ought to have explained* (=but you did not).
- You say that someone **ought not to do** something: *She ought not to go.*
- You say that someone **ought not to have done** something: *She ought not to have gone* (=but she did go).
- You can also use **oughtn't**: *She oughtn't to go.* | *She oughtn't to have gone.*
- You ask **ought** someone **to do** something: *Ought we to tell them?*
- You ask **ought** someone **to have done** something: *Ought we to have told them?*

GRAMMAR GUIDE MODAL VERBS

Oui·ja board /ˈwiːdʒə bɔːd $ ˈwiːdʒiː bɔːrd/ *n* [C] *trademark* a board with letters and signs on it, which some people believe can be used to receive messages from dead people

ounce /aʊns/ ●●● S3 W3 *n* [C] (*written abbreviation* **oz**)

1 a unit for measuring weight, equal to 28.35 grams. There are 16 ounces in a pound. → FLUID OUNCE

2 an ounce of sense/truth/decency etc any sense, truth etc at all: *If you had an ounce of sense you wouldn't believe him!*

3 every (last) ounce of courage/energy/strength etc all the courage, energy etc that you have: *Every ounce of attention was focused on our common goal.*

4 an ounce of prevention (is worth a pound of cure) used to say that it is better to prevent a problem before it happens than to try to solve it after it has happened

5 not an ounce of fat (on sb) if there is not an ounce of fat on someone, they are thin and usually look healthy

our /aʊə $ aʊr/ ●●● S1 W1 *determiner* [possessive form of 'we']

1 belonging to or connected with us: *a picture of our grandchildren* | *You can stay at our house.* | *We must preserve our natural environment.* | *We must each take responsibility for **our own** actions.*

2 *spoken* used to show that the person mentioned is your child, brother, or sister – used in northern England: *Our Sharon did really well in her exams.*

ours /aʊəz $ aʊrz/ ●●● S1 *pron* [possessive form of

'we'] used to refer to something that belongs to or is connected with us: *I'll show you to your room. Ours is next door.* | *The main difference between our brains and those of monkeys is that ours are bigger.* | *No, that's not ours.* | **of ours** *The Thackers are* ***friends of ours.***

our·selves /aʊə'selvz $ aʊr-/ ●●● S1 W3 *pron*
1 used by the person speaking to show that they and one or more other people are affected by their own action: *We prepared ourselves for the long journey ahead.* | *It was strange seeing ourselves on television.*
2 a) used to emphasize 'we' or 'us': *We built the house ourselves.* | *As parents ourselves, we understand the problem.* **b)** used after 'as', 'like', or 'except' instead of 'us': *More help is needed for people like ourselves.*
3 (all) by ourselves a) alone: *We weren't supposed to play by ourselves near the pond.* **b)** without help from anyone else: *I knew that Tim and I wouldn't be able to do the whole job by ourselves.*
4 (all) to ourselves without having to share something with any other people: *We had the house to ourselves.*

-ous /əs/ *suffix* [in adjectives] describes something that has a particular quality: *dangerous* (=full of danger) | *spacious* (=with a lot of space)

oust /aʊst/ *v* [T] to force someone out of a position of power, especially so that you can take their place SYN **remove**: **oust sb from sth** *The Communists were finally ousted from power.*

ous·ter /'aʊstə $ -ər/ *n* [U] *AmE* when someone is removed from a position of power or from a competition – used in news reports: **sb's ouster/the ouster of sb** *the ouster of the brutal dictatorship*

out¹ /aʊt/ ●●● S1 W1 *adv*
1 FROM INSIDE from inside an object, container, building, or place OPP **in**: *She opened her suitcase and took out a pair of shoes.* | *Lock the door on your way out.* | *Charlotte went to the window and looked out.* | *Out you go* (=used to order someone to leave a room)! | **[+of]** *The keys must have fallen out of my pocket.* | *Get out of here!* | *Someone had torn several pages out of her diary.* | *I don't think I'd have the courage to jump out of a plane.* | *All the roads out of the city were snowbound.* | **out came/jumped etc** *The egg cracked open and out came a baby chick.*
2 OUTSIDE not inside a building SYN **outside**: *Many of the homeless have been sleeping out for years.* | *Children were out playing in the snow.* | *Brrr, it's cold out there.* THESAURUS ▸ OUTSIDE
3 NOT AT HOME **a)** away from your home, office etc, especially for a short time OPP **in**: *Did anyone call while I was out?* | *My parents are both out at the moment.* | *He went out at 11 o'clock.* **b)** to or in a place that is not your home, in order to enjoy yourself: *You should get out and meet people.* | *Let's eat out tonight* (=eat in a restaurant). | *At first he was too shy to ask her out.* | **be/get out and about** (=go to places where you can meet people) *Most teenagers would rather be out and about with their friends.*
4 DISTANT PLACE **a)** in or to a place that is far away or difficult to get to: *He went out to New Zealand.* | *They've rented a farmhouse* ***right out*** *in the country.* **b)** used to say how far away something is: *The Astra Satellite is travelling some 23,000 miles out in space.* | **[+of]** *a little village about five miles out of Birmingham*
5 GIVEN TO MANY PEOPLE used to say that something is given to many people: *The examination will start when all the question papers have been handed out.* | *Have you sent out the invitations yet?*
6 GET RID OF STH used to say that someone gets rid of something or makes it disappear: *Have you thrown out yesterday's paper?* | *Mother used washing soda to get the stains out.*
7 NOT BURNING/SHINING a fire or light that is out is no longer burning or shining: *Turn the lights out when you go to bed.* | *The firefighters arrived, and within minutes the fire was out.*
8 SUN/MOON ETC if the sun, moon, or stars are out, they have appeared in the sky: *When the sun came out, a rainbow formed in the sky.*
9 FLOWERS if the flowers on a plant are out, they have opened: *It's still February and already the primroses are out.*
10 COMPLETELY/CAREFULLY used to say that something is done carefully or completely: *I spent all morning cleaning out the kitchen cupboards.* | *In the summer months the soil dries out quickly.*
11 NOT INCLUDED not included in a team, group, competition etc: *The Welsh team was surprisingly knocked out in the semi-finals.* | **[+of]** *Daniels will be out of the team until he recovers from his injury.*
12 COME FROM STH used to say where something comes from or is taken from: **[+of]** *A lot of good music came out of the hippy culture in the 1960s.* | *The money is automatically taken out of your bank account every month.*
13 AWAY FROM THE EDGE OF STH away from the main part or edge of something: *I swam out into the middle of the lake.* | *A long peninsula juts out into the sea.* | **[+of]** *She stuck her head out of the window to see what was happening.*
14 NOT WORKING *especially AmE* if a machine, piece of equipment etc is out, it is not working: *I don't believe it – the elevator's out again!* → **be out of order** at ORDER¹(8)
15 PRODUCT used to say that a product is available to be bought: *Is the new Harry Potter book out yet?* | *Sony have brought out a new portable music system.*
16 NOT IN A SITUATION no longer in a particular state or situation: **[+of]** *She's not completely cured, but at least she's out of danger.* | *This whole situation is getting out of control.* | *How long have you been out of work now?* | *Karen waved until the car was* ***out of sight*** (=too far away to be seen).
17 HAVING LEFT AN INSTITUTION **a)** having left the institution where you were: **[+of]** *a kid just out of college* | *His wife isn't out of hospital yet.* **b)** no longer in prison: *Once he was out, he returned to a life of crime.*
18 NOT FASHIONABLE no longer fashionable OPP **in**: *You can't wear that – maxi skirts have been out for years.*
19 NOT SECRET no longer a secret: *Her secret was out.* | *The word's out that Mel Gibson is in town.* | *Eventually the truth came out.*
20 read/shout etc sth out (loud) to say something in a voice that is loud enough for others to hear: *Someone called out my name.* | *We all listened as he read the statement out loud.*
21 UNCONSCIOUS not conscious: *She fainted – she was out for about ten minutes.* | *How hard did you hit him? He's* ***out cold.***
22 NONE LEFT used to say that there is none of something left because you have used it all, sold it all etc: *The album was sold out within minutes.* | **[+of]** *We're out of milk.* | *They've run out of ideas.*
23 before the day/year etc is out before the day, year etc has ended: *Don't cry, I'll be back before the week's out.*
24 NOT CORRECT if a measurement, result etc is out, it is wrong because the numbers have not been calculated correctly: *He was out in his calculations, so there was a lot of carpet left over.* | *The bill was out by over £10.* | *Their forecast was* ***way out.*** → **not far off/out/wrong** at FAR¹(2)
25 be out for sth/be out to do sth *informal* to have a particular intention: *Andrew's just out for a good time.* | *I was convinced he was out to cheat me.*
26 NOT IN POWER used to say that someone, especially a political party, no longer has power or authority OPP **in**: *It's time we voted the Republicans out.* | **[+of]** *The party has been out of office for a long time.*
27 ON STRIKE *BrE* used to say that someone has stopped working as a way of protesting about something: *The railway workers have come out in sympathy with the miners.*
28 HOMOSEXUAL if a HOMOSEXUAL is out, they have told people that they are homosexual
29 NOT POSSIBLE *spoken* if a particular suggestion or activity is out, it is not possible: *We don't have enough money to rent a car, so that's out.*
30 SEA when the TIDE is out, the sea by the shore is at its lowest level OPP **in**: *You can walk across the sands when the tide is out.*
31 SPORT **a)** a player or team that is out in a game such as CRICKET or baseball is no longer allowed to BAT: *Sussex*

were all out for 365. **b)** a ball that is out in a game such as tennis or BASKETBALL is not in the area of play OPP **in**

32 out with it! *spoken* used to tell someone to say something which they have been unwilling to say or have difficulty saying: *OK, out with it! What really happened?*

33 REASON because of a particular feeling that you have: **[+of]** *They obeyed him out of fear rather than respect.* | *Just out of curiosity, why did you take that job?*

34 MADE OF STH used to say what substance or materials a particular thing is made of: **[+of]** *a tombstone carved out of black marble* | *toy boats made out of old tin cans*

35 HOW MANY OF A GROUP used to say how common something is, or how large a part of a group you are talking about: **nine out of ten/three out of four etc** *Nine out of ten students pass the test first time.* | *Apparently they've lost three games out of seven already.*

36 out of it *informal* **a)** slightly unhappy because you feel different from the rest of a group of people and cannot share their fun, conversation etc: *I felt a bit out of it because I was the only one who couldn't speak French.* **b)** unable to think clearly because you are tired or drunk, or have taken drugs: *You were really out of it last night. What were you drinking?*

37 out there a) in a place that could be anywhere except here: *My real father is out there and one day I plan to find him.* **b)** where someone or something can be noticed by many people: *Jerry Lewis is out there all the time raising money for disabled kids.* **c)** *informal* an idea, work of art etc that is out there is so unusual that it might seem silly or extreme: *He's brilliant, but some of his ideas are really out there.*

38 out front *especially AmE* **a)** in front of something, especially a building, where everyone can see you: *There's a blue car out front.* **b)** taking a leading position: *As a civil rights leader, he was always out front.* **c)** *informal* very honest and direct: *Molly is very out front in talking about her mistakes.* → **out of your mind** at MIND[1](24), → **out of the blue** at BLUE[2](4), → **out of luck** at LUCK[1](10), → **out of this world** at WORLD[1](15), → **be out of the question** at QUESTION[1](9), → **out front** at FRONT[1](8), → **out back** at BACK[2](2), → **out of sorts** at SORT[1](10)

out² ●●● S1 W2 *prep especially AmE informal* from the inside to the outside of something – many teachers of British English consider it incorrect to use 'out' as a PREPOSITION: *Karen looked out the window at the back yard.* | *Get out the car and push with the rest of us!*

out³ *v* **1** [T] to publicly say that someone is HOMOSEXUAL when that person would prefer to keep it secret: *Several politicians have been outed in recent months.* **2** [T] to let the public know a fact about someone that they would prefer to keep secret: **out sb as sth** *He was outed as a supporter of the far-right party.* **3 murder/the truth etc will out!** used to say that it is difficult to hide a murder, the truth etc

out⁴ *n* **1** [singular] an excuse to avoid doing an activity or to avoid being blamed for something: *I'm busy on Sunday, so that gives me an out.* **2** [C] an act of making a player in baseball lose the chance to score a point **3 on the outs (with sb)** *AmE informal* arguing or not agreeing with someone: *Wilson is on the outs with his family because of his relationship with that woman.* → INS AND OUTS

out- /aʊt/ *prefix* **1** used to form nouns and adjectives from verbs that are followed by 'out': *an outbreak of flu* (=from 'break out') | *outspoken comments* (=from 'speak out') **2** [in nouns and adjectives] outside or beyond something: *an outbuilding* (=small building away from the main building) | *outlying areas* (=far from the centre) **3** [in verbs] being or becoming bigger, further, greater etc than someone or something else: *He's outgrown his clothes* (=become too big for them). | *She outlived her brother* (=he died before her). **4** [in verbs] doing better than someone, so that you defeat them: *I can out-argue you any day.* | *She outran him.*

out·age /ˈaʊtɪdʒ/ *n* [C] *AmE* a period of time during which a service such as the electricity supply cannot be provided SYN **power cut** *BrE*: *a power outage*

ˌout-and-ˈout *adj* [only before noun] used to emphasize that someone is definitely a particular kind of person or thing SYN **complete**: *he's an out-and-out liar*

out·back /ˈaʊtbæk/ *n* **the outback** the Australian countryside far away from cities, where few people live

out·bid /aʊtˈbɪd/ *v* (*past tense and past participle* **outbid**, *present participle* **outbidding**) [T] to offer a higher price than someone else, especially at an AUCTION

out·board mo·tor /ˌaʊtbɔːd ˈməʊtə $ -bɔːrd ˈmoʊtər/ *n* [C] a motor attached to the back end of a small boat

out·bound /ˈaʊtbaʊnd/ *adj* moving away from you or away from a town, country etc OPP **inbound**: *outbound traffic* | *the outbound flight*

out·box, **out box** /ˈaʊtbɒks $ -bɑːks/ *n* [C] **1** the place in a computer email program where messages that you have not sent yet are stored → INBOX **2** *AmE* a container on an office desk that is used to hold letters, documents etc that have been dealt with and are ready to be taken away by someone such as a secretary SYN **out tray** *BrE*

out·break /ˈaʊtbreɪk/ ●●○ *n* [C] if there is an outbreak of fighting or disease in an area, it suddenly starts to happen: *a cholera outbreak* | **[+of]** *outbreaks of fighting* | *the outbreak of World War II* → **break out** at BREAK[1]

out·build·ing /ˈaʊtˌbɪldɪŋ/ *n* [C] a building near a main building, for example a BARN or SHED: *a farmhouse with a few outbuildings*

out·burst /ˈaʊtbɜːst $ -bɜːrst/ ●○○ *n* [C]
1 something you say suddenly that expresses a strong emotion, especially anger: *He later apologized for his outburst.* | **emotional/violent/angry outburst** *his father's violent outbursts of temper* | **[+of]** *an outburst of anger*
2 a sudden short increase in an activity: **[+of]** *an outburst of creative energy* | *outbursts of violence*

out·cast /ˈaʊtkɑːst $ -kæst/ *n* [C] someone who is not accepted by the people they live among, or who has been forced out of their home SYN **pariah**: *Smokers often feel as though they are being treated as social outcasts.* —**outcast** *adj*

out·class /aʊtˈklɑːs $ -ˈklæs/ *v* [T] to be or do something much better than someone or something else: *He won his next race, completely outclassing his rivals.*

out·come /ˈaʊtkʌm/ ●●○ W3 AWL *n* [C] the final result of a meeting, discussion, war etc – used especially when no one knows what it will be until it actually happens SYN **result**: **[+of]** *It was impossible to predict the outcome of the election.* | *People who had heard the evidence at the trial were surprised at the outcome.* THESAURUS RESULT

> **REGISTER**
> **Outcome** is slightly formal and is used mostly in writing. In everyday English, people are more likely to talk about **what happened**: *It was impossible to predict* ***what would happen*** *in the election.*

out·crop /ˈaʊtkrɒp $ -krɑːp/ (*also* **out·crop·ping** /-krɒpɪŋ $ -krɑː-/ *AmE*) *n* [C] a rock or group of rocks above the surface of the ground: *Below us was a pool surrounded by rocky outcrops.*

out·cry /ˈaʊtkraɪ/ *n* [C usually singular, U] an angry protest by a lot of ordinary people: *The closure of the local hospital has caused a huge* ***public outcry.*** | **[+against/about/over]** *a national outcry about the lack of gun control laws* | **[+from]** *The proposed changes* ***caused*** *an* ***angry*** *outcry from residents.*

out·dat·ed /ˌaʊtˈdeɪtɪd◂/ *adj* **1** if something is outdated, it is no longer considered useful or effective, because something more modern exists → **old-fashioned**: *outdated teaching methods* | *a factory with outdated equipment* | *His writing style is now boring and outdated.* THESAURUS OLD-FASHIONED **2** outdated information is not recent and may no longer be correct: *This estimate was made on the basis of outdated figures.*

out·did /aʊtˈdɪd/ *v* the past tense of OUTDO

out·dis·tance /aʊtˈdɪstəns/ *v* [T] to run, ride etc faster than other people, especially in a race, so that you are far ahead SYN **outstrip**: *Lewis quickly outdistanced the other runners.*

out·do /aʊtˈduː/ *v* (*past tense* **outdid** /-ˈdɪd/, *past participle* **outdone** /-ˈdʌn/, *third person singular* **outdoes** /-ˈdʌz/) [T] **1** to be better or more successful than someone else at doing something: *When it comes to speed of response, a small firm can outdo a big company.* | **outdo sb in sth** *skaters trying to outdo each other in grace and speed* **2 not to be outdone** in order not to let someone else do better or seem better than you: *Not to be outdone, other computer manufacturers are also donating machines to schools.*

out·door /ˌaʊtˈdɔː◂ $ -ˈdɔːr◂/ ●●○ *adj*
1 [only before noun] existing, happening, or used outside, not inside a building OPP **indoor**: *a huge outdoor market* | *outdoor recreational activities* | *outdoor clothing* | *a healthy outdoor life*
2 outdoor type someone who enjoys camping, walking in the countryside etc

USAGE: Outdoor, outdoors
Outdoor is an adjective and **outdoors** is an adverb.
You say: *an outdoor swimming pool* ✗ Don't say: *an outdoors swimming pool*
You say: *They could play outdoors.* ✗ Don't say: *They could play outdoor.*

out·doors[1] /ˌaʊtˈdɔːz $ -ˈdɔːrz/ ●●○ *adv* outside, not in a building SYN **out of doors** OPP **indoors**: *It's warm enough to eat outdoors tonight.* | *He wants a job that will let him work outdoors.*

outdoors[2] *n* **the (great) outdoors** the countryside far away from buildings and cities: *a woman with a taste for adventure in the great outdoors*

out·door·sy /aʊtˈdɔːzi $ -ˈdɔːr-/ *adj informal* an outdoorsy person enjoys outdoor activities

out·er /ˈaʊtə $ -ər/ ●●○ *adj* [only before noun]
1 on the outside of something OPP **inner**: *Remove the tough outer leaves before cooking.*
2 further from the centre of something OPP **inner**: *the outer suburbs*
3 relating to objects, activities etc that are part of the world, as opposed to your own thoughts and feelings OPP **inner**: *His inner conflict is related to struggles in the outer world.*

out·er·most /ˈaʊtəməʊst $ -tərmoʊst/ *adj* [only before noun] furthest from the middle OPP **innermost**: *the outermost stars*

ˌouter ˈspace *n* [U] the space outside the Earth's air, where the PLANETS and stars are: *creatures from outer space* (=from another planet)

out·er·wear /ˈaʊtəweə $ -tərwer/ *n* [U] clothes such as coats that are worn over other clothes

out·face /aʊtˈfeɪs/ *v* [T] *formal* to deal bravely with a difficult situation or opponent

out·fall /ˈaʊtfɔːl/ *n* [C] a place where water flows out, especially from a DRAIN or river: *a sewage outfall*

out·field /ˈaʊtfiːld/ *n* **the outfield a)** the part of a CRICKET or baseball field furthest away from the player who is hitting the ball OPP **infield b)** the players in this part of the field —**outfielder** *n* [C]

out·fit[1] /ˈaʊtfɪt/ ●●○ *n* [C]
1 a set of clothes worn together, especially for a special occasion: *She bought a new outfit for the party.* | *a cowboy outfit*
2 *informal* a group of people who work together as a team or organization: *My outfit was sent to Italy during the war.* | *a small advertising outfit in San Diego*
3 *BrE* a set of equipment that you need for a particular purpose or job SYN **kit**: *a tyre repair outfit*

outfit[2] *v* (**outfitted**, **outfitting**) [T] to provide someone or something with a set of clothes or equipment, especially ones that are needed for a particular purpose SYN **kit out**: **outfit sb/sth with sth** *a car outfitted with dual controls for driver training* | **outfit sb in sth** *Members outfit themselves in Civil War clothing.*

out·fit·ter /ˈaʊtfɪtə $ -ər/ *n* [C] **1** *BrE old-fashioned* a shop that sells men's clothes **2** *AmE* a shop that sells equipment for outdoor activities such as camping

out·flank /aʊtˈflæŋk/ *v* [T] **1** to gain an advantage over an opponent, especially in politics: *The Tories found themselves outflanked by Labour on the issue of law and order.* **2** to go around the side of a group of enemies during a battle and attack them from behind

out·flow /ˈaʊtfləʊ $ -floʊ/ *n* [C] **1** when money, goods etc leave a bank, country etc: **[+of]** *the outflow of capital from the developed countries* **2** the flow of water or air from something: **[+of]** *an outflow of gas escaping from the main duct* | *the outflow valve*

out·fox /aʊtˈfɒks $ -ˈfɑːks/ *v* [T] to gain an advantage over someone by using your intelligence SYN **outsmart**

out·go·ing /ˌaʊtˈgəʊɪŋ◂ $ -ˈgoʊ-/ ●○○ *adj*
1 someone who is outgoing likes to meet and talk to new people: *We're looking for someone with an outgoing personality.*
2 outgoing president/chancellor etc someone who will soon finish their time as president etc
3 [only before noun] going out or leaving a place OPP **incoming**: *the tray for outgoing mail* | *outgoing phone calls*

out·go·ings /ˈaʊtˌgəʊɪŋz $ -ˌgoʊ-/ *n* [plural] *BrE* the money that you have to spend regularly, for example on rent or food: *List all your outgoings for a month.*

out·grow /aʊtˈgrəʊ $ -ˈgroʊ/ *v* (*past tense* **outgrew** /-ˈgruː/, *past participle* **outgrown** /-ˈgrəʊn $ -ˈgroʊn/) [T] **1** to grow too big for something SYN **grow out of**: *They outgrow their clothes so quickly.* | *Harry outgrew his cot when he was about two.* **2** to no longer do or enjoy something that you used to do, because you have grown older and changed: *Most children eventually outgrow a tendency toward travel sickness.* **3** if a business outgrows a building, it begins to have too many people or too much work to fit into the building: *His furniture-making business soon outgrew his garage.* **4** to grow or increase faster than someone or something else: *a population outgrowing its resources*

out·growth /ˈaʊtgrəʊθ $ -groʊθ/ *n* [C] **1** something that develops from something else, as a natural result of it: **[+of]** *Crime is often an outgrowth of poverty.* **2** *technical* something that grows out of something else

out·house /ˈaʊthaʊs/ *n* [C] **1** *BrE* a small building which is near to and belongs to a larger main building SYN **outbuilding 2** *AmE* a small building over a hole in the ground that is used as a toilet, in a camping area or, in the past, behind a house SYN **privy** *BrE*

out·ing /ˈaʊtɪŋ/ ●○○ *n*
1 [C] a short trip that a group of people take for pleasure: **a family/school etc outing** *a class outing to the ballet* | **[+to]** *an outing to the beach* | **on an outing** *They had* ***gone on an outing*** *to the pool for Robert's birthday.*
2 [C,U] when someone publicly says that someone else is HOMOSEXUAL, when that person does not want anyone to know

out·land·ish /aʊtˈlændɪʃ/ *adj* strange and unusual: *outlandish clothes* | *Her story seemed so outlandish.*

out·last /aʊtˈlɑːst $ -ˈlæst/ *v* [T] to continue to exist or be effective for a longer time than something else: *Smith outlasted his rivals in the council to become leader in 1996.* | *A leather sofa will usually outlast a cloth one.* → OUTLIVE

out·law[1] /ˈaʊtlɔː $ -lɒː/ *v* [T] to completely stop something by making it illegal: *The bill would have outlawed several types of guns.*

outlaw[2] *n* [C] someone who has done something illegal, and who is hiding in order to avoid punishment – used especially about criminals in the past

out·lay /ˈaʊtleɪ/ *n* [C,U] the amount of money that you have to spend in order to start a new business, activity etc → **expense**, **cost**: **small/modest/considerable/large etc outlay** *For a relatively small outlay, you can start a home hairdressing business.* | **[+on]** *House buyers usually have a large initial outlay on carpets and furniture.*

out·let /ˈaʊtlet, -lɪt/ ●●○ *n* [C]
1 a way of expressing or getting rid of strong feelings: **[+for]** *Is football a good outlet for men's aggression? | an outlet for creativity*
2 a) *formal* a shop, company, or organization through which products are sold: *Benetton has* ***retail outlets*** *in every major European city. | a fast-food outlet* **b)** a shop that sells things for less than the usual price, especially things from a particular company or things of a particular type
3 *AmE* a place on a wall where you can connect electrical equipment to the supply of electricity SYN **power point** *BrE* → see picture at PLUG[1]
4 a pipe or hole through which something such as a liquid or gas can flow out: *a waste water outlet*

ˈoutlet ˌmall *n* [C] *AmE* a SHOPPING MALL where clothes are sold for less than the usual price, often because they are no longer fashionable or are slightly damaged

ˈoutlet store *n* [C] a store where clothes or other goods are sold for less than the usual price, often because they are no longer fashionable or are slightly damaged, or because the factory made too many of them to sell in normal stores

ˈoutlet ˌvillage *n* [C] an area, usually outside a town or city, where there are a lot of outlet stores all in one place

out·li·er /ˈaʊtˌlaɪə $ -ər/ *n* [C] *technical* a number that is a lot higher or lower than all the other numbers in a set of numbers that represent facts or measurements: *In the set {3, 5, 4, 6, 2, 25, 5, 6}, 25 is an outlier*

out·line[1] /ˈaʊtlaɪn/ ●●○ *n*
1 [C,U] the main ideas or facts about something, without the details: *a research proposal outline* | **[+of]** *an outline of world history* | **broad/rough/general outline** *a broad outline of the committee's plans* | **in outline** *A debt reduction scheme was agreed in outline* (=people agreed on its main points).
2 [C,U] a line around the edge of something which shows its shape: **[+of]** *The outlines of animals were cut into the rock. | an* ***outline map*** *of Europe* | **in outline** *figures drawn in outline*
3 [C] a plan for a piece of writing in which each new idea or fact is separately written down: *Always write an outline for your essays.*

outline[2] ●●○ *v* [T]
1 to describe something in a general way, giving the main points but not the details: *The new president outlined plans to deal with crime, drugs, and education.*
2 to show the edge of something, or draw around its edge, so that its shape is clear: *a map with our property outlined in red | trees outlined against the sky*
GRAMMAR **Outline** is usually passive in this meaning.

out·live /aʊtˈlɪv/ *v* [T] **1** to remain alive after someone else has died: *She outlived her husband by 20 years.* **2** to continue to exist after something else has ended or disappeared → **outlast**: *Good books have a way of outliving those who want to ban them.* **3 outlive its/your usefulness** to become no longer useful: *The docks have outlived their usefulness.*

out·look /ˈaʊtlʊk/ ●●○ *n* [C]
1 your general attitude to life and the world: **[+on]** *He's got a good* ***outlook on life****. | Exercise will improve your looks and your outlook.* | **positive/optimistic outlook** *She still has an optimistic outlook for the future.*
2 [usually singular] what is expected to happen in the future: **[+for]** *The outlook for the weekend is unsettled, with periods of heavy rain. | The outlook for sufferers from this disease is bleak.* | **economic/financial/political etc outlook** *a gloomy economic outlook in Western Europe*
3 a view from a particular place: *a very pleasing outlook from the bedroom window*

out·ly·ing /ˈaʊtˌlaɪ-ɪŋ/ *adj* [only before noun] far from the centre of a city, town etc or from a main building: *one of the outlying suburbs*

out·ma·noeu·vre *BrE*, **outmaneuver** *AmE* /ˌaʊtməˈnuːvə $ -ər/ *v* [T] to gain an advantage over someone by using cleverer or more skilful plans or methods SYN **outwit**: *He believed he could outmanoeuvre and trap the English king.*

out·mod·ed /aʊtˈməʊdɪd $ -ˈmoʊ-/ *adj* no longer fashionable or useful SYN **outdated**: *outmoded ideas*

out·num·ber /aʊtˈnʌmbə $ -ər/ *v* [T] to be more in number than another group: *Flats outnumber houses in this area. | His troops were hopelessly outnumbered.* | **outnumber sb/sth by sth** *In nursing, women still outnumber men by four to one.* | **vastly/greatly/heavily outnumber** *Men in prison vastly outnumber women.*

ˌout-of-body exˈperience *n* [C] the feeling that you are outside your body and looking down on it from above, which people sometimes have when they are close to death

ˌout-of-court ˈsettlement *n* [C] an agreement to end a legal argument, in which one side agrees to pay money to the other so that the problem is not brought to court → **settle sth out of court** at COURT[1](1)

ˌout-of-ˈdate ●○○ *adj*
1 if information is out-of-date, it is not recent and may no longer be correct SYN **outdated**: *The information in the tourist guide is already out-of-date.* THESAURUS OLD-FASHIONED
2 if something is out-of-date, it is no longer considered useful or effective, because something more modern exists SYN **outdated**: *Their manufacturing methods are hopelessly out-of-date.*
3 an official document that is out-of-date cannot be used because the period of time for which it was effective has finished → **invalid**: *an out-of-date passport*

ˌout of ˈdoors *adv* outside, not in a building SYN **outdoors** OPP **indoors**: *The kids spent all their time out of doors.*

ˌout-of-pocket exˈpenses *n* [plural] small amounts of money that you have to spend as part of your job, and get back from your employer

ˌout-of-ˈstate *adj AmE* to, from, or in another state: *an out-of-state driver's license*

ˌout-of-the-ˈway, **out of the way** *adj* **1** an out-of-the-way place is in an area where there are few people → **remote**: *an out-of-the-way spot for a picnic | It's a great little pub, but a bit out of the way.* **2** *BrE* unusual or strange: *Her taste in music is a bit out-of-the-way.*

ˌout-of-ˈtown *adj* [only before noun] **1** to, from, or in another town: *out-of-town visitors* **2** *BrE* on the edge of a town: *out-of-town shopping centres*

ˌout of ˈwork, **out-of-work** *adj* unemployed: *out-of-work actors | He's been out of work for six months.*

out·pace /aʊtˈpeɪs/ *v* [T] to go faster, do better, or develop more quickly than someone or something else SYN **outstrip**: *Job openings were outpacing the supply of qualified workers.*

out·pa·tient /ˈaʊtˌpeɪʃənt/ *n* [C] someone who goes to a hospital for treatment but does not stay for the night → **inpatient**: *an outpatient clinic | a routine examination in* ***outpatients*** (=the outpatient department of a hospital)

out·per·form /ˌaʊtpəˈfɔːm $ -pərˈfɔːrm/ *v* [T] to be more successful than someone or something else: *Stocks generally outperform other investments.*

out·place·ment /ˈaʊtˌpleɪsmənt/ *n* [C,U] a service that a company provides to help its workers find new jobs when it cannot continue to employ them

out·play /aʊtˈpleɪ/ *v* [T] to beat an opponent in a game by playing with more skill than they do

out·point /aʊtˈpɔɪnt/ *v* [T] to defeat an opponent in BOXING by gaining more points

out·post /ˈaʊtpəʊst $ -poʊst/ *n* [C] a group of buildings in a place far from cities or towns, usually established as a military camp or a place for trade: *a remote outpost of the empire*

out·pour·ing /ˈaʊtpɔːrɪŋ/ *n* [C] **1** an expression of strong feelings: **[+of]** *an outpouring of grief* **2** a lot of something that is produced suddenly: **[+of]** *an outpouring of creative energy*

out·put¹ /ˈaʊtpʊt/ ●●○ W3 AWL *n* [C,U]
1 the amount of goods or work produced by a person, machine, factory etc → **production**: *Output is up 30% on last year.* | **manufacturing/industrial/agricultural etc output** *Korea's agricultural output* | **[+of]** *the world's output of carbon dioxide*
2 the information produced by a computer OPP **input**
3 *technical* the amount of electricity produced by a GENERATOR

output² AWL *v* (*past tense and past participle* **output**, *present participle* **outputting**) [T] if a computer outputs information, it produces it

out·rage¹ /ˈaʊtreɪdʒ/ ●○○ *n*
1 [U] a feeling of great anger and shock: *The response to the jury's verdict was one of outrage.* | *a sense of* ***moral outrage*** | **[+at/over]** *environmentalists' outrage at plans to develop the coastline* | **public/popular outrage** *The case generated public outrage.*
2 [C] an event that produces great anger and shock, especially because it is cruel or violent: *bomb outrages in London* | *This is an outrage!*

outrage² ●○○ *v* [T] to make someone feel very angry and shocked: *Customers were outraged by the price increases.* GRAMMAR **Outrage** is usually passive.

out·ra·geous /aʊtˈreɪdʒəs/ ●○○ *adj*
1 very shocking and extremely unfair or offensive: *outrageous prices* | *an outrageous attack on his policies* | **it is outrageous (that)** *It's outrageous that the poor should pay such high taxes.*
2 extremely unusual and slightly amusing or shocking: *an outrageous hairstyle* | *He says the most outrageous things.*
—**outrageously** *adv*

out·ran /aʊtˈræn/ *v* the past tense of OUTRUN

out·rank /aʊtˈræŋk/ *v* [T] **1** to have a higher rank than someone else in the same group **2** to be more important than something else

ou·tré /ˈuːtreɪ $ uːˈtreɪ/ *adj literary* strange, unusual, and slightly shocking

out·reach /ˈaʊtriːtʃ/ *n* [U] when help, advice, or other services are provided for people who would not otherwise get these services easily: **outreach program/service/center etc** *outreach centers for drug addicts*

out·ride /aʊtˈraɪd/ *v* (*past tense* **outrode** /-ˈrəʊd $ -ˈroʊd/, *past participle* **outridden** /-ˈrɪdn/) [T] to ride faster or further than someone else

out·rid·er /ˈaʊtˌraɪdə $ -ər/ *n* [C] a guard or police officer who rides on a MOTORCYCLE or horse beside or in front of a vehicle in which an important person is travelling

out·rig·ger /ˈaʊtˌrɪɡə $ -ər/ *n* [C] **1** a long piece of wood that is attached to the side of a boat, especially a CANOE, to prevent it from turning over in the water **2** a boat with an outrigger

out·right¹ /ˈaʊtraɪt/ ●○○ *adj* [only before noun]
1 clear and direct: *an outright refusal* | *an outright attack on his actions*
2 complete and total: *an outright victory* | *an outright ban on the sale of tobacco*
3 the outright winner/victor someone who has definitely and easily won

out·right² /aʊtˈraɪt/ *adv* **1** clearly and directly, without trying to hide your feelings or intentions: *If she* ***asked*** *me* ***outright****, I'd tell her.* **2** clearly and completely: *She won outright.* | *They* ***rejected*** *the deal* ***outright***. **3 buy/own sth outright** to own something such as a house completely because you have paid the full price with your own money **4** immediately and without any delay: *The passenger was* ***killed outright***. | *They fired her outright.*

out·rode /aʊtˈrəʊd $ -ˈroʊd/ *v* the past tense of OUTRIDE

out·run /aʊtˈrʌn/ *v* (*past tense* **outran** /-ˈræn/, *past participle* **outrun**, *present participle* **outrunning**) [T] **1** to run faster or further than someone else **2** to develop more quickly than something else: *The company's spending was outrunning its income.*

out·sell /aʊtˈsel/ *v* (*past tense and past participle* **outsold** /-ˈsəʊld $ -ˈsoʊld/) [T] **1** to be sold in larger quantities than something else: *It may outsell his previous novels.* **2** to sell more goods or products than a competitor: *Australia now outsells the US in wines.*

out·set /ˈaʊtset/ ●○○ *n* **at/from the outset** at or from the beginning of an event or process → **set out**: *It was clear from the outset that there were going to be problems.* | *It's better to get something in writing right at the outset.* | **[+of]** *A person with higher qualifications can get a better paid job at the outset of their career.*

out·shine /aʊtˈʃaɪn/ *v* (*past tense and past participle* **outshone** /aʊtˈʃɒn $ -ˈʃoʊn/) [T] to be better or more impressive than someone or something else: *Several new players outshone the veterans.*

out·side¹ /aʊtˈsaɪd/ ●●● S1 W1 *adv, prep*
1 a) not inside a building SYN **outdoors** OPP **inside**: *When we got up, it was still dark outside.* | *Go and play outside.* **b)** not inside a building or room but close to it: *Could you wait outside please.* | *I'll meet you outside the theatre at two o'clock.* | **[+of]** *AmE*: *Several people were standing in the hallway outside of his room.* **c)** out of a building or room: *We went outside to see what was happening.* | *I opened the door and looked outside.*
2 a) not in a particular city, country etc: *She often travels outside the UK.* **b)** close to a place, city etc but not in it: *We camped a few miles outside the town.* | *Bolton is a mill town* ***just outside*** *Manchester.* | **[+of]** *AmE*: *Maritza, 19, lives in Everett, outside of Boston.*
3 beyond the limits or range of a situation, activity etc OPP **within** → **beyond**: *It's outside my experience, I'm afraid.* | **[+of]** *especially AmE*: *children born outside of marriage*
4 if someone is outside a group of people, an organization etc, they do not belong to it: *Few people outside the government realized what was happening.* | **from outside (sth)** *The university administrators ignored criticism from outside.* | *Management consultants were brought in from outside the company.*
5 outside of sb/sth *especially AmE informal* apart from a particular person or thing SYN **except**: *Outside of love, the best thing you can give a child is attention.* | *I'm taking one big trip this summer, but outside of that I'll be around.*
6 if the time that someone takes to do something, especially finish a race, is outside a particular time, it is greater than that time: *He finished in 10 minutes 22.4 seconds, 4 seconds outside the record.*

THESAURUS

outside not inside a building, but usually close to it: *Why don't you go outside and play?* | *He was standing outside, smoking a cigarette.*
out outside – used mainly before the following prepositions or adverbs: *We slept* ***out under*** *the stars.* | *Don't stand* ***out in*** *the rain – come inside.* | *I can hear somebody* ***out there***.
outdoors/out of doors away from buildings and in the open air – used especially when talking about pleasant or healthy things you do outside: *In the summer, we like to eat outdoors.* | *Kids should spend as much time out of doors as possible.*
in the open air outside where the air is fresh: *It's good to exercise in the open air.* | *Leave the wood to dry slowly in the open air.*
al fresco outside – used when talking about eating outside: *We prefer to dine al fresco.*

out·side² /ˈaʊtsaɪd/ ●●● S2 W2 *adj* [only before noun]
1 not inside a building OPP **inside**: *We turned off the outside lights and went to bed.* | *The house will need a lot of outside repairs before we can sell it.*
2 involving people who do not belong to the same group or organization as you: *Outside observers said the election*

was free and fair. | *Consultants were brought in to provide some outside advice.*
3 the outside world the rest of the world: *The city is largely cut off from the outside world.* | *computers linked by modems to the outside world*
4 outside interests/experiences etc interests, experiences etc that are not part of your work or studying: *Children should be encouraged to take up outside interests, such as music or sport.*
5 an outside chance a very small possibility that something will happen: *Ireland still have an outside chance of winning.*
6 outside line/call etc a telephone line or telephone call which is to or from someone who is not inside a particular building or organization: *Dial '9' before the number when making outside calls.*
7 an outside figure/estimate etc a number or amount that is the largest something could possibly be
8 the outside lane *BrE* the LANE that is nearest the middle of the road SYN **fast lane** OPP **the inside lane, inside lane**

out·side[3] /aʊtˈsaɪd, ˈaʊtsaɪd/ ●●● S3 *n*
1 the outside a) the part or surface of something that is furthest from the centre OPP **inside**: **[+of]** *The outside of the house was painted white.* **b)** the area around something such as a building, vehicle etc OPP **inside**: **from the outside** *From the outside, it looked like any other big warehouse.* **c)** someone who is on or from the outside is not involved in an activity or does not belong to a particular group, organization etc OPP **inside**: **from the outside** *Influences from the outside can undermine the values you want to teach your children.* | **on the outside** *To anyone on the outside, our marriage seemed perfect.*
2 on the outside a) used to describe the way someone appears to be or to behave: *Ken was furious, but forced himself to appear calm on the outside.* **b)** not in prison: *Life on the outside was not as easy as he'd first thought.* **c)** *BrE* if a car passes another car on the outside, it passes on the driver's side
3 at the (very) outside used to say that a particular number or amount is the largest something could possibly be, and it might be less SYN **at the most**: *It's only a 20-minute walk, half an hour at the outside.*

out·sid·er /aʊtˈsaɪdə $ -ər/ ●○○ *n* [C]
1 someone who is not accepted as a member of a particular social group → **insider**: *I'm an outsider, the only foreign woman in the group.* | **to an outsider** *To an outsider, the system seems complex and confusing.*
2 someone who does not belong to a particular company or organization or who is not involved in a particular activity → **insider**: *a political outsider who is running for governor*
3 someone who does not seem to have much chance of winning a race or competition: **rank outsider** *BrE*: *Last year he was a rank outsider for the title.*

out·size /ˈaʊtsaɪz/, **out·sized** /-saɪzd/ *adj* **1** larger than normal: *a woman in outsize glasses* **2** made for people who are very large or fat: *outsize clothes*

out·skirts /ˈaʊtskɜːts $ -ɜːr-/ ●○○ *n* [plural] the parts of a town or city that are furthest from the centre: **on the outskirts (of sth)** *They live on the outskirts of Paris.* **THESAURUS** ▸ EDGE

out·smart /aʊtˈsmɑːt $ -ˈsmɑːrt/ *v* [T] to gain an advantage over someone using tricks or your intelligence SYN **outwit**: *The older kids outsmart the young ones when trading cards.*

out·sold /aʊtˈsəʊld $ -ˈsoʊld/ the past tense and past participle of OUTSELL

out·sour·cing /ˈaʊtˌsɔːsɪŋ $ -ˌɔːr-/ *n* [U] when a company uses workers from outside the company to do a job: *the outsourcing of the marketing to a specialist firm* —**outsource** *v* [T]

out·spend /aʊtˈspend/ *v* (*past tense and past participle* **outspent** /-ˈspent/) [T] to spend more money than another person or organization: *In the Senate race, the Republican outspent his rival by nearly $2 million.*

out·spo·ken /aʊtˈspəʊkən $ -ˈspoʊ-/ *adj* expressing your opinions honestly and directly, even when doing this might annoy some people OPP **reticent**: *an outspoken critic of the education reforms* —**outspokenly** *adv* —**outspokenness** *n* [U]

out·spread /ˌaʊtˈspred◂/ *adj* spread out flat or completely → **spread out**: *He was lying on the beach with arms outspread.* | *a bird with its wings outspread*

out·stand·ing /aʊtˈstændɪŋ/ ●●○ W3 *adj*
1 extremely good: *an* **outstanding example** *of a 13th-century castle* | *an outstanding success* | *His performance was outstanding.* **THESAURUS** ▸ GOOD
2 not yet done, solved, or paid: *We've got quite a few debts still outstanding.* | *an outstanding issue*
3 very great or clear: *The question of who is in charge is of outstanding importance.*

out·stand·ing·ly /aʊtˈstændɪŋli/ *adv* extremely well: *He played outstandingly.* | *She performed outstandingly well in her examinations.* | *an outstandingly talented musician*

out·stay /aʊtˈsteɪ/ *v* [T] to stay somewhere longer than someone else → **outstay your welcome** at WELCOME[4](3)

out·stretched /ˌaʊtˈstretʃt◂/ *adj* stretched out to full length: **outstretched arms/hands/fingers** *She ran to meet them with outstretched arms.*

out·strip /aʊtˈstrɪp/ *v* (**outstripped**, **outstripping**) [T]
1 to do something better than someone else or be more successful: *We outstripped all our competitors in sales last year.* **2** to be greater in quantity than something else: *Demand for new aircraft production is outstripping supply.*
3 to run or move faster than someone or something else: *Speeding at 90 mph, Denny outstripped police cars for an hour.*

out·ta /ˈaʊtə/ *prep AmE informal* used in writing to represent the spoken form 'out of': *I've got to get outta here.*

ˈ**out-take** (*also* **out·take** *AmE*) /ˈaʊt-teɪk/ *n* [C] a piece of a film or television show that is removed before it is broadcast, especially because it contains a mistake

ˈ**out tray** *n* [C] a box on an office desk where you put work and letters which are ready to be posted or put away → **in tray**

out·vote /aʊtˈvəʊt $ -ˈvoʊt/ *v* [T] to defeat a person by winning more votes than them: *France was outvoted on that issue.* GRAMMAR **Outvote** is usually passive.

out·ward /ˈaʊtwəd $ -wərd/ ●○○ *adj*
1 [only before noun] relating to how a person or situation seems to be, rather than how it really is OPP **inward**: *The economy and* **outward appearance** *of the area have changed considerably.* | *His clenched fist was the only* **outward sign** *of his anger.*
2 outward journey/voyage etc a journey in which you are travelling away from home
3 [only before noun] directed towards the outside or away from a place: *the outward flow of oil*

out·ward·ly /ˈaʊtwədli $ -wərd-/ *adv* according to the way people or things seem OPP **inwardly**: *Calvin remained outwardly calm, but inside he was very angry.* | *Outwardly, at least, he was an optimist.*

out·wards /ˈaʊtwədz $ -wərdz/ ●○○ (*also* **outward** *AmE*) *adv* towards the outside or away from the centre of something OPP **inwards**: *The door opens outwards.* | **facing/looking/spreading etc outwards** *Stand with your elbows pointing outwards.*

out·weigh /aʊtˈweɪ/ ●○○ *v* [T] to be more important or valuable than something else: *The benefits of the scheme outweigh the disadvantages.*

out·wit /aʊtˈwɪt/ *v* (**outwitted**, **outwitting**) [T] to gain an advantage over someone using tricks or clever plans: *a wolf that had outwitted hunters for years*

out·work /ˈaʊtwɜːk $ -wɜːrk/ *n* [U] work for a business that is done by people at home —**outworker** *n* [C]

out·worn /ˌaʊtˈwɔːn◂ $ -ˈwɔːrn◂/ *adj* [only before noun] old-fashioned, and no longer useful or important → **worn out**: *outworn traditions*

O

ou·zo /ˈuːzəʊ $ -zoʊ/ *n* [U] a Greek alcoholic drink that is drunk with water

o·va /ˈəʊvə $ ˈoʊ-/ *n* the plural form of OVUM

o·val /ˈəʊvəl $ ˈoʊ-/ ●○○ *n* [C] a shape like a circle, but wider in one direction than the other → **elliptical** —**oval** *adj*: *an oval mirror*

ˌOval ˈOffice *n* **the Oval Office** the office of the US president, in the White House in Washington D.C.

o·var·i·an /əʊˈveəriən $ oʊˈver-/ *adj* relating to the ovary: *ovarian cancer*

O

o·va·ry /ˈəʊvəri $ ˈoʊ-/ *n* (*plural* **ovaries**) [C] **1** the part of a female that produces eggs **2** the part of a female plant that produces seeds

o·va·tion /əʊˈveɪʃən $ oʊ-/ *n* [C] *formal* if a group of people give someone an ovation, they CLAP to show approval: *The Chancellor's entrance was greeted with a* ***standing ovation*** (=everyone stood up). | *Fans* ***gave*** *the rock group a thunderous* ***ovation***.

ov·en /ˈʌvən/ ●●● S3 *n* [C]
1 a piece of equipment that food is cooked inside, shaped like a metal box with a door on the front → **cooker**, **stove**: *Preheat the oven to 200 degrees C.* | *Press the mixture onto the bread and bake in a hot oven for ten minutes.*
2 like an oven *informal* uncomfortably hot → **have a bun in the oven** at BUN(5)

ov·en·proof /ˈʌvənpruːf/ *adj* ovenproof dishes, plates etc will not be harmed by the high temperatures in an oven

ˌoven-ˈready *adj BrE* oven-ready food is already prepared when you buy it, so you only have to cook it: *a five-pound oven-ready turkey*

ov·en·ware /ˈʌvənweə $ -wer/ *n* [U] cooking pots that can be put in a hot oven without cracking

o·ver¹ /ˈəʊvə $ ˈoʊvər/ ●●● S1 W1 *prep*
1 ABOVE above or higher than something, without touching it OPP **under**: *A lamp hung over the table.* | *She leaned over the desk to answer the phone.* | *The sign over the door said 'Mind your head'.* | *We watched a helicopter flying low over the harbour.*
2 COVERING on something or covering it OPP **under**: *Over the body lay a thin white sheet.* | *She wore a large jacket over her sweater.* | *Mind you don't spill coffee over my best tablecloth.*
3 ACROSS from one side of something to the other side of it: *Somehow the sheep had jumped over the fence.* | *The road over the mountains is steep and dangerous.* | *a bridge over the River Thames* | *Their house has a magnificent view over the bay.*
4 ON THE OTHER SIDE on the opposite side of something from where you already are: *There's a bus stop just over the road.* | *They live over the river in Richmond.*
5 DOWN FROM STH down from the edge of something: *The car plunged over a cliff.*
6 IN MANY PARTS OF STH in or to many parts of a particular place, organization, or thing: *He used to wander over the moors, losing all track of time.* | **all over (sth)** (=in every part) *They said they had cleaned up but there were bottles all over the place.* | *Scientists from all over the world gather here.*
7 NO LONGER AFFECTED if you are over an illness or a bad experience or situation, you are no longer affected by it → **recover**: *I think we're over the worst of the crisis now.* | *He had a fever last night, but he seems to be over it now.* | *Sybil has never got over the shock of her mother's death.* | *I'm over him now* (=I am no longer in love with him).
8 MORE THAN more than a particular number, amount, or level OPP **under**: *The Japanese were producing over 100 million tons of steel.* | *toys suitable for children over the age of three* | *drivers who go over the speed limit* | **the over-30s/50s etc** (=people who are more than a particular age) *a social club for the over-60s*
9 DURING during: *Will you be home over the summer vacation?* | *Over a period of ten years he stole a million pounds from the company.* | *Can we talk about this over dinner?* **THESAURUS** ▸ DURING
10 CONCERNING about a particular subject, person, or thing: *He's having problems over his income tax.* | *a row over public expenditure* | *There is concern over the bad image of the legal profession.*
11 CONTROLLING in control of or influencing someone or something: *Genghis ruled over an empire that stretched from Persia across to China.* | *She had great personal influence and power over her followers.*
12 BETTER used to say that someone or something is more successful or better than someone or something else: *Ipswich's 3-1 win over Manchester City* | *Can Labour maintain its lead over the Conservatives?* | *It has one great advantage over its rivals.*
13 BY TELEPHONE/RADIO using something such as a telephone or radio: *I don't want to talk about this over the telephone.* | *I heard the news over the radio.*
14 over and above in addition to something: *He gets a travel allowance over and above his existing salary.*
15 LOUDER THAN STH making a sound louder than another sound: *'What?' he yelled over the noise of the engine and the wind.*
16 PREFERRING if you choose one thing over another, you choose that thing rather than the other: *What is your main reason for choosing one restaurant over another?*

over² ●●● S1 W1 *adv, adj*
1 FALLING DOWN from an upright position into a position of lying on a surface: *He was so drunk he fell over in the road.* | *Mind you don't knock the candle over.* | *Engineers are working to prevent the tower from toppling over.*
2 BENDING/FOLDING so that someone or something is no longer straight or flat, but is bent or folded in the middle: *As Sheila bent over, a sudden pain shot up her back.* | *He folded the paper over and put it in his pocket.*
3 ACROSS **a)** from one side of an object, space, or area to the other side: *There are only three canoes so some people will have to swim over.* | *The wall was crumbling where children had climbed over.* | *I went over* (=crossed the room, street etc) *to say hello, but Vincent didn't recognize me.* | **[+to]** *We flew over to the US to visit my Aunt Polly.* | **[+from]** *One of my cousins is coming over from France with his wife and daughter.* | *Come* ***over here*** *and see what I've found.* **b)** in a place that is on the other side of a space or area: *Bill lives over on the other side of town.* | *She was standing over by the window.* | *Do you see that building* ***over there****?*
4 IN OR TO A PLACE in or to a particular house, city etc: *You really should come over and see our new house.* | *I spent the whole day over at Gabby's place.* | *We could drive over to Oxford this afternoon.*
5 FINISHED if an event or period of time is over, it has finished: *Is the meeting over yet?* | **over (and done) with** (=used about something unpleasant) *I'm so glad the mid-term exams are over and done with.* | *You'd better give them the bad news. Do it now – get it over with.*
6 TO THE SIDE towards one side: *The bus pulled over to the side of the road.* | *Would you move over, so I can sit next to you.*
7 GIVING from one person or group to another: *The attacker was ordered to hand over his weapon.* | *Most of the money has been signed over to his children.*
8 CHANGING from one position or system to another: *The guards change over at midnight.* | *We switched over from electricity to gas because it was cheaper.*
9 TURNING so that the bottom or the other side of something can now be seen: *Turn the box over and open it at that end.* | *Josh rolled over and went back to sleep.*
10 MORE THAN more than or higher than a particular number, amount, or level OPP **under**: *Almost 40% of women are size 14* ***or over***. | *People earning £33,000* ***and over*** *will pay the higher rate of tax.*
11 VERY/TOO used before an adjective or adverb to mean 'very' or 'too': *She didn't seem over pleased when I asked her to wait.* | *Perhaps we were all over enthusiastic about the project.*
12 REMAINING an amount of something that is over is what remains after some of it has been used: *There should*

be some money over when I've paid all the bills. | There was a little food left over from the party.*
13 COVERED used to show that something is completely covered with a substance or material: *Most of the windows have been boarded over. | Parts of the river were iced over.* | **[+with]** *The door had been painted over with a bright red varnish.*
14 ABOVE above someone or something: *We stood on the roof watching the planes fly over.*
15 TALKING/THINKING/READING in a detailed and careful way: *After talking it over with my wife, I've decided to retire. | I'll need time to read the contract over before I sign. | Think it over carefully before you make a decision.*
16 AGAIN *AmE* if you start or do something over, you do it again: *I got mixed up and had to start over.*
17 over and over (again) many times: *The way to learn the script is to say it to yourself over and over again.*
18 twice over/three times over etc a) used to say how many times the same thing happens: *He sings each song twice over. | The pattern is repeated many times over.* **b)** used to say by how much an amount is multiplied: *Trade between the two countries has increased five times over.*
19 all over again used to emphasize that you do the whole of something again from the beginning, or that the same thing happens again: *Their first plan had gone wrong, so they had to start all over again. | We had quarrelled about the money before, and now it was happening all over again.*
20 over to sb used to say that it is now someone else's turn to do something, to speak etc: *I've done my best. Now it's over to the professionals.*
21 RADIO MESSAGE *spoken* used when communicating by radio to show that you have finished speaking: *Are you hearing me loud and clear? Over.*
22 over against sth *formal* used to say what something is compared to or preferred to: *The Celtic Church maintained the Greek calendar over against that of Rome.*
23 it's not over until the fat lady sings (*also* **it's not over until it's over**) used during a game, election etc to say that, although a particular result seems likely, the situation could still change

over³ *n* [C] the period of time in the game of CRICKET during which six or eight balls are thrown by the same BOWLER in one direction

over- /ˌəʊvə $ ˌoʊvər/ *prefix* **1** too much: *overpopulation | overcooked vegetables | overweight* **2** above; beyond; across: *overhanging branches | overhead telephone wires | the overland route* (=not by sea or air) **3** outer: *an overcoat* **4** additional: *We were working overtime* (=working beyond the usual time).

ˌover-aˈchiever *n* [C] someone who works very hard to be successful, and is very unhappy if they do not achieve everything they want to OPP **underachiever**

o·ver·act /ˌəʊvərˈækt $ ˌoʊ-/ *v* [I] to act in a play with too much emotion or movement – used to show disapproval —**overacting** *n* [U]

o·ver·ac·tive /ˌəʊvərˈæktɪv◂ $ ˌoʊv-/ *adj* too active, in a way that produces a bad result OPP **underactive**: *an overactive thyroid gland | Such fears are nothing more than the product of an* ***overactive imagination****.*

ˌover-ˈage *adj* too old for a particular purpose or activity OPP **under-age**: *Leyton was over-age for recruitment into the army.*

o·ver·all¹ /ˌəʊvərˈɔːl◂ $ ˌoʊvərˈɒːl◂/ ●●○ S3 W2 AWL *adj* [only before noun] considering or including everything: *The overall cost of the exhibition was £400,000. | The overall result is an increase in population. | An overall winner and a runner-up were chosen. | We don't want all the details now, just the overall picture.*

overall² ●●○ AWL *adv*
1 considering or including everything: *Williams came fifth overall. | What will it cost, overall?*
2 [sentence adverb] generally: *Overall, prices are still rising.*

o·ver·all³ /ˈəʊvərɔːl $ ˈoʊvərɒːl/ *n* **1** [C] *BrE* a loose-fitting piece of clothing like a coat, that is worn over clothes to protect them **2 overalls** [plural] *AmE* heavy cotton trousers with a piece covering your chest, held up by pieces of cloth that go over your shoulders SYN **dungarees** *BrE* **3 overalls** [plural] *BrE* a piece of clothing like a shirt and trousers in one piece that is worn over other clothes to protect them SYN **coveralls** *AmE*

ˌoverall maˈjority *n* [C] *BrE* **1** more votes than all the other political parties together: *The Conservatives had a huge overall majority in the House of Commons.* **2** the difference between the number of votes gained by the winning party and the total votes gained by all the other parties: *an overall majority of 28*

o·ver·arch·ing /ˌəʊvərˈɑːtʃɪŋ◂ $ ˌoʊvərˈɑːr-/ *adj* [only before noun] including or influencing every part of something: *The crisis gave an overarching justification to the government's policy.*

o·ver·arm /ˈəʊvərɑːm $ ˈoʊvərɑːrm/ *adj, adv especially BrE* an overarm throw in a sport is when you throw the ball with your arm high above your shoulder → **underarm**

o·ver·awe /ˌəʊvərˈɔː $ ˌoʊvərˈɒː/ *v* [T] to make someone feel respect or fear, so that they are nervous or unable to say or do anything: *He was overawed by his father.* —**overawed** *adj*

o·ver·bal·ance /ˌəʊvəˈbæləns $ ˌoʊvər-/ *v* [I,T] **1** *BrE* to fall over or nearly fall over because you lose balance **2** *AmE* OUTWEIGH

o·ver·bear /ˌəʊvəˈbeə $ ˌoʊvərˈber/ *v* (*past tense* **overbore** /-ˈbɔː $ -ˈbɔːr/, *past participle* **overborne** /-ˈbɔːn $ -ˈbɔːrn/) [T] to defeat someone or something: *She is independent-minded enough not to be easily overborne by her husband.*

o·ver·bear·ing /ˌəʊvəˈbeərɪŋ $ ˌoʊvərˈber-/ *adj* always trying to control other people without considering their wishes or feelings SYN **domineering**: *a bossy overbearing wife*

o·ver·bid /ˌəʊvəˈbɪd $ ˌoʊvər-/ *v* (*past tense and past participle* **overbid**, *present participle* **overbidding**) **1** [I + for] to offer too high a price for something, especially at an AUCTION **2** [I,T] to offer more than the value of your cards in a card game such as BRIDGE

o·ver·bite /ˈəʊvəbaɪt $ ˌoʊvərˈbaɪt/ *n* [C] a condition in which someone's upper teeth are too far in front of their lower teeth

o·ver·blown /ˌəʊvəˈbləʊn◂ $ ˌoʊvərˈbloʊn/ *adj* made to seem greater or more impressive than something really is SYN **exaggerated**: *He's not really a scientist; he's just an overblown technician.*

o·ver·board /ˈəʊvəbɔːd $ ˈoʊvərbɔːrd/ *adv* **1** over the side of a ship or boat into the water: *One of the crew* ***fell overboard*** *and drowned. | Man overboard* (=said when someone falls off a boat)*!* **2 go overboard** to do or say something that is too extreme for a particular situation: *I hope politicians will not go overboard in trying to control the press.* **3 throw sth overboard** to get rid of an idea, system etc that is considered to be useless or unnecessary

o·ver·book /ˌəʊvəˈbʊk $ ˌoʊvər-/ *v* [I,T] to sell more tickets for a theatre, plane etc than there are seats available: *overbooked hotels*

o·ver·bur·den /ˌəʊvəˈbɜːdn $ ˌoʊvərˈbɜːrdn/ *v* [T] to give an organization, person, or system more work or problems than they can deal with: *Health services have been overburdened and are unable to care for many older people. | a manager overburdened with work*

o·ver·came /ˌəʊvəˈkeɪm $ ˌoʊvər-/ *v* the past tense of OVERCOME

o·ver·ca·pa·ci·ty /ˌəʊvəkəˈpæsəti $ ˌoʊvər-/ *n* [singular, U] the situation in which an industry or factory cannot sell as much as it produces

o·ver·cast /ˌəʊvəˈkɑːst◂ $ ˌoʊvərˈkæst◂/ ●○○ *adj* dark with clouds: *a chilly overcast day | The sky was overcast and a light rain began to fall.*

o·ver·charge /ˌəʊvəˈtʃɑːdʒ $ ˌoʊvərˈtʃɑːrdʒ/ *v* **1** [I,T] to charge someone too much money for something OPP **undercharge**: *They were being overcharged for cheap beer.* **2** [T] to put too much power into a BATTERY or electrical system

o·ver·charged /ˌəʊvəˈtʃɑːdʒd $ ˌoʊvərˈtʃɑːrdʒd/ *adj* [I] full of emotion or excitement: *the stadium's overcharged atmosphere*

o·ver·coat /ˈəʊvəkəʊt $ ˈoʊvərkoʊt/ *n* [C] a long thick warm coat

o·ver·come /ˌəʊvəˈkʌm $ ˌoʊvər-/ ●●○ W3 *v* (*past tense* **overcame** /-ˈkeɪm/, *past participle* **overcome**) [T]
1 to successfully control a feeling or problem that prevents you from achieving something: *He struggled to overcome his shyness.* | *Her financial problems could no longer be overcome.*
2 if someone is overcome by smoke or gas, they become extremely sick or unconscious because they breathe it: *The engineer was working on the freezer when he was overcome by gas.* GRAMMAR **Overcome** is usually passive in this meaning.
3 if someone is overcome by emotion, they cannot behave normally because they feel the emotion so strongly: **be overcome by/with sth** *Charles was overcome with grief.* GRAMMAR **Overcome** is usually passive in this meaning.
4 to fight and win against someone or something SYN **defeat**: *Australia overcame the Netherlands 2–1.*

o·ver·com·pen·sate /ˌəʊvəˈkɒmpənseɪt, -pen- $ ˌoʊvərˈkɑːm-/ *v* [I] to try to correct a weakness or mistake by doing too much of the opposite thing: **[+for]** *Zoe overcompensates for her shyness by talking a lot.* —**overcompensation** /ˌəʊvəkɒmpənˈseɪʃən, -pen- $ ˌoʊvərkɑːm-/ *n* [U]

o·ver·cook /ˌəʊvəˈkʊk $ ˌoʊvər-/ *v* [T] to cook food for too long OPP **undercook**: *overcooked chicken*

o·ver·crowd·ed /ˌəʊvəˈkraʊdɪd◂ $ ˌoʊvər-/ ●○○ *adj* filled with too many people or things: *Staff had to work in* ***overcrowded conditions***. | *overcrowded housing*

o·ver·crowd·ing /ˌəʊvəˈkraʊdɪŋ $ ˌoʊvər-/ *n* [U] when there are too many people or things in one place: **relieve/ease/reduce overcrowding** *There are plans to relieve overcrowding in the village.* | *the prison's chronic overcrowding problem*

o·ver·de·vel·oped /ˌəʊvədɪˈveləpt◂ $ ˌoʊvər-/ *adj* **1** if a city or area is overdeveloped, too many houses, buildings, roads etc have been built there: *an overdeveloped country* **2** too great or large: *You have an overdeveloped sense of duty.*

o·ver·do /ˌəʊvəˈduː $ ˌoʊvər-/ *v* (*past tense* **overdid** /-ˈdɪd/, *past participle* **overdone** /-ˈdʌn/, *third person singular* **overdoes** /-ˈdʌz/) [T] **1** to do something more than is suitable or natural: *Analysts believe that worries about the economy are overdone.* | *Use a few drawings and photographs, but* ***don't overdo it***. **2 overdo it** to work too hard or be too active so that you become tired: *You mustn't overdo it - if you're tired, just sit down and start again.* **3** to use too much of something: *I think I overdid the salt.*

o·ver·done /ˌəʊvəˈdʌn◂ $ ˌoʊvər-/ *adj* cooked too much OPP **underdone**: *The beef was overdone.*

o·ver·dose¹ /ˈəʊvədəʊs $ ˈoʊvərdoʊs/ *n* [C] **1** too much of a drug taken at one time: **[+of]** *a massive overdose of heroin* | *She* ***took an overdose*** *and died two days later.* **2** too much of something, especially something harmful: **[+of]** *an overdose of sun*

o·ver·dose² /ˌəʊvəˈdəʊs $ ˌoʊvərˈdoʊs/ *v* [I] (*abbreviation* **OD**) to take too much of a drug at one time, so that it harms you or kills you: **[+on]** *She overdosed on sleeping pills.*

o·ver·draft /ˈəʊvədrɑːft $ ˈoʊvərdræft/ *n* [C] *BrE* the amount of money you owe to a bank when you have spent more money than you had in your account: *a £250 overdraft* | *Many students have a free* ***overdraft facility*** (=agreement with their bank to have an overdraft up to a particular limit).

o·ver·drawn /ˌəʊvəˈdrɔːn $ ˌoʊvərˈdrɒːn/ *adj* [not before noun] if you are overdrawn or if your bank account is overdrawn, you have spent more than you had in your account and so you owe the bank money: *I try not to* ***go overdrawn*** *if possible.* | **[+by]** *My account is overdrawn by £300.*

o·ver·dressed /ˌəʊvəˈdrest◂ $ ˌoʊvər-/ *adj* dressed in clothes that are too formal for the occasion OPP **underdressed**: *She felt overdressed in her smart suit.* —**overdress** *v* [I]

o·ver·drive /ˈəʊvədraɪv $ ˈoʊvər-/ *n* [U] **1** an additional GEAR which allows a car to go fast while its engine produces the least power necessary **2 go into overdrive/be in overdrive** to start being very active or working very hard: *Her career has gone into overdrive.*

o·ver·due /ˌəʊvəˈdjuː◂ $ ˌoʊvərˈduː◂/ ●○○ *adj*
1 not done, paid, returned etc by the time expected: *an overdue gas bill* | *The library books are overdue.* | *The baby was a week overdue* (=it was expected to be born a week ago). THESAURUS ▸ LATE
2 something that is overdue should have happened or been done a long time ago: **[+for]** *He was overdue for a shave.* | *We welcome this announcement and think it's* ***long overdue***.

o·ver·eat /ˌəʊvərˈiːt $ ˌoʊ-/ *v* (*past tense* **overate** /-ˈet,-ˈeɪt $ -ˈeɪt/, *past participle* **overeaten** /-ˈiːtn/) [I] to eat too much, or eat more than is healthy

o·ver·egg /ˌəʊvərˈeg $ ˌoʊ-/ *v* **overegg the pudding** *BrE informal* to do more than is necessary, or add something that is not needed

o·ver·em·pha·size (*also* **-ise** *BrE*) /ˌəʊvərˈemfəsaɪz $ ˌoʊ-/ *v* [T] to give something more importance than it deserves or than is suitable: *In the past the exam had been overemphasized.* | *The importance of adequate preparation* ***cannot be overemphasized*** (=used to say that something is very important). THESAURUS ▸ EMPHASIZE —**overemphasis** /-fəsɪs/ *n* [singular]: *There has been an overemphasis on content rather than methodology.*

o·ver·es·ti·mate¹ /ˌəʊvərˈestɪmeɪt $ ˌoʊ-/ ●○○ AWL *v* [T]
1 to think something is better, more important etc than it really is OPP **underestimate**: *He tends to overestimate his own abilities.* | *The importance of training in health and safety* ***cannot be overestimated*** (=is extremely important).
2 to guess an amount or value that is too high OPP **underestimate**: *Most patients overestimated how long they had had to wait to see a doctor.*

o·ver·es·ti·mate² /ˌəʊvərˈestəmət $ ˌoʊ-/ AWL *n* [C] a calculation, judgment, or guess that is too large: *The figure of 30% is clearly an overestimate.*

o·ver·ex·cit·ed /ˌəʊvərɪkˈsaɪtɪd $ ˌoʊ-/ *adj* someone who is overexcited is very excited and not behaving sensibly: *Some of the boys became overexcited.*

o·ver·ex·pose /ˌəʊvərɪkˈspəʊz $ ˌoʊvərɪkˈspoʊz/ *v* [T] **1** to allow too much light to reach the film when taking or developing a photograph → **underexpose 2 be overexposed** to appear too many times on television, in the newspapers etc, so that people lose interest in you and you become less popular

ˌover-exˈposure *n* [U] **1** when too much light, RADIATION etc reaches someone's skin, a photographic film etc and is harmful **2** when someone receives too much attention from television, the newspapers etc

o·ver·ex·tend /ˌəʊvərɪkˈstend $ ˌoʊ-/ *v* [T] **1** to try to do or use too much of something, causing problems, illness, or damage: **overextend yourself** *Be careful not to overextend yourself. You've been very ill.* **2** to spend more money than you actually have: *Jackson's company became overextended financially.* —**overextended** *adj*

o·ver·feed /ˌəʊvəˈfiːd $ ˌoʊvər-/ *v* (*past tense and past participle* **overfed** /-ˈfed/) [T] to give someone too much food

o·ver·fill /ˌəʊvəˈfɪl $ ˌoʊvər-/ *v* [T] to put too much of something into a container: *He had overfilled the jug.*

o·ver·fish·ing /ˌəʊvəˈfɪʃɪŋ $ ˌoʊvər-/ *n* [U] the process of taking too many fish from the sea, a river etc, so that the number of fish in it becomes too low

o·ver·flow¹ /ˌəʊvəˈfləʊ $ ˌoʊvərˈfloʊ/ *v* [I,T] **1** if a river, lake, or container overflows, it is so full that the liquid or material inside flows over its edges: *The drains flooded and water overflowed down the main street.* | *The river had* overflowed its banks. | **[+with]** *waste bins overflowing with plastic cups* **2** to have a lot of something: **[+with]** *The garden overflows with colour.* | *He was overflowing with good ideas.* **3** if a place overflows with people or people overflow into a place, there are too many of them to fit into it: **[+with]** *Hospitals were reported to be overflowing with dead and wounded.* | **[+into]** *The house was full and people were overflowing into the street.* **4** to have a very strong feeling: **[+with]** *My heart was overflowing with gratitude.* **5 be filled to overflowing (with sth)** to be completely full: *One wall was filled to overflowing with books.*

o·ver·flow[2] /ˈəʊvəfləʊ $ ˈoʊvərfloʊ/ *n* **1** [singular] the amount of something or the number of people that cannot be contained in a place because it is already full: *The overflow will be accommodated in another hotel.* | **[+of]** *the overflow of water from the lake* **2** [C] a pipe through which water flows out of a container when it becomes too full

o·ver·fly /ˌəʊvəˈflaɪ $ ˌoʊvər-/ *v* (*past tense* **overflew** /-ˈfluː/, *past participle* **overflown** /-ˈfləʊn $ -ˈfloʊn/, *present participle* **overflying**, *third person singular* **overflies**) [T] to fly over an area or country in an aircraft

o·ver·ground /ˈəʊvəgraʊnd $ ˈoʊvər-/ *adj* [only before noun] used to describe a train system that runs on the surface of the ground rather than below it OPP **underground**: *an overground railway*

o·ver·grown /ˌəʊvəˈgrəʊn◂ $ ˌoʊvərˈgroʊn◂/ *adj* **1** covered with plants that have grown in an uncontrolled way: **[+with]** *The garden will be overgrown with weeds by the time we get back.* **2** when grass or plants are overgrown, they have grown in an uncontrolled way: *a lawn with overgrown grass* **3 overgrown schoolboy/child** an adult who behaves like a child – used to show disapproval: *Stop acting like an overgrown schoolboy.*

o·ver·growth /ˈəʊvəgrəʊθ $ ˈoʊvərgroʊθ/ *n* [U] plants and branches of trees growing above your head, usually in a forest

o·ver·hand /ˈəʊvəhænd $ ˈoʊvər-/ *adj, adv AmE* an overhand throw in a sport is when you throw the ball with your arm above the level of your shoulder → **underhand**

o·ver·hang[1] /ˌəʊvəˈhæŋ $ ˌoʊvər-/ *v* (*past tense and past participle* **overhung** /-ˈhʌŋ/) [I,T] to hang over something or stick out above it

o·ver·hang[2] /ˈəʊvəhæŋ $ ˈoʊvər-/ *n* [C, usually singular] **1** a rock, roof etc that hangs over something else: *We stood under the overhang while it rained.* **2** the amount by which something hangs over something else: *a five-foot overhang*

o·ver·haul[1] /ˌəʊvəˈhɔːl $ ˌoʊvərˈhɒːl/ *v* [T] **1** to repair or change the necessary parts in a machine, system etc that is not working correctly: *A mechanic is coming to overhaul the engine.* **2** to change a system or method in order to improve it: *All the community's decision-making institutions need to be overhauled.*

o·ver·haul[2] /ˈəʊvəhɔːl $ ˈoʊvərhɒːl/ *n* [C] **1** necessary changes or repairs made to a machine or system: *The car needs a* ***complete overhaul.*** **2** when a system or method is changed in order to improve it: **[+of]** *an overhaul of the tax system*

o·ver·head[1] /ˌəʊvəˈhed◂ $ ˌoʊvər-/ ●●○ *adv* above your head or in the sky: *Bullets whizzed overhead.* | *A plane flew overhead.* —**overhead** *adj*: *overhead wires*

o·ver·head[2] /ˈəʊvəhed $ ˈoʊvər-/ *n* **1** [U] *AmE*, **overheads** *BrE* [plural] money spent regularly on rent, insurance, electricity, and other things that are needed to keep a business operating: *Their offices are in London so the overheads are very high.* **2** [C] a piece of transparent material used with an overhead projector to show words, pictures etc

ˌoverhead proˈjector *n* [C] (*abbreviation* **OHP**) a piece of electrical equipment used when giving a talk, which shows words or pictures on a wall or large screen so that many people can see them

o·ver·hear /ˌəʊvəˈhɪə $ ˌoʊvərˈhɪr/ ●○○ *v* (*past tense and past participle* **overheard** /-ˈhɜːd $ -ˈhɜːrd/) [T] to accidentally hear what other people are saying, when they do not know that you have heard: *I overheard part of their conversation.* | **overhear sb saying sth** *She overheard the management discussing pay rises.* | **overhear sb say (that)** *We overheard the teacher say there would be a pop quiz today.* | *I* ***couldn't help overhearing*** *your argument.* THESAURUS HEAR → EAVESDROP

o·ver·heat /ˌəʊvəˈhiːt $ ˌoʊvər-/ *v* [I,T] **1** to become too hot, or to make something too hot: *I think the engine's overheating again.* | *Try not to overheat the sauce.* **2** if a country's ECONOMY overheats, or if something overheats it, it grows too fast and this leads to increases in prices, salaries, interest rates etc

o·ver·heat·ed /ˌəʊvəˈhiːtɪd◂ $ ˌoʊvər-/ *adj* **1** too hot: *an overheated waiting room* **2** an overheated ECONOMY grows too fast, leading to increases in prices, salaries, interest rates etc **3** too full of anger or excitement: *her* ***overheated imagination***

o·ver·hung /ˌəʊvəˈhʌŋ $ ˌoʊvər-/ the past tense and past participle of OVERHANG[1]

o·ver·in·dulge /ˌəʊvərɪnˈdʌldʒ $ ˌoʊ-/ *v* **1** [I] to eat or drink too much: *It's hard not to overindulge at Christmas.* **2** [T] to let someone have everything they want, or always let them do what they want → **spoil**: *Penny was overindulged by her parents.* —**overindulgence** *n* [U]

o·ver·joyed /ˌəʊvəˈdʒɔɪd $ ˌoʊvər-/ *adj* [not before noun] extremely pleased or happy: **overjoyed to hear/find/see etc sth** *He was overjoyed to see his mother again.* | **[+at]** *She wasn't exactly overjoyed at the prospect of looking after two small boys.* | **overjoyed (that)** *Her parents were overjoyed that she'd been found alive.* THESAURUS HAPPY

o·ver·kill /ˈəʊvəkɪl $ ˈoʊvər-/ *n* [U] more of something than is necessary or desirable: *More television coverage of the election would be overkill.*

o·ver·la·den /ˌəʊvəˈleɪdn◂ $ ˌoʊvər-/ *adj* filled with too many people or things: *overladen buses*

o·ver·laid /ˌəʊvəˈleɪd $ ˌoʊvər-/ the past tense and past participle of OVERLAY

o·ver·land /ˌəʊvəˈlænd◂ $ ˌoʊvər-/ *adv* across land, not by sea or air: *They plan to travel overland to China.* —**overland** *adj*: *an overland route*

o·ver·lap[1] /ˌəʊvəˈlæp $ ˌoʊvər-/ ●○○ AWL *v* (**overlapped, overlapping**) [I,T]

1 if two or more things overlap, part of one thing covers part of another thing: *One of Jilly's front teeth overlaps the other.* | *The tiles on the roof overlap.*

2 if two subjects, ideas etc overlap, they include some but not all of the same things: *Maxwell's responsibilities overlap yours, so you will be sharing some of the work.* | **[+with]** *The study of sociology overlaps with the study of economics.* | *two great men with overlapping interests*

3 if two activities or periods of time overlap, the second one starts before the first one has finished: *The second phase of development overlaps the first.* | **[+with]** *My vacation overlaps with yours.*

o·ver·lap[2] /ˈəʊvəlæp $ ˈoʊvər-/ ●○○ AWL *n* [C,U] the amount by which two activities, ideas, things etc overlap: **[+between]** *There is* ***considerable overlap*** *between the girls' and boys' test results.* | **[+of]** *an overlap of about two centimetres* | *a large* ***degree of overlap***

o·ver·lay[1] /ˌəʊvəˈleɪ $ ˌoʊvər-/ *v* (*past tense and past participle* **overlaid**) [T] **1** to cover or be on top of something: **be overlaid with sth** *The wood is overlaid with silver.* **2** if one quality, sound etc overlays another, it is added to it and is often stronger or more noticeable: *The roar of the engines was overlaid by a loud banging.*

o·ver·lay[2] /ˈəʊvəleɪ $ ˈoʊvər-/ *n* [C] **1** something which covers something else: *the brass fire surround with its decorative overlay* **2** a transparent sheet with a picture or drawing on it which is put on top of another picture to change it **3** an additional quality or feeling: *sad stories with an overlay of humour*

o·ver·leaf /ˌəʊvəˈliːf $ ˈoʊvərliːf/ *adv* on the other side of the page: *See the diagram overleaf.*

o·ver·lie /ˌəʊvəˈlaɪ $ ˌoʊvər-/ *v* (*past tense* **overlay** /-ˈleɪ/, *past participle* **overlain** /-ˈleɪn/, *present participle* **overlying**)

[T] *technical* to lie over something: *Clay overlies chalk in the southern mountains.*

o·ver·load /ˌəʊvəˈləʊd $ ˌoʊvərˈloʊd/ *v* (*past participle* **overloaded** *or* **overladen** /-ˈleɪdn/) [T] **1** to put too many things or people on or into something: *Be careful not to overload the washing machine.* | **be/become overloaded with sth** *The bus was overloaded with tourists and their luggage.* **2** to put too much electricity through an electrical system or piece of equipment: *Don't overload the lighting circuit.* **3** to give someone too much work or information to deal with: **be/become overloaded with sth** *All the staff are overloaded with work.* —**overload** /ˈəʊvələʊd $ ˈoʊvərloʊd/ *n* [C,U]: *the modern day* ***information overload*** | *an* ***overload of*** *urgent daily business*

o·ver·long, **over-long** /ˌəʊvəˈlɒŋ◂ $ ˌoʊvərˈlɒːŋ◂/ *adj* continuing for too long: *an overlong performance*

o·ver·look /ˌəʊvəˈlʊk $ ˌoʊvər-/ ●●○ *v* [T]
1 to not notice something, or not see how important it is SYN **miss**: *It is easy to overlook a small detail like that.* | *Nobody could* ***overlook the fact that*** *box office sales were down.*
2 to forgive someone's mistake, bad behaviour etc and take no action: *She found him entertaining enough to overlook his faults.*
3 if a house, room etc overlooks something, it has a view of it, usually from above: *Our room overlooks the ocean.*

o·ver·lord /ˈəʊvəlɔːd $ ˈoʊvərlɔːrd/ *n* [C] someone with great power over a large number of people, especially in the past

o·ver·ly /ˈəʊvəli $ ˈoʊvər-/ ●○○ *adv* too or very: *Your views on economics are overly simplistic.* | *I'm not overly fond of cats.*

o·ver·man·ning /ˌəʊvəˈmænɪŋ $ ˌoʊvər-/ *n* [U] a situation in which a company, industry etc has more workers than are needed SYN **overstaffing** —**overmanned** *adj*

o·ver·much /ˌəʊvəˈmʌtʃ $ ˌoʊvər-/ *adv literary* too much or very much: *At his age, he didn't care overmuch about impressing people.*

o·ver·night¹ /ˌəʊvəˈnaɪt $ ˌoʊvər-/ ●●○ *adv*
1 for or during the night: *Pam's* ***staying overnight*** *at my house.*
2 suddenly or surprisingly quickly: *He became a millionaire overnight.* | **happen/appear/change overnight** *Reputations are not changed overnight.* ⚠ Do not talk about 'an overnight' because **overnight** is never a noun. It is either an adverb or an adjective.

o·ver·night² /ˈəʊvənaɪt $ ˈoʊvər-/ ●●○ *adj*
1 happening during the night or for the night: *an overnight flight to Chicago* | *overnight accommodation in London*
2 happening surprisingly quickly: *The show was an overnight success.* | *his overnight decision to become a vegetarian*

ˈovernight ˌbag *n* [C] a bag containing everything you need for a night away from home: *He* ***packed*** *an* ***overnight bag*** *and left.*

ˌover-optiˈmistic *adj* expecting that things will be better than is possible or likely: *over-optimistic forecasts of economic growth*

o·ver·paid /ˌəʊvəˈpeɪd $ ˌoʊvər-/ *adj* given more money for a job than you deserve OPP **underpaid**: *grossly overpaid football players*

o·ver·pass /ˈəʊvəpɑːs $ ˈoʊvərpæs/ *n* [C] *AmE* a structure like a bridge that allows one road to go over another road → see picture at BRIDGE¹

o·ver·pay /ˌəʊvəˈpeɪ $ ˌoʊvər-/ *v* (*past tense and past participle* **overpaid**) **1** [T] to pay someone more money than they deserve OPP **underpay**: *Most big companies continue to overpay their top executives.* **2** [I,T] to pay too much money for something OPP **underpay**: *Try to recover any tax you have overpaid.* —**overpayment** *n* [C,U]

o·ver·play /ˌəʊvəˈpleɪ $ ˌoʊvər-/ *v* [T] **1** to make something seem more important than it is OPP **underplay**: *His role in the group's success has been overplayed.* **2 overplay your hand** to behave too confidently because you think you are in a stronger position than you actually are: *The unions overplayed their hand in the end and failed to get the pay rise they wanted.*

o·ver·pop·u·la·tion /ˌəʊvəpɒpjəˈleɪʃən $ ˌoʊvərpɑːp-/ *n* [U] when there are too many people living in a particular place: *efforts to reduce overpopulation* —**overpopulated** /ˌəʊvəˈpɒpəleɪtɪd $ ˌoʊvərˈpɑːp-/ *adj*: *our overpopulated cities*

o·ver·pow·er /ˌəʊvəˈpaʊə $ ˌoʊvərˈpaʊr/ *v* [T] **1** to take control of someone physically because you are stronger: *The security guards soon overpowered the man.* **2** if a smell, taste, or emotion overpowers you, it affects you very strongly: *Her scent overpowered his senses.* | *She was overpowered by grief.*

o·ver·pow·er·ing /ˌəʊvəˈpaʊərɪŋ◂ $ ˌoʊvərˈpaʊr-/ *adj* **1** very strong → **intense**: *an overpowering smell of rotten flesh* | *He felt an overpowering desire to slap her.* **2** someone who is overpowering has such a strong character that they make other people feel uncomfortable or afraid SYN **overbearing** —**overpoweringly** *adv*

o·ver·priced /ˌəʊvəˈpraɪst◂ $ ˌoʊvər-/ *adj* something that is overpriced is more expensive than it should be **THESAURUS** ▸ EXPENSIVE

o·ver·print /ˌəʊvəˈprɪnt $ ˌoʊvər-/ *v* [T] to print additional words over a document, stamp etc that already has printing on it

o·ver·pro·duc·tion /ˌəʊvəprəˈdʌkʃən $ ˌoʊvər-/ *n* [U] the act of producing more of something than people want or need: *the systematic overproduction of food*

o·ver·pro·tec·tive /ˌəʊvəprəˈtektɪv◂ $ ˌoʊvər-/ *adj* so anxious to protect someone from harm that you restrict their freedom: *overprotective parents*

o·ver·qual·i·fied /ˌəʊvəˈkwɒlɪfaɪd◂ $ ˌoʊvərˈkwɑː-/ *adj* if you are overqualified for a particular job, you have more experience or training than is needed OPP **underqualified**: *I'm having trouble finding another job - everyone says I'm overqualified.*

o·ver·ran /ˌəʊvəˈræn $ ˌoʊ-/ *v* the past tense of OVERRUN

o·ver·rated /ˌəʊvəˈreɪtɪd◂ $ ˌoʊ-/ *adj* not as good or important as some people think or say OPP **underrated**: *a* ***vastly overrated*** *film* —**overrate** *v* [T]

o·ver·reach /ˌəʊvəˈriːtʃ $ ˌoʊ-/ *v* **overreach yourself** to try to do more than you have the power, ability, or money to do SYN **overstretch**: *The company overreached itself financially.*

o·ver·re·act /ˌəʊvəriˈækt $ ˌoʊ-/ *v* [I] to react to something with too much emotion, or by doing something that is unnecessary: **[+to]** *You always overreact to criticism.* | *Many investors overreacted to the stock market crash.* —**overreaction** /-riˈækʃən/ *n* [singular, U]: *Their response was an overreaction.*

o·ver·ride /ˌəʊvəˈraɪd $ ˌoʊ-/ ●○○ *v* (*past tense* **overrode** /-ˈrəʊd $ -ˈroʊd/, *past participle* **overridden** /-ˈrɪdn/) [T]
1 to use your power or authority to change someone else's decision: *The EU commission exercised its power to override British policy.*
2 to be regarded as more important than something else: *The needs of the mother should not override the needs of the child.*
3 to stop a machine doing something that it does by itself: *Can you override the automatic locking system?* —**override** /ˈəʊvəraɪd $ ˈoʊ-/ *n* [C]: *a manual override*

o·ver·rid·ing /ˌəʊvəˈraɪdɪŋ◂ $ ˌoʊ-/ *adj* [only before noun] more important than anything else: *a question of overriding importance* | *Their overriding concern is with efficient crime control.*

o·ver·ripe /ˌəʊvəˈraɪp◂ $ ˌoʊ-/ *adj* overripe fruit and vegetables are past the point of being ready to eat and are too soft: *overripe bananas*

o·ver·rule /ˌəʊvəˈruːl $ ˌoʊ-/ *v* [T] to change an order or decision that you think is wrong, using your official power: *The House of Lords overruled the decision of the Court of Appeal.* | *They have the power to overrule the local council.*

o·ver·run¹ /ˌəʊvəˈrʌn $ ˌoʊ-/ *v* (*past tense* **overran**

/-'ræn/, *past participle* **overrun**, *present participle* **overrunning**) **1** [I,T] to take more time or money than intended: *The final speaker overran by at least half an hour.* **2** [T] if a place is overrun by unwanted things or people, they spread over it in great numbers: **be overrun by/with sth** *a tiny island overrun by tourists | The house was overrun with mice.* **3** [T] if a place is overrun by soldiers, they take control of it: *Poland was overrun by the Russian army.*

o·ver·run² /'əʊvərʌn $ 'oʊ-/ *n* [C] an amount of time or money that is larger than was planned or intended: *cost overruns of £2 billion*

o·ver·seas¹ /ˌəʊvə'siːz◂ $ ˌoʊvər-/ ●●○ W3 AWL *adv* to or in a foreign country that is across the sea → **abroad**: *Chris is going to work overseas. | Most applications came from overseas.*

o·ver·seas² /'əʊvəsiːz $ 'oʊvər-/ ●○○ AWL *adj* [only before noun] coming from, existing in, or happening in a foreign country that is across the sea → **home**: *overseas students | overseas investment*

o·ver·see /ˌəʊvə'siː $ ˌoʊvər-/ *v* (*past tense* **oversaw** /-'sɔː $ -'sɒː/, *past participle* **overseen** /-'siːn/) [T] to be in charge of a group of workers and check that a piece of work is done satisfactorily SYN **supervise**: *A team leader was appointed to oversee the project.*

o·ver·seer /'əʊvəsɪə $ 'oʊvərsiːər/ *n* [C] someone who is in charge of a project, group of workers etc, and who makes sure that the job is done properly SYN **supervisor**

o·ver·sell /ˌəʊvə'sel $ ˌoʊvər-/ *v* (*past tense and past participle* **oversold** /-'səʊld $ -'soʊld/) [T] **1** to praise someone or something too much: *Tourism on the island is oversold.* **2** to sell more of something than is actually available

o·ver·sen·si·tive /ˌəʊvə'sensətɪv◂ $ ˌoʊvər-/ *adj* easily upset or offended: *Don't you think you're being a bit oversensitive?*

o·ver·sexed /ˌəʊvə'sekst◂ $ ˌoʊvər-/ *adj* having more interest in or desire for sex than is usual

o·ver·shad·ow /ˌəʊvə'ʃædəʊ $ ˌoʊvər'ʃædoʊ/ *v* [T] **1** to make someone or something else seem less important: *Her interest in politics began to overshadow her desire to be a poet. | The achievement of the men's team was overshadowed by the continuing success of the women's team.* **2** to make an occasion or period of time less enjoyable by making people feel sad or worried: *The threat of war overshadowed the summer of 1939.* **3** if a tall building, mountain etc overshadows a place, it is very close to it and much taller than it: *a dark valley overshadowed by towering peaks*

o·ver·shar·ing /ˌəʊvə'ʃeərɪŋ $ ˌoʊvər'ʃer-/ *n* [U] the process of giving too many details about your private life, so that it embarrasses the people listening

o·ver·shoe /'əʊvəʃuː $ 'oʊvər-/ *n* [C] a rubber shoe that you wear over an ordinary shoe to keep your feet dry

o·ver·shoot /ˌəʊvə'ʃuːt $ ˌoʊvər-/ *v* (*past tense and past participle* **overshot** /-'ʃɒt $ -'ʃɑːt/) [I,T] **1** to accidentally go a little further than you intended: *The plane overshot the runway and plunged into a ditch.* **2** to spend more money than you had intended: *The school has overshot its cash limit.* —**overshoot** /'əʊvəʃuːt $ 'oʊvər-/ *n* [C]

o·ver·sight /'əʊvəsaɪt $ 'oʊvər-/ ●○○ *n* [C,U]
1 a mistake in which you forget something or do not notice something: *I assure you that this was purely an oversight on my part.* THESAURUS ▸ MISTAKE
2 have oversight of sth to be in charge of something: *He has general oversight of all training courses.*

o·ver·sim·pli·fy /ˌəʊvə'sɪmplɪfaɪ $ ˌoʊvər-/ *v* (**oversimplified**, **oversimplifying**, **oversimplifies**) [I,T] to describe something in a way that is too simple and ignores many facts: *To describe all these people as refugees is to oversimplify the situation.* —**oversimplification** /ˌəʊvəsɪmplɪfɪ'keɪʃən $ ˌoʊvər-/ *n* [C,U]

o·ver·sized /ˌəʊvə'saɪzd◂ $ ˌoʊvər-/, **o·ver·size** /-'saɪz◂/ *adj* bigger than usual or too big: *an oversized jacket*

o·ver·sleep /ˌəʊvə'sliːp $ ˌoʊvər-/ *v* (*past tense and past participle* **overslept** /-'slept/) [I] to sleep for longer than you intended: *Sorry I'm late. I overslept.* THESAURUS ▸ SLEEP
→ **sleep in** at SLEEP¹

o·ver·spend /ˌəʊvə'spend $ ˌoʊvər-/ *v* (*past tense and past participle* **overspent** /-'spent/) [I,T] to spend more money than you can afford: *The hospital has overspent its budget by £70,000.* —**overspend** /'əʊvəspend $ 'oʊvər-/ *n* [C]: *an overspend of £200,000*

o·ver·spill /'əʊvəˌspɪl $ 'oʊvər-/ *n* [singular, U] *BrE* people who move out of a big city because there are too many people living there, and go to live in new houses outside the city: *an overspill of workers from London*

O

o·ver·staffed /ˌəʊvə'stɑːft◂ $ ˌoʊvər'stæft◂/ *adj* an overstaffed company, organization etc has more workers than it needs OPP **understaffed**

o·ver·state /ˌəʊvə'steɪt $ ˌoʊvər-/ *v* [T] to talk about something in a way that makes it seem more important, serious etc than it really is SYN **exaggerate** OPP **understate**: *To say that all motorists speed in residential areas is* ***overstating the case****. | The importance of a child's early years* ***cannot be overstated*** (=is very important). —**overstatement** *n* [C,U]: *It's an overstatement to say that the man's a fool.*

o·ver·stay /ˌəʊvə'steɪ $ ˌoʊvər-/ *v* [T] to stay somewhere longer than you are allowed to SYN **outstay**: *They overstayed their visas and were arrested.* → **overstay your welcome** at WELCOME⁴(3)

o·ver·step /ˌəʊvə'step $ ˌoʊvər-/ *v* (**overstepped**, **overstepping**) [T] **1 overstep the limits/bounds/boundaries** to do something that is not acceptable or allowed: *He has overstepped the bounds of acceptable behaviour.* **2 overstep the mark** to offend someone by doing or saying things that you should not do or say: *She overstepped the mark and lost her job.*

o·ver·stock /ˌəʊvə'stɒk $ ˌoʊvər'stɑːk/ *v* [I,T] to obtain more of something than is needed —**overstock** /'əʊvəstɒk $ 'oʊvərstɑːk/ *n* [C]

o·ver·stretch /ˌəʊvə'stretʃ $ ˌoʊvər-/ *v* [T] to try to do more than you are able to, or to use more money, supplies etc than you have: *an overstretched social services department* | **overstretch yourself** *Problems only arise when people overstretch themselves.*

o·ver·sub·scribed /ˌəʊvəsəb'skraɪbd◂ $ ˌoʊvər-/ *adj* if something is oversubscribed, too many people have said that they want to use it or have it: *All good schools are oversubscribed.*

o·ver·sup·ply /'əʊvəsəplaɪ $ 'oʊvər-/ *n* (*plural* **oversupplies**) [C,U] the state of having more of something than you need or can sell: *an oversupply of computers*

o·vert /'əʊvɜːt, əʊ'vɜːt $ 'oʊvɜːrt, oʊ'vɜːrt/ ●○○ *adj* overt actions are done publicly, without trying to hide anything OPP **covert**: *an overt attempt to silence their political opponents | Overt race discrimination is illegal.* —**overtly** *adv*: *an overtly political message*

o·ver·take /ˌəʊvə'teɪk $ ˌoʊvər-/ ●○○ *v* (*past tense* **overtook** /-'tʊk/, *past participle* **overtaken** /-'teɪkən/)
1 [I,T] to go past a moving vehicle or person because you are going faster than them and want to get in front of them: *He pulled out to overtake the van. | Never try to overtake on a bend.*
2 [T] to develop or increase more quickly than someone or something else and become more successful, more important, or more advanced than them: *Television soon overtook the cinema as the most popular form of entertainment. | Hingis has now overtaken her in the world tennis rankings.*
3 [T] if something bad, especially a feeling, overtakes you, it happens to you suddenly and has a strong effect on you → **overcome**: **be overtaken by sth** *She was overtaken by emotion and started to cry. | A terrible sense of panic overtook him.*
4 be overtaken by events if you are overtaken by events, the situation changes, so that your plans or ideas are not useful anymore: *The diplomatic negotiations were soon overtaken by events.*

o·ver·tax /ˌəʊvəˈtæks $ ˌoʊvər-/ *v* [T] **1** to make someone do more than they are really able to do, so that they become very tired: **overtax yourself** *Be careful you don't overtax yourself.* **2** to make people pay too much tax

ˌover-the-ˈcounter *adj* [only before noun] **1** over-the-counter drugs can be obtained without a PRESCRIPTION (=a written order) from a doctor **2** *AmE* (*abbreviation* **OTC**) over-the-counter business shares are ones that do not appear on an official STOCK EXCHANGE list

ˌover-the-ˈtop *adj BrE informal* (*abbreviation* **OTT**) remarks, behaviour etc that are over-the-top are so extreme or unreasonable that they seem stupid or offensive: *It's a bit over-the-top to call him a fascist.*

o·ver·throw¹ /ˌəʊvəˈθrəʊ $ ˌoʊvərˈθroʊ/ ●○○ *v* (*past tense* **overthrew** /-ˈθruː/, *past participle* **overthrown** /-ˈθrəʊn $ -ˈθroʊn/) [T]
1 to remove a leader or government from power, especially by force SYN **oust**: *Rebels were already making plans to overthrow the government.*
2 to get rid of the rules, ideas, or systems of a society

o·ver·throw² /ˈəʊvəθrəʊ $ ˈoʊvərθroʊ/ *n* [U] the defeat and removal from power of a leader or government, especially by force: **[+of]** *The organization was dedicated to the overthrow of capitalism.* | *the overthrow of Mussolini*

o·ver·time /ˈəʊvətaɪm $ ˈoʊvər-/ ●○○ *n* [U]
1 time that you spend working in your job in addition to your normal working hours: *six hours' overtime* | *They're **working overtime** to get the job finished.* | *He's been **doing** a lot of **overtime** recently.* | *Many employees work countless hours of **unpaid overtime**.* | *Many of our offices will be working **on overtime** until the end of the year.*
2 the money that you are paid for working more hours than usual: *He earns £450 a week, including overtime.*
3 be working overtime *informal* to be very active: *As she put down the phone, her brain was working overtime.* | *His senses were working overtime.*
4 *AmE* a period of time added to the end of a sports game to give one of the two teams a chance to win SYN **extra time** *BrE*: **in overtime** *Steve Smith scored all nine of the Hawks' points in overtime.*

o·ver·tired /ˌəʊvəˈtaɪəd $ ˌoʊvərˈtaɪrd/ *adj* very tired, so that you cannot think or do things normally and become annoyed easily

o·ver·tone /ˈəʊvətəʊn $ ˈoʊvərtoʊn/ *n*
1 overtones [plural] signs of an emotion or attitude that is not expressed directly → **undertone**: **[+of]** *There were overtones of anger in his voice.* | **racial/sexual etc overtones** *football songs with violent overtones* | **political/religious overtones** (=having a connection to politics or religion that is not directly expressed) *The decision may have political overtones.* **2** [C] *technical* a higher musical note that sounds together with the main note

o·ver·took /ˌəʊvəˈtʊk $ ˌoʊvər-/ *v* the past tense of OVERTAKE

o·ver·top /ˌəʊvəˈtɒp $ ˌoʊvərˈtɑːp/ *v* (**overtopped**, **overtopping**) [T] *formal* to be higher or more important than something

o·ver·ture /ˈəʊvətjʊə, -tʃʊə, -tʃə $ ˈoʊvərtjʊr, -tʃʊr, -tʃər/ *n* **1** [C] a short piece of music written as an introduction to a long piece of music, especially an OPERA **2 overtures** [plural] an attempt to begin a friendly relationship with a person, country etc: *They began **making overtures to** the Irish government.* | *She had rejected his overtures.* **3 be an overture** if an event is an overture to a more important event, it happens just before it and makes you expect it

o·ver·turn /ˌəʊvəˈtɜːn $ ˌoʊvərˈtɜːrn/ ●●○ *v*
1 [I,T] if you overturn something, or if it overturns, it turns upside down or falls over on its side: *Leslie jumped to her feet, overturning her chair.* | *His car overturned, trapping him inside.*
2 overturn a decision/verdict etc to change a decision or result so that it becomes the opposite of what it was before: *His conviction was overturned by the Court of Appeal.*
3 [T] to suddenly remove a government from power, especially by using violence SYN **overthrow**

o·ver·use /ˌəʊvəˈjuːz $ ˌoʊvər-/ *v* [T] to use something too much, especially so that it is not effective anymore or it is damaged: *Students tend to overuse certain words.* —**overuse** /-ˈjuːs/ *n* [U]: *the overuse of natural resources*

o·ver·val·ue /ˌəʊvəˈvæljuː $ ˌoʊvər-/ *v* [T] to believe or say that something is more valuable or more important than it really is —**overvaluation** /ˌəʊvəvæljuˈeɪʃən $ ˌoʊvər-/ *n* [U]

o·ver·view /ˈəʊvəvjuː $ ˈoʊvər-/ ●○○ *n* [C] a short description of a subject or situation that gives the main ideas without explaining all the details: **[+of]** *an overview of the issues involved* | **provide/give an overview** *The document provides a general overview of the bank's policies.* | **broad/general overview** *This chapter gives a broad overview of the main concerns facing employers.*

o·ver·ween·ing /ˌəʊvəˈwiːnɪŋ◂ $ ˌoʊvər-/ *adj formal* too proud and confident - used to show disapproval SYN **arrogant**: *overweening ambition* —**overweeningly** *adv*

o·ver·weight /ˌəʊvəˈweɪt◂ $ ˌoʊvər-/ ●●○ *adj*
1 someone who is overweight is too heavy and fat → **underweight**: **10 kilos/20 pounds etc overweight** *Sally was 50 pounds overweight.* | *He is slightly overweight.*
THESAURUS ▸ FAT
2 something such as a package that is overweight weighs more than it is supposed to weigh → **underweight**: *My luggage was overweight by five kilos.*

o·ver·whelm /ˌəʊvəˈwelm $ ˌoʊvər-/ ●○○ *v* [T]
1 EMOTION if someone is overwhelmed by an emotion, they feel it so strongly that they cannot think clearly: **be overwhelmed by sth** *Harriet was overwhelmed by a feeling of homesickness.* | **be overwhelmed with sth** *The children were overwhelmed with excitement.* | *Grief overwhelmed me.*
2 TOO MUCH if work or a problem overwhelms someone, it is too much or too difficult to deal with: **be overwhelmed by sth** *We were overwhelmed by the number of applications.* | **be overwhelmed with sth** *They would be overwhelmed with paperwork.*
3 SURPRISE SB to surprise someone very much, so that they do not know how to react: **be overwhelmed by sth** *I was completely overwhelmed by his generosity.* | *We were overwhelmed by the sheer size of the place.*
4 DEFEAT SB to defeat an army completely: *In 1532 the Spaniards finally overwhelmed the armies of Peru.*
5 WATER *literary* if water overwhelms an area of land, it covers it completely and suddenly

o·ver·whelm·ing /ˌəʊvəˈwelmɪŋ $ ˌoʊvər-/ ●○○ *adj*
1 having such a great effect on you that you feel confused and do not know how to react: *an overwhelming sense of guilt* | *She felt an overwhelming desire to hit him.* | *She found the city quite overwhelming when she first arrived.*
2 very large or greater, more important etc than any other: *There is overwhelming evidence that smoking damages your health.* | *An **overwhelming majority** of the members were against the idea.* | *The proposal has been given overwhelming support.* | *The British Air Force succeeded despite **overwhelming odds** against them.*

o·ver·whelm·ing·ly /ˌəʊvəˈwelmɪŋli $ ˌoʊvər-/ ●○○ *adv* used to emphasize the great amount or degree of something: *Congress voted overwhelmingly in favor of the bill.* | *The response was overwhelmingly positive.*

o·ver·win·ter /ˌəʊvəˈwɪntə $ ˌoʊvərˈwɪntər/ *v* [I,T] to live through the winter, or to make it possible for something to live through the winter: *These birds generally overwinter in tropical regions.*

o·ver·work¹ /ˌəʊvəˈwɜːk $ ˌoʊvərˈwɜːrk/ *v* [I,T] to work too much or to make someone work too much: *You've been overworking - why don't you take a week off?* | *Have they been overworking you again?*

overwork² *n* [U] too much hard work: *a heart attack brought on by overwork*

o·ver·worked /ˌəʊvəˈwɜːkt◂ $ ˌoʊvərˈwɜːrkt◂/ *adj* **1** made to work too hard: *an overworked doctor* | *They're overworked and understaffed.* **2** a word or phrase that is overworked is used too much and has become less effective: *overworked metaphors*

o·ver·write /ˌəʊvəˈraɪt $ ˌoʊ-/ *v* (*past tense* **overwrote** /-ˈrəʊt $ -ˈroʊt/, *past participle* **overwritten** /-ˈrɪtn/) [T] to replace the information in a computer document with new information from another document: *Do you want to overwrite the file?*

o·ver·wrought /ˌəʊvəˈrɔːt◂ $ ˌoʊvəˈrɒːt◂/ *adj* very upset, nervous, and worried: *Clara was tired and overwrought after all the problems of the last few days.*

o·ver·zeal·ous /ˌəʊvəˈzeləs◂ $ ˌoʊvər-/ *adj* too eager about something you believe in strongly: *overzealous fans*

o·vi·duct /ˈəʊvidʌkt $ ˈoʊvə-/ *n* [C] *technical* one of the two tubes in a woman or female animal through which eggs pass to the WOMB

o·vip·a·rous /əʊˈvɪpərəs $ oʊ-/ *adj technical* an animal, a fish, a bird etc that is oviparous produces eggs that develop outside its body

o·void /ˈəʊvɔɪd $ ˈoʊ-/ *adj formal* shaped like an egg —**ovoid** *n* [C]

ov·u·late /ˈɒvjəleɪt $ ˈɑːv-/ *v* [I] when a woman or female animal ovulates, she produces eggs inside her body —**ovulation** /ˌɒvjəˈleɪʃən $ ˌɑːv-/ *n* [U]

o·vum /ˈəʊvəm $ ˈoʊ-/ *n* (*plural* **ova** /-və/) [C] *technical* an egg, especially one that develops inside the mother's body

ow /aʊ/ *interjection* used to express sudden pain: *'Ow, that hurts!'*

owe /əʊ $ oʊ/ ●●● (S2) (W3) *v* [T]
1 MONEY to need to pay someone for something that they have done for you or sold to you, or to need to give someone back money that they have lent you → **borrow**, **lend**: **owe sb money/£10 etc** *I owe my brother $50.* | **owe sb for sth** *I still owe you for the taxi.* | *How much do I owe you* (=often used to show that you want to pay for something)*?* | **owe sth to sb** *the money owed to credit card companies*
2 STH DONE/GIVEN to feel that you should do something for someone or give someone something, because they have done something for you or given something to you: *He asked for help from a colleague who* **owed** *him* **a favour**. | **owe sb a drink/letter etc** *I owe Shaun a letter; I must write soon.* | *Thanks a lot for being so understanding about all this –* ***I owe you one*** (=used to thank someone who has helped you, and to say that you are willing to help them in the future)*!* | **owe sb** (=be in a position in which someone has helped you, so that you should help them) *Let's go and see Joe – he owes me!*
3 owe sb an explanation/apology to feel that you should give someone an explanation of why you did something, or say you are sorry: *You owe him an apology.*
4 HELP TO ACHIEVE STH **a)** to have something or achieve something because of what someone else has done: **owe sth to sb** *He probably owes his life to her prompt action.* **b)** to know that someone's help has been important to you in achieving something: **owe sb a lot/owe sb a great deal** *'I owe my parents a lot,' he admitted.* | *He owes a great deal to his publishers.* | **owe it all to sb/owe everything to sb** *I owe it all to you.* | **owe sb a debt (of gratitude)** *the debt that we owe to our teachers*
5 GOOD EFFECT to be successful because of the good effect or influence of something or someone: **[+to]** *Their success* **owes more to** *good luck than to careful management.* | *Pearson's work* **owed much to** *the research of his friend, Hugh Kingsmill.*
6 owe it to sb to do sth to feel you should do something for someone, because they have helped you or given you support: *You owe it to your supporters not to give up now.*
7 owe it to yourself to do sth to feel you should try to achieve something because it is what you deserve: *You owe it to yourself to take some time off.*
8 owe loyalty/allegiance etc to sb to have a duty to obey someone: *provinces owing allegiance to the Emperor*
9 think that the world owes you a living to be unwilling to work in order to get things, and expect them to be provided for you – used to show disapproval

ow·ing /ˈəʊɪŋ $ ˈoʊ-/ *adj* [not before noun] *especially BrE* if money is owing, it has not yet been paid to the person who should receive it → **outstanding**: *You need to pay the amount owing, plus the interest.*

ˈow·ing to ●○○ *prep formal* because of something: *Owing to a lack of funds, the project will not continue next year.* | *Flight BA213 has been delayed owing to fog.*

owl /aʊl/ ●●○ *n* [C] a bird with large eyes that hunts at night → see picture at BIRD OF PREY

owl·et /ˈaʊlɪt/ *n* [C] a young owl

owl·ish /ˈaʊlɪʃ/ *adj* looking like an owl and seeming serious and clever: *He was an owlish man, with little round glasses.* —**owlishly** *adv*

own¹ /əʊn $ oʊn/ ●●● (S1) (W1) *adj, pron* [always after a possessive]
1 used to emphasize that something belongs to or is connected with a particular person or thing and not any other: *Bring your own equipment.* | *Every dance has its own rhythm.* | *The yacht was intended for the King's own personal use.* | *His face was only a few inches from her own.* | **of your own** *We have problems of our own.* | *I'd like to have a place of my own* (=my own home). | **your very own** (=used to add more emphasis) *One day I want to have a horse of my very own.* | **sth to call your own/which you can call your own** (=something that belongs to you) *She just wanted a place to call her own.*
2 used to emphasize that someone did or made something without the help or involvement of anyone else: *She makes a lot of her own clothes.* | *We encourage students to develop their own ideas.* | *It's your* **own fault** *for leaving the window open.*
3 (all) on your own a) alone: *I've been living on my own for four years now.* | *He didn't want to be* **left on** *his* **own**. **b)** without anyone's help: *You can't expect him to do it all on his own.* | *I can manage on my own, thanks.*
4 for your own good/safety/benefit etc if you do something for someone's own good etc, you do it to help them even though they might not like it or want it: *I'm only telling you this for your own good.* | *He was kept away from the other prisoners for his own safety.*
5 too nice/clever etc for your own good used to say that someone has too much of a good quality so that it may be a disadvantage: *Stephen can be too generous for his own good.*
6 get your own back (on sb) *informal* to do something bad to someone who has harmed you, as a way of punishing them → **revenge**: *She wanted to get her own back on Liz for ruining her party.*
7 be your own man/woman to have strong opinions and intentions that are not influenced by other people: *Hilary's very much her own woman.*
8 make sth your own to change or deal with something in a way that makes it seem to belong to you: *Great singers can take an old song and make it their own.* → **come into your own** at COME¹(6), → **hold your own** at HOLD¹(24)

GRAMMAR

- You say **my own, her own, their own** etc: *They miss their own country.* | *The town has its own station.*
✗ Don't say: *They miss the own country.* | *The town has an own station.*
- You can also say **of my own, of her own, of their own** etc: *I want to have a room of my own.* | *Each house has a garden of its own.*

own² ●●● (S2) (W2) *v* [T]
1 to have something which belongs to you, especially because you have bought it, been given it etc and it is legally yours → **possess**: *The building is owned by the local council.* | *You need to get permission from the farmer who owns the land.* | *Many more people now own their own homes.* | *the cost of owning a car* | **publicly/privately owned** *BrE* (=belonging to the government or a private organization) *a privately owned company*
2 as if/as though/like you own the place *informal* to behave in a way that is too confident and upsets other people:

She acts like she owns the place! | *They walked in as if they owned the place.*
3 *old-fashioned* to admit that something is true: **own (that)** *I own that I judged her harshly at first.* | **[+to]** *I must own to a feeling of anxiety.*
4 *informal* to defeat someone very easily or by a large amount: *Our team totally owned them!*

O

GRAMMAR: Using the progressive

Own is not used in the progressive. You say: *They own several cars.* ✗ Don't say: *They are owning several cars.*

GRAMMAR GUIDE ▶ VERBS

THESAURUS

own if you own something, it legally belongs to you: *They live in a flat but they don't own it.* | *The land is owned by farmers.* | *a privately owned plane*
have [not in passive] to own something – used when focussing on the fact that someone has the use of something, rather than the fact that they legally own it: *How many students have a cell phone?* | *I wish I had a sports car.*
possess [not in passive] *formal* to own something: *It is illegal to possess a firearm in Britain.* | *I don't even possess a smart suit!*
belong to sb/sth [not in passive] if something belongs to you, you own it: *The ring belonged to my grandmother.*
hold to own shares in a company: *One man holds a third of the company's shares.*
be the property of sb/sth *formal* to be owned by someone – written on signs, labels etc: *This camera is the property of the BBC.*

own up *phr v* to admit that you have done something wrong, especially something that is not serious: *Come on, own up. Who broke it?* | **own up to (doing) sth** *No one owned up to breaking the window.* | *He was too frightened to own up to his mistake.* | *He still wouldn't own up to the fact that he'd lied.*

ˌown ˈbrand *adj BrE* own brand goods are specially produced and sold by particular shops and have the name of the shop on them SYN **store brand** *AmE*: *Tesco's own brand tomato sauce*

own·er /ˈəʊnə $ ˈoʊnər/ ●●● S2 W2 *n* [C] someone who owns something: **[+of]** *I met the owner of the local hotel.* | **original/previous/new owner** *the club's new owners* | *He was now* ***the proud owner of*** *a bright red sports car.* | **car-owner/dog-owner etc** *Dog-owners have been warned to keep their animals under control.* | **home-owner** (=someone who owns their house)

ˌowner-ˈoccupied *adj* houses, apartments etc that are owner-occupied are lived in by the people who own them: *Most of these properties are owner-occupied.* —**owner-occupier** *n* [C]

own·er·ship /ˈəʊnəʃɪp $ ˈoʊnər-/ ●●○ W3 *n* [U] the fact of owning something: **[+of]** *a dispute over the ownership of the land* | **public/private/state ownership** *The company was returned to private ownership in mid-1987.* | *The price of* ***home ownership*** *is increasing.*

ˌown ˈgoal *n* [C] *BrE* **1** a GOAL that you accidentally score against your own team without intending to in a game of football, HOCKEY etc **2** *informal* an action or remark that has the opposite effect from what you intended: *The minister's admission turned out to be a spectacular own goal.*

ˌown ˈlabel *adj BrE* OWN BRAND

ox /ɒks $ ɑːks/ *n* (*plural* **oxen** /ˈɒksən $ ˈɑːk-/) [C] **1** a BULL whose sex organs have been removed, often used for working on farms **2** a large cow or BULL

Ox·bridge /ˈɒksˌbrɪdʒ $ ˈɑːks-/ *n* [U] the universities of Oxford and Cambridge → **redbrick**

ox·cart /ˈɒkskɑːt $ ˈɑːkskɑːrt/ *n* [C] a vehicle pulled by oxen that was used in the past

ˈox-eye *n* [C] a yellow flower like a DAISY

Ox·fam, **OXFAM** /ˈɒksfæm $ ˈɑːks-/ a CHARITY organization in the UK which helps people in poorer countries, for example by providing training in farming methods or operating educational programmes, and also by providing medicine at times of serious shortage. Oxfam gets some of its money by selling goods in its own shops all over the UK. These shops are especially known for selling used clothes, books etc: *He always looks as if he buys his clothes from Oxfam.*

ox·ford /ˈɒksfəd $ ˈɑːksfərd/ *n AmE* **1 oxfords** [plural] a type of leather shoes that fasten with SHOELACES **2** [C] a type of shirt made of thick cotton

ox·ide /ˈɒksaɪd $ ˈɑːk-/ *n* [C,U] a substance which is produced when a substance is combined with oxygen: *iron oxide*

ox·i·dize (*also* **-ise** *BrE*) /ˈɒksədaɪz $ ˈɑːk-/ *v* [I,T] *technical* to combine with oxygen, or make something combine with oxygen, especially in a way that causes RUST —**oxidation** /ˌɒksəˈdeɪʃən $ ˌɑːk-/ (*also* **oxidization** /ˌaksədaɪˈzeɪʃən $ ˌɑːksədə-/) *n* [U]

Ox·on /ˈɒksɒn $ ˈɑːksɑːn/ used after the title of a degree from Oxford University: *David Jones BA (Oxon)*

ox·tail /ˈɒksteɪl $ ˈɑːks-/ *n* [U] the meat from the tails of cattle, used especially in soup

ox·y·a·cet·y·lene /ˌɒksiəˈsetəliːn◂ $ ˌɑːksiəˈsetl-iːn◂, -ən◂/ *n* [U] *technical* a mixture of oxygen and ACETYLENE that produces a hot white flame that can cut steel

ox·y·gen /ˈɒksɪdʒən $ ˈɑːk-/ ●●○ *n* [U] a gas that has no colour or smell, is present in air, and is necessary for most animals and plants to live. It is a chemical ELEMENT: symbol O

ox·y·gen·ate /ˈɒksɪdʒəneɪt $ ˈɑːk-/ *v* [T] *technical* to add oxygen to something —**oxygenation** /ˌɒksɪdʒəˈneɪʃən $ ˌɑːk-/ *n* [U]

ˈoxygen bar *n* [C] a bar where you pay to breathe pure oxygen, or oxygen that has a pleasant smell, so that you can relax and have more energy

ˈoxygen ˌdebt *n* [U] a temporary medical condition in which not enough oxygen is going to the muscles in your body, caused by doing physical exercise that takes a lot of strength or effort

ˈoxygen mask *n* [C] a piece of equipment that fits over someone's mouth and nose to provide them with oxygen → see picture at **MASK**[1]

ˈoxygen tent *n* [C] a piece of equipment shaped like a tent that is put around people who are very ill in hospital, to provide them with oxygen

ox·y·mo·ron /ˌɒksiˈmɔːrɒn $ ˌɑːksiˈmɔːrɑːn/ *n* [C] *technical* a deliberate combination of two words that seem to mean the opposite of each other, such as 'cruel kindness'

o·yez /əʊˈjez $ oʊ-/ *interjection* a word used by law officials or by TOWN CRIERS in the past to get people's attention

oy·ster /ˈɔɪstə $ -ər/ *n* [C] **1** a type of SHELLFISH that can be eaten cooked or uncooked, and that produces a jewel called a PEARL → see picture at **SHELLFISH** **2 the world is your oyster** used to tell someone that they can achieve whatever they want

ˈoyster bed *n* [C] an area at the bottom of the sea where oysters live

oz *BrE*, **oz.** *AmE* the written abbreviation of ***ounce*** or ***ounces***

Oz /ɒz $ ɑːz/ *n BrE, AusE informal* a short way of saying Australia

o·zone /ˈəʊzəʊn $ ˈoʊzoʊn/ *n* [U] **1** *technical* a poisonous blue gas that is a type of oxygen **2** *informal* air near the sea, thought to be fresher and healthier

ˌozone-ˈfriendly *adj* not containing chemicals that damage the ozone layer: *an ozone-friendly aerosol*

ˈozone ˌlayer *n* [singular] a layer of gases in the sky that prevents harmful RADIATION from the sun from reaching the Earth: *the hole in the ozone layer*

Pp

P¹, **p** /piː/ *n* (*plural* **P's**, **p's**) [C,U] the 16th letter of the English alphabet → **mind your p's and q's** at MIND²(23)

P² *BrE* the written abbreviation of ***provisional***, used on cars to show that the driver is a learner and has a PROVISIONAL LICENCE → **P-PLATE**

p. (*also* **p** *BrE*) **1** the written abbreviation of ***page*** → **PP.** **2** *BrE* the abbreviation of ***penny*** or ***pence***: *The bus fare was only 50p.* **3** used in written music to show that a part should be played or sung quietly

pa /pɑː/ *n* [C] *old-fashioned informal* father – used by children or when speaking to children

p.a. the written abbreviation of ***per annum***

PA /ˌpiː ˈeɪ/ *n* [C] **1** [usually singular] (***public address system***) electronic equipment that makes someone's voice loud enough to be heard by large groups of people **2** *BrE* (***personal assistant***) someone who works as a secretary for one person

PAC /ˌpiː eɪ ˈsiː, pæk/ *n* [C] *AmE* the abbreviation of ***political action committee***

pace¹ /peɪs/ ●●○ W3 *n*

1 SPEED OF EVENTS/CHANGES [singular] the speed at which something happens or is done: **[+of]** *The pace of change in our lives is becoming faster and faster.* | **at a steady/slow etc pace** *Public spending continues to rise at a steady pace.*

2 WALK/RUN [singular] the speed at which someone walks, runs, or moves: **[+of]** *You need to step up the pace of your exercises.* | **at a slow/leisurely/brisk etc pace** *Lucy set off at a leisurely pace back to the hotel.* | *He* ***quickened*** *his* ***pace****, longing to be home.* | *Traffic slowed to a* ***walking pace****.*

3 STEP [C] a single step when you are running or walking, or the distance you move in one step: **[+backwards/towards/forwards etc]** *He* ***took*** *a* ***pace*** *towards the door.* | *Rebecca walked a few paces behind her mum.*

4 keep pace (with sth/sb) to change or increase as fast as something else, or to move as fast as someone else: *Salaries have not always kept pace with inflation.* | *The supply of materials cannot keep pace with demand.* | *Slow down! I can't keep pace with you.*

5 go through your paces (*also* **show your paces**) to show how well you can do something

6 put sb/sth through their paces to make a person, vehicle, animal etc show how well they can do something: *The test driver puts all the cars through their paces.*

7 set the pace a) if a company sets the pace, it does something before its competitors or to a better standard: **[+in]** *Japanese firms have been setting the pace in electronic engineering.* **b)** (*also* **set a brisk/cracking etc pace** *BrE*) to go faster than the other competitors in a race, who then try to achieve the same speed: *The Italians set the pace for the first eight laps.*

8 force the pace to make something happen or develop more quickly than it would do normally: **[+on]** *measures designed to force the pace on alternative energy policies*

9 be able to stand the pace to be able to deal with situations where you are very busy and have to think and act very quickly: *If you can stand the pace, working in advertising pays well.*

COLLOCATIONS

ADJECTIVES/NOUN + pace

rapid/fast *The rapid pace of change creates uncertainty.*
slow *The pace of life in the countryside is slower.*
a steady pace *The economy was growing at a slow but steady pace.*
at your own pace (=at the pace that suits you) *This allows each child to learn at his or her own pace.*
at a snail's pace (=very slowly) *Reform is proceeding at a snail's pace.*
a breakneck pace (=extremely fast) *Singapore prospered and modernized at a breakneck pace.*
a hectic/frantic pace (=a very fast and hurried speed)

VERBS

the pace quickens/accelerates *The pace of change is quickening.*
the pace slows/slackens *After a surge in exports, the pace slackened considerably the following year.*
gather pace (=happen more quickly) *Support for the campaign is gathering pace.*
keep up the pace (=continue to do something or happen as quickly as before)

PHRASES

the pace of change *The pace of change accelerated dramatically in the early 1980s.*
the pace of life *Here, the sun shines every day and the pace of life is slower.*
the pace of development | **the pace of reform**

COMMON ERRORS

⚠ Don't say 'in your own pace' or 'on your own pace'. Say **at your own pace**.

pace² *v* **1** [I always + adv/prep, T] to walk first in one direction and then in another many times, especially because you are nervous: *I found Mark at the hospital,* ***pacing*** *restlessly* ***up and down****.* | **pace the floor/room** *Sam stood up and paced the floor, deep in thought.* THESAURUS ▸ WALK **2 pace yourself a)** to control the speed that you move at in a race, so that you still have energy left near the end: *Nicky paced herself and came through the ranks to win.* **b)** to organize your life and activities so that you do not have too much to do: *You need to pace yourself and decide which tasks are the most important.* **3** [T] (*also* **pace sth ↔ off**, **pace sth ↔ out**) to measure a distance by walking across it with steps of equal length: *The director paced out the length of the stage.*

pace·mak·er /ˈpeɪsˌmeɪkə $ -ər/ *n* [C] **1** a small machine that is placed inside someone's chest in order to help their heart beat regularly **2** (*also* **pacesetter**) a person or horse who goes to the front in a race and sets the speed that the others must try to achieve

pace·set·ter /ˈpeɪsˌsetə $ -ər/ (*also* **pacemaker**) *n* [C] **1** a person or team that is winning in a competition, and that others have to try to defeat: *That left him three strokes behind the pacesetter, Parry.* **2** a person or company that is considered to be a leader in a particular area of activity: *a new company, now seen as the industry's pacesetter* **3** PACEMAKER(2)

pa·chin·ko /pəˈtʃɪŋkəʊ $ -koʊ/ *n* [U] a game that is popular in Japan, in which you can win money or prizes by making balls fall into particular places in a special machine

pach·y·derm /ˈpækɪdɜːm $ -dɜːrm/ *n* [C] *technical* an animal with thick skin, such as an ELEPHANT

pa·cif·ic /pəˈsɪfɪk/ *adj literary* peaceful and loving or wanting peace: *a normally pacific community*

pac·i·fi·er /ˈpæsəfaɪə $ -faɪər/ *n* [C] **1** *AmE* a rubber object that you give a baby to suck so that it does not cry SYN **dummy** *BrE* **2** something that makes people calm

pac·i·fis·m /ˈpæsəfɪzəm/ *n* [U] the belief that war and violence are always wrong

pac·i·fist /ˈpæsɪfɪst/ *n* [C] someone who believes that wars are wrong and who refuses to use violence —**pacifist** *adj* [only before noun]: *the pacifist movement*

pac·i·fy /ˈpæsɪfaɪ/ *v* (**pacified**, **pacifying**, **pacifies**) [T] **1** to make someone calm, quiet, and satisfied after they have been angry or upset: *'You're right,' Rita said, in order to pacify him.* **2** to stop groups of people from fighting or protesting, often by using force: *Economic reforms are needed to pacify and modernize the country.*

pack¹ /pæk/ ●●● S2 W3 *v*
1 CLOTHES [I,T] (*also* **pack up**) to put things into cases, bags etc ready for a trip somewhere: *I forgot to pack my razor.* | *Have you finished packing yet?* | **pack your things/belongings** *Kelly packed her things before breakfast.* | **pack a bag/case** *You'd better pack your bags. We're leaving in an hour.* | **pack sb sth** *Shall I pack us a picnic?*
2 GOODS [T] (*also* **pack up**) to put something into a box or other container, so that it can be moved, sold, or stored: **pack sth in/into sth** *Now wild mushrooms are available all year, packed in handy 25 g boxes.*
3 CROWD [I always + adv/prep, T] to go in large numbers into a space, or to make people or animals do this, until the space is too full: **[+into/in/onto]** *Fifty thousand fans packed into the stadium.* | *The sheep had been packed into a truck and transported without food or water.*
4 PROTECT STH [T] to cover or fill an object with soft material so that it does not get damaged: **[+in/with]** *Glass must be packed in several layers of paper.*
5 SNOW/SOIL ETC to press snow, soil, sand etc down so that it becomes hard and firm: **pack sth down** *Pack the soil down firmly.*
6 pack your bags *informal* to leave a place and not return, especially because of a disagreement
7 pack a gun *AmE informal* to carry a gun
8 pack a (hard/hefty/strong etc) punch (*also* **pack a wallop**) *informal* to have a very strong or impressive effect: *The Spanish wine, with the flavour of honey, packed quite a punch.* → **send sb packing** at SEND(11)
pack sth ↔ **away** *phr v* to put something back in a box, case etc where it is usually kept: *Christmas was over and the decorations packed away.*
pack in *phr v*
1 pack sth ↔ in (*also* **pack sth into sth**) to do a lot in a limited period of time, or fit a lot of information, ideas etc into a limited space: *We packed a lot of sightseeing into two weeks.* | *In an essay of 2,000 words, you can pack a lot in.*
2 pack sb ↔ in *informal* if a film, play etc packs people in, it attracts large numbers to come and see it: *Any film starring Tom Cruise always packs them in.*
3 pack sth ↔ in *BrE informal* to stop doing a job or activity that you are not enjoying: *After one year, I packed in university.* | *Sometimes I feel like* ***packing it all in*** *and going off travelling.*
4 pack it in *BrE spoken* used to tell someone to stop doing something that is annoying you
5 *BrE informal* if a machine packs in, it stops working because there is something wrong with it SYN **pack up**: *Halfway to the airport, the engine packed in.*
pack sb/sth **off** *phr v informal* to send someone to stay somewhere for a period of time: **[+to]** *My parents used to pack us off to camp every summer.*
pack up *phr v*
1 to put things into cases, bags etc ready for a trip somewhere: *Most of the holidaymakers had packed up and gone.* | **pack sth ↔ up** *I gave her a hand packing up her clothes and stuff.*
2 pack sth ↔ up to put something into a box or other container, so that it can be moved, sold, or stored: *Don't worry. The removal men will pack everything up.*
3 *informal* to finish work at the end of the day: *'What time do you pack up?' 'Oh, about six.'*
4 *BrE informal* if a machine packs up, it stops working because there is something wrong with it SYN **pack in**: *The photocopier's packed up again.*
5 pack sth ↔ up *BrE informal* to stop doing something, especially a job: *He packed up his teaching job after only three months.*

pack² ●●● S2 W3 *n* [C]
1 THINGS WRAPPED TOGETHER something wrapped in paper or packed in a box and then sent by post or taken somewhere: **[+of]** *a pack of three T-shirts* | *Send away for your free* ***information pack*** *today.* → SIX-PACK(1)
2 SMALL CONTAINER *especially AmE* a small container, usually made of paper, that something is sold in SYN **packet** *BrE*: **[+of]** *a pack of cigarettes* | *a 10 oz pack of frozen peas*
3 BAG *especially BrE* a bag that you carry on your back, especially when climbing or walking, used to carry equipment, clothes etc SYN **rucksack** *BrE*, **backpack**
4 CARDS (*also* **pack of cards**) a complete set of PLAYING CARDS SYN **deck**
5 ANIMALS a group of wild animals that hunt together, or a group of dogs trained to hunt together: *a wolf pack* | **[+of]** *a pack of hounds* THESAURUS ▸ GROUP
6 GROUP OF PEOPLE a group of the same type of people, especially a group who you do not approve of: **[+of]** *A pack of reporters were waiting outside.*
7 be leading the pack/be ahead of the pack to be more successful than the other people or companies you are competing against
8 pack of lies *informal* something you are told that is completely untrue: *Don't believe what it says in the paper – it's a pack of lies.*
9 Cub/Brownie pack a group of children who belong to a particular children's organization → CUB SCOUT, BROWNIE, GIRL SCOUT
10 ON A WOUND a thick soft piece of cloth that you press on a wound to stop the flow of blood SYN **compress** → ICE PACK

pack·age¹ /ˈpækɪdʒ/ ●●● S2 W2 *n* [C]
1 something wrapped in paper, packed in a box, and then sent by mail or delivered SYN **parcel** *BrE*: *There's a package here for a Miami Lakes address.*
2 *AmE* the paper or plastic container that food or other goods are sold in SYN **packet** *BrE*: **[+of]** *a package of meat*
3 a set of ideas or services that are suggested or offered all together as a group: **package of measures/proposals/incentives etc** *The government has announced a package of measures to assist affected areas.* | **aid/financial/benefits etc package** *Many banks are offering financial packages for students.*
4 a set of related programs sold together for use on a computer: **software/word-processing/graphics etc package**

package² *v* [T] **1** (*also* **package up**) to put food or other goods into a bag, box etc ready to be sold or sent: *The code informs us where and when a product was packaged.* | *The videos were packaged up, ready for distribution.* GRAMMAR **Package** is usually passive in this meaning. **2** to prepare something for sale, especially by making it attractive or interesting to a particular group of people: *They try to package their product to give it mass appeal.*

ˈpackage deal *n* [C] **1** (*also* **package holiday** *BrE*) a holiday organized by a company at a fixed price that includes the cost of travel, hotel etc: *a cheap package deal to Tenerife* **2** an offer or agreement which includes several things that you must buy or accept together: *The Commission attempted to bring all three proposals into one package deal.*

ˈpackage tour *n* [C] a PACKAGE DEAL(1)

pack·ag·ing /ˈpækɪdʒɪŋ/ ●○○ *n* [U]
1 the container or material that a product is sold in: *plastic packaging*
2 the process of wrapping something for sale: *the date of packaging*
3 a way of making something seem attractive and interesting to people: *the packaging of the company image*

ˈpack ˌanimal *n* [C] an animal used for carrying heavy loads, for example a horse → **pack horse**

packed /pækt/ ●○○ *adj*
1 extremely full of people: *a packed courtroom* | **[+with]** *The island was packed with tourists.* THESAURUS ▸ FULL
2 packed with/full of sth containing a lot of a particular type of thing: *a new magazine packed with exciting recipes*
3 [not before noun] if you are packed, you have put everything you need into cases ready to go somewhere
4 tightly/loosely/densely packed pressed, arranged etc closely or not closely together: *houses tightly packed in rows*

ˌpacked ˈlunch *n* [C] *BrE* food such as sandwiches and fruit that you take with you to work, school etc for LUNCH

ˌpacked ˈout *adj* [not before noun] *BrE informal* a cinema, restaurant etc that is packed out is completely full of people

pack·er /ˈpækə $ -ər/ *n* [C] someone who works in a factory, putting things into containers

pack·et /ˈpækɪt/ ●●● S2 *n* [C]
1 a) *BrE* a container made of paper, plastic, or CARDBOARD that something is sold in: **[+of]** *a packet of envelopes* | *a packet of cigarettes* | *a cereal packet* **b)** *AmE* a small flat paper or plastic container that a liquid or powder is sold in SYN **sachet** *BrE*: *packets of ketchup and mustard* → see picture at **CONTAINER**
2 *especially BrE* a small flat package that is sent by post or delivered to someone: *Paul tore open the packet as soon as it arrived.* → **PAY PACKET**
3 cost a packet *BrE informal* to cost a lot of money: *I bet that car cost him a packet.*
4 *technical* a quantity of information that is sent as a single unit from one computer to another on a network or on the Internet

ˈpacket boat *n* [C] *old-fashioned* a boat that carries letters, packages etc and usually passengers at regular times

ˈpacket-ˌswitching *n* [C] a method of sending information stored on a computer, usually across the Internet. Long messages are broken into pieces and put together again when they are received.

ˈpack horse *n* [C] a horse used for carrying heavy loads

ˈpack ice *n* [U] a mass of ice floating in the sea

pack·ing /ˈpækɪŋ/ *n* [U] **1** when you put things into cases or boxes so that you can send or take them somewhere: *I can* ***do*** *my* ***packing*** *the night before we leave.* **2** the material used for packing things so that they can be sent somewhere: *Use plenty of packing.*

ˈpacking case *n* [C] a large strong wooden box in which things are packed to be sent somewhere → **crate** → see picture at **CASE**[1]

ˈpack rat *n* [C] *AmE informal* someone who collects and stores things that they do not really need

ˈpack trip *n* [C] *AmE* a trip through the countryside on horses, for fun or as a sport SYN **pony-trekking** *BrE*

pact /pækt/ ●○○ *n* [C] a formal agreement between two groups, countries, or people, especially to help each other or to stop fighting SYN **treaty**: *the Warsaw pact* | **make/sign a pact** *The two countries signed a non-aggression pact.* | **[+with]** *a defence pact with the USA* | **[+between]** *a peace pact between the rebels and the government* → **SUICIDE PACT**

pad[1] /pæd/ ●●○ S3 *n* [C]
1 SOFT MATERIAL a thick flat object made of cloth or rubber, used to protect or clean something, or to make something more comfortable: **[+of]** *Press on the wound with a large pad of cotton wool.* | *Use an abrasive pad for stubborn stains.* | **knee/elbow/shin/shoulder pad** (=a pad that you wear to protect a part of your body when you are playing a sport) → see picture at **SPORT**[1]
2 PAPER several sheets of paper fastened together, used for writing or drawing: **writing/sketch/memo/legal etc pad** *a box of paints and a sketch pad* | *Keep a telephone pad and a pen to hand.* | *a pad of paper*
3 FLAT GROUND a piece of flat ground where small aircraft can land: **launch/landing/helicopter pad** *The hospital has built a helicopter pad.*
4 ANIMAL'S FOOT the flesh on the bottom of the foot of a cat, dog etc
5 APARTMENT *old-fashioned informal* someone's apartment or the room where they live
6 WATER PLANT the leaf of a WATER LILY → **LAUNCH PAD**, **HELICOPTER PAD**

pad[2] *v* (**padded**, **padding**) **1** [I always + adv/prep] to walk softly and quietly: **[+across/through/along etc]** *The cat came padding silently back to its home.* | *She padded barefoot down the stairs.* THESAURUS WALK **2** [T] (*also* **pad (sth) out** *BrE*) to fill or cover something with a soft material in order to protect it or make it more comfortable: **pad sth with sth** *jackets padded out with a soft cotton filling* **3** [T] *AmE* to dishonestly make bills more expensive than they should be: ***padding*** *the* ***bills*** *of Medicare patients* **4** [T] (*also* **pad (sth) out**) to make a speech or piece of writing longer by adding unnecessary words or details: *Don't pad out your answer to make it seem impressive.* | **[+with]** *His autobiography is padded with boring anecdotes.*

pad·ded /ˈpædɪd/ *adj* filled or covered with a soft material to make it thicker or more comfortable: *The shoes are padded to protect the foot.* | *a padded headrest*

ˌpadded ˈcell *n* [C] a special room in a hospital for people who are mentally ill. The room has thick soft material on the walls so that the person in it cannot get hurt.

pad·ding /ˈpædɪŋ/ *n* [U] **1** soft material used to fill or cover something: *a helmet with protective padding* **2** unnecessary and uninteresting details or words that are added to make a sentence, speech etc longer – used to show disapproval

pad·dle[1] /ˈpædl/ ●○○ *n*
1 [C] a short pole that is wide and flat at the end, used for moving a small boat in water → **oar**
2 [singular] *BrE* when you walk for pleasure without shoes or socks in water that is not very deep: *If it's not too cold, we can* ***go for a paddle****.*
3 [C] *AmE* a small round flat BAT with a short handle, used for hitting the ball in TABLE TENNIS: *a ping-pong paddle* → see picture at **SPORT**[1]
4 [C] a tool like a flat spoon, used for mixing food → **DOG PADDLE**

paddle[2] *v* (**paddled**, **paddling**) **1** [I,T] to move a small light boat through water, using one or more paddles: **[+along/upstream/towards etc]** *I desperately tried to paddle for the shore.* | *She and her husband paddled a canoe down the Mississippi.* → **ROW**[2] **2** [I] *BrE* to walk for pleasure without shoes or socks in water that is not very deep SYN **wade** *AmE*: *children* ***paddling in the sea*** **3** [I] to swim with short quick movements: *The dog was paddling furiously after the ducks.* **4** [T] *AmE informal* to hit a child with a piece of wood as a punishment **5 paddle your own canoe** *BrE informal* to do things yourself, without help from anyone else

pad·dle·board·ing /ˈpædlˌbɔːdɪŋ $ -ˌbɔːr-/ (*also* **stand-up paddleboarding**) *n* [U] the activity of moving along on water by using a paddle while standing on a long board

ˈpaddle ˌsteamer (*also* **ˈpaddle boat**) *n* [C] *BrE* a large old-fashioned boat that moves by using steam to drive a large wheel attached to the side

ˈpaddling pool *n* [C] *BrE* a small pool or plastic container of water which is not very deep, for children to play in SYN **wading pool** *AmE*

pad·dock /ˈpædək/ *n* [C] **1** *especially BrE* a small field in which horses are kept **2** a piece of ground where horses are brought together before a race so that people can look at them

pad·dy /ˈpædi/ *n* (*plural* **paddies**) [C] **1** (*also* **paddy field**) a field in which rice is grown in water SYN **rice paddy** **2** *BrE informal* a state of being angry or upset: *The news put Mum in a bit of a paddy.*

Paddy *n* (*plural* **Paddies**) [C] *taboo* a very offensive word for someone from Ireland. Do not use this word.

ˈpaddy ˌwagon *n* [C] *AmE informal* a police vehicle used to carry prisoners

pad·lock /ˈpædlɒk $ -lɑːk/ *n* [C] a lock that you can put on a gate, door, bicycle etc: *He undid the padlock and eased back the lid.* → see picture at **LOCK**[2] —**padlock** *v* [T]

pa·dre /ˈpɑːdreɪ, -ri/ *n* [C] *informal* a priest, especially one in the army

pae·an /ˈpiːən/ *n* [C] *literary* a happy song of praise, thanks, or victory

paed·e·rast *BrE*, **pederast** *AmE* /ˈpedəræst/ *n* [C] *formal* a man who has sex with a young boy → **paedophile** —**paederasty** *n* [U]

pae·di·a·tri·cian *BrE*, **pediatrician** *AmE* /ˌpiːdiəˈtrɪʃən/ *n* [C] a doctor who deals with children and their illnesses

pae·di·at·rics *BrE*, **pediatrics** *AmE* /ˌpiːdiˈætrɪks/ *n* [U]

P

the area of medicine that deals with children and their illnesses —**paediatric** *adj*: *a paediatric hospital*

pae·do·phile *BrE*, **pedophile** *AmE* /ˈpiːdəfaɪl/ *n* [C] someone who is sexually attracted to children → **paederast**

pa·el·la /paɪˈelə $ pɑː-/ *n* [U] a Spanish dish made with rice, pieces of meat, fish, and vegetables

pa·gan[1] /ˈpeɪgən/ *adj* pagan religious beliefs and customs do not belong to any of the main religions of the world, and may come from a time before these religions: *ancient pagan temples*

pagan[2] *n* [C] **1** (*also* **Pagan**) someone who believes in a pagan religion **2** someone with few or no religious beliefs - used humorously —**paganism** *n* [U]

P

page[1] /peɪdʒ/ ●●● S1 W1 *n* [C]

1 PAPER one side of a piece of paper in a book, newspaper, document etc, or the sheet of paper itself: *The full address is given* **on page** *15.* | *You will find the answers* **over the page***.* | *a 400-page novel* | *We took out a* **full page advertisement** *in the 'Village Voice'.*

2 COMPUTER all the writing etc that you can see at one time on a computer screen: *a* **web page** (=a single screen of writing, pictures etc on a website)

3 YOUNG PERSON *AmE* a student or young person who works as a helper to a member of the US Congress

4 on the same page if a group of people are on the same page, they are working well together and have the same aims: *We need to get environmentalists and businesses on the same page to improve things.*

5 BOY **a)** a boy who served a KNIGHT during the Middle Ages as part of his training **b)** a PAGEBOY(2)

6 SERVANT a boy who in the past served a person of high rank

7 a page in history an important event or period of time

GRAMMAR: Patterns with page

- Something is **on a page**: *I stared at the words on the page.*
- Something is **on the first/last/next etc page**: *The answer is on the next page.* ✗ Don't say: *The answer is in the next page.*
- Something is **on page 1/10 etc**: *There is a diagram on page 35.* ✗ Don't say: *There is a diagram on the page 35.* | *There is a diagram in page 35.*

COLLOCATIONS

ADJECTIVES

the next/previous page *I glanced back to the previous page.*
the opposite/facing page *See the diagram on the opposite page.*
the left-hand/right-hand page *The answers are on the right-hand page.*
the front/back page (=of a newspaper) | **the sports/arts/financial etc pages** (=the part of a newspaper that deals with sport, art etc) | **a blank page** (=with nothing on it) | **a new/fresh page** (=which has not yet been written on) | **a full page**

VERBS

turn a page *I turned the page in order to find out what happened next.*
turn to/see page 22/45 etc *Turn to page 8 for more details.*
flick/flip/leaf through the pages of sth (=turn them quickly)
jump/leap off the page (=be very noticeable) *One mistake jumped off the page.*

PHRASES

the top of the page *Write your name at the top of the page.*
the bottom/foot of the page *See the note at the bottom of page 38.*

page[2] *v* [T] **1** to call someone's name out in a public place, especially using a LOUDSPEAKER, in order to find them: *She hurried to the reception desk and asked the girl to page her husband.* **2** to send a message to someone's PAGER asking them to go somewhere or telephone someone: *He was constantly being paged during meetings.* | *the paging network*

page down *phr v* to press a special key on a computer that makes the screen show the page after the one you are reading OPP **page up**: *It's not there, so page down and see if you can find it.*

page through sth *phr v AmE* to look at a book, magazine etc by turning the pages quickly

page up *phr v* to press a special key on a computer that makes the screen show the page before the one you are reading OPP **page down**

pag·eant /ˈpædʒənt/ *n* [C] **1** an organized public show, often performed outdoors, where people dress in decorated or unusual clothes: *a colourful pageant of Scotland's past* **2** *AmE* a public competition for young women in which their appearance, and sometimes other qualities, are compared and judged SYN **beauty contest 3 the pageant of sth** *literary* a series of historical events that are interesting and important: *the pageant of African history*

pag·eant·ry /ˈpædʒəntri/ *n* [U] impressive ceremonies or events, involving many people wearing special clothes: **[+of]** *the pageantry of a military ceremony*

page·boy /ˈpeɪdʒbɔɪ/ *n* [C] **1** *BrE* a boy who helps the BRIDE as part of a wedding ceremony → **bridesmaid 2** *old-fashioned* a young man who works in a hotel, club etc, delivering messages, carrying bags etc **3** a woman's HAIRSTYLE in which very straight hair is cut shorter at the front than at the back, and turned under at the ends

ˈpage-jack *v* [T] *informal* to steal a WEBPAGE and send it to a SEARCH ENGINE under a different name and address, so that anyone who goes to that webpage is sent straight to a different website, often a PORNOGRAPHIC website —**page-jacking** *n* [U]

pag·er /ˈpeɪdʒə $ -ər/ *n* [C] a small machine you can carry in your pocket that can receive signals from a telephone. It tells you when someone has sent you a message, or wants you to telephone them, for example by making a noise. SYN **beeper** → **page**

ˈpage ˌtraffic *n* [U] *technical* the number of people who read a page in a magazine, newspaper etc

pa·gi·na·tion /ˌpædʒəˈneɪʃən/ *n* [U] *technical* the process of giving a number to each page of a book, magazine etc —**paginate** /ˈpædʒəneɪt/ *v* [T]

pa·go·da /pəˈgəʊdə $ -ˈgoʊ-/ *n* [C] a Buddhist TEMPLE (=religious building) that has several levels with a decorated roof at each level

pah /pɑː/ *interjection BrE* used to show that you disapprove strongly of something

paid /peɪd/ the past tense and past participle of PAY → **put paid to sth** at **PUT(15)**

ˌpaid-ˈup *adj BrE informal* **1 a fully paid-up member of sth** if someone is a fully paid-up member of a particular group, they strongly support what that group likes or believes in: *a fully paid-up member of the celebrity circuit* **2 paid-up member** someone who has paid the money needed to be a member of a club, political party etc: *The competition is open to all paid-up members of the Women's Institute.*

pail /peɪl/ *n* [C] *especially AmE* **1** a metal or wooden container with a handle, used for carrying liquids SYN **bucket**: *a milk pail* | **[+of]** *a pail of water* **2** (*also* **pailful** /-fʊl/) the amount of liquid a pail will hold

pain[1] /peɪn/ ●●● S2 W2 *n*

1 [C,U] the feeling you have when part of your body hurts: *The pain is getting worse.* | **[+in]** *She felt a sharp pain in her leg.* | *Greg was in* **a lot of pain***.* → **GROWING PAINS(2)**

2 [C,U] the feeling of unhappiness you have when you are sad, upset etc: *the* **pain and grief** *of bereavement* | **cause (sb) pain/inflict pain on sb** *She hated to say the words, for fear of causing pain.*

3 be a pain (in the neck) (*also* **be a pain in the ass/arse/backside/butt** *not polite*) *spoken* to be very annoying: *There*

were times when Joe could be a real pain in the neck. | It's a pain, having to go upstairs to make the coffee every time.
4 take/go to (great) pains to do sth (*also* **take pains with/over sth**) to make a special effort to do something: *He's taken great pains to improve his image.*
5 be at pains to do sth to be especially careful to make sure people understand what you are saying or what you plan to do: *Roy was at pains to point out that English was the only exam he'd ever failed.*
6 for your pains as a reward for something you worked to achieve – used especially when this is disappointing: *I fetched the file, and all I* ***got for*** *my* ***pains*** *was a dirty look from Simon.*
7 no pain, no gain used to say that you can only achieve something, for example become fitter, by suffering or working hard
8 on/under pain of death at the risk of being killed as punishment, if you do not obey: *Communist activity was prohibited on pain of death.*

COLLOCATIONS

ADJECTIVES

bad *Later that evening, the pain was really bad.*
terrible/awful *I woke up with a terrible pain in my side.*
severe/intense *Ever since the accident, Mike's suffered from severe back pain.*
excruciating (=very severe) *The pain in my eye was excruciating.*
a sharp pain (=short but severe) *She felt a sharp pain in the back of her throat.*
a slight pain (=not severe) | **a dull pain** (=a slight but continuous pain) | **a nagging pain** (=felt all the time) | **chronic pain** (=pain that you suffer from for long periods of time) | **a shooting pain** (=a severe pain that goes from one part of your body to another) | **a searing pain** (=very severe, as if you have been burnt) | **back/chest/stomach etc pain** | **abdominal pain** | **physical pain**

VERBS

have a pain *I've got a terrible pain in my stomach.*
feel pain *The dentist told me that I wouldn't feel any pain.*
be in pain *Despite being in great pain, he managed to call for help.*
suffer (from) pain *She suffers from chronic pain in her legs.*
inflict pain *The guards enjoyed inflicting pain on them.*
relieve/ease pain (*also* **alleviate pain** *formal*) (=make it less severe) *Exercise can help to relieve lower back pain.*
experience pain *formal* | **complain of pain** (=say that you have a pain in a part of your body) | **the pain gets worse** | **the pain goes away** (*also* **the pain subsides** *formal*) (=becomes less severe)

pain + NOUN

pain relief (=a drug or treatment that makes pain less severe) | **sb's pain threshold** (=their ability to bear pain)

PHRASES

aches and pains *Everyone has a few aches and pains when they get older.*

COMMON ERRORS

⚠ Don't say 'big pain'. Say **terrible pain** or **severe pain**.

THESAURUS

pain *n* [C,U] the feeling when part of your body hurts: *A broken leg can cause a lot of pain. | He felt a sharp pain in his chest.*
ache *n* [C,U] a continuous pain, especially one that is not very bad. Most commonly used in compounds such as **headache**, **toothache**, and **backache**: *I felt an ache in my back after decorating all day. | Driving gives me a* ***headache***.
twinge *n* [C] a sudden slight pain that comes and then disappears quickly: *When I bent down I felt a twinge in my back.*
discomfort *n* [U] *formal* an uncomfortable feeling in your body, or a slight pain: *The procedure takes five minutes and only causes slight discomfort.*
agony *n* [U] a feeling of great pain, or a situation in which you feel a lot of pain: *the agony of childbirth | I was* ***in agony*** *by the time I got to the hospital.*

pain² *v* [T] **it pains sb to do sth** *formal* used to say that it is very difficult and upsetting for someone to have to do something

ˈpain ˌbarrier *n* **the pain barrier** in sport, the point that you reach when you continue trying to do something, even though you are in pain, very tired, or injured: *Iona reached the final, but she had to* ***go through the pain barrier*** *to get there.*

pained /peɪnd/ *adj* **pained expression/look/voice etc** someone's expression, voice etc that shows they are worried, upset, or slightly annoyed: *He sat stiffly,* ***with a pained expression on his face***.

pain·ful /ˈpeɪnfəl/ ●●● W2 *adj*
1 if a part of your body is painful, it hurts: *stiff painful joints | Is your arm very painful? | The neck becomes swollen and* ***painful to the touch*** (=hurts when you touch it).
2 making you feel very upset, or very difficult and unpleasant for you OPP **painless**: **painful memories/experience etc** *He sobbed as he recalled the painful memory. | Venice was a* ***painful reminder of*** *her marriage. | He and his wife took the* ***painful decision*** *to switch off their son's life support machine. | the long and* ***painful process*** *of growing up* | **painful to do sth** *It can be painful to leave the house in which you were born.* | **[+for/to]** *The divorce was painful for both of us. | Even hearing his name was painful to her.*
3 causing physical pain: *a painful blow on the head* | **excruciatingly/extremely painful** *an excruciatingly painful death* | **painful to do sth** *He was finding it painful to breathe.*
4 if someone's behaviour or a performance is painful, it is so bad that it embarrasses people: **painful to watch/listen to/hear etc** *It's painful to watch her making the best of a terrible script.* ⚠ Do not use **painful** to mean 'feeling pain': *He didn't feel much pain (NOT feel very painful) at first.*

THESAURUS

WHEN A PART OF YOUR BODY HURTS

painful used for describing a part of the body that hurts: *Her leg is still painful where she broke it. | painful joints*
tender painful when touched: *The skin around the wound is very tender.*
stiff painful and difficult to move: *I've got a stiff neck. | Her body was stiff from sitting in the car for so long.*
sore painful as a result of a wound, infection, or too much exercise: *sore muscles | a sore throat | The wound was sore and red.*

pain·ful·ly /ˈpeɪnfəli/ ●○○ *adv*
1 very – used to emphasize a bad or harmful quality that someone or something has: *painfully thin arms | As a teenager, I was painfully shy. | The road to peace is a painfully slow process. | We are only too* ***painfully aware*** *of the damage his actions have caused.* | **painfully obvious/clear/evident/apparent** *It was painfully obvious he'd rather not see her again.*
2 with pain or causing pain: *Robyn swallowed painfully.*
3 needing a lot of effort: *all the knowledge that he had so painfully acquired*

pain·kill·er /ˈpeɪnˌkɪlə $ -ər/ ●○○ *n* [C] a medicine which reduces or removes pain: *an overdose of painkillers*

pain·kill·ing /ˈpeɪnˌkɪlɪŋ/ *adj* [only before noun] able to reduce or remove pain: *painkilling drugs*

P

pain·less /ˈpeɪnləs/ ●○○ *adj*
1 causing no pain OPP **painful**: *a painless death*
2 not difficult or unpleasant to do OPP **painful**: *The train is a quick and painless way to travel.* | *The interview was **relatively painless**.* THESAURUS EASY —**painlessly** *adv*

pains·tak·ing /ˈpeɪnzˌteɪkɪŋ/ ●○○ *adj* [usually before noun] very careful and thorough SYN **meticulous**: *The work had been done with painstaking attention to detail.* | *Chris described in painstaking detail what had happened.* THESAURUS CAREFUL —**painstakingly** *adv*: *The old painting was painstakingly restored.*

paint¹ /peɪnt/ ●●● S2 W2 *n* [U]
1 a liquid that you put on a surface, using a brush to make the surface a particular colour: *a can of blue paint* | *Wet paint* (=used as a warning on signs when something has just been painted) | *The whole house could do with a fresh **coat of paint**.* | **peeling/flaking paint** (=old paint that is starting to come off the surface) | *All this room needs is **a lick of paint*** (=paint used to make a place more attractive).
2 paints tubes or dry blocks of a coloured substance, used for painting pictures: *acrylic and oil paints*

paint² ●●● S2 W3 *v*
1 [I,T] to put paint on a surface: *The ceiling needs painting.* | ***brightly painted** houses* | **paint sth (in) blue/red/green etc** *We painted the door blue.* | *Paint the walls in a contrasting colour.* | *The living room was painted in pastel shades of pink and blue.*
2 [I,T] to make a picture, design etc using paint: *A white cross was painted on the door.* | *Turner is famous for painting landscapes.* | **paint in oils/watercolours etc** (=paint using a particular type of paint) *He paints mainly in acrylics.*
3 [T] to put a coloured substance on part of your face or body to make it different or more attractive: *The children's faces were painted to look like animals.* | *She'd painted her toenails with red nail polish.*
4 [T] to describe someone or something in a particular way: **paint sb/sth as sth** *She's often been painted as a tough businesswoman.* | **paint a grim/rosy/gloomy picture of sb/sth** *Dickens painted a grim picture of Victorian life.* | *The article **painted** him **in a bad light*** (=described him in a way that made him seem bad).
5 paint the town (red) *informal* to go out to bars, clubs etc to enjoy yourself → **not be as black as you are painted** at BLACK¹(10)

paint sth ↔ **out** *phr v* to cover part of a picture or sign with paint so that it can no longer be seen: *The name of the firm had been partially painted out.*

paint over sth *phr v* to cover a picture or surface with new paint: *Much of the original decoration was painted over.*

paint·ball /ˈpeɪntbɔːl $ -bɒːl/ *n* [U] a game in which you shoot small containers of paint at people

paint·box /ˈpeɪntbɒks $ -bɑːks/ *n* [C] a small box containing dry paint that you mix with water

paint·brush /ˈpeɪntbrʌʃ/ ●○○ *n* [C] a brush for spreading paint on a surface → see picture at BRUSH¹

paint·er /ˈpeɪntə $ -ər/ ●●○ *n* [C]
1 someone who paints pictures SYN **artist**: *Gerry's ambition was to become a portrait painter.*
2 someone whose job is painting houses or other buildings: **painter and decorator** *BrE*

paint·er·ly /ˈpeɪntəli $ -tər-/ *adj written* typical of painters or painting: *painterly images*

paint·ing /ˈpeɪntɪŋ/ ●●● S3 W2 *n*
1 [C] a painted picture that you put on a wall for people to see: *a collection of valuable paintings* | **[+of]** *There was a large painting of his father on the wall.* | *Can you help me **hang** this **painting*** (=put it on a wall)? → OIL PAINTING
2 [U] the act or skill of making a picture, using paints: *Degas' style of painting* | *the Cubist school of painting* (=a particular style used by a group of people)
3 [U] the work of covering a wall, house etc with paint: **painting and decorating** *BrE*

ˈpaint job *n* [singular] *informal* if a car has a paint job, it is painted again: *old cars that are given a quick paint job before being sold*

PAINTINGS

abstract

landscape

still life

portrait

ˈpaint ˌstripper *n* [U] a powerful chemical substance used to remove paint from walls, doors etc

paint·work /ˈpeɪntwɜːk $ -wɜːrk/ *n* [U] paint on a car, house etc: *She noticed the peeling paintwork.*

pair¹ /peə $ per/ ●●● S2 W2 *n* (*plural* **pairs** *or* **pair**) [C]
1 JOINED TOGETHER an object that is made from two similar parts that are joined together: **pair of trousers/scissors/glasses etc** *two pairs of jeans* | *a pair of black tights*
2 BELONGING TOGETHER two things of the same type that are used together: **[+of]** *a new pair of sandals* | **pair of hands/eyes/legs etc** *She felt as if every pair of eyes in the room was on her.* | *earrings, £5 a pair* | *a pair of skis* | *We have five pairs of free tickets to give away.*
3 in pairs in groups of two: *We **worked in pairs** for the role-play exercise.* | *The leaves of the tree are arranged in pairs.*
4 TWO PEOPLE two people who are standing or doing something together, or who have some type of connection with each other: *The pair are looking for sponsorship from local businesses.* | **[+of]** *a pair of dancers* ⚠ Do not use **pair** to talk about a husband and wife (or two people in a similar relationship). Use **couple**: *They're a nice couple (NOT pair).*
5 the pair of you/them *BrE spoken* used when you are angry or annoyed with two people: *Oh, get out, the pair of you.*
6 TWO ANIMALS **a)** a male and a female animal that come together in order to BREED: **[+of]** *a pair of doves* | *a breeding pair* **b)** *old use* two horses that work together
7 I've only got one pair of hands *spoken* used to say that you are busy and cannot do any more than you are already doing
8 an extra pair of hands someone who helps you do something when you are busy: *Having an extra pair of hands during busy periods can take the pressure off.*
9 a safe pair of hands someone you can trust and depend on because they are sensible – used especially in news reports: *Colleagues regard him as a safe pair of hands.*

pair² *v* **1** [I,T] to put people or things into groups of two, or to form groups of two: **be paired with sb** *We were each* paired with a newcomer to help with training. GRAMMAR **Pair** is usually passive in this meaning, when used as a transitive verb. **2** (*also* **pair up**) [I] if animals pair, they come together in order to BREED

pair off *phr v* to come together or bring two people together to have a romantic relationship: *All the others were pairing off and I was left on my own.* | **pair sb off with sb** *My aunt was forever pairing me off with unsuitable men.*

pair up *phr v* **1** *BrE* to become friends and start to have a relationship: *We learned later that he and Tanya had paired up.* **2** to work together to do something or to put two people together to do something: *They first paired up in the screen adaptation of 'Grease'.* | **pair sb ↔ up** *They have paired up writers and artists, and commissioned linked works.* **3** if animals pair up, they come together in order to BREED

pais·ley /ˈpeɪzli/ *n* [U] a pattern consisting of curved shapes used on cloth: *a paisley shawl* → see picture at **PATTERN**[1]

pa·ja·mas /pəˈdʒɑːməz $ -ˈdʒɑː-, -ˈdʒæ-/ *n* [plural] the American spelling of PYJAMAS

pak choi /ˌpæk ˈtʃɔɪ $ ˌpɑːk-/ *BrE*, **bok choy** *AmE n* [U] a green vegetable similar to CABBAGE that is used in Chinese cooking → see picture at **VEGETABLE**[1]

Pa·ki /ˈpæki/ *n* [C] *BrE taboo* a very offensive word for someone from Pakistan or India. Do not use this word.

Pak·i·sta·ni[1] /ˌpækɪˈstɑːni◂ $ -ˈstæni/ *adj* relating to Pakistan or its people

Pakistani[2] *n* [C] someone from Pakistan: *a 20-year-old Pakistani*

pal[1] /pæl/ *n* [C] **1** *informal* a close friend → **mate**: *We've been pals since we were at school.* | *an* **old pal** (=a friend you have had for a long time) THESAURUS FRIEND **2** *spoken* used to speak to a man in an unfriendly way: *Look, pal, I don't want you hanging around.*

pal[2] *v* (**palled, palling**)

pal around *phr v AmE* if you pal around with someone, you do things together as friends: **[+with]** *It was nice having someone to pal around with.*

pal up *phr v BrE* to become someone's friend: **[+with]** *She palled up with Neil while travelling round Europe.*

pal·ace /ˈpælɪs/ ●●○ W3 *n* [C]

1 the official home of a person of very high rank, especially a king or queen – often used in names: *Buckingham Palace*

2 the Palace *especially BrE* the people who live in a palace – used in news reports: *The Palace has announced that the Duke and Duchess are to separate.*

3 a large beautifully decorated house: *the splendid palaces of Florence*

ˌpalace revoˈlution (*also* **ˌpalace ˈcoup**) *n* [C] a situation in which the people who work for a leader take control and remove that leader's power: *He deposed his father in a palace coup.*

pal·a·din /ˈpælədɪn/ *n* [C] a KNIGHT (=a soldier of high rank) in the Middle Ages who was very brave and loyal

palaeo- /pæliəʊ, peɪ- $ peɪlioʊ/ *prefix* a British spelling of PALEO-

pal·ae·o·lith·ic /ˌpæliəʊˈlɪθɪk◂, ˌpeɪ- $ ˌpeɪliə-/ *adj* a British spelling of PALEOLITHIC

pal·ae·on·tol·o·gy /ˌpæliɒnˈtɒlədʒi, ˌpeɪ- $ ˌpeɪliɑːnˈtɑː-/ *n* [U] a British spelling of PALEONTOLOGY

Pal·ae·o·zo·ic *BrE*, **Paleozoic** *AmE* /ˌpæliəˈzəʊɪk, ˌpeɪ- $ ˌpeɪliəˈzoʊ-/ *adj* belonging or relating to the period of time in the Earth's history, from about 570 million years ago to about 245 million years ago, when fish, insects, REPTILES and some plants first started to exist → **mesozoic**

pal·at·a·ble /ˈpælətəbəl/ *adj* **1** palatable food or drink has a pleasant or acceptable taste OPP **unpalatable**: *a very palatable wine* **2** an idea, suggestion etc that is palatable is acceptable OPP **unpalatable**: **[+to]** *They changed the wording of the advertisement to* **make** *it more* **palatable** *to women.* | *The truth, as always, is slightly less palatable.*

pal·ate /ˈpælət/ *n* **1** [C] the ROOF (=top inside part) of your mouth → **CLEFT PALATE, SOFT PALATE 2** [C,U] the sense of taste, and especially your ability to enjoy or judge food: *It tasted very strange, at least to my untrained palate.* | *a collection of dishes to tempt your palate*

pa·la·tial /pəˈleɪʃəl/ *adj* a palatial building etc is large and beautifully decorated: *a palatial country residence*

pa·lat·i·nate /pəˈlætənət/ *n* [C] in the past, an area which was controlled by someone who represented the ruler

pa·la·ver /pəˈlɑːvə $ -ˈlævər/ *n* [singular, U] *especially BrE informal* unnecessary trouble and anxiety that makes something seem more important than it really is SYN **fuss**: *We could have done without all this palaver.* | ***What a palaver*** *over nothing!*

pale[1] /peɪl/ ●●○ W3 *adj*

1 having a skin colour that is very white, or whiter than it usually is: *He looked very pale and drawn.* | **turn/go pale** *He suddenly went pale.* | *Sharon went* **deathly pale** *and looked as if she might faint.* | *an elderly* **pale-faced** *woman*

2 a pale colour has more white in it than usual OPP **deep** SYN **light**: *pale blue curtains* THESAURUS COLOUR

3 pale light is not bright: *the pale gray dawn*

4 pale imitation (of sth) something that is similar to, but not as good as, something else: *The cheese is a pale imitation of real Parmesan.*

pale[2] *v* [I] **1** *literary* if your face pales, it becomes whiter than usual because you have had a shock: *Kent's face paled when he saw that Rob had a knife.* **2 pale into insignificance** to seem much less important when compared to something bigger, worse, more serious etc: *The amounts of money involved pale into insignificance when compared with the sums spent each year on research.* **3 pale in/by comparison** to seem small or unimportant compared to something else: **[+to/with]** *Today's economic problems pale in comparison with those of the 1930s.*

pale[3] *n* **beyond the pale** offensive or unacceptable: *His opinions are entirely beyond the pale.*

ˌpale ˈale *n* [C,U] *BrE old-fashioned* a type of light-coloured beer that is sold in bottles

paleo- (*also* **palaeo-** *BrE*) /pæliəʊ, peɪ- $ peɪlioʊ/ *prefix technical* relating to very ancient times

pal·e·o·lith·ic (*also* **palaeolithic** *BrE, often* **Paleolithic**) /ˌpæliəʊˈlɪθɪk◂, ˌpeɪ- $ ˌpeɪlioʊ-/ *adj* relating to the STONE AGE (=the period of time thousands of years ago when people used stone tools and weapons): *a paleolithic axe* → **NEOLITHIC**

pal·e·on·tol·o·gy (*also* **palaeontology** *BrE*) /ˌpæliɒnˈtɒlədʒi, ˌpeɪ- $ ˌpeɪliɑːnˈtɑː/ *n* [U] the study of FOSSILS (=ancient bones, plants etc that have been preserved in rock) —**paleontologist** *n* [C]

pal·ette /ˈpælət/ *n* [C] **1** a thin curved board that an artist uses to mix paints, holding it by putting his or her thumb through a hole at the edge **2** [usually singular] the colours that a particular artist uses or the colours in a particular painting **3** the choice of colours or shapes that are available in a computer program

ˈpalette knife *n* [C] a knife that bends easily and is not sharp, used for spreading a substance, for example in cooking or painting → see picture at **KNIFE**[1]

pa·li·mo·ny /ˈpæləməni $ -moʊni/ *n* [U] *especially AmE* an amount of money that a law court orders someone to pay regularly to a former partner that they were living with but were not married to

pal·imp·sest /ˈpæləmpsest/ *n* [C] *technical* an ancient document on which the original writing has been covered over with new writing

pal·in·drome /ˈpæləndrəʊm $ -droʊm/ *n* [C] a word or phrase such as 'deed' or 'level', which is the same when you spell it backwards

pal·ing /ˈpeɪlɪŋ/ *n* [C,U] a wooden or metal post that is pointed at the top, or a fence made of these posts: *A new paling had been erected around the yard.* | *iron palings*

pal·i·sade /ˌpæləˈseɪd/ *n* [C] **1** a strong fence made of pointed posts **2** (*also* **palisades** *AmE*) a line of high straight cliffs, especially beside water

pall[1] /pɔːl $ pɒːl/ *v* [I] *literary* if something palls, it becomes less interesting or enjoyable because you have experienced it before: *Gradually, the novelty of city life began to pall.*

pall² *n* [C] **1** [usually singular] a thick dark cloud of smoke, dust etc: **pall of smoke/dust/ash etc** *A pall of thick grey smoke hung over the buildings.* **2 a pall of sth** *literary* an unpleasant quality that seems to be in a place or situation: *The area is enveloped in a pall of neglect.* **3** a cloth used to cover a COFFIN (=a box containing a dead body)

pal·la·di·um /pəˈleɪdiəm/ *n* [U] a soft silver-white metal that is often combined with gold and silver, and used to cover an object with a very thin layer of metal. It is a chemical ELEMENT: symbol Pd

pall·bear·er /ˈpɔːlˌbeərə $ ˈpɒːlˌberər/ *n* [C] someone who helps to carry a COFFIN at a funeral

pal·let /ˈpælɪt/ *n* [C] **1** a large frame, used for storing or carrying heavy things: *wooden pallets* **2** a rough cloth bag filled with STRAW, used in the past for sleeping on

pal·li·ate /ˈpælieɪt/ *v* [T] *formal* to reduce the effects of illness, pain etc without curing them: *Chosen carefully, the oils may not only palliate but also cure the condition.*

pal·li·a·tive /ˈpæliətɪv $ -ətɪv, -eɪtɪv/ *n* [C] **1** *formal* something done to make a bad situation seem better, but which does not solve the problem: *short-term economic palliatives* **2** *medical* a medical treatment that will not cure an illness but will reduce the pain —**palliative** *adj* [usually before noun]: *palliative care*

pal·lid /ˈpælɪd/ *adj* **1** very pale, especially in a way that looks weak or unhealthy: *pallid cheeks* **2** not very interesting: *a pallid performance*

pal·lor /ˈpælə $ -ər/ *n* [singular, U] when someone's skin is very pale in a way that makes them look weak or unhealthy: *A sleepless night had added to her pallor.*

pal·ly /ˈpæli/ *adj* [not before noun] *BrE informal* very friendly with someone: *She's pally with Steven.*

palm¹ /pɑːm $ pɑːm, pɑːlm/ ●●○ *n* [C]

1 PART OF HAND the inside surface of your hand, in which you hold things: **in sb's palm** *She looked at the coins in her palm.* | *He held the pebble* ***in the palm of his hand.*** → see picture at HAND¹

2 TREE (*also* **palm tree**) a tropical tree which grows near beaches or in deserts, with a long straight trunk and large pointed leaves at the top: *coconut palms*

3 hold/have sb in the palm of your hand to have a strong influence on someone, so that they do what you want them to do

4 read sb's palm to tell someone what is going to happen to them in the future by looking at the lines on their hand → **cross sb's palm (with silver)** at CROSS¹(18), → **grease sb's palm** at GREASE²(2)

palm² *v* [T] to hide something in the palm of your hand, especially when you are performing a magic trick or stealing something

palm sth ↔ **off** *phr v* to persuade someone to accept or buy something that is not of good quality or is not the thing that they really want: **[+on/onto]** *He tried to palm off his old books onto me.* | **[+as]** *Dealers sometimes palm off fakes as genuine works of art.*

palm sb **off with** sth *phr v* to give someone an explanation that is not true but that you hope they will accept

Palm·cor·der /ˈpɑːmˌkɔːdə $ ˈpɑːmˌkɔːrdər, ˈpɑːlm-/ *n* [C] *trademark* a small video camera that you can hold in your hand

palm·ist /ˈpɑːmɪst $ ˈpɑːm-, ˈpɑːlm-/ *n* [C] *BrE* someone who claims they can tell what will happen to a person by looking at the lines on the palm of their hand SYN **palm reader**

palm·ist·ry /ˈpɑːməstri $ ˈpɑːm-, ˈpɑːlm-/ *n* [U] the art of looking at the palm of a person's hand to tell what will happen to them in the future

ˈpalm oil *n* [U] the oil obtained from the nut of an African PALM TREE

ˈpalm phone *n* [C] a MOBILE PHONE which is also a small computer that can store information, send emails, or connect you to the Internet

ˈpalm ˌreader *n* [C] a PALMIST

ˈpalm-sized *adj* **palm-sized computer/PC/PDA** a palm-sized computer, PC etc is small enough to fit in your hand → **palmtop**

ˌPalm ˈSunday *n* the Sunday before Easter in the Christian Church

palm·top /ˈpɑːmtɒp $ ˈpɑːmtɑːp, ˈpɑːlm-/ *n* [C] a very small computer that you can hold in your hand → **laptop**, **notebook**

ˈpalm tree (*also* **palm**) *n* [C] a tropical tree which grows near beaches or in deserts, with a long straight trunk and large pointed leaves at the top

pal·o·mi·no /ˌpæləˈmiːnəʊ◂ $ -noʊ◂/ *n* (*plural* **palominos**) [C] a horse that is a golden or cream colour, with a white MANE and tail

pal·pa·ble /ˈpælpəbəl/ *adj formal* **1** a feeling that is palpable is so strong that other people notice it and can feel it around them OPP **impalpable**: *There was a palpable sense of relief among the crowd.* **2** [only before noun] complete: *What he said is palpable nonsense.* —**palpably** *adv*: *This was palpably untrue.*

pal·pate /pælˈpeɪt $ ˈpælpeɪt/ *v* [T] *medical* to touch part of someone's body in order to examine it

pal·pi·tate /ˈpælpɪteɪt/ *v* [I] if your heart palpitates, it beats quickly in an irregular way

pal·pi·ta·tions /ˌpælpəˈteɪʃənz/ *n* [plural] if you have palpitations, your heart beats quickly in an irregular way

pal·sy /ˈpɔːlzi $ ˈpɒːl-/ *n* [U] **1** an illness that makes your arms and legs shake because you cannot control your muscles **2** *old use* PARALYSIS → **CEREBRAL PALSY**

pal·sy-wal·sy /ˌpælzi ˈwælzi/ *adj BrE spoken* very friendly with someone - used especially when you disapprove of this

pal·try /ˈpɔːltri $ ˈpɒːl-/ *adj* **1** a paltry amount of something is too small to be useful or important: ***paltry sum*** *of money* | *He received only a paltry £25 a day.* **2** *formal* unimportant or worthless SYN **trivial**: *paltry issues*

pam·pas /ˈpæmpəs, -pəz/ *n* **the pampas** the large flat areas of land covered with grass in some parts of South America

ˈpampas grass *n* [U] a type of tall grass with silver-white feathery flowers

pam·per /ˈpæmpə $ -ər/ *v* [T] to look after someone very kindly, for example by giving them the things that they want and making them feel warm and comfortable SYN **spoil**: *She spent her childhood as the pampered daughter of a wealthy family.* | **pamper yourself** *Pamper yourself with a stay in one of our luxury hotels.*

pam·phlet /ˈpæmflɪt/ ●○○ *n* [C] a very thin book with paper covers, that gives information about something → **leaflet**: *a political pamphlet*

pam·phle·teer /ˌpæmfləˈtɪə $ -ˈtɪr/ *n* [C] someone who writes pamphlets giving political opinions

Pan, Peter → **PETER PAN**

pan¹ /pæn/ ●●● S3 W3 *n* [C]

1 FOR COOKING a round metal container that you use for cooking, usually with one long handle and a lid SYN **saucepan**: *a frying pan* | *pots and pans* | *Cook the pasta in a large pan of boiling water.*

2 FOR BAKING CAKES ETC *AmE* a metal container for baking things in SYN **tin** *BrE*: *a cake pan*

3 OPEN CONTAINER *AmE* a wide, usually round, open container with low sides, used for holding liquids

4 TOILET *BrE* the bowl of a toilet

5 go down the pan *BrE informal* to be wasted or become useless or ruined: *The business is rapidly going down the pan.* → **WARMING PAN**, → **a flash in the pan** at FLASH²(5)

pan² *v* (**panned, panning**)

1 CRITICIZE [T] *informal* to strongly criticize a film, play etc in a newspaper or on television or radio: *The movie was panned by the critics.* THESAURUS CRITICIZE

2 CAMERA **a)** [I always + adv/prep] if a film or television camera pans in a particular direction, it moves in that direction and follows the thing that is being filmed: *The*

camera panned slowly across the crowd. **b)** [I,T] to move a camera in this way
3 GOLD [I,T] to wash soil in a metal container in order to separate gold from other substances: **[+for]** *panning for gold in Alaska*
pan out *phr v* to happen or develop in a particular way: *We'll have to see how things pan out.*
pan-, **Pan-** /pæn/ *prefix* including all people: *pan-African unity*
pan·a·cea /ˌpænəˈsɪə/ *n* [C] something that people think will make everything better and solve all their problems SYN **cure-all** → **solution**: **[+for]** *There is no panacea for the country's economic problems.*
pa·nache /pəˈnæʃ, pæ-/ *n* [U] a way of doing things that makes them seem easy and exciting, and makes other people admire you → **style**: **with panache** *They played and sang with great panache.*
pan·a·ma hat /ˌpænəmɑː ˈhæt/ (*also* **panama** /ˌpænəˈmɑː◂, ˈpænəmɑː/) *n* [C] a light hat for men, made from STRAW
pan·cake /ˈpænkeɪk/ ●●● S3 *n*
1 [C] a thin flat round cake made from flour, milk, and eggs, that has been cooked in a flat pan and is eaten hot → **crêpe**
2 [U] very thick MAKE-UP for your face, that is worn especially by actors

PANCAKE
maple syrup

ˈ**Pancake Day** (*also* ˌ**Pancake** ˈ**Tuesday**) *n* [C,U] *BrE* SHROVE TUESDAY, when people in Britain traditionally eat pancakes
pan·cre·as /ˈpæŋkriəs/ *n* [C] a GLAND inside your body, near your stomach, that produces INSULIN and a liquid that helps your body to use the food that you eat —**pancreatic** /ˌpæŋkriˈætɪk◂/ *adj*
pan·da /ˈpændə/ *n* [C] **1** a large black and white animal that looks like a bear and lives in the mountains of China → see picture at **BEAR²** **2** a small animal with red-brown fur and a long tail that lives in the southeastern Himalayas
ˈ**Panda car** *n* [C] *BrE informal* a small black and white police car
pan·dem·ic /pænˈdemɪk/ *n* [C] *technical* a disease that affects people over a very large area or the whole world → **endemic**, **epidemic**: *the AIDS pandemic* —**pandemic** *adj*
pan·de·mo·ni·um /ˌpændəˈməʊniəm $ -ˈmoʊ-/ *n* [U] a situation in which there is a lot of noise because people are angry, confused or frightened SYN **chaos**: ***There was** complete **pandemonium** in the kitchen.* | *When the verdict was read **pandemonium broke out** in the courtroom.*
pan·der /ˈpændə $ -ər/ *v*
pander to sb/sth *phr v* to give someone anything they want in order to please them, even if it seems unreasonable or unnecessary – used to show disapproval: *Some newspapers feel they have to pander to the prejudices of their readers.* | *Highly trained staff will **pander to** your **every whim**.*
Pan·do·ra's box /pænˌdɔːrəz ˈbɒks $ -ˈbɑːks/ *n* **open a Pandora's box** to do or start something that will cause a lot of other problems: *The report could open up a Pandora's box of claims from similar cases.*
p & p *BrE* the written abbreviation of ***postage and packing***: *Please send 80p to cover p & p.*
pane /peɪn/ *n* [C] a piece of glass used in a window or door: *a window pane* | *a pane of glass* → **WINDOWPANE**
pan·e·gyr·ic /ˌpænəˈdʒɪrɪk/ *n* [C] *old-fashioned formal* a speech or piece of writing that praises someone or something a lot
pan·el /ˈpænl/ ●●○ S3 W3 AWL *n* [C]
1 GROUP OF PEOPLE **a)** a group of people with skills or SPECIALIST knowledge who have been chosen to give advice or opinions on a particular subject: **[+of]** *A panel of experts has looked at the proposal.* | **on a panel** *There will be at least three senior doctors on the panel.* **b)** a group of well-known people who answer questions on a radio or television programme → **panellist**: **on a panel** *We have two senior politicians on our panel tonight.* **c)** *AmE* a group of people who are chosen to listen to a case in a court of law and to decide the result SYN **jury**: *The panel spent 14 hours going over the evidence.*

GRAMMAR: Singular or plural verb?
• In this meaning, **panel** is usually followed by a singular verb: *The panel **has** reached a decision.*
• In British English, you can also use a plural verb: *The panel **have** reached a decision.*
GRAMMAR GUIDE ▸ **NOUNS**

2 PIECE OF SOMETHING **a)** a flat piece of wood, glass etc with straight sides, which forms part of a door, wall, fence etc: *a stained glass panel* | *There were a few panels missing from the fence.* **b)** a piece of metal that forms part of the outer structure of a vehicle: *One of the door panels was badly damaged and had to be replaced.* **c)** a piece of material that forms part of a piece of clothing: *a skirt made in six panels*
3 **instrument/control panel** a board in a car, plane, boat etc that has the controls on it
4 PICTURE a thin board with a picture painted on it → **SOLAR PANEL**
pan·elled *BrE*, **paneled** *AmE* /ˈpænld/ *adj* covered or decorated with flat pieces of wood: **[+with/in]** *The walls were panelled with oak.*
pan·el·ling *BrE*, **paneling** *AmE* /ˈpænəl-ɪŋ/ *n* [U] long or square pieces of wood that are used to cover and decorate walls
pan·el·list *BrE*, **panelist** *AmE* /ˈpænəl-ɪst/ *n* [C] one of a group of well-known people who answer questions on a radio or television programme
ˈ**panel pin** *n* [C] *BrE* a short thin nail that is used for fastening thin pieces of wood together
ˈ**panel show** (*also* ˈ**panel game**) *n* [C] a television programme in which famous people sit and take part in a game or QUIZ, and usually say humorous things
ˈ**panel truck** *n* [C] *AmE* a small motor vehicle used for delivering goods
pang /pæŋ/ *n* [C] a sudden feeling of pain, sadness etc: **pang of jealousy/guilt/remorse/regret** *She felt a sudden pang of guilt.* | ***hunger pangs***
pan·han·dle¹ /ˈpænˌhændl/ *n* [C] *AmE* a long thin area of land that sticks out from a larger area: *the Texas panhandle*

panhandle² *v* [I] *especially AmE informal* to ask for money in the streets SYN **beg**: *homeless people panhandling in the subway* —**panhandler** *n* [C]

pan·ic¹ /ˈpænɪk/ ●●○ S3 *n*
1 [C usually singular, U] a sudden strong feeling of fear or nervousness that makes you unable to think clearly or behave sensibly: **in (a) panic** *The children fled in panic.* | *a feeling of* **sheer panic** (=complete panic) | *She* **got into a panic** *when she couldn't find the tickets.* | *The whole nation is* **in a state of panic** *following the attacks.* | *She suffers from terrible* **panic attacks**. THESAURUS ▸ FEAR
2 [C usually singular, U] a situation in which people are suddenly made very anxious, and make quick decisions without thinking carefully: **[+over/about]** *the recent panic over the safety of baby milk* | **panic buying/selling** *a wave of panic selling in Hong Kong*
3 [singular] *especially BrE* a situation in which you have a lot to do and not much time to do it in → **rush**: *the usual* **last minute panic** *just before the deadline*
4 panic stations *BrE* a situation in which everyone is busy and anxious because something needs to be done urgently: *It was panic stations here on Friday.*

panic² ●●○ *v* (**panicked**, **panicking**) [I,T] to suddenly feel so frightened that you cannot think clearly or behave sensibly, or to make someone do this: *He started to panic when he saw the gun.* | **Don't panic!** *We'll soon get you out of there.* | **panic sb into doing sth** *The protests became more violent and many people were panicked into leaving the country.*

ˈpanic ˌbutton *n* [C] **1** a button that you can press to call for help if you are being attacked **2 press/push the panic button** *BrE* to do something quickly without thinking enough about it, because something unexpected or dangerous has suddenly happened

pan·ic·ky /ˈpænɪki/ *adj informal* very nervous and anxious: *By ten o'clock she was starting to get a bit panicky.*

ˈpanic-ˌstricken *adj* so frightened that you cannot think clearly or behave sensibly: *Lucy suddenly looked panic-stricken.*

pan·ni·er /ˈpæniə $ -ər/ *n* [C] **1** one of a pair of baskets or bags that you carry one on each side of an animal or a bicycle → **saddlebag 2** a basket in which someone carries a load on their back

pan·o·ply /ˈpænəpli/ *n* [singular] *formal* **1** an impressive show of special clothes, decorations etc, especially at an important ceremony: **[+of]** *a glorious panoply of colours* **2** a large number of people or things: **[+of]** *a panoply of men in grey suits* | **full/entire/whole panoply of sth** (=the whole range of something)

pan·o·ra·ma /ˌpænəˈrɑːmə $ -ˈræmə/ *n* [C usually singular] **1** an impressive view of a wide area of land: **[+of]** *The tower offers a panorama of the city.* | *a breathtaking panorama of mountains* THESAURUS ▸ SIGHT **2** a description or series of pictures that shows all the features of a subject, historical period etc: **[+of]** *a panorama of life in England 400 years ago* —**panoramic** /ˌpænəˈræmɪk◂/ *adj*: *a* **panoramic view** *of the valley*

pan·pipes /ˈpænpaɪps/ *n* [plural] a simple musical instrument made of short wooden pipes of different lengths, that you play by blowing across their open ends

pan·sy /ˈpænzi/ *n* (*plural* **pansies**) [C] **1** a small garden plant with brightly coloured flowers **2** *informal not polite* an offensive word for a man who seems weak and too much like a woman

pant /pænt/ ●○○ *v*
1 [I] to breathe quickly with short noisy breaths, for example because you have been running or because it is very hot: *He came in panting after running up the steps.* | *He was* **panting for breath**. | *The dog lay panting on the doorstep.* THESAURUS ▸ BREATHE
2 [T] to say something while you are panting: *'I can't run any farther,' she panted.* —**pant** *n* [C]

pant for sth *phr v* to want something very much: *He came in panting for a cup of tea.*

pan·ta·loons /ˌpæntəˈluːnz/ *n* [plural] *old-fashioned* long trousers with wide legs, that become tight at the bottom of your legs

pan·tech·ni·con /pænˈteknɪkən $ -kɑːn/ *n* [C] *BrE old-fashioned* a REMOVAL VAN

pan·the·is·m /ˈpænθi-ɪzəm/ *n* [U] the religious idea that God and the universe are one thing and that God is present in all natural things —**pantheist** *n* [C] —**pantheistic** /ˌpænθiˈɪstɪk◂/ *adj*

pan·the·on /ˈpænθiən $ -θiɑːn/ *n* [C] **1** all the gods of a particular people or nation: *the Roman pantheon* **2** *literary* a group of famous and important people: **[+of]** *a leading figure in the pantheon of 20th-century artists* **3** a religious building that is built in honour of all gods

pan·ther /ˈpænθə $ -ər/ *n* [C] **1** a large wild animal that is black and a member of the cat family → see picture at BIG CAT **2** *AmE* a COUGAR

pan·ties /ˈpæntiz/ *n* [plural] *especially AmE* a piece of women's underwear that covers the area between their waist and the top of their legs SYN **knickers** *BrE*: *a pair of lacy panties* → see picture at UNDERWEAR

pan·ti·hose /ˈpæntihəʊz $ -hoʊz/ *n* [plural] *AmE* another spelling of PANTYHOSE

pan·tile /ˈpæntaɪl/ *n* [C usually plural] *BrE* a curved TILE used for covering a roof

pan·to /ˈpæntəʊ $ -toʊ/ *n* (*plural* **pantos**) [C,U] *BrE informal* pantomime

pan·to·graph /ˈpæntəgrɑːf $ -græf/ *n* [C] *technical* **1** an instrument used to make a smaller or larger exact copy of a drawing, plan etc **2** a thing on top of an electric train which takes electric power from an electric power line above it

pan·to·mime /ˈpæntəmaɪm/ *n* **1** [C,U] a type of play for children that is performed in Britain around Christmas, in which traditional stories are performed with jokes, music, and songs **2** [C,U] a method of performing using only actions and not words, or a play performed using this method SYN **mime 3** [C] *BrE* a situation or behaviour that is silly

pan·try /ˈpæntri/ *n* (*plural* **pantries**) [C] a very small room in a house where food is kept SYN **larder**

pants¹ /pænts/ ●●● S3 *n* [plural]
1 *especially AmE* a piece of clothing that covers you from your waist to your feet and has a separate part for each leg SYN **trousers** *BrE*: *She was wearing dark blue pants and a white sweater.*
2 *BrE* a piece of underwear that covers the area between your waist and the top of your legs SYN **underpants** *AmE* → **knickers**, **briefs**, **boxer shorts**
3 bore/scare etc the pants off sb *informal spoken* to make someone feel very bored, very frightened etc: *She always bores the pants off me.*
4 beat the pants off sb *AmE spoken* to defeat someone very easily in a game or competition SYN **thrash**
5 sb puts his pants on one leg at a time *AmE spoken* used to say that someone is just like everyone else: *Go on, ask him for his autograph – he puts his pants on one leg at a time just like you do.*
6 (since sb was) in short pants *BrE informal* since someone was a very young boy: *I've known Eric since he was in short pants.* → **do sth by the seat of your pants** at SEAT¹(10), → **catch sb with their pants down** at CATCH¹(6), → **wear the pants/trousers** at WEAR¹(7)

pants² *adj* [not before noun] *BrE spoken informal* very bad: *The concert was pants.*

pant·suit /ˈpæntsuːt, -sjuːt $ -suːt/ *n* [C] *AmE* a woman's suit consisting of a jacket and matching trousers

pan·ty·hose, **pantihose** /ˈpæntihəʊz $ -hoʊz/ *n* [plural] *AmE* a very thin piece of women's clothing that covers their legs from the toes to the waist and is usually worn with dresses or skirts SYN **tights** *BrE*

pan·ty·lin·er /ˈpæntilaɪnə $ -ər/ *n* [C] a very thin SANITARY PAD

pap¹ /pæp/ *n* [U] **1** films, programmes, books etc that are badly made or badly written, are intended for entertainment only, and have no serious value: *Hollywood* *produces a lot of pap.* **2** *especially BrE* very soft food that does not have a strong taste, like the food that babies eat → PAP SMEAR

pap² *v* (**papped**, **papping**) [T] *informal* if a famous person is papped, one of the PAPARAZZI takes a photograph of them without asking them, for a newspaper or magazine: *The singer was papped coming out of a nightclub.*

pa·pa /pəˈpɑː $ ˈpɑːpə/ *n* [C] *old-fashioned* a way of talking to or about your father: *Good morning, Papa!*

pa·pa·cy /ˈpeɪpəsi/ *n* **1 the papacy** the position and authority of the Pope **2** [U] the time during which a pope is in power

pap·a·dum /ˈpæpədəm $ ˈpɑː-/ *n* [C] another spelling of POPPADOM

pa·pal /ˈpeɪpəl/ *adj* [only before noun] relating to the Pope: *a challenge to papal authority*

pap·a·raz·zi /ˌpæpəˈrætsi $ ˌpɑːpəˈrɑː/ *n* [plural] photographers who follow famous people in order to take photographs they can sell to newspapers

pa·pa·ya /pəˈpaɪə/ *n* [C] the large yellow-green fruit of a tropical tree → see picture at FRUIT¹

pa·per¹ /ˈpeɪpə $ -ər/ ●●● S1 W1 *n*

1 FOR WRITING/WRAPPING [U] material in the form of thin sheets that is used for writing on, wrapping things etc: *I'll get you a piece of paper so you can write the number down.* | *Do you have a pen and paper?*

2 NEWSPAPER [C] a newspaper: *Have you seen today's paper?* | *You'll read about it in tomorrow's papers.* | *the **Sunday papers*** THESAURUS NEWSPAPER

3 DOCUMENTS/LETTERS **papers** [plural] **a)** pieces of paper with writing on them that you use in your work, at meetings etc: *I left some important papers in my briefcase.* **b)** documents and letters concerning someone's private or public life: *While I was organizing Simon's papers I came across his diaries.* **c) divorce papers** documents concerning a DIVORCE **d)** official documents such as your PASSPORT, IDENTITY CARD etc: *My papers are all in order* (=they are legal and correct). → WHITE PAPER, GREEN PAPER, ORDER PAPER

4 on paper a) if you put ideas or information on paper, you write them down: **put/get sth down on paper** *You need to get some of these thoughts down on paper.* **b)** if something seems true on paper, it seems to be true as an idea, but may not be true in a real situation SYN **in theory**: *It's a nice idea on paper, but you'll never get it to work.*

5 EXAMINATION [C] *BrE* a set of printed questions used as an examination in a particular subject, and the answers people write: *an exam paper* | *I have a stack of papers to mark.* | **history/French etc paper** *The geography paper was really easy.* THESAURUS TEST

6 SPEECH/PIECE OF WRITING [C] a piece of writing or a talk on a particular subject by someone who has made a study of it: *a scientific paper* | **[+on]** *a paper on psychology* | *Professor Usborne **gave** a **paper** on recent developments in his field.*

7 PIECE OF SCHOOLWORK [C] *especially AmE* a piece of writing that is done as part of a course at school or university SYN **essay**: **[+on]** *a paper on the Civil War*

8 OFFICIAL PUBLICATION [C] a report prepared by a government or committee on a question they have been considering or a proposal for changes in the law: *We will publish a **discussion paper** on the future of the BBC.* | **[+on]** *the 1998 White Paper on political reform* | *a **working paper*** (=a report that is not final) *on funding the Health Service*

9 FOR WALLS [C,U] paper for covering and decorating the walls of a room SYN **wallpaper**: *a floral paper*

10 FINANCIAL [C,U] STOCKS and SHARES that can be bought and sold on a financial market

11 TOILET [U] soft thin paper used for cleaning yourself after you have used the toilet SYN **toilet paper, toilet roll**

12 not worth the paper it is written on/printed on if something such as a contract is not worth the paper it is written on, it has no value because whatever is promised in it will not happen → **put/set pen to paper** at PEN¹(3), → WASTE PAPER

COLLOCATIONS

PHRASES

a sheet of paper *Each recipe was written down on a separate sheet of paper.*
a piece of paper *Can I have another piece of paper?*
a scrap/slip of paper (=a small piece)

ADJECTIVES/NOUN + paper

writing/note paper (=good quality paper for writing letters) *Can you fetch me a piece of writing paper and a pen?*
plain paper (=with nothing written or printed on it) *The package was wrapped in plain brown paper.*
lined paper (=printed with horizontal lines, for writing) | **wrapping paper** (=coloured paper for wrapping presents) | **tissue paper** (=very thin paper for wrapping things) | **recycled paper** (=paper made from waste paper)

COMMON ERRORS

⚠ Don't say 'write on a paper'. Say **write on a piece of paper.**

paper² ●●● S3 W2 *adj* [only before noun]

1 made of paper: *a paper bag*

2 written or printed on paper: *The brochure is available in electronic and paper versions.*

3 paper qualifications an expression meaning documents showing that you have passed particular examinations, used specially when you think that experience and knowledge are more important: *Paper qualifications are no guide to ability.*

4 existing only as an idea but not having any real value: *paper profits* (=a record of the value of something, that is not real until the thing is sold) | *paper promises*

paper³ *v* [T] **1** to decorate the walls of a room by covering them with special paper SYN **wallpaper** **2 paper over the cracks** to try to hide disagreements or difficulties: *We need to discuss disagreements honestly without papering over the cracks.*

pa·per·back /ˈpeɪpəbæk $ -ər-/ ●○○ *n* [C] a book with a stiff paper cover → **hardback**: *a shelf full of paperbacks* | **in paperback** *Her first novel sold over 20,000 copies in paperback.* THESAURUS BOOK

pa·per·boy /ˈpeɪpəbɔɪ $ -ər-/ *n* [C] a boy who delivers newspapers to people's houses → **paper girl**

ˈpaper chase *n* [C] *informal* an official process that prevents you from doing something quickly because it involves writing or reading a lot of documents → **bureaucracy, red tape**

pa·per·clip /ˈpeɪpəklɪp $ -ər-/ *n* [C] a small piece of curved wire used for holding sheets of paper together → see picture at STATIONERY

ˈpaper ˌfastener *n* [C] *BrE* a small metal object like a button used to hold several pieces of paper together

ˈpaper girl *n* [C] a girl who delivers newspapers to people's houses → **paperboy**

ˈpaper knife *n* [C] *BrE* a knife for opening envelopes → see picture at KNIFE¹

ˌpaper ˈmoney *n* [U] money made of paper, not coins → **note**

ˈpaper-ˌpusher *n* [C] someone whose job is doing unimportant office work SYN **pen pusher** *BrE*, **pencil pusher** *AmE*

ˈpaper round *BrE*, **ˈpaper route** *AmE* *n* [C] the job of delivering newspapers to a group of houses

ˈpaper shop *n* [C] *BrE* a shop that sells newspapers and magazines, and also things such as tobacco, sweets, and cards SYN **newsagent** *BrE*

ˌpaper-ˈthin *adj* very thin: *paper-thin walls* THESAURUS THIN

ˌpaper ˈtiger *n* [C] an enemy or opponent who seems powerful but actually is not

ˌpaper ˈtowel *n* [C] a sheet of soft thick paper that you

P

use to dry your hands or to clean up small amounts of liquid, food etc

ˈpaper trail *n* [C usually singular] documents and records that show what someone has done, especially ones proving that someone is guilty of a crime: *The paper trail led investigators straight to the White House.*

pa·per·weight /ˈpeɪpəweɪt $ -ər-/ *n* [C] a small heavy object used to hold pieces of paper in place

pa·per·work /ˈpeɪpəwɜːk $ -pərwɜːrk/ ●○○ *n* [U]
1 work such as writing letters or reports, which must be done but is not very interesting: *Police work involves so much paperwork these days.*
2 the documents that you need for a business deal, a journey etc: *I'm leaving the solicitors to sort out the paperwork.*

P

pa·per·y /ˈpeɪpəri/ *adj* something such as skin or leaves that is papery is very dry and thin and a little stiff

pap·ier mâ·ché /ˌpæpieɪ ˈmæʃeɪ, ˌpeɪpər- $ ˌpeɪpər məˈʃeɪ, ˌpæpjeɪ-/ (*also* **paper-mâché** /ˌpeɪpə- $ ˌpeɪpər/ *AmE*) *n* [U] a soft substance made from a mixture of paper, water, and glue, which becomes hard when it dries and is used for making pots and other objects

pa·pist /ˈpeɪpɪst/ *n* [C] an insulting word for a member of the Roman Catholic Church, used especially by Protestants

pa·poose /pəˈpuːs $ pæ-/ *n* [C] **1** *BrE* a type of bag attached to a frame, which you use to carry a baby on your back **2** *old use* a Native American baby or young child

pap·ri·ka /ˈpæprɪkə, pəˈpriːkə $ pəˈpriːkə/ *n* [U] a red powder made from a type of sweet PEPPER, used for giving a slightly hot taste to meat and other food

ˈPap smear *n* [C] *AmE* a medical test that takes cells from a woman's CERVIX and examines them for signs of CANCER SYN **smear test** *BrE*

pa·py·rus /pəˈpaɪrəs/ *n* (*plural* **papyruses** *or* **papyri** /-raɪ/) **1** [U] a plant like grass that grows in water **2** [C,U] a type of paper made from papyrus and used in ancient Egypt, or a piece of this paper

par /pɑː $ pɑːr/ *n* [U] **1 be on a par (with sth)** to be at the same level or standard: *The wages of clerks were on a par with those of manual workers.* | *We will have Christmas decorations on a par with anything on show at the Metro Centre.* **2 be below/under par a)** to feel a little ill or lacking in energy: *I've been feeling a little under par the last couple of weeks.* **b)** (*also* **not be up to par**) to be less good than usual or below the proper standard: *None of the people who'd auditioned were really up to par.* | *The champion was playing well below par.* **3 be par for the course** to be what you would normally expect to happen – used to show disapproval: *Long hours and tough working conditions are often par for the course in catering.* **4** the number of STROKES a good player should take to hit the ball into a hole in the game of GOLF: *The last hole is a par five.* **5** (*also* **par value** *technical*) the value of a STOCK or BOND that is printed on it when it is first sold: *bonds sold at 97% of their par value* | **at/above/below/under par** *The notes are currently trading at 10% above par.* → PAR EXCELLENCE

par·a¹ /ˈpærə/ *n* [C] *BrE informal* a PARATROOPER

para² (*also* **par**) the written abbreviation of ***paragraph***

para- /pærə/ *prefix* **1** beyond: *the paranormal* (=strange unnatural events, beyond normal experience) **2** very similar to something: *terrorists wearing paramilitary uniforms* **3** relating to a profession and helping more highly trained people: *a paramedic* (=someone who helps a doctor) | *a paralegal* (=someone who helps a lawyer) **4** relating to PARACHUTES: *a paratrooper* | *paragliding*

par·a·ben /ˈpærəben/ *n* [C] one of a group of chemicals used as PRESERVATIVES in substances such as COSMETICS

par·a·ble /ˈpærəbəl/ *n* [C] a short simple story that teaches a moral or religious lesson, especially one of the stories told by Jesus in the Bible

pa·rab·o·la /pəˈræbələ/ *n* [C] *technical* a curve in the shape of the imaginary line an object makes when it is thrown high in the air and comes down a little distance away —**parabolic** /ˌpærəˈbɒlɪk◂ $ -ˈbɑː-/ *adj*

par·a·ce·ta·mol /ˌpærəˈsiːtəmɒl, -ˈset- $ -mɑːl, -mɒːl/ *n* (*plural* **paracetamol** *or* **paracetamols**) [C,U] *BrE* a common drug used to reduce pain, which does not contain ASPIRIN

par·a·chute¹ /ˈpærəʃuːt/ ●○○ *n* [C] a piece of equipment fastened to the back of people who jump out of planes, which makes them fall slowly and safely to the ground: *a parachute jump*

parachute² *v* **1** [I always + adv/prep] to jump from a plane using a parachute: **[+into]** *They parachuted into Vietnam in 1968.* **2** [T always + adv/prep] to drop something from a plane with a parachute: **parachute sth to/into sth** *Supplies have been parachuted into the area.*

par·a·chut·ist /ˈpærəʃuːtɪst/ *n* [C] someone who jumps from a plane with a parachute

pa·rade¹ /pəˈreɪd/ ●●○ *n* [C]
1 a public celebration when musical bands, brightly decorated vehicles etc move down the street: *a victory parade* | *the St Patrick's Day parade*
2 a military ceremony in which soldiers stand or march together so that important people can examine them: *a military parade* | **on parade** (=be standing or marching in a parade) *troops on parade*
3 a line of people moving along so that other people can watch them: *a fashion parade*
4 a series of people, events etc that seems to never end: **[+of]** *She had a constant parade of young men coming to visit her.*
5 *BrE* a street with a row of small shops → IDENTIFICATION PARADE, HIT PARADE

parade² *v*
1 PROTEST/CELEBRATE [I always + adv/prep] to walk or march together to celebrate or protest about something: **[+around/past etc]** *The marchers paraded peacefully through the capital.*
2 SHOW STH [T] if you parade your skills, knowledge, possessions etc, you show them publicly in order to make people admire you SYN **show off**: *Young athletes will get a chance to parade their skills.*
3 WALK AROUND [I always + adv/prep] to walk around, especially in a way that shows that you want people to notice and admire you: **[+around/past etc]** *A trio of girls in extremely tight shorts paraded up and down.*
4 SHOW SB [T always + adv/prep] if prisoners are paraded on television or through the streets, they are shown to the public, in order to prove that the people holding them are important or powerful: *The prisoners were paraded in front of the TV cameras.*
5 PROUDLY SHOW [T] to proudly show something or someone to other people, because you want to look impressive to them SYN **show off**: *She paraded her new team.* | *war medals paraded for public admiration*
6 SOLDIERS [I,T] if soldiers parade, or if an officer parades them, they march together so that an important person can watch them
7 parade as sth/be paraded as sth if something parades as something else that is better, someone is pretending that it is the other better thing – used to show disapproval: *It's just self-interest parading as concern for your welfare.*

paˈrade ˌground *n* [C] a place where soldiers practise marching or standing together in rows

par·a·digm /ˈpærədaɪm/ ●○○ AWL *n* [C]
1 *technical* a model or example that shows how something works or is produced: **[+of]** *the basic paradigm of the family tree*
2 *formal* a very clear or typical example of something: **[+of]** *Pius XII remained the paradigm of what a pope should be.* —**paradigmatic** /ˌpærədɪgˈmætɪk◂/ *adj* —**paradigmatically** /-kli/ *adv*

ˈparadigm ˌshift *n* [C] an important change in which the usual way of thinking or doing something is replaced by another way of thinking or doing something

par·a·dise /ˈpærədaɪs/ ●●○ *n*
1 [U] a place or situation that is extremely pleasant,

beautiful, or enjoyable: *a beautiful tropical paradise | The hotel felt like paradise after two weeks of camping. | A home near the sea is my idea of paradise.*
2 [singular] a place that has everything you need for doing a particular activity: *The market is a shopper's paradise. |* **[+for]** *Hawaii is a paradise for surfers.*
3 Paradise [singular] **a)** in some religions, a perfect place where people are believed to go after they die, if they have led good lives → **heaven b)** according to the Bible, the garden where the first humans, Adam and Eve, lived → BIRD OF PARADISE, → **be living in a fool's paradise** at FOOL[1](9)

par·a·dox /ˈpærədɒks $ -dɑːks/ ●○○ *n*
1 [C] a situation that seems strange because it involves two ideas or qualities that are very different: *It's a paradox that in such a rich country there can be so much poverty.*
2 [C] a statement that seems impossible because it contains two opposing ideas that are both true: *The paradox is that fishermen would catch more fish if they fished less.*
3 [U] the use of statements that are a paradox in writing or speech —**paradoxical** /ˌpærəˈdɒksɪkəl◂ $ -ˈdɑːk-/ *adj*

par·a·dox·i·cally /ˌpærəˈdɒksɪkli $ -ˈdɑːk-/ ●○○ *adv* in a way that is surprising because it is the opposite of what you would expect: *Paradoxically, the prohibition of liquor caused an increase in alcoholism.*

par·af·fin /ˈpærəfɪn/ *n* [U] **1** *BrE* a kind of oil used for heating and in lamps, made from PETROLEUM or coal SYN **kerosene** *AmE* **2** (*also* **paraffin wax** *BrE*) a soft white substance used for making CANDLES, made from PETROLEUM or coal

par·a·glid·ing /ˈpærəˌglaɪdɪŋ/ *n* [U] a sport in which you jump off a hill or out of a plane and use a PARACHUTE to fly for long distances before floating back down to the ground

par·a·gon /ˈpærəgən $ -gɑːn/ *n* [C] someone who is perfect or is extremely brave, good etc – often used humorously: **[+of]** *a* ***paragon of virtue***

par·a·graph /ˈpærəgrɑːf $ -græf/ ●●● S2 AWL *n* [C] part of a piece of writing which starts on a new line and contains at least one sentence: *the opening paragraphs of the novel* —**paragraph** *v* [T]

par·a·keet /ˈpærəkiːt/ *n* [C] a small brightly coloured bird with a long tail

par·a·le·gal /ˌpærəˈliːgəl/ *n* [C] *AmE* someone whose job is to help lawyers do their work

par·al·lel[1] /ˈpærəlel/ ●●○ AWL *adj*
1 two lines, paths etc that are parallel to each other are the same distance apart along their whole length: *Lines AB and CD are parallel. | two parallel roads |* **[+to]** *She was travelling parallel to her previous route. |* **[+with]** *The railway is parallel with the canal. | Take the road* ***running parallel*** *to the main road just after the village.*
2 *formal* similar and happening at the same time: *Social changes in Britain are matched by parallel trends in some other countries.*

parallel[2] ●○○ AWL *n* [C]
1 a relationship or similarity between two things, especially things that exist or happen in different places or at different times: **[+with]** *Entering the world of fine art, she found many parallels with the world of fashion. |* **[+between]** *There are many parallels between Yeats and the Romantic poets. | books that attempt to* ***draw parallels*** *between brains and computers*
2 in parallel with sb/sth together with and at the same time as something else: *She wanted to pursue her own career in parallel with her husband's.*
3 have no parallel/be without parallel be greater, better, worse etc than anything else: *The poverty of hill farmers had no parallel.*
4 an imaginary line drawn on a map of the Earth, that is parallel to the EQUATOR: *the 38th parallel*

parallel[3] AWL *v* (**paralleled, paralleling** *also* **parallelled, parallelling** *BrE*) [T] *written* if one thing parallels another, they happen at the same time or are similar, and seem to be related: *The rise in greenhouse gases parallels the reduction in the ozone layer. | His career parallels that of his father.*

ˌparallel ˈbars *n* [plural] two wooden bars that are held parallel to each other on four posts, used in GYMNASTICS

par·al·lel·is·m /ˈpærəlelɪzəm/ *n* [singular, U] *written* the state of being PARALLEL with something: *There is a parallelism between fatigue and the ability to sleep.*

par·al·lel·o·gram /ˌpærəˈleləgræm/ *n* [C] a flat shape with four sides in which each side is the same length as the side opposite it and parallel to it → **rectangle**

ˌparallel ˈprocessing *n* [U] *technical* when several computers work on a single problem at one time, or the process by which a single computer can perform several operations at the same time

Par·a·lym·pics /ˌpærəˈlɪmpɪks/ (*also* **ˌParalympic ˈGames**) *n* [plural] an international sports event held every four years for DISABLED athletes who cannot use a part of their body properly. It is held after the OLYMPIC GAMES, in the same city.

par·a·lyse *BrE*, **paralyze** *AmE* /ˈpærəlaɪz/ *v* [T]
1 if something paralyses you, it makes you lose the ability to move part or all of your body, or to feel it: *Her legs were partly paralysed in the crash.* **2** to make something unable to operate normally: *Fear of unemployment is paralysing the economy. | Motor traffic was paralysed in much of the city.*

par·a·lysed *BrE*, **paralyzed** *AmE* /ˈpærəlaɪzd/ *adj*
1 unable to move part or all of your body or feel it: *The accident left him permanently paralysed. |* **paralysed from the neck/chest/waist down 2** unable to think clearly or deal with a situation: **[+by/with]** *paralysed by fear | paralyzed with shock | He stood paralysed for a moment, and then ran away.*

pa·ral·y·sis /pəˈrælɪsɪs/ *n* [U] **1** the loss of the ability to move all or part of your body or feel things in it: *paralysis of the lower body | The snake's poison causes paralysis.* **2** a state of being unable to take action, make decisions, or operate normally: *a period of political paralysis* → INFANTILE PARALYSIS

par·a·lyt·ic[1] /ˌpærəˈlɪtɪk◂/ *adj* **1** [not before noun] *BrE informal* very drunk **2** [only before noun] suffering from paralysis —**paralytically** /-kli/ *adv*

paralytic[2] *n* [C] *old-fashioned* someone who is PARALYSED

par·a·lyze /ˈpærəlaɪz/ *v* [T] the American spelling of PARALYSE

par·a·med·ic /ˌpærəˈmedɪk/ *n* [C] someone who has been trained to help people who are hurt or to do medical work, but who is not a doctor or nurse THESAURUS DOCTOR —**paramedical** *adj* [usually before noun]

pa·ram·e·ter /pəˈræmɪtə $ -ər/ ●○○ AWL *n* [C usually plural] a set of fixed limits that control the way that something should be done: *The inquiry has to stay within the parameters laid down by Congress.*

par·a·mil·i·ta·ry /ˌpærəˈmɪlətəri◂ $ -teri◂/ *adj* [usually before noun] **1** a paramilitary organization is an illegal group that is organized like an army: *extremist paramilitary groups* **2** relating to or helping a military organization: *the paramilitary police* —**paramilitary** *n* [C]

par·a·mount /ˈpærəmaʊnt/ ●○○ *adj formal* more important than anything else: *During a war the interests of the state are paramount, and those of the individual come last. | Women's role as mothers is* ***of paramount importance*** *to society.* THESAURUS IMPORTANT —**paramountcy** *n* [U]

par·a·mour /ˈpærəmʊə $ -mʊr/ *n* [C] *literary* someone who you have a romantic or sexual relationship with, but who you are not married to SYN **lover**

par·a·noi·a /ˌpærəˈnɔɪə/ *n* [U] **1** an unreasonable belief that you cannot trust other people, or that they are trying to harm you or have a bad opinion of you **2** *medical* a mental illness that makes someone believe that they are very important and that people hate them and are trying to harm them

par·a·noi·ac /ˌpærəˈnɔɪæk◂/ *adj* paranoid —**paranoiac** *n* [C]

P

par·a·noid /ˈpærənɔɪd/ *adj* **1** believing unreasonably that you cannot trust other people, or that they are trying to harm you or have a bad opinion of you: **be/become/get paranoid** *Malcolm got really paranoid, deciding that there was a conspiracy out to get him.* | **[+about]** *He has always been paranoid about his personal security.* **2** *medical* suffering from a mental illness that makes you believe that other people are trying to harm you: *a patient suffering from paranoid schizophrenia*

par·a·nor·mal /ˌpærəˈnɔːməl◂ $ -ˈnɔːr-/ *adj* **1** paranormal events cannot be explained by science and seem strange and mysterious → **supernatural**: *ghosts and other paranormal phenomena* **2 the paranormal** strange and mysterious events in general: *researchers investigating the paranormal*

par·a·pet /ˈpærəpət, -pet/ *n* [C] **1** a low wall at the edge of a high roof, bridge etc **2** a protective wall of earth or stone built in front of a TRENCH in a war **3 put/stick your head above the parapet** *BrE* to take a risk

par·a·pher·na·li·a /ˌpærəfəˈneɪliə $ -fər-/ *n* [U] **1** a lot of small things that belong to someone, or are needed for a particular activity: *an electric kettle and all the paraphernalia for making tea and coffee* | *travelling paraphernalia* **2** the things and events that are connected with a particular activity, especially those which you think are unnecessary: *all the usual paraphernalia of bureaucracy*

par·a·phrase¹ /ˈpærəfreɪz/ ●○○ *v* [T] to express in a shorter, clearer, or different way what someone has said or written → **summarize**: *To paraphrase Finkelstein, mathematics is a language, like English.*

paraphrase² ●○○ *n* [C] a statement that expresses in a shorter, clearer, or different way what someone has said or written → **summary**

par·a·ple·gia /ˌpærəˈpliːdʒə, -dʒiə/ *n* [U] inability to move your legs and the lower part of your body → **paralysis**

par·a·ple·gic /ˌpærəˈpliːdʒɪk◂/ *n* [C] someone who is unable to move the lower part of their body, including their legs → **paralysed** —**paraplegic** *adj*

par·a·psy·chol·o·gy /ˌpærəsaɪˈkɒlədʒi $ -ˈkɑː-/ *n* [U] the scientific study of mysterious abilities that some people claim to have, such as knowing what will happen in the future

par·a·quat /ˈpærəkwɒt $ -kwɑːt/ *n* [U] a strong poison used to kill WEEDS → **weed killer**

par·a·sail·ing /ˈpærəˌseɪlɪŋ/ *n* [U] a sport in which you wear a PARACHUTE and are pulled behind a motor boat so that you fly through the air

par·as·cend·ing /ˈpærəˌsendɪŋ/ *n* [U] a sport in which you wear a PARACHUTE, and are pulled along by a car so that you go up into the sky and float back down to the ground

par·a·site /ˈpærəsaɪt/ *n* [C] **1** a plant or animal that lives on or in another plant or animal and gets food from it **2** *informal* a lazy person who does not work but depends on other people – used to show disapproval

par·a·sit·ic /ˌpærəˈsɪtɪk◂/ (*also* **par·a·sit·i·cal** /-ˈsɪtɪkəl/) *adj* **1** living in or on another plant or animal and getting food from them: *parasitic fungi* **2** a parasitic person is lazy, does no work, and depends on other people **3** a parasitic disease is caused by parasites —**parasitically** /-kli/ *adv*

par·a·sol /ˈpærəsɒl $ -sɔːl, -sɑːl/ *n* [U] a type of UMBRELLA used to provide shade from the sun

par·a·troop·er /ˈpærəˌtruːpə $ -ər/ *n* [C] a soldier who is trained to jump out of a plane using a PARACHUTE

par·a·troops /ˈpærətruːps/ *n* [plural] a group of paratroopers who fight together as a military unit

par·boil /ˈpɑːbɔɪl $ ˈpɑːr-/ *v* [T] to boil something until it is partly cooked

par·cel¹ /ˈpɑːsəl $ ˈpɑːr-/ ●●○ S3 *n* [C]
1 *especially BrE* an object that has been wrapped in paper or put in a special envelope, especially so that it can be sent by post SYN **package**: *The parcel was delivered last week.* | *He sends regular food parcels to his family in Libya.* | **[+of]** *a parcel of clothes and blankets*
2 an area of land that is part of a larger area which has been divided up: **[+of]** *a parcel of farmland*
3 *BrE* a small quantity of food that has been wrapped up, usually in PASTRY → **be part and parcel of sth** at PART¹(28)

parcel² *v* (**parcelled**, **parcelling** *BrE*, **parceled**, **parceling** *AmE*)

parcel sth ↔ **off** *phr v AmE* to divide something into small parts so that it can be sold: *The new owner has parceled off many of the company's assets.*

parcel sth ↔ **out** *phr v* to divide or share something among several people: *They didn't want the federal government parceling out food supplies.*

parcel sth ↔ **up** *phr v BrE* **1** to make something into a parcel by wrapping it up: *She parcelled up the photos.* **2** to divide something into small parts, especially so that it is easier to deal with: *University education is often parcelled up into specialist teaching units.*

ˈparcel ˌbomb *n* [C] *BrE* a bomb which is wrapped like a parcel and sent by post, and is intended to explode when it is opened → **letter bomb**

ˈparcel post *n* [U] the slowest and cheapest system of sending parcels by post in the US

parch /pɑːtʃ $ pɑːrtʃ/ *v* [T] if the sun or wind parches something, it makes it very dry

parched /pɑːtʃt $ pɑːrtʃt/ *adj* **1** very dry, especially because of hot weather: *the parched African landscape* | *He raised the water bottle to his parched lips.* **2 be parched** *informal* to be very thirsty

Par·chee·si /pɑːˈtʃiːzi $ pɑːr-/ *n* [U] *trademark AmE* a children's game in which you move a small piece of plastic around a board after throwing DICE

parch·ment /ˈpɑːtʃmənt $ ˈpɑːr-/ *n* **1** [U] a material used in the past for writing on, made from the skin of a sheep or a goat **2** [U] thick yellow-white writing paper, sometimes used for official documents **3** [C] a document written on parchment

pard·ner /ˈpɑːdnə $ ˈpɑːrdnər/ *n AmE spoken* used humorously when speaking to someone you know well: *Howdy, pardner!*

par·don¹ /ˈpɑːdn $ ˈpɑːrdn/ ●●● S2 (*also* **ˌpardon ˈme**) *interjection*
1 used when you want someone to repeat something because you did not hear it: *'Hurry up Jonathan!' 'Pardon?' 'I said hurry up!'*
2 *BrE* used to say 'sorry' after you have made an impolite sound such as a BURP SYN **excuse me**

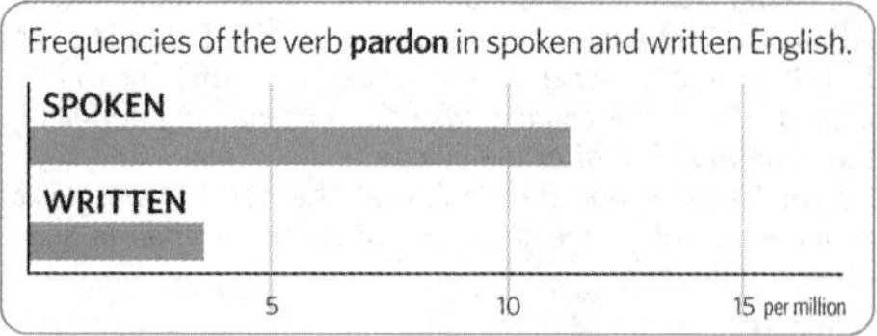

pardon² ●●○ *v* [T]
1 to officially allow someone who has been found guilty of a crime to go free without being punished: *The two spies were pardoned yesterday by the president.*
2 [not in progressive] *formal* to forgive someone for behaving badly SYN **forgive**: **pardon sb for sth** *He could never pardon her for the things she had said.*
3 sb may be pardoned for doing sth used to say that it is easy to understand why someone has done something or why they think something: *Anyone reading the advertisement might be pardoned for thinking that the offer was genuine.*
4 pardon me *spoken* **a)** used to say 'sorry' politely when you have accidentally pushed someone or interrupted them: *Oh, pardon me, I didn't mean to disturb you.* **b)** used to say 'sorry' politely after you have made an impolite sound such as a BURP **c)** used before you politely correct someone or disagree with them: *James, if you'll pardon me,*

you've got it all wrong. **d)** used to politely get someone's attention in order to ask them a question SYN **excuse me**: *Pardon me, can you direct me to City Hall?*
5 pardon me for interrupting/asking/saying *spoken* used to politely ask if you can interrupt someone, ask them a question, or tell them something: *Pardon me for saying so, but you don't look well.*
6 pardon my ignorance/rudeness etc *spoken* used when you want to say something which you think may make you seem not to know enough or not to be polite enough: *Pardon my ignorance, but what does OPEC stand for?*
7 if you'll pardon the expression *spoken* used when you are saying that you are sorry for using an impolite phrase: *It was a bit of a cock-up, if you'll pardon the expression.*
8 pardon my French *spoken* used humorously to say that you are sorry for using a swear word
9 pardon me for breathing/living *spoken* used when you are annoyed because you think someone has answered you angrily for no good reason: *'Shut up, Callum!' 'Well, pardon me for breathing.'*

pardon[3] ●●○ *n* [C]
1 an official order allowing someone who has been found guilty of a crime to go free without being punished: **grant/give sb a pardon** *Tyler was convicted but was granted a* ***royal pardon*** (=one given by a king or queen).
2 ask/beg sb's pardon (for sth) *old-fashioned* to ask someone to forgive you: *Walter begged her pardon for all the pain he had caused her.* → **I beg your pardon** at BEG(4)

par·don·a·ble /ˈpɑːdənəbəl $ ˈpɑːr-/ *adj formal* pardonable mistakes are not very bad and can be forgiven SYN **forgivable**: *He had made the pardonable mistake of trusting the wrong person.* —**pardonably** *adv*

pare /peə $ per/ *v* [T] **1** to cut off the outer layer of something, using a sharp knife: *Pare the rind from the fruit.* **2** to reduce the amount, number, or size of something as much as you can: *The firm has not been able to pare costs fast enough to match competitors.* | *The country's defences have been* ***pared to the bone*** (=reduced as far as possible).
pare sth ↔ **down** *phr v* to reduce something, especially by making a lot of small reductions: *The list was pared down for the final interviews.* —**pared-down** *adj*: *Even in its pared-down form, the contract was unacceptable.*

par·ent /ˈpeərənt $ ˈper-/ ●●● S1 W1 *n* [C]
1 the father or mother of a person or animal: *Children under 14 should be accompanied by a parent.* | *The eggs are guarded by both parents.* | *Melissa's spending the weekend at her parents' house.* → BIRTH PARENT, → **foster parents** at FOSTER[2](3), → **lone parent** at LONE(2), → ONE-PARENT FAMILY, SINGLE PARENT
2 something that produces other things of the same type: *New shoots appear near the parent plant.*
3 a company which owns a smaller company or organization: *Land Rover's new parent*

par·ent·age /ˈpeərəntɪdʒ $ ˈper-/ *n* [U] someone's parents and the country and social class they are from: *an English-born man with Irish parentage* | *He was born in France in 1670* ***of unknown parentage*** (=nobody knows who his parents were).

pa·rent·al /pəˈrentl/ ●○○ *adj* relating to being a parent and especially to being responsible for a child's safety and development: *parental responsibility* | *Opening a new school will increase parental choice.* | *Parental consent is required before the operation can take place.*

paˌrental ˈleave *n* [U] time that a parent is allowed to spend away from work with his or her baby → **paternity leave**

ˈparent ˌcompany *n* [C] a company that controls a smaller company or organization

pa·ren·the·sis /pəˈrenθɪsɪs/ ●○○ *n* (*plural* **parentheses** /-siːz/) [C usually plural]
1 a round BRACKET: **in parentheses** *The figures in parentheses refer to page numbers.*
2 in parenthesis *BrE*, **in parentheses** *AmE* if you say something in parenthesis, you say it while you are talking about something else in order to add information or explain something: *In parenthesis, I should add that the results have not yet been proven.* → PUNCTUATION MARK

par·en·thet·i·cal /ˌpærənˈθetɪkəl◂/ (*also* **par·en·thet·ic** /-ˈθetɪk◂/) *adj formal* said or written while you are talking or writing about something else in order to explain something or add information: *parenthetical references to his childhood* —**parenthetically** /-kli/ *adv*

par·ent·hood /ˈpeərənthʊd $ ˈper-/ *n* [U] the state of being a parent → **motherhood**: *Story-reading should be one of the great joys of parenthood.*

par·ent·ing /ˈpeərəntɪŋ $ ˈper-/ *n* [U] the skill or activity of looking after your own children: *The program aims to teach young men parenting skills.*

ˈparents-in-ˌlaw *n* [plural] the parents of your husband or wife → **mother-in-law**

ˌparent-ˈteacher associˌation *n* [C] a PTA

par ex·cel·lence /ˌpɑːr ˈeksəlɑːns $ -eksəˈlɑːns/ *adj* [only after noun] the very best of a particular thing: *Auguste Escoffier, master chef par excellence*

par·fait /pɑːˈfeɪ $ pɑːr-/ *n* [U] *AmE* a sweet food made of layers of ICE CREAM and fruit

pa·ri·ah /pəˈraɪə, ˈpæriə/ *n* [C] someone who everyone hates and avoids SYN **outcast**

par·i·mu·tu·el /ˌpæriˈmjuːtʃuəl/ *n* **1** [U] a system in which the money that people have risked on a horse race is shared between the people who have won: *parimutuel betting* **2** [C] *AmE* a machine used to calculate the amount of money that people can win when they risk it on horse races

par·ings /ˈpeərɪŋz $ ˈper-/ *n* [plural] *especially BrE* thin narrow pieces of something that have been cut off → **pare**: *nail parings* | *cheese parings*

par·ish /ˈpærɪʃ/ *n* [C] **1** the area that a priest in some Christian churches is responsible for: *Father Doyle moved to a new parish.* **2** *BrE* a small area, especially a village, that has its own local government: *elections to the* ***parish council***

ˌparish ˈchurch *n* [C] *BrE* the main Christian church in a particular area

ˌparish ˈclerk *n* [C] *BrE* an official who works for a Christian church in a particular town or area

pa·rish·ion·er /pəˈrɪʃənə $ -ər/ *n* [C] someone who lives in a parish, especially someone who regularly goes to a Christian church there

ˌparish ˈpump *adj* [only before noun] *BrE old-fashioned* concerned only with what happens in a small local area: *parish pump politics*

ˌparish ˈregister *n* [C] *BrE* an official record of the births, deaths, and marriages in a parish

Pa·ris·i·an /pəˈrɪziən $ pəˈrɪʒən, -ˈriː-/ *n* [C] someone from the city of Paris in France —**Parisian** *adj*

par·i·ty /ˈpærəti/ *n* [U] **1** the state of being equal, especially having equal pay, rights, or power SYN **equality**: **[+with]** *Women workers are demanding parity with their male colleagues.* **2** *technical* equality between the units of money from two different countries

park[1] /pɑːk $ pɑːrk/ ●●● S1 W2 *n* [C]
1 a large open area with grass and trees, especially in a town, where people can walk, play games etc: *Let's go for a walk in the park.* | *a park bench* | *a flat overlooking Hyde Park*
2 a large area of land in the country which has been kept in its natural state to protect the plants and animals there: **national/state/county park** *the Lake District National Park*
3 *BrE* a large enclosed area of land, with grass and trees, around a big house in the countryside
4 the park *BrE informal* the field where a game of football or RUGBY is played SYN **the pitch**: *He was easily the best player on the park.*
5 *AmE informal* the field where a game of baseball is played → AMUSEMENT PARK, BALL PARK(1), CAR PARK, NATIONAL PARK, SAFARI PARK, SCIENCE PARK, THEME PARK, TRAILER PARK

P

park² ●●● S2 *v*
1 [I,T] to put a car or other vehicle in a particular place for a period of time: *You can't park here – it's private property.* | *I couldn't find anywhere to park.* | *She parked the car on the drive.* | *a line of parked cars*
2 [T] *spoken* to put something in a particular place for a period of time, especially in a way that annoys someone: **park sth on/in etc sth** *He parked a load of papers on my desk.*
3 park yourself *informal* to sit down in a particular place, especially with the intention of staying a long time: **[+on/in etc]** *Connie parked herself on the sofa.*
park up *phr v* to put a car or other vehicle in a particular place for a period of time SYN **park**

par·ka /ˈpɑːkə $ ˈpɑːrkə/ *n* [C] a thick warm jacket with a HOOD → **anorak**

ˌpark and ˈride *n* [U] a system in which you leave your car outside a busy town and then take a special bus to the centre of the town

park·ing /ˈpɑːkɪŋ $ ˈpɑːr-/ ●●● S3 *n* [U]
1 the act of parking a car or other vehicle: *No Parking* (=used on signs) | *a £45 parking fine* | **parking space/place/spot** *I couldn't find a parking space near the shops.*
2 spaces in which you can leave a car or other vehicle: *Free parking is available at the hotel.*

ˈparking ˌbrake *n* [C] *AmE* a piece of equipment in a car which prevents it from moving when it is parked SYN **handbrake** *BrE*

ˈparking ˌgarage / $ ˈ...ˌ./ *n* [C] *AmE* a building with open sides in a public place where cars can be parked

ˈparking ˌlight *n* [C] *AmE* one of two small lights next to each of the main lights at the front of a car → see picture at CAR

ˈparking lot ●●● S3 *n* [C] *AmE* an open area for cars to park in SYN **car park** *BrE*

ˈparking ˌmeter *n* [C] a machine at the side of a road which you have to put money into if you park your car next to it

ˈparking ˌticket *n* [C] an official notice fixed to a vehicle, saying that you have to pay money because you have parked your car in the wrong place or for too long

Par·kin·son's dis·ease /ˈpɑːkənsənz dɪˌziːz $ ˈpɑːr-/ (*also* **Parkinson's**) *n* [U] a serious illness in which your muscles become very weak and your arms and legs shake

ˈParkinson's ˌlaw *n* [U] the idea that the amount of work you have to do increases to fill the amount of time you have to do it in – used humorously

ˈpark ˌkeeper *n* [C] someone whose job is to look after a public park in British towns

park·land /ˈpɑːk-lænd $ ˈpɑːrk-/ *n* [U] **1** *BrE* an area of land with grass and trees, surrounding a big house in the countryside: *The hotel is set in ten acres of parkland.* **2** land with grass and trees which is used as a park: *a narrow strip of parkland*

par·kour /pɑːˈkʊə $ pɑːrˈkʊr/ *n* [U] the sport of running through city streets and jumping between buildings SYN **freerunning**

ˈpark ˌranger *n* [C] *AmE* a RANGER(1)

park·way /ˈpɑːkweɪ $ ˈpɑːrk-/ *n* [C] **1** *AmE* a wide road with an area of grass and trees in the middle or along the sides **2** *BrE* used to talk about railway stations that have large areas for cars to park

par·ky /ˈpɑːki $ ˈpɑːrki/ *adj BrE informal* cold SYN **chilly**: *It's a bit parky outside today.*

par·lance /ˈpɑːləns $ ˈpɑːr-/ *n* **1 in medical/advertising etc parlance** expressed in the words that a particular group of people would use: *In military parlance this is known as a fast retreat.* **2 in common parlance** expressed in the words that most people use: *These schemes are known in common parlance as 'private pensions'.*

par·lay /ˈpɑːli $ ˈpɑːrleɪ/ *v* [T] *AmE* to use advantages that you already have, such as your skills, experience, or money, and increase their value by using all your opportunities well: **parlay sth into sth** *He owned five movie theaters, which he eventually parlayed into hotels.*

par·ley /ˈpɑːli $ ˈpɑːrli/ *n* [C] *old-fashioned* a discussion in which enemies try to achieve peace —**parley** *v* [I]

par·lia·ment /ˈpɑːləmənt $ ˈpɑːr-/ ●●● W2 *n*
1 [C] the group of people who are elected to make a country's laws and discuss important national affairs → **government**, **MP**: *They demanded a free parliament and press.*
2 Parliament the main law-making institution in the UK, which consists of the HOUSE OF COMMONS and the HOUSE OF LORDS: **in Parliament** *The government has actually increased its majority in Parliament.* → **HUNG PARLIAMENT**
3 [C] the period during which the British Parliament meets: *We expect to get these laws passed during the present parliament.*

GRAMMAR: Singular or plural verb?

- In meanings 1 and 2, **parliament** is usually followed by a singular verb: *Parliament* ***has*** *been unable to agree.*
- In British English, you can also use a plural verb: *Parliament* ***have*** *been unable to agree.*

GRAMMAR GUIDE ▸ **NOUNS**

COLLOCATIONS – MEANINGS 1 & 2

VERBS

be elected to parliament *She was elected to parliament in 1997.*
stand for parliament (=try to be elected) *Ms Jackson stood for Parliament as a Labour candidate.*
enter/get into parliament (=be elected as a member of parliament) *Tony Blair first entered Parliament in 1983.*
a bill is passed by parliament (=it is made into a law) | **a bill goes through parliament** (=it goes through the process of being made a law) | **go before/be put before parliament** (=be considered by parliament) | **dissolve parliament** *formal* (=officially end parliament before holding an election)

PHRASES

a member of parliament *He was the Conservative member of Parliament for Edgbaston.*
an act of parliament (=a law that has been passed by parliament) *Their rights are guaranteed by Act of Parliament.*
a seat in parliament (=a position as member of parliament) | **a session of parliament** (=when its members are working)

par·lia·men·tar·i·an /ˌpɑːləmənˈteəriən $ ˌpɑːrləmənˈter-/ *n* [C] a member of a parliament, especially one who is very experienced → **MP**

par·lia·men·ta·ry /ˌpɑːləˈmentəri◂ $ ˌpɑːr-/ ●○○ *adj* relating to or governed by a parliament: *the world's oldest parliamentary democracy*

par·lour *BrE*, **parlor** *AmE* /ˈpɑːlə $ ˈpɑːrlər/ *n* [C] **1 ice-cream/funeral/tattoo parlour** a shop or type of business that provides a particular service **2** *old-fashioned* a room in a house which has comfortable chairs and is used for meeting guests → **MILKING PARLOUR**

ˈparlour game *n* [C] *BrE old-fashioned* a game that can be played indoors, such as a guessing game or a word game

ˈparlour maid *n* [C] *BrE* a female servant who was employed in large houses in the past to clean the rooms and serve guests

par·lous /ˈpɑːləs $ ˈpɑːr-/ *adj formal* in a very bad or dangerous condition: *The country's police force was in a* ***parlous state*** *in 1990.*

Par·me·san /ˌpɑːmɪˈzæn◂ $ ˈpɑːrməzɑːn, -zæn/ (*also* **ˌParmesan ˈcheese**) *n* [U] a hard Italian cheese

pa·ro·chi·al /pəˈrəʊkiəl $ -ˈroʊ-/ *adj* **1** only interested in things that affect your local area – used to show disapproval: *Local newspapers tend to be very parochial.* **2** [only before noun] relating to a particular church and the area around it: *the parochial church council* —**parochialism** *n* [U]

pa'rochial ˌschool *n* [C] *AmE* a private school which is run by or connected with a church

par·o·dy¹ /ˈpærədi/ ●○○ *n* (*plural* **parodies**)
1 [C,U] a piece of writing, music etc or an action that copies someone or something in an amusing way: **[+of]** *a brilliant parody of classical dance* | **in a parody of sth** *He swung the door wide open in a parody of welcome.* | *Her performance contains a strong element of* ***self-parody*** (=when someone makes fun of their own style).
2 [C] something that is not a correct or acceptable example of something: **[+of]** *Although his comment was a parody of the truth, Diana was upset by it.* | *The trial was a* ***parody of justice*** (=very unfair).

parody² *v* (**parodied**, **parodying**, **parodies**) [T] to copy someone or something in a way that makes people laugh: *His style has often been parodied.* —**parodist** *n* [C]

pa·role¹ /pəˈrəʊl $ -ˈroʊl/ *n* [U] permission for someone to leave prison, on the condition that they promise to behave well: **on parole** *He was* ***released on parole*** *after serving two years.* | *She will become* ***eligible for parole*** *in 19 months.*

parole² *v* [T] to allow someone to leave prison on the condition that they promise to behave well

pa'role ˌboard *n* [C] the people who decide if a prisoner should get permission to leave prison

par·ox·ys·m /ˈpærəksɪzəm/ *n* [C] **1** a sudden expression of strong feeling that you cannot control: **[+of]** *Had she cut her wrists in a paroxysm of guilt?* **2** a sudden, short attack of pain, coughing, shaking etc

par·quet /ˈpɑːkeɪ, ˈpɑːki $ pɑːrˈkeɪ/ *n* [U] small flat blocks of wood fitted together in a pattern that cover the floor of a room: *a parquet floor*

par·ri·cide /ˈpærɪsaɪd/ *n* [U] *formal* the crime of killing your father, mother, or any other close relative → **matricide**, **patricide**

par·rot¹ /ˈpærət/ ●●○ *n* [C]
1 a tropical bird with a curved beak and brightly coloured feathers that can be taught to copy human speech
2 parrot fashion *BrE* if you learn something parrot fashion, you repeat what someone has just said without understanding it → **by heart**: *We recited poems parrot fashion.*
→ **sick as a parrot** at SICK¹(10)

parrot² *v* [T] to repeat someone else's words or ideas without really understanding what you are saying – used to show disapproval: *He just parroted his father's opinions.*

par·ry /ˈpæri/ *v* (**parried**, **parrying**, **parries**) **1** [I,T] to defend yourself against someone who is attacking you by pushing their weapon or hand to one side SYN **deflect**: *It is far easier to parry a direct blow than to stop it forcibly.* **2** [T] to avoid answering a question that is difficult to answer or that someone does not want to answer: *He parried all her questions about his work.* —**parry** *n* [C]

parse /pɑːz $ pɑːrs/ *v* [T] *technical* to describe the grammar of a word when it is in a particular sentence, or the grammar of the whole sentence —**parser** *n* [C]

Par·see, **Parsi** /pɑːˈsiː $ ˈpɑːrsiː/ *n* [C] a member of an ancient Persian religious group in India —**Parsee** *adj*

par·si·mo·ni·ous /ˌpɑːsəˈməʊniəs◂ $ ˌpɑːrsəˈmoʊ-/ *adj formal* extremely unwilling to spend money —**parsimoniously** *adv* —**parsimony** /ˈpɑːsəməni $ ˈpɑːrsəmoʊni/ *n* [U]

pars·ley /ˈpɑːsli $ ˈpɑːr-/ *n* [U] a herb with curly leaves, used in cooking or as decoration on food

pars·nip /ˈpɑːsnɪp $ ˈpɑːr-/ *n* [C,U] a vegetable with a thick white or yellowish root → see picture at VEGETABLE¹

par·son /ˈpɑːsən $ ˈpɑːr-/ *n* [C] *old-fashioned* a Christian priest or minister

par·son·age /ˈpɑːsənɪdʒ $ ˈpɑːr-/ *n* [C] the house where a parson lives

ˌparson's 'nose *n* [C] *BrE informal* the piece of flesh at the tail end of a bird, usually a chicken, that has been cooked SYN **pope's nose** *AmE*

part¹ /pɑːt $ pɑːrt/ ●●● S1 W1 *n*
1 PIECE [C] a piece or feature of something such as an object, area, event, or period of time: **[+of]** *The front part of the car was damaged.* | *In parts of Canada, French is the first language.* | *The cost of living is becoming unbearable for retired people in our* ***part of the world*** (=where we live). | *More heat is lost through the head than any other* ***part of the body***. | **the early/later/latter/last part** *in the early part of the 19th century* | **the best/worst part** *The best part of the holiday was the food.* | **the first/final/last part etc** *You can see the final part of that series on Tuesday.* | **part two/three etc** *I shall be explaining this further in Part Two.* | **the hard/easy part** *Getting Dad to agree will be the hard part.* | **different parts/all parts of sth** *The jobs attracted people from all parts of the world.* | **integral/vital/important part** *the traditions that are an integral part of Jewish life* | **in parts** *The film is very violent in parts.*
2 MACHINE/OBJECT [C] one of the separate pieces that something such as a machine or piece of equipment is made of: *Lay all the parts out before you start assembling the model.* | *engine parts* | **spare parts** (=kept for when a part breaks, needs replacing etc)
3 NOT ALL **part of sth** some, but not all, of a particular thing: *Part of the money will be spent on a new playground.* | *Part of the castle was destroyed by fire.* | *For part of the day, you will be outside doing practical work.* | **part of me/him etc** *Part of me hates him* (=I partly hate him). | **(only) part of the story/problem/explanation etc** *Poor working conditions are only part of the problem.* ⚠ Don't say '(the) most part of'. Say **most of**: *We spent most of (NOT most part of) the morning shopping.*
4 INVOLVEMENT **play a part** if something or someone plays a part in something else, they are involved in it: **[+in]** *Health education will play a part in preparing us for old age.* | *Britain should* ***play its full part*** *in the negotiations.* | **play a big/important part in sth** *Pictures play an important part in publishing.*
5 have a part to play (in sth) to have a particular job or be responsible for something: *The church used to have a more important part to play in the community.*
6 take part to be involved in an activity, sport, event etc with other people: **[+in]** *About 400 students took part in the protest.* | *She wanted to take part but she was too ill.* | **take an active/leading part** *At college I took an active part in student politics.* ⚠ Don't say 'take a part in' something. Say **take part in** something.
7 take/have/play no part in sth to not be involved in something: *She took no part in the fighting.*
8 want no part of sth to not want to be involved in something: *There was a plan to change the production style, and he wanted no part of it.*
9 the best/better part of sth nearly all of something: *We waited for the best part of an hour.*
10 a good/large part of sth a lot or more than half of something: *A large part of the budget will be spent on advertising.*
11 the greater/major part of sth most of something: *They controlled the greater part of North Africa.*
12 in part to some degree, but not completely SYN **partly**: *His reluctance to help could, in part, be explained by his poor eyesight.*
13 in large part/for the most part mostly, or in most places: *Success was due in large part to good teamwork.* | *For the most part he worked patiently.*
14 be (a) part of sth to be included or involved in something: *Falling over is part of learning how to ski.* | *If you decide to work for our organisation, you will be part of a great team.*
15 form (a) part of sth to be one of the things that make up something larger or more important: *Practical work* ***forms an integral part of*** *the course.*
16 HAIR [C usually singular] *AmE* a PARTING
17 ACTING [C] the words and actions of a particular character in a play or film SYN **role**: *Could someone* ***take the part of*** *Romeo, please?* | *Katharine's* ***playing the part of*** *Mary in the school play.*
18 MUSIC [C] the music that one type of instrument or

voice within a group plays or sings: *The violin part is difficult.* | *The choir sings in four-part harmony.*
19 QUANTITY [C] used to say how much of each substance there is or should be in a mixture: *Prepare the glue with one **part** powder **to** three **parts** water.* | *The sulphur dioxide level in the air was 32 parts per billion.*
20 look the part a) to look like a typical person of a particular type: *In his smart suit, he certainly looked the part.* **b)** to perform well and seem likely to be successful – used in sports reports: *He's beginning to look the part on the soccer field.*
21 dress the part to wear suitable clothes for something: *She's got a new high-powered job, and she's certainly dressing the part.*
22 sb's part in sth what a particular person did in an activity that was shared by several people, especially something bad: *He was imprisoned for six years for his part in the murder.*
23 in/round these parts in the particular area that you are in: *We don't get many tourists in these parts.*
24 take sb's part *BrE formal* to support someone in a quarrel or argument (SYN) **take sb's side**: *Dad always takes my brother's part when we argue.*
25 for my/his part etc *formal* used when saying what a particular person thinks or does, as opposed to other people: *For my part, I prefer living in the country.*
26 on sb's part/on the part of sb used when describing a particular person's feelings or actions: *It was probably just a mistake on her part.* | *There has never been any jealousy on my part.*
27 take sth in good part *old-fashioned* to accept jokes or criticism about you without being upset
28 be part and parcel of sth to be a necessary feature of something: *Working irregular hours is all part and parcel of being a journalist.*
29 be/become part of the furniture to have been in a place for so long that people no longer notice you
30 man/woman of many parts someone who is able to do many different things: *He was a man of many parts: writer, literary critic and historian.*

THESAURUS

part something that together with other things forms a whole: *It looks like part of a car engine.* | *The best part of the movie was the end.* | *The hardest part is getting started.*
bit *especially BrE informal* a small part of something: *Some bits of the book are really funny.* | *I didn't read the bottom bit.*
piece one of several different parts that you join together to make something: *One of the pieces of the jigsaw puzzle was missing.* | *The furniture comes in several pieces.*
component a part of a machine or process: *The company supplies engine components for trucks.* | *Education is a major component in a child's growth and development.*
section a part of something that is clearly different and separate from other parts: *The test is divided into two sections.* | *the reference section of the library* | *the string section of the orchestra*
chapter one of the numbered parts that a book is divided into: *The opening chapter of the book sets the scene.*
scene one of the parts that a film or play is divided into: *Some scenes had to be cut because they were too violent.* | *act 1, scene 2 of the play*
episode a part of a story on the television or the radio, which is told in separate parts: *I missed last week's episode.*

part² ●○○ *v*
1 [I,T] *written* to move the two sides of something apart, or to move apart, making a space in the middle: *When he parted the curtains, the sunlight flooded into the room.* | *The crowd parted to let him through.* | *Ralph's lips parted in a delighted smile.*
2 [I] *written* to separate from someone, or end a relationship with them: *They parted on amicable terms.* | **[+from]** *He has parted from his wife.*
3 be parted (from sb) to be prevented from being with someone: *They were hardly ever parted in 30 years of marriage.* | *He hates being parted from the children.*
4 part company (with sb) a) to go in different directions after having gone in the same direction: *The two women parted company outside their rooms.* **b)** to end a relationship with someone: *George parted company with the band in 1996.* **c)** to disagree with someone about something: *He parted company with Lloyd George over post-war diplomacy.*
5 [T] if you part your hair, you comb some of your hair in one direction and the rest in the other direction
part with sth *phr v* to give something to someone else, although you do not want to: *I'm reluctant to part with any of the kittens, but we need the money.*

part³ *adv* **1 part sth, part sth** if something is part one thing, part another, it consists of both of those things: *The exams are part written, part practical.* | *The room is part sitting room, part bedroom.* **2** not completely (SYN) **partly**: *The project is part funded by the council.* | *The object was part hidden by the grass.*

part⁴ *adj* **1 part payment** payment of only a part of something, not all of it: *I gave them £10 in part payment.* **2 part owner** someone who is one of the people who own something

par·take /pɑːˈteɪk $ pɑːr-/ *v* (*past tense* **partook** /-ˈtʊk/, *past participle* **partaken** /-ˈteɪkən/) [I] *formal* **1** to eat or drink something: **[+of]** *Grandmother likes to partake of a small glass of sherry before lunch.* **2** to take part in an activity or event (SYN) **participate**: **[+in]** *a woman's fundamental right to partake in club affairs*
partake of sth *phr v formal* to have a certain amount of a particular quality

par·terre /pɑːˈteə $ pɑːrˈter/ *n* [C] *formal* a part of a garden with areas of flowers surrounded by low HEDGES in a formal pattern

ˌpart exˈchange *n* [C,U] *BrE* a way of buying a new car, television etc in which you give your old car, television etc as part of the payment (SYN) **trade in** *AmE*: *The company **takes** the buyer's property **in part exchange**.*

par·the·no·gen·e·sis /ˌpɑːθɪnəʊˈdʒenɪsɪs $ ˌpɑːrθənoʊ-/ *n* [U] *technical* the production of a new plant or animal from a female without the sexual involvement of the male

par·tial /ˈpɑːʃəl $ ˈpɑːr-/ ●○○ *adj*
1 not complete: *The exhibition was only a partial success.* | *a partial solution to traffic congestion in Oxford*
2 be partial to sth *formal* to like something very much: *I'm very partial to cream cakes.*
3 unfairly supporting one person or one group against another (OPP) **impartial**

par·ti·al·i·ty /ˌpɑːʃiˈæləti $ ˌpɑːr-/ *n* [U] **1** unfair support of one person or one group against another (SYN) **bias**: *the problem of partiality in news reporting* **2 partiality for sth** *formal* a special liking for something: *a partiality for Moorish architecture*

par·tial·ly /ˈpɑːʃəli $ ˈpɑːr-/ ●○○ *adv formal* not completely (SYN) **partly**: *The operation was only partially successful.* | *Remember that you are partially responsible for their unhappiness.*

ˌpartially ˈsighted *adj* unable to see well → **blind**: *Reading aids have been provided for partially sighted pupils.*

par·tic·i·pant /pɑːˈtɪsəpənt $ pɑːr-/ ●●○ (AWL) *n* [C] someone who is taking part in an activity or event: **[+in]** *an **active participant** in the negotiations*

par·tic·i·pate /pɑːˈtɪsəpeɪt $ pɑːr-/ ●●○ (W3) (AWL) *v* [I] *formal* to take part in an activity or event: *Some members refused to participate.* | **[+in]** *Everyone in the class is expected to **participate actively** in these discussions.* | *They welcomed the opportunity to **participate fully** in the life of the village.* ⚠ **Participate** is never followed immediately by a noun, or by 'on' or 'to'. Say that you **participate in** something: *More people should participate in elections (NOT More people should participate elections).*

THESAURUS

participate *formal* to do an activity together with other people: *He always participates in classroom activities. | The people should have the right to participate in discussions about their future.*
take part to participate in something. **Take part** is less formal that **participate** and is more common in everyday English: *Nearly 500 teams took part in the competition. | She was asked to take part in a TV debate on drugs. | Anyone who is over 18 can take part.*
play a part/role to take part in something in a useful way: *Everyone can play a part in improving the security of their neighborhood. | Schneider played a key role in getting the organization started.*
be involved to take part in an activity in some way: *He has denied being involved in the murder. | It was a big project and many people were involved.*
be active in sth to actively take part in the work of an organization such as a political group or church: *He is very active in the church's work with homeless people. | She is no longer active in politics.*
compete to take part in a competition or race: *Athletes from all over the world will be competing. | She's hoping to compete in the Olympic Games.*

par·ti·ci·pa·tion /pɑːˌtɪsəˈpeɪʃən $ pɑːr-/ ●●○ AWL *n* [U] the act of taking part in an activity or event SYN **involvement**: *Thank you for your participation.* | **[+in]** *We want more participation in the decision-making. | entertainment with plenty of* ***audience participation***

par·ti·ci·pa·tory /pɑːˌtɪsəˈpeɪtəri◂ $ pɑːrˈtɪsəpətɔːri/, **participative** /pɑːˌtɪsəpeɪtɪv/ AWL *adj* [usually before noun] *formal* a participatory way of organizing something, making decisions etc is one that involves everyone who will be affected: *a participatory democracy*

par·ti·cip·i·al /ˌpɑːtəˈsɪpiəl $ ˌpɑːr-/ *adj technical* using a participle, or having the form of a participle

par·ti·ci·ple /ˈpɑːtəsɪpəl, pɑːˈtɪsəpəl $ ˈpɑːr-/ ●●○ *n* [C] *technical* one of the forms of a verb that are used to make tenses. In English, PRESENT PARTICIPLES end in -ing and PAST PARTICIPLES usually end in -ed or -en.

par·ti·cle /ˈpɑːtɪkəl $ ˈpɑːr-/ ●○○ *n* [C]
1 a very small piece of something: *dust particles* | **[+of]** *tiny particles of soil*
2 not a particle of truth/evidence etc no truth etc at all: *There's not a particle of truth in what he says.*
3 one of the very small pieces of matter that an atom consists of
4 *technical* an adverb or PREPOSITION that can combine with a verb to form a PHRASAL VERB

ˈparticle acˌcelerator *n* [C] a machine used in scientific studies which makes the very small pieces of matter that atoms are made of move at high speeds

ˈparticle ˌphysics *n* [U] the study of the way that parts of atoms develop and behave

par·tic·u·lar¹ /pəˈtɪkjələ $ pərˈtɪkjələr/ ●●● S1 W1 *adj*
1 [only before noun] a particular thing or person is the one that you are talking about, and not any other → **certain**, **specific**: *In this particular case, no one else was involved. | Most students choose one particular area for research. | a particular type of food*
2 special or great: *You should pay particular attention to spelling. | For* ***no particular reason****, he quit the job.* | **of particular interest/concern/importance etc** *Of particular concern is the rising cost of transportation.* | **anything/nothing/something particular** *I had nothing particular planned.*
3 very careful about choosing exactly what you like and not easily satisfied SYN **fussy**: **[+about]** *Marty's very particular about his food.*

particular² ●●○ *n*
1 in particular especially: *It was a good concert – I enjoyed the last song in particular.* | **anything/anyone/anywhere in particular** *Was there anything in particular that you wanted to talk about?* | **nothing/no one/nowhere in particular** *'What did you want?' 'Oh, nothing in particular.'*
2 particulars [plural] the facts and details about a job, property, legal case etc: **[+of]** *You may be required to* ***give particulars*** *of the change in your financial position. | For* ***further particulars****, contact the College secretary. | Send your particulars* (=details such as your name, address, profession etc) *to the address above.*
3 in every particular/in all particulars *formal* in every detail: *The documents were identical in almost every particular.*

par·tic·u·lar·i·ty /pəˌtɪkjəˈlærəti $ pər-/ *n* (*plural* **particularities**) *formal* **1** [U] a quality that makes something different from all others: *the particularity of her style of writing* **2** [U] the quality of being exact and paying attention to details **3** [C] a detail

par·tic·u·lar·ize (*also* **-ise** *BrE*) /pəˈtɪkjələraɪz $ pər-/ *v* [I,T] *formal* to give the details of something SYN **itemize**

par·tic·u·lar·ly /pəˈtɪkjələli $ pərˈtɪkjələrli/ ●●● S1 W1 *adv*
1 more than usual or more than others SYN **especially**: *Steve was in a particularly bad mood when he got back. | The restaurant is particularly popular with young people. | We are hoping to expand our business, particularly in Europe. | British farmers, particularly those producing lamb, are very worried.*
2 not particularly a) not very: *I'm not particularly impressed with their performance.* **b)** *spoken* not very much: *'Do you want to come to the party?' 'Not particularly.'*

par·tic·u·lates /pəˈtɪkjələts, -leɪts $ pər-/ *n* [plural] harmful dust in the air, especially produced by car engines

part·ing¹ /ˈpɑːtɪŋ $ ˈpɑːr-/ *n* **1** [C,U] an occasion when two people leave each other: *an emotional parting at the airport | the moment of parting* | **on parting** *He gave her a light kiss on parting.* **2** [C] *BrE* the line on your head made by dividing your hair with a comb SYN **part** *AmE*: *a centre parting* **3 parting of the ways** the point at which two people or organizations decide to separate

parting² *adj* **1 a parting kiss/gift/glance etc** a kiss etc that you give someone as you leave **2 parting shot** an unpleasant remark that you make just as you are leaving, especially at the end of an argument: *As her parting shot, she told me never to phone her again.*

par·ti·san¹ /ˌpɑːtɪˈzæn $ ˈpɑːrtəzən, -sən/ *adj* **1** strongly supporting a particular political party, plan, or leader, usually without considering the other choices carefully: *British newspapers are* ***highly partisan****.* **2** relating to the fighting of an armed group against an enemy that has taken control of its country: *the nature of partisan warfare*

partisan² *n* [C] **1** someone who strongly supports a political party, plan, or leader: *a media campaign to represent Democrats as angry partisans* **2** a member of an armed group that fights against an enemy that has taken control of its country —**partisanship** *n* [U]

par·ti·tion¹ /pɑːˈtɪʃən $ pər-, pɑːr-/ *n* **1** [C] a thin wall that separates one part of a room from another **2** [U] the action of separating a country into two or more independent countries: **[+of]** *the partition of India*

partition² *v* [T + into] to divide a country, building, or room into two or more parts

partition sth ↔ **off** *phr v* to divide part of a room from the rest by using a partition: *They partitioned off part of the living room to make a study.*

par·ti·tive /ˈpɑːtətɪv $ ˈpɑːr-/ *n* [C] *technical* a word which comes before a noun and shows that only part of something is being described, for example the word 'some' in the phrase 'some of the cake' —**partitive** *adj*

part·ly /ˈpɑːtli $ ˈpɑːr-/ ●●● S2 W2 *adv* to some degree, but not completely OPP **wholly**: *The poor weather was* ***partly responsible*** *for the crash. | The company's problems are* ***partly due to*** *bad management. | It is* ***partly because***

of her sick mother that she hasn't taken the job abroad. | *The group is funded partly by the government.*

part·ner¹ /ˈpɑːtnə $ ˈpɑːrtnər/ ●●● S2 W2 AWL *n* [C]

1 MARRIAGE ETC one of two people who are married, or who live together and have a sexual relationship → **husband**, **wife**: *Discuss your worries with your partner.* | *Only 29% of lone parents receive financial support from their **former partners**.* | *a sexual partner* THESAURUS MARRIED

2 BUSINESS one of the owners of a business: *She's a partner in a law firm.* | *The **senior partner** has retired.* → SLEEPING PARTNER

3 DANCING/GAMES ETC someone you do a particular activity with, for example dancing or playing a game against two other people: *Clare's my tennis partner.* | ***Take** your **partners** for the next dance.*

4 COUNTRY/ORGANIZATION a country or organization that another country or organization has an agreement with: *Nigeria is our principal **trading partner** in Africa.* | *The group is a **junior partner*** (=less important group) *in the PLO's governing coalition.*

5 partners in crime two people who have planned and done something together, especially something that slightly annoys other people – used humorously → SPARRING PARTNER

partner² *v* [T] to be someone's partner in a dance, game etc: *I used to partner him in tennis matches.*

part·ner·ship /ˈpɑːtnəʃɪp $ ˈpɑːrtnər-/ ●●○ W3 AWL *n*

1 [U] the state of being a partner in business: **be/work in partnership (with sb)** *I've been in partnership with her for five years.* | *She's **gone into partnership with** two local doctors.*

2 [C] a business owned by two or more people: *It's one of the most **successful partnerships** in the country.*

3 [C,U] a relationship between two people, organizations, or countries: *Several youth charities have **formed a partnership** to help these homeless teenagers.* | **[+between]** *The **close partnership** between Britain and the US will continue.*

ˌpart of ˈspeech ●●○ *n* (*plural* **parts of speech**) [C] *technical* one of the types into which words are divided in grammar according to their use, such as noun, verb, or adjective

par·took /pɑːˈtʊk $ pɑːr-/ *v* the past tense of PARTAKE

par·tridge /ˈpɑːtrɪdʒ $ ˈpɑːr-/ *n* [C] a fat brown bird with a short tail which is shot for sport and food

ˈpart-song *n* [C] *technical* a song that consists of several voice parts, usually singing without a piano etc

ˌpart-ˈtime ●●○ *adj* [only before noun] someone who has a part-time job works for only part of each day or week: *a part-time job* | *women wishing to return to work **on a part-time basis*** —**part-time** *adv*: *She wants to **work part-time** after she's had the baby.* —**part-timer** *n* [C] → FULL-TIME(1)

part·way /ˈpɑːtweɪ $ ˈpɑːrt-/ *adv informal* for some of the distance or after some of the time has passed → **halfway**: *I got the bus partway.* | **[+through/along/down]** *She left partway through the two-year contract.*

par·ty¹ /ˈpɑːti $ ˈpɑːrti/ ●●● S1 W1 *n* (*plural* **parties**) [C]

1 FOR FUN a social event when a lot of people meet together to enjoy themselves by eating, drinking, dancing etc: *We're **having** a small **party** this evening to celebrate our wedding anniversary.* | **throw/give a party** *The university threw a party to welcome them.* | **go/come to a party** *Are you going to the party tonight?* | **at a party** *I met John at a party a couple of months ago.* | *the **party spirit*** (=the way someone feels when they are really enjoying a party) → HEN PARTY, HOUSE PARTY, STAG PARTY, PARTY ANIMAL → see Thesaurus box on p. 1327

2 IN POLITICS a political organization with particular beliefs and aims, which you can vote for in elections: *I have always voted for the Labour Party.* | *He failed to win the party's nomination for president.* | *The conference is open to all party members.* → PARTY LINE THESAURUS ORGANIZATION

3 GROUP OF PEOPLE a group of people who go somewhere together or do a job together: **[+of]** *a party of tourists* | *There were several students in our party.* | *A **search party** was sent out to look for the missing climbers.* | *a **rescue party*** | *Admission is free for **school parties**.* → WORKING PARTY THESAURUS GROUP

GRAMMAR: Singular or plural verb?

- In meanings 2 and 3, **party** is usually followed by a singular verb: *The party **has** accepted the need for change.*
- In British English, you can also use a plural verb: *The party **have** accepted the need for change.*

GRAMMAR GUIDE NOUNS

4 IN AN ARGUMENT/LAW *law or formal* one of the people or groups who are involved in a legal argument or agreement: *helping the two parties to reach an agreement* | **guilty/innocent party** *He sees himself as the innocent party in this dispute.* → THIRD PARTY¹

5 be (a) party to sth *formal* to be involved in an activity or decision: *I was not a party to this discussion.*

COLLOCATIONS – MEANING 2

ADJECTIVES/NOUN + party

a political party *The Labour Party and the Conservative Party are the two main political parties in Britain.*
the Labour/Democratic etc Party *The leadership race within the Republican Party is almost over.*
an opposition party (=a party that is not in power) *The tax increase was criticized by opposition parties.*
the ruling party (=the party in power) | **a right-wing/left-wing party**

party + NOUN

a party member *He's been a Conservative party member for 20 years.*
the party leader *He met with opposition party leaders.*
a party candidate (=someone who represents a political party in an election) | **the party faithful** (=strong supporters of a party) | **a party activist** (=someone who works hard for a party) | **party policy** (=a political party's official plan or position on important subjects) | **a party conference** | **the party chairman** *BrE*

VERBS

a party wins/loses an election *Do you think the Labour Party can win the next election?*
join a party | **form/found a party**

PHRASES

a party is in power *From 1945 until 1951 the Labour Party was in power in Britain.*
a party comes to power (=begins to be the government)

party² *v* (**partied**, **partying**, **parties**) [I] *informal* to enjoy yourself with a group of other people by drinking alcohol, eating, dancing etc: *Let's party!*

ˈparty ˌanimal *n* [C] *informal* someone who enjoys going to parties and drinking a lot of alcohol, and behaving in a loud and often rude way

ˈparty ˌfavor *n* [C] *AmE* a small gift that people give to children at a party

par·ty·go·er /ˈpɑːtiˌgəʊə $ ˈpɑːrtiˌgoʊər/ *n* [C] someone who is at a party: *young partygoers*

ˈparty line *n* [singular] the official opinion of a political party or other organization, which its members are expected to agree with and support: **follow/toe the party line** (=to support the official opinion) *He refused to toe the party line.*

ˈparty ˌpiece *n* [C] *BrE* a song, dance etc that you often perform to entertain people at parties

ˌparty poˈlitical *adj* [only before noun] *BrE* relating to activities in which people try to get support for one political party in a country: *a **party political broadcast** on television* | *party political propaganda*

ˌparty ˈpolitics *n* [U] activities that are concerned with getting support for one political party in a country: *The decision was influenced by party politics.*

party poop·er /ˈpɑːti ˌpuːpə $ ˈpɑːrti ˌpuːpər/ *n* [C] *informal* someone who spoils other people's fun

ˌparty ˈwall *n* [C] a dividing wall between two houses, apartments etc

par·ve·nu /ˈpɑːvənjuː $ ˈpɑːrvənuː/ *n* [C] *formal old-fashioned* an insulting word for someone from a low social position who has suddenly become rich and powerful

pas de deux /ˌpɑː də ˈdɜː $ -ˈduː/ *n* (*plural* **pas de deux** (*same pronunciation*)) [C] a dance in BALLET performed by a man and a woman

pash·mi·na /pæʃˈmiːnə/ *n* [C] a piece of soft cloth that is worn by women around their shoulders → **shawl**

pass¹ /pɑːs $ pæs/ ●●● S1 W1 *v*

1 GO PAST [I,T] to come up to a particular place, person, or object and go past them: *The crowd parted to let the truck pass.* | *He gave me a smile as he passed.* | *We passed a group of students outside the theatre.* | *I pass the sports centre on the way to work.*

2 MOVE/GO [I always + adv/prep] to go or travel along or through a place: *He passed along the corridor to a small room at the back of the building.* | *We passed through the gates into a courtyard behind.* | *We were **just passing through*** (=travelling through a place) *and thought we'd drop in to see you.*

3 PUT [T always + adv/prep] to put something around, through, or across something else: *He passed the rope carefully around the post.*

4 ROAD/RIVER ETC [I always + adv/prep, T] a road, river, or railway line that passes a place goes through or near the place: *The road **passes** right **through** the town centre.* | *The main railway line passes just north of Manchester.*

5 GIVE [T] to hold something in your hand and give it to someone else: *Pass the salt, please.* | **pass sb sth** *Can you pass me that bag by your feet?* | **pass sth to sb** *She passed a cup of tea to the headmaster.* | *I passed the note back to her.* → **pass around**

6 GIVE INFORMATION [T always + adv/prep] to give information or a job to another person so that they can deal with it: **pass sth (on/over/back) to sb** *I'll pass the information on to our sales department.* | *They've passed the enquiry over to the police.*

7 TIME **a)** [I] if time passes, it goes by: *The days passed slowly.* | *She became more ambitious as the years passed.* | *They sat in silence while the minutes passed.* | ***Hardly a day passes without*** more bad news about the economy (=there is bad news almost every day). **b)** [T] if you pass time or pass your life in a particular way, you spend it in that way: *We passed the winter pleasantly enough.* | *We played cards **to pass the time*** (=to help us stop feeling bored).

> **REGISTER**
> In everyday English, people usually say that they **spend** time doing something rather than **pass** time:
> *I **spent** the whole day watching TV.*

8 EXAM/TEST **a)** [I,T] to succeed in an examination or test OPP **fail**: *Did you pass all your exams?* | *He hasn't passed his driving test yet.* | *She **passed with flying colours*** (=got very high marks). **b)** [T] to officially decide that someone has succeeded in an examination or test OPP **fail**: *The examiners will only pass you if they feel that you have done the work properly.*

9 LAW/PROPOSAL **a)** [T] to officially accept a law or proposal, especially by voting: *Plans to extend the hotel have now been passed.* | *The motion was passed by 16 votes to 11.* | **pass a law/bill/act** *The first Transport Act was passed in 1907.* | *The government has **passed** new **legislation** to protect consumers.* | *The United Nations Security Council has **passed a resolution** asking the two countries to resume peace negotiations.* **b)** [I,T] *especially AmE* if a law or proposal passes an official group, it is officially accepted by that group: *The bill failed to pass the House of Representatives.* THESAURUS ▶ APPROVE

10 HAPPEN [I always + adv/prep] *written* if something passes between people, they speak to each other or do something together: **[+between]** *A glance of recognition passed between them.* | *Please say nothing of what has passed here today.*

11 SAY **pass a remark/comment** to say something that gives your opinion: *I'm afraid I can't pass any comment on this matter.* | *He passed some remark about doctors being paid too much.*

12 **let sth pass** to deliberately not say anything when someone says or does something that you do not like: *Carla made some comment about my work but I decided to **let it pass**.*

13 END [I] to end or stop: *After a couple of hours the storm passed.* | *The feeling of sickness soon passed.*

14 SPORT [I,T] to kick, throw, or hit a ball to a member of your own team during a game: **[+to]** *He passed to Beckham on the edge of the penalty area.* | **pass sth to sb** *Are you allowed to pass the ball back to the goalkeeper?* → see picture at BASKETBALL THESAURUS ▶ THROW

15 MORE THAN [T] to become more than a particular number or amount: *The number of unemployed has **passed** the two million **mark** for the first time.*

> **THESAURUS: party**
>
> **party** a social event when a lot of people meet together to enjoy themselves by eating, drinking, dancing etc: *We're having a party for Sarah's 40th birthday.*
> **get-together** an informal party: *Christmas is the perfect time for a family get-together.*
> **ball** a large formal party where people dance: *the end of term ball*
> **reception** a large formal party, especially one after a wedding or to welcome an important person: *The wedding reception is at a nearby hotel.* | *a reception for the Thai Foreign Minister*
> **function** a large formal or official party: *He has been asked to play at many corporate functions* (=an official party held by a company).
> **celebration** a party or special event that is organized in order to celebrate something: *the country's 50th anniversary celebrations*
> **bash** *informal* a party, especially a big one that a lot of famous people go to – used especially in journalism: *the star's birthday bash* | *a picture of him at a Hollywood bash*
> **do** *BrE informal* a party: *We're having a do to celebrate Margaret's birthday.*
> **dinner party** a party where people are invited to someone's house for an evening meal: *I met him at a dinner party.*
> **house-warming (party)** a party that you have when you move into a new house
> **cocktail party** (*also* **drinks party** *BrE*) a party that people go to in order to talk and have a drink together for a few hours
> **fancy-dress party** *BrE*, **costume party** *AmE* a party where people dress in special clothes, for example to look like a famous person or a character in a story
> **hen party** *especially BrE* a social event just before a wedding, for a woman who is getting married and her female friends
> **stag night** *BrE*, **bachelor party** *AmE* a social event just before a wedding, for a man who is getting married and his male friends
> **baby/wedding shower** *AmE* an event at which people give presents to a woman who is going to have a baby or get married

P

16 pass unnoticed to happen without anyone noticing or saying anything: *His resignation passed largely unnoticed.*
17 pass the time of day (with sb) to talk to someone for a short time in order to be friendly
18 CHANGE CONTROL [I always + prep] *formal* to change from being controlled or owned by one person to being controlled or owned by someone else: **[+to]** *The land will pass to my son when I die.* | *Control of these services has now **passed into the hands of** the local authorities.*
19 CHANGE [I always + prep] *formal* to change from one state or condition into another: **[+from/to]** *The chemical passes from a liquid to a solid state during the cooling process.*
20 pass (a) sentence (on sb) to officially decide how a criminal will be punished, and to announce what the punishment will be: *Judges no longer have the power to pass the death sentence.*
21 pass judgment (on sb) to give your opinion about someone's behaviour: *I don't want to pass judgment on my colleagues.*
22 GIVE NO ANSWER [I] to give no answer to a question because you do not know the answer: *'Who won the World Cup in 1998?' 'Pass.'*
23 NOT ACCEPT [I] to not accept an invitation or offer: **[+on]** *I'm afraid I'll have to pass on that offer of coffee.*
24 not pass sb's lips *humorous* **a)** used to say that someone does not talk about something that is secret: *Don't worry. Not a word of this will pass my lips.* **b)** used to say that someone does not eat or drink a particular thing: *Not a drop of liquor has passed my lips.*
25 WASTE MATTER [T] *medical* to let out a waste substance from your BLADDER or BOWELS: *See your doctor immediately if you pass any blood.* | *He was having difficulty **passing water*** (=letting out URINE).
26 come to pass *literary or biblical* to happen → **pass muster** at MUSTER[2](1), → **pass the buck** at BUCK[1](3)
pass sth ↔ **around** (*also* **pass sth ↔ round** *BrE*) *phr v* to offer or show something to each person in a group: *Pass the cookies around, would you?* → **pass the hat round/around** at HAT(6)
pass as sb/sth *phr v* if someone or something can pass as someone or something, they are similar enough to be accepted as that type of person or thing: *His French is so good that he can pass as a Frenchman.*
pass away *phr v* to die – use this when you want to avoid saying the word 'die'
pass by *phr v*
1 pass by (sb/sth) to go past a person, place, vehicle etc: *They all waved as they passed by.* | *Will you be passing by the supermarket on your way home?* → PASSERBY
2 pass sb by if something passes you by, it happens but you are not involved in it: *She felt that life was passing her by.*
pass sth ↔ **down** *phr v* to give or teach something to people who are younger than you or live after you: **be passed down (from sb) to sb** *The tradition has been passed down from father to son for generations.* GRAMMAR **Pass down** is usually passive.
pass for sb/sth *phr v* if something passes for another thing, it is so similar to that thing that people think that is what it is: *With my hair cut short, I could have passed for a boy.*
pass off *phr v*
1 pass off well/badly etc if an event passes off well, badly etc, it happens in that way: *The visit passed off without any serious incidents.*
2 pass sb/sth off as sth to make people think that someone or something is another thing: *They bought up pieces of old furniture and passed them off as valuable antiques.* | *He passed himself off as a doctor.*
pass on *phr v*
1 pass sth ↔ on to give someone a piece of information that someone else has given to you: **[+to]** *She said she'd pass the message on to the other students.*
2 pass sth ↔ on a) to give something, especially a disease, to your children through your GENES **b)** to give a slight illness to someone else: **[+to]** *One catches the virus and they pass it on to the rest.*
3 pass sth ↔ on to make someone else pay the cost of something: **[+to]** *Any increase in our costs will have to be passed on to the consumer.*
4 to die – use this when you want to avoid saying the word 'die'
pass out *phr v*
1 to become unconscious: *I nearly passed out when I saw all the blood.*
2 *especially BrE* to finish a course of study at a military school or police college
3 pass sth ↔ out to give something, such as books or papers, to everyone in a group SYN **hand out, distribute**
pass over *phr v*
1 pass sb ↔ over if you are passed over for a job, someone else who is younger or lower in the organization than you is chosen for it: *This is the second time I've been **passed over for promotion*** (=someone else has been given a higher job instead of me).
2 pass over sth if you pass over a remark or subject, you do not spend any time discussing it: *I want to pass over this quite quickly.* | *I think we'd better pass over that last remark.*
pass sth ↔ **up** *phr v* to not make use of a chance to do something: **pass up a chance/opportunity/offer** *I don't think you should pass up the opportunity to go to university.*

pass² ●●● S2 W3 *n* [C]
1 DOCUMENT an official piece of paper which shows that you are allowed to enter a building or travel on something without paying: *The guard checked our passes.* | *They issued us with free passes to the theatre.* | *You can buy a cheap one-day **bus pass**.*
2 EXAM/TEST a successful result in an examination OPP **fail**: *You will need at least three passes to get onto the course.* | **[+in]** *Did you get a pass in English?* | *The **pass mark*** (=the mark you need to be successful) *is 55%.*
3 SPORT when you kick, throw, or hit a ball to another member of your team during a game: *That was a brilliant pass by Holden.* → see picture at AMERICAN FOOTBALL
4 make a pass at sb *informal* to try to kiss or touch another person with the intention of starting a sexual relationship with them
5 ROAD/PATH a high road or path that goes between mountains to the other side: *a narrow, winding mountain pass*
6 STAGE one part of a process that involves dealing with the whole of a group or thing several times: *On the first pass we eliminated all the candidates who didn't have the right experience.*
7 AIRCRAFT a movement in which an aircraft flies once over a place which it is attacking
8 come to a pretty/sorry pass *old-fashioned informal* if things have come to a pretty or sorry pass, a situation has become very bad

pass·a·ble /ˈpɑːsəbəl $ ˈpæ-/ *adj* **1** *formal* fairly good, but not excellent: *The food was excellent and the wine was passable.* | *He can do a passable imitation of the maths teacher.* THESAURUS SATISFACTORY **2** a road or river that is passable is not blocked, so you can travel along it or across it OPP **impassable**

pass·a·bly /ˈpɑːsəbli $ ˈpæs-/ *adv* in a way that is fairly good, but not excellent: *There were one or two passably funny jokes but it was mostly dull.*

pas·sage /ˈpæsɪdʒ/ ●●○ W2 *n*
1 IN A BUILDING [C] a long narrow area with walls on either side which connects one room or place to another → **corridor**: *My office is just along the passage.* | *We walked down a narrow passage to the back of the building.* | *an underground passage*
2 FROM A BOOK ETC [C] a short part of a book, poem, speech, piece of music etc: **[+from/of]** *He read out a short passage from the Bible.*
3 MOVEMENT [U] *formal* the movement of people or vehicles along a road or across an area of land: **[+of]** *The bridge isn't strong enough to allow the passage of heavy*

vehicles. | *Both sides agreed to allow the* ***free passage*** *of medical supplies into the area.* | *He was guaranteed* ***safe passage*** *out of the country.*
4 OF A LAW [U] when a new law is discussed and accepted by a parliament or Congress: **[+through]** *The bill was amended several times during its passage through Congress.* | *They are expecting the new legislation to have quite a* ***rough passage*** (=be discussed and criticized a lot) *through Parliament.*
5 JOURNEY [C] *old-fashioned* a journey on a ship: **[+to]** *My parents couldn't afford the passage to America.*
6 INSIDE SB'S BODY [C] a tube in your body that air or liquid can pass through: *the nasal passages*
7 WAY THROUGH [singular] a way through something: **[+through]** *The police forced a passage through the crowd.*
8 the passage of time the passing of time: *With the passage of time, things began to look more hopeful.* → **rite of passage** at RITE(2)

pas·sage·way /ˈpæsɪdʒweɪ/ *n* [C] a PASSAGE(1): *He led me down a narrow passageway.*

pass·book /ˈpɑːsbʊk $ ˈpæs-/ *n* [C] a book in which a record is kept of the money you put into and take out of a bank account

pas·sé /ˈpæseɪ, ˈpɑː- $ pæˈseɪ/ *adj formal* no longer modern or fashionable

pas·sel /ˈpæsəl/ *n* [C] *AmE old-fashioned* a group of people or things: **[+of]** *a whole passel of kids*

pas·sen·ger /ˈpæsɪndʒə, -sən- $ -ər/ ●●● S3 W2 *n* [C]
1 someone who is travelling in a vehicle, plane, boat etc, but is not driving it or working on it: *Neither the driver nor the passengers were hurt.* | **passenger train/plane/ship** *a crash involving a passenger train* | **bus/rail/airline passengers** *Rail passengers now face even longer delays.*
THESAURUS TRAVEL
2 *BrE* someone in a group who does not do their share of the group's work: *The company can't afford to carry any passengers.*

ˈ**passenger ˌseat** *n* [C] the seat in the front of a vehicle next to the driver

pass·er·by /ˌpɑːsəˈbaɪ $ ˌpæsər-/ *n* (*plural* **passersby**) [C] someone who is walking past a place by chance: *They sell drinks to passersby.*

pas·sim /ˈpæsɪm/ *adv formal* used to show that a person or subject is referred to many times in a book or article

pass·ing¹ /ˈpɑːsɪŋ $ ˈpæ-/ ●●○ *n* [U]
1 the passing of time/the years the process of time going by: *Most of the old traditions have died out with the passing of time.* | *The passing of the years had done nothing to improve his temper.*
2 mention/note sth in passing if you say something in passing, you mention it while you are mainly talking about something else: *He did mention his brother's wife, but only in passing.*
3 the passing of something is the fact that it has ended: *The old regime was defeated, and few people mourned its passing.*
4 the passing of a person is their death – use this when you want to avoid using the word 'death': *Nothing could fill the gap in her life left by his passing.*

passing² ●●○ *adj* [only before noun]
1 going past a place or person: *Michael watched the passing cars.* | *A passing motorist stopped to help.*
2 passing days/weeks/years etc *literary* the days, weeks, years etc that pass: *Her grief became less intense with the passing years.* | *With each passing day she grew stronger.*
3 a passing thought or feeling is short and not very serious: *He had only ever shown a* ***passing interest*** *in sport.*
THESAURUS SHORT
4 a passing remark is one that you make while you are talking about something else: *He made only a passing reference to her achievements.*

pas·sion /ˈpæʃən/ ●●○ W3 *n*
1 [C,U] a very strong feeling of sexual love → **desire**: *His eyes were burning with passion.* | **[+for]** *her passion for a married man*
2 [C,U] a very strong belief or feeling about something: **with passion** *He spoke with considerable passion about the importance of art and literature.* | *The issue arouses* ***strong passions***.
3 [C] a very strong liking for something: **[+for]** *his passion for football* | *Gardening was her great passion.*
4 fly into a passion *literary* to suddenly become very angry
→ **crime of passion** at CRIME(5)

Passion *n* **the Passion** the suffering and death of Jesus Christ

pas·sion·ate /ˈpæʃənət/ ●●○ *adj*
1 showing or involving very strong feelings of sexual love: *He had a brief but passionate love affair with an older woman.* | *a very passionate young man* | *a passionate lover* | *a passionate kiss*
2 someone who has a passionate belief believes something very strongly: *a passionate supporter of women's rights* | *He had a* ***passionate belief*** *in justice.*
3 if you are passionate about something, you like it a lot: *She developed a* ***passionate interest*** *in wild flowers.* | **[+about]** *I've always been passionate about football.*
—**passionately** *adv*: *He kissed her passionately.* | *Peter is passionately involved in environmental issues.*

pas·sion·flow·er /ˈpæʃənˌflaʊə $ -ˌflaʊr/ *n* [C] a climbing plant with large attractive flowers

ˈ**passion fruit** *n* [C,U] a small fruit which has a brown skin and many seeds → see picture at FRUIT¹

pass·ion·less /ˈpæʃənləs/ *adj* with no strong feelings of love: *a dull, passionless marriage*

ˈ**passion play** *n* [C] a play that tells the story of the suffering and death of Jesus Christ

pas·sive¹ /ˈpæsɪv/ ●●○ AWL *adj*
1 someone who is passive tends to accept things that happen to them or things that people say to them, without taking any action → **impassive**: *Kathy seems to take a very passive role in the relationship.* | *their passive acceptance of their fate*
2 *technical* a passive verb or sentence has as its subject the person or thing to which an action is done, as in 'His father was killed in a car accident.' → ACTIVE¹(6)
—**passively** *adv*: *He listened passively as his sentence was read out.* —**passivity** /pæˈsɪvəti/ *n* [U]

passive² ●●○ AWL *n* **the passive** *technical* the passive form of a verb, for example 'was destroyed' in the sentence 'The building was destroyed during the war.' → ACTIVE²

ˌ**passive reˈsistance** *n* [U] a way of protesting against something or opposing a government without using violence: *They tried to achieve their aims by passive resistance.*

ˌ**passive ˈsmoking** *n* [U] *especially BrE* the act of breathing in smoke that is in the air around you when someone else is smoking cigarettes

ˈ**passive ˌvoice** *n* [singular] the PASSIVE²

pas·siv·ize (*also* **-ise** *BrE*) /ˈpæsɪvaɪz/ *v* [I,T] *technical* to make a verb PASSIVE, or to become passive

pass·key /ˈpɑːs-kiː $ ˈpæs-/ *n* [C] a key that will open several different locks in a building

Pass·o·ver /ˈpɑːsəʊvə $ ˈpæsoʊvər/ *n* [U] (*also* **the Passover**) a Jewish religious holiday when people remember the escape of the Jews from Egypt

pass·port /ˈpɑːspɔːt $ ˈpæspɔːrt/ ●●○ *n* [C]
1 a small official document that you get from your government, that proves who you are, and which you need in order to leave your country and enter other countries: *I have an Irish passport.* | *They need to check that your passport is in order.*
2 passport to success/health/romance etc something that makes it easy for you to achieve success, good health etc: *She saw a good diet as a passport to good health.* | *Don't assume that winning a talent contest is a passport to success.*

COLLOCATIONS

VERBS

have/hold a passport *I have a Canadian passport.*
apply for a passport *You can apply for an Italian passport if your parents are Italian.*
get a passport (*also* **obtain a passport** *formal*) | **renew a passport**

ADJECTIVES

a British/American etc passport *She was born in India but has a British passport.*
a valid passport (=one that is officially acceptable) *For travel abroad, you must have a valid passport.*
a false/forged passport (*also* **a fake passport** *informal*)

passport + NOUN

a passport photograph/photo | **a passport holder** (=someone who has a passport) | **a passport application**

P

ˈpassport conˌtrol *n* [U] the place where your passport is checked when you leave or enter a country → **immigration**: *It took us ages to get through passport control.*

pass·word /ˈpɑːswɜːd $ ˈpæswɜːrd/ ●●● S2 W2 *n* [C]
1 a secret group of letters or numbers that you must type into a computer before you can use a system or program: *Enter your password, then click on the 'proceed' icon.* | *Give your user name and password.*
2 a secret word or phrase that someone has to say before they are allowed to enter a place such as a military camp

past¹ /pɑːst $ pæst/ ●●● S1 W1 *adj*
1 PREVIOUS [only before noun] done, used, or experienced before now: *Judging by her past performance, Jane should do very well.* | *From past experience she knew that it was no use arguing with him.* | *Study some past exam papers to get an idea of the questions.*
2 RECENT [only before noun] used to refer to a period up until now: *the events of the past year* | *During the past two weeks, 12 people have died of the disease.* | *She has been feeling tired for the past few days.*
3 FINISHED finished or having come to an end: *Winter is past and spring has come at last.* | *writers from past centuries* | *a tradition rooted in times **long past***
4 FORMER [only before noun] having held a particular position in the past or achieved a particular honour in the past: **past president/member/winner etc** *a past president of the golf club* | *a celebration for past and present employees of the newspaper* | *Bruce Jenner, a past Olympic champion*
5 GRAMMAR [only before noun] relating to the PAST TENSE

past² ●●● S1 W2 *prep, adv*
1 later than a particular time: *It's ten past nine.* | *I should be finished by half past* (=30 minutes after the hour). | *It was past midnight when the party ended.* | *Come on Annie, it's **long past** your bedtime.*
2 further than a particular place: *The hospital's just up this road, about a mile past the school.* | *There are parking spaces over there, **just past*** (=a little further than) *the garage.*
3 up to and beyond a person or place, without stopping: *She waved as she drove past.* | *Will you be going past my house on your way home?* | **straight/right past** (=used to emphasize that someone passes close to you and does not stop) *Monica hurried straight past me and down the steps.*
4 if a period of time goes past, it passes: *Weeks went past without any news.* | *The hours seemed to fly past.*
5 beyond or no longer at a particular point or stage: *The roses were already past their best.* | *Reid never really got past the stage of copying other artists.* | *a pot of yoghurt **well past** its sell-by date* | *an Italian singer who was then past her prime* (=no longer strong and active) | *I'm past caring about my appearance* (=I do not care about it anymore).
6 I wouldn't put it past sb (to do sth) *spoken* used to say that you would not be surprised if someone did something bad or unusual because it is typical of them to do that type of thing: *I wouldn't put it past Colin to cheat.*
7 past it *BrE spoken* too old to be able to do what you used to do, or too old to be useful: *People seem to think that just because I'm retired, I'm past it.*
8 be past due *AmE* something that is past due has not been paid or done by the time it should have been

past³ ●●● S1 W2 *n*
1 the past a) the time that existed before the present: **in the past** *The lake was smaller in the past.* | *Good manners have become **a thing of the past*** (=something that does not exist anymore). | *It's time she stopped **living in the past*** (=thinking only about the past) *and began to think about her future.* | **the recent/immediate/distant past** *She allowed her mind to drift towards the recent past.* | *I did a law degree some time **in the dim and distant past*** (=a long time ago). **b)** the PAST TENSE
2 all in the past *spoken* used to say that an unpleasant experience has ended and can be forgotten: *You mustn't think about it. It's all in the past now.*
3 [singular] the past life or existence of someone or something: *At some time in its past the church was rebuilt.* | *The woman who ran the bar had a very **shady past*** (=events in her past which might be considered bad).

pas·ta /ˈpæstə $ ˈpɑː-/ ●●● S2 *n* [U] an Italian food made from flour, eggs, and water and cut into various shapes, usually eaten with a sauce: *I eat a lot of pasta.*

paste¹ /peɪst/ ●●○ *v*
1 [T always + adv/prep] to stick something to something else using glue: *A notice had been pasted to the door.*
2 [I,T] to make words that you have removed or copied appear in a new place on a computer screen → **copy**, **cut**: *Data can be pasted into word processing documents.*
→ PASTE-UP, PASTING

paste² ●●○ *n*
1 meat/fish/tomato etc paste a soft smooth food, made by crushing meat, fish etc
2 [C,U] a soft thick mixture that can easily be shaped or spread: *Mix the powder with enough water to make a smooth paste.*
3 [C,U] a type of glue that is used for sticking paper onto things: *wallpaper paste*
4 [U] pieces of glass that are used in jewellery to look like valuable stones

paste·board /ˈpeɪstbɔːd $ -bɔːrd/ *n* [U] flat stiff CARDBOARD made by sticking sheets of paper together

pas·tel¹ /ˈpæstl $ pæˈstel/ *n* **1 a)** [C,U] a small coloured stick for drawing pictures with, made of a substance like CHALK **b)** [C] a picture drawn with pastels **2** [C usually plural] a light colour such as pale blue or pink: *a room beautifully furnished in **soft pastels***

pastel² *adj* [only before noun] **1** pastel colours are light and pale: *pastel blue* | *The walls were painted in pastel shades.* THESAURUS COLOUR **2** drawn using pastels: *a set of four small pastel drawings*

ˈpaste-up *n* [C] a piece of paper with writing and pictures stuck on it that shows what a page will look like when a book or magazine is produced

pas·teur·ized (*also* **-ised** *BrE*) /ˈpɑːstʃəraɪzd, -stə- $ ˈpæs-/ *adj* a liquid, usually milk, that is pasteurized has been heated using a special process in order to kill any harmful BACTERIA in it —**pasteurize** *v* [T] —**pasteurization** /ˌpɑːstʃəraɪˈzeɪʃən -stə- $ ˌpæstʃərə-/ *n* [U]

pas·tiche /pæˈstiːʃ/ *n* **1** [C] a piece of writing, music, film etc that is deliberately made in the style of someone or something else → **parody**: **[+of]** *The film is a pastiche of the Hollywood Wild West.* **2** [C] a work of art that consists of a variety of different styles put together **3** [U] the practice of making a piece of writing, music, film etc using the style of something else or using a variety of different styles

pas·tille /pæˈstiːl/ *n* [C] *especially BrE* a small round sweet, sometimes containing medicine for a sore throat SYN **lozenge**: *fruit pastilles*

pas·time /ˈpɑːstaɪm $ ˈpæs-/ ●○○ *n* [C] something

that you do because you think it is enjoyable or interesting → **hobby**: *Reading was her favourite pastime.*

past·ing /ˈpeɪstɪŋ/ *n* **1** [U] the activity of moving words from one place to another on a computer screen: *cutting and pasting* **2** [singular] *informal* an easy defeat of someone in a game or competition **3** [singular] *BrE informal* a severe beating

ˌpast ˈmaster *n* [C] someone who is very skilled at doing something and has done it many times before SYN **expert**: **past master at (doing) sth** *She's a past master at exploiting other people.*

pas·tor /ˈpɑːstə $ ˈpæstər/ *n* [C] a Christian priest in some Protestant churches: *the pastor of Carr's Lane Congregational church | Pastor Martin Niemoller*

pas·tor·al /ˈpɑːstərəl $ ˈpæ-/ *adj* **1** relating to the duties of a priest, minister etc towards the members of their religious group: *his pastoral work among the congregation* **2** *literary* typical of the simple peaceful life in the country: *a charming pastoral scene* **3** relating to the duties of a teacher in advising students about their personal needs rather than their schoolwork: *pastoral care at the school*

ˌpast ˈparticiple ●●○ *n* [C] *technical* the form of a verb used with the verb 'to have' in PERFECT tenses (for example 'eaten' in 'I have eaten'), or with the verb 'to be' in the PASSIVE (for example 'changed' in 'it was changed'), or sometimes as an adjective (for example 'broken' in 'a broken leg')

ˌpast ˈperfect *n* [singular] *technical* the form of a verb that shows that the action described by the verb was completed before a particular time in the past, formed in English with 'had' and a past participle —**past perfect** *adj*

pas·tra·mi /pəˈstrɑːmi/ *n* [U] smoked BEEF that contains a lot of spices

pas·try /ˈpeɪstri/ ●●○ *n* (*plural* **pastries**)
1 [U] a mixture of flour, butter, and milk or water, used to make the outer part of baked foods such as PIES
2 [C] a small sweet cake, made using pastry: *a Danish pastry*

ˌpast ˈtense *n* [C] a form of a verb that shows that something happened or existed before the present time, typically a form such as 'walked', as in 'I walked away'

pas·tur·age /ˈpɑːstʃərɪdʒ $ ˈpæs-/ *n* [U] pasture

pas·ture¹ /ˈpɑːstʃə $ ˈpæstʃər/ *n* [C,U] **1** land or a field that is covered with grass and is used for cattle, sheep etc to feed on: *large areas of rough upland pasture | the lush pastures of the southern counties* **2 put sth/sb out to pasture a)** to move cattle, horses etc into a field to feed on the grass **b)** *informal* to make someone leave their job because you think they are too old to do it well **3 pastures new/greener pastures** a new and exciting or better job, place, or activity – used humorously: *I'd like to say goodbye to Paul who leaves us for pastures new.*

pasture² *v* **1** [T] to put animals outside in a field to feed on the grass **2** [I + on] if animals pasture on a particular area of land, they eat the grass that is growing there

pas·ture·land /ˈpɑːstʃəlænd $ ˈpæstʃər-/ *n* [U] pasture

past·y¹ /ˈpeɪsti/ *adj* a pasty face looks very pale and unhealthy

past·y² /ˈpæsti/ *n* (*plural* **pasties**) [C] *BrE* a small PASTRY case filled with meat, vegetables etc and baked: *a Cornish pasty*

pasty-faced /ˈpeɪsti feɪst/ *adj* having a very pale face that looks unhealthy

pat¹ /pæt/ ●●○ *v* (**patted**, **patting**) [T]
1 to lightly touch someone or something several times with your hand flat, especially to give comfort → **stroke**: *He patted the dog affectionately.* THESAURUS TOUCH
2 pat sb/yourself on the back to praise someone or yourself for doing something well: *You can pat yourselves on the back for a job well done.*

pat² *n* [C] **1** a friendly act of touching someone with your hand flat: *Mrs Dodd* ***gave*** *the child a* ***pat*** *on the head.* **2 pat of butter** a small flat amount of butter **3 a pat on the back** *informal* praise for something that you have done well: *Alex deserves a pat on the back for all his hard work.*
→ COWPAT

pat³ *adj* [usually before noun] a pat answer or explanation seems too quick and too simple and sounds as if it has been used before: *There are no pat answers to these questions.*

pat⁴ *adv* **1 have sth off pat** *BrE*, **have sth down pat** *AmE* to know something thoroughly so that you can say it, perform it etc immediately without thinking about it SYN **(off) by heart 2 stand pat** *AmE* to refuse to change your opinion or decision

PATCHES

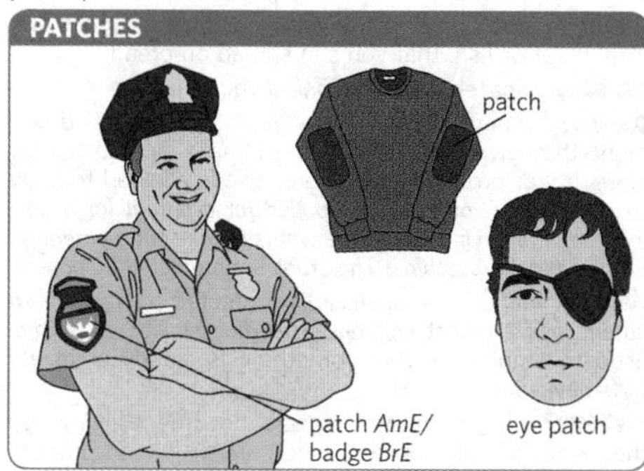

patch¹ /pætʃ/ ●●○ *n* [C]
1 PART OF AN AREA a small area of something that is different from the area around it: **[+of]** *We finally found a patch of grass to sit down on. | Belinda watched a patch of sunlight move slowly across the wall. | Look out for icy patches on the road. | a cat with a white patch on its chest | He combs his hair over his* ***bald patch****.*
2 OVER A HOLE a small piece of material that is sewn on something to cover a hole in it: *a jacket with leather patches at the elbows*
3 FOR GROWING STH a small area of ground for growing fruit or vegetables: *a strawberry patch*
4 COMPUTER a small computer program that is added to software to solve problems
5 EYE a piece of material that you wear over your eye to protect it when it has been hurt: *He had a black patch over one eye.*
6 DECORATION *AmE* a small piece of cloth with words or pictures on it that you can sew onto clothes SYN **badge** *BrE*
7 a bad/difficult/sticky/rough patch *informal* a period of time when you are having a lot of difficulty: *Gemma's* ***going through*** *a* ***bad patch*** *right now.*
8 sb's patch *BrE informal* an area that someone knows very well because they work or live there SYN **turf**: *Policemen know what's going on in their* ***home patch****.*
9 not be a patch on sb/sth *BrE informal* to be much less attractive, good etc than something or someone else: *The second film isn't a patch on the first.*

patch² (*also* **patch up**) *v* [T + with] to repair a hole in something by putting a piece of something else over it

patch sth ↔ **together** *phr v* to make something quickly or carelessly from a number of different pieces or ideas: *A new plan was quickly patched together.*

patch sth/sb ↔ **up** *phr v* **1** to end an argument because you want to stay friendly with someone: *Try to* ***patch up*** *your* ***differences*** *before he leaves.* | **patch it/things up (with sb)** *He went back to patch things up with his wife.* **2** to repair a hole in something by putting a piece of something else over it: *We'll have to patch up the hole in the roof.* **3** to give quick and basic medical treatment to someone who is hurt: *We patched up the wounded as best we could.*

pa·tchou·li /pəˈtʃuːli/ *n* [U] a type of PERFUME made from the leaves of a South East Asian bush

patch·work /ˈpætʃwɜːk $ -wɜːrk/ *n* **1** [U] a type of sewing in which many coloured squares of cloth are stitched together to make one large piece: *a* ***patchwork quilt*** **2** [singular] something that is made up of a lot of different things: **[+of]** *a patchwork of woods and fields, typical of the*

P

English countryside | *The area was a patchwork of local industries.*

patch·y /ˈpætʃi/ *adj* **1** happening or existing in some areas but not in others: *patchy fog* **2** not complete enough to be useful: *His knowledge of French remained pretty patchy.* | *There is only patchy evidence of the animal's existence.* **3** *especially BrE* good in some parts but bad in others: *I thought the performance was patchy.* —**patchiness** *n* [U]

pate /peɪt/ *n* [C] *old use* the top of your head: *his bald pate*

pâ·té /ˈpæteɪ $ pɑːˈteɪ, pæ-/ *n* [C,U] a soft food made from meat or fish, that you can spread on bread

pa·tel·la /pəˈtelə/ *n* [C] *technical* your KNEE CAP

pa·tent¹ /ˈpeɪtnt, ˈpæ- $ ˈpæ-/ *n* [C,U] a special document that gives you the right to make or sell a new INVENTION or product that no one else is allowed to copy → **copyright**: **[+on/for]** *He **applied for** a **patent** for a new method of removing paint.* | *He wants to **take out** a **patent** on his new type of dustbin.* | *The drugs are protected by patent.*

patent² *adj* [only before noun] **1** protected by a patent: *a patent lock* **2 patent lie/nonsense/impossibility etc** *formal* used to emphasize that something is clearly a lie etc SYN **obvious** → PATENTLY

patent³ *v* [T] to obtain a special document giving you the right to make or sell a new INVENTION or product → **copyright**

patent leath·er /ˌpeɪtnt ˈleðə◂ $ ˌpætnt ˈleðər/ *n* [U] thin shiny leather, usually black: *patent leather shoes*

pa·tent·ly /ˈpeɪtntli $ ˈpæ-/ *adv formal* very clearly: *The treatment is patently not working.* | **patently false/untrue** *To say that the proposal has no disadvantages at all is patently untrue.* | *It's **patently obvious** that you're in love with her.*

patent medi·cine /ˌpeɪtnt ˈmedsən $ ˌpætnt ˈmedəsən/ *n* [C] a medicine which can be bought without a PRESCRIPTION (=a written order from your doctor) SYN **over-the-counter**

pa·ter /ˈpeɪtə $ -ər/ *n* [C] *BrE old-fashioned* father

pa·ter·fa·mil·ias /ˌpeɪtəfəˈmiːliæs $ ˌpɑːtərfəˈmiːliəs/ *n* [C] *formal* a father or a man who is the head of a family

pa·ter·nal /pəˈtɜːnl $ -ɜːr-/ *adj* **1** paternal feelings or behaviour are like those of a kind father towards his children: *Dan took a paternal interest in my work.* **2 paternal grandmother/uncle etc** your father's mother, brother etc —**paternally** *adv* → MATERNAL

pa·ter·nal·is·m /pəˈtɜːnəl-ɪzəm $ -ɜːr-/ *n* [U] when people in charge of an organization or society protect the members and give them what they need but do not allow them any freedom or responsibility —**paternalistic** /pəˌtɜːnəlˈɪstɪk◂ $ -ɜːr-/ (*also* **paternalist** /pəˈtɜːnəlɪst $ -ɜːr-/) *adj*

pa·ter·ni·ty /pəˈtɜːnəti $ -ɜːr-/ *n* [U] *law* the fact of being the father of a particular child, or the question of who the child's father is: *The paternity of the child is in dispute.*

paˈternity ˌleave *n* [U] a period of time that the father of a new baby is allowed away from work → **maternity leave**, **parental leave**

paˈternity ˌsuit *n* [C] a legal action in which a mother asks a court of law to find proof that a particular man is the father of her child, usually in order to claim financial support from him

path /pɑːθ $ pæθ/ ●●● S2 W2 *n* (*plural* **paths** /pɑːðz $ pæðz/) [C]

1 TRACK a track that has been made deliberately or made by many people walking over the same ground: *I walked nervously up the **garden path** towards the front door.* | *a well-worn path across the grass* | ***Follow** the **path** along the river to the bridge.* | *a **path leading** to the summer house*

2 WAY THROUGH STH the space ahead of you as you move along: **[+through]** *Police cleared a path through the protesters.* | *Damian blocked their path.*

3 DIRECTION the direction or line along which something or someone is moving: **in sth's/sb's path** *The tornado destroyed **everything in its path**.* | **into the path of sth** *She walked into the path of an oncoming vehicle.*

4 PLAN a plan or series of actions that will help you achieve something, especially over a long period of time: *a career path* | **path to freedom/success/independence etc** *She saw a college degree as her path to success.* | **the same/a different path** *I hope you will choose a different path.*

5 sb's paths cross if two people's paths cross, they meet by chance: *Our paths did not cross again.* → **beat a path (to sb's door)** at BEAT¹(16), → **off the beaten path** at BEATEN(1), → FLIGHT PATH, → **lead sb up the garden path** at LEAD¹(12), → **stand in sb's path** at STAND¹(30)

pa·thet·ic /pəˈθetɪk/ ●●○ *adj*

1 something or someone that is pathetic is so useless, unsuccessful, or weak that they annoy you: *You're pathetic! Here, let me do it.* | *I know it sounds pathetic now, but at the time I was frightened.* | *Vic made a pathetic attempt to apologise.*

2 making you feel pity or sympathy: *The child looked a pathetic sight.* —**pathetically** /-kli/ *adv*: *She whimpered pathetically.*

paˌthetic ˈfallacy *n* [U] *technical* the idea of describing the sea, rocks, weather etc in literature as if they were human

path·find·er /ˈpɑːθˌfaɪndə $ ˈpæθˌfaɪndər/ *n* [C] *especially AmE* **1** someone who goes ahead of a group and finds the best way through unknown land **2** a person who discovers new ways of doing things SYN **trailblazer**

path·o·gen /ˈpæθədʒən, -dʒen/ *n* [C] *technical* something that causes disease in your body → **germ** —**pathogenic** /ˌpæθəˈdʒenɪk◂/ *adj*

path·o·log·i·cal /ˌpæθəˈlɒdʒɪkəl◂ $ -ˈlɑː-/ *adj* **1** pathological behaviour or feelings happen regularly, and are strong, unreasonable, and impossible to control: *a pathological hatred of women* | *a pathological liar* **2** a mental or physical condition that is pathological is caused by disease: ***pathological conditions** such as cancer* **3** relating to pathology —**pathologically** /-kli/ *adv*: *Stephen was almost pathologically jealous of his brother.*

pa·thol·o·gy /pəˈθɒlədʒi $ -ˈθɑː-/ *n* [U] the study of the causes and effects of illnesses —**pathologist** *n* [C]

pa·thos /ˈpeɪθɒs $ -θɑːs/ *n* [U] the quality that a person, situation, film, or play has that makes you feel pity and sadness: *the pathos of the woman trying to keep her lover*

path·way /ˈpɑːθweɪ $ ˈpæθ-/ *n* [C] **1** a path **2** a series of nerves that pass information to each other

pa·tience /ˈpeɪʃəns/ ●●○ S3 *n* [U]

1 the ability to continue waiting or doing something for a long time without becoming angry or anxious OPP **impatience**: *I wouldn't **have** the **patience** to sit sewing all day.* | **infinite/unlimited/endless patience** *a good listener who has infinite patience*

2 the ability to accept trouble and other people's annoying behaviour without complaining or becoming angry: *You'll need patience and understanding if you're going to be a teacher.* | **have little/no patience with sb** *She has no patience with time-wasters.* | **lose/run out of patience (with sb)** (=stop being patient and get angry) *I'm beginning to lose patience with you people.* | *It will **take** time and **patience** to get these changes accepted.* | *Celia's **patience** suddenly **snapped** and she told them to shut up.* | **the patience of Job/the patience of a saint** (=very great patience when someone is annoying you) | *Henry's negative attitude is beginning to **try** my **patience*** (=make me lose my patience).

3 (have) patience used to tell someone to wait calmly: *Patience, my dear. Some things take time.*

4 *BrE* a card game for one player SYN **solitaire** *AmE*

pa·tient¹ /ˈpeɪʃənt/ ●●● S2 W1 *n* [C] someone who is receiving medical treatment from a doctor or in a hospital THESAURUS CUSTOMER

patient² ●●● W3 *adj* able to wait calmly for a long time or to accept difficulties, people's annoying behaviour etc without becoming angry OPP **impatient**: *You'll just have to **be patient** and wait till I'm off the phone.* |

[+with] *Louise was very patient with me.* —**patiently** *adv*: *He* ***waited patiently*** *for Katherine to speak.*

pat·i·na /ˈpætənə $ pəˈtiːnə/ *n* [singular] **1** a greenish layer that forms naturally on the surface of COPPER or BRONZE **2** a smooth shiny surface that gradually develops on wood, leather etc **3 a patina of wealth/success etc** the appearance of being wealthy, successful etc

pat·i·o /ˈpætiəʊ $ -oʊ/ *n* (*plural* **patios**) [C] a flat hard area near a house, where people sit outside

ˈpatio ˌdoors *n* [plural] *especially BrE* glass doors that open from a living room onto a patio

pa·tis·se·rie /pəˈtiːsəri, -ˈtɪs-/ *n* [C] a shop that sells cakes and PIES, especially French cakes, or the cakes it sells

pa·tois /ˈpætwɑː/ *n* (*plural* **patois** /-twɑːz/) [C,U] a spoken form of a language used by the people of a small area and different from the national or standard language

pa·tri·arch /ˈpeɪtriɑːk $ -ɑːrk/ *n* [C] **1** an old man who is respected as the head of a family or tribe → MATRIARCH **2** a BISHOP in the early Christian church **3** a BISHOP of the Orthodox Christian churches who is very high in rank

pa·tri·arch·al /ˌpeɪtriˈɑːkəl◂ $ -ˈɑːr-/ *adj* **1** ruled or controlled only by men: *a* ***patriarchal society*** **2** relating to being a patriarch, or typical of a patriarch → **matriarchal**

pa·tri·arch·y /ˈpeɪtriɑːki $ -ɑːr-/ *n* (*plural* **patriarchies**) [C,U] **1** a social system in which men have all the power **2** a social system in which the oldest man rules his family and passes power and possessions on to his sons → MATRIARCHY

pa·tri·cian /pəˈtrɪʃən/ *adj* **1** typical of a member of the highest class in society: *a patrician manner* **2** belonging to the high class of people that governed in ancient Rome —**patrician** *n* [C] → PLEBEIAN[1]

pat·ri·cide /ˈpætrɪsaɪd/ *n* [U] the crime of murdering your father → **matricide**, **parricide**

pat·ri·mo·ny /ˈpætrəməni $ -moʊni/ *n* [singular, U] *formal* property given to you after the death of your father, which was given to him by your grandfather etc SYN **inheritance**

pat·ri·ot /ˈpætriət, -triɒt, ˈpeɪ- $ ˈpeɪtriət, -triɑːt/ *n* [C] someone who loves their country and is willing to defend it – used to show approval

pat·ri·ot·ic /ˌpætriˈɒtɪk◂, ˌpeɪ- $ ˌpeɪtriˈɑːtɪk◂/ ●○○ *adj* having or expressing a great love of your country → **nationalistic**: *patriotic songs* | *I'm not very patriotic.* —**patriotism** /ˈpætriətɪzəm, ˈpeɪ- $ ˈpeɪ-/ *n* [U]

pa·trol[1] /pəˈtrəʊl $ -ˈtroʊl/ ●○○ *v* (**patrolled**, **patrolling**) [T]
1 to go around the different parts of an area or building at regular times to check that there is no trouble or danger: *Armed guards patrolled the grounds.* | *an area patrolled by special police units*
2 to drive or walk around an area in a threatening way: *Gangs of youths patrolled the streets at night.*

patrol[2] ●○○ *n*
1 [C,U] when someone goes around different parts of an area at regular times to check that there is no trouble or danger: **on patrol** *police on patrol in the city centre* | *The security forces increased their patrols in the area.*
2 [C] a group of police, soldiers, vehicles, planes etc sent out to search a particular area: *a US border patrol* | **patrol boat/car** (=used by the army or police)
3 [C] a small group of BOY SCOUTS or GUIDES → HIGHWAY PATROL

paˈtrol car *n* [C] a police car that drives around the streets of a city

pa·trol·man /pəˈtrəʊlmən $ -ˈtroʊl-/ *n* (*plural* **patrolmen** /-mən/) [C] **1** *AmE* a police officer who regularly walks or drives around a particular area to try to prevent crime **2** someone employed by a car owners' association in Britain who goes to give help to drivers by the road

pa·tron /ˈpeɪtrən/ ●○○ *n* [C]
1 someone who supports the activities of an organization, for example by giving money: *a wealthy patron* | **[+of]** *a patron of the arts*
2 a famous person who is officially involved with an organization, such as a CHARITY, and whose name is used to help advertise it → **patroness**
3 *formal* someone who uses a particular shop, restaurant, or hotel SYN **customer**: *facilities for disabled patrons*
THESAURUS CUSTOMER

pat·ron·age /ˈpætrənɪdʒ $ ˈpeɪ-, ˈpæ-/ *n* [U] **1** the support, especially financial support, that is given to an organization or activity by a patron **2** *AmE formal* the support that you give a particular shop, restaurant etc by buying their goods or using their services SYN **custom** *BrE*: *Thank you for your patronage.* **3** a system by which someone in a powerful position gives people help or important jobs in return for their support

pa·tron·ess /ˈpeɪtrənəs/ *n* [C] a woman who supports the activities of a person or organization, by giving money or using their name in advertising → **patron**

pat·ron·ize (*also* **-ise** *BrE*) /ˈpætrənaɪz $ ˈpeɪ-, ˈpæ-/ *v* [T] **1** to talk to someone in a way which seems friendly but shows that you think they are not as intelligent or do not know as much as you: *Don't patronize me!* | *The program focuses on kids' interests without patronizing them.* **2** *formal* to use or visit a shop, restaurant etc **3** to support or give money to an organization or activity

pat·ro·niz·ing (*also* **-ising** *BrE*) /ˈpætrənaɪzɪŋ $ ˈpeɪ-, ˈpæ-/ ●○○ *adj* someone who is patronizing talks to you in a way that shows they think you are less intelligent or important than them SYN **condescending**: *a patronizing attitude* | *a patronizing tone* | *I don't mean to sound patronizing.* —**patronizingly** *adv*

ˌpatron ˈsaint *n* [C] a Christian SAINT who people believe gives special protection to a particular place, activity, or person: **[+of]** *St. Christopher, the patron saint of travellers*

pat·sy /ˈpætsi/ *n* (*plural* **patsies**) [C] *especially AmE informal* someone who is easily tricked or deceived, especially so that they take the blame for someone else's crime

pat·ter[1] /ˈpætə $ -ər/ *v* [I] if something, especially water, patters, it makes quiet sounds as it keeps hitting a surface lightly and quickly: **[+on]** *rain pattering on the window panes*

patter[2] *n* **1** [singular] the sound made by something as it keeps hitting a surface lightly and quickly: **[+of]** *the patter of footsteps* | *the* ***pitter-patter*** *of raindrops* **2** [singular, U] fast, continuous, and usually amusing talk, used by someone telling jokes or trying to sell something: *It's difficult to look at the cars without getting the* ***sales patter***. **3 the patter of tiny feet** used humorously to mean that someone is going to have a baby: *Are we going to hear the patter of tiny feet?*

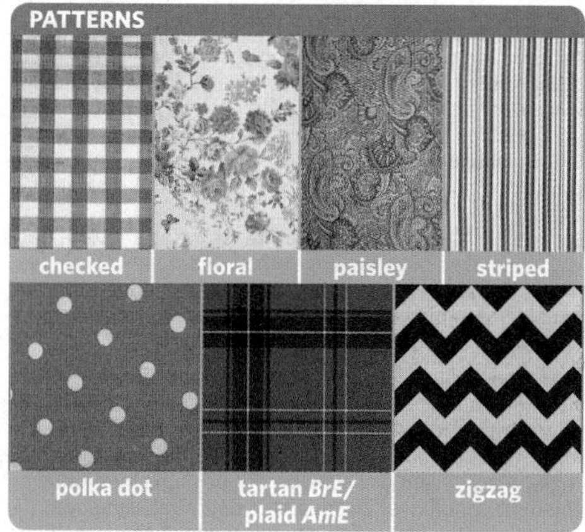

pat·tern[1] /ˈpætən $ ˈpætərn/ ●●● S2 W1 *n* [C]
1 the regular way in which something happens, develops,

or is done: *Weather patterns have changed in recent years.* | **[+of]** *changing* ***patterns of behaviour*** *among students* | *The child showed a normal* ***pattern of development****.* | **[+in]** *They noticed patterns in the data.* | *A general* ***pattern*** *began to* ***emerge****.* | *Their descriptions seemed to* ***follow a set pattern*** (=always develop in the same way). | *His behavior* ***fits*** *a* ***pattern*** *of violent acts.*
2 a) a regularly repeated arrangement of shapes, colours, or lines on a surface, usually as decoration: *a black and white striped pattern* | **[+of]** *a* ***pattern of dots*** **b)** a regularly repeated arrangement of sounds or words: *A sonnet has a fixed rhyming pattern.*
3 [usually singular] a thing, idea, or person that is an example to copy: *The book* ***set the pattern for*** *over 40 similar historical romances.*
4 a shape used as a guide for making something, especially a thin piece of paper used when cutting material to make clothes: *a dress pattern*
5 a small piece of cloth, paper etc that shows what a larger piece will look like SYN **sample**

pattern² *v* [T] **1 be patterned on/after sth** to be designed or made in a way that is copied from something else: *The exam system is patterned after the one used in Japan.* **2** *literary* to form a pattern on something: *Tiny white flowers patterned the ground like confetti.*

pat·terned /ˈpætənd $ -ərnd/ *adj* decorated with a pattern: *a patterned carpet* | *a brightly patterned dress* | **[+with]** *wallpaper patterned with roses*

pat·tern·ing /ˈpætənɪŋ $ -tər-/ *n* [U] **1** *technical* the development of particular ways of behaving, thinking, doing things etc that are the result of copying and repeating actions, language etc: *cultural patterning* | **[+of]** *the patterning of parent-child relationships* **2** patterns of a particular kind, especially on an animal's skin

pat·ty /ˈpæti/ *n* (*plural* **patties**) [C] small flat pieces of cooked meat or other food: *a beef patty*

pau·ci·ty /ˈpɔːsəti $ ˈpɒː-/ *n* [singular] *formal* less than is needed of something SYN **lack**: **[+of]** *a paucity of information*

paunch /pɔːntʃ $ pɒːntʃ/ *n* [C] a man's fat stomach —**paunchy** *adj*

pau·per /ˈpɔːpə $ ˈpɒːpər/ *n* [C] *old-fashioned* someone who is very poor

pause¹ /pɔːz $ pɒːz/ ●●● W2 *v*
1 [I] to stop speaking or doing something for a short time before starting again: **[+for]** *She paused for a moment.* | *He* ***paused for breath****, then continued up the hill.* | *'No,' he replied, without* ***pausing for thought****.* | **pause to do sth** *Joe paused to consider his answer.* **THESAURUS** ▸ STOP
2 [I,T] to push a button on a CD PLAYER, DVD PLAYER etc in order to make a CD, DVD etc stop playing for a short time

pause² ●●● W2 *n* [C]
1 a short time during which someone stops speaking or doing something before starting again: *There was a pause while Alice changed the tape.* | *After a* ***long pause****, she went on.* | **[+in]** *an awkward pause in the conversation*
2 (*also* **pause button**) a control which allows you to stop a CD PLAYER, DVD PLAYER etc for a short time and start it again
3 a mark (𝄐) over a musical note, showing that the note is to be played or sung longer than usual
4 give sb pause (for thought) to make someone stop and consider carefully what they are doing: *an avoidable accident that should give us all pause for thought*

pave /peɪv/ *v* [T] **1** to cover a path, road, area etc with a hard level surface such as blocks of stone or CONCRETE: **be paved with sth** *The city centre streets are paved with dark local stone.* | *a paved courtyard* **2 pave the way for sth** to make a later event or development possible by producing the right conditions: *The Supreme Court decision paved the way for further legislation on civil rights.* **3 the streets are paved with gold** used to say that it is easy to become rich quickly in a particular place

pave·ment /ˈpeɪvmənt/ ●●○ *n*
1 [C] *BrE* a hard level surface or path at the side of a road for people to walk on SYN **sidewalk** *AmE*: *A small group of journalists waited on the pavement outside her house.* | *a pavement café*
2 [U] *AmE* the hard surface of a road: *As she fell off the bike, her head hit the pavement.*
3 [C,U] any paved surface or area SYN **paving**
4 pound/hit the pavement to work very hard to get something, especially a job, by going to a lot of different places: *He spent the next six months pounding the pavement in search of a job.*

pa·vil·ion /pəˈvɪljən/ *n* [C] **1** a temporary building or tent which is used for public entertainment or EXHIBITIONS and is often large with a lot of space and light: *the German pavilion at the World Trade Fair* **2** *BrE* a building beside a sports field, especially a CRICKET field, used by the players and people watching the game **3** *AmE* a very large building with big open areas used for sports and other public events: *victory before a home crowd at Maples Pavilion*

pav·ing /ˈpeɪvɪŋ/ *n* **1** [U] material used to form a hard level surface on a path, road, area etc: *brick paving* **2** [U] an area covered in a hard level surface such as blocks of stone or CONCRETE **3** [C] a paving stone

ˈpaving stone (*also* **ˈpaving slab** *BrE*) *n* [C] one of the flat pieces of stone that are used to make a hard surface to walk on

pav·lo·va /pævˈləʊvə $ pɑːvˈloʊ-/ *n* [C,U] *BrE* a light cake made of MERINGUE, cream, and fruit

paw¹ /pɔː $ pɒː/ ●●○ *n* [C]
1 an animal's foot that has nails or CLAWS: *a lion's paw*
2 *informal* someone's hand – used when you are annoyed or angry: *Keep your filthy paws off me!*

paw² *v* [I,T] **1** if an animal paws a surface, it touches or rubs one place several times with its paw: **[+at]** *The dog's pawing at the door again – let him out.* | *His horse pawed the ground.* **2** *informal* to feel or touch someone in a rough or sexual way that is offensive: *He'd had too much to drink and started pawing me.*

pawn¹ /pɔːn $ pɒːn/ *n* [C] **1** one of the eight smallest and least valuable pieces which each player has in the game of CHESS → see picture at **CHESS** **2** someone who is used by a more powerful person or group and has no control of the situation: **[+in]** *They became pawns in the political battle.*

pawn² *v* [T] to leave something valuable with a pawnbroker in order to borrow money from them
pawn sth ↔ **off** *phr v AmE* **1** *informal* to persuade someone to buy or accept something that you want to get rid of, especially something of low quality: **[+on]** *Don't let him pawn off an old bike on you – get a new one.* **2 pawn sb/sth ↔ off as sth** to present something in a dishonest way: *The tabloids often pawn off gossip and trivia as real news.*

pawn·bro·ker /ˈpɔːnˌbrəʊkə $ ˈpɒːnˌbroʊkər/ *n* [C] someone whose business is to lend people money in exchange for valuable objects. If the money is not paid back, the pawnbroker can sell the object.

pawn·shop /ˈpɔːnʃɒp $ ˈpɒːnʃɑːp/ *n* [C] a pawnbroker's shop

paw·paw /ˈpɔːpɔː $ ˈpɒːpɒː/ *n* [C] *especially BrE* the large yellow-green fruit of a tall tropical tree SYN **papaya**

pay¹ /peɪ/ ●●● S1 W1 *v* (*past tense and past participle* **paid** /peɪd/)
1 GIVE MONEY [I,T] to give someone money for something you buy or for a service: *How would you like to pay?* | **[+for]** *Mum paid for my driving lessons.* | **pay (in) cash** *You'd get a discount for paying cash.* | **pay by cheque/credit card** *Can I pay by credit card?* | **pay sb for sth** *He didn't even offer to pay me for the ticket.* | **pay sb to do sth** *Ray paid some kids to wash the car.* | **pay sb sth** *I paid him $5 to cut the grass.* | **pay (sb) in dollars/euros etc** *He wanted to be paid in dollars.*

GRAMMAR: Patterns with pay
• You **pay** an amount or you **pay** a person: *We paid $700.* | *Pay the delivery man.*

• You **pay for** something that you buy: *I'll pay for the tickets.* ✗ Don't say: *I'll pay the tickets.*
• You **pay** an amount or a person **for** something that you buy: *I paid £100 for this jacket.* | *She paid me for the drinks.*
• You **pay** someone an amount: *They paid the owner €3,000.*
• You **pay in** a type of money: *Can I pay in euros?*
• You **pay by** a particular method: *You can pay by credit card.*

2 BILL/TAX/RENT [T] to pay money that you owe to a person, company etc: *I forgot to* ***pay*** *the gas* ***bill***! | *You pay tax at the basic rate.* | *Is it okay if I pay you what I owe you next week?*
3 WAGE/SALARY [I,T] to give someone money for the job they do: *How much do they pay you?* | **pay sb $100 a day/£200 a week etc** *They're only paid about £4 an hour.* | *Some lawyers* ***get paid*** *over $400 an hour.* | **be paid weekly/monthly** (*also* **get paid weekly/monthly**) *We get paid weekly on Fridays.* | **well/badly/poorly paid** *Many of the workers are very badly paid.* | **paid work** (=work you are paid to do) | **paid holiday/leave** (=time when you are not working but are still paid)
4 pay attention (to sb/sth) to watch, listen to, or think about someone or something carefully: *I'm sorry, I wasn't paying attention to what you were saying.* | *They* ***paid no attention to*** (=ignored) *him.*
5 LEGAL COST [T] to give money to someone because you are ordered to by a court as part of a legal case: *She had to* ***pay*** *a £35* ***fine*** *for speeding.* | **pay (sth in) compensation/damages** (=give someone money because you have done something against them) *The company were forced to* ***pay*** *£5,000* ***in compensation***. | *Martins was ordered to pay court costs of £1,500.*
6 SAY STH GOOD [T] to say something good or polite about or to someone: *The minister* ***paid tribute to*** *the work of the emergency services.* | *I came by to* ***pay my respects*** (=visit or send a polite greeting to someone) *to Mrs Owens.* | *I was just trying to* ***pay*** *her* ***a compliment***.
7 GOOD RESULT [I] if a particular action pays, it brings a good result or advantage for you: *Crime doesn't pay.* | ***It pays to*** *get some professional advice before you make a decision.* | ***It would pay you to*** *ask if there are any jobs going at the London office.* | *Getting some qualifications now will* ***pay dividends*** (=bring a lot of advantages) *in the long term.*
8 PROFIT [I] if a shop or business pays, it makes a profit: *If the pub doesn't start to pay, we'll have to sell it.* | *The farm just manages to* ***pay its way*** (=make as much profit as it costs to run).
9 pay the penalty/price to experience something unpleasant because you have done something wrong, made a mistake etc: **pay the penalty/price for (doing) sth** *Williams is now paying the price for his early mistakes.*
10 pay (sb) a call/visit to visit a person or place: *I decided to pay my folks a visit.* | **[+to]** *If you have time, pay a visit to the City Art Gallery.*
11 put paid to sth *BrE* to stop something from happening or spoil plans for something: *Bad exam results put paid to his hopes of a university place.*
12 BE PUNISHED [I] to suffer or be punished for something you have done wrong: *I'll* ***make*** *him* ***pay***! | **[+for]** *They* ***paid dearly*** *for their mistakes.*
13 pay your way to pay for everything that you want without having to depend on anyone else for money: *Sofia worked to pay her way through college.*
14 pay for itself if something you buy pays for itself, the money it saves over a period of time is as much as the product cost to buy: *A new boiler would pay for itself within two years.*
15 the devil/hell to pay used to say that someone will be in a lot of trouble about something: *If the boss finds out you were late again, there's going to be hell to pay.*
16 pay through the nose (for sth) *spoken* to pay much more for something than it is really worth
17 sb has paid their debt to society used to say that someone who has done something illegal has been fully punished for it
18 pay court (to sb) *old-fashioned* to treat someone, especially a woman, carefully and with respect, so that they will like you or help you
19 he who pays the piper calls the tune *old-fashioned* used to say that the person who gives the money for something can decide how it will be used
20 pay it forward to do something nice for someone because someone else did something nice for you → **pay lip service to** at LIP SERVICE, → **pay your dues** at DUE³(2)

THESAURUS

pay to give someone money for something you are buying from them, or a service they are providing: *I paid a lot of money for that computer.* | *You have to pay to park your car.*
meet the cost of sth to pay for something for someone else, or to provide the money needed to do something: *We will meet the cost of your travelling expenses.*
foot the bill to pay for something for someone else, especially when you do not want to, or do not think that you should: *As usual, the taxpayer will have to foot the bill.*
pick up the tab *informal* to pay for something: *My company will pick up the tab for all moving costs.*
fork out/shell out *informal* to pay a lot of money for something because you have to and not because you want to: *He had to fork out £500 to get his car fixed.*
settle the bill to pay the bill after eating a meal, staying in a hotel etc: *She went down to the hotel lobby to settle the bill.*
give *especially spoken* to pay a particular amount of money for something – used especially when saying how much you are willing to pay: *How much will you give me for the car?* | *I'll give you $50 for the lot* (=for everything).
sth is on sb *spoken* used when saying that someone else will pay for your meal, drinks etc: *Order whatever you like – this is on me!* | *The drinks* ***are on the house*** (=the bar, restaurant etc will let you have them for free).

pay sb/sth ↔ **back** *phr v*
1 to give someone the money that you owe them SYN **repay**: *I'll pay you back on Friday.* | *We're paying back the loan over 15 years.*
2 to make someone suffer for doing something wrong or unpleasant: **pay sb back for sth** *I'll pay Jenny back for what she did to me!*
pay sth ↔ **in** (*also* **pay sth into sth**) *phr v* to put money in your bank account etc: *Did you remember to pay that cheque in?* | *I've paid $250 into my account.*
pay off *phr v*
1 pay sth ↔ off to give someone all the money you owe them: *I'll* ***pay off*** *all my* ***debts*** *first.* | *He finally paid his overdraft off.*
2 if something you do pays off, it is successful or has a good result: *Teamwork paid off.*
3 pay sb ↔ off *BrE* to pay someone their wages and tell them they no longer have a job: *Two hundred workers have been paid off.*
4 pay sb ↔ off to pay someone not to say anything about something illegal or dishonest → PAYOFF(2)
pay out *phr v*
1 pay out (sth) to pay a lot of money for something: *Why is it always me who has to pay out?* | **[+for]** *Altogether he had paid out almost £5000 for the improvements.*
2 pay out (sth) if a company or organization pays out, it gives someone money as a result of an insurance claim, INVESTMENT, competition etc: *Insurance companies were slow paying out on claims for flood damage.* → PAYOUT
3 pay sth ↔ out to let a piece of rope unwind
pay sth ↔ **over** *phr v* to make an official payment of money: **[+to]** *Clancy's share of the inheritance was paid over to him.*
pay up *phr v* to pay money that you owe, especially when you do not want to or you are late: *She refused to pay up.* → PAID-UP

P

pay² ●●● S1 W2 *n* [U]
1 money that you are given for doing your job: *Staff have been working without pay for the last month.* | *The tax is deducted from your pay every week.* | *He was suspended* ***on full pay*** *until the hearing.* THESAURUS ▸ SALARY
2 **in the pay of sb** *written* someone who is in someone else's pay is working for them, often secretly: *an informer in the pay of the police*

COLLOCATIONS

ADJECTIVES/NOUN + pay

low *Nurses often work long hours for relatively low pay.*
good *The work was steady and the pay was pretty good.*
higher/better *Workers demanded higher pay.*
equal pay (=the same pay for the same type of work) *The women at the factory went on strike for equal pay.*
basic pay *BrE*, **base pay** *AmE* (=not including overtime pay or bonuses) | **take-home pay** (=after tax etc has been taken away) | **overtime pay** (=for extra hours that you work) | **holiday pay** *BrE*, **vacation pay** *AmE* (=pay when you are on holiday) | **sick pay** (=pay when you are ill) | **maternity pay** (=pay while a woman takes time off to have a baby) | **redundancy pay** *BrE*, **severance pay** *AmE* (=pay when there is no longer a job for you) | **full pay** | **half pay**

pay + NOUN

a pay increase *Teachers will be awarded a 6% pay increase this year.*
a pay rise *BrE*, **pay raise** *AmE* *If you get promoted, will you get a pay rise?*
a pay cut *Staff were asked to take a 10% pay cut.*
a rate of pay (*also* **a pay rate**) (=the amount paid every hour, week etc) *Many workers in the catering industry are on low rates of pay.*
a pay cheque *BrE*, **a paycheck** *AmE* (=the money you earn every week or month) | **a pay freeze** (=when no one's pay is increased) | **a pay claim** *BrE* (=official request for more pay) | **a pay dispute** (=disagreement between an employer and employees about pay)

COMMON ERRORS

⚠ Don't say 'the salary pay'. Just say **the pay**.

pay·a·ble /ˈpeɪəbəl/ *adj* [not before noun] **1** a bill, debt etc that is payable must be paid: **[+on]** *Tax is payable on the interest.* | **[+by]** *a fee of £49, payable by the tenant* | **[+to]** *State pensions become payable to women at age 60.* | *The rent is* ***payable in advance.*** **2** **payable to sb** a cheque etc that is payable to someone has that person's name written on it and should be paid to them: *Cheques should be* ***made payable to*** *the National Trust.*

ˌpay-as-you-ˈgo *adj* [only before noun] a pay-as-you-go MOBILE PHONE or Internet service is one that you must pay for before you can use it → **pre-pay**

pay·back /ˈpeɪbæk/ *n* **1** [C] the money or advantage you gain from a business, project, or something you have done: *The immediate payback for them is publicity.* **2** [U] *AmE informal* when you do something to make someone suffer because of something they have done to harm you → **revenge**: *I guess* ***it's payback time.*** **3** **payback period a)** the period of time in which you will make a profit on an INVESTMENT **b)** the period of time over which you must pay back money you have borrowed

pay·cheque *BrE*, **paycheck** *AmE* /ˈpeɪ-tʃek/ *n* [C] **1** a cheque that someone receives as payment for their wages: *a weekly paycheque* **2** *especially AmE* the amount of wages someone earns SYN **pay packet** *BrE*: *a nice fat paycheck*

pay·day /ˈpeɪdeɪ/ *n* [U] the day on which you get your wages

ˈpayday ˌlender *n* [C] a person or organization that offers payday loans

ˈpayday ˌloan *n* [C] an amount of money that is lent for a short period of time, usually at a high rate of interest and because someone needs money until they get paid again from their job

pay·dirt /ˈpeɪdɜːt $ -dɜːrt/ *n* [U] **hit/strike paydirt** *AmE informal* to make a valuable or useful discovery, especially one that makes you rich or successful

PAYE /ˌpiː eɪ waɪ ˈiː/ *n* [U] *BrE* (***pay as you earn***) a system for paying tax in which tax is taken from workers' wages and paid directly to the government

pay·ee /peɪˈiː/ *n* [C] the person or organization to whom money, especially a cheque, must be paid

pay·er /ˈpeɪə $ -ər/ *n* [C] someone who pays someone or something: *tax payers*

ˌpaying-ˈin book *n* [C] *BrE* a book containing forms that you use when you put money into your bank account

ˌpaying-ˈin slip *n* [C] *BrE* a form that you use when you put money into your bank account SYN **deposit slip** *AmE*

pay·load /ˈpeɪləʊd $ -loʊd/ *n* **1** [C,U] the amount of goods or passengers that can be carried by a vehicle, or the goods that a vehicle is carrying → **cargo**: **[+of]** *The helicopter is designed to carry a payload of 2,640 pounds.* **2** [C] the amount of explosive that a MISSILE can carry

pay·mas·ter /ˈpeɪˌmɑːstə $ -ˌmæstər/ *n* [C] **1** a powerful person or organization that secretly pays and controls another person or organization: *The assassin's paymasters were never identified.* **2** someone who is responsible for giving people their wages that they are owed, for example an official in a factory or the army

pay·ment /ˈpeɪmənt/ ●●● S2 W1 *n*
1 [C] an amount of money that has been or must be paid: *You can make a payment in any bank.* | *They fell behind on their mortgage payments.*
2 [U] the act of paying for something: **[+of]** *There are severe penalties for late payment of taxes.* | **[+in]** *Most hotels here accept payment in dollars.* | ***Payment*** *can be* ***made*** *by cheque or credit card.* | *We do accept* ***payment in instalments*** (=paying in small amounts over a period of time). | *She demanded* ***payment in advance.*** | **in payment for sth** (=in order to pay for something) *cheques received in payment for goods supplied* | **on payment of sth** (=when an amount has been paid) *Any item can be reserved on payment of a deposit.*
3 **payment in kind** a way of paying for something with goods or services instead of money

COLLOCATIONS

VERBS

make (a) payment *He was supposed to make payments of $250 a month.*
receive (a) payment *You will receive a cash payment on your 65th birthday.*
meet/keep up the payments (on sth) (=be able to make regular payments) *He was having trouble meeting the interest payments.*
fall behind on the payments (*also* **fall behind with the payments** *BrE*) (=not make payments when you should)

ADJECTIVES/NOUN + payment

a monthly payment *Home buyers have seen their monthly payments go up by more than 50 percent.*
a cash payment (=a payment in cash) *He provided pills to athletes in return for cash payments.*
a down payment (=a small payment for something you are buying, when you will pay the rest later) *We were able to put a down payment on an apartment.*
an interest payment (=a payment of interest on a loan) | **a mortgage payment** (=a payment towards a loan on your house) | **an interim payment** (=a payment that is made before something is finished or settled) | **a bonus payment** (=an additional payment because success has been achieved)

pay·off /ˈpeɪɒf $ -ɒːf/ *n* [C] **1** an advantage or profit that you get as a result of doing something: *With electric cars* *there is a big environmental payoff.* **2** a payment that is made to someone, often illegally, in order to stop them from causing you trouble → **bribe**: *Union leaders allegedly received huge payoffs from the company's bosses.* **3** a payment made to someone when they are forced to leave their job → **redundancy**: *The average payoff to staff was about £2000.*

pay·o·la /peɪˈəʊlə $ -ˈoʊlə/ *n* [U] *especially AmE informal* **1** the illegal practice of paying someone to use their influence to make people buy what your company is selling **2** the money that is paid to someone to use their influence

pay·out /ˈpeɪ-aʊt/ *n* [C] a large payment of money to someone, for example from an insurance claim or from winning a competition: *There should be a big payout on this month's lottery.* | *Some of the victims have been offered massive* ***cash payouts****.*

ˈpay ˌpacket *n* [C] *BrE* **1** the amount of money someone earns **2** an envelope containing someone's wages

ˌpay-per-ˈread *n* [U] a method of reading books and other material on the Internet, and paying only for what you read —**pay-per-read** *adj* [only before noun]

ˌpay-per-ˈview *adj* [only before noun] a pay-per-view television CHANNEL makes people pay for each programme they watch → **pay TV** —**pay-per-view** *n* [U]

ˈpay phone *n* [C] a public telephone that you can use when you put in a coin or a CREDIT CARD

ˈpay rise *BrE*, **ˈpay raise** *AmE n* [C] an increase in the amount of money you are paid for doing your job: *Some company directors have awarded themselves huge pay rises.* | *a 4% pay raise*

pay·roll /ˈpeɪrəʊl $ -roʊl/ *n* **1 on the payroll** if someone is on the payroll of a company, they are employed by that company: *The company now has 350 people on the payroll.* **2** [U] the activity of managing salary payments for workers in a company: *the payroll department* | *a computerized payroll system* **3** [C,U] the total amount of wages paid to all the people working in a particular company or industry: *the annual payroll was $88 million*

ˈpayroll ˌtax *n* [C,U] a tax that is taken from someone's wages and given directly to the government → **income tax**

pay·slip /ˈpeɪslɪp/ *BrE*, **ˈpay stub** *AmE n* [C] a piece of paper that an employed person gets every time they are paid, showing the amount they have been paid and the amount that has been taken away for tax

ˌpay TˈV (*also* **ˌpay teleˈvision**) *n* [U] television CHANNELS that you must pay to watch → **pay-per-view**

pay·wall /ˈpeɪwɔːl $ -wɒːl/ *n* [C] a feature of a website that means people have to pay to see part or all of the website, rather than seeing it for free: *Most of the magazine's website content is hidden behind a paywall.*

PC¹ /ˌpiː ˈsiː◂/ ●●○ *n* [C]
1 (***personal computer***) a computer that is used by one person at a time, either at home or at work: *People can use their PCs to do their banking from home.*
2 *BrE* (***police constable***) a police officer of the lowest rank

PC² ●○○ *adj* (***politically correct***) used to describe language, behaviour, and attitudes that are carefully chosen so that they do not offend or insult anyone: *It's not PC to describe people as disabled.*

PˈC ˌCard *n* [C] *trademark* (***personal computer card***) a small flat object which stores information that can be added to some computers

pcm (***per calendar month***) used in writing when stating the amount of rent to be paid each month

PCP /ˌpiː siː ˈpiː/ *n* [C] *AmE* (***primary care physician***) a doctor you go to when you are ill, who may treat you or advise you to see a SPECIALIST (=a doctor who deals with a particular part of the body)

PCSO /ˌpiː siː es ˈəʊ $ -ˈoʊ/ *n* [C] (***police community support officer***) someone whose job with the police is to PATROL (=walk around) an area in order to make the people who live or work there feel safer, and to find out about criminal activity in that area. PCSOs do not have the same rights and duties as an ordinary police officer.

PDA /ˌpiː diː ˈeɪ/ *n* **1** [C] (***personal digital assistant***) a very small light computer that you can carry with you, and that you use to store information such as telephone numbers, addresses, and APPOINTMENTS. Some PDAs can send and receive email, and connect to the Internet. **2** [C,U] (***public display of affection***) *informal* when someone kisses or touches their boyfriend, girlfriend, partner etc in public in a way that shows that they love them: *She and her new boyfriend engaged in a pretty obvious PDA at the celebrity party.*

PDF /ˌpiː diː ˈef/ *n* [U] *technical* (***portable document format***) a way of storing computer FILES so that they can be easily read when they are moved from one computer to another

PDQ /ˌpiː diː ˈkjuː/ *adv informal* (***pretty damn quick***) used to say that something should be done immediately

PE *BrE*, **P.E.** *AmE* /ˌpiː ˈiː/ ●●○ *n* [U] (***physical education***) sport and physical activity taught as a school subject: *a PE teacher*

pea /piː/ ●●● S3 *n* [C]
1 a round green seed that is cooked and eaten as a vegetable, or the plant on which these seeds grow: *roast chicken with peas and carrots* → see picture at **VEGETABLE¹**
2 like two peas in a pod *informal* exactly the same in appearance, behaviour etc

ˈpea-brained *adj informal* stupid: *a pea-brained idiot*

peace /piːs/ ●●● S2 W2 *n*
1 NO WAR [singular, U] a situation in which there is no war or fighting: *The country is* ***at peace with*** *its neighbours for the first time in years.* | *By the end of the century, France had* ***made peace with*** *Britain.* | *a city where people of different religions have* ***lived*** *together* ***in peace*** *for centuries* | *efforts to* ***bring peace*** *to the region* | *a dangerous situation which threatens* ***world peace*** | **[+between]** *a* ***lasting peace*** *between the two sides* | *An* ***uneasy peace*** *continued until 1939.* | *the Northern Ireland* ***peace talks*** | *an international* ***peace conference*** | *the* ***peace treaty*** *that ended the First World War* | *the Middle East* ***peace process***
2 NO NOISE/INTERRUPTIONS [U] a very quiet and pleasant situation in which you are not interrupted: **in peace** *I'll leave you now and let you get dressed in peace.* | *I wish she would just* ***leave*** *me* ***in peace****.* | *All I want is some* ***peace and quiet****.*
3 CALM/NOT WORRIED [U] a feeling of being calm, happy, and not worried: *the search for* ***inner peace*** | *Having household insurance is supposed to give you* ***peace of mind****.* | *Lynn seems to* ***be*** *more* ***at peace with herself*** *these days* (=calm, satisfied, no longer worried about anything).
4 make (your) peace with sb to end a quarrel with a person or group, especially by telling them you are sorry: *Ann wanted to make her peace with her father before he died.*
5 keep the peace to stop people from fighting, arguing, or causing trouble: *The US is sending troops overseas in order to keep the peace.*
6 hold/keep your peace *formal old-fashioned* to keep quiet even though you would like to say something
7 disturb the peace *law* to behave in a noisy or violent way: *Macklin was charged with disturbing the peace.* → **breach of the peace** at **BREACH¹(5)**
8 rest in peace words that are said during a funeral service for someone who has died, or written on a GRAVESTONE → **RIP**

peace·a·ble /ˈpiːsəbəl/ *adj literary* **1** someone who is peaceable does not like fighting or arguing → **pacifist** OPP **violent, aggressive**: *He's always been a very peaceable man.* **2** a peaceable situation or way of doing something is calm, without any violence or fighting: *We are now hoping for a peaceable end to this dispute.* —**peaceably** *adv*: *The two communities live together quite peaceably.*

ˈPeace Corps, the a US government organization that helps poorer countries, by sending them VOLUNTEERS (=people who work without payment), especially young people, who teach skills in education, health, farming etc

ˈpeace ˌdividend *n* [singular] the money that is saved on weapons and is available for other purposes, when a government reduces its military strength because the risk of war has been reduced

peace·ful /ˈpiːsfəl/ ●●○ S3 *adj*
1 a peaceful time, place, or situation is quiet and calm without any worry or excitement: *We had a peaceful afternoon without the children.* | *It's very peaceful out here in the woods.* THESAURUS QUIET
2 not involving war, fighting, or violence: **peaceful protest/demonstration** *There was a large but peaceful demonstration outside the US Embassy.* | **peaceful solution/conclusion/settlement** *We must try to find a peaceful solution to the conflict.* | **peaceful means/way/manner/method** *a political change achieved by peaceful and democratic means* | *the use of nuclear power for peaceful purposes* | *The countries in Europe have established a* **peaceful co-existence** (=they exist together without fighting).
3 peaceful people do not like violence and do not behave in a violent way → **non-violent**: *a noisy but peaceful group of demonstrators* —**peacefully** *adv*: *She was sleeping peacefully.* —**peacefulness** *n* [U]

peace·keep·ing /ˈpiːsˌkiːpɪŋ/ *adj* [only before noun] **peacekeeping force/troops etc** a group of soldiers who are sent to a place in order to stop two opposing groups from fighting each other: *The United Nations has decided to send a peacekeeping force into the area.* —**peacekeeper** *n* [C]: *a group of UN peacekeepers*

ˈpeace-ˌloving *adj* believing strongly in peace rather than war: *a peace-loving nation*

peace·mak·er /ˈpiːsmeɪkə $ -ər/ *n* [C] someone who tries to persuade other people or countries to stop fighting: *The US sees itself as a peacemaker in the region.*

ˈpeace ˌoffering *n* [C] something you give to someone to show them that you are sorry and want to be friendly, after you have annoyed or upset them

ˈpeace pipe *n* [C] a pipe which Native Americans use to smoke tobacco, which is shared in a ceremony as a sign of peace SYN **pipe of peace**

peace·time /ˈpiːstaɪm/ *n* [U] a period of time when a country is not fighting a war OPP **wartime**: **in peacetime** *the highest military award given in peacetime*

peach¹ /piːtʃ/ ●●● S3 *n*
1 [C] a round juicy fruit that has a soft yellow or red skin and a large hard seed in the centre, or the tree that this fruit grows on → see picture at FRUIT¹
2 [U] a pale pinkish-orange colour
3 [singular] *old-fashioned* something or someone that you think is very good: *Anderton scored* **a peach of a** *goal.* | *Jan's* **a real peach**.
4 peaches and cream used to describe skin that is an attractive pink colour: *a peaches and cream complexion*

peach² *adj* pinkish-orange in colour: *peach curtains*

Peach Mel·ba, **peach Melba** /ˌpiːtʃ ˈmelbə/ *n* [C,U] half a peach served with ice cream and RASPBERRY juice

peach·y /ˈpiːtʃi/ *adj* **1** tasting or looking like a peach: *a delicious peachy flavour* **2** *AmE informal* very good or pleasant

pea·cock /ˈpiːkɒk $ -kɑːk/ *n* [C] a large bird, the male of which has long blue and green tail feathers that it can lift up and spread out → **peahen**

pea·fowl /ˈpiːfaʊl/ *n* [C] a peacock or peahen

ˌpea ˈgreen *n* [U] a light green colour —**pea green** *adj*

pea·hen /ˈpiːhen/ *n* [C] a female PEACOCK

peak¹ /piːk/ ●●○ W3 *n* [C]
1 TIME [usually singular] the time when something or someone is best, greatest, highest, most successful etc: **at sth's peak** *The British Empire was at its peak in the mid 19th century.* | *Sales this month have* **reached** *a new* **peak**. | *Most athletes* **reach** *their* **peak** *in their mid-20s.* | *He's* **past** *his* **peak** *as a tennis player.* | *Oil production is down from its peak of two years ago.* | **at the peak of sth** *Hotel rooms are difficult to find at the peak of the holiday season.* | *the* **peaks and troughs** *of the US economy* (=high and low points)
2 MOUNTAIN **a)** the sharply pointed top of a mountain: *snow-capped* **mountain peaks** | *jagged peaks* **b)** a mountain → **summit**: *Mount McKinley is Alaska's highest peak.*
3 POINT a part that forms a point above a surface or at the top of something: *Whisk the egg whites until they form stiff peaks.*
4 HAT *especially BrE* the flat curved part of a cap that sticks out in front above your eyes SYN **visor** *AmE*

peak² ●○○ *v* [I] to reach the highest point or level: *Sales peaked in August, then fell sharply.* | **[+at]** *Wind speeds peaked at 105 mph yesterday.*

peak³ ●○○ *adj* [only before noun]
1 used to talk about the best, highest, or greatest level or amount of something: *Gasoline prices are 14% below the peak level they hit in November.* | *a shampoo designed to keep your hair* **in peak condition** | *If you phone during the day you pay the* **peak rate** *for calls.* | *periods of* **peak demand** *for electricity*
2 *BrE* the peak time or period is when the greatest number of people are doing the same thing, using the same service etc: *Extra buses run at* **peak times**. | *Hotel prices rise during the* **peak season**.
3 peak oil/coal/gas the time when the rate of getting oil, coal, or gas out of the ground has reached its highest level, after which it will gradually begin to get lower: *Some scientists believe we have already reached peak oil.*

peak·ed¹ /ˈpiːkɪd/ *adj AmE* looking pale and ill SYN **peaky** *BrE*: *You're* **looking** *a little* **peaked** *this morning.*

peaked² /piːkt/ *adj BrE* a peaked cap or hat has a flat curved part at the front above the eyes → see picture at HAT

pea·ky /ˈpiːki/ *adj BrE informal* looking pale and ill SYN **peaked** *AmE*: *He's* **looking** *a bit* **peaky** *today.*

peal¹ /piːl/ *n* [C] **1** a sudden loud sound of laughter: **[+of]** *We could hear* **peals of laughter** *coming from the hall.* **2** a loud sound of thunder SYN **clap**: **[+of]** *A loud* **peal of thunder** *crashed directly overhead.* **3** the loud ringing sound made by a bell: *A sudden* **peal of bells** *broke the silence.* **4** *technical* a musical pattern made by ringing a number of bells one after the other

peal² *v* [I] **1** (*also* **peal out**) if bells peal, they ring loudly: *The bells pealed out on Christmas Day.* **2** *literary* to make a loud sound: *Lightning flashed and thunder pealed.*

pea·nut /ˈpiːnʌt/ ●●● S3 *n*
1 [C] a pale brown nut in a thin shell which grows under the ground SYN **groundnut**: *a packet of roasted peanuts* → see picture at NUT¹
2 peanuts *informal* a very small amount of money: *The hotel workers get* **paid peanuts**. | *I'm tired of* **working for peanuts**.

ˌpeanut ˈbutter / $ ˈ.. ˌ../ *n* [U] a soft food made from crushed peanuts, which is eaten on bread or used in cooking

pear /peə $ per/ ●●● S3 *n* [C] a sweet juicy fruit that has a round base and is thinner near the top, or the tree that produces this fruit → see picture at FRUIT¹

pearl /pɜːl $ pɜːrl/ ●●○ *n*
1 JEWEL [C] a small round white object that forms inside an OYSTER, and is a valuable jewel: *a* **pearl necklace** | *a* **string of pearls** (=a NECKLACE made of pearls)
2 HARD SUBSTANCE [U] a hard shiny substance of various colours formed inside some SHELLFISH, which is used for making buttons or to make objects look attractive SYN **mother-of-pearl**
3 pearls of wisdom wise remarks – used especially when you really think that someone's remarks are slightly stupid: *Thank you for those pearls of wisdom, Emma.*
4 cast/throw pearls before swine *formal* to give something valuable to someone who does not understand its value
5 LIQUID [C] *literary* a small round drop of liquid: *the pearls of the morning dew*
6 EXCELLENT THING/PERSON [C usually singular] *old-fashioned* someone or something that is especially good or valuable: **[+among]** *She's a pearl among women.*

ˌpearl ˈbarley *n* [U] small grains of BARLEY that are used in cooking

ˌPearl ˈHarbor an important US naval base in Hawaii, which was suddenly attacked by Japanese planes in December 1941. Many warships were destroyed or damaged, and this caused great shock and anger in the US, and made the US start fighting in World War II.

pearl·y /ˈpɜːli $ ˈpɜːrli/ *adj* pale in colour and shiny, like a pearl: *pearly white teeth | a pearly grey jacket*

ˌpearly ˈgates *n* **the pearly gates** [plural] the entrance to heaven - often used humorously

ˈpear-shaped *adj* **1 go pear-shaped** *BrE informal* if an activity or situation goes pear-shaped, it goes wrong: *The whole thing went pear-shaped.* **2** someone who is pear-shaped has wide HIPS and a fairly small chest

peas·ant /ˈpezənt/ *n* [C] **1** a poor farmer who owns or rents a small amount of land, either in past times or in poor countries: *Most villagers are peasant farmers.* **2** *old-fashioned informal* an insulting word for someone who does not behave politely in social situations or is not well educated

peas·ant·ry /ˈpezəntri/ *n* **the peasantry** all the peasants of a country

pease pud·ding /ˌpiːz ˈpʊdɪŋ/ *n* [U] *BrE* a dish made of dried PEAS, boiled with HAM to make a thick yellow substance that is eaten hot or cold

pea·shoot·er /ˈpiːʃuːtə $ -ər/ *n* [C] a small tube used by children to blow small objects, especially dried PEAS, at someone or something

pea·soup·er /ˌpiːˈsuːpə $ -ər/ *n* [C] *BrE old-fashioned* a very thick FOG

peat /piːt/ *n* [U] a black substance formed from decaying plants under the surface of the ground in some areas, which can be burned as a FUEL, or mixed with soil to help plants grow well —**peaty** *adj*: *a rich, peaty soil*

peb·ble /ˈpebəl/ ●○○ *n* [C] a small smooth stone found especially on a beach or on the bottom of a river: *The beach was covered with smooth white pebbles.* —**pebbly** *adj*: *a pebbly beach* → see picture at **STONE**[1]

peb·ble·dash /ˈpebəldæʃ/ *n* [U] *BrE* a surface for the outside walls of houses, made of CEMENT with a lot of very small round stones in it

pe·can /pɪˈkæn, ˈpiːkən $ pɪˈkɑːn, pɪˈkæn/ *n* [C] a long thin sweet nut with a dark red shell, or the tree that it grows on → see picture at **NUT**[1]

pec·ca·dil·lo /ˌpekəˈdɪləʊ $ -loʊ/ *n* (*plural* **peccadilloes** *or* **peccadillos**) [C] something bad which someone does, especially involving sex, which is not regarded as very serious or important: *The public is willing to forgive him for his peccadillos.*

pec·ca·ry /ˈpekəri/ *n* (*plural* **peccaries**) [C] a wild animal like a pig that lives in Central and South America

peck[1] /pek/ *v* **1** [I,T] if a bird pecks something or pecks at something, it makes quick repeated movements with its beak to try to eat part of it, make a hole in it etc: **[+at]** *birds pecking at breadcrumbs on the pavement* **2 peck sb on the cheek/forehead etc** to kiss someone quickly and lightly: *She pecked her father lightly on the cheek.*

peck at sth *phr v* to eat only a little bit of a meal because you are not interested in it or not hungry: *She pecked at her food in silence.*

peck[2] *n* [C] **1** a quick light kiss: *He* ***gave*** *her a quick* ***peck on the cheek***. **2** an action in which a bird pecks someone or something with its beak

peck·er /ˈpekə $ -ər/ *n* [C] **1 keep your pecker up** *BrE old-fashioned informal* used to tell someone to stay cheerful even when it is difficult to do so **2** *AmE informal* PENIS

ˈpecking ˌorder *n* [singular] a social system within a group of people or animals in which each member knows who has a higher or lower rank than themselves: *Nobody wants to be* ***at the bottom of the pecking order***.

peck·ish /ˈpekɪʃ/ *adj BrE informal* slightly hungry: *She was* ***feeling*** *a bit* ***peckish***.

pecs /peks/ *n* [plural] *informal* PECTORALS

pec·tin /ˈpektɪn/ *n* [U] a chemical substance that is found in some fruits and is sometimes added to JAM and JELLY to make it less liquid

pec·to·rals /ˈpektərəlz/ *n* [plural] your chest muscles —**pectoral** *adj*: *pectoral muscles*

pe·cu·li·ar /pɪˈkjuːliə $ -ər/ ●●○ *adj*
1 strange, unfamiliar, or a little surprising: *There was a peculiar smell in the kitchen. | Something peculiar is going on. |* ***It*** *seems very* ***peculiar that*** *no one noticed Kay had gone.*
THESAURUS ▸ STRANGE
2 be peculiar to sb/sth if something is peculiar to a particular person, place, or situation, it is a feature that only belongs to that person or only exists in that place or situation: *The problem of racism* ***is not peculiar to*** *this country.*
3 behaving in a strange and slightly crazy way: *He's been a little peculiar lately. | She's a very peculiar child.*
4 feel peculiar/come over all peculiar *BrE informal* to feel slightly ill

pe·cu·li·ar·i·ty /pɪˌkjuːliˈærəti/ *n* (*plural* **peculiarities**)
1 [C] something that is a feature of only one particular place, person, situation etc: **[+of]** *The lack of a written constitution is a peculiarity of the British political system.*
2 [C] a strange or unusual habit, quality etc: *Margaret regarded her mother's peculiarities with a fond tolerance.*
3 [U] the quality of being strange or unfamiliar: **[+of]** *She was well aware of the peculiarity of her own situation.*

pe·cu·li·ar·ly /pɪˈkjuːliəli $ -ər-/ *adv* **1 peculiarly British/female/middle-class etc** something that is peculiarly British etc is a typical feature only of British people etc: *a peculiarly American idea* **2** in a strange or unusual way: *Theo had been behaving peculiarly.* **3** especially: *a peculiarly difficult question*

pe·cu·ni·a·ry /pɪˈkjuːniəri $ -nieri/ *adj formal* relating to or consisting of money → **financial**: *He was trying to get a* ***pecuniary advantage*** *for himself.*

ped·a·go·gi·cal /ˌpedəˈgɒdʒɪkəl $ -ˈgɑː-/ (*also* **ped·a·go·gic** /-ˈgɒdʒɪk $ -ˈgɑː-/) *adj formal* relating to teaching methods or the practice of teaching → **educational** —**pedagogically** /-kli/ *adv*

ped·a·gogue /ˈpedəgɒg $ -gɑːg/ *n* [C] *formal* a teacher, especially one who thinks they know a lot and is strict in the way they teach

ped·a·go·gy /ˈpedəgɒdʒi $ -goʊ-/ *n* [U] *formal* the practice of teaching or the study of teaching → **education**

ped·al[1] /ˈpedl/ ●●○ *n* [C]
1 (*also* **bicycle pedal**) one of the two parts of a bicycle that you push round with your feet to make the bicycle go forward → see picture at **BICYCLE**
2 a part in a car or on a machine that you press with your foot to control it: *She put her foot down on the accelerator pedal.*
3 a part on a piano or organ that you press with your foot to change the quality of the sound → see picture at **PIANO**[1]
4 put/press/push the pedal to the metal *AmE* **a)** to drive a car, truck etc very fast **b)** to work harder or faster, especially so that you can win a game

pedal[2] *v* (**pedalled**, **pedalling** *BrE*, **pedaled**, **pedaling** *AmE*) [I,T] **1** [always + adv/prep] to ride a bicycle → **cycle**, **ride**: **[+up/along/down etc]** *Andrew pedalled up the road towards the town centre.* **2** to turn or push the pedals on a bicycle or other machine with your feet: *She was* ***pedalling furiously*** (=very fast).

ˈpedal bin *n* [C] *BrE* a container for waste that has a lid which is opened by pressing part of it with your foot → see picture at **BIN**[1]

ped·a·lo /ˈpedələʊ $ -loʊ/ *n* (*plural* **pedalos**) [C] *BrE* a small boat that you move forward by pushing pedals round with your feet

ped·ant /ˈpednt/ *n* [C] someone who pays too much attention to rules or to small unimportant details, especially someone who criticizes other people in an extremely annoying way: *'That's not exactly what it means.' 'Pedant.'* —**pedantry** *n* [U]

pe·dan·tic /pɪˈdæntɪk/ *adj* paying too much attention to rules or to small unimportant details: **[+about]** *Some* *people can be very pedantic about punctuation.* —**pedantically** /-kli/ *adv*

ped·dle /ˈpedl/ *v* [T] **1** to sell goods to people, especially goods that people disapprove of because they are illegal, harmful, or of not very high quality → **push**, **deal**: *They were accused of* ***peddling drugs****.* | *people who peddle cigarettes to young children* **2** to try to sell things to people, especially by going from place to place: *Farmers come to Seoul to peddle rice.* | *a door-to-door salesman* ***peddling his wares*** (=selling his goods) **THESAURUS** SELL **3** to try to persuade people to accept an opinion or idea which is wrong or false: *politicians peddling instant solutions to long-standing problems*

ped·dler /ˈpedlə $ -ər/ *n* [C] **1** the American spelling of PEDLAR **2** *old-fashioned* someone who sells illegal drugs → **pusher**, **dealer**

P

ped·e·rast /ˈpedəræst/ *n* [C] *formal* a man who has sex with a young boy —**pederasty** *n* [U]

ped·es·tal /ˈpedəstəl/ *n* [C] **1** the base on which a PILLAR or STATUE stands: *a Grecian bust on a pedestal* **2** a solid vertical post that supports something such as a table: *the pedestal of the dentist's chair* | **pedestal basin** *BrE* (=a bowl to wash your hands in, supported by a pedestal) **3 put/place sb on a pedestal** to admire someone so much that you treat them or talk about them as though they are perfect: *Women are both put on a pedestal and treated like second-class citizens.*

pe·des·tri·an[1] /pəˈdestriən/ ●●○ *n* [C] someone who is walking, especially along a street or other place used by cars → **motorist**

pedestrian[2] *adj* **1** ordinary and uninteresting and without any imagination: *a painting that is pedestrian and unimaginative* | *a rather pedestrian student* **2** [only before noun] relating to pedestrians or used by pedestrians: *pedestrian traffic* | *a pedestrian walkway*

peˌdestrian ˈcrossing ●●○ *n* [C] *BrE* a specially marked place for people to walk across the road (SYN) **crosswalk** *AmE* → PELICAN CROSSING, ZEBRA CROSSING

pe·des·tri·a·nize (*also* **-ise** *BrE*) /pəˈdestriənaɪz/ *v* [T] to change a street or shopping area so that cars and trucks are no longer allowed —**pedestrianization** /pəˌdestriənaɪˈzeɪʃən $ -nə-/ *n* [U]

peˌdestrian ˈprecinct *BrE*, **peˌdestrian ˈmall** *AmE* *n* [C] a shopping area in the centre of a town where cars, trucks etc cannot go

pe·di·a·tri·cian /ˌpiːdiəˈtrɪʃən/ *n* [C] the American spelling of PAEDIATRICIAN

pe·di·at·rics /ˌpiːdiˈætrɪks/ *n* [U] the American spelling of PAEDIATRICS

ped·i·cure /ˈpedɪkjʊə $ -kjʊr/ *n* [C] a treatment for feet and toenails, to make them more comfortable or beautiful —**pedicurist** *n* [C] → MANICURE

ped·i·gree[1] /ˈpedəgriː/ *n* [C,U] **1** the parents and other past family members of an animal or person, or an official written record of this **2** the history and achievements of something or someone, especially when they are good and should be admired → **background**: *Founded in 1781, the school has an excellent pedigree.* | *a scientist's academic pedigree*

pedigree[2] *BrE*, **ped·i·greed** /ˈpedəgriːd/ *AmE* *adj* [only before noun] a pedigree animal comes from a family that has been recorded for a long time and is considered to be of a very good BREED: *a pedigree greyhound* → PUREBRED, THOROUGHBRED

ped·i·ment /ˈpedəmənt/ *n* [C] a three-sided part above the entrance to a building, especially on the buildings of ancient Greece

ped·lar /ˈpedlə $ -ər/ *n* [C] *BrE* someone who, in the past, walked from place to place selling small things → **peddle** (SYN) **peddler** *AmE*

pe·dom·e·ter /pəˈdɒmətə, pe- $ -ˈdɑːmɪtər/ *n* [C] an instrument that measures how far you walk

pe·do·phile /ˈpiːdəfaɪl/ *n* [C] the American spelling of PAEDOPHILE

pee[1] /piː/ *v* [I] *informal* to pass liquid waste from your body (SYN) **urinate**

pee[2] *n informal* **1** [U] liquid waste passed from your body (SYN) **urine 2** [singular] an act of passing liquid waste from your body: **go for a pee/have a pee** *BrE*, **take a pee** *AmE not polite*: *Have I got time to go for a pee before we leave?*

peek /piːk/ *v* [I] **1** to look quickly at something, or to look at something from behind something else, especially something that you are not supposed to see → **peep**: **[+at/through/into etc]** *Carefully he peeked through the glass window in the door.* | *Paula opened the box and peeked inside.* | *Shut your eyes and don't peek!* **THESAURUS** LOOK **2** [always + adv/prep] if something peeks from somewhere, you can just see a small amount of it: *The moon peeked out from behind the clouds.* —**peek** *n* [C]: *Diane* ***took a*** *quick* ***peek*** *at herself in the mirror.*

peek·a·boo /ˌpiːkəˈbuː $ ˈpiːkəbuː/ *interjection*, *n* [U] a game you play to amuse young children, in which you hide your face and then show it again, or the word you say when you play this game: *Peekaboo! I see you!*

peel[1] /piːl/ ●●○ *v*

1 [T] to remove the skin from fruit or vegetables: *Peel and dice the potatoes.* **THESAURUS** CUT

2 [I] if skin, paper, or paint peels, it comes off, usually in small pieces: **[+from/off]** *The paper was peeling from the wall.* | *New skin grows, and the damaged skin peels off.*

3 [I] to lose an outer layer or surface: *The walls were peeling from the damp.*

4 [T always + adv/prep] to remove the outer layer from something: **peel sth away/off/back** *Peel away the waxed paper from the bottom of the cake.* → **keep your eyes peeled** at EYE[1](18)

peel off *phr v*

1 peel sth ↔ **off** to take your clothes off: *Tom peeled off his wet T-shirt and shorts.*

2 peel off $20/£50 etc *informal* to take a piece of paper money from the top of a pile of paper money: *Manville peeled off a 20, and pressed it into the man's hand.*

3 to leave a moving group of vehicles, aircraft etc and go in a different direction: *Two motorcycles peeled off from the line.*

peel[2] ●●○ *n* [C,U] the skin of some fruits and vegetables, especially the thick skin of fruits such as oranges, which you do not eat → **rind**, **zest**: *orange peel* → see picture at FRUIT[1]

peel·er /ˈpiːlə $ -ər/ *n* [C] a special type of knife for removing the skin from fruit or vegetables

peel·ings /ˈpiːlɪŋz/ *n* [plural] pieces of skin that have been removed from fruit or vegetables: *Put the potato peelings on the compost heap.*

peep[1] /piːp/ *v* **1** [I] to look at something quickly and secretly, especially through a hole or opening (SYN) **peek** → **peer**: **[+into/through/out etc]** *The door was ajar and Helen peeped in.* | *Henry peeped through the window into the kitchen.* **THESAURUS** LOOK **2** [I always + adv/prep] if something peeps from somewhere, you can just see a small amount of it: **[+through/from/out etc]** *I could see her toes peeping out from under the sheet.* **3** [T] *informal* to look at something because it is interesting or attractive: *On our website you can peep our video interview with R&B's newest supergroup.*

peep[2] *n* [C] **1** a quick or secret look at something: **[+at/into]** *Jon* ***took a peep*** *at his watch.* **2 a peep** *informal* a sound that someone makes, or something that they say, especially a complaint: *There has* ***not*** *been* ***a peep out of*** *them since bedtime.* | *a peep of protest* **3** a short high sound, like the sound a mouse or a young bird makes: *the peep of a chick* | *loud peeps from the smoke alarm* **4** (*also* **peeps**) *informal* a word meaning 'people', used in magazines

peep·bo /ˈpiːpbəʊ $ -boʊ/ *interjection*, *n* [U] PEEKABOO

peep·hole /ˈpiːphəʊl $ -hoʊl/ *n* [C] a small hole in a door or wall that you can see through → **spy hole**

peeping Tom /ˌpiːpɪŋ ˈtɒm $ -ˈtɑːm/ *n* [C] someone who secretly watches people, especially people who are taking off their clothes, having sex etc → **voyeur**

peep·show /ˈpiːpʃəʊ $ -ʃoʊ/ *n* [C] **1** a type of show in which a man pays for a woman to take her clothes off while he watches through a window **2** a box containing moving pictures that you look at through a small hole

peer[1] /pɪə $ pɪr/ ●●○ *n* [C]
1 [usually plural] *formal* your peers are the people who are the same age as you, or who have the same type of job, social class etc: *American children did less well in math than their peers in Japan.* | *Staff members are trained by their peers.* → PEER GROUP, PEER PRESSURE
2 a member of the British NOBILITY → **House of Lords**, **peerage** → LIFE PEER

peer[2] ●●○ *v* [I always + adv/prep] to look very carefully at something, especially because you are having difficulty seeing it: *He was peering through the wet windscreen at the cars ahead.* | *Philippa peered into the darkness.* THESAURUS LOOK

peer·age /ˈpɪərɪdʒ $ ˈpɪr-/ *n* **1 the peerage** all the British peers considered as a group **2** [C] the rank of a British peer

peer·ess /ˈpɪərɪs $ ˈpɪr-/ *n* [C] a woman who is a member of the British NOBILITY → **peer**

ˈpeer group *n* [C] a group of people, especially people who are the same age, social class etc as yourself: *the TV shows that are popular with his peer group*

peer·less /ˈpɪələs $ ˈpɪr-/ *adj written* better than any other SYN **incomparable**: *the peerless blues musician B.B. King*

ˈpeer ˌpressure *n* [U] a strong feeling that you must do the same things as other people of your age if you want them to like you: *Teenagers often start smoking because of peer pressure.*

ˌpeer-to-ˈpeer (*also* **P2P**) *adj* **peer-to-peer architecture/network/technology etc** a computer system etc in which all of the computers are connected to each other and they do not need a SERVER (=a main computer that controls all the others): *How will peer-to-peer technology be important to the average Internet user?*

peeve /piːv/ *n* → **pet hate/pet peeve** at PET[3](2)

peeved /piːvd/ *adj informal* annoyed: **[+at]** *Peeved at his silence, she left.*

peev·ish /ˈpiːvɪʃ/ *adj* easily annoyed by small and unimportant things → **bad-tempered**: *The kids were peevish after so long in the car.* —**peevishly** *adv* —**peevishness** *n* [U]

pee·wit /ˈpiːwɪt/ *n* [C] a LAPWING

peg[1] /peg/ ●○○ *n* [C]
1 SHORT STICK a short piece of wood, metal, or plastic that is attached to a wall or fits into a hole, used especially to hang things on or to fasten things together: *Sarah hung her coat on the peg.* | *a table fitted together with pegs* | *a pattern made with coloured pegs on a board*
2 HANGING WET CLOTHES *BrE* a small plastic or wooden object used to fasten wet clothes to a thin rope to dry SYN **clothes peg**, **clothespin** *AmE*
3 TENT a pointed piece of wood or metal that you push into the ground in order to keep a tent in the correct position → see picture at TENT
4 take/bring sb down a peg (or two) to make someone realize that they are not as important or skilled as they think they are: *Evans is an arrogant bully who needs taking down a peg or two.*
5 MUSICAL INSTRUMENT a wooden screw used to make the strings of a VIOLIN, GUITAR etc tighter or looser SYN **tuning peg**
6 a peg to hang sth on *BrE* something that is used as a reason for doing, discussing, or believing something: *As a peg to hang it on, the tournament had the 100th anniversary of Nehru's birth.*
7 DRINK *BrE old-fashioned* a small amount of strong alcoholic drink, especially WHISKY or BRANDY → **square peg in a round hole** at SQUARE[1](12)

peg[2] *v* (**pegged**, **pegging**) [T] **1** to set prices, wages etc at a particular level, or set them in relation to something else: **peg sth at sth** *The dividend was pegged at 6.1p.* | **peg sth to sth** *a currency pegged to the American dollar* **2** to fasten something somewhere with a peg: *The tent flap was pegged open.* | *Outside, a woman was pegging sheets to a washing line.*

peg sb/sth **as** sth *phr v* to believe or say that someone has a particular type of character, or that a situation has particular qualities: *I'd* ***had*** *him* ***pegged as*** *a troublemaker.*

peg away *phr v BrE informal* to work hard and with determination: **[+at]** *She pegged away at her essay.*

peg sb/sth ↔ **back** *phr v BrE* to stop someone from winning in a sport or from increasing the amount by which they are winning – used in news reports: *They were pegged back by an equaliser from Jameson.*

peg out *phr v* **1** *BrE informal* to die, or to fall down because you are tired **2 peg sth ↔ out** *BrE* to fasten wet clothes to a washing line to dry **3 peg sth ↔ out** to mark a piece of ground with wooden sticks

peg·board, **peg board** /ˈpegbɔːd $ -bɔːrd/ *n* [C,U] thin board with holes in it, into which you can put pegs or hooks to hang things on

ˈpeg leg *n* [C] *informal* an artificial leg, especially a wooden one

pe·jo·ra·tive /pɪˈdʒɒrətɪv $ -ˈdʒɔː-, -ˈdʒɑː-/ *adj formal* a word or expression that is pejorative is used to show disapproval or to insult someone: *For hard-line Republicans, the word 'liberal' had become a pejorative term.* —**pejoratively** *adv*

peke /piːk/ *n* [C] *informal* a Pekinese dog

Pe·kin·ese, **Pekingese** /ˌpiːkəˈniːz◂/ *n* (*plural* **Pekinese**, **Pekingese**) [C] a very small dog with a short flat nose and long silky hair

pe·lag·ic /pəˈlædʒɪk/ *adj technical* relating to or living in the deep sea, far from shore: *pelagic fish*

pel·i·can /ˈpelɪkən/ *n* [C] a large water bird that catches fish for food and stores them in a deep bag of skin under its beak

ˌpelican ˈcrossing *n* [C] a place on some roads in Britain where someone who wants to cross the road can stop the traffic by pushing a button that changes the TRAFFIC LIGHTS → ZEBRA CROSSING

pel·lag·ra /pəˈlægrə/ *n* [U] a disease that makes you feel tired and that causes problems with your skin and CENTRAL NERVOUS SYSTEM, caused by a lack of a type of B VITAMIN

pel·let /ˈpelɪt/ *n* [C] **1** a small ball of a substance: *food pellets for rabbits* **2** a small ball of metal made to be fired from a gun: *shotgun pellets*

pell-mell /ˌpel ˈmel◂/ *adv old-fashioned* quickly and in an uncontrolled way: *The children ran pell-mell out of school.*

pel·lu·cid /pɪˈluːsɪd/ *adj literary* very clear SYN **transparent**: *a pellucid stream*

pel·met /ˈpelmɪt/ *n* [C] *BrE* a narrow piece of wood or cloth above a window that hides the rod that the curtains hang on SYN **valance** *AmE*

pelt[1] /pelt/ *v* **1** [T] to attack someone by throwing a lot of things at them: **pelt sb with sth** *The marchers were pelted with rocks and bottles.* **2** [I,T] to be raining very heavily → **pour**: *Rain pelted the windows.* | ***It's pelting down*** *out there.* | *the cold wind and* ***pelting rain*** **3** [I always + adv/prep] *informal* to run somewhere very fast: *Three huge dogs came pelting into the street.*

pelt[2] *n* [C] **1** the skin of a dead animal, especially with the fur or hair still on it → **hide 2** the fur or hair of a living animal **3 (at) full pelt** *BrE* moving as fast as possible: *Nancy ran at full pelt to the school.*

pel·vic /ˈpelvɪk/ *adj* in or relating to the pelvis

pel·vis /ˈpelvɪs/ *n* [C] the set of large wide curved bones at the base of your SPINE, to which your legs are joined → see picture at SKELETON

pem·mi·can /ˈpemɪkən/ *n* [U] dried meat, beaten into small pieces and pressed into flat round shapes

pen[1] /pen/ ●●● S2 *n*
1 [C,U] an instrument for writing or drawing with ink

→ **pencil**, **biro**: *a ballpoint pen | a felt-tip pen |* **in pen** *Please fill out the form in pen. | a* ***pen and ink*** *drawing* → see picture at STATIONERY
2 [C] a small piece of land enclosed by a fence to keep farm animals in: *a sheep pen* → PLAYPEN
3 put/set pen to paper to begin to write
4 [C] *AmE informal* a short form of PENITENTIARY
5 [C] *BrE informal* a PENALTY, used especially when talking about football

pen² *v* (**penned**, **penning**) [T] *literary* to write something such as a letter, a book etc, especially using a pen: *a song penned by George Clinton*

pen sb/sth ↔ **up/in** *phr v* **1** to shut an animal in a small enclosed area **2 be penned up/in** to be restricted or forced to remain in a small place: *Norma felt restless and penned in.*

P

pe·nal /ˈpiːnl/ *adj* **1** [only before noun] relating to the legal punishment of criminals, especially in prisons: *the penal system |* **penal colony/settlement** (=a special area of land where prisoners are kept) **2 penal servitude** *law* when someone is punished by being kept in prison and made to do hard physical work **3** *BrE* very severe: *penal rates of interest*

ˈpenal ˌcode *n* [C] a set of laws and the punishments for not obeying those laws

pe·nal·ize (*also* **-ise** *BrE*) /ˈpiːnəl-aɪz $ ˈpiː-, ˈpe-/ *v* [T] **1** to punish someone or treat them unfairly: **penalize sb for (doing) sth** *Two students were penalized very differently for the same offence. | Women feel professionally penalized for taking time off to raise children.* **2** to punish a team or player in sports by giving an advantage to the other team: *The team was penalized for wasting time.*

pen·al·ty /ˈpenlti/ ●●○ W3 *n* (*plural* **penalties**) [C]
1 a punishment for breaking a law, rule, or legal agreement: *No littering. Penalty $500. | Withdrawing the money early will result in a 10% penalty. |* **[+for]** *The penalty for a first offense is a fine. |* **severe/stiff/heavy penalty** *Drug dealers face severe penalties. | If he is convicted, he could receive* ***the death penalty*** (=be killed as a punishment).
THESAURUS ▸ PUNISHMENT
2 something bad that happens to you because of something you have done or because of the situation you are in: **penalty of (doing) sth** *One of the penalties of being famous is the loss of privacy. | If you don't do the job right, you will* ***pay the penalty****.*
3 a disadvantage in sports given to a player or team for breaking a rule: *Woodson received a penalty.*
4 a chance to kick the ball or hit the PUCK into the GOAL in a game of football, RUGBY, or ICE HOCKEY, given because the other team has broken a rule: *Townsend* ***kicked*** *a* ***penalty*** (=in a rugby game) *in the last minute. | Leeds were awarded a penalty.*

ˈpenalty ˌarea *n* [C] the area in front of the GOAL in football. The team opposing you is given a PENALTY if you break a rule there. → see picture at FOOTBALL

ˈpenalty ˌbox *n* [C] **1** an area off the ice where a player in ICE HOCKEY must wait after not obeying a rule **2** a penalty area

ˈpenalty ˌclause *n* [C] the part of a contract which says what someone will have to pay or do if they do not obey the agreement, for example if they do not complete work on time

ˈpenalty ˌkick *n* [C] a PENALTY(4)

ˈpenalty ˌpoint *n* [C] *BrE* a note made on a driver's LICENCE to show that they have done something wrong while they were driving. If someone gets 12 penalty points, they are no longer allowed to drive a car.

ˌpenalty ˈshoot-out *n* [C] an occasion when each team in a football match takes penalty kicks until one team misses the GOAL – used as a way of deciding which team will win when the ordinary part of the match has ended in a DRAW

pen·ance /ˈpenəns/ *n* **1** [C usually singular, U] something that you must do to show that you are sorry for something you have done wrong, especially in some religions: **do/perform penance** *We prayed and did penance together. |* **[+for]** *as a penance for his sins* **2** [singular] something that you have to do but do not enjoy doing: *Working in the garden was a kind of penance.*

pence /pens/ *n BrE* (*abbreviation* **p**) a plural of PENNY: *a few pence | a 20 pence stamp*

pen·chant /ˈpɒnʃɒn, ˈpentʃənt $ ˈpentʃənt/ *n* **a/sb's penchant for sth** if you have a penchant for something, you like that thing very much and try to do it or have it often: *a penchant for fast cars*

pen·cil¹ /ˈpensəl/ ●●● S2 *n* [C,U] an instrument that you use for writing or drawing, consisting of a wooden stick with a thin piece of a black or coloured substance in the middle: *a sharp pencil | a blue pencil |* **in pencil** *a note written in pencil | a pencil sketch* → EYEBROW PENCIL → see picture at STATIONERY

pencil² *v* (**pencilled**, **pencilling** *BrE*, **penciled**, **penciling** *AmE*) [T] to write something or make a mark with a pencil: *a name pencilled on the envelope*

pencil sb/sth ↔ **in** *phr v* to make an arrangement for a meeting or other event, knowing that it might have to be changed later: *Pickford has been pencilled in as Robson's replacement.*

ˈpencil case (*also* **ˈpencil box**) *n* [C] a bag or box to carry pens and pencils in → see picture at CASE¹

ˈpencil ˌpusher *n* [C] *AmE* someone who has a boring unimportant job in an office

ˈpencil ˌsharpener *n* [C] a small instrument with a blade inside, used to make pencils sharp → see picture at STATIONERY

ˈpencil ˌskirt *n* [C] a long narrow straight skirt

pen·dant /ˈpendənt/ *n* [C] a jewel, stone etc that hangs from a thin chain that you wear around your neck → **necklace**: *a ruby pendant* → see picture at JEWELLERY

pen·dent /ˈpendənt/ *adj literary or technical* hanging from something: *a pendent lamp*

pend·ing¹ /ˈpendɪŋ/ ●○○ *prep formal* while waiting for something, or until something happens: *Sales of the drug have been stopped, pending further research.*

pending² *adj* **1** *formal* not yet decided or settled: *Many trade disputes are pending, awaiting the outcome of the talks.* **2** *formal* something that is pending is going to happen soon: *the pending election* **3 pending file/tray** *BrE* a container for keeping papers, letters etc that have not yet been dealt with → **in-tray**, **out-tray**

ˈpen drive *n* [C] a small piece of electronic equipment that uses FLASH MEMORY to store information and can be fitted into a computer SYN **flash drive, USB drive**

pen·du·lous /ˈpendjələs $ -dʒə-/ *adj literary* hanging down loosely and swinging freely: *pendulous breasts*

pen·du·lum /ˈpendjələm $ -dʒə-/ *n* [C] **1** a long metal stick with a weight at the bottom that swings regularly from side to side to control the working of a clock **2 the pendulum** used to talk about the tendency of ideas, beliefs etc to change regularly to the opposite: *After several years of Republican government,* ***the pendulum*** *will undoubtedly* ***swing*** *back and voters will elect a Democrat. |* **[+of]** *the pendulum of fashion*

PENDULUM

pen·e·trate /ˈpenətreɪt/ ●○○ *v*
1 GO THROUGH [I,T] to enter something and pass or spread through it, especially when this is difficult → **pierce**: *bullets that penetrate thick armour plating | Sunlight barely penetrated the dirty windows. |* **[+into]** *Explorers penetrated deep into unknown regions.*
2 BUSINESS [T] to start to sell things to an area or country, or to have an influence there: *Few U.S. companies have successfully penetrated the Japanese electronics market.*

3 ORGANIZATION [T] to succeed in becoming accepted into a group or an organization, sometimes in order to find out their secrets: *KGB agents had penetrated most of their intelligence services.*
4 UNDERSTAND *formal* **a)** [T] to succeed in understanding something: *Science has penetrated the mysteries of nature.* **b)** [I,T] to be understood, with difficulty: *What could I say that would* ***penetrate*** *his thick* ***skull****?*
5 SEX [T] if a man penetrates someone, he puts his PENIS into a woman's VAGINA or into someone's ANUS when having sex
6 SEE THROUGH [T] to see into or through something when this is difficult: *My eyes couldn't penetrate the gloom.*

pen·e·trat·ing /ˈpenətreɪtɪŋ/ *adj* **1 penetrating look/eyes/gaze etc** a look etc which makes you feel uncomfortable and seems to see inside your mind: *a pair of penetrating dark eyes | He gave her a penetrating stare.* **2** showing an ability to understand things quickly and completely: *questions that are intelligent and penetrating | a penetrating analysis of the issue* **3** spreading and reaching everywhere: *the penetrating cold* **4** a penetrating sound is loud, clear, and often unpleasant: *a high, penetrating voice* —**penetratingly** *adv*

pen·e·tra·tion /ˌpenəˈtreɪʃən/ *n* **1** [C,U] when something or someone enters or passes through something, especially when this is difficult: *Cover the entire device to prevent water penetration.* | **[+of]** *The attack failed to lead to any deep penetration of enemy territory.* **2** [C,U] the degree to which a product is available or sold in an area: **[+of]** *the rise in import penetration of the domestic market* **3** [U] when a system of beliefs enters a society and becomes accepted: **[+of]** *the penetration of Marxism into Latin America* **4** [U] when someone joins and gets accepted by an organization, business etc in order to find out secret information: **[+of]** *foreign penetration of the British secret service* **5** [U] when a man puts his PENIS into a woman's VAGINA or into someone's ANUS **6** [U] a special ability to understand things very clearly and completely

pen·e·tra·tive /ˈpenətrətɪv $ -treɪtɪv/ *adj* **1 penetrative sex** sex in which a man puts his PENIS into a woman's VAGINA or into someone's ANUS **2** able to get into or through something easily: *penetrative missiles* **3** showing an ability to understand things quickly and completely: *penetrative observations*

ˈpen friend, pen·friend /ˈpenfrend/ *n* [C] *BrE* someone you write friendly letters to, especially someone in another country who you have never met SYN **pen pal**

pen·guin /ˈpeŋgwɪn/ ●●○ *n* [C] a large black and white Antarctic sea bird, which cannot fly but uses its wings for swimming

pen·i·cil·lin /ˌpenɪˈsɪlɪn/ *n* [U] a type of medicine that is used to treat infections caused by BACTERIA

pe·nile /ˈpiːnaɪl/ *adj medical* relating to the PENIS

pe·nin·su·la /pəˈnɪnsjələ $ -sələ/ ●○○ *n* [C] a piece of land almost completely surrounded by water but joined to a large area of land: *the Korean peninsula* —**peninsular** *adj* → see picture at ISLAND

pe·nis /ˈpiːnɪs/ *n* [C] the outer sex organ of men and male animals, which is used for sex and through which waste water comes out of the body

pen·i·tent[1] /ˈpenɪtənt/ *adj formal* feeling sorry because you have done something wrong, and are intending not to do it again SYN **repentant**: *a penitent expression* —**penitently** *adv* —**penitence** *n* [U]

penitent[2] *n* [C] someone who is doing PENANCE

pen·i·ten·tial /ˌpenəˈtenʃəl◂/ *adj formal* relating to being sorry for having done something wrong: *penitential journeys to famous shrines*

pen·i·ten·tia·ry /ˌpenəˈtenʃəri/ *n* (*plural* **penitentiaries**) [C] *AmE* a prison - used especially in the names of prisons: *the North Carolina state penitentiary* **THESAURUS** PRISON

pen·knife /ˈpen-naɪf/ *n* (*plural* **penknives** /-naɪvz/) [C] a small knife with blades that fold into the handle, usually carried in your pocket SYN **jackknife** → see picture at KNIFE[1]

pen·light /ˈpenlaɪt/ *n* [C] an electric light that you can carry in your hand and that is almost as small as a pen → FLASHLIGHT, TORCH[1](1)

pen·man·ship /ˈpenmənʃɪp/ *n* [U] *formal* the art of writing by hand, or skill in this art: *children practicing their penmanship*

ˈpen name *n* [C] a name used by a writer instead of their real name SYN **pseudonym, nom de plume**

pen·nant /ˈpenənt/ *n* [C] **1** a long narrow pointed flag used on ships or by schools, sports teams etc **2 the pennant** the prize given to the best team in the American and National League baseball competitions

pen·nies /ˈpeniz/ a plural of PENNY

pen·ni·less /ˈpenɪləs/ *adj* someone who is penniless has no money → **broke**: *Uncle Charlie was jobless and penniless.* **THESAURUS** POOR

pen·non /ˈpenən/ *n* [C] a long narrow pointed flag, especially one carried on the end of a long pole by soldiers on horses in the Middle Ages

pen·n'orth /ˈpenəθ $ -ərθ/ *n* [singular] *BrE old-fashioned* a PENNYWORTH

pen·ny /ˈpeni/ ●●● S1 *n* [C]
1 a) (*plural* **pence**) (*abbreviation* **p**) a small unit of money in Britain. There are 100 pence in one pound: *The bus fare is 80 pence. | a 50p piece (=coin) | A loaf of bread costs 70p.* **b)** (*plural* **pennies**) a coin worth one penny: *I've only got a few pennies left.*
2 (*plural* **pennies**) a coin that is worth one CENT in the US or Canada. One hundred pennies are equal to $1.
3 (*plural* **pennies** *or* **pence**) (*written abbreviation* **d**) a British unit of money or coin used until 1971. There were 12 pennies in one SHILLING: **twopence/threepence etc** *a book costing only sixpence* | **fourpenny/sixpenny etc** *a fourpenny cigar | a threepenny bit (=coin)*
4 not a penny used to emphasize that someone has no money or that something did not cost any money: *I haven't got a penny on me. | It didn't* ***cost*** *me* ***a penny****. | He died* ***without a penny to*** *his* ***name****.*
5 every penny all of an amount of money: *The hotel was expensive but it was* ***worth every penny****.* | **[+of]** *He was determined to go to Australia even if it took every penny of his savings.*
6 every penny counts used to say that money is needed and even a small amount is important: *Every penny counts in the battle to save the rain forests.*
7 the/your last penny the only money that is left: *She's* ***down to*** *her* ***last penny****.*
8 a penny for your thoughts/a penny for them *spoken* used to ask someone who is silent what they are thinking about
9 in for a penny, in for a pound *spoken* used to say that because you are already involved in something, you will complete it whatever time, money, or effort is needed: *Oh well, it's done now. In for a penny, in for a pound.*
10 the penny (has) dropped *BrE informal* used to say that someone has finally understood something that they had not understood before
11 be two/ten a penny *BrE* to be very common and easy to get, or cheap - used to show disapproval: *Rings like these are ten a penny.*
12 turn up like a bad penny *BrE* if someone you dislike turns up like a bad penny, they appear when they are not wanted → HALFPENNY, → **spend a penny** at SPEND[1](5), → **cost a pretty penny** at PRETTY[2](6)

ˈpenny ˌante *adj AmE informal* involving very small amounts of money, and not important: *penny ante schemes to make money*

ˌpenny-ˈfarthing *n* [C] *BrE* a bicycle with a very large front wheel and a very small back wheel, used in the late 19th century

ˈpenny-ˌpinching *adj* unwilling to spend or give money → **mean**: *penny-pinching governments* —**penny pinching** *n* [U]

ˌpenny ˈwhistle *n* [C] a musical instrument like a small pipe with six holes, that you play by blowing SYN **tin whistle**

pen·ny·worth /ˈpenɪwəθ $ -wərθ/ *n* [singular] *old-fashioned* the amount of something that you could buy with a penny in the past: **[+of]** *a pennyworth of sweets*

pe·nol·o·gy /piːˈnɒlədʒi $ -ˈnɑːl-/ *n* [U] the study of prisons and the punishment of criminals —**penologist** *n* [C]

ˈpen pal *n* [C] someone you make friends with by writing letters, especially someone who lives in another country and who you have never met SYN **pen friend** *BrE*

ˈpen ˌpusher *n* [C] *BrE informal* someone who has a boring unimportant job in an office

P

pen·sion¹ /ˈpenʃən/ ●●○ S3 W2 *n* [C] an amount of money paid regularly by the government or company to someone who does not work anymore, for example because they have reached the age when people stop working or because they are ill: *At what age can you start* ***drawing*** *your* ***pension****? | If you are self-employed, you should think about* ***taking out*** *a* ***private pension****. | Many people find it hard to live on a basic* ***state pension****. | She* ***pays*** *a quarter of her salary* ***into*** *a* ***pension plan****.*

pension² *v BrE*

pension sb/sth ↔ **off 1** to make someone leave their job when they are old or ill, and pay them a pension: *Not everyone wants to be pensioned off at 65.* **2** *informal* to get rid of something because it is old or not useful anymore: *Many of the old ships have been pensioned off.*

pen·si·on³ /ˈpɒnsiɒn $ pɑːnˈsjoʊn/ *n* [C] a small cheap hotel in France and some other European countries

pen·sion·a·ble /ˈpenʃənəbəl/ *adj BrE* **1** giving someone the right to receive a pension: *36% of the population were of* ***pensionable age****.* **2 pensionable pay/salary etc** pay from which money is regularly taken for a pension: *The employee's contribution is 5% of pensionable salary.*

ˈpension ˌbook *n* [C] a book that the British government gives to pensioners, which allows them to collect their pensions

pen·sion·er /ˈpenʃənə $ -ər/ ●●○ *n* [C] someone who receives a pension SYN **senior citizen**, **OAP** *BrE* → **retire**: *old age pensioners*

ˈpension fund *n* [C] a large amount of money that a company INVESTS and uses to pay PENSIONS

ˈpension plan (*also* **ˈpension scheme** *BrE*) *n* [C] an arrangement in which you pay money regularly into a pension fund while you are working, so that you will receive a PENSION

ˈpension scheme *n* [C] *BrE* a PENSION PLAN

pen·sive /ˈpensɪv/ *adj* thinking a lot about something, especially because you are worried or sad → **thoughtful**: *Jan looked pensive.* —**pensively** *adv*

pentagon *n* [C] a flat shape with five sides and five angles → see picture at SHAPE¹ —**pentagonal** /penˈtægənəl/ *adj*

pen·ta·gram /ˈpentəgræm/ *n* [C] a shape like a star with five points, often used as a magic sign

pen·tam·e·ter /penˈtæmɪtə $ -ər/ *n* [C,U] a line of poetry with five beats, or the beat of a poem like this → IAMBIC PENTAMETER

pen·tath·lon /penˈtæθlən/ *n* [singular, U] a sports event involving five different sports

Pen·te·cost /ˈpentɪkɒst $ -kɔːst, -kɑːst/ *n* [C,U] **1** (*also* **Whitsun** *BrE*) the seventh Sunday after Easter, when Christians celebrate the appearance of the Holy Spirit to the APOSTLES **2** a Jewish religious holiday 50 days after Passover

Pen·te·cos·tal /ˌpentɪˈkɒstl◂ $ -ˈkɔːs-, -ˈkɑːs-/ (*also* **Pentecostalist**) *adj* relating to a group of Christian churches that believe in the Holy Spirit's power, such as the power to cure diseases —**Pentecostalist** *n* [C]

pent·house /ˈpenthaʊs/ *n* [C] a very expensive and comfortable apartment or set of rooms on the top floor of a building: *a £7 million London penthouse* | **penthouse apartment/flat/suite**

pent-up /ˌpent ˈʌp◂/ *adj* pent-up feelings or energy have not been expressed or used for a long time: *years of pent-up anger and frustration*

pe·nul·ti·mate /peˈnʌltəmət, pə-/ *adj* [only before noun] not the last, but immediately before the last SYN **last but one** → **ultimate**: *the penultimate chapter* THESAURUS ▸ LAST

> **REGISTER**
> In everyday English, people usually say **the next to last** or, in British English, **the last but one** rather than use **penultimate**: *the* ***next to last*** *chapter | the* ***last but one*** *chapter*

pe·num·bra /pəˈnʌmbrə/ *n* [C] *technical* an area of slight darkness

pen·u·ry /ˈpenjəri/ *n* [U] *formal* the state of being very poor SYN **poverty**: *He died in penury in 1644.* —**penurious** /pəˈnjʊəriəs $ -ˈnʊr-/ *adj*

pe·on /ˈpiːən/ *n* [C] *AmE* **1** *informal* someone who does boring or physically hard work for low pay – used humorously **2** someone in Mexico or South America who works as a type of slave to pay back debts

pe·o·ny /ˈpiːəni/ *n* (*plural* **peonies**) [C] a garden plant with large round flowers that are dark red, white, or pink

peo·ple¹ /ˈpiːpəl/ ●●● S1 W1 *n*

1 PERSONS [plural] used as the plural of 'person' to refer to men, women, and children: *How many people were at the meeting? | At least 40 people were killed. | the people who live next door*

2 PEOPLE IN GENERAL [plural] people in general, or people other than yourself: *I don't care what people think. | People can be really mean sometimes.* | **theatre/business etc people** (=people who work or are involved in the theatre etc) *The hotel was full of business people.*

3 COUNTRY/RACE [C] the people who belong to a particular country, race, or area: **the British/American etc people** *He pledged that he would never lie to the American people.* | **[+of]** *the Basques, a people of northwestern Spain | the peoples of Europe*

4 the people [plural] **a)** all the ordinary people in a country or a state, not the government or ruling class: *The people rebelled. | Rice formed the staple food of the* ***common people****. | The party try to portray the prime minister as* ***a man of the people*** (=someone in power who understands or is like ordinary people). | **the people's party/army etc** (=belonging to or popular with the ordinary people) *the People's Liberation Army | Diana – the people's princess* **b)** *AmE* used in court cases to represent the government of the US or of a particular state: *The People vs. Romero*

5 sb's people [plural] **a)** the people that a king or leader rules or leads: *The king ordered his people to prepare for war.* **b)** the people who work for a person or organization: *A manager's job is to make his or her people feel part of the system.* **c)** *old-fashioned* your relatives, especially your parents, grandparents etc: *Do your people live round here?*

6 of all people *spoken* used to say that someone is the person you would least or most expect to do something: *Why should he, of all people, get a promotion? | You of all people should have known better.*

7 TO GET ATTENTION [plural] *AmE spoken informal* used to get the attention of a group of people: *Listen up, people!* → LITTLE PEOPLE

> **GRAMMAR: Singular or plural verb?**
> **People** is followed by a plural verb: *The American people* ***are*** *proud of their democracy.* ✗ Don't say: *The American people is proud of its democracy.*

people² *v* [T] *formal* **1** if a country or area is peopled by people of a particular type, they live there SYN **inhabit**: **be peopled by/with sb** *an island peopled by hardy sea folk* **2** if a story or someone's imagination is peopled by people of a particular type, it is full of them: **be peopled by/with sb** *Her* world was peopled with imaginary friends. GRAMMAR **People** is usually passive.

ˈpeople ˌcarrier (*also* **ˈpeople ˌmover**) *n* [C] a large car with about eight seats, used especially by people with families SYN **mini-van** *AmE*

ˈpeople skills *n* [plural] the ability to deal with people well: *A doctor needs people skills as well as technical knowledge.*

pep[1] /pep/ *v* (**pepped, pepping**)
pep sb/sth ↔ **up** *phr v informal* to make something or someone more active or interesting: *The team needs a few new players to pep it up.*

pep[2] *n* [U] *informal* physical energy: *an enthusiastic player, full of pep* → PEP TALK

pep·per[1] /ˈpepə $ -ər/ ●●● S3 *n*
1 [U] a powder that is used to add a hot taste to food: *salt and pepper* → BLACK PEPPER, WHITE PEPPER
2 [C] a hollow red, green, or yellow vegetable, eaten either raw or cooked with other food SYN **bell pepper** *AmE* → SWEET PEPPER, CAYENNE PEPPER, RED PEPPER, see picture at VEGETABLE[1]

pepper[2] *v* [T] **1** if something is peppered with things, it has a lot of those things in it or on it: **be peppered with sth** *a speech peppered with amusing stories | The surface of the Moon is peppered with craters.* **2** if bullets pepper something, they hit it several times: *Machine gun fire peppered the front of the building.* **3 pepper sb with questions** *AmE* to ask someone a lot of questions, one after the other: *Reporters peppered him with questions.* **4** to add pepper to food: *Pepper the steak well. | peppered salami*

ˌpepper-and-ˈsalt (*also* **salt-and-pepper**) *adj* pepper-and-salt hair is starting to become grey

pep·per·corn /ˈpepəkɔːn $ ˈpepərkɔːrn/ *n* [C] the small dried fruit that is crushed to make pepper

ˌpeppercorn ˈrent *n* [C] *BrE* a very low rent

ˈpepper mill *n* [C] a piece of kitchen equipment used to crush peppercorns to make pepper

PEPPER MILL

pep·per·mint /ˈpepəˌmɪnt $ -ər-/ *n*
1 [U] a plant with a strong taste and smell, often used in sweets **2** [C] a sweet with the taste of peppermint

pep·pe·ro·ni /ˌpepəˈrəʊni $ -ˈroʊ-/ *n* [C,U] an Italian SAUSAGE with a strong taste

ˈpepper pot *BrE*, **ˈpepper ˌshaker** *AmE n* [C] a small container with little holes in the top, used for shaking pepper onto food

ˈpepper ˌspray *n* [C,U] a substance used especially by the police for controlling people. It contains red pepper and is SPRAYed into people's eyes to make them blind for a short time.

pep·per·y /ˈpepəri/ *adj* **1** tasting or smelling of pepper **2** *informal* becoming annoyed easily SYN **irritable**

ˈpep pill *n* [C] *informal* a PILL containing a drug that gives you more energy or makes you feel happier for a short time

ˈpep ˌrally *n* [C] *AmE* a meeting at a school before a sports event, when CHEERLEADERS lead the students in encouraging their team to win

pep·sin /ˈpepsɪn/ *n* [U] *technical* a liquid in your stomach that changes food into a form that your body can use

ˈpep squad *n* [C] *AmE* a group of CHEERLEADERS who perform at school sports events or pep rallies

ˈpep talk *n* [C] *informal* a short speech intended to encourage someone to work harder, win a game etc: *Alam* ***gave*** *the Pakistani team a* ***pep talk***.

pep·tic ul·cer /ˌpeptɪk ˈʌlsə $ -ər/ *n* [C] a painful ULCER inside someone's stomach

per /pə; *strong* pɜː $ pər *strong* pɜːr/ ●●● S3 W1 *prep*
1 per hour/day/week etc during each hour etc: *The park attracts four million visitors per year.* | **miles/kilometres per hour** (=used for measuring speed) *a speed limit of 40 miles per hour*
2 for each: *How much does it cost per kilo? | rooms costing £40 per night | Admission is £9.95 per adult. | My car does 12 miles per litre* (=for each litre of petrol). | *The meal cost $25* ***per head*** (=for or by each person).
3 as per sth *formal* according to something: *The work was carried out as per your instructions.*
4 as per usual/normal *spoken* used when something annoying happens which has often happened before: *Jenny was late, as per usual.* → PER ANNUM, PER CAPITA

per·am·bu·la·tion /pəˌræmbjəˈleɪʃən/ *n* [C] *old-fashioned* a walk around a place, especially a slow walk for pleasure —**perambulate** /pəˈræmbjʊleɪt/ *v* [I,T]

per·am·bu·la·tor /pəˈræmbjəleɪtə $ -ər/ *n* [C] *BrE old-fashioned* a PRAM

per an·num /pər ˈænəm/ ●○○ (*written abbreviation* **p.a.**) *adv formal* for each year: *a salary of $40,000 per annum*

per·cale /pəˈkeɪl $ pər-/ *n* [C,U] a type of cotton cloth, used especially for making sheets

per cap·i·ta /pə ˈkæpɪtə $ pər-/ *adj, adv formal* used to describe the average amount of something in a particular place, calculated according to the number of people who live there: *the country's per capita income | the number of crimes that occur per capita*

per·ceive /pəˈsiːv $ pər-/ ●●○ W3 AWL *v* [T]
1 *written* to understand or think of something or someone in a particular way → **perception**: **perceive sth/sb as sth** *Even as a young woman she had been perceived as a future chief executive.* | **perceive sth/sb to be sth** *Often what is perceived to be aggression is simply fear. | Children who do badly in school tests often perceive themselves to be failures.*
2 *formal* to notice, see, or recognize something → **perceptive**: *That morning, he perceived a change in Franca's mood. | Cats are not able to perceive colour.* | **perceive that** *He perceived that there was no other way out of the crisis.*
THESAURUS NOTICE

GRAMMAR: Using the progressive
Perceive is not used in the progressive. You say: *I perceive a slight difference.* ✗ Don't say: *I am perceiving a slight difference.*
GRAMMAR GUIDE VERBS

per·cent[1] (*also* **per cent** *BrE*) /pəˈsent $ pər-/ ●●● W1 AWL *adj, adv*
1 5 percent (5%)/10 percent (10%) etc equal to five, ten etc parts out of a total of 100 parts: *a 10% increase in house prices | a company with a 40 percent stake in the project*
2 a/one hundred percent completely: *I agree with you a hundred percent.*

percent[2] (*also* **per cent** *BrE*) ●●● S3 W2 AWL *n* **5 percent (5%)/10 percent (10%) etc** an amount equal to five, ten etc parts out of a total of 100 parts: *The bank charges interest at 14%.* | **[+of]** *Eighty percent of the population voted.* ⚠ **Percent** is only used after a number. If you are referring more generally to part of an amount, use **percentage**: *A high percentage (NOT percent) of the population was illiterate.*

per·cen·tage /pəˈsentɪdʒ $ pər-/ ●●○ W3 AWL *n*
1 [C,U] an amount expressed as if it is part of a total which is 100: **[+of]** *The percentage of school leavers that go to university is about five per cent. | Tax is paid as a percentage of total income.* | **high/low/small percentage** *A high percentage of married women have part-time jobs. | Interest rates fell by six* ***percentage points*** (=6%). | *The numbers are small* ***in percentage terms*** (=when calculated as a percentage). | **percentage change/increase etc** *Crime figures showed significant percentage increases.*

GRAMMAR: Singular or plural verb?
If the noun that follows **a percentage of** is plural, use a plural verb after it: *Only a small percentage of* ***people are*** *interested in politics.*

2 [C usually singular] a share of the profits: *She gets a percentage for every record sold.*
3 there is no percentage in doing sth *BrE informal* used to say that doing something is not going to help or be useful: *There's no percentage in worrying.*

per·cen·tile /pəˈsentaɪl $ pər-/ *n* [C] *technical* one of 100 equal-sized parts that a group of people can be divided into - used especially when comparing people's scores in a test or levels of health

per·cep·ti·ble /pəˈseptəbəl $ pər-/ *adj formal* something that is perceptible can be noticed, although it is very small OPP **imperceptible**: *a small but perceptible change | The sound was* ***barely perceptible****.* —**perceptibly** *adv: the light dimmed perceptibly*

per·cep·tion /pəˈsepʃən $ pər-/ ●●○ W3 AWL *n*
1 [C,U] the way you think about something and your idea of what it is like: **[+of]** *children's perceptions of the world | the* ***public perception*** *of the government's performance*
2 [U] the way that you notice things with your senses of sight, hearing etc: *drugs that alter perception | visual perception*
3 [U] the natural ability to understand or notice things quickly: *Ross shows unusual perception for a boy of his age.*

per·cep·tive /pəˈseptɪv $ pər-/ *adj* someone who is perceptive notices things quickly and understands situations, people's feelings etc well - used to show approval: *a perceptive young man | highly perceptive comments | You're right.* ***That's*** *very* ***perceptive of*** *you.* —**perceptively** *adv* —**perceptiveness** *n* [U]

perch[1] /pɜːtʃ $ pɜːrtʃ/ ●○○ *v*
1 be perched on/above etc sth to be in a position on top of something or on the edge of something: *a house perched on a cliff above the town*
2 perch (yourself) on sth to sit on top of something or on the edge of something: *Bobby had perched himself on a tall wooden stool.* **THESAURUS** ▸ **SIT**
3 [I + on] if a bird perches on something, it flies down and sits on it

perch[2] *n* [C] **1** a branch or stick where a bird sits **2** *informal* a high place or position, especially one where you can sit and watch something: *She watched the parade from her perch on her father's shoulders.* **3** a type of fish that lives in lakes and rivers

per·chance /pəˈtʃɑːns $ pərˈtʃæns/ *adv old use or literary* **1** perhaps: *One day perchance I shall tell you.* **2** by chance: *Leave now, lest perchance he find you.*

per·cip·i·ent /pəˈsɪpiənt $ pər-/ *adj formal* quick to notice and understand things SYN **perceptive** —**percipience** *n* [U]

per·co·late /ˈpɜːkəleɪt $ ˈpɜːr-/ *v* **1** [I] if an idea, feeling, or piece of information percolates through a group, it gradually spreads: **[+through/down]** *The message has begun to percolate through the organization. | These ideas were slow to percolate.* **2** [I always + adv/prep] if liquid, light, or air percolates somewhere, it passes slowly through a material that has very small holes in it: **[+through/down/into]** *Rainwater percolates down through the rock.* **3** [I,T] (*also* **perk**) if coffee percolates, or if you percolate it, you make it in a special pot in which hot water goes up through a tube and then passes down through crushed coffee beans —**percolation** /ˌpɜːkəˈleɪʃən $ ˌpɜːr-/ *n* [C,U]

per·co·la·tor /ˈpɜːkəleɪtə $ ˈpɜːrkəleɪtər/ *n* [C] a special pot in which coffee is percolated

per·cus·sion /pəˈkʌʃən $ pər-/ *n* [U] **1** musical instruments such as drums, bells etc which you play by hitting them: *Tonight we have Paul Duke* ***on percussion*** (=playing a percussion instrument). *| a range of* ***percussion instruments*** → BRASS(2), STRINGED INSTRUMENT, WIND INSTRUMENT, WOODWIND **2 the percussion (section)** the people in an ORCHESTRA or band who play musical instruments such as drums, bells etc **3** *formal* the sound or effect of two things hitting each other with great force —**percussionist** *n* [C]

per·cus·sive /pəˈkʌsɪv $ pər-/ *adj* [usually before noun] relating to or sounding like percussion instruments: *On the piano such chords have a fine percussive effect.*

per di·em[1] /pə ˈdiːəm $ pər-/ *n* [C] *AmE* **1** an amount of money that an employer pays a worker for each day that is worked **2** an amount of money that a worker is allowed to spend when doing his or her job, for example on a business trip: *a per diem allowance*

per diem[2] *adv AmE formal* for each day or on each day: *workers who are paid per diem*

per·di·tion /pəˈdɪʃən $ pər-/ *n* [U] *old use* **1** punishment after death **2** complete destruction or failure: *an alcoholic on the road to perdition*

per·e·gri·na·tion /ˌperəgrəˈneɪʃən/ *n* [C] *literary* a long journey: *His peregrinations took him to India.*

per·e·grine fal·con /ˌperəgrən ˈfɔːlkən $ -ˈfɔːl-, -ˈfɑːl-/ (*also* **peregrine**) *n* [C] a hunting bird with a black and white spotted front

pe·remp·to·ry /pəˈremptəri/ *adj formal* peremptory behaviour, speech etc is not polite or friendly and shows that the person speaking expects to be obeyed immediately: *a peremptory demand for silence* —**peremptorily** *adv*

pe·ren·ni·al[1] /pəˈreniəl/ *adj* **1** continuing or existing for a long time, or happening again and again: *Lack of resources has been a* ***perennial problem*** *since the beginning. | Teddy bears are a* ***perennial favorite*** *with children.* **2** a plant that is perennial lives for more than two years → **annual** —**perennially** *adv*

perennial[2] *n* [C] a plant that lives for more than two years → **annual** → HARDY PERENNIAL(1)

per·e·stroi·ka /ˌperəˈstrɔɪkə/ *n* [U] a Russian word meaning 'rebuilding', used to describe the social, political, and economic changes that happened in the former USSR in the 1980s, just before the end of the Communist government → **glasnost**

per·fect[1] /ˈpɜːfɪkt $ ˈpɜːr-/ ●●● S2 W2 *adj*
1 not having any mistakes, faults, or damage OPP **imperfect**: *His English was perfect. | The car was in perfect condition. | You're very lucky to have perfect teeth. | a perfect performance |* ***In a perfect world****, we wouldn't need an army.*
2 as good as possible, or the best of its kind: *The weather was perfect the whole week. | a perfect example of Gothic architecture | The clothes were a perfect fit. | a perfect solution to the problem | Ronnie was in perfect health. |* **perfect timing** (=used when something happens at exactly the right time) *Good, you're home. Perfect timing - dinner's on the table.*
3 exactly what is needed for a particular purpose, situation, or person SYN **ideal**: *That's perfect! Just the way I wanted it to look. | Crusty bread is the perfect accompaniment to this soup. |* **[+for]** *The land is perfect for sheep farming. |* **perfect way/place/time etc to do sth** *She thought she'd found the perfect place to live. |* **perfect day/place/person etc for sth** *a perfect day for a picnic | the perfect actor for the part*
4 nobody's perfect *spoken* said when you are answering someone who has criticized you or someone else: *So I made a mistake! Nobody's perfect.*
5 have a perfect right to do sth used to emphasize that it is reasonable for someone to do something: *He has a perfect right to know what's happening.*
6 perfect stranger/fool/angel etc used to emphasize that someone has a particular quality completely SYN **complete, total**: *I felt a perfect idiot.*
7 perfect storm a very bad event that happens because a number of things happen at the same time, which is unusual: *The economy has been hit by a perfect storm.* → PERFECTLY, → **practice makes perfect** at PRACTICE(9), → PRESENT PERFECT, PAST PERFECT

per·fect² /pəˈfekt $ pər-/ ●○○ *v* [T] to make something as good as you are able to: *Mock trials help students perfect their legal skills.*

per·fect³ /ˈpɜːfɪkt $ ˈpɜːr-/ *n* **the perfect** *technical* the form of a verb which is used when talking about a period of time up to and including the present. In English, it is formed with 'have' and the past participle. SYN **present perfect** → PAST PERFECT

per·fec·ti·ble /pəˈfektəbəl $ pər-/ *adj* able to be improved or made perfect —**perfectibility** /pəˌfektəˈbɪləti $ pər-/ *n* [U]

per·fec·tion /pəˈfekʃən $ pər-/ ●○○ *n* [U]
1 the state of being perfect: *My father expected perfection from all of us.* | *the search for technical perfection* | **to perfection** (=perfectly) *The beef was cooked to perfection.*
2 the process of making something perfect: **[+of]** *the perfection of his golf swing*
3 be perfection to be perfect: *Her performance was pure perfection.*

per·fec·tion·ist /pəˈfekʃənɪst $ pər-/ *n* [C] someone who is not satisfied with anything unless it is completely perfect: *Many top athletes are perfectionists who drive themselves to excel.* —**perfectionist** *adj* —**perfectionism** *n* [U]

per·fect·ly /ˈpɜːfɪktli $ ˈpɜːr-/ ●●● S2 W3 *adv*
1 completely – used to emphasize what you are saying: *It's perfectly normal to be nervous before a performance.* | *The sale was perfectly legal.* | *You can get a perfectly good coat at Sears for a lot less money.*
2 in a perfect way: *The plan worked perfectly.* | *The steaks were perfectly cooked.*

ˌperfect ˈparticiple *n* [C] the PAST PARTICIPLE

ˌperfect ˈpitch *n* [U] the ability to correctly name any musical note that you hear, or to sing any note at the correct PITCH without the help of an instrument

per·fid·i·ous /pəˈfɪdiəs $ pər-/ *adj literary* someone who is perfidious is not loyal and cannot be trusted SYN **treacherous**

per·fi·dy /ˈpɜːfədi $ ˈpɜːr-/ *n* [U] *literary* when someone is not loyal to another person who trusts them SYN **treachery**

per·fo·rate /ˈpɜːfəreɪt $ ˈpɜːr-/ *v* [T] to make a hole or holes in something: *A broken rib had perforated her lung.*

per·fo·rat·ed /ˈpɜːfəreɪtɪd $ ˈpɜːr-/ *adj* something that is perforated has a hole or holes cut or torn in it: *a perforated eardrum* | *perforated coupons*

per·fo·ra·tion /ˌpɜːfəˈreɪʃən $ ˌpɜːr-/ *n formal* **1** [C usually plural] a small hole in something, especially one of a line of holes made in a piece of paper so that it can be torn easily: *the perforations in a sheet of stamps* **2** [U] when something makes a hole or holes

per·force /pəˈfɔːs $ pərˈfɔːrs/ *adv literary* because it is necessary

per·form /pəˈfɔːm $ pərˈfɔːrm/ ●●● S3 W2 *v*
1 [I,T] to do something to entertain people, for example by acting a play or playing a piece of music: *Chenier and the band are performing at the Silver Palace tomorrow.* | *The children perform two plays each school year.* ⚠ Do not use **perform** to say what person an actor pretends to be in a play, film etc. Use **play**: *John Wayne played (NOT performed) a Roman soldier in the film.*
2 [T] to do something, especially something difficult or useful SYN **carry out**: *Surgeons performed an emergency operation.* | *The official opening ceremony was performed by Princess Margaret.* | **perform a study/experiment/analysis etc** *An analysis of the survey data was performed.* | **perform a task/job/duty** *She was fired for not performing the duties outlined in her contract.* | **perform a function/role** *software that performs a specific function* | *The leadership cannot be expected to* ***perform miracles*** (=improve a situation in a way that seems impossible).

REGISTER
In everyday English, people usually say that someone **carries out** an operation, a study etc rather than use **perform**: *The operation was* ***carried out*** *by a team of surgeons.*

3 perform well/badly etc a) to work or do something well, badly etc → **underperform**: *Many religious schools perform well academically.* | *The team performed poorly on Saturday.* **b)** if a product, business etc performs well or badly, it makes a lot of money or very little money: *The economy is performing well.*

per·form·ance /pəˈfɔːməns $ pərˈfɔːr-/ ●●● S2 W1 *n*
1 [C] when someone performs a play or a piece of music: **[+of]** *Their performance of Mozart's Concerto in E flat was finely controlled and dramatic.* | *This evening's performance will begin at 8.00 pm.*
2 [C,U] how well or badly a person, company etc does a particular job or activity: *Sean's performance at school has greatly improved.* | *I was impressed by the team's performance.* | *The country's economic performance so far this year has been good.* | *Shareholders blamed him for the company's* ***poor performance***. | *her* ***disappointing performance*** *in the Olympics* | *Exam results are used as* ***performance indicators*** (=things that show how well something is done) *for schools.*
3 [U] the act of doing a piece of work, duty etc: **[+of]** *the performance of his official duties*
4 [U] how well a car or other machine works: *The car's performance on mountain roads was impressive.* | *an imaging system using* ***high-performance*** (=very effective) *technology*
5 a performance *BrE spoken* a process that takes a lot of unnecessary time and effort: *Shopping at the markets turned out to be quite a performance.*

COLLOCATIONS

VERBS

give a performance *Samuel Jackson gives a terrific performance as Elijah.*
go to a performance (*also* **attend a performance** *formal*) *We can go to the evening performance if you prefer.*

ADJECTIVES

a fine/great performance *There are fine performances by Kathy Bates and Daryl Hannah.*
a memorable performance (=good and easy to remember) *There were memorable performances from Madonna and U2.*
a brilliant/magnificent/superb performance | **a virtuoso performance** (=one showing great skill) | **a live performance** (=one performed for people who are watching) | **a solo performance** (=one performed by a single musician, not a group)

COMMON ERRORS

⚠ Don't say 'have a performance' or 'make a performance'. Say **give a performance**.

perˈformance ˌart *n* [U] a type of art that can combine acting, dance, painting, film etc to express an idea —**performance artist** *n* [C]

perˈformance-enˌhancing *adj* **performance-enhancing drug/product/supplement etc** a drug or product that is used illegally by people competing in sports events to improve their performance

perˌformance-related ˈpay *n* [U] money that you earn for your work, which is increased if you do your work very well

per·form·er /pəˈfɔːmə $ pərˈfɔːrmər/ ●●○ *n* [C]
1 an actor, musician etc who performs to entertain people: *circus performers* | *He was a better songwriter than performer.*
2 good/top/poor etc performer a) someone who does a particular job or activity well or badly: *Star performers are rewarded with bonuses.* **b)** a product, business etc that makes a lot of money, or that makes very little money: *Newcastle Brown Ale is an outstanding performer in the British beer market.*

per,forming 'arts *n* **the performing arts** arts such as dance, music, or DRAMA

per·fume¹ /ˈpɜːfjuːm $ ˈpɜːr-/ ●●○ *n* [C,U]
1 a liquid with a strong pleasant smell that women put on their skin or clothing to make themselves smell nice SYN **scent**: *She was* ***wearing*** *the* ***perfume*** *that he'd bought her.* → see picture at BOTTLE¹ THESAURUS SMELL
2 a sweet or pleasant smell SYN **scent**: *It had the delicate perfume of roses.* —**perfumed** *adj*: *perfumed soap*

per·fume² /ˈpɜːfjuːm $ pərˈfjuːm/ *v* [T] **1** *literary* to make a place have a sweet pleasant smell: *Lilacs perfumed the air.* **2** to put perfume on something

per·fum·er·y /pəˈfjuːməri $ pər-/ *n* (*plural* **perfumeries**) *old-fashioned* **1** [C] a place where perfumes are made or sold **2** [U] the process of making perfumes

per·func·to·ry /pəˈfʌŋktəri $ pər-/ *adj formal* a perfunctory action is done quickly, and is only done because people expect it: *She gave him a perfunctory smile.* | *The applause was perfunctory.* —**perfunctorily** *adv*

per·go·la /ˈpɜːgələ $ ˈpɜːr-/ *n* [C] a structure made of posts built for plants to grow over in a garden

per·haps /pəˈhæps, præps $ pər-, præps/ ●●● S1 W1 *adv*
1 used to say that something may be true, but you are not sure SYN **maybe**: *Perhaps she's next door.* | *Perhaps it will snow tomorrow.* | *It won't take so long next time, perhaps.* | *'I don't think you understand.' 'Well,* ***perhaps not****.'*

> REGISTER
> In everyday English, people usually use **may** or **might** rather than use **perhaps it/she/they etc will**: *It* ***might*** *snow tomorrow.*

2 used to give your opinion, when you do not want to be too definite SYN **maybe**: *This is perhaps her finest novel yet.* | *The industrial revolution was, perhaps, the most important event in history.*
3 used to say that a number is only a guess SYN **maybe**: *The room was large, perhaps 20 feet square.* | *Perhaps 200 people were there.*
4 *spoken* used to politely ask or suggest something, or say what you are going to do SYN **maybe**: *I thought perhaps we'd have lunch in the garden.*

per·il /ˈperəl/ ●○○ *n*
1 [U] *literary or formal* great danger, especially of being harmed or killed: **in peril** *They put their own lives in peril to rescue their friends.* | **great/grave/serious peril** *The economy is now in grave peril.* | *a voyage that was* ***fraught with peril*** (=full of danger)
2 [C usually plural] *literary or formal* a danger or problem in a particular activity or situation: *the perils posed by mountaineering* | **[+of]** *the perils of the sea*
3 do sth at your peril used to say that what someone is intending to do is dangerous or could cause them problems: *Politicians ignore this issue at their peril.*

per·il·ous /ˈperələs/ *adj literary or formal* very dangerous: *a perilous journey across the mountains* THESAURUS DANGEROUS

per·il·ous·ly /ˈperələsli/ *adv literary or formal* in a way that is dangerous and likely to result in something bad soon SYN **dangerously**: *Karpov, the champion, came* ***perilously close*** *to losing.*

pe·rim·e·ter /pəˈrɪmɪtə $ -ər/ *n* [C] **1** the border around an enclosed area such as a military camp: **[+of]** *the perimeter of the airfield* | **perimeter fence/wall** *A mine blew a hole in the perimeter wall.* THESAURUS EDGE **2** the whole length of the border around an area or shape: **[+of]** *Calculate the perimeter of the rectangle.* → CIRCUMFERENCE

pe·ri·na·tal /ˌperəˈneɪtl◂/ *adj technical* at or around the time of birth → **antenatal**, **post natal**: *a high rate of perinatal mortality*

pe·ri·od¹ /ˈpɪəriəd $ ˈpɪr-/ ●●● S1 W1 AWL *n* [C]
1 LENGTH OF TIME a particular length of time with a beginning and an end: *Tomorrow's weather will be dry with sunny periods.* | **[+of]** *His playing improved in a very short* ***period of time****.* | *a brief period of silence* | *The drug was tested over a five-week period.* | *They adopted the system for a* ***trial period*** (=time in which something is tested to see if it works well).
2 LIFE/HISTORY a particular time in someone's life or in history → **era**: *the conflict of the Cold War period* | *Van Gogh's early period* | *the Jurassic period* | *the behaviour of children during the period of adolescence*
3 BLOOD the flow of blood that comes from a woman's body each month → **menstrual period**: *I was 12 years old when I* ***started*** *my* ***periods****.*
4 MARK *AmE* the mark (.) used in writing to show the end of a sentence or of an ABBREVIATION SYN **full stop** *BrE*
5 SCHOOL one of the equal parts that the school day is divided into SYN **lesson** *BrE*: *What class do you have first period?* | **[+of]** *a double period of Science*
6 SPORTS one of the equal parts that a game is divided into in a sport such as ICE HOCKEY: *The Bruins scored twice in the first period.*
7 FOR EMPHASIS **period!** *AmE spoken* used to emphasize that you have made a decision and that you do not want to discuss the subject any more SYN **full stop!**: *I'm not going, period!*

> **THESAURUS**
> **A PERIOD IN HISTORY**
> **period** a particular time in history, especially one studied as a subject: *the late Victorian period* | *the interwar period* | *During that period many people moved from the countryside to the towns.*
> **time** a period of years, months, days etc: *The 1960s were a time of great social change.* | *the biggest earthquake in modern times* | *Verdun was an important city in Roman times.*
> **age** a long period, especially one that represents a particular stage in the development of civilization or technology: *the industrial age* | *We are now in the age of the Internet.* | *the Stone Age* (=when people used tools made of stone)
> **era** a long period that has a particular character or that is marked by particular events: *We live in an era of breathtaking change.* | *the post-war era* | *De Gaulle's death marked* ***the end of an era****.*
> **epoch** /ˈiːpɒk $ ˈepək/ *formal* means the same as era, but sounds more formal and important: *We are now entering a new epoch in human history.* | *the colonial epoch* | *It was the* ***end of an epoch****.*

period² *adj* **period costume/furniture etc** clothes, furniture etc in the style of a particular time in history: *actors dressed in period costume*

pe·ri·od·ic /ˌpɪəriˈɒdɪk◂ $ -ˌpɪriˈɑː-/ ●○○ AWL (*also* **periodical**) *adj* [only before noun] happening a number of times, usually at regular times: *periodic home visits by nurses* —**periodically** /-kli/ *adv*: *Teachers meet periodically to discuss progress.*

pe·ri·od·i·cal /ˌpɪəriˈɒdɪkəl $ ˌpɪriˈɑː-/ AWL *n* [C] a magazine, especially one about a serious or technical subject

ˌperiodic ˈtable *n* **the periodic table** a list of ELEMENTS (=simple chemical substances) arranged according to their atomic structure

per·i·o·don·tal /ˌperiəʊˈdɒntl $ -oʊˈdɑːn-/ *adj technical* relating to the part of the mouth at the base of the teeth: *periodontal disease*

ˈperiod pain *n* [C,U] *especially BrE* pain that a woman gets when she has her PERIOD SYN **cramps** *AmE*

ˈperiod piece *n* [C] **1** an old piece of furniture or work of art: *a house furnished with period pieces* **2** a film, play, book etc whose story takes place during a particular period in history: *a period piece based on a book by E.M. Forster*

per·i·pa·tet·ic /ˌperəpəˈtetɪk◂/ *adj formal* travelling from place to place, especially in order to do your job: *a peripatetic music teacher*

pe·riph·e·ral[1] /pəˈrɪfərəl/ ●○○ *adj*
1 *formal* not as important as other things or people in a particular activity, idea, or situation: *a diplomat who had a peripheral role in the negotiations | Her involvement in the case was peripheral.* | **[+to]** *The romance is peripheral to the main plot of the movie.*
2 *formal* in the outer area of something, or relating to this area: *the city's peripheral suburbs | the peripheral nervous system*
3 peripheral vision your ability to see things to the side of you when you look straight ahead
4 *technical* peripheral equipment can be connected to a computer and used with it —**peripherally** *adv*

peripheral[2] *n* [C] *technical* a piece of equipment that is connected to a computer and used with it, for example a PRINTER

pe·riph·e·ry /pəˈrɪfəri/ *n* (*plural* **peripheries**) *formal* **1** [C usually singular] the edge of an area: **[+of]** *the periphery of the crowd* | **on/at the periphery** *a residential area on the periphery of the city* → OUTSKIRTS **2 on/at the periphery (of sth)** a person or thing that is on the periphery of something is not one of the main people or things involved in it: *extremists on the periphery of the animal rights movement | Homeopathy is on the periphery of medical practice.*

pe·riph·ra·sis /pəˈrɪfrəsɪs/ *n* (*plural* **periphrases** /-siːz/) [C,U] **1** *formal* when someone uses long words or phrases that are not necessary **2** *technical* the use of AUXILIARY words instead of INFLECTED forms —**periphrastic** /ˌperəˈfræstɪk◂/ *adj*

per·i·scope /ˈperəskəʊp $ -skoʊp/ *n* [C] a long tube with mirrors fitted in it, used to look over the top of something, especially to see out of a SUBMARINE

per·ish /ˈperɪʃ/ *v* **1** [I] *formal or literary* to die, especially in a terrible or sudden way: *Hundreds perished when the ship went down.* THESAURUS ▸ DIE **2** [I,T] *especially BrE* if rubber or leather perishes, it decays **3 perish the thought!** *spoken old-fashioned* used to say that you hope what someone has suggested will never happen: *If we lose, perish the thought, Watford will take first place.*

per·ish·a·ble /ˈperɪʃəbəl/ *adj* food that is perishable is likely to decay quickly: *perishable goods such as butter, milk, fruit and fish* —**perishables** *n* [plural]

per·ished /ˈperɪʃt/ *adj BrE spoken* feeling very cold: *I wish I'd brought a jacket - I'm perished!*

per·ish·er /ˈperɪʃə $ -ər/ *n* [C] *BrE old-fashioned informal* a child that behaves badly

per·ish·ing /ˈperɪʃɪŋ/ *adj BrE spoken* **1** very cold: *It was perishing in the tent. | Let's go indoors. I'm perishing!* **2** [only before noun] *old-fashioned informal* used to describe someone or something that is annoying you: *Tell those perishing kids to shut up!* —**perishingly** *adv*

per·i·style /ˈperəstaɪl/ *n* [C] *technical* a row of PILLARS around an open space in a building, or the open space itself

per·i·to·ni·tis /ˌperɪtəˈnaɪtɪs $ -tnˈaɪ-/ *n* [U] *technical* a serious condition in which the inside wall of someone's ABDOMEN (=part around and below your stomach) becomes infected and painful

per·i·win·kle /ˈperɪwɪŋkəl/ *n* **1** [C] a small plant with light blue or white flowers that grows close to the ground **2** [C] a small sea animal that lives in a shell and can be eaten SYN **winkle**

per·jure /ˈpɜːdʒə $ ˈpɜːrdʒər/ *v* **perjure yourself** *law* to tell a lie after promising to tell the truth in a court of law —**perjured** *adj*: *perjured evidence* —**perjurer** *n* [C]

per·ju·ry /ˈpɜːdʒəri $ ˈpɜːr-/ *n* [U] *law* the crime of telling a lie after promising to tell the truth in a court of law, or a lie told in this way: *Hall was found guilty of perjury.*

perk[1] /pɜːk $ pɜːrk/ *n* [C usually plural] something that you get legally from your work in addition to your wages, such as goods, meals, or a car: *theatre tickets and other perks* | **[+of]** *the perks of working at a large law firm | I only eat here because it's free -* ***one of the perks*** *of the job.*

perk[2] *v* [I,T] *informal* to PERCOLATE(3)

perk up *phr v informal* **1** to become more cheerful, active, and interested in what is happening around you, or to make someone feel this way: *She seemed kind of tired, but she perked up when Helen came over.* | **perk sb ↔ up** *There's no doubt coffee perks you up.* **2** to become more active, more interesting, more attractive etc, or to make something do this: **perk sth ↔ up** *A little chili will perk up the sauce.*

perk·y /ˈpɜːki $ ˈpɜːrki/ *adj informal* confident, happy, and active: *a perky salesgirl* —**perkily** *adv* —**perkiness** *n* [U]

perm[1] /pɜːm $ pɜːrm/ *n* [C] a process in which you make straight hair curly by using chemicals, or hair that has been treated in this way SYN **permanent** *AmE*: *a very curly perm*

perm[2] *v* [T] **1** to make straight hair curly by using chemicals: *I'm going to* ***have*** *my* ***hair permed****. | her blonde permed hair* **2** *BrE* to choose and combine a number of football games from the list given in the FOOTBALL POOLS in order to try to win money —**perming** *n* [U]: *a home perming kit*

per·ma·frost /ˈpɜːməfrɒst $ ˈpɜːrməfrɔːst/ *n* [U] a layer of soil that is always frozen in countries where it is very cold

per·ma·nent[1] /ˈpɜːmənənt $ ˈpɜːr-/ ●●● S2 W2 *adj* continuing to exist for a long time or for all the time in the future OPP **temporary**: *He gave up a permanent job in order to freelance. | a permanent change in your eating habits | The blindness that the disease causes will be permanent. | Miller soon became a* ***permanent fixture*** (=someone or something that is always there) *on the team.* —**permanence** (*also* **permanency**) *n* [U]: *the permanence of parental love | our desire for some sense of permanence*

> **THESAURUS**
>
> **permanent** continuing forever, for a very long time, or for the rest of your life: *She has permanent damage to her eyesight. | the search for a permanent solution to the problem | They've offered her the job on a permanent basis.*
>
> **lasting** continuing for a very long time - used especially when something continues to affect someone or something for a long time: *The experience left a lasting impression on him. | Things that happen in early childhood can have a lasting effect on your life. | Shelley was to have a lasting influence on him. | Is there any hope for a lasting peace in the Middle East?*
>
> **never-ending** continuing so long that you think it will never end - used especially when something needs a lot of effort: *Keeping the house clean is a never-ending battle. | It was a never-ending task. | The search was never-ending.*
>
> **perpetual** a perpetual state or feeling seems to be there all the time - used especially about something that is very annoying, worrying, or tiring: *For many working mothers, balancing the demands of children and job is a perpetual challenge. | The people live in a perpetual state of fear.*
>
> **everlasting** continuing forever - used especially in the following phrases: *Gold is the symbol of* ***everlasting love****. | He promised them* ***everlasting life****.*
>
> **eternal** continuing forever - used especially in the following phrases: *Do you believe in* ***eternal life****? | the secret of* ***eternal youth*** *| She has my* ***eternal gratitude*** (=I will always be grateful to her).

permanent[2] *n* [C] *AmE* a PERM[1]

per·ma·nent·ly /ˈpɜːmənəntli $ ˈpɜːr-/ ●●○ *adv* always, or for a very long time OPP **temporarily**: *The accident left him permanently disabled.* THESAURUS ▸ ALWAYS

ˌpermanent ˈpress *n* [U] a process used to treat cloth so that it does not WRINKLE easily, or cloth that has been treated in this way

ˌpermanent ˈwave *n* [C] *old-fashioned* a PERM[1]

per·ma·tanned /ˈpɜːməˌtænd $ ˈpɜːr-/ *adj BrE* a permatanned person is a white person who always has brown skin because they use SUNBEDS or products that colour their skin: *a permatanned chat show host* —**permatan** *n* [C]: *He has dyed hair and a permatan.*

per·me·a·ble /ˈpɜːmiəbəl $ ˈpɜːr-/ *adj technical* material that is permeable allows water, gas etc to pass through it OPP **impermeable**: *the permeable cell membrane* —**permeability** /ˌpɜːmiəˈbɪləti $ ˌpɜːr-/ *n* [U]

per·me·ate /ˈpɜːmieɪt $ ˈpɜːr-/ *v* **1** [I always + adv/prep, T] if liquid, gas etc permeates something, it enters it and spreads through every part of it: *The smell of diesel oil permeated the air.* | **[+through/into]** *Rain permeates through the ground to add to ground water levels.* **2** [T] if ideas, beliefs, emotions etc permeate something, they are present in every part of it: *Racism continues to permeate our society.* | *An emotional intensity permeates every one of O'Connor's songs.*

per·mis·si·ble /pəˈmɪsəbəl $ pər-/ *adj formal* allowed by law or by the rules SYN **allowable** OPP **impermissible**: *the maximum permissible level of radiation*

per·mis·sion /pəˈmɪʃən $ pər-/ ●●● S2 W3 *n* [U] if you have permission to do something, you are officially allowed to do it: **[+from]** *You'll have to get permission from your parents if you want to come.* | **[+for]** *The Council refused permission for the development.* | *Photographs should only be taken* ***with the permission of*** *the subject.* → PLANNING PERMISSION

GRAMMAR: Countable or uncountable?

- **Permission** is normally used as an uncountable noun: *Permission was granted for the interview.* ✗ Don't say: *a permission was granted* | *the permission was granted*
- The plural form **permissions** is also sometimes used when talking about official written statements allowing someone to do something: *The company needs to obtain all the necessary permissions before it can start drilling for oil.*

COLLOCATIONS

VERBS

have permission to do sth *They did not have permission to build on the land.*
ask (for) permission (*also* **request permission** *formal*) *Tommy asked for permission to go to the bathroom.*
apply for permission (=ask for official written permission) *The company has applied for permission to drill for oil.*
get permission (*also* **obtain/receive permission** *formal*) *We'll need to get permission to film in the museum.*
give permission (*also* **grant sb permission** *formal*) | **refuse/deny (sb) permission** | **seek permission** *formal* (=ask someone for permission)

ADJECTIVES

written permission *Doctors need written permission from the patient before they can operate.*
special permission | **official permission** | **planning permission** (=official permission to build a new building or change an existing one)

PHRASES

without permission *Pages should not be copied without the permission of the publisher.*
with sb's permission *With your permission, I'd like to talk to your son alone.*
by kind permission of sb *formal* (=used for thanking someone for allowing something) *This photograph is reproduced by kind permission of Country Living.*

per·mis·sive /pəˈmɪsɪv $ pər-/ *adj* not strict, and allowing behaviour that many other people would disapprove of: *parents who are too permissive* | *a* ***permissive society*** —**permissiveness** *n* [U]: *permissiveness in education*

Frequencies of the verbs **let**, **allow** and **permit** in spoken and written English.

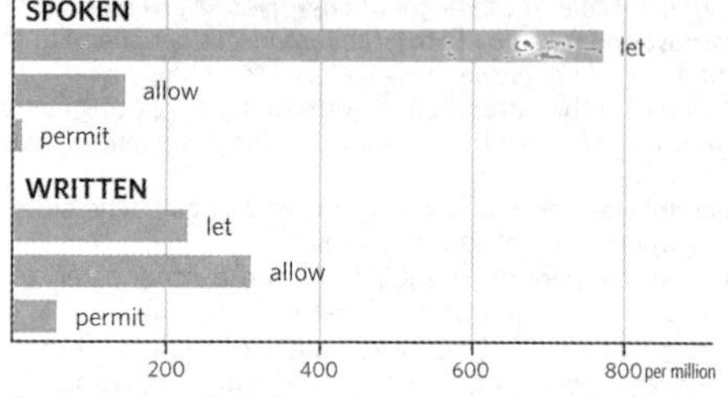

This graph shows that **let** is much more common in spoken English than **allow** and **permit**. **Allow** is more common in written English. **Permit** is more formal than **let** and **allow**, and is used especially when talking about rules or laws.

per·mit¹ /pəˈmɪt $ pər-/ ●●○ W3 *v* (**permitted**, **permitting**) *formal*
1 [T] to allow something to happen, especially by an official decision, rule, or law: *Smoking is only permitted in the public lounge.* | **be permitted to do sth** *As a punishment, she was not permitted to attend any school activities.* | **be permitted in/near etc sth** *Dogs are not permitted inside the shop.* | **permit sb sth** *The bill would permit workers 12 weeks of unpaid leave for family emergencies.* | *He had more than the permitted level of alcohol in his blood.* THESAURUS ALLOW

REGISTER

Permit is a formal word, which is used especially about someone being officially allowed to do something. In everyday situations, people usually say **let sb do sth** or **allow sb to do sth**: *His parents won't* ***let*** *him watch TV after ten o'clock.*

2 [I,T] to make it possible for something to happen: *The large windows permit a clear view of the lake.* | **permit sb to do sth** *The moon permitted me to see a little way into the distance.* | *I'll see you after the meeting,* ***if time permits*** (=if it finishes early enough). | *We'll have a picnic at the beach,* ***weather permitting*** (=if the weather is good enough).

GRAMMAR: Comparison

permit
- Something **is permitted**: *Working from home is permitted.*
- Someone **is permitted to do** something: *Employees are permitted to work from home.*
- Someone **is permitted** something: *Women were not permitted a vote.*

Permit is usually used in the passive in this meaning.

allow
- You **allow** someone **to do** something: *Her boss allows her to work from home.*
- Something **is allowed**: *Working from home is allowed.*
- Someone **is allowed** something: *You are allowed one piece of hand luggage.*

Allow is often used in the passive.

let
- You **let** someone **do** something: *Her boss lets her work from home.* ✗ Don't say: *let someone to do something*

Let is not used in the passive.

per·mit² /ˈpɜːmɪt $ ˈpɜːr-, pərˈmɪt/ ●●○ *n* [C] an official written statement giving you the right to do something: **[+for]** *A permit is required for fishing in the canal.* | **travel/parking/export etc permit** *Hikers need a camping permit for overnight stays in the park.* → WORK PERMIT

per·mu·ta·tion /ˌpɜːmjʊˈteɪʃən $ ˌpɜːr-/ *n* [C] one of the different ways in which a number of things can be arranged: *a sandwich shop that sells every possible permutation of meat and bread* → COMBINATION

per·ni·cious /pəˈnɪʃəs $ pər-/ *adj formal* very harmful or evil, often in a way that you do not notice easily: *the pernicious effects of poverty | the media's pernicious influence* THESAURUS ▸ HARMFUL —**perniciously** *adv*

perˌnicious aˈnaemia *n* [U] *medical* a severe form of ANAEMIA (=too few red blood cells in the blood)

per·nick·e·ty /pəˈnɪkəti $ pər-/ *adj BrE informal* worrying too much about small and unimportant things SYN **fussy**

per·o·ra·tion /ˌperəˈreɪʃən/ *n* [C] **1** *technical* the last part of a speech, in which the main points are repeated **2** *formal* a long speech that sounds impressive but does not have much meaning

pe·rov·skite /pəˈrɒfskaɪt $ -ˈrɒːf-/ *n* [U] a mineral that contains various types of metals that are used in industry

per·ox·ide /pəˈrɒksaɪd $ -ˈrɑːk-/ *n* [U] a liquid chemical used to make hair light in colour or to kill BACTERIA: *her waist-length* **peroxide blonde** *hair* (=hair made light yellow using peroxide)

perp /pɜːp $ pɜːrp/ *n* [C] *AmE informal* a person who has committed a particular crime - used especially by police officers

per·pen·dic·u·lar¹ /ˌpɜːpənˈdɪkjələ◂ $ ˌpɜːrpənˈdɪkjələr◂/ *adj* **1** not leaning to one side or the other but exactly vertical → **vertical, horizontal**: *a perpendicular line | a perpendicular wall of rock* **2 be perpendicular to sth** if one line is perpendicular to another line, they form an angle of 90 degrees SYN **at right angles to**: *a road perpendicular to the highway* **3 Perpendicular** in the style of 14th- and 15th-century English churches, which are decorated with straight upright lines —**perpendicularly** *adv*

perpendicular² *n* [singular] an exactly vertical position or line

per·pe·trate /ˈpɜːpətreɪt $ ˈpɜːr-/ *v* [T] *formal* to do something that is morally wrong or illegal → **commit**: *Who could have perpetrated such a dreadful crime?* —**perpetration** /ˌpɜːpəˈtreɪʃən $ ˌpɜːr-/ *n* [U]

per·pe·tra·tor /ˈpɜːpətreɪtə $ ˈpɜːrpətreɪtər/ *n* [C] *formal* someone who does something morally wrong or illegal → **culprit**: *The perpetrators were never caught.* | **[+of]** *The perpetrators of racially motivated violence must be punished.*

per·pet·u·al /pəˈpetʃuəl $ pər-/ ●○○ *adj* [usually before noun]
1 continuing all the time without changing or stopping SYN **continuous**: *the perpetual noise of the machines | a little girl with a perpetual smile* THESAURUS ▸ PERMANENT
2 repeated many times in a way that annoys you SYN **continual**: *my mother's perpetual nagging*
3 *literary* permanent: *the perpetual snows of the mountaintops* —**perpetually** *adv*

perˌpetual ˈmotion *n* [U] the ability of a machine to always continue moving without getting energy from anywhere else, which is not considered possible

per·pet·u·ate /pəˈpetʃueɪt $ pər-/ ●○○ *v* [T] to make a situation, attitude etc, especially a bad one, continue to exist for a long time: *an education system that perpetuates the divisions in our society* —**perpetuation** /pəˌpetʃuˈeɪʃən $ pər-/ *n* [U]

per·pe·tu·i·ty /ˌpɜːpəˈtjuːəti $ ˌpɜːrpɪˈtuː-/ *n* **in perpetuity** *law* for all future time SYN **forever**: *The land had been promised to the Indian tribes in perpetuity.*

per·plex /pəˈpleks $ pər-/ *v* [T] if something perplexes you, it makes you feel confused and worried because it is difficult to understand SYN **puzzle**: *Shea's symptoms perplexed the doctors.* —**perplexing** *adj*: *a perplexing problem*

per·plexed /pəˈplekst $ pər-/ *adj* confused and worried by something that you do not understand SYN **puzzled**: *The student looked at him, perplexed. | Perplexed investors tried to work out what the deal meant.* —**perplexedly** /pəˈpleksədli, -ˈplekstli $ pər-/ *adv*

per·plex·i·ty /pəˈpleksəti $ pər-/ *n* (*plural* **perplexities**) **1** [U] the feeling of being confused or worried by something you cannot understand **2** [C usually plural] something that is complicated or difficult to understand: *moral perplexities*

per·qui·site /ˈpɜːkwəzɪt $ ˈpɜːr-/ *n* [C] *formal* a PERK¹

per·ry /ˈperi/ *n* [U] *especially BrE* an alcoholic drink made from PEARS

per se /ˌpɜː ˈseɪ $ ˌpɜːr ˈsiː, -ˈseɪ, ˌper ˈseɪ/ *adv formal* used to say that something is being considered alone, not with other connected things: *The color of the shell per se does not affect the quality of the egg.*

per·se·cute /ˈpɜːsɪkjuːt $ ˈpɜːr-/ *v* [T] **1** to treat someone cruelly or unfairly over a period of time, especially because of their religious or political beliefs: *The Puritans left England to escape being persecuted.* **2** to deliberately cause difficulties for someone by annoying them often SYN **harass**: *Like many celebrities, she complained of being persecuted by the press.* —**persecutor** *n* [C]

per·se·cu·tion /ˌpɜːsɪˈkjuːʃən $ ˌpɜːr-/ ●○○ *n* [C,U] cruel or unfair treatment of someone over a period of time, especially because of their religious or political beliefs: *the persecution of writers who criticize the government | They are refugees who are fleeing religious persecution.*

perseˈcution ˌcomplex *n* [C] a mental illness in which someone believes that other people are trying to harm them

per·se·ver·ance /ˌpɜːsəˈvɪərəns $ ˌpɜːrsəˈvɪr-/ *n* [U] determination to keep trying to achieve something in spite of difficulties - use this to show approval: *It took perseverance to overcome his reading problems.*

per·se·vere /ˌpɜːsəˈvɪə $ ˌpɜːrsəˈvɪr/ *v* [I] to continue trying to do something in a very determined way in spite of difficulties - use this to show approval: *It can be tricky at first, but persevere.* | **[+with]** *He persevered with his task until he had succeeded in collecting an armful of firewood.* | **persevere in (doing) sth** *She had persevered in her claim for compensation.* THESAURUS ▸ CONTINUE —**persevering** *adj*

Per·sian¹ /ˈpɜːʃən, -ʒən $ ˈpɜːrʒən/ *adj* relating to Iran, its people, or its language, especially in the time when it was called Persia: *the Persian Empire | a Persian carpet*

Persian² *n* **1** [C] someone from Iran, especially in the time when it was called Persia **2** [U] the language used in Iran SYN **Farsi**

ˌPersian ˈcat *n* [C] a cat with long silky hair

per·sim·mon /pəˈsɪmən $ pər-/ *n* [C] a soft orange-coloured fruit that grows in hot countries

PERSIMMON

per·sist /pəˈsɪst $ pər-/ ●●○ AWL *v*
1 [I,T] to continue to do something, although this is difficult, or other people oppose it: **persist in (doing) sth** *He persisted in his refusal to admit responsibility.* | **[+with]** *She persisted with her studies in spite of financial problems. | 'I don't think it's right,' John persisted.*

GRAMMAR

You **persist in doing** something: *She persisted in asking the question.* ✗ Don't say: *She persisted to ask the question.*
GRAMMAR GUIDE ▸ VERBS

2 [I] if something bad persists, it continues to exist or happen: *If the pain persists, you must see a doctor.* THESAURUS ▸ CONTINUE

per·sis·tence /pəˈsɪstəns $ pər-/ ●○○ AWL *n* [U]
1 determination to do something even though it is difficult or other people oppose it: *Her persistence paid off when she was offered the job of manager. | 'Why can't I come?' repeated Will with* **dogged persistence**.

2 when something continues to exist or happen, especially for longer than is usual or desirable: **[+of]** *the persistence of high unemployment in the post-war years*

per·sis·tent /pəˈsɪstənt $ pər-/ ●○○ AWL *adj*
1 [usually before noun] continuing to exist or happen, especially for longer than is usual or desirable: *persistent rumours | persistent headaches | a persistent problem | persistent rain*
2 continuing to do something, although this is difficult, or other people warn you not to do it: *If she hadn't been so persistent she might not have gotten the job. | persistent efforts | **Persistent offenders*** (=people who often break the law) *face a prison sentence.* —**persistently** *adv*: *persistently low rainfall*

perˌsistent ˈvegetative ˌstate *n* [C] *medical* a condition in which someone's brain is so damaged that they cannot move or talk, and their condition is unlikely to improve

per·snick·e·ty /pəˈsnɪkəti $ pər-/ *adj AmE* worrying too much about details that are not important - used to show disapproval

per·son /ˈpɜːsən $ ˈpɜːr-/ ●●● S1 W1 *n* [C]
1 (*plural* **people** /ˈpiːpəl/) a human being, especially considered as someone with their own particular character: *He was a very nice person, always pleasant and friendly. | The only person who really said anything helpful was Jack.* | **kind/type/sort of person** *David was not the sort of person who found it easy to talk about his feelings. | I like her **as a person**, but not as a boss. | I still know quite a lot of people in the village. | a group of young people* | **city/cat/night etc person** (=someone who likes a particular kind of thing) *I'm not a morning person.*
2 in person if you do something in person, you go somewhere and do it yourself, instead of doing something by letter, asking someone else to do it etc: *You have to sign for it in person.*
3 businessperson/salesperson etc someone who works in business, who sells things etc → CHAIRPERSON, SPOKESPERSON
4 (*plural* **persons**) *formal or law* someone who is not known or not named: *The police are appealing for any person who was in the area at this time to contact them. | murder by **person or persons unknown** | All 115 persons on board were killed.*
5 on/about your person *formal* if you have something on or about your person, you have it in your pockets or attached to you: *Customs officers found a gun concealed about his person.*
6 in the person of sb *formal* used before the name of someone who you have just mentioned in a more general way: *I was met by the police in the person of Sergeant Black.*
→ FIRST PERSON, MISSING PERSON, PERSON-TO-PERSON, SECOND PERSON, THIRD PERSON

USAGE: People, persons
• The plural of **person** is usually **people**: *There are 25 people in the class.* ✗ Don't say: *There are 25 persons in the class.*
• The plural **persons** is used in official English, for example in official notices, documents, or statements: *All persons born in the United States are citizens of the United States. | The maximum number of persons in each group is 14.*

per·so·na /pəˈsəʊnə $ pərˈsoʊ-/ *n* (*plural* **personae** /-niː/ *or* **personas**) [C] the way you behave when you are with other people or in a particular situation, which gives people a particular idea about your character: *Joel has a cheerful **public persona** but in private he's different.*

per·son·a·ble /ˈpɜːsənəbəl $ ˈpɜːr-/ *adj* someone who is personable is attractive and pleasant

per·son·age /ˈpɜːsənɪdʒ $ ˈpɜːr-/ *n* [C] *formal* a person, usually someone famous or important: *a royal personage*

per·son·al /ˈpɜːsənəl $ ˈpɜːr-/ ●●● S1 W1 *adj*
1 [only before noun] belonging or relating to one particular person, rather than to other people or to people in general: *My **personal view** is that we shouldn't offer him the job. | Style and colour are a matter of **personal taste**. | She took full personal responsibility for all the arrangements. | When I went to her room all her **personal belongings** had gone. | After Nelson's death, his mother received his **personal effects**. | I know **from personal experience** that you can't trust Trevor. | the **personal qualities** needed to be successful in business | The car is **for personal use** only.* | **On a personal level** *he felt sympathy for them, but he had a job to do. | celebrities with their own **personal trainer***
2 relating to the private areas of your life: *I don't answer questions about my **personal life**. | May I ask you a **personal question**? | the records will include other **personal details** such as nationality, date of birth and address | He's got a few **personal problems** at the moment. | The envelope was marked 'Personal and Confidential'. | We're not allowed to make personal phone calls at work.* THESAURUS▸ PRIVATE
3 involving rude or upsetting criticism of someone: *It's unprofessional to make such personal remarks. | a bitter personal attack on the president | There's no need to **get personal**!* | **(it's) nothing personal** (=used to tell someone that you are not criticizing them) *It's nothing personal, I just have to go home now.*
4 if you give something your personal care or attention, you deal with it yourself instead of asking someone else to do it: *Small companies can devote more personal attention to each project. | As you get promoted in a firm you lose that personal contact* (=meeting and dealing with people yourself).
5 personal friend someone who you know well, especially a famous or important person: **[+of]** *Apparently the director is a personal friend of hers.*
6 [only before noun] relating to your body or the way you look: *Grant was always fussy about his **personal appearance**. | the importance of **personal hygiene***
7 personal touch something you do to make something special, or that makes someone feel special: *It's those extra personal touches that make our service better.*
8 personal best the fastest time, most points etc that a SPORTSMAN or SPORTSWOMAN has ever achieved: *I ran 20.51 seconds for a personal best.*
9 personal development improvements in your character and skills

ˈpersonal ˌad *n* [C] a short advertisement put in a newspaper or magazine by someone who wants a friend or LOVER → **lonely hearts**

ˌpersonal alˈlowance *n* [C] *BrE* the amount of money that you can earn each year before you must pay INCOME TAX

ˌpersonal asˈsistant *n* [C] (*abbreviation* **PA**) **1** someone who works for one person and helps them do their job **2** *BrE* someone who works as a secretary for one person

ˈpersonal ˌcolumn *n* [C] *BrE* a part of a newspaper in which people can have private or personal messages printed

ˌpersonal comˈmunicator *n* [C] a small computer that you can carry with you and use to send, store, and receive FAXes, or spoken or written messages

ˌpersonal comˈputer *n* [C] a PC

ˌpersonal ˈdata ˌorganizer *n* [C] a PDA

ˌpersonal ˌdigital asˈsistant *n* [C] a PDA

ˌpersonal elecˌtronic deˈvice *n* [C] a piece of electronic equipment, such as a LAPTOP computer or a MOBILE PHONE, that is small and easy to carry

ˌpersonal exˈemption *n* [C] *AmE* the amount of money that you can earn each year before you must pay INCOME TAX

ˌpersonal identifiˈcation ˌnumber *n* [C] a PIN

per·son·al·i·ty /ˌpɜːsəˈnæləti $ ˌpɜːr-/ ●●● S3 W3 *n* (*plural* **personalities**)
1 [C,U] someone's character, especially the way they behave towards other people: *Despite their different personalities, they became the best of friends. | Unfortunately,*

the illness can lead to changes in personality. → SPLIT PERSONALITY
2 [C] someone who is very famous and often appears in the newspapers, on television etc, especially an entertainer or sports person → **celebrity**: **TV/radio/sports personality** *one of the most well-liked TV personalities*
THESAURUS STAR
3 [U] the qualities of character that make someone interesting or enjoyable to be with: *He's honest but he lacks personality.*
4 [C usually singular] someone who has a very strong character and is very different from other people: *He was a dynamic personality in the business world.*
5 [C usually singular] the qualities which make a place or thing different and interesting: *It's partly the architecture which gives the town its personality.*

COLLOCATIONS

ADJECTIVES

a strong personality *Mercer has a strong personality and always tells you his opinion.*
a forceful personality *The architect's forceful personality ensured that the work progressed rapidly.*
a dominant personality (=controlling other people) | **a warm personality** (=friendly and kind to people) | **an outgoing/extrovert personality** (=liking to talk to people)

personality + NOUN

a personality trait *formal* (=a part of your personality) *She shares many of her mother's personality traits.*
a personality disorder (=a mental illness affecting someone's personality) | **a personality clash** (=when people cannot work together because they are so different)

person'ality ˌcult (*also* **cult of personality**) *n* [C] a situation in which people are encouraged to admire and praise a famous person, especially a political leader – used to show disapproval

per·son·al·ize (*also* **-ise** *BrE*) /ˈpɜːsənəlaɪz $ ˈpɜːr-/ *v* [T] **1** to put your name or INITIALS on something, or to decorate it in your own way, to show that it belongs to you: *Why not do something to personalize your office?* **2** to design or change something so that it is suitable for a particular person: *All the products can be personalized to the client's exact requirements.* **3** to discuss a subject by talking about or criticizing the people who are involved in it, rather than talking about it in a more general way: *the mass media's tendency to personalize politics* —**personalized** *adj*: *a personalized number plate*

per·son·al·ly /ˈpɜːsənəli $ ˈpɜːr-/ ●●● S2 *adv*
1 [sentence adverb] *spoken* used to emphasize that you are only giving your own opinion about something: *Personally, I don't think much of the idea.* | *I personally think it's too cold to go out.*
2 if you do something personally, you do it yourself rather than getting someone else to do it SYN **in person**: *The managing director wrote personally to thank me.* | *All important work is personally approved by him.* | *I'll see to it personally.*
3 used to show that one particular person is involved, rather than a group of people: *I'm **holding** you **personally responsible** for this mess!* | *She clearly blamed me personally for the difficulties she'd been having.*
4 take sth personally to get upset by the things other people say or do, because you think that their remarks or behaviour are directed at you in particular: *Don't take it personally; she's rude to everyone.*
5 as a friend, or as someone you have met: *I don't **know** her **personally**, but I like her work.*
6 in a way that criticizes someone's character or appearance: *Members of the Senate rarely attack each other personally.*
7 in relation to someone's private life, rather than to their work, business, or official duties: *She had a lasting impact on his life both personally and professionally.*

ˌpersonal ˈorganizer *n* [C] a small book with loose sheets of paper, or a very small computer, for recording information, addresses, meetings etc

ˌpersonal ˈpronoun *n* [C] *technical* a PRONOUN such as 'I', 'you', or 'they'

per·son·als /ˈpɜːsənəlz $ ˈpɜːr-/ *n AmE* **the personals** the part of a newspaper in which people can have private or personal messages printed

ˌpersonal ˈshopper *n* [C] someone whose job is to help people decide what to buy, or to go shopping for them

ˌpersonal ˈspace *n* [U] the distance that you like to keep between you and other people in order to feel comfortable, for example when you are talking to someone or travelling on a bus or train: *She objected to this **invasion of** her **personal space**.*

ˌpersonal ˈstereo *n* [C] a small MP3 PLAYER, CD PLAYER, or radio which you carry around with you and listen to through small HEADPHONES

ˌpersonal ˈtrainer *n* [C] someone whose job is to help people decide what type of exercise is best for them and show them how to do it

persona non gra·ta /pəˌsəʊnə nɒn ˈɡrɑːtə $ pərˌsoʊnə nɑːn ˈɡrætə/ *n formal* **be/become/be declared persona non grata** to be not welcome in a particular place because of something that you have done – used especially when a foreign government orders you to go home

per·son·i·fi·ca·tion /pəˌsɒnɪfɪˈkeɪʃən $ pərˌsɑː-/ *n* **1 the personification of sth** someone who is a perfect example of a quality because they have a lot of it: *He became the personification of the financial excess of the 1980s.* **2** [C,U] the representation of a thing or a quality as a person, in literature or art: **[+of]** *the personification of rivers in fifth-century art*

per·son·i·fy /pəˈsɒnɪfaɪ $ pərˈsɑː-/ *v* (**personified, personifying, personifies**) [T] **1** to have a lot of a particular quality or be a typical example of something: *Carter personifies the values of self-reliance and hard work.* | **kindness/generosity etc personified** *Bertha was kindness personified.* **2** to think of or represent a quality or thing as a person: **personify sth as sb** *Time is often personified as an old man.*

per·son·nel /ˌpɜːsəˈnel $ ˌpɜːr-/ ●●○ W3 *n*
1 [plural] the people who work in a company, organization, or military force → **staff**: **military/medical/technical etc personnel** *senior military personnel* | *doctors and other medical personnel* | *All personnel are to receive security badges.*
2 [U] the department in a company that chooses people for jobs and deals with their complaints, problems etc SYN **human resources**: *A copy should then be sent to Personnel for our files.* | *the personnel department*

person'nel ˌcarrier *n* [C] a vehicle for carrying soldiers

ˌperson-to-ˈperson *adj* [only before noun] involving communication between people: *Email provides a way of sending person-to-person messages almost instantaneously.*

per·spec·tive /pəˈspektɪv $ pər-/ ●●○ W3 AWL *n*
1 [C] a way of thinking about something, especially one which is influenced by the type of person you are or by your experiences → **viewpoint**: **[+on]** *His father's death gave him a whole new perspective on life.* | **from sb's perspective** *The novel is written from a child's perspective.* | **from a feminist/Christian/global etc perspective** *We have to look at everything from an international perspective.* | *a much-needed **historical perspective*** | **wider/broader perspective** *Our work in Uganda and Romania adds a wider perspective.*
2 [U] a sensible way of judging and comparing situations so that you do not imagine that something is more serious than it really is: *I think Viv's **lost** all **sense of perspective**.* | *The figures have to be **put into perspective**.* | **get/keep sth in perspective** (=judge the importance of something correctly)

3 [U] a method of drawing a picture that makes objects look solid and shows distance and depth, or the effect this method produces in a picture: *the artist's use of perspective*
4 [C] *formal* a view, especially one in which you can see a long way into the distance

Per·spex /ˈpɜːspeks $ ˈpɜːr-/ *n* [U] *trademark BrE* a strong type of plastic that can be used instead of glass

per·spi·ca·cious /ˌpɜːspɪˈkeɪʃəs◂ $ ˌpɜːr-/ *adj formal* good at judging and understanding people and situations SYN **perceptive** —**perspicaciously** *adv* —**perspicacity** /-ˈkæsəti/ *n* [U]

per·spi·ra·tion /ˌpɜːspəˈreɪʃən $ ˌpɜːr-/ *n* [U] *formal* liquid that appears on your skin when you are hot or nervous SYN **sweat** → **antiperspirant**: *He wiped the* ***beads of perspiration*** (=drops) *from his brow.*

P

per·spire /pəˈspaɪə $ pərˈspaɪr/ *v* [I] *formal* if you perspire, parts of your body become wet, especially because you are hot or have been doing hard work SYN **sweat**: *Willie was* ***perspiring heavily****.*

per·suade /pəˈsweɪd $ pər-/ ●●● S3 W2 *v* [T]
1 to make someone decide to do something, especially by giving them reasons why they should do it, or asking them many times to do it: **persuade sb to do sth** *I finally managed to persuade her to go out for a drink with me.* | **persuade sb into doing sth** *Don't let yourself be persuaded into buying things you don't want.* | **try/manage/fail to persuade sb** *I'm trying to persuade your dad to buy some shares.* | **attempt/effort to persuade sb** *Leo wouldn't agree, despite our efforts to persuade him.* | **little/a lot of/no persuading** *He took a lot of persuading to come out of retirement* (=it was hard to persuade him). | *He was fairly* ***easily persuaded****.*
2 to make someone believe something or feel sure about something SYN **convince**: *I am not persuaded by these arguments.* | **persuade sb (that)** *She'll only take me back if I can persuade her that I've changed.* | **persuade sb of sth** *McFadden must persuade the jury of her innocence.*

THESAURUS

persuade to make someone decide to do something, especially by giving them reasons why they should do it, or asking them many times to do it: *I persuaded her to change her mind.* | *Do you think you can persuade him to lend us the money?*
talk sb into (doing) sth to persuade someone to do something, especially something they do not really want to do: *Why did I let you talk me into this?* | *He finally talked her into going on a date with him.*
get sb to do sth to make someone do something by persuading or asking them: *If we can't get a taxi I'll get Joe to pick us up.* | *I know how to get you to kiss me.*
convince to persuade someone that they should do something, because it is the best or the right thing to do. Some British speakers think this use is incorrect, and prefer to use **persuade**: *It would be difficult to convince him to move.*
encourage to try to persuade someone to do something, especially because you think it will be good for them: *Children should be encouraged to read all kinds of books.*
influence to have an effect on what someone decides to do: *What influences you to buy clothes?*
coax to persuade someone to do something by talking gently and kindly: *I tried to coax him to eat a little.*
cajole /kəˈdʒəʊl $ -ˈdʒoʊl/ to persuade someone to do something by praising them or making promises to them: *He hoped to cajole her into selling her house.*
put sb up to sth to persuade or encourage someone to do something wrong or stupid: *Who put you up to this?*
dissuade *formal* to persuade someone not to do something: *How do you dissuade young people from experimenting with drugs?*

per·sua·sion /pəˈsweɪʒən $ pər-/ ●○○ *n*
1 [U] the act of persuading someone to do something: *After a little* ***gentle persuasion****, Debbie agreed to let us in.* | *It had taken a great deal of persuasion to get him to accept.* | *She used all her* ***powers of persuasion*** (=skill at persuading people) *to convince Tilly that it was the right thing to do.*
2 [C] *formal* a particular type of belief, especially a political or religious one: **political/religious persuasion** *We need people with talent, whatever their political persuasions.* | *politicians* ***of all persuasions***
3 of the ... persuasion *formal* of a particular type – often used humorously: *an ancient bed of the iron persuasion*

per·sua·sive /pəˈsweɪsɪv $ pər-/ ●○○ *adj* able to make other people believe something or do what you ask → **convincing**: *Trevor can be very persuasive.* | **persuasive argument/evidence** *a persuasive argument against capital punishment* —**persuasively** *adv* —**persuasiveness** *n* [U]

pert /pɜːt $ pɜːrt/ *adj* **1** a girl or woman who is pert is amusing, but slightly disrespectful: *Angie gave him one of her pert little glances.* **2** a pert part of the body is small, firm, and attractive: *a pert bottom* —**pertly** *adv* —**pertness** *n* [U]

per·tain /pəˈteɪn $ pər-/ *v*
pertain to sth *phr v formal* to relate directly to something: *legislation pertaining to employment rights*

per·ti·na·cious /ˌpɜːtəˈneɪʃəs◂ $ ˌpɜːr-/ *adj formal* continuing to believe something or to do something in a very determined way SYN **tenacious** —**pertinaciously** *adv* —**pertinacity** /-ˈnæsəti/ *n* [U]

per·ti·nent /ˈpɜːtɪnənt $ ˈpɜːr-/ *adj formal* directly relating to something that is being considered SYN **relevant**: *He asked me a lot of very* ***pertinent questions****.* | **[+to]** *The last point is particularly pertinent to today's discussion.* —**pertinently** *adv* —**pertinence** *n* [U]

per·tur·ba·tion /ˌpɜːtəˈbeɪʃən $ ˌpɜːrtər-/ *n*
1 [C,U] *technical* a small change in the movement, quality, or behaviour of something: *climatic perturbations*
2 [U] *formal* worry about something that has happened or will happen

per·turbed /pəˈtɜːbd $ pərˈtɜːrbd/ *adj formal* worried about something that has happened or will happen: *William looked a little perturbed.* | **[+by/at/about]** *He didn't seem perturbed by the noises outside.* | **perturbed that** *He was perturbed that she didn't look happy.* —**perturb** *v* [T]: *My unexpected arrival didn't perturb him in the least.*

pe·ruse /pəˈruːz/ *v* [T] *formal* to read something, especially in a careful way: *She leant forward to peruse the document more closely.* —**perusal** *n* [C,U]

perv /pɜːv $ pɜːrv/ *n* [C] *BrE spoken informal* a PERVERT —**pervy** *adj*

per·vade /pəˈveɪd $ pər-/ *v* [T] *formal* if a feeling, idea, or smell pervades a place, it is present in every part of it: *A spirit of hopelessness pervaded the country.*

per·va·sive /pəˈveɪsɪv $ pər-/ *adj* existing everywhere: *the pervasive influence of television* | *the* ***all-pervasive*** *mood of apathy* —**pervasiveness** *n* [U]

per·verse /pəˈvɜːs $ pərˈvɜːrs/ *adj* behaving in an unreasonable way, especially by deliberately doing the opposite of what people want you to do → **bizarre**: *He gets perverse satisfaction from embarrassing people.* —**perversely** *adv*: *Perversely, she was irritated by his kindness.*

per·ver·sion /pəˈvɜːʃən, -ʒən $ pərˈvɜːrʒən/ *n* [C,U]
1 a type of sexual behaviour that is considered unnatural and unacceptable **2** the process of changing something that is natural and good into something that is unnatural and wrong, or the result of such a change: **[+of]** *a perversion of the true meaning of democracy*

per·ver·si·ty /pəˈvɜːsəti $ pərˈvɜːr-/ *n* [U] the quality of being perverse: *Max refused the money out of sheer perversity.*

per·vert[1] /pəˈvɜːt $ pərˈvɜːrt/ *v* [T] **1** to change something in an unnatural and often harmful way: *Genetic* *scientists are often accused of perverting nature.* **2** to influence someone so that they begin to think or behave in an immoral way SYN **corrupt**: *TV violence perverts the minds of young children.* **3 pervert the course of justice** *law* to deliberately prevent a fair examination of the facts about a crime

per·vert² /ˈpɜːvɜːt $ ˈpɜːrvɜːrt/ *n* [C] someone whose sexual behaviour is considered unnatural and unacceptable

per·vert·ed /pəˈvɜːtɪd $ pərˈvɜːr-/ *adj* **1** morally wrong: *He derives a perverted pleasure from hurting other people.* | *the perverted logic of terrorism* **2** sexually unacceptable or unnatural

pe·se·ta /pəˈseɪtə/ *n* [C] the standard unit of money used in Spain before the EURO

pes·ky /ˈpeski/ *adj* [only before noun] *especially AmE informal* annoying: *Those pesky kids!*

pe·so /ˈpeɪsəʊ $ -soʊ/ *n* (*plural* **pesos**) [C] the standard unit of money in the Philippines and in various Latin American countries including Mexico, Cuba, and Colombia

pes·sa·ry /ˈpesəri/ *n* (*plural* **pessaries**) [C] **1** a small block of medicine which a woman puts into her VAGINA in order to cure an infection or to stop herself becoming PREGNANT **2** an instrument put into a woman's VAGINA to support her WOMB

pes·si·mi·sm /ˈpesəmɪzəm/ *n* [U] a tendency to believe that bad things will happen OPP **optimism**: **[+about/over]** *There is deep pessimism about the future.*

pes·si·mist /ˈpesəmɪst/ *n* [C] someone who always expects that bad things will happen OPP **optimist**: *Don't be such a pessimist!*

pes·si·mis·tic /ˌpesəˈmɪstɪk◂/ ●○○ *adj* expecting that bad things will happen in the future or that something will have a bad result OPP **optimistic**: *a pessimistic view of life* | **[+about]** *He remains deeply pessimistic about the peace process.* —**pessimistically** /-kli/ *adv*

pest /pest/ ●○○ *n* [C]
1 a small animal or insect that destroys crops or food supplies → **vermin**: *a chemical used in pest control*
2 *informal* an annoying person, especially a child

pes·ter /ˈpestə $ -ər/ *v* [I,T] to annoy someone, especially by asking them many times to do something → **harass**: *She'd been pestered by reporters for days.* | **pester sb for sth** *I can't even walk down the street without being continually pestered for money.* | **pester sb to do sth** *The kids have been pestering me to buy them new trainers.* THESAURUS ASK

ˈpester ˌpower *n* [U] the ability that children have to make their parents buy things or do things for them by asking them again and again

pes·ti·cide /ˈpestɪsaɪd/ ●○○ *n* [C,U] a chemical substance used to kill insects and small animals that destroy crops → **herbicide**

pes·ti·lence /ˈpestələns/ *n* [C,U] *literary* a disease that spreads quickly and kills a lot of people SYN **plague**

pes·ti·len·tial /ˌpestəˈlenʃəl◂/ (*also* **pes·ti·lent** /ˈpestələnt/) *adj* **1** *literary* extremely unpleasant and annoying **2** *old use* causing disease

pes·tle /ˈpesəl, ˈpestl/ *n* [C] a short stick with a heavy round end, used for crushing things in a MORTAR (=a special bowl)

pes·to /ˈpestəʊ $ -oʊ/ *n* [U] a sauce made from BASIL, GARLIC, PINE NUTS, OLIVE OIL, and cheese

pet¹ /pet/ ●●● S2 *n*
1 [C] an animal such as a cat or a dog which you keep and care for at home: *They* ***have*** *two* ***pets*** *- a cat and a dog.* | *We weren't allowed to* ***keep pets*** *at school.* | *Rabbits* ***make good pets.*** | **pet rabbit/bird etc** *He got bitten by his pet rabbit.* | ***pet food*** | *a* ***pet shop***
2 *BrE spoken* used when speaking to someone you like or love: *Don't cry, pet.* → TEACHER'S PET

pet² *v* (**petted, petting**) [T] to touch and move your hand gently over someone, especially an animal or a child → **stroke**: *Our cat loves being petted.* THESAURUS TOUCH → PETTING

pet³ *adj* **1 pet project/theory/subject** a plan, idea, or subject that you particularly like or are interested in **2 pet hate** *BrE*, **pet peeve** *AmE* something that you strongly dislike because it always annoys you: *TV game shows are one of my pet hates.* → PET NAME

pet·a·byte /ˈpetəbaɪt/ *n* [C] 1000 TRILLION BYTES

pet·a·flop /ˈpetəflɒp $ -flɑːp/ *n* [C usually plural] a unit that measures how fast a computer works. One petaflop is one million BILLION operations every second.

pet·al /ˈpetl/ ●●○ *n* [C] one of the coloured parts of a flower that are shaped like leaves: *rose petals* | *The flower has seven petals.* → see picture at TREE

pe·tard /pəˈtɑːd $ -ɑːrd/ *n* → **be hoist with/by your own petard** at HOIST¹(2)

ˈpet door *n* [C] *AmE* a CATFLAP

pe·ter /ˈpiːtə $ -ər/ *v*
peter out *phr v* to gradually become smaller, less, weaker etc and then come to an end: *The road became narrower and eventually petered out.* | *Public interest in the environment is in danger of petering out.*

Peter → **rob Peter to pay Paul** at ROB(2)

ˌPeter ˈPan a man who never seems to become older or grow up. The name comes from the main character in the play *Peter Pan* (1904) by J. M. Barrie. Peter Pan is a young boy who never grows up, but lives in a magic place called Never-Never Land and can fly: *He is considered to be the Peter Pan of the music business.*

peth·i·dine /ˈpeθədiːn/ *n* [U] a drug used to reduce severe pain, given especially to women who are giving birth

pet·it bour·geois /ˌpeti ˈbʊəʒwɑː, -bʊəˈʒwɑː $ ˌpeti bʊrˈʒwɑː, pəˌtiː-/ *adj* another spelling of PETTY BOURGEOIS

pe·tite /pəˈtiːt/ *adj* a woman who is petite is short and attractively thin SYN **slim** THESAURUS SHORT

pet·it four /ˌpeti ˈfʊə, -ˈfɔː $ -ˈfʊr, -ˈfɔːr/ *n* (*plural* **petits fours**) [C] a small sweet cake or BISCUIT served with coffee

pe·ti·tion¹ /pəˈtɪʃən/ ●○○ *n* [C]
1 a written request signed by a lot of people, asking someone in authority to do something or change something: **[+for/against]** *a petition against the new road* | *They wanted me to* ***sign*** *a* ***petition*** *against experiments on animals.* | *Local residents have* ***drawn up*** *a* ***petition*** *to protest the hospital closure.* | ***petition drive*** *AmE* (=an attempt to get a lot of people to sign a petition)
2 *law* an official letter to a law court, asking for a legal case to be considered: **[+for]** *She is threatening to* ***file*** *a* ***petition*** *for divorce.*
3 *formal* a formal prayer or request to someone in authority or to God

petition² *v* [I,T] **1** to ask the government or an organization to do something by sending them a petition: **petition sb to do sth** *Villagers petitioned the local authority to provide better bus services.* | **[+against/for]** *Residents are petitioning against the new road.* **2** *law or formal* to make a formal request to someone in authority, to a court of law, or to God: **[+for]** *More and more couples are* ***petitioning for*** *divorce.*

pe·ti·tion·er /pəˈtɪʃənə $ -ər/ *n* [C] **1** someone who writes or signs a petition **2** *law* someone who asks for a legal case to be considered in a court of law

petit mal /ˌpeti ˈmæl/ *n* [U] *medical* a form of EPILEPSY which is not very serious → GRAND MAL

ˌpet ˈname *n* [C] a special name you call someone who you like very much

pet·rel /ˈpetrəl/ *n* [C] a black and white sea bird

Pe·tri dish /ˈpiːtri dɪʃ/ *n* [C] a small clear dish with a cover which is used by scientists, especially for growing BACTERIA

pet·ri·fied /ˈpetrɪfaɪd/ *adj* **1** extremely frightened, especially so frightened that you cannot move or think: **[+of]**

I'm petrified of spiders. | **petrified with fright/fear** *He was petrified with fear when he saw the gun.* **THESAURUS** FRIGHTENED **2 petrified wood/trees etc** wood, trees etc that have changed into stone over a long period of time —**petrify** *v* [T]

pet·ro·chem·i·cal /ˌpetrəʊˈkemɪkəl $ -troʊ-/ *n* [C] any chemical substance obtained from PETROLEUM or natural gas: *the petrochemical industry*

pet·ro·dol·lars /ˈpetrəʊˌdɒləz $ -troʊˌdɑːlərz/ *n* [plural] money earned by the sale of oil: *the flow of petrodollars into the American economy*

pet·rol /ˈpetrəl/ ●●● S3 *n* [U] *BrE* a liquid obtained from PETROLEUM that is used to supply power to the engine of cars and other vehicles SYN **gasoline** *AmE*: *unleaded petrol* | *petrol prices* | *The petrol tank is leaking.*

ˈpetrol bomb *n* [C] *BrE* a simple bomb consisting of a bottle filled with petrol and a lighted cloth SYN **Molotov cocktail**

pe·tro·le·um /pəˈtrəʊliəm $ -ˈtroʊ-/ *n* [U] oil that is obtained from below the surface of the Earth and is used to make petrol, PARAFFIN, and various chemical substances: *petroleum-based products*

peˌtroleum ˈjelly *n* [U] VASELINE

pet·rol·head /ˈpetrəlhed/ *n* [C] *BrE informal* someone who loves cars, especially fast cars

ˈpetrol ˌstation *n* [C] *BrE* a place where you can take your car and fill it with petrol SYN **filling station**, **gas station** *AmE*

PET scan /ˈpet skæn/ *n* [C] *medical* (***positron emission tomography scan***) a type of medical test that can produce a picture of areas in your body where cells are very active, for example the brain or where a TUMOUR is growing

pet·ti·coat /ˈpetikəʊt $ -koʊt/ *n* [C] *BrE* a piece of women's underwear like a thin skirt or dress that is worn under a skirt or dress SYN **slip**

pet·ti·fog·ging /ˈpetiˌfɒgɪŋ $ -ˌfɑː-, -ˌfɒː-/ *adj BrE old-fashioned* too concerned with small details

pet·ting /ˈpetɪŋ/ *n* [U] **1** the activity of kissing and touching someone as part of a sexual activity → HEAVY PETTING **2** the action of touching and moving your hand gently over an animal → PET²

ˈpetting zoo *n* [C] *AmE* part of a ZOO which has animals in it for children to touch

pet·tish /ˈpetɪʃ/ *adj* PETULANT —**pettishly** *adv*

pet·ty /ˈpeti/ ●○○ *adj*

1 a petty problem, detail etc is small and unimportant SYN **trivial**: *petty squabbles* | *petty restrictions*

2 unkind and caring too much about small unimportant things: *How can she be so petty?* | *petty jealousy and spitefulness*

3 petty crime a crime that is not serious, for example stealing things that are not very valuable

4 petty criminal/thief etc a criminal whose crimes are not very serious

5 a petty official is not important – used especially when they use their power as if they were important: *Some petty bureaucrat wanted all the documents in triplicate.* —**pettiness** *n* [U]: *the pettiness of Hollywood*

ˌpetty ˈbourgeois (*also* **petit bourgeois**) / $ ˌ...ˈ./ *adj* **1** paying too much attention to things such as social position, money, and possessions – used to show disapproval **2** belonging to the group of lower MIDDLE CLASS people —**petty bourgeois** *n* [C]

ˌpetty ˈcash *n* [U] a small amount of money that is kept in an office for making small payments

ˌpetty ˈlarceny *n* [U] *law* the crime of stealing things that are worth only a small amount of money → **grand larceny**

ˌpetty ˈofficer *n* [C] an officer of low rank in the Navy

pet·u·lant /ˈpetʃələnt/ *adj* behaving in an unreasonably impatient and angry way, like a child —**petulantly** *adv*: *'Which one?' he demanded petulantly.* —**petulance** *n* [U]

pe·tu·ni·a /pəˈtjuːniə $ pɪˈtuː-/ *n* [C] a garden plant which has pink, purple, or white TRUMPET-shaped flowers

pew¹ /pjuː/ *n* [C] **1** a long wooden seat in a church **2 take a pew** *BrE spoken* used humorously to invite someone to sit down

PEW

pew² *interjection AmE spoken* used when something smells very bad

pew·ter /ˈpjuːtə $ -ər/ *n* [U] a grey metal made by mixing LEAD and TIN: *a pewter plate*

PG /ˌpiː ˈdʒiː/ *n* [singular, U] (***parental guidance***) used to show that a film includes parts that parents may feel are not suitable for young children

PGCE /ˌpiː dʒiː siː ˈiː/ *n* [C] *BrE* (***Postgraduate Certificate of Education***) a course and examination in teaching done by someone who already has a university degree: *I came to Birmingham to* ***do a PGCE****.*

pH /piː ˈeɪtʃ/ (*also* **pˈH ˌvalue**) *n* [singular] a number on a scale of 0 to 14 which shows how acid or ALKALINE a substance is → **litmus test**: **[+of]** *soil with a pH of 3.1*

phab·let /ˈfæblət/ *n* [C] a piece of equipment that has the abilities of a SMARTPHONE and a TABLET computer

pha·lanx /ˈfælæŋks $ ˈfeɪ-/ *n* (*plural* **phalanxes**) [C] *formal* a large group of people or things standing close together so that it is difficult to go through them: **[+of]** *A solid phalanx of policemen blocked the road.*

phal·lic /ˈfælɪk/ *adj* like or relating to a phallus: *phallic symbols*

phal·lus /ˈfæləs/ *n* [C] **1** a model of the male sex organ, used to represent sexual power **2** the male sex organ SYN **penis**

phan·tas·m /ˈfæntæzəm/ *n* [C,U] *literary* something that exists only in your imagination SYN **illusion**

phan·tas·ma·go·ri·a /ˌfæntæzməˈgɒriə $ fænˌtæzməˈgɔːriə/ *n* [C] *literary* a scene that is confused, changing, and strange, like something from a dream —**phantasmagorical** /-ˈgɒrɪkəl $ -ˈgɔː-/ *adj*

phan·ta·sy /ˈfæntəsi/ *n* an old spelling of FANTASY

phan·tom¹ /ˈfæntəm/ *n* [C] *literary* **1** the image of a dead person or strange thing that someone thinks they see SYN **ghost 2** something that exists only in your imagination

phantom² *adj* [only before noun] **1** *literary* seeming to appear to someone: *a phantom ship* **2** not real, but seeming real to the person affected: *a phantom pregnancy* | **phantom limb** (=an arm or leg that someone feels they still have after it has been cut off) | **phantom fat** (=fat that someone believes they still have after they have lost weight) **3** made to seem real in order to deceive people: *Phantom contracts were used to make the company seem more successful than it was.* **4** used humorously to describe an unknown person that you blame for something annoying: *The phantom pen stealer strikes again!*

Pha·raoh, **pharaoh** /ˈfeərəʊ $ ˈferoʊ/ *n* [C] a ruler of ancient Egypt

Phar·i·see /ˈfærɪsiː/ *n* **1 the Pharisees** [plural] a group of Jews who lived at the time of Christ and who believed in strictly obeying religious laws **2** [C] someone who pretends to be religious or morally good, but who is not sincere —**Pharisaic** /ˌfærɪˈseɪ-ɪk◂/ *adj*

phar·ma /ˈfɑːmə $ ˈfɑːr-/ *n* [U] the pharmaceutical industry – used in business: *jobs in pharma*

phar·ma·ceu·ti·cal /ˌfɑːməˈsjuːtɪkəl◂ $ ˌfɑːrməˈsuː-/ ●○○ *adj* [only before noun] relating to the production of drugs and medicines: *the pharmaceutical industry* | *pharmaceutical products*

phar·ma·ceu·ti·cals /ˌfɑːməˈsjuːtɪkəlz $ ˌfɑːrməˈsuː-/ *n* [plural] *technical* drugs and medicines

phar·ma·cist /ˈfɑːməsɪst $ ˈfɑːr-/ *n* [C] someone whose job is to prepare medicines in a shop or hospital

phar·ma·col·o·gy /ˌfɑːməˈkɒlədʒi $ ˌfɑːrməˈkɑː-/ *n* [U] the scientific study of drugs and medicines —**pharmacologist** *n* [C] —**pharmacological** /ˌfɑːməkəˈlɒdʒɪkəl◂ $ ˌfɑːrməkəˈlɑː-/ *adj*

phar·ma·co·poe·ia /ˌfɑːməkəˈpiːə $ ˌfɑːr-/ *n* [C] *technical* an official book giving information about medicines

phar·ma·cy /ˈfɑːməsi $ ˈfɑːr-/ ●●● S3 *n* (*plural* **pharmacies**)
1 [C] a shop or a part of a shop where medicines are prepared and sold SYN **chemist** *BrE*: *an all-night pharmacy*
2 [C] the place where medicines are prepared in a hospital
3 [U] the study or practice of preparing drugs and medicines

pharm·ing /ˈfɑːmɪŋ $ ˈfɑːr-/ *n* [U] a technology in which an animal's DNA is changed so that the animal produces substances, especially PROTEINS, that scientists can use to make medicines for people

phar·yn·gi·tis /ˌfærɪnˈdʒaɪtɪs/ *n* [U] a medical condition in which you have a sore swollen pharynx

phar·ynx /ˈfærɪŋks/ *n* (*plural* **pharynges** /fəˈrɪndʒiːz/) [C] the tube that goes from the back of your mouth to the place where the tube divides for food and air

phase[1] /feɪz/ ●●○ W2 AWL *n* [C]
1 one of the stages of a process of development or change: *a new drug that is in the experimental phase* | **[+of]** *The first phase of renovations should be finished by January.* | **in phases** *The work will be carried out in phases.* | *It's just **a phase** he's **going through**.*
2 out of phase (with sth) *BrE* not happening together in the right way: *Nizan's views were out of phase with the political climate of the time.*
3 in phase (with sth) *BrE* happening together in the right way: *The electrical work will be carried out in phase with the other renovations.*
4 *technical* one of a fixed number of changes in the appearance of the Moon or a PLANET when it is seen from the Earth

phase[2] AWL *v* [T] to make something happen gradually in a planned way: *The closure of the regional offices was phased over an 18-month period.* | *a phased withdrawal of military forces*

phase sth ↔ **in** *phr v* to gradually start using a new system, law, process etc: *The new tests will be phased in over the next two years.*

phase sth ↔ **out** *phr v* to gradually stop using or providing something: *The subsidy for company cars is to be phased out next year.* GRAMMAR **Phase (in/out)** is usually passive.

phat /fæt/ (*also* **ˈphat-ass** *AmE*) *adj informal* fashionable, attractive, or desirable – used by young people: *a phat song* | *These shoes are just so phat.*

PhD *BrE*, **Ph.D.** *AmE* /ˌpiː eɪtʃ ˈdiː/ *n* [C] (***Doctor of Philosophy***) a university degree of a very high level, which involves doing advanced RESEARCH: **[+in]** *He's got a PhD in Biochemistry.* | *Jacqueline Hope, PhD* | **do/start/finish a PhD**

pheas·ant /ˈfezənt/ *n* [C,U] a large bird with a long tail, often shot for food, or the meat of this bird

phe·nom /fɪˈnɒm $ -ˈnɑːm/ *n* [C] *AmE informal* a PHENOMENON(2): *a 16-year-old guitar phenom*

phe·nom·e·nal /fɪˈnɒmɪnəl $ -ˈnɑː-/ ●○○ AWL *adj* very great or impressive: *the **phenomenal success** of computer games in recent years* | **phenomenal growth/rise/increase** *California had experienced a phenomenal growth in population.* | *He has learned a phenomenal amount in the last two years.* | *The results have been phenomenal.* —**phenomenally** *adv*: *The group have been phenomenally successful in Europe.*

phe·nom·e·nol·o·gy /fɪˌnɒməˈnɒlədʒi $ fɪˌnɑːməˈnɑː-/ *n* [U] the part of PHILOSOPHY that deals with people's feelings, thoughts, and experiences

phe·nom·e·non /fɪˈnɒmənən $ fɪˈnɑːmənɑːn, -nən/ ●●○ W3 AWL *n* (*plural* **phenomena** /-nə/) [C]
1 something that happens or exists in society, science, or nature, especially something that is studied because it is difficult to understand: **[+of]** *the growing phenomenon of telecommuting* | *Homelessness is not a **new phenomenon**.* | **natural/historical/social etc phenomenon** *Language is a social and cultural phenomenon.* THESAURUS ▸ EVENT
2 something or someone that is very unusual because of a rare quality or ability that they have

pher·o·mone /ˈferəməʊn $ -moʊn/ *n* [C usually plural] a chemical that is produced by people's and animals' bodies and is thought to influence the behaviour of other people or animals

phew /fjuː/ *interjection* used when you feel tired, hot, or RELIEVED: *Phew! We finally did it.*

phi·al /ˈfaɪəl/ *n* [C] a small bottle, especially for liquid medicines SYN **vial**: **[+of]** *a phial of morphine*

Phi Be·ta Kap·pa /ˌfaɪ ˌbiːtə ˈkæpə $ -ˌbeɪtə-/ *n* an American society for university and college students who have done well in their studies

-phil /fɪl/ *suffix* another form of the suffix -PHILE

phi·lan·derer /fəˈlændərə $ -ər/ *n* [C] *old-fashioned* a man who has sex with many women, without intending to have any serious relationships → **playboy** —**philandering** *adj* —**philandering** *n* [U]

phil·an·throp·ic /ˌfɪlənˈθrɒpɪk◂ $ -ˈθrɑː-/ *adj* a philanthropic person or institution gives money and help to people who are poor or in trouble —**philanthropically** /-kli/ *adv*

phi·lan·thro·pist /fɪˈlænθrəpɪst/ *n* [C] a rich person who gives a lot of money to help poor people

phi·lan·thro·py /fəˈlænθrəpi/ *n* [U] the practice of giving money and help to people who are poor or in trouble

phi·lat·e·ly /fəˈlætəli/ *n* [U] the activity of collecting stamps for pleasure SYN **stamp collecting** —**philatelic** /ˌfɪləˈtelɪk◂/ *adj* —**philatelist** /fəˈlætəlɪst/ *n* [C]

-phile /faɪl/ (*also* **-phil**) *suffix* [in nouns] someone who likes something: *a bibliophile* (=someone who likes books) | *an Anglophile* (=someone who likes English or British things)

Phil·har·mon·ic /ˌfɪləˈmɒnɪk◂, ˌfɪlhɑː- $ ˌfɪlərˈmɑː-, ˌfɪlhɑːr-/ *adj, n* [C] used in the names of ORCHESTRAS: *the Berlin Philharmonic*

-philia /fɪliə/ *suffix* [in nouns] **1** *technical* a tendency to feel sexually attracted in a way that is not approved of or not normal: *necrophilia* (=a sexual attraction to dead bodies) **2** a love of something: *Francophilia* (=a love of French things)

-philiac /fɪliæk/ *suffix* [in nouns] *technical* someone who feels sexually attracted in a way that is not approved of: *a necrophiliac*

phi·lip·pic /fəˈlɪpɪk/ *n* [C] *literary* a strong angry speech publicly attacking someone

phil·is·tine /ˈfɪləstaɪn $ -stiːn/ *n* [C] someone who does not like or understand art, literature, music etc: *When it comes to art, the man's a philistine.* —**philistine** *adj* —**philistinism** *n* [U]

phi·lol·o·gy /fəˈlɒlədʒi $ -ˈlɑː-/ *n* [U] *old-fashioned* the study of words and of the way words and languages develop —**philologist** *n* [C] —**philological** /ˌfɪləˈlɒdʒɪkəl◂ $ -ˈlɑː-/ *adj* → LINGUISTICS

phi·los·o·pher /fəˈlɒsəfə $ -ˈlɑːsəfər/ ●○○ AWL *n* [C]
1 someone who studies and develops ideas about the nature and meaning of existence, truth, good and evil etc: *Plato, Aristotle, and other Greek philosophers*
2 someone who thinks deeply about the world, life etc

phiˌlosopher's ˈstone *n* [singular] an imaginary substance that was thought in the past to have the power to change any other metal into gold

phil·o·soph·i·cal /ˌfɪləˈsɒfɪkəl◂ $ -ˈsɑː-/ ●○○ AWL (*also* **phil·o·soph·ic** /-ˈsɒfɪk $ ˈsɑː-/) *adj*
1 relating to philosophy: *the philosophical problem of whether there is free will* | *a philosophical argument*
2 calmly accepting a difficult or unpleasant situation which cannot be changed: **[+about]** *Some old people are philosophical about death.* | *He was by nature a philosophical person.* —**philosophically** /-kli/ *adv*

phi·los·o·phize (*also* **-ise** *BrE*) /fəˈlɒsəfaɪz $ -ˈlɑː-/ AWL v [I] to talk about serious subjects in detail or for a long time

phi·los·o·phy /fəˈlɒsəfi $ -ˈlɑː-/ ●●● W3 AWL *n* (*plural* **philosophies**)
1 [U] the study of the nature and meaning of existence, truth, good and evil etc: *Emma studies philosophy at university.* | **[+of]** *the philosophy of science*
2 [C] the views of a particular philosopher or group of philosophers: **[+of]** *the philosophy of Aristotle*
3 [C] the attitude or set of ideas that guides the behaviour of a person or organization: *The company explained their management philosophy.* | *The idea that you should treat others as you would like them to treat you is a fine* ***philosophy of life***. → NATURAL PHILOSOPHY

phil·tre (*also* **philter** *AmE*) /ˈfɪltə $ -ər/ *n* [C] *literary* a magic drink that makes someone fall in love

phish·ing /ˈfɪʃɪŋ/ *n* [U] the criminal activity of sending emails or having a website that is intended to trick someone into giving away information such as their bank account number or their computer PASSWORD. This information is then used to get money or goods. THESAURUS STEAL

phle·bi·tis /flɪˈbaɪtɪs/ *n* [U] *medical* a condition in which there is swelling and roughness on the inside surface of a VEIN (=tube that carries blood through your body)

phlegm /flem/ *n* [U] **1** the thick yellowish substance produced in your nose and throat, especially when you have a cold SYN **mucus 2** unusual calmness in worrying, frightening, or exciting situations

phleg·mat·ic /flegˈmætɪk/ *adj* calm and not easily excited or worried: *The taxi driver, a phlegmatic man in middle age, showed no surprise at this request.* —**phlegmatically** /-kli/ *adv*

phlox /flɒks $ flɑːks/ *n* [C,U] **1** a tall garden plant with pink, purple, or white flowers **2** *AmE* a low spreading plant with pink or white flowers

-phobe /fəʊb $ foʊb/ *suffix* [in nouns] someone who dislikes or hates something: *a xenophobe* (=someone who hates foreigners) | *a technophobe* (=someone who dislikes and fears modern technology such as computers)

pho·bi·a /ˈfəʊbiə $ ˈfoʊ-/ *n* [C,U] a strong unreasonable fear of something: **[+about]** *Owen* ***has*** *a* ***phobia*** *about snakes.* | *Some children* ***suffer from*** *school* ***phobia***. THESAURUS FEAR —**phobic** *adj*

-phobia /fəʊbiə $ foʊ-/ *suffix* [in nouns] **1** *technical* a strong unreasonable dislike or fear of something, which may be part of a mental illness: *claustrophobia* (=fear of being in a small enclosed space) | *aquaphobia* (=fear of water) **2** a dislike or hatred of something: *Anglophobia* (=a dislike of English or British things)

-phobic /fəʊbɪk $ foʊ-/ *suffix technical* **1** [in nouns] someone who has a strong unreasonable fear of something: *He's a claustrophobic* (=he fears small enclosed places). **2** [in adjectives] suffering from or connected with a strong unreasonable fear of something: *I'm a bit agoraphobic* (=I am afraid of crowds and open places).

phoe·nix /ˈfiːnɪks/ *n* [C] **1** a magic bird that is born from a fire, according to ancient stories **2 rise like a phoenix from the ashes** to become successful again after seeming to have failed completely

phon- /fən, fəʊn, fɒn $ fən, foʊn, fɑːn/ *prefix* another form of the prefix PHONO-

phone[1] /fəʊn $ foʊn/ ●●● S1 W2 *n* [C]
1 a telephone: *Much of his work is done* ***by phone***. | *Who was that* ***on the phone***? | *I wish Amy would get* ***off the phone***. → CELLPHONE, MOBILE PHONE, PAY PHONE

GRAMMAR

You say: *She's on the phone.* | *She's talking on her phone.* ✗ Don't say: *at the phone*

2 the part of a telephone into which you speak SYN **receiver**: *He* ***put the phone down on*** *me* (=ended the call before I had finished speaking).

COLLOCATIONS – MEANINGS 1 & 2

VERBS

use the phone *Do you mind if I use your phone?*
the phone rings *Around three o'clock, the phone rang.*
answer the phone (*also* **pick up the phone**) *My dad answered the phone.*
put the phone down *I only remembered his name after I had put the phone down.*
talk/speak (to sb) on the phone *We talk on the phone every day.*
come to the phone *I'm sorry, she can't come to the phone right now.*
be on the phone to sb (=be talking to someone on the phone) *I was on the phone to my mother all morning.*
call sb on the phone | **get on the phone to sb** (=call them)

phone + NOUN

a phone number *Can I have your phone number?*
a phone line (=a telephone wire or connection) | **a phone bill** (=a bill for phone calls) | **a phone company** (=one that provides a telephone service) | **a phone conversation**

PHRASES

the phone is busy (*also* **the phone is engaged** *BrE*) (=the person you are calling is already speaking to someone else) *I tried you earlier, but your phone was engaged.*
the phone goes/is dead (=the phone line stops working or is not working) | **the phone is off the hook** (=it cannot be used because it is not connected or is already being used)

phone[2] ●●● S1 (*also* **phone up**) *v* [I,T] to speak to someone by telephone: *I'll phone you this evening.* | *Why didn't they phone the police?* | *For information phone 8279-3772.* | *Stevie phoned to say that he was going to be late.* | *I kept phoning her up, asking to meet her.* | *Tell him to phone back* (=telephone again at a later time) *tomorrow.*
⚠ You do not 'phone to' someone or 'phone to' a number. **Phone** is followed immediately by a noun or number: *She phoned her friend Judy.* | *Phone 01279-623772 and ask to speak to Elaine.*

THESAURUS

phone to speak to someone by telephone. **Phone** is more common in British English than American English: *I'll phone you tomorrow.*
call to phone someone. **Call** is used in both British and American English: *One of the neighbors called the police.* | *Call me later.*
ring *BrE spoken* to phone someone. **Ring** is more informal than **phone** or **call**: *I can ring her at the office tomorrow.*
give sb a call (*also* **give sb a ring**) *spoken* to phone someone: *If you ever come to Seattle, give me a call.* | *I'll give the hospital a ring and see how he is.*
telephone *formal* to phone someone: *Angry listeners telephoned the BBC to complain.*
Skype /skaɪp/ *trademark* to make a telephone call using special software that allows you to make calls over the Internet: *I Skyped her last night and we spoke for hours.*

phone in *phr v*
1 to telephone the place where you work, especially in order to report something: *I'll phone in and let them know.* | **phone sth ↔ in** *I'll phone the report in tomorrow morning.* | *She* ***phoned in sick*** (=telephoned to say that she was ill and could not come to work).
2 to telephone a radio or television show to give your opinion or ask a question: *There's still time to phone in before the end of the programme.* → PHONE-IN

-phone /fəʊn $ foʊn/ *suffix* **1** [in nouns] an instrument or machine relating to sound or hearing, especially a musical instrument: *earphones* (=for listening to a radio etc) | *a saxophone* **2** [in nouns] *technical* someone who speaks a particular language: *a Francophone* (=someone who speaks French) **3** [in adjectives] speaking a particular language: *Francophone nations* (=nations where French is spoken)

ˈ**phone book** *n* [C] a book that contains an alphabetical list of the names, addresses, and telephone numbers of all the people who have a telephone in a particular area SYN **telephone directory**

ˈ**phone booth** *n* [C] a small structure that is partly or completely enclosed, containing a public telephone

ˈ**phone box** *n* [C] *BrE* a small structure that is partly or completely enclosed, containing a public telephone

ˈ**phone call** *n* [C] when you speak to someone on the telephone SYN **call**, **telephone call**: *I need to **make a** quick **phone call**.* | *I **got a phone call** from someone called Mike.* | *obscene phone calls*

phone·card /ˈfəʊnkɑːd $ ˈfoʊnkɑːrd/ *n* [C] a plastic card that can be used in some public telephones instead of money

ˈ**phone ˌhacking** *n* [U] the illegal practice of calling someone's MOBILE PHONE and using a special number so that you can listen to messages left on it, or getting private information in other ways from it

ˈ**phone-in** *n* [C] a radio or television programme in which you hear ordinary people expressing opinions or asking questions over the telephone

pho·neme /ˈfəʊniːm $ ˈfoʊ-/ *n* [C] *technical* the smallest unit of speech that can be used to make one word different from another word, such as the 'b' and the 'p' in 'big' and 'pig' → **morpheme** —**phonemic** /fəˈniːmɪk/ *adj* —**phonemically** /-kli/ *adv*

pho·ne·mics /fəˈniːmɪks/ *n* [U] *technical* the study and description of the phonemes of languages

ˈ**phone sex** *n* [U] the activity of talking with someone on the telephone about sex in order to become sexually excited: *She claimed the relationship consisted mainly of him calling her up to **have phone sex**.*

ˈ**phone-ˌtapping** *n* [U] the activity of listening secretly to other people's telephone conversations using special electronic equipment

pho·net·ic /fəˈnetɪk/ *adj technical* **1** relating to the sounds of human speech **2** using special signs, often different from ordinary letters, to represent the sounds of speech: *a phonetic alphabet* | *phonetic symbols*

pho·net·ics /fəˈnetɪks/ *n* [U] the science and study of speech sounds —**phonetician** /ˌfəʊnəˈtɪʃən, ˌfɒn- $ ˌfoʊ-/ *n* [C]

GRAMMAR: Singular or plural verb?

Phonetics is followed by a singular verb: ***Phonetics is** a branch of linguistics.*

GRAMMAR GUIDE ▸ NOUNS

ˈ**phone tree** *n* [C] *informal* a list of all the telephone numbers of the people in an organization, showing who should call who if there is important information that everyone should know

pho·ney (*also* **phony** *AmE*) /ˈfəʊni $ ˈfoʊ-/ *adj informal* **1** false or not real, and intended to deceive someone SYN **fake**: *a phoney American accent* THESAURUS ▸ FALSE **2** someone who is phoney is insincere and pretends to be something they are not —**phoney** *n* [C]: *He's a complete phoney!* —**phoniness** *n* [U]

ˌ**phoney** ˈ**war** *n* [singular] a period during which a state of war officially exists but there is no actual fighting

phon·ic /ˈfɒnɪk, ˈfəʊ- $ ˈfɑː, ˈfoʊ-/ *adj technical* **1** relating to sound **2** relating to speech sounds

phon·ics /ˈfɒnɪks, ˈfəʊ- $ ˈfɑː-, ˈfoʊ-/ *n* [U] a method of teaching people to read in which they are taught to recognize the sounds that letters represent

phono- *prefix* /fəʊnəʊ, -nə, fɒnə $ foʊnoʊ, -nə, fɑːnə/ (*also* **phon-**) *technical* **1** relating to the voice or speech: *phonetics* (=the science of speech sounds) **2** relating to sound: *a phonoreceptor* (=a hearing organ)

pho·no·graph /ˈfəʊnəgrɑːf $ ˈfoʊnəgræf/ *n* [C] *AmE old-fashioned* a RECORD PLAYER

pho·nol·o·gy /fəˈnɒlədʒi $ -ˈnɑː-/ *n* [U] *technical* the study of the system of speech sounds in a language, or the system of sounds itself —**phonologist** *n* [C] —**phonological** /ˌfəʊnəˈlɒdʒɪkəl◂, ˌfɒn- $ ˌfoʊnəˈlɑː-/ *adj* —**phonologically** /-kli/ *adv*

pho·ny /ˈfəʊni $ ˈfoʊ-/ *adj* the usual American spelling of PHONEY THESAURUS ▸ FALSE

phoo·ey /ˈfuːi/ *interjection* used to express strong disbelief or disappointment

phos·gene /ˈfɒzdʒiːn $ ˈfɑːz-/ *n* [U] a poisonous gas used in war and in industry

phos·phate /ˈfɒsfeɪt $ ˈfɑːs-/ *n* [C,U] **1** one of the various forms of a SALT of PHOSPHORUS, often used in industry **2** [usually plural] a substance containing a phosphate used for making plants grow better

phos·pho·res·cence /ˌfɒsfəˈresəns $ ˌfɑːs-/ *n* [U] a slight steady light that can only be noticed in the dark

phos·pho·res·cent /ˌfɒsfəˈresənt◂ $ ˌfɑːs-/ *adj* shining slightly in the dark but producing little or no heat: *a strange phosphorescent light*

phos·pho·rus /ˈfɒsfərəs $ ˈfɑːs-/ *n* [U] a poisonous yellowish chemical substance that starts to burn when it is in the air, and shines in the dark. It is a chemical ELEMENT: symbol P —**phosphoric** /fɒsˈfɒrɪk $ fɑːsˈfɔː-, fɑːsˈfɑː-, ˈfɑːsfərɪk/ *adj*: ***phosphoric acid***

pho·to /ˈfəʊtəʊ $ ˈfoʊtoʊ/ ●●● S3 W3 *n* (*plural* **photos**) [C] *informal* a photograph: **[+of]** *I'll send Mom a photo of Sammy.* | *Can you **take a photo** of me and Rachel?*

photo- /fəʊtəʊ, -tə $ foʊtoʊ, -tə/ *prefix technical* **1** relating to light: *photosensitive paper* (=paper that changes when light touches it) **2** relating to photography: *photojournalism* (=the use of photographs in reporting news)

pho·to·bomb·ing /ˈfəʊtəʊˌbɒmɪŋ $ ˈfoʊtoʊˌbɑː-/ *n* [U] the activity of deliberately getting into the background of someone else's photograph and spoiling it by doing something such as making a silly expression with your face

ˈ**photo booth** *n* [C] a small structure in which you can sit to have photographs taken by a machine

pho·to·call /ˈfəʊtəʊkɔːl $ ˈfoʊtoʊˌkɒːl/ *n* [C] an occasion during which a professional photographer takes pictures of a famous person or group of people

pho·to·cop·i·er /ˈfəʊtəʊˌkɒpiə $ ˈfoʊṭəˌkɑːpiər/ *n* [C] a machine that makes photographic copies of documents

pho·to·cop·y[1] /ˈfəʊtəʊˌkɒpi $ ˈfoʊṭəˌkɑːpi/ ●●○ *n* (*plural* **photocopies**) [C] a photographic copy, especially of something printed, written, or drawn: *I sent him the original document, not a photocopy.*

photocopy[2] ●●○ *v* (**photocopied**, **photocopying**, **photocopies**) [T] to make a photographic copy of something: *Leave the papers with me and I'll get them photocopied.* THESAURUS ▸ COPY —**photocopying** *n* [U]: *Could you **do** some **photocopying** for me tomorrow?*

pho·to·e·lec·tric /ˌfəʊtəʊ-ɪˈlektrɪk◂ $ ˌfoʊtoʊ-/ *adj* using an electrical current that is controlled by light

ˌ**photoelectric** ˈ**cell** *n* [C] **1** an electronic instrument that changes light into electricity **2** an electronic instrument that uses light to start an electrical effect, often used in BURGLAR ALARMS

ˌ**photo** ˈ**finish** *n* [C] the end of a race in which the leading runners finish so close together that a photograph of it has to be examined to decide which is the winner

Pho·to·fit /ˈfəʊtəʊfɪt $ ˈfoʊtoʊ-/ *n* [U] *trademark BrE* a way of making a picture of a face using photographs of parts of different faces, used to help the police catch a criminal

pho·to·gen·ic /ˌfəʊtəˈdʒenɪk◂, ˌfəʊtəʊ- $ ˌfoʊtə-/ *adj* always looking attractive in photographs: *Helen is very photogenic.*

pho·to·graph[1] /ˈfəʊtəgrɑːf $ ˈfoʊtəgræf/ ●●● S2 W2 (*also* **photo** *informal*) *n* [C] a picture obtained by

P

using a camera and film that is sensitive to light: *a colour photograph* | *a black and white photograph* | **[+of]** *I wish I had a photograph of Thomas.* | *He* ***took*** *a* ***photograph*** *of the hotel.* | *Tim was looking through an old* ***photograph album*** (=book in which you put photographs). | *Did you see Leo's photograph* (=a photograph of Leo) *in the newspaper?*

> REGISTER
> In everyday English, people usually say **photo** or **picture** rather than **photograph**: *This is my dad in this* ***photo***. | *Who took the* ***picture***?

photograph² ●●○ *v*
1 [T] to take a photograph of someone or something: *Kate agreed to let me photograph her.* | *He stood by the tree to be photographed.*

> REGISTER
> In everyday English, people usually say **take a photo** or **take a picture of someone or something** rather than **photograph someone or something**: *She agreed to let me* ***take her photo***. | *He stood there waiting to* ***have his picture taken***.

2 photograph well to look attractive in photographs: *Celia does not photograph well.*

pho·tog·ra·pher /fəˈtɒɡrəfə $ -ˈtɑːɡrəfər/ ●●○ *n* [C] someone who takes photographs, especially as a professional or as an artist: *a fashion photographer*

pho·to·graph·ic /ˌfəʊtəˈɡræfɪk◂ $ ˌfoʊ-/ ●●○ *adj* relating to photographs, using photographs, or used in producing photographs: *photographic film* | *photographic equipment* | *The software allows you to scan photographic images on your personal computer.* —**photographically** /-kli/ *adv*

ˌphotographic ˈmemory *n* [C] if you have a photographic memory, you can remember exactly every detail of something you have seen

pho·tog·ra·phy /fəˈtɒɡrəfi $ -ˈtɑː-/ ●●○ *n* [U] the art, profession, or method of producing photographs or the scenes in films: *He did fashion photography for 'Vogue' magazine.* | *the National Museum of Photography*

pho·to·jour·nal·is·m /ˌfəʊtəʊˈdʒɜːnəl-ɪzəm $ ˌfoʊtoʊˈdʒɜːr-/ *n* [U] the job or activity of reporting news stories in newspapers and magazines using mainly photographs instead of words

pho·ton /ˈfəʊtɒn $ ˈfoʊtɑːn/ *n* [C] *technical* a unit of ENERGY that carries light and has zero MASS

ˈphoto opporˌtunity *n* [C] a chance for someone such as a politician to be photographed for a newspaper in a way that will make them look good

pho·to·sen·si·tive /ˌfəʊtəʊˈsensətɪv◂ $ ˌfoʊtəˈsen-/ *adj* reacting to light, for example by changing colour or producing an electrical current: *photosensitive paper*

pho·to·sen·si·tize (*also* **-ise** *BrE*) /ˌfəʊtəʊˈsensətaɪz $ ˌfoʊtəˈsen-/ *v* [T] to make something photosensitive

ˈphoto shoot *n* [C] an occasion during which a professional photographer takes pictures of a fashion model or an actor for advertisements

Pho·to·stat /ˈfəʊtəstæt $ ˈfoʊ-/ *n* [C] *trademark* a photographic copy of a document, or a type of machine used for making one.

ˈphoto stream, **photostream** *n* [C] a group of photographs that you put on the Internet so that other people can see them

pho·to·syn·the·sis /ˌfəʊtəʊˈsɪnθɪsɪs $ ˌfoʊtəˈsɪn-/ *n* [U] *technical* the production by a green plant of special substances like sugar that it uses as food, caused by the action of sunlight on CHLOROPHYLL (=the green substance in leaves) —**photosynthesize** *v* [I,T]

pho·to·vol·ta·ic pan·el /ˌfəʊtəʊvɒlteɪ-ɪk ˈpænl $ ˌfoʊtoʊvɑːl-/ *n* [C] *technical* a SOLAR PANEL

phras·al /ˈfreɪzəl/ *adj* consisting of or relating to a phrase or phrases

ˌphrasal ˈverb ●●○ *n* [C] a group of words that is used like a verb and consists of a verb with an adverb or PREPOSITION after it, for example 'set off' or 'look after'. In this dictionary, phrasal verbs are marked 'phr v'.

phrase¹ /freɪz/ ●●● S3 W3 *n* [C]
1 a group of words that have a particular meaning when used together, or which someone uses on a particular occasion: *Who first used the phrase 'survival of the fittest'?* | *Shakespeare's plays are full of* ***well-known phrases***. THESAURUS ▸ WORD
2 *technical* a group of words without a FINITE verb, especially when they are used to form part of a sentence, such as 'walking along the road' and 'a bar of soap' → CLAUSE(2), SENTENCE¹(1)
3 a short group of musical notes that is part of a longer piece → **to coin a phrase** at COIN²(2), → **a turn of phrase** at TURN²(11), → **turn a phrase** at TURN¹(20)

> **THESAURUS**
> **phrase** a group of words that have a particular meaning when used together, or which someone uses on a particular occasion: *What was the phrase he used to describe her?* | *I've never heard of the phrase before.*
> **expression** a fixed phrase which is used in a language and has a particular meaning: *a* ***colloquial expression*** (=an informal expression used in everyday spoken language) | *The old-fashioned expression 'in the family way' means pregnant.*
> **idiom** a group of words that has a special meaning which you cannot guess from the meanings of each separate word: *'Under the weather' is an idiom which means 'ill'.*
> **cliché** a phrase that is boring and no longer original because people use it a lot: *The phrase 'at the end of the day' has become a real cliché.*
> **saying/proverb** a well-known phrase that gives advice about life: *Do you know the saying 'A problem shared is a problem halved'?* | *There is an old Chinese proverb which states 'A journey of a thousand miles starts with a single step'.*
> **slogan** a short phrase that is easy to remember, especially one that is used in advertising: *advertising slogans* | *Protesters were shouting anti-government slogans.*
> **motto** a phrase that expresses a person's or organization's beliefs and aims: *The school motto was 'Truth and Honour'.*

phrase² *v* [T] **1** to express something in a particular way: *Polly tried to think how to phrase the question.* | *Sorry, I phrased that badly.* **2** to perform music in order to produce the full effect of separate musical phrases

phrase·book /ˈfreɪzbʊk/ *n* [C] a book that explains phrases of a foreign language, for people to use when they travel to other countries

phra·se·ol·o·gy /ˌfreɪziˈɒlədʒi $ -ˈɑː-/ *n* [U] the way that words and phrases are chosen and used in a particular language or subject

phras·ing /ˈfreɪzɪŋ/ *n* [U] **1** the way that something is said: *I don't remember her exact phrasing.* **2** a way of playing music, reading poetry etc that separates the notes, words, or lines into phrases

phre·nol·ogy /frəˈnɒlədʒi $ -ˈnɑː-/ *n* [U] the study of the shape of people's heads as a way of finding out what their characters and abilities are, which was popular in the 19th century —**phrenologist** *n* [C]

phut /fʌt/ *n* **go phut** *BrE informal* if a machine goes phut, it stops working completely: *The microwave's gone phut.*

phwoar /fwɔː/ *interjection BrE informal* used to show that you think someone is sexually attractive: *Phwoar! Look at her!*

phyl·lo /ˈfiːləʊ $ -loʊ/ *n* [U] another spelling of FILO

phy·lum /ˈfaɪləm/ *n* (*plural* **phyla** /-lə/) [C] *technical* one of the large groups into which scientists divide plants, animals, and languages → **species**

physi- /fɪzi/ *prefix* another form of PHYSIO-

phys·i·cal¹ /ˈfɪzɪkəl/ ●●● S2 W1 AWL *adj*
1 BODY NOT MIND related to someone's body rather than their mind or emotions → **mental**, **emotional**: *She was in constant physical pain.* | *the physical and emotional needs of young adults* | *people with severe physical disabilities* | *Don't be put off by his* ***physical appearance***. | *He was obsessed with* ***physical fitness***.
2 SEX a physical relationship involves sex rather than just friendship: *My attraction to him was totally physical.* | *Their physical relationship had never been very good.*
3 PERSON *informal* someone who is physical likes touching people a lot: *She's a very physical person.*
4 VIOLENT involving touching someone in a rough or violent way: *Football can be a very physical game.* | *I was a bit worried that the argument might become physical.*
5 REAL/SOLID relating to real objects that you can touch, see, or feel: *the physical world around us* | *the physical environment* | *They were kept in appalling physical conditions.*
6 NATURAL relating to or following natural laws: *a physical explanation for this phenomenon*
7 SCIENCE [only before noun] a physical science is an area of scientific study that is related to PHYSICS: *physical chemistry* —**physicality** /ˌfɪzɪˈkæləti/ *n* [U]: *the physicality of sport* → PHYSICALLY

physical² (*also* ˌ**physical examinˈation**) *n* [C] a thorough examination of someone's body by a doctor, in order to discover whether they are healthy or have any illnesses or medical problems

ˌ**physical eduˈcation** *n* [U] (*abbreviation* **PE**) sport and physical exercise that are taught as a school subject

ˌ**physical geˈography** *n* [U] the study of the Earth's surface and of its rivers, mountains etc

phys·i·cally /ˈfɪzɪkli/ ●●○ S3 AWL *adv*
1 in relation to your body rather than your mind or emotions → **mentally**, **emotionally**: *She is young and physically fit.* | *Do you find him physically attractive?* | *I felt physically sick at the thought.* | *children who have been physically abused*
2 physically possible/impossible possible or not possible according to the laws of nature: *It would be physically impossible to carry everything at once.*

ˌ**physically ˈchallenged** *adj AmE* someone who is physically challenged has a problem with their body that makes it difficult for them to do things that other people can do easily SYN **disabled**

ˌ**physical ˈscience** *n* [U] (*also* **the physical sciences**) [plural] the sciences, for example CHEMISTRY and PHYSICS, that are concerned with studying things that are not living

ˌ**physical ˈtherapist** *n* [C] *AmE* someone whose job is to give physical therapy SYN **physiotherapist** *BrE*

ˌ**physical ˈtherapy** *n* [U] *AmE* a treatment that uses special exercises, rubbing, heat etc to treat medical conditions and problems with muscles SYN **physiotherapy** *BrE*

phy·si·cian /fəˈzɪʃən/ ●●○ *n* [C] *especially AmE formal* a doctor THESAURUS ▸ DOCTOR

phys·i·cist /ˈfɪzɪsɪst/ ●○○ *n* [C] a scientist who has special knowledge and training in PHYSICS

phys·ics /ˈfɪzɪks/ ●●● S3 *n* [U] the science concerned with the study of physical objects and substances, and of natural forces such as light, heat, and movement

GRAMMAR: Singular or plural verb?

Physics is followed by a singular verb: *To me,* ***physics is*** *a fascinating subject.*
GRAMMAR GUIDE ▸ NOUNS

phys·i·o /ˈfɪziəʊ $ -zioʊ/ *n* (*plural* **physios**) **1** [C] *informal* a PHYSIOTHERAPIST **2** [U] PHYSIOTHERAPY

physio- /fɪziəʊ, -ziə $ -zioʊ, -ziə/ (*also* **physi-**) *prefix* **1** relating to nature and living things: *physiology* (=study of how the body works) **2** physical: *physiotherapy* (=treatment using exercises etc)

phys·i·og·no·my /ˌfɪziˈɒnəmi $ -ˈɑː-, -ˈɑːg-/ *n* (*plural* **physiognomies**) [C] *technical* the general appearance of a person's face

phys·i·ol·o·gy /ˌfɪziˈɒlədʒi $ -ˈɑː-/ *n* [U] **1** the science that studies the way in which the bodies of living things work: *a book on biochemistry and physiology* **2** the way the body of a person or an animal works → **anatomy**: *the physiology of the brain* —**physiological** *adj*

phys·i·o·ther·a·pist /ˌfɪziəʊˈθerəpɪst $ -zioʊ-/ *n* [C] someone whose job is to give physiotherapy SYN **physical therapist** *AmE*

phys·i·o·ther·a·py /ˌfɪziəʊˈθerəpi $ -zioʊ-/ *n* [U] a treatment that uses special exercises, rubbing, heat etc to treat medical conditions and problems with muscles SYN **physical therapy** *AmE*

phy·sique /fəˈziːk/ *n* [C] the size and appearance of someone's body: *She didn't have the physique to be a dancer.* | *He had good health and a strong physique.*

pi /paɪ/ *n* [U] *technical* a number that is represented by the Greek letter (π) and is equal to the distance around a circle, divided by its width

pi·a·nis·si·mo /ˌpiːəˈnɪsəməʊ $ -moʊ/ *adj, adv technical* played or sung very quietly OPP **fortissimo**

pi·a·nist /ˈpiːənɪst $ piˈænəst, ˈpiːə-/ ●○○ *n* [C] someone who plays the piano

PIANOS

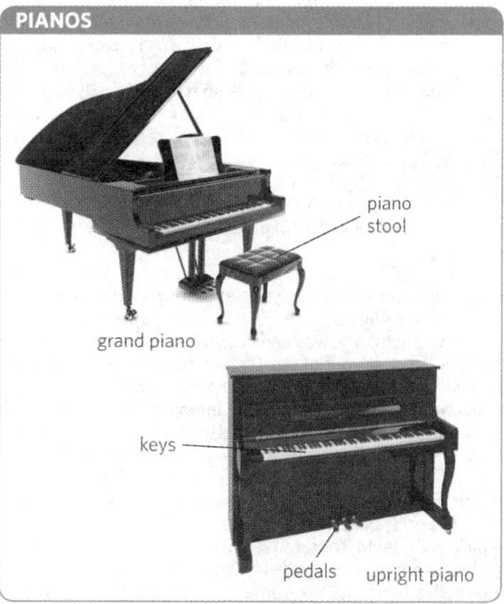

pi·an·o¹ /piˈænəʊ $ -noʊ/ ●●● S3 *n* (*plural* **pianos**) [C] a large musical instrument that has a long row of black and white KEYS. You play the piano by sitting in front of it and pressing the keys: *Jean accompanied her* ***on the piano***. | **a piano lesson/teacher etc** *a wonderful piano player*

piano² *adj, adv technical* played or sung quietly OPP **forte**

piˌano acˈcordion *n* [C] *BrE* an ACCORDION

piˈano ˌbar *n* [C] a bar where someone plays the piano for entertainment

pi·an·o·for·te /piˌænəʊˈfɔːti $ -noʊˈfɔːrteɪ/ *n* [C] *old-fashioned* a piano

pi·a·no·la /ˌpiːəˈnəʊlə $ -ˈnoʊ-/ *n* [C] *trademark* a piano that is played by machinery inside it. A long roll of paper with holes cut in it gradually turns and works the machinery, pressing down the KEYS on the piano to produce music. SYN **player piano**

piˈano stool *n* [C] a small seat that you sit on while you play the piano

pi·az·za /piˈætsə $ -ˈɑːt-/ *n* [C] a large square open area between the houses in a town or city, where people often meet or sit together

pic /pɪk/ *n* [C] *informal* a picture or film

pic·a·dor /ˈpɪkədɔː $ -dɔːr/ *n* [C] a man in a BULLFIGHT who rides a horse, and annoys and weakens the BULL by sticking a long spear into it

pic·a·resque /ˌpɪkəˈresk◂/ *adj* a picaresque story tells the amusing and unlikely adventures of a character who travels to a lot of different places

pic·a·yune /ˌpɪkəˈjuːn/ *adj AmE written* small and unimportant SYN **trivial**: *A few cuts and bruises are picayune compared to what might have happened.*

ˌPiccadilly ˈCircus a round open area in central London, where several streets join together, famous for being very busy, for its advertising signs made of NEON LIGHTS, and for the statue of Eros in its centre. People sometimes say that a place is like Piccadilly Circus to mean that it is very busy.

pic·ca·lil·li /ˌpɪkəˈlɪli/ *n* [U] *BrE* a hot-tasting sauce that is made with small pieces of vegetables and eaten with cold meat

pic·co·lo /ˈpɪkələʊ $ -loʊ/ *n* (*plural* **piccolos**) [C] a musical instrument that looks like a small FLUTE → see picture at **WOODWIND**

pick¹ /pɪk/ ●●● S1 W1 *v* [T]

1 CHOOSE STH to choose a person or thing, for example because they are the best or most suitable: *Students have to pick three courses from a list of 15.* | *I don't know which colour to pick.* | *Who's going to* **pick the team** *for the match on Saturday?* | **pick sb/sth for sth** *I wasn't picked for the hockey team.* | **pick sb/sth as sth** *The hotel was picked as the best small hotel in the area.* | **pick sb to do sth** *He was picked to run in the 100 metres.* | *Russell spoke slowly,* **picking** *his* **words** (=choosing what to say) *very carefully.* → **PICKED**

THESAURUS ► **CHOOSE**

2 FLOWERS/FRUIT ETC to remove a flower, fruit, nut etc from a plant or tree: *We picked some blackberries to eat on the way.* | *Amy picked a small bunch of wild flowers.* | *a dish of* **freshly picked** *peas*

3 REMOVE STH [always + adv/prep] to remove something carefully from a place, especially something small: **pick sth from sth** *Ahmed picked the melon pips from his teeth.* | **pick sth off (sth)** *She was nervously picking bits of fluff off her sweater.* | **pick sth out of sth** *The goalkeeper spent a lot of his time picking the ball out of the back of the net.*

4 pick your way through/across/among etc sth to walk in a slow careful way, choosing exactly where to put your feet down: *She picked her way between the puddles.* | *He picked his way down the narrow staircase.*

5 pick your nose to remove MUCUS from your nose with your finger: *Don't pick your nose!*

6 pick your teeth to remove bits of food from between your teeth with your finger or a small pointed object

7 pick sb's brains to ask someone who knows a lot about something for information and advice about it: *Have you got a minute? I need to pick your brains.*

8 pick a quarrel/fight (with sb) to deliberately start a quarrel or fight with someone: *I could see he was trying to pick a fight with me.*

9 pick and choose to choose only the best people or things, or only the ones that you really like: *Come on, you haven't got time to pick and choose.*

10 pick a lock to use something that is not a key to unlock a door, drawer etc: *It's quite easy to pick the lock on a car door.*

11 pick a hole in sth to make a hole in something by pulling it with your fingers: *He had picked a hole in his jumper.*

12 pick holes in sth *informal* to criticize an idea or a plan by saying what its weak points are: *It's easy to pick holes in her argument.*

13 pick sth clean to remove all the meat from a bone when you are eating

14 pick sb's pocket to quietly steal something from someone's pocket → **pickpocket**

15 pick a winner *informal* to choose someone or something very good

16 pick sth to pieces *informal* to criticize something very severely and in a very detailed way: *I'm fed up with having my work picked to pieces.*

17 MUSICAL INSTRUMENT *AmE* to play a musical instrument by pulling at its strings with your fingers SYN **pluck**

→ **have a bone to pick with sb** at **BONE¹(10)**

pick at sth *phr v*

1 to eat only small amounts of food because you do not feel hungry or do not like the food: *Paige could only pick at her meal, forcing down a mouthful or two.*

2 to touch something many times with your fingers, pulling it slightly: *She was picking at her skirt.*

pick sb/sth ↔ **off** *phr v* to point a weapon carefully at one person or animal in a group, and then shoot them: *There were gunmen in some of the buildings who picked off our men as they went past.*

pick on sb/sth *phr v spoken*

1 to behave in an unfair way to someone, for example by blaming them or criticizing them unfairly: *Why don't you pick on someone else for a change?*

2 *BrE* to choose a particular person or thing: *Just pick on one job and try to get that finished.*

pick sb/sth ↔ **out** *phr v*

1 CHOOSE to choose someone or something from a group: *She picked out a navy blue dress.* | *His story was picked out as the best by the judges.*

2 RECOGNIZE to recognize someone or something in a group of people or things: *She was able to pick out her father at the other side of the room.* | *I picked out Valerie's voice from among the general conversation.*

3 SEE if you can pick something out, you can see it but not very clearly: *I could just pick out some letters carved into the stone.*

4 SHOWN CLEARLY if something is picked out, it is in a different colour or material from the background, so that it can be clearly seen: *His name was picked out in gold lettering.*

5 PLAY A TUNE to play a tune on a musical instrument slowly or with difficulty: *He sat at the piano and picked out a simple tune.*

pick over sth *phr v* to examine a group of things very carefully in order to choose the ones you want: *She was sitting at the kitchen table picking over a pile of mushrooms.*

pick through sth *phr v* to search through a pile of things to find things that you want: *Police are still picking through the rubble looking for clues to the cause of the explosion.*

pick up *phr v*

1 LIFT STH/SB UP **pick sth/sb ↔ up** to lift something or someone up: *He picked up the letter and read it.* | *The phone rang and I picked it up.* | *Mummy, can you pick me up?*

2 pick yourself up to get up from the ground after you have fallen: *Carol picked herself up and brushed the dirt off her coat.*

3 TIDY STH **pick sth ↔ up** *AmE* to make a room or building tidy: *Pick up your room before you go to bed.*

4 GET STH **pick sth ↔ up** *informal* **a)** to get or win something: *He's already picked up three major prizes this year.* **b)** to buy something or get it from a shop etc: *I picked up an evening paper on the way home.* | *For more details, pick up a leaflet in your local post office.* **c)** to get an illness: *I picked up a virus while I was in America.*

5 COLLECT **pick sth ↔ up** to collect something from a place: *I'll pick my things up later.* | *She just dropped by to pick up her mail.*

6 LET SB INTO A VEHICLE **pick sb ↔ up** to let someone get into your car, boat etc and take them somewhere: *I'll pick you up at the station.* | *The survivors were picked up by fishing boats from nearby villages.*

7 LEARN **pick sth ↔ up** to learn something by watching or listening to other people: *I picked up a few words of Greek when I was there last year.* | *Mary watched the other dancers to see if she could pick up any tips.*

8 NOTICE **pick sth ↔ up** to notice something that is not easy to notice, such as a slight smell or a sign of something: *I picked up a faint smell of coffee.* | *The dogs picked up the scent and raced off.* | *We* **picked up** *their* **tracks** *again on the other side of the river.*

9 RADIO/SIGNALS **pick sth ↔ up** if a machine picks up a sound, movement, or signal, it is able to notice it or

receive it: *The sensors pick up faint vibrations in the earth.* | *I managed to pick up an American news broadcast.*
10 SEX **pick sb ↔ up** to become friendly with someone you have just met because you want to have sex with them: *young women sitting around in bars waiting to be picked up*
11 START AGAIN **a)** if you pick up where you stopped or were interrupted, you start again from that point: *We'll meet again in the morning and we can **pick up where** we **left off**.* **b) pick sth ↔ up** if you pick up an idea that has been mentioned, you return to it and develop it further: *I'd like to pick up what you said earlier.* | *This same theme is picked up in his later works.*
12 IMPROVE **a)** if a situation picks up, it improves: *Her social life was picking up at last.* | *The economy is finally beginning to pick up again.* | *We've been through a bit of a bad patch, but **things are picking up** again now.* **b) pick sb up** if a medicine or drink picks you up, it makes you feel better → **pick-me-up**
13 ROAD **pick sth ↔ up** if you pick up a road, you go onto it and start driving along it: *We take the A14 to Birmingham and then pick up the M5.*
14 TRAIN/BUS **pick sth ↔ up** if you pick up a train, bus etc, you get onto it and travel on it
15 pick up speed/steam to go faster: *The train was gradually picking up speed.*
16 pick up the bill/tab (for sth) *informal* to pay for something: *Why should the taxpayer pick up the tab for mistakes made by a private company?*
17 WIND if the wind picks up, it increases or grows stronger
18 COLOUR **pick sth ↔ up** if one thing picks up a colour in something else, it has an amount of the same colour in it so that the two things look nice together: *I like the way the curtains pick up the red in the rug.*
19 CRIMINAL **pick sb ↔ up** if the police pick someone up, they take them somewhere to answer questions or to be locked up: *He was picked up by police as he was trying to leave the country.*
20 pick up the pieces (of sth) to try to make your life normal again after something very bad has happened to you: *Thousands of victims of the earthquake are now faced with the task of picking up the pieces of their lives.*
21 pick up the threads (of sth) if you pick up the threads of something that you were doing, you try to return to it and start doing it again after it stopped or was changed: *Now that the war was over they could pick up the threads of their lives again.*
22 pick your feet up *spoken* used to tell someone to walk properly or more quickly

pick up after sb *phr v informal* to tidy things that someone else has left untidy: *I'm tired of picking up after you!*

pick up on sth *phr v*
1 to notice something about the way someone is behaving or feeling, even though they are trying not to show it: *Children pick up on our worries and anxieties.*
2 to return to a point or an idea that has been mentioned and discuss it more: *I'd like to pick up on a point that Steven made earlier.*
3 pick sb up on sth to criticize someone slightly for something they have said: *I knew he was lying and I should have picked him up on it.*

pick² ●○○ *n*
1 [U] if you can have your pick or take your pick of different things, you can choose which one you want: *Have a look at the menu and **take** your **pick**.* | *He knew he **could take** his **pick of** any of the girls in the office.* | *Sarah **could have** her **pick of** any university in the country.* | **have/get first pick (of sth)** *She always gets first pick of the videos.*
2 the pick of sth *informal* the best things in a group: *In tonight's programme we'll be discussing the pick of this month's new movies.* | *There were fifteen candidates for the job, and he was **the pick of the bunch*** (=the best one).
3 [C] *informal* your pick is the person or thing that you have chosen from a group SYN **choice**: *There are a lot of good horses in the race, but Archimedes would be my pick.*
4 [C] a PICKAXE
5 [C] *informal* a small flat object that you use for pulling at the strings of a musical instrument such as a GUITAR SYN **plectrum** → ICE PICK

ˌpick-and-ˈmix *adj BrE* if something is pick-and-mix, you are free to choose the things or parts that you want and not choose the rest: *Students can select parts of the course on a pick-and-mix basis.*

pick·axe *BrE*, **pickax** *AmE* /ˈpɪk-æks/ *n* [C] a large tool that you use for breaking up the ground. It consists of a curved iron bar with a sharp point on each end and a long handle.

picked /pɪkt/ *adj* [only before noun] picked people have been specially chosen because they are very suitable for a particular job → **handpicked**

pick·er /ˈpɪkə $ -ər/ *n* [C] **cotton picker/fruit picker etc** a person or machine that picks fruit or vegetables

pick·et¹ /ˈpɪkɪt/ *n* [C] **1 a)** when a group of people stand or march in front of a shop, factory, government building etc to protest about something or to stop people from going in during a STRIKE: *There was a **mass picket*** (=one involving a lot of people) *by students outside the main office of the university.* | **[+of]** *They organized a picket of the power station.* **b)** a person or the group of people involved in a picket: *The pickets persuaded some drivers not to enter the factory.* → FLYING PICKET **2** a soldier or a group of soldiers with the special duty of guarding a military camp: *He's **on picket duty** tonight.*

picket² *v* **1** [I,T] to stand or march in front of a shop, factory, government building etc to protest about something or to stop people from going in during a STRIKE: *Protesters are still picketing outside the White House gates.* | *a group of picketing miners* **2** [T] to place soldiers around or near a place as guards —**picketing** *n* [U]: *The new law will still allow peaceful picketing.*

ˈpicket ˌfence *n* [C] *AmE* a fence made up of a line of strong pointed sticks that are fixed in the ground

ˈpicket ˌline *n* [C] a group of people who stand outside a factory and try to prevent people from going in or coming out during a STRIKE: **on a picket line** *So far, there has been very little violence on the picket line.* | *Very few workers were willing to **cross** the **picket line**.*

pick·ings /ˈpɪkɪŋz/ *n* [plural] *informal* money or profits that you can get easily from a situation: *There were **rich pickings*** (=a lot of money) *to be had from the stock market.* | *There are **easy pickings** for thieves at these big outdoor concerts.* | **slim/lean/meagre pickings** *Companies are put off investing in poor areas because of the meagre pickings to be had.*

pick·le¹ /ˈpɪkəl/ *n* **1** [C,U] *BrE* a thick cold sauce that is made from pieces of vegetables preserved in VINEGAR. It is usually eaten with cold meat or cheese: *cheese and pickle sandwiches* | *a selection of cold meats and pickles* **2** [C] *AmE* a CUCUMBER preserved in VINEGAR or salt water, or a piece of this SYN **gherkin** *BrE* **3 be in a (pretty) pickle** *old-fashioned* to be in a very difficult situation and not know what to do

pickle² *v* [T] to preserve food in VINEGAR or salt water

pick·led /ˈpɪkəld/ *adj* **1** pickled vegetables or fruits have been preserved in VINEGAR or salt water: *pickled onions* **2** *old-fashioned informal* drunk

ˈpick-me-up *n* [C] *informal* a drink or medicine that makes you feel happier and gives you more energy

pick·pock·et /ˈpɪkˌpɒkɪt $ -ˌpɑːk-/ *n* [C] someone who steals things from people's pockets, especially in a crowd
THESAURUS ▸ THIEF

ˈpick-up *n*
1 VEHICLE [C] *especially AmE* a small truck with low sides that is used for carrying goods → see picture at **TRUCK**
2 IMPROVEMENT [C] an improvement in something which will be good for economic success: **[+in]** *There are signs of a pick-up in high street spending.*
3 COLLECTION [C,U] an occasion when someone or something is collected from a place: *The price includes travel from your local **pick-up point** in the UK to your hotel in Paris.* | *trash pick-up*

P

4 PERSON [C] *informal* a stranger that you meet in a bar, at a party etc and have sex with
5 MUSIC [C] an electronic part on a musical instrument, especially an electric GUITAR, that makes the sound louder
6 SPEED [U] *AmE* the rate at which a vehicle can increase its speed SYN **acceleration**: *It was a small car, but it had good pick-up.*

ˈpick-up ˌgame *n* [C] *AmE* a game of BASKETBALL, baseball, etc that is played by anyone who wants to play when the game is starting

ˈpick-up ˌtruck *n* [C] *AmE* a PICK-UP(1) → see picture at TRUCK[1]

pick·y /ˈpɪki/ *adj informal* someone who is picky only likes particular things and not others, and so is not easy to please SYN **fussy**: *He's a very* ***picky eater***.

pic·nic[1] /ˈpɪknɪk/ ●●● S3 *n* [C]
1 if you have a picnic, you take food and eat it outdoors, especially in the country: *We decided to* ***have*** *a* ***picnic*** *down by the lake.* | **go on/for a picnic** *We could go on a picnic today.* | *a picnic table* | *There is free parking for visitors, as well as a restaurant and* ***picnic area*** (=a special area with tables where people can have a picnic). | **picnic site/spot/place** (=a place that is suitable or pleasant for a picnic) *We found a lovely picnic spot by the river.* | **picnic basket/hamper** (=a container in which you can carry food for a picnic) ⚠ Don't say 'do a picnic' or 'make a picnic'. Say **have a picnic**.
2 *BrE* the food that you take to eat outdoors on a picnic: *We'll* ***take*** *a* ***picnic*** *with us.* | **picnic lunch/tea/supper** *We ate our picnic lunch by the river.*
3 be no picnic *informal* if something is no picnic, it is very difficult and needs a lot of effort or hard work: *Bringing up six children is no picnic!*

picnic[2] *v* (**picnicked**, **picnicking**) [I] to have a picnic: *We picnicked on the beach.* —**picnicker** *n* [C]: *The area is very popular with picnickers.*

pic·to·gram /ˈpɪktəgræm/ *n* [C] **1** a picture that represents a word or phrase **2** a mathematical drawing that shows numbers or amounts in the form of pictures

pic·to·ri·al /pɪkˈtɔːriəl/ *adj* using or relating to paintings, drawings, or photographs: *a pictorial record of their journey*

pic·ture[1] /ˈpɪktʃə $ -ər/ ●●● S1 W1 *n*
1 PAINTING/DRAWING [C] shapes, lines etc painted or drawn on a surface, showing what someone or something looks like: *The room had several pictures on the walls.* | *a book with pictures in it* | **[+of]** *I like that picture of the two horses.* | **draw/paint a/sb's picture** *Draw a picture of your house.* | *He asked her permission to paint her picture* (=paint a picture of her).
2 PHOTOGRAPH [C] a photograph: **[+of]** *That's a great picture of you, Dad!* | **take sb's picture/take a picture of sb** *I asked the waiter if he'd mind taking our picture.* | **wedding/holiday etc pictures** *Would you like to see the wedding pictures?*
3 TELEVISION [C] an image that appears on a television or cinema screen: **[+of]** *upsetting pictures of the famine in Africa* | *satellite pictures from space*
4 DESCRIPTION/IDEA [C usually singular] a description or idea of what something is like: **[+of]** *The book* ***gives*** *you a good* ***picture*** *of what life was like in Japan in the early 19th century.* | *The article* ***paints*** *a rather bleak* ***picture*** *of the future of our planet.* | *Detectives are trying to* ***build up a picture*** *of the kidnapper.* | *The description in the guidebook showed rather a* ***rosy picture*** (=one that makes you think that something is better than it really is). | *I now have a* ***vivid picture*** (=very clear picture) *in my mind.*
5 SITUATION [singular] the general situation in a place, organization etc: *The worldwide picture for tribal people remains grim.* | *the wider political picture* | *Checks throughout the region revealed a similar picture everywhere.* | **big/bigger/wider picture** *We were so caught up with the details, we lost sight of the big picture* (=the situation considered as a whole).
6 MENTAL IMAGE [C usually singular] an image or memory that you have in your mind: *Sarah had a* ***mental picture*** *of Lisbon.* | *He had a* ***vivid picture*** *in his mind.*
7 put/keep sb in the picture to give someone all the information they need to understand a situation, especially one that is changing quickly: *I'm just going now, but Keith will put you in the picture.*
8 get the picture *informal* to understand a situation: *You've said enough. I get the picture.*
9 out of the picture if someone is out of the picture, they are no longer involved in a situation: *Injury has effectively* ***put*** *Woods* ***out of the picture*** *as far as international matches are concerned.*
10 FILM **a)** [C] a film: *It was voted the year's best picture.* **b) the pictures** [plural] *BrE* the cinema: *Would you like to go to the pictures?*
11 be the picture of health/innocence/despair etc to look very healthy etc: *Head bowed and sobbing, she was the picture of misery.*
12 be/look a picture to look beautiful → **pretty as a picture** at PRETTY[2](7)

picture[2] ●●○ *v* [T]
1 to imagine something by making an image in your mind: *Tom, picturing the scene, smiled.* | **picture sb/sth as sth** *Rob had pictured her as serious, but she wasn't like that.* | **picture sb doing sth** *I can't picture him skiing. He's so clumsy!* | **picture what/how** *Picture what it would be like after a nuclear attack.* THESAURUS ▸ IMAGINE
2 to show someone or something in a photograph, painting, or drawing: *She is pictured with her mum Christine and sister Kelly.* GRAMMAR **Picture** is usually passive in this meaning.
3 to describe something in a particular way: **be pictured as sth** *She's been pictured as a difficult, demanding woman.* GRAMMAR **Picture** is usually passive in this meaning.

ˈpicture book *n* [C] a book for children with many pictures in it

ˈpicture card *n* [C] *BrE* a COURT CARD

ˈpicture ˌmessaging *n* [U] the activity of sending a photo from one MOBILE TELEPHONE to another

ˌpicture-ˈperfect *adj AmE* exactly right in appearance or quality: *The bride looked picture-perfect.*

ˌpicture ˈpostcard *n* [C] a POSTCARD with a photograph or picture on it

ˈpicture-postcard *adj* [only before noun] a picture-postcard place is very pretty: *picture-postcard villages*

ˈpicture rail *n* [C] *BrE* a long narrow piece of wood fixed high on a wall, used for hanging pictures from → see picture at RAIL[1]

pic·tur·esque /ˌpɪktʃəˈresk◂/ ●○○ *adj*
1 a picturesque place is pretty and interesting in an old-fashioned way: *a quiet fishing village with a picturesque harbour* THESAURUS ▸ BEAUTIFUL
2 picturesque language uses unusual, interesting, or sometimes rude words to describe something: *a picturesque account of his trip to New York*

ˈpicture ˌwindow *n* [C] a large window made of a single piece of glass

pid·dle /ˈpɪdl/ *v* [I] *informal* to URINATE
piddle around *phr v* to waste time doing things that are not important

pid·dling /ˈpɪdlɪŋ/ *adj informal* small and unimportant SYN **trivial**

pid·gin /ˈpɪdʒɪn/ *n* [C,U] **1** a language that is a mixture of two other languages, which people who do not speak each other's languages well use to talk to each other **2 pidgin English/French etc** English, French etc that is mixed with the words or grammar of another language

pie /paɪ/ ●●● S2 *n* [C,U]
1 fruit baked inside a PASTRY covering: **slice/piece of pie** *Would you like another piece of apple pie?* → see picture at DESSERT
2 *BrE* meat or vegetables baked inside a PASTRY or potato covering: *I had steak and kidney pie with chips.*
3 slice/share/piece of the pie a share of something such as money, profits etc: *The smaller companies want a bigger share of the pie.*
4 pie in the sky something good that someone says will

happen, but which you think is impossible or unlikely: *Hope of a cure is just pie in the sky.* → MUD PIE, PIE CHART, → **easy as pie** at EASY[1](1), → **eat humble pie** at HUMBLE[1](6), → **have a finger in every pie** at FINGER[1](7), → **be as nice as pie** at NICE(11)

pie·bald /ˈpaɪbɔːld $ -bɒːld/ *adj* a piebald animal has black and white areas on its body: *a piebald horse*

piece[1] /piːs/ ●●● (S1) (W1) *n* [C]

1 AMOUNT an amount of something that has been separated from the main part: **[+of]** *He broke off a piece of bread and gave it her.* | *Cut off a piece of wood 5 cm in length.* | *His trousers were held up with a piece of string.* | *Would you like a small or a large piece?* | **cut/divide etc sth into pieces** *She cut the cake into four equal pieces.* | *Chop the potato into bite-sized pieces.* → see Thesaurus box on *p. 1366*

2 PART one of the parts that something divides or breaks into: **[+of]** *a piece of broken glass* | *Individual pieces of text can be cut and pasted to their correct position.* | **in pieces** *The china dish lay in pieces on the floor.* | *jigsaw pieces* | *His father had taught him how to* ***take*** *a gun* ***to pieces****.* | *The shelving* ***comes to pieces*** (=divides into separate parts) *for easy transport.* | *The shower head just* ***came to pieces*** (=broke into separate parts) *in my hand.* | *The fireplace was carefully dismantled* ***piece by piece*** (=one part at a time). THESAURUS ▸ PART

3 SINGLE ITEM a single thing of a particular type, or something that is one of several similar things: **[+of]** *Pass me another piece of paper.* | *You should eat three pieces of fruit a day.* | *She was wearing a single piece of jewellery.* | *You need to examine every piece of evidence first.* | *an excellent piece of work* | *a major piece of legislation* | *a piece of equipment* | **four-piece/60-piece etc** (=consisting of four, 60 etc separate parts) *a five-piece band* | *a* ***three-piece suite*** (=two chairs and a SOFA)

4 SMALL AMOUNT [usually singular] a small amount of something that is interesting, useful, or unusual in some way: **piece of advice/information/gossip etc** *Let me give you a piece of advice.* | *We're witnessing a piece of history in the making.* | **piece of luck/good fortune** *It really was an extraordinary piece of luck.*

5 LAND an area of land: **[+of]** *a piece of waste ground* | *a dispute about a piece of land*

6 fall to pieces a) to become old and in bad condition: *All my clothes are falling to pieces.* | *They've let that lovely old house fall to pieces around them.* **b)** to no longer be successful or working well: *The economy is falling to pieces.*

7 go to pieces if a person or what they do goes to pieces, they are so upset or nervous that they cannot live, work, or perform as they should: *He just went to pieces after his wife died.* | *Her performance goes to pieces when her father is watching.*

8 smash/rip/tear sth to pieces to damage something badly by breaking it into many parts: *His arm was ripped to pieces by a shark.* | *Wear thick gloves, otherwise you'll tear your fingers to pieces.*

9 pull/rip/tear sb/sth to pieces to criticize someone or their ideas very severely: *Donna could tear your work to pieces, and frequently did.*

10 ART/MUSIC ETC something that has been produced by an artist, musician, or writer: **piece of music/writing/sculpture etc** *some unusual pieces of sculpture* | *The LSO will perform a much-loved concert piece.* THESAURUS ▸ MUSIC

11 NEWS ITEM a short ARTICLE in a newspaper or magazine or part of a television or radio programme that is about a particular subject: **[+about/on]** *Did you read that piece in 'The Observer' about censorship?* | *Robert* ***wrote*** *a short* ***piece*** *on the earthquake.*

12 in one piece *informal* if you arrive somewhere in one piece, you are not injured: *Cheer up. At least you're* ***still in one piece****.* | *Ring Mum and let her know we* ***got here in one piece****.*

13 give sb a piece of your mind *informal* to tell someone that

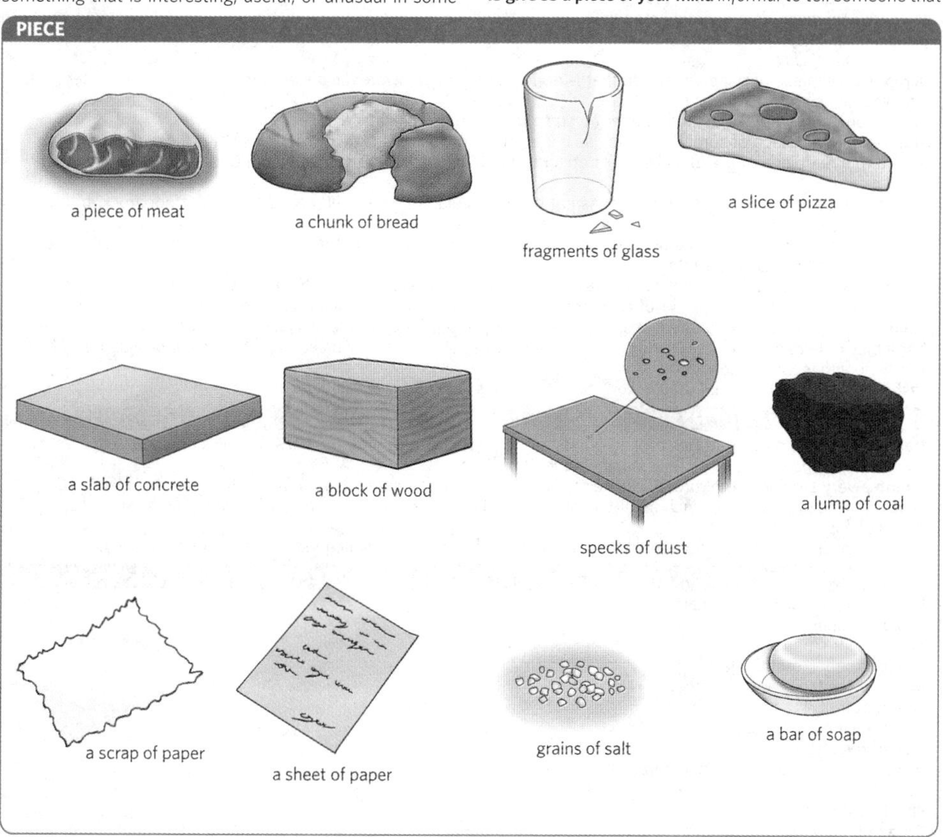

P

you are very angry with them: *After the game he gave the players a piece of his mind.*
14 be a piece of cake *informal* to be very easy to do: *Landing this type of aircraft is a piece of cake for an experienced pilot.*
15 be a piece of piss *BrE spoken not polite* to be very easy to do
16 a piece of the action *informal* a share of the money from a business activity: *And will foreign firms* ***get a piece of the action****?*
17 be (all) of a piece a) if the things someone says or does are all of a piece, they are part of the typical behaviour of that person: **[+with]** *Sexist language is all of a piece with the way some men treat women.* **b)** to be the same or similar in all parts: *The architecture here is all of a piece.*
18 MONEY **a)** a coin of a particular value: **ten pence/50-cent etc piece** *Have you change for a 50-cent piece?* **b)** *old use* a coin: *Robert slipped two gold pieces into the man's hand.*
19 GAMES a small object used in a game such as CHESS → see picture at **BOARD GAME**
20 GUN *AmE informal* a small gun
21 across the piece in all parts of an organization, system, activity etc SYN **across the board**: *We will be making changes across the piece.*
22 be a (real) piece of work *spoken informal especially AmE* to be someone who does nasty things or deceives people in order to get what they want
23 be a piece of shit/crap *spoken not polite* used to show that you do not respect someone or something they say
24 piece of ass *AmE informal not polite* an offensive expression for a woman. Do not use this expression. → **how long is a piece of string?** at **LONG**[1](9)

piece[2] ●○○ *v*
piece sth ↔ **together** *phr v*
1 to use all the information you have about a situation in order to discover the truth about it: *Police are trying to piece together his movements before the murder.* | *Her early life has been pieced together from several different sources.*
2 to put all the separate parts of an object into the correct order or position: *He slowly pieced together the torn fragments of a letter.*

pi·èce de ré·sis·tance /piˌes də reziːˈstɑːns/ *n* [singular] the best or most important thing in a series, which comes after everything else: *The pièce de résistance was a stunning goal in the last minute of the match.*

piece·meal /ˈpiːsmiːl/ *adj* a process that is piecemeal happens slowly and in stages that are not regular or planned properly: *The buildings have been adapted* ***in a piecemeal fashion****.* | *a piecemeal approach to the problem* —**piecemeal** *adv*: *The new fire regulations have been introduced piecemeal.*

piece·work /ˈpiːswɜːk $ -wɜːrk/ *n* [U] work for which you are paid according to the number of things you produce rather than the number of hours that you spend working: *bargaining over piecework rates*

ˈpie ˌchart *n* [C] a circle divided into parts by lines coming from the centre to show how big the different parts of a total amount are

pied /paɪd/ *adj* [only before noun] used in the names of birds that are black and white: *a pied wagtail*

pied-à-terre /ˌpjeɪd æ ˈteə $ piˌed ɑː ˈter/ *n* [singular] a small apartment or house, often in the centre of a city or town, that is not your main home but which you own and

THESAURUS: piece

piece an amount of something that has been cut or separated from the main part: *Could I have another piece of cake?* | *a piece of broken glass*
bit a piece. Bit is more informal than **piece** and is often used about smaller pieces: *The notes were written on bits of paper.* | *He threw a bit of wood onto the fire.*
lump a small piece of something solid or firm that does not have a regular shape: *two lumps of sugar* | *a lump of coal* | *a lump of clay*
scrap a small piece of paper, cloth etc that is no longer needed: *I wrote the phone number on a scrap of paper.* | *The dog was eating scraps of food off the floor.*
strip a long narrow piece of cloth, paper etc: *a strip of cloth* | *The leather had been cut into strips.*
sheet a thin flat piece of something such as paper, glass, or metal: *a blank sheet of paper* | *a sheet of aluminium*
slice a thin flat piece of bread, cake, meat etc cut from a larger piece: *a slice of pizza* | *Cut the tomatoes into thin slices.*
chunk a piece of something solid that does not have a regular shape - used especially about food, rock, or metal: *The fruit was cut into large chunks.* | *a chunk of bread*
hunk a large piece with rough edges, which has been cut or has broken off a bigger piece of food, rock etc: *a big hunk of cheese* | *hunks of concrete*
block a piece of something solid, which has straight sides: *concrete blocks* | *a block of cheese* | *a block of ice*
slab a thick flat piece of stone, or of cake, meat etc: *The floor had been made from stone slabs.* | *a slab of beef*
cube a piece that has six square sides - used especially about food: *a cube of sugar* | *ice cubes*
bar a block of soap, chocolate, candy, or metal, which has straight sides: *a chocolate bar* | *a bar of soap* | *gold bars worth more than £26 million*
rasher *BrE* a slice of bacon: *I usually have two rashers of bacon for breakfast.*

A SMALL PIECE

fragment a small piece that has broken off something, especially something hard: *The window shattered, covering them with fragments of glass.* | *They found fragments of bone.*
crumb a very small piece of bread, cake etc: *There were just a few crumbs left on the plate.*
speck a piece of something such as dirt or dust which is so small you almost cannot see it: *She brushed the specks of dust from the table.*
drop a very small amount of a liquid: *There were drops of blood on the floor.* | *I felt a drop of rain.*

COLLOCATIONS CHECK

lump of sugar/rock/metal/earth
scrap of paper
strip of cloth/paper
sheet of paper/metal/glass
slice of bread/pizza/cake/meat
chunk of fruit/bread
block of ice/stone/wood
slab of rock/stone/meat
bar of soap/chocolate/candy/metal
rasher of bacon
speck of dirt/dust
drop of blood/rain/liquid

stay in sometimes: *They kept a pied-à-terre in London for theatre evenings.*

ˌpie-ˈeyed *adj old-fashioned informal* very drunk

pier /pɪə $ pɪr/ ●○○ *n* [C]
1 a structure that is built over and into the water so that boats can stop next to it or people can walk along it: *a yacht moored at a pier | strolling along Brighton Pier*
2 a thick stone, wooden, or metal post that is used to support something

pierce /pɪəs $ pɪrs/ ●○○ *v*
1 [T] to make a small hole in or through something, using an object with a sharp point: *Steam the corn until it can easily be pierced with a fork. | Rose underwent emergency surgery after a bullet pierced her lung.* | **pierce a hole in/through sth** *Pierce small holes in the base of the pot with a hot needle.*
2 have your ears/nose etc pierced to have a small hole made in your ears, nose etc so that you can wear jewellery through the hole: *I had my belly-button pierced. | pierced ears*
3 [I,T always + adv/prep] *literary* if sound or light pierces something, you suddenly hear or see it: *The darkness was pierced by the beam from the lighthouse. | A sudden scream pierced the silence.* | **[+through]** *The men's lanterns pierced through the dense mist.*
4 pierce sb's heart to make someone feel a strong emotion such as pain, sadness, or love: *Her memories sometimes pierced her heart.*
5 [T] to force a way through something: *Leicester rarely threatened to pierce the Manchester United defence.*

pierc·ing¹ /ˈpɪəsɪŋ $ ˈpɪr-/ *adj*
1 EYES/LOOK *literary* someone with piercing eyes is looking at you and seems to know what you are thinking: *There was mockery now in those piercing blue eyes. | She felt foolish and unsure under his* ***piercing gaze****. | He gave her a* ***piercing look****.*
2 SOUND a sound that is piercing is high, sharp, and unpleasant: *He grinned and let out a piercing whistle. | a piercing scream* **THESAURUS** HIGH, LOUD
3 WIND a piercing wind is very cold
4 PAIN causing a lot of pain: *She felt a piercing sensation in her arm.*
5 EMOTION [only before noun] affecting your feelings very deeply in a sad way: *a piercing moment of regret* —**piercingly** *adv*: *It was piercingly cold. | She looked at him piercingly.*

piercing² *n* [C,U] a hole made through part of your body so that you can put jewellery there, or the process of making these holes

pi·e·ty /ˈpaɪəti/ *n* [U] when you behave in a way that shows respect for your religion → **pious**: *an act of Christian piety*

pif·fle /ˈpɪfəl/ *n* [U] *old-fashioned informal* nonsense

pif·fling /ˈpɪflɪŋ/ *adj BrE old-fashioned informal* piffling amounts are very small and therefore useless SYN **trivial**

pig¹ /pɪg/ ●●● S2 *n* [C]
1 ANIMAL a farm animal with short legs, a fat body, and a curved tail. Pigs are kept for their meat, which includes PORK, BACON, and HAM. SYN **hog** *AmE*: *He kept pigs and poultry.*
2 PERSON *spoken* **a)** someone who eats too much or eats more than their share: *You* ***greedy pig****, you ate all the candy! | I* ***made*** *a bit of* ***a pig of myself*** (=ate too much) *at dinner.* **b)** someone who is unpleasant in some way, for example unkind or very untidy: *They live like pigs in that house over the road. | You can tell him from me he's an ignorant pig.* | **(male) chauvinist pig** (=a man who thinks women are not equal to men)
3 POLICE *taboo informal* an offensive word for a police officer. Do not use this word.
4 a pig (of a sth) *BrE spoken* something that is very difficult or unpleasant to do: *They're improving, and they're a pig of a team to beat.*
5 make a pig's ear of sth *BrE spoken* to do something very badly: *Someone's made a right pig's ear of these repairs.*
6 in a pig's eye *AmE spoken informal* used to show that you do not believe what someone is saying
7 pig in a poke *spoken* something you bought without seeing it first and that is not as good or valuable as you expected: *What if the car you buy* ***turns out to be a pig in a poke****?*
8 pigs might fly *BrE*, **when pigs fly** *AmE spoken* used to say that you do not think something will happen: *'Someone might have handed in your pass.' 'Yes, and pigs might fly.'*

pig² *v* (**pigged**, **pigging**)
pig out *phr v informal* to eat a lot of food all at once: **[+on]** *I found Sam in front of the TV, pigging out on pizza and fries.*

pi·geon /ˈpɪdʒɪn/ ●○○ *n* [C] a grey bird with short legs that is common in cities → CARRIER PIGEON, CLAY PIGEON SHOOTING, HOMING PIGEON

ˌpigeon-ˈchested *adj* someone who is pigeon-chested has a very narrow chest that sticks out

pi·geon·hole¹ /ˈpɪdʒənhəʊl $ -hoʊl/ *n* [C] one of a set of small open boxes fixed to a wall. You leave letters, messages etc for particular people in the boxes.

pigeonhole² *v* [T] to unfairly consider a person, activity etc as belonging to a particular type or group SYN **label**: **pigeonhole sb/sth as sth** *Patsy was pigeonholed as a Country and Western singer, but that's too simple.*

ˌpigeon-ˈtoed *adj* someone who is pigeon-toed has feet that turn towards each other as they walk

pig·ge·ry /ˈpɪgəri/ *n* (*plural* **piggeries**) [C] *BrE* a pig farm, or the place on a farm where pigs are kept

pig·gy¹ /ˈpɪgi/ *n* (*plural* **piggies**) [C] **1** a pig – used by children or when you are talking to children **2 piggy in the middle** *BrE* **a)** *informal* someone who is involved in an argument between two opposing sides, but does not know who they should support: *What have I got myself into? I'm piggy in the middle between Guido and Silvia!* **b)** a game in which two people throw a ball backwards and forwards between them, while a third person in the middle tries to catch it SYN **keep-away** *AmE*

piggy² *adj* **piggy eyes** small unattractive eyes: *His little piggy eyes were red with hatred.*

pig·gy·back¹ /ˈpɪgibæk/ (*also* **ˈpiggyback ˌride**) *n* [C] if you give someone, especially a child, a piggyback, you carry them high on your shoulders, supporting them with your hands under their legs —**piggyback** *adv*

PIGGYBACK

piggyback² *v* [I] *informal* **1** to use something that is bigger, better, or more successful in order to help another product or project succeed: **[+on/onto]** *videos that piggyback onto the success of proven TV programs* **2** to use someone else's WI-FI connection to the Internet, without their knowledge or permission: **[+on/onto]** *How can I prevent other people from piggybacking onto my connection?* —**piggybacking** *n* [U]

ˈpiggy-bank *n* [C] a small container, usually in the shape of a pig, in which children can save coins

pig·head·ed /ˌpɪgˈhedɪd◂/ *adj* determined to do things the way you want and refusing to change your mind, even when there are good reasons to do so SYN **stubborn**: *Never have I met a woman so obstinate, so pigheaded!* —**pigheadedness** *n* [U]: *It was just* ***sheer pigheadedness*** *on his part.*

ˈpig ˌiron *n* [U] a form of iron that is not pure

pig·let /ˈpɪglɪt/ *n* [C] a young pig

pig·ment /ˈpɪgmənt/ *n* [C,U] a natural substance that makes skin, hair, plants etc a particular colour: *Melanin is the dark brown pigment of the hair, skin and eyes. | The artist Sandy Lee uses* ***natural pigments*** *in her work.*

pig·men·ta·tion /ˌpɪɡmənˈteɪʃən/ *n* [U] *technical* the natural colour of living things: *The dark pigmentation gives protection from the sun's rays.*

pig·my /ˈpɪɡmi/ *n* [C] another spelling of PYGMY

pig·pen /ˈpɪɡpen/ *n* [C] *AmE* **1** a building where pigs are kept SYN **pigsty 2** *informal* a very dirty or untidy place SYN **pigsty**

Pigs, Bay of → BAY OF PIGS, THE

pig·skin /ˈpɪɡˌskɪn/ *n* **1** [U] leather made from the skin of a pig: *a pigskin suitcase* **2** [singular] *AmE informal* the ball used in American football: *We started tossing the pigskin around.*

pig·sty /ˈpɪɡstaɪ/ *n* (*plural* **pigsties**) [C] **1** a building where pigs are kept SYN **pigpen** *AmE* → see picture at HOME[1] **2** *informal* a very dirty or untidy place SYN **pigpen** *AmE*: *The house was a pigsty, as usual.*

pig·swill /ˈpɪɡˌswɪl/ *n* [U] *BrE* waste food that is fed to pigs

pig·tail /ˈpɪɡteɪl/ *n* [C] lengths of hair that have been twisted together into a PLAIT: **in pigtails** *She wore her hair in pigtails.* → BUNCH[1](5), → PLAIT[1], BRAID[1](2), PONYTAIL, → see picture at HAIRSTYLE

pike /paɪk/ *n* [C] **1** (*plural* **pike**) a large fish that eats other fish and lives in rivers and lakes **2** a long-handled weapon with a sharp blade, used in the past **3 come down the pike** *AmE* to happen or become known: *The world is being turned upside down by the string of multimedia technologies coming down the pike.* **4** *AmE spoken* a TURNPIKE

pik·er /ˈpaɪkə $ -ər/ *n* [C] *AusE* someone who avoids difficult situations, especially ones involving money

pike·staff /ˈpaɪkstɑːf $ -stæf/ *n* **as plain as a pikestaff** *BrE old-fashioned* very clear and easy to understand: *None of us worked it out, though it was as plain as a pikestaff when you thought about it.*

pi·laff, **pilaf** /ˈpiːlæf $ pɪˈlɑːf/ *n* [C,U] a pilau

pi·las·ter /pəˈlæstə $ -ər/ *n* [C] a flat square COLUMN attached to the wall of a building for decoration

Pi·la·tes /pɪˈlɑːtiz/ *n* [U] a type of exercise based on YOGA and dance that you do with special equipment which makes you push, pull, and stretch, so that your body moves more easily and becomes stronger

pi·lau /ˈpiːlaʊ $ pɪˈloʊ/ *n* [C,U] *BrE* a dish made of rice, vegetables, and sometimes meat: *mushroom pilau*

pil·chard /ˈpɪltʃəd $ -ərd/ *n* [C] *BrE* a small fish that lives in the sea and that can be eaten

PILE

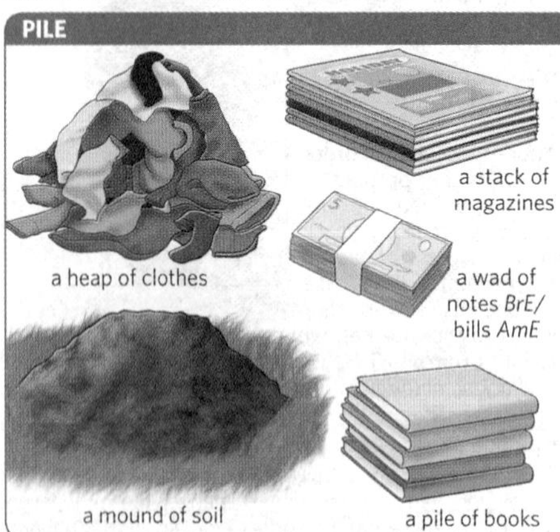

pile[1] /paɪl/ ●●● S2 *n*

1 ARRANGEMENT OF THINGS [C] a group of several things of the same type that are put on top of each other SYN **stack**: **[+of]** *His mother came in carrying a pile of ironing in her arms.* | *Flora shuffled through a pile of magazines.* | **put sth in/into a pile** *She tidied up the books and put them in* **neat piles**. | *He balanced the plate* **on the top of a pile** *of books.*

2 LARGE AMOUNT [C] a large amount of something arranged in a shape that looks like a small hill: **[+of]** *piles of melting snow* | *All that remained of the old house was a pile of rubble.* | *Sophie stooped to throw another branch on the pile.* | *He began to* **sweep** *the pieces of glass* **into a pile**.

3 a pile of sth (*also* **piles of sth**) *informal* a lot of something: *We've had piles of letters from viewers.* | *another pile of directives from the EU*

4 the bottom of the pile *BrE* the weakest or least important position in a society or organization: *I soon discovered I was at the bottom of the pile in the office hierarchy.* | *She always puts her own needs to the bottom of the pile.*

5 the top of the pile *BrE* the best or highest position in a society or organization: *It's been 20 years since a British tennis player was at the top of the pile.*

6 HOUSE [C] a very large old house: *They've just bought an 18th-century pile in Surrey.*

7 MATERIAL [C,U] the soft surface of short threads on a CARPET or some types of cloth: **thick/deep pile** *Her feet sank into the thick pile of the rug.* | *a deep pile carpet* → NAP[1](2)

8 POST [C] *technical* a heavy wooden, stone, or metal post, used to support something heavy

9 make a/your pile *informal* to make a lot of money: *He had made his pile in the wholesale business.*

10 piles [plural] painfully swollen BLOOD VESSELS near a person's ANUS

pile[2] ●○○ *v* [T]

1 [always + adv/prep] to fill a place or container or cover a surface with a large amount of things: **pile sth into/onto etc sth** *He piled bread and milk into his basket.* | *Melissa piled spaghetti onto her plate.* | **be piled with sth** *a chair piled with velvet cushions* | *The room was* **piled high** *with boxes* (=filled with a lot of boxes).

2 (*also* **pile up**) to arrange things in a pile: *Ma stacked the cups and piled the plates.* | **pile sth on/onto sth** *She brushed her hair and piled it carefully on top of her head.*

pile in (*also* **pile into sth**) *phr v* if people pile in, they get into a vehicle very quickly: *Pierre came to pick them up, and they all piled in.*

pile sth ↔ **on** *phr v informal*

1 pile it on/pile on the drama to talk about something in a way that makes it seem much worse than it really is SYN **exaggerate**: *I know I'm piling it on a bit, but there is a serious point to be made.*

2 pile on the pressure/agony to show that you are much better than your opponent in a game: *England piled on the pressure from the start.*

3 pile on the pounds to gain a lot of body weight: *She slimmed down a couple of years ago but has piled on the pounds again.*

pile out *phr v* if people pile out, they leave a place or get out of a vehicle quickly and in a disorganized way: *Edward parked by the river and we all piled out.*

pile up *phr v*

1 to increase in quantity or amount, in a way that is difficult to manage: *It wasn't long before the debts were piling up.* | *The traffic starts piling up around this time.* | *The work has a tendency to pile up if I'm not careful.*

2 pile sth ↔ up to arrange things in a pile: *tiny doughnuts piled up in a dish* → PILEUP

ˈpile ˌdriver *n* [C] **1** a machine for pushing heavy posts into the ground **2** *BrE informal* a very hard hit

ˈpileup, **pile-up** *n* [C] a traffic accident involving many vehicles: *a motorway pile-up* THESAURUS ACCIDENT

pil·fer /ˈpɪlfə $ -ər/ *v* [I,T] to steal things that are not worth much, especially from the place where you work: **[+from]** *She was sacked after being caught pilfering from the till.* —**pilferer** *n* [C]: *an office pilferer* —**pilfering** *n* [U]

pil·grim /ˈpɪlɡrɪm/ *n* [C] a religious person who travels a long way to a holy place: *pilgrims visiting a holy shrine*

pil·grim·age /ˈpɪlɡrəmɪdʒ/ ●○○ *n* [C,U]

1 a journey to a holy place for religious reasons: **make a pilgrimage/go on (a) pilgrimage** *the chance to go on pilgrimage to Mecca* THESAURUS JOURNEY

2 a journey to a place connected with someone or something famous: *Presley's home has become a* **place of pilgrimage**.

pill[1] /pɪl/ ●●● S3 *n*
1 [C] a small solid piece of medicine that you swallow whole: *He has to* ***take pills*** *to control his blood pressure.* | ***sleeping pills*** | *a bottle of* ***vitamin pills*** → see picture at BOTTLE[1]
2 the Pill/the pill a pill taken regularly by some women in order to prevent them having babies: **on the Pill** *My doctor advised me to go on the pill* (=start taking it regularly).
3 sugar/sweeten the pill to do something to make an unpleasant job or situation less unpleasant for the person who has to accept it
4 be a pill *AmE informal* if someone, especially a child, is a pill, they are annoying: *Luke can be a real pill sometimes.* → **a bitter pill (to swallow)** at BITTER[1](7), → **MORNING-AFTER PILL**

pill[2] *v* [I] *AmE* if a piece of clothing pills, especially a SWEATER, it forms little balls on the surface of the cloth after it has been worn or washed

pil·lage /ˈpɪlɪdʒ/ *v* [I,T] if soldiers pillage a place in a war, they steal a lot of things and do a lot of damage SYN **plunder** —**pillage** *n* [U] —**pillager** *n* [C]

pil·lar /ˈpɪlə $ -ər/ ●●○ *n* [C]
1 a) a tall upright round post used as a support for a roof or bridge: *Eight massive stone pillars supported the roof.* **b)** a tall upright round post, usually made of stone, put up to remind people of an important person or event
2 pillar of society/the community/the church etc somebody who is an important and respected member of a group, and is involved in many public activities: *Mr Fitzwilliam had been seen as a pillar of the community.*
3 a very important part of a system of beliefs or ideas: **[+of]** *One of the pillars of a civilized society must be that everyone has equal access to the legal system.*
4 be driven/pushed from pillar to post to have to go from one person or situation to another without achieving much or being able to settle: *The poor kid has been pushed from pillar to post.*
5 be a pillar of strength if someone is a pillar of strength, they are there to give you help and support at a difficult time: *Christine's been a pillar of strength to me.*
6 pillar of dust/smoke/flame etc a tall upright mass of dust, smoke, flame etc

ˈpillar box *n* [C] *BrE old-fashioned* a large red tube-shaped box for posting letters that stands on streets in Britain SYN **postbox** → **letterbox**

ˌpillar-box ˈred *n* [U] *BrE* a very bright red colour —**pillar-box red** *adj*

pill·box /ˈpɪlbɒks $ -bɑːks/ *n* [C] **1** a small round box for holding PILLS **2** a small strong usually circular shelter with a gun inside it, built as a defence **3** (*also* **ˌpillbox ˈhat**) a small round hat for a woman

pil·lion /ˈpɪljən/ *n* [singular] *BrE* the seat behind the driver of a MOTORCYCLE: *a pillion passenger* —**pillion** *adv*: *Tom had never* ***ridden pillion*** *before.*

pil·lock /ˈpɪlək/ *n* [C] *BrE informal* a very stupid person

pil·lo·ry[1] /ˈpɪləri/ *v* (**pilloried**, **pillorying**, **pillories**) [T] if someone is pilloried, they are publicly criticized by a lot of people, especially in newspapers etc: *The education secretary was pilloried by the press for his latest proposals.*
GRAMMAR **Pillory** is usually passive.

pillory[2] *n* (*plural* **pillories**) [C] a wooden frame with holes for someone's head and hands to be locked into, used in the past as a way of publicly punishing someone → **the stocks** at STOCK[1](9)

pil·low[1] /ˈpɪləʊ $ -loʊ/ ●●● S3 *n* [C]
1 a cloth bag filled with soft material that you put your head on when you are sleeping: *I'll be asleep as soon as my head hits the pillow.* → CUSHION[1](1)
2 pillow fight a game in which children hit each other with pillows
3 pillow talk *informal* conversation between lovers in bed

pillow[2] *v* [T always + adv/prep] *literary* to rest your head somewhere: *His head was pillowed on his arm.*

pil·low·case, **ˈpillow case** /ˈpɪləʊkeɪs $ -loʊ-/ *n* [C] a cloth cover for a pillow

pi·lot[1] /ˈpaɪlət/ ●●● W3 *n* [C]
1 someone who operates the controls of an aircraft or spacecraft: *an airline pilot* | *a fighter pilot* | *The official report into the accident says that it was caused by* ***pilot error*** (=a mistake by the pilot).
2 someone with a special knowledge of a particular area of water, who is employed to guide ships across it: *a harbour pilot*
3 pilot study/project/scheme etc a small study, project etc which is carried out as a test to see if an idea, product etc will be successful: *a pilot scheme which could be extended to other areas*
4 a television programme that is made in order to test whether people like it and would watch it: *a pilot for a new sitcom* → **AUTOMATIC PILOT**

pilot[2] *v* [T] **1** to guide an aircraft, spacecraft, or ship as its pilot **2** to test a new idea, product etc on people to find out whether it will be successful: *The new exams are currently being piloted in a number of areas.* **3** *literary* to help someone to go to a place **4** *BrE* to be responsible for making sure that a new law or plan is officially approved: **pilot sth through sth** *The Bill was piloted through Parliament by the health minister.*

ˈpilot light *n* [C] a small gas flame that burns all the time and is used for lighting larger gas burners

ˈpilot ˌofficer *n* [C] a middle rank in the Royal Air Force, or someone who has this rank

ˈpilot ˌwhale *n* [C] a small WHALE with black skin

pi·men·to /pəˈmentəʊ $ -toʊ/ (*also* **pim·i·en·to** /-ˈmjentəʊ $ -toʊ/) *n* (*plural* **pimentos**) [C,U] a small red PEPPER which does not have a very strong taste

pimp[1] /pɪmp/ *n* [C] a man who makes money by controlling PROSTITUTES

pimp[2] *v* **1** [I,T] to find customers for a PROSTITUTE **2** (*also* **pimp out**) [T] *informal* to improve something or make it more attractive: *You can pimp your car with these stickers.*

pim·per·nel /ˈpɪmpənel $ -ər-/ *n* [C] a small wild plant with flowers in various colours, especially red

pim·ple /ˈpɪmpəl/ *n* [C] a small raised red spot on your skin, especially on your face —**pimply** *adj*: *a pimply 18-year-old* → **GOOSE PIMPLES**

pin[1] /pɪn/ ●●● S3 *n* [C]
1 FOR JOINING/FASTENING **a)** a short thin piece of metal with a sharp point at one end, used especially for fastening together pieces of cloth while making clothes **b)** a thin piece of metal used to fasten things together, especially broken bones
2 JEWELLERY *AmE* a piece of metal, sometimes containing jewels, that you fasten to your clothes to wear as a decoration SYN **brooch** *BrE*
3 ELECTRICAL *BrE* one of the pieces of metal that sticks out of an electric PLUG: *a three-pin plug* → see picture at PLUG[1]
4 BOWLING one of the bottle-shaped objects that you try to knock down in a game of BOWLING
5 you could hear a pin drop *spoken* used to say that it is very quiet and no one is speaking
6 PART OF BOMB a short piece of metal which you pull out of a HAND GRENADE to make it explode a short time later
7 GOLF a metal stick with a flag at the top which marks the holes on a GOLF COURSE
8 for two pins I'd ... *BrE old-fashioned* used to say that you would like to do something to someone because they have annoyed you: *For two pins, I'd just send them all home.*
9 pins [plural] *BrE informal* legs → **DRAWING PIN, PIN MONEY, PINS AND NEEDLES(1), ROLLING PIN, SAFETY PIN**

pin[2] ●●○ *v* (**pinned**, **pinning**) [T always + adv/prep]
1 to fasten something somewhere, or to join two things together, using a pin: **pin sth to/on sth** *Can you pin this to the notice board?* | *He pinned the name tag on his jacket.* | **pin sth up** *She had photos of her kids pinned up next to her desk.*
2 to make someone unable to move by putting a lot of pressure or weight on them: **pin sb/sth to sth** *He pinned her arms to her sides.* | **pin sb against sth** *Albert got him*

pinned against the wall. | **pin sb down** *They managed to pin him down until the police arrived.* | **be pinned under/beneath sth** *Her body was pinned under the weight of the car.*

pin sb/sth ↔ **down** *phr v*
1 to make someone give clear details or make a definite decision about something: **[+to]** *Did you manage to pin him down to a definite date?* | *He's impossible to pin down.*
2 to understand something clearly or be able to describe it exactly: **hard/difficult to pin down** *The flavour was hard to pin down.*
3 if soldiers etc involved in fighting are pinned down, they cannot move from their position because someone is shooting at them: *The rebels have been pinned down in a camp to the south of the river.*

pin sth **on** sb/sth *phr v*
1 to blame someone for something, often unfairly: *Don't try to* ***pin the blame on*** *me!* | *They're trying to pin the murder on the boyfriend.*
2 pin your hopes/faith on sth/sb to hope that something will happen or someone will help you, because all your plans depend on this: *Chris is pinning his hopes on getting into Yale.*

PIN /pɪn/ (*also* **ˈPIN ˌnumber**) *n* [C] (***personal identification number***) a number that you use when you get money from a machine using a plastic card

pi·ña co·la·da /ˌpiːnə kəˈlɑːdə/ *n* [C,U] an alcoholic drink made from COCONUT juice, PINEAPPLE juice, and RUM

pin·a·fore /ˈpɪnəfɔː $ -fɔːr/ *n* [C] **1** (*also* **ˈpinafore ˌdress** *BrE*) a dress that does not cover your arms and under which you wear a shirt or BLOUSE SYN **jumper** *AmE* **2** (*also* **pinny** *BrE informal*) a loose piece of clothing that does not cover your arms, worn over your clothes to keep them clean → **apron**

pi·ña·ta /pɪˈnjɑːtə/ *n* [C] a decorated paper container filled with sweets or toys. It is hung up at a party and children try to break it open with a stick.

pin·ball /ˈpɪnbɔːl $ -bɒːl/ *n* [U] a game played on a machine with a sloping board which a ball rolls down while the player tries to prevent it reaching the bottom

pin·board /ˈpɪnbɔːd $ -bɔːrd/ *n* [C] **1** a board on a wall which notices, pictures etc can be pinned to **2** a WEB PAGE where users can put images

pince-nez /ˌpæns ˈneɪ, ˌpɪns-/ *n* [plural] glasses worn in the past that were held in position on the nose by a spring, instead of by pieces fitting round the ears

pin·cer /ˈpɪnsə $ -ər/ *n* **1** [C usually plural] one of the pair of CLAWs that some SHELLFISH and insects have, used for holding and cutting food, and for fighting **2 pincers** [plural] a tool made of two crossed pieces of metal used for holding things tightly

ˈpincer ˌmovement *n* [C] a military attack in which two groups of soldiers come from opposite directions in order to trap the enemy between them

pinch¹ /pɪntʃ/ ●○○ *v*
1 [T] to press a part of someone's skin very tightly between your finger and thumb, especially so that it hurts: *We have to stop her pinching her baby brother.* | *He pinched her cheek.* THESAURUS ▸ HURT
2 [T] *BrE informal* to steal something, especially something small or not very valuable: *Someone's pinched my coat!* THESAURUS ▸ STEAL
3 [T] to press something between your finger and thumb: *Pinch the edges of the pastry together to seal it.*
4 [I,T] if something you are wearing pinches you, it presses painfully on part of your body, because it is too tight: *Her new shoes were pinching.*
5 sb has to pinch themselves used when a situation is so surprising that the person involved needs to make sure that they are not imagining it: *Sometimes she had to pinch herself to make sure it was not all a dream.*
6 [T] *BrE old-fashioned* to ARREST someone

pinch sth ↔ **out** *phr v* to remove a small part of a plant with your fingers: *Pinch out any side shoots to make the plant grow upwards.*

pinch² *n* [C] **1 pinch of salt/pepper etc** a small amount of salt, pepper etc that you can hold between your finger and thumb: *Add a pinch of salt to taste.* **2** when you press someone's skin between your finger and thumb: *She gave him a playful pinch.* **3 at a pinch** *BrE*, **in a pinch** *AmE* used to say that you could do something if necessary in a difficult or urgent situation: *There's space for three people. Four at a pinch.* | *If you're in a pinch, I'm sure they'd look after Jenny for a while.* **4 take sth with a pinch of salt** used to say that you should not always completely believe what a particular person says: *You have to take what he says with a pinch of salt.* **5 feel the pinch** to have financial difficulties, especially because you are not making as much money as you used to make: *Local stores and businesses are beginning to feel the pinch.*

pinched /pɪntʃt/ *adj* a pinched face looks thin and unhealthy, for example because the person is ill, cold, or tired: *She had a small pinched face with sad eyes.*

ˈpinch-hit *v* [I + for] *AmE* **1** to do something for someone else because they are suddenly not able to do it **2** to HIT for someone else in baseball —**pinch-hitter** *n* [C]

pin·cush·ion /ˈpɪnˌkʊʃən/ *n* [C] a soft filled bag for sticking pins in until you need to use them

pine¹ /paɪn/ ●●○ *n*
1 [C,U] (*also* **pine tree**) a tall tree with long hard sharp leaves that do not fall off in winter: *an ancient pine forest*
2 [U] the pale wood of pine trees, used to make furniture, floors etc: *a pine table*

pine² *v* [I] to become sad and not continue your life as normal because someone has died or gone away: *Six months after he left, she was still pining.*

pine away *phr v* to become less active, weaker, and often ill, especially because you miss someone who has died or gone away

pine for sb/sth *phr v* **1** if you pine for a place or for something, you miss it a lot and wish you could be there or have it again: *After two months in France I was pining for home.* **2** if you pine for someone, you feel very unhappy because they are not with you: *Karen had been pining for her friends back home in Colorado.*

pine·ap·ple /ˈpaɪnæpəl/ ●●○ *n* [C,U] a large yellow-brown tropical fruit or its sweet juicy yellow flesh: *pineapple chunks* | *pineapple juice* → see picture at **FRUIT¹**

ˈpine ˌmarten *n* [C] a small thin furry animal that lives in forests in Europe

ˈpine ˌneedle *n* [C] a leaf of the PINE tree, which is thin and sharp like a needle → see picture at **NEEDLE¹**

ˈpine nut *n* [C] a small seed that grows on some PINE trees and is eaten as food → see picture at **NUT¹**

ˈpine tree *n* [C] a tall tree with long hard sharp leaves that do not fall off in winter SYN **pine**

pine·wood /ˈpaɪnwʊd/ *n* **1** [C] a forest of pine trees **2** [U] the wood from a pine tree

ping¹ /pɪŋ/ *n* [C] a short high ringing sound: *The microwave* ***goes ping*** *when the food's ready.*

ping² *v* **1** [I] to make a short high ringing sound **2** [T] *informal* to send an email to someone, telephone them etc: *We'll ping you with confirmation of your booking.* **3** [T] to send a message to a computer, usually in order to find out if a connection is working

ping·back /ˈpɪŋbæk/ *n* [C,U] *technical* an AUTOMATIC message which tells you that a website has made a LINK to your website, or the system of sending these messages

ˈPing-Pong *n* [U] *trademark* an indoor game played on a table by two people with a small plastic ball and two BATS SYN **table tennis**

pin·head /ˈpɪnhed/ *n* [C] the small round part at one end of a pin

pin·hole /ˈpɪnhəʊl $ -hoʊl/ *n* [C] a very small hole in something, especially one made by a pin

pin·ion¹ /ˈpɪnjən/ *v* [T always + adv/prep] to hold or tie someone's arms or legs very tightly, so that they cannot move freely: *My arms were pinioned behind me by the policemen.*

pinion² *n* [C] a small wheel, with teeth on its outer

edge, that fits into a larger wheel and turns it or is turned by it

pink¹ /pɪŋk/ ●●● S2 *adj*
1 pale red: ***bright pink*** *lipstick | Hannah's face went pink.* → SHOCKING PINK
2 [only before noun] *BrE* relating to people who are HOMOSEXUAL → **be tickled pink** at TICKLE¹(3)

pink² ●●● S2 *n*
1 [C,U] a pale red colour: *Her room was decorated in* ***bright pinks*** *and purples. | She had arrived dressed in pink.*
2 [C] a garden plant with pink, white, or red flowers
3 in the pink *old-fashioned* in very good health

ˌpink-ˈcollar *adj* **pink-collar jobs/workers/industries etc** *especially AmE* low-paid jobs done mainly by women, for example in offices and restaurants, or the women who do these jobs → WHITE-COLLAR, BLUE-COLLAR

ˌpink ˈgin *n* [C,U] a pink alcoholic drink made of GIN and a strong bitter liquid

pink·ie, pinky /ˈpɪŋki/ *n* [C] *especially AmE* your smallest finger SYN **little finger**

ˈpinking ˌshears (*also* **ˈpinking ˌscissors**) *n* [plural] a special type of scissors with blades that have V-shaped teeth, used for cutting cloth

pink·ish /ˈpɪŋkɪʃ/ *adj* slightly pink: *the pinkish glow of the fire*

pink·o /ˈpɪŋkəʊ $ -koʊ/ *n* (*plural* **pinkos**) [C] **1** *AmE* an insulting word for a SOCIALIST or COMMUNIST **2** *BrE* someone who has slightly LEFT-WING ideas, but is not a strong believer in SOCIALISM → **red** —**pinko** *adj*: *pinko liberals*

ˌpink ˈpound *n* [singular] *BrE* the money that people who are HOMOSEXUAL have available to spend: *Companies are trying to attract the pink pound.*

ˌpink ˈslip *n* [C] *AmE informal* **1** an official document that proves that you own a particular car **2** a written warning you get when your job is going to end because there is not enough work

pink·y /ˈpɪŋki/ *n* [C] a PINKIE

ˈpin ˌmoney *n* [U] *BrE* a small amount of extra money which someone earns to spend on things which they want but do not really need: *She helped her uncle out sometimes just to earn a bit of pin money.*

pin·na·cle /ˈpɪnəkəl/ *n* **1** [singular] the most successful, powerful, exciting etc part of something: *the pinnacle of academic achievement |* **[+of]** *She had* ***reached the pinnacle*** *of her political career. |* **at the pinnacle of sth** *The bank was then at the pinnacle of England's financial system.* **2** [C] *literary* a high mountain top **3** [C] a pointed stone decoration, like a small tower, on a building such as a church or castle

pin·ny /ˈpɪni/ *n* (*plural* **pinnies**) [C] *BrE informal* a PINAFORE(2)

pi·noch·le /ˈpiːnʌkəl/ *n* [U] an American card game

pin·point¹ /ˈpɪnpɔɪnt/ *v* [T] **1** to discover or explain exactly the real facts about something or the cause of a problem: *It's difficult to pinpoint the cause of the accident. |* **pinpoint what/how/why etc** *They need to pinpoint exactly what skills are necessary.* **2** to find or show the exact position of something: *Rescue teams have now* ***pinpointed*** *the* ***location*** *of the ship.*

pinpoint² *n* [C] **1** a very small area or DOT of something: **[+of]** *tiny pinpoints of light* **2 with pinpoint accuracy** very exactly: *The missiles can hit targets with pinpoint accuracy.*

pin·prick /ˈpɪnˌprɪk/ *n* [C] **1** a very small area or DOT of something: **[+of]** *a pinprick of light* **2** a very small hole in something, similar to one made by a pin **3** something that slightly annoys you: *These problems were pinpricks compared with what was to come.*

ˌpins and ˈneedles *n* [U] **1** an uncomfortable feeling, often in your foot or your leg, which you get especially when you have not moved part of your body for a long time, and the supply of blood has stopped flowing properly: *I'll have to move because I'm starting to* ***get pins and needles*** *in my foot.* **2 be on pins and needles** *AmE* to be very nervous and unable to relax, especially because you are waiting for something important SYN **be on tenterhooks**

pin·stripe /ˈpɪnstraɪp/ *n* [C] **1** one of the thin pale lines that form a pattern on cloth against a darker background **2 pinstripe suit** a suit made from cloth with a pinstripe pattern, worn especially by business people: *a navy-blue pinstripe suit* —**ˈpin-striped** *adj*

pint /paɪnt/ ●●○ *n* [C]
1 (*written abbreviation* **pt**) a unit for measuring an amount of liquid, especially beer or milk. In Britain a pint is equal to 0.568 litres, and in the US it is equal to 0.473 litres: **[+of]** *Add two pints of water to the mixture. | half a pint of milk | a pint glass* (=a glass which will hold a pint of liquid)
2 *BrE* a pint of beer, especially one that you drink in a bar → **half**: *He's gone down the pub for a quick pint.*

pin·to /ˈpɪntəʊ $ -toʊ/ *n* (*plural* **pintos**) [C] *AmE* a horse with irregular patterns of two or more colours SYN **piebald** *BrE*

ˈpinto bean *n* [C] a small light-brown bean

ˈpint-sized *adj* [only before noun] small - usually used humorously: *the pint-sized child star*

ˈpin-up *n* [C] **1** a picture of an attractive person, often not wearing many clothes, that is put up on a wall to be looked at and admired: *a pin-up of her favourite boy band* **2** someone who appears in pin-up pictures or who is considered attractive by a particular group of people: *He's becoming the thinking woman's pin-up.*

pin·wheel /ˈpɪnwiːl/ *n* [C] *AmE* a toy consisting of a stick with curved pieces of plastic at the end which turn around when they are blown SYN **windmill** *BrE*

pi·o·neer¹ /ˌpaɪəˈnɪə $ -ˈnɪr/ ●○○ *n* [C]
1 someone who is important in the early development of something, and whose work or ideas are later developed by other people: **[+of]** *John Whitney was a pioneer of computer animation. | He was a* ***pioneer in the field of*** *biotechnology.*
2 one of the first people to travel to a new country or area and begin living there, farming etc: *the early pioneers of the Dakota territory*

pioneer² ●○○ *v* [T] to be the first person to do, invent, or use something: *The new cancer treatment was pioneered in the early eighties by Dr Sylvia Bannerjee.*

pi·o·neer·ing /ˌpaɪəˈnɪərɪŋ◂ $ -ˈnɪr-/ *adj* [only before noun] introducing new and better methods or ideas for the first time: **pioneering work/research/efforts etc** *the pioneering work of NASA scientists | She played a* ***pioneering role*** *in opening higher education to women.*

pi·ous /ˈpaɪəs/ *adj* **1** having strong religious beliefs, and showing this in the way you behave → **piety**: *He was a quiet, pious man.* **2** if you describe what someone says as pious talk, words etc, you mean that they are trying to sound good or moral but you do not believe that they are sincere or will really do what they say: *pious speeches by politicians about 'family values'* **3 pious hope/wish** something that you want to be true or to happen, but that is very unlikely: *All these agreements and ideas remain little more than pious hopes in the present climate.* —**piously** *adv*

pip¹ /pɪp/ *n* [C] *BrE* **1** a small seed from a fruit such as an apple or orange: *an apple pip | Have these oranges got pips in?* → see picture at FRUIT¹ **2** a high note that is part of a series of short sounds, used for example on the radio to show the time, or on a public telephone line to show that your money has almost finished SYN **beep** *AmE*: *The pips are going so I'd better say goodbye.* **3** *old-fashioned* one of the stars on the shoulders of the coats of army officers that shows their rank

pip² *v* (**pipped, pipping**) [T] *BrE informal* **1 pip sb at the post** to beat someone at the last moment in a race, competition etc, when they were expecting to win: *The Maclaren team were narrowly pipped at the post by Ferrari.* **2** to beat someone in a race, competition etc, by only a small amount: **pip sb to/for sth** *Jackson just pipped him for the gold.*

P

pipe[1] /paɪp/ ●●● S2 W3 *n* [C]

1 TUBE a tube through which a liquid or gas flows: *a* ***water pipe*** | *a frozen* ***waste pipe*** | *copper pipes* | *A* ***pipe*** *had* ***burst*** *in the kitchen and flooded the floor.* → DRAINPIPE, WINDPIPE, → **exhaust pipe** at EXHAUST[2](2)

2 FOR SMOKING a thing used for smoking tobacco, consisting of a small tube with a container shaped like a bowl at one end: *Dad was there,* ***smoking*** *his* ***pipe****.* | *pipe tobacco*

3 MUSIC a) a simple musical instrument like a tube, that you play by blowing → PANPIPES **b)** one of the metal tubes that air passes through when you play an ORGAN **c) the pipes** BAGPIPES → see picture at **ORGAN**

4 pipe dream a hope, idea, plan etc that is impossible or will probably never happen: *In many parts of the country, democratic elections are simply a pipe dream.*

5 put/stick that in your pipe and smoke it *spoken* used to say that someone must accept what you have just said, even though they do not like it

PIPES

pipe[2] *v*

1 SEND LIQUID/GAS [T] to send a liquid or gas through a pipe to another place: **be piped into/from/out of etc sth** *Eighty per cent of sewage is piped directly into the sea.* | **be piped in/out/up etc** *A lot of oil is piped in from Alaska.* | *villages with no* ***piped water*** GRAMMAR **Pipe** is usually passive in this meaning.

2 MAKE MUSIC [I,T] to make a musical sound, using a pipe

3 FOOD [T] to decorate food, especially a cake, with lines of ICING or cream

4 SPEAK [T] *literary* to speak or sing something in a high voice: *'Morning!' he piped with a cheery voice.*

pipe down *phr v spoken* to stop talking or making a noise, and become calmer and less excited: *Everybody pipe down. There's no need to shout.*

pipe sth ↔ **in** (*also* **pipe sth into sth**) *phr v* to send radio signals or recorded music into a room or building: *tunes piped in over an acoustic system*

pipe up *phr v informal* to suddenly say something, especially when you have been quiet until then: *Mum suddenly piped up 'No!'*

ˈpipe ˌcleaner *n* [C] a length of wire covered with soft material, used to clean the inside of a tobacco pipe

ˌpiped ˈmusic *n* [U] quiet recorded music played continuously in shops, hotels, restaurants etc

ˈpipe ˌfitter *n* [C] someone who puts in and repairs pipes for water, gas etc

pipe·line /ˈpaɪp-laɪn/ ●○○ *n* [C]

1 a line of connecting pipes, often under the ground, used for sending gas, oil etc over long distances

2 be in the pipeline if a plan, idea, or event is in the pipeline, it is being prepared and it will happen or be completed soon: *More job losses are in the pipeline.*

ˌpipe of ˈpeace *n* [C] a PEACE PIPE

ˈpipe ˌorgan *n* [C] an ORGAN

pip·er /ˈpaɪpə $ -ər/ *n* [C] someone who plays a PIPE or the BAGPIPES

pi·pette /pɪˈpet $ paɪ-/ *n* [C] a thin glass tube for sucking up exact amounts of liquid, used especially in chemistry

pipe·work /ˈpaɪpwɜːk $ -wɜːrk/ *n* [U] the pipes that are part of a building, machine, or structure: *The houses all have lead pipework.*

pip·ing[1] /ˈpaɪpɪŋ/ *n* [U] **1** a thin tube of cloth, usually with string inside, sewn onto clothing, furniture etc as decoration **2** several pipes, or a system of pipes, used to send liquid or gas in or out of a building

piping[2] *adv* **piping hot** piping hot liquid or food is very hot: *piping hot coffee*

pip·it /ˈpɪpɪt/ *n* [C] a small brown or grey singing bird

pip·pin /ˈpɪpɪn/ *n* [C] a small sweet apple

pip·squeak /ˈpɪpskwiːk/ *n* [C] *old-fashioned* someone that you think is not worth respecting or paying attention to, especially because they are small or young

pi·quant /ˈpiːkənt/ *adj* **1** having a pleasantly spicy taste: *a piquant wild mushroom sauce* THESAURUS TASTE **2** interesting and exciting —**piquantly** *adv* —**piquancy** *n* [U]: *The production retains its original piquancy.*

pique[1] /piːk/ *n* [U] **1** a feeling of being annoyed or upset, especially because someone has ignored you or insulted you: *He stormed out* ***in a fit of pique****.* **2** (*also* **piqué**) a type of material made of cotton, silk, or RAYON

pique[2] *v* **1** [T] to make someone feel annoyed or upset, especially by ignoring them or making them look stupid: *Privately, Zarich was piqued that his offer was rejected.* **2 pique your interest/curiosity** *especially AmE* to make you feel interested in something or someone: *She was hostile to him, which piqued his curiosity.*

pi·ra·cy /ˈpaɪərəsi $ ˈpaɪrə-/ *n* [U] **1** the crime of illegally copying and selling books, tapes, videos, computer programs etc → **pirate**: *software piracy* **2** the crime of attacking and stealing from ships at sea **3** the crime of making illegal television or radio broadcasts

pi·ra·nha /pəˈrɑːnə $ -ˈrɑːnjə, -ˈrænə/ *n* [C] a South American fish with sharp teeth that lives in rivers and eats flesh

pi·rate[1] /ˈpaɪərət $ ˈpaɪrət/ ●○○ *n* [C]

1 someone who sails on the seas, attacking other boats and stealing things from them → **piracy**

2 someone who dishonestly copies and sells another person's work → **piracy**: *Computer game pirates cost the industry twenty million pounds a year.* | **pirate videos/CDs/software etc**

3 pirate radio/TV (station) illegal radio or television broadcasts, or the station sending them out —**piratical** /paɪˈrætɪkəl, pə-/ *adj literary*

pirate[2] *v* [T] to illegally copy and sell another person's work such as a book, DVD, or computer program: *pirated copies of the best-selling computer games* THESAURUS COPY

pir·ou·ette /ˌpɪruˈet/ *n* [C] a dance movement in which the dancer turns very quickly, standing on one toe or the front part of one foot —**pirouette** *v* [I]

pis·ca·to·ri·al /ˌpɪskəˈtɔːriəl◂/ *adj formal* relating to fishing or people who go fishing

Pis·ces /ˈpaɪsiːz/ *n* **1** [U] the 12th sign of the ZODIAC, represented by two fish, which some people believe affects the character and life of people born between February 20 and March 20 **2** [C] (*also* **Piscean**) someone who was born between February 20 and March 20 —**Piscean** /ˈpaɪsiən, paɪˈsiːən/ *adj*

piss[1] /pɪs/ *v* [I] *spoken not polite* **1** to URINATE **2 piss in the wind** to waste time or effort trying to do something that is impossible **3 it is pissing down (with rain)** *BrE* used to say that it is raining very heavily **4 piss yourself (laughing)** *BrE* to laugh a lot, especially when you cannot stop laughing: *They were all copying my accent and pissing themselves laughing.* **5 piss all over sb** *BrE* to thoroughly defeat a person or a team **6 not have a pot to piss in** to be extremely poor **7 go piss up a rope!** *AmE* used to tell someone to go away

piss about/around *phr v BrE spoken not polite* **1** to waste time doing stupid things with no purpose or plan SYN **mess about/around**: *Stop pissing about and get some work done!* **2 piss sb about/around** to treat someone badly by not doing what you have promised to do, or by not being honest with them SYN **mess sb about/around**: *I wish he'd say yes or no – he's been pissing me around for weeks.*

piss sth ↔ **away** *phr v spoken not polite* to waste something in a very stupid way: *I was earning quite a lot but I pissed it all away.*

piss off *phr v spoken not polite* **1 piss sb ↔ off** to annoy someone very much: *The way she treats me really pisses* me off. **2** *BrE* to go away – used especially to tell someone to go away: *Now piss off and leave me alone!* | *He pissed off before we got there.* **3** *BrE* used to say no or to refuse to do something

piss² *n spoken not polite* **1** [singular] an act of URINATING: **go for/have/take a piss** *I need to have a piss.* **2** [U] URINE **3 take the piss (out of sb/sth)** *BrE* to annoy someone by laughing at them or making them seem stupid → **piss-take**: *The kids always take the piss out of some teachers.* **4 be on the piss** *BrE* to be at a PUB or club, drinking a lot of alcohol: *'Where's Jo?' 'Out on the piss somewhere.'* **5 be full of piss and vinegar** *AmE* to be full of energy → **be a piece of piss** at PIECE¹(15)

'piss-ant, **piss·ant** /ˈpɪsænt/ *n* [C] *AmE informal not polite* an offensive word for an annoying person with a weak character

'piss ˌartist *n* [C] *BrE informal not polite* a very offensive word for someone who drinks a lot of alcohol

pissed /pɪst/ *adj* [not before noun] *informal not polite* **1** *BrE* drunk: *They rolled in pissed at three in the morning.* | **pissed as a newt/pissed out of your head** (=extremely drunk) **2** *AmE* PISSED OFF

ˌpissed 'off (*also* **pissed** *AmE*) *adj* [not before noun] *informal not polite* annoyed, disappointed, or unhappy: *You* **get** *really* **pissed off** *applying for jobs all the time.* | **[+with/at]** *I was pissed off with the way some people were behaving.* | *Judy's pissed at Carol.*

pis·ser /ˈpɪsə $ -ər/ *n* [C] *informal not polite* an offensive word for a difficult job or activity, or a bad or annoying situation: *The real pisser was investing so much time and effort for zero return.*

piss·head /ˈpɪshed/ *n* [C] *BrE informal not polite* a very offensive word for someone who drinks a lot of alcohol

ˌpiss-'poor *adj informal not polite* very bad in quality: *All the local beers were piss-poor imitations.*

'piss-take *n* [C usually singular] *BrE informal not polite* something you do to make people laugh at someone, especially by copying them in a funny way SYN **spoof**: *The record is a piss-take of people who have a high opinion of themselves.* → **take the piss out of sb/sth** at PISS²(3)

'piss-up *n* [C] *BrE informal not polite* an occasion when people drink a lot of alcohol together: *We had a good piss-up on my birthday.*

pis·sy /ˈpɪsi/ *adj* [not before noun] *informal not polite* **1** angry or annoyed and treating people badly: *Stacey gets pissy if we tease her.* **2** small or unimportant and annoying

pis·ta·chi·o /pəˈstɑːʃiəʊ $ pəˈstæʃioʊ/ *n* (*plural* **pistachios**) [C] a small green nut: *pistachio ice cream* → see picture at NUT¹

piste /piːst/ *n* [C] *BrE* **1** a snow-covered slope which has been prepared for people to SKI down → **OFF-PISTE** **2 across the piste** in all parts of an organization, system, activity etc SYN **across the board**: *We will be making changes across the piste.*

pis·til /ˈpɪstl/ *n* [C] *technical* the female part of a flower that produces seeds → **stamen**

pis·tol /ˈpɪstl/ ●●○ *n* [C] a small gun you can use with one hand → **handgun**, **revolver**

'pistol-whip *v* (**pistol-whipped**, **pistol-whipping**) [T] to hit someone many times with a pistol

pis·ton /ˈpɪstən/ *n* [C] a part of an engine consisting of a short solid piece of metal inside a tube, which moves up and down to make the other parts of the engine move

'piston ring *n* [C] a circular metal spring used to stop gas or liquid escaping from between a piston and the tube that it moves in

pit¹ /pɪt/ ●●○ *n* [C]

1 HOLE **a)** a hole in the ground, especially one made by digging: *The female* **digs** *a* **pit** *in which to lay the eggs.* | *a five-foot deep pit* → **SANDPIT** **b)** a large hole in the ground from which stones or minerals are obtained by digging: **gravel/sand/chalk pit**

2 MINE *especially BrE* a coal mine: *Dad first* **went down** *the* **pit** (=worked in a coal mine) *when he was 15 years old.* | *a national strike against* **pit closures**

3 MARK a small hollow mark in the surface of something, especially on your skin as the result of a disease: *the deep pits left by smallpox*

4 UNTIDY PLACE [usually singular] *informal* a house or room that is dirty, untidy, or in bad condition

5 be the pits *informal* to be extremely bad: *The company refused to pay – I think it's the pits.*

6 in/at the pit of your stomach if you have a feeling in the pit of your stomach, you have a sick or tight feeling in your stomach, usually because you are nervous or afraid: *I had a feeling in the pit of my stomach that something terrible was going to happen.*

7 CAR RACING **the pits** the place beside the track in a car race where cars can come in for petrol, new tyres etc → **PIT STOP**

8 IN A THEATRE an ORCHESTRA PIT

9 IN A GARAGE a hole in the floor of a garage that lets you get under a car to repair it: *an* ***inspection pit***

10 a/the pit of sth *literary* a situation which makes you feel very bad: *Just thinking about the future plunged her into* ***a pit of despair***.

11 IN FRUIT *especially AmE* the single large hard seed in some fruits SYN **stone** *BrE*: *a peach pit* → see picture at **FRUIT¹**

12 BODY PART *informal* an ARMPIT

13 BUSINESS *AmE* the area of a STOCK EXCHANGE where people buy and sell shares SYN **floor** *BrE*

pit² *v* (**pitted**, **pitting**) **1** [T] to put small marks or holes in the surface of something: **be pitted with sth** *The whole street was pitted with potholes.* GRAMMAR **Pit** is usually passive in this meaning. **2** [T] *especially AmE* to take out the single hard seed inside some fruits SYN **stone**: *Peel and pit two avocados.* **3** [I] *AmE* to stop in a car race to get petrol or have your car repaired → **PITTED**

pit sb/sth **against** sb/sth *phr v* to test someone's strength, ability, power etc in a competition or fight against someone or something else: *We'll be pitting our team against the champions.* | **pit your wits against sb** (=compete against someone using your intelligence or knowledge) *Pit your wits against family or friends!* | **pit yourself against sth/sb** *The men had to pit themselves against the forces of nature.*

pit out *phr v AmE informal* to SWEAT so much that your clothes become wet under your arms

pit·a bread /ˈpɪtə bred $ ˈpiː-/ *n* [C,U] the American spelling of PITTA BREAD → see picture at **BREAD**

'pit-a-ˌpat *adv informal* PITTER-PATTER

ˌpit bull 'terrier (*also* **'pit bull**) *n* [C] a small but extremely strong and sometimes violent fighting dog

pitch¹ /pɪtʃ/ ●●○ S3 W3 *n*

1 SPORTS FIELD [C] *BrE* a marked out area of ground on which a sport is played SYN **field**: **football/cricket/rugby etc pitch** *the world-famous Wembley football pitch* | *He ran the length of the pitch and scored.* | **on the pitch** (=playing a sport) *Jack was on the pitch for his school in the Senior Cup Final.*

2 STRONG FEELINGS/ACTIVITY [singular, U] a strong level of feeling about something or a high level of an activity or a quality: *The controversy* **reached** *such a* **pitch** (=become so strong) *that the paper devoted a whole page to it.* | **a pitch of excitement/excellence/perfection etc** (=a high level of excitement etc) *He screamed at her in a pitch of fury.* | *The goal roused the crowd to* **fever pitch** (=a very excited level).

3 MUSIC **a)** [singular, U] how high or low a note or other sound is: *Ultrasonic waves are at a higher pitch than the human ear can hear.* **b)** [U] the ability of a musician to play or sing a note at exactly the correct level: *She's got* ***perfect pitch***.

4 PERSUADING [C] *informal* the things someone says to persuade people to buy something, do something, or accept an idea: *an aggressive salesman with a fast-talking* ***sales pitch*** | **make a/sb's pitch (for sth)** (=try to persuade people to do something) *He made his strongest pitch yet for standardized testing in schools.*

P

5 BASEBALL [C] a throw of the ball, or a way in which it can be thrown: *His first pitch was high and wide.* → see picture at BASEBALL
6 BLACK SUBSTANCE [U] a black sticky substance that is used on roofs, the bottoms of ships etc to stop water coming through: *The night was **as black as pitch*** (=very dark). → PITCH-BLACK, PITCH-DARK
7 SHIP/AIRCRAFT [U] an up and down movement of a ship or an aircraft → **roll**: *the **pitch and roll** of the ship*
8 SLOPE [singular, U] the degree to which a roof slopes or the sloping part of a roof: *the steep pitch of the roof*
9 STREET/MARKET [C] *BrE* a place in a public area where someone goes to sell things or where an entertainer goes to perform: *We found the boy at his usual pitch at the bottom of the Acropolis.* → **queer sb's pitch/queer the pitch for sb** at QUEER[3]

P

pitch² ●○○ *v*
1 THROW [T always + adv/prep] to throw something with a lot of force, often aiming carefully: *She crumpled up the page and pitched it into the fire.* THESAURUS ▸ THROW
2 BALL GAMES **a)** [I,T] to aim and throw a ball in baseball: **[+to]** *Stanton pitched to two batters in the ninth inning.* **b)** [I] if a ball pitches in CRICKET or golf, it hits the ground **c)** [T] to hit the ball in a high curve in golf **d)** [T] to make the ball hit the ground when you are BOWLing in CRICKET → see picture at BASEBALL
3 FALL [I,T always + adv/prep] to fall or be moved suddenly in a particular direction, or to make someone or something do this: **pitch (sb/sth) forward/backward/over etc** *She slipped and pitched forward onto the ground.* | **pitch sb/sth into/onto/through etc sth** *Without a seat belt, you can easily be pitched right through the windscreen.*
4 SHIP/PLANE [I] if a ship or an aircraft pitches, it moves up and down in an uncontrolled way with the movement of the water or air → ROLL²(4), → YAW
5 SET A LEVEL [T] **a)** to set a speech, examination, explanation etc at a particular level of difficulty: **pitch sth at a high level/the right level etc** *You have to pitch your writing at the right level.* | *Some questions were pitched too high for intermediate students.* **b)** *BrE* to set prices at a particular level: **be pitched at sth** *Room rates are pitched at £69 for a single.* GRAMMAR **Pitch** is often passive in this meaning.
6 AIM PRODUCT [T] to aim a product at a particular type of organization, group of people etc, or to describe it in a particular way, in order to sell it: **be pitched at sb/sth** *The new machine will be pitched at users in the hotel and air reservation business.* | **be pitched as sth** *It is pitched as a cheaper alternative to other workstations.*
7 BUSINESS DEALS [I,T] *informal* to try to persuade someone to do business with you, buy something etc: **pitch for business/contracts/custom etc** *Booksellers are keen to pitch for school business.* | **[+to]** *For many companies, pitching to investors has become almost a full-time job.* | *sales reps pitching new gadgets*
8 VOICE/MUSIC [T always + adv/prep] if you pitch your voice or another sound at a particular level, the sound is produced at that level: **pitch sth high/low etc** *Her voice is pitched a little too high.* → HIGH-PITCHED, LOW-PITCHED
9 **pitch a tent/pitch camp** to set up a tent or a camp for a short time: *Try and pitch your tent on level ground.*
10 SLOPE [I always + adv/prep] to slope down: **pitch gently/steeply etc** *The roof pitches sharply to the rear of the house.* → PITCHED
11 **pitch sb a line** *AmE informal* to tell someone a story or give them an excuse that is difficult to believe: *She pitched me some line about a bomb scare on the metro.*

pitch in *phr v informal*
1 to join others and help with an activity: *If we all pitch in, we'll have it finished in no time.* | **[+with]** *Everyone pitched in with efforts to entertain the children.*
2 to join others and pay part of the money towards something: *They all pitched in and the money was collected within a few days.*
3 *BrE* to start to eat hungrily: *Pitch in – there's plenty.*

pitch into sb/sth *phr v BrE informal*
1 to suddenly start criticizing someone or hitting them: *She pitched into me as soon as I started to speak.*
2 to start doing something, especially quickly and eagerly: *Rick pitched into decorating the house at once.*

pitch up *phr v BrE spoken* to arrive somewhere SYN **turn up**: *Wait a bit longer – Bill hasn't pitched up yet.*

ˌpitch-and-ˈputt *n* [U] *BrE* a game of golf played on a very small course

ˌpitch-ˈblack *adj* completely black or dark: *The lights were off and it was pitch-black.* —**pitch-black** *n* [U]

pitch·blende /ˈpɪtʃblend/ *n* [U] a dark shiny substance dug from the earth, from which URANIUM and RADIUM are obtained

ˌpitch-ˈdark *adj* completely dark: *Outside it was pitch-dark and pouring with rain.* THESAURUS ▸ DARK

pitched /pɪtʃt/ *adj* a pitched roof is sloping rather than flat

ˌpitched ˈbattle *n* [C] **1** a big battle between armies or large groups of people: *a pitched battle between the rival groups* **2** an angry and usually long argument: *She wanted to avoid another pitched battle with her son.* → SKIRMISH

pitch·er /ˈpɪtʃə $ -ər/ *n* [C] **1** the player in baseball who throws the ball → see picture at BASEBALL **2** *AmE* a container for holding and pouring a liquid, with a handle and a shaped part to help the liquid flow out SYN **jug** *BrE*: *a pitcher of water* **3** *BrE* a large clay container with two handles, used in the past for holding and pouring a liquid

pitch·fork¹ /ˈpɪtʃfɔːk $ -fɔːrk/ *n* [C] a farm tool with a long handle and two long curved metal points, used especially for lifting HAY (=dried grass)

pitchfork² *v* [T] *BrE* to put someone suddenly into a situation for which they are not properly prepared: **pitchfork sb into sth** *She was pitchforked into power by the early death of her husband James V.*

pitch·out /ˈpɪtʃaʊt/ *n* [C] a ball in baseball that the PITCHER deliberately throws too far to the side for it to be hit

ˈpitch pine *n* [C,U] a type of PINE tree that grows in North America, or the wood from this tree

pit·e·ous /ˈpɪtiəs/ *adj literary* expressing suffering and sadness in a way that makes you feel pity: *She gave a long piteous cry.* —**piteously** *adv*

pit·fall /ˈpɪtfɔːl $ -fɒːl/ *n* [C usually plural] a problem or difficulty that is likely to happen in a particular job, course of action, or activity: **[+of]** *He gave me advice on how to **avoid** the **pitfalls** of the legal process.* | *the pitfalls associated with the purchase of a used car*

pith /pɪθ/ *n* [U] **1** a white substance just under the outside skin of oranges and similar fruit: *Peel the oranges with a sharp knife to remove all pith.* **2** a soft white substance that fills the stems of some plants

pit·head /ˈpɪt-hed/ *n* [C] *BrE* the entrance to a coal mine and the buildings around it

ˌpith ˈhelmet *n* [C] a large light hat worn especially in the past in hot countries, to protect your head from the sun

pith·y /ˈpɪθi/ *adj* if something that is said or written is pithy, it is intelligent and strongly stated, without wasting any words OPP **long-winded**: *Press releases must be short and pithy.* | *a series of pithy quotations* —**pithily** *adv*

pit·i·a·ble /ˈpɪtiəbəl/ *adj formal* making you feel pity: *the pitiable victims of war* —**pitiably** *adv*

pit·i·ful /ˈpɪtɪfəl/ *adj* **1** someone who is pitiful looks or sounds so sad and unfortunate that you feel very sorry for them → **pity**: *The refugees were a **pitiful sight**.* **2** a pitiful amount is very small: *The fee was pitiful – only about £60.* **3** very bad in quality SYN **awful**: *His performance was pitiful – five goals flew past him.* —**pitifully** *adv*: *The dog was pitifully thin.*

pit·i·less /ˈpɪtɪləs/ *adj* **1** showing no pity and not caring if people suffer SYN **cruel**: *a pitiless tyrant* | *the pitiless bombing of Guernica* **2** *literary* pitiless wind, rain, or sun is very severe and shows no sign of changing: *a night of pitiless rain* —**pitilessly** *adv*

pi·ton /ˈpiːtɒn $ -tɑːn/ *n* [C] a piece of metal used in

ROCK CLIMBING that you attach onto a rock to hold the rope → **crampon**

ˈpit ˌpony *n* [C] a small horse that was used in the past for moving coal in a mine in Britain

ˈpit stop *n* [C] **1** a time when a driver in a car race stops in the PITS to get more petrol or have repairs done **2 make a pit stop** *AmE informal* to stop when driving on a long journey, for food, petrol, or to go to the toilet

pit·ta bread *BrE*, **pita bread** *AmE* /ˈpɪtə bred $ ˈpiːtə-/ *n* [C,U] a type of bread which is flat and hollow. It can be cut open and filled with food. → see picture at BREAD

pit·tance /ˈpɪtəns/ *n* [singular] a very small amount of money, especially wages, that is less than someone needs or deserves OPP **fortune**: **earn/be paid a pittance** *The musicians earn a pittance.* | **work/be sold for a pittance** *The crop was sold for a pittance.* | *She raised three children on a pittance.*

pit·ted /ˈpɪtɪd/ *adj* **1** covered with small marks or holes on the surface: *a red-faced man with pitted cheeks* | **[+with]** *The desert roads are pitted with potholes.* **2** a pitted fruit has had the single hard seed removed from it: *pitted olives*

pit·ter-pat·ter /ˈpɪtə ˌpætə $ ˈpɪtər ˌpætər/ *adv literary* with quick light beats or steps: *Anna's heart **went pitter-patter** as she opened the letter.* —**pitter-patter** *n* [singular]: *the pitter-patter of small feet running up the stairs*

pi·tu·i·ta·ry /pəˈtjuːətəri $ -ˈtuːəteri/ (*also* **piˈtuitary ˌgland**) *n* (*plural* **pituitaries**) [C] the small organ at the base of your brain which produces HORMONES that control the growth and development of your body —**pituitary** *adj*

pit·y¹ /ˈpɪti/ ●●○ S3 *n*

1 a pity *spoken* used to show that you are disappointed about something and you wish things could happen differently SYN **shame**: **(it's a) pity (that)** *It's a pity that he didn't accept the job.* | *It's a **great pity** Joyce wasn't invited.* | *I like Charlie. Pity he had to marry that awful woman.* | *A pity we can't find the guy who did it.* | **what/that's a pity** *'Are you married?' 'No.' 'What a pity.'* | **it's a pity to do sth** *It would be a pity to give up now – you've nearly finished.*

2 [U] sympathy for a person or animal who is suffering or unhappy → **piteous**, **pitiable**, **pitiful**, **pitiless**: **[+for]** *He looked exhausted, but Marie felt no pity for him.* | *I listened to Jason's story with pity.* | *I hated the thought of being an **object of pity*** (=someone who other people feel sorry for). | **take/have pity on sb** (=feel sorry for someone and treat them with sympathy) *He sounded so upset that Leah started to take pity on him.*

3 for pity's sake *BrE spoken* used to show that you are very annoyed and impatient: *For pity's sake just shut up and let me drive!*

4 more's the pity *spoken especially BrE* used after describing a situation, to show that you wish it was not true: *Sue's not coming, more's the pity.*

pity² ●●○ *v* (**pitied**, **pitying**, **pities**) [T not usually in progressive] to feel sorry for someone because they are in a very bad situation: *I pity anyone who has to feed a family on such a low income.* | *Sam pitied his grandmother there alone, never going out.* | *Pity the poor teachers who have to deal with these kids.*

> **REGISTER**
> In everyday English, people usually say that they **feel sorry for** someone rather than **pity** them: *I **feel sorry for** his wife.*

pit·y·ing /ˈpɪtiɪŋ/ *adj* **pitying look/smile/glance** a look or smile that shows you feel pity for someone → **sympathetic**: *Ellen gave me a pitying look.*

piv·ot¹ /ˈpɪvət/ *n* [C] **1** a central point or pin on which something balances or turns **2** [usually singular] (*also* **pivot point**) the most important thing in a situation, system etc, which other things depend on or are based on: **the pivot on/around which sth turns/revolves** *Iago's lie is the pivot on which the play turns.* | **[+of]** *West Africa was the pivot of the chocolate trade.*

pivot² *v* **1** [I,T] to turn or balance on a central point, or to make something do this: **[+on]** *The table-top pivots on two metal pins.* **2** [I] to turn quickly on your feet so that you face in the opposite direction: *Magee pivoted and threw the ball to first base.*

pivot on/around sth *phr v* to depend on or be based on one important thing, event, or idea: *His argument will pivot on the growing cost of legal fees.*

piv·ot·al /ˈpɪvətəl/ *adj* more important than anything else in a situation, system etc SYN **key**: *The Bank of England has a **pivotal role** in the London money market.* | **[+to]** *The talks are pivotal to the success of the country.*

pix /pɪks/ *n* [plural] *informal* pictures or photographs

pix·el /ˈpɪksəl/ *n* [C] *technical* the smallest unit of an image on a computer screen

pix·e·lat·ed, **pixellated** /ˈpɪksɪleɪtɪd/ *adj technical* consisting of pixels, especially large pixels that produce an unclear image: *pixelated photographs* —**pixelate** *v* [T]: *Their faces had been pixelated to hide their identities.*

pix·ie, **pixy** /ˈpɪksi/ *n* [C] an imaginary creature that looks like a very small human being, has magical powers, and likes to play tricks on people

piz·za /ˈpiːtsə/ ●●● S2 *n* [C,U] a food made of thin flat round bread, baked with tomato, cheese, and sometimes vegetables or meat on top → **pizzeria**: *a slice of pizza*

ˈpizza ˌparlor *n* [C] *AmE* a restaurant that serves pizza SYN **pizzeria**

piz·zazz /pəˈzæz/ *n* [U] *informal* something that has pizzazz is exciting and has a strong interesting style: *Their new album has plenty of pizzazz.*

piz·ze·ri·a /ˌpiːtsəˈriːə/ *n* [C] a restaurant that serves pizza

piz·zi·ca·to /ˌpɪtsɪˈkɑːtəʊ $ -toʊ/ *n* [U] musical notes played by pulling on the strings of an instrument —**pizzicato** *adv, adj*

pj's, **PJ's** /ˌpiː ˈdʒeɪz/ *n* [plural] *informal* the abbreviation of ***pyjamas***

Pk *BrE*, **Pk.** *AmE* the written abbreviation of ***park***

pkg. *AmE* the written abbreviation of ***package***

pkt the written abbreviation of ***packet***

pl. (*also* **pl** *BrE*) the written abbreviation of ***plural***

Pl. (*also* **Pl** *BrE*) the written abbreviation of ***Place***, used in addresses: *3 Palmerston Pl., Edinburgh*

plac·ard /ˈplækɑːd $ -ərd/ *n* [C] a large notice or advertisement on a piece of card, which is put up or carried in a public place: *a huge placard saying 'Welcome to Derbyville'* → see picture at SIGN¹

pla·cate /pləˈkeɪt $ ˈpleɪkeɪt/ *v* [T] *formal* to make someone stop feeling angry SYN **appease** OPP **rile**: *These changes did little to placate the unions.* —**placatory** /pləˈkeɪtəri, ˈplækətəri $ ˈpleɪkətɔːri/ *adj*: *a placatory smile*

place¹ /pleɪs/ ●●● S1 W1 *n* [C]

1 AREA/SPACE/BUILDING ETC a space or area, for example a particular point on a surface or in a room, building, town, city etc: *Make sure you keep the key in a safe place.* | *I've spent the day dashing about from place to place.* | *The place was full of screaming children.* | *He was threatening to burn the place down.* | *She had never been back to the place where the accident happened.* | *The theatre bar was our usual meeting place.* | *We were living then in a place called Alberiga.* | *The wall was quite damp **in places*** (=in some places). | **[+for]** *This is a great place for a holiday.* | **a place to do sth** *I couldn't find a place to park.* | *Did the accident happen at your **place of work*** (=the place where you work)? | *The Great Mosque has been a **place of worship** for Muslims for centuries.*

2 HOME *informal* a house or apartment where someone lives: *They've got quite a big place on the outskirts of Leeds.* | **sb's place** *Do you want to come back to my place for coffee?* | *It took us ages to find a **place to live**.* | *He's staying with us until he can find a **place of** his **own**.* **THESAURUS** ▸ HOME

3 take place to happen, especially after being planned or arranged: *The next meeting will take place on Thursday.* | *Talks between the two sides are still taking place.* | *Major changes are taking place in society.*

4 SPACE TO SIT OR PUT STH a space where someone can

sit, or a space where you can put something: *I might arrive a bit late, so could you save me a place?* | *There are still a few places left on the coach.* | *Make sure you put everything back in its proper place.* | **[+for]** *Can you find a good place for this vase?*

5 POINT IN BOOK/SPEECH a point that you have reached in a book or a speech: *This would be a good place to stop and answer any questions that people have.* | *I used a bookmark so that I wouldn't* ***lose*** *my* ***place*** (=forget the point that I had reached).

6 OPPORTUNITY TO DO STH if someone has a place somewhere, they have the opportunity to go there or join in an activity: **[+in]** *If you don't come to training you might lose your place in the team.* | *We've been trying to find her a place in a residential home.* | **[+on]** *He was offered a place on the management committee.* | *There are still a couple of places left on the course.* | **[+at]** *I've been offered a place at York University.*

7 ROLE/POSITION the ROLE or important position that someone or something has in a situation or in society: **sb's place** *the old idea that a woman's place is in the home* | **[+in]** *He finally reached the summit of Everest and secured his place in history.* | *Working has a very important place in all our lives.*

8 in place a) in the correct position: *The chairs for the concert were nearly all in place.* | *The glass was* ***held in place*** *by a few pieces of sellotape.* **b)** existing and ready to be used: *Funding arrangements are already in place.*

9 in place of sb/sth (*also* **in sb's/sth's place**) instead of someone or something else: *In place of our advertised programme, we will have live coverage of the special memorial service.* | *The company flag had been taken down and in its place hung the Union Jack.* | *If I refused to go, they would send someone else in my place.*

10 take the place of sb/sth (*also* **take sb's/sth's place**) to exist or be used instead of someone or something else SYN **replace**: *Natural methods of pest control are now taking the place of chemicals.* | *I had to find someone to take Jenny's place.*

11 in sb's place used to talk about what you would do if you were in someone else's situation: *What would you do in my place?* | *Try to* **put yourself in** *my* **place** *and think how you would feel.*

12 be no place for sb to be a completely unsuitable place for someone: *This is no place for a child.*

13 first/second/third etc place first, second etc position in a race or competition: *He* ***took*** *second* ***place*** *in the long jump.* | **in first/second etc place** *I* ***finished in*** *third* ***place***.

14 in the first place a) used to introduce a series of points in an argument, discussion etc: *In the first place, I'm too busy, and in the second I don't really want to go.* **b)** used to talk about what someone did or should have done at the start of a situation: *I wish I'd never got involved in the first place!*

15 take second place (to sb/sth) to be less important than someone or something else: *She wasn't prepared to take second place in his life.*

16 take your places used to tell people to go to the correct place or position that they need to be in for an activity: *If you would like to take your places, the food will be served shortly.*

17 all over the place *informal* **a)** everywhere: *There was blood all over the place.* **b)** in a very untidy state: *She came in with her hair all over the place.*

18 put sb in their place to show someone that they are not as clever or important as they think they are: *I soon put him in his place.*

19 out of place a) not suitable for a particular situation or occasion: *He never seemed to feel out of place at social functions.* | *The paintings looked strangely out of place.* **b)** not in the correct or usual position: *The kitchen was spotlessly clean, with nothing out of place.*

20 it is not sb's place (to do sth) if it is not your place to do something, you do not have the duty or right to do it: *It's not your place to criticize me!*

21 have no place *formal* to be completely unacceptable: **[+in]** *Capital punishment has no place in a modern society.*

22 fall into place a) if things fall into place in your mind, you suddenly realize and understand what is really happening: *Things were beginning to fall into place in my mind.* | *Everything suddenly fell into place.* **b)** if plans or events fall into place, they start to happen in the way that you hoped they would: *Eventually I got a job, and my life began to fall into place.*

23 be going places *informal* to start becoming successful in your life: *William is a young man who is definitely going places.*

24 be in a good/bad etc place *AmE informal* to be in a good, bad etc situation → **a/my/your etc happy place** at HAPPY(10), → **have/take pride of place** at PRIDE[1](6)

USAGE: Place, space

- You use **place** when talking about a particular position or location. **Place** is always countable. You say: *We visited some beautiful places.* | *I found a place to put my boots.* ✗ Don't say: *I found some place to put my boots.*
- You use **space** about the area that is available for doing something. In this meaning, **space** is uncountable. You say: *We don't have enough space for a washing machine.* ✗ Don't say: *We don't have enough place for a washing machine.* You say: *The children need more space to play.* ✗ Don't say: *The children need more place to play.*
- You also use **space** about an area that you can use for doing something. In this meaning, **space** is countable: *There are very few parking spaces left.* | *I found a space at the back of the bus.*
- **Someplace** means 'somewhere' and is used especially in American English: *I can't find my keys - I must have left them someplace.*

THESAURUS

place a point or area, especially one that you visit or use for a particular purpose: *He's been to lots of places.* | *a good meeting place*

position the exact place where someone or something is, in relation to other things: *She showed me the position of the village on the map.* | *I changed the position of the mirror slightly.*

point a particular place on a line or surface: *At this point the path gets narrower.* | *No cars are allowed beyond this point.*

spot a place, especially a particular kind of place, or a place where something happens. **Spot** sounds rather informal: *She chose a sunny spot.* | *The area is a favourite spot for windsurfers.*

location a place where someone or something is, or where something happens. **Location** sounds more formal than **place**: *your exact location* | *The prisoners were taken to an undisclosed location.*

site a place, especially one that will be used for a particular purpose, or where something important happened: *the site of a great battle* | *There are plans to develop the site for housing.*

venue a place where something such as a meeting, concert, game etc takes place: *the venue for the next Olympic Games* | *The hotel is a popular wedding venue.*

scene the place where something bad such as an accident or crime happened: *the scene of the crime* | *Ambulance crews were at the scene within minutes.*

setting the place and the area around it, where something is or where something happens: *The hotel is in a beautiful setting.* | *the setting for the film 'A Room With a View'*

whereabouts the place where someone or something is - used especially when you do not know this or do not want to tell people: *The whereabouts of the painting is unknown.* | *He refused to disclose his whereabouts.*

place[2] ●●○ S3 W2 *v*

1 POSITION [T always + adv/prep] to put something somewhere, especially with care SYN **put**: *She poured the doctor* *a cup of tea and placed it on the table.* | *He carefully placed the folder back in his desk drawer.* THESAURUS PUT

2 SITUATION [T always + adv/prep] to put someone or something in a particular situation SYN **put**: *The government is being placed under pressure to give financial help to farmers.* | *Children must not be placed at risk.* | *Some areas of the city have been placed under curfew.* | *This places me in a very difficult position.*

3 IN A JOB/HOME [T] *formal* to find a suitable job or home for someone: *Some unemployed people can be very difficult to place.* | *He was later placed with a foster family.*

4 ARRANGE STH [T] to arrange for something to be done: *He **placed** an **advertisement** in the local paper.* | *You can **place orders** by telephone.* | *I had no idea which horse I should **place** a **bet** on.*

5 HOW GOOD/IMPORTANT [T always + adv/prep] to say how good or important you think someone or something is: *I would place health quite high on my list of priorities.* | **place sb/sth above/before sb/sth** *Some museums seem to place profit above education.*

6 place value/importance/emphasis etc on sth to decide that something is important: *Most people place too much value on money.* | *The company places a lot of emphasis on training.*

7 can't place sb to recognize someone, but be unable to remember where you have met them before: *I've seen her somewhere before, but I can't quite place her.*

8 be well/ideally etc placed a) to be in a good situation where you have the ability or opportunity to do something: **be well/ideally placed to do sth** *The company is now well placed to compete in Europe.* **b)** *BrE* to be in a good place or position: **[+for]** *The hotel is well placed for most of London's theatres.*

9 RACES **be placed first/second etc** to be first, second etc in a race or competition

> REGISTER
> **Place** is slightly formal in most of its meanings. In everyday English, people usually use **put** instead: *She **put** the cup on the table.* | *Innocent people were **put** at risk.* | *They **put** an ad in the paper.*

pla·ce·bo /plə'siːbəʊ $ -boʊ/ *n* (*plural* **placebos**) [C] **1** a harmless substance given to a sick person instead of medicine, without telling them it is not real. Placebos are often used in tests in which some people take real medicine and others take a placebo, so that doctors can compare the results to see if the real medicine works properly. **2 placebo effect** when someone feels better after taking a placebo, even though it has not had any effect on their body

'place card *n* [C] a small card with someone's name on it, which is put on a table to show where they are going to sit

'place kick *n* [C] in RUGBY or AMERICAN FOOTBALL, an occasion when the ball is kicked after it has been placed or held on the ground → see picture at **AMERICAN FOOTBALL**

'place mat *n* [C] a board or piece of cloth that you put on a table for each person who is eating there, so that the table is protected from the plates, knives etc

place·ment /'pleɪsmənt/ ●○○ *n* [C,U]
1 the act of finding a place for someone to live or work: *The centre provides a **job placement** service.* | **[+of]** *the placement of children in foster homes* | *They lived on campus, but this was just a temporary placement.*
2 *BrE* a job, usually as part of a course of study, which gives you experience of a particular type of work: **on placement** *Students are sent out on placement for training.* | *a forty-five day placement in a factory*
3 when something is placed somewhere or when you decide where something should go: **[+of]** *the placement of fire hydrants along the city's streets*

'place name *n* [C] the name of a particular place, such as a town, mountain etc: *Many of the place names are Scottish in origin.*

pla·cen·ta /plə'sentə/ *n* [C] an organ that forms inside a woman's UTERUS to feed an unborn baby —**placental** *adj* [only before noun]: *placental blood*

'place ˌsetting *n* [C] an arrangement on a table of knives, forks, glasses etc to be used by one person

plac·id /'plæsɪd/ *adj* **1** a placid person does not often get angry or upset and does not usually mind doing what other people want them to: *a large, placid baby* | *She sat still, placid and waiting.* **2** calm and peaceful: *The lake was placid and still under the moonlight.* —**placidly** *adv*: *Dobbs stood at the entrance, placidly smoking his pipe.* —**placidity** /plə'sɪdəti/ *n* [U]

plac·ing /'pleɪsɪŋ/ *n* [C] *BrE* the position of someone or something in a competition or ordered list: *Hancock and Smith took the top two placings.*

pla·gia·ris·m /'pleɪdʒərɪzəm/ ●○○ *n*
1 [U] when someone uses another person's words, ideas, or work and pretends they are their own: *The journal accused the professor of plagiarism.*
2 [C] an idea, phrase, or story that has been copied from another person's work, without stating where it came from: *claims that there are plagiarisms in the new software* —**plagiarist** *n* [C]

pla·gia·rize (*also* **-ise** *BrE*) /'pleɪdʒəraɪz/ ●○○ *v* [I,T] to take words or ideas from another person's work and use them in your work, without stating that they are not your own: *He accused other scientists of plagiarizing his research.*

plague¹ /pleɪg/ ●○○ *n*
1 [C] a disease that causes death and spreads quickly to a large number of people: *drops in population levels due to plagues and famines*
2 [U] (*also* **the plague**) a very infectious disease that produces high fever and swollen places on the body, and often leads to death, especially BUBONIC PLAGUE → **Black Death**: *The plague caused 100,000 deaths in London alone in the 1600s.*
3 a plague of rats/locusts etc an uncontrolled and harmful increase in the numbers of a particular animal or insect: *A plague of squirrels is threatening our forests.* → **avoid sb/sth like the plague** at **AVOID(2)**

plague² *v* [T] **1** to cause pain, suffering, or trouble to someone, especially for a long period of time: **be plagued by/with sth** *He was plagued by eye troubles.* | *Financial problems continued to plague the company.* **2** to annoy someone, especially by asking for something many times or asking them many questions: **plague sb with sth** *The kids have been plaguing me with questions.*

plaice /pleɪs/ *n* (*plural* **plaice**) [C,U] a flat sea fish that is eaten

plaid /plæd/ *n* **1** [U] a pattern of crossed lines and squares, used especially on cloth SYN **tartan** *BrE*: *a plaid shirt* → see picture at **PATTERN¹ 2** [C] a piece of plaid cloth worn over the shoulder and across the chest by people from Scotland as part of their NATIONAL COSTUME

plain¹ /pleɪn/ ●●● S2 W3 *adj*
1 CLEAR very clear, and easy to understand or recognize SYN **obvious**: **it is plain (that)** *It was plain that Giles was not going to agree.* | *The advantages were plain to see.* | *You have made your feelings plain enough.* | *Let me **make** it **plain*** (=state it clearly). *We do not want you here.* | **make yourself plain** (=make what you are saying clear) *If you do that again you will be severely punished. Do I make myself plain?* | **as plain as day/the nose on your face** (=very clear)
2 in plain English/language in clear and simple words, without using technical language: *The document, written in plain English, tells you about your new policy.*
3 SIMPLE without anything added or without decoration SYN **simple**: *a plain white blouse* | *a plain wooden table* | *plain yoghurt* | *a plain gold wedding ring* | *Your essay should be written on **plain paper*** (=paper with no lines on it).
4 HONEST showing clearly and honestly what is true or what you think about something SYN **frank**, **candid**: *Let's have some plain, truthful answers.* | *I don't know, and that's **the plain truth**.* | ***The plain fact is** people still buy books.*
5 EMPHASIS [only before noun] *spoken* used to emphasize

that a particular type of behaviour, attitude etc is involved, usually a bad one: *His motive was plain greed.* | *When you told him his house was too cold that was just plain bad manners.*
6 NOT BEAUTIFUL not beautiful or attractive - often used because you want to avoid saying this directly: *Mrs Jones was a rather plain woman.* | **plain Jane** (=used to talk about a woman who is not beautiful)
7 in plain clothes police officers in plain clothes are not wearing uniform → PLAIN-CLOTHES
8 (just) plain Mr/Mrs etc *spoken* used to show that someone does not have or use a special title: *I don't call him Uncle - just plain Bill.*
9 be plain sailing to be very easy to do or achieve: *If you can answer the first question, the rest of the test should be plain sailing.*
10 in plain sight *AmE* if something is in plain sight, it is easy to see or notice, especially when it should be hidden: *Don't leave your valuables in plain sight.* —**plainness** *n* [U]

P

plain² ●●○ *n*
1 (*also* **plains**) [C] a large area of flat dry land → **prairie**: *The grassy plain gave way to an extensive swamp.* | *the vast plains of central China*
2 [U] the ordinary stitch in KNITTING

plain³ *adv informal* used to emphasize an adjective, usually one referring to a bad quality: *It's just plain crazy to spend all your pay as soon as you get it.*

plain·chant /ˈpleɪntʃɑːnt $ -tʃænt/ *n* [U] PLAINSONG

ˌ**plain ˈchocolate** *n* [U] *BrE* chocolate made without milk and with very little sugar SYN **dark chocolate**

ˌ**plain-ˈclothes** *adj* [only before noun] plain-clothes police are police who wear ordinary clothes so that they can work without being recognized

ˌ**plain ˈflour** *n* [U] *BrE* flour that contains no BAKING POWDER → **self-raising flour**

plain·ly /ˈpleɪnli/ ●○○ *adv*
1 in a way that is easy to understand or recognize: *Mrs Gorman was plainly delighted.* | *The first part of that argument is plainly true.* | *We could hear Tom's voice plainly over the noise of the crowd.* | [sentence adverb] *Plainly the laws are not effective.*
2 speaking honestly, and without trying to hide the truth: *She told him plainly that she had no intention of marrying him.*
3 simply or without decoration: *a plainly dressed young girl* | *The room was very plainly furnished.*

plain·song /ˈpleɪnsɒŋ $ -sɒːŋ/ (*also* **plainchant**) *n* [U] a type of old Christian church music in which people sing a simple tune without musical instruments

plain·spo·ken /ˌpleɪnˈspəʊkən◂ $ -ˈspoʊ-/ *adj* saying exactly what you think, especially in a way that people think is honest rather than rude: *a straightforward, plain-spoken man*

plain·tiff /ˈpleɪntɪf/ *n* [C] someone who brings a legal action against another person in a court of law SYN **complainant** *BrE* → **defendant**

plain·tive /ˈpleɪntɪv/ *adj* a plaintive sound is high, like someone crying, and sounds sad: **plaintive cry/voice/sound etc** *the plaintive cry of the seagull* —**plaintively** *adv*

plait¹ /plæt $ pleɪt, plæt/ *v* [T] *BrE* to twist three long pieces of hair or rope over and under each other to make one long piece SYN **braid** *AmE*: *She plaited her hair hurriedly.* | *a plaited leather belt*

plait² *n* [C] *BrE* a length of something, usually hair, that has been plaited SYN **braid** *AmE*: **in plaits** *Jenni wore her hair in plaits.* → see picture at **HAIRSTYLE**

plan¹ /plæn/ ●●● S1 W1 *n* [C]
1 INTENTION something you have decided to do: *His plan is to get a degree in economics and then work abroad for a year.* | *Do you* ***have*** *any* ***plans*** *for the weekend?* | *There's been a* ***change of plan*** *- we're not going to Ibiza after all.* | **the best plan** *BrE* (=the best course of action) *Your best plan would be to take a taxi.*
2 METHOD/ARRANGEMENT a set of actions for achieving something in the future, especially a set of actions that has been considered carefully and in detail: **[+for]** *The chairman outlined the company's plans for achieving a 10% growth in sales.* | **plan to do sth** *There are plans to turn the site of the factory into a park.*
3 MAP a drawing similar to a map, showing roads, towns, and buildings: **[+of]** *a street plan of London*
4 DRAWING **a)** *technical* a drawing of a building, room, or machine as it would be seen from above, showing the shape, size, and position of the walls, windows, and doors → ELEVATION(4), SECTION¹(7), GROUND PLAN(1) **b)** a drawing that shows exactly how something will be arranged: *I have to organise a* ***seating plan*** *for the dinner.*
5 plan A, Plan A your first plan, which you will use if things happen the way you expect: *We're going to find a restaurant and buy a meal. That's Plan A.*
6 plan B, Plan B your second plan, which you can use if things do not happen the way you expect: *It's time to put Plan B into action.*

COLLOCATIONS - MEANING 2

VERBS

have a plan *Don't worry - I have a plan.*
make plans (=prepare for something) *Mary has been busy making plans for her wedding.*
come up with a plan (=think of a plan) *The chairman must come up with a plan to get the club back on its feet.*
carry out a plan (=do what has been planned) *The bombers were arrested by the security forces before they could carry out their plans.*
keep to/stick to a plan *We're sticking to our original plan.*
abandon/scrap a plan (=decide not to continue with it) *The plan was scrapped because it was too expensive.*
announce/unveil a plan (=officially tell people about it) | **approve a plan** | **reject a plan** | **outline a plan** (=describe it in a general way) | **implement a plan** *formal* (=to do what has been agreed as part of an official plan)

ADJECTIVES/NOUN + plan

ambitious *The plan was very ambitious, but it worked.*
detailed *The generals drew up detailed plans for the invasion.*
cunning/clever/ingenious | *They devised a cunning plan to get back their money.*
a five-year/ten-year etc plan *Unesco has a 25-year plan to provide basic education to all.*
a grand plan (=a plan that involves doing a lot of things in order to achieve something big) *Marrying the countess was all part of his grand plan.*
a master plan (=a detailed plan for dealing with a complicated situation) | **a business plan** | **a peace plan** | **a rescue plan** (=a plan for saving a company, economy etc) | **an action plan**

PHRASES

go according to plan (=happen in the way that was arranged) *If everything goes according to plan, we'll finish in January.*
a plan of action *Ministers are discussing a plan of action to deal with the crisis.*
a plan of attack (=a plan to attack or achieve something) | **a plan of campaign** *BrE* (=a plan to achieve something)

COMMON ERRORS

⚠ Don't say 'do a plan'. Say **make a plan.**

THESAURUS - MEANING 2

plan a set of actions for achieving something in the future, especially a set of actions that has been considered carefully and in detail: *Leaders outlined a plan to end the fighting.*

plot/conspiracy a secret plan to do something bad or illegal, made by a group of people: *There was a plot to assassinate the president.* | *a terrorist conspiracy*
scheme *BrE* an official plan that is intended to help people: *The government has introduced a new scheme to help young people find work.*
strategy a carefully designed plan which is intended to achieve a particular purpose over a long period of time: *the company's business strategy* | *The government's economic strategy has been criticized by many experts.*
initiative a new plan for dealing with a particular problem or for achieving a particular aim: *a peace initiative* | *a major new initiative to tackle street crime*
policy a plan that members of a government, political party, company etc agree on, that states how they intend to deal with a particular subject or problem: *the government's immigration policy* | *It's company policy to allow people to work from home.*
programme *BrE*, **program** *AmE* a series of activities that a government or organization organizes, which aims to achieve something important and will continue for a long time: *a five-year programme which will create 2,000 new jobs* | *federal programs for low-income housing*

plan² ●●● S1 W1 *v* (**planned**, **planning**)
1 [I,T] to think carefully about something you want to do, and decide how and when you will do it: *He immediately began planning his escape.* | *Talks are planned for next week.* | *The wedding was fine and everything* **went as planned** (=happened the way it had been planned). | **plan to do sth** *Maria didn't plan to kill Fiona. It was an accident.* | **plan ahead/plan for the future** *Now that you're pregnant you'll have to plan ahead.*
2 [T] to intend to do something: **plan to do sth** *He said he planned to write his essay tonight.* | **plan on doing sth** *When do you plan on going to Geneva?* | *The former president is planning a return to politics.*
3 [T] to think about something you are going to make, and decide what it will be like SYN **design**: *Planning a small garden is often difficult.* | *The system needs to be planned carefully.*
plan *sth* ↔ **out** *phr v* to plan something carefully, considering all the possible problems: *I'll get the maps so we can plan out our route.* → PLANNING

PLANE

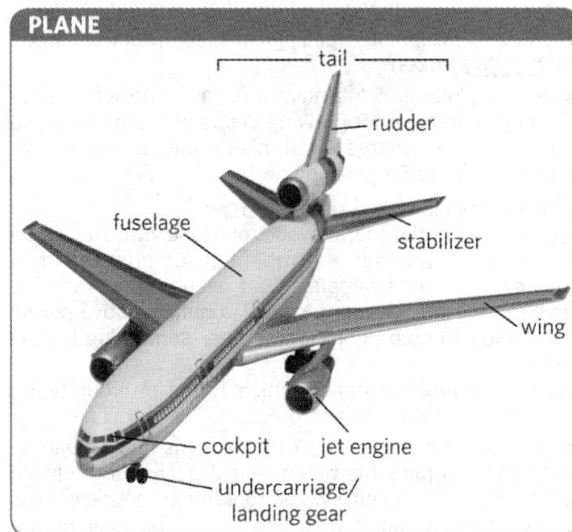

plane¹ /pleɪn/ ●●● S2 W2 *n* [C]
1 AIRCRAFT a vehicle that flies in the air and has wings and at least one engine: *It is a big airline with a large fleet of planes.* | *It's much quicker to go* **by plane**. | *She slept* **on the plane**.
2 LEVEL a level or standard of thought, conversation etc: *The two newspapers are on completely different intellectual planes.*
3 TOOL a tool that has a flat bottom with a sharp blade in it, used for making wooden surfaces smooth
4 TREE a PLANE TREE
5 SURFACE *technical* a completely flat surface in GEOMETRY

GRAMMAR: Patterns with plane

- You usually say **get on a plane**: *I got on a plane at 6.15 and arrived in Chicago at 10.*
- You can also say **get in a plane**: *Everyone got in the plane and found their seats.*
- You usually say **get off a plane**: *We were tired when we got off the plane.* 'Get out of' is much less common.
- You usually say that someone is **on a plane**: *Take something to read on the plane.*
- You can also say they are **in a plane**: *Have you ever flown in a plane?*
- You go somewhere **by plane**: *It takes five hours by rail or an hour by plane.*
- Say **go by plane** or just **fly**. ✗ Don't say: *fly by plane*

COLLOCATIONS

VERBS
catch/take a plane *She caught the first plane back to New York.*
get on a plane (*also* **board a plane**) *We got on the plane and found our seats.*
a plane takes off (=goes into the air) *The flight attendants served drinks shortly after the plane took off.*
a plane lands (=moves safely down onto the ground) *Because of the fog, our plane had to land at Luton.*
a plane touches down (=lands safely on the ground) *As soon as the plane touched down on the runway, I felt better.*
a plane flies | **a plane crashes** | **a plane crash-lands** (=lands in a sudden and dangerous way because of a problem) | **fly/pilot a plane** | **land a plane** (=bring it safely down onto the ground) | **bring a plane down** (=land it) | **get off a plane**

ADJECTIVES/NOUN + plane
a private plane *He flew to Vegas in his private plane.*
a cargo plane (=for carrying goods) | **a transport plane** (=for carrying military equipment and soldiers) | **a military plane** | **a fighter plane** (=a small fast military plane) | **a spy plane**

plane + NOUN
a plane crash *Over 200 people died in the plane crash.*

plane² *v* [T] if you plane a piece of wood, you make it smoother or smaller, using a plane: *He planed the edge of the door.*

plane³ *adj* [only before noun] *technical* completely flat and smooth: *a plane surface*

ˈplane geˌometry *n* [U] the study of lines, shapes etc that are TWO-DIMENSIONAL (=with measurements in only two directions, not three)

plane·load /ˈpleɪnləʊd $ -loʊd/ *n* [C] the number of people or amount of something that an aircraft will hold: *planeloads of food aid*

plan·er /ˈpleɪnə $ -ər/ *n* [C] an electric tool with a flat bottom and a sharp blade, used for making wooden surfaces smooth

plan·et /ˈplænɪt/ ●●● W3 *n* [C]
1 a very large round object in space that moves around the Sun or another star: *Mercury is the smallest of all the planets.* | *Is there life on other planets?* | *the future of planet Earth* ⚠ Don't say 'in a planet'. Say **on a planet**.
2 sb is (living) on another planet/what planet is sb on? *spoken* used humorously to say that someone's ideas are not at all practical or sensible: *He thinks motherhood is glamorous – what planet is he on?*
3 the planet the world – used especially when talking about the environment: *a safer future for the planet*
—**planetary** *adj* [only before noun]: *the planetary system*

P

plan·e·tar·i·um /ˌplænəˈteəriəm $ -ˈter-/ *n* [C] a building where lights on a curved ceiling show the movements of planets and stars

ˈplane tree *n* [C] a large tree with broad leaves that is often planted along streets

plan·gent /ˈplændʒənt/ *adj* [usually before noun] *literary* a plangent sound is loud and deep and sounds sad: *the plangent sound of the violin* —**plangently** *adv* —**plangency** *n* [U]

plank /plæŋk/ *n* [C] **1** a long narrow piece of wooden board, used especially for making structures to walk on: *a long* ***plank of wood*** | *a bridge made of planks* **2** one of the main features or principles of an argument etc → **platform**: **plank of an argument/policy/campaign etc** *the* ***main plank*** *of their argument* | *a* ***central plank*** *of our policy* | *a five-plank campaign including raising the minimum wage* → **walk the plank** at WALK[1](13), → **as thick as two short planks** at THICK[1](7)

plank·ing /ˈplæŋkɪŋ/ *n* [U] **1** *BrE* wood that has been cut into planks, especially when it is used to make a floor, bridge, or fence **2** the activity of lying face down with your body straight and stiff, in an unusual place or on something unusual, so that a photograph of this can be shown on the Internet

plank·ton /ˈplæŋktən/ *n* [U] the very small forms of plant and animal life that live in water, especially the sea, and are eaten by fish

ˌplanned obsoˈlescence *n* [U] when a product is deliberately made so that it will soon be replaced by something more fashionable or more technically advanced. This is done so that people will want to buy new things more often.

plan·ner /ˈplænə $ -ər/ ●○○ *n* [C] someone who plans and makes important decisions about something, especially someone whose job is to plan the way towns grow and develop: **urban/city planner** *City planners are looking for ways to ease traffic.* | *Many* ***financial planners*** *will help you shop for insurance.*

plan·ning /ˈplænɪŋ/ *n* [U] the process of thinking about and deciding on a plan for achieving or making something: **good/bad/careful etc planning** *A little careful planning is important in gardening.* | *'How did you manage to be so late?' 'Just bad planning.'* | *A little* ***forward planning*** (=thinking about how to do something before doing it) *can save you a lot of expense.* | *Good financial planning is vital to business success.* → TOWN PLANNING, FAMILY PLANNING

ˈplanning perˌmission *n* [U] *BrE* official permission to build a new building or change an existing one

plant[1] /plɑːnt $ plænt/ ●●● S2 W1 *n*
1 LIVING THING [C] a living thing that has leaves and roots and grows in earth, especially one that is smaller than a tree: *Don't forget to water the plants.* → HOUSEPLANT
2 FACTORY [C] a factory or building where an industrial process happens: *a huge chemical plant* → POWER PLANT
3 MACHINERY [U] *BrE* heavy machinery that is used in industrial processes: *a plant hire business*
4 STH HIDDEN [C usually singular] something illegal or stolen that is hidden in someone's clothes or possessions to make them seem guilty of a crime
5 PERSON [C] someone who is put somewhere or sent somewhere secretly to find out information

COLLOCATIONS

ADJECTIVES/NOUN + plant

rare *Many rare plants were collected from India and China.*
common *These plants are common in British gardens.*
wild plants *Many wild plants are in danger of dying out.*
garden plants (=plants that are grown in gardens) | **exotic/tropical plants** | **medicinal plants** (=plants that can be used in medicine) | **a potted/pot plant** *BrE* (=a plant that is grown in a container) | **a climbing plant** (=one that grows up things) | **a trailing plant** | **a tomato/potato/bean etc plant**

VERBS

a plant grows *The plant grows to a height of about 20 inches.*
a plant thrives/flourishes (=grows well) *A lot of plants thrive in partial shade.*
a plant flowers *The plants are flowering earlier this year.*
grow a plant *It is not an easy plant to grow.*
water a plant

plant + NOUN

plant life (=plants) *All but the dirtiest of rivers support some plant life.*
plant material *They feed on decaying plant material.*

plant[2] ●●○ *v* [T]
1 PLANTS/SEEDS to put plants or seeds in the ground to grow: *Residents have helped us plant trees.* | *We've planted tomatoes and carrots in the garden.* | **plant a field/garden/area etc (with sth)** *a hillside planted with fir trees*
2 PUT STH SOMEWHERE [always + adv/prep] *informal* to put something firmly in or on something else: **plant sth in/on etc sth** *He came up to her and planted a kiss on her cheek.* | *She planted her feet firmly to the spot and refused to move.*
3 HIDE ILLEGAL GOODS *informal* to hide stolen or illegal goods in someone's clothes, bags, room etc in order to make them seem guilty of a crime: **plant sth on sb** *She claims that the police planted the drugs on her.*
4 BOMB **plant a bomb** to put a bomb somewhere: *Two men are accused of planting a bomb on the plane.*
5 PERSON to put or send someone somewhere, especially secretly, so that they can find out information: *The police had planted undercover detectives at every entrance.*
6 plant an idea/doubt/suspicion (in sb's mind) to make someone begin to have an idea, especially so that they do not realize that you gave them the idea: *Someone must have planted the idea of suicide in his mind.*

plant sth ↔ **out** *phr v* to put a young plant into the soil outdoors, so that it has enough room to grow: *The seedlings should be planted out in May.*

plan·tain /ˈplæntɪn/ *n* **1** [C,U] a kind of BANANA that is cooked before it is eaten, or the plant on which it grows **2** [C] a common wild plant with small green flowers and wide leaves

plan·ta·tion /plænˈteɪʃən, plɑːn- $ plæn-/ ●○○ *n* [C]
1 a large area of land in a hot country, where crops such as tea, cotton, and sugar are grown: *a rubber plantation*
2 a large group of trees grown to produce wood
THESAURUS ▸ FOREST

plant·er /ˈplɑːntə $ ˈplæntər/ *n* [C] **1** an attractive, usually large, container for growing plants in **2** someone who owns or is in charge of a plantation: *a tea planter* **3** a machine used for planting

plaque /plɑːk, plæk $ plæk/ ●○○ *n*
1 [C] a piece of flat metal, wood, or stone with writing on it, used as a prize in a competition or attached to a building to remind people of an event or person: *The team's coach was given a plaque.* | **commemorative plaque** (=a plaque to help people remember something important)
2 [U] a harmful substance which forms on your teeth, which BACTERIA can live and breed in

plas·ma /ˈplæzmə/ *n* [U] **1** the yellowish liquid part of blood that contains the blood cells **2** *technical* the living substance inside a cell SYN **protoplasm 3** *technical* a gas that contains about the same numbers of positive and negative electric CHARGES and is found in the Sun and most stars

ˈplasma screen *n* [C] a type of television or computer screen that is wider and taller than most regular screens, but that shows pictures using a different type of technology which makes it possible for the screen to be thinner than other types of screens

plas·ter[1] /ˈplɑːstə $ ˈplæstər/ ●○○ *n*
1 [U] a substance used to cover walls and ceilings with a smooth even surface. It consists of LIME, water, and sand.

2 [U] PLASTER OF PARIS
3 [C,U] *BrE* a piece of thin material that is stuck on to the skin to cover a small wound SYN **bandaid** *AmE* → see picture at **FIRST AID KIT**
4 in plaster *BrE* if you have a leg or arm in plaster, you have a PLASTER CAST around it because a bone is broken and needs to be kept in place while it mends

plaster² *v* [T] **1** to put a wet usually sticky substance all over a surface so that it is thickly covered: **be plastered with sth** *Her face was plastered with make-up.* **2** to completely cover a surface with something, especially large pieces of paper, pictures etc: **be plastered with sth** *The windows were plastered with notices.* | *The news of the wedding* ***was plastered all over the papers*** (=was the main story in the newspapers). **3** to put wet plaster on a wall or ceiling: *We're plastering the bathroom.* **4** to make your hair lie flat or stick to your head: **be plastered to sth** *His hair was plastered to his forehead with sweat.* | **be plastered down/back** *Her hair had been plastered down by the rain.*

plaster sth ↔ **over** *phr v* to cover a hole or an old surface by spreading plaster over it: *The original brickwork has been plastered over.*

plas·ter·board /ˈplɑːstəbɔːd $ ˈplæstərbɔːrd/ *n* [U] *BrE* board made of large sheets of thick paper held together with plaster, used to cover walls and ceilings inside a house SYN **drywall** *AmE*

ˈplaster cast *n* [C] **1** a cover made from PLASTER OF PARIS, put around an arm, leg etc to keep a broken bone in place while it mends SYN **cast 2** a copy of something that is made of PLASTER OF PARIS

plas·tered /ˈplɑːstəd $ ˈplæstərd/ *adj* [not before noun] *informal* very drunk: *Chris was plastered after five beers.*

plas·ter·er /ˈplɑːstərə $ ˈplæstərər/ *n* [C] *BrE* someone whose job is to cover walls and ceilings with PLASTER

plaster of Par·is /ˌplɑːstər əv ˈpærɪs $ ˌplæs-/ *n* [U] a mixture of a white powder and water that dries fairly quickly and is used for making plaster casts and to decorate buildings

plas·tic¹ /ˈplæstɪk/ ●●● S2 W2 *adj*
1 made of plastic: *a plastic spoon* | *plastic bags*
2 *technical* a plastic substance can be formed into many different shapes and keeps the shape it is formed into until someone changes it
3 something that is plastic looks or tastes artificial or not natural: *plastic food* | *I hate that plastic smile of hers.*

plastic² ●●● S3 W2 *n*
1 [C,U] a light strong material that is produced by a chemical process, and which can be made into different shapes when it is soft: *children's toys made of plastic* | *the plastics industry*
2 [U] *informal* small plastic cards that are used to pay for things instead of money SYN **credit cards**: *'I haven't got any cash.' 'Don't worry, I'll stick it on the plastic* (=pay for it using a credit card).*'* | *Do they take plastic?* (=can you pay using a credit card?)

ˌplastic ˈbullet *n* [C] a large bullet made of hard plastic that is intended to injure but not kill

ˌplastic exˈplosive *n* [C,U] an explosive substance that can be shaped using your hands, or a small bomb made from this

Plas·ti·cine /ˈplæstəsiːn/ *n* [U] *trademark BrE* a soft substance like clay, that comes in many different colours and is used by children for making models → **play dough**

plas·tic·i·ty /plæˈstɪsəti/ *n* [U] *technical* the quality of being easily made into any shape, and of staying in that shape until someone changes it

ˌplastic ˈsurgery *n* [U] the medical practice of changing the appearance of people's faces or bodies, either to improve their appearance or to repair injuries —**ˌplastic ˈsurgeon** *n* [C]

ˌplastic ˈwrap *n* [U] *AmE* thin transparent plastic used to cover food to keep it fresh SYN **clingfilm** *BrE*

plat du jour /ˌplɑː dʊ ˈʒʊə $ -ˈʒʊr/ *n* (*plural* **plats du jour** *(same pronunciation)*) [C] *BrE* a dish that a restaurant prepares specially on a particular day in addition to its usual food

plate¹ /pleɪt/ ●●● S2 W2 *n*
1 FOOD [C] **a)** a flat and usually round dish that you eat from or serve food on: *The plates were piled high with rice.* | *a dinner plate* **b)** (*also* **plateful**) the amount of food that is on a plate: **[+of]** *He's eaten a whole plate of french fries.*
⚠ Do not use **plate** when you mean 'food cooked in a particular way as a meal'. Use **dish**: *the chef who created this dish (NOT this plate)*
2 SIGN [C] a flat piece of metal with words or numbers on it, for example on a door or a car: *The brass plate on the door said 'Dr Rackman'.* | **number/license/registration plate** (=on a car) *Did anyone see the car's license plate?* → **L-PLATE, NAMEPLATE**
3 have a lot/enough on your plate *informal* to have a lot of problems to deal with or problems to worry about
4 PROTECTIVE COVERING [C] **a)** *technical* one of the thin sheets of bone, horn etc that covers and protects the outside of some animals **b)** a thin sheet of metal used to protect something: **metal/steel/iron plates** *The shoes had metal plates attached to the heels.*
5 EARTH'S SURFACE [C] *technical* one of the very large sheets of rock that form the surface of the Earth → **PLATE TECTONICS**
6 GOLD/SILVER a) gold/silver plate ordinary metal with a thin covering of gold or silver **b)** [U] things such as plates, cups, forks, or knives made of gold or silver
7 hand/give/offer sb sth on a plate to let someone get or achieve something easily, without much effort from them: *I worked hard for what I've got. It wasn't handed to me on a plate.*
8 PICTURES/PHOTOS [C] **a)** a sheet of metal that has been cut or treated in a special way so that words or pictures can be printed from its surface: *copper printing plates* **b)** a picture in a book, printed on good-quality paper and usually coloured **c)** a thin sheet of glass used especially in the past in photography, with chemicals on it that are sensitive to light
9 BASEBALL [C usually singular] the place where the person hitting the ball stands
10 COMPETITION the ... Plate used in the names of sports competitions or races in which the winner gets a silver plate: *This horse won the Galway Plate.*
11 TEETH [C] **a)** a thin piece of plastic shaped to fit inside a person's mouth, into which FALSE TEETH are fixed **b)** *BrE* a thin piece of plastic with wires fixed to it, that some people wear in their mouth to make their teeth straight SYN **brace** *BrE* → **HOTPLATE**

plate² *v* [T] **be plated with sth a)** to be covered with a thin covering of gold or silver: *a beautiful necklace, plated with 22-carat gold* | **gold-plated/silver-plated** *a gold-plated watch* **b)** to be covered in sheets of a hard material such as metal: *The ship had been heavily plated with protective sheets.*

plat·eau¹ /ˈplætəʊ $ plæˈtoʊ/ ●○○ *n* (*plural* **plateaus** *or* **plateaux** /-təʊz $ -ˈtoʊz/) [C]
1 a large area of flat land that is higher than the land around it
2 a period during which the level of something does not change, especially after a period when it was increasing: *Inflation rates have reached a plateau.*

plateau² *v* [I] if something plateaus, it reaches and then stays at a particular level: *The athletic footwear market has not yet plateaued.*

plate·ful /ˈpleɪtfʊl/ *n* [C] all the food that is on a plate: **[+of]** *a plateful of toast*

ˌplate ˈglass *n* [U] big pieces of glass made in large thick sheets, used especially in shop windows

plate·let /ˈpleɪtlɪt/ *n* [C] one of the very small flat round cells in your blood that help it become solid when you bleed, so that you stop bleeding

ˌplate tecˈtonics *n* [U] *technical* the study of the forming and movement of the large sheets of rock that form the surface of the Earth

P

plat·form /ˈplætfɔːm $ -fɔːrm/ ●●○ S3 W3 *n* [C]
1 TRAIN *especially BrE* the raised place beside a railway track where you get on and off a train in a station: *The Edinburgh train will depart from platform six.*
2 FOR SPEECHES a stage for people to stand on when they are making a speech, performing etc: *a small raised platform at one end of the room*
3 POLITICS **a)** [usually singular] the main ideas and aims of a political party, especially the ones that they state just before an election → **plank**: *a strong women's rights platform | the Labour party platform* **b)** a chance for someone to express their opinions, especially their political opinions: **[+for]** *The conference provides a platform for people on the left wing of the party.*
4 STRUCTURE a tall structure built so that people can stand or work above the surrounding area: *an oil exploration platform*
5 COMPUTERS the type of computer system or software that someone uses: *the UNIX platform | a multimedia platform*
6 EXPRESS IDEAS an opportunity to express your ideas to a large number of people: **[+for]** *We mustn't give these groups a platform for their propaganda.*
7 BUS *BrE* the open part at the back of some DOUBLE-DECKER buses, where passengers get on and off
8 SHOES **platforms** (*also* **platform shoes**) [plural] shoes that have a raised thick SOLE (=flat bottom part) and a high heel → see picture at **SHOE**[1]

ˈplatform ˌgame *n* [C] *technical* a computer game in which the action happens against a background that does not move

plat·ing /ˈpleɪtɪŋ/ *n* [U] a thin layer of metal that covers another metal surface: *gold plating*

plat·i·num /ˈplætənəm/ *n* [U] **1** a silver-grey metal that does not change colour or lose its brightness, and is used in making expensive jewellery and in industry. It is a chemical ELEMENT: symbol Pt: *a platinum ring* **2** if a music recording goes platinum, at least a million copies of it have been sold: *Eight of Denver's albums **went platinum**. | a **platinum disc***

ˌplatinum ˈblonde *n* [C] *informal* a woman whose hair is a silver-white colour, especially because it has been coloured with chemicals —**platinum blonde** *adj*

plat·i·tude /ˈplætɪtjuːd $ -tuːd/ *n* [C] *formal* a statement that has been made many times before and is not interesting or clever – used to show disapproval: *His excuse was the platitude 'boys will be boys'.* —**platitudinous** /ˌplætɪˈtjuːdɪnəs◂ $ -ˈtuː-/ *adj*

pla·ton·ic /pləˈtɒnɪk $ -ˈtɑː-/ *adj* a relationship that is platonic is just friendly and is not a sexual relationship: *a platonic friendship*

pla·toon /pləˈtuːn/ *n* [C] a small group of soldiers which is part of a COMPANY and is led by a LIEUTENANT

plat·ter /ˈplætə $ -ər/ *n* [C] **1** *especially AmE* a large plate from which food is served: *a serving platter* | **[+of]** *a platter of turkey and vegetables* **2 chicken/seafood etc platter** chicken, fish etc with vegetables or other foods on a large plate, served in a restaurant

plat·y·pus /ˈplætəpəs/ *n* [C] a small furry Australian animal that has a beak and feet like a duck, lays eggs, and produces milk for its young

plau·dits /ˈplɔːdəts $ ˈplɒː-/ *n* [plural] *formal* praise and admiration: **win/draw/receive etc plaudits** *Her performance won plaudits from the critics.*

plau·si·ble /ˈplɔːzəbəl $ ˈplɒː-/ ●○○ *adj*
1 reasonable and likely to be true or successful OPP **implausible**: *His story certainly sounds plausible. | a plausible explanation*
2 someone who is plausible is good at talking in a way that sounds reasonable and truthful, although they may in fact be lying: *a plausible liar* —**plausibly** *adv* —**plausibility** /ˌplɔːzəˈbɪləti $ ˌplɒː-/ *n* [U]

play[1] /pleɪ/ ●●● S1 W1 *v*
1 CHILDREN [I,T] when children play, they do things that they enjoy, often with other people or with toys: *Kids were playing and chasing each other.* | **play catch/house/tag/school etc** *Outside, the children were playing cowboys and Indians.* | **[+with]** *Did you like to play with dolls when you were little? | Parents need to spend time just playing with their children.*
2 SPORTS/GAMES **a)** [I,T] to take part or compete in a game or sport: *Karen began playing basketball when she was six. | If you feel any pain, you shouldn't play. | Men were sitting in the park, playing cards.* | **[+against]** *Bristol will play against Coventry next week. | She's playing Helen Evans in the semi-final* (=playing against her). | **[+for]** *Moxon played for England in ten test matches.* **b)** [T] to use a particular piece, card, person etc in a game or sport: *Harrison played a ten of spades. | The Regents played Eddie at center* (=used him as a player in that position) *in the game against Arizona.* **c)** [I,T] to take a particular position on a team: *Garvey played first base for the Dodgers.* **d)** [T] to hit a ball in a particular way or to a particular place in a game or sport: *She played the ball low, just over the net.*
3 MUSIC [I,T] to perform a piece of music on a musical instrument: *He's learning to play the piano. | She played a Bach prelude. | Haden has played with many jazz greats. | A small orchestra was playing.*
4 RADIO/CD ETC [I,T] if a radio, CD etc plays, or if you play it, it produces sound, especially music: *The bedside radio played softly.* | **play a record/CD/tape etc** *DJs playing the latest house and techno tracks*
5 THEATRE/FILM **a)** [T] to perform the actions and say the words of a particular character in a theatre performance, film etc: *Streep plays a shy, nervous woman.* | **play a role/part/character etc** *Playing a character so different from herself was a challenge.* **b)** [I] if a play or film is playing at a particular theatre, it is being performed or shown there: *'Macbeth' is playing at the Theatre Royal in York.* **c)** [T] if actors play a theatre, they perform there in a play
6 play a part/role to have an effect or influence on something: **[+in]** *A good diet and fitness play a large part in helping people live longer.*
7 play ball a) to throw, kick, hit, or catch a ball as a game or activity: *Jim and Karl were playing ball in the backyard.* **b)** to do what someone wants you to do: *So far, the company has refused to play ball, preferring to remain independent.*
8 PRETEND [linking verb] to behave as if you are a particular kind of person or have a particular feeling or quality, even though it is not true: *the accusation that scientists are **playing God** | Some snakes fool predators by **playing dead**. | 'What do you mean?' 'Don't **play dumb*** (=pretend you do not know something).' | *Don't **play the innocent*** (=pretend you do not know about something) *with me – we both know what happened.* | **play the idiot/the teacher etc** *Susan felt she had to play the good wife. | He **played the fool*** (=behaved in a silly way) *at school instead of working.*
9 BEHAVE [T always + adv/prep] to behave in a particular way in a situation, in order to achieve the result or effect that you want: *How do you want to play this meeting? | **Play it safe*** (=avoid risks) *and make sure the eggs are thoroughly cooked.* | **play it carefully/cool etc** *If you like him, play it cool, or you might scare him off.*
10 play games to hide your real feelings or wishes in order to achieve something in a clever or secret way – used to show disapproval: *Stop playing games, Luke, and tell me what you want.*
11 play sth by ear a) to decide what to do according to the way a situation develops, without making plans before that time: *We'll see what the weather's like and **play it by ear**.* **b)** if someone can play a musical instrument by ear, they can play a tune without looking at written music
12 play a joke/trick/prank on sb to do something to someone as a joke or trick
13 play the game a) to do things in the way you are expected to do them or in a way that is usual in a particular situation: *If you want a promotion, you've got to play the game.* **b)** *BrE* to behave in a fair and honest way
14 play the race/nationalist/environmentalist etc card to use

a particular subject in politics in order to gain an advantage: *a leader who is skilfully playing the nationalist card to keep power*
15 play your cards right to say or do things in a situation in such a way that you gain as much as possible from it: *Who knows? **If you play your cards right**, maybe he'll marry you.*
16 play your cards close to your chest to keep secret what you are doing in a situation
17 play into sb's hands to do what someone you are competing with wants you to do, without realizing it: *If we respond with violence, we'll be playing into their hands, giving them an excuse for a fight.*
18 play for time to try to delay something so that you have more time to prepare for it or prevent it from happening: *The rebels may be playing for time while they try to get more weapons.*
19 play tricks (on you) if your mind, memory, sight etc plays tricks on you, you feel confused and not sure about what is happening: *It happened a long time ago, and my memory might be playing tricks on me.*
20 play the market to risk money on the STOCK MARKET as a way of trying to earn more money
21 play the system to use the rules of a system in a clever way, to gain advantage for yourself: *Accountants know how to play the tax system.*
22 play second fiddle (to sb) (*also* **play second banana** *informal*) to be in a lower position or rank than someone else
23 play hard to get to pretend that you are not sexually interested in someone so that they will become more interested in you
24 SMILE [I always + adv/prep] *written* if a smile plays about someone's lips, they smile slightly
25 play hooky *AmE*, **play truant** *BrE* to stay away from school without permission
26 play with fire to do something that could have a very dangerous or harmful result: *Dating the boss's daughter is playing with fire.*
27 play to your strengths to do what you are able to do well, rather than trying to do other things: *It is up to us to play to our strengths and try to control the game.*
28 LIGHT [I always + adv/prep] *written* if light plays on something, it shines on it and moves on it: *the sunlight playing on the water*
29 WATER [I] *written* if a FOUNTAIN plays, water comes from it
30 play a hose/light on sth to point a HOSE or light towards something so that water or light goes onto it
31 play the field to have sexual relationships with a lot of different people
32 play fast and loose with sth to not be careful about what you do, especially by not obeying the law or a rule: *They played fast and loose with investors' money.*
33 play happy families *BrE* to spend time with your family, doing normal things, especially so that your family appears to be happy when it is not

play around (*also* **play about** *BrE*) *phr v*
1 to have a sexual relationship with someone who is not your usual partner: **[+with]** *Wasn't she playing around with another man?* | *It was years before I realized he'd been playing around.*
2 to try doing something in different ways, to see what would be best, especially when this is fun: **[+with]** *Play around with the ingredients if you like.*
3 to behave in a silly way or waste time, when you should be doing something more serious SYN **fool around**: *When the teacher wasn't looking, we used to play about a lot.*

play around with sth (*also* **play about with sth** *BrE*) *phr v* to keep moving or making changes to something in your hands SYN **fiddle with**: *Will you stop playing around with the remote control!*

play along *phr v*
1 to pretend to agree to do what someone wants, in order to avoid annoying them or to get an advantage: *She felt she had to play along or risk losing her job.*
2 play sb along *BrE* to tell someone something that is not true because you need their help in some way

play at sth *phr v*
1 What is sb playing at? *BrE spoken* used when you do not understand what someone is doing or why they are doing it, and you are surprised or annoyed: *What do you think you're playing at?*
2 if you play at doing something, you do not do it properly or seriously: **play at doing sth** *He's still playing at being an artist.*
3 *BrE* if children play at doctors, soldiers etc, they pretend to be doctors, soldiers etc: **play at being sth** *a 14-year-old playing at being a grown woman*

play sth ↔ **back** *phr v* to play something that has been recorded on a machine so that you can listen to it or watch it: *He played back his answering machine messages.*

play sth ↔ **down** *phr v* to try to make something seem less important or less likely than it really is: *Management has been playing down the possibility of job losses.* | **play down the importance/seriousness/significance of sth** *The White House spokeswoman sought to play down the significance of the event.*

play off *phr v*
1 *BrE* if people or teams play off, they play the last game in a sports competition, in order to decide who is the winner: *The top two teams will play off at Twickenham for the county title.*
2 play off sb/sth *AmE* to deliberately use a fact, action, idea etc in order to make what you are doing better or to get an advantage: *The two musicians **played off each other** in a piece of inspired improvisation.*

play sb **off against** sb *phr v* to encourage one person or group to compete or argue with another, in order to get some advantage for yourself: *The house seller may try to play one buyer off against another, to raise the price.*

play on/upon sth *phr v* to use a feeling, fact, or idea in order to get what you want, often in an unfair way: *The ad plays on our emotions, showing a doctor holding a newborn baby.*

play sth ↔ **out** *phr v*
1 if an event or situation is played out or plays itself out, it happens: *It will be interesting to see how the election **plays itself out**.*
2 if people play out their dreams, feelings etc, they express them by pretending that a particular situation is really happening: *The weekend gives you a chance to play out your fantasies.*

play up *phr v*
1 play sth ↔ up to emphasize something, sometimes making it seem more important than it really is: *Play up your strongest arguments in the opening paragraph.*
2 play (sb) up *BrE informal* if children play up, they behave badly: *Jordan's been playing up in school.* | *I hope the kids don't play you up.*
3 play (sb) up *BrE informal* to hurt you or cause problems for you: *My knee's been playing me up this week.* | *The car's playing up again.*

play up to sb *phr v* to behave in a very polite or kind way to someone because you want something from them: *Connie always plays up to her parents when she wants money.*

play with sb/sth *phr v*
1 to keep touching something or moving it: *Stop playing with the light switch!*
2 to try doing something in different ways to decide what works best: *Play with the design onscreen, moving text and pictures until you get a pleasing arrangement.*
3 to consider an idea or possibility, but not always very seriously SYN **toy with**: *After university, I **played with the idea of** teaching English in China.*
4 money/time/space etc to play with money, time etc that is available to be used: *The budget is very tight, so there isn't much money to play with.*
5 play with yourself to touch your own sex organs for pleasure SYN **masturbate**
6 play with words/language to use words in a clever or amusing way

play² ●●● S1 W2 *n*
1 THEATRE [C] a story that is written to be performed by

P

actors, especially in a theatre: *a play by Chekhov* | *This is a major theme of Miller's plays.* | **[+about]** *Edward Bond's play about class war*
2 AMUSEMENT [U] things that people, especially children, do for amusement rather than as work: *Play is very important to a child's development.* | *a play area* | **through play** *The program aims to teach road safety through play.* | **at play** *the happy shouts of children at play*
3 EFFECT [U] the effect or influence of something: *the free play of competition in the building industry* | **at play** *There are a number of factors at play* (=having an effect) *in the current recession.* | **bring/put sth into play** (=use something or make it have an effect) *A complex system of muscles is brought into play for each body movement.* | *Political considerations do **come into play** (=have an effect) when making policy.*
4 ACTION IN A GAME OR SPORT **a)** [U] the actions of the people who are playing a game or sport: *Rain stopped play after only an hour.* **b)** [C] one particular action or set of actions during a game: *On the next play, Johnson ran 15 yards for a touchdown.*
5 in play/out of play if a ball is in play or out of play, it is inside or outside the area in which the rules of the game allow you to hit, kick, catch etc the ball: *He kicked the ball out of play.*
6 play on words a use of a word that is interesting or amusing because it can be understood as having two very different meanings SYN **pun**
7 play of light patterns made by light as it moves over a surface: *the play of light on the water*
8 make a play for sth to make an attempt to gain something: *He made a play for the leadership last year.*
9 make a play for sb to try to begin a romantic or sexual relationship with someone: *It's obvious he was making a play for her.*
10 LOOSENESS [U] if there is some play in something, it is loose and can be moved: *There's too much play in the rope.*
→ FAIR PLAY, FOUL PLAY

COLLOCATIONS

VERBS

write a play *So far, he has written three plays.*
go to (see) a play *While we were in New York, we went to a play.*
see a play *I've never seen the play.*
watch a play *Some of the audience were talking instead of watching the play.*
perform a play *The play was performed by Brighton Youth Theatre.*
act/perform/appear in a play | **be in a play** (=be performing in a play) | **put on a play** (=arrange for it to be performed) | **direct a play** (=tell the actors what to do) | **produce/stage a play** (=arrange its performance) | **rehearse a play** (=practise it)

ADJECTIVES/NOUN + play

a stage play (=a play in a theatre) *I occasionally write reviews of local stage plays.*
a TV/radio play (=a play written to be performed on TV/radio) | **a school play**

COMMON ERRORS

⚠ Don't say 'give a play'. Say **put on a play**.

play·a /ˈpleɪjʌ/ (*also* **player**) *n* [C] *spoken informal* a man who is good at meeting women and persuading them to have sex with him

play·a·ble /ˈpleɪəbəl/ *adj* **1** a piece of ground used for sports that is playable is in good condition and suitable for playing on: *Despite the frost, the pitch was playable.* **2** something that is playable can be played: **[+on]** *The disks are playable on home computers.* | *an old guitar that is still playable*

ˈplay-ˌacting *n* [U] behaviour in which someone pretends to be serious or sincere, but is not —**play-act** *v* [I]

play·back /ˈpleɪbæk/ *n* [C usually singular, U] the act of playing a film, a piece of music, or a message has been recorded on a machine and watching or listening to it again: *the playback button on an answering machine*

ˈplayback ˌsinger *n* [C] a singer who records songs which are later used in films, especially Bollywood films. The actors in the films pretend that they are singing the songs themselves.

play·bill /ˈpleɪbɪl/ *n* [C] a printed piece of paper advertising a play

play·boy /ˈpleɪbɔɪ/ *n* [C] a rich man who does not work and who spends his time enjoying himself with beautiful women, fast cars etc: *a middle-aged playboy*

ˌplay-by-ˈplay *n* [C usually singular] *AmE* a report on what is happening in a sports game, given at the same time as the game is being played

ˈplay date *n* [C] *AmE* a time that is arranged for children to meet together to play

ˈPlay-Doh *n* [U] *trademark* a type of PLAY DOUGH

ˈplay dough *n* [U] a soft coloured substance similar to clay, that children use for making models or shapes → **Plasticine**

ˌplayed-ˈout *adj* an idea, a situation etc that is played out is finished or no longer has influence → **play out** at PLAY[1]

play·er /ˈpleɪə $ -ər/ ●●● S2 W1 *n* [C]
1 someone who takes part in a game or sport: *a basketball player*
2 one of the important people, companies, countries etc that is involved in and influences a situation, especially one involving competition: **a major/dominant/key etc player** *a firm that is a dominant player on Wall Street* | **[+in/on]** *a key player in world affairs*
3 a CD/record/video etc player a machine that is used to play CDs, videos etc
4 someone who plays a musical instrument: *a guitar player*
5 a man who has sexual relationships with many different women
6 *old-fashioned* an actor → **key mover/player** at KEY[1]

ˌplayer piˈano *n* [C] a piano that is played by machinery inside it. A long roll of paper with holes cut in it gradually turns and works the machinery, pressing down the KEYs on the piano to produce music. SYN **pianola**

play·ful /ˈpleɪfəl/ *adj* **1** very active, happy, and wanting to have fun: *a playful little dog* | *Babies are playful and alert when they first wake up.* **2** intended to be fun rather than serious, or showing that you are having fun: *a playful kiss on the cheek* —**playfully** *adv* —**playfulness** *n* [U]

play·go·er /ˈpleɪˌgəʊə $ -ˌgoʊər/ *n* [C] someone who often goes to see plays

play·ground /ˈpleɪgraʊnd/ ●●● S3 *n* [C]
1 an area for children to play, especially at a school or in a park, that often has special equipment for climbing on, riding on etc: *children shouting and running in the playground*
2 a place where a particular group of people go to enjoy themselves: **[+of]** *the playground of the rich*

play·group, **ˈplay group** /ˈpleɪgruːp/ *n* [C,U] **1** *BrE* a type of school where children between two and four years old meet to learn and play SYN **preschool** *AmE*: *a playgroup at the community centre* **2** *AmE* a group of children, usually between two and four years old, whose parents meet each week so that the children can play together

play·house /ˈpleɪhaʊs/ *n* [C] **1** a theatre – used in the name of theatres: *the Oxford Playhouse* **2** a small structure like a little house for children to play in

ˈplaying card *n* [C] *formal* a CARD[1](7a)

ˈplaying field *n* [C] a large piece of ground with areas marked out for playing football, CRICKET etc SYN **pitch** → **level playing field** at LEVEL[1](8)

play·list /ˈpleɪlɪst/ *n* [C] the list of songs that a radio station plays

play·mate /ˈpleɪmeɪt/ *n* [C] a friend that a child plays with

ˈplay-off *n* [C] **1** *BrE* a game played to decide who will win after a previous game has ended with two teams or players having equal points **2** [usually plural] *AmE* a game, usually one of a series of games, played by the best teams or players in a competition in order to decide the final winner: *The Lakers will meet the Bulls in the playoffs.*

play·pen /ˈpleɪpen/ *n* [C] an enclosed area in which a very small child can play safely, that is like an open box with sides made of bars or a net

play·room /ˈpleɪrʊm, -ruːm/ *n* [C] a room for children to play in

play·school, ˈ**play school** /ˈpleɪskuːl/ *n* [C,U] *BrE* a PLAYGROUP

play·suit /ˈpleɪsuːt/ *n* [C] **1** a piece of clothing like a top and a pair of shorts joined together, worn by women **2** a piece of clothing that covers the body, arms, and legs, worn by babies and young children

play·thing /ˈpleɪˌθɪŋ/ *n* [C] **1** *formal* a toy **2** someone that you use for your own amusement or advantage, without caring about them: *men who treat women as playthings*

play·time /ˈpleɪtaɪm/ *n* [U] **1** a period of time during which a child can play: *Don't let TV take up too much of your child's playtime.* **2** *BrE* a period of time at a school when children can go outside and play SYN **recess** *AmE*

play·wright /ˈpleɪraɪt/ ●○○ *n* [C] someone who writes plays SYN **dramatist**

pla·za /ˈplɑːzə $ ˈplæzə/ *n* [C] **1** a public square or market place surrounded by buildings, especially in towns in Spanish-speaking countries **2** a group of shops and other business buildings in a town, usually with outdoor areas between them → MALL

plc, **PLC** /ˌpiː el ˈsiː/ *n* [C] *BrE* (***public limited company***) a large company in Britain which has shares that the public can buy: *Marks & Spencer plc*

plea /pliː/ ●○○ *n*

1 [C] a request that is urgent or full of emotion: **[+for]** *a plea for help* | *Caldwell **made** a **plea** for donations.* | **[+to]** *The parents made an emotional plea to their child's kidnappers.*

2 [C usually singular] a statement by someone in a court of law saying whether they are guilty or not: *a guilty plea* | **make/enter a plea** *Adams entered a plea of 'not guilty'.*

3 [singular] an excuse for something: *He refused the appointment on a plea of illness.*

ˈ**plea ˌbargaining** *n* [U] when someone agrees to admit in court that they are guilty of one crime, in exchange for not being charged with a more serious crime —**plea bargain** *v* [I,T] —**plea bargain** *n* [C]

plead /pliːd/ ●●○ *v*

1 [I,T] to ask for something that you want very much, in a sincere and emotional way SYN **beg**: *'Don't go!' Robert pleaded.* | **[+for]** *Civil rights groups pleaded for government help.* | **plead with sb (to do sth)** *Moira pleaded with him to stay.* THESAURUS ASK

2 (*past tense and past participle* **pleaded** *also* **pled** /pled/ *especially AmE*) [I,T] *law* to state in a court of law whether or not you are guilty of a crime: **plead guilty/not guilty/innocent** *Henderson pled guilty to burglary.*

3 (*past tense and past participle* **pleaded** *also* **pled** *AmE*) **plead ignorance/illness/insanity etc** *formal* to give a particular excuse for your actions: *She stayed home from work, pleading illness.*

4 [T] *written* to give reasons why you think something is true or why something should be done: **plead that** *Managers pleaded that there was not enough time to make the changes.* | *Residents successfully **pleaded** their **case** at a council meeting.*

plead·ing·ly /ˈpliːdɪŋli/ *adv written* in an emotional way that shows you very much want someone to do something: *Kathleen looked at him pleadingly.*

pleas·ant /ˈplezənt/ ●●○ S3 W3 *adj*

1 enjoyable or attractive and making you feel happy SYN **nice** → **pleasure**: *It had been a pleasant evening.* | *the pleasant climate of Southern California* | *The restaurant was large and pleasant.* | *Kate! What a **pleasant surprise**!* | **it is pleasant to do sth** *It was pleasant to sit in a sidewalk cafe and watch people pass.*

2 friendly, polite, and easy to talk to: *Nick seemed very pleasant on the phone.* | *a pleasant-looking woman* | **[+to]** *He's always been very pleasant to me.* THESAURUS NICE

—**pleasantly** *adv*: *He smiled pleasantly.*

> **REGISTER**
> In everyday English, people usually say something or someone is **nice** rather than **pleasant**: *It was a really **nice** day.* | *They were all very **nice** to me.*

pleas·ant·ry /ˈplezəntri/ *n* (*plural* **pleasantries**) [C usually plural] *formal* things that you say to someone in order to be polite, but which are not very important: *Stephen and Mr Illing **exchanged pleasantries**.*

please[1] /pliːz/ ●●● S1 W2 *interjection*

1 used to be polite when asking someone to do something: *Could you please clean up the living room?* | *Sit down, please.* | *Please be quiet!*

2 used to be polite when asking for something: *I'd like a cup of coffee, please.* | *Please can I go to Rebecca's house?*

3 said in order to politely accept something that someone offers you: *'More wine?' 'Yes, please.'*

4 Please! *informal* **a)** said when you think what someone has just said or asked is not possible or reasonable: *Oh, please, he'd never do that.* **b)** used to ask someone to stop behaving badly: *Alison! Please!*

5 please Sir/Mrs Towers etc *BrE spoken* used by children to get an adult's attention

please[2] ●●● W3 *v*

1 [I,T] to make someone happy or satisfied: *a business that wants to please its customers* | *She did everything she could to please him.* | *Most children are **eager to please**.* | **be hard/easy/impossible etc to please** *She's hard to please. Everything has to be perfect.*

> **GRAMMAR: Using the progressive**
> **Please** is not used in the progressive. You say: *I do it because it pleases me.* ✗ Don't say: *I do it because it is pleasing me.*
> GRAMMAR GUIDE VERBS

2 [I] used in some phrases to show that someone can do or have what they want: *She does **what** she **pleases**.* | **however/whatever etc you please** *You can spend the money however you please.* | *With the Explorer pass, you can get on and off the bus **as you please**.*

3 please yourself *spoken* used when telling someone to do whatever they like, even though really you think they are making the wrong choice: *'I don't think I'll go.' 'Okay, please yourself.'*

4 if you please *old-fashioned* **a)** *formal* used to politely ask someone to do something: *Close the door, if you please.* **b)** *BrE* used to show that you are surprised, angry, or annoyed about something: *He asked me, in my own house if you please, to leave the room!*

5 bold/calm/cool etc as you please *BrE spoken* very BOLD, calm etc, in a way that is surprising: *He just walked in and sat down, as bold as you please.*

6 please God used to express a very strong hope or wish: *Everything will be all right, please God.*

pleased /pliːzd/ ●●● S2 W3 *adj*

1 happy or satisfied: *Your dad will be so pleased.* | **pleased by sth** *She seemed pleased by the compliment.* | **pleased about sth** *I could tell they were pleased about the news.* | **pleased with sth** *Gwinn was pleased with the results.* | **pleased for sb** *That's wonderful! I'm really pleased for you.* | **pleased (that)** *Her mother was pleased that she chose a college close to home.* | **pleased to hear/see/report etc** *I'm pleased to tell you that you've got the job.* THESAURUS HAPPY, SATISFIED

2 (I'm) pleased to meet you *spoken formal* used as a polite greeting when you meet someone for the first time

3 pleased to help/assist very willing or happy to help: *If there's anything we can do, we'd be pleased to help.*

4 pleased with yourself feeling proud or satisfied because you think you have done something clever, often in a way that annoys other people: *Miranda, pleased with herself for getting it right, sat down.*

pleas·er /ˈpliːzə $ -ər/ *n* **crowd-pleaser/audience-pleaser etc** someone or something that people like a lot: *A chocolate dessert is a sure crowd-pleaser.*

pleas·ing /ˈpliːzɪŋ/ *adj formal* giving pleasure, enjoyment, or satisfaction: *a pleasing sound* | **[+to]** *a design that is pleasing to the eye* —**pleasingly** *adv*: *a pleasingly relaxed atmosphere*

plea·sur·a·ble /ˈpleʒərəbəl/ *adj formal* enjoyable OPP **unpleasant**: *a pleasurable experience* **THESAURUS** NICE —**pleasurably** *adv*

plea·sure /ˈpleʒə $ -ər/ ●●● S2 W2 *n*

1 [U] the feeling of happiness, enjoyment, or satisfaction that you get from an experience → **pleasant**: **with pleasure** *She sipped her drink with obvious pleasure.* | **for pleasure** *Are you taking the trip for business or pleasure?* **THESAURUS** FUN

2 [C] an activity or experience that you enjoy very much → **pleasant**: *the simple pleasures of life* | **be a pleasure to read/work with/watch etc** *Carol was a pleasure to work with.*

3 (it's) my pleasure *spoken* used when someone has thanked you for doing something and you want to say that you were glad to do it

4 [singular] *spoken formal* used to be polite when you are meeting someone, asking for something, agreeing to do something etc: **have the pleasure of (doing) sth** *May I have the pleasure of seeing you again?* | ***It's been a pleasure*** *to meet you.* | **It'll be a pleasure/With pleasure** (=used to respond to a request) *'Give the kids a hug for me.' 'With pleasure.'*

5 at your pleasure *formal* if you can do something at your pleasure, you can do it when you want to and in the way you want to

6 at His/Her Majesty's pleasure *BrE law* if someone is put in prison at His or Her Majesty's pleasure, there is no fixed limit to the time they have to spend there

COLLOCATIONS

VERBS

take pleasure in (doing) sth *He takes great pleasure in boasting about his big salary.*
get pleasure from/out of sth *Young children get a lot of pleasure from dressing up.*
find pleasure in (doing) sth *I find great pleasure in reading.*
give (sb) pleasure *Over the years, painting has given me a lot of pleasure.*
bring pleasure to sb (=give someone pleasure) | **derive pleasure from sth** *formal* (=get pleasure from it)

ADJECTIVES

great/enormous/immense pleasure *Steinbeck's books have brought enormous pleasure to many people.*
sheer/pure pleasure

PHRASES

a source of pleasure *Her garden was a constant source of pleasure.*

THESAURUS

pleasure the feeling you have when you are doing something you enjoy or when something very nice has happened to you: *Most craftsmen get a lot of pleasure out of making things.* | *His music has brought pleasure to people all over the world.*
happiness the feeling you have when you are happy: *Happiness is more important than money.* | *Pauline was willing to do anything for her children's happiness.*
joy *especially written* a deep feeling of great happiness, because something good has happened: *It's hard to describe the joy we felt, seeing each other again after so many years.* | *They* ***danced with joy*** *when they heard the news.*
delight great happiness and excitement, because of something good that has happened: ***To*** *the audience's* ***delight****, she agreed to play another song.* | *Imagine my delight when I found out that the house was for sale.*
contentment a quietly happy and satisfied feeling, especially because you are happy with your work, your life etc: *He moved to the country and found contentment for the first time in his life.*
euphoria /juːˈfɔːria $ jʊ-/ an extremely strong feeling of happiness and excitement that continues for a short time: *The whole country experienced a period of euphoria after the war ended.* | *the euphoria that parents feel after the birth of a child*
elation /ɪˈleɪʃən/ *formal* a strong feeling of happiness and excitement, especially because you have achieved something: *After she had made her first landing, she experienced a great sense of elation.* | *The troops' sense of elation at the victory was not to last.*

ˈpleasure ˌboat (*also* **ˈpleasure ˌcraft**) *n* [C] a boat that someone uses for fun rather than for business

ˈpleasure ˌseeker *n* [C] *written* someone who does things just for enjoyment without considering other people

pleat /pliːt/ *n* [C usually plural] a flat narrow fold in a skirt, a pair of trousers, a dress etc

pleat·ed /ˈpliːtɪd/ *adj* a pleated skirt, dress etc has a lot of flat narrow folds

pleath·er /ˈpleðə $ -ər/ *n* [U] an artificial material that looks like leather and is used to make clothes: *a pleather jean jacket*

pleb /pleb/ *n* [C usually plural] *BrE informal* an insulting word meaning someone who is from a low social class – often used humorously: *Plebs like me could never have such perfect manners.* —**plebby** *adj*

plebe /pliːb/ *n* [C] *AmE informal* a student in their first year at a military college

ple·be·ian¹ /plɪˈbiːən/ *adj* relating to ordinary people and what they like, rather than to people from a high social class – used to show disapproval: *a man with plebeian tastes*

plebeian² *n* [C] **1** an insulting word for someone who is from a low social class **2** an ordinary person who had no special rank in ancient Rome OPP **patrician**

pleb·is·cite /ˈplebəsət $ -saɪt/ *n* [C,U] *formal* a system by which everyone in a country or area votes on an important decision that affects the whole country or area: **[+on]** *a plebiscite on independence* → **referendum**

plec·trum /ˈplektrəm/ *n* [C] *especially BrE* a small thin piece of plastic, metal, or wood that you use for playing some musical instruments with strings, such as a GUITAR SYN **pick**

pled /pled/ *AmE* a past tense and past participle of PLEAD

pledge¹ /pledʒ/ ●○○ *n* [C]

1 PROMISE *formal* a serious promise or agreement, especially one made publicly or officially: **[+of]** *a pledge of support for the plan* | **pledge to do sth** *the government's pledge to make no deals with terrorists* | **make/take/give a pledge** *Parents make a pledge to take their children to rehearsals.* | **keep/fulfil/honour a pledge** *Eisenhower fulfilled his election pledge to end the war in Korea.*

2 MONEY a promise to give money to an organization: *Donors have* ***made pledges*** *totaling nearly $4 million.* | **[+of]** *a pledge of $200 to the public TV station*

3 SOMETHING VALUABLE something valuable that you leave with someone else as proof that you will do what you have agreed to do

4 US COLLEGES someone who has promised to become a member of a FRATERNITY or SORORITY at an American university

pledge² ●○○ *v* [T]

1 PROMISE to make a formal, usually public, promise that you will do something: **pledge sth to sth/sb** *Moore pledged $100,000 to the orchestra at the fund-raising dinner.* | **pledge to do sth** *The new governor pledged to reduce crime.* | **pledge that** *Herrera pledged that his company would give aid to* *schools.* | **pledge (your) support/loyalty/solidarity etc** *He pledged his cooperation.* | **pledge yourself to (do) sth** *Trade unions pledged themselves to resist the government plans.* **THESAURUS** PROMISE

2 MAKE SB PROMISE to make someone formally promise something: *Employees were **pledged to secrecy**.*

3 LEAVE STH to leave something with someone as a PLEDGE[1](3)

4 US COLLEGES to promise to become a member of a FRATERNITY or SORORITY at an American university

Pleis·to·cene /ˈplaɪstəsiːn/ *adj* belonging to the period in the Earth's history that started about two million years ago and ended about 10,000 years ago, when much of the Earth was covered with ice

ple·na·ry /ˈpliːnəri/ *adj* [only before noun] *formal* **1** involving all the members of a committee, organization etc: *The conference ended with a plenary debate.* **2** plenary powers are complete powers with no limit: *He was given plenary powers to negotiate with the rebels.* —**plenary** *n* [C]

plen·i·po·ten·tia·ry /ˌplenəpəˈtenʃəri $ -ʃieri/ *n* (*plural* **plenipotentiaries**) [C] *formal or technical* someone who has full power to take action or make decisions, especially as a representative of their government in a foreign country —**plenipotentiary** *adj*

plen·i·tude /ˈplenɪtjuːd $ -tuːd/ *n* [U] *literary* **1** **a plenitude of sth** a large amount of something: *a plenitude of wealth* **2** completeness or fullness

plen·te·ous /ˈplentiəs/ *adj literary* plentiful

plen·ti·ful /ˈplentɪfəl/ *adj* more than enough in quantity: *a plentiful supply of food* —**plentifully** *adv*

plen·ty[1] /ˈplenti/ ●●● S1 W1 *pron* a large quantity that is enough or more than enough: **[+of]** *Make sure she gets plenty of fresh air.* | *No need to hurry – you've got plenty of time.* | **plenty to do/say/eat etc** *There's plenty to do and see in New York.* | *There are **plenty more** chairs in the next room.* **THESAURUS** ENOUGH

> **REGISTER**
> In written English, people sometimes prefer to use **ample** rather than **plenty of**, as it sounds more formal: *They were given **ample** time to complete the work.*

> **GRAMMAR**
> • You use **plenty of** before an uncountable noun: ***There is** plenty of **evidence** that he is guilty.* ✗ Don't say: *There is a plenty of evidence.*
> • You also use **plenty of** before a plural noun: ***There are** plenty of **opportunities** to improve your skills.* ✗ Don't say: *There is plenty of opportunities.*
> • You say that something **has plenty of** a thing, quality etc: *The town has plenty of nightlife.* ✗ Don't say: *The town is plenty of nightlife.*

plenty[2] *adv informal* **1** **plenty big/fast/warm etc enough** used to emphasize that something is more than big enough, fast enough etc: *This apartment's plenty big enough for two.* **2** *AmE* a lot or very: *I'd practiced plenty.* | *I was plenty nervous.*

plenty[3] *n* [U] *formal* **1** a situation in which there is a lot of food and goods available for people: *a land of plenty* **2** **in plenty** in large supply or more than enough: *There was food and wine in plenty.*

pleth·o·ra /ˈpleθərə/ *n* **a plethora of sth** *formal* a very large number of something, usually more than you need: *a plethora of suggestions*

pleu·ri·sy /ˈplʊərəsi $ ˈplʊr-/ *n* [U] a serious illness which affects your lungs, causing severe pain in your chest

Plex·i·glas, **plexiglass** /ˈpleksiglɑːs $ -glæs/ *n* [U] *trademark AmE* a strong clear type of plastic that can be used instead of glass SYN **Perspex** *BrE*

plex·us /ˈpleksəs/ *n* → SOLAR PLEXUS

pli·a·ble /ˈplaɪəbəl/ *adj* **1** able to bend without breaking or cracking: *a shoe made of soft pliable leather* **2** easily influenced and controlled by other people: *Senior officials would have preferred a more pliable government.* —**pliability** /ˌplaɪəˈbɪləti/ *n* [U]

pli·ant /ˈplaɪənt/ *adj* **1** soft and moving easily in the way that you want: *Isabel was pliant in his arms.* | *her pliant lips* **2** easily influenced and controlled by other people: *Pliant judges have been a problem in the past.* —**pliantly** *adv* —**pliancy** *n* [U]

pli·ers /ˈplaɪəz $ -ərz/ *n* [plural] a small tool made of two crossed pieces of metal, used to hold small things or to bend and cut wire: *a **pair of pliers*** → see picture at TOOL[1]

plight[1] /plaɪt/ ●○○ *n* [usually singular] a very bad situation that someone is in: **[+of]** *the **desperate plight** of the flood victims* | *the country's **economic plight***

plight[2] *v* **plight your troth** *old use* to promise someone that you will marry them

plim·soll /ˈplɪmsəl, -səʊl $ -səl, -soʊl/ *n* [C] *BrE* a cotton shoe with a flat rubber SOLE SYN **sneaker** *AmE*

ˈPlimsoll line (*also* **ˈPlimsoll mark**) *n* [C] *BrE* a line painted on the outside of a ship, showing how low in the water it can safely be when it is loaded

plinth /plɪnθ/ *n* [C] *especially BrE* a square block, usually made of stone, that is used as the base for a PILLAR or STATUE → see picture at STAND[2]

Pli·o·cene /ˈplaɪəsiːn/ *adj* belonging to the period in the Earth's history that started about five million years ago and continued until about three million years ago

plod /plɒd $ plɑːd/ *v* (**plodded**, **plodding**) [I always + adv/prep] to walk along slowly, especially when this is difficult: **[+through/up/across etc]** *The horse plodded up the hill.* | **[+on/along/back]** *Jake kept plodding on.* **THESAURUS** WALK

plod on/along *phr v* to work slowly or make slow progress, especially in a way that is boring: *For years he had plodded along in a series of boring office jobs.*

plod·der /ˈplɒdə $ ˈplɑːdər/ *n* [C] *informal* **1** *BrE* someone who works slowly and is not very clever **2** someone who walks or does something slowly

plod·ding /ˈplɒdɪŋ $ ˈplɑː-/ *adj* slow or thorough and not exciting: *plodding research*

plonk[1] /plɒŋk $ plɑːŋk, plɒːŋk/ *v* [T always + adv/prep] *especially BrE informal* **1** (*also* **plonk sth down**) to put something down somewhere, especially in a noisy and careless way SYN **plunk** *AmE*: *You can plonk those bags down anywhere in my room.* | **plonk sth on/onto/beside etc sth/sb** *He plonked a couple of glasses on the table.* **2** **plonk yourself (down)** to sit down heavily and then relax: *We plonked ourselves down in front of the telly and opened a couple of beers.*

plonk[2] *n* [U] *BrE informal* cheap wine

plonk·er /ˈplɒŋkə $ ˈplɑːŋkər, ˈplɒːŋ-/ *n* [C] *BrE informal not polite* an offensive word for a stupid person

plop[1] /plɒp $ plɑːp/ *n* [C] the sound made by something when it falls or is dropped into liquid: **with a plop** *The soap fell into the bath with a loud plop.* **THESAURUS** SOUND

plop[2] *v* (**plopped**, **plopping**) **1** [I always + adv/prep] to fall somewhere, making a sound like something dropping into water: **[+into/out of/onto etc]** *The frog plopped back into the pond.* **2** [T] to drop something, especially into a liquid, so that it makes a sound: **plop sth into sth** *I plopped a couple of ice cubes into the drink.* **3** **plop (yourself) down** to sit down or lie down heavily: *She plopped down on the sofa beside me.*

plo·sive /ˈpləʊsɪv $ ˈploʊ-/ *n* [C] *technical* a CONSONANT sound that is made by completely stopping the flow of air out of your mouth and then suddenly letting it out, as when saying /b/ or /t/ —**plosive** *adj*

plot[1] /plɒt $ plɑːt/ ●●○ W3 *n* [C]

1 PLAN a secret plan by a group of people to do something harmful or illegal: **plot to do sth** *a plot to bomb the UN headquarters* | **[+against]** *a plot against the king* | *The court heard how she and her lover **hatched** a **plot*** (=planned a plot) *to kill her husband.* | *The **plot** to overthrow the military*

government was ***foiled*** (=prevented from being successful). | *an* ***assassination plot*** THESAURUS ▸ PLAN
2 STORY/FILM the events that form the main story of a book, film, or play: *The plot was a little confusing.* | *We discover that Jack isn't as innocent as he seems, as the* ***plot unfolds*** (=gradually becomes clearer).
3 the plot thickens used to say that events seem to be becoming more complicated – often used humorously
4 PIECE OF LAND **a)** a small piece of land for building or growing things on: *a two-acre* ***plot of land*** | *a* ***vegetable plot*** **b)** a piece of land that a particular family owns in a CEMETERY, in which members of the family are buried when they die: *a* ***burial plot***
5 DRAWING *AmE* a drawing that shows the plan of a building at ground level SYN **ground plan** → **lose the plot** at LOSE(14)

P

plot² ●○○ *v* (**plotted**, **plotting**)
1 [I,T] to make a secret plan to harm a person or organization, especially a political leader or government: **plot to do sth** *They had plotted to blow up the White House.* | **[+against]** *He suspected that the military were* ***secretly plotting*** *against him.* | *The minister was found guilty of plotting the downfall of the government.* | *the story of a woman who plots revenge*
2 [T] (*also* **plot out**) to draw marks or a line to represent facts, numbers etc: *We* ***plotted*** *a* ***graph*** *to show the increase in sales figures this year.* | **plot sth on sth** *You can plot all these numbers on one diagram for comparison.*
3 [T] (*also* **plot out**) to mark, calculate, or follow the path of an aircraft or ship, for example on a map: *We* ***plotted*** *a* ***course*** *across the Pacific.*

plot·ter /ˈplɒtə $ ˈplɑːtər/ *n* [C] **1** someone who makes a secret plan to harm a person or organization, especially a political leader or government: *The plotters were caught and executed.* **2** a computer program that turns facts, numbers etc into a GRAPH or CHART

plough¹ (*also* **plow** *AmE*) /plaʊ/ *n* [C] **1** a piece of farm equipment used to turn over the earth so that seeds can be planted **2 under the plough** *BrE formal* land that is under the plough is used for growing crops → SNOW PLOUGH(1)

plough² (*also* **plow** *AmE*) *v* **1** [I,T] to turn over the earth using a plough so that seeds can be planted: *In those days the land was plowed by oxen.* | *a* ***ploughed field*** THESAURUS ▸ DIG **2** [I always + adv/prep] to move with a lot of effort or force: **[+through/up/across etc]** *We ploughed through the thick mud.* **3 plough a lonely/lone furrow** *BrE literary* to do a job or activity that is different from those done by other people, or to do it alone

plough ahead *phr v* to continue to do something in spite of opposition or difficulties: **[+with]** *The government will plough ahead with tests this year, despite a boycott from teachers.*

plough sth ↔ **back** *phr v* to use money that you have earned from a business to make the business bigger and more successful: **[+into]** *Companies can* ***plough back*** *their* ***profits*** *into new equipment.*

plough into sb/sth *phr v* to crash into something or someone, especially while driving, because you are unable to stop quickly enough: *I plowed into the car in front.*

plough on *phr v* to continue doing something that is difficult or boring: **[+with]** *Julia ploughed on with the endless exam papers.* | *He looked displeased but she* ***ploughed on regardless.***

plough through sth *phr v* to read all of something, even though it is boring and takes a long time: *Most staff will never want to plough through the manuals that come with the software.*

plough sth ↔ **up** *phr v* to break up the surface of the ground by travelling over it many times: *Horses plough up the paths and make them muddy for walkers.*

plough·man /ˈplaʊmən/ *n* (*plural* **ploughmen** /-mən/) [C] *BrE old use* a man whose job was to guide a plough that was being pulled by a horse

ˌploughman's ˈlunch *n* [C] *BrE* a simple meal that people eat especially in PUBS, consisting of bread, cheese, SALAD, and PICKLE

plough·share *BrE*, **plowshare** *AmE* /ˈplaʊʃeə $ -ʃer/ *n* [C] **1** the broad curved metal blade of a PLOUGH, which turns over the soil **2 turn/beat swords into ploughshares** to stop fighting and start living in peace

plov·er /ˈplʌvə $ -ər/ *n* [C] a small bird that lives near the sea

plow /plaʊ/ *n, v* the usual American spelling of PLOUGH

ploy /plɔɪ/ *n* [C] a clever and dishonest way of tricking someone so that you can get an advantage: *His usual ploy is to pretend he's ill.* | **ploy to do sth** *a smart ploy to win votes*

PLS, **pls** the written abbreviation of ***please***, used in email or TEXT MESSAGES

pluck¹ /plʌk/ ●○○ *v*
1 PULL STH [T] *written* to pull something quickly in order to remove it: **pluck sth from/off etc sth** *He plucked a couple of plastic bags from the roll.* | *Reaching up, she plucked an apple off the tree.*
2 pluck your eyebrows to make your EYEBROWS the shape you want, by pulling out some of the hairs
3 TAKE SB/STH AWAY [T always + adv/prep] to take someone away from a place or situation that is dangerous or unpleasant in a quick and unexpected way: **pluck sb/sth from/out of sth** *Some refugee children were plucked out of the country in a number of mercy missions.* | *She was* ***plucked from obscurity*** (=made suddenly famous) *by a Hollywood film producer.* | *Three survivors were* ***plucked to safety*** *after being in the sea for 7 hours.*
4 CHICKEN [T] to pull the feathers off a dead chicken or other bird before cooking it
5 pluck up (the) courage (to do sth) to force yourself to be brave and do something you are afraid of doing: *He finally plucked up enough courage to ask her out.*
6 MUSIC [I,T] to pull the strings of a musical instrument: **[+at]** *Someone was plucking at the strings of an old guitar.*
7 pluck sth out of the air (*also* **pluck something out of thin air**) to say or suggest a number, name etc that you have just thought of, without thinking about it carefully: *I'm plucking a figure out of the air here, but let's say it'll cost about $15,000.*

pluck at sth *phr v* to pull something quickly several times with your fingers, especially because you are nervous or to attract attention: *Kitty's hands plucked at her black cotton skirt.* | *The little boy plucked at her sleeve.*

pluck² *n* [U] *old-fashioned* courage and determination: *It* ***takes*** *a lot of* ***pluck*** *to stand up to a bully.*

pluck·y /ˈplʌki/ *adj informal* brave and determined – often used in newspapers: *Plucky Denise saved her younger sister's life.*

PLUGS

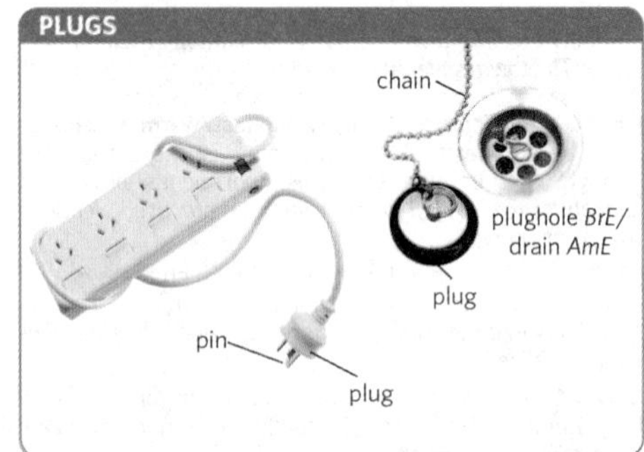

plug¹ /plʌg/ ●●● S3 *n* [C]
1 ELECTRICITY **a)** a small object at the end of a wire that is used for connecting a piece of electrical equipment to the main supply of electricity: *The plug on my iron needs changing.* | *an* ***electric plug*** **b)** *especially BrE informal* a place on a wall where electrical equipment can be connected to the main electricity supply SYN **socket**, **outlet** *AmE*
2 BATH a round flat piece of rubber used for stopping the water flowing out of a bath or SINK: *the* ***bath plug***

3 ADVERTISEMENT *informal* a way of advertising a book, film etc by mentioning it publicly, especially on television or radio: **put/get in a plug (for sth)** *During the show she managed to put in a plug for her new book.*
4 IN AN ENGINE *informal* the part of a petrol engine that makes a SPARK, which makes the petrol start burning SYN **spark plug**: *Change the plugs every 10,000 miles.*
5 pull the plug (on sth) *informal* to prevent a plan, business etc from being able to continue, especially by deciding not to give it any more money: *The Swiss entrepreneur has pulled the plug on any further investment in the firm.*
6 TO FILL A HOLE an object or substance that is used to fill or block a hole, tube etc: **[+of]** *You can fill any holes with plugs of matching wood.* → **EARPLUG**
7 FOR HOLDING SCREWS *BrE* a small plastic tube put in a hole to hold a screw tightly
8 A PIECE OF STH a piece of something pressed tightly together: *a plug of tobacco*

plug² ●●● S3 *v* (**plugged**, **plugging**) [T]
1 (*also* **plug up**) to fill or block a small hole: *We used mud to plug up the holes in the roof.*
2 to advertise a book, film etc by mentioning it on television or radio: *Arnie was on the show to plug his new movie.*
3 plug the gap to provide something that is needed, because there is not enough: *With so few trained doctors, paramedics were brought in to plug the gap.*
4 *AmE old-fashioned* to shoot someone

plug away *phr v* to keep working hard at something: **[+at]** *If you keep plugging away at it, your English will improve.*

plug sth ↔ **in** *phr v* to connect a piece of electrical equipment to the main supply of electricity, or to another piece of electrical equipment: *'Is your printer working?' 'Wait a minute – it's not plugged in.'*

plug into sth *phr v*
1 plug (sth) into sth to connect one piece of electrical equipment to another, or to be connected: *Your phone can be plugged into the cigarette lighter socket in your car.* | *Games consoles plug into the back of the TV.*
2 *informal* to realize that something is available to be used and use it: *A lot of students don't plug into all the research facilities we have.*

ˌplug and ˈplay *n* [U] *technical* the ability of a computer and a new piece of equipment to be used together as soon as they are connected

plug·hole /ˈplʌghəʊl $ -hoʊl/ *n* [C] *BrE* **1** the hole in a bath or SINK that the water flows out of, and which you can put a plug into SYN **drain** *AmE* → see picture at **PLUG¹**
2 go down the plughole *informal* **a)** if work or effort goes down the plughole, it is completely wasted: *Two years of hard work went right down the plughole.* **b)** if a business goes down the plughole, it fails and has to close

ˈplug-in¹ *adj* [only before noun] able to be connected to the electricity supply, or to another piece of electrical equipment: *a plug-in microphone*

plug-in², **plug·in** /ˈplʌgɪn/ *n* [C] *technical* a piece of computer software that can be used in addition to existing software in order to make particular programs work properly

plum¹ /plʌm/ ●●○ *n*
1 [C] a small round juicy fruit which is dark red, purple, or yellow and has a single hard seed, or the tree that produces this fruit: *juicy ripe plums* → see picture at **FRUIT¹**
2 [U] a dark purple-red colour
3 [C] *informal* something very good that other people wish they had, such as a good job or a part in a play: *The first job I had was a real plum.* → **PLUM PUDDING**

plum² *adj* **1 plum job/role/assignment etc** *informal* a good job etc that other people wish they had: *He landed a plum role in a TV mini-series.* **2** having a dark purple-red colour

plum·age /ˈpluːmɪdʒ/ *n* [U] the feathers covering a bird's body: *the parrot's brilliant blue plumage*

plumb¹ /plʌm/ *v* [T] **1 plumb the depths (of despair/misery/bad taste etc)** to feel an unpleasant emotion in a very extreme way, or to behave in a way that is extremely unpleasant or morally bad: *When his wife left him, Matt plumbed the very depths of despair.* | *That night they plumbed the depths of treachery and horror, and murdered the king as he slept.* **2** to succeed in understanding something completely SYN **fathom**: *Psychologists try to plumb the deepest mysteries of the human psyche.*

plumb sth ↔ **in** *phr v* to connect a piece of equipment such as a washing machine to the water supply

plumb² *adv* **1** [always + adv/prep] *informal* exactly: *The bullet hit him plumb between the eyes.* **2** *AmE informal* completely – often used humorously: *The whole idea sounds plumb crazy to me.*

plumb³ *adj technical* **1** exactly upright or level **2 out of plumb** not exactly upright or level

plumb·er /ˈplʌmə $ -ər/ ●●○ *n* [C] someone whose job is to repair water pipes, baths, toilets etc

plumb·ing /ˈplʌmɪŋ/ *n* [U] **1** the pipes that water flows through in a building: *We keep having problems with the plumbing.* **2** the work of fitting and repairing water pipes, baths, toilets etc

ˈplumb line *n* [C] a piece of string with a small heavy object tied to one end, used for measuring the depth of water, or for checking whether something such as a wall is built exactly upright

plume¹ /pluːm/ *n* [C] **1** a cloud of smoke, dust etc which rises up into the air: **plume of smoke/dust/gas/spray etc** *A black plume of smoke rose above the city.* **2** a large feather or bunch of feathers, especially one that is used as a decoration on a hat → **NOM DE PLUME**

plume² *v* [I] *literary* to rise or come out in a cloud: *No smoke plumed out of the factory's great chimneys.*

plumed /pluːmd/ *adj* [only before noun] decorated with feathers: *a knight with a plumed helmet*

plum·met /ˈplʌmɪt/ (*also* **plummet down**) *v* [I] **1** to suddenly and quickly decrease in value or amount SYN **plunge**: **plummet from sth to sth** *Profits plummeted from £49 million to £11 million.* | *House prices have plummeted down.* THESAURUS **DECREASE** **2** to fall suddenly and quickly from a very high place SYN **plunge**: *The plane plummeted towards the Earth.*

plum·my /ˈplʌmi/ *adj* **1** *BrE informal* a plummy voice sounds very UPPER-CLASS **2** like a PLUM in taste, colour etc: *a plummy wine*

plump¹ /plʌmp/ ●○○ *adj*
1 slightly fat in a fairly pleasant way – used especially about women or children, often to avoid saying the word 'fat': *The nurse was a cheerful plump woman.* | *The baby's nice and plump.* THESAURUS **FAT**
2 round and full in a way that looks attractive: *plump soft pillows* | *plump juicy tomatoes* —**plumpness** *n* [U]

plump² *v* **1** (*also* **plump up**) [T] to gently hit CUSHIONS or PILLOWS in order to make them rounder and softer **2 plump (yourself) down** to sit down suddenly and heavily SYN **plonk** **3** [T always + adv/prep] to put something down suddenly and carelessly SYN **plonk**: *Plump the bags down anywhere you like.* **4** (*also* **plump up**) [I,T] if dried fruit plumps up, or if you plump it up, it becomes fatter and softer when in liquid: *Soak the apricots and raisins until the fruit plumps up.*

plump for sth/sb *phr v BrE informal* to choose something or someone after thinking carefully about it: *Finally we plumped for a bottle of champagne.*

ˌplum ˈpudding *n* [C,U] *BrE* CHRISTMAS PUDDING

ˈplum toˌmato *n* [C] a type of tomato shaped like a PLUM, often used in cooking

plun·der¹ /ˈplʌndə $ -ər/ *v written* **1** [I,T] to steal large amounts of money or property from somewhere, especially while fighting in a war: *The rich provinces of Asia Minor were plundered by the invaders.* **2** [T] to use up all or most of the supplies of something in a careless way: *Unlicensed fishermen have plundered tuna stocks.* | *the egotism of man as he plunders our planet* —**plunderer** *n* [C]

plunder² *n* [U] *written* **1** things that have been stolen during a violent attack, especially during a war: *Henry's army returned loaded down with plunder.* **2** the act of plundering: *fear of invasion and plunder*

P

plunge¹ /plʌndʒ/ ●○○ *v*
1 [I,T always + adv/prep] to move, fall, or be thrown suddenly forwards or downwards: **[+off/into etc]** *Her car swerved and plunged off the cliff.* | *Both the climbers had* ***plunged to*** *their* ***deaths****.*
2 [I] if a price, rate etc plunges, it suddenly decreases by a large amount: *The unemployment rate plunged sharply.* | **[+to]** *Oil prices have* ***plunged to a new low****.* | *In the recession, the company's profits plunged 60%.*
3 [I] *literary* if a ship plunges, it moves violently up and down because of big waves THESAURUS▸ DECREASE
plunge in (*also* **plunge into sth**) *phr v*
1 to start talking or doing something quickly and confidently, especially without thinking about it first: *It's a difficult situation. You can't just plunge in and put everything right.* | *'I don't agree,' she said, plunging into the conversation.*
2 to jump or DIVE into water: *He stripped off and plunged into the sea.*
3 plunge sth ↔ in (*also* **plunge sth into sth**) to push something firmly and deeply into something else: *He opened the bag and plunged his hand in.* | *Plunge the pasta into boiling water.* | *Repeatedly she* ***plunged*** *the* ***knife*** *into his chest.* THESAURUS▸ PUT
plunge (sb/sth) **into** sth *phr v* to suddenly experience a difficult or unpleasant situation, or to make someone or something do this: *A strike would plunge the country into chaos.* | *The house was suddenly* ***plunged into darkness****.* | *After the war, the family plunged into debt.*

plunge² *n* **1 take the plunge** to decide to do something important or risky, especially after thinking about it for a long time: *We took the plunge and set up our own business.* **2** [C] a sudden large decrease in the price, value etc of something: **[+in]** *a* ***dramatic plunge*** *in house prices* **3** [C usually singular] a sudden movement down or forwards: *The plane began a* ***headlong plunge*** *towards the Earth.* **4** [C usually singular] when someone suddenly becomes involved in something new: **[+into]** *his sudden plunge into marriage* **5** [C usually singular] a jump or DIVE into water, or a quick swim: **[+in/into]** *a quick plunge in the lake*

plung·er /ˈplʌndʒə $ -ər/ *n* [C] **1** a tool for clearing waste that is blocking a kitchen or bathroom pipe. It consists of a straight handle with a rubber cup on the end. **2** *technical* a part of a machine that moves up and down

ˌplunging ˈneckline *n* [C] if a woman's dress or shirt has a plunging neckline, the top part at the front is very low

plunk /plʌŋk/ *v* [T always + adv/prep] *AmE informal* **1** (*also* **plunk sth down**) to put or place something somewhere, especially in a noisy, sudden, or careless way SYN **plonk** *BrE*: **plunk sth in/on etc sth** *plans to plunk a theme park on the island* **2 plunk (yourself) down** to sit down suddenly or heavily and then relax SYN **plonk** *BrE*: *Why don't you plunk yourself down with a good book?*
plunk sth **↔ down** *phr v* to spend an amount of money on something: *She plunked down $250 for a silver necklace.*

plu·per·fect /pluːˈpɜːfɪkt $ -ɜːr-/ *n* **the pluperfect** *technical* the PAST PERFECT tense of a verb

plu·ral¹ /ˈplʊərəl $ ˈplʊr-/ ●●● *n* [C] a form of a word that shows you are talking about more than one thing, person etc. For example, 'dogs' is the plural of 'dog' OPP **singular**: **in the plural** *'Sheep' remains the same in the plural.* | **[+of]** *What's the plural of 'mouse'?*

plural² ●●● *adj*
1 a plural word or form shows you are talking about more than one thing, person etc. For example, 'we' is a plural PRONOUN. OPP **singular**
2 *formal* a plural society, system, or culture is one with people from many different religions, races etc: *Britain has developed into a plural society.*

plu·ral·is·m /ˈplʊərəlɪzəm $ ˈplʊr-/ *n* [U] *formal* when people of many different races, religions, and political beliefs live together in the same society, or the belief that this can happen successfully: *a nation characterized by cultural pluralism* —**pluralist** *n* [C] —**pluralistic** /ˌplʊərəˈlɪstɪk◂ $ ˌplʊr-/ —**pluralist** *adj*: *a* ***pluralist society***

plu·ral·i·ty /plʊˈræləti/ *n* (*plural* **pluralities**) **1** [C usually singular] *formal* a large number of different things: **[+of]** *the plurality of factors affecting the election* **2** [C,U] *especially AmE technical* if one person or party receives a plurality in an election, they receive more votes than any of the other people or parties, but fewer votes than the total number of votes that all the others receive together: *The Democrats won only a plurality of the votes cast.* **3** [U] *technical* when a noun is plural

plus¹ /plʌs/ ●●● S1 W2 AWL *prep*
1 used to show that one number or amount is added to another OPP **minus**: *Three plus six equals nine (3 + 6 = 9).* | *The total cost was $10,000, plus 14% interest.*
2 and also: *There are numerous clubs, plus a casino.*
3 plus or minus used to say that a number may be more or less by a certain amount: *There may be a variation of plus or minus 5% in the prices that are quoted.*

plus² ●●○ AWL *n* [C]
1 *informal* something that is an advantage: **major/definite/big etc plus** *Some knowledge of Spanish is a definite plus in this job.*
2 a PLUS SIGN OPP **minus**

plus³ ●○○ AWL *adj*
1 [only before noun] used to talk about an advantage or good feature of a thing or situation OPP **minus**: *Another of the Beach Club's* ***plus points*** *is that it's right in the middle of town.* | *This is not an exciting car to drive, but* ***on the plus side*** *it is extremely reliable.*
2 used after a number to mean an amount which is more than that number: *an income of $50,000 plus* | *Most children start school when they're five plus.*
3 more than zero – used especially when talking about temperatures OPP **minus**: *Daytime temperatures barely reached plus 5°.*
4 A plus/B plus etc a mark used in a system of judging students' work. An 'A plus' is slightly higher than an 'A'.

plus⁴ ●○○ *conjunction informal* used to add more information: *He's been studying hard for exams. Plus he's been working in a bar at night.*

ˌplus ˈfours *n* [plural] short loose trousers that are fastened just below the knee. Men wore them in the past, especially when playing golf.

plush¹ /plʌʃ/ *adj informal* very comfortable, expensive, and of good quality: *a plush hotel* | *Their casino is the plushest in town.*

plush² *n* [U] a silk or cotton material with a thick soft surface: *plush curtains*

plus-ˈone *n* [C] *informal* someone who you take with you to an event when you have received an invitation for yourself and one other person, who is not named on the invitation: *He asked her to come to the wedding with him as his plus-one.*

ˈplus sign (*also* **plus** *especially BrE*) *n* [C] the sign (+), showing that you should add two or more numbers together, or that a number is more than zero

ˈplus-size *adj* plus-size clothes are for people who are larger than average

Plu·to /ˈpluːtəʊ $ -toʊ/ *n* an object that goes around the Sun, usually beyond Neptune, which was called a PLANET until 2006: *the discovery of Pluto in 1930*

plu·toc·ra·cy /pluːˈtɒkrəsi $ -ˈtɑːk-/ *n* (*plural* **plutocracies**) [C] a ruling class or government that consists of rich people, or a country that is governed by rich people

plu·to·crat /ˈpluːtəkræt/ *n* [C] someone who has power because they are rich – used to show disapproval: *champagne-drinking plutocrats* —**plutocratic** /ˌpluːtəˈkrætɪk◂/ *adj*

plu·to·ni·um /pluːˈtəʊniəm $ -ˈtoʊ-/ *n* [U] a RADIOACTIVE metal that is used in the production of NUCLEAR power, and in nuclear weapons. It is a chemical ELEMENT: symbol Pu

ply¹ /plaɪ/ *v* (**plied, plying, plies**) **1 ply your trade** *literary* to work at your business, especially buying and selling things on the street: *In some areas, drug dealers openly ply their trade on street corners.* **2** [I,T always + adv/prep] *written* if a ship, bus etc plies between two places or across a place, it does that journey regularly: **[+between/across etc]** *Two ferries ply between Tripoli and Malta every day.* **3 ply for hire/trade** *BrE* to try to get customers or passengers, in order to do business: *Continental airlines ply for trade in the UK.* **4** [T] *old use or literary* to use a tool skilfully

ply sb **with** sth *phr v* **1** to keep giving someone large quantities of food or drink: *The local people plied me with beer, until I could barely move.* **2 ply sb with questions** to keep asking someone questions

ply² *n* (*plural* **ply**) [C] a unit for measuring the thickness of thread, rope, plywood etc, based on the number of threads or layers that it has: *a sweater in four-ply yarn*

ply·wood /ˈplaɪwʊd/ *n* [U] a material made of several thin layers of wood that are stuck together to form a strong board

p.m. (*also* **pm** *BrE*) /ˌpiː ˈem/ ●●● W2 used after numbers expressing the time, to show that it is between NOON and MIDNIGHT → **a.m.**: *The meeting starts at 2.30 pm.*

PM /ˌpiː ˈem/ *n* [C] *BrE informal* the PRIME MINISTER: *a meeting with the PM*

PMP /ˌpiː em ˈpiː/ *n* [C] the abbreviation of ***portable media player***

PMS /ˌpiː em ˈes/ *n* [U] (***premenstrual syndrome***) the unpleasant physical and emotional feelings that many women have before their PERIOD starts

PMT /ˌpiː em ˈtiː/ *n* [U] *BrE* (***premenstrual tension***) the unpleasant physical and emotional feelings that many women have before their PERIOD starts

pneu·mat·ic /njuːˈmætɪk $ nʊ-/ *adj* [usually before noun] **1** *technical* filled with air: *pneumatic tyres* **2** worked by air pressure: *a pneumatic pump*

pneuˌmatic ˈdrill *n* [C] *especially BrE* a large powerful tool worked by air pressure and used for breaking up hard materials, especially road surfaces SYN **jackhammer** *AmE*

pneu·mo·ni·a /njuːˈməʊniə $ nʊˈmoʊ-/ *n* [U] a serious illness that affects your lungs and makes it difficult for you to breathe: *She was taken to hospital, suffering from pneumonia.*

PO *BrE*, **P.O.** *AmE* **1** the written abbreviation of ***post office*** → PO BOX **2** *BrE* the written abbreviation of ***postal order***

poach /pəʊtʃ $ poʊtʃ/ *v*

1 COOK [T] **a)** to cook an egg in or over gently boiling water, without its shell: *poached eggs on toast* **b)** to gently cook food, especially fish, in a small amount of boiling water, milk etc: *Poach the salmon in white wine and water.* → see picture at EGG¹ THESAURUS COOK

2 ANIMALS [I,T] to illegally catch or shoot animals, birds, or fish, especially on private land without permission: *Deer have been poached here for years.*

3 PEOPLE [T] to persuade someone who belongs to another organization, team etc to leave it and join yours, especially in a secret or dishonest way: *That company's always poaching our staff.* | **[+from]** *Several of their reporters were poached from other papers.*

4 STEAL IDEAS [T] to take and use someone else's ideas unfairly or illegally: **[+from]** *characters poached from Shakespeare*

5 poach on sb's territory/preserve *BrE* to do something that is someone else's responsibility, especially when they do not want you to do it —**poaching** *n* [U]: *the poaching of elephants for their ivory tusks*

poach·er /ˈpəʊtʃə $ ˈpoʊtʃər/ *n* [C] **1** someone who illegally catches or shoots animals, birds, or fish, especially on private land without permission THESAURUS THIEF **2 poacher turned gamekeeper** *BrE* someone who used to do illegal things or have a bad attitude to authority, and who has now changed completely – used especially of someone who is now in a position of authority **3** *BrE* a pan with small containers shaped like cups used for poaching eggs

PO Box *BrE*, **P.O. Box** *AmE* /ˈpiː əʊ bɒks $ -oʊ bɑːks/ *n* [C] (***post office box***) used before a number as an address at a post office where letters to you can be sent: *Write to P.O. Box 714, Key Largo, Florida.*

pocked /pɒkt $ pɑːkt/ *adj* covered with small holes or marks SYN **pockmarked**: **[+with]** *His face was pocked with scars.*

pock·et¹ /ˈpɒkɪt $ ˈpɑː-/ ●●● S2 W2 *n* [C]

1 IN CLOTHES a type of small bag in or on a coat, trousers etc that you can put money, keys etc in: *Luke came in with his hands in his pockets.* | **jacket/trouser etc pocket** *The keys are in my trouser pocket.* | **[+of]** *the* ***inside pocket*** *of his jacket* | *The policeman told me to* ***turn out*** *my* ***pockets*** (=take everything out of them).

2 MONEY the amount of money that you have to spend: *There are eight hotels, with a price range to* ***suit every pocket***. | **from/out of/into your own pocket** *Dan had to pay for the repairs out of his own pocket.* | *He was accused of diverting some of the firm's money into his own pocket.* | *The deepening recession has* ***hit*** *people's* ***pockets***. | *For investors with* ***deep pockets*** (=a lot of money), *the Berlin property market is attractive.*

3 SMALL CONTAINER a small bag or piece of material fastened to something so that you can put things into it: *Please read the air safety card in the pocket of the seat in front.*

4 SMALL AREA/AMOUNT a small area or amount of something that is different from what surrounds it: **[+of]** *In some parts, there are still pockets of violence and unrest.* | *pockets of air inside the hull of the ship*

5 be in sb's pocket to be controlled or strongly influenced by someone in authority, and willing to do whatever they want: *The judge was in the defense lawyer's pocket.*

6 have sth in your pocket to be certain to win something such as a competition or an election: *The Democrats had the election in their pocket.*

7 out of pocket *especially BrE informal* if you are out of pocket, you have less money than you should have, especially as a result of making a mistake or being unlucky: *If he loses the deal, he'll be badly out of pocket.*

8 be/live in each other's pockets *BrE informal* if two people are in each other's pockets, they are together too much

9 GAME a small net on a POOL, SNOOKER, or BILLIARD table, which you try to hit balls into → **AIR POCKET**, → **burn a hole in your pocket** at BURN¹(17), → **line your own pockets** at LINE²(4), → **pick sb's pocket** at PICK¹(14), → see picture at POOL¹

pocket² *v* [T] **1** to put something into your pocket: *Maggie locked the door and pocketed the keys.* **2** to steal money, especially money that you are responsible for: *One inspector had pocketed up to $500,000 in bribes.* **3** to get a large amount of money, win a prize etc, especially in a way that seems very easy or slightly dishonest: *Johnston pocketed $2,500 in prize money.* **4** to hit a ball into a pocket in the game of POOL, SNOOKER or BILLIARDS SYN **pot**

pocket³ *adj* [only before noun] small enough to be carried in your pocket: *a pocket dictionary*

ˌpocket ˈbattleship *n* [C] a fairly small fighting ship

pock·et·book /ˈpɒkətbʊk $ ˈpɑː-/ *n* [C] **1** *AmE* the amount of money that you have, or your ability to pay for things SYN **pocket** *BrE*: *The aim was to provide a car* ***for every*** *age and* ***pocketbook***. | *Older voters are most concerned about* ***pocketbook issues*** (=that concern money). **2** *AmE old-fashioned* a HANDBAG **3** *AmE old-fashioned* a WALLET **4** *BrE old-fashioned* a NOTEBOOK

ˌpocket ˈcalculator *n* [C] a small piece of electronic equipment that you use to do calculations

ˈpocket ˌchange *n* [U] *AmE* **1** a small or unimportant amount of money: *The money is nothing – pocket change to them.* **2** coins that you carry in your pocket

pock·et·ful /ˈpɒkətfʊl $ ˈpɑː-/ *n* [C] the amount that can fit in a pocket: **[+of]** *a pocketful of coins*

ˌpocket ˈhandkerchief *n* [C] *old-fashioned* a HANDKERCHIEF

P

ˌpocket-ˈhandkerchief *adj* [only before noun] *BrE informal* a pocket-handkerchief garden or area of land is very small and usually square

ˈpocket knife *n* (*plural* **pocket knives**) [C] a small knife with one or more blades that fold into the handle SYN **penknife**

ˈpocket ˌmoney *n* [U] **1** *BrE* a small amount of money that parents give regularly to their children, usually every week or month SYN **allowance** *AmE*: *How much pocket money do you get?* **2** *informal* a small amount of extra money that you earn in order to spend it on things you want: *I give a few private lessons too, for pocket money.*

ˈpocket-sized, **ˈpocket-size** *adj* [usually before noun] *BrE* small enough to fit into your pocket or be carried easily: *pocket-sized dictionaries*

ˌpocket ˈveto *n* [C] a method used by the US president to stop a BILL (=proposal for a new law). The president keeps the proposal without signing it until Congress is not working anymore.

pock·mark /ˈpɒkmɑːk $ ˈpɑːkmɑːrk/ *n* [C] a hollow mark on someone's skin or on the surface of something

pock·marked /ˈpɒkmɑːkt $ ˈpɑːkmɑːrkt/ *adj* covered with hollow marks or holes: *a pockmarked skin*

pod /pɒd $ pɑːd/ *n* [C] **1** a long narrow seed container that grows on various plants, especially PEAS and beans: *a pea pod* → **like two peas in a pod** at PEA(2) **2** a part of a space vehicle that can be separated from the main part: *a space pod* **3** a long narrow container for petrol or other substances, especially one carried under an aircraft wing **4** a group of sea animals, such as WHALES or DOLPHINS, that swim together **5** a container which holds the eggs of some types of insects

p.o.'d /ˌpiː ˈəʊd $ -ˈoʊd/ *adj AmE spoken* very annoyed: *She was really p.o.'d when she didn't get the job.*

pod·cast¹ /ˈpɒdkɑːst $ ˈpɑːdkæst/ ●●○ *n* [C] a radio programme that can be DOWNLOADed from the Internet THESAURUS ▸ PROGRAMME

podcast² *v* (*past tense and past participle* **podcast**) [T] to make a radio programme available to be DOWNLOADed from the Internet: *The show is to be podcast.*

podg·y /ˈpɒdʒi $ ˈpɑː-/ *adj BrE* another form of PUDGY

po·di·a·trist /pəˈdaɪətrɪst/ *n* [C] *especially AmE* a doctor who takes care of people's feet and treats foot diseases SYN **chiropodist** *BrE* —**podiatry** *n* [U]

po·di·um /ˈpəʊdiəm $ ˈpoʊ-/ *n* [C] **1** a small raised area for a performer, speaker, or musical CONDUCTOR to stand on **2** *AmE* a high sloping surface for putting an open book or notes on while you are giving a speech to a lot of people – some people think that this use is incorrect SYN **lectern**: *Several speakers* ***took the podium*** (=spoke from it) *that night.*

po·dunk /ˈpəʊdʌŋk $ ˈpoʊ-/ *adj AmE informal* a podunk place is small and unimportant: *Bob's from some podunk town in Iowa.*

po·em /ˈpəʊɪm $ ˈpoʊ-/ ●●● S3 W3 *n* [C] a piece of writing that expresses emotions, experiences, and ideas, especially in short lines using words that RHYME (=end with the same sound): **[+about]** *I decided to write a poem about how I felt.*

po·et /ˈpəʊɪt $ ˈpoʊ-/ ●●● W3 *n* [C] someone who writes poems → **poem**, **poetry**

po·et·ess /ˌpəʊəˈtes◂ $ ˈpoʊɪtɪs/ *n* [C] *old-fashioned* a female poet

po·et·ic /pəʊˈetɪk $ poʊ-/ ●○○ (*also* **po·et·ic·al** /-ˈetɪkəl/) *adj*
1 relating to poetry, or typical of poetry: *poetic expression*
2 having qualities of deep feeling or graceful expression: *poetic language* —**poetically** /-kli/ *adv*

poˌetic ˈjustice *n* [U] a situation in which someone suffers, and you think they deserve it because they did something bad: *After the way she treated Sam, it's only poetic justice that Dave left her.*

poˌetic ˈlicence *BrE*, **poetic license** *AmE* *n* [U] the freedom that poets and other artists have to change facts, ignore grammar rules etc, because what they are making is poetry or art

ˌpoet ˈlaureate *n* (*plural* **poets laureate**) [C] a poet who is chosen by a king, queen, president etc to write poems on important national occasions

po·et·ry /ˈpəʊətri $ ˈpoʊ-/ ●●● W3 *n* [U]
1 poems in general, or the art of writing them → **poem**, **poet**: *He reads a lot of poetry.* | *a poetry magazine* | **modern/lyric/love etc poetry** *a selection of religious poetry*
2 a quality of beauty, gracefulness, and deep feeling: **pure/sheer poetry** *The way she moves on the court is sheer poetry.* | *His golf swing is* ***poetry in motion***.

po-faced /ˌpəʊ ˈfeɪst◂ $ ˌpoʊ-/ *adj BrE informal* having an unfriendly disapproving expression on your face SYN **stern**

po·go stick /ˈpəʊgəʊ stɪk $ ˈpoʊgoʊ-/ *n* [C] a toy used for jumping, that consists of a pole with a spring near the bottom, a bar across the pole that you stand on, and a handle at the top

pog·rom /ˈpɒgrəm $ pəˈgrɑːm/ *n* [C] a planned killing of large numbers of people, usually done for reasons of race or religion

poi·gnant /ˈpɔɪnjənt/ *adj* making you feel sad or full of pity: **poignant reminder/image/moment etc** *a poignant reminder of our nation's great sacrifices* —**poignancy** *n* [U] —**poignantly** *adv*: *a poignantly expressed tribute to his father*

poin·set·ti·a /pɔɪnˈsetiə/ *n* [C] a tropical plant with groups of large red or white leaves that look like flowers

point¹ /pɔɪnt/ ●●● S1 W1 *n*
1 IDEA [C] a single fact, idea, or opinion that is part of an argument or discussion: *That's a very interesting point.* | *She made some extremely good points.* | *There are three important points we must bear in mind.* | *This brings me to my next point.* | **[+about]** *I agree with John's point about keeping the costs down.* THESAURUS ▸ COMMENT
2 MAIN MEANING/IDEA **the point** the most important fact or idea: ***The point is****, at least we're all safely back home.* | *Nobody knows exactly how it works. That's* ***the whole point****.* | *He may not have stolen the money himself, but* ***that's not the point****.* | *I wish you'd* ***get to the point*** (=talk about the most important thing). | *I'll* ***come*** *straight* ***to the point*** (=talk about the most important thing first). | *I need to find out who killed Alf, and* ***more to the point*** (=what is more important) *I need to do it before anyone else gets killed.* | *We all like him, but that's* ***beside the point*** (=not the most important thing). | *I think you've* ***missed the point*** (=you have not understood the most important thing).
3 PURPOSE [U] the purpose or aim of something: *I suppose we could save one or two of the trees, but* ***what's the point****?* | **[+of]** *What's the point of this meeting anyway?* | ***The whole point*** *of this legislation is to protect children.* | ***There's no point in*** *worrying.* | *We're going to lose anyway, so I* ***can't see the point of*** *playing.* | *I* ***didn't see the point in*** *moving to London.*
4 PLACE [C] a particular place or position: *The accident happened at the point where the A15 joins the M1.* | *No cars are allowed beyond this point.* | *a border crossing point* | *Cairo is a convenient* ***departure point*** *for tours.* | *Dover is a* ***point of entry*** *into Britain.* THESAURUS ▸ PLACE
5 IN TIME/DEVELOPMENT [C] an exact moment, time, or stage in the development of something: *I had* ***reached*** *a* ***point*** *in my career where I needed to decide which way to go.* | *She had* ***got to the point where*** *she felt that she could not take any more.* | *Their win over old rivals Manchester United was the* ***high point*** (=best part) *in their season.* | *Sales reached a* ***low point*** *in 1996.* | *We will take last week's riots as a* ***starting point*** *for our discussion.* | ***At one point****, I thought he was going to burst into tears.* | *Maybe* ***at this point*** *we should move onto some of the practical experiments.* | ***At that point****, I was still living at home and had no job.* | *You will probably sell the car* ***at some point*** *in the future.* | *It is impossible to give a definite answer* ***at this point in time****.* | *Some children are bullied* ***to the point of*** *suicide* (=until they reach this stage). THESAURUS ▸ TIME
6 QUALITY/FEATURE [C usually plural] a particular quality or

feature that something or someone has: **sb's/sth's good/bad points** *Sometimes she had to remind herself of his good points.* | **[+of]** *They would spend hours discussing* ***the finer points*** (=small details about qualities and features) *of various cars.* | *The low price is one of its main* ***selling points*** (=features that will help to sell it). | *Driving was not one of Baxter's* ***strong points****.* | *One of the club's* ***plus points*** *is that it is central.* | *There were some* ***weak points*** *in his argument.*

7 GAMES/SPORT [C] one of the marks or numbers that shows your score in a game or sport: *He is three points behind the leader.* | *Leeds United are now six points clear at the top of the table.* | *She had to* ***win*** *this* ***point****.* | *You* ***get*** *three* ***points*** *for a win and one point for a draw.* | *You* ***lose*** *a* ***point*** *if you do not complete the puzzle on time.* | *The fight went the full fifteen rounds, and in the end the American* ***won on points****.*

8 SHARP END [C] a sharp end of something: *the sharp point of a spear*

9 boiling point/freezing point/melting point etc the temperature at which something boils, freezes, melts etc: *Heat the water until it reaches boiling point.*

10 the point of no return a stage in a process or activity when it becomes impossible to stop it or do something different: **reach/pass the point of no return** *I was aware that we had passed the point of no return.*

11 point of departure an idea which you use to start a discussion: *He takes the idea of personal freedom as his point of departure.*

12 be on the point of (doing) sth to be going to do something very soon: *I was on the point of giving up the search when something caught my eye in the bushes.* | *The country's economy is on the point of collapse.*

13 up to a point partly, but not completely: *I agree with you up to a point.* | *That is true, but only up to a point.*

14 to the point dealing only with the important subject or idea, and not including any unnecessary discussions: *Her comments were brief and to the point.*

15 make a point of doing sth to do something deliberately, even when it involves making a special effort: *He made a point of spending Saturdays with his children.* | *I always make a point of being early.*

16 when/if it comes to the point *BrE* used to talk about what happens when someone is in a difficult situation and has to make a difficult decision: *I'm sure that if it came to the point, he would do what is expected of him.*

17 in point of fact *formal* used when saying that something is true, although it may seem unlikely: *We were assured that the prisoners were being well treated, when in point of fact they were living in terrible conditions.*

18 not to put too fine a point on it *especially BrE* used when you are saying something in a very direct way: *She's lying, not to put too fine a point on it.*

19 NUMBERS [C] a sign (.) used to separate a whole number from any DECIMALs that follow it

20 MEASURE ON A SCALE [C] a mark or measure on a scale: *The stock market has fallen by over 200 points in the last week.*

21 SMALL SPOT [C] a very small spot of light or colour: *The stars shone like* ***points of light*** *in the sky.*

22 DIRECTION [C] one of the marks on a COMPASS that shows direction: *Soldiers were advancing on us from all points of the compass.*

23 PIECE OF LAND [C] a long thin piece of land that stretches out into the sea: *We sailed round the point into a small, sheltered bay.*

24 ELECTRICITY [C] *BrE* a piece of plastic with holes in it which is attached to a wall and to which electrical equipment can be connected: *a telephone point* | *an electrical point*

25 RAILWAYS **points** [plural] *BrE* a piece of railway track that can be moved to allow a train to cross over from one track to another: *The train rattled over the points.* → POINTE

COLLOCATIONS

ADJECTIVES

a good point *I think that's a very good point.*
an interesting point *He has made an interesting point.*
an important point *That's an important point to bear in mind.*
a serious point *He's making a joke but there is a serious point there as well.*
a valid point *She raised a number of valid points.*
a general point *I'd like to make one further general point.*
a similar point | the main point | one final/last point

VERBS

make a point *He makes the point that predicting behaviour is not easy.*
put/get your point across (=make people understand it) *I think we got our point across.*
raise a point (=mention it) *I was going to raise that point.*
illustrate/demonstrate a point *A simple example will illustrate the point.*
prove your/a point (=prove that what you say is right) *He was determined to prove his point.*
understand a point *I'm sorry, I don't understand your point.*
see/take/get sb's point (=understand or agree with it) *OK, I take your point. But it's not that easy.*
have a point (=have made a good point) *Maybe she has a point.*
labour the point *BrE*, **belabor the point** *AmE* (=keep saying something)

PHRASES

point taken (=used to say to someone that you accept what they say) *All right, point taken – I should have asked you first.*
the finer points of sth (=the small details)

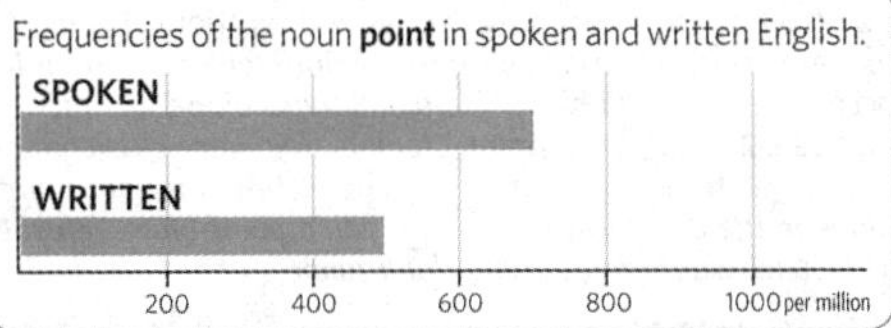

point² ●●● S2 W2 *v*

1 SHOW STH WITH YOUR FINGER [I,T] to show something to someone by holding up one of your fingers or a thin object towards it: *'Look!' she said and pointed.* | **[+at]** *I could see him pointing at me and telling the other guests what I had said.* | **[+to/towards]** *She was pointing to a small boat that was approaching the shore.* | **[+with]** *The driver pointed with his whip.* | *She* ***pointed in the direction of*** *the car park.* | *He stood up and* ***pointed*** *his* ***finger*** *at me.* THESAURUS ▸ LEAD

2 AIM STH [T always + adv/prep] to hold something so that it is aimed towards a person or thing: **point sth at sb/sth** *He stood up and pointed his gun at the prisoner.* | *She produced a camera and pointed it at me.*

3 FACE IN ONE DIRECTION [I always + adv/prep] to face or be aimed in a particular direction: *The arrow always points north.* | *There were flashlights all around us, pointing in all directions.* | **[+at]** *There were TV cameras pointing at us.* | **[+to/towards]** *The hands of the clock pointed to a quarter past one.* | *We found footprints pointing towards the back door.*

4 SHOW SB WHERE TO GO [T always + adv/prep] to show someone which direction they should go in: *She pointed me towards an armchair.* | *Could you* ***point*** *me* ***in the direction of*** *the bathroom, please?*

5 SUGGEST WHAT SB SHOULD DO [T always + adv/prep] to suggest what someone should do: *My teachers were all pointing me towards university.* | *A financial adviser should be able to* ***point*** *you* ***in the right direction****.*

6 SUGGEST THAT STH IS TRUE [I always + adv/prep] to suggest that something is true: *Everything seemed to point in one direction.* | **[+to/towards]** *All the evidence pointed*

towards Blake as the murderer. | *Everything points to her having died from a drugs overdose.*
7 WALLS/BUILDINGS [T] *BrE* to put new CEMENT between the bricks of a wall
8 point your toes to stretch the ends of your feet downwards
9 point the/a finger at sb to blame someone or say that they have done something wrong: *I knew that they would point the finger at me.* | *I don't want to* ***point*** *a* ***finger of blame*** *at anyone.*
10 point the way a) to show the direction that something is in: **[+to/towards]** *An old-fashioned signpost pointed the way to the restaurant.* **b)** to show how something could change or develop successfully: **[+forward/forwards]** *This report points the way forward for the water industry.* | **[+to/towards]** *a government paper which points the way towards reform*

point sth ↔ **out** *phr v*
1 to tell someone something that they did not already know or had not thought about: *He was always very keen to point out my mistakes.* | *The murder was obviously well planned, as the inspector had pointed out.* | **point out that** *Some economists have pointed out that low inflation is not necessarily a good thing.* | **point sth out to sb** *Thank you for pointing this out to me.*
2 to show something to someone by pointing at it: *Luke pointed out two large birds by the water's edge.* | **point sb/sth out to sb** *I'll point him out to you if we see him.*

point to sth *phr v* to mention something because you think it is important: *Many politicians have pointed to the need for a written constitution.*

point sth ↔ **up** *phr v formal* to make something seem more important or more noticeable: *These cases point up the complete incompetence of some government departments.*

ˌpoint-ˈblank *adv* **1** if you say or refuse something point-blank, you do it directly and without trying to explain your reasons: *He* ***refused point-blank*** *to identify his accomplices.* | *I told him point-blank that I didn't want to get involved.* **2** a gun fired point-blank is fired very close to the person or thing it is aimed at: *The victim was shot point-blank in the chest.* —**point-blank** *adj*: *a* ***point-blank refusal*** | *The bullet was fired at* ***point-blank range.***

pointe, **pointes** /pwænt $ pwɑːnt/ *n* [U] if BALLET dancers are on pointe, they are dancing on the ends of their toes with their feet in a vertical position

point·ed /ˈpɔɪntɪd/ ●●○ *adj* [usually before noun]
1 having a point at the end: *a pointed beard*
2 a pointed question/look/remark a direct question, look etc that deliberately shows that you are annoyed, bored, or disapprove of something: *a pointed remark about my being late*

point·ed·ly /ˈpɔɪntɪdli/ *adv* in a way that is deliberately meant to show that you are annoyed, bored, or disapprove of something: *She looked pointedly at the clock on the kitchen wall.* | **say/add/ask etc pointedly** *'I thought you were leaving,' she said pointedly.*

point·er /ˈpɔɪntə $ -ər/ ●○○ *n* [C]
1 ADVICE a useful piece of advice or information that helps you to do or understand something SYN **tip**: **[+on]** *Ralph* ***gave*** *me some* ***pointers*** *on my golf swing.* | **practical/useful/helpful pointers** *a few useful pointers about using the technique*
2 SIGN *BrE* something that shows how a situation is developing, or is a sign of what might happen in the future SYN **indicator**: **[+to]** *an encouraging pointer to an improvement in the economy* | *The local elections were seen as a pointer to the general elections.*
3 COMPUTER the small symbol, usually an ARROW, that you move using a computer's MOUSE to point to the place on the screen where you want to work, start a program etc: *Position the mouse pointer and click.*
4 STICK a long stick used to point at things on a map, board etc
5 SHOWS NUMBER/DIRECTION ETC a thin piece of metal that points to a number or direction on a piece of equipment, for example on a measuring instrument: *The pointer was between 35 and 40 pounds.*
6 DOG a hunting dog that stands very still and points with its nose to where birds or animals are hiding

poin·til·lis·m /ˈpwæntɪlɪzəm, ˈpɔɪn-/ *n* [U] a style of painting popular in the late 19th century that uses small spots of colour all over the painting, rather than brush strokes —**pointillist** *adj* —**pointillist** *n* [C]

point·ing /ˈpɔɪntɪŋ/ *n* [U] *BrE* the substance that is put in the spaces between the bricks or stones in a wall, or the way that this substance is put in the spaces SYN **mortar**

point·less /ˈpɔɪntləs/ ●○○ *adj* worthless or not likely to have any useful result: *Life just seemed pointless to me.* | *a pointless quarrel* | **it is pointless doing sth** *It's pointless telling her to clean her room – she'll never do it.* | **it is pointless to do sth** *I think it would be pointless to discuss this issue again.* —**pointlessly** *adv* —**pointlessness** *n* [U]

ˈpoint man *n AmE* **1** [singular] someone with a very important job or a lot of responsibility for a particular subject in a company or organization: **[+on]** *the administration's point man on health care* **2** [C] a soldier who goes ahead of a group to see if there is any danger

ˌpoint of ˈorder *n* (*plural* **points of order**) [C] *formal* a rule used to organize an official meeting: **on a point of order** (=according to a rule) *One MP raised an objection on a point of order.*

ˌpoint of ˈreference *n* (*plural* **points of reference**) [C] something you already know about that helps you understand a situation

ˌpoint of ˈsale (*also* **ˌpoint of ˈpurchase**) *n* [singular] the place or shop where a product is sold: *Under the new law, cigarette advertising will only be allowed at the point of sale.*

ˌpoint of ˈview ●●○ *n* (*plural* **points of view**) [C]
1 a particular way of thinking about or judging a situation: **scientific/technical/business etc point of view** *From an economic* ***point of view****, the new development will benefit the town greatly.*
2 someone's own personal opinion or attitude about something: *I respect your point of view, but I'm not sure I agree with you.* | **from sb's point of view** *From my point of view, there is no way they can win.* GRAMMAR ✗ Don't say: *in my point of view*

point·y /ˈpɔɪnti/ *adj informal* POINTED(1)

poise[1] /pɔɪz/ *n* [U] **1** a calm confident way of behaving, combined with an ability to control your feelings or reactions in difficult situations: *Louisa seems to have much more poise and confidence.* **2** a graceful way of moving or standing, so that your body seems balanced and not awkward: *the poise of a dancer* | *She's pretty, but lacks poise.*

poise[2] *v* [T always + adv/prep] to put or hold something in a carefully balanced position, especially above something else: **poise sth over/above sth** *He poised the bottle over her glass. 'More wine?'*

poised /pɔɪzd/ ●○○ *adj*
1 [not before noun] not moving, but ready to move or do something at any moment: **[+for]** *She waited by the door like a small animal poised for flight.* | **[+on]** *His finger was poised on the camera's shutter release.* | **poised to do sth** *He stood on the edge of the roof, poised to jump.*
2 [not before noun] completely ready to do something or for something to happen, when it is likely to happen soon: **poised to do sth** *Spain was poised to become the dominant power in Europe.* | **poised on the brink/edge of sth** *The economy is poised on the edge of collapse.*
3 poised between sth and sth to be in a position or situation in which two things have an equally strong influence: *The world stood poised between peace and war.*
4 behaving in a calm confident way, and able to control your feelings and reactions: *Abigail walked to the microphone, poised and confident.*

poi·son[1] /ˈpɔɪzən/ ●●○ *n*
1 [C,U] a substance that can cause death or serious illness if you eat it, drink it etc: *Belladonna and red arsenic*

are ***deadly poisons.*** | *a box of* ***rat poison*** (=poison to kill rats) | *He swallowed some type of poison.*
2 [C] something such as an emotion or idea that makes you behave badly or become very unhappy: *Hatred is a poison that will destroy your life.*
3 what's your poison? *old-fashioned spoken* a humorous way of asking which alcoholic drink someone would like
→ **one man's meat is another man's poison** at MEAT(4)

poison² ●○○ *v* [T]
1 to give someone poison, especially by adding it to their food or drink, in order to harm or kill them: *She was accused in 1974 of poisoning her second husband, Charles.* | *He killed several people by poisoning their tea.* | **poison sb with sth** *Helms attempted to poison his whole family with strychnine.*
2 if a substance poisons someone, it makes them sick or kills them: *Thousands of children were poisoned by radiation.*
3 to make land, rivers, air etc dirty and dangerous, especially by the use of harmful chemicals: *Pesticides are poisoning our rivers.*
4 to have very harmful and unpleasant effects on someone's mind, emotions, or a situation: *Her childhood had been poisoned by an abusive stepfather.* | *The law will only serve to poison relations between the US and Mexico.* | *Television violence is* ***poisoning*** *the* ***minds*** *of young people.* **THESAURUS** ▸ **SPOIL**
5 poisoned chalice an important job that someone is given, which is likely to cause them a lot of trouble —**poisoner** *n* [C]

ˌpoison ˈgas *n* [U] gas that causes death or serious injury, used especially against an enemy in a war: *There are reports that poison gas is being used against the rebels.*

poi·son·ing /ˈpɔɪzənɪŋ/ *n* [C,U] **1** illness caused by swallowing, touching, or breathing in a poisonous substance: **alcohol/lead/radiation etc poisoning** (=caused by a particular substance) *a case of alcohol poisoning* **2** the act of giving poison to someone: *An autopsy revealed no evidence of poisoning.* → **FOOD POISONING**

ˌpoison ˈivy *n* [U] a North American plant that has an oily substance on its leaves that makes your skin hurt and ITCH if you touch it

ˌpoison ˈoak *n* [U] a North American plant with leaves similar to an OAK tree's, that makes your skin hurt and ITCH if you touch it

poi·son·ous /ˈpɔɪzənəs/ ●●○ *adj*
1 containing poison or producing poison: *Some mushrooms are extremely poisonous.* | *poisonous gases such as hydrogen sulfide* | *poisonous substances* | *She was bitten on the ankle by a* ***poisonous snake.*** | **[+to]** *The berries are poisonous to birds.*
2 full of bad and unfriendly feelings: *the poisonous atmosphere of the office*
3 *BrE* someone who is poisonous seems to get pleasure from causing arguments, unhappiness etc: *That poisonous bastard Lucett told Morris I was seeing his wife.* —**poisonously** *adv*

ˌpoison-ˈpen letter *n* [C] a letter that is not signed and that says bad things about the person it has been sent to

ˌpoison ˈpill *n* [C] *technical informal* something in a company's financial or legal structure that is intended to make it difficult for another company to take control of it

POKE

poke¹ /pəʊk $ poʊk/ ●●○ *v*
1 WITH A FINGER/STICK ETC [I,T] to quickly push your finger or some other pointed object into something or someone: **poke sb/sth with sth** *Andy poked the fish with his finger to see if it was still alive.* | **poke sb in the eye/arm/ribs etc** *Be careful with that umbrella or you'll poke someone in the eye.* | **[+at]** *He was poking at the dust with a stick, making little patterns.* **THESAURUS** ▸ **PUSH**
2 THROUGH A SPACE/HOLE [T always + adv/prep] to move or push something through a space or opening: **poke sth in/into/through sth** *He poked a hand into one of his pockets.* | *One of the nurses* ***poked*** *her* ***head*** *around the door.*
3 BE SEEN [I always + adv/prep] if something is poking through or out of something else, you can see part of it but not all of it: **[+out]** *Ella looked at the tiny face poking out of the blanket.* | **[+through]** *Weeds had started poking through the cracks in the patio.*
4 poke a hole to make a hole or hollow area in something by pushing something pointed into or through it: **[+into/in/through]** *Poke a hole in the dough, and then form it into a rounded shape.*
5 poke holes in sth to find mistakes or problems in a plan or in what someone has said: *Defense attorneys tried to poke holes in Rodger's story.*
6 poke fun at sb to make fun of someone in an unkind way: *Some of the kids were poking fun at Judy because of the way she was dressed.*
7 poke your nose into sth *informal* to take an interest or get involved in someone else's private affairs, in a way that annoys them: *I'm sick of your mother poking her nose into our marriage.*
8 poke the fire to move coal or wood in a fire with a stick to make it burn better
9 ON THE INTERNET [T] to show someone on a SOCIAL NETWORKING SITE that you want to communicate with them
10 SEX [T] *spoken not polite* to have sex with a woman

poke along *phr v AmE informal* to move very slowly: *He kept the car in the slow lane, poking along at about 40 miles an hour.*

poke around (*also* **poke about** *BrE*) *phr v informal*
1 to look for something, especially by moving a lot of things around: **[+in]** *James began poking about in the cupboard, looking for the sugar.*
2 to try to find out information about other people's private lives, business etc, in a way that annoys them: **[+in]** *Stop poking around in my business!*
3 poke around (sth) to spend time in shops, markets etc looking at nothing in particular SYN **browse**: *I spent Sunday afternoon poking around an old bookshop.*

poke into sth *phr v informal* to try to find out information about other people's private lives, business etc, in a way that annoys them

poke² *n* [C] **1 give sb/sth a poke** to quickly push your fingers, a stick etc into something or someone: *Vanessa gave me a playful poke in the ribs.* **2** *AmE informal* a criticism of someone or something: *Bennett* ***took a poke at*** *the president's refusal to sign the bill.* **3** the act of showing someone on a SOCIAL NETWORKING SITE that you want to communicate with them

pok·er /ˈpəʊkə $ ˈpoʊkər/ *n* **1** [U] a card game that people usually play for money: *Can you* ***play poker?*** **2** [C] a metal stick used to move coal or wood in a fire to make it burn better

ˌpoker-ˈfaced *adj* showing no expression on your face: *a poker-faced officer* —**poker face** *n* [singular]

po·ker·work /ˈpəʊkəwɜːk $ ˈpoʊkərwɜːrk/ *n* [U] pictures or patterns burned onto the surface of wood or leather with hot tools, or the art of making these pictures

pok·ey /ˈpəʊki $ ˈpoʊ-/ *n* [C] *AmE old-fashioned informal* a prison

pok·y, pokey /ˈpəʊki $ ˈpoʊ-/ *adj informal* **1** *BrE* too small and not very pleasant or comfortable: *The whole family was crammed into two poky little rooms.* **THESAURUS** ▸ **SMALL**
2 *AmE* doing things very slowly, especially in a way that is annoying: *I got behind some poky driver on the freeway.*

pol /pɒl $ pɑːl/ *n* [C] *AmE informal* a politician – used in newspapers: *He's just another Washington pol.*

Po·lack, Polak /ˈpəʊlæk $ ˈpoʊ-/ *n* [C] *AmE taboo* a very offensive word for someone from Poland. Do not use this word.

po·lar /ˈpəʊlə $ ˈpoʊlər/ *adj* **1** close to or relating to the North Pole or the South Pole: *As our climate warms up, the polar ice caps will begin to melt.* **2 polar opposite/extreme** something that is the complete or exact opposite of something else: *Ortega's cheerful landscapes are the polar opposites of Miller's dark, troubled portraits.* **3** *technical* relating to one of the POLES of a MAGNET

ˌpolar ˈbear / $ ˈ.../ *n* [C] a large white bear that lives near the North Pole → see picture at **BEAR²**

po·lar·ise /ˈpəʊləraɪz $ ˈpoʊ-/ *v* [I,T] a British spelling of POLARIZE

po·lar·i·ty /pəˈlærəti/ *n* (*plural* **polarities**) [C,U] **1** *formal* a state in which people, opinions, or ideas are completely different or opposite to each other: **[+between]** *the polarity between the intellect and the emotions* **2** *technical* the state of having either a positive or negative electric charge

po·lar·ize (*also* **-ise** *BrE*) /ˈpəʊləraɪz $ ˈpoʊ-/ *v* [I,T] *formal* to divide into clearly separate groups with opposite beliefs, ideas, or opinions, or to make people do this: *The issue has polarized the country.* —**polarization** /ˌpəʊləraɪˈzeɪʃən $ ˌpoʊlərə-/ *n* [U]

Po·lar·oid /ˈpəʊlərɔɪd $ ˈpoʊ-/ *n* [C] *trademark* **1** in the past, a camera that used a special film to produce a photograph very quickly **2** a photograph taken with a Polaroid camera

pole¹ /pəʊl $ poʊl/ ●●● W3 *n* [C]

1 STICK/POST a long stick or post usually made of wood or metal, often set upright in the ground to support something: *a telephone pole*

2 the most northern or most southern point on a PLANET, especially the Earth: *the distance from pole to equator* | **the North/South Pole** *Amundsen's expedition was the first to reach the South Pole.*

3 be poles apart two people or things that are poles apart are as different from each other as it is possible to be: *Both are brilliant pianists, though they're poles apart in style.*

4 OPPOSITE IDEAS/BELIEFS one of two situations, ideas, or opinions that are the complete opposite of each other: **at one pole/at opposite poles** *We have enormous wealth at one pole, and poverty and misery at the other.* | *Washington and Beijing are at opposite poles* (=think in two completely different ways) *on this issue.*

5 ELECTRICAL **a)** one of two points at the ends of a MAGNET where its power is the strongest **b)** one of the two points at which wires can be attached to a BATTERY in order to use its electricity

pole² *v* [I,T] *BrE* to push a boat along in the water using a pole

Pole *n* [C] someone from Poland

pole·axed /ˈpəʊlækst $ ˈpoʊl-/ *adj* [not before noun] *especially BrE* **1** *informal* very surprised and shocked: *I was poleaxed when I heard I'd passed the exam.* **2** unable to stand because something has hit you very hard: *He staggered and collapsed as if poleaxed.*

pole·cat /ˈpəʊlkæt $ ˈpoʊl-/ *n* [C] **1** a small dark brown wild animal that lives in northern Europe and can defend itself by producing a bad smell **2** *AmE informal* a SKUNK

ˈpole ˌdancing *n* [U] the activity of dancing around a long upright metal post in a sexually exciting way, done by women wearing few or no clothes, in order to entertain people in some clubs or bars

po·lem·ic /pəˈlemɪk/ *n formal* **1** [C] a written or spoken statement that strongly criticizes or defends a particular idea, opinion, or person: *Before long, the dispute degenerated into fierce polemics.* **2** [U] (*also* **polemics**) the practice or skill of making written or spoken statements that strongly criticize or defend a particular idea, opinion, or person

po·lem·i·cal /pəˈlemɪkəl/ (*also* **polemic**) *adj formal* using strong arguments to criticize or defend a particular idea, opinion, or person: *The reforms were attacked in a highly polemical piece in the 'New Yorker'.* —**polemically** /-kli/ *adv*

po·len·ta /pəˈlentə/ *n* [U] **1** crushed MAIZE that is used in Italian cooking **2** a yellow food made from crushed MAIZE

ˈpole poˌsition *n* [C,U] the front position at the beginning of a car or bicycle race

ˈPole Star *n* **the Pole Star** a star that is almost directly over the North Pole and that can be seen from the northern part of the world

ˈpole vault *n* **the pole vault** the sport of jumping over a high bar using a long pole —**pole vaulter** *n* [C] —**pole vaulting** *n* [U]

po·lice¹ /pəˈliːs/ ●●● S1 W1 *n* [plural]

1 the people who work for an official organization whose job is to catch criminals and make sure that people obey the law: *Police surrounded the courthouse.*

2 the police the official organization whose job is to catch criminals and make sure that people obey the law: *Quick! Call the police!* | *By the time the police arrived the man had fled.* | *He was arrested by the police for dangerous driving.* | *He plans to join the police when he leaves school.* → **MILITARY POLICE, SECRET POLICE**

GRAMMAR: Singular or plural verb?

- **Police** is a plural noun and is followed by a plural verb: *The police **are** investigating the case.* ✗ Don't say: *The police is investigating the case.*
- When talking about someone who works for the police, you say a **police officer**, a **policeman**, or a **policewoman**. ✗ Don't say: *a police*

COLLOCATIONS – MEANINGS 1 & 2

VERBS

call the police *Staff called the police when they noticed a broken window.*
tell the police (*also* **inform the police** *formal*) *I think we should tell the police.*
report sth to the police *Why are so many crimes not reported to the police?*
the police investigate sth *Sussex Police are investigating a break-in at the club.*
the police catch sb | **the police arrest sb/make an arrest** | **the police question/interview sb** | **the police charge sb** (=officially say that someone will be judged in a court for committing a crime) | **the police hold sb** (*also* **the police detain sb** *formal*) (=keep them at a police station) | **the police release sb**

ADJECTIVES/NOUN + police

armed police *Armed police surrounded the house.*
uniformed police *Uniformed police and plainclothes detectives were present in large numbers.*
riot police | **traffic police** *BrE*

police + NOUN

a police investigation *Despite a police investigation, no arrests were made.*
a police raid (=a surprise visit made by the police to search for something illegal) *Six people were arrested in a police raid on the bar.*
a police escort (=a police officer or officers that go with someone to guard or protect them) | **the police force** | **a police officer** | **a police station** (=building where the police work) | **a police car** | **a police dog**

police² ●○○ *v* [T]

1 to keep control over a particular area in order to make sure that laws are obeyed and that people and property are protected, using a police or military force: *The army was brought in to police the city centre.*

2 to control a particular activity or industry by making sure that people follow the correct rules for what they do: *The agency was set up to police the nuclear power industry.* → **POLICING**

po͵lice com͵munity supˈport ͵officer *n* [C] *BrE* a COMMUNITY SUPPORT OFFICER

po͵lice ˈconstable *n* [C] *BrE formal* (*abbreviation* **PC**) a police officer of the lowest rank

poˈlice de͵partment *n* [C] *AmE* the official police organization in a particular area or city

poˈlice dog *n* [C] a dog trained by the police to find hidden drugs or catch criminals

poˈlice force *n* [C] the official police organization in a country or area: *Jones joined the police force in 1983.*

po·lice·man /pəˈliːsmən/ ●●● S2 W3 *n* (*plural* **policemen** /-mən/) [C] a male police officer → **policewoman**

poˈlice ͵officer ●●● S3 W2 *n* [C] a member of the police

poˈlice state *n* [C] a country where the government strictly controls people's freedom to meet, write, or speak about politics, travel etc

poˈlice ͵station ●●○ *n* [C] the local office of the police in a town, part of a city etc

po·lice·wom·an /pəˈliːs͵wʊmən/ *n* (*plural* **policewomen** /-͵wɪmɪn/) [C] a female police officer → **policeman**

po·lic·ing /pəˈliːsɪŋ/ *n* [U] **1** the way that the police are used to keep control over a particular area and to protect people and property: *The community is demanding a less aggressive style of policing.* | **[+of]** *the policing of the city* **2** the way that an industry or activity etc is controlled in order to make sure that people obey the rules: *In the last twenty years the industry has had no oversight or policing.* → POLICE[1]

pol·i·cy /ˈpɒləsi $ ˈpɑː-/ ●●● S3 W1 AWL *n* (*plural* **policies**)
1 [C,U] a way of doing something that has been officially agreed and chosen by a political party, a business, or another organization: **foreign/economic/public etc policy** *a foreign policy adviser* | *The company has adopted a strict no-smoking policy.* | **[+on/towards]** *government policy on higher education* | *US policy towards China* | **it is (sb's) policy to do sth** *It is hospital policy to screen all mothers with certain risk factors.* THESAURUS▸ PLAN
2 [C] a contract with an insurance company, or an official written statement giving all the details of such a contract: *an* ***insurance policy*** | *There's a clause in the policy that I'd like to discuss.* | *I've just* ***renewed*** *the* ***policy*** (=arranged for it to continue). | *Does the* ***policy cover*** *theft and fire?* | *You can* ***take out*** *a* ***policy*** (=buy one) *for as little as $11.00 a month.*
3 [C] a particular principle that you believe in and that influences the way you behave: **it is sb's policy to do sth** *It's always been my policy not to gossip.*

pol·i·cy·hold·er /ˈpɒləsi͵həʊldə $ ˈpɑːləsi͵hoʊldər/ *n* [C] someone who has bought insurance for something

pol·i·cy·mak·er /ˈpɒləsi͵meɪkə $ ˈpɑːləsi͵meɪkər/ *n* [C] someone who decides what an organization's or government's policies will be

po·li·o /ˈpəʊliəʊ $ ˈpoʊlioʊ/ (*also* **po·li·o·my·e·li·tis** /͵pəʊliəʊmaɪəˈlaɪtɪs $ ͵poʊlioʊ-/ *technical*) *n* [U] a serious infectious disease of the nerves in the SPINE, that often results in someone being permanently unable to move particular muscles

pol·i sci /͵pɒli ˈsaɪ $ ͵pɑː-/ *n* [U] *AmE informal* the abbreviation of ***political science***

pol·ish¹ /ˈpɒlɪʃ $ ˈpɑː-/ ●●● S3 *v* [T]
1 to make something smooth, bright, and shiny by rubbing it: *I spent all afternoon polishing the silver.* | **polish sth with sth** *Polish the lenses with a piece of tissue.*
2 to improve a piece of writing, a speech etc by making slight changes to it before it is completely finished: *Your essay is good, you just need to polish it a bit.* —**polishing** *n* [U]

polish sb/sth ↔ **off** *phr v informal* **a)** to finish food, work etc quickly or easily: *Sam polished off the rest of the pizza.* **b)** *AmE* to kill or defeat a person or animal when they are weak or wounded: *He was polished off with a shotgun blast to the face.*

polish sth ↔ **up** *phr v*
1 (*also* **polish up on sth**) to improve a skill or an ability by practising it: *You should polish up your Spanish before you go to Chile.*
2 to make something seem better or more attractive to other people: *The company needs to polish up its image.*
3 to polish something

polish² ●●● S3 *n*
1 [C,U] a liquid, powder, or other substance that you rub into a surface to make it smooth and shiny: **furniture/shoe/floor etc polish** → FRENCH POLISH
2 [singular] *especially BrE* an act of polishing a surface to make it smooth and shiny: *An occasional polish will keep wall tiles looking good.*
3 [U] a high level of skill or style in the way someone performs, writes, or behaves: *Carla's writing has potential, but it lacks polish.*
4 [singular] the smooth shiny appearance of something produced by polishing → **spit and polish** at SPIT²(5)

Pol·ish¹ /ˈpəʊlɪʃ $ ˈpoʊ-/ *adj* relating to Poland, its people, or its language

Polish² *n* **1 the Polish** [plural] people from Poland **2** [U] the language used in Poland

pol·ished /ˈpɒlɪʃt $ ˈpɑː-/ *adj* **1** shiny because of being rubbed, usually with polish: *highly polished boots* **2** done with great skill and style: *a polished performance* | *a polished piece of writing* **3** polite, confident, and graceful: *a polished and confident man*

pol·ish·er /ˈpɒlɪʃə $ ˈpɑːlɪʃər/ *n* [C] a machine used to polish something: *an electric floor polisher*

pol·it·bu·ro /ˈpɒlɪtbjʊərəʊ, $ ˈpɑːlətbjʊroʊ/ *n* (*plural* **politburos**) [C] the most important decision-making committee of a Communist party or Communist government

po·lite /pəˈlaɪt/ ●●● S3 *adj*
1 behaving or speaking in a way that is correct for the social situation you are in, and showing that you are careful to consider other people's needs and feelings OPP **rude, impolite**: *She's always very polite.* | *polite, well-behaved children* | *a clear but polite request* | **it is polite (of sb) to do sth** *We left the party as soon as it was polite to do so.* | *It's not polite to talk with your mouth full.*
2 you make polite conversation, remarks etc because it is considered socially correct to do this, but not necessarily because you believe what you are saying: **polite remarks/conversation/interest etc** *While they ate, they made polite conversation about the weather.* | *Jan expressed polite interest in Edward's stamp collection.* | *I know Ian said he liked her singing, but he was* ***only being polite.***
3 in polite society/circles/company among people who are considered to have a good education and correct social behaviour – often used humorously: *You can't use words like that in polite company.* —**politely** *adv*: *'Can I help you?' she asked politely.* —**politeness** *n* [U]

THESAURUS

polite behaving or speaking in a way that is correct for the social situation you are in, and showing that you are careful to consider other people's needs and feelings: *He was too polite to ask how old she was.* | *'Excuse me, sir,' she said in a polite voice.*
well-mannered having good manners and knowing the correct way to behave in social situations: *She was beautifully dressed and very well-mannered.*
well-behaved polite and not causing any trouble – used about children or animals: *The children were very well-behaved.*
courteous /ˈkɜːtiəs $ ˈkɜːr-/ polite and respectful, and behaving rather formally: *The hotel staff were very courteous and helpful.* | *a courteous reply*
respectful polite and treating someone with respect: *He was very respectful towards all my relatives.* | *'Thank you,' he said with a respectful bow.*
civil polite in a formal way, especially when you do not feel very friendly towards someone: *She'd never*

P

liked her father-in-law, but she forced herself to be civil to him.
deferential *formal* polite towards someone, especially because they are in a more important social position: *In those days women were expected to be deferential to men.*

pol·i·tic /'pɒlətɪk $ 'pɑː-/ *adj formal* sensible and likely to gain you an advantage SYN **prudent**: **it is politic to do sth** *It would not be politic to ignore the reporters.* → POLITICS, BODY POLITIC

po·lit·i·cal /pə'lɪtɪkəl/ ●●● S2 W1 *adj*
1 relating to the government, politics, and public affairs of a country → **politically**: *Education is now a major political issue.* | *a time of political and social change* | **political party/system/institutions** *The U.S. has two main political parties.* | *The UN is seeking a political solution rather than a military one.* | *political jokes* | *the workers' struggle for political power*
2 relating to the ways that different people have power within a group, organization etc: *a purely political decision* | *The appointment was given to Wellington, mainly for political reasons.*
3 [not before noun] interested in or active in politics: *Most students aren't very political.*
4 political football a difficult problem which opposing politicians argue about or which each side deals with in a way that will bring them advantage: *Funding of the health service has become a political football.*

po,litical 'action com,mittee *n* [C] *AmE* (*abbreviation* **PAC**) an organization formed by a business, UNION, or INTEREST GROUP to help raise money for politicians who support their ideas

po,litical a'sylum *n* [U] the right to stay in another country if you cannot live safely in your own country because of the political situation there: *Refugees were* ***seeking political asylum*** *in Britain.* | *No country would* ***grant*** (=give) *him* ***political asylum.***

po,litical cor'rectness *n* [U] language, behaviour, and attitudes that are carefully chosen so that they do not offend or insult anyone – used especially when you think someone is too careful in what they say or how they behave → **PC, politically correct**: *Political correctness has had an impact on the language people use to describe women.*

po,litical e'conomy *n* [U] the study of the way nations organize the production and use of wealth

po,litical ge'ography *n* [U] the study of the way the Earth's surface is divided up into different countries, rather than the way it is marked by rivers, mountains etc → **physical geography**

po·lit·ic·ally /pə'lɪtɪkli/ ●●○ *adv* in a political way: *Women were becoming more politically active.* | *a politically sensitive issue* | [sentence adverb] *Politically, raising the minimum wage is good for the Democrats.*

po,litically cor'rect *adj* (*abbreviation* **PC**) language, behaviour, and attitudes that are politically correct are carefully chosen so that they do not offend or insult anyone OPP **politically incorrect**: *politically correct textbooks*

po,litically incor'rect *adj* language, behaviour, or attitudes that are politically incorrect might offend or insult someone: *politically incorrect jokes*

po,litical ma'chine *n* [singular] *AmE* the system used by people with the same political interests to make sure that political decisions give advantages to themselves or to their group: *the Chicago mayor's political machine*

po,lit,ical 'prisoner *n* [C] someone who is in prison because they have opposed or criticized the government of their own country

po,litical 'science *n* [U] the study of politics and government —**political scientist** *n* [C]

pol·i·ti·cian /,pɒlə'tɪʃən $,pɑː-/ ●●● W2 *n* [C]
1 someone who works in politics, especially an elected member of the government: *politicians who are trying to get the minority vote* | *a British Labour politician*
2 someone who is skilled at dealing with people or using the situation within an organization to gain an advantage: *the office politician*

po·li·ti·cize (*also* **-ise** *BrE*) /pə'lɪtɪsaɪz/ *v* [T] **1** to make a subject or a situation more political: *The Olympic Games should not be politicized.* **2** to make someone become more involved in political activities: *He* ***became politicised*** *during his years in prison.* —**politicized** *adj*: *Abortion is a* ***highly politicized*** *issue.* —**politicization** /pə,lɪtəsaɪ'zeɪʃən $ -sə-/ *n* [U]

pol·i·tick·ing /'pɒlətɪkɪŋ $ 'pɑː-/ *n* [U] political activity, usually done to gain support for yourself or your political group: *the politicking at the party conference*

po·lit·i·co /pə'lɪtɪkəʊ $ -koʊ/ *n* [C] a politician or someone who is active in politics – usually used to show disapproval: *a slick politico*

politico- /pəlɪtɪkəʊ $ -koʊ/ *prefix* [used in adjectives] relating to both politics and something else: *politico-economic factors*

pol·i·tics /'pɒlətɪks $ 'pɑː-/ ●●● S2 W2 *n*
1 [U] ideas and activities relating to gaining and using power in a country, city etc → **political, politician**: *a good understanding of politics in China* | *modern American politics* | *Politics have always interested Anita.* | **national/local etc politics** *Brooke's been involved in city politics since college.* | *The president should stand above* ***party politics*** (=working only for your political PARTY).

GRAMMAR: Singular or plural verb?
- In this meaning, **politics** is usually followed by a singular verb: ***Politics plays*** *no part in this decision.*
- In British English, you can also use a plural verb: ***Politics play*** *no part in this decision.*

GRAMMAR GUIDE ▸ NOUNS

2 [U] the profession of being a politician: *Flynn retired from politics in 1986.* | *Her father's trying to* ***enter politics.*** | *Smith* ***went into politics*** *in his early twenties.*
3 [plural] the activities of people who are concerned with gaining personal advantage within a group, organization etc: *I'm tired of dealing with all of the* ***office politics.*** | *Her art examines* ***sexual politics*** (=how power is shared between men and women). | **the politics of sth** *the politics of race and class at American universities*
4 [plural] someone's political beliefs and opinions: *I assume her politics must be fairly conservative.*
5 [U] *especially BrE* the study of political power and systems of government SYN **political science**: *Tom is studying for a degree in politics.*

pol·i·ty /'pɒləti $ 'pɑː-/ *n* (*plural* **polities**) [C,U] *formal* a particular form of political or government organization, or a condition of society in which political organization exists

pol·ka /'pɒlkə, 'pəʊlkə $ 'poʊlkə/ *n* [C] a very quick simple dance for people dancing in pairs, or a piece of music for this dance —**polka** *v* [I]

'polka dot *n* [C] one of a number of round spots that form a pattern, especially on cloth used for clothing: *a white scarf with red polka dots* → see picture at PATTERN[1] —**polka-dot** *adj*: *a polka-dot dress*

poll[1] /pəʊl $ poʊl/ ●●○ W3 *n*
1 [C] the process of finding out what people think about something by asking many people the same question, or the record of the result SYN **opinion poll, survey**: *A recent poll found that 80% of Californians support the governor.* | *Polls indicate that education is the top issue with voters.* | *Labour is ahead in the polls.* | *The latest* ***public opinion poll*** *showed that 25% of us consider ourselves superstitious.* | **conduct/carry out/do a poll** *a poll conducted by 'USA Today'* | **[+on]** *a poll on eating habits* | **[+of]** *a poll of 1,000 people*
2 go to the polls to vote in an election: *Ten million voters went to the polls.*
3 [singular] *BrE* the process of voting in an election, or the number of votes recorded: *Labour won the election with*

40% of the poll. | *The result of the poll won't be known until around midnight.*
4 the polls the place where you can go to vote in an election: *The polls will close in an hour.*

poll² *v* [T] **1** to ask a lot of people the same questions in order to find out what they think about a subject: *18% of the women we polled said their husbands had a drinking problem.* THESAURUS ASK **2** to get a particular number of votes in an election: *Labour polled just 4% of the vote.*

pol·lard /ˈpɒləd, -lɑːd $ ˈpɑːlərd/ *v* [T] *BrE* to cut the top off a tree in order to make the lower branches grow more thickly: *pollarded limes* GRAMMAR **Pollard** is usually passive.

pol·len /ˈpɒlən $ ˈpɑː-/ *n* [U] a fine powder produced by flowers, which is carried by the wind or by insects to other flowers of the same type, making them produce seeds

ˈpollen count *n* [C] a measure of the amount of pollen in the air, usually given as a guide for people who are made ill by it: *The* ***pollen count*** *was* ***high*** *yesterday.*

pol·li·nate /ˈpɒləneɪt $ ˈpɑː-/ *v* [T] to give a flower or plant pollen so that it can produce seeds: *flowers pollinated by bees* —**pollination** /ˌpɒləˈneɪʃən $ ˌpɑː-/ *n* [U]

poll·ing /ˈpəʊlɪŋ $ ˈpoʊ-/ *n* [U] **1** when people vote in a political election: *Polling started at 8.00 this morning.* | **heavy/light polling** (=with many or few people voting) **2** when a person or an organization asks a lot of people the same questions in order to find out what they think about a subject

ˈpolling booth *n* [C] *BrE* a small partly enclosed place in a polling station where you can vote secretly in an election

ˈpolling day *n* [C] *BrE* the day on which people vote in an election

ˈpolling ˌstation *BrE*, **ˈpolling ˌplace** *AmE n* [C] the place where people go to vote in an election

poll·ster /ˈpəʊlstə $ ˈpoʊlstər/ *n* [C] someone who works for a company that prepares and asks questions to find out what people think about a particular subject

ˈpoll tax *n* [C] a tax of a particular amount that is collected from every citizen of a country SYN **council tax**

pol·lut·ant /pəˈluːtənt/ *n* [C] a substance that makes air, water, soil etc dangerously dirty, and is caused by cars, factories etc: **air/environmental/water etc pollutants** *New regulations will reduce hazardous air pollutants.* | *a dumping ground for* ***toxic pollutants*** | **chemical/industrial etc pollutants** *industrial pollutants in the lake*

pol·lute /pəˈluːt/ ●●○ *v* [T]
1 to make air, water, soil etc dangerously dirty and not suitable for people to use: *beaches polluted by raw sewage* | *The factory pollutes the air and water.* | **heavily/severely/badly etc polluted** *The island has been seriously polluted by a copper mine.* | **pollute sth with sth** *The rivers had been polluted with aluminium.*
2 to spoil or ruin something that used to be good: *an artist spiritually polluted by money and fame*
3 pollute sb's mind to give someone immoral thoughts and spoil their character: *Violence on television is polluting the minds of our children.*

pol·lut·ed /pəˈluːtɪd/ *adj* dangerously dirty and not suitable for people to use: *one of the most polluted areas in the world* | **polluted air/water/rivers etc** *The project's aim is to clean up polluted land.* | **heavily/seriously/severely polluted** *The lake is seriously polluted.* THESAURUS DIRTY

pol·lut·er /pəˈluːtə $ -ər/ *n* [C] a person or organization that causes pollution: *The polluter should pay for the cost of the clean-up.* | **big/major/main etc polluter** *a list of Canada's worst polluters*

pol·lu·tion /pəˈluːʃən/ ●●○ S3 W2 *n* [U]
1 the process of making air, water, soil etc dangerously dirty and not suitable for people to use, or the state of being dangerously dirty: *California's tough anti-pollution laws* | **air/water/soil pollution** *air pollution from traffic fumes* | **pollution prevention/standards/control** *The costs of pollution control must be considered.*
2 substances that make air, water, soil etc dangerously dirty: *a plan to* ***reduce pollution*** | **industrial/chemical etc pollution** *the effects of industrial pollution on the population* | *The chemicals have been identified as a* ***source of pollution.***
→ NOISE POLLUTION

> **GRAMMAR: Countable or uncountable?**
> **Pollution** is an uncountable noun and is not used in the plural. You say: *The air is full of pollution.* ✗ Don't say: *The air is full of pollutions.*

Pol·ly·an·na /ˌpɒliˈænə $ ˌpɑː-/ *n* [C usually singular] someone who is always happy and always thinks something good is going to happen

po·lo /ˈpəʊləʊ $ ˈpoʊloʊ/ *n* [U] a game played between two teams of players who ride on horses and hit a small ball with long-handled wooden hammers → WATER POLO

ˈpolo neck *n* [C] *BrE* a shirt or SWEATER that has a high collar that folds down and fits closely around the neck SYN **turtleneck** *AmE*: *a polo-neck sweater* → see picture at NECK¹

ˈpolo shirt *n* [C] a shirt with a collar and a few buttons near the neck, that is pulled on over the head

pol·ter·geist /ˈpɒltəgaɪst $ ˈpoʊltər-/ *n* [C] a GHOST that makes objects move around and causes strange noises

pol·y /ˈpɒli $ ˈpɑːli/ *n* (*plural* **polys**) [C] *BrE informal* a POLYTECHNIC

poly- /pɒlɪ $ pɑː-/ *prefix* many: *polysyllabic* (=with three or more SYLLABLES)

pol·y·clin·ic /ˈpɒlɪˌklɪnɪk $ ˈpɑː-/ *n* [C] a large building where many medical services are provided, but where you do not stay the night for treatment

pol·y·es·ter /ˈpɒliestə, ˌpɒliˈestə◂ $ ˈpɑːliestər/ *n* [U] an artificial material used to make cloth: *a blue polyester shirt*

pol·y·eth·y·lene /ˌpɒliˈeθəliːn $ ˌpɑː-/ *n* [U] *AmE* a strong light plastic used to make bags, sheets for covering food, small containers etc SYN **polythene** *BrE*

po·lyg·a·my /pəˈlɪgəmi/ *n* [U] the practice of having more than one husband or wife at the same time → **bigamy**, **monogamy** —**polygamous** *adj*: *polygamous societies*

pol·y·glot /ˈpɒlɪglɒt $ ˈpɑːlɪglɑːt/ *adj formal* speaking or using many languages SYN **multilingual**: *a polyglot population* —**polyglot** *n* [C]

pol·y·gon /ˈpɒlɪgən $ ˈpɑːlɪgɑːn/ *n* [C] *technical* a flat shape with three or more sides —**polygonal** /pəˈlɪgənəl/ *adj*

pol·y·graph /ˈpɒlɪgrɑːf $ ˈpɑːlɪgræf/ *n* [C] a piece of equipment that is used by the police to find out whether someone is telling the truth SYN **lie detector**: *The suspect was given a* ***polygraph test.***

pol·y·he·dron /ˌpɒlɪˈhiːdrən $ ˌpɑː-/ *n* [C] *technical* a solid shape with many sides

pol·y·math /ˈpɒlɪmæθ $ ˈpɑː-/ *n* [C] *formal* someone who has a lot of knowledge about many different subjects

pol·y·mer /ˈpɒlɪmə $ ˈpɑːlɪmər/ *n* [C] a chemical COMPOUND that has a simple structure of large MOLECULES

pol·y·mor·phous /ˌpɒlɪˈmɔːfəs◂ $ ˌpɑːlɪˈmɔːr-/ (*also* **pol·y·mor·phic** /-fɪk◂/) *adj technical* having many forms, styles etc during the stages of development

pol·y·no·mi·al /ˌpɒlɪˈnəʊmiəl $ ˌpɑːlɪˈnoʊ-/ *n* [C] *technical* a statement in ALGEBRA that contains several different numbers and signs which are equal to a specific amount: *polynomial equations*

pol·yp /ˈpɒlɪp $ ˈpɑː-/ *n* [C] **1** a small lump that grows inside your body because of an illness, but is not likely to harm you **2** a very simple sea animal that has a body like a tube: *a coral polyp*

po·lyph·o·ny /pəˈlɪfəni/ *n* [U] a type of music in which several different tunes or notes are sung or played together at the same time —**polyphonic** /ˌpɒlɪˈfɒnɪk◂ $ ˌpɑːlɪˈfɑː-/ *adj*

pol·y·pro·py·lene /ˌpɒlɪˈprəʊpəliːn $ ˌpɑːliˈproʊ-/ *n* [U] a hard light plastic material

po·lys·e·mous /pəˈlɪsəməs, ˌpɒlɪˈsiːməs $ ˌpɑːliˈsiːməs◂/

adj technical a polysemous word has two or more different meanings —**polysemy** /pəˈlɪsəmi, ˈpɒləsiːmi $ ˈpɑːləsiːmi, pəˈlɪsəmi/ *n* [U]

pol·y·sty·rene /ˌpɒlɪˈstaɪriːn◂ $ ˌpɑː-/ *n* [U] *BrE* a soft light plastic material that prevents heat or cold from passing through it, used especially for making containers

pol·y·syl·lab·ic /ˌpɒlisɪˈlæbɪk◂ $ ˌpɑː-/ *adj technical* a polysyllabic word has three or more SYLLABLES → **monosyllabic** —**polysyllable** /ˈpɒliˌsɪləbəl $ ˈpɑː-/ *n* [C]

pol·y·tech·nic /ˌpɒlɪˈteknɪk $ ˌpɑː-/ *n* [C] **1** a type of British college similar to a university, which provided training and degrees in many subjects, and existed until 1993 **2** a word used in the names of high schools or colleges in the US, where you can study technical or scientific subjects: *Baltimore Polytechnic Institute*

P

pol·y·the·is·m /ˈpɒlɪθiːɪzəm $ ˈpɑː-/ *n* [U] the belief that there is more than one god → **monotheism** —**polytheistic** /ˌpɒlɪθiˈɪstɪk◂ $ ˌpɑː-/ *adj*

pol·y·thene /ˈpɒləθiːn $ ˈpɑː-/ *n* [U] *BrE* a strong light plastic used to make bags, sheets for covering food, small containers etc SYN **polyethylene** *AmE*

pol·y·tun·nel /ˈpɒliˌtʌnl $ ˈpɑː-/ *n* [C] a long structure consisting of a frame covered in plastic, used for growing plants in

pol·y·un·sat·u·ra·ted /ˌpɒliʌnˈsætʃəreɪtɪd $ ˌpɑː-/ *adj* polyunsaturated fats or oils come from vegetables and plants, and are considered to be better for your health than animal fats → **saturated fat** —**polyunsaturate** /-rət/ *n* [C]

pol·y·u·re·thane /ˌpɒlɪˈjʊərəθeɪn $ ˌpɑːlɪˈjʊr-/ *n* [U] a plastic used to make paints and VARNISH

pom /pɒm $ pɑːm/ (*also* **pommy**, **pommie**) *n* [C] an offensive word for someone from Britain, used in Australia and New Zealand

po·made /pəˈmeɪd, pəˈmɑːd $ poʊˈmeɪd/ *n* [U] a sweet-smelling oily substance men used to rub on their hair to make it smooth, especially in the past

po·man·der /pəˈmændə, pəʊ- $ ˈpoʊmændər/ *n* [C] a box or ball that contains dried flowers and HERBS and is used to make clothes or a room smell pleasant → **pot-pourri**

pom·e·gran·ate /ˈpɒməgrænət $ ˈpɑːmə-/ *n* [C] a round fruit that has a lot of small juicy red seeds that you can eat and a thick reddish skin

pom·mel /ˈpʌməl/ *n* [C] **1** the high rounded part at the front of a horse's SADDLE **2** the round end of a sword handle

ˈpommel horse *n* [C] a piece of equipment used in GYMNASTICS that has two handles on top, which you hold on to when you jump or swing over it

pom·my, **pommie** /ˈpɒmi $ ˈpɑː-/ *n* (*plural* **pommies**) [C] a POM

pomp /pɒmp $ pɑːmp/ *n* [U] *formal* all the impressive clothes, decorations, music etc that are traditional for an important official or public ceremony: *The Queen's birthday was celebrated with great* ***pomp and ceremony***. | *all the* ***pomp and circumstance*** (=an impressive ceremony) *of a treaty signing*

POMPOM

pom·pom /ˈpɒmpɒm $ ˈpɑːmpɑːm/, **pom·pon** /-pɒn $ -pɑːn/ *n* [C] **1** a small soft ball used as a decoration on clothing, especially hats **2** a large round ball of loose plastic strings connected to a handle, used by CHEERLEADERS

pom·pous /ˈpɒmpəs $ ˈpɑːm-/ *adj* someone who is pompous thinks that they are important, and shows this by being very formal and using long words – used to show disapproval: *He seems rather pompous.* | *the book's pompous style* THESAURUS▸ PROUD —**pompously** *adv* —**pomposity** /pɒmˈpɒsəti $ pɑːmˈpɑː-/ (*also* **pompousness**) /ˈpɒmpəsnəs ˈpɑːm-/ *n* [U]

ponce¹ /pɒns $ pɑːns/ *n* [C] *BrE informal* **1** *taboo* an offensive word for a man who dresses or behaves in a way that is typical of women or who people think is a HOMOSEXUAL. Do not use this word. **2** a PIMP

ponce² *v*

ponce about/around *phr v BrE informal* to waste time doing silly things: *He's been poncing about all day.*

pon·cho /ˈpɒntʃəʊ $ ˈpɑːntʃoʊ/ *n* (*plural* **ponchos**) [C] a type of coat consisting of one large piece of cloth, with a hole in the middle for your head

ponc·y, **poncey** /ˈpɒnsi $ ˈpɑː-/ *adj BrE informal not polite* an offensive word used about people or things that seem typical of HOMOSEXUAL men: *a poncy suit*

pond /pɒnd $ pɑːnd/ ●●○ S3 *n* [C]

1 a small area of fresh water that is smaller than a lake, that is either natural or artificially made

2 across the pond (*also* **on the other side of the pond**) *informal* on the other side of the Atlantic Ocean in the US or in Britain: *my cousins from across the pond*

pon·der /ˈpɒndə $ ˈpɑːndər/ ●○○ *v* [I,T] *formal* to spend time thinking carefully and seriously about a problem, a difficult question, or something that has happened SYN **consider**: *He continued to ponder the problem as he walked home.* | **[+on/over/about]** *The university board is still pondering over the matter.* | **ponder how/what/whether** *Jay stood still for a moment, pondering whether to go or not.* THESAURUS▸ THINK

pon·der·ous /ˈpɒndərəs $ ˈpɑːn-/ *adj* **1** slow or awkward because of being very big and heavy: *an elephant's ponderous walk* **2** boring, very serious, and seeming to progress very slowly: *a ponderous and difficult book* | *The system, though ponderous, works.* —**ponderously** *adv* —**ponderousness** *n* [U]

ˈpond scum *n* [U] **1** *AmE informal* someone that you do not like, respect, or trust: *He's lower than pond scum.* **2** ALGAE

pong /pɒŋ $ pɑːŋ/ *n* [C usually singular] *BrE informal* an unpleasant smell: *an awful pong in the fridge* THESAURUS▸ SMELL —**pong** *v* [I]

pon·tiff /ˈpɒntɪf $ ˈpɑːn-/ *n* [C] *formal* the Pope

pon·tif·i·cal /pɒnˈtɪfɪkəl $ pɑːn-/ *adj formal* **1** relating to the Pope **2** speaking as if you think your judgment or opinion is always right

pon·tif·i·cate¹ /pɒnˈtɪfɪkeɪt $ pɑːn-/ *v* [I] to give your opinion about something in a way that shows you think you are always right: **[+about/on]** *Politicians are always pontificating about education.*

pon·tif·i·cate² /pɒnˈtɪfɪkət $ pɑːn-/ *n* [C] the position or period of being Pope

pon·toon /pɒnˈtuːn $ pɑːn-/ *n* **1** [C] one of several metal containers or boats that are fastened together to support a floating bridge **2** [C] one of two hollow metal containers fastened to the bottom of a plane so that it can come down onto water and float **3** [U] *BrE* a card game, usually played for money SYN **blackjack** *AmE*

ponˈtoon bridge *n* [C] a floating bridge which is supported by several pontoons

po·ny¹ /ˈpəʊni $ ˈpoʊ-/ ●●○ *n* (*plural* **ponies**) [C] a small horse → PIT PONY, SHETLAND PONY

pony² *v* (**ponied**, **ponying**, **ponies**)

pony up (sth) *phr v AmE informal* to find or produce a particular amount of money: *All investors had to pony up a minimum of $5000.*

po·ny·tail /ˈpəʊniteɪl $ ˈpoʊ-/ *n* [C] hair tied together at the back of your head and falling like a horse's tail → see picture at HAIRSTYLE

ˈpony-ˌtrekking *n* [U] *BrE* the activity of riding through the countryside on ponies

poo /puː/ *n informal* **1** [C,U] solid waste from the BOWELS SYN **poop** *AmE* **2** [C usually singular] the act of passing waste from the BOWELS SYN **poop** *AmE* —**poo** *v* [I,T] *informal*

pooch /puːtʃ/ *n* [C] *informal* a dog – often used humorously

poo·dle /ˈpuːdl/ *n* [C] **1** a dog with thick curly hair **2 be sb's poodle** *BrE informal* if someone is another person's poodle, they always do what the other person tells them to do

poof[1] /pʊf, puːf/ (*also* **poof·ter** /ˈpʊftə, ˈpuːf- $ -ər/) *n* [C] *BrE taboo informal* a very offensive word for a HOMOSEXUAL man. Do not use this word.

poof[2] *interjection* used when talking about something that happened suddenly: *Then poof! She was gone.*

poof·y /ˈpʊfi, ˈpuːfi/ *adj* **1** *AmE* poofy hair or clothes look big and soft or filled with air: *a blouse with big poofy sleeves* **2** *BrE informal not polite* an offensive word meaning typical of a HOMOSEXUAL man

pooh /puː/ *interjection* **1** *BrE* used when there is a very unpleasant smell SYN **pew** *AmE* **2** *old-fashioned* used when you think an idea, suggestion, effort etc is stupid or not very good: *Pooh! You can't finish that paper by tomorrow.*

pooh-bah /ˈpuː bɑː/ *n* [C] *informal* someone who is important or powerful – used to show that you do not respect them very much: *the pooh-bahs of the technology industry*

ˌpooh-ˈpooh *v* [T] *informal* to say that you think that an idea, suggestion, effort etc is silly or not very good: *He pooh-poohed herbal remedies at first.*

POOL

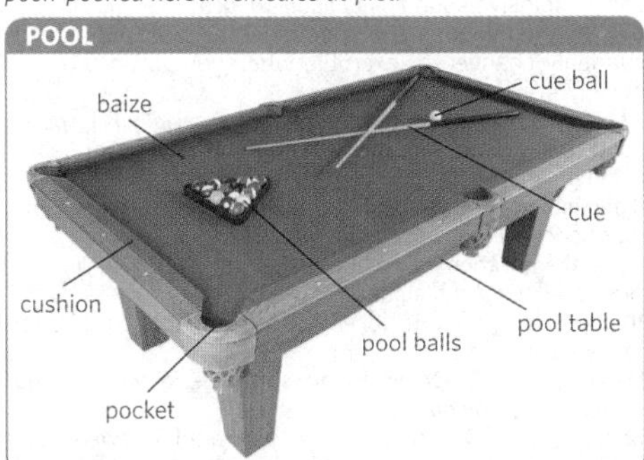

pool[1] /puːl/ ●●● S2 W2 *n*

1 FOR SWIMMING [C] a hole or container that has been specially made and filled with water so that people can swim or play in it SYN **swimming pool**: *They have a nice pool in their backyard.* | *a shallow pool suitable for children*

2 AREA OF WATER [C] a small area of still water in a hollow place: *pools of water with tiny fish in them* | *Mosquitoes breed in stagnant pools of water.*

3 pool of water/blood/light etc a small area of liquid or light on a surface: *A guard found him lying in a pool of blood.* | *a pool of light formed by the street lamp above*

4 GAME [U] a game in which you use a stick to hit numbered balls into holes around a table, which is often played in bars: **shoot/play pool** *We went to the pub and played pool.*

5 GROUP OF PEOPLE [C] a group of people who are available to work or to do an activity when they are needed: **[+of]** *a pool of talented applicants to choose from* | *The region has a large and talented* ***labour pool***.

6 SHARED MONEY/THINGS [C usually singular] a number of things that are shared or an amount of money that is shared by a group of people: *Both partners put money into a common pool.*

7 the pools a system in Britain in which people try to win money each week by guessing the results of football games: *I* ***do the pools*** *sometimes.* | *Dad* ***won*** *£40* ***on the pools***.

8 SPORTS [C] *AmE* a game in which people try to win money by guessing the result of a sports game, or the money that is collected from these people for this: *the office basketball pool*

pool[2] *v* [T] to combine your money, ideas, skills etc with those of other people so that you can all use them: *Investors agreed to* ***pool*** *their* ***resources*** *to develop the property.* | *The students worked together, pooling their knowledge.*

ˈpool hall *n* [C] *AmE* a building where people go to play pool

pool·room /ˈpuːlrʊm, -ruːm/ *n* [C] a room used for playing pool, especially in a bar

pool·side /ˈpuːlsaɪd/ *adj* [only before noun] near or on the side of a swimming pool: *a poolside bar* —**poolside** *n* [singular]: *We met down at the poolside.*

poop[1] /puːp/ *n* **1** [U] *AmE informal* solid waste from the BOWELS SYN **poo** *BrE* **2** [singular] *AmE informal* the act of passing waste from the BOWELS SYN **poo** *BrE*

poop[2] *v* [I] *AmE informal* to pass solid waste from the BOWELS SYN **poo** → **PARTY POOPER**

poop out *phr v AmE informal* **1** to stop trying to do something because you are tired, bored etc: *Dan pooped out about halfway through the race.* **2** to decide not to do something you have already said you would do, because you are tired or not interested: **[+on]** *'Is Bill coming along?' 'Nah, he's pooping out on us.'* **3** if a machine or piece of equipment poops out, it stops working: *The laptop's battery pooped out after only two hours.*

ˈpoop deck *n* [C] the floor on the raised part at the back of an old sailing ship

pooped /puːpt/ (*also* **ˌpooped ˈout**) *adj* [not before noun] *AmE informal* very tired SYN **exhausted**: *I was really pooped by the end of the day.*

poop·er scoop·er /ˈpuːpə ˌskuːpə $ -pər ˌskuːpər/ *n* [C] *informal* a small SPADE and a container, used by dog owners for removing their dogs' solid waste from the streets

ˈpoo-poo *n* [C,U] *informal* POO

ˈpoop sheet *n* [C] *AmE informal* written official instructions or information

poor /pɔː $ pʊr/ ●●● S1 W1 *adj* (*comparative* **poorer**, *superlative* **poorest**)

1 NO MONEY **a)** having very little money and not many possessions OPP **rich**: *Her family were so poor they couldn't afford to buy her new clothes.* | *an area where poor people lived* | *one of the poorest countries in the world* | *a poor part of Chicago* (=where a lot of poor people live) | *My grandparents grew up* ***dirt poor*** (=very poor). | **desperately/extremely poor** *Many of the families are desperately poor.* **b) the poor** [plural] people who are poor: *It's the government's responsibility to help the poor.* | **the rural/urban/working poor** *tax relief for the working poor*

2 NOT GOOD not as good as it could be or should be: *The soil in this area is very poor.* | *poor rates of pay* | *He blames himself for the team's* ***poor performance***. | **of poor quality** (=not made well or not made of good materials) *The jacket was of very poor quality.* | **poor hearing/eyesight/memory** *Her hearing is poor, so speak fairly loudly.* | **make/do a poor job of doing sth** *The builders did a really poor job of fixing our roof.* THESAURUS ▸ BAD

3 SYMPATHY [only before noun] *spoken* used to show sympathy for someone because they are so unlucky, unhappy etc: *Poor kid, he's had a rough day.* | *You* ***poor thing***, *you've had a hard time of it, haven't you?* | ***Poor old*** *Ted was sick for weeks.*

4 NOT GOOD AT STH not good at doing something: *a poor public speaker* | **[+at]** *He's poor at sports.*

5 HEALTH someone whose health is poor is ill or weak for a long period of time: *My parents are both* ***in*** *rather* ***poor health***.

6 poor in sth lacking something that is needed: *The country is poor in natural resources.*
7 a poor second/third etc the act of finishing a race, competition etc a long way behind the person ahead of you: *McLean won easily, and Benson was a poor second.* | **come (in) a poor second/third etc** *BrE*: *The Socialists came a poor second with 26.5% of the vote.*
8 the poor man's sb used to say that someone is like a very famous performer, writer etc but is not as good as they are: *He was the poor man's Elvis Presley.*
9 the poor man's sth used to say that something can be used for the same purpose as something else, and is much cheaper: *Herring is the poor man's salmon.*
10 poor relation *BrE* someone or something that is not treated as well as other members of a group or is much less successful than they are: **[+of]** *Theatre musicians tend to be the poor relations of the musical profession.* → **be in bad/poor taste** at TASTE[1](6), POORLY[1]

P

THESAURUS

poor having very little money and not many possessions - used about people or places: *Many families were too poor to pay for education.* | *poor countries*
hard up/broke (*also* **skint** *BrE*) [not before noun] *informal* having very little money, especially for a short period of time. **Skint** is more informal than the other words: *I'm a bit hard up at the moment* | *We were so broke we couldn't afford to go out to the cinema.*
deprived [usually before noun] much poorer than other people in a country, and not having the things that are necessary for a comfortable or happy life - used about people and areas: *The charity works with deprived children in the inner city.* | *one of the most deprived areas of London*
disadvantaged *especially written* used about groups of people in society who have much less chance of being successful because they are poor: *An increase in the minimum wage would help the most disadvantaged Americans.*
needy having very little money, and so needing help - used about groups of people: *More help should be given to needy families.* | *We offer scholarships for needy students.*
destitute *especially written* having no money or possessions and nowhere to live - used when someone is in a very bad situation: *Her family was left destitute after her father died.*
impoverished *formal* impoverished people and places are very poor: *out-of-work miners and their impoverished families* | *The children come from impoverished neighbourhoods.*
poverty-stricken *written* extremely poor: *poverty-stricken areas* | *They were left poverty-stricken.*
penniless *especially literary* having no money: *She died penniless.* | *a penniless student*

COLLOCATIONS CHECK

deprived area/children/homes/background
disadvantaged groups/children/students/background
needy children/students/families
impoverished families/areas/countries
poverty-stricken areas/countries/people

ˈpoor boy (*also* **po' boy**) /ˈpɔː bɔɪ/ *n* [C] *AmE* a sandwich made with a long bread roll - used especially in the southern US SYN **submarine sandwich**

poor·house /ˈpɔːhaʊs $ ˈpʊr-/ *n* [C] **1** the state of not having any money: *If Jimmy keeps spending like this, he's going to* ***end up in the poorhouse***. **2** a building where very poor people in the past could live and be fed, which was paid for with public money SYN **workhouse**

poor·ly[1] /ˈpɔːli $ ˈpʊrli/ ●●○ *adv* badly: *Jana's doing poorly in school.* | *poorly educated workers* | *The article was poorly written.*

poorly[2] ●●○ *adj BrE informal* ill: *Matt's wife's been very poorly.* THESAURUS ILL

ˌpoorly ˈoff *adj* [not before noun] *BrE* someone who is poorly off does not have very much money OPP **well off**

Poo·ter, Mr /ˈpuːtəʳ/ the main character in the humorous book *The Diary of a Nobody* (1892) by George Grossmith. Mr Pooter is a very ordinary man, and he describes his daily life in the book. He is sometimes not sure about the socially correct way to behave, and he often makes mistakes that make him feel very embarrassed. The word 'Pooterish' can be used to describe someone who takes themselves too seriously.

poo·tle /ˈpuːtl/ *v* [I + about/around] *BrE spoken* to spend time pleasantly, doing things that are not very important

pop[1] /pɒp $ pɑːp/ ●●○ S3 *v* (**popped, popping**)
1 COME OUT/OFF [I always + adv/prep] to come suddenly or unexpectedly out of or away from something: **[+out/off/up etc]** *The top button popped off my shirt.* | *The ball popped out of Smith's hands and onto the ground.* | **out/up popped sth** *The egg cracked open and out popped a tiny head.* | *The lid* ***popped open*** *and juice spilled all over the floor.*
2 GO QUICKLY [I always + adv/prep] *spoken* to go somewhere for a short time: **[+in/out/by etc]** *Why don't you pop by the next time you're in town?* | *I need to pop into the drugstore for a second.* | **[+round]** *BrE*: *Could you pop round to the shop for some bread?*
3 QUICKLY PUT STH [T always + adv/prep] *informal* to quickly put something somewhere, usually for a short time: **pop sth in/around/over etc** *I'll just pop these cookies into the oven.* | **pop sth round sth** *BrE*: *Barry popped his head round the door to say hello.* THESAURUS PUT
4 SHORT SOUND [I,T] to make a short sound like a small explosion, or to make something do this: *The wood sizzled and popped in the fire.*
5 BURST [I,T] to burst, or to make something burst, with a short explosive sound: *A balloon popped.*
6 EARS [I] if your ears pop, you feel the pressure in them suddenly change, for example when you go up or down quickly in a plane
7 sb's eyes popped (out of their head) *especially BrE spoken* used to say that someone looked extremely surprised or excited
8 pop into your head/mind to suddenly think of something: *All at once an idea popped into her head.*
9 pop the question *informal* to ask someone to marry you: *Hasn't Bill popped the question yet?*
10 pop pills *informal* to take PILLS too often, or to take too many at one time
11 HIT [T] *AmE spoken* to hit someone: *If you say that again, I'll* ***pop you one***.
12 POPCORN [I,T] to cook POPCORN until it swells and bursts open, or to be cooked in this way
13 pop your clogs *BrE humorous* to die
pop off *phr v informal* to die suddenly
pop sth ↔ **on** *phr v BrE spoken*
1 to quickly put on a piece of clothing: *Here, pop on your pyjamas and then we'll read a story.*
2 to quickly turn on a piece of electrical equipment: *Pop the kettle on, would you?*
pop out *phr v informal* if words pop out, you suddenly say them without thinking first: *I didn't mean to say it like that - it just popped out.*
pop up *phr v* to appear, sometimes unexpectedly: *Click here, and a list of files will pop up.* | *Her name keeps popping up in the newspapers.* → POP-UP[1]

pop[2] ●●○ S3 W3 *n*
1 MUSIC [U] modern music that is popular, especially with young people, and usually consists of simple tunes with a strong beat → **pop music**: *a new pop record* | *a pop star* | *a pop festival*
2 SOUND [C] a sudden short sound like a small explosion: *the pop of a champagne cork* | *The balloon* ***went pop*** (=made a sudden short sound).
3 DRINK [C,U] *informal* a sweet drink with bubbles but no alcohol, or a glass or can of this drink SYN **soda**: *a bottle of pop* | *Can you get me a pop while you're up?*

4 take a pop at sb *BrE informal* to criticize someone in public: *When you're a professional footballer, you expect people to take a pop at you now and again.*
5 $7/$50/25¢ etc a pop *AmE spoken* used when each of something costs a particular amount of money: *Tickets for the show are a hundred bucks a pop.*
6 FATHER [C] (*also* **Pops**) *AmE old-fashioned* father – used especially when you are talking to your father
7 pops *AmE* CLASSICAL music that most people know, especially people who do not usually like this type of music: *a pops concert | the Boston Pops Orchestra*

pop. the written abbreviation of ***population***

ˈpop art *n* [U] a type of art that was popular in the 1960s, which shows ordinary objects, such as advertisements, or things you see in people's homes

pop·corn /ˈpɒpkɔːn $ ˈpɑːpkɔːrn/ ●●● S3 *n* [U] a kind of corn that swells and bursts open when heated, and is usually eaten warm with salt or sugar as a SNACK

ˈpop ˌculture *n* [U] music, films, products etc in a particular society that are familiar to and popular with most ordinary people in that society

Pope, **pope** /pəʊp $ poʊp/ *n* [C] **1** the leader of the Roman Catholic Church → **papal**: *The pope will visit El Salvador this year. | Pope John XXIII* **2 Is the Pope (a) Catholic?** *informal* used to say that something is clearly true or certain – used humorously: *'Do you think they'll win?' 'Is the Pope Catholic?'*

pop·e·ry /ˈpəʊpəri $ ˈpoʊ-/ *n* [U] *taboo especially BrE* an offensive word for the Roman Catholic religion. Do not use this word.

ˌpop-ˈeyed *adj informal* **1** having your eyes wide open, because you are surprised, excited, or angry **2** having eyes that stick out slightly

ˈpop fly *n* [C] a type of hit in baseball in which the ball is hit straight up into the air

ˈpop group *n* [C] *especially BrE* a group of people who sing and perform POP MUSIC

ˈpop-gun *n* [C] a toy gun that fires small objects, such as CORKS, with a loud noise

pop·ish /ˈpəʊpɪʃ $ ˈpoʊ-/ *adj taboo especially BrE* an offensive word for something that is related to the Roman Catholic religion. Do not use this word.

pop·lar /ˈpɒplə $ ˈpɑːplər/ *n* [C] a very tall straight thin tree that grows very fast

pop·lin /ˈpɒplɪn $ ˈpɑːp-/ *n* [U] a strong shiny cotton cloth

ˈpop ˌmusic *n* [U] modern music that is popular, especially with young people, and usually consists of simple tunes with a strong beat

pop·o·ver /ˈpɒpəʊvə $ ˈpɑːpoʊvər/ *n* [C] *AmE* a light hollow MUFFIN (=small cake) made with eggs, milk, and flour

pop·pa /ˈpɒpə $ ˈpɑːpə/ *n AmE* another spelling of PAPA

pop·pa·dom, **poppadum** /ˈpɒpədəm $ ˈpɑː-/ *n* [C] a large circular piece of very thin flat Indian bread cooked in oil

pop·per /ˈpɒpə $ ˈpɑːpər/ *n* **1** [C] *BrE informal* a small metal thing that is used to fasten clothes, which works when you press its two parts together SYN **snap** *AmE*
2 poppers [plural] *informal* an illegal drug in the form of a liquid, which people take for pleasure by breathing it in

pop·pet /ˈpɒpɪt $ ˈpɑː-/ *n* [C] *BrE spoken* used to talk to or about a child or animal you like very much: *Come here, poppet.*

ˌpop psyˈchology *n* [U] ways of dealing with personal problems that are made popular on television or in books, but are not considered scientific

pop·py /ˈpɒpi $ -ˈpɑː-/ *n* (*plural* **poppies**) [C] a plant that has brightly coloured, usually red, flowers and small black seeds

pop·py·cock /ˈpɒpikɒk $ ˈpɑːpikɑːk/ *n* [U] *old-fashioned* nonsense

pop·py·seed /ˈpɒpisiːd $ ˈpɑː-/ *n* [U] the small black seeds of the poppy plant, used in cakes, bread etc

ˈpop quiz *n* [C] *AmE* a short test that a teacher gives without any warning, in order to check whether students have been studying

Pop·si·cle /ˈpɒpsɪkəl $ ˈpɑːp-/ *n* [C] *trademark AmE* a food made of juice that is frozen onto sticks SYN **ice lolly** *BrE*

ˈpop star *n* [C] a famous and successful entertainer who plays or sings POP MUSIC

pop·u·lace /ˈpɒpjələs $ ˈpɑː-/ *n* [singular] *formal* the people who live in a country: *the effects of the war on the local populace*

pop·u·lar /ˈpɒpjələ $ ˈpɑːpjəposlər/ ●●● S2 W1 *adj*
1 liked by a lot of people OPP **unpopular**: *Hilary was popular at school. | a popular holiday resort | Coffee is probably the most popular drink in the world.* | **hugely/enormously/immensely etc popular** *Guerrero's music is hugely popular in Latin America.* | **[+with/among]** *The president is very popular with Jewish voters.*
2 [only before noun] done by a lot of people in a society, group etc: *the closest popular vote in U.S. presidential history | The government has little **popular support** among women voters. | Kaplan's latest recording has received considerable **popular acclaim*** (=it is liked by a lot of people). | **popular belief/opinion/view** (=a belief, opinion etc that a lot of people have) *a survey of Hispanic-American popular opinion* | ***Contrary to popular belief*** (=in spite of what many people believe), *gorillas are basically shy, gentle creatures. | a **popular movement** for democracy*
3 [only before noun] relating to ordinary people, or intended for ordinary people: *Wintour's writing is full of references to American **popular culture**. | Steele was ridiculed by the popular press.* → **POP MUSIC**

pop·u·lar·i·ty /ˌpɒpjəˈlærəti $ ˌpɑː-/ ●●○ *n* [U] when something or someone is liked or supported by a lot of people: **[+of]** *The popularity of the Internet has soared. | The president's **popularity** has **declined** considerably.* | **gain/grow/increase in popularity** (=start to be liked by many people) *Country music is growing in popularity.*

pop·u·lar·ize (*also* **-ise** *BrE*) /ˈpɒpjələraɪz $ ˈpɑː-/ *v* [T] **1** to make something well known and liked: *Bob Marley popularized reggae music in the 1970s.* **2** to make a difficult subject or idea able to be easily understood by ordinary people who have no special knowledge about it: *Skinner was the psychologist who popularized behavior modification.* —**popularization** /ˌpɒpjələraɪˈzeɪʃən $ ˌpɑːpjələrə-/ *n* [U]

pop·u·lar·ly /ˈpɒpjələli $ ˈpɑːpjələr-/ *adv* by most or many people: *The president of Korea is popularly elected every five years.* | **popularly believed/thought/called etc** *Vitamin C is popularly believed to prevent colds. | The Church of Jesus Christ of Latter-Day Saints is **popularly known as** the Mormon Church.*

pop·u·late /ˈpɒpjəleɪt $ ˈpɑː-/ *v* [T] **1** if an area is populated by a particular group of people, they live there: *The highlands are populated mainly by peasant farmers.* | **densely/heavily/highly/thickly populated** (=with a lot of people) *one of the most densely populated areas in the world* | **sparsely/thinly/lightly populated** (=with very few people) GRAMMAR **Populate** is usually passive.
2 *technical* to fill a computer DATABASE or TABLE with information

pop·u·la·tion /ˌpɒpjəˈleɪʃən $ ˌpɑː-/ ●●● S2 W1 *n*
1 [C] the number of people living in a particular area, country etc: **[+of]** *India has a population of more than one billion. | Nearly 70 percent of the population still live in the countryside.*
2 [C usually singular] all of the people who live in a particular area: *Most of the world's population doesn't get enough to eat.* | **white/French/urban etc population** (=part of the group of people who live in a particular area who are white, French etc) *South Florida has a large Jewish population.*
3 centre of population/population centre a city, town etc: *Cromer is the main centre of population in this area.*

P

P

COLLOCATIONS - MEANINGS 1 & 2

ADJECTIVES/NOUN + population

the total/whole/entire population *The entire population will be celebrating.*
the world's population *Sixty percent of the world's population live in areas that are at risk from sea-level rises.*
the general population *Ethnic minorities suffer more than the general population.*
the local population *The local population gave them a warm welcome.*
the black/white population (=black or white people who live in a place) *Unemployment is greater among the black population.*
the Jewish/Muslim/Asian etc population (=the people of a particular nationality or religion who live in a place) *the city's 4,000-strong Asian population*
the indigenous population *formal* (=the people who have always lived in a place) *His new book assesses the impact of Spanish culture on the indigenous population of Mexico.*
the urban population (=the people who live in towns or cities) *The region's urban population will more than double in the next two decades.*
the rural population (=the people who live in the countryside) *Agricultural reforms must address the needs of the rural population.*
the adult population *A third of the adult population pay no tax at all.*
the elderly population *Should the entire elderly population be regularly screened for this disease?*
an ageing population (=gradually becoming older on average) *The rapidly ageing population will put a strain on the country's health care system.*
a large population *California is a big state with a large population.*
a prison population (=the number of people in prisons in a country or area) *A quarter of the prison population is under 21.*
a student population *The university has a student population of almost 5,000.*

VERBS

a population grows/increases/rises *Between these years the population grew by 40%.*
a population falls/declines/decreases *The population in many rural areas has continued to fall.*
a population reaches *Nigeria 's population will reach 532 million in the middle of this century.*

population + NOUN

population growth *Rapid population growth intensifies competition for land.*
population increase *The population increase in the region is a cause for concern.*
a population explosion/boom (=when the population increases quickly and by a large amount) *What will be the long-term effects of this population explosion?*
population density (=the degree to which an area is filled with people) *Australia has a low population density.*
population control (=controlling how many children people have) *It is argued that population control is essential to limit the depletion of natural resources.*

pop·u·list /ˈpɒpjəlɪst $ ˈpɑː-/ *adj* relating to or representing ordinary people, rather than rich or very highly educated people: *a populist campaign* —**populist** *n* [C] —**populism** *n* [U]

pop·u·lous /ˈpɒpjələs $ ˈpɑː-/ *adj formal* a populous area has a large population in relation to its size: *Hong Kong is one of the most populous areas in the world.*

ˈpop-under *n* [C] a WINDOW containing an advertisement, that suddenly appears under another window on a computer screen when you are looking at a website → **pop-up**

ˈpop-up¹ *adj* **1 pop-up book/card etc** a book, card etc with a picture that stands up when you open the pages **2 pop-up menu/window** a MENU or WINDOW that can appear suddenly on a computer screen while you are using it **3 pop-up restaurant/bar/shop etc** a restaurant, bar, shop etc that is opened somewhere for a short, limited period of time

POP-UP

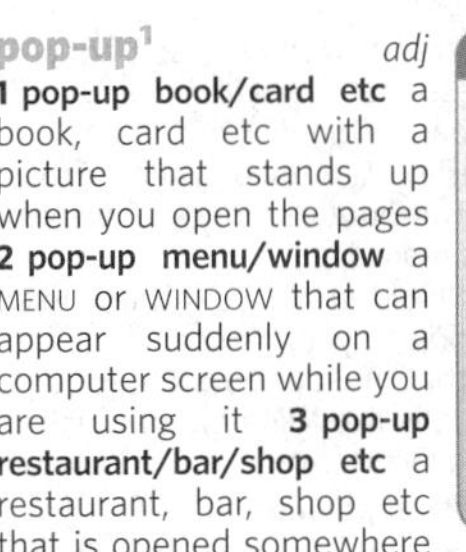

a pop-up book

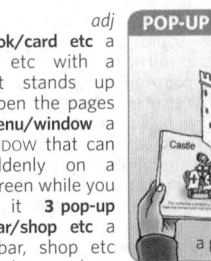

pop-up² *n* [C] **1** a WINDOW, often containing an advertisement, that suddenly appears on a computer screen, especially when you are looking at a website **2** a restaurant, bar, shop etc that is opened somewhere for a short, limited period of time

porce·lain /ˈpɔːslɪn $ ˈpɔːrsəlɪn/ *n* [U] **1** a hard shiny white substance that is used for making expensive plates, cups etc → **china**: *a porcelain vase* **2** plates, cups etc made of this → **china**

porch /pɔːtʃ $ pɔːrtʃ/ ●●● S3 *n* [C]
1 *BrE* an entrance covered by a roof outside the front door of a house or church
2 *AmE* a structure built onto the front or back entrance of a house, with a floor and a roof but no walls

por·cine /ˈpɔːsaɪn $ ˈpɔːr-/ *adj formal* looking like or relating to pigs

por·cu·pine /ˈpɔːkjəpaɪn $ ˈpɔːr-/ *n* [C] an animal with long sharp parts growing all over its back and sides

pore¹ /pɔː $ pɔːr/ *n* [C] one of the small holes in your skin that liquid, especially SWEAT, can pass through, or a similar hole in the surface of a plant

pore² *v*
pore over sth *phr v* to read or look at something very carefully for a long time: *She was poring over a book.*

pork /pɔːk $ pɔːrk/ ●●● S3 *n* [U]
1 the meat from pigs: *pork chops*
2 *AmE informal* government money spent in a particular area in order to get political advantages - used to show disapproval: *a bill filled with pork projects*

ˈpork ˌbarrel *n* [singular, U] *AmE informal* a government plan to increase the amount of money spent in a particular area, done in order to gain a political advantage - used to show disapproval: *pork-barrel spending*

pork·er /ˈpɔːkə $ ˈpɔːrkər/ *n* [C] **1** a young pig that is made fat before being killed for food **2** *informal* a fat person - often used humorously

ˌpork ˈpie *n* [C] *BrE* a small round PIE which contains pieces of cooked pork

ˌpork ˈrinds *n* [plural] *AmE* small pieces of pig fat that have been cooked in hot oil and are eaten as a SNACK

pork·y¹ /ˈpɔːki $ ˈpɔːrki/ *adj informal* fat - often used humorously

porky² (*also* **ˈporky pie**) *n* (*plural* **porkies**) [C] *BrE informal* a lie: *Was he **telling porkies** again?*

porn /pɔːn $ pɔːrn/ *n* [U] *informal* **1** (*also* **porn·o** /ˈpɔːnəʊ $ ˈpɔːrnoʊ/) pornography: *the porn industry | a porno movie* **2 property/food/car etc porn** television programmes, advertisements, magazines, or books about homes, food, cars etc, which people enjoy looking at because they contain attractive images of things they would like to have - used humorously or to show disapproval → **HARD PORN, SOFT PORN**

por·nog·ra·phy /pɔːˈnɒɡrəfi $ pɔːrˈnɑːɡ-/ *n* [U] magazines, films etc that show sexual acts and images in a way that is intended to make people feel sexually excited —**pornographer** *n* [C] —**pornographic** /ˌpɔːnəˈɡræfɪk◂ $ ˌpɔːr-/ *adj*: *pornographic websites*

po·rous /ˈpɔːrəs/ *adj* **1** allowing liquid, air etc to pass slowly through many very small holes: *porous material* **2** easy to pass through or get into something: *the porous border between Haiti and the Dominican Republic*

por·poise /ˈpɔːpəs $ ˈpɔːr-/ *n* [C] a sea animal that looks similar to a DOLPHIN and breathes air

por·ridge /ˈpɒrɪdʒ $ ˈpɑː-, ˈpɔː-/ *n* [U] **1** OATS that are cooked with milk or water and served hot for breakfast SYN **oatmeal** *AmE* **2** *BrE informal* a period of time spent in prison: **do porridge** (=spend time in prison)

port¹ /pɔːt $ pɔːrt/ ●●● W2 *n*

1 WHERE SHIPS STOP [C,U] a place where ships can be loaded and unloaded: **be in port** *We'll have two days ashore while the ship is in port.* | **come into port/leave port** *The ferry was about to leave port.*

2 TOWN [C] a town or city with a HARBOUR or DOCKS where ships can be loaded or unloaded: *Britain's largest port*

3 COMPUTER [C] a part of a computer where you can connect another piece of equipment, such as a PRINTER

4 WINE [U] strong sweet Portuguese wine that is usually drunk after a meal: *a glass of port*

5 SIDE OF SHIP [U] the left side of a ship or aircraft when you are looking towards the front OPP **starboard**: *on the port side* | **to port** *The plane tilted to port.*

6 any port in a storm *spoken* used to say that you should take whatever help you can when you are in trouble, even if it has some disadvantages → PORT OF CALL

port² *v* [T] to move software from one computer system to another: **port sth from/to sth** *Can Windows applications be ported to Unix?* —**porting** *n* [U]

por·ta·ble¹ /ˈpɔːtəbəl $ ˈpɔːr-/ ●●○ *adj*

1 able to be carried or moved easily: *a portable radio*

2 a portable computer program can be used on different computer systems

3 portable benefits *AmE* health insurance, PENSION PLANS etc that workers can keep when they move from one job to another —**portability** /ˌpɔːtəˈbɪləti $ ˌpɔːr-/ *n* [U]

portable² *n* [C] a piece of electronic equipment that can be easily carried or moved: *Get a portable, not a big TV.*

ˌportable ˈmedia ˌplayer *n* [C] (*abbreviation* **PMP**) a small machine that can store and play DIGITAL music and videos and show digital photographs

port·age /ˈpɔːtɪdʒ $ ˈpɔːr-/ *n* [U] when people carry small boats over land from one river to another

Por·ta·kab·in /ˈpɔːtəkæbɪn $ ˈpɔːr-/ *n* [C] *trademark BrE* a very small building that can be used as a temporary office, CLASSROOM etc, and can be moved by truck

por·tal /ˈpɔːtl $ ˈpɔːrtl/ *n* [C] **1** a website that helps you find other websites **2** [usually plural] *literary* a tall and impressive gate or entrance to a building

Port·a·loo /ˈpɔːtəluː $ ˈpɔːr-/ *n* [C] *trademark BrE* a toilet that is in a small plastic building that can be moved

Por·ta Pot·ti, **porta-potty** /ˈpɔːtə ˌpɒti $ ˈpɔːrtə ˌpɑːti/ *n* [C] *trademark AmE* a toilet that is in a small plastic building that can be moved

port·cul·lis /pɔːtˈkʌlɪs $ pɔːrt-/ *n* [C] a strong iron gate that can be lowered over the entrance of a castle

por·tend /pɔːˈtend $ pɔːr-/ *v* [T] *literary* to be a sign that something is going to happen, especially something bad: *strange events that portend disaster*

por·tent /ˈpɔːtent $ ˈpɔːr-/ *n* [C] *literary* a sign or warning that something is going to happen SYN **omen**: **[+of]** *Some people believe the raven is a portent of death.*

por·ten·tous /pɔːˈtentəs $ pɔːr-/ *adj* **1** *literary* showing that something important is going to happen, especially something bad: *Recent developments are as portentous as the collapse of the Berlin Wall.* **2** trying to appear important and serious: *a portentous film*

por·ter /ˈpɔːtə $ ˈpɔːrtər/ *n* **1** [C] someone whose job is to carry people's bags at railway stations, airports etc **2** [C] *BrE* someone in charge of the entrance to a hotel, hospital etc **3** [C] *BrE* someone whose job is to carry heavy goods at markets **4** [C] *AmE* someone whose job is to look after the part of a train where people sleep **5** [C] *AmE* someone whose job is to look after a building by cleaning it, repairing things etc **6** [U] *old-fashioned* a dark brown bitter beer

por·ter·house steak /ˌpɔːtəhaʊs ˈsteɪk $ ˌpɔːrtər-/ *n* [C,U] a thick flat piece of high-quality BEEF

port·fo·li·o /pɔːtˈfəʊliəʊ $ pɔːrtˈfoʊlioʊ/ ●○○ *n* (*plural* **portfolios**) [C]

1 a large flat case used especially for carrying pictures, documents etc

2 a set of pictures or other pieces of work that an artist, photographer etc has done: *You'll need to prepare a portfolio of your work.*

3 a group of STOCKS owned by a particular person or company: *an investment portfolio*

4 *BrE* the work that a particular government official is responsible for: *the foreign affairs portfolio*

port·hole /ˈpɔːthəʊl $ ˈpɔːrthoʊl/ *n* [C] a small round window on the side of a ship or plane → see picture at WINDOW

por·ti·co /ˈpɔːtɪkəʊ $ ˈpɔːrtɪkoʊ/ *n* (*plural* **porticoes** *or* **porticos**) [C] a covered entrance to a building, consisting of a roof supported by PILLARS

por·tion¹ /ˈpɔːʃən $ ˈpɔːr-/ ●●○ AWL *n*

1 [C] a part of something larger, especially a part that is different from the other parts: **[+of]** *The front portion of the rocket breaks off.* | *The rent on his portion of the apartment was $500 a month.* | **significant/substantial/major/good portion** *The main character's childhood takes up a good portion of the film.*

2 [C] an amount of food for one person, especially when served in a restaurant SYN **serving**, **helping**: *Do you have any children's portions?* | **[+of]** *a huge portion of roast beef* | *He served* ***generous portions*** (=large portions) *of soup from a black pot.*

3 [usually singular] a share of something, such as responsibility, blame, or a duty, that is divided between a small number of people: **[+of]** *The other driver must bear a portion of the blame for the accident.*

portion² *v*

portion sth ↔ **out** *phr v BrE* to divide something into parts and give it to several people: **[+among]** *The money was portioned out among them.*

port·ly /ˈpɔːtli $ ˈpɔːr-/ *adj written* someone who is portly, especially an old man, is fat and round: *a portly old gentleman* THESAURUS ▸ FAT

port·man·teau /pɔːtˈmæntəʊ $ pɔːrtˈmæntoʊ/ *n* (*plural* **portmanteaus** *or* **portmanteaux** /-təʊz $ -toʊz/) [C] *old-fashioned* a very large SUITCASE that opens into two parts

portˈmanteau ˌword *n* [C] *technical* a portmanteau word is made by combining the sound and meaning of two other words, for example 'edutainment' combines 'education' and 'entertainment'

ˌport of ˈcall *n* (*plural* **ports of call**) [C usually singular] **1** *informal* one of a series of places that you visit: *My* ***first port of call*** *will be the post office.* **2** a port where a ship stops on a journey from one place to another

ˌport of ˈentry *n* (*plural* **ports of entry**) [C] a place, such as a port or airport, where people or goods can enter a country

Por·ton Down /ˌpɔːtn ˈdaʊn $ ˌpɔːr-/ a place in the south of England where there is a government LABORATORY used for studying chemical weapons and BIOLOGICAL weapons (=weapons that use BACTERIA to kill people by giving them diseases)

por·trait¹ /ˈpɔːtrɪt $ ˈpɔːr-/ ●●○ *n* [C]

1 a painting, drawing, or photograph of a person: *a family portrait* | **[+of]** *the artist's portrait of his mother* | *She's been commissioned to* ***paint*** *Jackson's* ***portrait***. → see picture at PAINTING

2 a description or representation of something: **[+of]** *a portrait of working life in America* → SELF-PORTRAIT

portrait² *adj* if a piece of paper, a page, a photograph etc is in a portrait position, it is placed on a surface or hung on a wall with its longer edges at the sides OPP **landscape**

por·trai·ture /ˈpɔːtrətʃə $ ˈpɔːrtrətʃər/ *n* [U] *formal* the art of painting or drawing pictures of people

P

por·tray /pɔːˈtreɪ $ pɔːr-/ ●●○ *v* [T]
1 portray sb/sth as sth to describe or show someone or something in a particular way, according to your opinion of them SYN **depict**: *Romantic artists portrayed nature as wild and powerful.* | *The president likes to portray himself as a friend of working people.* THESAURUS ▸ DESCRIBE
2 to describe or represent something or someone SYN **depict**: *His most famous painting portrayed the death of Nelson.* | *Religion was portrayed in a negative way.*
3 to act the part of a character in a play, film, or television programme SYN **play**: *She portrays a dancer in the hit film.*

por·tray·al /pɔːˈtreɪəl $ pɔːr-/ ●○○ *n* [C,U] the way someone or something is described or shown in a book, film, play etc: **[+of]** *the newspapers' portrayal of Islamic culture* | **accurate/realistic etc portrayal** *The film is not an accurate portrayal* (=correct portrayal) *of his life.*

P

Por·tu·guese[1] /ˌpɔːtʃəˈgiːz◂ $ ˌpɔːr-/ *adj* relating to Portugal, its people, or its language

Portuguese[2] *n* **1 the Portuguese** [plural] people from Portugal **2** [U] the language used in Portugal, Brazil, and some other countries

ˌPortuguese man-of-ˈwar *n* [C] a very large poisonous JELLYFISH

pose[1] /pəʊz $ poʊz/ ●●○ W3 AWL *v*
1 CAUSE PROBLEM [T] to exist in a way that may cause a problem, danger, difficulty etc: **pose a threat/danger/risk** *Officials claim the chemical poses no real threat.* | **pose sth to/for sb/sth** *The events pose a challenge to the church's leadership.* | *Rising unemployment is* ***posing*** *serious* ***problems*** *for the administration.*
2 PICTURE [I] to sit or stand in a particular position in order to be photographed or painted, or to make someone do this: **[+for]** *We posed for photographs.*
3 pose a question to ask a question, especially one that needs to be carefully thought about: *In her book she poses the question 'How much do we need to be happy?'.*
4 pose as sb to pretend to be someone else, in order to deceive people: *Bryce was caught posing as a lawyer.*
5 TO IMPRESS PEOPLE [I] to dress or behave like a rich and fashionable person in order to make other people notice you or admire you

pose[2] AWL *n* [C] **1** the position in which someone stands or sits, especially in a painting, photograph etc: **in a pose** *a painting of the Duchess in a dramatic pose* | *Ann* ***struck a pose*** (=stood or sat in a particular position) *and smiled for the camera.* **2** behaviour in which someone pretends to have a quality or social position they do not really have, usually in order to make other people notice them or admire them: *Her confidence was merely a pose to hide her uncertainty.*

pos·er /ˈpəʊzə $ ˈpoʊzər/ *n* [C] *informal* **1** *BrE* (*also* **po·seur** /pəʊˈzɜː $ poʊˈzɜːr/) someone who pretends to have a quality or social position they do not really have, usually in order to make people notice or admire them: *You meet a lot of posers in this job.* **2** a difficult question: *That's a real poser.*

posh[1] /pɒʃ $ pɑːʃ/ ●○○ *adj informal*
1 a posh restaurant, hotel, car etc is expensive and looks as if it is used or owned by rich people: *a posh private school*
2 *BrE* upper class: *Her parents are terribly posh.*

posh[2] *adv BrE informal* **talk posh** to talk in an upper-class way

pos·it /ˈpɒzɪt $ ˈpɑː-/ *v* [T] *formal* to suggest that a particular idea should be accepted as a fact: **posit that** *He posited that each planet moved in a perfect circle.*

po·si·tion[1] /pəˈzɪʃən/ ●●● S1 W1 *n*
1 WAY OF STANDING/SITTING ETC [C] the way someone is standing, sitting, or lying: *Lie in a* ***comfortable position***. | *Frankie* ***shifted*** *his* ***position*** *so that his knees would not become cramped.* | **sitting/kneeling/standing position** *I struggled up into a sitting position.*
2 SITUATION [C usually singular] the situation that someone is in, especially when this affects what they can and cannot do: *I'm not sure what I would do if I were* ***in*** *your position.* | **be in a position to do sth** *Next week we will be in a much better position to comment.* | **be in the position of doing sth** *She is in the enviable position of having three job offers.* | *You're putting me in rather a difficult position.*
3 PLACE WHERE SB/STH IS [C] the place where someone or something is, especially in relation to other objects and places: **[+of]** *the position of the sun in the sky* | *Our hotel was in a superb* ***central position*** *near St Mark's Square.* | *the* ***strategic position*** (=useful or important position) *of Egypt in relation to the Arabian peninsula*
4 CORRECT PLACE [C,U] the place where someone or something is needed or supposed to be: **into position** *He pulled the ladder into position.* | **in/out of position** *All parking signs have now been placed in position.*
5 DIRECTION [C] the direction in which an object is pointing: **vertical/upright/horizontal position** *Make sure the container remains in an upright position.* | *She turned the switch to the 'on' position.* THESAURUS ▸ PLACE
6 OPINION [C] an opinion or judgment on a particular subject, especially the official opinion of a government, a political party, or someone in authority SYN **attitude**: **[+on]** *What's the party's position on tax reform?* | *The principal* ***took*** *the* ***position that*** *the students didn't need music classes.* | *I hope you'll* ***reconsider*** *your* ***position***.
7 JOB [C] *formal* a job: **sb's position as sth** *Bill* ***took up*** *his new* ***position*** *as Works Director in October.* | **[+of]** *She has* ***held*** *the* ***position*** *of Chief Financial Officer since 1992.* | *Bruce is thinking of* ***applying for*** *the* ***position***. | *I'm sorry, the* ***position has been filled*** (=someone has been found to do the job). THESAURUS ▸ JOB
8 LEVEL/RANK [C,U] someone's or something's level, authority, or importance in a society or organization: **the position of sb** *the position of women in society* | **position of power/authority/influence etc** *Many of his supporters used their positions of power for personal advantage.* | *As a priest, he was in a* ***position of trust***. | **abuse your position as sth** (=use your authority wrongly)
9 be in a position to do sth to be able to do something because you have the ability, money, or power to do it: *When I know all the facts, I'll be in a position to advise you.*
10 be in no position to do sth to be unable to do something because you do not have the ability, money, or power to do it: *You're unemployed and in no position to support a family.* | *Ned says I'm always late? He's* ***in no position to talk*** (=should not criticize because he does the same thing).
11 RACE/COMPETITION [C,U] the place of someone or something in a race or competition in relation to the other people or things: **(in) 2nd/3rd/4th etc position** *Alesi* ***finished*** *in third* ***position***.
12 SPORTS [C] the area where someone plays in a sport, or the type of actions they are responsible for doing: *What* ***position*** *do you* ***play***?
13 jockey/manoeuvre/jostle for position to try to get an advantage over other people who are all trying to succeed in doing the same thing: *Firms adopt different strategies as they jockey for position.*
14 ARMY [C usually plural] a place where an army has put soldiers, guns etc: *an attack on the enemy positions*

COLLOCATIONS – MEANING 2

ADJECTIVES

the same position *A lot of people are in the same position.*
a similar position *You can ask to be put in contact with others in a similar position.*
a strong/good position (=a situation in which you have an advantage) *A victory tonight will put them in a very strong position to win the cup.*
a unique position (=a situation that no one else is in) *Their close knowledge of the area places them in a unique position to advise on social policy.*
a difficult/awkward position *I was in the difficult position of having to choose between them.*
an enviable position (=a situation that other people would like to be in) *He is in the enviable position of not needing to work.*

an impossible position (=a very difficult situation) *She was furious with Guy for putting her in such an impossible position.*
a weak position (=a situation in which you have a disadvantage) *Someone who is desperate to sell their house is in a weak position.*
a vulnerable position (=a situation in which you might be harmed) *Today we are in the vulnerable position of producing barely half our own food.*
the present/current position *The following statistics indicate the present position.*
the legal position (=the situation from a legal point of view) *The legal position is far from clear.*
sb's financial position *Has your financial position changed recently?*
a bargaining/negotiating position (=someone's ability to bargain/negotiate) *The new law has strengthened workers' bargaining position.*

VERBS

be in a strong/weak etc position *We are in a good position to help.*
find yourself in a similar/awkward etc position *The refugee organizations now found themselves in a difficult position.*
reach a position *It has taken two years to reach the position we are now in.*
put/place sb in a good/awkward etc position *I'm sorry if I put you in an awkward position.*
strengthen sb's position (=give someone a bigger advantage) *People said that he used the conflict to strengthen his own position.*
weaken sb's position (=give someone a bigger disadvantage) *The prime minister's position had been weakened by allegations of financial mismanagement.*
sb's position improves *By March, the Democrats' position had improved.*

PHRASES

a position of strength (=a strong position) *By now they were negotiating from a position of strength.*

position² ●○○ *v* [T always + adv/prep]
1 to carefully put something in a particular position: *Position the cursor before the letter you want to delete.* | **position yourself** *I positioned myself where I could see the door.* THESAURUS ▸ PUT
2 be well/ideally/perfectly positioned to be in a situation in which you will be able to do something successfully: *We are ideally positioned to take advantage of the growth in demand.*

pos·i·tion·al /pəˈzɪʃənəl/ *adj* [only before noun] relating to the position or job of someone or something: *positional power or authority*

poˈsition ˌpaper *n* [C] a written statement that shows how a department, organization etc intends to deal with something

pos·i·tive¹ /ˈpɒzətɪv $ ˈpɑː-/ ●●● S2 W2 AWL *adj*
1 ATTITUDE if you are positive about things, you are hopeful and confident, and think about what is good in a situation rather than what is bad OPP **negative**: **[+about]** *You've got to be more positive about your work.* | **positive attitude/approach/outlook etc** *She's got a really positive attitude to life.* | *the power of* **positive thinking** | **'Think positive**!' *she advised herself.*
2 GOOD THING good or useful OPP **negative**: *At least* **something positive** *has come out of the situation.* | *Write down all the* **positive things** *about your life.* | *The rural environment was having a* **positive effect** *on the children's health.* | *It's been a very* **positive experience** *for her.* | *TV can* **be a positive influence**. | *the* **positive contribution** *to the community* **made** *by many older people* | *It's been a difficult time but,* **on the positive side**, *I feel physically fine.* | *Women should be portrayed* **in a** *more* **positive light**.
3 ACTION if you take positive action, you do something definite in order to try to achieve something: *We need to* **take positive steps** *to improve the situation of families in poverty.* | **Positive action** *was required.* | *It's a relief to know that* **something positive** *is being done.*
4 SUPPORT expressing support, agreement, or approval OPP **negative**: **positive response/reaction** *The response we've had from the public has been very positive.* | *We've had a lot of* **positive feedback** *from the people of this city.* | **[+about]** *Most people have been very positive about the show.*
5 SURE [not before noun] very sure, with no doubt at all that something is right or true SYN **certain**: **positive (that)** *Are you* **absolutely positive** *you locked the door?* | *'Are you sure about that?' 'Positive.'* THESAURUS ▸ SURE
6 SIGN showing that something is likely to succeed or improve: *The fact that he's breathing on his own again is a* **positive sign**.
7 PROOF positive proof/evidence/identification etc proof etc that shows that there is no doubt that something is true: *The witness made a positive identification.*
8 SCIENTIFIC TEST showing signs of the medical condition or chemical that is being looked for OPP **negative**: *kThe test results came back positive.* | *athletes who had* **tested positive** *for banned substances* | *children who are HIV positive*
9 EMPHASIS [only before noun] *spoken* used to emphasize how good or bad something is SYN **total**: *The journey was a positive nightmare.*
10 NUMBER *technical* a positive number is more than zero OPP **negative**
11 ELECTRICITY *technical* having the type of electrical charge that is carried by PROTONS OPP **negative**: *a* **positive charge**

positive² *n* [C] a quality or feature that is good or useful OPP **negative**: *You can find positives in any situation.* | *Always emphasise* **the positive**. → FALSE POSITIVE

ˌpositive discrimiˈnation *n* [U] *BrE* the practice of giving a particular number of jobs, places at university etc to people who are often treated unfairly because of their race, sex etc SYN **affirmative action** *AmE*

pos·i·tive·ly /ˈpɒzətɪvli $ ˈpɑː-/ ●○○ AWL *adv*
1 used to emphasize that something is true, especially when this seems surprising: *Some holiday destinations are* **positively dangerous**.
2 in a way that shows you agree with something or want it to succeed OPP **negatively**: *It is hoped that the industry will respond positively to this new initiative.*
3 in a way that shows you are thinking about what is good in a situation rather than what is bad: *They're encouraged to* **think positively** *about themselves and their future.* | *Change should be accepted and be viewed positively.*
4 in a way that leaves no doubt: *'You certainly won't!' Katherine said positively.* | *The blood was never* **positively identified** *as the victim's.*
5 *spoken* used to emphasize that you really mean what you are saying SYN **definitely**: *This is positively the last time you'll hear me say this.*
6 positively charged *technical* having the type of electrical charge that is carried by PROTONS

pos·i·tiv·is·m /ˈpɒzətɪvɪzəm $ ˈpɑː-/ *n* [U] a type of PHILOSOPHY based only on facts which can be scientifically proved, rather than on ideas —**positivist** *adj, n* [C]

pos·i·tron /ˈpɒzətrɒn $ ˈpɑːzətrɑːn/ *n* [C] *technical* a very small piece of matter that has the same mass as an ELECTRON but has a positive electrical CHARGE

poss /pɒs $ pɑːs/ *adj BrE informal* **1 if poss** if possible: *Please send a photo if poss.* **2 as soon as poss** as soon as possible: *I need them back as soon as poss.*

pos·se /ˈpɒsi $ ˈpɑːsi/ *n* [C] **1** *informal* a group of the same kind of people: **[+of]** *I was surrounded by a posse of photographers.* **2** a group of men gathered together by a SHERIFF (=local law officer) in the US in past times to help catch a criminal **3** *AmE informal* **a)** someone's group of friends – used especially by young people **b)** a group of friends from a particular place who share an interest in RAP, HIP-HOP, or HOUSE music SYN **massive** *BrE*

pos·sess /pəˈzes/ ●●○ W3 *v* [T]
1 *formal* to have a particular quality or ability: *Different*

workers possess different skills. | *He no longer possessed the power to frighten her.*

> **REGISTER**
> In everyday English, people usually say that someone **has** or **has got** something rather than **possesses** it: *They all **have** different skills.*

2 *formal or law* to have or own something: *Neither of them possessed a credit card.* | *Campbell was found guilty of possessing heroin.* **THESAURUS** ▸ **OWN**
3 what possessed sb (to do sth)? *spoken* used to say that you cannot understand why someone did something stupid: *What on earth possessed her to do it?*
4 *literary* if a feeling possesses you, you suddenly feel it very strongly and it affects your behaviour: *A mad rage possessed her.*

> **GRAMMAR: Using the progressive**
> **Possess** is not used in the progressive when it means 'have' or 'own'. You say: *He possesses many good qualities.* ✗ Don't say: *He is possessing many good qualities.*
> **GRAMMAR GUIDE** ▸ **VERBS**

pos·sessed /pəˈzest/ *adj* **1** if someone is possessed, their mind is controlled by something evil: *She was convinced he was **possessed by the devil**.* | **like a man/woman possessed** *literary* (=with a lot of energy or violence) **2 be possessed of sth** *literary* to have a particular quality, ability etc: *She was possessed of a fine and original mind.* → **SELF-POSSESSED**

pos·ses·sion /pəˈzeʃən/ ●●○ W3 *n*
1 HAVING STH [U] *formal* if something is in your possession, you own it, or you have obtained it from somewhere: **in sb's possession** *The house has been in the family's possession since the 1500s.* | *That information is not in our possession.* | **in possession of sth** *She was found in possession of stolen goods.* | *How did the painting **come into** your **possession*** (=how did you get it)? | *The finance company now **has possession of** the house.* | *We didn't **take possession of*** (=get and start using) *the car until a few days after the auction.*
2 STH YOU OWN [C usually plural] something that you own or have with you at a particular time SYN **belongings**: *He had sold all his possessions and left the country.* | *I packed my remaining possessions into the trunk.* | **treasured/prized/precious possession** (=one that is very important to you) *This old violin had been her father's most treasured possession.* | *Prisoners were allowed no **personal possessions**.*
3 CRIME [U] *law* the crime of having illegal drugs or weapons with you or in your home: **[+of]** *He was arrested and **charged with possession** of cocaine.*
4 SPORT [U] when a person or team has control of the ball in some sports: **win/lose/gain etc possession** *Pittsburgh got possession and scored.*
5 COUNTRY [C usually plural] a country controlled or governed by another country: *France's former **colonial possessions***
6 EVIL SPIRITS [U] a situation in which someone's mind is being controlled by something evil: *Was it a case of demonic possession?*
7 in (full) possession of your faculties/senses able to think in a clear and intelligent way, and not crazy or affected by old age
8 possession is nine-tenths of the law used to say that if you have something, you are likely to be able to keep it, even if it is not yours

pos·ses·sive¹ /pəˈzesɪv/ *adj* **1** wanting someone to have feelings of love or friendship for you and no one else: **[+of/about]** *She was terribly possessive of our eldest son.* **2** unwilling to let other people use something you own: **[+of/about]** *He's so possessive about his new car.* **3** *technical* used in grammar to show that something belongs to someone or something: **possessive pronoun/form/case etc** *the possessive pronouns 'ours' and 'mine'* —**possessively** *adv* —**possessiveness** *n* [U]

possessive² *n* [C] *technical* an adjective, PRONOUN, or form of a word that shows that something belongs to someone or something

pos·ses·sor /pəˈzesə $ -ər/ *n* [C] *formal* someone who owns or has something – often used humorously: **[+of]** *He's now **the proud possessor** of two satellite dishes.*

pos·si·bil·i·ty /ˌpɒsəˈbɪləti $ ˌpɑː-/ ●●● S2 W2 *n* (*plural* **possibilities**)
1 [C,U] if there is a possibility that something is true or that something will happen, it might be true or it might happen: *There's always **a possibility that** he might go back to Seattle.* | *the **possibility of** an enemy attack* | *There was **no possibility of** changing the voting procedure.* | *A peace settlement now looks like **a real possibility**.* | *Tomorrow, there's a **remote possibility** of snow on high ground.* | *They might get married – it's **not beyond the bounds of possibility**.* | *The study **raises the possibility** that dieting is bad for your health.*
2 [C usually plural] an opportunity to do something, or something that can be done or tried: **possibilities for/of (doing) sth** *exciting possibilities for reducing costs* | *Archer began to **explore the possibilities** of opening a club in the city.* | *The US has not yet **exhausted** all diplomatic **possibilities*** (=tried everything possible). | *the range of **possibilities offered** to students*
3 have possibilities if something has possibilities, it could be made into something much better SYN **have potential**: *The house has great possibilities.*

pos·si·ble¹ /ˈpɒsəbəl $ ˈpɑː-/ ●●● S1 W1 *adj*
1 if something is possible, it can be done or achieved OPP **impossible**: ***Is it possible to** get tickets for the game?* | ***It might be possible for** the documents **to** be sent over.* | *Computer technology **makes it possible for** many people **to** work from home.* | *I want to avoid the rush hour traffic **if possible**.* | *I walk or use public transport **whenever possible**.* | *We are doing **everything possible** to track down the killer.* | *Our staff will help you **in every way possible**.* | *Even if it were **technically possible**, we do not have the money to do it.* | *She decided to stay as far away from him as was **humanly possible**.*
2 as soon/quickly/much etc as possible as soon, quickly etc as you can: *I need the money as soon as possible.* | *Sharon always does as little work as possible.* | *The original features of the house have been preserved **as far as possible*** (=as much as possible).
3 a possible answer, cause etc might be true: *There seem to be only two **possible explanations**.* | *the **possible causes** of a child's learning difficulties* | **it is possible (that)** *It's possible that the letter got lost in the post.*
4 a possible event or thing might happen or exist: *Heavy rain is possible later in the day.* | *the possible effect on the health of local people* | *You need to look at the **possible consequences** of your actions.* | *In Hollywood, **anything is possible*** (=anything can happen, even though it may seem very unlikely).
5 the best/biggest/fastest etc possible the best etc that can exist or be achieved: *Try to get the best possible price.* | *What is the worst possible thing that could happen?*
6 would it be possible (for sb) to do sth? *spoken* used when asking politely if you can do or have something: *Would it be possible to speak to Oliver?*

> **THESAURUS**
> **possible** if something is possible, it can be done or achieved: *I think it's possible that we could win the race.* | *I want to get back by 5 o'clock if possible.* | *Please let me know your answer as soon as possible.*
> **feasible** if an idea or plan is feasible, it is possible and you can find a practical way of doing it: *We need to find out first if the idea is technically feasible.* | *It is not feasible to have security cameras in every part of the building.*
> **viable** possible and likely to be successful, and therefore worth doing: *Nuclear energy is the only viable alternative to coal or gas.* | *The product needs to be commercially viable.* | *The company was no longer financially viable* (=it could not make enough money to be able to continue).

workable a workable plan, system, or solution is one that can be done or used: *By early morning, they had arrived at a workable and safe solution.* | *The company would have a tough job convincing people that the deal was workable.*
doable *informal* if something is doable, you have enough money, energy, or skill to do it: *This exercise programme is doable for most people.*
achievable (*also* **attainable** *formal*) able to be achieved: *A 15% cut in carbon emissions is achievable.* | *Perfect democracy is not attainable, nor is perfect freedom or perfect justice.*
realistic if something is realistic, it seems sensible to think that it can be done or achieved: *a realistic target* | *Their expectations didn't seem very realistic.*

possible² *n* [C] someone or something that might be suitable or acceptable for a particular purpose: *Frank's a possible for the job.*

pos·si·bly /ˈpɒsəbli $ ˈpɑː-/ ●●● S1 W2 *adv*
1 used when saying that something may be true or likely, although you are not completely certain SYN **perhaps**, **maybe**: *This last task is possibly the most difficult.* | *It will take three weeks, possibly longer.* | *'Will you be here tomorrow?' 'Possibly.'* | *'Was it murder?' '**Quite possibly** (=it is very likely).'*
2 *spoken* used to emphasize that you are very surprised or shocked by something, or you cannot understand it: ***How could** anyone **possibly** do such a thing?*
3 could/can you possibly *spoken* used when making a polite request: *Could you possibly close that window?*
4 used to emphasize that someone will do or has done everything they can to help or to achieve something: *We shall be contributing **as much as** we **possibly can** to the campaign.* | *Doctors did **everything** they **possibly could** to save his life.*
5 used to emphasize that you cannot do something, or that something cannot or could not happen or be done: **can't/couldn't possibly** *I can't possibly allow you to go home in this weather.* | *She couldn't possibly have heard what was said.*

pos·sum /ˈpɒsəm $ ˈpɑː-/ (*also* **opossum**) *n* [C] **1** one of various types of small furry animals that climb trees and live in America or Australia **2 play possum** *informal* to pretend to be asleep or dead so that someone will not annoy or hurt you

post¹ /pəʊst $ poʊst/ ●●● S2 W2 *n*
1 JOB [C] *formal* a job, especially an important one in a large organization SYN **position**: *I **applied for the post** and was asked to attend an interview.* | *She was **offered** the **post** of ambassador to India.* | *He will **take up** his **post** as Head of Modern Languages in September.* | *Goddard has **held** the **post** since 1998.* | *Unfortunately they were unable to find a suitable person to **fill** the **post**.* | *Mr Thomson **resigned** his £50,000 a year **post** in April.* | *She now holds a **senior post** in the Department of Education.* | *the creation of 4,000 new **teaching posts*** THESAURUS ➤ JOB
2 POSTAL SYSTEM **the post** *BrE* the official system for carrying letters, packages etc from one place to another SYN **mail**: **by post** *The winners will be notified by post.* | **in the post** *Your letter must have got **lost in the post**.* | *I'll **put** a copy of the book **in the post** (=send it).* | **through the post** *A parcel arrived through the post.*
3 LETTERS [U] *BrE* letters, packages etc that are sent and delivered SYN **mail**: *Was there any post for me today?* | *Emma was **opening** her **post**.*
4 COLLECTION/DELIVERY [singular, U] *BrE* when letters are collected or delivered SYN **mail**: *What time does **the post go** (=get collected)?* | **(the) first/second/last post** (=the first, second etc collection or delivery of letters each day) *Applications must arrive by first post on September 23.* | **catch/miss the post** (=post your letter in time for it to be collected, or not in time) → **by return (of post)** at RETURN²(12)
5 PIECE OF WOOD/METAL [C] a strong upright piece of wood, metal etc that is fixed into the ground, especially to support something: *a **fence post*** → BEDPOST, GATEPOST(1), LAMP-POST, SIGNPOST¹(1)
6 FOOTBALL/HOCKEY ETC [C] one of the two upright pieces of wood between which players try to kick or hit the ball in football, HOCKEY etc SYN **goalpost**: *The ball hit the post and bounced off.*
7 NEWSPAPER [singular] used in the names of some newspapers: *the 'Washington Post'*
8 SOLDIER/GUARD ETC **sb's post** the place where a soldier, guard etc is expected to be in order to do their job: **at sb's post** *By 5 am the soldiers were already at their posts.* | *No one was allowed to **leave** their **post**.*
9 border/military/customs/police post a place, especially one on a border, where soldiers or police are guarding, checking etc something
10 RACE **the post** (*also* **the finishing post**) the place where a race finishes, especially a horse race: *Mr Magic was first **past the post**.*
11 INTERNET MESSAGE [C] (*also* **posting**) a message sent to an Internet discussion group so that all members of the group can read it: *There was post after post criticizing the Minister.* → **as deaf as a post** at DEAF(1), → **be driven/passed from pillar to post** at PILLAR(4), → **pip sb at the post** at PIP²(1), → FIRST-PAST-THE-POST

post² ●●● S3 *v* [T]
1 LETTER *BrE* to send a letter, package etc by post SYN **mail**: *She's just gone to **post** a **letter**.* | **post sth (off) to sb** *Did you remember to post the card to my parents?* | **post sb sth** *I posted Barry the cheque last Friday.*
2 post sth through sb's door/letterbox *BrE* to push something through someone's LETTERBOX: *I'll post the key through your letterbox when I leave.*
3 JOB if you are posted somewhere, your employer sends you to work there, usually for several years: **be posted to France/London etc** *He joined the British Army and was posted to Germany.* | **be posted abroad/overseas** GRAMMAR **Post** is usually passive in this meaning.
4 PUBLIC NOTICE (*also* **post up**) to put up a public notice about something on a wall or notice board: *The exam results were posted on the bulletin board yesterday.*
5 GUARD to make someone be in a particular place in order to guard a building, check who enters or leaves a place, watch something etc SYN **station**: *Guards were to be posted around nuclear power stations.*
6 keep sb posted *spoken* to regularly tell someone the most recent news about something: **[+on]** *I'll keep you posted on his progress.*
7 PROFIT/LOSS ETC *especially AmE* to officially record and announce information about a company's financial situation or a country's economic situation: *Cisco Systems **posted** record **profits** and **sales** for the third fiscal quarter.*
8 INTERNET MESSAGE to put a message or computer document on the Internet so that other people can see it: *Could you post those new flyers on David's website?*
9 be posted missing *BrE* if a soldier is posted missing, it is announced officially that they have disappeared
10 post bail *law especially AmE* to pay a specific amount of money in order to be allowed to leave prison before your TRIAL

post- /pəʊst $ poʊst/ *prefix* later than or after something: *the post-war years* (=the years after a particular war) | *the post-1979 Conservative government*

post·age /ˈpəʊstɪdʒ $ ˈpoʊs-/ *n* [U] the money charged for sending a letter, package etc by post: *How much is the postage for a postcard?* | **postage and packing** *BrE*, **postage and handling** *AmE* (=the charge for packing and sending something you have bought) *It's yours for £13.99, including postage and packing.*

ˈpostage ˌmeter *n* [C] *AmE* a machine used by businesses which puts a mark on letters and packages to show that postage has been paid SYN **franking machine** *BrE*

ˈpostage stamp *n* [C] *formal* a stamp

post·al /ˈpəʊstl $ ˈpoʊs-/ *adj* [only before noun] **1** relating to the official system which takes letters from one place to another: *the U.S. **postal service*** | ***postal workers*** | *an*

P

increase in postal charges **2** relating to sending things by post: *Candidates are chosen by a* ***postal ballot*** *of all party members.* | **postal vote** *BrE*: *Housebound voters should register early for a postal vote.* **3 go postal** *AmE informal* to become very angry and behave in a violent way

ˈpostal ˌorder *n* [C] *BrE* an official document that you buy in a post office and send to someone so that they can then exchange it for money SYN **money order** *AmE*

post·bag /ˈpəʊstbæg $ ˈpoʊst-/ *n BrE* **1** [singular] all the letters received by an important person, television programme etc on a particular occasion: *We've had an enormous postbag on the recent programme changes.* **2** [C] a bag for carrying letters, used by the person who delivers them SYN **mailbag** *AmE*

post·box /ˈpəʊstbɒks $ ˈpoʊstbɑːks/ *n* [C] *BrE* a box in a public place, into which you put letters that you want to send SYN **letterbox** *BrE*, **mailbox** *AmE*

POSTBOX

UK postbox US mailbox

post·card /ˈpəʊstkɑːd $ ˈpoʊstkɑːrd/ ●●● S3 *n* [C] a card that can be sent in the post without an envelope, especially one with a picture on it: *Don't forget to send us a postcard!*

post·code /ˈpəʊstkəʊd $ ˈpoʊstkoʊd/ ●●○ *n* [C] *BrE* a group of numbers and letters that you write at the end of an address on an envelope, package etc. The postcode shows the exact area where someone lives and helps the post office deliver the post more quickly SYN **zip code** *AmE*

ˈpostcode ˌlottery *n* [singular] *BrE* a situation in which different things or services are provided by the health service, local government etc in different parts of the country - used to show disapproval: *Some sufferers are denied treatment because of the postcode lottery.*

post-coital /ˌpoʊst ˈkəʊɪtəl, -ˈkɔɪt- $ ˈkoʊətəl/ *adj* happening or done after having sex

post·date /ˌpəʊstˈdeɪt $ ˌpoʊst-/ *v* [T] **1** if you postdate a cheque, you write it with a date that is later than the actual date, so that it will not become effective until that time → **backdate 2** to happen, live, or be made later in history than something else → **predate**: *Some of the mosaics postdate this period.*

ˌpost ˈdoctoral *adj* [only before noun] relating to study done after a PHD: *post doctoral research*

post·er /ˈpəʊstə $ ˈpoʊstər/ ●●● S3 *n* [C] a large printed notice, picture, or photograph, used to advertise something or as a decoration: *A team of volunteers were* ***putting up posters****.* | *a poster campaign for the election* | **[+for]** *the poster for the exhibition* | **[+of]** *posters of old movie stars* → see picture at SIGN[1] THESAURUS ADVERTISEMENT

ˈposter ˌchild *n* [C usually singular] *AmE* **1** a child with a particular illness or physical problem whose picture appears on a poster advertising the work of an organization that helps children with that problem **2** someone or something that represents a particular quality, idea etc - often used humorously: *Dillon is the poster child for wasted talent.*

poste res·tante /ˌpəʊst ˈrestɒnt $ ˌpoʊst reˈstɑːnt/ *n* [U] *BrE* a post office department which keeps letters for people who are travelling, until they arrive to collect them

pos·te·ri·or[1] /pɒˈstɪəriə $ pɑːˈstɪriər/ *adj* [only before noun] *technical* near or at the back of something OPP **anterior**: *the posterior part of the brain*

posterior[2] *n* [C] the part of the body you sit on - used humorously SYN **buttocks**, **bottom**

pos·ter·i·ty /pɒˈsterəti $ pɑː-/ *n* [U] *formal* all the people in the future who will be alive after you are dead: **preserve/record/keep etc sth for posterity** *a priceless work of art that must be kept for posterity*

ˈposter paint *n* [C,U] brightly coloured paint that contains no oil, used especially by children to paint pictures

post·game /ˌpəʊstˈgeɪm◂ $ ˌpoʊst-/ *adj* [only before noun] *AmE* happening after a sports game: *postgame celebrations*

ˌpost-ˈgrad *n* [C] *BrE informal* a postgraduate —**post-grad** *adj*

post·grad·u·ate[1] /ˌpəʊstˈgrædjuət $ ˌpoʊstˈgrædʒuət/ *n* [C] *especially BrE* someone who is studying at a university to get a MASTER'S DEGREE or a PHD SYN **graduate student** *AmE*

postgraduate[2] *adj* [only before noun] **1** *especially BrE* relating to studies done at a university after completing a first degree SYN **graduate** *AmE*: *postgraduate degrees* **2** *AmE* relating to studies done after completing a PHD SYN **post doctoral**

ˌpost-ˈhaste *adv literary* very quickly: *He departed post-haste for Verdun.*

post·hu·mous /ˈpɒstjəməs $ ˈpɑːstʃə-/ *adj* happening, printed etc after someone's death: *a posthumous collection of his articles* —**posthumously** *adv*: *He was* ***posthumously awarded*** *the Military Cross.*

post·ie /ˈpəʊsti $ ˈpoʊ-/ *n* [C] *BrE informal* a POSTMAN

ˌpost-inˈdustrial *adj* relating to the period in the late 20th century when the older types of industry became less important, and computers became more important: *the* ***post-industrial*** *information-based* ***society***

post·ing /ˈpəʊstɪŋ $ ˈpoʊs-/ *n* [C] **1** if a soldier, a representative of a country etc gets a posting somewhere, they are sent there to do their job: **[+to]** *shortly before his posting to South Africa* | *a* ***diplomatic posting*** THESAURUS JOB **2** (*also* **post**) a message sent to an Internet discussion group so that all members of the group can read it **3** *AmE* a public notice, especially one advertising a job: *job postings*

ˈPost-it (*also* **ˈPost-it ˌnote**) *n* [C] *trademark* a small piece of coloured paper that sticks to things, used for leaving notes for people

post·man /ˈpəʊstmən $ ˈpoʊst-/ *n* (*plural* **postmen** /-mən/) [C] *BrE* someone whose job is to collect and deliver letters SYN **mailman** *AmE*

post·mark /ˈpəʊstmɑːk $ ˈpoʊstmɑːrk/ *n* [C] an official mark made on a letter, package etc to show when and where it was posted —**postmark** *v* [T]: *The letter was postmarked Iowa.*

post·mas·ter /ˈpəʊstˌmɑːstə $ ˈpoʊstˌmæstər/ *n* [C] someone who is in charge of a post office → **postmistress**

post·men·o·paus·al /ˌpəʊstmenəˈpɔːzəl $ ˌpoʊstmenəˈpɒː-/ *adj* a postmenopausal woman has gone through the MENOPAUSE (=when she stops having her monthly flow of blood)

post·mis·tress /ˈpəʊstˌmɪstrɪs $ ˈpoʊst-/ *n* [C] *old-fashioned* a woman who is in charge of a post office → **postmaster**

post·mod·ern /ˌpəʊstˈmɒdn◂ $ ˌpoʊstˈmɑːdərn◂/ *adj* **1** relating to or influenced by postmodernism: *postmodern architecture* **2** used to describe styles, attitudes etc that are typical of the social life that is found in many western countries now, in which television and the buying of goods and services etc are very important: *postmodern culture*

post·mod·ern·is·m /ˌpəʊstˈmɒdən-ɪzəm $ ˌpoʊstˈmɑːdərn-/ *n* [U] a style of building, painting, writing etc, developed in the late 20th century, that uses a mixture of old and new styles as a reaction against MODERNISM —**postmodernist** *adj*: *postmodernist fiction* —**postmodernist** *n* [C]

post-mor·tem, **post·mor·tem** /ˌpəʊstˈmɔːtəm $ ˌpoʊstˈmɔːr-/ *n* [C] **1** (*also* **postˌmortem examinˈation**) an examination of a dead body to discover why the person died SYN **autopsy**: **[+on]** *A post-mortem on the body revealed that the victim had been strangled.* | **do/carry out/conduct a post-mortem 2** *especially BrE* an examination of a plan or event that failed, done to discover why it failed: **[+on]** *a post-mortem on the company's poor results*

post·na·tal /ˌpəʊstˈneɪtl◂ $ ˌpoʊst-/ *adj* [only before noun] relating to the time after a baby is born OPP **prenatal**: *postnatal care* | ***postnatal depression*** (=an illness in which a woman feels very unhappy and tired after her baby is born)

ˈpost ˌoffice ●●● S3 *n*
1 [C] a place where you can buy stamps, send letters and packages etc
2 the Post Office the national organization which is responsible for collecting and delivering letters

ˈpost office ˌbox *n* [C] *formal* a PO BOX

ˌpost-ˈoperative *adj* [only before noun] relating to the time after someone has had a medical operation: *post-operative care*

post·paid /ˌpəʊstˈpeɪd◂ $ ˌpoʊst-/ *adj* costing nothing to send because the amount has already been paid: *The kit costs $33.95 postpaid.*

post·par·tum /ˌpəʊstˈpɑːtəm◂ $ ˌpoʊstˈpɑːr-/ *adj technical* relating to the time immediately after a woman has a baby SYN **postnatal**

post·pone /pəʊsˈpəʊn $ poʊsˈpoʊn/ ●●○ *v* [T] to change the date or time of a planned event or action to a later one SYN **put back** OPP **bring forward**: *The match had to be **postponed until** next week.* | **postpone doing sth** *They've decided to postpone having a family for a while.* | *His trial has been **postponed indefinitely*** (=no one knows when it will happen). **THESAURUS** CANCEL, DELAY —**postponement** *n* [C,U]

post·pran·di·al /ˌpəʊstˈprændiəl◂ $ ˌpoʊst-/ *adj* [only before noun] *especially BrE formal* happening immediately after a meal – often used humorously: *a postprandial nap*

post·script /ˈpəʊsˌskrɪpt $ ˈpoʊs-/ *n* [C] (*written abbreviation* **PS**) **1** a message written at the end of a letter after you have signed your name **2** extra details or information that you add after a story or an account: **[+to]** *There's an interesting postscript to this tale.*

post·sea·son /ˈpəʊstˌsiːzən◂ $ ˈpoʊst-/ *adj* [only before noun] *AmE* relating to the time after the usual sports season is over OPP **preseason**: *a postseason game* —**postseason** *n* [singular]

post·sec·ond·a·ry /ˌpəʊstˈsekəndəri $ ˌpoʊstˈsekənderi/ *adj* relating to schools or education after you have finished HIGH SCHOOL

ˌpost-traumatic ˈstress disˌorder *n* [U] *medical* (*abbreviation* **PTSD**) a mental illness which can develop after a very bad experience such as a plane crash

pos·tu·late¹ /ˈpɒstjəleɪt $ ˈpɑːstʃə-/ *v* [T] *formal* to suggest that something might have happened or be true → **hypothesize**: **postulate that** *It has been postulated that the condition is inherited.* —**postulation** /ˌpɒstjəˈleɪʃən $ ˌpɑːstʃə-/ *n* [C,U]

pos·tu·late² /ˈpɒstjələt $ ˈpɑːstʃə-/ *n* [C] *formal* something believed to be true, on which an argument or scientific discussion is based → **hypothesis**: **[+of]** *the basic postulates of Marxism*

pos·tur·al /ˈpɒstʃərəl $ ˈpɑːs-/ *adj* [only before noun] *formal* relating to the way you sit or stand: *postural problems*

pos·ture /ˈpɒstʃə $ ˈpɑːstʃər/ ●○○ *n*
1 [C,U] the way you position your body when sitting or standing: **good/bad etc posture** *Poor posture can lead to muscular problems.* | *her **upright posture***
2 [singular] the way you behave or think in a particular situation: **[+towards]** *He tends to **adopt a** defensive **posture** towards new ideas.*

pos·tur·ing /ˈpɒstʃərɪŋ $ ˈpɑːs-/ *n* [C,U] *formal* **1** when someone pretends to have a particular opinion or attitude: *He dismissed the Senator's comments as '**political posturing**'.* **2** when someone stands or moves in a way that they hope will make other people notice and admire them —**posture** *v* [I]

ˌpost-ˈwar *adj* [only before noun] happening or existing after a war, especially the Second World War OPP **pre-war**: *post-war Britain* | **post-war period/years/era** *food rationing in the **immediate post-war** years* —**post-war** *adv*

po·sy /ˈpəʊzi $ ˈpoʊ-/ *n* (*plural* **posies**) [C] a small BUNCH of flowers → see picture at **BOUQUET**

POTS

pot¹ /pɒt $ pɑːt/ ●●● S2 W2 *n*
1 COOKING [C] a container used for cooking which is round, deep, and usually made of metal: ***pots and pans*** | **[+of]** *There was a big pot of soup on the stove.*
2 FOR A PLANT [C] a container for a plant, usually made of plastic or baked clay: *herbs growing in pots*
3 TEA/COFFEE [C] a container with a handle and a small tube for pouring, used to make tea or coffee: *Is there any tea left in the pot?* | **[+of]** *I'll make a pot of coffee.* → **COFFEE POT**, **TEAPOT**
4 FOR FOOD, PAINT ETC [C] *BrE* a round container for storing foods such as JAM that are slightly liquid, or for substances such as glue or paint: **[+of]** *a pot of blue paint* | **jam/paint/yoghurt etc pot**
5 BOWL/DISH ETC [C] a dish, bowl, plate, or another container that is made by shaping clay and then baking it → **pottery**: *an earthenware pot*
6 go to pot *informal* if something such as a place or an organization goes to pot, it becomes much worse or fails because no one is taking care of it: *The government has **let** the whole country **go to pot**.*
7 pots of money *BrE informal* a lot of money: *They've got pots of money in the bank.* | *He's hoping to **make pots of money** from the deal.*
8 MONEY **the pot a)** money that is available to do something, especially money that people have collected: **in the pot** *So far we've got £150 in the pot.* **b)** all the money that people have risked in a card game, and which can be won: **in the pot** *There was $1000 in the pot.*
9 DRUG [U] *old-fashioned informal* MARIJUANA: *Michael was **smoking pot** with some friends.*
10 (a case of) the pot calling the kettle black *informal* used humorously to say that you should not criticize someone for something, because you have done the same thing or have the same fault
11 STOMACH [C] a POTBELLY
12 HIT A BALL [C] *BrE* the act of hitting a ball into one of the POCKETS (=holes at the edge of the table) in games such as BILLIARDS, POOL, and SNOOKER
13 TOILET [C] *informal* a toilet → **CHAMBER POT**, **CHIMNEY POT**, **FLOWERPOT**, **LOBSTERPOT**, **MELTING POT**

pot² *v* (**potted**, **potting**) [T] **1** (*also* **pot up** *BrE*) to put a plant into a pot filled with soil: *Pot the seedlings after 2-3 weeks.* **2** *BrE* to hit a ball into one of the POCKETS (=holes at the edge of the table) in games such as BILLIARDS, POOL, and SNOOKER SYN **pocket**

po·ta·ble /ˈpəʊtəbəl $ ˈpoʊ-/ *adj formal* potable water is safe to drink SYN **drinkable**

pot·ash /ˈpɒtæʃ $ ˈpɑː-/ *n* [U] a type of potassium used especially in farming to make the soil better

P

po·tas·si·um /pəˈtæsiəm/ *n* [U] a common soft silver-white metal that usually exists in combination with other substances, used for example in farming. It is a chemical ELEMENT: symbol K

po·ta·to /pəˈteɪtəʊ $ -toʊ/ ●●● S2 *n* (*plural* **potatoes**) **1** [C,U] a round white vegetable with a brown, red, or pale yellow skin, that grows under the ground: **roast/fried/boiled/mashed potato** | **jacket potato** (=cooked in its skin) *Marie stood at the sink, **peeling potatoes*** (=cutting off the skin). → see picture at VEGETABLE[1]
2 [C] a plant that produces potatoes

poˈtato ˌcrisp *BrE*, **poˈtato ˌchip** *AmE n* [C] a very thin round piece of potato cooked in oil and eaten cold, sold in packages

poˈtato ˌpeeler *n* [C] a small tool like a knife, used for removing the skin of a potato

ˌpotbellied ˈstove *n* [C] *AmE* a small round metal STOVE that you burn wood or coal in for heating or cooking, used especially in the past

pot·bel·ly /ˈpɒtˌbeli $ ˈpɑːt-/ *n* (*plural* **potbellies**) [C] a large round unattractive stomach that sticks out —**potbellied** [adj]

pot·boil·er /ˈpɒtˌbɔɪlə $ ˈpɑːtˌbɔɪlər/ *n* [C] a book or film that is produced quickly to make money and which is not of very high quality, especially one that is exciting or romantic

pot·bound /ˈpɒtbaʊnd $ ˈpɑːt-/ *adj BrE* a plant that is potbound cannot grow any more because its roots have grown to fill the pot it is in

po·teen /pəˈtʃiːn, -ˈtiːn/ *n* [U] Irish WHISKY made secretly and illegally to avoid paying tax

po·ten·cy /ˈpəʊtənsi $ ˈpoʊ-/ *n* [singular, U] **1** the power that something has to influence people: **[+of]** *the potency of his arguments* | *The myth of male superiority was losing its potency.* **2** the strength of something, especially a drug, on your mind or body: **[+of]** *the potency of the drug* **3** (*also* **sexual potency**) the ability of a man to have sex: *loss of potency after age 40*

po·tent /ˈpəʊtənt $ ˈpoʊ-/ ●○○ *adj*
1 having a very powerful effect or influence on your body or mind SYN **powerful**: *potent drugs* | *a **potent symbol** of oppression* | *Advertising is a **potent force** in showing smoking as a socially acceptable habit.* | *A good company pension scheme remains a **potent weapon** for attracting staff.*
2 powerful and effective: *The treaty requires them to get rid of their most potent weapons.*
3 a man who is potent is able to have sex or able to make a woman PREGNANT OPP **impotent** —**potently** *adv*

po·ten·tate /ˈpəʊtənteɪt $ ˈpoʊ-/ *n* [C] *literary* a ruler in the past, who had great power over his people

po·ten·tial[1] /pəˈtenʃəl/ ●●● S3 W2 AWL *adj* [only before noun] likely to develop into a particular type of person or thing in the future SYN **possible**: **potential customer/buyer/client** *new ways of attracting potential customers* | **potential benefit/problem** *the potential benefits of the new system* | **potential danger/threat/risk** *the potential risks to health associated with the drug*

potential[2] ●●○ W3 AWL *n* [U]
1 the possibility that something will develop in a particular way, or have a particular effect: **[+for]** *The company certainly has the potential for growth.* | **[+of]** *the potential of the Internet to create jobs*
2 if people or things have potential, they have a natural ability or quality that could develop to make them very good: **have/show potential** *She has the potential to become a champion.* | **with potential** *a young player with great potential* | **achieve/fulfil/realize your (full) potential** (=succeed as well as you possibly can)
3 *technical* the difference in VOLTAGE between two points on an electrical CIRCUIT

poˌtential ˈenergy *n* [U] *technical* the energy that something has because of its position or state, rather than because it is moving → **kinetic energy**

po·ten·ti·al·i·ty /pəˌtenʃiˈæləti/ *n* (*plural* **potentialities**) [C] *formal* an ability or quality that could develop in the future

po·ten·tial·ly /pəˈtenʃəli/ ●●○ AWL *adv* [+adj/adv] something that is potentially dangerous, useful etc is not dangerous etc now, but may become so in the future: *a potentially dangerous situation*

pot·ful /ˈpɒtfʊl $ ˈpɑːt-/ *n* [C] the amount a pot can contain

pot·hold·er /ˈpɒtˌhəʊldə $ ˈpɑːtˌhoʊldər/ *n* [C] a piece of thick material that you use to protect your hands when you pick up a hot cooking pan

pot·hole /ˈpɒthəʊl $ ˈpɑːthoʊl/ *n* [C] **1** a large hole in the surface of a road, caused by traffic and bad weather, which makes driving difficult or dangerous **2** *BrE* a long hole that goes deep under the ground, formed by natural processes —**potholed** *adj*

pot·hol·ing /ˈpɒtˌhəʊlɪŋ $ ˈpɑːtˌhoʊl-/ *n* [U] *BrE* the sport of climbing down POTHOLES and underground CAVES SYN **caving** —**potholer** *n* [C]

po·tion /ˈpəʊʃən $ ˈpoʊ-/ *n* [C] **1** *literary* a drink intended to have a special or magical effect on the person who drinks it, or which is intended to poison them: *a magic potion* | *a love potion* **2** a medicine, especially one that seems strange or old-fashioned

ˌpot ˈluck *BrE*, **pot·luck** *AmE* /ˌpɒtˈlʌk◂ $ ˌpɑːt-/ *n* **1 take pot luck a)** to choose something without knowing very much about it, and hope that it will be what you want: *We hadn't booked a hotel so we had to take pot luck.* **b)** to have a meal at someone's home in which you eat whatever they have available, rather than food which has been specially bought for the occasion: *I'm not sure what there is in the fridge – you'll have to take pot luck.* **2** [C] *AmE* a meal in which everyone who is invited brings something to eat: *Can you bring a salad? It's a potluck.* | **potluck meal/dinner etc** *a potluck supper at the church*

ˌpot ˈpie *n* [C] *AmE* meat and vegetables covered with PASTRY and baked in a deep dish

ˈpot plant *n* [C] *BrE* a plant that is grown indoors in a pot

pot·pour·ri /ˌpəʊpʊˈriː $ ˌpoʊ-/ *n* **1** [U] a mixture of pieces of dried flowers and leaves kept in a bowl to make a room smell pleasant **2** [singular] a mixture of things that are not usually put together, for example different pieces of music or writing: **[+of]** *a potpourri of literary styles*

ˈpot roast *n* [C] a dish that consists of a piece of meat cooked slowly in a pan with potatoes and other vegetables

ˈpot shot *n* **take a pot shot at sb/sth a)** to shoot at someone or something without aiming very carefully: *The boy took a pot shot at a pigeon with his air gun.* **b)** to criticize someone or something unfairly without thinking carefully about it: *He enjoys taking pot shots at the government whenever the opportunity arises.*

pot·ted /ˈpɒtɪd $ ˈpɑː-/ *adj* [only before noun] **1** growing indoors in a pot: *a **potted plant*** **2 potted history/biography/version** *BrE* a short and simple explanation or description that gives only the most important facts about someone or something **3** *BrE* potted meat or fish has been cooked and stored in a container, usually in the form of a PASTE for spreading on bread

pot·ter[1] /ˈpɒtə $ ˈpɑːtər/ *n* [C] someone who makes pots, dishes etc out of clay

potter[2] (*also* **potter about/around**) *v* [I] *BrE* to spend time doing pleasant things that are not important without hurrying SYN **putter** *AmE*: *I spent the morning pottering about in the garden.* —**potterer** *n* [C]

ˌpotter's ˈwheel *n* [C] a piece of equipment that turns around, onto which wet clay is placed so that it can be shaped by hand into a pot

pot·ter·y /ˈpɒtəri $ ˈpɑː-/ ●●○ *n* (*plural* **potteries**)
1 [U] objects made out of baked clay: *Native American pottery*
2 [U] clay that has been shaped and baked in order to make pots, dishes etc: *a pottery bowl*

3 [U] the activity of making pots, dishes etc out of clay: *a pottery class*
4 [C] a factory where pottery objects are made

ˈpotting shed *n* [C] *BrE* a small building, usually made of wood, where garden tools, seeds etc are kept → **tool shed**

pot·ty¹ /ˈpɒti $ ˈpɑːti/ *adj BrE informal* **1** crazy or silly: *What a potty idea!* | *You must be potty!* **2 drive sb potty** if something or someone is driving you potty, they are annoying you, especially if they are making it difficult for you to continue what you are doing **3 be potty about sb/sth** to like someone very much, or be very interested in something: *She's potty about riding.* —**pottiness** *n* [U]

potty² *n* (*plural* **potties**) [C] **1** a container used by very young children as a toilet **2 go potty** *AmE* to use the toilet - used by young children or when speaking to them: *Do you need to go potty?* **3 potty mouth** *AmE informal* someone who has or is a potty mouth uses offensive words **4 potty break** *AmE informal* a time when you stop what you are doing, especially when driving a car, so that you can use the toilet - used humorously

ˈpotty mouth *n* [C] *informal* someone who is or has a potty mouth uses a lot of rude words

ˈpotty-mouthed *adj informal* using a lot of rude or offensive words

ˈpotty-ˌtraining *n* [U] the process of teaching a very young child to use a potty or toilet —**potty-train** *v* [T] —**potty-trained** *adj*

pouch /paʊtʃ/ *n* [C] **1** a small leather, cloth, or plastic bag that you can keep things in, and which is sometimes attached to a belt: **[+of]** *a leather pouch of tobacco* | *a money pouch* **2** *especially AmE* a large bag for carrying letters or papers: *a mail pouch* **3** a pocket in the side of a bag such as a RUCKSACK **4** a pocket of skin on the stomach which MARSUPIALS such as KANGAROOS use for carrying their babies **5** a fold of skin like a bag which animals such as HAMSTERS or SQUIRRELS have inside each cheek to carry and store food

pouffe, **pouf** /puːf/ *n* [C] *BrE* a soft piece of furniture like a large CUSHION, which you can sit on or rest your feet on

poul·tice /ˈpəʊltɪs $ ˈpoʊl-/ *n* [C] something that is put on someone's skin to make it less swollen or painful, often made of a wet cloth with milk, herbs, or clay on it

poul·try /ˈpəʊltri $ ˈpoʊl-/ ●○○ *n*
1 [plural] birds such as chickens and ducks that are kept on farms in order to produce eggs and meat
2 [U] meat from birds such as chickens and ducks

POUNCE

pounce /paʊns/ ●○○ *v* [I] to suddenly move forward and attack someone or something, after waiting to attack them: *The cat was hiding in the bushes, ready to pounce.* | **[+on]** *Kevin pounced on Liam and started hitting him.* —**pounce** *n* [C]

pounce on sb/sth *phr v*
1 to criticize someone's mistakes or ideas very quickly and eagerly: *Teachers are quick to pounce on students' grammatical errors.*
2 to eagerly take an opportunity as soon as it becomes available: *When they offered O'Leary the chance to become manager, he pounced on it.*

pound¹ /paʊnd/ ●●● S1 W2 *n*
1 WEIGHT [C] (*written abbreviation* **lb**) a unit for measuring weight, equal to 16 OUNCES or 0.454 kilograms: **[+of]** *a pound of apples* | *Moira **weighs** about 130 **pounds**.* | *The grapes **cost** $2 **a pound**.*
2 MONEY [C] (*also* **pound sterling**) **a)** **£** the standard unit of money in Britain, which is divided into 100 pence: *They spent over a thousand pounds.* | *a multi-million pound business* | *a five pound note* **b) the (British) pound** the value of British money compared with the value of the money of other countries: *The pound was up against the dollar.* **c)** the standard unit of money in various other countries, such as Egypt and the Sudan
3 FOR DOGS AND CATS [C usually singular] a place where dogs and cats that have been found on the street are kept until their owners come to get them
4 FOR CARS [C] a place where cars that have been illegally parked are kept until their owners pay money to get them back
5 get/take/demand etc your pound of flesh to get the full amount of work, money etc that someone owes you, even though it makes them suffer and you do not really need it. The phrase comes from Shylock, a character in the play *The Merchant of Venice* by William Shakespeare. He is a Jewish money-lender who lends money to Antonio. When Antonio is unable to pay the money back, Shylock says he has the right to cut a pound of flesh from Antonio's body.
6 TELEPHONE [U] *AmE* the POUND KEY

pound² ●○○ *v*
1 HIT [I,T] to hit something very hard several times and make a lot of noise, damage it, break it into smaller pieces etc: *He began pounding the keyboard of his computer.* | **[+against/on]** *Thomas pounded on the door with his fist.* | *Waves pounded against the pier.* | **pound sth against/on sth** *Green pounded his fist on the counter.* THESAURUS ▸ HIT
2 HEART [I] if your heart or blood is pounding, your heart is beating very hard and quickly: **[+with]** *Patrick rushed to the door, his heart pounding with excitement.* | *She ran, her **heart pounding in her chest**.*
3 HEAD [I] if your head is pounding, it feels painful, especially because you have a headache or you have been using a lot of effort
4 MOVE [I always + adv/prep, T] to walk or run quickly with heavy loud steps: **[+along/through/down etc]** *I could hear him pounding up the stairs.* | *a policeman pounding his beat* | *Runners will be pounding the pavement this weekend during the London Marathon.*
5 ATTACK WITH BOMBS [T] to attack a place continuously for a long time with bombs: *Enemy forces have been pounding the city for over two months.*

pound sth ↔ **out** *phr v* to play music loudly: *The Rolling Stones were pounding out one of their old numbers.*

pound·age /ˈpaʊndɪdʒ/ *n* [U] **1** *technical* an amount charged for every pound in weight, or for every British £1 in value **2** *informal* weight

ˈpound cake *n* [C] a heavy cake made from flour, sugar, and butter

pound·er /ˈpaʊndə $ -ər/ *n* **a 3-pounder/24-pounder/185-pounder etc a)** an animal, fish, or person that weighs 3 pounds, 24 pounds etc **b)** a gun that fires a SHELL that weighs 3 pounds, 24 pounds etc

pound·ing /ˈpaʊndɪŋ/ *n* **1** [singular, U] the action or the sound of something hitting a surface very hard many times: **[+of]** *the pounding of the waves on the rocks below* **2** [singular, U] the action or sound of your heart beating **3 take a pounding a)** to be completely defeated: *Manchester United took a real pounding.* **b)** to be hit or attacked many times and often badly damaged: *The ship had taken a pounding on the rocks.*

ˈpound key *n* [C] *AmE* the button on a telephone that has the SYMBOL (#) on it

ˈpound sign *n* [C] **1** *BrE* the SYMBOL (£), used for a pound in British money **2** *AmE* the SYMBOL (#), used especially on a telephone SYN **hash** *BrE*

ˌpound ˈsterling *n* [singular] the standard unit of money in Britain, which is divided into 100 pence

pour /pɔː $ pɔːr/ ●●● S2 W3 *v*
1 LIQUID [T] to make a liquid or other substance flow out of or into a container by holding it at an angle: *She poured coffee for everyone.* | **pour sth into/out/down etc (sth)** *Pour the oil into a frying pan and heat.* | **pour sth away** (=get rid of something) *The wine was so bad I just poured it away.* | **pour sb sth** *Why don't you* **pour** *yourself another* **drink**?
2 LIQUID/SMOKE [I always + adv/prep] if a lot of liquid or smoke pours out, it comes out from somewhere in very large amounts: **[+from/down/out]** *Smoke was pouring out of the upstairs windows.* | *Blood was pouring from his nose.*
3 RAIN [I] (*also* **pour down**) **it pours** to rain heavily without stopping: ***It's pouring*** *now.* | ***It poured*** *all night.* | **it's pouring with rain/it poured with rain** *BrE*: *It was pouring down with rain at three o'clock.*
4 PEOPLE OR THINGS [I always + adv/prep] if a lot of people or things pour into or out of a place, a lot of them arrive or leave at the same time: **[+into/out of/from etc]** *The crowds began pouring out of the stadium.* | *Offers of help poured in from all over the country.*
5 LIGHT [I always + adv/prep] if light is pouring into or out of a place, a lot of light is coming in or out: **[+into/out of]** *Light was pouring into the courtyard.*
6 pour cold water over/on sth to criticize someone's plan, idea, or desire to do something so much that they no longer feel excited about it
7 pour scorn on sb/sth to say that something or someone is stupid and not worth considering
8 pour oil on troubled waters to try to stop a quarrel, for example by talking to people and making them calmer
9 pour it on a) to behave or talk in a particular way in order to make people like you or feel sorry for you **b)** *AmE informal* to try very hard in order to do something, especially in order to win a game: *The Raiders really poured it on in the second quarter.*
10 pour on the charm to behave in a very nice and polite way, in order to make someone like you
pour sth **into** sth *phr v* if people pour money into something, they provide a lot of money for it over a period of time, in order to make it successful: *They've poured thousands of pounds into developing the business.*
pour sth ↔ **out** *phr v* if you pour out your thoughts, feelings etc, you tell someone all about them, especially because you feel very unhappy: *She poured out all her troubles to him.* | **pour out your heart/soul** (=tell someone all your feelings, including your most secret ones)

pour·ing /ˈpɔːrɪŋ/ *adj* pouring rain is very heavy rain

pout /paʊt/ *v* [I,T] to push out your lower lip because you are annoyed or unhappy, or in order to look sexually attractive: *He sounded like a pouting child.* | *Her full* **lips pouted** *slightly.* —**pout** *n* [C] —**pouty** *adj*

pov·er·ty /ˈpɒvəti $ ˈpɑːvərti/ ●●○ W3 *n*
1 [U] the situation or experience of being poor → **poor**, **impoverished**: *Millions of elderly people* **live in poverty**. | *We need an effective strategy to* **fight poverty**. | *continued efforts to* **alleviate poverty** *and raise living standards* | *scenes of* **abject poverty** | *the causes of* **urban poverty**
2 the poverty line (*also* **the poverty level** *AmE*) the income below which a person or a family is officially considered to be very poor and in need of help: *20% of the population now live* **below the poverty line**.
3 the poverty trap a situation in which a poor person without a job cannot afford to take a low-paying job because they would lose the money they receive from the government
4 [singular, U] *formal* a lack of a particular quality: **[+of]** *The novel shows a surprising poverty of imagination.*

ˈpoverty-ˌstricken *adj* extremely poor: *poverty-stricken families* **THESAURUS** ▸ **POOR**

pow /paʊ/ *interjection* used to represent the sound of a gun firing, an explosion, or someone hitting another person hard, especially in children's COMICS

POW /ˌpiː əʊ ˈdʌbəljuː $ -oʊ-/ *n* [C] a PRISONER OF WAR

pow·der¹ /ˈpaʊdə $ -ər/ ●●○ *n*
1 [C,U] a dry substance in the form of very small grains: *curry powder* | *talcum powder* | ***Grind*** *the sugar* ***into a powder***. | *The paint is supplied* **in powder form**. | **milk/custard etc powder** (=a powder that you add water to in order to change it into a liquid)
2 [U] (*also* **face powder**) a type of powder that you put on your face in order to make it look smoother and to give it more colour → see picture at **MAKE-UP**
3 a powder keg a dangerous situation or place where violence or trouble could suddenly start: *Since the riot, the city has been a powder keg waiting to explode.*
4 [U] (*also* **powder snow**) dry light snow: *There's a foot of powder on the slopes.*
5 [U] GUNPOWDER
6 keep your powder dry to wait calmly until you see how a situation develops before deciding what to do

powder² *v* **1** [T] to put powder on something, especially your skin: *She was* **powdering** *her* **face**. **2 powder your nose** an expression meaning to go to the TOILET, used by women to avoid saying this directly: *She's just gone to powder her nose.*

ˌpowder ˈblue *n* [U] a pale blue colour —**powder blue** [adj]

pow·dered /ˈpaʊdəd $ -ərd/ *adj* **1** produced or sold in the form of a powder: *powdered milk* **2** covered with powder

ˌpowdered ˈsugar *n* [U] *AmE* sugar in a powder form SYN **icing sugar** *BrE*

ˈpowder puff *n* [C] a small round piece of soft material used by women to spread POWDER on their face or body

ˈpowder room *n* [C] a room with a toilet for women, especially in a public place - used to avoid saying this directly

pow·der·y /ˈpaʊdəri/ *adj* **1** like powder or easily broken into powder: *powdery snow* **2** covered with powder

pow·er¹ /ˈpaʊə $ paʊr/ ●●● S1 W1 *n*
1 CONTROL [U] the ability or right to control people or events → **powerful**, **powerless**: **[+over]** *People should have more power over the decisions that affect their lives.* | **power-mad/power-crazy/power-hungry** (=wanting too much power) *power-hungry politicians*
2 GOVERNMENT [U] the position of having political control of a country or government: **in power** *The voters have once again shown their support for the party in power.* | **come/rise to power** (=start having political control) *De Gaulle came to power in 1958.* | *They* **seized power** *in a military coup.*
3 INFLUENCE [U] the ability to influence people or give them strong feelings → **powerful**, **powerless**: **[+of]** *the power of his writing* | *the immense power of television* | *the* **pulling power** (=ability to attract people or attention) *of major celebrities* | **student/black/consumer etc power** (=the political or social influence a particular group has)
4 RIGHT/AUTHORITY [C,U] the right or authority to do something: *The police have been given special powers to help them in the fight against terrorism.* | **power to do sth** *The committee has the power to order an enquiry.* | **power of arrest/veto etc** *The chairman has the power of veto on all decisions.*
5 ABILITY [C,U] a natural or special ability to do something: *After the accident she lost the* **power of speech** (=ability to speak). | **powers of observation/concentration/persuasion** *a writer's powers of observation* | *your mental powers* | *a stone with magical powers*
6 ENERGY [U] energy that can be used to make a machine work or to make electricity: **nuclear/wind/solar etc power** *Many people are opposed to the use of nuclear power.* | *the search for renewable* **sources of power** | **under power** *The ship was able to leave port* **under its own power** (=without help from another machine, ship etc).
7 earning/purchasing/bargaining etc power the ability to earn money, buy things etc: *Property in the city is beyond the purchasing power of most people.* | *your bargaining power in pay negotiations*
8 STRENGTH [U] the physical strength or effect of something → **powerful**: *the power of a cheetah's long legs* | *The power of the explosion smashed windows across the street.*

9 ELECTRICITY [U] electricity that is used in houses, factories etc: *Make sure the power is switched off first.* | **power cut/failure/outage** (=a short time when the electricity supply is not working) *Parts of the country have had power cuts because of the storms.* | *The power came back on.*

10 air/sea power the number of planes or ships that a country has available to use in a war

11 STRONG COUNTRY [C] a country that is strong and important and can influence events, or that has a lot of military strength → **powerful**, **powerless**: *Egypt is still a major power in the Middle East.* | **world power** (=a country that can influence events in different parts of the world) THESAURUS ➤ COUNTRY

12 be in/within sb's power (to do sth) if it is in someone's power to do something, they have the authority or ability to do it: *I wish it was within my power to change the decision.* | **do everything/all in your power** *The ambassador promised to do everything in his power to get the hostages released.*

13 be beyond sb's power (to do sth) if it is beyond someone's power to do something, they do not have the authority or ability to do it: *It's beyond the power of the court to make such a decision.*

14 be in sb's power *literary* to be in a situation in which someone has complete control over you

15 do sb a power of good *BrE informal* to make someone feel more healthy, happy, and hopeful about the future: *It looks as if your holiday has done you a power of good.*

16 MATHEMATICS [C] if a number is increased to the power of three, four, five etc, it is multiplied by itself three, four, five etc times

17 the powers that be the unknown people who have important positions of authority and power, and whose decisions affect your life: *The powers that be don't want the media to get hold of the story.*

18 LENS [U] *technical* the ability of a LENS, for example in a pair of GLASSES or a MICROSCOPE, to make things look bigger

19 the powers of good/evil/darkness unknown or magical forces that people believe can influence events in a good or evil way

20 a power in the land *old-fashioned* someone who has a lot of power and influence in a country

21 the power behind the throne someone who secretly controls and influences decisions made by the leader or government of a country, but who does not have an official government position

22 power trip *informal* if you are on a power trip, you are enjoying your power or authority in a way that other people think is unpleasant → STAYING POWER, BALANCE OF POWER, HIGH-POWERED

COLLOCATIONS

VERBS

have power *People who have power never seem to use it to help others.*
get/gain power *Women were trying to gain power in a male-dominated world.*
use your power (*also* **exercise (your) power** *formal*) *The party will use all its power and influence to raise the issue in the Senate.*
wield power *formal* (=use power - used when someone has a lot of power) *The Church still wields enormous power in the country.*

ADJECTIVES

great/huge/enormous *The central banks have huge power.*
limited *The king's power was limited.*
political/economic/military power *countries with little economic power*
absolute power (=total power, with no limits) | **real power**

PHRASES

a power struggle (=a situation in which groups or leaders try to get control) *The country is locked in a power struggle between forces favouring and opposing change.*
the balance of power *There has been a shift in the balance of power between the two countries.*
a position of power (=a job or role that gives someone power) | **an abuse of power** (=a wrong or unfair use of power)

power² ●○○ *v*
1 [T] to supply power to a vehicle or machine: *It's powered by a Ferrari V12 engine.* GRAMMAR **Power** is usually passive in this meaning.
2 [I always + adv/prep] to move with a lot of force and speed: *His strong body powered through the water.* → HIGH-POWERED

power sth ↔ **up** *phr v* to make a machine start working: *Never move a computer while it is powered up.*

power³ *adj* [only before noun] **1** driven by an electric motor: *power tools* | *power shower* **2 power breakfast/lunch etc** *informal* a meal at which people meet to discuss business **3 power suit** *informal* clothes which you wear at work to make you look important or confident

ˌpower-assisted ˈsteering *n* [U] POWER STEERING

ˈpower base *n* [C] an area or group of people whose support makes a politician or leader powerful: *the party's traditional power base*

pow·er·boat /ˈpaʊəbəʊt $ ˈpaʊrboʊt/ *n* [C] a powerful MOTORBOAT that is used for racing → **speedboat**

ˈpower ˌbroker, **power-broker** *n* [C] someone who controls or influences which people get political power in an area —**power-broking** *n* [U]

ˈpower cut *n* [C] *BrE* a period of time when there is no electricity supply SYN **power failure**, **power outage** *AmE*

ˈpower ˌdressing *n* [U] when you wear a particular style of clothes in order to emphasize how important or powerful you are, especially at work

ˈpower drill *n* [C] a tool for making holes that works by electricity

pow·ered /ˈpaʊəd $ paʊrd/ *adj* working or moving using a means of power such as electricity, a motor etc: *a powered wheelchair* | **battery-powered/nuclear-powered/mains powered** *a nuclear-powered submarine* | **high-powered/low-powered** *a high-powered engine* → HIGH-POWERED

ˈpower ˌfailure *n* [C] a period of time when there is no electricity supply

pow·er·ful /ˈpaʊəfəl $ ˈpaʊr-/ ●●● S3 W2 *adj*
1 IMPORTANT a powerful person, organization, group etc is able to control and influence events and other people's actions → **powerless**: *He was one of the most powerful men in Bohemia.* | *a very influential and powerful family* | *rich and powerful nations*
2 SPEECH/FILM ETC having a strong effect on someone's feelings or opinions: *a powerful speech* | **powerful reasons/arguments** (=reasons that make you think that something must be true) | *Good teamwork is a* **powerful tool** (=very effective method) *for effective management.*
3 FEELING/EFFECT a powerful feeling or effect is very strong or great: *Immigrants have had a* **powerful influence** *on the local culture.* | *a powerful sense of tradition*
4 MACHINE/WEAPON ETC a powerful machine, engine, weapon etc is very effective and can do a lot: *a new generation of more powerful PCs* | *a machine that is* **immensely powerful** | *a powerful 24-valve engine* | *a powerful telescope*
5 PHYSICALLY STRONG physically strong: *Jed was a powerful, well-built man.* | *The females are smaller and less powerful than the males.* THESAURUS ➤ STRONG
6 A LOT OF FORCE a powerful blow, explosion etc has a lot of force: *an explosion ten times more powerful than the Hiroshima bomb* | *a powerful right-foot shot on goal* | *winds powerful enough to uproot trees*
7 MEDICINE a powerful medicine or drug has a very strong effect on your body
8 TEAM/ARMY ETC a powerful team, army etc is very

P

strong and can easily defeat other teams or armies: *a powerful fighting force*

9 QUALITY very strong, bright, loud etc: *a powerful singing voice | the powerful headlights* —**powerfully** *adv*: *Christie is very powerfully built.* → ALL-POWERFUL

THESAURUS

powerful a powerful person, organization, group etc is able to control and influence events and other people's actions: *the world's most powerful nation | Parliament had become more powerful than the King.*
influential having a lot of power to influence what happens, because people pay attention to what you say: *a highly influential fashion designer | He's one of the most influential figures in international politics.*
strong powerful – used about people or groups in politics who have a lot of supporters: *The communists were particularly strong in the big industrial cities.*
dominant more powerful than other people, groups, countries etc: *She was the dominant force in women's tennis for many years. | The company has a dominant position in the market.*

P

pow·er·house /ˈpaʊəhaʊs $ ˈpaʊr-/ *n* [C] *informal* **1** an organization or place where there is a lot of activity or where a lot of things are produced: *Europe's industrial powerhouse* **2** someone who is very strong or has a lot of energy: *a powerhouse of a man*

pow·er·less /ˈpaʊələs $ ˈpaʊr-/ ●○○ *adj* unable to stop or control something because you do not have the power, strength, or legal right to do so → **powerful**: *He felt so powerless.* | **powerless to do sth** *Local police were powerless to stop them doing it again.* | **[+against]** *The villagers were powerless against the rising flood water.* —**powerlessly** *adv* —**powerlessness** *n* [U]: *a sense of frustration and powerlessness*

ˈpower line *n* [C] a large wire carrying electricity above or under the ground: *overhead power lines*

ˈpower-nap *n* [C] a short sleep in the middle of the day that helps you to have more energy, do your job better, and make better decisions

ˌpower of atˈtorney *n* (*plural* **powers of attorney**) [C,U] *law* the legal right to make financial decisions, sign documents etc for another person

ˈpower ˌoutage *n* [C] *AmE* a period of time when there is no electricity supply SYN **power failure, power cut** *BrE*

ˈpower ˌpack *n* [C] something that is easily carried from which a piece of electrical equipment can get power, for example a BATTERY

ˈpower plant *n* [C] **1** a building where electricity is produced to supply a large area SYN **power station** **2** the machine or engine that supplies power to a factory, plane, car etc

ˈpower point *n* [C] *BrE* a place on a wall where electrical equipment can be connected to the electricity supply SYN **socket**

ˈpower ˌpolitics *n* [U] when a country or person attempts to get power and influence by using or threatening to use force or other actions, especially against another country

ˈpower-ˌsharing *n* [U] an arrangement in which different groups, such as political parties, share the power to make decisions: *proposals for power-sharing between Catholics and Protestants in Northern Ireland*

ˈpower ˌstation *n* [C] *especially BrE* a building where electricity is produced to supply a large area: *Chernobyl nuclear power station* | **coal-fired/gas-fired power station**

ˈpower ˌsteering (*also* **power-assisted steering**) *n* [U] a system for STEERing a vehicle which uses power from the vehicle's engine and so needs less effort from the driver: *Most new cars now have power steering.*

ˈpower ˌstructure *n* [C] the way in which the group of people who control a country, society, or organization are organized: *There have been significant changes in the power structure of the company.*

ˈpower tool *n* [C] a tool that works by electricity → **hand tool**

ˈpow-wow *n* [C] **1** a meeting or discussion – used humorously **2** a meeting or council of Native Americans

pox /pɒks $ pɑːks/ *n old use* **1 the pox a)** the disease SYPHILIS **b)** the disease SMALLPOX **2 a pox on sb** used to show that you are angry or annoyed with someone → CHICKEN POX

pox·y /ˈpɒksi $ ˈpɑː-/ *adj BrE informal* used to show that you do not like something, or do not think it is big or important: *We've had such poxy weather lately. | a poxy little room*

pp. (*also* **pp** *BrE*) **1** the written abbreviation of ***pages***: *See pp 15–17.* **2** written before the name of another person when you are signing a letter instead of them

P-plate /ˈpiː pleɪt/ *n* [C] a flat white square with a green letter P on it, that is attached to the car of someone in Britain who has passed their driving test but who is not very experienced → **L-plate**

PPP /ˌpiː piː ˈpiː/ *n* [U] (***public-private partnership***) a system of providing money for transport systems, hospitals, schools etc where the government pays some money and private INVESTORs provide the rest of it

PPS /ˌpiː piː ˈes/ *n* [C] **1** (*also* **P.P.S.** *AmE*) a note added after a PS in a letter or message **2** (***Parliamentary Private Secretary***) a member of the British Parliament whose job is to help a minister

PR /ˌpiː ˈɑː $ -ˈɑːr/ *n* [U] **1** (***public relations***) the work of explaining to the public what an organization does, so that they will understand it and approve of it: **PR agency/firm/consultant** *a large PR firm | The band have been getting a lot of **good PR** recently. | Many say it was no more than a **PR exercise*** (=something done to make people think something is good). **2** *BrE* the abbreviation of ***proportional representation***

prac·ti·ca·ble /ˈpræktɪkəbəl/ *adj* a practicable way of doing something is possible in a particular situation OPP **impracticable**: *The only practicable course of action is to sell the company. | It is their duty to ensure, so far as is reasonably practicable, that the equipment is safe.* | **it is practicable (for sb) to do sth** *It may not always be practicable to follow exactly the recommendations.* —**practicably** *adv* —**practicability** /ˌpræktɪkəˈbɪləti/ *n* [U]

prac·ti·cal¹ /ˈpræktɪkəl/ ●●● S3 W2 *adj*

1 REAL relating to real situations and events rather than ideas, emotions etc → **theoretical**: *Candidates should have training and **practical experience** in basic electronics. | the **practical problems** of old age | They provide financial and **practical help** for disabled students. | a combination of theoretical and practical training | They haven't thought about the practical consequences of the new regulations. | **In practical terms**, this means spending more time with each student.*

2 EFFECTIVE practical plans, methods etc are likely to succeed or be effective in a situation OPP **impractical**: *It doesn't sound like a very practical solution. | a **practical way** of achieving greater efficiency | Unfortunately, there's no **practical alternative** to driving. | a **practical guide** to buying and selling a house*

3 CLEAR THINKING a practical person is good at dealing with problems and making decisions based on what is possible and what will really work OPP **impractical**: *She's a very **practical person**. | I was very shocked, but tried to be practical and think what to do.*

4 SUITABLE useful or suitable for a particular purpose or situation OPP **impractical**: *Skirts aren't very practical in my kind of work.*

5 USING YOUR HANDS good at repairing or making things: *I'm not very practical – I can't even change a light bulb.*

6 for/to all practical purposes used to say what the real effect of a situation is: *The time you spend on it doesn't, for all practical purposes, affect the final result.*

7 practical certainty/disaster/sell-out etc something that is almost certain, almost a DISASTER etc: *Sampras looks a practical certainty to win Wimbledon this year.*

practical² *n* [C] *BrE* a lesson or examination in science, cooking etc in which you have to do or make something yourself rather than write or read about it: *a chemistry practical* THESAURUS ➤ TEST

prac·ti·cal·i·ty /ˌpræktɪˈkæləti/ *n* **1 practicalities** [plural] the real facts of a situation rather than ideas about how it might be: **[+of]** *the practicalities of everyday life for someone in a wheelchair* **2** [U] how suitable something is, or whether it will work: *doubts about the practicality of your suggestion* | *You need to think about comfort and practicality when choosing walking shoes.* **3** [U] the quality of being sensible and basing your plans on what you know will work

ˌpractical ˈjoke *n* [C] a trick that is intended to give someone a surprise or shock, or to make them look stupid —**practical joker** *n* [C]

prac·ti·cally /ˈpræktɪkli/ ●●○ *adv*
1 *especially spoken* almost: *I've read* ***practically all*** *of his books.* | *She sees him* ***practically every*** *day.* | *It's practically impossible to predict what will happen.* | *The two designs were practically identical.* THESAURUS ➤ ALMOST
2 in a sensible way which takes account of problems: *'But how can we pay for it?' said John practically.*

ˈpractical ˌnurse *n* [C] *AmE* someone who has been trained and is allowed to do some of the same work as a nurse, but who has less training than a REGISTERED NURSE

prac·tice /ˈpræktɪs/ ●●● S2 W1 *n*
1 A SKILL [C,U] when you do a particular thing, often regularly, in order to improve your skill at it: *It takes hours of practice to learn to play the guitar.* | *With a little more practice you should be able to pass your test.* | *We have choir practice on Tuesday evening.* | **in practice for sth** *Schumacher crashed out in practice for the Australian grand prix.* | **football/rugby/basketball etc practice** *John's at baseball practice.* ⚠ In British English, the verb is always spelled **practise** (see separate entry). In American English, both noun and verb are spelled **practice**.
2 in practice used when saying what really happens rather than what should happen or what people think happens: *In practice women receive much lower wages than their male colleagues.* | *The journey should only take about 30 minutes, but in practice it usually takes more like an hour.*
3 STH DONE OFTEN [C,U] something that people do often, especially a particular way of doing something or a social or religious custom: *religious beliefs and practices* | *dangerous* ***working practices*** | **the practice of doing sth** *the practice of dumping waste into the sea* THESAURUS ➤ HABIT
4 DOCTOR/LAWYER [C] the work of a doctor or lawyer, or the place where they work: **medical/legal practice** *Mary Beth had a busy legal practice in Los Angeles.* → GENERAL PRACTICE, PRIVATE PRACTICE
5 be common/standard/normal practice to be the usual and accepted way of doing something: ***It's common practice*** *in many countries* ***for*** *pupils to repeat a year if their grades are low.* | ***It's standard practice to*** *seek parents' permission wherever possible.*
6 good/best/bad practice an example of a good or bad way of doing something, especially in a particular job: *It's not considered good practice to reveal clients' names.*
7 put sth into practice if you put an idea, plan etc into practice, you start to use it and see if it is effective: *It gave him the chance to put his ideas into practice.*
8 be out of practice to have not done something for a long time, so that you are not able to do it well
9 practice makes perfect used to say that if you do an activity regularly, you will become very good at it

prac·tise *BrE*, **practice** *AmE* /ˈpræktɪs/ ●●● S3 W3 *v*
1 [I,T] to do an activity, often regularly, in order to improve your skill or to prepare for a test: *They moved the furniture back to practise their dance routine.* | *It gives students the opportunity to practice their speaking skills.* | **practise doing sth** *Today we're going to practise parking.* | **[+for]** *She's practicing for her piano recital.* | **practise sth on sb** *Everybody wants to practise their English on me.*

GRAMMAR

Practise is followed by an **-ing** form, not an infinitive. You say: *We practised hitting the ball.* ✗ Don't say: *We practised to hit the ball.*
GRAMMAR GUIDE ➤ VERBS

2 [T] to use a particular method or custom: *This technique is* ***widely practised*** *in Europe* (=many people use it).
3 [I,T] to work as a doctor or lawyer: *When she has completed her training, she intends to practise in the UK.* | **[+as]** *Gemma is now practising as a dentist.*
4 [T] if you practise a religion, system of ideas etc, you live your life according to its rules: *They are free to practice their religion openly.*
5 practise what you preach to do the things that you advise other people to do: *She didn't always practise what she preached.*

THESAURUS

practise *BrE*, **practice** *AmE* *v* [I,T] to do an activity many times in order to improve your skill or to prepare for a test: *The course will give you a chance to practise your language skills.* | *He was practising his golf swing.*
train *v* [I] to practise physical movements or activities in preparation for a race or game: *He's training for the Olympics.*
rehearse *v* [I,T] to practise a play, speech, or music in preparation for a public performance: *She's in New York where she's rehearsing her new play.* | *The band are currently rehearsing for their world tour.*
work on sth to practise a particular skill so that your general performance improves: *You need to work on your listening comprehension.*
go/run through sth to practise something such as a speech, play, or piece of music by reading or playing it from the beginning to the end: *I'll just run through the speech one more time.*

prac·tised *BrE*, **practiced** *AmE* /ˈpræktɪst/ *adj* **1** someone who is practised in a particular job or skill is good at it because they have done it many times before: *a practised performer* | **practised in (doing) sth** *He was already well practiced in giving acceptance speeches.* | **to the practised eye** (=to someone who has seen something many times and knows a lot about it) **2** [only before noun] a practised action has been done so often that it now seems very easy: *He faced the television cameras* ***with practised ease***.

prac·tis·ing *BrE*, **practicing** *AmE* /ˈpræktəsɪŋ/ *adj* **1 a practising Catholic/Muslim/Jew etc** someone who follows the rules and customs of a particular religion OPP **lapsed 2 a practising doctor/lawyer/teacher etc** someone who is working as a doctor, lawyer etc: *Few practicing teachers have time for such research.*

prac·ti·tion·er /prækˈtɪʃənə $ -ər/ AWL *n* [C] **1** someone who works as a doctor or a lawyer: **medical/legal practitioner** | *a practitioner of alternative medicine* → GENERAL PRACTITIONER **2** someone who regularly does a particular activity: *one of golf's most experienced practitioners* | **[+of]** *a practitioner of Taoist philosophy*

prae·sid·i·um /prɪˈsɪdiəm, -ˈzɪ-/ *n* [C] another spelling of PRESIDIUM

prag·mat·ic /prægˈmætɪk/ ●○○ *adj* dealing with problems in a sensible practical way instead of strictly following a set of ideas → **dogmatic**: *Williams took a more pragmatic approach to management problems.* —**pragmatically** /-kli/ *adv*

prag·mat·ics /prægˈmætɪks/ *n* [U] *technical* the study of how words and phrases are used with special meanings in particular situations

prag·ma·tis·m /ˈprægmətɪzəm/ *n* [U] a way of dealing with problems in a sensible practical way instead of following a set of ideas: *a politician known for his pragmatism* —**pragmatist** *n* [C]

prai·rie /ˈpreəri $ ˈpreri/ *n* [C] a wide open area of fairly

P

flat land in North America which is covered in grass or wheat

ˈprairie dog *n* [C] a small animal with a short tail, which lives in holes on the prairies

praise[1] /preɪz/ ●●● W2 *v* [T]
1 to say that you admire and approve of someone or something, especially publicly OPP **criticize**: *Jane was praised by her teacher.* | **praise sb/sth for (doing) sth** *The mayor praised the rescue teams for their courage.* | *a* ***highly praised*** *novel* | **praise sb/sth to the skies** (=praise someone or something very much)
2 to give thanks to God and show your respect to Him, especially by singing in a church
3 God/Heaven be praised (*also* **Praise the Lord**) used to say that you are pleased something has happened and thank God for it

P

THESAURUS

praise to say that you admire and approve of someone or something, especially publicly: *The film was praised by the critics when it first came out.* | *The report praises staff in both schools.*
congratulate to tell someone that you think it is good that they have achieved something: *I congratulated him on his success.* | *The government should be congratulated for what they have achieved.*
compliment to say to someone that you like how they look, or you like something they have done: *She complimented me on my new hairstyle.* | *He complimented my cooking.*
flatter to praise someone in order to please them or get something from them, even though you do not mean it: *He had persuaded her to buy it by flattering her and being charming.* | *You're just flattering me!*
rave about sth (*also* **enthuse about sth** *formal*) to talk about something you enjoy or admire in an excited way, and say that it is very good. **Rave** is rather informal, whereas **enthuse** is much more formal and is used mainly in written English: *Everyone is raving about the movie.* | *She enthused about the joys of motherhood.*
applaud *formal* to publicly praise a decision, action, idea etc: *Business leaders applauded the decision.* | *A spokesperson applauded the way the festival had been run.*
commend *formal* to praise someone or something, especially officially: *After the battle, Andrew Jackson commended him for 'his courage and fidelity'.* | *The officers should be commended for their prompt action.*
hail sb/sth as sth *especially written* to describe someone or something in a way that shows you have a very good opinion of them, especially in newspapers, on television reports etc: *The book was hailed as a masterpiece.* | *Journalists and music writers hailed the band as 'the next big thing'.* | *He is being hailed as the new James Dean.*

praise[2] ●●● W3 *n* [U]
1 words that you say or write in order to praise someone or something OPP **criticism**: *It's important to* ***give*** *children plenty of* ***praise*** *and encouragement.* | *Her teacher* ***was full of praise for*** *her work.* | *His first novel* ***received high praise****.* | *Gregory was singled out* (= he was chosen in particular) *for* ***special praise****.* | *The film has* ***won praise*** *from audiences and critics alike.* | **in praise of sb/sth** *He wrote a poem in praise of his hero.*
2 the expression of respect and thanks to God: *Let us give praise unto the Lord.* | *songs of praise*
3 praise be! *old-fashioned* used when you are very pleased about something that has happened → **sing sb's praises** at SING(4)

praise·wor·thy /ˈpreɪzwɜːði $ -ɜːr-/ *adj* something that is praiseworthy deserves praise, even though it may not have been completely successful: *the council's praiseworthy attempts to improve efficiency* —**praiseworthiness** *n* [U]

pra·line /ˈprɑːliːn/ *n* [C,U] a sweet food made of nuts cooked in boiling sugar

pram /præm/ *n* [C] *BrE* a small vehicle with four wheels in which a baby can lie down while it is being pushed SYN **baby carriage** *AmE* → **buggy**: *a young woman* ***pushing a pram***

prance /prɑːns $ præns/ *v* [I] **1** [always + adv/prep] to walk or dance with high steps or large movements, especially in a confident way: **[+around]** *We used to prance around our bedroom pretending to be pop stars.* **2** if a horse prances, it moves with high steps

prang /præŋ/ *v* [T] *BrE informal* to damage a vehicle in an accident —**prang** *n* [C]

prank /præŋk/ *n* [C] a trick, especially one which is played on someone to make them look silly: *a childish prank*

prank·ster /ˈpræŋkstə $ -ər/ *n* [C] someone who plays tricks on people to make them look silly

prate /preɪt/ *v* [I] *old use* to talk in a meaningless boring way about something

prat·fall /ˈprætfɔːl $ -fɔːl/ *n* [C] **1** an embarrassing accident or mistake: *another one of the vice-president's pratfalls* **2** an act of falling down, especially when this is funny or embarrassing

prat·tle /ˈprætl/ *v* [I] to talk continuously about silly and unimportant things: **[+away/on]** *What's Sarah prattling on about?* THESAURUS TALK —**prattle** *n* [U] —**prattler** *n* [C]

prawn /prɔːn $ prɒːn/ ●○○ *n* [C] *especially BrE* a small pink SHELLFISH that can be eaten SYN **shrimp** *AmE*: *a prawn sandwich* | *prawn cocktail* (=a small dish of prawns in a sauce with some salad) → see picture at SHELLFISH

pray[1] /preɪ/ ●●○ S3 W3 *v* [I,T]
1 to speak to God in order to ask for help or give thanks → **prayer**: *They went to the mosque to pray.* | **[+for]** *Let us pray for peace.* | **[+to]** *Martha prayed to God for help.* | **pray (that)** *He prayed that his sight might be restored.*
2 to wish or hope very strongly that something will happen or is true: **pray (that)** *Paul was praying that no one had noticed his absence.* | *I* ***hope and pray*** *that this is a misunderstanding.* | **[+for]** *We're praying for good weather tomorrow.*

pray[2] *adv* [sentence adverb] *old-fashioned* used when politely asking a question or telling someone to do something SYN **please**: *Pray be seated.* | *And who,* ***pray tell****, is this?*

prayer /preə $ prer/ ●●● S3 W3 *n*
1 [C] words that you say when praying to God or gods: *Our thoughts and prayers are with you at this difficult time.* | *The children* ***said*** *their* ***prayers*** *and got into bed.* | *God has* ***answered*** *your* ***prayer****.* | **[+for]** *a prayer for the dead* → **LORD'S PRAYER**
2 [U] when someone prays, or the regular habit of praying: *the power of prayer* | *a* ***prayer meeting*** | **in prayer** *The congregation knelt in prayer.*
3 [C] a wish or hope that something will happen: *Her prayer was that she would pass her exams.*
4 prayers [plural] a regular religious meeting in a church, school etc, at which people pray together: *Prayers are at eight o'clock.*
5 not have a prayer (of doing sth) *informal* to have no chance of succeeding: *He tried hard, but he didn't have a prayer.* | *They don't have a prayer of winning.*
6 an/the answer to sb's prayers *informal* something that someone wants or needs very much: *The job was an answer to my prayers.* → **on a wing and a prayer** at WING[1](10)

ˈprayer book *n* [C] a book containing prayers that is used in some Christian church services

ˈprayer mat (*also* **ˈprayer rug**) *n* [C] a small cloth on which Muslims kneel when praying

ˈprayer wheel *n* [C] a drum-shaped object with prayers on it or inside it, which Tibetan Buddhists turn on a pole as a way of praying

ˌpraying ˈmantis (*also* **mantis**) *n* [C] a large insect that eats other insects

pre- /priː/ *prefix* **1** before someone or something → **ante-**: *pre-war* (=before a war) **2** in preparation: *a prearranged signal | Preset the video.*

preach /priːtʃ/ ●○○ *v*
1 [I,T] to talk about a religious subject in a public place, especially in a church during a service: **[+to]** *Christ began preaching to large crowds.* | **[+on/about]** *The vicar **preached** a **sermon** about the prodigal son.* | *He traveled the southern states, **preaching the gospel**.*
2 [T] to talk about how good or important something is and try to persuade other people about this: *Alexander has been preaching patience.* | **preach the virtues/merits/benefits of sth** *a politician preaching the virtues of a free market*
3 [I] to give someone advice, especially about their behaviour, in a way that they think is boring or annoying: **[+about]** *grown-ups preaching about the evils of drugs*
4 preach to the converted/choir to talk about what you think is right or important to people who already have the same opinions as you → **practise what you preach** at PRACTISE(5)

preach·er /ˈpriːtʃə $ -ər/ ●○○ *n* [C] someone who talks about a religious subject in a public place, especially at a church

preach·y /ˈpriːtʃi/ *adj informal* trying too much to persuade people to accept a particular opinion - used to show disapproval: *a preachy TV show*

pre·am·ble /priˈæmbəl $ ˈpriːæmbəl/ *n* [C,U] *formal* a statement at the beginning of a book, document, or talk, explaining what it is about: **[+to]** *the preamble to the American Constitution | Harding gave him the news **without preamble*** (=without saying anything else before it).

pre·ar·ranged /ˌpriːəˈreɪndʒd◂/ *adj* planned or decided before: *At a prearranged signal, everyone stood up.* —**prearrangement** *n* [U]

pre·but·tal /prɪˈbʌtl/ *n* [C] a statement that a politician makes saying that a criticism of them is false or unfair, before the criticism has been made → **rebuttal**: *Wiggins issued a prebuttal against his opponent's speech, even before the text was delivered to reporters.*

Pre·cam·bri·an /priːˈkæmbriən/ *adj* belonging or relating to the period of time in the Earth's history from about 4,600 million years ago, when the hard outer surface of the Earth first formed, until about 570 million years ago, when simple forms of life first appeared on the Earth: *Precambrian rocks*

pre·car·i·ous /prɪˈkeəriəs $ -ˈker-/ *adj* **1** a precarious situation or state is one which may very easily or quickly become worse: *Her health remained precarious, despite the treatment.* | *the company's **precarious** financial **position***
2 likely to fall, or likely to cause someone to fall: *a precarious mountain trail* —**precariously** *adv*: *a cup of tea **balanced precariously** on her knee* —**precariousness** *n* [U]

pre·cast /ˌpriːˈkɑːst◂ $ -ˈkæst◂/ *adj* precast CONCRETE is already formed into the shapes needed to build something

pre·cau·tion /prɪˈkɔːʃən $ -ˈkɒː-/ ●○○ *n* [C usually plural] something you do in order to prevent something dangerous or unpleasant from happening: *Fire precautions were neglected.* | **as a precaution** *The traffic barriers were put there as a **safety precaution**.* | **[+against]** *Save your work often as a precaution against computer failure.* | **wise/sensible precaution** *The trails are well marked, but carrying a map is a wise precaution.* | *Vets **took precautions** to prevent the spread of the disease.* | **take the precaution of doing sth** *I took the precaution of insuring my camera.*

> **REGISTER**
> In everyday English, people usually say **just in case** rather than **as a precaution**: *I'm going to take my umbrella **just in case**.*

pre·cau·tion·a·ry /prɪˈkɔːʃənəri $ -ˈkɒːʃəneri/ *adj* done in order to prevent something dangerous or unpleasant from happening: *More troops were sent to the area as a **precautionary measure**.*

pre·cede /prɪˈsiːd/ ●○○ AWL *v* [T] *formal*
1 to happen or exist before something or someone, or to come before something else in a series → **preceding**: *a type of cloud that precedes rain | Lunch will be preceded by a short speech from the chairman.*
2 to go somewhere before someone else: *The guard preceded them down the corridor.*

pre·ce·dence /ˈpresɪdəns/ AWL *n* [U] when someone or something is considered to be more important than someone or something else, and therefore comes first or must be dealt with first SYN **priority**: **[+over]** *Do we want a society where appearance **takes precedence** over skill or virtue?* | *Guests were seated **in order of precedence**.* | *Safety must be **given precedence**.*

pre·ce·dent /ˈpresɪdənt/ ●○○ AWL *n*
1 [C] an action or official decision that can be used to give support to later actions or decisions: *a **legal precedent*** | **set/create a precedent** *UN involvement in the country's affairs would set a dangerous precedent.* | **[+for]** *precedents for what courts will accept as 'fair'*
2 [C,U] something of the same type that has happened or existed before: **[+for]** *There's not much precedent for men taking leave when their baby is born.* | **without precedent** *An epidemic on this scale is without precedent.*
3 [U] the way that things have always been done: **break with precedent** (=do something in a new way)

pre·ced·ing /prɪˈsiːdɪŋ/ AWL *adj* [only before noun] *formal* happening or coming before the time, place, or part mentioned SYN **previous** OPP **following**: **preceding days/weeks/months/years** *income tax paid in preceding years* | **preceding chapter/paragraph/page etc** *the diagram in the preceding chapter*

pre·cept /ˈpriːsept/ *n* [C] *formal* a rule on which a way of thinking or behaving is based: *basic moral precepts*

pre·cinct /ˈpriːsɪŋkt/ *n* **1** [C] **shopping/pedestrian precinct** *BrE* an area of a town where people can walk and shop, and where cars are not allowed **2** [C] *AmE* one of the areas that a town or city is divided into, so that elections or police work can be organized more easily **3** [C] *AmE* the main police station in a particular area of a town or city **4 precincts** [plural] the area that surrounds an important building: *the precincts of the cathedral*

pre·cious¹ /ˈpreʃəs/ ●●○ *adj*
1 something that is precious is valuable and important and should not be wasted or used without care: **precious seconds/minutes/hours/time** *We cannot afford to waste precious time.* | *planes delivering precious supplies of medicine and food | our planet's **precious resources***
2 rare and worth a lot of money: **precious gem/stone/jewel** *a statue covered with precious jewels* → see picture at STONE
3 precious memories or possessions are important to you because they remind you of people you like or events in your life: **[+to]** *The doll is cracked and worn, but it's precious to me because it was my mother's.* **THESAURUS** VALUABLE
4 [only before noun] *spoken* used to show that you are annoyed that someone seems to care too much about something: *I never touched your precious car!*
5 *spoken* used to speak to someone you love, especially a baby or small child: *Come sit by me, precious.*
6 *AmE spoken* used in order to describe someone or something that is small and pretty SYN **cute**: *The kids gave me that ornament. Isn't it precious?*
7 *formal* too concerned about style or detail in your writing or speech, so that it does not seem natural: *His early work is rather precious and juvenile.* —**preciously** *adv* —**preciousness** *n* [U]

precious² *adv informal* **precious little/few** very little or very few: *I had precious little time for reading.*

ˌprecious ˈmetal *n* [C,U] a rare and valuable metal such as gold or silver

ˌprecious ˈstone *n* [C] a rare and valuable jewel such as a DIAMOND or an EMERALD → **semi-precious** → see picture at STONE¹

pre·ci·pice /ˈpresɪpɪs/ *n* [C] **1** a very steep side of a high rock, mountain, or cliff: *A loose rock tumbled over the* precipice. **2** a dangerous situation in which something very bad could happen: *The stock market is **on the edge of a precipice**.*

pre·cip·i·tate¹ /prɪˈsɪpɪteɪt/ *v* **1** [T] *formal* to make something serious happen suddenly or more quickly than was expected SYN **hasten**: *The riot was precipitated when four black men were arrested.* THESAURUS ▸ CAUSE **2** [I,T + out] *technical* to separate a solid substance from a liquid by chemical action, or to be separated in this way

precipitate sb **into** sth *phr v formal* to force someone or something into a particular state or condition: *The drug treatment precipitated him into a depression.*

pre·cip·i·tate² /prəˈsɪpətət/ *n* [C] *technical* a solid substance that has been chemically separated from a liquid

precipitate³ *adj formal* happening or done too quickly, and not thought about carefully SYN **hasty**: *a precipitate decision* —**precipitately** *adv*

pre·cip·i·ta·tion /prɪˌsɪpɪˈteɪʃən/ *n* **1** [U] *technical* rain, snow etc that falls on the ground, or the amount of rain, snow etc that falls **2** [C,U] *technical* a chemical process in which a solid substance is separated from a liquid **3** [U] *formal* the act of doing something too quickly in a way that is not sensible

pre·cip·i·tous /prɪˈsɪpɪtəs/ *adj* **1** very sudden: *a precipitous decline in stock prices* **2** dangerously high or steep: *a precipitous path* **3** *formal* happening or done too quickly, and not thought about carefully: *a precipitous marriage* —**precipitously** *adv*

pré·cis /ˈpreɪsiː $ preɪˈsiː/ *n* (*plural* **précis** /-siːz $ -ˈsiːz/) [C] *especially BrE* a statement which gives the main idea of a piece of writing, speech etc SYN **summary**, **abstract** *AmE*: *a précis of the report* —**précis** *v* [T]

pre·cise /prɪˈsaɪs/ ●●○ W3 AWL *adj*
1 precise information, details etc are exact, clear, and correct SYN **exact**: *precise sales figures* | *It was difficult to get precise information.* | *'She's a lot older than you, isn't she?' 'Fifteen years, **to be precise**.'*
2 [only before noun] used to emphasize that you are referring to an exact thing SYN **exact**: *At that precise moment, her husband walked in.* | *The precise cause of the disease is unknown.* | *the precise location of the ship* | *the precise nature of their agreement*
3 someone who is precise is very careful about small details or about the way they behave: *a precise careful woman* | *with precise movements of his hands*

pre·cise·ly /prɪˈsaɪsli/ ●●○ W3 AWL *adv*
1 exactly and correctly SYN **exactly**: *Temperature can be measured precisely.* | *He arrived at precisely four o'clock.* | **precisely what/how/where etc** *It is difficult to **know precisely** how much impact the changes will have.* | *What, precisely, does that mean?* | *Lathes make wheels, or, **more precisely**, they make cylindrical objects.* THESAURUS ▸ EXACTLY
2 used to emphasize that a particular thing is completely true or correct: *Women in these jobs are paid less **precisely because** most of the jobs are held by women rather than men.* | *She's precisely the kind of person we're looking for.*
3 *spoken formal* used to say that you agree completely with someone: *'It needs to be dealt with now.' 'Precisely, before it gets any worse.'*

pre·ci·sion¹ /prɪˈsɪʒən/ ●○○ AWL *n* [U] the quality of being very exact or correct: **with precision** *The work was carried out with **military precision*** (=the work was done in a carefully planned and exact way).

precision² AWL *adj* [only before noun] **1** made or done in a very exact way: *precision engineering* | *precision bombing* **2 precision tool/instrument** a precision tool or instrument is used for making or measuring something in a very exact way

pre·clude /prɪˈkluːd/ ●○○ *v* [T] *formal* to prevent something or make something impossible: *rules that preclude experimentation in teaching methods* | **preclude sb from doing something** *Age alone will not preclude him from standing as a candidate.*

pre·co·cious /prɪˈkəʊʃəs $ -ˈkoʊ-/ *adj* a precocious child shows intelligence or skill at a very young age, or behaves in an adult way – sometimes used to show disapproval in British English: *a **precocious child** who walked and talked early* —**precociously** *adv* —**precociousness** (*also* **precocity**) /prɪˈkɒsəti $ -ˈkɑː-/ *n* [U]

pre·cog·ni·tion /ˌpriːkɒgˈnɪʃən $ -kɑːg-/ *n* [U] *formal* the knowledge that something will happen before it actually does

pre·con·ceived /ˌpriːkənˈsiːvd◂/ *adj* [only before noun] preconceived ideas, opinions etc are formed before you really have enough knowledge or experience: *preconceived notions about art* | *We started from scratch with no preconceived ideas.*

pre·con·cep·tion /ˌpriːkənˈsepʃən/ *n* [C] a belief or opinion that you have already formed before you know the actual facts, and that may be wrong: **[+about/of]** *I **had** the same **preconceptions** about life in South Africa that many people have.*

pre·con·di·tion /ˌpriːkənˈdɪʃən/ *n* [C] something that must happen or exist before something else can happen: **[+of/for]** *A ceasefire is a precondition for talks.*

pre·cooked /ˌpriːˈkʊkt◂/ *adj* precooked food has been partly or completely cooked before it is sold so that it can be quickly heated up later —**precook** *v* [T]

pre·cur·sor /prɪˈkɜːsə $ -ˈkɜːrsər/ *n* [C] *formal* something that happened or existed before something else and influenced its development: **[+of/to]** *a precursor of modern jazz*

pre·date /priːˈdeɪt/ *v* [T] to happen or exist earlier in history than something else: *The kingdom predates other African cultures by over 3,000 years.*

pre·da·tion /prɪˈdeɪʃən/ *n* [U] *technical* when an animal kills and eats another animal

pred·a·tor /ˈpredətə $ -ər/ ●○○ *n* [C]
1 an animal that kills and eats other animals → **prey**
2 someone who tries to use another person's weakness to get advantages: *a sexual predator*

pred·a·to·ry /ˈpredətəri $ -tɔːri/ *adj* **1** a predatory animal kills and eats other animals for food **2** trying to use someone's weakness to get advantages for yourself – used to show disapproval: *predatory pricing*

pre·de·ces·sor /ˈpriːdəsesə $ ˈpredəsesər/ ●○○ *n* [C]
1 someone who had your job before you started doing it OPP **successor**: *Kennedy's predecessor as president was the war hero Dwight Eisenhower.*
2 a machine, system etc that existed before another one in a process of development OPP **successor**: *The new BMW has a more powerful engine than its predecessor.*

pre·des·ti·na·tion /prɪˌdestəˈneɪʃən, ˌpriːdes-/ *n* [U] the belief that God has decided everything that will happen and that people cannot change this

pre·des·tined /prɪˈdestɪnd/ *adj* something that is predestined is certain to happen because it has been decided by God or FATE: **predestined to do sth** *They believed that kings were predestined to rule.*

pre·de·ter·mined /ˌpriːdɪˈtɜːmɪnd $ -ɜːr-/ ●○○ *adj formal* decided or arranged before something happens, so that it does not happen by chance: **predetermined level/limit/amount etc** *a predetermined level of spending* —**predetermine** *v* [T]: *The colour of your eyes is predetermined by the colours of your parents' eyes.* —**predetermination** /ˌpriːdɪtɜːməˈneɪʃən $ -ɜːr/ *n* [U]

pre·de·ter·min·er /ˌpriːdɪˈtɜːmənə $ -ˈtɜːrmənər/ *n* [C] *technical* a word that is used before a DETERMINER (=a word such as 'the', 'that', 'his' etc). In the phrases 'all the boys' and 'both his parents', the words 'all' and 'both' are predeterminers.

pre·dic·a·ment /prɪˈdɪkəmənt/ *n* [C] a difficult or unpleasant situation in which you do not know what to do, or in which you have to make a difficult choice: *the country's economic predicament* | *She went to the office to **explain** her **predicament**.* | **in a predicament** *Other married couples are in a similar predicament.*

pred·i·cate¹ /ˈpredɪkət/ *n* [C] *technical* the part of a sentence that makes a statement about the subject, such as 'swim' in 'Fish swim' and 'is an artist' in 'She is an artist' → **subject**

pred·i·cate² /ˈpredɪkeɪt/ *v* **be predicated on/upon sth** *formal* if an action or event is predicated on a belief or situation, it is based on it or depends on it: *The company's expansion was predicated on the assumption that sales would rise.*

pre·dic·a·tive /prɪˈdɪkətɪv $ ˈpredəkeɪ-/ *adj technical* a predicative adjective or phrase comes after a verb, for example 'happy' in the sentence 'She is happy' —**predicatively** *adv*

pre·dict /prɪˈdɪkt/ ●●● W3 AWL *v* [T] to say that something will happen, before it happens → **prediction**: *Sales were five percent lower than predicted.* | **predict (that)** *Newspapers predicted that Davis would be re-elected.* | **predict whether/what/how etc** *It is difficult to predict what the long-term effects of the accident will be.* | ***As Liz had predicted**, the rumours were soon forgotten.* | **be predicted to do sth** *Unemployment is predicted to increase to 700,000 by the end of the year.*

GRAMMAR: Patterns with predict

- You **predict** that something **will** happen: *Experts predict that the economic situation will improve.*
- You **predicted** that something **would** happen: *Experts predicted that the economic situation would improve.*
- You **predict** that something **might** or **could** happen: *No one could have predicted that she might do something like that.*
- You say that something **is predicted to** happen: *The population is predicted to increase.*
- You say **it is predicted that** something **will** happen: *It is predicted that the population will increase.*
- You say that someone **is predicting** something.

Predict is often used in the progressive: *They are predicting another hot summer.*

THESAURUS

predict to say that something will happen, before it happens: *In the future, it may be possible to predict earthquakes.* | *Scientists are trying to predict what the Amazon will look like in 20 years' time.*

forecast to say what is likely to happen in the future, especially in relation to the weather or the economic or political situation: *They're forecasting a hard winter.* | *Economists forecast that there would be a recession.*

project to say what the amount, size, cost etc of something is likely to be in the future, using the information you have now: *The world's population is projected to rise by 45%.*

can say *especially spoken* be able to know what will happen in the future: ***No one can say** what the next fifty years will bring.* | *I can't say exactly how much it will cost.*

foretell to say correctly what will happen in the future, using special religious or magical powers: *The woman claimed that she had the gift of foretelling the future.* | *It all happened as the prophet had foretold.*

prophesy to say that something will happen because you feel that it will, or by using special religious or magical powers: *He's one of those people who are always prophesying disaster.* | *The coming of a great Messiah is prophesied in the Bible.*

foresee to know that something is going to happen before it happens: *They should have foreseen these problems.* | *No one foresaw the outcome of the war.*

have a premonition to have a strange feeling that something is about to happen, especially something bad, usually just before it happens: *Suddenly I had a strange premonition of danger ahead.*

pre·dict·a·ble /prɪˈdɪktəbəl/ ●●○ AWL *adj* if something or someone is predictable, you know what will happen or what they will do – sometimes used to show disapproval: *The snow had a predictable effect on traffic.* | *an entertaining but predictable film* | *Logan's reaction was predictable.* —**predictably** *adv* [sentence adverb]: *Predictably, no one was home when I called.* —**predictability** /prɪˌdɪktəˈbɪləti/ *n* [U]

pre·dic·tion /prɪˈdɪkʃən/ ●●○ AWL *n* [C,U] a statement about what you think is going to happen, or the act of making this statement: **[+of]** *predictions of a Republican victory* | *The data can be used to **make** useful economic **predictions**.*

pre·dict·ive /prɪˈdɪktɪv/ *adj* [usually before noun] *formal* relating to the ability to show what is going to happen in the future: *Dreams, even vivid ones, have little predictive value.*

preˌdictive ˈtext (*also* **preˌdictive ˈtexting**) *n* [U] a system on a MOBILE PHONE that suggests a word when you start writing a word in a TEXT MESSAGE

pre·dic·tor /prɪˈdɪktə $ -ər/ *n* [C] *formal* something that shows what will happen in the future: **[+of]** *High blood pressure is a strong predictor of heart attacks.*

pre·di·lec·tion /ˌpriːdɪˈlekʃən $ ˌpredlˈek-/ *n* [C] *formal* if you have a predilection for something, especially something unusual, you like it very much SYN **liking**: **[+for]** *Mrs Lane's predilection for gossip*

pre·dis·pose /ˌpriːdɪsˈpəʊz $ -ˈpoʊz/ *v* [T] **1** to make someone more likely to suffer from a particular health problem: **predispose sb to sth** *Diabetes predisposes patients to infections.* **2** to make someone more likely to behave or think in a particular way: **predispose sb to sth** *Parents who smoke predispose children to smoking.* —**predisposed** *adj*: *genetically predisposed to gain weight*

pre·dis·po·si·tion /ˌpriːdɪspəˈzɪʃən/ *n* [C] a tendency to behave in a particular way or suffer from a particular illness: **[+to/towards]** *a predisposition towards alcoholism*

pre·dom·i·nance /prɪˈdɒmənəns $ -ˈdɑː-/ AWL *n* **1** [singular] if there is a predominance of one type of person or thing in a group, there are more of that type than of any other type: **[+of]** *a predominance of boys in the class* **2** [U] someone or something that has predominance has the most power or importance in a particular group or area: *Britain's naval predominance*

pre·dom·i·nant /prɪˈdɒmɪnənt $ -ˈdɑː-/ AWL *adj* more powerful, more common, or more easily noticed than others: *the predominant group in society* | *In this painting, the predominant colour is black.* THESAURUS▸ MAIN

pre·dom·i·nant·ly /prɪˈdɒmənəntli $ -ˈdɑː-/ ●●○ AWL *adv* mostly or mainly: *The city's population is predominantly Irish.*

pre·dom·i·nate /prɪˈdɒməneɪt $ -ˈdɑː-/ AWL *v* [I] *formal* **1** if one type of person or thing predominates in a group or area, there are more of this type than any other: *Pine trees predominate in this area of forest.* **2** to have the most importance or influence, or to be most easily noticed: *In this type of case, the rights of the parent predominate.*

pree·mie /ˈpriːmi/ *n* [C] *AmE informal* a PREMATURE baby

pre-em·i·nent, **preeminent** /priˈemɪnənt/ *adj* much more important, more powerful, or better than any others of its kind: *his pre-eminent position in society* —**pre-eminently** *adv* —**pre-eminence** *n* [U]

pre-empt, **pre·empt** /priˈempt/ *v* [T] **1** to make what someone has planned to do or say unnecessary or ineffective by saying or doing something first: *The deal pre-empted a strike by rail workers.* **2** *AmE* to replace a television show with a special programme or report: *Regular programming was preempted by a report on the war.* —**pre-emption** /-ˈempʃən/ *n* [U]

pre-emp·tive, **preemptive** /priˈemptɪv/ *adj* a pre-emptive action is done to prevent something from happening, especially something that will harm you: **pre-emptive strike/attack** *a series of pre-emptive strikes on guerrilla bases*

preen /priːn/ *v* [I,T] **1** if a bird preens or preens itself, it cleans itself and makes its feathers smooth using its beak **2** to spend time making yourself look tidier and more attractive: **preen yourself** *a girl preening herself in the mirror*

3 to look proud and feel pleased because of something you have done: **preen yourself** *He enjoyed the applause, preening himself like a pop star.*

pre-existing, **pre·ex·ist·ing** /ˌpriːɪɡˈzɪstɪŋ◂/ *adj* [only before noun] *formal* existing before a particular time or event: *Inform your doctor of any* ***pre-existing*** *medical* ***condition***.

pre·fab /ˈpriːfæb $ ˌpriːˈfæb/ *n* [C] *informal* a small prefabricated building

pre·fab·ri·cat·ed /priːˈfæbrɪkeɪtɪd/ *adj* built from parts which are made in standard sizes so that they can be put together anywhere: *a prefabricated house* —**prefabrication** /priːˌfæbrɪˈkeɪʃən/ *n* [U]

pref·ace¹ /ˈprefɪs/ ●○○ *n* [C] an introduction at the beginning of a book or speech

preface² *v* [T] *formal* to say or do something before the main part of what you are going to say: *The book is prefaced by a quotation from Faulkner.*

pref·a·to·ry /ˈprefətəri $ -tɔːri/ *adj* [only before noun] *formal* forming a preface or introduction SYN **introductory**: *a few prefatory remarks*

pre·fect /ˈpriːfekt/ *n* [C] **1** an older student in some British schools, who has special duties and helps to control younger students **2** a public official in some countries etc who is responsible for a particular area

pre·fec·ture /ˈpriːfektʃʊə $ -tʃər/ *n* [C] a large area which has its own local government in some countries: *Saitama prefecture*

pre·fer /prɪˈfɜː $ -ˈfɜːr/ ●●● S2 W2 *v* (**preferred**, **preferring**) [T]

1 to like someone or something more than someone or something else, so that you would choose it if you could → **preference**: *This type of owl prefers a desert habitat.* | *She prefers her coffee black.* | *the government's preferred option* | **prefer sb/sth to sb/sth** *a child that prefers his imaginary world to reality* | *Employees said they would prefer more flexible working hours.* | **prefer to do sth** *I prefer to wear clothes made of natural fibers.* | *Or,* ***if you prefer***, *you can email us.* | **prefer doing sth** *Chantal prefers travelling by train.* | **prefer that** *We prefer that our teachers have a degree in early childhood education.*

> **REGISTER**
> In everyday English, people often say they **would rather** do something instead of using **prefer**: *I* ***prefer to*** *travel by train.* → *I'****d rather*** *travel by train.*

2 I would prefer it if *spoken* **a)** used to say that you wish a situation was different: *Sales have gone down, and obviously we'd prefer it if that didn't happen.* **b)** used when telling someone politely not to do something: *I'd prefer it if you didn't smoke in front of the children.*

3 prefer charges *BrE law* to make an official statement that someone has done something illegal

> **GRAMMAR**
> **Patterns with prefer**
> • You **prefer to** do something: *I prefer to read a book.*
> ✗ Don't say: *I prefer read a book.*
> • You **prefer doing** something: *We prefer going abroad for our vacation.* ✗ Don't say: *We prefer go abroad.*
> • You say that you **would prefer it if** someone **did** something: *We would prefer it if you didn't tell anyone.* ✗ Don't say: *We would prefer it if you don't tell anyone.*
> **Using the progressive**
> **Prefer** is not used in the progressive in meaning 1. You say: *I prefer the blue one.* ✗ Don't say: *I am preferring the blue one.*
> GRAMMAR GUIDE ▸ VERBS

pref·e·ra·ble /ˈprefərəbəl/ ●○○ *adj* better or more suitable: *For this dish, fresh herbs and garlic are preferable.* | *In warm weather, clothes made of natural fabrics are* ***infinitely preferable*** (=much better). | **preferable to (doing) sth** *Being taught in a small group is* ***far preferable*** *to being in a large, noisy classroom.* THESAURUS ▸ BETTER

pref·e·ra·bly /ˈprefərəbli/ ●○○ *adv* used in order to show which person, thing, place, or idea you think would be the best choice: *Students must take two years of a foreign language, preferably Spanish.*

pref·e·rence /ˈprefərəns/ ●●○ W3 *n*

1 [C,U] if you have a preference for something, you like it more than another thing and will choose it if you can → **prefer**: *Do you* ***have*** *a colour* ***preference***? | **[+for]** *a cultural preference for boy babies* | *Parents may be able to* ***express*** *a* ***preference*** *as to the school their child will attend.* | *The amount of sugar you add will depend on* ***personal preference***. | *Many elderly people expressed a* ***strong preference*** *to live in their own homes.* | **in preference to sth** (=rather than something) *Use clear English in preference to technical language.*

2 [C,U] when someone is treated more favourably than other people, often when he or she has been treated unfairly in the past: *Racial preferences are a way to make up for years of discrimination against minorities.* | **give/show preference (to sb)** *In allocating housing, preference is given to families with young children.*

3 sexual preference someone's sexual preference is whether they want to have sex with men or women

pref·e·ren·tial /ˌprefəˈrenʃəl◂/ *adj* [only before noun] preferential treatment, rates etc are deliberately different in order to give an advantage to particular people: *preferential credit terms for reliable borrowers* —**preferentially** *adv*

pre·fer·ment /prɪˈfɜːmənt $ -ɜːr-/ *n* [U] *formal* when someone is given a more important job

pre·fig·ure /ˌpriːˈfɪɡə $ -ɡjər/ *v* [T] *formal* to be a sign that something will happen later

pre·fix¹ /ˈpriːfɪks/ *n* [C] **1** *technical* a group of letters that is added to the beginning of a word to change its meaning and make a new word, such as 'un' in 'untie' or 'mis' in 'misunderstand' → **affix**, **suffix** **2** a number or letter that comes before other numbers or letters, especially a group of numbers that comes before a telephone number when you are calling someone in a different area **3** *old-fashioned* a title such as 'Ms' or 'Dr' used before someone's name SYN **title**

prefix² *v* [T] **1** to add a prefix to a word, name, or set of numbers **2** *formal* to say something before the main part of what you have to say

pre·gam·ing /ˈpriːˌɡeɪmɪŋ/ *n* [U] the practice of drinking alcohol at home before you go out to a party, club, or bar SYN **preloading**

preg·nan·cy /ˈpreɡnənsi/ ●●○ *n* (*plural* **pregnancies**) [C,U] when a woman is pregnant (=has a baby growing inside her body): *This drug should not be taken during pregnancy.* | *her third pregnancy* | *teenage pregnancies* | *a* ***pregnancy test***

preg·nant /ˈpreɡnənt/ ●●○ S3 *adj*

1 if a woman or female animal is pregnant, she has an unborn baby growing inside her body → **pregnancy**: *medical care for pregnant women* | *I knew right away that I was pregnant.* | *I thought I was too old to* ***get pregnant***. | **twenty weeks/three months etc pregnant** *She's about five months pregnant.* | **[+with]** *Maria was pregnant with her second child.* | *I didn't mean to* ***get*** *her* ***pregnant*** (=make her pregnant). | *His wife was* ***heavily pregnant*** (=almost ready to give birth).

2 pregnant pause/silence a pause or silence which is full of meaning or emotion: *He stopped, and there was a pregnant pause.*

3 pregnant with sth *formal* containing a lot of a quality: *Every phrase in this poem is pregnant with meaning.*

pre·heat /ˌpriːˈhiːt/ *v* [T] to heat an OVEN to a particular temperature before it is used to cook something: ***Preheat the oven*** *to 375 degrees.*

pre·hen·sile /prɪˈhensaɪl $ -səl/ *adj technical* a prehensile tail, foot etc can curl around things and hold on to them

pre·her·i·tance /priːˈherətəns/ *n* [C,U] money or property that you receive from a member of your family while they are still alive rather than after they die, so that you do not have to pay tax on it → **inheritance**

pre·his·tor·ic /ˌpriːhɪˈstɒrɪk◂ $ -ˈstɔː-, -ˈstɑː-/ *adj* **1** relating to the time in history before anything was written down: *prehistoric burial grounds* | *prehistoric animals* **2** very old-fashioned – used humorously: *a prehistoric attitude towards women*

pre·his·to·ry /priːˈhɪstəri/ *n* [U] the time in history before anything was written down

pre·judge /ˌpriːˈdʒʌdʒ/ *v* [T] to form an opinion about someone or something before you know or have considered all the facts – used to show disapproval: *Shepherd's case was prejudged by the media before her trial.* —**prejudgment** *n* [C,U]

prej·u·dice¹ /ˈpredʒədɪs/ ●●○ *n*
1 [C,U] an unreasonable dislike and distrust of people who are different from you in some way, especially because of their race, sex, religion etc – used to show disapproval: *Women still face prejudice in the workplace.* | *It takes a long time to overcome these kinds of prejudices.* | **[+against]** *a cultural prejudice against fat people* | **racial/sexual prejudice** *Asian pupils complained of racial prejudice at the school.*
2 [C,U] strong and unreasonable feelings which make you like some things but not others: *irrational prejudices* | *Interviewers are often influenced too much by their personal prejudices.*
3 without prejudice (to sth) *law* without harming or affecting something: *He was able to turn down the promotion without prejudice, and applied again several years later.*
4 to the prejudice of sth *formal* in a way that has a harmful effect or influence on something

THESAURUS

prejudice an unreasonable dislike and distrust of people who are different from you in some way, especially because of their race, sex, religion etc: *racial prejudice* | *prejudice against women*
discrimination the practice of treating one group of people differently from another in an unfair way: *There is widespread discrimination against older people.* | *the laws on sex discrimination*
intolerance an unreasonable refusal to accept beliefs, customs, and ways of thinking that are different from your own: *religious intolerance* | *There is an atmosphere of intolerance in the media.*
bigotry a completely unreasonable hatred for people of a different race, religion etc, based on strong and fixed opinions: *religious bigotry* | *the bigotry directed at Jews and other ethnic groups*
racism/racial prejudice unfair treatment of people because they belong to a different race: *Many black people have been the victims of racism in Britain.*
sexism the belief that one sex, especially women, is weaker, less intelligent etc than the other, especially when this results in someone being treated unfairly: *sexism in language* | *She accused him of sexism.*
ageism (*also* **agism** *AmE*) unfair treatment of people because they are old: *The new law aims to stop ageism in the workplace.*
homophobia prejudice towards or hatred of gay people: *homophobia in the armed forces*
xenophobia /ˌzenəˈfəʊbiə $ -ˈfoʊ-/ hatred and fear of foreigners: *the xenophobia of the right-wing press*
anti-Semitism a strong feeling of hatred toward Jewish people: *Is anti-Semitism on the increase?*
Islamophobia hatred and fear of Muslims: *the rise of Islamophobia and right-wing extremism in Europe*
gay/union/America etc bashing unfair public criticism of gay people, union members, the American government etc: *The minister was accused of union bashing.*

prejudice² *v* [T] **1** to influence someone so that they have an unfair or unreasonable opinion about someone or something: *There was concern that reports in the media would prejudice the jury.* | **prejudice sb against sth** *My own schooldays prejudiced me against all formal education.* **2** to have a bad effect on the future success or situation of someone or something: *A criminal record will* ***prejudice*** *your* ***chances*** *of getting a job.* | *He refused to comment, saying he did not wish to* ***prejudice the outcome*** *of the talks.*
THESAURUS ▸ HARM

prej·u·diced /ˈpredʒədɪst/ ●●○ *adj*
1 having an unreasonable dislike of someone or something, especially a dislike of a group of people who belong to a different race, sex, or religion – used to show disapproval: *Some officers were* ***racially prejudiced.*** | *an intolerant and prejudiced man* | **[+against]** *The early Christian church was prejudiced against the Jews.* | *Environmentalists are prejudiced against the dam.*
2 seriously affected by a bad situation: *The council must provide housing for young people whose welfare is seriously prejudiced.*

prej·u·di·cial /ˌpredʒəˈdɪʃəl◂/ *adj formal* having a bad effect on something: *prejudicial testimony*

prel·ate /ˈprelət/ *n* [C] a BISHOP, CARDINAL, or other important priest in the Christian church

pre·lim·i·na·ry¹ /prɪˈlɪmənəri $ -neri/ ●○○ AWL *adj* [only before noun] happening before something that is more important, often in order to prepare for it: *the* ***preliminary stages*** *of the competition* | *a preliminary draft* | **[+to]** *The discussions were preliminary to preparing a policy paper.*

preliminary² AWL *n* (*plural* **preliminaries**) [C usually plural] **1** something that is said or done first, to introduce or prepare for something else: **[+to]** *Pilot studies are a useful preliminary to large research projects.* | *After* ***the usual preliminaries****, the chairman made his announcement.* **2** one of the games in the first part of a competition, when it is decided who will go on to the main competition: *Four teams will be eliminated in the preliminaries.*

pre·lit·e·rate /priːˈlɪtərət/ *adj* a society that is preliterate has not developed a written language → **illiterate**

pre·load·ing /ˈpriːˌləʊdɪŋ $ -ˌloʊ-/ *n* [U] another word for PREGAMING —**preload** *v* [I]

pre-loved /ˌpriː ˈlʌvd◂/ *adj* a pre-loved house, pet etc has already been owned by someone else – used especially in advertisements to suggest the previous owner cared strongly about the object, animal etc

prel·ude /ˈpreljuːd/ *n* [C] **1 a prelude to sth** if an event is a prelude to a more important event, it happens just before it and makes people expect it: *Living together as a prelude to marriage is now considered acceptable in many countries.* **2** a short piece of music, especially one played at the beginning of a longer musical piece or before a church ceremony: *Chopin's Preludes* | *an organ prelude*

pre·mar·i·tal /priːˈmærətəl/ *adj* happening or existing before marriage: *premarital sex*

pre·ma·ture /ˈpremətʃə, -tʃʊə, ˌpreməˈtʃʊə $ ˌpriːməˈtʃʊr◂/ ●○○ *adj*
1 happening before the natural or proper time: *his premature death due to cancer* | *premature ageing of the skin*
2 a premature baby is born before the usual time of birth: *a premature birth* | *The baby was six weeks premature.*
3 done too early or too soon: *a premature order to attack* | *Any talk of a deal is premature.* | **it is premature (for sb) to do sth** *It would be premature to accuse anyone until the investigation is complete.* —**prematurely** *adv*: *The baby was born prematurely.*

pre·med, **pre-med** /ˌpriːˈmed/ *adj AmE* relating to classes that prepare a student for medical school, or to the students who are taking these classes: *a premed student* —**premed**, **pre-med** /ˈpriːmed/ *n* [U]

pre·med·i·tat·ed /priːˈmedɪteɪtɪd $ prɪ-/ *adj* a premeditated crime or attack is planned in advance and done deliberately: *premeditated murder*

pre·med·i·ta·tion /priːˌmedɪˈteɪʃən $ prɪ-/ *n* [U] the

act of thinking about something and planning it before you actually do it

pre·men·stru·al /priːˈmenstruəl/ *adj* happening or relating to the time just before a woman's PERIOD (=the time each month when blood flows from her body)

preˌmenstrual ˈsyndrome *n* [U] (*abbreviation* **PMS**) the tiredness, headache, bad temper etc experienced by some women in the days before their PERIOD SYN **premenstrual tension** *BrE*

preˌmenstrual ˈtension *n BrE* [U] (*abbreviation* **PMT**) the tiredness, headache, bad temper etc experienced by some women in the days before their PERIOD

prem·i·er[1] /ˈpremiə $ prɪˈmɪr/ ●○○ *adj* [only before noun] *formal* best or most important: *one of Dublin's premier hotels*

premier[2] *n* [C] a PRIME MINISTER – used in news reports: *the Irish Premier*

prem·i·ere, **première** /ˈpremieə $ prɪˈmɪr/ *n* [C] the first public performance of a film, play, or piece of music: *Rossini's work had its premiere at the Paris Opera.* | *a movie premiere* | *the play's* ***world premiere*** (=the first performance in the world) —**premiere** *v* [I,T]: *The movie premiered on December 21, 1937.*

prem·i·er·ship /ˈpremiəʃɪp $ prɪˈmɪrʃɪp/ *n* [C,U] the period when someone is PRIME MINISTER

prem·ise /ˈpremɪs/ ●●○ W3 *n*

1 premises [plural] the buildings and land that a shop, restaurant, company etc uses: *Schools may earn extra money by renting out their premises.* | *business premises* | **off the premises** *The manager escorted him off the premises.* | **on the premises** *The wonderful desserts are made on the premises.*

2 [C] (*also* **premiss** *BrE*) a statement or idea that you accept as true and use as a base for developing other ideas: *The idea that there is life on other planets is the central premise of the novel.* | **premise that** *the premise that an accused person is innocent until they are proved guilty*

prem·ised /ˈpremɪst/ *adj* **be premised on/upon sth** to be based on a particular idea or belief: *The program is premised on the idea that drug addiction can be cured.*

pre·mi·um[1] /ˈpriːmiəm/ ●○○ *n*

1 [C] the cost of insurance, especially the amount that you pay each year: *insurance premiums*

2 [C] an additional amount of money, above a standard rate or amount: *Consumers are prepared to* ***pay a premium*** *for organically grown vegetables.* | *Top quality cigars are being* ***sold at a premium***.

3 be at a premium if something is at a premium, people need it or want it, but there is little of it available or it is difficult to get: *During the Olympic Games, accommodation will be at a premium.* | **space/time is at a premium** *Foldaway furniture is the answer where space is at a premium.*

4 put/place a premium on sth to consider one quality or type of thing as being much more important than others: *Modern economies place a premium on educated workers.*

5 [U] *especially AmE* good quality petrol

premium[2] *adj* **1** of very high quality: *premium ice cream* | *the current consumer trend for premium products* | ***premium quality*** *British potatoes* **2 premium price/rate** premium prices and rates are higher than usual ones: *People are prepared to pay premium prices for quality products.* | *Calls are charged at the premium rate of 60p per minute.*

ˈpremium ˌbond *n* [C] a document that you buy from the government in Britain, which gives you the chance to win a large amount of money each month

ˈpremium rate *adj BrE* **premium rate number/line/service** a telephone connection to a particular service or company that costs a lot more than the usual rate when you call it because the company you are calling takes some of the money that you pay

pre·mo·ni·tion /ˌpreməˈnɪʃən, ˌpriː-/ *n* [C] a strange feeling that something, especially something bad, is going to happen: **[+of]** *a premonition of death* | **premonition that** *When Anne didn't arrive, Paul* ***had*** *a* ***premonition*** *that she was in danger.*

pre·mon·i·to·ry /prɪˈmɒnətəri $ -ˈmɑːnətɔːri/ *adj formal* giving a warning that something unpleasant is going to happen: *premonitory symptoms of the disease*

pre·na·tal /ˌpriːˈneɪtl◂/ *adj* [only before noun] relating to unborn babies and the care of PREGNANT women OPP **postnatal** SYN **antenatal** *BrE*: *prenatal care* | *prenatal screening* —**prenatally** *adv*

pre·nup·tial a·gree·ment /priːˌnʌpʃəl əˈgriːmənt/ (*also* **pre-nup** /ˈpriːnʌp/ *informal*) *n* [C] a legal document that is written before a man and a woman get married, in which they agree things such as how much money each will get if they DIVORCE

pre·oc·cu·pa·tion /priːˌɒkjəˈpeɪʃən $ -ˌɑːk-/ ●○○ *n*

1 [singular, U] when someone thinks or worries about something a lot, with the result that they do not pay attention to other things: **[+with]** *the current preoccupation with sex and scandal* | *The management's preoccupation with costs and profits resulted in a drop in quality and customer service.*

2 [C] something that you give all your attention to: **main/chief/central etc preoccupation** *Their main preoccupation was how to feed their families.*

pre·oc·cu·pied /priːˈɒkjəpaɪd $ -ˈɑːk-/ *adj* thinking about something a lot, with the result that you do not pay attention to other things: *What's wrong with Cindy? She seems a little preoccupied.* | **[+with]** *He's completely preoccupied with all the wedding preparations at the moment.*

pre·oc·cu·py /priːˈɒkjəpaɪ $ -ˈɑːk-/ *v* (**preoccupied**, **preoccupying**, **preoccupies**) [T] *formal* if something preoccupies someone, they think or worry about it a lot

pre·op·e·ra·tive /priˈɒpərətɪv $ -ˈɑːp-/ *adj medical* relating to the time before a medical operation OPP **post-operative**: *the patient's preoperative assessment*

pre·or·dained /ˌpriːɔːˈdeɪnd◂ $ -ɔːr-/ *adj formal* if something is preordained, it is certain to happen in the future because God or FATE has decided it: *Is everything we do preordained?*

pre-owned /ˌpriː ˈəʊnd◂ $ -ˈoʊnd◂/ *adj* if something that is for sale is pre-owned, it has been owned and used by someone else before – used especially in advertisements to make something not sound old SYN **second-hand** *BrE*, **used** *AmE*: *pre-owned cars*

prep[1] /prep/ *n* [U] *BrE informal* work that is done by students on their own, after classes have finished – used in private schools SYN **homework**

prep[2] *v* (*past participle* **prepped**, *present participle* **prepping**) *AmE informal* **1** [T] to prepare someone for an operation or an examination **2** [T] to prepare food for cooking in a restaurant **3** [I] to prepare for something that you are going to do: *I have to prep for my afternoon class.*

prep. (*also* **prep** *BrE*) the written abbreviation of ***preposition***

pre·pack·aged /ˌpriːˈpækɪdʒd◂/ *adj* prepackaged foods have already been prepared when you buy them, so that they are ready to eat, or only have to be heated: *prepackaged microwave meals*

pre·packed /ˌpriːˈpækt◂/ *adj* prepacked food or other goods are wrapped before they are sent to the shop where they are sold: *prepacked vegetables*

pre·paid /ˌpriːˈpeɪd◂/ *adj* if something is prepaid, it is paid for before it is needed or used: *The shipping charges are prepaid.* | *a prepaid envelope*

prep·a·ra·tion /ˌprepəˈreɪʃən/ ●●○ S3 W3 *n*

1 [singular, U] the process of preparing something or preparing for something: *This dish is good for dinner parties because much of the preparation can be done ahead of time.* | **[+for]** *Business training is a good preparation for any career.* | **[+of]** *the preparation of the budget* | **do sth in preparation for sth** (=in order to prepare for something) *He is practising every day, in preparation for the ice-skating championship.* | *Plans for the new school* ***are now in preparation***. | *a course in food service and* ***food preparation***

2 preparations [plural] arrangements for something that is going to happen: **[+for]** *Preparations for the upcoming Olympic Games are nearing completion.* | ***Preparations*** *are*

being ***made*** *for the president's visit.* | *The festival was a great success, and* ***preparations are underway*** (=have started) *for another one next summer.*
3 [C] *formal* a mixture that has been prepared and that is used for a particular purpose, especially as a medicine or to make your skin more attractive: *a new preparation for cleansing the skin*

pre·par·a·to·ry /prɪˈpærətəri $ -tɔːri/ *adj* **1** [only before noun] done in order to get ready for something: *preparatory talks to clear the way for a peace settlement* | *preparatory drawings* | *A lot of preparatory work still needs to be done.* **2 preparatory to sth** *formal* before something else and in order to prepare for it: *The partners held several meetings preparatory to signing the agreement.*

preˈparatory ˌschool *n* [C] **1** a private school in Britain for children between the ages of 8 and 13 **2** a private school in the US that prepares students for college

Frequencies of **prepare, get ready** and **make preparations** in spoken and written English.

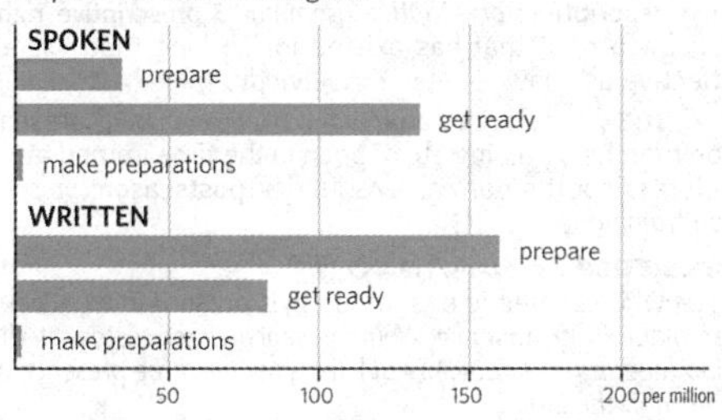

Make preparations is less general than **prepare** and **get ready**, and is usually used to talk about making a large number of arrangements for something important that is going to happen.

pre·pare /prɪˈpeə $ -ˈper/ ●●● S1 W1 *v*
1 MAKE STH [T] **a)** to make a meal or a substance: *Prepare the sauce while the pasta is cooking.* | *When we got home, Stephano was busy preparing dinner.* **b)** to write a document, make a programme etc: *Health and safety officers will investigate the site and prepare a report.* | *Green set himself the task of preparing a map of this remote area.* **THESAURUS** ▸ COOK
2 MAKE PLANS/ARRANGEMENTS [I,T] to make plans or arrangements for something that will happen in the future SYN **get ready**: **[+for]** *The 45-year-old explorer has been preparing for his latest expedition to the Arctic.* | **prepare to do sth** *Her parents were busy preparing to go on holiday.* | *The prosecution wanted more time to prepare their case.*
3 MAKE STH READY [T] to make something ready to be used: *Prepare the soil, then plant the seedlings eight inches apart.* | **prepare sth for sb/sth** *Coulthard's team were up all night preparing the car for the race.*
4 MAKE YOURSELF READY [T] to make yourself mentally or physically ready for something that you expect to happen soon: **prepare yourself (for sth)** *The letter arrived, and we prepared ourselves for bad news.* | *Can you just give me a couple more moments to prepare myself?* | **prepare yourself for a race/fight etc** *The Chicago Bears are busy preparing themselves for the big game.* | **prepare to do sth** *Buy the album, and prepare to be amazed.*
5 MAKE SB READY [T] to provide someone with the training, skills, experience etc that they will need to do a job or to deal with a situation: **prepare sb for sth** *a course that prepares students for English examinations* | *Schools should do more to prepare children for the world of work.* | *What does a coach do to prepare his team for the Superbowl?*
6 prepare the way/ground for sb/sth to make it possible for something to be achieved, or for someone to succeed in doing something: *Curie's research prepared the way for the work of modern nuclear scientists.*

THESAURUS

TO PREPARE FOR AN EVENT

prepare to make plans or arrangements for something that will happen in the future so that you will be ready when it happens: *He only had a few hours to prepare for the interview.* | *The family are preparing to move to Queensland.*
get ready to prepare for something. **Get ready** is less formal than **prepare** and is the usual phrase to use in everyday English: *Smith has been busy getting ready for the race.* | *The army was getting ready to attack.*
make preparations to prepare for an event that needs a lot of planning: *The couple are making preparations for their wedding next year.*
gear up to prepare for an important event - used about companies, organizations, cities etc: *Stores are gearing up for the busy Christmas shopping period.* | *The city is gearing up for the Olympics.*

TO PREPARE SOMETHING SO IT CAN BE USED

prepare to make something ready to be used: *Have you prepared your speech?* | *Groundsmen were preparing the pitch for tomorrow's game.*
get sth ready to prepare something. **Get sth ready** is less formal than **prepare** and is the usual phrase to use in everyday English: *They were getting the ship ready to sail.*
set (sth) up to prepare equipment so that it is ready to be used: *It will take a few minutes to set the camera up.* | *The band was setting up on the stage.*

pre·pared /prɪˈpeəd $ -ˈperd/ ●●○ *adj*
1 be prepared to do sth to be willing to do something, especially something difficult or something that you do not usually do: *You have to be prepared to take risks in this kind of work.* | *How much is she prepared to pay?*
2 READY TO DEAL WITH STH [not before noun] ready to do something or deal with a situation: **[+for]** *I wasn't prepared for all their questions.* | **well/fully/inadequately etc prepared** *Luckily, we were well prepared for the storm.* | **ill-prepared** (=not ready to deal with a difficult situation) *The country was ill-prepared to fight another war.* | *There was no news and we were* ***prepared for the worst*** (=expected something very bad). **THESAURUS** ▸ READY
3 I'm not prepared to do sth *spoken* used when saying strongly that you refuse to do something: *I'm not prepared to sit here and listen to this rubbish!*
4 MADE EARLIER planned, made, or written at an earlier time, so that it is ready when it is needed: *The president read out a* ***prepared statement***.

pre·pared·ness /prɪˈpeədnəs, -ˈpeərəd- $ -ˈperəd-, -ˈperd-/ *n* [U] *formal* **1** when someone is ready for something: *the country's lack of military preparedness* **2** when someone is willing to do something: *their preparedness to break the law*

pre·pay /priːˈpeɪ/ *v* (*past tense and past participle* **prepaid**) [I,T] to pay for something before you need it or use it —**prepayment** *n* [C,U]

pre-pay /ˈpriː peɪ/ *adj* [only before noun] pre-pay MOBILE PHONE systems make you pay before you use the service, rather than sending you a demand for money after you have been using it → **pay-as-you-go**

pre·pon·de·rance /prɪˈpɒndərəns $ -ˈpɑːn-/ *n formal* **1 a preponderance of sth** if there is a preponderance of people or things of a particular type in a group, there are more of that type than of any other: *There is a preponderance of female students in the music department.* **2 a preponderance of the evidence** *law* most of the EVIDENCE in a law case

pre·pon·de·rant /prɪˈpɒndərənt $ -ˈpɑːn-/ *adj formal* main, most important, or most frequent —**preponderantly** *adv*: *the preponderantly female staff at the factory*

pre·pon·de·rate /prɪˈpɒndəreɪt $ -ˈpɑːn-/ *v* [I] *formal* to be more important or frequent than something else

prep·o·si·tion /ˌprepəˈzɪʃən/ ●●● *n* [C] a word that is used before a noun, PRONOUN, or GERUND to show place, time, direction etc. In the phrase 'the trees in the park', 'in' is a preposition. —**prepositional** *adj*

ˌprepositional ˈphrase *n* [C] *technical* a phrase beginning with a preposition, such as 'in bed' or 'at war'

P

pre·pos·sess·ing /ˌpriːpəˈzesɪŋ◂/ *adj formal* looking attractive or pleasant: *a prepossessing smile*

pre·pos·ter·ous /prɪˈpɒstərəs $ -ˈpɑːs-/ *adj formal* completely unreasonable or silly SYN **absurd**: *The whole idea sounds absolutely preposterous!* —**preposterously** *adv* —**preposterousness** *n* [U]

prep·py /ˈprepi/ *adj AmE informal* preppy clothes or styles are very neat, in a way that is typical of students who go to expensive private schools in the US

ˈprep school *n* [C,U] *informal* a PREPARATORY SCHOOL

pre·pu·bes·cent /ˌpriːpjuːˈbesənt◂/ *adj formal* relating to the time just before a child reaches PUBERTY

pre·quel /ˈpriːkwəl/ *n* [C] a book, film etc that tells you what happened before the story told in a previous popular book or film → **sequel**: **[+to]** *'The Phantom Menace' is a prequel to 'Star Wars'.*

Pre-Raph·ae·lite /ˌpriː ˈræfəlaɪt $ -ˈræfiə-/ *adj* **1** relating to the members of a group of late 19th-century English painters and artists: *a Pre-Raphaelite painting* **2** used to describe a woman's hair that is long and curly —**Pre-Raphaelite** *n* [C]

pre·re·cord /ˌpriːrɪˈkɔːd $ -ˈkɔːrd/ *v* [T] to record music, a radio programme etc on a machine so that it can be used later: *a prerecorded interview* —**prerecording** *n* [C,U]

pre·req·ui·site /priːˈrekwəzət/ *n* [C] *formal* something that is necessary before something else can happen or be done: **[+for/of/to]** *A reasonable proficiency in English is a prerequisite for the course.*

pre·rog·a·tive /prɪˈrɒgətɪv $ -ˈrɑː-/ *n* [C usually singular] a right that someone has, especially because of their importance or social position: **[+of]** *Education was once the prerogative of the elite.* | *Arriving late is* ***a woman's prerogative***. | ***the royal prerogative*** (=the rights of kings and queens)

pres. (*also* **pres** *BrE*) **1** the written abbreviation of ***present*** **2** the written abbreviation of ***president***

pres·age /ˈpresɪdʒ, prəˈseɪdʒ/ *v* [T] *formal* to be a sign that something is going to happen, especially something bad: *The large number of moderate earthquakes that have occurred recently could presage a larger quake soon.* —**presage** *n* [C]: *a presage of doom*

Pres·by·te·ri·an /ˌprezbəˈtɪəriən◂ $ -ˈtɪr-/ *n* [C] a member of a Protestant church, which is one of the largest churches in the US, and is the national church of Scotland —**Presbyterian** *adj* —**Presbyterianism** *n* [U]

pres·by·ter·y /ˈprezbətəri $ -teri/ *n* (*plural* **presbyteries**) [C] **1** a local court or council of the Presbyterian church or the area controlled by that church **2** a house in which a Roman Catholic priest lives **3** the eastern part of a church, behind the area where the CHOIR (=singers) sits

pre·school¹, **pre-school** /ˈpriːskuːl/ *adj* relating to the time in a child's life before they are old enough to go to school: *preschool children*

preschool² *n* [C,U] *AmE* a school for children between two and five years of age SYN **kindergarten** *BrE*

preschool·er /ˌpriː ˈskuːlə $ -ər/ *n* [C] *AmE* a child who does not yet go to school, or who goes to preschool

pre·sci·ent /ˈpresiənt $ ˈpreʃənt, ˈpriː-/ *adj formal* able to imagine or know what will happen in the future —**prescience** *n* [U]

pre·scribe /prɪˈskraɪb/ ●●○ *v* [T]

1 to say what medicine or treatment a sick person should have → **prescription**: **prescribe sb sth** *If these don't work I may have to prescribe you something stronger.* | **prescribe sth for sth** *the drugs prescribed for his stomach pains*

2 *formal* to state officially what should be done in a particular situation: *What punishment does the law prescribe for this crime?*

pre·scribed /prɪˈskraɪbd/ *adj* decided by a rule: *All schools must follow the prescribed curriculum.*

pre·script /ˈpriːˌskrɪpt/ *n* [C] *formal* an official order or rule

pre·scrip·tion /prɪˈskrɪpʃən/ ●●○ *n* [C]

1 a piece of paper on which a doctor writes what medicine a sick person should have, so that they can get it from a PHARMACIST → **prescribe**: **[+for]** *a prescription for sleeping pills* | *We are trying to cut the price of* ***prescription drugs***. | *a* ***repeat prescription*** (=one that you have regularly) | **fill a prescription** *AmE* (=get the drugs a doctor has written that you need) *I got the prescription filled on the way home.*

2 a particular medicine or treatment ordered by a doctor for a sick person: *If you're pregnant, you can get free prescriptions.*

3 on prescription *BrE*, **by prescription** *AmE* a drug that you get on prescription can only be obtained with a written order from the doctor → **over the counter**

4 an idea or suggestion about how you should behave, or how to make a situation, activity etc successful: **[+for]** *The party's main prescription for educational problems was to give schools more money.*

pre·scrip·tive /prɪˈskrɪptɪv/ *adj* **1** saying how something should or must be done, or what should be done: *prescriptive teaching methods* **2** stating how a language should be used, rather than describing how it is used OPP **descriptive**: *prescriptive grammar* **3 prescriptive right** *BrE law* a right that has existed for so long that it is as effective as a law —**prescriptively** *adv*

pre·sea·son /ˌpriːˈsiːzən◂/ *adj* [only before noun] preseason matches, training etc happen in the time immediately before a sport's normal SEASON OPP **postseason**: *preseason training*

pres·ence /ˈprezəns/ ●●○ W3 *n*

1 [U] when someone or something is present in a particular place OPP **absence**: *Your presence is requested at the club meeting on Friday.* | **[+of]** *Tests revealed the presence of poison in the blood.*

2 in the presence of sb (*also* **in sb's presence**) *formal* with someone or in the same place as them: *He was determined not to complain in the presence of the nurse.* | *I asked you not to smoke in my presence.*

3 APPEARANCE/MANNER [U] the ability to appear impressive to people because of your appearance or the way you behave: *a man of great presence*

4 OFFICIAL GROUP [singular] a group of people, especially soldiers, who are in a place to control what is happening: *We will increase* ***police presence*** *in local communities.* | *Soldiers still maintain a* ***military presence*** *in the area.*

5 BUSINESS [C usually singular] the ability to gain sales because your business is strong or noticeable: *a company with a strong presence in all major world markets*

6 SPIRIT [C usually singular] a spirit or influence that cannot be seen but is felt to be near: *They felt a strange presence in the deserted house.*

7 make your presence felt to have a strong and noticeable effect on the people around you or the situation you are in: *She was a very pretty girl and made her presence felt almost at once.*

ˌpresence of ˈmind *n* [U] the ability to deal with a dangerous situation calmly and quickly: **have the presence of mind to do sth** *I'm glad she had the presence of mind to take down the car's registration number.*

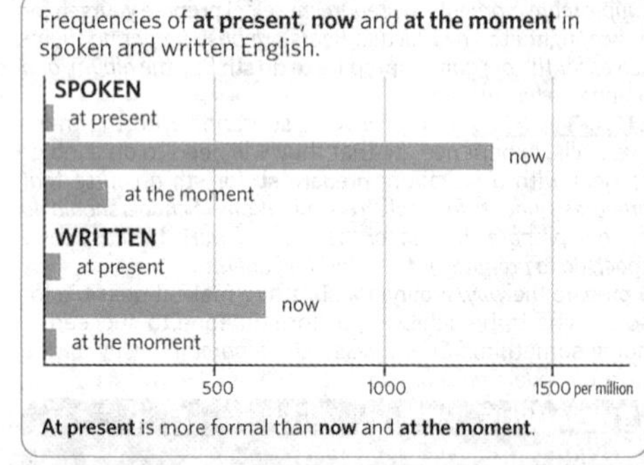

pres·ent¹ /ˈprezənt/ ●●● S2 W2 *adj*

1 PLACE [not before noun] in a particular place OPP **absent**:

[+at/in] *Foreign observers were present at the elections.* | *the gases present in the Earth's atmosphere*
2 MEMORY [not before noun] to be felt strongly or remembered for a long time: **[+in]** *The memory of her brother's death is still present in her mind.*
3 TIME [only before noun] happening or existing now: *the **present situation** of the millions of people who are suffering poverty and disease* | ***At the present time** we have no explanation for this.*
4 the present day (*also* **the present**) in the time now, or modern times: *The practice has continued from medieval times to the present day.*
5 all present and correct *BrE*, **all present and accounted for** *AmE* used to say that everyone who is supposed to be in a place, at a meeting etc is now here
6 present company excepted *spoken* used when you are criticizing a group of people and you want to tell the people you are with that they are not included in the criticism: *Women are never satisfied with anything! Present company excepted, of course.* → PRESENTLY

pre·sent² /prɪˈzent/ ●●● S2 W2 *v*
1 GIVE [T] to give something to someone, for example at a formal or official occasion: **present sb with sth** *He was presented with a bottle of champagne.* | *She was **presented** with an **award**.* | **present sth to sb/sth** *The computer centre presented a cheque for £500 to cancer research.* **THESAURUS** ▸ GIVE
2 CAUSE STH TO HAPPEN [T] to cause something to happen or exist: **present sb with sth** *I knew I had presented her with an impossible task.* | **present a problem/difficulty** *Large classes present great problems to many teachers.*
3 present yourself to talk and behave in a particular way when you meet people: *He presents himself well.*
4 DESCRIPTION [T] to show or describe someone or something: *The artist was determined to present an accurate picture.* | *We'll present the information using a chart.* | **present sb as sth** *Shakespeare presents the hero as a noble man doomed to make mistakes.* | **present yourself as sth** *The government presents itself as being sensitive to environmental issues.*
5 SPEECH [T] to give a speech in which you offer an idea, plan etc to be considered or accepted: *Our manager is due to present the report at the end of the month.* | **present sth to sb** *On January 3 the company will present its plans to the bank.*
6 DOCUMENT/TICKET [T] to show something such as an official document or ticket to someone in an official position: *You must present your passport to the customs officer.*
7 THEATRE/CINEMA [T] to give a performance in a theatre, cinema etc, or broadcast a programme on television or radio: *Edinburgh Theatre Company presents 'The Wind in the Willows'.*
8 TELEVISION/RADIO [T] *BrE* if you present a television or radio programme, you introduce its different parts SYN **host** *AmE*: *Thursday's 'The Late Show' was presented by Cynthia Rose.*
9 APPEARANCE [T] to give something or someone a particular appearance or style: *The restaurant likes to present food with style.*
10 sth presents itself if a situation, opportunity etc presents itself, it suddenly happens or exists: *I'll tell her as soon as the **opportunity presents itself**.*
11 FORMALLY INTRODUCE SB [T] to formally introduce someone to another person, especially to someone of a very high rank: *I was presented to the Queen in 1964.*
12 present your apologies/compliments etc *formal* used to greet someone, say sorry to them etc very politely: *Mrs. Gottlieb presents her apologies and regrets she will not be able to attend.*
13 ILLNESS [I,T] *medical* to show an illness by having a particular SYMPTOM (=sign of an illness): *The doctor asked whether any of the children had been presenting any unusual symptoms.* | *Three of the five patients presented with fever and severe headaches.*
14 present arms when soldiers present arms, they hold their guns straight up in front of them while an officer or other important person walks past

pres·ent³ /ˈprezənt/ ●●● S2 W3 *n*
1 [C] something you give someone on a special occasion or to thank them for something SYN **gift**: *I'm looking for a present for Mark.*
2 the present a) the time that is happening now: *Stop worrying about the past and live in the present.* | *The film is set sometime between 1995 and the present.* | *'When do you want to start?' 'Well, there's **no time like the present*** (=used to say that if you are going to do something at all, you should do it now).' **b)** *technical* the form of the verb that shows what exists or is happening now SYN **the present tense**
3 at present at this time SYN **now**: *The item you want is not available at present.* | *At present, the airport handles 110 flights a day.*

> REGISTER
> In everyday English, people usually say **at the moment** rather than **at present**: *I'm looking for a new job **at the moment**.*

4 for the present something that exists or will be done for the present exists now and will continue for a while, though it may change in the future: *The company is still in business, at least for the present.*

> REGISTER
> In everyday English, people usually say **for now**, rather than **for the present**: *That's all we have time for, **for now**.*

> **COLLOCATIONS**
> **VERBS**
> **give sb a present** *He gave everyone a present.*
> **give sth as a present** *I was given this book as a present.*
> **buy sb a present** (*also* **get sb a present** *informal*) *I want to buy a present for Lucy but I'm not sure what she'd like.* | *Did you get Bill a birthday present?*
> **get a present** (=receive a present) *Children soon learn to enjoy giving presents as well as getting them.*
> **wrap a present** *She spent the afternoon wrapping Christmas presents.*
> **open/unwrap a present** *Can we open our presents now?*
> **ADJECTIVES/NOUN + present**
> **a birthday present** *Thanks for the birthday present.*
> **a Christmas present** *What would Dad like as a Christmas present?*
> **a wedding present** *His wedding present to her had been a diamond necklace.*
> **COMMON ERRORS**
> ⚠ Don't say 'unpack a present'. Say **open a present**.

pre·sent·a·ble /prɪˈzentəbəl/ *adj* tidy and attractive enough to be seen or shown to someone: *She's a presentable young woman.* | *Let's tidy up and **make** the house a bit more **presentable**.* | *I must go and **make myself presentable**.* —**presentably** *adv*

pre·sen·ta·tion /ˌprezənˈteɪʃən $ ˌpriːzen-, -zən-/ ●●○ S3 *n*
1 GIVE PRIZE [C] the act of giving someone a prize or present at a formal ceremony: *the presentation ceremony* | *Dr Evans thanked him for coming to **make** the **presentations**.* | **[+of]** *the presentation of prizes*
2 TALK [C] an event at which you describe or explain a new product or idea: *We will begin a series of presentations to help the public fully understand our system.* | **make/give a presentation** *I'm going to ask each of you to make a short presentation.* **THESAURUS** ▸ SPEECH
3 WAY OF SAYING/SHOWING [U] the way in which something is said, offered, shown, or explained to others: **[+of]**

desktop devices for the presentation of information | the presentation of evidence
4 PROOF [U] when you show something to someone so that it can be checked or considered: **[+of]** *the presentation of the identity documents* | **on presentation of sth** *Club members will be admitted on presentation of their membership cards.*
5 PERFORMANCE [C] the act of performing a play: **[+of]** *I went to see the National Theatre's presentation of Arthur Miller's 'The Last Yankee'.*
6 BABY [C,U] *medical* the position in which a baby is lying in its mother's body just before it is born: *a breech presentation*
7 presentation copy a book that is given to someone, especially by the writer or PUBLISHER —**presentational** *adj*

ˈpresent-day *adj* [only before noun] modern or existing now: *present-day Sicily*

pres·en·tee·is·m /ˌprezənˈtiːɪzəm/ *n* [U] a situation when people spend a lot of time at work, even if they are ill or could take a holiday, because they want their employers to see that they are working very hard → **absenteeism**

pre·sent·er /prɪˈzentə $ -ər/ ●○○ *n* [C] *BrE* someone who introduces the different parts of a television or radio show SYN **host** *AmE*: *the presenter of BBC 2's 'Newsnight'*

pre·sen·ti·ment /prɪˈzentəmənt/ *n* [C] *formal* a strange feeling that something is going to happen, especially something bad SYN **premonition**: **[+of]** *a presentiment of disaster*

pres·ent·ly /ˈprezəntli/ ●○○ *adv formal*
1 in a short time SYN **soon**: *The doctor will be here presently.* | *Presently, I fell asleep.*
2 *especially AmE* at the present time SYN **now**: *The range of courses* ***presently available*** *has grown.* | *Your case is presently being investigated.*

ˌpresent ˈparticiple ●●○ *n* [C] *technical* a PARTICIPLE that is formed in English by adding 'ing' to the verb, as in 'sleeping'. It can be used in COMPOUND forms of the verb to show CONTINUOUS tenses, as in 'she's sleeping', or as an adjective, as in 'the sleeping child'.

ˌpresent ˈperfect ●●○ *n* **the present perfect** the form of a verb that shows what happened during a period of time up to and including the present, formed in English with the present tense of the verb 'have' and a PAST PARTICIPLE, as in 'he has gone'

ˌpresent ˈtense ●●○ *n* **the present tense** *technical* the form of the verb that shows what exists or is happening now SYN **the present**

pres·er·va·tion /ˌprezəˈveɪʃən $ -zər-/ ●○○ *n* [U]
1 when something is kept in its original state or in good condition → **preserve**: **[+of]** *Eliot campaigned for the preservation of London's churches.* | *We are working for the preservation of the environment.* | *the preservation of our cultural heritage* | *methods of food preservation*
2 the act of making sure that a situation continues without changing: **[+of]** *the preservation of peace in the region*
3 the degree to which something has remained unchanged or unharmed by weather, age etc: *The arena is in an exceptionally fine* ***state of preservation.***
→ SELF-PRESERVATION

pres·er·va·tion·ist /ˌprezəˈveɪʃənɪst $ -zər-/ *n* [C] someone who works to prevent historical places, buildings etc from being destroyed

preserˈvation ˌorder *n* [C] in Britain, an official order that something, especially an area of countryside or an old building, must be preserved and not damaged: *a tree preservation order*

pre·ser·va·tive /prɪˈzɜːvətɪv $ -ɜːr-/ *n* [C,U] a chemical substance that is used to prevent things from decaying, for example food or wood: *food that contains no* ***artificial preservatives***

pre·serve¹ /prɪˈzɜːv $ -ɜːrv/ ●●○ W3 *v* [T]
1 to save something or someone from being harmed or destroyed → **preservation**: *We must encourage the planting of new trees and preserve our existing woodlands.* THESAURUS PROTECT
2 to make something continue without changing: *the responsibility of the police to preserve the peace* | *Norma tried to preserve a normal family life in difficult circumstances.*
3 to store food for a long time after treating it so that it will not decay: *black olives preserved in brine* —**preservable** *adj* —**preserver** *n* [C] → WELL-PRESERVED

preserve² *n* **1** [C usually plural] a substance made from boiling fruit or vegetables with sugar, salt, or VINEGAR: *homemade fruit preserves* **2** [singular] an activity that is only suitable or allowed for a particular group of people: *Banking used to be a* ***male preserve.*** | **[+of]** *The civil service became the preserve of the educated middle class.* **3** [C] an area of land or water that is kept for private hunting or fishing

pre-set /ˌpriː ˈset◂/ *adj* [usually before noun] decided or set at an earlier time: *The heating automatically switches on and off at pre-set temperatures.*

pre-shrunk /ˌpriː ˈʃrʌŋk◂/ *adj* pre-shrunk clothes are sold after they have been made smaller by being washed → **shrink**: *pre-shrunk jeans*

pre·side /prɪˈzaɪd/ *v* [I] to be in charge of a formal event, organization, ceremony etc: *I shall be pleased to preside at your meetings.* | *Mr Justice Waller, presiding judge for the north east*

preside over sth *phr v* **1** to be in a position of authority at a time when important things are happening: *The government seemed to be presiding over large-scale unemployment.* **2** to be the head of a company or organization: *Finch presided over the company for 30 years.* **3** to be in charge of a meeting or activity: *The chairman will preside over an audience of architects and developers.*

pres·i·den·cy /ˈprezədənsi/ ●○○ *n* (*plural* **presidencies**) [C] the position of being the president of a country or organization, or the period of time during which someone is president: *Roosevelt was elected four times to the presidency of the US.* | *There were few real improvements during his presidency.*

Pres·i·dent, president /ˈprezɪdənt/ ●●● S2 W2 *n* [C]
1 the official leader of a country that does not have a king or queen → **vice-president**: **[+of]** *the president of France* | *President Bush*
2 the person who has the highest position in a company or organization → **vice-president**: **[+of]** *the president of General Motors*

ˌpresident-eˈlect *n* [singular] someone who has been elected as a new president, but who has not yet started the job

pres·i·den·tial /ˌprezɪˈdenʃəl◂/ ●●○ *adj* [usually before noun] relating to a president: *a presidential election* | *the party's presidential candidate*

pre·sid·i·um, praesidium /prɪˈsɪdiəm, -ˈzɪ-/ *n* (*plural* **presidia** /-diə/) [C] a committee chosen to represent a large political organization, especially in a COMMUNIST country

press¹ /pres/ ●●● S2 W1 *n*
1 NEWS **a) the press** people who write reports for newspapers, radio, or television: *the* ***freedom of the press*** | *The press has been very nasty about him.*

> **GRAMMAR: Singular or plural verb?**
> • **The press** is usually followed by a singular verb: *The press* ***does*** *not always report the whole story.*
> • In British English, you can also use a plural verb: *The press* ***do*** *not always report the whole story.*
> GRAMMAR GUIDE NOUNS

b) reports in newspapers and on radio and television: *To judge from the press, the concert was a great success.* | **press reports** | *The band has received good* ***press coverage*** (=the reports written about something in newspapers). | **local/national etc press** *The story was widely covered in the national press.* | **tabloid/popular etc press**

2 get/be given a bad press to be criticized in the newspapers or on radio or television: *The government's policy on mental health care is getting an increasingly bad press.*
3 get/have a good press to be praised in the newspapers or on radio or television: *Our recycling policy is getting a good press.*
4 PRINTING [C] **a)** a business that prints and sometimes also sells books: *the Clarendon Press* **b)** (*also* **printing press**) a machine that prints books, newspapers, or magazines
5 MACHINE [C] a piece of equipment used to put weight on something in order to make it flat or to force liquid out of it: *a trouser press | a flower press*
6 PUSH [C, usually singular] *especially BrE* a light steady push against something small: *Give the button another press.*
7 go to press if a newspaper, magazine, or book goes to press, it begins to be printed: *All information was correct at the time we went to press.*
8 CROWD [singular + of] *especially BrE* a crowd of people pushing against each other

press² ●●● S1 W2 *v*
1 AGAINST STH [T always + adv/prep] to push something firmly against a surface SYN **push**: *Manville kept his back pressed flat against the wall. | She pressed the gas pedal and the car leapt forwards. | He pressed a card into her hand before leaving.*
2 BUTTON [T] to push a button, switch etc to make a machine start, a bell ring etc SYN **push**: *Lily* ***pressed*** *the* ***switch*** *and plunged the room into darkness. | Press control, alt, delete to log on to the computer.*
3 CLOTHES [T] to make clothes smooth using a hot iron SYN **iron**: *I'll need to press my suit.*
4 CROWD [I always + adv/prep] to move in a particular direction by pushing: *The car rocked as the crowd pressed hard against it.*
5 PERSUADE [I,T] to try hard to persuade someone to do something, especially by asking them many times: *I felt that if I had pressed him he would have lent me the money.* | **press sb to do sth** *The police pressed her to remember all the details.* | **press sb for sth** *The manufacturers are pressing the government for action.* | **[+for]** *We must continue to press for full equality. | I was* ***pressing*** *my* ***claim*** *for custody of the child.*
6 HEAVY WEIGHT [T] to put pressure or a weight on something to make it flat, crush it etc: *pressed flowers | At this stage the grapes have to be pressed.*
7 HOLD SB/STH CLOSE [T] to hold someone or something close to you: **press sb/sth to you** *He reached out and pressed her to him.*
8 press sb's hand/arm to hold someone's hand or arm tightly for a short time, to show friendship, sympathy etc: *Sometimes he was too ill to speak, and just pressed my hand.*
9 press charges to say officially that someone has done something illegal and must go to court
10 be pressed for time/cash etc to not have enough time, money etc: *a government department that is pressed for both time and money*
11 GIVE [T] to offer something to someone and try to make them take it: **press sth on sb** *I pressed money on him, but he refused to take it.*
12 EXERCISE [T] to push a weight up from your chest using only your arms, without moving your legs or feet
13 press sb/sth into service to persuade someone to help you, or to use something to help you do something because of an unexpected problem or need: *The army was pressed into service to fight the fires.*
14 press the flesh to shake hands with a lot of people – used humorously: *The president reached into the crowd to press the flesh.*
15 press sth home a) to push something into its place: *Jane slammed the door and pressed the bolt home.* **b)** to repeat or emphasize something, so that people remember it: *He decided it was time to* ***press*** *his* ***point*** *home.*
16 press home your advantage to try to succeed completely, using an advantage that you have gained
17 RECORD [T] to make a copy of a record, CD etc → **be hard pressed to do sth** at HARD²(5)
press on (*also* **press ahead** *phr v*) to continue doing something, especially working, in a determined way: *We'll talk about your suggestion later – now let's just press on.* | **[+with]** *Shall we press ahead with the minutes of the last meeting?*

ˈpress ˌagency *n* [C] an organization that gets news from a country and supplies it to newspapers, television news etc all over the world

ˈpress ˌagent *n* [C] someone whose job is to supply photographs or information about a particular actor, musician etc to newspapers, radio, or television

ˈpress ˌbaron *n* [C] *BrE* someone who owns and controls one or more important national newspapers

ˈpress box *n* [C] an area at a sports STADIUM where people from newspapers, radio, or television sit

ˈpress ˌconference *n* [C] a meeting held by a person or group at which they answer questions from people who write or present news reports: *The Green Party* ***held a press conference*** *the next day.*

ˈpress corps *n* [C] a group of news REPORTERS working at the place where something important is happening: *the White House press corps*

ˈpress ˌcutting (*also* **ˈpress ˌclipping**) *n* [C] a short piece of writing or a picture, cut out from a newspaper or magazine

pressed /prest/ *adj* **be pressed for time/money etc** to not have enough time, money etc

ˈpress ˌgallery *n* [C] an area above or at the back of a hall, used by news REPORTERS

ˈpress-gang¹ *v* [T] **1 press-gang sb into doing sth** *informal* to force someone to do something: *I don't want to press-gang you into doing something you're not happy with.* **2** to force men to work on a ship, by taking them from the streets – done in the past

press-gang² *n* [C] a group of people in the past who took young men away using force in order to make them come to work on a ship

pres·sie, **prezzie** /ˈprezi/ *n* [C] *BrE spoken* a present

press·ing¹ /ˈpresɪŋ/ ●○○ *adj* needing to be discussed or dealt with very soon SYN **urgent**: **pressing problem/matter/need etc** *Poverty is a more pressing problem than pollution.*

pressing² *n* **1** [C] a thing or group of things, especially records or CDs, that have been made by pressing plastic or metal into shape: *The CD, released in October, sold out a first pressing of 1,500 in just four months.* **2** [C,U] the act of pressing something: *The olives are heat treated during the second pressing.*

press·man /ˈpresmæn/ *n* (*plural* **pressmen** /-men/) [C] *BrE informal* someone who writes news reports

ˈpress ˌoffice *n* [C] the office of an organization or government department which gives information to the newspapers, radio, or television —**press officer** *n* [C]

ˈpress reˌlease *n* [C] an official statement giving information to the newspapers, radio, or television

ˈpress ˌsecretary *n* [C] a secretary to an important organization or person, who gives information about them to the newspapers, radio, or television

ˈpress stud *n* [C] *BrE* a small metal thing that is used to fasten clothes, which works when you press its two parts together SYN **popper** *BrE*, **snap** *AmE*

ˈpress-up *n* [C] *BrE* a type of exercise in which you lie facing the ground, and push your body up with your arms SYN **push-up** *AmE* → see picture at GYM

pres·sure¹ /ˈpreʃə $ -ər/ ●●● S1 W1 *n*
1 PERSUADE [U] an attempt to persuade someone by using influence, arguments, or threats: *They are* ***putting pressure on*** *people to vote yes.* | **be/come under pressure to do sth** *The minister was under pressure to resign.* | **be/come under pressure from sb (to do sth)** *I was under pressure from my parents to become a teacher. | The Labour government came under pressure from the trade unions.* | **[+for]** *Pressure*

P

for change has become urgent. | **[+on]** *the pressure on all of us to keep slim* | *He* ***exerts pressure on*** *his kids to get them to do as he wants.* | *You must never* ***give in to pressure****.*

2 ANXIETY/OVERWORK [C,U] a way of working or living that causes you a lot of anxiety, especially because you feel you have too many things to do: **[+of]** *I feel I'm not able to cope well with the pressures of life.* | **[+on]** *The pressure on doctors is increasing steadily.* | **under pressure** *I'm under constant pressure at work.* | *The* ***pressures of work*** *can make you ill.* | *a* ***high pressure*** *job* | *athletes who show* ***grace under pressure*** (=who behave well when they are anxious)

3 CAUSING CHANGE [C,U] events or conditions that cause changes and affect the way a situation develops, especially in ECONOMICS or politics: *inflationary pressures* | *Analysts expect the pound to* ***come under pressure****.* | **relieve/reduce pressure (on sb/sth)** *Slowing the arms race relieved pressure on the Soviet economic system.* | *The 1990s* ***brought*** *increased economic* ***pressure to bear on*** *all business activities.*

4 WEIGHT [U] the force or weight that is being put on to something: **[+of]** *The pressure of the water turns the wheel.* | *the pressure of his hand on my arm*

5 GAS/LIQUID [C,U] the force produced by the quantity of gas or liquid in a place or container: *The gas containers burst* ***at high pressure****.*

6 WEATHER [C,U] a condition of the air in the Earth's ATMOSPHERE, which affects the weather: **high/low pressure** *A ridge of high pressure is building up strongly over the Atlantic.* → PEER PRESSURE

pressure² *v* [T] *especially AmE* to try to make someone do something by making them feel it is their duty to do it SYN **pressurize** *BrE*: **pressure sb into doing sth** *You want to enjoy food, not to be pressured into eating the right things.* | **pressure sb to do sth** *Don't feel we are pressuring you to give what you can't afford.* THESAURUS FORCE

ˈpressure ˌcooker *n* [C] **1** a tightly covered cooking pot in which food is cooked very quickly by the pressure of hot steam **2** a situation or place that causes anxiety or difficulties: *the pressure cooker of soccer management*

pres·sured /ˈpreʃəd $ -ərd/ *adj* feeling worried, or making you feel worried, because of the number of things you have to do SYN **pressurized** *BrE*: *a highly pressured job*

ˈpressure group *n* [C] a group or organization that tries to influence the opinions of ordinary people and persuade the government to do something → **interest group**: *environmental pressure groups*

ˈpressure point *n* [C] **1** a place or situation where there may be trouble: *a pressure point for racial tension* **2** a place on the body that can be pressed, either to stop bleeding or to help make you feel better

ˈpressure ˌwasher *n* [C] a piece of equipment that forces water or another liquid out of a container very quickly, used to clean things such as cars, engines, machines etc

pres·sur·ize (*also* **-ise** *BrE*) /ˈpreʃəraɪz/ *v* [T] to persuade someone to do something by making them feel it is their duty to do it SYN **pressure**: **pressurize sb into doing sth** *It is not a good idea to pressurize children into playing a musical instrument.* | **pressurize sb to do sth** *Everyone is being pressurized to vote.*

pres·sur·ized (*also* **-ised** *BrE*) /ˈpreʃəraɪzd/ *adj* **1** if a container or space is pressurized, the air, gas, or liquid inside it is kept at a controlled pressure: *a pressurized aircraft cabin* | *a pressurized water reactor* **2** *BrE* feeling worried, or making you feel worried, because of the number of things you have to do SYN **pressured**: *I feel very pressurized at the moment.*

pres·tige¹ /preˈstiːʒ/ ●○○ *n* [U] the respect and admiration that someone or something gets because of their success or important position in society: **[+of]** *the prestige of having your work shown at a top London gallery* | *The king wanted to* ***enhance*** *his* ***prestige*** *through war.* | *This little-known British firm has now* ***gained*** *considerable* ***prestige****.* | *the personal prestige attached to owning a large property* THESAURUS REPUTATION

prestige² *adj* [only before noun] a prestige project, product etc is one of high quality that people respect you for having or being involved in: *tiny roles in prestige films* | *a prestige car*

pres·ti·gious /preˈstɪdʒəs $ -ˈstiː-, -ˈsti-/ ●○○ *adj* admired as one of the best and most important: *a prestigious literary award* | *a* ***highly prestigious*** *university*

pres·to¹ /ˈprestəʊ $ -toʊ/ *adj, adv technical* played or sung very quickly

presto² *n* (*plural* **prestos**) [C] *technical* a piece of music, or part of one, that is played or sung very quickly

presto³ *interjection AmE* said when something happens suddenly in a way that seems unbelievable or magical SYN **hey presto** *BrE*: *You just press a button and presto! A drink appears.*

pre-stressed /ˌpriː ˈstrest◂/ *adj* pre-stressed CONCRETE has been made stronger by having wires put inside it

pre·su·ma·bly /prɪˈzjuːməbli $ -ˈzuː-/ ●●○ S3 W3 AWL *adv* used to say that you think something is probably true: *It's raining, which presumably means that your football match will be cancelled.* | [sentence adverb] *He's dead now, presumably?*

pre·sume /prɪˈzjuːm $ -ˈzuːm/ ●●○ S3 AWL *v*

1 [T] to think that something is true, although you are not certain SYN **assume**: *Each of you will make a speech, I presume?* | *'Are his parents still alive?'* ***'I presume so.'*** | **presume that** *I presume we'll be there by six o'clock.* | **presume sb/sth to be sb/sth** *From the way he talked, I presumed him to be your boss.* | **be presumed to do sth** *The temple is presumed to date from the first century BC.*

2 [T] to accept something as true until it is shown to not be true, especially in law SYN **assume**: *We must presume innocence until we have evidence of guilt.* | **be presumed dead/innocent etc** *Their nephew was missing, presumed dead.*

3 [I] *formal* to behave without respect or politeness by doing something that you have no right to do: **presume to do something** *I would never presume to tell you what to do.*

4 [T usually in present tense] *formal* to accept something as being true and base something else on it SYN **presuppose**: *The Ancient History course presumes some knowledge of Greek.* | **presume that** *I presume that someone will be there to meet us when we arrive.*

5 presume on/upon sb's friendship/generosity etc to unfairly ask someone for more than you should, because they are your friend, are generous etc: *It would be presuming on his generosity to ask him for money.*

pre·sump·tion /prɪˈzʌmpʃən/ ●○○ AWL *n*

1 [C] something that you think is true because it is very likely: **presumption that** *the presumption that their wealth is the result of crime* | **on the presumption that** *On the presumption that the doctor knows best, I took the medicine.*

2 [C,U] *law* the act of thinking something is true, bad, or good until it is shown to not be true, bad, or good: **[+of]** *the presumption of innocence* | **[+against/in favour of]** *a strong presumption against development in national parks*

3 [U] *formal* behaviour that seems rude and too confident: *She was enraged by his presumption.*

pre·sump·tive /prɪˈzʌmptɪv/ *adj formal or technical* based on a reasonable belief about what is likely to be true: *a presumptive diagnosis* —**presumptively** *adv*

pre·sump·tu·ous /prɪˈzʌmptʃuəs/ *adj formal* doing something that you have no right to do and that seems rude: **is it presumptuous (of sb) to do sth** *Would it be presumptuous of me to ask why you are so miserable?* —**presumptuously** *adv* —**presumptuousness** *n* [U]

pre·sup·pose /ˌpriːsəˈpəʊz $ -ˈpoʊz/ *v* [T] *formal* **1** to depend on something that is believed to exist or to be true SYN **assume**: *The idea of heaven presupposes the existence of God.* | **presuppose that** *Your argument presupposes that Dickens was a social reformer.* **2** to have to happen if something is true: *Without struggle there can be no progress, and struggle presupposes winners and losers.*

pre·sup·po·si·tion /ˌpriːsʌpəˈzɪʃən/ *n formal* **1** [C] something that you think is true, although you have no proof SYN **assumption**: **presupposition that** *Hick's presupposition is that all religions believe in the same God.* **2** [U] when you think something is true even though you have no proof

pre-tax /ˌpriː ˈtæks◂/ *adj* pre-tax profits or losses are the profits or losses of a company before tax has been taken away: ***Pre-tax profits*** *fell 26.6% to £3.1 million.* —**pre-tax** *adv*

pre·teen /ˌpriːˈtiːn◂/ *adj* relating to or made for children who are 11 or 12 years old: *preteen clothing* —**preteen** /ˈpriːtiːn/ *n* [C]

pre·tence *BrE*, **pretense** *AmE* /prɪˈtens $ ˈpriːtens/ *n* [singular, U] **1** a way of behaving which is intended to make people believe something that is not true: **pretence that** *the pretence that the old system could be made to work* | **pretence of/at (being/doing) sth** *a pretence at seriousness* | *Tollitt* ***made no pretense of*** *being surprised.* | *How long are you going to* ***keep up the pretence*** *of being ill?* | **abandon/give up/drop a pretence** *Abandoning any pretense at politeness, they ran for the door.* | **under the pretence of (doing) sth** *John waited for her under the pretence of tying his shoelaces.* | *It was all an* ***elaborate pretence***. **2 under/on false pretences** without telling the truth about yourself or your intentions: *You brought me here under false pretences!*

This graph shows how common the different grammar patterns of the verb **pretend** are.

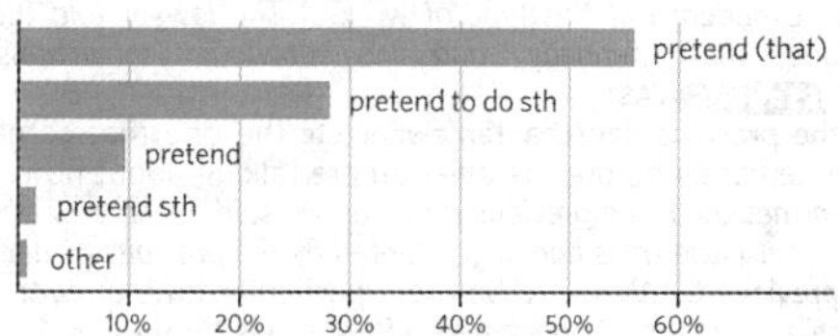

pre·tend¹ /prɪˈtend/ ●●● S2 W3 *v*
1 [I,T] to behave as if something is true when in fact you know it is not, in order to deceive people or for fun: **pretend (that)** *We can't go on pretending that everything is OK.* | *Let's pretend we're on the Moon.* | **pretend to do sth** *She pretended not to notice.* | *He's not asleep – he's just pretending.* | *To* ***pretend ignorance*** *of the situation would be irresponsible.* | *I can't marry her and to* ***pretend otherwise*** *would be wrong.*
2 [T usually in negatives] to claim that something is true, when it is not: **pretend (that)** *I can't pretend I understand these technical terms* (=I admit I do not understand them). | **pretend to do/be sth** *The book doesn't pretend to be for beginners.*

THESAURUS

pretend /prɪˈtend/ to deliberately behave as though something is true when it is not, either for fun or to deceive someone: *Mark closed his eyes and pretended to be asleep.* | *She shouted but he pretended that he hadn't heard her.*
act to behave in a particular way – often used when saying that someone is pretending that something is true, when it is not: *Paul* ***acted as if*** *nothing was wrong.* | *He enjoyed* ***acting the fool*** (=pretending to be stupid) *and couldn't care less about his studies.*
make out sth *informal* to pretend that something is true, in order to avoid doing something or to deceive someone: *I didn't want to go, so I made out I was busy.* | *She always makes out that she doesn't have any money.*
be putting it on *informal* to be pretending to be ill, hurt etc, especially in order to avoid doing something, or to make other people feel sympathy for you: *She's not really upset, she's just putting it on.*
feign interest/surprise/ignorance/illness etc *formal* to pretend that you are interested, surprised etc: *'Oh really!' he said, trying to feign interest.* | *Sometimes it's best just to feign ignorance* (=pretend that you do not know).
keep up appearances to pretend that your life is happy and successful, especially when you have suffered some kind of trouble or loss: *Although we were poor, our family always tried to keep up appearances.* | *She did her best to keep up appearances after her husband left her.*

pretend² *adj* imaginary or not real – used especially by children: *We sang songs around a pretend campfire.*

pre·tend·ed /prɪˈtendɪd/ *adj* something that is pretended appears to be real but is not: *Her eyes widened in pretended astonishment.*

pre·tend·er /prɪˈtendə $ -ər/ *n* [C] someone who claims to have a right to be king, leader etc, when this is not accepted by many people: **[+to]** *the pretender to the English throne*

pre·tense /prɪˈtens $ ˈpriːtens/ *n* [singular, U] the American spelling of PRETENCE

pre·ten·sion /prɪˈtenʃən/ *n* [C usually plural, U] **1** an attempt to seem more important, more intelligent, or of a higher class than you really are: **[+to]** *Lilith resented Adam's pretensions to superiority.* | *the humbleness and* ***lack of pretension*** *of Jordan's cafe* **2** a claim to be or do something: **pretension(s) to be sth** *The group don't* ***have any pretensions*** *to be pop stars.* | **[+to]** *a large village with pretensions to the status of a small town*

pre·ten·tious /prɪˈtenʃəs/ ●○○ *adj* if someone or something is pretentious, they try to seem more important, intelligent, or high class than they really are in order to be impressive OPP **unpretentious**: *a pretentious film* —**pretentiously** *adv* —**pretentiousness** *n* [U]

pret·er·ite (*also* **preterit** *AmE*) /ˈpretərət/ *n* **the preterite** *technical* the tense or verb form that expresses a past action or condition —**preterite** *adj*

pre·ter·nat·u·ral /ˌpriːtəˈnætʃərəl◂ $ -tər-/ *adj formal* **1** beyond what is usual or normal: *He felt possessed of a preternatural strength and fearlessness.* **2** strange, mysterious, and unnatural: *the preternatural green light* —**preternaturally** *adv*: *The town was preternaturally quiet.*

pre·text /ˈpriːtekst/ *n* [C] a false reason given for an action, in order to hide the real reason: **[+for]** *The incident* ***provided*** *the* ***pretext*** *for war.* | **on/under the pretext of doing sth** *Tom called at her apartment on the pretext of asking for a book.* | **on/under the pretext that** *He left immediately on the pretext that he had a train to catch.* | *He'll phone* ***on some pretext*** *or other.* **THESAURUS** ▸ REASON

pret·ti·fy /ˈprɪtɪfaɪ/ *v* (**prettified**, **prettifying**, **prettifies**) [T] to change something with the intention of making it more attractive, but often with the effect of spoiling it: *attempts to prettify the harbour*

pret·ty¹ /ˈprɪti/ ●●● S1 W3 *adv* [+adj/adv] *spoken*
1 fairly or more than a little: *I'm pretty sure he'll say yes.* | *She still looks pretty miserable.*

REGISTER
In written English, people usually avoid **pretty** and use **fairly** instead: *The consequences of this are* ***fairly*** *obvious.*

2 very: *Dinner at Luigi's sounds pretty good to me.*
3 pretty well/much almost completely: *He hit the ball pretty well exactly where he wanted it.* | *The guard left us pretty much alone.* | *They're all pretty much the same.*
4 pretty nearly (*also* **pretty near** *AmE*) almost: *The shock of Pat's death pretty near killed Roy.* → **be sitting pretty** at SIT(9)

pretty² ●●● S2 W3 *adj* (*comparative* **prettier**, *superlative* **prettiest**)
1 a woman or child who is pretty has a nice attractive face: *a pretty little girl* | *Maria looks much prettier with her hair cut short.* **THESAURUS** ▸ BEAUTIFUL
2 something that is pretty is pleasant to look at or listen to but is not impressive: *a pretty dress* | *The tune is pretty.* | *What a pretty little garden!*
3 not a pretty sight very unpleasant to look at – sometimes

used humorously: *After a night's drinking, Al was not a pretty sight.*
4 not just a pretty face *spoken* used humorously to say that someone is intelligent, when people think this is surprising: *I'm not just a pretty face, you know!*
5 come to a pretty pass *old-fashioned* used to say that a very bad situation has developed: ***Things have come to a pretty pass****, if you can't say what you think without causing a fight.*
6 cost a pretty penny *old-fashioned* to cost a lot of money
7 pretty as a picture *old-fashioned* very pretty —**prettily** *adv*: *Charlotte sang very prettily.* —**prettiness** *n* [U]

pret·zel /ˈpretsəl/ *n* [C] a hard salty type of bread baked in the shape of a stick or a loose knot

pre·vail /prɪˈveɪl/ ●○○ *v* [I] *formal*
1 if a belief, custom, situation etc prevails, it exists among a group of people at a certain time: **[+in/among etc]** *the economic conditions which prevail in England and Wales | I admired the creativity which prevailed among the young writers.*
2 if a person, idea, or principle prevails in a fight, argument etc, they are successful in the end: *Justice will prevail.* | **common sense prevails/reason prevails** (=a sensible decision is made) *He considered lying, but then common sense prevailed.* | **[+over/against]** *Your inner strength will enable you to prevail over life's obstacles.*
prevail on/upon sb *phr v formal* to persuade someone: **prevail on/upon sb to do sth** *She prevailed upon her father to say nothing.*

pre·vail·ing /prɪˈveɪlɪŋ/ ●○○ *adj* [only before noun]
1 existing or accepted in a particular place or at a particular time SYN **current**: *The **prevailing mood** of public opinion remained hostile.* | *the **prevailing** economic **conditions** in Northern Ireland*
2 prevailing wind a wind that blows over a particular area most of the time

prev·a·lence /ˈprevələns/ ●○○ *n* [singular, U] the fact that something is prevalent: **[+of]** *the prevalence of deafness in older age groups*

prev·a·lent /ˈprevələnt/ ●○○ *adj* common at a particular time, in a particular place, or among a particular group of people: **[+in/among etc]** *Solvent abuse is especially prevalent among younger teenagers.* | *the prevalent belief in astrology* THESAURUS COMMON

pre·var·i·cate /prɪˈværɪkeɪt/ *v* [I,T] *formal* to try to hide the truth by not answering questions directly: *'I'm not sure,' he prevaricated.* —**prevarication** /prɪˌværɪˈkeɪʃən/ *n* [C,U]

pre·vent /prɪˈvent/ ●●● S2 W1 *v* [T] to stop something from happening, or stop someone from doing something: *The rules are intended to prevent accidents.* | **prevent sb/sth (from) doing sth** *His back injury may prevent him from playing in tomorrow's game.* | *We were prevented from entering the site.* | *Wrap small ornaments in paper to prevent them being damaged.* —**preventable** *adj*: *preventable diseases | Every one of these deaths is preventable.*

> **REGISTER**
> In everyday English, people usually say **stop sb/sth (from) doing sth** rather than **prevent sb/sth (from) doing sth**: *This barrier is to **stop** people from coming in without a ticket.*

pre·vent·a·tive /prɪˈventətɪv/ *adj* PREVENTIVE: *preventative measures* —**preventatively** *adv*

pre·ven·tion /prɪˈvenʃən/ ●●○ *n* [U] when something bad is stopped from happening: **[+of]** *Educating new drivers is important for the **prevention of accidents**.* | **crime/accident/fire etc prevention** *Effective crime prevention must be our main goal.* | *a fire prevention officer* | *You know what they say, **prevention is better than cure*** (=it is better to stop something bad from happening than to remove the problem once it has happened).

pre·vent·ive /prɪˈventɪv/ (*also* **preventative**) *adj* [only before noun] intended to stop something you do not want to happen, such as illness, from happening: *preventive health programs* | **preventive action/measure** *While travelling abroad, take preventive measures to avoid illness.* —**preventively** *adv*

preˌventive deˈtention *n* [U] *BrE law* a system in which people who are guilty of many crimes are kept in prison for a long time

preˌventive ˈmedicine *n* [U] medical treatment, advice, and health education that is designed to prevent disease happening rather than cure it

pre-verb·al /ˌpriːˈvɜːbəl◂ $ -ɜːr-/ *adj* [only before noun] *technical* happening before a child has learned to speak: *the pre-verbal stages*

pre·view¹ /ˈpriːvjuː/ *n* [C] **1** an occasion when you can see a film, play, painting etc before it is shown to the public: **[+of]** *a **sneak preview** of the new fashions for autumn* | *the press preview of the show* (=when people who write for newspapers, television etc could see it) **2** a description of a film, television programme, show etc that people will be able to see soon

preview² *v* [T] **1** to see or describe something before it is shown to the public: *Journalists will be able to preview the exhibition tomorrow.* **2** to show or perform something before it is shown to the public: *The band will preview their new album on 2nd March.*

pre·vi·ous /ˈpriːviəs/ ●●● S1 W1 AWL *adj*
1 [only before noun] having happened or existed before the event, time, or thing that you are talking about now: *I've met him before on two previous occasions.* | *She has two children from a previous marriage.* | *Do you have any previous experience of this type of work?* | *The lawyer told the judge that Kennedy had no previous convictions.* THESAURUS LAST
2 the previous day/chapter/owner etc the one that came immediately before the one you are talking about now: *I had met them the previous day.* | *as we said in the previous chapter* | *The trees had been planted by the previous owner.*
3 previous to sth *formal* before a particular time or event: *There were almost no women MPs previous to 1945.*

pre·vi·ous·ly /ˈpriːviəsli/ ●●● S3 W2 AWL *adv* before now or before a particular time: *Almost half the group had previously been heavy smokers.* | **two days/three years etc previously** (=two days, three years etc before) *Six months previously he had smashed up his car.* THESAURUS BEFORE

pre-war /ˌpriː ˈwɔː◂ $ -ˈwɔːr◂/ *adj* [usually before noun] happening or existing before a war, especially the Second World War OPP **post-war**: *pre-war Britain*

prey¹ /preɪ/ *n* **1** [singular, U] an animal, bird etc that is hunted and eaten by another animal OPP **predator**: *a tiger stalking its prey* **2 bird/beast of prey** a bird or animal which lives by killing and eating other animals **3 be/fall prey to sb/sth** if someone falls prey to someone or something bad, they are harmed or affected by them: *Street children in this part of the world often fall prey to drug dealers.* | *They are prey to nameless fears.* **4 easy prey a)** someone who can easily be deceived or harmed: *He was easy prey for the two conmen who called at his house.* **b)** an animal which is easily caught by another: *Fish at the surface of the water are easy prey for eagles.*

prey² *v*
prey on sb/sth *phr v* **1** if an animal or bird preys on another animal or bird, it hunts and eats it → **predator**: *Cats prey on birds and mice.* **2** to try to deceive or harm weaker people: *religious cults that specialize in preying on young people* **3 prey on sb's mind** to make someone worry continuously: *The accident has been preying on my mind all week.*

prez·zie /ˈprezi/ *n* [C] *BrE spoken* a present

price¹ /praɪs/ ●●● S1 W1 *n*
1 [C,U] the amount of money you have to pay for something: **[+of]** *The price of fuel keeps going up.* | **[+for]** *We agreed a price for the bike.* | *Supermarkets often offer you two products for the price of one.* → ASKING PRICE, COST PRICE, LIST PRICE, MARKET PRICE THESAURUS COST
2 [singular] something unpleasant that you must suffer in

order to be successful, free etc, or that you suffer because of a mistake or bad action: **[+of]** *He's never at home, but that's the price of success.* | *The awful boat journey was* ***a small price to pay*** *for freedom.* | *They may* ***pay a high price*** *for their few years of glory.* | *The country will* ***pay a heavy price*** *for the government's failure.* | *She was finally made senior executive, but* ***at what price****!*
3 half/full price used to talk about half the usual price of something, or the actual usual price: *I bought these jeans at half price in the sale.*
4 at a price for a lot of money: *You can get goat's cheese at the local delicatessen - at a price!*
5 at any price whatever the cost and difficulties may be: *She was determined to have a child at any price.*
6 not at any price used to say that you would not do something, even for a lot of money: *Sorry, that painting's not for sale at any price.*
7 put a price on sth to give something a financial value: *You can't put a price on what a mother does for her children.*
8 What price fame/glory etc? *usually spoken* used to suggest that something was not worth achieving because too many bad things have happened as a result: *What price progress?*
9 be beyond price to be extremely valuable or important
10 price on sb's head a reward for catching or killing someone
11 everyone has their price used to say that you can persuade people to do anything if you give them what they want → **cheap at the price** at CHEAP[1](8), → **name your price** at NAME[2](7), → **pay the price** at PAY[1](9)

COLLOCATIONS

ADJECTIVES/NOUN + price

high *House prices in the UK are very high.*
low *With such low prices, there are lots of eager buyers.*
reasonable (=not too high) *The price was reasonable for such good food.*
fair *I am sure we can agree on a fair price.*
astronomical (=extremely high) *Many fans paid astronomical prices for their tickets.*
exorbitant/extortionate (=much too high) *£10,000 seemed an exorbitant price for the rug.*
house/food/oil etc prices *A poor harvest led to higher food prices.*
a good price (=quite high) *Did you get a good price for your car?*
a bargain price (*also* **a knockdown/giveaway price**) (=much lower than usual) *We sell quality cars at bargain prices.*
the market price (=the price of something on a market at a particular time) | **the asking price** (=the amount of money that someone is asking for when they are selling something, especially a house) | **the purchase price** *formal* (=the price that someone pays when they buy something, especially a house) | **the retail price** (=the price that the public pays for something in a shop) | **the wholesale price** (=the price that a business such as a shop pays to buy something)

VERBS

a price goes up/rises/increases *When supplies go down, prices tend to go up.*
a price goes down/falls/decreases *In real terms, the price of clothes has fallen over the last ten years.*
a price shoots up/soars/rockets (=increases quickly by a large amount) *The price of oil soared in the 1970s.*
prices fluctuate (=keep going up and down) *Gas prices have continued to fluctuate in recent months.*
put up/increase/raise a price *Manufacturers have had to put their prices up.*
cut/lower/reduce a price *The company recently cut the price of its best-selling car.*
slash a price (=reduce it by a very large amount) *Many carpet stores have slashed prices to bring in customers.*
fix a price (=decide on it, sometimes illegally with others) *Publishers are not permitted to fix prices with one another.*
agree on a price | **pay a good/low etc price** | **get a good/reasonable etc price** (=be paid a particular amount for something) | **fetch a good/high etc price** *BrE*, **bring a good, high etc price** *AmE* (=be sold for a particular amount of money)

price + NOUN

a price rise/increase *Consumers are facing more fuel price rises.*
a price cut/reduction *Holiday sales were down, even with drastic price cuts.*
a price freeze (=when prices are kept at the same level by a company or by the government)

PHRASES

a fall/drop in prices *Poor demand led to a sharp drop in prices.*
a rise in prices *The sharp rise in wholesale food prices will have to be passed onto customers.*
in/outside sb's price range (=used when saying that someone can/cannot afford to pay for something) *Unfortunately, there was nothing in our price range.*

COMMON ERRORS

⚠ Don't say 'a convenient price'. Say **a reasonable price** or **a fair price**.

price² ●●○ *v* [T]
1 to decide the price of something that is for sale: *a* ***reasonably priced*** *apartment* | **be priced at sth** *Tickets are priced at £75 each.* GRAMMAR **Price** is usually passive in this meaning.
2 to put the price on goods to show how much they cost
3 to compare the prices of things: *We spent Saturday morning pricing microwaves.*
4 price yourself out of the market to demand too much money for the services or goods that you are selling

ˈprice conˌtrol *n* [C,U] a system in which the government decides the prices of things

ˈprice ˌfixing *n* [U] **1** a system in which the government decides the prices of things SYN **price control 2** an agreement between producers and sellers of a product to set its price at a high level

ˈprice ˌindex *n* [C] a list of particular goods and services and how much their prices change each month → RETAIL PRICE INDEX

price·less /ˈpraɪsləs/ ●○○ *adj*
1 extremely valuable: *priceless antiques* THESAURUS VALUABLE
2 a quality or skill that is priceless is extremely important or useful: *The ability to motivate people is a priceless asset.*
3 *informal* extremely funny or silly: *The look on his face was priceless.*

ˈprice list *n* [C] a list of prices for things being sold

ˈprice supˌport *n* [U] a system in which the government keeps the price of a product at a particular level by giving the producer money or buying the product itself

ˈprice tag *n* [C] **1** a piece of paper with a price on it that is attached to something in a shop **2** the amount that something costs: *It's difficult to* ***put*** *a* ***price tag on*** *such a project* (=say how much it costs).

ˈprice war *n* [C] a situation in which several companies reduce the prices of what they sell, because they are all trying to get the most customers

pric·ey, **pricy** /ˈpraɪsi/ *adj informal* expensive: *The clothes are beautiful but very pricey.* THESAURUS EXPENSIVE

pric·ing /ˈpraɪsɪŋ/ *n* [U] the act of deciding the price of something that you sell: *a competitive* ***pricing policy***

prick¹ /prɪk/ *v* **1** [T] to make a small hole in something using something sharp: *Prick the sausages before you grill them.* | **prick yourself/prick your finger** (=accidentally make a hole in your skin) *She had pricked her finger on a rose*

P

thorn. **2** [I,T] if something pricks a part of your body, or if it pricks, you feel small sharp pains → **prickle**: *Angry tears pricked her eyes.* | *a curious pricking sensation* **3 prick sb's conscience** if something pricks someone's conscience or their conscience pricks them, they feel guilty or ashamed: *Her conscience pricked her as she told the lie.* **4 prick (up) its ears** if an animal pricks up its ears, it raises them to listen to a sound: *The rabbit stopped suddenly, pricking up its ears.*
5 prick (up) your ears if you prick up your ears or your ears prick up, you listen carefully because you have heard something interesting: *Jay pricked up his ears when I mentioned a vacation.*
prick sth↔ **out** *phr v BrE* to place young plants in soil after you have grown them from seed

prick² *n* [C]
1 PERSON *taboo spoken* a very offensive word for a stupid unpleasant man. Do not use this word.
2 SEX ORGAN *informal not polite* a PENIS
3 POINT ENTERING **a)** a slight pain you get when something sharp goes into your skin: *I didn't feel the prick of the needle.* **b)** *BrE* an act of pricking something: *Give the sausages a prick.* → PINPRICK
4 EMOTION a sudden slight feeling you get when you are unhappy about something: **[+of]** | *She felt a prick of resentment when she saw them together.*
5 prick of conscience an uncomfortable feeling that you have done something wrong

prick·le¹ /ˈprɪkəl/ *n* [C] **1** a long thin sharp point on the skin of some animals or the surface of some plants **2** if you feel a prickle of fear, anger, or excitement, you feel slightly afraid, angry, or excited in a way that makes your skin feel slightly cold and uncomfortable: **[+of]** *She felt a prickle of fear as she realized that she was alone.*

prickle² *v* **1** [I,T] if something prickles your skin, it makes it sting slightly: *A cold breeze prickled his face.* | *His hair prickled my neck.* | **[+on]** *He felt sweat prickle on his forehead.* **2** [I] if your skin prickles, it begins to sting slightly: *Her skin was prickling uncomfortably.* **3** [I] *BrE* if your eyes prickle, they sting slightly because you are going to cry: *She felt her eyes prickle. 'It was awful,' she whispered.* | *My eyes* **prickled with tears**. **4** [I] if you prickle, you feel slightly angry, excited, or afraid: **[+with]** *The thought of meeting him made her prickle with excitement.* | **[+at]** *She felt herself prickle* (=become angry) *at his tone of voice.*

prick·ly /ˈprɪkli/ *adj* **1** covered with thin sharp points: *a plant with prickly leaves* THESAURUS▸ SHARP **2** if your skin feels prickly, it stings slightly: *His skin felt painful and prickly.* | *The base of my neck was prickly with sweat.* **3** something that is prickly makes your skin sting slightly: *a prickly woollen sweater* **4** *informal* someone who is prickly gets annoyed or offended easily: *She was prickly and sharp with me.* | *As she got older, she became more prickly and forgetful.* **5** a prickly subject causes a lot of disagreements and difficulties: *We finally turned to the prickly question of who was going to pay.* —**prickliness** *n* [U]

ˌprickly ˈheat *n* [U] a skin condition in which you get uncomfortable red spots on your skin. Prickly heat is caused by too much strong sun on your skin.

ˌprickly ˈpear *n* [C,U] a type of CACTUS that has yellow flowers and red fruit. The fruit is also called a prickly pear.

pric·y /ˈpraɪsi/ *adj* another spelling of PRICEY

pride¹ /praɪd/ ●●● S3 W3 *n*
1 FEELING OF PLEASURE [U] a feeling that you are proud of something that you or someone connected with you has achieved → **proud**: *He wore his medals with pride.* | **[+in]** *He* **takes great pride in** *his children's achievements.* | *The people have a* **sense of pride** *in their community.* | *His heart* **swelled with pride** *when his daughter came in.* | *She felt a* **glow of pride** *when her name was announced for the prize.* | *Success in sport is a source of* **national pride**.
2 RESPECT [U] a feeling that you like and respect yourself and that you deserve to be respected by other people → **proud**: **sb's pride** *It* **hurt** *his* **pride** *when his wife left him.* | *I think that getting a job would* **give** *him his* **pride back**. | *She didn't try to hide her anger and* **injured pride**. | **It's a matter of pride** *for some men that their wives don't have to work.*
3 TOO MUCH PRIDE [U] a belief that you are better than other people and do not need their help or support → **proud**: **sb's pride** *His pride wouldn't allow him to ask for help.* | *She ought to* **swallow** *her* **pride** (=ignore or forget her feelings of pride) *and call him.*
4 take pride in your work/appearance etc to do something very carefully and well, in a way that gives you a lot of satisfaction: *Your should take more pride in your work.* | *She took great pride in her appearance.*
5 sb's pride and joy a person or thing that someone is very proud of: *His garden is his pride and joy.*
6 the pride of sth a) the thing or person that the people in a particular place are most proud of: *Wigan's rugby team was the pride of the town.* **b)** the best thing in a group: *a beautiful Japanese sword that is the pride of our collection*
7 have/take pride of place if something has or takes pride of place, it is put in the best place for people to see because it is the thing you are most proud of: *A large photograph of the children had pride of place on the sitting room wall.*
8 LIONS [C] a group of lions: *A young lion had strayed some distance from the pride.*

pride² *v* **pride yourself on (doing) sth** to be especially proud of something that you do well, or of a good quality that you have: *a restaurant that prides itself on speed of service* | *She prides herself on being a good listener.*

priest /priːst/ ●●● W3 *n* [C]
1 someone who is specially trained to perform religious duties and ceremonies in the Christian church
2 a man with religious duties and responsibilities in some non-Christian religions

priest·ess /ˈpriːstes/ *n* [C] a woman with religious duties and responsibilities in some non-Christian religions

priest·hood /ˈpriːsthʊd/ *n* **1 the priesthood** if someone is in the priesthood, they are a Christian priest: *He is celebrating 30 years in the priesthood.* | *There has been a decline in the number of people joining the priesthood.* **2** [C usually singular, U] all the priests of a particular religion or country: *an attempt to reduce the influence of the priesthood in the country*

priest·ly /ˈpriːstli/ *adj* [usually before noun] like a priest, or relating to a priest: *priestly robes*

prig /prɪg/ *n* [C] someone who behaves in a morally good way and shows that they disapprove of the way other people behave – used to show disapproval: *Don't be such a prig! It's only a bit of harmless fun!* —**priggish** *adj*: *a rather priggish, old-fashioned man* —**priggishness** *n* [U]

prim /prɪm/ *adj* **1** very formal and careful in the way you speak and behave, and easily shocked by anything rude: *She looked prim and nervous in her best hat and coat.* | *a very* **prim and proper** *young lady* **2** prim clothes are neat and formal: *a prim suit* —**primly** *adv*

pri·ma bal·le·ri·na /ˌpriːmə bæləˈriːnə/ *n* [C] the main woman dancer in a group of BALLET dancers

pri·ma·cy /ˈpraɪməsi/ AWL *n* [singular, U] *formal* if someone or something has primacy, they are the best or most important person or thing: **[+of]** *the primacy of the family* | *We must* **give primacy to** *education.*

prima don·na /ˌpriːmə ˈdɒnə $ -ˈdɑːnə/ *n* [C]
1 the most important woman singer in an OPERA company
2 someone who thinks that they are very good at what they do, and demands a lot of attention and praise from other people: *In my view, football players are a bunch of over-paid prima donnas.*

pri·mae·val /praɪˈmiːvəl/ *adj* a British spelling of PRIMEVAL

pri·ma fa·cie /ˌpraɪmə ˈfeɪʃi $ -ʃə/ *adj* [only before noun] *law* based on what seems to be true when you first consider a situation, even though it may later be proved to be untrue: *prima facie evidence* | *a prima facie case of professional misconduct*

pri·mal /ˈpraɪməl/ *adj* [only before noun] *formal* primal feelings or actions seem to belong to a part of people's character that is ancient and animal-like: *a primal fear of the unknown*

pri·ma·ri·ly /ˈpraɪmərəli $ praɪˈmerəli/ ●●○ W3 AWL *adv* mainly: *The advertisement is aimed primarily at children.*

pri·ma·ry¹ /ˈpraɪməri $ -meri/ ●●○ W2 AWL *adj*
1 [usually before noun] most important SYN **main**: *Our primary concern is to provide the refugees with food and health care.* | *Many of the villagers rely on fishing as their primary source of income.* | **primary purpose/aim/objective** *Their primary objective is to make money.* | *Personal safety is* ***of primary importance.*** **THESAURUS** ▶ IMPORTANT, MAIN
2 [only before noun] *especially BrE* relating to the education of children between 5 and 11 years old SYN **elementary** *AmE* → **secondary**: *a primary teacher* | *primary education* | *teaching at primary level*
3 happening or developing before other things: *a primary tumour* | *Counselling was given as a primary therapy for depression.*

primary² *n* (*plural* **primaries**) [C] **1** a primary election **2** *BrE* a primary school

ˌprimary ˈcare *n* [U] basic medical treatment that you receive from a doctor who is not a SPECIALIST: *a primary care physician* (=a doctor who provides primary care)

ˌprimary ˈcolour *n* [C] one of the three colours red, yellow, and blue, which you can mix together to make any of the other colours

ˌprimary eˈlection *n* [C] an election in the US at which people vote to decide who will be a party's CANDIDATE for a political position in the main election

ˌprimary ˈhealth care (*also* **primary care**) *n* [U] the medical care that someone receives first when they become ill or have an accident

ˈprimary ˌschool ●●○ *n* [C] *BrE* a school for children between 5 and 11 years old in England and Wales SYN **elementary school** *AmE*

ˌprimary ˈsource *n* [C] a document, book etc that contains information that has been obtained from people's experiences and not taken from other documents, books etc → **secondary source**

ˌprimary ˈstress *n* [C,U] *technical* the strongest force that is put on a part of a long word when you say it, like the force given to 'pri' in 'primary'. It is shown in this dictionary by the mark (ˈ).

pri·mate /ˈpraɪmeɪt/ *n* [C] a member of the group of animals that includes humans and monkeys

Pri·mate /ˈpraɪmət/ *n* [C] the most important priest in a country, especially in the Church of England SYN **archbishop**

prime¹ /praɪm/ ●○○ AWL *adj* [only before noun]
1 most important SYN **main**: *Smoking is the prime cause of lung disease.* | *Our prime concern is providing jobs for all young school leavers.* | *He was named as the* ***prime suspect*** *in the murder investigation.* | *Good management is* ***of prime importance*** *in business.* **THESAURUS** ▶ MAIN
2 of the very best quality or kind: *prime rib of beef* | *prime agricultural land* | *The hotel is in a prime location overlooking the valley.*
3 be a prime candidate/target (for sth) to be the person or thing that is most suitable or most likely to be chosen for a particular purpose: *The school is a prime candidate for closure.* | *Old people are a prime target for thieves.*
4 prime example a very typical example of something: *Blakey Hall is a prime example of a 19th-century building.*

prime² ●○○ *n* [singular] the time in your life when you are strongest and most active: **in your prime** *She's now 40 and still in her prime.* | *He is now* ***past*** *his* ***prime***. | *a man* ***in the prime of life*** | *a young singer who was tragically* ***cut off in*** *her* ***prime*** (=died while she was in her prime)

prime³ *v* [T]
1 PREPARE SB to prepare someone for a situation so that they know what to do: **prime sb with sth** *Did you prime her with what to say?* | **prime sb for sth** *He had a shower and primed himself for action.* | **prime sb to do sth** *He had been primed to say nothing about it.*
2 A GUN to prepare a gun or bomb so that it can fire or explode
3 PAINT to put a special layer of paint on a surface, in order to prepare it for the next layer: *All metal surfaces will have to be primed.*
4 prime the pump *informal* to encourage a business, industry, or activity to develop by putting money or effort into it
5 WATER to pour water into a water pump in order to make it ready to work

ˌPrime ˈMinister, **prime minister** ●●○ *n* [C] (*abbreviation* **PM**) the most important minister and leader of the government in some countries which have a parliament: *the British prime minister* | *He first became prime minister in 1982.* | **[+of]** *the prime minister of Turkey*

ˌprime ˈmover *n* [C] **1** someone who helps to make something happen and has great influence in the way it develops: **[+in/of/behind]** *He was a prime mover in the bid to get better pay for West Indian cricketers.* | *She was a prime mover of social change in the 19th century.* **2 Prime Mover** a way of referring to God

ˌprime ˈnumber *n* [C] a number that can be divided only by itself and the number one. For example, three and seven are prime numbers.

prim·er /ˈpraɪmə $ -ər/ *n* **1** [C,U] paint that you put on the surface of wood, metal etc before you put on the main layer of paint **2** [C] a tube that contains explosive and is used to fire a gun or explode a bomb **3** [C] *AmE* a book that contains basic information about something: **[+on/of]** *a primer on Italian wines* | *a primer of good management techniques* **4** [C] *old-fashioned* a school book that contains very basic facts about a subject

ˈprime ˌrate *n* [C] the lowest rate of interest at which companies can borrow money from a bank → **base rate**

ˈprime ˌtime *n* [U] the time in the evening when the largest number of people are watching television: *a prime time entertainment programme* | *prime time television* | *prime time audiences* | *a speech that was broadcast live during prime time*

pri·me·val (*also* **primaeval** *BrE*) /praɪˈmiːvəl/ *adj*
1 belonging to the earliest time in the existence of the universe or the Earth: *Primeval clouds of gas formed themselves into stars.* **2** very ancient: *primeval forests* **3** primeval feelings are very strong and seem to come from a part of people's character that is ancient and animal-like: *the primeval urge to reproduce*

prim·i·tive¹ /ˈprɪmətɪv/ ●●○ *adj*
1 WAY OF LIFE belonging to a simple way of life that existed in the past and does not have modern industries and machines OPP **advanced**, **modern**: *a primitive society* | *a primitive nomadic tribe* | *the tools used by primitive man* | *primitive art*
2 NOT MODERN something that is primitive is very simple and does not have the extra modern parts that would make it faster, better, more comfortable etc OPP **advanced**, **modern**: *The first station buildings were quite primitive.* | *The local hospital care is primitive and unreliable.* | *Conditions at the camp are very primitive.* | *a primitive steam engine*
3 ANIMALS/PLANTS a primitive animal or plant has a simple structure or body: *primitive life-forms that live deep in the ocean* | *a primitive single-celled creature*
4 FEELINGS primitive feelings are not based on reason, and seem to come from a part of people's character that is ancient and animal-like: *the primitive instinct of survival* | *primitive desires* —**primitively** *adv* —**primitiveness** *n* [U]

primitive² *n* [C] an artist who paints simple pictures like those of a child

pri·mo·gen·i·ture /ˌpraɪməʊˈdʒenətʃə $ -moʊˈdʒenətʃər/ *n* [U] *law* the system by which property that is owned by a man goes to his oldest son after his death

P

pri·mor·di·al /praɪˈmɔːdiəl $ -ˈmɔːr-/ *adj formal* **1** existing at the beginning of time or the beginning of the Earth: *the primordial seas* **2** primordial feelings are very strong and seem to come from the part of people's character that is ancient and animal-like: *He was driven on by a primordial terror.* **3 the primordial soup** the mixture of gases and other substances that people believe existed before the beginning of life on Earth

primp /prɪmp/ *v* [I,T] *old-fashioned* to make yourself look attractive by arranging your hair, putting on MAKE-UP etc: *She spends hours primping in front of the mirror.*

prim·rose /ˈprɪmrəʊz $ -roʊz/ *n* **1** [C] a small wild plant with pale yellow flowers, or the flower from this plant: *a bunch of primroses* **2** (*also* **primrose yellow**) [U] a pale yellow colour **3 the primrose path** *literary* a way of life that is full of pleasure but causes you harm after a period of time

P

prim·u·la /ˈprɪmjələ/ *n* [C] a small wild or garden plant with brightly coloured flowers

Pri·mus /ˈpraɪməs/ (*also* **ˈPrimus stove**) *n* [C] *trademark BrE* a small STOVE (=a piece of equipment for cooking) that burns oil and can be easily carried around, used especially when camping

prince /prɪns/ ●●● W3 *n* [C]
1 the son of a king, queen, or prince → **princess**: *Prince William*
2 a male ruler of a small country or state: *Prince Rainier of Monaco*
3 the prince of sth/a prince among sth *literary* the man who is best at something: *the prince of sculptors*

ˌPrince ˈCharming *n* [C] a perfect man who a young woman might dream about meeting – often used humorously. The name comes from a character who appears in various FAIRY TALES and rescues a DAMSEL IN DISTRESS (=woman who is in danger): *She is still waiting to find her Prince Charming.*

ˌprince ˈconsort *n* [C] a title that is sometimes given to the husband of a ruling queen

prince·ly /ˈprɪnsli/ *adj* [only before noun] **1** a princely amount of money is very large – often used humorously to mean a very small amount of money: *My savings had now reached* **the princely sum of** *£30.* | *a far from princely salary* **2** *formal* impressive or generous: *princely buildings* | *A princely welcome awaited them.* **3** belonging or relating to a prince: *a princely state*

prin·cess /ˌprɪnˈses◂ $ ˈprɪnsəs/ ●●● W3 *n* [C]
1 a close female relation of a king and queen, especially a daughter → **prince**: *Princess Anne*
2 the wife of a prince

prin·ci·pal¹ /ˈprɪnsəpəl/ ●●○ W2 AWL *adj* [only before noun] most important SYN **main**: *His principal reason for making the journey was to visit his family.* | *Teaching is her principal source of income.* | *the principal character in the book* THESAURUS IMPORTANT, MAIN → PRINCIPALLY

principal² ●●○ *n*
1 SCHOOL [C] *AmE* someone who is in charge of a school SYN **headteacher** *BrE*: *a small school with just three teachers and the principal* THESAURUS TEACHER
2 UNIVERSITY/COLLEGE [C] *BrE* someone who is in charge of a university or college
3 BUSINESS [C] *AmE* the main person in a business or organization, who can make important business decisions and is legally responsible for them: *The principal of the business has an office in New York.*
4 PERFORMER [C] the main performer in a play or in a group of musicians, dancers etc: *She later became a principal with the Royal Ballet.*
5 MONEY [singular] *technical* the original amount of money that is lent to someone, not including any of the INTEREST

ˌprincipal ˈboy *n* [C] *BrE* the main male character in a PANTOMIME, usually played by a young woman

prin·ci·pal·i·ty /ˌprɪnsəˈpæləti/ *n* (*plural* **principalities**) [C] **1** a country that is ruled by a prince **2 the Principality** *BrE* Wales

prin·ci·pally /ˈprɪnsəpli/ ●○○ AWL *adv* mainly: *The money is principally invested in stocks and shares.* | *He was principally a landscape painter.* | *We met principally to discuss the future of the school.*

prin·ci·ple /ˈprɪnsəpəl/ ●●● S2 W1 AWL *n*
1 MORAL RULE [C,U] a moral rule or belief about what is right and wrong, that influences how you behave: *Schools try to teach children a set of principles.* | *He's got no principles at all!* | *It's against my principles to accept gifts from clients.*
2 IDEA BEHIND STH [C] the basic idea that a plan or system is based on: *The* ***general principle*** *is that education should be available to all children up to the age of 16.* | **basic/fundamental/guiding principle** *the basic principles of business management* | **[+of]** *the principles of French law* | **principle that** *Reflexology is based on the principle that specific areas on the feet correspond to different parts of the body.* | **on a principle** *The project worked on the principle that each person's experience was equally valuable.* | **[+behind]** *the principles behind government policies* | *He called for a return to* ***first principles*** (=the most important ideas) *of road safety for children.* | *Similar* ***principles apply*** *in the case of older children* (=the principles are the same as others that have been mentioned).
3 in principle a) if something is possible in principle, there is no good reason why it should not happen, but it has not actually happened yet SYN **theoretically**: *In principle, the new software should make the accounting system a lot simpler.* **b)** if you agree to something in principle, you agree about a general plan or idea but have not yet considered the details: *They have accepted the idea in principle.* | *The government has* ***agreed in principle*** *to a referendum.*
4 RULES OF A PROCESS [C] a rule which explains the way something such as a machine works, or which explains a natural force in the universe: *Archimedes' principle* | **[+of]** *the basic principles of physics* ⚠ Do not confuse the noun **principle** with the noun and adjective **principal**: *a former principal of the college* | *her principal tasks*

COLLOCATIONS

ADJECTIVES

strict principles *Rosa is a woman of strict moral principles.*
strong principles (=that someone believes in very strongly) *a man of strong principles*
high principles (=strong beliefs about right and wrong) *Dunn's high principles and pleasant manner won him the real affection of his colleagues.*
moral principles *Criminal law should be used to protect and reinforce moral principles.*
religious/political principles *Doesn't working on Sunday conflict with your religious principles?*

VERBS

have principles *I may have no money and no power but I have principles.*
stick to your principles (=act according to them, even when this is difficult) *Throughout this time, he stuck to his principles and spoke out against injustice.*
betray/compromise your principles (=do something that is against your principles) *I knew I could lie to help him, but it would be betraying my principles.*
abandon your principles (=stop believing in them or trying to act by them) *It has been said that he abandoned his basic political principles while he was in power.*

PHRASES

be against sb's principles *It's against my principles to eat meat.*
as a matter of principle (=because of moral beliefs about right and wrong) *As a matter of principle one should never yield to terrorism.*
a man/woman of principle (=someone with strong moral ideas) *He is the only candidate who has demonstrated that he is a man of principle.*

prin·ci·pled /ˈprɪnsəpəld/ AWL *adj formal* **1** someone who is principled has strong opinions about what is morally right and wrong: **principled stand/opposition/objection etc** *He took a principled stand against the legislation.* **2** based on clear and definite ideas: *an attempt to reduce prison sentences in a principled way*

print¹ /prɪnt/ ●●● S2 W3 *v*
1 WORDS **a)** [I,T] to produce words, numbers, or pictures on paper, using a machine which puts ink onto the surface: *I need to make a few changes before I print the document.* | *The company's name was printed in bold letters across the top of the page.* | *a printed letter* | *The printer's switched on but it won't print.* | *As a newspaper publisher he understood the power of* ***the printed word*** (=words that are printed on paper). **b)** [I] when a computer document prints, a printed copy of it is produced: *Press return, then the document should print.*
2 BOOKS/NEWSPAPERS [T] to produce many printed copies of a book, newspaper etc: *Over five million copies of the paper are printed every day.* | *When the book was first written no publisher would print it.*
3 IN A NEWSPAPER [T] to print a report of something or a letter, speech etc in a newspaper or magazine SYN **publish**: *'The Express' was the first paper to print the story.* | *'The Telegraph' has printed numerous articles on this subject over the last three years.* | *I wrote to the newspaper but my letter wasn't printed.*
4 PHOTOGRAPH [T] to produce a photograph from a photographic film: *It usually takes a couple of hours for the pictures to be developed and printed.*
5 CLOTH [T] to decorate cloth with a pattern that is put all over its surface by a machine: *a skirt printed with brightly coloured flowers* | *a printed silk shirt*
6 WRITE [I,T] to write words by hand without joining the letters: *Please print your name clearly in the top right-hand corner of the page.*
7 MAKE A MARK [T] to make a mark on a surface or in a soft substance by pressing something on to it: **print sth on/in sth** *The mark of the man's shoe was printed in the mud.*
→ **a licence to print money** at LICENCE(6)
print sth ↔ **off/out** *phr v* to produce a printed copy of a computer document: *Could you print a copy off for me?* | *I'll print the file out and then we can look at it.*

print² ●●○ W3 *n*
1 BOOKS/NEWSPAPERS [U] writing that has been printed, for example in books or newspapers: *There was no print at all on the backs of the tickets.* | **in print** (=printed in a book, newspaper etc) *It must be really exciting to see your work in print.* | *the pleasure of seeing my name in print* | *Very little of his poetry actually* ***got into print*** (=was printed).
2 be in print if a book is in print, new copies of it are still being printed: *After fifty years, the book is still in print.*
3 be out of print if a book is out of print, it is no longer being printed and you cannot buy new copies
4 LETTERS [U] the letters in which something is printed: *The book is also available in* ***large print***. | *The print quality of the new printer is excellent.*
5 the small/fine print the details of a legal document, which are often printed in very small writing: *Always read the small print before signing anything.*
6 MARK [C] a mark that is made on a surface by something that has been pressed onto it: *His feet left deep prints in the soft soil.*
7 prints [plural] the marks that are made by the pattern of lines on the ends of your fingers SYN **fingerprints**: *The police found a set of prints on the car door.*
8 CLOTH [C,U] cloth, especially cotton, on which a coloured pattern has been printed: *a lovely selection of floral prints* | *She was wearing a cotton print dress.*
9 PHOTOGRAPH [C] a photograph that has been produced from a film: *Why don't you order an extra* ***set of prints***? | *a colour print*
10 PICTURE [C] **a)** a picture that is made by cutting lines onto a piece of metal or wood and then printing it onto paper **b)** a copy of a painting that is produced by taking a photograph of it and printing it onto paper

print·a·ble /ˈprɪntəbəl/ *adj* suitable to be printed and read by everyone OPP **unprintable**: *Her remarks were scarcely printable* (=were very rude).

ˌprinted ˈcircuit *n* [C] a set of connections in a piece of electrical equipment consisting of thin lines of metal on a board

ˈprinted ˌmatter *n* [U] printed articles – used especially about advertisements that can be sent by post at a cheap rate

print·er /ˈprɪntə $ -ər/ ●●● S3 W3 *n* [C]
1 a machine which is connected to a computer and can make a printed record of computer information: *a laser printer* | *a colour printer*
2 someone who is employed in the trade of printing

print·ing /ˈprɪntɪŋ/ *n* **1** [U] the act or process of making a book, magazine etc using a machine that puts ink onto paper: *the invention of printing* | *the printing industry* | *a printing error* **2** [C] an act of printing a number of copies of a book: *The first printing of her book was 10,000 copies.* **3** [U] a method of writing when you write each letter separately rather than joining the letters of a word

ˈprinting ink *n* [U] a type of ink that dries very quickly and is used in printing books and newspapers etc

ˈprinting press (*also* **ˈprinting maˌchine**) *n* [C] a machine that prints newspapers, books etc SYN **press**

print·out /ˈprɪntˌaʊt/ *n* [C,U] a sheet or length of paper with printed information on it, produced by a computer

ˈprint run *n* [C] the number of books or magazines that are printed at the same time

pri·on /ˈpraɪɒn, ˈpriː- $ -ɑːn/ *n* [C] a very small piece of PROTEIN that is thought to cause some brain diseases such as BSE

pri·or¹ /ˈpraɪə $ praɪr/ ●●○ W3 AWL *adj*
1 existing or arranged before something else or before the present situation SYN **previous**: *You do not need any prior knowledge of the subject.* | *Changes may not be made without the prior approval of the council.* | *Vegetarian meals are provided by prior agreement.* | *Some prior experience with the software is needed.*
2 prior warning/notice a warning or announcement made before something happens: *The society must* ***give*** *customers* ***prior notice*** *before changing the cost.* | *The bomb exploded* ***without*** *any* ***prior warning***.
3 prior to sth *formal* before: *All the arrangements should be completed prior to your departure.*
4 prior claim a person's right to something which is considered more important than another person's right to the same thing: *His own children have a prior claim to the business.*

prior² *n* [C] **1** the man in charge of a PRIORY **2** the priest next in rank to the person in charge of an ABBEY **3** *informal* a previous occasion when someone was found guilty of a crime: *two priors for homicide*

pri·or·ess /ˈpraɪərɪs/ *n* [C] the woman in charge of a PRIORY

pri·o·ri·tize (*also* **-ise** *BrE*) /praɪˈɒrətaɪz $ -ˈɔːr-/ ●○○ AWL *v* [T]
1 to put several things, problems etc in order of importance, so that you can deal with the most important ones first: *You need to prioritize your tasks.*
2 to deal with one thing first, because it is the most important: *The public wants to see the fight against crime prioritized.* —**prioritization** /praɪˌɒrətaɪˈzeɪʃən $ -ˌɔːrətə-/ *n* [U]

pri·or·i·ty¹ /praɪˈɒrəti $ -ˈɔːr-/ ●●○ S3 W2 AWL *n* (*plural* **priorities**)
1 [C,U] the thing that you think is most important and that needs attention before anything else: *The club's priority is to win the League.* | **first/top/main priority** *The children are our first priority.* | *After several burglaries in the area, security is now a* ***high priority*** (=very important and needing attention soon). | *With so little money available, repairs must remain a* ***low priority*** (=not important and not needing attention soon). | *The customer is high on our* ***list of***

priorities. | *List your tasks* ***in order of priority*** (=most important first).

2 [U] the right to be given attention first and before other people or things: **[+over]** *Buses should* ***have priority*** *over other road users.* | *A young person who has finished the course will be* ***given priority*** *over one who has not.* | *I want to start work on the garden but the house must* ***take priority****.*

3 get your priorities right (*also* **get your priorities straight** *AmE*) to know what is most important and needs attention first: *We need to get our priorities right.*

priority² *adj* before other people or things: *Members receive priority bookings and reduced ticket prices to all concerts.*

pri·o·ry /ˈpraɪəri/ *n* (*plural* **priories**) [C] a building where a group of MONKS or NUNS (=men or women living a religious life) live, which is smaller and less important than an ABBEY → **monastery**

Priory, The one of the mental health treatment centres in the UK run by a company called the Priory Group, best known for helping rich and famous people with drug or alcohol problems

prise *BrE*, **prize** *AmE* /praɪz/ *v* [T always + adv/prep] to move or lift something by pushing it away from something else: *I tried to prise the lid off.*

prise sth **out of** sb (*also* **prise sth from sb**) *phr v* to get something such as information or money from someone when they do not want to give it to you: *I more or less had to prise it out of him.*

pris·m /ˈprɪzəm/ *n* [C] **1** a transparent block of glass that breaks up white light into different colours **2** *technical* a solid object with matching ends and several sides which are the same width all the way up → see picture at SHAPE¹

pris·mat·ic /prɪzˈmætɪk/ *adj* **1** using or containing a PRISM: *a prismatic compass* **2** a prismatic colour is very clear and bright

pris·on /ˈprɪzən/ ●●● S2 W2 *n*

1 [C,U] a building where people are kept as a punishment for a crime, or while they are waiting to go to court for their TRIAL SYN **jail** → **prisoner, imprison**: *He visits his dad* ***in prison*** *every week.* | *Ricky has been* ***out of prison*** *for three years now.* | *They'll probably* ***put*** *him* ***in prison*** *for a long time.* | *Helen was* ***sent to prison*** *for attacking a man with a knife.* | *The two men were arrested only a week after they were* ***released from prison****.* | *Three terrorists* ***escaped from*** *Brixton* ***Prison****.* | *an increase in the number of women* ***going to prison*** | *Mr Gunn received a ten-year* ***prison sentence****.*

2 [U] the system that deals with keeping people in a prison: *the* ***prison service*** | *Does prison deter criminals from offending again?*

3 [C] an unpleasant place or situation which it is difficult to escape from: *The farm felt like a prison to her.*

GRAMMAR

• You use **prison** without 'the' when talking in general about someone being kept somewhere as a punishment: *He is in prison for murder.* | *The judge sent him to prison.*

• You use **the prison** when talking about a particular place: *There are about 600 prisoners in the prison.* | *Visitors to the prison are carefully checked.*

GRAMMAR GUIDE ▸ NOUNS

THESAURUS

prison a large building where people are kept as a punishment for a crime or while they are waiting to go to court for their trial: *He was sentenced to five years in prison.* | *Wandsworth Prison*

jail a prison, or a similar smaller building where prisoners are kept for a short time: *He was taken to a cell in the Los Angeles County Jail.*

gaol /dʒeɪl/ *BrE* another way of spelling **jail**: *He spent the night in gaol.*

penitentiary /ˌpenəˈtenʃəri/ *AmE* a large prison for people who are guilty of serious crimes: *the Ohio State Penitentiary*

correctional facility *AmE formal* an official word for a prison: *1,000 prisoners rioted at the North County Correctional Facility.*

detention centre *BrE*, **detention center** *AmE* a place where young people who have done something illegal are kept, because they are too young to go to prison. Also used about a place where people who have entered a country illegally are kept: *a juvenile detention center*

open prison *BrE* a prison in which prisoners have more freedom than in an ordinary prison, usually because their crimes were less serious

cell a small room in a prison or police station, where someone is kept as a punishment: *a prison cell*

ˈprison camp *n* [C] a special prison in which prisoners of war are kept

pris·on·er /ˈprɪzənə $ -ər/ ●●● S3 W2 *n* [C]

1 someone who is kept in a prison as a legal punishment for a crime or while they are waiting for their TRIAL → **guard, imprison**: *Relationships between the staff and the prisoners are good.* | *Prisoners here only serve short sentences.* | **remand prisoner** *BrE* (=someone who is in prison waiting for their trial) | *The organization is arguing for the release of* ***political prisoners*** (=people in prison because of their political opinions).

2 someone who is taken by force and kept somewhere SYN **captive**: **hold/keep sb prisoner** *The guerrillas kept her prisoner for three months.* | *He was being held prisoner.* | *Our pilot was* ***taken prisoner****.* | *The army advanced,* ***taking*** *200,000* ***prisoners****.*

3 someone who is in a place or situation from which they cannot escape: *He is a prisoner of his own past.*

ˌprisoner of ˈconscience *n* [C] someone who is put in prison because of their political ideas

ˌprisoner of ˈwar *n* [C] a soldier, member of the navy etc who is caught by the enemy during a war and kept as a prisoner

ˌprison ˈvisitor *n* [C] someone who visits prisoners in Britain to help them

pris·sy /ˈprɪsi/ *adj informal* behaving very correctly and easily shocked by anything rude – used to show disapproval —**prissily** *adv* —**prissiness** *n* [U]

pris·tine /ˈprɪstiːn/ *adj* **1** extremely fresh or clean: *a pristine white shirt* THESAURUS ▸ CLEAN **2** something that is pristine is in the same condition as when it was first made: *The car has been restored to* ***pristine condition****.* **3** not spoiled or damaged in any way: *pristine African rainforest*

prith·ee /ˈprɪði/ *interjection old use* please

priv·a·cy /ˈprɪvəsi, ˈpraɪ- $ ˈpraɪ-/ ●●○ *n* [U]

1 the state of being able to be alone, and not seen or heard by other people: *With seven people squashed in one house, you don't get much privacy.*

2 the state of being free from public attention: *each individual's right to privacy*

pri·vate¹ /ˈpraɪvət/ ●●● S1 W1 *adj*

1 NOT FOR THE PUBLIC for use by one person or group, not for everyone OPP **public**: *Morris has a private jet.* | *He made some notes for his private use.* | *Many communists objected to any form of* ***private property****.*

2 NOT GOVERNMENT [only before noun] not related to, owned by, or paid for by the government OPP **public**: *a private hospital* | *There is private ownership of property in a market economy.* | *private education* | **go private** *BrE* (=pay for medical treatment instead of getting it free at a public hospital)

3 FOR ONLY A FEW a private meeting, conversation etc involves only two people or a small number of people, and is not for other people to know about: *I need to have a private discussion with you.* | *Are you alone? I just wanted a private word.*

4 SECRET private feelings, information, or opinions are personal or secret and not for other people to know about: *Jack's private opinion was that she was selfish.* | *Don't read that – it's private.*

5 NOT PUBLICLY KNOWN used about someone who is not known to the public or not working for the government or another organization: *a private citizen | The painting was sold to a private collector. | Seven police and three* ***private individuals*** *needed medical attention.*
6 NOT WORK separate from and not related to your work or your official position: *The president is paying a private visit to Europe. | He enjoys everything he does in both his professional and his* ***private life****.*
7 QUIET PLACE quiet and without a lot of people: *Why don't we go upstairs where it's more private?*
8 PERSON [only before noun] a private person is one who likes being alone, and does not talk much about their thoughts or feelings: *He's a very private man.*
9 **private joke** a joke made between friends, family members etc that other people do not understand → **privately**

THESAURUS

private if something is private, you do not want most people to know about it because it concerns your feelings, your relationships etc: *He didn't want to discuss his private life. | What happens in the bedroom is strictly private.*
personal relating to your private life - used especially about problems, feelings, and questions: *They asked a lot of personal questions. | She talked about her own personal feelings. | I'd rather not talk about it - it's personal.*
secret [only before noun] used about feelings and thoughts that you do not tell anyone about: *Barclay had a secret desire to become an actor. | His secret fear was that Jenny would leave him.*
intimate very private - used about things relating to your relationships and sexual feelings: *an intimate conversation | Many people share intimate details of their lives on the Internet.*
innermost [only before noun] your innermost feelings, thoughts etc are your most private ones: *Counselling often encourages you to reveal your innermost thoughts.*
be none of sb's business if something is none of your business, it is private and you should not ask about it: *It's none of your business how much I earn.*

private² *n* **1 in private** without other people being present: *I need to speak to you in private.* **2** [C] a soldier of the lowest rank **3 privates** [plural] *informal* PRIVATE PARTS

ˌprivate deˈtective *n* [C] someone who can be employed to look for information or missing people, or to follow people and report on what they do

ˌprivate eduˈcation *n* [U] education which parents pay for, rather than free education provided by the government

ˌprivate ˈenterprise *n* [U] the economic system in which private businesses are allowed to compete freely with each other, and the government does not control industry → **private sector**

pri·va·teer /ˌpraɪvəˈtɪə $ -ˈtɪr/ *n* [C] **1** an armed ship in the past that was not in the navy but attacked and robbed enemy ships carrying goods **2** someone who sailed on a privateer

ˌprivate ˈeye *n* [C] *informal* a PRIVATE DETECTIVE

ˌPrivate ˈEye *trademark* a British SATIRICAL magazine which is known for criticizing and making jokes about famous people, and for printing stories about dishonest or embarrassing behaviour by people in public life

ˌprivate ˈincome *n* [C,U] money that someone gets regularly, not from working but because they own part of a business or have money which earns INTEREST

ˌprivate inˈvestigator *n* [C] a PRIVATE DETECTIVE

ˈprivate ˌlaw *n* [U] *law* the part of the law relating to ordinary people, private property, and relationships

ˌprivate ˌlimited ˈcompany *n* [C] a company whose shares are not bought and sold on the STOCK MARKET and can only pass to another person with the agreement of other SHAREHOLDERS

pri·vate·ly /ˈpraɪvətli/ ●○○ *adv*
1 with no one else present SYN **in private**: *I must talk to you privately.*
2 if you feel or think something privately, you do not tell anyone about it: *Laura praised the pictures, though she privately thought they were rather ordinary.* | [sentence adverb] *Privately, Harriet had to agree.*
3 not publicly or as part of your work: [sentence adverb] *Privately, senior officials agreed that not many people had voted.*
4 *especially BrE* using or involving private rather than government institutions: *Both children are privately educated. | a privately owned company*

ˌprivate ˈmedicine *n* [U] *BrE* the system in which medical treatment and advice is not provided by the government but is paid for by the patient or their insurance company → **NHS**

ˌprivate ˈmember *n* [C] *BrE* a Member of Parliament who is not a minister in the government

ˌprivate ˈmember's ˌbill *n* [C] a law introduced to the British Parliament by a Member of Parliament who is not a minister in the government

ˌprivate ˈparts *n* [plural] the sex organs - used when you want to avoid naming them directly

ˌprivate ˈpatient *n* [C] *BrE* someone who pays for medical treatment or advice, rather than receiving it free through the government's system

ˌprivate ˈpractice *n* [C,U] **1** the business of a professional person that is independent of a bigger or government-controlled organization: *Richard set up in private practice.* **2** *AmE* the business of a professional person, especially a doctor, who works alone rather than with others

ˈprivate school *n* [C] a school that is not supported by government money, where education must be paid for by the children's parents → **public school, state school**

ˌprivate ˈsecretary *n* [C] **1** a secretary who is employed to help one person, especially with personal business **2** *BrE* a CIVIL SERVANT whose job is to help a government minister: *a parliamentary private secretary*

ˌprivate ˈsector *n* **the private sector** the industries and services in a country that are owned and run by private companies, and not by the government → **public sector**: *pay increases in the private sector*

ˌprivate ˈsoldier *n* [C] *BrE formal* a soldier of the lowest rank SYN **private**

ˌprivate ˈview (*also* **ˌprivate ˈviewing**) *n* [C] an occasion when a few people are invited to see a show of paintings before the rest of the public

pri·va·tion /praɪˈveɪʃən/ *n* [C,U] *formal* a lack or loss of the things that everyone needs, such as food, warmth, and shelter: *the privations of wartime*

pri·vat·i·za·tion (*also* **-isation** *BrE*) /ˌpraɪvətaɪˈzeɪʃən $ -tə-/ *n* [C,U] the act of privatizing something OPP **nationalization**

pri·vat·ize (*also* **-ise** *BrE*) /ˈpraɪvətaɪz/ *v* [T] if a government privatizes an organization, industry, or service that it owns or controls, it sells it → **nationalize**

priv·et /ˈprɪvɪt/ *n* [U] a bush with leaves that stay green all year, often grown to form a HEDGE

priv·i·lege¹ /ˈprɪvəlɪdʒ/ ●●○ W3 *n*
1 [C] a special advantage that is given only to one person or group of people: *He had no* ***special privileges*** *and was treated just like every other prisoner.* | **[+of]** *the privilege of a good education*
2 [singular] something that you are lucky to have the chance to do, and that you enjoy very much: **the privilege of doing sth** *Today, we* ***have*** *the* ***privilege*** *of listening to two very unusual men.* | **the privilege to do sth** *I* ***had*** *the great* ***privilege*** *to play for Yorkshire. | It is a privilege to hear her play.*
3 [U] a situation in which people who are rich or of a high social class have many more advantages than other people: *wealth and privilege*
4 [U] a situation in which doctors, lawyers etc are

allowed to keep information about their discussions with their patients or CLIENTS secret from other people
5 [C,U] the right to do or say something unacceptable without being punished, especially in Parliament: **breach of privilege** (=a breaking of the rules about what a Member of Parliament can do or say)

privilege² *v* [T] *formal* to treat some people or things better than others

priv·i·leged /ˈprɪvəlɪdʒd/ ●●○ *adj*
1 a) having advantages because of your wealth, social position etc OPP **underprivileged**: *Students from a privileged background have an advantage at university.* | *Only the* ***privileged few*** *can afford private education.* **b) the privileged** [plural] people who are privileged THESAURUS ➤ RICH
2 having a special advantage or a chance to do something that most people cannot do: *Kylie feels fortunate to be in such a* ***privileged position*** *because of her successful TV career.* | **be privileged to do sth** *I was privileged to lead the team.*
3 *law* privileged information is private and is not allowed to be made public by law

priv·y¹ /ˈprɪvi/ *adj* **1 be privy to sth** sharing in the knowledge of facts that are secret: *Colby was privy to the committee's decisions.* **2** *old use* secret and private —**privily** *adv*

privy² *n* (*plural* **privies**) [C] a toilet, especially one outside a house in a small separate building

ˌPrivy ˈCouncil *n* **the Privy Council** a group of important people in Britain who advise the king or queen on political affairs —**Privy Councillor** *n* [C]

ˌprivy ˈpurse, Privy Purse *n* **the privy purse** money given by the British government to the king or queen for their personal use

prix fixe /ˌpriː ˈfiːks, -ˈfɪks/ *adj AmE* a prix fixe meal is a complete meal served for a fixed price

prize¹ /praɪz/ ●●● S2 W2 *n* [C]
1 something that is given to someone who is successful in a competition, race, game of chance etc: *In this month's competition you could* ***win*** *a* ***prize*** *worth £3,000.* | *The* ***first prize*** *has gone to Dr John Gentle.* | **[+for]** *The prize for best photography has been won by a young Dutch photographer.* | *Scientists from Oxford shared the Nobel Prize for Medicine in 1945.* | *The* ***prizes*** *are* ***awarded*** (=given) *every year to students who have shown original thinking in their work.* | *The total* ***prize money*** *was £30,000.*
2 something that is very valuable to you or that it is very important to have: *Fame was the prize.*
3 no prizes for guessing sth *spoken* used to say that it is very easy to guess something: *No prizes for guessing what she was wearing.*

prize² ●○○ *v* [T]
1 to think that someone or something is very important or valuable: *He is someone who prizes truth and decency above all things.* | *The company's shoes are* ***highly prized*** *by fashion conscious youngsters.*
2 the American spelling of PRISE

prize³ *adj* [only before noun] **1** good enough to win a prize or having won a prize: *He has spent months cultivating what he hopes are prize flowers.* → PRIZE-WINNING **2** very good or important: *The Picasso painting is a prize exhibit in the museum.* **3 a prize idiot/fool** *informal* a complete idiot, fool etc

prized /praɪzd/ *adj* extremely important or valuable to someone: *The child held the bag as tightly as if it were her most* ***prized possession.*** THESAURUS ➤ VALUABLE

ˈprize day *n* [C] *BrE* an occasion at a school, usually once a year, when prizes are given to children who have done well in particular subjects

prize·fight /ˈpraɪzfaɪt/ *n* [C] **1** *BrE* a public BOXING match in which two men fight each other without boxing gloves, in order to win money **2** *AmE* a professional BOXING match —**prizefighter** *n* [C] —**prizefighting** *n* [U]

ˈprize-ˌgiving *n* [C] *BrE* a ceremony at which people are given prizes, especially at a school: *the annual school prize-giving* | *a glittering prize-giving ceremony*

ˈprize-ˌwinning *adj* [only before noun] a prize-winning thing or person has won a prize: *a prize-winning novel* | *a prize-winning pianist* —**prize winner** *n* [C]

pro¹ /prəʊ $ proʊ/ ●●○ *n* (*plural* **pros**) [C]
1 someone who is paid to do something, especially play a sport, that other people do for pleasure SYN **professional** OPP **amateur**: *a tennis pro* | *the small gap between top amateurs and pros in golf*
2 *informal* (*also* **old pro**) someone who has had a lot of experience with a particular type of situation: *Cathy's an old pro at organizing raffles.*
3 pros and cons the advantages and disadvantages of something: **the pros and cons of (doing) sth** *We discussed the pros and cons of going to university.*
4 *BrE old-fashioned informal* a PROSTITUTE → **PRO FORMA, PRO RATA**

pro² *adj informal* **1** paid to do something, especially play a sport, that other people do for pleasure SYN **professional**: **turn/go pro** *Most young talented players are determined to turn pro.* **2** *AmE* played or done by people who are paid for what they do: *pro basketball*

pro³ *prep* if you are pro an idea, suggestion etc, you support it: *As a party, they had always been pro family.*

pro- /prəʊ $ proʊ/ *prefix* **1** supporting or approving of something OPP **anti-**: *pro-American* | *the pro-choice lobby* **2** *technical* doing a job instead of someone: *the pro-vice-chancellor*

pro·ac·tive /prəʊˈæktɪv $ proʊ-/ *adj* making things happen or change rather than reacting to events: *a proactive approach to staffing requirements*

pro-am /ˌprəʊ ˈæm◂ $ ˌproʊ-/ *n* [C] a competition, especially in golf, for PROFESSIONALS (=people who play for money) and AMATEURS (=people who play just for pleasure) —**pro-am** *adj*

prob·a·bil·i·ty /ˌprɒbəˈbɪləti $ ˌprɑː-/ ●●○ *n*
1 [C,U] how likely something is, sometimes calculated in a mathematical way SYN **likelihood, chance**: **the probability of (doing) sth** *The probability of winning the lottery is really very low.* | **probability that** *There is a 95% probability that she will not have the disease.* | **high/strong probability** *There's a high probability that the children will follow a different career.* | *You must decide whether,* ***on the balance of probabilities,*** *he committed the crime.*
2 [singular] what is likely or something that is likely: *The probability is that smaller businesses will not have to pay the tax.* | *A peace agreement now seems a probability rather than a possibility.*
3 in all probability very probably: *Mistakes could and, in all probability, would occur.*

prob·a·ble¹ /ˈprɒbəbəl $ ˈprɑː-/ ●●○ *adj* likely to exist, happen, or be true: *The probable cause of the fire was faulty wiring.* | *Success is* ***highly probable.*** | **it is probable (that)** *It seems probable that the accident has damaged her brain.* | **probable outcome/consequence/result** *The probable result of global warming will be a rise in sea levels.*

probable² *n* [C] someone who is likely to be chosen for a team, to win a race etc

prob·a·bly /ˈprɒbəbli $ ˈprɑː-/ ●●● S1 W1 *adv* used to say that something is likely to happen, likely to be true etc: *It will probably take about a week.* | *This would probably be a good time to take a break.* | *It's probably the best movie I have ever seen.* | [sentence adverb] *'Are you going to be able to do this?' 'Yes, probably.'* | *'Is she going to send it back?'* ***'Probably not****, no.'* | **very/most probably** *The building will be replaced, most probably by a modern sports centre.*

pro·bate¹ /ˈprəʊbeɪt, -bət $ ˈproʊbeɪt/ *n* [U] *law* the legal process of deciding that someone's WILL has been properly made

probate² *v* [T] *AmE law* to prove that a WILL is legal

pro·ba·tion /prəˈbeɪʃən $ proʊ-/ *n* [U] **1** a system that allows some criminals not to go to prison or to leave prison, if they behave well and see a probation officer regularly, for a particular period of time: *The judge sentenced Jennings to three years' probation.* | **(put/place sb) on probation** *He pleaded guilty and was placed on probation.*

2 a period of time, during which an employer can see if a new worker is suitable: *a three-month probation period* | **on probation** *Some people are appointed on probation.* **3** *AmE* a period of time in which you must improve your work or behave well so that you will not have to leave your job: *I'm afraid I have no choice but to* ***put*** *you* ***on probation***. —**probationary** *adj*: *a probationary period*

pro·ba·tion·er /prəˈbeɪʃənə $ proʊˈbeɪʃənər/ *n* [C] **1** someone who has recently started a job, especially nursing or teaching, and who is being tested to see whether they are suitable for it **2** someone who has broken the law, and has been put on probation

pro'bation ˌofficer *n* [C] someone whose job is to watch, advise, and help people who have broken the law and are on probation

probe[1] /prəʊb $ proʊb/ ●○○ *v* [I,T]
1 to ask questions in order to find things out, especially things that other people do not want you to know: **[+into]** *I don't want to probe too deeply into your personal affairs.* | *Police probed claims that he had sold drugs.*
2 to look for something or examine something, using a long thin object: *Jules probed the mud gingerly with a stick.*

probe[2] *n* [C] **1** a long thin metal instrument that doctors and scientists use to examine parts of the body **2** a SPACE PROBE **3** an INVESTIGATION in which many questions are asked to discover the truth about something: *a police corruption probe*

prob·ing /ˈprəʊbɪŋ $ ˈproʊ-/ *adj* **1** designed to find things out, especially things that other people do not want you to know: *probing questions* **2** watching carefully and intelligently: *his probing eyes* —**probingly** *adv*

pro·bi·ot·ic /ˌprəʊbaɪˈɒtɪk◂ $ ˌproʊbaɪˈɑː-/ *n* [C,U] a food or other substance that contains BACTERIA and is used in a positive way to improve health, or the use of this type of food to improve health: *Probiotics have been reported to enhance digestion.* | *probiotic yoghurt*

pro·bi·ty /ˈprəʊbəti $ ˈproʊ-/ *n* [U] *formal* complete honesty: *I have always found Bentner to be a model of probity in our dealings.*

prob·lem /ˈprɒbləm $ ˈprɑː-/ ●●● S1 W1 *n* [C]
1 DIFFICULTY a situation that causes difficulties: *She was older than me, but that wasn't really a problem.* | **[+of]** *The problem of street crime is getting worse every year.* | **[+with]** *I've been having a few problems with my car.*

> **REGISTER**
> In writing, people sometimes prefer to use the word **issue** rather than **problem**, as it sounds more neutral and less negative: *the* ***issue*** *of race relations*

2 something wrong with your health or with part of your body: **health problem/problem with your health** *Does she have any long-term health problems?* | **back/heart/kidney etc problem** *If you have back problems you should avoid lifting heavy objects.* | **hearing problem** *Many people with hearing problems try to hide their condition.* | **weight problem** *She refuses to admit to herself that she has a weight problem.* | **emotional/psychological problem** *Is this a sign of some kind of deeper psychological problem?* THESAURUS ILLNESS
3 QUESTION a question for which you have to find the right answer, using mathematics or careful thought: *She gave us 20* ***mathematical problems*** *to solve.*
4 no problem *spoken* **a)** used to say that you are happy to do something or for someone else to do something: *'Can I bring a friend?' 'Sure, no problem.'* **b)** used after someone has said thank you or said that they are sorry: *'Thanks for all your help.' 'No problem!'*
5 have no problem (in) doing sth to do something easily: *I've had no problem recruiting staff.*
6 the (only) problem is (that) ... *spoken* used before saying what the main difficulty in a situation is: *The problem is, there isn't enough time.*
7 that's your/his etc problem *spoken* used to say rudely that someone else is responsible for dealing with a situation, not you: *If you miss the train, that's your problem.*
8 it's/that's not my problem *spoken* used to say rudely that you are not responsible for dealing with a particular problem and are not willing to help: *'We've got a serious staffing shortage.' 'That's not my problem.'*
9 What's your/his etc problem? *spoken informal* used when you think that someone is behaving in a way that is unreasonable
10 Do you have a problem with that? *spoken informal* used to ask someone why they seem to disagree with you, in a way that shows that you are annoyed
11 problem child/family/drinker etc a child etc whose behaviour causes problems for other people

> **COLLOCATIONS**
> **VERBS**
> **have a problem** *We saw water rushing in and realised we had a serious problem.*
> **cause/create a problem** *The building's lack of parking space could cause problems.*
> **present/pose a problem** (=cause it or make it have to be considered) *A shortage of trained nurses is posing major problems.*
> **deal with/sort out a problem** *The state has failed to deal with the problem of violence against women.*
> **tackle/address a problem** (=deal with it) *There is more than one way to tackle this problem.*
> **solve/resolve a problem** (*also* **fix a problem** *informal*) | **overcome a problem** | **face a problem** | **raise a problem** (=mention it, so that people can discuss it) | **encounter/experience a problem**
> **a problem arises/occurs** (*also* **a problem comes up**) (=it happens) *Problems may arise when the family wants to move house.*
> **the problem lies in/with sth** *The problem lies in the design of the rocket.*
> **ADJECTIVES/NOUN + problem**
> **big/major/serious** *The school's biggest problem is a shortage of cash.*
> **little/small/minor** *Old cars often develop minor engine problems.*
> **the main problem** *The main problem for the climbers was lack of sleep.*
> **a real problem** *They quickly found that their real problem lay with marketing.*
> **a difficult problem** | **a fundamental problem** (=relating to the most basic and important parts of something) | **a pressing problem** (=one that needs to be dealt with very soon) | **personal problems** (=relating to your private life and relationships) | **financial/money problems** | **economic problems** | **a technical problem** | **a practical problem**
> **COMMON ERRORS**
> ⚠ It is more usual to say **a big problem, a major problem** or **a serious problem**, instead of saying 'an important problem'.

> **THESAURUS**
> **setback** a problem that stops you from making progress: *The space program suffered a major setback when the space shuttle, Discovery, exploded.*
> **snag** *informal* a problem, especially one that you had not expected: *There's a snag – I don't have his number.*
> **hitch** a small problem that delays or prevents something: *There have been a few last-minute hitches.*
> **trouble** when something does not work in the way it should: *The plane developed engine trouble.*
> **hassle** *spoken* a situation that is annoying because it causes problems: *Just trying to store all this stuff is a hassle.*

prob·lem·at·ic /ˌprɒbləˈmætɪk◂ $ ˌprɑː-/ ●○○ *adj* involving problems and difficult to deal with: *The reforms could turn out to be* ***highly problematic***.

prob·lem·a·tize (*also* **-ise** *BrE*) /ˈprɒbləmətaɪz $ ˈprɑː-/ *v* [T] *formal* to regard or treat something as a problem, when it may not be a problem: *Teachers sometimes problematize the different learning styles of foreign students.*

ˈproblem page *n* [C] *BrE* a page in a magazine where letters are printed about people's personal problems, and answers are suggested

ˈproblem-ˌsolving *n* [U] when you find ways of doing things, or answers to problems: *tasks that involve problem-solving | employees with good problem-solving skills*

pro bo·no /ˌprəʊ ˈbəʊnəʊ $ ˌproʊ ˈboʊnoʊ/ *adj, adv* used to describe work that someone, especially a lawyer, does without getting paid

pro·bos·cis /prəˈbɒsɪs $ -ˈbɑː-/ *n* (*plural* **probosces** /-siːz/ *or* **proboscises**) [C] **1** a long thin tube that forms part of the mouth of some insects and WORMS **2** the long thin nose of some animals such as an ELEPHANT

P

probs /prɒbz $ prɑːbz/ *n* **no probs** *BrE spoken informal* used to say that you will be able to do something easily and with no problems: *It'll be ready by six – no probs.*

pro·ce·du·ral /prəˈsiːdʒərəl/ AWL *adj* [only before noun] *formal* connected with a procedure, especially in a law court: *procedural rules*

pro·ce·dure /prəˈsiːdʒə $ -ər/ ●●○ W3 AWL *n* [C,U]
1 a way of doing something, especially the correct or usual way → **process**: **[+for]** *What's the procedure for applying for a visa?* | **correct/proper/normal etc procedure** *This is standard procedure for getting rid of toxic waste.* | **legal/court/parliamentary etc procedures** *All schools have disciplinary* ***procedures*** *they must* ***follow****.* | *On board, we were given the usual talk on* ***safety procedures*** (=what to do if an accident happens, or to prevent an accident).
2 a medical treatment or operation: *Liposuction is a minor* ***surgical procedure****.*

pro·ceed /prəˈsiːd/ ●●○ S3 W3 AWL *v* [I]
1 *formal* to continue to do something that has already been planned or started: **[+with]** *The government was determined to proceed with the election.* | *Before proceeding further, we must define our terms.*

> **REGISTER**
> In everyday English, people usually say **go ahead** rather than **proceed**: *They decided to* ***go ahead with*** *the project.*

2 *formal* to continue: *Work is* ***proceeding according to plan****.*
3 proceed to do sth to do something after doing something else first – used sometimes to express surprise or annoyance: *Sammy took off his coat and proceeded to undo his boots.*
4 [always +adv/prep] *formal* to move in a particular direction: **[+to/towards/into etc]** *Passengers for Miami should proceed to gate 25.* ⚠ Do not confuse with **precede** (=happen before or go before): *the period of illness that preceded his death*

proceed against sb *phr v law* to begin a legal case against someone

proceed from sth *phr v formal* to happen or exist as a result of something: *ideas that proceed from a disturbed state of mind*

proceed to sth *phr v formal* if you proceed to the next part of an activity, job etc, you do or take part in the next part of it SYN **go on to**: *players who proceed to the finals of the competition*

pro·ceed·ing /prəˈsiːdɪŋ/ ●○○ AWL *n*
1 the proceedings (*also* **the proceeding**) an event or a series of things that happen: *We watched the proceedings in the street below.* | *At this point in the proceedings, my doctor offered me a choice.*
2 [C usually plural] when someone uses a court of law to deal with a legal case: **begin/open/take proceedings (against sb)** *She has begun* ***divorce proceedings****.* | *John is taking* ***legal proceedings*** *against his ex-partner.*
3 the proceedings *formal* the official written records of a meeting, society etc: **[+of]** *the proceedings of the conference*

pro·ceeds /ˈprəʊsiːdz $ ˈproʊ-/ ●○○ AWL *n* [plural] *formal* the money that is obtained from doing something or selling something → **profit**: *We sold the business and bought a villa in Spain with the proceeds.* | **[+of/from]** *The proceeds of the concert will go to charity.*

pro·cess¹ /ˈprəʊses $ ˈprɑː-/ ●●● S1 W1 AWL *n* [C]
1 a series of actions that are done in order to achieve a particular result: *the Israeli–Egyptian* ***peace process*** | *Repetition can help the learning process.* | **[+of]** *the process of economic change* | **slow/lengthy/laborious etc process** *Getting fit again has been a long slow process.* | *the* ***mental processes*** *involved in decision-making*
2 a series of things that happen naturally and result in gradual change: **[+of]** *the* ***natural process*** *of evolution* | *Coal forms by a* ***slow process*** *of chemical change.* | *the digestive process*
3 be in the process of (doing) sth to have started doing something and not yet be finished: *The company is in the process of moving to new offices.*
4 be in process if something is in process, it is happening now: *There was an armed revolt in process.*
5 in the process while you are doing something or something is happening: *I spilt the coffee, burning myself in the process.*
6 process of elimination a way of finding the right answer, the truth etc by gradually deciding that none of the other answers etc are possible: **by (a) process of elimination** *I solved the problem by a process of elimination.*
7 a method of making or producing goods: *the car* ***production process*** | *Recycling is an industrial process.* → DUE PROCESS

process² ●●○ AWL *v* [T]
1 to make food, materials, or goods ready to be used or sold, for example by preserving or improving them in some way: *Goats' cheese may be processed in many ways.* | *Two million workers are employed processing goods for electronic firms.*
2 to deal with an official document, request etc in the usual way: **process an application/claim/transaction etc** *All university applications are processed through this system.* THESAURUS ▸ DEAL
3 to deal with information using a computer: *The new network will enable data to be processed more speedily.*
4 to print a picture from a photographic film → DATA PROCESSING, WORD PROCESSOR

pro·cess³ /prəˈses/ *v* [I always + adv/prep] *formal* to walk or move along in a very slow and serious way, especially as part of a group

pro·cessed /ˈprəʊsest $ ˈprɑː-/ AWL *adj* [only before noun] processed food has substances added to it before it is sold, in order to preserve it, improve its colour etc: **processed cheese/meat/fish etc** | *the artificial colourings and flavourings in processed foods*

pro·ces·sion /prəˈseʃən/ ●○○ *n*
1 [C,U] a line of people or vehicles moving slowly as part of a ceremony → **parade**: **funeral/wedding/carnival etc procession** | *They* ***marched in procession*** *to the Capitol building.*
2 [C] several people or things of the same type, appearing or happening one after the other: **[+of]** *an endless procession of visitors*

pro·ces·sion·al /prəˈseʃənəl/ *adj* [only before noun] relating to or used in a procession

pro·ces·sor /ˈprəʊsesə $ ˈprɑːsesər/ ●○○ *n* [C]
1 the central part of a computer that deals with the commands and information it is given SYN **central processing unit**
2 a machine or person that processes food or other materials before they are sold or used: *US tuna processors* → FOOD PROCESSOR

ˌpro-ˈchoice *adj* someone who is pro-choice believes that women have a right to have an ABORTION → **pro-life**: *the pro-choice lobby*

pro·claim /prəˈkleɪm $ proʊ-/ ●○○ *v* [T] *formal*
1 to say publicly or officially that something important is true or exists → **proclamation**: *The president proclaimed the*

republic's independence. | **proclaim that** *Protesters proclaimed that the girl was innocent.* | **proclaim sb sth** *His son was immediately proclaimed king.*
2 to show something clearly or be a sign of something: *The stripes on her uniform proclaimed her seniority.*

proc·la·ma·tion /ˌprɒkləˈmeɪʃən $ ˌprɑː-/ *n* [C,U] an official public statement about something that is important, or when someone makes such a statement → **proclaim**: *The authorities* ***issued*** *a* ***proclamation*** *forbidding public meetings.* | **[+of]** *the proclamation of Lithuania's independence*

pro·cliv·i·ty /prəˈklɪvəti $ proʊ-/ *n* (*plural* **proclivities**) [C] *formal* a tendency to behave in a particular way, or to like a particular thing - used especially about something bad: **[+to/towards/for]** *The child* ***showed no proclivity*** *towards aggression.* | *his sexual proclivities*

pro·con·sul /prəʊˈkɒnsəl $ proʊˈkɑːn-/ *n* [C] someone who governed a part of the ancient Roman Empire

pro·con·su·late /prəʊˈkɒnsjələt $ proʊˈkɑːnsəl-/ (*also* **pro·con·sul·ship** /-səlʃɪp/) *n* [C] the rank of a proconsul, or the time when someone was a proconsul

pro·cras·ti·nate /prəˈkræstəneɪt/ *v* [I] *formal* to delay doing something that you ought to do, usually because you do not want to do it SYN **put off**: *People often procrastinate when it comes to paperwork.* **THESAURUS** DELAY
—**procrastination** /prəˌkræstəˈneɪʃən/ *n* [U]

pro·cre·ate /ˈprəʊkrieɪt $ ˈproʊ-/ *v* [I,T] *formal* to produce children or baby animals SYN **reproduce**
—**procreation** /ˌprəʊkriˈeɪʃən $ ˌproʊ-/ *n* [U]

proc·tor /ˈprɒktə $ ˈprɑːktər/ *n* [C] *AmE* someone who watches students in an examination to make sure that they do not cheat SYN **invigilator** *BrE* —**proctor** *v* [T]

pro·cu·ra·tor /ˈprɒkjəreɪtə $ ˈprɑːkjəreɪtər/ *n* [C]
1 an official with legal powers, especially in the former Soviet Union, the Roman Catholic Church or the ancient Roman Empire: *the Procurator General of the Ukraine*
2 procurator fiscal an official in Scotland who decides whether someone should be sent to court for a TRIAL

pro·cure /prəˈkjʊə $ proʊˈkjʊr/ *v* [T] *formal* **1** to obtain something, especially something that is difficult to get: **procure sth for sb** *He was accused of procuring weapons for terrorists.* **2** to provide a PROSTITUTE for someone —**procurable** *adj* —**procurement** *n* [U]: *the procurement of raw materials from abroad* —**procurer** *n* [C]

prod¹ /prɒd $ prɑːd/ *v* (**prodded**, **prodding**) [I,T]
1 to quickly push something or someone with your finger or a pointed object SYN **poke**: *'Don't go to sleep,' she said, prodding me in the ribs.* | **[+at]** *Theo prodded at the dead snake.* **2** to make someone do something by persuading or reminding them that it is necessary, especially when they are lazy or unwilling: **prod sb into (doing) sth** *It had prodded Ben into doing something about it.* | *The strike may* ***prod*** *the government* ***into action***. —**prodding** *n* [U]: *He's a bright kid, but he needs prodding.*

prod² *n* [C usually singular] **1** *especially BrE* a quick pushing movement, using your finger or a pointed object SYN **poke**: *'Go on,' he whispered,* ***giving*** *me a* ***prod*** *in the back.* **2** *BrE* when you persuade or remind someone to do something: *Why don't you ring the shop and* ***give*** *them a* ***prod***? **3** a pointed instrument used for pushing animals, to make them move: *a* ***cattle prod***

prod·i·gal¹ /ˈprɒdɪɡəl $ ˈprɑː-/ *adj* [usually before noun] *formal* **1 prodigal son/daughter** someone who leaves their family and home without the approval of their family, but who is sorry later and returns **2** spending money, wasting time etc in a careless way SYN **extravagant**: *a prodigal lifestyle*

prodigal² *n* [C] *literary* someone who spends money carelessly and wastes their time - used humorously

pro·di·gious /prəˈdɪdʒəs/ *adj* [usually before noun] very large or great in a surprising or impressive way: **prodigious amounts/quantities of sth** *Some galaxies seem to release prodigious amounts of energy.* | *the artist's prodigious output* —**prodigiously** *adv*

prod·i·gy /ˈprɒdɪdʒi $ ˈprɑː-/ *n* (*plural* **prodigies**) [C] a young person who has a great natural ability in a subject or skill → **genius**: **child/infant prodigy** | *Mozart was a musical prodigy.*

pro·duce¹ /prəˈdjuːs $ -ˈduːs/ ●●● S1 W1 *v* [T]
1 CAUSE to cause a particular result or effect → **product**: *New drugs are* ***producing*** *remarkable* ***results***. | *a rise in sea level produced by climatic change* | *As a policy, it did not* ***produce the desired effect***.
2 CREATE/MAKE to make, write etc something to be bought, used, or enjoyed by people → **product**, **production**: *The factory produces an incredible 100 cars per hour.* | *How did you manage to produce a meal so quickly?*
→ MASS-PRODUCED **THESAURUS** MAKE
3 MAKE NATURALLY to grow something or make it naturally → **product**, **production**: *This region produces the grapes used in champagne.* | *Plants produce oxygen.*
4 SHOW if you produce an object, you bring it out or present it, so that people can see or consider it: *When challenged, he produced a gun.* | *They were unable to produce any statistics to verify their claims.*
5 PLAY/FILM if someone produces a film or play, they find the money for it and control the way it is made → **producer**: *Costner produced and directed the film.*
6 BABY to give birth to a baby or young animals: *An adult cat may produce kittens three times a year.*

prod·uce² /ˈprɒdjuːs $ ˈproʊduːs/ ●○○ *n* [U] food or other things that have been grown or produced on a farm to be sold: **agricultural/organic etc produce** ***fresh*** *local* ***produce*** | **dairy produce** *BrE* (=milk, butter, cheese etc)

pro·duc·er /prəˈdjuːsə $ -ˈduːsər/ ●●● W3 *n* [C]
1 someone whose job is to control the preparation of a play, film, or broadcast, but who does not direct the actors: **television/film/theatre producer** | *Hollywood producers and movie stars*
2 (*also* **record producer**) someone whose job is to organize and direct the recording and production of a record
3 a person, company, or country that makes or grows goods, foods, or materials → **consumer**: **[+of]** *South Carolina is the fourth largest producer of tobacco.* | **coffee/wine/car etc producer** *leading oil producers*

prod·uct /ˈprɒdʌkt $ ˈprɑː-/ ●●● S1 W1 *n*
1 [C,U] something that is grown or made in a factory in large quantities, usually in order to be sold: **agricultural/dairy/software etc products** *consumer products such as VCRs* | *The London factory assembles* ***the finished product***. | *He works in marketing and product development.*
2 the product of sth a) if someone is the product of a particular background or experience, their character is typical of that background or the result of that experience: *Paula was the product of a sheltered middle-class home.* **b)** if something is the product of a particular situation, process etc, it is the result of that situation or process: *The report was the product of four years' hard work.*
3 [C] *technical* the number you get by multiplying two or more numbers in MATHEMATICS
4 [C] something that is produced through a natural or chemical process: *Hemoglobin is a product of red blood cells.*

THESAURUS

product *n* [C] something that is made or produced in large quantities, usually in order to be sold: *consumer products such as mobile phones* | *dairy products*
goods *n* [plural] things that are produced in order to be sold, especially for use in the home: *They sell furniture and other* ***household goods***. | ***electrical goods*** | ***white goods*** (=large electrical goods used in the home such as washing machines and refrigerators)
commodity *n* [C] *formal* a type of product or raw material that can be bought and sold - used especially about basic food products, metals, and fuels: *The decline in prices for agricultural commodities made the economic situation worse.* | *All metal was a valuable commodity and was rarely wasted.*

P

merchandise *n* [U] *formal* things that are being sold, especially in shops: *Customers are not allowed to handle the merchandise.* | *Sales of books, videos, and other merchandise have increased.*
wares *n* [plural] *written* things that are offered for sale, especially in a market or on the street: *In the market, the traders began selling their wares.* | *Merchants brought their wares from all over the world.*
export *n* [C often plural] a product that is sent to a foreign country in order to be sold: *US exports rose to $11.935 billion.* | *At the moment, oil is their biggest export.*
import *n* [C often plural] goods that are brought from one country into another to be sold there: *The UK clothing industry cannot compete with foreign imports on price.*

P

pro·duc·tion /prəˈdʌkʃən/ ●●● S1 W1 *n*
1 [U] the process of making or growing things to be sold, especially in large quantities → **produce**, **product**: **[+of]** *the production of consumer goods* | **food/oil/milk etc production** *agricultural production and distribution* | **production costs/facilities/processes etc** *high-tech production methods* | **be in production** (=being produced) *By September, the new motors were in production.* | **go into/out of production** (=begin to be produced in large numbers, or stop being produced) *The new model will go into production next year.*
2 [U] the amount of goods that are made or grown: **increase/rise/fall etc in production** *a drop in oil and gas production* | **production levels/targets etc**
3 [U] when something is produced through a natural process: **[+of]** *the skin's natural production of oil*
4 [C,U] a play, film, broadcast etc that is produced for the public, or the process of producing it: *the new Shakespeare production at the Arts Theatre* | *In 1992, Green moved into video production.*
5 on/upon (the) production of sth *formal* when you show something: *Entrance is only permitted on production of a ticket.*

proˈduction ˌline *n* [C] a line of machines and workers in a factory, each doing one job in the process of making a product before passing it to the next machine or worker SYN **assembly line**

proˈduction ˌnumber *n* [C] a scene in a MUSICAL with a lot of people singing and dancing

pro·duc·tive /prəˈdʌktɪv/ ●●○ *adj*
1 producing or achieving a lot OPP **unproductive**: *Most of us are more productive in the morning.* | *a **highly productive** meeting*
2 [only before noun] relating to the production of goods, crops, or wealth: *the economy's productive capacity*
3 productive of sth *formal* causing or resulting in something: *The meeting was productive of several good ideas.*
—**productively** *adv*

prod·uc·tiv·i·ty /ˌprɒdʌkˈtɪvəti, -dək- $ ˌprɑː-/ ●○○ *n* [U] the rate at which goods are produced, and the amount produced, especially in relation to the work, time, and money needed to produce them: **increase/improve/raise productivity** *ways of increasing productivity* | ***high productivity** levels in manufacturing* | *It cost the country $4 million in **lost productivity**.*

ˈproduct ˌplacement *n* [U] a form of advertising in which a company arranges for one or more of its products to appear in a television programme or film

prof /prɒf $ prɑːf/ *n* [C] **1** *informal* a PROFESSOR **2 Prof.** the written abbreviation of ***professor***, used in front of names

pro·fane¹ /prəˈfeɪn/ *adj formal* **1** showing a lack of respect for God or holy things: *profane language* **2** related to ordinary life, not religion or holy things SYN **secular** OPP **sacred**: *sacred and profane art*

profane² *v* [T] *formal* to treat something holy with a lack of respect

pro·fan·i·ty /prəˈfænəti/ *n* (*plural* **profanities**) **1** [C usually plural] offensive words or religious words used in a way that shows you do not respect God or holy things **2** [U] *formal* behaviour that shows you do not respect God or holy things

pro·fess /prəˈfes/ *v* [T] *formal* **1** to say that you do, are etc something, especially when it is not really true: **profess to do/be sth** *The government professes to care about the poor.* | *He professed to be an expert on Islamic art.* **2 profess your innocence** to say that you did not do something bad, especially a crime: *In court, the man was still professing his innocence.* **3** to state a personal feeling or belief openly: *He finally made up his mind to **profess** his **love** for her.* | **profess yourself (to be) sth** *He professed himself satisfied with the results.* **4** to have a religion or belief: *Matt professed no religion.*

pro·fessed /prəˈfest/ *adj* [only before noun] *formal* **1** used to describe a belief that someone has stated openly: *a professed atheist* **2** used to describe a feeling or attitude that someone says they have, but which may not be true: *Their professed aim is to encourage democracy.*

pro·fes·sion /prəˈfeʃən/ ●●○ W3 *n*
1 [C] a job that needs a high level of education and training: **the legal/medical/teaching etc profession** *members of the teaching profession* | **enter/go into/join a profession** *Some students enter other professions such as arts administration.* | *people who work in **the professions*** (=doctors, lawyers etc) | **by profession** *Johnson was a barrister by profession.* | *nurses, social workers, and other people in **the caring professions*** (=ones that involve looking after people) THESAURUS ▸ JOB
2 [singular] all the people who work in a particular profession: *the **medical profession***

GRAMMAR: Singular or plural verb?
- In this meaning, **profession** is usually followed by a singular verb: *Our profession **has** been keen to use new technology.*
- In British English, you can also use a plural verb: *Our profession **have** been keen to use new technology.*

GRAMMAR GUIDE ▸ NOUNS

3 [C] *formal* a statement of your belief, opinion, or feeling: **[+of]** *a profession of faith*
4 the oldest profession the job of being a PROSTITUTE – used humorously

pro·fes·sion·al¹ /prəˈfeʃənəl/ ●●● S2 W1 AWL *adj*
1 JOB [only before noun] **a)** relating to a job that needs special education and training: *What professional qualifications does he have?* | *It is essential to get good **professional advice**.* | *You may need to seek **professional help**.* **b)** relating to your job or work and not to your private life: *professional contacts*
2 WELL TRAINED showing that someone has been well trained and is good at their work: *This business plan looks very professional.* | *a more professional approach to work*
3 PAID doing a job, sport, or activity for money, rather than just for fun → **amateur**: *a professional tennis player* | *a professional army* | **turn/go professional** (=start to do something as a job)
4 TEAM/EVENT done by or relating to people who are paid to do a sport or activity → **amateur**: *a professional hockey team* | *The golf tournament is a professional event.*
5 professional person/man/woman etc someone who works in a profession, or who has an important position in a company or business: *We'd prefer to rent the house to a professional couple.*
6 professional liar/complainer etc someone who lies or complains too much – used humorously
—**professionalization** /prəˌfeʃənəlaɪˈzeɪʃən $ -lə-/ *n* [U]: *the increasing professionalization of childcare services*
—**professionalize** /prəˈfeʃənəlaɪz/ *v* [T]

professional² ●●○ W3 AWL *n* [C]
1 someone who earns money by doing a job, sport, or activity that many other people do just for fun → **amateur**: *Hurd signed as a professional in 1998.* | *top snooker professionals*

2 someone who works in a job that needs special education and training, such as a doctor, lawyer, or ARCHITECT: ***health professionals*** (=doctors, nurses etc)
3 someone who has a lot of experience and does something very skilfully: *You sing like a real professional.*
4 tennis/golf/swimming etc professional someone who is very good at a sport and is employed by a private club to teach its members

pro,fessional 'foul *n* [C] in football, if someone commits a professional foul, they deliberately do something that is against the rules in order to prevent another player from scoring

pro·fes·sion·al·is·m /prəˈfeʃənəlɪzəm/ AWL *n* [U] **1** the skill and high standards of behaviour expected of a professional person: *the dedication and professionalism of our staff* **2** *BrE* the practice of using professional players in sports: *Professionalism has raised the standard of rugby immensely.*

pro·fes·sion·al·ly /prəˈfeʃənəli/ AWL *adv* **1** as part of your work: *Do you need to use English professionally?* **2** in a way that shows high standards and good training: *The magazine wasn't very professionally designed.* **3** as a paid job rather than just for fun: *a chance to play football professionally* **4** by someone who has the necessary skills and training: *The carpet should be professionally fitted.*

pro,fessional 'wrestling *n* [U] a form of entertainment in which people, usually men, fight each other in a way that has been planned before the event —**professional wrestler** *n* [C]

pro·fes·sor /prəˈfesə $ -ər/ ●●● S3 W3 *n* [C]
1 *BrE* a teacher of the highest rank in a university department: *Professor Barclay* | **professor of Chinese/economics/religion etc** *She's been named the professor of English.*
THESAURUS ▸ TEACHER
2 *AmE* a teacher at a university or college: *Ted's a **college professor**.* | **biology/history/French etc professor** *Who's your chemistry professor?* → ASSISTANT PROFESSOR, ASSOCIATE PROFESSOR

pro·fes·so·ri·al /ˌprɒfəˈsɔːriəl◂ $ ˌprɑː-/ *adj* relating to the job of a professor, or considered typical of a professor: *a new professorial chair* | *His beard gives him a very professorial look.* —**professorially** *adv*

pro·fes·sor·ship /prəˈfesəʃɪp $ -sər-/ *n* [C] the job or position of a university or college professor: *a professorship in Japanese*

prof·fer /ˈprɒfə $ ˈprɑːfər/ *v* [T] *formal* **1** to offer something to someone, especially by holding it out in your hands: *Sarah took the glass proffered by the attendant.* | **proffer sb sth** *Poirot proffered him a cigarette.* **2** to give someone advice, an explanation etc: *the proffered invitation*

pro·fi·cien·cy /prəˈfɪʃənsi/ *n* [U] a good standard of ability and skill: **[+in/with/at]** *a high level of proficiency in English* | *Nick's proficiency with computers is well known.*

pro·fi·cient /prəˈfɪʃənt/ *adj* able to do something well or skilfully: **[+in/at]** *Martha's proficient in Swedish.* | *There's only one way to become proficient at anything – practice!* | *a proficient typist* —**proficiently** *adv*

pro·file¹ /ˈprəʊfaɪl $ ˈproʊ-/ ●●○ W3 *n* [C]
1 HEAD a side view of someone's head: *Dani has a lovely profile.* | **in profile** *I only saw her face in profile.*
2 DESCRIPTION a short description that gives important details about a person, a group of people, or a place: *a job profile* | **[+of]** *a short profile of the actor*

PROFILE
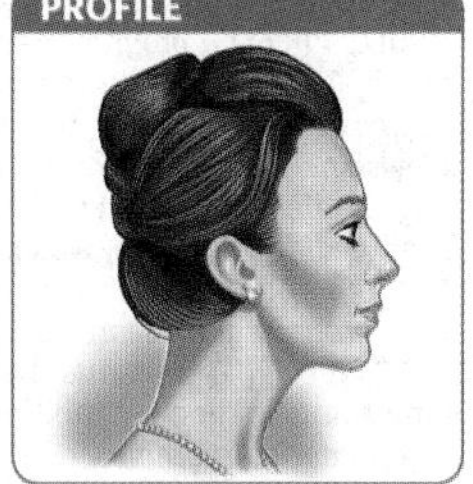

3 high profile something that is high profile is noticed by many people or gets a lot of attention: *Jack runs a department with a high public profile.* | *The star **has a high profile** in Britain.*
4 keep a low profile to behave quietly and avoid doing things that will make people notice you
5 raise sb's profile if a person or an organization raises its profile, it gets more attention from the public: *an advertising campaign designed to raise the bank's profile*
6 SHAPE an edge or a shape of something seen against a background: *the sharp profile of the western foothills against the sky*

profile² *v* [T] to write or give a short description of someone or something: *The new Chief Executive was profiled in yesterday's newspaper.*

pro·fil·ing /ˈprəʊfaɪlɪŋ $ ˈproʊ-/ *n* [U] **1 offender profiling** *BrE* the process of studying a crime, especially a murder, and making judgments about the character of the person who committed it **2** *AmE* when people who belong to a particular race or group are stopped and searched, for example by the police or at airports, because the police think that they are more likely to commit crimes: *racial profiling* **3** when companies collect information about people that they wish to sell something to

prof·it¹ /ˈprɒfɪt $ ˈprɑː-/ ●●● S1 W1 *n*
1 [C,U] money that you gain by selling things or doing business, after your costs have been paid OPP **loss** → **revenue**: *The shop's daily profit is usually around $500.* | *She sold the business and bought a farm with the profits.* | *They sold their house **at a** healthy **profit**.*
2 [U] *formal* an advantage that you gain from doing something: *There's no profit in letting meetings drag on.* → NON-PROFIT

COLLOCATIONS

ADJECTIVES

a big/huge profit *Drug companies make huge profits.*
a quick profit (=happening quickly) *They were only interested in a quick profit.*
a good profit *There is a good profit to be made in selling cars.*
a substantial profit | **a healthy/handsome/tidy profit** (=big) | **a small/modest profit**

VERBS

make a profit *We are in business to make a profit.*
turn/earn a profit (=make a profit) *Without the liquor sales, the store could not turn a profit.*
profits are up/down *Pre-tax profits were up 21.5%.*
profits rise/increase/grow | **profits fall**

THESAURUS

profit money that you gain by selling things or doing business, after your costs have been paid: *Our profits are down this year.* | *The big oil companies have made enormous profits following the rise in oil prices.*
earnings the profit that a company makes: *The company said it expected fourth-quarter earnings to be lower than last year's results.* | *Pre-tax earnings have grown from $6.3 million to $9.4 million.*
return the profit that you get from an investment: *You should get a good return on your investment.* | *We didn't get much of a return on our money.* | *They're promising high returns on investments of over $100,000.*
turnover the amount of business done during a particular period: *The illicit drugs industry has an annual turnover of some £200bn.*
takings the money that a business, shop etc gets from selling its goods in a day, week, month etc: *He counted the night's takings.* | *This week's takings are up on last week's.*
interest money paid to you by a bank or other financial institution when you keep money in an account there: *They are offering a high rate of interest on deposits of over £3,000.* | *The money is still earning interest in your account.*
dividend a part of a company's profit that is divided among the people who have shares in the company:

Shareholders will receive a dividend of 10p for each share. | The company said it will pay shareholders a final dividend of 700 cents a share.

profit² ●○○ *v* [I,T]
1 *formal* to be useful or helpful to someone: **profit sb to do sth** *It might profit you to learn about the company before your interview.* | **[+by/from]** *There are lessons in these stories that all children can profit by.*
2 to get money from doing something: **[+by/from]** *Some industries, such as shipbuilding, clearly profited from the war.*

prof·it·a·bil·i·ty /ˌprɒfətəˈbɪləti $ ˌprɑː-/ *n* [U] when a business or an activity makes a profit, or the amount of profit it makes: *a decline in company profitability*

prof·it·a·ble /ˈprɒfətəbəl $ ˈprɑː-/ ●●○ *adj* producing a profit or a useful result OPP **unprofitable**: *The advertising campaign proved very profitable.* | *a **highly profitable** business* | *a profitable afternoon* —**profitably** *adv*

ˌ**profit and ˈloss acˌcount** *n* [C] *BrE* a financial statement showing a company's income, spending, and profit over a particular period

prof·it·eer·ing /ˌprɒfəˈtɪərɪŋ $ ˌprɑːfəˈtɪr-/ *n* [U] the process of making unfairly large profits, especially by selling things that are very difficult to get at very high prices —**profiteer** *n* [C]: *black market profiteers* —**profiteer** *v* [I]

pro·fit·e·role /prəˈfɪtərəʊl $ -roʊl/ *n* [C] *BrE* a small round PASTRY with a sweet filling and chocolate on the top

prof·it·less /ˈprɒfətləs $ ˈprɑː-/ *adj formal* not making a profit, or not useful to do OPP **profitable** —**profitlessly** *adv*

ˈ**profit-ˌmaking** *adj* [usually before noun] a profit-making organization or business makes a profit OPP **non-profit-making**

ˈ**profit ˌmargin** *n* [C] the difference between the cost of producing something and the price at which you sell it

ˈ**profit ˌsharing** *n* [U] a system by which all the people who work for a company receive part of its profits

ˈ**profits ˌwarning** *n* [C] *BrE technical* an occasion when a company announces that its profit for a particular period of time will be less than expected

prof·li·gate /ˈprɒflɪɡət $ ˈprɑː-/ *adj formal* **1** wasting money or other things in a careless way SYN **wasteful**: *profligate spending* | *the profligate use of energy resources*
2 behaving in an immoral way and not caring that your behaviour is bad —**profligacy** *n* [U] —**profligate** *n* [C]

pro for·ma /ˌprəʊ ˈfɔːmə $ ˌproʊ ˈfɔːr-/ *adj, adv formal* if something is approved, accepted etc pro forma, this is part of the usual way of doing things and does not involve any actual choice or decision: *pro forma approval*

pro ˌforma ˈinvoice *n* [C] *BrE* a document like a bill that is sent to the customer to show what a price would be if he or she made an order SYN **quotation**

pro·found /prəˈfaʊnd/ ●●○ *adj*
1 having a strong influence or effect: **profound effect/influence/impact/consequence etc** *Tolstoy's experiences of war had a profound effect on his work.* | *The mother's behaviour has a profound impact on the developing child.* | *profound changes in society*
2 showing strong serious feelings SYN **deep**: *a **profound sense of** guilt*
3 showing great knowledge and understanding SYN **deep**: *a profound question* | *Jenner is a profound thinker.*
4 *literary* deep or far below the surface of something SYN **deep**: *Her work touches something profound in the human psyche.*
5 complete: *profound deafness*

pro·found·ly /prəˈfaʊndli/ ●○○ *adv*
1 extremely: **profoundly affected/influenced** *He was profoundly affected by his time in the army.* | *The experience had been profoundly disturbing.*
2 profoundly deaf physically unable to hear anything at all

pro·fun·di·ty /prəˈfʌndəti/ *n* (*plural* **profundities**) *formal* **1** [U] when someone or something shows great knowledge and understanding, or strong serious feelings SYN **depth**: *The cartoon version lacks the profundity of the original text.* **2** [C usually plural] something that someone says that shows great knowledge and understanding: *the profundities of her speech*

pro·fuse /prəˈfjuːs/ *adj* produced or existing in large quantities: *He made **profuse apologies**.* | *Profuse sweating is one of the symptoms of heat exhaustion.* —**profusely** *adv*: *The wound was bleeding profusely.* —**profuseness** *n* [U]

pro·fu·sion /prəˈfjuːʒən/ *n* [singular, U] *formal* a very large amount of something: **[+of]** *The house was overflowing with a profusion of strange ornaments.* | **in profusion** *Cornflowers grow in profusion in the fields.*

pro·gen·i·tor /prəʊˈdʒenɪtə $ proʊˈdʒenɪtər/ *n* [C] **1** *formal* someone who first thought of an idea: **[+of]** *a progenitor of cubism* **2** *technical* a person or animal that lived in the past, to whom someone or something living now is related SYN **ancestor**

prog·e·ny /ˈprɒdʒɪni $ ˈprɑː-/ *n* [U] **1** *formal* the babies of animals or plants SYN **offspring 2** someone's children – used humorously SYN **offspring**: *Sarah with her numerous progeny* **3** something that develops from something else: **[+of]** *Connolly's book is the progeny of an earlier TV series.*

pro·ges·ter·one /prəʊˈdʒestərəʊn $ proʊˈdʒestəroʊn/ *n* [U] a female sex HORMONE which prepares the body for having a baby, and which is also used in CONTRACEPTIVE drugs → **oestrogen**

prog·na·thous /prɒɡˈneɪθəs $ prɑːɡ-/ *adj technical* having a jaw that sticks out more than the rest of the face

prog·no·sis /prɒɡˈnəʊsɪs $ prɑːɡˈnoʊ-/ *n* (*plural* **prognoses** /-siːz/) [C] **1** a doctor's opinion of how an illness or disease will develop → **diagnosis**: **good/poor prognosis** *Doctors said Blake's long-term prognosis is good.* **2** *formal* a judgment about the future, based on information or experience: **[+of]** *a hopeful prognosis of the country's future development*

prog·nos·ti·ca·tion /prɒɡˌnɒstɪˈkeɪʃən $ prɑːɡˌnɑːs-/ *n* [C,U] *formal* a statement about what you think will happen in the future SYN **forecast**: *gloomy prognostications* —**prognosticate** /prɒɡˈnɒstɪkeɪt $ prɑːɡˈnɑːs-/ *v* [T]

pro·gram¹ /ˈprəʊɡræm $ ˈproʊ-/ ●●● W1 *n* [C]
1 a set of instructions given to a computer to make it perform an operation: *a word-processing program*
2 the American spelling of PROGRAMME

program² *v* (**programmed**, **programming**) [T] **1** to give a computer a set of instructions that it can use to perform a particular operation: **program sth to do sth** *attempts to program computers to produce and understand speech* | *Any large high-speed computer can be programmed to learn.*
2 the American spelling of programme → **PROGRAMMER**

pro·gram·ma·ble /ˈprəʊɡræməbəl $ ˈproʊ-/ *adj* able to be controlled by a computer or an electronic program: *a programmable heating system*

pro·gramme¹ *BrE*, **program** *AmE* /ˈprəʊɡræm $ ˈproʊ-/ ●●● S1 W1 *n* [C]
1 PLAN a series of actions which are designed to achieve something important: *the US space program* | **programme to do sth** *a United Nations programme to control the spread of AIDS* | **[+of]** *a programme of economic reforms*
2 TELEVISION/RADIO something that you watch on television or listen to on the radio: *What's your favourite **television programme**?* | *news and current affairs programmes* | **[+about/on]** *There's a programme about killer whales next.* | **see/watch a programme**
3 EDUCATION *AmE* a course of study: *Stanford University's MBA program* | *a research program*
4 IMPROVEMENTS actions that have been planned to keep something in good condition or improve something: *a new fitness programme*
5 PLAY/CONCERT a small book or piece of paper that gives information about a play, concert etc and who the performers are: *a theatre programme*
6 LIST OF EVENTS a series of planned activities or events, or a list showing what order they will come in: **[+for]**

What's the programme for tomorrow? | **[+of]** *a programme of exhibitions throughout the year* **THESAURUS** ▸ PLAN

7 MACHINE a series of actions done in a particular order by a machine such as a washing machine: *The light goes off when it finishes the programme.*

8 get with the program *spoken informal especially AmE* used to tell someone to pay attention to what needs to be done, and to do it → PROGRAM[1]

THESAURUS

programme *BrE*, **program** *AmE* /ˈprəʊɡræm/ something that you watch on television, or listen to on the radio: *What's your favourite television programme?* | *I watched an interesting programme about Egypt last night.*

show /ʃəʊ/ a programme on television or the radio, especially an informal one in which people talk together, take part in a game etc: *a late-night talk show* | *game shows* | *She hosts a weekly call-in radio show called 'Got a question?'*

documentary /ˌdɒkjəˈmentəri◂ $ ˌdɑːk-/ a programme that gives you facts and information about a serious subject, such as history, science, or social problems: *a documentary about homeless people* | *a 50-minute television documentary*

soap opera/soap /ˈsəʊp ˌɒpərə $ -ˌɑː-, səʊp/ a television or radio programme that tells an imaginary story about a group of people and their lives, and is often broadcast regularly for many years: *the Australian soap opera 'Neighbours'*

sitcom /ˈsɪtkɒm $ -kɑːm/ an amusing programme in which there is a different story each week about the same group of people: *the American sitcom 'Friends'*

reality TV television programmes that show real people in funny situations or situations in which they must compete with each other. Often the people are filmed continuously for weeks or months: *the reality TV show 'Big Brother'*

webcast a programme, event etc that is broadcast on the Internet: *Universities may record and broadcast some lectures as webcasts.*

podcast a file of recorded sound and sometimes pictures that you can DOWNLOAD from the Internet: *The interview is available as a podcast.*

programme[2] *BrE*, **program** *AmE* *v* [T] **1** to set a machine to operate in a particular way: **programme sth to do sth** *The computers are programmed to search for key words and numbers.* → PROGRAM[2] **2 be programmed** if a person or an animal is programmed socially or biologically to do something, they do it without thinking: **be programmed to do sth** *All birds of this species are programmed to build their nests in the same way.* **3** to arrange for something to happen as part of a series of planned events or activities: *What's programmed for this afternoon?*

ˌprogrammed ˈlearning (*also* **ˌprogrammed inˈstruction**) *n* [U] a method of learning in which the subject to be learned is divided into small parts, and you have to get one part right before you can go on to the next

pro·gram·mer /ˈprəʊɡræmə $ ˈproʊɡræmər/ ●○○ *n* [C] someone whose job is to write computer programs

pro·gram·ming /ˈprəʊɡræmɪŋ $ ˈproʊ-/ ●○○ *n* [U]
1 the activity of writing programs for computers, or something written by a programmer: *a course in computer programming*
2 television or radio programmes, or the planning of these broadcasts: *The Winter Olympics received over 160 hours of television programming.*

pro·gress[1] /ˈprəʊɡres $ ˈprɑː-/ ●●● S2 W2 *n* [U]
1 the process of getting better at doing something, or getting closer to finishing or achieving something: **[+of]** *The police are disappointed by the slow progress of the investigation.* | **[+in]** *There has been significant progress in controlling heart disease.* | **[+towards]** *We are making steady progress towards a peaceful settlement.* | **[+on]** *Little progress has been made on human rights issues.*
2 slow or steady movement somewhere: *We* ***made good progress*** *despite the snow.* | **[+through]** *They watched the ship's slow progress through the heavy seas.*
3 change which is thought to lead to a better society, because of developments in science or fairer methods of social organization: *Mankind is destroying the planet,* ***all in the name of progress*** (=because people want progress). | *Under communism, nothing was allowed to get in the way of* ***the great march of progress.***
4 in progress *formal* happening now, and not yet finished: *A lecture was in progress in the main hall.* | **work/research in progress** *They looked in periodically to check the work in progress.*

GRAMMAR: Countable or uncountable?

- **Progress** is an uncountable noun: *She is making good progress.* ✗ Don't say: *She is making a good progress.*
- **Progress** is not used with 'a'.

COLLOCATIONS

VERBS

make progress *The country has made significant economic progress.*

hinder sb's progress (=make it slower) *Language problems might hinder a child's progress at school.*

achieve progress *The talks ended with no real progress having been achieved.*

check (on) sb's progress *A social worker calls regularly to check on the children's progress.*

follow/monitor/chart sb's progress (=keep checking it)

ADJECTIVES

slow *The task remains difficult and progress has been slow.*

steady *Steady progress has been made towards our objectives.*

good *He is out of hospital and making good progress.*

significant/real progress *Significant progress has been made in reducing nuclear weapons.*

great progress | **substantial/considerable progress** | **satisfactory progress**

THESAURUS

progress *n* [U] /ˈprəʊɡres $ ˈprɑː-/ the process of getting better at doing something, or getting closer to finishing or achieving something: *a test of the students' progress* | *We have made good progress towards meeting our objectives.*

advance *n* [C usually plural] /ədˈvɑːns $ ədˈvæns/ a discovery, invention, or change that brings progress: *the technological advances of the twentieth century*

breakthrough *n* [C] /ˈbreɪkθruː/ an important discovery or achievement that makes progress possible, especially one that happens suddenly after a long period of trying: *The breakthrough in the investigation came when police found a stolen car.*

make headway to make progress towards achieving something – used especially when it is difficult to make progress: *After several months of discussion, the committee had made little headway.*

NO PROGRESS

stalemate/deadlock /ˈsteɪlmeɪt/ [C,U] a situation in which no further progress can be made because two groups or organizations cannot find a way to end a disagreement: *The negotiations ended in deadlock.* | *At that point the strike appeared to have reached a stalemate.*

impasse /æmˈpɑːs $ ˈɪmpæs/ [singular] *formal* a situation in which progress has stopped completely, especially because people cannot agree on what to do next: *The continuing impasse over the budget.*

grind to a halt to slowly stop making any progress: *The economy seems to be grinding to a halt.*

pro·gress² /prəˈgres/ ●●○ *v*
1 [I] to improve, develop, or achieve things so that you are then at a more advanced stage OPP **regress**: *I asked the nurse how my son was progressing.* | **[+to]** *She started with a cleaning job, and progressed to running the company.* | **[+towards]** *We must progress towards full integration of Catholic and Protestant pupils in Ireland.* | **[+beyond]** *Last year the team didn't progress beyond the opening round.*
2 [I,T] if an activity such as work or a project progresses, or you progress it, it continues: *Work on the ship progressed quickly.* | *We're hoping to progress the Lane project more quickly next week.*
3 [I] if time or an event progresses, time passes: *As the meeting progressed, Nina grew more and more bored.* | *Time is progressing, so I'll be brief.*
4 [I] to move forward: *Our taxi seemed to be progressing very slowly.*

P

pro·gres·sion /prəˈgreʃən/ ●○○ *n*
1 [singular, U] a gradual process of change or development: **[+of]** *the* ***natural progression*** *of the disease* | **[+through]** *his career progression through the organization* | **[+from/to]** *the* ***logical progression*** *from accountant to financial controller* | **[+towards]** *Europe's progression towards economic and monetary union*
2 [C] a number of things coming one after the other → **ARITHMETIC PROGRESSION, GEOMETRIC PROGRESSION**

pro·gres·sive¹ /prəˈgresɪv/ ●○○ *adj*
1 supporting new or modern ideas and methods, especially in politics and education: *a progressive administration* | *progressive and forward-looking policies*
2 happening or developing gradually over a period of time: **progressive decline/reduction/increase etc** *the progressive increase in population* | *Britain's progressive decline as a world power*
3 *technical* the progressive form of a verb is used to show that an action or activity is continuing to happen. In English, it consists of the verb 'be' followed by the PRESENT PARTICIPLE, as in 'I was waiting for the bus'. SYN **continuous** —**progressiveness** *n* [U] —**progressivism** *n* [U]

progressive² *n* [C] someone with modern ideas who wants to change things

pro·gres·sive·ly /prəˈgresɪvli/ ●○○ *adv* gradually over a period of time: *The situation became progressively worse.*

proˌgressive ˈtax *n* [singular] a tax that takes more money from people with higher incomes than from people with lower incomes OPP **regressive tax**

ˈprogress reˌport *n* [C] a statement about how something, especially work, is developing

prog rock /ˈprɒg rɒk $ ˈprɑːg rɑːk/ (*also* **progressive rock**) *n* [U] a type of rock music that was produced especially in the 1970s. Prog rock ALBUMS typically have an impressive sound involving electronic KEYBOARDS or ORCHESTRAL instruments, and are often based on a particular idea or story

pro·hib·it /prəˈhɪbɪt $ proʊ-/ ●●○ AWL *v* [T]
1 to say that an action is illegal or not allowed SYN **ban, forbid**: *Smoking is strictly prohibited inside the factory.* | **be prohibited from doing sth** *They are prohibited from revealing details about the candidates.* GRAMMAR **Prohibit** is usually passive in this meaning. THESAURUS ▶ FORBID
2 *formal* to make something impossible or prevent it from happening

pro·hi·bi·tion /ˌprəʊhəˈbɪʃən $ ˌproʊ-/ ●○○ AWL *n*
1 [U] the act of saying that something is illegal: **[+of]** *the prohibition of the sale of firearms*
2 [C] an order stopping something: **[+on/against]** *a prohibition on Sunday trading*

Prohibition *n* the period from 1919 to 1933 in the US when the production and sale of alcoholic drinks was illegal

pro·hi·bi·tion·ist /ˌprəʊhɪˈbɪʃənɪst $ ˌproʊ-/ *n* [C] someone who supported Prohibition

pro·hib·i·tive /prəˈhɪbətɪv $ proʊ-/ AWL *adj* **1** prohibitive costs are so high that they prevent people from buying or doing something: *The cost of land in Tokyo is prohibitive.* **2** a prohibitive rule prevents people from doing things: *prohibitive regulations* —**prohibitively** *adv*: *Moving house would be prohibitively expensive.*

pro·hib·i·to·ry /prəˈhɪbətəri $ proʊˈhɪbətɔːri/ *adj formal* intended to stop something

proj·ect¹ /ˈprɒdʒekt $ ˈprɑː-/ ●●● S1 W1 AWL *n* [C]
1 a carefully planned piece of work to get information about something, to build something, to improve something etc: *The project aims to provide an analysis of children's emotions.* | *a three-year* ***research project*** | *The scheme will now be extended after a successful* ***pilot project*** (=a small trial to test if an idea will be successful). | **project to do sth** *a project to develop a substitute for oil* | *The project is funded by Wellcome plc.* | *a* ***project manager***
2 a part of a school or college course that involves careful study of a particular subject over a period of time: **[+on]** *We're* ***doing*** *a* ***project*** *on pollution.* | *a geography project*
3 (*also* **the projects** *AmE informal*) a HOUSING PROJECT

pro·ject² /prəˈdʒekt/ AWL *v*
1 CALCULATE [T] to calculate what something will be in the future, using the information you have now: *The company projected an annual growth rate of 3%.* | *projected sales figures* | **be projected to do sth** *Total expenditure is projected to rise by 25%.*
2 STICK OUT [I] to stick out beyond an edge or surface SYN **protrude**: **[+out/from/through etc]** *Four towers projected from the main building.* | *projecting teeth*
3 FILM [T] to make the picture of a film, photograph etc appear in a larger form on a screen or flat surface: **project sth onto sth** *She projected the slide onto the wall.*
4 YOURSELF [T] to try to make other people have a particular idea about you: *I hope the team will* ***project*** *a smart professional* ***image***. | **project yourself (as sth)** *his attempts to project himself as a potential leader*
5 PLAN **be projected** to be planned to happen in the future: *the projected closure of the hospital* THESAURUS ▶ PREDICT
6 project your voice to speak clearly and loudly so that you can be heard by everyone in a big room
7 SEND [T] to make something move up or forwards with great force: *The plant projects its seeds over a wide area.*
8 SUCCESS [T] to make someone quickly have success or a much better job: **project sb into/onto etc sth** *His success projected him onto Channel 4's comedy series 'Packet of Three'.*
9 FEELING [T] to imagine that someone else is feeling the same emotions as you: **project sth on/onto sb** *You're projecting your insecurity onto me.*

pro·jec·tile /prəˈdʒektaɪl $ -tl/ *n* [C] *formal* **1** an object that is thrown at someone or is fired from a gun or other weapon, such as a bullet, stone, or SHELL
2 projectile vomiting *informal* when someone VOMITS with a lot of force, especially because they have drunk too much alcohol - used humorously

pro·jec·tion /prəˈdʒekʃən/ ●○○ AWL *n*
1 CALCULATION [C] a statement or calculation about what something will be in the future or was in the past, based on information available now: **[+of]** *projections of declining natural gas production* | **[+for]** *population projections for the next 25 years* | *He declined to* ***make projections*** *about fourth quarter earnings.* | *Early projections show a three-point lead for the Socialists.*
2 STH STICKING OUT [C] *formal* something that sticks out from a surface: *small projections of weathered rock on the hillside*
3 FILM [U] the act of projecting a film or picture onto a screen: *projection equipment*
4 FEELING [U] *technical* the act of imagining that someone else is feeling the same emotions as you
5 PICTURE [C] *technical* a representation of something solid on a flat surface: *a map projection*
6 IMAGINED QUALITIES [C] something that you imagine to have particular qualities because of your wishes or feelings: **[+of]** *The Devil is a projection of our fears and insecurities.* → **MERCATOR PROJECTION**

pro·jec·tion·ist /prəˈdʒekʃənɪst/ *n* [C] someone whose job is to show films by operating a projector

pro·jec·tor /prəˈdʒektə $ -ər/ *n* [C] a piece of equipment that makes a film or picture appear on a screen or flat surface

pro·lapse /ˈprəʊlæps, prəʊˈlæps $ proʊˈlæps, ˈproʊlæps/ *n* [C] *medical* the slipping of an inner part of your body, such as the WOMB, from its usual position

prole /prəʊl $ proʊl/ *n* [C] *BrE old-fashioned not polite* an offensive word for a working-class person

pro·le·tar·i·at /ˌprəʊləˈteəriət $ ˌproʊləˈter-/ *n* **the proletariat** [+ singular or plural verb] the class of workers who own no property and work for wages, especially in factories, building things etc - used in SOCIALIST writings —**proletarian** *adj* —**proletarian** *n* [C]

ˌpro-ˈlife *adj* someone who is pro-life is opposed to ABORTION and uses this word to describe their opinion → **pro-choice**: *a pro-life activist*

pro·lif·e·rate /prəˈlɪfəreɪt/ *v* [I] if something proliferates, it increases quickly and spreads to many different places: *Computer courses continue to proliferate.*

pro·lif·e·ra·tion /prəˌlɪfəˈreɪʃən/ *n* **1** [singular, U] a sudden increase in the amount or number of something: **[+of]** *the proliferation of global media networks* **2** [U] the very fast growth of new parts of a living thing, such as cells

pro·lif·ic /prəˈlɪfɪk/ *adj* **1** a prolific artist, writer etc produces many works of art, books etc: *Handel's prolific output of opera* **2** a prolific sports player produces a lot of runs, GOALS etc: *the most prolific goalscorer this decade* **3** an animal or plant that is prolific produces many babies or many other plants **4** existing in large numbers: *the prolific bird life* —**prolifically** /-kli/ *adv*

pro·lix /ˈprəʊlɪks $ proʊˈlɪks/ *adj formal* a prolix piece of writing has too many words and is boring SYN **wordy**

pro·logue /ˈprəʊlɒg $ ˈproʊlɔːg, -lɑːg/ *n* [C usually singular] **1** the introduction to a play, a long poem etc → **epilogue** **2** *literary* an act or event that leads to a more important event: **[+to]** *a prologue to the final abandonment of trams in London*

pro·long /prəˈlɒŋ $ -ˈlɔːŋ/ ●○○ *v* [T]
1 to deliberately make something such as a feeling or an activity last longer SYN **lengthen**: *I was trying to think of some way to prolong the conversation.*
2 prolong the agony *informal* to make an unpleasant or anxious time last longer, especially when people are waiting for news: *There's no point in prolonging the agony any longer.*

pro·lon·ga·tion /ˌprəʊlɒŋˈgeɪʃən $ ˌproʊlɔːŋ-/ *n* **1** [singular, U] the act of making something last longer: **[+of]** *the prolongation of life* **2** [C] something added to another thing which makes it longer

pro·longed /prəˈlɒŋd $ -ˈlɔːŋd/ ●○○ *adj* continuing for a long time: *prolonged exposure to the sun* | *a prolonged period of time* THESAURUS ▶ LONG

prom /prɒm $ prɑːm/ *n* [C] **1** *AmE* a formal dance party for HIGH SCHOOL students, often held at the end of a school year **2** *BrE informal* a PROMENADE(1) **3** *BrE informal* a PROMENADE CONCERT

prom·e·nade /ˌprɒməˈnɑːd◂, ˈprɒmənɑːd $ ˌprɑːməˈneɪd◂/ *n* [C] **1** *BrE* a wide road next to the beach, where people can walk for pleasure **2** *old-fashioned* a walk for pleasure in a public place: *an evening promenade*

promeˈnade ˌconcert *n* [C] *BrE* a concert at which many of the people who are listening stand rather than sit

promeˈnade deck *n* [C] the upper level of a ship, where people can walk for pleasure

prom·i·nence /ˈprɒmənəns $ ˈprɑː-/ ●○○ *n*
1 [U] the fact of being important and well known: **[+of]** *the prominence of pressure groups as political forces* | **come to/rise to/achieve prominence (as sth)** *She first came to prominence as an artist in 1989.*
2 give sth prominence/give prominence to sth to treat something as specially important: *Every newspaper gave prominence to the success of England's cricketers.*
3 [C] *formal* a part or place that is higher than what is around it

prom·i·nent /ˈprɒmɪnənt $ ˈprɑː-/ ●○○ *adj*
1 important: *a prominent Russian scientist* | **play a prominent part/role (in sth)** *Mandela played a prominent role in the early years of the ANC.* | *The World Cup will have a* ***prominent place*** *on the agenda.*
2 something that is in a prominent place is easily seen: **prominent place/position** *The statue was in a prominent position outside the railway station.*
3 something that is prominent is large and sticks out: *a prominent nose* —**prominently** *adv*: *Her photo was prominently displayed on his desk.*

pro·mis·cu·ous /prəˈmɪskjuəs/ *adj* **1** having many sexual partners: *the risks of promiscuous sexual behaviour* **2** *old use* involving a wide range of different things —**promiscuously** *adv* —**promiscuity** /ˌprɒməˈskjuːəti $ ˌprɑː-/ *n* [U]: *sexual promiscuity*

prom·ise¹ /ˈprɒmɪs $ ˈprɑː-/ ●●● S2 W2 *v*
1 [I,T] to tell someone that you will definitely do or provide something or that something will happen: *Last night the headmaster promised a full investigation.* | **promise to do sth** *She's promised to do all she can to help.* | **promise (that)** *Hurry up - we promised we wouldn't be late.* | **promise sb (that)** *You promised me the car would be ready on Monday.* | *'Promise me you won't do anything stupid.' 'I promise.'* | **promise sth to sb** *I've promised that book to Ian, I'm afraid.* | **promise sb sth** *The company promised us a bonus this year.* | *'I'll be back by 1.00.'* ***'Promise****?' 'Yes! Don't worry.'* | *He reappeared two hours later,* ***as promised****.*
2 [T] to show signs of something: **promise to be sth** *Tonight's meeting promises to be a difficult one.* | *dark clouds promising showers later*
3 promise sb the moon/the earth to promise to give someone something that is impossible for you to give
4 I can't promise (anything) *spoken* used to tell someone that you will try to do what they want, but may not be able to: *I'll try my best to get tickets, but I can't promise anything.*
5 I promise you *spoken* used to emphasize a promise, warning, or statement: *I promise you, it does work!*

GRAMMAR: Patterns with promise

- You **promise to** do something: *He promised to help.*
- You **promise** that you **will** do something: *I promise that I will come to your party.*
- You **promise** someone that you **will** do something: *I promise you that I will come.*
- You **promised** that you **would** do something: *She promised that she would come.*
- You **promised** someone that you **would** do something: *My parents promised me that they would buy me a new car.* ✗ Don't say: *My parents promised me to buy a new car.*
- You can also **promise** someone something: *My parents promised me a new car.*

THESAURUS

promise to tell someone that you will definitely do something, or that something will happen: *He promised to give the book back.* | *The organisers have promised that this year's event will take place.*
swear to make a very serious and sincere promise, for example in a law court: *He had sworn to tell the truth.* | *I would never do that, I swear.*
give sb your word *especially spoken* to promise sincerely that you will do something or that something is true - often used when you are trying to persuade someone that they can trust you: *I give you my word that your money is safe with me.*
vow to make a very serious promise, often to yourself: *She vowed that she would never drink alcohol again.* | *They vowed to carry on their campaign for justice.*

assure to promise someone that something will happen or that something is true, in order to try to make them feel less worried: *Police have assured the public that they are doing everything they can to find the killer.*
guarantee to promise that you will make sure that something will definitely happen, so that there is no question of it not happening: *I guarantee that you will have the documents by tomorrow. | How can you guarantee that this won't happen again?*
pledge to promise publicly or officially that you will do something, for example to give help or money: *The government has pledged to increase overseas aid to $4 billion over the next five years.*
undertake *formal* to make an official or legal promise to do something: *The government undertook to keep price increases to a minimum. | The two sides undertook to respect each other's territory.*
commit to sth *formal* to make a firm and definite promise to do something important, which will affect you for a long time and which could result in serious effects if you fail: *Bobby felt unready to commit to a romantic relationship. | A group of 11 companies has committed to developing a new passenger plane.*

promise² ●●● S3 W2 *n*
1 [C] a statement that you will definitely do or provide something or that something will definitely happen: **[+of]** *We received promises of support from several MPs.* | **[+to]** *He would never break his promise to his father.* | **promise to do sth** *She made a promise to visit them once a month.* | **promise that** *I received a promise that this would not happen again.*
2 [U] signs that something or someone will be good or successful: *a young man full of promise* | *Bill* ***shows*** *great* ***promise*** *as a goalkeeper.* | *She didn't* ***fulfil*** *her* ***early promise****.*
3 [singular, U] a sign that something, usually something good, may happen: **[+of]** *the promise of spring* | *The letter gave a promise of greater happiness.*

COLLOCATIONS
VERBS
make a promise *I made a promise to my mother that I'd look after Dad.*
keep a promise (*also* **fulfil a promise** *BrE*, **fulfill a promise** *AmE formal*) (=do what you promised to do) *She said she would come back, and she kept her promise.*
break a promise (=not do what you promised to do) *Once again, the government has broken its promises.*
ADJECTIVES/NOUN + promise
a solemn promise *As governor, I made a solemn promise to defend the laws of the Republic.*
a firm promise (=definite) | **a vague promise** (=not definite) | **a false/empty/hollow promise** (=one that will not be kept) | **a broken promise** (=one that has not been kept)

ˌPromised ˈLand a) the land of Canaan, which was promised by God to Abraham and his people in the Bible **b)** a place where people want to go because they will be safe and happy there, or a situation that people would like to be true or happen

prom·is·ing /ˈprɒməsɪŋ $ ˈprɑː-/ ●○○ *adj* showing signs of being successful or good in the future: *a promising career in law* | *a promising young actor* | *a promising start* THESAURUS ▸ SUCCESSFUL —**promisingly** *adv*

prom·is·so·ry note /ˈprɒməsəri ˌnəʊt $ ˈprɑːməsɔːri ˌnoʊt/ *n* [C] *technical* a document promising to pay money before a particular date

pro·mo /ˈprəʊməʊ $ ˈproʊmoʊ/ *n* (*plural* **promos**) [C] *informal* a short film that advertises an event or product: *a promo video*

prom·on·to·ry /ˈprɒməntəri $ ˈprɑːməntɔːri/ *n* (*plural* **promontories**) [C] a long narrow piece of land which sticks out into the sea: *a rocky promontory*

pro·mote /prəˈməʊt $ -ˈmoʊt/ ●●○ W2 AWL *v* [T]
1 ENCOURAGE to help something to develop or increase: *a meeting to promote trade between Taiwan and the UK* | *Fertilizer promotes leaf growth.*
2 BETTER JOB to give someone a better more responsible job in a company OPP **demote**: **promote sb to sth** *Helen was promoted to senior manager.* GRAMMAR **Promote** is often passive in this meaning.
3 SELL to help sell a new product, film etc by offering it at a reduced price or by advertising it: *She's in London to promote her new book.*
4 SPORT *BrE* if a sports team is promoted, they play in a better group of teams the next year OPP **relegate**: **be promoted to sth** *They have been promoted to the First Division.* GRAMMAR **Promote** is usually passive in this meaning.
5 PERSUADE to try to persuade people to support or use something: *John Major promoted the idea of a classless society.*
6 ARRANGE to be responsible for arranging a large public event such as a concert or a sports game

pro·mot·er /prəˈməʊtə $ -ˈmoʊtər/ AWL *n* [C] **1** someone who arranges and advertises concerts or sports events: *a boxing promoter* **2** someone who tries to persuade people to support or use something: *promoters of solar energy*

pro·mo·tion /prəˈməʊʃən $ -ˈmoʊ-/ ●●○ S3 W3 AWL *n*
1 [C,U] a move to a more important job or position in a company or organization: *I want a job with good prospects for promotion.* | **[+to]** *Your promotion to Senior Editor is now official.*
2 [C,U] an activity intended to help sell a product, or the product that is being promoted: *a winter sales promotion* THESAURUS ▸ ADVERTISEMENT
3 [U] the activity of persuading people to support something: **[+of]** *the promotion of energy conservation*
4 [U] the activity of helping something to develop or increase: **[+of]** *the promotion of international environmental cooperation*
5 [U] *BrE* when a sports team moves into a better group of teams OPP **relegation**

pro·mo·tion·al /prəˈməʊʃənəl $ -ˈmoʊ-/ *adj* promotional films, events etc advertise something: *a promotional video*

prompt¹ /prɒmpt $ prɑːmpt/ ●●○ W3 *v*
1 [T] to make someone decide to do something: **prompt sb to do sth** *What prompted you to buy that suit?*
2 [T] to make people say or do something as a reaction: *The decision prompted an outcry among prominent US campaigners.*
3 [T] to help a speaker who pauses, by suggesting how to continue: *'I can't decide,' said Beatrice. 'Decide what?' prompted Marlon.*
4 [T] to ask someone to do something on a computer: *A message will appear which will prompt you for certain information.*
5 [I,T] to remind an actor of the next words in a speech

prompt² ●●○ *adj*
1 done quickly, immediately, or at the right time: *Prompt action must be taken.* | *Prompt payment is requested.* | *a prompt response*
2 [not before noun] someone who is prompt arrives or does something at the right time and is not late: *Lunch is at two. Try to be prompt.* —**promptness** *n* [U]

prompt³ ●○○ *n* [C]
1 a word or words said to an actor in a play, to help them remember what to say
2 a sign on a computer screen which shows that the computer has finished one operation and is ready to begin the next

prompt⁴ *adv BrE informal* at the time mentioned and no later SYN **sharp** *AmE*: *The bus will leave at 8 o'clock prompt.*

prompt·er /ˈprɒmptə $ ˈprɑːmptər/ *n* [C] someone who tells actors in a play what words to say when they forget

prompt·ly /ˈprɒmptli $ ˈprɑː-/ ●○○ *adv*
1 at the right time without being late SYN **on time**: *She arrived promptly.*
2 immediately: *She turned off the alarm and promptly went back to sleep.*
3 without delay: *A reply came very promptly.*

prom·ul·gate /ˈprɒməlgeɪt $ ˈprɑː-/ *v* [T] *formal* **1** to spread an idea or belief to as many people as possible **2** to make a new law come into effect by announcing it officially —**promulgator** *n* [C] —**promulgation** /ˌprɒməlˈgeɪʃən $ ˌprɑː-/ *n* [U]

pron. (*also* **pron** *BrE*) the written abbreviation of ***pronoun***

prone /prəʊn $ proʊn/ ●●○ *adj*
1 likely to do something or suffer from something, especially something bad or harmful: **[+to]** *Some plants are very prone to disease.* | **prone to do sth** *Kids are all prone to eat junk food.* | **accident-prone/injury-prone etc** *He's always been accident-prone.*
2 *formal* lying down with the front of your body facing down SYN **prostrate**: *His eyes shifted to the prone body on the floor.* —**proneness** *n* [U] —**prone** *adv*: *Jack lay prone on his bed.*

prong /prɒŋ $ prɒːŋ/ *n* [C] **1** a thin sharp point of something such as a fork that has several points: *sticking out like the prongs of a garden fork* **2** one of two or three ways of achieving something which are used at the same time: **[+of]** *the second prong of the attack* —**pronged** *adj*: *a two-pronged fork*

pro·nom·i·nal /prəʊˈnɒmɪnəl $ proʊˈnɑː-/ *adj technical* related to or used like a PRONOUN —**pronominally** *adv*

pro·noun /ˈprəʊnaʊn $ ˈproʊ-/ ●●● *n* [C] a word that is used instead of a noun or noun phrase, such as 'he' instead of 'Peter' or 'the man' → **DEMONSTRATIVE PRONOUN, PERSONAL PRONOUN**

pro·nounce /prəˈnaʊns/ ●●● S3 *v*
1 [T] to make the sound of a letter, word etc, especially in the correct way → **pronunciation**: *How do you pronounce your name?*
2 [T] to officially state that something is true: **pronounce sb/sth sth** *The victim was pronounced dead on arrival.* | *I now pronounce you man and wife.*
3 [I,T] to give a judgment or opinion: *The scheme was pronounced a failure.* | **[+on/upon]** *He used to pronounce on matters he knew nothing about.*
4 [I,T] *law* to give a legal judgment: **pronounce sentence** (=tell a court of law what punishment a criminal will have)

pro·nounce·a·ble /prəˈnaʊnsəbəl/ *adj* a word, name etc that is pronounceable is easy to say

pro·nounced /prəˈnaʊnst/ *adj* very great or noticeable: *a pronounced Polish accent* | *This disability is more pronounced in men.* —**pronouncedly** /prəˈnaʊnsɪdli/ *adv*

pro·nounce·ment /prəˈnaʊnsmənt/ *n* [C] *formal* an official public statement: **[+on]** *the pope's last pronouncement on birth control*

pron·to /ˈprɒntəʊ $ ˈprɑːntoʊ/ *adv spoken informal* quickly or immediately: *You'd better get back here pronto.*

pro·nun·ci·a·tion /prəˌnʌnsiˈeɪʃən/ ●●● S3 *n*
1 [C,U] the way in which a language or a particular word is pronounced: **[+of]** *Do you know the* ***correct pronunciation*** *of these Gaelic names?*
2 [singular] a particular person's way of pronouncing a word or words

proof¹ /pruːf/ ●●○ S3 W3 *n*
1 EVIDENCE [C,U] facts, information, documents etc that prove something is true: **[+of]** *proof of the existence of life on other planets* | *This latest interview was further proof of how good at her job Cara was.* | **proof (that)** *Do you have any proof that this man stole your bag?* | *There is no proof that the document is authentic.*
2 COPY [C usually plural] *technical* a copy of a piece of writing or a photograph that is checked carefully before the final printing is done: *Can you check these proofs?*
3 MATHEMATICS [C] **a)** a test in mathematics of whether a calculation is correct **b)** a list of reasons that shows a THEOREM (=statement) in GEOMETRY to be true
4 the proof of the pudding (is in the eating) used to say that you can only know whether something is good or bad after you have tried it
5 ALCOHOL [U] a measurement of the strength of some types of alcoholic drink, especially SPIRITS: *70% proof vodka* (=that contains 70% pure alcohol) *BrE* | *70 proof vodka* (=that contains 35% pure alcohol) *AmE*

COLLOCATIONS

VERBS

have proof *The newspaper claimed it had proof that I worked for the CIA.*
provide/give proof *You will be required to provide proof of your identity.*
need proof *He needed proof to back up those allegations.*
there is proof *There is now proof that giant squid do exist.*

ADJECTIVES

further proof (=additional proof) *He showed his driving licence as further proof of his identity.*
scientific proof *They say they have scientific proof that the treatment works.*
living proof (=someone whose existence or experience proves something) *She is living proof that stress need not necessarily be ageing.*
clear proof *His indecision is clear proof of his inability to handle the situation.*
conclusive/tangible proof (=definite proof)

PHRASES

proof of identity (=something that proves who you are) *Do you have any proof of identity, such as a passport?*
proof of purchase (=something that proves you bought something from a particular place) | **proof of ownership**
proof positive (=definite proof that cannot be doubted) *Here is proof positive that she's wrong.*
the burden/onus of proof *law* (=the need to prove that you are right in a legal case) *The burden of proof is on the prosecution.*

proof² *adj* **be proof against sth** *literary* to be too strong or good to be affected by something bad: *Their defences are proof against most weapons.*

proof³ *v* [T] *BrE* **1** to treat a material with a substance in order to protect it against water, oil etc: **be proofed against sth** *climbing gear proofed against water* **2** to proofread something: *Do you want me to proof those documents for you?*

-proof /pruːf/ *suffix* **1** [in adjectives] used to describe something which a particular thing cannot harm or pass through, or which protects people against that thing: *a bulletproof car* | *a waterproof jacket* | *an ovenproof dish* (=that cannot be harmed by heat) **2** [in adjectives] used to describe something which cannot easily be affected or damaged by someone or something: *a childproof container* | *vandal-proof* **3** [in verbs] to treat or make something so that a particular thing cannot harm it or pass through it, or so that it gives protection against it: *soundproof a room* (=so that sound cannot get into or out of it)

proof·read /ˈpruːfriːd/ (*also* **proof**) *v* (*past tense and past participle* **proofread** /-red/) [I,T] to read through something that is written or printed in order to correct any mistakes in it —**proofreader** *n* [C] —**proofreading** *n* [U]: *a proofreading job*

prop¹ /prɒp $ prɑːp/ *v* (**propped**, **propping**) [T always + adv/prep] to support something by leaning it against something, or by putting something else under, next to, or behind it: **prop sth against/on sth** *He propped his bike against a tree.* | *Can we* ***prop*** *the window* ***open*** *with something?*

prop sth ↔ **up** *phr v* **1** to prevent something from falling by putting something against it or under it: *The builders* *are trying to prop up the crumbling walls of the church.* | **[+against]** *paintings propped up against the wall* **2** to help an ECONOMY, industry, or government so that it can continue to exist, especially by giving money: *The government introduced measures to prop up the stock market.* **3 prop yourself up** to hold your body up by leaning against something: **[+on/against/with]** *She propped herself up on one elbow.*

prop² *n* [C] **1** an object placed under or against something to hold it in a particular position **2** [usually plural] a small object such as a book, weapon etc, used by actors in a play or film: *Anna looks after costumes and props.* | *stage props* **3** something or someone that helps you to feel strong: *She was becoming an emotional prop for him.* **4** *informal* a PROPELLER **5** (*also* **prop forward**) one of the players in a RUGBY team, who is large and strong and holds up the SCRUM

prop·a·gan·da /ˌprɒpəˈgændə $ ˌprɑː-/ ●●○ *n* [U] information which is false or which emphasizes just one part of a situation, used by a government or political group to make people agree with them: *the spreading of* ***political propaganda*** | **Nazi/Communist etc propaganda** | **propaganda exercise/campaign** (=something done to show one political opinion) *They have mounted a propaganda campaign against Western governments.* | *the government* ***propaganda machine*** (=people who produce propaganda) —**propagandize** (*also* **-ise** *BrE*) *v* [I,T] —**propagandist** *n* [C]

prop·a·gate /ˈprɒpəgeɪt $ ˈprɑː-/ *v formal* **1** [T] *formal* to spread an idea, belief etc to many people: *The group launched a website to* ***propagate*** *its* ***ideas***. **2** [I,T] if you propagate plants, or if they propagate, they start to grow from a parent plant to produce new plants: *Propagate your plants in fresh soil.* **3** [T] if an animal, insect etc propagates itself or is propagated, it increases in number SYN **reproduce** —**propagation** /ˌprɒpəˈgeɪʃən $ ˌprɑː-/ *n* [U]

prop·a·gat·or /ˈprɒpəgeɪtə $ ˈprɑːpəgeɪtər/ *n* [C] **1** someone who spreads ideas, beliefs etc **2** a covered box of soil in which young plants or seeds are placed so that they can grow

pro·pane /ˈprəʊpeɪn $ ˈproʊ-/ *n* [U] a colourless gas used for cooking and heating

pro·pel /prəˈpel/ *v* (**propelled**, **propelling**) [T] **1** to move, drive, or push something forward → **propulsion**: *a boat propelled by a small motor* | *One of our students was unable to propel her wheelchair up the ramp.* | **propel yourself along/through etc** *She used the sticks to propel herself along.* **2** *written* to make someone move in a particular direction, especially by pushing them: *He took her arm and propelled her towards the door.* **3** to move someone into a new situation or make them do something: **propel sb to/into sth** *The film propelled her to stardom.* | *Company directors were propelled into action.*

pro·pel·lant /prəˈpelənt/ *n* [C,U] **1** an explosive for firing a bullet or ROCKET **2** gas which is used in an AEROSOL to SPRAY out a liquid —**propellant** *adj*

pro·pel·ler /prəˈpelə $ -ər/ *n* [C] a piece of equipment consisting of two or more blades that spin around, which makes an aircraft or ship move

proˌpelling ˈpencil *n* [C] *BrE* a pencil made of plastic or metal, in which the LEAD (=the part used for making marks) can be pushed out as it is used SYN **mechanical pencil** *AmE*

pro·pen·si·ty /prəˈpensəti/ *n* (*plural* **propensities**) [C usually singular] *formal* a natural tendency to behave in a particular way: **propensity to do sth** *the male propensity to fight* | **[+for]** *He seems to* ***have*** *a* ***propensity*** *for breaking things.*

prop·er¹ /ˈprɒpə $ ˈprɑːpər/ ●●● S1 W2 *adj*
1 [only before noun] right, suitable, or correct: *Everything was in its* ***proper place*** (=where it should be). | *the* ***proper way*** *to clean your teeth* | *The* ***proper name for*** *Matthew's condition is hyperkinetic syndrome.* **THESAURUS** SUITABLE
2 socially or legally correct and acceptable OPP **improper**: **it is proper (for sb) to do sth** *I don't feel that it would be proper for me to give you that information.* | ***It is only right and proper*** *that an independent inquiry should take place.*
3 [only before noun] *BrE spoken* real, or of a good and generally accepted standard SYN **decent, real** *AmE*: *When are you going to settle down and get a* ***proper job***? | *Try to eat* ***proper meals*** *instead of fast-food takeaways.*
4 [only after noun] the real or main part of something, not other parts before, after, or near to it: *The friendly chat which comes before the interview proper is intended to relax the candidate.* | *the city centre proper*
5 proper to sth *formal* **a)** belonging to one particular type of thing: *the reasoning abilities proper to our species* **b)** suitable for something: *dressed in a way that was proper to the occasion*
6 [only before noun] *BrE spoken* complete SYN **real**: *He's made a proper fool of himself this time!*
7 very polite, and careful to do what is socially correct: *She was very formal and proper.* → PROPERLY

proper² *adv BrE spoken* **1 good and proper** completely: *We beat 'em good and proper.* **2** used by some people to mean PROPERLY, although most people think that this is incorrect

ˌproper ˈfraction *n* [C] a FRACTION such as ¾, in which the number above the line is smaller than the one below it → **improper fraction**

prop·er·ly /ˈprɒpəli $ ˈprɑːpərli/ ●●● S1 W2 *adv*
1 *especially BrE* correctly, or in a way that is considered right SYN **right** *AmE*: *The brakes don't seem to be working properly.* | *Then he's not doing his job properly.* | *Parents should teach their children to behave properly in public.* | *properly trained staff*
2 *especially BrE* completely or fully SYN **thoroughly**: *Is the chicken properly defrosted?* | *The allegations were never properly investigated.*
3 *formal* really: *Documents properly belonging to the family were taken away.* | **properly speaking** *BrE* (=really) *It isn't, properly speaking, a real science.*
4 used to say that someone is right to do something SYN **rightly**: **quite/very/perfectly properly** *People are, quite properly, proud of their homes.*

ˌproper ˈnoun (*also* **ˌproper ˈname** *especially BrE*) *n* [C] a noun such as 'James', 'New York', or 'China' that is the name of one particular thing and is written with a CAPITAL letter → **noun**

prop·er·tied /ˈprɒpətid $ ˈprɑːpər-/ *adj* [only before noun] *formal* owning a lot of property or land: *the propertied classes*

prop·er·ty /ˈprɒpəti $ ˈprɑːpər-/ ●●● S2 W1 *n* (*plural* **properties**)
1 [U] the thing or things that someone owns: *The hotel is not responsible for any loss or damage to guests'* ***personal property***. | *Some of the* ***stolen property*** *was found in Mason's house.*
2 [C,U] a building, a piece of land, or both together: ***Property prices*** *have shot up recently.* | *the* ***property market*** | *a sign saying '****Private Property****. Keep Out.'* | *property taxes* | **commercial/residential property**
3 [C usually plural] a quality or power that a substance, plant etc has SYN **quality, characteristic**: *a herb with healing properties* | **physical/chemical etc properties** *the chemical properties of a substance* → LOST PROPERTY, REAL PROPERTY, INTELLECTUAL PROPERTY

ˈproperty deˌveloper *n* [C] someone who makes money by buying land and building on it

proph·e·cy /ˈprɒfəsi $ ˈprɑː-/ *n* (*plural* **prophecies**) **1** [C] a statement that something will happen in the future, especially one made by someone with religious or magic powers → **prophet**: **prophecy (that)** *The* ***prophecy*** *that David would become king was* ***fulfilled***. | **[+of]** *the prophecy of Isaiah* **2** [U] the power or act of making statements about what will happen in the future: *She had the gift of prophecy.* → **self-fulfilling prophecy** at SELF-FULFILLING

proph·e·sy /ˈprɒfəsaɪ $ ˈprɑː-/ *v* (**prophesied**, **prophesying**, **prophesies**) [I,T] to say what will happen in the future, especially using religious or magical knowledge SYN **foretell**: **prophesy that** *He prophesied that a flood would cover the earth.* | *There was a great war between the countries, just as the elders had prophesied.* THESAURUS ▸ PREDICT

proph·et /ˈprɒfɪt $ ˈprɑː-/ ●○○ *n* [C]
1 a man who people in the Christian, Jewish, or Muslim religion believe has been sent by God to lead them and teach them their religion: *the prophet Elijah*
2 the Prophet Muhammad, who began the Muslim religion: *followers of the Prophet*
3 the Prophets the Jewish holy men whose writings form part of the Old Testament (=first part of the Bible), or the writings themselves
4 someone who claims that they know what will happen in the future: **prophet of doom/disaster** (=someone who says that bad things will happen) | **false prophet** (=someone whose claims about the future are not true)
5 someone who introduces and spreads a new idea: **[+of]** *Gandhi was the prophet of non-violent protest.*

proph·et·ess /ˌprɒfəˈtes $ ˈprɑːfɪtəs/ *n* [C] a woman who people believe has been sent by God to lead them

pro·phet·ic /prəˈfetɪk/ *adj* correctly saying what will happen in the future: *It turned out to be a prophetic piece of journalism.* | *Lundgren's warnings* ***proved prophetic.*** —**prophetically** /-kli/ *adv*

pro·phet·i·cal /prəˈfetɪkəl/ *adj literary* like a prophet, or related to the things a prophet says or does

pro·phy·lac·tic[1] /ˌprɒfəˈlæktɪk◂ $ ˌprɑː-/ *adj technical* intended to prevent disease: *prophylactic antibiotics*

prophylactic[2] *n* [C] **1** *technical* something used to prevent disease **2** *AmE formal* a CONDOM – often used humorously

pro·phy·lax·is /ˌprɒfɪˈlæksɪs $ ˌprɑː-/ *n* [C,U] *technical* a treatment for preventing disease

pro·pin·qui·ty /prəˈpɪŋkwəti/ *n* [U + of/to] *formal* the fact of being near someone or something, or of being related to someone SYN **proximity**

pro·pi·ti·ate /prəˈpɪʃieɪt/ *v* [T] *formal* to make someone who has been unfriendly or angry with you feel more friendly by doing something to please them SYN **appease** —**propitiation** /prəˌpɪʃiˈeɪʃən/ *n* [U]

pro·pi·ti·a·to·ry /prəˈpɪʃiətəri $ -tɔːri/ *adj formal* intended to please someone and make them feel less angry and more friendly: *a propitiatory gift of flowers*

pro·pi·tious /prəˈpɪʃəs/ *adj formal* good and likely to bring good results: *a propitious moment* | **[+for]** *Conditions after the 1905 revolution were propitious for stable development.* —**propitiously** *adv*

pro·po·nent /prəˈpəʊnənt $ -ˈpoʊ-/ ●○○ *n* [C] someone who supports something or persuades people to do something SYN **advocate** → **opponent**: **[+of]** *Steinem has always been a* ***strong proponent*** *of women's rights.* | **leading/main/major proponent** *Dr George is one of the leading proponents of this view.*

pro·por·tion[1] /prəˈpɔːʃən $ -ˈpɔːr-/ ●●○ W2 AWL *n*
1 PART OF STH [C usually singular] a part of a number or an amount, considered in relation to the whole: **[+of]** *The proportion of women graduates has increased in recent years.* | *Every parent is asked to contribute a proportion of the total cost.* | **high/large/small etc proportion** *The decision affects a significant proportion of the population.* | *Although the majority of offenders are men, a small proportion – about five percent – are women.* THESAURUS ▸ AMOUNT

GRAMMAR: Singular or plural verb?
- In this meaning, **proportion** is usually followed by a singular verb: *A small proportion* ***disagrees.***
- In British English, you can also use a plural verb: *A small proportion* ***disagree.***

GRAMMAR GUIDE ▸ NOUNS

2 RELATIONSHIP [C,U] the relationship between two things in size, amount, importance etc: **the proportion of sth to sth** *What's the proportion of boys to girls in your class?* | **in proportion to sth** *The rewards you get in this job are* ***in direct proportion to*** *the effort you put in.*
3 CORRECT SCALE [U] the correct or most suitable relationship between the size, shape, or position of the different parts of something: *Builders must learn about scale and proportion.* | **in proportion** *Reduce the drawing so that all the elements stay in proportion.* | **in proportion to sth** *Her feet are small in proportion to her height.* | **out of proportion with sth** *The porch is out of proportion with* (=too big or too small when compared with) *the rest of the house.*
4 proportions [plural] **a)** the size or importance of something: *Try to reduce your tasks to more* ***manageable proportions.*** | **of immense/huge/massive etc proportions** *an ecological tragedy of enormous proportions* | **of epic/heroic/mythic proportions** *For most of us, Scott was a hero of mythic proportions.* | **crisis/epidemic proportions** *The flu outbreak has* ***reached*** *epidemic* ***proportions.*** **b)** the relative sizes of the different parts of a building, object etc: *a building of classic proportions* | *the elegant proportions of the living room*
5 out of (all) proportion too big, great, or strong in relation to something: **[+to/with]** *The fear of violent crime has now risen out of all proportion to the actual risk.* | **get/blow sth out of proportion** (=treat something as more serious than it really is) *Aren't you getting things rather out of proportion?* | *The whole issue has been blown out of all proportion.*
6 keep sth in proportion to react to a situation sensibly, and not think that it is worse or more serious than it really is → **perspective**: *Let's keep things in proportion.*
7 sense of proportion the ability to judge what is most important in a situation: **have/keep/lose a sense of proportion** *You can protest by all means, but keep a sense of proportion.*
8 MATHEMATICS [U] *technical* equality in the mathematical relationship between two sets of numbers, as in the statement '8 is to 6 as 32 is to 24' → **ratio**

proportion[2] *v* [T] *formal* to put something in a particular relationship with something else according to their relative size, amount, position etc: **be proportioned to sth** *The amount of damages awarded are proportioned to the degree of injury caused.*

pro·por·tion·al /prəˈpɔːʃənəl $ -ˈpɔːr-/ AWL *adj* something that is proportional to something else is in the correct or most suitable relationship to it in size, amount, importance etc OPP **disproportionate**: **[+to]** *The punishment should be proportional to the crime.* | *The fee charged by the realtor is* ***directly proportional*** *to the price of the property.* | *a proportional increase in costs* —**proportionally** *adv*

proˌportional represenˈtation *n* [U] *especially BrE* (*abbreviation* **PR**) a system of voting in elections by which all political parties are represented in the government according to the number of votes they receive in the whole country

pro·por·tion·ate /prəˈpɔːʃənət $ -ˈpɔːr-/ AWL *adj formal* PROPORTIONAL —**proportionately** *adv*

pro·por·tioned /prəˈpɔːʃənd $ -ˈpɔːr-/ *adj* used to talk about how correct, attractive, suitable etc something is in its size or shape: **well/badly/beautifully etc proportioned** *Arnold's* ***perfectly proportioned*** *body* | *a beautifully proportioned room*

pro·pos·al /prəˈpəʊzəl $ -ˈpoʊ-/ ●●○ S3 W3 *n* [C]
1 a plan or suggestion which is made formally to an official person or group, or the act of making it → **propose**: **[+for]** *the government's proposals for regulation of the industry* | **proposal to do sth** *The committee put forward a proposal to reduce the time limit.* | **proposal that** *They rejected proposals that the president should be directly elected.*
2 when you ask someone to marry you: **marriage proposal/proposal of marriage** *She politely declined his proposal of marriage.*

COLLOCATIONS

VERBS

make a proposal *I'd like to make a proposal.*

put forward/submit a proposal *They put forward a proposal for a joint research project.*
come up with a proposal (=think of one) *The sales staff came up with an innovative proposal.*
draw up a proposal *A committee of experts drew up proposals for a constitution.*
approve/accept a proposal *The proposal was approved by the committee.*
support/back a proposal | reject a proposal | consider a proposal | discuss a proposal | vote on a proposal

ADJECTIVES/NOUN + proposal

a detailed proposal *They drew up a detailed proposal and submitted it to the Department of Energy.*
a specific/concrete proposal *The report will make specific proposals for further investigation.*
a research proposal *Applicants should submit a short research proposal on their chosen topic.*
a budget/tax proposal (=a budget/tax plan) | **a peace proposal** (=a plan to achieve peace)

P

pro·pose /prəˈpəʊz $ -ˈpoʊz/ ●●○ W2 *v*
1 SUGGEST [T] *formal* to suggest something as a plan or course of action → **proposal**: *The changes were first proposed last year.* | *the proposed budget cuts* | **propose (that)** *In his speech he proposed that the UN should set up an emergency centre for the environment.* | **propose doing sth** *The report also proposes expanding the airport.* | **propose sth to sb** *He proposed a compromise to me.* THESAURUS ▸ SUGGEST

REGISTER
In everyday English, people usually say that someone **puts forward** plans, ideas etc, rather than **proposes** them: *The idea was first* ***put forward*** *by a German scientist.*

2 MEETING [T] to formally suggest a course of action at a meeting and ask people to vote on it: **propose a motion/amendment/resolution etc** *The resolution was proposed by the chairman of the International Committee.* | **propose sb for sth** *Mr Leesom proposed Mrs Banks for the position of Treasurer* (=he suggested formally that she should be the treasurer).
3 THEORY [T] to suggest an idea, method etc as an answer to a scientific question or as a better way of doing something: *A number of theories have been proposed to explain the phenomenon.*
4 INTEND [T] *formal* to intend to do something: **propose to do sth** *How does he propose to deal with the situation?* | **propose doing sth** *We still don't know how the company proposes raising the money.*
5 MARRIAGE **a)** [I] to ask someone to marry you, especially in a formal way: **[+to]** *Shaun proposed to me only six months after we met.* **b) propose marriage** *formal* to ask someone to marry you
6 propose a toast (to sb) to formally ask a group of people at a social event to join you in wishing someone success, happiness, etc as they raise and drink a glass of wine: *I'd like to propose a toast to the bride and groom.*

GRAMMAR: Patterns with propose

• In everyday English, you **propose that** someone **does** something: *I propose that Ms Hallam is appointed.*
• In more formal English, you **propose that** someone **do** something, using the base form of the verb (=infinitive without 'to'): *I propose that Ms Hallam be appointed.* ✗ Don't say: *I propose Ms Hallam to be appointed.*
• You can also use the base form when talking about the past: *I proposed that Ms Hallam be appointed.*
• You **propose** that someone **should do** something: *He proposed that we should have another meeting.* This pattern is used especially in British English.
• You say **it was proposed that** someone **(should) do** something: *It was proposed that we (should) have another meeting.*
GRAMMAR GUIDE ▸ VERBS

pro·posed /prəˈpəʊzd $ -ˈpoʊzd/ ●●○ W3 *adj* [only before noun] a proposed change, plan, development etc is one that has been formally suggested to an official person or group: *The document supplies details of the proposed changes.* | *The government is set to vote on the proposed reforms tomorrow.*

pro·pos·er /prəˈpəʊzə $ -ˈpoʊzər/ *n* [C] *formal* a person who formally suggests a plan, course of action etc at a meeting for people to vote on → **seconder**

prop·o·si·tion¹ /ˌprɒpəˈzɪʃən $ ˌprɑː-/ ●○○ *n* [C]
1 STATEMENT a statement that consists of a carefully considered opinion or judgment: **proposition that** *Most people accept the proposition that we have a duty to protect endangered animals.* | *The theory is founded on two basic propositions.*
2 SUGGESTION a suggestion, or something that is suggested or considered as a possible thing to do: *He telephoned Stuart with a proposition.* | **attractive/interesting/practical etc proposition** *The offer of two tickets for the price of one* ***makes*** *it a very attractive* ***proposition***. | *It doesn't sound like a very* ***viable proposition*** *to me.* | *I've got a* ***proposition*** *to* ***put to*** *you.*
3 be a different/tricky/simple etc proposition used to say how easy someone or something will be to deal with: *My new boss is a very different proposition.*
4 LAW (*also* **Proposition**) a suggested change or addition to the law of a state of the US, which citizens vote on: *Proposition 147*
5 MATHEMATICS *technical* something that must be proved, or a question to which the answer must be found – used in GEOMETRY —**propositional** *adj*

proposition² *v* [T] *formal* to suggest to someone that they have sex with you: *Here, prostitutes constantly proposition tourists.*

pro·pound /prəˈpaʊnd/ *v* [T] *formal* to suggest an idea, explanation etc for other people to consider: *The theory of natural selection was first propounded by Charles Darwin.*

prop·py /ˈprɒpi $ ˈprɑːpi/ *adj AusE* unable to walk or run well SYN **lame**

pro·pri·e·ta·ry /prəˈpraɪətəri $ -teri/ *adj formal*
1 *especially BrE* a proprietary product is one that is sold under a TRADE NAME OPP **generic**: *a* ***proprietary brand*** *of insecticide* | *proprietary software products* **2** relating to who owns something: *They have* ***proprietary rights*** *to the data.* | *He has no* ***proprietary interest*** *in the farm* (=he does not own any part of it). **3** proprietary behaviour makes it seem that you think you own something or someone

pro·pri·e·tor /prəˈpraɪətə $ -ər/ *n* [C] *formal* an owner of a business: **[+of]** *the proprietor of a small hotel and restaurant* | **newspaper/garage/cafe etc proprietor**

pro·pri·e·to·ri·al /prəˌpraɪəˈtɔːriəl/ *adj* behaving or feeling as if you own something or someone: **[+about]** *She* ***felt proprietorial*** *about the valley.* —**proprietorially** *adv*

pro·pri·e·tress /prəˈpraɪətrɪs/ *n* [C] *old-fashioned* a woman who owns a business

pro·pri·e·ty /prəˈpraɪəti/ *n formal* **1** [singular, U] correctness of social or moral behaviour OPP **impropriety**: **[+of]** *They discussed the propriety of treating ill children against the wishes of the parents.* | **with propriety** *They conducted themselves with propriety.* **2 the proprieties** *especially BrE* the accepted rules of correct social behaviour: *strict in observing the proprieties*

props /prɒps $ prɑːps/ *interjection informal* used when you want to say publicly that someone has done something good: **props to sb for (doing) sth** *Props to Chris for all of his volunteer work.*

pro·pul·sion /prəˈpʌlʃən/ *n* [U] *technical* the force that drives a vehicle forward → **propel**: **rocket/wind/nuclear/jet propulsion** | *research into liquid hydrogen as a* ***means of propulsion*** —**propulsive** /-sɪv/ *adj*

pro ra·ta /prəʊ ˈrɑːtə $ proʊ ˈreɪtə/ *adj* [only before noun] *especially BrE* a payment or share that is pro rata is calculated according to how much of something is used, how much work is done etc: *Fees are calculated* ***on a pro rata basis***. —**pro rata** *adv*

pro·rate /prəʊ'reɪt $ proʊ-/ *v* [T] *AmE* to calculate a charge, price etc according to the actual amount of service received rather than by a standard sum: *The costs should be prorated.* GRAMMAR **Prorate** is usually passive.

pro·sa·ic /prəʊ'zeɪ-ɪk, prə- $ proʊ-, prə-/ *adj* boring or ordinary: *a prosaic writing style* | *The reality, however, is probably more prosaic.* —**prosaically** /-kli/ *adv*

pro·sce·ni·um /prə'siːniəm, prəʊ- $ prə-, proʊ-/ *n* [C] *technical* the part of a theatre stage that is in front of the curtain: *the* ***proscenium arch*** (=the arch over the stage where the curtain can be attached)

pro·scribe /prəʊ'skraɪb $ proʊ-/ *v* [T] *formal* to officially say that something is not allowed to exist or be done SYN **forbid**, **prohibit**: *The Act proscribes discrimination on the grounds of race.* **THESAURUS** FORBID —**proscription** /-'skrɪpʃən/ *n* [C,U]

prose /prəʊz $ proʊz/ ●○○ *n* [U] written language in its usual form, as opposed to poetry

pros·e·cute /'prɒsɪkjuːt $ 'prɑː-/ ●●○ *v*
1 [I,T] to charge someone with a crime and try to show that they are guilty of it in a court of law: *Shoplifters will be prosecuted.* | **prosecute sb for (doing) sth** *Buxton is being prosecuted for assault.* | **prosecute sb under a law/Act etc** *The company is to be prosecuted under the Health and Safety Act.*
2 [I,T] if a lawyer prosecutes a case, he or she tries to prove that the person charged with a crime is guilty → **defend**: *Mrs Lynn Smith, prosecuting, said the offence took place on January 27.*
3 [T] *formal* to continue doing something: *We cannot prosecute the investigation further.*

pros·e·cu·tion /ˌprɒsɪ'kjuːʃən $ ˌprɑː-/ ●●○ W3 *n*
1 [C,U] when a charge is made against someone for a crime, or when someone is judged for a crime in a court of law: *a* ***criminal prosecution*** | **[+for]** *Walters could* ***face prosecution*** *for his role in the robbery.* | **[+of]** *the prosecution of war criminals* | *The evidence is not sufficient to* ***bring*** *a* ***prosecution against*** *him.*
2 the prosecution the lawyers who try to prove in a court of law that someone is guilty of a crime → **defence**: *the chief* ***witness for the prosecution***
3 [U] *formal* when you do something that is your job: *the prosecution of her duties*

pros·e·cu·tor /'prɒsɪkjuːtə $ 'prɑːsɪkjuːtər/ ●○○ *n* [C] a lawyer who is trying to prove in a court of law that someone is guilty of a crime

pros·e·lyt·ize (*also* **-ise** *BrE*) /'prɒsələtaɪz $ 'prɑː-/ *v* [I,T] *formal* to try to persuade someone to join a religious group, political party etc – used especially when you disapprove of this —**proselytizer** *n* [C] —**proselytizing** *n* [U]

pros·o·dy /'prɒsədi $ 'prɑː-/ *n* [U] *technical* the patterns of sound and RHYTHM in poetry and spoken language, or the rules for arranging these patterns —**prosodic** /prə'sɒdɪk $ -'sɑː-/ *adj*

pros·pect¹ /'prɒspekt $ 'prɑː-/ ●●○ W3 AWL *n*
1 [C,U] the possibility that something will happen: **prospect of doing sth** *I see* ***no prospect*** *of things improving here.* | *There is* ***every prospect*** (=a strong possibility) *of the weather remaining dry this week.* | **[+for]** *There are good prospects for growth in the retail sector.* | **prospect that** *There's a* ***real prospect*** *that England will not qualify for the World Cup.* **THESAURUS** FUTURE
2 [singular] a particular event which will probably or definitely happen in the future – used especially when you want to talk about how you feel about it: **[+of]** *The prospect of marriage terrified Alice.* | *Greeks* ***face the prospect*** *of new general elections next month.* | *He* ***relishes the prospect*** *of a fight.* | **daunting/exciting etc prospect** | **be excited/alarmed/concerned etc at the prospect (of sth)** *She wasn't exactly overjoyed at the prospect of looking after her niece.*
3 prospects [plural] chances of future success: *I had no job, no education, and* ***no prospects***. | **job/career prospects** *Job prospects for graduates don't look good.*
4 [C] a person, job, plan etc that has a good chance of success in the future
5 in prospect *formal* likely to happen in the near future: *A new round of trade talks is in prospect.*
6 [C usually singular] *formal* a view of a wide area of land, especially from a high place

pro·spect² /prə'spekt $ 'prɑːspekt/ *v* [I] **1** to examine an area of land or water, in order to find gold, silver, oil etc → **prospector**: **[+for]** *The company is prospecting for gold in Alaska.* **2** to look for something, especially business opportunities: **[+for]** *salesmen prospecting for new customers*

pro·spec·tive /prə'spektɪv/ ●○○ AWL *adj* [only before noun]
1 prospective employee/candidate/buyer etc someone who is likely to do a particular thing or achieve a particular position
2 likely to happen: *the prospective costs of providing pensions*

pro·spec·tor /prə'spektə $ 'prɑːspektər/ *n* [C] someone who looks for gold, minerals, oil etc

pro·spec·tus /prə'spektəs/ ●○○ *n* [C]
1 *especially BrE* a small book that advertises a school, college, new business etc
2 a document produced by a company that wants the public to buy its shares

pros·per /'prɒspə $ 'prɑːspər/ ●○○ *v* [I] if people or businesses prosper, they grow and develop in a successful way, especially by becoming rich or making a large profit: *Businesses across the state are prospering.*

pro·sper·i·ty /prɒ'sperəti $ prɑː-/ ●○○ *n* [U] when people have money and everything that is needed for a good life: *a time of* ***economic prosperity*** | **[+of]** *the future prosperity of the country*

pros·per·ous /'prɒspərəs $ 'prɑː-/ ●○○ *adj formal* rich and successful: *a prosperous landowner* **THESAURUS** RICH

> **REGISTER**
> In everyday English, people usually say **rich** or **well-off** rather than **prosperous**: ***well-off*** *neighborhoods such as Lakeview*

pros·tate /'prɒsteɪt $ 'prɑː-/ (*also* **'prostate ˌgland**) *n* [C] an organ in the body of male MAMMALS that is near the BLADDER and that produces a liquid in which SPERM are carried

pros·the·sis /prɒs'θiːsɪs $ prɑːs-/ *n* (*plural* **prostheses** /-siːz/) [C] *medical* an artificial leg, tooth, or other part of the body which takes the place of a missing part —**prosthetic** /-'θetɪk/ *adj*

pros·ti·tute¹ /'prɒstɪtjuːt $ 'prɑːstɪtuːt/ *n* [C] someone, especially a woman, who earns money by having sex with people

prostitute² *v* **1** [T] if someone prostitutes a skill, ability, important principle etc, they use it in a way that does not show its true value, usually to earn money: *Friends from the theater criticized him for* ***prostituting*** *his* ***talent*** *in the movies.* **2 prostitute yourself** to work as a prostitute

pros·ti·tu·tion /ˌprɒstɪ'tjuːʃən $ ˌprɑːstə'tuːʃən/ *n* [U] the work of prostitutes

pros·trate¹ /'prɒstreɪt $ 'prɑː-/ *adj* **1** lying on your front with your face towards the ground: *They found him* ***lying prostrate*** *on the floor.* | **prostrate body/figure/form** **2** too shocked, upset, weak etc to be able to do anything: **[+with]** *Julie was prostrate with grief after her father's death.* —**prostration** /prɒ'streɪʃən $ prɑː-/ *n* [C,U]

pro·strate² /prə'streɪt $ 'prɑːstreɪt/ *v* **1 prostrate yourself** to lie on your front with your face towards the ground, especially as an act of religious WORSHIP or as a sign of your willingness to obey someone **2** [T] to make someone too shocked, upset, or weak to be able to do anything: *They were prostrated by grief.* GRAMMAR **Prostrate** is usually passive in this meaning.

pro·tag·o·nist /prəʊ'tægənɪst $ proʊ-/ *n* [C] *formal*

1 the most important character in a play, film, or story SYN **main character** **2** one of the most important people taking part in a competition, battle, or struggle: *the* ***main protagonists*** *in the conflict* **3** one of the most important supporters of a social or political idea: **[+of]** *a protagonist of educational reform*

pro·te·an /ˈprəʊtiən, prəʊˈtiːən $ ˈproʊtiən, proʊ-/ *adj literary* able to keep changing or to do many things

pro·tect /prəˈtekt/ ●●● S2 W2 *v*

1 [I,T] to keep someone or something safe from harm, damage, or illness → **protection, protective**: *Are we doing enough to protect the environment?* | **protect sb/sth from sth** *The cover protects the machine from dust.* | **protect sb/sth against sth** *Physical exercise can protect you against heart disease.* | **protect against sth** *Waxing your car will help protect against rust.*

2 [T] if an insurance company protects your home, car, life etc, it agrees to pay you money if things are stolen or damaged or you are hurt or killed SYN **cover**: *Unemployment insurance means that you are partially protected if you lose your job.* GRAMMAR **Protect** is usually passive in this meaning.

3 [T] to help the industry and trade of your own country by taxing or restricting foreign goods

THESAURUS

protect to keep someone or something safe from harm, damage, or illness: *Don't worry, I'll protect you.* | *The government wants to protect the environment.* | *Eating healthily helps to protect against many diseases.*

give/offer/provide protection to protect someone from something harmful: *Wearing a hat offers some protection from the sun.* | *The drug can give protection against cancer.*

guard to protect a person, place, or object by staying near them and watching them: *Police officers guarded the entrance to the building.* | *He is guarded by armed men.*

save to protect someone or something when they are in danger of being harmed or destroyed: *Local people are fighting to save the theatre from demolition.* | *Emergency aid could save millions of people who are threatened with starvation.*

preserve to keep something, especially buildings or the environment, from being harmed, destroyed, or changed too much: *The organization works to preserve forests.* | *There is little money for preserving historic buildings.*

safeguard to protect something important, such as people's rights, interests, jobs, health etc: *The deal will safeguard 200 jobs at the factory.* | *Laws should do more to safeguard the rights of victims.*

shield to put something in front of something else to protect it. Also used to talk about protecting people from unpleasant situations: *He lifted his hand to shield his eyes from the light.* | *They thought the public should be shielded from the truth.*

shelter to provide a place where someone or something is protected from the weather or from danger: *The village is sheltered by a belt of trees.* | *His family had sheltered Jews during the war.*

harbour *BrE*, **harbor** *AmE* to help and protect someone who has done something illegal, and prevent the police from finding them: *He is accused of harbouring suspected terrorists.*

pro·tect·ed /prəˈtektɪd/ *adj* a protected animal, plant, area, or building is one that it is illegal to harm or damage: *Spotted owls are a* ***protected species****.*

pro·tec·tion /prəˈtekʃən/ ●●● S2 W2 *n*

1 [U] when someone or something is protected: **[+of]** *the protection of the environment* | **[+against/from]** *evidence that vitamin C* ***gives protection*** *against cancer* | **[+for]** *This law* ***provides protection*** *for threatened animals and plants.* | **for protection** *The police were issued with body armour for extra protection.*

2 [C,U] something that protects: **as (a) protection (against sth)** *Magee pulled up his collar as protection against the breeze.*

3 [U] the promise of payment from an insurance company if something bad happens SYN **coverage**

4 [U] CONTRACEPTION: *Do you have any protection?*

5 [U] when criminals threaten to damage your property or hurt you unless you pay them money: *protection money* | *a* ***protection racket*** (=the illegal activity of demanding money for protection)

pro·tec·tion·is·m /prəˈtekʃənɪzəm/ *n* [U] when a government tries to help industries in its own country by taxing or restricting foreign goods —**protectionist** *adj* —**protectionist** *n* [C]

pro·tec·tive /prəˈtektɪv/ ●○○ *adj*

1 [only before noun] used or intended for protection: *protective clothing* | *Sunscreen provides a protective layer against the sun's harmful rays.*

2 wanting to protect someone from harm or danger: **[+towards]** *I can't help feeling protective towards my kids.* | **[+of]** *He's very protective of his younger brother.*

3 intended to give an advantage to your own country's industry: *protective tariffs* —**protectively** *adv* —**protectiveness** *n* [U]

proˌtective ˈcustody *n* [U] a situation in which the police make you stay somewhere to protect you from people who could harm you: **in/into protective custody** *The children were* ***taken into protective custody****.*

pro·tec·tor /prəˈtektə $ -ər/ *n* [C] someone or something that protects someone or something else

pro·tec·tor·ate /prəˈtektərət/ *n* [C] a country that is protected and controlled by a more powerful country

prot·é·gé /ˈprɒtəʒeɪ $ ˈproʊ-/ *n* [C] someone, especially a young person, who is taught and helped by someone who has influence, power, or more experience: *She attempted to encourage her young protégé.*

pro·tein /ˈprəʊtiːn $ ˈproʊ-/ ●●○ *n* [C,U] one of several natural substances that exist in food such as meat, eggs, and beans, and which your body needs in order to grow and remain strong and healthy

pro tem /ˌprəʊ ˈtem $ ˌproʊ-/ (*also* **pro tem·po·re** /-ˈtempəreɪ/) *adj* [only after noun] *formal* happening or existing now, but only for a short time: *the president pro tem of the Senate*

pro·test¹ /ˈprəʊtest $ ˈproʊ-/ ●●○ W3 *n*

1 [C,U] something that you do to show publicly that you think that something is wrong and unfair, for example taking part in big public meetings, refusing to work, or refusing to buy a company's products: **[+against]** *Students held a protest march against the war.* | *Five thousand employees came out on strike* ***in protest at*** *the poor working conditions.*

2 [C] words or actions that show that you do not want someone to do something or that you dislike something very much: **[+from]** *I turned off the TV, despite* ***loud protests*** *from the kids.* | **without protest** *He accepted his punishment without protest.* | *She* ***ignored his protests*** *and walked away.* | *The programme caused a* ***storm of protest*** (=a lot of angry protest). | *The announcement was met with* ***howls of protest****.*

3 do sth under protest to do something while making it clear that you do not want to do it: *The bill was eventually paid under protest.*

COLLOCATIONS

VERBS

hold/stage/mount a protest *Opponents of the plan have staged several protests.*

lead to/spark (off) protests (=cause them) *The arrests sparked off violent street protests.*

protests erupt (=start suddenly)

ADJECTIVES/NOUN + protest

a public/popular protest *The announcement led to widespread public protests.*

political protest *Lee spent five years in prison for his involvement in political protest.*

a peaceful protest *Some 5,000 students and others began a peaceful protest.*
a violent/angry protest | **a mass protest** (=one involving a lot of people) | **a student protest** | **a street protest**

protest + NOUN

a protest group/movement *Students at the heart of the protest movement have called for a general strike.*
a protest march | **a protest rally** (=a large outdoor public meeting to protest about something)

pro·test² /prəˈtest $ ˈprə-/ ●●○ *v*
1 [I,T] to come together to publicly express disapproval or opposition to something: **[+against/at/about]** *Thousands of people blocked the street, protesting against the new legislation.* | **protest sth** *AmE*: *Students protested the decision.*
2 [I,T] to say that you strongly disagree with or are angry about something because you think it is wrong or unfair: *'I don't see why I should take the blame for this!' she protested.* | **protest that** *Clive protested that he hadn't been given enough time to do everything.* THESAURUS ➤ COMPLAIN
3 [T] to state very firmly that something is true, when other people do not believe you: **protest (that)** *Sarah protested that she wasn't Mick's girlfriend.* | *Years later, he is still* ***protesting*** *his* ***innocence***.

Prot·es·tant /ˈprɒtəstənt $ ˈprɑː-/ *n* [C] a member of a part of the Christian Church that separated from the Roman Catholic Church in the 16th century —**Protestant** *adj* —**Protestantism** *n* [U]

prot·es·ta·tion /ˌprɒtəˈsteɪʃən ˌprəʊ- $ ˌprɑː-, ˌproʊ-/ *n* [C] *formal* a strong statement saying that something is true or not true, when other people believe the opposite: **[+of]** *protestations of innocence*

pro·test·er, **protestor** /prəˈtestə $ -ər/ ●●○ *n* [C] someone who takes part in a public activity such as a DEMONSTRATION in order to show their opposition to something

proto- /prəʊtəʊ, -tə $ proʊtoʊ, -tə/ *prefix technical* existing or coming before other things of the same type: *a proto-fascist group* | *a prototype*

pro·to·col /ˈprəʊtəkɒl $ ˈproʊtəkɒːl, -kɑːl/ ●○○ AWL *n*
1 [U] a system of rules about the correct way to behave on an official occasion: *a breach of* ***diplomatic protocol***
2 [C] *formal* **a)** an international agreement between two or more countries: *the Montreal Protocol on the protection of the ozone layer* **b)** a written record of a formal or international agreement, or an early form of an agreement
3 [C] *technical* an established method for connecting computers so that they can exchange information
4 [C] *technical* a set of rules that are followed when doing a scientific EXPERIMENT or giving someone medical treatment

pro·ton /ˈprəʊtɒn $ ˈproʊtɑːn/ *n* [C] a very small piece of matter with a positive electrical CHARGE that is in the central part of an atom → **electron**, **neutron** → see picture at ATOM

pro·to·plas·m /ˈprəʊtəplæzəm $ ˈproʊ-/ *n* [U] *technical* the colourless substance that forms the cells of plants and animals

pro·to·type /ˈprəʊtətaɪp $ ˈproʊ-/ ●○○ *n* [C]
1 the first form that a new design of a car, machine etc has, or a model of it used to test the design before it is produced: **[+of/for]** *a* ***working prototype*** *of the new car*
2 someone or something that is one of the first and most typical examples of a group or situation

pro·to·typ·i·cal /ˌprəʊtəˈtɪpɪkəl◂ $ ˌproʊ-/ *adj* very typical of a group or type: *prototypical behaviour*

pro·to·zo·an /ˌprəʊtəˈzəʊən $ ˌproʊtəˈzoʊən/ (*also* **pro·to·zo·on** /-ˈzəʊɒn $ -ˈzoʊɑːn/) *n* (*plural* **protozoa** /-ˈzəʊə $ -ˈzoʊə/ *or* **protozoans**) [C] a very small living thing that has only one cell —**protozoan** *adj*

pro·trac·ted /prəˈtræktɪd/ *adj* used to describe something that continues for a long time, especially if it takes longer than usual, necessary, or expected SYN **lengthy**: **protracted negotiations/discussions/debate etc** *the expense of a protracted legal battle* THESAURUS ➤ LONG

pro·trac·tor /prəˈtræktə $ proʊˈtræktər/ *n* [C] a piece of plastic in the shape of a half-circle, which is used for measuring and drawing angles → **set square** → see picture at MATHEMATICS

pro·trude /prəˈtruːd $ proʊ-/ *v* [I] *written* to stick out from somewhere: **[+from]** *The envelope was protruding from her bag.*

REGISTER
In everyday English, people usually say **stick out** rather than **protrude**: *The envelope was* ***sticking out*** *of her bag.* | *His front teeth* ***stick out***.

pro·tru·sion /prəˈtruːʒən $ proʊ-/ *n* [C] *formal* something that sticks out

pro·tu·be·rance /prəˈtjuːbərənt $ -ˈtuː-/ *n* [C] *formal* something that sticks out: *This dinosaur is recognizable by the protuberance on the top of its head.* —**protuberant** *adj*

proud /praʊd/ ●●● S2 W3 *adj* (*comparative* **prouder**, *superlative* **proudest**)
1 PLEASED feeling pleased about something that you have done or something that you own, or about someone or something you are involved with or related to → **pride** OPP **ashamed**: **[+of]** *Her parents are very proud of her.* | *You should be proud of yourself.* | *His past record is certainly* ***something to be proud of***. | **be justly/rightly proud of sth** (=have good reasons for being proud) *The company is justly proud of its achievements.* | **proud to do/be sth** *Seven-year-old Ian is proud to have earned his red belt in karate.* | **proud (that)** *She was proud that the magazine had agreed to publish one of her stories.* | *Seth was the* ***proud owner*** *of a new sports car.*

GRAMMAR: Prepositions with proud
You are **proud of** someone or something: *He's proud of his son.* ✗ Don't say: *He's proud for his son.*

2 proudest moment/achievement/possession the moment etc that makes you feel most proud: *His proudest moment was winning the European Cup final.*
3 TOO HIGH OPINION thinking that you are more important, skilful etc than you really are – used to show disapproval → **pride**: *a proud man who would not admit his mistakes*
4 GREAT SELF-RESPECT having respect for yourself, so that you are embarrassed to ask for help when you are in a difficult situation → **pride**: *Some farmers were too proud to ask for government help.*
5 do sb proud a) *informal* to make people feel proud of you by doing something well: *I tried to do my country proud.* **b)** *old-fashioned* to treat someone well by providing them with good food or entertainment
6 IMPRESSIVE *literary* tall and impressive —**proudly** *adv*

THESAURUS

proud very pleased with what you, your family, or your country have achieved, or of something you own: *I felt so proud when my son graduated from college.* | *Judith's very proud of her new Ferrari.*
pleased with yourself feeling pleased because something good has happened, especially because you think you have been very clever, skilful etc: *He was smoking a big cigar and was obviously pleased with himself.* | *I'd made a big profit and was feeling pretty pleased with myself.*
arrogant *disapproving* behaving in an unpleasant and annoying way, because you think you are better or know more than other people, and that your opinions are always right: *He was arrogant and regarded people who disagreed with him as fools.* | *his arrogant attitude to women*

P

vain *disapproving* too proud of your appearance, in a way that annoys other people: *He's so vain – he thinks all the girls fancy him.*
conceited/big-headed *disapproving* proud of yourself because you think you are very intelligent, skilful, beautiful etc, especially without good reason and in a way that annoys people: *Stewart's the most arrogant conceited person I've ever known.* | *She was offered a brilliant job and became incredibly big-headed overnight.*
pompous *disapproving* thinking that you are much more important than you really are, and using very long and formal words to try to sound important: *The clerk was a pompous little man with glasses.* | *a pompous speech*
smug *disapproving* pleased with yourself in a quiet but annoying way because you think you are in a better position than other people: *Milly was looking very smug about coming top of the class.* | *a smug expression*
self-satisfied *disapproving* pleased with what you have achieved and showing it clearly in an annoying way: *She glared angrily into his self-satisfied face.* | *a self-satisfied grin*

P

prove /pruːv/ ●●● S2 W1 *v* (*past tense* **proved**, *past participle* **proved** *or* **proven** /ˈpruːvən/ *especially AmE*)
1 SHOW STH IS TRUE [T] to show that something is true by providing facts, information etc → **proof**: *You're wrong, and I can prove it.* | **prove (that)** *Tests have proved that the system works.* | **prove sth to sb** *I knew he had done it, but there was no way I could prove it to Eddie.* | **prove sb's guilt/innocence** *He claims the police destroyed records that could prove the officer's guilt.* | **prove sb wrong/innocent etc** *They say I'm too old, but I'm going to prove them all wrong.* | *To* **prove his point** (=show that he was right), *he mentioned several other experiments which had produced similar results.*

GRAMMAR

You **prove** something **to** someone: *I will prove to you that I'm right.* ✗ Don't say: *I will prove you that I'm right.*

2 BE [linking verb] if someone or something proves difficult, helpful, a problem etc, they are difficult, helpful, a problem etc: *The recent revelations may prove embarrassing to the president.* | **prove to be sth** *The design proved to be a success.*

GRAMMAR: Linking verbs

Prove is a linking verb in this meaning. This type of verb links the subject of the sentence with an adjective or noun: *The task proved difficult.* | *He has proved a loyal friend.* You can also say: *The task proved to be difficult.* | *He has proved to be a loyal friend.*

3 prove yourself/prove something (to sb) to show how good you are at doing something: *When I first started this job, I felt I had to prove myself.*
4 prove yourself (to be) sth to show other people that you are a particular type of person: *She's proved herself to be a very reliable worker.*
5 what is sb trying to prove? *spoken* said when you are annoyed by someone's actions and do not understand them
6 prove a point if someone does something to prove a point, they do it to show that they are right or that they can do something: *I'm not going to run the marathon just to prove a point.*
7 BREAD [I] if DOUGH (=unbaked bread mixture) proves, it rises and becomes light because of the YEAST in it
8 LAW [T] *law* to show that a WILL has been made in the correct way —**provable** *adj*

prov·en¹ /ˈpruːvən, ˈprəʊvən $ ˈproʊvən, ˈpruːvən/ ●○○ *adj* [usually before noun] tested and shown to be true or good, or shown to exist: *a player of proven ability* | *a telephone system with a* **proven track record** (=past performance showing how good it is) *of reliability*

prov·en² /ˈpruːvən/ *especially AmE* a past participle of PROVE

prov·e·nance /ˈprɒvənəns $ ˈprɑː-/ *n* [U] *formal* the place where something originally came from SYN **origin**: *The provenance of the paintings is unknown.* | **(of) dubious/doubtful provenance** (=used to suggest that something may have been stolen) *artworks of doubtful provenance*

prov·erb /ˈprɒvɜːb $ ˈprɑːvɜːrb/ ●●○ *n* [C] a short well-known statement that gives advice or expresses something that is generally true. 'A penny saved is a penny earned' is an example of a proverb. → **saying**
THESAURUS PHRASE

pro·ver·bi·al /prəˈvɜːbiəl $ -ɜːr-/ *adj* **1 the proverbial sth** used when you describe something using part of a well-known expression: *The store had everything including the proverbial kitchen sink.* **2** relating to a proverb: *a* ***proverbial expression*** **3** well known by a lot of people: *His modesty is proverbial.* —**proverbially** *adv*

pro·vide /prəˈvaɪd/ ●●● S1 W1 *v* [T]
1 to give something to someone or make it available to them, because they need it or want it → **provision**: *Tea and biscuits will be provided.* | **provide sth for sb** *The hotel* ***provides*** *a shoe-cleaning* ***service*** *for guests.* | **provide sb with sth** *The project is designed to provide young people with work.*
2 to produce something useful as a result: *We are hoping the enquiry will provide an explanation for the accident.* | **provide sb with sth** *The search provided the police with several vital clues.*
3 provide that *formal* if a law or rule provides that something must happen, it states that it must happen

GRAMMAR: Patterns with provide

• You **provide** something **for** someone: *We provide information for parents.*
• You **provide** someone **with** something: *We provide parents with information.* ✗ Don't say: *We provide parents information.*

provide against sth *phr v formal* to make plans in order to deal with a bad situation that might happen: *Health insurance will provide against loss of income if you become ill.*
provide for sb/sth *phr v*
1 to give someone the things they need to live, such as money, food etc: *Without work, how can I provide for my children?*
2 *formal* if a law, rule, or plan provides for something, it states that something will be done and makes it possible for it to be done: *The new constitution provides for a 650-seat legislature.*
3 *formal* to make plans in order to deal with something that might happen in the future: *Commanders failed to provide for an attack by sea.*

pro·vid·ed /prəˈvaɪdɪd/ ●●○ S3 W2 (*also* **proˈvided that**) *conjunction* used to say that something will only be possible if something else happens or is done SYN **providing**: *He can come with us, provided he pays for his own meals.*

Prov·i·dence, **providence** /ˈprɒvɪdəns $ ˈprɑː-/ *n* [U] *literary* a force which is believed by some people to control what happens in our lives and to protect us → **fate**: *divine providence*

prov·i·dent /ˈprɒvɪdənt $ ˈprɑː-/ *adj formal* careful and sensible in the way you plan things, especially by saving money for the future

prov·i·den·tial /ˌprɒvɪˈdenʃəl◂ $ ˌprɑː-/ *adj formal* a providential event is a lucky one —**providentially** *adv*

pro·vid·er /prəˈvaɪdə $ -ər/ ●○○ *n* [C]
1 a company or person that provides a service: *an Internet service provider*
2 someone who supports a family: *A widow, she is the* ***sole provider*** (=the only one) *for her family.*

pro·vid·ing /prəˈvaɪdɪŋ/ ●●○ S3 (*also* **proˈviding that**) *conjunction* used to say that something will only be possible if something else happens or is done SYN **provided**: *You can borrow the car, providing I can have it back by six o'clock.*

prov·ince /ˈprɒvəns $ ˈprɑː-/ ●●○ *n*
1 (*also* **Province**) [C] one of the large areas into which some countries are divided, and which usually has its own local government: *a Chinese province*
2 the provinces the parts of a country that are not near the capital
3 [singular] *formal* a subject that someone knows a lot about or something that only they are responsible for: **[+of]** *Computers were once the exclusive province of scientists and mathematicians.*

pro·vin·cial¹ /prəˈvɪnʃəl/ ●○○ *adj*
1 [only before noun] relating to or coming from a province: *a provincial election | the* ***provincial government*** *of Quebec*
2 relating to or coming from the parts of a country that are not near the capital: *a* ***provincial town***
3 old-fashioned and not interested in anything new or different – used to show disapproval: *provincial attitudes*

provincial² *n* [C] someone who comes from a part of a country that is not near the capital, especially someone who is not interested in anything new or different – often used to show disapproval

pro·vin·cial·is·m /prəˈvɪnʃəlɪzəm/ *n* [U] provincial attitudes

ˈproving ground *n* [C] **1** a place or situation in which something new is tried or tested: **[+for]** *High-crime areas are proving grounds for new police officers.* **2** *technical* an area for scientific testing, especially of vehicles

pro·vi·sion¹ /prəˈvɪʒən/ ●●○ *n*
1 [C usually singular, U] when you provide something that someone needs now or in the future: **[+of]** *the provision of childcare facilities* | **[+for]** *provision for people with disabilities | He* ***made provisions for*** *his wife and his children in his will.*
2 provisions [plural] food, drink, and other supplies, especially for a journey: *We had enough provisions for two weeks.*
3 [C] a condition in an agreement or law: *The agreement includes a provision for each side to check the other side's weapons.* | **under the provisions of sth** *Under the provisions of the Act, employers must supply safety equipment.*

provision² *v* [T] *formal* to provide someone or something with a lot of food and supplies, especially for a journey

pro·vi·sion·al /prəˈvɪʒənəl/ ●○○ *adj formal* likely or able to be changed in the future: *a* ***provisional government*** | *We accept provisional bookings by phone.* —**provisionally** *adv*: *The meeting has been provisionally arranged for the end of May.*

proˌvisional ˈlicence *n* [C] *BrE* an official document that you must have when you are learning to drive SYN **learner's permit** *AmE*

pro·vi·so /prəˈvaɪzəʊ $ -zoʊ/ *n* (*plural* **provisos**) [C] *formal* a condition that you ask for before you will agree to something: **with the proviso that** *The money was given to the museum with the proviso that it should be spent on operating costs.*

prov·o·ca·tion /ˌprɒvəˈkeɪʃən $ ˌprɑː-/ *n* [C,U] an action or event that makes someone angry or upset, or is intended to do this → **provoke**: **without provocation** *She claims that Graham attacked her without any provocation. | He was accused of* ***deliberate provocation****. | Julie has a tendency to burst into tears* ***at the slightest provocation****.*

pro·voc·a·tive /prəˈvɒkətɪv $ -ˈvɑː-/ ●○○ *adj*
1 provocative behaviour, remarks etc are intended to make people angry or upset, or to cause a lot of discussion: **provocative comment/remark/statement** *The minister's provocative remarks were widely reported in the press. | a* ***provocative act*** *by a terrorist group | She was accused of being* ***deliberately provocative****.*
2 provocative clothes, movements, pictures etc are intended to make someone sexually excited: ***provocative images*** *of young girls* —**provocatively** *adv*

pro·voke /prəˈvəʊk $ -ˈvoʊk/ ●●○ *v* [T]
1 to cause a reaction or feeling, especially a sudden one → **provocation**: **provoke a protest/an outcry/criticism etc** *The proposal provoked widespread criticism. | The decision to invade provoked storms of protest.* | **provoke debate/discussion** | *The novel has provoked fierce debate in the US.* | **provoke sb into (doing) sth** *She hopes her editorial will provoke readers into thinking seriously about the issue.* | **provoke sb to do sth** *Emma, though still at school, was provoked to help too.*
2 to make someone angry, especially deliberately: *The dog would not have attacked if it hadn't been provoked.* | **provoke sb into (doing) sth** *Paul tried to provoke Fletch into a fight.*

Prov·ost, provost /ˈprɒvəst $ ˈproʊvoʊst/ *n* [C] **1** the person in charge of a college in some British universities, especially at Oxford or Cambridge **2** an important official at a university in the US **3** *old use* the leader of the council in some Scottish towns and cities

prow /praʊ/ *n* [C] *especially literary* the front part of a ship or boat

prow·ess /ˈpraʊɪs/ *n* [U] *formal* great skill at doing something: *his physical prowess | military prowess*

prowl¹ /praʊl/ *v* [I,T] **1** if an animal prowls, it moves around an area quietly, especially because it is hunting another animal **2** if someone prowls, they move around an area slowly and quietly, especially because they are involved in a criminal activity or because they are looking for something: *gangs of teenagers* ***prowling the streets*** | **[+around/about]** *BrE*: *Irene prowled restlessly around the room.*

prowl² *n* **be/go on the prowl (for sth/sb) a)** if an animal is on the prowl, it is hunting **b)** if someone is on the prowl, they are moving around different places, looking for an opportunity to do something: *local men* ***out on the prowl*** (=looking for people to have a sexual relationship with) *in the city's bars and nightclubs | She's always on the prowl for bargains.*

prowl·er /ˈpraʊlə $ -ər/ *n* [C] a person who follows someone or hides near their house, especially at night, in order to frighten or harm them or to steal something: *The police were called after a prowler was spotted near their home.*

prox·i·mate /ˈprɒksəmət $ ˈprɑːk-/ *adj formal* **1** a proximate cause is a direct one **2** nearest in time, order, or family relationship SYN **close**

prox·im·i·ty /prɒkˈsɪməti $ prɑːk-/ ●○○ *n* [U] *formal* nearness in distance or time: **[+to]** *We chose the house for its proximity to the school.* | **[+of]** *the proximity of the Bahamas to the States | Here the rich and the poor live* ***in close proximity*** (=very near to each other).

prox·y¹ /ˈprɒksi $ ˈprɑːksi/ *n* (*plural* **proxies**) **1 by proxy** if you do something by proxy, you arrange for someone else to do it for you: *You can vote by proxy.* **2** [C,U] someone who you choose to represent you, especially to vote for you: **[+for]** *a husband acting as proxy for his wife* **3** [C + for] *formal* something used to represent something else that you want to measure

proxy² *adj* [only before noun] involving the use of a proxy: *a* ***proxy vote***

prude /pruːd/ *n* [C] someone who is very easily shocked by anything relating to sex – used to show disapproval → **prudish**

pru·dence /ˈpruːdəns/ *n* [U] a sensible and careful attitude that makes you avoid unnecessary risks: *financial prudence*

pru·dent /ˈpruːdənt/ ●○○ *adj* sensible and careful, especially by trying to avoid unnecessary risks: *prudent house buyers* | **it is prudent (for sb) to do sth** *It might be prudent to get a virus detector for the network.*

pru·den·tial /pruːˈdenʃəl/ *adj old-fashioned* PRUDENT

prud·er·y /ˈpruːdəri/ *n* [U] the behaviour or attitude of people who are too easily shocked by things relating to sex – used to show disapproval

prud·ish /ˈpruːdɪʃ/ *adj* very easily shocked by things relating to sex – used to show disapproval → **prudery**: *American culture is in many ways still fairly prudish.* —**prudishly** *adv* —**prudishness** *n* [U]

prune¹ /pruːn/ *v* [T] **1** (*also* **prune sth ↔ back**) to cut

P

off some of the branches of a tree or bush to make it grow better: *The roses need pruning.* **2** *especially BrE* to make something smaller by removing parts that you do not need or want: *The company is pruning staff in order to reduce costs.* | *The original version of the text has been pruned quite a bit.*

prune² *n* [C] a dried PLUM, often cooked before it is eaten: *stewed prunes*

pru·ri·ent /ˈprʊəriənt $ ˈprʊr-/ *adj formal* having or showing too much interest in sex - used to show disapproval: *prurient interests* —**pruriently** *adv* —**prurience** *n* [U]

prus·sic ac·id /ˌprʌsɪk ˈæsɪd/ *n* [U] a very poisonous acid

pry /praɪ/ *v* (**pried**, **prying**, **pries**) **1** [I] to try to find out details about someone else's private life in an impolite way: *I* ***don't want to pry****, but I need to ask you one or two questions.* | **[+into]** *reporters prying into the affairs of celebrities* **2** [T always + adv/prep] *especially AmE* to force something open, or force it away from something else SYN **prize** *BrE*: **pry sth open/away/off etc** *We finally managed to pry the door open with a screwdriver.* **3 away from prying eyes** in private, where people cannot see what you are doing

pry sth **out of** sb/sth *phr v AmE* to get money or information from someone with a lot of difficulty: *If you want to know his name, you'll have to pry it out of her.*

PS (*also* **P.S.** *AmE*) /ˌpiː ˈes/ ●●○ *n* [C] (***postscript***) a note written at the end of a letter, adding more information → **PPS**: *She added a PS to say 'hi' to my brother.* | *Best wishes, Julie. PS Maggie sends her love.*

psalm /sɑːm $ sɑːm, sɑːlm/ *n* [C] a song or poem praising God, especially in the Bible

psalm·ist /ˈsɑːmɪst $ ˈsɑːm-, ˈsɑːlm-/ *n* [C] someone who has written a psalm

psal·ter /ˈsɔːltə $ ˈsɒːltər/ *n* [C] a book containing the psalms from the Bible

psal·ter·y /ˈsɔːltəri $ ˈsɒːl-/ *n* (*plural* **psalteries**) [C] an ancient musical instrument with strings stretched over a board

pse·phol·o·gy /seˈfɒlədʒi $ siːˈfɑː-/ *n* [U] *BrE technical* the study of how people vote in elections —**psephologist** *n* [C]

pseud /sjuːd $ suːd/ *n* [C] *BrE* a person who pretends to know a lot about a subject and talks about it in a complicated way in order to make other people admire them - used to show disapproval

pseudo- /sjuːdəʊ $ suːdoʊ/ *prefix* false or not real: *pseudo-intellectuals* (=people who pretend to be clever) | *She dismisses astrology as pseudo-science.*

pseu·do·nym /ˈsjuːdənɪm $ ˈsuː-/ *n* [C] an invented name that a writer, artist etc uses instead of their real name SYN **nom de plume**: **under a pseudonym** *He wrote under the pseudonym 'Silchester'.* —**pseudonymous** /sjuːˈdɒnɪməs $ suːˈdɑː-/ *adj*: *He was the pseudonymous author.* —**pseudonymously** *adv*

pso·ri·a·sis /səˈraɪəsɪs/ *n* [U] a skin disease that causes rough red areas where the skin comes off in small pieces

psst /pst/ *interjection* a sound people make when they want to attract someone's attention without other people noticing: *Psst! Guess what?*

PST /ˌpiː es ˈtiː/ the abbreviation of ***Pacific Standard Time***

psych¹ /saɪk/ *v*

psych sb ↔ **out** *phr v informal* to do or say things that will make your opponent in a game or competition feel nervous or confused, so that it is easier for you to win

psych sb **up** *phr v informal* if you psych yourself up or if someone psychs you up, you get mentally prepared before doing something so that you feel confident: **psych yourself up (for sth)** *We both knew we had to psych ourselves up for the race.*

psych² *n spoken informal* **1** [U] a short form of PSYCHOLOGY: *I'm a psych major now.* **2** [C] a short form of PSYCHIATRIST

psy·che /ˈsaɪki/ *n* [C usually singular] *technical or formal* someone's mind, or their deepest feelings, which control their attitudes and behaviour: *Freud's account of* ***the human psyche*** | *A characteristic of the feminine psyche is to seek approval from others.*

psy·che·del·ic /ˌsaɪkəˈdelɪk◂/ *adj* [usually before noun] **1** psychedelic drugs such as LSD make you HALLUCINATE (=see things that do not exist) **2** having or using bright colours or strange sounds, and representing the experiences people have when they use drugs such as LSD: *a psychedelic light show* | *Fashion designers look back to the 1960s with dazzling psychedelic prints.* —**psychedelically** /-kli/ *adv* —**psychedelia** /-ˈdiːliə/ *n* [U]: *sixties psychedelia*

psy·chi·at·ric /ˌsaɪkiˈætrɪk◂/ ●●○ *adj* relating to the study and treatment of mental illness: *a psychiatric hospital* | *a psychiatric nurse* | *Charles was suffering from a* ***psychiatric disorder*** (=mental illness). —**psychiatrically** /-kli/ *adv*

psy·chi·a·trist /saɪˈkaɪətrɪst $ sə-/ ●●○ *n* [C] a doctor trained in the treatment of mental illness → **psychologist** THESAURUS▸ DOCTOR

psy·chi·a·try /saɪˈkaɪətri $ sə-/ *n* [U] the study and treatment of mental illnesses → **psychology**

psy·chic¹ /ˈsaɪkɪk/ *adj* [no comparative] **1** (*also* **psy·chi·cal** /ˈsaɪkɪkəl/) relating to the power of the human mind to do strange or surprising things that cannot be explained by reason: *a spiritual healer with* ***psychic powers*** | *a documentary on psychic phenomena* **2** someone who is psychic has the ability to know what other people are thinking or what will happen in the future → **clairvoyant**: *You don't have to be psychic to know what Maggie is thinking.* **3** (*also* **psychical**) affecting the mind rather than the body: *psychic disorders* (=illnesses) —**psychically** /-kli/ *adv*

psychic² *n* [C] someone who has mysterious powers, especially the ability to receive messages from dead people or to know what will happen in the future

psy·cho /ˈsaɪkəʊ $ -koʊ/ *n* (*plural* **psychos**) [C] *informal* someone who is mentally ill and who may behave in a violent or strange way —**psycho** *adj*

psycho- /saɪkəʊ, -kə $ -koʊ, -kə/ (*also* **psych-**) *prefix technical* relating to the mind and the mental processes, rather than the body: *a psychoanalyst*

psy·cho·ac·tive /ˌsaɪkəʊˈæktɪv◂ $ -koʊ-/ *adj* psychoactive drugs have an effect on your mind

psy·cho·a·nal·y·sis /ˌsaɪkəʊ-əˈnælɪsɪs $ -koʊ-/ *n* [U] medical treatment that involves talking to someone about their life, feelings etc in order to find out the hidden causes of their problems —**psychoanalytic** /ˌsaɪkəʊænəˈlɪtɪk◂ $ -koʊænlˈɪtɪk◂/ *adj*: *psychoanalytic theory* —**psychoanalytical** *adj* —**psychoanalytically** /-kli/ *adv*

psy·cho·an·a·lyst /ˌsaɪkəʊˈænəl-ɪst $ -koʊ-/ *n* [C] someone who treats patients using psychoanalysis

psy·cho·an·a·lyze (*also* **-yse** *BrE*) /ˌsaɪkəʊˈænəlaɪz $ -koʊ-/ *v* [T] to treat someone using psychoanalysis

psy·cho·bab·ble /ˈsaɪkəʊˌbæbəl $ -koʊ-/ *n* [U] *informal* language that sounds scientific but is not really, that some people use when talking about their emotional problems - used to show disapproval

psy·cho·bi·ol·o·gy /ˌsaɪkəʊbaɪˈɒlədʒi $ -koʊbaɪˈɑː-/ *n* [U] the study of the body in relation to the mind

psy·cho·drama /ˈsaɪkəʊˌdrɑːmə $ -koʊˌdrɑːmə,-ˌdræmə/ *n* **1** [C,U] a way of treating mental illness in which people are asked to act in a situation together to help them understand their emotions **2** [C] a serious film, play etc that examines the minds and feelings of the characters, rather than what happens

psy·cho·ki·ne·sis /ˌsaɪkəʊkaɪˈniːsɪs $ -koʊkə-/ *n* [U] the moving of solid objects using only the power of the mind, which some people believe is possible —**psychokinetic** /-kaɪˈnetɪk◂ $ -kəˈne-/ *adj* —**psychokinetically** /-kli/ *adv*

psy·cho·log·i·cal /ˌsaɪkəˈlɒdʒɪkəl◂ $ -ˈlɑː-/ ●●○ W3 AWL *adj*
1 relating to the way that your mind works and the way that this affects your behaviour SYN **mental**: *Sleep disorders are a serious* ***psychological problem****. | Freud's psychological theories | What was the patient's* ***psychological state****?*
2 relating to what is in someone's mind rather than what is real: *Max says he's ill, but I'm sure it's psychological.*
3 psychological warfare behaviour intended to make your opponents lose confidence or feel afraid
4 the psychological moment *BrE informal* the exact time in a situation when you have the best chance to achieve what you want —**psychologically** /-kli/ *adv*: *psychologically disturbed patients*

psy·chol·o·gist /saɪˈkɒlədʒɪst $ -ˈkɑː-/ ●●○ AWL *n* [C] someone who is trained in psychology → **psychiatrist**: *a clinical psychologist* THESAURUS DOCTOR

psy·chol·o·gy /saɪˈkɒlədʒi $ -ˈkɑː-/ ●●○ W3 AWL *n* (*plural* **psychologies**)
1 [U] the study of the mind and how it influences people's behaviour: **educational/social etc psychology** *experts in the field of developmental psychology*
2 [U] the mental processes involved in believing in something or doing a certain activity: **[+of]** *research into the psychology of racism*
3 [C,U] what someone thinks or believes, and how this affects what they do: *the psychology of three-year-olds | mob psychology | You have to use psychology to get people to stop smoking.*

psy·cho·met·ric /ˌsaɪkəʊˈmetrɪk◂ $ -koʊ-/ *adj* relating to the measurement of mental abilities and qualities: *psychometric tests*

psy·cho·path /ˈsaɪkəpæθ/ *n* [C] someone who has a serious and permanent mental illness that makes them behave in a violent or criminal way → **sociopath** —**psychopathic** /ˌsaɪkəˈpæθɪk◂/ *adj*: *a psychopathic personality* —**psychopathically** /-kli/ *adv*

psy·cho·sis /saɪˈkəʊsɪs $ -ˈkoʊ-/ *n* (*plural* **psychoses** /-siːz/) [C,U] a serious mental illness that can change your character and make you unable to behave in a normal way → **psychotic**

psy·cho·so·mat·ic /ˌsaɪkəʊsəˈmætɪk◂ $ -kəsə-/ *adj medical* **1** a psychosomatic illness is caused by fear or anxiety rather than by a physical problem: **psychosomatic illness/symptoms/disorder etc** *Children are just as susceptible to psychosomatic conditions as adults.* **2** relating to the relationship between the mind and physical illness —**psychosomatically** /-kli/ *adv*

psy·cho·ther·a·py /ˌsaɪkəʊˈθerəpi $ -koʊ-/ *n* [U] the treatment of mental illness, for example DEPRESSION, by talking to someone and discussing their problems rather than giving them drugs —**psychotherapist** *n* [C]

psy·chot·ic /saɪˈkɒtɪk $ -ˈkɑː-/ *adj* suffering from or caused by psychosis: *psychotic patients | psychotic illness* —**psychotic** *n* [C]: *Like most psychotics, she was very dependent on others.* —**psychotically** /-kli/ *adv*

psy·cho·tro·pic /ˌsaɪkəˈtrəʊpɪk◂ $ -ˈtroʊ-/ *adj* psychotropic drugs have an effect on your mind

pt. (*also* **pt** *BrE*) **1** the written abbreviation of ***part*** **2** *BrE* the written abbreviation of ***payment*** **3** the written abbreviation of ***pint*** or ***pints*** **4** (*also* **Pt**) the written abbreviation of ***point*** **5** (*also* **Pt**) the written abbreviation of ***port***: *Pt Moresby*

PT¹ /ˌpiː ˈtiː/ *n* [U] *BrE* (***physical training***) activities involving organized games, exercises etc at school: *a PT instructor | PT lessons at school*

PT², **P/T** the written abbreviation of ***part-time*** → **FT**

PTA /ˌpiː tiː ˈeɪ/ *n* [C] *especially BrE* (***parent-teacher association***) an organization of parents and teachers that tries to help and improve a particular school SYN **PTO** *AmE*: *an active member of the PTA*

Pte *BrE* a written abbreviation of ***private***, the lowest military rank in the army

pter·o·dac·tyl /ˌterəˈdæktɪl $ -tl, -tɪl/ *n* [C] a large flying animal that lived many millions of years ago

PTO¹ /ˌpiː tiː ˈəʊ $ -ˈoʊ/ (***please turn over***) written at the bottom of a page to tell the reader to look at the next page

PTO² *n* [C] *AmE* (***Parent-Teacher Organization***) an organization of parents and teachers that tries to help and improve a particular school SYN **PTA** *BrE*

pto·maine /ˈtəʊmeɪn, təʊˈmeɪn $ ˈtoʊmeɪn, toʊ-/ *n* [C,U] a poisonous substance formed by BACTERIA in decaying food

PTSD /ˌpiː tiː es ˈdiː/ *n* [U] the abbreviation of ***post-traumatic stress disorder***

P2P /ˌpiː tə ˈpiː/ *adj* **1** (***peer-to-peer***) peer-to-peer computer systems make it possible to exchange files, software etc between two computers, even though they are not connected to each other
2 (***person-to-person***) person-to-person methods of paying for something allow the person buying something on the Internet to pay the person who is selling it: *P2P payments*

pty the written abbreviation of ***proprietary***, used in Australia, New Zealand, and South Africa after the name of a business company: *Australian Wine Growers Pty*

pub /pʌb/ ●●● S2 W3 *n* [C] a building in Britain where alcohol can be bought and drunk, and where meals are often served → **bar**: *Do you fancy going to the pub? | a pub lunch | the pub landlord*

ˈpub-crawl *n* [C] *BrE informal* a visit to several pubs, one after the other, during which you have a drink in each pub: *a Saturday night pub-crawl*

pu·ber·ty /ˈpjuːbəti $ -ər-/ *n* [U] the stage of physical development during which you change from a child to an adult and are able to have children: *Fourteen is a fairly normal age for a girl to* ***reach puberty****.*

pubes /pjuːbz/ *n* [plural] *informal* PUBIC hair (=hair around the sexual organs)

pu·bes·cent /pjuːˈbesənt/ *adj* [usually before noun] a pubescent boy or girl is going through puberty

pu·bic /ˈpjuːbɪk/ *adj* [only before noun] related to or near the sexual organs: *pubic hair*

pub·lic¹ /ˈpʌblɪk/ ●●● S1 W1 *adj*
1 ORDINARY PEOPLE [only before noun] relating to all the ordinary people in a country, who are not members of the government or do not have important jobs: *We have to show that publishing this story is* ***in the public interest*** (=helpful or useful to ordinary people). | *full* ***public access*** *to information |* ***Public opinion*** *is gradually shifting in favor of the imprisoned men. | There was a* ***public outcry*** (=expression of anger by a lot of people) *about the shooting. | Their activities have been hidden from* ***the public gaze*** (=people's eyes or attention).
2 FOR ANYONE [only before noun] available for anyone to use OPP **private**: *a public telephone | a public footpath | proposals to ban smoking in* ***public places*** *| a public library |* **public transport** *BrE*, **public transportation** *AmE* (=buses, trains etc)
3 GOVERNMENT [only before noun] relating to the government and the services it provides for people OPP **private**: *the Government's* ***public spending*** *plans | We do not believe he is fit for* ***public office*** (=a job in the government). | *efforts to control public expenditure | public funding for the arts* → PUBLIC SERVICE
4 KNOWN ABOUT known about by most people: *Details of the highly sensitive information have not been* ***made public****. | Although not a* ***public figure*** (=famous person), *he was a man of great influence.*
5 NOT HIDDEN intended for anyone to know, see, or hear OPP **private**: *Today the school finds itself in the midst of a very public debate.* | **public display of grief/affection etc** (=showing your emotions so that everyone can see) *She was acutely embarrassed by his public display of temper. | There will be a* ***public inquiry*** *into the sinking of the oil tanker. | a fear of* ***public speaking***
6 PLACE WITH A LOT OF PEOPLE a public place usually has a lot of people in it OPP **private**: *Let's go somewhere less public where we can talk.*

P

7 public life work that you do, especially for the government, that makes you well known to many people: *Howard seems to have retired from public life.*
8 public image the public image of a famous person or organization is the character or attitudes that most people think they have: **[+of]** *attempts to improve the public image of the police*
9 go public a) to tell everyone about something that was secret: **[+on/with]** *The planners are almost ready to go public on the road-building scheme.* **b)** to become a PUBLIC COMPANY: *Many partnerships went public in the 1980s to secure extra capital.*
10 public appearance a visit by a famous person in order to make a speech, advertise something etc: *She is paid £10,000 for the briefest of public appearances.*
11 the public eye someone who is in the public eye is seen a lot on television, written about in newspapers etc: *It is a job that brings him constantly into the public eye.*
12 public property a) something that is provided for anyone to use, and is usually owned by the government: *The army was called out to protect public property.* **b)** something that everyone has a right to know about: *Our lives seem to have become public property.*
13 public enemy number one the criminal, problem etc that is considered the most serious threat to people's safety: *Drugs have become public enemy number one.*

public² ●●● S2 W2 *n*
1 the public ordinary people who do not work for the government or have any special position in society: *The meeting will be open to* ***the general public****.* | *Police warned* ***members of the public*** *not to approach the man, who may be armed.* | *On the whole, the public is conservative about education.*
2 in public if you do something in public, you do it where anyone can see OPP **in private**: *Her husband was always nice to her in public.* → **wash/air your dirty linen/laundry (in public)** at DIRTY¹(7)
3 [singular, U] the people who like a particular singer, writer etc: *He is adored by his public.* | *The theatre-going public are very demanding.*

GRAMMAR: Singular or plural verb?
- **Public** is usually followed by a singular verb: *The public* ***needs*** *to be better informed.*
- In British English, you can also use a plural verb: *The public* ***need*** *to be better informed.*

GRAMMAR GUIDE ▸ NOUNS

ˌpublic ˈaccess ˌchannel *n* [C] a television CHANNEL provided by CABLE television companies in the US on which anyone can broadcast a programme

ˌpublic-adˈdress ˌsystem *n* [C] a PA

ˌpublic afˈfairs *n* [plural] events and questions, especially political ones, which have an effect on most people: *He took an active part in public affairs.*

pub·li·can /ˈpʌblɪkən/ *n* [C] *BrE formal* someone who is in charge of a PUB SYN **landlord**

pub·li·ca·tion /ˌpʌblɪˈkeɪʃən/ ●○○ AWL *n*
1 [U] the process of printing a book, magazine etc and offering it for sale → **publish**: **[+of]** *She was in England for the publication of her new book.* | **for publication** (=intended to be published) *He spent his holiday writing reviews for publication.*
2 [C] a book, magazine etc: *He was the author of 70 major scientific publications.* | *a weekly publication*
3 [U] when information is printed in a book, magazine etc so that the public can read it → **publish**: **[+of]** *the publication of the company's annual results*

ˌpublic ˈbar *n* [C] in PUBs in Britain, a room with plain furniture where you can buy drinks more cheaply than in the other rooms → **lounge bar**

ˌpublic ˈcompany *n* [C] a company that offers its SHARES for sale on the STOCK EXCHANGE SYN **public corporation** *AmE*

ˌpublic conˈvenience *n* [C] *formal BrE* a toilet in a public place

ˌpublic corpoˈration *n* [C] **1** *AmE* a PUBLIC COMPANY **2** *BrE* a business that is run by the government

ˌpublic deˈfender *n* [C] *AmE* a lawyer who is paid by the government to defend people in court, because they cannot pay for a lawyer themselves → **district attorney**

ˌpublic doˈmain *n* [singular] *law* something that is in the public domain is available for anyone to have or use: *The information* ***is*** *not currently* ***in the public domain****.* | *Public domain software is sometimes called shareware.*

ˌpublic ˈhealth *n* [U] **1** in Britain, health care provided by the government, including medical care and public cleaning services **2** the health of all the people in an area: *a danger to public health*

ˌpublic ˈholiday ●●○ *n* [C] a special day when people do not go to work or school SYN **holiday** *AmE*

ˌpublic ˈhouse *n* [C] *BrE formal* a PUB

ˌpublic ˈhousing *n* [U] in the US, houses or apartments built by the government for poor people

pub·li·cist /ˈpʌblɪsɪst/ *n* [C] someone whose job is to make sure that people know about a new product, film, book etc or what a famous person is doing

pub·lic·i·ty /pʌˈblɪsəti/ ●●○ S3 W3 *n* [U]
1 the attention that someone or something gets from newspapers, television etc: *Standards in education have* ***received*** *much* ***publicity*** *over the last few years.* | **bad/good/unwelcome etc publicity** *It's important to gain good publicity for the school.* | *The adverse publicity had damaged sales.*
2 the business of making sure that people know about a new product, film etc or what a particular famous person is doing: *Who's going to do the show's publicity?* | *The Government has launched a* ***publicity campaign****.* | *Is their much-reported romance just a* ***publicity stunt*** (=something that is only done to get publicity)?

pub·li·cize (*also* **-ise** *BrE*) /ˈpʌblɪsaɪz/ *v* [T] to give information about something to the public, so that they know about it: *television's failure to publicize the unemployment issue* | **well/widely/highly publicized** (=receiving a lot of attention) *His visit was highly publicized.*

ˌpublic ˌlimited ˈcompany *n* [C] (*abbreviation* **plc**) a British company owned by at least two people and whose SHARES can be bought by everyone

pub·lic·ly /ˈpʌblɪkli/ ●●○ *adv*
1 in a way that is intended for anyone to know, see, or hear: *She and her family agreed never to discuss the matter publicly.*
2 done or controlled by the government: *a publicly funded health service*
3 a company that is publicly owned has sold its SHARES to people who are not part of the company
4 involving the ordinary people in a country or city: *publicly elected bodies*

ˌpublic ˈnuisance *n* [C] **1** *law* an action that is harmful to everyone **2** someone who does things that annoy a lot of people

ˌpublic oˈpinion *n* [U] the opinions or beliefs that ordinary people have about a particular subject: *Public opinion is shifting in favor of the new law.* | *the pressure of public opinion*

ˌpublic ˈownership *n* [U] businesses, property etc in public ownership are owned by the government: *The Opposition intends to bring the industry back into public ownership.*

ˌpublic ˈprosecutor *n* [C] *BrE* a lawyer who works for the government, and tries to prove in a court of law that someone has done something illegal SYN **district attorney** *AmE*

ˌpublic reˈlations *n* **1** [U] the work of explaining to the public what an organization does, so that they will understand it and approve of it: *They ran their own successful public relations business in London.* **2** [plural] the relationship between an organization and the public: *The project has been disastrous for the bank in terms of public relations.* | *a* ***public relations exercise*** (=done in order to improve the relationship between the public and an organization)

GRAMMAR: Singular or plural verb?

- In meaning 1, **public relations** is followed by a singular verb: ***Public relations is*** *an interesting field to work in.*
- In meaning 2, **public relations** is followed by a plural verb: *Our* ***public relations are*** *handled by Lisa Holden.*

GRAMMAR GUIDE ▸ NOUNS

ˌpublic ˈschool *n* [C] **1** in Britain, a private school for children aged between 13 and 18, whose parents pay for their education. The children often live at the school while they are studying → **state school 2** a free local school, especially in the US and Scotland, controlled and paid for by the government → **private school**

ˈpublic ˌsector *n* **the public sector** the industries and services in a country that are owned and run by the government → **the private sector**: **in the public sector** *a job in the public sector | public sector workers | public sector housing*

ˌpublic ˈservant *n* [C] someone who works for the government

ˌpublic ˈservice *n* **1** [C usually plural] a service, such as transport or health care, that a government provides: *efforts to improve quality in public services* **2** [C,U] a service provided to people because it will help them, and not for profit: *Local TV stations ran the ads as a public service.* **3** [singular, U] the government or its departments: *staff cuts in the public service | He left the public service and embarked on a career in the City.*

ˌpublic-ˈspirited *adj* willing to do things that are helpful for everyone in society: *Any public-spirited citizen would have done the same.*

ˌpublic ˈtelevision *n* [U] a television service or programme in the US which is paid for by the government, large companies, and the public

ˌpublic ˈtransport *BrE*, **ˌpublic transporˈtation** *AmE* ●●○ *n* [U] buses, trains etc that are available for everyone to use

ˌpublic uˈtility *n* [C] a private company that is allowed by the government to provide important services such as gas, electricity, water etc

ˌpublic ˈworks *n* [plural] buildings such as hospitals, roads, PORTS etc that are built and paid for by the government: *the public works department*

pub·lish /ˈpʌblɪʃ/ ●●● S3 W1 AWL *v*

1 [T] to arrange for a book, magazine etc to be written, printed, and sold → **publication**: *The first edition was published in 1765. | They are publishing the dictionary on CD-ROM.*

2 [T] if a newspaper or magazine publishes a letter, article etc, it prints it for people to read → **publication**: *We love reading your letters and we try to publish as many as possible.*

3 [T] to make official information such as a report available for everyone to read → **publication**: *The latest unemployment figures will be published tomorrow.* GRAMMAR **Publish** is often passive in this meaning.

4 [I,T] if a writer, musician etc publishes their work, they arrange for it to be printed and sold: *University teachers must publish regularly to gain promotion.*

5 publish and be damned *BrE* used to say that you should take a risk in saying what you think is true, although the result may be harmful to you

pub·lish·er /ˈpʌblɪʃə $ -ər/ ●●○ W3 AWL *n* [C] a person or company whose business is to arrange the writing, production, and sale of books, newspapers etc

pub·lish·ing /ˈpʌblɪʃɪŋ/ ●●○ AWL *n* [U] the business of producing books and magazines: *Tony wants to get a job in publishing. | a new* ***publishing house*** (=publishing company) → DESKTOP PUBLISHING

puce /pjuːs/ *adj* dark brownish purple in colour —**puce** *n* [U]

puck /pʌk/ *n* [C] a hard flat circular piece of rubber that you hit with the stick in the game of ICE HOCKEY

puck·er /ˈpʌkə $ -ər/ (*also* **pucker up**) *v* **1** [I,T] if part of your face puckers, or if you pucker it, it becomes tight or stretched, for example because you are going to cry or kiss someone: *Her mouth puckered, and she started to cry.* **2** [I] if cloth puckers, it gets lines or folds in it and is no longer flat —**pucker** *n* [C] —**puckered** *adj*

puck·ish /ˈpʌkɪʃ/ *adj* [usually before noun] *literary* showing that you are amused by other people, and like to make jokes about them: *a puckish grin* —**puckishly** *adv*

pud /pʊd/ *n* [C,U] *BrE informal* a PUDDING: *What's for pud?*

pud·ding /ˈpʊdɪŋ/ ●●● S3 *n* [C,U]

1 *especially BrE* a hot sweet dish, made from cake, rice, bread etc with fruit, milk, or other sweet things added

2 *especially AmE* a thick sweet creamy dish, usually made with milk, eggs, sugar, and flour, and served cold: *chocolate pudding*

3 *BrE* a sweet dish served at the end of a meal: **for pudding** *There's ice cream for pudding.* → DESSERT

4 *BrE* a hot dish made of a mixture of flour, fat etc, with meat or vegetables inside: ***steak and kidney pudding*** → BLACK PUDDING, CHRISTMAS PUDDING, MILK PUDDING, PLUM PUDDING, YORKSHIRE PUDDING, → **the proof of the pudding is in the eating** at PROOF[1](4)

ˈpudding ˌbasin *n* [C] *BrE* a deep round dish in which puddings are cooked

pud·dle /ˈpʌdl/ ●●○ *n* [C] a small pool of liquid, especially rainwater: *Children splashed through the puddles.* | **[+of]** *He had fallen asleep, his head resting in a puddle of beer.* —**puddle** *v* [I] *literary*: *Rain trickled down the glass, puddling on the window sills.*

pu·den·dum /pjuːˈdendəm/ *n* (*plural* **pudenda** /-də/) [C] *technical* the sexual organs on the outside of the body, especially a woman's

pudg·y /ˈpʌdʒi/ *adj* fairly fat: *the baby's pudgy little legs* —**pudginess** *n* [U]

pueb·lo /ˈpwebləʊ $ -loʊ/ *n* (*plural* **pueblos**) [C] a small town, especially in the southwest U.S.

puer·ile /ˈpjʊəraɪl $ ˈpjʊrəl/ *adj formal* silly and stupid SYN **childish**: *a puerile joke* —**puerility** /pjʊˈrɪləti/ *n* [U]

puff[1] /pʌf/ ●○○ *v*

1 [I] to breathe quickly and with difficulty after the effort of running, carrying something heavy etc: *George* ***puffed and panted*** *as he tried to keep up.* | **[+along/up etc]** *An old man puffed up to them. | He caught up with Gary,* ***puffing for breath.*** → **huff and puff** at HUFF[1](1)

2 [I,T] (*also* **puff away**) to breathe in and out while smoking a cigarette or PIPE: **[+at/on]** *Kinane sat in silence, puffing thoughtfully at his pipe.*

3 [I always + adv/prep, T] if smoke, steam etc puffs from somewhere, or if something puffs it, it comes out in little clouds: *Steam puffed out of the chimney. | The boiler was puffing thick black smoke. | Don't puff smoke into my face.*

4 [I always + adv/prep] to move in a particular direction, sending out little clouds of steam or smoke: *The train puffed steadily across the bridge.*

puff sth ↔ **out** *phr v* **puff out your cheeks/chest** to make your cheeks or chest bigger by filling them with air: *Henry puffed out his chest proudly.*

puff up *phr v*

1 to become bigger by increasing the amount of air inside, or to make something bigger in this way: *The pastry will puff up while it bakes.* | **puff sth ↔ up** *Birds puff up their feathers to keep warm.*

2 if a part of your body puffs up, it swells painfully because of injury or infection: *My eye had puffed up because of a mosquito bite.*

puff[2] *n* **1** [C] the action of taking the smoke from a cigarette, PIPE etc into your LUNGS: **[+on/at]** *He laughed and* ***took a puff*** *on his cigar.* **2** [C] a sudden small movement of wind, air, or smoke: **puff of smoke/wind/air/steam etc** *The dragon disappeared in a puff of smoke.* **3 cheese/jam/cream etc puff** a piece of light PASTRY with a soft mixture inside **4** [U] *BrE informal* your breath: *I* ***was out of puff*** (=had difficulty breathing). **5** [C] (*also* **puff piece**) a piece of writing or a speech that praises someone too much – used to show disapproval

puff·ball /ˈpʌfbɔːl $ -bɒːl/ *n* [C] a type of round white FUNGUS that bursts to send out its seeds

puffed /pʌft/ *adj* [not before noun] *BrE informal* breathing quickly because you have been using a lot of energy: *I'm too puffed to dance anymore.*

ˌpuffed ˈup *adj* [not before noun] behaving in a way that shows you are too pleased with yourself and your achievements – used to show disapproval: *I was so puffed up with my own importance in those days.*

puff·er /ˈpʌfə $ -ər/ *n* [C] **1** *BrE informal* a small piece of equipment containing medicine which you breathe in through your mouth, to help you breathe more easily SYN **inhaler**: *Asthma can be made worse by using puffers too often.* **2** a type of tropical fish that can fill itself with air so that it looks almost round

puf·fin /ˈpʌfɪn/ *n* [C] a North Atlantic seabird with a black and white body and a large brightly coloured beak

PUFFIN

ˌpuff ˈpastry *n* [U] a type of very light PASTRY made of many thin layers

puff·y /ˈpʌfi/ *adj* **1** if a part of your body is puffy, it is swollen: *Her eyes were puffy from crying.* **2** soft and full of air: *puffy white clouds* —**puffiness** *n* [U]

pug /pʌg/ *n* [C] a small short-haired dog with a wide flat face, a very short nose, and a curly tail

pu·gi·lis·t /ˈpjuːdʒɪlɪst/ *n* [C] *old-fashioned formal* a BOXER —**pugilism** *n* [U] —**pugilistic** /ˌpjuːdʒəˈlɪstɪk◂/ *adj*

pug·na·cious /pʌgˈneɪʃəs/ *adj formal* very eager to argue or fight with people: *The professor had been pugnacious and irritable.* —**pugnaciously** *adv* —**pugnacity** /pʌgˈnæsəti/ *n* [U]

puke¹ /pjuːk/ (*also* **puke up**) *v* [I,T] *informal* **1** to bring food back up from your stomach through your mouth SYN **vomit**: *He puked all over the carpet.* **2 make you (want to) puke** *informal* to make you feel very angry: *That kind of greed makes me puke!*

puke² *n* [U] *informal* food brought back up from your stomach through your mouth SYN **vomit**

puk·ey, **puky** /ˈpjuːki/ *adj informal* very unpleasant or unattractive

puk·ka, **pukha** /ˈpʌkə/ *adj BrE informal* real or properly made and of good quality: *pukka food*

pul·chri·tude /ˈpʌlkrɪtjuːd $ -tuːd/ *n* [U] *formal* physical beauty

Pul·it·zer Prize /ˈpʊlɪtsə ˌpraɪz $ -sər-/ *n* [C] one of the 21 prizes given every year in the US to people who have produced especially good work in JOURNALISM (=writing for newspapers), literature, or music. The prizes were started by the US newspaper owner Joseph Pulitzer (1847–1911), and winning a Pulitzer Prize is regarded as a great honour. → **MAN BOOKER PRIZE, THE**

pull¹ /pʊl/ ●●● S1 W1 *v*

1 MOVE STH TOWARDS YOU [I,T] to use your hands to make something or someone move towards you or in the direction that your hands are moving OPP **push**: *Mom! Davey's pulling my hair!* | **pull sb/sth into/away from/over etc sth** *He pulled her down into her seat.* | **pull sth open/shut** *She pulled open the door and hurried inside.*

2 REMOVE [T] to use force to take something from the place where it is fixed or held: *She has to have two teeth pulled.* | **pull sth out/off/away etc** *Vicky had pulled the arm off her doll.*

3 MAKE STH FOLLOW YOU [T] to be attached to something or hold something and make it move behind you in the direction you are going: *a tractor pulling a trailer*

4 TAKE STH OUT [T always + adv/prep] to take something out of a bag, pocket etc with your hand: *He pulled out his wallet and said 'let me pay'.* | *Ben pulled a pen from his pocket.* | **pull a gun/knife (on sb)** (=take one out, ready to use it)

5 CLOTHING [T always + adv/prep] to put on or take off a piece of clothing, usually quickly: **[+on/off/up/down etc]** *He pulled off his damp shirt.*

6 MOVE YOUR BODY a) [I,T always + adv/prep] to move your body or part of your body away from someone or something: **pull sth away/free** *She tried to pull her hand free, but it was held fast.* | **pull sth out of/from sth** *She struggled fiercely, trying to pull her arm out of his grasp.* | **[+away/back]** *She pulled away from him.* **b) pull yourself up/to your feet etc** to hold onto something and use your strength to move your body towards it: *Benny pulled himself up from the floor with difficulty.*

7 MUSCLE [T] to injure one of your muscles by stretching it too much during physical activity SYN **strain**: *Paul pulled a muscle trying to lift the freezer.* **THESAURUS** ▸ **HURT**

8 pull strings to secretly use your influence with important people in order to get what you want or to help someone else: *Francis pulled strings to get him out of trouble.*

9 pull the/sb's strings to control something or someone, especially when you are not the person who is supposed to be controlling them: *It was widely believed that Montagu was secretly pulling the strings behind the prime minister.*

10 TRICK/CRIME [T] *informal* to succeed in doing something illegal or dishonest or in playing a trick on someone: *The gang have pulled another bank robbery.* | *He was trying to **pull a fast one*** (=deceive you) *when he told you he'd paid.* | **pull a stunt/trick/joke** *Don't you ever pull a stunt like that again!*

11 pull sb's leg to tell someone something that is not true, as a joke: *I haven't won, have I? You're pulling my leg.*

12 pull the other one (it's got bells on) *BrE spoken* used to tell someone that you think they are joking or not telling the truth: *Your dad's a racing driver? Pull the other one!*

13 SWITCH [T] to move a control such as a switch, LEVER, or TRIGGER towards you to make a piece of equipment work: *She raised the gun, and pulled the trigger.*

14 pull the curtains/blinds to open or close curtains or BLINDS: *It was already getting dark so he pulled the curtains.*

15 CROWD/VOTES ETC [T] if an event, performer etc pulls crowds or a politician pulls a lot of votes, a lot of people come to see them or vote for them: *Muhammad Ali can still pull the crowds.*

16 ATTRACT/INFLUENCE [T] to attract or influence someone or their thoughts or feelings: *The city's reputation for a clean environment has pulled new residents from other states.*

17 SEXUALLY ATTRACT [I,T] *BrE spoken* to attract someone in order to have sex with them or spend the evening with them: *He knew he could pull any girl he wanted.*

18 STOP EVENT [T] to stop a planned event from taking place: *They pulled the concert.*

19 pull sb's licence *informal* to take away someone's LICENCE to do something, especially to drive a car, because they have done something wrong

20 STOP A VEHICLE [I,T] to drive a vehicle somewhere and stop, or to make a vehicle gradually slow down and stop: **pull sth into/towards/down etc sth** *She pulled the car into a side street.* | *The bus **pulled to a halt**.*

21 CAR [I] if a car pulls to the left or right as you are driving, it moves in that direction because of a problem with its machinery

22 sth is like pulling teeth used to say that it is very difficult or unpleasant to persuade someone to do something: *Getting him to do his homework is like pulling teeth.*

23 BEER [T] *BrE* to get beer out of a BARREL by pulling a handle: *The barman laughed and began to pull a couple of pints.*

24 pull a punch to deliberately hit someone with less force than you could do, so that it hurts less → **not pull any punches** at **PUNCH²(6)**

25 CRICKET/GOLF/BASEBALL [I,T] to hit the ball in CRICKET, golf, or baseball so that it does not go straight but moves to one side

26 ROW A BOAT [I,T] to make a boat move by using OARS

→ **pull/make a face** at FACE[1](2), → **pull your finger out** at FINGER[1](12), → **pull rank (on sb)** at RANK[1](5), → **pull the rug (out) from under sb's feet** at RUG(3), → **pull the plug (on sth)** at PLUG[1](5), → **pull your socks up** at SOCK[1](3), → **pull your weight** at WEIGHT[1](12), → **pull the wool over sb's eyes** at WOOL(4)

THESAURUS

pull to make something or someone move in the direction that your hands are moving: *He pulled her towards him and kissed her.* | *Sam was pulling on his socks.*
tug to pull something suddenly with a short quick movement, often to get someone's attention: *'Look,' he said, tugging at his brother's sleeve.* | *I tugged at the drawer but it wouldn't open.*
drag to pull something along the ground, especially because it is heavy: *If we can't lift the piano, we'll have to drag it.*
haul to pull something big and heavy using a lot of effort, especially upwards and using a rope: *They hauled their boats further up the beach.* | *fishermen hauling in their nets*
heave to pull or lift something very heavy, especially with one movement: *He heaved the sack of sand onto his shoulder.*
draw *formal* to pull something or someone gently in a particular direction: *Lisa reached for his hand but he drew it away.*
pull to be attached to a vehicle or piece of machinery and make it move behind you in the direction you are going: *Ten dogs were pulling a sledge over the ice.* | *a tractor pulling a plough*
tow to pull a vehicle behind – used about a vehicle, a boat, or a horse pulling something using a rope or chain: *The car in front of us was towing a caravan.* | *Horses were used to tow the boats along the canals.*
draw to pull a vehicle such as a carriage – used especially about horses doing this: *a carriage drawn by four horses* | *a horse-drawn cart*

pull ahead *phr v* if one vehicle pulls ahead of another, it gets in front of it by moving faster: *Schumacher pulled ahead of Montoya as the two drivers approached the first corner of the race.*
pull apart *phr v*
1 pull sth ↔ apart to separate something into pieces: *Pull the meat apart with two forks.*
2 pull sb ↔ apart to make the relationships between people in a group bad or difficult: *His drinking pulled the family apart.*
3 pull sth ↔ apart to carefully examine or criticize something: *The selection committee pulled each proposal apart.*
4 pull sb/sth ↔ apart to separate people or animals when they are fighting: *The fight ended only when the referee pulled the two players apart.*
5 if something pulls apart, it breaks into pieces when you pull on it
pull at/on sth *phr v*
1 to take hold of something and pull it several times: *Mary was pulling nervously at her hair.*
2 to take smoke from a pipe or cigarette into your lungs: *He pulled hard on the cigarette.*
3 to take a long drink from a bottle or glass
pull away *phr v*
1 to start to drive away from a place where you had stopped: *He waved as he pulled away.*
2 to move ahead of a competitor by going faster or being more successful: **[+from]** *Nkoku is pulling away from the other runners.*
pull back *phr v*
1 to decide not to do or become involved in something: **[+from]** *In the end, he pulled back from financing the film.*
2 to get out of a bad situation or dangerous place, or to make someone else do this: **[+from]** *Many banks are pulling back from international markets.* | **pull sb ↔ back** *They are preparing to pull back their forces.*
3 pull sth ↔ back *BrE* if a team that is losing pulls back a GOAL or some points, it succeeds in scoring a goal or some points: *Our play improved and we pulled back two goals.*
pull down *phr v*
1 pull sth ↔ down to destroy something or make it stop existing: *My old school was pulled down.*
2 pull down sth to earn a particular amount of money: *Real estate stocks pulled down total returns of 35.7 percent.*
3 pull sb down to make someone less successful, happy, or healthy: *Her problems have really pulled her down.*
4 pull down a menu to make a computer program show you a list of the things it can do
pull for sb/sth *phr v informal* to encourage a person or team to succeed: *The crowd were pulling for me to do well.*
pull in *phr v*
1 if a driver pulls in, they move to the side of the road and stop: *She pulled in to let the ambulance pass.*
2 if a train pulls in, it arrives at a station OPP **pull out**
3 pull sb/sth ↔ in to attract business, money, people etc: *a publicity stunt to pull in the crowds*
4 pull in sth *informal* if you pull in a lot of money, you earn it
5 pull sb ↔ in if a police officer pulls someone in, they take them to a police station because they think that person may have done something wrong
pull off *phr v*
1 pull sth ↔ off *informal* to succeed in doing something difficult: *The goalkeeper pulled off six terrific saves.*
2 pull off (sth) to drive a car off a road in order to stop, or to turn into a smaller road: *We pulled off the road to get some food.*
pull on sth *phr v* to PULL AT something
pull out *phr v*
1 a) to drive onto a road from another road or from where you have stopped: *Don't pull out! There's something coming.* **b)** to drive over to a different part of the road in order to get past a vehicle in front of you: *I pulled out to overtake a bus.*
2 if a train pulls out, it leaves a station OPP **pull in**
3 to stop doing or being involved in something, or to make someone do this: *McDermott pulled out with an injury at the last minute.* | **[+of]** *They are trying to pull out of the agreement.* | **pull sb out of sth** *He threatened to pull his son out of the team.*
4 to get out of a bad situation or dangerous place, or to make someone or something do this: *Jim saw that the firm was going to be ruined, so he pulled out.* | **pull sb/sth ↔ out** *Most of the troops have been pulled out.* | **[+of]** *when the country was still pulling out of a recession* → **pull out all the stops** at STOP[2](7)
pull over *phr v* to drive to the side of the road and stop your car, or to make someone else do this: *The policeman signalled to him to pull over.* | **pull sb/sth ↔ over** *He pulled the car over.* | *A cop pulled him over and gave him a speeding ticket.*
pull (sb) **through** *phr v*
1 to stay alive after you have been very ill or badly injured, or to help someone do this: *His injuries are severe but he's expected to pull through.* → **bring (sb) through** at BRING
2 to succeed in doing something very difficult, or to help someone to do this: *He relied on his experience to pull him through.*
pull together *phr v*
1 if a group of people pull together, they all work hard to achieve something: *If we all pull together, we'll finish on time.*
2 pull yourself together to force yourself to stop behaving in a nervous, frightened, or uncontrolled way: *With an effort Mary pulled herself together.*
3 pull sth together to improve something by organizing it more effectively: *We need an experienced manager to pull the department together.*
pull up *phr v*
1 to stop the vehicle that you are driving: *He pulled up in front of the gates.*
2 pull up a chair/stool etc to get a chair etc and sit down next to someone who is already sitting

3 pull sb up *especially BrE* to stop someone who is doing something wrong and tell them you do not approve: **[+on]** *I felt I had to pull her up on her lateness.* → **pull sb up short** at SHORT³(7)

pull² ●○○ *n*

1 ACT OF MOVING STH [C] an act of using force to move something towards you or in the same direction that you are moving OPP **push**: *He **gave** her a sharp **pull** forward.*

2 FORCE [C usually singular] a strong physical force that makes things move in a particular direction: *the gravitational pull of the Moon*

3 ATTRACTION [C usually singular] the ability to attract someone or have a powerful effect on them: **[+of]** *After about a year I gave in to the pull of fatherhood.*

4 INFLUENCE [singular, U] *informal* special influence or power over other people: *His family's name gives him a lot of pull in this town.*

5 CLIMB [singular] *BrE* a difficult climb up a steep road: *It was a long pull up the hill.*

6 MUSCLE [C usually singular] an injury to one of your muscles, caused by stretching it too much during exercise: *a groin pull*

7 SMOKE/DRINK [C] an act of taking the smoke from a cigarette, pipe etc into your LUNGS or of taking a long drink of something: **[+on/at]** *She took a long pull on her cigarette.*

8 HANDLE [C] a rope or handle that you use to pull something: *He popped the ring pull on another can of lager.*

9 CRICKET/GOLF/BASEBALL [C] a way of hitting the ball in CRICKET, golf, or baseball so that it does not go straight, but moves to one side

10 on the pull *BrE informal* trying to find someone who will take part in sexual activity with you

pull·back /ˈpʊlbæk/ *n* **1** [C] the act of moving soldiers away from the area where they were fighting: **[+from]** **2** [C] a reduction in the value, amount, or level of something: *a significant pullback in the stock market* **3** [U] the action of a plane moving backwards, away from an airport TERMINAL (=building where people wait to get on the plane)

ˌpull-down ˈmenu *n* [C] a list of things a computer program can do. You make a pull-down menu appear on the computer screen by CLICKing on a special word with a MOUSE.

pul·let /ˈpʊlɪt/ *n* [C] a young chicken that is in its first year of laying eggs

pul·ley /ˈpʊli/ *n* [C] a piece of equipment consisting of a wheel over which a rope or chain is pulled to lift heavy things

ˈpulling ˌpower *n* [U] *BrE* the ability of someone or something to attract people: *Madonna's pulling power filled the Arena for 10 nights.*

Pull·man /ˈpʊlmən/ *n* [C] a very comfortable train carriage, or a train made up of these carriages

ˈpull-on *adj* [only before noun] pull-on clothes or shoes do not have any buttons, ZIPs etc, so you just pull them on to wear them

ˈpull-out, **pull·out** /ˈpʊlaʊt/ *n* [C] **1** the act of an army, business etc leaving a particular place: *The pull-out of troops will begin soon.* **2** part of a book or magazine that is designed to be removed and read separately: *a pull-out on home PCs*

pull·o·ver /ˈpʊlˌəʊvə $ -ˌoʊvər/ *n* [C] a piece of WOOLLEN clothing without buttons that you wear on the top half of your body SYN **sweater**

ˈpull tab *n* [C] *AmE* a small piece of metal attached to a can of food, drink etc that you pull in order to open it SYN **ring-pull** *BrE*

ˈpull-up *n* [C] *BrE* an exercise in which you use your arms to pull yourself up towards a bar above your head SYN **chin-up** *AmE*

pul·mo·na·ry /ˈpʊlmənəri, ˈpʌl- $ -neri, ˈpʌl-/ *adj* [only before noun] *medical* relating to the lungs, or having an effect on the lungs

pulp¹ /pʌlp/ *n*

1 SOFT SUBSTANCE [singular, U] a very soft substance that is almost liquid, made by crushing plants, wood, vegetables etc: ***Mash** the bananas **to a pulp**.* | *timber grown for **wood pulp*** (=used for making paper) | *a soft pulp of leaves and mud*

2 FRUIT/VEGETABLE [U] the soft inside part of a fruit or vegetable: *Halve the melon and scoop out the pulp.*

3 BOOKS/FILMS ETC [U] *AmE* books, magazines, films etc that are badly written and that contain lots of sex, violence etc: *an ad in a pulp magazine* | ***pulp fiction***

4 beat sb to a pulp *informal* to seriously injure someone by hitting them many times

5 TOOTH [U] part of the inside of a tooth —**pulpy** *adj*: *Cook slowly until soft and pulpy.*

pulp² *v* [T] **1** to beat or crush something until it becomes very soft and almost liquid: *pulped apples* **2** to beat or hit someone's face or body very badly: *His body was pulped by the impact of the train.* **3** to make wood or old books and newspapers into paper: *Unsold novels are sent to be pulped.* | *wood pulping techniques*

pul·pit /ˈpʊlpɪt/ *n* [C usually singular] a raised structure inside a church that a priest or minister stands on when they speak to the people: **in/from the pulpit** *Rev. Dawson addressed the congregation from the pulpit.*

pul·sar /ˈpʌlsɑː $ -sɑːr/ *n* [C] an object like a star that is far away in space and produces RADIATION and RADIO WAVES → **quasar**

pul·sate /pʌlˈseɪt $ ˈpʌlseɪt/ *v* [I] **1** to make sounds or movements that are strong and regular like a heart beating: *I could see the veins in his neck pulsating.* | *pulsating music* **2** *literary* to be strongly affected by a powerful emotion or feeling: **[+with]** *The whole city seemed to pulsate with excitement.*

pul·sa·tion /pʌlˈseɪʃən/ *n* [C,U] *technical* a beat of the heart or any regular movement that can be measured: *the pulsations of the baby's heart* | *muscular pulsation*

pulse¹ /pʌls/ ●○○ *n*

1 HEART [C usually singular] the regular beat that can be felt, for example at your wrist, as your heart pumps blood around your body → **heartbeat**: *His breathing was shallow and his **pulse** was **weak**.* | **take sb's pulse** (=count the beats of their pulse, usually by feeling their wrist) | **check/feel sb's pulse** *The doctor listened to his breathing and checked his pulse.* | **find a pulse** (=be able to feel a pulse, which shows that someone is alive) *I held his wrist, trying to find a pulse.* | *She felt his neck. There was no pulse.* | **pulse rate** (=the number of beats that can be felt in a minute) *If your pulse rate is between 90 and 100, it is likely that you are unfit.* | *Her **pulse raced*** (=beat very quickly) *with excitement.*

2 MUSIC [C,U] a strong regular beat in music: *the distant pulse of a steel band*

3 SOUND/LIGHT/ELECTRICITY [C] an amount of sound, light, or electricity that continues for a very short time

4 FEELINGS/OPINIONS [U] the ideas, feelings, or opinions that are most important to a particular group of people or have the greatest influence on them at a particular time: *Clinton had an uncanny ability to sense the pulse of the nation.*

5 FOOD **pulses** [plural] seeds such as beans, PEAS, and LENTILs that you can eat → **have/keep your finger on the pulse** at FINGER¹(6)

pulse² *v* **1** [I] to move or flow with a steady quick beat or sound: *She felt the blood **pulsing through** her **veins**.* | *Colored lights pulsed in time to the music.* **2** [I] if a feeling or emotion pulses through someone, they feel it very strongly: **[+through]** *Excitement pulsed through the crowd.* **3** [I,T] to push a button on a FOOD PROCESSOR to make the machine go on and off regularly, rather than work continuously: *Pulse several times until the mixture looks like oatmeal.*

pul·ver·ize (*also* **-ise** *BrE*) /ˈpʌlvəraɪz/ *v* [T] **1** to crush something into a powder: *The seeds can be used whole or pulverized into flour.* **2** *informal* to completely defeat someone: *Stewart completely pulverized the opposition.*

—**pulverized** *adj*: *pulverized coal* —**pulverization** /ˌpʌlvəraɪˈzeɪʃən $ -rə-/ *n* [U]

pu·ma /ˈpjuːmə/ *n* [C] a COUGAR → see picture at **BIG CAT**

pum·ice /ˈpʌmɪs/ (*also* ˈ**pumice stone**) *n* **1** [U] very light grey rock from a VOLCANO that is crushed to a powder and used for cleaning **2** [C] a piece of pumice stone that you rub on your skin to clean it or make it soft

pum·mel /ˈpʌməl/ *v* (**pummelled**, **pummelling** *BrE*, **pummeled**, **pummeling** *AmE*) [T] **1** to hit someone or something many times quickly, especially using your FISTS (=closed hands) SYN **beat**: *Diane leaned over and pummeled the pillows.* | **pummel sth with sth** *She flew at him, pummelling his chest with her fists.* | **[+at]** *The cook pummelled at the dough.* | *The platoon was pummeled by heavy machine-gun fire.* **2** *informal* to completely defeat someone at a sport

pump¹ /pʌmp/ ●●○ *n*
1 [C] a machine for forcing liquid or gas into or out of something: **water/air/beer etc pump** (=for moving water, air etc) | **hand/foot pump** (=operated by your hand or foot) | **petrol pump/gas pump** (=for putting petrol into cars) | **stomach pump** (=for removing the contents of someone's stomach) → see picture at **BICYCLE**
2 [C usually plural] **a)** *BrE* a flat light shoe for dancing, exercise, sport etc **b)** *AmE* a woman's plain shoe with no LACES, BUCKLES etc: *a pair of leather pumps* → see picture at **SHOE¹**
3 [C] an act of pumping → **HEAT PUMP**, → **all hands to the pumps** at **HAND¹**(39), → **prime the pump** at **PRIME³**(4), → **PARISH PUMP**

pump² ●●○ *v*
1 MOVE IN A DIRECTION [T always + adv/prep] to make liquid or gas move in a particular direction, using a pump: **pump sth into/out of/through sth** *The fire department is still pumping floodwater out of the cellars.*
2 MOVE FROM UNDER GROUND [T] to bring a supply of water, oil etc to the surface from under the ground: *We were able to pump clean water from several of the wells.* | **pump gas** *AmE* (=put gasoline into a car) *He got a job pumping gas for the hotel guests.*
3 MOVE IN AND OUT [I] (*also* **pump away**) to move very quickly in and out or up and down: *My heart was pumping fast.*
4 USE A PUMP [I] (*also* **pump away**) to operate a pump: **[+at]** *The furnace man's job was to pump away furiously at the bellows.*
5 COME OUT [I always + adv/prep] if a liquid pumps from somewhere, it comes out suddenly in small amounts: **[+from/out of]** *Blood pumped from the wound.*
6 ASK QUESTIONS [T] *informal* to ask someone a lot of questions in order to get information from them: **pump sb for sth** *I tried to pump him for information about their other contacts.*
7 DRUGS **pump sb full of sth** *informal* to put a lot of drugs into someone's body: *athletes pumped full of steroids*
8 EXERCISE **pump iron** *informal* to do exercises by lifting heavy weights
9 MEDICAL TREATMENT **have your stomach pumped** to have a medical treatment to remove things you have swallowed, using a pump

pump sth **into** sb/sth *phr v*
1 pump bullets into sb/sth *informal* to shoot someone several times
2 pump money into sth to put a lot of money into a project, INVESTMENT etc

pump out *phr v*
1 if something such as music, information, or a supply of products pumps out, or if someone pumps it out, a lot of it is produced: *Music pumped out from the loudspeakers.* | **pump sth ↔ out** *propaganda pumped out by the food industry*
2 pump sth ↔ out to remove liquid from something, using a pump: *You'll have to pump the boat out.*

pump sth/sb ↔ **up** *phr v*
1 to fill a tyre, AIRBED etc with air until it is full SYN **inflate**
2 *informal* to increase the value, amount, or level of something: *The US was able to pump up exports.* | *Come on, pump up the volume* (=play music louder)*!*
3 to increase someone's excitement, interest etc

ˈ**pump-ˌaction** *adj* [only before noun] a pump-action piece of equipment is operated by pulling or pressing a part in or out so that the contents come out in short bursts: **pump-action shotgun/rifle**

pumped /pʌmpt/ (*also* ˌ**pumped** ˈ**up**) *adj* [not before noun] *especially AmE informal* very excited about something: *I'm really pumped about this opportunity.*

pum·per·nick·el /ˈpʌmpənɪkəl $ ˈpʌmpər-/ *n* [U] a heavy dark brown bread

pump·kin /ˈpʌmpkɪn/ ●●○ *n*
1 [C,U] a very large orange fruit that grows on the ground, or the inside of this fruit: *pumpkin pie* → see picture at **VEGETABLE¹**
2 *AmE* used when speaking to someone you love

ˈ**pump-ˌpriming** *n* [U] the process of trying to help a business, industry, or country to develop by giving it money

pun¹ /pʌn/ ●●○ *n* [C] an amusing use of a word or phrase that has two meanings, or of words that have the same sound but different meanings SYN **play on words**: **forgive/excuse/pardon the pun** (=used to show you know you are making a pun) | **no pun intended** (=used to show you do not mean to make a joke about something) *The clergy prey (no pun intended) on bereaved families.*

pun² *v* (**punned**, **punning**) [I] to make a pun: **[+on]** *In this line, Hamlet puns on the meaning of 'saw'.*

punch¹ /pʌntʃ/ ●●● S3 *v* [T]
1 HIT to hit someone or something hard with your FIST (=closed hand): *He punched me and knocked my teeth out.* | **punch sb on/in sth** *He punched Jack in the face.*
THESAURUS ▸ HIT
2 MAKE HOLES to make a hole in something, using a metal tool or other sharp object: *The guard punched my ticket and I got on.* | *These bullets can* **punch** *a* **hole** *through 20 mm steel plate.*
3 PUSH BUTTONS to push a button or key on a machine: *Just punch the button to select a track.*
4 punch holes in sb's argument/idea/plans etc to criticize someone's views, idea, plans etc by showing why they are wrong
5 punch the air to make a movement like a punch towards the sky, to show that you are very pleased: *He punched the air in triumph.*
6 punch sb's lights out *informal* to hit someone hard in the face
7 punch the clock *AmE informal* to record the time that you start or finish work by putting a card into a special machine
8 CATTLE *AmE old-fashioned* to move cattle from one place to another
9 punch above your weight *informal* if businesses, organizations, teams etc punch above their weight, they are successful in an activity or task which usually needs more money, power, skill etc than they seem to have – used especially in newspapers

punch in *phr v*
1 *AmE* to record the time that you arrive at work, by putting a card into a special machine SYN **clock in** *BrE*
2 punch sth ↔ in to put information into a computer by pressing buttons or keys

punch out *phr v AmE*
1 to record the time that you leave work, by putting a card into a special machine SYN **clock out** *BrE*
2 punch sb out to hit someone so hard that they become unconscious

punch² ●●○ *n*
1 [C] a quick strong hit made with your FIST (=closed hand): **[+in/on]** *a punch in the kidneys* | *I managed to* **land a punch** *on his chin.* | *The two men started* **throwing punches** (=trying to hit each other).
2 [singular, U] a strong effective way of expressing things

that makes people interested: *Thirty years after it was written, Orton's 'Entertaining Mr Sloane' still* ***packs a punch****.*
3 [C,U] a drink made from fruit juice, sugar, water, and usually some alcohol: *a glass of hot punch*
4 [C] a metal tool for cutting holes or for pushing something into a small hole
5 a one-two punch two bad events that happen close together: *A meteorite collided with Earth at the same time, delivering a one-two punch to the magnetic field.*
6 not pull any/your punches to express disapproval or criticism clearly, without trying to hide anything: *The inquiry report doesn't pull any punches in apportioning blame.*
7 beat sb/sth to the punch *informal* to do or get something before anyone else does: *Hitachi has beaten its competitors to the punch with its new palmtop.*
8 as pleased as punch *old-fashioned* very happy: *He's as pleased as punch about the baby.* → **pack a (hard) punch** at PACK[1](8)

P

Punch and Ju·dy show /ˌpʌntʃ ən ˈdʒuːdi ʃəʊ $ -ʃoʊ/ *n* [C] a traditional type of entertainment for children, especially at British SEASIDE towns, that uses PUPPETS

punch·bag /ˈpʌntʃbæg/ *BrE*, **ˈpunching bag** *AmE n* [C] **1** a heavy leather bag hung from a rope, that is punched for exercise or training **2** a person who is hit, criticized strongly, or blamed, even though they have done nothing wrong: *a young wife whose husband* ***used*** *her* ***as a punching bag***

ˈpunch bowl *n* [C] a large bowl in which punch (=a mixed drink) is served

ˈpunch-drunk *adj* **1** *informal* very confused, especially because you have had a lot of bad luck or have been treated badly **2** a BOXER who is punch-drunk is suffering brain damage from being hit on the head

ˈpunched card (*also* **ˈpunch card**) *n* [C] a card with a pattern of holes in it that was used in the past for putting information into a computer

punch·line, **ˈpunch line** /ˈpʌntʃlaɪn/ *n* [C usually singular] the last few words of a joke or story, that make it funny or surprising

ˈpunch-up *n* [C] *BrE informal* a fight

punch·y /ˈpʌntʃi/ *adj* a punchy piece of writing or speech is short but very clear and effective —**punchiness** *n* [U]

punc·til·i·ous /pʌŋkˈtɪliəs/ *adj formal* very careful to behave correctly and follow rules: **[+about]** *Joe was always punctilious about repaying loans.* —**punctiliously** *adv* —**punctiliousness** *n* [U]

punc·tu·al /ˈpʌŋktʃuəl/ *adj formal* arriving, happening, or being done at exactly the time that has been arranged SYN **on time**: *She's always very punctual for appointments.* | *the punctual payment of invoices* —**punctually** *adv* —**punctuality** /ˌpʌŋktʃuˈæləti/ *n* [U]

punc·tu·ate /ˈpʌŋktʃueɪt/ *v* **1** [T] to divide written work into sentences, phrases etc using COMMAS, FULL STOPS etc **2** [T] *literary* to interrupt something, especially when this is repeated: *The silence was occasionally punctuated by laughter.* GRAMMAR **Punctuate** is usually passive in this meaning.

punc·tu·a·tion /ˌpʌŋktʃuˈeɪʃən/ ●●○ *n* [U] the marks used to divide a piece of writing into sentences, phrases etc

ˌpunctuˈation mark ●●○ *n* [C] a sign, such as a COMMA or QUESTION MARK, used to divide a piece of writing into sentences, phrases etc

punc·ture¹ /ˈpʌŋktʃə $ -ər/ *n* [C] **1** *BrE* a small hole made accidentally in a tyre SYN **flat** *AmE*: *She was cycling home when she* ***had a puncture****.* | **slow puncture** (=one that lets air out very slowly) THESAURUS HOLE **2** a small hole made by a sharp point, especially in someone's body: *puncture wounds*

puncture² *v* **1** [I,T] if a tyre punctures, or if you puncture it, a small hole appears in it: *A piece of glass punctured the back tyre.* **2** [T] to make a small hole in something: *One bullet punctured his lung.* | *Pressurized container – do not puncture.* **3** [T] to interrupt a period of silence by making a noise: *There was a stunned silence, punctured by shrill laughter.* **4** [T] to suddenly destroy someone's hopes or beliefs, making them feel unhappy, embarrassed, or confused: *He wasn't hurt, but his dignity was punctured.*

pun·dit /ˈpʌndɪt/ *n* [C] someone who is often asked to give their opinion publicly of a situation or subject: **political/media/TV etc pundits** *If you believe the fashion pundits, we'll all be wearing pink this year.*

pun·gent /ˈpʌndʒənt/ *adj* **1** having a strong taste or smell: **pungent smell/aroma/odour etc** *the pungent odour of garlic* **2** *formal* pungent speech or writing is clever and direct, and usually criticizes someone or something strongly: *He expressed some fairly pungent criticisms.* —**pungently** *adv* —**pungency** *n* [U]

pun·ish /ˈpʌnɪʃ/ ●●○ *v* [T]
1 to make someone suffer because they have done something wrong or broken the law → **punishment**, **punitive**: *Smacking is not an acceptable way of punishing a child.* | *He promised to* ***punish severely*** *any officials found guilty of electoral fraud.* | **punish sb for (doing) sth** *It's unfair to punish a whole class for the actions of one or two students.* | *They* ***deserve to be punished*** *for putting passengers at risk.* | *I felt I was being punished for what my mother had done.* | **punish sb by doing sth** *My parents decided to punish me by withdrawing financial support.* | **punish sb with sth** *The House voted to punish the senator with a formal reprimand.*
2 if a crime is punished in a particular way, anyone who is guilty of it is made to suffer in that way → **punishment**, **punitive**: **be punished by/with sth** *In some societies, theft is punished by death.* GRAMMAR **Punish** is usually passive in this meaning.
3 punish yourself to make yourself feel guilty or bad for something you have done: *If you fail, don't punish yourself.*

pun·ish·a·ble /ˈpʌnɪʃəbəl/ *adj* in law, a punishable act can be punished: *a* ***punishable offence*** | **[+by/with]** *a crime punishable by death*

pun·ish·ing /ˈpʌnɪʃɪŋ/ *adj* [usually before noun] difficult, tiring, or extreme: *He set himself a* ***punishing schedule*** *of conferences.* | *a series of punishing defeats* | *a punishing exercise regime*

pun·ish·ment /ˈpʌnɪʃmənt/ ●●● W3 *n*
1 [C,U] something that is done in order to punish someone, or the act of punishing them → **punitive**: **[+for]** *The punishment for treason is death.* | **as a punishment** *I was sent to bed as a punishment.*
2 [U] *informal* rough physical treatment: *tough plants that can* ***take*** *any amount of* ***punishment*** → CAPITAL PUNISHMENT

COLLOCATIONS

ADJECTIVES

harsh/severe *The court decided the original punishment was too severe.*
light *The punishment seemed very light.*
just/fitting (=appropriate and right) *Death would be a just punishment.*
physical punishment *Children respond more to affection than to physical punishment.*
corporal punishment (=when someone punishes a child by hitting them) | **capital punishment** (=death as a punishment for a crime) | **the maximum punishment**

VERBS

give sb a punishment *He deserved the punishment he was given.*
hand out punishments (=give people punishments) *The courts are handing out harsher punishments to reckless drivers.*
receive a punishment *He received the maximum punishment.*
escape/avoid punishment *The thieves managed to escape punishment.*
carry a punishment (=used when saying what the punishment for something is) *The offence carries a punishment of up to 10 years in prison.*
inflict a punishment (on sb) (=punish someone, especially physically)

PHRASES

the punishment should fit the crime (=it should be appropriate) *The public believe that the punishment should fit the crime.*

THESAURUS

punishment something that is done in order to punish someone, or the act of punishing them: *I don't think they deserved such a severe punishment.* | *The usual punishment is life in prison.*
sentence a punishment given by a judge in a court: *He was given a long prison sentence.* | *They asked for the maximum sentence.*
fine an amount of money that you must pay as a punishment: *I got an £80 fine for speeding.* | *There are **heavy fines** for drink-driving.*
penalty a general word for a punishment given to someone who has broken a law, rule, or agreement: *What's the penalty if you get caught?* | *He called for **stiffer penalties** for crimes involving guns.*
the death penalty (*also* **capital punishment**) the system in which people are killed as a punishment for crimes: *If he is found guilty, he faces the death penalty.* | *A number of states have abolished capital punishment.*
community service unpaid work helping other people that someone does as punishment for a crime: *He was given a choice between doing 200 hours of community service, or a big fine.*
corporal punishment the punishment of children by hitting them: *I don't agree with corporal punishment.* | *Corporal punishment was abolished in schools in 1987.*

pu·ni·tive /ˈpjuːnətɪv/ ●○○ *adj* [usually before noun]
1 intended to punish someone: **punitive action/measures etc** *The agency sent a letter, but took no punitive action.* | *The jury awarded **punitive damages*** (=money paid to someone who is the victim of a crime). | *The government is expected to **take punitive steps** against offenders.*
2 punitive taxes/price increases etc taxes etc that are so high that it is difficult for people to pay them: *The US could impose **punitive tariffs** on exports.*

Pun·ja·bi /pʌnˈdʒɑːbi/ *n* **1** [U] the language used in the Punjab **2** [C] someone from the Punjab —**Punjabi** *adj*

punk /pʌŋk/ *n* **1** [U] (*also* ˌ**punk ˈrock**) a type of loud music popular in the late 1970s and 1980s **2** [C] (*also* **punk rocker**) someone who likes punk music and wears things that are typical of it, such as torn clothes, metal chains, and coloured hair: *punk hairstyles* **3** [C] *AmE informal* a young man who fights and breaks the law **4** [U] *AmE* a substance that burns without a flame that is used to light FIREWORKS etc

pun·kah /ˈpʌŋkə/ *n* [C] in the past, a large FAN that was hung across a room and was swung backwards and forwards by hand

pun·net /ˈpʌnɪt/ *n* [C] *BrE* a small square box used to hold soft fruits such as STRAWBERRIES

punt¹ /pʌnt/ *n*
1 BOAT [C] a long thin boat with a flat bottom that you move by pushing a long pole against the bottom of the river
2 a punt the activity of travelling in a punt: *a punt down the river*
3 KICK [C usually singular] in RUGBY or American football, the action of kicking the ball after dropping it from your hands: *a 45-yard punt* → see picture at AMERICAN FOOTBALL
4 MONEY [C] the standard unit of money used in the Republic of Ireland before the EURO

punt² *v* **1** [I,T] to go on a river in a punt: **[+along/down/past etc]** *Pete punted us back to the boatyard.* **2** [T] **a)** in RUGBY or American football, to drop the ball from your hands and kick it: *He punted the ball 40 yards.* **b)** to kick a ball hard so that it goes a long way

punt·er /ˈpʌntə $ -ər/ *n* [C] **1** *BrE informal* someone who buys a product or service SYN **customer**: **average/typical/ordinary punter** *The technical details mean nothing to the average punter.* | *You need something to **pull in the punters*** (=attract them). **2** *BrE informal* someone who BETs on the result of a horse race etc **3** the player who punts the ball in American football

pu·ny /ˈpjuːni/ *adj* **1** a puny person is small, thin, and weak: *a **puny little** guy* | *puny arms* THESAURUS▸ WEAK
2 not effective or impressive: **puny effort/attempt** *a puny attempt at humour* | *Our efforts look puny beside Fred's.*
3 a puny amount of money is too small: *She was awarded a puny £1,000 in compensation.*

pup /pʌp/ *n* [C] **1** a young dog SYN **puppy**: *a spaniel pup* | *a **litter of pups*** (=several pups born to the same mother at the same time) **2** a young SEAL or OTTER **3** *old-fashioned* a young man who is rude or too confident **4 be sold a pup/buy a pup** *BrE old-fashioned* to be tricked into buying something that is not worth what you paid for it

pu·pa /ˈpjuːpə/ *n* (*plural* **pupae** /-piː/ *also* **pupas** *AmE*) [C] an insect at the stage before it becomes adult, when it is protected by a special cover: *moth pupae* —**pupal** *adj* [only before noun]: *the pupal stage*

pu·pate /pjuːˈpeɪt $ ˈpjuːpeɪt/ *v* [I] *technical* to become a pupa

pu·pil /ˈpjuːpəl/ ●●● S2 W1 *n* [C]
1 *especially BrE* someone who is being taught, especially a child: *About 20 pupils study music here.* | *staff and pupils* | *a **star pupil*** (=a very good one) | *a third-grade pupil* THESAURUS▸ STUDENT
2 the small black round area in the middle of your eye → **iris** → see picture at EYE¹

pup·pet /ˈpʌpɪt/ ●○○ *n* [C]
1 a model of a person or animal that you move by pulling wires or strings, or by putting your hand inside it: **puppet show/theatre/play** *a 20-minute puppet show* | **glove/hand/finger puppet** → see picture at MARIONETTE
2 a person or organization that allows other people to control them and make their decisions: **[+of]** *The government is in danger of becoming a mere puppet of the military.* | **puppet government/regime/state** (=a government etc controlled by a more powerful country or organization)

pup·pe·teer /ˌpʌpəˈtɪə $ -ˈtɪr/ *n* [C] someone who performs with puppets

pup·pet·ry /ˈpʌpətri/ *n* [U] the art of performing with puppets

pup·py /ˈpʌpi/ ●●● S3 *n* (*plural* **puppies**) [C]
1 a young dog: *a six-month-old puppy*
2 this/that puppy *AmE spoken informal* used instead of the name of a thing, especially when you do not know the name: *How do you turn this puppy off?*

ˈ**puppy fat** *n* [U] *BrE informal* fat on a child's body, that disappears as they get older SYN **baby fat** *AmE*: *Carol had shed her puppy fat and was now very elegant.*

ˈ**puppy love** *n* [U] a young person's romantic love for someone, which other people do not think is serious: *a bad case of puppy love*

ˈ**pup tent** *n* [C] *AmE* a small TENT for two people

pur·chase¹ /ˈpɜːtʃɪs $ ˈpɜːr-/ ●●○ W3 AWL *v* [T] *formal* to buy something: *You can purchase insurance online.* | *the growing demand to purchase goods on credit* | *Where did you purchase the car?* | **[+from]** *Tickets may be purchased in advance from the box office.* THESAURUS▸ BUY —**purchasable** *adj* —**purchaser** *n* [C]: *France was the no. 1 purchaser of Iraqi oil.*

purchase² ●○○ AWL *n*
1 [C,U] *formal* something you buy, or the act of buying it: *She paid for her purchases and left.* | **day/date/time of purchase** *This product should be consumed on the day of purchase.* | *I enclose my receipt as **proof of purchase**.* | **[+of]** *a loan towards the purchase of a new car* | *She **made** two **purchases** from my stall.* → HIRE PURCHASE, PURCHASE PRICE
2 [singular] *formal* a firm hold on something: **gain/get a purchase on sth** *The ice made it impossible to get a purchase on the road.*

P

ˈ**purchase price** *n* [singular] *formal* the price that has to be paid for something, especially a house: *We borrowed 80% of the purchase price.*

ˈ**purchasing ˌpower** *n* [U] **1** the amount of money that a person or group has available to spend: *increases in purchasing power* **2** the amount that a unit of money can buy: *The purchasing power of the local currency has halved.*

pur·dah /ˈpɜːdə, -dɑː $ ˈpɜːr-/ *n* [U] **1** the custom in some Muslim and Hindu societies in which women stay indoors or cover their faces so that men cannot see them: **in purdah** *The bride remains in purdah until the wedding.* **2** a period of being alone, especially to keep something secret: *18 months of self-imposed purdah*

pure /pjʊə $ pjʊr/ ●●● S3 W3 *adj*

1 NOT MIXED [usually before noun] a pure substance or material is not mixed with anything OPP **impure**: **pure silk/cotton/wool etc** *pure wool blankets* | *rings made of* ***pure gold*** | *Our beef patties are* ***100% pure****.*

2 COMPLETE [only before noun] complete and total SYN **sheer**: *a work of pure genius* | *a smile of pure joy* | *My mother's life was pure hell.* | **pure chance/luck/coincidence etc** *By pure chance, I met Sir Malcolm that morning.* | *The chairman dismissed the report as pure speculation.*

3 CLEAN clean and not containing anything harmful OPP **impure**: *We had trouble finding a* ***pure water*** *supply.* | *Up here the* ***air*** *was* ***purer****.* **THESAURUS** CLEAN

4 pure and simple used to emphasize that there is only one thing involved or worth considering: *He wanted revenge, pure and simple.*

5 MORALLY GOOD *literary* without any sexual experience or evil thoughts OPP **impure**: *a pure young girl* | *They're too pure and innocent to know what's really going on.*

6 COLOUR OR SOUND very clear and beautiful: *a cloudless sky of the purest blue* | *Her voice, clear and pure, soared up to the roof.*

7 TYPICAL [only before noun] typical of a particular style: *His music is pure New York.*

8 BREED/RACE bred from only one group or race: *My husband is pure Japanese and traces his family back 800 years.* | *The Highland is the oldest and purest breed of cattle in Britain.*

9 ART OR STUDY [usually before noun] done according to an accepted standard or pattern: *Gothic architecture in its* ***purest form***

10 pure science/maths etc work in science etc that increases our knowledge of the subject rather than using it for practical purposes

11 be as pure as the driven snow to be morally perfect – used humorously to say someone is not like this at all → PURELY

pure·bred /ˈpjʊəbred $ ˈpjʊr-/ *adj* a purebred animal has parents that are both the same breed SYN **pedigree** → **thoroughbred**: *purebred Irish wolfhounds* —**purebred** *n* [C]

pu·ree, **purée** /ˈpjʊəreɪ $ pjʊˈreɪ/ *v* [T] if you puree food, you crush it so that it is almost liquid: *Use a processor to puree the apricots.* | *puréed potatoes* —**puree, purée** *n* [C,U]: *tomato purée*

pure·ly /ˈpjʊəli $ ˈpjʊrli/ ●●○ S3 W3 *adv* completely and only: *a decision made* ***for purely political reasons*** | *The building was closed* ***purely on the grounds of*** *safety.* | *It happened* ***purely by chance****.* | *I do it* ***purely and simply*** *for the money.*

pur·ga·tive /ˈpɜːɡətɪv $ ˈpɜːr-/ *n* [C] *old-fashioned* a substance that makes your BOWELS empty

pur·ga·tory /ˈpɜːɡətəri $ ˈpɜːrɡətɔːri/ *n* **1** [U] something that makes you suffer – used humorously: *Sewing is relaxation for some, purgatory for others.* **2 Purgatory** in Roman Catholic belief, a place where the souls of dead people suffer until they are pure enough to enter heaven —**purgatorial** /ˌpɜːɡəˈtɔːriəl◂ $ ˌpɜːr-/ *adj*

purge¹ /pɜːdʒ $ pɜːrdʒ/ *v* **1** [T] to force people to leave a place or organization because the people in power do not like them: **purge sth of sb/sth** *He sought to purge the Democrat party of conservatives.* | **purge sb/sth from sth** *plans to purge ethnic minorities from rebel-controlled areas* **2** [T] to remove something that is thought to be harmful or unacceptable: **purge sth of sb/sth** *an initiative to purge the PC market of software pirates* | *Local languages were purged of Russian words.* | **purge sb/sth from sth** *It's hard to imagine now that Lawrence's novels were purged from public libraries.* **3** [T] to destroy something that is no longer needed: *The system automatically purges unread emails after two weeks.* **4** [T] *literary* to remove bad feelings: **purge sb/sth of sth** *We have to begin by purging our minds of prejudice.* | *Any doubts about his leadership were purged by the courage of his performance.* **5** [T] to take a substance that makes your BOWELS empty: *Anorexics may overeat before* ***purging themselves*** *or vomiting.* **6** [I] to force yourself to bring food up from your stomach and out of your mouth, especially because you have BULIMIA

purge² *n* [C] **1** an action to remove your opponents or the people who disagree with you from an organization or a place: *the Stalinist purges* | **[+of/on]** *a purge of military commanders* | *a purge on tax dodgers* **2** a substance used to make you empty your BOWELS

pu·ri·fi·er /ˈpjʊərəfaɪə $ ˈpjʊrɪfaɪər/ *n* [C] something used to remove dirty or harmful substances: **air/water purifier**

pu·ri·fy /ˈpjʊərɪfaɪ $ ˈpjʊr-/ *v* (**purified, purifying, purifies**) [T] **1** to remove dirty or harmful substances from something: *chemicals used to purify the water* **2** to make someone pure by removing evil from their soul: *They prayed to God to purify them.* —**purification** /ˌpjʊərɪfɪˈkeɪʃən $ ˌpjʊr-/ *n* [U]: ***water purification*** *tablets*

pur·ist /ˈpjʊərɪst $ ˈpjʊr-/ *n* [C] someone who believes that something should be done in the correct or traditional way, especially in the areas of art, sport, music, and language: ***The purists*** *won't like it, but opera on TV certainly brings in the audiences.* | *Architects with* ***purist views*** *were suspicious of his work.*

pu·ri·tan /ˈpjʊərətən $ ˈpjʊr-/ *n* [C] **1** someone with strict moral views who thinks that pleasure is unnecessary and wrong **2 Puritan** a member of a Protestant religious group in the 16th and 17th centuries, who wanted to make religion simpler —**puritan** *adj*: *the Puritan work ethic*

pu·ri·tan·i·cal /ˌpjʊərəˈtænɪkəl◂ $ ˌpjʊr-/ *adj* very strict about moral matters, especially sex – used to show disapproval: *a puritanical father who wouldn't let his children watch television* | *The atmosphere at the school was oppressively puritanical.*

pu·ri·tan·is·m /ˈpjʊərətənɪzəm $ ˈpjʊr-/ *n* [U] strict religious and moral attitudes – used to show disapproval: *a harsh and repressive sexual puritanism*

pu·ri·ty /ˈpjʊərəti $ ˈpjʊr-/ ●○○ *n* [U] the quality or state of being pure: *the purity of tap water* | ***spiritual purity*** → IMPURITY

purl /pɜːl $ pɜːrl/ *n* [U] a type of stitch that you use when you KNIT (=make clothes from wool) —**purl** *v* [I,T]

pur·lieus /ˈpɜːljuːz $ ˈpɜːrluːz/ *n* [plural] *literary* the area in and around a place

pur·loin /pɜːˈlɔɪn, ˈpɜːlɔɪn $ -ɜːr-/ *v* [T] *formal* to obtain something without permission – often used humorously: *He must have purloined a key from somewhere.*

pur·ple¹ /ˈpɜːpəl $ ˈpɜːr-/ ●●● S3 W3 *n* [U] a dark colour that is a mixture of red and blue

purple² ●●● S3 W3 *adj*

1 having a dark colour that is a mixture of red and blue

2 purple with rage/purple in the face etc with a face that is dark red, caused by anger: *His face* ***turned purple*** *with rage.*

3 purple patch a time when you are very successful – used especially in news reports: *Steve's purple patch continued with a second victory on Tuesday.*

4 purple prose/passage writing that uses difficult or unusual words – used to show disapproval

ˌ**Purple ˈHeart** *n* [C] a MEDAL given to US soldiers who have been wounded

pur·plish /ˈpɜːplɪʃ $ ˈpɜːr-/ *adj* slightly purple

pur·port¹ /pɜːˈpɔːt $ pɜːrˈpɔːrt/ *v* [I,T] *formal* to claim to be or do something, even if this is not true: **purport to do**

sth *Two undercover officers purporting to be dealers infiltrated the gang.* | **be purported to be sth** *The document is purported to be 300 years old.* —**purportedly** *adv*: *a portrait purportedly of Shakespeare*

pur·port² /ˈpɜːpɔːt, -pət $ ˈpɜːrpɔːrt/ *n* [U] *formal* the general meaning of what someone says

pur·pose /ˈpɜːpəs $ ˈpɜːr-/ ●●● S2 W2 *n*
1 [C] the purpose of something is what it is intended to achieve: **[+of]** *The purpose of this meeting is to elect a new chairman.* | *What is the purpose of your visit?* | **the purpose of doing sth** *The purpose of conducting a business is to make money.* | **for the purpose of doing sth** *Troops were sent solely for the purpose of assisting refugees.* | **for medical/political/decorative etc purposes** *It should be legitimate to use cannabis for medical purposes.* | **sole/primary/main etc purpose** *The protection of children is the primary purpose of this legislation.* | **serve a purpose** (=achieve something) *It would* ***serve no useful purpose*** *to re-open the investigation.*
2 [C] a plan or aim: *Nick* ***had no particular purpose in mind*** *when he started.* | **sb's purpose in doing sth** *Attending the race was not my purpose in coming to Indianapolis.* | **with the purpose of doing sth** *He came here with the purpose of carrying out the attack.*
3 for ... purposes in a particular situation or when being considered in a particular way: ***For tax purposes****, you will be treated as a married couple.* | *The details are,* ***for the present purposes****, irrelevant.* | **for the purposes of sth** *For the purposes of this book, America is taken to include the continent north of Mexico.*
4 on purpose deliberately: **do sth on purpose** *You make it sound as if I did it on purpose!*
5 FEELING [U] a feeling of determination to achieve things in life: *It's so important to have a* ***sense of purpose*** *that it underlies human happiness.* | *My football career was over and I* ***had no purpose in life****.* | *He possessed* ***great strength of purpose****.*
6 for all practical purposes (*also* **to all intents and purposes**) used to say that something is so close to the truth that it can be considered to be the truth: *The war, to all intents and purposes, was over.* | *We have a secretary of state for Scotland who is for all practical purposes a Scottish prime minister.*
7 serve its purpose if something has served its purpose, it has done what you needed it to do: *We delete the data once it has served its purpose.*
8 defeat the purpose to fail to achieve the result you want: *Anxiety will cause tension, which* ***defeats the purpose of the exercise*** (=the activity or plan).
9 to no purpose *formal* without any useful results: *She called after them, but to no purpose.*
10 to the purpose *old-fashioned* useful or helpful
→ PURPOSELY, CROSS-PURPOSES

THESAURUS

purpose the reason you do something, and the thing you want to achieve when you do it: *What is the purpose of your visit to England?* | *The plant is used for medicinal purposes.*
aim what you want to achieve when you do something: *The main aims of the project are as follows.* | *Their ultimate aim is to find a cure for cancer.*
goal something that you hope to achieve in the future, even though this may take a long time: *It took Mandela over forty years to achieve his goal of a democratic South Africa.* | *the goal of ending child poverty*
objective something that you are working hard to achieve, especially in business or politics: *The bank achieved its objective of increasing its share of the market.* | *The government's long-term objective is to cut CO^2 emissions by 50%.*
the object of sth *formal* the specific purpose of an activity: *The object of the game is to get as many points as possible.* | *The students will benefit, and that must be* ***the object of the exercise*** (=the main thing that you are trying to do).
the point the purpose of doing something and the reason why it is right or necessary: *At fourteen, I couldn't see the point of going to school.* | ***What's the point*** *in waiting?* (=I don't think it is useful or necessary)
intention the purpose that you have in your mind when you do something: *He kept his real intentions well hidden.* | *Although we made a lot of money, this wasn't our original intention.*
ends the result that someone is trying to achieve – used especially when you disapprove of what someone is doing: *They are using religion for political ends.* | ***The ends do not justify the means*** (=you should not use violence, cruelty, dishonest behaviour etc to achieve your aims).

ˌpurpose-ˈbuilt *adj BrE* designed and made for a particular purpose: *purpose-built toilets for disabled people*

pur·pose·ful /ˈpɜːpəsfəl $ ˈpɜːr-/ *adj* having a clear aim or purpose SYN **determined** OPP **purposeless**: *a purposeful and consistent foreign policy* | *a purposeful movement* —**purposefully** *adv*: *He walked purposefully to his desk.* —**purposefulness** *n* [U]

pur·pose·less /ˈpɜːpəsləs $ ˈpɜːr-/ *adj* not having a clear aim or purpose OPP **purposeful**: *hours of purposeless activity* —**purposelessly** *adv* —**purposelessness** *n* [U]

pur·pose·ly /ˈpɜːpəsli $ ˈpɜːr-/ *adv* deliberately SYN **on purpose**: *A clause in the contract had been left purposely vague.*

purr /pɜː $ pɜːr/ *v* **1** [I] if a cat purrs, it makes a soft low sound in its throat to show that it is pleased **2** [I] if the engine of a vehicle or machine purrs, it works perfectly and makes a quiet smooth sound: *The big Bentley purred along the road.* **3** [I,T] to speak in a soft low SEXY voice: *'That feels good,' she purred.* —**purr** *n* [C]

PURSE

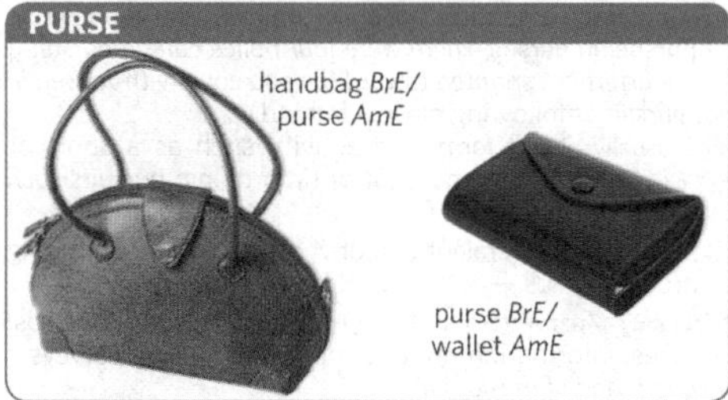

purse¹ /pɜːs $ pɜːrs/ ●●● S3 *n*
1 [C] **a)** *especially BrE* a small bag in which women keep paper money, coins, cards etc SYN **wallet** *AmE*: *Julie opened her handbag and took out her purse.* **b)** (*also* **change purse**, **coin purse** *AmE*) a small bag used to hold coins, used especially by women
2 [C] *AmE* a bag in which a woman carries her money and personal things SYN **handbag** *BrE*: *I locked the door and dropped the keys in my purse.* → see picture at BAG¹
3 [singular] *formal* the amount of money that a person, organization, or country has available to spend: *Election expenses are met from* ***the public purse*** (=money controlled by the government). | *A visit to the new county museum will set the family purse back by around £12.*
4 [C] the amount of money given to someone who wins a sports event, such as a BOXING match or a car race: *They will compete for a $100,000 purse.*
5 the purse strings used to refer to the control of spending in a family, company, country etc: **hold/control the purse strings** *It all comes down to who holds the purse strings.* | *She keeps tight control over the purse strings.*

purse² *v* [T] if you purse your lips, you bring them together tightly into a small circle, especially to show disapproval or doubt: *Mrs Biddell pursed her lips and shook her head.*

purs·er /ˈpɜːsə $ ˈpɜːrsər/ *n* [C] an officer on a ship who is responsible for money and the passengers' rooms, comfort etc

pur·su·ance /pəˈsjuːəns $ pərˈsuː-/ *n* **in pursuance of sth** *formal* with the aim of doing or achieving something, or while doing something: *In pursuance of this objective, 8,000 letters were sent.*

pur·su·ant /pəˈsjuːənt $ pərˈsuː-/ *adj formal* **pursuant to sth** done according to a particular law, rule, contract etc: *The boy was provided with an interpreter, pursuant to the Individuals with Disabilities Act.*

pur·sue /pəˈsjuː $ pərˈsuː/ ●●○ S3 W2 AWL *v* [T]
1 to continue doing an activity or trying to achieve something over a long period of time → **pursuit**: *She plans to **pursue** a **career** in politics.* | *Students should **pursue** their own **interests**, as well as do their school work.* | **pursue a goal/aim/objective etc** *companies that pursue the traditional goal of profits* | *a campaign promise to **pursue policies** that will help the poor*
2 pursue the matter/argument/question etc to continue trying to find out about or persuade someone about a particular subject: *Janet did not dare **pursue the matter further**.* | *The defence pursued the question of Dr Carrington's state of mind.*
3 to chase or follow someone or something, in order to catch them, attack them etc → **pursuit**: *Briggs ran across the field with one officer pursuing him.* **THESAURUS** FOLLOW
4 to keep trying to persuade someone to have a relationship with you: *I was pleased, but somewhat embarrassed, when she pursued me.*

pur·su·er /pəˈsjuːə $ pərˈsuːər/ *n* [C] someone who is chasing you: *They managed to escape their pursuers.*

pur·suit /pəˈsjuːt $ pərˈsuːt/ ●○○ AWL *n*
1 [U] when someone tries to get, achieve, or find something in a determined way → **pursue**: **[+of]** *the pursuit of liberty and happiness* | *the pursuit of war criminals* | **in (the) pursuit of sth** *People are having to move to other areas in pursuit of work.*
2 [U] when someone chases or follows someone else → **pursue**: **in pursuit** *There were four police cars in pursuit.* | *The quarterback sprinted toward the end zone with Jansen **in hot pursuit*** (=following closely behind).
3 [C usually plural] *formal* an activity such as a sport or HOBBY, which you spend a lot of time doing: *pursuits such as swimming and tennis*

pu·ru·lent /ˈpjʊərələnt $ ˈpjʊr-/ *adj technical* containing or producing PUS —**purulence** *n* [U]

pur·vey /pɜːˈveɪ $ pɜːr-/ *v* [T] *formal* to supply goods, services, information etc to people: *DJ Dominic purveys a unique brand of music.*

pur·vey·or /pɜːˈveɪə $ pɜːrˈveɪər/ *n* [C usually plural] *formal* a business that supplies goods, services, or information: *purveyors of farmyard-fresh poultry*

pur·view /ˈpɜːvjuː $ ˈpɜːr-/ *n* **within/outside the purview of sb/sth** *formal* within or outside the limits of someone's job, activity, or knowledge: *This matter comes within the purview of the Department of Health.*

pus /pʌs/ *n* [U] a thick yellowish liquid produced in an infected part of your body → **pustule**: *a wound oozing pus*

push¹ /pʊʃ/ ●●● S1 W1 *v*
1 MOVE [I,T] to make someone or something move by pressing them with your hands, arms etc OPP **pull**: *It didn't move, so she pushed harder.* | *I promised to push him on the swings for as long as he wanted.* | *shoppers pushing their grocery carts* | **push sb/sth away/back/aside etc** *She pushed him away.* | *Maria pushed her hair back from her forehead.* | **push sb/sth towards/into etc sth** *Philip pushed him towards the door.* | **push sth open/shut** *I slowly pushed the door open.*
2 BUTTON/SWITCH [I,T] to press a button, switch etc in order to make a piece of equipment start or stop working SYN **press**: *I got in and pushed the button for the fourth floor.* | *Push the green button to start the engine.*
3 TRY TO GET PAST [I] to use your hands, arms etc to make people or things move, so that you can get past them: *Don't push. Everyone will get a turn.* | **push (your way) past/through/into etc** *A fat man pushed past me in his rush to leave.* | *She pushed her way to the front.*
4 ENCOURAGE [T] to encourage or force someone to do something or to work hard: *Encourage your kids to try new things, but try not to **push** them too **hard**.* | *athletes who **push** their bodies **to the limit*** | **push yourself** *He's been pushing himself too hard, working 12-hour days.* | **push sb into (doing) sth** *My husband pushed me into leaving the job.* | **push sb to do sth** *The teachers pushed the students to achieve.*
5 PERSUADE [I,T] to try to persuade people to accept your ideas, opinions etc in order to achieve something: *The president is trying to push his agenda in Congress.* | **[+for]** *He was **pushing hard** for welfare reform.* | **push to do sth** *Company representatives are pushing to open foreign markets to their products.* | **push sth on sb** *We don't try to push our religion on anyone.*
6 CHANGE [T always + adv/prep] to change someone's situation, or to make a situation change, especially when some people do not want it to change: *The law would push even more children into poverty.* | *attempts to push the peace process forward*
7 INCREASE/DECREASE [T always + adv/prep] to increase or decrease an amount, value, or number: **push sth up/down** *Slow sales have pushed down orders.* | **push sth higher/lower** *New technology has pushed the cost of health care even higher.*
8 ARMY [I always + adv/prep] if an army pushes somewhere, it moves in that direction: *The army was pushing north.* | *We pushed deep into enemy territory.*
9 ADVERTISE [T] *informal* to try to sell more of a product by advertising it a lot: *Sports stars earn big bucks for pushing everything from shoes to soft drinks.*
10 DRUGS [T] *informal* to sell illegal drugs → PUSHER
11 be pushing 40/50 etc *informal* to be nearly 40, 50 etc years old
12 push your luck/push it *informal* to do something or ask for something, especially something you have done or asked for before, when this is likely to annoy someone or involves a risk: *If she doesn't want to go, don't push it.* | *It's 26 miles, so you're pushing your luck if you try to hike it in a day.*
13 push sth out of your mind (*also* **push sth to the back of your mind**) to try not to think about something, especially something bad or worrying: *He pushed the thought out of his mind and tried to concentrate.*
14 push (sb's) buttons *informal* to make someone feel strong emotions: *Movies shouldn't be afraid to push a few buttons.*
15 push the boat out *BrE informal* to spend more money than you usually do, on something special: *Push the boat out and get tickets to the theatre or ballet.*
16 push the point to keep trying to make someone accept your opinion in a way that they think is annoying
17 push the envelope *AmE* to do something that is new and that goes beyond the limits of what has already been done in a particular area of activity: **[+of/on]** *ideas that push the envelope of design and construction*
18 be pushing up (the) daisies *informal* to be dead - used humorously
19 *technical* [T] to AUTOMATICALLY send your email to your SMARTPHONE, so that you receive it immediately → **PUSHED**, **PUSHING**

THESAURUS

push to make something or someone move by pressing them with your hands, arms etc: *Push the door, don't pull it.* | *She pushed him away and walked out.*
shove to push someone or something in a rough or careless way: *People were shoving to get to the front of the queue.* | *Tom shoved his suitcase under the bed.*
stuff *informal* to push something quickly and carelessly into a small space: *She stuffed a few clothes into a bag and left.*
poke to push someone or something with your finger or something sharp: *I poked the snake with a stick but it was dead.*
nudge to push someone beside you gently with your elbow to get their attention: *Toby nudged me and pointed out of the window.*

roll to push something round or something on wheels so that it moves forward: *They rolled the logs down the hill.* | *The car still didn't start so we tried to roll it off the road.*
wheel to push something with wheels, for example a bicycle or a TROLLEY, so that it moves forward, while guiding it with your hands: *Rob wheeled his bike round the back of the house.*

push ahead *phr v* to continue with a plan or an activity, especially in a determined way: **[+with]** *Quinlan decided to push ahead with the deal.*
push along *phr v* **must/should etc be pushing along** *BrE spoken* used to say that you think it is time for you to leave a place: *It's getting late – I think we should be pushing along.*
push sb **around** (*also* **push sb about** *BrE*) *phr v* to tell someone what to do in an impolite or threatening way: *Europeans sometimes feel the Americans are trying to push them around.*
push sb/sth **aside** *phr v*
1 push sth ↔ aside to try to forget about something, especially something unpleasant, so that you can give your attention to what you are doing: *She pushed aside her anger, forcing herself to focus on her work.*
2 to force someone out of their job or position, taking the job in their place: *Primakov was pushed aside but later became head of Intelligence.*
push yourself **forward** *phr v BrE* to try to make other people notice you: *Rupert was a quiet type, not one to push himself forward.*
push in *phr v BrE informal* to go in front of other people who are already waiting in a line for something, instead of going to the back of the line: *A couple of boys pushed in at the head of the queue.*
push off *phr v*
1 to start moving in a boat, on a bicycle, or when swimming or jumping, by pushing against something with your arms, legs etc: *Dad pushed off and jumped into the rowboat.*
2 *BrE spoken* used to tell someone rudely to go away
push on *phr v*
1 to continue travelling somewhere, especially after you have had a rest: *We decided to push on a little further.*
2 to continue doing an activity: **[+with]** *Nixon pushed on with the weapons development program.*
push sb/sth **↔ over** *phr v* to make someone or something fall to the ground by pushing them: *He went wild, pushing over tables and chairs.*
push sth **↔ through** (*also* **push sth through sth**) *phr v* to get a plan, law etc officially accepted, especially quickly: *The planning application was pushed through as quickly as possible.*

push² ●●○ *n*
1 PUSHING MOVEMENT [C] when someone pushes something OPP **pull**: *Jodi had stopped swinging. 'Want a push?' her dad asked.* | *If the door's stuck, just **give** it a **push**.* | **at/with the push of a button** (=used to emphasize how easy a machine is to use) *Files can be attached to your email at the push of a button.*
2 EFFORT [C] when someone, especially a business, tries to get or achieve something: *the pre-Christmas advertising push* | **[+into]** *The company has recently **made** a big **push** into the Japanese market.* | **[+for]** *the push for improved productivity* | **push to do sth** *a push to attract new members*
3 ENCOURAGEMENT [singular] if someone gives someone else a push, they encourage or persuade them to try something: *She just needed a gentle push to get her to join in.*
4 ARMY [C] a planned military movement into the area where the enemy is: **[+into]** *The army has made another big push into enemy territory.*
5 give sb the push/get the push *BrE informal* **a)** if your employer gives you the push, they make you leave your job: *I was scared I'd get the push.* **b)** if someone you are having a romantic relationship with gives you the push, they tell you that they no longer want to continue the relationship
6 when/if push comes to shove (*also* **if it comes to the push** *BrE*) *spoken* if a situation becomes very difficult or action needs to be taken: *If push comes to shove, you can always sell the car.*
7 at a push *BrE informal* if you can do something at a push, it will be difficult, but you will be able to do it: *We have room for five people, maybe six at a push.*
8 it'll be a push *BrE spoken* used to say that something will be difficult because you do not have enough time to do it: *I'll do my best, but it'll be a bit of a push.*

ˈpush-bike *n* [C] *BrE informal* a BICYCLE

ˈpush-button *adj* [only before noun] operated by pressing a button with your finger: *a push-button telephone*

push·cart /ˈpʊʃkɑːt $ -kɑːrt/ *n* [C] a large flat container like a box with wheels, used especially by people who sell goods in the street

push·chair /ˈpʊʃ-tʃeə $ -tʃer/ *n* [C] *BrE* a small seat on wheels, in which a young child sits and is pushed along SYN **stroller** *AmE*

pushed /pʊʃt/ *adj* [not before noun] *BrE informal* **1 be pushed for time/money etc** to not have much time, money etc SYN **pressed**: *I'm a bit pushed for time today.* **2** too busy: *I'd love to help, but I'm a bit pushed at the moment.* **3 be (hard) pushed to do sth** to have a lot of difficulty doing something: *I was hard pushed to keep my mind on my work.*

push·er /ˈpʊʃə $ -ər/ *n* [C] *informal* someone who sells illegal drugs

push·ing /ˈpʊʃɪŋ/ *prep* **be pushing 40/60 etc** *spoken* to be nearly 40, 60 etc years old – used only about older people: *Sheila must be pushing 40 by now.*

push·o·ver /ˈpʊʃˌəʊvə $ -ˌoʊvər/ *n informal* **be a pushover a)** to be easy to persuade, influence, or defeat: *They aren't the best team in the league, but they're **no pushover**, either.* | **[+for]** *Tony's a pushover for blondes.* **b)** *BrE* to be very easy to do or win: *The exam was a pushover.*

ˈpush-start *v* [T] to push a vehicle in order to make the engine start —**push-start** *n* [C]

ˈpush techˌnology *n* [C,U] *technical* a type of technology by which information or a message is sent from the Internet to someone's computer or SMARTPHONE without them asking for it each time

ˈpush-up *n* [C usually plural] *AmE* an exercise in which you lie on the floor on your chest and push yourself up with your arms SYN **press-up** *BrE* → see picture at **GYM**

push·y /ˈpʊʃi/ *adj* someone who is pushy does everything they can to get what they want from other people – used to show disapproval: *a pushy salesman* —**pushiness** *n* [U]

pu·sil·lan·i·mous /ˌpjuːsɪˈlænɪməs/ *adj formal* frightened of taking even small risks SYN **cowardly** —**pusillanimity** /ˌpjuːsələˈnɪməti/ *n* [U]

puss /pʊs/ *n BrE spoken* used to talk to or call a cat SYN **kitty** *AmE*: *Come here, puss, puss, puss!*

pus·sy /ˈpʊsi/ *n* (*plural* **pussies**) [C] *informal* **1** *BrE* a cat – used especially by or to children **2** *taboo* a very offensive word meaning a woman's sex organs. Do not use this word. **3** *AmE not polite* an offensive word for a man who is weak or not brave SYN **coward**

pus·sy·cat /ˈpʊsikæt/ *n* [C] **1** a cat – used especially by or to children **2** [usually singular] someone who is very nice and gentle – used especially when they do not seem this way: *Greg? He's a pussycat, really.*

pus·sy·foot /ˈpʊsifʊt/ *v* [I] (*also* **pussyfoot around/about**) *informal* to be too careful and frightened to do something, such as making firm decisions or telling someone exactly what you think: *You can't pussyfoot around when it comes to keeping kids safe.*

ˈpussy ˌwillow *n* [C,U] a tree with white flowers that are soft like fur

pus·tule /ˈpʌstjuːl $ -tʃuːl/ *n* [C] *medical* a small raised spot on your skin containing PUS

put /pʊt/ ●●● S1 W1 *v* (*past tense and past participle* **put**, *present participle* **putting**) [T]

1 MOVE TO PLACE [always + adv/prep] to move something to a particular place or position, especially using your hands SYN **place**: *He put the coffee on the table.* | *Where did you put the programmes?*

2 CHANGE SB'S SITUATION/FEELINGS [always + adv/prep] to make someone be in a situation or have a feeling: *Don't put yourself into a situation you can't handle.* | **put sb in a good/bad etc mood** (=make them feel happy/annoyed etc) *The long delay had put us all in a bad mood.* | *I don't want to* **put** *you* **in danger**. | *Pit closures have* **put** *thousands of miners* **out of a job** (=made them lose their job). | **put sb in control/command/charge etc** (=give someone authority over a group, activity, or organization) *His boss resigned and Murphy was put in charge.* | *Politics* **puts** *me* **to sleep**. | *A knee injury* **put** *him* **out of action** *for three months.*

3 WRITE/PRINT STH to write or print something or to make a mark with a pen or pencil: **put sth in/on/under etc sth** *Put your name at the top of each answer sheet.* | **put sth to sth** *He put his signature to the contract* (=he signed it to show he agreed with it). THESAURUS ▸ WRITE

4 EXPRESS [always + adv/prep] to say or write something using words in a particular way: **put sth well/cleverly/simply etc** *The question was well put.* | *So it was an accident, an 'act of God' if you want to* **put it like that**. | *When women joined the organization, it 'took on a new look',* **as** *news reports* **put it**. | *It is hard to* **put into words** (=express) *how I feel now.* | *He's not very musical,* **to put it mildly** (=he's not musical at all). | *We get on each other's nerves,* **to put it bluntly** (=to say exactly what I mean). | *It's fairly risky. Or* **to put it another way** (=say it in different words)*, don't try this at home.* | *The subject matter makes the painting a little,* **how shall I put it** (=how can I say it politely?)*, undesirable for public display.*

5 put a stop/an end to sth to stop an activity that is harmful or unacceptable: *We must put an end to their threats.*

6 put sth into action/effect/practice to start using a plan, idea, knowledge etc: *James was keen to put some of the things he had learned into practice.*

7 ASK/SUGGEST to ask a question or make a suggestion, especially to get someone's opinion or agreement: **put a proposition/proposal/case etc to sb** *He put the proposal to his wife.* | **put sth before sb** *The budget was put before the board of directors.* | *Can I* **put a question to** *you?* | *I* **put it to you that** *this proposal has to be considered.*

8 put sth right to make a situation better, especially after someone has made a mistake or behaved badly: *He has a chance to put things right by admitting a mistake was made.*

9 put sb straight/right (*also* **set sb straight/right**) to tell someone the true facts when they have made a mistake that annoys you: *A young man was in here asking for 'Miss' Whalby, but I put him right on that one.*

10 put sth straight to make something look clean and tidy: *It took us all weekend to put the garden straight.*

11 MAKE SB/STH DO STH to make someone or something work or do something, or to use it: *a scheme to* **put** *unemployed people* **to work** *on government construction projects* | *If you have a spare room,* **put** *it* **to work** *for you – take in a lodger.* | *Computer games are being* **put to use** *in the classroom.* | *We* **put** *15 rain jackets* **to the test** (=we tested them).

12 HAVE IMPORTANCE/QUALITY [always + adv/prep] to consider something as having a particular level of importance or quality: **put sb as/among/in etc sth** *A recent poll put Dr Martens among the world's top thirty designer labels.* | **put sb/sth before sb/sth** *Some companies put profit before safety.* | **put sb/sth first/second etc** *The job's important to him, but he puts his family first.*

13 SEND SB SOMEWHERE [always + adv/prep] to arrange for someone to go to a place, or to make them go there: **put sb in (sth)** *The company is putting in new management.* | *Pneumonia put him in the hospital for a week.* | **Put** *the boys* **to bed** *around eight o'clock.*

14 put sb on a train/plane etc to take someone to a plane, train etc to start a journey: *I put her on the plane for London.*

15 put paid to sth *BrE* to spoil and end your hopes or plans completely: *A car accident put paid to his chances of taking part in the race.*

16 I wouldn't put it past sb (to do sth) *spoken* used to say that you think someone could easily do something wrong or illegal: *I wouldn't put it past him to use force.*

17 put sb to trouble/inconvenience *especially BrE* to make extra work or cause problems for someone

18 put it there *spoken* used to tell someone to put their hand in yours, either as a greeting or after making an agreement with them: *$500? OK, it's a deal. Put it there!*

19 THROW to throw a SHOT (=a heavy metal ball) in a sports competition → **put your finger on sth** at FINGER[1](4), → **put your foot down** at FOOT[1](13), → **put your foot in it** at FOOT[1](15), → **put the record straight** at RECORD[1](11), → **put sth to (good) use** at USE[2](4), → **put your back into it** at BACK[2](19)

put about *phr v*

1 put sth about *BrE informal* to give other people news or information, especially when it is unpleasant or untrue:

THESAURUS: put

put to move something to a particular place: *I've put the wine in the fridge.* | *Where have you put my grey shirt?*
place to put something somewhere carefully: *'It's beautiful,' he said, placing it back on the shelf.*
lay to put someone or something down carefully on a flat surface: *He laid all the money on the table.* | *She laid the baby on his bed.*
position to carefully put something in a suitable position: *Position the microphone to suit your height.* | *Troops were positioned around the city.*
slip to put something somewhere with a quick movement: *He slipped his arm around her waist.* | *Carrie quickly slipped the money into her bag.*
shove to put something into a space or container quickly or carelessly: *Shove anything you don't want in that sack.* | *I've ironed those shirts so don't just shove them in a drawer.*
stick (*also* **bung** *BrE*) *informal* to put something somewhere quickly or carelessly: *I stuck the address in my pocket and I can't find it now.* | *Could you bung those clothes in the washing machine?*
dump to put something down somewhere in a careless and untidy way: *Don't just dump all your bags in the kitchen.* | *People shouldn't dump rubbish at the side of the street.*
pop *informal* to quickly put something somewhere, usually for a short time: *Pop it in the microwave for a minute.*
thrust *literary* to put something somewhere suddenly or forcefully: *'Hide it,' he said, thrusting the watch into her hand.*

TO PUT SOMETHING INTO A LIQUID

dip to put something into a liquid for a very short time and take it out again: *She dipped her hand in the water to see how hot it was.* | *Prawns are delicious dipped in a spicy sauce.*
plunge to put something quickly, firmly, and deeply into a liquid: *Plunge the pasta into a pan of boiling water.* | *I had to plunge my arm in up to the elbow to reach the keys.*
dunk to put something such as a piece of bread or cake into a hot drink or soup before eating it: *I love biscuits dunked in coffee.*
immerse to put something deep into a liquid so that it is completely covered: *If the plant's leaves look dry, immerse the roots in water for a while.*

P

After he was fired, he **put it about that** *he was fed up with working for such a large company.*

2 put (sth) about *technical* if a ship puts about or if you put it about, it changes direction

3 put yourself about *BrE informal* to have sexual relationships with a lot of different people

put sth ↔ **across** *phr v*

1 to explain your ideas, beliefs etc in a way that people can understand: *He was trying to put across a serious point.*

2 put yourself across *BrE* to explain your ideas and opinions clearly so that people understand them and realize what sort of person you are: *Sue's never been very good at putting herself across at interviews.*

3 to sing, play music, or act in a film or play in a clear effective way: *She can really put a song across.*

put sth ↔ **aside** *phr v*

1 to try to stop thinking about a problem, argument, or disagreement, because you want to achieve something: *You must put aside your pride and apologise to him.*

2 to save money regularly, usually for a particular purpose: *She put at least £30 a week aside for food.*

3 to put down something you are reading or working with, in order to start doing something else: *He glanced at the note, put it aside and went on with the meeting.*

4 to keep a period of time free in order to be able to do something: *If you're planning a trip to the museum, be sure to put aside at least an hour and a half.*

put sth **at** sth *phr v* to calculate or guess an amount, number, age etc, without being very exact: *Her fortune was put at £5.5 million.*

put sb/sth **away** *phr v*

1 put sth ↔ away to put something in the place where it is usually kept: *He put his toys away every night.*

2 put sth ↔ away to save money: *We're putting some money away for expenses.*

3 put sb away *informal* to put someone in a prison or in a mental hospital: *If you are found guilty, the judge is going to put you away for life.*

4 put sth ↔ away *informal* to eat or drink a lot: *It's amazing the amount that child can put away.*

5 put sth ↔ away *informal* to score a GOAL, especially after other failed attempts: *He seized the opportunity to put the ball away.*

6 put sth ↔ away *AmE informal* to defeat your opponent in a sports competition: *Two plays later, Smith scored to put the game away.*

put sth **back** *phr v*

1 put sb/sth ↔ back to put people or things in the place or situation they were in before: *She put the saucepan back on the stove.* | *Our win today put us back into third place in the league.*

2 put sth ↔ back to arrange for an event to start at a later time or date SYN **postpone**: **[+to]** *The meeting has been put back to next Thursday.*

3 put sth ↔ back to delay a process or activity by a number of weeks, months etc: *This fire could put back the opening date by several weeks.*

4 to make someone or something have something that they used to have before: *The win put a smile back on his face.*

5 put a clock/watch back *BrE* to make a clock or watch show an earlier time SYN **set back** *AmE* → **put the clock back** at CLOCK[1](3)

put sth **behind** you *phr v* to try to forget about an unpleasant event or experience and think about the future: *She had dealt with the guilt years ago and put it behind her.*

put sth ↔ **by** *phr v* to save money regularly in order to use it later: *We're trying to put a little by each month for a new car.*

put down *phr v*

1 PLACE **put sth/sb ↔ down** to put something or someone that you are holding or carrying onto a surface: *Put those heavy bags down for a minute.*

2 CRITICIZE **put sb ↔ down** to criticize someone and make them feel silly or stupid SYN **belittle**: *I hate the way Dave puts me down the whole time.* | **put yourself down** *Stop putting yourself down.*

3 WRITE **put sth ↔ down** to write something, especially a name or number, on a piece of paper or on a list SYN **write down**: *Put down your name and address.*

4 put down a revolution/revolt/rebellion etc to stop a REVOLUTION etc by using force: *The uprising was put down by the police and the army.*

5 PAY **put sth ↔ down** to pay part of the total cost of something, so that you can pay the rest later: **[+on]** *They put down a deposit on the goods until Christmas.*

6 BABY **put sb down** to put a baby in its bed: *We try to put Amy down at six every evening.*

7 put the phone down to put the RECEIVER back onto the telephone when you have finished speaking to someone SYN **hang up**: **[+on]** *She put the phone down on me* (=suddenly ended the conversation).

8 KILL **put sth ↔ down** to kill an animal without causing it pain, usually because it is old or sick SYN **put sth to sleep**: *We had to have the dog put down.*

9 I couldn't put it down *spoken* used to say that you found a book, game etc extremely interesting: *Once I'd started reading it I just couldn't put it down.*

10 AIRCRAFT **put (sth) down** if an aircraft puts down or if a pilot puts it down, it lands, especially because of an EMERGENCY: *The engine failed and the plane put down in the sea.*

11 put down a motion/an amendment to suggest a subject, plan, change in the law etc for a parliament or committee to consider

12 LEAVE PASSENGER **put sb down** *BrE* to stop a vehicle so that passengers can get off at a particular place: *He asked the taxi to put him down at the end of the road.*

put sb **down as** sth *phr v* to guess what someone is like or what they do, without having much information about them: *I didn't think he was unfriendly. I put him down as shy.*

put sb **down for** sth *phr v*

1 to put someone's name on a list so that they can take part in an activity, join an organization etc: *They put themselves down for a training course.*

2 put sb down for £5/£20 etc *especially BrE* to write someone's name on a list with an amount of money that they have promised to give

put sth **down to** sth *phr v*

1 to think that something is caused by something else: *I was having difficulty reading, which I put down to the poor light.*

2 put it down to experience to try not to feel too upset about failure, especially when you learn something useful from it: *Everyone gets rejected from time to time; put it down to experience.*

put forth sth *phr v*

1 to suggest an idea, explanation etc, especially one that other people later consider and discuss SYN **submit**: *Arguments were put forth for changing some of the rules of the game.*

2 put forth leaves/shoots/roots etc *formal* if a tree or bush puts forth leaves etc, it begins to grow them

put sb/sth ↔ **forward** *phr v*

1 to suggest a plan, proposal, idea etc for other people to consider or discuss SYN **propose**: *They put forward a number of suggestions.*

2 to suggest formally that you or someone else should be considered for a particular job, membership of an organization etc: *Her name was put forward for the lead role in the play.*

3 to arrange for an event to start at an earlier time or date: **[+to]** *The men's final has been put forward to 1:30.*

4 put a clock/watch forward *BrE* to make a clock or watch show a later time SYN **set forward** *AmE*

put in *phr v*

1 put sth ↔ in to fix a piece of equipment somewhere and connect it so that it is ready to be used SYN **install**: *We decided to have a new bathroom put in.*

2 put sth ↔ in to spend time or use energy working or practising something: *Dorothy had put in a lot of hard work during her six years as chairperson.*
3 put in sth *written* to interrupt someone in order to say something: *'How old are you?' 'Sixteen.' 'I'm sixteen too,' put in Dixie.*
4 put sth ↔ in to ask for something in an official way: *She put in an insurance claim.* | *We must put in an order by tonight.* | **put in for sth** *I put in for a pay increase.*
5 put your faith/trust/confidence in sb/sth to trust someone or something or believe that they can do something: *I'm putting my faith in the appeal judges.*
6 put in sth to do something in a particular way, especially a performance in a play, film, race etc: *He put in a brilliant performance in the British Grand Prix.*
7 put in an appearance to go to a social event, meeting etc for a short time: *There was an hour yet before she needed to put in an appearance at the restaurant.*
8 if a ship puts in, it enters a port

P

put sth **into** sth *phr v*
1 to make money available to be used for a particular purpose: *The government appears to be putting more money into education.*
2 to use a lot of energy etc when you are doing an activity: *Candidates put a lot of time and effort into gaining qualifications.*
3 to add a quality to something: *These simple recipes put more fun into eating.*

put sb/sth **off** *phr v*
1 put sth ↔ off to delay doing something or to arrange to do something at a later time or date, especially because there is a problem or you do not want to do it now SYN **delay, procrastinate**: *The match has been put off until tomorrow because of bad weather.* | **put off doing sth** *I put off going to the doctor but I wish I hadn't.*
2 put sb ↔ off *BrE* to make you dislike something or not want to do something: *Don't let the restaurant's decor put you off – the food is really good.* | **put sb off (doing) sth** *Don't let your failures put you off trying harder.*
3 put sb off to make someone wait because you do not want to meet them, pay them etc until later SYN **stall**: *When he calls, put him off as long as you can.*
4 put sb off (sth) *BrE* to make it difficult for someone to pay attention to what they are doing by talking, making a noise, moving etc: *It puts me off when you watch me all the time.*
5 put sb off (sth) *BrE* to let someone leave a vehicle at a particular place: *I'll put you off at the supermarket.*

put sb/sth **on** *phr v*
1 CLOTHES **put sth ↔ on** to put a piece of clothing on your body OPP **take off**: *He took off his uniform and put on a sweater and trousers.* | *I'll have to put my glasses on; I can't read the sign from here.*
2 ON SKIN **put sth ↔ on** to put MAKE-UP, cream etc on your skin: *I've got to put this cream on twice a day.*
3 AFFECT/INFLUENCE STH **put sth on sth** to do something that affects or influences someone or something else: *The government put a limit on imports of textiles.* | *Pat was* ***putting pressure on*** *him to leave his wife.*
4 START EQUIPMENT **put sth ↔ on** to make a light or a piece of equipment start working by pressing or turning a button or switch SYN **switch on, turn on**: *He got up and put on the light.* | *Shall I put the kettle on?*
5 MUSIC **put sth ↔ on** to put a record, tape, or CD into a machine and start playing it: *She put on some music while they ate.*
6 PRETEND **put sth ↔ on** to pretend to have a particular feeling, opinion, way of speaking etc especially in order to get attention: *Sheila's not really that upset; she's just putting it on.* | *Leaving the court, the families all tried to* ***put on a brave face*** (=not show that they were sad or worried).
7 put on weight/12 lbs/4 kg etc to become fatter and heavier SYN **gain**: *Rosie's put on five kilos since she quit smoking.*
8 EVENT/CONCERT/PLAY ETC **put sth ↔ on** to arrange for a concert, play etc to take place, or to perform in it: *One summer the children put on a play.*
9 SHOW WHAT YOU CAN DO **put sth ↔ on** to show what you are able to do or what power you have: *The team need to put on another world-class performance.*
10 COOK **put sth ↔ on** to start cooking something: *Shall I put the pasta on now?*
11 PROVIDE STH **put sth ↔ on** *BrE* to provide a service for people, especially a special one: *BA is putting on extra flights to cover the Christmas rush.*
12 you're putting me on! *AmE spoken* used to tell someone that you think they are joking: *He wouldn't do that – you're putting me on.*
13 RISK MONEY **put sth on sth** to risk an amount of money on the result of a game, race etc SYN **bet**: *We put £50 on Brazil to win the Cup.*
14 ADD **put sth on sth** to add an amount of money or tax onto the cost of something: *Can smokers really complain if more tax is put on cigarettes?*
15 TELEPHONE **put sb ↔ on** to give someone the telephone so that they can talk to someone who is telephoning: *Can you put Janet on?*

put sb **onto** sb/sth *phr v BrE informal* to give someone information about something interesting or useful that they did not know about: *Jo put us onto this fantastic French restaurant.*

put out *phr v*
1 FIRE/CIGARETTE ETC **put sth ↔ out** to make a fire etc stop burning SYN **extinguish**: *The rescue services are still trying to put out the fires.*
2 LIGHT **put sth ↔ out** to make a light stop working by pressing or turning a button or switch SYN **switch off**
3 MAKE AVAILABLE **put sth ↔ out** to put things where people can find and use them: *The girls helped her to put out the cups and plates.*
4 feel/be put out to feel upset or offended: *We were a little put out at not being invited to the wedding.*
5 MAKE EXTRA WORK **put sb out** to make extra work or cause problems for someone: *Mary can't come to dinner tonight. She hopes it won't put you out.*
6 put yourself out to make an effort to do something that will help someone: *They had put themselves out to entertain her during her visit.*
7 TAKE OUTSIDE **put sth ↔ out** to take something outside your house and leave it there: *Remember to put the cat out before you go to bed.* | **put the rubbish/garbage etc out** (=put unwanted things outside your house to be taken away) | **put the washing out** (=put clothes outside to dry)
8 put your tongue out to push your tongue out of your mouth, especially as a rude sign to someone
9 put your hand/foot/arm out to move your hand etc forward and away from your body: *He put out his hand toward her.*
10 MAKE UNCONSCIOUS **put sb out** to make someone unconscious before a medical operation
11 put your back out to injure your back
12 PRODUCE STH **put sth ↔ out** to broadcast or produce something for people to read or listen to: *They put out a half-hour programme on young refugees.*
13 put out feelers to try to discover information or opinions by listening to people or watching what is happening: *He had already put out feelers with local employers but they hadn't been interested.*
14 SHIP if a ship puts out, it starts to sail
15 HAVE SEX *AmE informal* if a woman puts out, she has sex with a man
16 BASEBALL **put sb out** to prevent a baseball player from running around the BASES, for example by catching the ball that they have hit

put sth **↔ over** *phr v*
1 *BrE* to succeed in telling other people your ideas, opinions, feelings etc: *The advert puts over the message clearly and simply: nuclear power is clean.*
2 put one/sth over on sb *informal* to deceive someone into believing something that is not true or that is useless: *Nobody could put one over on him.*

put through *phr v*
1 put sb/sth ↔ through to connect someone to someone else on the telephone: **[+to]** *Could you put me through to Eddie?*
2 put sb through school/college/university to pay for someone to study at school, college etc: *She worked as a waitress and put herself through school.*
3 put sb through sth to make someone do or experience something difficult or unpleasant: *The soldiers were put through eight weeks of basic training.* | *They really* ***put*** *me* ***through it*** *at the interview.*
4 put sth ↔ through to do what is necessary in order to get a plan or suggestion accepted or approved: *Production will start up again when these changes have been put through.*
put sth ↔ **together** *phr v*
1 to prepare or produce something by collecting pieces of information, ideas etc: *It took all morning to put the proposal together.*
2 to form people or things into a group: *We are currently putting together a sales and marketing team.*
3 to make a machine, model etc by joining all the different parts SYN **assemble**: *I can't work out how to put this table together.*
4 more ... than the rest/the others/everything else put together used to say that one amount is greater than the total of a set of amounts: *Paul seemed to have more money than the rest of us put together.*
put sth **towards** sth *phr v* to use some money in order to pay part of the cost of something: *Alec put the money towards a trip to Australia.*
put sb **under** *phr v* if a doctor puts you under, they give you drugs to make you unconscious before SURGERY
put up *phr v*
1 BUILD **put sth ↔ up** to build something such as a wall, fence, building etc SYN **erect**: *They're putting up several new office blocks in the centre of town.*
2 FOR PEOPLE TO SEE **put sth ↔ up** to put a picture, notice etc on a wall so that people can see it: *Can I put up some posters?* | *The shops have started to put up Christmas decorations.*
3 ATTACH STH **put sth ↔ up** to attach a shelf, cupboard etc to a wall: *My dad put up five shelves.*
4 INCREASE **put sth ↔ up** *BrE* to increase the cost or value of something SYN **raise**: *Most big stores admit they daren't put prices up for fear of losing their customers.*
5 RAISE **put sth ↔ up** to raise something to a higher position: *I put up my hand and asked to leave the room.* | *Philip put his hood up because it was raining.*
6 LET SB STAY **put sb up** to let someone stay in your house and give them meals: *I was hoping Kenny could put me up for a few days.*
7 STAY SOMEWHERE *BrE* to stay in a place for a short time: **[+at/in/with]** *We can put up at a hotel for the night.*
8 put up a fight/struggle/resistance to show great determination to oppose something or get out of a difficult situation: *Gina put up a real fight to overcome the disease.* | *The rebels have put up fierce resistance.*
9 put up sth to give an amount of money for a particular purpose: *The paper put up a reward for information on the murder.*
10 MAKE AVAILABLE **put sth up** to make something or someone available for a particular purpose: **[+for]** *They* ***put*** *their house* ***up for sale***. | *The baby was* ***put up for adoption***.
11 put up a proposal/argument/case etc to explain a suggestion or idea so that other people can think about it or discuss it: *If you can put up a good enough case, the board will provide the finance.*
12 ELECTIONS **put sb ↔ up** to suggest someone as a suitable person to be elected to a position: *I was put up for the committee.*
13 put up or shut up *spoken informal* used to tell someone that they should either do what needs to be done or stop talking about it
put sb **up to** sth *phr v* to encourage someone to do something stupid or dangerous: *'Did Shirley put you up to this?' 'No, it was my own idea.'*
put up with sb/sth *phr v* to accept an unpleasant situation or person without complaining: *She put up with his violent temper.*

> **REGISTER**
> In written English, people usually prefer to use **tolerate**, which is more formal: *They had to* ***tolerate*** *many hardships.*

pu·ta·tive /ˈpjuːtətɪv/ *adj* [only before noun] *formal* believed or accepted by most people: *the putative father of her child*
ˈput-down *n* [C usually singular] something you say that is intended to make someone feel stupid or unimportant SYN **snub**: *She was tired of his put-downs.*
ˈput-on *n* [C usually singular] *AmE informal* something you say or do to try to make someone believe something that is not true
ˌput ˈout *adj* [not before noun] *BrE* upset or offended: *She felt put out that she hadn't been consulted.*
pu·tre·fy /ˈpjuːtrəfaɪ/ *v* (**putrefied**, **putrefying**, **putrefies**) [I] *formal* if a dead animal or plant putrefies, it decays and smells very bad —**putrefaction** /ˌpjuːtrəˈfækʃən/ *n* [U]
pu·trid /ˈpjuːtrɪd/ *adj* **1** dead animals, plants etc that are putrid are decaying and smell very bad: *the putrid smells from the slaughterhouses* **2** *informal* very unpleasant: *a putrid green colour*
putsch /pʊtʃ/ *n* [C] a secretly planned attempt to remove a government by force: *the communist putsch*
putt /pʌt/ *v* [I,T] to hit a golf ball lightly a short distance along the ground towards the hole —**putt** *n* [C] —**putting** *n* [U]: *I was practising my putting.* → see picture at GOLF
put·tee /ˈpʌti $ pʌˈtiː/ *n* [C usually plural] a long piece of cloth that soldiers wrapped around each leg from the knee down, as part of their uniform in the past
put·ter¹ /ˈpʌtə $ -ər/ *n* [C] a type of GOLF CLUB (=stick), used to hit the ball a short distance towards or into the hole
putter² *v* [I always + adv/prep] **1** *AmE* (*also* **putter around**) to spend time doing things that are not very important in a relaxed way SYN **potter** *BrE*: *I puttered around for a while, cleaning up the kitchen.* **2** *AmE* to walk or move slowly and without hurrying: *A little boy puttered along the sidewalk.* **3** *BrE informal* to make the low sound that a vehicle makes when it is moving slowly: *A motor boat puttered by.*
ˈputting green *n* [C] **1** (*also* **green**) one of the smooth areas of grass on a GOLF COURSE where you hit the ball along the ground into the hole **2** *BrE* a smooth area of grass with special holes in it for playing a simple type of golf
put·ty /ˈpʌti/ *n* [U] **1** a soft whitish substance that becomes hard when it dries and that is used to fix glass into window frames **2 be putty in sb's hands** to be easily controlled or influenced by someone
ˈput-up job *n* [C usually singular] *informal* an event that seems real but has actually been arranged in order to deceive someone: *It's been suggested the kidnapping was a put-up job.*
ˈput-upon *adj informal* someone who feels put-upon thinks that other people are treating them unfairly by expecting them to do too much
putz¹ /pʌts/ *n* [C] *AmE informal not polite* **1** an offensive word for someone, especially a man, who is stupid, annoying, and unpleasant **2** a PENIS
putz² /pʌts, pʊts/ *v*
putz around *phr v AmE informal* to spend time doing very little, or not doing anything important SYN **mess around**: *I've just been putzing around this morning.*
puz·zle¹ /ˈpʌzəl/ ●●● S3 *n* [C]
1 a game or toy that has a lot of pieces that you have to fit together → **jigsaw**: *a child's wooden puzzle*
2 a game in which you have to think hard to solve a difficult question or problem: *a crossword puzzle*

3 [usually singular] something that is difficult to understand or explain: **[+of]** *the puzzle of how the sun works* | *The meaning of the poem has always been a puzzle.* | *He thought he had* ***solved*** *the* ***puzzle***.
4 piece of the puzzle a piece of information that helps you to understand part of a difficult question, mystery etc

puzzle² ●●○ *v* [T] to confuse someone or make them feel slightly anxious because they do not understand something: *a question that continues to puzzle scientists* | *He was puzzled by the reactions to his remark.* | *What puzzles me is why his books are so popular.*
puzzle sth ↔ **out** *phr v* to solve a confusing or difficult problem by thinking about it carefully: *He lay looking at the ceiling, trying to puzzle things out.*
puzzle over sth *phr v* to think for a long time about something because you cannot understand or solve it: *The class puzzled over a poem by Shakespeare.*

P

puz·zled /ˈpʌzəld/ ●●○ *adj* confused and unable to understand something: *'Dinner?' Sam asked, looking puzzled.* | **[+about/as to/at]** *John seemed puzzled about what the question meant.* | **puzzled that** *Harry was puzzled that Nicholas didn't seem to recognize him.* | **puzzled look/expression/frown etc** *Alice read the letter with a puzzled expression on her face.* THESAURUS▸ CONFUSED

puz·zle·ment /ˈpʌzəlmənt/ *n* [U] *formal* a feeling of being confused and unable to understand something

puz·zler /ˈpʌzlə $ -ər/ *n* [C] *informal* something that is difficult to understand or explain

puz·zling /ˈpʌzlɪŋ/ ●●○ *adj* confusing and difficult to understand or explain: *a puzzling fact* | *Gary found her reaction puzzling.*

PVC /ˌpiː viː ˈsiː◂/ *n* [U] a type of plastic, used to make pipes, window frames, clothes etc

PVR /ˌpiː viː ˈɑː $ -ˈɑːr/ *n* [C] (***personal video recorder***) a piece of equipment that can record television programmes for you DIGITALLY

pvt. *AmE* a written abbreviation of ***private***, the lowest military rank in the army

p.w. *BrE* (***per week***) used in writing to show that something happens, is paid etc each week: *Rent is £55 p.w.*

PX /ˌpiː ˈeks/ *n* [C] a shop selling food and other supplies on a US military base

pyg·my¹, **pigmy** /ˈpɪgmi/ *n* (*plural* **pygmies**, **pigmies**) [C]
1 (*also* **Pygmy**) someone who belongs to a race of very small people, especially one of the tribes of central Africa
2 someone who is not as good, intelligent, strong etc as other people in the same group – used to show disapproval: *a literary pygmy*

pygmy² *adj* [only before noun] used to describe a type of animal or plant that is much smaller than other similar types: *a pygmy elephant*

py·ja·mas *BrE*, **pajamas** *AmE* /pəˈdʒɑːməz $ -ˈdʒæ-, -ˈdʒɑː-/ ●●○ *n* [plural]
1 a soft pair of trousers and a top that you wear in bed: *striped pyjamas*
2 loose trousers that are tied around the waist, worn by Muslim men or women —**pyjama** *adj* [only before noun]: *pyjama bottoms* → **the cat's pyjamas** at CAT(5)

py·lon /ˈpaɪlən $ -lɑːn, -lən/ *n* [C] **1** a tall metal structure that supports wires carrying electricity
2 *AmE* one of a set of plastic CONES placed on a road to control traffic and protect people working there

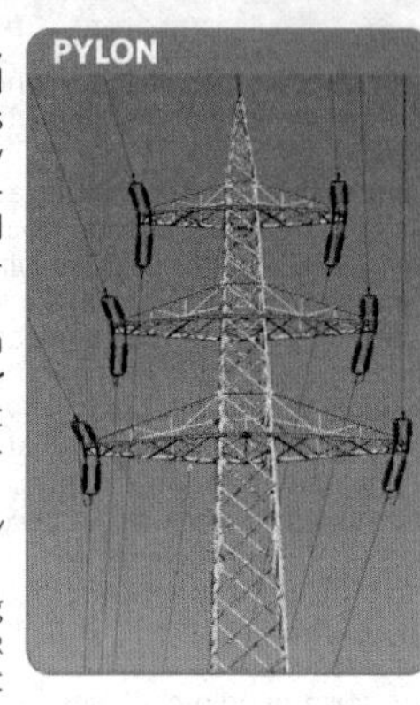

PYO *BrE* the written abbreviation of ***pick your own***, used by farms that let people pick fruit and vegetables to buy

pyr·a·mid /ˈpɪrəmɪd/ ●○○ *n* [C]
1 a large stone building with four TRIANGULAR (=three-sided) walls that slope in to a point at the top, especially in Egypt and Central America → see picture at SHAPE¹
2 [usually singular] a system, society, company etc that is organized in different levels, so that there is a small number of people at the top and a much larger number of people at the bottom: *different levels of the management pyramid* | *At the bottom of the pyramid are the poor.*
3 a pile of objects that have been put into the shape of a pyramid: **[+of]** *a pyramid of oranges*
4 an object shaped like a pyramid —**pyramidal** /pɪˈræmɪdl/ *adj*

ˈpyramid ˌscheme (*also* **Pon·zi scheme** /ˈpɒnzi skiːm $ ˈpɑːn-/) *n* [C] a dishonest and often illegal way of selling INVESTMENTS, in which money from people who INVEST later is used to pay people in the system who have already invested

ˈpyramid ˌselling *n* [U] a business activity in which the main income comes from people who buy the right to sell products, rather than from the sale of the products themselves. Pyramid selling is illegal in many places.

pyre /paɪə $ paɪr/ *n* [C] a high pile of wood on which a dead body is placed to be burned in a funeral ceremony: *a funeral pyre*

Py·rex /ˈpaɪreks/ *n* [U] *trademark* a special type of strong glass that does not break when it gets very hot and that is used to make cooking dishes, plates etc

py·ri·tes /paɪˈraɪtiːz $ pə-/ *n* [U] a mix of SULPHUR with a type of metal, usually iron, or iron and COPPER → **fool's gold**: *iron pyrites*

py·ro·ma·ni·ac /ˌpaɪrəʊˈmeɪniæk $ -rə-/ *n* [C] *medical* someone who suffers from a mental illness that gives them a strong desire to start fires —**pyromania** *n* [U]

py·ro·tech·nics /ˌpaɪrəʊˈteknɪks $ -rə-/ *n*
1 [plural] *formal or technical* a public show of FIREWORKS
2 [U] *technical* the skill or business of making FIREWORKS
3 [plural] an impressive show of someone's skill as a public performer, musician etc: *the guitar pyrotechnics of Eric Clapton* —**pyrotechnic** *adj*: *a pyrotechnic display*

Pyr·rhic vic·to·ry /ˌpɪrɪk ˈvɪktəri/ *n* [C] a victory in which the person who wins suffers so much that the victory was hardly worth winning

py·thon /ˈpaɪθən $ -θɑːn, -θən/ *n* [C] a large tropical snake that kills animals for food by winding itself around them and crushing them

Qq

Q, **q** /kjuː/ *n* (*plural* **Q's, q's**) [C,U] the 17th letter of the English alphabet → **mind your p's and q's** at MIND²(23), → Q-TIP

Q., **q.** (*also* **Q**, **q** *BrE*) the written abbreviation of ***question***: *a Q and A session* (=a time when people can ask questions and get answers) → FAQ

QB *AmE* the written abbreviation of ***quarterback***

QC /ˌkjuː ˈsiː/ *n* [C] (***Queen's Counsel***) a BARRISTER of high rank in the British legal system → **KC**

QED /ˌkjuː iː ˈdiː/ the abbreviation of the Latin phrase ***quod erat demonstrandum***, used to say that a fact or event proves that what you say is true

QR code /kjuː ˈɑ kəʊd $ -ˈɑːr koʊd/ *n* [C] (***Quick Response code***) a square pattern of small black and white squares, which is put on a product, advertisement etc. It contains information that can be read by a MOBILE PHONE or SCANNER.

qt *BrE*, **qt.** *AmE* the written abbreviation of ***quart*** or ***quarts***

q.t. /ˌkjuː ˈtiː/ *n* **on the q.t.** *old-fashioned* secretly

Q-tip /ˈkjuː tɪp/ *n* [C] *trademark AmE* a short stick with cotton at each end, used especially for cleaning your ears SYN **cotton bud** *BrE*

qtr. the written abbreviation of ***quarter***

qua /kwɑː, kweɪ $ kwɑː/ *prep formal* used to show you are talking about the basic nature or job of someone or something: *Money, qua money, cannot provide happiness.* → SINE QUA NON

quack¹ /kwæk/ *v* [I] to make the sound a duck makes

quack² *n* [C] **1** the sound a duck makes **2** someone who pretends to be a doctor – used to show disapproval → **quackery**: *quacks selling weight-loss drugs* **3** *BrE informal* a doctor: *You'd better go and see the quack with that burn.*

quack³ *adj* [only before noun] relating to the activities or medicines of someone who pretends to be a doctor → **quackery**: *a quack remedy*

quack·er·y /ˈkwækəri/ *n* [U] the activities of someone who pretends be a doctor

quad /kwɒd $ kwɑːd/ *n* [C] *informal* **1** a square open area with buildings all around it, especially in a school or college **2** a QUADRUPLET **3** **quads** [plural] QUADRICEPS

ˈ**quad bike** *n* [C] *BrE* a small vehicle, similar to a MOTORCYCLE but with four wide wheels, usually ridden on rough paths or fields SYN **four wheeler** *AmE*

quadr- /kwɒdr $ kwɑːdr/ *prefix* another form of QUADRI-

quad·ran·gle /ˈkwɒdræŋɡəl $ ˈkwɑː-/ *n* [C] **1** *formal* a square open area with buildings all around it, especially at a school or college SYN **quad** **2** *technical* a flat shape that has four straight sides

quad·rant /ˈkwɒdrənt $ ˈkwɑː-/ *n* [C] **1** a quarter of a circle **2** an instrument for measuring angles, used when sailing or looking at the stars

quad·ra·phon·ic, **quadrophonic** /ˌkwɒdrəˈfɒnɪk◂ $ ˌkwɑːdrəˈfɑː-/ *adj* using a system of sound recording, broadcasting etc in which sound comes from four different SPEAKERS at the same time → **mono, stereo**

quad·rat·ic e·qua·tion /kwɒˌdrætɪk ɪˈkweɪʒən $ kwɑː-/ *n* [C] *technical* an EQUATION such $ax^2+by+c = z$, which includes numbers or quantities multiplied by themselves

quadri- /kwɒdrə $ kwɑː-/ (*also* **quadru-**, **quadr-**) *prefix* four or four times: *a quadrilateral* (=shape with four straight sides) | *a quadruped* (=animal with four legs)

quad·ri·ceps /ˈkwɒdrəseps $ ˈkwɑː-/ *n* (*plural* **quadriceps**) [C] the large muscle at the front of your THIGH → **bicep**

quad·ri·lat·er·al /ˌkwɒdrəˈlætərəl◂ $ ˌkwɑː-/ *n* [C] *technical* a flat shape with four straight sides —**quadrilateral** *adj*

qua·drille /kwəˈdrɪl $ kwɑː-/ *n* [C] a dance, popular especially in the 19th century, in which the dancers form a square

qua·dril·lion /kwɒˈdrɪljən $ kwɑː-/ *number* **1** the number one followed by 15 zeros **2** *BrE old use* the number one followed by 24 zeros

quad·ri·ple·gic /ˌkwɒdrəˈpliːdʒɪk◂ $ ˌkwɑː-/ *n* [C] someone who is permanently unable to move any part of their body below their neck → **paraplegic**: *A car accident left him a quadriplegic.* —**quadriplegia** *n* [U] —**quadriplegic** *adj*

quad·ro·phon·ic /ˌkwɒdrəˈfɒnɪk◂ $ ˌkwɑːdrəˈfɑː-/ *adj* another spelling of QUADRAPHONIC

quadru- /kwɒdrʊ $ kwɑː-/ *prefix* another form of QUADRI-

quad·ru·ped /ˈkwɒdrʊped $ ˈkwɑːdrə-/ *n* [C] *technical* an animal that has four legs → **biped**

quad·ru·ple¹ /ˈkwɒdrʊpəl, kwɒˈdruː- $ kwɑːˈdruː-/ *v* [I,T] to increase and become four times as big or as high, or to make something increase in this way → **double, triple**: *Food prices quadrupled during the war.* | *The company has quadrupled its profits in just three years.*

quadruple² *adj, predeterminer* **1** four times as big or as many → **double, triple**: *The subjects were given quadruple the normal dosage of the drug.* **2** involving four things of the same kind: *a quadruple murder*

quad·ru·plet /ˈkwɒdrʊplɪt $ kwɑːˈdruːp-/ *n* [C] one of four babies born at the same time to the same mother SYN **quad**

quaff /kwɒf, kwɑːf $ kwɑːf, kwæf/ *v* [T] *literary* to drink a lot of something quickly SYN **knock back**: *Wedding guests quaffed champagne.*

quag·mire /ˈkwæɡmaɪə, ˈkwɒɡ- $ ˈkwæɡmaɪr/ *n* [C usually singular] **1** an area of soft wet muddy ground: *In the rainy season the roads become a quagmire.* **2** a difficult or complicated situation: *The Balkan situation became a political and military quagmire.*

quail¹ /kweɪl/ *n* [C,U] a small fat bird with a short tail that is hunted for food or sport, or the meat from this bird

quail² *v* [I] *literary* to be afraid and show it by shaking a little bit or moving back slightly SYN **shrink**: **[+at]** *She quailed visibly at the sight of the prison walls.*

quaint /kweɪnt/ ●○○ *adj* unusual and attractive, especially in an old-fashioned way: *a quaint little village in Yorkshire*

quake¹ /kweɪk/ *v* [I] **1** to shake or tremble, usually because you are very frightened: **quake with fear/fright/anger etc** *Richmond was quaking with fury.* **2** **quake in your boots** *informal* to feel very afraid – used humorously **3** if the earth, a building etc quakes, it shakes violently: *The explosion made the whole house quake.*

quake² *n* [C] an EARTHQUAKE

Quak·er /ˈkweɪkə $ -ər/ *n* [C] a member of the Society of Friends, a Christian religious group that meets without any formal ceremony or priests and that is opposed to violence —**Quaker** *adj*

qual·i·fi·ca·tion /ˌkwɒlɪfɪˈkeɪʃən $ ˌkwɑː-/ ●●○ W3 *n* **1** [C usually plural] if you have a qualification, you have passed an examination or course to show you have a particular level of skill or knowledge in a subject: *He left school without any qualifications.* | **[+in]** *We are looking for graduates with qualifications in maths or science.*
2 [C usually plural] a skill, personal quality, or type of experience that makes you suitable for a particular job or position: **[+for]** *health and fitness qualifications for membership in the Territorial Army* | **qualification to do sth** *There have been questions about his qualifications to lead the company.* | *Does he have the right qualifications to become a Supreme Court Justice?*
3 [U] when a person or team reaches a necessary standard, for example by passing an examination or defeating

another team: *Upon qualification, you can expect to find work abroad fairly easily.* | **[+for]** *the US qualification for the World Cup*
4 [C,U] something that you add to a statement to limit its effect or meaning SYN **reservation**: *I welcome without qualification the Minister's proposal.*

COLLOCATIONS

VERBS

have a qualification (*also* **hold a qualification** *formal*) *You don't need to have any qualifications for this job.*
lack qualifications *40 percent of the prisoners lack any qualifications.*
get a qualification *BrE* (*also* **gain/obtain a qualification** *formal*) *I want to get the qualifications so that I can become a doctor.*

ADJECTIVES/NOUN + qualification

academic qualifications *Eva had excellent academic qualifications.*
educational qualifications *Too many children leave school without any educational qualifications.*
a teaching/medical/legal etc qualification *BrE*: *She has a degree and a teaching qualification.*
a professional qualification *BrE* (=one relating to a professional job, such as a teacher, lawyer etc) | **a vocational qualification** *BrE* (=one relating to a skilled job, such as a nurse or a builder) | **formal qualifications** (=official qualifications rather than experience) | **paper qualifications** *BrE often disapproving* (=documents showing that you have passed exams, rather than actual experience of doing something)

qual·i·fied /ˈkwɒlɪfaɪd $ ˈkwɑː-/ ●●○ *adj*
1 having suitable knowledge, experience, or skills, especially for a particular job: **well/suitably/highly qualified** *Dawn is well qualified for her new role.* | **qualified to do sth** *The guides are qualified to lead groups into the mountains.* | *If you don't speak German, you're not qualified to comment.*
2 having passed a professional examination: **qualified doctor/teacher/accountant etc** *There are qualified instructors on hand to advise you.* | **highly/fully qualified** *a fully qualified nurse* | *a* ***professionally qualified*** *social worker* | *Are you* ***medically qualified****?* | **qualified to do sth** *He's qualified to teach biology at high school level.*
3 [usually before noun] limited in some way → **partial**: **qualified approval/support** *The proposal received qualified approval.* | *The program was considered a* ***qualified success****.* | *Is it worth the money? The answer is a* ***qualified yes****.*

qual·i·fi·er /ˈkwɒləfaɪə $ ˈkwɑːlɪfaɪər/ *n* [C] **1** someone who has reached the necessary standard for entering a competition, especially by defeating other competitors: *He's among the qualifiers for the Lancome Trophy at Paris.* **2** a game that you have to win in order to be able to take part in a competition: *the World Cup qualifier against the Netherlands* **3** *technical* a word or phrase that limits or adds to the meaning of another word or phrase

qual·i·fy /ˈkwɒlɪfaɪ $ ˈkwɑː-/ ●●○ S3 W3 *v* (**qualified, qualifying, qualifies**)
1 HAVE A RIGHT [I,T] to have the right to have or do something, or to give someone this right: *Free school lunches are given to children who qualify.* | **[+for]** *You may qualify for unemployment benefit.* | **qualify sb/sth for sth** *Membership qualifies you for a discount on purchases.*
2 PASS EXAM [I] to pass an examination or finish a course of study that you need in order to do something: **[+as]** *I finally qualified as a pilot.* | *After qualifying, doctors spend at least two years working in hospitals.*
3 BE CONSIDERED STH [I] to have all the necessary qualities to be considered to be a particular thing: **[+as]** *It doesn't qualify as a date if you bring your children with you.*
4 GIVE SB SKILLS/KNOWLEDGE [T] if something qualifies you to do something, you have the necessary skills, knowledge, ability etc to do it: **qualify sb for sth** *Fluency in three languages qualifies her for work in the European Parliament.* | **qualify sb to do sth** *The certificate qualifies you to work as a dental assistant.*
5 SPORT [I] to reach the necessary standard to enter or continue in a competition or sports event: **[+for]** *She qualified for a spot on the U.S. Olympic speed skating team.*
6 ADD SOMETHING [T] to add to something that has already been said, in order to limit its effect or meaning: *Could I just qualify that last statement?*
7 GRAMMAR [T] if a word or phrase qualifies another word or phrase, it limits or adds to the meaning of it → **qualifier**

qual·i·ta·tive /ˈkwɒlətətɪv $ ˈkwɑːləteɪ-/ ●○○ AWL *adj formal* relating to the quality or standard of something rather than the quantity: **a qualitative analysis/study** *a qualitative study of educational services* | **qualitative research** —**qualitatively** *adv*: *Women's experiences are qualitatively different from men's.* → **quantitative**

qual·i·ty¹ /ˈkwɒləti $ ˈkwɑː-/ ●●● S1 W1 *n* (*plural* **qualities**)
1 [C,U] how good or bad something is: *Much of the land was of poor quality.* | *Use only high quality ingredients.* | **[+of]** *The quality of the water is reasonably good.*
2 [C usually plural] something that people may have as part of their character, for example courage or intelligence → **characteristic**: *He shows strong* ***leadership qualities****.* | *the* ***personal qualities*** *necessary to be a successful salesman* | **[+of]** *the qualities of honesty and independence*
3 [C] something that is typical of one thing and makes it different from other things, for example size, colour etc: *the drug's addictive quality* | **[+of]** *the physical and chemical qualities of the rock*
4 [U] a high standard: *his pride in the quality of his craftsmanship* | *wines of quality*
5 quality of life how good or bad your life is, shown for example by whether or not you are happy, healthy, able to do what you want etc: *drugs that improve the quality of life for very ill patients*

COLLOCATIONS

ADJECTIVES/NOUN + quality

good/high *I was impressed that the quality of their work was so high.*
poor/low *The magazine is printed on low quality paper.*
excellent/outstanding *The T-shirts are only $10 and the quality is excellent.*
superior *formal* (=good or better quality) *These speakers offer superior quality sound.*
top quality *Our chef uses only top quality ingredients.*
water/air quality *Scientists took samples to test the water quality.*
sound quality | **picture quality** (*also* **image quality**)

VERBS

improve/enhance the quality *The measures will improve the quality of the water in the river.*
affect the quality *Lack of sleep started to affect the quality of his work.*
test/check/monitor the quality *The equipment is used to monitor the city's air quality.*
maintain the quality | **the quality goes up/down** | **the quality suffers** (=it is badly affected by something)

quality + NOUN

quality standards *Greater investment is needed to meet the European Union's strict quality standards.*

COMMON ERRORS

⚠ Don't say 'living quality' or 'life quality'. Say **quality of life**.

quality² *adj* [only before noun] **1** [no comparative] very good – used especially by people who are trying to sell something: *quality childcare at prices people can afford* | *quality double glazing* **2 quality newspapers/press etc** *BrE* newspapers etc intended for educated readers

ˈquality asˌsurance *n* [U] the practice of checking the quality of goods or services that a company sells, so that the standard continues to be good

ˈquality conˌtrol *n* [U] the practice of checking goods as they are produced to be sure that their quality is good enough —**quality controller** *n* [C]

ˈquality ˌtime *n* [U] the time that you spend giving someone your full attention, especially time that you spend with your children when you are not busy: *Do you spend enough quality time with your children?*

qualm /kwɑːm $ kwɑːm, kwɑːlm/ *n* [C usually plural] a feeling of slight worry or doubt because you are not sure that what you are doing is right: *Despite my qualms, I took the job.* | *The manager* ***has*** *no* ***qualms about*** *dropping players who do not perform well.*

quan·da·ry /ˈkwɒndəri $ ˈkwɑːn-/ *n* (*plural* **quandaries**) [C] a difficult situation or problem, especially one in which you cannot decide what to do SYN **dilemma**: **in a quandary** *Kate was in a quandary over whether to go or not.*

quan·go /ˈkwæŋgəʊ $ -goʊ/ *n* (*plural* **quangos**) [C] an independent organization in Britain, started by the government but with its own legal powers THESAURUS ORGANIZATION

quan·ta /ˈkwɒntə $ ˈkwɑːn-/ *n* the plural of QUANTUM

quan·ti·fi·er /ˈkwɒntəfaɪə $ ˈkwɑːntɪfaɪər/ *n* [C] *technical* a word or phrase such as 'much', 'few', or 'a lot of' that is used with a noun to show quantity

quan·ti·fy /ˈkwɒntɪfaɪ $ ˈkwɑːn-/ ●○○ *v* (**quantified, quantifying, quantifies**) [T] to calculate the value of something and express it as a number or an amount: *an attempt to quantify the region's social and economic decline* | **difficult/impossible to quantify** *The damage caused to the tourist industry is difficult to quantify.* —**quantifiable** *adj: The cost of unemployment to the government is quite easily quantifiable.*

quan·ti·ta·tive /ˈkwɒntətətɪv $ ˈkwɑːntəteɪ-/ ●○○ *adj formal* relating to amounts rather than to the quality or standard of something → **qualitative**: **quantitative analysis/methods/data etc** *We need to do a proper quantitative analysis of this problem.* —**quantitatively** *adv*

ˌquantitative ˈeasing *n* [U] *technical* a way of putting money into a country's financial system. The national bank creates new money and buys things such as BONDS from banks, so that the banks have more money to lend.

quan·ti·ty /ˈkwɒntəti $ ˈkwɑːn-/ ●●● S3 W2 *n* (*plural* **quantities**)

1 [C,U] an amount of something that can be counted or measured: **[+of]** *The police also found a quantity of ammunition in the flat.* | *Add 50 grams of butter, and the same quantity of sugar.* | **a large/small/vast etc quantity of sth** *He had consumed a large quantity of alcohol.* | *Huge quantities of oil were spilling into the sea.* | **in large/small/sufficient etc quantities** *Buy vegetables in small quantities, for your immediate use.* | *Your work has improved in quantity and quality this term.* ⚠ Don't say 'a big quantity'. Say **a large quantity.** THESAURUS AMOUNT

2 [U] the large amount of something: *The sheer quantity of text meant that people did not read the whole of their newspaper.*

3 in quantity in large amounts: *It's a lot cheaper if you* ***buy*** *it* ***in quantity***. → **be an unknown quantity** at UNKNOWN[1](4)

ˈquantity surˌveyor *n* [C] *BrE* someone whose job is to calculate the amount of materials needed to build something, how long it will take to build, and how much it will cost

quan·tum /ˈkwɒntəm $ ˈkwɑːn-/ *n* (*plural* **quanta** /-tə/) [C] *technical* a unit of energy in NUCLEAR PHYSICS

ˌquantum comˈputer *n* [C] a very advanced and powerful type of computer that is being developed, which uses the principles of QUANTUM MECHANICS

ˌquantum ˈleap (*also* **ˌquantum ˈjump**) *n* [C] a very large and important development or improvement: **[+in]** *There has been a quantum leap in the range of the wines sold in the UK.* | *The treatment of breast cancer has* ***taken a quantum leap*** *forward.*

ˌquantum meˈchanics *n* [U] the scientific study of the way that atoms and smaller parts of things behave

ˈquantum ˌtheory *n* [U] the idea that energy, especially light, travels in separate pieces and not in a continuous form

quar·an·tine[1] /ˈkwɒrəntiːn $ ˈkwɔː-/ *n* [U] a period of time when a person or animal is kept apart from others in case they are carrying a disease: **in quarantine** *The monkeys were* ***kept in quarantine*** *for 31 days.*

quarantine[2] *v* [T] to keep a person or animal apart from others for a period of time in case they are carrying a disease

quark /kwɑːk, kwɔːk $ kwɔːrk, kwɑːrk/ *n* [C] *technical* a very small part of something, which is smaller than an atom

quar·rel[1] /ˈkwɒrəl $ ˈkwɔː-, ˈkwɑː-/ ●●○ *n* [C] *especially BrE*

1 an angry argument or disagreement: **[+with]** *Jacob left after a quarrel with his wife.* | **[+about/over]** *They had a quarrel about some girl.* | **[+between]** *Had there been any quarrel between you?* THESAURUS ARGUMENT

2 a reason to disagree with something or argue with someone: **[+with]** *My only quarrel with this plan is that it's going to take far too long.* | *I* ***have no quarrel with*** *the court's verdict.*

COLLOCATIONS

VERBS

have a quarrel *We had a terrible quarrel last night.*
pick a quarrel (=deliberately start it) *Members of the gang were picking quarrels with strangers.*
patch up a quarrel *BrE* (=end it) *The brothers eventually patched up their quarrel.*
a quarrel breaks out (=starts to happen) *A fresh quarrel broke out between the players.*

ADJECTIVES/NOUN + quarrel

a family quarrel *Your family quarrels are none of my concern.*
a lovers' quarrel *Outside, two teenagers were having a lovers' quarrel.*
bitter (=involving strong feelings of anger or hatred) *They are locked in a bitter quarrel over ownership of the land.*
violent | **serious** | **an old quarrel** (=one that has existed for a long time)

quarrel[2] ●●○ *v* (**quarrelled, quarrelling** *BrE*, **quarreled, quarreling** *AmE*) [I] to have an argument: *I wish you two would stop quarreling.* | **[+with]** *I always seem to be quarrelling with my parents.* | **[+about]** *We're not going to quarrel about a few dollars.* THESAURUS ARGUE

quarrel with sth *phr v* to disagree with something or complain about something: *Nobody could quarrel with the report's conclusions.*

GRAMMAR: Reciprocal verbs

Quarrel is a reciprocal verb. This type of verb is used when saying that two or more people do something that involves both or all of them: *The brothers quarrelled.* You can also say: *The brothers quarrelled with each other.* | *He quarrelled with his brother.*
GRAMMAR GUIDE VERBS

quar·rel·some /ˈkwɒrəlsəm $ ˈkwɔː-, ˈkwɑː-/ *adj especially BrE* someone who is quarrelsome quarrels a lot with people SYN **argumentative**: *He became quarrelsome after drinking too much.*

quar·ry[1] /ˈkwɒri $ ˈkwɔː-, ˈkwɑː-/ *n* (*plural* **quarries**) **1** [C] a place where large amounts of stone or sand are dug out of the ground: *a slate quarry* **2** [singular] the person or animal that you are hunting or chasing: *Briefly, the hunter and his quarry glared at each other.*

quarry[2] *v* (**quarried, quarrying, quarries**) [T] to dig stone or sand from a quarry: **quarry sth for sth** *The rock here is quarried for building stones.* | **quarry sth from sth** *Chalk is quarried from the surrounding area.* —**quarrying** *n* [U]

Q

ˈquarry ˌtile *n* [C usually plural] a clay TILE that has not been GLAZED. Quarry tiles are used to cover floors.

quart /kwɔːt $ kwɔːrt/ *n* [C] (*written abbreviation* **qt**) a unit for measuring liquid, equal to two PINTS. In Britain this is 1.14 litres, and in the US it is 0.95 litres.

quar·ter[1] /ˈkwɔːtə $ ˈkwɔːrtər/ ●●● S1 W2 *n* [C]
1 AMOUNT one of four equal parts into which something can be divided → **half**, **third**: **a/one quarter (of sth)** *a quarter of a mile* | *roughly one quarter of the city's population* | *It's about a page and a quarter.* | **three quarters (of sth)** (=75%) *three quarters of a million pounds* | **the first/second etc quarter** *in the last quarter of the 19th century* | ***Cut** the cake **into quarters**.* ⚠ Say **a quarter of** something, not 'quarter of' something.
2 PART OF AN HOUR a period of 15 minutes: *I'll meet you in **a quarter of an hour**.* | *She arrived **three quarters of an hour*** (=45 minutes) *late.* | **(a) quarter to (sth)** (*also* **(a) quarter of (sth)** *AmE*) (=15 minutes before the hour) *It's a quarter of two.* | **(a) quarter past (sth)** *BrE* (*also* **(a) quarter after (sth)** *AmE*) (=15 minutes after the hour) *I'll meet you at a quarter past ten.*
3 MONEY a coin used in the US and Canada worth 25 cents
4 THREE MONTHS a period of three months, used especially when discussing business and financial matters: **the first/second/third/fourth quarter** *The company's profits rose by 11% in the first quarter of the year.* | *Our database is updated every quarter.* → QUARTERLY[1]
5 SPORT one of the four equal periods of time into which games of some sports are divided: **the first/second/third/fourth quarter** *The home side took the lead in the second quarter.*
6 PART OF A CITY [usually singular] an area of a town: *I found a small flat in the student quarter.* | *Granada's ancient Arab quarter* | *a historic quarter of the city* **THESAURUS** AREA
7 HOME **quarters** [plural] the rooms that are given to someone to live in as part of their job, especially servants or soldiers: *The top floor provided **living quarters** for the kitchen staff.* | *Most of the officers live in **married quarters*** (=houses where soldiers live with their wives).
8 COLLEGE *AmE* one of the four periods into which a year at school or college is divided, continuing for 10 to 12 weeks → **semester**: *What classes are you taking this quarter?*
9 MOON the period of time twice a month when you can see a quarter of the moon's surface
10 in/from ... quarters among or from different groups of people: *Offers of financial help came from several quarters.* | *Doubts were expressed in many quarters.*
11 all quarters of the Earth/globe *literary* everywhere in the world
12 give/receive no quarter *literary* if someone gives no quarter, they do not show any pity or gentleness when dealing with someone, especially an enemy: *It was a fight to the death, with no quarter given.* → **at close quarters** at CLOSE[2](20)

quarter[2] *v* [T] **1** to cut or divide something into four parts → **halve**: *Quarter the tomatoes and place them round the dish.* **2** *formal* to provide someone with a place to sleep and eat, especially soldiers: *Our troops were quartered in Boston until June.*

quar·ter·back[1] /ˈkwɔːtəbæk $ ˈkwɔːrtər-/ *n* [C] **1** the player in American football who directs the team's attacking play and passes the ball to the other players at the start of each attack → see picture at AMERICAN FOOTBALL **2 Monday morning quarterback** *AmE informal* someone who gives advice about something only after it has happened

quarterback[2] *v AmE* **1** [I] to play in the position of quarterback in American football **2** [T] *informal* to organize or direct an activity, event etc: *She quarterbacked the new sales campaign.*

ˈquarter day *n* [C] *technical BrE* a day which officially begins a three-month period of the year, and on which payments are made, for example at the STOCK EXCHANGE

quar·ter·deck /ˈkwɔːtədek $ ˈkwɔːrtər-/ *n* [C] the back part of the upper level of a ship, which is used mainly by officers

ˌquarter-ˈfinal *BrE*, **quar·ter·fi·nal** *AmE* /ˌkwɔːtəˈfaɪnl $ ˌkwɔːrtər-/ *n* [C] one of the four games near the end of a competition, whose winners play in the two SEMI-FINALS

quar·ter·ly[1] /ˈkwɔːtəli $ ˈkwɔːrtər-/ ●○○ *adj, adv* produced or happening four times a year → **monthly**, **annually**: *We publish a quarterly journal.* | *The rent is payable quarterly.*

quarterly[2] *n* (*plural* **quarterlies**) [C] a magazine that is produced four times a year

quar·ter·mas·ter /ˈkwɔːtəˌmɑːstə $ ˈkwɔːrtərˌmæstər/ *n* [C] **1** a military officer in charge of providing food, uniforms etc **2** a ship's officer in charge of signals and guiding the ship on the right course

ˈquarter note *n* [C] *AmE* a musical note which continues for a quarter of the length of a WHOLE NOTE SYN **crotchet** *BrE*

ˈquarter ˌsessions *n* [plural] an English law court that was held in the past once every three months

quar·ter·staff /ˈkwɔːtəstɑːf $ ˈkwɔːrtərstæf/ *n* [C] a long wooden pole that was used as a weapon in the past

quar·tet /kwɔːˈtet $ kwɔːr-/ *n* [C] **1** four singers or musicians who sing or play together: *a **string quartet*** (=four people playing musical instruments with strings, such as violins) **2** a piece of music written for four performers **3** four people or things of the same type: **[+of]** *a quartet of short films set in the 1920s* → **quintet**, **trio**

quar·to /ˈkwɔːtəʊ $ ˈkwɔːrtoʊ/ *n* (*plural* **quartos**) [C] *technical* the size of paper made by folding a normal large sheet of paper twice to produce four sheets

quartz /kwɔːts $ kwɔːrts/ *n* [U] a hard mineral substance that is used in making electronic watches and clocks: *quartz crystals* | *a quartz watch*

qua·sar /ˈkweɪzɑː $ -ɑːr/ *n* [C] *technical* an object in space that is similar to a star and that shines very brightly → **pulsar**

quash /kwɒʃ $ kwɑːʃ, kwɒːʃ/ *v* [T] *formal* **1** to officially say that a legal judgment or decision is no longer acceptable or correct SYN **overturn**: *The High Court later **quashed** his **conviction** for murder.* | *The decision was quashed by the House of Lords.* **2** to say or do something to stop something from continuing: *A hospital chief executive has **quashed rumours** that people will lose their jobs.* | *The government immediately moved to quash the revolt.*

quasi- /kweɪzaɪ, kwɑːzi/ *prefix* like something else or trying to be something else: *a quasi-scientific approach* | *a quasi-governmental organization*

quat·er·cen·te·na·ry /ˌkwætəsenˈtiːnəri $ ˌkwɑːtərsenˈten-/ *n* (*plural* **quatercentenaries**) [C] the day or year exactly 400 years after a particular event: **[+of]** *the quatercentenary of Shakespeare's birth*

quat·rain /ˈkwɒtreɪn $ ˈkwɑː-/ *n* [C] *technical* a group of four lines in a poem

qua·ver[1] /ˈkweɪvə $ -ər/ *v* [I,T] if your voice quavers, it shakes as you speak, especially because you are nervous or upset: *'It's not true,' she said, in a quavering voice.* | *'No,' he quavered.* —**quavery** *adj*

quaver[2] *n* [C] **1** *BrE* a musical note which continues for an eighth of the length of a SEMIBREVE SYN **eighth note** *AmE* **2** a shaking sound in your voice

quay /kiː $ keɪ, kiː/ *n* [C] a place in a town or village where boats can be tied up or can stop to load and unload goods

quay·side /ˈkiːsaɪd/ *n* [C] the area next to a quay: *people strolling along the quayside* | *a quayside restaurant*

quea·sy /ˈkwiːzi/ *adj* **1** feeling that you are going to VOMIT: *The sea got rougher, and I began to **feel queasy**.* **2** *AmE* feeling uncomfortable because an action seems morally wrong: **[+about]** *Many Democrats **felt queasy** about the issue.*

queen[1] /kwiːn/ ●●● S2 W2 *n* [C]
1 RULER (*also* **Queen**) **a)** the female ruler of a country

→ **king**: **[+of]** *Cleopatra, Queen of Egypt | Queen Elizabeth | At 18, Victoria was **crowned queen*** (=officially became ruler). **b)** the wife of a king: *the future queen*
2 CARD a playing card with a picture of a queen on it: *the queen of diamonds*
3 the queen of sth the woman or place that is considered the best in a particular area or activity: *With 42 albums, she was the queen of pop. | Paris, the queen of fashion*
4 COMPETITION *AmE* the woman who wins a beauty competition, or who is chosen to represent a school, area etc: *the carnival queen*
5 INSECT a large female BEE, ANT etc, which lays the eggs for a whole group
6 queen bee a woman who behaves as if she is the most important person in a place
7 HOMOSEXUAL *taboo informal* an offensive word for a male HOMOSEXUAL who behaves very like a woman. Do not use this word.
8 CHESS the most powerful piece in the game of CHESS
→ **BEAUTY QUEEN, DRAG QUEEN**

queen² *v* [T] **1** *technical* to change a PAWN into a queen in the game of CHESS **2 queen it over sb** *BrE informal* if a woman queens it over other people, she behaves as if she is more important than them, in an annoying way

queen·ly /ˈkwiːnli/ *adj* like a queen or suitable for a queen: *She gave a queenly wave as she rode past.*

ˌQueen ˈMother *n* [singular] the mother of the ruling king or queen

ˌQueen's ˈCounsel *n* a QC

ˌQueen's ˈEnglish *n BrE* **speak the Queen's English** to speak very correctly and in a way that is typical of people who belong to the highest social class → **KING'S ENGLISH**

ˌQueen's ˈevidence *n BrE* **turn Queen's evidence** if a criminal turns Queen's evidence, they agree to help the police and law courts to catch other criminals by giving them information → **KING'S EVIDENCE, STATE'S EVIDENCE**

ˈqueen-size *adj* a queen-size bed, sheet etc is a bed, sheet etc for two people that is larger than the standard size → **DOUBLE BED, KING-SIZE**(1), → **SINGLE¹**(6)

ˌQueen's ˈspeech, the a speech given by the Queen at the official opening of the British Parliament each year, usually in October. The speech is actually written by the government, and it gives details of the government's plans for the next year, including the new laws it intends to make.

queer¹ /kwɪə $ kwɪr/ *adj* **1** *taboo* an offensive word used to describe someone who is HOMOSEXUAL, especially a man. Do not use this word. **2** *old-fashioned* strange or difficult to explain: *She gave a queer laugh. | Hank was beginning to feel a little queer.* **3 queer in the head** *old-fashioned* slightly crazy —**queerly** *adv*: *Sue looked at him queerly.*

queer² *n* [C] *taboo* an offensive word for a HOMOSEXUAL person, especially a man. Do not use this word.

queer³ *v* **queer sb's pitch/queer the pitch for sb** *BrE informal* to make it difficult for someone to do something that they had planned to do

ˈqueer ˌbashing *n* [U] *informal* physical violence against people because they are HOMOSEXUAL

quell /kwel/ *v* [T] *formal* **1** to end a situation in which people are behaving violently or protesting, especially by using force SYN **put down**: **quell the violence/disturbance/riot etc** *Police used live ammunition to quell the disturbances.*
2 *literary* to reduce or stop unpleasant feelings such as fear, doubt, or worry: *'Jerry?' she called, trying to quell the panic inside her.*

quench /kwentʃ/ *v* [T] *formal* **1 quench your thirst** to stop yourself feeling thirsty, by drinking something: *We stopped at a small bar to quench our thirst.* **2 quench a fire/flames** to stop a fire from burning: *a desperate bid to quench the raging flames*

quer·u·lous /ˈkwerələs/ *adj formal* someone who is querulous complains about things in an annoying way: *'But why can't I go?' he said in a **querulous voice**.* —**querulously** *adv*

que·ry¹ /ˈkwɪəri $ ˈkwɪri/ ●●○ *n* (*plural* **queries**) [C] a question that you ask to get information, or to check that something is true or correct: **[+about]** *Give us a ring if you **have** any **queries** about the contract. | Staff are always available to **answer** your **queries**.* THESAURUS ▶ QUESTION

query² ●○○ *v* (**queried, querying, queries**) [T]
1 to express doubt about whether something is true or correct: *Both players queried the umpire's decision.* | **query whether** *Many people are querying whether the tests are accurate.*
2 to ask a question: *'What time are we leaving?' Maggie queried.*

quest /kwest/ ●○○ *n* [C] *literary*
1 a long search for something that is difficult to find: **[+for]** *his long quest for truth | the quest for human happiness | World leaders are now united in their quest for peace.*
2 in quest of sth trying to find or get something: *They journeyed to the distant Molucca islands in quest of spices.*

ques·tion¹ /ˈkwestʃən/ ●●● S1 W1 *n*
1 ASKING FOR INFORMATION [C] a sentence or phrase that is used to ask for information or to test someone's knowledge OPP **answer**: *Can I ask you a question? | I'm afraid I can't answer that question.* | **[+about/on]** *They asked me quite a lot of difficult questions about my job. | The survey included questions on age and smoking habits.* | **in answer to sb's question** *In answer to your last question, 'Yes'.*
2 SUBJECT/PROBLEM [C] a subject or problem that needs to be discussed or dealt with SYN **issue**: **[+of]** *We discussed the question of confidentiality. | This **raises the question** of government funding. | an urgent need to **address the question** of crime | Several **questions** have still not been **resolved**. | **The question is** should I take the job in Japan, or should I stay here? | Some important **questions remain unanswered*** (=still have not been dealt with or explained).
3 DOUBT [C,U] if there is some question about something, there is doubt about it, or people feel uncertain about it: *The exact cause of death is still* **open to question** (=not certain). | **call/bring/throw sth into question** (=make people doubt something) *This has called into question people's right to retire at 60. | He's by far the best candidate, there's **no question about it*** (=it is completely certain). | ***There is no question that*** (=it is completely certain that) *the government knew about the deal.* | **beyond question** (=completely certain or definite) *Her efficiency and intelligence are beyond question.* | **questions about/over sth** *There are questions about the system's practicality.*
4 without question a) used to emphasize that what you are saying is true or correct: *Marilyn was, without question, a very beautiful woman.* **b)** if you accept or obey something without question, you do it without expressing any doubt about whether it is correct or necessary: *Clara accepted his decision without question.*
5 there is no question of sth happening/sb doing sth used to say that there is no possibility of something happening: *There is no question of the project being postponed.*
6 in question a) the things, people etc in question are the ones that are being discussed: *Where were you during the evening in question?* **b)** if something is in question, there is doubt about it: *I'm afraid his honesty is now in question.*
7 be a question of sth used to say what the most important fact, part, or feature of something is: *Dance is a question of control and creative expression. | I would love to come, but it's a question of time.*
8 it's just/only/simply a question of doing sth *spoken* used to say that what needs doing is easy or not complicated: *It's just a question of putting in a couple of screws.*
9 be out of the question if something is out of the question, it is definitely not possible or not allowed: *You can't go in that old shirt – it's out of the question.*
10 (that's a) good question! *spoken* used to admit that you do not know the answer to a question: *'How can we afford this?' 'Good question!'*
11 pop the question *informal* to ask someone to marry you – used humorously → **leading question** at LEADING¹(4),

→ **rhetorical question** at RHETORICAL(1), → **beg the question** at BEG(6)

COLLOCATIONS

VERBS

ask (sb) a question *Don't be afraid to ask questions.*
have a question (=want to ask a question) *I just have one question: is the treatment effective?*
pose a question *formal* (=ask a question) *He poses the question, 'What should we teach our children?'*
put a question to sb (=ask a question in a formal situation) *I recently put some of these questions to a psychologist.*
answer a question *You haven't answered my question.*
avoid/evade/dodge a question (=not give a direct answer) | **rephrase a question** (=ask it in a different way) | **bombard sb with questions** (=ask someone a lot of questions)

ADJECTIVES/NOUN + question

difficult/hard *Some of the questions in the last section were very difficult.*
easy *These questions should be easy for you.*
a good question (=interesting or difficult to answer) *That's a good question.*
a stupid/silly question (=one whose answer is obvious) *Did you win, or is that a stupid question?*
an awkward question (=one that someone does not want to answer) *How can we keep the press from asking awkward questions?*
a tricky/tough question (=one that is difficult to answer) *That's a really tricky question.*
a personal question (=one relating to someone's private life) *Can I ask you a personal question?*
a simple question (=one that is easy to answer) | **a direct question** (=one that asks for information in a very direct way) | **an exam/a test question** | **a rhetorical question** (=one that you ask without expecting an answer, in order to make a point)

THESAURUS

question something that you ask someone, either when speaking or when writing: *Would anyone like to ask any questions?* | *I've emailed the hotel with one or two questions.*
query /ˈkwɪəri $ ˈkwɪri/ *especially BrE* a question that you ask when you are not sure you have understood something or that the information you have is correct: *If you have any queries, please contact your travel agent.* | *Our staff are always available to answer customers' queries.*
inquiry (*also* **enquiry** *especially BrE*) /ɪnˈkwaɪəri $ ɪnˈkwaɪri, ˈɪŋkwəri/ a question you ask in order to get information or find out the details about something: *We've advertised the house, and we've already received lots of enquiries.* | *The police have been making some inquiries in the area.*
request a polite or formal question asking for something that you want or need: *The bank said 'no' to our request for more money.* | *You must make your request in writing.*

question² ●●● S2 W3 *v* [T]
1 to ask someone questions in order to get information about something such as a crime → **interrogate**: *Two men have been arrested and questioned.* | **question sb about sth** *She hates being questioned about her past.* | *Joseph **questioned** the doctors **closely*** (=asked them a lot of questions). THESAURUS ASK
2 to have or express doubts about whether something is true, good, necessary etc: **question what/how/when etc** *Are you questioning what I'm saying?* | *No one dared to question his decisions.* | **question whether** *One questions whether he's telling the truth.*

ques·tion·a·ble /ˈkwestʃənəbəl/ ●○○ *adj*
1 not likely to be true or correct: *The statistics are **highly questionable**.* | **it is questionable whether** *It is questionable whether the taxpayer receives value for money.*
2 not likely to be good, honest, or useful: *I suspected that his motives for helping us were questionable.* | *He was a man of questionable character.*

ques·tion·er /ˈkwestʃənə $ -ər/ *n* [C] someone who is asking a question, for example in a public discussion

ques·tion·ing /ˈkwestʃənɪŋ/ *adj* a questioning look or expression shows that you have doubts about something or need some information: *Mrs Carson gave Ruth a questioning look.* —**questioningly** *adv*

ˈquestion mark ●●○ *n* [C]
1 the mark (?) that is used at the end of a question
2 there is a question mark over sth/a question mark hangs over sth used to say that there is a possibility that something will not be successful or will not continue to exist: *A big question mark hangs over the company's future.*

ˈquestion ˌmaster *n* [C] *BrE* the person who asks the questions in a QUIZ game on television or radio SYN **quizmaster**

ques·tion·naire /ˌkwestʃəˈneə, ˌkes- $ -ˈner/ ●●○ *n* [C] a written set of questions which you give to a large number of people in order to collect information: **fill in/fill out/complete a questionnaire** (=answer all the questions in it) *All staff were asked to fill in a questionnaire about their jobs.*

ˈquestion tag *n* [C] *technical* a phrase such as 'isn't it?', 'won't it?', or 'does she?' that you add to the end of a statement to make it a question or to check that someone agrees with you, as in the sentence: 'You're from Hamburg, aren't you?'

queue¹ /kjuː/ ●●○ S3 *n* [C]
1 *BrE* a line of people waiting to enter a building, buy something etc, or a line of vehicles waiting to move SYN **line** *AmE*: **be/stand/wait in a queue** *We stood in a queue for half an hour.* | *You'll have to **join the queue**.* | **[+of]** *a queue of people waiting for the bus* | **[+for]** *the queue for the toilets* | **queue to do sth** *There was a long queue to get into the cinema.* | **the front/head/back/end of a queue** *At last we got to the front of the queue.*
2 *BrE* all the people who are waiting to have or get something: *You'll have to join the housing queue.* | **[+for]** *the queue for kidney transplant operations* | *It is possible to **jump the queue*** (=get something before people who have been waiting longer) *if you are prepared to pay for your treatment.*
3 *technical* a list of jobs that a computer has to do in a particular order: *the print queue*
4 a number of telephone calls to a particular number that are waiting to be answered → **the dole queue** at DOLE¹(2)

queue² ●○○ *v* (*also* **queue up**) [I] *BrE*
1 to form or join a line of people or vehicles waiting to do something or go somewhere SYN **line up** *AmE*: **[+for]** *Some of the people queuing for tickets had been there since dawn.* | **queue (up) to do sth** *We had to queue up for ages to get served.*
2 if people are queuing up to do something, they all want to do it very much: **queue up to do sth** *The school is one of the best, and parents are queuing up to send their children there.* | **queue up for sth** *Actresses are queuing up for the part.*

ˈqueue-ˌjumping *n* [U] *BrE* when someone unfairly gets something before other people who have been waiting longer —**queue-jump** *v* [I]

quib·ble¹ /ˈkwɪbəl/ *v* [I] to argue about small unimportant details: **[+about/over]** *Let's not quibble over minor details.*

quibble² *n* [C] a small complaint or criticism about something unimportant: *I've just got a few **minor quibbles**.*

quiche /kiːʃ/ *n* [C,U] a PIE without a top, filled with a mixture of eggs, cheese, vegetables etc

QUICHE
quiche
pie

quick¹ /kwɪk/ ●●● S1 W2 *adj* (*comparative* **quicker**, *superlative* **quickest**)
1 SHORT TIME lasting for or taking only a short time: *That was quick! I thought you'd be another hour.* | *It's probably quicker by train.* | *Have we got time for a quick drink?* | *What's the quickest way to the station?* | *We stopped to have a quick look at the church.* | *Three bombs went off* ***in quick succession*** (=quickly, one after the other). THESAURUS▸ SHORT
2 FAST moving or doing something fast: *She walked with short, quick steps.* | *They were great people to work with – very quick, very efficient.* | *Boxers have to be* ***quick on*** *their* ***feet*** (=able to move about quickly). THESAURUS▸ FAST
3 NO DELAY happening very soon, without any delay SYN **speedy**: *I had to make a* ***quick decision***. | *We've put the house on the market and we're hoping for a* ***quick sale***. | *We need a* ***quick response*** *from the government.* | *Robertson's* ***quick thinking*** *had saved the little girl's life.*
4 CLEVER able to learn and understand things fast: *Jane's very witty and very quick.* | *She's a* ***quick learner***. | *He's a good interviewer, tough and* ***quick on the uptake*** (=able to understand quickly what someone is saying).
5 be quick used to tell someone to hurry: *If you want to come with me you'll have to be quick – I'm leaving in ten minutes.* | *'Can I just finish this first?' 'OK, but* ***be quick about it***.*'*
6 be quick to do sth to react quickly to what someone says or does: *The government was quick to deny any involvement in the attacks.*
7 quick fix *informal* a solution to a problem that can be done quickly, but is not a good or permanent solution: *There's no quick fix for stopping pollution.* | *Congress is trying to avoid quick-fix solutions.*
8 have a quick temper to get angry very easily
9 be quick on the draw a) to be able to pull a gun out quickly in order to shoot **b)** *AmE informal* to be good at reacting quickly and intelligently to difficult questions or in difficult situations —**quickness** *n* [U] → QUICKLY

quick² ●●● S1 *interjection* used to tell someone to hurry or come quickly: *Quick! We'll miss the bus!*

quick³ ●●○ S3 *adv* quickly – many teachers think this is not correct English SYN **fast**: *Come quick! Larry's on TV!* | *It all happened pretty quick.* | ***Quick as a flash*** (=very quickly) *she replied, 'That's not what I've heard!'* THESAURUS▸ QUICKLY

quick⁴ *n* **1 the quick** the sensitive flesh under your fingernails and toenails: *Her* ***nails*** *were* ***bitten to the quick***. **2 cut/sting/pierce sb to the quick** if a remark or criticism cuts you to the quick, it makes you feel extremely upset: *She was cut to the quick by the accusation.* **3 the quick and the dead** *biblical* all people, including those who are alive and those who are dead

quick·en /ˈkwɪkən/ *v* [I,T] **1** *written* to become quicker or make something quicker: *Ray glanced at his watch and* ***quickened*** *his* ***pace*** (=began to walk faster). | *Companies are finding it hard to cope with the quickening pace of technological change.* | **your heart/pulse/breathing quickens** (=your heart beats faster because you are afraid, excited etc) *She caught sight of Rob and felt her heart quicken.* **2** *formal* if a feeling quickens, or if something quickens it, it becomes stronger or more active SYN **increase**: *This policy served only to quicken anti-government feeling.*

quick·en·ing /ˈkwɪkənɪŋ/ *n* [U] the first movements of a baby that has not been born yet

quick·fire /ˈkwɪkfaɪə $ -faɪr/ *adj* [only before noun] done very quickly, one after the other: *Contestants have to answer a series of quickfire questions.*

quick·ie /ˈkwɪki/ *n* [C] *informal* **1** something that you can do quickly and easily: *I've got a question for you – it's just a quickie.* **2** a sexual act that you do quickly – used humorously —**quickie** *adj* [only before noun]: *a quickie divorce*

quick·lime /ˈkwɪk-laɪm/ *n* [U] a white powder that is made by heating LIMESTONE

quick·ly /ˈkwɪkli/ ●●● S1 W1 *adv*
1 fast: *We need to get this finished as quickly as possible.* | *Kids grow up so quickly these days.*

> **REGISTER**
> In everyday English, people usually use a verb such as **rush**, **run**, or **hurry** rather than say **go quickly**: *She* ***went quickly*** *to fetch the doctor.* → *She* ***ran*** *to fetch the doctor.*

2 after only a very short time SYN **soon**: *I realized fairly quickly that this wasn't going to be easy.*
3 for a short time: *I'll just quickly nip into that shop.* | *'Have you talked to Vera about it yet?' 'Just quickly.'*

> **THESAURUS**
> **quickly** at a high speed or without taking much time: *The stream was flowing quite quickly.* | *They quickly became friends.*
> **fast** at a high speed – used especially when talking about how something moves: *You're driving too fast!* | *He ran home as fast as he could.*
> **quick** *spoken* quickly – used in exclamations or in comparatives: *Quick! There's a mouse!*
> **swiftly** *written* quickly: *The government acted swiftly.* | *She was surprised that he agreed so swiftly.*
> **rapidly** quickly – used especially about changes, increases, improvements etc: *The population is growing rapidly.* | *a rapidly changing world*
> **speedily** quickly and therefore efficiently: *All problems were speedily dealt with.*
> **briskly** quickly and energetically: *He walked briskly back along the path.*
> **at high/great speed** at a very fast speed – used especially in technical descriptions: *The molecules are travelling at great speed.*
> **at a rapid rate** *especially written* quickly – used about changes, increases, improvements etc: *Internet shopping is growing at a rapid rate.*
> **as quick as a flash/in a flash** extremely quickly: *As quick as a flash, I was back in my bed and under the covers.*
> **like lightning** moving extremely quickly: *Like lightning, the cat darted under the bushes.*
> **flat out** *especially BrE* at the fastest speed possible: *The car was going flat out.*

quick·sand /ˈkwɪksænd/ *n* [C,U] **1** wet sand that is dangerous because you sink down into it if you try to walk on it **2** a bad situation that keeps getting worse, and that you cannot escape from

quick·sil·ver /ˈkwɪkˌsɪlvə $ -ər/ *n* [U] **1** *old use* the metal MERCURY **2** *literary* something that is like quicksilver changes or moves quickly in a way that you do not expect: *His mood changed like quicksilver.* —**quicksilver** *adj*: *his quicksilver temperament*

quick·step /ˈkwɪkstep/ *n* [C] a dance with fast movements of the feet, or music for this dance

ˌquick-ˈtempered *adj* someone who is quick-tempered becomes angry very easily SYN **bad-tempered** OPP **easy-going**

ˌquick-ˈwitted *adj* able to think and understand things quickly OPP **slow-witted**: *Toby was quick-witted and entertaining.* | *a quick-witted reply*

quid /kwɪd/ *n* (*plural* **quid**) [C] *BrE informal* **1** one pound in money: *She earns at least 600 quid a week.* **2 be quids in** to make a good profit: *If this deal comes off, we'll be quids in.*

Q

quid pro quo /ˌkwɪd prəʊ ˈkwəʊ $ -proʊ ˈkwoʊ/ *n* (*plural* **quid pro quos**) [C] something that you give or do in exchange for something else, especially when this arrangement is not official: **[+for]** *There's a quid pro quo for everything in politics – you'll soon learn that.*

qui·es·cent /kwiˈesənt, kwaɪ-/ *adj formal* not developing or doing anything, especially when this is only a temporary state

qui·et¹ /ˈkwaɪət/ ●●● S2 W2 *adj* (*comparative* **quieter**, *superlative* **quietest**)
1 MAKING NO NOISE not making much noise, or making no noise at all: *We'll have to be quiet so as not to wake the baby.* | *It's a nice car. The engine's really quiet.* | *I'll be* ***as quiet as a mouse*** (=very quiet).
2 NOT SPEAKING **a)** not saying much or not saying anything: *You're very quiet, Mom – is anything the matter?* | *I didn't know anything about it so I just* ***kept quiet****.* | *The crowd* ***went quiet****.* | **quiet confidence/satisfaction/desperation** (=having a particular feeling but not talking about it) *a woman whose life of quiet desperation threatens to overwhelm her* | **quiet authority/dignity** (=not saying much but making other people have a particular feeling about you) *Jack's air of quiet authority* **b)** someone who is quiet does not usually talk very much: *a strange, quiet girl*
3 (be) quiet! *spoken* used to tell someone to stop talking or making a noise: *Tanya, be quiet! I'm on the phone.* | *Quiet, you lot!*
4 keep sth quiet/keep quiet about sth to keep information secret: *You're getting married? You kept that quiet!*
5 PLACE WITH NO NOISE a place that is quiet has no noise or not much noise: *Our hotel room was comfortable and quiet.* | *When they walked into the pub, the place* ***went quiet****.*
6 NO ACTIVITY/PEOPLE without much activity or without many people: *It was a Sunday, about three o'clock, and the streets were quiet.* | *I'd love to go on holiday somewhere where it's* ***nice and quiet****.* | *Anthony met her in the bar, and they found a* ***quiet corner*** *where they could talk.* | *I'm going to have a* ***quiet night in*** (=an evening when you stay at home and relax). | *He wants a* ***quiet life****, while she wants to go out partying.*
7 BUSINESS if business is quiet, there are not many customers SYN **slack**: *August is a quiet time of year for the retail trade.*
8 keep sb quiet to stop someone from talking, complaining, or causing trouble: *Give the kids some crayons – that will keep them quiet for a while.*
9 have a quiet word (with sb) *especially BrE* to talk to someone privately when you want to criticize them or tell them about something serious: *Brian's just not keeping up with the workload. Can you have a quiet word?* ⚠ Do not confuse **quiet** with **quite** (=fairly). —**quietness** *n* [U]
→ QUIETLY

quiet² *n* [U] **1** the state of being quiet, calm, and peaceful: *We were enjoying* ***the quiet*** *of the forest.* | *I've had an awful day – now I just want some* ***peace and quiet****.* **2** silence: *Can I have some quiet, please?* **3 on the quiet** *BrE informal* secretly: *We found out he'd been doing some freelance work on the quiet.*

qui·et·en /ˈkwaɪətn/ *BrE*, **quiet** *AmE* *v* **1** [I,T] (*also* **quieten down** *BrE*) to become calmer and less noisy or active, or to make someone or something do this: *Javed Miandad appealed for calm, but he failed to quieten the protesters.* | *Quiet down and get ready for bed!* | *Things tend to quieten down after Christmas.* **2** [T] to reduce a feeling such as fear or worry: *I managed to quieten her fears.*

qui·et·is·m /ˈkwaɪətɪzəm/ *n* [U] *formal* when you accept situations and do not try to change them

qui·et·ly /ˈkwaɪətli/ ●●● S3 W3 *adv*
1 without making much noise: *Rosa shut the door quietly.* | *'I'm sorry,' she said quietly.* | *a* **quietly-spoken** *man* (=one who always speaks quietly)
2 in a way that does not attract attention: *The mayor had been aiming to quietly turn over control of the city's water to private business interests.* | *The government hoped that their early mishandling of the crisis could be* ***quietly forgotten****.*
3 without protesting, complaining, or fighting: *Now are you gonna* ***come quietly****, or do I have to use force?* | *Speculation is growing that Grogan will be replaced at the end of the season, and he is unlikely to* ***go quietly****.*
4 quietly confident *especially BrE* fairly confident of success, but without talking proudly about it: *Adam came out of the interview feeling quietly confident.*

qui·e·tude /ˈkwaɪətjuːd $ -tuːd/ *n* [U] *formal* calmness, peace, and quiet SYN **calm**

qui·e·tus /kwaɪˈiːtəs, kwiˈeɪtəs $ kwaɪˈiːtəs/ *n* [singular] *formal* **1** the death of a person **2** the end of something

THESAURUS: quiet

A QUIET SOUND OR VOICE

quiet not making a loud sound: *I heard a quiet voice behind me.* | *a car with a quiet engine*
low quiet – especially because you do not want people to hear or be disturbed: *Doug was on the phone, speaking in a low voice.* | *I turned the volume down low.*
soft quiet and pleasant to listen to: *Soft music was playing in the background.* | *His voice was soft and gentle.*
silent not making any sound at all: *a silent prayer* | *silent laughter* | *The machines were virtually silent.*
hushed deliberately quiet because you do not want people to hear – used about people's voices: *They were talking about money in hushed tones.* | *The doctor's voice was hushed and urgent.*
faint quiet and difficult to hear because it comes from a long way away: *The men went ahead and their voices got fainter and fainter.* | *the faint sound of bells*
muffled difficult to hear, for example because the sound comes from another room or someone's mouth is covered by something: *Muffled voices were coming from downstairs.* | *the muffled sound of someone crying*
inaudible too quiet to hear: *The sound is inaudible to the human ear.* | *Her answer came in an almost inaudible whisper.*

A QUIET PLACE

quiet without much noise: *It's so quiet here at night.* | *This is the quietest room in the house to work in.*
silent with no noise at all: *The room* ***fell silent*** (=became silent).
peaceful (*also* **tranquil** *especially written*) quiet in a pleasant and relaxing way: *Life's more peaceful in the countryside.* | *The hotel is set in tranquil surroundings.*
sleepy [only before noun] quiet – used about a town or village where there are not many people and very little happens: *a sleepy fishing village*

NOT SAYING MUCH

quiet not saying much: *He's a quiet boy who loves reading.* | *You're very quiet tonight, Suzy – are you OK?*
silent not saying anything: *Her husband was a big silent man.* | *Everyone was arguing but I decided to remain silent.*
taciturn /ˈtæsətɜːn $ -ɜːrn/ *formal* not talking much and seeming a little unfriendly or bad-tempered: *He found Vaughn a taciturn and rather difficult person.*
reticent unwilling to talk to other people, especially about a particular subject: *She's always been reticent about her early life.*
a man/woman of few words someone who does not talk much, especially because they only speak when there is something important to say: *My father was a man of few words, but when he spoke everyone listened.*

quiff /kwɪf/ *n* [C] *BrE* a part of a man's hairstyle where the hair stands up at the front above his forehead

quill /kwɪl/ *n* [C] **1** (*also* **quill pen**) a pen made from a large bird's feather, used in the past **2** a stiff bird's feather **3** one of the long pointed things that grow on the back of a PORCUPINE

QUILL

quilt /kwɪlt/ ●○○ *n* [C] a warm thick cover for a bed, made by sewing two layers of cloth together, with feathers or a thick material in between them → **duvet**

quilt·ed /ˈkwɪltɪd/ *adj* quilted cloth consists of layers held together by lines of stitches that cross each other: *a quilted bath robe*

quilt·ing /ˈkwɪltɪŋ/ *n* [U] the work of making a quilt, or the material and stitches that you use

quin /kwɪn/ *n* [C] *BrE informal* a QUINTUPLET

quince /kwɪns/ *n* [C,U] a hard yellow fruit like a large apple, used in cooking

quin·ine /ˈkwɪniːn $ ˈkwaɪnaɪn/ *n* [U] a drug used for treating fevers, especially MALARIA

qui·no·a /kiːˈnəʊə, ˈkiːnwɑː $ -ˈnoʊə/ *n* [U] the seeds of a plant from South America, which can be cooked like rice

quint /kwɪnt/ *n* [C] *AmE informal* a QUINTUPLET

quin·tes·sence /kwɪnˈtesəns/ *n* **the quintessence of sth** *formal* a perfect example of something: *John is the quintessence of good manners.*

quin·tes·sen·tial /ˌkwɪntəˈsenʃəl◂/ *adj* being a perfect example of a particular type of person or thing SYN **typical**: *'Guys and Dolls' is the quintessential American musical.* **THESAURUS** TYPICAL —**quintessentially** *adv*: *a place that is quintessentially English*

quin·tet /kwɪnˈtet/ *n* [C] **1** five singers or musicians who perform together **2** a piece of music written for five performers → **quartet**, **sextet**, **trio**

quin·tu·plet /ˈkwɪntjʊplət, kwɪnˈtjuːp- $ kwɪnˈtʌp-/ *n* [C] one of five babies born to the same mother at the same time → **quadruplet**, **sextuplet**

quip /kwɪp/ *v* (**quipped**, **quipping**) [T] to say something clever and amusing: *'Giving up smoking is easy,' he quipped. 'I've done it hundreds of times.'* **THESAURUS** COMMENT —**quip** *n* [C]: *an amusing quip*

quire /kwaɪə $ kwaɪr/ *n* [C] *technical* 24 sheets of paper

quirk /kwɜːk $ kwɜːrk/ *n* [C] **1** something strange that happens by chance: **[+of]** *Years later, **by a strange quirk of fate**, she found herself sitting next to him on a plane.* **2** a strange habit or feature of someone's character, or a strange feature of something: *Like every computer, this one has its little quirks.*

quirk·y /ˈkwɜːki $ -ɜːr-/ *adj* unusual, especially in an interesting way: *I like his quirky sense of humour.* —**quirkily** *adv* —**quirkiness** *n* [U]

quis·ling /ˈkwɪzlɪŋ/ *n* [C] *old-fashioned* someone who helps an enemy country that has taken control of their own country

quit /kwɪt/ ●●○ S3 *v* (*past tense and past participle* **quit**, *also* **quitted** *BrE*, *present participle* **quitting**)

1 [I,T] *informal* to leave a job, school etc, especially without finishing it completely: *He quit his job after an argument with a colleague.* | *I quit school at 16.* | *She has decided to quit show business.* | *People are now calling on the chairman to quit.*

2 [I,T] *especially AmE* to stop doing something, especially something that is bad or annoying → **give up**: *The majority of smokers say that they would like to quit the habit.* | *Quit it, Robby, or I'll tell mom!* | *We've done what we can. Let's quit.* | **quit doing sth** *He's been given six months to live if he doesn't quit drinking.* | *I wish you'd all quit complaining.* **THESAURUS** STOP

3 [I,T] *BrE law* to leave a house or apartment that you have been renting: *The landlord gave them **notice to quit** the premises within seven days.*

4 be quit of sth *BrE formal* to no longer have to suffer or be involved with something bad: *The people now long to be quit of war.*

5 [T] *formal* to leave a place: *It was ten years since he had quit Russia.*

quite /kwaɪt/ ●●● S1 W1 *predeterminer, adv*

1 *especially AmE* very, but not extremely → **pretty**: *The food in the cafeteria is usually quite good.* | *His hair is quite thin on top now.* | *Amy's at college, and she's doing quite well.* | **quite a sth** *He's quite a good soccer player.*

GRAMMAR: Word order

You say **quite a** before an adjective and a noun: *It took quite a long time to answer the questions.* ✗ Don't say: *It took a quite long time.*

2 *especially BrE* fairly, or to a small extent, but not very → **pretty**: *The film was quite good, but the book was much better.* | *I got a letter from Sylvia quite recently.* | **quite like/enjoy** *I quite like Chinese food.*

3 quite a lot/bit/few a fairly large number or amount: *He's got quite a lot of friends.* | *Quite a few towns are now banning cars from their shopping centres.*

4 [+adj/adv] *BrE* completely: *I'm sorry. That's **quite impossible**.* | *What she's suggesting is quite ridiculous!* | *I think you've had **quite enough** to drink already!* | *That's quite a different matter.*

5 not quite not completely: *They weren't quite ready so we waited in the car.* | *I'm not quite sure where she lives.* | *Dinner's **almost** ready, but **not quite**.*

6 not quite why/what/where etc not exactly why, what, where etc: *The play wasn't quite what we expected.*

7 quite a sth/quite some sth *BrE* used before a noun to emphasize that something is very good, large, interesting etc: *That was quite a party you had.* | *The engines make quite a noise.* | *It's quite some distance away.*

8 quite a/some time *especially BrE* a fairly long time: *We've been waiting for quite some time now.*

9 quite right *BrE* used to show that you agree strongly with someone: *'I refuse to do any more work.' 'Quite right. They can't expect you to work for nothing.'*

10 that's quite all right *BrE* used to reply to someone that you are not angry about something they have done: *'I'm sorry we're so late.' 'That's quite all right.'*

11 quite/quite so *BrE formal* used to show that you agree with what someone is saying SYN **exactly**: *'They really should have thought of this before.' 'Yes, quite.'*

12 quite something *especially BrE* used to say that someone or something is very impressive: ***It's quite something** to walk out on stage in front of 20,000 people.*

quits /kwɪts/ *adj informal* **1 be quits** *BrE* if two people are quits, neither one owes anything to the other SYN **straight**: *I'll give you £10, and then we're quits.* **2 call it quits a)** to agree that a debt or argument is settled: *Just give me $20 and we'll call it quits.* **b)** to stop doing something: *After 25 years as a teacher, he's decided to call it quits.*

quit·ter /ˈkwɪtə $ -ər/ *n* [C] *informal* someone who does not have the determination or courage to finish something that is difficult

quiv·er[1] /ˈkwɪvə $ -ər/ *v* [I] to shake slightly because you are cold, or because you feel very afraid, angry, excited etc SYN **tremble**: *The child was quivering in her arms.* | *Her mouth quivered slightly as she turned away.* | **quiver with indignation/anger etc** *I lay there quivering with fear.* | *His voice was quivering with rage.*

quiver[2] *n* [C] **1** a slight trembling: **quiver of fear/anxiety/anticipation etc** *I felt a quiver of excitement run through me.* **2** a long case for carrying ARROWS

quix·ot·ic /kwɪkˈsɒtɪk $ -ˈsɑː-/ *adj* quixotic ideas or plans are not practical and are based on unreasonable hopes of improving the world: *This is a vast, exciting, and perhaps quixotic project.*

quiz¹ /kwɪz/ ●●● S3 *n* (*plural* **quizzes**) [C]
1 a competition or game in which people have to answer questions: *a love quiz in a magazine* | *a* **general knowledge quiz** | **quiz show** *especially BrE*: *I get fed up with television quiz shows.* | **quiz night** *BrE*: *a quiz night held in the local pub*
2 *AmE* a short test that a teacher gives to a class: *a biology quiz* → POP QUIZ THESAURUS TEST

quiz² *v* (**quizzed**, **quizzing**) [T] to ask someone a lot of questions SYN **question**: **quiz sb about sth** *Four men have been quizzed about the murder, but no one has yet been charged.* | **quiz sb on/over sth** *They quizzed me on my involvement in the scheme.*

quiz·mas·ter /ˈkwɪzˌmɑːstə $ -ˌmæstər/ *n* [C] *BrE* someone who asks people questions during a quiz SYN **question master**

quiz·zi·cal /ˈkwɪzɪkəl/ *adj* a quizzical expression is one that shows that you do not understand something and perhaps think it is slightly amusing: **a quizzical look/expression/smile** *He sat and watched her, a quizzical look on his face.* —**quizzically** /-kli/ *adv*

quo /kwəʊ $ kwoʊ/ → QUID PRO QUO, STATUS QUO

quoit /kwɔɪt, kɔɪt/ *n* **1 quoits** [U] a game in which you throw rings over a small upright post **2** [C] the ring that you throw in this game **3** [C] a small circle made of large vertical stones in ancient times

Quon·set hut /ˈkwɒnset ˌhʌt $ ˈkwɑːn-/ *n* [C] *trademark AmE* a long metal building with a curved roof where soldiers live or things are stored

Quorn /kwɔːn $ kwɔːrn/ *n* [U] *trademark BrE* a vegetable substance you can use in cooking instead of meat

quo·rum /ˈkwɔːrəm/ *n* [singular] the smallest number of people who must be present at a meeting so that official decisions can be made: *We need a quorum of seven.*

quo·ta /ˈkwəʊtə $ ˈkwoʊ-/ ●○○ *n* [C]
1 an official limit on the number or amount of something that is allowed in a particular period: **[+on]** *The government has* **imposed quotas** *on the export of timber.* | *The government has decided to* **scrap quotas** *on car imports.* | **[+for]** *Several countries have now* **set quotas** *for cod fishing.* | *There are plans to introduce* **strict** *immigration* **quotas**. THESAURUS AMOUNT
2 an amount of something that someone is expected to do or achieve: **[+of]** *Each person was given a quota of tickets to sell.* | **[+for]** *In the 1990s the Navy couldn't* **fill** *its* **quota** *for new recruits.* | **meet/make/achieve a quota** *Workers only get paid if they make their quota.* | **sales/production quota** *They're worried that they won't achieve this year's sales quota.*
3 an amount of something that you think is fair, right, or normal SYN **fair share**: **[+of]** *The committee has had* **more than** *its* **quota** *of problems.* | *I think I've had my quota of coffee for the day.*
4 *BrE* a particular number of votes that someone needs to get to be elected in an election

quot·a·ble /ˈkwəʊtəbəl $ ˈkwoʊ-/ *adj* a quotable remark or statement is interesting, clever, or amusing: *a speech full of witty, quotable phrases*

quo·ta·tion /kwəʊˈteɪʃən $ kwoʊ-/ ●●○ AWL *n*
1 [C] a sentence or phrase from a book, speech etc which you repeat in a speech or piece of writing because it is interesting or amusing SYN **quote**: **[+from]** *a quotation from the Bible* | *The following quotation is taken from a nineteenth century travel diary.* | *a dictionary of quotations*
2 [C] a written statement of exactly how much money something will cost → **estimate**: **[+for]** *Ask the builder to* **give** *you a written* **quotation** *for the job.* | *a quotation for car insurance* | **Get** *a couple of* **quotations** *from different companies before you decide which one to use.*
3 [U] the act of quoting something that someone else has written or said

quoˈtation ˌmark ●●○ *n* [C usually plural] one of a pair of marks (' ') or (" ") that are used in writing to show that you are recording what someone has said SYN **inverted comma** *BrE*

quote¹ /kwəʊt $ kwoʊt/ ●●○ S3 W3 AWL *v*
1 [I,T] to repeat exactly what someone else has said or written: **[+from]** *She quoted from a newspaper article.* | *He* **quoted** *a short* **passage** *from the Bible.* | *A military spokesman was* **quoted as saying** *that the border area is now safe.* | **quote sb on sth** *Can I quote you on that?*
2 [T] to give a piece of information that is written down somewhere: *You can order by phoning our hotline and quoting your credit card number.* | *He quoted a figure of 220 deaths each year from accidents in the home.*
3 [T] to give something as an example to support what you are saying SYN **cite**: *Mr Jackson quoted the case of an elderly man who had been evicted from his home.* | **quote sth as sth** *He quoted the example of France as a country with a good rail service.* | *The nurses' union was* **quoted as an example of** *a responsible trade union.*
4 [T] to tell a customer the price you will charge them for a service or product: *They quoted a price of £15,000.* | **quote sth for sth** *The firm originally quoted £6,000 for the whole job.*
5 [T] to give the price of a share or CURRENCY: *The pound was quoted this morning at just under $1.46.* | *The company is now* **quoted on the stock exchange** (=people can buy and sell shares in it).
6 (I) quote *spoken* used when you are going to repeat what someone else has said, to emphasize that it is exactly the way they said it: *The minister said, quote: 'There will be no more tax increases this year.'*
7 quote ... unquote *spoken* used at the beginning and end of a word or phrase that someone else has said or written, to emphasize that you are repeating it exactly

quote² ●●○ AWL *n* [C]
1 a sentence or phrase from a book, speech etc which you repeat in a speech or piece of writing because it is interesting or amusing SYN **quotation**: **[+from]** *a quote from the minister's speech*
2 in quotes words that are in quotes are written with QUOTATION MARKS around them to show that someone said those words
3 a statement of how much it will probably cost to build or repair something SYN **estimate**: *Always get a quote before proceeding with repair work.*

quoth /kwəʊθ $ kwoʊθ/ *v* [T] *old use* **quoth I/he/she etc** a way of saying 'I said', 'he said' etc

quo·tid·i·an /kwəʊˈtɪdiən $ kwoʊ-/ *adj literary* ordinary, and happening every day

quo·tient /ˈkwəʊʃənt $ ˈkwoʊ-/ *n* [C] **1** the amount or degree of a quality, feeling etc in a person, thing, or situation: *Is all this healthy food supposed to increase my happiness quotient?* **2** *technical* the number which is obtained when one number is divided by another

Qu·ran, the (*also* **the Qur'an**, **the Koran**) /kɔːˈrɑːn, kə- $ kəˈræn, -ˈrɑːn/ the holy book of the Muslims

q.v. (*quod vide*) used to tell readers to look in another place in the same book for a piece of information

qwert·y /ˈkwɜːti $ ˈkwɜːrti/ *adj especially BrE* a qwerty KEYBOARD on a computer or TYPEWRITER has the keys arranged in the usual way for English-speaking countries, with Q,W,E,R,T, and Y on the top row

Rr

R¹, **r** /ɑː $ ɑːr/ *n* (*plural* **R's**, **r's**) **1** [C,U] the 18th letter of the English alphabet **2** [singular, U] *AmE* used to describe a film that has been officially approved as only suitable for people over 17 → THREE RS

R² **1** *AmE* the written abbreviation of ***Republican***, used after a politician's name to show that he or she belongs to the Republican Party in the US → **D**: *Steve Gunderson (R)* **2** *BrE* the written abbreviation of ***regina*** (=queen), used after the name of the queen of the United Kingdom: *Elizabeth R* **3** (*also* **R.**) the written abbreviation of river, used especially on maps → R & B, R & D, R & R

rab·bi /ˈræbaɪ/ *n* [C] a Jewish priest

rab·bi·nate /ˈræbənət, -neɪt/ *n* **the rabbinate** rabbis considered together as a group

rab·bin·i·cal /rəˈbɪnɪkəl/ *adj* relating to the writings or teaching of rabbis

rab·bit¹ /ˈræbɪt/ ●●● (S3) *n*
1 [C] a small animal with long ears and soft fur, that lives in a hole in the ground
2 [U] the fur or meat of a rabbit

rabbit² *v*

rabbit on *phr v BrE informal* to talk for a long time in an uninteresting or annoying way (SYN) **go on**: **[+about]** *He kept rabbiting on about the environment.*

ˈrabbit punch *n* [C] *BrE* a quick hit on the back of the neck, done with the side of your hand

ˈrabbit ˌwarren *n* [C] **1** an area under the ground where a lot of wild rabbits live (SYN) **warren** → **burrow 2** a building with a lot of narrow passages, or a place with a lot of narrow streets, where you can easily get lost (SYN) **warren**

rab·ble /ˈræbəl/ *n* [singular] a noisy crowd of people: **[+of]** *a rabble of angry youths* THESAURUS ▸ GROUP

ˈrabble-ˌrousing *n* [U] when someone deliberately makes a crowd of people angry and violent, especially in order to achieve political aims: *He accused union leaders of rabble-rousing.* —**rabble-rousing** *adj*: *a rabble-rousing speech* —**rabble-rouser** *n* [C]

rab·id /ˈræbəd, ˈreɪ-/ *adj* **1** having very extreme and unreasonable opinions: *a group of rabid right-wing fanatics* **2** a rabid animal is suffering from rabies —**rabidly** *adv*

ra·bies /ˈreɪbiːz/ *n* [U] a very dangerous disease that affects dogs and other animals, and that you can catch if you are bitten by an infected animal → **rabid**

> **GRAMMAR: Singular or plural verb?**
> **Rabies** is followed by a singular verb: ***Rabies is** almost always fatal if not treated early.*
> GRAMMAR GUIDE ▸ NOUNS

rac·coon, **racoon** /rəˈkuːn, ræ- $ ræ-/ *n* **1** [C] a small North American animal with black fur around its eyes and black and grey rings on its tail **2** [U] the skin and thick fur of a raccoon: *a raccoon coat*

race¹ /reɪs/ ●●● (S2) (W2) *n*
1 SPORT [C] a competition in which people or animals compete to run, drive etc fastest and finish first: **in a race** *He will be the youngest runner in the race.* | *Over 80 cars will take part in the race.* | **[+between]** *the annual boat race between Oxford and Cambridge Universities*
2 PEOPLE **a)** [C,U] one of the main groups that humans can be divided into according to the colour of their skin and other physical features → **ethnic group**: *The school welcomes children **of all races**.* | *a person of **mixed race*** | *The law forbids discrimination on the grounds of race or religion.* → HUMAN RACE **b)** [singular] *informal* a group of people who are similar in some way: **[+of]** *The 1960s produced a new race of young novelists.* | *Are schools breeding* (=producing) *a race of children incapable of making decisions for themselves?*
3 GET/DO STH FIRST [singular] a situation in which one group of people tries to obtain or achieve something before another group does: **the race to do sth** *More and more drug companies are joining the race to beat cancer.* | ***The race is on** to develop more environmentally friendly forms of energy.* → ARMS RACE, RAT RACE
4 DO STH QUICKLY [singular] a situation in which you have to do something very quickly because you have very little time available: **a race to do sth** *It is now a race to find the killer.* | **race against time/against the clock** *The pilot then began a desperate race against time to land the plane before it ran out of fuel.*
5 PRIZE/POWER [singular] a situation in which people are competing with each other to win a prize or obtain a position of power: **[+for]** *Mr Bird has now officially joined the race for the White House.* | *He **is** no longer **in the race for** academic awards.* | **race to do sth** *the race to host the next Olympic Games*
6 HORSE RACE **the races** an occasion when horse races are held: **at the races** *We spent a day at the races.* → **play the race card** at PLAY¹(14)

> **COLLOCATIONS**
> **VERBS**
> **compete in a race** (*also* **take part in a race**) *He is competing in his first race this year.*
> **have a race** *Let's have a race!*
> **hold a race** *The race will be held on February 25th.*
> **win/lose a race** *He did not win another race that season.*
> **come first/last etc in a race** (*also* **finish first/last etc in a race**) *She came third in the race.*
> **lead the race** (=be ahead of everyone else) | **finish the race** | **run a race**
> **ADJECTIVES/NOUN + race**
> **tough/hard** *He said he expected the race to be tough.*
> **the big race** (=an important race) *There are only three days to go until the big race.*
> **a 3000 metres/10 km etc race** *He finished first in the 100 metres race.*
> **a horse/boat/bike etc race** | **a road race** (=when people run, cycle etc on ordinary roads)

race² ●●● (S3) (W3) *v*
1 SPORT **a)** [I,T] to compete against someone or something in a race: **[+against]** *She'll be racing against some of the world's top athletes.* | **[+in]** *Stevens will not be racing in the final due to a knee injury.* | **race sb up/down sth etc** *I'll race you to the end of the road.* **b)** [T] to use an animal or a vehicle to compete in a race: *He will be racing a Ferrari in this year's Formula One championships.*
2 MOVE QUICKLY [I,T always + adv/prep] to move very quickly or take someone or something to a place very quickly: *He raced into the village on his bike.* | *I had to race home for my bag.* | **race sb to sth etc** *She was raced to hospital.* | **race to do sth** *He raced to meet her.* THESAURUS ▸ RUN
3 DO STH QUICKLY [I] to try to do something very quickly because you want to be the first to do it, or because there is very little time available: **race to do sth** *Investors are racing to buy shares in the new hi-tech companies.* | **race against time/the clock** *The astronauts are racing against time to repair the spaceship.*
4 HEART/MIND [I] if your heart or mind races, it works harder and faster than usual, for example because you are afraid or excited: *My heart was racing and my knees shook uncontrollably.* | *My mind was racing, trying to think where I had seen him before.*
5 ENGINE [I] if an engine races, it runs too fast

ˈrace car *n* [C] *AmE* a RACING CAR

race·card /ˈreɪskɑːd $ -kɑːrd/ *n* [C] *BrE* a list of the races that will happen at a horse racing event, and the horses that will take part in each race

race·course /ˈreɪs-kɔːs $ -kɔːrs/ *n* [C] *BrE* a grass track on which horses race SYN **racetrack** *AmE*

race·go·er /ˈreɪsɡəʊə $ -ɡoʊər/ *n* [C] *BrE* someone who goes regularly to watch horse races

race·horse /ˈreɪshɔːs $ -hɔːrs/ *n* [C] a horse specially bred and trained for racing

ˈrace ˌmeeting *n* [C] *BrE* an occasion when horse races are held at a particular place

rac·er /ˈreɪsə $ -ər/ *n* [C] someone who competes in a race

ˈrace reˌlations *n* [plural] the relationship that exists between people from different countries, religions etc who are now living in the same place: *We need to do more to promote good race relations.* | *Community leaders are working to improve race relations in the city.*

ˈrace ˌriot *n* [C] violent fighting between people of different countries, religions etc who now live in the same country

race·track /ˈreɪs-træk/ *n* [C] **1** a track on which runners or cars race **2** *AmE* a grass track on which horses race SYN **racecourse** *BrE*

ra·cial /ˈreɪʃəl/ ●●○ *adj*
1 [only before noun] relating to the relationships between different races of people who now live in the same country or area: *a victim of* ***racial discrimination*** | *This part of the community needs to be protected from* ***racial prejudice****.* | *evidence of* ***racial harassment*** | *the campaign for* ***racial equality*** | *the need for tolerance and* ***racial harmony***
2 relating to the various races that humans can be divided into → **ethnic**: *a broad range of racial and ethnic groups* | *people of different* ***racial origin*** —**racially** *adv*: *They live in a* ***racially mixed*** *area.* | *Police officers believe the attack was* ***racially motivated****.*

ra·cial·is·m /ˈreɪʃəlɪzəm/ *n* [U] *BrE old-fashioned* RACISM —**racialist** *n, adj*

rac·ing¹ /ˈreɪsɪŋ/ ●○○ *n* [U]
1 the sport of racing horses SYN **horse racing**: *watching the racing on television* | *today's racing results* → FLAT RACING
2 car/bike/greyhound etc racing the sport of racing cars etc

racing² *adj* [only before noun] designed or bred to go very fast and be used for racing: *racing pigeons* | *a racing yacht*

ˈracing car *n* [C] a very fast car that is specially designed for races

ra·cis·m /ˈreɪsɪzəm/ ●●○ *n* [U]
1 unfair treatment of people, or violence against them, because they belong to a different race from your own: *The government has promised to continue the fight against racism.* | *the problem of racism in schools*
2 the belief that some races of people are better than other races

rac·ist /ˈreɪsɪst/ ●○○ *n* [C] someone who believes that people of their own race are better than others, and who treats people from other races unfairly and sometimes violently - used to show disapproval: *He denied being a racist.* —**racist** *adj*: *the victim of a racist attack* | *racist violence* | *racist remarks*

rack¹ /ræk/ ●●○ *n* [C]
1 a frame or shelf that has bars or hooks on which you can put things: *a wine rack* | *a magazine rack* → LUGGAGE RACK, ROOF-RACK
2 the rack a piece of equipment that was used in the past to make people suffer severe pain by stretching their bodies: *Thousands of people were tortured on the rack.*
3 on the rack *BrE informal* in a very difficult situation: *The company is now well and truly on the rack.*
4 go to rack and ruin if a building goes to rack and ruin, it gradually gets into a very bad condition because no one has looked after it: *The house had been left to go to rack and ruin.*
5 *AmE* a three-sided frame used for arranging the balls at the start of a game of SNOOKER or POOL
6 a rack of lamb/pork a fairly large piece of meat from the side of an animal, that contains several RIB bones

RACKS

wine rack

magazine rack

luggage rack

7 off the rack *AmE* if you can buy something off the rack, you can buy it in a shop rather than having it specially made SYN **off the peg** *BrE*: *A lot of designer clothes are now available off the rack.*

rack² *v* **1** [T] to make someone suffer great mental or physical pain: *Great sobs* ***racked*** *her* ***body****.* | **be racked by/with sth** *Her face was racked with pain.* | *Liza was racked by guilt.* **2 rack your brains** to try very hard to remember or think of something: *I racked my brains, trying to remember his name.*

rack sth ↔ **up** *phr v informal* to get a number or amount of something, especially a number of points in a competition: *He racked up 41 points.*

rack·et /ˈrækɪt/ ●●○ *n*
1 [singular] *informal* a loud noise: *The old machine used to* ***make*** *an awful* ***racket****.*
2 [C] *informal* a dishonest way of obtaining money, such as by threatening people or selling them illegal goods: **drugs/gambling/smuggling etc racket** *Police believe he is involved in an international smuggling racket.* → **protection racket** at PROTECTION(5)
3 [C] (*also* **racquet**) a specially shaped piece of wood or metal that you use for hitting the ball in games such as tennis, that has a circle filled with tight strings at one end → **bat**: *a tennis racket* → see picture at SPORT¹

rack·e·teer /ˌrækəˈtɪə $ -ˈtɪr/ *n* [C] someone who earns money through crime and illegal activities

rack·e·teer·ing /ˌrækəˈtɪərɪŋ $ -ˈtɪr-/ *n* [U] when someone earns money through crime and illegal activities: *people involved in smuggling and racketeering* | *He has been arrested on racketeering charges.*

rac·on·teur /ˌrækɒnˈtɜː $ -kɑːnˈtɜːr/ *n* [C] *formal* someone who is good at telling stories in an interesting and amusing way

ra·coon /rəˈkuːn, ræ- $ ræ-/ *n* [C,U] another spelling of RACCOON

rac·quet /ˈrækɪt/ *n* [C] another spelling of RACKET(3)

rac·quet·ball /ˈrækətbɔːl $ -bɒːl/ *n* [U] an indoor game in which two or four players hit a small ball against the four walls of the court → **squash**

rac·y /ˈreɪsi/ *adj* racy writing is exciting and entertaining and often about sex: *a racy novel*

rad /ræd/ *adj informal* exciting or interesting: *Have you guys seen Wendy's new place? It's so rad.*

ra·dar /ˈreɪdɑː $ -ɑːr/ ●○○ *n*
1 [C,U] a piece of equipment that uses radio waves to find the position of things and watch their movement → **sonar**: *The coastline can now be monitored by radar.* | *We could see the plane quite clearly on the radar screen.*
2 on sb's/the radar (screen) if something is on your radar, you have noticed it and are giving it some attention: *This is one of the issues on our radar.*
3 fly/slip under sb's/the radar to not be noticed by someone: *How did this band slip under the radar?*

ˈradar gun *n* [C] a small piece of radar equipment that is used to find out how fast things, especially cars, are going

ˈradar trap *n* [C] a place on a road where police wait with radar equipment in order to catch drivers who are going too fast SYN **speed trap**

rad·dled /ˈrædld/ *adj BrE* someone who looks raddled looks old or tired: *her raddled face*

ra·di·al /ˈreɪdiəl/ *adj* arranged in a circular shape with bars or lines coming from the centre: *radial roads leading out of the city centre*

ˌradial ˈtyre *BrE*, **radial tire** *AmE n* [C] a car tyre with wires inside the rubber that go completely around the wheel to make it stronger and safer

ra·di·ance /ˈreɪdiəns/ *n* [U] *literary* **1** great happiness that shows in someone's face and makes them look attractive: *a young face full of radiance* **2** a soft gentle light: *the moon's radiance*

ra·di·ant /ˈreɪdiənt/ *adj* **1** full of happiness and love, in a way that shows in your face and makes you look attractive: *She looked radiant in a white silk dress.* | *a* ***radiant smile*** | **[+with]** *They were both radiant with happiness.* **2** [only before noun] *literary* very bright: *a lovely day with clear blue skies and radiant sun* **3** [only before noun] *technical* radiant heat or energy is sent out in the form of waves —**radiantly** *adv*: *She looked radiantly beautiful.*

ra·di·ate /ˈreɪdieɪt/ *v* **1** [I,T] if someone radiates a feeling, or if it radiates from them, it is very easy to see that this is how they feel: *He radiated calm confidence.* | **[+from]** *Kindness radiated from her.* **2** [I always + adv/prep, T] if something radiates light or heat, or if light or heat radiates from something, the light or heat is sent out in all directions: *The log fire radiated a warm cosy glow.* | **[+from]** *Heat radiated from the glowing coals.* **3** [I always + adv/prep] if things radiate from a central point, they spread out in different directions from that point: **[+out/from]** *There were tiny lines radiating from the corners of her eyes.*

ra·di·a·tion /ˌreɪdiˈeɪʃən/ ●○○ *n* [U]
1 a form of energy that comes especially from NUCLEAR reactions, which in large amounts is very harmful to living things: *An accident at the power station could result in large amounts of radiation being released.* | *a lethal dose of radiation*
2 energy in the form of heat or light that is sent out as waves that you cannot see: *Sun creams work by blocking harmful ultraviolet radiation.*

radiˈation ˌsickness *n* [U] an illness that is caused when your body receives too much radiation

ra·di·a·tor /ˈreɪdieɪtə $ -ər/ ●●○ *n* [C]
1 a thin metal container that is fastened to a wall and through which hot water passes to provide heat for a room
2 the part of a car or aircraft which stops the engine from getting too hot

rad·i·cal¹ /ˈrædɪkəl/ ●●○ W3 AWL *adj*
1 CHANGE/DIFFERENCE a radical change or difference is very big and important OPP **slight**: *They are proposing* ***radical changes*** *to the way the company is run.* | *a radical reform of the tax system* | *There are radical differences between the two organizations.*
2 OPINIONS radical ideas are very new and different, and are against what most people think or believe → **conservative**: *He has put forward some very* ***radical ideas.*** | *I was shocked by her radical views.* | *a radical approach to education*
3 PEOPLE someone who is radical has ideas that are very new and different, and against what most people think or believe: *a radical left-wing politician* | *a radical feminist*
4 GOOD *AmE informal* very good or enjoyable: *That was one radical party last night!*

radical² ●○○ AWL *n* [C] someone who has new and different ideas, especially someone who wants complete social and political change → **conservative**: *radicals on the extreme left wing of the party* —**radicalism** *n* [U]

rad·i·cal·ize (*also* **-ise** *BrE*) /ˈrædɪkəlaɪz/ *v* [T] to make people accept new and different ideas, especially ideas about complete social and political change

rad·i·cally /ˈrædɪkli/ ●○○ AWL *adv* if something changes radically, it changes a lot in an important way: *The situation is* ***radically different*** *from that of ten years ago.* | *a* ***radically new*** *approach to the problem* | **radically change/alter** *Mozart radically altered the structure of the opera.*

ra·dic·chi·o /ræˈdiːtʃiəʊ, -kiəʊ $ -kioʊ/ *n* [U] a type of plant used in SALADS that is red and has a bitter taste

rad·i·i /ˈreɪdiaɪ/ the plural of RADIUS

ra·di·o¹ /ˈreɪdiəʊ $ -dioʊ/ ●●● S1 W2 *n*
1 a) [C] a piece of electronic equipment which you use to listen to programmes that are broadcast, such as music and news: **turn/switch the radio on/off** *I sat down and turned on the radio.* **b)** [U] programmes that are broadcast on the radio: *I don't really* ***listen to the radio*** *very much.* | **on the radio** *Did you hear the interview with the prime minister on the radio this morning?* | **radio programme/show** *He's got his own radio show now.* | **local/national radio** *She works for a local radio station.*
2 a) [C] a piece of electronic equipment, for example on a plane or ship, which can send and receive spoken messages: **over the radio** *We received a call for help over the ship's radio.* **b)** [U] when messages are sent or received in this way: **by radio** *We should be able to reach them by radio.* | *We've lost* ***radio contact*** *with the plane.*

GRAMMAR
- You listen to **the radio**: *I often listen to the radio in my car.* ✗ Don't say: listen to radio
- You say that someone or something is **on the radio**: *My mother heard the news on the radio.* ✗ Don't say: *on radio*

GRAMMAR GUIDE ▸ NOUNS

radio² *v* [I,T] to send a message using a radio: **[+for]** *The ship radioed for help.* | **radio sb for sth** *We radioed London for permission to land.*

radio- /reɪdiəʊ $ -dioʊ/ *prefix technical* using radio waves: *radiopaging* (=calling people by radio)

ra·di·o·ac·tive /ˌreɪdiəʊˈæktɪv◂ $ -dioʊ-/ ●○○ *adj* a radioactive substance is dangerous because it contains RADIATION (=a form of energy that can harm living things): *the problem of how to dispose of* ***radioactive waste*** | *a consignment of* ***highly radioactive*** *plutonium*

ˌradioactive ˈdating *n* [U] *AmE* a scientific method of calculating the age of a very old object by measuring the amount of a certain substance in it SYN **carbon dating** *BrE*

ˌradioactive ˈwaste *n* [U] harmful radioactive substances that remain after energy has been produced in a NUCLEAR REACTOR SYN **nuclear waste**

ra·di·o·ac·tiv·i·ty /ˌreɪdiəʊækˈtɪvəti $ -dioʊ-/ *n* [U] the sending out of RADIATION (=a form of energy) when the NUCLEUS (=central part) of an atom has broken apart: *the discovery of radioactivity* | *high levels of radioactivity*

ˈradio ˌbeacon *n* [C] a tower that sends out radio signals to help aircraft stay on the correct course

ra·di·o·car·bon dat·ing /ˌreɪdiəʊkɑːbən ˈdeɪtɪŋ $ -dioʊkɑːr-/ *n* [U] *formal* CARBON DATING

ˌradio-conˈtrolled *adj* controlled from far away using radio signals: *a radio-controlled toy car*

ra·di·o·gram /ˈreɪdiəʊgræm $ -dioʊ-/ *n* [C] *BrE* a piece of furniture, popular in the 1950s, which contained a radio and a record player

ra·di·og·ra·pher /ˌreɪdiˈɒgrəfə $ -ˈɑːgrəfər/ *n* [C] someone whose job is to take X-RAY photographs of the inside of people's bodies, or who treats people for illnesses using an X-ray machine

ra·di·og·ra·phy /ˌreɪdiˈɒgrəfi $ -ˈɑːg-/ *n* [U] the taking of X-RAY photographs of the inside of people's bodies for medical purposes

ra·di·ol·o·gist /ˌreɪdiˈɒlədʒɪst $ -ˈɑː-/ *n* [C] a hospital doctor who is trained in the use of RADIATION to treat people

R

ra·di·ol·o·gy /ˌreɪdiˈɒlədʒi $ -ˈɑː-/ *n* [U] the study and medical use of RADIATION

ˌradio-ˈtelephone *n* [C] a telephone that works by sending and receiving radio signals and can be used in a car, boat etc

ˌradio ˈtelescope *n* [C] a piece of equipment that collects RADIO WAVES from space and is used to find stars and other objects in space

ra·di·o·ther·a·py /ˌreɪdiəʊˈθerəpi $ -dioʊ-/ *n* [U] the treatment of illnesses using RADIATION —**radiotherapist** *n* [C]

ˈradio ˌwave *n* [C usually plural] a form of electric energy that can move through air or space

rad·ish /ˈrædɪʃ/ *n* [C] a small vegetable whose red or white root is eaten raw and has a strong spicy taste → see picture at **VEGETABLE[1]**

ra·di·um /ˈreɪdiəm/ *n* [U] a white metal that is RADIOACTIVE and is used in the treatment of diseases such as CANCER. It is a chemical ELEMENT: symbol Ra

ra·di·us /ˈreɪdiəs/ ●○○ *n* (*plural* **radii** /-diaɪ/) [C]
1 the distance from the centre to the edge of a circle, or a line drawn from the centre to the edge → **diameter** → see picture at **VEGETABLE[1]**
2 an area that covers a particular distance in all directions from a central point: *The shock of the explosion was felt over a radius of forty miles.* | **within a 10-mile/200-metre etc radius** *There are more than a dozen golf courses within a 15-mile radius of St Andrews.*
3 *technical* the outer bone of the lower part of your arm → see picture at **SKELETON**

ra·don /ˈreɪdɒn $ -dɑːn/ *n* [U] a RADIOACTIVE gas that is used in the treatment of diseases such as CANCER. It is a chemical ELEMENT: symbol Rn

rad·waste /ˈrædweɪst/ *n* [U] *AmE* RADIOACTIVE WASTE

RAF, the /ˌɑːr eɪ ˈef, ræf/ (***the Royal Air Force***) the British air force

raf·fi·a /ˈræfiə/ *n* [U] a soft substance like string that comes from the leaves of a PALM tree and is used for making baskets, hats, MATS etc

raf·fish /ˈræfɪʃ/ *adj literary* behaving or dressing in a way which is not respected by many people but which is still confident and attractive: *an interesting character with a raffish air* —**raffishly** *adv* —**raffishness** *n* [U]

raf·fle[1] /ˈræfəl/ *n* [C] a competition or game in which people buy numbered tickets and can win prizes: *a woman selling* ***raffle tickets***

raffle[2] (*also* **raffle off**) *v* [T] to offer something as a prize in a raffle

raft /rɑːft $ ræft/ ●○○ *n* [C]
1 a flat floating structure, usually made of pieces of wood tied together, used as a boat
2 a raft of sth a large number of things: *The company has launched a whole raft of new software products.*
3 a flat floating structure that you can sit on, jump from etc when you are swimming
4 a small flat rubber boat filled with air, used for example if a boat sinks

RAFT

raf·ter /ˈrɑːftə $ ˈræftər/ *n* [C usually plural] one of the large sloping pieces of wood that form the structure of a roof: *The club was* ***packed to the rafters*** (=very full).

raft·ing /ˈrɑːftɪŋ $ ˈræf-/ *n* [U] the activity of travelling on a raft, especially as a sport: *white-water rafting*

rag[1] /ræg/ ●○○ *n*
1 CLOTH [C,U] a small piece of old cloth, for example one used for cleaning things: *He wiped his boots dry with an old rag.* | *an oily rag*
2 NEWSPAPER [C] *informal* a newspaper, especially one that you think is not particularly important or of good quality: *He writes for the* ***local rag***.
3 in rags wearing old torn clothes: *Children in rags begged money from the tourists.*
4 from rags to riches becoming very rich after starting your life very poor: *He likes to tell people of his rise from rags to riches.* → **RAGS-TO-RICHES**
5 MUSIC [C] a piece of RAGTIME music
6 STUDENTS' EVENT [C] *BrE* an event organized by students every year in order to make money for people who are poor, sick etc: *rag week* → **glad rags** at **GLAD(7)**, → **like a red rag to a bull** at **RED[1](5)**, → **lose your rag** at **LOSE(11)**

rag[2] *v* (**ragged, ragging**) [T] *BrE old-fashioned* to laugh at someone or play tricks on them SYN **tease**

ra·ga /ˈrɑːgə/ *n* [C] **1** a piece of Indian music based on an ancient pattern of notes **2** one of the ancient patterns of notes that are used in Indian music

rag·a·muf·fin /ˈrægəˌmʌfɪn/ *n* [C] *literary* a dirty young child wearing torn clothes

ˌrag-and-ˈbone-man *n* (*plural* **rag-and-bone-men**) [C] *BrE* a man who goes around the streets buying and collecting old clothes and other things that people no longer want

rag·bag /ˈrægbæg/ *n* [singular] *BrE* a mixture of very different things that do not seem to fit together well: **[+of]** *a ragbag of leftover bits of food*

ˌrag ˈdoll / $ ˈ../ *n* [C] a soft DOLL made of cloth

rage[1] /reɪdʒ/ ●●○ *n*
1 [C,U] a strong feeling of uncontrollable anger: *Sobbing with rage, Carol was taken to the hospital.* | **in a rage** *Sam became quite frightening when he was in a rage.* | **cry/scream/roar etc of rage** *Just then, she heard Mr Evan's bellow of rage.* | **red/dark/purple with rage** *His face was red with rage.* | **trembling/shaking with rage** *Forester stared at his car, trembling with rage.* | **seething/incandescent with rage** (=as angry as a person can possibly be) *Animal rights supporters were incandescent with rage.* | *Richens was 17 when he* ***flew into a rage*** *and stabbed another teenager.*
2 be all the rage *informal* to be very popular or fashionable: *DiCaprio became all the rage after starring in the film 'Titanic'.*
3 rage for sth a situation in which something is very popular or fashionable: *The rage for cycling has been growing.*

rage[2] *v* **1** [I,T] *written* to feel very angry about something and show this in the way you behave or speak: **[+at/against]** *He was sorry he had raged at her earlier.* | *'How was I to know!' Jenny raged.* **2** [I] if something such as a battle, a disagreement, or a storm rages, it continues with great violence or strong emotions: *Civil war has been raging in the country for years.* | *A debate is raging about what form pensions should take.* | *Outside, a storm was raging.* | **[+on]** *The battle raged on* (=continued). **3** [I] if a fire or illness rages, it spreads fast and is hard to control: *The fire raged for twelve hours and fifteen people died.* | *A great cholera epidemic raged across Europe in 1831.* **4** [I] *informal* to have fun with a group of people in a wild and uncontrolled way: *We couldn't wait to go out and rage.*

-rage /reɪdʒ/ *suffix* [in nouns] **road-rage/air-rage etc** when someone becomes extremely angry and violent while they are driving, on a plane etc: *He was attacked in a road-rage incident.*

rag·ga /ˈrægə/ *n* [U] a form of popular music from the West Indies

rag·ged /ˈrægɪd/ *adj*
1 CLOTHES ETC (*also* **rag·ged·y** /ˈrægədi/ *especially AmE*) torn and in bad condition: *the ragged blankets on the bed* | *a raggedy hat*
2 PEOPLE wearing clothes that are old and torn: *Crowds of ragged children played among the rocks.*
3 UNEVEN (*also* **raggedy**) having a rough uneven edge or surface: *The old photograph looked a little ragged at the edges.* | *a ragged hole* | *raggedy hair*
4 NOT REGULAR not regular or together: *The crowd gave a ragged cheer.* | *ragged breathing*
5 TIRED *informal* tired after using a lot of effort: *He looked*

R

ragged, so I told him to go to bed. | *He* ***ran*** *United's defence* ***ragged*** (=made them do a lot of work).
6 be on the ragged edge *AmE informal* to be feeling very tired or upset —**raggedly** *adv*: *raggedly dressed* | *She was breathing raggedly.* —**raggedness** *n* [U]

rag·ing /ˈreɪdʒɪŋ/ *adj* [only before noun] **1** very great and hard to control: *a raging appetite* | *I was in a raging temper.* **2** continuing strongly and showing no signs of ending: *a raging debate* | *raging inflation* | *The show was a raging success.* **3** a raging headache etc is very painful: *Richard developed a raging headache and had to lie down.* | *a raging fever* (=a very high body temperature) **4** continuing or moving with great natural force: *a raging storm* | *a raging sea* | *The fire had become a raging blaze.*

rag·lan /ˈræglən/ *adj* if a coat, SWEATER etc has raglan sleeves, the sleeves are joined with a sloping line from the arm to the neck

ra·gout /ræˈguː, ˈræguː $ ræˈguː/ *n* [C,U] a mixture of vegetables and meat boiled together SYN **stew**

ˌrags-to-ˈriches *adj* [only before noun] a rags-to-riches story is about someone who becomes very rich after starting life very poor

rag·tag /ˈrægtæg/ *adj* [only before noun] *informal* a ragtag group is not tidy or properly organized: *a ragtag fighting force*

rag·time /ˈrægtaɪm/ *n* [U] a type of music and dancing that has a strong beat and was popular in the US in the early part of the 20th century

ˈrag trade *n* **the rag trade** *BrE informal* the business of making and selling clothes, especially women's clothes SYN **the fashion industry**

rag·weed /ˈrægwiːd/ *n* [U] a North American plant that produces a substance which causes HAY FEVER

rag·wort /ˈrægwɜːt $ -wɜːrt/ *n* [U] a common plant with yellow flowers, and leaves with uneven edges

rai /raɪ/ *n* [U] a style of Algerian popular music

raid¹ /reɪd/ ●●○ *n* [C]
1 a short attack on a place by soldiers, planes, or ships, intended to cause damage but not take control: *a bombing raid* | *an* ***air raid*** *warning siren* | **[+on/against]** *The colonel led a successful raid against a rebel base.* | **launch/carry out/stage a raid** *The army launched several cross-border raids last night.* → AIR RAID
2 a surprise visit made to a place by the police to search for something illegal: *a police raid* | *an FBI raid* | **[+on]** *Four people were arrested during a raid on a house in London.* | *a* ***dawn raid*** (=one made very early in the morning)
3 an attack by criminals on a building where they believe they can steal money or drugs: *a bank raid* | **[+on]** *an armed raid on a shop in Glasgow* → RAM-RAIDING
4 *technical* an attempt by a company to buy enough SHARES in another company to take control of it

raid² ●●○ *v* [T]
1 if police raid a place, they make a surprise visit to search for something illegal: *Police found weapons when they raided his home.*
2 to make a sudden military attack on a place: *air bases on the mainland from which the island could be raided* | **raiding party** (=a group taking part in an attack)
3 to go into a place and steal things: *The gang raided three homes in the area.*
4 to go to a place that has supplies of food or drink and take some because you are hungry: *Peter went into the kitchen to raid the fridge.*

raid·er /ˈreɪdə $ -ər/ *n* [C] someone who goes into a place and steals things: *an armed raider* | *Masked raiders carried out a bank robbery today.*

rail¹ /reɪl/ ●●● S2 W2 *n*
1 [U] the railway system → **train**: *the American* ***rail system*** | *a high-speed* ***rail network*** | *Passengers want a better* ***rail service.*** | *the Channel Tunnel and its* ***rail links*** *with London* | **by rail** *We continued our journey by rail.* | *I need to buy a* ***rail ticket.*** | *cheap* ***rail fares***
2 [C] one of the two long metal tracks fastened to the ground that trains move along

RAILS

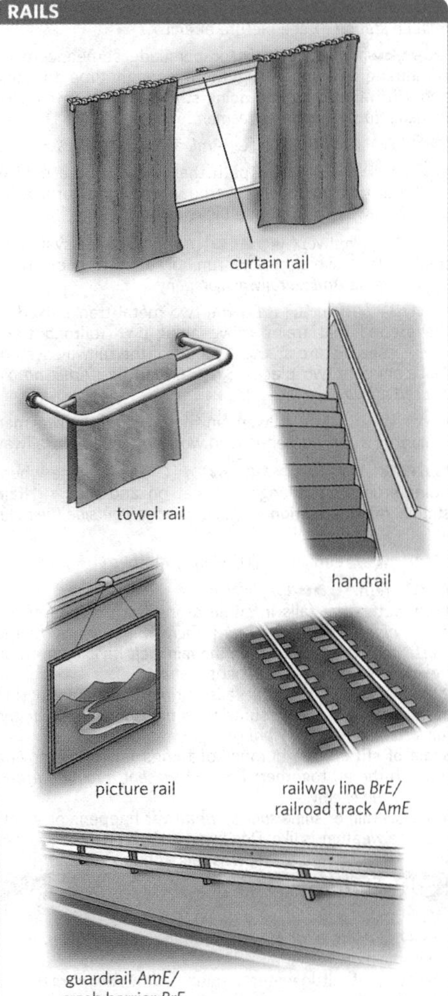

3 [C] a bar that is fastened along or around something, especially to stop you from going somewhere or from falling: *Several passengers were leaning against the ship's rail.* → GUARDRAIL, HANDRAIL
4 [C] a bar that you use to hang things on: *a* ***towel rail*** | *a* ***curtain rail***
5 go off the rails *informal* to start behaving in a strange or socially unacceptable way: *At 17 he suddenly went off the rails and started stealing.*
6 back on the rails happening or functioning normally again: *The coach was credited with putting the team back on the rails.*

rail² *v* **1** [T] to enclose or separate an area with rails → **cordon off**: **rail sth off/in** *The police railed off the area where the accident happened.* **2** [I,T] *formal* to complain angrily about something, especially something that you think is very unfair: **[+against/at]** *Consumers rail against the way companies fix prices.*

rail·head /ˈreɪlhed/ *n* [C] the end of a railway line

rail·ing /ˈreɪlɪŋ/ *n* [C] **1** (*also* **railings** [plural]) a metal fence that is made of a series of upright bars: *a small park surrounded by railings* → see picture at FENCE¹ **2** one of the bars in some railings

rail·le·ry /ˈreɪləri/ *n* [U] *formal* friendly joking about someone: *affectionate raillery*

rail·road¹ /ˈreɪlrəʊd $ -roʊd/ ●●○ *n* [C] *AmE* a railway or the railway: *The supplies were sent on the railroad.* | *a railroad station* → see picture at **RAIL**

railroad² *v* [T] to force or persuade someone to do something without giving them enough time to think about it: **railroad sb into doing sth** *The workers were railroaded into signing the agreement.*

'railroad ˌcrossing *n* [C] *AmE* a LEVEL CROSSING

'rail trail *n* [C] *AmE* a path that used to be a railway track but that has been covered with a hard surface for people to walk, run, or ride bicycles on

rail·way /ˈreɪlweɪ/ ●●● S2 W2 *n* [C] *BrE* a system of tracks along which trains run, or a system of trains SYN **railroad** *AmE*: *a railway company*

'railway line *n* [C] *BrE* **1** the two metal tracks fixed to the ground that trains move along SYN **railroad track** *AmE* → see picture at **RAIL** **2** a part of the railway system that connects two places SYN **railroad line** *AmE*: *an old disused railway line*

rail·way·man /ˈreɪlweɪmən/ *n* (*plural* **railwaymen** /-mən/) [C] *BrE* someone who works on a train or railway

'railway ˌstation ●●● S3 *n* [C] *BrE* a place where trains stop for passengers to get on and off SYN **train station, railroad station** *AmE*: *I'll meet you outside the main railway station.*

rai·ment /ˈreɪmənt/ *n* [U] *literary* clothes

R

rain¹ /reɪn/ ●●● S2 W2 *n*

1 [U] water that falls in small drops from clouds in the sky: *a night of wind and rain* | *There will be heavy rain in most parts of the country.* | **in the rain** *I left my bicycle out in the rain.* → **ACID RAIN, RAIN DROP, RAINY**

2 the rains heavy rain that falls during a particular period in the year in tropical countries → **monsoon**: *Last year, the rains came on time in April.*

3 rain of sth a large number of things falling or moving through the air together: *The archers sent a rain of arrows towards the enemy.*

4 (come) rain or shine *spoken* whatever happens or whatever the weather is like: *Don't worry. We'll be there – rain or shine.* —**rainless** *adj* → **right as rain** at **RIGHT¹(9)**

COLLOCATIONS

ADJECTIVES/NOUN + rain

heavy (=with a lot of water coming down) *The rain became more heavy.*
light (=with little water coming down) *A light rain began to fall.*
torrential (=very heavy) *I woke to the sound of torrential rain.*
pouring rain (=very heavy rain) *He left us standing in the pouring rain.*
driving rain (=heavy rain that is falling fast or being blown along) *They struggled to walk against driving rain.*
freezing rain (=extremely cold rain) | **fine rain** (=very gentle rain) | **acid rain** (=rain which contains pollution from factories)

VERBS

the rain falls *The rain was still falling steadily.*
the rain comes down (=it falls) *If the rain starts coming down, we can always go inside.* | *The monsoon rain comes down in sheets.*
the rain stops *They went into a cafe and waited for the rain to stop.*
the rain eases off (=it starts to rain less) | **the rain pours down** (=a lot of rain comes down) | **the rain beats/lashes** (=it falls or hits something with a lot of force) | **the rain patters on sth** (=drops of rain hit something and make a sound) | **get caught in the rain** (=be outside when it starts raining)

PHRASES

it is pouring with rain *BrE*, **it is pouring rain** *AmE* (=a lot of rain is falling) *When we went outside it was pouring with rain.*
it looks like rain (=rain appears likely because there are dark clouds in the sky) *We ate indoors because it looked like rain.*
a drop of rain *Robert felt a drop of rain on his face.*
an inch/25mm etc of rain *Two inches of rain fell in twelve hours.*
outbreaks of rain (=short periods of rain – used in weather forecasts) *Outbreaks of rain will spread across northern parts.*
a rain shower (*also* **a shower of rain** *BrE*) (=a short period of rain) | **sheets of rain** (=large moving masses of heavy rain) | **a rain cloud**

THESAURUS

rain *n* [U] water that falls in small drops from clouds in the sky: *The rain has stopped at last.* | *There had been heavy rain during the night.*
drizzle *n* [U] light rain with very small drops of water: *A light drizzle was falling as I left the house.*
shower *n* [C] a short period of rain that can be heavy or light: *More heavy showers are forecast for tonight.* | *a light shower of rain*
downpour *n* [C usually singular] a short period of very heavy rain that starts suddenly: *A sudden downpour sent us running for shelter.* | *a torrential downpour*
hail *n* [U] frozen rain that falls in the form of HAILSTONES (=small balls of ice): *The hail and high winds have destroyed many of the county's crops.*
sleet *n* [U] a mixture of snow and rain: *The rain had turned to sleet.* | *Sleet and snow fell.*
the rains *n* [plural] heavy rain that falls during a particular period in the year in tropical countries: *The farmers are waiting for the rains to come.*
monsoon *n* [C] the heavy rain that falls between April and October in India and other southern Asian countries: *The monsoon is late this year.* | *the monsoon season*

rain² ●●● S3 *v*

1 it rains if it rains, drops of water fall from clouds in the sky: *Outside it was still raining.* | *It's starting to rain.* | **rain heavily/hard** *It must have rained quite hard last night.* | **it's raining cats and dogs** *spoken* (=it is raining very hard)

2 rain (down) blows/blows rain down if you rain blows onto someone, you hit them many times: *She attacked the man, raining blows on his head and shoulders.*

3 it never rains but it pours *spoken* used to say that as soon as one thing goes wrong, a lot of other things go wrong as well

THESAURUS

it's raining drops of water are falling from the sky: *It's raining – you'd better take an umbrella.*
it's pouring (down) *BrE*, **it's pouring (rain)** *AmE* it is raining very heavily: *We stayed at home because it was pouring down all day.*
it's chucking it down *BrE informal* it is raining very heavily: *Outside it was chucking it down and the streets were deserted.*
it's drizzling very gentle rain is falling: *It's only drizzling – let's go for a walk anyway.*
it's hailing frozen rain in the form of small balls of ice are falling: *It had been hailing and the roads were still slippery.*

rain down *phr v* to fall in large quantities: **[+on]** *Bombs rained down on the city.*

be rained off *BrE*, **be rained out** *AmE phr v* if an event or activity is rained off or rained out, it has to stop because there is too much rain: *The match was rained off.*

'rain boots *n* [plural] *AmE* rubber boots that stop your feet getting wet SYN **wellingtons** *BrE*

rain·bow /ˈreɪnbəʊ $ -boʊ/ ●●○ *n* [C] a large curve of different colours that can appear in the sky when there is both sun and rain

'rain check *n* **1 take a rain check (on sth)** *informal especially AmE* used to say that you will do something in the future but not now: *'Care for a drink?' 'I'll take a rain check, thanks.'* **2** [C] *AmE* a ticket for an outdoor event, such as a sports game, that you can use again if it rains and the action stops

rain·coat /ˈreɪnkəʊt $ -koʊt/ ●●○ *n* [C] a coat that you wear to protect yourself from rain

ˈrain drop, rain·drop /ˈreɪndrɒp $ -drɑːp/ *n* [C] a single drop of rain

rain·fall /ˈreɪnfɔːl $ -fɒːl/ *n* [C,U] the amount of rain that falls on an area in a particular period of time: *We've had a long period of low rainfall. | The city has received only half its average rainfall of four inches.*

ˈrain ˌforest, rain·for·est /ˈreɪnfɒrɪst $ -fɔː-, -fɑː-/ ●○○ *n* [C,U] a tropical forest with tall trees that are very close together, growing in an area where it rains a lot: *the destruction of the rain forest*

ˈrain gauge *n* [C] an instrument that is used for measuring the amount of rain that falls somewhere

rain·proof /ˈreɪnpruːf/ *adj* able to keep rain out → **waterproof**: *a rainproof jacket*

rain·storm /ˈreɪnstɔːm $ -ɔːrm/ *n* [C] a sudden heavy fall of rain SYN **downpour**

rain·wa·ter /ˈreɪnwɔːtə $ -wɒːtər, -wɑː-/ *n* [U] water that has fallen as rain

rain·y /ˈreɪni/ ●●● S3 *adj*

1 a rainy period of time is one when it rains a lot SYN **wet**: *a cold* ***rainy day*** *in October | I hate* ***rainy weather***. *| the* ***rainy season***

2 save sth for a rainy day to save something, especially money, for a time when you will need it

raise¹ /reɪz/ ●●● S1 W1 *v* [T]

1 MOVE HIGHER to move or lift something to a higher position, place, or level: *Can you raise the lamp so I can see? | William raised his hat and smiled at her. |* ***Raise*** *your* ***hand*** *if you know the right answer.* THESAURUS ▸ LIFT

> **REGISTER**
> In everyday British English, people usually say **lift** something **up** rather than **raise** something: *Can you* ***lift up*** *the lamp a bit?*
> British English speakers usually say **put up your hand** rather than **raise your hand**: ***Put your hand up*** *if you know the right answer.*

2 INCREASE to increase an amount, number, or level OPP **lower**: *Many shops have raised their prices. | The university is working to raise the number of students from state schools. | a campaign to* ***raise awareness*** *of meningitis | Dr Hayward intends to* ***raise*** *the museum's* ***profile*** (=make it more well-known). THESAURUS ▸ INCREASE

> **REGISTER**
> In everyday British English, people usually say **put up** an amount, a price etc rather than **raise** it: *They've* ***put*** *the price of fuel* ***up*** *again.*

3 COLLECT MONEY to collect money that you can use to do a particular job or help people: *The Trust hopes to raise $1 million to buy land. | They are* ***raising funds*** *to help needy youngsters. | a concert to* ***raise money*** *for charity* → FUNDRAISING

4 IMPROVE to improve the quality or standard of something: *Changing the law cannot raise standards. | The team need to raise their game.*

5 START A SUBJECT to begin to talk or write about a subject that you want to be considered or a question that you think should be answered SYN **bring up**: *He did not raise the subject again. | I'd like to raise the issue of publicity. | Betty* ***raised*** *the important* ***question*** *of who will be in charge.* THESAURUS ▸ MENTION

6 CAUSE A REACTION to cause a particular emotion or reaction: *This attack* ***raises fears*** *of increased violence against foreigners. | The way the research was carried out* ***raises doubts*** *about the results.*

7 MOVE EYES OR FACE to move your eyes, head, or face so that you are looking up OPP **lower**: *Albert raised his eyes and stared at Ruth. | 'No,' he said without raising his head.*

8 MOVE UPRIGHT (*also* **raise up**) to move or lift yourself into an upright position OPP **lower**: **raise yourself** *Adele raised herself from the pillows. | He raised himself up on one elbow to watch.*

9 CHILDREN *especially AmE* to look after your children and help them grow SYN **bring up** *BrE*: *Stan's dad died, leaving his mother to raise three sons alone. | It was time for Dean to settle down and* ***raise*** *a* ***family***. *| Anne married a Jew, despite being raised a Catholic. | The new generation was the first to be raised on processed food. | Camus was* ***born and raised*** *in Algeria.*

10 ANIMALS OR PLANTS to look after animals or grow plants so that they can be sold or used as food: *He raised cattle in Nebraska when he was young. | Jim retired to raise raspberries.*

11 COLLECT PEOPLE to collect together a large group of people, especially soldiers: *The rebels quickly raised an army.*

12 raise a smile to smile when you are not feeling happy, or to make someone smile when they are not feeling happy: *I couldn't raise a smile.*

13 raise your eyebrows to show surprise, doubt, disapproval etc by moving your EYEBROWS upwards: *Blanche raised her eyebrows in surprise.*

14 raise eyebrows if something raises eyebrows, it surprises people: *The band's new sound will raise some eyebrows.*

15 raise your voice to speak loudly or shout because you are angry: *He's never raised his voice to me. | I could hear raised voices in the next room.*

16 raise your glass *spoken* to celebrate someone's happiness or success by holding up your glass and drinking from it: *Ladies and gentlemen, will you raise your glasses to the bride and groom.*

17 raise the alarm *BrE* to warn people about a danger so that they can take action: *Sam stayed with his injured friend while a passing motorist raised the alarm.*

18 raise the spectre of sth *literary* to make people feel afraid that something frightening might soon happen: *The violence has raised the spectre of civil war.*

19 raise its (ugly) head if a question or problem raises its head, it appears and has to be dealt with: *Another problem then raised its ugly head.*

20 raise the bar to do, produce, or be something better than anyone before, so that other people then feel they have to do better themselves: *He has raised the bar for other filmmakers.*

21 CARD GAME to make a higher BID than an opponent in a card game: *I'll raise you $100.*

22 raise hell *informal* to complain in a very angry way about something you think is not acceptable: *I'll raise hell with whoever is responsible for this mess.*

23 raise hell/Cain *especially AmE* to behave in a wild, noisy way that upsets other people: *The kids next door were raising hell last night.*

24 raise the roof to make a very loud noise when singing, celebrating etc

25 SPEAK TO SB to speak to someone on a piece of radio equipment SYN **contact, get**: *They finally managed to raise him at Miller's sheep farm.*

26 WAKE SB *literary* to wake someone who is difficult to wake: *Try as he might he could not raise her.*

27 DEAD PERSON *biblical* to make someone who has died live again: *Jesus raised Lazarus from the grave.*

28 raise a siege/embargo *formal* to allow goods to go in and out of a place again after they have been stopped by force or by a law

29 BUILD *formal* to build something such as a MONUMENT SYN **erect**

30 raise 2/4/10 etc to the power of 2/3/4 etc *technical* to multiply a number by itself a particular number of times: *2 raised to the power of 3 is 8.*

raise² ●○○ *n* [C] *AmE* an increase in the money you earn SYN **rise** *BrE*

R

raised /reɪzd/ *adj* higher than the surrounding area or surface: *a raised platform*

rai·sin /ˈreɪzən/ *n* [C] a dried GRAPE

rai·son d'être /ˌreɪzɒn ˈdetrə $ -zoʊn-/ *n* [singular] the reason why something exists, why someone does something etc: *Commerce was the town's raison d'être.*

ra·jah, **raja** /ˈrɑːdʒə/ *n* [C] the king or ruler of an Indian state

rake[1] /reɪk/ *n* **1** [C] a gardening tool with a row of metal teeth at the end of a long handle, used for making soil level, gathering up dead leaves etc: *a garden rake* → see picture at GARDEN **2** [C] *old-fashioned* a man who has many sexual relationships, drinks too much alcohol etc **3** [singular] the angle of a slope: *the rake of the stage*

rake[2] *v* **1** [I,T] to move a rake across a surface in order to make the soil level, gather dead leaves etc: **rake sth over/up** *She raked the soil over to loosen the weeds.* **2** [I always + adv/prep] to search a place very carefully for something: **[+through/around]** *I've been raking through my drawers looking for those tickets.* **3** [T] to point something such as a gun, camera, or strong light, and keep moving it across an area SYN **sweep**: *The searchlight raked the open ground around the prison.* | **rake sth with sth** *They raked the room with gunfire.* **4** [T] to push a stick backwards and forwards in a fire in order to remove ASHes **5 rake over the past/old coals** to keep talking about something that happened in the past that people would prefer you not to mention **6 rake your fingers (through sth)** to pull your fingers through something or across a surface: *Ken raked his fingers through his hair.*

rake sth ↔ **in** *phr v informal* to earn a lot of money without trying very hard: *Lou's been raking in the dollars since he opened his business.* | *If someone opened a burger bar, they'd really* ***rake it in.***

rake sth ↔ **up** *phr v informal* **1** to talk about something from the past that people would prefer you not to mention SYN **dredge up**: *It upsets Dad when that story is raked up again.* **2** (*also* **rake sth ↔ together**) to collect things or people together for a purpose, but with difficulty: *They could only rake up $300.*

ˈrake-off *n* [C] *informal* a dishonest share of profits → **cut**: *The taxi driver gets a rake-off from the hotel.*

rak·ish /ˈreɪkɪʃ/ *adj* **1** if a man looks rakish, or wears rakish clothes, he dresses nicely and looks confident and relaxed SYN **stylish**: *a rakish uniform* **2 at a rakish angle** if you wear a hat at a rakish angle, you do not wear it straight, and this makes you look relaxed and confident **3** *old-fashioned* a rakish man has a lot of sexual relationships, wastes money, and drinks too much alcohol —**rakishly** *adv*

ral·ly[1] /ˈræli/ ●○○ *n* (*plural* **rallies**) [C]

1 a large public meeting, especially one that is held outdoors to support a political idea, protest etc: *About 1,000 people* ***attended*** *the* ***rally*** *in Hyde Park.* | *We decided to* ***hold a rally*** *to put pressure on the government.* | *a* ***mass rally*** (=large rally) *in support of the pay claim* | **political/election/peace etc rally** *He was shot dead while addressing an election rally.* → PEP RALLY **THESAURUS** MEETING

2 a car race on public roads: *a* ***rally driver***

3 an occasion when something, especially the value of shares, becomes stronger again after a period of weakness or defeat: *a late rally in the Tokyo stock market*

4 a continuous series of hits of the ball between players in a game such as tennis

rally[2] *v* (**rallied**, **rallying**, **rallies**) **1** [I,T] to come together, or to bring people together, to support an idea, a political party etc: **[+to]** *Fellow Republicans rallied to the president's defense.* | **rally to do sth** *Surely the local business community could have rallied to raise the cash.* | *an attempt to* ***rally support*** *for the party* **2** [I] to become stronger again after a period of weakness or defeat → **recover**: *After a shaky start, he rallied and won the title in style.* | *The Tokyo stock market rallied later in the day.*

rally around (sb) (*also* **rally round (sb)** *BrE*) *phr v informal* if a group of people rally round, they all try to help you when you are in a difficult situation: *Her friends all rallied round when she was ill.*

ˈrallying ˌcry *n* [singular] a word or phrase used to unite people in support of an idea: *'Land and Liberty' was the rallying cry of revolutionary Mexico.*

ˈrallying ˌpoint *n* [singular] an idea, event, person etc that makes people come together to support something they believe in: **[+for]** *a rallying point for the struggle against apartheid*

ram[1] /ræm/ *v* (**rammed**, **ramming**) **1** [I,T] to run or drive into something very hard: *In the latest raid, thieves used his van to ram a police car.* | **[+into]** *He lost control of his truck and rammed into a van, killing two people.* **2** [T always + adv/prep] to push something into a position, using great force: *First, you'll have to ram the posts into the ground.* | *I rammed my foot down on the brake.* **3 ram sth down sb's throat** to try to make someone accept an idea or opinion by repeating it many times, especially when they are not interested **4 ram sth home** to make sure someone fully understands something by emphasizing it and by providing a lot of examples, proof etc: *a police video ramming home the dangers of driving fast in fog*

ram[2] *n* [C] **1** an adult male sheep → **ewe 2** a BATTERING RAM **3** a machine that hits something again and again to force it into a position

RAM /ræm/ *n* [U] *technical* (***random access memory***) the part of a computer that acts as a temporary store for information so that it can be used immediately → **ROM**: *a model with 128 MB of RAM*

Ram·a·dan /ˈræmədæn, -dɑːn, ˌræməˈdɑːn, -ˈdæn/ *n* [U] the ninth month of the Muslim year, during which Muslims do not eat or drink anything between SUNRISE and SUNSET

ram·ble[1] /ˈræmbəl/ *v* [I] **1** to talk for a long time in a way that does not seem clearly organized, so that other people find it difficult to understand you: *She's getting old and she tends to ramble a bit.* **2** [always + adv/prep] *BrE* to go on a walk in the countryside for pleasure → **hike**: *There's plenty to discover as you ramble around this little island.* **3** a plant that rambles grows in all directions

ramble on *phr v BrE* to talk or write for a long time in a way that other people find boring SYN **go on**: **[+about]** *My father kept rambling on about the war.*

ramble[2] *n* [C] *BrE* **1** a walk in the countryside for pleasure → **hike**: *I quite like the idea of* ***going for a ramble*** *one weekend.* **2** a speech or piece of writing that is very long and does not seem to be clearly organized: *In a ten-page ramble, Barre explains why he wrote the book.*

ram·bler /ˈræmblə $ -ər/ *n* [C] **1** *BrE* someone who goes for walks in the countryside for pleasure **2** a plant, especially a rose, that grows in all directions

ram·bling[1] /ˈræmblɪŋ/ *adj* [usually before noun] **1** a rambling building has an irregular shape and covers a large area: *a rambling old farmhouse* **2** rambling speech or writing is very long and does not seem to have any clear organization or purpose: *a long rambling letter*

rambling[2] *n* [U] *BrE* the activity of going for walks in the countryside for pleasure

ram·blings /ˈræmblɪŋz/ *n* [plural] speech or writing that goes on for a long time and does not seem to have any clear organization or purpose: *He refused to listen to their mad ramblings.*

Ram·bo /ˈræmbəʊ/ a character played by Sylvester Stallone in several US films, called *First Blood, Rambo: First Blood II* etc. Rambo was a strong, very violent soldier who fought against the US's enemies, especially the COMMUNISTS. His name is often used to describe anyone who thinks fighting and violence are the only ways of settling disagreements: *Several European politicians condemned America's Rambo-style approach to Saddam Hussein.* —**Ramboesque** *adj*: *Ramboesque violence*

ram·bunc·tious /ræmˈbʌŋkʃəs/ *adj AmE* noisy, full of energy, and behaving in a way that cannot be controlled: *three rambunctious kids*

ram·e·kin /ˈræmɪkɪn, ˈræmkɪn/ *n* [C] a small dish in which food for one person can be baked and served

ram·i·fi·ca·tion /ˌræmɪfɪˈkeɪʃən/ *n* [C usually plural] *formal* an additional result of something you do, which may not have been clear when you first decided to do it → **implications, implication**: *an agreement which was to* **have** *significant* **ramifications** *for British politics* | **[+of]** *the practical ramifications of taking on a new job* | **legal/political/economic etc ramifications** *the environmental ramifications of the road-building program*

ramp¹ /ræmp/ ●○○ *n* [C]
1 a slope that has been built to connect two places that are at different levels: *Ramps are needed at exits and entrances for wheelchair users.*
2 *AmE* a road for driving onto or off a large main road SYN **slip road** *BrE*: *Take the Lake Drive ramp at Charles Street.* | **off-/on-ramp** *They missed the off-ramp to Manhattan.*

ramp² *v*
ramp sth ↔ **up** *phr v* **1** to try to persuade people that a company's SHARES are worth more than they really are: *To ramp up a share price during a takeover bid is unacceptable.* **2** if a company ramps up an activity, it increases it: *Producers can quickly ramp up production.* —**ramp-up** *n* [C usually singular]

ram·page¹ /ræmˈpeɪdʒ, ˈræmpeɪdʒ/ *v* [I] to rush about in groups, acting in a wild or violent way: **[+through]** *Drunken football fans rampaged through the streets.*

rampage² *n* **on the rampage** rushing about in a wild and violent way, often causing damage: *gangs of youths on the rampage* | *Rioters* **went on the rampage** *through the town.*

ram·pant /ˈræmpənt/ *adj* **1** if something bad, such as crime or disease, is rampant, there is a lot of it and it is very difficult to control → **rife, widespread**: *Pickpocketing is rampant in the downtown area.* | **rampant inflation** **2** a plant that is rampant grows and spreads quickly, in a way that is difficult to control —**rampantly** *adv*

ram·part /ˈræmpɑːt $ -ɑːrt/ *n* [C usually plural] a wide pile of earth or a stone wall built to protect a castle or city in the past

ˈram-ˌraiding *n* [U] *BrE informal* the crime of driving a car into a shop window in order to steal goods from the shop —**ram-raid** *n* [C]: *a ram-raid on a jeweller's shop* —**ram-raider** *n* [C]

ram·rod /ˈræmrɒd $ -rɑːd/ *n* [C] **1 straight/stiff as a ramrod** sitting or standing with your back straight and your body stiff **2** a stick for cleaning a gun or pushing GUNPOWDER into an old-fashioned gun

ram·shack·le /ˈræmʃækəl/ *adj* a ramshackle building or vehicle is in bad condition and in need of repair SYN **tumbledown**: *a ramshackle old cottage*

ran /ræn/ *v* the past tense of RUN

ranch /rɑːntʃ $ ræntʃ/ ●●○ *n* [C]
1 a very large farm in the western US and Canada where sheep, cattle, or horses are bred
2 a RANCH HOUSE

ranch·er /ˈrɑːntʃə $ ˈræntʃər/ *n* [C] someone who owns or works on a ranch

ˈranch house *n* [C] **1** *AmE* a house built on one level, usually with a roof that does not slope very much → **bungalow** → see picture at **HOUSE** **2** a house on a ranch in which the rancher lives

ranch·ing /ˈrɑːntʃɪŋ $ ˈræn-/ *n* [U] the activity or business of operating a ranch: *cattle ranching*

ran·cid /ˈrænsɪd/ *adj* oily or fatty food that is rancid smells or tastes unpleasant because it is no longer fresh: *rancid butter*

ran·cour *BrE*, **rancor** *AmE* /ˈræŋkə $ -ər/ *n* [U] *formal* a feeling of hatred and anger towards someone you cannot forgive because they harmed you in the past → **resentment**: **without rancour** *He spoke openly about the war without a trace of rancour.*

rand /rænd/ *n* (*plural* **rand**) [C] the standard unit of money in South Africa

R & B /ˌɑːr ən ˈbiː/ *n* [U] (***rhythm and blues***) a style of popular music that is a mixture of BLUES, JAZZ and SOUL

R & D /ˌɑːr ən ˈdiː/ *n* [U] (***research and development***) the part of a business concerned with studying new ideas and planning new products

ran·dom /ˈrændəm/ ●●○ AWL *adj*
1 happening or chosen without any definite plan, aim, or pattern: *The company has introduced random drug testing of its employees.* | *A few random shots were fired.* | *We looked at a* **random sample** *of 120 families.* | *a* **random selection** *of women who were in the shop*
2 at random without any definite plan, aim, or pattern: **choose/select/pick sth at random** *The gang picked their victims at random.*
3 *informal* strange, unusual, or unexpected: *She's great - she's just so random!* —**randomly** *adv*: *seven* **randomly chosen** *numbers* —**randomness** *n* [U]

ˌrandom ˈaccess ˌmemory *n* [U] *technical* RAM

ran·dom·ize (*also* **-ise** *BrE*) /ˈrændəmaɪz/ *v* [T] *technical* to choose things in a way that is not carefully controlled or planned in order to do a scientific test: *The numbers have been randomized.* | *a randomized trial of a new drug*

R & R /ˌɑːr ənd ˈɑː $ -ˈɑːr/ *n* [U] *especially AmE* (***rest and relaxation***) a holiday, especially one given to people in the army, navy etc after a long period of hard work or during a war: *He was enjoying a few hard-earned days of R and R.*

rand·y /ˈrændi/ *adj BrE informal* full of sexual desire SYN **horny**: *She was* **feeling** *very* **randy**.

rang /ræŋ/ *v* the past tense of RING

range¹ /reɪndʒ/ ●●● S1 W1 AWL *n*
1 VARIETY OF THINGS/PEOPLE [C usually singular] a number of people or things that are all different, but are all of the same general type: **[+of]** *a range of services* | *The drug is effective against a range of bacteria.* | **wide/broad/whole/full range of sth** *students from a wide range of backgrounds* | *advice on a whole range of subjects* | **narrow/limited range of sth** *A fairly narrow range of people are responsible for key decisions.*
2 LIMITS [C] the limits within which amounts, quantities, ages etc vary: **age/price/temperature etc range** *toys suitable for children in the pre-school age range* | *a temperature range of 72–85°,* | **in/within a ... range** *Your blood pressure's well within the normal range.* | **in the range (of) sth to sth** *a salary in the range of $25,000 to $30,000* | *Even the cheapest property was* **out of** *our* **price range** (=too expensive for us).
3 PRODUCTS [C] a set of similar products made by a particular company or available in a particular shop: **[+of]** *a new range of kitchenware* | *A company from Darlington has just launched its latest range of fashion jewellery.* | *The watches in this range are priced at £24.50.* | *We have a very large* **product range**. → MID-RANGE, TOP-OF-THE-RANGE
4 DISTANCE **a)** [C,U] the distance over which a particular weapon can hit things: **[+of]** *missiles with a range of 3000 km* | **within range (of sth)** *We waited until the enemy was within range.* | **out of/beyond range (of sth)** *I ducked down to get out of range of the gunshots.* | **at close/short/point-blank range** (=from very close) *Both men had been* **shot at point-blank range**. → LONG-RANGE, SHORT-RANGE **b)** [C,U] the distance within which something can be seen or heard: **within range (of sth)** *a handsome man who drew admiring glances from any female within range* | *any spot within range of your radio signal* | **out of/beyond range (of sth)** *Joan hoped that the others were out of range of her mother's voice.* | *One way to see birds* **at close range** *is to attract them into your own garden.* **c)** [C] the distance which a vehicle such as an aircraft can travel before it needs more FUEL etc: **[+of]** *The plane has a range of 3,600 miles.*
5 MUSIC [C usually singular] all the musical notes that a particular singer or musical instrument can make: *His* **vocal range** *is amazing.*
6 MOUNTAINS/HILLS [C] a group of mountains or hills, usually in a line: *a land of high* **mountain ranges** *and deep valleys* | **range of mountains/hills** *the longest range of hills in the Lake District*
7 PLACE FOR SHOOTING [C] an area of land where you can

practise shooting or where weapons can be tested: *a **rifle range** | the police **shooting range***
8 ABILITY [C,U] the number of different things that someone, especially an actor or actress, does well: *an actor of extraordinary range and intensity*
9 LAND [C,U] *AmE* a large area of land covered with grass, on which cattle are kept
10 COOKING [C] **a)** *AmE* a COOKER **b)** *BrE* a large piece of kitchen equipment in which you make a fire and use this heat to cook food → **stove**: *a coal-fired **kitchen range***
→ FREE-RANGE

range² ●●○ W3 AWL *v*
1 INCLUDE [I always + adv/prep] **a)** to include a variety of different things or people in addition to those mentioned: **range from sth to sth** *The show had a massive audience, ranging from children to grandparents.* **b)** if prices, levels, temperatures etc range from one amount to another, they include both those amounts and anything in between: **range from sth to sth** *There were 120 students whose ages ranged from 10 to 18.* | **range between sth and sth** *The population of these cities ranges between 3 and 5 million.* | **range in age/size/price etc** *The shoes range in price from $25 to $100.*
2 DEAL WITH MANY SUBJECTS [I] to deal with a wide range of subjects or ideas in a book, speech, conversation etc: **[+over]** *The conversation had ranged over a variety of topics, from sport to current affairs.* | *The discussion **ranged widely**.*
3 MOVE AROUND [I always + adv/prep] to move around in an area without aiming for a particular place SYN **wander**: **[+over/through]** *Cattle ranged over the pastures in search of food.*
4 range yourself with/against sb/sth *formal* to publicly state your agreement with, or opposition to, a particular group's beliefs and ideas: *individuals who had ranged themselves against the authorities*
5 ARRANGE *BrE* [T always + adv/prep] *formal* to put things in a particular order or position: *In the dining room, team photographs were ranged along the wall.*

rang·er /ˈreɪndʒə $ -ər/ *n* [C] **1** someone whose job is to look after a forest or area of countryside: *a park ranger* **2** (*also* **ranger guide**) a girl who belongs to a part of the Guide Association in Britain, for girls between the ages of 14 and 19

rang·y /ˈreɪndʒi/ *adj* with long thin strong legs: *a tall, rangy boy*

rank¹ /ræŋk/ ●●● W3 *n*
1 POSITION IN ARMY/ORGANIZATION [C,U] the position or level that someone holds in an organization, especially in the police or the army, navy etc: **[+of]** *officers below the rank of Colonel* | *He **held** (=had) the **rank** of Chief Inspector.* | **rise to/be promoted to/attain the rank of sth** *During the war Harold had risen to the rank of major.* | **high/senior/low/junior rank** *an officer of junior rank* | *He was sentenced to prison and **stripped of** his **rank*** (=had his rank taken from him).
2 the ranks a) the people who belong to a particular organization or group: **in/within ... ranks** *There were splits in the party ranks on this issue.* | *The Democrats now face opposition from within their own ranks.* | **[+of]** *Most are recruited from the ranks of people who studied Latin and Greek at university.* | *That summer I left school and **joined the ranks of*** (=became one of) *the unemployed.* **b)** all the members of the army, navy etc who are not officers: *He **rose from the ranks** to become a Field Marshal* (=he became an officer after starting as an ordinary soldier).
3 break ranks to behave in a way which is different from other members of a group, especially when they expect your support: **[+with]** *He was the first to break ranks with Ceausescu and publicly criticise his policies.*
4 LINE [C] a rank of people or things is a line or row of them: **[+of]** *Silently, ranks of police edged closer to the crowds.* | *Everyone lines up in ranks, all facing the instructor.* | **rank after rank/rank upon rank** (=a lot of things or people in a row) *On the shelves were rank after rank of liquor bottles.*
5 pull rank (on sb) *informal* to use your authority over someone to make them do what you want, especially unfairly: *You may just have to pull rank and tell them.*
6 QUALITY [singular] the degree to which something or someone is of high quality: *While none of these pictures is **of the first rank*** (=of the highest quality), *some are of interest.*
7 SOCIAL CLASS [C,U] someone's position in society: *people of all ranks in society* | *He came from a **family of rank*** (=one from a high social class).
8 TAXI [C] (*also* **taxi rank**) a place where taxis wait in a line to be hired: *I called a taxi from the rank outside.* → **close ranks** at CLOSE¹(17)

rank² ●●● W3 *v*
1 a) [I always + adv/prep, not in progressive] to have a particular position in a list of people or things that have been put in order of quality or importance: **[+as/among]** *Today's match ranks as one of the most exciting games that these two have ever played.* | *We rank among the safest countries in the world.* | **[+with/alongside]** (=be of the same importance or quality) *Cuvier wanted to turn natural history into a science that would rank with physics and chemistry.* | **rank high/low** *He ranked high among the pioneers of 20th century chemical technology.* **b)** [T] to decide the position of someone or something on a list based on quality or importance: **be ranked fourth/number one etc** *Agassi was at that time ranked sixth in the world.* | *It is not always easy to **rank** the students **in order of** ability.*
2 [T] *AmE* to have a higher rank than someone else SYN **outrank**: *A general ranks a captain.*
3 [T] to arrange objects in a line or row: *There were several pairs of riding boots ranked neatly in the hall.*

rank³ *adj* **1** if something is rank, it has a very strong unpleasant smell: **rank smell/odour** *the rank odour of sweat and urine* **2** [only before noun] used to emphasize a bad or undesirable quality SYN **total**: *an example of this government's rank stupidity* | *They make us look like **rank amateurs*** (=not at all good or professional). **3** rank plants are too thick and have spread everywhere: *rank grass and weeds*

ˌrank and ˈfile *n* **the rank and file** the ordinary members of an organization rather than the leaders: *The rank and file of the party had lost confidence in the leadership.* —**rank-and-file** *adj* [only before noun]: *the **rank-and-file members** of the trade union*

rank·ing¹ /ˈræŋkɪŋ/ *n* [C] a position on a scale that shows how good someone or something is when compared with others: *She is now fifth in the **world rankings**.*

ranking² *adj* [only before noun] *especially AmE* a ranking person has a high, or the highest, position in an organization or is one of the best at an activity: *the panel's ranking Democrat, William Clay* | *He's the ship's **ranking officer*** (=the one with the highest rank).

-ranking /ræŋkɪŋ/ *suffix* used to say where someone or something is on a scale that shows how good they are, or what position they have, compared with other people or things: **high/top/low/middle-ranking** *a top-ranking tennis player*

ran·kle /ˈræŋkəl/ *v* [I,T] if something rankles, you still remember it angrily because it upset you or annoyed you a lot: *His comments still rankled.*

ran·sack /ˈrænsæk/ *v* [T] **1** to go through a place, stealing things and causing damage: *The whole flat had been ransacked.* **2** to search a place very thoroughly, often making it untidy: **ransack sth for sth** *She ransacked the wardrobe for something to wear.*

ran·som¹ /ˈrænsəm/ *n* [C] **1** an amount of money that is paid to free someone who is held as a prisoner: *The kidnappers were **demanding** a **ransom** of $250,000.* | *The government refused to **pay** the **ransom**.* | **ransom demand/note** *There has still been no ransom demand.* | *He's got the **ransom money**.* **2 hold sb for ransom** (*also* **hold sb to ransom** *BrE*) to keep someone prisoner until money is paid: *His daughter was kidnapped and held for ransom.* **3 hold sb to ransom** *BrE* to put someone in a situation where they have no choice and are forced to agree to your demands: *He has accused the nurses of holding the government to ransom by threatening to strike.*

ransom² *v* [T] to pay an amount of money so that someone who is being held as a prisoner is set free: *They were all ransomed and returned unharmed.*

rant /rænt/ *v* [I,T] to talk or complain in a loud excited and rather confused way because you feel strongly about something: **[+about]** *She was still ranting about the unfairness of it all.* | *Why don't you stop* ***ranting and raving*** *for a minute and listen?* —**rant** *n* [C]: *a 15-minute rant about the evils of modern society*

rant·ings /ˈræntɪŋz/ *n* [plural] a long speech in which someone complains about something in a loud excited and rather confused way

rap¹ /ræp/ *n*

1 MUSIC [C,U] (*also* **rap music**) a type of popular music in which the words of a song are not sung, but spoken in time to music with a steady beat: *a popular rap song*

2 KNOCK [C] a series of quick sharp hits or knocks → **tap**: *She was woken by a sharp rap on the door.*

3 CRIME [C] *AmE informal* a statement by the police saying that someone is responsible for a serious crime SYN **charge**: **murder/robbery etc rap** *The kid's been cited twice on drunk-driving raps.* → RAP SHEET

4 take the rap (for sth) to be blamed or punished for a mistake or crime, especially unfairly: *Bo was left to take the rap for Victor's murder.*

5 beat the rap *AmE informal* to avoid being punished for a crime

6 a rap on/over the knuckles a) *informal* a punishment or criticism that is not very severe: *The New York Post received an official rap over the knuckles for the way it reported the story.* **b)** if someone gives a child a rap on the knuckles, they hit them on the back of their hand as a punishment

7 a bum/bad rap *especially AmE informal* unfair treatment or punishment: *Cleveland always* ***gets a bum rap*** *in the press.*

rap² *v* (**rapped**, **rapping**)

1 HIT [I,T] to hit or knock something quickly several times → **tap**: *She rapped the table with her pen.* | **[+on/at]** *Angrily she rapped on his window.* THESAURUS HIT

2 MUSIC [I] to say the words of a rap song

3 CRITICIZE [T] to criticize someone angrily – used especially in news reports SYN **slam**: *a film rapped by critics for its excessive violence*

4 SAY (*also* **rap out**) [T] to say something loudly, suddenly, and in a way that sounds angry: *'Come on,' he rapped impatiently.*

5 rap sb on/over the knuckles (*also* **rap sb's knuckles**) **a)** to punish or criticize someone for something, but not very severely: *He had his knuckles rapped sharply for meddling in foreign policy.* **b)** to punish a child by hitting them on the back of their hand

ra·pa·cious /rəˈpeɪʃəs/ *adj formal* always wanting more money, goods etc than you need or have a right to SYN **greedy**: *rapacious landlords* —**rapaciously** *adv* —**rapacity** /rəˈpæsəti/ *n* [U]

rape¹ /reɪp/ ●●○ *v* [T] to force someone to have sex, especially by using violence → **rapist**: *She had been raped and stabbed.*

rape² ●●○ *n*

1 [C,U] the crime of forcing someone to have sex, especially by using violence: *Police are investigating a series of violent rapes in the town.* | *He was arrested and charged with rape.* | *He always denied that he was guilty of rape.* | *a* ***rape victim*** | *the* ***gang rape*** *of a 17-year-old girl* | *He was convicted of* ***attempted rape***. THESAURUS CRIME

2 [U] (*also* **oilseed rape**) a European plant with yellow flowers, grown as animal food and for its oil SYN **canola** *AmE*

3 the rape of sth the unnecessary destruction of something, especially the environment: *companies which profit from the rape of the Earth*

rap·id /ˈræpɪd/ ●●○ W3 *adj* happening or done very quickly and in a very short time → **fast**, **quick**: *The patient made a rapid recovery.* | **rapid growth/expansion/development/increase** *rapid population growth* | *a period of* ***rapid decline*** | *He fired three times* ***in rapid succession*** (=one after another). THESAURUS FAST —**rapidity** /rəˈpɪdəti/ *n* [U]: *Their debts mounted with alarming rapidity.*

ˈrapid-fire *adj* [only before noun] **1** rapid-fire questions, jokes etc are said quickly, one after another **2** a rapid-fire gun fires shots quickly, one after another

rap·id·ly /ˈræpɪdli/ ●●○ W3 *adv* very quickly and in a very short time: *The disease was spreading more rapidly than expected.* | **rapidly growing/changing/expanding etc** *the rapidly changing world of technology* THESAURUS QUICKLY

ˌrapid-reˈsponse *adj* [only before noun] **1** relating to a person or group of people whose job is to react quickly to a dangerous or important situation, such as a military attack, and find a solution to the problem: **rapid-response forces/team/unit etc 2** relating to something which allows someone to react quickly to information they have received: *a rapid-response system* —**rapid response** *n* [U]

rap·ids /ˈræpədz/ *n* [plural] part of a river where the water looks white because it is moving very fast over rocks

ˌrapid ˈtransit ˌsystem (*also* **ˌrapid ˈtransit**) *n* [C] *AmE* a system for moving people quickly around a city using trains

ra·pi·er /ˈreɪpiə $ -ər/ *n* [C] a long thin sword with two sharp edges

rap·ist /ˈreɪpɪst/ *n* [C] a person who has RAPEd someone (=forced them to have sex, especially using violence): *She later found out that he was a convicted rapist.*

rap·pel /ræˈpel/ *v* (**rappelled**, **rappelling**) [I] *AmE* to go down a cliff or rock by sliding down a rope and touching the rock or cliff with your feet SYN **abseil** *BrE* —**rappel** *n* [C]

rap·per /ˈræpə $ -ər/ *n* [C] someone who speaks the words of a RAP song

rap·port /ræˈpɔː $ -ɔːr/ *n* [singular, U] friendly agreement and understanding between people → **relationship**: **[+with/between]** *He had an excellent rapport with his patients.* | **establish/build up/develop (a) rapport** *He built up a good rapport with the children.*

rap·proche·ment /ræˈprɒʃmɒŋ, ræˈprəʊʃ- $ ˌræproʊʃˈmɑːŋ/ *n* [singular, U] *formal* the establishment of a good relationship between two countries or groups of people, after a period of unfriendly relations: **[+between/with]** *I hope for a rapprochement between our two countries.*

ˈrap sheet *n* [C] *AmE informal* a list kept by the police of someone's criminal activities

rapt /ræpt/ *adj written* so interested in something that you do not notice anything else: *They listened with* ***rapt attention***. | *the* ***rapt expression*** *on his face*

rap·ture /ˈræptʃə $ -ər/ *n* [U] **1** *literary* great excitement and happiness: *The boys gazed up at him in rapture.* **2 be in raptures/go into raptures** *BrE formal* to express or feel great pleasure and happiness about something: **[+over/about/at]** *She went into raptures about the climate, the food, the spring flowers.*

rap·tu·rous /ˈræptʃərəs/ *adj* [usually before noun] expressing great happiness or admiration – used especially in news reports: *She was greeted with* ***rapturous applause***. | **rapturous reception/welcome** *He was given a rapturous welcome.* —**rapturously** *adv*

rare /reə $ rer/ ●●● S3 W2 *adj* (*comparative* **rarer**, *superlative* **rarest**)

1 not seen or found very often, or not happening very often OPP **common** → **unusual**: *This species of plant is becoming increasingly rare.* | *I only saw Helen on the* ***rare occasions*** *when I went into her shop.* | **it is rare (for sb/sth) to do sth** *It is rare to find such an interesting group of people.* | *It is very rare for her to miss a day at school.* THESAURUS UNUSUAL

2 meat that is rare has only been cooked for a short time and is still red → **underdone**, **well-done**: *I like my steak rare.*

3 [only before noun] *BrE old-fashioned* very good or surprising: *We had a* ***rare old*** *time at the party.*

R

rar·e·fied /ˈreərɪfaɪd $ ˈrer-/ *adj* [usually before noun] **1** a rarefied place, organization, or type of activity is only available to or understood by a small group of people – used to show disapproval: *the rarefied atmosphere of academia* **2** rarefied air is the air in high places, which has less oxygen than usual

rare·ly /ˈreəli $ ˈrerli/ ●●● W2 *adv* not often OPP **frequently**: *She very rarely complains.* | *This method is rarely used in modern laboratories.*

GRAMMAR: Word order

• **Rarely** usually comes before a verb: *He **rarely plays** any sports.*
• **Rarely** usually comes after the verb 'be': *She **is rarely** wrong.*
• **Rarely** usually comes after an auxiliary verb such as 'do' or 'have': *I **have rarely** seen someone eat so much.*
• In written English, **rarely** is sometimes used at the beginning of a sentence before an auxiliary, to emphasize that something seems surprising or special: ***Rarely has** a film looked so striking.* | ***Rarely does** such a good investment opportunity arise.*
GRAMMAR GUIDE ▸ ADVERBS

THESAURUS

rarely not often: *These geese are rarely found on inland waters.* | *50% of Britons say they rarely eat meat.*
not (very) often often used in everyday English instead of saying **rarely**: *Tina's not often late.* | *I don't go there very often.* | *It's not often that you get a chance like this.*
seldom rarely. Seldom is more formal than **rarely** and is used especially in written English: *He seldom slept well.* | *They seldom went out.*
hardly ever/scarcely ever almost never: *Ben's nineteen and he's hardly ever at home these days.* | *For some reason, her name was scarcely ever mentioned.*
very occasionally used when you want to emphasize that something only happens a few times over a long period of time: *Very occasionally the temperature drops to below 30.*

rar·ing /ˈreərɪŋ $ ˈrer-/ *adj informal* **1 raring to go** very eager to start an activity: *They woke up early and were raring to go.* **2 raring to do sth** *BrE* very eager to do something: *The children were raring to get outdoors.*

rar·i·ty /ˈreərəti $ ˈrer-/ *n* (*plural* **rarities**) **1 be a rarity** to not happen or exist very often: *Visitors were a rarity in the village.* **2** [C] something that is valuable or interesting because it is rare: *Some of these plants are national rarities.* **3** [U] the quality of being rare: *Such stamps are expensive because of their rarity.*

ras·cal /ˈrɑːskəl $ ˈræs-/ *n* [C] **1** a child who behaves badly but whom you still like **2** *old-fashioned* a dishonest man SYN **scoundrel**

rash[1] /ræʃ/ *adj* if you are rash, you do things too quickly, without thinking carefully about whether they are sensible or not → **foolish**: *Please Jessie, don't do anything rash.* | *Don't go making any **rash decisions** about your future!* | ***It was** rather **rash of** you to lend them your car.* —**rashly** *adv*: *I rashly agreed to look after the children.* —**rashness** *n* [U]

rash[2] *n* [C] **1** a lot of red spots on someone's skin, caused by an illness: *She had a nasty rash on her arm.* | **come/break out in a rash** (=get a rash) *My mother comes out in a rash if she eats seafood.* | **nappy rash** *BrE*, **diaper rash** *AmE*) | *Most babies get nappy rash at some stage.* | *a **heat rash*** (=a rash caused by heat) **2 rash of sth** *informal* a large number of unpleasant events, changes etc within a short time SYN **spate of sth**: *There's been a rash of car thefts in the city centre.*

rash·er /ˈræʃə $ -er/ *n* [C] *BrE* a thin piece of BACON or HAM: **[+of]** *a rasher of bacon* THESAURUS ▸ PIECE

rasp[1] /rɑːsp $ ræsp/ *v* **1** [I,T] to make a rough unpleasant sound: *my father's rasping voice* | *'Stop!' he rasped.* **2** [T] to rub a surface with something rough

rasp[2] *n* **1** [singular] a rough unpleasant sound: **[+of]** *the harsh rasp of her breathing* **2** [C] a metal tool with a rough surface that is used for shaping wood or metal

rasp·ber·ry /ˈrɑːzbəri $ ˈræzberi/ ●●● S3 *n* (*plural* **raspberries**) [C]
1 a soft sweet red berry, or the bush that this berry grows on: *a bowl of fresh raspberries* | *raspberry jam* → see picture at FRUIT[1]
2 *informal* a rude sound that you make by putting your tongue out and blowing: **blow a raspberry** (*also* **give a raspberry** *AmE*): *She blew a raspberry at him as he drove off.*

Ras·ta /ˈræstə/ *n* [C] *informal* a Rastafarian

Ras·ta·fa·ri·an /ˌræstəˈfeəriən◂ $ -ˈfer-/ *n* [C] someone who believes in a religion that is popular in Jamaica, which has Haile Selassie as its religious leader, and has the belief that one day black people will return to Africa —**Rastafarian** *adj* —**Rastafarianism** *n* [U]

Ras·ta·man /ˈræstəmæn/ *n* (*plural* **Rastamen** /-men/) [C] *informal* a male Rastafarian

rat[1] /ræt/ ●●○ *n* [C]
1 an animal that looks like a large mouse with a long tail
2 *spoken* someone who has been disloyal to you or deceived you: *But you promised to help us, you rat!*
3 look like a drowned rat to look very wet and uncomfortable
4 (like) rats leaving the sinking ship used to describe people who leave a company, organization etc when it is in trouble → RAT RACE, RATS, → **smell a rat** at SMELL[2](7)

rat[2] *v* (**ratted**, **ratting**) [I] *informal* **1** if someone rats on you, they tell someone in authority about something wrong that you have done SYN **grass**: **[+on]** *They'll kill you if they find out you've ratted on them!* **2** *BrE* to not do what you had promised to do SYN **go back on**, **renege on**: **[+on]** *He accused the government of ratting on its promises to the disabled.*

rat sb ↔ **out** *AmE informal* if someone rats you out, they are disloyal to you, especially by telling someone in authority about something wrong that you have done: *You can't rat out your teammates.*

ˈrat-arsed *adj BrE informal* extremely drunk

ˌrat-a-ˈtat (*also* **ˌrat-a-tat-ˈtat**) *n* [singular] the sound of knocking, especially on a door

rat·bag /ˈrætbæg/ *n* [C] *BrE informal* an unpleasant person

ratch·et[1] /ˈrætʃɪt/ *n* [C] a machine part consisting of a wheel or bar with teeth on it, which allows movement in only one direction

ratchet[2] *v*

ratchet up *phr v* to increase something by a small amount, especially after a series of increases, or to increase in this way: **ratchet sth ↔ up** *Raising the minimum wage would ratchet up real incomes in general.* | *The debate will ratchet up a notch on Wednesday when the Commission publishes its report.*

rate[1] /reɪt/ ●●● S1 W1 *n* [C]
1 NUMBER the number of times something happens, or the number of examples of something within a certain period: **birth/unemployment/crime etc rate** *Australia's unemployment rate rose to 6.5% in February.* | *a rapid increase in the divorce rate* | **high/low rate of sth** *areas with high rates of crime* | **success/failure rate** (=the number of times that something succeeds or fails) *It's a new technique and the failure rate is quite high.* | *Immediately his **heart rate** (=the number of beats per minute) increased.* | **at a rate of sth** *Asylum seekers were entering Britain at a rate of 1,600 per day.* → BIRTHRATE, DEATH RATE
2 MONEY a charge or payment that is set according to a standard scale: **at (a) ... rate** *people who pay tax at the highest rate* | **at a rate of sth** *They only pay tax at a rate of 5%.* | **interest/exchange/mortgage etc rate** *another reduction in the mortgage rate* | **rate of pay/tax/interest etc** *Nurses are demanding higher rates of pay.* | **special/reduced/lower rate** *Some hotels offer special rates for children.* | **hourly/weekly rate** (=the amount someone is paid per hour or week) *What's the hourly rate for cleaning?* | *$20 an hour is **the going rate*** (=the usual

amount paid) *for private tuition.* → BASE RATE, → **cut-rate** at CUT-PRICE, EXCHANGE RATE, INTEREST RATE, PRIME RATE THESAURUS COST

3 SPEED the speed at which something happens over a period of time: **[+of]** *an attempt to slow down the **rate of** economic **growth*** | **at (a) ... rate** *Children learn at different rates.* | *Our money was running out **at an alarming rate**.* | **at a rate of sth** *Iceland is getting wider at a rate of about 0.5 cm per year.*

4 at any rate *spoken* **a)** used when you are stating one definite fact in a situation that is uncertain or unsatisfactory SYN **anyway**: *They've had technical problems - at any rate that's what they told me.* **b)** used to introduce a statement that is more important than what was said before SYN **anyway**: *Well, at any rate, the next meeting will be on Wednesday.*

5 at this rate *spoken* used to say what will happen if things continue to happen in the same way as now: *At this rate we won't ever be able to afford a holiday.*

6 first-rate/second-rate/third-rate of good, bad, or very bad quality: *a cheap third-rate motel*

7 at a rate of knots *BrE informal* very quickly: *Jack's getting through the ironing at a rate of knots!*

8 rates [plural] a local tax, paid before 1990 by owners of buildings in Britain

rate² ●○○ *v*

1 a) [T] to think that someone or something has a particular quality, value, or standard: *The company seems to **rate** him very **highly*** (=think he is very good). | **be rated (as) sth** *Rhodes is currently rated the top junior player in the country.* **b)** [I] to be considered as having a particular quality, value, or standard: **[+as]** *That rates as one of the best meals I've ever had.*

2 [T] *BrE informal* if you rate someone or something, you think they are very good: *I never rated him.*

3 rate sb's chances (of doing sth) *BrE spoken* if you do not rate someone's chances of achieving something, you do not think that it is likely that they will achieve it: *I don't rate your chances of getting a ticket for the Leeds game.* | *How do you rate your chances* (=do you think you will be successful?) *tomorrow?*

4 [T] *informal especially AmE* to deserve something: *They rate a big thank-you for all their hard work.* | *a local incident that didn't **rate a mention** in the national press*

5 be rated G/U/PG/X etc if a film is rated G, U etc, it is officially judged to be suitable or unsuitable for people of a particular age to see → X-RATED

ˌrate of exˈchange *n* [C] the EXCHANGE RATE

ˌrate of reˈturn *n* [singular] a company's profit for a year, expressed as a PERCENTAGE of the money that the company has spent during the year

rate·pay·er /ˈreɪtpeɪə $ -ər/ *n* [C] *BrE* someone who pays taxes that are used to provide local services

ra·ther /ˈrɑːðə $ ˈræðər/ ●●● S1 W1 *predeterminer, adv*

1 fairly or to some degree: *I was rather surprised to see him with his ex-wife.* | *He was limping rather badly.* | *My own position is **rather different**.* | *Abigail's always been **rather a** difficult child.* BrE | *Isn't it rather late* (=a little too late) *to start changing all the arrangements?* | *Actually I **rather like** the new style of architecture.* BrE | *It was a nice house, but **rather too** small for a family of four.* BrE | *The task proved to be **rather more** difficult than I had expected.* BrE

2 would rather used to say that you would prefer to do or have something: *I'd rather have a quiet night in front of the TV.* | *We could eat later if you would rather do that.* | *'I think you'd better ask her.' **'I'd rather not*** (=I do not want to).*'* | **would rather ... than ...** *I'd rather die than apologize to Helen.* | *I'd rather you didn't go out alone* (=I do not want you to go).

3 rather than instead of: *I think you'd call it a lecture rather than a talk.* | *Rather than go straight on to university why not get some work experience first?* | *Bryson decided to quit rather than accept the new rules.*

4 or rather used before correcting something that you have said, or giving more specific information: *We all went in Vic's car, or rather his father's.*

5 not ... but rather ... used to say that one thing is not true but a different thing is true: *The problem is not their lack of funding, but rather their lack of planning.*

6 rather you/him/her/them than me *spoken* used to say that you are glad that you are not going to be doing something that someone else will be doing

7 Rather! *BrE spoken old-fashioned* used to agree with someone

GRAMMAR: Patterns with rather

- You say that you **would rather do** something: *I would rather play than study.* ✗ Don't say: *I would rather to play than study.*
- You say that you **would rather be** something: *I would rather be rich than poor.* ✗ Don't say: *I would rather to be rich than poor.*
- You say that you **would rather** someone **did** something: *I would rather you **came** in spring.*
- You say that you **would rather** someone **did not do** something, when you don't want them to do it in the future: *I would rather you **didn't say** that.*
- You say that you **would rather** someone **had not done** something, when criticizing them for something they have done in the past: *I would rather you **hadn't said** that.*

rat·i·fy /ˈrætɪfaɪ/ *v* (**ratified**, **ratifying**, **ratifies**) [T] to make a written agreement official by signing it: **ratify a treaty/an agreement/a decision etc** *We hope that the republics will be willing to ratify the treaty.* THESAURUS APPROVE —**ratification** /ˌrætɪfɪˈkeɪʃən/ *n* [U]: *an attempt to delay ratification of the treaty*

R

rat·ing /ˈreɪtɪŋ/ ●●○ *n*

1 [C] a level on a scale that shows how good, important, popular etc someone or something is: *By the end of the year the prime minister's **approval rating*** (=how many people agreed with his policies) *had fallen as low as 12 percent.* → CREDIT RATING

2 the ratings a list that shows which films, television programmes etc are the most popular: *CBS will end the series if it continues to drop in the ratings.*

3 [singular] a letter that shows whether or not a film is suitable for children: *'The Godfather' had an X-rating when it was first shown.*

4 [C] *BrE* a SAILOR in the navy who is not an officer

ra·ti·o /ˈreɪʃiəʊ $ ˈreɪʃoʊ/ ●●○ W3 AWL *n* (*plural* **ratios**) [C] a relationship between two amounts, represented by a pair of numbers showing how much bigger one amount is than the other → **proportion**: **the ratio of sth to sth** *The ratio of nursing staff to doctors is 2:1.* | **[+between]** *the ratio between profits and incomes*

ra·tion¹ /ˈræʃən $ ˈræ-, ˈreɪ-/ ●○○ *n*

1 [C,U] a fixed amount of something that people are allowed to have when there is not enough, for example during a war: **food/clothes/meat etc ration** *the weekly meat ration* | *a coal ration of 4 kg a month* | **on ration** *Even wool was on ration in the war.*

2 rations [plural] a fixed amount of food given to a soldier or member of a group: *emergency food rations* | *The prisoners were queuing for their **meagre rations*** (=small rations). | *We were **on short rations*** (=given a smaller amount than usual).

3 [singular] an amount of something that you think is reasonable or normal: **[+of]** *holidaymakers who like a generous ration of open-air activity*

ration² *v* [T] **1** to control the supply of something because there is not enough: *Fuel was rationed during the war.* GRAMMAR **Ration** is usually passive in this meaning. **2** to allow someone only a small amount of something: *the need to ration health care resources* | *diets which ration fat* | **ration sb/sth to sth** *He rationed himself to 4 cigarettes a day.* | *I try to ration the children's television viewing to an hour a day.*

ra·tion·al /ˈræʃənəl/ ●●○ AWL *adj*
1 rational thoughts, decisions etc are based on reasons rather than emotions OPP **irrational**: *Parents need to be fully informed so they can make a rational decision.* | *I'm sure there's a* ***rational explanation*** *for all this.* | *It's impossible to have a rational conversation with him.*
2 a rational person is able to think calmly and sensibly OPP **irrational**: *Culley was quite rational at the time of her baby's death.*
3 *formal* able to make sensible judgments: *Man is a rational animal.* —**rationally** *adv*: *We were too shocked to* ***think rationally****.* —**rationality** /ˌræʃəˈnæləti/ *n* [U]

ra·tio·nale /ˌræʃəˈnɑːl $ -ˈnæl/ ●○○ *n* [C usually singular] *formal* the reasons for a decision, belief etc: **[+behind/for/of]** *The rationale behind the changes is not at all evident.* | *The rationale for using this teaching method is to encourage student confidence.* THESAURUS ▸ REASON

ra·tion·al·is·m /ˈræʃənəlɪzəm/ AWL *n* [U] *technical* the belief that your actions should be based on scientific thinking rather than emotions or religious beliefs: *philosophers who accept scientific rationalism*

ra·tion·al·ist /ˈræʃənəlɪst/ *n* [C] someone who bases their actions on rationalism —**rationalist**, **rationalistic** /ˌræʃənəˈlɪstɪk◂/ *adj*

ra·tion·al·ize (*also* **-ise** *BrE*) /ˈræʃənəlaɪz/ AWL *v* [I,T] **1** if you rationalize behaviour that is wrong, you invent an explanation for it so that it does not seem as bad: *When he fouls up, Glen always finds a way to rationalize what he's done.* **2** *BrE* to make a business more effective by removing unnecessary workers, equipment etc: *Our systems will be rationalized over the coming months.* —**rationalization** /ˌræʃənəlaɪˈzeɪʃən $ -lə-/ *n* [C,U]: *a major rationalization of the aircraft industry*

ra·tion·ing /ˈræʃənɪŋ/ *n* [U] when the amount of food, petrol etc that people are allowed to have is limited by the government: **fuel/clothes/food etc rationing** *News of bread rationing created panic buying.*

ˈrat race *n* **the rat race** the unpleasant situation experienced by people working in big cities, when they continuously compete for success and have a lot of STRESS in their lives: **get out of/quit the rat race** *the story of a couple who quit the rat race*

ˈrat run *n* [C] *BrE* a quiet street that drivers use as a quick way of getting to a place, rather than using a main road → **short cut**: *The road has become a rat run for traffic avoiding the town centre.*

rats /ræts/ *interjection informal* used to show annoyance: *Rats! I forgot to buy any bread.*

ˈrats' tails *n BrE* **in rats' tails** if your hair is in rats' tails, it hangs down in separate pieces because it is wet or dirty

rat·tan /rəˈtæn/ *n* [U] the plant used to make WICKER furniture: *rattan chairs*

rat·tle¹ /ˈrætl/ ●○○ *v*
1 [I,T] if you rattle something, or if it rattles, it shakes and makes a quick series of short sounds: *Dan banged on her door and rattled the handle.* | *The window rattled in the wind.* | *Bottles rattled as he stacked the beer crates.*
2 [I] if a vehicle rattles somewhere, it travels there while making a rattling sound: **[+along/past/over etc]** *The cart rattled along the stony road.* | *An old blue van rattled into view.*
3 [T] *informal* to make someone lose confidence or become nervous: *His mocking smile rattled her more than his anger.* | *It was hard not to* ***get rattled*** *when the work piled up.* | *His confidence was rattled by the accident.*
4 rattle sb's cage *spoken informal* to annoy someone – used humorously: *Who rattled your cage?*
rattle around *phr v BrE* to live in a building that is much too big for you: **[+in]** *Dad and I rattled around miserably in the house after Mum died.*
rattle sth ↔ **off** *phr v* to say several pieces of information or a list quickly and easily from memory: *Chris rattled off some statistics about the teams.*
rattle on *phr v BrE informal* to talk quickly for a long time about boring things SYN **go on**: **[+about]** *Nancy would rattle on for hours about her grandchildren.*
rattle through sth *phr v BrE informal* to do something quickly because you want to finish it
rattle up sth *phr v BrE* if a sports player rattles up a number of points, they get that number of points very quickly: *The West Indies had rattled up 411 for 5 when rain stopped play.*

rattle² *n* **1** [C,U] a short repeated sound, made when something shakes: *They listened anxiously to every rattle and creak in the house.* | **[+of]** *the rattle of chains* | *the faint rattle of distant gunfire* → DEATH RATTLE THESAURUS ▸ SOUND
2 [C] a baby's toy that makes a noise when it is shaken
3 [C] *BrE* an object that people shake to make a loud noise and show excitement or encouragement, for example at ceremonies or sports games

rat·tler /ˈrætlə $ -ər/ *n* [C] *informal* a rattlesnake

rat·tle·snake /ˈrætlsneɪk/ *n* [C] a poisonous American snake that shakes its tail to make a noise when it is angry

rat·tle·trap /ˈrætlˌtræp/ *adj* [only before noun] *AmE* a rattletrap vehicle is old and in bad condition

rat·tling /ˈrætlɪŋ/ *adv* **a rattling good yarn/story/read** *BrE old-fashioned* a good exciting story

rat·ty /ˈræti/ *adj* **1** *BrE informal* becoming annoyed quickly or easily SYN **irritable**: *I feel guilty about* ***getting ratty*** *with the children.* **2** *AmE informal* dirty and in bad condition → **shabby**: *a ratty old sofa* | *ratty hair*

rau·cous /ˈrɔːkəs $ ˈrɒː-/ *adj* **1** sounding unpleasantly loud: *He burst into* ***raucous laughter****.* | *raucous cheers* THESAURUS ▸ LOUD **2** impolite, noisy, and violent: *A group of raucous students spilled out of the bar.* | *The atmosphere became increasingly raucous.* —**raucously** *adv*

raunch·y /ˈrɔːntʃi $ ˈrɒː-/ *adj informal* intended to be sexually exciting, in a way that seems immoral or shocking → **sexy**: *a raunchy magazine* | *The show was quite raunchy.*

rav·age /ˈrævɪdʒ/ *v* [T] to damage something very badly: *a country ravaged by civil war* | *His health was gradually ravaged by drink and drugs.* GRAMMAR **Ravage** is usually passive.

rav·ag·es /ˈrævɪdʒɪz/ *n literary* **the ravages of sth** the damage caused by something: *a building that has survived* ***the ravages of time*** | *the ravages of war*

rave¹ /reɪv/ *v* [I] **1 rave about/over sth** to talk about something you enjoy or admire in an excited way SYN **enthuse**: *Now I understand why travelers rave about Lapland.* | *The customers were raving over our homemade chili.* **2** to talk in an angry, uncontrolled, or crazy way: **[+at]** *He started raving at me* | **[+on]** *BrE*: *Lisa raved on about how awful it all was.* | *He was still* ***ranting and raving*** *the next morning.*

rave² *n* [C] **1** a big event where people dance to loud music with a strong beat and often take drugs: *an all-night rave* | *rave music* | *rave parties* → RAVER
2 strong praise for a new play, book etc: *The play got raves from the critics.*

rave³ *adj* **rave reviews/notices/reports** strong praise for a new play, book etc, especially in a newspaper or magazine: **win/receive/earn rave reviews** *The performance earned them rave reviews from critics.*

ra·ven¹ /ˈreɪvən/ *n* [C] a large shiny black bird

raven² *adj* [only before noun] *literary* raven hair is black and shiny

rav·e·ning /ˈrævənɪŋ/ *adj literary* ravening animals are hungry and dangerous: *a pack of ravening wolves*

rav·e·nous /ˈrævənəs/ *adj* very hungry → **starving**: *I'm absolutely ravenous.* | *a ravenous appetite* —**ravenously** *adv*: *I was* ***ravenously hungry****.*

rav·er /ˈreɪvə $ -ər/ *n* [C] *BrE informal* **1** someone who goes to a RAVE: *Police believe many of the ravers were on drugs.* **2** someone who has an exciting social life and goes to a lot of parties

ra·vine /rəˈviːn/ *n* [C] a deep narrow valley with steep sides SYN **gorge**

rav·ing¹ /ˈreɪvɪŋ/ *adj* [only before noun] *informal* **1** talking or behaving in a crazy way: *a **raving lunatic*** **2** *especially BrE* used to emphasize that someone or something has a lot of a particular quality: *She was no **raving beauty**, but at least she looked smart.*

raving² *adv* **(stark) raving mad/bonkers** *informal* completely crazy

rav·ings /ˈreɪvɪŋz/ *n* [plural] crazy things that someone says: **[+of]** *the ravings of a demented man*

rav·i·o·li /ˌræviˈəʊli $ -ˈoʊli/ *n* [U] small PASTA squares filled with meat or cheese

rav·ish /ˈrævɪʃ/ *v* [T] *literary* **1** to force a woman to have sex SYN **rape** **2** to badly harm something: *a landscape ravished by drought*

rav·ish·ing /ˈrævɪʃɪŋ/ *adj literary* very beautiful SYN **stunning**: *She looked ravishing.* | *a ravishing smile* —**ravishingly** *adv*

raw¹ /rɔː $ rɒː/ ●●● W3 *adj*

1 FOOD not cooked: *raw meat* | *grated raw carrots* | *Cabbage can be eaten raw.*

2 SUBSTANCES raw substances are in a natural state and not treated or prepared for use → **refined**: *raw silk* | *In its raw state, cocoa is very bitter.* | *Raw sewage had been dumped in the river.* | *The cost of our **raw materials** has risen significantly.*

3 INFORMATION raw information is collected but not organized, examined, or developed: *software to convert **raw data** into usable information* | *His time here provided the **raw material** for his novel.* | *Warhol used everyday items as the **raw ingredients** of his art.*

4 EMOTIONS raw feelings are strong and natural, but not fully controlled: *raw passion* | *Linda didn't want to see Roy while her emotions were still raw.* | *It took raw courage to admit she was wrong.*

5 BODY if a part of your body is raw, the skin there is red and painful: *The skin on my feet was rubbed raw.*

6 INEXPERIENCED not experienced or not fully trained: *Most of our soldiers are raw recruits.*

7 touch/hit a raw nerve to upset someone by something you say: *Seeing his face, Joanne realized she'd touched a raw nerve.*

8 raw deal unfair treatment: *Customers are getting a raw deal and are rightly angry.*

9 WEATHER very cold: *She shivered in the raw morning air.*

10 ART music, art, language etc that is raw is simple, direct, and powerful, but not fully developed: *Her voice has a raw poetic beauty.* | *His early sketches are raw and unpretentious.*

11 raw talent someone with raw talent is naturally good at something, but has not developed their ability yet: *He has the raw talent to become a star.*

12 raw edge the edge of a piece of material before it has been sewn: *Turn over the raw edges and stitch.* —**rawness** *n* [U]

raw² *n* **1 in the raw a)** seen in a way that does not hide cruelty and violence: *He went on the streets to experience **life in the raw**.* | *It was my first exposure to India in the raw.* **b)** *informal* not wearing any clothes SYN **in the nude**: *sunbathing in the raw* **2 catch/touch sb on the raw** *BrE* to say or do something that upsets someone: *She flinched, caught on the raw by his question.*

raw·hide /ˈrɔːhaɪd $ ˈrɒː-/ *n* [U] leather that is in its natural state

ray /reɪ/ ●○○ *n* [C]

1 a straight narrow beam of light from the sun or moon: *The room darkened as a cloud hid the sun's rays.* | **[+of]** *Rays of light filtered through the trees.*

2 a beam of heat, electricity, or other form of energy → COSMIC RAY, GAMMA RAY, X-RAY¹

3 a ray of hope/light etc something that provides a small amount of hope or happiness in a difficult situation: *a treatment that offers a ray of hope for cancer sufferers*

4 a ray of sunshine someone who is happy and makes a difficult situation seem better

5 catch some/a few rays *informal* to sit or lie in the sun: *Let's go out and catch a few rays.*

6 a large flat sea fish with a long pointed tail

ray·on /ˈreɪɒn $ -ɑːn/ *n* [U] a smooth artificial cloth used for making clothes: *a rayon shirt*

raze /reɪz/ *v* [T] to completely destroy a town or building: *In 1162 Milan was **razed to the ground** by imperial troops.* GRAMMAR **Raze** is usually passive.

ra·zor /ˈreɪzə $ -ər/ ●○○ *n*

1 [C] a tool with a sharp blade, used to remove hair from your skin → **shaver**: *an electric razor* | *a disposable razor*

2 be on a razor/razor's edge *BrE* to be in a difficult position where a mistake could be dangerous: *Politically we are on a razor edge.*

ˈrazor blade *n* [C] a small flat blade with a very sharp edge, used in a razor

ˌrazor-ˈsharp *adj* **1** very sharp: *razor-sharp teeth* THESAURUS▸ SHARP **2** intelligent and able to think quickly: *He has a razor-sharp mind.*

ˌrazor-ˈthin *adj AmE* **razor-thin victory/margin** in an election, a razor-thin victory is won by only a small number of votes

ˈrazor ˌwire *n* [U] strong wire with sharp edges, used to keep people out of a building, area of land etc

razz /ræz/ *v* [T] *AmE informal* to make jokes that insult or embarrass someone SYN **tease**: *Eddie was razzed by his teammates after the game.*

raz·zle /ˈræzəl/ *n* **be/go (out) on the razzle** *BrE spoken informal* to go somewhere such as a party, bar etc to enjoy yourself

razz·ma·tazz /ˌræzməˈtæz/ (*also* **raz·za·ma·tazz** /ˌræzə-/) (*also* **ˈrazzle-ˌdazzle**) *n* [U] noisy exciting activity that is intended to attract people's attention: *the razzmatazz of show business*

RC the written abbreviation of ***Roman Catholic***

-rd /d $ rd/ *suffix* used with ORDINAL numbers ending in 3, except 13: *the 3rd* (=third) *of June* | *his 53rd birthday*

Rd. (*also* **Rd** *BrE*) the written abbreviation of ***Road***, used in addresses

R.D. /ˌɑː ˈdiː $ ˌɑːr-/ *n* [U] *AmE* (***rural delivery***) the postal system for country areas

RDA /ˌɑː diː ˈeɪ $ ˌɑːr-/ *n* [singular] (***recommended daily allowance***) the amount of substances such as VITAMINS that you should have every day

re¹ /riː/ *prep written formal* used in business letters to introduce the subject: *re your enquiry of the 19th October* THESAURUS▸ ABOUT

re² /reɪ/ *n* [singular] the second note in a musical SCALE → SOL-FA

re- /riː/ *prefix* **1** again: *They're rebroadcasting the play.* **2** again in a better way: *She asked me to redo the essay.* **3** back to a former state: *After years of separation they were finally reunited.*

're /ə $ ər/ the short form of 'are'

RE /ˌɑːr ˈiː/ *n* [U] *BrE* (***Religious Education***) a subject taught in schools

reach¹ /riːtʃ/ ●●● S1 W1 *v*

1 DEVELOPMENT [T] if someone or something reaches a particular point in their development or in a process or competition, they get to that point: *Chelsea could reach the final of the European Cup.* | **reach the point/level/stage etc** *I had reached the point where I was earning a good salary.* | *The kids have reached the age when they can care for themselves.*

> **REGISTER**
> In everyday English, people often use **get to** rather than **reach**: *The kids have **got to** the age where they can care for themselves.*

2 RATE/AMOUNT [T] if something reaches a particular rate, amount etc, it increases until it is at that rate or amount: *By 2008, that figure is expected to reach 7 million.* | *wind speeds reaching up to 180 mph* | *Prices rose steadily to **reach record levels**.*

3 AGREE [T] to agree on something or decide something

R

after a lot of discussion or thought: **reach a decision/agreement etc** *The theatre has reached an agreement with striking actors.* | *It took the jury three days to **reach** a **verdict**.* | *The talks will continue until a **conclusion** is **reached**.*
4 reach a target/goal to achieve what you wanted to achieve: *We hope to reach our £1 million target by the autumn.*
5 TOUCH **a)** [I,T always + adv/prep] to move your arm in order to touch or lift something with your hand: *She reached into her bag and produced a business card.* | *He reached down to help her to her feet.* | **[+for]** *Kelly reached for his gun.* | *Luisa **reached out** her **hand** to stroke the cat.* **b)** [I,T not in progressive] to touch something by stretching out your arm: *It's no good – I can't reach.* | *She's too small to reach the table.* **c)** [T] to get something from a high place by stretching up your arm: **reach sth down** *She fell while reaching down a vase from the top shelf.*
6 LENGTH/HEIGHT [I always + adv/prep, T not in progressive] to be big enough, long enough etc to get to a particular point: *The phone lead isn't long enough to reach the bedroom.* | *a skirt that reaches halfway down her legs* | **reach as far as sth/reach down to sth** *Her hair reaches down to her waist.*
7 ARRIVE [T] to arrive at a place: *We reached London late at night.* | *The pyramids can be reached by public transport.*
THESAURUS ARRIVE

REGISTER
In everyday English, people often use **get to** rather than **reach**: *We **got to** the airport just in time.* | *You can **get to** the pyramids by public transport.*

8 SPEAK TO SB [T] if you reach someone, you succeed in speaking to them on the telephone SYN **contact**: *I can probably reach him on his mobile.*
9 BE SEEN/HEARD [T] if a message, television programme etc reaches a lot of people, they hear it or see it: *Cable TV **reaches** a huge **audience**.*
10 INFORMATION [T] if information reaches you, you hear about it: *The news reached us in Lahore.*
11 COMMUNICATE [T] to succeed in making someone understand or accept what you tell them SYN **get through to**: *I just can't seem to reach Ed anymore.*
12 reach for the stars to aim for something that is very difficult to achieve
reach out to sb *phr v* to show people that you are interested in them and want to listen to them: *So far, his administration has failed to reach out to hard line Republicans.*

GRAMMAR: Comparison

reach
- You **reach** a city, country, or other place: *The climbers reached the summit of the mountain.*
- You **reach here/there**: *You should reach there around 9.45 a.m.*
- You **reach home**: *She finally reached home late at night.* ✗ Don't say: *reach to a place* | *reach to here/there* | *reach to home*

arrive
- You **arrive in** a city or country: *We arrived in London at 2 a.m.*
- You **arrive at** a place such as a house, hotel, or airport: *They arrived at the airport at 10.30.*
- You **arrive home**: *He arrived home at midnight.*
- You **arrive here/there/back**: *Call me when you arrive there.* ✗ Don't say: *arrive to a place* | *arrive to home* | *arrive to here/there*

get
- You **get to** a city, country, or other place: *We got to London at 2 a.m.* | *We got to the airport at 10.30.*
- You **get home**: *He got home at midnight.*
- You **get here/there/back**: *Call me when you get there.* ✗ Don't say: *get to home* | *get to here/there*

reach² ●○○ *n*
1 [singular, U] the distance that you can stretch out your arm to touch something: **out of/beyond (sb's) reach** *Keep chemicals out of the reach of children.* | **within reach (of sb)** *Keep a glass of water within reach.*
2 [singular, U] **within (easy) reach of sth** close to a place: *The beach is within easy reach of the hotel.*
3 [singular, U] the limit of someone's power or ability to do something: **beyond the reach of sb** *He lives in Paraguay, well beyond the reach of the British authorities.*
4 reaches [plural] **a)** the parts of a place that are furthest from the centre: **the further/outer reaches of sth** *the further reaches of the jungle* **b)** the straight part of a river between two bends: *the **upper reaches of** the Nile*
5 the higher/lower reaches of sth the high or low levels of an organization or system: *They lingered in the lower reaches of the Football League.*

re·act /riˈækt/ ●●● S3 W3 AWL *v* [I]
1 BEHAVIOUR/FEELINGS to behave in a particular way or show a particular emotion because of something that has happened or been said → **respond**: **[+to]** *How did Wilson react to your idea?* | *He **reacted angrily** to the suggestion that he had lied.* | *She **reacted** very **badly** (=was very upset) when her parents split up.* | *You have to **react quickly** to circumstances.* | **react by doing sth** *The government reacted by declaring all strikes illegal.* → OVERREACT
2 CHEMICALS *technical* if a chemical substance reacts, it changes when it is mixed with another chemical substance: **[+with]** *The calcium reacts with sulphur in the atmosphere.*
3 PRICES if prices or financial markets react to something that happens, they increase or decrease in value because of it: **[+to]** *Oil prices **reacted sharply** (=reacted a lot) to news of the crisis in the Middle East.* | *The market reacted favourably to the announcement.*
4 BECOME ILL to become ill when a chemical or drug goes into your body, or when you eat a particular kind of food → **respond**: **[+to]** *Quite a lot of children **react badly** to antibiotics.*
react against sth *phr v* to show that you dislike someone else's ideas or ways of doing something, by deliberately doing the opposite: *He **reacted strongly** against his religious upbringing.*

re·ac·tion /riˈækʃən/ ●●● S2 W2 AWL *n*
1 TO A SITUATION/EVENT [C,U] something that you feel or do because of something that has happened or been said → **response**: *What was Jeff's reaction when you told him about the job?* | **[+to]** *the government's reaction to the fuel crisis* | **in reaction to sth** *An emergency fund was set up in reaction to the famine.*
2 MOVING QUICKLY **reactions** [plural] your ability to move quickly when something dangerous happens suddenly: *a skilled driver with very **quick reactions***
3 TO FOOD/DRUGS [C] if you have a reaction to a drug or to something you have eaten, it makes you ill: **[+to]** *a reaction to the immunization* | **have/suffer a reaction** *She had a **severe allergic reaction** to the drug.* | **cause/bring on/trigger a reaction** *Certain foods are more likely than others to cause **allergic reactions**.*
4 SCIENCE [C,U] **a)** a chemical change that happens when two or more substances are mixed together: *a **chemical reaction** in the soil* **b)** a physical force that is the result of an equally strong physical force in the opposite direction
5 CHANGE [singular] a change in people's attitudes, behaviour, fashions etc that happens because they disapprove of the way in which things were done in the past: **[+against]** *a reaction against the traditional values of the nineteenth century*
6 AGAINST CHANGE [U] *formal* strong and unreasonable opposition to all social and political changes: *The revolutionary movement was crushed by **the forces of reaction**.*
→ CHAIN REACTION

COLLOCATIONS

ADJECTIVES/NOUN + reaction

sb's first/initial/immediate reaction *His first reaction was to laugh.*

sb's gut reaction *informal* (=what they feel or decide immediately, before thinking) *You must trust your gut reactions.*
sb's instinctive reaction (=what they do immediately, before thinking) *Often your instinctive reaction is to blame someone else.*
a natural reaction *Anger is a natural reaction if you feel undervalued.*
a knee-jerk reaction (=an immediate reaction that happens without sensible thinking) *Environmentalists have a knee-jerk reaction against any development.*
an emotional reaction (=showing strong emotion, especially by crying) *I was surprised by her emotional reaction to the news.*
a positive/favourable reaction (=showing that someone agrees or likes something) | **a negative reaction** (=showing that someone disagrees or dislikes something) | **mixed reactions** (=some positive and some negative reactions) | **a violent/angry reaction** | **a delayed reaction** (=a reaction that comes some time after an event) | **the public reaction** (=what the public think about something that happens)

VERBS

provoke/produce/bring a reaction *The decision provoked an angry reaction from the local tourist industry.*
get a reaction *We didn't know what kind of reaction we would get.*
gauge sb's reaction (=judge or find out someone's reaction)

re·ac·tion·a·ry[1] /riˈækʃənəri $ -ʃəneri/ AWL *adj* very strongly opposed to any social or political change – used to show disapproval: *reactionary attitudes*

reactionary[2] AWL *n* (*plural* **reactionaries**) [C] someone who strongly opposes any social or political change – used to show disapproval

re·ac·tiv·ate /riˈæktɪveɪt/ AWL *v* [T] to make something start working again

re·ac·tive /riˈæktɪv/ AWL *adj* **1** reacting to events or situations rather than starting or doing new things yourself: *a reactive foreign policy* **2** *technical* a reactive substance changes when it is mixed with another substance: *a highly reactive chemical*

re·ac·tor /riˈæktə $ -ər/ ●○○ AWL *n* [C] a NUCLEAR REACTOR

read[1] /riːd/ ●●● S1 W1 *v* (*past tense and past participle* **read** /red/)
1 WORDS/BOOKS [I,T] to look at written words and understand what they mean: *I can't read your writing.* | *She picked up the letter and read it.* | *Read the instructions carefully before you start.* | *children who are just learning to read and write* | *Her books are quite **widely read*** (=read by a lot of people). | *When I was young, I **read** every one of his books **from cover to cover*** (=read all of something because you are very interested).
2 FIND INFORMATION [I,T not in progressive] to find out information from books, newspapers etc: *You can't believe everything you read in the papers.* | **[+about]** *Did you read about what happened to that guy in Florida?* | **[+of]** *I was shocked when I read of his death.* | **read (that)** *I read last week that the disease is on the increase.*
3 READ AND SPEAK [I,T] to say the words in a book, newspaper etc so that people can hear them: **read sb sth** *Daddy, will you read me a story?* | **read (sth) to sb** *Our mother reads to us every evening.* | *Teachers should read more poetry to children.* | *He glanced at the letter and began to **read** it **aloud**.*
4 MUSIC/MAPS ETC [T] to look at signs or pictures and understand what they mean: *He plays the violin very well but can't actually read music.* | *Are you any good at map reading?*
5 COMPUTER [T] *technical* if a computer can read a DISK, it can take the information that is on the disk and put it into its memory
6 UNDERSTAND STH IN A PARTICULAR WAY [T always + adv/prep] to understand a situation, remark etc in one of several possible ways SYN **interpret**: *I wasn't sure how to read his silence.* | **read sth as sth** *She shook her head, and I read this as a refusal.* | *The poem can be read as a protest against war.* | **read sth well/accurately** (=understand something correctly) *He had accurately read the mood of the nation.*
7 HAVE WORDS ON [T not in progressive] used to say what words are on a sign, in a letter etc SYN **say**: *A sign on the outer door read: 'No Entry'.*
8 STYLE OF WRITING [I] if something reads well, badly etc, it has been written well, badly etc: *I think in general the report **reads well**.*
9 read sth as/for sth to replace one word or number with another one, usually with the correct one: *Please read £50 as £15.* | *For 'November'* (=instead of November) *on line 6, read 'September'.*
10 MEASURING [T] **a)** to look at the number or amount shown on a measuring instrument: *Someone should be coming to read the gas meter.* **b)** if a measuring instrument reads a particular number, it shows that number: *The thermometer read 46 degrees.*
11 AT UNIVERSITY [I,T] *BrE* to study a subject at a university: *I read history at Cambridge.* | **[+for]** *He wants to read for a law degree.*

REGISTER
In everyday British English, people usually say that someone **does** a subject at university: *I **did** history at Cambridge.* | *He wants to **do** a law degree.*

12 take it as read (that) *especially BrE* to feel certain that something is true although no one has told you it is true SYN **assume**: *You can take it as read that we will support the project.*
13 take sth as read to accept that a report or statement is correct without reading it or discussing it: *We'll take the secretary's report as read.*
14 read between the lines to guess someone's real feelings from something they say or write, when they do not tell you directly: *Reading between the lines, I'd say Robert's not very happy.*
15 read sb's mind/thoughts to guess what someone else is thinking: *'Want some coffee?' 'You read my mind.'*
16 can read sb like a book if you can read someone like a book, you know them so well that you immediately know what they are thinking or feeling
17 read sb's palm to look carefully at someone's hand, in order to find out about their future
18 read sb's lips to understand what someone is saying by watching the way their lips move. People who cannot hear do this. → LIP-READ
19 read my lips *spoken* used to tell someone that you really mean what you are saying: *Read my lips: I will not let you down.*
20 do you read me? *spoken* used to ask someone whether they can hear you when you are speaking to them by radio
21 well-read/widely-read someone who is well-read has read a lot of books and knows a lot about many subjects: *She is intelligent and extremely well-read.* → READING, → **read (sb) the riot act** at RIOT[1](4)

GRAMMAR: Patterns with read

read sth in sth
• You **read** something **in** a book, newspaper, magazine etc: *I read the interview in the newspaper.*
✗ Don't say: *read something on a book, newspaper, magazine etc*
• You **read** something **in** a particular chapter of a book, or **in** the introduction: *In this chapter you can read about different types of diet.*
• You **read** something **in** the instructions or **in** a recipe: *I read in the instructions that you are supposed to boil the pasta for six minutes.*

read sth on sth
• You **read** something **on** the Internet or **on** a website: *She read the story on the Internet.*

R

• You **read** something **on** a page: *You can read about his life story on page 12.*
• You **read** something **on** a train, bus, plane etc: *I like reading on the train – it helps to pass the time.* ✗ Don't say: *read something in a train, bus, plane etc*

THESAURUS

read to look at and understand the words in a book, magazine, letter etc for interest, enjoyment, or study: *What book are you reading at the moment? | I usually read the newspaper on the way to work.*
flick/flip/leaf through sth to turn the pages of a book, magazine etc quickly, looking for things that might interest you: *While I was waiting, I flicked through a magazine.*
browse through sth to spend time looking through a book, magazine etc without any clear purpose, looking for things that might interest you: *Would you like to browse through our holiday brochure?*
skim/scan (through) sth to read something quickly to get the main ideas or find a particular piece of information: *I want you to skim through the article and write a short summary of it. | Tony scanned the menu for a vegetarian option.*
pore over sth to read something very carefully for a long time: *They spent weeks poring over guidebooks and planning their holiday.*
devour sth /dɪˈvaʊə $ -ˈvaʊr/ to read something quickly and eagerly: *Her young fans devour her books.*
dip into sth to read short parts of something: *It's a book you can dip into rather than read from cover to cover.*
plough/wade through sth to read something long and boring: *He's upstairs ploughing through financial reports. | I can't possibly wade through all this.*
surf the Net/Internet/Web to look quickly through information on the Internet, stopping to read what interests you: *He surfed the Net, looking for jobs.*

read sth ↔ **back** *phr v* to read out loud something that you have just written down: **[+to]** *Can you read that last bit back to me?*
read for sth *phr v* to say some of the words that are said by a particular character in a play, as a test of your ability to act
read sth **into** sth *phr v* to think that a situation, action etc has a meaning or importance that it does not really have: *It was only a casual remark. I think you're reading too much into it.*
read sth ↔ **out** *phr v* to read and say words that are written down, so that people can hear: *Why don't you read out the name of the winner?* | **[+to]** *He read the last few sentences out to me.*
read sth ↔ **through/over** *phr v* to read something carefully from beginning to end in order to check details or find mistakes SYN **check over/through**: *Read the contract over carefully before you sign it. | Spend a couple of minutes just reading through your essay.*
read up on sth (*also* **read sth ↔ up** *BrE*) *phr v* to read a lot about something because you will need to know about it: *You'll enjoy traveling more if you read up on the history of the countries you'll be visiting.*

read² *n* [singular] *informal* **1** *BrE* if you have a read, you spend time reading: *I sat down to* ***have a*** *nice quiet* ***read****.* | **[+of]** *I had a quick read of the report before I left.* **2 a good read** something that you enjoy reading: *I thought his last book was a really good read.*

read·a·ble /ˈriːdəbəl/ *adj* **1** interesting and enjoyable to read, and easy to understand OPP **unreadable**: **very/highly/eminently readable** *The book is informative and highly readable.* **2** writing or print that is readable is clear and easy to read SYN **legible** —**readability** /ˌriːdəˈbɪləti/ *n* [U] → MACHINE-READABLE

read·er /ˈriːdə $ -ər/ ●●● S3 W2 *n* [C]
1 SB WHO READS someone who reads books, or who reads in a particular way: *The book will appeal to young readers. | I've always been an* ***avid reader*** (=someone who reads a lot). | **[+of]** *He's a great reader of crime fiction.* | **a fast/slow reader**
2 OF A NEWSPAPER/MAGAZINE someone who reads a particular newspaper or magazine regularly: *The newspaper gradually lost readers during the 1980s.*
3 BOOK an easy book for children who are learning to read or for people who are learning a foreign language
4 TEACHER **Reader** an important teacher in a British university: **[+in]** *a Reader in Sociology at Bristol University*
5 EQUIPMENT *technical* a piece of electronic equipment that can read information that is stored or recorded somewhere, for example on a card → MIND READER, NEWSREADER

read·er·ship /ˈriːdəʃɪp $ -ər-/ *n* [C,U] **1** all the people who read a particular newspaper or magazine regularly: **[+of]** *a magazine with a readership of 60,000 | They are hoping that the paper will have quite a* ***wide readership****.* **2** the job that a Reader has in a British university: *a readership in linguistics*

read·i·ly /ˈredəli/ ●●○ W3 *adv*
1 quickly and easily: *Boats are* ***readily available*** *to visitors. | The information is* ***readily accessible*** *on the Internet.*
2 quickly, willingly, and without complaining: *Jack readily agreed to help.*

read·i·ness /ˈredinəs/ *n* **1** [U] when you are prepared for something, or when something is ready to be used: **in readiness (for sth)** *They stacked the firewood in readiness for the evening campfire.* **2** [singular, U] willingness to do something: **readiness to do sth** *He stressed the government's readiness to take tough action against terrorists.*

read·ing /ˈriːdɪŋ/ ●●● W2 *n*
1 ACTIVITY/SKILL [U] the activity or skill of understanding written words: *She loves reading. | Reading is taught using a combination of several methods.*
2 BOOKS [U] books and other things that you can read: *Her main reading seems to be mystery novels. | a bit of* ***light reading*** (=things that are easy and enjoyable to read) *for my holiday | There's a list of* ***further reading*** (=other things you can read) *at the end of each chapter. | a supply of interesting* ***reading material***
3 ACT OF READING [singular] when you read something: *The book is quite difficult* ***on first reading****. | a* ***close reading*** *of the text* (=when you read it very carefully)
4 UNDERSTANDING [C] your way of understanding what a particular statement, situation, event etc means SYN **interpretation**: **[+of]** *What's your reading of the government's response to this crisis?*
5 TO A GROUP [C] **a)** an occasion when a piece of literature is read to a group of people: *a poetry reading at the bookstore* **b)** a piece of writing, especially from the Bible, that is read to a group of people: *The first reading is from Corinthians I, Chapter 3.*
6 make (for) interesting/fascinating/compelling etc reading to be interesting etc to read: *Your report made fascinating reading.*
7 MEASUREMENT [C] a number or amount shown on a measuring instrument: *We* ***take*** *temperature* ***readings*** *every two hours.*
8 IN PARLIAMENT [C] one of the occasions in the British Parliament or the US Congress when a suggested new law is discussed: *the second reading of the Energy Bill*

re·ad·just /ˌriːəˈdʒʌst/ AWL *v* **1** [I] to get used to a new situation, job, or way of life: *It takes time to readjust after a divorce.* | **[+to]** *Former soldiers often struggle to readjust to life outside the army.* **2** [T] to make a small change to something or to its position: *He readjusted his glasses. | We may need to readjust these figures slightly.* —**readjustment** *n* [C,U]

ˌread-only ˈmemory *n* [U] *technical* ROM

ˈread-out *n* [C] information that is produced by a computer and shown on a screen → **printout**: *a read-out of all the sales figures*

read·y[1] /ˈredi/ ●●● S1 W2 *adj*
1 PREPARED [not before noun] if you are ready, you are prepared for what you are going to do: *Come on. Aren't you ready yet?* | *When the doorbell rang he was* ***ready and waiting***. | **ready to do sth** *Everything's packed, and we're ready to leave.* | *Why does it take you so long to* ***get ready*** *to go out?* | **ready for sth** *I don't feel that I'm ready for my driving test yet.* | *I felt strong, fit, and* ***ready for anything***. | **ready with sth** *At the end of the lecture, I was ready with questions.* | **make ready** (=prepare to start doing something) *We made ready for our journey home.* | **when you're ready** (=said to tell someone that you are ready for them to start doing something) | **ready when you are** (=said to tell someone that you are ready to do what you have arranged to do together) → PREPARE
2 FOR IMMEDIATE USE [not before noun] if something is ready, someone has prepared it and you can use it immediately: *When will supper be ready?* | **ready to use/eat etc** *The computer is now set up and ready to use.* | **ready for sth** *Is everything ready for the exhibition?* | *I've got to* ***get*** *a room* ***ready*** *for our guests.*
3 have sth ready to have something near you so that you can use it if you need to: *I had my calculator ready.*
4 be/feel ready for sth *spoken* to need or want something as soon as possible: *I'm really ready for a vacation.*
5 be ready to do sth *informal* to be likely to do something soon: *She looked ready to burst into tears.*
6 WILLING [not before noun] very willing to do something: **ready to do sth** *He was always ready to help us.* | *She was* ***ready and willing*** *to work hard.*
7 QUICK [only before noun] available or coming without delay: *They need to have ready access to police files.* | *a* ***ready supply*** *of drink* | *I had no* ***ready answer*** *to his question.* | *an intelligent man with* ***a ready wit***
8 ready money/cash money that you can spend immediately: *The company is short of ready cash.*
9 ready, steady, go! *BrE*, **get ready, get set, go!** *AmE spoken* used to tell people to start a race → READILY, READINESS, → **rough and ready** at ROUGH[1](15)

THESAURUS

ready [not before noun] having done everything that needs to be done in order to prepare for something: *Are you ready? The taxi's here.* | *I don't feel that I'm ready for the test yet.*
prepared [not before noun] ready to deal with a situation, because you are expecting it or have made careful preparations: *The police were prepared for trouble.* | *The team looked* ***well-prepared*** *for the game.*
be all set to be ready to start doing something that you have planned to do, and be just about to do it: *We were all set for a barbecue when it started to rain.*
be good to go *AmE informal* be ready to start doing something after completing all the necessary preparations: *We just need to get you a pair of skis and you're good to go.*
be in place if the arrangements or the equipment for doing something are in place, they are ready to start being used: *The television cameras were in place for the wedding.* | *All the arrangements are in place for a new constitution and democratic elections.*
be standing by if people are standing by, they are ready to take action and help if they are needed – used especially about medical teams, police, the army etc: *Officers in full riot gear were standing by outside the police station.* | *Several ambulances were standing by.*

ready[2] *v* (**readied**, **readying**, **readies**) [T] *formal* to make something or someone ready for something SYN **prepare**: **ready sb/sth for sth** *I tried to ready him for the bad news.*

ready[3] *n* **1 at the ready** available to be used immediately: *Soldiers stood around with weapons at the ready.* **2 the readies** *BrE informal* money that you can use immediately: *I'm getting a new car as soon as I can scrape together the readies.*

ready[4] *adv* **ready cooked/prepared etc** already cooked, prepared etc by someone else: *They seem to live on ready cooked meals.*

ˌready-ˈmade *adj* [only before noun] **1** ready-made food or goods are already prepared or made, and ready for you to use immediately: *a ready-made spaghetti sauce* **2** ready-made ideas or reasons are provided for you, so that you do not have to think of them yourself: *The rain gave us a ready-made excuse to stay at home.*

ˌready ˈmeal *n* [C] *BrE* a meal that has already been cooked and is sold ready to eat

ˌready-to-ˈwear *adj old-fashioned* ready-to-wear clothes are made in standard sizes, not made specially to fit one person OPP **made-to-measure**

re·af·firm /ˌriːəˈfɜːm $ -ɜːrm/ *v* [T] to formally state an opinion, belief, or intention again, especially when someone has questioned you or expressed a doubt SYN **reiterate**: *The party reaffirmed its commitment to nuclear disarmament.* | **reaffirm that** *The government has reaffirmed that education is a top priority.* —**reaffirmation** /ˌriːæfəˈmeɪʃən $ -fər-/ *n* [C,U]

re·af·for·es·ta·tion /ˌriːəfɒrəˈsteɪʃən $ -fɔː, -fɑː-/ *n* [U] *BrE technical* REFORESTATION

re·a·gent /riˈeɪdʒənt/ *n* [C] *technical* a substance that shows that another substance in a COMPOUND exists, by causing a chemical REACTION

real[1] /rɪəl/ ●●● S1 W1 *adj*
1 IMPORTANT something that is real exists and is important: *There is a real danger that the disease might spread.* | *We need to tackle the real problems of unemployment and poverty.* | *There is* ***no real*** *reason to worry.*
2 NOT ARTIFICIAL something that is real is actually what it seems to be and not false or artificial OPP **fake**: *a coat made of real fur* | *She had never seen a* ***real live*** *elephant before.* | *Artificial flowers can sometimes look better than* ***the real thing***. THESAURUS GENUINE
3 NOT IMAGINARY something that is real actually exists and is not just imagined: *The children know that Santa Claus isn't a real person.* | *Dreams can sometimes seem very real.* | *Things don't happen quite that easily* ***in real life***.
4 the real world used to talk about the difficult experience of living and working with other people, rather than being protected at home, at school, or at college: *the shock of leaving university and going out into the real world*
5 TRUE [only before noun] actual and true, not invented: *That's not her real name.* | *What was the* ***real reason*** *you quit your job?*
6 FEELINGS a real feeling or emotion is one that you actually experience and is strong SYN **genuine**: *There was a look of real hatred in her eyes.* | *I got a real sense of achievement when my work was first published.*
7 RIGHT QUALITIES [only before noun] a real thing has all the qualities you expect something of that type to have: *I remember my first real job.* | *Simon was her first real boyfriend.*

SPOKEN PHRASES
8 FOR EMPHASIS [only before noun] used to emphasize how stupid, beautiful, terrible etc someone or something is: *Thanks – you've been a real help.* | *The house was a real mess.*
9 for real seriously, not just pretending: *After two trial runs we did it for real.*
10 are you for real? *AmE* used when you are very surprised or shocked by what someone has done or said
11 get real! used to tell someone that they are being very silly or unreasonable
12 keep it real to behave in an honest way and not pretend to be different from how you really are

13 MONEY [only before noun] a real increase or decrease in an amount of money is one you calculate by including the general decrease in the value of money over a period of time: *a real increase of 6% in average wages* | *The average value of salaries has fallen* ***in real terms*** (=calculated in this way).

R

real² ●●● [S2] *adv AmE spoken* very: *He's real cute.* | *It was real nice to see you again.*

ˌreal ˈale *n* [C,U] *BrE* beer that has been made in the traditional way, not in a large factory

ˈreal esˌtate ●○○ *n* [U] *especially AmE*
1 property in the form of land or houses: *a fall in the value of real estate*
2 the business of selling houses or land

ˈreal estate ˌagent *n* [C] *AmE* someone whose job is to sell houses or land for other people [SYN] **estate agent** *BrE*

re·a·lign /ˌriːəˈlaɪn/ *v* [T] **1** to change the way in which something is organized [SYN] **reorganize**: *The company is planning to realign its sales operations.* **2 realign yourself with sb** to begin to support and work together with someone again: *They have tried to realign themselves with the communists.* **3** to change the position of something slightly so that it is in the correct position in relation to something else: *You'll have to realign your text columns.*

re·a·lign·ment /ˌriːəˈlaɪnmənt/ *n* [C,U] **1** when something is changed and organized in a different way [SYN] **reorganization**: **[+of]** *a realignment of the company's management structure* **2** when people stop supporting one group and start to support and work together with a different group: **[+of]** *There is now a need for a realignment of political parties.* **3** when the parts of something are arranged so that they return to their correct positions in relation to each other: *the realignment of several major roads*

R

real·is·m /ˈrɪəlɪzəm/ ●○○ *n* [U]
1 the ability to accept and deal with difficult situations in a practical way, based on what is possible rather than what you would like to happen: *He has hope, but also a scientist's sense of realism.*
2 the quality of being or seeming real: *the realism of the horses on the carousel*
3 (*also* **Realism**) the style of art and literature in which things, especially unpleasant things, are shown or described as they really are in life → **idealism**, **romanticism**: *the tough realism of his early works*

real·ist /ˈrɪəlɪst/ ●○○ *n* [C]
1 someone who accepts that things are not always perfect, and deals with problems or difficult situations in a practical way: *She had always been a realist, not a dreamer.*
2 a writer, painter etc who shows or describes things, especially unpleasant things, as they really are in life

rea·lis·tic /rɪəˈlɪstɪk/ ●●○ [S3] *adj*
1 judging and dealing with situations in a practical way according to what is actually possible rather than what you would like to happen [OPP] **unrealistic**: **it is not realistic to do sth** *It's just not realistic to expect a promotion so soon.* | **[+about]** *You need to be realistic about the amount you can do in a day.* **THESAURUS** ▸ POSSIBLE
2 a realistic aim or hope is something that it is possible to achieve [OPP] **unrealistic**: *Is this a realistic target?* | *I don't think they have a* ***realistic chance*** *of winning.*
3 realistic pictures or stories show things as they are in real life: *a realistic portrayal of life in Victorian Britain*

rea·lis·tic·ally /rɪəˈlɪstɪkli/ *adv* **1** if you think about something realistically, you think about it in a practical way and according to what is actually possible: *You can't realistically expect to win the whole competition.* | [sentence adverb] *Realistically, we're not going to get this finished this week.* **2** if you describe or show something realistically, you describe or show it as it is in real life: *realistically painted toy soldiers* | *The novel realistically depicts immigrant life at the beginning of the last century*

re·al·i·ty /riˈæləti/ ●●● [S2] [W2] *n* (*plural* **realities**)
1 [C,U] what actually happens or is true, not what is imagined or thought: *the distinction between fantasy and reality* | *TV is used as an* ***escape from reality.*** | *I think the government has* ***lost touch with reality*** (=no longer understands what is real or true). | *political realities* | **harsh/grim/stark reality** *Millions of people live with the harsh realities of unemployment.* | **the reality is that** *The reality is that young people will not go into teaching until salaries are higher.* | *The paperless office may one day* ***become a reality.***
2 in reality used to say that something is different from what people think: *In reality, violent crimes are still extremely rare.*
3 [U] the fact that something exists or is happening: *She had never accepted the reality of her pregnancy.* → VIRTUAL REALITY

reˈality ˌcheck *n* [C usually singular] *informal* an occasion when you consider the facts of a situation, as opposed to what you would like or what you have imagined: *It's time for a reality check. The Bears aren't as good a team as you think.*

reˌality TˈV *n* [U] television programmes that feature real people doing real things, for example police officers chasing after stolen cars, or people who have been put in different situations and filmed continuously over a period of weeks or months

rea·liz·a·ble (*also* **-isable** *BrE*) /ˈrɪəlaɪzəbəl/ *adj* **1** possible to achieve [SYN] **achievable**: *Is this a realizable goal?* **2** in a form that can be changed into money easily: *the company's realizable assets*

re·a·li·za·tion (*also* **-isation** *BrE*) /ˌrɪəlaɪˈzeɪʃən $ -lə-/ ●○○ *n* [singular, U]
1 when you understand something that you had not understood before: **[+of]** *I was shocked by the realization of what I had done.* | **realization that** *the realization that she might never recover from her illness* | *There is a* ***growing realization*** *that we must manage the Earth's resources more carefully.*
2 *formal* when you achieve something that you had planned or hoped for [SYN] **achievement**: **[+of]** *the realization of his dreams*
3 *technical* when you change something into money by selling it: *the realization of assets*

rea·lize (*also* **-ise** *BrE*) /ˈrɪəlaɪz/ ●●● [S1] [W1] *v* [T]
1 UNDERSTAND to know and understand something, or suddenly begin to understand it: **realize (that)** *I suddenly realized that the boy was crying.* | *Do you realize you're an hour late?* | **realize who/what/how etc** *I'm sorry, I didn't realize who you were.* | *It took us a while to realize the extent of the tragedy.* | *It was only later that I realized my mistake.*
⚠ Do not say that you 'realize about/of something'. Say that you **realize something**.

GRAMMAR: Using the progressive
- In this meaning, **realize** is not usually used in the progressive. You say: *Nobody realizes how important this is.* ✗ Don't say: *Nobody is realizing how important this is.*
- In spoken English, people sometimes say **I'm realizing** to say that they have recently begun to realize something: *Now I'm a parent, I'm realizing what my parents went through.*

GRAMMAR GUIDE ▸ VERBS

2 ACHIEVE *formal* to achieve something that you were hoping to achieve: *She never* ***realized*** *her* ***ambition*** *of winning an Olympic gold medal.* | *a young singer who has not yet* ***realized*** *her full* ***potential*** (=achieved as much as she can achieve)
3 sb's worst fears were realized used to say that the thing that you were most afraid of has actually happened: *His worst fears were realized when he heard that Chris had been arrested.*
4 MONEY **a)** *formal* to obtain or earn an amount of money: *The campaign realized $5000.* | *We realized a small profit on the sale of the house.* **b) realize an asset** *technical* to change something that you own into money by selling it

ˈreal-life *adj* [only before noun] actually happening in life, not invented in a book: *a real-life drama* | *real-life problems*

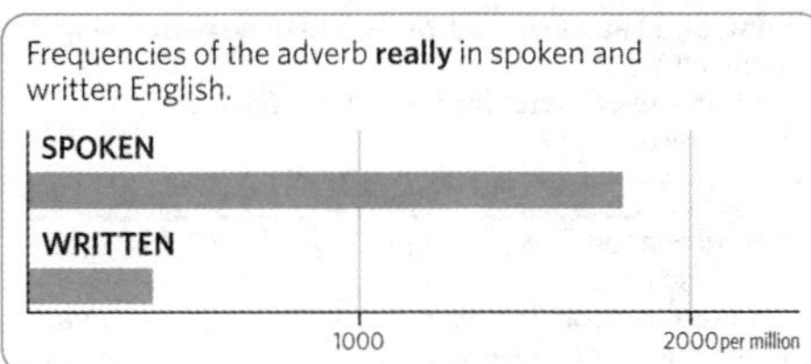

real·ly /ˈrɪəli/ ●●● (S1) (W1) *adv*
1 VERY very (SYN) **extremely**: *a really good film* | *It was really cold last night.* | *He walks really slowly.* | *I'm really, really sorry.*

> **REGISTER**
> **Really** is especially frequent in spoken English. In writing, people usually prefer to use **very** or **extremely** to emphasize an adjective, or **very much** to emphasize a verb: *a **really** dangerous activity* → *a **very** dangerous activity* | *I **really** enjoyed the play.* → *I enjoyed the play **very much**.*

2 THE REAL SITUATION used when you are talking about what actually happened or is true, rather than what people might wrongly think: *Why don't you tell us what really happened?* | *Oliver's not really her brother.* | *I never know what he's really thinking.* | *She seems unfriendly at first, but she's really very nice.*

SPOKEN PHRASES
3 DEFINITELY used to emphasize something you are saying: *We really need that extra money.* | *I really don't mind.* | *I'm absolutely fine, Dad – really.*
4 NOT TRUE used in questions when you are asking someone if something is true and suggesting that you think it is not true (SYN) **honestly**: *Do you really think she's doing this for your benefit?* | *Do you really expect me to believe that?*
5 a) really? used to show that you are surprised by what someone has said: *'He's Canadian.' 'Really?'* **b) really?** used in conversation to show that you are listening to or interested in what the other person is saying: *'We had a great time in Florida.' 'Really? How lovely.'* **c)** *AmE* used to show that you agree with someone: *'Glen can be such a jerk.' 'Yeah, really!'* **d)** *especially BrE* used to show that you are angry or disapprove of something: *Really, Larry, you might have told me!*
6 not really used to say 'no' or 'not' in a less strong way: *'Do you want to come along?' 'Not really.'* | *I don't really know what he's doing now.*
7 should/ought really used to say what someone should do, especially when they are probably not going to do it: *You should really go and see a doctor.*
8 really and truly (*also* **really, truly** *AmE*) used to emphasize a statement or opinion: *He was really and truly a brilliant comedian.*

realm /relm/ ●○○ *n* [C]
1 *written* a general area of knowledge, activity, or thought: *the spiritual realm* | **[+of]** *an idea that belongs in the realm of science fiction*
2 within the realms of possibility (*also* **not beyond the realm(s) of possibility**) used, often humorously, to say that something is possible even though you think it is not very likely: *I suppose it's not beyond the realms of possibility.*
3 *literary* a country ruled by a king or queen

re·al·pol·i·tik /reɪˈɑːlpɒlɪtiːk $ -pɑː-/ *n* [U] politics based on practical situations and needs rather than on moral principles or ideas

ˌreal ˈproperty *n* [U] *law* REAL ESTATE(1)

ˈreal-time *adj* [only before noun] *technical* a real-time computer system deals with information as fast as it receives it: *a real-time operating system* —**real time** *n* [U]: *The images are created in real time.*

Real·tor, **realtor** /ˈrɪəltə, -tɔː $ -ər, -ɔːr/ *n* [C] *trademark AmE* a REAL ESTATE AGENT

real·ty /ˈrɪəlti/ *n* [U] *AmE* REAL ESTATE

ream¹ /riːm/ *n* [C] **1 reams** [plural] *informal* a large amount of writing on paper: **[+of]** *reams of notes* **2** *technical* a standard amount of paper, 500 pieces in the US or 480 pieces in Britain

ream² *v* [T] *AmE informal* to treat someone badly, especially by cheating

re·an·i·mate /riːˈænɪmeɪt/ *v* [T] *formal* to give new strength to someone or something or the energy to start again

reap /riːp/ ●○○ *v*
1 [T] to get something, especially something good, as a result of what you have done: **reap the benefit/reward/profit (of sth)** *Those who do take risks often reap the rewards.*
2 you reap what you sow used to say that if you do bad things, bad things will happen to you, and if you do good things, good things will happen to you
3 [I,T] *old-fashioned* to cut and collect a crop of grain → **harvest** —**reaper** *n* [C] →

re·ap·pear /ˌriːəˈpɪə $ -ˈpɪr/ ●○○ *v* [I] to appear again after not being seen for some time: *In March, his cancer reappeared.* | *Many of these ideas reappear in his later books.* —**reappearance** *n* [C,U]

re·ap·praise /ˌriːəˈpreɪz/ *v* [T] to examine something again in order to consider whether you should change it or your opinion of it (SYN) **reassess**: *People began to reappraise their values.* —**reappraisal** *n* [C,U]

rear¹ /rɪə $ rɪr/ ●●○ *adj* [only before noun] at or near the back of something, especially a vehicle (OPP) **front**: *the rear door of the car* | *Knock at the rear entrance.*

rear² ●●○ *n*
1 *formal* **the rear** the back part of an object, vehicle, or building, or a position at the back of an object or area (OPP) **front**: **at/to the rear (of sth)** *a garden at the rear of the house* | *The hotel overlooks the river to the rear.* | **in the rear (of sth)** *a passenger travelling in the rear of a car*
2 [C] (*also* **rear end**) *informal* the part of your body which you sit on (SYN) **bottom**
3 bring up the rear to be at the back of a line of people or in a race: *Carole was left to bring up the rear.*

rear³ ●○○ *v*
1 [T] to look after a person or animal until they are fully grown (SYN) **raise**: *It's a good place to rear young children.* | *The birds have been successfully reared in captivity.*
2 [I] (*also* **rear up**) if an animal rears, it rises up to stand on its back legs → **buck**: *The horse reared and threw me off.*
3 [I] (*also* **rear up**) if something rears up, it appears in front of you and often seems to be leaning over you in a threatening way: *A large rock, almost 200 feet high, reared up in front of them.*
4 be reared on sth to be given a particular kind of food, books, entertainment etc regularly while you are a child: *children reared on TV and video games*
5 rear its ugly head if a problem or difficult situation rears its ugly head, it appears and is impossible to ignore: *The problem of drug-taking in sport has reared its ugly head again.*

ˌrear ˈadmiral *n* [C] a high rank in the navy

rear·guard /ˈrɪəgɑːd $ ˈrɪrgɑːrd/ *n* **1 fight a rearguard action a)** to make a determined effort to prevent a change that you think is bad, although it seems too late to stop it: *They have been fighting a rearguard action to stop a supermarket being built on the land.* **b)** if an army fights a rearguard action, it defends itself at the back against an enemy that is chasing it **2** [singular] the group of soldiers who defend the back of an army against an enemy that is chasing it

re·arm /riːˈɑːm $ -ˈɑːrm/ *v* [I,T] to obtain weapons again or provide someone else with new weapons: *They returned to base to rearm.* —**rearmament** *n* [U]

rear·most /ˈrɪəməʊst $ ˈrɪrmoʊst/ *adj* [only before noun] furthest back (SYN) **last**: *the rearmost seats*

re·ar·range /ˌriːəˈreɪndʒ/ *v* [T] **1** to change the position or order of things: *She set about rearranging the furniture in the living room.* **2** to change the time of a meeting etc: *My*

R

secretary will phone to rearrange the appointment. **3 be rearranging the deckchairs on the Titanic** to be making small and useless changes when something very bad is about to happen and there is little chance of preventing it: *These attempts to reduce climate change just amount to rearranging the deckchairs on the Titanic.* —**rearrangement** *n* [C,U]

rear·view mir·ror /ˌrɪəvjuː ˈmɪrə $ ˌrɪrvjuː ˈmɪrər/ *n* [C] a mirror inside a car etc that lets the driver see the area behind the car → **wing mirror** → see picture at CAR

rear·ward /ˈrɪəwəd $ ˈrɪrwərd/ *adj* in or towards the back of something —**rearward, rearwards** *adv*

rea·son¹ /ˈriːzən/ ●●● S1 W1 *n*
1 CAUSE [C] why something happens, or why someone does something: **[+for]** *People give different reasons for wanting to change jobs.* | **[+why]** *We'd like to know the reason why she didn't accept the job.* | **[+(that)]** *The reason I called was to ask about the plans for Saturday.* | **[+behind]** *He explained the reasons behind the decision.* | **for reasons of sth** *The bridge is closed for reasons of safety.* | **reason to do sth** *This work gives me a reason to live.* | **there is no reason to do sth** *There is no reason whatsoever to doubt her story.* | **by reason of sth** *formal* (=because of something) *a person disqualified by reason of age*
2 GOOD OR FAIR [U] a fact that makes it right or fair for someone to do something: **(no) reason to do sth** *There is no reason to panic.* | *She **has reason** to feel guilty.* | *We **have reason to believe that** the goods were stolen.* | *I know I'm late, but **that's no reason** to shout at me.* | *Under the circumstances, we **had every reason*** (=had very good reasons) *to be suspicious.* | **with (good) reason** (=based on something sensible) *Natalie was alarmed by the news, and with reason.*
3 all the more reason why/to do sth *spoken* used to say that what has just been mentioned is an additional reason for doing what you have suggested: *But surely that's all the more reason to act quickly.*
4 GOOD JUDGMENT [U] sensible judgment and understanding SYN **sense**: *There's reason in what he says.* | *They're not prepared to **listen to reason*** (=be persuaded by someone's sensible advice). | *There's no way of making my grandfather **see reason*** (=accept advice and make a sensible decision).
5 within reason within sensible limits: *You can go anywhere you want, within reason.*
6 go/be beyond (all) reason to be more than is acceptable or reasonable: *Their demands go beyond all reason.*
7 ABILITY TO THINK [U] the ability to think, understand, and form judgments that are based on facts: *the human **power of reason*** | **lose your reason** *old-fashioned* (=become mentally ill)
8 no reason *spoken* used when someone asks you why you are doing something and you do not want to tell them: *'Why d'you want to go that way?' 'Oh, no reason.'* → **no rhyme or reason** at RHYME¹(4), → **it stands to reason** at STAND¹(32)

GRAMMAR: Comparison

reason
• You say the **reason for** something: *What do you think was the reason for their success?* ✗ Don't say: *the reason of their success*
• You say the **reason why** something happens: *Can you tell me the reason why you did this?*

cause
• You say the **cause of** something: *There will be a police investigation into the cause of the fire.* ✗ Don't say: *the cause for the fire*
• You say there is **cause for concern/alarm/complaint/worry etc**: *The doctor said there was no cause for concern.*

COLLOCATIONS

VERBS
have a reason *We had many reasons to celebrate.*
give a reason *No reason was given for the change.*
think of a reason/see a reason *I see no reason why it shouldn't work.*
explain the reasons for sth *Explain the reasons for your choice.*

ADJECTIVES
a good reason *There is usually a good reason why the price is so cheap.*
the main reason *The main reason for the decline in the railways is lack of investment.*
a major reason (*also* **a big reason** *informal*) *His personality was a major reason for his success.*
the real reason *What do you think was the real reason for their decision?*
a valid/legitimate reason (=a good and acceptable reason) *An employer can't fire someone without a valid reason.*
a compelling reason (=a very good reason for doing something) | **a simple reason** (=one that is easy to understand) | **a logical reason** | **the only reason**

PHRASES
for legal/political/medical etc reasons *The boy cannot be named for legal reasons.*
for security reasons *The road will be closed for security reasons.*
for personal reasons *He resigned for personal reasons.*
for sentimental reasons (=because you like someone or something very much) | **for obvious reasons** | **for no apparent reason** (=for no obvious reason) | **for some reason (or other)** (*also* **for some unknown reason**) (=for a reason that you do not know) | **for reasons best known to sb** (=used when you do not understand someone's behaviour) | **have your reasons** (=have a secret reason for doing something)

THESAURUS

reason why something happens, or why someone does something: *What was the reason for the delay?* | *I don't know the reason why he left his last job.*
cause the reason why something happens, especially something bad: *What was the cause of his death?* | *We studied the causes of the First World War.*
explanation a set of reasons that helps you to understand why something happens, especially when it seems difficult to understand: *There are various possible explanations for climate change.* | *Is there any explanation for his behavior?*
motive a reason that makes someone decide to do something - often used about crimes: *Police say that there is no obvious motive for the attack.*
justification a good reason for doing something that seems wrong: *There is never any justification for torture or abuse.* | *They try to use the situation in the Middle East as a justification for killing innocent civilians.*
grounds a reason that makes it right or fair to do something, especially according to legal, official, or moral rules: *The court will decide if she has grounds for divorce.* | *They claim the war is justified on moral grounds* (=because of moral reasons).
basis the main ideas or reasons on which something is based: *The doctor makes his decisions purely on the basis of clinical observation.* | *What do you think is the basis for this advice?*
rationale /ˌræʃəˈnɑːl $ -ˈnæl/ *formal* a set of reasons that are used to explain why someone does something in a particular way: *the rationale behind the government's economic reforms*

A REASON THAT DOES NOT SEEM BELIEVABLE
excuse a reason that you give to explain why you have done something bad, or not done something that you should have done - especially one that is not completely true: *She said she couldn't come because she had to work late, but it was just an*

excuse. | *a feeble excuse* (=one that is hard to believe)
pretext *especially written* an untrue reason that you give for doing or not doing something, in order to hide the real reason: *He would often find some pretext to go out in the evening alone.* | *They used this as a pretext for taking military action.*

reason² ●○○ *v*
1 [T] to form a particular judgment about a situation after carefully considering the facts: **reason (that)** *They reasoned that other businesses would soon copy the idea.*
2 [I] to think and make judgments: *the ability to reason*
reason sth ↔ **out** *phr v* to find an explanation or solution to a problem, by thinking of all the possibilities SYN **work out**
reason with sb *phr v* to talk to someone in an attempt to persuade them to be more sensible: *I tried to reason with her.*

rea·son·a·ble /ˈriːzənəbəl/ ●●● S1 W2 *adj*
1 fair and sensible OPP **unreasonable**: *a reasonable request* | ***Be reasonable*** *– you can't expect her to do all the work on her own!* | *I thought it was a* ***perfectly reasonable*** (=completely reasonable) *question.* | **it is reasonable to do sth** *It seems reasonable to assume they've been tested.* | *He had* ***reasonable grounds*** (=good reasons but no proof) *for believing the law had been broken.* | **a reasonable explanation/excuse** *It sounded like a* ***reasonable enough*** *excuse to me.* THESAURUS FAIR
2 fairly good, but not especially good SYN **average**: *She has a reasonable chance of doing well in the exam.* THESAURUS SATISFACTORY
3 a reasonable amount is fairly large: *I've got a reasonable amount of money saved.*
4 reasonable prices are not too high SYN **fair**: *good food at a reasonable price* THESAURUS CHEAP
5 beyond (a) reasonable doubt *law* if something is proved beyond reasonable doubt, it is shown to be almost certainly true —**reasonableness** *n* [U]

rea·son·a·bly /ˈriːzənəbli/ ●●○ S3 W3 *adv*
1 [+adj/adv] quite or to a satisfactory degree, but not completely: *The car is in reasonably good condition.* | *He's doing reasonably well at school.*
2 in a way that is right or fair: *He can't reasonably be expected to have known that.*
3 in a sensible way: *Despite her anger, she had behaved very reasonably.*

rea·soned /ˈriːzənd/ *adj* [only before noun] based on careful thought, and therefore sensible SYN **logical**: *reasoned argument*

rea·son·ing /ˈriːzənɪŋ/ ●○○ *n* [U] a process of thinking carefully about something in order to make a judgment: **scientific/logical/legal reasoning** | **[+behind]** *What is the reasoning behind this decision?*

re·as·sem·ble /ˌriːəˈsembəl/ *v* **1** [T] to bring together the different parts of something to make a whole again, after they have been separated: *The equipment had to be dismantled and reassembled at each new location.* **2** [I] if a group of people reassemble, they meet together again after a period apart: *Parliament reassembled after a seven-week break.*

re·as·sert /ˌriːəˈsɜːt $ -ˈsɜːrt/ *v* [T] **1 reassert your authority/power/control** to do or say something to make your position stronger after a period when it seemed weak: *The prime minister aimed to reassert his authority.* **2** to state a fact or opinion again, often more strongly or more clearly: *He used the opportunity to reassert his position on energy policy.* **3 reassert itself** if something reasserts itself, it returns or becomes stronger after a period when it was missing or weak: *At last, common sense had reasserted itself.*

re·as·sess /ˌriːəˈses/ AWL *v* [T] to think about something again carefully in order to decide whether to change your opinion or judgment about it SYN **reappraise**: *This has caused us to reassess the way we approach our planning.* —**reassessment** *n* [C,U]

re·as·sur·ance /ˌriːəˈʃʊərəns $ -ˈʃʊr-/ ●○○ *n* [C,U] something that is said or done which makes someone feel calmer and less worried or frightened about a problem: *Parents are looking for reassurance about their children's safety.* | **give/offer/provide reassurance** *They are offering practical help and reassurance.* | **reassurance that** *We have been given reassurances that the water is safe to drink.*

re·as·sure /ˌriːəˈʃʊə $ -ˈʃʊr/ ●●○ *v* [T] to make someone feel calmer and less worried or frightened about a problem or situation: *Teachers reassured anxious parents.* | **reassure sb (that)** *He tried to reassure me that my mother would be okay.*

re·as·sur·ing /ˌriːəˈʃʊərɪŋ◂ $ -ˈʃʊr-/ ●●○ *adj* making you feel less worried or frightened SYN **comforting**: *a reassuring smile* | **it is reassuring (for sb) to do sth** *It's reassuring to know that problems are rare.* —**reassuringly** *adv*

re·bate /ˈriːbeɪt/ *n* [C] an amount of money that is paid back to you when you have paid too much tax, rent etc: *You may be entitled to a tax rebate.*

reb·el¹ /ˈrebəl/ ●●○ *n* [C]
1 someone who opposes or fights against people in authority: *Anti-government rebels attacked the town.* | **rebel forces/soldiers** | *the rebel leader*
2 someone who refuses to do things in the normal way, or in the way that other people want them to: *Alex has always been a bit of a rebel.*

re·bel² /rɪˈbel/ ●○○ *v* (**rebelled, rebelling**) [I]
1 to oppose or fight against someone in authority or against an idea or situation which you do not agree with: **[+against]** *teenage boys rebelling against their parents*
2 *written* if your stomach, legs, mind etc rebel, you cannot do or believe something you think you should: *He knew he ought to eat, but his stomach rebelled.*

re·bel·lion /rɪˈbeljən/ ●●○ *n* [C,U]
1 an organized attempt to change the government or leader of a country, using violence → **coup, revolution**: *an armed rebellion* | **[+against]** *a rebellion against the military regime* | **in rebellion** *The Bretons rose in rebellion against the King.* | **suppress/crush a rebellion** (=use violence to stop it) THESAURUS REVOLUTION
2 when someone opposes or fights against people in authority or ideas which they do not agree with: *a rebellion by right-wing members of the party* | **[+against]** *rebellion against traditional values*

re·bel·lious /rɪˈbeljəs/ ●○○ *adj*
1 deliberately not obeying people in authority or rules of behaviour: *rebellious teenagers* | *He's always had a* ***rebellious streak*** (=a tendency to rebel).
2 fighting against the government of your own country: *rebellious minorities* —**rebelliously** *adv* —**rebelliousness** *n* [U]

re·birth /ˌriːˈbɜːθ $ -ɜːrθ/ *n* **1** [singular] *formal* when an important idea, feeling, or organization becomes strong or popular again: **[+of]** *a rebirth of nationalism in the region* **2** [U] when something or someone becomes alive again after dying → **reborn**: *the cycle of birth, death and rebirth*

re·boot /ˌriːˈbuːt/ *v* [I,T] if you reboot a computer, or if it reboots, you start it up again

re·born /riːˈbɔːn $ -ˈbɔːrn/ *v literary* **be reborn a)** to become active or popular again: *In the past decade, the city has been reborn.* **b)** to be born again, especially according to some beliefs, ancient stories etc

re·bound¹ /rɪˈbaʊnd/ *v* **1** [I] if a ball or other moving object rebounds, it moves quickly back away from something it has just hit → **ricochet**: **[+off]** *His shot on goal rebounded off the post.* **2** [I] if prices, values etc rebound, they increase again after decreasing SYN **recover**: *Share prices rebounded today after last week's losses.* **3** [I,T] to catch a BASKETBALL after a player has tried but failed to get a point
rebound on/upon sb *phr v* if something bad or unpleasant you have done rebounds on you, it has a bad effect on you SYN **backfire**

R

re·bound² /ˈriːbaʊnd/ *n* **1 on the rebound a)** someone who is on the rebound is upset or confused because their romantic relationship has just ended: *He first met me when I was on the rebound, after splitting up with Mark.* **b)** a ball that is on the rebound has just hit something and is moving back through the air: *I caught the ball on the rebound.* **c)** something that is on the rebound is starting to increase or improve again: *The market seems to be on the rebound.* **2** [C] *technical* an act of catching a BASKETBALL after a player has tried but failed to get a point

re·buff /rɪˈbʌf/ *n* [C] *formal* an unkind or unfriendly answer to a friendly suggestion or offer of help SYN **snub**: *He received a humiliating rebuff from his manager.* THESAURUS REFUSE —**rebuff** *v* [T]: *He rebuffed all her suggestions.*

re·build /riːˈbɪld/ ●○○ *v* (*past tense and past participle* **rebuilt** /-ˈbɪlt/) [T]
1 to build something again, after it has been damaged or destroyed: *The church was completely rebuilt in the last century.*
2 to make something strong and successful again: *The first priority is to rebuild the area's manufacturing industry.* | *We try to help them **rebuild** their **lives*** (=live normally again after something bad has happened).

re·buke /rɪˈbjuːk/ ●○○ *v* [T] *formal* to speak to someone severely about something they have done wrong SYN **reprimand**: **rebuke sb for doing sth** *Members of the jury were sharply rebuked for speaking to the press.* —**rebuke** *n* [C,U]: *a rebuke from the president*

re·but /rɪˈbʌt/ *v* (**rebutted, rebutting**) [T] *formal* to prove that a statement or a charge made against you is false SYN **refute** —**rebuttal** *n* [C,U]: *his firm rebuttal of the accusations*

re·cal·ci·trant /rɪˈkælsətrənt/ *adj formal* refusing to do what you are told to do, even after you have been punished SYN **unruly**: *a recalcitrant pupil* —**recalcitrance** *n* [U]

re·call¹ /rɪˈkɔːl $ ˈriːkɔːl/ ●●○ S3 W3 *v*
1 REMEMBER STH [I,T not in progressive] to remember a particular fact, event, or situation from the past: *You don't happen to recall his name, do you?* | **recall (that)** *I seem to recall I've met him before somewhere.* | **recall doing sth** *I don't recall seeing any cars parked outside.* | **recall what/how/where etc** *I can't recall who gave me the information.* | ***As I recall**, it was you who suggested this idea in the first place.* THESAURUS REMEMBER
2 PERSON [T] to officially tell someone to come back to a place or group: **recall sb to sth** *Cole was recalled to the squad to replace the injured Quinn.* | **recall sb from sth** *The Ambassador was recalled from Washington.*
3 PRODUCT [T] if a company recalls one of its products, it asks people who have bought it to return it because there may be something wrong with it: *The cars had to be recalled due to an engine fault.*
4 COMPUTER [T] to bring information back onto the screen of a computer
5 BE SIMILAR TO STH [T] if something recalls something else, it makes you think of it because it is very similar: *The furnishings recall the 1960s.*
6 POLITICS [T] *AmE* to vote to remove someone from their political position

re·call² /rɪˈkɔːl, ˈriːkɔːl $ -ɒːl/ *n*
1 MEMORY [U] the ability to remember something that you have learned or experienced: *A child's recall is usually accurate.* | *He had **total recall*** (=remembered everything) *of every play in the game.*
2 ORDER TO RETURN [singular, U] an official order telling someone to return to a place, especially before they expected to: **[+of]** *the recall of their ambassador*
3 beyond recall impossible to bring back or remember
4 PRODUCT [C] when a company asks people to return a product they have bought because there may be something wrong with it
5 POLITICS [singular, U] *AmE* a vote to remove someone from their political position, or the act of being removed by a vote: **[+of]** *the recall of four city council members*

re·cant /rɪˈkænt/ *v* [I,T] *formal* to say publicly that you no longer have a political or religious belief that you had before —**recantation** /ˌriːkænˈteɪʃən/ *n* [C,U]

re·cap /ˈriːkæp, riːˈkæp/ *v* (**recapped, recapping**) [I,T] to repeat the main points of something that has just been said: *Let me just recap what's been discussed so far.* | **[+on]** *to recap on the previous lecture* —**re·cap** /ˈriːkæp/ *n* [C]

re·ca·pit·u·late /ˌriːkəˈpɪtʃəleɪt/ *v* [I,T] *formal* to repeat the main points of something that has just been said SYN **recap** —**recapitulation** /ˌriːkəpɪtʃəˈleɪʃən/ *n* [C,U]

re·cap·ture /riːˈkæptʃə $ -ər/ *v* [T] **1** to bring back the same feelings or qualities that you experienced in the past: *The film really recaptures the atmosphere of those days.* **2** to catch a prisoner or animal that has escaped: *He was recaptured after nearly two weeks on the run.* **3** to take control of a place again by fighting for it SYN **retake**: *an attempt to recapture the city* —**recapture** *n* [U]

re·cast /ˌriːˈkɑːst $ -ˈkæst/ *v* (*past tense and past participle* **recast**) [T] **1** to give something a new shape or a new form of organization: *an attempt to recast the statement in less formal language* **2** to give parts in a play or film to different actors —**recasting** *n* [C,U]

rec·ce /ˈreki/ *n* [C,U] *BrE informal* RECONNAISSANCE: *a quick recce of the area* —**recce** *v* [I,T]

recd. (*also* **recd** *BrE*) the written abbreviation of ***received***

re·cede /rɪˈsiːd/ ●○○ *v* [I]
1 if something you can see or hear recedes, it gets further and further away until it disappears: **[+into]** *footsteps receding into the distance*
2 if a memory, feeling, or possibility recedes, it gradually goes away: *The pain in his head gradually receded.*
3 if water recedes, it moves back from an area that it was covering: *The flood waters finally began to recede in November.*
4 if your hair recedes, you gradually lose the hair at the front of your head: *He was in his mid-forties, with a **receding hairline**.*
5 receding chin a chin that slopes backwards

re·ceipt /rɪˈsiːt/ ●●● S2 *n*
1 [C] a piece of paper that you are given which shows that you have paid for something: *Keep your receipt in case you want to bring it back.* | **[+for]** *Make sure you get receipts for everything.* | *Can you give me a receipt?*
2 [U] *formal* when someone receives something: **[+of]** *the closing date for receipt of applications* | **on/upon receipt of sth** *The booking will be made on receipt of a deposit.* | **be in receipt of sth** (=to have received something)
3 receipts [plural] *technical* the money that a business, bank, or government receives: *total revenue receipts of $18.4 million*

re·ceiv·a·ble /rɪˈsiːvəbəl/ *adj* needing or waiting to be paid: *the company's **accounts receivable*** (=sales that have been made but not yet paid for)

re·ceiv·a·bles /rɪˈsiːvəbəlz/ *n* [plural] amounts of money that are owed to a company

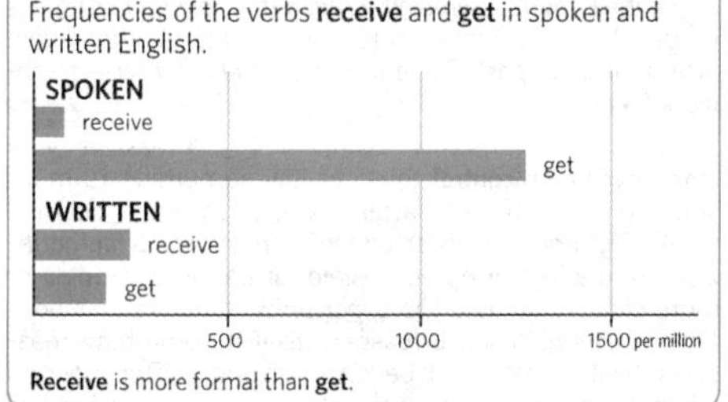

re·ceive /rɪˈsiːv/ ●●● S1 W1 *v* [T]
1 BE GIVEN STH to be given something SYN **get**: *All the children will receive a small gift.* | **receive sth from sb** *She received an honorary degree from Harvard.* | **receive attention/affection/support** *She received no support from her parents.* | **receive payment/money/a pension etc** *They*

will be entitled to receive unemployment benefit. | **receive a prize/award/gift etc** *He went up to receive his award from the mayor.* | **receive education/training** *16 to 18-year-olds receiving full-time education* | *Lee* ***received*** *324* ***votes*** (=324 people voted for him).

> REGISTER
> **Receive** is a rather formal word, which is used especially in written English. In everyday English, people usually use **get**. *What did you* ***get*** *for your birthday?* | *She* ***got*** *a degree from York University.*

2 BE SENT STH *formal* to get a letter, message, or telephone call, or something which someone has sent you: **receive sth from sb** *He received a letter from his insurance company.* | *If you would like to* ***receive*** *further* ***information****, return the attached form.* | *We have* ***received*** *numerous* ***complaints*** *about the noise.*
3 TREATMENT *formal* if you receive a particular type of medical treatment, it is done to you: *He* ***received*** *hospital* ***treatment*** *for a cut over his eye.*
4 REACTION TO STH to react in a particular way to a suggestion, idea, performance etc → **reception**: *The film was* ***well received*** *by critics* (=they said it was good). | *He received the news in silence.* GRAMMAR **Receive** is often passive in this meaning.
5 be on/at the receiving end (of sth) to be the person who is affected by someone else's actions, usually in an unpleasant way: *She found herself on the receiving end of racist abuse.*
6 receive an injury/blow *formal* to be injured or hit
7 PEOPLE *formal* to officially accept someone as a guest or member of a group: **receive guests/visitors** *She isn't well enough to receive visitors yet.* | **receive sb into sth** *She was later received into the Church.*
8 BY RADIO **a)** if a radio or television receives radio waves or other signals, it makes them become sounds or pictures **b)** to be able to hear a radio message that someone is sending: *'Receiving you loud and clear!'*

re·ceived /rɪˈsiːvd/ *adj* [only before noun] *formal* accepted or considered to be correct by most people: **received opinion/wisdom etc** (=the opinion most people have) *The received wisdom is that he will retire within the next year.*

Reˌceived Pronunciˈation *n* [U] RP

re·ceiv·er /rɪˈsiːvə $ -ər/ ●●○ *n* [C]
1 TELEPHONE the part of a telephone that you hold next to your mouth and ear → **handset**: **pick up/lift the receiver** *She picked up the receiver and dialled his number.* | **put down/replace the receiver**
2 BUSINESS *BrE* someone who is officially in charge of a business or company that is BANKRUPT: **an official/administrative receiver** | *The business is* ***in the hands of the receivers****.*
3 STOLEN PROPERTY someone who buys and sells stolen property
4 RADIO *formal* a radio or television, or other equipment which receives signals: *a satellite receiver*
5 AMERICAN FOOTBALL a player in American football who is in a position to catch the ball

re·ceiv·er·ship /rɪˈsiːvəʃɪp $ -vər-/ *n* [U] if a business is in receivership, it is controlled by an official receiver because it has no money: *The company* ***went into receivership*** *with massive debts.*

re·ceiv·ing /rɪˈsiːvɪŋ/ *n* [U] *BrE* the crime of buying and selling stolen goods

re·cent /ˈriːsənt/ ●●● S2 W1 *adj* having happened or started only a short time ago: *Irving's most recent book* | *recent research into the causes of cancer* | **in recent years/months/times etc** *The situation has improved in recent years.* | *the recent past* THESAURUS ▸ NEW

> REGISTER
> In everyday English, people usually say **in the last/past few** weeks/months/years etc rather than **in recent** weeks/months etc: *Things have been pretty busy* ***in the last few weeks****.*

re·cent·ly /ˈriːsəntli/ ●●● S1 W1 *adv* not long ago: *He has recently been promoted to Assistant Manager.* | *a recently published biography* | *Jerry lived in Cairo* ***until*** *quite* ***recently****.* | ***More recently****, he's appeared in a number of British films.*

> THESAURUS
> **recently** not long ago, especially a few days, weeks, or months ago: *The president has recently returned from a tour of South America.* | *A new species of plant was recently discovered in Brazil.*
> **lately** *especially spoken* during the recent past, especially during the weeks or days closest to now: *I've been really busy lately so I haven't been out much.* | *There hasn't been much in the news lately.*
> **just** *especially spoken* a very short time ago, especially only a few minutes, hours, days, or weeks ago: *John's just gone out.* | *They've just had a new baby.*
> **a short/little while ago** *especially spoken* not long ago – often used when you are not sure exactly when: *That house was sold a short while ago.* | *I looked in on her a little while ago and she was fast asleep.*
> **the other day** *spoken* recently, especially only a few days ago: *I met Lucy in town the other day.* | *You'll never guess what happened to me the other day.*
> **freshly** made, prepared, done etc not long ago – used especially about food and drink. Also used about things that have just been painted, washed, or dug: *freshly baked bread* | *freshly squeezed orange juice* | *The boat had been freshly painted.*
> **newly** created, built, married etc not long ago: *the newly created position of Chief Designer* | *a newly married couple* | *their newly elected president*

re·cep·ta·cle /rɪˈseptəkəl/ *n* [C] *formal* a container for putting things in: *a trash receptacle*

re·cep·tion /rɪˈsepʃən/ ●●○ W3 *n*
1 WELCOME/REACTION [C usually singular] a particular type of welcome for someone, or a particular type of reaction to their ideas, work etc → **receive**: *She was unsure of her reception after everything that had happened.* | **a warm/good/enthusiastic reception** *The delegates* ***gave*** *him a warm* ***reception****.* | **a hostile/cool/frosty reception** *His ideas met with a hostile reception.* | **receive/have/get/meet with a ... reception** *He got a great reception from the crowd.* | *The plans received a* ***mixed reception*** *from unions* (=some people liked them, others did not).
2 HOTEL/OFFICE [U] **a)** the desk or office where visitors arriving in a hotel or large organization go first: *Please leave your key at the* ***reception desk****.* | *I asked the man at reception.* **b)** *BrE* the area around or in front of this desk or office SYN **lobby**: *I'll wait for you in reception.* | *the* ***reception area***
3 PARTY [C] a large formal party to celebrate an event or to welcome someone: *It's an ideal location for a* ***wedding reception****.* | *The occasion was marked by a* ***civic reception****.* THESAURUS ▸ PARTY
4 SIGNALS [U] the act of receiving radio, television, or other signals, or the quality of signals you receive: *Mobile phone users have complained of* ***poor reception*** *in the area.*
5 FOOTBALL [C] the act of catching the ball in American football

reˈception ˌcentre *n* [C] *BrE* a place where people who have no home, especially people who have had to leave their homes, can go for food, help etc and to stay for a short time

reˈception ˌclass *n* [C] *BrE* the first class of a PRIMARY SCHOOL, which children go to aged 4 or 5

re·cep·tion·ist /rɪˈsepʃənɪst/ ●●○ *n* [C] someone whose job is to welcome and deal with people arriving in a hotel or office building, visiting a doctor etc

reˈception ˌroom *n* [C] *BrE* a room in a private house that is not a kitchen, bedroom, or bathroom – used by people who sell houses

re·cep·tive /rɪˈseptɪv/ *adj* willing to consider new ideas or listen to someone else's opinions: *You might find them in a more* ***receptive mood*** *tomorrow.* | *a* ***receptive audience*** |

R

[+to] *a workforce that is receptive to new ideas* —**receptiveness** (*also* **receptivity** /ˌriːsepˈtɪvəti/) *n* [U]

re·cep·tor /rɪˈseptə $ -ər/ *n* [C] a nerve ending which receives information about changes in light, heat etc and causes the body to react in particular ways

re·cess[1] /rɪˈses, ˈriːses $ ˈriːses, rɪˈses/ *n* **1** [C,U] a time during the day or year when no work is done, especially in parliament, law courts etc: *Parliament's summer recess* **2** [U] *AmE* a short period of time between lessons at a school when children can go outdoors and play SYN **break** *BrE*: *Her favorite things at school are music and recess.* **3** [C] a space in the wall of a room, especially for shelves, cupboards etc SYN **alcove 4 the recesses of sth** the inner hidden parts of something: *the deep recesses of the cave | fears hidden away in the darker recesses of her mind*

re·cess[2] /rɪˈses $ ˈriːses, rɪˈses/ *v* [I] *especially AmE* if a government, law court etc recesses, it officially stops work for a period of time

re·cessed /rɪˈsest $ ˈriːsest, rɪˈsest/ *adj* fitted into a part of a wall that is further back than the rest of the wall: *a recessed bookshelf*

re·ces·sion /rɪˈseʃən/ ●○○ *n* [C,U] a difficult time when there is less trade, business activity etc in a country than usual: *the* ***economic recession*** *of the early 1980s | There is* ***deep recession*** *in the UK.* | **into/out of recession** *attempts to pull the country out of recession*

R

re·ces·sion·a·ry /rɪˈseʃənəri $ -ʃəneri/ *adj* relating to a recession or likely to cause one: *recessionary pressures*

re·ces·sive /rɪˈsesɪv/ *adj technical* a recessive GENE is passed to children from their parents only if both parents have the gene OPP **dominant**

re·charge /ˌriːˈtʃɑːdʒ $ -ɑːr-/ *v* [T] **1** to put a new supply of electricity into a BATTERY **2 recharge your batteries** *informal* to get back your strength and energy again: *I'm going to spend a week in the mountains to recharge my batteries.* —**rechargeable** *adj*: ***rechargeable batteries***

re·charg·er /riːˈtʃɑːdʒə $ -ˈtʃɑːrdʒər/ *n* [C] a machine that recharges a BATTERY

re·cher·ché /rəˈʃeəʃeɪ $ rəʃerˈʃeɪ/ *adj formal* a recherché subject, idea, word etc is uncommon and has been chosen to make people admire your knowledge

re·chip /riːˈtʃɪp/ *v* (**re-chipped**, **re-chipping**) [T] to put a new computer CHIP into a piece of electronic equipment such as a MOBILE PHONE or a computer games machine so that you can use software that you are not supposed to use, or use a service that you have not paid for

re·cid·i·vist /rɪˈsɪdɪvɪst/ *n* [C] *technical* a criminal who starts doing illegal things again, even after he or she has been punished —**recidivism** *n* [U]

re·ci·pe /ˈresəpi/ ●●● S3 *n*
1 [C] a set of instructions for cooking a particular type of food: **[+for]** *a recipe for tomato soup | a* ***recipe book***
2 be a recipe for sth to be likely to cause a particular result, often a bad one: *She said that five small boys on skis was a* ***recipe for disaster****, not a holiday.*

re·cip·i·ent /rɪˈsɪpiənt/ ●○○ *n* [C] *formal* someone who receives something: **[+of]** *the recipient of the Nobel Peace Prize*

re·cip·ro·cal /rɪˈsɪprəkəl/ ●○○ *adj formal* a reciprocal arrangement or relationship is one in which two people or groups do or give the same things to each other → **mutual**: *He spoke of the necessity for a* ***reciprocal relationship*** *that would be useful for all sides. | Such treaties provide reciprocal rights and obligations.* —**reciprocally** /-kli/ *adv*

re·cip·ro·cate /rɪˈsɪprəkeɪt/ *v* **1** [I,T] *formal* to do or give something, because something similar has been done or given to you: *When he spoke I was expected to reciprocate with some remark of my own.* **2** [T] to feel the same about someone as they feel about you: *It was a hopeless love that could not possibly be reciprocated.* —**reciprocation** /rɪˌsɪprəˈkeɪʃən/ *n* [U]

re·ci·pro·ci·ty /ˌresəˈprɒsəti $ -ˈprɑː-/ *n* [U] *formal* a situation in which two people, groups, or countries give each other similar kinds of help or special rights

re·cit·al /rɪˈsaɪtl/ *n* [C] **1** a performance of music or poetry, usually given by one performer: *a piano recital |* **[+of]** *a recital of classical favourites* **2** *formal* a spoken description of a series of events: **[+of]** *a long recital of her adventures*

re·ci·ta·tion /ˌresɪˈteɪʃən/ *n* [C,U] **1** an act of saying a poem, piece of literature etc that you have learned, for people to listen to: *recitations from the great poets* **2** a spoken description of an event or a series of events: **[+of]** *He went into a recitation of his life from the earliest years.*

re·ci·ta·tive /ˌresətəˈtiːv/ *n* [C,U] *technical* a speech set to music that is sung by one person and continues the story of an OPERA (=musical play) between the songs

re·cite /rɪˈsaɪt/ ●○○ *v*
1 [I,T] to say a poem, piece of literature etc that you have learned, for people to listen to: *She recited a poem that she had learnt at school.*
2 [T] to tell someone a series or list of things: *Len recited the breakfast menu - cereal, bacon and eggs, and toast.* —**reciter** *n* [C]

reck·less /ˈrekləs/ ●○○ *adj* not caring or worrying about the possible bad or dangerous results of your actions: *He was accused of causing death by* ***reckless driving****. | a* ***reckless disregard*** *for safety | He ran into the burning house with* ***reckless abandon*** (=without caring about the danger). THESAURUS CARELESS —**recklessly** *adv* —**recklessness** *n* [U]

reck·on /ˈrekən/ ●●○ S3 *v* [T]
1 *spoken* to think or suppose something: **reckon (that)** *Do you reckon he'll agree to see us? | The police reckon that whoever killed Dad was with him earlier that day. | 'There's nothing we can do about it.' 'You reckon* (=used to express doubt or disagreement)*?'*
2 to guess a number or amount, without calculating it exactly: **reckon (that)** *We reckon that sitting in traffic jams costs us around $9 billion a year in lost output.* | **reckon sth to be sth** *The average selling price for flats in the area was reckoned to be around £200,000.*
3 to think that someone or something is a particular kind of person or thing: **be reckoned to be sth** *The Lowsons were reckoned to be very good farmers. | Moving house is reckoned to be nearly as stressful as divorce.* | **be reckoned as sth** *An earthquake of magnitude 7 is reckoned as a major quake.* GRAMMAR **Reckon** is usually passive in this meaning.
4 *formal* to calculate an amount: *The expression 'full moon' means the fourteenth day of the moon reckoned from its first appearance.*

GRAMMAR: Using the progressive

Reckon is not used in the progressive. You say: *I reckon he's going to win.* ✗ Don't say: *I'm reckoning he's going to win.*

GRAMMAR GUIDE VERBS

reckon on sth *phr v BrE* to expect something to happen, when you are making plans: *We were reckoning on a profit of about half a million a year.* | **reckon on doing sth** *I was reckoning on getting at least 60% of the votes.*

reckon sth ↔ **up** *phr v BrE old-fashioned* to add up amounts, costs etc in order to get a total SYN **calculate**: *Pat was reckoning up the cost of everything in her mind.*

reckon with sb/sth *phr v*
1 sb/sth to be reckoned with someone or something that is powerful and must be regarded seriously as a possible opponent, competitor, danger etc: *Barcelona will be a* ***force to be reckoned with*** *this season. | The principal was certainly a woman to be reckoned with.*
2 not reckon with sb/sth to not consider a possible problem when you are making plans: *I had not reckoned with the excitement in the popular press.*
3 have sb/sth to reckon with to have to deal with someone or something powerful: *Any invader would have the military might of NATO to reckon with.*

reckon without sb/sth *phr v BrE* if you are reckoning without something, you do not expect it and are not prepared for it: *They doubted that Fiona could finish the course, but they reckoned without her determination.*

reck·on·ing /ˈrekənɪŋ/ *n* **1** [U] calculation that is based on a careful guess rather than on exact knowledge: **by sb's reckoning** *By my reckoning, we have 12,000 clients.* **2** [C usually singular, U] a time when you are judged or punished for your actions, or when they have results that affect you: *We know that you will not forget their crimes when their **day of reckoning** comes.* | *In the **final reckoning**, the president failed to achieve his major goals.* **3 in/into/out of the reckoning** *BrE* among or not among those who are likely to win or be successful, especially in sport: *He had a knee injury, which put him out of the reckoning.* → DEAD RECKONING

re·claim /rɪˈkleɪm/ ●○○ *v* [T]
1 to get back an amount of money that you have paid SYN **claim back**: *You may be entitled to reclaim some tax.*
2 to make an area of desert, wet land etc suitable for farming or building: *This land will be reclaimed for a new airport.*
3 to get back something that you have lost or that has been taken away from you: *I want to reclaim the championship that I lost in 1999.*
4 to obtain useful products from waste material → **recycle**: *You can reclaim old boards and use them as shelves.*
—**reclamation** /ˌrekləˈmeɪʃən/ *n* [U]: *land reclamation*

re·cline /rɪˈklaɪn/ *v* **1** [I] *formal* to lie or lean back in a relaxed way: **[+in/on]** *I spent Sunday reclining in a deckchair.* | *A solitary figure was reclining on the grass.* **2** [I,T] if you recline a seat, or if it reclines, you lower the back of the seat so that you can lean back in it: **reclining seat/chair**

re·clin·er /rɪˈklaɪnə $ -ər/ *n* [C] *especially AmE* a chair in which you can lean back at different angles

re·cluse /rɪˈkluːs $ ˈrekluːs/ *n* [C] someone who chooses to live alone, and does not like seeing or talking to other people: *She became a recluse after her two sons were murdered.* —**reclusive** /rɪˈkluːsɪv/ *adj*

rec·og·ni·tion /ˌrekəgˈnɪʃən/ ●●○ W3 *n*
1 [singular, U] the act of realizing and accepting that something is true or important: **[+of]** *Don's recognition of the importance of Suzy in his life* | **recognition that** *There is general recognition that the study techniques of many students are weak.* | **formal/official recognition** *official recognition of the need for jail reform*
2 [singular, U] public respect and thanks for someone's work or achievements: *He has **achieved recognition** and respect as a scientist.* | *The importance of voluntary organizations in the economy still needs to be **given recognition**.* | **in recognition of sth** *He was presented with a gold watch in recognition of his service to the company.*
3 [U] the act of knowing someone or something because you have known or learned about them in the past: *He stared at her, but there was no **sign of recognition**.* | **change beyond/out of all recognition** (=change completely) *The bakery business has changed beyond all recognition in the last 10 years.*
4 [U] the act of officially accepting that an organization, government, person etc has legal or official authority: **[+of]** *the recognition of Latvia as an independent state* | **international/diplomatic recognition** *the government's failure to achieve international recognition*
5 speech recognition the ability of a computer to recognize speech: *speech recognition systems*

rec·og·nize (*also* **-ise** *BrE*) /ˈrekəgnaɪz, ˈrekən-/ ●●● S1 W1 *v* [T]
1 to know who someone is or what something is, because you have seen, heard, experienced, or learned about them in the past: *I didn't recognize you in your uniform.* | *It was malaria, but Dr Lee hadn't recognized the symptoms.*
2 to officially accept that an organization, government, document etc has legal or official authority: *British medical qualifications are recognized in Canada.* | **recognize sth as sth** *The World Health Organization has recognized alcoholism as a disease since 1951.*
3 to accept or admit that something is true: **recognize (that)** *One must recognise that homesickness is natural.* | **recognize what/how/who etc** *It is important to recognize how little we know about this disease.*
4 if something is recognized by people, they realize that it is important or very good: *Alexander tried to get his work recognized by the medical profession.* | **be recognized as sth** *Lawrence's novel was eventually recognized as a work of genius.* | *a recognized authority on Roman pottery*
5 to officially and publicly thank someone for something they have done, by giving them a special honour: *He was recognized for having saved many lives.* —**recognizable** /ˈrekəgnaɪzəbəl, -kən- ˌrekəgˈnaɪ-/ *adj*: *His face was **instantly recognizable**.* —**recognizably** *adv*

GRAMMAR: Using the progressive

Recognize is not used in the progressive. You say: *I recognize that woman.* ✗ Don't say: *I am recognizing that woman.*

GRAMMAR GUIDE ▸ VERBS

THESAURUS

recognize to know who someone is or what something is, especially because you have seen or heard them before: *I hadn't seen her for ten years, but I recognized her immediately.* | *Do you recognize this song?*

identify to recognize someone or something and say who or what they are: *As they came closer, I was able to identify two of the group.* | *It's delicious but I can't quite identify the taste.*

distinguish to recognize and understand the difference between two or more things or people: *By this age, kids can usually distinguish between right and wrong.* | *It's often difficult to distinguish identical twins from each other.*

make sth/sb out to be able to see or hear something or someone - used when it is very difficult to do this: *In the distance, I could just make out the outline of an island.* | *He whispered something but I couldn't make out what it was.*

discern /dɪˈsɜːn $ -ɜːrn/ *formal* to notice or understand something by looking carefully or thinking about it carefully: *I thought I discerned a faint gleam of hope in his eyes.* | *A number of differences can be discerned in the data for the three countries.*

know to recognize someone or something. Know is often used in everyday English instead of **recognize**: *How do you know that it is real gold?* | *I **know** him **from somewhere**.* | *I can't remember his name, but I **know his face**.*

can tell to be able to recognize someone or something: *I could tell that it was him by his voice.* | *Can you tell that it's not real leather?* | *It's difficult to be able to **tell them apart*** (=to recognize that they are different).

re·coil /rɪˈkɔɪl/ *v* [I] **1** to move back suddenly and quickly from something you do not like or are afraid of: **[+from/at]** *She recoiled from his touch as if she had been slapped.* **2** to feel such a strong dislike of a particular situation that you want to avoid it: **[+from/at]** *He recoils from everything in life that demands hard work.* | *We **recoil in horror** from the thought of subjecting someone to extreme pain.* **3** if a gun recoils, it moves backwards very quickly after it has been fired —**recoil** /ˈriːkɔɪl/ *n* [singular, U]: *The recoil of the gun sent him flying backwards.*

rec·ol·lect /ˌrekəˈlekt/ *v* [T] to be able to remember something SYN **remember**: *All I recollect is a grey sky.* | **recollect that** *She recollected sadly that she and Ben used to laugh a lot.* | **recollect how/when/what etc** *Can you recollect how your brother reacted?* | **recollect doing sth** *I recollect seeing Ryder some years ago in Bonn.* THESAURUS ▸ REMEMBER

rec·ol·lec·tion /ˌrekəˈlekʃən/ ●○○ *n formal*
1 [C] something from the past that you remember: *My earliest recollections are of my mother bending over my cot.*

2 [U] an act of remembering something: **have no recollection (of sth)** (=not remember) *I have no recollection of how I found my way there in the dark.* | **to (the best of) my recollection** (=used when you are unsure if you remember correctly) *To the best of my recollection, she drives a Mercedes.* | *No one, to my recollection, gave a second thought to the risks involved.*

re·com·mence /ˌriːkəˈmens/ *v* [I,T] to begin something again after it has stopped

rec·om·mend /ˌrekəˈmend/ ●●● S2 W2 *v* [T]
1 to advise someone to do something, especially because you have special knowledge of a situation or subject: **recommend (that)** *I recommend that you get some professional advice.* | *Doctors* ***strongly recommend*** *that fathers should be present at their baby's birth.* | **recommend doing sth** *I would never recommend using a sunbed on a regular basis.* | *Sleeping tablets are not recommended in this case.* | *It is dangerous to exceed the* ***recommended dose***. | **recommend sb to do sth** *Students are recommended to make an appointment with a counselor.* **THESAURUS** ADVISE
2 to say that something or someone is good, or suggest them for a particular purpose or job: *I recommend the butter chicken – it's delicious.* | *Can you recommend a good lawyer?* | **recommend sth to sb** *I recommend this book to anyone with an interest in chemistry.* | **recommend sth for sth/sb** *Which type of oil do you recommend for my car?* | **recommend sb for sth** *I have decided to recommend you for the directorship.* | **highly/thoroughly recommend** *The hotel is highly recommended.* **THESAURUS** SUGGEST
3 sth has much/little/nothing to recommend it used to say that something has many, few, or no good qualities: *The town itself has little to recommend it.*

GRAMMAR

Patterns with recommend (meaning 1)

- In everyday English, you **recommend that** someone **does** something: *I recommend that she speaks to a lawyer.* 'That' can be omitted: *I recommend she speaks to a lawyer.*
- In more formal English, you **recommend that** someone **do** something, using the base form of the verb (=the infinitive without 'to'): *I recommend that she speak to a lawyer.* ✗ Don't say: *I recommend her to speak to a lawyer.*
- In more formal English, you also use the base form of the verb when talking about the past: *I recommended that she speak to a lawyer.*
- You **recommend** that someone **should do** something: *I recommended that they should get insurance.*
- You can say **it is recommended that** someone **(should) do** something: *It is recommended that everyone (should) take the test.*

Patterns with recommend (meaning 2)

- You **recommend** something **to** someone: *I recommended a book to her.* ✗ Don't say: *I recommended her a book.*

GRAMMAR GUIDE VERBS

THESAURUS

recommend to advise someone to do something, especially when you have special knowledge of a situation or subject: *I would strongly recommend buying a good quality bicycle rather than a cheap one.* | *The report recommended stricter supervision of the trade in live animals.*
tell to tell someone that you think they should do something, especially in order to avoid problems: *We've been told that we should start revising early.* | *I told you not to drink the water here.*
urge to strongly advise someone to do something because you think it is very important: *Her doctor has urged her to see a specialist.* | *Police are urging drivers not to come into London this weekend.*
advocate to say publicly that something should be done, often something that a lot of people disagree about: *In 1984, he advocated the use of force against Nicaragua.* | *I am surprised that dentists don't advocate the use of fluoride tablets.*
endorse to say in an advertisement that you like a product and think that people should use it: *A lot of companies use sports stars to endorse their products.*

rec·om·men·da·tion /ˌrekəmenˈdeɪʃən/ ●●○ S3 W3 *n*
1 [C] official advice given to someone, especially about what to do: *We will review the case and* ***make a recommendation*** *to the client.* | **[+for]** *recommendations for school reform* | **[+of]** *the main recommendations of the report* | **recommendation that** *We are making no recommendation that children should use Standard English.* | **recommendation to do sth** *a recommendation to replace the existing system*
2 [U] a suggestion to someone that they should choose a particular thing or person that you think is very good: **on sb's recommendation** *Academic staff are appointed on the recommendation of a committee.*
3 [C] (*also* **letter of recommendation**) *especially AmE* a formal letter or statement saying that someone would be a suitable person to do a job, take a course of study etc: *Try to get letters of recommendation from bosses and colleagues.*

ˌrecommenˈdation ˌengine *n* [C] a piece of software that makes suggestions about products or services that you may like, based on things you have chosen before or things chosen by people who like the same things as you SYN **suggestion engine**

rec·om·pense[1] /ˈrekəmpens/ *v* [T] *formal* to give someone a payment for trouble or losses that you have caused them, or a reward for their efforts to help you SYN **compensate**: **recompense sb for sth** *The charge recompenses the bank for the costs involved.*

recompense[2] *n* [singular, U] *formal* something that you give to someone for trouble or losses that you have caused them, or as a reward for their help SYN **compensation**: **[+for]** *financial recompense for the victims of violence*

re·con /ˈriːkɒn $ -kɑːn/ *n* [C,U] *AmE informal* RECONNAISSANCE

rec·on·cile /ˈrekənsaɪl/ ●○○ *v*
1 [T] if you reconcile two ideas, situations, or facts, you find a way in which they can both be true or acceptable: *The possibility remains that the two theories may be reconciled.* | **reconcile sth with sth** *Bevan tried to reconcile British socialism with a wider international vision.*
2 be reconciled (with sb) to have a good relationship again with someone after you have quarrelled with them: *Jonah and his youngest son were, on the surface at least, reconciled.*

REGISTER
In everyday English, people usually say that two people **make up** rather than saying that they **are reconciled**: *They had a fight, but they seem to have* ***made up*** *now.*

reconcile sb **to** sth *phr v* to make someone able to accept a difficult or unpleasant situation: *He tried to reconcile his father to the idea of the wedding.* | **reconcile yourself to sth** *Henry had more or less reconciled himself to Don's death.*

rec·on·cil·i·a·tion /ˌrekənsɪliˈeɪʃən/ ●○○ *n* [singular, U]
1 a situation in which two people, countries etc become friendly with each other again after quarrelling: *Her ex-husband had always hoped for a reconciliation.* | **[+between/with]** *The meeting achieved a reconciliation between the groups.* | *his reconciliation with his brother* | *The treaty has brought a new spirit of reconciliation on both sides.* | *The leadership announced a programme of national reconciliation* (=an attempt by all sides to end a war or trouble in a country).
2 the process of finding a way that two beliefs, facts etc that are opposed to each other can both be true or successful: **[+between]** *a reconciliation between environment and development*

rec·on·dite /ˈrekəndaɪt, rɪˈkɒn- $ ˈrekən-, rɪˈkɑːn-/ *adj formal* recondite facts or subjects are not known about or understood by many people SYN **obscure**

re·con·di·tion /ˌriːkənˈdɪʃən/ *v* [T] to repair something, especially an old machine, so that it works like a new one: *a reconditioned engine*

re·con·nais·sance /rɪˈkɒnəsəns $ rɪˈkɑː-/ *n* [C,U] the military activity of sending soldiers and aircraft to find out about the enemy's forces: *reconnaissance aircraft | a reconnaissance mission | wartime roles such as observation and reconnaissance*

re·con·noi·tre *BrE*, **reconnoiter** *AmE* /ˌrekəˈnɔɪtə $ ˌriːkəˈnɔɪtər/ *v* [I,T] **1** to try to find out the position and size of your enemy's army, for example by flying planes over land where their soldiers are **2** to find out information about an area: *All morning, the world's top cyclists have been reconnoitring the course.*

re·con·sid·er /ˌriːkənˈsɪdə $ -ər/ ●○○ *v* [I,T] to think again about something in order to decide if you should change your opinion or do something different: *He should* ***reconsider*** *his* ***decision*** *to resign. | We want you to come. Please reconsider.* —**reconsideration** /ˌriːkənsɪdəˈreɪʃən/ *n* [U]

re·con·sti·tute /riːˈkɒnstɪtjuːt $ riːˈkɑːnstɪtuːt/ *v* [T] **1** to form an organization or a group again in a different way: *The committees will be reconstituted after the election.* | **reconstitute sth as sth** *In 1832 the firm was reconstituted as Mills and Co.* **2** to change dried food back to its original form by adding water to it: *reconstituted milk* —**reconstitution** /ˌriːkɒnstɪˈtjuːʃən $ -kɑːnstɪˈtuː-/ *n* [U]

re·con·struct /ˌriːkənˈstrʌkt/ ●○○ AWL *v* [T]
1 to produce a complete description or copy of an event by collecting together pieces of information: *Police were reconstructing the movements of the murdered couple.*
2 to build something again after it has been destroyed or damaged SYN **rebuild**: *The task ahead is to reconstruct the building.*

re·con·struc·tion /ˌriːkənˈstrʌkʃən/ ●○○ AWL *n*
1 [U] the work that is done to repair the damage to a city, industry etc, especially after a war: **[+of]** *the reconstruction of Western Europe after the war*
2 [C usually singular] a description or copy of an event or a place, which you produce by collecting information about it: **[+of]** *Detectives want to* ***stage*** *a* ***reconstruction*** *of events. | a reconstruction of a Roman villa*

re·con·struct·ive /ˌriːkənˈstrʌktɪv◂/ *adj* [only before noun] a reconstructive operation is one done to make a part of someone's body the right shape, for example after a bad injury or a previous operation: *He's recovering well from* ***reconstructive surgery*** *on his nose.*

re·con·vene /ˌriːkənˈviːn/ *v* [I,T] if a meeting, a court etc reconvenes, or if you reconvene it, it meets again after a break

rec·ord[1] /ˈrekɔːd $ -ərd/ ●●● S1 W1 *n*
1 INFORMATION [C] information about something that is written down or stored on computer, film etc so that it can be looked at in the future: **[+of]** *I try to keep a record of everything I spend. | According to official records, five people were killed last year near that road junction.*
2 HIGHEST/BEST EVER [C] the fastest speed, longest distance, highest or lowest level etc that has ever been achieved or reached, especially in sport: *The American team set a new world record in the sprint relay.*
3 MUSIC [C] a round flat piece of plastic with a hole in the middle that music and sound are stored on → **vinyl**: *I spent a lot of time* ***listening to records****. | My dad's got a huge* ***record collection****. | a major British* ***record company*** → RECORD PLAYER
4 PAST ACTIVITIES [singular] the facts about how successful, good, bad etc someone or something has been in the past: **record of/in (doing) sth** *Chemistry graduates have a good record in finding employment. | the company's* ***track record*** *in improving conditions* | **[+on]** *Mr Davis defended the government's record on unemployment* (=what they have done about unemployment).
5 CRIME [C] (*also* **criminal/police record**) information kept by the police that shows someone has committed a crime: *He's only 18 and he already has a record. | They won't employ anyone with a criminal record.*
6 the record books if someone is in the record books, they have achieved more than anyone else in a particular way: *She hopes to get into the record books by becoming the youngest woman to hold a pilot's licence.*
7 in record time very quickly: *She was out of bed and ready for school in record time that morning.*
8 off the record if you say something off the record, you do not want people to repeat what you say, for example in newspapers or meetings: *May I talk to you, strictly off the record?*
9 be/go on (the) record as saying (that) to say something publicly or officially, so that it may be written down and repeated: *She is on record as saying that teachers are under too much pressure.*
10 for the record *spoken* used to tell someone that what you are saying should be remembered or written down: *For the record, the police never charged me.*
11 set/put the record straight to tell people the truth about something, because you want to be sure that they understand what the truth really is: *I would like to set the record straight on a few points.*

COLLOCATIONS – MEANING 1

VERBS

the records show sth *Official records show that 44 businesses have stopped trading in the last 12 months.*
keep a record *Teachers keep a record of students' progress.*
place/put sth on record (=officially say something or write it down) *I wish to put on record my objection to the scheme.*
access records (*also* **have/gain access to records**) (=be able to look at them)

ADJECTIVES/NOUN + record

a written record *Where written records do survive, they are incomplete.*
historical records *Using historical records, we have produced an image of the temple.*
official records *This has been the wettest winter since official records began.*
an accurate record *Many hospitals did not keep accurate records.*
a detailed record | **medical/hospital/health etc records** | **financial records** | **public records** (=records of births, deaths etc, that the public are allowed to look at)

PHRASES

the biggest/highest etc on record *Last summer was one of the hottest on record.*

COLLOCATIONS – MEANING 2

VERBS

break/beat a record (=do better or be greater than an existing record) *He broke the world record twice.*
hold a record (=have it) *Davies holds the record for most points in a season.*
set a record (=achieve it for the first time) *The twenty-year-old set a new British record of 44.47 secs.*
equal a record (*also* **tie a record** *AmE*) (=do as well as the record)

ADJECTIVES

an all-time record *The price of oil has hit an all-time record.*
a world record *Powell equalled the 100 metres world record with a time of 9.77 seconds.*
an Olympic record | **a British/American/Italian etc record**

record + NOUN

a record number/level/time etc *Pollution in the lake has reached record levels.*
a record high/low *The stock market reached a record high on August 21.*

re·cord² /rɪˈkɔːd $ -ɔːrd/ ●●● S3 W2 *v*
1 [T] to write information down or store it in a computer or on film so that it can be looked at in the future: *Her husband made her record every penny she spent.* | **record that** *He recorded that the operation was successful.* | *In 1892* ***it** is* **recorded that** *the weather became so cold that the river froze over.* | *The coroner* **recorded** *a* **verdict** *of accidental death.*
2 [I,T] to store music, sound, television programmes etc on a DISC or tape so that people can listen to them or watch them again: *The group has just recorded a new album.* | *Is the machine still recording?* | *I'll record the film and we can all watch it later.*
3 [T] if an instrument records the size, speed, temperature etc of something, it measures it and keeps that information: *Wind speeds of up to 100 mph have been recorded.*

ˈrecord-ˌbreaking *adj* [only before noun] a record-breaking number, level, performance, or person is the highest, lowest, biggest, best etc of its type that has ever happened or existed: *his record-breaking flight across the Atlantic* —**record-breaker** *n* [C]

reˌcorded deˈlivery *n* [U] *BrE* if you send a letter or package by recorded delivery, you send it using a service which records that it has been sent and delivered SYN **certified mail** *AmE*

re·cord·er /rɪˈkɔːdə $ -ˈkɔːrdər/ ●●○ *n* [C]
1 cassette recorder/tape recorder/video recorder etc a piece of electrical equipment that records music, films etc → FLIGHT RECORDER
2 a simple wooden or plastic musical instrument like a tube with holes in it, which you play by blowing into it and covering different holes with your fingers to change the notes → see picture at WOODWIND
3 a judge in a city court, in some areas of Britain and the US

ˈrecord-ˌholder *n* [C] the person who has achieved the fastest speed, the longest distance etc in a sport: *the world long-jump record-holder*

re·cord·ing /rɪˈkɔːdɪŋ $ -ɔːr-/ ●●○ W3 *n*
1 [C] music, sound, or images that have been stored on a DISC, computer file, or tape: **[+of]** *Have you heard the new recording of Mozart's Requiem?* | *a video recording of the interview*
2 [U] the act of storing sound or images on tape or DISCS: **recording studio/equipment etc** (=a studio etc used for recording music)

ˈrecord ˌplayer *n* [C] a piece of equipment for playing records

re·count¹ /rɪˈkaʊnt/ ●○○ *v* [T] *formal* to tell someone a story or describe a series of events: **recount how/what** *Alan recounted how he and Joyce had met.* THESAURUS TELL

re·count² /ˈriːkaʊnt/ *n* [C] a second count of votes that happens in an election because the result was very close —**recount** /riːˈkaʊnt/ *v* [T]

re·coup /rɪˈkuːp/ *v* [T] to get back an amount of money you have lost or spent SYN **recover**: *The movie will have to be a huge hit to recoup its cost.* | *He was desperate to try and recoup his losses.*

re·course /rɪˈkɔːs $ ˈriːkɔːrs/ *n* [singular, U] *formal* something that you do to achieve something or deal with a situation, or the act of doing it: *We may conclude that he never* ***had recourse to*** *this simple experiment.* | **without recourse to sth** (=without using or doing something) *a way of solving disputes without recourse to courts of law* | *Surgery may be the only recourse.*

re·cov·er /rɪˈkʌvə $ -ər/ ●●● W2 AWL *v*
1 [I] to get better after an illness, accident, shock etc: *After a few days of fever, she began to recover.* | **[+from]** *He's in hospital, recovering from a heart attack.*

> **GRAMMAR**
> **Recover** is never transitive in this meaning. You say: *I've recovered from my cold.* ✗ Don't say: *I've recovered my cold.*
> GRAMMAR GUIDE VERBS

2 [I] to return to a normal condition after a period of trouble or difficulty: *The tourist industry is recovering to pre-war levels.* | **[+from]** *Yesterday morning shares seemed to recover from Monday's collapse.*
3 [T] to get back something that was taken from you, lost, or almost destroyed: *Four paintings stolen from the gallery have been recovered.* | **recover sth from sth** *Two bodies were recovered from the wreckage.*
4 [T] to get back an amount of money that you have spent or lost SYN **recoup**: *He was entitled to* **recover damages** *from the defendants.*
5 [T] to get back an ability, a sense, or control over your feelings, movements etc after a period without it SYN **regain**: *It was some hours before she* **recovered consciousness**. | *Once she stumbled, but somehow she* **recovered** *her* **balance** *and carried on running.* | **recover yourself** *He recovered himself enough to speak calmly.* —**recoverable** *adj*

> **THESAURUS**
> **recover** to become healthy again after you have been seriously ill or injured, or had a bad experience: *My mother's been very ill, and she's still in hospital recovering.* | *She needed time to recover from the shock.*
> **get better** to recover from an injury or illness. In everyday English, people usually say **get better** rather than **recover**: *I hope you get better soon.* | *My back's been quite bad recently, but it's getting better slowly.*
> **get over sth** to recover from a bad experience, or a minor illness. In everyday English, people usually say **get over** rather than **recover**: *She never got over his death.* | *I'm getting over my cold.*
> **get well** to recover from an illness or operation – used especially when you are writing to encourage someone to recover: *Get well soon – we all miss you!* | *I hope you get well quickly.*
> **be back on your feet** to have recovered and be able to live life as usual again: *It may take a week or two until you're back on your feet.*
> **be on the mend** to be showing definite signs of recovering after an illness or injury: *I'm glad to see you're on the mend again.*
> **recuperate** *formal* to spend time resting and getting your health or energy back, after you have had an illness or had a difficult or tiring experience: *It had been a hard year, and I needed a few weeks in the sun in order to recuperate.* | *He is recuperating from a heart attack.*
> **convalesce** /ˌkɒnvəˈles $ ˌkɑːn-/ *formal* to spend a long period of time recovering from a serious illness, especially by resting in a comfortable or warm place: *She was at home convalescing after major surgery.*

re·cov·er·y /rɪˈkʌvəri/ ●●○ W3 AWL *n*
1 [singular, U] the process of getting better after an illness, injury etc: **make a full/good/remarkable etc recovery** *Doctors expect him to make a full recovery.* | **[+from]** *Ann made a quick recovery from her operation.*
2 [singular, U] the process of returning to a normal condition after a period of trouble or difficulty: *Hopes of* **economic recovery** *are fading.*
3 [U] when you get something back that has been taken or lost: **[+of]** *the recovery of the stolen money*

reˈcovery ˌprogram *n* [C] *AmE* a course of treatment for people who are ADDICTED to drugs or alcohol

reˈcovery room *n* [C] a room in a hospital where people first wake up after an operation

re·cre·ate /ˌriːkriˈeɪt/ ●○○ AWL *v* [T] to make something from the past exist again in a new form or be experienced again SYN **recapture**: *You can never recreate the feeling of winning for the first time.*

rec·re·a·tion /ˌrekriˈeɪʃən/ ●●○ *n* [C,U] an activity that you do for pleasure or amusement → **hobby**, **pastime**, **leisure**: *His only recreations are drinking beer and watching football.* | *the provision of* **recreation facilities** (=places or equipment for people to use to enjoy themselves) |

recreation ground/area/room *a recreation area for children to play in* THESAURUS ▸ FUN —**recreational** *adj*: *recreational activities*

ˌrecreational ˈvehicle *n* [C] *AmE* an RV

recreˈation ˌground *n* [C] *BrE* an area of public land used for sports and games SYN **playing field**

recreˈation ˌroom *n* [C] **1** a public room, for example in a hospital, used for social activities or games **2** *AmE* a room in a private house, where you can relax, play games etc SYN **games room** *BrE*

re·crim·i·na·tion /rɪˌkrɪməˈneɪʃən/ *n* [C usually plural, U] when you blame or criticize someone for something that has happened: *Bitter accusations and recriminations followed the disaster.*

rec room /ˈrek ruːm, -rʊm/ *n* [C] *AmE informal* a RECREATION ROOM

re·cruit¹ /rɪˈkruːt/ ●●○ *v*
1 [I,T] to find new people to work in a company, join an organization, do a job etc: *We're having difficulty recruiting enough qualified staff.* | *Many government officials were recruited from private industry.*
2 [I,T] to get people to join the army, navy etc → **conscript**: *Most of the men in the village were recruited that day.*
3 [T] to persuade someone to do something for you: **recruit sb to do sth** *I recruited three of my friends to help me move.* —**recruiter** *n* [C]

recruit² ●○○ *n* [C]
1 someone who has just joined the army, navy, or air force → **conscript**: **new/raw/fresh recruit** (=one who is completely untrained) *Drill sergeants have eight weeks to turn fresh recruits into soldiers.*
2 someone who has recently joined an organization, team, group of people etc: *New recruits are sent to the Atlanta office for training.*

re·cruit·ment /rɪˈkruːtmənt/ ●●○ *n* [U] the process of finding new people to join a company, organization, the army etc: **[+of]** *the recruitment of nurses* | *A* ***recruitment drive*** *to attract new members is underway.* | *a recruitment agency*

rec·tal /ˈrektəl/ *adj medical* relating to the RECTUM

rec·tan·gle /ˈrektæŋɡəl/ ●●● *n* [C] a shape that has four straight sides, two of which are usually longer than the other two, and four 90° angles at the corners → **square** → see picture at SHAPE¹

rec·tan·gu·lar /rekˈtæŋɡjələ $ -ər/ ●○○ *adj* having the shape of a rectangle

rec·ti·fy /ˈrektɪfaɪ/ ●○○ *v* (**rectified**, **rectifying**, **rectifies**) [T] *formal* to correct something that is wrong SYN **put right**: *I did my best to rectify the situation, but the damage was already done.* —**rectification** /ˌrektɪfɪˈkeɪʃən/ *n* [C,U]

rec·ti·lin·e·ar /ˌrektəˈlɪniə◂ $ -ər◂/ *adj technical* consisting of straight lines

rec·ti·tude /ˈrektɪtjuːd $ -tuːd/ *n* [U] *formal* behaviour that is honest and morally correct

rec·tor /ˈrektə $ -ər/ *n* [C] **1** a priest in some Christian churches who is responsible for a particular area, group etc → **vicar** **2** the person in charge of certain colleges and schools

rec·to·ry /ˈrektəri/ *n* (*plural* **rectories**) [C] a house where the priest of the local church lives → **vicarage**

rec·tum /ˈrektəm/ *n* (*plural* **rectums** *or* **recta** /-tə/) [C] *medical* the lowest part of your BOWELS → **rectal**

re·cum·bent /rɪˈkʌmbənt/ *adj formal* lying down on your back or side

re·cu·pe·rate /rɪˈkjuːpəreɪt, -ˈkuː-/ *v* **1** [I] to get better again after an illness or injury SYN **recover**: **[+from]** *Coles is recuperating from a sprained ankle.* THESAURUS ▸ RECOVER **2** [T] *especially BrE* to get back money that you have spent or lost in business SYN **recoup**, **recover**: *We've recuperated our losses.* **3** [I] to return to a more normal condition after a difficult time SYN **recover**: *Winston proposed several ways for the industry to recuperate.* —**recuperation** /rɪˌkjuːpəˈreɪʃən, -ˌkuː-/ *n* [U]

re·cu·pe·ra·tive /rɪˈkjuːpərətɪv, -ˈkuː- $ -pəreɪtɪv/ *adj* [only before noun] recuperative powers, abilities etc help someone or something get better again, especially after an illness: *a recuperative vacation*

re·cur /rɪˈkɜː $ -ɜːr/ ●○○ *v* (**recurred**, **recurring**) [I]
1 if something, especially something bad or unpleasant, recurs, it happens again: *There is a danger that the disease may recur.* | *Love is a* ***recurring theme*** *in the book.* | **recurring dream/nightmare**
2 *technical* if a number or numbers after a DECIMAL POINT recur, they are repeated for ever in the same order

re·cur·rence /rɪˈkʌrəns $ -ˈkɜːr-/ ●○○ *n* [C usually singular, U] *formal* an occasion when something that has happened before happens again: **[+of]** *after the recurrence of a back problem* | *Measures must be taken to stop a recurrence of last night's violence.*

re·cur·rent /rɪˈkʌrənt $ -ˈkɜːr-/ *adj* happening or appearing several times: *recurrent minor illnesses* | *Political revolution is a* ***recurrent theme*** *in Riley's books.* —**recurrently** *adv*

re·cy·cla·ble /ˌriːˈsaɪkləbəl/ *adj* used materials or substances that are recyclable can be recycled: *recyclable cardboard packaging* —**recyclables** *n* [plural]

re·cy·cle /ˌriːˈsaɪkəl/ ●●○ *v*
1 [I,T] to put used objects or materials through a special process so that they can be used again: *We take all our bottles to be recycled.* | *packaging made of* ***recycled paper***
2 [T] to use something such as an idea, writing etc again instead of developing something new: *The fashion world just keeps recycling old ideas.*

re·cy·cling /riːˈsaɪklɪŋ/ ●●○ *n*
1 [U] the process of treating used objects or materials so that they can be used again: *Recycling is important to help protect our environment.* → see picture at BIN¹
2 [singular] *AmE informal* things that are to be recycled: *Don't forget to take out the recycling.*

red¹ /red/ ●●● S1 W1 *adj* (*comparative* **redder**, *superlative* **reddest**)
1 COLOUR having the colour of blood: *We painted the door* ***bright red.*** | *a red balloon* → BLOOD-RED, → **cherry red** at CHERRY(3), SCARLET
2 HAIR hair that is red has an orange-brown colour
3 FACE if you go red, your face becomes a bright pink colour, especially because you are embarrassed or angry: **go/turn red** *Every time you mention his name, she goes bright red.*
4 WINE red wine is a red or purple colour → **white**
5 like a red rag to a bull *BrE* (*also* **like waving a red flag in front of a bull** *AmE*) very likely to make someone angry or upset: *Just mentioning his ex-wife's name was like a red rag to a bull.*
6 roll out the red carpet/give sb the red carpet treatment to give special treatment to an important visitor
7 not one red cent *AmE informal* used to emphasize that you mean no money at all: *I wouldn't give him one red cent for that car.*
8 POLITICS *informal* COMMUNIST or extremely LEFT-WING political views - used to show disapproval —**redness** *n* [U] → **paint the town red** at PAINT²(5)

red² ●●● S2 W2 *n*
1 [C,U] the colour of blood: *I like the way the artist uses red in this painting.* | *the reds and yellows of the trees* | *The corrections were marked in red* (=in red ink).
2 [C,U] red wine → **white**: *a nice bottle of red*
3 be in the red *informal* to owe more money than you have OPP **be in the black** → **overdrawn**: *This is the airline's fourth straight year in the red.*
4 [C] *informal* someone who has COMMUNIST or very LEFT-WING political opinions - used especially in the past to show disapproval → **see red** at SEE¹(34)

re·dac·tion /rɪˈdækʃən/ *n* [C,U] the action of changing, removing, or putting black marks over parts of an official document before it is published in order to keep information secret: *There were complaints about the redaction of details of MPs' expenses claims.* —**redact** /rɪˈdækt/ *v* [T]

ˌred aˈlert *n* [C usually singular, U] a warning that there is

R

very great danger: **be (put/placed) on red alert** *All the hospitals are on red alert.*

ˌred ˈblood cell (*also* **ˌred ˈcorpuscle**) *n* [C] one of the cells in your blood that carry oxygen to every part of your body → **white blood cell**

ˌred-ˈblooded *adj* **red-blooded male/Englishman/American etc** used to emphasize that someone has all of the qualities that a typical man, Englishman etc is supposed to have – used humorously

red·brick /ˈredbrɪk/ *adj* a redbrick university is one of the British universities built in the late 19th or early 20th century, rather than an older university → **Oxbridge**

red ˈbutton *n* [C] a red button on a television REMOTE CONTROL which you press if you want to use INTERACTIVE TV services

ˌred ˈcard *n* [C] a red card held up by the REFEREE in a football match, to show that a player has done something against the rules and will not be allowed to play for the rest of the game → **yellow card**

ˌred-ˈcarpet *adj* [only before noun] relating to or suitable for an important event which guests arrive at by walking along a red carpet: *The Oscar ceremony is the year's biggest red-carpet event.* | *a red-carpet dress*

red·coat /ˈredkəʊt $ -koʊt/ *n* [C] a British soldier during the 18th and 19th centuries

ˌRed ˈCrescent *n* **the Red Crescent** an organization in Muslim countries that helps people who are suffering as a result of war, floods, disease etc

ˌRed ˈCross *n* **the Red Cross** an international organization that helps people who are suffering as a result of war, floods, disease etc

red·cur·rant /ˌredˈkʌrənt◂ $ -ˈkɜːr-/ *n* [C] a very small red fruit that grows on bushes in northern Europe

red·den /ˈredn/ *v* [I,T] *written* to become red, or to make something red: *Sue's face reddened.*

red·dish /ˈredɪʃ/ *adj* slightly red: *reddish-brown lipstick*

re·dec·o·rate /riːˈdekəreɪt/ *v* [I,T] to change the way a room looks by painting it, changing the curtains etc —**redecoration** /riːˌdekəˈreɪʃən/ *n* [U]

re·deem /rɪˈdiːm/ ●○○ *v* [T] *formal*

1 IMPROVE STH to make something less bad SYN **make up for**: *Olivier's performance redeemed an otherwise second-rate play.* | **redeeming quality/feature etc** (=the one good thing about an unpleasant person or thing) *The hotel had a single redeeming feature – it was cheap.*

2 redeem yourself to do something that will improve what other people think of you, after you have behaved badly or failed: *He spent the rest of the game trying to redeem himself after a first-minute mistake.*

3 GET MONEY FOR STH to exchange a piece of paper representing an amount of money for that amount of money or for goods equal in cost to that amount of money: *You can redeem the coupon at any store.*

4 RELIGION to free someone from the power of evil, especially in the Christian religion → REDEEMER

5 redeem a promise/pledge *formal* to do what you promised to do: *The government found itself unable to redeem its election pledges.*

6 GET STH BACK to buy back something which you left with someone you borrowed money from: **redeem sth from sth** *He finally redeemed his watch from the pawnbroker.*

re·deem·a·ble /rɪˈdiːməbəl/ *adj* able to be exchanged for money or goods: *Stamps are redeemable for merchandise or cash.*

Re·deem·er /rɪˈdiːmə $ -ər/ *n literary* **the Redeemer** Jesus Christ

re·demp·tion /rɪˈdempʃən/ *n* [U] **1** the state of being freed from the power of evil, believed by Christians to be made possible by Jesus Christ **2** the act of exchanging a piece of paper worth a particular amount of money for money, goods, or services **3 past/beyond redemption** too bad to be saved, repaired, or improved **4** *technical* the exchange of SHARES, BONDS etc for money —**redemptive** /-tɪv/ *adj*

re·de·ploy /ˌriːdɪˈplɔɪ/ *v* [T] to move someone or something to a different place or job: *There are plans to redeploy 200 employees in the next six months.* —**redeployment** *n* [U]

re·de·vel·op /ˌriːdɪˈveləp/ *v* [T] to make an area more modern by putting in new buildings or changing or repairing the old ones: *The old docks are being redeveloped as a business park.*

re·de·vel·op·ment /ˌriːdɪˈveləpmənt/ *n* [C,U] the act of redeveloping an area, especially in a city: *redevelopment of the city's downtown area*

ˈred eye *n* **take the red eye** *AmE informal* to take a journey in a plane that continues all night: *I took the red eye to LA.*

ˌred-ˈfaced *adj* embarrassed or ashamed: *Red-faced officials ordered an investigation into the accident.* THESAURUS EMBARRASSED

ˌred ˈflag *n* [C] *AmE* something that shows or warns you that something might be wrong, illegal etc

ˌred ˈgiant *n* [C] a large star that is near the middle of its life and shines with a reddish light

ˌred-ˈhanded *adj* **catch sb red-handed** to catch someone at the moment when they are doing something wrong: *Earl was caught red-handed taking the money.*

red·head /ˈredhed/ *n* [C] someone who has red hair

ˌred ˈherring *n* [C] a fact or idea that is not important but is introduced to take your attention away from the points that are important → **distraction**

ˌred-ˈhot *adj* **1 a)** metal or rock that is red-hot is so hot that it shines red: *The poker glowed red-hot in the fire.* **b)** *informal* very hot: *Be careful with those plates – they're red-hot.* **2** *informal* extremely active, exciting, or interesting: *a red-hot news story* | *The Braves have been red-hot in the last few games.* **3** a red-hot feeling is very strong: *red-hot anger* **4 red-hot favourite** *BrE* the team or person who most people believe will win a competition

re·dial /ˌriːˈdaɪəl/ *v* (**redialled**, **redialling** *BrE*, **redialed**, **redialing** *AmE*) [I,T] to DIAL a telephone number again

re·di·rect /ˌriːdaɪˈrekt, -də-/ *v* [T] **1** to use something for a different purpose: *She was good at redirecting the children's energy into something useful.* **2** to send something in a different direction: *The flight was redirected to Cleveland.* **3** *BrE* to send someone's letters to their new address from an address that they have left SYN **forward** —**redirection** /-ˈrekʃən/ *n* [U]

re·dis·trib·ute /ˌriːdɪˈstrɪbjuːt/ AWL *v* [T] to give something to each member of a group so that it is divided up in a different way from before: **redistribute income/wealth/resources etc** *a programme to redistribute wealth from the rich to the poor*

re·dis·tri·bu·tion /ˌriːdɪstrəˈbjuːʃən/ AWL *n* [U] the act of redistributing something, especially money or land: **[+of]** *a major redistribution of land*

ˌred-ˈletter day *n* [C] *informal* a day that you will always remember because something special happened that made you very happy

ˌred-ˈlight ˌdistrict *n* [C] the area of a town or city where there are many PROSTITUTES

ˌred ˈmeat *n* [U] dark coloured meat such as BEEF or LAMB → **white meat**

red·neck /ˈrednek/ *n* [C] *AmE informal* a person who lives in a country area of the US, is uneducated, and has strong unreasonable opinions – used to show disapproval: *a redneck bar*

ˌRed ˈNose ˌDay a day every other year on which a lot of money is collected for people who need help in the UK and other countries. Red Nose Day is organized by the CHARITY organization Comic Relief, and people often wear plastic red noses or put them on the front of their cars to show their support.

re·do /riːˈduː/ *v* (*past tense* **redid** /-ˈdɪd/, *past participle* **redone** /-ˈdʌn/, *third person singular* **redoes** /-ˈdʌz/) [T] **1** to do something again: *You'll have to redo this piece of work.* **2** to change the way a room is decorated SYN **redecorate**: *We're having the kitchen redone.*

red·o·lent /ˈredəl-ənt/ *adj* **1** *formal* making you think of something SYN **reminiscent**: **[+of]** *a style redolent of the sixties* **2** *literary* smelling strongly of something: **[+of/with]** *The bar was redolent with the smell of stale cigarette smoke.*

re·doub·le /riːˈdʌbəl/ *v* **redouble your efforts** to greatly increase your effort as you try to do something: *Both sides redoubled their efforts to end the war.*

re·doubt /rɪˈdaʊt/ *n* [C] *formal* a small hidden place, for example where soldiers hide themselves when they are fighting

re·doubt·a·ble /rɪˈdaʊtəbəl/ *adj literary* someone who is redoubtable is a person you respect or fear: *He had never met a more redoubtable fighter.*

re·dound /rɪˈdaʊnd/ *v* **redound to sb's credit/honour etc** *formal* to improve people's opinion of someone

ˌred ˈpepper *n* **1** [C] a red vegetable which you can eat raw or use in cooking: *stuffed red peppers* **2** [U] a spicy red powder used in cooking SYN **cayenne pepper**

re·dress¹ /rɪˈdres/ *v* [T] *formal* to correct something that is wrong or unfair: *Little could be done to* ***redress the situation***. | *Affirmative action was meant to* ***redress the balance*** (=make the situation fair) *for minorities.*

re·dress² /rɪˈdres $ ˈriːdres/ *n* [U] *formal* money that someone pays you because they have caused you harm or damaged your property SYN **compensation**: *The only hope of redress is in a lawsuit.*

ˌred ˈtape *n* [U] official rules that seem unnecessary and prevent things from being done quickly and easily → **bureaucracy**: *a procedure surrounded by bureaucracy and red tape* | *The new rules should help* ***cut the red tape*** *for farmers.*

ˈred-top *n* [C] *BrE informal* a British newspaper that has its name in red at the top of the front page. Red-tops have a lot of readers, but are not considered to be as serious as other newspapers. → **tabloid**

re·duce /rɪˈdjuːs $ rɪˈduːs/ ●●● S1 W1 *v*
1 [T] to make something smaller or less in size, amount, or price SYN **cut** → **reduction**: *The governor announced a new plan to reduce crime.* | *The helmet law should reduce injuries in motorcycle accidents.* | *Small businesses will need to reduce costs in order to survive.* | **reduce sth by sth** *The workforce has been reduced by half.* | **reduce sth (from sth) to sth** *All the shirts were reduced to £10.* | *The new bridge should reduce travelling time from 50 minutes to 15 minutes.*
2 [I,T] if you reduce a liquid, or if it reduces, you boil it so that there is less of it
3 [I] *especially AmE* to become thinner by losing weight → **diet**
4 be in reduced circumstances *old-fashioned* to be poorer than you were before

THESAURUS

TO REDUCE PRICES, NUMBERS, OR AMOUNTS

reduce to make the price, amount, or size of something less or smaller: *The price was reduced by 50%.* | *We need to reduce the amount of salt in our diet.*
cut to reduce something, especially by a large amount – used about prices, costs, jobs, or the time needed to do something: *Companies are always looking for ways to cut costs.* | *The journey time will be cut to under 2 hours.*
lower to reduce the level, limit, or amount of something. **Lower** sounds rather formal: *The voting age was lowered to 18.* | *The government decided to lower interest rates by 0.5%.*
bring sth down to reduce something such as prices or costs, or reduce the level of something. **Bring sth down** is less formal than **lower**: *The government wants to bring down the level of inflation.* | *The company is trying to bring its costs down.*
slash *informal* to reduce an amount or price by a very large amount – used especially in newspapers and advertisements: *Public spending has been slashed over the past two years.* | *Prices slashed for one week only!*
cut sth back to reduce the amount of something – used especially about people deciding to spend less, do less, or use less of something: *The education budget has been cut back again.* | *I need to cut back on my workload.*
downsize to reduce the number of people employed in order to reduce costs – used about a company or organization: *The company is planning to downsize its European operations.*

reduce sb/sth **to** sth *phr v*
1 reduce sb to tears/silence etc to make someone cry, be silent etc: *She was reduced to tears in front of her students.*
2 reduce sb to doing sth to make someone do something they would rather not do, especially when it involves behaving or living in a way that is not as good as before: *Eventually Charlotte was reduced to begging on the streets.*
3 reduce sth to ashes/rubble/ruins to destroy something, especially a building, completely: *A massive earthquake reduced the city to rubble.*
4 to change something into a shorter simpler form: *Many jobs can be reduced to a few simple points.*

re·duc·i·ble /rɪˈdjuːsəbəl $ rɪˈduːs-/ *adj* [not before noun] *formal* able to be considered simply as something: **[+to]** *Things do not happen according to plan, and they are not reducible to tidy models.*

re·duc·tion /rɪˈdʌkʃən/ ●●● S3 W2 *n* [C,U] a decrease in the size, price, or amount of something, or the act of decreasing something OPP **increase**: *strategies for noise reduction* | **[+in]** *a slight reduction in the price of oil* | **[+of]** *the reduction of interest rates* | **[+on]** *substantial reductions on children's clothes* | *The company promised they would* ***make*** *no staff* ***reductions*** *for at least two years.*

re·duc·tion·is·m /rɪˈdʌkʃənɪzəm/ *n* [U] *formal* when someone tries to explain complicated ideas or systems in very simple terms – often used to show disapproval —**reductionist** *adj*

re·dun·dan·cy /rɪˈdʌndənsi/ *n* (*plural* **redundancies**)
1 [C,U] *BrE* a situation in which someone has to leave their job, because they are no longer needed SYN **layoff**: *The closure of the export department resulted in over 100 redundancies.* | *Two thousand workers now face redundancy.* | *An employee is not eligible for a* ***redundancy payment*** *unless he has been with the company for two years.* | **voluntary/compulsory redundancy** *We were offered a £3,000 cash bonus to take voluntary redundancy.*
2 [U] when something is not used because something similar or the same already exists

reˈdundancy ˌpay *n* [U] *BrE* money you get from your employer when you are made redundant SYN **severance pay** *AmE*

re·dun·dant /rɪˈdʌndənt/ ●●○ *adj*
1 *BrE* if you are redundant, your employer no longer has a job for you: *Seventy factory workers were* ***made redundant*** *in the resulting cuts.* | **make a job/position etc redundant** *As the economy weakens, more and more jobs will be made redundant.* **THESAURUS** UNEMPLOYED
2 not necessary because something else means or does the same thing: *the removal of redundant information*

red·wood /ˈredwʊd/ *n* [C,U] a very tall tree that grows in California and Oregon, or the wood from this tree

reed /riːd/ *n* **1** [C,U] a type of tall plant like grass that grows in wet places: *Reeds grew in clumps all along the river bank.* **2** [C] a thin piece of wood that is attached to a musical instrument such as an OBOE or CLARINET, and that produces a sound when you blow over it

re·ed·u·cate /riːˈedjəkeɪt $ -dʒə-/ *v* [T] to teach someone to think or behave in a different way: *Young criminals must be re-educated.* —**re-education** /riːˌedjəˈkeɪʃən $ -dʒə-/ *n* [U]

reed·y /ˈriːdi/ *adj* **1** a voice that is reedy is high and unpleasant to listen to **2** a place that is reedy has a lot of reeds growing there

reef¹ /riːf/ *n* [C] a line of sharp rocks, often made of

R

CORAL, or a raised area of sand near the surface of the sea: *a proposal to protect several miles of thousand-year-old **coral reef***

reef² (*also* **reef in**) *v* [T] *technical* to tie up part of a sail in order to make it smaller

ree·fer /ˈriːfə $ -ər/ *n* [C] *old-fashioned* a cigarette containing the drug MARIJUANA SYN **joint**

ˈ**reef knot** *n* [C] *especially BrE* a double knot that cannot come undone easily SYN **square knot** *AmE*

reek /riːk/ *v* [I] to have a strong bad smell SYN **stink**: *This room absolutely reeks.* | **[+of]** *He reeked of sweat.* —**reek** *n* [singular]: *the reek of cigarettes and beer*

reek of sth *phr v* to seem very clearly to have a particular quality or be connected with something bad: *The whole business reeks of dishonesty.*

reel¹ /riːl/ *v* [I] **1** to be confused or shocked by a situation: *Norman's brain was reeling, but he did his best to appear calm.* | **[+from]** *The party is still reeling from its recent election defeat.* **2** (*also* **reel back**) to step backwards suddenly and almost fall over, especially after being hit or getting a shock: *Diane reeled back in amazement.* | *The force of the punch sent him reeling against the wall.* **3** [always + adv/prep] to walk in an unsteady way and almost fall over, as if you are drunk: *Andy reeled away from the bar and knocked over his stool.* **4** to seem to go around and around: *The room reeled before my eyes and I fainted.*

R

reel sb/sth ↔ **in** *phr v* **1** to wind the reel on a fishing rod so that a fish caught on the line comes towards you: *It took almost an hour to reel the fish in.* **2** to get or attract a large number of people or things SYN **pull in**: *The programme reels in more than 13 million viewers a show.*

reel sth ↔ **off** *phr v* **1** to repeat a lot of information quickly and easily: *Jack reeled off a list of names.* **2** *informal* to do something again and again: *The Yankees reeled off 14 straight wins.*

REEL

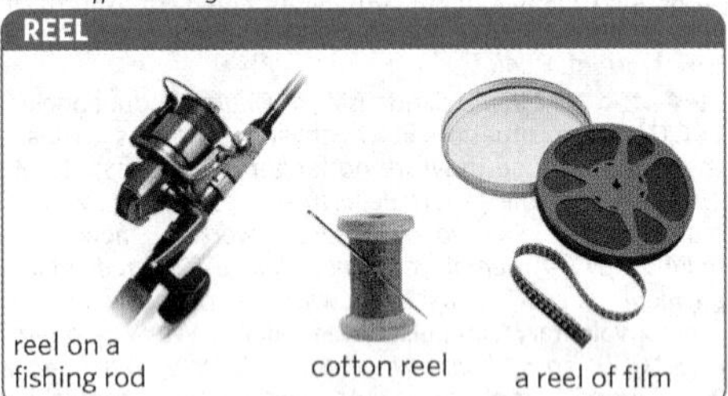

reel on a fishing rod | cotton reel | a reel of film

reel² *n* [C] **1 a)** a round object onto which film, wire, a special string for fishing etc can be wound: *a cotton reel* | *a fishing rod and reel* **b)** the amount that one of these objects will hold: *a reel of film* **2** one of the parts of a cinema film that is contained on a reel: *the final reel* **3** a quick FOLK dance, especially one from Scotland or Ireland, or the music for this

re-e·lect /ˌriː ɪˈlekt/ *v* [T] to elect someone again: *Morris was re-elected for a third term.* —**re-election** /-ˈlekʃən/ *n* [C,U]: *Barnes is **seeking re-election**.*

re-enact /ˌriː ɪˈnækt/ *v* [T] to perform the actions of a story, crime etc that happened in the past: *At the church, children re-enacted the Christmas story.* —**re-enactment** *n* [C]: *a re-enactment of the crime*

re-en·gi·neer (*also* **re-engineer**) /ˌriːendʒəˈnɪə $ -ˈnɪr/ *v* [T] **1** to change the structure of an activity, organization etc so that it performs better: *They reengineered the department, and cut nearly 400 jobs.* **2** to improve the design of a product: *Radio networks are being reengineered to give digital operation.* —**reengineering** *n* [U]

re-en·try /riˈentri/ *n* (*plural* **re-entries**) [C,U] **1** when someone starts being involved in something again or enters a place again: **[+into]** *America's successful re-entry into the Japanese auto market* **2** when a spacecraft enters the Earth's ATMOSPHERE again: *The satellite burned up on re-entry.* —**re-enter** *v* [I,T]

reeve /riːv/ *n* [C] **1** the official who is in charge of the town governments in some Canadian PROVINCES **2** an English law officer in the past

ref /ref/ *n* [C] *informal* a REFEREE

ref. (*also* **ref** *BrE*) the written abbreviation of ***reference***

re·fec·to·ry /rɪˈfektəri/ *n* (*plural* **refectories**) [C] *BrE* a large room in a school, college etc where meals are served and eaten SYN **cafeteria** *AmE*

re·fer /rɪˈfɜː $ -ɜːr/ ●●● S1 W1 *v* (**referred, referring**)

refer to sb/sth *phr v*

1 to mention or speak about someone or something: *We agreed never to refer to the matter again.* | *Although she didn't mention any names, everyone knew who she was referring to.* | **[+as]** *He likes to be referred to as 'Doctor Khee'.* | **[+by]** *The hospital now refers to patients by name, not case number.*

GRAMMAR

You always **refer to** someone or something: *He referred to my letter.* ✗ Don't say: *He referred about my letter.* | *He referred my letter.*

2 to look at a book, map, piece of paper etc for information: *He gave the speech without referring to his notes.*

3 if a statement, number, report etc refers to someone or something, it is about that person or thing: *The figures refer to our sales in Europe.*

4 refer sb/sth to sb to send someone or something to a person or organization to be helped or dealt with: *My doctor is referring me to a dermatologist.* | *My complaint was referred to the manufacturers.*

5 refer sb to sth *formal* to tell someone where to find information: *Readers are referred to the bibliography for further information.*

re·fer·a·ble /rɪˈfɜːrəbəl/ *adj* [+to] *formal* something that is referable to something else can be related to it

ref·er·ee¹ /ˌrefəˈriː/ ●●○ *n* [C]

1 someone who makes sure that the rules of a sport such as football, BASKETBALL, or BOXING, are followed → **umpire** → see pictures at **BASKETBALL**, **FOOTBALL**, **UMPIRE¹**

2 *BrE* someone who provides information about you when you are trying to get a job: *His headmaster agreed to act as his referee.*

3 someone who is asked to settle a disagreement

4 someone who judges an article or RESEARCH idea before it is PUBLISHed or money is provided for it

referee² *v* (**refereed, refereeing**) [I,T] to be the referee of a game

ref·er·ence¹ /ˈrefərəns/ ●●● S2 W1 *n*

1 [C,U] part of something you say or write in which you mention a person or thing: **[+to]** *There is no direct reference to her own childhood in the novel.* | *The article **made** no **reference** to previous research on the subject.* | *The governor made only a **passing reference** to the problem of unemployment* (=he mentioned it quickly).

2 [U] the act of looking at something for information: **for easy/quick reference** *A vocabulary index is included for easy reference.* | *Keep their price list on file **for future reference*** (=so that it can be looked at in the future). | *The book will become a standard **work of reference*** (=a book that people look at for information).

3 reference point (*also* **point/frame of reference**) **a)** an idea, fact, event etc that you already know, which helps you understand or make a judgment about another situation: *Lee's case will be the reference point for lawyers in tomorrow's trial.* | *She used her work experience as a frame of reference for her teaching.* **b)** something that you can see that helps you to know where you are when you are travelling in an area

4 in/with reference to sth *formal* used to say what you are writing or talking about, especially in business letters: *I am writing to you in reference to the job opening in your department.*

5 [C] **a)** (*also* **letter of reference**) a letter containing information about you that is written by someone who knows you well, and is usually intended for a new

employer: *We will need references from your former employers.* **b)** a person who provides information about your character and abilities SYN **referee**: *Ask your teacher to act as one of your references.*
6 [C] a book, article etc from which information has been obtained: *a comprehensive list of references*
7 [C] a number that tells you where you can find the information you want in a book, on a map etc: *a list of towns, each with a* ***map reference*** → CROSS-REFERENCE, → **terms of reference** at TERM[1](11)

reference² *v* [T] *written* to mention another book, article etc that contains information connected with the subject you are writing about: *The book does not reference anything written in the last 10 years.*

ˈreference book *n* [C] a book such as a dictionary or ENCYCLOPEDIA that you look at to find information

ˈreference ˌlibrary *n* [C] a public library or a room in a library, that contains books that you can read but not take away → **lending library**

ref·e·ren·dum /ˌrefəˈrendəm/ ●○○ *n* (*plural* **referenda** /-də/ *or* **referendums**) [C,U] when people vote in order to make a decision about a particular subject, rather than voting for a person: **[+on]** *a referendum on independence | The city council agreed to* ***hold*** *a* ***referendum*** *on the issue in November.* THESAURUS ELECTION

re·fer·ral /rɪˈfɜːrəl/ *n* [C,U] *formal* when someone sends someone or something to another person to be helped or dealt with: **[+to]** *The doctor will give you a referral to a specialist in your area. | Only 39 percent of patients were seen within four weeks of referral.*

re·fill¹ /ˌriːˈfɪl/ *v* [T] to fill something again: *The waitress refilled our coffee cups.* THESAURUS FILL —**refillable** *adj*: *a refillable lighter*

re·fill² /ˈriːfɪl/ *n* [C] **1** a container filled with a particular substance, such as ink or petrol, that you use to fill or replace an empty container, or the substance itself: *a refill for his pen* **2** another drink of the same kind: *Would you like a refill? | a free refill*

re·fi·nance /riːˈfaɪnæns $ -fəˈnæns/ *v* [T] to borrow money from a bank etc in order to pay back an existing amount that you owe: *As interest rates fall, homeowners are likely to refinance their loans.* —**refinancing** *n* [U]

re·fine /rɪˈfaɪn/ ●○○ AWL *v* [T]
1 to improve a method, plan, system etc by gradually making slight changes to it: *Car makers are constantly refining their designs.*
2 to make a substance purer using an industrial process → **refinery**: *oil refining*

re·fined /rɪˈfaɪnd/ AWL *adj* **1** [usually before noun] a substance that is refined has been made pure by an industrial process → **raw**, **crude** OPP **unrefined**: **refined sugar/oil/petroleum** **2** someone who is refined is polite and seems to be well-educated or to belong to a high social class – sometimes used humorously: *a refined way of speaking* **3** a method or process that is refined has been improved to make it more effective → **sophisticated**: *Laser surgery has become much more refined over the last decade.*

re·fine·ment /rɪˈfaɪnmənt/ AWL *n* **1** [C] an improvement, usually a small one, to something: *The new model has a number of refinements.* **2** [C] something which is an improved VERSION of an existing product, system etc: **[+of]** *The new theory is a refinement of Corbin's theory of personality development.* **3** [U] the process of improving something: *Some further refinement is needed.* **4** [U] the process of making a substance more pure: *sugar refinement |* **[+of]** *the refinement of cocaine* **5** [U] the quality of being polite and well-educated, in a way that is typical of someone from a high social class: *a woman of great refinement*

re·fin·e·ry /rɪˈfaɪnəri/ *n* (*plural* **refineries**) [C] a factory where something such as oil or sugar is made purer → **refine**: **oil/petroleum/sugar refinery**

re·fit /ˌriːˈfɪt/ *v* (**refitted**, **refitting**) [I,T] to make a ship, aircraft, building etc ready to be used again, by doing repairs and putting in new machinery: *The ship was completely refitted five years ago.* —**refit** /ˈriːfɪt/ *n* [C,U]

re·fla·tion /riːˈfleɪʃən/ *n* [U] *technical* the process of increasing the amount of money being used in a country in order to increase trade → **inflation**, **deflation** —**reflate** /riːˈfleɪt/ *v* [I,T] —**reflationary** *adj*

re·flect /rɪˈflekt/ ●●● S2 W1 *v*
1 IMAGE [T] if a person or a thing is reflected in a mirror, glass, or water, you can see an image of the person or thing on the surface of the mirror, glass, or water: **be reflected in sth** *She could see her face reflected in the car's windshield.* GRAMMAR **Reflect** is usually passive in this meaning.
2 BE A SIGN OF STH [T] to show or be a sign of a particular situation or feeling: *The drop in consumer spending reflects concern about the economy.* | **be reflected in sth** *The increasing racial diversity of the US is reflected in the latest census statistics.* | **reflect who/what/how etc** *How much you're paid reflects how important you are to the company you work for.*
3 LIGHT/HEAT/SOUND **a)** [T] if a surface reflects light, heat, or sound, it sends back the light etc that reaches it: *Wear something white – it reflects the heat.* **b)** [I always + adv/prep] if light, heat, or sound reflects off something it reaches, it comes back from it
4 THINK ABOUT STH [I,T] to think carefully about something, or to say something that you have been thinking about: **[+on]** *He had time to reflect on his successes and failures.* | **reflect that** *Moe reflected that he had never seen Sherry so happy.*

reflect on/upon sb/sth *phr v* to influence people's opinion of someone or something, especially in a bad way: *If my children are rude, that reflects on me as a parent.* THESAURUS THINK

reˌflected ˈglory *n* [U] respect or admiration that is given to someone, not because of what they are or what they have done, but because of what someone they know has done: *I certainly don't want to* ***bask in*** *any* ***reflected glory***.

re·flec·tion /rɪˈflekʃən/ ●●○ W3 *n*
1 [C] an image that you can see in a mirror, glass, or water: *Can you see your reflection in the glass?*
2 [C,U] careful thought, or an idea or opinion based on this: ***A moment's reflection*** *will show the stupidity of this argument.* | **on/upon reflection** *At first I disagreed, but on reflection* (=after thinking carefully about it), *I realized she was right.*
3 [C] something that shows what something else is like, or that is a sign of a particular situation: **[+of]** *His speech was an accurate reflection of the public mood.* | **be a reflection on sb/sth** (=show how good or bad someone or something is) *On some level, a student's grades are a reflection on the teacher.*
4 [U] the action or process of light, heat, or sound being thrown back from a surface

re·flec·tive /rɪˈflektɪv/ *adj* **1** a reflective surface reflects light: *Stick reflective tape on your school bag.* **2** thinking quietly about something: *She was in a reflective mood.* **3** showing that something is true about a situation: **[+of]** *TV is reflective of society's more liberal views on sex.* —**reflectively** *adv* —**reflectiveness** *n* [U]

re·flec·tor /rɪˈflektə $ -ər/ *n* [C] **1** a small piece of plastic that is fastened to a bicycle or to a piece of clothing, so that it can be seen more easily at night. All bicycles sold in the UK must be fitted with reflectors. → see picture at BICYCLE **2** a surface that reflects light

re·flex /ˈriːfleks/ *n* [C] **1 reflexes** [plural] **a)** the natural ability to react quickly and well to sudden situations: **have good/quick/slow reflexes** *A tennis player needs to have very quick reflexes.* **b)** a sudden uncontrolled movement that your muscles make as a natural reaction to a physical effect: *Doctor Mulholland* ***tested*** *Jennifer's* ***reflexes*** (=especially by hitting her knee with a special rubber hammer). **2 reflex action** something that you do without thinking, as a reaction to a situation

re·flex·ive /rɪˈfleksɪv/ *adj technical* a reflexive verb or PRONOUN shows that the action in a sentence affects the

R

person or thing that does the action. In the sentence 'I enjoyed myself', 'myself' is reflexive. —**reflexive** *n* [C] —**reflexively** *adv*

re·flex·ol·o·gy /ˌriːflekˈsɒlədʒi $ -ˈsɑː-/ *n* [U] a type of ALTERNATIVE medicine in which areas of the feet are touched or rubbed in order to cure medical problems in other parts of the body

re·for·est·a·tion /riːˌfɒrəˈsteɪʃən $ -ˌfɔː-, -ˌfɑː-/ *n* [U] the practice of planting trees in an area where they were previously cut down, in order to grow them for industrial use or to improve the environment OPP **deforestation**

re·form[1] /rɪˈfɔːm $ -ɔːrm/ ●●○ W3 *n* [C,U] a change or changes made to a system or organization in order to improve it: **[+of]** *a reform of the legal system* | **economic/political/educational reform** *The government announced a much-needed programme of economic reform.* | ***Reforms** were **made** to revive the economy.* | **far-reaching/sweeping/radical reforms** *The prime minister is calling for sweeping reforms of the NHS.*

reform[2] ●●○ *v*
1 [T] to improve a system, law, organization etc by making a lot of changes to it, so that it operates in a fairer or more effective way: *plans to radically reform the tax system*
2 [I,T] to change your behaviour and become a better person, or to make someone do this: *Greeley says he's a genuinely **reformed character**.* | *a reformed criminal*

re-form /ˌriː ˈfɔːm $ -ɔːrm/ *v* [I,T] to start to exist again or to make something start to exist again: *At the end of the year, the company re-formed.*

re·for·mat /ˌriːˈfɔːmæt $ -ɔːr-/ *v* (**reformatted**, **reformatting**) [T] if you reformat a document, you change the way it is organized or arranged, for example the amount of space between lines: *The first seven books will all be condensed and reformatted for electronic reading.*

ref·or·ma·tion /ˌrefəˈmeɪʃən $ -fər-/ *n* **1** [C,U] *formal* when something is completely changed in order to improve it **2 the Reformation** the religious changes in Europe in the 16th century, that resulted in the Protestant churches being established

re·for·ma·to·ry /rɪˈfɔːmətəri $ rɪˈfɔːrmətɔːri/ *n* (*plural* **reformatories**) [C] *AmE old use* a REFORM SCHOOL

re·form·er /rɪˈfɔːmə $ -ɔːrmər/ *n* [C] someone who works to improve a social or political system: *a great social reformer*

re·form·ist /rɪˈfɔːmɪst $ -ɔːr-/ *adj* wanting to change systems or situations, especially in politics: *the reformist wing of the party* —**reformist** *n* [C]

reˈform school *n* [C] *AmE* a special school where young people who have broken the law are sent: *If you're not careful, you'll end up in reform school.*

re·fract /rɪˈfrækt/ *v* [T] *technical* if glass or water refracts light, the light changes direction when it passes through the glass or water —**refraction** /rɪˈfrækʃən/ *n* [U]

re·frac·to·ry /rɪˈfræktəri/ *adj* **1** *formal* deliberately not obeying someone in authority and being difficult to deal with or control SYN **unruly 2** *medical* a refractory disease or illness is hard to treat or cure

re·frain[1] /rɪˈfreɪn/ ●○○ *v* [I] *formal* to not do something that you want to do → **abstain**: **refrain from (doing) sth** *Please refrain from smoking in this area.*

refrain[2] *n* [C] **1** part of a song or poem that is repeated, especially at the end of each VERSE → **chorus 2** *formal* a remark or idea that is often repeated: *Our proposal met with the constant refrain that the company could not afford it.*

re·fresh /rɪˈfreʃ/ ●○○ *v*
1 [T] to make someone feel less tired or less hot: *A shower will refresh you.* | **refresh yourself (with sth)** *He refreshed himself with a glass of iced tea.*
2 refresh sb's memory to make someone remember something: *I looked at the map to refresh my memory of the route.*
3 refresh sb's drink *AmE* to add more of an alcoholic drink to someone's glass SYN **top sb up** *BrE*: *Can I refresh your drink?*
4 [I,T] *technical* if you refresh your computer screen while you are connected to the Internet, you make the screen show any new information that has arrived since you first began looking at it SYN **update** —**refreshed** *adj*: *Jen returned from vacation feeling relaxed and refreshed.*

reˈfresher ˌcourse (*also* **re·fresh·er** /rɪˈfreʃə $ -ər/) *n* [C] a training course, usually a short one, that teaches you about new developments in a particular subject or skill, especially one that you need for your job

re·fresh·ing /rɪˈfreʃɪŋ/ *adj* **1** making you feel less tired or less hot: *a refreshing drink* | *The breeze felt refreshing.* **2** pleasantly different from what is familiar and boring: *It made a **refreshing change** to talk to someone new.* —**refreshingly** *adv*

re·fresh·ment /rɪˈfreʃmənt/ ●○○ *n formal*
1 refreshments [plural] small amounts of food and drink that are provided at a meeting, sports event etc: *Refreshments will be served after the meeting.*
2 [U] food and drink in general: *We worked all day without refreshment.* | **liquid refreshment** (=alcoholic drink - used humorously) *I was in need of some liquid refreshment.*
3 [U] the experience of being made to feel less tired or hot

re·fried beans /ˌriːfraɪd ˈbiːnz/ *n* [plural] a Mexican dish in which beans that have already been cooked are crushed and then FRIED with spices

re·fri·ge·rate /rɪˈfrɪdʒəreɪt/ *v* [T] to make something such as food or liquid cold in a refrigerator in order to preserve it → **freeze**: *Refrigerate the mixture overnight.* —**refrigeration** /rɪˌfrɪdʒəˈreɪʃən/ *n* [U]

re·fri·ge·ra·tor /rɪˈfrɪdʒəreɪtə $ -ər/ ●●● S3 *n* [C] *BrE formal or AmE* a large piece of electrical kitchen equipment, shaped like a cupboard, used for keeping food and drink cool SYN **fridge** → **freezer**

re·fu·el /ˌriːˈfjuːəl/ *v* (**refuelled**, **refuelling** *BrE*, **refueled**, **refueling** *AmE*) **1** [I,T] to fill a plane or vehicle with FUEL before continuing a journey: *The plane was refuelled in Dubai.* **2** [T] to make feelings, emotions, or ideas stronger: *The attack refuelled fears of war.*

ref·uge /ˈrefjuːdʒ/ ●○○ *n*
1 [U] shelter or protection from someone or something: **take/seek refuge (in sth)** *During the frequent air-raids, people took refuge in their cellars.*
2 [C] a place that provides shelter, or protection from danger: *a **wildlife refuge*** | **[+from]** *A huge oak tree provided a refuge from the storm.* | **[+for]** *a refuge for battered wives*

ref·u·gee /ˌrefjʊˈdʒiː/ ●●○ *n* [C] someone who has been forced to leave their country, especially during a war, or for political or religious reasons: *Refugees were streaming across the border.* | ***refugee camps***

re·fund[1] /ˈriːfʌnd/ ●●○ *n* [C]
1 an amount of money that is given back to you if you are not satisfied with the goods or services that you have paid for: *They refused to **give** me a **refund**.* | *Return your purchase within 14 days for a **full refund**.* | *You should go down there and demand a refund.*
2 tax refund money that you get back from the government when it has taken too much money in taxes from your salary

re·fund[2] /rɪˈfʌnd/ ●○○ *v* [T] to give someone their money back, especially because they are not satisfied with the goods or services they have paid for → **reimburse**: *I took the radio back, and they **refunded** my **money**.*

re·fur·bish /ˌriːˈfɜːbɪʃ $ -ɜːr-/ *v* [T] *especially BrE* **1** to decorate and repair something such as a building or office in order to improve its appearance → **renovate**: *The Grand Hotel has been completely refurbished.* **2** to change and improve a plan, idea, or skill —**refurbishment** *n* [C,U]

R

re·fus·al /rɪˈfjuːzəl/ ●●○ *n* [C,U] when you say firmly that you will not do, give, or accept something: **refusal to do sth** *His refusal to pay the fine got him into even more trouble.* | **flat/blunt/point-blank refusal** (=an immediate direct refusal) *His request was met with a blunt refusal.* | **[+of]** *They couldn't understand her refusal of a scholarship to Yale.*

re·fuse[1] /rɪˈfjuːz/ ●●● S2 W1 *v*
1 [I] to say firmly that you will not do something that someone has asked you to do: *She asked him to leave, but he refused.* | **refuse to do sth** *The chairman refused to answer any more questions.* | **flatly refuse/refuse point-blank (to do sth)** (=refuse immediately and directly without giving a reason) *Mom flatly refused to go back into the hospital.*
2 [I,T] to say no to something that you have been offered SYN **turn down**: *She refused a second piece of cake.* | *The offer seemed* ***too good to refuse***. | *When they offered all that money, I* ***could hardly refuse***, *could I?* (=it was very unlikely that you would refuse)
3 [T] to not give or allow someone something that they want, especially when they have asked for it officially: **refuse sb sth** *She was refused a work permit.*

ref·use[2] /ˈrefjuːs/ *n* [U] *formal* waste material that has been thrown away SYN **rubbish** *BrE*, **trash, garbage** *AmE*: *a refuse dump* | **household/domestic refuse** | *refuse collection*

re·fuse·nik /rɪˈfjuːznɪk/ *n* [C] someone who refuses to take part in something or obey a law: *Around 250,000 refuseniks have not paid the tax.*

re·fute /rɪˈfjuːt/ *v* [T] *formal* **1** to prove that a statement or idea is not correct SYN **rebut**: **refute a hypothesis/a claim/an idea etc** *an attempt to refute Darwin's theories* **2** to say that a statement is wrong or unfair SYN **deny**: **refute an allegation/a suggestion etc** *She refuted any allegations of malpractice.* —**refutable** *adj* —**refutation** /ˌrefjʊˈteɪʃən/ *n* [C,U]

reg. (*also* **reg** *BrE*) /redʒ/ **1** the written abbreviation of ***registration*** **2 L reg./M reg. etc** *BrE* used to show what year a car was first REGISTERed, based on the first letter of its NUMBER PLATE: *a Y reg. BMW*

re·gain /rɪˈɡeɪn/ ●●○ *v* [T]
1 to get something back, especially an ability or quality, that you have lost SYN **recover**: *The family never quite regained its former influence.* | *He somehow managed to* ***regain*** *his* ***balance***. | *Government forces have* ***regained control*** *of the city.* | *When she* ***regained consciousness*** (=woke up after being unconscious), *she was lying on the floor.* | *He looked stunned, but he soon* ***regained*** *his* ***composure*** (=became calm again). | *The doctors don't know if he will ever regain the use of his legs.*
2 *literary* to reach a place again

re·gal /ˈriːɡəl/ *adj formal* typical of a king or queen, suitable for a king or queen, or similar to a king or queen in behaviour, looks etc: *a ceremony of regal splendour* | *James watched with regal detachment.* —**regally** *adv*

re·gale /rɪˈɡeɪl/ *v*
regale sb **with** sth *phr v written* to entertain someone by telling them about something: *Bailey regaled the customers with tales of our exploits.*

re·ga·li·a /rɪˈɡeɪliə/ *n* [U] traditional clothes and decorations, used at official ceremonies: *the royal regalia* (=worn by a king or queen) | *a pipe band* ***in full regalia*** (=wearing all their traditional clothes, decorations etc)

re·gard[1] /rɪˈɡɑːd $ -ɑːrd/ ●●○ W3 *n*
1 ADMIRATION/RESPECT [U] respect and admiration for someone or something: **[+for]** *Jan's regard for his great talent* | *Burt* ***had high regard*** *for his old law professor, Dr. Finch* (=he respected him a lot). | *The voters* ***hold*** *her* ***in high regard*** (=respect or admire her). | *Teachers are held in low regard in this society* (=are not respected or admired).
2 ATTENTION/CONSIDERATION [U] *formal* attention or consideration that is shown towards someone or something: **[+for]** *She has no regard for other people's feelings.* | **pay/show regard** *One must show proper regard for the law.* | **little/no/scant regard (for sb/sth)** *The present administration has demonstrated little regard for environmental issues.* | *All students must have access to quality education* ***without regard to*** *wealth or class.*
3 with/in regard to sth *formal* relating to a particular subject: *US foreign policy with regard to Cuba*
4 in this/that regard *formal* relating to something you have just mentioned: *The company's problems, in this regard, are certainly not unique.*
5 regards [plural] good wishes – used when sending your good wishes to someone or when ending a short letter or message: *My husband* ***sends his regards***. | *Hope to see you soon. Regards, Chris* | **(with) kind/best regards** (=used to end a letter in a friendly but rather formal way)
6 [singular] *literary* a long look without moving your eyes

regard[2] ●●○ W3 *v* [T]
1 [not in progressive] to think about someone or something in a particular way: **regard sb/sth as sth** *Paul seemed to regard sex as sinful and immoral.* | *Edith was* ***widely regarded as*** (=considered by many people to be) *eccentric.* | *His work is* ***highly regarded*** (=regarded as very good) *by art experts.*
2 *formal* to look at someone or something in a particular way: *She stood back and regarded him coldly.* THESAURUS ▸ LOOK
3 as regards sth *formal* relating to a particular subject – use this when you want to talk or write about a particular subject: *As regards a cure for the disease, very few advances have been made.*

re·gard·ing /rɪˈɡɑːdɪŋ $ -ɑːr-/ ●●○ *prep formal* a word used especially in letters or speeches to introduce the subject you are writing or talking about SYN **concerning, with regard to**: *Regarding your recent inquiry, I have enclosed a copy of our new brochure.* THESAURUS ▸ ABOUT

THESAURUS: refuse

refuse to say firmly that you will not do something that someone has asked you to do: *I asked the bank for a loan, but they refused.* | *When they refused to leave, we had to call the police.*
say no *spoken* to say that you will not do something when someone asks you: *They asked me so nicely that I couldn't really say no.*
turn sb/sth down to refuse to accept an offer or invitation, or a formal request: *They offered me the job but I turned it down.* | *The board turned down a request for $25,000 to sponsor an art exhibition.*
reject to refuse to accept an idea, offer, suggestion, or plan: *They rejected the idea because it would cost too much money.* | *The Senate rejected a proposal to limit the program to two years.*
decline *formal* to politely refuse to accept an offer or invitation, or refuse to do something: *She has declined all offers of help.* | *A palace spokesman declined to comment on the rumours.*
deny to refuse to allow someone to do something or enter somewhere: *They were denied permission to publish the book.* | *He was denied access to the US.*
veto to officially refuse to allow a law or plan, or to refuse to accept someone's suggestion: *Congress vetoed the bill.* | *The suggestion was quickly vetoed by the other members of the team.*
disallow to officially refuse to accept something because someone has broken the rules, or not done it in the correct way: *The goal was disallowed by the referee.* | *The court decided to disallow his evidence.*
rebuff *formal* to refuse to accept someone's offer, request, or suggestion: *The company raised its offer to $6 billion, but was rebuffed.* | *He was politely rebuffed when he suggested holding the show in Dublin.*
give sb/sth the thumbs down *informal* to refuse to allow or accept a plan or suggestion: *The plan was given the thumbs down by the local authority.* | *They gave us the thumbs down.*

R

GRAMMAR: Comparison

regarding

• You use **regarding** followed directly by a noun: *I am writing regarding your English course for foreign students.* ✗ Don't say: *I am writing regarding to your English course.*

concerning

• You use **concerning** followed directly by a noun: *They called concerning our subscription.* ✗ Don't say: *They called concerning to our subscription.*

with regard to

• You use **with regard to** followed by a noun: *With regard to your invoice, it will be paid as soon as possible.*

re·gard·less /rɪˈɡɑːdləs $ -ɑːr-/ ●●○ *adv*
1 without being affected or influenced by something: **[+of]** *The law requires equal treatment for all, regardless of race, religion, or sex.*
2 if you continue doing something regardless, you do it in spite of difficulties or other people telling you not to: **carry on/go on regardless** *BrE* (=continue what you are doing) *You get a lot of criticism, but you just have to carry on regardless.*

re·gat·ta /rɪˈɡætə/ *n* [C] a sports event at which there are races for rowing boats or sailing boats

re·gen·cy /ˈriːdʒənsi/ *n* (*plural* **regencies**) [C,U] a period of government by a REGENT (=person who governs instead of a king or queen)

Regency *adj* Regency buildings, furniture etc are from or in the style of the period 1811–1820 in Britain

re·gen·e·rate /rɪˈdʒenəreɪt/ *v* **1** [T] *formal* to make something develop and grow strong again: *efforts to regenerate the US economy | The Marshall Plan sought to regenerate the shattered Europe of 1947.* **2** [I,T] *technical* to grow again, or make something grow again: *Small nodules form as the liver cells regenerate.* —**regenerative** /-nərətɪv/ *adj*: *a regenerative process* —**regeneration** /rɪˌdʒenəˈreɪʃən/ *n* [U]: *a new strategy for* ***urban regeneration***

re·gent /ˈriːdʒənt/ *n* [C] someone who governs instead of a king or queen, because the king or queen is ill, absent, or still a child → **regency** —**regent** *adj* [only after noun]: *the Prince Regent*

reg·gae /ˈreɡeɪ/ *n* [U] a kind of popular music originally from Jamaica, with a strong regular beat

re·gi·cide /ˈredʒɪsaɪd/ *n formal* **1** [U] the crime of killing a king or queen **2** [C] someone who kills a king or queen

re·gime /reɪˈʒiːm/ ●○○ AWL *n* [C]
1 a government, especially one that was not elected fairly or that you disapprove of for some other reason: *The regime got rid of most of its opponents.* | **military/totalitarian/fascist regime** | **brutal/oppressive/corrupt regime** THESAURUS ▸ GOVERNMENT
2 a particular system – used especially when talking about a previous system, or one that has just been introduced: **under a regime** *Under the new regime, all sheep and cattle will be regularly tested for disease.*
3 a special plan of food, exercise etc that is intended to improve your health SYN **regimen**: *a dietary regime*

reˈgime ˌchange *n* [U] a change in the government of a country that happens because another country forces that government out of power → **revolution**, **coup d'etat**

re·gi·men /ˈredʒɪmɪn/ *n* [C] *formal* a special plan of food, exercise etc that is intended to improve your health SYN **regime**: **[+of]** *a regimen of morning stretching exercises | Patients maintain a strict dietary regimen.*

re·gi·ment¹ /ˈredʒəmənt/ ●○○ *n* [C]
1 a large group of soldiers, usually consisting of several BATTALIONS
2 a large number of people, animals, or things: **[+of]** *a regiment of ants* —**regimental** /ˌredʒəˈmentl◂/ *adj*: *the regimental commander*

re·gi·ment² /ˈredʒəment/ *v* [T] to organize and control people firmly and usually too strictly: *the regimented routine of boarding school* —**regimentation** /ˌredʒəmenˈteɪʃən/ *n* [U]

re·gion /ˈriːdʒən/ ●●● S1 W1 AWL *n* [C]
1 a large area of a country or of the world, usually without exact limits SYN **area**: *efforts to bring peace to the region |* **[+of]** *the Choco region of Columbia |* **coastal/border/central etc region** *Flooding is likely in some coastal regions of the Northeast during the early part of the week.* THESAURUS ▸ AREA
2 a particular part of someone's body SYN **area**: *the lower back region |* **[+of]** *a region of the brain*
3 **(somewhere) in the region of sth** used to describe an amount of time, money etc without being exact: *a grant somewhere in the region of £2,500*
4 **the regions** *BrE* the parts of a country that are away from the capital city: *a government policy to relocate jobs from the capital to the regions*

re·gion·al /ˈriːdʒənəl/ ●●● S1 W2 AWL *adj* [usually before noun] relating to a particular region or area → **local**: *local and regional government | regional variations in farming practice | a slight regional accent* —**regionally** *adv*: *goods sold locally and regionally*

re·gion·al·is·m /ˈriːdʒənəlɪzəm/ *n* [U] loyalty to a particular region of a country and the desire for it to be more independent politically

re·gis·ter¹ /ˈredʒɪstə $ -ər/ ●●○ S3 W3 AWL *n*
1 OFFICIAL LIST [C] an official list of names of people, companies etc, or a book that has this list: **[+of]** *the official register of births, deaths, and marriages | Have you signed the* ***hotel register****? | Police want a* ***national register*** *of DNA samples.* | **the electoral register** (=official list of voters) | **call/take the register** *BrE old-fashioned* (=say the names of the students in a class, to check who is there)
2 LANGUAGE STYLE [C,U] *technical* the words, style, and grammar used by speakers and writers in a particular situation or in a particular type of writing: **formal/informal register** *letters written in a formal register*
3 MUSIC [C] *technical* the range of musical notes that someone's voice or a musical instrument can reach: **the upper/middle/lower register** *the upper register of the cello*
4 MACHINE [C] a CASH REGISTER
5 HEATING CONTROL [C] *AmE* a movable metal plate that controls the flow of air in a HEATING or COOLING SYSTEM SYN **vent**

register² ●●○ S3 W3 AWL *v*
1 ON A LIST [I,T] to put someone's or something's name on an official list: *The tanker is registered in Rotterdam.* | **[+for]** *How many students have registered for English classes?* | **[+with]** *You must bring your insurance card with you when you register with a dentist or doctor.* | **register a birth/death/marriage** *The baby's birth was registered this morning.* | **be registered (as) unemployed/disabled etc** *BrE* (=be on an official list of a particular group)
2 STATE YOUR OPINION [T] *formal* to officially state your opinion about something so that everyone knows what you think or feel: *The delegation* ***registered*** *a formal* ***protest*** *with US embassy officials Wednesday.*
3 REALIZE [I usually in negatives, T] if something registers, or if you register it, you realize or notice it, and then remember it: *She had told me her name before, but I guess it didn't register. | I'd been standing there for several minutes before he registered my presence.*
4 MEASUREMENT [I,T] if an instrument registers an amount or if something registers on it, the instrument shows that amount: *The thermometer registered 98.6°. | The earthquake registered 7.2 on the Richter scale.*
5 SHOW A FEELING [T] *formal* to show or express a feeling: *Her face registered shock and anger.*
6 MAIL [T] *BrE* to send a package, letter etc by REGISTERED POST: *Did you register the parcel?*

ˌregistered ˈoffice *n* [C] the office of a company in Britain, to which all letters and official documents must be sent

ˌregistered ˈpost *n* [U] *BrE* a way of insuring something that you send by post in case it gets lost or damaged SYN **certified mail** *AmE*

ˈregister ˌoffice *n* [C] *BrE* a REGISTRY OFFICE

re·gis·trar /ˌredʒəˈstrɑː◂ $ ˈredʒəstrɑːr/ *n* [C] **1** someone who is in charge of official records of births, marriages, and deaths **2** an official of a college or university who deals with the running of the college **3** *BrE* a hospital doctor who has finished his or her training but is of a lower rank than a CONSULTANT

re·gis·tra·tion /ˌredʒəˈstreɪʃən/ ●●○ S3 AWL *n*
1 [U] the act of recording names and details on an official list: **[+of]** *the registration of motor vehicles* | *Student registration* (=for a course of study) *starts the first week in September.* | *The* ***registration fee*** *is $75.*
2 [C] *AmE* an official piece of paper containing details about a motor vehicle and the name of its owner: *May I see your* ***license and registration****, ma'am?*

regiˈstration ˌnumber *n* [C] *BrE* the official set of numbers and letters shown on the front and back of a vehicle on the NUMBER PLATE

re·gis·try /ˈredʒəstri/ *n* (*plural* **registries**) [C] **1** a place where information used by an organization is kept, especially official records or lists **2** *BrE technical* used when saying where something, especially a ship, is officially REGISTERed: *the registry of the vessel*

ˈregistry ˌoffice *n* [C] a local government building in Britain where you can get married, and where births, marriages, and deaths are officially recorded

re·gress /rɪˈgres/ *v* [I] *technical* to go back to an earlier and worse condition, or to a less developed way of behaving OPP **progress**: *The patient had regressed to a state of childish dependency.*

re·gres·sion /rɪˈgreʃən/ *n* [C,U] **1** the act of returning to an earlier condition that is worse or less developed OPP **progression** **2** *technical* the act of thinking or behaving as you did at an earlier time of your life, such as when you were a child

re·gres·sive /rɪˈgresɪv/ *adj* returning to an earlier, less advanced state, or causing something to do this – used to show disapproval OPP **progressive**: *Many considered the changes to the welfare laws a regressive step.*

reˈgressive ˌtax *n* [C] a tax that has less effect on the rich than on the poor

re·gret¹ /rɪˈgret/ ●●○ W3 *v* (**regretted**, **regretting**) [T]
1 to feel sorry about something you have done and wish you had not done it: *Don't do anything you might regret.* | **regret doing sth** *I regret leaving school so young.* | **regret (that)** *He was beginning to regret that he'd come along.*
2 [not in progressive] *formal* used in official letters or statements when saying that you are sorry or sad about something: *We regret any inconvenience caused to our customers.* | **regret (that)** *I regret that I will be unable to attend.* | **regret to say/inform/tell** *I regret to inform you that your contract will not be renewed.*

COLLOCATIONS

ADVERBS

deeply/greatly *I deeply regretted what had happened.*
bitterly (=with a feeling of great sadness) *I bitterly regretted my decision to leave.*
sincerely *The airline sincerely regrets any delays to passengers.*
very much *We very much regret that there will be job losses.*

PHRASES

live to regret sth (=regret it in the future) *If you don't go, you may live to regret it.*

regret² ●○○ *n*
1 [C usually plural, U] sadness that you feel about something, especially because you wish it had not happened: **[+about]** *I* ***have*** *no* ***regrets*** *about leaving.* | **great/deep regret** *She has already* ***expressed*** *deep* ***regret*** *for what happened.* | **with regret** *I decided with some regret that it was time to move on.* | *It is* ***with great regret*** *that I must decline your offer.* | **to sb's regret** *I lost touch with her, much to my regret.*
2 give/send your regrets *formal* to say that you are unable to go to a meeting, accept an invitation etc: *My father was ill and had to send his regrets.*

re·gret·ful /rɪˈgretfəl/ *adj* someone who is regretful feels sorry or disappointed: *She apologized and sounded genuinely regretful.*

re·gret·ful·ly /rɪˈgretfəli/ *adv* **1** feeling sad because you do not want to do what you are doing: *'I must go,' he said regretfully.* **2** [sentence adverb] *formal* used to talk about a situation that you wish was different or that you are sorry about SYN **regrettably**: *Regretfully, we do not have time to continue this discussion now.*

re·gret·ta·ble /rɪˈgretəbəl/ *adj* something that is regrettable is unpleasant, and you wish things could be different SYN **unfortunate**: *This was a very regrettable error.* | **it is regrettable that** *It's regrettable that classical music receives so little attention.*

re·gret·ta·bly /rɪˈgretəbli/ *adv* used to talk about a situation that you wish was different or that you are sorry about SYN **regretfully**: [sentence adverb] *Regrettably, he will not be able to come.*

re·group /ˌriːˈgruːp/ *v* **1** [I,T] to form a group again in order to be more effective, or to make people do this: *The Allies regrouped and launched a new attack.* | *The Russians retreated, needing to regroup their forces.* **2** [I] *AmE* to stop and think about something, so that you can start to do something again in a better way: *I paused for a minute to regroup.*

reg·u·lar¹ /ˈregjələ $ -ər/ ●●● S2 W2 *adj*
1 EVERY HOUR/DAY/WEEK ETC happening every hour, every week, every month etc, usually with the same amount of time in between OPP **irregular**: *The company holds regular meetings with employees.* | *His breathing was slow and regular.* | *Trains will run* ***at regular intervals*** *from 11am to 4pm.* | *We hear from him* ***on a regular basis****.* | *He phones us every Sunday at six,* ***regular as clockwork*** (=always at the same time). | *a* ***regular job*** (=a job that you do during normal working hours)
2 OFTEN [only before noun] happening or doing something very often OPP **irregular**: *a regular occurrence* | *Regular exercise helps keep your weight down.* | **regular customer/visitor** *He's one of the bar's regular customers.* | *Penn Station was* ***in regular use*** (=people used it often) *until the 1960s.*
3 USUAL [only before noun] *especially AmE* normal or usual: *He has returned to his regular duties.* | *Our regular opening hours are 10am to 7pm.*
4 EQUAL DISTANCE with the same amount of space between each thing and the next OPP **irregular**: *The pipes were placed* ***at regular intervals****.* | *a carpet with a* ***regular pattern*** *of flowers*
5 ORDINARY *especially AmE* ordinary, without any special feature or qualities: *a regular type of guy*
6 NORMAL SIZE [only before noun] *especially AmE* of a normal or standard size: *a regular Coke*
7 SHAPE evenly shaped with parts or sides of equal size: *a regular hexagon* | *He's very handsome, with strong* ***regular features*** (=an evenly shaped face).
8 GRAMMAR *technical* a regular verb changes its forms in the same way as most verbs, for example its past tense and past participle end in 'ed'. The verb 'dance' is regular, but the verb 'be' is not. OPP **irregular**
9 EMPHASIZING [only before noun] *BrE informal* used to emphasize what you think someone is like SYN **real**: *He's a regular little dictator!*
10 regular army/troops/soldier a regular army etc is permanent, and exists whether there is a war or not
11 be/keep regular *informal* **a)** to get rid of waste from your BOWELs often enough to be healthy **b)** a woman who is regular has her MENSTRUAL PERIOD at the same time each month

regular² *n* **1** [C] *informal* someone who often goes to the same bar, restaurant etc or who takes part in an activity very often: *The barman knows all the regulars by name.* **2** [C] a soldier whose permanent job is in the army **3** [U] *AmE* petrol that contains LEAD

ˌregular ˈfooted *adj* if you ride a SKATEBOARD or SNOWBOARD regular footed, you ride with your left foot at the front of the board and your right foot at the back → **goofy footed**

re·gu·lar·i·ty /ˌregjəˈlærəti/ *n* (*plural* **regularities**) **1** [U] when the same thing keeps happening often, especially with the same amount of time between each occasion when it happens: *Climate change is disrupting the regularity of the seasons.* | **with alarming/increasing etc regularity** *Our team kept losing with monotonous regularity* (=in a way that seems boring or annoying). **2** [C,U] when something is arranged in an even way: *the regularity of his features*

reg·u·lar·ize (*also* **-ise** *BrE*) /ˈregjələraɪz/ *v* [T] to make a situation that has existed for some time legal or official —**regularization** /ˌregjələraɪˈzeɪʃən $ -rə-/ *n* [U]

reg·u·lar·ly /ˈregjələli $ -ərli/ ●●● S3 W3 *adv*
1 at the same time each day, week, month etc: *We meet regularly, once a month.*
2 often: *I see them pretty regularly.* | *It's important to exercise regularly.*
3 evenly arranged or shaped: *The plants are regularly spaced.* | *regularly shaped crystals*

reg·u·late /ˈregjəleɪt/ ●○○ AWL *v* [T]
1 to control an activity or process, especially by rules: *strict rules regulating the use of chemicals in food*
2 to make a machine or your body work at a particular speed, temperature etc: *People sweat to regulate their body heat.*

reg·u·la·tion¹ /ˌregjəˈleɪʃən/ ●●○ W3 AWL *n*
1 [C] an official rule or order: *There seem to be so many* ***rules and regulations*** *these days.* | **[+on]** *new regulations on imports* | *regulations governing the safety of toys* | **building/planning/fire/health regulations** *The local authority is introducing new planning regulations.* | *All companies must* ***comply with*** *the* ***regulations***. | **under ... regulations** *Under the new regulations, all staff must have safety training.* **THESAURUS** RULE
2 [U] control over something, especially by rules: **[+of]** *the regulation of public spending*

regulation² *adj* [only before noun] used or worn because of official rules: *The girls were all wearing regulation shoes.*

reg·u·la·tor /ˈregjəleɪtə $ -ər/ AWL *n* [C] **1** an instrument for controlling the temperature, speed etc of something: *a heat regulator* **2** someone who makes sure that a system operates properly or fairly: *traffic safety regulators*

reg·u·la·to·ry /ˌregjəˈleɪtəri $ ˈregjələtɔːri/ AWL *adj formal* a regulatory authority has the official power to control an activity and to make sure that it is done in a satisfactory way: **regulatory body/authority/agency** *New drugs have been approved by the regulatory authority.*

re·gur·gi·tate /rɪˈgɜːdʒɪteɪt $ -ɜːr-/ *v* [T] *formal* **1** to bring food that you have already swallowed, back into your mouth → **vomit**: *Some birds and animals regurgitate food to feed their young.* **2** to repeat facts, ideas etc that you have read or heard without thinking about them yourself – used to show disapproval: *She tries to get students to think critically, not just regurgitate facts.* —**regurgitation** /rɪˌgɜːdʒɪˈteɪʃən $ -ɜːr-/ *n* [U]

re·hab /ˈriːhæb/ *n* [U] the process of curing someone who has an alcohol or drugs problem: *a rehab program* | **in rehab** *I spent three months in rehab.*

re·ha·bil·i·tate /ˌriːhəˈbɪlɪteɪt/ *v* [T] **1** to help someone to live a healthy, useful, or active life again after they have been seriously ill or in prison: *a special unit for rehabilitating stroke patients* **2** to make people think that someone or something is good again after a period when people had a bad opinion of them: *The prime minister seems to be trying to rehabilitate the former defence secretary.* **3** to improve a building or area so that it returns to the good condition it was in before → **renovate**: *A lot of the older houses have now been rehabilitated.* —**rehabilitation** /ˌriːhəbɪlɪˈteɪʃən/ *n* [U]: *the rehabilitation of mentally ill patients*

re·hash /riːˈhæʃ/ *v* [T] **1** to use the same ideas again in a new form that is not really different or better – used to show disapproval: *He simply rehashed the same story.* **2** to repeat something that was discussed earlier, especially in an annoying way: *This issue has been rehashed so many times already.* —**rehash** /ˈriːhæʃ/ *n* [C]: *It was just a rehash of last year's show.*

re·hears·al /rɪˈhɜːsəl $ -ɜːr-/ ●○○ *n*
1 [C,U] a time when all the people in a play, concert etc practise before a public performance: **[+for/of]** *a rehearsal for 'Romeo and Juliet'* | **in rehearsal** *The dialogue was worked out by actors in rehearsal.* → DRESS REHEARSAL
2 [C] a time when all the people involved in a big event practise it together before it happens: *a wedding rehearsal*

re·hearse /rɪˈhɜːs $ -ɜːrs/ ●○○ *v*
1 [I,T] to practise or make people practise something such as a play or concert in order to prepare for a public performance: *I think we need to rehearse the first scene again.* | **[+for]** *The band was rehearsing for their world tour.* **THESAURUS** PRACTISE
2 [T] to practise something that you plan to say to someone: *She had carefully rehearsed her resignation speech.*
3 [T] *formal* to repeat an opinion that has often been expressed before

re·heat /ˌriːˈhiːt/ *v* [T] to make a meal or drink hot again: *I reheated some soup for lunch.*

re·home /ˌriːˈhəʊm $ -ˈhoʊm/ *v* [T] to arrange for a pet to have a new owner and home, especially a pet that has been looked after in a SHELTER: *The kittens have been rehomed.*

re·house /ˌriːˈhaʊz/ *v* [T] to put someone in a new or better home: *All flood victims will be rehoused as soon as possible.*

reign¹ /reɪn/ ●○○ *n* [C]
1 the period when someone is king, queen, or EMPEROR: **[+of]** *changes that took place during Charlemagne's reign* | *the reign of James I*
2 the period when someone is in charge of an organization, team etc: *during his reign at the Education Department*
3 a period during which something is the most powerful or most important feature of a place: **[+of]** *the reign of Stalinism in Russia*
4 reign of terror a period when a ruler or a government kills many of their political opponents

reign² ●○○ *v* [I]
1 to rule a nation or group of nations as their king, queen, or EMPEROR: *George VI reigned from 1936 to 1952.* | **[+over]** *Pharaohs reigned over Egypt for centuries.*
2 *literary* if a feeling or quality reigns, it exists strongly for a period of time: *For several minutes* ***confusion reigned***. | ***Silence reigned*** *while we waited for news.*
3 reigning champion the most recent winner of a competition: *Can he defeat the reigning Wimbledon champion?*
4 reign supreme if someone or something reigns supreme, they are the most important part of a situation or time: *It was a time when romance reigned supreme.*

re·im·burse /ˌriːəmˈbɜːs $ -ɜːrs/ *v* [T] *formal* to pay money back to someone when their money has been spent or lost: **reimburse sb for sth** *The company will reimburse you for travel expenses.* —**reimbursement** *n* [C,U]

rein¹ /reɪn/ *n* **1** [C usually plural] a long narrow band of leather that is fastened around a horse's head in order to control it → **bridle 2 give (full/free) rein to sth** to allow an emotion or feeling to be expressed freely: *He gave free rein to his imagination.* **3 give sb (a) free rein** to give someone complete freedom to do a job in whatever way they choose **4 keep a tight rein on sb/sth** to control something strictly: *The finance director keeps a tight rein on spending.* **5 take/hand over the reins** to take or give someone control over an organization or country: *Owens will officially take over the reins in a few weeks.*

rein² *v*
rein sth ↔ **in** (*also* **rein sth** ↔ **back** *BrE*) *phr v* **1** to start to control a situation more strictly: *The government is reining in public expenditure.* **2** to make a horse go more slowly by pulling on the reins

re·in·car·nate /ˌriːɪnˈkɑːneɪt $ -ɑːr-/ *v* **be reincarnated** to be born again in another body after you have died

re·in·car·na·tion /ˌriːɪnkɑːˈneɪʃən $ -ɑːr-/ *n* **1** [U] the belief that after someone dies their soul lives again in another body **2** [C] the person or animal that contains the soul of a dead person or animal: **[+of]** *She thinks she is a reincarnation of Cleopatra.*

rein·deer /ˈreɪndɪə $ -dɪr/ *n* (*plural* **reindeer**) [C] a large DEER with long wide ANTLERS (=horns), that lives in cold northern areas

re·in·force /ˌriːənˈfɔːs $ -ˈfɔːrs/ ●●○ W3 AWL *v* [T]
1 to give support to an opinion, idea, or feeling, and make it stronger: *The film reinforces the idea that women should be pretty and dumb.*
2 to make part of a building, structure, piece of clothing etc stronger
3 to make a group of people, especially an army, stronger by adding people, equipment etc

ˌreinforced ˈconcrete *n* [U] CONCRETE with metal bars in it to make it stronger

re·in·force·ment /ˌriːɪnˈfɔːsmənt $ -ˈfɔːrs-/ AWL *n* **1 reinforcements** [plural] more soldiers, police etc who are sent to a battle, fight etc to make their group stronger: *The police **called for reinforcements**.* **2 positive/negative reinforcement** positive reinforcement is when you give someone praise or rewards for their behaviour or work, so they want to continue doing well. Negative reinforcement is when you give someone punishments or criticism when their behaviour or work is bad, so that they want to improve to avoid punishments again: *We need to **give** students plenty of **positive reinforcement**.* **3** [U] the act of making something stronger: *The bridge needs some structural reinforcement.*

re·in·state /ˌriːɪnˈsteɪt/ *v* [T] **1** if someone is reinstated, they are officially given back their job after it was taken away **2** to make something such as a law, system, or rule exist again: *California reinstated the death penalty in 1977.* —**reinstatement** *n* [C,U]

re·in·sure /ˌriːɪnˈʃʊə $ -ˈʃʊr/ *v* [T] *technical* to share the insurance of something between two or more companies, so that there is less risk for each —**reinsurance** *n* [U] —**reinsurer** *n* [C]

re·in·ter·pret /ˌriːɪnˈtɜːprɪt $ -ˈtɜːrp-/ *v* [T] *formal* to think about something, show something, perform something etc in a new way: *The book reinterprets the Dracula legend.* —**reinterpretation** /ˌriːɪntɜːprəˈteɪʃən/ *n* [C,U]

re·in·tro·duce /ˌriːɪntrəˈdjuːs $ -ˈduːs/ *v* [T] to start using something again or bring something back to an area after it has not been used or has not existed there for some time SYN **bring back**: *plans to reintroduce a capital-gains tax on securities* —**reintroduction** /-ˈdʌkʃən/ *n* [U]

re·in·vent /ˌriːɪnˈvent/ *v* [T] **1** to make changes to an idea, method, system etc in order to improve it or make it more modern SYN **reform**: *plans to reinvent the American educational system* **2 reinvent yourself** to do something differently from before, especially in order to improve or change the way people think of you: *Bowie has constantly reinvented himself during his long career.* **3 reinvent the wheel** *informal* to waste time trying to find a way to do something when someone else has already discovered the best way to do it

re·in·vest /ˌriːɪnˈvest/ AWL *v* [I,T] to use money you have earned from INVESTMENTS to buy additional investments: **reinvest sth in sth** *She reinvested the dividends in mutual funds.* —**reinvestment** *n* [U]

re·is·sue /ˌriːˈɪʃuː, -ˈɪsjuː $ -ˈɪʃuː/ *v* [T] to produce a record, book etc again, after it has not been available for some time: *an early jazz record reissued on CD* —**reissue** *n* [C]

re·it·e·rate /riːˈɪtəreɪt/ ●○○ *v* [T] *formal* to repeat a statement or opinion in order to make your meaning as clear as possible SYN **restate**: *Let me reiterate the most important points.* | **reiterate that** *Lawyers reiterated that there was no direct evidence against Mr Evans.* —**reiteration** /riːˌɪtəˈreɪʃən/ *n* [C,U]: *a reiteration of his previous statement*

re·ject¹ /rɪˈdʒekt/ ●●○ W2 AWL *v* [T]
1 OFFER/SUGGESTION/IDEA to refuse to accept, believe in, or agree with something OPP **accept**: *Sarah rejected her brother's offer of help.* | **reject sth as sth** *Gibson rejected the idea as 'absurd'.* | *Dexter **flatly rejected*** (=completely rejected) *calls for his resignation.* | *His proposal was **rejected outright*** (=completely rejected). THESAURUS REFUSE
2 NOT CHOOSE SB to not choose someone for a job, course of study etc OPP **accept**: *It's obvious why his application was rejected.*
3 PRODUCT to throw away something that has just been made, because its quality is not good enough: *If inspectors find a defective can, the batch is rejected.*
4 NOT LOVE SB to refuse to give someone any love or attention: *Children feel abandoned or rejected if they don't see their parents regularly.*
5 ORGAN if your body rejects an organ, after a TRANSPLANT operation, it does not accept that organ

re·ject² /ˈriːdʒekt/ *n* [C] **1** a product that has been rejected because there is something wrong with it: *a shop selling cheap rejects* **2** someone who is not accepted or liked by another person, or by other people: *They felt that they were society's rejects.*

re·jec·tion /rɪˈdʒekʃən/ ●●○ AWL *n*
1 [C,U] the act of not accepting, believing in, or agreeing with something OPP **acceptance**: **[+of]** *What are the reasons for his rejection of the theory?*
2 [C,U] the act of not accepting someone for a job, school etc OPP **acceptance**: *They sent me a rejection letter.*
3 [U] a situation in which someone stops giving you love or attention: *He was left with a feeling of rejection and loss.*

re·jig /riːˈdʒɪɡ/ *BrE*, **re·jig·ger** /riːˈdʒɪɡə $ -ər/ *AmE v* (**rejigged**, **rejigging**) [T] *informal* to arrange or organize something in a different way SYN **reorganize**: *plans to rejig the schedule*

re·joice /rɪˈdʒɔɪs/ *v* [I] **1** *literary* to feel or show that you are very happy: **[+at/over/in]** *His family rejoiced at the news.* | *We rejoiced in our good fortune.* **2 rejoice in the name/title (of) sth** *BrE* to have a name or title that is silly or amusing: *He rejoices in the name of Pigg.*

re·joic·ing /rɪˈdʒɔɪsɪŋ/ *n* [U] (*also* **rejoicings** [plural]) *literary* a situation in which a lot of people are very happy because they have had good news: **[+at/over]** *There was **great rejoicing** at the victory.*

re·join¹ /ˌriːˈdʒɔɪn/ *v* [T] to go back to a group of people, organization etc that you were with before: *She rejoined her friends in the lounge.* | *In 1938 he rejoined the Socialists.*

re·join² /rɪˈdʒɔɪn/ *v* [T] *literary* to say something in reply, especially rudely or angrily SYN **retort**: *'I don't care!' she rejoined.*

re·join·der /rɪˈdʒɔɪndə $ -ər/ *n* [C] *formal* a reply, especially a rude one: *He tried to think of a snappy rejoinder.*

re·ju·ve·nate /rɪˈdʒuːvəneɪt/ *v* [T] **1** to make something work much better or become much better again: *plans to rejuvenate the inner city areas* **2** to make someone look or feel young and strong again: *I came back from holiday feeling rejuvenated.* —**rejuvenation** /rɪˌdʒuːvəˈneɪʃən/ *n* [singular, U]

re·kin·dle /riːˈkɪndl/ *v* [T] to make someone have a particular feeling, thought etc again SYN **reawaken**: *The trial has rekindled painful memories of the war.*

re·laid /riːˈleɪd/ the past tense and past participle of RELAY³

re·lapse¹ /rɪˈlæps/ *v* [I] **1** to become ill again after you have seemed to improve: **[+into]** *We were afraid he might relapse into a coma.* **2** to start to behave badly again: **[+into]** *Clara soon relapsed into her old ways.*

re·lapse² /rɪˈlæps $ ˈriːlæps/ *n* [C,U] when someone becomes ill again after having seemed to improve: *She **had a relapse** and died soon after.*

re·late /rɪˈleɪt/ ●●● S2 W1 *v*
1 [I] if two things relate, they are connected in some way SYN **connect**: *I don't understand how the two ideas relate.* |

[+to] *The charges of fraud relate to events that took place over ten years ago.*

> **REGISTER**
> In everyday English, people often say something **has (something) to do with** another thing, rather than **relates to** it: *The changes* ***have to do with*** *events that took place over ten years ago. | I don't understand what the two ideas* ***have to do with*** *each other.*

2 [T] if you relate two different things, you show how they are connected: **relate sth to sth** *The report seeks to relate the rise in crime to an increase in unemployment.*
3 [T] *formal* to tell someone about events that have happened to you or to someone else: **relate sth to sb** *He later related the whole story to me.* THESAURUS ▸ TELL
4 [I] to feel that you understand someone's problem, situation etc: **[+to]** *Laurie finds it difficult to relate to children. | I know he feels upset, and I can relate to that.*

re·lat·ed /rɪˈleɪtɪd/ ●●● S2 W3 *adj*
1 things that are related are connected in some way: *Police now believe that the three crimes could be related. | the problem of drug abuse and other related issues |* **[+to]** *He suffers with memory loss related to his disease. |* **closely/directly/strongly etc related** *Education levels are strongly related to income. |* **drug-/pollution-/stress-related etc** *people suffering from tobacco-related illnesses*
2 [not before noun] connected by a family relationship: *Are you two related? |* **[+to]** *I might be related to him.*
3 animals, plants, languages etc that are related belong to the same group: *Dolphins and porpoises are closely related.*

> **THESAURUS**
> **related/connected** *adj* used about things that have a connection with each other. **Connected** is not used before a noun: *Physics and Maths are closely related. | The two problems are connected. | homelessness and other related issues*
> **linked** *adj* having a direct connection – often used when one thing is the cause of the other: *Skin cancer is directly linked to sun exposure and damage. | Two closely linked factors produced this result.*
> **interrelated/interconnected** *adj* used about two or more things that are connected with each other and affect each other in a complicated series of ways: *The various parts of society are closely interrelated. | The book consists of a series of interconnected essays.*
> **interdependent** used about two or more things, countries, people etc that depend on each other, and cannot exist or continue without each other: *The two countries' economies have become increasingly interdependent. | interdependent relationships between species*
> **relevant** *adj* related to what is being discussed or to a particular area of activity: *The exam tests the way you select and organize information relevant to the question. | Applicants should have several years' relevant experience.*
> **be bound up with sth** to be very closely connected – used about two things that need to be considered together: *The history of the city has long been bound up with the sea. | Your professional development is closely bound up with personal growth.*

reˈlating to *prep* about or concerning: *documents relating to immigration laws*

re·la·tion /rɪˈleɪʃən/ ●●● S2 W1 *n*
1 BETWEEN PEOPLE/COUNTRIES **relations** [plural] **a)** official connections between countries, companies, organizations etc: **[+with]** *Britain threatened to break off diplomatic relations with the regime. |* **[+between]** *Relations between the two countries have improved recently.* **b)** the way in which people or groups of people behave towards each other: **[+between]** *Relations between workers and management are generally good.* → PUBLIC RELATIONS
2 in relation to sth *formal* **a)** used to talk about something that is connected with or compared with the thing you are talking about: *Women's earnings are still low in relation to men's.* **b)** *formal* concerning: *latest developments in relation to the disease*
3 CONNECTION [C,U] a connection between two or more things SYN **relationship**: **[+between]** *the relation between prices and wages | The price the meat is sold for* ***bears no relation to*** (=is not connected to) *the price the farmer receives.*
4 FAMILY [C] a member of your family SYN **relative**: *We have relations in Canada and Scotland. |* **[+of/to]** *What relation are you to Jessica? |* **close/distant relation** *Steve is a distant relation of my wife.* → BLOOD RELATION, → **poor relation** at POOR THESAURUS ▸ RELATIVE
5 have (sexual) relations (with sb) *old-fashioned* to have sex with someone

> **COLLOCATIONS**
> **ADJECTIVES/NOUN + relations**
> **close** *Many Japanese favor closer relations with the U.S.*
> **good** *Relations between neighbours on the estate are very good.*
> **friendly** *He had begun to establish friendly relations with his co-workers.*
> **race relations** (=relations between people from different races who live in the same place) | **industrial relations** (*also* **labour relations** *BrE*, **labor relations** *AmE*) (=relations between managers and workers) | **diplomatic relations** (*also* **international/foreign relations**) (=official relations between two countries) | **community relations** (=relations between different groups in society)
> **VERBS**
> **break off relations** *After the incident, Croatia broke off all relations with Serbia.*
> **establish/develop relations** *The company has tried to establish relations with several universities.*
> **restore/resume relations** (=begin them again after they were stopped or interrupted) | **improve relations** | **sour relations** (=make them less friendly)

re·la·tion·ship /rɪˈleɪʃənʃɪp/ ●●● S1 W1 *n*
1 [C] the way in which two people or two groups feel about each other and behave towards each other: **[+with]** *I have quite a good relationship with my parents. |* **[+between]** *the special relationship between Britain and the US*
2 [C,U] the way in which two or more things are connected and affect each other: **[+between]** *the relationship between diet and health problems |* **[+to]** *He's studying politics and its relationship to the media. | The lessons* ***bear little relationship*** (=they are not connected to) *the children's needs.*
3 [C] a situation in which two people spend time together or live together, and have romantic or sexual feelings for each other: *He's never had a* ***sexual relationship*** *before. |* **[+with]** *She doesn't really want a relationship with me. |* **in a relationship** *Are you in a relationship right now?*
4 [U] the way in which you are related to someone in your family: **[+to]** *'What's your relationship to Sue?' 'She's my cousin.'*

> **COLLOCATIONS**
> **VERBS**
> **have a relationship** *We've always had a good relationship with our neighbours.*
> **develop/form/build a relationship** *By that age, children start developing relationships outside the family.*
> **forge a relationship** (=develop a strong relationship) *We want to forge closer relationships with our allies.*
> **cement a relationship** (=make it firm and strong)
> **ADJECTIVES/NOUN + relationship**
> **good/great** *Over the years, we've developed a good relationship.*

R

close *Laura had a very close relationship with her grandmother.*
friendly/harmonious *My friendly relationship with Scott's family continued after his death.*
strong *Our relationship is strong enough to survive anything.*
a love-hate relationship (=when someone both likes and dislikes someone else) *The local people have a love-hate relationship with tourists.*
a special relationship (=a particularly close relationship) | **a working relationship** (=a relationship appropriate for people who work together) | **family relationships** | **a personal relationship** | **a business/professional relationship** | **the doctor-patient/parent-child/teacher-student etc relationship**

rel·a·tive[1] /ˈrelətɪv/ ●●● S3 W3 *n* [C] a member of your family SYN **relation**: *a gathering of friends and relatives* | **a close/distant relative** *Her boyfriend is a distant relative of mine.*

THESAURUS

relative a member of your family, especially one who does not live with you: *Most of her relatives were able to come to the wedding.* | *We have some* ***distant relatives*** *in Australia.*
relation a member of your family. **Relation** means the same as **relative**. It is often used when talking about whether someone is in the same family as another person: *Big cities can be lonely places if you have no friends or relations there.* | *'****What relation is she to you****?' 'She's my half sister.'* | *He's no relation to the singer.*
descendant someone who is a family member of a person who lived and died a long time ago, for example the great-grandchild of that person: *The people are the descendants of slaves who were brought over from Africa.*
ancestor a member of your family who lived a long time ago, especially hundreds of years ago: *My ancestors originally came from Ireland.*
forefathers *especially written* people in your family who lived a long time ago - often used in historical descriptions: *His forefathers came to America over a century ago.*
extended family a family group that consists not only of parents and children, but also includes grandparents, aunts etc: *Extended families rarely live together in Britain, but they are still important.*
folks *especially AmE informal* your family, especially your parents: *Are you going to see your folks at Christmas?*
next of kin the person or people who are most closely related to you, for example your husband or mother, and who need to be told if something serious happens to you: *The next of kin must be notified of his death before his name is released to the press.*

relative[2] ●●○ W3 *adj*
1 having a particular quality when compared with something else: *The relative merits of both approaches have to be considered.* | *her opponent's relative lack of experience* | *You may think you're poor, but* ***it's all relative*** (=you are not poor compared to some people).
2 relative to sth *formal* connected with a particular subject: *facts relative to this issue*

ˌrelative ˈclause ●●○ *n* [C] *technical* a part of a sentence that has a verb in it, and is joined to the rest of the sentence by 'who', 'which', 'where' etc, for example the phrase 'who lives next door' in the sentence 'The man who lives next door is a doctor.'

rel·a·tive·ly /ˈrelətɪvli/ ●●○ S3 W2 *adv*
1 something that is relatively small, easy etc is fairly small, easy etc compared to other things: *The system is relatively easy to use.* | *E-commerce is a relatively recent phenomenon.*
2 relatively speaking used when comparing something with all similar things: *Relatively speaking, land prices are still pretty cheap here.*

ˌrelative ˈpronoun *n* [C] *technical* a PRONOUN such as 'who', 'which', or 'that' by which a relative clause is connected to the rest of the sentence

rel·a·tiv·is·m /ˈrelətɪvɪzəm/ *n* [U] *technical* the belief in PHILOSOPHY that nothing is absolutely true and that things can only be judged in comparison with one another

rel·a·tiv·i·ty /ˌreləˈtɪvəti/ *n* [U] the relationship in PHYSICS between time, space, and movement according to Einstein's THEORY

re·launch /ˈriːlɔːntʃ $ -lɒːntʃ/ *n* [C] a new effort to sell a product that is already on sale —**relaunch** /riːˈlɔːntʃ $ -ˈlɒːntʃ/ *v* [T]: *The product is being relaunched with a new name.*

re·lax /rɪˈlæks/ ●●● S3 W3 AWL *v*
1 REST [I,T] to rest or do something that is enjoyable, especially after you have been working: *I just want to sit down and relax.* | *What Robyn needed was a drink to relax her.* | *A hot bath should help to relax you.*
2 BECOME CALM [I,T] to become quiet and calm after you have been upset or nervous, or to make someone do this: *Once out of danger, he started to relax.* | *Relax! Everything's fine.*
3 MUSCLE [I,T] if you relax a part of your body or it relaxes, it becomes less stiff or less tight: *Gentle exercise can relax stiff shoulder muscles.*
4 RULES/LAWS [T] to make a rule or law less strict: **relax rules/regulations/controls** *Hughes believes that immigration controls should not be relaxed.*
5 relax your hold/grip a) to hold something less tightly than before: **[+on]** *He relaxed his grip on my arm.* **b)** to become less strict in the way you control something: **[+on]** *The party has no intention of relaxing its hold on the country.*
6 relax your concentration/vigilance etc to reduce the amount of attention you give to something

THESAURUS

relax to rest or do something that is enjoyable after you have been working: *In the evenings, I like to relax with some music and a nice meal.* | *In two weeks' time I'll be relaxing on a beach in Greece.*
rest to stop working or stop being active, and sit down or lie down so that you become less tired: *If you're tired, we'll stop and rest for a while.* | *The doctor told me to take some time off work and try to rest.*
unwind to gradually relax after you have been working hard or feeling anxious: *It had been a bad day and he just wanted to get home and unwind.*
take it/things easy to relax and not do very much, especially after working very hard or being ill: *Now that you've finished your exams, you can take it easy.* | *The doctor said he'll have to take things easy for while.*
put your feet up *informal* to rest for a short time after a tiring activity, especially by sitting with your feet resting on something: *Kate poured herself a drink and put her feet up.* | *When you're pregnant and doing a full-time job, you must find time to put your feet up.*
chill out/chill *informal* to relax completely, or stop worrying and getting annoyed about things - used mainly by young people: *We spent the day chilling out by the pool.* | *Hey dude, chill out! It's only a car!* | *Let's go back to my place and chill.*

re·lax·a·tion /ˌriːlækˈseɪʃən/ ●●○ AWL *n*
1 [C,U] a way of resting and enjoying yourself: *I play the piano for relaxation.* | *Meditation allows you to enter a state of* ***deep relaxation***. THESAURUS▸ FUN
2 [U] the process of making rules on the control of something less strict: **[+of]** *a relaxation of government regulations*

re·laxed /rɪˈlækst/ ●●● S2 W3 *adj*
1 feeling calm, comfortable, and not worried or annoyed:

R

Gail was lying in the sun looking very relaxed and happy. | **[+about]** *I feel more relaxed about my career than I used to.* THESAURUS ➔ CALM
2 a situation that is relaxed is comfortable and informal: *There's a very* ***relaxed atmosphere*** *in the school.*
3 not strict, or not feeling that you have to do something in the way that other people think you should do it: **a relaxed attitude/manner/style etc** *She has a fairly relaxed approach to housework.*

re·lax·ing /rɪˈlæksɪŋ/ ●●○ *adj* making you feel relaxed OPP **stressful**: *a relaxing evening at home*

re·lay¹ /ˈriːleɪ/ ●○○ *n*
1 in relays if people do something in relays, several small groups of them do it, one group after another, so that the activity is continuous
2 [C] a relay race: *the 100 metres relay*
3 [C,U] a piece of electrical equipment that receives radio or television signals and sends them on

re·lay² /riːˈleɪ $ rɪˈleɪ, ˈriːleɪ/ *v* (*past tense and past participle* **relayed**) [T] **1** to pass a message from one person or place to another SYN **pass on**: **relay sth to sb** *He quickly relayed this news to the other members of staff.* **2** if radio or television signals are relayed, they are received and sent, especially so that they can be heard on the radio or seen on television: *The broadcasts were relayed by satellite.*

re·lay³ /riːˈleɪ/ *v* (*past tense and past participle* **relaid**) [T] to lay something on the ground again because it was not done well enough before: *The carpet will have to be relaid.*

R

ˈrelay ˌrace *n* [C] a running or swimming race between two or more teams in which each member of the team takes part one after another

re·lease¹ /rɪˈliːs/ ●●● S3 W1 AWL *v* [T]
1 LET SB GO to let someone go free, after having kept them somewhere ➔ **free, discharge**: *Police arrested several men, who were later released.* | *The bears are eventually released into the wild.* | **release sb from sth** *He was released from the hospital yesterday.*
2 MAKE PUBLIC to let news or official information be known and printed SYN **publish**: *The new trade figures have just been released.*
3 FILM/RECORD to make a CD, film, computer game etc available for people to buy or see: *A version of the game for Mac computers will be released in February.*
4 STOP HOLDING/DROP to stop holding or drop something: *Thousands of bombs were released over Dresden.* | **release your grip/hold (on sb/sth)** *The sudden noise made him release his hold on her arm.*
5 FEELINGS to express or get rid of feelings such as anger or worry: *Physical exercise is a good way of releasing stress.*
6 CHEMICAL to let a substance flow out: **release sth into sth** *Oil was released into the sea.*
7 FROM A DUTY to allow someone not to do their duty or work: *Because of rising costs, the company released 10% of their workforce.* | **release sb from sth** *Williams asked to be released from her contract.*
8 MACHINERY to allow part of a piece of machinery or equipment to move from the position in which it is fastened or held: *Release the handbrake first.*

release² ●●○ S3 W3 AWL *n*
1 FROM PRISON [singular, U] when someone is officially allowed to go free, after being kept somewhere: *Before release, the sea lions are fitted with electronic tracking devices.* | **[+from]** *Simon has obtained early release from prison.*
2 RECORD/FILM **a)** [C] a new CD, film, computer game etc that is available to buy or see: *the band's latest release* **b) be on (general) release** if a film is on release, you can go and see it in a cinema: *The film is on general release.*
3 FEELINGS [singular, U] **a)** freedom to show or express your feelings: *Playing an instrument can be a form of emotional release.* **b)** a feeling that you are free from the worry or pain that you have been suffering: *treatment that will bring a release from pain*
4 CHEMICALS [U] when a chemical, gas etc is allowed to flow out of its usual container: **[+into]** *the release of toxic waste into the rivers*
5 OFFICIAL STATEMENT [C,U] an official statement, report etc that is made available to be printed or broadcast, or the act of making it available SYN **publication**: *October 22nd is the date set for the report's release.* ➔ PRESS RELEASE
6 MACHINE [C] a handle, button etc that can be pressed to allow part of a machine to move

rel·e·gate /ˈrelɪgeɪt/ *v* [T] **1** *formal* to give someone or something a less important position than before: **relegate sb/sth to sth** *Women tended to be relegated to typing and filing jobs.* **2** *BrE* if a sports team is relegated, it is moved into a lower DIVISION OPP **promote**: **relegate sth/sb to sth** *We were relegated to the Fourth Division last year.* —**relegation** /ˌreləˈgeɪʃən/ *n* [U]

re·lent /rɪˈlent/ *v* [I] *formal* to change your attitude and become less strict or cruel towards someone SYN **give in**: *At last her father relented and came to visit her.*

re·lent·less /rɪˈlentləs/ ●○○ *adj*
1 strict, cruel, or determined, without ever stopping: *her relentless determination to succeed* | *a regime that was relentless in its persecution of dissidents*
2 something bad that is relentless continues without ever stopping or getting less severe SYN **endless**: *the relentless crying of a small baby* | *a family facing relentless financial problems* —**relentlessly** *adv*: *He questioned her relentlessly.*

rel·e·vance /ˈreləvəns/ ●●○ AWL (*also* **rel·e·van·cy** /ˈreləvənsi/) *n* [U] the quality of directly relating to something that is being discussed or considered OPP **irrelevance**: **[+of]** *He didn't realize the relevance of what he had seen.* | **[+to]** *They have no relevance to the story.* | **of relevance to sth/sb** *This book will be of particular relevance to chemists.*

rel·e·vant /ˈreləvənt/ ●●● S2 W2 AWL *adj* directly relating to the subject or problem being discussed or considered OPP **irrelevant**: *Relevant documents were presented in court.* | *We received all the relevant information.* | **[+to]** *What experience do you have that is relevant to this position?* —**relevantly** *adv*

re·li·a·ble /rɪˈlaɪəbəl/ ●●○ AWL *adj* someone or something that is reliable can be trusted or depended on SYN **dependable** ➔ **rely**: *a birth control method that is cheap and reliable* | *Miller was a quiet and reliable man.* —**reliably** *adv* —**reliability** /rɪˌlaɪəˈbɪləti/ *n* [U]

re·li·ance /rɪˈlaɪəns/ AWL *n* [singular, U] when someone or something is dependent on someone or something else SYN **dependence**: **[+on/upon]** *the country's reliance on imported oil* | *the country's* ***heavy reliance*** *on trade*

re·li·ant /rɪˈlaɪənt/ ●○○ AWL *adj* dependent on someone or something: **[+on/upon]** *Most companies are now reliant on computer technology.* ➔ SELF-RELIANT

rel·ic /ˈrelɪk/ ●○○ *n* [C]
1 an old object or custom that reminds people of the past or that has lived on from a past time: *Roman relics found in a field* | **[+of]** *the books and photos, relics of Rob's university days* | *Everything in the house seemed old and untouched, like relics of an ancient time.*
2 a part of the body or clothing of a holy person which is kept after their death because it is thought to be holy

re·lief /rɪˈliːf/ ●●○ W2 *n*
1 COMFORT [singular, U] a feeling of comfort when something frightening, worrying, or painful has ended or has not happened ➔ **relieve**: *I felt a huge surge of relief and happiness.* | **with relief** *He watched with relief as the girl nodded.* | **in relief** *He laughed in relief.* | *No one was hurt, and we all* ***breathed a sigh of relief***. | **it is a relief to see/have/know etc sth** *I hate to say it, but it was a relief to have him out of the house.* | **to sb's relief** *To my relief, they spoke English.* | **what a relief/that's a relief** *The doctor said it was just the flu. What a relief!*
2 REDUCTION OF PAIN [U] when something reduces someone's pain or unhappy feelings: *Marijuana can provide* ***pain relief*** *for some cancer patients.* | **[+of]** *the relief of suffering* | **[+from]** *The cool room provided relief from the terrible heat outdoors.*
3 HELP [U] money, food, clothes etc given to people who are poor or hungry: *money raised for the* ***relief effort*** |

disaster/famine/flood etc relief *famine relief for victims of the drought*
4 REPLACEMENT [U] a person or group of people that replaces another one and does their work after they have finished: *the relief for the military guard | a relief driver*
5 DECORATION [C,U] a way of decorating wood, stone etc with a shape or figure that is raised above the surface, or the decoration itself → **bas relief**: **in relief** *figures carved in relief*
6 bring/throw sth into relief (*also* **stand out in relief**) to make something very noticeable, or to be very noticeable: **sharp/stark relief** *The tree stood out in stark relief against the snow. | The article throws into sharp relief the differences between the two theories.*
7 light/comic relief a funny moment during a serious film, book, or situation: *a moment of comic relief*
8 MONEY [U] *old-fashioned especially AmE* money given by the government to help people who are poor, old, unemployed etc SYN **welfare**: **on relief** *families on relief during the Depression*
9 WAR [U] *formal* the act of freeing a town when it has been surrounded by an enemy: **[+of]** *the relief of Mafeking*
10 MAP **in relief** if you show a part of the Earth's surface in relief, you show the differences in height between different parts of it → TAX RELIEF

re'lief map *n* [C] a map that shows the different heights of mountains, valleys etc by printing them in a different colour or by raising some parts

re'lief road *n* [C] *BrE* a road that vehicles use to avoid heavy traffic, usually built for this purpose: *an eastern relief road for city traffic*

re·lieve /rɪˈliːv/ ●●○ S3 *v* [T]
1 PAIN to reduce someone's pain or unpleasant feelings → **relief**: *Drugs helped to relieve the pain.* | **relieve tension/pressure/stress etc** *Some people eat for comfort, to relieve their anxieties.*
2 PROBLEM to make a problem less difficult or serious: *programs aimed at relieving unemployment*
3 REPLACE SB to replace someone when they have completed their duty or when they need a rest: *The guard will be relieved at midnight.*
4 relieve yourself a polite expression meaning to URINATE – often used humorously
5 BORING to make something less dull and boring: *a plain wall relieved by flecks of blue and yellow* | **relieve the boredom/monotony** *The books helped relieve the boredom of waiting.*
6 WAR *formal* to free a town which an enemy has surrounded

relieve sb **of** sth *phr v*
1 *formal* to help someone by taking something from them, especially a job they do not want to do or something heavy that they are carrying: *A secretary was hired to relieve her of some of the administrative work. | He rose and relieved her of her bags.*
2 relieve sb of their post/duties/command etc *formal* to take away someone's job because they have done something wrong: *After the defeat General Meyer was relieved of his command.*
3 to steal something from someone – used humorously: *A couple of guys relieved him of his wallet.*

re·lieved /rɪˈliːvd/ ●●○ *adj* feeling happy because you are no longer worried about something → **relief**: **greatly/immensely/extremely etc relieved** *She looked immensely relieved when she heard the news.* | **relieved to see/hear/know sth** *His mother was relieved to see him happy again.* | **relieved (that)** *I felt relieved that Ben would be there. | A relieved smile spread over his face.*

re·li·gion /rɪˈlɪdʒən/ ●●● S2 W2 *n*
1 [U] a belief in one or more gods: *The U.S. Constitution promises freedom of religion. | a course on philosophy and religion*
2 [C] a particular system of this belief and all the ceremonies and duties that are related to it: *people **of different religions** | the Islamic religion | The tribe **practised a religion** that mixed native beliefs and Christianity.*
3 find/get religion to suddenly become interested in religion in a way that seems strange to other people: *Miller found religion in prison.*
4 sth is (like) a religion used when saying that something is very important to someone and they are extremely interested in it and spend a lot of time doing it, watching it etc: *Football was a religion in my family.*

re·li·gious /rɪˈlɪdʒəs/ ●●● S2 W2 *adj*
1 relating to religion in general or to a particular religion: *I don't share her **religious beliefs**. | a religious school | the dates of major religious observances such as Easter or Christmas*
2 believing strongly in your religion and obeying its rules carefully: *a **deeply religious** person* —**religiosity** /rɪˌlɪdʒiˈɒsəti $ -ˈɑːs-/ *n* [U]

THESAURUS

RELATING TO RELIGION

religious relating to religion: *the country's religious leaders | the importance of religious freedom*
spiritual relating to matters of the human spirit, rather than the physical world: *The Dalai Lamai is the exiled spiritual leader of Tibet. | We tend to ignore people's spiritual needs, and focus too much on material things. | spiritual values*
holy [usually before noun] connected with God and religion, and therefore treated in a special way – used especially in the following phrases: *the Holy Bible | the holy city of Mecca | a Hindu holy man | They believe they are fighting a holy war. | The priest puts some holy water on the child's head.*
sacred connected with God and religion, and therefore treated in a special way – used especially in the following phrases: *This place is **sacred to** both Jews and Muslims. | In India, cows are **considered sacred**. | the Hindu sacred texts | sacred music | a sacred ritual*
theological relating to the study of religion or to religious beliefs: *a theological debate | theological training*
secular not relating to religion or controlled by a religious authority: *secular education | secular matters | In the UK we live in a much more secular society.*

BELIEVING IN A RELIGION

religious believing strongly in a religion and obeying its rules: *My father was a very religious man. | Are you religious?*
devout having a very strong belief in a religion: *a devout Catholic*
orthodox believing in the traditional beliefs, laws, and practices of a religion: *orthodox Jews*

NOT BELIEVING IN GOD OR RELIGION

atheist *n, adj* someone who does not believe that God exists: *She says she is an atheist. | atheist propaganda*
agnostic *n, adj* someone who believes that people cannot know whether God exists or not: *I think I'd describe myself as an agnostic. | a group of prominent agnostic scientists*

re·li·gious·ly /rɪˈlɪdʒəsli/ *adv* **1** if you do something religiously, you are always very careful to do it: *He exercises religiously every morning.* **2** in a way that is related to religion: *a religiously diverse country*

reˌligious 'right *n* **the religious right** people who belong to Christian churches and who support CONSERVATIVE political ideas and have very traditional moral beliefs, for example not approving of HOMOSEXUALITY and ABORTION

re·lin·quish /rɪˈlɪŋkwɪʃ/ *v* [T] *formal* to let someone else have your position, power, or rights, especially unwillingly SYN **give up**: *No one wants to relinquish power once they have it.* | **relinquish sth to sb** *Stultz relinquished control to his subordinate.*

rel·i·qua·ry /ˈreləkwəri $ -kweri/ *n* (*plural* **reliquaries**) [C] *technical* a container for religious objects that are related to holy people

R

rel·ish¹ /ˈrelɪʃ/ ●○○ *v* [T] to enjoy an experience or the thought of something that is going to happen: **relish the prospect/thought/idea** *I don't relish the thought of you walking home alone.* | **relish the chance/opportunity** *He relishes the chance to play Hamlet.*

relish² *n* **1** [U] great enjoyment of something: **with relish** *I ate **with great relish**, enjoying every bite.* **2** [C,U] a thick spicy sauce made from fruits or vegetables, and usually eaten with meat: *a hot dog with mustard and relish*

re·live /ˌriːˈlɪv/ *v* [T] to remember or imagine something that happened in the past so clearly that you experience the same emotions again: *The girls watch the tape, eager to relive their victory against UCLA.*

re·load /ˌriːˈləʊd $ -ˈloʊd/ *v* [I,T] **1** to put something into a container again, especially bullets into a gun **2** if you reload a page on the Internet, you ask for the information shown on that page to be sent to your computer again, usually because there has been a problem or because you want the information to be as new as possible SYN **refresh**

re·lo·cate /ˌriːləʊˈkeɪt $ riːˈloʊkeɪt/ ●○○ AWL *v* [I,T] if a person or business relocates, or if they are relocated, they move to a different place: **[+to]** *A lot of firms are relocating to the North of England.* | **[+in]** *businesses that relocate in depressed areas* | **relocate sb/sth to sth** *The residents were relocated to temporary accommodation while the work was being done.* —**relocation** /ˌriːləʊˈkeɪʃən $ -loʊ-/ *n* [U]

R

re·luc·tance /rɪˈlʌktəns/ ●○○ AWL *n* [singular, U] when someone is unwilling to do something, or when they do something slowly to show that they are not very willing: *Wells finally agreed, but with reluctance.* | **reluctance to do sth** *a reluctance to share information*

re·luc·tant /rɪˈlʌktənt/ ●●○ AWL *adj* slow and unwilling OPP **willing**: *She gave a reluctant smile.* | **reluctant to do sth** *Maddox was reluctant to talk about it.* —**reluctantly** *adv*: *Reluctantly, he agreed.*

re·ly /rɪˈlaɪ/ ●●● S3 W2 AWL *v* (**relied, relying, relies**)
rely on/upon sb/sth *phr v*
1 to trust or depend on someone or something to do what you need or expect them to do → **reliable**, **reliance**: *I knew I could rely on David.* | **rely on sb/sth to do sth** *Many working women rely on relatives to help take care of their children.* | **[+for]** *Many people now rely on the Internet for news.*
2 to depend on something in order to continue to live or exist: *The company **relies heavily** on only a few contracts.* | **[+for]** *They have to rely on the river for their water.*

Frequencies of the verbs **remain** and **stay** in spoken and written English.

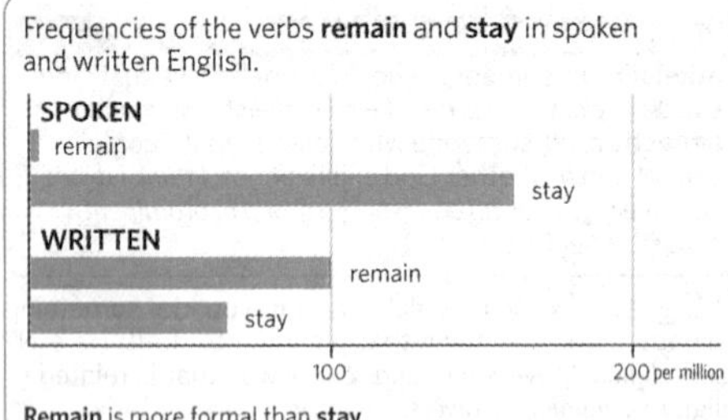

Remain is more formal than **stay**.

re·main /rɪˈmeɪn/ ●●● S1 W1 *v*
1 [I always + adv/prep, linking verb] to continue to be in the same state or condition: *Please remain seated until all the lights are on.* | *We remained friends.* | *The boy **remained silent**.* | **[+as]** *Despite the job losses, Parker remained as manager.* | **remain unclear/unchanged/unanswered etc** *Many scientists remain unconvinced by the current evidence.*

> **REGISTER**
> In everyday English, people usually say something or someone **stays** in a particular state, condition, or place, rather than **remains** in it: *We **stayed** friends.*

> **GRAMMAR: Linking verbs**
> **Remain** is a linking verb in this meaning. This type of verb links the subject of the sentence with an adjective or noun: *He remains undecided about what to do.* | *Traffic congestion remains a problem.*

2 [I] *formal* to stay in the same place without moving away SYN **stay**: **[+at/in/with etc]** *She was too ill to remain at home.* | *The refugees were allowed to remain in the UK.*
THESAURUS ▸ STAY
3 [I] to continue to exist or be left after others have gone, been used, or been destroyed: *Little of the original building remains.* | *The score is tied, with fifteen minutes remaining.* | ***What remains of** his original art collection is now in the city museum.*

> **REGISTER**
> In everyday English, people usually say that something **is left** rather than **remains**. *Not much of the old town **is left**.*

4 [I] to be left after other things have been dealt with: **remain to be done** *Several points remain to be settled.* | ***There remained** a few jobs still to be finished.* | ***The fact remains that** racism is still a considerable problem.*
5 it remains to be seen used to say that it is still uncertain whether something will happen or is true: *It remains to be seen whether the operation was successful.*

re·main·der /rɪˈmeɪndə $ -ər/ ●○○ *n*
1 the remainder the part of something that is left after everything else has gone or been dealt with SYN **the rest**: *The remainder must be paid by the end of June.* | **[+of]** *He spent the remainder of his police career behind a desk.*
2 [C] **a)** the number you get when you subtract one number from another number **b)** the number that is left when you divide one number by another number: *Fifteen divided by four gives you a remainder of 3.*

re·main·ing /rɪˈmeɪnɪŋ/ ●●○ *adj* [only before noun] the remaining people or things are those that are left when the others have gone, been used, or been dealt with: *The few remaining guests were in the kitchen.* | *Add the remaining ingredients and simmer for 30 minutes.* | *The only remaining question is whether we can raise the money.*

re·mains /rɪˈmeɪnz/ ●●○ W3 *n* [plural]
1 the parts of something that are left after the rest has been destroyed or has disappeared: **[+of]** *On the table were the remains of the evening meal.* | *extensive Roman remains* (=of ancient buildings) *at Arles*
2 the body of someone who has died: *Her remains are buried in Westminster.*

re·make¹ /ˈriːmeɪk/ *n* [C] a record or film that has the same music or story as one that was made before: **[+of]** *a remake of 'Cape Fear'*

re·make² /ˌriːˈmeɪk/ *v* (*past tense and past participle* **remade** /-ˈmeɪd/) [T] **1** to film a story or record a piece of music again: *It was remade as a musical.* **2** to build or make something again: *She remade her wedding dress to fit her daughter.*

re·mand¹ /rɪˈmɑːnd $ rɪˈmænd/ *v* [T] *law* **1** *BrE* to send someone back from a court of law, to wait for their TRIAL: *Smith was **remanded in custody*** (=kept in prison) *until Tuesday.* | *He's been **remanded on bail** for a month* (=allowed to leave the law court and go home to wait for trial). GRAMMAR **Remand** is usually passive in this meaning. **2** *AmE* to send a case to be dealt with in another court: *The court remanded the case for trial.*

remand² *n* [U] *BrE* the period of time that someone spends in prison before their TRIAL: **on remand** *Evans committed suicide while on remand in Parkhurst prison.* | *remand prisoners*

reˈmand ˌcentre *n* [C] *BrE* a place like a prison where people are kept while waiting for a TRIAL

reˈmand ˌhome *n* [C] *BrE* a place like a prison where young people are kept while waiting for a TRIAL

re·mark¹ /rɪˈmɑːk $ -ɑːrk/ ●●● W3 *n*
1 [C] something that you say when you express an opinion or say what you have noticed SYN **comment**: *Unfortunately, a local journalist overheard the remark.* THESAURUS COMMENT
2 remarks [plural] the things you say in a formal speech: **introductory/opening/concluding remarks** *the chairman's introductory remarks* | **in sb's remarks** *Caldwell, in his remarks, emphasized the need for cooperation.*

COLLOCATIONS

VERBS

make a remark *I'm sorry, I shouldn't have made that remark.*
ignore a remark *He ignored my remark and carried on working.*

ADJECTIVES

a casual/throwaway remark (=one that you do not think about carefully) *I didn't mean to upset you – it was just a throwaway remark.*
a chance remark (=one that is not planned or intended) *I found out about their relationship from a chance remark Teddy made at dinner.*
a personal remark (=a remark about someone's appearance or behaviour, especially an offensive one) *He kept making personal remarks about Tom.*
a racist/sexist remark (=an offensive remark showing racist/sexist attitudes) | **a disparaging remark** (=one that shows you do not think someone or something is very good) | **a rude remark** | **a witty remark** (=one that is clever and amusing)

remark² ●●○ *v* [T] to say something, especially about something you have just noticed: *'This house must be very old,' he remarked.* | **remark that** *Anderson left the table, remarking that he had some work to do.* | **[+on/upon]** *He remarked on the difference in security measures at the two airports.* THESAURUS SAY

re·mark·a·ble /rɪˈmɑːkəbəl $ -ɑːr-/ ●●○ W3 *adj* unusual or surprising and therefore deserving attention or praise: *She has made remarkable progress.* | *a remarkable coincidence* | **remarkable feat/achievement/accomplishment** *It's a remarkable achievement for the company.* | **it is remarkable that** *It is remarkable that women did not have the vote until that time.* | **[+for]** *His drawings are remarkable for their accuracy.* | *He's a* ***remarkable man.***

re·mark·a·bly /rɪˈmɑːkəbli $ -ɑːr-/ ●●○ *adv* in an amount or to a degree that is unusual or surprising SYN **surprisingly**: [+adj/adv] *She plays the violin remarkably well.* | [sentence adverb] *Remarkably, all of the passengers survived the crash.*

re·mar·ry /ˌriːˈmæri/ *v* (**remarried**, **remarrying**, **remarries**) [I,T] to marry again: *Widowed in 1949, Mrs Hayes never remarried.* —**remarriage** /riːˈmærɪdʒ/ *n* [C]

re·mas·ter /riːˈmɑːstə $ -ˈmæstər/ *v* [T] *technical* to make a musical recording sound better or a film look better by using a computer to improve the original: *an album with 15* ***digitally remastered*** *songs*

re·match /ˈriːmætʃ/ *n* [C usually singular] when two teams or people compete against each other a second time, especially when there was no clear winner in the first competition SYN **replay**: *Both teams are preparing for the rematch.*

re·me·di·a·ble /rɪˈmiːdiəbəl/ *adj formal* able to be corrected or cured: *remediable problems*

re·me·di·al /rɪˈmiːdiəl/ *adj* **1 remedial course/class/teacher etc** a special course etc that helps students who have difficulty learning something **2** intended to improve something that is wrong: *Some remedial work needs to be done on the foundations.* **3** intended to cure a problem with someone's health: *remedial mental health therapies*

rem·e·dy¹ /ˈremədi/ ●●○ *n* (*plural* **remedies**) [C]
1 a way of dealing with a problem or making a bad situation better SYN **solution**: *The problems in our schools do not have a simple remedy.* | **[+for]** *The program is one remedy for discrimination.*
2 a medicine to cure an illness or pain that is not very serious SYN **cure**: **cold/cough remedy** | **[+for]** *a remedy for colds* | **herbal/natural remedy** *a natural remedy that helps insomnia* | *a home remedy* (=one that you make at home) *for sore throats* | *The herb is used as a folk remedy* (=a traditional medicine, rather than one a doctor gives you) *for a baby's teething pains.*
3 beyond/without remedy *formal* if a situation is beyond remedy, nothing can be done to make it better: *She felt as if her marital problems were beyond remedy.*

remedy² ●○○ *v* (**remedied**, **remedying**, **remedies**) [T] to deal with a problem or improve a bad situation SYN **put right**: *To remedy the situation, the water must be chemically treated.*

re·mem·ber /rɪˈmembə $ -ər/ ●●● S1 W1 *v*
1 THE PAST [I,T] to have a picture or idea in your mind of people, events, places etc from the past → **forget**: *Do you remember Rosa Davies?* | *I* ***can't remember*** *her exact words.* | **remember (that)** *I remember you two couldn't stand each other at first!* | **remember (sb) doing sth** *I remember meeting her at a party once.* | *I remember my father bringing home a huge Christmas tree.* | *I* ***remember*** *it* ***well****; I'd never seen my mother so angry.* | *She* ***clearly remembers*** *the excitement as they boarded the train.* | *I* ***vaguely remember*** *reading something about it in the paper.* | *They had three children,* ***if I remember rightly.*** | *They've lived here* ***for as long as I can remember.*** | *No one got drunk* ***as far as I can remember.***

GRAMMAR

Using the progressive

• The verb **remember** is not usually used in the progressive in this meaning. You say: *Yes, I remember him.* ✗ Don't say: *Yes, I am remembering him.*
• You often say someone **can remember** something when describing what they remember: *Yes, I can remember him.*

Patterns with remember

• Do not use 'remember about' in this meaning. You say: *Do you remember that day?* ✗ Don't say: *Do you remember about that day?*
GRAMMAR GUIDE VERBS

2 INFORMATION/FACTS [I,T] to bring information or facts that you know into your mind → **forget**: *You left your keys on the table, remember?* | *I can't remember her phone number.* | **remember (that)** *I suddenly remembered that I'd left the stove on.* | **remember what/how/why etc** *I called the office, but I don't remember who I spoke to.*
3 TO DO/GET STH [I,T] to not forget something that you must do, get, or bring: *I hope he remembers the wine.* | **remember to do sth** *Remember to take your P.E. clothes to school.*
4 KEEP STH IN MIND [T] to keep a particular fact about a situation in your mind: *Remember, processed food is usually full of salt and sugar.* | **remember that** *Remember that not everyone has as much money as you.* | **it should/must be remembered (that)** *It should be remembered that a lot of work went into this event.*
5 HONOUR THE DEAD [T] to think with respect about someone who has died, often in a ceremony: *On this day we remember the dead of two world wars.*
6 be remembered for/as sth to be famous for something important that you did in the past: *He is best remembered for his travel books.* | *Johnson wanted to be remembered as 'the education president.'*
7 GIVE SB A PRESENT [T] to give someone a present on a particular occasion: *Lilian always remembers me at Christmas.* | **remember sb in your will** (=arrange for someone to have something of yours after you die)

R

8 remember me to sb *spoken* used to ask someone to give a greeting from you to someone else

THESAURUS

remember to form an idea in your mind of people, events, places etc from the past: *I remember Janine – she lived in that house on the corner. | I can't remember how the film ends.*
recall to remember a particular fact, event, or situation, especially in order to tell someone about it: *Can you recall where your husband was that night? | She recalled that he had seemed a strange, lonely man.*
recollect *formal* to remember an event or situation: *Harry smiled as he recollected the scene. | She tried to recollect what had happened next in her dream.*
memorize to learn facts, a piece of writing or music etc, so that you can remember them later: *He's trying to memorize his speech.*
think back/look back to think about something that happened in the past: *I thought back to when I was his age. | Looking back, I should have been more patient with her.*
reminisce /ˌreməˈnɪs/ to talk about pleasant events, people, experiences etc from the past, because you want to remember them or enjoy talking about them: *They were reminiscing about old times.*
bear sth in mind to remember something important when you are doing something, because it could affect what you do: *Bear in mind that this is the first time he's done this.*
sth is on the tip of your tongue used to say that you know a word or a name but that you have difficulty remembering it at this exact moment: *His name's on the tip of my tongue. I'll think of it in a minute.*
remind sb of sth to make you think of another person, thing, or time, because they are similar: *It reminds me of the time when I first started teaching. | The taste reminded him of school dinners.*

re·mem·brance /rɪˈmembrəns/ *n* **1** [singular, U] when people remember and give honour to someone who has died: **in remembrance of sth** *a service in remembrance of those killed in the war | a Holocaust remembrance* **2** [C,U] *formal* a memory that you have of a person or event: **[+of]** *Trillin's remembrances of his childhood*

Reˈmembrance ˌDay (*also* **Reˌmembrance ˈSunday**) *n* the Sunday nearest to November 11th, when a ceremony is held in Britain to remember people who were killed in the two world wars

re·mind /rɪˈmaɪnd/ ●●● S1 W2 *v* [T]
1 to make someone remember something that they must do: *Yes, I'll be there. Thanks for reminding me.* | **remind sb about sth** *The girls constantly had to be reminded about their chores.* | **remind sb to do sth** *Remind me to buy some milk tonight.* | **remind sb (that)** *Mrs Welland reminded her son that they still had several people to see.* | **that reminds me** (=used when something has just made you remember something you were going to say or do) *Oh, that reminds me, I saw Jenny in town today.* | **remind yourself** *I reminded myself to watch them closely. | He made a few notes to remind himself of what he wanted to say.*
2 to make someone remember someone that they know or something that happened in the past: **remind sb of sth** *That song always reminds me of our first date.* | **remind sb (of) what/how etc** *I was reminded how lucky I was.*
3 don't remind me *spoken* used in a joking way when someone has mentioned something that embarrasses or annoys you: *'We've got a test tomorrow.' 'Don't remind me!'*
4 let me remind you/may I remind you (that) *spoken formal* used to emphasize a warning or criticism: *Let me remind you that you are expected to arrive on time.*
remind sb **of** sb/sth *phr v* to seem similar to someone or something else: *The landscape reminded her of Scotland. | Corinne reminds me of myself when I was her age.*

GRAMMAR: Using the progressive

Remind someone **of** is not used in the progressive. You say: *He reminds me of Pete.* ✗ Don't say: *He is reminding me of Pete.*
GRAMMAR GUIDE ▶ **VERBS**

re·mind·er /rɪˈmaɪndə $ -ər/ ●●○ *n* [C]
1 something that makes you notice, remember, or think about something: **[+of]** *a reminder of the dangers of drinking and driving* | **reminder that** *Occasional bursts of gunfire are a reminder that the rebels are still active.* | **constant/painful/vivid etc reminder** *The damaged church was preserved as a stark reminder of the horrors of war. | The drop in stock prices* ***serves as a reminder*** (=is a reminder) *that investing is a form of gambling.*
2 something, for example a letter, that reminds you to do something which you might have forgotten: *a reminder from the dentist for your check-up*

rem·i·nisce /ˌreməˈnɪs/ *v* [I] to talk or think about pleasant events in your past: **[+about]** *a group of former students reminiscing about their college days* THESAURUS ▶ **REMEMBER**

rem·i·nis·cence /ˌreməˈnɪsəns/ *n* [C,U often plural] a spoken or written story about events that you remember → **memoir**: **[+of/about]** *reminiscences of the war*

rem·i·nis·cent /ˌreməˈnɪsənt/ ●○○ *adj*
1 reminiscent of sth reminding you of something: *a style* ***strongly reminiscent*** *of Virginia Woolf's novels*
2 *literary* thinking about the past: *Her face wore a reminiscent smile.*

re·miss /rɪˈmɪs/ *adj* [not before noun] *formal* careless because you did not do something that you ought to have done SYN **negligent**: **[+in]** *parents who are remiss in their duties* | **it was remiss of sb to do sth** *It was remiss of the social services not to notify the police.*

re·mis·sion /rɪˈmɪʃən/ *n* **1** [C,U] a period when a serious illness improves for a time: **in remission** *The chemotherapy was successful, and she is now in remission. | The cancer has* ***gone into remission***. **2** [C,U] *BrE* a reduction of the time that someone has to spend in prison: *He was given six months' remission for good behaviour.* **3** [U] *formal* when you allow someone to keep the money they owe you: *remission of debts* **4 the remission of sins** *formal* forgiveness from God for the bad things that you have done

re·mit¹ /rɪˈmɪt/ *v* (**remitted**, **remitting**) *formal* **1** [I,T] to send a payment: *Please remit payment by cheque.* **2** [T] to free someone from a debt or punishment → **unremitting**
remit sth **to** sb/sth *phr v formal* to send a proposal, plan, or problem back to someone for them to make a decision about: *The court remitted the matter to the agency for reconsideration.*

re·mit² /ˈriːmɪt $ rɪˈmɪt, ˈriːmɪt/ *n* [singular, U] *BrE formal* the particular piece of work that someone has been officially asked to deal with: *the remit of a senior member of staff* | **be within/outside sb's remit** *Marketing is outside our remit.*

re·mit·tance /rɪˈmɪtəns/ *n* **1** [C] *formal* an amount of money that you send to pay for something **2** [U] when you send money: **on remittance of sth** *We will forward the goods on remittance of £10.*

re·mix /ˈriːmɪks/ *n* [C] a different VERSION of a popular song, in which someone has added to or changed the original recording: *a disco remix* —**remix** /riːˈmɪks/ *v* [T] —**remixer** *n* [C]

rem·nant /ˈremnənt/ ●○○ *n* [C]
1 [usually plural] a small part of something that remains after the rest of it has been used, destroyed, or eaten: **[+of]** *The remnants of a meal stood on the table.*
2 a small piece of cloth left from a larger piece and sold cheaply

re·mod·el /ˌriːˈmɒdl $ -ˈmɑːdl/ *v* (**remodelled**, **remodelling** *BrE*, **remodeled**, **remodeling** *AmE*) [I,T] to change the shape, structure, or appearance of something, especially a building: *The airport terminals have been extensively remodelled.* —**remodelling** *n* [U]

re·mold /ˌriːˈməʊld $ -ˈmoʊld/ *v* [T] *formal* the American spelling of REMOULD

re·mon·strance /rɪˈmɒnstrəns $ rɪˈmɑːn-/ *n* [C,U] *formal* a complaint or protest: *angry remonstrances*

rem·on·strate /ˈremənstreɪt $ rɪˈmɑːn-/ *v* [I] *formal* to tell someone that you strongly disapprove of something they have said or done: **[+with]** *The Everton manager remonstrated angrily with the referee.* —**remonstrative** /rɪˈmɒnstrətɪv $ -ˈmɑːn-/ *adj* —**remonstration** /ˌremənˈstreɪʃən/ *n* [C,U]

re·morse /rɪˈmɔːs $ -ɔːrs/ *n* [U] a strong feeling of being sorry that you have done something very bad → **regret**: *Throughout the trial, he had* ***shown*** *no* ***remorse****.* | **[+for]** *She felt a pang of remorse for what she had done.* | **be full of remorse/be filled with remorse** *Filled with remorse, Dillon decided to resign.* —**remorseful** *adj* —**remorsefully** *adv*

re·morse·less /rɪˈmɔːsləs $ -ˈmɔːr-/ *adj* **1** something bad or threatening that is remorseless continues to happen and seems impossible to stop SYN **relentless**: *the remorseless winter winds* **2** cruel, and not caring how much other people are hurt SYN **merciless**: *a remorseless murderer* —**remorselessly** *adv*

re·mort·gage /ˌriːˈmɔːɡɪdʒ $ -ɔːr-/ *v* [T] to borrow money by having a second MORTGAGE on your house, or increasing the one you have: *We may have to remortgage the house.*

re·mote¹ /rɪˈməʊt $ -ˈmoʊt/ ●●○ W3 *adj*

1 FAR AWAY far from towns or other places where people live SYN **isolated**: *a remote border town* | *a fire in a remote mountain area* THESAURUS ▸ FAR

2 NOT LIKELY if a chance or possibility of something happening is remote, it is not very likely to happen SYN **slight**: **remote chance/possibility** *There's a remote chance that you can catch him before he leaves.* | *The prospect of peace seems remote.*

3 TIME far away in time SYN **distant**: *the remote time when dinosaurs walked the earth* | **a remote ancestor** (=someone related to you, who lived a long time ago)

4 DIFFERENT very different from something: **[+from]** *The Heights was quiet and clean and remote from the busy daily life of the city.*

5 PERSON unfriendly, and not interested in people SYN **distant**: *His father was a remote, quiet man.*

6 not have the remotest idea/interest/intention etc *especially BrE* used to emphasize that you do not know something, are not interested in something, do not intend to do something etc: *He hasn't the remotest interest in sport.* | **[+what/where/who etc]** *I haven't the remotest idea what you mean.* —**remoteness** *n* [U]

remote² *n* [C] a REMOTE CONTROL: *Give me the remote.*

reˌmote ˈaccess *n* [U] a system that allows you to use information on a computer that is far away from your computer

reˌmote conˈtrol ●○○ *n*

1 [C] a thing you use for controlling a piece of electrical or electronic equipment without having to touch it, for example for turning a television on or off SYN **zapper**

2 [U] the process of controlling equipment from a distance, using radio or electronic signals: *a missile guided by remote control*

3 [U] a type of computer software that lets you use a particular computer by connecting it to another one that is far away —**remote-controlled** *adj*

reˌmote interroˈgation *n* [U] the process of calling your own telephone when you are away from your home or office so that you can listen to messages that people have left on your ANSWERING MACHINE

re·mote·ly /rɪˈməʊtli $ -ˈmoʊt-/ *adv* **1** by only a small amount SYN **slightly**: *The brew tasted only remotely of beer.* **2 not remotely interested/funny/possible etc** used to emphasize that someone or something is not at all interested, funny etc: *There was nothing remotely new in this idea.* **3** from far away: *remotely operated vehicles*

reˌmote ˈsensing *n* [U] the use of SATELLITES to obtain pictures and information about the Earth

reˌmote ˈworking *n* [U] when people do their work at home, using a computer that is connected to the computer system in an office SYN **homeworking**

re·mould¹ *BrE*, **remold** *AmE* /ˌriːˈməʊld $ -ˈmoʊld/ *v* [T] *formal* to change an idea, system, way of thinking etc: *Mergers have forced organizations to remould themselves.*

re·mould² /ˈriːməʊld $ -moʊld/ *n* [C] *BrE* an old tyre with a new surface, that you can use again

re·mount /ˌriːˈmaʊnt/ *v* [I,T] to get onto a horse, bicycle etc again

re·mov·a·ble /rɪˈmuːvəbəl/ AWL *adj* easy to remove: *a sofa with removable cloth covers*

re·mov·al /rɪˈmuːvəl/ ●●○ AWL *n* [C,U]

1 when something is taken away from, out of, or off the place where it is → **remove**: **[+of]** *the removal of rubbish*

2 when you get rid of something so that it does not exist any longer: *stain removal*

3 when someone is forced out of an important position or dismissed from a job: **[+from]** *the mayor's removal from office*

4 *BrE* the process of taking furniture from your old house to your new one: **removal company/man etc** *The removal men have been in and out all day.*

reˈmoval van *n* [C] *BrE* a large vehicle used for moving furniture and other things from one house to another

re·move¹ /rɪˈmuːv/ ●●● S2 W1 AWL *v* [T]

1 TAKE AWAY to take something away from, out of, or off the place where it is: *Remove the old wallpaper and fill any holes in the walls.* | **remove sth from sth** *Reference books may not be removed from the library.*

2 GET RID OF to get rid of something so that it does not exist any longer: *a cleaner that will remove wine stains* | *The college removed rules that prevented women from enrolling.*

3 FROM A JOB to force someone out of an important position or dismiss them from a job: **remove sb from sth** *Congress could remove the president from office.*

4 CLOTHES *formal* to take off a piece of clothing: *He removed his hat and gloves.*

> **REGISTER**
> In everyday English, people usually say that someone **takes** clothing **off** rather than **removes** it: *Is it OK if I* ***take*** *my coat* ***off****?*

5 be far removed from sth to be very different from something: *The events in the newspaper article were far removed from reality.*

6 cousin once/twice etc removed the child, GRANDCHILD etc of your COUSIN, or your parent's, grandparent's etc cousin

THESAURUS - MEANING 2

remove to make something no longer exist, especially something that was causing problems: *Some stains are difficult to remove with ordinary washing powder.* | *All the obstacles to an agreement have now been removed.*

get rid of sb/sth to remove someone or something that you do not want. **Get rid of** is much more common than **remove** in everyday English, but is usually only used in active sentences: *They managed to get rid of all the weeds.* | *It was almost impossible to get rid of him.*

eliminate to completely get rid of something that you do not want, especially because it is unnecessary or causing problems: *If you book online, this eliminates the need for a ticket.* | *The new system will help to eliminate costly delays.*

eradicate to completely get rid of a disease or a problem: *The disease has been eradicated from most of Europe.* | *Street crime has almost been eradicated.*

delete to remove something that has been written on a computer, or stored in a computer: *Do you want to delete this file?*

erase to remove recorded sounds or pictures from a tape, or writing from paper: *Shall I erase this video?* | *It's better to cross out a mistake than to try to erase it.*

R

cut to remove a part from a film, book, speech etc: *The most violent scenes were cut.* | *Parts of his original speech were cut.*

remove² AWL *n* [C,U] *especially BrE formal* a distance or amount by which two things are separated: **at a remove** *The X-ray operator works at a safe remove in a separate room.*

re·mov·er /rɪˈmuːvə $ -ər/ *n* [C,U] **paint/nail varnish/stain etc remover** a substance that removes paint marks etc

REM sleep /ˈrem sliːp/ *n* [U] *technical* (***rapid eye movement sleep***) a period during sleep when your eyes move quickly, when you are dreaming

re·mu·ne·ra·tion /rɪˌmjuːnəˈreɪʃən/ *n* [C,U] *formal* the pay you give someone for something they have done for you: *high rates of remuneration* —**remunerate** /rɪˈmjuːnəreɪt/ *v* [T]

re·mu·ne·ra·tive /rɪˈmjuːnərətɪv $ -nəreɪtɪv/ *adj formal* making a lot of money

re·nais·sance /rɪˈneɪsəns $ ˈrenəˌsɑːns/ *n* [singular] a new interest in something, especially a particular form of art, music etc, that has not been popular for a long period: **[+in]** *a renaissance in wood carving over the last few years*

Renaissance *n* **1 the Renaissance** the period of time in Europe between the 14th and 17th centuries, when art, literature, PHILOSOPHY, and scientific ideas became very important and a lot of new art etc was produced **2 Renaissance art/furniture/architecture etc** art, furniture etc belonging to the Renaissance period

ReˌnaissanceˈMan / $,... './, **ReˌnaissanceˈWoman** / $,... '../ *n* [C] a man or woman who can do many things well, such as writing and painting, and who knows a lot about many different subjects

re·nal /ˈriːnl/ *adj* [only before noun] *technical* relating to the KIDNEYS: *acute renal failure*

re·name /ˌriːˈneɪm/ *v* [T] to give something a new name: **be renamed sth** *Myddleton Way was renamed Allende Avenue.* GRAMMAR **Rename** is usually passive.

re·nas·cent /rɪˈnæsənt/ *adj* [only before noun] *formal* becoming popular, strong, or important again: *Voters have come back to a renascent Labour Party.*

rend /rend/ *v* (*past tense and past participle* **rent** /rent/) [T] *literary* to tear or break something violently into pieces

ren·der /ˈrendə $ -ər/ ●○○ *v* [T]

1 to cause someone or something to be in a particular condition: **render sb/sth impossible/harmless/unconscious etc** *He was rendered almost speechless by the news.* | *The blow to his head was strong enough to render him unconscious.*

2 *formal* to give something to someone or do something, because it is your duty or because someone expects you to: *an obligation to **render assistance** to those in need* | **render a decision/opinion/judgment etc** *It is unlikely that the court will render an opinion before November 5.* | *a bill of $3200 **for services rendered*** (=for something you have done)

3 to express or present something in a particular way: **render sth as sth** *She made a sound that in print is rendered as 'harrumph'.* | **render sth sth** *Infrared film renders blue skies a deep black.* | **render sth in sth** *a sculpture rendered in bronze*

4 render sth into English/Russian/Chinese etc *formal* to translate something into English, Russian etc

5 *technical* to spread PLASTER or CEMENT on the surface of a wall: *a brick wall that has been rendered and whitewashed*

6 to melt the fat of an animal as you cook it: *Steam the goose to render some of the fat.*

ren·der·ing /ˈrendərɪŋ/ *n* **1** [C] someone's performance of a play, piece of music etc SYN **rendition**: **[+of]** *a spirited rendering of the national anthem* **2** [C] the way an expression, piece of writing etc is translated or explained, or the way an event, situation etc is described: **accurate/literal etc rendering of sth** *a faithful rendering of historical events* **3** [C,U] *BrE* a material made of CEMENT and sand, used on the outside walls of buildings

ren·dez·vous¹ /ˈrɒndəvuː, -deɪ- $ ˈrɑːndeɪ-/ *n* (*plural* **rendezvous** /-vuːz/) **1** [C] an arrangement to meet someone at a particular time and place, often secretly: **[+with]** *He **made** a **rendezvous** with her in Times Square.* | *plans for a **secret rendezvous*** THESAURUS ▸ MEETING **2** [C usually singular] a place where two or more people have arranged to meet: *Boats picked us up at pre-arranged rendezvous.* **3** [C] a bar, restaurant etc where people like to meet: *a popular rendezvous for media people*

rendezvous² *v* [I] **1** to meet someone at a time or place that was arranged earlier SYN **meet up**: **[+with]** *We'll rendezvous with James in Nicosia.* **2** if two spacecraft, aircraft, or military vehicles rendezvous, they meet, for example to move supplies from one to the other

ren·di·tion /renˈdɪʃən/ *n* **1** [C usually singular, U] someone's performance of a play, piece of music etc: *He gave a moving rendition of Lennon's 'Imagine'.* **2** [C] a translation of a piece of writing: **[+of]** *an English rendition of a Greek poem*

ren·e·gade /ˈrenəgeɪd/ *n* [C] *literary* someone who leaves one side in a war, politics etc in order to join the opposing side – used to show disapproval: *a renegade army unit*

re·nege /rɪˈniːg, rɪˈneɪg $ rɪˈnɪg, rɪˈniːg/ *v* [I] *formal* **renege on an agreement/deal/promise etc** to not do something you have promised or agreed to do SYN **go back on**: *They reneged on a pledge to release the hostages.*

re·new /rɪˈnjuː $ rɪˈnuː/ ●○○ *v* [T]

1 to arrange for an agreement or official document to continue for a further period of time: **renew sb's contract/licence/membership etc** *I need to renew my passport this year.*

2 *formal* to begin doing something again after a period of not doing it SYN **resume**: *Local people have renewed their efforts to save the school.* | *Police renewed their appeal for witnesses.* | **renew a friendship/acquaintance etc** (=become friendly with someone again)

3 to remove something that is old or broken and put a new one in its place SYN **replace**: *The window frames need to be renewed.*

4 renew a book to arrange to borrow a library book for a further period of time

re·new·a·ble /rɪˈnjuːəbəl $ rɪˈnuː-/ ●○○ *adj*

1 if an agreement or official document is renewable, you can make it continue for a further period of time after it ends OPP **non-renewable**: *It's a six-month lease but it's renewable.* | *a renewable visa*

2 [usually before noun] renewable energy replaces itself naturally, or is easily replaced because there is a large supply of it: ***renewable energy** such as solar power* | *an industry based on **renewable resources*** THESAURUS ▸ ENVIRONMENTALLY FRIENDLY

re·new·a·bles /rɪˈnjuːəbəlz $ -ˈnuː-/ *n* [plural] renewable ways of producing energy: *We must expand the use of renewables.*

re·new·al /rɪˈnjuːəl $ -ˈnuː-/ ●○○ *n* [singular, U]

1 when an activity, situation, or process begins again after a period when it had stopped: **[+of]** *a renewal of the recent conflict* | *Spring is a time of renewal.*

2 when you make an agreement or official document continue for a further period of time after it ends: **[+of]** *the renewal of our annual licence* | *Mark's contract **comes up for renewal** at the end of this year.*

3 inner city/urban renewal when the poor areas of towns are improved by making new jobs, industries, homes etc

re·newed /rɪˈnjuːd $ -ˈnuːd/ ●○○ *adj*

1 [only before noun] starting again, especially with increased interest or strength: **renewed interest/confidence/enthusiasm etc** *renewed concern about farming methods* | *The festival went ahead, despite renewed protests.*

2 [not before noun] feeling healthy and relaxed again, after feeling ill or tired

ren·net /ˈrenɪt/ *n* [U] a substance used for making milk thicker in order to make cheese

re·nounce /rɪˈnaʊns/ *v* [T] **1** if you renounce an official position, title, right etc, you publicly say that you will not keep it anymore SYN **give up**: *Edward renounced his claim to the French throne.* | *She renounced her citizenship.* **2** to publicly say or show that you no longer believe in something, or will no longer behave in a particular way SYN **reject** → **renunciation**: *These groups must renounce violence if there is to be progress towards peace.* | *Young people renounced capitalism in favour of peace and love.*

ren·o·vate /ˈrenəveɪt/ *v* [T] to repair a building or old furniture so that it is in good condition again: *The hotel has been renovated and redecorated.* THESAURUS REPAIR —**renovation** /ˌrenəˈveɪʃən/ *n* [C,U]

re·nown /rɪˈnaʊn/ *n* [U] *formal* when you are famous and a lot of people admire you for a special skill, achievement, or quality SYN **acclaim**: **international/public etc renown** *He has **won** world **renown** for his films.* | *He **achieved** some **renown** as a football player.*

re·nowned /rɪˈnaʊnd/ ●○○ *adj* known and admired by a lot of people, especially for a special skill, achievement, or quality SYN **famous**: **[+for]** *an island renowned for its beauty* | **[+as]** *He's renowned as a brilliant speaker.* | **renowned author/actor/photographer etc** *a world renowned expert in the field* THESAURUS FAMOUS

rent[1] /rent/ ●●● S2 W3 *v*
1 [I,T] to regularly pay money to live in a house or room that belongs to someone else, or to use something that belongs to someone else: *Most students rent rooms in their second year.* | *I'd rather have my own house than rent.* | **rent sth from sb** *Some farmers rent their land from the council.*
2 (*also* **rent out**) [T] to let someone live in a house, room etc that you own, or use your land, in return for money SYN **let** *BrE*: **rent sth (out) to sb** *She rents out two rooms to students.*
3 [T] *especially AmE* to pay money for the use of something for a short period of time SYN **hire** *BrE*: *Will you rent a car while you're in Spain?*
rent at/for sth *phr v* if a house rents at or for an amount of money, that is how much you must pay to use it: *Houses here rent for at least $1,500 a week.*

rent[2] ●●● S2 W3 *n*
1 [C,U] the money that someone pays regularly to use a room, house etc that belongs to someone else: *I pay the rent at the beginning of every month.* | **[+of]** *an annual rent of £8,000* THESAURUS COST
2 [C,U] *especially AmE* an amount of money that you pay to use a car, boat etc that belongs to someone else: *The rent was only $20 an hour.*
3 for rent available to be rented: *Luxury villas for rent.*
4 [C] *formal* a large tear in something made of cloth: *huge rents in the curtains*

COLLOCATIONS

ADJECTIVES/NOUN + rent

high *Rents in the city centre are very high.*
low *Our workers get low rents and other advantages.*
exorbitant (=extremely high) *Some landlords charge exorbitant rents.*
fixed *The rent is fixed for three years.*
affordable (=which people can easily pay) *The government plans to provide more homes at affordable rents.*
the annual/monthly/weekly rent | **ground rent** *BrE* (=rent paid to the owner of the land that a house, office etc is built on)

VERBS

pay the rent *She couldn't afford to pay the rent.*
increase/raise the rent (*also* **put up the rent** *BrE*) *The landlord wants to put up the rent.*
fall behind with the rent/get behind on the rent (=fail to pay your rent on time) | **collect the rent** | **the rent increases/goes up**

rent + NOUN

a rent increase *How can they justify such big rent increases?*
rent arrears *BrE* (=money that you owe because you have not paid your rent) | **a rent book** *BrE* (=a book that shows the payments you have made in rent)

rent[3] the past tense and past participle of REND

rent-a- /ˈrent ə/ *prefix informal* used to describe or refer to someone who is always willing to do something – used to show disapproval: *a rent-a-mob* (=people who are always willing to go and protest somewhere) | *a rent-a-quote politician* (=one who is always willing to make a statement about a subject)

rent·al /ˈrentl/ ●●○ *n*
1 [C usually singular, U] the money that you pay to use a car, television, or other machine over a period of time: **car/television/telephone etc rental** *The price includes accommodation and car rental.* | *Video rental is usually £3.* | **line rental** *BrE* (=the money that you pay to use a telephone line)
2 [C,U] an arrangement to rent something for a period of time, or the act of doing this: **rental contract/scheme/service etc** *Could you sign the rental agreement?*
3 [C] *especially AmE* something that you rent, especially a house or car: *companies that provide rentals*

ˈrent boy *n* [C] *BrE informal* a young man who has sex with other men in return for money

ˈrent conˌtrol *n* [U] when a city or a state uses laws to control the cost of renting houses and apartments

rent·ed /ˈrentɪd/ *adj* **rented accommodation/housing/apartment etc** houses etc that people pay rent for

ˌrent-ˈfree *adj, adv* without payment of rent: *rent-free accommodation* | *He lives there rent-free.*

ˈrent ˌrebate *n* [C] *BrE* money that some people get from the local government to help them pay their rent

ˈrent strike *n* [C] an occasion when all the people living in a group of houses or apartments refuse to pay their rent, as a protest against something

re·nun·ci·a·tion /rɪˌnʌnsiˈeɪʃən/ *n* [C,U] *formal* when someone makes a formal decision to no longer believe in something, live in a particular way etc → **renounce**: **[+of]** *Eastern Europe's renunciation of Communism*

re·o·pen /riˈəʊpən $ -ˈoʊ-/ ●○○ *v* [I,T]
1 if a theatre, restaurant etc reopens, or if it is reopened, it opens again after a period when it was closed: *The swimming pool will reopen in May.*
2 if you reopen a discussion, law case etc, or if it reopens, you begin it again after it had stopped: **reopen a case/question/debate etc** *attempts to reopen the issue of the power station's future*
3 if a government reopens the border of their country, or if the border reopens, people are allowed to pass through it again after it had been closed

re·or·der /riˈɔːdə $ -ˈɔːrdər/ *v* [I,T] **1** to order a product to be supplied again: *Could you reorder more of this fabric?* **2** to change the way that things are ordered or arranged: *The whole system needs reordering.*

re·or·gan·ize (*also* **-ise** *BrE*) /riːˈɔːgənaɪz $ -ˈɔːr-/ *v* [I,T] to arrange or organize something in a new way: *Our office is being completely reorganized.* —**reorganization** /riˌɔːgənaɪˈzeɪʃən $ -ˌɔːrgənə-/ *n* [C,U]: *a major reorganization of childcare services*

rep /rep/ *n* **1** [C] *informal* a SALES REPRESENTATIVE **2** [C] someone who speaks officially for a company, organization, or group of people SYN **representative**: **staff/union/company etc rep** *You need to speak to the students' rep.* | ***Safety reps** have the right to stop the job when workers are in danger.* **3** [C] *AmE* a REPRESENTATIVE **4** [C,U] REPERTORY, or a repertory theatre or company: *Most actors start off in rep.* **5** [C] *AmE spoken* a REPUTATION **6** [C] one exercise that you do in a series of exercises SYN **repetition**: *Do 15 reps of each exercise.*

Rep. **1** the written abbreviation of ***Representative***, used before names: *Rep. Bud Shuster* **2** the written abbreviation of ***Republican***

re·paid /rɪˈpeɪd/ the past tense and past participle of REPAY

re·pair¹ /rɪˈpeə $ -ˈper/ ●●○ *v* [T]
1 to fix something that is damaged, broken, split, or not working properly SYN **mend** *BrE*: *Dad was up the ladder, repairing the roof.* | *Where can I **get** my shoes **repaired**?*
2 *formal* to do something to remove harm that you have caused SYN **mend** *BrE*: *Neil tried to **repair the damage** that his statements had caused.* → IRREPARABLE

repair to sth *phr v old-fashioned* to go to a place: *Shall we repair to the drawing room?* —**repairer** *n* [C]

THESAURUS

repair to do some work on something that is damaged or not working properly, so that it is in good condition again: *The builders are coming to repair the roof.* | *Have you had the washing machine repaired yet?*
fix *especially AmE* to repair something: *I'm taking the car in to get it fixed.* | *The chain on the bike needs fixing.*
mend *especially BrE* to repair something that is damaged, torn, or not working: *I've found someone who'll mend the fence.* | *Can you mend this sweater for me?*
service to check a vehicle or machine and repair it if necessary, especially regularly: *You should have your car serviced every six months.*
renovate to repair an old building so that it looks in good condition again: *They bought an old house and renovated it themselves.*
restore to repair something old and valuable, especially a building, piece of furniture, painting etc, so that it looks the same as it did originally: *Many paintings were damaged in the fire but have now been restored.*
do up *BrE informal*, **fix up** *AmE informal* to repair an old building or vehicle, so that it looks in good condition again: *He does up old cars and sells them.*
patch sth up to quickly repair something that has a hole in it, by putting a piece of material on it, especially temporarily: *They patched up the wall with bits of cement.*
darn to repair holes in clothes: *Are you any good at darning socks?*

repair² ●●○ *n*
1 [C,U] something that you do to fix a thing that is damaged, broken, or not working: **[+to]** *repairs to the roads* | **make/carry out/do repairs** *His job is to make minor repairs on all the machines.* | *The church tower is **in need of repair**.* | **structural/housing/motorway etc repairs** *an extensive programme of building repairs* | **beyond repair** *Many of the paintings were beyond repair* (=so damaged that they could not be mended). | **under repair** (=being repaired) *Is the bridge still under repair?* | *They did a good repair job on the roof.*
2 in good/poor etc repair in good or bad condition: *Garden tools should be **kept in good repair**.*

re·pair·a·ble /rɪˈpeərəbəl $ -ˈper-/ *adj* [not before noun] able to be fixed

re·pair·man /rɪˈpeəmæn $ -ˈper-/ *n* (*plural* **repairmen** /-men/) [C] someone whose job is to repair things: *the TV repairman*

rep·a·ra·tion /ˌrepəˈreɪʃən/ *n formal*
1 reparations [plural] money paid by a defeated country after a war, for all the deaths, damage etc it has caused: *The government agreed to **pay reparations** to victims.*
2 [C,U] when you give something to someone or do something for them because you have done something wrong to them in the past: **make reparation (to sb) for sth** *Offenders must make reparation for their crimes through community service.*

rep·ar·tee /ˌrepɑːˈtiː $ ˌrepərˈtiː/ *n* [U] conversation which is fast and full of intelligent and amusing remarks and replies: *witty repartee*

re·past /rɪˈpɑːst $ rɪˈpæst/ *n* [C] *formal* a meal

re·pat·ri·ate /riːˈpætrieɪt $ riːˈpeɪ-/ *v* [T] **1** to send someone back to their own country → **deport**: *After the war, prisoners were repatriated.* **2** to send profits or money you have earned back to your own country

re·pay /rɪˈpeɪ/ ●●○ *v* (*past tense and past participle* **repaid**) [T]
1 to pay back money that you have borrowed: **repay a loan/debt etc** *Your mortgage will be repaid over 25 years.* | **repay sb sth** *I'll repay you the money you lent me next week.*

REGISTER
In everyday English, people usually say that someone **pays** money **back** rather than **repays** it: *I'll **pay** you **back** the money at the end of the week.*

2 to do something for someone, or give them something, in return for helping you: **repay sb for sth** *How can we repay him for everything he's done?* | *I'd like to buy them something to repay all their kindness.*
3 if something repays your time, effort etc, it is worth the time or effort you have spent

re·pay·a·ble /rɪˈpeɪəbəl/ *adj* [not before noun] money that is repayable at a particular time has to be paid back by that time: **[+over]** *a loan repayable over 10 years*

re·pay·ment /rɪˈpeɪmənt/ ●○○ *n*
1 [U] when you pay back money that you have borrowed: **[+of]** *the **repayment** of **debt***
2 [C usually plural] an amount of money that you pay regularly until you do not owe any more: *monthly **mortgage repayments** of £330* | *Do you worry about **meeting*** (=paying) *your loan **repayments?***

re·peal /rɪˈpiːl/ *v* [T] if a government repeals a law, it officially ends that law —**repeal** *n* [U]

re·peat¹ /rɪˈpiːt/ ●●● S2 W2 *v* [T]
1 SAY AGAIN to say or write something again: *Can you repeat your question?* | *Sorry – could you repeat that?* | **repeat that** *Nick patiently repeated that he had to work that day.* | *It is not, I repeat not, my fault.* | *'I promise,' she repeated.* | **repeat yourself** (=say something that you have said before, usually by mistake) *Elderly people tend to repeat themselves.*
2 DO AGAIN to do something again: *Repeat the exercises twice a day.* | *We must not repeat the mistakes of the past.* | **repeat a class/grade/year** (=do the same class at school again the following year) | *The team are hoping to **repeat** their **success*** (=achieve the same good result) *of last season.*
3 LEARN to say something that someone else has just said, especially in order to learn it: **repeat (sth) after sb** *Repeat after me: amo, amas, amat ...*
4 TELL to tell someone something that you have heard, especially something secret: *Here's what happened, but don't repeat it.*
5 BROADCAST to broadcast a television or radio programme again: *The series will be repeated in the autumn.*
6 sth doesn't bear repeating used to say that you do not want to repeat what someone has said, especially because it is rude: *Her comments don't bear repeating!*
→ **history repeats itself** at HISTORY(8)

repeat on sb *phr v BrE* if food repeats on you, its taste keeps coming back into your mouth after you have eaten it

repeat² ●●○ *n* [C]
1 [usually singular] an event that is very like something that happened before: **[+of]** *The match was basically a repeat of last year's game at Wembley.* | *It was a terrible journey – I hope we don't have a **repeat performance*** (=have the same thing happen again) *on the way home.*
2 a television or radio programme that has been broadcast before: *'Is it a repeat?' 'No, it's a new series.'*
3 repeat order/prescription *BrE* an order of goods or a PRESCRIPTION of medicine that is the same as one you had before
4 *technical* the sign that tells a performer to play a piece of music again, or the music that is played again

re·peat·a·ble /rɪˈpiːtəbəl/ *adj* [not usually before noun]

1 not repeatable too rude to repeat - used about something someone says SYN **unrepeatable 2** able to be repeated: *I hope these results are repeatable.*

re·peat·ed /rɪˈpiːtɪd/ ●○○ *adj* [only before noun] done or happening again and again: *repeated calls for change | repeated attempts to kill him*

re·peat·ed·ly /rɪˈpiːtɪdli/ ●●○ *adv* many times: *Graham was repeatedly warned not to work so hard.*

re·peat·er /rɪˈpiːtə $ -ər/ *n* [C] *technical* a gun that you can fire several times before you have to load it again

re·pel /rɪˈpel/ *v* (**repelled, repelling**) **1** [T] if something repels you, it is so unpleasant that you do not want to be near it, or it makes you feel ill → **repulsive**: *The smell repelled him.* **2** [T] to make someone who is attacking you go away, by fighting them: *The army was ready to repel an attack.* **3** [T] to keep something or someone away from you: *a lotion that repels mosquitoes* **4** [I,T] *technical* if two things repel each other, they push each other away with an electrical force OPP **attract**: *Two positive charges repel each other.*

re·pel·lent¹ /rɪˈpelənt/ *adj* very unpleasant → **repulsive**: *She found him physically repellent.* | **[+to]** *The sight of blood is repellent to some people.*

repellent², **repellant** *n* [C,U] a substance that keeps insects away: **insect/mosquito/bug etc repellent**

re·pent /rɪˈpent/ *v* [I,T] *formal* to be sorry for something and wish you had not done it - used especially when considering your actions in a religious way: **[+of]** *He repented of his sins before he died.*

re·pen·tance /rɪˈpentəns/ *n* [U] when you are sorry for something wrong that you have done

re·pen·tant /rɪˈpentənt/ *adj formal* sorry for something wrong that you have done OPP **unrepentant**

re·per·cus·sion /ˌriːpəˈkʌʃən $ -pər-/ *n* [C usually plural] the effects of an action or event, especially bad effects that continue for some time → **consequence**: **[+for]** *The collapse of the company **had repercussions** for the whole industry.* | **[+on]** *There were **serious repercussions** on his career.* | **[+of]** *the repercussions of the crisis* | **political/social/economic etc repercussions**

rep·er·toire /ˈrepətwɑː $ -pərtwɑːr/ ●○○ *n* [C usually singular]
1 all the plays, pieces of music etc that a performer or group knows and can perform: **in sb's repertoire** *The group include some techno in their repertoire.* | **[+of]** *a **wide repertoire** of songs*
2 the total number of things that someone or something is able to do: *the behavioural repertoire of infants*

rep·er·to·ry /ˈrepətəri $ ˈrepərtɔːri/ *n* (*plural* **repertories**)
1 [U] a type of theatre work in which actors perform different plays on different days, instead of doing the same play for a long time: *a repertory company*
2 [C] *formal* a repertoire

rep·e·ti·tion /ˌrepəˈtɪʃən/ ●●○ *n*
1 [U] doing or saying the same thing many times: **[+of]** *The job involved the **constant repetition** of the same movements.* | *Children used to learn by repetition.*
2 [C,U] something that happens again, especially something bad: **[+of]** *a repetition of the same problem*

rep·e·ti·tious /ˌrepəˈtɪʃəs◂/ *adj* involving the same actions or using the same words many times, in a way that is boring: *repetitious work*

re·pet·i·tive /rɪˈpetətɪv/ *adj* done many times in the same way, and boring: **repetitive work/tasks/jobs** *repetitive tasks like washing and ironing* | *The song was dreary and repetitive.* —**repetitively** *adv*

reˌpetitive ˈstrain ˌinjury *n* [U] *medical* (*abbreviation* **RSI**) pains in your hands, arms etc caused by doing the same hand movements many times, especially by using a computer KEYBOARD or MOUSE → **carpal tunnel syndrome**

re·phrase /ˌriːˈfreɪz/ *v* [T] to say or write something again using different words to express what you mean in a way that is clearer or more acceptable: *OK. Let me **rephrase** the **question**.*

re·place /rɪˈpleɪs/ ●●● S2 W1 *v* [T]
1 to start doing something instead of another person, or start being used instead of another thing: *I'm replacing Sue on the team.* | *Lectures have replaced the old tutorial system.*
2 to remove someone from their job or something from its place, and put a new person or thing there: *Two of the tyres had to be replaced.* | **replace sth with sth** *They replaced the permanent staff with part-timers.*
3 if you replace something that has been broken, stolen etc, you get a new one → **irreplaceable**: *I'll replace the vase I broke as soon as possible.*
4 to put something back where it was before: *He replaced the book on the shelf.* —**replaceable** *adj*

> **REGISTER**
> In everyday English, people usually say **put** something **back** rather than **replace** something: *Don't forget to **put** the books **back** when you've finished.*

re·place·ment /rɪˈpleɪsmənt/ ●●○ W3 *n*
1 [U] when you get something that is newer or better than the one you had before: *Our old car is badly in need of replacement.* | *replacement windows*
2 knee/hip/joint replacement an artificial knee etc that replaces a damaged one, given to people in a medical operation
3 [C] someone or something that replaces another person or thing: **[+for]** *It was difficult to find a replacement for Ted.*

re·plat·form /ˌriːˈplætfɔːm $ -fɔːrm/ *v BrE* **be replatformed** if a train is replatformed, passengers have to get on it in a different part of the station from the one they were originally told to go to: *The replatformed 19:47 to Leeds will now leave from platform six.*

re·play¹ /ˈriːpleɪ/ ●○○ *n* [C]
1 a game that is played again because neither team won the first time: *Milan won the semi-final replay 3–0.*
2 the playing again of an important part of a sports event being shown on television, usually at a slower speed so that it can be examined it more clearly: *You can see on the replay that the goalkeeper was fouled.* → ACTION REPLAY
3 *informal* something that is done exactly as it was before: **[+of]** *a replay of the same old mistakes*

re·play² /ˌriːˈpleɪ/ *v* [T] **1** to play a game again because neither team won the first time: *The match will be replayed on Wednesday.* **2** to show again on television something that has been recorded: *Highlights of the race were replayed on the news.* GRAMMAR **Replay** is often used in the passive.

re·plen·ish /rɪˈplenɪʃ/ *v* [T] *formal* to put new supplies into something, or to fill something again: *More vaccines are needed to replenish our stocks.* THESAURUS FILL —**replenishment** *n* [U]

re·plete /rɪˈpliːt/ *adj* [not before noun] **1** *formal* full of something: **[+with]** *Literature is replete with tales of power.* **2** *old-fashioned* very full of food or drink

rep·li·ca /ˈreplɪkə/ *n* [C] an exact copy of something, especially a building, a gun, or a work of art: **[+of]** *an **exact replica** of the Taj Mahal* | *replica guns*

rep·li·cate /ˈreplɪkeɪt/ ●○○ *v*
1 [T] *formal* if you replicate someone's work, a scientific study etc, you do it again, or try to get the same result again: *There is a need for further research to replicate these findings.*
2 [I,T] *technical* if a VIRUS or a MOLECULE replicates, or if it replicates itself, it divides and produces exact copies of itself: *the ability of DNA to replicate itself* —**replication** /ˌreplɪˈkeɪʃən/ *n* [C,U]

re·ply¹ /rɪˈplaɪ/ ●●● W2 *v* (**replied, replying, replies**)
1 [I,T] to answer someone by saying or writing something: *I asked Clive where he was going, but he didn't reply.* | *Sorry it took me so long to reply.* | *'Did you see Simon today?'*

'Of course,' Nathalie replied with a smile. | **[+to]** *Has Ian replied to your letter yet?* | **reply that** *Mills replied that he was staying at his parents' flat.* **THESAURUS** ANSWER

> REGISTER
> **Reply** is used especially in written English. In everyday English, people usually say **answer**: *You haven't **replied to** my question.* → *You haven't **answered** my question.*

2 [I] to react to an action by doing something else: **reply (to sth) with sth** *The rebel troops replied to government threats with increased violence.*

reply² ●●● S3 W3 *n* (*plural* **replies**) [C]
1 something that is said, written, or done as a way of replying SYN **answer**: *I tried calling, but there was no reply.* | **[+to]** *We still haven't received a reply to our letter.* | *Stephen **made no reply**.*

> REGISTER
> **Reply** is used especially in written English. In everyday English, people usually say **answer**: *I tried calling but there was no **answer**.*

2 in reply (to sth) *formal* as a way of replying to something: *I am writing in reply to your letter of 1st June.*
3 without reply *BrE* if a sports team gets a number of points or GOALS without reply, their opponents do not score

re,ply-'paid *adj BrE* a reply-paid envelope is one which you can send back to an organization without a stamp because they have already paid for this

re·po man /ˈriːpəʊ mæn $ -poʊ/ *n* [C] *AmE informal* someone whose job is to REPOSSESS (=take away) cars that have not been paid for

re·port¹ /rɪˈpɔːt $ -ɔːrt/ ●●● S2 W1 *n* [C]
1 a written or spoken description of a situation or event, giving people the information they need → **account**: **[+of/on/about]** *Colleges have to provide a written report on the progress of each student during the year.*
2 a piece of writing in a newspaper about something that is happening, or part of a news programme → **reporter**: *According to recent **news reports**, two of the victims are Americans.* | **[+on/of]** *media reports of the food shortages*
3 an official document that carefully considers a particular subject: **[+on]** *a recent report on child abuse*
4 information that something has happened, which may or may not be true: **[+of]** *Police **received reports** of a bomb threat at the airport at 11:28 p.m.* | *Government officials have **denied reports** of rebel advances.* | **report that** *a report that he had been killed*
5 *BrE* a written statement by teachers about a child's work at school, which is sent to his or her parents SYN **report card** *AmE*
6 *BrE* someone who works for a particular manager: *Only Gordon's **direct reports** are attending the course.*
7 *formal* the noise of an explosion or shot: *a loud report*

> **COLLOCATIONS**
> **VERBS**
> **write a report** *Her social worker has written a report on the case.*
> **make a report** *We make regular progress reports to our manager.*
> **give a report** (=make a report, usually a spoken one) *He came to the office to give his report in person.*
> **prepare a report** *The surveyor will view the property and prepare a full report.*
> **submit a report** *formal* (=give a written report to someone) *Doctors will have to submit weekly reports.*
> **a report says/states (that)** *The report said that it would cost another £250 million to repair the damage.*
> **ADJECTIVES**
> **a full/detailed report** *A full report will be prepared for the next committee meeting.*
> **an official/formal report** *Black graduates still face discrimination from employers, according to an official report.*
> **a written report** *Mr Thomas asked me to send him a written report.*
> **a confidential report** (=one that only a few people see)

report² ●●● S2 W1 *v*
1 NEWS [I,T] to give people information about recent events, especially in newspapers and on television and radio → **reporter**: *This is Gavin Williams, reporting from the United Nations in New York.* | *We aim to report the news as fairly as possible.* | *The incident was widely reported in the national press.* | **[+on]** *The Times sent her to Bangladesh to report on the floods.* | **report that** *Journalists in Cairo reported that seven people had been shot.* | **report doing sth** *Witnesses reported seeing three people flee the scene.*

> **GRAMMAR**
> In more formal English, you say **it is reported that** something is true: *It is reported that there has been an explosion.*

2 be reported to be/do sth used to say that a statement has been made about someone or something, but you do not know if it is true → **allege**: *The stolen necklace is reported to be worth $57,000.*
3 JOB/WORK [I,T] to tell someone about what has been happening, or what you are doing as part of your job: **report (to sb) on sth** *I've asked him to come back next week and report on his progress.* **THESAURUS** TELL
4 PUBLIC STATEMENT [T] to officially give information to the public: *Doctors have reported a 13% increase in the number of people with heart disease.*
5 CRIME/ACCIDENT [T] to tell the police or someone in authority that an accident or crime has happened: *I'd like to report a theft.* | **report sth to sb** *All accidents must be reported to the safety officer.* | **report sb/sth missing/injured/killed** *The plane was reported missing.*
6 COMPLAIN [T] to complain about someone to people in authority: **report sb for sth** *Polish referee Ryszard Wojoik reported two Leeds United players for violent conduct.* | **report sb to sb** *Hadley's drinking problem led co-workers to report him to the supervisor.*
7 ARRIVAL [I] to go somewhere and officially state that you have arrived: **[+to]** *All visitors must report to the site office.* | *All soldiers were required to **report for duty** (=arrive and be ready for work) on Friday.*
8 report sick to officially tell your employers that you cannot come to work because you are ill

report back *phr v* to give someone information about something that they asked you to find out about: **[+to]** *The committee has 60 days to report back to Congress.* | **[+on]** *Students were asked to report back on their results.*

report to sb *phr v* to be responsible to someone at work and be managed by them: *He will report to Greg Carr, Boston Technology's chief executive.*

re·port·age /rɪˈpɔːtɪdʒ, ˌrepɔːˈtɑːʒ $ -ɔːr-/ *n* [U] *formal* the reporting or describing of events in newspapers, on television, or on the radio → **reporting**

re'port card *n* [C] *AmE* a written statement by teachers about a child's work at school, which is sent to his or her parents SYN **report** *BrE*

re·port·ed·ly /rɪˈpɔːtɪdli $ -ɔːr-/ *adv* [sentence adverb] according to what some people say: *Her husband's assets are reportedly worth over $15 million.*

re,ported 'speech ●○○ *n* [U] *technical* in grammar, words that are used to tell what someone says without repeating their actual words. 'She said she didn't feel well' is an example of reported speech SYN **indirect speech** OPP **direct speech**

re·port·er /rɪˈpɔːtə $ -ˈpɔːrtər/ ●●● S3 *n* [C] someone whose job is to write about news events for a newspaper, or to tell people about them on television or on the radio → **correspondent**, **journalist**: *a news reporter*

R

re·port·ing /rɪˈpɔːtɪŋ $ -ɔːr-/ *n* [U] the activity of writing about news events for a newspaper or telling people about them on television or on the radio → **reportage**: *news reporting*

re·pose¹ /rɪˈpəʊz $ -ˈpoʊz/ *n* [U] *formal or literary* a state of calm or comfortable rest: **in repose** *His face looked less hard in repose.*

repose² *v* [I always + adv/prep] *formal or literary* **1** if something reposes somewhere, it has been put there **2** if someone reposes somewhere, they rest there **3 repose your trust/hope etc in sb** to trust someone to help you

re·pos·i·to·ry /rɪˈpɒzətəri $ rɪˈpɑːzətɔːri/ *n* (*plural* **repositories**) [C] *formal* **1** a place or container in which large quantities of something are stored SYN **store**: **[+of/for]** *a fire-proof repository for government papers* **2** a person or book that has a lot of information: **[+of/for]** *Bob is a repository of football statistics.*

re·pos·sess /ˌriːpəˈzes/ *v* [T] to take back cars, furniture, or property from people who had arranged to pay for them over a long time, but cannot now continue to pay for them → **bailiff**, **repo man**: *Eventually the bailiffs came to repossess the flat.* —**repossession** /-ˈzeʃən/ *n* [C,U]

rep·re·hen·si·ble /ˌreprɪˈhensəbəl/ *adj formal* reprehensible behaviour is very bad and deserves criticism: *I find their behaviour **morally reprehensible**.*

rep·re·sent /ˌreprɪˈzent/ ●●● S2 W1 *v*
1 SPEAK FOR SB [T] to officially speak or take action for another person or group of people: *Mr Kobayashi was chosen to represent the company at the conference.*
2 IN COURT [T] to speak officially for someone in a court of law: **represent yourself** *She decided to represent herself* (=speak for herself without a lawyer) *during the trial.*
3 BE STH [linking verb] to form or be something → **amount to**: *European orders represented 30 percent of our sales last year.* | **represent a change/an advance/an increase etc** *This treatment represents a significant advance in the field of cancer research.*
4 GOVERNMENT [T] to have been elected to a parliament, council etc by the people in a particular area: *He represents the Congressional District of Illinois.*
5 SIGN [T] to be a sign or mark that means something SYN **stand for**: *Brown areas represent deserts on the map.*
6 SYMBOL [T] to be a symbol of something SYN **symbolize**: *He hated the school and everything it represented.*
7 SPORTS [T] if you represent your country, school, town etc in a sport, you take part in a sports event for that country etc: *Her greatest ambition was to represent her country at the Olympics.*
8 be represented if a group, organization, area etc is represented at an event, people from it are at the event: *All the local clubs were represented in the parade.*
9 DESCRIBE [T] to describe someone or something in a particular way, especially in a way that is not true SYN **portray** → **depict**: **represent sb/sth as sth** *The article represents the millionaire as a simple family man.* | *He had represented himself as an employee in order to gain access to the files.* THESAURUS DESCRIBE
10 ART [T] if a painting, STATUE, piece of music etc represents something or someone, it shows them: *Paintings representing religious themes were common in medieval times.*

re-pre·sent /ˌriː prɪˈzent/ *v* [T] to give, offer, or send something again, especially an official document: *The phone company re-presented the bill for payment.*

rep·re·sen·ta·tion /ˌreprɪzenˈteɪʃən/ ●●○ W3 *n*
1 [U] when you have someone to speak, vote, or make decisions for you: *Minority groups need more effective parliamentary representation.* | *There has been a decline in union representation in the auto industry.* → PROPORTIONAL REPRESENTATION
2 [C] a painting, sign, description etc that shows something: **[+of]** *The clock in the painting is a symbolic representation of the passage of time.*
3 [U] the act of representing someone or something: **[+of]** *She received praise for her effective representation of Garcia during the trial.*
4 [C usually plural] *formal especially BrE* a formal complaint or statement: **[+about]** *A group of students **made representations** to the college about the poor standard of the accommodation.*
5 make false representations *law* to describe or explain something in a way that you know is not true

rep·re·sen·ta·tion·al /ˌreprɪzenˈteɪʃənəl/ *adj* a representational painting or style of art shows things as they actually appear in real life SYN **figurative**

rep·re·sen·ta·tive¹ /ˌreprɪˈzentətɪv◂/ ●●○ W3 *n* [C]
1 someone who has been chosen to speak, vote, or make decisions for someone else SYN **delegate**: *a union representative* | **[+of]** *an elected representative of the people*
2 Representative a member of the House of Representatives, the Lower House of Congress in the United States

representative² ●○○ *adj*
1 typical of a particular group or thing: **[+of]** *The latest incident is representative of a wider trend.* THESAURUS TYPICAL
2 including examples of all the different types of something in a group: *The pollsters asked a **representative sample** of New York residents for their opinions.*
3 a representative system of government allows people to vote for other people to represent them in the government: *a representative democracy*

re·press /rɪˈpres/ ●○○ *v* [T]
1 to stop yourself from doing something you want to do: *Brenda repressed the urge to shout at him.* | *I repressed a smile.*
2 if someone represses upsetting feelings, memories etc, they do not allow themselves to express or think about them: *He had long ago repressed the painful memories of his childhood.*
3 to control a group of people by force → **suppress**, **oppress**: *The police were widely criticized for their role in repressing the protest movement.*

re·pressed /rɪˈprest/ *adj* **1** having feelings or desires that you do not allow yourself to express or think about, especially sexual feelings SYN **frustrated**: *a repressed middle-aged woman* **2** repressed feelings or desires are ones which you do not allow yourself to express or think about: *repressed anger*

re·pres·sion /rɪˈpreʃən/ ●○○ *n* [C,U]
1 when someone does not allow themselves to express feelings or desires which they are ashamed of, especially sexual ones – used when you think someone should express these feelings: ***sexual repression*** | **[+of]** *the repression of desire*
2 cruel and severe control of a large group of people → **suppression**, **oppression**: **[+of]** *brutal repression of members of the Communist party*

re·pres·sive /rɪˈpresɪv/ *adj* **1** a repressive government or law controls people in a cruel and severe way SYN **oppressive**: *a repressive regime* | *repressive measures* **2** not allowing the expression of feelings or desires, especially sexual ones —**repressively** *adv* —**repressiveness** *n* [U]

re·prieve¹ /rɪˈpriːv/ *n* [C] **1** a delay before something bad happens or continues to happen → **respite**: **[+from]** *Shoppers will get a temporary reprieve from the new sales tax.* **2** an official order stopping the killing of a prisoner as a punishment: **give/grant sb a reprieve** *The US Supreme Court voted against granting Smith a reprieve* (=against giving him one).

reprieve² *v* [T] **1** to officially stop a prisoner from being killed as a punishment **2** to change a decision to close a factory, school etc or get rid of something GRAMMAR **Reprieve** is usually passive.

rep·ri·mand /ˈreprəmɑːnd $ -mænd/ *v* [T] to tell someone officially that something they have done is very wrong → **scold**, **tell off**: **reprimand sb for (doing) sth** *The military court reprimanded him for failing to do his duty.* —**reprimand** *n* [C]: *a **severe reprimand***

R

re·print¹ /ˌriːˈprɪnt/ *v* [T] to print a book, story, newspaper article etc again

re·print² /ˈriːprɪnt/ *n* [C] **1** an occasion when more copies of a book are printed because all the copies of it have been sold **2** a book that is printed again

re·pri·sal /rɪˈpraɪzəl/ *n* [C,U] something violent or harmful which you do to punish someone for something bad they have done to you → **revenge**, **retaliation**: *They didn't tell the police* ***for fear of reprisal***. | **[+against]** *There were reprisals against unarmed civilians.* | **in reprisal (for sth)** *Alfred was shot in reprisal for the killing of a rival gang member.*

re·prise¹ /rɪˈpriːz/ *n* [C] when all or part of something, especially a piece of music, is repeated

reprise² *v* [T] to act the same part again, play the same tune again etc

re·proach¹ /rɪˈprəʊtʃ $ -ˈproʊtʃ/ *n formal* **1** [U] criticism, blame, or disapproval: *'You don't need me,' she said quietly, without reproach.* **2** [C] a remark that expresses criticism, blame, or disapproval: *He argued that the reproaches were unfair.* **3 above/beyond reproach** impossible to criticize SYN **perfect**: *His behaviour throughout this affair has been beyond reproach.* **4 a reproach to sb/sth** something that should make a person, society etc feel bad or ashamed: *These derelict houses are a reproach to the city.*

reproach² *v* [T] **1** *formal* to blame or criticize someone in a way that shows you are disappointed at what they have done: **reproach sb for/with sth** *He publicly reproached his son for his behavior.* **2 reproach yourself** to feel guilty about something that you think you are responsible for: **[+for/with]** *You've got nothing to reproach yourself for – it was his own decision.*

re·proach·ful /rɪˈprəʊtʃfəl $ -ˈproʊtʃ-/ *adj* a reproachful look, remark etc shows that you are criticizing someone or blaming them: *She gave her daughter a reproachful glance.* —**reproachfully** *adv*

rep·ro·bate /ˈreprəbeɪt/ *n* [C] *formal* someone who behaves in an immoral way – often used humorously —**reprobate** *adj*

re·pro·cess /riːˈprəʊses $ -ˈprɑː-/ *v* [T] to treat a waste substance so that it can be used again

re·pro·duce /ˌriːprəˈdjuːs $ -ˈduːs/ ●○○ *v*
1 [I,T] if an animal or plant reproduces, or reproduces itself, it produces young plants or animals: *The turtles return to the coast to reproduce.*
2 [T] to make a photograph or printed copy of something: *Klimt's artwork is reproduced in this exquisite book.* **THESAURUS▸ COPY**
3 [T] to make something happen in the same way as it happened before SYN **repeat** → **copy**: *British scientists have so far been unable to reproduce these results.*
4 [T] to make something that is just like something else → **copy**: *With a good set of speakers, you can reproduce the orchestra's sound in your own home.* —**reproducible** *adj*

re·pro·duc·tion /ˌriːprəˈdʌkʃən◂/ ●○○ *n*
1 [U] the act or process of producing babies, young animals, or plants: *Scientists studied the reproduction, diet, and health of the dolphins.* | ***sexual reproduction***
2 [U] the act of producing a copy of a book, picture, piece of music etc: **[+of]** *Unauthorized reproduction of this publication is strictly forbidden.*
3 [C] a copy of a work of art, piece of furniture etc: **[+of]** *a reproduction of Vincent Van Gogh's 'Sunflowers'* | **reproduction furniture/chairs etc** *a reproduction Louis XIV table*

re·pro·duc·tive /ˌriːprəˈdʌktɪv◂/ *adj* [only before noun] **1** relating to the process of producing babies, young animals, or plants: *the human* ***reproductive system*** | *reproductive organs* **2** relating to the copying of books, pictures, music etc

re·proof /rɪˈpruːf/ *n formal* **1** [U] blame or disapproval: *She greeted me with a look of cold reproof.* **2** [C] a remark that blames or criticizes someone: *a mild reproof*

re·prove /rɪˈpruːv/ *v* [T] *formal* to criticize someone for something that they have done SYN **tell off**: **reprove sb for (doing) sth** *Employees were reproved for smoking in the building's restrooms.*

re·prov·ing /rɪˈpruːvɪŋ/ *adj formal* expressing criticism of something that someone has done SYN **disapproving** —**reprovingly** *adv*

REPTILES

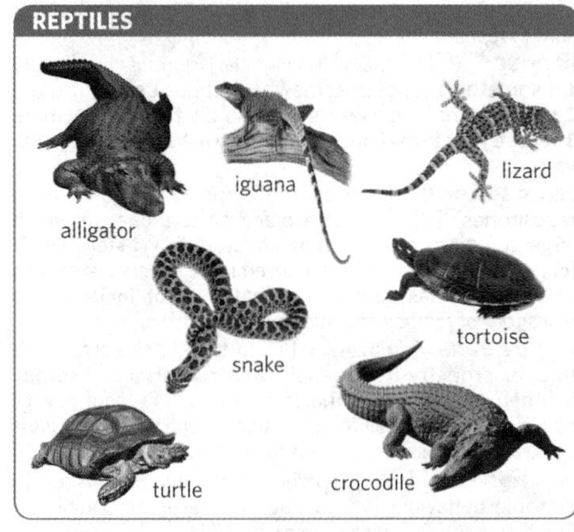

rep·tile /ˈreptaɪl $ ˈreptl/ *n* [C] **1** a type of animal, such as a snake or LIZARD, whose body temperature changes according to the temperature around it, and that usually lays eggs to have babies **2** *informal* someone who is unpleasant or cannot be trusted —**reptilian** /repˈtɪliən/ *adj*

re·pub·lic, **Republic** /rɪˈpʌblɪk/ ●●● W2 *n* [C] a country governed by elected representatives of the people, and led by a president, not a king or queen → **democracy**, **monarchy**: *the former Federal Republic of Germany* | *Nine republics took part in the referendum.* **THESAURUS▸ GOVERNMENT**

re·pub·li·can¹ /rɪˈpʌblɪkən/ *n* [C] **1** someone who believes in government by elected representatives only, with no king or queen **2 Republican** a member or supporter of the Republican Party in the US → **Democrat** **3 Republican** someone from Northern Ireland who believes that Northern Ireland should become part of the Republic of Ireland, not the United Kingdom → **loyalist** —**republicanism** *n* [U]

republican² *adj* relating to or supporting a system of government that is not led by a king or queen → **democratic**

re·pu·di·ate /rɪˈpjuːdieɪt/ *v* [T] *formal* **1** to refuse to accept or continue with something SYN **reject**: *He repudiated all offers of friendship.* **2** to state or show that something is not true or correct: *The book repudiates the racist stereotypes about black women.* —**repudiation** /rɪˌpjuːdiˈeɪʃən/ *n* [U]

re·pug·nance /rɪˈpʌgnəns/ *n* [U] *formal* a strong feeling of dislike for something SYN **disgust**

re·pug·nant /rɪˈpʌgnənt/ *adj formal* very unpleasant and offensive SYN **repellent**: **deeply/utterly/wholly etc repugnant** | *I find his political ideas totally repugnant.* | **[+to]** *Animal experiments are* ***morally repugnant*** *to many people.*

re·pulse /rɪˈpʌls/ *v* [T] *formal* **1** if something or someone repulses you, you think that they are extremely unpleasant SYN **disgust**: *The very thought of his cold clammy hands repulsed me.* **2** to fight someone and successfully stop their attack on you: *Government troops repulsed an attack by rebel forces.* **3** to refuse an offer of friendship or help in a way that is rude —**repulse** *n* [singular]

re·pul·sion /rɪˈpʌlʃən/ *n* **1** [singular,U] a feeling that you want to avoid something or move away from it, because it is extremely unpleasant SYN **revulsion**: *I felt a mixture of amazement and repulsion.* **2** [U] *technical* the electric or MAGNETIC force by which one object pushes another one away from it

re·pul·sive /rɪˈpʌlsɪv/ ●○○ *adj*
1 extremely unpleasant, in a way that almost makes you feel sick SYN **revolting**, **disgusting**: *Many people find slugs repulsive.*
2 *technical* repulsive forces push objects away from each other —**repulsively** *adv* —**repulsiveness** *n* [U]

re·pur·pose /ˌriːˈpɜːpəs $ -ˈpɜːr-/ *v* [T] if something such as equipment, a building, or a document is repurposed, it is used in a new way that is different from its original use, without having to be changed very much → **adapt**: *We put a lot of material up on our website simply by repurposing our existing catalog.*

rep·u·ta·ble /ˈrepjətəbəl/ *adj* respected for being honest or for doing good work SYN **reliable** OPP **disreputable**: **reputable firm/company** *If you have a burglar alarm fitted, make sure it is done by a reputable company.* THESAURUS HONEST

rep·u·ta·tion /ˌrepjəˈteɪʃən/ ●●○ W3 *n* [C] the opinion that people have about someone or something because of what has happened in the past: **[+for]** *Judge Kelso has a reputation for being strict but fair.* | **[+as]** *In her last job she gained a reputation as a hard worker.*

COLLOCATIONS

VERBS

have a good/bad etc reputation *The law firm has an excellent reputation.*
get a reputation (*also* **gain/acquire a reputation** *formal*) *Over the years, the company has gained a reputation for making quality products.*
earn/win a reputation *As a young publisher, she earned a reputation for toughness.*
enjoy a reputation (=have it) *The hotel enjoys a good reputation.*
live up to its reputation (=be as good as people say it is) *New York certainly lived up to its reputation as an exciting city.*
establish a reputation (=make people accept that you are good at doing something) *By then Picasso was already establishing his reputation as an artist.*
enhance sb's reputation (=make it better) | **build/develop a reputation** | **damage sb's reputation** | **tarnish sb's reputation** (=make it worse) | **destroy/ruin sb's reputation**

ADJECTIVES

good/excellent *The university has a very good reputation.*
bad/poor *The city doesn't deserve its bad reputation.*
an international/worldwide reputation *The department has a worldwide reputation for its research.*
a formidable reputation (=one that makes people have a lot of respect for someone or something, or be afraid of them) | **an enviable reputation** (=a good one that others would like to have) | **a well-deserved reputation**

THESAURUS

reputation *n* [C] the opinion that people have about a person, organization etc because of what has happened in the past: *She was a good lawyer with a reputation for honesty and diligence.* | *The school had an excellent reputation.*
image *n* [C] the idea that people have about what something is like, especially when this is created through newspaper stories, advertising etc: *A PR campaign was launched in an effort to improve the company's image.* | *Boxing has rather a* ***negative image****.*
name *n* [singular] the reputation that a person, organization etc has – used especially in the following phrases: *The company is anxious to protect its* ***good name****.* | *Cyclists who ignore traffic rules give other cyclists* ***a bad name****.* | *Electrolux* ***has a name for*** *making top quality vacuum cleaners.*
standing *n* [U] someone's reputation and position compared to other people in a group or society, based on other people's opinion of them: *The class system in Great Britain encourages people to be very aware of their* ***social standing****.* | *He needs to improve his standing among female voters.*
prestige *n* [U] the good reputation that a company, organization, group etc has, which makes people respect and admire them: *the prestige of a carmaker such as Rolls-Royce* | *Does Stanford University* ***carry*** *the same* ***prestige*** *as Harvard or Yale?*
stature *n* [U] *formal* the importance and respect that a person or organization has, because of their achievements or their influence: *As he got older, Picasso's stature as an artist increased.* | *an actor* ***of international stature***

re·pute /rɪˈpjuːt/ *n* [U] *formal* reputation: **of good/high/international etc repute** *a man of high repute* | **of (some) repute** (=having a good reputation) *a hotel of some repute*

re·put·ed /rɪˈpjuːtɪd/ *adj* according to what some people say, but not definitely: **be reputed to be/do sth** *She is reputed to be extremely wealthy.* | *the reputed leader of the Crips gang* | *The painting was sold for a reputed $3 million.*

re·put·ed·ly /rɪˈpjuːtɪdli/ *adv* [sentence adverb] according to what some people say SYN **reportedly** → **allegedly**: *The committee had reputedly spent over $3000 on 'business entertainment'.*

re·quest[1] /rɪˈkwest/ ●●● S3 W2 *n* [C]
1 a polite or formal demand for something: **[+for]** *They have made an urgent request for international aid.* | **[+from]** *requests from customers for more information* | **[+that]** *Anderson repeated his request that we postpone the meeting.* | **at sb's request** (=because someone asked for it to be done) *The study was done at the request of the Chairman.* | **on request** (=if you ask for it) *Further details will be sent on request.* | **by request** *There were no flowers at the funeral, by request.* THESAURUS QUESTION
2 a piece of music that is played on the radio because someone has asked for it

COLLOCATIONS

VERBS

make a request *I'd like to make a request.*
submit/put in a request (=make a formal request) *The request was first submitted a number of months ago.*
agree to a request (*also* **grant sb's request** *formal*) *The judge granted his request.*
refuse/reject a request (*also* **turn down sb's request**) *He rejected their request for a meeting.*
receive a request | **consider a request** | **respond to a request** | **ignore a request**

ADJECTIVES

a formal request *The government made a formal request for food aid.*
a special request *Do you have any special requests?*
an urgent request *The family made an urgent request on television for help in finding their daughter.*
a reasonable request | **a strange/unusual request** | **a written request** | **repeated requests**

request[2] ●●○ *v* [T] *formal* to ask for something in a polite or formal way: *To request more information, please call our toll-free number.* | *You have to request permission if you want to take any photographs.* | **request that** *The prosecution has requested that all charges against Hodgkins be dropped.* | **request sb to do sth** *All club members are requested to attend the annual meeting.* | **request sth from sb** *The Police Committee requested a grant from the Government to cover the extra expense.* THESAURUS ASK

GRAMMAR: Patterns with request

- You **request** something: *I requested permission to leave early.*
- In everyday English, you **request that** someone **does** something: *They* ***request that*** *he* ***finishes*** *the work by Friday.*
- In more formal English, you **request that** someone

R

do something, using the base form of the verb (=the infinitive without 'to'): *She **requested that** she **be** allowed to leave.*
• You say that someone **is requested to do** something. This pattern is used especially on official notices and announcements: *Passengers are requested not to throw things out of the window.*
GRAMMAR GUIDE ▸ VERBS

req·ui·em /ˈrekwiəm, -em/ (*also* ˌ**requiem ˈmass**) *n* [C] **1** a Christian ceremony in which prayers are said for someone who has died **2** a piece of music written for a requiem

Frequencies of the verbs **require** and **need** in spoken and written English.

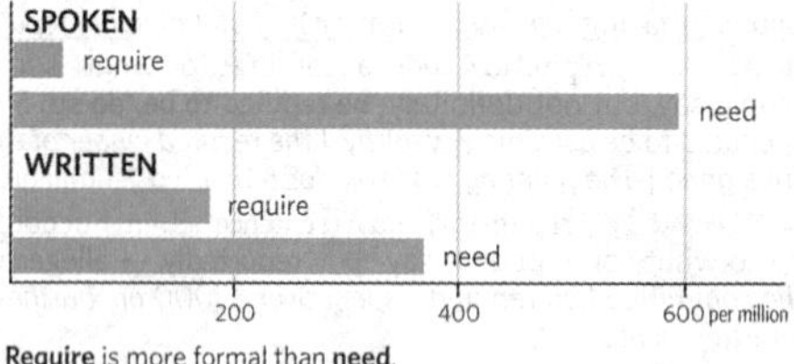

Require is more formal than **need**.

re·quire /rɪˈkwaɪə $ -ˈkwaɪr/ ●●● S1 W1 AWL *v* [T not in progressive]
1 to need something: *Campbell's broken leg will probably require surgery.* | *What's required is a complete reorganization of the system.* | *Most houseplants require regular watering.*

REGISTER
Require is used especially in written English. In everyday English, people usually say **need**: *His leg will probably **need** surgery.*

2 if you are required to do or have something, a law or rule says you must do it or have it: **be required to do sth** *You are required by law to wear a seat belt.* | **require that** *Regulations require that students attend at least 90% of the lectures.* | *The bill failed to get the required number of votes.*
THESAURUS ▸ INSIST

GRAMMAR: Using the progressive
Require is not used in the progressive. You say: *The project requires considerable investment.* ✗ Don't say: *The project is requiring considerable investment.*
GRAMMAR GUIDE ▸ VERBS

re·quire·ment /rɪˈkwaɪəmənt $ -ˈkwaɪr-/ ●●● S2 W2 AWL *n* [C usually plural]
1 something that someone needs or asks for: *The refugees' main requirements are food and shelter.* | **[+of]** *Potatoes can provide one-third of our daily requirement of vitamin C.* | **meet/fulfil/satisfy a requirement** (=have or do what is necessary) *The new computer system will meet all our requirements.* | **surplus to requirements** *BrE* (=more than is needed) *The increase in gas-fired power stations means traditional coal ones are becoming surplus to requirements.*
2 something that must be done because of a law or rule: *If you are installing a new bathroom, it has to **meet** the **requirements** of the Building Regulations.* | *Two measures have been introduced as **legal requirements**.*
3 something, especially good examination results, that a college, employer etc says you must have in order to do something: **[+for]** *English 4 is a requirement for English majors.* | *To find out about **entry requirements** for students, write to the college admissions board.* | *The **minimum requirement** for the post was a degree in engineering.*

req·ui·site¹ /ˈrekwəzət/ *adj* [only before noun] *formal* needed for a particular purpose SYN **necessary**, **required**: *He lacks the requisite qualifications.* THESAURUS ▸ NECESSARY

requisite² *n* [C usually plural] *formal* something that is needed for a particular purpose: **[+of/for]** *He lacked the moral requisites for marriage.* → PREREQUISITE

req·ui·si·tion /ˌrekwəˈzɪʃən/ *v* [T] if someone in authority, especially the army, requisitions a building, vehicle, or food, they officially demand to have it during an EMERGENCY such as a war SYN **commandeer**: *The building was requisitioned as a military hospital for the duration of the war.* —**requisition** *n* [C,U]

re·quite /rɪˈkwaɪt/ *v* [T] *formal* to give or do something in return for something done or given to you

re-re·lease /ˌriː rɪˈliːs/ *v* [T] if a CD, record, or film is re-released, it is produced and sold or shown for a second time, usually with small changes —**re-release** /ˈriː rɪliːs/ *n* [C]

re·route /ˌriː ˈruːt $ -ˈruːt, -ˈraʊt/ *v* [T] to send vehicles, planes, telephone calls etc to a different place from the one where they were originally going SYN **redirect**

re·run¹ /ˈriːrʌn/ *n* [C] **1** a film or television programme that is being shown again on television SYN **repeat**: *We watched a rerun of 'I Love Lucy.'* **2** something that happens in the same way as something that happened before SYN **repeat**: *The government wants to avoid a rerun of last year's crisis.*

re·run² /riːˈrʌn/ *v* (*past tense* **reran** /-ˈræn/, *past participle* **rerun**, *present participle* **rerunning**) [T] **1** to show a film or television programme again on television SYN **repeat** **2** to do something in the same way as before SYN **repeat** **3** to arrange for a race or competition to be held again SYN **repeat**

re·sale /ˈriːseɪl/ *n* [U] the activity of selling goods that you have bought from someone else → **resell**

re·sched·ule /ˌriːˈʃedjuːl $ -ˈskedʒʊl, -dʒəl/ AWL *v* [T] **1** to arrange for something to happen at a different time from the one that was previously planned: **reschedule sth for sth** *The press conference had to be rescheduled for March 19.* **2** *technical* to arrange for a debt to be paid back later than was previously agreed —**rescheduling** *n* [singular, U]

re·scind /rɪˈsɪnd/ *v* [T] to officially end a law, or change a decision or agreement

res·cue¹ /ˈreskjuː/ ●●○ S3 W3 *v* [T] to save someone or something from a situation of danger or harm: *Survivors of the crash were rescued by helicopter.* | **rescue sb/sth from sb/sth** *She died trying to rescue her children from the blaze.* —**rescuer** *n* [C]

THESAURUS
rescue to remove someone from a dangerous, difficult, or unpleasant situation: *Firefighters worked for two hours to rescue people from the building.* | *Will you rescue me if I get stuck talking to Sam?*
come to the rescue/sb's rescue to come and rescue or help someone: *It was an embarrassing moment, but fortunately Paul came to the rescue.*
save to prevent someone from being killed, harmed, or losing something, or to make it possible for something to continue: *Wearing a seat belt can help save your life.* | *They saved the hospital from closure.*
pick sb up to rescue someone from a dangerous place by taking them away in a boat or aircraft: *A lifeboat picked them up two miles from the coast.*
bail sb out to rescue a person, company etc from a difficult situation, by providing them with the money they need: *A number of state-owned enterprises have been bailed out by the central bank.*

rescue² ●●○ *n* [C,U]
1 when someone or something is rescued from danger: *a daring rescue at sea* | **[+of]** *Storms delayed the rescue of the crash victims.* | *Rescue workers arrived at the scene two hours later.* | **rescue mission/operation** *The rescue operation proved successful.*
2 come to the/sb's rescue a) to save someone who is in a dangerous situation: *A lifeboat came to the yachtsman's rescue.* **b)** to help someone who is having problems or difficulties: *Carol's brother came to the rescue and sent her $1000.*

re·search¹ /rɪˈsɜːtʃ, ˈriːsɜːtʃ $ -ɜːr-/ ●●● S2 W1 AWL *n* [U] (*also* **researches** [plural] *formal*)
1 serious study of a subject, in order to discover new facts or test new ideas: **[+into/on]** *research into the causes of cancer* | *Gould was helped in his researches by local naturalists.*
2 the activity of finding information about something that you are interested in or need to know about: *It's a good idea to* ***do*** *some* ***research*** *before you buy a house.* → **investigation** → MARKET RESEARCH

COLLOCATIONS

VERBS

do/carry out research (*also* **conduct research** *formal*) *The research was carried out by a team of scientists at Edinburgh University.*
undertake research *formal* (=start or do research) *They are planning to undertake research into the genetic causes of the disease.*

ADJECTIVES

scientific research *Our conclusions are based on scientific research.*
medical research *The charity raises money for medical research.*
historical research *This is a fascinating piece of historical research.*
basic research (=the most important or most necessary area of research) *He wants to conduct basic research into the nature of human cells.*
extensive research (=research that examines a lot of information and details) | **painstaking research** (=very careful and thorough research) | **pioneering research** (=research that produces completely new information)

research + NOUN

a research project/programme *The research project will be funded by the Medical Research Council.*
research findings (=what is discovered by a piece of research) *He will present his research findings at the conference.*
research work | **a research team** | **a research student** | **a research grant** (=money for doing research)

PHRASES

an area/field of research *This is a very exciting area of research.*
a piece of research

COMMON ERRORS

⚠ Don't say 'make research'. Say **do research** or **carry out research**.

re·search² /rɪˈsɜːtʃ $ -ɜːr-/ ●●○ AWL *v* [I,T]
1 to study a subject in detail, especially in order to discover new facts or test new ideas → **investigate**: *He's been researching material for a documentary.* | **[+into]** *Ten years ago I began researching into the role of women in trade unions.*

REGISTER

In everyday English, people often use the expression **do research** rather than the verb **to research**:
She's been ***doing some research*** *into the history of the area.*

2 to get all the necessary facts and information for something: *This book has been very well researched.*

reˌsearch and deˈvelopment *n* [U] R & D

re·search·er /rɪˈsɜːtʃə $ -ˈsɜːrtʃər/ ●●○ AWL *n* [C] someone who studies a subject in detail in order to discover new facts or test new ideas: *medical researchers* | *Researchers have found links between stress and heart disease.*

re·sell /ˌriːˈsel/ *v* (*past tense and past participle* **resold** /ˈsəʊld $ -ˈsoʊld/) [T] to sell something that you have bought → **resale**: *The retailer resells the goods at a higher price.*

re·sem·blance /rɪˈzembləns/ ●○○ *n* [C,U] if there is a resemblance between two people or things, they are similar, especially in the way they look → **similarity**: **[+between]** *The resemblance between Susan and her sister was remarkable.* | **bear a (close/striking/uncanny etc) resemblance to sb/sth** (=look like) *Tina bears a striking resemblance to her mother.* | **bear little/no resemblance to sb/sth** *What happens in the film bears little resemblance to what actually happened.*

re·sem·ble /rɪˈzembəl/ ●○○ *v* [T] to look like or be similar to someone or something: *It's amazing how* ***closely*** *Brian and Steve* ***resemble*** *each other.* | *He grew up to resemble his father.*

GRAMMAR: Using the progressive

Resemble is not used in the progressive. You say: *The flower resembles a rose.* ✗ Don't say: *The flower is resembling a rose.*
GRAMMAR GUIDE ▶ VERBS

re·sent /rɪˈzent/ ●○○ *v* [T] to feel angry or upset about a situation or about something that someone has done, especially because you think that it is not fair: **resent (sb) doing sth** *I resented having to work such long hours.* | **bitterly/deeply/strongly resent** *She bitterly resented his mother's influence over him.* | *Paul* ***resented the fact that*** *Carol didn't trust him.*

re·sent·ful /rɪˈzentfəl/ *adj* feeling angry and upset about something that you think is unfair SYN **bitter**: **[+of/about/at etc]** *She felt resentful at not being promoted.* —**resentfully** *adv* —**resentfulness** *n* [U]

re·sent·ment /rɪˈzentmənt/ ●○○ *n* [U] a feeling of anger because something has happened that you think is unfair SYN **bitterness**: **[+at/against/of etc]** *She was filled with* ***deep resentment*** *at being passed over for promotion.* | **feel/harbour/bear resentment** *He felt considerable resentment towards Sheila for making him work late.*

res·er·va·tion /ˌrezəˈveɪʃən $ -zər-/ ●●● S3 W3 *n*
1 [C] an arrangement which you make so that a place in a hotel, restaurant, plane etc is kept for you at a particular time in the future → **booking**: *a dinner reservation* | *Customers are advised to* ***make*** *seat* ***reservations*** *well in advance.*
2 [C,U] a feeling of doubt because you do not agree completely with a plan, idea, or suggestion: **have/express reservations (about sth)** *I had* ***serious reservations*** *about his appointment as captain.* | *We condemn their actions* ***without reservation*** (=completely).
3 [C] an area of land in the US kept separate for Native Americans to live on: *a Navajo reservation*
4 [C] *AmE* an area of land where wild animals can live without being hunted SYN **reserve**, **preserve** *AmE*: *a wildlife reservation*

re·serve¹ /rɪˈzɜːv $ -ɜːrv/ ●●● W3 *v* [T]
1 to arrange for a place in a hotel, restaurant, plane etc to be kept for you to use at a particular time in the future → **book**: **reserve sth for sb/sth** *I'd like to reserve a table for two.* | *Do you have to reserve tickets in advance?*
2 to keep something so that it can be used by a particular person or for a particular purpose SYN **set aside**: **reserve sth for sb/sth** *A separate room is reserved for smokers.* | *reserved parking spaces*
3 *especially written* to keep part of something for use at a later time during a process – used especially when describing how to cook something SYN **keep**, **save**: *Reserve a little of the mixture to sprinkle over the top of the pie.*
4 to use or show something only in one particular situation: **reserve sth for sb/sth** *She spoke in a tone of voice she usually reserved for dealing with officials.*
5 reserve the right to do sth *formal* if you reserve the right to do something, you will do it if you think it is necessary – used especially in notices or official documents: *The management reserves the right to refuse admission.*
6 reserve (your) judgment (on sth) *spoken* to not give your

opinion about something until a later time when you have more information

reserve² ●●○ *n*

1 SUPPLY [C usually plural] a supply of something kept to be used if it is needed: *$10 million in cash reserves | oil reserves |* **[+of]** *Somehow Debbie maintained an inner reserve of strength.*

2 in reserve ready to be used if needed: *We always* ***keep*** *some money* ***in reserve****, just in case.*

3 PERSONAL QUALITY [U] a quality in someone's character that makes them not like expressing their emotions or talking about their problems → **shyness**: *She overcame her own* ***natural reserve****.*

4 PLAYER [C] an extra player who plays in a team if one of the other players is injured or ill → **substitute**

5 TEAM **the reserves** *BrE* a team that plays when the usual team cannot do so

6 MILITARY **the reserve** (*also* **the reserves**) an extra military force that a country has in addition to its usual army, navy etc which can be used if needed → **reservist**

7 FOR ANIMALS/PLANTS [C] *BrE* an area of land where wild animals and plants are protected SYN **reservation**, **preserve** *AmE*: *a* ***wildlife reserve*** → NATURE RESERVE

8 FOR NATIVE AMERICANS [C] a RESERVATION

9 PRICE [C] (*also* **reserve price**) a price below which something will not be sold, especially in an AUCTION

re·served /rɪˈzɜːvd $ -ɜːr-/ ●○○ *adj* unwilling to express your emotions or talk about your problems → **shy**: *Ellen was a shy, reserved girl.* THESAURUS ▸ SHY

re·serv·ist /rɪˈzɜːvɪst $ -ɜːr-/ *n* [C] someone in the RESERVE

res·er·voir /ˈrezəvwɑː $ -ərvwɑːr, -vɔːr/ ●●○ *n* [C]

1 a lake, especially an artificial one, where water is stored before it is supplied to people's houses

2 a large amount of something that is available and has not yet been used: **[+of]** *She found she had reservoirs of unexpected strength.*

3 *technical* a part of a machine or engine where a liquid is kept before it is used

re·set¹ /ˌriːˈset/ *v* (*past tense and past participle* **reset**, *present participle* **resetting**) [T] **1** to change a clock, control, machine etc so that it shows a different time or number, or is ready to be used again **2** to put a broken bone back into its correct place so that it grows back together correctly **3** to restart a computer without switching the power off → **reboot** **4** to put a jewel into a new piece of jewellery —**reset** /ˈriːset/ *n* [C,U]

re·set² /ˈriːset/ *adj* **reset button/switch** a control that is used to make a machine or instrument ready to work again

re·set·tle /riːˈsetl/ *v* **1** [I,T] to go to live in a new country or area, or to help people do this: *The tribesmen were forcibly resettled by the government.* **2** [T] to start using an area again as a place to live: *The area was resettled in the latter half of the century.* —**resettlement** *n* [U]

re·shuffle /riːˈʃʌfəl, ˈriːʃʌfəl/ *n* [C] *especially BrE* when the jobs of people who work in an organization are changed around, especially in a government SYN **reorganize**: *a* ***Cabinet reshuffle*** —**reshuffle** /ˌriːˈʃʌfəl/ *v* [T]

re·side /rɪˈzaɪd/ ●○○ AWL *v* [I always + adv/prep] *formal* to live in a particular place: *He spent most of his time in Rutherglen, where his family resided.* THESAURUS ▸ LIVE

reside in sth/sb *phr v formal*

1 to be present in or consist of something: *Joe's talent resides in his storytelling abilities.*

2 (*also* **reside within sth/sb**) if a power, right etc resides in something or someone, it belongs to them: *Executive power resides in the president.*

res·i·dence /ˈrezɪdəns/ ●○○ AWL *n*

1 [C] *formal* a house, especially a large or official one: *the ambassador's* ***official residence*** THESAURUS ▸ HOME

2 [U] legal permission to live in a country for a certain period of time SYN **residency**: *a residence permit |* **permanent/temporary residence** *Jeff has permanent residence in Canada, but is still a US citizen.*

3 [U] *formal* the state of living in a place SYN **residency**: *Rome was his main* ***place of residence****.*

4 artist/writer etc in residence an artist etc who has been officially chosen by a college or other institution to work there

5 take up residence *formal* to start living in a place: *He took up residence in Chicago.*

6 in residence *formal* living in a place at a particular time: *The emperor was in residence at his summer palace.*

ˈresidence ˌhall *n* [C] *AmE* a large building where many students live at a university SYN **dormitory** *AmE*, **hall of residence** *BrE*

res·i·den·cy /ˈrezədənsi/ *n* (*plural* **residencies**) **1** [U] legal permission to live in a country for a certain period of time SYN **residence** **2** [C,U] when an artist, writer, musician etc does work at a college or other institution for a period of time SYN **residence** **3** [U] the state of living in a place SYN **residence** **4** [U] *especially AmE* a period of time when a doctor receives special training in a particular type of medicine, especially at a hospital

res·i·dent¹ /ˈrezɪdənt/ ●●○ S3 W3 AWL *n* [C]

1 someone who lives or stays in a particular place: *the residents of Westville*

2 *AmE* a doctor working at a hospital where he or she is being trained SYN **registrar** *BrE*

resident² ●○○ AWL *adj*

1 *formal* living in a place: **[+in]** *Many retired British people are now resident in Spain.*

2 [only before noun] living or working in a particular place or institution: *a resident tutor | The resident population of mental hospitals has fallen by 20%.*

3 [only before noun] belonging to a particular group of people – used humorously: *He's our* ***resident expert*** *on computer games.*

res·i·den·tial /ˌrezɪˈdenʃəl◂/ ●●○ W3 AWL *adj*

1 a residential part of a town consists of private houses, with no offices or factories → **suburban**: *a quiet residential neighbourhood*

2 relating to homes rather than offices or businesses → **domestic**: *telephone services for residential customers*

3 residential course/school etc *especially BrE* if you are on a residential course, you are living in the institution where you are studying

ˌresidential ˈcare *n* [U] a system in which people who are old or ill live together in a special house and are looked after by professionals

ˌresidential ˈhome *n* [C] a special house in which old or ill people live and are looked after by professionals SYN **nursing home**

ˌresidential ˈtreatment faˌcility (*also* **ˌresidential ˈtreatment ˌcenter**) *n* [C] *formal especially AmE* a place that gives treatment to people with mental problems or problems with drugs or alcohol

ˌresident phyˈsician *n* [C] *AmE* a RESIDENT¹(2)

ˈresidents' associˌation *n* [C] *BrE* a group of people who meet to discuss the problems and needs of the area where they live

re·sid·u·al /rɪˈzɪdʒuəl/ ●○○ *adj* [only before noun] *formal* remaining after a process, event etc is finished: *the residual effects of drug treatment |* **residual income** (=the money left from what you earn after you have paid your taxes)

re·sid·u·als /rɪˈzɪdʒuəlz/ *n* [plural] money that is paid to an actor, writer etc when their work is broadcast again → **royalty**

re·sid·u·a·ry /rɪˈzɪdʒuəri $ -eri/ *adj* [only before noun] *BrE law* relating to all the money and property that remains after a person has died, and after any bills have been paid

res·i·due /ˈrezədjuː $ -duː/ ●○○ *n*

1 [C,U] a substance that remains on a surface, in a container etc and cannot be removed easily, or that remains after a chemical process: **[+from]** *residue from sewage*

treatment plants | *The flies* **leave** *a sticky* **residue** *on crops.* | *Rinse off any soap residue.*
2 [C] *formal* the part of something that is left after the rest has gone or been taken away: **[+of]** *The residue of the stock was sold.*

re·sign /rɪˈzaɪn/ ●●○ W3 *v* [I,T]
1 to officially announce that you have decided to leave your job or an organization → **quit**: **[+from]** *She resigned from the government last week.* | **[+as]** *He resigned as governor of Punjab in August.* | **resign your post/seat/position etc** *Tom has since resigned his membership of the golf club.*
2 resign yourself to (doing) sth to make yourself accept something that is bad but cannot be changed → **resigned**: *Josh resigned himself to the long walk home.* | *At sixteen, I resigned myself to the fact that I'd never be a dancer.*

res·ig·na·tion /ˌrezɪgˈneɪʃən/ ●●○ W3 *n*
1 [C,U] an occasion when you officially announce that you have decided to leave your job or an organization, or a written statement that says you will be leaving → **notice**: *Illness forced his resignation.* | *Further resignations are expected later this week.*
2 [U] when someone calmly accepts a situation that cannot be changed, even though it is bad: *She gave a sigh of resignation.* | **with resignation** *He accepted her decision with resignation.*

COLLOCATIONS

VERBS

call for sb's resignation (=publicly ask for it) *After the defeat, there were calls for the coach's resignation.*
demand sb's resignation (=ask for it forcefully) *His political opponents demanded his resignation.*
hand in your resignation (=say that you are going to leave an organization) *I'm thinking of handing in my resignation.*
offer your resignation (*also* **tender/submit your resignation** *formal*) | **accept sb's resignation** | **reject/turn down sb's resignation**

PHRASES

a letter of resignation *He immediately wrote a letter of resignation.*

re·signed /rɪˈzaɪnd/ *adj* **1 be resigned to (doing) sth** to calmly accept a situation that is bad, but cannot be changed: *She's resigned to spending Christmas on her own.* | *Sam was* **resigned to the fact that** *he would never be promoted.* **2** a resigned look, voice etc shows that you are making yourself accept something that you do not like: *'We'll have to leave,' she said with a resigned sigh.* —**resignedly** /rɪˈzaɪnɪdli/ *adv*

re·sil·i·ence /rɪˈzɪliəns/ (*also* **re·sil·i·en·cy** /-ənsi/) *n* [U]
1 the ability to become strong, happy, or successful again after a difficult situation or event → **toughness**: **[+of]** *the resilience of youth* | *People* **showed** *remarkable* **resilience** *during the war.* **2** the ability of a substance such as rubber to return to its original shape after it has been pressed or bent

re·sil·i·ent /rɪˈzɪliənt/ *adj* **1** able to become strong, happy, or successful again after a difficult situation or event → **tough**: *Children are often very resilient.* | *The company proved* **remarkably resilient** *during the recession.*
2 strong and not easily damaged by being pulled, pressed etc: *boots with tough resilient soles* | *Any chemical treatment will leave hair less resilient than before.* —**resiliently** *adv*

res·in /ˈrezɪn/ *n* **1** [U] a thick sticky liquid that comes out of some trees → **sap** **2** [C,U] a type of plastic —**resinous** *adj*

re·sist /rɪˈzɪst/ ●●○ W3 *v*
1 [I,T usually in negatives] to stop yourself from having something that you like very much or doing something that you want to do: **cannot resist (doing) sth** *I just can't resist chocolate.* | *She can never resist buying new shoes.* | **it is hard/difficult/impossible to resist sth** *It's hard to resist an invitation like that.* | **resist the temptation/urge to do sth** *She resisted the temptation to laugh.* | *They only wanted 3 dollars for it, so how could I resist?*
2 [T] to try to prevent a change from happening, or prevent yourself from being forced to do something: *He resisted pressure to resign.* | **resist doing sth** *For months the company has resisted changing its accounts system.* | **strongly/fiercely/vigorously etc resist** *The proposal was strongly resisted by the police.*
3 [I,T] to use force to stop something from happening: **strongly/fiercely/firmly etc resist** *Demonstrators violently resisted attempts to remove them from the building.* | *He was charged with trying to* **resist arrest**.
4 [T] to not be changed or harmed by something: *your ability to resist infection*

re·sist·ance /rɪˈzɪstəns/ ●●○ S3 W3 *n*
1 AGAINST CHANGE [singular, U] a refusal to accept new ideas or changes: **[+to]** *people's resistance to change* | **[+from]** *The no-smoking policy was introduced with little resistance from staff.*
2 FIGHTING [singular, U] fighting against someone who is attacking you: **put up/offer resistance** *Rebel gunmen have put up strong resistance.*
3 AGAINST INFECTION/ILLNESS [singular, U] the natural ability of a person, animal, or plant to stop diseases or difficult conditions from harming them: **[+to]** *the body's resistance to infection* | *disease resistance*
4 wind/air/water resistance the way in which wind, air, or water can cause a moving object such as a car, plane, or boat to slow down
5 ELECTRICITY [U] the ability of a substance to stop the flow of an electric current through it
6 the resistance (*also* **the Resistance**) an organization that secretly fights against an enemy that controls their country
7 the line/path of least resistance if you follow the path of least resistance, you avoid making difficult decisions and choose the easiest solution to a problem - often used to show disapproval: *Many people don't make changes because they're* **following the path of least resistance**. | *Kirk always just* **takes the line of least resistance**. → PASSIVE RESISTANCE

re·sis·tant /rɪˈzɪstənt/ ●○○ *adj*
1 not damaged or affected by something → **proof**: **[+to]** *an infection that's resistant to antibiotics* | **heat-resistant/stain-resistant/fire-resistant etc** *shock-resistant rubber*
2 opposed to something and wanting to prevent it from happening: **[+to]** *Many managers are resistant to change.*

re·sis·tor /rɪˈzɪstə $ -ər/ *n* [C] a piece of wire or other material used for increasing electrical resistance

re·sit /ˌriːˈsɪt/ *v* (*past tense and past participle* **resat** /-ˈsæt/, *present participle* **resitting**) [T] *BrE* to take an examination again, because you failed it or did not do well enough SYN **retake** —**re·sit** /ˈriːsɪt/ *n* [C]

re·skill·ing /ˌriː ˈskɪlɪŋ/ *n* [U] *BrE* the practice of teaching people new skills, to help them find a new job

res·o·lute /ˈrezəluːt/ *adj* doing something in a very determined way because you have very strong beliefs, aims etc OPP **irresolute**: *resolute opposition* | *resolute leadership* | *She remained resolute in her belief that the situation would improve.* THESAURUS DETERMINED —**resolutely** *adv*: *Mia resolutely refused to talk about her illness.*

res·o·lu·tion /ˌrezəˈluːʃən/ ●○○ AWL *n*
1 DECISION [C] a formal decision or statement agreed on by a group of people, especially after a vote: **pass/adopt/approve a resolution** *The resolution was passed by a two-thirds majority.* | *a* **resolution calling for** *a ban on dumping nuclear waste* | *They have failed to comply with the resolution.*
2 SOLUTION [singular, U] when someone solves a problem, argument, or difficult situation: **[+of]** *a forum for the resolution of commercial disputes*
3 PROMISE [C] a promise to yourself to do something → **resolve**: **resolution to do sth** *Carol* **made a resolution** *to work harder at school.* | **New Year's resolution** (=a resolution made on January 1st)

R

4 DETERMINATION [U] strong belief and determination: *Then, with sudden resolution, she stood up.*
5 CLEAR PICTURE [C,U] the power of a television, camera, MICROSCOPE etc to give a clear picture: **high/low resolution** (=how clear or unclear the picture is)

re·solve[1] /rɪˈzɒlv $ rɪˈzɑːlv, rɪˈzɒːlv/ ●●○ W3 AWL *v* [T]
1 to find a satisfactory way of dealing with a problem or difficulty SYN **solve** → **settle**: **resolve a dispute/conflict/problem etc** *The crisis was resolved by negotiations.* | *Barnet was desperate for money to resolve his financial problems.*
2 *formal* to make a definite decision to do something: **resolve to do sth** *After the divorce she resolved never to marry again.* | **resolve that** *Mary resolved that she would stop smoking.* THESAURUS DECIDE
3 to make a formal decision, especially by voting: **resolve to do sth** *The Senate resolved to accept the president's proposals.*
4 *technical* to separate something into its different parts: *DNA samples were extracted and resolved.*
resolve (sth) **into** sth *phr v*
1 *technical* to separate into parts, or to separate something: *This mixture will resolve into two separate compounds.*
2 resolve (itself) into sth *formal* to gradually change into something else SYN **become**: *The argument resolved itself into an uneasy truce.*

resolve[2] ●○○ AWL *n* [U] *formal* strong determination to succeed in doing something: *Recent events* ***strengthened*** *her* ***resolve*** *to find out the truth.*

res·o·nance /ˈrezənəns/ *n* **1** [U] the resonance of a sound is its quality of being deep and loud and continuing for a long time **2** [C,U] *formal* the special meaning or importance that something has for you because it relates to your own experiences: *a tradition that* ***has*** *little* ***resonance*** *in the 21st century* | *His words will have resonance for many musicians.* **3** [C,U] *technical* sound that is produced or increased in one object by sound waves from another object

res·o·nant /ˈrezənənt/ *adj* **1** a resonant sound is deep, loud, and clear, and continues for a long time: *the violin's smooth, resonant tone* **2 resonant with sth** *literary* filled with a particular meaning, quality, or sound: *prints resonant with traditions of Russian folk art* **3** *technical* resonant materials increase any sound produced inside them —**resonantly** *adv*

res·o·nate /ˈrezəneɪt/ *v* [I] **1** if something such as an event or a message resonates, it seems important or good to people, or continues to do this: **[+with]** *an idea that resonates with many voters* **2** to make a deep loud clear sound that continues for a long time → **resound**: *The music resonated through the streets.* **3** to make a sound that is produced as a reaction to another sound
resonate with sth *phr v* **1** *formal* to be full of a particular meaning or quality: *literature that resonates with biblical imagery* **2** to be full of a particular sound: *a hall resonating with laughter*

res·o·na·tor /ˈrezəneɪtə $ -ər/ *n* [C] a piece of equipment that makes the sound of a musical instrument louder

re·sort[1] /rɪˈzɔːt $ -ɔːrt/ ●●○ W3 *n*
1 [C] a place where a lot of people go for holidays: **seaside/beach/ski etc resort** *Aspen, a ski resort in Colorado* | *Lagoon Reef is one of the best resort hotels.*
2 last/final resort what you will do if everything else fails: **as a last resort** *Drug treatment should only be used as a last resort.* | **of last resort** *a weapon of last resort* | **in the last resort** *BrE*: *Economic sanctions will be used only in the last resort.*
3 first resort what you will do first before you try other things: *In the past, your family was the first resort when looking for a job.*
4 resort to sth *formal* when you must use or depend on something because nothing better is available: **without resort to sth** *We hope they will be able to resolve the situation without resort to force.*

resort[2] ●○○ *v*
resort to sth *phr v* to do something bad, extreme, or difficult because you cannot think of any other way to deal with a problem: *Officials fear that extremists may* ***resort to violence.*** | **resort to doing sth** *Vets have had to resort to killing the animals.*

re·sound /rɪˈzaʊnd/ *v* [I] **1** if a place resounds with a sound, it is full of that sound: **[+with]** *The stadium resounded with cheers.* | **[+to]** *By now, the whole room was resounding to the sound of the team's chants.* **2** if a sound such as a musical note resounds, it continues loudly and clearly for quite a long time → **resonate**: **[+through/around etc]** *a horn resounding through the forest* **3** *formal* to be mentioned or talked about a lot: *The war still resounds in the country's folklore.*

re·sound·ing /rɪˈzaʊndɪŋ/ *adj* **1 resounding success/victory/defeat etc** a very great or complete success, victory etc: *The show was a resounding success.* **2** [only before noun] a resounding noise is so loud that it seems to continue for a few seconds: *a resounding thud* THESAURUS LOUD —**resoundingly** *adv*

re·source[1] /rɪˈzɔːs, -ˈsɔːs $ ˈriːsɔːrs/ ●●● S2 W1 AWL *n*
1 LAND/OIL/COAL ETC [C usually plural] something such as useful land, or minerals such as oil or coal, that exists in a country and can be used to increase its wealth: *Canada's vast mineral resources* | *a country rich in* ***natural resources***
2 MONEY/PROPERTY ETC **resources** [plural] all the money, property, skills etc that you have available to use when you need them: *She had no* ***financial resources.*** | *Only* ***limited resources*** *are available to the police.* | **pool your resources** (=put together all the resources that each of you can provide) → HUMAN RESOURCES
3 PERSONAL QUALITIES **resources** [plural] personal qualities, such as courage and determination, that you need to deal with a difficult situation: *He proved that he has considerable* ***inner resources.***
4 EDUCATIONAL [C] something such as a book, film, or picture used by teachers or students to provide information: *resources for learning* | *a valuable new computer resource* | **resource room/centre**
5 PRACTICAL ABILITY [U] *formal* the ability to deal with practical problems SYN **resourcefulness**: *a man of great resource*

re·source[2] /rɪˈzɔːs, -ˈsɔːs $ -ˈsɔːrs/ AWL *v* [T] to provide money or other resources for something: *The program wasn't adequately resourced.* GRAMMAR **Resource** is usually passive.

re·source·ful /rɪˈzɔːsfəl, -ˈsɔːs- $ -ɔːr-/ AWL *adj* good at finding ways of dealing with practical problems: *a woman who is energetic and resourceful* —**resourcefully** *adv* —**resourcefulness** *n* [U]

re·spawn /ˌriːˈspɔːn $ -ɒːn/ *v* [I,T] if a character in a computer game respawns or is respawned, they are born again after being killed

re·spect[1] /rɪˈspekt/ ●●● S3 W2 *n*
1 ADMIRATION [U] a feeling of admiring someone or what they do, especially because of their personal qualities, knowledge, or skills → **admiration**: **[+for]** *I have the greatest respect for Jane's work.*
2 CONSIDERATION [U] the belief that something or someone is important and should not be harmed, treated rudely etc OPP **disrespect**: **[+for]** *Out of respect for the wishes of her family, the affair was not reported in the media.* | *The boys showed a complete* ***lack of respect*** *for authority.* | **with respect** *Your mother should be treated with respect.*
3 with (the greatest) respect/with (all) due respect *spoken formal* say this before disagreeing with someone when you want to be polite: *With respect, I think you're wrong.*
4 FOR DANGER [singular, U] a careful attitude towards something or someone that could be dangerous: **[+for]** *My fear turned into a respect for the sea.* | *People should have a* ***healthy respect*** *for alcohol* (=a sensible careful attitude towards it).
5 in one respect/in some respects etc used to say that something is true in one way, in some ways etc: *In many*

respects the new version is not as good as the old one. | *Mum is very stubborn, and Kim takes after her in that respect.*
6 GREETINGS **respects** [plural] *formal* polite greetings: **give/send your respects (to sb)** *Give my respects to your wife.* | **pay your respects (to sb)** *BrE* (=make a polite visit) *I've come to pay my respects to Mrs O'Hara.*
7 pay your last respects (to sb) to go to someone's funeral
8 in respect of sth *formal* concerning or in relation to something: *This is especially true in respect of the UK.*
9 with respect to sth *formal* **a)** concerning or in relation to something: *the freedom of a property owner to make a contract with respect to his property* **b)** used to introduce a new subject, or to return to one that has already been mentioned: *With respect to your request, I am not yet able to agree.* → SELF-RESPECT

COLLOCATIONS

VERBS

have respect for sb *I have a lot of respect for my boss.*
win/earn/gain respect (=start to be respected) *Morris eventually won the respect of his fellow workers.*
command respect (=be respected) *Lady Thatcher commanded huge respect from everyone she worked with.*
deserve respect | **lose respect for sb** (=no longer respect them) | **lose sb's respect** (=no longer be respected by them)

ADJECTIVES

great respect *Rex and Joe had great respect for his judgement.*
the utmost respect *I have the utmost respect for the prime minister.*
mutual respect (=when two people respect each other) | **grudging respect** (=when you respect someone or something unwillingly)

respect² ●●● S3 W2 *v* [T]
1 [not in progressive] to admire someone because they have high standards and good qualities such as fairness and honesty → **admire**: **respect sb for (doing) sth** *She respected him for his honesty.* | *I respect his views, although I do not agree with them.* THESAURUS ADMIRE
2 to be careful not to do anything against someone's wishes, rights etc: *She said she wanted to leave, and her father **respected** her **wishes**.* | *I would like you to respect my privacy.* | *the need to respect human rights* THESAURUS OBEY
3 to not break a rule or law: *The president is expected to respect the constitution.*

re·spect·a·ble /rɪˈspektəbəl/ ●●○ *adj*
1 someone who is respectable behaves in a way that is considered socially acceptable: *hard-working, respectable people* | *a respectable family* | *Put a tie on – it'll make you look more respectable.*
2 good or satisfactory SYN **decent**: *a respectable income* | *Her exam results were respectable enough.* —**respectably** *adv* —**respectability** /rɪˌspektəˈbɪləti/ *n* [U]

re·spect·ed /rɪˈspektɪd/ *adj* admired by many people because of your good work or achievements: *He's one of the most respected managers in the game.* | **highly/well/widely/greatly respected** *a highly respected journalist*

re·spect·er /rɪˈspektə $ -ər/ *n* **1 be no respecter of persons** *formal* to affect all people in the same way, whether or not they are rich or powerful: *Disease is no respecter of persons.* **2 be a respecter of sth** to have respect for something such as a law or organization: *She is a respecter of the rights of all religious groups.*

re·spect·ful /rɪˈspektfəl/ ●○○ *adj* feeling or showing respect OPP **disrespectful**: *They listened in respectful silence.* | **[+of]** *He was always respectful of my independence.* THESAURUS POLITE —**respectfully** *adv* —**respectfulness** *n* [U]

re·spect·ing /rɪˈspektɪŋ/ *prep formal* about or relating to something: *A discussion took place respecting the provision of science teaching.*

re·spec·tive /rɪˈspektɪv/ ●●○ *adj* [only before noun] used before a plural noun to refer to the different things that belong to each separate person or thing mentioned: *We all went back to our respective homes to wait for news.* | *the respective roles of teachers and students*

re·spec·tive·ly /rɪˈspektɪvli/ ●●○ W3 *adv* in the same order as the things you have just mentioned: *The cups and saucers cost £5 and £3 respectively.*

res·pi·ra·tion /ˌrespəˈreɪʃən/ *n* [U] *technical* the process of breathing → ARTIFICIAL RESPIRATION

res·pi·ra·tor /ˈrespəreɪtə $ -ər/ *n* [C] **1** a piece of equipment that pumps air in and out of someone's lungs if they are too ill or weak to breathe SYN **ventilator**: *The baby was immediately put on a respirator.* **2** a piece of equipment that you wear over your nose and mouth to help you breathe in a place where there is harmful gas, smoke etc → **gas mask**

re·spi·ra·to·ry /rɪˈspɪrətəri, ˈrespəreɪtəri, rɪˈspaɪərə- $ ˈrespərətɔːri, rɪˈspaɪrə-/ *adj formal or technical* relating to breathing or your lungs: *respiratory disease*

re·spire /rɪˈspaɪə $ -ˈspaɪr/ *v* [I] *technical* to breathe

res·pite /ˈrespɪt, -paɪt $ -pɪt/ *n* [singular, U] **1** a short time when something bad stops happening, so that the situation is temporarily better: **[+from]** *The trip was a welcome respite from the pressures of work.* | *a **brief respite** from persecution* | **without respite** *The pain went on without respite.* **2** a short period of time before you have to do something that you do not like: *We have a few days' respite before we have to pay them.*

ˈrespite ˌcare *n* [U] temporary care for people who are too old or ill to look after themselves, which allows the people who usually look after them to rest

re·splen·dent /rɪˈsplendənt/ *adj formal* very beautiful, bright, and impressive in appearance: **[+in]** *She looked resplendent in a silk dress.* —**resplendently** *adv*

re·spond /rɪˈspɒnd $ rɪˈspɑːnd/ ●●● S2 W2 AWL *v*
1 [I] to do something as a reaction to something that has been said or done SYN **react**: **[+to]** *Responding to the news, Mr Watt appealed for calm.* | **respond by doing sth** *The US responded by sending troops into Laos.* | **[+with]** *Villagers responded with offers of help.*
2 [I,T] to say or write something as a reply: **respond that** *He responded that he didn't want to see anyone.* | **[+to]** *Dave didn't respond to any of her emails.* THESAURUS ANSWER
3 [I] to improve as a result of a particular kind of treatment: **[+to]** *She has responded well to treatment.* | *Colds do not respond to antibiotics.*

re·spon·dent /rɪˈspɒndənt $ rɪˈspɑːn-/ AWL *n* [C] **1** *formal* someone who answers questions, especially in a SURVEY: *Only 62 percent of respondents said they were satisfied.* **2** *law* someone who has to defend their own case in a law court, especially in a DIVORCE case

re·sponse /rɪˈspɒns $ rɪˈspɑːns/ ●●● S1 W1 AWL *n*
1 [C,U] something that is done as a reaction to something that has happened or been said: **[+to]** *the public's response to our appeal for help* | **in response to sth** *The law was passed in response to public pressure.* | **positive/favourable/negative etc response** *The exhibition has received a positive response from visitors.* | **an emotional/angry response** *The decision provoked an angry response from residents.* | *His **immediate response** was one of disbelief.* | *Emmett's new exhibition has **met with** a favourable **response** from critics.*
2 [C] something that is said or written as a reply: **[+to]** *'Sure, why not?' was his response to all of Billie's suggestions.* | *Carl **made** no **response**, and carried on with his meal.* | **in response (to sth)** *I am writing in response to your letter of June 12.* | *Ronni merely groaned in response.* → RAPID-RESPONSE

re·spon·si·bil·i·ty /rɪˌspɒnsəˈbɪləti $ rɪˌspɑːn-/ ●●● S2 W1 *n* (*plural* **responsibilities**)
1 [U] a duty to be in charge of someone or something, so that you make decisions and can be blamed if something bad happens: *Kelly's promotion means more money and more responsibility.* | **+for** *The Minister has responsibility for the National Health Service.* | **with responsibility for sth** *a*

R

manager with responsibility for over 100 staff | **it is sb's responsibility to do sth** *It's your responsibility to inform us of any changes.*
2 [U] blame for something that has happened: *The firm is* ***denying*** *all* ***responsibility****.* | **[+for]** *No one wants to* ***take responsibility*** *for the problem.* | *The surgeon* ***accepted full responsibility*** *for the error that led to her death.* | *So far no one has* ***claimed responsibility*** (=said that they are responsible) *for the bombings.*
3 [C] something that you must do as part of your job or duty: *My responsibilities include answering the phone and dealing with customer enquiries.* | **family/professional/parental etc responsibilities** *a single parent struggling to balance work and family responsibilities*
4 [C] something that you ought to do because it is morally or socially right SYN **duty**: **a responsibility to do sth** *We all* ***have a responsibility*** *to protect the environment.* | *Parents need to encourage* ***a sense of responsibility*** *in their children* (=the ability to behave sensibly in a way that will not harm themselves or other people). | **moral/social/legal etc responsibility** *The company saw it as part of its social responsibility to provide education for its workers.*
5 responsibility to sb a duty to help someone because of your work or position in society: *A doctor's first responsibility is to her patients.*
6 do sth on your own responsibility *formal* to do something without being told to do it or officially allowed to do it
→ DIMINISHED RESPONSIBILITY

COLLOCATIONS

VERBS

have responsibility for (doing) sth *The Council has responsibility for maintaining the streetlights.*
take responsibility for (doing) sth *Who do you trust to take responsibility for our country's defence?*
take on responsibility (*also* **assume responsibility** *formal*) (=start to have responsibility for something) *These days men tend to take on more responsibility at home.*
shoulder responsibility (=agree to start having a difficult or unpleasant duty) | **shirk responsibility** (=not accept a duty you should accept) | **exercise responsibility** *formal* (=take action because you have responsibility for something) | **abdicate responsibility** *formal* (=refuse to have responsibility for something you used to have responsibility for) | **the responsibility lies with sb** (=they are responsible for it)

ADJECTIVES

personal responsibility *So far, no one had taken personal responsibility for the project.*
overall responsibility *The Department of Education has overall responsibility for schools and universities.*
direct responsibility (=when no other person is involved) *He has direct responsibility for all the programmes on Radio 1.*
sole responsibility (=not shared with others) | **collective responsibility** (=shared equally by a group of people) | **primary responsibility** (=most important responsibility) | **ultimate responsibility** (=responsibility for making a final decision)

PHRASES

a burden of responsibility (=a lot of responsibility, that worries you) *Being the only wage earner put a great burden of responsibility on my father.*
a position of responsibility (=a job in which people depend on you to tell them what they should do)

re·spon·si·ble /rɪˈspɒnsəbəl $ rɪˈspɑːn-/ ●●● S2 W2 *adj*
1 GUILTY [not before noun] if someone is responsible for an accident, mistake, crime etc, it is their fault or they can be blamed: **[+for]** *Police believe that the same man is responsible for three other murders in the area.* | **hold sb responsible (for sth)** *If anything goes wrong, I will hold you* ***personally responsible****.* | **the person/people etc responsible** *We are determined to bring the people responsible to justice.*
THESAURUS GUILTY
2 IN CHARGE OF [not before noun] having a duty to be in charge of or to look after someone or something: **[+for]** *Mills is responsible for a budget of over $5 million.* | *The airline is* ***legally responsible*** *for the safety of its passengers.* | **responsible for doing sth** *He is responsible for recruiting and training new staff.*
3 CAUSE [not before noun] if something is responsible for a change, problem, event etc, it causes it: **[+for]** *The floods were responsible for over a hundred deaths.*
4 SENSIBLE sensible and able to make good judgments, so that you can be trusted OPP **irresponsible** → **reliable**: *You can leave the children with Billy – he's very responsible.* | **responsible adult/citizen** *It's time you started acting like a responsible adult.*
5 responsible job/position a job in which the ability to make good judgments and decisions is needed
6 be responsible to sb if you are responsible to someone, that person is in charge of your work and you must explain what you have done to them: *Cabinet members are* ***directly responsible*** *to the president.*

GRAMMAR

• **Responsible** is always an adjective, never a noun: *Who is responsible?* ✗ Don't say: *Who is the responsible?*
• The **person/man/woman etc responsible** is the person who has done something, usually something bad: *We will catch the person responsible.* ✗ Don't say: *We will catch the responsible.* | *We will catch the responsible person.*
• You say that someone is **responsible for** something: *Who is responsible for this mess?* | *Claire is responsible for marketing.* ✗ Don't say: *be responsible of something*

re·spon·si·bly /rɪˈspɒnsəbli $ rɪˈspɑːn-/ *adv* in a sensible way which makes people trust you OPP **irresponsibly**: **act/behave responsibly** *Can I rely on you to behave responsibly while I'm away?*

re·spon·sive /rɪˈspɒnsɪv $ rɪˈspɑːn-/ ●○○ AWL *adj*
1 reacting quickly, in a positive way: *a car with* ***highly responsive*** *steering* | **[+to]** *We try to be responsive to the needs of the customer.* | *Her condition is not responsive to drug therapy.*
2 eager to communicate with people, and to react to them in a positive way: *I tried to get him talking, but he wasn't* ***very responsive****.* —**responsively** *adv* —**responsiveness** *n* [U]

re·spray /ˌriːˈspreɪ/ *v* [T] *BrE* to change the colour of a car by putting new paint on it —**respray** /ˈriːspreɪ/ *n* [C]

rest[1] /rest/ ●●● S1 W1 *n*
1 RELAXING [C,U] a period of time when you are not doing anything tiring and you can relax or sleep: *You look exhausted! Why don't you take a rest?*
2 the rest what is left after everything or everyone else has gone or been used, dealt with, or mentioned → **remainder**, **leftovers**: *You carry these two bags, and I'll bring the rest.* | *Two of the attackers were killed, and the rest escaped.* | **[+of]** *Does anyone want the rest of this pizza?* | *He'll be in a wheelchair for* ***the rest of his life****.*

GRAMMAR: Singular or plural verb?

• You use a singular verb after **the rest** when referring to an uncountable noun: *The rest of the money* ***is*** *for you.* | *I've eaten some cheese – the rest* ***is*** *in the fridge.*
• You use a plural verb after **the rest** when referring to a group of people or things: *Two of the terrorists were captured and the rest* ***were*** *killed.*

3 put/set sb's mind at rest to make someone feel less anxious or worried: *Why don't you talk to him, and put his mind at rest.*
4 come to rest a) to stop moving: *The aircraft skidded across the runway and finally came to rest in a cornfield.* **b)** if your eyes come to rest on something, you stop looking

around and look at that one thing: **[+on]** *My eyes came to rest on a photograph of a young man.*
5 give it a rest *spoken especially BrE* used to tell someone to stop talking about something because they are annoying you: *Give it a rest, Jack!*
6 give sth a rest *spoken* to stop doing an activity: *I gave the acting a rest for a while.*
7 at rest a) an expression meaning dead, and free from pain and problems **b)** *technical* not moving
8 and all the rest of it *BrE spoken* used at the end of a short list to mean other things of a similar type: *I was paying the rent and the bills and all the rest of it.*
9 and the rest *BrE spoken* used to emphasize in a humorous way that a number or amount is really much higher than someone thinks: *'I'd say she's about 40.' 'Yeah, and the rest!'*
10 lay/put sth to rest *formal* to stop people from worrying about or believing something: *The minister resigned, and the government hoped that the scandal would finally be laid to rest.*
11 lay sb to rest an expression meaning to bury someone, used when you want to avoid saying this directly: *She was laid to rest beside her husband.*
12 MUSIC [C] **a)** a period of silence of a particular length in a piece of music **b)** a written sign that shows how long the period of silence should be → HEADREST, FOOTREST, BACKREST, → **and the rest is history** at HISTORY(10)

COLLOCATIONS

VERBS

have/take a rest *I'm going upstairs to have a rest.*
get some rest *You'd better get some rest if you're driving back tonight.*
deserve a rest *I think we deserve a rest after all that hard work.*

ADJECTIVES

a well-earned/well-deserved rest (=a rest after working hard) *Our players are taking a well-earned rest before the start of the new season.*
a complete rest *The doctor had advised a complete rest for a fortnight.*
a little/short rest | a long rest | a good rest (=a complete rest that relaxes you)

rest + NOUN

a rest day/period *The crew had a three hour rest period before their next flight.*

rest² ●●● S3 W3 *v*
1 RELAX [I] to stop working or doing an activity for a time and sit down or lie down to relax: *If you're tired, we'll stop and rest for a while.*
2 SUPPORT STH [I,T always + adv/prep] to support an object or part of your body by putting it on or against something, or to be supported in this way → **lean**: **rest (sth) against/on sth** *Rest your head on my shoulder.* | *Brassard rested his elbows on the table and leaned forward.* | *Their bikes were resting against the wall.*
3 rest your feet/legs/eyes etc to stop using a part of your body because it is feeling sore or tired: *I need to sit down and rest my legs.*
4 let the matter rest (*also* **let it rest**) to stop discussing or dealing with something: *The man apologized, but Aunt Matilda refused to let the matter rest.*
5 rest assured (that) *formal* used to tell someone not to worry, because what you say about a situation is true: *You may rest assured that it will be ready on time.*
6 sb will not rest until ... if you will not rest until something happens, you will not be satisfied until it happens: *We will not rest until the murderer is found.*
7 DEAD PERSON [I always + adv/prep] *literary* if a dead person rests somewhere, they are buried there: *My mother rests beside my father in the family graveyard.* | **sb's last/final resting place** (=the place where someone is buried) | **rest in peace** (=often written on a grave)
8 rest on your laurels to be satisfied with what you have done, so that you do not make any further effort
9 I rest my case *spoken* **a)** *formal* used by a lawyer when they have finished trying to prove something in a court of law **b)** used when something happens or is said which proves that you were right - used humorously
10 rest easy to relax and stop worrying: *I can rest easy, knowing everything's under control.*
rest on/upon sth *phr v*
1 *formal* to depend on something: *Success in management ultimately rests on good judgment.*
2 *formal* to be based on a particular idea or set of facts: *The case against my client rests entirely on circumstantial evidence.*
3 if your eyes rest on something, you notice it and look at it: *His eyes rested on a small figure in the distance.*
rest with sb *phr v* if a decision rests with someone, they are responsible for it: *The final decision rests with the president.*

ˈrest ˌarea *n* [C] *especially AmE* a place near a road where you can stop and rest, go to the toilet etc

re·start /ˌriːˈstɑːt $ -ˈstɑːrt/ *v* [I,T] to start something such as a machine, process etc again after it has stopped: *attempts to restart the peace process* —**restart** /ˈriːstɑːt $ -stɑːrt/ *n* [C usually singular]

re·state /ˌriːˈsteɪt/ *v* [T] to say something again in a different way, so that it is clearer or more strongly expressed: *He is not changing the rules; he is simply restating the policy that was established last year.* —**restatement** *n* [C,U]

res·tau·rant /ˈrestərɒnt $ -rənt, -rɑːnt/ ●●● S2 W2 *n* [C] a place where you can buy and eat a meal: **Chinese/French/Mexican etc restaurant** *We went to a little Italian restaurant near Leicester Square.* | *He took her out for a five-course dinner in a fancy restaurant.* | *The company runs a chain of restaurants.* | *A new restaurant has just opened across the road.*

ˈrestaurant car *n* [C] a carriage on a train where meals are served SYN **dining car**

res·tau·ra·teur /ˌrestərəˈtɜː $ -ˈtɜːr/ (*also* **res·tau·ran·teur** /ˌrestərɒnˈtɜː $ -rɑːnˈtɜːr/) *n* [C] someone who owns and manages a restaurant

rest·ed /ˈrestɪd/ *adj* [not before noun] feeling healthier, stronger, or calmer because you have had time to relax: *We came back from holiday feeling rested and relaxed.*

rest·ful /ˈrestfəl/ *adj* peaceful and quiet, making you feel relaxed: *restful music* —**restfully** *adv*

ˈrest home *n* [C] a place where old or sick people can live and be taken care of SYN **nursing home**

res·ti·tu·tion /ˌrestɪˈtjuːʃən $ -ˈtuː-/ *n* [U] *formal* the act of giving back something that was lost or stolen to its owner, or of paying for damage → **compensation**: **[+of]** *the restitution of art treasures missing since World War II* | *The offender must* ***make restitution*** *for the hurt that he or she has caused.*

res·tive /ˈrestɪv/ *adj written* dissatisfied or bored with your situation, and impatient for it to change: *Communist leaders struggled to rule over increasingly restive populations.* —**restively** *adv* —**restiveness** *n* [U]

rest·less /ˈrestləs/ ●○○ *adj*
1 unwilling to keep still or stay where you are, especially because you are nervous or bored SYN **fidgety**: **become/grow/get restless** *The children had been indoors all day, and were getting restless.*
2 unwilling to stay in one place, and always wanting new experiences: *After a few weeks in Marseille, I grew restless and decided to move on.*
3 restless night a night during which you cannot sleep or rest —**restlessly** *adv* —**restlessness** *n* [U]

re·stock /ˌriːˈstɒk $ -ˈstɑːk/ *v* [I,T] to bring in more supplies to replace those that have been used

res·to·ra·tion /ˌrestəˈreɪʃən/ ●●○ AWL *n* [C,U]
1 when you repair something such as an old building or a piece of furniture, so that it looks the same as when it was first built or made: **[+of]** *a fund for the restoration of historic buildings* | *Major* ***restoration work*** *will begin in May.*

2 the act of bringing back a law, tax, or system of government: **[+of]** *They're fighting for the restoration of democratic rights.* | *the restoration of the monarchy in Spain*
3 the Restoration the return of Charles II as king of England in 1660, and the period afterwards: **Restoration comedy/drama** (=plays written during this time in England)
4 the act of officially giving something back to its former owner SYN **return**: **[+of]** *an attempt to secure the restoration of their lands*

re·sto·ra·tive /rɪˈstɔːrətɪv/ *adj formal* making you feel healthier or stronger: *the restorative power of sleep*

re·store /rɪˈstɔː $ -ɔːr/ ●●○ W3 AWL *v* [T]
1 FORMER SITUATION to make something return to its former state or condition: **restore sth to sth** *The government promises to restore the economy to full strength.* | *She was hoping that the Mediterranean climate would restore her to full health.* | *The National Guard was called in to* ***restore order*** (=make people stop fighting and breaking the law) *when riots broke out.* | *initiatives to* ***restore peace*** *in the Middle East* | **restore (diplomatic) relations with sb** *Vietnam restored diplomatic relations with South Korea on December 22.* | **restore sb's sight/hearing** (=make someone who cannot hear or who is blind, hear or see again)
2 POSITIVE FEELING to bring back a positive feeling that a person or a group of people felt before: *measures aimed at* ***restoring*** *public* ***confidence*** *in the education system* | *a man whose kindness and sincerity really restored my faith in human nature* (=helped me to believe that people can be good)
3 REPAIR to repair an old building, piece of furniture, or painting etc so that it is in its original condition: *The church was carefully restored after the war.* | *a Victorian fireplace* ***restored to its former glory*** **THESAURUS** ▶ REPAIR
4 GIVE STH BACK *formal* to give back to someone something that was lost or taken from them SYN **return**: **restore sth to sb** *The treaty restored Okinawa to Japan.*

> **REGISTER**
> In everyday English, people usually say that someone **gives** something **back** to its former owner, rather than **restores** it: *The treaty* ***gave*** *Okinawa* ***back*** *to Japan.*

5 BRING BACK A LAW to bring back a law, tax, right etc: *a campaign to restore the death penalty*
6 restore sb to power/the throne *formal* make someone king, queen, or president again, after a period when they have not been in power

re·stored /rɪˈstɔːd $ -ɔːrd/ AWL *adj* [not before noun] feeling better and stronger: *After a cup of tea, she felt quite restored.*

re·stor·er /rɪˈstɔːrə $ -ər/ *n* [C] **1** a person whose job is repairing old things: *an art restorer* **2** someone who brings back something that existed before: *He was described as a restorer of peace and order.*

re·strain /rɪˈstreɪn/ ●○○ AWL *v* [T]
1 to stop someone from doing something, often by using physical force: **restrain sb from doing sth** *I had to restrain her from running out into the street.* | *He had to be restrained from using violence.*
2 to control your own emotions or behaviour: *Renwick restrained a feeling of annoyance.* | **restrain yourself (from doing something)** *She could barely restrain herself from hitting him.*
3 to control or limit something that is increasing too much: *Price rises should restrain consumer spending.*

re·strained /rɪˈstreɪnd/ *adj* **1** behaviour that is restrained is calm and controlled: *a restrained and cool-headed response to their criticisms* **2** not too brightly coloured or decorated: *The interior decoration is quite restrained.*

reˈstraining ˌorder *n* [C] an official legal document that prevents someone from doing something

re·straint /rɪˈstreɪnt/ ●○○ AWL *n*
1 [U] calm sensible controlled behaviour, especially in a situation when it is difficult to stay calm SYN **self-control**: *The police were praised for their restraint in handling the demonstrators.* | **show/exercise restraint** *He urged the millions of protesters to exercise restraint.*
2 [C usually plural, U] a rule or principle that limits what people can do: **[+on]** *Opposition politicians have called for restraints on public spending.* | *The government has* ***imposed restraints*** *on corporate mergers.*
3 [U] *formal* physical force that is used to hold someone back, especially because they are likely to be violent: *Sometimes police officers have to use physical restraint to control dangerous prisoners.*
4 [C] something that prevents someone from moving freely, such as a rope or a SEAT BELT

re·strict /rɪˈstrɪkt/ ●●○ W3 AWL *v* [T]
1 to limit or control the size, amount, or range of something: *The new law restricts the sale of hand guns.* | *You may need to restrict access to certain files* (=limit the number of people who can read them). | *The agreement will restrict competition.* | **restrict sth to sth** *In future we will restrict class sizes to 20 students.*
2 to limit someone's actions or movements: *The cramped living conditions severely restricted the children's freedom to play.*
3 restrict yourself/sb to (doing) sth to allow yourself to have or do only a particular thing or amount of something: *I'm restricting myself to two cigarettes a day.*

re·strict·ed /rɪˈstrɪktɪd/ ●○○ AWL *adj*
1 small or limited in size, area, or amount: *It's difficult trying to work in such a restricted space.*
2 limited or controlled, especially by laws or rules: *Press freedom is severely restricted.* | **[+to]** *The sale of alcohol is restricted to people over the age of 18.* | *There is restricted access to this information* (=only certain people can have it).
3 limited in your movements or in what you are able to do: *The accident left her with restricted movement in her right leg.* | *In those days women led very restricted lives.*
4 a restricted area, document, or information can only be seen or used by a particular group of people because it is secret or dangerous: *No Entry –* ***restricted area*** *for army personnel only.*
5 be restricted to sb/sth to only affect a limited area, group etc: *The damage is restricted to the left side of the brain.* | *Eligibility for five weeks' holiday is restricted to senior management.*

re·stric·tion /rɪˈstrɪkʃən/ ●●○ W3 AWL *n*
1 [C] a rule or law that limits or controls what people can do: **[+on]** *restrictions on immigration* | *a 50 mph* ***speed restriction*** | **trade/travel restrictions** | **impose/place restrictions on sth** *The law imposed new financial restrictions on private companies.* | **strict/tough/tight restriction** *tougher restrictions on alcohol advertising* | **lift/remove a restriction** *Restrictions on trade were lifted.* **THESAURUS** ▶ RULE
2 [U] when you restrict the size, amount, or range of something

re·stric·tive /rɪˈstrɪktɪv/ ●○○ AWL *adj* something that is restrictive stops people doing what they want to do SYN **limiting**: *Many members thought the rules were too restrictive.* | *a restrictive policy on admission to the college*

reˌstrictive ˈclause (*also* **reˌstrictive ˌrelative ˈclause**) *n* [C] *technical* a part of a sentence that says which particular person or thing you are talking about. For example in 'the man who came to dinner', the phrase 'who came to dinner' is a restrictive clause OPP **non-restrictive clause**

reˌstrictive ˈpractices *n* [plural] **1** unreasonable rules that are used by a TRADE UNION to limit the kind of work that members of other trade unions are allowed to do for a company **2** an unfair trade agreement between companies that limits the amount of competition there is

ˈrest room *n* [C] *AmE* a room with a toilet in a place such as a restaurant or cinema SYN **toilet** *BrE*

re·struc·ture /ˌriːˈstrʌktʃə $ -ər/ ●○○ AWL *v* [T] to change the way in which something such as a government, business, or system is organized: *proposals to* ***radically restructure*** *Britain's electronics industry* —**restructuring** *n* [C,U]: *the* ***major restructuring*** *of our armed forces*

ˈrest stop *n* [C] a place near a road where you can stop and rest, use the toilet etc

re·sult¹ /rɪˈzʌlt/ ●●● S1 W1 *n*

1 HAPPENING BECAUSE OF STH [C,U] something that happens or exists because of something that happened before → **consequence**: **[+of]** *Accidents are the inevitable result of driving too fast.* | *High unemployment is a* ***direct result*** *of the recession.* | **end/final/net result** (=the result at the end of a long process) *The net result of all these changes is that schools should be able to deliver a better service to pupils.* | *Growing plants from seed can* ***produce*** *disappointing* ***results****.* | *With a little effort you should* ***achieve*** *the desired* ***result****.* | **as a result (of sth)** *As a result of the pilots' strike, all flights have had to be cancelled.* | **with the result that** *Sara wasn't at school last week, with the result that she missed an important test.*

2 SPORTS/ELECTIONS [C] the final number of points, votes etc at the end of a competition, game, or election: *The results will be announced at midnight.* | *the football results* | **[+of]** *A lot depends on the result of this match.*

3 SCIENTIFIC TESTS [C] the answers that are produced by a scientific study or test: *Results suggest that diet is very important.* | **[+of]** *Police are awaiting the results of a forensic examination.* | **positive/negative/inconclusive results** *The experiments gave positive results in all cases.* THESAURUS CONCLUSION

4 EXAMINATIONS [C] *BrE* the mark you get in an examination SYN **grade** *AmE*: *When do we get our* ***exam results****?*

5 SUCCESS [C] the achievement of something: *She certainly knows how to* ***get results****.* | ***For best results****, always use fresh ingredients when you are cooking.*

6 BUSINESS **results** [plural] the accounts of a business that show how successful it has been over a period of time, usually a year: *British Airways has announced disappointing results for the first half of the year.*

7 get a result *BrE informal* to win a victory in a sports match: *They were lucky to get a result on Saturday.*

THESAURUS

result something that happens because of something else: *The fire at the house was the result of a dropped cigarette.* | *Many people find that herbal remedies produce a good result.*

consequence something important that happens as the result of a decision or action: *Global warming will have serious consequences for the environment.* | *Rising prices are the inevitable consequence of the grain shortage.*

repercussions the bad effects that happen later as a result of an event, often a long time afterwards: *The economic crisis in the US is likely to have serious repercussions for the rest of the world.* | *The scandal could have major repercussions for his career.*

outcome the final result of a meeting, election, war etc: *The final outcome of the election remained in doubt for several days.* | *So, what is the likely outcome for Spain?*

the upshot the final result of a situation, especially when this was unexpected: *The upshot of all this was that the trial had to be delayed.*

the fruits of sth *literary* the things that have been achieved as a result of someone's efforts – used especially in the following phrases: *He did not live to see* ***the fruits of his labours****.* | *They can now enjoy* ***the fruits of their success****.*

result² ●●○ W2 *v* [I] if something results from something else, it is caused by it: **[+from]** *We are still dealing with problems resulting from errors made in the past.* | *How would you cope with unemployment and the resulting loss of income?*

result in sth *phr v* to make something happen SYN **cause**: *an accident that resulted in the death of two passengers*

result³ *interjection informal* **Result!** said when you have just done something successfully

re·sul·tant /rɪˈzʌltənt/ *adj* [only before noun] *formal* happening or existing because of something: *She is still trying to get over the attack and the resultant injuries.*

re·sume¹ /rɪˈzjuːm $ rɪˈzuːm/ ●●○ *v formal*

1 [T] to start doing something again after stopping or being interrupted: *She hopes to resume work after the baby is born.* | *The rebels have resumed hostilities against government troops.* | **resume doing sth** *He will resume training as soon as the injury is better.* THESAURUS START

2 [I] if an activity or process resumes, it starts again after a pause: *Peace talks will resume tomorrow.*

3 resume your seat/place/position to go back to the seat, place, or position where you were before: *Will the delegates please resume their seats?*

re·su·me², **résumé** /ˈrezjʊmeɪ, ˈreɪ- $ ˌrezʊˈmeɪ/ ●●○ *n* [C]

1 a short account of something such as an article or speech which gives the main points but no details SYN **summary**: *a brief résumé of the day's events*

2 *AmE* a short written account of your education and your previous jobs that you send to an employer when you are looking for a new job SYN **CV** *BrE*

re·sump·tion /rɪˈzʌmpʃən/ *n* [singular, U] *formal* the act of starting an activity again after stopping or being interrupted → **resume**: **[+of]** *Both countries are now hoping for a quick resumption of diplomatic relations.*

re·sur·face /ˌriːˈsɜːfɪs $ -ɜːr-/ *v* **1** [I] to appear again after being lost or missing: *One of the missing paintings suddenly resurfaced.* THESAURUS APPEAR **2** [I] if an idea or problem resurfaces, it becomes important again: *Nationalist tensions have resurfaced here.* **3** [T] to put a new surface on a road **4** [I] to come back up to the surface of the water

re·sur·gence /rɪˈsɜːdʒəns $ -ɜːr-/ *n* [singular, U] the reappearance and growth of something that was common in the past: **[+of]** *There has been a* ***resurgence of interest*** *in religion over the last ten years.* | **[+in]** *a resurgence in the popularity of 60s music*

re·sur·gent /rɪˈsɜːdʒənt $ -ɜːr-/ *adj* [usually before noun] growing and becoming more popular, after a period of quietness: *resurgent fascism*

res·ur·rect /ˌrezəˈrekt/ *v* [T] to bring back an old activity, belief, idea etc that has not existed for a long time: *The Home Office have resurrected plans to build a new prison just outside London.* | *another failed attempt to resurrect his career*

res·ur·rec·tion /ˌrezəˈrekʃən/ *n* [singular] *formal* a situation in which something old or forgotten returns or becomes important again: *a resurrection of old jealousies*

re·sus·ci·tate /rɪˈsʌsɪteɪt/ *v* [T] to make someone breathe again or become conscious after they have almost died → **revive**: *Doctors managed to resuscitate him.* —**resuscitation** /rɪˌsʌsɪˈteɪʃən/ *n* [U]: ***mouth-to-mouth resuscitation*** (=when you breathe air into someone's mouth to make them breathe)

re·tail¹ /ˈriːteɪl/ ●○○ *n* [U] the sale of goods in shops to customers, for their own use and not for selling to anyone else → **wholesale**: **the retail trade/business** *a manager with twenty years' experience in the retail business* | **retail outlet/shop/store/chain** *We are looking for more retail outlets for our products.* | *a* ***retail price*** *of £8.99* | *The* ***retail value*** *would be around $500.* | ***Retail sales*** *fell by 1.3% in January.*

re·tail² /ˈriːteɪl/ *v* **1** [I] *technical* to be sold for a particular price in a shop: **[+at/for]** *The wine retails at £6.95 a bottle.* | *The decoder is expected to retail for under $300.* **2** [T] *technical* to sell goods in shops: *Their products are retailed all over Britain.*

re·tail³ /ˈrɪteɪl $ rɪˈteɪl, ˈriːteɪl/ *v* [T] *formal* to give other people private information about someone or something

R

re·tail⁴ /ˈriːteɪl/ *adv* if you buy or sell something retail, you buy or sell it in a shop: *We only deal with wholesalers – we don't sell any of our goods retail.*

re·tail·er /ˈriːteɪlə $ -ər/ ●○○ *n* [C] a person or business that sells goods to customers in a shop

re·tail·ing /ˈriːteɪlɪŋ/ *n* [U] the business of selling goods to customers in shops: *There may be many job losses in retailing.*

ˈretail park *n* [C] *BrE* an area outside a town with many large shops and space for cars to park

ˌretail ˈprice ˌindex *n* (*abbreviation* **RPI**) **the retail price index** a list of certain goods and services and how much their prices change each month

ˈretail ˌtherapy *n* [U] the act of buying things that you do not need when you are unhappy because you think it will make you feel better – often used humorously → **shopaholic**: *What you need is a bit of retail therapy!*

re·tain /rɪˈteɪn/ ●●○ W3 AWL *v* [T] *formal*
1 to keep something or continue to have something: *You have the right to retain possession of the goods.* | *The state wants to retain control of food imports.*

> **REGISTER**
> In everyday English, people usually say **keep** rather than **retain**: ***Keep** all your receipts.*

2 to store or keep something inside something else: *A lot of information can be retained in your computer.* | *Limestone is known to retain moisture.*
3 to remember information: *I find it very difficult to retain facts.*
4 if you retain a lawyer or other specialist, you pay them to work for you now and in the future: *He has retained a lawyer to challenge the court's decision.* | *We had to pay a **retaining fee*** (=an amount of money to keep someone working for you).
5 if a company retains workers, it continues to employ them for a long time: *It's increasingly difficult to recruit and retain good staff.*

re·tain·er /rɪˈteɪnə $ -ər/ AWL *n* [C] **1** an amount of money paid to someone, especially a lawyer, so that they will continue to work for you in the future **2** *BrE* a reduced amount of rent that you pay for a room, flat etc when you are not there, so that it will still be available when you return **3** *AmE* a plastic and wire object that you wear in your mouth to make your teeth stay straight SYN **brace** *BrE* **4** *old use* a servant

reˈtaining ˌwall *n* [C] a wall that is built to prevent land from slipping or moving

re·take¹ /ˌriːˈteɪk/ *v* (*past tense* **retook** /-ˈtʊk/, *past participle* **retaken** /-ˈteɪkən/) [T] **1** to get control of an area again in a war SYN **recapture**: *an attempt to retake the city* **2** to take an examination again because you have previously failed it SYN **resit** *BrE*

re·take² /ˈriːteɪk/ *n* [C] **1** an act of filming or photographing something again: *They had to do several retakes before the director was satisfied.* **2** *BrE* an examination or test that you take again because you failed it

re·tal·i·ate /rɪˈtælieɪt/ *v* [I] to do something bad to someone because they have done something bad to you → **hit back**: **retaliate by doing sth** *The British government retaliated by breaking off diplomatic relations.* | **[+against]** *The army began to retaliate against the civilian population.*

re·tal·i·a·tion /rɪˌtæliˈeɪʃən/ *n* [U] action against someone who has done something bad to you → **revenge**: **in retaliation (for sth)** *This action was undoubtedly in retaliation for last week's bomb attack.* | **[+against]** *the threat of **massive retaliation** against British troops*

re·tal·i·a·to·ry /rɪˈtæliətəri $ -tɔːri/ *adj* [usually before noun] *formal* done against someone because they have harmed you: *a retaliatory attack*

re·tard¹ /rɪˈtɑːd $ -ɑːrd/ *v* [T] *formal* to delay the development of something, or to make something happen more slowly than expected SYN **slow down**: *Cold weather retards the growth of many plants.*

re·tard² /ˈriːtɑːd $ -ɑːrd/ *n* [C] *spoken not polite* an offensive word for a stupid person

re·tard·ed /rɪˈtɑːdɪd $ -ɑːr-/ *adj old-fashioned* less mentally developed than other people of the same age. Many people think that this word is offensive.

retch /retʃ/ *v* [I] to try to VOMIT SYN **gag**: *The smell made her retch.*

re·tell /ˌriːˈtel/ *v* (*past tense and past participle* **retold** /-ˈtəʊld $ -ˈtoʊld/) [T] to tell a story again, often in a different way or in a different language

re·ten·tion /rɪˈtenʃən/ ●○○ AWL *n* [U]
1 *formal* the act of keeping something: **[+of]** *The UN will vote on the retention of sanctions against Iraq.*
2 *technical* the ability or tendency of something to hold liquid, heat etc within itself: *Many people with heart problems suffer from fluid retention.*
3 the ability to keep something in your memory: *I have a real problem with retention of information.*

re·ten·tive /rɪˈtentɪv/ AWL *adj* a retentive memory or mind is able to hold facts and remember them → ANAL(2) —**retentiveness** *n* [U]

re·think /riːˈθɪŋk/ *v* (*past tense and past participle* **rethought** /-ˈθɔːt $ -ˈθɒːt/) [I,T] to think about a plan or idea again in order to decide if any changes should be made SYN **reconsider**: *an opportunity to rethink our policy on advertising* —**rethink** /ˈriːθɪŋk/ *n* [singular]: *It's time for a **complete rethink** of the way we farm our countryside.*

ret·i·cent /ˈretəsənt/ *adj* unwilling to talk about what you feel or what you know SYN **reserved**: **[+about]** *She's strangely reticent about her son.* THESAURUS▸ QUIET —**reticence** *n* [U]

re·tic·u·la·ted /rɪˈtɪkjəleɪtɪd/ *adj technical* forming or covered with a pattern of squares and lines that looks like a net

ret·i·na /ˈretənə/ *n* [C] the area at the back of your eye that receives light and sends an image of what you see to your brain

ˌretinal ˈscanner *n* [C] computer equipment that is used to examine someone's retina in order to IDENTIFY them. Retinal scanners are used by the police and IMMIGRATION officials at some airports to check the information on someone's PASSPORT or ID CARD.

ret·i·nue /ˈretɪnjuː $ -nuː/ *n* [C] a group of people who travel with someone important to help and support them: **[+of]** *He travelled with a huge retinue of servants.*

re·tire /rɪˈtaɪə $ -ˈtaɪr/ ●●○ S3 W3 *v*
1 WORK **a)** [I] to stop working, usually because you have reached a certain age: *Most people retire at 65.* | *He was forced to **retire early** because of poor health.* | **[+from]** *I retired from teaching three years ago.* | *her decision to retire from her position as librarian of the law society* | *Her drink problem has forced her to **retire from public life**.* | **[+as]** *He retired as a GP last year.* **b)** [T] to ask someone to stop doing their job, usually because of ill health: *He became ill and was retired early.* GRAMMAR **Retire** is usually passive when used as a transitive verb.
2 QUIET PLACE [I] *formal* to go away to a quiet place: **[+to]** *I retired to my room to think.*
3 JURY [I] when a JURY in a law court retires, they go away to consider whether someone is guilty or not
4 GAME/RACE [I] to stop competing in a game or race because you are losing or injured: *He had to retire with a neck injury in the second half.*
5 BED [I] *literary* to go to bed
6 ARMY [I] to move back from a battle after being defeated

re·tired /rɪˈtaɪəd $ -ˈtaɪrd/ ●●○ *adj* having stopped working, usually because of your age: *a retired teacher* | *Both my parents are retired now.*

re·tir·ee /rɪˌtaɪəˈriː $ -ˌtaɪˈriː/ *n* [C] *AmE* someone who has stopped working, usually because of their age → **pensioner**

re·tire·ment /rɪˈtaɪəmənt $ -ˈtaɪr-/ ●●○ S3 W3 *n*
1 [C,U] when you stop working, usually because of your age: **[+from]** *He became a keen golfer after his retirement*

from politics. | **[+as]** *He announced his retirement as chief executive of the company.* | *She* ***took early retirement*** (=retired at an earlier age than usual) *last year.* | *Dad's approaching* ***retirement age****.*
2 [singular, U] the period after you have stopped work: *I hope you enjoy a long and happy retirement.* | **in retirement** *Will you be able to support yourself in retirement?* | *a retirement pension*

re'tirement ˌhome *n* [C] an OLD PEOPLE'S HOME

re'tirement ˌplan *n* [C] *AmE* a system for saving money for when you stop work, done either through your employer or arranged by you SYN **pension plan**

re·tir·ing /rɪ'taɪərɪŋ $ -'taɪrɪŋ/ *adj* **1** someone who is retiring does not want to be with other people, especially people they do not know SYN **shy**: *As a child, Elizabeth was very shy and retiring.* THESAURUS▸ SHY **2 the retiring president/manager/director etc** a president etc who is soon going to leave their job

re·tool /ˌriː'tuːl/ *v* **1** [T] *AmE informal* to organize something in a new way: *The College Board has retooled the admission exams.* **2** [I,T] to change or replace the machines or tools in a factory

re·tort¹ /rɪ'tɔːt $ -ɔːrt/ ●○○ *v* [T] to reply quickly, in an angry or humorous way: *'It's all your fault!' he retorted.* THESAURUS▸ ANSWER

retort² *n* [C] **1** a short angry or humorous reply: *He was about to make a* ***sharp retort****.* **2** a bottle with a long narrow bent neck, used for heating chemicals

re·touch /ˌriː'tʌtʃ/ *v* [T] to improve a picture or photograph by painting over marks or making other small changes → **airbrush**: *postcards that have been retouched to cover the grey skies*

re·trace /rɪ'treɪs, riː-/ *v* [T] **1 retrace your steps/path/route etc** to go back exactly the way you have come: *After a few minutes, he turned around and began to retrace his steps.* **2** to repeat exactly the same journey that someone else has made: *We shall be retracing the route taken by Marco Polo.* **3** to find out where someone went: *an investigation to retrace the dead man's last known movements*

re·tract /rɪ'trækt/ *v formal* **1** [T] if you retract something that you said or agreed, you say that you did not mean it SYN **withdraw**: *He confessed to the murder but later retracted his statement.* **2** [I,T] if part of a machine or an animal's body retracts or is retracted, it moves back into the main part: *The sea otter can retract the claws on its front feet.*

re·tract·a·ble /rɪ'træktəbəl/ *adj* a retractable part of something can be pulled back into the main part: *a knife with a retractable blade*

re·trac·tion /rɪ'trækʃən/ *n formal* **1** [C] an official statement that something which you said previously is not true: **[+of]** *The newspaper was forced to publish a retraction of its allegations.* **2** [U] the act of pulling one part of something back inside the main part

re·train /ˌriː'treɪn/ *v* [I,T] to learn or to teach someone the skills that are needed to do a different job: *One solution is to retrain the long-term unemployed.* | **[+as]** *She's hoping to retrain as a teacher.* —**retraining** *n* [U]

re·tread /'riːtred/ *n* [C] **1** a old tyre which is given a new rubber surface SYN **remould** **2** *AmE informal* something that is made or done again, with a few changes added - used to show disapproval: *retreads of old TV shows* **3** *AmE informal* someone who has been trained to do work which is different from what they did before

re·treat¹ /rɪ'triːt/ ●○○ *v* [I]
1 ARMY to move away from the enemy after being defeated in battle OPP **advance**: *The rebels retreated to the mountains.* | *They were attacked and forced to retreat.*
2 MOVE BACK *written* **a)** to move away from someone or something: *He saw her and retreated, too shy to speak to her.* | **[+to/from/into etc]** *Perry lit the fuse and retreated to a safe distance.* | *It was not a conscious choice to retreat from public life.* **b)** if an area of water, snow, or land retreats, it gradually gets smaller: *The flood waters are slowly retreating.*
3 CHANGE YOUR MIND *written* to decide not to do something you were planning to do, because it was unpopular or too difficult: **[+from]** *The Canadian government has retreated from a plan to kill 300 wolves.*
4 QUIET PLACE to go away to a place that is quiet or safe: **[+from/into/to]** *After the noise of the city he was glad to retreat to his hotel room.*
5 retreat into yourself/your shell/fantasy etc to ignore what is happening around you and give all your attention to your private thoughts
6 FINANCE *technical* if shares etc retreat, their value falls to a lower level

retreat² ●○○ *n*
1 OF AN ARMY [C,U] a movement away from the enemy after a defeat in battle OPP **advance**: *Napoleon's retreat from Moscow* | *The rebel forces are* ***in full retreat*** (=retreating very fast). | *The bugler sounded the retreat* (=gave a loud signal for retreat).
2 MOVEMENT BACK [singular, U] a movement away from someone or something: **[+from]** *Ten thousand years ago the ice began its retreat from Scotland.*
3 beat a retreat *informal* to leave a place quickly: *I saw my aunt coming and* ***beat a hasty retreat****.*
4 CHANGE OF INTENTION [singular, U] when you change your mind about something because your idea was unpopular or too difficult: **[+from]** *a retreat from hard-line policies*
5 PLACE [C] a place you can go to that is quiet or safe: *a country retreat*
6 THOUGHT AND PRAYER [C,U] a period of time that you spend praying or studying religion in a quiet place: **on (a) retreat** *I spent three weeks on retreat in Scotland.*
7 FINANCE [singular, U] *technical* a situation in which the value of shares etc falls to a lower level

re·trench /rɪ'trentʃ/ *v* [I] *formal* if a government or organization retrenches, it spends less money SYN **economize** —**retrenchment** *n* [C,U]: *a government policy of retrenchment*

re·tri·al /ˌriː'traɪəl,'riːtraɪəl $ ˌriː'traɪəl/ *n* [C] a process of judging a law case in court again → **retry**: *The jury was dismissed and the judge ordered a retrial.*

ret·ri·bu·tion /ˌretrə'bjuːʃən/ *n* [singular, U] severe punishment for something very serious: **[+for]** *Victims are demanding retribution for the terrorist attacks.* | ***divine retribution*** (=punishment by God)

re·triev·al /rɪ'triːvəl/ *n* [U] **1** *technical* the process of getting back information stored on a computer system: *a new system that should speed up information retrieval* **2** the act of getting back something you have lost or left somewhere **3 be beyond/past retrieval** if a situation is beyond retrieval, it has become so bad that it cannot be made right again

re·trieve /rɪ'triːv/ ●○○ *v* [T]
1 *formal* to find something and bring it back → **recover**: *She bent down to retrieve her earring.* | **retrieve sth from sth** *It took four days to retrieve all the bodies from the crash.*
2 *technical* to get back information that has been stored in the memory of a computer: *The new version of the software automatically retrieves digital information.*
3 retrieve a situation *BrE* to make a situation satisfactory again after there has been a serious mistake or problem: *The general made one last desperate effort to retrieve the situation.* —**retrievable** *adj*

re·triev·er /rɪ'triːvə $ -ər/ *n* [C] a type of dog that can be trained to find and bring back birds that its owner has shot

ret·ro¹ /'retrəʊ $ -troʊ/ *adj* based on styles of fashion and design from the recent past: *retro '60s fashions*

retro² *n* (*plural* **retros**) [C] *AmE informal* a RETROSPECTIVE

retro- /retrəʊ, -trə $ -troʊ, -trə/ *prefix* back towards the past or an earlier state: *retroactive legislation* (=laws which have an effect on things already done) | *a retrograde step* (=returning to a worse state)

ret·ro·ac·tive /ˌretrəʊ'æktɪv◂ $ -troʊ-/ *adj formal* a law

R

or decision that is retroactive is effective from a particular date in the past SYN **retrospective**: *a retroactive pay increase* | **[+to]** *The legislation is retroactive to 1st June.* —**retroactively** *adv*

ret·ro·fit /ˈretrəʊfɪt $ -troʊ-/ *v* (**retrofitted**, **retrofitting**) [T] to improve a machine, piece of equipment, building etc by putting new and better parts in it after it has been used for some time: *plans to retrofit oil boilers* —**retrofit** *n* [C] —**retrofitting** *n* [U]

ret·ro·flex /ˈretrəfleks/ *adj technical* a retroflex speech sound is made with the end of your tongue pointing backwards and upwards

ret·ro·grade /ˈretrəgreɪd/ *adj* **1** *formal* involving a return to an earlier and worse situation SYN **backward**: *The closure of the factories is seen as a* ***retrograde step***. **2** *technical* moving backwards SYN **backward**

ret·ro·gres·sive /ˌretrəˈgresɪv◂/ *adj formal* returning to an earlier and worse situation SYN **regressive**: *retrogressive legislation* —**retrogress** *v* [I] —**retrogression** /-ˈgreʃən/ *n* [singular, U]

ret·ro·spect /ˈretrəspekt/ *n* **in retrospect** thinking back to a time in the past, especially with the advantage of knowing more now than you did then: *In retrospect, I wonder if we should have done more.*

ret·ro·spec·tion /ˌretrəˈspekʃən/ *n* [U] *formal* thinking about the past

ret·ro·spec·tive[1] /ˌretrəˈspektɪv◂/ *adj* [usually before noun] **1** related to or thinking about the past: *a retrospective study of 110 patients* **2** *BrE* a law or decision that is retrospective is effective from a particular date in the past SYN **retroactive**: *retrospective legislation* | *Teachers settled for a 4.2% pay rise* ***with retrospective effect*** *from 1 April.* —**retrospectively** *adv*: *The new rule will be applied retrospectively.*

retrospective[2] *n* [C] a show of the work of an ARTIST, actor, FILM-MAKER etc that includes examples of all the kinds of work they have done: *a Hitchcock retrospective* | **[+of]** *a retrospective of painter Hans Hofmann*

ret·ro·vi·rus /ˈretrəʊˌvaɪərəs $ -troʊˌvaɪrəs/ *n* [C] *technical* a VIRUS of a type that includes some CANCER viruses and the AIDS virus, but that also has a quality that makes it useful for GENETIC ENGINEERING

re·try /ˌriːˈtraɪ/ *v* (**retried**, **retrying**, **retries**) [T] **1** to judge a person or a law case again in court → **retrial 2** to do an action on a computer again after it has failed

ret·si·na /retˈsiːnə/ *n* [U] a Greek wine that tastes of the RESIN (=juice) of certain trees

Frequencies of **return**, **get/go/come back**, and **get/go/come home** in spoken and written English.

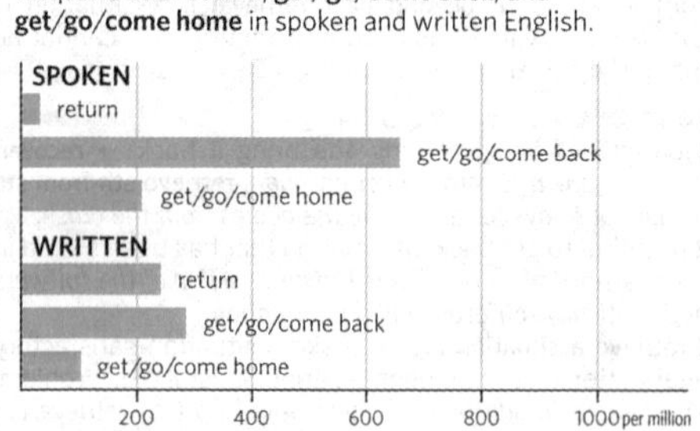

This graph shows that is much more usual in spoken English to use **get/go/come back** or **get/go/come home** rather than **return**. **Return** is much more common in written English than in spoken English.

re·turn[1] /rɪˈtɜːn $ -ɜːrn/ ●●● S2 W1 *v*

1 GO BACK [I] to go or come back to a place where you were before SYN **go back**, **come back**: *It was forty five minutes before she returned.* | **[+to]** *Are you planning to return to Spain?* | **[+from]** *I have just returned from five months in Zimbabwe.* | *Alison decided to* ***return home***. | *He left his country,* ***never to return***.

2 GIVE BACK [T] to give or send something back, or to put something back in its place SYN **give back**, **put back**: **return sth to sth/sb** *Carson returned the notebook to his pocket.* | *I returned the books to the library unread.* | *Please complete the enclosed application form and return it in the envelope attached.*

> **REGISTER**
> In everyday English, people usually say that they **take** something **back**, **put** it **back**, or **bring** it **back**, rather than **return** it: *He* ***put*** *the key* ***back*** *in his pocket.* | *Did you* ***take*** *the books* ***back*** *to the library?*

3 FEELING/SITUATION [I] if a feeling, situation etc returns, it starts to exist or happen again SYN **come back**: *If the pain returns, take two of the tablets with some water.* | *David could feel his anger returning.* | **[+to]** *when peace finally returns to this country*

4 DO THE SAME [T] to do something to someone because they have done the same thing to you: *He smiled at her warmly and she returned his smile.* | *I phoned him twice on Friday and left messages, but he never* ***returned*** *my* ***call*** (=he didn't phone me). | *Thanks very much. I'll* ***return the favour*** (=do something to help you) *some day.* | *The police did not* ***return fire*** (=shoot back at someone who shot at them).

5 ANSWER [T] *written* to answer someone: *'Yes,' he returned. 'I'm a lucky man.'*

6 BALL [T] to hit the ball back to your opponent in a game such as tennis

7 ELECT [T] *BrE* to elect someone to a political position, especially to represent you in parliament: **be returned to sth** *Yeo was returned to Parliament with an increased majority.* | **be returned as sth** *At the election, she was returned as MP for Brighton.* GRAMMAR **Return** is usually passive in this meaning.

8 return a verdict when a JURY return their VERDICT, they say whether someone is guilty or not

9 PROFIT [T] to make a profit: *The group returned increased profits last year.*

> **GRAMMAR: Patterns with return**
> • You **return to** a place: *The writer returned to his home town many years later.* | *Hardy returned to his house in the country.* ✗ Don't say: *The writer returned his home town.* | *Hardy returned his house.*
> • You **return home**: *When she returned home that night, there was a letter for her.* ✗ Don't say: *when she returned to home*

> **THESAURUS**
> **return** to go back or come back to a place where you were before. **Return** sounds more formal than **go back** or **come back**, and is more commonly used in written English: *She returned to the hotel hoping to find a message.* | *Alastair returned from the office late that night.*
> **go back** to go to the place where you were before, or to the place where you usually live: *It's cold out here – shall we go back inside?* | *When are you going back to Japan?*
> **go home** to go to your home again, or to the country where you were born, after you have been away from it: *I did a bit of shopping and then went home.* | *Are you going home to Hong Kong when the course finishes?*
> **come back** to come to the place where you are again, after going away from it: *I'll be away for two days – coming back on Thursday night.* | *He's just come back from a vacation in Miami.*
> **get back** to arrive somewhere where you were before, especially your home or the place where you are staying: *We got back at about 9 o'clock.* | *She couldn't wait to get back to London.*
> **turn back** to turn around and go back in the direction you came from: *We took the wrong road and had to turn back.* | *He ordered the soldiers to turn back and march south.*

return to sth *phr v*
1 to change back to a previous state or situation, or to change something back: *David waited for a moment to let his breathing* ***return to normal.*** | **return sth to sth** *The new chairman made the cuts necessary to return the company to profitability.*
2 to start doing an activity, job etc that you were doing before you stopped or were interrupted SYN **go back**: *Nicholas looked up, grinned, then returned to his newspaper.* | *The children return to school next week.* | *Ellie needed to* ***return to work*** *soon after the birth.*
3 *formal* to start discussing or dealing with a subject that you have already mentioned: *I will return to this problem in a moment.*

return² ●●● S2 W2 *n*
1 COMING BACK [singular] the act of returning from somewhere, or your arrival back in a place: *We're all looking forward to your return!* | **[+from]** *I need to know the date of her return from Europe.* | **[+to]** *Malcolm decided to delay his return to York.* | **on/upon sb's return** *On his return from Canada, he joined the army.*
2 GIVING BACK [singular] the act of giving, putting, or sending something back: **[+of]** *A mother is appealing for the safe return of her baby son.* | *Police have arranged for the return of the stolen goods.*
3 CHANGING BACK [singular] a change back to a previous state or situation: **[+to]** *The United States called for a return to democracy.* | *a return to normal*
4 STARTING AGAIN [singular] when someone starts an activity again after they had stopped: **[+to]** *Rose's return to the teaching profession* | *Jean is well enough now to consider her* ***return to work.***
5 PROFIT [C,U] the amount of profit that you get from something: *The markets are showing extremely poor returns.* | **[+on]** *How can you get the best return on your investment?* | **[+from]** *The returns from farming are declining.* | *The average* ***rates of return*** *were 15%.*
THESAURUS ▸ PROFIT
6 in return (for sth) as payment or reward for something: *He is always helping people without expecting anything in return.* | *We offer an excellent all-round education to our students. In return, we expect students to work hard.* | *Liz agreed to look after the baby in return for a free room.*
7 COMPUTER [U] the key that you press on a computer at the end of an instruction or to move to a new line SYN **enter**: *Key in the file name and press return.*
8 TICKET [C] *BrE* (*also* **return ticket**) a ticket for a journey from one place to another and back again OPP **single** SYN **round trip** *AmE*: *Can I have a return to London please?* → DAY RETURN
9 FEELING/SITUATION [singular] when a feeling, situation etc starts to exist or happen again: **[+of]** *She felt a return of her old anxiety.* | *David had noticed the return of worrying symptoms in the last few days.*
10 STATEMENT [C] a statement giving written information in reply to official questions: *an analysis of the 1851 census returns* → TAX RETURN
11 VOTE [C] *technical* a vote in an election: *What are the returns from last night's voting?*
12 by return (of post) *BrE* if you reply to a letter by return, you send your reply almost immediately → **the point of no return** at POINT¹(10)

return³ *adj* [only before noun] used or paid for a journey from one place to another and back again → **single** SYN **round trip** *AmE*: *a return ticket* | *a return fare*

re·turn·a·ble /rɪˈtɜːnəbəl $ -ɜːr-/ *adj* **1** something that is returnable can be taken back to a shop and used again OPP **non-returnable 2** an amount of money that is returnable will be given back to you later SYN **refundable** OPP **non-returnable**: *a returnable deposit of £50*

reˌturn adˈdress / $ ˌ.ˈ. ˈ../ *n* [C] the address of the person who is sending a letter or package, that is written on the envelope or package

re·tur·nee /rɪˌtɜːˈniː $ -ˌtɜːr-/ *n* [C] a person who returns to their own country after living in another country

re·turn·er /rɪˈtɜːnə $ -ˈtɜːrnər/ *n* [C] *BrE* someone who goes back to work after a long time away, especially a woman who left work to look after her children

reˈturning ˌofficer *n* [C] the official in each town or area of Britain who arranges an election to Parliament and announces the result

reˌturn ˈmatch *n* [C] *BrE* the second of two matches that are played by the same teams or players

reˌturn ˈvisit *n* [C] a visit to someone who has visited you, or to a place where you have been before

re·tweet /riːˈtwiːt/ *v* [T] to send other people a message that you received using the SOCIAL NETWORKING service Twitter: *His tweets on the subject have been retweeted by thousands of people.*

re·u·nify /riːˈjuːnɪfaɪ/ *v* (**reunified, reunifying, reunifies**) [T] to join the parts of something together again, especially a country that was divided —**reunification** /riːˌjuːnɪfɪˈkeɪʃən/ *n* [U]: *German reunification* → REUNITE

re·u·nion /riːˈjuːnjən/ ●○○ *n*
1 [C] a social meeting of people who have not met for a long time, especially people who were at school or college together: *an* ***annual reunion*** | *a* ***family reunion*** | *a high-school reunion*
2 [U] when people are brought together again after a period of being separated: **[+with]** *Joseph's eventual reunion with his brother*

re·u·nite /ˌriːjuːˈnaɪt/ *v* [I,T] to come together again or to bring people, parts of an organization, political party, or country together again: **be reunited with sb** *The children were finally reunited with their families.* | *The band will reunite for a US tour.* GRAMMAR **Reunite** is usually passive when used as a transitive verb.

re·use /ˌriːˈjuːz/ *v* [T] to use something again: *The bottles are designed to be reused up to 20 times.* —**reusable** *adj*: *reusable containers* —**reuse** /ˌriːˈjuːs/ *n* [U]: *to purify water for reuse*

rev¹ /rev/ (*also* **rev up**) *v* (**revved, revving**) [I,T] if you rev an engine, or if an engine revs, you make it work faster
rev up *phr v informal* if you rev up a system or organization, or if it revs up, it becomes more active: **[+for]** *They are revving up for one of the biggest fund-raising events ever organized.* | **rev sth ↔ up** *Investors keep putting money in U.S. companies, revving up the economy even more.*

rev² *n* [C] *informal* a complete turn of a wheel or engine part, used as a unit for measuring the speed of an engine SYN **revolution**

Rev *BrE*, **Rev.** *AmE* (*also* **Revd** *BrE*) (***Reverend***) a title used before the name of a minister of the Christian church: *Rev D Macleod*

re·val·ue /ˌriːˈvæljuː/ *v* [T] **1** to examine something again in order to calculate its present value: *The company's land has been revalued at £16.9m.* **2** to increase the value of a country's money in relation to that of other countries OPP **devalue**: *The dollar has just been revalued.* GRAMMAR **Revalue** is usually passive. —**revaluation** /riːˌvæljuˈeɪʃən/ *n* [C,U]

re·vamp /riːˈvæmp/ *v* [T] *informal* to change something in order to improve it and make it seem more modern: *Many older companies are revamping their image.* —**revamp** /ˈriːvæmp/ (*also* **revamping**) *n* [C]

Revd a British form of REV

re·veal¹ /rɪˈviːl/ ●●● W1 AWL *v* [T]
1 to make known something that was previously secret or unknown OPP **conceal**: *He may be prosecuted for revealing secrets about the security agency.* | *a test that can reveal a teacher's hidden skills* | **reveal (that)** *He revealed that he had been in prison twice before.* | **reveal yourself (as/to be sth)** *The violinist revealed himself as a talented interpreter of classical music.*
2 to show something that was previously hidden OPP **conceal**: *The curtain opened to reveal the grand prize.*
THESAURUS ▸ SHOW

THESAURUS

reveal to let someone know about something that is secret or has not been known until now: *Doctors are*

R

not allowed to reveal confidential information. | *It was revealed that he had smoked marijuana at college.*
tell to talk about something to someone, so that they know about it: *Don't tell anyone about this just yet.* | *Shall I tell you a secret?*
disclose *formal* to publicly reveal something such as a fact or a name that has been kept secret: *The terms of the agreement have not yet been disclosed.*
divulge /daɪˈvʌldʒ, də-/ *formal* to reveal important or personal information which was previously secret or unknown: *The bank has refused to divulge its plans.* | *I'm afraid I cannot divulge what was said to me.*
make sth public to tell people about important information, especially after it has been kept secret: *Apparently they were engaged for some time before making it public.*
leak to deliberately give secret information to a newspaper, television company etc, when a government or other organization wants to keep it secret: *The contents of the email were leaked to the press.*
give sth away (*also* **spill the beans** *informal*) to tell someone something that you want to keep secret: *He was careful not to give away any trade secrets.* | *I'm not going to give away how much I paid for it!*
let slip *informal* to accidentally tell someone about something: *He let slip that he was envious of his older brother.*

R

reveal[2] *n* [singular] the time, especially on a television programme, when something that was previously secret or unknown is shown or made known, or when a changed person or thing is shown: *After the garden makeover, it was time to bring the owners back for the big reveal.*

re·veal·ing /rɪˈviːlɪŋ/ AWL *adj* **1** a remark or event that is revealing shows you something interesting or surprising about a situation or someone's character: *a revealing insight into her life* **2** revealing clothes allow parts of your body to be seen which are usually kept covered → **low-cut**: *a very revealing dress* —**revealingly** *adv*

re·veil·le /rɪˈvæli $ ˈrevəli/ *n* [singular, U] a special tune played as a signal to wake soldiers in the morning, or the time at which it is played

rev·el /ˈrevəl/ *v* (**revelled**, **revelling** *BrE*, **reveled**, **reveling** *AmE*) [I] *old use* to spend time dancing, eating, drinking etc, especially at a party —**revel** *n* [C usually plural]

revel in sth *phr v* to enjoy something very much: *He revelled in his new-found fame.*

rev·e·la·tion /ˌrevəˈleɪʃən/ ●○○ AWL *n*
1 [C] a surprising fact about someone or something that was previously secret and is now made known: **[+about/concerning]** *He resigned after revelations about his affair.* | ***startling revelations** about his background* | **revelation that** *revelations that two senior officers had lied in court*
2 [U] the act of suddenly making known a surprising fact that had previously been secret: **[+of]** *the revelation of previously unknown facts*
3 [C] *informal* something that is surprisingly good, enjoyable, or useful: **[+to]** *Alice Walker's novel was a real revelation to me.*
4 [C,U] an event, experience etc that is considered to be a message from God —**revelatory** /ˌrevəˈleɪtəri $ ˈrevələtɔːri/ *adj*: *His playing has many moments of revelatory insights.*

rev·el·ler *BrE*, **reveler** *AmE* /ˈrevələ $ -lər/ *n* [C usually plural] someone who is having fun singing, dancing etc in a noisy way

rev·el·ry /ˈrevəlri/ *n* [U] (*also* **revelries** [plural]) wild noisy dancing, eating, drinking etc, usually to celebrate something → **celebration**

re·venge[1] /rɪˈvendʒ/ ●●○ *n* [U]
1 something you do in order to punish someone who has harmed or offended you: **[+for]** *She wanted revenge for the insult.* | **[+against/on]** *At his wife's funeral, he vowed revenge against her killer.* | **in revenge for sth** *a bomb attack in revenge for the imprisonment of the terrorists*
2 the defeat of someone who has previously defeated you in a sport: **[+for]** *The Australians **took revenge** for their defeat here last time.* | *a revenge match* —**revengeful** *adj*

COLLOCATIONS

VERBS
take revenge *He dreamed of taking revenge on his father's killers.*
get (your) revenge *Louise eventually got her revenge by reporting him to the immigration service.*
have your revenge *One day I'll have my revenge.*
seek revenge | **want revenge** | **exact/wreak revenge** *formal* (=take revenge) | **vow revenge** (=promise to take revenge)

ADJECTIVES
a terrible/awful revenge *Caesar returned to Rome to exact a terrible revenge.*

revenge + NOUN
a revenge attack *The camp was burned down, apparently in a revenge attack.*
a revenge killing

PHRASES
an act of revenge *The men were shot dead in an act of revenge for Khan's assassination.*
revenge is sweet (=said when someone feels good because they have got revenge) *It took me a long time, but revenge is sweet.*

revenge[2] *v* [T] *formal* to punish someone who has done something to harm you or someone else: **revenge yourself on sb** *The terrorist group is still looking to revenge itself on its attackers.* | *The poor murdered girl must be revenged.*

rev·e·nue /ˈrevənjuː $ -nuː/ ●○○ AWL *n* [U] (*also* **revenues** [plural])
1 money that a business or organization receives over a period of time, especially from selling goods or services → **income**: *advertising revenue* | *Strikes have cost £20 million in **lost revenues**.*
2 money that the government receives from tax: *an increase in **tax revenues** of 8.4%* → INTERNAL REVENUE SERVICE

re·ver·be·rate /rɪˈvɜːbəreɪt $ -ɜːr-/ *v* [I] **1** if a loud sound reverberates, it is heard many times as it is sent back from different surfaces SYN **echo**: **[+through/around etc]** *The bang reverberated through the house.* **2** if a room, building etc reverberates, it seems to shake because of a loud sound: **[+with]** *The room reverberated with laughter.* **3** if an event, action, or idea reverberates, it has a strong effect over a wide area and for a long time: **[+through/around etc]** *The events of 9/11 will reverberate through history.*

re·ver·be·ra·tion /rɪˌvɜːbəˈreɪʃən $ -ɜːr-/ *n* **1** [C usually plural] a severe effect that is caused by a particular event and continues for a long time SYN **repercussion**: *the scandal's political reverberations* **2** [C,U] a loud sound that is heard again and again as it is sent back from different surfaces → **echo**

re·vere /rɪˈvɪə $ -ˈvɪr/ *v* [T usually passive] *formal* to respect and admire someone or something very much: **be revered as sth** *He is revered as a national hero.* GRAMMAR **Revere** is usually passive. **THESAURUS** ADMIRE

rev·e·rence /ˈrevərəns/ *n* [U] *formal* great respect and admiration for someone or something: **[+for]** *reverence for tradition*

rev·e·rend /ˈrevərənd/ *n* [C] a minister of a Christian church

Reverend *n* a title of respect used before the name of a minister in the Christian church

ˌReverend ˈMother *n* a title of respect for the woman in charge of a CONVENT SYN **Mother Superior**

rev·e·rent /ˈrevərənt/ *adj formal* showing a lot of respect and admiration OPP **irreverent**: *a hushed reverent voice* —**reverently** *adv*

rev·e·ren·tial /ˌrevəˈrenʃəl◂/ *adj formal* showing a lot of respect and admiration: *He spoke in reverential tones.* —**reverentially** *adv*

rev·e·rie /'revəri/ *n* [C,U] a state of imagining or thinking about pleasant things, that is like dreaming → **daydream**: *She was startled out of her reverie by a loud crash.*

re·vers·al /rɪ'vɜːsəl $ -ɜːr-/ ●○○ AWL *n*
1 [C,U] a change to an opposite arrangement, process, or way of doing something → **turnaround**: **[+of/in]** *a sudden reversal of government policy* | **dramatic/sudden/complete reversal** *a dramatic reversal in population decline* | *Some Internet firms have suffered a painful* ***reversal of fortune*** (=they were successful but now they are not). | *Some carers and dependants find it difficult to adapt to a* ***role reversal****.*
2 [C] a failure or other problem that prevents you from being able to do what you want: *In spite of setbacks and reversals, his business was at last making money.*

re·verse¹ /rɪ'vɜːs $ -ɜːrs/ ●●○ W3 AWL *v*
1 OPPOSITE [T] to change something, such as a decision, judgment, or process so that it is the opposite of what it was before: **reverse a decision/verdict/policy etc** *The decision was reversed on appeal.* | **reverse a trend/process/decline etc** *More changes are required to reverse the trend towards centralised power.*
2 CAR [I,T] *especially BrE* if a vehicle or its driver reverses, they go backwards SYN **back up** *AmE*: **[+out of/into etc]** *Bob reversed into a parking space.* | **reverse sth into/out of sth** *I reversed the car into a side road.*
3 CHANGE POSITION/PURPOSE [T] to change around the usual order of the parts of something, or the usual things two people do SYN **swap**: **reverse roles/positions** *Our roles as child and guardian had now been reversed.*
4 TURN STH OVER [T] to turn something over or around, in order to show the back of it: *Reverse the paper in the printer.*
5 reverse yourself *AmE* to change your opinion or position in an argument: *Suddenly, he reversed himself completely.*
6 reverse the charges *BrE* to make a telephone call which is paid for by the person you are telephoning SYN **call collect** *AmE*

reverse² ●○○ AWL *n*
1 OPPOSITE **the reverse** the exact opposite of what has just been mentioned: **quite/just/precisely/exactly the reverse** *I didn't mean to insult her – quite the reverse* (=in fact, I meant to praise her). | *I owe you nothing. If anything,* ***the reverse is true*** (=you owe me).
2 in reverse in the opposite way to normal or to the previous situation → **vice versa**: *US video recorders cannot play European tapes, and the same applies in reverse.*
3 go into reverse/put sth into reverse to start to happen or to make something happen in the opposite way: *The incident threatened to put the peace process into reverse.*
4 CAR [U] the position of the GEARS in a vehicle that makes it go backwards: **into/in reverse** *Put the car into reverse.*
5 DEFEAT [C] *formal* a defeat or a problem that delays your plans SYN **setback**: *Losing the Senate vote was a serious reverse for the president.*
6 OTHER SIDE [singular] the less important side or the back of an object that has two sides: **on the reverse** *The British ten-pence coin has a lion on the reverse.*

reverse³ ●○○ AWL *adj* [only before noun]
1 reverse order/situation/process etc the opposite order etc to what is usual or to what has just been stated: *The results were read out in reverse order* (=with the worst first and the best last).
2 the reverse side the back of something

reˌverse discrimiˈnation *n* [U] the practice of giving unfair treatment to a group of people who usually have advantages, in order to be fair to the group of people who were unfairly treated in the past → **positive discrimination**

reˌverse engiˈneering *n* [U] *technical* a situation in which a product is examined to see how it is made, so that it can be copied —**reverse engineer** *v* [T]

reˌverse ˈgear *n* [C,U] the position of the GEARS in a vehicle that makes it go backwards

reˌverse ˈsnobbery *n* [U] the idea that things that well-educated or upper-class people like must be bad SYN **inverted snobbery** *BrE*: *There's a lot of reverse snobbery about opera.*

re·vers·i·ble /rɪ'vɜːsəbəl $ -ɜːr-/ AWL *adj* **1** a change that is reversible can be changed back to how it was before OPP **irreversible**: *A lot of chemical reactions are reversible.* **2** a piece of clothing or material that is reversible can be worn with either side showing on the outside: *a reversible jacket*

reˈversing ˌlight *n* [C] *BrE* a light on the back of a car which comes on when the car is going backwards → **taillight** → see picture at CAR

re·ver·sion /rɪ'vɜːʃən $ rɪ'vɜːrʒən/ *n* [singular, U] *formal*
1 a return to a former condition or habit: **[+to]** *the country's reversion to a traditional monarchy* **2** *law* the return of property to a former owner

re·vert /rɪ'vɜːt $ -ɜːrt/ ●○○ *v*
revert to sb/sth *phr v*
1 to change back to a situation that existed in the past SYN **go back to**: *The city reverted to its former name of St Petersburg.* | *After a few weeks, everything* ***reverted to normal****.*
2 *formal* to return to an earlier subject of conversation SYN **go back to**: *To revert to the question of exams, I'd like to explain further.*
3 *law* if land or a building reverts to its former owner, it becomes their property again

re·vet·ment /rɪ'vetmənt/ *n* [C] *technical* a surface of stone or other building material added for strength to a wall that holds back loose earth, water etc

re·view¹ /rɪ'vjuː/ ●●● S2 W2 *n*
1 [C,U] a careful examination of a situation or process → **evaluation, analysis**: **[+of]** *She sent us her review of the research.* | **carry out/conduct/undertake a review** *The company hired Bob to conduct an independent review of their workplace procedures.* | **review body/committee/panel/board** *the Teachers' Pay Review Body* | **under review** *We're keeping this policy under review* (=we are continuing to examine it). | *The policy* ***comes up for review*** (=will be reviewed) *in April.* | *All fees are* ***subject to review*** (=may be reviewed). | *Mr Crowther asked for* ***judicial review*** *of the decision* (=an examination of the decision by a judge).
2 [C] an article in a newspaper or magazine that gives an opinion about a new book, play, film etc: *a film review* | **[+of]** *The paper published a review of her book.* | **good/bad/mixed review** *The band's new album has had very good reviews.* | *The film opened to* ***rave reviews*** (=reviews that praised it a lot).
3 [U] the work of writing reviews for a newspaper or magazine: **for review** *The book was sent to the press for review in September.* | *The journal receives* ***review copies*** (=free copies to review) *of most new software products.*
4 [C] a report on a series of events or a period of time, that mentions the most important parts: **[+of]** *a review of the year*
5 [C] an official show of the army, navy etc so that a king, president, or officer of high rank can see them: *a naval review*

review² ●●● S3 W3 *v* [T]
1 to examine, consider, and judge a situation or process carefully in order to see if changes are necessary → **evaluate, analyse**: *We will review your situation and decide how we can help you.* | *The decision will be reviewed by the Supreme Court.* | *The team manager's position will be reviewed at the end of the season.* THESAURUS EXAMINE
2 to write a short article describing and judging a new book, play, film etc: *Bradman will review the best of the new children's books.*
3 *AmE* to look again at something you have studied, such as notes, reports etc SYN **revise** *BrE*
4 to examine and describe the most important parts of a series of events or period of time: *a journalist who will review the events of the past six months*
5 to officially watch a group of soldiers, ships etc at a military show: *The president will review the soldiers on parade.*

re·view·er /rɪ'vjuːə $ -ər/ ●○○ *n* [C] someone who

R

writes about new books, plays, films etc in a newspaper or magazine SYN **critic**

re·vile /rɪˈvaɪl/ v [T] *written* to express hatred of someone or something SYN **hate**: *The president was now reviled by the same party he had helped to lead.*

re·vise /rɪˈvaɪz/ ●●○ AWL v
1 [T] to change something because of new information or ideas: *The college has revised its plans because of local objections.* | *We have revised our estimates of population growth.* | **revise sth upwards/downwards** *Forecasts of economic growth are being revised downwards.*
2 [I,T] *BrE* to study facts again, in order to learn them before an examination SYN **review, study** *AmE*: *I've got to revise my geography.* | **[+for]** *She's revising for her history exam.* **THESAURUS** LEARN, STUDY
3 [T] to change a piece of writing by adding new information, making improvements, or correcting mistakes → **amend**: *A couple of sections of the book will need to be revised.*

re·vi·sion /rɪˈvɪʒən/ ●○○ AWL n
1 [C,U] the process of changing something in order to improve it by correcting it or including new information or ideas → **amendment**: **[+of]** *The judge wants to see a revision of the procedures.* | **[+to]** *I'm* ***making*** *some* ***revisions*** *to the book for the new edition.*
2 [C] a piece of writing that has been improved and corrected
3 [U] *BrE* the work of studying facts again in order to learn them: *I know I haven't* ***done*** *enough* ***revision*** *for tomorrow's exam.*

re·vi·sion·is·m /rɪˈvɪʒənɪzəm/ n [U] ideas which are changing away from the main beliefs of a political system, especially a Marxist system —**revisionist** *adj*: *revisionist writings* —**revisionist** *n* [C]

re·vis·it /ˌriːˈvɪzɪt/ v [T] **1** *written* to return to a place you once knew well: *Ten years later, I revisited the school to find out what had changed.* **2** *formal* to consider or discuss something again: *We need to revisit this proposal as soon as the budget is clearer.*

re·vi·tal·ize (*also* **-ise** *BrE*) /riːˈvaɪtəlaɪz/ v [T] to put new strength or power into something → **revive**: *They hope to revitalize the neighborhood by providing better housing.* | *a revitalizing massage* —**revitalization** /riːˌvaɪtəlaɪˈzeɪʃən $ -tl-ə-/ n [U]

re·vi·val /rɪˈvaɪvəl/ ●○○ n
1 [C,U] a process in which something becomes active or strong again: *The US and the UK have expectations of economic revival.* | **[+of]** *A revival of the timber industry is needed.* | *There has been a* ***revival of interest*** *in Picasso's work.*
2 [C,U] when something becomes popular again: **[+of/in]** *the recent revival in medieval music* | *a revival of organized religion* | *Traditional English food seems to be* ***enjoying a revival*** *at the moment.*
3 [C] a new production of a play that has not been performed for a long time: *Neeson was excellent in a revival of Eugene O'Neill's 'Anna Christie'.*
4 [C] a REVIVAL MEETING

re·vi·val·is·m /rɪˈvaɪvəlɪzəm/ n [U] organized attempts to make a religion more popular —**revivalist** *adj*

reˈvival ˌmeeting n [C] a public religious meeting with music, famous speakers etc, which is intended to make people interested in Christianity

re·vive /rɪˈvaɪv/ ●○○ v
1 [T] to bring something back after it has not been used or has not existed for a period of time: *Local people have decided to revive this centuries-old tradition.*
2 [I,T] to become healthy and strong again, or to make someone or something healthy and strong again → **recover**: *The economy is beginning to revive.* | *an attempt to revive the steel industry* | *The doctors revived her with injections of glucose.*
3 [T] to produce a play again after it has not been performed for a long time: *A London theatre has decided to revive the 1950s musical 'In Town'.*

re·viv·i·fy /riːˈvɪvɪfaɪ/ v (**revivified, revivifying, revivifies**) [T] *formal* to give new life and health to someone or something: *The aim was to strengthen and revivify the Labour Party.*

rev·o·ca·tion /ˌrevəˈkeɪʃən/ n [C,U] *formal* the act of revoking a law, decision, or agreement → **revoke**

re·voke /rɪˈvəʊk $ -ˈvoʊk/ v [T] to officially state that a law, decision, or agreement is no longer effective → **revocation**: *Their work permits have been revoked.*

re·volt¹ /rɪˈvəʊlt $ -ˈvoʊlt/ ●○○ n [C,U]
1 a refusal to accept someone's authority or obey rules or laws SYN **rebellion**: *The prime minister is now facing a revolt by members of his own party.* | **[+against]** *a revolt against authority* | **[+over]** *a revolt over the proposed spending cuts* | **in revolt** *French farmers are in revolt over cheap imports.* **THESAURUS** REVOLUTION
2 strong and often violent action by a lot of people against their ruler or government SYN **rebellion** → **revolution**: *the Polish revolt of 1863* | **[+against]** *a revolt against the central government* | **[+of]** *the successful revolt of the American colonies* | **put down/crush a revolt** (=use military force to stop it) *Troops loyal to the president crushed the revolt.*

revolt² v **1** [I] if people revolt, they take strong and often violent action against the government, usually with the aim of taking power away from them SYN **rebel** → **revolution**: **[+against]** *It was feared that the army would revolt against the government.* **2** [I] to refuse to accept someone's authority or obey rules or laws SYN **rebel**: **[+against]** *Some members of the government may revolt against this proposed legislation.* **3** [T] if something revolts you, it is so unpleasant that it makes you feel sick and shocked → **revulsion**: *He was revolted by the smell.*

re·volt·ing /rɪˈvəʊltɪŋ $ -ˈvoʊl-/ ●○○ *adj* extremely unpleasant SYN **disgusting**: *The food was revolting!* | *What a revolting colour!* **THESAURUS** HORRIBLE, TASTE —**revoltingly** *adv*

rev·o·lu·tion /ˌrevəˈluːʃən/ ●●○ W3 AWL n
1 [C] a complete change in ways of thinking, methods of working etc: **[+in]** *In the last ten years there has been a revolution in education.* | **social/cultural/sexual etc revolution** *the biggest social revolution we have had in this country* | *the sexual revolution of the 1960s* → INDUSTRIAL REVOLUTION, THE
2 [C,U] a time when people change a ruler or political system by using force or violence → **revolt, rebellion**: *the French Revolution of 1789* | *The role of women has changed since the revolution.* | *The country seems to be heading towards revolution.* → COUNTER-REVOLUTION
3 a) [C,U] a circular movement around something → **revolve**: **[+around]** *the planets' revolution around the Sun* **b)** [C] one complete circular spinning movement, made by something such as a wheel attached to a central point → **revolve**: *a speed of 100 revolutions per minute*

THESAURUS

revolt/rebellion/uprising an attempt by a large group of people at revolution: ***a popular uprising*** (=involving ordinary people, not the army)

coup /kuː/ an occasion when a group of people, especially soldiers, suddenly take control of a country: *a military coup*

rev·o·lu·tion·a·ry¹ /ˌrevəˈluːʃənəri◂ $ -ʃəneri◂/ ●○○ AWL *adj*
1 completely new and different, especially in a way that leads to great improvements: *The new cancer drug is a revolutionary breakthrough.* | *a* ***revolutionary new*** *drug* **THESAURUS** NEW
2 [only before noun] relating to a political or social revolution: *a revolutionary leader*

revolutionary² AWL n (*plural* **revolutionaries**) [C] someone who joins in or supports a political or social revolution → **rebel**: *a band of young revolutionaries*

ˌRevolutionary ˈWar, the the American Revolutionary War in which the US became independent of Britain

rev·o·lu·tion·ize (*also* **-ise** *BrE*) /ˌrevəˈluːʃənaɪz/ ●○○ AWL *v* [T] to completely change the way people do something or think about something: *New technology is going to revolutionize everything we do.* | *His work revolutionized the treatment of this disease.*

re·volve /rɪˈvɒlv $ rɪˈvɑːlv/ ●○○ *v* [I,T] to move around like a wheel, or to make something move around like a wheel → **revolution**, **turn**: *The wheel began to revolve.* | *The restaurant slowly revolves, giving excellent views of the city.* | *Using graphics software, you can revolve the image on the screen.*

revolve around sb/sth (*also* **revolve round sb/sth** *BrE*) *phr v*
1 [not in progressive] to have something as a main subject or purpose: *Jane's life revolves around her children.* | *The argument revolved around costs.* | *She seems to think that* ***the world revolves around*** *her* (=that she is the only important person).
2 to move in circles around something: *The Moon revolves around the Earth.*

re·volv·er /rɪˈvɒlvə $ rɪˈvɑːlvər/ *n* [C] a type of small gun. The bullets are in a case which turns around as you fire the gun, so that when you fire one bullet the next bullet is ready to be fired. → **handgun**, **pistol**

re·volv·ing /rɪˈvɒlvɪŋ $ -ˈvɑːl-/ *adj* a revolving object is designed so that it turns with a circular movement: *The theatre has a revolving stage.*

reˌvolving ˈdoor *n*
1 [C] a type of door in the entrance of a large building, which goes around and around as people go through it **2** [singular] used to say that the people involved in a situation, organization etc change often: *The park director position has been a revolving door for seven appointees.* **3** [singular] used to say that people return to a situation, position etc often, but usually for a different reason: *This could mean that we end up with a revolving door Congress, in which former members return as lobbyists.*

REVOLVING DOOR

re·vue /rɪˈvjuː/ *n* [C] a show in a theatre that includes songs, dances, and jokes about recent events

re·vul·sion /rɪˈvʌlʃən/ *n* [U] a strong feeling of shock and very strong dislike SYN **disgust** → **revolt**: *News of the atrocities produced a wave of anger and revulsion.*

re·ward¹ /rɪˈwɔːd $ -ˈwɔːrd/ ●●● W3 *n*
1 [C,U] something that you get because you have done something good or helpful or have worked hard → **prize**, **benefit**: *The school has a system of rewards and punishments to encourage good behaviour.* | **reward for (doing) sth** *Parents often give their children rewards for passing exams.*
2 [C,U] money that is offered to people for helping the police to solve a crime or catch a criminal: **[+of]** *A reward of $20,000 has been offered.* | **[+for]** *a reward for information leading to the capture of the murderers*

COLLOCATIONS

ADJECTIVES

great/big/high *The rewards for those who invested at the right time are high.*
little reward *They have to work very hard for very little reward.*
financial/economic reward (*also* **monetary reward** *formal*) *It's a difficult job, but the financial rewards are considerable.*
material rewards (=money or possessions that you get) | **tangible rewards** (=things that are obviously worth having) | **rich rewards** (=great rewards) | **personal reward**

VERBS

get/receive your reward *If you work hard, you will get your reward.*
reap rewards (=get them) *She is now reaping the rewards of all her hard work.*
bring rewards (=cause someone to get rewards) | **deserve a reward**

reward² ●●○ *v* [T]
1 to give something to someone because they have done something good or helpful or have worked for it → **award**: **reward sb with sth** *The club's directors rewarded him with a free season ticket.* | **reward sb for (doing) sth** *She wanted to reward the cleaners for their efforts.* | *He gave the children some chocolate to reward them for behaving well.*
2 be rewarded (with sth) to achieve something through hard work and effort: *The team have worked hard and their* ***efforts*** *have been* ***rewarded*** *with success.* | *Finally, Molly's patience was rewarded.*

re·ward·ing /rɪˈwɔːdɪŋ $ -ɔːr-/ ●○○ *adj* making you feel happy and satisfied because you feel you are doing something useful or important, even if you do not earn much money → **satisfying**, **worthwhile**: *Teaching can be a very rewarding career.*

re·wind /riːˈwaɪnd/ *v* (*past tense and past participle* **rewound** /-ˈwaʊnd/) [T] to make a CASSETTE tape or VIDEO go backwards in order to see or hear it again → **fast forward**

re·wire /ˌriːˈwaɪə $ -ˈwaɪr/ *v* [T] to put new electric wires in a building, machine, light etc

re·word /ˌriːˈwɜːd $ -ˈwɜːrd/ *v* [T] to say or write something again in different words, in order to make it easier to understand or more suitable SYN **rephrase**: *Let me reword my question.*

re·work /ˌriːˈwɜːk $ -ˈwɜːrk/ *v* [T] to make changes in something such as music or a piece of writing SYN **revise**: *I plan to rework the whole song.*

re·write /ˌriːˈraɪt/ ●○○ *v* (*past tense* **rewrote** /-ˈrəʊt $ -ˈroʊt/, *past participle* **rewritten** /-ˈrɪtn/) [T] to change something that has been written, especially in order to improve it, or because new information is available SYN **revise**: *I'll have to rewrite most of the essay.* —**rewrite** /ˈriːraɪt/ *n* [C]: *Software packages may need complete rewrites to match new hardware.*

Rex /reks/ *n BrE* **1** a title used in official writing after the name of a king, when the king's name has been written in Latin: *Henricus Rex* (=King Henry) **2** *law* a word meaning the state, used in the names of law cases in Britain when a king is ruling → **regina**: *Rex v Jones*

rhap·so·dize (*also* **-ise** *BrE*) /ˈræpsədaɪz/ *v* [I] *formal* to talk about something in an eager, excited, and approving way SYN **enthuse**: **[+about/over]** *I could hear Sophie rhapsodizing about her new job.*

rhap·so·dy /ˈræpsədi/ *n* (*plural* **rhapsodies**) [C]
1 a piece of music that is written to express emotion, and does not have a regular form: *Gershwin's Rhapsody in Blue*
2 *formal* an expression of eager and excited approval: *The performance was greeted with rhapsodies of praise.*

Rhe·sus fac·tor /ˈriːsəs ˌfæktə $ -tər/ *n* [singular] a substance that some people have in their blood

rhesus mon·key /ˈriːsəs ˌmʌŋki/ *n* [C] a small monkey from northern India that is often used in medical tests

rhet·o·ric /ˈretərɪk/ ●○○ *n* [U]
1 language that is used to persuade or influence people, especially language that sounds impressive but is not actually sincere or useful: *The speech was dismissed by some people as merely* ***political rhetoric****.* | **[+of]** *the rhetoric of socialism*
2 the art of speaking or writing to persuade or influence people

rhe·tor·i·cal /rɪˈtɒrɪkəl $ -ˈtɔː-, -ˈtɑː-/ *adj*
1 rhetorical question a question that you ask as a way of making a statement, without expecting an answer
2 using speech or writing in special ways in order to

persuade people or to produce an impressive effect: *a speech full of rhetorical phrases* —**rhetorically** /-kli/ *adv*

rhet·o·ri·cian /ˌretəˈrɪʃən/ *n* [C] *formal* someone who is trained or skilful in the art of persuading or influencing people through speech or writing → **orator**

rheu·mat·ic /ruːˈmætɪk/ *adj* **1** relating to rheumatism: *a rheumatic disease | rheumatic pain* **2** *old-fashioned* suffering from rheumatism: *He's old and rheumatic and can't manage the stairs any longer.*

rheuˌmatic ˈfever *n* [U] a serious infectious disease that causes fever, swelling in your joints, and sometimes damage to your heart

rheu·ma·tis·m /ˈruːmətɪzəm/ *n* [U] a disease that makes your joints or muscles painful and stiff → **arthritis**

rheu·ma·toid ar·thri·tis /ˌruːmətɔɪd ɑːˈθraɪtɪs $ -ɑːr-/ *n* [U] a disease that continues for many years and makes your joints painful and stiff, and often makes them lose their proper shape

RH fac·tor /ˌɑːr ˈeɪtʃ ˌfæktə $ -tər/ *n* [singular] the RHESUS FACTOR

rhine·stone /ˈraɪnstəʊn $ -stoʊn/ *n* [C,U] a jewel made from glass or a transparent rock that is intended to look like a diamond

rhi·no /ˈraɪnəʊ $ -noʊ/ *n* (*plural* **rhinos**) [C] *informal* a rhinoceros

rhi·no·ce·ros /raɪˈnɒsərəs $ -ˈnɑː-/ *n* (*plural* **rhinoceros** *or* **rhinoceroses**) [C] a large heavy African or Asian animal with thick skin and either one or two horns on its nose → **hippopotamus**

R

rhi·no·plas·ty /ˈraɪnəʊˌplæsti $ -noʊ-/ *n* [U] *medical* PLASTIC SURGERY on your nose → **nose job**

rhi·zome /ˈraɪzəʊm $ -zoʊm/ *n* [C] *technical* the thick stem of some plants, which lies under the ground and has roots and leaves growing out of it

rho·do·den·dron /ˌrəʊdəˈdendrən $ ˌroʊ-/ *n* [C] a bush with bright flowers which keeps its leaves in winter

rhom·boid[1] /ˈrɒmbɔɪd $ ˈrɑːm-/ *n* [C] *technical* a shape with four sides whose opposite sides are equal in length SYN **parallelogram**

rhomboid[2] (*also* **rhom·boid·al**) /rɒmˈbɔɪdl $ rɑːm-/ *adj technical* shaped like a rhombus

rhom·bus /ˈrɒmbəs $ ˈrɑːm-/ *n* [C] *technical* a shape with four equal straight sides, especially one that is not a square → see picture at SHAPE[1]

rhu·barb /ˈruːbɑːb $ -ɑːrb/ *n* [U] **1** a plant with broad leaves. It has thick red stems that can be cooked and eaten. → see picture at FRUIT[1] **2** *spoken* a word repeated by actors to make a sound like many people talking

rhyme[1] /raɪm/ ●○○ *n*
1 [C] a short poem or song, especially for children, using words that rhyme: *a collection of traditional rhymes with illustrations* → NURSERY RHYME
2 [C] a word that rhymes with another word: **[+for]** *Can you think of a rhyme for 'bicycle'?*
3 [U] words or lines of poetry that rhyme: *I love his use of rhyme and rhythm.* | **in rhyme** *The whole story is written in rhyme.*
4 no rhyme or reason no sensible reason or organization: *There seems to be no rhyme or reason for the school's behaviour.*

rhyme[2] ●○○ *v*
1 [I] if two words or lines of poetry rhyme, they end with the same sound, including a vowel: **[+with]** *'Hat' rhymes with 'cat'.* | *The song has* ***rhyming couplets*** (=pairs of lines that end in words that rhyme).

GRAMMAR: Using the progressive
• **Rhyme** is not used in the progressive. You say: *'Fruit' rhymes with 'toot'.* ✗ Don't say: *'Fruit' is rhyming with 'toot'.*
• However, the participle **rhyming** is used as an adjective: *Underline the rhyming words.*
GRAMMAR GUIDE ▸ VERBS

2 [T] to put two or more words together to make them rhyme: **rhyme sth with sth** *You can't rhyme 'box' with 'backs'.*

ˌrhyming ˈslang *n* [U] *BrE* a way of talking, used especially by COCKNEYS (=people from east London), in which you use words or phrases that rhyme with the words you mean, instead of using the normal words. For example, 'plates of meat' is rhyming slang for 'feet'.

rhyth·m /ˈrɪðəm/ ●●○ W3 *n* [C,U]
1 a regular repeated pattern of sounds or movements → **metre**: *Drums are basic to African rhythm.* | *complicated dance rhythms* | **[+of]** *She started moving to the rhythm of the music.* | *the steady rhythm of her heartbeat*
2 a regular pattern of changes: *the body's natural rhythms* | **[+of]** *Jim liked the rhythm of agricultural life.*

ˌrhythm and ˈblues *n* [U] R & B (=a type of popular music)

rhyth·mic /ˈrɪðmɪk/ ●○○ (*also* **rhyth·mic·al** /-mɪkəl/) *adj* having a strong rhythm: *the rhythmic thud of the bass drum* —**rhythmically** /-kli/ *adv*

ˈrhythm ˌmethod *n* [singular] a method of BIRTH CONTROL which depends on having sex only at a time when the woman is not likely to become PREGNANT

ˈrhythm ˌsection *n* [C] the part of a band that provides a strong RHYTHM with drums and other similar instruments → **percussion**

ri·al, **riyal** /riˈɑːl $ riˈɒːl, -ˈɑːl/ *n* [C] the standard unit of money in Saudi Arabia and some other Arab countries

rib[1] /rɪb/ ●●○ *n* [C]
1 one of the 12 pairs of curved bones that surround your chest: *She was taken to hospital with a broken arm and ribs.* | *He was punched and kicked in the ribs.* → see picture at SKELETON
2 a piece of meat that includes an animal's rib: *a rib of beef* | *barbecued ribs* → SPARE RIBS
3 a curved piece of wood, metal etc that is used as part of the structure of something such as a boat or building

rib[2] *v* (**ribbed**, **ribbing**) [T] *informal* to make jokes and laugh at someone so that you embarrass them, but in a friendly way SYN **tease**

rib·ald /ˈrɪbəld/ *adj* ribald remarks or jokes are humorous, rude, and about sex: *a ribald remark* | *ribald humour*

rib·ald·ry /ˈrɪbəldri/ *n* [U] ribald remarks or jokes

ribbed /rɪbd/ *adj* something that is ribbed has raised lines on it: *a ribbed woollen sweater*

rib·bing /ˈrɪbɪŋ/ *n* [U] **1** friendly jokes and laughter about someone: *He* ***took*** *a lot of* ***ribbing*** *from other members of the crew.* **2** raised lines, especially on a piece of woollen clothing

RIBBON

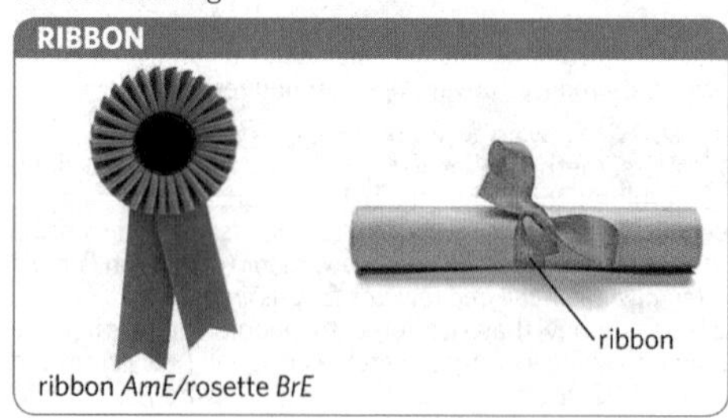

ribbon *AmE*/rosette *BrE*

rib·bon /ˈrɪbən/ ●●○ *n*
1 PIECE OF CLOTH [C,U] a narrow piece of attractive cloth that you use, for example, to tie your hair or hold things together → **bow**: *little girls with ribbons in their hair* | *a bundle of letters tied with pale blue ribbon* | *The ribbon was cut and the new station was officially open.* → see picture at BAG
2 MILITARY HONOUR [C] a piece of ribbon with a special pattern on it that you wear to show that you have received a military honour
3 PRIZE [C] *AmE* a length of coloured ribbon, sometimes arranged in the form of a flat flower, that is given as a prize in a competition SYN **rosette** *BrE*: *For the second time she won the* ***blue ribbon*** (=first prize).

4 STH NARROW [singular] *written* something that is long and narrow: **[+of]** *a winding ribbon of water*
5 be cut/torn to ribbons to be cut or torn in a lot of places: *Her legs were bruised and her feet were cut to ribbons.*
6 INK [C] a long narrow piece of cloth or plastic with ink on it that is used in a TYPEWRITER

ˈribbon deˌvelopment *n* [C,U] *BrE* long lines of houses along the sides of a main road leading out of a town or city

ˈrib cage *n* [C] the structure of RIBS in your chest → see picture at **SKELETON**

ri·bo·fla·vin /ˌraɪbəʊˈfleɪvɪn $ ˌraɪbə-/ *n* [U] *technical* VITAMIN B2, a substance that exists in meat, milk, and some vegetables, and that is important for your health

rice /raɪs/ ●●● S3 *n* [U]
1 a food that consists of small white or brown grains that you boil in water until they become soft enough to eat → **risotto, pilau**: *a tasty sauce served with rice or pasta | a plate of* ***brown rice*** *| Serve with plain* ***boiled rice****. | a few* ***grains of rice***
2 the plant that produces rice: *Rice is the main crop grown in the area. | rice fields*

ˈrice ˌpaddy *n* (*plural* **rice paddies**) [C] a field in which rice is grown

ˈrice ˌpaper *n* [U] **1** a type of thin paper that is made especially in China and used by painters there **2** a type of thin paper that can be eaten and is used in cooking

ˌrice ˈpudding *n* [U] a sweet dish made of rice, milk, and sugar cooked together

rich /rɪtʃ/ ●●● S2 W2 *adj* (*comparative* **richer**, *superlative* **richest**)
1 WEALTHY **a)** someone who is rich has a lot of money and valuable possessions OPP **poor**: *one of the richest women in America | She found herself a rich husband. | He thought this was the easiest way to* ***get rich****. | the rich nations of the world |* **fabulously rich** *BrE*: *She was both beautiful and fabulously rich. | His brother's* ***stinking rich*** (=very rich, in a way that you do not approve of). **b) the rich** [plural] people who are rich: *houses belonging to the rich and famous*
2 LARGE AMOUNT containing a lot of something: **[+in]** *Citrus fruits are rich in vitamin C.* | **oxygen-rich/nutrient-rich/protein-rich etc** *Pregnant women should eat protein-rich foods. | Rich mineral deposits have been found in the sea bed. | Red meat is a* ***rich source*** *of iron.*
3 FULL OF INTEREST full of interesting or important facts, events, or ideas: *the rich literary tradition of England | The area has a very rich history.* | **[+in]** *a story that was rich in detail*
4 FOOD rich food contains a lot of butter, cream, or eggs, which make you feel full very quickly OPP **light**: *a rich fruit cake | The sauce was very rich.*
5 SMELL/FLAVOUR a rich smell or flavour is strong and pleasant: *the rich scent of the pine trees | meat with a wonderfully rich flavour | a rich, fruity wine*
6 COLOUR a rich colour is strong and attractive: *a rich dark brown colour* THESAURUS ▸ COLOUR
7 SOUND a rich sound is low and pleasant: *the rich tone of a cello | He laughed with a rich, throaty chuckle.*
8 SOIL rich soil is good for growing plants in OPP **poor**: *Vegetables grow well in the rich, black soil.*
9 CLOTH rich cloth is expensive and beautiful: *She stroked the rich velvet of the dress enviously.*
10 that's rich (coming from him/you etc) *BrE spoken* used to say that what someone has said is unreasonable and that they are criticizing you for doing something that they do themselves: *He accused me of being dishonest, which was a bit rich coming from him.*

THESAURUS

rich having a lot of money – used about people and places: *She married a rich Greek shipowner. | one of the world's richest nations*
wealthy rich – used about people and places, especially when they have been rich for a long time: *wealthy landowners | Orange County is a very wealthy area.*
affluent *formal* rich – used about societies, groups of people, or areas where people live, where people have nice houses and a lot of expensive possessions: *today's affluent society | affluent young professionals | an affluent suburb of Boston*
prosperous *formal* rich – used about places and groups of people, especially when their money is related to success in business: *Sales have grown fastest in the more prosperous areas of the south. | prosperous merchants and bankers*
well-off fairly rich compared to other people, so that you can live very comfortably: *Her parents are pretty well-off.*
well-to-do *written* rich – used especially in the past about families and people who had a fairly high position in society: *Only well-to-do families could afford to send their children to university.*
privileged having special advantages because your family have a lot of money and a high position in society: *He comes from a privileged background. | The sport was only played by* ***a privileged few****.*
comfortably off [not before noun] having enough money to have a nice life without having to worry about money: *I wouldn't say that we were rich – just comfortably off.*
be rolling in it/be loaded *informal* to be extremely rich: *They've got two houses and a boat – they must be rolling in it.*

COLLOCATIONS CHECK

wealthy person/family/area
affluent society/area/family/lifestyle
prosperous area/economy/middle class
well-to-do family
privileged person/background/few/elite

rich·es /ˈrɪtʃɪz/ *n* [plural] *literary* expensive possessions and large amounts of money SYN **wealth**: *He was enjoying his new-found riches. | the story of her rise* ***from rags to riches*** (=from being poor to being rich)

rich·ly /ˈrɪtʃli/ *adv* **1** if something is richly decorated, it is decorated a lot, in a way that is beautiful: *a richly carved ceiling | a cloak richly embroidered with gold thread* **2** if someone is richly dressed, they are dressed in expensive clothes **3 richly coloured** having beautiful strong colours: *the richly coloured mosaic* **4 richly flavoured/scented** having a strong pleasant taste or smell: *richly scented flowers* **5 richly deserve** to completely deserve something such as success or punishment: *They got the punishment they so richly deserved.* **6** containing large amounts of something: *a richly wooded valley | an area that is richly endowed with wildlife* **7 richly rewarding** giving you a strong feeling of pleasure: *It was a richly rewarding relationship.*

rich·ness /ˈrɪtʃnəs/ *n* [U] **1** if something has richness, it contains a lot of interesting things: **[+of]** *the richness and diversity of the Amazonian rain forests | a literary work of remarkable richness and vitality* **2** the richness of a colour, taste, smell, or sound is the quality that makes it rich: **[+of]** *the richness of the autumn colours*

Rich·ter scale /ˈrɪktə ˌskeɪl, ˈrɪx- $ -tər-/ *n* **the Richter scale** a system of numbers used for measuring how powerful an EARTHQUAKE is: *a severe earthquake* ***measuring 7.2 on the Richter scale***

ˈrich world *n* **the rich world** rich industrial countries SYN **first world**: *He said that people in the rich world should eat less meat.* —**rich-world** *adj*: *rich-world diseases*

ri·cin /ˈraɪsɪn/ *n* [U] a very strong poison, which has sometimes been used by TERRORISTS

rick[1] /rɪk/ *n* [C] a large pile of STRAW or grass that is kept in a field until it is needed SYN **haystack**

rick[2] *v* [T] *BrE* **rick your back/neck** to twist and slightly injure your back or neck SYN **wrench** *AmE*: *I ricked my back moving the furniture around.*

rick·ets /ˈrɪkəts/ *n* [U] a disease that children get in which their bones become soft and bent, caused by a lack of VITAMIN D

rick·et·y /ˈrɪkəti/ *adj* a rickety structure or piece of furniture is in very bad condition, and likely to break easily: *a rickety old wooden chair | a rickety bridge* **THESAURUS** WEAK

rick·shaw /ˈrɪkʃɔː $ -ʃɒː/ *n* [C] a small vehicle used in South East Asia for carrying one or two passengers. It is pulled by someone walking or riding a bicycle.

ric·o·chet¹ /ˈrɪkəʃeɪ/ *v* [I] if a bullet, stone, or other object ricochets, it changes direction when it hits a surface at an angle: **[+off]** *Bullets ricocheted off the boulders around him.*

ricochet² *n* [C] something such as a bullet or a stone that has ricocheted: *He was hit in the arm by a ricochet.*

ri·cot·ta /rɪˈkɒtə $ -ˈkɑː-/ *n* [U] a type of soft white Italian cheese

rid¹ /rɪd/ ●●○ S3 *adj*
1 get rid of sb/sth a) to throw away or destroy something you do not want anymore: *It's time we got rid of all these old toys. | Governments should be encouraged to get rid of all nuclear weapons.* **b)** to take action so that you no longer have something unpleasant that you do not want: *I can't get rid of this cough. | He opened the windows to get rid of the smell.* **c)** to make someone leave because you do not like them or because they are causing problems: *Are you trying to get rid of me? | It can be difficult for schools to get rid of poor teachers.*
2 be rid of sb/sth to have taken action so that something or someone is no longer there to worry or annoy you: *The clerical part of his job was tedious, and he was glad to be rid of it. | He was a bully, and we're* ***well rid*** *of him* (=it is good that he has gone).
3 want rid of sb/sth to want to get rid of someone or something that is annoying you: *I could tell that he wanted rid of me.*

rid² *v* (**rid, ridding**)
rid sb/sth **of** sth *phr v written* to take action so that a person, place etc is no longer affected by something bad or no longer has it → **overcome**: *a promise to rid the country of nuclear weapons | Will science finally rid us of this disease?* | **rid yourself of sth** *He struggled to rid himself of his fears.*

rid·dance /ˈrɪdns/ *n* **good riddance (to sb)** *spoken* a rude way of saying you are glad someone has left: *She was awful. Good riddance to her, I say!*

-ridden /rɪdn/ *suffix* [in adjectives] very full of something unpleasant: *mosquito-ridden swamps | disease-ridden slums*

rid·dle¹ /ˈrɪdl/ *n* [C] **1** a question that is deliberately very confusing and has a humorous or clever answer → **puzzle**: *See if you can* ***solve*** *this* ***riddle***. **2** something that you do not understand and cannot explain SYN **puzzle, mystery**: **[+of]** *The police have been unable to* ***solve*** *the* ***riddle*** *of her disappearance.* **3 talk/speak in riddles** to say things in a mysterious way that other people cannot understand: *Stop talking in riddles and explain what's going on!* **4** a wire container with holes in it that is used to separate earth from stones

riddle² *v* [T] **1** to make a lot of small holes in something: *Two gunmen riddled the bus with gunfire.* **2** to shake the coal or wood in a fire, in order to remove ASHes

rid·dled /ˈrɪdld/ *adj* **1 riddled with sth** very full of something bad or unpleasant: *The whole house was riddled with damp. | By this time her body was riddled with cancer.*
2 riddled with holes full of small holes: *The wall of the fort was riddled with bullet holes.*

ride¹ /raɪd/ ●●● S2 W2 *v* (*past tense* **rode** /rəʊd $ roʊd/, *past participle* **ridden** /ˈrɪdn/)
1 ANIMAL [I,T] to sit on an animal, especially a horse, and make it move along: *She learned to ride when she was seven. | He was riding a large grey mare.* | **[+on]** *She arrived riding on a white horse.* | **[+away/across/through etc]** *He rode away across the marshes.*
2 BICYCLE/MOTORBIKE [I always + adv/prep, T] to travel on a bicycle or MOTORBIKE: *He had never learned to ride a bicycle. | They mounted their bikes and rode off.*
3 VEHICLE [I always + adv/prep, T] *especially AmE* to travel in a bus, car, or other vehicle that you are not driving: *We got onto the bus and rode into San Francisco.* | **[+in]** *The kids were riding in the back.* | **ride a bus** *AmE*: *Ann rides the bus to work.* ⚠ Do not use **ride** to talk about someone controlling a car or other vehicle. Use **drive**: *the man who was driving the stolen car*
4 IN A LIFT [I always + adv/prep, T] *AmE* to travel up or down in a LIFT: **[+up/down]** *He* ***rode the elevator*** *down to the first floor. | I rode up to the tenth floor.*
5 WATER/AIR **a)** [I always + adv/prep] to be floating in water or in the air: *The smaller boat was lighter and rode higher in the water. | The moon was riding high in the sky. | There was a large ship* ***riding at anchor*** *in the bay.* **b) ride a wave** to float on a wave and move forward with it: *surfboarders riding the waves*
6 be riding high to feel very happy and confident: *They were still riding high after their election victory.*
7 let sth ride *spoken* to take no action about something that is wrong or unpleasant: *What he had said was wrong, and I knew I shouldn't just let it ride.*
8 ride roughshod over sth to ignore someone else's feelings or ideas because you have the power or authority to do this: *The planning authorities should not ride roughshod over the wishes of local people.*
9 ANNOY SB [T] *AmE spoken* to annoy someone by often criticizing them or asking them to do things: *Why are you riding her so hard?*
10 ride on sb's shoulders/back if a child rides on someone's shoulders or back, they are carried in that way
11 ride a punch/blow to move back slightly when someone hits you, so that you are not hit with so much force: *He managed to ride the punch.*
12 be riding for a fall *informal* to be doing something unwise which could result in failure: *I had a feeling he was riding for a fall, and tried to tell him so.*

ride on sth *phr v* if one thing is riding on another, it depends on it: *He knew he had to win – his reputation was riding on it. | There's a lot riding on this match.*

ride sth ↔ **out** *phr v*
1 if a ship rides out a storm, it manages to keep floating until the storm has ended
2 if you ride out a difficult situation, you are not badly harmed by it: *Most large companies should be able to ride out the recession.*

ride up *phr v* if a piece of clothing rides up, it moves upwards so that it is no longer covering your body properly

ride² ●●● S3 *n* [C]
1 CAR/TRAIN ETC a journey in a vehicle, when you are not driving → **lift**: **[+in]** *He invited me to* ***go for a ride*** *in his new car. | Can you* ***give*** *me a* ***ride*** *back to town? | Sammy had promised to* ***take*** *me* ***for a ride*** *in his truck. | I managed to* ***get a ride*** *down to the station. | We* ***hitched a ride*** (=got a free ride from a passing vehicle) *into town.* | **car/bus/train etc ride** *A fifteen minute taxi ride will take you to the airport.* | **a smooth/comfortable/bumpy etc ride** *The new model offers a lovely smooth, comfortable ride.* **THESAURUS** JOURNEY
2 HORSE/BICYCLE a journey on a bicycle, a horse, or a similar animal: **[+on]** *Can I* ***have a ride*** *on your bike?* | **a bike/bicycle ride** *Shall we* ***go for a bike ride*** *this afternoon?*
3 a rough/easy ride *informal* if people give someone, especially someone in authority, a rough or an easy ride, they make a situation difficult or easy for them: *Journalists* ***gave*** *the prime minister* ***a rough ride*** *at the press conference. | The chairman will face a rough ride from shareholders. | The president will not* ***have an easy ride*** *when he gives his account of events.*
4 a bumpy ride *informal* if something has a bumpy ride, it experiences a lot of problems: *Shares* ***had a bumpy ride*** *yesterday, falling by an average of 15%. | The new bill could* ***be in for a bumpy ride*** *when it is put before parliament.*
5 take sb for a ride *spoken* to trick someone, especially in order to get money from them: *I'd just begun to realise he was taking me for a ride.*

R

6 come/go along for the ride *spoken* to join what other people are doing just for pleasure, not because you are seriously interested in it: *A couple of friends had come along for the ride.*
7 MACHINE AT A FAIR a large machine that people ride on for fun at a FAIR: *We* ***went on*** *loads of* ***rides***.
8 PATH *literary* a path for riding on a horse in the country-side: *a grassy ride*

rid·er /ˈraɪdə $ -ər/ ●●○ *n* [C]
1 someone who rides a horse, bicycle etc → **cyclist**: *a horse and rider*
2 an extra or more detailed piece of information that is added to an official document and changes it slightly

ridge /rɪdʒ/ ●○○ *n* [C]
1 a long area of high land, especially at the top of a mountain: *We made our way carefully along the ridge.*
2 a) something long and thin that is raised above the things around it: *A small ridge of sand separated the field from the beach.* | *The ridges on the soles give the shoes a better grip.* **b)** the part at the top of a roof, where the two sides meet
3 ridge of high pressure *technical* a long area of high air pressure in the ATMOSPHERE, which has an effect on the weather

ridged /rɪdʒd/ *adj* something that is ridged has ridges on its surface: *the ridged sand of the river bottom*

rid·i·cule¹ /ˈrɪdəkjuːl/ *n* [U] unkind laughter or remarks that are intended to make someone or something seem stupid: *the ridicule of his peers* | *The government's proposals were* ***held up to ridicule*** (=suffered ridicule) *by opposition ministers.* | *He had become an* ***object of ridicule*** *among the other teachers.*

ridicule² *v* [T] to laugh at a person, idea etc and say that they are stupid SYN **mock**: *At the time, his ideas were ridiculed.*

ri·dic·u·lous /rɪˈdɪkjələs/ ●●○ S3 *adj* very silly or unreasonable: *That's a ridiculous idea!* | *Don't be ridiculous!* | *I'd* ***look ridiculous*** *in a dress like that.* | **absolutely/totally/utterly ridiculous** *It's an absolutely ridiculous decision.* | **it is ridiculous that** *It's ridiculous that we have to wait six weeks.* THESAURUS STUPID —**ridiculously** *adv*: *a ridiculously expensive jacket* | *ridiculously low prices* —**ridiculousness** *n* [U]

GRAMMAR
Ridiculous is not used with 'very'. You say: *I think it's absolutely ridiculous.* ✗ Don't say: *I think it's very ridiculous.*
GRAMMAR GUIDE ADJECTIVES

rid·ing /ˈraɪdɪŋ/ *n* [U] the sport or activity of riding horses: *horse riding* | *Shall we* ***go riding*** *on Saturday?* | **riding school/stables** (=place where people learn to ride horses)

rife /raɪf/ *adj* **1** [not before noun] if something bad or unpleasant is rife, it is very common: *Violent crime is rife in our inner cities.* THESAURUS COMMON **2 rife with sth** full of something bad or unpleasant: *The crowded factories are rife with disease.* **3 run rife** to spread quickly in an uncontrolled way: *No one knew exactly what he had done, but speculation ran rife.*

riff¹ /rɪf/ *n* [C] **1** a repeated series of notes in popular or JAZZ music: *a guitar riff* **2** a piece of speech in which someone talks about a subject in an entertaining way that does not seem planned: *He* ***goes off on a riff*** *about the problems of being middle-aged.*

riff² *v* [I] **1** to play different notes related to the main tune in popular or JAZZ music: *He was riffing on his guitar.* **2** to talk about a subject in an entertaining way that does not seem planned: *During her show, she riffs about everything from her family to global warming.*

rif·fle /ˈrɪfəl/ (*also* **riffle through**) *v* [T] to move and quickly look at pieces of paper or the pages of a book, magazine etc → **flip through**: *He riffled through the papers on his desk.*

riff-raff /ˈrɪf ræf/ *n* [plural] an insulting word for people who are noisy, badly-behaved, or of low social class: *We charge high prices to keep the riff-raff out.*

ri·fle¹ /ˈraɪfəl/ ●●○ *n* [C] a long gun which you hold up to your shoulder to shoot → **pistol**

rifle² (*also* **rifle through**) *v* [T] to search a place or container quickly because you are looking for something, especially something to steal: *Sally rifled through her wardrobe looking for a dress.* | *The killer had rifled his wallet and stolen £200.*

ri·fle·man /ˈraɪfəlmən/ *n* (*plural* **riflemen** /-mən/) [C] a man who uses a rifle

ˈrifle range *n* [C] a place where people practise shooting with rifles

rift /rɪft/ ●○○ *n* [C]
1 a situation in which two people or groups have had a serious disagreement and begun to dislike and not trust each other SYN **split**: **[+between/with]** *Party officials have denied that there is any rift between ministers.* | **[+over]** *Today's announcement could lead to a further rift over public spending.* | *He set out to* ***heal*** *the* ***rifts*** *in the party.*
2 a crack or narrow opening in a large mass of rock, cloud etc

ˈrift ˌvalley *n* [C] a valley with very steep sides, formed by the cracking and moving of the Earth's surface

rig¹ /rɪg/ *v* (**rigged**, **rigging**) [T] **1** to dishonestly arrange the result of an election or competition before it happens SYN **fix**: *Some international observers have claimed the election was rigged.* **2** if people rig prices or rig financial markets, they unfairly agree with each other the prices that will be charged SYN **fix** → **cartel**: *Two of the largest oil companies have been accused of rigging prices.* | *Some investors feel that the market is rigged.* **3** to put ropes, sails etc on a ship: *The ship was fully rigged and ready to sail.* GRAMMAR **Rig** is usually passive in this meaning.

rig sb ↔ **out** *phr v BrE informal* to dress someone in special or unusual clothes: *young children who are rigged out in designer clothes*

rig sth ↔ **up** *phr v informal* to make a piece of equipment, furniture etc quickly from objects that you find around you: *We rigged up a simple shower at the back of the cabin.*

rig² *n* [C] **1** a large structure that is used for getting oil from the ground under the sea **2** *AmE informal* a large truck: *We drove the rig down to Baltimore.* **3** the way in which a ship's sails are arranged

rig·a·ma·role /ˈrɪgəmərəʊl $ -roʊl/ *n* [singular, U] an American spelling of RIGMAROLE

rig·a·to·ni /ˌrɪgəˈtəʊni $ -ˈtoʊni/ *n* [U] a type of PASTA in the shape of short tubes

rig·ging /ˈrɪgɪŋ/ *n* [U] all the ropes, posts, and chains that hold up a ship's sails

right¹ /raɪt/ ●●● S1 W1 *adj*
1 TRUE/CORRECT **a)** a statement or piece of information that is right is correct and based on true facts SYN **correct** OPP **wrong**: *Yes, that's the* ***right answer***. | *Is that the* ***right time***? | *I* ***got*** *most of the questions* ***right***. | *His ideas have now been* ***proved right***. **b)** [not before noun] if you are right, you have said something that is correct and based on true facts OPP **wrong**: *I think you're right. We should have set out earlier.* | **[+about]** *You were right about the hotel being too crowded.* | *I think the prime minister is only* ***half right***. | *Am I* ***right in thinking that*** *you two have met before?*
2 SUITABLE the right thing, person, method etc is the one that is most suitable or effective OPP **wrong**: *I think you've made the right decision.* | *I think she's definitely the* ***right person*** *for the job.* | **[+for]** *A huge development like this isn't right for such a small village.* THESAURUS SUITABLE
3 SIDE [only before noun] **a)** your right side is the side with the hand that most people write with OPP **left**: *He had a knife in his right hand.* | *a scar on the* ***right side*** *of her face* **b)** on the same side of something as your right side OPP **left**: *Take the next right turn.* | *the right bank of the river*
4 PROBLEMS something that is not right is not in the state it should be in: *The engine's not quite right.* | *This cheese doesn't smell right.* | *Things haven't been right between me and James for some time.* | **put/set sth right** (=correct

something) *It didn't take long to find the fault and put it right.*
5 MORALLY if someone is right to do something, their action is morally correct or sensible OPP **wrong**: **right to do sth** *Do you think I was right to report them to the police? | It can't be right to keep lying to your family.* | **it is right that** *I think it's right that the people who work hardest should earn the most.* | *It's **only right*** (=completely right) *that he should get his share of the money.* | *The company wants to **do the right thing** and offer compensation to all the injured workers.*
6 that's right *spoken* **a)** used to agree with what someone says or to answer 'yes' to a question: *'I gather you work in the sales department?' 'That's right.'* | *'Some people find it very difficult to work quickly.' 'That's right, and they often find exams very stressful.'* **b)** used when you are telling someone that you are angry about what they are doing: *That's right! Just blame me for everything, as usual!*
7 right you are *BrE spoken* used to say 'yes' to a request, order, or suggestion
8 EMPHASIS [only before noun] *BrE spoken* used to emphasize how bad someone or something is SYN **total**, **complete**: *He sounds like a right idiot!* | *The house was in a right mess when we got back.*
9 HEALTH *spoken* if you are not feeling right, you are not feeling completely well: *I haven't been feeling right all day.* | *A few days in bed will soon **put** you **right**.* | *You'll soon be **as right as rain*** (=completely healthy). → **put sb right/straight** at PUT(9)
10 SOCIALLY the right people, places, schools etc are considered to be the best or most important: *Sonia's always careful to be seen with the right people.*
11 be in the right place at the right time to be in the place where something useful becomes available or is being offered: *Being a news photographer is all about being in the right place at the right time.* —**rightness** *n* [U]: *He was convinced of the rightness of his cause.* → **put sth right** at PUT(8)

THESAURUS

right not wrong – used about something someone says, or about the person who says it: *the right answer* | *You were right about the colour.* | *'He's about thirty, isn't he?' 'That's right.'*
correct right. **Correct** sounds more formal than **right**: *the correct answer* | *He is absolutely correct.* | *Unfortunately, this information is not correct.*
accurate right – used about information, measurements, descriptions etc: *Make sure that your measurements are accurate.* | *an accurate description of the suspect*
exact an exact number, amount, or time is completely correct, and is no more and no less than it should be: *The exact time is 9.28 a.m.* | *The exact weight of the baby was 3.3 kilos.*
spot-on *BrE spoken informal* exactly right – used especially about guesses or things people say: *His answer was spot-on.* | *You're spot-on.*

right² ●●● S1 W1 *adv*
1 EXACTLY exactly in a particular position or place: **right in/in front of/by etc sth** *She was standing right in the middle of the room.* | *There's the house, right in front of you.* | **right here/there** *I left my bags right here.* THESAURUS ▸ EXACTLY
2 IMMEDIATELY immediately and without any delay SYN **straight**: *It's on **right after** the six o'clock news.* | *I'll phone him **right away*** (=immediately). | *I could tell **right off** that something was wrong.* | **right off the bat** *AmE* (=immediately, without having to think carefully) *Kay answered right off the bat.*
3 CORRECTLY correctly: *We guessed right; they'd gone.* | *'I thought you'd be cross.' 'You thought right!'*
4 WELL *informal* in a way that is good or satisfactory: *Everything's **going right** for him at the moment.* | *It'll work out right in the end.*
5 DIRECTION/SIDE towards the direction or side that is on the right OPP **left**: *Turn right at the crossroads.*
6 right now now, or immediately: *Do you need me right now?* | *We need to deal with this problem right now.*
7 right along/through/around etc all the way along, through etc: *Go right to the end of the road.* | *We don't have to go right into town.* | *I slept soundly right through the night.*
8 be right behind sb *spoken* to completely support someone in their ideas or in what they are trying to achieve: *We're all right behind you.*
9 I'll be right with you/right there/right back *spoken* used to ask someone to wait because you are coming or returning very soon: *'Lunch is ready!' 'I'll be right there.'* | *Don't go away; I'll be right back.*
10 be right up there (with sb/sth) *informal* to be as good or as important as the very best: *He's definitely right up there with all the world-class footballers.*
11 right, left, and centre *BrE*, **right and left** *AmE* everywhere or in every way: *The company's losing money right, left and centre.*

right³ ●●● S1 W1 *n*
1 ALLOWED [C] something that you are morally, legally, or officially allowed to do or have: **[+of]** *The new charter establishes the rights and duties of citizens.* | **[+to]** *Everyone should have the right to freedom of expression.* | **right to do sth** *You have the right to consult a lawyer.* | **by right** *The money is yours by right.* | **within your rights** (=legally or morally allowed) *You would be within your rights to sue the company for negligence.* → CIVIL RIGHTS, HUMAN RIGHT
2 have a right to be angry/concerned/suspicious etc to have a good reason for being angry, concerned etc: *I think you have a right to feel very disappointed.* | *You had **every right** to be angry with them.*
3 have no right to do sth used to say that someone's action is completely unreasonable or unfair: *You had no right to take money from my purse!* | *He has no right to speak to me like that!*
4 SIDE **the right/sb's right** the side of your body that has the hand that most people write with, or this side of anything else OPP **left**: **on/to the right (of sth)** *Our car is just to the right of that white van.* | *Take the first turning on the right.* | **on/to sb's right** *The school is on your right as you come into the village.*
5 POLITICS **the right/the Right** political parties or groups that support the ideas and beliefs of CAPITALISM. They usually want low taxes and to encourage private business rather than businesses owned by the state OPP **left** → **right-wing**: *The campaign is being supported by the Right.* | *The Conservative Party seems to be moving even further to the right.* | **extreme/far right** *politicians on the extreme right*
6 CORRECT BEHAVIOUR [U] behaviour that is morally good and correct: *Some kids don't seem to know the difference between **right and wrong**.* | *The protesters believe that they have right on their side.*
7 BOOKS/TV ETC **rights** [plural] if someone has the rights to a book, film, television programme etc, they are allowed to sell it or show it → **copyright**: **[+to]** *The studio bought the rights to his new book.* | *The company paid £2 million for **film rights** to the book.* | *the **television rights** to the Olympic Games*
8 be in the right to have the best reasons, arguments etc in a disagreement with someone else: *Both sides are convinced that they are in the right.*
9 by rights *spoken* used to describe what should happen if things are done fairly or correctly: *By rights, the house should be mine now.*
10 in your own right used to say that you have something or achieve something on your own, without depending on other people: *She's a very wealthy woman in her own right.*
11 put sth to rights to make a place or situation return to normal again: *It took ages to put the room to rights again.*
12 the rights and wrongs of sth the subject of what or who is right or wrong in a situation: *I don't want to spend ages discussing the rights and wrongs of all this.*
13 [C] a hit made with your right hand OPP **left**

COLLOCATIONS

VERBS

have a right *People have a right to know the truth.*
violate sb's rights *formal* (=stop them doing

something they have a right to do) *Imprisoning the men without trial violated their rights.*
exercise a right *formal* (=do what you have a right to do) *The insurance company decided not to exercise its right of appeal.*
deny sb a right (=not allow them to do something they have the right to do) | **demand a right** (=ask for it firmly) | **defend a right** (=take action to stop a right being taken away) | **uphold sb's rights** (=defend their rights)

ADJECTIVES/NOUN + right

human rights (=the rights that everyone should have) *This company always operates with respect for human rights.*
civil rights (=the rights that every person in a society should have) *As a young man, he was deeply involved in the struggle for civil rights.*
equal rights *Women demanded equal rights.*
a fundamental/basic right | **a legal right** | **a constitutional right** | **political rights** | **women's rights** | **workers' rights** | **gay/lesbian rights** | **animal rights**

PHRASES

a right of appeal (=the right to ask for an official decision to be changed) *In these circumstances, there is no right of appeal.*
the right to privacy (=the right to be free from public attention) *The judge decided that the media's actions violated the couple's right to privacy.*
a right of access (=the right to enter a place, use something, or see someone) | **a right of reply** (*also* **the right to reply**) (=the right to say or write something in answer to a criticism)

right[4] ●●● S2 *interjection*
1 used to show that you have understood or agree with what someone has just said: *'You need to be there by ten o'clock.' 'Right.'*
2 *BrE* used to get someone's attention before starting to say or do something: *Right, open your books on page 16. | Right, is everyone listening? | Right, I think we're ready to go.*
3 used to check if what you have said is correct: *So we're meeting in the pub, right?*
4 used to check that the person you are speaking to is listening and understands what you are saying: *So I handed him the camera, right, and asked him to take our photograph.*

right[5] *v* [T] **1 right a wrong** to do something to prevent a bad situation from continuing: *He seems to think he can right all the wrongs of the world.* **2** to put something back into the state or situation that it should be in: *We must try to right the balance between taxation and government spending.* **3** to put something, especially a boat, back into its correct upright position: *I finally managed to right the canoe. | She righted herself and picked up her bag.*

ˈright ˌangle ●○○ *n* [C]
1 an angle of 90°, like the angles at the corners of a square
2 at right angles (to sth) if two things are at right angles, they make a 90° angle where they touch: *Hold the brush at right angles to the surface.* —**right-angled** *adj*: *a right-angled bend*

ˌright-angled ˈtriangle *n* [C] *BrE* a TRIANGLE which has an angle of 90° SYN **right triangle** *AmE* → see picture at TRIANGLE

ˌright-ˈclick *v* [I] to press the right-hand button on a computer MOUSE to make the computer do something OPP **left-click**: **[+on]** *Right-click on the image to save it.*

right·eous /ˈraɪtʃəs/ *adj* **1 righteous indignation/anger etc** strong feelings of anger when you think a situation is not morally right or fair: *He was full of righteous indignation about the attack.* **2** *formal* morally good and fair: *a righteous God* —**righteously** *adv* —**righteousness** *n* [U] → SELF-RIGHTEOUS

right·ful /ˈraɪtfəl/ *adj* [only before noun] *formal* according to what is correct or what should be done legally or morally: *George sat at the head of the table, in his **rightful place** as their leader. | I'll return the money to **its rightful owner**. | the **rightful heir** to the throne* —**rightfully** *adv*: *I'm only claiming what is rightfully mine.*

ˌright-ˈhand ●●○ *adj* [only before noun] on the right side of something OPP **left-hand**: *the **right-hand side** of the body* | **top/bottom right-hand corner** *the bottom right-hand corner of the page*

ˌright-hand ˈdrive *adj* [only before noun] *BrE* a right-hand drive vehicle is one in which the driver sits on the right OPP **left-hand drive**

ˌright-ˈhanded ●●○ *adj* a right-handed person uses their right hand for writing, throwing etc OPP **left-handed**

ˌright-ˈhander *n* [C] **1** someone who uses their right hand for writing, throwing etc OPP **left-hander**: *He was the only right-hander among his team's top six batsmen.* **2** a hit using your right hand

ˌright-hand ˈman *n* [singular] the person who supports and helps you the most, especially in your job: *John is Bill's right-hand man and has put a lot of time into the team.*

ˈRight ˌHonourable *adj BrE* used when formally announcing or talking about a member of the British Parliament: *the Right Honourable Giles Williams MP*

right·ist /ˈraɪtɪst/ *adj* supporting RIGHT-WING ideas or groups OPP **leftist**: *rightist demonstrators* —**rightist** *n* [C]

right·ly /ˈraɪtli/ ●●○ *adv*
1 correctly, or for a good reason OPP **wrongly**: *I was, as you **rightly said**, the smallest boy in the class. | As you so **rightly pointed out**, things are getting worse. | They have been treated badly, and they are rightly upset.* | **quite rightly** *BrE*: *There's a lot of talk, quite rightly, about the dangers of smoking. | This photo was taken in Paris, **if I remember rightly**.*
2 rightly or wrongly used to emphasize that someone else thinks that something they did was right, but you think it was wrong: *The prime minister was widely judged, rightly or wrongly, to be an honest man.*
3 and rightly so *spoken* used to say that a decision or action you have just described is fair and morally right, in your opinion: *A lot of people round here were furious, and rightly so.*
4 I can't rightly say/don't rightly know *spoken* used to say that you are not sure whether something is correct or not

ˌright-ˈminded *adj* a right-minded person has opinions, principles, or standards of behaviour that you approve of SYN **right-thinking**: *All right-minded people will support us.*

right-o /ˌraɪtˈəʊ $ -ˈoʊ/ (*also* **ˌright ˈoh**) *interjection BrE informal* used to show that you agree with a suggestion that someone has made SYN **OK**: *Righto, I'll see you at six.*

ˌright of apˈpeal *n* (*plural* **rights of appeal**) [C] *law* the legal right to ask for a court's decision to be changed

ˌright-of-ˈcentre *adj* supporting ideas and aims that are between the centre and the right in politics OPP **left-of-centre**

ˌright of ˈway *n* (*plural* **rights of way**) **1** [U] the right to drive into or across a road before other vehicles: *I never know who **has right of way** at this junction.* *BrE | The law here says that pedestrians always **have the right of way**.* **2** [C] *BrE* **a)** the right to walk across someone else's land: *Walkers are often quite aggressive about their rights of way.* **b)** a path that people have the right to use: *The path is not a **public right of way**.*

ˌright ˈon *adj informal* **1** *BrE* someone who is right on supports social justice, equal rights, the protection of the environment etc - often used to show disapproval because someone does this in an extreme way → **PC**, **politically correct**: *It's one of those annoyingly right-on magazines about the environment.* **2** *AmE* someone is right on when they say something that is correct or that you completely agree with: *Parker's column on teenage sexuality is right on.* **3** *AmE spoken old-fashioned* used to emphasize that you agree with what someone says or does: *'Power to the people!' 'Yeah, right on.'*

ˈrights ˌissue *n* [C] *BrE technical* an offer of company

SHARES at a cheaper price than usual, to people who own some already

right·size /ˈraɪtsaɪz/ *v* [I,T] if a company or organization rightsizes, or if it rightsizes its operations, it reduces the number of people it employs in order to reduce costs – used especially by companies to make the reduction in the number of workers sound good and sensible → **downsize**: *They have been given one year to rightsize their workforce.* —**rightsizing** *n* [U]: *Many workers lost their jobs as a result of rightsizing.*

ˌright-ˈthinking *adj* a right-thinking person has opinions, principles, or standards of behaviour that you approve of SYN **right-minded**: *I condemn this killing, as all right-thinking people must.*

ˌright-to-ˈdie *adj* [only before noun] supporting the right of people who are extremely ill, injured, or unconscious to refuse to use machines or methods that would keep them alive → **euthanasia**: *the growing right-to-die lobby within the USA*

ˌright to ˈlife *n* [singular] if you talk about a baby's right to life, you mean that a baby has the right to be born, even if there are problems → **pro-life**: *Every unborn child has a right to life.*

ˌright ˈtriangle *n* [C] *AmE* a TRIANGLE which has an angle of 90° SYN **right-angled triangle** *BrE*

right·ward /ˈraɪtwəd $ -wərd/ *adj* [only before noun] on or towards the right OPP **leftward**: *a rightward glance*

right·wards /ˈraɪtwədz $ -wərdz/ *especially BrE*, **rightward** *AmE adv* on or towards the right OPP **leftwards**: *The plane's course was veering rightwards.*

ˌright-ˈwing ●○○ *adj* a right-wing person or group supports the ideas and beliefs of CAPITALISM OPP **left-wing**: *right-wing parties | The organization is very right-wing.* —**right wing** *n* [C]: *the right wing of the Conservative party* —**right-winger** *n* [C]: *a prominent right-winger in the party*

ri·gid /ˈrɪdʒɪd/ ●●○ AWL *adj*
1 rigid methods, systems etc are very strict and difficult to change OPP **flexible**: *rigid and authoritarian methods of education*
2 someone who behaves in a rigid way is very unwilling to change their ideas or behaviour OPP **flexible**: *rigid adherence to old-fashioned ideas | She maintained rigid control over her emotional and sexual life.*
3 stiff and not moving or bending OPP **flexible**: *rigid plastic*
THESAURUS HARD
4 used to describe someone who cannot move, especially because they are very frightened, shocked, or angry: **[+with]** *I heard a noise and woke up rigid with terror.* —**rigidly** *adv*: *rigidly opposed to all new ideas* —**rigidity** /rɪˈdʒɪdəti/ *n* [U]

rig·ma·role /ˈrɪgmərəʊl $ -roʊl/ (*also* **rigamarole** *AmE*) *n* [singular, U] a long confusing process or description: *I don't want to* ***go through the rigmarole of*** *taking him to court.*

rig·or /ˈrɪgə $ -ər/ *n* the American spelling of RIGOUR

rig·or mor·tis /ˌrɪgə ˈmɔːtəs, ˌraɪgɔː- $ ˌrɪgər ˈmɔːr-/ *n* [U] the condition in which someone's body becomes stiff after they die

rig·or·ous /ˈrɪgərəs/ ●○○ *adj*
1 careful, thorough, and exact: *a rigorous analysis of defence needs | the rigorous standards required by the college*
2 very severe or strict: *rigorous army training* —**rigorously** *adv*

rig·our *BrE*, **rigor** *AmE* /ˈrɪgə $ -ər/ *n* **1 the rigours of sth** the problems and difficulties of a situation: *all the rigors of a Canadian winter | the stresses and rigours of modern life*
2 [U] great care and thoroughness in making sure that something is correct: *Their research seems to me to be lacking in rigour.*

rile /raɪl/ *v* [T] *informal* to make someone extremely angry: *He was the calmest guy I ever knew – nothing ever riled him. | That class gets me so* ***riled up***.

rim¹ /rɪm/ ●○○ *n* [C]
1 the outside edge of something circular: **[+of]** *the rim of a glass | plates with a gold band around the rim* → see picture at EDGE¹ THESAURUS EDGE
2 gold-rimmed/red-rimmed etc with a gold, red etc rim: *gold-rimmed spectacles | red-rimmed eyes* —**rimless** *adj*: *rimless glasses*

rim² *v* (**rimmed**, **rimming**) [T] *literary* to be around the edge of something: *His eyes were rimmed with fatigue.*

rime /raɪm/ *n* [U] *literary* FROST (=powdery ice)

rind /raɪnd/ *n* [C,U] **1** the thick outer skin of some types of fruit, such as oranges → **peel**, **zest**: *grated lemon rind*
2 the thick outer skin of some foods, such as BACON or cheese

ring¹ /rɪŋ/ ●●● S1 W2 *n* [C]
1 JEWELLERY a piece of jewellery that you wear on your finger: *a* ***diamond ring*** *| a plain silver ring* → **engagement ring** at ENGAGEMENT(1), SIGNET RING, WEDDING RING
2 CIRCLE **a)** an object in the shape of a circle: *a rubber ring for children to go swimming with | onion rings | a key ring* → NAPKIN RING **b)** a circular line or mark: **[+around]** *She left a dirty ring around the bath.* | **[+round]** *BrE*: *a ring round the moon* **c)** a group of people or things arranged in a circle: **[+of]** *A ring of armed troops surrounded the building. | The city was overlooked by a ring of high-rise buildings.*
3 give sb a ring *BrE informal* to make a telephone call to someone: *I'll give you a ring later in the week.*
4 BELLS the sound made by a bell or the act of making this sound: *a ring at the doorbell*
5 CRIMINALS a group of people who illegally control a business or criminal activity: *Are you aware that a* ***drugs ring*** *is being operated in the club? | Secret files reveal an Oxford* ***spy ring***.
6 have the/a ring of sth if a statement or argument has a ring of truth, confidence etc, it seems as if it has this quality: *His explanation has the ring of truth.*
7 have a familiar ring if something has a familiar ring, you feel that you have heard it before: *His voice had a strangely familiar ring.*
8 run rings around sb *informal* to be able to do something much better than someone else can: *I'm sure you can run rings around him.*
9 COOKING *BrE* one of the circular areas on top of a COOKER that is heated by gas or electricity → **hob** SYN **burner** *AmE*: *a gas ring*
10 SPORT **a)** a small square area surrounded by ropes, where people BOX or WRESTLE → **RINGSIDE** **b) the ring** the sport of BOXING: *He retired from the ring at 34.*
11 ENTERTAINMENT a large circular area surrounded by seats at a CIRCUS

ring² /rɪŋ/ ●●● S1 W2 *v* (*past tense* **rang** /ræŋ/, *past participle* **rung** /rʌŋ/)
1 BELL **a)** [I,T] to make a bell make a sound, especially to call someone's attention to you or to call someone to help you: *I rang the doorbell but no one came.* | **[+for]** *The sign said, 'Ring for service'. | Instead of ringing for the maid, she made the tea herself.* **b)** [I] if a bell rings, it makes a noise: *The bell rang for the end of break.*
2 TELEPHONE **a)** [I,T] *BrE* to make a telephone call to someone SYN **call**, **phone**: *I was going to ring you but I don't have your number.* | **[+for]** *Sally rang for a taxi.* **b)** [I] if a telephone rings, it makes a sound to show that someone is telephoning you: *The phone hasn't stopped ringing all day.*
THESAURUS PHONE
3 SOUNDS [I] **a)** if your ears ring, they make a continuous sound that only you can hear, after you have been somewhere very noisy or heard a loud sound: *The explosion made our ears ring.* **b)** *literary* if a place rings with a sound, it is full of that sound: **[+with]** *The whole room rang with their laughter.*
4 ring a bell *informal* if something rings a bell, it reminds you of something, but you cannot remember exactly what it is: *Her name rings a bell but I can't remember her face.*
5 not ring true if something does not ring true, you do not believe it, even though you are not sure why: *It was a possible explanation, but it didn't quite ring true.*

6 ring the changes *BrE* to make changes to something, not because it needs changing but just in order to make it more interesting, more attractive etc: *Choose a variety of foods and ring the changes with meals.*
7 ring hollow if something that someone says rings hollow, you do not feel that it is true or sincere: *Assurances that things have changed ring hollow in many ears.*
8 ring in your ears if a sound or remark rings in your ears, you continue to remember it very clearly, exactly as it sounded, after it has finished: *He left Washington with the president's praises ringing in his ears.*

GRAMMAR

Ring belongs to a group of verbs where the same noun can be the subject of the verb or its object.
• You can say: *The teacher rang the bell.* In this sentence, 'the bell' is the object of **ring**.
• You can say: *The bell rang.* In this sentence, 'the bell' is the subject of **ring**.
GRAMMAR GUIDE ▸ VERBS

ring (sb) back *phr v BrE* to telephone someone again, or to telephone someone because you were not available when they telephoned you SYN **call (sb) back**: *I'll ring back as soon as I find out anything.* | *John rang, and he wants you to ring him back.*
ring in *phr v*
1 *BrE* to telephone the place where you work: *Jane's rung in to say she'll be late.* | *He* ***rang in sick*** (=telephoned to say he was ill) *every morning for a week.*
2 ring in the New Year to celebrate the beginning of the New Year
ring off *phr v BrE* to end a telephone call → **hang up**: *He rang off without giving his name.*
ring out *phr v*
1 a voice, bell etc that rings out is loud and clear: *The sound of a shot rang out.*
2 ring out the Old Year to celebrate the end of the year
ring round (sb) *phr v BrE* to make telephone calls to a group of people, in order to organize something, find out information etc: *I'll ring round to see whether anyone's interested in coming with us.* | *She rang round all the agencies.*
ring up *phr v*
1 *BrE* to telephone someone SYN **call (sb) up**: **ring sb ↔ up** *I'll ring the manager up tomorrow.* | *I rang up and made an appointment.*
2 ring sth ↔ up to press buttons on a CASH REGISTER to record how much money is being put inside: *The cashier rang up £300 by mistake.*

ring³ *v (past tense and past participle* **ringed***)* [T] **1** to surround something: *Thousands of people ringed the court building to demand the release of Mr Cox.* | **be ringed with sth** *Her eyes were ringed with stiff black lashes.* **2** *BrE* to draw a circular mark around something SYN **circle**: *Ring the mistakes in red.*

ring·back /ˈrɪŋbæk/ *n* [U] a telephone service that you can use when you call someone who is already using their telephone. The service arranges for their telephone to ring yours as soon as their line is free.

ˈring ˌbinder *n* [C] *BrE* a FILE for holding papers, in which metal rings go through the edges of the pages, holding them in place → see picture at **STATIONERY**

ring·er /ˈrɪŋə $ -ər/ *n* [C] **1** someone who rings church bells or hand bells **2** a piece of equipment that makes a ringing noise: *Turn down the ringer on your phone.* **3** someone who pretends not to have a skill that they really have, in order to play on a team, enter a competition etc → **DEAD RINGER**

ring·fence /ˈrɪŋfens/ *v* [T] *BrE* to decide officially that something, especially money, can only be used for a particular purpose: *OK, so this £20,000 is ringfenced as the training budget.*

ˈring ˌfinger *n* [C] the finger, next to the smallest finger on your hand, that you traditionally wear your WEDDING RING on → **index finger** → see picture at **HAND¹**

ring·ing /ˈrɪŋɪŋ/ *adj* **1** a ringing sound or voice is loud and clear: *She pronounced her final words in ringing tones.* **2 a ringing endorsement** a statement that is made with a lot of force in support of something: *a ringing endorsement of the proposals*

ring·lead·er /ˈrɪŋˌliːdə $ -ər/ *n* [C] someone who leads a group that is doing something illegal or wrong: *the ringleader of a new international drugs ring* THESAURUS ▸ LEADER

ring·let /ˈrɪŋlɪt/ *n* [C usually plural] a long curl of hair that hangs down → see picture at **HAIRSTYLE**

ring·mas·ter /ˈrɪŋˌmɑːstə $ -ˌmæstər/ *n* [C] the person who introduces the performers and animals in a CIRCUS

ˈring-pull *n* [C] *BrE* the ring on the top of a can of drink that you pull to open it

ˈring road *n* [C] *BrE* a road that goes around a large town to keep the traffic away from the centre → **bypass**

ring·side /ˈrɪŋsaɪd/ *n* [singular] **1** the area nearest to the performance in a CIRCUS, a BOXING match etc → **ring** **2 ringside seat** a seat very near to the performers in a CIRCUS, a BOXING match etc → **ring**

ring·tone /ˈrɪŋtəʊn $ -toʊn/ *n* [C] the sound made by a telephone, especially a MOBILE PHONE, when someone is calling it

ring·worm /ˈrɪŋwɜːm $ -wɜːrm/ *n* [U] a skin infection that causes red rings, especially on your head

rink /rɪŋk/ *n* [C] **1** a specially prepared area of ice that you can SKATE on SYN **ice rink** **2** a special area with a smooth surface where you can go around on ROLLER SKATES SYN **skating rink**

rinse¹ /rɪns/ ●●○ *v* [T]
1 to wash clothes, dishes, vegetables etc quickly with water, especially running water, and without soap: *Let me just rinse my hands.* | *Rinse the vegetables under a cold tap.* | **rinse sth out** *Don't forget to rinse out your swimsuit.* THESAURUS ▸ CLEAN
2 to remove soap, dirt etc from something by washing it quickly with water: **rinse sth off/out/away etc** *Leave the shampoo for two minutes, then rinse it off with warm water.* | *I rinsed the mud out under the tap.* | *The cream rinses off easily.*
3 to put colour into your hair SYN **dye**
4 if you rinse your mouth, or rinse your mouth out, you wash it by filling it with water and then spitting (SPIT) the water out → **gargle**

rinse² *n* **1** [C] when you rinse something: *I* ***gave*** *my hands a quick* ***rinse***. **2** [C,U] a product you use to change the colour of your hair or to make it more shiny SYN **dye**: *a blue rinse for grey hair*

ri·ot¹ /ˈraɪət/ ●●○ *n*
1 [C] a situation in which a large crowd of people are behaving in a violent and uncontrolled way, especially when they are protesting about something: *urban riots* | *prison riots* | *His murder triggered vicious* ***race riots*** (=caused by a problem between different races). | *police wearing* ***riot gear*** (=the special clothing and equipment worn by police officers during a riot) | *police in bullet-proof vests and carrying* ***riot shields*** (=a piece of very hard plastic which police officers stand behind to protect them)
2 run riot a) if your imagination, emotions, thoughts etc run riot, you cannot or do not control them: *Manufacturers have* ***let*** *their* ***imaginations run riot*** *to create new computer games.* **b)** if people run riot, they behave in a violent, noisy, and uncontrolled way: *Some people let their children run riot.* **c)** if a plant runs riot, it grows very quickly
3 a riot of colour something with many different bright colours: *The garden is a riot of colour in spring.*
4 read (sb) the riot act to give someone a strong warning that they must stop causing trouble – used humorously: *If the kids don't settle down soon, I'll go up and read them the riot act.*

riot² *v* [I] if a crowd of people riot, they behave in a violent and uncontrolled way, for example by fighting the police and damaging cars or buildings: *University students rioted in protest at tuition fees.* —**rioting** *n* [U] —**rioter** *n* [C]

R

ri·ot·ous /ˈraɪətəs/ *adj* [usually before noun] *formal* **1** noisy, exciting, and enjoyable in an uncontrolled way SYN **wild**: *a riotous party* **2** noisy or violent, especially in a public place: *Their* ***riotous behaviour*** *led to their arrest.* —**riotously** *adv*

ˈriot poˌlice *n* [plural] police whose job is to stop riots: *Riot police fired tear gas into the crowd.*

rip¹ /rɪp/ ●●○ S3 *v* (**ripped**, **ripping**)
1 [I,T] to tear something or be torn quickly and violently: *Her clothes had all been ripped.* | *The sails ripped under the force of the wind.* | *Impatiently, Sue* ***ripped*** *the letter* ***open***. THESAURUS TEAR
2 [T always + adv/prep] to remove something quickly and violently, using your hands: **rip sth out/off/away/down** *Gilly ripped out a sheet of paper from her notebook.* | *The buttons had been ripped off.*
3 rip sth/sb to shreds a) to destroy something or damage it badly by tearing it in many places: *Jill's kitten is ripping her sofa to shreds.* **b)** *informal* to strongly criticize someone, or criticize their opinions, remarks, behaviour etc: *I expected to have my argument ripped to shreds.*
4 [T] to copy music from a CD to an MP3 PLAYER or computer
5 let rip *informal* to speak or behave violently or emotionally: *Fran took a slow deep breath, then let rip, yelling and shouting at him.*
6 let it/her rip *informal* to make a car, boat etc go as fast as it can: *Put your foot on the gas and let her rip!*
rip sth ↔ **apart** *phr v* to tear or pull something to pieces: *He was ripped apart by savage beasts in the forest.*
rip sb/sth ↔ **off** *phr v informal*
1 to charge someone too much money for something SYN **overcharge**: *The agency really ripped us off.*
2 to steal something: *Somebody had come in and ripped off the TV and stereo.*
3 to take words, ideas etc from someone else's work and use them in your own work as if they were your own ideas SYN **plagiarize** → RIP-OFF(2)
rip on sb/sth *phr v AmE informal* to complain a lot about someone or something
rip through sth *phr v* to move through a place quickly and with violent force: *A wave of bombings ripped through the capital's business district.*
rip sth ↔ **up** *phr v* to tear something into pieces: *Sue ripped his photo up into tiny bits.*

rip² *n* [C] a long tear or cut: *a green leather jacket with a rip in the sleeve*

RIP /ˌɑːr aɪ ˈpiː/ the abbreviation of ***Rest in Peace***, written on a GRAVESTONE

rip·cord /ˈrɪpkɔːd $ -kɔːrd/ *n* [C] the string that you pull to open a PARACHUTE

ripe /raɪp/ ●●○ *adj* (*comparative* **riper**, *superlative* **ripest**)
1 ripe fruit or crops are fully grown and ready to eat OPP **unripe**: *Those tomatoes aren't ripe yet.*
2 be ripe for sth to be ready for a change to happen, especially when it should have happened sooner: *The police forces are ripe for reform.* | *The former dock area is ripe for development.*
3 the time is ripe (for sth) used to say it is a very suitable time for something to happen, especially when it should have happened sooner: *The time is ripe for a review of progress up to now.*
4 ripe old age a) if you live to a ripe old age, you are very old when you die: *Eat less and exercise more if you want to* ***live to a ripe old age***. **b)** used to show that you find it surprising or impressive that someone is doing something or has achieved something at a very young age – used humorously: *She was put in charge* ***at the ripe old age of*** *twenty-nine.*
5 ripe cheese has developed a strong taste and is ready to eat SYN **mature**
6 *especially BrE* a ripe smell is strong and unpleasant – used humorously: *We were pretty ripe after a week of walking.* —**ripeness** *n* [U]

rip·en /ˈraɪpən/ *v* [I,T] to become ripe or to make something ripe: *The apples were ripening on the trees.*

ˈrip-off *n* [C] **1** *informal* something that is unreasonably expensive: *The meal was a rip-off and the service was appalling.* **2** music, art, films etc that are rip-offs copy something else without admitting that they are copies: **[+of]** *a rip-off of a hit movie* → **rip off** at RIP¹

ri·poste /rɪˈpɒst, rɪˈpəʊst $ rɪˈpoʊst/ *n* [C] *formal* a quick, clever reply to something that someone has said: *a suitably witty riposte*

rip·ple¹ /ˈrɪpəl/ *v* **1** [I,T] to move in small waves, or to make something move in this way: *fields of grain rippling in the soft wind* | *I could see the muscles rippling under his shirt.* **2** [I always + adv/prep] to pass from one person to another like a wave: **[+through]** *Panic rippled through Hollywood as the murders were discovered.* | **[+around]** *Enthusiastic applause rippled around the tables.* **3** [I always + adv/prep] if a feeling ripples through you, you feel it strongly: **[+through]** *Anger was rippling through him so fiercely that his whole body shook.* **4** [I] to make a noise like water that is flowing gently: *The water rippled over the stones.* | *a rippling brook*

ripple² *n* [C] **1** a small low wave on the surface of a liquid: *ripples on the surface of the pond* | *She dived into the pool, making scarcely a ripple.* **2** a sound that gets gradually louder and softer: *A* ***ripple of laughter*** *ran through the audience.* | *a ripple of applause* **3** a feeling that spreads through a person or a group because of something that has happened: *A ripple of excitement went through the crowd as he came on stage.* **4** a shape or pattern that looks like a wave: *ripples on the sand* **5 raspberry ripple/chocolate ripple etc** a type of ICE CREAM that has different coloured bands of fruit, chocolate etc in it **6 ripple effect** a situation in which one action causes another, which then causes a third etc SYN **domino effect**: *The increase* ***had a ripple effect*** *through the whole financial market.*

ˌrip-ˈroaring *adj, adv informal* exciting and full of energy: *Micky had a rip-roaring time spending his first wage packet.*

rise¹ /raɪz/ ●●● S2 W1 *v* (*past tense* **rose** /rəʊz $ roʊz/, *past participle* **risen** /ˈrɪzən/) [I]
1 INCREASE to increase in number, amount, or value SYN **go up** OPP **fall**: **[+by]** *Sales rose by 20% over the Christmas period.* | **[+from/to]** *The research budget rose from £175,000 in 1999 to £22.5 million in 2001.* | **[+above]** *Temperatures rarely rise above freezing.* | **rise dramatically/sharply/rapidly/steeply etc** *The number of people seeking asylum in Britain has risen sharply.* | *The divorce rate has* ***risen steadily*** *since the 1950s.* | **rising crime/unemployment/inflation etc** *The country faces economic recession and rising unemployment.* | *The police seem unable to cope with the* ***rising tide of*** (=large increase in) *car crime.* THESAURUS INCREASE

> **REGISTER**
> In everyday English, people usually say an amount or level **goes up** rather than **rises**: *Prices have* ***gone up*** *a lot.*

2 GO UPWARDS to go upwards OPP **fall**: *The floodwaters began to rise again.* | *She watched the bubbles rise to the surface.* | *the problems caused by climate change and rising sea levels* | **[+from]** *Smoke rose from the chimney.* | *The road* ***rises steeply*** *from the village.* | *The waves* ***rose and fell***.
3 STAND *formal* to stand up: *Then she picked up her bag and rose to leave.* | **rise from the table/your chair etc** *The chairman rose from his chair and came forward to greet her.* | *He put down his glass and* ***rose to his feet***. THESAURUS STAND
4 BECOME SUCCESSFUL to become important, powerful, successful, or rich OPP **fall**: **[+to]** *He* ***rose to the rank of*** *major.* | **rise to prominence/fame/power** *He had swiftly risen to prominence during the 1950s.* | *Mussolini rose to power in Italy in 1922.* | *people who* ***rise to the top*** *in their chosen professions* | **rise to do sth** *He rose to become chairman of the company.* | *She had joined the company as a secretary and*

risen through the ranks (=made progress from a low position to a high position) *to become a senior sales director.*
5 BE TALL (*also* **rise up**) to be very tall: **[+above]** *The cliffs rose above them.* | **[+from]** *huge rocks rising from the sea* | *The bridge* ***rose majestically*** *into the air.*
6 VOICE/SOUND **a)** to be loud enough to be heard: **[+from]** *The sound of traffic rose from the street below.* | **[+above]** *Her voice rose above the shouts of the children.* **b)** to become louder or higher: *His voice rose in frustration.*
7 SUN/MOON/STAR to appear in the sky OPP **set**: *The sun rises in the east.*
8 EMOTION if a feeling or emotion rises, you feel it more and more strongly: *She could sense her temper rising again.* | *There was an atmosphere of rising excitement in the school.* | *The doctor sounded optimistic and John's* ***hopes rose.***
9 rise to the occasion/challenge to deal successfully with a difficult situation or problem, especially by working harder or performing better than usual: *a young athlete who can certainly rise to the occasion* | *The team rose to the challenge.*
10 AGAINST A GOVERNMENT/ARMY (*also* **rise up**) if a large group of people rise, they try to defeat the government, army etc that is controlling them: *They rose up and overthrew the government.* | **[+against]** *The prisoners rose against the guards and escaped.* | **rise in revolt/rebellion** *They rose in rebellion against the king.*
11 BREAD/CAKES ETC if bread, cakes etc rise, they become bigger because there is air inside them
12 BED *literary* to get out of bed in the morning
13 ALIVE AGAIN to come alive after having died → **resurrection**: **rise from the dead/grave** *On the third day Jesus rose from the dead.*
14 COURT/PARLIAMENT if a court or parliament rises, that particular meeting is formally finished
15 WIND *formal* if the wind rises, it becomes stronger: *The wind had risen again and it was starting to rain.*
16 RIVER *literary* if a river rises somewhere, it begins there: *The Rhine rises in Switzerland.*
17 rise and shine *spoken* used humorously to tell someone to wake up and get out of bed
rise above sth *phr v* if someone rises above a bad situation or bad influences, they do not let these things affect them because they are mentally strong or have strong moral principles: *You expect a certain amount of criticism, but you have to rise above it.* | *I try to rise above such prejudices.*
rise to sth *phr v* if you rise to a remark, you reply to it rather than ignoring it, especially because it has made you angry: *You shouldn't rise to his comments.* | *He refused to* ***rise to the bait*** (=react in the way someone wanted him to).

rise² ●●● S3 W2 *n*
1 INCREASE [C] an increase in number, amount, or value SYN **increase** OPP **fall**: **[+in]** *We are expecting a rise in interest rates.* | *an alarming rise in unemployment* | **[+of]** *Profits went up to £24 million, a rise of 16%.*
2 WAGES [C] *BrE* an increase in wages SYN **raise** *AmE*: *He's been promised a rise next year.* | *The railworkers were offered a 3%* ***pay rise.***
3 SUCCESS/POWER [singular] the achievement of importance, success, or power OPP **fall**: **[+of]** *the rise of fascism* | *the rise of Napoleon* | **[+to]** *Thatcher's rise to power in the late 70s* | *The band's sudden* ***rise to fame*** *took everyone by surprise.* | *his swift* ***rise to prominence*** | *the* ***rise and fall*** *of the Roman Empire*
4 give rise to sth *formal* to be the reason why something happens, especially something bad or unpleasant → **provoke**: *His speech gave rise to a bitter argument.* | *The president's absence has given rise to speculation about his health.*
5 MOVEMENT UP [singular] a movement upwards OPP **fall**: **[+in]** *a sudden rise in sea levels* | *She watched the steady* ***rise and fall*** *of his chest.*
6 SLOPE [C] an upward slope or a hill: *There's a slight rise in the road.* | *They topped the rise* (=reached the top of the hill) *and began a slow descent towards the town.*
7 get a rise out of sb *informal* to make someone become annoyed or embarrassed by making a joke about them → **make fun of sb**: *She enjoys getting a rise out of you.*

COLLOCATIONS

ADJECTIVES/NOUN + rise

sharp/steep (=great and sudden) *There's been a sharp rise in house prices.*
dramatic (=great and sudden) *The meter showed a dramatic rise in the level of radioactivity.*
huge/massive *The result was a huge rise in unemployment.*
substantial/significant *Manufacturers claimed the increase would mean a substantial rise in costs.*
rapid | **steady** | **a 10%/40% etc rise** | **a price rise** | **a rent rise** *BrE* | **a temperature rise**

PHRASES

a rise in the number of sth *There has been a rise in the number of arrests for drug offences.*

ris·er /ˈraɪzə $ -ər/ *n* [C] **1 early/late riser** someone who usually gets out of bed very early or very late **2** *technical* the upright part of a step on a set of stairs **3 risers** [plural] *AmE* a set of wooden or metal steps that can be moved from place to place, used for a group of people to stand on: *The school choir stood on risers behind the orchestra.*

ris·i·ble /ˈrɪzəbəl/ *adj formal* something that is risible is so stupid that it deserves to be laughed at SYN **ridiculous**: *a risible suggestion* —**risibility** /ˌrɪzəˈbɪləti/ *n* [U]

ris·ing¹ /ˈraɪzɪŋ/ ●○○ *adj*
1 [only before noun] becoming more important or famous: *Francesca was a* ***rising star*** *in the cinema.*
2 the rising generation *BrE* young people who will soon be old enough to vote, have jobs etc: *The rising generation of students are optimistic about the future.*

rising² *n* [C] *BrE* a sudden attempt by a large group of people to violently remove a government or ruler SYN **uprising**, **rebellion**

ˌrising ˈdamp *n* [U] *BrE* a condition where water comes up from the ground and gets into the walls of a building

risk¹ /rɪsk/ ●●● S2 W1 *n*
1 [C,U] the possibility that something bad, unpleasant, or dangerous may happen SYN **danger** → **chance**: **[+of]** *Skiers always face the risk of serious injury.* | **[+(that)]** *There is a risk that the disease may spread further.* | **[+to]** *There is no risk to public health.*
2 [C] an action that might have bad results → **gamble**: *It was a risk, sending a letter to my house.* | **take a risk** (=do something that might have bad results) *Isn't he taking a bit of a risk in coming here?* | **take the risk of doing sth** *I couldn't take the risk of leaving him alone even for a short time.* | **calculated risk** (=a risk you take because you think a good result is quite likely)
3 [C] something or someone that is likely to cause harm or danger: **[+to]** *Polluted water supplies are a risk to public health.* | *Meat from the infected animals is regarded as a serious* ***health risk*** (=something likely to harm people's health). | *The tyre dump is a major* ***fire risk*** (=something that could cause a dangerous fire). | *She's becoming a* ***security risk*** (=someone who may tell important secrets to an enemy).
4 at risk in a situation where you may be harmed: *We must stop these rumours; the firm's reputation is at risk.* | **[+from]** *Women are more at risk from the harmful effects of alcohol than men.* | **[+of]** *Their children are also at* ***high risk*** *of developing the disease.* | *That would mean* ***putting*** *other children* ***at risk.***
5 run a risk to be in a situation where there is a possibility that something bad could happen to you: **run the risk of doing sth** *Anyone travelling without a passport runs the risk of being arrested.*
6 at the risk of doing sth used when you think that what you are going to say or do may have a bad result, may offend or annoy people etc: *At the risk of sounding stupid,*

can I ask a question? | Will they go ahead with their plans, even at the risk of offending the Americans?

7 at your own risk if you do something at your own risk, you do it when you understand the possible dangers and have been warned about them: *You can use it, but it's at your own risk.* | *All personal belongings are left at the owner's risk.*

8 [C] a person or business judged according to the danger involved in giving them insurance or lending them money: **good/bad/poor risk** *Drivers under 21 are regarded as poor risks by insurance companies.*

COLLOCATIONS

ADJECTIVES

high *Professional sport involves a relatively high risk of injury.*
low *The risks of failure are quite low.*
considerable (=fairly large) *Starting up your own business involves considerable risks.*
a big/great/huge risk *There is a great risk that the wound will become infected.*
an increased/reduced risk *Those who smoke have an increased risk of heart disease.*
a real risk | **a serious/grave risk** (=real and big) | **a potential risk** | **attendant risks** *formal* (=risks involved in something)

VERBS

carry a risk (=might be dangerous) *Most medical operations carry some risk.*
pose a risk (=might be dangerous) *Climate change poses serious risks to the environment.*
involve/entail risk *Investments that provide a high return generally entail more risk.*
reduce/minimize a risk *This diet could reduce your risk of certain cancers.*
increase a risk | **eliminate risk** (=remove risk completely) | **avoid a risk** | **face a risk**

risk + NOUN

a risk factor (=something that increases a risk) | **risk assessment** (=a calculation of how much risk is involved in something)

PHRASES

there is a risk *There is always a risk that mistakes will be made.*
an element/degree of risk (=some risk, but not much) *There is always an element of risk in flying.*
be worth the risk *Don't walk home alone at night - it's not worth the risk.*
the risks involved/the risks associated with sth *The soldiers were well aware of the risks involved.*
the benefits outweigh the risks (=they are more important than the possible risks)

risk² ●●○ *v* [T]

1 to put something in a situation in which it could be lost, destroyed, or harmed → **gamble**: *When children start smoking, they don't realize that they're risking their health.* | **risk sth to do sth** *He's prepared to risk everything to avoid this war.* | **risk sth on sth** *You'd be crazy to risk your money on an investment like that!* | *He* ***risked*** *his* ***life*** *helping others to escape.* | *I'm not going to* ***risk*** *my* ***neck*** (=risk my life) *just to save a common criminal.* | *Why* ***risk life and limb*** (=risk your life and health) *jumping out of a plane just to raise money for charity?*

2 to get into a situation where something unpleasant may happen to you → **endanger**: **risk doing sth** *They may even risk losing their homes.* | **risk defeat/death etc** *He would prefer not to risk another embarrassing defeat.* | *Some people are prepared to risk imprisonment for what they believe.* | **risk being seen/caught/arrested etc** *Workers who broke the strike risked being attacked when they left the factory.*

3 to do something that you know may have dangerous or unpleasant results: **risk doing sth** *Are you prepared to risk traveling without an armed guard?* | *She risked a glance back over her shoulder.* | *You could slip out of school between classes, but I wouldn't* ***risk it***.

GRAMMAR

Risk is followed by an **-ing** form, not an infinitive. You say: *They risk being shot if they are caught.* ✗ Don't say: *They risk to be shot.*
GRAMMAR GUIDE ▸ VERBS

ˈrisk aˌverse *adj* not willing to take risks: *Shareholders are more risk averse than they used to be.*

ˈrisk ˌmanagement *n* [U] **1** a system to prevent or reduce dangerous accidents or mistakes **2** *technical* the practice of managing INVESTMENTS in ways that produce as much profit as possible while limiting the danger of losses

ˈrisk-ˌtaking *n* [U] when people do things that involve risks in order to achieve something —**risk-taker** *n* [C]

risk·y /ˈrɪski/ ●●○ *adj* involving a risk that something bad will happen SYN **dangerous**: *Doctors say it's* ***too risky*** *to try and operate.* | *Buying a secondhand car is a* ***risky business***.
THESAURUS ▸ DANGEROUS —**riskiness** *n* [U]

ri·sot·to /rɪˈzɒtəʊ $ -ˈsɔːtoʊ/ *n* (*plural* **risottos**) [C,U] a hot meal made from rice mixed with cheese, vegetables, or pieces of meat

ris·qué /ˈrɪskeɪ $ rɪˈskeɪ/ *adj* a joke, remark etc that is risqué is slightly shocking, because it is about sex

ris·sole /ˈrɪsəʊl $ -soʊl/ *n* [C] *BrE* cooked meat cut into very small pieces, mixed with potato or bread, and cooked in hot fat

rite /raɪt/ ●○○ *n* [C]

1 a ceremony that is always performed in the same way, usually for religious purposes → **ritual**: *funeral rites* | *ancient fertility rites* | *These traditional* ***rites*** *are* ***performed*** *only by the women of the village.*

2 rite of passage a special ceremony or action that is a sign of a new stage in someone's life, especially when a boy starts to become a man → **coming of age**

3 last rites final prayers or religious ceremonies for someone who is dying: *A priest came to* ***give*** *him* ***the last rites***.

rit·u·al¹ /ˈrɪtʃuəl/ ●○○ *n* [C,U]

1 a ceremony that is always performed in the same way, in order to mark an important religious or social occasion → **rite**: *ancient pagan rituals* | *the importance of religion and ritual in our lives* | *The lady of the house* ***performs*** *the sacred* ***ritual*** *of lighting two candles.*

2 something that you do regularly and in the same way each time → **routine**: **[+of]** *the* ***daily ritual*** *of mealtimes* | *He* ***went through the ritual*** *of lighting his cigar.*

ritual² ●○○ *adj* [only before noun]

1 done as part of a rite or ritual: *ritual dances*

2 done in a fixed and expected way, but without real meaning or sincerity: *The police issued the usual ritual apology.* —**ritually** *adv*: *Animals are brought in and ritually slaughtered.*

rit·u·al·is·tic /ˌrɪtʃuəˈlɪstɪk◂/ *adj* ritualistic words or behaviour always follow the same pattern, especially because they form part of a ritual: *a ritualistic procession* | *the ritualistic marking of birth, marriage and death* —**ritualistically** /-kli/ *adv*

ritz·y /ˈrɪtsi/ *adj informal* fashionable and expensive SYN **fancy**: *a ritzy restaurant*

ri·val¹ /ˈraɪvəl/ ●●○ W3 *n* [C]

1 a person, group, or organization that you compete with in sport, business, a fight etc SYN **competitor**: *This gives the company a competitive advantage over its rivals.* | **[+for]** *his chief rival for the job* | *He finished 39 seconds ahead of his* ***main rival***. | *She was 2 minutes faster than her* ***nearest rival***. | *a game against their* ***old rivals***, *Manchester United* | *They still remain* ***bitter rivals*** (=hate each other). | *Their sales have now overtaken those of their* ***arch-rival*** (=main or strongest rival). | **rival company/firm/team etc** *Sheena left her job and went to work for a rival company.*

2 one of a group of things that people can choose between: *The newest model has several advantages over its rivals.*

R

rival² ●○○ *v* (**rivalled**, **rivalling** *BrE*, **rivaled**, **rivaling** *AmE*) [T] to be as good or important as someone or something else → **unrivalled**: *The college's facilities rival those of Harvard and Yale.* | *a stadium to rival any in the world*

ri·val·ry /ˈraɪvəlri/ ●○○ *n* (*plural* **rivalries**) [C,U] a situation in which two or more people, teams, or companies are competing for something, especially over a long period of time, and the feeling of competition between them → **competition**: **[+between]** *There has always been **intense rivalry** between New Zealand and Australia.* | *The two players have developed a **friendly rivalry**.* | *She had never overcome her feelings of **sibling rivalry*** (=rivalry between brothers and sisters).

riv·en /ˈrɪvən/ *adj formal* **1** if a group of people are riven, they are divided by disagreements, especially in a violent way: **[+by/with]** *a community riven by religious differences* **2** if an object is riven, it is divided into two or more parts

riv·er /ˈrɪvə $ -ər/ ●●● S2 W2 *n* [C]
1 a natural and continuous flow of water in a long line across a country into the sea → **stream**: *the Mississippi River* | *the River Thames* | **on a river** *There were several boats on the river.* | **along a river** *We went for a walk along the river.* | **up/down (a) river** *a ship sailing up river* | *They drifted slowly down river.* | **across a river** *a bridge across the river*
2 a large amount of moving liquid: **[+of]** *a river of hot lava flowing from the volcano* → **sell sb down the river** at SELL¹

GRAMMAR: Patterns with river

in the river
• You use **in the river** to talk about things that happen in the water: *In summer we swim in the river.* | *There was something floating in the river.*

on the river
• You use **on the river** to talk about things that happen on the surface of a river or very close to the edge of a river: *We went boating on the river.* | *There's a nice pub on the river.*

along the river
• You use **along the river** to talk about things that happen on land next to a river: *They strolled along the river.* | *There are houses built all along the river.*

USAGE: Word order with names of rivers

• In Britain and Europe, the name usually comes after the word 'river'. You usually say: *the River Thames, the River Seine, the River Rhone, the River Nile, the River Ganges.*
• In the US and outside Europe, the name usually comes before the word 'river'. You usually say: *the Yangtze River, the Amazon River, the Congo River, the Hudson River, the Mississippi River, the Colorado River.*

COLLOCATIONS

VERBS

a river flows *The River Avon flows through the town of Stratford.*
a river runs (=it flows in a particular direction) *the place where the river runs into the sea*
a river winds (=it turns and curves, rather than going in a straight line) *He could see the river winding across the plain.*
a river floods | **a river dries up** | **a river narrows** (=it becomes narrower) | **a river rises somewhere** *formal* (=it starts there) | **cross a river** | **ford a river** (=cross a river on foot, in a vehicle, or on a horse, without using a bridge) | **navigate a river** (=travel along a river in a boat)

ADJECTIVES

wide/broad *We crossed the wide River Rhone the following morning.*
long *The Severn is the longest river in Britain.*
swollen/high (=containing more water than usual) *After the rains, the river was swollen.*
fast-flowing *The child fell into a fast-flowing river.*
a mighty river (=very big and impressive) *Cairo sits at the mouth of the mighty river Nile.*
a river is navigable (=people are able to travel along it in a boat)

river + NOUN

the river bank *Crowds lined the river banks to watch the boat race.*
a river bed (=the bottom of a river) | **a river valley**

PHRASES

the banks of a river (=the land near a river) *He bought a house on the banks of the River Wye.*
the mouth of a river (=where it joins the sea) *The Statue of Liberty stands at the mouth of the Hudson River.*
the source of a river (=the place where it starts) | **the upper/lower etc reaches of a river** (=the upper, lower etc parts) | **a bend in a river** | **a river is in spate** *BrE* (=it is very full and the water is flowing very quickly)

ˈriver ˌbasin *n* [C] an area from which all the water flows into the same river

ˈriver bed *n* [C] the ground at the bottom of a river → **sea bed**

riv·er·side /ˈrɪvəsaɪd $ -ər-/ *n* **the riverside** the land along the sides of a river: *We had a picnic by the riverside.* —**riverside** *adj*: *a riverside inn*

riv·et¹ /ˈrɪvɪt/ *v* **1 be riveted on/to/by sth** if your attention is riveted on something, you are so interested or so frightened that you keep looking at it: *All eyes were riveted on her in horror.* **2 be riveted to the spot** to be so shocked or frightened that you cannot move **3** [T] to fasten something with rivets

rivet² *n* [C] a metal pin used to fasten pieces of metal together → **bolt**

riv·et·ing /ˈrɪvətɪŋ/ *adj* something that is riveting is so interesting or exciting that you cannot stop watching it or listening to it SYN **fascinating**: *a riveting performance* | *His story makes riveting listening.* THESAURUS ▸ INTERESTING

Ri·vi·e·ra /ˌrɪviˈeərə $ -ˈerə/ *n* **the French/Italian/English Riviera** a warm coast that is popular with people who are on holiday, especially the Mediterranean coast of France

riv·u·let /ˈrɪvjəlɪt/ *n* [C] *written* a very small stream of water or liquid: **[+of]** *rivulets of rain running down the window*

ri·yal /riˈɑːl $ riˈɒːl, -ˈɑːl/ *n* [C] another spelling of RIAL

RN /ˌɑːr ˈen/ **1** the abbreviation of ***registered nurse*** **2** *BrE* the abbreviation of ***Royal Navy***: *Captain Anstruther, RN*

RNA /ˌɑːr en ˈeɪ/ *n* [U] an important chemical that exists in all living cells → **DNA**

roach /rəʊtʃ $ roʊtʃ/ *n* [C] **1** *AmE informal* a COCKROACH **2** a type of European fish **3** *informal* the end part of a MARIJUANA cigarette that has been smoked

road /rəʊd $ roʊd/ ●●● S1 W1 *n*
1 [C,U] a specially prepared hard surface for cars, buses, bicycles etc to travel on → **street**, **motorway**, **freeway**: **along the road** *I was driving along the road when a kid suddenly stepped out in front of me.* | **up the road** *You'll see the library a bit further up the road.* | **down the road** *I ran down the road to see what was happening.* | *My sister lives just down the road.* | **in the road** *Protestors sat down in the road to stop the lorries.* | **in the middle of the road** *Someone was standing in the middle of the road.* | **across the road** *I ran across the road to meet him.* | **by road** *The college is easily accessible by road.* | **on the road** *There are far more cars on the road now than there used to be.* | *There were lots of cars parked on the road.*
2 Road (*written abbreviation* **Rd.**) used in addresses after the names of roads and streets: *65 Maple Road* | *He lives on Dudley **Road**.*
3 on the road a) travelling in a car, especially for long distances: *I've been on the road since 5:00 a.m. this morning.* **b)** if a group of actors or musicians are on the road,

they are travelling from place to place giving performances: *They're on the road for six months out of every year.* **c)** if your car is on the road, you have paid for the repairs, tax etc necessary for you to drive it legally: *It would cost too much to put it back on the road.*
4 the road to sth if you are on the road to something, you will achieve it soon, or it will happen to you soon: *The doctor says she's* ***well on the road to*** *recovery.* | *It was this deal that* ***set*** *him* ***on the road to*** *his first million.* | *the first* ***step along the road to*** *democracy*
5 go down a/this road to choose a particular course of action: *Is there any scope for going down that road in the future?* | *It depends which road you want to go down.*
6 along/down the road in the future, especially at a later stage in a process: *You can always upgrade a bit further down the road if you want.* | *Somewhere down the road, they're going to clash.*
7 one for the road *spoken* a last alcoholic drink before you leave a party, PUB etc
8 road to Damascus a situation in which someone experiences a sudden and complete change in their opinions or beliefs. The phrase is based on the story in the New Testament of the Bible, in which St Paul saw a blinding light and heard God's voice while he was travelling on the road to Damascus. He immediately became a Christian.
→ **the end of the road** at END[1](16), → **hit the road** at HIT[1](13)

USAGE: Up/down the road
You often use the phrases **up the road** and **down the road** when saying that someone or something is not far away, on the same road: *She lives just up the road from us.*| *The post office is down the road on the right.*

COLLOCATIONS
ADJECTIVES/NOUN + road
busy (=with a lot of traffic) *The children have to cross a busy road to get to school.*
quiet (=with little traffic) *At that time of night, the roads were quiet.*
clear (=with no traffic or nothing blocking it) *Before you overtake, make sure the road is clear.*
a main road (=an important road that is used a lot) | **a minor road** | **a side road/a back road** (=a small road that is not used much) | **a country road** | **a mountain road** | **the coast road** | **the open road** (=a road without much traffic or anything to stop you getting somewhere)
VERBS
cross a road *She was standing on the pavement waiting to cross the road.*
run out into a road *He had to swerve when a child ran out into the road.*
a road leads/goes/runs somewhere *We turned into the road leading to the village.*
a road winds (=it turns and curves, rather than going in a straight line) | **a road forks** (=it starts going ahead in two different directions) | **a road narrows/widens**
road + NOUN
a road accident *Her husband was killed in a road accident.*
road safety *We share parents' concern for road safety.*
road sense (=knowledge of how to behave safely near traffic)
PHRASES
the side of the road *We stopped and had something to eat by the side of the road.*
the road ahead (=in front of you) *The road ahead was completely flooded.*
a fork in the road (=a place where a road goes in two different directions)

ˈroad ˌatlas *n* (*plural* **road atlases**) [C] a map that shows the roads in a particular country or area: *a road atlas of Europe*

road·block /ˈrəʊdblɒk $ ˈroʊdblɑːk/ *n* [C] **1** a place where the police are stopping traffic → **check point**: *The police have* ***set up roadblocks*** *to try and catch the two men.* **2** *AmE* something that stops the progress of a plan: *mental roadblocks that get in the way of success*

ˈroad hog *n* [C] *informal* someone who drives badly or too fast without thinking about other people's safety

road·house /ˈrəʊdhaʊs $ ˈroʊd-/ *n* [C] *AmE* a restaurant or bar on a main road outside a city

road·ie /ˈrəʊdi $ ˈroʊ-/ *n* [C] *informal* someone whose job is moving equipment for rock musicians

road·kill /ˈrəʊdkɪl $ ˈroʊd-/ *n* [U] *AmE informal* animals that have been killed by cars on the road

ˈroad ˌmanager *n* [C] someone who makes arrangements for entertainers when they are travelling

ˈroad map *n* **1 a road map to peace** an official plan to achieve peace in the future, that sets out what each country, government, group etc should try to do at particular stages along the way **2 a road map to sth** a guide telling you about something, or telling you how to use or do something: *a road map to the United States Constitution*

ˈroad ˌpricing *n* [U] a system in which drivers have to pay to use the roads at particular times → **toll road**: *road pricing schemes for congested cities*

ˈroad rage *n* [U] violence and angry behaviour by car drivers towards other car drivers: *Road rage seems to be on the increase.* | *a road rage attack*

road·run·ner /ˈrəʊdrʌnə $ ˈroʊdrʌnər/ *n* [C] a small bird that runs very fast and lives mainly in deserts

road·show /ˈrəʊdʃəʊ $ ˈroʊdʃoʊ/ *n* [C] a group of people who travel around the country entertaining the public, advertising, or providing a service

road·side /ˈrəʊdsaɪd $ ˈroʊd-/ *n* **the roadside** the edge of the road: **on/by/at the roadside** *a van parked by the roadside* —**roadside** *adj*: *a roadside snack bar*

ˈroad sign *n* [C] a sign next to a road that gives information to drivers

ˈroad tax *n* [U] a tax in Britain that the owner of a vehicle must pay in order to drive it legally → **tax disc**

ˈroad test *n* [C] a test to check that a vehicle is in good condition and safe to drive → **MOT** —**roadtest** /ˈrəʊdtest $ ˈroʊd-/ *v* [T]: *All our vehicles are roadtested before they are sold.*

ˈroad trip *n* [C] *AmE* a long trip that you take in a car, usually with friends

ˈroad ˌwarrior *n* [C] *informal* someone who uses computers, MOBILE PHONES, PAGERS etc in a place other than their home or office

road·way /ˈrəʊdweɪ $ ˈroʊd-/ *n* [C] the part of the road used by vehicles

road·works /ˈrəʊdwɜːks $ ˈroʊdwɜːrks/ *n* [plural] *BrE* repairs that are being done to a road: *There were roadworks on the motorway.*

road·wor·thy /ˈrəʊdˌwɜːði $ ˈroʊdˌwɜːr-/ *adj* a vehicle that is roadworthy is in good condition and safe enough to drive —**roadworthiness** *n* [U]

roam /rəʊm $ roʊm/ ●○○ *v*
1 [I,T] to walk or travel, usually for a long time, with no clear purpose or direction → **wander**: **[+over/around/about etc]** *The dogs are allowed to roam around.* | *Chickens and geese* ***roam freely*** *in the back yard.* | *You shouldn't let your children* ***roam the streets***. | **roam the countryside/desert/forests etc** *Wild sheep roam the hills.* **THESAURUS** TRAVEL
2 [I always + adv/prep, T] if your eyes roam over something, you look slowly at all parts of it: *Her eyes roamed the room.* | **[+over]** *His eyes roamed over the bookshelves.*
3 [I] to use your MOBILE PHONE in a different country or area from usual by connecting to a different network: *Some pay-as-you-go phones do not allow you to roam.*

roam·ing /ˈrəʊmɪŋ $ ˈroʊ-/ *n* [U] the process that a MOBILE PHONE uses when it is in a different country or area from usual, and has to connect to a different network

roan /rəʊn $ roʊn/ *n* [C] a horse with some white hairs, giving it a light colour —**roan** *adj*

roar¹ /rɔː $ rɔːr/ ●●○ *v*
1 [I] to make a deep, very loud noise → **growl**: *We heard a lion roar.* | *The engines roared.*
2 [I,T] to shout something in a deep powerful voice: *'Get out of my house!' he roared.* | *The crowd roared in delight.* THESAURUS ▸ SHOUT
3 [I] to laugh loudly and continuously: *By this time, Michael was **roaring with laughter**.*
4 [I always + adv/prep] if a vehicle roars somewhere, it moves very quickly and noisily: *The car roared off down the road.*
roar back *phr v* if a competitor or team that was losing roars back, they start performing much better – used in sports reports: *In the second half Leeds **came roaring back** with two goals in five minutes.*

roar² ●○○ *n* [C]
1 a deep, loud noise made by an animal such as a lion, or by someone's voice → **growl**: *the roar of the crowd* | *He let out a **roar of laughter**.*
2 a continuous loud noise, especially made by a machine or a strong wind: *the roar of the traffic* THESAURUS ▸ SOUND

roar·ing /ˈrɔːrɪŋ/ *adj* **1** [only before noun] making a deep, very loud, continuous noise: *the roaring wind and waves* **2 roaring fire** a fire that burns with a lot of flames and heat **3 do a roaring trade (in sth)** *BrE informal* to sell a lot of something very quickly: *The stallholders were doing a roaring trade in burgers.* **4 be a roaring success** *BrE informal* to be extremely successful: *The new musical has been a roaring success.* **5 roaring drunk** *BrE informal* very drunk and noisy

roast¹ /rəʊst $ roʊst/ ●●○ *v* [I,T]
1 to cook something, such as meat, in an OVEN or over a fire, or to cook in this way → **grill**, **bake**: *Are you going to roast the chicken?* | *the delicious smell of meat roasting* | *We caught a rabbit and roasted it over an open fire.* THESAURUS ▸ COOK
2 to heat nuts, coffee beans etc quickly in order to dry them and give them a particular taste: *dry-roasted peanuts*

roast² ●●○ *adj* [only before noun] roasted: *roast chicken*

roast³ *n* [C] **1** a large piece of roasted meat: *a traditional Sunday roast* **2 hot dog roast/oyster roast etc** *AmE* an outdoor party at which food is cooked on an open fire **3** *AmE* an occasion at which people celebrate a special event in someone's life by telling funny stories or giving speeches about them: *a celebrity roast*

roast·ing¹ /ˈrəʊstɪŋ $ ˈroʊ-/ *adj* **1** (*also* ˌ**roasting** ˈ**hot**) *informal* very hot, especially so that you feel uncomfortable: *a roasting hot day* | *I'm absolutely roasting in this suit.* **2** [only before noun] used for roasting food: *a roasting dish* → see picture at **PAN¹**

roasting² *n* **give sb/get a roasting** *BrE informal* if you give someone a roasting, you tell them angrily that you disapprove of their behaviour: *He got a roasting from angry fans.*

rob /rɒb $ rɑːb/ ●●○ S3 *v* (**robbed**, **robbing**) [T]
1 to steal money or property from a person, bank etc → **steal**, **burgle**: *They killed four policemen while robbing a bank.* | *A 77-year-old woman was robbed at knifepoint.* | **rob sb of sth** *They threatened to shoot him and robbed him of all his possessions.* ⚠ You say that someone **robs** a person or place. Do not say that someone robs an object or an amount of money. Use **steal**: *He stole cash and valuables worth $500,000.* THESAURUS ▸ STEAL
2 rob Peter to pay Paul to take money away from someone or something that needs it in order to pay someone else or use it for something else: *Taking money out of the hospital's budget for this is simply robbing Peter to pay Paul.*
3 rob sb blind *informal* to steal everything someone has: *The minute your back's turned, they'll rob you blind.*
4 I/we was robbed! *BrE spoken* used when you think that you were beaten unfairly in a sport
5 rob the cradle *AmE* to have a sexual relationship with someone who is a lot younger than you – used humorously SYN **cradle-snatch** *BrE*
rob sb/sth **of** sth *phr v literary* to take away an important quality, ability etc from someone or something: *The illness robbed him of a normal childhood.*

rob·ber /ˈrɒbə $ ˈrɑːbər/ ●●○ *n* [C] someone who steals money or property → **thief**, **burglar**: *Armed robbers broke into the shop and demanded money from the till.* | *a bank robber* THESAURUS ▸ THIEF

ˌ**robber** ˈ**baron** *n* [C] a powerful person who uses their money and influence to get more money, business, land etc in a way that is slightly dishonest

rob·ber·y /ˈrɒbəri $ ˈrɑː-/ ●●○ *n* (*plural* **robberies**) [C,U] the crime of stealing money or things from a bank, shop etc, especially using violence → **theft**, **burglary**: *Police are investigating a series of **bank robberies** in South Wales.* | *He received a 10 year prison sentence for **armed robbery** (=robbery using a gun).* | *He admitted **attempted robbery** and was given a suspended sentence.* THESAURUS ▸ CRIME → **daylight robbery** at DAYLIGHT(5), → **highway robbery** at HIGHWAY(3)

robe /rəʊb $ roʊb/ ●●○ *n* [C]
1 (*also* **robes**) a long loose piece of clothing, especially one worn for official ceremonies: *a priest's robes*
2 *especially AmE* a long loose piece of clothing that you wear over your night clothes or after a bath SYN **bathrobe**, **dressing gown** *BrE*

robed /rəʊbd $ roʊbd/ *adj formal* wearing long loose clothing: *a robed figure* | **[+in]** *a man robed in black*

Robert the Bruce → BRUCE, ROBERT (THE)

rob·in /ˈrɒbɪn $ ˈrɑː-/ *n* [C] **1** a small European bird with a red breast and brown back **2** a North American bird like a European robin, but larger

ˌ**Robin** ˈ**Hood** in old English stories, a man who lived as an OUTLAW in Sherwood Forest in central England, with his followers, known as his 'Merry Men'. These included Friar Tuck, Little John, and Maid Marian. His enemy is the evil Sheriff of Nottingham, who is always trying to catch him. Robin Hood is usually shown dressed in green clothes, holding a BOW. He is remembered especially for robbing the rich and giving to the poor, and people use his name to describe a situation in which money is taken from rich people and given to poor people: *a new higher-rate tax that will have a 'Robin Hood effect' on income distribution*

ˌ**Robin** ˈ**Hood tax** *n* [singular] *BrE* a suggested tax on the buying and selling of SHARES, BONDS etc, in order to get money to help poor people and countries

Robinson Cru·soe /ˌrɒbənsən ˈkruːsəʊ $ ˌrɑː-/ the main character in the book *Robinson Crusoe* by Daniel Defoe. When Robinson Crusoe's ship sinks, he manages to reach a DESERT ISLAND (=a small tropical island with no people living on it) where he builds a home. Later he meets a black man who he calls Man Friday and who becomes his servant and friend. They are both finally discovered by a British ship and taken home. If someone lives alone on an island, people sometimes compare them to Robinson Crusoe: *The explorer is a latter-day Robinson Crusoe.*

ro·bo·call /ˈrəʊbəʊkɔːl $ ˈroʊboʊkɒːl/ *n* [C] *especially AmE* a telephone call with a recorded message that is made AUTOMATICALLY

ro·bo·dial·er /ˈrəʊbəʊˌdaɪələ $ ˈroʊboʊˌdaɪələr/ *n* [C] *AmE* an AUTODIALLER

ro·bot /ˈrəʊbɒt $ ˈroʊbɑːt, -bət/ ●●○ *n* [C] a machine that can move and do some of the work of a person, and is usually controlled by a computer: *cars built by robots*

ro·bot·ic /rəʊˈbɒtɪk $ roʊˈbɑː-/ *adj* **1** [only before noun] robotic equipment etc is related to robots or is part of a robot: *the space shuttle's robotic arm* **2** someone who is robotic acts like a robot by making stiff movements, not showing any human feelings etc

ro·bo·tics /rəʊˈbɒtɪks $ ˈroʊbɑː-/ *n* [U] the study of how robots are made and used

ro·bust /rəˈbʌst, ˈrəʊbʌst $ rəˈbʌst, ˈroʊ-/ ●○○ *adj*
1 a robust person is strong and healthy: *a robust man of six feet four* THESAURUS ▸ HEALTHY

2 a robust system, organization etc is strong and not likely to have problems: *The formerly robust economy has begun to weaken.*
3 a robust object is strong and not likely to break SYN **sturdy**: *a robust metal cabinet* THESAURUS▸ STRONG
4 showing determination or strong opinions: *a typically robust performance by the prime minister*
5 robust food or FLAVOURS have a good strong taste: *a robust cheese* —**robustly** *adv* —**robustness** *n* [U]

rock[1] /rɒk $ rɑːk/ ●●● S2 W2 *n*
1 STONE **a)** [U] the hard substance that forms the main surface of the Earth → **stone**: *To build the tunnel, they had to cut through 500 feet of* **solid rock**. | *Most of the country is desert and* **bare rock**. | *massive* **rock formations** (=shapes made naturally from rock) | *ancient dark* **volcanic rock** **b)** [C] a piece of rock, especially a large one that sticks up from the ground: *Jack stood on a rock for a better view.* | *During the storm a ship had been driven onto* **the rocks** (=a line of rocks under or next to the sea). → see picture at STONE[1]
2 MUSIC [U] (*also* **rock music**) a type of popular modern music with a strong loud beat, played using GUITARS and drums: **rock band/group** *Komuro formed a rock band with some friends while in college.* | *the late rock star, Freddie Mercury* | *The stadium has hosted numerous* **rock concerts**. → HARD ROCK, → **punk rock** at PUNK(1)
3 (as) solid/steady as a rock a) very strongly built or well supported and not likely to break or fall: *a large sofa, solid as a rock* **b)** someone who is as solid or steady as a rock is very strong and calm in difficult situations and you can depend on them → ROCK-SOLID
4 [singular] someone who always gives you support and who you can depend on: *My sister has always been my rock.*
5 be on the rocks *informal* a relationship or business that is on the rocks is having a lot of problems and is likely to fail soon SYN **in trouble**: *I'm afraid Tim's marriage is on the rocks.*
6 scotch/vodka etc on the rocks *informal* an alcoholic drink that is served with ice but no water
7 SWEET FOOD [U] *BrE* a hard sweet made in long round pieces: *a* **stick of rock**
8 DRUG **a)** [U] a very pure form of the illegal drug COCAINE that some people use for pleasure **b)** [C] a small amount of this drug
9 be (stuck) between a rock and a hard place to have a choice between two things, both of which are unpleasant or dangerous
10 get your rocks off *informal not polite* if a man gets his rocks off, he has sex
11 JEWEL [C usually plural] *old-fashioned informal* a DIAMOND or other jewel

rock[2] ●○○ *v*
1 [I,T] to move gently backwards and forwards or from side to side, or to make something do this → **sway**: *She covered her face,* **rocking to and fro** *in her grief.* | *The waves* **rocked** *the boat* **from side to side**. | *Paul sat gently rocking the child in his arms.* | *Jim* **rocked with laughter** *when he heard what had happened.* THESAURUS▸ MOVE
2 [T] **a)** to make the people in a place or organization feel very shocked – used in news reports SYN **shake**: *The scandal rocked the nation.* **b)** to make the future of something seem less certain or steady than it was before, especially because of problems or changes SYN **shake**: *Another financial blow has rocked the industry.* | *The theory* **rocked the foundations** *of social and moral life.*
3 rock the boat *informal* to cause problems for other members of a group by criticizing something or trying to change the way something is done: *He kept his feelings to himself, not wanting to rock the boat.*
4 [T] if an explosion or EARTHQUAKE rocks an area, it makes it shake: *Residents had only a few minutes to escape before the blast rocked their houses.*
5 sb/sth rocks *spoken informal* said to show that you strongly approve of someone or something
6 rock sb's world *informal* to cause someone to think about something or someone in a completely new way
7 rock a trend/look etc to look good when wearing something fashionable – used especially in magazines: *We'll tell you how to rock this season's hottest looks.*

rock·a·bil·ly /ˈrɒkəbɪli $ ˈrɑːk-/ *n* [U] a type of music that combines rock music and traditional country music

ˌrock and ˈroll *n* [U] ROCK 'N' ROLL

ˌrock ˈbottom *n* **hit/reach rock bottom** *informal* to become as unhappy, unpleasant, or unsuccessful as it is possible to be: *My personal life had hit rock bottom.*

ˈrock-bottom *adj* [only before noun] a rock-bottom price is as low as it can possibly be: *bargain holidays at* **rock-bottom prices**

ˈrock ˌclimbing *n* [U] the sport of climbing up very steep rock surfaces such as the sides of mountains —**rock climber** *n* [C]

rock·er /ˈrɒkə $ ˈrɑːkər/ *n* [C] **1** *AmE* a ROCKING CHAIR **2** one of the curved pieces of wood fixed to the bottom of a ROCKING CHAIR, that allows it to move backwards and forwards if you push it **3 be off your rocker** *spoken informal* to be crazy **4** a member of a group of young people in Britain in the 1960s who wore leather jackets, rode MOTORCYCLES, and listened to ROCK 'N' ROLL music → **mod**, **greaser 5** a musician who plays ROCK 'N' ROLL music, or someone who likes this kind of music: *ageing rockers*

rock·e·ry /ˈrɒkəri $ ˈrɑː-/ *n* (*plural* **rockeries**) [C] *BrE* part of a garden where there are rocks with small plants growing between them SYN **rock garden**

rock·et[1] /ˈrɒkɪt $ ˈrɑː-/ ●●○ *n*
1 [C] a vehicle used for travelling or carrying things into space, which is shaped like a big tube → **spacecraft**: *The* **rocket** *was* **launched** *from a space research base.* | *a* **space rocket**
2 [C] a weapon shaped like a big tube that is fired at things → **missile**: *anti-tank rockets*
3 [C] a FIREWORK that goes high into the air before exploding into coloured lights
4 [U] *BrE* a plant with green leaves and a strong taste, eaten raw in SALADS SYN **arugula** *AmE*

rocket[2] *v* [I] **1** (*also* **rocket up**) if a price or amount rockets, it increases quickly and suddenly: *Interest rates rocketed up.* | **rocket (from sth) to sth** *Car sales rocketed from 180 to 2000 a year.* **2** [always + adv/prep] to move somewhere very fast SYN **shoot**: *The train rocketed through the tunnel.* | *Larsson's shot rocketed into the back of the net.* **3** [always + adv/prep] to achieve a successful position very quickly SYN **shoot**: **[+to]** *Their new album rocketed to number one in the charts.* | *Beatty rocketed to stardom after his first film.*

ˈrocket ˌscience *n* **sth is not rocket science** *informal* used to say that something is not difficult to do or understand: *Designing a website may be a lot of work but it's not rocket science.*

ˈrocket ˌscientist *n* [C] **1 it doesn't take a rocket scientist (to do sth)** *informal* used humorously to emphasize that something is easy to do or understand: *It doesn't take a rocket scientist to work out that doubling productivity will improve profits.* **2** someone who is extremely clever **3** a scientist whose work is related to rockets

ˈrock face *n* [C] a very steep surface of rock on the side of a mountain

rock·fall /ˈrɒkfɔːl $ ˈrɑːkfɒːl/ *n* [C] a pile of rocks that are falling or have fallen

ˈrock ˌgarden *n* [C] a ROCKERY

ˌrock-ˈhard *adj* **1** extremely hard: *The bread was stale and rock-hard.* **2** *BrE* strong and not afraid of anyone – used humorously

ˈrocking chair *n* [C] a chair that has two curved pieces of wood fixed under its legs, so that it moves backwards and forwards smoothly → see picture at CHAIR[1]

ˈrocking horse *n* [C] a wooden horse for children that moves backwards and forwards when you sit on it

ˈrock ˌmusic *n* [U] a type of popular modern music with a strong loud beat, played using GUITARS and drums

rock 'n' roll /ˌrɒk ən ˈrəʊl $ ˌrɑːk ən ˈroʊl/ *n* [U] **1** a style of music with a strong loud beat played on GUITARS and drums, which first became popular in the 1950s: *Elvis, the king of rock 'n' roll* **2 sth is the new rock 'n' roll** *BrE* used to say that a particular activity has become very popular and fashionable and is being discussed a lot on television, in newspapers etc: *Hadn't Mark heard that cooking was the new rock 'n' roll?*

'rock pool *n* [C] *BrE* a small pool of water between rocks by the sea SYN **tide pool** *AmE*

'rock salt *n* [U] a type of salt which is obtained from under the ground → **sea salt**

ˌrock-'solid, rock solid *adj* **1** rock-solid things can be depended on and trusted not to change: *a rock-solid guarantee* **2** very hard and not likely to break

rock·y /ˈrɒki $ ˈrɑːki/ ●○○ *adj*
1 covered with rocks or made of rock: *a rocky cliff | They hurried over the rough* ***rocky ground***.
2 *informal* a relationship or situation that is rocky is difficult and may not continue or be successful: *Rangers got off to a* ***rocky start*** *this season. | The company faces a* ***rocky road*** *ahead.*

ro·co·co /rəˈkəʊkəʊ $ rəˈkoʊkoʊ/ *adj* rococo buildings and furniture have a lot of curly decoration and were fashionable in Europe in the 18th century

rod /rɒd $ rɑːd/ ●○○ *n* [C]
1 a long thin pole or bar: **steel/iron/wooden etc rod** *The walls are reinforced with steel rods. | a measuring rod*
2 a long thin pole used with a line and hook for catching fish SYN **fishing rod** → HOT ROD, LIGHTNING ROD, → **rule sb/sth with a rod of iron** at RULE²(5)

rode /rəʊd $ roʊd/ *v* the past tense of RIDE

ro·dent /ˈrəʊdənt $ ˈroʊ-/ *n* [C] any small animal of the type that has long sharp front teeth, such as a rat or a rabbit

ro·de·o /ˈrəʊdiəʊ, rəʊˈdeɪ-əʊ $ ˈroʊdioʊ, roʊˈdeɪ-oʊ/ *n* (*plural* **rodeos**) [C] a type of entertainment in which COWBOYS ride wild horses, catch cattle with ropes, and ride in races

roe /rəʊ $ roʊ/ *n* [C,U] fish eggs eaten as a food → **caviar**

'roe deer *n* (*plural* **roe deer**) [C] a small European and Asian DEER that lives in forests

ROFL (*rolling on the floor laughing*) used by people communicating on the Internet to say that they are very amused by something that someone else has written SYN **ROTFL**

ro·ger¹ /ˈrɒdʒə $ ˈrɑːdʒər/ *interjection* used in radio conversations to say that a message has been understood

roger² *v* [T] *BrE informal not polite* to have sex with someone

rogue¹ /rəʊg $ roʊg/ *n* [C] **1** a man or boy who behaves badly, but who you like in spite of this – often used humorously: *What's the old rogue done now, I wonder? | a lovable rogue* **2** *BrE old-fashioned* a man who is dishonest and has a bad character

rogue² *adj* [only before noun] **1** not behaving in the usual or accepted way and often causing trouble: *rogue moneylenders | Officials are concerned about rogue regimes that may have nuclear weapons. | What happens when a spy* ***goes rogue***? **2** a rogue wild animal lives apart from the main group and is often dangerous

rogu·ish /ˈrəʊgɪʃ $ ˈroʊ-/ *adj* someone with a roguish expression or smile looks amused, especially because they have done something slightly dishonest or wrong —**roguishly** *adv*

Ro·hyp·nol /rəʊˈhɪpnɒl $ roʊˈhɪpnɒːl/ *n* [U] *trademark* a drug that makes you sleep, which is sometimes used to make someone unable to defend themselves against RAPE

role /rəʊl $ roʊl/ ●●● S2 W1 AWL *n* [C]
1 the way in which someone or something is involved in an activity or situation, and how much influence they have on it: **[+in]** *women's role in society | the role of diet in the prevention of disease* | **[+of]** *They want to limit the role of government.*
2 the character played by an actor in a play or film SYN **part**: **[+of]** *Matthews* ***plays*** *the* ***role*** *of a young doctor suspected of murder.* | **the lead/leading/starring role** (=the most important role) *A young actor named Johnny Depp was given the leading role.* | **major/minor role** *It was Johansson's first major movie role.* | **the title role** (=the role of the character whose name is in the title of a film or play) *The film features Paul Schofield in the title role.*
3 role reversal a situation in which two people, especially a man and a woman, each do what is traditionally expected of the other

COLLOCATIONS

VERBS

play/have a role *He played a prominent role in the company's success.*
take on a role (*also* **assume a role** *formal*) (=start having it) *Mr Jones took on the role of spokesperson for the organization.*
take a role *Britain began to take a more active role in the affairs of Europe.*
give sb a role

ADJECTIVES

an important/major role *She played an important role in her husband's political career.*
a key/central role *The report recognized the key role of teachers.*
a vital/crucial/essential role *Every member of the team has a vital role to play.*
an active role (=when you do practical things to achieve particular aims) *She took an active role in the community.*
a leading role (=the most important role) | **a significant role** | **a prominent role** | **a dual role** (=when someone or something does two things) | **sb's traditional role** (=one based on ideas that have existed for a long time, without changing)

'role ˌmodel ●○○ *n* [C] someone whose behaviour, attitudes etc people try to copy because they admire them: *I want to be a* ***positive role model*** *for my sister.*

'role-play *n* [C,U] an exercise in which you pretend to be in a particular situation, especially to help you learn a language or deal with problems: *Language teachers often use role-play in the classroom.* —**role-play** *v* [I,T]

roll¹ /rəʊl $ roʊl/ ●●● S1 W2 *v*
1 ROUND OBJECT [I always + adv/prep, T] if something rolls, especially something round, or if you roll it, it moves along a surface by turning over and over: **[+down/into/through etc]** *The ball rolled into the street. | One of the eggs rolled off the counter.* | **roll sth along/in/onto etc sth** *Roll the chicken breasts in flour.*
2 PERSON/ANIMAL [I,T always + adv/prep] (*also* **roll over**) to turn your body over one or more times while lying down, or to turn someone else's body over: **[+down/onto/off etc]** *The children rolled down the hill, laughing. | Ralph rolled onto his stomach.* | **roll sb onto/off sth** *I tried to roll him onto his side.*
3 SHAPE OF TUBE/BALL [T] (*also* **roll up**) to make something into the shape of a tube or ball: **roll sth into a ball/tube** *Roll the dough into small balls. | Would you like the paper rolled or folded?*
4 MAKE STH FLAT [T] to make something flat by rolling something heavy over it → **rolling pin**: *Pizza dough should be rolled thinly.*
5 CLOTHES [T] (*also* **roll up**) to fold the sleeves or legs of something that you are wearing upwards, so that they are shorter: *His sleeves were rolled above his elbows.*
6 STH WITH WHEELS [I,T always + adv/prep] to move on wheels, or make something that has wheels move: **[+into/forwards/past etc]** *Her car was slowly rolling away from the curb.* | **roll sth to/around etc sth** *The waitress rolled the dessert trolley over to our table.* THESAURUS ▸ PUSH
7 DROP OF LIQUID [I always + adv/prep] to move over a surface smoothly without stopping: **[+down/onto etc]** *Tears rolled down her cheeks.*

R

8 WAVES/CLOUDS [I always + adv/prep] to move continuously in a particular direction: **[+into/towards etc]** *Mist rolled in from the sea.* | *We watched the waves rolling onto the beach.*
9 GAME [I,T] if you roll DICE, you throw them as part of a game
10 SOUND [I] if drums or THUNDER roll, they make a long low series of sounds: *Thunder rolled in the distance.*
11 MACHINE/CAMERA [I] if a machine such as a film camera or a PRINTING PRESS rolls, it operates: *There was silence as the cameras started to roll.*
12 SHIP/PLANE [I] if a ship or plane rolls, it leans one way and then another with the movement of the water or air
13 CIGARETTE [T] to make your own cigarette, using tobacco or MARIJUANA and special paper → **roll-up**: *Ben* ***rolled*** *a* ***joint*** (=a cigarette containing marijuana) *and lit it.* | *It's cheaper to* ***roll*** *your* ***own*** (=make your own cigarettes).
14 SHOULDERS [T] to move your shoulders forward, up, and back down: *He rolled his shoulders back.*
15 EYES [T] to move your eyes around and up, especially in order to show that you are annoyed or think something is silly: *Lucy rolled her eyes as Tom sat down beside her.*
16 ATTACK [T] *AmE informal* to rob someone, especially when they are drunk and asleep: *Kids on the streets rolled drunks for small change.*
17 (all) rolled into one if someone or something is several different things rolled into one, they include or do the work of all those things: *Mum was cook, chauffeur, nurse, and entertainer all rolled into one.*
18 get (sth) rolling to start happening or make something start happening in a smooth and successful way: *The business didn't really get rolling until 1975.* | *Have a good breakfast to get your day rolling.*
19 be rolling in money/dough/cash/it to have or earn a lot of money: *'He's rolling in it,' said the girl, pointing at Lewis.*
20 be rolling in the aisles if people in a theatre, cinema etc are rolling in the aisles, they are laughing a lot
21 be ready to roll *spoken* to be ready to start doing something: *The car was packed and we were ready to roll.*
22 let's roll *spoken* used to suggest to a group of people that you all begin doing something or go somewhere
23 roll with the punches to deal with problems or difficulties by doing whatever you need to do, rather than by trying only one method: *Strong industries were able to roll with the punches during the recession.*
24 roll on sth *BrE spoken* used to say that you wish a time or event would come quickly: *Roll on the weekend!*
25 roll your r's to pronounce the sound /r/ using your tongue in a way that makes the sound very long
26 a rolling stone gathers no moss used to say that someone who often changes jobs, moves to different places etc is not able to have any permanent relationships or duties
27 that's how I roll/it's how I roll *spoken* used to say that what you are doing is how you like to do things or live your life → **set/start/keep the ball rolling** at BALL[1](5), → **heads will roll** at HEAD[1](36), → **let the good times roll** at LET[1](20)

roll around (*also* **roll round** *BrE*) *phr v* if a time, event etc that happens regularly rolls around, it arrives or takes place again: ***By the time*** *Wednesday* ***rolled around****, I still hadn't finished.*

roll sth ↔ **back** *phr v*
1 to reduce the influence or power of a law, system, government etc: *a threat to roll back the legislation of the past 12 years*
2 *especially AmE* to reduce a price, cost etc: *the administration's promise to roll back taxes* → ROLLBACK
3 to force your opponents in a war to move back from their position
4 roll back the years *BrE* to make someone remember something from the past: *Looking at those old photos really rolled back the years.*

roll sth ↔ **down** *phr v*
1 roll a window down to open a car window
2 to unfold the ends of your sleeves or trouser legs so that they are their usual length: *He rolled down his sleeves and buttoned the cuffs.*

roll in *phr v*
1 to happen or arrive in large numbers or quantities: *As the result of our appeal, the money came rolling in.*
2 to arrive, especially later than usual or expected: *Chris finally rolled in at about 4:00 am.*
3 if mist, clouds etc roll in, they begin to cover an area of the sky or land: *Fog rolled in from the sea.*

roll out *phr v*
1 roll sth ↔ out to make food that you are preparing flat and thin by pushing a ROLLING PIN over it: *Roll out the dough on a floured surface.*
2 roll sth ↔ out to make a new product available for people to buy or use SYN **launch**: *The company expects to roll out the new software in September.* → ROLL-OUT
3 to leave a place, especially later than expected: **[+of]** *We used to hear people rolling out of the pubs at closing time.* | *He finally rolled out of bed at noon.*
4 roll sth ↔ out to put something flat on the ground or a surface, when it was previously rolled into a tube shape: *We rolled out our sleeping bags under the stars.*
5 roll out the red carpet to make special preparations for an important visitor

roll (sb) **over** *phr v* to turn your body over once so that you are lying in a different position, or to turn someone's body over: *Ben rolled over and kissed her.* | **[+onto]** *The guards rolled him over onto his front.*

roll up *phr v*
1 to make something into the shape of a tube or ball, or to become this shape: **roll sth ↔ up** *Painters arrived and rolled up the carpet.* | **[+into]** *Many animals roll up into a ball for warmth.*
2 roll your sleeves/trousers etc up to turn the ends of your sleeves or trouser legs over several times so that they are shorter
3 roll your sleeves up to start doing a job even though it is difficult or you do not want to do it: *It's time to roll up our sleeves and get some work done on the basics.*
4 roll a window up to close the window of a car
5 to arrive somewhere, especially late or when you were not expected: *Max rolled up just after 9 o'clock.*
6 roll up! *BrE spoken* used to call people to come and watch or buy things at a CIRCUS or FAIR

roll[2] ●●○ *n* [C]
1 PAPER/FILM/MONEY ETC a piece of paper, camera film, money etc that has been rolled into the shape of a tube: **[+of]** *I used up three rolls of film on holiday.* | *There's a new roll of silver foil in there.* | *wallpaper costing £3 a roll* → KITCHEN ROLL, TOILET ROLL
2 BREAD a small round LOAF of bread for one person → **bun**: *hot soup served with crusty rolls* | ***bread rolls*** *with butter* | **ham/cheese etc roll** *BrE* (=one that is filled with ham, cheese etc) → see picture at BREAD
3 LIST OF NAMES an official list of names SYN **register**: **on the roll** *BrE*: *a school with 300 pupils on the roll* | **call/take the roll** (=say the list of names to check who is there) *The teacher called the roll.* | *Three senators missed the roll call.* | **the electoral roll** *BrE*, **the (voter) rolls** *AmE* (=a list of the people who are allowed to vote) | **welfare rolls** *AmE* (=a list of people without jobs who claim money from the state) *Thompson said he had cut welfare rolls by 39%.* → ROLL OF HONOUR, HONOR ROLL
4 be on a roll *informal* to be having a lot of success with what you are trying to do: *Midvale High was on a roll, having won their last six basketball games.*
5 GAME the action of throwing DICE as part of a game: *If you get a 7 or 11 on your first roll, you win.*
6 SKIN/FAT a thick layer of skin or fat, usually just below your waist: **[+of]** *the rolls of fat on her stomach*
7 PHYSICAL MOVEMENT **a)** *BrE* a movement in which you roll forward or back in a controlled way with your body curled so that your head is near your feet, often done as part of a sport SYN **somersault**: *a forward roll* | *gymnasts* ***doing rolls*** *and handsprings* **b)** *especially BrE* the action of turning your body over one or more times while lying down: *a young horse* ***having a roll*** *in the field*

8 DRUMS/GUNS/THUNDER a long low fairly loud sound made by drums etc: *There was a* ***roll of thunder****, and the rain started pelting down.* | *a* ***drum roll***
9 SHIP/PLANE the movement of a ship or plane when it leans from side to side with the movement of the water or air
10 a roll in the hay *old-fashioned informal* when you have sex with someone – used humorously → **ROCK 'N' ROLL, SAUSAGE ROLL, SPRING ROLL, SWISS ROLL**

roll·back /ˈrəʊlbæk $ ˈroʊl-/ *n* [C,U] *especially AmE* an occasion when a tax, price, law etc is reduced to a previous level or changed so that it is the way it used to be → **roll back** at **ROLL[1]**

ˈroll-call *n* [C,U] the act of reading out an official list of names to check who is there

roll·er /ˈrəʊlə $ ˈroʊlər/ *n* [C] **1** a piece of equipment consisting of a tube-shaped piece of wood, metal etc that rolls over and over, used for painting, crushing, making things smoother etc: *a paint roller* | *a garden roller* → **STEAMROLLER[1](1)** **2** [usually plural] a tube-shaped piece of metal or wood, used for moving heavy things that have no wheels: *The boats are taken down to the sea on rollers.* **3** a small plastic or metal tube used for making hair curl SYN **curler** **4** a long powerful wave: *great Atlantic rollers*

Roll·er·blade /ˈrəʊləbleɪd $ ˈroʊlər-/ *n* [C] *trademark* a special boot with a single row of wheels fixed under it, used for SKATING on hard surfaces → **ROLLER SKATE, IN-LINE SKATE**

ˈroller blind *n* [C] *BrE* a piece of cloth or other material that can be rolled up and down to cover a window → **venetian blind** → see picture at **BLIND[3]**

ˈroller ˌcoaster *n* [C] **1** a track with very steep slopes and curves, which people ride on in small carriages at FAIRS and AMUSEMENT PARKS **2** a situation that changes often: *Their relationship was an emotional roller coaster.*

ˈroller skate *n* [C] a special boot with four wheels fixed under it, used for SKATING on hard surfaces → **ROLLERBLADE, IN-LINE SKATE** —**roller-skate** *v* [I] —**roller skating** *n* [U] → see picture at **SKATE[1]**

rol·lick·ing[1] /ˈrɒlɪkɪŋ $ ˈrɑː-/ *adj* [only before noun] *old-fashioned* noisy and cheerful: *a rollicking song*

rollicking[2] *n* **give sb a rollicking** *BrE informal* to criticize someone angrily for something they have done

roll·ing /ˈrəʊlɪŋ $ ˈroʊ-/ *adj* [only before noun] **1** rolling hills have many long gentle slopes **2** done or happening regularly over a period of time, not all at once: *We recommend a* ***rolling programme*** *of machine upgrading.*

ˈrolling pin *n* [C] a long tube-shaped piece of wood used for making PASTRY flat and thin before you cook it

ˈrolling stock *n* [U] all the trains, carriages etc that are used on a railway

ˌroll of ˈhonour *n* [C] *BrE* a list of people who are officially praised, especially because they were brave in battle SYN **honor roll** *AmE*: *the roll of honour on the war memorial*

ˈroll-on (*also* **ˌroll-on deˈodorant**) *n* [C] a bottle which contains liquid that you rub under your arms in order to stop your SWEAT from smelling unpleasant

ˌroll-on ˈroll-off *adj* [only before noun] *BrE* a roll-on roll-off ship is one that vehicles can drive straight on and off: *a roll-on roll-off car ferry*

ˈroll-out *n* [C,U] an occasion when a new product is made available for people to buy or use SYN **launch**: *Sun had to cancel the intended roll-out of the 514 model.*

roll·ov·er /ˈrəʊləʊvə $ ˈroʊloʊvər/ *n* **1 a)** [C] when money is moved from one bank account or INVESTMENT to another without any tax or other FEES having to be paid: *Many CD rollovers happen in October.* **b)** [C,U] the action of making a bank account, INVESTMENT etc do this: **[+of]** *The law allows a rollover of retirement money from a company pension to an IRA.* **2** [C] *BrE* if there is a rollover in a competition or LOTTERY, nobody wins the biggest prize that week, and the money is added to the prize that can be won the following week **3** [C] an accident in which a car turns over onto its roof **4** [U] *technical* a way of making the images change whenever someone using a MOUSE moves it over a particular word or picture on a computer screen

Rolls-Royce /ˌrəʊlz ˈrɔɪs◂ $ ˌroʊlz-/ *n trademark* **1** [C] a very expensive and comfortable car made by a British company **2 the Rolls-Royce of sth** *BrE informal* something that is regarded as the highest quality example of a particular type of product: *the Rolls-Royce of beers*

ˈroll-up *n* [C] *BrE informal* a cigarette that you make yourself

ro·ly-po·ly[1] /ˌrəʊli ˈpəʊli◂ $ ˌroʊli ˈpoʊ-/ *adj informal* a roly-poly person is round and fat

roly-poly[2] *n* (*plural* **roly-polies**) [C,U] a British sweet food made of JAM that is rolled up inside PASTRY

ROM /rɒm $ rɑːm/ *n* [U] *technical* (***read-only memory***) the part of a computer where permanent instructions and information are stored → **RAM**

ro·maine /rəʊˈmeɪn $ roʊ-/ *n* [U] *AmE* a type of bitter-tasting LETTUCE with long leaves

ro·man /ˈrəʊmən $ ˈroʊ-/ *n* [U] *technical* the ordinary style of printing that uses small upright letters, like the style used for printing these words → **font, italics**

Roman *adj* [usually before noun] **1** relating to ancient Rome or the Roman Empire: *an old Roman road* | *the Roman occupation of Britain* **2** relating to the city of Rome —**Roman** *n* [C]

ro·man à clef /rəʊˌmən æ ˈkleɪ $ roʊˌmɑːn ɑː-/ *n* [C] *formal* a NOVEL based on the actions of real people, who are given different names in the novel so that they seem to be invented characters and not real

ˌRoman ˈalphabet *n* **the Roman alphabet** the alphabet used in English and many other European languages, which begins with the letters A, B, C

ˌRoman ˈCatholic *adj* (*abbreviation* **RC**) belonging or relating to the part of the Christian religion whose leader is the Pope SYN **Catholic** → **Protestant**: *a Roman Catholic priest* —**Roman Catholic** *n* [C] —**ˌRoman Caˈtholicism** *n* [U]

ro·mance[1] /rəʊˈmæns, ˈrəʊmæns $ roʊˈmæns, ˈroʊ-/ ●●○ *n*
1 [C] an exciting and often short relationship between two people who love each other → **affair**: **[+with]** *Hemingway's romance with his nurse inspired him to write 'A Farewell to Arms'.* | *Michelle married him after a* ***whirlwind romance*** (=one that happens very suddenly and quickly). | **holiday romance** *BrE*, **summer romance** *AmE* (=one that happens during a holiday) *a short holiday romance*
2 [U] love, or a feeling of being in love: *The romance had gone out of their relationship.*
3 [U] the feeling of excitement and adventure that is related to a particular place, activity etc: **[+of]** *the romance of Hollywood*
4 [C] a story about the love between two people: *romance novels*
5 [C] a story that has brave characters and exciting events: *a Medieval romance*

romance[2] *v* **1** [I] to describe things that have happened in a way that makes them seem more important, interesting etc than they really were: **[+about]** *an old man romancing about the past* **2** [T] *old-fashioned* to try to persuade someone to love you

Roˈmance ˌlanguage *n* [C] a language that comes from Latin, for example French or Spanish

Ro·man·esque /ˌrəʊməˈnesk◂ $ ˌroʊ-/ *adj* in the style of building that was popular in Western Europe in the 11th and 12th centuries, and had many round ARCHes and thick PILLARS

ˌRoman ˈlaw *n* [U] *law* CIVIL LAW

ˌRoman ˈnose *n* [C] a nose that curves out near the top → **aquiline**

ˌroman ˈnumeral *n* [C] a number in a system first used in ancient Rome that uses combinations of the letters I, V, X, L, C, D, and M to represent numbers → **Arabic numeral**

R

Romano- /rəmɑːnəʊ $ -noʊ/ *prefix* [in nouns and adjectives] ancient Roman and something else: *Romano-British society*

ro·man·tic¹ /rəʊˈmæntɪk, rə- $ roʊ, rə-/ ●●○ *adj*
1 SHOWING LOVE showing strong feelings of love: *'Tom always sends me red roses on my birthday.' 'How romantic!'*
2 RELATING TO LOVE relating to feelings of love or a loving relationship: *After dinner, they took a romantic stroll by the sea.* | *real old-fashioned* ***romantic love*** | *I'm not ready for a romantic relationship.*
3 STORY/FILM a romantic story or film is about love: *a romantic comedy*
4 BEAUTIFUL beautiful in a way that affects your emotions and makes you think of love or adventure: *romantic music* | *The castle is set in one of England's most romantic landscapes.*
5 NOT PRACTICAL romantic ideas are not practical or not based on reality OPP **realistic**: **romantic notion/view/idea etc** *romantic notions about becoming a famous actress* | *Like many New Yorkers, he had a romantic image of country life.*
6 Romantic art/literature etc art or literature that is based on the ideas of romanticism —**romantically** /-kli/ *adv*

romantic² *n* [C] **1** someone who shows strong feelings of love and likes doing things that are related to love such as buying flowers, presents etc **2** someone who is not practical, and bases their ideas too much on an imagined idea of the world OPP **realist**: *a romantic who longed for adventure* **3** (*also* **Romantic**) a writer, painter etc whose work is based on romanticism

R

roˌmantic ˈcomedy *n* [C] a film which is intended to make people laugh and which involves a love story

ro·man·ti·cis·m /rəʊˈmæntəsɪzəm, rə- $ roʊ-, rə-/ *n* [U] **1** (*also* **Romanticism**) a way of writing or painting that was popular in the late 18th and early 19th century, in which feelings, imagination, and wild natural beauty were considered more important than anything else **2** ideas which are not practical or not based on reality OPP **realism**

ro·man·ti·cize (*also* **-ise** *BrE*) /rəʊˈmæntəsaɪz, rə- $ roʊ-, rə-/ *v* [T] to talk or think about things in a way that makes them seem more romantic or attractive than they really are: *a romanticized image of life during the war*

Ro·ma·ny /ˈrəʊməni $ ˈrɑː-/ *n* (*plural* **Romanies**) **1** [C] a GYPSY **2** [U] the language traditionally used by the GYPSY people —**Romany** *adj*

rom com /ˈrɒm kɒm $ ˈrɑːm kɑːm/ *n* [C] *informal* a ROMANTIC COMEDY

ro·me·o, **Romeo** /ˈrəʊmiəʊ $ ˈroʊmioʊ/ *n* (*plural* **romeos**) [C] a man who tries to attract all the women he meets in a ROMANTIC or sexual way – often used humorously → **Casanova**

ˌRomeo and ˈJuliet one of William Shakespeare's best-known plays, a sad romantic story about two young people, Romeo and Juliet, who fall in love although their families are great enemies. They marry secretly, but are prevented from being together, and finally they both kill themselves. They are considered to be typical examples of unlucky young lovers.

romp¹ /rɒmp $ rɑːmp/ *v* [I] **1** [always + adv/prep] to play in a noisy way, especially by running, jumping etc: **[+around/about]** *They could hear the children romping around upstairs.* **2** to win a race, competition, election etc very easily: **romp to a win/victory** *The women's team romped to a 132-81 win over Ireland.* | *In 1906 the Liberal Party romped back to power.* | **romp home** *BrE*: *The favourite, Badawi, romped home in the first race.*

romp through sth *phr v BrE informal* to succeed in doing or finishing something quickly and easily

romp² *n* [C] **1** *informal* a piece of amusing entertainment which has a lot of exciting scenes: *'A Royal Scandal' is an hour-long romp that pokes fun at British royal marriages.* **2** *BrE informal* a period of sexual activity – used humorously, especially in newspapers **3** when one sports team defeats another one very easily – used in newspapers: **[+over]** *the Yankees' 12–1 romp over the Red Sox*

ron·do /ˈrɒndəʊ $ ˈrɑːndoʊ/ *n* (*plural* **rondos**) [C] a piece of music in which the main tune is repeated several times

Ron·seal test /ˈrɒnsiːl test $ ˈrɑːn-/ *n BrE informal* **the Ronseal test** if something passes the Ronseal test, it successfully does what it claims it can do: *Will the new legislation pass the Ronseal test?*

ˈrood screen *n* [C] *technical* a decorated wooden or stone wall in a Christian church which divides the part where the CHOIR sit from the part where other people sit

ROOF

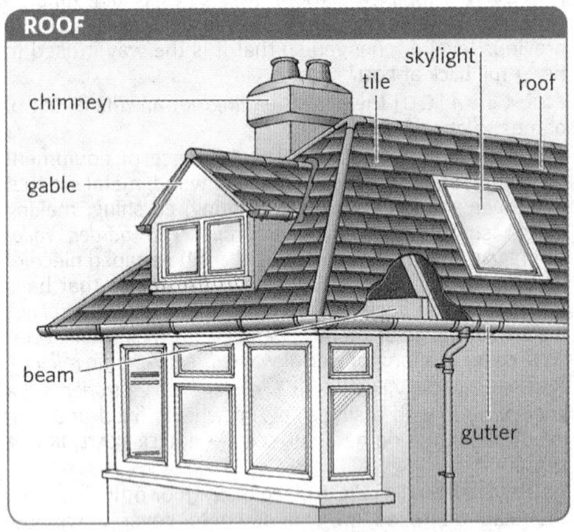

roof¹ /ruːf $ ruːf, rʊf/ ●●● S2 W2 *n* [C]
1 the structure that covers or forms the top of a building, vehicle, tent etc: *They finally found the cat up on the roof.* | **[+of]** *We can probably strap the cases to the roof of her car.* | **slate/tiled/thatched etc roof** | *a flat roof* | *a* ***pitched roof*** (=sloping roof) | **red-roofed/metal-roofed etc** *a wooden-roofed theatre*
2 the top of a passage under the ground: *Suddenly, the whole tunnel roof caved in.*
3 a roof over your head somewhere to live: *I may not have a job, but at least I've got a roof over my head.*
4 go through the roof *informal* **a)** (*also* **hit the roof**) to suddenly become very angry: *Put that back before Dad sees you and hits the roof!* **b)** if a price, cost etc goes through the roof, it increases to a very high level
5 the roof of sb's mouth the hard upper part of the inside of your mouth
6 under the same roof/under one roof in the same building or home: *If we're going to* ***live under the same roof****, we need to get along.* | *Here you can buy food, clothes, and electrical goods all under one roof.*
7 under sb's roof *spoken* in your home: *As long as you live under my roof, you'll do as I say.*
8 the roof falls/caves in *informal especially AmE* if the roof falls in or caves in, something bad suddenly happens to you when you do not expect it → **raise the roof** at RAISE¹(24), → SUNROOF

roof² *v* [T] to put a roof on a building: **be roofed with sth** *a cottage roofed with the local slate* GRAMMAR **Roof** is usually passive.

roof sth ↔ **in/over** *phr v BrE* to cover an open space by putting a roof over it: *We're going to roof in the yard to make a garage.*

roof·ies /ˈruːfiz $ ˈruːf-,ˈrʊf-/ *n* [plural] *informal* an illegal drug that is sometimes used to make someone unconscious so they can be RAPED

roof·ing /ˈruːfɪŋ $ ˈruːf-, ˈrʊf-/ *n* [U] **1** material used for making or covering roofs **2** the job of building or repairing roofs

ˈroof-rack *n* [C] *BrE* a metal frame fixed on top of a car and used for carrying bags, cases etc SYN **luggage rack** *AmE*

roof·top /ˈruːftɒp $ ˈruːftɑːp, ˈrʊf-/ *n* [C] the upper surface of a roof: *Spectators stood on rooftops to watch the parade.* → **shout sth from the rooftops** at SHOUT¹(3)

rooi·bos /ˈrɔɪbɒs $ -bɒːs/ *n* [U] (*also* **rooibos tea**) a type of tea made from the leaves of a South African plant

rook /rʊk/ *n* [C] **1** a large black European bird like a CROW **2** one of the pieces in a game of CHESS SYN **castle** → see picture at **CHESS**

rook·ie /ˈrʊki/ *n* [C] **1** *especially AmE* someone who has just started doing a job and has little experience: *rookie cops* **2** *AmE* someone who is in their first year of playing a professional sport

room¹ /ruːm, rʊm/ ●●● S1 W1 *n*

1 IN A BUILDING [C] a part of the inside of a building that has its own walls, floor, and ceiling: *I looked around the room.* | *She nodded toward a man who was standing across the room* (=on the other side of the room). | *Someone was laughing in* ***the next room*** (=the one beside the one you are in). | **sb's room** (=someone's bedroom) *Beth, it's time to clean up your room.* | **bathroom/dining room/meeting room etc** *the doctor's waiting room* | **one-room(ed)/two-room(ed) etc** *a three-room apartment* | **single/double room** (=a room in a hotel for one person or for two) *I'd like to book a double room for two nights.* | *Here's your key – room 348.* → **FRONT ROOM, LIVING ROOM, SITTING ROOM**

2 SPACE [U] space somewhere for a particular thing, person, or activity: **[+in]** *I hope* ***there's*** *going to be enough* ***room*** *in the fridge.* | **[+for]** *My suitcase was so full I didn't* ***have room*** *for anything else.* | **room to do sth** *The museum doesn't have enough room to show everything in their collection.* | **plenty of room/enough room** *There's plenty of room in the boot for your luggage.* | *I'm trying to* ***make room*** *for a vegetable garden in the backyard.* | *Step back,* ***leave room*** *for people to get past.* | *The old wardrobe* ***took up*** *too much* ***room****.* | **leg-room/head-room** (=space for your legs or head in a vehicle) → **elbow-room** at **ELBOW¹(5)**

3 OPPORTUNITY/POSSIBILITY [U] the chance to do something, or the possibility that something exists or can happen: **[+for]** ***There's*** *little* ***room*** *for innovation.* | **room for doubt/debate/argument etc** *The evidence was clear, and there was little room for doubt.* | **room for manoeuvre** *BrE*, **room for maneuver** *AmE* (=the possibility of changing what you do or decide) *Teachers feel they have little room for manoeuvre when the curriculum is so demanding.* | **room to do sth** *Children need to* ***have room*** *to develop their natural creativity.* | ***Make room*** *in your day for exercise.*

4 there's room for improvement used to say that something is not perfect and needs to be improved: *The report shows that there is room for improvement.*

5 there's not enough room to swing a cat used humorously to say that an area or room is not very big

6 APARTMENT **rooms** [plural] *old-fashioned especially BrE* two or more rooms that you rent in a building, or stay in at a college

7 PEOPLE [singular] all the people in a room: ***The whole room*** *started singing 'Happy Birthday'.*

room² ●○○ *v* [I] *AmE* to rent and live in a room somewhere

room with sb *phr v* to share a room or house with someone, especially at college: *I roomed with Al at UCSD.*

ˌroom and ˈboard *n* [U] a room to sleep in, with food provided: *You'll receive free room and board with the job.*

room·er /ˈruːmə, ˈrʊm- $ -ər/ *n* [C] *AmE* someone who pays rent to live in a house with its owner SYN **lodger** *BrE*

room·ful /ˈruːmfʊl, ˈrʊm-/ *n* [C] a large number of things or people that are all together in one room: **[+of]** *a roomful of reporters*

ˈrooming house *n* [C] *AmE* a house where people can rent a room to live in

room·mate, **ˈroom-mate** /ˈruːmˌmeɪt, ˈrʊm-/ ●●○ *n* [C]

1 someone who you share a room with, especially at college: *one of my college roommates*

2 *AmE* someone you share an apartment or house with SYN **flatmate** *BrE*

ˈroom ˌservice *n* [U] a service provided by a hotel, by which food and drinks can be sent to a guest's room

ˈroom ˌtemperature *n* [U] the normal temperature inside a house: *The wine should be served at room temperature.*

room·y /ˈruːmi/ *adj* a house, car etc that is roomy is large and has a lot of space inside it SYN **spacious** OPP **cramped**

roost¹ /ruːst/ *n* [C] a place where birds rest and sleep → **rule the roost** at **RULE²(4)**

roost² *v* [I] **1** if a bird roosts, it rests or sleeps somewhere **2 sb's chickens come home to roost** (*also* **sth comes home to roost**) used to say that someone's past mistakes are causing problems for them now: *After years of overspending, the chickens have come home to roost.*

roost·er /ˈruːstə $ -ər/ *n* [C] a male chicken SYN **cock** *BrE*

root¹ /ruːt/ ●●● S2 W2 *n* [C]

1 PLANT the part of a plant or tree that grows under the ground and gets water from the soil: *tree roots* | *These plants produce a number of thin roots.* → **ROOT CROP, ROOT VEGETABLE**, see picture at **TREE**

2 CAUSE OF A PROBLEM the main cause of a problem: **be/lie at the root of sth** (=be the cause of something) *Allergies are at the root of a lot of health problems.* | *The love of money is* ***the root of all evil****.* | *A competent mechanic should be able to get to the root of* ***the problem*** (=find out the cause of a problem). | *the* ***root causes*** *of crime*

3 ORIGIN/MAIN PART the origin or main part of something such as a custom, law, activity etc, from which other things have developed: **[+in]** *a legal system with roots in English common law* | *Jazz* ***has its roots in*** *the folk songs of the southern states of the US.* | **be/lie at the root of sth** *the liberal economic policies which lie at the root of American power*

4 FAMILY CONNECTION **sb's roots** your relation to a place because you were born there, or your family used to live there: *immigrants keeping in touch with their cultural roots* | *Alex Haley's story about his* ***search for*** *his* ***roots*** *became a bestseller.*

5 put down roots if you put down roots somewhere, you start to feel that a place is your home and to have relationships with the people there: *Because of her husband's job, they'd moved too often to put down roots anywhere.*

6 TOOTH/HAIR ETC the part of a tooth, hair etc that connects it to the rest of your body: *She'd pulled some of Kelly's hair out by the roots.*

7 take root a) if an idea, method, activity etc takes root, people begin to accept or believe it, or it begins to have an effect: *Economists believe that economic recovery will begin to take root next year.* **b)** if a plant takes root, it starts to grow where you have planted it

8 have a (good) root round *BrE informal* to search for something by moving other things around

9 LANGUAGE *technical* the basic part of a word which shows its main meaning, to which other parts can be added. For example, the word 'coldness' is formed from the root 'cold' and the SUFFIX 'ness'. → **stem**

10 MATHEMATICS *technical* a number that, when multiplied by itself a certain number of times, equals the number that you have: *2 is the fourth root of 16.*

11 root and branch if you destroy or change something root and branch, you get rid of it or change it completely and permanently because it is bad: *a root and branch reform of the electoral system* → **CUBE ROOT, SQUARE ROOT, GRASS ROOTS**

root² *v*

1 PLANT a) [I] to grow roots: *New shrubs will root easily in summer.* **b)** [T] if a plant is rooted somewhere, it is held in the ground firmly by its roots: *a bush firmly rooted in the hard ground* | **root itself** *Clumps of thyme had rooted themselves between the rocks.* GRAMMAR **Root** is either passive or reflexive in this meaning.

2 be rooted in sth to have developed from something and be strongly influenced by it: *The country's economic troubles are rooted in a string of global crises.* | *This feeling of rejection is often* ***deeply rooted in*** *childhood.*

R

3 SEARCH [I always + adv/prep] to search for something by moving things around SYN **rummage**: **root through/in/amongst sth (for sth)** *Leila rooted through her handbag for a pen.*
4 PIGS [I usually + adv/prep] if a pig roots somewhere, it looks for food under the ground: **[+for]** *pigs rooting for truffles*
5 rooted to the spot/floor/ground etc so shocked, surprised, or frightened that you cannot move: *She stood rooted to the spot, staring at him.*
root for sb *phr v informal*
1 to want someone to succeed in a competition, test, or difficult situation: *You can do it – I'm rooting for you.*
2 *especially AmE* to support a sports team or player by shouting and cheering: *the Los Angeles fans rooting for the Lakers*
root sth ↔ **out** *phr v*
1 to find out where a particular kind of problem exists and get rid of it: *Action is being taken to root out corruption in the police force.*
2 to find something by searching for it: *I'll try and root out something for you to wear.*
root sth ↔ **up** *phr v* to dig or pull a plant up with its roots
ˈroot beer *n* [C,U] a sweet brown non-alcoholic drink made from the roots of some plants, drunk especially in the US
ˈroot caˌnal *n* [C] the space inside the root of a tooth: *root canal treatment* (=treatment in which a DENTIST removes a diseased area in the root of a tooth)
ˈroot crop *n* [C] a vegetable or plant that is grown so that its roots can be sold
root·le /ˈruːtl/ (*also* **rootle around/about**) *v* [I] *BrE informal* to search for something by moving many other things around —**rootle** *n* [singular]
root·less /ˈruːtləs/ *adj* having nowhere that you feel is really your home: *rootless people* —**rootlessness** *n* [U]
ˈroots ˌreggae (*also* **ˈroots ˌrock ˌreggae**) *n* [U] a popular style of REGGAE which is a mixture of Jamaican SKA and American styles such as POP MUSIC, ROCK AND ROLL, and RHYTHM AND BLUES
root·sy /ˈruːtsi/ *adj* rootsy music is music that is played in the traditional way for a particular style of music: *a rootsy blues album*
ˈroot ˌvegetable *n* [C] a vegetable such as a potato or CARROT that grows under the ground

ROPE

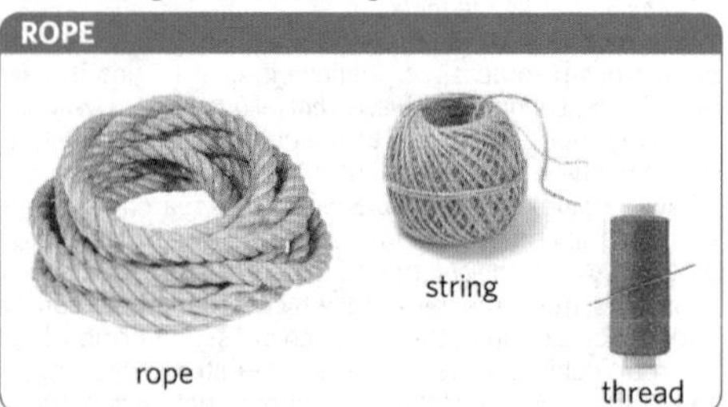

rope¹ /rəʊp $ roʊp/ ●●● S3 W3 *n*
1 [C,U] very strong thick string, made by twisting together many thinner strings: *They tied a rope around my waist and pulled me up.* | *The man was coiling a length of rope.*
2 the ropes [plural] **a)** all the things someone needs to know to do a job or deal with a system: *I spent the first month just **learning the ropes**.* | *He works repairing streets, and **knows the ropes** when it comes to safety.* | *Miss McGinley will **show** you **the ropes** and answer any questions.* **b)** the rope fence that surrounds an area used for BOXING or WRESTLING
3 be on the ropes *informal* to be in a very bad situation, in which you are likely to be defeated: *The army says the rebels are on the ropes.*
4 be at/near etc the end of your rope *especially AmE* to have no more PATIENCE or strength left to deal with a problem or a difficult situation: *My son is causing endless problems, and I'm close to the end of my rope.*
5 give sb some/enough etc rope to give someone a lot of freedom to do something in the way they want to do it: *Managers have to decide how much rope to give their subordinates.*
6 give sb enough rope to hang themselves to give someone freedom to do what they want to do, because you think they will cause problems for themselves and you want them to look stupid
7 a rope of pearls PEARLS on a string, worn around your neck as jewellery → JUMP ROPE, SKIPPING ROPE, TIGHTROPE, TOWROPE, → **money for old rope** at MONEY(17)
rope² *v* [T] **1** [always + adv/prep] to tie things together using rope: **rope sth to sth** *Suitcases were roped to the top of the car.* | **rope sb/sth together** *Mountaineers rope themselves together for safety.* **2** *AmE* to catch an animal using a circle of rope: *The calves are roped and branded.*
rope sb **into** sth (*also* **rope sb ↔ in** *BrE*) *phr v informal* to persuade someone to help you in a job or join in an activity, especially when they do not want to: **rope sb into doing sth** *Denise roped me into selling tickets.* | **rope sb in to do sth** *Anyone who could sing was roped in to help.* | *Have you been roped in too?*
rope sth ↔ **off** *phr v* to surround an area with ropes, especially in order to separate it from another area: *The stairs were roped off.*
ˈrope ˌladder *n* [C] a LADDER made of two long ropes connected by wooden pieces that you stand on
rop·ey, ropy /ˈrəʊpi $ ˈroʊ-/ (*comparative* **ropier**, *superlative* **ropiest**) *adj BrE informal* **1** in bad condition or of bad quality: *ropey old furniture* **2** [not before noun] slightly ill: *I'm feeling a bit ropey this morning.*
ro-ro /ˈrəʊ rəʊ $ ˈroʊ roʊ/ *n* (*plural* **ro-ros**) [C] *BrE informal* a ROLL-ON ROLL-OFF ship
Ror·schach test /ˈrɔːʃɑːk test $ ˈrɔːr-/ *n* [C] a method of testing someone's character, by making them say what they think spots of ink with various shapes look like
ro·sa·ry /ˈrəʊzəri $ ˈroʊ-/ *n* (*plural* **rosaries**) [C] **1** a string of BEADS used by Roman Catholics for counting prayers **2 the rosary/the Rosary** the set of prayers that are said by Roman Catholics while counting rosary BEADS: **say/recite the rosary** *Three nuns knelt there, reciting the rosary.*
ro·sé /ˈrəʊzeɪ $ roʊˈzeɪ/ *n* [C,U] pink wine
rose¹ /rəʊz $ roʊz/ ●●● S3 *n*
1 FLOWER [C] a flower that often has a pleasant smell, and is usually red, pink, white, or yellow, or the bush that this flower grows on: *a dozen red roses* | *A large bouquet of roses arrived on her desk.* | ***rose bushes*** → see picture at FLOWER¹
2 COLOUR [U] a pink colour
3 sth is not a bed of roses (*also* **sth is not all roses** *BrE*) *informal* if a job or situation is not a bed of roses, it is not always pleasant and there are difficult things to deal with: *It's no bed of roses teaching in a secondary school.*
4 put the roses back in sb's cheeks *BrE informal* to make someone look healthy again
5 be coming up roses *informal* to be happening or developing in the best possible way
6 come out of sth/come up smelling of roses *informal* to do well or get an advantage from a situation, when you could have been blamed, criticized, or harmed by it: *She managed to come out of the deal smelling of roses.*
7 FOR WATER [C] *BrE* a circular piece of metal with holes in it that is attached to the end of a pipe or WATERING CAN so that liquid comes out in several thin streams
rose² *v* the past tense of RISE
rose³ *adj* pink in colour: *rose velvet curtains*
ro·se·ate /ˈrəʊziət $ ˈroʊ-/ *adj literary* pink: *the **roseate** glow of the evening sun*
ˈRose ˌBowl, the **1** an American football game held in January every year in Pasadena, California between two of the best college football teams in the US **2** the STADIUM where this game is played. The Rose Bowl is also used for other American football games, as well as other sports games, such as soccer.

rose·bud /ˈrəʊzbʌd $ ˈroʊz-/ *n* [C] **1** the flower of a rose before it opens **2** **rosebud mouth/lips** a mouth or lips that have a small round shape and are very red

ˈrose-ˌcoloured *BrE*, **rose-colored** *AmE* *adj* **1** pink **2** **rose-coloured glasses** (*also* **rose-coloured spectacles** *BrE*) if you see or view something through rose-coloured glasses, you think it is better than it really is

ˈrose hip *n* [C] the small red fruit produced by some kinds of rose bushes, used in medicines and juices

rose·ma·ry /ˈrəʊzməri $ ˈroʊzmeri/ *n* [U] the narrow leaves of a bush, used as a herb, or the bush that these leaves come from

ˈrose-ˌtinted *adj BrE* ROSE-COLOURED

Roˈsetta Stone, the a large ancient stone that was found in Egypt in 1799, which had the same piece of writing on it in three different writing systems: Greek letters, Egyptian letters, and ancient Egyptian HIEROGLYPHICS. This important discovery made it possible for people to translate hieroglyphics for the first time. The stone is now kept in the British Museum. Something that could provide the answer to a problem, especially in a particular area of science, is sometimes called a Rosetta Stone: *The study of genes in mice could be the Rosetta Stone for establishing the functions of human genes.*

ro·sette /rəʊˈzet $ roʊ-/ *n* [C] **1** *BrE* a circular BADGE made of coloured RIBBON that is given to the winner of a competition, or that people in Britain wear to show support for a particular football team or political party → see picture at **RIBBON** **2** a shape like a round flat flower that has been made in stone or wood

rose·wa·ter /ˈrəʊzˌwɔːtə $ ˈroʊzˌwɒːtər, -ˌwɑː-/ *n* [U] a liquid made from roses which has a pleasant smell

ˌrose ˈwindow *n* [C] a circular window in a church, especially one with coloured glass in it

rose·wood /ˈrəʊzwʊd $ ˈroʊz-/ *n* [U] a hard dark red wood, used for making expensive furniture

Rosh Ha·sha·nah /ˌrɒʃ həˈʃɑːnə $ ˌrɒːʃ həˈʃɒːnə/ *n* [U] the Jewish new year holiday

ros·in /ˈrɒzɪn $ ˈrɑː-/ *n* [U] a solid slightly sticky substance that you rub on the BOW of a VIOLIN etc, to help it move smoothly on the strings —**rosin** *v* [T]

ros·ter¹ /ˈrɒstə $ ˈrɑːstər/ *n* [C] **1** a list of the names of people on a sports team, in an organization etc: **on a roster** *The club has outstanding players on the roster.* | **[+of]** *The campaign has a roster of 500 volunteers.* **2** a list that shows when each person in a group must do a particular job SYN **rota** *BrE*: *duty roster*

roster² *v* [T] to put someone's name on a roster

ros·trum /ˈrɒstrəm $ ˈrɑː-/ *n* [C] a small PLATFORM that you stand on when you are making a speech or CONDUCTing musicians SYN **podium**

ros·y /ˈrəʊzi $ ˈroʊ-/ *adj* (*comparative* **rosier**, *superlative* **rosiest**) **1** seeming to offer hope of success or happiness: *a company that sees a* ***rosy future*** *for itself* | *Letters to relatives in Europe* ***painted a rosy picture*** *of life in the United States.* **2** pink: *the kids'* ***rosy cheeks***

rot¹ /rɒt $ rɑːt/ ●●○ *v* (**rotted**, **rotting**)

1 [I,T] to decay by a gradual natural process, or to make something do this: *Candy will rot your teeth.* | *The trees were cut and* ***left to rot***. | **[+away]** *All the woodwork was rotting away.*

2 **rot in hell/jail** to suffer or be punished for a long time – used especially when you are angry with someone: *I hope the people who did this rot in hell.*

rot² *n* **1** [U] the natural process of decaying, or the part of something that has decayed: *the smell of rot* | *wood that is soft with rot* → **DRY ROT** **2** [singular, U] a state in which something becomes bad or does not work as well as it should: *He criticized the talk shows as 'cultural rot'.* | **stop the rot** *BrE* (=stop a bad situation getting worse) *The team has enough good players to stop the rot.* | **the rot set in** *BrE* (=a situation started to get worse) *It was after he left the company that the rot set in.* **3** [U] *BrE old-fashioned* nonsense: *You do talk rot!*

ro·ta /ˈrəʊtə $ ˈroʊ-/ *n* [C] *BrE* a list that shows when each person in a group must do a particular job SYN **roster**: *a cleaning rota*

ro·ta·ry¹ /ˈrəʊtəri $ ˈroʊ-/ *adj* [only before noun] **1** turning in a circle around a fixed point, like a wheel: *the rotary movement of the helicopter blades* **2** having a main part that turns like a wheel: *a rotary engine*

rotary² *n* (*plural* **rotaries**) [C] *AmE* a ROUNDABOUT

ˈRotary Club, the an organization of business people in a town who work together to raise money for people who are poor or sick

ro·tate /rəʊˈteɪt $ ˈroʊteɪt/ ●○○ *v*

1 [I,T] to turn with a circular movement around a central point, or to make something do this SYN **revolve** → **spin**: *The Earth rotates on its axis once every 24 hours.* | *Rotate the pan halfway through the baking time.*

2 [I,T] if a job rotates, or if people rotate jobs, they each do a particular job for a particular period of time: *The chairmanship of the committee rotates annually.* | *Employers may rotate duties to give staff wider experience.*

3 [I,T] to change the places of things or people, or to change places, especially in a circular direction: *Rotating the tyres every few months helps them last longer.*

4 [T] *technical* to regularly change the crops grown on a piece of land, in order to preserve the quality of the soil → **crop rotation**

ro·ta·tion /rəʊˈteɪʃən $ roʊ-/ ●○○ *n*

1 [U] when something turns with a circular movement around a central point: **[+of]** *the rotation of the Earth on its axis* | **[+about/around]** *the planet's rotation around the Sun*

2 [C] one complete circular turn around a central point SYN **revolution**: *The blades spin at 100 rotations per minute.*

3 [U] the practice of regularly changing the thing that is being used or done, or the person who does a particular job: *job rotation* | **in rotation** *Three plays will be performed in rotation during the drama festival.*

4 [C] *AmE* a period of time spent doing a particular job, when you will soon change to a different job for the same employer: *a young doctor on a rotation in the children's ward*

5 [C] *AmE* the people who each take a turn to do a particular job in a regular order: *The rotation included two rookies, Hernandez and Saunders.* —**rotational** *adj*

rote /rəʊt $ roʊt/ *n* [U] *formal* when you learn something by repeating it many times, without thinking about it carefully or without understanding it: *In old-fashioned schools, much* ***learning*** *was* ***by rote***. | *the* ***rote learning*** *of facts*

ROTFL (***rolling on the floor laughing***) used by people communicating on the Internet to say that they are very amused by something that someone else has written SYN **ROFL**

rot·gut /ˈrɒtɡʌt $ ˈrɑːt-/ *n* [U] *informal* strong cheap low-quality alcohol

ro·tis·ser·ie /rəʊˈtɪsəri $ roʊ-/ *n* [C] a piece of equipment for cooking meat by turning it around and around on a metal rod over heat → **grill**

ro·tor /ˈrəʊtə $ ˈroʊtər/ *n* [C] *technical* **1** a part of a machine that turns around on a central point **2** (*also* **rotor blade**) the long flat part that turns around and around on top of a HELICOPTER

rot·ten¹ /ˈrɒtn $ ˈrɑːtn/ ●●○ *adj*

1 badly decayed and no longer good to use: *the smell of rotten eggs* | *Some of the wood was completely rotten.* | *The apples* ***went rotten*** *very quickly.*

2 *informal* very bad SYN **terrible**: *What* ***rotten luck***! | *a rotten idea* | *The service was rotten.* | *He's a rotten driver.*

3 *informal* if someone is rotten, they are unpleasant, unkind, or dishonest: *Why are you being so rotten?* | *a* ***rotten little*** *brat*

4 **feel rotten** **a)** to feel ill **b)** to feel unhappy and guilty about something: *I felt rotten about lying to him.*

5 [only before noun] *spoken* used when you are angry: *I don't want your rotten money!*

6 **rotten to the core** extremely dishonest: *The whole government is rotten to the core.*

7 **a rotten apple** one bad person who has a bad effect on all the others in a group —**rottenness** *n* [U]

R

rotten² *adv informal* **1 spoil sb rotten** to treat someone too well or too kindly, especially a child, so that they think they should always have what they want: *He was the favorite, and his mother spoiled him rotten.* **2 fancy sb rotten** *BrE* to be extremely attracted to someone in a sexual way - used humorously

rot·ter /ˈrɒtə $ ˈrɑːtər/ *n* [C] *BrE old-fashioned* an unpleasant person who treats other people badly

rott·wei·ler /ˈrɒtvaɪlə, -waɪlə $ ˈrɑːtwaɪlər/ *n* [C] a type of strong and dangerous dog, often used as a guard dog

ro·tund /rəʊˈtʌnd $ roʊ-/ *adj* having a fat round body - used humorously SYN **stout** —**rotundity** *n* [U]

ro·tun·da /rəʊˈtʌndə $ roʊ-/ *n* [C] a round building or hall, especially one with a DOME

rou·ble *BrE*, **ruble** *AmE* /ˈruːbəl/ *n* [C] the standard unit of money in Russia and Belarus

rou·é /ˈruːeɪ $ ruːˈeɪ/ *n* [C] *literary* a man who believes that pleasure is the most important thing in life - used to show disapproval

rouge /ruːʒ/ *n* [U] *old-fashioned* pink or red powder or cream that women put on their cheeks SYN **blusher** —**rouge** *v* [T]: *heavily rouged cheeks*

rough¹ /rʌf/ ●●● S2 W3 *adj* (*comparative* **rougher**, *superlative* **roughest**)

1 NOT SMOOTH having an uneven surface OPP **smooth**: *Her hands were rough from hard work.* | *the **rough terrain** at the base of the mountains* | *We were bumping over the **rough ground**.*

2 NOT EXACT [usually before noun] not exact, not containing many details, or not in a final form SYN **approximate**: *a rough sketch of the house* | *a rough translation* | *Could you give me a **rough idea** what time you'll be home?* | *a **rough estimate** of the cost* | *First do a **rough draft** of your essay.*

3 PROBLEMS/DIFFICULTIES a rough period is one in which you have a lot of problems or difficulties SYN **tough**: *The first year was rough, but things have gotten better.* | *Sounds like you had a **rough day**.* | *We've been through some **rough times** together.* | *My boyfriend and I were **going through a rough patch**.* | *The bill **is in for a rough ride** in the Senate.* | *It's been **rough going**, but we've almost finished now.*

4 NOT GENTLE using force, anger, or violence OPP **gentle**: *Rugby is a very rough sport.* | *Don't be too rough - she's only little.* | *Paul gave her a rough shake.* | *equipment capable of withstanding **rough treatment*** | *The referee won't allow any **rough stuff*** (=violent behaviour). | **be rough on sb** (=treat someone unkindly or criticize them in an angry way) *Don't you think you were a little rough on her?* THESAURUS ▸ VIOLENT

5 TOWN/AREA ETC a rough area is a place where there is a lot of violence or crime: *a rough part of town*

6 WEATHER/SEA with strong wind or storms OPP **calm**: *The ship went down in **rough seas**.*

7 VOICE/SOUND **a)** not sounding soft or gentle, and often rather unpleasant or angry: *Barton's deep, rough voice* **b)** having an unpleasant sound, especially because there is something wrong with a machine: *The clutch sounds rough - better get it checked.*

8 SIMPLE/NOT WELL MADE simple and often not very well made: *a rough wooden table*

9 NOT COMFORTABLE uncomfortable, and with difficult conditions: *The journey was long and rough.*

10 have rough edges (*also* **be rough around the edges**) **a)** to have some parts that are not as good as they should be, but that are not a serious problem: *The team has a few rough edges, but they're winning more games.* **b)** if a person is rough around the edges, they are not very polite, educated etc

11 rough night a night when you did not sleep well: *Mickey **had a rough night** last night.*

12 a rough deal something that happens to you that is unfair or unpleasant: *He's **had a rough deal** with his wife leaving him like that.*

13 feel rough *BrE informal* to feel ill

14 look rough *BrE informal* to look untidy, dirty, or unhealthy: *After travelling for two days we must have looked pretty rough.*

15 rough and ready not perfect, but good enough for a particular purpose: *The tests are only a rough and ready guide to a pupil's future development.*

16 rough justice punishment that is not decided in a court in the usual legal way, and that is often severe or unfair: *Gangs practise a kind of rough justice on their members.* —**roughness** *n* [U] → ROUGH DIAMOND, ROUGH PAPER, ROUGHLY

THESAURUS

rough having a surface that is not flat or smooth: *rough ground* | *a rough mountain path* | *The walls were all rough.* | *Her hands were rough and work-hardened.*

uneven an uneven surface has areas that are not flat or not all at the same level: *The floor was uneven.* | *She climbed the uneven steps with great care.*

bumpy a bumpy road, path, or area of land has a lot of holes and raised parts in it: *the bumpy track down to the farm* | *The field was too bumpy to play football on.* | *a bumpy journey* (=on a road that has a very rough surface)

coarse having a rough surface that feels slightly hard - used especially about materials such as cloth or wool: *coarse woollen blankets* | *coarse grass*

rugged /ˈrʌɡəd/ land that is rugged is very rough and uneven and is often in a high place: *the rugged terrain near the mountains*

COLLOCATIONS CHECK

rough ground/sea/stone/skin
uneven surface/floor/pavement
bumpy road/field/journey
coarse cloth/wool/paper/grass
rugged terrain/mountain/landscape/coastline

rough² *n* **1 the rough** uneven ground with long grass on an area where people play golf OPP **green** → see picture at GOLF **2 take the rough with the smooth** to accept the bad things in life as well as the good ones: *You have to learn to take the rough with the smooth.* **3** [C] a picture drawn very quickly, not showing all the details SYN **sketch**: *a rough of the proposed housing development* **4 in rough** *BrE* if you write or draw something in rough, you do it without paying attention to details or tidiness, because you are going to do it again later: *It's best to work in rough first, and then write it out neatly.* **5 a bit of rough** *BrE informal* someone from a lower social class than you, with whom you have a sexual relationship → DIAMOND IN THE ROUGH

rough³ *v* **rough it** *informal* to live for a short time in conditions that are not very comfortable: *I don't mind roughing it for a while.*

rough sth ↔ **out** *phr v BrE* to draw or write something without including all the details: *a diagram the engineer had roughed out on his notepad*

rough sb ↔ **up** *phr v informal* to attack someone and hurt them by hitting them

rough⁴ *adv* **1 sleep rough** *BrE* to sleep outside with nothing to protect you from the weather, especially because you have no home to live in: *the number of people sleeping rough on the street* **2 play rough** to play in a fairly violent way → **cut up rough** at CUT¹(6)

rough·age /ˈrʌfɪdʒ/ *n* [U] a substance contained in some vegetables, fruits, and grains that helps your BOWELS to work SYN **fibre**

ˌrough and ˈtumble *n* **1** [U] a situation in which people compete with each other, often in a cruel way: **[+of]** *the rough and tumble of public life* **2** [singular, U] noisy rough behaviour when playing or fighting, especially by children —**rough-and-tumble** *adj* [only before noun]: *Most boys enjoy rough-and-tumble play.*

rough·cast /ˈrʌfkɑːst $ -kæst/ *n* [U] a rough surface on the outside of a building, made of PLASTER mixed with little stones or broken shells —**roughcast** *adj*

ˌrough ˈdiamond *n* [C] *BrE informal* someone who seems rude, rough, or unfriendly, but is actually nice and generous SYN **diamond in the rough** *AmE*

rough·en /ˈrʌfən/ *v* [I,T] to become rough, or to make something rough: *hands roughened by work*

ˌrough-ˈhewn *adj* rough-hewn wood or stone has been cut without much care and its surface is not yet smooth

rough·house /ˈrʌfhaʊs/ *v* [I] *AmE* to play roughly or pretend to fight: *Okay, guys, slow down. No more rough-housing.*

rough·ly /ˈrʌfli/ ●●● S2 *adv*
1 not exactly SYN **about, approximately**: *There were roughly 200 people there.* | *Azaleas flower at roughly the same time each year.* | **roughly equal/comparable/equivalent** *two rocks of roughly equal size* | **roughly speaking** (=used when saying something without giving exact details or information) *Roughly speaking, I'd say we need about $500.*
THESAURUS ▸ APPROXIMATE
2 not gently or carefully: *He grabbed her roughly.*

rough·neck /ˈrʌfnek/ *n* [C] *especially AmE informal* **1** someone who works on an OIL WELL **2** a man who usually behaves in a rough, rude, or angry way

ˌrough ˈpaper *n* [U] *BrE* paper that is used for writing or drawing things that will later be changed or copied more neatly

rough·shod /ˈrʌfʃɒd $ -ʃɑːd/ *adv* **ride roughshod over sb/sth** *especially BrE*, **run roughshod over sb/sth** *AmE* to behave in a way that ignores other people's feelings or opinions: *We cannot ride roughshod over the concerns of the local community.*

rou·lette /ruːˈlet/ *n* [U] a game in which a small ball is spun around on a moving wheel, and people try to win money by guessing which hole the ball will fall into

round¹ /raʊnd/ ●●● S2 W2 *especially BrE* (*also* **around**) *adv, prep*
1 surrounding or on all sides of something or someone: *We sat round the table playing cards.* | *Gather round! I have an important announcement to make.* | *He put his arm gently round her waist.* | *I kept the key on a chain round my neck.* | *The ballroom's huge, with windows **all the way round**.* | *There was a lovely courtyard with tables **all round**.*
2 used to say that someone or something turns so that they face in the opposite direction: *When he turned round I recognised him immediately.* | *Graham glanced round, startled by the voice behind him.*
3 in or to many places or parts of an area: *Reggie went round making sure all the lights were off.* | *Leah showed me round on my first day at the office.* | *A guide took us round the palace and gardens.* | *He spent a whole year travelling round Europe.* | *She looked round the room as though leaving it for the last time.* | *changes that are affecting the weather **all round** the world*
4 moving in a circle: *She watched the clock hands go round.* | *An aeroplane was circling round far overhead.* | *Until the 16th century people believed that the Sun went round the Earth.* | *He stared at the washing machine, just watching the clothes go **round and round**.* | *a shoal of tiny fish swimming **round in circles***
5 *informal* if you go round to someone's house, you go to their house, usually to visit them: *I might go round to Nigel's this evening.* | *He's invited us round for dinner.* | *We'll be round* (=will arrive) *at seven.*
6 to other people or positions: *A big box of chocolates was handed round.* | *He'd moved his furniture round.*
7 on the other side of something, or to the other side of it without going through it or over it: *He ran round to open Kate's door for her.* | *There must be another entrance round the back.* | *I watched the two boys disappear **round the corner**.* | **[+to]** *She came round to his side of the desk.*
8 in the area near a particular place: *Much of the countryside round Hinkley Point is given over to agriculture.* | *Do you live **round here**?* | *He owned all the land **round about*** (=in the surrounding area).
9 round about *spoken informal* (*also* **round**) used when guessing a number, amount, time etc without being exact SYN **approximately**: *We got there round about half past nine.* | *He's round about the same age as my son.* | *It must have been round midnight when I saw him.*
10 used to show that someone spends time in a place without doing anything useful: *People were just standing round and not doing anything to help.*
11 if something is organized round a particular person or thing, it is organized according to their needs, wishes, ideas etc: *Working from home, she could arrange her hours round her children.* | *He had built his whole existence round her.*
12 a way round a difficult situation or problem is a way to solve it or avoid it: *She's going to have to buy a car. I can't see any other way round it.* | *strategies to **get round*** (=solve) *the **problem***
13 used to show the length of a line surrounding something: *The park was about five miles round.* → ALL ROUND, → **go round in circles** at CIRCLE¹(5), → **(a)round the clock** at CLOCK¹(2), → **(just) around/round the corner** at CORNER¹(9), → **first/second time round** at TIME¹(3), → **way round** at WAY¹(24)

round² ●●● S1 W2 *adj*
1 shaped like a circle: *a big round table* | *Jamie's eyes grew round with delight.*
2 shaped like a ball: *small round berries*
3 fat and curved: *round chubby cheeks*
4 [only before noun] a round number or figure is a whole number, often ending in 0 → **round up**: *Let's make it a round figure: say £50?* | **in round figures** (=expressed as the nearest 10, 100, 1,000 etc) *Altogether, in round figures, there are about three thousand students here.* | **a round hundred/dozen etc** (=a complete hundred etc) → **a square peg in a round hole** at SQUARE¹(12) —**roundness** *n* [U]

round³ ●●○ *n* [C]
1 SERIES a round of events is a series of related events, which are part of a longer process: **[+of]** *a third round of peace talks* | *the Government's latest round of expenditure cuts*
2 COMPETITION one of the parts of a competition that you have to finish or win before you can go on to the next part → **heat, stage**: **the first/final/next/qualifying etc round** *I got beaten in the first round.* | *Two of their candidates made it through to the next round.* | **[+of]** *the final round of the championship*
3 REGULAR ACTIVITIES **round of sth** a round of activities is a regular series of activities, especially activities that are not very exciting: *an **endless round** of meetings and interviews* | *He continued with his **usual round** of private and business engagements.* | *the **daily round** of commuting and shopping*
4 VISITS **rounds** [plural] the usual visits that someone, especially a doctor, regularly makes as part of their job: **be (out) on your rounds** *I'm sorry. The doctor is out on her rounds.*
5 round of applause when people CLAP for a short time to show that they enjoyed something or approve of something: *She **got** a big **round of applause**.* | *The passengers **gave** the pilot a **round of applause**.*
6 GOLF a complete game of golf: *I **played a round of golf** on Sunday morning.*
7 BOXING/WRESTLING one of the periods of fighting in a BOXING or WRESTLING match
8 DRINKS if you buy a round of drinks in a bar, you buy drinks for all the people in your group: **it's my/your etc round** (=used to say whose turn it is to buy drinks for all the people in your group) *What are you having? It's my round.*
9 do the rounds *BrE informal*, **make the rounds** *AmE* (*also* **go the rounds** *BrE*) if a story, idea, or illness does the rounds, it is passed on from one person to another: *a joke doing the rounds*
10 do the rounds of sth *BrE*, **make the rounds of sth** *AmE* to go around from one place to another, especially looking for work or advertising something: *Ryan is making the rounds of talk shows to promote her new movie.*
11 GUN SHOT a single shot from a gun, or a bullet for one shot: *I've only got ten **rounds of ammunition** left.* | *Richards **fired** a few **rounds**.*
12 CIRCLE something that has a circular shape: *Slice the potatoes into rounds.*
13 FOOD/NEWSPAPERS/LETTERS ETC *BrE* a regular visit to a

number of houses, offices etc to deliver or sell things: **paper/milk round** (=a job in which you deliver newspapers, milk etc to people's houses) *I used to* ***do*** *a paper* ***round***.

14 SONG a song for three or four singers, in which each one sings the same tune, starting at a different time

15 round of sandwiches *BrE* SANDWICHes made from two whole pieces of bread

16 round of toast *BrE* one whole piece of bread that has been TOASTed

17 in the round a play that is performed in the round is performed on a central stage surrounded by the people watching it

round⁴ ●○○ *v*

1 [T] to go round something such as a bend or the corner of a building: *As they* ***rounded*** *the* ***bend*** *and came in sight of the river, Philip took her hand.* | *The tide was coming in as he rounded the rocks.*

2 [T] to make something into a round shape: *The stones were then rounded, polished and engraved.*

3 [I] *written* if your eyes round, you open them wide because you are shocked, frightened etc: *Barbara's eyes rounded in surprise.* → **ROUNDED**, **WELL-ROUNDED**

round sth ↔ **down** *phr v* to reduce an exact figure to the nearest whole number → **round up**: *For the 1841 census it was decided to round down ages over fifteen to the nearest five.*

round sth ↔ **off** *phr v*

1 to do something as a way of ending an event, performance etc in a suitable or satisfactory way SYN **finish**: **[+with]** *You can round off the evening with a visit to the nightclub.* | *She rounded off the meal with some cheese.* | *It was the perfect way to round off the season.*

2 to take the sharp or rough edges off something: *Round off the corners with a pair of scissors.*

3 to change an exact figure to the nearest whole number: **[+to]** *Prices are rounded off to the nearest dollar.*

round on sb *phr v BrE* to suddenly turn and attack someone when they do not expect it, either with words or physically: *When the door closed, Crabb rounded on Edwards. 'You stupid idiot!'*

round sth ↔ **out** *phr v* to make an experience more thorough or complete: *African percussion and Native American flute round out the show.*

round sb/sth ↔ **up** *phr v*

1 if police or soldiers round up a particular group of people, they find them and force them to go to prison: *Thousands of men were rounded up and jailed.*

2 to find and gather together a group of people, animals, or things: *See if you can round up a few friends to help you!* | *His dog Nell started to round up the sheep.*

3 to increase an exact figure to the next highest whole number → **round down**

round·a·bout¹ /ˈraʊndəbaʊt/ *n* [C] *BrE* **1** a raised circular area where three or more roads join together and which cars must drive around SYN **traffic circle** *AmE*: *Turn left at the first roundabout.* → **MINI-ROUNDABOUT** **2** a round structure for children to play on in a park. Children sit on it while someone pushes it around and around. SYN **merry-go-round** *AmE* **3** a MERRY-GO-ROUND → **swings and roundabouts** at **SWING²(9)**

roundabout² *adj* [only before noun] **1** a roundabout way of saying something is not clear, direct, or simple SYN **indirect** OPP **direct**: **roundabout way/fashion** *It was a roundabout way of telling us to leave.* **2** a roundabout way of getting somewhere is longer and more complicated than necessary: *The bus took a very long and* ***roundabout route***.

round·ed /ˈraʊndɪd/ *adj* **1** having a round shape SYN **curved** **2** having a wide range of qualities that make someone or something pleasant, balanced, and complete: *Psychology tests found me to be thoroughly rounded in skills and attitudes.* → **ROUND²**, **WELL-ROUNDED**

round·el /ˈraʊndəl/ *n* [C] a circular design, for example one used to make a military aircraft recognizable

roun·ders /ˈraʊndəz $ -ərz/ *n* [U] a British ball game, similar to baseball, in which players hit the ball and then run around the edge of an area

ˌround-ˈeyed *adj* having eyes which are wide open because of shock, fear etc

round·ly /ˈraʊndli/ *adv* **roundly condemn/criticize etc** to CONDEMN, criticize etc someone strongly and severely: *All the major political parties roundly condemned the attack.*

ˌround ˈrobin *n* [C] a competition in which every player or team plays against every other player or team: *a round robin tournament*

ˌround-ˈshouldered *adj* someone who is round-shouldered has shoulders that are bent forwards or slope downwards

ˌround-ˈtable *adj* [only before noun] a round-table discussion is one in which everyone can talk about things in an equal way: **round-table discussion/meeting/talks**

ˌRound ˈTable, the **1** the table at which King Arthur and his KNIGHTS sat, according to old stories. As it was round, all the places at it were equal. The expression 'round table' is used to describe a peaceful way of reaching an agreement: *The treaty was signed following a round table discussion.* **2** a CHARITY organization for men under 40, who hold meetings and do work for their local areas. It is related to the Rotary Club, whose members are usually a little older.

ˌround-the-ˈclock *adj* [only before noun] happening all the time, both day and night: *round-the-clock medical care* → **round the clock** at **CLOCK¹(6)**

ˈround-trip¹ *n* [C] a journey to a place and back again: *a round-trip ticket from Los Angeles to New York* | **30 mile/360 kilometre/2 hour etc round trip** *A coachload of supporters* ***made*** *the 700-mile* ***round trip*** *to South Devon.* | **[+of]** *It's a round trip of 90 miles.*

round-trip² *adj* [only before noun] *AmE* a round-trip ticket includes the journey to a place and back again OPP **one-way** SYN **return** *BrE* —**round trip** *adv*

ˈround-up *n* [C] **1** a short description of the main parts of the news, on the radio or on television SYN **summary**: **[+of]** *First, with a round-up of the day's local news, here's Paul Kirby.* | **news/sports round-up** *our Friday sports round-up* **2** when people or animals of a particular type are all brought together, often using force: **[+of]** *a round-up of suspected drug-dealers* | *the annual cattle round-up* → **round up** at **ROUND⁴**

round·worm /ˈraʊndwɜːm $ -wɜːrm/ *n* [C] a small round PARASITE that lives in the bodies of animals and sometimes humans → **tapeworm**, **worm**

rouse /raʊz/ *v* [T] **1** *formal* to wake someone who is sleeping deeply: *His banging roused the neighbours.* | **rouse sb from sleep/dreams etc** *A persistent ringing roused Christina from a pleasant dream.* **2** to make someone start doing something, especially when they have been too tired or unwilling to do it: **rouse yourself** *She roused herself stiffly from her chair.* | **rouse sb to sth/to do sth** *a campaign designed to rouse the younger generation to action* **3** to make someone feel a particular emotion, such as anger or fear → **arouse**: *We don't want to rouse any suspicions.* | **rouse sb to sth** *Paul strode forward, roused to anger.*

roused /raʊzd/ *adj* [not before noun] angry: ***When roused****, he could be violent.*

rous·ing /ˈraʊzɪŋ/ *adj* [only before noun] a rousing song, speech etc makes people feel excited and eager to do something: *a rousing chorus of 'Happy Birthday'*

roust /raʊst/ *v* [T] *AmE* to make someone move from a place: *We rousted him out of bed.*

rous·ta·bout /ˈraʊstəbaʊt/ *n* [C] *especially AmE* a man who does work for which he needs to be strong but not skilled, especially in a port, an OILFIELD, or a CIRCUS

rout¹ /raʊt/ *v* [T] to defeat someone completely in a battle, competition, or election

rout² *n* [C usually singular, U] a complete defeat in a battle, competition, or election: *The battle turned into a rout.* | **put sb to rout** (=defeat someone completely)

R

route[1] /ruːt $ ruːt, raʊt/ ●●● S3 W2 AWL *n* [C]
1 a way from one place to another: **[+to/from]** *What's the best route to Cambridge?* | **take/follow a route** (=use a route) *We weren't sure about which route we should take.* | *the most direct route home*
2 a way between two places that buses, planes, ships etc regularly travel: **bus/air/shipping etc route** *Is your office on a bus route?* | **cycle route** (=a way between two places that only people on bicycles can use)
3 a way of doing something or achieving a particular result: **[+to]** *the surest route to disaster* | *Kennedy arrived at the same conclusion by a different route.*
4 Route 66/54 etc used to show the number of a main road in the US → PAPER ROUTE

route[2] AWL *v* [T] to send something somewhere using a particular route: **route sth through/via sth** *They had to route the goods through Germany.* → RE-ROUTE

Route 66 /ˌruːt sɪksti ˈsɪks $ ˌruːt-, ˌraʊt-/ a famous road in the US that is mentioned in books, films, and songs. It was built in the early 1930s, and was the first road to go across the US, from Chicago to Los Angeles.

ˈroute march *n* [C] a long march done by soldiers when they are training

rout·er /ˈruːtə $ -ər/ *n* [C] *technical* a piece of electronic equipment that makes sending messages between different computers or between different networks easier and faster

rou·tine[1] /ruːˈtiːn/ ●●○ W3 *n*
1 [C,U] the usual order in which you do things, or the things you regularly do: *John's departure had upset their* ***daily routine****.* | *Try to* ***get into*** *a* ***routine*** (=develop a fixed order of doing things). | *my daily* ***exercise routine*** | *Dressing is a task which we do every day as a* ***matter of routine*** (=done regularly and not unusual).
2 [C] a set of movements, jokes etc that form part of a performance: *a* ***dance routine***
3 [C] *technical* a set of instructions given to a computer so that it will do a particular operation —**routinize** /ruːˈtiːnaɪz, ˈruːtiːnaɪz/ *v* [T] *AmE*

rou·tine[2] /ˌruːˈtiːn◂/ ●●○ *adj*
1 happening as a normal part of a job or process: *You mustn't worry. These are just routine enquiries.* | *routine maintenance work* | *a routine operation* THESAURUS NORMAL
2 ordinary and boring: **routine jobs/tasks** *routine tasks such as washing up*

rou·tine·ly /ruːˈtiːnli/ ●○○ *adv* if something is routinely done, it is done as a normal part of a process or job SYN **regularly**: *This vaccine is already routinely used.*

roux /ruː/ *n* (*plural* **roux** /ruːz/) [C,U] a mixture of flour, butter, and milk that is used for making sauces

rove /rəʊv $ roʊv/ *v* **1** [I,T] *written* to travel from one place to another SYN **roam**: *a salesman roving the country* **2 roving reporter** someone who works for a newspaper or television company and moves from place to place **3** [I] if someone's eyes rove, they look continuously from one part of something to another: **[+over/around]** *Benedict's eyes roved boldly over her sleeping body.* **4 have a roving eye** *old-fashioned* to always be looking for a chance to have romantic relationships - often used humorously

row[1] /rəʊ $ roʊ/ ●●● S2 W2 *n* [C]
1 a line of things or people next to each other → **column**: **[+of]** *a row of houses* | *rows of trees* | **in a row** *The children were asked to stand in a row.* | ***row upon row*** (=many rows) *of shelves stacked with books*
2 a line of seats in a theatre or cinema: *We sat in the front row.*
3 in a row happening a number of times, one after the other SYN **consecutively**: **4 nights/3 weeks etc in a row** *She's been out four nights in a row.* | *I've beaten her three* ***times in a row****.*
4 used in the name of some roads: *22 Church Row*
5 a hard/tough row to hoe used to say that a particular situation is difficult

row[2] /rəʊ $ roʊ/ ●●○ *v* [I,T] to make a boat move across water using OARS: **[+away/towards/across]** *She rowed across the lake.* | *Jenny used to row at college* (=as a sport). —**row** *n* [singular]: *Why don't we* ***go for a row****?* —**rower** *n* [C]

row[3] /raʊ/ *n BrE* **1** [C] a short angry argument, especially between people who know each other well SYN **quarrel**: **[+with]** *He had just* ***had*** *a* ***row*** *with his wife.* | **[+about]** *What was the row about?* | *a* ***family row*** | *a* ***blazing row*** (=a very angry argument) THESAURUS ARGUMENT
2 [C] a situation in which people disagree strongly about important public matters SYN **controversy**: **[+about/over]** *a new row over government secrecy* **3** [singular] a loud unpleasant noise that continues for a long time SYN **racket**: *Stop that row - I'm trying to get to sleep!*

row[4] /raʊ/ *v* [I] *BrE* to argue in an angry way: **[+about]** *They rowed about money all the time.*

ro·wan /ˈrəʊən $ ˈroʊ-/ *n* [C] a small tree with red berries

row·boat /ˈrəʊbəʊt $ ˈroʊboʊt/ *n* [C] *AmE* a small boat that you move through the water with OARS SYN **rowing boat** *BrE*

row·dy[1] /ˈraʊdi/ *adj* behaving in a noisy rough way that is likely to cause arguments and fighting: *gangs of rowdy youths* THESAURUS LOUD —**rowdily** *adv* —**rowdiness** *n* [U] —**rowdyism** *n* [U]

rowdy[2] *n* (*plural* **rowdies**) [C usually plural] *old-fashioned* someone who behaves in a rough noisy way

row house /ˈrəʊ haʊs $ ˈroʊ-/ *n* [C] *AmE* a house that is part of a line of houses that are joined to each other SYN **terraced house** *BrE*

row·ing /ˈrəʊɪŋ $ ˈroʊ-/ *n* [U] the sport or activity of making a boat move through water with OARS

rowing boat /ˈrəʊɪŋ bəʊt $ ˈroʊɪŋ boʊt/ *n* [C] *BrE* a small boat that you move through the water with OARS (=long poles that are flat at the end) SYN **row boat** *AmE*

ˈrowing maˌchine *n* [C] a piece of exercise equipment on which you perform the action of rowing a boat → see picture at GYM

row·lock /ˈrɒlək $ ˈroʊlɑːk/ *n* [C] *BrE* one of the U-shaped pieces of metal that holds the OARS of a rowing boat

roy·al[1] /ˈrɔɪəl/ ●●● S3 W1 *adj* [only before noun]
1 relating to or belonging to a king or queen → **regal**: *the royal palace* | *the royal family*
2 used in the names of organizations that serve or are supported by a king or queen: *the Royal Navy* | *the Royal College of Music*
3 very impressive, as if done for a king or queen: *a royal welcome*
4 the royal 'we' *BrE* the use of the word 'we' instead of 'I' by the Queen or King —**royally** *adv*

royal[2] *n* [C] *informal* a member of a royal family OPP **commoner**

ˌRoyal ˈAscot a four-day horse-racing event at Ascot, England, that takes place every June. It is known as a social event, especially for UPPER-CLASS people, where women wear expensive fashionable clothes and hats.

ˌroyal ˈblue *n* [U] a bright deep blue colour —**royal blue** *adj*

ˌRoyal Comˈmission *n* [C] a group of people chosen by the British government to make suggestions about a subject that the government thinks may need new laws

ˌroyal ˈflush *n* [C usually singular] a set of cards that someone has in a card game, which are the five most important cards in a SUIT (=one of the four different types of card)

ˌRoyal ˈHighness *n* [C] **your/his/her Royal Highness** used when speaking about or to a royal person, especially a prince or princess

roy·al·ist /ˈrɔɪəlɪst/ *n* [C] someone who supports their country's king or queen, or believes that a country should be ruled by kings or queens OPP **republican** —**royalist** *adj*

ˌRoyal ˈMail, the the British organization which is responsible for collecting and delivering letters

R

roy·al·ty /ˈrɔɪəlti/ *n* (*plural* **royalties**) **1** [U] members of a royal family: *At school the other children* ***treated*** *them* ***like royalty***. **2** [C usually plural] a payment made to the writer of a book or piece of music depending on how many books etc are sold, or to someone whose idea, invention etc is used by someone else to make money: *the royalties from his latest book | royalty payments*

RP /ˌɑː ˈpiː $ ˌɑːr-/ *n* [U] (***Received Pronunciation***) the form of British pronunciation that many educated people in Britain use, and that is thought of as the standard form

rpm /ˌɑː piː ˈem $ ˌɑːr-/ (***revolutions per minute***) used to describe the speed at which something turns, especially an engine or a RECORD PLAYER

RR, **R.R.** /ˌɑːr ˈɑː $ ˌɑːr-/ (***rural route***) used in addresses in country areas of the US, to show which postal delivery area a letter should go to

RSI /ˌɑːr es ˈaɪ/ *n* [U] *medical* (***repetitive strain injury***) pains in your hands, arms etc caused by doing the same movements many times, especially by using a computer KEYBOARD or MOUSE

RSS /ˌɑːr es ˈes/ *n* [U] (***Rich Site Summary*** *or* ***Really Simple Syndication***) software that tells an Internet user when a website has new information on it: *Our free RSS feeds include headlines and news summaries.*

RSVP /ˌɑːr es viː ˈpiː/ used on invitations to ask someone to reply

RTF /ˌɑː tiː ˈef $ ˌɑːr-/ *n* [U] *technical* (***rich text format***) a system used to arrange and show the information in computer documents

Rt Hon *BrE* the written abbreviation of ***Right Honourable***

rub¹ /rʌb/ ●●● S2 *v* (**rubbed**, **rubbing**)

1 [I,T] to move your hand, or something such as a cloth, backwards and forwards over a surface while pressing firmly → **stroke**: **rub your nose/chin/eyes/forehead etc** *She yawned and rubbed her eyes.* | **rub sth with sth** *She began rubbing her hair with a towel.* | *You'll have to rub harder if you want to get it clean.* | *I hurriedly rubbed myself dry.* THESAURUS ▸ TOUCH

2 [I,T] to make something press against something else and move it around: **rub sth against/on sth** *She stood by the oven, rubbing one bare foot against the other.* | **[+against]** *The cat purred loudly, rubbing against her legs.* | **rub sth together** *We tried to make a fire by rubbing two pieces of wood together.* | *He* ***rubbed*** *his* ***hands together*** *with embarrassment.*

3 [I,T] if shoes, clothes, or parts of a machine rub, they move around while pressing against another surface, often causing pain or damage: *Badly fitting shoes are bound to rub.* | **[+against/on]** *The front left fender was smashed and rubbing against the wheel.* | *The skin under my sock was rubbed raw* (=the skin had come off).

4 [T always + adv/prep] to put a substance into or onto a surface by pressing it and moving it about with your fingers or something such as a cloth: *Can you rub some sun cream on my back for me?*

5 rub shoulders with sb *informal* (*also* **rub elbows with sb** *AmE*) to meet and spend time with people, especially rich and famous people: *As a reporter he gets to rub shoulders with all the big names in politics.*

6 rub salt into the wound *informal* to make a bad situation even worse for someone

7 rub sb up the wrong way *BrE informal*, **rub sb the wrong way** *AmE informal* to annoy someone by the things you say or do, usually without intending to

8 be rubbing your hands *informal* to be pleased because something has happened which gives you an advantage, especially because something bad has happened to someone else

9 rub sb's nose in it/in the dirt *informal* to keep reminding someone about something they did wrong or failed to do, especially in order to punish them

10 not have two pennies/halfpennies/beans to rub together *BrE old-fashioned* to not have any money

rub along *phr v BrE informal* to have a friendly relationship with someone SYN **get along**: *We rub along well most of the time.* | **[+with/together]** *By and large the Poles and Germans of the city had shown that they could rub along together.*

rub sth/sb ↔ **down** *phr v*

1 to make a surface smooth by rubbing it with SANDPAPER: *That door needs rubbing down before you paint it.*

2 to dry a person or animal by rubbing them with a cloth, TOWEL etc: *The groom rubbed down the horses.*

3 to MASSAGE someone, especially after exercise

rub sth ↔ **in** *phr v informal* to remind someone about something they want to forget, especially because they are embarrassed about it: *Was he trying to rub in the fact that he didn't think much of me?* | *I know I should have been more careful, but there's no need to keep* ***rubbing it in***.

rub off *phr v*

1 to remove something from a surface by rubbing it, or to come off a surface because of being rubbed: **rub sth off sth** *Jack rubbed the mud off his face.* | **rub sth ↔ off** *She rubbed off her lipstick and eye shadow.* | *Some of the gold paint had begun to rub off.*

2 if a feeling, quality, or habit rubs off on you, you start to have it because you are with another person who has it: **[+on]** *She refused to give up, and her confidence rubbed off on the others.*

rub sth/sb ↔ **out** *phr v*

1 *BrE* to remove writing, a picture etc from a surface by rubbing it with a piece of rubber, a cloth etc SYN **erase**: *Draw the outline lightly with a soft pencil. This can be rubbed out later.*

2 *AmE old-fashioned informal* to murder someone

rub² *n* **1 give sb/sth a rub** to rub something or MASSAGE someone for a short time: *Give the table a good rub with a damp cloth.* **2 there's/here's the rub** *literary* used when saying that a particular problem is the reason why a situation is so difficult – often used humorously

rub·ber /ˈrʌbə $ -ər/ ●●○ S3 *n*

1 [U] a substance used to make tyres, boots etc, which is made from the juice of a tropical tree or artificially: *a rubber ball*

2 [C] *BrE* **a)** a small piece of rubber or similar material used for removing pencil marks from paper SYN **eraser** *AmE* **b)** an object used for cleaning marks from a BLACKBOARD SYN **eraser** *AmE* → see picture at **STATIONERY**

3 [C] *AmE informal* a CONDOM

4 rubbers [plural] *AmE old-fashioned* rubber shoes or boots that you wear over ordinary shoes when it rains or snows SYN **galoshes**

5 [C] a series of games of BRIDGE or CRICKET

6 [C] the piece of white rubber where the PITCHER (=person who throws the ball) stands in a baseball game

ˌrubber ˈband *n* [C] a thin circular piece of rubber used for fastening things together SYN **elastic band** *BrE*

ˈrubber boot *n* [C] *AmE* a tall boot made of rubber that keeps your feet and the lower part of your legs dry SYN **wellington boot** *BrE*

ˌrubber ˈbullet *n* [C] a bullet made of rubber that is not intended to seriously hurt or kill people, but is used to control violent crowds → **plastic bullet**

ˌrubber ˈchicken ˌcircuit *n* [singular] public dinners where someone makes a speech, especially ones held in order to raise money for a political party: *She is in demand on the rubber chicken circuit.*

ˌrubber ˈdinghy *n* [C] a small rubber boat that is filled with air

rub·ber·neck /ˈrʌbənek $ -ər-/ *v* [I] *informal* to look around at something, especially something such as an accident while you are driving past – used to show disapproval: *People rubbernecking in the southbound lane caused a second accident.* —**rubbernecker** *n* [C]

ˈrubber plant *n* [C] a plant with large shiny dark green leaves that is often grown indoors

ˌrubber ˈstamp *n* [C] a small piece of rubber with a handle, used for printing dates or names on paper

ˌrubber-ˈstamp *v* [T] to give official approval to something without really thinking about it – used to show disapproval: *The committee has already rubber-stamped the scheme.* THESAURUS ▸ APPROVE

rub·ber·y /ˈrʌbəri/ *adj* **1** looking or feeling like rubber: *rubbery eggs* | *rubbery lips* **THESAURUS** ▸ **HARD** **2** if your legs or knees are rubbery, they feel weak or unsteady

rub·bing /ˈrʌbɪŋ/ *n* [C] a copy of a shape or pattern made by rubbing WAX, CHALK etc onto a piece of paper laid over it: *a* ***brass rubbing***

ˈrubbing ˌalcohol *n* [U] *AmE* a type of alcohol used for cleaning wounds or skin SYN **surgical spirit** *BrE*

Frequencies of the nouns **rubbish**, **garbage**, and **trash** in British and American English.

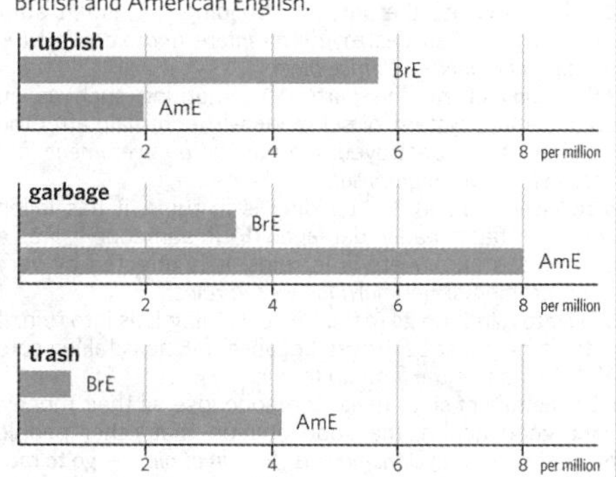

In British English **rubbish** is commonly used to mean something that is thrown away, or something that is silly, wrong, or of bad quality. In American English **garbage** and **trash** are commonly used for these meanings. In British English **trash** is only used to mean something of bad quality, and **garbage** is only used to mean words, ideas etc that are stupid.

rub·bish¹ /ˈrʌbɪʃ/ ●●● S2 *n* [U] *especially BrE*
1 food, paper etc that is no longer needed and has been thrown away SYN **garbage**, **trash** *AmE*: *a* ***rubbish bin*** | ***household rubbish*** | **rubbish tip/dump** (=a place to take rubbish)
2 *informal* objects, papers etc that you no longer use and should throw away: *I've got so much rubbish on my desk it's unbelievable.*
3 *informal* an idea, statement etc that is rubbish is silly or wrong and does not deserve serious attention SYN **nonsense**, **garbage** *AmE*: *You do* ***talk rubbish*** *sometimes.* | *That's* ***a load of rubbish***. | *The suggestion is* ***absolute rubbish***. | **rubbish!** *spoken* (=used to tell someone that what they have just said is completely wrong)
4 *informal* a film, book etc that is rubbish is very bad: *the usual Hollywood rubbish*

rubbish² *v* [T] *BrE* to say something is bad or useless

rubbish³ *adj BrE informal* not skilful at a particular activity: *a rubbish team*

rub·bish·y /ˈrʌbɪʃi/ *adj BrE informal* silly or of a very low quality SYN **trashy**: *rubbishy magazines*

rub·ble /ˈrʌbəl/ *n* [U] broken stones or bricks from a building or wall that has been destroyed

rub·down /ˈrʌbdaʊn/ *n* [C] **1** *especially AmE* if you give someone a rubdown, you rub their body to make them relaxed, especially after exercise SYN **massage** **2** if you give a surface a rubdown, you rub it to make it smooth or clean → **rub down** at RUB¹

rube /ruːb/ *n* [C] *AmE informal* someone, usually from the country, who has no experience of other places and thinks in a simple way – used to show disapproval SYN **bumpkin**

ru·bel·la /ruːˈbelə/ *n* [U] *medical* an infectious disease that causes red spots on your body, and can damage an unborn child SYN **German measles**

Ru·bi·con /ˈruːbɪkən, -kɒn $ -kɑːn/ *n* **cross the Rubicon** to do something that will have extremely important effects in the future and that you cannot change

ru·bi·cund /ˈruːbɪkənd/ *adj literary* someone who is rubicund is fat and has a red face

ru·ble /ˈruːbəl/ *n* [C] the American spelling of ROUBLE

ru·bric /ˈruːbrɪk/ *n* [C] **1** *formal* a set of instructions or an explanation in a book, examination paper etc **2** a title under which particular things are mentioned or discussed: *The names were listed under the rubric 'Contributors'.*

ru·by /ˈruːbi/ *n* (*plural* **rubies**) **1** [C] a red jewel **2** (*also* **ˌruby ˈred**) [U] a dark red colour —**ruby** *adj*

ruched /ruːʃt/ *adj* a ruched curtain or piece of clothing has parts of it gathered together so that it has folds in it

ruck¹ /rʌk/ *n* **1** [C] a group of RUGBY players trying to get the ball when it is lying on the ground **2 the ruck** *formal* ordinary events or people, which seem rather boring compared to the lives of rich or famous people: *Obtaining a good education was seen as a way out of the ruck.* **3** [singular] a group of people standing very closely together or fighting **4** [C] *BrE informal* a fight

ruck² *v*
ruck up *phr v* if a piece of cloth rucks up, or if you ruck it up, it forms folds in an untidy way: **ruck sth ↔ up** *Your coat's all rucked up at the back.*

ruck·sack /ˈrʌksæk/ ●●○ *n* [C] *especially BrE* a bag used for carrying things on your back, especially by people on long walks SYN **backpack** → see picture at BAG¹

ruck·us /ˈrʌkəs/ *n* [singular] *especially AmE informal* a noisy argument or confused situation SYN **rumpus**

ruc·tions /ˈrʌkʃənz/ *n* [plural] *informal especially BrE* angry talk and complaints because many people are annoyed about a situation

rud·der /ˈrʌdə $ -ər/ *n* [C] a flat part at the back of a ship or aircraft that can be turned in order to control the direction in which it moves → see picture at PLANE¹

rud·der·less /ˈrʌdələs $ -dər-/ *adj* without someone to lead you or give you an aim or direction: *a company left rudderless by the resignation of its CEO*

rud·dy /ˈrʌdi/ *adj* **1** a ruddy face looks pink and healthy OPP **sallow**: *a ruddy complexion* | *ruddy cheeks* **2** *literary* red: *The fire cast a ruddy glow over the room.* **3** [only before noun] *BrE informal* used to emphasize what you are saying, especially when you are annoyed with someone or something SYN **bloody**, **damn**: *I wish that ruddy dog would stop barking!* —**ruddiness** *n* [U] —**ruddy** *adv*

rude /ruːd/ ●●● S3 *adj* (*comparative* **ruder**, *superlative* **rudest**)
1 speaking or behaving in a way that is not polite and is likely to offend or annoy people SYN **impolite** OPP **polite**: *a rude remark* | *I didn't mean to be rude, but I had to leave early.* | **[+to]** *Why are you so rude to her?* | **it is rude to do sth** *It's rude to stare.*
2 rude jokes, words, songs etc are about sex SYN **dirty** *AmE* → see Thesaurus box on *p. 1592*
3 rude awakening/shock a situation in which you suddenly realize something unpleasant: *If they expect the match to be friendly, they're in for a rude awakening.*
4 in rude health *BrE old-fashioned* very healthy
5 *literary* made in a simple basic way: *a rude wooden hut* —**rudely** *adv*: *We were rudely awakened by the storm.* | *He answered me very rudely.* —**rudeness** *n* [U]

ru·di·men·ta·ry /ˌruːdəˈmentəri◂/ *adj* **1** a rudimentary knowledge or understanding of a subject is very simple and basic OPP **sophisticated**: *Gradually, I acquired a rudimentary knowledge of music.* | *my rudimentary German* **2** rudimentary equipment, methods, systems etc are very basic and not advanced: *subsistence farming in its most* ***rudimentary form*** | *The classroom equipment is pretty rudimentary.*

ru·di·ments /ˈruːdəmənts/ *n* [plural] *formal* the most basic parts of a subject, which you learn first SYN **basics**: **[+of]** *the rudiments of windsurfing*

rue /ruː/ *v* [T] *literary* to wish that you had not done something SYN **regret**: *She learned to* ***rue the day*** *she had met Henri.*

rue·ful /ˈruːfəl/ *adj* feeling or showing that you wish you had not done something: *a rueful smile* —**ruefully** *adv*: *He smiled ruefully.*

ruff /rʌf/ *n* [C] **1** a stiff circular white collar, worn in the 16th century **2** a circle of feathers or fur around the neck of an animal or bird

ruf·fi·an /ˈrʌfiən/ *n* [C] *old-fashioned* a violent man, involved in crime: *a gang of ruffians* —**ruffianly** *adj*

ruf·fle[1] /ˈrʌfəl/ *v* [T] **1** (*also* **ruffle sth ↔ up**) to make a smooth surface uneven: *He* ***ruffled*** *her* ***hair*** *affectionately.* | *A light wind ruffled the water.* **2** to offend or upset someone slightly: *Louise's sharp comments had ruffled his pride.* | **ruffle sb's feathers** (=offend someone)

ruffle[2] *n* [C] a band of thin cloth sewn in folds as a decoration around the edge of something such as a collar

rug /rʌg/ ●●● S3 *n* [C]
1 a piece of thick cloth or wool that covers part of a floor, used for warmth or as a decoration → **mat**, **carpet**
2 *BrE* a large piece of material that you can wrap around yourself, especially when you are travelling
3 pull the rug (out) from under sb/sb's feet *informal* to suddenly take away something that someone was depending on to achieve what they wanted
4 a TOUPÉE – used humorously

rug·by /ˈrʌgbi/ ●●● S3 (*also* ˌ**rugby** ˈ**football**) *n* [U] an outdoor game played by two teams with an OVAL (=egg-shaped) ball that you kick or carry

ˌ**Rugby** ˈ**League** *n* [U] a type of rugby played by teams of 13 players

ˌ**Rugby** ˈ**Union** *n* [U] a type of rugby played by teams of 15 players

rug·ged /ˈrʌgɪd/ ●○○ *adj*
1 land that is rugged is rough and uneven: *a rugged coastline* | *the rugged beauty of the Highlands* THESAURUS ROUGH
2 a man who is rugged is good-looking and has strong features which are often not perfect: *his rugged good looks*
3 a vehicle or piece of equipment that is rugged is strongly built and not likely to break easily SYN **sturdy**
4 rugged behaviour is confident and determined but not always polite: *rugged individualism* —**ruggedly** *adv* —**ruggedness** *n* [U]

rug·ger /ˈrʌgə $ -ər/ *n* [U] *BrE informal* Rugby Union

ru·in[1] /ˈruːɪn/ ●●○ S3 *v* [T]
1 to spoil or destroy something completely: *This illness has ruined my life.* | *His career would be ruined.* | *All this mud's going to ruin my shoes.* THESAURUS DESTROY, SPOIL
2 to make someone lose all their money: *Jefferson was ruined by the lawsuit.* → RUINED

ruin[2] ●●○ *n*
1 [U] a situation in which you have lost all your money, your social position, or the good opinion that people had about you: *small businesses facing* ***financial ruin*** | **be on the road to ruin** (=be doing something that will make you lose your money, position etc)
2 [C] (*also* **ruins**) the part of a building that is left after the rest has been destroyed: *an interesting old ruin* | *the ruins of a bombed-out office block*
3 the ruins of sth the parts of something such as an organization, system, or set of ideas that remain after the rest have been destroyed: *the ruins of a government that once held so much promise*
4 be/lie in ruins a) if a building is in ruins, it has fallen down or been badly damaged **b)** if someone's life, a country's ECONOMY etc is in ruins, it is affected by very great problems: *Her marriage was in ruins.*
5 fall into ruin (*also* **go to ruin**) if something falls into ruin, it gets damaged or destroyed because no one is taking care of it: *He had let the farm go to ruin.*
6 be the ruin of sb to make someone lose all their money, their good health, the good opinion that other people have of them etc: *Drinking was the ruin of him.* → **go to rack and ruin** at RACK[1](4)

ru·in·a·tion /ˌruːəˈneɪʃən/ *n* [U] *old-fashioned* a process in which someone or something is ruined, or the cause of this – often used humorously

ru·ined /ˈruːɪnd/ *adj* [only before noun] a ruined building has been almost completely destroyed: *a ruined castle* → RUIN[2]

ru·in·ous /ˈruːɪnəs/ *adj* **1** causing a lot of damage or problems: *a ruinous civil war* **2** costing much more than you can afford: *ruinous rates of interest* **3** *formal* a building that is ruinous has been almost completely destroyed SYN **ruined**: *an old ruinous chapel* | **ruinous state/condition** *the ruinous state of the city walls* —**ruinously** *adv*: *ruinously expensive*

rule[1] /ruːl/ ●●● S1 W1 *n*
1 ABOUT WHAT IS ALLOWED [C] an official instruction that

THESAURUS: rude

rude not following the rules of good social behaviour or treating other people with a lack of respect: *It's rude to interrupt.* | *He's the rudest man I've ever met.* | *rude remarks about her stomach*
impolite/not polite not following the rules of good social behaviour. **Impolite** sounds rather formal: *It is impolite to stare.* | *It's not polite to talk with your mouth full of food.*
cheeky *BrE*, **smart/sassy** *AmE* behaving in a way that is a little rude, especially when this is amusing or annoying – used especially about children: *a cheeky grin* | *Let go, you cheeky monkey* (=cheeky child)*!* | *Don't get smart with me!*
tactless saying things that are likely to upset or embarrass someone, without intending to: *a tactless remark* | *How could you be so tactless?*
offensive speaking or behaving in a way that is likely to upset or offend someone: *His remarks are offensive to African-Americans.* | *offensive language*
insulting speaking or behaving in a way that is very rude and offensive to someone: *comments that are insulting to women* | *The article was full of insulting language.*
discourteous /dɪsˈkɜːtiəs $ -ɜːr-/ *formal* rather rude. **Discourteous** sounds very formal and is often used when talking about being careful not to upset someone's feelings: *He did not wish to appear discourteous towards his host.* | *It would seem discourteous to refuse her offer.*
ill-mannered (*also* **bad-mannered**) *especially written* behaving in a rude way, especially because you have never been taught how to behave politely: *Ill-mannered movie-goers talked throughout the entire picture.*
disrespectful not showing the proper respect for someone or something: *I felt her comments were disrespectful to all the people who have worked so hard on this project.*
impertinent *formal* not showing a proper respect for someone, especially by asking or talking about subjects that you do not have a right to know about: *an impertinent question about his private life* | *an impertinent young man*
insolent *formal* behaving in a way that is deliberately very rude to someone in authority: *The girl's only response was an insolent stare.* | *Don't be so insolent!*

COLLOCATIONS CHECK

cheeky boy/monkey/grin
impertinent question
insulting behaviour/remark/comment/language
insolent stare/tone
tactless remark/question/attempt

says how things must be done or what is allowed, especially in a game, organization, or job: **[+of]** *the rules of the game* | **under the rules/according to the rules** *Under the rules, the company must publish its annual accounts.*

2 ABOUT WHAT YOU SHOULD DO [C] what you should do in a particular situation, or a statement about this: *There are no* ***hard and fast rules*** (=clear and definite rules) *about what to wear to classes.* | **[+of]** *There are two basic rules of survival.* | ***The rule is****: if you feel any pain you should stop exercising immediately.*

3 NORMAL/USUAL [singular] something that is normal or usually true: **as a (general) rule** *As a general rule most students finish their coursework by the end of May.* | *Early marriage used to* **be the rule** *in that part of the world.* | *A series of payments used to be* **the exception rather than the rule**. | *Unfortunately there is an* **exception** *to every* **rule**.

4 GOVERNMENT [U] the government of a country or area by a particular group of people or using a particular system: **under ... rule** *people living under communist rule* | *the end of* **colonial rule** | *a period of* **military rule** | **direct rule** *from Westminster* | *the restoration of* **majority rule** (=government by the party that most people have voted for) *to Northern Ireland*

5 IN GRAMMAR/SCIENCE ETC [C] a statement about what is usually allowed in a particular system, such as the grammar of a language, or a science: **[+of]** *the rules of English punctuation*

6 the rule of law a situation in which the laws of a country are obeyed: *We are here to uphold the rule of law.*

7 the rules of natural justice what people believe to be right and fair: *The governor failed to observe the rules of natural justice.*

8 rule of thumb a rough figure or method of calculation, based on practical experience: *As a general rule of thumb, children this age should not spend more than one hour on homework.*

9 make it a rule (to do sth) to try to make sure that you always do something: *I make it a rule never to mix business with pleasure.*

10 FOR MEASURING [C] *old-fashioned* a RULER → **GOLDEN RULE, GROUND RULES, HOME RULE, SLIDE RULE,** → **work to rule** at **WORK**[1](32)

COLLOCATIONS

VERBS

break a rule (*also* **violate a rule** *formal*) (=not obey it) *He had clearly broken the official rules.*
obey/follow a rule *She wasn't going to obey their silly rules.*
comply with/abide by/observe a rule *formal* (=obey it) *All members must comply with the rules of the organization.*
stick to/go by the rules *informal* (=obey them) *We all have to stick to the rules.*
make the rules *I'm only an assistant manager – I don't make the rules.*
the rule says ... *The rule says that you must be standing inside the line.*
the rule applies to sb/sth (=it concerns them) | **play by the rules** (=do what is expected and agreed) | **bend/stretch the rules** (=allow someone to do something that is not normally allowed) | **relax the rules** (=make them less strict) | **tighten (up) the rules** (=make them stricter) | **enforce a rule** (=make sure that it is obeyed)

ADJECTIVES/NOUN + rule

strict *They have very strict rules about gambling.*
simple *The rules of the game are quite simple.*
petty (=unreasonable rules about unimportant things) *There are hundreds of petty rules.*
a school/prison/club etc rule *He had broken one of the school rules.*
an unwritten rule (=a rule of behaviour that everyone in a group understands)

PHRASES

be against the rules (=not be allowed) *It was against the rules to talk in class.*
the rules concerning/governing/relating to sth *formal* (=the rules about something) *the rules governing food labeling*
a change in the rules | **rules and regulations** | **rules are rules** *spoken* (=a rule must be obeyed)

THESAURUS

rule an instruction that says what people are allowed to do or not allowed to do, for example in a game, school, or company: *the rules of baseball* | *He disobeyed the school rules.*
law an official rule that everyone in a country, city, or state must obey: *It is against the law to carry a concealed weapon.*
regulation an official rule or order, which is part of a set of rules made by a government or organization: *the regulations for applying for a passport* | *building regulations*
restriction an official rule that limits what people can do: *new restrictions on immigration* | *The government is planning to impose regulations on the amount of alcohol you can bring into the country.*
guidelines rules or instructions about the best way to do something: *the Department of Health's guidelines for a healthy diet*
code a set of rules that people or organizations agree to obey but are not forced to obey: *The school has a* **dress code** *for its students.* | *the company's* **code of conduct**
statute *formal* a law that has been officially approved by a parliament, council etc, and written down: *The statute banned corporal punishment.*

rule² ●●● W2 *v*

1 GOVERNMENT [I,T] to have the official power to control a country and the people who live there → **govern**: *Queen Victoria ruled England for 64 years.* | *African tribal societies were traditionally ruled by a council of elders.* | **[+over]** *Alexander the Great ruled over a huge empire.* | *He announced that henceforth he would* **rule by decree** (=make all the important decisions himself). THESAURUS CONTROL

2 CONTROL/INFLUENCE [T] if a feeling or desire rules someone, it has a powerful and controlling influence on their actions: *the passion for power and success which* **rules** *her* **life**

3 COURT/LAW [I always + adv/prep, T] to make an official decision about something, especially a legal problem → **decree**: **rule that** *The judge ruled that she should have custody of the children.* | **[+on]** *The Supreme Court has yet to rule on the case.* | **rule in favour of/against sb/sth** *The tribunal ruled in her favour.* | **be ruled illegal/unlawful etc** *This part of the bill was ruled unconstitutional.* → RULING[1]

4 rule the roost *informal* to be the most powerful person in a group: *His wife rules the roost in their house.*

5 rule sb/sth with a rod of iron *also* **rule sb with an iron fist/hand** to control a group of people in a very severe way: *Although he was a fair man, he ruled us with an iron fist.*

6 sb/sth rules *informal* used to say that the team, school, place etc mentioned is better than any other: *Arsenal rules OK. BrE* | *graffiti saying 'Poheny High rules'*

7 DRAW A LINE [T] to draw a line using a ruler or other straight edge: *Rule a line under each answer.* → OVERRULE, → **let your heart rule your head** at HEART[1](2)

rule *sth/sb* ↔ **out** *phr v*

1 to decide that something is not possible or suitable: *The police have ruled out suicide.* | *She has refused to* **rule out the possibility** *of singing again.*

2 to make it impossible for something to happen: *The mountainous terrain rules out most forms of agriculture.*

3 to state that someone will not be able to take part in a sports event: **[+of]** *He has been ruled out of the match with a knee injury.*

R

rule·book /ˈruːlbʊk/ *n* **1 go by the rulebook** *informal* to obey exactly the rules about how something should be done: *If I went by the rulebook, I'd have to report this conversation.* **2** [C] a book of rules, especially one that is given to workers in a job

ruled /ruːld/ *adj* ruled paper has parallel lines printed across it SYN **lined**

rul·er /ˈruːlə $ -ər/ ●●● W3 *n* [C]
1 someone such as a king or queen who has official power over a country or area THESAURUS ➤ LEADER
2 a long flat straight piece of plastic, metal, or wood that you use for measuring things or drawing straight lines: *a 12-inch ruler* → see picture at MATHEMATICS

rul·ing¹ /ˈruːlɪŋ/ ●○○ *n* [C] an official decision, especially one made by a court: **[+on]** *the recent Supreme Court ruling on defendants' rights*

ruling² *adj* [only before noun] **1** the ruling group in a country or organization is the group that controls it: *A* ***ruling class*** *clearly existed.* | *the* ***ruling body*** *of American golf* **2** a ruling interest or emotion interests someone more than anything else: *Football remains the* ***ruling passion*** *of many men.*

rum¹ /rʌm/ *n* [C,U] a strong alcoholic drink made from sugar, or a glass of this drink

rum² *adj old-fashioned* unusual or strange

rum·ba /ˈrʌmbə/ *n* [C,U] a popular dance from Cuba, or music for this dance

rum·ble¹ /ˈrʌmbəl/ *v* **1** [I] to make a series of long low sounds, especially a long distance away from you: *We could hear thunder rumbling in the distance.* **2** [I always + adv/prep] to move slowly along while making a series of long low sounds: *We watched the tanks rumbling past the window.* **3** [I] if your stomach rumbles, it makes a noise, especially because you are hungry **4** [T] *BrE informal* to find out what someone is secretly intending to do: *How did you rumble them?* **5** [I,T] *AmE old-fashioned* to fight with someone

rumble on *phr v* if a disagreement rumbles on, it continues for a long time SYN **drag on**: *The row about pay is still rumbling on.*

rumble² *n* [singular] a series of long low sounds: **[+of]** *the* ***low rumble*** *of traffic in the distance* | *the* ***distant rumble*** *of gunfire* THESAURUS ➤ SOUND

ˈrumble ˌstrip *n* [C] a number of raised lines across a road which make a loud noise when you drive over them to warn you to slow down

rum·bling /ˈrʌmblɪŋ/ *n* **1 rumblings** [plural] remarks that show that people are starting to become annoyed, or that a difficult situation is developing: *rumblings of discontent* | *There have been rumblings about the need for better computers.* **2** [C usually singular] a series of long low sounds: *We heard a rumbling behind us.*

rum·bus·tious /rʌmˈbʌstʃəs/ *adj* full of energy, fun, and noise SYN **rambunctious** *AmE*: *rumbustious football fans*

ru·mi·nant /ˈruːmɪnənt/ *n* [C] *technical* an animal such as a cow that has several stomachs and eats grass

ru·mi·nate /ˈruːməneɪt/ *v* [I] **1** *formal* to think carefully and deeply about something: **[+on/over]** *He sat alone, ruminating on the injustice of the world.* **2** *technical* if animals such as cows ruminate, they bring food back into their mouths from their stomachs and CHEW it again —**rumination** /ˌruːməˈneɪʃən/ *n* [C,U]

ru·mi·na·tive /ˈruːmənətɪv $ -neɪtɪv/ *adj formal* thinking deeply and carefully about something: *a typically ruminative speech* —**ruminatively** *adv*

rum·mage¹ /ˈrʌmɪdʒ/ *v* [I always + adv/prep] (*also* **rummage around/about**) to search for something by moving things around in a careless or hurried way: **[+in/through etc]** *Looks like someone's been rummaging around in my desk.*

rummage² *n* **1** [C usually singular] *informal* a careless or hurried search for something: ***Have a rummage*** *in my jewellery box and see if you can find something you like.* **2** [U] *especially AmE* old clothes, toys etc that you no longer want SYN **jumble** *BrE*

ˈrummage sale *n* [C] *AmE* an event at which old clothes, toys etc are sold as a way of getting money, for example to help a school or church SYN **jumble sale** *BrE*

rum·my /ˈrʌmi/ *n* [U] a simple card game in which players try to collect series of cards

ru·mour *BrE*, **rumor** *AmE* /ˈruːmə $ -ər/ ●●○ *n* [C,U]
1 information or a story that is passed from one person to another and which may or may not be true: **[+about/of]** *I've heard all sorts of rumours about him and his secretary.* | **rumour that** *There's an unsubstantiated rumour that Eddie is bankrupt.*
2 the rumour mill the people, considered as a group, who discuss something and pass rumours to each other: *His name has come up in the rumour mill as a possible director for the project.*

COLLOCATIONS

VERBS

a rumour spreads *A rumour spread that he had been killed.*
a rumour goes around (*also* **a rumour circulates** *formal*) (=a rumour is passed among people) *There are a lot of rumors going around that they're going to sell the company.*
rumour has it (=it is being said) *Rumour has it that they plan to get married.*
hear a rumour *I heard a rumour that she was leaving.*
spread a rumour *Someone has been spreading rumours about us.*
deny a rumour | **confirm a rumour** (=say that it is true)

ADJECTIVES

false/unfounded *He says that the rumours are completely unfounded.*
rumours are rife (=are talked about by a lot of people) *Rumours were rife that the band had refused to play.*
a widespread rumour *The arrests followed widespread rumours of police corruption.*
a persistent rumour (=one that keeps being repeated for a long time) *Despite persistent rumours of an affair, his wife stood by him.*
a strong rumour (=a rumour that is likely to be true) | **a wild rumour** (=one that is completely untrue) | **a malicious rumour** (=a false one that someone spreads to make trouble) | **an unsubstantiated rumour** (=one that has not been proved to be true) | **a scurrilous rumour** *formal* (=a damaging and false rumour)

COMMON ERRORS

⚠ Don't say 'a rumour spreads out'. Say **a rumour spreads**.

THESAURUS

rumour *BrE*, **rumor** *AmE n* [C,U] information or a story that is passed from one person to another and which may or may not be true: *The band denied the rumours that they may be splitting up.* | *The truth finally came out after months of rumour.*
speculation *n* [U] a situation in which a lot of people are talking about something that is happening, especially something that is happening in politics or public life, and trying to guess what the truth is: *There was a great deal of speculation about a possible merger involving Belgium's largest banks.* | *The report* ***fuelled speculation*** (=caused more speculation) *that he was about to resign.*
gossip *n* [U] things that people say about what they think has happened in other people's private lives, which is usually not true: *She tells me all the latest gossip from the office.* | *The magazine was full of gossip about celebrities.* | *You shouldn't believe every* ***piece of gossip*** *you hear.*
talk *n* [U] something that people talk about a lot but which is not official: *The government has dismissed*

talk of a military strike on the country. | *There's been a lot of talk of him resigning.*
hearsay *n* [U] something that you have heard from someone else, but cannot prove whether it is true or untrue – often used in legal contexts: *All the accounts were based on hearsay rather than eye-witness reports.* | *hearsay evidence*

ru·moured *BrE*, **rumored** *AmE* /ˈruːməd $ -ərd/ *v* **be rumoured** if something is rumoured to be true, people are saying secretly or unofficially that it may be true → **alleged**: **it is rumoured that** *It was rumoured that Johnson had been poisoned.* | **be rumoured to be sth** *She was rumoured to be a millionaire.* | *a young man* ***widely rumoured*** *to be her lover*

ru·mour·mon·ger *BrE*, **rumormonger** *AmE* /ˈruːməˌmʌŋɡə $ -mərˌmɑːŋɡər, -ˌmʌŋ-/ *n* [C] someone who tells other people rumours – used to show disapproval

rump /rʌmp/ *n* **1** [C] the part of an animal's back that is just above its legs **2 rump steak** good quality meat that comes from the rump of a cow **3** [C] the part of your body that you sit on – used humorously SYN **bottom** **4** [singular] *BrE* the part of a group or government that remains after most of the other members have left

rum·ple /ˈrʌmpəl/ *v* [T] to make hair, clothes etc less tidy: *He rumpled her hair playfully.* —**rumpled** *adj*: *the slightly rumpled bed* | *a rumpled linen suit*

rum·pus /ˈrʌmpəs/ *n* [singular] *informal* a lot of noise, especially made by people quarrelling: *There's a real rumpus going on upstairs.*

ˈrumpus room *n* [C] *AmE* a room in a house that is used by the family for games, parties etc

rump·y pump·y /ˌrʌmpi ˈpʌmpi/ *n* [U] *BrE* sexual activity – used humorously

run¹ /rʌn/ ●●● S1 W1 *v* (*past tense* **ran** /ræn/, *past participle* **run**, *present participle* **running**)

1 MOVE QUICKLY USING YOUR LEGS **a)** [I] to move very quickly, by moving your legs more quickly than when you walk: **[+down/up/to/towards etc]** *I ran down the stairs as fast as I could.* | *He was running towards the door.* | *She turned and ran away.* | *The boys ran off into the crowd.* | **run to do sth** *Several people ran to help her when she fell.* | *The children* ***came running*** *out of the house.* | *Women* ***ran screaming***, *with children in their arms.* | *Jane struggled free and* ***ran for*** *her* ***life*** (=ran in order to avoid being killed). | *Hurry!* ***Run for it*** (=run as quickly as possible in order to escape)! | *He picked up the child and* ***ran like hell*** (=ran very quickly, especially in order to escape). *not polite* **b)** [T] to run a particular distance: *Firefighters are to run 500km to raise money for a children's charity.* | *He ran the length of the corridor.*

2 RACE **a)** [I,T] to run in a race: *I'd never run a marathon before.* | **[+in]** *Murray has said she will consider running in the 3000 metres.* **b)** [T] if a race is run at a particular time or in a particular place, it happens at that time or in that place: *The Derby will be run at 3 o'clock.* GRAMMAR **Run** is usually passive in this meaning.

3 ORGANIZE/BE IN CHARGE OF [T] to organize or be in charge of an activity, business, organization, or country: *For a while, she ran a restaurant in Boston.* | *Many people don't care who runs the country.* | *Courses are currently being run in London and Edinburgh.* | *Many people belong to a pension scheme run by their employers.* | **well/badly run** *The hotel is well-run and extremely popular.* | *a* ***state-run*** (=controlled by the government) *television station* THESAURUS CONTROL

4 DO STH/GO SOMEWHERE QUICKLY [I] to do something or go somewhere quickly: *Run and ask your mother where she's put the keys.* | **[+to]** *I need to run to the store for some more milk.*

5 BUSES/TRAINS ETC **a)** [I] if a bus, train etc service runs, it takes people from one place to another at fixed times: *The buses don't run on Sundays.* | **[+to]** *The number 61 bus runs to the city centre.* **b)** [T] if a company or other organization runs a bus, train etc service, they make it operate: *They're running special trains to and from the exhibition.*

6 COMPUTERS **a)** [I] if a computer program runs, it operates: **[+on]** *The software will run on any PC.* **b)** [T] if you run a program, you make it operate: *The RS8 system runs both Unix and MPX-32.*

7 MACHINE/ENGINE **a)** [I] if a machine or engine runs, it operates: *She got out of the car and left the engine running.* | **run on electricity/gas/petrol etc** (=get its power from electricity etc) *Most cars run on unleaded fuel.* | **run off sth** (=use something for power) *It runs off batteries.* **b)** [T] if you run a machine or engine, you make it operate: *You shouldn't* ***keep the engine running*** *when the car is standing still.* | *I often run the washing machine more than once a day.*

8 TAPE **a)** [I] if a tape is running, it is recording: *She didn't realize the tape was running as she spoke.* GRAMMAR **Run** is usually used in the progressive in this meaning. **b)** [T] if you run a tape, you make it move backwards or forwards: *Run the tape back to the beginning.*

9 NEWSPAPER/TELEVISION **a)** [T] to print something in a newspaper or magazine, or broadcast something on television: *The company is running a series of advertisements in national newspapers.* | *A local TV station ran her story.* **b)** [I] if a program runs on television, it is shown. If a story runs in a newspaper or magazine, it is printed: *The series ran for 20 episodes and was extremely popular.* | *Conan Doyle's stories ran in 'The Strand' magazine.*

10 FAST/OUT OF CONTROL [I always + adv/prep] to move too fast or in an uncontrolled way: *Her car ran off the road and into a tree.* | *The truck* ***ran out of control*** *and hit a house.*

11 USE A VEHICLE [T] *especially BrE* to own and use a vehicle: *I can't afford to run a car.* | *A bicycle is relatively cheap to buy and run.*

12 TAKE SB IN YOUR CAR [T always + adv/prep] *informal* to take someone somewhere in your car SYN **drive**: *Shall I run you home?* | **run sb to sth** *Let me run you to the station.*

13 IN AN ELECTION [I] *especially AmE* to try to be elected in an election SYN **stand** *BrE*: **[+for]** *Salinas is running for a second term as president.* | *an attempt to encourage more women to* ***run for office*** | **[+against]** *Feinstein will win if she runs against Lungren.*

14 STH LONG [I,T always + adv/prep] if something long such as a road or wire runs in a particular direction, that is its position, or that is where you put it: *The road runs along a valley.* | *Developers want to run a road right through his farm.* | *Run the cables under the carpet.* | *The Sierra mountain range* ***runs the length of*** *the north west coast of Majorca.*

15 MOVE STH ON A SURFACE [T always + adv/prep] to move something lightly along a surface: *Charles ran his fingers through her hair.* | *Run the scanner over the bar codes.*

16 FLOW [I always + adv/prep] to flow in a particular direction or place: *Tears started to run down her cheeks.* | *Water was running off the roof.*

17 TAP [I,T] if a TAP is running, water is coming out of it, or if you run a tap, you make water come out of it: *Did you leave the tap running?* | *He ran the tap until the water was really hot.*

18 run a bath to fill a bath with water: *I could hear her running a bath upstairs.* | **run sb a bath** *Could you run me a nice hot bath while I finish my meal?*

19 SB'S NOSE [I] if someone's nose is running, liquid is flowing out of it

20 OFFICIAL PAPERS [I] if something runs for a particular length of time, it can officially be used for that time: *The contract runs for a year.* | *My car insurance only has another month to run.*

21 PLAY/FILM [I] to continue being performed regularly in one place: *The play ran for two years.*

22 HAPPEN [I] to happen in a particular way or at a particular time: *Andy kept things* ***running smoothly*** (=happening in the way they should) *while I was away.* | *He was given a further three month prison sentence to run concurrently.* | *The course runs over a three year period.*

23 AMOUNT/PRICE [I] to be at a particular level, amount, or price: **[+at]** *Inflation was running at 5%.* | **[+to]** *The cost of repairing the damage could run to $5000.*

24 STORY/ACCOUNT ETC [I,T] if a story, discussion etc runs in a particular way, it has those particular words or events: *The story runs that someone offered Lynch a further $500.* | *'President's marriage really over' ran the headline in a national newspaper.*
25 run its course if something runs its course, it continues in the way you expect until it has finished: *Recession in the country has run its course and left an aftermath of uncertainty.*
26 sth will run and run *BrE* if a subject, discussion, event etc will run and run, people will continue to be interested in it for a long time: *This is a story that will run and run.*
27 THOUGHTS/FEELINGS [I always + adv/prep] if a feeling runs through you, or a thought runs through your mind, you feel it or think it quickly: **[+through/down]** *A feeling of excitement ran through her body as they touched.* | *The same thought kept running through his mind.* | *A cold shiver ran down my back.* | *I felt a sharp pain run down my leg.*
28 run high if feelings run high, people are very angry, upset, excited etc: *Tension ran high and fights broke out among the crowd.* | *Feelings have been running high in the town, following the murder of a young girl.*
29 run sb's life *informal* to keep telling someone what they should do all the time, in a way that annoys them: *Don't try to run my life!*
30 run for cover a) to run towards a place where you will be safe, especially to avoid bullets: *He was shot in the leg as he ran for cover.* **b)** to try to protect yourself from a bad situation or from being criticized: *His success at backing winning horses has had the bookmakers running for cover.*
31 COLOUR IN CLOTHES [I] if colour runs, it spreads from one piece of clothing or one area of cloth to another when the clothes are wet: *The T-shirt ran and made all my other clothes pink.*
32 PAINT/INK [I] if paint runs, it moves onto an area where you did not intend it to go
33 run a check/test/experiment etc to arrange for someone or something to be checked or tested: **[+on]** *Ask your doctor to run a test on your blood sugar levels.*
34 HOLE IN CLOTHES [I] if a hole in TIGHTS or STOCKINGS runs, it gets bigger in a straight line
35 run drugs/guns to bring drugs or guns into a country illegally in order to sell them → **DRUG RUNNER**, **GUN-RUNNING**
36 run in the family if something such as a quality, disease, or skill runs in the family, many people in that family have it: *Diabetes appears to run in families.*
37 run a temperature/fever to have a body temperature that is higher than normal, because you are ill
38 run a mile *informal* to try very hard to avoid a particular situation or person because you do not want to deal with them: *If someone asked me to marry them, I'd probably run a mile.*
39 run late/early/on time to arrive, go somewhere, or do something late, early, or at the right time: *I'm running late, so I'll talk to you later.* | *If the train runs on time, we'll be there by ten.*
40 be running scared to feel worried because someone who you are competing against is becoming very successful or powerful: *The party are running scared.*
41 come running a) *informal* to react in a very eager way when someone asks or tells you to do something: *He thinks he's only got to look at me and I'll come running.* **b)** *especially spoken* to ask someone for help, advice, or sympathy when you have a problem: **[+to]** *Well I warned you, so don't come running to me when it all goes wrong!*
42 run your eyes over/along etc sth to look quickly at something: *He ran his eyes along the books on the shelf.*
43 run before you can walk to try to do something difficult before you have learned the basic skills you need: *A lot of language students want to run before they can walk.*
44 run a (red) light *informal* to drive quickly through a red TRAFFIC LIGHT instead of stopping → **RUNNING**[1], → **cut and run** at CUT[1](38), → **be/run/go counter to sth** at COUNTER[3], → **run deep** at DEEP[2](4), → **run dry** at DRY[1](4), → **run low** at LOW[1](4), → **run sb ragged** at RAGGED(5), → **run rings around sb** at RING[1](8), → **run riot** at RIOT[1](2), → **be running short** at SHORT[3](2), → **run sb/sth to earth** at EARTH[1](14), → **run to fat** at FAT[2](6), → **run sb/sth to ground** at GROUND[1](19), → **run to seed** at SEED[1](4), → **run wild** at WILD[2](1), → **be up and running** at UP[1](22)

THESAURUS

run to move very quickly, by moving your legs more quickly than when you walk: *My five-year-old son runs everywhere.* | *I go running twice a week.*
jog to run quite slowly for exercise over a long distance: *A few people were jogging in the park.*
race/dash to run somewhere as quickly as you can, especially because you have to do something urgently: *He dashed across the road to the police station.* | *We raced to the bus stop and got there just in time.*
sprint to run as fast as you can for a short distance: *I saw the runners sprinting past.* | *He sprinted up the stairs.*
tear to run very quickly and without really looking where you are going, because you are in a hurry: *He tore down the street and around the corner.*
charge to run quickly and with a lot of energy, so that you might knock down anyone or anything that gets in your way: *They all charged out of the school gates at 4 o'clock.*
take to your heels to start running away very quickly, especially to escape or because you are afraid: *The men took to their heels as soon as they saw the police.*

ANIMALS RUNNING

trot to run fairly slowly, taking short steps - used especially about horses and dogs: *A little dog was trotting behind her.*
gallop if a horse gallops, it runs very quickly: *The horse galloped off across the field.*
bolt to suddenly run somewhere very fast, especially in order to escape: *Suddenly a fox bolted out from beneath a hedge.*

run across sb/sth *phr v* to meet someone or find something by chance: *I ran across him at a conference in Milan.* | *I ran across some old love letters while I was clearing out a cupboard.*
run after sb/sth *phr v*
1 to chase someone or something: *He ran after her, calling her name.*
2 *informal* to try to start a sexual relationship with someone: *He's always running after younger women.*
3 *spoken* to do a lot of things for someone else as though you were their servant: *I can't keep running after you all day!*
run along *phr v spoken* used to tell a child to leave, or to tell someone that you must leave: *Run along now! I've got work to finish.* | *Oh, it's late. I'd better be running along.*
run around (*also* **run round** *BrE*) *phr v*
1 to run in an area while you are playing: *The children were running around in the garden.*
2 *informal* to be very busy doing many small jobs: *Maria was running around trying to get the house tidy.* | *We were all **running around like headless chickens*** (=trying to do a lot of things, in an anxious or disorganized way). → **RUNAROUND**
run around after sb *phr v informal* to do a lot of things for someone else as though you were their servant: *I've spent all day running around after the kids.*
run around with sb *phr v informal* to spend a lot of time with someone, especially someone that other people disapprove of: *He started running around with a gang of teenagers.*
run away *phr v*
1 to leave a place, especially secretly, in order to escape from someone or something: **[+from]** *Toby ran away from home at the age of 14.* → **RUNAWAY**[2]
2 to try to avoid dealing with a problem or difficult situation: **[+from]** *You can't just run away from your responsibilities.*
3 to secretly go away with someone in order to marry

them or live with them: *They ran away together to get married.*

run away with sb/sth *phr v*

1 to secretly go away with someone in order to marry them or live with them – usually used to show disapproval: *His wife has run away with another man.*

2 run away with you if your feelings, ideas etc run away with you, they start to control how you behave: *Don't let your imagination run away with you!*

3 your tongue runs away with you if your tongue runs away with you, you say something that you did not intend to say

4 run away with the idea/impression (that) *spoken* to think that something is true when it is not: *Don't run away with the impression that he doesn't care.*

5 *informal* to win a competition or sports game very easily: *The Reds ran away with the championship.*

run sth **by/past** sb *phr v*

1 to tell someone something so that they can give you their opinion: *Let me run some figures by you.* | *I just wanted to run it past you and see what you thought.*

2 run that by me again *spoken* used to ask someone to repeat what they have just said because you did not completely understand it

run down *phr v*

1 run sb/sth ↔ down to drive into a person or animal and kill or injure them: *Their daughter was run down by a car.*

2 run sb/sth ↔ down *informal* to criticize someone or something in a way that is unfair: *There's a lot of good things about homeopathic treatment. I'm certainly not running it down.*

3 if a clock, machine, BATTERY etc runs down, it has no more power and stops working

4 to make a company, organization etc gradually reduce in size, especially in order to close it in the future, or to gradually reduce in size: **run sth ↔ down** *Many smaller local hospitals are being run down.* | *The business had been running down for a long time.*

5 if a supply of something runs down, or if you run it down, there gradually becomes less of it: *Crude oil reserves are running down.* | **run sth ↔ down** *Electricity generating companies are running down stocks and cutting purchases.*

6 run down sth to read a list of people or things: *Let me just run down the list of people who've been invited.*

7 run sb/sth down to find someone or something after searching for a long time: *I finally ran him down at his new office in Glendale.* → **RUNDOWN, RUN-DOWN**

run sb/sth ↔ **in** *phr v BrE*

1 to drive a new car slowly and carefully for a period of time so you do not damage its engine

2 *old-fashioned* if the police run a criminal in, they catch him or her

run into sb/sth *phr v*

1 to start to experience a difficult or unpleasant situation: *He ran into criticism after remarks he made in a television interview.* | **run into trouble/problems/difficulties** *The business ran into financial difficulties almost immediately.*

2 run into hundreds/thousands etc to reach an amount of several hundred, several thousand etc: *The cost of repairing the damage could run into millions.* | *The list ran into hundreds of pages.*

3 to hit someone or something with a vehicle SYN **crash into**: *He ran into the back of another car.*

4 *informal* to meet someone by chance: *Guess who I ran into in town today!* → **run yourself into the ground** at **GROUND**[1](13)

run off *phr v*

1 to leave a place or person in a way that people disapprove of: *Amy's husband had run off and left her with two children to bring up.*

2 run sth ↔ off to quickly print several copies of something: *I'll run off a few more copies before the meeting.*

3 run sb off sth to force someone to leave a place: *Someone tried to run me off the road.* | *Smith had run them off his property with a rifle.*

4 run sth ↔ off to write a speech, poem, piece of music etc quickly and easily: *He could run off a five-page essay in an hour.*

5 run off at the mouth *AmE informal* to talk too much

6 run sth ↔ off to get rid of weight or energy by running: *I'm trying to run off some of the calories in that chocolate cake!*

run off with sb/sth *phr v informal*

1 to secretly go away with someone in order to marry them or live with them – used to show disapproval: *Liz shocked us all by running off with a married man.*

2 to steal something and go away: *a conman who makes a habit of running off with people's savings*

run on *phr v* to continue happening for longer than expected or planned: *These things always run on longer than people imagine.*

run out *phr v*

1 a) to use all of something and not have any more left: *I've got money you can borrow if you run out.* | **[+of]** *They ran out of money and had to abandon the project.* | *He'd run out of ideas.* **b)** if something is running out, there will soon be none left: *We must act now because time is running out.* | *My patience was running out.* | *His luck had run out* (=there was none left).

2 if an agreement, official document etc runs out, the period for which it is legal or has an effect ends SYN **expire**: *My contract runs out in September.*

3 run out of steam *informal* (*also* **run out of gas** *AmE*) to have no more energy or no longer be interested in what you are doing: *The team seemed to have run out of gas.*

4 run sb out of town *old-fashioned* to force someone to leave a place, because they have done something wrong

5 run sb ↔ out to end a player's INNINGS in the game of CRICKET by hitting the STUMPS with the ball while they are running

run out on sb *phr v* to leave someone when they are in a difficult situation – used to show disapproval: *He ran out on her when she became pregnant.*

run over *phr v*

1 run sb/sth ↔ over to hit someone or something with a vehicle, and drive over them: *He was run over and killed by a bus.* | *She* ***got run over*** *outside the school.*

2 run over sth to think about something: *Mark's mind raced, running over all the possibilities.*

3 run over sth to explain or practise something quickly: *I'll just run over the main points again.*

4 run over (sth) to continue happening for longer than planned: *The meeting ran over.* | *The talks have run over the 15 November deadline.*

5 if a container runs over, there is so much liquid inside that some flows out SYN **overflow**

run sth **past** sb *phr v* to RUN something BY someone

run round *phr v BrE* to RUN AROUND

run through *phr v*

1 run through sth to repeat something in order to practise it or make sure it is correct: *Let's run through the first scene again.*

2 run through sth to read, look at, or explain something quickly: *Briefly, she ran through details of the morning's events.*

3 run through sth if a quality, feature etc runs through something, it is present in all of that thing: *This theme runs through the whole book.*

4 run sb through *literary* to push a sword completely through someone → **RUN-THROUGH**

run to sb/sth *phr v*

1 to reach a particular amount: *The cost of repairing the damage could run to $1 million.* | *The treaty ran to 248 pages.*

2 [usually in negatives] *BrE* to be or have enough money to pay for something: *Our budget won't run to replacing all the computers.*

3 to ask someone to help or protect you: *You can't keep running to your parents every time you have a problem.*

4 sb's taste runs to sth if someone's taste runs to something, that is what they like: *His taste ran to action movies and thrillers.*

run up sth *phr v*

1 run up a debt/bill etc to use so much of something, or

borrow so much money, that you owe a lot of money: *She ran up an enormous phone bill.*
2 to achieve a particular score or position in a game or competition: *He quickly ran up a big lead in the polls.*
3 run sth ↔ up to make something, especially clothes, very quickly: *She can run up a dress in an evening.*
4 run sth ↔ up to raise a flag on a pole
run up against sth/sb *phr v* to have to deal with unexpected problems or a difficult opponent: *The museum has run up against opposition to its proposals.*
run with sth *phr v* to be covered with a liquid that is flowing down: *His face was running with blood.*

run² ●●● S1 W1 *n*
1 ON FOOT [C] a period of time spent running, or a distance that you run → **jog**, **sprint**: *a five-mile run | She usually* ***goes for*** *a* ***run*** *before breakfast. | He was still following me, and in a panic I* ***broke into a run****.* | **at a run** *Sarah left the house at a run.*
2 in the long run later in the future, not immediately → **long-term**: *Moving to Spain will be better for you in the long run.*
3 in the short run in the near future → **short-term**: *Sufficient supply, in the short run, will be a problem.*
4 the usual/normal/general run of sth the usual type of something: *The place was very different from the normal run of street cafes.*
5 SERIES [C usually singular] a series of successes or failures → **string**, **streak**: *an unbeaten run of 19 games* | **run of good/bad luck** *Losing my job was the start of a run of bad luck that year.* | **a run of defeats/victories etc** *His extraordinary run of successes has been stopped.*
6 AMOUNT PRODUCED [C] an amount of a product produced at one time: *a limited run of 200 copies*
7 be on the run a) to be trying to escape or hide, especially from the police: **[+from]** *wanted criminals on the run from police* **b)** if an army or opponent is on the run, they will soon be defeated **c)** to be very busy and continuously rushing about: *Typical of stress is this feeling of being continuously on the run.*
8 do sth on the run to do something while you are on your way somewhere or doing something else: *I always seem to eat on the run these days.*
9 make a run for it to suddenly start running, in order to escape
10 the run of sth if you have the run of a place, you are allowed to go anywhere and do anything in it: *We* ***had the run of*** *the house for the afternoon.*
11 a run on sth a) a situation in which lots of people suddenly buy a particular product → **rush**: *There's always a run on roses before Valentine's Day.* **b) a run on the dollar/pound etc** a situation in which lots of people sell dollars etc and the value goes down **c) a run on the bank** an occasion when a lot of people take their money out of a bank at the same time
12 give sb a (good) run for their money to make your opponent in a competition use all their skill and effort to defeat you: *They've given some of the top teams a run for their money this season.*
13 have a (good) run for your money *informal* to succeed in doing something successfully for a long time: *Investors have also had a good run for their money.*
14 ILLNESS **the runs** *informal* DIARRHOEA
15 PLAY/FILM [C] a continuous series of performances of a play, film etc in the same place: *His first play had a three-month run in the West End.*
16 JOURNEY [singular] **a)** a journey by train, ship, truck etc made regularly between two places: *It's only a 55-minute run from London to Brighton. | the daily* ***school run*** (=the journey that parents make each day taking their children to and from school) *BrE* **b)** *informal* a short journey in a car, for pleasure: *Let's take the car out for a run.*
17 FOR ANIMALS [C] an enclosed area where animals such as chickens or rabbits are kept: *a chicken run*
18 SPORT [C] a point won in CRICKET or baseball: *Jones* ***made*** *32* ***runs*** *this afternoon.*
19 WINTER SPORTS [C] a special area or track on a mountain for people to SKI or SLEDGE down: *a ski run*
20 ELECTION [C usually singular] *AmE* an attempt to be elected to an important position: **[+for]** *He is preparing a run for the presidency.*
21 IN CLOTHES [C] *AmE* a line of torn stitches in TIGHTS or STOCKINGS SYN **ladder** *BrE*
22 MUSIC [C] a set of notes played or sung quickly up or down a SCALE in a piece of music
23 CARD GAMES [C] a set of cards with numbers in a series, held by one player → **DRY RUN, DUMMY RUN, FUN RUN, MILK RUN, PRINT RUN, TRIAL RUN**

run·a·bout /ˈrʌnəbaʊt/ *n* [C] *informal* a small car used for short journeys

run·a·round /ˈrʌnəˌraʊnd/ *n* **give sb the runaround** *informal* to deliberately avoid giving someone a definite answer, especially when they are asking you to do something: *Every time we ask the landlord about fixing the roof, he gives us the runaround.* → **run around** at RUN¹

run·a·way¹ /ˈrʌnəweɪ/ *adj* [only before noun] **1** a runaway vehicle or animal is out of control: *a runaway horse* **2** happening very easily or quickly, and not able to be controlled: *The film was a* ***runaway success****. |* ***runaway inflation*** *| a runaway victory* **3** a runaway person has left the place where they are supposed to be → **run away**

runaway² *n* [C] someone, especially a child, who has left home without telling anyone and does not intend to come back → **run away** at RUN¹

run·down /ˈrʌndaʊn/ *n* [singular] **1** the process of making a business or industry smaller and less important: **[+of]** *the rundown of British Steel's activities in Scotland* **2** a quick report or explanation of an idea, situation etc: **[+on]** *Connors promised to give me a rundown on local police activity.*

ˌrun-ˈdown *adj* **1** a building or area that is run-down is in very bad condition: *a run-down inner-city area* **2** [not before noun] someone who is run-down is tired and not healthy: *You look a bit run-down.*

rune /ruːn/ *n* [C] *technical* **1** one of the letters of the alphabet used in the past by people in Northern Europe **2** a magic song or written sign —**runic** *adj*

rung¹ /rʌŋ/ *v* the past participle of RING²

rung² *n* [C] **1** one of the bars that form the steps of a ladder **2** *informal* a particular level or position in an organization or system: **[+of/on]** *Humans are on the highest rung of the evolutionary ladder.*

ˈrun-in *n* [C] an argument or disagreement, especially with someone in an official position: **[+with]** *Michael got drunk and* ***had a run-in*** *with the police.*

run·nel /ˈrʌnl/ *n* [C] a small stream or passage that water flows along

run·ner /ˈrʌnə $ -ər/ ●●○ *n* [C]
1 someone who runs for sport or pleasure → **jogger**: *a long-distance runner | a marathon runner*
2 a horse that runs in a race: *The runners and riders appear in Friday's Racing Post.*
3 do a runner *BrE informal* to leave somewhere quickly in order to avoid paying for something or having to meet someone: *By the time the police got there, the boys had done a runner.*
4 one of the two thin pieces of metal under a SLEDGE, or the single piece of metal under a SKATE
5 the bar of wood or metal that a drawer or curtain slides along
6 *technical* a stem on a plant that grows along the ground and then puts down roots to form a new plant
7 a long narrow piece of cloth or CARPET → **DRUG RUNNER**, → **gun runner** at **GUN-RUNNING**, **FRONT-RUNNER**

ˌrunner ˈbean *n* [C] *BrE* a vegetable that grows as a long green POD (=seed container) on a climbing plant

ˌrunner-ˈup *n* (*plural* **runners-up**) [C] the person or team that comes second in a race or competition

run·ning¹ /ˈrʌnɪŋ/ ●●● S3 *n* [U]
1 the activity or sport of running → **jogging**: *Did you* ***go running*** *this morning? | New facilities include a pool and a running track. | running shoes*
2 the running of sth the process of managing or organizing

a business, home, organization etc: *Brian took over the **day-to-day running** of the company while his father was away.* | *He praised the **smooth running** of the election.*
3 be in the running/out of the running to have some hope or no hope of winning a race or competition: *Who's in the running for the world title this year?*
4 make (all) the running *BrE informal* to be the person who makes most of the suggestions in a relationship, plan, activity etc

running² *adj* [only before noun] **1 running water a)** if a house has running water, it has pipes which provide water to its kitchen, bath, toilet etc **b)** water that is flowing or moving: *the sound of running water* | *Rinse the vegetables thoroughly under running water.* **2 running commentary** a spoken description of an event, especially a race or game, made while the event is happening: *She **gave us a running commentary** on what was happening in the street.* **3 running total** a total that keeps being increased as new costs, amounts etc are added: *Keep a running total of your expenses as you go along.* **4 running battle/joke** an argument or joke that continues or is repeated over a long period of time **5 running sore** a sore area on your skin that has liquid coming out of it **6 in running order** a machine that is in running order is working correctly **7 the running order** the order in which the different parts of an event have been arranged to take place **8 take a running jump** *spoken* used to tell someone to go away and stop annoying you

running³ *adv* **three years/five times etc running** for three years etc without a change or interruption SYN **in a row**: *She won the prize for the fourth year running.*

ˈrunning costs *n* [plural] the amount of money needed to operate an organization, system, machine etc

ˈrunning mate *n* [C usually singular] the person chosen by someone who is trying to become president, leader etc to help win an election, and be the second most important political person if they are elected

ˌrunning reˈpairs *n* [plural] small things that you do to something to keep it in good working order

ˈrunning ˌtime *n* [U] the length of time that a film or television programme takes to run from beginning to end

run·ny /ˈrʌni/ *adj informal* **1** a runny nose, runny eyes etc have liquid coming out of them, usually because you have a cold **2** food that is runny is not as solid or thick as normal or as desired: *The butter had gone runny in the heat.*

ˈrun-off *n* **1** [C] a second competition or election that is arranged when there is no clear winner of the first one → PLAY-OFF, → **run off** at RUN¹ **2** [U] *technical* rain or other liquid that flows off the land into rivers

ˌrun-of-the-ˈmill *adj* not special or interesting in any way SYN **ordinary**: *a run-of-the-mill performance*

ˈrun-on ˌsentence *n* [C] *especially AmE* a sentence that has two main CLAUSES without connecting words or correct PUNCTUATION

ˈrun rate *n* [C] a calculation of how much money a company or project will spend or earn in a year. It is usually made by looking at how much it has spent or earned in a three-month period and multiplying that by four.

runt /rʌnt/ *n* [C] **1** the smallest and least developed baby animal of a group born at the same time: **[+of]** *the runt of the litter* **2** *informal* a small, unpleasant, or unimportant person

ˈrun-through *n* [C] a short practice before a performance, test etc → **rehearsal**: *a final run-through of the play*

ˈrun-up *n* **1 the run-up to sth** the period of time just before an important event: *in the run-up to the election* **2** [C] the act of running, or the distance that you run, before you kick a ball, jump over a pole etc

run·way /ˈrʌnweɪ/ ●●○ *n* [C]
1 a long specially prepared hard surface like a road on which aircraft land and take off
2 *AmE* a long narrow part of a stage that stretches out into the area where the AUDIENCE sits SYN **catwalk** *BrE*

ru·pee /ruːˈpiː/ *n* [C] the standard unit of money in India, Pakistan, and some other countries

ru·pi·ah /ruːˈpiːə/ *n* [C] the standard unit of money in Indonesia

rup·ture¹ /ˈrʌptʃə $ -ər/ *n* **1** [C,U] an occasion when something suddenly breaks apart or bursts: **[+of]** *the rupture of a blood vessel* **2** [C] a situation in which two countries, groups of people etc suddenly disagree and often end their relationship with each other: **[+between]** *The eleventh century saw the formal rupture between East and West.* | **[+with]** *The rupture with his father was absolute.* **3** [C] a medical condition in which an organ of the body, especially one near the ABDOMEN, sticks out through the wall of muscle that normally surrounds it SYN **hernia**

rupture² *v* **1** [I,T] to break or burst, or to make something break or burst: *The pipe will rupture at its weakest point.* | *His liver was ruptured when a brick wall collapsed on him.* **2** [T] to damage good relations between people or a peaceful situation: *The noise ruptured the tranquility of the afternoon.* **3 rupture yourself** to cause an organ of the body, especially one near the ABDOMEN, to stick out through the wall of muscle that normally surrounds it

ru·ral /ˈrʊərəl $ ˈrʊr-/ ●●○ S3 W2 *adj*
1 happening in or relating to the countryside, not the city OPP **urban**: *a rural setting* | *rural bus routes* THESAURUS COUNTRY
2 like the countryside or reminding you of the countryside: *It's very rural round here, isn't it?*

ˌrural deˈlivery *n* [U] *AmE* R.D.

ruse /ruːz $ ruːs, ruːz/ *n* [C] a clever trick used to deceive someone: *Agnes tried to think of a ruse to get Paul out of the house.*

rush¹ /rʌʃ/ ●●● S2 W3 *v*
1 MOVE QUICKLY [I always + adv/prep] to move very quickly, especially because you need to be somewhere very soon SYN **hurry**: *A small girl rushed past her.* | *Mo rushed off down the corridor.* THESAURUS HURRY
2 rush to do sth to do something very quickly and without delay: *I rushed to pack my suitcase before she came back.* | *He rushed to help his comrade.*
3 DO STH TOO QUICKLY [I,T] to do or decide something too quickly, especially so that you do not have time to do it carefully or well: *He does not intend to rush his decision.* | **[+into]** *I'm not rushing into marriage again.* | **[+through]** *She rushed through her script.* | **rush it/things** *When we first met, neither of us wanted to rush things.*
4 TAKE/SEND URGENTLY [T always + adv/prep] to take or send someone or something somewhere very quickly, especially because of an unexpected problem: **rush sb/sth to sth** *The Red Cross rushed medical supplies to the war zone.* | *Dan was **rushed to hospital** with serious head injuries.*
5 MAKE SB HURRY [T] to try to make someone do something more quickly than they want to: *I'm sorry to rush you, but we need a decision by Friday.* | **rush sb into (doing) sth** *They felt they were being rushed into choosing a new leader.*
6 LIQUID [I always + adv/prep] if water or another liquid rushes somewhere, it moves quickly: *Water rushed through the gorge.*
7 BLOOD **blood rushes to sb's face/cheeks** used to say that someone's face becomes red because they feel embarrassed: *I felt the blood rush to my face as I heard my name.*
8 ATTACK [T] to attack a person or place suddenly and in a group: *They rushed the guard and stole his keys.*
9 AMERICAN UNIVERSITIES *AmE* **a)** [T] to give parties for students, have meetings etc, in order to decide whether to let them join your FRATERNITY or SORORITY (=type of club) **b)** [I,T] to go through the process of trying to be accepted into one of these clubs
10 AMERICAN FOOTBALL [I,T] to carry the ball forward

rush around (*also* **rush about** *BrE*) *phr v* to try to do a lot of things in a short period of time: *Get things ready early so that you don't have to rush around at the last minute.*

rush sth ↔ **out** *phr v* to make a new product, book etc available for sale very quickly: *The new edition was rushed out just before Christmas.*

R

rush sth ↔ **through** *phr v* to deal with official or government business more quickly than usual: **rush sth through sth** *The legislation was rushed through parliament.*

rush² ●●○ *n*
1 FAST MOVEMENT [singular] a sudden fast movement of things or people: **rush of air/wind/water** *She felt a cold rush of air as she wound down her window.* | **in a rush** *Her words came out in a rush.* | *At five past twelve there was a* ***mad rush*** *to the dinner hall.*
2 HURRY [singular, U] a situation in which you need to hurry: *I knew there would be a* ***last-minute rush*** *to meet the deadline.* | *Don't worry,* ***there's no rush****. We don't have to be at the station until 10.* | **do sth in a rush** (=do something quickly because you need to hurry) *I had to do my homework in a rush because I was late.* | **be in a rush** *I'm sorry, I can't talk now – I'm in a rush.*
3 BUSY PERIOD **the rush** the time in the day, month, year etc when a place or group of people is particularly busy → **peak**: *The café is quiet until the lunchtime rush begins.* | *the Christmas rush* → RUSH HOUR
4 PEOPLE WANTING STH [singular] a situation in which a lot of people suddenly try to do or get something: **[+on]** *There's always a rush on swimsuits in the hot weather.* | **rush to do sth** *the rush to put computers in all schools* → GOLD RUSH
5 FEELING [singular] **a)** *informal* a sudden strong, usually pleasant feeling that you get from taking a drug or from doing something exciting → **high**: *The feeling of power gave me such a rush.* | *an* ***adrenalin rush*** **b) rush of anger/excitement/gratitude etc** a sudden very strong feeling of anger etc: *I felt a rush of excitement when she arrived.* | *A rush of jealousy swept through her.*
6 PLANT [C usually plural] a type of tall grass that grows in water, often used for making baskets → see picture at FLOWER¹
7 FILM **rushes** [plural] the first prints of a film before it has been EDITed SYN **dailies** *AmE*
8 AMERICAN STUDENTS [U] *AmE* the time when students in American universities who want to join a FRATERNITY or SORORITY (=type of club) go to a lot of parties in order to try to be accepted: *rush week*

rushed /rʌʃt/ *adj* **1** done very quickly or too quickly, because there was not enough time: *We did have a meeting, but it was a bit rushed.* **2** *BrE* if you are rushed, you are very busy because you have a lot of things to do quickly: *I'll talk to you later – I'm a bit rushed at the moment.* | *I've been* ***rushed off*** *my* ***feet*** (=extremely busy) *all day.*

ˈrush hour ●●○ *n* [C,U] the time of day when the roads, buses, trains etc are most full, because people are travelling to or from work: *I got caught in the morning rush hour.* | *heavy rush hour traffic*

rusk /rʌsk/ *n* [C] *BrE* a hard sweet dry bread for babies to eat

rus·set /ˈrʌsɪt/ *n* [U] *literary* a reddish brown colour —**russet** *adj*

Rus·sian¹ /ˈrʌʃən/ *adj* relating to Russia, its people, or its language

Russian² *n* **1** [C] someone from Russia **2** [U] the language used in Russia

ˌRussian rouˈlette *n* [U] a game in which you risk killing yourself by shooting at your head with a gun that has six spaces for bullets but only one bullet in it

rust¹ /rʌst/ ●○○ *n* [U]
1 the reddish-brown substance that forms on iron or steel when it gets wet → **rusty**: *There were large patches of rust on the car.*
2 a plant disease that causes reddish-brown spots

rust² *v* [I,T] to become covered with rust, or to make something become covered in rust: *The metal had begun to rust.* | *The gate was old and badly rusted.*

rust away *phr v* to be gradually destroyed by rust: *The blades of the swords have rusted away.*

ˈRust Belt, the *AmE* an area in the northern US, including parts of the states such as Illinois, Michigan, Indiana, Ohio, and Wisconsin, where many large older industries, especially the steel and car industries, have become less successful and many factories have closed down

rus·tic¹ /ˈrʌstɪk/ *adj* **1** simple, old-fashioned, and not spoiled by modern developments, in a way that is typical of the countryside: *The village had a certain* ***rustic charm****.* **2** [only before noun] roughly made from wood: *a rustic chair* —**rusticity** /rʌˈstɪsəti/ *n* [U]

rustic² *n* [C] *literary* someone from the country, especially a farm worker

rus·tle¹ /ˈrʌsəl/ *v* **1** [I,T] if leaves, papers, clothes etc rustle, or if you rustle them, they make a noise as they rub against each other: *She moved nearer, her long silk skirt rustling around her.* | *He rustled the papers on his desk.* **2** [T] to steal farm animals such as cattle, horses, or sheep

rustle sth ↔ **up** *phr v informal* to make a meal quickly: *I'll rustle up a couple of steaks on the barbecue.*

rustle² *n* [singular] the noise made when something rustles: **[+of]** *the rustle of leaves in the wind* **THESAURUS** SOUND

rus·tler /ˈrʌslə $ -ər/ *n* [C] someone who steals farm animals such as cattle, horses, or sheep

rust·proof /ˈrʌstpruːf/ *adj* metal that is rustproof will not RUST

rust·y /ˈrʌsti/ ●○○ *adj*
1 metal that is rusty is covered in RUST: *a rusty nail* | *a new metal that will never* ***go rusty***
2 if you are rusty, you are not as good at something as you used to be, because you have not practised it for a long time: *My French is a bit rusty.*

rut /rʌt/ *n* **1** [C] a deep narrow track left in soft ground by a wheel **2 in a rut** living or working in a situation that never changes, so that you feel bored: *I was* ***stuck in a rut*** *and decided to look for a new job.* **3** [U] (*also* **the rut**) *technical* the period of the year when some male animals, especially DEER, are sexually active: **in rut** *a stag in rut*

ru·ta·ba·ga /ˌruːtəˈbeɪɡə/ *n* [C] *AmE* a large round yellow vegetable that grows under the ground SYN **swede** *BrE* → see picture at VEGETABLE¹

ruth·less /ˈruːθləs/ ●○○ *adj*
1 so determined to get what you want that you do not care if you have to hurt other people in order to do it: *a ruthless dictator* | *They have shown a ruthless disregard for basic human rights.* **THESAURUS** DETERMINED
2 determined and firm when making unpleasant decisions: *He ran the company with ruthless efficiency.* | *Throw away clothes you don't wear – be ruthless.* —**ruthlessly** *adv*: *The uprising was ruthlessly suppressed.* —**ruthlessness** *n* [U]

rut·ted /ˈrʌtɪd/ *adj* a surface that is rutted has deep narrow tracks in it left by the wheels of vehicles → **uneven**

RV /ˌɑː ˈviː $ ˌɑːr-/ *n* [C] *AmE* (***recreational vehicle***) a large vehicle, usually with cooking equipment and beds in it, that a family can use for travelling or camping → **mobile home**, **caravan** → see picture at HOUSE¹

Rx *AmE* the written abbreviation of ***prescription***

ˈRyder Cup, ˌthe an important golf competition held every two years, in which two teams compete, one representing Europe and the other the US

rye /raɪ/ *n* [U] **1** a type of grain that is used for making bread and WHISKY: *rye bread* **2** (*also* **ˌrye ˈwhiskey** *AmE*) a type of American WHISKY made from rye

rye·grass /ˈraɪɡrɑːs $ -ɡræs/ *n* [U] a type of grass that is grown as food for animals

Ss

S¹, s /es/ *n* (*plural* **S's, s's**) [C,U] the 19th letter of the English alphabet

S² **1** the written abbreviation of ***south*** or ***southern*** **2** the written abbreviation of ***small***, used on clothes to show the size

-s /z, s/ *suffix* **1** forms the plural of nouns: *a cat and two dogs* **2** forms the third person singular of the present tense of most verbs: *he plays* | *she sits*

-s' /z, s/ *suffix* forms the plural POSSESSIVE of most nouns: *the girls' dresses* | *the islands' inhabitants*

-'s¹ /z, s/ **1** the short form of 'is': *John's here.* | *What's that?* | *She's writing a letter.* **2** the short form of 'has': *Polly's gone out.* | *A spider's got eight legs.* **3** a short form of 'us' used only in 'let's' **4** *spoken* a short form of 'does', used in questions after 'who', 'what' etc that many people think is incorrect: *How's he plan to do that?*

-'s² *suffix* **1** forms the POSSESSIVE of singular nouns, and of plural nouns that do not end in -s: *my sister's husband* | *Mary's generosity* | *yesterday's lesson* | *the children's bedroom* **2** *BrE* the shop or home of someone: *I bought it at the baker's* (=at the baker's shop). | *I met him at Mary's* (=at Mary's house).

Sab·bath /ˈsæbəθ/ *n* **1 the Sabbath a)** Sunday, considered as a day of rest and prayer by most Christian churches **b)** Saturday, considered as a day of rest and prayer in the Jewish religion and some Christian churches **2 keep/break the Sabbath** to obey or not obey the religious rules of the Sabbath

sab·bat·i·cal /səˈbætɪkəl/ *n* [C,U] a period when someone, especially someone in a university job, stops doing their usual work in order to study or travel: *She* ***took*** *a long* ***sabbatical***. | **on sabbatical** *Dr Watson's away on sabbatical.*

sa·ber /ˈseɪbə $ -ər/ *n* [C] the American spelling of SABRE

sa·ble¹ /ˈseɪbəl/ *n* [C,U] an expensive fur used to make coats etc, or the small animal that this fur comes from

sable² *adj literary* black or very dark in colour

sab·o·tage¹ /ˈsæbətɑːʒ/ *v* [T] **1** to secretly damage or destroy equipment, vehicles etc that belong to an enemy or opponent, so that they cannot be used: *Every single plane had been sabotaged.* **THESAURUS** ▸ DAMAGE **2** to deliberately spoil someone's plans because you do not want them to succeed: *Demonstrators have sabotaged the conference.*

sabotage² *n* [U] deliberate damage that is done to equipment, vehicles etc in order to prevent an enemy or opponent from using them: *The terrorists were planning* ***acts of sabotage*** *to destabilize the country.* | *industrial sabotage*

sab·o·teur /ˌsæbəˈtɜː $ -ˈtɜːr/ *n* [C] someone who deliberately damages, destroys, or spoils someone else's property or activities, in order to prevent them from doing something: *The lorries were wrecked by saboteurs.* → HUNT SABOTEUR

sa·bre *BrE*, **saber** *AmE* /ˈseɪbə $ -ər/ *n* [C] **1** a light pointed sword with one sharp edge used in FENCING **2** a heavy sword with a curved blade, used in past times

ˈsabre-ˌrattling *n* [U] when someone threatens to use force but you do not think they are very frightening or serious: *What the situation calls for is calm discussion, not sabre-rattling.*

sac /sæk/ *n* [C] *technical* a part inside a plant or animal that is shaped like a bag and contains liquid or air

sac·cha·rin /ˈsækərɪn/ *n* [U] a chemical substance that tastes sweet and is used instead of sugar in drinks

sac·cha·rine /ˈsækəriːn/ *adj formal* too romantic in a way that seems silly and insincere: *I hated the movie's saccharine ending.*

sach·et /ˈsæʃeɪ $ sæˈʃeɪ/ *n* [C] **1** *BrE* a small plastic or paper package containing a liquid or powder SYN **packet** *AmE*: **[+of]** *a sachet of shampoo* → see picture at CONTAINER **2** a small bag containing dried herbs or flowers that smell pleasant: *a lavender sachet*

sack¹ /sæk/ ●●○ S3 *n* [C]

1 a) a large bag made of strong rough cloth or strong paper, used for storing or carrying flour, coal, vegetables etc: **[+of]** *a sack of potatoes* **b)** (*also* **sackful**) the amount that a sack can contain: **[+of]** *We need about a sack of rice.* → see picture at BAG¹

2 the sack *BrE informal* when someone is dismissed from their job: *They've never actually* ***given*** *anyone* ***the sack***. | *He* ***got the sack*** *for stealing.* | *She claimed she'd been threatened with the sack.*

3 hit the sack *old-fashioned informal* to go to bed: *It's one o'clock – time to hit the sack.*

4 in the sack *informal* in bed – used to talk about sexual activity: *I bet she's great in the sack.*

5 the sack of sth *formal* a situation in which an army goes through a place, destroying or stealing things and attacking people: *the sack of Rome in 1527*

sack² *v* [T] **1** *BrE informal* to dismiss someone from their job SYN **fire**: *They couldn't sack me – I'd done nothing wrong.* | **sack sb from sth** *He was sacked from every other job he had.* | **sack sb for (doing) sth** *He was sacked for being drunk.*

> **REGISTER**
> In written and formal British English, people often prefer to use **dismiss** rather than **sack**: *People can be* ***dismissed*** *for misusing the Internet at work.*

2 to knock down the QUARTERBACK in American football **3** if soldiers sack a place, they go through it destroying or stealing things and attacking people: *The Goths sacked Rome.*

sack out *phr v AmE informal* to go to sleep: *He sacked out on the sofa.*

sack·cloth /ˈsæk-klɒθ $ -klɔːθ/ (*also* **sack·ing** /ˈsækɪŋ/) *n* [U] **1** rough cloth used for making sacks **2 wear sackcloth and ashes** *BrE* to behave in a way that shows everyone you are sorry about something wrong you have done

ˈsack race *n* [C] a race in which the competitors, usually children, have to jump forwards with both legs inside a SACK

sac·ra·ment /ˈsækrəmənt/ *n* [C] **1 the Sacrament** the bread and wine that are eaten at COMMUNION (=an important Christian ceremony) **2** one of the important Christian ceremonies, such as marriage or COMMUNION —**sacramental** /ˌsækrəˈmentl◂/ *adj*

sa·cred /ˈseɪkrɪd/ ●●○ *adj*

1 relating to a god or religion: *a sacred vow* | *the miraculous powers of sacred relics* | *Certain animals were considered sacred.* | **[+to]** *The land is sacred to these tribesmen.* **THESAURUS** ▸ RELIGIOUS

2 very important or greatly respected: *Human life is sacred.* | *Frontiers which have held for over forty years are no longer sacred.* | **[+to]** *Few things were sacred to Henry, but local history was one of them.* | *He had no respect for everything I* ***held sacred***.

3 is nothing sacred? *spoken* used to express shock when something you think is valuable or important is being changed or harmed —**sacredness** *n* [U]: *the sacredness of human life*

ˌsacred ˈcow *n* [C] a belief, custom, system etc that is so important to some people that they will not let anyone criticize it: *In New York's show business scene, money, fame and power are sacred cows.*

sac·ri·fice¹ /ˈsækrəfaɪs/ ●●○ *n*

1 [C,U] when you decide not to have something valuable, in order to get something that is more important: *The minister stressed the need for economic sacrifice.* | *The workforce were willing to* ***make sacrifices*** *in order to preserve* *jobs.* | *She brought three children up single-handedly, often at great* ***personal sacrifice.***

2 a) [C,U] the act of offering something to a god, especially in the past, by killing an animal or person in a religious ceremony: *They* ***made sacrifices*** *to ensure a good harvest.* **b)** [C] an animal, person, or object offered to a god in sacrifice: **[+to]** *In those days, an animal was offered as a sacrifice to God.* | *a* ***human sacrifice*** (=a person killed as a sacrifice)

3 *literary* **the final/supreme/ultimate sacrifice** the act of dying while you are fighting for a principle or in order to help other people: *Captain Oates* ***made the ultimate sacrifice*** *in a bid to save his colleagues.*

sacrifice² ●●○ *v*
1 [T] to willingly stop having something you want or doing something you like in order to get something more important: **sacrifice sth for sth** *A Labour government chose to sacrifice defence for welfare.* | **sacrifice sth to do sth** *He sacrificed a promising career to look after his kids.* | **sacrifice yourself (for sth)** *mothers who sacrifice themselves for their children*

> **REGISTER**
> In everyday English, people often say **give up** rather than **sacrifice**: *He* ***gave up*** *a promising career to look after his kids.*

2 [I,T] to kill an animal or person and offer them to a god in a religious ceremony

sac·ri·fi·cial /ˌsækrɪˈfɪʃəl◂/ *adj* [usually before noun] relating to or offered as a sacrifice: *a sacrificial ceremony* | *a sacrificial lamb*

sac·ri·lege /ˈsækrəlɪdʒ/ *n* [C,U] **1** when someone treats something holy in a way that does not show respect **2** when someone treats something that another person thinks is very important or special without enough care or respect: **it is sacrilege (for sb) to do sth** *It's sacrilege to even think of destroying that lovely building.* —**sacrilegious** /ˌsækrəˈlɪdʒəs◂/ *adj*

sac·ris·tan /ˈsækrəstən/ *n* [C] someone whose job is to take care of the holy objects in a church

sac·ris·ty /ˈsækrəsti/ *n* (*plural* **sacristies**) [C] a small room in a church, where holy cups and plates are kept, and where priests put on their ceremonial clothes SYN **vestry**

sac·ro·sanct /ˈsækrəʊsæŋkt $ -roʊ-/ *adj* something that is sacrosanct is considered to be so important that no one is allowed to criticize or change it SYN **sacred**: *Weekends are sacrosanct in our family.*

sad /sæd/ ●●● S2 W3 *adj* (*comparative* **sadder**, *superlative* **saddest**)
1 FEELING UNHAPPY not happy, especially because something unpleasant has happened OPP **happy**: **feel/look/sound sad** *Dad looked sad and worried as he read the letter.* | **be sad to hear/see/read etc sth** *I was very sad to hear that he had died.* | **sad that** *Lilly felt sad that Christmas was over.* | **[+about]** *I was sad about the friends I was leaving behind.* | **sad smile/face/expression etc** *There was such a sad look in her eyes.*
2 MAKING YOU UNHAPPY a sad event, situation etc makes you feel unhappy: *Sorry to hear the* ***sad news.*** | *It was a* ***sad case.*** *The boy ended up in prison.* | **sad story/song/film etc** *a story with a sad ending* | **it is sad to see/hear etc sth** *It was sad to see them arguing.* | **sad time/day/moment etc** *This is a sad day for us all.*
3 NOT SATISFACTORY very bad or unacceptable: *There aren't enough teachers, which is a* ***sad state of affairs*** (=bad situation). | **it's sad that/when/if ...** *It's sad if people are too afraid to go out alone at night.* | **the sad fact is (that)** *spoken: The sad fact is that prejudice still exists.* | ***Sad to say*** (=unfortunately), *the country is heading towards civil war.*
4 LONELY a sad person has a dull, unhappy, or lonely life: *She's a sad character – without any friends at all.*
5 BORING *informal* boring or not deserving any respect: *Stay in on Saturday night? What a sad idea!*
6 sadder and/but wiser having learned something from an unpleasant experience: *He came out of the relationship sadder but wiser.* → SADNESS

> **THESAURUS**
> **sad** not happy: *She felt sad as she waved goodbye.* | *a sad and lonely figure* | *a sad face* | *a sad film*
> **unhappy** sad, especially for a long time – used about people and periods of time: *I was unhappy at school.* | *an unhappy childhood*
> **homesick** [not before noun] sad because you are away from your home, family, and friends: *She sometimes felt homesick when she first arrived in Japan.*
> **down** [not before noun] *informal* feeling sad for a few hours or days, often for no reason: *Whenever I'm feeling down, I go out and buy myself some new clothes.*
> **gloomy** looking or sounding sad and without hope – used about people, places, and weather: *Why are you all looking so gloomy?* | *the gloomy immigration office* | *a gloomy afternoon in February*
> **dejected/downcast** looking sad and disappointed because something you hoped for did not happen: *'I didn't pass,' he said, looking dejected.* | *a downcast expression*
> **mournful** *especially literary* looking or sounding sad: *the dog's big mournful eyes* | *the mournful sound of the church bell*
>
> **VERY SAD**
> **miserable** very sad, especially because you are lonely, cold, ill, or upset – used about people and periods of time: *I felt miserable and blamed myself for what had happened.* | *Her life was miserable.*
> **depressed** very sad and without hope for a long time, because things are wrong in your life or because of a medical condition: *After his wife left him, he became depressed and refused to talk to anyone.*
> **heartbroken** extremely sad because of something that has happened to someone or something that you care about very much: *She was heartbroken when her dog died.*
> **distressed/distraught** very upset because of something bad that has happened, so that you cannot think clearly: *She was very distressed when he left her.* | *The boy's hospital bed was surrounded by distraught relatives.*
> **devastated** [not before noun] extremely sad and shocked, because something very bad has happened: *The whole town was devastated by the tragedy.*
>
> **COLLOCATIONS CHECK**
> **sad** person/expression/story/song/film
> **unhappy** person/expression/childhood/marriage
> **gloomy** person/expression/place/weather
> **dejected/downcast** person/expression
> **mournful** sound/eyes/expression

SAD /sæd/ *n* [U] *medical* the abbreviation of ***seasonal affective disorder***

sad·den /ˈsædn/ *v* [T] *formal* to make someone feel sad: *Those who knew him are saddened by his death.* | **it saddens sb that** *It saddened him that they no longer trusted him.* —**saddening** *adj*

sad·dle¹ /ˈsædl/ ●●○ *n* [C]
1 a leather seat that you sit on when you ride a horse
2 a seat on a bicycle or a MOTORCYCLE → see pictures at MOTORBIKE, BICYCLE
3 in the saddle *informal* **a)** riding a horse: *We did six or eight hours in the saddle every day.* **b)** in a position in which you have power or authority: *He always has to be in the saddle, controlling everything.*
4 saddle of lamb/hare/venison a large joint of meat taken from the middle of the animal's back

saddle² *v* [T] to put a saddle on a horse

saddle up *phr v* to put a saddle on a horse: **saddle sth ↔ up** *He was in the stable, saddling up his horse.*

saddle sb **with** sth *phr v* to make someone have a job or problem that is difficult or boring and that they do not want: *I've been saddled with organizing the whole party!* | *Many farms were saddled with debts.*

'saddle bag *n* [C] a bag for carrying things, fixed to the saddle on a horse or bicycle

sad·dler /'sædlə $ -ər/ *n* [C] someone who makes saddles and other leather products, or a shop where these are sold

sad·dler·y /'sædləri/ *n* [U] saddles and leather goods made by a saddler

'saddle shoe *n* [C] *AmE* a shoe that has a toe and heel of one colour, with a different colour in the middle

'saddle-sore *adj* [not before noun] feeling stiff and sore after riding a horse or bicycle

sad·do /'sædəʊ $ -oʊ/ *n* (*plural* **saddos**) [C] *informal* someone who you do not respect, especially because you think their interests are boring or strange: *a bunch of saddos dressed up as science fiction characters*

sa·dhu /'sɑːduː/ *n* [C] a Hindu holy man who lives a very simple life

sa·dis·m /'seɪdɪzəm/ *n* [U] **1** behaviour in which someone gets pleasure from hurting other people or making them suffer → **masochism**: *There seemed to be an element of sadism in the training regime.* **2** when someone gets sexual pleasure from hurting someone → **masochism**

sa·dist /'seɪdɪst/ *n* [C] someone who enjoys hurting other people or making them suffer → **masochist**

sa·dis·tic /sə'dɪstɪk/ *adj* cruel and enjoying making other people suffer → **masochistic**: *He took* ***sadistic pleasure*** *in humiliating her.* | *sadistic fantasies* **THESAURUS** CRUEL, UNKIND —**sadistically** /-kli/ *adv*

sad·ly /'sædli/ ●●○ *adv*

1 in a way that shows that you are sad SYN **unhappily**: *Peter shook his head sadly.*

2 [sentence adverb] unfortunately: *Sadly, the business failed.*

3 very much – used when talking about bad situations or states: *The garden's been sadly neglected.* | *Good restaurants were sadly lacking.* | *He was a popular man who will be sadly missed.* | *I'm afraid you're going to be sadly disappointed.* | *If you think you'll get any money from him, you're sadly mistaken.*

sad·ness /'sædnəs/ ●●○ *n* [U] the state of feeling sad SYN **unhappiness**: **great/deep sadness** *She sensed Beth's deep sadness.* | *It was with great sadness that we learned of his death.* | *There was* ***a touch of sadness*** *in his voice* (=he sounded a little sad). | *His relief* ***was tinged with sadness*** (=he also felt rather sad).

sa·do·mas·o·chis·m /ˌseɪdəʊ'mæsəkɪzəm $ -doʊ-/ *n* [U] (*abbreviation* **S & M**) when someone gets sexual pleasure from hurting someone or being hurt —**sadomasochist** *n* [C] —**sadomasochistic** /ˌseɪdəʊmæsə'kɪstɪk◂ $ -doʊ-/ *adj*

sae /ˌes eɪ 'iː/ *n* [C] *BrE* (***stamped addressed envelope*** *or* ***self-addressed envelope***) an envelope on which you have written your own name and address, and usually put a stamp, so that someone else can send you something SYN **SASE** *AmE*: *For further details, send an sae to the following address.*

sa·fa·ri /sə'fɑːri/ *n* [C] **1** a trip to see or hunt wild animals, especially in Africa: **on safari** *They* ***went on safari*** *in Kenya.* **2 safari suit/jacket** a suit or jacket that is made of light material, usually with a belt, and pockets on the chest

sa'fari park *n* [C] an enclosed area of land where wild animals are kept, so that people can drive round to look at them

safe¹ /seɪf/ ●●● S2 W2 *adj* (*comparative* **safer**, *superlative* **safest**)

1 NOT IN DANGER [not before noun] not in danger of being harmed, lost, or stolen OPP **unsafe** → **safety**: *She doesn't* ***feel safe*** *in the house on her own.* | **[+from]** *The birds' nests are high up, safe from predators.* | *Make sure you* ***keep*** *these documents* ***safe***. | **be (as) safe as houses** *BrE* (=be completely safe) *Your money will be as safe as houses.*

2 NOT HARMED OR LOST not harmed, lost, or stolen: *Your family are all safe.* | **safe and sound/well** (=unharmed, especially after being in danger) *The missing children were found safe and sound.*

3 NOT CAUSING HARM not likely to cause any physical injury or harm OPP **dangerous**: *Flying is one of the safest forms of travel.* | *Don't go near the edge – it isn't safe.* | *a safe working environment* | **it is safe (for sb) to do sth** *Is it safe to swim here?* | **safe to use/drink/eat etc** *The water is treated to* ***make*** *it* ***safe*** *to drink.* | **[+for]** *play areas that are safe for children* | **(at/from) a safe distance** *We watched from a safe distance.* | *Drivers should* ***keep a safe distance*** *from the car in front.* | **safe driver** *Women are safer drivers than men.*

4 NO RISK not involving any risk and very likely to be successful: *a safe investment* | *a safe method of contraception* | **it's safe to say/assume (that)** *I think it's safe to say that the future is looking pretty good.*

5 safe place a place where something is not likely to be stolen or lost: **keep/put sth in a safe place** *Keep your credit cards in a safe place.*

6 safe journey/arrival/return etc a journey etc when someone or something is not harmed or lost: *His family celebrated his safe return home.* | **safe journey** *BrE* (=said to someone when they start a long journey) *Dad rang to wish me a safe journey.*

7 SUBJECT a safe subject of conversation is not likely to upset anyone or make people argue: *I kept to safe subjects, like the weather.*

8 to be on the safe side *spoken* to do something in order to be certain to avoid an unpleasant situation: *I'd take an umbrella, just to be on the safe side.*

9 be in safe hands to be with someone who will look after you very well: *Everyone wants to feel that their children are in safe hands.*

10 better (to be) safe than sorry *spoken* used to say that it is better to be careful, even if this takes time, effort etc, than take a risk that may have a bad result: *Set the alarm clock – better safe than sorry!*

11 safe in the knowledge that ... completely certain that something is true or will happen: *She went out, safe in the knowledge that no one else was awake.*

12 a safe pair of hands someone you can trust to do a difficult job without making mistakes

13 safe! *BrE spoken informal* used by young people to show approval of something: *'Alex is having a party.' 'Oh, safe!'*

14 NO PROBLEM *BrE spoken informal* used to say that something is good and that there is no problem: *'How's your new boss?' 'She's safe.'* → **play it safe** at PLAY¹(9), → **it's a safe bet (that)** at BET²(4), → **safe seat** at SEAT¹(2), → **sb's secret is safe (with sb)** at SECRET²(1)

safe² ●○○ *n* [C] a strong metal box or cupboard with special locks where you keep money and valuable things

safe³ *interjection BrE informal* said by young people as a greeting

ˌsafe 'conduct *n* [C,U] SAFE PASSAGE

ˌsafe-deposit ˌbox *n* [C] a SAFETY-DEPOSIT BOX

safe·guard¹ /'seɪfgɑːd $ -gɑːrd/ ●○○ *v* [T] to protect something from harm or damage: **safeguard sb's interests/rights/welfare etc** *The industry has a duty to safeguard consumers.* | *technology that will safeguard the environment* | **safeguard sth against sth** *a program for safeguarding the computer system against viruses* **THESAURUS** PROTECT

safeguard² ●○○ *n* [C] a rule, agreement etc that is intended to protect someone or something from possible dangers or problems: *International safeguards prevent the increase of nuclear weapons.* | **[+against]** *safeguards against the exploitation of children*

ˌsafe 'haven *n* [C] a place where someone can go in order to escape from possible danger or attack SYN **refuge**: **provide/offer/create a safe haven (for sb)** *The prime minister wanted to create a safe haven for the refugees.*

ˌsafe 'house *n* [C] a house where someone can hide and be protected. Safe houses are used especially by criminals hiding from the police, or by people who are being protected by the police.

safe·keep·ing /ˌseɪfˈkiːpɪŋ/ *n* [U] the state of being kept safe, or the action of keeping something safe: **for safekeeping** *My passport was in the inner pocket of my bag, for safekeeping.*

safe·ly /ˈseɪfli/ ●●○ *adv* in a way that is safe: *Drive safely!* | *I think we can safely assume that she will pass the exam.*

ˌsafe ˈpassage (*also* **safe conduct**) *n* [C,U] official protection for someone when they are in danger or passing through a dangerous area: **permit/promise/guarantee etc safe passage (to/for sb)** *The government offered safe passage to militants taking up their offer of peace talks.*

ˌsafe ˈsex *n* [U] ways of having sex that reduce the risk of spreading AIDS and other sexual diseases, especially by using a CONDOM

SAFETY

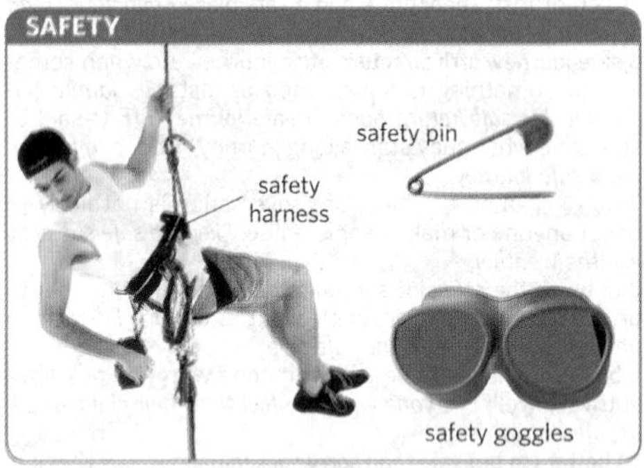

safe·ty /ˈseɪfti/ ●●● S2 W2 *n* (*plural* **safeties**)

1 NOT IN DANGER [U] when someone or something is safe from danger or harm: **[+of]** *measures to improve the* ***health and safety*** *of employees* | **in safety** *We were able to watch the lions in complete safety.* | **for safety** *For safety, always climb with a partner.* | *You shouldn't travel alone,* ***for safety's sake****.* | ***For*** *your* ***own safety****, please do not smoke inside the plane.*

2 HARMFUL/NOT HARMFUL [U] how safe something is to use, do etc: **[+of]** *Campaigners have challenged the safety of genetically modified foods.* | **safety standards/regulations/precautions etc** (=things that are done in order to make sure that something is safe) *The device meets safety standards.* | *Lower speed limits are part of a new road safety campaign.*

3 sb's safety how safe someone is in a particular situation: *The boy had been missing for five days and there were fears for his safety.*

4 SAFE PLACE [U] a place where you are safe from danger: **[+of]** *Thirty thousand people fled to the safety of the capital.* | **get/lead/drag etc sb to safety** *Firefighters led the children to safety.* | *They* ***reached safety*** *seconds before the bomb went off.*

5 there is safety in numbers used to say that it is safer to be in a group than alone

6 SPORT [C] a way of getting two points in American football by making the other team put the ball down in its own GOAL

7 GUN [C] *AmE* a lock on a gun that stops anyone from shooting it by accident SYN **safety catch** *BrE*

8 safety harness/helmet/glasses etc equipment etc that keeps you safe when you are doing something dangerous

ˈsafety belt *n* [C] a SEAT BELT

ˈsafety catch *n* [C] *BrE* a lock on a gun that stops anyone from shooting it by accident SYN **safety** *AmE*

ˈsafety ˌcurtain *n* [C] a thick curtain at the front of a theatre stage that prevents fire from spreading

ˈsafety-deposit ˌbox (*also* **safe-deposit box**) *n* [C] a small box used for storing valuable objects, usually kept in a special room in a bank

ˈsafety glass *n* [U] strong glass that breaks into very small pieces that are not sharp, used, for example, in car windows

ˈsafety lamp *n* [C] a special lamp used by MINERS, with a flame which will not make underground gases explode

ˈsafety match *n* [C] a match that you can light only by rubbing it along a special surface on the side of its box

ˈsafety net *n* [C] **1** a large net that is placed below an ACROBAT who is performing high above the ground, in order to catch them if they fall **2** a system or arrangement that exists to help you if you have serious problems or get into a difficult situation: **[+for]** *State support should provide a safety net for the very poor.*

ˈsafety ˌofficer *n* [C] someone in an organization who is responsible for the safety of the people who work there

ˈsafety pin *n* [C] a metal pin for fastening things together. The point of the pin fits into a cover so that it cannot hurt you.

ˈsafety ˌrazor *n* [C] a RAZOR that has a cover over part of the blade to protect your skin

ˈsafety valve *n* [C] **1** a part of a machine that allows gas, steam etc to escape when the pressure becomes too great **2** something that allows you to get rid of strong feelings without doing any harm: *Being able to express emotion is a healthy safety valve for the relationship.*

saf·fron /ˈsæfrən/ *n* [U] **1** a bright yellow spice that is used in cooking to give food a special taste and colour. It is sold as a powder or in thin pieces. **2** a bright orange-yellow colour

sag /sæɡ/ *v* (**sagged**, **sagging**) [I] **1** to hang down or bend in the middle, especially because of the weight of something SYN **droop**: *The branch sagged under the weight of the apples.* | *The skin around my eyes is starting to sag.* | *a sagging roof* **2** to become weaker or less valuable OPP **flourish**: *attempts to revive the sagging economy* —**sag** *n* [C,U]: *a sag in the mattress*

sa·ga /ˈsɑːɡə/ *n* [C] **1** a long and complicated series of events, or a description of this: *The whole saga began back in May.* | **[+of]** *She launched into the saga of her on-off engagement.* **2** a long story about events that happen over many years: **[+of]** *a saga of four generations of the Coleman family* THESAURUS ▶ STORY **3** one of the stories written about the Vikings of Norway and Iceland

sa·ga·cious /səˈɡeɪʃəs/ *adj formal* able to understand and judge things very well SYN **wise** —**sagaciously** *adv*

sa·ga·ci·ty /səˈɡæsəti/ *n* [U] *formal* good judgment and understanding SYN **wisdom**

sage[1] /seɪdʒ/ *n* **1** [U] a herb with grey-green leaves **2** [C] *literary* someone, especially an old man, who is very wise

sage[2] *adj literary* very wise, especially as a result of a lot of experience: *sage advice* —**sagely** *adv*

sage·brush /ˈseɪdʒbrʌʃ/ *n* [U] a small plant that is very common in dry areas in the western US

sag·gy /ˈsæɡi/ *adj informal* something that is saggy hangs down or bends more than it should: *The bed was saggy in the middle.*

Sa·git·tar·i·us /ˌsædʒəˈteəriəs $ -ˈter-/ *n* **1** [U] the ninth sign of the ZODIAC, represented by an animal that is half horse and half human, which some people believe affects the character and life of people born between November 23 and December 21 **2** (*also* **Sagittarian**) [C] someone who was born between November 23 and December 21 —**Sagittarian** *adj*

sa·go /ˈseɪɡəʊ $ -ɡoʊ/ *n* [U] *BrE* small white grains obtained from some PALM trees, used to make sweet dishes with milk

sahib /sɑːb $ ˈsɑːɪb/ *n* used in India, especially during the period of British rule, when talking to a man in authority: *Good morning, sahib!*

said[1] /sed/ the past tense and past participle of SAY[1]

said[2] *adj* [only before noun] *law* mentioned before SYN **aforementioned**: *The said weapon was later found in the defendant's home.*

sail¹ /seɪl/ ●●● S3 *v*
1 [I always + adv/prep, T] to travel on or across an area of water in a boat or ship: **[+across/into/out of etc]** *the first Europeans to sail across the Atlantic | Three tall ships sailed past. | She always wanted to* ***sail around the world****.* | **sail the Pacific/the Atlantic etc** *We're taking two months off to sail the Caribbean.*
2 [I] to start a journey by boat or ship: *We sail at dawn.* | **[+for]** *They're sailing for Antigua next week.*
3 [I,T] to direct or control the movement of a boat or ship that has a sail: *Blake sailed the ship safely through the narrow passage. | My father taught me to sail.*
4 [I always + adv/prep] to move quickly and smoothly through the air: **[+through/over/into etc]** *A ball came sailing over the fence.*
5 [I always + adv/prep] to move forwards gracefully and confidently: *She sailed into the room.*
6 sail close to the wind *BrE* to do or say something that is nearly wrong, illegal, or dishonest
sail through sth *phr v* to succeed very easily in a test, examination etc: *Adam sailed through his final exams.*

sail² ●●○ *n*
1 [C] a large piece of strong cloth fixed onto a boat, so that the wind will push the boat along: *a yacht with white sails* | **hoist/lower the sails** (=put the sails up or down)
2 set sail to begin a journey by boat or ship: **[+for/from]** *The following week the 'Queen Elizabeth' set sail for Jamaica.*
3 under sail *literary* moving along on a ship or boat that has sails

sail·board /ˈseɪlbɔːd $ -bɔːrd/ *n* [C] a flat board with a sail, that you stand on in the sport of WIND-SURFING SYN **wind-surfer**

sail·boat /ˈseɪlbəʊt $ -boʊt/ *n* [C] *AmE* a small boat with one or more sails

sail·ing /ˈseɪlɪŋ/ *n* **1** [U] the sport or activity of travelling in or directing a small boat with sails: *Bud has invited us to* ***go sailing*** *this weekend.* **2** [C] a time when a ship leaves a port: *Luckily, there was another sailing at 2 o'clock.* → **be plain sailing** at PLAIN¹(9)

ˈsailing boat *n* [C] *BrE* a small boat with one or more sails

ˈsailing ship *n* [C] a large ship with sails

sail·or /ˈseɪlə $ -ər/ ●●○ *n* [C]
1 someone who works on a ship: *Six British sailors drowned. | We were both experienced sailors.*
2 bad/good sailor someone who does or does not feel sick when they are on a boat or ship

ˈsailor suit *n* [C] a blue and white suit that looks like an old-fashioned sailor's uniform, worn by small boys

saint /seɪnt/ ●●○ *n* [C]
1 (*written abbreviation* **St** *or* **St.**) someone who is given the title 'saint' by the Christian Church after they have died, because they have been very good or holy: *Saint Patrick | Statues of saints lined the walls of the church.*
2 *informal* someone who is extremely good, kind, or patient: *His wife must have been a saint to put up with him for all those years.*
3 the patience of a saint a very large amount of patience: *You need the patience of a saint for this job.*

saint·ed /ˈseɪntɪd/ *adj literary* **1** having been made a saint by the Christian church **2** *old-fashioned* used when talking about a dead person: *my sainted mother, God rest her soul* **3 my sainted aunt!** *BrE old-fashioned* used to express surprise or shock

saint·hood /ˈseɪnthʊd/ *n* [U] the state of being a saint

saint·ly /ˈseɪntli/ *adj* completely good and honest, with no faults: *She led a saintly and blameless life.* —**saintliness** *n* [U]

ˈsaint's day *n* [C] the day of the year when the Christian church remembers a particular saint

saith /seθ/ *v biblical* says

sake¹ /seɪk/ ●●○ S3 *n* [U]
1 for the sake of sb/sth (*also* **for sb's/sth's sake**) in order to help, improve, or please someone or something: *He moved to the seaside for the sake of his health. | I only went for Kay's sake. | I hope he's told the truth* **for** *his* **own sake** (=because it will be good for him).
2 for God's/Christ's/goodness'/Heaven's/Pete's sake *spoken* **a)** used when you are telling someone how important it is to do something or not to do something: *For goodness' sake, don't be late!* **b)** used to show that you are angry or annoyed: *What is it now, for God's sake?*
3 for the sake of it if you do something for the sake of it, you do it because you want to and not for any particular reason: *She likes spending money just for the sake of it.*
4 for its own sake (*also* **sth for sth's sake**) if something is done for its own sake, it is done for the value of the experience itself, not for any advantage it will bring: *art for art's sake*
5 for the sake of argument *spoken* if you say something for the sake of argument, what you say may not be true but it will help you to have a discussion: *Let's say, just for the sake of argument, that you've got £200 to invest.*

sa·ke² /ˈsɑːki/ *n* [U] a Japanese alcoholic drink made from rice

sal·a·ble /ˈseɪləbəl/ *adj* another spelling of SALEABLE

sa·la·cious /səˈleɪʃəs/ *adj formal* showing too much interest in sex: *the media's love of* ***salacious gossip*** —**salaciously** *adv* —**salaciousness** *n* [U]

sal·ad /ˈsæləd/ ●●● S2 *n* [C,U]
1 a mixture of raw vegetables, especially LETTUCE, CUCUMBER, and tomato: *Would you like some salad with your pasta? | a spinach salad* | **toss a salad** (=mix it all together, usually with a dressing)
2 raw or cooked food cut into small pieces and served cold: **fruit/potato salad**

ˈsalad bar *n* [C] a place in a restaurant, with different vegetables that you can choose to make your own salad

ˈsalad cream *n* [U] *BrE* a thick light-coloured liquid, similar to MAYONNAISE, that you put on salad

ˈsalad days *n* [plural] *old-fashioned* the time of your life when you are young and not very experienced SYN **youth**

ˈsalad ˌdressing *n* [C,U] a liquid mixture made from oil and VINEGAR, for putting on salads

sal·a·man·der /ˈsælmændə $ -ər/ *n* [C] a small animal similar to a LIZARD, which lives on land and in the water

sa·la·mi /səˈlɑːmi/ *n* [C,U] a large SAUSAGE with a strong taste that is eaten cold

saˈlami ˌslicing *n* [U] the action of gradually removing or reducing something, by taking a small amount away at a time: *The budget cuts have been made by a process of salami slicing.*

sal·a·ried /ˈsælərid/ *adj* receiving money every month for the work you do, rather than for every week or every hour: *salaried workers*

sal·a·ry /ˈsæləri/ ●●● S2 W3 *n* (*plural* **salaries**) [C,U] money that you receive as payment from the organization you work for, usually paid to you every month → **wage**, **pay**: *The average salary for a teacher is $39,000 a year.*

COLLOCATIONS

VERBS

earn/get/receive a salary *She's now earning a good salary as an interpreter.*
be on a salary *BrE* (=be earning a salary) *He won't tell me what salary he's on.*
pay sb a salary | offer sb a salary

ADJECTIVES

high/good *She moved to a job with a higher salary.*
low *It sounds an interesting job, but the salary is too low.*
a six-figure salary (=one over £100,000 or $100,000)
annual salary *His annual salary is $200,000.*
monthly salary *What's your monthly salary?*
current salary | basic/base salary (=the basic amount that someone is paid) | **starting salary** (=the salary someone gets when they start a job)

salary + NOUN

a salary increase *He was given a huge salary increase.*
a salary cut (=a decrease in someone's salary) | **the salary scale/structure** (=the list of increasing salaries that someone in a job can earn)

THESAURUS

salary *n* [C] the money that you receive regularly for doing your job, usually paid to you every month. Salary is usually used for professional jobs such as teachers, managers, doctors etc: *Nurses earn a basic salary of £21,250.* | *Her salary is paid directly into her bank account.*
pay *n* [U] the money you receive for doing a job: *The pay is pretty good.* | *Teachers are asking for higher pay.*
wages *n* [plural] (*also* **wage** [singular]) the money that someone is paid every week by their employer, especially someone who works in a shop or factory: *Practically all my wages go on housing and transport to work.* | *The average weekly wage was £350.* | *a wage increase*
income *n* [C,U] the money that you receive regularly for doing your job, and from things such as a business or investments: *The amount of tax you have to pay depends on your income.* | *People* ***on low incomes*** *are finding it difficult to pay their fuel bills.*
earnings *n* [plural] the total amount of money you earn from any job you do – used especially when the amount is different each month or year: *The average worker's earnings have not kept up with inflation.*

sal·a·ry·man /ˈsælərimæn/ *n* (*plural* **salarymen** /-men/) [C] a man who works in an office, often for many hours each day, and receives a salary as payment, especially in Japan

sale /seɪl/ ●●● S1 W1 *n*
1 [C,U] when you sell something: **[+of]** *The use and sale of marijuana remains illegal.* | *Harvey gets a $50 commission every time he* ***makes a sale*** (=sells something as part of his job). | *Car salesmen will often bring down the price rather than* ***lose a sale*** (=fail to sell something). | *arms sales to Iran*
2 sales a) [plural] the total number of products that are sold during a particular period of time: *Britain's* ***retail sales*** (=all the things sold to the public in shops) *jumped 3.2 percent in April.* | **[+of]** *Sales of automobiles are up this year.* | *We did not reach our summer* ***sales targets***. | *The company no longer releases its* ***sales figures*** (=how much money it makes or loses from sales). | **in sales** *We grossed more than $500,000 in sales last year.* **b)** [U] the part of a company that deals with selling products: *She found a job in sales.* | *a sales manager* | *a worldwide* ***sales force*** *of 1,100*
3 for sale available to be bought: *Excuse me, are these for sale?* | *There was a 'for sale' sign in the yard.* | *Reluctantly, they* ***put*** *the family home* ***up for sale*** (=made it available to be bought).
4 on sale a) available to be bought in a shop: *A wide range of postcards and other souvenirs are on sale in the visitors' centre.* | *Stephen King's new novel will* ***go on sale*** (=will begin to be sold) *next week.* **b)** *especially AmE* available to be bought at a lower price than usual: *These gloves were on sale for only $9.*
5 [C] a period of time when shops sell their goods at lower prices than usual: *Marsdon's department store is* ***having a sale*** *this week.* | **the sales** *BrE* (=when all the shops have a sale) *I picked up some real bargains in the January sales this year.*
6 [C] an event at which things are sold to the person who offers the highest price SYN **auction**: *a sale of 17th-century paintings*
7 sales drive/campaign when a company makes a special effort to try to increase the amount of its products that it sells: *a new sales campaign*
8 sales pitch/talk the things that someone says when they are trying to persuade you to buy something
9 (on) sale or return *BrE* if a shop buys something on sale or return, it can return the goods that it is unable to sell → BILL OF SALE, JUMBLE SALE, POINT OF SALE

COLLOCATIONS – MEANING 2

ADJECTIVES/NOUN + sales

strong (=good) *The company has reported continuing strong sales.*
disappointing *Sales for the first three months of this year were disappointing.*
record sales (=better than ever before) *The Ford Fiesta has achieved record sales in Italy.*
car/ticket/book etc sales *Car sales have fallen every month for the past two years.*
annual sales *The company has annual sales of over $300 million.*
worldwide sales | **retail sales** (=sales of things to the public in shops) | **export sales** (=sales of things to other countries) | **high-street sales** *BrE* (=in shops in towns and cities)

VERBS

sales increase/rise/grow/go up *Sales rose by 9% last year.*
sales fall/drop/go down (=become lower) *European sales have fallen by 12%.*
sales soar (=increase quickly and by a large amount) | **sales slump** (=decrease quickly and by a large amount)

sales + NOUN

sales figures *The company said its sales figures continued to show growth.*
a sales target *It achieved only 20% of its sales target.*
the sales force (=the people who sell a company's products) *The sales force had grown from 40 to 270.*
sales performance (=how much a company sells) | **the sales forecast** (=how much a company expects to sell)

PHRASES

an increase/growth in sales *The company is expecting a 20% increase in sales next year.*
a fall/drop in sales | **the volume of sales** (=the amount of goods a company sells)

sale·a·ble, **salable** /ˈseɪləbəl/ *adj* something that is saleable can be sold, or is easy to sell: *a saleable commodity* —**saleability** /ˌseɪləˈbɪləti/ *n* [U]

sale·room /ˈseɪlrʊm, -ruːm/ *n* [C] *BrE* a room where things are sold by AUCTION

ˈsales asˌsistant *n* [C] someone who sells things in a shop SYN **shop assistant**

sales·clerk /ˈseɪlzklɑːk $ -klɜːrk/ *n* [C] *AmE* someone who sells things in a shop SYN **shop assistant** *BrE*

sales·girl /ˈseɪlzɡɜːl $ -ɡɜːrl/ *n* [C] *old-fashioned* a young woman who sells things in a shop

sales·man /ˈseɪlzmən/ ●●○ *n* (*plural* **salesmen** /-mən/) [C] a man whose job is to persuade people to buy his company's products: **computer/car/insurance etc salesman**

sales·man·ship /ˈseɪlzmənʃɪp/ *n* [U] the skill or ability to persuade people to buy things as part of your job

sales·per·son /ˈseɪlzˌpɜːsən $ -pɜːr-/ ●●○ *n* (*plural* **salespeople** /-ˌpiːpəl/) [C] someone whose job is selling things

ˈsales repreˌsentative (*also* **ˈsales rep**) *n* [C] someone who travels around, usually within a particular area, selling their company's products

ˈsales slip *n* [C] *AmE* a small piece of paper that you are given in a shop when you buy something SYN **receipt**

ˈsales tax *n* [C,U] a tax that you have to pay in addition to the cost of something you are buying → VAT

sales·wom·an /ˈseɪlzˌwʊmən/ *n* (*plural* **saleswomen** /-ˌwɪmɪn/) [C] a woman whose job is selling things

sa·li·ent /ˈseɪliənt/ *adj formal* the salient points or features of something are the most important or most noticeable parts of it: *the salient points of the report* —**salience** *n* [U]

sa·line¹ /ˈseɪlaɪn/ *adj medical* containing or consisting of salt: *saline solution* —**salinity** /səˈlɪnəti/ *n* [U]

saline² *n* [U] a special mixture of water and salt

sa·li·va /səˈlaɪvə/ *n* [U] the liquid that is produced naturally in your mouth SYN **spit**

saˈlivary ˌgland *n* [C] a part of your mouth that produces saliva

sal·i·vate /ˈsælɪveɪt/ *v* [I] **1** to produce more saliva in your mouth than usual, especially because you see or smell food **2** to look at or show interest in something or someone in a way that shows you like or want them very much – used to show disapproval SYN **drool**: **[+at/over]** *The media are salivating over the story.* —**salivation** /ˌsæləˈveɪʃən/ *n* [U]

sal·low /ˈsæləʊ $ -loʊ/ *adj* sallow skin looks slightly yellow and unhealthy: **sallow face/skin/complexion** *a woman with dark hair and a sallow complexion* —**sallowness** *n* [U]

sal·ly¹ /ˈsæli/ *n* (*plural* **sallies**) [C] *formal* **1** a sudden quick attack and return to a position of defence **2** an intelligent remark that is intended to amuse people

sally² *v* (**sallied, sallying, sallies**)

sally forth *phr v literary* to go out in order to do something, especially something that you expect to be difficult or dangerous – often used humorously: *Each morning they sallied forth in search of jobs.*

salm·on /ˈsæmən/ ●●○ *n*
1 (*plural* **salmon**) [C] a large fish with silver skin and pink flesh that lives in the sea but swims up rivers to lay its eggs
2 [U] this fish eaten as food: **fresh/smoked salmon**
3 [U] a pink-orange colour

sal·mo·nel·la /ˌsælməˈnelə/ *n* [U] a kind of BACTERIA in food that makes you ill: *a case of* ***salmonella poisoning***

sal·on /ˈsælɒn $ səˈlɑːn/ ●○○ *n* [C]
1 a place where you can get your hair cut, have beauty treatments etc SYN **hairdresser's**: **hair/beauty salon** *an exclusive hair salon*
2 a shop where fashionable and expensive clothes are sold
3 *old-fashioned* a room in a very large house, where people can meet and talk
4 a regular meeting of famous people at which they talk about art, literature, or music, popular in the past in France: *a literary salon*

sa·loon /səˈluːn/ *n* [C] **1** a public place where alcoholic drinks were sold and drunk in the western US in the 19th century SYN **bar 2** (*also* **saloon bar**) *BrE* a comfortable room in a PUB SYN **lounge bar 3** (*also* **saloon car**) *BrE* a car that has a separate enclosed space for your bags etc SYN **sedan** *AmE*: *a four-door family saloon* → ESTATE CAR **4** a large comfortable room where passengers on a ship can sit and relax

sal·o·pettes /ˌsæləˈpets/ *n* [plural] special trousers that are worn by SKIERS. They reach up to your chest and have STRAPS that go over your shoulders.

sal·sa /ˈsælsə $ ˈsɑːl-/ *n* [U] **1** a type of Latin American dance music **2** a sauce made from onions, tomatoes, and CHILLIES, that you put on Spanish or Mexican food

salt¹ /sɔːlt $ sɒːlt/ ●●● S2 W3 *n*
1 [U] a natural white mineral that is added to food to make it taste better or to preserve it: *This might need some salt and pepper.* | *a* ***pinch of salt*** (=a very small amount) | *Could you pass the salt?*
2 the salt of the earth someone who is ordinary but good and honest
3 take sth with a pinch/grain of salt *informal* to not completely believe what someone tells you, because you know that they do not always tell the truth: *Most of what he says should be taken with a pinch of salt.*
4 [C] *technical* a type of chemical substance that is formed when an acid is combined with a BASE → EPSOM SALTS, SMELLING SALTS, OLD SALT, → **rub salt into the wound** at RUB¹(7), → **worth his/her salt** at WORTH¹(10)

salt² *v* [T] **1** to add salt to food to make it taste better: *salted peanuts* **2** (*also* **salt down**) to add salt to food to preserve it: **salted pork/meat/fish** | *The meat is salted to store it through the winter.* **3** to put salt on the roads to prevent them from becoming icy

salt sth ↔ **away** *phr v* to save money for the future, especially dishonestly by hiding it: *She salted the money away in a secret account.*

salt³ *adj* [only before noun] **1** preserved with salt: *salt pork* **2 salt water** water that contains salt, especially naturally in the sea **3** consisting of salt water: *a salt lake*

ˈsalt ˌcellar *n* [C] *BrE* a small container for salt SYN **salt shaker** *AmE*

salt·pe·tre *BrE*, **saltpeter** *AmE* /ˌsɔːltˈpiːtə $ ˌsɒːltˈpiːtər/ *n* [U] a substance used in making GUNPOWDER (=powder that causes explosions) and matches

ˈsalt ˌshaker *n* [C] *AmE* a small container for salt SYN **salt cellar** *BrE*

ˈsalt truck *n* [C] *AmE* a large vehicle that puts salt or sand on the roads in winter to make them less icy SYN **gritter** *BrE*

salt·wa·ter /ˈsɔːltˌwɔːtə $ -ˌwɒːtər, -ˌwɑː-/ *adj* [only before noun] **1** living in salty water or in the sea OPP **freshwater**: *saltwater fish* **2** containing salt water OPP **freshwater**: *a saltwater lake*

salt·y /ˈsɔːlti $ ˈsɒːlti/ ●●○ *adj*
1 tasting of or containing salt: *a slightly salty taste* | *salty foods* THESAURUS▸ TASTE
2 *AmE old-fashioned* language, a story, or a joke that is salty is amusing and often about sex

sa·lu·bri·ous /səˈluːbriəs/ *adj formal* a salubrious area or place is pleasant and clean, especially compared to other places – often used humorously: *the less salubrious area near the docks*

sal·u·ta·ry /ˈsæljətəri $ -teri/ *adj formal* a salutary experience is unpleasant but teaches you something: **salutary experience/lesson/reminder etc** *Losing money in this way taught young Jones a salutary lesson.*

sal·u·ta·tion /ˌsæljəˈteɪʃən/ *n formal* **1** [C] a word or phrase used at the beginning of a letter or speech, such as 'Dear Mr Smith' **2** [C,U] something you say or do when greeting someone

sa·lute¹ /səˈluːt/ *v* **1** [I,T] to move your right hand to your head, especially in order to show respect to an officer in the army, navy etc: *The two soldiers saluted Lieutenant Cecil.* | *The men jumped to their feet and saluted.* **2** [T] *formal* to praise someone for the things they have achieved, especially publicly: **salute sb as sth** *James Joyce was saluted as the greatest writer of the 20th century.* **3** [T] *old-fashioned* to greet someone in a polite way, especially by moving your hand or body

salute² *n* **1** [C] an act of raising your right hand to your head as a sign of respect, usually done by a soldier to an officer: *As they left, the corporal gave them a respectful salute.* | **in salute** *The officer raised his hand in salute.* **2** [C,U] something that expresses praise to someone for something they have achieved, or that expresses honour or respect to someone or something: **in salute** *Everyone at the table raised their glasses in salute.* | **[+to]** *His first words were a salute to the people of South Africa.* **3** [C] an occasion when guns are fired into the air in order to show respect for someone important: *a 21-gun salute*

sal·vage¹ /ˈsælvɪdʒ/ *v* [T] **1** to save something from an accident or bad situation in which other things have already been damaged, destroyed, or lost: *Divers hope to salvage some of the ship's cargo.* | **salvage sth from sth** *They managed to salvage only a few of their belongings from the fire.* **2** to make sure that you do not lose something completely, or to make sure that something does not fail completely SYN **save**: *He fought to* ***salvage*** *the company's* ***reputation***.

salvage² *n* [U] **1** when you save things from a situation in which other things have already been damaged,

S

destroyed, or lost: *a massive* ***salvage operation*** **2** things that have been saved from an accident, especially when a ship has sunk

sal·va·tion /sælˈveɪʃən/ *n* [U] **1** something that prevents or saves someone or something from danger, loss, or failure: **be sb's/sth's salvation** *A drug treatment program was Ron's salvation.* | **[+of]** *The Internet turned out to be the salvation of the company.* **2** in the Christian religion, the state of being saved from evil

Salˌvation ˈArmy *n* **the Salvation Army** a Christian organization that tries to help poor people

salve¹ /sælv, sɑːv $ sæv/ *n* [C,U] a substance that you put on sore skin to make it less painful SYN **balm**: *lip salve*

salve² *v* [T] *formal* **salve your conscience** if you do something to salve your conscience, you do it to make yourself feel less guilty SYN **ease**

sal·ver /ˈsælvə $ -ər/ *n* [C] a large metal plate used for serving food or drink at a formal meal: *a silver salver*

sal·vo /ˈsælvəʊ $ -voʊ/ *n* (*plural* **salvos** *or* **salvoes**) [C usually singular] *formal* **1** [+of] when several guns are fired during a battle or as part of a ceremony **2 opening salvo** the first in a series of questions, statements etc that you use to try to win an argument: *Congressman Saunders* ***fired the opening salvo*** *during a heated debate on capital punishment.* **3** sudden laughter, APPLAUSE etc from many people at the same time

sal·war ka·meez /ˌsælwɑː kæˈmiːz $ -wɑːr-/ *n* [C] SHALWAR KAMEEZ

Sa·mar·i·tan /səˈmærətən/ *n* [C] **good Samaritan** someone, especially a stranger, who helps you when you have problems or need something

sam·ba /ˈsæmbə/ *n* [C,U] a fast dance from Brazil, or the type of music played for this dance

S

same¹ /seɪm/ ●●● S1 W1 *adj* [only before noun]

1 NOT DIFFERENT **a)** the same person, place, thing etc is one particular person etc and not a different one: *He sits in the same chair every night.* | *They went to the same school.* | **[+as]** *She was born on the same day as me.* | *It is* ***those same people*** *who voted for the Democrats who now complain about their policies.* | **the very same** (=the same person or thing and not a different one - used to emphasize that what you are saying seems surprising) *We stood in front of the very same house in which Shakespeare wrote his plays.* **b)** used to say two or more people, things, events etc are exactly like each other: *Both women were wearing the same dress.* | *The same thing could happen again.* | **[+as]** *He gets the same pay as me but he gets his own office.* | **just/exactly the same sth** *That's funny - Simon said exactly the same thing.* | *The furniture is made in* ***much the same*** (=almost the same) *way as it was 200 years ago.*

> **REGISTER**
> In written English, people often prefer to say that two amounts or values are **equal** rather than **the same**: *They demanded* ***equal*** *pay for work of* ***equal*** *value.*

2 NOT CHANGING used to say that a particular person or thing does not change: *Her perfume has always had the same effect on me.* | *He's* ***the same old*** *Peter - moody and irritable.*

3 at the same time a) if two things happen at the same time, they both happen together: *Kate and I both went to live in Spain at the same time.* **b)** used when you want to say that something else is also true: *We don't want to lose him. At the same time, he needs to realise that company regulations must be obeyed.*

4 amount/come to the same thing to have the same result or effect: *It doesn't matter whether she was happy to leave or not. It amounts to the same thing - she's gone.*

5 the same old story/excuse etc *informal* something that you have heard many times before - used especially to show disapproval: *It's the same old story - his wife didn't really love him.*

6 same old same old *spoken* used to say that a situation has not changed, when this is boring or annoying but you did not really expect it to change: *Nothing interesting's going on - just same old same old.*

7 same difference *spoken* used to say that different actions, behaviour etc have the same result or effect: *'I could mail the letter or send a fax in the morning.' 'Same difference. It still won't get there on time.'*

8 by the same token *formal* for the same reasons - used when you want to say that something else is also true, especially something very different or surprising: *I realise that he hasn't come up with any new ideas, but by the same token we haven't needed any.*

9 be in the same boat to be in the same difficult situation that someone else is in: *Others in her profession are in the same boat.*

> **THESAURUS**
> **the same** used to say that two people, things, events etc are exactly like each other: *The houses on the street all look the same.* | *They were doing the same jobs as the men, but being paid less.*
> **just like/exactly like** *especially spoken* used to say that there is very little difference between two people, things etc: *He's just like his father.* | *There are insects that look exactly like green leaves.*
> **identical** identical things are exactly the same in every way: *The tablets were identical in size, shape, and colour.* | *identical names*
> **indistinguishable** two things that are indistinguishable are so similar that it is impossible to know which is which or to see any differences between them: *The copy was indistinguishable from the original painting.*
> **equal** two or more amounts, totals, levels etc that are equal are the same as each other: *Spend an equal amount of time on each essay question.*
> **be no different from sb/sth** to be the same, even though you expect them to be different: *People often think that movie stars are special, but really they're no different from anybody else.*
> **can't tell the difference** (*also* **can't tell sb/sth apart**) *especially spoken* if you can't tell the difference between two people or things, or if you can't tell them apart, they look, sound, or seem exactly the same to you: *Emma and Louise sound so alike on the phone that I can't tell the difference.*

same² ●●● S1 W1 *pron*

1 the same a) used to say that two or more people or things are exactly like each other: *The coins may look the same but one's a forgery.* | **[+as]** *Your measurements are* ***exactly the same*** *as Dana's.* | *Thanks for your help - I'll do the same for you one day.* **b)** used to say that a particular person or thing does not change: *Things just won't be the same without Sam.*

> **REGISTER**
> In written English, people often prefer to say that an amount or level **remains constant** rather than **stays the same**.

2 (and the) same to you! *spoken* **a)** used as a reply to a greeting: *'Merry Christmas!' 'And the same to you, Ben.'* **b)** used as an angry reply to a rude remark: *'Up yours!' 'Same to you!'*

3 just/all the same in spite of a particular situation, opinion etc: *I realise she can be very annoying, but I think you should apologise all the same.*

4 all the same in spite of something that you have just mentioned: *I'm not likely to run out of money but, all the same, I'm careful.*

5 it's all the same to sb used to say that someone does not mind what decision is made, would be pleased with any choice, or does not really care: *If it's all the same to you, I'll go this weekend.*

6 same here *spoken* used to say that you feel the same way as someone else: *'I'm exhausted.' 'Same here!'*

7 (the) same again used to ask for another drink of the same kind

8 more of the same another person, thing etc like the one just mentioned: *He has produced a string of thrillers, and this movie is just more of the same.* → **one and the same** at ONE²(17)

GRAMMAR: Patterns with same

- You usually say **the same**: *They both gave the same reason for leaving.* | *I'd like the same sort of car.* | *The buildings all look the same.* ✗ *They both gave a same reason.* | *I'd like a same sort of car.*
- You say **the same as**: *His answer was the same as mine.* ✗ Don't say: *the same like mine* | *the same with mine*
- You can also say **this same** or **that same** followed by a noun, to emphasize it: *At that same moment, the telephone rang.*

same³ ●●● S1 W1 *adv*
1 the same (as) in the same way: *'Rain' and 'reign' are pronounced the same, even though they are spelt differently.* | *Everyone had to dress the same as a well-known historical figure.*
2 same as sb *spoken* just like someone else: *I have my pride, same as anyone else.*

same·ness /ˈseɪmnəs/ *n* [U] a boring lack of variety, or the quality of being very similar to something else

ˌsame-ˈsex *adj* **same-sex couple/relationship etc** a couple, relationship etc involving two men or two women SYN **homosexual**

ˌsame-sex ˈmarriage *n* [C] a marriage between two men or two women

same·y /ˈseɪmi/ *adj BrE informal* boring and having very little variety: *His novels tend to be very samey.*

sa·mo·sa /səˈməʊsə $ -ˈmoʊ-/ *n* [C] a type of Indian food made from meat or vegetables covered in thin PASTRY and cooked in hot oil

sam·o·var /ˈsæməvɑː $ -vɑːr/ *n* [C] a large metal container used in Russia to boil water for making tea

sam·pan /ˈsæmpæn/ *n* [C] a small boat used in China and Southeast Asia

sam·ple¹ /ˈsɑːmpəl $ ˈsæm-/ ●●● S3 W2 *n* [C]
1 a small part or amount of something that is examined in order to find out something about the whole: **[+of]** *I'd like to see some samples of your work.* | *They took a* ***blood sample*** *to test for hepatitis.*
2 a small amount of a product that people can try in order to find out what it is like: **[+of]** *free samples of a new shampoo*
3 a small group of people who have been chosen from a larger group to give information or answers to questions: *The sample consisted of 98 secondary school teachers.* | *Out of a* ***random sample*** *of drivers, 21% had been in an accident in the previous year.* | *a nationally* ***representative sample*** *of over 950 elderly persons*
4 a small part of a song from a CD or record that is used in a new song: *Her latest album makes extensive use of samples from a wide range of acid jazz tracks.*

sample² ●●○ *v* [T]
1 to taste food or drink in order to see what it is like: *a chance to sample the local food*
2 to choose some people from a larger group in order to ask them questions or get information from them: *18% of the adults sampled admitted having had problems with alcohol abuse.*
3 to try an activity, go to a place etc in order to see what it is like: *Here's your chance to* ***sample the delights of*** *country life.*
4 to use a small part of a song from a CD or record in a new song: *Many of his songs have been sampled by other artists.*

sam·pler /ˈsɑːmplə $ ˈsæmplər/ *n* [C] **1** a machine that can record sounds or music so that you can change them and use them for a new piece of music **2** a piece of cloth with different stitches on it, made to show how good someone is at sewing

sam·u·rai /ˈsæmʊraɪ/ *n* (*plural* **samurai**) [C] a member of a powerful military class in Japan in the past —**samurai** *adj*: *a samurai sword*

san·a·to·ri·um /ˌsænəˈtɔːriəm/ *n* (*plural* **sanatoria** /-riə/ *or* **sanatoriums**) [C] *old-fashioned* a type of hospital for sick people who are getting better after a long illness but still need rest and a lot of care SYN **sanitarium** *AmE*

sanc·ti·fy /ˈsæŋktɪfaɪ/ *v* (**sanctified, sanctifying, sanctifies**) [T] **1** to make something seem morally right or acceptable or to give something official approval: *The rule of the czar was sanctified by the Russian Orthodox Church.* **2** to make something holy —**sanctification** /ˌsæŋktɪfɪˈkeɪʃən/ *n* [U]

sanc·ti·mo·ni·ous /ˌsæŋktəˈməʊniəs◂ $ -ˈmoʊ-/ *adj formal* behaving as if you are morally better than other people, in a way that is annoying - used to show disapproval SYN **self-righteous**: *sanctimonious politicians preaching about family values* —**sanctimoniously** *adv* —**sanctimoniousness** *n* [U]

sanc·tion¹ /ˈsæŋkʃən/ ●○○ *n*
1 sanctions [plural] official orders or laws stopping trade, communication etc with another country, as a way of forcing its leaders to make political changes → **embargo**: **[+against]** *US sanctions against Cuba* | *a resolution to* ***impose sanctions*** (=start using sanctions) *on North Korea* | *the threat of* ***trade sanctions*** | *The UN Security Council may impose* ***economic sanctions****.* | *Any talk about* ***lifting sanctions*** (=ending them) *is premature.*
2 [U] *formal* official permission, approval, or acceptance SYN **approval**: *Apparently, the aide had acted without White House sanction.*
3 [C] *formal* a form of punishment that can be used if someone disobeys a rule or law SYN **punishment**: *the harshest possible sanction which could be imposed*

sanction² ●○○ *v* [T] *formal*
1 to officially accept or allow something SYN **approve**: *The church refused to sanction the king's second marriage.* THESAURUS ALLOW
2 be sanctioned by sth to be made acceptable by something: *a barbaric custom, but one sanctioned by long usage*

sanc·ti·ty /ˈsæŋktəti/ *n* [U] **1 the sanctity of life/marriage etc** the quality that makes life, marriage etc so important that it must be respected and preserved: *the sanctity of the Constitution* **2** *formal* the holy or religious character of a person or place → **sacred**: *an aura of sanctity*

sanc·tu·a·ry /ˈsæŋktʃuəri, -tʃəri $ -tʃueri/ ●○○ *n* (*plural* **sanctuaries**)
1 [C] an area for birds or animals where they are protected and cannot be hunted SYN **refuge**: **bird/wildlife etc sanctuary** *The park is the largest wildlife sanctuary in the US.* | **[+for]** *a sanctuary for tigers*
2 [C,U] a peaceful place that is safe and provides protection, especially for people who are in danger SYN **refuge**: **find/seek sanctuary** *Fleeing refugees found sanctuary in Geneva.* | **[+for]** *a sanctuary for battered women*
3 [C] the part of a religious building that is considered to be the most holy
4 [C] *AmE* the room in a religious building where religious services take place
5 [U] the right that people had under Christian law, especially in the past, to be protected from police, soldiers etc by staying in a church

sanc·tum /ˈsæŋktəm/ *n* [C] **1 inner sanctum** a private place or room that only a few important people are allowed to enter - often used humorously: *Occasionally, she would be allowed into the inner sanctum of his office.* **2** a holy place inside a temple

sand¹ /sænd/ ●●● S3 W3 *n*
1 [U] a substance consisting of very small pieces of rocks and minerals, that forms beaches and deserts: *a mixture of sand and cement* | *I have sand in my shoe.*
2 [C,U] an area of beach: *miles of golden sands* | *We were just sitting on the sand.*
3 the sands of time *literary* moments of time that pass quickly

sand² (*also* **sand down**) *v* [I,T] to make a surface smooth

S

by rubbing it with SANDPAPER or using a special piece of equipment

san·dal /ˈsændl/ ●●○ *n* [C] a light shoe that is fastened onto your foot by bands of leather or cloth, and is worn in warm weather: *a pair of sandals* → see picture at SHOE[1]

san·dal·wood /ˈsændlwʊd/ *n* [U] pleasant-smelling wood from a southern Asian tree, or the oil from this wood

sand·bag[1] /ˈsændbæg/ *n* [C] a bag filled with sand, used for protection against floods, explosions etc

sandbag[2] *v* (**sandbagged**, **sandbagging**) **1** [I,T] to put sandbags around a building in order to protect it from a flood or explosion **2** [T] to treat someone unfairly in order to prevent them from doing something or being successful

sand·bank /ˈsændbæŋk/ *n* [C] a raised area of sand in a river, ocean etc

ˈsand bar *n* [C] a long pile of sand in a river or the ocean, formed by the movement of the water

sand·blast /ˈsændblɑːst $ -blæst/ *v* [T] to clean or polish metal, stone, glass etc with a machine that sends out a powerful stream of sand

sand·board /ˈsændbɔːd $ -bɔːrd/ *n* [C] a long wide board made of plastic, which people stand on to go down SAND DUNES as sport

sand·board·ing /ˈsændbɔːdɪŋ $ -ɔːr-/ *n* [U] the sport of going down SAND DUNES on a sandboard → **snowboarding** —**sandboarder** *n* [C]

sand·box /ˈsændbɒks $ -bɑːks/ *n* [C] *AmE* a small box filled with sand for children to play in SYN **sandpit** *BrE*

sand·cas·tle /ˈsændˌkɑːsəl $ -ˌkæ-/ *n* [C] a small model of a castle, made out of sand by children playing on a beach

ˈsand dune *n* [C] a hill formed of sand in a desert or near the sea

sand·er /ˈsændə $ -ər/ (*also* **ˈsanding maˌchine**) *n* [C] an electric tool with a rough surface that moves very quickly, used for making surfaces smooth, especially the surface of wood

ˈsand fly *n* [C] a small fly that bites people and lives on beaches

S & L /ˌes ənd ˈel/ *n* [C] *AmE informal* the abbreviation of ***savings and loan association***

sand·lot /ˈsændlɒt $ -lɑːt/ *n* [C] *AmE* an area of empty land in a town or city, where children often play sports or games: *a sandlot ball game*

S & M /ˌes ənd ˈem/ *n* [U] the abbreviation of ***sadomasochism***

sand·man /ˈsændmæn/ *n* [singular] an imaginary man who is supposed to make children go to sleep

sand·pa·per[1] /ˈsændˌpeɪpə $ -ər/ *n* [U] strong paper covered on one side with sand or a similar substance, used for rubbing wood in order to make the surface smooth

sandpaper[2] *v* [T] to rub something with sandpaper

sand·pip·er /ˈsændˌpaɪpə $ -ər/ *n* [C] a small bird with long legs and a long beak that lives near the shore

sand·pit /ˈsændˌpɪt/ *n* [C] *BrE* a box or special area filled with sand for children to play in SYN **sandbox** *AmE*

sand·stone /ˈsændstəʊn $ -stoʊn/ *n* [U] a type of soft yellow or red rock, often used in buildings

sand·storm /ˈsændstɔːm $ -stɔːrm/ *n* [C] a storm in the desert, in which sand is blown around by strong winds

sand·trap /ˈsændtræp/ *n* [C] *AmE* a hollow place on a golf course, filled with sand, from which it is difficult to hit the ball SYN **bunker** *BrE*

sand·wich[1] /ˈsænwɪdʒ $ ˈsændwɪtʃ, ˈsænwɪtʃ/ ●●● S2 *n*

1 [C] two pieces of bread with cheese, meat, cooked egg etc between them: *a ham sandwich*

2 [C] *BrE* a cake consisting of two layers with JAM and cream between them: *a raspberry sponge sandwich* → CLUB SANDWICH, OPEN SANDWICH

sandwich[2] *v* [T] to put something in a very small space between two other things: **be sandwiched in between sb/sth** *A layer of transparent material is sandwiched between the pieces of glass.*

ˈsandwich board *n* [C] two boards with advertisements on them that hang in front of and behind someone who is paid to walk around in public

ˈsandwich course *n* [C] *BrE* a course of study at a British college or university that includes periods spent working in industry or business

ˈsandwich geneˌration *n* [singular] people who have both children and parents who need looking after

sand·y /ˈsændi/ *adj* **1** covered with sand, or containing a lot of sand: *The soil is quite sandy.* **2** hair that is sandy is a yellowish-brown colour —**sandiness** *n* [U]

sane /seɪn/ ●○○ *adj*

1 able to think in a normal and reasonable way OPP **insane**, **mentally ill** → **sanity**: *He seems* ***perfectly sane*** (=completely sane) *to me.* | *No sane person would want to kill a baby.*

2 reasonable and based on sensible thinking: *a sane and sensible approach to gun control*

3 keep sb sane (*also* **enable sb to stay/remain sane**) to stop someone from thinking about their problems and becoming upset: *The only thing that kept me sane was music.* —**sanely** *adv*

sang /sæŋ/ *v* the past tense of SING

sang-froid /ˌsɒŋ ˈfrwɑː $ ˌsɑːŋ-/ *n* [U] *literary* courage and the ability to keep calm in dangerous or difficult situations

san·gri·a /sæŋˈgriːə, sæn-, ˈsæŋgriə/ *n* [U] a Spanish drink made from red wine, fruit, and fruit juice

san·gui·na·ry /ˈsæŋgwənəri $ -neri/ *adj literary* involving violence and killing

san·guine /ˈsæŋgwɪn/ *adj formal* happy and hopeful about the future SYN **optimistic**: **[+about]** *Other economists are more sanguine about the possibility of inflation.* | *a sanguine view*

san·i·tar·i·um /ˌsænəˈteəriəm $ -ˈter-/ *n* [C] an American spelling of SANATORIUM

san·i·ta·ry /ˈsænətəri $ -teri/ *adj* **1** [only before noun] relating to the ways that dirt, infection, and waste are removed, so that places are clean and healthy for people to live in SYN **hygienic**: *Diseases were spread through poor* ***sanitary conditions***. | *a prison with no proper* ***sanitary facilities*** (=toilets) **2** clean and not causing any danger to people's health OPP **insanitary**: *Often, the camps were not very sanitary.*

ˈsanitary ˌpad (*also* **ˈsanitary ˌtowel** *BrE*, **ˈsanitary ˌnapkin** *AmE*) *n* [C] a special piece of soft material that a woman wears in her underwear for the blood when she has her PERIOD

san·i·ta·tion /ˌsænɪˈteɪʃən/ *n* [U] the protection of public health by removing and treating waste, dirty water etc: *Overcrowding and* ***poor sanitation*** *are common problems in prisons.*

saniˈtation ˌworker *n* [C] *AmE formal* someone who removes waste material that people put outside their houses SYN **garbage man**

san·i·tize (*also* **-ise** *BrE*) /ˈsænətaɪz/ *v* [T] **1** to remove particular details from a report, story etc in order to make it less offensive, unpleasant, or embarrassing – used especially to show disapproval: *the sanitized version of events which was reported in the government-controlled media* **2** to clean something thoroughly, removing dirt and BACTERIA

san·i·ty /ˈsænəti/ *n* [U] **1** the condition of being mentally healthy OPP **insanity** → **sane**: *I began to doubt his sanity.* | *She wondered if she was* ***losing*** *her* ***sanity***. **2** when someone or something is being reasonable and sensible → **sane**: *Sanity appears to be returning to the stock market.* | **regain/get back/recover your sanity** *I took a vacation to try to recover my sanity.*

sank /sæŋk/ the past tense of SINK

sans /sænz/ *prep* without – usually used humorously: *He came to the door sans shirt.*

San·skrit /ˈsænskrɪt/ *n* [U] an ancient language of India

sans ser·if /ˌsæn ˈserəf, ˌsænz-/ *n* [U] *technical* a style of printing in which letters have no SERIFS

San·ta Claus /ˈsæntə klɔːz $ ˈsænti klɒːz, ˈsæntə-/ (*also* **Santa**) *n* [singular] an imaginary old man with red clothes and a long white BEARD who, children believe, brings them presents at Christmas SYN **Father Christmas** *BrE*

sap¹ /sæp/ *n* **1** [U] the watery substance that carries food through a plant **2** [C] *informal* a stupid person who is easy to deceive or treat badly

sap² *v* (**sapped**, **sapping**) [T] to make something weaker or destroy it, especially someone's strength or their determination to do something SYN **weaken**: **sap sb's strength/courage/energy** *Her long illness was gradually sapping Charlotte's strength.*

sa·pi·ent /ˈseɪpiənt/ *adj literary* very wise

sap·ling /ˈsæplɪŋ/ *n* [C] a young tree

sap·per /ˈsæpə $ -ər/ *n* [C] *BrE* a soldier whose job involves digging and building

sap·phic /ˈsæfɪk/ *adj literary* LESBIAN

sap·phire /ˈsæfaɪə $ -faɪr/ *n* [C,U] a transparent bright blue jewel

sap·py /ˈsæpi/ *adj* **1** *AmE* expressing love and emotions in a way that seems silly SYN **soppy** *BrE*: *a sappy song* **2** full of SAP (=liquid in a plant)

sap·wood /ˈsæpwʊd/ *n* [U] the younger outer wood in a tree, that is paler and softer than the wood in the middle

Sar·a·cen /ˈsærəsən/ *n* [C] *old use* a Muslim – used in the Middle Ages

Sa·ran Wrap /səˈræn ræp/ *n* [U] *trademark AmE* thin transparent plastic, used for wrapping food SYN **clingfilm** *BrE*

sar·cas·m /ˈsɑːkæzəm $ ˈsɑːr-/ ●○○ *n* [U] a way of speaking or writing that involves saying the opposite of what you really mean in order to make an unkind joke or to show that you are annoyed: *'Good of you to arrive on time,' George said, with* ***heavy sarcasm*** (=very clear sarcasm). | **hint/trace/edge/touch of sarcasm** *There was just a touch of sarcasm in her voice.*

sar·cas·tic /sɑːˈkæstɪk $ sɑːr-/ ●○○ *adj* saying things that are the opposite of what you mean, in order to make an unkind joke or to show that you are annoyed: *Was she being sarcastic?* | **sarcastic remark/comment/question** *He can't help making sarcastic comments.* | **sarcastic manner/smile/laugh etc** *'I thought so,' she said with a sarcastic smile.* —**sarcastically** /-kli/ *adv*

sar·coph·a·gus /sɑːˈkɒfəgəs $ sɑːrˈkɑː-/ *n* (*plural* **sarcophagi** /-gaɪ/) [C] a decorated stone box for a dead body, used in ancient times

sar·dine /ˌsɑːˈdiːn◂ $ ˌsɑːr-/ *n* **1** [C] a small young fish that is often packed in flat metal boxes when it is sold as food → see picture at **FISH¹** **2 be packed like sardines** to be crowded tightly together in a small space: *commuters packed like sardines on the evening train*

sar·don·ic /sɑːˈdɒnɪk $ sɑːrˈdɑː-/ *adj written* showing that you do not have a good opinion of someone or something, and feel that you are better than them: *He looked at her with sardonic amusement.* —**sardonically** /-kli/ *adv*

sarge /sɑːdʒ $ sɑːrdʒ/ *n* [singular] *spoken* SERGEANT

sa·ri /ˈsɑːri/ *n* [C] a long piece of cloth that you wrap around your body like a dress, worn especially by women from India

sar·ky /ˈsɑːki $ ˈsɑːr-/ *adj BrE informal* SARCASTIC

sar·nie /ˈsɑːni $ ˈsɑːr-/ *n* [C] *BrE informal* a SANDWICH

sa·rong /səˈrɒŋ $ səˈrɒːŋ, səˈrɑːŋ/ *n* [C] a loose skirt consisting of a long piece of cloth wrapped around your waist, worn especially by people in Malaysia and Indonesia

Sars, **SARS** /sɑːz $ sɑːrz/ *n* [U] (***Severe Acute Respiratory Syndrome***) an infectious illness caused by a VIRUS (=small living thing) which makes it difficult for people to breathe and can kill them if it is not treated quickly

sarsa·pa·ril·la /ˌsɑːspəˈrɪlə $ ˌsæs-/ *n* [U] a sweet drink without alcohol, made from the root of the SASSAFRAS plant

sar·to·ri·al /sɑːˈtɔːriəl $ sɑːr-/ *adj formal* relating to clothes, especially the style of clothes that a man wears – used especially humorously: *a man of great* ***sartorial elegance*** —**sartorially** *adv*

SAS /ˌes eɪ ˈes/ *n* **the SAS** (***the Special Air Service***) a British military force that is specially trained to do secret and dangerous work

SASE /ˌes eɪ es ˈiː/ *n* [C] *AmE* (***self-addressed stamped envelope***) an envelope that you put your name, address, and a stamp on, so that someone else can send you something SYN **sae** *BrE*

sash /sæʃ/ *n* [C] **1** a long piece of cloth that you wear around your waist like a belt **2** a long piece of cloth that you wear over one shoulder and across your chest

sa·shay /sæˈʃeɪ/ *v* [I always + adv/prep] to walk in a confident way, moving your body from side to side, especially so that people look at you: **[+around/along/down etc]** *Models sashayed down the aisle.*

sa·shi·mi /sæˈʃiːmi/ *n* [U] a type of Japanese food consisting of small pieces of fresh fish that have not been cooked

ˈsash ˌwindow *n* [C] *BrE* a window consisting of two frames that you open by sliding one up or down, behind or in front of the other → see picture at **WINDOW**

sass /sæs/ *v* [T] *AmE informal* to talk in a rude way to someone you should respect: *Don't you sass me, young lady!*

sas·sa·fras /ˈsæsəfræs/ *n* [C,U] a small Asian or North American tree, or the pleasant-smelling roots of this tree that are used in food and drink

Sas·se·nach /ˈsæsənæk/ *n* [C] an English person – used by Scottish people in a humorous way or to show disapproval

sas·sy /ˈsæsi/ *adj AmE* **1** a child who is sassy is rude to someone they should respect SYN **cheeky** *BrE* **2** someone, especially a woman, who is sassy is confident and does not really care what other people think about her SYN **feisty**

sat /sæt/ the past tense and past participle of SIT

Sat. (*also* **Sat** *BrE*) the written abbreviation of ***Saturday***

SAT /sæt, ˌes eɪ ˈtiː/ *n* [C] **1** *trademark* (***Scholastic Aptitude Test***) an examination that American high school students take before they go to college: ***SAT scores*** *have been steadily decreasing.* **2 SATs** (***Standard Assessment Tests***) examinations that students in England and Wales take at the ages of 7, 11, and 14, to see if they have reached the NATIONAL CURRICULUM standard

Sa·tan /ˈseɪtn/ *n* the Devil, considered to be the main evil power and God's opponent

sa·tan·ic /səˈtænɪk/ *adj* **1** relating to practices that treat the Devil like a god: **satanic ritual/cult/rite** *The children were abused as part of a satanic ritual.* **2** *literary* extremely cruel or evil: *satanic laughter* —**satanically** /-kli/ *adv*

sa·tan·is·m /ˈseɪtənɪzəm/ *n* [U] the practice of worshipping Satan —**satanist** *n* [C] —**satanist** *adj*

satch·el /ˈsætʃəl/ *n* [C] a leather bag that you carry over your shoulder, used especially in the past by children for carrying books to school → see picture at **BAG¹**

sat·ed /ˈseɪtɪd/ *adj literary* feeling that you have had enough or too much of something, especially food or pleasure SYN **full** —**sate** *v* [T]: *He had sated his lust.*

S

sat·el·lite /ˈsætəlaɪt/ ●●○ W3 *n* [C]
1 a machine that has been sent into space and goes around the Earth, Moon etc, used for radio, television, and other electronic communication: *the launch of a communications and weather satellite* | **via/by satellite** (=using a satellite) *This broadcast comes live via satellite from New York.*
2 a natural object that moves around a PLANET: *The Moon is a satellite of the Earth.*
3 a country, area, or organization that is controlled by or is dependent on another larger one: *the former Soviet satellite country of Lithuania*
4 a town that has developed next to a large city: *We stayed in Aurora, a satellite suburb of Chicago.* → SAT-NAV, SATPHONE

SATELLITE

satellite

satellite dish

ˈsatellite ˌdish *n* [C] a large circular piece of metal that receives satellite television broadcasts

ˌsatellite ˈtelevision (*also* **ˌsatellite TˈV**) *n* [U] television programmes that are broadcast using satellites in space, and which you need a special piece of equipment to be able to watch

sa·ti·ate /ˈseɪʃieɪt/ *v* [T] *literary* to satisfy a desire or need for something such as food or sex, especially so that you feel you have had too much —**satiated** *adj* —**satiation** /ˌseɪʃiˈeɪʃən/ *n* [U]

sa·tiet·y /səˈtaɪəti/ *n* [U] *formal* the condition of feeling that you have had enough of something, for example food: *physical feelings of hunger and satiety*

sat·in[1] /ˈsætɪn $ ˈsætn/ *n* [U] a type of cloth that is very smooth and shiny: *a red satin ribbon*

satin[2] *adj* having a smooth shiny surface: *The new paints are available in gloss and satin finishes.*

sat·in·y /ˈsætɪni $ ˈsætni/ *adj* smooth, shiny, and soft: *women in tight, satiny dresses*

sat·ire /ˈsætaɪə $ -taɪr/ ●○○ *n*
1 [U] a way of criticizing something such as a group of people or a system, in which you deliberately make them seem funny so that people will see their faults: *the characteristic use of satire in Jonson's work* | **political/social satire** *a comedy group that does political satire*
2 [C] a piece of writing, film, play etc that uses this type of criticism: **[+on]** *a satire on American politics* | **savage/stinging/vicious/biting satire** *a biting satire of the television industry* —**satirical** /səˈtɪrɪkəl/ *adj*: *a well-known satirical magazine* —**satiric** *adj* —**satirically** /-kli/ *adv*

sat·i·rist /ˈsætɪrɪst/ *n* [C] someone who writes satire

sat·ir·ize (*also* **-ise** *BrE*) /ˈsætəraɪz/ *v* [T] to use satire to make people see someone's or something's faults: *a play satirizing the fashion industry*

sat·is·fac·tion /ˌsætəsˈfækʃən/ ●●○ W3 *n*
1 [C,U] a feeling of happiness or pleasure because you have achieved something or got what you wanted OPP **dissatisfaction**: *She got great satisfaction from helping people to learn.* | *'I've passed all my exams,' he announced with satisfaction.* | **[+with]** *Finance officials expressed satisfaction with the recovery of the dollar.* | **the satisfaction of knowing/seeing/having etc** *I didn't want to give him the satisfaction of knowing that I was jealous.* | **for your own satisfaction** (=because you want to be sure about something) *For her own satisfaction, she checked through the figures again.*
2 to sb's satisfaction if something is done to someone's satisfaction, it is done as well or as completely as they want, so they are pleased: *The question could not be resolved, at least not to my satisfaction.*
3 [U] when you get money or an APOLOGY from someone who has treated you badly or unfairly: *I* ***got no satisfaction*** *from the customer complaints department.*
4 [U] *formal* when someone gets something that they want, need, or have demanded: **[+of]** *the satisfaction of basic human needs* | *sexual satisfaction*

COLLOCATIONS

ADJECTIVES/NOUN + satisfaction

great/deep satisfaction *It was hard work, but it gave her great satisfaction.*
real satisfaction (=great satisfaction) *There is real satisfaction in helping other people to overcome their problems.*
complete satisfaction *They expressed complete satisfaction with the agreement.*
personal satisfaction (=happiness with your own life or achievements) | **quiet satisfaction** (=satisfaction that you express in a quiet, not very obvious way) | **job satisfaction** (=enjoyment of your job) | **customer/patient/voter etc satisfaction** (=among customers/patients/voters etc)

VERBS

get satisfaction from sth (*also* **gain/derive satisfaction from sth** *formal*) *I get a lot of satisfaction from teaching.*
find satisfaction in sth *They found satisfaction in helping others achieve their goals.*
take satisfaction in/from sth *He took great satisfaction in doing his job well.*
have the satisfaction of doing sth *They have the satisfaction of knowing that the company needs them.*
sth gives/brings sb satisfaction *To have won both awards in the same year gives us great satisfaction.*
feel satisfaction *As she looked at what she had created, she felt a quiet satisfaction.*
express satisfaction

PHRASES

a sense/feeling of satisfaction *Performing such a difficult piece gave her a deep sense of satisfaction.*
a smile/sigh/look of satisfaction *He allowed himself a little smile of satisfaction.*
the level of satisfaction (=the number of people who feel satisfied) *Research shows a high level of satisfaction with the system.*
a source of satisfaction (=something that gives you a feeling of satisfaction)

sat·is·fac·to·ry /ˌsætəsˈfæktəri◂/ ●●○ *adj* something that is satisfactory seems good enough for you, or good enough for a particular situation or purpose OPP **unsatisfactory**: *His progress this term has been satisfactory.* | **[+to/for]** *an arrangement that is satisfactory to both sides* | **satisfactory explanation/answer** *There seems to be no satisfactory explanation.* | **perfectly/entirely/wholly satisfactory** *None of the solutions was entirely satisfactory.* | **satisfactory result/outcome/resolution** —**satisfactorily** *adv*: *The question has not been satisfactorily answered.*

THESAURUS

satisfactory good enough – often used when something reaches a fairly good standard, but is not of a high standard: *Her grades are satisfactory.* | *For a beginner, this camera produces satisfactory results.*
all right/OK *spoken* not bad, but not very good: *The meal was all right, but rather expensive.* | *'How was the film?' 'It was OK.'*
reasonable fairly good: *a reasonable standard of living* | *The quality of the food was reasonable.*
acceptable if something is acceptable to you, you think it is good enough and you are willing to take it: *an acceptable offer* | *an acceptable level of risk* | *They can't find a solution that is acceptable to both sides.*
adequate enough in quantity, or of a good enough standard. **Adequate** sounds rather formal and is used especially in official contexts: *an adequate*

supply of drinking water | adequate standards of hygiene
decent *especially spoken* good enough in quality – used especially when something is as good as most other things: *I want my kids to get a decent education.* | *Where can I get a decent cup of coffee?*
passable satisfactory, but not of the best quality – used especially about food and drink, or someone's skill at doing something. **Passable** sounds rather formal: *a passable French wine* | *His Japanese was passable.*
be up to scratch *informal* to be of a good enough standard: *His work wasn't up to scratch.*
will do *informal* to be good enough for a particular purpose: *Any kind of paper will do.* | *'How about Ken?' 'I suppose he'll do.'*

sat·is·fied /ˈsætəsfaɪd/ ●●● S3 *adj*
1 feeling that something is as good as it should be, or that something has happened in the way that you want OPP **dissatisfied**: *a satisfied smile* | *They have plenty of **satisfied customers**.* | *Will she ever be satisfied?* | **[+with]** *I'm not satisfied with the way he cut my hair.* | **completely/fully/totally/entirely satisfied** *If you're not completely satisfied, you can get your money back.*

GRAMMAR
Someone is **satisfied with** something: *They were not satisfied with the room.* ✗ Don't say: *They were not satisfied about the room.*

2 feeling sure that something is right or true: **[+that]** *He was satisfied that he had done nothing wrong.* **THESAURUS** SURE
3 (are you) satisfied? *spoken* **a)** used to say in an annoyed way that you agree to do something that you do not really want to do: *Okay, okay, I'll ask him this afternoon. Satisfied?* **b)** used when you are annoyed with someone because they have done something that has a bad result: *Dad's said neither of us can go now. Are you satisfied?* → SELF-SATISFIED

THESAURUS
satisfied feeling that something is as good as it should be, or that something has happened in the way that you want: *The teacher is satisfied with his progress.* | *another satisfied customer*
happy [not before noun] satisfied. **Happy** is very commonly used instead of **satisfied** in everyday English: *The boss seems happy with my work.* | *I'm happy to work part-time until the kids are older.*
pleased [not before noun] very satisfied: *I'm pleased with the results.* | *He came out looking pleased with himself.*
content [not before noun] satisfied with what you are doing, so that you do not want to change anything: *She seemed content to just sit and watch the others.* | *Sam was quite content with his life on the farm.*
fulfilled [not usually before noun] feeling that you have achieved enough in your life, and that you do not need things that are more interesting, important, or useful: *I enjoy being a mother, but to feel fulfilled I need to work too.*

sat·is·fy /ˈsætəsfaɪ/ ●●○ W2 *v* (**satisfied**, **satisfying**, **satisfies**) [T]
1 to make someone feel pleased by doing what they want: *Nothing I did would ever satisfy my father.*
2 if you satisfy someone's needs, demands etc, you provide what they need or want: **satisfy sb's needs/demands/desires** *The program is designed to satisfy the needs of adult learners.* | **satisfy sb's hunger/appetite** (=give someone enough food to stop them from feeling hungry) *A salad won't be enough to satisfy my appetite.* | *Just to **satisfy** my **curiosity*** (=find out something), *how much did it cost?*
3 *formal* to make someone feel sure that something is right or true SYN **convince**: **satisfy sb of sth** *Jackson tried to satisfy me of his innocence.* | **satisfy yourself (that)** *Having satisfied herself that no one was there, she closed the door.*
4 *formal* to be good enough for a particular purpose, standard etc SYN **meet**: *Have you **satisfied** all the **requirements** for the general degree?*

sat·is·fy·ing /ˈsætəsfaɪ-ɪŋ/ ●●○ *adj*
1 making you feel pleased and happy, especially because you have got what you wanted OPP **unsatisfying**: *a **deeply satisfying** feeling* | **it is satisfying (to do sth)** *It can be very satisfying to work in the garden.*
2 food that is satisfying makes you feel that you have eaten enough: *a satisfying meal*

sat-nav, **Sat-Nav** /ˈsæt næv/ *n* [U] *informal* (***satellite navigation***) a piece of electronic equipment in a car. It can tell you which way you need to go by using information received from a SATELLITE: *The Audi A6 comes with sat-nav and climate control as standard.*

sat·phone /ˈsætfəʊn $ -foʊn/ *n* [C] *informal* (***satellite telephone***) a special telephone that sends and receives its signal through a SATELLITE that is moving around the Earth

sat·su·ma /sætˈsuːmə/ *n* [C] a fruit like a small orange, that has no seeds, and a loose skin you can pull off easily → see picture at FRUIT[1]

sat·u·rate[1] /ˈsætʃəreɪt/ *v* [T] **1** *formal* to make something very wet SYN **soak** OPP **dry**: *Water poured through the hole, saturating the carpet.* **2** to put a lot of something into a particular place, especially so that you could not add any more: **saturate sth with sth** *Our culture is saturated with television and advertising.* **3 saturate the market** to offer so much of a product for sale that there is more than people want to buy **4** *technical* to mix as much of a solid into a chemical mixture as possible

sat·u·rate[2] /ˈsætʃərət/ *n* [C usually plural] a type of fat from meat or milk products that is thought to be less healthy than other kinds of fat from vegetables or fish SYN **saturated fat**: *Choose a type of spread that's lower in saturates than butter.*

sat·u·rat·ed /ˈsætʃəreɪtɪd/ *adj* **1** extremely wet SYN **soaked** OPP **dry**: **[+with]** *a T-shirt saturated with sweat* **THESAURUS** WET **2** *technical* if a chemical mixture is saturated, it has had as much of a solid mixed into it as possible

ˌsaturated ˈfat *n* [C,U] a type of fat from meat and milk products that is thought to be less healthy than other kinds of fat from vegetables or fish

sat·u·ra·tion /ˌsætʃəˈreɪʃən/ *n* [U] **1** when an event or person is given so much attention by newspapers, television etc that everyone has heard about it: *The trial was given **saturation coverage** by the press.* | *saturation advertising* **2 saturation bombing** a military attack in which a whole area is bombed **3** *technical* the degree to which something has been mixed into something else: *Keep saturation below 80%.* **4** when something is made completely wet

satuˈration ˌpoint *n* [C usually singular] **1** a situation in which no more people or things can be added because there are already too many: *The number of summer tourists in the area has **reached saturation point**.* **2** *technical* the state that a chemical mixture reaches when it has had as much of a solid substance mixed into it as possible

Sat·ur·day /ˈsætədi, -deɪ $ -ər-/ ●●● S2 W2 *n* [C,U] (*written abbreviation* **Sat.**) the day between Friday and Sunday: **on Saturday** *We went for a picnic on Saturday.* | *The festivities begin Saturday. AmE* | **Saturday morning/afternoon etc** *They arrived in Paris on Saturday evening.* | **last Saturday** *I saw Sally last Saturday at the mall.* | **this Saturday** *What are you doing this Saturday?* | **next Saturday** (=Saturday of next week) *Ask her yourself next Saturday.* | **a Saturday** (=one of the Saturdays in the year) *It was a crazy idea to go to the store on a Saturday.*

Sat·urn /ˈsætən $ -ərn/ *n* the PLANET that is sixth in order from the Sun and is surrounded by large rings

sat·ur·na·li·a /ˌsætəˈneɪliə $ -tər-/ *n* [C] *literary* an occasion when people enjoy themselves in a very wild and uncontrolled way

S

sat·ur·nine /ˈsætənaɪn $ -ər-/ *adj literary* looking sad and serious, especially in a threatening way: *his lean saturnine face*

sat·yr /ˈsætə $ -ər/ *n* [C] *literary* a god in ancient Greek stories, represented as half human and half goat

sauce /sɔːs $ sɒːs/ ●●● S3 *n*
1 [C,U] a thick cooked liquid that is served with food to give it a particular taste: **tomato/cheese/wine etc sauce** *vanilla ice cream with chocolate sauce | spaghetti sauces*
2 [U] *BrE old-fashioned* rude remarks made to someone that you should respect: *Less of your sauce, my girl!*
3 what's sauce for the goose is sauce for the gander used to say that if one person is treated in a particular way, other people should be treated in the same way

ˈ**sauce boat** *n* [C] *BrE* a container that has a handle and is shaped like a boat, used for serving sauce with a meal

sauce·pan /ˈsɔːspən $ ˈsɒːspæn/ ●●○ *n* [C] a deep round metal container with a handle that is used for cooking SYN **pan**: *Heat the oil and garlic in a large saucepan.* → see picture at PAN[1]

sau·cer /ˈsɔːsə $ ˈsɒːsər/ ●●○ *n* [C] a small round plate that curves up at the edges, that you put a cup on: *a china cup and saucer* → FLYING SAUCER → see picture at CUP

sauc·y /ˈsɔːsi $ ˈsɒːsi/ *adj old-fashioned* saucy jokes, remarks etc are about sex in a way that is amusing but not shocking: *saucy postcards* —**saucily** *adv* —**sauciness** *n* [U]

sau·er·kraut /ˈsaʊəkraʊt $ -ər-/ *n* [U] a German food made from CABBAGE (=a round green vegetable) that has been left in salt so that it tastes sour

sau·na /ˈsɔːnə $ ˈsɒːnə, ˈsaʊnə/ *n* [C] **1** a room that is heated to a very high temperature by hot air, where people sit because it is considered healthy **2** a period of time when you sit or lie in a room like this: **have/take a sauna** *I have a sauna and massage every week.*

saun·ter /ˈsɔːntə $ ˈsɒːntər/ *v* [I always + adv/prep] to walk in a slow relaxed way, especially so that you look confident or proud → **stroll**: **[+along/around/in etc]** *He came sauntering down the road with his hands in his pockets.* —**saunter** *n* [singular]

saus·age /ˈsɒsɪdʒ $ ˈsɒː-/ ●●● S3 *n* [C,U]
1 a small tube of skin filled with a mixture of meat, spices etc, eaten hot or cold after it has been cooked: *pork sausages*
2 not a sausage! *BrE old-fashioned informal* nothing at all: *'Have you heard from Tom yet?' 'No, not a sausage!'*

ˈ**sausage dog** *n* [C] *BrE informal* a DACHSHUND

ˈ**sausage meat** *n* [U] the soft meat mixture that is used to make sausages

ˌ**sausage** ˈ**roll** *n* [C] *BrE* a piece of sausage meat surrounded by PASTRY

sau·té /ˈsəʊteɪ $ soʊˈteɪ/ *v* [T] to cook something in a little hot oil or fat → **fry**: *Sauté the onions for 5 minutes.* THESAURUS COOK —**sauté** *adj BrE*: *sauté potatoes*

sav·age[1] /ˈsævɪdʒ/ ●○○ *adj*
1 VIOLENT very violent or cruel SYN **vicious**: *a savage dog | a savage murder* THESAURUS VIOLENT
2 CRITICIZING criticizing someone or something very severely OPP **mild**: *a savage attack on the government*
3 SEVERE very severe: *The government has announced savage cuts in spending. | a savage storm*
4 PEOPLE [only before noun] *old-fashioned not polite* an offensive word used to describe people who have a simple traditional way of life → **primitive**: *a savage tribe* —**savagely** *adv*: *He was savagely attacked and beaten.* —**savageness** *n* [U]

savage[2] *n* [C] *old-fashioned not polite* a very offensive word for someone who has a simple traditional way of life

savage[3] *v* [T] **1** if an animal such as a dog savages someone, it attacks them and injures them badly SYN **maul** **2** to criticize someone or something very severely SYN **attack**: *The prime minister was savaged by the press for failing to take action quickly enough.*

sav·ag·e·ry /ˈsævɪdʒəri/ *n* (*plural* **savageries**) [C,U] extremely cruel and violent behaviour: *Local people were shocked by the savagery of the attack.*

sa·van·na, **savannah** /səˈvænə/ *n* [C,U] a large flat area of grassy land, especially in Africa

sav·ant /ˈsævənt $ səˈvɑːnt, sæ-/ *n* [C] *formal* **1** someone who knows a lot about a subject **2** someone who has mental problems and may have lower intelligence than average, but who can do one thing very well, such as adding numbers very quickly

save[1] /seɪv/ ●●● S1 W1 *v*
1 FROM HARM/DANGER [T] to make someone or something safe from danger, harm, or destruction → **rescue**: *Emergency aid could save millions threatened with starvation. | a new treatment that could* **save** *his* **life** *| She was determined to save her marriage. | the campaign to save the rain forests* | **save sb/sth from sth** *He saved the child from drowning.* THESAURUS PROTECT, RESCUE
2 MONEY [I,T] (*also* **save up**) to keep money in a bank so that you can use it later, especially when you gradually add more money over a period of time: *He managed to save enough to buy a small house. | So far, I've saved about £500.* | **[+for]** *I'm saving up for a new car.* → SAVER
3 NOT WASTE [T] (*also* **save on sth**) to use less money, time, energy etc so that you do not waste any OPP **waste**: *We'll save a lot of time if we go by car. | Everyone is being encouraged to save energy. | ways to save money on heating bills* | **energy-saving/time-saving etc** *money-saving ideas*
4 TO USE LATER [T] to keep something so that you can use or enjoy it in the future: *We'll save the rest of the food and have it later.* | **save sth for sth** *I had a bottle of champagne which I'd been saving for a special occasion.*
5 COLLECT [T] (*also* **save sth ↔ up**) to keep all the objects of a particular kind that you can find, so that you can use them: *I'm saving up vouchers to get a cheap air ticket to the States.*
6 HELP TO AVOID [T] to help someone by making it unnecessary for them to do something that they do not want to do: *If you lent me £5, it would save me a trip to the bank.* | **save sb doing sth** *I'll take the shopping home in the car to save you carrying it.* | **save sb the trouble/bother (of doing sth)** *I'll get a taxi from the station to save you the trouble of coming to collect me.*
7 KEEP FOR SB [T] to stop people from using something so that it is available for someone else: *Will you save me a seat?* | **save sth for sb** *We'll save some dinner for you if you're late.*
8 COMPUTER [I,T] to make a computer keep the work that you have done on it: *Don't forget to save before you close the file. | Did you save the changes that you made?*
9 SPORT [I,T] to stop the other team from scoring in a game such as football: *The goalkeeper just managed to save the shot.* → see picture at FOOTBALL
10 you saved my life *spoken* used to thank someone who has helped you out of a difficult situation or solved a problem for you: *Thanks again for the loan – you really saved my life.*
11 save sb's skin/neck/bacon *informal* to help someone to escape from an extremely difficult or dangerous situation: *He lied in court to save his own skin.*
12 save the day to stop things from going badly and make a situation end successfully: *A local businessman saved the day by donating £30,000 to the school.*
13 save face to do something that will stop you from looking stupid or feeling embarrassed: *A compromise must be found which will allow both sides in the dispute to save face.* → FACE-SAVING
14 saving grace the one good thing that makes someone or something acceptable: *His sense of humour was his only saving grace.*
15 sb can't do sth to save his/her life *informal* to be completely unable to do something: *He couldn't draw to save his life!*
16 save your breath *spoken* used to tell someone that it is not worth saying anything, because nothing they say will make any difference to the situation: *I tried to explain, but she told me to save my breath.*
17 save sb from themselves to prevent someone from doing

something that they want to do but that you think is harmful

18 RELIGION [I,T] in the Christian church, to free someone from the power of evil and bring them into the Christian religion: *Jesus came to save sinners.*

save² *n* [C] an action in which a player in a game such as football prevents the other team from scoring: *Martin* ***made*** *a brilliant* ***save*** *from Nichol's shot.*

save³ (*also* **'save for**) *prep formal* except: *She answered all the questions save one.* | **save that** *Little is known about his early life, save that he had a brother.* **THESAURUS** EXCEPT

sav·er /ˈseɪvə $ -ər/ *n* [C] someone who saves money in a bank: *Mutual funds have been attractive to* ***small savers*** (=people who save small amounts of money).

Sav·ile Row /ˌsævəl ˈrəʊ◂ $ -ˈroʊ/ a street in London, known for having many expensive clothes shops for men which sell traditional, often hand-made, suits: *a Savile Row suit*

sav·ing /ˈseɪvɪŋ/ ●●○ S3 W3 *n*

1 savings [plural] all the money that you have saved, especially in a bank: *Buying a house had taken all their savings.*

2 [C] an amount of money that you have not spent, or an amount of something that you have not used: *The new engines will lead to savings in fuel.* | **[+of]** *This represents a saving of £60,000.* | *All small companies will need to* ***make savings*** *if they are to survive.*

3 [U] when you save money rather than spend it → SAVE¹(2)

ˈsavings acˌcount *n* [C] a bank account in which you keep money that you want to save for a period of time, and which pays you INTEREST on the money you have in it → **checking account**, **current account**

ˌsavings and ˈloan association *n* [C] *AmE* a business, similar to a bank, that lends money, and into which you pay money that you want to save SYN **building society** *BrE*

ˈsavings bank *n* [C] a bank where people can save small amounts of money and receive INTEREST on it

ˈsavings bond *n* [C] *technical* a BOND that is sold by the US government and that cannot be sold from one person to another

sa·viour *BrE*, **savior** *AmE* /ˈseɪvjə $ -ər/ *n* [C] someone who saves you from a difficult or dangerous situation: **[+of]** *He was seen by many as the saviour of the organization.*

Saviour *BrE*, **Savior** *AmE* *n* **the/sb's Saviour** Jesus Christ – used by Christians

ˈsaviour ˌsibling *n* [C] a child that is born so that cells from its body can be used to treat a sick brother or sister

sav·oir-faire /ˌsævwɑː ˈfeə $ -wɑːr ˈfer/ *n* [U] *formal* the ability to do and say the right things in social situations

sa·vor /ˈseɪvə $ -ər/ *v, n* the American spelling of SAVOUR

sa·vo·ry¹ /ˈseɪvəri/ *adj* the American spelling of SAVOURY

savory² *n* [U] a plant that is used in cooking to add taste to meat and other food

sa·vour¹ *BrE*, **savor** *AmE* /ˈseɪvə $ -ər/ *v* [T] **1** to fully enjoy the taste or smell of something: *She sipped her wine, savouring every drop.* **2** to fully enjoy a time or experience: *She savoured her few hours of freedom.* | *He hesitated, savouring the moment.*

savour of sth *phr v formal* to seem to involve something bad or to have some of a bad quality: *We must avoid anything that savours of corruption.*

savour² *BrE*, **savor** *AmE* *n* [singular, U] *formal* **1** a pleasant taste or smell: *the sweet savour of wood smoke* **2** interest and enjoyment: *Life seemed to have* ***lost its savour*** *for him.*

sa·vour·y¹ *BrE*, **savory** *AmE* /ˈseɪvəri/ *adj* **1** *BrE* savoury food tastes of salt OPP **sweet**: *savoury party snacks* | *pancakes with sweet and savoury fillings* **2** a savoury smell or taste is strong and pleasant but is not sweet **3 not very savoury/none too savoury** unpleasant or morally unacceptable → **unsavoury**: *Some of the customers in the pub looked none too savoury.*

savoury² *n* (*plural* **savouries**) [C] *BrE* a small piece of food with a salty taste that is served at a party: *plates of cakes and savouries*

sav·vy¹ /ˈsævi/ *n* [U] *informal* practical knowledge and ability SYN **know-how**: *He's obviously got a lot of political savvy.*

savvy² *adj AmE informal* someone who is savvy is clever and knows how to deal with situations successfully: *savvy consumers*

saw¹ /sɔː $ sɒː/ *v* the past tense of SEE

saw² ●●○ *n* [C]

1 a tool that you use for cutting wood. It has a flat blade with an edge cut into many V shapes.

2 a short familiar phrase or sentence that is considered to contain some truth about life SYN **proverb**, **saying**: *That reminds me of the* ***old saw*** *about being careful about what you wish for.*

saw³ ●●○ *v* (*past tense* **sawed**, *past participle* **sawn** /sɔːn $ sɒːn/ *or* **sawed** *AmE*) [I,T] to cut something using a saw: *She was in the backyard sawing logs.* | **[+through]** *He sawed through a power cable by mistake.* **THESAURUS** CUT

saw at sth *phr v* to cut something with a repeated backwards and forwards movement: *He sawed at the loaf with a blunt knife.*

saw sth ↔ **off** *phr v* to remove something by cutting it off with a saw: *We sawed off the dead branches.*

saw sth ↔ **up** *phr v* to cut something into many pieces, using a saw: *The tree was cut down and sawn up for logs.*

saw·buck /ˈsɔːbʌk $ ˈsɒː-/ *n* [C] *AmE old-fashioned informal* a piece of paper money worth $10

saw·dust /ˈsɔːdʌst $ ˈsɒː-/ *n* [U] very small pieces of wood that are left when you have been cutting wood

saw·mill /ˈsɔːmɪl $ ˈsɒː-/ *n* [C] a factory where trees are cut into flat pieces that can be used as wood

ˌsawn-off ˈshotgun *BrE*, **ˌsawed-off ˈshotgun** *AmE* *n* [C] a SHOTGUN whose BARREL (=long thin tube) has been cut short so that it is easier to hide

Sax·on /ˈsæksən/ *n* [C] a member of the race of people from northern Europe that came to live in England in the 5th century —**Saxon** *adj*

sax·o·phone /ˈsæksəfəʊn $ -foʊn/ (*also* **sax** /sæks/ *informal*) *n* [C] a curved musical instrument made of metal that you play by blowing into it and pressing buttons, used especially in popular music and JAZZ → see picture at **WOODWIND**

sax·oph·o·nist /sækˈsɒfənɪst $ ˈsæksəfoʊnɪst/ *n* [C] someone who plays the saxophone

say¹ /seɪ/ ●●● S1 W1 *v* (*past tense and past participle* **said** /sed/, *third person singular* **says** /sez/)

1 EXPRESS STH IN WORDS [I only in negatives, T] to express an idea, feeling, thought etc using words: *'I'm so tired,' she said.* | *'Don't cry,' he said softly.* | *Don't believe anything he says.* | **say (that)** *A spokesman said that the company had improved its safety standards.* | *I always said I would buy a motorbike when I had enough money.* | **say how/why/who etc** *Did she say what happened?* | *I would like to say how much we appreciate your hard work.* | *'Why did she leave?' 'I don't know – she* ***didn't say****.'* | **say sth to sb** *What did you say to her?* | *'This is strange,' he said to himself.* | **a terrible/silly/strange etc thing to say** *What a silly thing to say!* | **say hello/goodbye/thank you etc** (=say something to greet someone, thank someone etc) *She left without saying goodbye.* | **say you're sorry** (=apologize) *I've said I'm sorry – what more do you want?* | **say yes/no (to sth)** (=agree or refuse) *Can I go, Mum? Oh, please say yes!* | **say nothing/anything/something (about sth)** *He looked as if he was going to say something.* | *I wished I had said nothing about Jordi.* | **have anything/nothing/something to say** *Does anyone else have anything to say?* | *Although he didn't* ***say so****, it was clear that he was in pain.* | ***What makes you say that*** (=why do you think that)? | **say to do sth** (=tell someone to do something) *Nina said to meet her at 4.30.* | *I'd like to* ***say a few***

S

words (=make a short speech). | *'So what are your plans now?' **'I'd rather not say.'*** → see Thesaurus box on p. 1617

REGISTER
In written English, people often avoid using **say** when referring to opinions or ideas expressed by another writer. Instead, they prefer to use a more formal verb such as **argue**, **assert**, **claim**, or **maintain**.

2 GIVE INFORMATION [T] to give information in the form of written words, numbers, or pictures – used about signs, clocks, letters, messages etc: *The sign said 'Back in 10 minutes.'* | *The clock said twenty past three.* | **say (that)** *He received a letter saying that the appointment had been cancelled.* | **say to do sth** (=give information about what you should do) *The label says to take one tablet before meals.* | **say who/what/how etc** *The card doesn't even say who sent the flowers.* | ***It says here** they have live music.*
3 MEAN [T] used to talk about what someone means: *What do you think the writer is **trying to say** in this passage?* | *So what you're saying is, there's none left.* | **be saying (that)** *Are you saying I'm fat?* | *I'm not saying it's a bad idea.* | ***All I'm saying is** that it might be better to wait a while.* GRAMMAR **Say** is usually used in the progressive in this meaning.
4 THINK THAT STH IS TRUE [T] used to talk about something that people think is true: **they say/people say/it is said (that)** *They say that she has been all over the world.* | *It is said that he was a spy during the war.* | **sb is said to be sth/do sth** *He's said to be the richest man in the world.* | *Well, **you know what they say** – blood's thicker than water.* | *The rest, **as they say**, is history.*
5 SHOW/BE A SIGN OF STH [T] **a)** to show clearly that something is true about someone or something's character: *The kind of car you drive says what kind of person you are.* | *The fact that she never apologized **says a lot about*** (=shows very clearly) *what kind of person she is.* | ***It said a lot for** the manager* (=it showed that he is good) *that the team remained confident despite losing.* | *These results **don't say much for** the quality of teaching* (=they show that it is not very good). **b)** to show what someone is really feeling or thinking, especially without using words: *The look on her face said 'I love you.'* | **sth says everything/says it all** *His expression said it all.*
6 SPEAK THE WORDS OF STH [T] to speak the words that are written in a play, poem, or prayer: *Can you say that line again, this time with more feeling?* | *I'll **say a prayer for** you.*
7 PRONOUNCE [T] to pronounce a word or sound: ***How do you say** your last name?*
8 SUGGEST/SUPPOSE STH [T] used when suggesting or supposing that something might happen or be true: **... say ...** *If we put out, say, twenty chairs, would that be enough?* | **let's say (that)/just say (that)** *Let's say your plan fails, then what?* | *Just say you won the lottery – what would you do?* GRAMMAR **Say** is usually used in the imperative or with **let's** in this meaning.
9 say to yourself to try to persuade yourself that something is true or not true: *I kept saying to myself that this wasn't really happening.*

SPOKEN PHRASES
10 I must say (*also* **I have to say**) used to emphasize what you are saying: *The cake does look good, I must say.* | *I have to say I was impressed.*
11 I can't say (that) used to say that you do not think or feel something: *I can't say I envy her being married to him!*
12 I would say used for giving your opinion even though other people may not agree: *I'd say he was jealous.*
13 I couldn't say used when you do not know the answer to something: *I couldn't say who will win.*
14 if I may say so (*also* **if I might say so**) *formal* used to be polite when saying something that may embarrass or offend the person you are talking to: *That's just the point, Mr Glover, if I may say so.*
15 having said that used to say that something is true in spite of what you have just said: *The diet can make you slim without exercise. Having said that, however, exercise is important too.*
16 wouldn't you say? used to ask someone whether they agree with the statement you have just made: *It seems very unlikely, wouldn't you say?*
17 what do you say? used to ask someone if they agree with a suggestion: *We could go into partnership – what do you say?* | ***What do you say we** all go to a movie?* | ***What would you say to** a meal out?*
18 say no more used to say that you understand what someone means, although they have not said it directly: *'I saw him leaving her house at 6.30 this morning.' 'Say no more!'*
19 you can say that again! used to say that you completely agree with someone: *'It's cold in here.' 'You can say that again!'*
20 you said it! a) used when someone says something that you agree with, although you would not have actually said it yourself because it is not polite: *'I was always stubborn as a kid.' 'You said it!'* **b)** *especially AmE* used to say that you agree with someone: *'Let's go home.' 'You said it! I'm tired.'*
21 who says? used to say that you do not agree with a statement, opinion etc: *Who says museum work doesn't pay?*
22 who can say? (*also* **who's to say?**) used to say that nobody can know something: *Who can say what will happen between now and then?* | *Many women believe that skin cream makes their skin look younger, and who's to say that they're wrong?*
23 you don't say! used to show you are surprised by what someone has told you – also often used when you are not at all surprised by what someone has told you
24 say when used to ask someone to tell you when to stop pouring them a drink or serving them food because they have got enough
25 say cheese used to tell people to smile when you are taking their photograph
26 (just) say the word used to tell someone that they have only to ask and you will do what they want: *Anywhere you want to go, just say the word.*
27 I'll say this/that (much) for sb used when you want to mention something good about someone, especially when you have been criticizing them: *I will say this for Tom – at least he's consistent.* | *You've got determination – I'll say that for you.*
28 say what you like *especially BrE* used when giving an opinion that you are sure is correct, even if the person you are talking to might disagree with you: *Say what you like about him, he's a very good writer.*
29 anything/whatever you say used to tell someone that you agree to do what they want, accept their opinion etc, especially because you do not want an argument
30 can't say fairer than that *BrE* used to say that you have made the best offer that you can: *If I win, I'll buy you a drink. Can't say fairer than that.*
31 I wouldn't say no (to sth) used to say that you would like something: *I wouldn't say no to a coffee.*
32 I'll say! used to say yes to a question, in a strong way: *'Was there a big argument?' 'I'll say!'*
33 let's just say used when you do not want to give a lot of details about something: *Let's just say she wasn't very pleased about it.*
34 shall I/we say used when you are not quite sure how to describe someone or something: *He is, shall we say, slightly unusual.*
35 what have you got to say for yourself? used to ask someone for an explanation when they have done something wrong
36 say what? *informal especially AmE* used when you did not hear what someone said or when you cannot believe that something is true
37 I say *BrE old-fashioned* **a)** used to get someone's attention: *I say, don't I know you?* **b)** used before giving your reaction to something: *'My husband's broken his leg.' 'I say! I'm sorry to hear that.'*

38 say sth to sb's face *informal* to criticize someone or say something unpleasant directly to them instead of saying it to someone else: *I knew they wanted me to leave, even though they wouldn't say it to my face.*

39 that's not saying much used to say that it is not surprising that someone or something is better than another person or thing because the other person or thing is so bad: *This version is better than the original, but that's not saying much.*
40 to say the least used to say that you could have described something, criticized someone etc a lot more severely than you have: *Jane could have been more considerate, to say the least.*
41 that is to say used before giving more details or being more exact about something: *They, that's to say Matt and John, were arguing about what to do.*
42 that is not to say used to make sure the person you are talking to does not think something that is not true: *I'm quite happy in my job but that's not to say I'm going to do it for the rest of my life.*
43 not to say *especially BrE* used when adding a stronger description of something: *The information is inadequate, not to say misleading.*
44 a lot/something/not much etc to be said for (doing) sth used to say that there are a lot of or not many advantages to something: *There's a lot to be said for taking a few days off now and then.* | *It was a town with very little to be said for it.*
45 to say nothing of sth used to mention another thing involved in what you have just been talking about: *It wasn't much for three years' work, to say nothing of the money it had cost.*
46 have something to say about sth to be angry about something: *Her father would have something to say about it.*
47 have a lot to say for yourself to talk a lot
48 not have much to say for yourself to not talk very much
49 what sb says goes used to emphasize who is in control in a situation: *My wife wants to go to Italy this year, and what she says goes!*
50 say your piece to give your opinion about something, especially something you do not like → **wouldn't say boo to a goose** at BOO²(3), → **easier said than done** at EASY²(4), → **enough said** at ENOUGH²(6), → **it goes without saying** at GO WITHOUT, → **needless to say** at NEEDLESS(1), → **no sooner said than done** at SOON(9), → **not say/breathe a word** at WORD¹(10), → **well said** at WELL¹(13), → **when all's said and done** at ALL¹(17)

GRAMMAR: Comparison

say

- You **say** something **to** someone: *The principal said a few words to us.* ✗ Don't say: *say someone something*
- You use **say** with speech marks ('...') when quoting the exact words that someone used: *'I'm sorry I'm late,' she said.* | *Joe said: 'I'll be back soon.'*
- You use **say (that)** when reporting what someone said: *She said that she **was** sorry she **was** late.* | *Joe said he **would** be back soon.* After **said**, the verb in the other clause is usually also in the past tense.

tell

- You **tell** someone something: *Diane told me the news.* | *He told us a long story.* ✗ Don't say: *tell something to someone*
- You **tell** someone **about** something that has happened: *She told me about the accident.* ✗ Don't say: *He told about the accident.*
- You use **tell** someone **(that)** when reporting what someone said: *I told them that I **was** sorry.* | *The teacher told me I **could** go home.* After **told**, the verb in the other clause is usually also in the past tense. ✗ Don't say: *He told that he was sorry.*

GRAMMAR GUIDE ▸ VERBS

say² ●●○ *n* [singular, U]
1 the right to take part in deciding something: **have some/no/little say in sth** *The workers had no say in how the factory was run.* | *The chairman **has the final say*** (=has the right to make the final decision about something).
2 have your say to have the opportunity to give your opinion about something: *You'll get a chance to have your*

S

THESAURUS: say

TO SAY SOMETHING

say to tell someone something, using words: *'I really ought to go,' she said.* | *Lauren said she'd probably be late.*
state to say something, especially in a definite or formal way – used in official contexts: *The witness stated that he had never seen the woman before.* | *Please state your name and address.*
announce to publicly tell people about something: *The chairman announced his resignation.* | *The results will be announced tomorrow.*
declare to say something very firmly: *'My personal life is none of your business,' she declared.*
mention to talk about someone or something, especially without giving many details: *Did Tom mention anything about what happened at school?* | *Your name was mentioned!*
express to let someone know your feelings by putting them into words: *Young children often find it difficult to express their emotions.*
comment to say what your opinion is about someone or something: *The prime minister was asked to comment on the crisis.*
note/remark *formal* to say that you have noticed that something is true – used especially in formal writing: *We have already noted that most old people live alone.* | *Someone once remarked that the problem with computers is that they only give you answers.*
add to say something more, after what has already been said: *He added that he thought it could be done fairly cheaply.*
point out to mention something that seems particularly important or relevant: *Dr Graham points out that most children show some signs of abnormal behaviour.* | *It's worth pointing out that few people actually die of this disease.*
air to talk about your opinions, worries, or the things you disagree about: **air your views/grievances/differences**: *The programme will give listeners the chance to air their views about immigration.* | *Workers were able to air their grievances.*

DIFFERENT WAYS OF SAYING SOMETHING

whisper to say something very quietly, using your breath rather than your full voice: *'Don't wake the baby,' Jenny whispered.*
mumble to say something quietly without pronouncing the words clearly: *He mumbled his thanks.*
mutter to say something quietly, especially when you are annoyed but do not want someone to hear you complaining: *'This is ridiculous,' he muttered under his breath.*
murmur to say something in a soft slow gentle voice: *She stroked his hair and murmured, 'Don't worry. You'll be all right.'*
growl to say something in a low angry voice: *'As I was saying,' Lewis growled, 'it needs to be finished today.'*
snarl to say something in a nasty angry way: *'Get out of my way!' he snarled.*
exclaim to say something suddenly and loudly: *'How beautiful!' she exclaimed.*
blurt out to suddenly say something without thinking, especially something embarrassing or secret: *It was partly nervousness that had made him blurt out the question.*
stammer/stutter to speak with a lot of pauses and repeated sounds, because you have a speech problem, or because you are nervous or excited: *'I'll, I'll only be a m-moment,' he stammered.*

say. | **[+in/on]** *Parents can have their say in the decision-making process.*

say³ *interjection AmE informal* used to express surprise, or to get someone's attention so that you can tell them something: *Say, haven't I seen you before somewhere?*

say·ing /ˈseɪ-ɪŋ/ ●●○ *n* [C] a well-known short statement that expresses an idea most people believe is true and wise SYN **proverb**: *You can't judge a book by its cover, as the old saying goes.* **THESAURUS** ▸ PHRASE

ˈsay-so *n informal* **1 sb's say-so** someone's permission to do something: *You can't leave the hospital without the say-so of the doctor.* **2 on sb's say-so** based on someone's personal statement without any proof: *She's hired a number of people on my say-so.*

S-bend /ˈes bend/ *n* [C] *BrE* **1** a bend in a road in the shape of an 'S' that can be dangerous to drivers SYN **S-curve** *AmE* **2** a bend in a waste pipe in the shape of an 'S'

scab /skæb/ *n* [C] **1** a hard layer of dried blood that forms over a cut or wound while it is getting better **2** an insulting word for someone who works while the other people in the same factory, office etc are on STRIKE

scab·bard /ˈskæbəd $ -ərd/ *n* [C] a metal or leather cover for the blade of a sword

scab·by /ˈskæbi/ *adj* scabby skin is covered with scabs

sca·bies /ˈskeɪbiz/ *n* [U] a skin disease caused by MITES (=small creatures like insects)

sca·brous /ˈskeɪbrəs, ˈskæb- $ ˈskæb-/ *adj literary* **1** rude or shocking, especially in a sexual way **2** scabrous skin is rough, not soft

scads /skædz/ *n informal* **scads of sth** large numbers or quantities of something: *They got scads of calls from reporters.*

scaf·fold /ˈskæfəld, -fəʊld $ -fəld, -foʊld/ *n* [C] **1** a structure built next to a wall, for workers to stand on while they build, repair, or paint a building **2** a raised structure which was used in the past as a place to kill criminals by hanging them or cutting off their heads **3** *AmE* a structure that can be moved up and down to help people work on high buildings SYN **cradle** *BrE*

scaf·fold·ing /ˈskæfəldɪŋ/ *n* [U] a set of poles and boards that are built into a structure for workers to stand on when they are working on the outside of a building

scag /skæg/ *n* [U] *informal* another spelling of SKAG

scal·a·bil·i·ty /ˌskeɪləˈbɪləti/ *n* [U] *technical* the degree to which a computer system is able to grow and become more powerful as the number of people using it increases

scal·a·ble /ˈskeɪləbəl/ *adj technical* if a piece of computer HARDWARE or software is scalable, it continues to work well even if it is made bigger or connected to a larger number of other pieces of equipment

scal·a·wag /ˈskæləwæg/ *n* [C] *AmE* a SCALLYWAG

scald¹ /skɔːld $ skɒːld/ *v* [T] to burn your skin with hot liquid or steam: *Don't scald yourself with that kettle!* **THESAURUS** ▸ BURN

scald² *n* [C] a burn on your skin caused by hot liquid or steam

scald·ing /ˈskɔːldɪŋ $ ˈskɒːl-/ *adj* **1** (*also* **scalding hot**) extremely hot: *a bowl of scalding water* | *a cup of scalding hot tea* **2** *literary* scalding tears feel hot on your skin: *Scalding tears poured down her face.*

scale¹ /skeɪl/ ●●● S2 W2 *n*

1 SIZE/LEVEL [singular, U] the size or level of something, or the amount that something is happening: **[+of]** *We had underestimated the scale of the problem.* | **on a large/small/grand etc scale** *There has been housing development on a massive scale since 1980.* | *Most alternative technologies work best on a small scale.* | *A structural survey revealed the* ***full scale*** *of the damage.* | *I was shocked by the* ***sheer scale*** (=very big scale) *of the destruction.* | **on a global/international/world scale** *Pollution could cause changes to weather patterns on a global scale.* | *Large firms benefit from* ***economies of scale*** (=ways of saving money because they are big).

2 RANGE [C usually singular] a whole range of different types of people or things, from the lowest level to the highest: *Some rural schools have 50 pupils, while* ***at the other end of the scale*** *are city schools with nearly 5,000 pupils.* | **up/down the scale** *She gradually made her way up* ***the social scale***. | *animals which are lower down* ***the evolutionary scale*** (=the range of animals that have developed gradually over a long time)

3 FOR WEIGHING **scales** [plural] *BrE*, **scale** [C] *AmE* a machine for weighing people or objects: *a set of kitchen scales* | *some new* ***bathroom scales*** (=scales that you use to weigh yourself) → **tip the balance/scales** at TIP²(6), → see picture at MEASURE¹

4 MEASURING SYSTEM [C] a system of numbers that is used for measuring the amount, speed, quality etc of something: **on a scale** *The earthquakes measured 7 on the Richter scale.* | *changes to the company's* ***pay scale*** | *Your performance will be judged* ***on a scale of*** *1* ***to*** *10.* | *We use a* ***sliding scale*** (=in which prices are not firmly fixed) *for charges.*

5 MEASURING MARKS [C] a set of marks with regular spaces between them on a tool that is used for measuring, or on the side of a mathematical drawing: *a ruler with a metric scale*

6 MAP/MODEL [C,U] the relationship between the size of a map, drawing, or model and the actual size of the place or thing that it represents: *a map with a scale of 1:250,000* | **to scale** *All our models are made to scale.* | **scale model/drawing etc** (=one done using a strict scale) *a scale drawing of the Eiffel Tower*

7 MUSIC [C] a series of musical notes that become higher or lower, with fixed distances between each note: *the scale of G major*

8 FISH [C usually plural] one of the small flat pieces of skin that cover the bodies of fish, snakes etc

9 TEETH [U] *BrE* a white substance that forms on your teeth

10 WATER PIPES [U] a white substance that forms around the inside of hot water pipes or containers in which water is boiled

11 the scales fell from sb's eyes *literary* used to say that someone suddenly realized something important → FULL-SCALE

scale² *v* **1** [T] to climb to the top of something that is high and difficult to climb: *Rescuers had to scale a 300-metre cliff to reach the injured climber.* **2 scale the heights** to be extremely successful: *By the age of 21, he had already scaled the heights in the academic world.* **3** [T] *technical* to make writing or a picture the right size for a particular purpose: **scale sth to sth** *The writing can be scaled to any size, depending on the paper.* **4** [I] if something will scale, it will continue to work well even if it is made bigger or comes to include more things: *Will this way of networking scale?*

scale *sth* ↔ **down/back** *phr v* to reduce the amount or size of something → **decrease**: *The emergency aid programme has now been scaled down.*

scale *sth* ↔ **up** *phr v* to increase the amount or size of something: *Production at the factory is being scaled up.*

sca·lene tri·an·gle /ˌskeɪliːn ˈtraɪæŋgəl/ *n* [C] *technical* a TRIANGLE whose sides are each a different length

scal·lion /ˈskæljən/ *n* [C] *AmE* a type of young onion with a small round end and a long green stem SYN **spring onion** *BrE*

scal·lop /ˈskɒləp, ˈskæ- $ ˈskɑː-/ *n* [C] **1** a small sea creature that you can eat, with a flat round shell made of two parts that fit together **2** [usually plural] one of a row of small curves that are used to decorate the edge of clothes, curtains etc

scal·loped /ˈskɒləpt, ˈskæ- $ ˈskɑː-/ *adj* **1** if the edge of something is scalloped, it is made into a row of small curves **2** scalloped potatoes, corn etc have been baked in a cream or cheese sauce

scal·ly /ˈskæli/ *n* (*plural* **scallies**) [C] *BrE spoken* someone

S

who causes trouble – often used humorously SYN **scallywag**: *You rude **little scally**!* —**scally** *adj* [only before noun]: *just some little scally kid*

scal·ly·wag /ˈskæliwæɡ/ *especially BrE* (*also* **scalawag** *AmE*) *n* [C] *old-fashioned* a child who causes trouble but not in a serious way – used when you are not angry with them SYN **rascal**

scalp[1] /skælp/ *n* [C] **1** the skin on the top of your head: *Massage the shampoo gently into your hair and scalp.* **2 sb's scalp** *informal* if you want someone's scalp, you want them to be completely defeated: *The board members were after the chairman's scalp.*

scalp[2] *v* [T] **1** *AmE informal* to buy tickets for an event and sell them again at a much higher price SYN **tout** *BrE* **2** to cut the hair and skin off the head of a dead enemy as a sign of victory

scal·pel /ˈskælpəl/ *n* [C] a small, very sharp knife that is used by doctors in operations → see picture at KNIFE[1]

scal·per /ˈskælpə $ -ər/ *n* [C] *AmE* someone who makes money by buying tickets for an event and selling them again at a very high price SYN **tout** *BrE*

scal·y /ˈskeɪli/ *adj* **1** a scaly animal or fish is covered with small flat pieces of hard skin **2** scaly skin is dry and rough

scam[1] /skæm/ *n* [C] *informal* a clever but dishonest way to get money: *He got involved in a credit card scam.*

scam[2] *v* [T] *informal* to deceive someone in order to get money from them —**scammer** *n* [C]

scamp /skæmp/ *n* [C] *old-fashioned* a child who has fun by tricking people

scam·per /ˈskæmpə $ -ər/ *v* [I always + adv/prep] to run with quick short steps, like a child or small animal

scam·pi /ˈskæmpi/ *n* [plural, U] *BrE* large PRAWNS (=sea creatures) that are covered in BREADCRUMBS and cooked in hot oil

scan[1] /skæn/ ●●○ *v* (**scanned**, **scanning**)
1 LOOK AT [T] to examine an area carefully but quickly, often because you are looking for a particular person or thing: *He scanned the horizon, but there was no sign of the ship.* | *She scanned his face, looking for signs of what he was thinking.* | *Video cameras scanned the car park.* | **scan sth for sth** *I scanned the street for people I knew.*
2 READ [I,T] (*also* **scan through**) to read something quickly SYN **skim**: **scan sth for sth** *I scanned the page for her name.* | *She scanned through the paper.*
3 SEE INSIDE [T] if a machine scans something, it passes an electrical beam over it to form a picture of what is inside it → **scanner**: *All luggage has to be scanned at the airport.* | *They scanned his brain for signs of damage.*
4 COMPUTER [T] if you scan a document or picture, you put it into a machine attached to a computer so that the information in the document can be taken into the computer and stored there → **scanner**: **scan sth into sth** *You scan the text into the computer, then edit it.*
5 POETRY [I] *technical* poetry that scans has a correct regular pattern of beats

scan[2] ●●○ *n*
1 [C] a medical test in which a special machine produces a picture of something inside your body: *The scan showed that she was expecting twins.* | *a brain scan*
2 [singular] when you read something quickly: **[+of]** *a quick scan of the newspapers*

scan·dal /ˈskændl/ ●●○ *n*
1 [C] an event in which someone, especially someone important, behaves in a bad way that shocks people: *It **caused** quite **a scandal** when he left his wife.* | *The college has recently been **involved in a** drugs **scandal**.* | *He has been **at the centre of** a political **scandal**.* | *a **major scandal** involving the government* | *a series of **financial scandals*** | *a **sex scandal** that ruined his reputation* | *They had already left the country when the **scandal broke**.*
2 [U] talk about dishonest or immoral things that famous or important people are believed to have done: *The magazine is full of gossip and scandal.*
3 be a scandal *BrE spoken* to be very shocking or unacceptable: *The price of petrol these days is an absolute scandal!*

scan·dal·ize (*also* **-ise** *BrE*) /ˈskændəl-aɪz/ *v* [T] to make people feel very shocked SYN **shock**: *His outspoken views scandalized the nation.*

scan·dal·mon·ger /ˈskændəlˌmʌŋɡə $ -ˌmɑːŋɡər, -ˌmʌŋ-/ *n* [C] someone who tells people untrue and shocking things about someone else

scan·dal·ous /ˈskændələs/ *adj* **1** completely unfair and wrong SYN **shocking**: *a scandalous waste of public money* | *scandalous behaviour* **2** involving stories about dishonest or immoral things that someone has done: *scandalous stories about the prime minister* —**scandalously** *adv*

Scan·di·na·vi·an /ˌskændəˈneɪviən◂/ *n* [C] someone from the area of northern Europe that consists of Norway, Sweden, Denmark, and usually Finland and Iceland —**Scandinavian** *adj*: *Scandinavian languages*

scan·ner /ˈskænə $ -ər/ ●●○ *n* [C]
1 a machine that passes an electrical beam over something in order to produce a picture of what is inside it → **scan**: *a high-tech body scanner*
2 a piece of computer equipment that allows written or printed information to be taken onto a computer and stored there → **scan**

scant /skænt/ *adj* [only before noun] **1** not enough: *The story has received **scant attention** in the press.* | *They produce goods with **scant regard** for quality.* **2 a scant cup/teaspoon etc** a little less than a full amount of a particular measurement

scant·y /ˈskænti/ *adj* **1** not enough: *There is only scanty evidence of his involvement.* **2** scanty clothes are small and do not cover very much of your body – used to show disapproval SYN **skimpy** —**scantily** *adv*: ***scantily clad** young women*

scape·goat /ˈskeɪpɡəʊt $ -ɡoʊt/ *n* [C] someone who is blamed for something bad that happens, even if it is not their fault: **[+for]** *She believed she had been **made a scapegoat** for what happened.* —**scapegoat** *v* [T]

scap·u·la /ˈskæpjələ/ *n* [C] *technical* one of the two flat bones on each side of your upper back SYN **shoulder blade** → SKELETON

scar[1] /skɑː $ skɑːr/ ●●○ *n* [C]
1 MARK ON SKIN a permanent mark that is left on your skin after you have had a cut or wound: *He had a long, curved scar on his right cheek.* | *a deep cut that could **leave** a permanent **scar***
2 FEELING a feeling of fear or sadness that remains with you for a long time after an unpleasant experience: *Her **mental scars** will take time to heal.* | *The war has **left** a deep **scar** on this community.*
3 DAMAGED AREA a place where the land or a building was damaged in the past: **[+of]** *The landscape still **bears the scars** of the war.*
4 CLIFF *BrE* a cliff on the side of a mountain

scar[2] *v* (**scarred**, **scarring**) [T] **1** if a wound or cut scars you, it leaves a permanent mark on your body: *His hands were **badly scarred** by the fire.* | *She will probably be **scarred for life**.* **2** if an unpleasant experience scars you, it leaves you with a feeling of sadness or fear that continues for a long time: *She was scarred by her father's suicide.* **3** to spoil the appearance of something SYN **deface**: *quarries that scar the landscape*

scar·ab /ˈskærəb/ (*also* **ˈscarab ˌbeetle**) *n* [C] a type of large black BEETLE

scarce[1] /skeəs $ skers/ ●●○ *adj* (*comparative* **scarcer**, *superlative* **scarcest**)
1 if something is scarce, there is not very much of it available: *Food was often scarce in the winter.* | *There was fierce competition for the **scarce resources**.*
2 make yourself scarce *informal* to leave a place, especially in order to avoid an unpleasant situation: *I decided it was time to make myself scarce.*

scarce[2] *adv literary* scarcely: *He could scarce believe it.*

scarce·ly /ˈskeəsli $ ˈsker-/ ●●○ *adv*
1 almost not or almost none at all SYN **hardly**: *The city had scarcely changed in 20 years.* | *The country had **scarcely any** industry.* | *He **scarcely ever** left the region.* | **can/could**

S

scarcely do sth *It was getting dark and she could scarcely see in front of her.* | **scarcely a day/year/moment etc** *Scarcely a day goes by when I don't think of him.*
2 only a moment ago SYN **hardly**, **barely**: *He **had scarcely** sat down **when** there was a knock at the door.*
3 definitely not or almost certainly not SYN **hardly**: *Early March is scarcely the time of year for sailing.*

GRAMMAR: Word order
- **Scarcely** usually comes before a main verb: *She **scarcely said** a word.*
- **Scarcely** comes after the first auxiliary verb: *I **can scarcely** believe he said that.* ✗ Don't say: *I scarcely can believe he said that.*
- **Scarcely** usually comes after the verb 'be' when it is used in simple tenses such as 'is' or 'was': *I **was scarcely** aware of the noise.*
- You can use **scarcely** at the beginning of a sentence before an auxiliary, to emphasize that one thing happens very soon after another thing: ***Scarcely had** they left the station than the train stopped.*

GRAMMAR GUIDE ADVERBS

scar·ci·ty /ˈskeəsəti $ ˈsker-/ *n* [singular] a situation in which there is not enough of something SYN **lack**: **[+of]** *the scarcity of employment opportunities*

scare¹ /skeə $ sker/ ●●● S2 *v*
1 [T] to make someone feel frightened SYN **frighten** → **afraid**: *Loud noises can scare animals or birds.* | **scare the life/living daylights/hell etc out of sb** (=scare someone very much) *The alarm scared the hell out of me.* | **scare the pants off sb** *informal* (=scare someone very much)
2 scare easily to be frightened by things that are not very frightening: *I don't scare easily, you know.*
scare sb **into** sth *phr v* to make someone do something by frightening them or threatening them: **scare sb into doing sth** *You can't scare me into telling you anything.*
scare sb/sth ↔ **off/away** *phr v*
1 to make an animal or person go away by frightening them: *She moved quietly to avoid scaring the birds away.*
2 to make someone uncertain or worried so that they do not do something they were going to do: *Rising prices are scaring off many potential customers.*
scare sth ↔ **up** *phr v AmE informal* to make something although you have very few things to make it from: *Let me see if I can scare up something for you to eat.*

scare² ●○○ *n*
1 [singular] a sudden feeling of fear: *You really **gave** us **a** scare!*
2 [C] a situation in which a lot of people become frightened about something: *a **bomb scare*** | *a **health scare***

scare·crow /ˈskeəkrəʊ $ ˈskerkroʊ/ *n* [C] an object in the shape of a person that a farmer puts in a field to frighten birds away

scared /skeəd $ skerd/ ●●● S3 *adj* frightened of something, or nervous about something SYN **afraid**: *At first, he was really scared.* | **scared of sb/sth** *I've always been scared of dogs.* | **scared of doing sth** *Don't be scared of asking for help.* | **scared (that)** *I wanted to ask her out, but was scared that she might refuse.* | **scared to do sth** *The boys were scared to cross the street.* | **scared stiff/scared to death/scared out of your wits** (=extremely frightened) *I was scared stiff at the thought of making a speech.* THESAURUS FRIGHTENED

REGISTER
Scared is slightly informal. In written English, people usually prefer to use **afraid** or **frightened**: *She was **afraid** of losing Anna in the crowd.*

scare·mon·ger·ing /ˈskeəˌmʌŋɡərɪŋ $ ˈskerˌmɑːŋ-, -ˌmʌŋ-/ *n* [U] *BrE* the practice of deliberately making people worried or nervous, especially in order to get a political or other advantage —**scaremonger** *n* [C]

ˈ**scare ˌstory** *n* [C] a report, especially in a newspaper, that makes a situation seem more serious or worrying than it really is: *Despite the scare stories in the media, no jobs will be lost at the factory.*

ˈ**scare ˌtactics** *n* [plural] methods of persuading people to do something by frightening them: *Employers **used scare tactics** to force a return to work.*

scare·y /ˈskeəri $ ˈskeri/ *adj* another spelling of SCARY

scarf¹ /skɑːf $ skɑːrf/ ●●● S3 *n* (*plural* **scarfs** *or* **scarves** /skɑːvz $ skɑːrvz/) [C] a piece of cloth that you wear around your neck, head, or shoulders, especially to keep warm

scarf² (*also* **scarf down/up**) *v* [T] *AmE informal* to eat something very quickly: *She scarfed down a bagel on her way to work.*

scar·i·fy /ˈskeərɪfaɪ, ˈskærɪfaɪ $ ˈsker-, ˈskær-/ *v* (**scarified**, **scarifying**, **scarifies**) [T] **1** to break and make loose the surface of a road or field using a pointed tool **2** *formal* to criticize someone very severely

scar·let /ˈskɑːlɪt $ -ɑːr-/ ●○○ *adj*
1 bright red
2 *BrE* if you go scarlet, your face becomes red, usually because you are embarrassed or angry SYN **blush**: **go/turn/flush/blush scarlet** *Eileen blushed scarlet at the joke.* —**scarlet** *n* [U]

ˌ**scarlet ˈfever** (*also* **scar·la·ti·na** /ˌskɑːləˈtiːnə $ ˌskɑːr-/) *n* [U] a serious infectious illness that mainly affects children, causing a sore throat and red spots on your skin

ˌ**scarlet ˈwoman** *n* [C] *old-fashioned* a woman who has sexual relationships with many different people

scarp /skɑːp $ skɑːrp/ *n* [C] a line of natural cliffs

scar·per /ˈskɑːpə $ ˈskɑːrpər/ *v* [I] *BrE informal* to run away: *They scarpered without paying their bill.*

SCART /skɑːt $ skɑːrt/ *n* [C] a piece of equipment used in some countries to connect electrical equipment so that video and sound signals can go from one piece of equipment to another, for example from a DVD PLAYER to a television: *a SCART cable*

scarves /skɑːvz $ skɑːrvz/ the plural of SCARF¹

scar·y, **scarey** /ˈskeəri $ ˈskeri/ ●●● S1 *adj* (*comparative* **scarier**, *superlative* **scariest**) *informal* frightening: *a scary moment* | *a scary movie* | *The book is both scary and funny.* THESAURUS FRIGHTENING

scat /skæt/ *n* [U] a style of JAZZ singing, in which the singer sings sounds rather than words

scath·ing /ˈskeɪðɪŋ/ *adj* a scathing remark criticizes someone or something very severely: **scathing attack/remark/comment etc** *a scathing attack on the government's planned tax increases* | **[+about]** *He's always been so scathing about psychiatrists.* —**scathingly** *adv*

scat·o·lo·gic·al /ˌskætəˈlɒdʒɪkəl◂ $ -ˈlɑː-/ *adj formal* too interested in or related to human waste, in a way that people find offensive: *scatological humour*

scat·ter /ˈskætə $ -ər/ ●●○ *v* [I,T]
1 if someone scatters a lot of things, or if they scatter, they are thrown or dropped over a wide area in an irregular way: **scatter (sth) over/around/across etc sth** *Scatter the onions over the fish.* | *The flowers fell and scattered on the ground.*
2 if a group of people or animals scatter, or if something scatters them, they move quickly in different directions: *The sound of gunfire made the crowd scatter in all directions.* → SCATTERED, SCATTERING

scat·ter·brained /ˈskætəbreɪnd $ -tər-/ *adj informal* not thinking in a practical way, so that you cannot do things or you forget or lose things —**scatterbrain** *n* [C]

ˈ**scatter ˌcushion** *n* [C] a small CUSHION that you put on SOFAS and chairs for decoration

scat·tered /ˈskætəd $ -ərd/ *adj* spread over a wide area or over a long period of time: **[+over/throughout/across/around etc]** *Broken glass lay scattered over the floor.* | **[+with]** *The sky was scattered with stars.* | *There will be some **scattered showers** (=short periods of rain) in the afternoon.* | *a **widely scattered** set of islands*

scat·ter·ing /ˈskætərɪŋ/ *n* **a scattering of sth** *written* a small number of things or people spread out over a large area: *a scattering of isolated farms*

scat·ty /ˈskæti/ *adj BrE informal* someone who is scatty often forgets or loses things because they are not sensible or practical

scav·enge /ˈskævəndʒ/ *v* [I,T] **1** if an animal scavenges, it eats anything that it can find: *Pigs scavenged among the rubbish.* | **[+for]** *rats scavenging for food* **2** if someone scavenges, they search through things that other people do not want, for food or useful objects: *There are people who live in the dump and scavenge garbage for a living.* | **[+for]** *Women were scavenging for old furniture.* —**scavenger** *n* [C]: *Foxes and other scavengers go through the dustbins.*

sce·na·ri·o /səˈnɑːriəʊ $ -ˈnærioʊ, -ˈne-/ ●○○ AWL *n* (*plural* **scenarios**) [C]
1 a situation that could possibly happen: *Imagine a scenario where only 20% of people have a job.* | **possible/likely/plausible scenario** *Under a likely scenario, world population will double by 2050.* | *a possible scenario* | **worst-case/nightmare scenario** (=the worst possible situation) *The worst-case scenario was that he would have to have an operation.*
2 *technical* a written description of the characters, place, and things that will happen in a film, play etc

scene /siːn/ ●●● S2 W2 *n*
1 PLAY/FILM [C] **a)** part of a play during which there is no change in time or place: *Hamlet, Act 5, Scene 2* | *the* ***opening scene*** **b)** a single piece of action that happens in one place in a film, book etc: ***battle scenes*** | *tender* ***love scenes*** | *The film contains some violent scenes.* | *colourful pictures depicting scenes from the Bible* THESAURUS ▸ PART
2 ACTIVITIES [singular] a particular set of activities and the people who are involved in them: *I'm not into the* ***club scene*** (=going to night clubs). | *LA's* ***music scene*** | *the* ***drug scene*** | *a newcomer to the* ***political scene***
3 ACCIDENT/CRIME [singular] the place where an accident, crime etc happened: *The police soon arrived at* ***the scene of the crime***. | **at the scene** *Investigators are now at the scene, searching for clues.* | **on the scene** *Journalists were on the scene within minutes.* THESAURUS ▸ PLACE
4 VIEW/PICTURE [C] a view of a place as you see it, or as it appears in a picture: *He photographed a wide range of street scenes.* | **[+of]** *She returned home to find a scene of devastation.* THESAURUS ▸ SIGHT
5 EVENT/SITUATION [C] what is happening in a place, or what can be seen happening: **[+of]** *There were scenes of rejoicing after the election.* | **bad scene** *AmE*: *'It's a bad scene here,' she said. 'Jamie is very sick.'*
6 ARGUMENT [C] a loud angry argument, especially in a public place: *There were angry scenes in parliament today.* | *I was mad, but I didn't want to* ***make a scene***.
7 not be your scene *informal* to not be the type of thing you like: *Loud discos aren't really my scene.*
8 behind the scenes secretly, while other things are happening publicly: *Behind the scenes, both sides are working towards an agreement.*
9 set the scene a) to provide the conditions in which an event can happen: **[+for]** *The prison riots have set the scene for major reform.* **b)** to describe the situation before you begin to tell a story: *A few words on the rules of English law will help to set the scene.*
10 be/come on the scene to be or become involved in a situation, activity etc: *By then, there was a boyfriend on the scene.* → **a change of scene** at CHANGE²(3), → **steal the scene** at STEAL¹(4)

sce·ne·ry /ˈsiːnəri/ ●●○ *n* [U]
1 the natural features of a particular part of a country that you can see, such as mountains, forests, deserts etc: *The best part of the trip was the fantastic scenery.* THESAURUS ▸ COUNTRY
2 the painted background, furniture etc used on a theatre stage SYN **set**

sce·nic /ˈsiːnɪk/ *adj* **1** surrounded by views of beautiful countryside: *a region of* ***scenic beauty*** **2 the scenic route** a longer way than usual, especially one that goes through beautiful or interesting areas – often used humorously: *Let's take the scenic route home.* —**scenically** /-kli/ *adv*

scent¹ /sent/ ●○○ *n*
1 [C] a pleasant smell that something has SYN **fragrance**: *a yellow rose with a lovely scent* | **[+of]** *the sweet scent of ripe fruit* THESAURUS ▸ SMELL
2 [C] the smell of a particular animal or person that some other animals, for example dogs, can follow
3 throw/put sb off the scent to give someone false information to prevent them from catching you or discovering something: *Was he trying to put me off the scent because I had come too close to the truth?*
4 [C,U] *especially BrE* a liquid that you put on your skin to make it smell pleasant SYN **perfume**

scent² *v* [T] **1** to give a particular smell to something → **perfume**: *Honeysuckle and roses scented the air.* **2** *written* to suddenly think that something is going to happen or exists: *We* ***scented danger*** *and decided to leave.* | *The press had immediately scented a story.* | *The trade unions have scented victory.* **3** if an animal scents another animal or a person, it knows that they are near because it can smell them

scent·ed /ˈsentɪd/ *adj* with a particular smell, especially a pleasant one: *scented soap* | **[+with]** *The dry cold air was scented with wood smoke.* | **rose-scented/vanilla-scented/pine-scented etc**

scep·ter /ˈseptə $ -ər/ *n* [C] the American spelling of SCEPTRE

scep·tic *BrE*, **skeptic** *AmE* /ˈskeptɪk/ *n* [C] a person who disagrees with particular claims and statements, especially those that are generally thought to be true: *Sceptics argued that the rise in prices was temporary.*

scep·ti·cal *BrE*, **skeptical** *AmE* /ˈskeptɪkəl/ ●○○ *adj* tending to disagree with what other people tell you SYN **doubtful**: **[+about/of]** *I'm extremely sceptical about what I read in the press.* | *Environmental groups are sceptical of the government's claims.* | **highly/deeply sceptical** *He is highly sceptical of the reforms.* | *'You can trust me,' he said. Jane looked sceptical.* —**sceptically** /-kli/ *adv*

scep·ti·cis·m *BrE*, **skepticism** *AmE* /ˈskeptɪsɪzəm/ ●○○ *n* [U] an attitude of doubting that particular claims or statements are true or that something will happen

scep·tre *BrE*, **scepter** *AmE* /ˈseptə $ -ter/ *n* [C] a decorated stick carried by kings or queens at ceremonies

scha·den·freu·de /ˈʃɑːdnˌfrɔɪdə/ *n* [U] *formal* a feeling of pleasure that you get when something bad happens to someone else

sched·ule¹ /ˈʃedjuːl, ˈske- $ ˈskedʒʊl, -dʒəl/ ●●● S2 W3 AWL *n* [C]
1 a plan of what someone is going to do and when they are going to do it: **on schedule** (=at the planned time) *The majority of holiday flights depart and arrive on schedule.* | **ahead of/behind schedule** (=before or after the planned time) *Meg's new book is still well ahead of schedule.* | *How can he fit everything into his* ***busy schedule***? | *I'm going to be working to a very* ***tight schedule*** (=including a lot of things that must be done in a short time).
2 *AmE* a list that shows the times that buses, trains etc leave or arrive at a particular place SYN **timetable** *BrE*
3 a formal list of something, for example prices: *a schedule of postal charges*

schedule² ●●● S3 AWL *v* [T] to plan that something will happen at a particular time: **be scheduled for June/Monday etc** *The elections are scheduled for mid-June.* | **be scheduled for release/publication/completion etc** *Her first album is scheduled for release in September.* | **be scheduled to do sth** *Meetings are scheduled to take place all over the country.* | **scheduled flight/service** (=a plane service that flies at the same time every day or every week) *Prices include scheduled flights from Heathrow.* | *We will not cancel your holiday less than eight weeks before the* ***scheduled departure date***. GRAMMAR **Schedule** is usually passive.

S

sche·ma /ˈskiːmə/ *n* (*plural* **schemas** *or* **schemata** /-mətə/) [C] *technical* a drawing or description of the main parts of something
sche·mat·ic /skiːˈmætɪk, skɪ-/ AWL *adj* showing the main parts of something in a simple way: *a schematic diagram of DNA*
sche·ma·tize (*also* **-ise** *BrE*) /ˈskiːmətaɪz/ *v* [T] *formal* to arrange something in a system
scheme¹ /skiːm/ ●●● S2 W1 AWL *n* [C]
1 *BrE* an official plan that is intended to help people in some way, for example by providing education or training SYN **program** *AmE*: *The money will be used for teacher training schemes.* | *a* ***pension scheme*** | **[+for]** *schemes for two new cross-city lines* | **scheme to do sth** *a new scheme to boost exports* | **pilot scheme** (=something that is done on a small scale in order to see if it is successful enough to be done on a larger scale) *The pilot scheme proved to be a great success.* **THESAURUS▸** PLAN
2 a clever plan, especially to do something that is bad or illegal – used to show disapproval: *a get-rich-quick scheme* | **scheme to do sth** *a scheme to pass false cheques*
3 a system that you use to organize information, ideas etc → **schematic**: *a* ***classification scheme***
4 in the scheme of things in the way things generally happen, or are organized: *the unimportance of man in the whole scheme of things* → COLOUR SCHEME
scheme² AWL *v* [I] to secretly make clever and dishonest plans to get or achieve something SYN **plot**: **scheme to do sth** *She schemed to kill him with poison.* | **[+against]** *He became aware that people were scheming against him and called an emergency meeting.* | *She's nothing but a lying, scheming little monster!* —**schemer** *n* [C]
scher·zo /ˈskeətsəʊ $ ˈskertsoʊ/ *n* (*plural* **scherzos**) [C] a happy piece of music that is meant to be played quickly
schil·ling /ˈʃɪlɪŋ/ *n* [C] the standard unit of money used in Austria before the EURO
schis·m /ˈskɪzəm, ˈsɪzəm/ *n* [C,U] the separation of a group into two groups, caused by a disagreement about its aims and beliefs, especially in the Christian church SYN **split** —**schismatic** /sɪzˈmætɪk, skɪz-/ *adj*
schist /ʃɪst/ *n* [U] a type of rock that naturally breaks apart into thin flat pieces
schiz·oid /ˈskɪtsɔɪd/ *adj* **1** *technical* typical of schizophrenia: *a schizoid personality disorder* **2** quickly changing between opposite opinions or attitudes: *Martin's latest play is as schizoid and erratic as its characters.*
schiz·o·phre·ni·a /ˌskɪtsəʊˈfriːniə, -sə- $ -soʊ-, -sə-/ *n* [U] a serious mental illness in which someone's thoughts and feelings are not based on what is really happening around them
schiz·o·phren·ic¹ /ˌskɪtsəʊˈfrenɪk◂, -sə- $ -soʊ-, -sə-/ *adj* **1** relating to schizophrenia **2** quickly changing from one opinion, attitude etc to another: *The film was an example of schizophrenic movie-making at its worst.*
schizophrenic² *n* [C] someone who has schizophrenia
schlep /ʃlep/ *v* (**schlepped**, **schlepping**) [T] *AmE informal* to carry or pull something heavy: **schlep sth down/out/along etc** *I schlepped his bag all the way to the airport and he didn't even thank me.*
schlep around (sth) *phr v* to spend your time lazily doing nothing useful: *I spent the afternoon schlepping around the house.*
schlock /ʃlɒk $ ʃlɑːk/ *n* [U] *AmE informal* things that are cheap and of poor quality: *The gift store sells both tasteful gifts and cheap schlock.*
schmaltz·y /ˈʃmɔːltsi, ˈʃmæltsi $ ˈʃmɒːltsi, ˈʃmɑːltsi/ *adj informal* a schmaltzy piece of music, book etc deals with emotions such as love and sadness in a way that seems silly and not serious enough: *a schmaltzy love song* —**schmaltz** *n* [U]
schman·cy /ˈʃmænsi/ (*also* **fancy-schmancy**) *adj AmE informal* expensive and fashionable in a way that is meant to be impressive – used to show disapproval: *a schmancy all-girls college*
schmo /ʃməʊ $ ʃmoʊ/ *n* (*plural* **schmoes**) [C] *AmE informal* a stupid or annoying person
schmooze /ʃmuːz/ *v* [I] *informal* to talk in a friendly way about unimportant things at a social event, especially because you want to gain an advantage for yourself later: **[+with]** *Politicians spent much of their time schmoozing with contributors.*
schmuck /ʃmʌk/ *n* [C] *AmE informal* a stupid person
schnapps /ʃnæps/ *n* [U] a strong alcoholic drink
schnit·zel /ˈʃnɪtsəl/ *n* [C,U] a small piece of VEAL (=meat from a young cow) covered with BREADCRUMBS and cooked in oil
schnook /ʃnʊk/ *n* [C] *AmE informal* a stupid person
schol·ar /ˈskɒlə $ ˈskɑːlər/ ●○○ *n* [C]
1 an intelligent and well-educated person: *the great Dutch scholar Erasmus*
2 someone who knows a lot about a particular subject, especially one that is not a science subject: *a Shakespearean scholar*
3 someone who has been given a scholarship to study at a school or college: *He was a King's scholar at Eton College.*
schol·ar·ly /ˈskɒləli $ ˈskɑːlərli/ *adj* **1** relating to serious study of a particular subject: *a scholarly journal* **2** someone who is scholarly spends a lot of time studying, and knows a lot about a particular subject
schol·ar·ship /ˈskɒləʃɪp $ ˈskɑːlər-/ ●○○ *n*
1 [C] an amount of money that is given to someone by an educational organization to help pay for their education: **[+to]** *She* ***won*** *a* ***scholarship*** *to Iowa State University.* | **on a scholarship** *He attended college on a drama scholarship.*
2 [U] the knowledge, work, or methods involved in serious studying: *Her latest publication is a fine piece of scholarship.*
scho·las·tic /skəˈlæstɪk/ *adj* [only before noun] *formal* **1** relating to schools or teaching → **academic**: *scholastic skills* **2** relating to scholasticism
scho·las·ti·cis·m /skəˈlæstɪsɪzəm/ *n* [U] a way of studying thought, especially religious thought, based on things written in ancient times
school¹ /skuːl/ ●●● S1 W1 *n*
1 WHERE CHILDREN LEARN [C,U] a place where children are taught: *His mother always used to pick him up from school.*
2 TIME AT SCHOOL [U] **a)** a day's work at school: *School begins at 8.30.* | **before/after school** *I'll see you after school.* **b)** the time during your life when you go to school: *He's one of my old friends from school.* | *Children start school between the ages of four and five.*
3 UNIVERSITY [C,U] **a)** *AmE* a college or university, or the time when you study there: *Their kids are away at school now.* | *She was going to school in Boston.* **b)** a department or group of departments that teaches a particular subject at a university: **[+of]** *the Harvard School of Public Health* | **law/medical/business/graduate school** *After two years of medical school, I thought I knew everything.*
4 ONE SUBJECT [C] a place where a particular subject or skill is taught: *a language school in Brighton* | **[+of]** *Amwell School of Motoring*
5 at school a) in the school building: *I can get some work done while the kids are at school.* **b)** *BrE* attending a school, rather than being at college or university or having a job: *We've got two children at school, and one at university.*
6 in school a) in the school building: *Sandra's not in school today.* **b)** *AmE* attending a school or university rather than having a job: *Are your boys still in school?*
7 ART [C] a number of people who are considered as a group because of their similar style of work: *the Impressionist school*
8 school of thought an opinion or way of thinking about something that is shared by a group of people: *There are two main schools of thought on the subject.*
9 of/from the old school with old-fashioned values or qualities: *a family doctor of the old school*
10 FISH [C] a large group of fish, WHALES, DOLPHINS etc that are swimming together: **[+of]** *a school of whales* **THESAURUS▸** GROUP

S

COLLOCATIONS - MEANINGS 1 & 2

VERBS

go to school *Did you go to school in Paris?*
start school *Children in Britain start school when they are five.*
leave school *He left school when he was 16.*

ADJECTIVES/NOUN + school

a state school *BrE*, **a public school** *AmE* (=a school that gets its money from the government) *Universities want to encourage more applicants from state schools.*
a private school (*also* **a public school** *BrE*) (=a school where students pay to study) *He was educated at a private school.*
sb's old school (=the school someone went to when they were young) *He went back to his old school to give a talk to the children.*
a local school (=a school near where someone lives) *They sent their kids to the local school.*
a boarding school (=a school where children also live and sleep) | **a nursery school** (=for children under 5) | **an infant school** *BrE* (=for children aged 5 to 7) | **a primary school** *BrE*, **an elementary school** *AmE* (=for children up to 11) | **a secondary school** (*also* **a high school** *BrE*) (=for children from 11 to 16 or 18) | **a high school** *AmE* (=a school for students aged 14 to 18) | **a comprehensive school** *BrE* (=a secondary school for all children) | **a grammar school** *BrE* (=a secondary school for children who have passed an exam when they are 11)

school + NOUN

school students (*also* **school pupils** *BrE*) *Most school students have musical interests of some kind.*
a school friend *She met some old school friends.*
a school uniform *He was still wearing his school uniform.*
the school holidays *BrE* | **the school run** *BrE* (=the journey taking children to and from school each day) | **the school playground** | **the school library** | **the school hall** | **the school bus** | **the school curriculum** | **school meals/lunches** (*also* **school dinners** *BrE*) | **a school governor** *BrE* (=an elected person who works with teachers to make decisions about how a school is organized) | **the school board** *AmE* (=the group of people who are elected to govern a school or group of schools) | **the school day**

school² *v* [T] **1** *old-fashioned* to train or teach someone to have a certain skill, type of behaviour, or way of thinking: **be schooled in (doing) sth** *She was schooled in hiding her emotions.* **2** to educate a child

ˈschool age *n* [U] the age at which a child is old enough to go to school: *children below school age* —**school-age** *adj*: *a school-age child*

ˌschool ˈboard *n* [C] a group of people, including some parents, who are elected to govern a school or group of schools in the US

school·book /ˈskuːlbʊk/ *n* [C] a book that is used in school classes SYN **textbook**

school·boy /ˈskuːlbɔɪ/ *n* [C] *especially BrE* **1** a boy attending school THESAURUS ▸ STUDENT **2 schoolboy humour** jokes that are silly and rude but not offensive

school·child /ˈskuːltʃaɪld/ *n* (*plural* **schoolchildren** /-tʃɪldrən/) [C] a child attending school THESAURUS ▸ STUDENT

school·day /ˈskuːldeɪ/ *n* [C] **1** a day of the week when children are usually at school **2 sb's schooldays** the time of your life when you go to school

ˈschool ˌdistrict *n* [C] an area in one state of the US that includes a number of schools which are governed together

ˈschool friend *n* [C] *especially BrE* a friend who goes to the same school as you

school·girl /ˈskuːlɡɜːl $ -ɡɜːrl/ *n* [C] *especially BrE* a girl attending school THESAURUS ▸ STUDENT

ˌschool ˈgovernor *n* [C] a member of a group of people in Britain who are elected to make decisions about how a school should be managed

school·house /ˈskuːlhaʊs/ *n* [C] a school building, especially for a small village school

school·ing /ˈskuːlɪŋ/ *n* [U] school education: *children in their final year of* ***compulsory schooling*** (=the time during which children have to attend school by law) | *Al's dad had only a few years of schooling.*

school·kid /ˈskuːlkɪd/ *n* [C] *informal* a child attending school

ˈschool-ˌleaver *n* [C] *BrE* someone who has just left school, especially to do or look for a job rather than going to college, university etc: *a shortage of jobs for school-leavers*

school·marm /ˈskuːlmɑːm $ -mɑːrm/ *n* [C] a woman who is considered to be old-fashioned, strict, and easily shocked

school·mas·ter /ˈskuːlˌmɑːstə $ -ˌmæstər/ *n* [C] *BrE* a male teacher, especially in a PRIVATE SCHOOL (=one that parents pay to send their children to)

school·mate /ˈskuːlmeɪt/ *n* [C] someone who goes or went to the same school as you

school·mis·tress /ˈskuːlˌmɪstrɪs/ *n* [C] *BrE* a female teacher, especially in a PRIVATE SCHOOL (=one that parents pay to send their children to)

ˈschool night *n* [C] **1** an evening before a day when a child must go to school: *The children are in bed by 8 o'clock on school nights.* **2** *humorous* an evening before a day when someone must go to work: *I left the pub at 10, since it was a school night.*

school·room /ˈskuːlruːm, -rʊm/ *n* [C] a room used for teaching in a small school SYN **classroom**

ˈschool run *n* [C usually singular] *BrE* when parents drive their children to school in the morning or home from school in the afternoon: *We hope to increase the safety of children who walk to school and cut the number of cars* ***doing the school run****.*

school·teach·er /ˈskuːlˌtiːtʃə $ -ər/ *n* [C] a TEACHER

ˌschool ˈtie *n* [C] **1** a special tie with a particular colour or pattern that children wear at some schools in Britain **2 the old school tie** *BrE informal* the unofficial system by which people who went to the same school, especially an expensive one, help each other to gain important positions later in their lives

school·work /ˈskuːlwɜːk $ -wɜːrk/ *n* [U] work done for or during school classes → **homework**

school·yard /ˈskuːljɑːd $ -jɑːrd/ *n* [C] *especially AmE* the area next to a school building where the children can go or play when they are not having lessons SYN **playground**

schoo·ner /ˈskuːnə $ -ər/ *n* [C] a fast sailing ship with two sails

schtick /ʃtɪk/ *n* [U] *AmE* another spelling of SHTICK

schtum, **schtoom**, **shtum** /ʃtʊm/ *adj* [not before noun] quiet or silent: *The boss of the failed company is* ***keeping schtum*** *about his role in the disaster.*

schwa /ʃwɑː/ *n* [C] *technical* **1** a vowel typically heard in parts of a word that are spoken without STRESS¹(4), such as the 'a' in 'about' **2** the sign (ə), used to represent the vowel schwa

sci·at·ic /saɪˈætɪk/ *adj technical* relating to the HIPS

sci·at·i·ca /saɪˈætɪkə/ *n* [U] pain in the lower back, HIPS, and legs

sci·ence /ˈsaɪəns/ ●●● S1 W1 *n*
1 [U] knowledge about the world, especially based on examining, testing, and proving facts: *Many leading scientists do not consider that science can give absolutely reliable knowledge.* | *the founder of modern science, Isaac Newton* | *developments in* ***science and technology***
2 [U] the study of science: *What did you do in science class today?*

S

3 [C] a particular part of science, for example BIOLOGY, CHEMISTRY, or PHYSICS: *the physical sciences*
4 sth is not an exact science used to say that something involves a lot of guessing and there is not just one right way to do it: *Advertising is not an exact science – you're always taking a risk.* → **DOMESTIC SCIENCE, INFORMATION SCIENCE, NATURAL SCIENCE, PHYSICAL SCIENCE, SOCIAL SCIENCE,** → **blind sb with science** at BLIND²(4), → **sth is not rocket science** at **ROCKET SCIENCE**

ˌscience ˈfiction ●●○ *n* [U] stories about events in the future which are affected by imaginary developments in science, for example about travelling in time or to other PLANETS with life on them

ˈscience park *n* [C] an area where there are a lot of companies or organizations that do scientific work

sci·en·tif·ic /ˌsaɪənˈtɪfɪk◂/ ●●● S3 W2 *adj*
1 [no comparative] about or relating to science, or using its methods: *We believe in investing in scientific research.* | *the limits of scientific knowledge* | *decisions based on scientific evidence* | *the international scientific community* (=scientists)
2 *informal* using an organized system: *I keep accounts for the business, but I'm not scientific about it.*
3 the scientific method the usual process of finding out information in science, which involves testing your ideas by performing EXPERIMENTS and making decisions based on the results —**scientifically** /-kli/ *adv*: *It hasn't been scientifically proven, though.*

sci·en·tist /ˈsaɪəntɪst/ ●●● S3 W2 *n* [C] someone who works or is trained in science

sci-fi /ˌsaɪ ˈfaɪ◂/ *n* [U] *informal* SCIENCE FICTION

scim·i·tar /ˈsɪmɪtə $ -ər/ *n* [C] a sword with a curved blade that was used in the past

S

scin·til·la /sɪnˈtɪlə/ *n* [singular] a very small amount of something: **[+of]** *There isn't a scintilla of evidence.*

scin·til·lat·ing /ˈsɪntəleɪtɪŋ/ *adj* interesting, clever, and amusing: *scintillating conversation* | *a scintillating performance*

sci·on /ˈsaɪən/ *n* [C] *literary* a young member of a famous or important family: **[+of]** *a scion of an ancient Scottish family*

scis·sors /ˈsɪzəz $ -ərz/ ●●● S3 *n* [plural] a tool for cutting paper, cloth etc, made of two sharp blades fastened together in the middle, with holes for your finger and thumb: *a **pair of scissors*** → see picture at **FIRST AID KIT**

scle·ro·sis /skləˈrəʊsɪs $ -ˈroʊ-/ *n* [U] *technical* a disease that causes an organ or soft part of your body to become hard —**sclerotic** /skləˈrɒtɪk $ -ˈrɑː-/ *adj* → **MULTIPLE SCLEROSIS**

scoff /skɒf $ skɒːf, skɑːf/ *v* **1** [I,T] to laugh at a person or idea, and talk about them in a way that shows you think they are stupid: **[+at]** *David scoffed at her fears.* | *Officials scoffed at the idea.* | *'You, a scientist!' he scoffed.* **2** [T] *BrE informal* to eat something very quickly: *She scoffed the plate of biscuits.*

scold /skəʊld $ skoʊld/ *v* [T] to angrily criticize someone, especially a child, about something they have done SYN **tell off**: *Do not scold the puppy, but simply and firmly say 'no'.* | **scold sb for (doing) sth** *Her father scolded her for upsetting her mother.* —**scolding** *n* [C,U]: *I got a scolding from my teacher.*

> **REGISTER**
> In everyday English, people usually say **tell** someone **off** rather than **scold** someone: *She **told** us **off** for making a mess.*

sconce /skɒns $ skɑːns/ *n* [C] an object that is attached to a wall and holds CANDLES or electric lights

scone /skɒn, skəʊn $ skoʊn, skɑːn/ *n* [C] a small round cake, sometimes containing dried fruit, which is usually eaten with butter: *tea and scones*

SCOOP

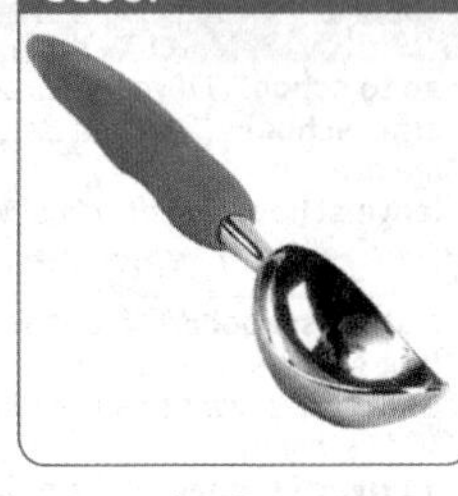

scoop¹ /skuːp/ ●○○ *n* [C]
1 an important or exciting news story that is printed in one newspaper or shown on one television station before any of the others know about it: *a journalist looking for a scoop*
2 a round deep spoon for serving food, for example ICE CREAM or MASHed potato
3 (*also* **scoopful**) an amount of food served with a scoop: **[+of]** *two scoops of ice cream*
4 *AmE informal* information about something: *the **inside scoop*** (=special information that other people do not have) *on the markets* | **what's the scoop?** (=used to ask for information or news)

scoop² ●○○ *v* [T]
1 [always + adv/prep] to pick something up or remove it using a scoop or a spoon, or your curved hand: *She bent down and scooped up the little dog.* | *Cut the tomato in half and scoop out the seeds with a teaspoon.*
2 to be the first newspaper to print an important news report: *Time and again, we have scooped our rivals.*
3 *BrE* to win a prize or AWARD: *Britain scooped the top prize in the over-50s category.*
scoop sth ↔ **up** *phr v* if a lot of people scoop something up, they buy it quickly so that soon there is none left: *Fans scooped up the trading cards in the first few hours of the sale.*

ˈscoop ˌneck (*also* **ˈscoop ˌneckline**) *n* [C] a round, quite low neck on a woman's TOP → see picture at **NECK¹**

scoot /skuːt/ *v informal* **1** [I] to move quickly and suddenly: *There's the bus – I'd better scoot!* | **[+off]** *She scooted off on her bike.* **2** [T] *especially AmE* to make someone or something move a short distance by pulling or pushing: *I scooted my chair over to their table.*
scoot over *phr v AmE informal* to move to one side, especially in order to make room for someone or something else: *He scooted over so I could sit down.*

SCOOTERS

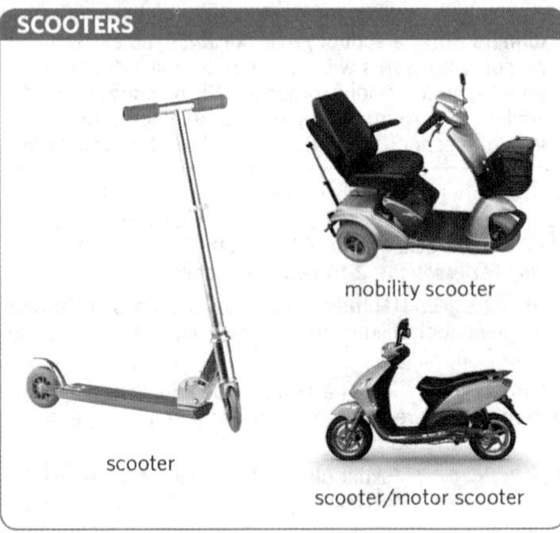

scoot·er /ˈskuːtə $ -ər/ ●●○ *n* [C]
1 (*also* **motor scooter**) a type of small, less powerful MOTORCYCLE with small wheels
2 a child's vehicle with two small wheels, an upright handle, and a narrow board that you stand on with one foot, while the other foot pushes against the ground

scope¹ /skəʊp $ skoʊp/ ●●○ W3 AWL *n*
1 [U] the range of things that a subject, activity, book etc deals with: **[+of]** *the need to define the scope of the investigation* | *measures to limit the scope of criminals' activities* | **beyond/outside/within the scope of sth** *A full discussion of that issue is beyond the scope of this book.* | **widen/broaden/extend etc the scope of sth** *Let us extend the scope of the study to examine more factors.* | **narrow/limit etc**

the scope of sth *The court's ruling narrowed the scope of the affirmative action program.* | **limited/wider etc in scope** *His efforts were too limited in scope to have much effect.*
2 [U] the opportunity to do or develop something: **[+for]** *The scope for successful gardening increases dramatically with a greenhouse.* | **there is considerable/great/little etc scope for sth** *There is considerable scope for further growth in the economy.*
3 [singular] *informal* a particular set of activities and the people who are involved in them SYN **scene**: **the music/cinema/club etc scope**

scope² *v*
scope sb/sth ↔ **out** *phr v AmE informal* to look at something or someone to see what they are like: *Let's go inside and scope out the menu.*

scorch¹ /skɔːtʃ $ skɔːrtʃ/ ●○○ *v*
1 [I,T] if you scorch something, or if it scorches, its surface burns slightly and changes colour: *The walls had been blackened and scorched by fire.* THESAURUS ▸ BURN
2 [T] if strong heat or wind scorches plants, it dries and damages them: *Direct sunlight will scorch the plant's leaves.*
3 [T] if strong heat scorches you, it burns you: *The hot sand scorched our feet.*
4 [I always + adv/prep] *BrE informal* to travel extremely fast: **[+along/down/across etc]** *He scorched out of the gate, almost crashing his new sports car.* —**scorched** *adj*

scorch² *n* **1** [C] a mark made on something where its surface has been burnt: *There were* ***scorch marks*** *on the kitchen worktop where a hot pan had been placed.* **2** [U] brown colouring on plants caused by some plant diseases

ˌscorched ˈearth ˌpolicy *n* [C] the destruction by an army of everything useful in an area, especially crops, so that the land cannot be used by an enemy

scorch·er /ˈskɔːtʃə $ ˈskɔːrtʃər/ *n* [C usually singular] *informal* an extremely hot day: *It was a scorcher of a day.*

scorch·ing /ˈskɔːtʃɪŋ $ ˈskɔːr-/ (*also* **scorching hot**) *adj* extremely hot: *the scorching desert heat* | *a scorching hot day*

score¹ /skɔː $ skɔːr/ ●●● S2 W2 *n* [C]
1 IN A GAME the number of points that each team or player has won in a game or competition: *At half-time the score was one all.* | *What's the score?* | *Is anybody* ***keeping score*** (=making a record of the score)? | *The* ***final score*** *was Southampton two, Leeds United nil.* | **[+of]** *a score of 3-2*
2 IN A TEST OR EXPERIMENT **a)** the number of points a student has earned for correct answers in a test: *The school's* ***test scores*** *have not improved.* | **[+of]** *a score of 90%* **b)** the number of points that a person or group of people gets in a scientific test or EXPERIMENT: **[+of]** *He had an IQ score of 120.*
3 MUSIC a written or printed copy of a piece of music, especially for a large group of performers, or the music itself: *a musical score* | *Who wrote the score for the movie?*
4 on that score *spoken* concerning the particular thing you have just mentioned: *As for the cost, you don't need to worry on that score.*
5 know the score *informal* to know the real facts of a situation, including any unpleasant ones: *We are trying to attract managers who know the score.*
6 settle a score to do something to harm or hurt someone who has harmed or hurt you in the past: *Jack came back after five years to* ***settle*** *some* ***old scores****.*
7 MARK a mark that has been cut onto a surface with a sharp tool: *deep scores in the wood*

score² ●●● S3 W2 *v*
1 WIN POINTS [I,T] to win a point in a sport, game, competition, or test: *Great cheers went up when he scored in the final minute of the game.* | *She scored an average of 9.9 in the test.* | **score a goal/point/run etc** *He has scored 12 goals so far this season.* → see picture at FOOTBALL
2 GIVE POINTS [T] to give a particular number of points in a game, competition, test, or EXPERIMENT SYN **mark**: *Each event will be scored separately.* | *Responses to the individual items are scored on a scale ranging from 0 to 12.*
3 score points a) (*also* **score off sb**) to say or do something in an attempt to prove that you are better or cleverer than someone else: *Too many MPs use debates as a chance to score political points.* | **[+over/off]** *Advertising may be used to score points off the competition.* **b)** *informal* to do or say something to please someone or to make them respect you: **[+with]** *You'll score points with your girlfriend if you send her roses.*
4 SUCCEED [I,T] *informal* to be very successful in something you do: *Her new book has* ***scored*** *a spectacular* ***success****.*
5 HAVE SEX [I] *informal* to have sex with someone, especially someone you have just met
6 LINE [T] to mark a line on a piece of paper, wood etc using a sharp instrument: *Scoring the paper first makes it easier to fold.*
7 MUSIC [T] to arrange a piece of music for a group of instruments or voices: **be scored for sth** *The piece is scored for a soprano voice and orchestra.* GRAMMAR **Score** is usually passive in this meaning.
8 GET DRUGS [I,T] *informal* to manage to buy or get illegal drugs
score off sb *phr v BrE* to say or do something in an attempt to prove that you are better or cleverer than someone else: *He liked scoring off his pupils in his days as a teacher.*
score sth ↔ **out/through** *phr v* to draw a line through something that has been written

score³ *number* **1** (*plural* **score**) a group of 20, or about 20, people or things: **a score of sth** *Our coach was escorted by a score of policemen.* | **three score years and ten** *old use* (=70 years, a person's expected length of life) **2 scores of sth** a lot of people or things: *Scores of victims were killed.* **3 by the score** in large numbers: *Friends came to help by the score.*

score·board /ˈskɔːbɔːd $ ˈskɔːrbɔːrd/ *n* [C] a board on which the points won in a game are recorded

score·card /ˈskɔːkɑːd $ ˈskɔːrkɑːrd/ *n* [C] **1** a printed card used by someone watching a sports match or race to record what happens **2** a system that is used for checking or testing something

ˈscore draw *n* [C] *BrE* a football match in which both teams score at least one GOAL and the final score is 1-1, 2-2, 3-3 etc

score·less /ˈskɔːləs $ ˈskɔːr-/ *adj* if a sports match or part of a sports match is scoreless, nobody scores any points or GOALS: *a scoreless first half*

score·line /ˈskɔːlaɪn $ ˈskɔːr-/ *n* [C] *BrE* the score or the final result in a football, RUGBY, or tennis match

scor·er /ˈskɔːrə $ -ər/ *n* [C] **1** (*also* **score·keep·er** /ˈskɔːkiːpə $ ˈskɔːrkiːpər/) someone who keeps an official record of the points won in a sports game **2** a player who wins a point or GOAL: **top/leading/highest scorer** *He was Palace's top scorer.*

score·sheet /ˈskɔːʃiːt $ ˈskɔːr-/ *n* [C] **1** a special piece of paper on which someone records the points won in a sports match **2 get (your name) on the scoresheet** *BrE* to score one or more GOALS or points in football, RUGBY, and some other sports

scorn¹ /skɔːn $ skɔːrn/ *n* [U] **1** the feeling that someone or something is stupid or does not deserve respect SYN **contempt**: **[+for]** *He felt scorn for his working-class parents.* | **with scorn** *Rachel looked at me with scorn.* **2 pour scorn on sb/sth** (*also* **heap scorn on sb/sth** *AmE*) to strongly criticize someone or something because you think they do not deserve respect: *Labour poured scorn on the Tory claim to be the party of law and order.*

scorn² *v* [T] **1** to show that you think that something is stupid, unreasonable, or not worth accepting: *Many women scorn the use of make-up.* **2** to criticize someone or something because you think they do not deserve respect: *He scorned the government's record in dealing with crime.*

scorn·ful /ˈskɔːnfəl $ ˈskɔːrn-/ *adj* feeling or showing scorn: *a scornful look* | **[+of]** *He was scornful of the women's movement.* —**scornfully** *adv*

S

Scor·pi·o /ˈskɔːpiəʊ $ ˈskɔːrpioʊ/ *n* (*plural* **Scorpios**) **1** [U] the eighth sign of the ZODIAC, represented by a SCORPION, which some people believe affects the character and life of people born between October 24 and November 22 **2** [C] someone who was born between October 24 and November 22

scor·pi·on /ˈskɔːpiən $ -ɔːr-/ *n* [C] a tropical animal like an insect, with a curving tail and a poisonous sting

Scot /skɒt $ skɑːt/ *n* [C] someone from Scotland

scotch /skɒtʃ $ skɑːtʃ/ *v* [T] to stop something happening by firmly doing something to prevent it: *He issued an announcement to scotch rumours of his death.*

Scotch¹ *n* [C,U] a strong alcoholic drink made in Scotland, or a glass of this → **whisky**: *Two Scotches, please.*

Scotch² *adj old-fashioned* SCOTTISH

ˌScotch ˈbroth *n* [U] *BrE* thick soup made from vegetables, meat, and BARLEY (=type of grain)

ˌScotch ˈegg *n* [C] *BrE* a cooked egg that is covered with sausage meat and BREADCRUMBS, then FRIED

ˌScotch ˈtape *n* [U] *trademark AmE* thin clear plastic tape that is sticky on one side, used for sticking light things such as paper together —**scotch tape** *v* [T]

scot-free /ˌskɒt ˈfriː $ ˌskɑːt-/ *adv* **get away/off scot-free** *informal* to avoid being punished although you deserve to be

Scot·land Yard /ˌskɒtlənd ˈjɑːd $ ˌskɑːtlənd ˈjɑːrd/ the part of the London police that deals with serious crimes, or their main office

Scots /skɒts $ skɑːts/ *adj* Scottish

Scots·man /ˈskɒtsmən $ ˈskɑːts-/ *n* (*plural* **Scotsmen** /-mən/) [C] a man from Scotland

Scots·wom·an /ˈskɒtsˌwʊmən $ ˈskɑːts-/ *n* (*plural* **Scotswomen** /-ˌwɪmɪn/) [C] a woman from Scotland

Scot·tish /ˈskɒtɪʃ $ ˈskɑːtɪʃ/ *adj* relating to Scotland or its people

ˈScottish ˌPlay, the a name for Shakespeare's play *Macbeth*, used by actors because they believe that it is unlucky to say 'Macbeth'

scoun·drel /ˈskaʊndrəl/ *n* [C] *old-fashioned* a bad or dishonest man, especially someone who cheats or deceives other people

scour /skaʊə $ skaʊr/ *v* [T] **1** to search very carefully and thoroughly through an area, a document etc: **scour sth for sth** *Her family began to scour the countryside for a suitable house.* **2** (*also* **scour out**) to clean something very thoroughly by rubbing it with a rough material SYN **scrub**: *Ada was scouring out the pans.* **3** (*also* **scour out**) to form a hole by continuous movement over a long period: *Over the years, the stream had scoured out a round pool in the rock.*

scour·er /ˈskaʊərə $ ˈskaʊrər/ (*also* **ˈscouring pad**) *n* [C] a small ball of wire or rough plastic for cleaning cooking pots and pans

scourge¹ /skɜːdʒ $ skɜːrdʒ/ *n* [C] **1** something that causes a lot of harm or suffering: **[+of]** *the scourge of unemployment* | *the scourge of war* **2** a WHIP used to punish people in the past

scourge² *v* [T] **1** to cause a lot of harm or suffering to a place or group of people **2** to hit someone with a whip as punishment in the past

Scouse /skaʊs/ *n* [U] *BrE* the way of speaking that is typical of people from Liverpool —**Scouse** *adj*

Scous·er /ˈskaʊsə $ -ər/ *n* [C] *BrE informal* someone from the city of Liverpool in England

scout¹ /skaʊt/ ●●○ *n* [C]

1 a) the Scouts an organization for boys that teaches them practical skills **b)** (*also* **boy scout**) a boy who is a member of this organization

2 (*also* **Girl Scout**) *AmE* a girl who is a member of an organization for girls that teaches them practical things SYN **guide** *BrE*

3 a soldier, plane etc that is sent to search the area in front of an army and get information about the enemy: *He sent three scouts ahead to take a look at the bridge.*

4 (*also* **talent scout**) someone whose job is to look for good sports players, musicians etc in order to employ them: *He was spotted by a scout at the age of 13.*

scout² *v* **1** [I] (*also* **scout around/round**) to look for something in a particular area: **[+for]** *I'm scouting round for a place to stay.* **2** [T] (*also* **scout out**) to examine a place or area in order to get information about it: *American companies are keen to scout out business opportunities in Vietnam.* **3** [I,T] to find out about the abilities of sports players, musicians etc in order to employ them

scout·ing /ˈskaʊtɪŋ/ *n* [U] the activities that Scouts take part in

scout·mas·ter /ˈskaʊtˌmɑːstə $ -ˌmæstər/ *n* [C] a man who is the leader of a group of Scouts

scowl¹ /skaʊl/ ●○○ *v* [I] to look at someone in an angry way → **frown**: *Patrick scowled, but did as he was told.* | **[+at]** *Mum scowled at him and refused to say anything.*

scowl² *n* [C] an angry or disapproving expression on someone's face → **frown**: *She looked at me with a scowl.*

scrab·ble /ˈskræbəl/ *v* [I always + adv/prep] to try to find or do something very quickly, usually by moving your hands or feet in an uncontrolled way: **[+for]** *He scrabbled for the light switch.* | **[+around/about]** *She was scrabbling around, searching for the door.*

Scrabble *n* [U] *trademark* a game in which players try to make words from the separate letters they have

scrag·gly /ˈskrægəli/ *adj informal* growing in a way that looks uneven and in bad condition: *his* ***scraggly*** *gray* ***beard***

scrag·gy /ˈskrægi/ *adj BrE* too thin SYN **skinny**: *a scraggy neck*

scram /skræm/ *v* (**scrammed**, **scramming**) [I usually in imperative] *informal* to leave a place very quickly, especially so that you do not get caught: *Scram, you two!*

scram·ble¹ /ˈskræmbəl/ ●●○ *v*

1 CLIMB [I always + adv/prep] to climb up, down, or over something quickly and with difficulty, especially using your hands to help you: **[+up/down/over etc]** *They tried to scramble up the cliff.* | *She scrambled down the tree as quickly as she could.*

2 MOVE QUICKLY [I always + adv/prep] to move somewhere in a hurried awkward way: **[+to/out/from etc]** *Alan scrambled out of the way.* | *Micky* ***scrambled to*** *his* ***feet*** (=stood up very quickly and awkwardly) *and hurried into the kitchen.*

3 DO STH QUICKLY [T] to try to do something difficult very quickly: **scramble to do sth** *They were scrambling to give the impression that the situation was under control.*

4 COMPETE [I] to struggle or compete with other people to get or reach something: **[+for]** *Thousands of people will be scrambling for tickets.*

5 INFORMATION/MESSAGE [T] to use special equipment to mix messages, radio signals etc into a different form, so that they cannot be understood by other people without the correct equipment: *Our conversation will be electronically scrambled.*

6 MIX [T] to mix words, ideas, sentences etc so that they are not in the right order and do not make sense: *The words in each sentence are scrambled.*

7 scramble an egg to cook an egg by mixing the white and yellow parts together and heating it in a pan

8 scramble sb's brains *informal* to make someone unable to think clearly or reasonably: *Maybe the alcohol has scrambled his brains.*

9 AIRCRAFT [I] if a military plane scrambles, it goes up into the air very quickly in order to escape or to attack an enemy

scramble² *n* **1** [singular] a difficult climb in which you have to use your hands to help you: *The village was a 20-minute scramble away.* **2** [singular] a situation in which people compete with and push each other in order to get what they want: **[+for]** *the usual scramble for the bathroom every morning* | **scramble to do sth** *a scramble to carry the baggage into the house* **3** [singular] a situation in which something has to be done very quickly, with a lot of rushing around: *It was a **mad scramble** trying to get things ready in time.* **4** [C] *BrE* a MOTORCYCLE race over rough ground

ˌscrambled ˈegg *n* [C,U] eggs cooked in a pan after the white and yellow parts have been mixed together → see picture at EGG¹

scram·bler /ˈskræmblə $ -ər/ *n* [C] a machine that mixes up a radio or telephone message so that it cannot be understood without special equipment

scram·bling /ˈskræmblɪŋ/ *n* [U] **1** the activity of climbing over rocks using your hands but no ropes **2** *BrE* the activity of racing on MOTORCYCLES over rough ground

scram·jet /ˈskræmˌdʒet/ *n* [C] a type of powerful engine that can make an aircraft fly at more than ten times the speed of sound

scrap¹ /skræp/ ●●○ *n*

1 PAPER/CLOTH [C] a small piece of paper, cloth etc: **[+of]** *He wrote his address on a scrap of paper.* | *a rug made out of old scraps of material* → see picture at PIECE¹ THESAURUS PIECE

2 OLD OBJECTS [U] materials or objects that are no longer used for the purpose they were made for, but can be used again in another way: *The equipment was **sold for scrap**.* | ***Scrap metal*** (=metal from old cars, machines etc) *fetched high prices after the war.*

3 FOOD **scraps** [plural] pieces of food that are left after you have finished eating: *My mother fed the dog on scraps to save money.* | **table/kitchen scraps** *AmE*

4 INFORMATION [C] a small amount of information, truth etc: **[+of]** *He obtained every scrap of information available.* | *There isn't a single scrap of evidence.*

5 FIGHT [C] *informal* a short fight or argument: *He's always getting into scraps with other dogs.*

scrap² *v* (**scrapped**, **scrapping**) **1** [T] to decide not to use a plan or system because it is not practical: *We believe that car tax should be scrapped.* **2** [T] to get rid of an old machine, vehicle etc, and use its parts in some other way: *Two aircraft carriers are being scrapped this year.* **3** [I] *informal* to have a short fight

scrap·book /ˈskræpbʊk/ *n* [C] a book with empty pages where you can stick pictures, newspaper articles, or other things you want to keep

scrape¹ /skreɪp/ ●●○ *v*

1 [T] to remove something from a surface using the edge of a knife, a stick etc: *Scrape the carrots and slice them thinly.* | **scrape sth away/off** *The earth was scraped away to uncover a trapdoor.* | **scrape sth off/into etc sth** *Teresa scraped the mud off her boots.* | *The two of them **scraped** their dishes **clean**.*

2 [I,T always + adv/prep] to rub against a rough surface in a way that causes slight damage or injury, or to make something do this → **graze**: *The coat was too long; the hem scraped the pavement.* | **[+against/on etc]** *I heard the side of the car scrape against the wall.* | **scrape sth against/on sth** *I scraped my knee painfully on the concrete.*

3 [I,T] to make a noise by rubbing roughly against a surface: *Chairs scraped loudly as they stood up.* | **scrape (sth) on/down/against sth** *He opened the gate quietly, trying not to let it scrape on the gravel.*

4 scrape home *especially BrE* to win a race, election, or competition by a very small amount: *The Tories may scrape home, but it's unlikely.*

5 scrape (the bottom of) the barrel *informal* to have to use something even though it is not very good, because there is nothing better available: *It was clear that the party was scraping the barrel for competent politicians.*

6 [T] *technical* if a computer program scrapes DATA, it collects it from a website → **bow and scrape** at BOW¹(5), → **scrape/scratch a living** at LIVING²(1)

scrape sth ↔ **back** *phr v* if you scrape your hair back, you pull it away from your face and tie it at the back: *Her blonde hair was scraped back into a ponytail.*

scrape by *phr v*

1 to have just enough money to live: *We can scrape by, thanks to what we grow ourselves.*

2 to only just succeed in passing an examination or dealing with a difficult situation

scrape in (*also* **scrape into sth**) *phr v* to only just succeed in getting a job, a place at university, a position in government etc: *Labour scraped in by a small majority.* | *He just scraped into college.*

scrape through (sth) *phr v* to only just succeed in passing an examination or dealing with a difficult situation: *I managed to scrape through the exam.*

scrape sth ↔ **together/up** *phr v* to get enough money for a particular purpose, when this is difficult: *She scraped together the last of her savings.* | *They could hardly scrape up enough money for the train fare.*

scrape² *n* **1** [C] a mark or slight injury caused by rubbing against a rough surface SYN **graze**: *I came away from the accident with only cuts and scrapes.* THESAURUS INJURY **2** [C] *informal* a situation in which you are in trouble or have difficulties: *He **got into** all sorts of **scrapes** as a boy.* **3** [singular] the noise made when one surface rubs roughly against another: **[+of]** *He heard the scrape of chairs being dragged across the floor.*

scrape·o·ver /ˈskreɪpəʊvə $ -oʊvər/ *n* [C] *AmE informal* a way of arranging a man's hair, in which a long piece of hair from one side is COMBed over the top of the head to hide the fact that the man is going BALD (=losing his hair) – used humorously SYN **combover** *BrE*

scrap·er /ˈskreɪpə $ -ər/ *n* [C] a tool used to remove something from a surface by rubbing: *a paint scraper*

scrap·heap /ˈskræphiːp/ *n* **1 on the scrapheap** *informal* not wanted or used anymore – used especially when this seems unfair: *Three years later he was on the political scrapheap.* **2** [C] a pile of unwanted things, especially pieces of metal

scra·pie /ˈskreɪpi/ *n* [U] a serious disease that sheep can get

scrap·ings /ˈskreɪpɪŋz/ *n* [plural] small pieces that have been SCRAPEd from a surface

ˈscrap ˌpaper *n* [U] paper, often paper that has already been used on one side, that you use for making notes, lists etc

scrap·py /ˈskræpi/ *adj* **1** *BrE* untidy or badly organized: *scrappy notes from the meeting* **2** *AmE informal* having a determined character and always willing to compete, argue, or fight: *a scrappy team that plays hard*

scratch¹ /skrætʃ/ ●●● S3 *v*

1 RUB YOUR SKIN [I,T] to rub your skin with your nails because it feels uncomfortable → **itch**: *John yawned and scratched his leg.* | *Try not to scratch.* | **[+at]** *He was scratching at the bites on his arm.* THESAURUS TOUCH

2 CUT SB'S SKIN [I,T] to cut someone's skin slightly with your nails or with something sharp: *She ran at him and scratched his face.* | *Don't scratch yourself on the thorns.*

3 MAKE A MARK [T] to make a small cut or mark on something by pulling something sharp across it: *I'm afraid I've scratched your car.* | *Some of the prisoners had scratched their names on the walls.*

4 ANIMALS [I always + adv/prep] if an animal scratches, it rubs its feet against something, often making a noise: *A few chickens scratched around in the yard.* | **[+at]** *a dog scratching at the door to be let in*

5 REMOVE STH [T always + adv/prep] to remove something from a surface by rubbing it with something sharp: **scratch sth off/away etc** *I scratched away a little of the paint with my fingernail.*

6 REMOVE WRITING [T always + adv/prep] to remove a word from a piece of writing by drawing a line through it SYN **cross out**: **scratch sth from/off sth** *I have scratched his name from the list.*

7 MAKE A NOISE [I always + adv/prep] to make a rough sound by moving something sharp across a surface: *His pen scratched away on the paper.*

8 scratch the surface to deal with only a very small part of a subject or problem: **[+of]** *I think we have only scratched the surface of this problem.*

9 scratch your head *informal* to think carefully about a

difficult question or problem: *This crisis has politicians scratching their heads and wondering what to do.*
10 STOP STH HAPPENING [T] *informal* if you scratch an idea or a plan, you decide that you will not do it SYN **abandon**
11 REMOVE FROM RACE [I,T] *informal* if someone scratches from a race, or if you scratch them from the race, they do not take part in it
12 you scratch my back, I'll scratch yours *spoken* used to say that you will help someone if they agree to help you → **scrape/scratch a living** at LIVING²(1)

scratch around (*also* **scratch about** *BrE*) *phr v* to try to find or get something which is difficult to find or get: **[+for]** *homeless people scratching around for a place to shelter*

scratch sth ↔ **out** *phr v* to remove a word from a piece of writing by drawing a line through it SYN **cross out**: *Emma's name had been scratched out.*

scratch² ●●○ *n*
1 CUT [C] a small cut on someone's skin: *There were* ***deep scratches*** *all over her face.* | *Don't worry, it's* ***only a scratch*** (=not a serious injury). | *She was unharmed apart from a few cuts and scratches.*
2 MARK [C] a thin mark or cut on the surface of something: *There was a big scratch on the car door.*
3 from scratch if you start something from scratch, you begin it without using anything that existed or was prepared before: *We had to* ***start*** *again* ***from scratch****.* | *He had* ***built*** *the business up* ***from scratch****.*
4 up to scratch *BrE informal* good enough for a particular standard: *Some of this work isn't up to scratch.* | **bring/get sth up to scratch** *We spent thousands of pounds getting the house up to scratch.*
5 RUB [singular] *especially BrE* when you rub part of your body with your nails because it feels uncomfortable: *He stretched and* ***had a scratch****.* | *He brushed his hair and* ***gave*** *his scalp a good* ***scratch****.*
6 SOUND [C] a sound made by something sharp or rough being rubbed on a hard surface: *I heard the scratch of an animal's claws on the door.*

scratch³ *adj* [no comparative] **1** a scratch team or group of people has been put together in a hurry, using anyone that is available **2** a scratch player in golf is very good and is not given any advantage in games

scratch·card, **scratch card** /ˈskrætʃkɑːd $ -kɑːrd/ *n* [C] *BrE* a small card you can buy which gives you a chance to win a prize. You rub off the surface of the card to find out whether you have won anything.

scratch·ing /ˈskrætʃɪŋ/ *n* [U] the activity of playing a record on a TURNTABLE and making new sounds by quickly spinning the record forwards and backwards with your finger while it is playing

scratch·ings /ˈskrætʃɪŋz/ *n* [plural] *BrE* small pieces of pig's skin that have been cooked in hot fat and are eaten cold SYN **pork rinds** *AmE*

scratch·mas·ter /ˈskrætʃˌmɑːstə $ -ˌmæstər/ *n* [C] a DJ who is skilful at scratching

scratch·pad /ˈskrætʃpæd/ *n* [C] **1** *AmE* several sheets of cheap paper that are joined together into a small book you can write notes in **2** a small screen on a MOBILE PHONE that lets you write short notes and stores them for you

ˈscratch ˌpaper *n* [U] *AmE* cheap paper, or paper that has already been used on one side, that you use for writing notes SYN **scrap paper**

scratch·y /ˈskrætʃi/ *adj* **1** something that is scratchy feels rough against your skin: *a scratchy woollen jumper* **2** a scratchy voice or musical sound is rough and not smooth and pleasant: *a scratchy old recording of some folk songs*

scrawl¹ /skrɔːl $ skrɒːl/ ●○○ *v* [T] to write in a careless and untidy way, so that your words are not easy to read → **scribble**: *He scrawled his name at the bottom.* THESAURUS▸ WRITE

scrawl² *n* [C,U] untidy careless writing: *The note was written in his usual illegible scrawl.*

scraw·ny /ˈskrɔːni $ ˈskrɒː-/ *adj* a scrawny person or animal looks very thin and weak SYN **skinny**: *a scrawny kid in jeans and a T-shirt* | *a few scrawny hens* THESAURUS▸ THIN

scream¹ /skriːm/ ●●● S3 *v*
1 [I] to make a loud high noise with your voice because you are hurt, frightened, excited etc SYN **shriek**: *After the first few shots, people started screaming.* | *a screaming baby* | **[+with/in]** *She jumped to her feet, screaming in terror.* | *The children were* ***screaming with laughter****.* | *She was* ***screaming her head off*** (=screaming a lot). | *She began to* ***scream blue murder*** (=scream very loudly). | *He was dragged* ***kicking and screaming*** *to a nearby van.* THESAURUS▸ SHOUT
2 [I,T] (*also* **scream out**) to shout something in a very loud high voice because you are angry or frightened SYN **yell**: *'Get out!' she screamed.* | *He screamed out her name.* | **[+for]** *I screamed for help.* | **[+at]** *He screamed at her to go away.* | *The crowd continued to* ***scream abuse*** *at him.*
3 [I] to make a very loud high noise: *The police car approached, its siren screaming.*

scream² ●●● S3 *n* [C]
1 a loud high sound that you make with your voice because you are hurt, frightened, excited etc SYN **shriek**: *We heard screams coming from the flat.* | *She saw the knife and* ***let out*** *a* ***scream****.* | **scream of laughter/terror etc** *He fell back with a scream of terror and pain.*
2 a very loud high sound: *the scream of a jet taking off*
3 a scream *informal* someone or something that is very funny: *The film was a scream!*

scream·ing·ly /ˈskriːmɪŋli/ *adv* extremely: *a screamingly funny film*

scree /skriː/ *n* [C] an area of loose soil and broken rocks on the side of a mountain: *a scree slope*

screech /skriːtʃ/ ●○○ *v*
1 [I,T] to shout loudly in an unpleasant high voice because you are angry, afraid, or excited SYN **shriek**, **scream**: *'Look out!' she screeched.* | *They* ***screeched with laughter****.* | **[+at]** *She screeched at me to take off my muddy shoes.*
2 [I] if a vehicle screeches, its wheels make a high unpleasant noise as it moves along or stops: *A van screeched onto the road in front of me.* | *The car* ***screeched to a halt****.* THESAURUS▸ SOUND —**screech** *n* [C]: *a screech of laughter* | *the screech of tyres*

screed /skriːd/ *n* [C] a very long boring piece of writing – used to show disapproval

screen¹ /skriːn/ ●●● S2 W2 *n*
1 TELEVISION/COMPUTER [C] the part of a television or computer where the picture or information appears → **monitor**: *a computer with an 18-inch colour screen* | *He went on staring at the* ***TV screen****.* | **on (a) screen** *Her picture appeared on the screen.* | *It's easy to change the text on screen before printing it.*
2 FILM **a)** [C] the large white surface that pictures are shown on in a cinema: *He was horrified at some of the images he saw on the screen.* **b)** [singular, U] films in general: *This is the first time the play has been adapted for* ***the big screen*** (=films). | *a star of* ***stage and screen*** (=the theatre and films) | **on screen** *his first appearance on screen* | *a well-known screen actor*
3 MOVABLE WALL [C] a piece of furniture like a thin wall that can be moved around and is used to divide one part of a room from another: *There was a screen around his bed.*
4 STH THAT HIDES **a)** [C] something tall and wide that hides a place or thing: **[+of]** *The house was hidden behind a screen of bushes.* **b)** [singular] something that hides what someone is doing: **[+for]** *The business was just a screen for his drug-dealing activities.*
5 TEST FOR ILLNESS [C] *BrE* a medical test to see whether someone has an illness SYN **screening** *AmE*: *The company is offering a free health screen to all employees.*
6 DOOR/WINDOW [C] a wire net fastened inside a frame in front of a window or door to keep insects out
7 CHURCH [C] a decorative wall in some churches
8 SPORTS [C] a player in a game such as BASKETBALL who protects the player who has the ball → SMOKESCREEN, SUNSCREEN

screen² ●●○ *v* [T]
1 TEST FOR ILLNESS to do tests on a lot of people to find out whether they have a particular illness: *All women over 50 will be regularly screened.* | **screen sb for sth** *It is now possible to screen babies for diabetes.*
2 HIDE STH if something screens something else, it is in front of it and hides it: **screen sth from sth** *A line of trees screened the house from the road.*
3 FILM/TELEVISION to show a film or television programme: *The film is being screened around the country.* | *The match will be screened live on television.*
4 TEST EMPLOYEES ETC to find out information about people in order to decide whether you can trust them: *Police are very careful when screening politicians' bodyguards.* | *Applicants are screened for security.*
5 CHECK THINGS to check things to see whether they are acceptable or suitable: *You can use an answerphone to* ***screen*** *your phone* ***calls*** *before you answer them.*
screen sth ↔ **off** *phr v* to separate one part of a room from the rest by putting a thin temporary wall or a curtain across it: *The back part of the room had been screened off.*
screen sth ↔ **out** *phr v*
1 to prevent something harmful from passing through SYN **filter out**: *Sun lotions screen out damaging ultraviolet light.*
2 to remove people or things that are not acceptable or not suitable SYN **filter out**: *An answering service can screen out nuisance calls.*

ˈscreen ˌdoor *n* [C] *AmE* a door with wire net fastened inside a frame, which is used outside the main door of a building to keep insects out

ˈscreen dump *n* [C] a picture of what is on a computer screen at a particular time, or the process of saving or printing this picture → **screenshot**

screen·ing /ˈskriːnɪŋ/ *n* **1** [C,U] the showing of a film or television programme: *a screening of Spielberg's new movie* **2** [U] medical tests that are done on a lot of people to make sure that they do not have a particular disease: **[+for]** *screening for breast cancer* **3** [U] tests or checks that are done to make sure that people or things are acceptable or suitable for a particular purpose: *security screening of airline passengers*

screen·play /ˈskriːnpleɪ/ *n* [C] the words that are written down for actors to say in a film, and the instructions that tell them what they should do SYN **script**

ˈscreen ˌprinting *n* [U] a way of printing pictures by forcing paint or ink through a specially prepared cloth onto paper or cloth —**screen print** *v* [T]

ˈscreen ˌsaver *n* [C] a computer program that makes a moving image appear on the screen when the image on it has not changed for a period of time, especially so that the screen does not become damaged

screen·shot /ˈskriːnʃɒt $ -ʃɑːt/ (*also* **screen capture**) *n* [C] *technical* a picture of what is on a computer screen at a particular time, which can be saved and put into a document or printed out

ˈscreen ˌtest *n* [C] an occasion when someone is filmed while they are performing, in order to see if they are suitable to act in a film

screen·writ·er /ˈskriːnˌraɪtə $ -ər/ *n* [C] someone who writes plays for film or television → **playwright**

SCREW
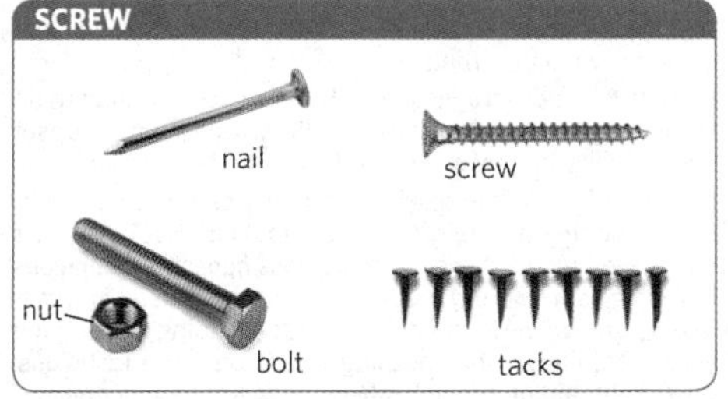

screw¹ /skruː/ ●●● S3 *n* [C]
1 a thin pointed piece of metal that you push and turn in order to fasten pieces of metal or wood together → **nail**: *Fix the frame in position and* ***tighten*** *the* ***screws***.
2 *informal not polite* **a)** an offensive word meaning an act of having sex **b) a good screw** a very offensive word for someone who is good at having sex
3 have a screw loose *informal* to be slightly crazy
4 put/tighten the screws on sb *informal* to force someone to do something by threatening them: *The government has started to tighten the screws on illegal share dealers.*
5 *BrE informal* a prison officer – used especially by prisoners

screw² ●●○ *v*
1 ATTACH [T always + adv/prep] to attach one thing to another using a screw → **nail**: **screw sth into/onto/to sth** *The chairs were screwed to the floor.* | *The wooden frame should be screwed onto the wall.*
2 CLOSE BY TURNING [I,T always + adv/prep] to fasten or close something by turning it, or to be fastened in this way OPP **unscrew**: **screw (sth) on/onto sth** *The lens screws onto the front of the camera.* | *She carefully screwed the cap back onto the toothpaste.*
3 PAPER/CLOTH [T always + adv/prep] (*also* **screw up**) to twist paper or cloth into a small round shape: *She screwed the letter up and threw it in the bin.* | **screw sth (up) into sth** *I screwed my handkerchief into a ball.*
4 SEX [I,T] *informal not polite* an offensive word meaning to have sex with someone
5 screw you/him etc *spoken not polite* an offensive expression used to show that you are very angry with someone
6 CHEAT [T] *not polite* to cheat someone in order to get money from them: **screw sb for sth** *They screwed us for $60 in the end.* → **have your head screwed on (straight)** at HEAD¹
screw around *phr v*
1 *informal* to do silly things that may cause trouble SYN **mess around**: *The kids were screwing around down by the bus station.*
2 *informal not polite* an offensive expression meaning to have sex with a lot of different people
screw up *phr v*
1 *informal* to make a bad mistake or do something very stupid SYN **mess up**: *You'd better not screw up this time.*
2 screw sth ↔ up *informal* to spoil something by doing something stupid SYN **mess sth up**: *She realized that she had screwed up her life.*
3 screw up your eyes/face to move the muscles in your face in a way that makes your eyes seem narrow: *He screwed up his eyes against the bright light.* | *Her face was screwed up with pain.*
4 screw sb ↔ up *informal* to make someone feel very unhappy, confused, or upset so that they have emotional problems for a long time SYN **mess sb up**: *It really screwed her up when her mother died.* → SCREWED UP
5 screw up the/enough courage to do sth (*also* **screw up your courage to do sth**) to be brave enough to do something you are very nervous about: *I finally screwed up enough courage to talk to her.*

screw·ball /ˈskruːbɔːl $ -bɒːl/ *n* [C] *especially AmE informal* someone who seems very strange or crazy

ˈscrewball ˌcomedy *n* [C] *AmE* a film or television programme that is funny because crazy things happen

screw·driv·er /ˈskruːˌdraɪvə $ -ər/ *n* [C] **1** a tool with a narrow blade at one end that you use for turning screws → see picture at TOOL¹ **2** an alcoholic drink made from VODKA and orange juice

ˌscrewed ˈup *adj informal* someone who is screwed up has a lot of emotional problems because of bad or unhappy experiences in the past

ˈscrew top *n* [C] a top for a bottle or other container that you fasten on by turning it —**screw-top** *adj* [only before noun]

screw·y /ˈskruːi/ *adj informal* an idea or plan that is screwy seems very strange or crazy

scrib·ble¹ /ˈskrɪbəl/ ●○○ *v*
1 [T] (*also* **scribble down**) to write something quickly and untidily: *I scribbled his phone number in my address book.* | *He scribbled down our names.* THESAURUS ▸ WRITE

2 [I] to draw marks that have no meaning: *Someone had scribbled all over my picture.* THESAURUS DRAW

scribble² *n* **1** [U] (*also* **scribbles** [plural]) meaningless marks or pictures, especially done by children **2** [singular, U] untidy writing that is difficult to read: *I couldn't read his scribble.*

scrib·bler /ˈskrɪbələ $ -ər/ *n* [C] *informal* a writer, especially an unimportant one

scribe /skraɪb/ *n* [C] **1** someone in the past whose job was to make written copies of official documents **2** a JOURNALIST - used humorously

scrim·mage /ˈskrɪmɪdʒ/ *n* [C] **1** *informal* a fight **2** *AmE* a practice game of football, BASKETBALL etc

scrimp /skrɪmp/ *v* [I] to try to save as much money as you can, even though you have very little: *They **scrimped and saved** for years to buy their own home.*

script /skrɪpt/ ●●○ S3 *n*

1 [C] the written form of a speech, play, film etc → **screenplay**: *They write all their own scripts.* | *a film script*

2 [C,U] the set of letters that are used in writing a language: *Arabic script*

3 [C] *BrE* a piece of work that a student writes in an examination

4 [singular, U] *formal* writing done by hand SYN **handwriting**: *a diary entry written in neat black script*

script·ed /ˈskrɪptɪd/ *adj* a speech or broadcast that is scripted has been written down before it is read

scrip·tur·al /ˈskrɪptʃərəl/ *adj* contained in the Bible or based on the Bible

scrip·ture /ˈskrɪptʃə $ -ər/ *n* **1 Scripture** [U] (*also* **the (Holy) Scriptures** [plural]) the Bible: *the way God is portrayed in Scripture* **2** [C,U] the holy books of a particular religion: *Hindu scriptures*

script·writ·er /ˈskrɪptˌraɪtə $ -ər/ *n* [C] someone who writes the stories and words for films or television programmes SYN **screenwriter** → **playwright**

scroll¹ /skrəʊl $ skroʊl/ *n* [C] **1** a long piece of paper that can be rolled up, and is used as an official document **2** a design shaped like a piece of rolled up paper

scroll² *v* [I always + adv/prep] to move information on a computer screen up or down so that you can read it: **[+through]** *He scrolled through the document.* | **[+up/down]** *Could you scroll down a few lines?*

ˈscroll bar *n* [C] a part on the side of a computer screen that you move using a MOUSE in order to move up or down

Scrooge, **scrooge** /skruːdʒ/ *n* [C] *informal* someone who hates spending money

scro·tum /ˈskrəʊtəm $ ˈskroʊ-/ *n* (*plural* **scrota** /-tə/ *or* **scrotums**) [C] the bag of skin that contains a man's TESTICLES

scrounge¹ /skraʊndʒ/ *v* [I,T] *informal* to get money or something you want by asking other people for it rather than by paying for it yourself: **[+for]** *a group of children scrounging for food* | **scrounge sth off/from sb** *I managed to scrounge some money off my dad.* | **scrounge around (for sth)** *AmE: Leroy would scrounge around for old car parts.* —**scrounger** *n* [C]

scrounge² *n* **be on the scrounge** *BrE informal* to be trying to get money or things you want by asking other people for them

scrub¹ /skrʌb/ ●●○ *v* (**scrubbed**, **scrubbing**)

1 [I,T] to rub something hard, especially with a stiff brush, in order to clean it: *She was on her hands and knees scrubbing the floor.* | *He scrubbed the dirt off his boots.* | *The table needs to be **scrubbed clean**.* | **[+at]** *She scrubbed at her face with a tissue.* → see picture at CLEAN² THESAURUS CLEAN

2 [T] *informal* to decide not to do something that you had planned SYN **cancel**: *We scrubbed the idea in the end.*

3 [T] to remove CARBON DIOXIDE from the gas that results from burning coal, before letting it out into the air: *The liquid is used to scrub carbon dioxide from power plant exhaust gases.*

scrub sth ↔ **out** *phr v* to clean the inside of a place thoroughly: *The rooms are all scrubbed out once a week.*

scrub up *phr v* to wash your hands and arms before doing a medical operation

scrub² *n* **1** [U] low bushes and trees that grow in very dry soil **2** [singular] *especially BrE* if you give something a scrub, you clean it by rubbing it hard: *I **gave** the floor a good **scrub**.*

scrub·ber /ˈskrʌbə $ -ər/ *n* [C] *BrE taboo old-fashioned informal* an offensive word for a woman who has sex for money, or has sex with a lot of different men. Do not use this word.

ˈscrubbing brush *especially BrE*, **ˈscrub brush** *AmE n* [C] a stiff brush that you use for cleaning things → see picture at BRUSH¹

scrub·by /ˈskrʌbi/ *adj* **1** scrubby land is covered by low bushes **2** scrubby trees and bushes are small and do not look very healthy

scrub·land /ˈskrʌblənd/ *n* [U] an area of land that is covered with low bushes

scruff /skrʌf/ *n* **1 by the scruff of the neck** if you hold a person or animal by the scruff of their neck, you hold the skin, fur, or clothes at the back of their neck **2** [C] *BrE informal* someone who looks untidy or dirty

scruf·fy /ˈskrʌfi/ *adj* dirty and untidy: *a scruffy old pair of jeans* | *scruffy shops* —**scruffily** *adv*: *a scruffily dressed man* —**scruffiness** *n* [U]

scrum /skrʌm/ *n* **1** [C] a part of a game of RUGBY when the players all push together in a circle, with their heads down, and try to get the ball **2** [singular] *BrE informal* a crowd of people who are all close together and pushing each other to try to get something: *He struggled through the scrum of people to the kitchen.*

scrum-half /ˌskrʌmˈhɑːf $ -ˈhæf/ *n* [C] a player in RUGBY who has to put the ball into the SCRUM

scrum·mage /ˈskrʌmɪdʒ/ *n* [C] a SCRUM(1)

scrum·my /ˈskrʌmi/ *adj BrE informal* food that is scrummy tastes very good SYN **scrumptious**

scrump /skrʌmp/ *v* [T] *BrE old-fashioned* to steal fruit from trees in people's gardens

scrump·tious /ˈskrʌmpʃəs/ *adj informal* food that is scrumptious tastes very good SYN **delicious**: *a scrumptious chocolate cake* | *That was **absolutely scrumptious**!*

scrum·py /ˈskrʌmpi/ *n* [U] *BrE* a strong alcoholic drink made from apples

scrunch /skrʌntʃ/ *v* [I] *informal* if stones, leaves etc scrunch as you walk on them, they make a noisy sound: *The dry leaves scrunched under our feet.* —**scrunch** *n* [singular]: *the scrunch of gravel*

scrunch sth ↔ **up** *phr v* **1** to crush and twist something into a small round shape: *I scrunched up the letter and threw it in the bin.* **2 scrunch up your face/eyes** to move the muscles in your face in a way that makes your eyes seem narrow: *He scrunched up his eyes and grinned.*

scrunch·y, **scrunchie** /ˈskrʌntʃi/ *n* (*plural* **scrunchies**) [C] a small circular piece of rubber covered loosely with cloth, which is used for holding hair together in a PONYTAIL

scru·ple¹ /ˈskruːpəl/ *n* [C usually plural, U] a belief about what is right and wrong that prevents you from doing bad things → **qualm**: **scruples about doing sth** *He **had** no **scruples** about selling faulty goods to people.* | *a man with no **moral scruples*** | **without scruple** *They made thousands of families homeless without scruple.*

scruple² *v* **not scruple to do sth** *literary* to be willing to do something even though it may be wrong or may upset people: *They did not scruple to bomb innocent civilians.*

scru·pu·lous /ˈskruːpjələs/ *adj* **1** very careful to be completely honest and fair OPP **unscrupulous**: *Not all lawyers are as scrupulous as she is.* | *scrupulous honesty* | **scrupulous in (doing) sth** *The organization will be scrupulous in maintaining the highest moral standards.* **2** doing something very carefully so that nothing is left out SYN **fastidious**: **scrupulous about (doing) sth** *He was not very scrupulous about keeping himself clean.* | *scrupulous attention to detail* —**scrupulously** *adv*: *scrupulously clean* | *scrupulously fair*

S

scru·ti·neer /ˌskruːtəˈnɪə $ -tnˈɪr/ *n* [C] *BrE* an official who checks that the votes in an election are counted fairly

scru·ti·nize (*also* **-ise** *BrE*) /ˈskruːtənaɪz/ *v* [T] to examine someone or something very carefully: *He scrutinized the document.* | *She scrutinized his face.* THESAURUS EXAMINE

scru·ti·ny /ˈskruːtɪni/ ●○○ *n* [U] careful and thorough examination of someone or something: **careful/close scrutiny** *Careful scrutiny of the company's accounts revealed a whole series of errors.* | *Their activities have* ***come under*** *police* ***scrutiny***.

SCSI /ˈskʌzi/ *n* [U] (***small computer systems interface***) something that helps a small computer work with another piece of electronic equipment, such as a PRINTER, especially when they are connected by wires: *a SCSI port*

scu·ba div·ing /ˈskuːbə ˌdaɪvɪŋ/ *n* [U] the sport of swimming under water while breathing through a tube that is connected to a container of air on your back —**scuba diver** *n* [C]

scud /skʌd/ *v* (**scudded**, **scudding**) [I always + adv/prep] *literary* if clouds scud across the sky, they move quickly

scuff /skʌf/ *v* [T] **1** to make a mark on a smooth surface by rubbing it against something rough: *His shoes were old and badly scuffed.* **2 scuff your feet/heels** to walk in a slow lazy way, not lifting your feet up very high

scuf·fle[1] /ˈskʌfəl/ *n* [C] a short fight that is not very violent SYN **tussle**: ***Scuffles broke out*** *between rival supporters during the match.* | **[+with/between]** *scuffles with police*

scuffle[2] *v* [I] **1** to have a short fight with someone, in a way that is not very serious or violent: **[+with]** *Some of the demonstrators scuffled with the police.* **2** [always + adv/prep] to walk quickly and make a noise as your feet rub on the ground

scuff·mark /ˈskʌfmɑːk $ -mɑːrk/ *n* [C] a mark made on something when it has rubbed against something rough

scull[1] /skʌl/ *n* [C] **1** a small light boat for only one person, used in races **2** one of a pair of OARS that you use to move along in a small light boat

scull[2] *v* [I,T] to make a small boat move along using a pair of OARS SYN **row**

scul·le·ry /ˈskʌləri/ *n* (*plural* **sculleries**) [C] a room next to the kitchen in a large house, where cleaning jobs were done in past times

sculpt /skʌlpt/ *v* [T] to make a particular shape from stone, wood, clay etc

sculpt·ed /ˈskʌlptɪd/ *adj* [only before noun] having a clear smooth shape that looks as though an artist has made it: *high sculpted cheekbones*

sculp·tor /ˈskʌlptə $ -ər/ *n* [C] someone who makes sculptures

sculp·tress /ˈskʌlptrɪs/ *n* [C] *old-fashioned* a woman who makes sculptures

sculp·ture /ˈskʌlptʃə $ -ər/ ●●○ *n*
1 [C,U] an object made out of stone, wood, clay etc by an artist: **[+of]** *a sculpture of an elephant* | *an exhibition of sculpture*
2 [U] the art of making objects out of stone, wood, clay etc

sculp·tured /ˈskʌlptʃəd $ -tʃərd/ *adj* [only before noun] **1** cut or formed from stone, wood, clay etc: *a row of sculptured animals* **2** having a smooth attractive shape: *her sculptured face*

ˈ**sculpture park** *n* [C] an area of land where there are a number of sculptures for the public to see

scum /skʌm/ *n* **1** [U] an unpleasant dirty substance that forms on the surface of water: *a pond covered with green scum* **2** [plural] *informal* nasty unpleasant people: *Scum like that should be locked away!* | *People like that are* ***the scum of the earth***. —**scummy** *adj*

scum·bag /ˈskʌmbæg/ *n* [C] *spoken informal not polite* a nasty unpleasant person

scup·per[1] /ˈskʌpə $ -ər/ *v* [T] *BrE* **1** to ruin someone's plans or chance of being successful – used especially in news reports SYN **scuttle** *AmE*: *Plans to build a private hospital have been scuppered after a government inquiry.* **2** to deliberately sink your own ship

scupper[2] *n* [C] *technical* a hole in the side of a ship that allows water to flow back into the sea

scur·ri·lous /ˈskʌrələs $ ˈskɜːr-/ *adj formal* scurrilous remarks, articles etc contain damaging and untrue statements about someone → **slanderous**: *a scurrilous attack on his integrity* —**scurrilously** *adv*

scur·ry /ˈskʌri $ ˈskɜːri/ *v* (**scurried**, **scurrying**, **scurries**) [I always + adv/prep] to move quickly with short steps, especially because you are in a hurry: *People were scurrying off to work.* —**scurry** *n* [singular]

S-curve /ˈes kɜːv $ -kɜːrv/ *n* [C] *AmE* a bend in the road in the shape of an 'S', that can be dangerous to drivers SYN **S-bend** *BrE*

scur·vy /ˈskɜːvi $ ˈskɜːr-/ *n* [U] a disease caused by not eating foods such as fruit and vegetables that contain VITAMIN C

scut·tle[1] /ˈskʌtl/ *v* **1** [I always + adv/prep] to move quickly with short steps, especially because you are afraid and do not want to be noticed: *A little lizard scuttled across the path.* **2** [T] *AmE* to ruin or end someone's plans or chance of being successful – used especially in news reports SYN **scupper** *BrE*: *The incident threatens to scuttle the peace process.* **3** [T] to sink a ship by making holes in the bottom, especially in order to prevent it being used by an enemy

scuttle[2] *n* [C] a container for carrying coal

scut·tle·butt /ˈskʌtlbʌt/ *n* [U] *AmE informal* stories about other people's personal lives, especially stories that are unkind or untrue SYN **gossip**

scuz·zy[1] /ˈskʌzi/ *adj informal* unpleasant and dirty SYN **disgusting**

scuzzy[2] *n* [U] *informal* SCSI: *What's the biggest scuzzy hard drive you have?*

scythe[1] /saɪð/ *n* [C] a farming tool that has a long curved blade attached to a long wooden handle, and is used to cut grain or long grass

scythe[2] *v* **1** [I,T] to move through or destroy something quickly and violently: *Bullets scythed through the crowd.* **2** [T] to cut with a scythe

SE the written abbreviation of ***southeast*** or ***southeastern***

sea /siː/ ●●● S2 W1 *n*
1 [C,U] *especially BrE* the large area of salty water that covers much of the Earth's surface SYN **ocean**: *Jay stripped his clothes off and ran into the sea.* | *The sea came up to my knees.* | *Most exports went* ***by sea*** (=on a ship). | *a little cottage* ***by the sea*** (=near the sea) | *He spent over 30 years* ***at sea*** (=working on ships or boats on the sea). | *They stood side by side looking* ***out to sea*** (=looking at the sea).
2 [C] a large area of salty water that is mostly enclosed by land: *the Mediterranean Sea*
3 sea of sth a very large number of people or things that all look similar: *He looked out at the sea of faces.*
4 (all) at sea confused or not sure what to do: *Living in a foreign country can mean you're always at sea about what's going on.*
5 the seas *literary* the sea – used especially when you are not talking about a particular ocean: **across the seas** (=far away) *They came from lands across the seas.*
6 [C] one of the broad areas that seem flat on the Moon and Mars

GRAMMAR: Patterns with sea

in the sea
• You use **in the sea** to talk about things that happen in the water: *We paddled in the sea.* | *Whales are mammals that live in the sea.*

on the sea
• You use **on the sea** to talk about things that happen on the surface of the water: *The boat floated on the calm sea.*

S

by the sea
• You use **by the sea** to talk about things that are on the land near the sea: *They live in a cottage by the sea.*

COLLOCATIONS

ADJECTIVES

blue *The sun shone brightly upon the clear blue sea.*
calm *The sea was perfectly calm.*
rough (=with big waves) *The sea was too rough to swim in.*
choppy (=with a lot of small waves) *The wind was starting to pick up and the sea was becoming choppy.*
heavy seas (=a rough sea) *The tanker split apart and sank in heavy seas.*
a stormy sea | **the open sea** (=the part of the sea that is far away from land)

VERBS

cross the sea *Our ancestors crossed the sea in small boats.*
go to sea (=go to work on a ship) *He went to sea when he was eighteen.*
put to sea (=sail a boat away from land) *The refugees put to sea in rickety rafts.*
be lost at sea *formal* (=be drowned in the sea) | **be swept out to sea** (=be taken far away from land by the sea)

sea + NOUN

sea water *Removing salt from sea water is an expensive process.*
a sea view *All the bedrooms have a sea view.*
sea level *Average sea levels are rising year on year.*
the sea air (=the air close to the sea) | **the sea bed** (*also* **the sea floor**) (=the land at the bottom of the sea)

sea 'air *n* [U] the air near the sea, which is considered to be clean, fresh, and good for your health

'sea a,nemone *n* [C] a small brightly coloured sea animal that sticks onto rocks and looks like a flower

sea·bed (*also* **'sea bed** *BrE*) /'si:bed/ *n* **the seabed** the land at the bottom of the sea SYN **sea floor**

sea·bird /'si:bɜ:d $ -bɜ:rd/ *n* [C] a bird that lives near the sea and finds food in it

sea·board /'si:bɔ:d $ -bɔ:rd/ *n* [C] the part of a country that is near the sea: **eastern/western/Pacific etc seaboard** *the eastern seaboard of the US*

sea·borne /'si:bɔ:n $ -bɔ:rn/ *adj* [only before noun] carried on or arriving in ships: *the threat of a seaborne invasion*

,sea 'breeze *n* [C] a light wind that blows from the sea onto the land

'sea ,captain *n* [C] the CAPTAIN of a ship

'sea change *n* [C] a very big change in something: **[+in]** *a sea change in attitudes*

'sea dog *n* [C] *literary* someone with a lot of experience of ships and sailing

sea·far·er /'si:,feərə $ -,ferər/ *n* [C] *old-fashioned or formal* a SAILOR or someone who travels regularly by ship

sea·far·ing /'si:,feərɪŋ $ -,fer-/ *adj* [only before noun] working or travelling on ships and the sea: *a seafaring man* —**seafaring** *n* [U]

,sea 'floor *BrE*, **sea·floor** *AmE* /'si:flɔ: $ -flɔ:r/ *n* **the sea floor** the land at the bottom of the sea SYN **seabed**

sea·food /'si:fu:d/ ●●○ *n* [U] animals from the sea that you can eat, for example fish and SHELLFISH: *a seafood restaurant*

sea·front /'si:frʌnt/ *n* [C usually singular] *especially BrE* the part of a town where the shops, houses etc are next to the beach: **on the seafront** *a hotel right on the seafront* | *a seafront café*

sea·go·ing /'si:,gəʊɪŋ $ -,goʊ-/ *adj* [only before noun] built to travel on the sea SYN **oceangoing**: *a seagoing ship*

,sea-'green *adj* bluish-green: *Jo's large sea-green eyes* —**sea-green** *n* [U]

sea·gull /'si:gʌl/ *n* [C] a large common grey or white bird that lives near the sea

sea·horse /'si:hɔ:s $ -hɔ:rs/ *n* [C] a small sea fish with a head and neck that look like those of a horse

seal¹ /si:l/ ●●○ S3 *n* [C]
1 a large sea animal that eats fish and lives around coasts
2 a) a mark that has a special design and shows the legal or official authority of a person or organization: *The document carried the seal of the governor's office.* **b)** the object that is used to make this mark
3 a piece of rubber or plastic that keeps air, water, dirt etc out of something: **airtight/watertight seal** *an airtight seal around the windows*
4 a piece of WAX, paper, wire etc that you have to break in order to open a container, document etc
5 seal of approval if you give something your seal of approval, you say that you approve of it, especially officially: *A number of employers have already* ***given*** *their* ***seal of approval*** *to the scheme.*
6 set the seal on sth *BrE* to make something definite or complete: *In 1972, Nixon himself went to China to set the seal on the new relationship.*

seal² ●●○ *v* [T]
1 (*also* **seal up**) to close an entrance or a container with something that stops air, water etc from coming in or out of it: *The window was sealed shut.* | **seal a joint/crack/opening/gap** *A quick way to seal awkward gaps is to use a foam filler.* | *Dried milk is kept in* ***hermetically sealed*** (=very tightly closed) *containers.* THESAURUS ▸ CLOSE
2 if a building, area, or country is sealed, no one can enter or leave it: *Authorities plan to seal the border.*
3 to close an envelope, package etc by using something sticky to hold its edges in place: *He wrote the address and sealed the envelope.*
4 to cover the surface of something with something that will protect it: *Wooden decks should be sealed to prevent cracking.*
5 seal sb's fate to make something, especially something bad, sure to happen: *The outbreak of war sealed the government's fate.*
6 seal a deal/bargain/pact etc to make an agreement more formal or definite
7 seal a victory/win/match to make a victory certain: *Smith's goal sealed the victory.* → **sb's lips are sealed** at LIP(5), → **all signed and sealed** at SIGN²(6)

seal sth ↔ **in** *phr v* to stop something that is inside something else from getting out: *Fry the meat quickly to seal in the juices.*

seal sth ↔ **off** *phr v* to stop people from entering an area or building, because it is dangerous: *Following a bomb warning, police have sealed off the whole area.*

'sea lane *n* [C] a path across the sea that ships regularly use

seal·ant /'si:lənt/ *n* [C,U] a substance that is put on the surface of something to protect it from air, water etc

sealed /si:ld/ *adj* **1** shut or protected with something that prevents air, water etc from getting in or out: *a sealed container* **2** sealed documents are closed so that they can only be read by a certain person or at a certain time: *Sealed bids* (=offers to pay a particular price for something) *should be sent to Richard Walker.*

'sea legs *n* [plural] the ability to walk normally, not feel ill etc when you are travelling on a ship: **find/get your sea legs** *I felt awful yesterday. But, thankfully, I've found my sea legs now.*

seal·er /'si:lə $ -ər/ *n* **1** [C,U] a substance that is put on the surface of something to protect it from air, water etc **2** [C] a person or ship that hunts SEALS

'sea ,level *n* [U] the average height of the sea, used as a standard for measuring other heights and depths, such as the height of a mountain: **above/below sea level** *1,000 m above sea level* | *changes in sea level*

seal·ing /'si:lɪŋ/ *n* [U] the activity of hunting or catching SEALS

'sealing wax *n* [U] a red substance that melts and

becomes hard again quickly, used for closing letters, documents etc, especially in the past

ˈsea ˌlion *n* [C] a large type of SEAL that lives near the coast in the Pacific Ocean

seal·skin /ˈsiːlˌskɪn/ *n* [U] the skin or fur of some types of SEAL, used for making leather or clothes

seam /siːm/ *n* [C] **1** a line where two pieces of cloth, leather etc have been stitched together: *She was repairing Billy's trousers, where the seam had come undone.* | *Join the shoulder seams together.* **2** a layer of a mineral under the ground: **seam of coal/iron etc 3 be coming/falling apart at the seams a)** if a plan, organization etc is coming apart at the seams, so many things are going wrong with it that it will probably fail: *The health service seems to be falling apart at the seams.* **b)** if a piece of clothing is coming apart at the seams, the stitches on it are coming unfastened **4 be bursting/bulging at the seams** if a room or building is bursting at the seams, it is so full of people that hardly anyone else can fit into it **5 a (rich) seam of sth** a thing, place, or group from which a type of thing can be obtained: *The 466-page book is a rich seam of statistical information.* **6** a line where two pieces of metal, wood etc have been joined together

sea·man /ˈsiːmən/ *n* (*plural* **seamen** /-mən/) [C] **1** a SAILOR on a ship or in the navy who is not an officer **2** someone who has a lot of experience of ships and the sea

sea·man·ship /ˈsiːmənʃɪp/ *n* [U] the skills and knowledge that an experienced sailor has

seamed /siːmd/ *adj* **1** having a seam: *seamed stockings* **2** *written* a seamed surface has many deep lines on it: *A gentle smile spread over her seamed face.*

ˈsea mile *n* [C] a unit for measuring distance at sea that is slightly longer than a land mile, and equals 1,853 metres SYN **nautical mile**

ˈsea mist *n* [U] a mist on land that comes in from the sea

seam·less /ˈsiːmləs/ *adj* **1** done or made so smoothly that you cannot tell where one thing stops and another begins: *the seamless integration of data, text, images, and sound* **2** without any SEAMS: *seamless stockings* —**seamlessly** *adv*

seam·stress /ˈsiːmstrəs, ˈsem- $ ˈsiːm-/ *n* [C] **1** *old-fashioned* a woman whose job is sewing and making clothes **2** a woman who is good at sewing

seam·y /ˈsiːmi/ *adj* involving unpleasant things such as crime, violence, or immorality: ***the seamy side of*** *the Internet*

se·ance /ˈseɪɑːns, -ɒns $ -ɑːns/ *n* [C] a meeting where people try to talk to or receive messages from the spirits of dead people

sea·plane /ˈsiːpleɪn/ *n* [C] a plane that can take off from and land on a body of water

sea·port /ˈsiːpɔːt $ -pɔːrt/ *n* [C] a large town on or near a coast, with a HARBOUR that big ships can use

ˈsea ˌpower *n* **1** [U] the size and strength of a country's navy **2** [C] a country with a powerful navy

sear /sɪə $ sɪr/ *v* **1** [I always + adv/prep, T] to burn something with a sudden powerful heat: *The heat seared their skin.* **2** [I always + adv/prep, T] to have a very strong sudden and unpleasant effect on you: *Pain was searing through her.* | *The image was seared into his brain.* **3** [T] to cook the outside of a piece of meat quickly at a high temperature, in order to keep its juices in: *seared tuna steaks*

search[1] /sɜːtʃ $ sɜːrtʃ/ ●●● S3 W2 *n*

1 [C usually singular] an attempt to find someone or something: **[+for]** *Bad weather is hampering the search for survivors.* | **[+of]** *Two more bodies were found after a search of the woods.*

2 [C] a series of actions done by a computer to find information: **[+of]** *a computerized search of 10,000 medical journals* | *A search found 46 websites.* | *an online search* | **perform/run/do a search** *Do a search on 'rabbit' and see what it brings up.*

3 in search of sth looking for something: *Mark* ***went in search of*** *water.*

4 [singular] an attempt to find an explanation or solution: **[+for]** *the search for a cure*

COLLOCATIONS

VERBS

carry out a search (*also* **conduct a search** *formal*) *Police have carried out a search of his home.*

launch/mount a search (=start a search) *A massive search was launched for the former soldier.*

call off/abandon a search *They called off the search when it got dark.*

ADJECTIVES/NOUN + search

a thorough/careful search *We conducted a thorough search of the building.*

a systematic search (=one done in an organized way) *They set about a systematic search of the ship.*

a desperate/frantic search | **a fruitless search** (=an unsuccessful one) | **a police search** | **a nationwide search** (=in every part of a country) | **a house-to-house search** (=a search of every house or building in an area) | **a fingertip search** *BrE* (=a careful search for clues by police officers)

PHRASES

the search is on (=people are trying to find someone or something) *The search is on for someone with the same blood type.*

a search is underway (=it has started)

search + NOUN

the search area *The search area has now been widened.*

Frequencies of **search**, **look for** and **try to find** in spoken and written English.

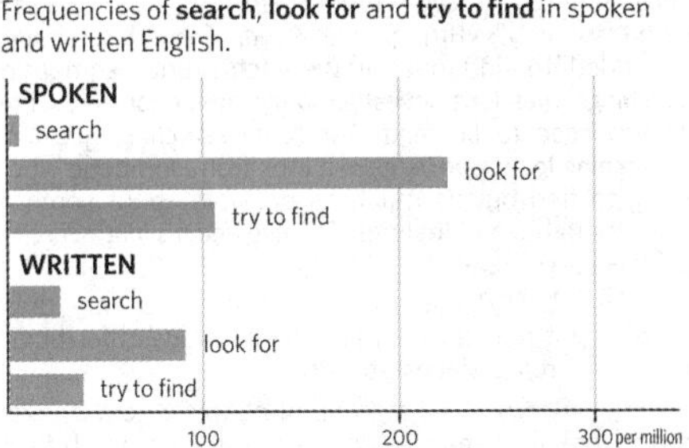

This graph shows that the expressions **look for** and **try to find** are much more common in both spoken and written English than the verb **search**. **Look for** and **try to find** are used in a very general way. **Search** is used when someone, often a group of people, spends time looking for someone or something in a careful, organized way.

search[2] ●●● W3 *v*

1 LOOKING [I,T] to try to find someone or something by looking very carefully: *It was too dark to search further.* | *The area was* ***thoroughly searched.*** | **search for sb/sth** *An RAF plane searched for the missing men.* | *I've* ***searched high and low*** (=everywhere) *for my glasses.* | **search sth for sb/sth** *Detectives are searching the yard for clues.* | **search in/under/through sth** *Alice bent to search through a heap of clothes.*

2 COMPUTER [T] to use a computer to find information: **search sth for sth** *Search the Web for cheap flights.*

3 PERSON [T] if someone in authority searches you or the things you are carrying, they look for things you might be hiding: **search sb for sth** *He was searched by the guards for weapons.*

4 SOLUTION [I] to try to find an explanation or solution: **[+for]** *Scientists are still searching for a cure.* | *She paused, searching for inspiration.*

5 search me! *spoken* used to tell someone that you do not know the answer to a question: *'Where is she?' 'Search me!'*

6 EXAMINE [T] to examine something carefully in order

to find something out, decide something etc: *Anya searched his face anxiously.* —**searcher** *n* [C]

THESAURUS

search to look carefully for someone or something: *Detectives continue to search for clues.* | *She searched through all his clothes.*
look for sb/sth to try to get someone or something you want or need: *I'm looking for something to wear for my sister's wedding.* | *The band is looking for a singer.* | *He's decided to look for a new career.*
try to find sb/sth used especially when someone or something is difficult to find: *I spent half an hour trying to find a parking space.*
seek *formal* to try to find something or someone – used especially about jobs, help, or information. Also used in newspaper advertisements when trying to find a suitable person: *They went there seeking work.* | *She decided to seek help.* | *Tall blond 18-year-old male seeks female 17+ for friendship.*
hunt to look for someone or something. Used when you look very carefully and thoroughly, or in the phrase **house/job/bargain hunting**: *I've hunted everywhere, but I can't find a recipe for French onion soup.* | *She's gone out bargain-hunting in the sales.*
be on the lookout for sb/sth to be continuously looking for someone or something: *I'm always on the lookout for a good bargain.*
leave no stone unturned to look for someone or something in every possible place: *The police say they will leave no stone unturned in their search for the killer.*

search sth ↔ **out** *phr v* to find something by searching: *We were too tired to search out extra blankets.*

S

ˈsearch ˌengine ●●○ *n* [C] a computer program that helps you find information on the Internet

search·ing /ˈsɜːtʃɪŋ $ ˈsɜːr-/ *adj* [only before noun] **1** intended to find out all the facts about something: **searching questions/investigation/examination etc** *Interviewees need to be ready for some searching questions.* **2 searching look/glance/gaze** a look from someone who is trying to find out as much as possible about someone else's thoughts and feelings: *She avoided his long searching look.* —**searchingly** *adv*

search·light /ˈsɜːtʃlaɪt $ ˈsɜːrtʃ-/ *n* [C] a very bright electric light that turns in any direction, used for finding people, guarding places etc

ˈsearch ˌparty *n* [C] a group of people who are organized to look for someone who is missing or lost: *Let's get going or they'll* ***send out*** *a* ***search party***.

ˈsearch ˌwarrant *n* [C] a legal document that gives the police official permission to search a building

sear·ing /ˈsɪərɪŋ $ ˈsɪr-/ *adj* **1** extremely hot: *the* ***searing heat*** *of the desert* **2** searing pain is severe and feels like a burn **3** searing words or attitudes criticize someone or something very strongly: *Adorno's searing analysis of mass culture* | *Emily felt a searing anger against her father.*

ˈsea salt *n* [U] a type of salt made from sea water, used in cooking

sea·scape /ˈsiːskeɪp/ *n* [C] a picture of the sea

sea·shell /ˈsiːʃel/ *n* [C] the empty shell of a small sea creature: *jewelry made out of seashells*

sea·shore /ˈsiːʃɔː $ -ʃɔːr/ *n* **the seashore** the land at the edge of the sea, consisting of sand and rocks → **beach**, **seaside**

sea·sick /ˈsiːˌsɪk/ *adj* feeling ill when you travel in a boat, because of the movement of the boat in the water: **get/feel/be seasick** *Hal was seasick almost at once.* —**seasickness** *n* [U]

sea·side¹ /ˈsiːsaɪd/ *n* **the seaside** *BrE* the areas or towns near the sea, where people go to enjoy themselves: *a trip to the seaside* | **at the seaside** *a day at the seaside*

seaside² *adj* [only before noun] relating to places that are near the sea: **seaside town/resort** *the popular seaside resort of Brighton* | *a seaside holiday*

sea·son¹ /ˈsiːzən/ ●●● S2 W1 *n*
1 TIME OF YEAR [C] one of the main periods into which a year is divided, each of which has a particular type of weather. The seasons are spring, summer, autumn, and winter: *the effect on plants as the seasons start to change*
2 USUAL TIME FOR STH [C usually singular] a period of time in a year during which a particular activity takes place, or during which something usually happens: *the first game of the season* | **the football/cricket etc season** *the end of the football season* | **the racing/fishing/hunting etc season** *The racing season starts in June.* | *Some footpaths are closed during the shooting season.* | **out of season** (=when an activity is not allowed) *He was caught fishing out of season.* | **[+for]** *The season for strawberries* (=when they are available to buy) *usually starts in early June.* | **the rainy/wet/dry season** (=the time when it rains a lot or does not rain at all) *African rivers turn to hard mud during the dry season.* | **the growing/planting etc season** *The planting season is in spring, with harvest in the fall.*
3 HOLIDAY [singular, U] the time of the year when most people take their holidays: **high/peak season** (=the busiest part of this time) *There are two boat trips a day, more in high season.* | **low/off season** (=the least busy part of this time) *An off-season break costs £114.* | **out of season** *It's quieter out of season.* | **tourist season** (*also* **holiday season** *BrE*): *We arrived at* ***the height of the tourist season*** (=the busiest time). | **the holiday season** *AmE* (=Thanksgiving to New Year, including Christmas, Hanukkah etc) | **the festive season** *BrE* (=Christmas and New Year)
4 FASHION [singular] the time in each year when new styles of clothes, hair etc are produced and become fashionable: *This season's look is fresh and natural.*
5 be in/out of season vegetables and fruit that are in season are cheap and easily available because it is the time of year when they are ready to eat. If they are out of season, they are expensive or not available: *Vine tomatoes are in season from April to October.*
6 FILMS, PLAYS ETC [C usually singular] a series of films, plays, television programmes etc that are shown during a particular period of time: **[+of]** *a new season of comedy on BBC1* | **summer/fall etc season** *The network has several new dramas lined up for the fall season.* | *Glyndebourne's* ***season opens*** *with a performance of Tosca.*
7 ANIMALS [singular] the time of the year when animals are ready to have sex: **the mating/breeding season** | *Their dog was* ***coming into season***.
8 season's greetings *written* used on cards to tell someone you hope they have a happy Christmas, Hanukkah etc
9 the season of goodwill *old-fashioned* the time around Christmas → CLOSE SEASON, OPEN SEASON, SILLY SEASON

season² *v* [T] **1** to add salt, pepper etc to food you are cooking: **season sth with sth** *Season the chicken with pepper.* | *Mix and* ***season to taste*** (=add the amount of salt etc that you think tastes right). **2** to prepare wood for use by gradually drying it

sea·son·a·ble /ˈsiːzənəbəl/ *adj formal* suitable or usual for a particular time of year OPP **unseasonable**: *seasonable temperatures*

sea·son·al /ˈsiːzənəl/ *adj* [usually before noun] happening, expected, or needed during a particular season: *heavy seasonal rains* | **seasonal workers/employment etc** *seasonal jobs in the tourist industry*

ˌseasonal afˌfective disˈorder *n* [U] an illness that makes people feel sad and tired in winter, because there is not enough light from the sun SYN **SAD**

sea·son·al·i·ty /ˌsiːzəˈnæləti/ *n* [U] the fact that something changes according to the time of the year: **[+of]** *the seasonality of sales of the product*

sea·son·al·ly /ˈsiːzənəli/ *adv* according to what is usual for a particular season: *bird migrations that occur seasonally* | **seasonally adjusted figures/rates/data etc** (=ones that are changed according to what usually happens at a particular time of year)

sea·soned /ˈsiːzənd/ *adj* **1** [only before noun] used to describe someone who has a lot of experience of a particular thing: **seasoned traveller/observer etc** *Artie was* *by then a seasoned musician with six albums to his credit.* **2** seasoned food has salt, pepper etc added to it: *a* ***highly seasoned*** *piece of fish* **3** seasoned wood has been prepared for use by drying

sea·son·ing /ˈsiːzənɪŋ/ *n* [C,U] salt, pepper, spices etc that give food a more interesting taste

ˈseason ˌticket *n* [C] a ticket that allows you to make a lot of journeys during a particular period of time, or go to all the games, concerts etc being held during a particular time. Season tickets cost less than it would cost to buy a ticket for each journey, game etc: *an annual season ticket* | **season ticket holder** (=someone who owns a season ticket)

seat¹ /siːt/ ●●● S2 W1 *n*

1 PLACE TO SIT [C] a place where you can sit, especially one in a vehicle or one from which you watch a performance, sports event etc: *I was in the back seat and Jo was driving.* | *a 10,000-seat stadium* | *People were shifting in their seats, looking uncomfortable.*

2 OFFICIAL POSITION [C] a position as an elected member of a government, or as a member of a group that makes official decisions: **[+in/on]** *a seat in the National Assembly* | *Promotion would mean a seat on the board of directors.* | **Parliamentary/Senate etc seat** *the Senate seat for Colorado* | **win/gain/lose a seat** (=at an election) *He predicts that his party will gain at least 12 seats.* | **hold a seat** (=have a seat) *The Republicans hold 235 seats and the Democrats have 197.* | **keep/hold onto a seat** *Mr Adams is expected to keep his seat.* | *Labour held onto the seat with a 7% majority.* | **safe seat** *BrE*: *one that a party will not lose* | **marginal seat** *BrE*: *one that another party might easily win*

3 PART OF A CHAIR [C usually singular] the flat part of a chair etc that you sit on: *Don't put your feet on the seat!* | *a wooden toilet seat* | *a broken bicycle seat*

4 baby/child/car seat a special seat that you put in a car for a baby or small child

5 seat of government/power *formal* a city where a country's government is based

6 seat of learning *formal* a university, college etc

7 CLOTHES [singular] the part of your trousers that you sit on: **[+of]** *a rip in the seat of his jeans*

8 take a back seat (to sb/sth) to have less influence or importance: *Foreign policy will take a back seat to domestic problems for a while.*

9 on the edge of your seat waiting excitedly to see what happens next: *a gripping movie that will* ***keep*** *you* ***on the edge of your seat***

10 do sth by the seat of your pants to do something by using only your own skill and experience, without any help from anyone or anything else, especially when this is risky or dangerous

11 in the driving seat *BrE*, **in the driver's seat** *AmE* controlling what happens in a situation, organization, or relationship: *We're trying to* ***put*** *young people* ***in the driving seat.***

12 in the hot seat (*also* **on the hot seat** *AmE*) *informal* in a difficult position where you have to make important decisions, answer questions etc

13 HOUSE [C] a home of a rich important family in the countryside: **family/country seat** → **back-seat driver** at BACK SEAT(2), → WINDOW SEAT

COLLOCATIONS

ADJECTIVES/NOUN + seat

free *Excuse me, is this seat free?*
an empty/vacant seat *Patrick spotted an empty seat near the back.*
the front/back/rear seat (=in a car) *Never leave bags on the back seat of a car.*
the driver's seat | **the passenger seat** | **a window/aisle seat** (=one next to the window or the space between seats, for example in a plane) | **a front-row seat** (=one at the front of a theatre, sports ground etc) | **a ringside seat** (=one in the front row at a sports event, especially a boxing match) | **a good seat** (=one from which you can see well)

VERBS

have a seat *We had really good seats, just in front of the stage.*
have/take a seat (=sit down) *Take a seat, please.*
book/reserve a seat *You can book seats online.*
show sb to their seat *A flight attendant showed them to their seats.*
go back to/return to your seat | **resume your seat** *formal* (=sit down again) | **save sb a seat** (=tell other people not to sit there)

PHRASES

bums on seats *BrE informal* (=used for saying that something or someone can attract a large audience) *He is an actor who will put bums on seats.*

seat² ●●○ *v* [T]

1 [not in progressive] if a place seats a number of people, it has enough seats for that number: *The arena seats 60,000.*

2 *formal* **seat yourself (in/on/beside etc sth)** to sit down somewhere: *She seated herself at her desk.*

3 to arrange for someone to sit somewhere: **seat sb beside/near etc sb/sth** *the old custom of seating boys and girls on opposite sides of the classroom* → SEATED

ˈseat belt ●●○ (*also* **safety belt**) *n* [C] a belt attached to the seat of a car or plane which you fasten around yourself for protection in an accident

seat·ed /ˈsiːtɪd/ *adj* [not before noun] *formal* **1** if someone is seated, they are sitting down: **[+at/near/beside etc]** *Paul was seated at his desk.* | ***Remain seated*** *until the aircraft has come to a complete stop.* **2 be seated** *spoken* used to ask people politely to sit down: *Please be seated.* → SEAT²

-seater /siːtə $ -ər/ *suffix* [in nouns] **4-seater/12-seater etc** a vehicle, piece of furniture etc with space for 4, 12 etc people to sit

seat·ing /ˈsiːtɪŋ/ *n* [U] **1** all the seats in a theatre, cinema etc: **[+for]** *a restaurant with seating for 40 customers* | *The hall has a* ***seating capacity*** *of 650.* **2** the places where people will sit, according to an arrangement: **seating plan/arrangements** *the seating plan for the wedding dinner*

seat·mate /ˈsiːtmeɪt/ *n* [C] *AmE* the person who sits next to you on a plane

ˈsea ˌurchin *n* [C] a small round sea animal with a hard shell covered in sharp points

sea·wall /ˌsiːˈwɔːl $ ˈsiːwɒːl/ *n* [C] a wall built beside the sea to stop the water from flowing onto the land

sea·ward /ˈsiːwəd $ -wərd/ *adj* [only before noun] facing towards the sea: *Keep to the seaward side of the path.* —**seaward, seawards** *adv*

sea·wa·ter, **sea water** /ˈsiːwɔːtə $ -wɒːtər, -wɑː-/ *n* [U] salty water from the sea

sea·weed /ˈsiːwiːd/ *n* [U] a plant that grows in the sea

sea·wor·thy /ˈsiːwɜːði $ -ɜːr-/ *adj* a ship that is seaworthy is in a suitable condition to sail

se·ba·ceous /səˈbeɪʃəs/ *adj technical* relating to a part of the body that produces oil: *sebaceous glands*

sec /sek/ *n* **1 a sec** *spoken informal* a very short period of time: **hang on a sec/hold on a sec/just a sec etc** (=wait a short time) *'Is Al there?' 'Hold on a sec, I'll check.'* | **in a sec** *I'll be with you in a sec.* **2** the written abbreviation of ***second***: *Journey time: 25 mins 14 secs.*

sec·a·teurs /ˈsekətɜːz $ ˌsekəˈtɜːrz/ *n* [plural] *BrE* strong scissors used for cutting plant stems: *a* ***pair of secateurs***

se·cede /sɪˈsiːd/ *v* [I] *formal* if a country or state secedes from another country, it officially stops being part of it and becomes independent OPP **accede**: **[+from]** *By 1861, 11 states had seceded from the Union.*

se·ces·sion /sɪˈseʃən/ *n* [C,U] when a country or state officially stops being part of another country and becomes independent OPP **accession**: *a vote in favor of secession* | **[+from]** *Croatia's secession from Yugoslavia*

S

se·ces·sion·ist /sɪˈseʃənɪst/ *n* [C] someone who wants their country or state to be independent of another country

se·clud·ed /sɪˈkluːdɪd/ *adj* very private and quiet: **secluded garden/spot/beach etc** *We sunbathed on a small secluded beach.* | *He's 80 years old now and lives a very secluded life.*

se·clu·sion /sɪˈkluːʒən/ *n* [U] the state of being private and away from other people: *They enjoyed ten days of peace and seclusion.* | **in seclusion** *He preferred to stay at home in seclusion.* | **[+of]** *the relative seclusion of the Norfolk countryside*

sec·ond[1] /ˈsekənd/ ●●● S1 W1 *number*
1 the second person, thing, event etc is the one that comes after the first: *the Second World War* | *the second of August* | *a second year student* | *his second wife* | *Clinton's second term in office* | *the second half of the year* | *the second time in three days*
2 the position in a competition or scale that comes after the one that is the best, most successful etc: *She won second prize.* | *They climbed to second place in the League.* | **second largest/most successful etc** *Africa's second highest mountain* | **be second only to sth** (=used to emphasize that something is nearly the largest, most important etc) *The euro will have a circulation second only to that of the dollar.*
3 another example of the same thing, or another in addition to the one you have: *We advertised for a second guitarist.* | *There was a second reason for his dismissal.* | *I asked the doctor for a* ***second opinion*** (=when you ask another person to repeat an examination, test etc for you).
4 every second year/person/thing etc a) the second, then the fourth, then the sixth year etc: *The nurse comes every second day.* **b)** used to emphasize that, in a group of similar things, there is too much of one particular thing: *Every second house seemed to be boarded up.*
5 be second to none to be the best: *The quality of Britain's overseas aid programme is second to none.*
6 second chance help given to someone who has failed, in the hope that they will succeed this time: *I just want to* ***give*** *these kids* ***a second chance****.*
7 have second thoughts to start having doubts about a decision you have made: *You're not having second thoughts, are you?* | **[+about]** *She'd had second thoughts about the whole project.*
8 on second thoughts *BrE*, **on second thought** *AmE spoken* used to say that you have changed your mind about something: *I'll call her tomorrow – no, on second thought, I'll try now.*
9 not give sth a second thought/without a second thought used to say that someone does not think or worry about something: *She dismissed the rumour without a second thought.*
10 not give sth a second glance/look (*also* **without a second glance/look**) to not look at something again, because you have not really noticed it or because it does not seem important: *No one gave the woman in the grey uniform a second glance.*
11 be/become second nature (to sb) something that is second nature to you is something you have done so often that you do it almost without thinking: *Driving becomes second nature after a while.*
12 second wind a new feeling of energy after you have been working or exercising very hard, and had thought you were too tired to continue: *He* ***got*** *his* ***second wind*** *and ran on.*

second[2] ●●● S1 W2 *n*
1 [C] a unit for measuring time. There are 60 seconds in a minute: *Hold your breath for six seconds.* | *The operation takes only 30 seconds.* | *Ultrasonic waves travel at around 300 metres* ***per second****.* | **within seconds** (=after only a few seconds) *Within seconds, Bev called back.*
2 [C] a very short period of time: *I'll be back in a second.* | ***Just a second*** (=wait a moment), *I'll come and help.* | *At least 30 shots were fired* ***in a matter of seconds*** (=in a very short time). → SPLIT SECOND
3 (at) any second (now) used to say that something will or may happen extremely soon: *He should be here any second.*
4 seconds [plural] **a)** *informal* another serving of food, after you have eaten your first serving **b)** clothes or other goods that are cheaper than usual because they are not perfect → SECOND HAND[1]
5 [C] *technical* one of the 60 parts into which a MINUTE of an angle is divided. It can be shown as a symbol after a number. For example, 78° 52' 11" means 78 degrees 52 minutes 11 seconds.
6 [C] someone who helps someone in a fight, especially in BOXING or, in the past, a DUEL
7 [U] *AmE informal* SECOND BASE

second[3] /ˈsekənd/ ●●● S2 W2 *adv*
1 next after the first one: **come/finish etc second** *I came second in the UK championships.* | *Tea is the most popular drink, while coffee ranks second* (=it is the second most popular drink).
2 [sentence adverb] used before you add information to what you have already said SYN **secondly**

second[4] *v* [T] to formally support a suggestion made by another person in a meeting → **propose**: **second a motion/proposal/amendment etc**

se·cond[5] /sɪˈkɒnd $ -ˈkɑːnd/ *v* [T] *BrE* to send someone to do someone else's job for a short time: **be seconded to sth** *Jill's been seconded to the marketing department while Dave's away.* GRAMMAR **Second** is usually passive. → SECONDMENT

sec·ond·a·ry /ˈsekəndəri $ -deri/ ●●○ S3 W2 *adj*
1 secondary education/schooling/teaching etc the education, teaching etc of children between the ages of 11 and 16 or 18 → **tertiary**
2 not as important as something else → **primary**: *the novel's secondary characters* | **[+to]** *Writing was always secondary to spending time with my family.* | **be of secondary importance/be a secondary consideration** *Cost is the important thing – any benefits for the user are a secondary consideration.* THESAURUS UNIMPORTANT —**secondarily** *adv*

ˌsecondary ˈmodern *n* [C] a type of school that existed in Britain until the 1960s, where children who had not passed a special examination were sent

ˈsecondary ˌschool *n* [C] a school for children between the ages of 11 and 16 or 18 → **primary school**

ˌsecondary ˈsource *n* [C] a book, article etc that ANALYSES something such as a piece of literature or a historical event and that can be used to support your ideas in an ESSAY

ˌsecondary ˈstress *n* [C,U] *technical* the second strongest STRESS that is put on a part of a long word when you speak it. It is shown in this dictionary by the mark (ˌ) → **primary stress**

ˌsecond ˈbase *n* [U] the second of the four places you have to run to in games such as baseball in order to get a point

ˌsecond ˈbest[1] *n* [U] something that you have to accept which is not perfect or not the best: *I'm not going to* ***settle for second best****.*

ˌsecond ˈbest[2] *adj* [only before noun], *adv* not quite as good as the best one: *Allie was the second best shooter on the rifle team.* | **come off second best** (=lose a game or competition, or not be as successful as someone else)

ˌsecond ˈchildhood *n* [U] someone who is in their second childhood is old, and their mental abilities are greatly reduced

ˌsecond ˈclass *n* [U] **1** a way of travelling on a ship or train that is cheaper and less comfortable than FIRST CLASS **2** a way of delivering letters etc in Britain that is cheaper and slower than FIRST CLASS **3** the system in the US for delivering newspapers, magazines, advertisements etc through the post

ˌsecond-ˈclass *adj* [only before noun]
1 PEOPLE considered to be less important and less valuable than other people: *Why should old people be treated like* ***second-class citizens****?*

2 LOWER STANDARD of a lower standard or quality than the best: *We will not accept a second-class education for our children.*
3 TRAVEL **second-class ticket/fare/compartment/cabin etc** tickets etc that are for cheaper, less comfortable seats on a train or ship
4 MAIL **second-class mail/post/stamp etc** relating to the system of delivering mail in Britain that is cheaper and slower
5 UNIVERSITY DEGREE used to describe a university degree in Britain that is good, but not the highest level: *a second-class honours degree* → FIRST CLASS(3) —**second class** *adv*: *He was travelling second class.*

ˌsecond-deˈgree *adj* **1 second-degree burns** the second most serious form of burns → **first-degree**, **third-degree** **2 second-degree murder/assault/burglary etc** *AmE* a crime that is less serious than the most serious type, especially because it was not planned → **first-degree**

sec·ond·er /ˈsekəndə $ -ər/ *n* [C] *formal* a person who supports a proposal etc in a formal meeting so that it can be discussed → **proposer**

ˌsecond-ˈguess *v* [T] **1** to try to say what will happen or what someone will do before they do it: *I'm not going to try and second-guess the committee's decisions.* **2** *AmE* to criticize something after it has already happened: *The decision has been made – there's no point in second-guessing it now.*

ˈsecond ˌhand[1] *n* [C] the long thin piece of metal that points to the seconds on a clock or watch

second ˈhand[2] *adv* **1** if you get something second hand, it is not new and has been used by other people before: **get/buy sth second hand** *We got most of our furniture second hand.* **2** if you hear something second hand, the person who tells you is not the person who originally said it: *It may not be true – I only* ***heard*** *it* ***second hand***. **3** if you experience something second hand, you experience it through other people, rather than directly → **(at) first hand** at FIRST[1](8)

ˌsecond-ˈhand, **sec·ond·hand** /ˌsekəndˈhænd◂/ ●●○ *adj*
1 second-hand things are not new when you get them, because they were owned by someone else before you: *second-hand clothes* | *a second-hand car* | **secondhand store/shop etc** (=a shop that sells second-hand things)
2 second-hand information or knowledge is told to you by someone who is not the person who originally said it – used to show disapproval OPP **first-hand**: **second-hand reports/accounts** *second-hand accounts of mass killings*

ˌsecond ˈhome *n* **1** [C] a house or apartment that you own as well as your main home and which you use, for example, for holidays: *town-dwellers who buy second homes in the countryside* **2** [singular] a place where you spend a large amount of time but which is not where you live: *I love Italy. It's my second home.* | *From then on, the hospital became my second home.*

ˌsecond-in-comˈmand *n* [C] the person who has the next highest rank to the leader of a group, especially in a military organization

ˌsecond ˈlanguage *n* [C usually singular] a language that you speak in addition to the language you learned as a child → **mother tongue**

ˌsecond lieuˈtenant *n* [C] a middle rank in several of the US and British military forces, or someone who has this rank

ˌSecond ˈLife *trademark* an ONLINE VIRTUAL WORLD. Users, called 'Residents', can talk to and meet each other, and take part in various activities.

sec·ond·ly /ˈsekəndli/ ●●○ S3 *adv* [sentence adverb] used when you want to give a second point or fact, or give a second reason for something → **firstly**: *Firstly, they are not efficient, and secondly, they are expensive to make.*

se·cond·ment /sɪˈkɒndmənt $ -ˈkɑːnd-/ *n* [singular, U] *BrE* a period of time that you spend away from your usual job, either doing another job or studying: **on secondment (from sth)** *a government adviser, on secondment from the Metropolitan Police*

ˈsecond ˌname *n* [C] **1** *BrE* a family name: *'What's your second name?' 'Jones.'* **2** a name that comes after your first name and before your family name: *Stephen's second name, Anthony, is after my brother.*

ˌsecond ˈperson *n* [singular] *technical* a form of a verb or PRONOUN that is used to show the person you are speaking to. For example, 'you' is a second person pronoun, and 'are' is the second person singular and plural of the verb 'to be'. → **FIRST PERSON, THIRD PERSON**

ˌsecond-ˈrate *adj* [usually before noun] not of the very best standard or quality → **first-rate**: *a second-rate artist*

ˌsecond ˈscreen *n* [C] an additional piece of equipment with a screen, such as a TABLET or SMARTPHONE, that you use while watching television or playing a computer game, and which shows extra information relating to the programme or game

ˌsecond ˈscreener *n* [C] someone who is using a second screen, for example in order to communicate with people about the television programme they are watching —**second screening** *n* [U]

ˌsecond ˈsight *n* [U] the ability to know what will happen in the future, or to know about things that are happening somewhere else, that some people claim to have SYN **clairvoyance**

ˌsecond-ˈstring *adj* [only before noun] not regularly part of a team, group etc, but sometimes taking someone else's place in it: *the Vikings' second-string quarterback*

se·cre·cy /ˈsiːkrəsi/ ●○○ *n* [U]
1 the process of keeping something secret, or when something is kept a secret → **secret**: *I must stress the need for* ***absolute secrecy*** *about the project.* | *His work was* ***shrouded in secrecy***. | *the* ***veil of secrecy*** *that covered the talks*
2 swear sb to secrecy to make someone promise not to repeat what you have told them

se·cret[1] /ˈsiːkrɪt/ ●●● S3 W2 *adj*
1 known about by only a few people and kept hidden from others → **secrecy**: *They* ***kept*** *their relationship* ***secret from*** *their parents.* | *agents on a secret mission* | *secret talks with the terrorists* | **secret compartment/passage etc** *The drugs were found in a secret compartment in Campbell's suitcase.* | **secret ingredient/recipe/formula** *The cookies are made to a secret recipe.*
2 [only before noun] secret feelings, worries, or actions are ones that you do not want other people to know about: *His secret fear was that Jenny would leave him.* | *Did you know you had a* ***secret admirer*** (=someone who is secretly in love with you)? **THESAURUS** PRIVATE
3 secret weapon something that will help you gain a big advantage over your competitors, that they do not know about
4 used to describe the behaviour of someone who is keeping their thoughts, intentions, or actions hidden from other people SYN **secretive**: **[+about]** *They're being very secret about it.* | *There was a* ***secret smile*** *on her face.*

THESAURUS

secret known about by only a few people, who have agreed not to tell anyone else: *a secret meeting place* | *The details of the proposal must remain secret.*
confidential used about information, especially in business or government, that is secret and not intended to be shown or told to other people: *a highly confidential report* | *Employees' personal details are treated as strictly confidential.*
classified used about information that the government has ordered to be kept secret from most people: *He was accused of passing on classified information to the Russians in the 1950s.*
sensitive used about information that is kept secret because there would be problems if the wrong people knew it: *A teenager managed to hack into sensitive US Air Force files.*
covert [only before noun] used about things that are

done secretly, especially by a government or official organization: *a CIA covert operation*
undercover [usually before noun] used about things that are done secretly by the police in order to catch criminals or find out information: *Detectives arrested the suspect after a five-day undercover operation.*
underground an underground organization or newspaper is one that operates or is produced secretly and opposes the government: *Her father was a member of the underground resistance movement in France during World War II.*
clandestine /klænˈdestɪn/ secret and often illegal or immoral: *clandestine meetings* | *his involvement in a clandestine operation to sell arms to Iran* | *a clandestine love affair*
hush-hush *informal* used about information or activities that are kept officially secret: *He was put in charge of some hush-hush military project.* | *I've no idea what he does – it's all very hush-hush.*

COLLOCATIONS CHECK

confidential information/document/report/letter/inquiry
classified information/document/material
sensitive information/files
covert operation/support/activities/war/aid
undercover agent/operation/investigation/work
underground organization/newspaper/economy
clandestine meeting/operation/organization/network
hush-hush research/project/experiment

S

secret² ●●● S3 W3 *n* [C]
1 something that is kept hidden or that is known about by only a few people → **secrecy**: *I can't tell you.* ***It's a secret.*** | ***It was no secret that*** *the two men hated each other.* | *Don't worry.* ***Your secret is safe with me*** (=I won't tell anyone about it).
2 in secret in a private way or place that other people do not know about: *The negotiations were conducted in secret.*
3 the secret a particular way of achieving a good result, that is the best or only way: **the secret to (doing) sth** *The secret to making good pastry is to use very cold water.* | *Your hair always looks so great –* ***what's your secret****?* | *What do you think is* ***the secret of*** *her* ***success****?*
4 make no secret of sth to make your opinions about something clear: *Louise made no secret of her dislike for John.*
5 the secrets of life/nature/the universe etc the things no one yet knows about life, nature etc

COLLOCATIONS

VERBS

have a secret *We have no secrets from each other.*
know a secret (=about someone else) *You can tell Tom that I know his secret.*
keep a secret (=not tell it to anyone) *Can you keep a secret?*
tell sb a secret *Shall I tell you a secret?*
let sb in on a secret (=tell them a secret) *Frank let me in on the secret.*
reveal/divulge a secret *formal* (=tell it to someone) *He was accused of revealing state secrets.*
give away a secret (=tell it to someone carelessly or by mistake) | **share a secret** (=tell it to someone because you trust them) | **discover/find out a secret**

ADJECTIVES/NOUN + secret

a big secret (=an important secret or one that very few people know) *The event was supposed to be a big secret, but everyone knew about it.*
a little secret (=a personal secret that very few people know) *You must promise me that this will be our little secret.*
a closely-guarded/well-kept secret (=a secret that few people are allowed to know) *The recipe is a closely-guarded secret.*
an open secret (=something that a lot of people know, but do not talk about because it is supposed to be a secret) *It was an open secret that he was having an affair.*
a dark/terrible secret (=a secret about something bad) *I'm sure every family has a few dark secrets.*
a guilty secret (=a secret that someone feels guilty about) | **a family secret** | **a state/official secret** (=a government secret) | **a trade secret** (=a company or business secret) | **military secrets**

COMMON ERRORS

⚠ Don't say 'say a secret' or 'say your secrets'. Say **tell sb a secret** or **tell sb your secrets**.

ˌsecret ˈagent *n* [C] someone whose job is to find out and report on the military and political secrets of other countries SYN **spy**

sec·re·tar·i·al /ˌsekrəˈteəriəl $ -ˈter-/ *adj* [usually before noun] relating to the work of a secretary: *a secretarial course* | *secretarial college*

sec·re·tar·i·at /ˌsekrəˈteəriət $ -ˈter-/ *n* [C] a government office or the office of a large international organization, especially one that has a SECRETARY GENERAL in charge of it: *the United Nations Secretariat in New York*

sec·re·ta·ry /ˈsekrətəri $ -teri-/ ●●● S2 W1 *n* (*plural* **secretaries**) [C]
1 someone who works in an office TYPING letters, keeping records, answering telephone calls, arranging meetings etc: *My secretary will fax you all the details.* | **medical/legal secretary**
2 a) (*also* **Secretary of State**) the head of an important department in the British government: *the Foreign Secretary* → **HOME SECRETARY b)** an official in charge of a large government department in the US: *the Secretary of Defense* **c)** a British official who works in a government department or EMBASSY and is below the rank of MINISTER or AMBASSADOR: *the First Secretary at the British Embassy* → **SECRETARY OF STATE, UNDERSECRETARY**
3 a member of a club or organization who takes notes in meetings, writes official letters etc: *the secretary of the tennis club*

ˌsecretary ˈgeneral *n* [C] the most important official in charge of a large organization, especially an international organization: *the UN Secretary General*

ˌSecretary of ˈState *n* (*plural* **Secretaries of State**) [C]
1 (*also* **Secretary**) the head of an important department in the British government: *the Secretary of State for Transport* **2** the head of the US government department that deals with the US's relations with other countries

ˌsecret ˈballot *n* [C,U] a way of voting in which people write their choices on a piece of paper in secret, or an act of voting in this way: **by secret ballot** *The chairman was elected by secret ballot.* | **in a secret ballot** *votes cast in a secret ballot*

se·crete /sɪˈkriːt/ *v* [T] **1** if a part of an animal or plant secretes a liquid substance, it produces it: *The toad's skin secretes a deadly poison.* **2** *formal* to hide something: *The money had been secreted in a Swiss bank account.*

se·cre·tion /sɪˈkriːʃən/ *n* **1** [C,U] a substance, usually liquid, produced by part of a plant or animal: *These secretions are used by the caterpillar as a defence.* **2** [U] the production of this substance: *the secretion of hormones by the pituitary gland*

se·cre·tive /ˈsiːkrətɪv, sɪˈkriːtɪv/ *adj* a secretive person or organization likes to keep their thoughts, intentions, or actions hidden from others OPP **open**: *The government has been accused of being secretive and undemocratic.* | **[+about]** *Carla was always very secretive about her work.* —**secretively** *adv* —**secretiveness** *n* [U]

se·cret·ly /ˈsiːkrɪtli/ ●●○ *adv*
1 if you do something secretly, you do it without other people knowing: *They started meeting secretly.*
2 if you feel something secretly, you do not tell anyone about your feelings: *She was secretly hoping that Dan*

would be at the party. | *Secretly, Beth admired Stella's strong character.*

ˌsecret poˈlice *n* **the secret police** a police force controlled by a government, that secretly tries to defeat the political enemies of that government

ˌsecret ˈservice *n* **the secret service a)** a British government organization that protects the country's military and political secrets, and obtains secrets about other countries **b)** a US government department that deals with special kinds of police work, especially protecting the president

sect /sekt/ ●○○ *n* [C] a group of people with their own particular set of beliefs and practices, especially within or separated from a larger religious group → **sectional**

sec·tar·i·an /sekˈteəriən $ -ˈter-/ *adj* **1 sectarian violence/conflict/murder etc** violence etc that is related to the strong feelings of people who belong to different religious groups: *people on both sides of the sectarian divide in Northern Ireland* **2** *AmE* supporting a particular religious group and its beliefs: *a sectarian school* —**sectarianism** *n* [U]

sec·tion¹ /ˈsekʃən/ ●●● S1 W1 AWL *n*

1 PLACE/OBJECT [C] one of the parts that something such as an object or place is divided into: **[+of]** *a busy section of road* | *the reference section of the library* | *The plane's tail section was found in a cornfield.* | *the smoking section* (=where you can smoke)

2 PART OF A WHOLE [C] one of the separate parts of a structure, piece of furniture etc that you fit together to form the whole: **in sections** *The boats were built in Scotland, and transported to Egypt in sections.* THESAURUS ▶ PART

3 BOOK/NEWSPAPER/REPORT [C] a separate part of a book, newspaper, document, report etc: *This issue will be discussed further in section two.* | **sports/style/business/travel etc section** (=particular part of a newspaper)

4 GROUP OF PEOPLE [C] a separate group within a larger group of people: **[+of]** *a large section of the American public*

5 brass/rhythm/woodwind/string etc section the people or person in a band or ORCHESTRA who play the BRASS, RHYTHM etc instruments

6 LAW [C] one of the parts of a law or a legal document: *Article I, Section 8 of the US Constitution*

7 SIDE/TOP VIEW [C,U] *technical* a picture that shows what a building, part of the body etc would look like if it were cut from top to bottom or side to side → **cross-section**: **in section** *Here's the outside view, and here are the floors in section.*

8 MEDICAL/SCIENTIFIC *technical* **a)** [C,U] a medical operation that involves cutting → **caesarean section** at CAESAREAN **b)** [C] a very thin flat piece that is cut from skin, a plant etc to be looked at under a MICROSCOPE

9 AREA OF LAND [C] *AmE* a square area of land in the US that is one mile long on each side

10 MATHEMATICS [C] *technical* the shape that is made when a solid figure is cut by a flat surface in mathematics

section² AWL *v* [T] **1** *BrE* to officially force someone with a mental illness to go to a PSYCHIATRIC hospital, because they are dangerous to themselves or other people **2** to separate something into parts: *Peel and section the oranges.* **3** *technical or medical* to cut a very thin flat piece from skin, a plant etc so that you can look at it under a MICROSCOPE **4** *medical* to cut a part of the body in a medical operation

section sth ↔ **off** *phr v* to divide an area into parts, especially by putting something between the parts: *The vegetable plots were sectioned off by a low wall.*

sec·tion·al /ˈsekʃənəl/ *adj* **1** concerned only with your own small group in society or in an organization, as opposed to being concerned about society or the institution as a whole: *community groups seeking to protect **sectional interests*** **2** a sectional drawing or view of something shows what it would look like if it were cut from top to bottom, or from side to side: *a sectional view of the building* **3** made up of sections that can be put together or taken apart: *a sectional sofa*

sec·tor /ˈsektə $ -ər/ ●●○ W3 AWL *n* [C]

1 a part of an area of activity, especially of business, trade etc: **[+of]** *the agricultural sector of the economy* | **public/private sector** (=business controlled by the government or by private companies)

2 one of the parts into which an area is divided, especially for military purposes

sec·tor·al /ˈsektərəl/ *adj* [usually before noun] *technical* relating to the various economic sectors of a society or to a particular economic sector

sec·u·lar /ˈsekjələ $ -ər/ ●○○ *adj*

1 not connected with or controlled by a church or other religious authority: *secular education* | *our modern secular society* THESAURUS ▶ RELIGIOUS

2 a secular priest lives among ordinary people, rather than with other priests in a MONASTERY

sec·u·lar·is·m /ˈsekjələrɪzəm/ *n* [U] **1** a system of social organization that does not allow religion to influence the government, or the belief that religion should not influence a government **2** the quality of behaving in a way that shows religion does not influence you: *the secularism of popular culture* —**secularist** *n* [C]

sec·u·lar·ize (*also* **-ise** *BrE*) /ˈsekjələraɪz/ *v* [T] to remove the control or influence of religious groups from a society or an institution —**secularization** /ˌsekjələraɪˈzeɪʃən $ -rə-/ *n* [U]

secure¹ ●●● W3 AWL *v* [T]

1 GET/ACHIEVE to get or achieve something that will be permanent, especially after a lot of effort: *Boyd's goal **secured** his team's **place** in the Cup Final.* | **secure a deal/contract** *The company secured a $20 million contract.* | *Negotiators are still working to secure the hostages' release.* | *Redgrave won his third Olympic gold medal, and **secured** his **place in history**.*

2 SAFE FROM HARM to make something safe from being attacked, harmed, or lost: *Troops were sent to secure the border.* | **secure sth against sb/sth** *They built a ten-foot high fence to secure the house against intruders.* | *an agreement to **secure** the **future** of the rainforest*

3 TIE FIRMLY to fasten or tie something firmly in a particular position: **secure sth to sth** *John secured the boat firmly to the jetty.*

4 BORROWING MONEY if you secure a debt or a LOAN, you legally promise that, if you cannot pay back the money you have borrowed, you will give the lender goods or property of the same value instead: *He used his house to **secure** the **loan**.*

se·cure² /sɪˈkjʊə $ -ˈkjʊr/ ●●○ S3 W3 AWL *adj*

1 PERMANENT/CERTAIN a situation that is secure is one that you can depend on because it is not likely to change OPP **insecure**: *There are no secure jobs these days.* | *We want a **secure future** for our children.* | *United's position at the top of the league seems relatively secure.*

2 PLACE/BUILDING locked or guarded so that people cannot get in or out or steal anything: *The house isn't very secure – we need some new locks.* | *Keep your passport in a **secure place**.* | **secure accommodation** *BrE* (=a type of prison) *In the last year, only three children under the age of 14 have had to be placed in secure accommodation.*

3 SAFE FROM HARM safe from and protected against damage or attack: *Companies can offer secure credit card transactions over the Internet.* | **[+from]** *These elephants are relatively secure from poachers.*

4 CONFIDENT feeling confident about yourself and your abilities OPP **insecure**: *We want our children to be secure and feel good about themselves.*

5 NOT WORRIED feeling confident and certain about a situation and not worried that it might change OPP **insecure**: *Workers no longer **feel secure** about the future.* | *It was enough money to make us feel **financially secure**.* | *We huddled together, **secure in the knowledge that** the rescue helicopter was on its way.*

6 FIRMLY FASTENED firmly fastened or tied, and not likely to fall down: *Are you sure that shelf is secure?*

se·cure·ly /sɪˈkjʊəli $ -ˈkjʊr-/ AWL *adv* **1** tied, fastened

S

etc tightly, especially in order to make something safe OPP **insecurely**: **securely locked/fastened/attached/held etc** *All firearms should be kept securely locked in a cabinet.* **2** in a way that protects something from being stolen or lost: *Customers can now buy products securely over the Internet.* **3** in a way that is likely to continue successfully and not change SYN **firmly**: *By that time, democracy had become **securely established** in Spain.*

se·cu·ri·ty /sɪˈkjʊərəti $ -ˈkjʊr-/ ●●● W1 AWL *n*

1 PROTECTION FROM DANGER [U] things that are done to keep a person, building, or country safe from danger or crime: *The trial was held under **tight security**. | **lax security** at airline check-in desks | terrorist activity that is a threat to **national security** | The prison was ordered to **tighten security** after a prisoner escaped yesterday. | The Security Commission investigates **breaches of security**. | We have been asked not to say anything **for security reasons**. | The **security forces** opened fire, killing two people. | The thief was caught on a **security camera**. | There are strict **security checks** on everyone entering the Opera House. | A large number of homes lack adequate **security measures**.*

2 PROTECTION FROM BAD SITUATIONS [U] protection from bad things that could happen to you OPP **insecurity**: *Parenting is about giving your child security and love. | Workers want greater **job security*** (=not being in danger of losing their jobs). *| This insurance plan offers your family **financial security** in the event of your death.*

3 GUARDS [U] the department of a company or organization that deals with the protection of its buildings and equipment: *One of the sales clerks called security.* → SECURITY GUARD

4 BORROWING MONEY [U] something such as property that you promise to give someone if you cannot pay back money you have borrowed from them: **[+for]** *Reiss used his Brooklyn home as security for the loan.*

5 securities [plural] STOCKS or SHAREs in a company

seˈcurity ˌblanket *n* [C] **1** a piece of material that a child likes to hold, to comfort himself or herself **2** something that you have had for a long time, and that you use to make yourself feel less anxious

seˈcurity ˌclearance *n* [C,U] official permission for someone to see secret documents etc, or to enter a building, after a strict checking process

seˈcurity deˌposit *n* [C] an amount of money that you give to a LANDLORD before you rent a house or apartment, and that is returned to you after you leave if you have not damaged the property

seˈcurity ˌguard *n* [C] someone whose job is to guard money or a building

seˈcurity ˌlight *n* [C] a light that turns on when someone tries to enter a building or area at night

seˈcurity ˌmom *n* [C] *AmE* an American mother who believes that protecting the US and its citizens from TERRORISM is the most important thing that the US government can do: *The soccer moms of the 1990s have become the security moms of today.*

seˈcurity ˌrisk *n* [C] **1** someone in a government or organization who you cannot trust with important secrets, because they might tell them to an enemy **2** a situation that could put people in danger: *After the bomb threat, it was considered too much of a security risk to let the races go ahead.*

seˈcurity ˌservice *n* [C] a government organization that protects a country's secrets against enemy countries, or protects the government against attempts to take away its power

se·dan /sɪˈdæn/ *n* [C] *AmE, AusE* a car that has four doors, seats for at least four people, and a BOOT SYN **saloon** *BrE*

seˌdan ˈchair *n* [C] a seat on two poles with a cover around it, used in the past to carry an important person

se·date¹ /sɪˈdeɪt/ *adj* **1** calm, serious, and formal: *a sedate seaside town | The wedding was rather a sedate occasion.* **2** *formal* moving slowly and calmly: *We continued our walk **at a sedate pace**.* —**sedately** *adv*

sedate² *v* [T] to give someone drugs to make them calm or to make them sleep: *He was still in shock, and **heavily sedated**.* GRAMMAR **Sedate** is often used in the passive.

se·da·tion /sɪˈdeɪʃən/ *n* [U] the use of drugs to make someone calm or go to sleep: **under sedation** *The patient was still **under** heavy **sedation**.*

sed·a·tive /ˈsedətɪv/ *n* [C] a drug used to make someone calm or go to sleep —**sedative** *adj*

sed·en·ta·ry /ˈsedəntəri $ -teri/ *adj* **1** *formal* spending a lot of time sitting down, and not moving or exercising very much: **sedentary life/job/lifestyle etc** *health problems caused by our sedentary lifestyles* **2** *technical* a sedentary group of people tend always to live in the same place: *a sedentary people living north of the Danube*

sedge /sedʒ/ *n* [U] a plant similar to grass that grows in wet ground and on the edge of rivers and lakes

sed·i·ment /ˈsedəmənt/ *n* [C,U] solid substances that settle at the bottom of a liquid: *a thick layer of sediment*

sed·i·men·ta·ry /ˌsedəˈmentəri◂/ *adj technical* made of the solid substances that settle at the bottom of the sea, rivers, lakes etc: *sedimentary rock | sedimentary deposits*

sed·i·men·ta·tion /ˌsedəmenˈteɪʃən, -mən-/ *n* [U] *technical* the natural process by which small pieces of rock, earth etc settle at the bottom of the sea etc and form a solid layer

se·di·tion /sɪˈdɪʃən/ *n* [U] *formal* speech, writing, or actions intended to encourage people to disobey a government: *Trade union leaders were charged with sedition.* —**seditious** *adj*: *a seditious speech*

se·duce /sɪˈdjuːs $ -ˈduːs/ ●○○ *v* [T]

1 to persuade someone to have sex with you, especially in a way that is attractive and not too direct: *The professor was sacked for seducing female students. | Are you trying to seduce me?*

2 to make someone want to do something by making it seem very attractive or interesting to them: *I was young and seduced by New York.* | **seduce sb into doing sth** *Leaders are people who can seduce other people into sharing their dream.* GRAMMAR **Seduce** is often passive in this meaning.

se·duc·er /sɪˈdjuːsə $ -ˈduːsər/ *n* [C] a man who persuades someone to have sex with him → **seductress**

se·duc·tion /sɪˈdʌkʃən/ *n* **1** [C,U] an act of persuading someone to have sex with you for the first time → **seduce**: **[+of]** *the seduction of a young girl* **2** [C usually plural] something that strongly attracts people, but often has a bad effect on their lives: **[+of]** *the seductions of power*

se·duc·tive /sɪˈdʌktɪv/ *adj* **1** someone, especially a woman, who is seductive is sexually attractive: *She used all of her **seductive charm** to try and persuade him.* **2** something that is seductive is very interesting or attractive to you, in a way that persuades you to do something you would not usually do: *the seductive power of advertising* —**seductively** *adv*: *She smiled seductively at him across the table.*

se·duc·tress /sɪˈdʌktrɪs/ *n* [C] a woman who persuades someone to have sex with her → **seducer**

see¹ /siː/ ●●● S1 W1 *v* (*past tense* **saw** /sɔː $ sɒː/, *past participle* **seen** /siːn/)

1 NOTICE/EXAMINE [T] to notice or examine someone or something, using your eyes: *The moment we saw the house, we knew we wanted to buy it. | He crouched down so he couldn't be seen. | Can I see your ticket, please? | I saw the offer advertised in the newspaper.* | **can/can't see** *You can see the Houses of Parliament from here.* | **see where/what/who etc** *Can you see where the marks are on the wall?* | **see (that)** *He saw that she was crying.* | **see sb/sth do sth** *I saw him leave a few minutes ago.* | **see sb/sth doing sth** *The suspect was seen entering the building.* | ***As you can see**, the house needs some work doing on it. | **Have you seen** Chris* (=do you know where he is)? *| The accommodation was so awful it **had to be seen to be believed*** (=you would not believe it if you did not see it yourself).

2 NOTICE STH IS TRUE [T] to notice that something is happening or that something is true: *More money must be invested if we are to see an improvement in services.* | *After a month's practice, you should see a difference in your playing.* | *Seeing his distress, Louise put her arm around him.* | *I would like to see changes in the way the course is run.* | *'You're not denying it, I see,' he said coldly.* | **see (that)** *I can see you're not very happy with the situation.*

3 ABILITY TO SEE [I,T] to be able to use your eyes to look at things and know what they are: **can/can't see** *From the tower, you can see for miles.* | *I can't see a thing without my glasses.* | **not see to do sth** *His eyes are so bad that he can't see to read anymore.*

4 FIND OUT INFORMATION [I,T] to find out information or a fact: **see what/how/when etc** *I'll call him and see how the job interview went.* | *She went outside to see what was happening.* | **see if/whether** *I've just come to see if you want to go out for a drink.* | *These chocolates are gorgeous. Try some and* ***see for yourself*** (=find out if it is true). | *By looking at this leaflet, you can* ***see at a glance*** (=find out very easily) *how much a loan will cost.* | **it can be seen that/we can see that** *From this graph, it can be seen that some people are more susceptible to the disease.* | ***As we have seen*** *in chapter four, women's pay is generally less than men's.*

5 IN THE FUTURE [I,T] to find out about something in the future: **see if/whether** *It will be interesting to see if he makes it into the team.* | **see how/what/when etc** *I might come – I'll see how I feel tomorrow.* | *Let's try it and see what happens.* | *'Can we go to the zoo, Dad?' '****We'll see****'* (=used when you do not want to make a decision immediately). | *'How long can you stay?' '****I'll have to see****. It depends* (=used when you cannot make a decision immediately).*'* | *We'll just have to* ***wait and see****.* | **see how it goes/see how things go** (=used when you are going to do something and will deal with problems if they happen) *I don't know. We'll just have to see how it goes on Sunday.* | *Things will work out,* ***you'll see*** (=you will find out that I am right).

6 WHERE INFORMATION IS [T] *especially written* used to tell you where you can find information: *See p. 58.* | *See press for details.* | **see above/below** *The results are shown in Table 7a (see below).* GRAMMAR **See** is always used in the imperative in this meaning.

7 UNDERSTAND [I,T] to understand or realize something: **see why/what/how etc** *I can't see why he's so upset.* | ***I see what*** *you* ***mean*** (=I understand what you are saying). | *'He lives here but works in London during the week.' 'Oh,* ***I see*** (=I understand).*'* | ***You see****, the thing is, I'm really busy right now* (=used when you are explaining something). | *You mix the flour and eggs like this,* ***see*** (=used to check that someone is listening and understands)? | *I* ***can't see the point of*** (=I do not understand the reason for) *spending so much money on a car.* | ***Do you see the point*** *I'm making* (=do you understand what I'm trying to say)? | *The other officers laughed, but Nichols couldn't* ***see the joke****.* | **see reason/sense** (=realize that you are wrong or doing something stupid) *I just can't get her to see reason!* **THESAURUS** **UNDERSTAND**

8 WATCH [T] to watch a television programme, play, film etc: *Did you see that programme on monkeys last night?* | *We're going to see 'Romeo and Juliet' tonight.*

9 CONSIDER SB/STH [T] to think about or consider someone or something in a particular way, or as having particular qualities: *Having a child makes you see things differently.* | *Violence is seen in different ways by different people.* | **as sb sees it/the way sb sees it** (=used to give someone's opinion) *As I see it, you don't have any choice.* | *The way I see it, we have two options.* | **see sb/sth as sth** *I see the job as a challenge.* | **see yourself as sth** *He saw himself as a failure.* | **be seen as (being) sth** *The peace talks are seen as a sign of hope.* | *This type of work is often seen as boring.* | **be seen to be (doing) sth** *Teachers need to be seen to be in control.* | *The government must be seen to be doing something about the rise in violent crime.*

10 see what sb/sth can do *spoken* **a)** to find out if someone can deal with a situation or problem: **[+about]** *I'll call them again and see what they can do about it.* **b)** to find out how good someone or something is at what they are supposed to be able to do: *Let's take the Porsche out to the racetrack and see what it can do!*

11 I'll see what I can do *spoken* used to say that you will try to help someone: *Leave the papers with me and I'll see what I can do.*

12 see you *spoken* used to say goodbye when you know you will see someone again: **see you tomorrow/at three/Sunday etc** *See you Friday – your place at 8:30.* | **see you later** (=see you soon, or later in the same day) | **see you in a bit** *BrE* (=see you soon) | **see you in a while** (=see you soon) | **(I'll) be seeing you!** (=see you soon)

13 VISIT [T] to visit or meet someone: *I'll be seeing her tomorrow night.* | *I haven't seen her since we left school.* | *She's too sick to see anyone right now.*

14 MEET BY CHANCE [T] to meet someone by chance: *I saw Jane while I was out.*

15 HAVE A MEETING [T] to have an arranged meeting with someone: *Mr Thomas is seeing a client at 2:30.* | *She was seen by a doctor but didn't need hospital treatment.* | **see sb about sth** (=see someone to discuss something) *I have to see my teacher about my grades.*

16 SPEND TIME WITH SB [T] to spend time with someone: *They've been* ***seeing a lot of*** *each other.* | **see more/less of sb** (=see someone more or less often) *They've seen more of each other since Dan moved to London.*

17 be seeing sb to be having a romantic relationship with someone: *Is she seeing anyone at the moment?*

18 IMAGINE [T] to imagine that something may happen in the future: *He could see a great future for her in music.* | **can't see sb/sth doing sth** *I can't see him winning, can you?* | *She's got a new book coming out, but I can't see it doing very well.* | **see sb as sth** (=be able to imagine someone being something) *I just can't see her as a ballet dancer.*

19 seeing as (how) *informal* (*also* **seeing that**) used before giving a reason for what you are saying: *'I might as well do something useful, seeing as I'm back,' she said.*

20 see sth for what it is (*also* **see sb for what they are**) to realize that someone or something is not as good or nice as they seem: *They are unimpressed with the scheme and rightly see it for what it is.*

21 MAKE SURE [T] to make sure or check that something is done: **see (that)** *It's up to you to see that the job's done properly.* | *Please see that the lights are switched off before you leave.* | *Don't worry – I'll* ***see to it****.* | *The hotel's owners* ***see to it that*** *their guests are given every luxury.*

22 EXPERIENCE STH [T] to experience something: *She was so sick that doctors didn't think she'd live to see her first birthday.* | *I never thought I'd* ***live to see the day*** *when women became priests.* | *She's* ***seen it all before*** (=has experienced so much that nothing surprises her) *in her long career.* → **been there, seen that, done that** at BEEN(3)

23 TIME/PLACE [T] if a time or place has seen a particular event or situation, it happened or existed in that time or place: *This year has seen a big increase in road accidents.* | *The city has seen plenty of violence over the years.*

24 let me see (*also* **let's see**) *spoken* used when you are trying to remember something: *Let me see ... where did I put that letter?*

25 I don't see why not *spoken* used to say 'yes' in answer to a request: *'Can we go to the park?' 'I don't see why not.'*

26 GO WITH SB [T always + adv/prep] to go somewhere with someone to make sure they are safe: *My mother used to see me across the road.* | *I'll get Nick to* ***see*** *you* ***home****.* | *Let me* ***see*** *you* ***to the door*** (=go with you to the door, to say goodbye).

27 be seeing things to imagine that you see someone or something which is not really there: *There's no one there – you must be seeing things.*

28 see double if you see double, something is wrong with your eyes, so that you see two things when there is only one

29 have seen better days *informal* to be in a bad condition: *Her hat had seen better days.*

30 be glad/pleased etc to see the back of sb/sth *BrE spoken* to be pleased when someone leaves or when you get rid of something, because you do not like them: *I'll be glad to see the back of him.*

31 see the last of sb/sth a) to not see someone or something again, especially someone or something you do not like: *I thought we'd seen the last of him.* | *It was a relief to see the last of them.* **b)** to not have to deal with something anymore: *Police hoped they'd seen the last of the joyriding.* | *We may not have seen the last of this controversy.*
32 see the light a) to realize that something is true: *She finally saw the light and ended the relationship.* **b)** to have a special experience that makes you believe in a religion
33 see the light of day a) if something sees the light of day, it is brought out so that people can see it: *This decision will ensure that the Pentagon Papers never see the light of day.* **b)** to start to exist: *This type of PC first saw the light of day in 1981.*
34 see red to become very angry: *The thought of Pierre with Nicole had made her see red.*
35 not see sb for dust *BrE informal* if you do not see someone for dust, they leave a place very quickly in order to avoid something
36 see eye to eye [usually in negatives] if two people see eye to eye, they agree with each other: *We didn't exactly see eye to eye.* | **[+with]** *I don't always see eye to eye with my father.* | **[+on/about]** *We don't see eye to eye on business issues.*
37 seen one ... seen them all *informal* used to say that something is boring because it is very similar to other things: *When you've seen one of these programmes, you've seen them all.*
38 see your way (clear) to doing sth *formal* to be able and willing to do something: *Small companies cannot see their way to taking on many trainees.*
39 (see and) be seen to look at or be noticed by important or fashionable people: *Royal Ascot is the place to see and be seen.*
40 not see the wood for the trees (*also* **not see the forest for the trees** *AmE*) to be unable to understand what is important in a situation because you are thinking too much about small details rather than the whole situation
41 see sth coming to realize that there is going to be a problem before it actually happens: *John's going to have a lot of trouble with him. You can see it coming.*
42 see sb coming (a mile off) *BrE spoken* to recognize that someone will be easy to trick or deceive: *You paid £500 for that! They must have seen you coming!*
43 see sb right *BrE spoken* to make sure that someone gets what they need or want, especially money: *Just do this for me and I'll see you right.* | *Tell the landlord I sent you and he'll see you right.*
44 not see that it matters *spoken* to think that something is not important: *I can't see that it matters what I think.*
45 GAME OF CARDS [T] to risk the same amount of money as your opponent in a CARD game → **it remains to be seen** at REMAIN(5), → **see fit (to do sth)** at FIT²(3), → **wouldn't be seen dead** at DEAD¹(12)

GRAMMAR: Using the progressive

- In meanings 1, 2, 3, 9, 14, and 18, **see** is not used in the progressive. You say: *I see Tina over there.* | *I suddenly saw the difference.* ✗ Don't say: *I am seeing Tina over there.* | *I was suddenly seeing the difference.*
- **See** is often used with **can**: *I can see Tina over there.* | *I could suddenly see the difference.*

GRAMMAR GUIDE ▸ VERBS

THESAURUS

see to notice something with your eyes, usually without planning to. Also used when saying that you watched a particular programme, film, game etc: *Have you seen my keys anywhere?* | *Did you see the basketball game last night?*
look at sb/sth to keep your eyes pointed toward someone or something, especially someone or something that is not moving: *I looked at the map.* | *She was looking at him in a strange way.*
notice to see something interesting or unusual: *I noticed a police car outside their house.*
spot to suddenly see something, especially something you are looking for: *Nick spotted the advertisement in the paper.*
catch sight of/catch a glimpse of (*also* **glimpse** *formal*) to suddenly see someone or something for a short time, usually not clearly: *I caught sight of him in the hotel lobby, and followed him out the door.* | *He glimpsed her face as she went into the courtroom.*
make out sb/sth to see something, but only with difficulty: *Ahead, I could just make out the figure of a woman.*
witness to see something happen, especially a crime or an accident: *The police are asking anyone who witnessed the attack to come forward.*
observe *formal* to see and pay attention to something: *Officers observed him driving at 100 mph.*
sight *especially written* to suddenly see something or someone from a long distance, especially when you have been looking for a long time: *The missing boys were sighted by a rescue helicopter.* | *The crew finally sighted land.*

see about sth *phr v*
1 to make arrangements or deal with something: *I'd better see about dinner.* | **see about doing sth** *Claire's gone to see about getting tickets for the concert.*
2 we'll see about that *spoken* **a)** (*also* **we'll have to see about that**) used to say that you do not know if something will be possible: *'I want to go to Joshua's tonight.' 'Well, we'll have to see about that.'* **b)** (*also* **we'll soon see about that**) used to say that you intend to stop someone from doing what they were planning to do
see sth **against** sth *phr v* to consider something together with something else: *The unemployment data must **be seen against the background of*** *world recession.* GRAMMAR **See against** is usually passive.
see around *phr v*
1 see sb around to notice someone regularly in places you go to, but not talk to them: *I don't know who he is, but I've seen him around.*
2 see you around *spoken* used to say goodbye to someone when you have not made a definite arrangement to meet again
3 see around/round sth *BrE* to visit a place and walk around looking at it: *Would you like to see round the house?*
see in *phr v*
1 not know what sb sees in sb (*also* **what does sb see in sb?**) used to say that you do not know why someone likes someone else: *I don't know what she sees in him.*
2 see sth in sb/sth to notice a particular quality in someone or something that makes you like them: *He saw a gentleness in Susan.*
3 see sb in to go with someone to make sure they arrive at a building or room: *He took her home and, after seeing her in, drove off without a word.*
4 see in the New Year to celebrate the beginning of a new year
see sb/sth ↔ **off** *phr v*
1 to defeat someone or stop them from competing against you: *To see off the threat, the company will have to cut its prices still further.* | *The team saw off their old rivals in last night's championship game.*
2 to go to an airport, train station etc to say goodbye to someone: *They've gone to the airport to see their son off.*
3 (*also* **see sb off sth**) to force someone to leave a place: *Security guards saw him off the premises.*
see sb/sth **out** *phr v*
1 to go to the door with someone to say goodbye to them when they leave: *I'll see you out.* | *Don't worry, I can* **see** ***myself out*** (=leave the building without anyone coming with me).
2 see sth ↔ out to continue doing something or being somewhere until a particular period of time or an unpleasant event is finished: *Connolly has promised to see out the remaining 18 months of his contract.* | *She saw out her last years at Sudeley Castle.*
see over sth *phr v BrE* to look at something large such as a house, especially in order to decide if you want to buy it

see through *phr v*
1 see through sb/sth to realize that someone is trying to deceive you: *I saw through his excuses.* | *I could never lie to her because I know she'd see through me straight away.* | *I can't bluff – she'd* ***see right through me****.*
2 see sth through to continue doing something until it is finished, especially something difficult or unpleasant: *It'll take a lot of effort to see the project through.*
3 see sb through (sth) to give help and support to someone during a difficult time: *Setting goals should help see you through.* | *I've got enough money to see me through six months of unemployment.*
4 see sth through sb's eyes to see something or think about it in the way that someone else does: *The world is very different when seen through the eyes of a child.*

see to sb/sth *phr v* to deal with something or do something for someone: *Go on, you go out. I'll see to the washing-up.* | **have/get sth seen to** *You should get that tooth seen to by a dentist.*

see² *n* [C] an area governed by a BISHOP

seed¹ /siːd/ ●●● S3 W3 *n*
1 PLANTS **a)** [C,U] a small hard object produced by plants, from which a new plant of the same kind grows: *a packet of sunflower seeds* | **plant/sow seeds** (=put them in the soil) *Sow the seeds one inch deep in the soil.* | **grow sth from seed** *We grew all our tomatoes from seed.* **b)** [U] a quantity of seeds: *Some of the poorest farmers don't have enough money to buy seed.*
2 IN FRUIT [C] *AmE* one of the small hard objects in a fruit such as an apple or orange, from which new fruit trees grow SYN **pip** *BrE*
3 seeds of sth *written* something that makes a new situation start to grow and develop: **seeds of change/victory** *The seeds of change in Eastern Europe were beginning to emerge.* | **seeds of doubt/disaster/destruction etc** (=something which makes a bad feeling or situation develop) *Something Lucy said began to* ***sow seeds of*** *doubt in his mind.*
4 go/run to seed a) if a plant or vegetable goes or runs to seed, it starts producing flowers and seeds as well as leaves **b)** if someone or something goes or runs to seed, they become less attractive or good, especially because they are getting old and have not been properly looked after: *The old central bus station is going to seed.*
5 number one/two/three etc seed [C] a player or team in a competition that is given a particular position, according to how likely they are to win: *He's been top seed for the past two years.*
6 SEX [U] *biblical* SEMEN or SPERM – often used humorously
7 FAMILY [U] *biblical* the group of people who have a particular person as their father, grandfather etc, especially when they form a particular race

seed² *v* **1** [T] to remove seeds from fruit or vegetables: *Add one lime, seeded and sliced.* **2** [T] to give a player or team in a competition a particular position, according to how likely they are to win: **be seeded 8th/18th etc** *Sharapova was seeded fifth at Wimbledon.* **3** [T] to plant seeds in the ground: *a newly seeded lawn* **4** [I] to produce seeds **5 seed itself** if a tree or plant seeds itself, it produces a new plant using its own seeds GRAMMAR **Seed** is usually passive when used as a transitive verb.

seed·bed /ˈsiːdbed/ *n* [C] **1** a place or condition that encourages something to develop: **[+for/of]** *Strong personal beliefs can become a seedbed for conflicts.* **2** an area of ground where young plants are grown from seeds before they are planted somewhere else

ˈseed ˌcapital *n* [U] SEED MONEY

ˈseed corn *n* [U] **1** *BrE* people or things that will develop to become useful or successful in the future: *Young people are the seed corn management of the future.* **2** grain that is used for planting next year's crops

seed·less /ˈsiːdləs/ *adj* seedless fruit has no seeds in it: *seedless grapes*

seed·ling /ˈsiːdlɪŋ/ *n* [C] a young plant or tree grown from a seed → see picture at TREE

ˈseed ˌmoney (*also* **ˈseed ˌcapital**) *n* [U] the money you have available to start a new business

ˈseed pearl *n* [C] a very small and often imperfect PEARL

seed·y /ˈsiːdi/ *adj informal* a seedy person or place looks dirty or poor, and is often connected with illegal or immoral activities: *a seedy nightclub* | *a seedy-looking old man*

see·ing /ˈsiːɪŋ/ *conjunction spoken* because a particular fact or situation is true: **[+as]** *I won't stay long, seeing as you're busy.* | *Oh, all right,* ***seeing as it's you*** (=used to agree humorously to someone's request).

ˌSeeing ˈEye ˌdog *n* [C] *trademark AmE* a dog trained to guide blind people SYN **guide dog** *BrE*

seek /siːk/ ●●● S2 W1 AWL *v* (*past tense and past participle* **sought** /sɔːt $ sɒːt/) [T]
1 *formal* to try to achieve or get something: *Do you think the president will* ***seek re-election****?* | **seek refuge/asylum/shelter etc** *Thousands of people crossed the border, seeking refuge from the war.* | **seek revenge/damages/compensation etc** *He sought revenge against Surkov for separating him from his wife and son.* | **seek to do sth** *Local schools are seeking to reduce the dropout rate.* | **attention-seeking/publicity-seeking**
2 seek (sb's) advice/help/assistance etc *formal* to ask someone for advice or help: *If the symptoms persist, seek medical advice.*
3 *written* to look for someone or something SYN **look for**: *new graduates seeking employment* | *Attractive woman, 27, seeks male, 25-35, for fun and friendship.* THESAURUS ▸ SEARCH

> **REGISTER**
> In everyday English, people usually say that they are **looking for** someone or something rather than **seeking** someone or something: *What kind of job are you* ***looking for****?*

4 seek your fortune *literary* to go to another place hoping to gain success and wealth: *Coles came to the Yukon in the 1970s to seek his fortune.*
5 to move naturally towards something or into a particular position: *Water seeks its own level.* → HEAT-SEEKING, HIDE-AND-SEEK, SELF-SEEKING, SOUGHT-AFTER

seek sb/sth ↔ **out** *phr v* to try to find someone or something, especially when this is difficult: *Our mission is to seek out the enemy and destroy them.*

seek·er /ˈsiːkə $ -ər/ *n* [C] someone who is trying to find or get something: **job-/attention-/publicity- etc seeker** *a brilliant politician and a ruthless power-seeker* → ASYLUM SEEKER

seem /siːm/ ●●● S1 W1 *v* [linking verb]
1 if something seems to be true, there are things that make people think it is true: **[+adj]** *Ann didn't seem very pleased.* | **[+adj+noun]** *It seems a foolish decision now.* | **[+like]** *The last few days had seemed like a dream.* | *Teri seemed like a nice girl.* | **it seems like/as if/as though** *It seems like you're catching a cold, Taylor.* | *It seemed as if the end of the world had come.* | **it seems (that)** *It seemed that Freeman had killed the man, and dumped the body in the lake.* | *It seems likely that he will miss the team's next game.* | **seem to do sth** *The rainbow seemed to end on the hillside.* | **seem to sb** *Doesn't that seem weird to you?* | **it seems to sb (that)** (=used when giving your opinion about something) *It seems to me you don't have much choice.* | **there seem(s) to be sth** (=used when saying what you think has happened or is true) *There seem to be a lot of people outside.* | **so it seems** (=it seems to be true) *'So Bill's leaving her?' 'So it seems.'*
2 can't/couldn't seem to do sth used to say that you have tried to do something but cannot do it: *I just can't seem to relax.*
3 used to make what you are saying less strong or certain, and more polite: **seem to do sth** *I seem to have lost my car keys.* | **it seems (that)/it would seem (that)** *It would seem that someone left the building unlocked.*

GRAMMAR

Linking verbs

Seem is a linking verb. This type of verb links the subject of the sentence with an adjective or noun: *She seemed satisfied with his explanation.* | *Their meeting seems a coincidence.*

Using the progressive

Seem is not used in the progressive. You say: *She seems very happy.* ✗ Don't say: *She is seeming happy.*

GRAMMAR GUIDE ▶ VERBS

seem·ing /ˈsiːmɪŋ/ *adj* [only before noun] *formal* appearing to be something, especially when this is not actually true SYN **apparent**: *a seeming piece of good luck, which later led to all kinds of trouble*

seem·ing·ly /ˈsiːmɪŋli/ ●○○ *adv*

1 appearing to have a particular quality, when this may or may not be true SYN **apparently**: *seemingly unrelated bits of information* | **seemingly endless/impossible etc** *The new minister was faced with a seemingly impossible task.* | **seemingly unaware/oblivious** *Alice was standing in the street, seemingly oblivious to the rain.*

2 [sentence adverb] *formal* according to the facts as you know them SYN **apparently**: *There is seemingly nothing we can do to stop the plans going ahead.*

seem·ly /ˈsiːmli/ *adj old-fashioned* suitable for a particular situation or social occasion, according to accepted standards of behaviour OPP **unseemly**: *It was not seemly for ladies to talk about money.*

seen /siːn/ *v* the past participle of SEE

seep /siːp/ *v* [I always + adv/prep] **1** to flow slowly through small holes or spaces: **[+into/through/down etc]** *Blood seeped down his leg.* **2** to move or spread gradually: **[+away/into/through etc]** *His tension was seeping away.*

seep·age /ˈsiːpɪdʒ/ *n* [C,U] a gradual flow of liquid or gas through small spaces or holes

seer /sɪə $ sɪr/ *n* [C] *especially literary* someone who can see into the future and say what will happen SYN **clairvoyant**

seer·suck·er /ˈsɪəˌsʌkə $ ˈsɪrˌsʌkər/ *n* [U] a light cotton cloth with an uneven surface and a pattern of lines on it

see·saw[1] /ˈsiːsɔː $ -sɒː/ *n* [C] **1** a piece of equipment that children play on, made of a board that is balanced in the middle, so that when one end goes up the other goes down SYN **teeter-totter** *AmE* **2** a repeated movement from one state or condition to another and back again SYN **oscillation**

seesaw[2] *v* [I] to keep changing from one state or condition to another and back again: *Before the election, the president seesawed in the polls.*

seethe /siːð/ *v* [I] **1** to feel an emotion, especially anger, so strongly that you are almost shaking SYN **fume**: **[+with]** *He was seething with anger.* | *I was absolutely seething.* **2 be seething (with sth)** if a place is seething with people, insects etc, there are a lot of them all moving quickly in different directions: *The cellar was seething with spiders.*

ˈsee-through *adj* a see-through material or surface allows you to see through it SYN **transparent**: *a see-through blouse*

seg·ment[1] /ˈsegmənt/ ●○○ *n* [C]

1 a part of something that is different from or affected differently from the whole in some way: **[+of]** *segments of the population*

2 a part of a fruit, flower, or insect that it naturally divides into: *Decorate with orange segments.*

3 *technical* the part of a circle that is separated from the rest of the circle when you draw a straight line across it

4 *technical* the part of a line or of a length of something between two points: **[+of]** *segments of DNA*

seg·ment[2] /segˈment/ *v* [T] to divide something into parts that are different from each other

seg·men·ta·tion /ˌsegmenˈteɪʃən, -mən-/ *n* [U] when something divides or is divided into smaller parts: **[+of]** *the segmentation of society*

seg·ment·ed /segˈmentɪd/ *adj* consisting of separate parts that are connected to each other: *segmented worms*

seg·re·gate /ˈsegrɪgeɪt/ *v* [T] **1** to separate one group of people from others, especially because they are of a different race, sex, or religion OPP **integrate**: **be segregated from sb** *Blacks were segregated from whites in schools.* THESAURUS ▶ SEPARATE **2** to separate one part of a place or thing from another: **be segregated from/into sth** *The coffee room had been segregated into smoking and non-smoking areas.* GRAMMAR **Segregate** is usually passive.

seg·re·gat·ed /ˈsegrɪgeɪtɪd/ ●○○ *adj* a segregated school or other institution can only be attended by members of one sex, race, religion etc OPP **integrated**: *a* ***racially segregated*** *education system*

seg·re·ga·tion /ˌsegrɪˈgeɪʃən/ ●○○ *n* [U] when people of different races, sexes, or religions are kept apart so that they live, work, or study separately OPP **integration**: ***racial segregation*** | **[+of]** *the segregation of men and women*

seg·re·ga·tion·ist /ˌsegrɪˈgeɪʃənɪst/ *adj* relating to the practice of keeping people of different races, sexes, or religions separate: *segregationist policies* —**segregationist** *n* [C]

seg·ue /ˈsegweɪ/ *v* (**segued**, **segueing**) [I] to move smoothly from one song, idea, activity, condition etc to another: **[+into/from]** *The conversation segued into banter about the Cup Final.* —**segue** *n* [C]

seis·mic /ˈsaɪzmɪk/ *adj* [only before noun] **1** *technical* relating to or caused by EARTHQUAKES: *increased seismic activity* **2** very great, serious, or important: *seismic changes in international relations*

seis·mo·graph /ˈsaɪzməgrɑːf $ -græf/ *n* [C] an instrument that measures and records the movement of the earth during an EARTHQUAKE

seis·mol·o·gy /saɪzˈmɒlədʒi $ -ˈmɑː-/ *n* [U] the scientific study of EARTHQUAKES —**seismologist** *n* [C]

sei·tan /ˈseɪtæn/ *n* [U] a Japanese food made from wheat, containing a lot of PROTEIN and usually eaten instead of meat

seize /siːz/ ●●○ W3 *v* [T]

1 to take hold of something suddenly and violently SYN **grab**: *Suddenly, he seized my hand.* | **seize sth from sb** *Maggie seized the letter from her.* THESAURUS ▶ HOLD

REGISTER

In everyday English, people usually say **grab** or **grab hold of** rather than **seize**: *She* ***grabbed hold of*** *his hand.*

2 to take control of a place suddenly and quickly, using military force: **seize power/control (of sth)** *The rebels have seized power.* | *A group of soldiers seized the airport.*

3 if the police or government officers seize something, for example illegal drugs, they take legal possession of it: *160,000 CDs were seized from illegal factories.* | *All of my* ***assets*** *were* ***seized****, including my home.*

4 to suddenly catch someone and make sure they cannot get away: *The gunmen were seized at 1 am.*

5 seize a chance/an opportunity/the initiative to quickly and eagerly do something when you have the chance to

6 be seized with/by terror/desire etc to suddenly be affected by an extremely strong feeling: *When she saw his face, she was seized by fear.*

seize on/upon sth *phr v* to suddenly become very interested in an idea, excuse, what someone says etc: *His every remark is seized upon by the press.*

seize up *phr v*

1 if an engine or part of a machine seizes up, its moving parts stop working and can no longer move, for example because of lack of oil: *The mechanism had seized up.*

2 if a part of your body, such as your back, seizes up, you suddenly cannot move it and it is very painful

sei·zure /ˈsiːʒə $ -ər/ ●○○ *n*

1 [C,U] the act of suddenly taking control of something,

especially by force: **[+of]** *the fascist seizure of power in 1922*
2 [C,U] when the police or government officers take away illegal goods such as drugs or guns: *drugs seizures*
3 [C] a sudden condition in which someone cannot control the movements of their body, which continues for a short time SYN **fit**: *He **had** an epileptic **seizure**.*

sel·dom /ˈseldəm/ ●●○ *adv* very rarely or almost never: *Karen had seldom seen him so angry.* THESAURUS RARELY

> **REGISTER**
> **Seldom** sounds rather literary. In everyday English, people usually say **rarely** or **not very often**: *I **seldom** go there.* → *I **don't** go there **very often**.*

> **GRAMMAR: Word order**
> In formal writing, **seldom** can be put first, followed by an auxiliary and the subject, to emphasize that something very rarely happens: *Seldom have I read an article that was so full of lies.*
> GRAMMAR GUIDE ADVERBS

se·lect¹ /səˈlekt/ ●●● S2 W2 AWL *v* [T] to choose something or someone by thinking carefully about which is the best, most suitable etc SYN **choose, pick**: *a group of students selected at random* | **select sb for sth** *He had hopes of being selected for the national team.* | **select sb/sth as sth** *York was selected as the site for the research centre.* | **select sb/sth from sth** *They selected the winner from six finalists.* | **select sb to do sth** *Simon's been selected to go to the conference.* THESAURUS CHOOSE

> **REGISTER**
> In everyday English, people usually say **choose** rather than **select**: *They **chose** the winner from six finalists.*

select² ●○○ AWL *adj formal*
1 a select group of people or things is a small special group that has been chosen carefully: *The party was small and select.* | *Honorary degrees are handed out to a **select few**.*
2 only lived in, visited, or used by a small number of rich people SYN **exclusive**: *a select block of flats*

se·lec·tion /səˈlekʃən/ ●●● S3 W2 AWL *n*
1 [singular, U] the careful choice of a particular person or thing from a group of similar people or things: *The judges have made their final selection.* | **[+of]** *the selection of a new leader* | **[+for]** *He had narrowly missed selection for the team.* | **[+as]** *Perlman's selection as the party's candidate*

SELECTION

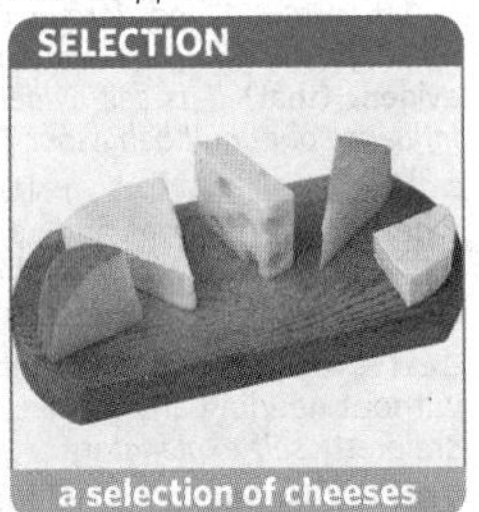

a selection of cheeses

2 [C] something that has been chosen from among a group of things SYN **choice**: *To order, just write your selections on the form.* | **[+from]** *These drawings represent a selection from a larger exhibition.*
3 [C usually singular] a group of things of a particular type, often of things that are for sale SYN **range**: *There's a **big selection** to choose from.* | **[+of]** *a **wide selection** of shellfish* | *They only have a **limited selection** of his books.* → NATURAL SELECTION

> **COLLOCATIONS**
> **VERBS**
> **make a selection** *Students should be able to make a selection from a range of reference materials.*
> **ADJECTIVES**
> **careful selection** *Adair emphasises the importance of careful selection of team members.*
> **random selection** (=choosing without any reason or order) *the random selection of genes*
> **the final selection** *The final selection will be based on local requirements.*
> **selection + NOUN**
> **the selection process/procedure** *Before the selection process begins, candidates need to be clear about what the job entails.*
> **the selection criteria** (=the set of reasons used for choosing something or someone) | **a selection committee** (=a group of people responsible for choosing something or someone)

se·lec·tive /səˈlektɪv/ ●○○ AWL *adj*
1 careful about what you choose to do, buy, allow etc → **non-selective**: **[+about/in]** *We're very selective about what we let the children watch.* | *selective schools* (=that choose which students to accept) | *He has a very **selective memory*** (=he chooses what he wants to remember and what to forget).
2 affecting or relating to the best or most suitable people or things from a larger group: *selective breeding*
—**selectively** *adv* —**selectivity** /səˌlekˈtɪvəti/ *n* [U]

se·lec·tor /səˈlektə $ -ər/ AWL *n* [C] **1** *BrE* a member of a committee that chooses the best people for something such as a sports team **2** *technical* a piece of equipment that helps you find the right thing, for example the correct GEAR in a car

se·le·ni·um /səˈliːniəm/ *n* [U] a poisonous chemical substance, used in electrical instruments to make them sensitive to light. It is a chemical ELEMENT: symbol Se

self /self/ ●●● S2 W3 *n* (*plural* **selves** /selvz/)
1 [C usually singular] the type of person you are, your character, your typical behaviour etc: **sb's usual/normal self** *Sid was not his usual smiling self.* | **be/look/feel (like) your old self** (=be the way you usually are again, especially after having been ill, unhappy etc) *Jim was beginning to feel like his old self again.* | **sb's true/real self** (=what someone is really like, rather than what they pretend to be like) *Peter was the only one to whom she showed her true self.*
2 sb's sense of self someone's idea that they are a separate person, different from other people: *a child's developing sense of self*
3 be a shadow/ghost of your former self to not be as healthy, strong etc as you used to be
4 [U] a word written in business letters, on cheques etc meaning yourself: *a cheque written to self*
5 [C] used to refer to a person: *a picture of a journalist and **your good self*** (=you)

self- /self/ *prefix* **1** by yourself or by itself: *a self-propelled vehicle* **2** of, to, with, or for yourself or itself: *a self-portrait*

ˌself-abˈsorbed *adj* interested only in yourself and the things that affect you: *Teenagers always seem so self-absorbed.* —**self-absorption** *n* [U]

ˌself-aˈbuse *n* [U] MASTURBATION - used to show disapproval

ˌself-ˈaccess *n* [U] *BrE* a method of learning in which students choose their own books, materials etc and study on their own: *a self-access centre*

self-ˌactualiˈzation (*also* **-isation** *BrE*) *n* [U] *technical* when someone achieves what they want through work or in their personal life

ˌself-adˈdressed *adj* a self-addressed envelope has the sender's address on it, so that information can be put in it and sent back to them → **SAE, SASE**

ˌself-adˈhesive *adj* a self-adhesive envelope, BANDAGE etc has a sticky surface and does not need liquid or glue to make it stay closed

ˌself-apˈpointed *adj* giving yourself a responsibility, job, position etc without the agreement of other people, especially those you claim to represent - used to show disapproval

ˌself-asˈsembly *adj* self-assembly furniture is sold as separate parts that you put together yourself at home

S

ˌself-asˈsertive *adj* very confident about saying what you think or want OPP **timid** —**self-assertiveness, self-assertion** *n* [U]

ˌself-asˈsessment *n* [U] **1** when you judge your own work or progress **2** *BrE* when someone who works for themselves calculates how much tax they should pay

ˌself-asˈsured *adj* calm and confident about what you are doing OPP **hesitant** THESAURUS▸ CONFIDENT —**self-assurance** *n* [U]

ˌself-aˈwareness *n* [U] knowledge and understanding of yourself SYN **self-knowledge** —**self-aware** *adj*

self-build, **self-build** /ˈselfbɪld/ *n* [U] when you build your own house rather than paying a professional builder to do it for you —**self-builder** *n* [C]

ˌself-ˈcatering *adj* [usually before noun] *BrE* relating to a holiday in which you stay in a place where you can cook your own food: **self-catering accommodation/apartment/cottage etc** —**self-catering** *n* [U]: *Prices start from £114 per person for seven nights' self-catering.*

ˌself-ˈcentred *BrE*, **self-centered** *AmE adj* paying so much attention to yourself that you do not notice what is happening to other people SYN **selfish** —**self-centredness** *n* [U]

ˌself-certifiˈcation *n* [U] *BrE* when you sign a form or note to say that you have been ill, to explain why you have not been at work or school for a short time

ˌself-ˈconcept *n* [C] the idea that someone has of what their own character is like

ˌself-conˈfessed *adj* [only before noun] admitting that you have a particular quality, especially one that is bad: *a self-confessed drug addict*

ˌself-ˈconfident *adj* sure that you can do things well, that people like you etc OPP **shy** THESAURUS▸ CONFIDENT —**self-confidently** *adv* —**self-confidence** *n* [U]

ˌself-congratuˈlation *n* [U] behaviour that shows in an annoying way that you think you have done very well at something —**ˌself-congratuˈlatory** / $ ˌ..ˈ...../ *adj*: *a smug, self-congratulatory smile*

ˌself-ˈconscious *adj* **1** worried and embarrassed about what you look like or what other people think of you: **[+about]** *Jerry's pretty self-conscious about his weight.* THESAURUS▸ EMBARRASSED, SHY **2** self-conscious art, writing etc shows that the artist etc is paying too much attention to how the public will react to their work —**self-consciously** *adv*: *The boys posed rather self-consciously for the photo.* —**self-consciousness** *n* [U]

ˌself-conˈtained *adj* **1** complete and not needing other things or help from somewhere else to work: *a self-contained database package* **2** someone who is self-contained does not seem to need other people or show their feelings **3** *BrE* a self-contained apartment has its own kitchen and bathroom

ˌself-contraˈdictory *adj* containing two opposite statements or ideas that cannot both be true

ˌself-conˈtrol *n* [U] the ability to behave calmly and sensibly even when you feel very excited, angry etc —**self-controlled** *adj*

ˌself-ˈcriticism *n* [U] when you judge your own behaviour or character, especially when you have done something bad —**self-critical** *adj*

ˌself-deˈception *n* [U] when you make yourself believe that something is true when it is not

ˌself-deˈfeating *adj* causing even more problems, or causing exactly the same problems and difficulties that you are trying to prevent or deal with: *Constant dieting can be self-defeating.*

ˌself-deˈfence *BrE*, **self-defense** *AmE n* [U] **1** something you do to protect yourself or your property: **in self-defence** *He shot him in self-defence.* **2** skills that you learn to protect yourself if you are attacked

ˌself-deˈnial *n* [U] when you do not do or have the things you enjoy, for moral or religious reasons —**self-denying** *adj*

ˌself-ˈdeprecating *adj* trying to make your own abilities or achievements seem unimportant: *self-deprecating humour* —**ˌself-depreˈcation** *n* [U]

self-de·struct /ˌself dɪˈstrʌkt◂/ *v* [I] if something such as a bomb self-destructs, it destroys itself, usually by exploding —**self-destruct** *adj*

ˌself-deˈstructive *adj* deliberately doing things that are likely to seriously harm or kill yourself: *a self-destructive alcoholic* —**self-destruction** *n* [U]

ˌself-determiˈnation *n* [U] the right of the people of a particular country to govern themselves and to choose the type of government they will have

ˌself-diˈrected *adj* responsible for judging and organizing your own work, rather than getting instructions from other people

ˌself-ˈdiscipline *n* [U] the ability to make yourself do the things you know you ought to do, without someone making you do them: *A lot of the kids seemed to lack self-discipline.* —**self-disciplined** *adj*

ˌself-ˈdoubt *n* [U] the feeling that you and your abilities are not good enough: *a moment of self-doubt*

ˌself-ˈdrive *adj* [only before noun] *BrE* **1** a self-drive car is one that you have HIREd to drive yourself **2** a self-drive holiday is one in which you use your own car to visit the holiday area

ˌself-ˈeducated *adj* having taught yourself by reading books, thinking about ideas etc, rather than learning things in school

ˌself-efˈfacing *adj* not wanting to attract attention to yourself or your achievements SYN **modest**: *a quiet self-effacing man* —**self-effacement** *n* [U]

ˌself-emˈployed *adj* working for yourself and not employed by a company: *a self-employed plumber* | *pension plans for* ***the self-employed*** (=people who are self-employed) —**self-employment** *n* [U]

ˌself-esˈteem *n* [U] the feeling of being satisfied with your own abilities, and that you deserve to be liked or respected → **self-respect**: **raise/build (up)/boost sb's self-esteem** *Playing a sport can boost a girl's self-esteem.* | *students'* ***sense of self-esteem*** | **low/poor self-esteem** (=not much self-esteem)

ˌself-ˈevident *adj formal* clearly true and needing no more proof SYN **obvious**: *self-evident truths* | **it is self-evident (that)** *It is self-evident that childhood experiences influence our adult behaviour.* THESAURUS▸ OBVIOUS

ˌself-examiˈnation *n* [U] **1** careful thought about whether your actions and your reasons for them are right or wrong **2** the practice of checking parts of your body for early signs of some illnesses

ˌself-exˈplanatory *adj* clear and easy to understand without needing any more explanation: *The video controls are pretty self-explanatory.*

ˌself-exˈpression *n* [U] the expression of your feelings or thoughts, especially through activities such as painting, writing, or acting: *Corporate dress codes don't give workers much room for self-expression.*

ˌself-fulˈfilling *adj* if a statement or belief about what will happen in the future is self-fulfilling, it becomes true because you expect it to be true and so behave in a way that will make it happen: *It's a* ***self-fulfilling prophecy****: expect things to go wrong, and they probably will.*

ˌself-ˈgoverning *adj* a country or organization that is self-governing is controlled by its own members rather than by someone from another country or organization: *self-governing states* —**self-government** *n* [U]

ˌself-ˈharm *n* [U] physical harm that someone deliberately does to their own body, for example cutting their skin with a knife

ˌself-ˈhelp *n* [U] the use of your own efforts to deal with your problems, instead of depending on other people: *a shelf of* ***self-help books*** | *Our program emphasizes self-help.* | *a* ***self-help group*** *for single parents*

sel·fie /ˈselfi/ *n* [C] *informal* a photograph you take of

S

yourself, usually so that you can put it on a SOCIAL NETWORKING SITE

ˌself-ˈimage *n* [C] the idea that you have of yourself, especially of your abilities, character, and appearance: **positive/good/poor/negative self-image** *Depression affects people with a poor self-image.*

ˌself-imˈportant *adj* behaving in a way that shows you think you are more important than other people - used to show disapproval: *a self-important pompous little man* —**self-importance** *n* [U] —**self-importantly** *adv*

ˌself-imˈposed *adj* [usually before noun] a self-imposed rule, duty etc is one that you have made for yourself, and which no one has asked you to accept: *She spent five years in* ***self-imposed exile*** *in Bolivia.*

ˌself-imˈprovement *n* [U] the process of trying to become a better and happier person, for example by gaining new knowledge

ˌself-inˈdulgent *adj* allowing yourself to have or do things that you enjoy but do not need, especially if you do this too often - used to show disapproval: *It feels self-indulgent spending so much on a pair of shoes.* | **self-indulgent novel/film etc** (=said when you think the book or film only expresses the author or DIRECTOR's own interests, which are not interesting to other people) —**self-indulgence** *n* [singular, U]: *My one self-indulgence is good coffee.* —**self-indulgently** *adv*

ˌself-inˈflicted *adj* self-inflicted pain, problems, illnesses etc are those you have caused yourself: *self-inflicted gunshot wounds* | *Stress is often self-inflicted.*

ˌself-ˈinterest *n* [U] when you only care about what is best for you, and do not care about what is best for other people: *His offer was motivated solely by self-interest.* —**self-interested** *adj*

self·ish /ˈselfɪʃ/ ●●○ *adj* caring only about yourself and not about other people - used to show disapproval: *How can you be so selfish?* | *selfish behaviour* —**selfishly** *adv*: *a small child behaving selfishly* —**selfishness** *n* [U]: *a lack of greed and selfishness*

ˌself-ˈknowledge *n* [U] an understanding of your own character and behaviour

self·less /ˈselfləs/ *adj* caring about other people more than about yourself - used to show approval: *selfless devotion to their work* —**selflessly** *adv* —**selflessness** *n* [U]

ˌself-ˈmade *adj* a self-made man or woman has become successful and rich by their own efforts, not by having money given to them: **self-made man/millionaire/businessman**

ˌself-oˈpinionated *adj* believing that your own opinions are always right and that everyone else should agree with you - used to show disapproval

ˌself-ˈpity *n* [U] the feeling of being sad and DEPRESSED because you think that something unfair or unpleasant has happened to you - used to show disapproval: *a note of self-pity in her voice* —**self-pitying** *adj*: *a self-pitying mood*

ˌself-ˈportrait *n* [C] a drawing, painting, or description that you do of yourself

ˌself-posˈsessed *adj* calm, confident, and in control of your feelings, even in difficult or unexpected situations - used to show approval: *She's a confident self-possessed public speaker.* —**self-possession** *n* [U]

ˌself-preserˈvation *n* [U] protection of yourself and your own life in a threatening or dangerous situation: *the instinct for self-preservation*

ˌself-proˈclaimed *adj* having given yourself a position or title without the approval or agreement of other people - used to show disapproval: *a self-proclaimed champion of the working class*

ˌself-raising ˈflour *n* [U] *BrE* a type of flour that contains BAKING POWDER SYN **self-rising flour** *AmE* → **plain flour**

self-reguˈlatory / $ ˌ. ˈ...../ (*also* **ˌself-ˈregulating**) *adj* a self-regulatory system, industry, or organization is one that controls itself, rather than having an independent organization or laws to make sure that rules are obeyed —ˌ**self-reguˈlation** *n* [U]

ˌself-reˈliant *adj* able to do or decide things by yourself, without depending on the help or advice of other people: *Our aim is to teach our son to become an independent self-reliant adult.* —**self-reliance** *n* [U]

ˌself-reˈspect *n* [U] a feeling of being happy about your character, abilities, and beliefs → **self-esteem**: *It's difficult to keep your self-respect when you have been unemployed for a long time.*

ˌself-reˈspecting *adj* [only before noun] having respect for yourself and your abilities and beliefs: **no/any self-respecting ... would do sth** *No self-respecting actor would appear in a porn movie.*

ˌself-reˈstraint *n* [U] the ability to stop yourself doing or saying something, even though you want to, because it is more sensible not to do or say it: **exercise/practise self-restraint** *The UN appealed for both sides to exercise self-restraint.*

ˌself-ˈrighteous *adj* proudly sure that your beliefs, attitudes, and MORALS are good and right, in a way that annoys other people - used to show disapproval SYN **sanctimonious**: *She's a vegetarian, but she's not at all self-righteous about it.* —**self-righteously** *adv* —**self-righteousness** *n* [U]

ˌself-rising ˈflour *n* [U] *AmE* a type of flour that contains BAKING POWDER SYN **self-raising flour** *BrE*

ˌself-ˈrule *n* [U] when a country or part of a country is governed by its own citizens

ˌself-ˈsacrifice *n* [U] when you decide not to do or have something you want or need, in order to help someone else: *several years of hard work and self-sacrifice* —**self-sacrificing** *adj*

self·same /ˈselfseɪm/ *adj* [only before noun] *written* exactly the same: *two great victories on* ***the selfsame*** *day*

ˌself-ˈsatisfied *adj* too pleased with yourself and what you have done - used to show disapproval: *A self-satisfied smile settled on his face.* **THESAURUS** ▸ **PROUD** —ˌ**self-satisˈfaction** *n* [U]: *a feeling of self-satisfaction*

ˌself-ˈseeking *adj* doing things only because they will give you an advantage that other people do not have - used to show disapproval: *a self-seeking politician*

ˌself-ˈservice *adj* a self-service restaurant, shop etc is one in which you get things for yourself and then pay for them —**self-service** *n* [U]

ˌself-ˈserving *adj* showing that you will only do something if it will gain you an advantage - used to show disapproval: *self-serving politicians*

ˌself-ˈstarter *n* [C] someone who is able to work successfully on their own without needing other people's help or a lot of instructions - used to show approval

ˈself-styled *adj* [only before noun] having given yourself a title or position without having a right to it - used to show disapproval: *a self-styled poet*

ˌself-sufˈficient *adj* able to provide all the things you need without help from other people: *a self-sufficient farm* | **[+in]** *Australia is 65% self-sufficient in oil.* —**self-sufficiency** *n* [U]

ˌself-supˈporting *adj* **1** able to earn enough money to support yourself: *The business will soon become self-supporting.* **2** able to stand or stay upright without support: *self-supporting fencing*

ˌself-ˈtaught *adj* having learned a skill or subject by reading about it, practising it etc yourself, rather than in a school: *She received some education at night school, but was largely self-taught.* | *a self-taught pianist*

ˌself-ˈwilled *adj* very determined to do what you want, whatever other people think - used to show disapproval SYN **obstinate**: *a wild and self-willed child* —**self-will** *n* [U]

self-wind·ing /ˌself ˈwaɪndɪŋ◂/ *adj* a self-winding watch is one that you do not have to WIND to make it work

ˌself-ˈworth *n* [U] the feeling that you deserve to be liked and respected → **self-esteem**: *Work gave me a sense of dignity and self-worth.*

S

sell¹ /sel/ ●●● S1 W1 *v* (*past tense and past participle* **sold** /səʊld $ soʊld/)

1 GIVE STH FOR MONEY [I,T] to give something to someone in exchange for money OPP **buy**: *If you offer him another hundred, I think he'll sell.* | *He regrets selling all his old records.* | **sell sth for £100/$50/30p etc** *Toni's selling her car for £700.* | **sell sb sth** *I won't sell you my shares!* | **sell sth to sb** *The vase was sold to a Dutch buyer.* | **sell sth at a profit/loss** (=make or lose money on a sale) *Tony had to sell the business at a loss.*

2 MAKE STH AVAILABLE [I,T] to offer something for people to buy: *Do you sell cigarettes?* | *a job selling advertising space* | **sell at/for £100/$50/30p etc** (=be offered for sale at £100/$50/30p etc) *Smoke alarms sell for as little as five pounds.*

3 MAKE SB WANT STH [T] to make people want to buy something: *Scandal sells newspapers.* | **sell sth to sb** *The car's new design will help sell it to consumers.*

4 BE BOUGHT [I,T] to be bought by people: *Tickets for the concert just aren't selling.* | *Her last book sold millions of copies.* | *All the new houses have been sold.* | **sell well/badly** (=be bought by a lot of people, or very few people) *Anti-age creams always sell well.*

5 sell like hot cakes to sell quickly and in large amounts

6 IDEA/PLAN [I,T] to try to make someone accept a new idea or plan, or to become accepted: *It's all right for Washington, but will it sell in small-town America?* | **sell sth to sb** *It's hard for any government to sell new taxes to the electorate.* | **sell sb sth** *managers selling employees the new working hours* | **be sold on (doing) sth** (=think an idea or plan is very good) *Joe's completely sold on the concept.*

7 sell yourself a) to make yourself seem impressive to other people: *If you want a promotion, you've got to sell yourself better.* **b)** (*also* **sell your body**) to have sex with someone for money

8 sell sb/sth short to not give someone or something the praise, attention, or reward that they deserve: *Don't sell yourself short – tell them about all your qualifications.*

9 sell your soul (to the devil) to agree to do something bad in exchange for money, power etc

10 sell sb down the river to do something that harms a group of people who trusted you, in order to gain money or power for yourself

11 sell your vote *AmE* to take money from someone who wants you to vote for a particular person or plan

THESAURUS

sell to give something to someone in exchange for money: *He sold his motorcycle.* | *The shop sells old furniture.* | *Do you sell books on gardening?*

export to send goods to another country to be sold: *Which countries export oil to the United States?*

deal in sth to buy and sell a particular type of goods as part of your business: *He deals in antiques.*

put sth up for sale/put sth on the market to make something available to be bought: *When the painting was first put up for sale, no one thought that it would be worth so much money.*

sell up *BrE* to sell your house or your business so that you can move to a different place or do something different: *They're thinking of selling up and moving to Canada.*

auction sth/sell sth at auction to sell things at a special event to the person who offers the most money: *The contents of his home will be auctioned.*

flog *BrE informal* to sell something, especially something that is of low quality: *A man at the market was flogging £10 watches.*

peddle to sell cheap things in the street. Also used about selling illegal drugs and PORNOGRAPHY: *Street vendors peddled American and British cigarettes.* | *People who peddle drugs to children should be severely punished.*

sell sth ↔ **off** *phr v*

1 to sell something, especially for a cheap price, because you need the money or because you want to get rid of it: *After the war, we had to sell off part of the farm.* | *We sell off leftover cakes before we close.*

2 to sell all or part of an industry or company: *The Leicestershire company has sold off many of its smaller branches to cut debts.*

sell out *phr v*

1 if a shop sells out of something, it has no more of that particular thing left to sell: **be/have sold out** *Sorry, we're sold out.* | **[+of]** *We've completely sold out of those shirts in your size, sir.*

2 if products, tickets for an event etc sell out, they are all sold and there are none left: *Wow! Those cakes sold out fast.* | **be/have sold out** *Tonight's performance is completely sold out.*

3 to change your beliefs or principles, especially in order to get more money or some other advantage – used to show disapproval: *ex-hippies who've sold out and become respectable businessmen*

4 to sell your business or your share in a business: *Wyman says he'll sell out if business doesn't pick up.* | **[+to]** *The T-mail Co. has sold out to San José-based DMX Inc for an undisclosed sum.*

sell up *phr v BrE* to sell most of what you own, especially your house or your business: *Liz decided to sell up and move abroad.*

sell² *n* **a hard/tough sell** (*also* **not an easy sell**) something that it is difficult to persuade people to buy or accept: *This tax increase is going to be a hard sell to voters.* → HARD SELL, SOFT SELL

ˈsell-by date *n* [C] *BrE* **1** the date stamped on a food product, after which it should not be sold: *a yoghurt two days* ***past*** *its* ***sell-by date*** **2** *informal* a time beyond which something or someone is no longer interesting or useful: *This type of games console is starting to look well* ***past*** *its* ***sell-by date.***

sell·er /ˈselə $ -ər/ ●●○ *n* [C]

1 someone who sells something OPP **buyer**

2 good/bad/poor etc seller a product that has been popular, not popular etc with customers → **bestseller**: *The album 'Thriller' remains one of the biggest sellers of all time.*

ˌseller's ˈmarket *n* [singular] a situation in which there is not much of a particular thing available, such as houses, so prices are high OPP **buyer's market**

sell·ing /ˈselɪŋ/ *n* [U] the job and skill of persuading people to buy things: *a career in selling*

ˈselling point *n* [C] a particular quality that something has which will make people want to buy it: *Small classes are a selling point for private schools.* → USP

ˈselling price *n* [C] the price at which something is actually sold → **asking price**

ˈsell-off *n* [C] **1** *BrE* the sale of an industry that the government owns, to private companies or other people **2** *AmE* the sale of a lot of STOCKS or SHARES, which makes the price decrease

Sel·lo·tape /ˈseləteɪp, -loʊ- $ -lə-, -loʊ-/ *n* [U] *trademark BrE* thin clear plastic tape that is sticky on one side, used for sticking things together: *a roll of Sellotape* —**sellotape** *v* [T]

ˈsell-out, sell-out /ˈselaʊt/ *n* [singular] **1** a performance, sports game etc for which all the tickets have been sold: *The concert was expected to be a sell-out.* | *a* ***sellout crowd*** *of 32,000* **2** *informal* a situation in which someone has not done what they promised to do or were expected to do by the people who trusted them: *a sellout of the poor for political reasons* **3** *informal* someone who has not done what they promised to do or who is not loyal to their friends or supporters, especially in order to become more popular, richer etc: *Many black students regarded him as a sellout.*

selt·zer /ˈseltsə $ -ər/ *n* [U] *AmE* water that contains small bubbles

sel·vedge, selvage /ˈselvɪdʒ/ *n* [C] the edge of a piece of cloth, made strong so that the threads will not come apart

selves /selvz/ the plural of SELF

se·man·tic /sɪˈmæntɪk/ ●○○ *adj formal* relating to the meanings of words —**semantically** /-kli/ *adv*

se·man·tics /sɪˈmæntɪks/ *n* [U] **1** the study of the meaning of words and phrases **2** *formal* the meaning of a word or expression

GRAMMAR: Singular or plural verb?

- In meaning 1, **semantics** is followed by a singular verb: ***Semantics is*** *not the same as syntax.*
- In meaning 2, **semantics** can be followed by a singular or plural verb: *The* ***semantics*** *of this phrase* ***is/are*** *difficult to pin down.*

GRAMMAR GUIDE ▸ NOUNS

sem·a·phore /ˈseməfɔː $ -fɔːr/ *n* [U] a system of sending messages using two flags, which you hold in different positions to represent letters and numbers

sem·blance /ˈsembləns/ *n* **a/some semblance of sth** a situation, condition etc that is close to or similar to a particular one, usually a good one: *She was trying to get her thoughts back into* ***some semblance of order****.* | *After the war, life returned to a semblance of normality.*

se·men /ˈsiːmən/ *n* [U] the liquid containing SPERM that is produced by the male sex organs in humans and animals

se·mes·ter /səˈmestə $ -ər/ ●●● S2 *n* [C] one of the two periods of time that a year at high schools and universities is divided into, especially in the US: *the fall semester* → **TERM**[1](5), **QUARTER**[1](8)

sem·i /ˈsemi/ *n* (*plural* **semis**) [C] **1** *BrE informal* a SEMI-DETACHED house: *a three-bedroomed semi* **2** *informal* a SEMI-FINAL **3** *AmE* a very large heavy truck consisting of two connected parts, which carries goods over long distances SYN **articulated lorry** *BrE*

semi- /semi/ *prefix* **1** exactly half: *a semicircle* **2** partly but not completely: *in the semi-darkness* | *semi-literate people* **3** happening, appearing etc twice in a particular period: *a semi-weekly visit* | *a semi-annual publication* → **BI-**

ˌsemi-autoˈmatic (*also* **sem·i·au·to·mat·ic** *AmE*) /ˌsemiɔːtəˈmætɪk◂ $ -ɒːtə-/ *adj* a semi-automatic weapon moves each bullet into position ready for you to fire, so that you can fire the next shot very quickly —**semi-automatic** *n* [C]

sem·i·breve /ˈsemibriːv/ *n* [C] *BrE* a musical note which continues for four BEATS SYN **whole note** *AmE*

sem·i·cir·cle /ˈsemiˌsɜːkəl $ -ɜːr-/ *n* [C] half a circle: **in a semicircle** *About 50 children sat in a semicircle around me.* —**semicircular** /ˌsemiˈsɜːkjələ◂ $ -ˈsɜːrkjələr◂/ *adj* → see picture at **CIRCLE**[1]

sem·i·co·lon, **ˌsemi-ˈcolon** /ˌsemiˈkəʊlən $ ˈsemiˌkoʊlən/ ●●○ *n* [C] a PUNCTUATION MARK (;) used to separate different parts of a sentence or list

sem·i·con·duc·tor /ˌsemikənˈdʌktə $ -ər/ *n* [C] a substance, such as SILICON, that allows some electric currents to pass through it, and is used in electronic equipment —**semiconducting** *adj* [only before noun]

ˌsemi-deˈtached *adj BrE* a semi-detached house is joined to another house on one side → **detached**, **terraced** → see picture at **HOUSE**[1]

ˌsemi-ˈfinal *BrE*, **sem·i·fi·nal** *AmE* /ˌsemiˈfaɪnl/ *n* [C] one of two sports games whose winners then compete against each other to decide who wins the whole competition

ˌsemi-ˈfinalist *BrE*, **sem·i·fi·nal·ist** *AmE* /ˌsemiˈfaɪnl-ɪst/ *n* [C] a person or team that competes in a semi-final

sem·i·nal /ˈsemɪnəl/ *adj* **1** *formal* a seminal article, book etc is important, and influences the way things develop in the future: *a seminal study of eighteenth-century France* **2** [only before noun] *technical* producing or containing SEMEN

sem·i·nar /ˈseməna: $ -naːr/ ●●○ *n* [C] **1** a class at a university or college for a small group of students and a teacher to study or discuss a particular subject: *a Shakespeare seminar* **2** a class on a particular subject, usually given as a form of training: *Publishers and writers from 13 countries* ***attended*** *the* ***seminar****.*

sem·i·na·ry /ˈsemənəri $ -neri/ *n* (*plural* **seminaries**) [C] **1** a college for training priests or ministers **2** *old-fashioned* a school

sem·i·ot·ics /ˌsemiˈɒtɪks $ -ˈɑːt-/ (*also* **sem·i·ol·o·gy** /ˌsemiˈɒlədʒi $ -ˈɑːl-/) *n* [U] *technical* the way in which people communicate through signs and images, or the study of this —**semiotic** *adj* —**semiotician** /ˌsemiəˈtɪʃən/ (*also* **semiologist**) *n* [C]

ˌsemi-ˈprecious *BrE*, **sem·i·pre·cious** *AmE* /ˌsemiˈpreʃəs◂/ *adj* a semi-precious jewel or stone is valuable, but not as valuable as a DIAMOND, RUBY etc

ˌsemi-proˈfessional, **sem·i·pro·fes·sion·al** /ˌsemiprəˈfeʃənəl◂/ (*also* **ˌsemi-ˈpro** *AmE informal*) *adj* a semi-professional sports player, musician etc is paid for doing a sport, playing music etc, but does not do it as their main job: *a semiprofessional boxer* —**semi-professional** (*also* **semi-pro** *informal AmE*) *n* [C]

sem·i·qua·ver /ˈsemiˌkweɪvə $ -ər/ *n* [C] *BrE* a musical note that continues for a sixteenth of the length of a SEMIBREVE SYN **sixteenth note** *AmE*

ˌsemi-reˈtired *BrE*, **sem·i·re·tired** *AmE* /ˌsemirɪˈtaɪəd◂ $ -ˈtaɪrd◂/ *adj* someone who is semi-retired continues to work, but not for as many hours as they used to, especially because they are getting older and want time to do other things

ˌsemi-ˈskilled, **sem·i·skilled** /ˌsemiˈskɪld◂/ *adj* **1** a semi-skilled worker has some skills related to the job they do, but is not fully skilled: *semi-skilled workers* **2** a semi-skilled job is one that you need some skills to do, but you do not have to be highly skilled: *a semi-skilled job*

ˌsemi-skimmed ˈmilk *n* [U] *BrE* milk that has had some of the fat removed SYN **two-percent milk** *AmE*

sem·i·sweet /ˌsemiˈswiːt◂/ *adj AmE* semisweet chocolate is only slightly sweet and has a darker colour than MILK CHOCOLATE

Se·mit·ic /səˈmɪtɪk/ *adj* **1 a)** belonging to the race of people that includes Jews, Arabs, and, in ancient times, Babylonians and Assyrians **b)** relating to any of the languages of these people **2** another word for JEWISH → **anti-Semitic** at **ANTI-SEMITE**

sem·i·tone /ˈsemitəʊn $ -toʊn/ *n* [C] *BrE* the difference in PITCH between any two notes that are next to each other on a piano SYN **half step** *AmE*

sem·i·trop·i·cal /ˌsemiˈtrɒpɪkəl $ -ˈtrɑː-/ *adj* SUBTROPICAL

ˈsemi-ˌvowel *n* [C] *technical* a sound made in speech that sounds like a vowel, but is in fact a CONSONANT, for example /w/

sem·o·li·na /ˌseməˈliːnə/ *n* [U] **1** small grains of crushed wheat, used especially in making sweet dishes and PASTA **2** *BrE* a sweet dish made with these grains and milk

Sem·tex /ˈsemteks/ *n* [U] *trademark* a powerful explosive often used illegally to make bombs

Sen. the written abbreviation of ***Senator***: *Sen. Biden*

sen·ate, **Senate** /ˈsenət/ ●○○ *n* **1 a) the Senate** the smaller and more important of the two parts of the government with the power to make laws, in countries such as the US, Australia, and France: *The Senate approved the bill.* **b)** [C] a similar part of the government in many US states: *the California state senate* **2 the Senate** the highest level of government in ancient Rome **3** [C] the governing council at some universities

sen·a·tor, **Senator** /ˈsenətə $ -tər/ ●●○ *n* [C] (*written abbreviation* **Sen.**) a member of the Senate or a senate: *Senator Kennedy* —**senatorial** /ˌsenəˈtɔːriəl◂/ *adj*

send /send/ ●●● S1 W1 *v* (*past tense and past participle* **sent** /sent/) **1** BY POST ETC [T] to arrange for something to go or be taken to another place, especially by post: *Lyn sent some pictures of the wedding.* | **send sb sth** *We sent Mom flowers for Mother's Day.* | *We sent her a letter of apology.* | **send sth**

to sb/sth *I'll send a copy to you.* | **send sth back/up/over etc** *He ordered coffee to be sent up.* | **send sth by post/sea/air etc** *Monday is the last day to send cards by post to arrive by Christmas.*

2 RADIO/COMPUTER ETC [T] to make a message, electronic signal etc go somewhere, using radio equipment, computers etc: **send sb sth** *I sent her an email yesterday.* | *Radio signals were sent into deep space.*

3 PERSON TO PLACE **a)** [T] to ask or tell someone to go somewhere, especially so that they can do something for you there: *The United Nations is sending troops.* | **send sb to sth** *A police officer was sent to Ryan's home.* | **send sb back/away/over/home etc** *Many of the refugees were sent back to Vietnam.* | *When Frank came, I told him I was ill and sent him away.* | *They sent me down to talk to Mr Strachan.* | *Mr Ellison is here. Shall I send him in* (=tell him to enter the room)? | **send sb to do sth** *The US offered to send ships to help in the rescue operation.* **b)** [T always + adv/prep] to arrange for someone to go to a place such as a school, prison, or hospital and spend some time there: **send sb to sth** *I can't afford to send my kid to private school.* | *He was sent to prison for five years.* | **send sb away/off** *I was sent away to school at the age of six.* | **send sb on sth** *New employees are sent on a training course.*

4 send (sb) a message/signal if something that someone does or says sends a particular message, it has that meaning: *Advertising sends the message that you have to be thin to be successful.*

5 send your love/regards/best wishes etc *spoken* to ask someone to give your greetings, good wishes etc to someone else: *Mother sends her love.*

6 CAUSE TO MOVE [T always + adv/prep] to make something move from one place to another: **send sth through/to/over etc sth** *The blaze sent smoke over much of the city.*

7 send sb/sth flying/sprawling/reeling etc to make someone or something move quickly through the air or across something: *The explosion sent glass flying everywhere.*

8 AFFECT [T always + adv/prep] to make someone or something start to be in a particular state: *His lectures always* ***send*** *me* ***to sleep.*** | **send sb/sth into sth** *The tail broke apart, sending the plane into a dive.*

9 send word *formal* to tell someone something by sending them a letter or message: **send word (to sb) that/of sth** *They sent word to the king of their arrival.*

10 send shivers/chills up (and down) your spine to make you feel very frightened or excited: *The eerie howl of the siren sent chills up her spine.*

11 send sb packing *informal* to tell someone who is not wanted that they must leave at once: *After his four years as governor, the voters sent him packing.*

send away for sth *phr v* to send a letter to a company or organization asking them to send something to you: *Send away for a free recipe booklet.*

send down *phr v*

1 send sth ↔ down to make something lose value: *The company's bad figures sent its share price down.*

2 send sb down *BrE informal* to send someone to prison: **[+for]** *He was sent down for possession of cocaine.*

3 be sent down *BrE old-fashioned* to be told to leave a university because of bad behaviour

send for sb/sth *phr v*

1 to ask or order that something be brought or sent to you, especially by writing a letter or by telephone: *Send for your free sample today!*

2 *old-fashioned* to ask or tell someone to come to you by sending them a message: *Charlie said he'd find a place to live and then send for me.* | *Get back into bed. I'll* ***send for the doctor.*** | *I've* ***sent for help.***

send sth/sb ↔ **in** *phr v*

1 to send something, usually by post, to a place where it can be dealt with: *I sent in a few job applications last week.*

2 to send soldiers, police etc somewhere to deal with a difficult or dangerous situation: *British troops were sent in as part of the peace-keeping force.*

send off *phr v*

1 send sth ↔ off to send something somewhere by post: *I sent off the letter this morning.*

2 send off for sth to send a letter to a company or organization asking them to post something to you: *I sent off for a copy of the photograph.*

3 send sb ↔ off *BrE* to order a sports player to leave the field because they have broken the rules: *One of Dundee's players was sent off for punching another player.*

send sth ↔ **on** *phr v*

1 *especially BrE* to send someone's letters or possessions to their new address from their old address SYN **forward**: *My flatmate said she'd send on all my post.*

2 to send something that has been received to another place so that it can be dealt with: **[+to]** *The data is then sent on to the Census Bureau.*

send out *phr v*

1 send sth/sb ↔ out to make a person or a group of people or things go from one place to various other places: *Information was sent out to interested students.* | *Search parties were sent out to look for survivors.*

2 send sth ↔ out to broadcast or produce a signal, light, sound etc: *The ship is sending out an SOS signal.*

3 send out for sth to ask a restaurant or food shop to deliver food to you at home or at work: *We sent out for sandwiches.*

send sth/sb ↔ **up** *phr v*

1 to make something increase in value: *The oil shortage is bound to send prices up.*

2 *BrE informal* to make someone or something seem silly by copying them in a funny way: *The film hilariously sends up Hollywood disaster movies.*

send·er /ˈsendə $ -ər/ *n* [C] the person who sent a particular letter, package, message etc: *a package marked* ***'return to sender'***

ˈsend-off *n* [C] *informal* a party or other occasion when people meet to say goodbye to someone who is leaving: *The department* ***gave*** *Tom a* ***send-off*** *he won't forget!*

ˈsend-up *n* [C] *informal* a film, article, show etc that copies someone or something in a way that makes them seem funny or silly SYN **take-off**: **[+of]** *a hilarious send-up of a Hollywood disaster movie*

se·nes·cent /səˈnesənt/ *adj technical* becoming old and showing the effects of getting older SYN **ageing**: *a senescent industry* —**senescence** *n* [U]

se·nile /ˈsiːnaɪl/ *adj* mentally confused or behaving strangely, because of old age: *a senile old man* | *She worries about* ***going senile.*** —**senility** /sɪˈnɪləti/ *n* [U]

ˌsenile deˈmentia *n* [U] a serious medical condition that affects the minds of some old people, and makes them confused and behave in a strange way

senior[1] ●●● W2 *adj*

1 having a higher position, level, or rank → **junior**: *the senior Democrat on the House committee* | *White men hold most of the jobs in* ***senior management.*** | *the* ***senior partner*** *in a law firm* | **[+to]** *He is also a diplomat, but senior to me.*

2 [only before noun] *BrE* a senior competition is for older people or for people at a more advanced level: *I won the 60-metre race, my first senior success.*

senior[2] ●○○ *n* [C]

1 *AmE* a student in their last year of HIGH SCHOOL or university → **freshman**, **junior**, **sophomore**: *Jen will be a senior this year.*

2 *especially AmE* a SENIOR CITIZEN: *Seniors can get a 10% discount.*

3 be two/five/ten etc years sb's senior to be two, five, ten etc years older than someone → **junior**: *Her husband was nine years her senior.*

4 *BrE* an adult or a person who has reached an advanced level in a particular sport → **junior**: *Juniors and seniors train together on Wednesdays.*

Se·ni·or /ˈsiːniə $ -ər/ (*written abbreviation* **Sr.** *AmE,* **Snr** *BrE*) used after the name of a man who has the same name as his son → **Junior**: *John J. Wallace, Sr.*

ˌsenior ˈcitizen ●○○ *n* [C] someone who is over 60 years old or who is RETIRED

ˌsenior ˈhigh school (*also* **ˌsenior ˈhigh**) *n* [C] *AmE* HIGH SCHOOL → **junior high school**

se·ni·or·i·ty /ˌsiːniˈɒrəti $ -ˈɔː-, -ˈɑː-/ *n* [U] **1** if you have seniority in a company or organization, you have worked there a long time and have some official advantages: *I **had** 15 years **seniority**, and they couldn't fire me.* **2** when you are older or higher in rank than someone else: *a position of seniority*

ˌsenior ˈmoment *n* [C] a time when you cannot remember something, because you are getting older – used humorously: *I **had a senior moment** and just couldn't think of his name.*

ˈsenior ˌschool *n* [C] *BrE* a SECONDARY SCHOOL

sen·na /ˈsenə/ *n* [U] a tropical plant with a fruit that is often used to make a medicine to help your BOWELs work

sen·sa·tion /senˈseɪʃən/ ●●○ *n*

1 [C,U] a feeling that you get from one of your five senses, especially the sense of touch: **burning/prickling/tingling etc sensation** *One sign of a heart attack is a tingling sensation in the left arm.* | **[+of]** *a sensation of heat*

2 [C] a feeling that is difficult to describe, caused by a particular event, experience, or memory: **sensation that** *Caroline had the sensation that she was being watched.* | **strange/curious/odd sensation** *It was a strange sensation – I felt I'd been there before.*

3 [U] the ability to feel things, especially through your sense of touch: *Jerry realized that he had no sensation in his legs.*

4 [C usually singular] extreme excitement or interest, or someone or something that causes this: **cause/create a sensation** *The sex scenes in the film caused a sensation.* | **pop/fashion/media etc sensation** *the latest pop sensation from England*

sen·sa·tion·al /senˈseɪʃənəl/ ●○○ *adj*

1 very interesting, exciting, and surprising: *a sensational discovery* | *The show was a sensational success.* | *a sensational 6–0 victory*

2 intended to interest, excite, or shock people – used to show disapproval: *sensational newspaper stories* | *sensational headlines*

3 *informal* very good SYN **stunning**: *She looked sensational.* —**sensationally** *adv*

sen·sa·tion·al·is·m /senˈseɪʃənəlɪzəm/ *n* [U] a way of reporting events or stories that makes them seem as strange, exciting, or shocking as possible – used to show disapproval —**sensationalist** *adj*

sen·sa·tion·al·ize (*also* **-ise** *BrE*) /senˈseɪʃənəlaɪz/ *v* [T] to deliberately make something seem as strange, exciting, or shocking as possible – used to show disapproval: *The media often sensationalizes crime.*

sense¹ /sens/ ●●● S1 W1 *n*

1 [C] a feeling about something: **[+of]** *Afterwards, I felt a great sense of relief.* | *A sense of panic has spread over the country.* | *Employees need the sense of being appreciated.* | **with a sense of sth** *He looked around the room with a sense of achievement.* | **sense that** *I had the sense that he was lying.*

2 [singular] the ability to understand or judge something: **sense of humour** *BrE*, **sense of humor** *AmE* (=the ability to understand and enjoy things that are funny) *I like Pam – she **has a** really **good sense of humour**.* | **sense of direction** (=the ability to judge which way you should be going, or what your aims should be) *It was dark and he had completely **lost** his **sense of direction**.* | **sense of proportion** (=the ability to judge what is important and what is not important) *Let's keep a sense of proportion, and not rush to any hasty conclusions.* | **sense of justice/fairness** *Kids have **a natural sense of justice**.* | **dress/clothes sense** (=the ability to judge which clothes look good)

3 [C] one of the five natural powers of sight, hearing, feeling, taste, and smell, that give us information about the things around us: **sense of smell/taste/touch etc** *She has a **good sense** of smell.* | *Cats have a very **acute sense** of hearing* (=very good, so that they can hear even the smallest sound). | *Combinations of flavors, textures, and color that can **delight the senses**.* | ***the five senses*** (=all of the senses) → SIXTH SENSE

4 [U] when someone makes sensible or practical decisions, or behaves in a sensible practical way: **have the sense to do sth** (=behave in a sensible way and do what is best in that situation) *You should have had the sense to turn off the electricity first.* | **there is no sense in (doing) sth** *spoken* (=it is not sensible to do something) *There's no sense in getting upset about it now.* | **see sense** (=realize what is the sensible thing to do) *I wish the politicians would see sense and stop the war.* | **talk/knock some sense into sb** (=try to make someone behave in a more sensible way) → COMMON SENSE

5 make sense a) to have a clear meaning and be easy to understand: *Read this and tell me if it makes sense.* **b)** to be a sensible thing to do: **it makes sense (for sb) to do sth** *It makes sense to save money while you can.* | *Would it make sense for the city authorities to further restrict parking?* **c)** if something makes sense, there seems to be a good reason or explanation for it: *Why did she do a thing like that? It doesn't seem to make sense.*

6 make (some) sense of sth to understand something, especially something difficult or complicated: *Can you make any sense of this article?*

7 [C] the meaning of a word, sentence, phrase etc: *The word 'record' has several different senses.* | *Any alteration would spoil the sense of the entire poem.*

8 [C] a way in which something can be true or real: **in a sense/in one sense/in some senses etc** (=in one way, in some ways etc) *What he says is right, in a sense.* | *The hotel was **in no sense*** (=not at all) *comfortable.* | *George was a big man **in every sense of the word*** (=in every way). | *This is true **in a general sense**.* | *Communication, **in any real sense*** (=of any real kind), *was extremely limited.* | **in a (very) real sense** (=used to emphasize that a statement or description is true) *A head of a school is a manager in a very real sense.*

9 your/her etc senses someone's ability to think clearly and behave sensibly – used in some expressions when you think that someone has lost this ability: **come to your senses** (=to start to think clearly and behave sensibly again) *One day he'll **come to his senses** and see what a fool he's been.* | *See if you can **bring her to her senses*** (=make someone think clearly and behave sensibly). | **be out of your senses** (=have lost the ability to think clearly and behave sensibly) *Are you completely out of your senses?* → **take leave of your senses** at LEAVE²(6)

10 talk sense *spoken* to say things that are reasonable or sensible – often used when you think someone has just said something silly: *Talk sense! There's no way we can afford a new car!*

11 regain your senses *old-fashioned* to stop feeling FAINT or slightly sick

COLLOCATIONS

ADJECTIVES

a strong/great sense of sth *He had a strong sense of responsibility.*

a real sense of sth (=a strong feeling) *Children need to feel a real sense of belonging.*

a deep sense of sth (=a very strong feeling) *He felt a deep sense of disappointment.*

a growing sense of sth (=becoming stronger) | **a vague/slight sense of sth** (=not very strong)

VERBS

feel/have a sense of sth *I felt a great sense of pride.*

give sb a sense of sth *The job gave her a sense of control over her life.*

PHRASES

a sense of relief/panic/guilt etc *We reached the medical centre with a sense of relief.*

a sense of purpose/direction (=a feeling that you know what you are trying to achieve) *Becoming a mother had given her a new sense of purpose.*

a sense of urgency (=a feeling that something is urgent) *The rescuers felt a real sense of urgency now.*

a sense of responsibility/duty (=a feeling that you must do something because it is right) *Parents try to give their children a sense of responsibility.*

a sense of loss (=a feeling of sadness for someone or something you no longer have) | **a sense of**

S

achievement/satisfaction (=a feeling that you have achieved something good) | **a sense of security** (=a feeling that you are safe) | **a false sense of security** (=a feeling that you are safe, which is not actually true) | **a sense of identity** (=a feeling of knowing who you are and how you belong to a community) | **a sense of belonging** (=a feeling that you belong to a group) | **a sense of occasion** (=a feeling that an event is special or important)

sense² ●●○ *v* [T]
1 if you sense something, you feel that it exists or is true, without being told or having proof: *Perhaps he sensed your distrust.* | **sense (that)** *I could sense that something was wrong.* | **sense what/how/who etc** *Hugo had already sensed how unhappy she was.* | **sense danger/trouble** *If a prairie dog senses danger, he whistles a warning.*
2 if a machine senses something, it discovers and records it: *an electronic device used for sensing intruders*

sense·less /ˈsensləs/ *adj* **1** happening or done for no good reason or with no purpose: *Her death seemed such a senseless waste of life.* | *a senseless crime* **2** unconscious: *He had been* ***beaten senseless****.* —**senselessly** *adv* —**senselessness** *n* [U]

ˈsense ˌorgan *n* [C] a part of your body through which you see, smell, hear, taste, or feel something

sen·si·bil·i·ty /ˌsensəˈbɪləti/ *n* (*plural* **sensibilities**) **1** [C,U] the way that someone reacts to particular subjects or types of behaviour: *her religious sensibilities* | **offend/wound sb's sensibilities** *Avoid using words that might offend someone's racial or moral sensibilities.* **2** [U] the ability to understand feelings, especially those expressed in literature or art: *the sensibility of the artist*

sen·si·ble /ˈsensəbəl/ ●●○ S3 W3 *adj*
1 reasonable, practical, and showing good judgment: *She seems very sensible.* | *sensible advice* | ***It's sensible*** *to keep a note of your passport number.* | *Moving house seemed like* ***the sensible thing to do****.* ⚠ A **sensible** person is reasonable and shows good judgment. A **sensitive** person is easily upset, or understands other people's feelings and problems.
2 suitable for a particular purpose, and practical rather than fashionable: *Eat a sensible diet and exercise daily.* | *an old woman in* ***sensible shoes*** *and a neat skirt*
3 *formal* noticeable: *a sensible increase in temperature*
4 be sensible of sth *literary* to know or realize that something exists or is true SYN **aware**: *He was very sensible of the difficult situation she was in.* —**sensibly** *adv*

sen·si·tive /ˈsensətɪv/ ●●○ S3 W3 *adj*
1 UNDERSTANDING PEOPLE able to understand other people's feelings and problems OPP **insensitive**: *a sensitive and intelligent young man* | **[+to]** *It's made me much more sensitive to the needs of the disabled.*
2 EASILY OFFENDED easily upset or offended by events or things that people say: *a very sensitive child* | **[+about]** *Laura's sensitive about her weight.* | **[+to]** *Throughout her career she remained very sensitive to criticism.* | **sensitive soul** *BrE* (=someone who is easily upset by small or unimportant things) → HYPERSENSITIVE
3 EASILY AFFECTED easily affected or damaged by something such as a substance or temperature: *Wetlands are environmentally sensitive areas.* | *a baby's sensitive skin* | **[+to]** *Older people tend to be very sensitive to cold.* | *Increasing numbers of people are sensitive to cow's milk.*
4 SITUATION/SUBJECT a situation or subject that is sensitive needs to be dealt with very carefully, because it is secret or because it may offend people: *Abortion is a very sensitive issue.* | *sensitive matters such as national security* | ***highly sensitive*** *information* THESAURUS ▸ SECRET
5 REACTING TO CHANGES reacting to very small changes in light, temperature, position etc: *a* ***highly sensitive*** *electronic camera* | **light-sensitive/heat-sensitive etc** *light-sensitive photographic paper*
6 ART/MUSIC ETC able to understand or express yourself through art, music, literature etc: *a very sensitive performance* —**sensitively** *adv*: *It is an issue which needs to be handled sensitively.*

sen·si·tiv·i·ty /ˌsensəˈtɪvəti/ ●○○ *n* (*plural* **sensitivities**)
1 UNDERSTANDING PEOPLE [singular, U] the ability to understand other people's feelings and problems: *His comments show a lack of sensitivity.* | *Interviewing victims of crime must be done with sensitivity.* | *a teacher with* ***great sensitivity*** | **[+to]** *She has always* ***shown*** *a* ***sensitivity*** *to audience needs and tastes.*
2 SITUATION/SUBJECT [U] when a situation or subject needs to be dealt with carefully because it is secret or may offend people: *It's a matter of great political sensitivity.*
3 BODY'S REACTION [C,U] when someone reacts badly to a particular food, substance, animal etc and becomes ill: *food sensitivity* | **[+to]** *Many children* ***have*** *a* ***sensitivity*** *to cow's milk.*
4 EASILY OFFENDED [U] when someone is easily upset or offended by things that people say
5 sensitivities [plural] someone's feelings and the fact that they could be upset or offended: *racial sensitivities*
6 ART/MUSIC ETC [C,U] the quality of being able to express emotions through art, literature etc
7 REACTION TO CHANGES [U] the ability to react to very small changes in light, heat, movement etc: *The sensitivity of the detector can be increased.*
8 REACTION TO NEW SITUATIONS [C,U] the fact of quickly reacting to new situations: *the market's price sensitivity*

sen·si·tize (*also* **-ise** *BrE*) /ˈsensətaɪz/ *v* [T] **1** to give someone some experience or knowledge of a particular problem or situation so that they can notice it and understand it easily: **sensitize sb to sth** *Volunteers need to be sensitized to the cultural differences they will meet in African countries.* **2** if someone is sensitized to a particular substance, their body has begun to have a bad reaction whenever they touch it, breathe it etc: **be sensitized to sth** *Many hospital workers have become sensitized to the latex in gloves.* GRAMMAR **Sensitize** is usually passive in this meaning. **3** *technical* to treat a material or a piece of equipment so that it will react to physical or chemical changes: *sensitized photographic paper* —**sensitization** /ˌsensətaɪˈzeɪʃən $ -tə-/ *n* [U]

sen·sor /ˈsensə $ -ər/ ●○○ *n* [C] a piece of equipment used for discovering the presence of light, heat, movement etc

sen·so·ry /ˈsensəri/ *adj* relating to or using your senses of sight, hearing, smell, taste, or touch: *sensory stimuli such as music* | *sensory deprivation* → ESP(1)

sen·su·al /ˈsenʃuəl/ *adj* **1** relating to the feelings of your body rather than your mind: *the* ***sensual pleasure*** *of good food* **2** interested in or making you think of physical pleasure, especially sexual pleasure: *the faint smile on his sensual mouth* | *a sensual woman* —**sensually** *adv* —**sensuality** /ˌsenʃuˈæləti/ *n* [U]

sen·su·al·ist /ˈsenʃuəlɪst/ *n* [C] someone who is only interested in physical pleasure

sen·su·ous /ˈsenʃuəs/ *adj* **1** pleasing to your senses: *the sensuous feeling of silk on her skin* | *sensuous music* **2** *literary* attractive in a sexual way: *full sensuous lips* | *a beautiful and sensuous young woman* —**sensuously** *adv* —**sensuousness** *n* [U]

sent /sent/ the past tense and past participle of SEND

sen·tence¹ /ˈsentəns/ ●●● S1 W2 *n* [C]
1 a group of words that usually contains a subject and a verb, and expresses a complete idea. Sentences written in English begin with a capital letter and usually end with a FULL STOP or a QUESTION MARK: *His voice dropped at the end of the sentence.* | **in a sentence** *It's difficult to sum it up in one sentence.* | **short/simple/full/complex etc sentence** *In a few short sentences, Quinn explained what he had done.*
2 a punishment that a judge gives to someone who is guilty of a crime: *She received an eight-year prison sentence.* | *He has just begun a life sentence for murder.* THESAURUS ▸ PUNISHMENT

COLLOCATIONS – MEANING 2

VERBS

get/receive a sentence (*also* **be given a sentence**) *She was given a three-year prison sentence.*
face a sentence (=be likely to receive a sentence) *He faces a long prison sentence if he is caught.*
serve a sentence (=spend time in prison) *Her husband is serving a two-year sentence for credit-card fraud.*
a crime carries a sentence (=that is the punishment for that crime) *Rape should carry an automatic life sentence.*
impose/hand down a sentence (=officially give someone a sentence) *The judge imposed a three-year sentence.*
pass sentence *formal* (=officially say what someone's punishment will be)

ADJECTIVES/NOUN + sentence

a stiff/long sentence (=a long time in prison) *Police officers are demanding stiffer sentences for offenders.*
a light/short sentence (=a short time in prison) *We're hoping that he gets off with a light sentence.*
a prison/jail sentence (*also* **a custodial sentence** *BrE formal*) *If found guilty, he faces a long jail sentence.*
a non-custodial sentence *BrE formal* (=a punishment in which a person does not go to prison) | **a five-year/eight-year etc sentence** (=five/eight etc years in prison) | **the maximum sentence** (=the most that can be given for a particular crime) | **a life sentence** (=prison for the rest of your life, or a very long time) | **a death sentence** (=a punishment of death) | **a suspended sentence** (=one which someone will serve only if they commit another crime)

sentence² ●●○ *v* [T] if a judge sentences someone who is guilty of a crime, they give them a punishment: **sentence sb to sth** *Sanchez was sentenced to three years in prison.*

ˈsentence ˌadverb *n* [C] an adverb that relates to the whole sentence that contains it

sen·ten·tious /senˈtenʃəs/ *adj formal* telling people how they should behave – used to show disapproval: *sententious remarks* —**sententiously** *adv*

sen·tient /ˈsenʃənt/ *adj formal or technical* able to experience things through your senses: *Man is a sentient being.*

sen·ti·ment /ˈsentəmənt/ ●○○ *n*
1 [C,U] *formal* an opinion or feeling you have about something: *Similar sentiments were expressed by many politicians.* | **popular/public sentiment** (=what most people think) *He was more in touch with public sentiment than many of his critics.* | **anti-American/anti-nationalistic/anti-religious etc sentiments** *the anti-immigrant sentiments expressed by some Americans* | *'After all, it's her decision.' '**My sentiments exactly** (=I agree).'*

REGISTER
In everyday English, people usually say **feeling** rather than **sentiment**: *They all expressed similar **feelings**.*

2 [U] feelings of pity, love, sadness etc that are often considered to be too strong or not suitable for a particular situation SYN **emotion**: *There's no place for sentiment in business!*

sen·ti·ment·al /ˌsentəˈmentl◂/ ●○○ *adj*
1 someone who is sentimental is easily affected by emotions such as love, sympathy, sadness etc, often in a way that seems silly to other people: *She said a sentimental goodbye.* | **[+about]** *People can be very sentimental about animals.*
2 based on or relating to your feelings rather than on practical reasons: *He wasn't the sort of person who kept things **for sentimental reasons**.* | *a **sentimental journey** to the place of his birth* | *The rings that were stolen were of great **sentimental value*** (=important because of your feelings or memories relating to them).
3 a story, film, book etc that is sentimental deals with emotions such as love and sadness, sometimes in a way that seems silly and insincere: *a sentimental story set in Russia* —**sentimentally** *adv*

sen·ti·men·tal·ist /ˌsentɪˈmentl-ɪst/ *n* [C] someone who behaves or writes in a sentimental way —**sentimentalism** *n* [U]

sen·ti·men·tal·i·ty /ˌsentəmenˈtæləti/ *n* [U] the quality of being sentimental

sen·ti·ment·al·ize (*also* **-ise** *BrE*) /ˌsentəˈmentl-aɪz/ *v* [I,T] to speak, write, or think about only the good or happy things about something, not the bad things: *novels that sentimentalize the past*

sen·ti·nel /ˈsentɪnəl/ *n* [C] *old-fashioned* a sentry

sen·try /ˈsentri/ *n* (*plural* **sentries**) [C] a soldier standing outside a building as a guard

ˈsentry box *n* [C] a tall narrow shelter with an open front where a soldier stands while guarding a building

SEO /ˌes iː ˈəʊ $ -ˈoʊ/ *n* [U] *technical* (***search engine optimization***) ways of making a website appear high up in results from a SEARCH ENGINE

Sep. (*also* **Sep** *BrE*) a written abbreviation of ***September***

sep·al /ˈsepəl $ ˈsiː-/ *n* [C] *technical* one of the small leaves directly under a flower

sep·a·ra·ble /ˈsepərəbəl/ *adj* two things that are separable can be separated or considered separately OPP **inseparable**: **[+from]** *Physical health is not always easily separable from mental health.*

sep·a·rate¹ /ˈsepərət/ ●●● S2 W2 *adj* [no comparative]
1 different: *Use separate knives for raw and cooked meat.* | *My wife and I have separate bank accounts.*
2 not related to or not affected by something else: *That's a separate issue.* | *He was attacked on two separate occasions.* | **[+from]** *He tries to **keep** his professional life completely **separate** from his private life.*
3 not joined to or touching something else: *The gym and the sauna are in separate buildings.* | **[+from]** ***Keep** the fish **separate** from the other food.*
4 go your separate ways a) if people go their separate ways, they stop being friends or lovers **b)** if people who have been travelling together go their separate ways, they start travelling in different directions —**separately** *adv*: *They did arrive together, but I think they left separately.*

sep·a·rate² /ˈsepəreɪt/ ●●● S2 W2 *v*
1 BE BETWEEN [T] if something separates two places or two things, it is between them so that they are not touching each other: **separate sth from sth** *The lighthouse is separated from the land by a wide channel.*
2 DIVIDE [I,T] to divide or split into different parts, or to make something do this: *This will keep your dressing from separating.* | **[+from]** *At this point, the satellite separates from its launcher.* | **separate sth into sth** *Separate the students into four groups.* | *First, **separate** the **eggs*** (=divide the white part from the yellow part).
3 STOP LIVING TOGETHER [I] if two people who are married or have been living together separate, they start to live apart: *Jill and John separated a year ago.* | **[+from]** *I decided to separate from my partner.*

GRAMMAR: Reciprocal verbs
Separate is a reciprocal verb. This type of verb is used when saying that two or more people or things do something that involves both or all of them: *She and her husband separated.* You can also say: *She separated from her husband.* | *She and her husband separated from each other.*
GRAMMAR GUIDE ▸ VERBS

4 RECOGNIZE DIFFERENCE [T] to recognize that one thing or idea is different from another: **separate sth from sth** *She finds it difficult to separate fact from fantasy.*
5 MOVE APART [I,T] if people separate, or if someone or something separates them, they move apart: *Ed stepped*

S

in to separate the two dogs. | **separate sb from sb/sth** *In the fog, they got separated from the group.*
6 MAKE SB/STH DIFFERENT [T] to be the quality or fact that makes someone or something different from other people or things: **separate sth from sth** *The capacity to think separates humans from animals.*
7 BETTER/OLDER [T] if an amount separates two things, one thing is better or older than the other by that amount: *Three points now separate the two teams.*
8 separate the men from the boys *informal* to show clearly which people are brave, strong, or skilled, and which are not
9 separate the sheep from the goats *BrE* (*also* **separate the wheat from the chaff**) to find out which people are intelligent, skilful, successful etc, and which are not: *This test should really separate the sheep from the goats.*

THESAURUS

TO MAKE SOMETHING SEPARATE

separate *v* [T] to divide something into two or more parts or groups, or to divide one type of thing from another. You use **separate** especially when saying that the parts are different from each other: *Motorola is planning to separate the company into two public companies.* | *The items are separated into recyclable and non-recyclable waste.*
divide *v* [T] to make something become two or more parts or groups: *The teacher divided us into groups.* | *The money was divided between them.* | *The house is divided into three apartments.*
split *v* [T] to separate something into two or more groups, parts etc – used especially when each part is equal in size: *The class was split into groups of six.*
break sth up *phr v* [T] to separate something into several smaller parts, especially to make it easier to deal with: *The phone company was broken up to encourage competition.* | *Police used tear gas to break up the crowd.*
segregate *v* [T] to separate one group of people from others because of race, sex, religion etc: *Schools were racially segregated.* | *Some prisons segregate prisoners who are infected with HIV.*

TO BECOME SEPARATE

separate *v* [I] to divide into different parts, especially in a natural way: *A watery liquid separates from the milk during cheesemaking.*
split *v* [I] to separate into two or more parts or groups – used especially when each part is equal in size: *What happens when an atom splits?*
break up *phr v* [I] to separate into several smaller parts: *In spring, the icebergs begin to break up.*

separate sb/sth ↔ **out** *phr v*
1 to divide a group of people or things into smaller groups: *We must separate out these different factors and examine each one.*
2 to remove one type of thing or person from a group: **[+from]** *Many older people may prefer not to be separated out from the rest of the adult population.*

sep·a·rat·ed /ˈsepəreɪtɪd/ *adj* not living with your husband, wife, or sexual partner anymore → **divorced**: *We've been separated for six months.* THESAURUS ▸ MARRIED

sep·a·rates /ˈsepərəts/ *n* [plural] women's clothing, such as skirts, shirts, and trousers, that can be worn in different combinations

sep·a·ra·tion /ˌsepəˈreɪʃən/ ●●○ *n*
1 [U] when something separates or is separate: *the separation of church and state* | **[+between]** *the zone of separation between the warring factions*
2 [C,U] a period of time that two or more people spend apart from each other: *the separation of families during wartime*
3 [C] a situation in which a husband and wife agree to live apart even though they are still married: *their separation and later divorce* → DIVORCE[1](1)

sep·a·ra·tist /ˈsepərətɪst/ *n* [C] someone who belongs to a group that wants to start a new country with its own government, by separating from the country that they belong to now —**separatism** *n* [U]

sep·a·ra·tor /ˈsepəreɪtə $ -ər/ *n* [C] a machine for separating liquids from solids, or cream from milk

se·pi·a /ˈsiːpiə/ *n* [U] **1** a dark reddish-brown colour **2 sepia photograph/print** a photograph, picture etc, especially an old one, that is dark reddish-brown **3** a dark reddish-brown ink used for drawing

sep·sis /ˈsepsɪs/ *n* [U] *medical* an infection in part of the body, in which PUS is produced

Sep·tem·ber /sepˈtembə $ -ər/ ●●● S2 W2 *n* [C,U] (*written abbreviation* **Sept.**) the ninth month of the year, between August and October: **next/last September** *I haven't heard from him since last September.* | **in September** *My birthday's in September.* | **on September 6th** *The meeting will be on September 6th.* | **on 6th September** *BrE*: *'When's the concert?' 'On 6th September.'* | **September 6** *AmE*: *They arrive September 6.*

sep·tet /sepˈtet/ *n* [C] **1** a group of seven singers or musicians who perform together **2** a piece of music written for seven performers

sep·tic /ˈseptɪk/ *adj especially BrE* a wound or part of your body that is septic is infected with BACTERIA: *a cut that* ***went septic***

sep·ti·cae·mi·a *BrE*, **septicemia** *AmE* /ˌseptəˈsiːmiə/ *n* [U] *medical* a serious condition in which infection spreads from a part of your body through your blood SYN **blood poisoning**

ˌseptic ˈtank *n* [C] a large container under the ground, for holding human waste from toilets

sep·tu·a·ge·nar·i·an /ˌseptʃuədʒəˈneəriən $ -ˈner-/ *n* [C] someone who is between 70 and 79 years old

se·pul·chral /səˈpʌlkrəl/ *adj literary* **1** sad, serious, and slightly frightening: *a sepulchral voice* **2** dark, empty, and slightly frightening: *in the sepulchral gloom of the church*

sep·ul·chre *BrE*, **sepulcher** *AmE* /ˈsepəlkə $ -kər/ *n* [C] *old use* a small room or building in which the bodies of dead people were put

se·quel /ˈsiːkwəl/ ●○○ *n*
1 [C] a book, film, play etc that continues the story of an earlier one, usually written or made by the same person → **prequel**: *'Star Wars' and its sequels* | **[+to]** *She's writing a sequel to her first novel.*
2 [C usually singular] an event that happens as a result of something that happened before

se·quence /ˈsiːkwəns/ ●●○ AWL *n*
1 [C,U] the order that something happens or exists in, or the order it is supposed to happen or exist in: **in a ... sequence** *The questions should be asked in a* ***logical sequence***. | *Be careful to perform the actions in the* ***correct sequence***. | **in sequence** *Number them in sequence, 1, 2, 3 etc.* | **out of sequence** *The chapters may be studied out of sequence.*
2 [C] a series of related events, actions etc that happen or are done in a particular order: **[+of]** *He's had a sequence of business failures.* | *the* ***sequence of events*** *leading up to the war*
3 [C] one part of a story, film etc that deals with a single subject or action SYN **scene**: *the dream sequence in the film*

se·quenc·ing /ˈsiːkwənsɪŋ/ AWL *n* [U] *formal* when things are arranged in an order, especially events or actions SYN **ordering** —**sequence** *v* [T]

se·quen·tial /sɪˈkwenʃəl/ AWL *adj formal* relating to or happening in a sequence —**sequentially** *adv*

se·ques·ter /sɪˈkwestə $ -ər/ *v* [T] *formal* **1** to keep a person or a group of people away from other people: *The jury were sequestered during the trial.* **2** *BrE* to sequestrate
GRAMMAR **Sequester** is usually passive.

se·ques·tered /sɪˈkwestəd $ -ərd/ *adj* [usually before noun] *literary* a sequestered place is quiet and far away from people SYN **remote**

se·ques·trate /sɪˈkwestreɪt, ˈsiːkwə-/ (*also* **se·ques·ter** /sɪˈkwestə $ -ər/) *v* [T] *BrE formal* to take property away from the person it belongs to because they have not paid their debts GRAMMAR **Sequestrate** is usually passive. —**sequestration** /ˌsiːkwəˈstreɪʃən/ *n* [C,U]

se·quin /ˈsiːkwɪn/ *n* [C] a small shiny flat piece of metal, sewn onto clothes for decoration —**sequined, sequinned** *adj*

se·quoi·a /sɪˈkwɔɪə/ *n* [C] a tree from the western US that can grow to be very tall SYN **redwood**

se·ra /ˈsɪərə $ ˈsɪrə/ a plural of SERUM

ser·aph /ˈserəf/ *n* (*plural* **seraphs** *or* **seraphim** /ˈserəfɪm/) [C] one of the ANGELS that protect the seat of God, according to the Bible → **cherub**

se·raph·ic /səˈræfɪk/ *adj literary* extremely beautiful or pure, like an ANGEL SYN **angelic**

ser·e·nade¹ /ˌserəˈneɪd/ *n* [C] **1** a song sung to someone, especially one that a man performs for the woman he loves while standing below her window at night **2** a piece of gentle music

serenade² *v* [T] if you serenade someone, you sing or play music to them, especially to show them that you love them

ser·en·dip·i·ty /ˌserənˈdɪpəti/ *n* [U] *literary* when interesting or valuable discoveries are made by accident → **luck**

se·rene /səˈriːn/ *adj* very calm or peaceful: *The child's face was serene and beautiful.* | *a serene mountain lake* —**serenely** *adv* —**serenity** /səˈrenəti/ *n* [U]

serf /sɜːf $ sɜːrf/ *n* [C] someone in the past who lived and worked on land that they did not own and who had to obey the owner of the land → **peasant** → SLAVE¹(1)

serf·dom /ˈsɜːfdəm $ ˈsɜːrf-/ *n* [U] the system of using serfs, or the state of being a serf → **feudalism**

serge /sɜːdʒ $ sɜːrdʒ/ *n* [U] strong woollen cloth used for making suits, trousers etc

ser·geant /ˈsɑːdʒənt $ ˈsɑːr-/ ●○○ *n* [C] a low rank in the army, air force, police etc, or someone who has this rank

ˌsergeant ˈmajor *n* [C] a military rank

se·ri·al¹ /ˈsɪəriəl $ ˈsɪr-/ *n* [C] a story that is broadcast or printed in several separate parts on television, in a magazine etc: *a television serial* | *a six-part serial*

serial² *adj* [only before noun] **1 serial killer/murderer etc** someone who commits the same crime several times: *a serial rapist* **2 serial killings/murders etc** crimes that are done in the same way several times **3** arranged or happening one after the other in the correct order: *Keep the questions* **in** *the same* **serial order**. **4** printed or broadcast in several separate parts: *cheap serial publications* —**serially** *adv*

se·ri·al·ize (*also* **-ise** *BrE*) /ˈsɪəriəlaɪz $ ˈsɪr-/ *v* [T] to print or broadcast a story in several separate parts: *His book was serialized in The New Yorker.* GRAMMAR **Serialize** is often used in the passive. —**serialization** /ˌsɪəriəlaɪˈzeɪʃən $ ˌsɪriələ-/ *n* [C,U]

ˌserial moˈnogamy *n* [U] when someone has a series of sexual relationships, rather than one long relationship or several relationships at one time - often used humorously

ˈserial ˌnumber *n* [C] a number put on things that are produced in large quantities, so that each one has its own different number: *Each computer has a serial number on it.*

se·ries /ˈsɪəriːz $ ˈsɪr-/ ●●● S2 W1 AWL *n* (*plural* **series**) [C usually singular]

1 series of sth several events or actions of a similar type that happen one after the other: *the series of events that led to the outbreak of war* | *The police are investigating a series of attacks in the area.* | *There's been* **a whole series of** *accidents on this road.*

2 PLANNED EVENTS a group of events or actions that are planned to happen one after the other: **[+of]** *This autumn the BBC will be showing a series of French films.* | *Staff will hold a series of meetings over the next few weeks.* | *a summer lecture series*

3 TV/RADIO a set of television or radio programmes that have the same characters or deal with the same type of subject, and are usually broadcast every week or several times a week: *a new comedy series*

4 BOOKS/ARTICLES ETC several books, articles etc that deal with the same subject or tell stories about the same characters: **[+of]** *a series of articles on community care* | *a science fiction series*

5 SIMILAR THINGS several things of the same kind: **[+of]** *a series of laws against discrimination* | *The area is linked by a series of canals.*

6 SPORT a set of sports games played between the same two teams: **the World Series** (=in baseball) | **Test series** (=in CRICKET)

7 in series *technical* being connected so that electricity passes through the parts of something electrical in the correct order

ser·if /ˈserɪf/ *n* [C] a short flat line at the top or bottom of some printed letters → **SANS SERIF**

se·ri·ous /ˈsɪəriəs $ ˈsɪr-/ ●●● S1 W1 *adj*

1 SITUATION/PROBLEM a serious situation, problem, accident etc is extremely bad or dangerous: *the serious problem of unemployment* | *Luckily, the damage was not serious.* | ***Serious crimes*** *have increased dramatically.* | **serious injury/illness/accident etc** *a serious accident on the freeway* | *Oil spills pose a serious threat to marine life.* | *The president was in* ***serious trouble***. → see Thesaurus box on *p. 1656*

2 IMPORTANT important and needing a lot of thought or attention: *This is a very* ***serious matter***. | *the* ***serious business*** *of earning a living* | *Be quiet, Jim. This is serious.*

3 NOT JOKING OR PRETENDING if someone is serious about something they say or plan to do, they really mean it and are not joking or pretending: *His voice suddenly became more serious.* | *a serious article* | **[+about]** *Is she serious about giving up her job?* | **deadly/dead serious** (=definitely not joking) *She sounded dead serious.* | *Marry Frank?* ***You can't be serious!***

4 CAREFUL **serious attention/consideration/thought** careful and thorough attention etc: *I'll give your suggestion serious consideration.*

5 QUIET/SENSIBLE someone who is serious is very quiet and sensible, and does not laugh and joke much: *a serious student*

6 WORRIED/UNHAPPY slightly worried or unhappy: *You look serious. What's wrong?*

7 ROMANTIC RELATIONSHIP a serious romantic relationship is likely to continue for a long time: *It's serious - they've been seeing each other for six months.* | **[+about]** *Are you really serious about her?* | **serious boyfriend/girlfriend**

8 SPORT/ACTIVITY [only before noun] very interested in an activity or subject, and spending a lot of time doing it: *He's become a serious golfer since he retired.* | *Chris is a serious photographer.*

9 VERY GOOD [only before noun] *informal* very good and often expensive: *He's got a serious car!*

10 LARGE AMOUNT [only before noun] *informal* used to emphasize that you are talking about a large amount of something: *In industry, you can earn* ***serious money***.

se·ri·ous·ly /ˈsɪəriəsli $ ˈsɪr-/ ●●● S2 W2 *adv*

1 very much or to a great degree: **seriously ill/injured/damaged etc** *Was she seriously hurt?* | *I'm seriously worried about Ben.* | *Something was* ***seriously wrong***.

2 a) in a way that is not joking, especially because something is important: *It's time we talked seriously about our relationship.* **b)** [sentence adverb] *spoken* used to show that what you say next is not a joke: ***Seriously though***, *I think Toby likes you.*

3 take sb/sth seriously to believe that someone or something is worth your attention or respect: *As a teacher, it's important that the kids take you seriously.* | *It's only a joke - don't take it seriously!*

4 seriously? *spoken* used to ask someone if they really mean what they have just said: *'The job's yours.' 'Seriously?'*

se·ri·ous·ness /ˈsɪəriəsnəs $ ˈsɪr-/ *n* [U] **1** the quality of being serious **2 in all seriousness a)** *spoken* used to show

S

that what you say next is not a joke, especially because it is important SYN **seriously**: *In all seriousness, if Tom does resign, a lot of other people will start leaving too.* **b)** in a way that is not joking: *'Playing with Richie was the highlight of my musical career,' said Sonny in all seriousness.*

ser·mon /ˈsɜːmən $ ˈsɜːr-/ ●○○ *n* [C]
1 a talk given as part of a Christian church service, usually on a religious or moral subject: **give/preach/deliver a sermon (on sth)** *The vicar gave a sermon on charity.* **THESAURUS▸** SPEECH
2 *informal* a long talk in which someone tries to give you moral advice that you do not want – used to show disapproval SYN **lecture**

ser·mon·ize (*also* **-ise** *BrE*) /ˈsɜːmənaɪz $ ˈsɜːr-/ *v* [I] to give a lot of moral advice to someone when they do not want it – used to show disapproval SYN **preach**

ser·o·to·nin /ˌserəˈtəʊnɪn $ -ˈtoʊ-/ *n* [U] *technical* a chemical in the body that helps carry messages from the brain and is believed to make you feel happy

ser·pent /ˈsɜːpənt $ ˈsɜːr-/ *n* [C] *literary* a snake, especially a large one

ser·pen·tine /ˈsɜːpəntaɪn $ ˈsɜːrpəntiːn/ *adj* [only before noun] *literary* **1** winding like a snake: *the serpentine course of the river* **2** complicated and difficult to understand: *a serpentine plot*

ser·ra·no /səˈrɑːnəʊ $ -oʊ/ *n* [C] a type of small green CHILLI PEPPER that is very hot

ser·rat·ed /səˈreɪtəd, se-/ *adj* [usually before noun] having a sharp edge made of a row of connected points like teeth: *Use a knife with a* ***serrated edge****.* **THESAURUS▸** SHARP

ser·ried /ˈserid/ *adj* [no comparative, usually before noun] *literary* standing or arranged closely together in rows: *the* ***serried ranks*** *of reporters waiting outside*

se·rum /ˈsɪərəm $ ˈsɪr-/ *n* (*plural* **serums** *or* **sera** /-rə/) [C,U] **1** *medical* a liquid containing substances that fight infection or poison, that is put into a sick person's blood → VACCINE **2** *technical* the thin part of blood or the liquid from a plant

ser·vant /ˈsɜːvənt $ ˈsɜːr-/ ●●○ *n* [C]
1 someone, especially in the past, who was paid to clean someone's house, cook for them, answer the door etc, and who often lived in the house: *Many young girls became* ***domestic servants****.*
2 servant of sb/sth someone who is controlled by someone or something – often used to show disapproval: *Are we the servants of computers?* → CIVIL SERVANT

serve¹ /sɜːv $ sɜːrv/ ●●● S1 W1 *v*
1 FOOD/DRINK [I,T] to give someone food or drink, especially as part of a meal or in a restaurant, bar etc: *The waiter was serving another table.* | *Sprinkle with cheese and serve immediately.* | **serve sth with sth** *Serve the soup with crusty bread.* | **serve breakfast/lunch/dinner** *Breakfast is served until 9 am.* | **serve sth to sb** *Meals can be served to you in your room.* | **serve sth hot/cold etc** *Teacakes should be served hot with butter.*
2 serve two/three/four etc (people) if food serves two, three etc, there is enough for that number of people
3 SHOP [I,T] to help the customers in a shop, especially by bringing them the things that they want: *There was only one girl* ***serving customers****.*
4 BE USEFUL/HELPFUL [I,T] to be useful or helpful for a particular purpose or reason: **[+as]** *The sofa had to serve as a bed.* | *The reforms served as a model for the rest of the Communist world.* | *A large cardboard box will* ***serve the purpose****.* | *Her talent for organization should* ***serve*** *her* ***well****.* | **serve the needs/interests of sb/sth** *research projects that serve the needs of industry*
5 DO USEFUL WORK [I,T] to spend a period of time doing useful work or official duties for an organization, country, important person etc: **[+as]** *Lord Herbert served as ambassador to France.* | **serve in the army/air force/navy etc** *He returned to Greece to serve in the army.* | **[+on]** *Ann serves on various local committees.* | *the women who* ***served*** *their* ***country*** *in the war*
6 HAVE AN EFFECT [I] *formal* to have a particular effect or result: **[+as]** *Her death should* ***serve as a warning*** *to other young people.* | **serve to do sth** *A single example serves to illustrate what I mean.*
7 PROVIDE STH [T] to provide an area or a group of people

THESAURUS: serious

VERY BAD

serious very bad – used about problems, accidents, illnesses, or crimes: *Violent crime is a serious problem in and around the capital.* | *The boy was taken to hospital with serious head injuries.* | *Fortunately, the damage to the car was not serious.*
severe very serious – used about problems, injuries, and illnesses: *He suffered severe injuries in a car crash.* | *The problem became so severe that they had to bring water in from other countries.* | *severe epilepsy*
grave used about a situation that is very serious and worrying, especially because it is dangerous or seems likely to get worse: *A thick fog descended and I knew that we were in grave danger.* | *The situation is grave – war now seems inevitable.*
acute used about an illness, problem, or situation that has become very serious or dangerous, and needs to be dealt with quickly: *She was taken to the hospital suffering from acute appendicitis.* | *In San Diego, the shortage of skilled workers is acute.*
desperate used about a situation or problem that is very serious or dangerous, especially because a lot of people need urgent help: *The situation is desperate – people here need aid before the harsh winter sets in.* | *The hospital is full of people in desperate need of medical attention.*
critical used about a situation that is very serious and dangerous and might get worse suddenly: *In 1991, the food supply situation became critical.* | *Eight people were killed and four are still in a critical condition.*
life-threatening used about a situation, illness, or condition in which someone could die: *Her child had a potentially life-threatening illness.* | *The situation was not life-threatening, but it was very worrying.*
be a matter of life and death *spoken* to be extremely serious – used when a situation is very urgent or important: *For people living with HIV, getting the right treatment is literally a matter of life and death.*

NOT JOKING

serious not joking or laughing, or not pretending: *His voice sounded serious.* | *They seem to be serious about their relationship.*
solemn very serious because of an important or sad occasion or ceremony: *My father looked solemn, the way grown-ups look at funerals.* | *The judge read the verdict in a solemn voice.*
grave *written* quiet and very serious – used especially about the way people look when something important or worrying happens: *She consulted Doctor Staples and returned looking grave.* | *He listened with a grave expression on his face.*
sombre *BrE* (*also* **somber** *AmE*) /ˈsɒmbə $ ˈsɑːmbər/ *written* sad, quiet, or serious because something unpleasant or worrying has happened or is going to happen: *They sat in sombre silence.* | *The meeting began in a sombre mood.*
earnest very serious and sincere – often used about someone who is young and not very experienced: *He was a rather earnest-looking young man.* | *'That's wrong,' she said, her voice sounding very earnest.*

with something that is necessary or useful: *Paris is served by two airports.* GRAMMAR **Serve** is usually passive in this meaning.
8 PRISON [T] to spend a particular period of time in prison: *He **served** an 18-month **sentence** for theft.* | *Did you know that Les is **serving time*** (=is in prison)?
9 SPORT [I,T] to start playing in a game such as tennis or VOLLEYBALL by throwing the ball up in the air and hitting it over the net
10 it serves sb right *spoken* used to say that you think someone deserves something unpleasant that happens to them, because they have been stupid or unkind: *'She kicked me!' 'It serves you right, teasing her like that.'*
11 serve an apprenticeship to learn a job or skill by working for a particular period of time for someone who has a lot of experience
12 serve a summons/writ etc to officially send or give someone a written order to appear in a court of law → **if my memory serves me (right/well/correctly)** at MEMORY(1)

serve sth ↔ **out** *phr v*
1 to complete a particular period of time in prison or doing a job: *Dillon's almost **served out** his **sentence*** (=in prison). | *The Senator's illness means he may not **serve out** his **term**.*
2 *BrE* to put food onto plates: *Serve out the rice, will you?*

serve sth ↔ **up** *phr v* to give food to someone as part of a meal: *What are you serving up tonight?*

serve² *n* [C] the action in a game such as tennis or VOLLEYBALL when you throw the ball in the air and hit it over the net → see picture at TENNIS

serv·er /ˈsɜːvə $ ˈsɜːrvər/ ●●○ *n* [C]
1 a) the main computer on a network, which controls all the others: *The server's down* (=not working) *again.* **b)** one of the computers on a network that provides a special service: **file/print server** *All data is stored on a central file server.*
2 the player who hits the ball to begin a game in tennis, VOLLEYBALL etc
3 a special spoon for putting a particular type of food onto a plate: *salad servers*
4 *AmE* someone whose job is to bring you your food in a restaurant SYN **waiter, waitress**

ˈ**server farm** *n* [C] an office which has a large amount of computer equipment holding all the software and information for websites

ˈ**server-side** *adj* [only before noun] relating to software that runs on a SERVER rather than on the user's own computer

ser·ve·ry /ˈsɜːvəri $ ˈsɜːr-/ *n* (*plural* **serveries**) [C] *BrE* the part of a restaurant where you get food to take back to your table SYN **buffet** *AmE*

ser·vice¹ /ˈsɜːvɪs $ ˈsɜːr-/ ●●● S1 W1 *n*
1 OFFICIAL SYSTEM/ORGANIZATION [C] the official system for providing something, especially something that everyone in a country needs to have, or the official organization that provides it: *the health service* | *the postal service* | *the police service* | *the prison service* | *Workers in **the emergency services*** (=the police, hospital, and the fire service) *are forbidden from striking.* | *There has been a decline in **public services** in recent years.* | ***the essential services*** (=the police, hospitals, fire service, and organizations that provide basic things such as water, gas, or electricity) → CIVIL SERVICE, DIPLOMATIC SERVICE, FIRE SERVICE, INTERNAL REVENUE SERVICE, NATIONAL HEALTH SERVICE, THE, SECRET SERVICE, SECURITY SERVICE
2 STH PROVIDED BY A COMPANY [C] a particular type of help or work that is provided by a business to customers, but not one that involves producing goods: *A wide range of **financial services** are available.* | **provide/offer a service** *Datapost offers a delivery service to over 160 countries.* | *Our aim is to provide the best service at the lowest price.* | *the supply of **goods and services*** → SERVICE INDUSTRY
3 IN A SHOP/RESTAURANT/BAR [U] the help that people who work in a shop, restaurant, bar etc give you: **good/bad/slow etc service** *The service was terrible and so was the food.* | **customer service** *At our bank, we insist on high standards of **customer service**.* | ***Service is included** in your bill* (=the charge for paying the people who serve you is included). → ROOM SERVICE, SELF-SERVICE, SERVICE CHARGE
4 WORK [U] (*also* **services** [plural]) the work that someone does for a person or organization, especially over a long period: **20/30 years etc of service** *Brian retired after 25 years of service to the company.* | *a long service award* | *a career in **public service*** (=work done for the public or the government) | **services to sb/sth** (=all the good work you have done for someone or something) *He received an award for services to sport.*
5 WORK DONE FOR SB **services** [plural] skilled work or advice from a particular type of worker who you use to help you do something: **sb's services/the services of sb** *Lydia **obtained the services** of a qualified nurse.* | **sb's services as sth** *Why don't you **offer** your **services** as a tennis coach?*
6 DUTY **jury/military/community etc service** something that ordinary people can be asked to do as a public duty or as a punishment: *Her attacker was sentenced to 120 hours' community service.*
7 BEING USED [U] used to talk about whether a piece of equipment, a vehicle etc is available to be used, or how long it can be used: **in service** (=being used or available to be used) *These trains have been in service for many years.* | **out of service** (=not being used or not available to be used) *The escalator is out of service.* | **give good/excellent etc service** (=work well and last a long time) *Steel tools give good service for years.*
8 RELIGIOUS CEREMONY [C] a formal religious ceremony, especially in church: **hold/conduct a service** *The service was held in the chapel.* | **marriage/funeral/christening etc service** *a memorial service for the disaster victims*
9 ARMY **the services** *BrE*, **the service** *AmE* a country's military forces, especially considered as a job: **join/go into the services** *Maybe you should join the services.* | *Her son is **in the services**.*
10 HELP [singular, U] *formal* help that you give to someone: **be at sb's service** (=be available to help someone, or for someone to use) *My secretary is at your service.* | **be of service (to sb)** (=help someone) *Can I be of any service?* | **do sb a service** (=do something that will help someone) *He did her a service by telling her the truth.*
11 CHECKS ON A CAR/MACHINE [C] an examination and repair of a machine or car to keep it working properly: *I'm getting the bus home – my car's **in for a service**.*
12 TENNIS/BALL GAME [C] an act of hitting a ball through the air in order to start a game, especially in tennis: *It's your service.*
13 ON A MOTORWAY **services** [plural] *BrE* a place near a MOTORWAY where you can stop and have a meal or drink, or buy food, petrol etc → **service station**: *How far is it to the next services?*
14 PLATES/CUPS ETC [C] a set of plates, bowls, cups etc that match each other
15 BUS/TRAIN/PLANE ETC [C usually singular] *BrE* a regular journey made by a bus, train, boat etc to a particular place at a particular time: *the 8:15 service to Cambridge*
16 be in service/go into service *BrE* to be working or start working as a servant in someone's house, especially in the past → DOMESTIC SERVICE
17 LEGAL DOCUMENT [U] *formal* when someone is given a legal document telling them that they must do something or that something is going to happen: *the service of a summons*
18 for services rendered *formal* for work you have done or help you have given: *payment for services rendered* → ACTIVE SERVICE, LIP SERVICE, → **press sb/sth into service** at PRESS²(13)

service² ●●○ *v* [T]
1 if someone services a machine or vehicle, they examine it and do what is needed to keep it working well: *The plumber came to service the boiler.* | **have sth serviced** *I'm having the car serviced next week.* → SERVICING THESAURUS REPAIR
2 to provide people with something they need or want: *schools that service local communities*
3 service a debt/loan *technical* to pay the INTEREST on a debt

S

ser·vice·a·ble /ˈsɜːvəsəbəl $ ˈsɜːr-/ *adj* ready or able to be used SYN **usable**: *Some of these old tools are still serviceable.*

ˈservice ˌarea *n* [C] *BrE* a place on a MOTORWAY where you can stop for petrol, food, toilets etc

ˈservice ˌcharge *n* [C] **1** *BrE* an amount of money that is added to a bill in a restaurant as an extra charge for the service of the waiters **2** *BrE* an amount of money paid to the owner of a block of FLATs for services such as cleaning the stairs **3** *AmE* an amount of money that is added to the price of something in order to pay for the services that you use when buying it SYN **booking fee** *BrE*: *There's a service charge for advance tickets.*

ˈservice ˌclub *n* [C] *AmE* a national organization made of smaller local groups in which members do things to help their COMMUNITY

ˈservice ˌindustry *n* [C,U] an industry that provides a service rather than a product, for example insurance or advertising

ser·vice·man /ˈsɜːvəsmən $ ˈsɜːr-/ *n* (*plural* **servicemen** /-mən/) [C] a man who is a member of the military

ˈservice ˌstation *n* [C] a place at the side of the road where you can stop to buy petrol, food, and other goods SYN **gas station** *AmE*

ser·vice·wom·an /ˈsɜːvəsˌwʊmən $ ˈsɜːr-/ *n* (*plural* **servicewomen** /-ˌwɪmɪn/) [C] a woman who is a member of the military

ser·vic·ing /ˈsɜːvəsɪŋ $ ˈsɜːr-/ *n* [U] when a machine or vehicle is examined and things are done to keep it working well: *The new model is quieter, needs less servicing, and is more fuel-efficient.*

ser·vi·ette /ˌsɜːviˈet $ ˌsɜːr-/ *n* [C] *BrE* a NAPKIN

ser·vile /ˈsɜːvaɪl $ ˈsɜːrvəl, -vaɪl/ *adj* **1** very eager to obey someone because you want to please them – used to show disapproval: *a servile attitude* **2** relating to SLAVES or to being a slave —**servility** /sɜːˈvɪləti $ sɜːr-/ *n* [U]

serv·ing¹ /ˈsɜːvɪŋ $ ˈsɜːr-/ *n* [C] an amount of food that is enough for one person SYN **helping**: *This should make enough for four servings.*

serving² *adj* [only before noun] **serving spoon/dish etc** a spoon, dish etc that is used to serve food

ser·vi·tude /ˈsɜːvɪtjuːd $ ˈsɜːrvɪtuːd/ *n* [U] *formal* the condition of being a SLAVE or being forced to obey someone else SYN **slavery**

ser·vo /ˈsɜːvəʊ $ ˈsɜːrvoʊ/ *n* (*plural* **servos**) [C] *technical* a part of a machine which passes on or increases a force or movement: *servo-assisted brakes*

ses·a·me /ˈsesəmi/ *n* [U] a tropical plant grown for its seeds and oil and used in cooking → **OPEN SESAME**

ses·sion /ˈseʃən/ ●●○ W2 *n* [C]

1 a period of time used for a particular activity, especially by a group of people: *a training session for teachers about computers* | *question-and-answer sessions* | **[+of]** *a session of group therapy* → **JAM SESSION**

2 a formal meeting or group of meetings, especially of a law court or parliament: **[+of]** *the first televised session of parliament* | **in session** (=meeting) *The court is now in session.* | *Board members met* ***in closed session*** (=with nobody else present).

3 *AmE* a part of the year when classes are given at a college or university → **semester**

set¹ /set/ ●●● S1 W1 *v* (*past tense and past participle* **set**, *present participle* **setting**)

1 PUT [T always + adv/prep] *written* to carefully put something down somewhere: **set sth (down) on sth** *She set the tray down on a table next to his bed.* | *Mark filled the pan and set it on the stove.* | **set sth down/aside** *The workmen set the box down carefully on the floor.* | *Remove the mushrooms and set them aside.*

2 PUT INTO SURFACE [T always + adv/prep] to put something into a surface: **be set into sth** *Gates should be hung on sturdy posts set well into the ground.* | **be set into the wall/floor/ceiling etc** (=be built into the surface of something so that it does not stick out) *an alarm button set into the wall beside the door* GRAMMAR **Set** is usually passive in this meaning.

3 STORY [T always + adv/prep] if a film, play, story etc is set in a particular place or period, the action takes place there or then: **be set in sth** *The novel is set in France.* | **be set against sth** *All this romance is* ***set against a backdrop*** *of rural Irish life.* GRAMMAR **Set** is usually passive in this meaning.

4 CONSIDER [T always + adv/prep] to consider something in relation to other things: **set sth against/beside sth** *These casualty totals have to be set against the continuing growth in traffic.* | *This debate should be* ***set in*** *an international* ***context***.

5 ESTABLISH STH [T] to establish a way of doing something that is then copied or regarded as good: **set the pattern/tone/trend etc (for sth)** *Art and literature flourished and this set the pattern for the whole of Europe.* | *The prime minister's fierce speech set the tone for the rest of the conference.* | *It is important that parents* ***set*** *an* ***example*** (=behave well). | *The outcome of the case will* ***set*** *a legal* ***precedent***. | *His photographs* ***set the standard*** *for landscapes.* | *Freud's views on sexuality* ***set the agenda*** *for much of the century* (=people paid attention to the subjects he dealt with).

6 START STH HAPPENING [T] to make something start happening or to make someone start doing something: **set sth in motion/progress/train** *A study by military experts was immediately set in motion.* | *The chief executive will* ***set in train*** *the* ***process*** *of finding a successor.* | **set sth on fire/alight/ablaze** (*also* **set fire to sth**) (=make something start burning) *Protesters set fire to two buses.* | **set sb/sth doing sth** *Her last remark has set me thinking.* | *The wind set the trees rustling.*

7 DECIDE STH [T] to decide and state when something will happen, how much something should cost, what should be done etc: **set a date/time (for sth)** *The government has still not set a date for the election.* | *International companies* ***set*** *the* ***price*** *of oil.* | **set standards/limits/guidelines etc** *high standards of hygiene set by the Department of Health*

8 START WORKING [I,T] to start doing something in a determined way, or to tell someone to start doing something: **set to work to do sth** *They set to work to paint the outside of the building.* | **set (sb) to work on sth** *He's about to set to work on a second book.* | **set (sb) to work doing sth** *The boys were set to work collecting firewood.* | **set sb to do sth** *Rocard set himself to reform public sector industry.*

9 MACHINE/CLOCK ETC [T] to move a switch on a machine, clock etc so that it will start or stop working at the time you want, or in the way you want: *Did you* ***set the alarm***? | *I set the oven to come on at 12.* | **set sth to/at/on sth** *Usually, the heating is set on 'low'.*

10 LIQUID/GLUE/CEMENT ETC [I] to become hard and solid: *How long does it take for the glue to set?*

11 SUN [I] when the sun sets, it moves down in the sky and disappears OPP **rise**

12 set (sb) a goal (*also* **set (sb) a task/challenge** *BrE*) to say what you or someone else will or must try to achieve: *It's best to set realistic goals that you can achieve.* | *He set himself the task of learning Japanese.*

13 set your heart/mind/sights on (doing) sth to want very much to have or achieve something, or to be determined to do something: *Ellen has completely set her heart on that house.* | *He set his sights on crossing the Pacific by balloon.*

14 set a record to achieve the best result in a sport, competition etc that has ever been achieved, by running fastest, jumping highest etc: *The Kenyan runner set a new Olympic Record in the 3,000 metres.*

15 set the table to arrange plates, knives, cups etc on a table so that it is ready for a meal SYN **lay the table** *BrE*

16 set a trap a) to make a trap ready to catch an animal **b)** to invent a plan to try and catch someone who is doing something wrong: *They decided to set a trap for him by leaving him in charge.*

17 set sb free/loose to allow a person or an animal to be free: *All the other hostages were finally set free.*

18 set sb straight/right to tell someone the right way to do something or the true facts about something: **[+on]** *I set* *him right on a few points of procedure.* → **set sth right** at RIGHT[1](4), → **set the record straight** at RECORD[1](11)

19 FACE [I] *written* if your face or mouth sets into a particular expression, you start to have an angry, sad, unfriendly etc expression: **[+into]** *His mouth set into a rather grim line.*

20 set your jaw to move your lower jaw forward in a way that shows your determination

21 BONE **a)** [T] if a doctor sets a broken bone, he or she moves it into position so that the bone can grow together again **b)** [I] if a broken bone sets, it joins together again

22 CLASS WORK [T] *BrE* to give a student in your class a piece of work to do: **set sb sth** *Mr Biggs has set us a 2,000-word essay.*

23 EXAMINATION [T] *BrE* to write the questions for an examination: *The head teacher* ***sets the questions*** *for the English exam.*

24 PRINTING [T] to arrange the words and letters of a book, newspaper etc so it is ready to be printed: *In those days, books had to be set by hand.*

25 HAIR [T] to arrange someone's hair while it is wet so that it has a particular style when it dries → **set sb at (their) ease** at EASE[1](2), → **set your face against sth** at FACE[1](21), → **set sth to music** at MUSIC(1), → **set the pace** at PACE[1](7), → **set pen to paper** at PEN[1](3), → **set sail** at SAIL[2](2), → **set the scene** at SCENE(9), → **set the stage for sth** at STAGE[1](7), → **set great store by/on sth** at STORE[1](6), → **set the world on fire/alight** at WORLD[1](22), → **set the world to rights** at WORLD[1](23)

set about sth/sb *phr v*

1 to start doing or dealing with something, especially something that needs a lot of time and effort: *A team of volunteers set about the task with determination.* | **set about doing sth** *How do senior managers set about making these decisions?*

2 *literary* to attack someone by hitting and kicking them: *They set about him with their fists.*

set sb/sth **against** sb/sth *phr v*

1 to make someone start to fight or quarrel with another person, especially a person who they had friendly relations with before: *The bitter civil war set brother against brother.*

2 set yourself against (doing) sth to decide that you are opposed to doing or having something: *She's set herself against going to university.*

3 set sth against tax to officially record the money you have spent on something connected with your job, in order to reduce the amount of tax you have to pay

set sb/sth **apart** *phr v*

1 if a quality sets someone or something apart, it makes them different from or better than other people or things: **[+from]** *Man's ability to reason sets him apart from other animals.*

2 to keep something, especially a particular time, for a special purpose: **be set apart for sth** *Traditionally, these days were set apart for prayer and fasting.* GRAMMAR **Set apart** is usually passive in this meaning.

set sth ↔ **aside** *phr v*

1 to keep something, especially money, time, or a particular area, for a special purpose: **[+for]** *Try to set aside some time each day for exercise.* | *a room that had been set aside for visitors*

2 to decide not to consider a particular feeling or thing because something else is more important: *Both sides agreed to set aside the question of independence.*

3 to officially state that a previous legal decision or agreement no longer has any effect: *The judge set aside the verdict of the lower court.*

4 if a farmer sets aside land, he or she agrees not to grow any crops on it, and accepts a payment from the government for this

set sb/sth **back** *phr v*

1 set sb/sth ↔ back to delay the progress or development of something, or delay someone from finishing something: *Environmental experts said the move would set back further research.* | *Illness had set me back a couple of weeks.*

2 *informal* to cost someone a lot of money: **set sb back $50/£100 etc** *This jacket set me back over £1,000.*

set sth/sb ↔ **down** *phr v*

1 to write about something so that you have a record of it: *I wanted to set my feelings down on paper.*

2 to state how something should be done in an official document or set of rules: *Clear guidelines have been set down for teachers.*

3 *BrE* to stop a car, bus etc and allow someone to get out: *The driver set her down at the station.*

set forth *phr v*

1 set sth ↔ forth *formal* to explain ideas, facts, or opinions in a clearly organized way in writing or in a speech SYN **set out**: *He set forth an idealistic view of society.*

2 *literary* to begin a journey: *They were about to set forth on a voyage into the unknown.*

set in *phr v* if something sets in, especially something unpleasant, it begins and seems likely to continue for a long time: *Winter seems to be setting in early this year.* | *Further economic decline set in during the 1930s.*

set off *phr v*

1 to start to go somewhere: *I'll set off early to avoid the traffic.* | **[+for]** *Jerry and I set off on foot for the beach.*

2 set sth ↔ off to make something start happening, especially when you do not intend to do so: *News that the claims might be true set off widespread panic.* | *Hong Kong's stock market fell, setting off a global financial crisis.*

> **REGISTER**
> In written English, people often say that something **triggers** a particular reaction or event, rather than **sets** it **off**, because it sounds more formal: *This could* ***trigger*** *a global financial crisis.*

3 set sth ↔ off to make an ALARM start ringing: *Smoke from a cigarette will not normally set off a smoke alarm.*

4 set sth ↔ off to make a bomb explode, or cause an explosion: *Any movement could have set off the bomb.*

5 set sth ↔ off if a piece of clothing, colour, decoration etc sets something off, it makes it look attractive: *The blue sundress set off her long blonde hair.*

6 set sb off to make someone start laughing, crying, or talking about something: *Don't mention what happened – you'll only set her off again.*

7 set sth off against tax to officially record the money you have spent on something connected with your job, in order to reduce the amount of tax you have to pay: *Some expenses can be set off against tax.*

set on sb *phr v BrE*

1 set sb/sth on sb to make people or animals attack someone: *The farmer threatened to set his dogs on us.*

2 if you are set on by people or animals, you are suddenly attacked by them: *A thirty-five-year-old man was set on by four youths last night.* GRAMMAR **Set on** is usually passive in this meaning.

3 set sb on/onto sb to give someone information about a person who you think has done something wrong, because you want that person to be found and caught: *If I refuse, he'll set the police onto me.*

set out *phr v*

1 to start a journey, especially a long journey: **[+for]** *Kate set out for the house on the other side of the bay.* | **set out on a journey/drive/voyage etc** *The band are setting out on a European tour in March.*

2 to start doing something or making plans to do something in order to achieve a particular result: **set out to do sth** *salesmen who deliberately set out to defraud customers* | **set out with the idea/purpose/intention etc of doing sth** *They set out with the aim of becoming the number one team in the league.*

3 set sth ↔ out to explain ideas, facts, or opinions in a clearly organized way, in writing or in a speech: *He set out the reasons for his decision in his report.*

4 set sth ↔ out to put a group of things down and arrange them: *The market traders began setting out their displays.*

S

5 set out on sth to start doing something, especially something new, difficult, or important: *My nephew is just setting out on a career in journalism.*

set to *phr v BrE* to start doing something eagerly and with determination: *If we all set to, we'll finish the job in half an hour.*

set up *phr v*

1 COMPANY/ORGANIZATION ETC to start a company, organization, committee etc SYN **establish**: **set sth ↔ up** *They want to set up their own import-export business.* | *new regulations for setting up political parties* | **set (yourself) up (as sth)** (=start your own business) *John decided to set up as a graphic designer.* | **set up shop/set up in business** (=begin operating a business) *Now Betterware plans to set up shop elsewhere in Europe.*

2 ARRANGE/ORGANIZE **set sth ↔ up** to make the arrangements that are necessary for something to happen: *I'll set up an appointment for you.* | *There was a lot of work involved in setting up the festival.*

3 EQUIPMENT to prepare the equipment that will be needed for an activity so that it is ready to be used: *The next band was already setting up on the other stage.* | **set sth ↔ up** *Can someone set the overhead projector up?*

4 BUILD/PUT UP **set sth ↔ up** to place or build something somewhere, especially something that is not permanent: *They've set up roadblocks around the city.*

5 TRICK SB **set sb ↔ up** *informal* to trick someone in order to achieve what you want, especially to make it appear that they have done something wrong or illegal: *Cox claimed that the police had tried to set him up.*

6 PROVIDE MONEY **set sb ↔ up** *BrE informal* to provide someone with money that they need, especially in order to start a business: *After he qualified as a doctor, his mother set him up in a practice of his own.* | *Selling her share of the company has* ***set*** *her* ***up for life****.*

7 HEALTHY/FULL OF ENERGY **set sb up** *BrE* to make you feel healthy and full of energy: *A good breakfast will* ***set*** *you* ***up for the day****.*

8 set yourself up as sth to deliberately make people believe that you have the authority and skill to do something, especially when this is not true: *politicians who set themselves up as moral authorities*

9 PUT SB IN POSITION **set sb up** to put someone in a position in which they are able to do something, or in which something is likely to happen to them: **[+for]** *If he won the fight, it would set him up for a title shot.* | *Anyone with public duties sets themselves up for attack.*

10 RELATIONSHIP **set sb ↔ up** *informal* to arrange for two people to meet, because you think they might start a romantic relationship: *'How did you meet Nick?' 'A friend set us up.'*

11 set up home/house (*also* **set up housekeeping** *AmE*) to get your own home, furniture etc, especially when you leave your parents' home to live with a wife, husband, or partner: *Many parents try to help their children set up home.*

12 set up a commotion/din/racket etc to start making a loud unpleasant noise: *The party guests were setting up a steady din.* → **set up camp** at CAMP[1](1)

set[2] ●●● S1 W1 *n*

1 GROUP OF THINGS [C] a group of similar things that belong together or are related in some way: **[+of]** *a set of tools* | *We face a new set of problems.* | *The older generation have a different set of values.* | *a chess set*

2 TELEVISION/RADIO [C] a television, or a piece of equipment for receiving radio signals: *a colour* ***television set***

3 FILM [C] a place where a film or television programme is filmed: **on set/on the set** *Cruise met Kidman on the set of 'Days of Thunder'.*

4 STAGE [C] the scenery, furniture etc used on a stage in a play or in the place where a film or television show is being made

5 SPORT [C] one part of a game such as tennis or VOLLEYBALL: *Nadal won the second set 6–4.*

6 PEOPLE [singular] a group of people who are similar in some way and spend time together socially: *a favourite meeting place of the smart set* (=rich and fashionable people) | *Val got in with a wild set at college.* → JET SET

7 the set of sb's face/jaw/shoulders etc the expression on your face or the way you hold your body, which tells people how you are feeling: *From the set of her shoulders, it was clear that Sue was exhausted.* | *the hard set of his face*

8 MUSIC [C] a performance by a singer, band, or DISC JOCKEY: *Sasha performed a three-hour set.*

9 MATHS [C] *technical* a group of numbers, shapes etc in MATHEMATICS: *The set (x, y) has two members.*

10 STUDENTS [C] *BrE* a group of children who are taught a particular school subject together because they have the same level of ability in that subject SYN **stream**: **top/bottom etc set** *Adam's in the top set for maths.*

11 ONION [C] a small onion that you plant in order to grow bigger ones: *onion sets*

set[3] ●○○ *adj*

1 PLACED [not before noun] being in the position that is mentioned: **[+in/on/back etc]** *a medieval village set high on a hill* | *a big house set back from the road*

2 BACKGROUND used to say that something is in front of a particular background, especially in a way that is attractive: **[+against]** *a small town of white buildings, set against a background of hills* | *pink petals set against dark green foliage*

3 FIXED [only before noun] a set amount, time etc is fixed and is never changed: *We were paid a set amount each week.* | *The evening meal is served at a set time.* | *Small children like a set routine.*

4 READY [not before noun] *informal* someone who is set for something is ready for it: **[+for]** *Are you* ***all set*** *for the trip?* | **set to do sth** *I was just set to go when the phone rang.* | ***Get set*** (=get ready) *for a night of excitement.* | ***On your marks, get set, go*** (=said to start a race).

5 set on/upon/against (doing) sth determined about something: *Nina's set on going to the party.* | *The government's* ***dead set*** (=completely determined) *against the plan.*

6 OPINIONS/HABITS ETC not likely to change: *People had very* ***set ideas*** *about how to bring up children.* | *Mark was 65 and rather* ***set in*** *his* ***ways*** (=habits).

7 have your heart/sights set on sth to want to do something very much, or to be aiming to do something: *She's got her heart set on going to France this summer.* | *Don has his sights set on a career in law.*

8 set to do sth likely to do something: *The weather is set to change.* | *This issue is set to cause some embarrassment.*

9 deep-set/wide-set/close-set eyes eyes whose position is deep in the face, far apart on the face, or close together on the face

10 be set with gems/jewels etc to be decorated with jewels: *a gold bracelet set with rubies*

11 MEAL [only before noun] *BrE* a set meal in a restaurant has a fixed price and a more limited choice than usual: **set lunch/dinner/menu** *The hotel does a very good set menu.*

12 set book/text etc *BrE* a book that must be studied for an examination

13 FIXED EXPRESSION *literary* if your face is set, it has a fixed expression on it, especially one that is angry, worried etc: *He stared at her, his face set.* | *Kate's face was set in a grim expression.* | **set smile/teeth/jaw** *'Damn you,' he said through set teeth.*

ˈset-aˌside *n* [C,U] **1** *BrE* an arrangement in the European Union in which a government pays farmers to leave some of their fields empty, in order to avoid producing too much of a crop and to keep the price higher **2** an arrangement in the US in which a local government helps small businesses to develop by making financial help available to them: *In 1976, Connecticut established one of the nation's first set-aside programs.* **3** an amount of money that is kept so that it can be used for a special purpose SYN **reserve**

set·back /ˈsetbæk/ ●○○ *n* [C] a problem that delays or prevents progress, or makes things worse than they were: **[+for]** *The December elections were a major setback for the party.* | *The team's hopes of playing in Europe* ***suffered*** *a* ***setback*** *last night.* **THESAURUS** PROBLEM → **set back** at SET[1]

ˌset ˈpiece *n* [C] **1** part of a play, piece of music, painting etc that follows a well-known formal pattern or style, and is often very impressive: *The trial scene is a classic set piece.* **2** *BrE* a move such as a FREE KICK or a CORNER in a game of football, HOCKEY etc

ˈset square *n* [C] *BrE* a flat piece of plastic or metal with three sides and one angle of 90°, used for drawing or testing angles SYN **triangle** *AmE* → see picture at **MATHEMATICS**

sett /set/ *n* [C] a passage in the ground made by a BADGER as a place to live

set·tee /seˈtiː/ *n* [C] *especially BrE* a long comfortable seat with a back and usually with arms, for more than one person to sit on SYN **sofa**

set·ter /ˈsetə $ -ər/ *n* [C] **1** a long-haired dog often trained to help hunters find where animals or birds are **2 style-setter/trend-setter/standard-setter etc** someone who does things that other people admire and try to copy: *Liz has always been a fashion-setter.* **3 exam-setter/policy-setter etc** *BrE* someone who decides or organizes something as part of a job: *Who's the question-setter for the quiz night?* → **set the pattern/tone/trend** at SET[1](5), **PACESETTER**, **TRENDSETTER**

set·ting /ˈsetɪŋ/ ●●○ *n* [C]
1 the place where something is or where something happens, and the general environment: **beautiful/perfect/magnificent/idyllic setting** *an old farmhouse in a beautiful setting* | **[+for]** *Cyprus is the perfect setting for a beach holiday.* | *I've worked with children in various settings, mainly in secondary school.* **THESAURUS** ▸ **PLACE**
2 the place or time where the events in a book, film etc happen: **[+for]** *Verona is best known as the setting for two of Shakespeare's plays.*
3 the position in which you put the controls on a machine or instrument: *The heating system was already **on its highest setting**.*
4 the metal that holds a stone in a piece of jewellery, or the way the stone is fixed: **in a ... setting** *a diamond ring in a gold setting*
5 music that is written to go with a poem, prayer etc
6 the setting of the sun *literary* the time when the sun goes down SYN **sunset** → **PLACE SETTING**

set·tle /ˈsetl/ ●●● S2 W2 *v*
1 END ARGUMENT [I,T] to end an argument or solve a disagreement: **settle a dispute/lawsuit/conflict/argument etc** *Rodman met with Kreeger to try and settle the dispute over his contract.* | *We hope the factions will be able to **settle** their **differences*** (=agree to stop arguing) *by peaceful means.* | *Forensic tests should **settle the question** of whether Bates was actually present at the scene of the crime.* | **[+with]** *She finally settled with her former employers for an undisclosed sum.* | *They might be willing to **settle out of court*** (=come to an agreement without going to a court of law).
2 DECIDE [T usually passive] to decide what you are going to do, especially so that you can make definite arrangements: *Nothing's settled yet.* | ***It's settled** then. I'll go back to the States in June.* | *'She's only 15.' '**That settles it*** (=that is enough information for a definite decision to be made)*! We're not taking her with us!'*
3 START LIVING IN A PLACE a) [I,T] to go to a place where no people have lived permanently before and start to live there: *This territory was settled in the mid-1850s by German immigrants.* GRAMMAR **Settle** is usually passive in this meaning, when used as a transitive verb. **b)** [I always + adv/prep] to go to live in a new place, and stay there for a long time: **[+in]** *Many Jewish people settled in the Lower East Side.*
4 COMFORTABLE [I,T always + adv/prep] to put yourself or someone else in a comfortable position: **settle yourself in/on etc sth** *Donna did not dare settle herself too comfortably into her seat, in case she fell asleep.* | *The dog settled on the grass to enjoy its bone.* | *A nurse settled the old man into a chair.* → **SETTLE BACK**
5 QUIET/CALM [I,T] (*also* **settle down**) to become quiet and calm, or to make someone quiet and calm: *When the children had settled, Miss Brown gave out the new reading books.* | *She breathed deeply to **settle** her **nerves*** (=stop herself from feeling worried or frightened).
6 MOVE DOWN [I] **a)** if dust, snow etc settles, it comes down and stays in one place: **[+on]** *Snow settled on the roofs.* **b)** if a bird, insect etc settles, it flies down and rests on something: **[+on]** *A fly kept trying to settle on his face.* **c)** if something such as a building or the ground settles, it sinks slowly to a lower level: *The crack in the wall is caused by the ground settling.*
7 PAY MONEY [I,T] to pay money that is owed: **settle a bill/account/claim** *I always settle my account in full each month.* | *These insurance companies take forever to settle a claim.* | **[+with]** *He was able to settle with his creditors, and avoid going to jail.*
8 ORGANIZE BUSINESS/MONEY [T] to deal with all the details of a business or of someone's money or property, so that nothing further needs to be done: *When it is finally settled, the Marshall estate may be worth no more than $100,000.* | *After her husband's death, Jackie went to the city to **settle** his **affairs**.*
9 settle a score/account to do something to hurt or cause trouble for someone because they have harmed or offended you: *Did he have any enemies – someone with an **old score** to **settle**?*
10 sb's eyes/gaze settles on sb/sth *written* if your eyes settle on someone or something, you notice them and look at them for a period of time: *Her gaze settled on a door, and she wondered what was on the other side of it.*
11 FEELING/QUALITY [I always + adv/prep] *written* if a quality or feeling settles over a place or person, it begins and has a strong effect: **[+over/on]** *An uneasy silence settled over the room.* | *Depression settled over her like a heavy black cloud.*
12 EXPRESSION [I always + adv/prep] *written* if a particular expression settles on your face, it stays there: *A disapproving frown settled on her face.*
13 STOMACH [I,T] if your stomach settles, or if something settles it, it stops feeling uncomfortable or making you sick: *Georgia had taken pills to settle her stomach, but she was still throwing up every hour.* → **let the dust settle/wait for the dust to settle** at DUST[1](5)

settle back *phr v* to lean back in a bed or chair, and relax and enjoy yourself: *Vera settled back to enjoy the film.*

settle down *phr v*
1 settle (sb) down to become quiet and calm, or to make someone quiet and calm: *Shh! Settle down, please! Now turn to page 57.* | *When Kyle was a baby, we used to take him for rides in the car to settle him down.*
2 to start living a quiet and calm life in one place, especially when you get married: *They'd like to see their daughter settle down, get married, and have kids.*
3 to start giving all of your attention to a job or activity: **[+to]** *I sorted out my mail, then settled down to some serious work.*
4 if a situation settles down, it becomes calmer and you are less busy or less worried: *It's been really hectic here. When **things settle down**, I'll give you a call.*

settle for sth *phr v* to accept something even though it is not the best, or not what you really want: *They want $2,500 for it, but they might settle for $2,000.* GRAMMAR **Settle for** is never passive.

settle in (*also* **settle into sth**) *phr v* to begin to feel happy and relaxed in a new situation, home, job, or school: *How's your new home? Are you settling in OK?* | *It takes a few months to settle into life at college.*

settle on/upon sb/sth *phr v*
1 to decide or agree on something: *They haven't settled on a name for the baby yet.*
2 settle sth on sb *BrE formal* to make a formal arrangement to give money or property to someone: *She settled a small yearly sum on each of her children.*

settle up *phr v* to pay what you owe on an account or bill: *We settled up and checked out of the hotel.* | **[+with]** *I'll settle up with the bartender, then let's go.*

set·tled /ˈsetld/ *adj* **1** remaining the same, and not likely to change: *She was tired of moving around and longed for a* *more settled existence.* **2** if you feel settled, you feel comfortable about your life, your job etc, because you have been living or working somewhere a long time and you like the place, people, company etc: **[+in]** *I still don't feel settled in my job.* **3** *BrE* if the weather is settled, it is dry and not likely to change OPP **changeable**

set·tle·ment /ˈsetlmənt/ ●●○ W3 *n*
1 OFFICIAL AGREEMENT [C] an official agreement or decision that ends an argument, a court case, or a fight, or the action of making an agreement: *Union leaders and company bosses will meet tomorrow in an attempt to* ***reach a settlement***. | *His lawyers are understood to be* ***negotiating a settlement***. | *Hopes grew that a workable* ***peace settlement*** *might emerge.* | **[+of]** *the search for a* ***peaceful settlement*** *of the Northern Ireland conflict* | *She got her home as part of the* ***divorce settlement***. | *The company paid out over $10 million in an* ***out-of-court settlement***.
2 PAYMENT [U] *formal* when you pay all the money that you owe: **[+of]** *the settlement of all his debts* | **in settlement (of sth)** *Wyatt had received the property in settlement of a bet.*
3 GROUP OF HOUSES [C] a group of houses and buildings where people live, especially in a place where few people have lived before: *The railway stations created new settlements.* | *an early Iron Age settlement*
4 NEW AREA/PLACES [U] when a lot of people move to a place in order to live there, especially in a place where not many people have lived before: **[+of]** *the settlement of the American West*
5 SINKING [U] *technical* the process in which a building or the ground slowly sinks downwards SYN **subsidence**

set·tler /ˈsetlə $ -ər/ ●○○ *n* [C] someone who goes to live in a country or area where not many people like them have lived before, and that is a long way from any towns or cities: *early settlers in Australia*

ˈset-to *n* [C usually singular] *informal* a short fight or quarrel SYN **argument**: *Tom and I* ***had*** *a bit of a* ***set-to*** *last night.* → **set to** at SET[1]

ˈset-top ˌbox *n* [C] *BrE* a piece of electronic equipment that is connected to your television to make it able to receive a different form of broadcasting, especially DIGITAL signals

ˈset-up, **set-up** /ˈsetʌp/ ●○○ *n*
1 [C usually singular] the way that something is organized or arranged: *the traditional classroom set-up*
2 [C usually singular] *informal* a dishonest plan that is intended to trick someone: *How do I know this isn't a set-up?*
3 [U] the act of organizing something, such as a business or a computer system: *The IT department will assist you with installation and setup.*
4 [C] several pieces of equipment that work together in a system: *'Do you use the school darkroom?' 'No, I've got my own setup at home.'* → **set up** at SET[1]

sev·en /ˈsevən/ ●●● S2 W2 *number*
1 the number 7: *The women visited cities in seven states.* | *We close the store at seven* (=seven o'clock). | *'How old's Sam?' 'He's seven* (=seven years old).*'*
2 the seven year itch the idea that after seven years of being married, many people start to want a relationship with someone new - used humorously → **at sixes and sevens** at SIX(3)

sev·en·teen /ˌsevənˈtiːn◂/ ●●● S3 W3 *number* the number 17: *a group of seventeen American military officers* | *I left home when I was seventeen* (=17 years old). —**seventeenth** *adj, pron*: *in the seventeenth century* | *her seventeenth birthday* | *I'm planning to leave on* ***the seventeenth*** (=the 17th day of the month).

sev·enth[1] /ˈsevənθ/ ●●● S3 W3 *adj*
1 coming after six other things in a series: *in the seventh century* | *her seventh birthday*
2 be in seventh heaven *informal* to be extremely happy —**seventh** *pron*: *I'm planning to leave on* ***the seventh*** (=the seventh day of the month).

seventh[2] *n* [C] one of seven equal parts of something

sev·en·ty /ˈsevənti/ ●●● *number* W3
1 the number 70
2 the seventies [plural] (*also* **the '70s, the 1970s**) the years from 1970 to 1979: *We lost touch during the seventies.* | **the early/mid/late seventies** *In the early seventies, Sag Harbor was still a peaceful village.*
3 be in your seventies to be aged between 70 and 79: **early/mid/late seventies** *Bill must be in his mid seventies now.*
4 in the seventies if the temperature is in the seventies, it is between 70 degrees and 79 degrees: **in the low/mid/high seventies** *sunny, with temperatures in the mid seventies* —**seventieth** *adj*: *her seventieth birthday*

ˌseventy-ˈeight *n* [C] an old-fashioned record that plays while turning around 78 times a minute

sev·er /ˈsevə $ -ər/ ●○○ *v formal*
1 [I,T] to cut through something completely, separating it into two parts, or to become cut in this way SYN **cut off**: *Martin's hand was severed in the accident.* | *a severed rope*
2 [T] to end a relationship with someone, or a connection with something, especially because of a disagreement SYN **break off**: **sever ties/relations/connections/links etc (with/between sb)** *The two countries severed diplomatic relations.* | *She had severed all contact with her ex-husband.*

> **REGISTER**
> In everyday English, people usually say **cut off** rather than **sever**: *The end of his finger had been* ***cut off***. | *The children's father had* ***cut off*** *all contact with them.*

sev·er·al[1] /ˈsevərəl/ ●●● S1 W1 *determiner, pron* a number of people or things that is more than a few, but not a lot: *I visited him in Kansas several times.* | *Several people have volunteered to go.* | **several hundred/thousand etc** *The bill came to several hundred pounds.* | *'Have you read any of his books?' 'Yes, several.'* | **[+of]** *Several of her colleagues agreed with her decision.* | *We had to wait* ***several more*** *weeks before the results arrived.*

several[2] *adj* [only before noun, no comparative] *formal* different and separate SYN **respective**: *They shook hands and* ***went*** *their* ***several ways*** (=went in different directions). —**severally** *adv*: *These issues can be considered severally, or as a whole.*

sev·er·ance /ˈsevərəns/ *n* [U] *formal* **1** when you end your relationship or connection with another person, organization, country etc, especially because of a disagreement: **[+of]** *the severance of diplomatic ties between the two countries* **2 severance pay/package** money or other things that you get when you have to leave a company because your employer no longer has a job for you: *Employees will get two weeks of severance pay for every year of service.*

se·vere /səˈvɪə $ -ˈvɪr/ ●●● S3 W3 *adj*
1 VERY SERIOUS severe problems, injuries, illnesses etc are very bad or very serious: *His injuries were quite severe.* | *She's suffering from severe depression.* | *The US faces severe economic problems.* | *The storm caused severe damage.* THESAURUS ▸ BAD, SERIOUS

> **REGISTER**
> In everyday English, people usually say an injury, a problem etc is **serious** rather than **severe**: *His injuries were quite* ***serious***.

2 WEATHER severe weather is very bad and very extreme, and very hot, dry, cold etc
3 PUNISHMENT a severe punishment is very strict or extreme: *Drug smugglers can expect severe penalties.*
4 CRITICISM severe criticism is very extreme and shows that you think someone has done something very badly: *The president came under severe criticism for his handling of the crisis.*
5 DIFFICULT very difficult and needing a lot of effort and skill: *The negotiations will be a severe test of his abilities.*
6 PERSON someone who is severe behaves in a way that

does not seem friendly or sympathetic, and is very strict or disapproving SYN **stern**: *His slightly severe expression softened.*
7 PLAIN very plain with little or no decoration: *a rather severe red-brick building* —**severity** /sə'verəti/ *n* [C,U]: *We didn't realize the severity of her illness.*

se·vere·ly /sə'vɪəli $ -'vɪr-/ ●●○ *adv*
1 very badly or to a great degree: *The town was severely damaged in the war.* | *She's now severely disabled.*
2 in a strict way: *Parents don't punish their children so severely these days.*
3 in a very unfriendly or disapproving way: *'Stop behaving like a fool!' she said severely.*
4 in a plain simple style with little or no decoration: *a severely dressed woman*

se·vi·che /sə'viːtʃeɪ/ *n* [U] another spelling of CEVICHE

sew /səʊ $ soʊ/ ●●● S3 *v* (*past tense* **sewed**, *past participle* **sewn** /səʊn $ soʊn/ *or* **sewed**) [I,T] to use a needle and thread to make or repair clothes or to fasten something such as a button to them: *I learned to sew at school.* | **sew sth on sth** *Can you sew a patch on my jeans?* | **sew sth together** *She sewed the two sides together.*

sew sth ↔ **up** *phr v*
1 to close or repair something by sewing it: *Could you sew up this hole in my trousers?*
2 *informal* to finish a business agreement or plan and get the result you want: *The deal should be sewn up in a week.* GRAMMAR **Sew up** is usually passive in this meaning.
3 have sth sewn up to have gained control over a situation so that you are sure to win or get what you want: *It looks like the Democrats have the election sewn up.*

sew·age /'sjuːɪdʒ, 'suː- $ 'suː-/ *n* [U] the mixture of waste from the human body and used water, that is carried away from houses by pipes under the ground: *Chlorine is used in sewage treatment.* | *The factory secretly dumped millions of gallons of* ***raw sewage*** (=sewage that had not been treated) *into the Ohio river.*

'sewage works *BrE*, **'sewage plant** *AmE*, **'sewage farm** *BrE n* [C] a place where sewage is treated to stop it being harmful

sew·er /'sjuːə,'suːə $ 'suːər/ *n* [C] a pipe or passage under the ground that carries away waste material and used water from houses, factories etc

sew·er·age /'sjuːərɪdʒ, 'suː- $ 'suː-/ *n* [U] the system by which waste material and used water are carried away in sewers and then treated to stop them being harmful

sew·ing /'səʊɪŋ $ 'soʊ-/ ●○○ *n* [U]
1 the activity or skill of making or repairing clothes or decorating cloth with a needle and thread
2 something you are sewing: *Imogen sighed and picked up her sewing.*

'sewing ma,chine *n* [C] a machine for stitching cloth or clothes together

sewn /səʊn $ soʊn/ a past participle of SEW

sex¹ /seks/ ●●● S1 W2 AWL *n*
1 [U] the physical activity that two people do together in order to produce babies, or for pleasure → **sexual**: *All you see on TV is sex and violence these days.* | *They* ***had sex*** *in the back seat of his car.* | *She no longer wanted to* ***have sex with*** *him.* | **premarital sex/sex before marriage** (=sex happening before marriage) | *the dangers of* ***casual sex*** (=having sex with someone without intending to have a serious relationship) | **safe sex** (=ways of having sex that reduce the spread of sexual diseases) | **unprotected sex** (=sex without a CONDOM)
2 [U] whether a person, plant, or animal is male or female: *Put your name and sex at the top of the form.*
3 [C] all men, considered as a group, or all women, considered as a group → **sexual**: *He found it difficult to talk to members of* ***the opposite sex*** (=people that were not his own sex). | *People of* ***both sexes*** (=both men and women) *buy her records.*
4 single-sex school/college etc *BrE* a school etc for either males or females, but not for both together

sex² *v* [T] *technical* to find out whether an animal is male or female

sex sth ↔ **up** *phr v informal* to change something in order to make it more exciting: *The organization is trying to sex up its image.*

sex·a·ge·na·ri·an /ˌseksədʒə'neəriən $ -'ner-/ *n* [C] someone who is between 60 and 69 years old

'sex ap,peal *n* [U] the quality of being sexually attractive: *She's young and pretty and full of sex appeal.*

'sex ,bias *n* [U] *especially AmE* treating people unfairly because they are women or because they are men SYN **sex discrimination**: *She has taken out a lawsuit against her employer, accusing them of sex bias.*

'sex change *n* [C usually singular] a medical operation or treatment which changes someone's body so that they look like someone of the other sex

'sex discrimi,nation *n* [U] treating people unfairly because they are women, or because they are men: *She is suing the company for sex discrimination.*

'sex drive *n* [C usually singular] someone's ability or need to have sex regularly

'sex edu,cation *n* [U] when young people are taught about sex, especially at school

,sexed-'up *adj* [only before noun] *informal* a sexed-up report, document etc has been changed so that it says what the writers want it to say, even though they know it is not completely true → **sex up**

'sex ,industry *n* [singular] the businesses and activities related to PROSTITUTION and PORNOGRAPHY

sex·is·m /'seksɪzəm/ ●○○ AWL *n* [U] the belief that one sex is weaker, less intelligent, or less important than the other, especially when this results in someone being treated unfairly: *sexism in the workplace* **THESAURUS** PREJUDICE

sex·ist /'seksɪst/ *n* [C] someone who believes that one sex is weaker, less intelligent, or less important than the other, and treats them unfairly because of this - used to show disapproval —**sexist** *adj*: *sexist attitudes*

sex·less /'seksləs/ *adj* **1** not involving sexual activity, in a way that does not seem normal or usual: *a sexless marriage* **2** neither male nor female

'sex life *n* [C] someone's sexual activities: *an active and fulfilling sex life*

'sex ,maniac *n* [C] someone who always thinks about or wants to have sex - often used humorously

'sex ,object *n* [C] someone who is thought about only as a way of satisfying another person's sexual desire, rather than as a whole person

'sex of,fender *n* [C] someone who is guilty of a crime related to sex —**sex offence** *BrE*, **sex offense** *AmE n* [U]

'sex ,organ *n* [C] a part of a person's or animal's body that is involved in producing babies

'sex shop *n* [C] *BrE* a shop selling goods, magazines etc related to sex and sexual activities

'sex ,symbol *n* [C] a famous person who is considered by many people to be very sexually attractive: *Hollywood's newest sex symbol*

sex·tant /'sekstənt/ *n* [C] a tool for measuring angles between stars in order to calculate the position of a ship or aircraft

sex·tet /seks'tet/ *n* [C] **1** a group of six singers or musicians performing together **2** a piece of music for six performers: *Mozart's sextet in B flat*

sex·ting /'sekstɪŋ/ *n* [U] the activity of sending sexual TEXT MESSAGES or sexual pictures of yourself to someone using a MOBILE PHONE —**sext** *v* [I,T] —**sext** *n* [C]

sex·ton /'sekstən/ *n* [C] someone whose job is to take care of a church building and the area around it, and do other related things, such as ring bells

'sex ,tourism *n* [U] the activity of travelling to other countries in order to have sex, especially of a type that is illegal in your own country —**sex tourist** *n* [C]

sex·tu·plet /sek'stjuːplɪt $ -'stʌ-/ *n* [C] one of six people

S

who are born at the same time and have the same mother

sex·u·al /ˈsekʃuəl/ ●●● S3 W2 AWL *adj*
1 relating to the physical activity of sex: *a disease passed on by sexual contact | allegations of sexual abuse | her first sexual experience | Many elderly people continue to have satisfying sexual relationships.*
2 relating to the social relationships between men and women, especially the differences between men and women: *sexual stereotypes* —**sexually** *adv*: *young people who are* ***sexually active*** (=who regularly have sex) | *I no longer found her sexually attractive. | She had been sexually assaulted.*

ˌsexual ˈharassment *n* [U] sexual remarks, looks, or touching done to someone who does not want it, especially from someone they work with

ˌsexual ˈintercourse *n* [U] *formal* the physical activity of two people having sex with each other

sex·u·al·i·ty /ˌsekʃuˈæləti/ ●●○ AWL *n* [U] the things people do, think, and feel that are related to their sexual desires: **male/female sexuality** *a study of male sexuality*

sex·u·a·lize (*also* **-ise** *BrE*) /ˈsekʃuəlaɪz/ *v* [T] to make someone or something sexual, especially in a way that is not suitable: *I worry about the fact that children are sexualized at such a young age.* —**sexualization** /ˌsekʃuəlaɪˈzeɪʃən $ -lə-/ *n* [U]

ˌsexually transˌmitted disˈease *n* [C,U] (*abbreviation* **STD**) a disease that one person passes to another through having sex, such as AIDS or HERPES

ˌsexual orienˈtation *n* [C,U] *formal* the fact that someone is HETEROSEXUAL or HOMOSEXUAL: *people of different sexual orientations*

ˌsexual ˈpolitics *n* [U] ideas and activities that are concerned with how power is shared between men and women, and how this affects their relationships

ˈsex ˌworker *n* [C] *formal* a PROSTITUTE – used to be polite or when you do not want to say this directly

sex·y /ˈseksi/ ●○○ *adj* (*comparative* **sexier**, *superlative* **sexiest**)
1 sexually exciting or sexually attractive: *sexy underwear | Don't you think he's sexy?*
2 *informal* sexy ideas, products etc are exciting, attractive, and interesting: *one of the sexiest companies in Seattle | a sexy investment* —**sexily** *adv* —**sexiness** *n* [U]

SF /ˌes ˈef/ an abbreviation of ***science fiction***

SGML /ˌes dʒiː em ˈel/ *n* [U] *technical* (***standard generalized markup language***) a way of writing a document on a computer so that its structure is clear, and so that it can easily be read on a different computer system

Sgt. (*also* **Sgt** *BrE*) the written abbreviation of ***sergeant***

sh, **shh** /ʃ/ *interjection* used to tell someone to be quiet: *Sh! I'm trying to sleep.*

shab·by /ˈʃæbi/ ●○○ *adj*
1 shabby clothes, places, or objects are untidy and in bad condition because they have been used for a long time: *Hugh's jacket was old and shabby. | a shabby little restaurant*
2 wearing clothes that are old and worn: *a shabby tramp*
3 old-fashioned unfair and unkind: *a shabby trick* —**shabbily** *adv* —**shabbiness** *n* [U]

shack¹ /ʃæk/ *n* [C] a small building that has not been built very well: *a tin shack*

shack² *v*
shack up *phr v informal* to start living with someone who you have sex with but are not married to – used to show disapproval: **[+with]** *She had shacked up with some guy from Florida.* | **be shacked up** *Is she shacked up with anyone?*

shack·le¹ /ˈʃækəl/ *n* [C] **1 the shackles of sth** *literary* the limits put on your freedom and happiness by something, especially a particular form of government – used to show disapproval: *They finally managed to throw off the shackles of communism.* **2** one of a pair of metal rings joined by a chain that are used for fastening together a prisoner's hands or feet, so that they cannot move easily or escape → HANDCUFFS

shackle² *v* [T] **1** to put many limits on what someone can do – used to show disapproval: *Industrial progress is being shackled by a mass of regulations.* **2** to put shackles on someone SYN **chain**: *He was blindfolded and shackled to a radiator.*

shade¹ /ʃeɪd/ ●●○ *n*
1 OUT OF SUNLIGHT [U] slight darkness or shelter from the direct light of the sun made by something blocking it: *a plant that needs a lot of shade* | **in the shade (of sth)** *She was sitting in the shade of a large oak tree. | The temperature was over 90 degrees in the shade.*
2 FOR BLOCKING LIGHT [C] **a)** something you use to reduce or block light: *The shade on the lamp was slightly crooked.* → LAMPSHADE **b)** *AmE* a covering that can be pulled down over a window SYN **blind**
3 shades [plural] *informal* SUNGLASSES
4 IN A PICTURE [U] the dark places in a picture: *strong contrasts of light and shade*
5 COLOUR [C] a particular type of red, green, blue etc: **[+of]** *a bright shade of pink* THESAURUS ▸ COLOUR
6 shade of meaning/opinion/feeling etc a meaning etc that is slightly different from other ones SYN **nuance**: *There is room in the Democratic Party for many shades of opinion.*
7 a shade *formal* very slightly: **a shade too big/hot/fast etc** *Matt's clothes were just a shade too big for me.* | **a shade better/quicker/faster etc** *The results were a shade better than we expected.* | **[+over/under/above etc]** *She was a shade under five feet tall.*
8 shades of sb/sth used to say that someone or something reminds you of another person or thing: *The food was horrible – shades of school dinners.*
9 put sb/sth in the shade to be so good or impressive that other similar things or people seem much less important or interesting: *They're planning a festival that will put all the others in the shade.*
10 have it made in the shade *AmE informal* to be extremely rich – used humorously

shade² *v* [T] **1** to protect something from direct light: *Shading her eyes, Anita scanned the horizon.* **2** (*also* **shade in**) to make part of a picture or drawing darker: *She shaded in the circles in the last two letters.*
shade into sth *phr v literary* if one thing shades into another, it is difficult to know where one stops and another starts: *His impatience shaded into anger.*

shad·ing /ˈʃeɪdɪŋ/ *n* **1** [U] the areas of a drawing or painting that have been made to look darker **2 shadings** [plural] slight differences: *He didn't understand the subtle shadings of legal language.*

shad·ow¹ /ˈʃædəʊ $ -doʊ/ ●●● S3 W2 *n*
1 DARK SHAPE [C] the dark shape that someone or something makes on a surface when they are between that surface and the light: *the long dark shadow of an old oak tree* | **in the shadow of sth** *It was hot, and we decided to walk in the shadow of the wall* (=along the wall, where its shadow would fall).
2 DARKNESS [U] (*also* **shadows** [plural]) darkness caused by something preventing light from reaching a place: **in shadow** *The room was half in shadow.* | **in the shadows** *In the shadows, something moved.*
3 BAD EFFECT/INFLUENCE [singular] the bad effect or influence that something has, which makes other things seem less enjoyable, attractive, or impressive: **in/under the shadow of sth** *For years, people had been living under the shadow of communism.* | **cast a shadow over/on sth** (=make something seem less enjoyable, attractive, or impressive) *The events of September 11th cast a shadow over the celebrations.*
4 without/beyond a shadow of a doubt used to say that something is definitely true: *Without a shadow of a doubt, he's the most talented player we have.*
5 in sb's shadow if you are in someone's shadow, they are much more famous and successful than you are: *Kate grew up in the shadow of her film star sister.*
6 be a shadow of your former self to be weaker, less powerful, or worse than you were before: *Lennox seemed like a shadow of his former self.*

S

7 shadows under your eyes small dark areas under your eyes that you have when you are very tired: *She looked pale, with deep shadows under her eyes.*
8 sb's shadow someone who follows someone else everywhere they go
9 afraid/frightened/scared etc of your own shadow easily frightened or very nervous → FIVE O'CLOCK SHADOW

COLLOCATIONS

VERBS

cast/throw a shadow (=make it appear) *The building cast a shadow across the narrow street.*
a shadow falls somewhere (=appears on something) *The footsteps came closer, and a shadow fell across the table.*
the shadows lengthen (=get longer, as it gets later in the day) *Already the shadows were lengthening.*

ADJECTIVES

a dark/black shadow *She saw the dark shadow of a man in the doorway.*
a long shadow | flickering shadows (=shadows that move about quickly)

shadow² *v* [T] **1** to follow someone closely in order to watch what they are doing: *Detectives shadowed him for weeks.* **2** *literary* to cover something with a shadow, or make it dark: *a narrow street which was shadowed by a huge Catholic church* GRAMMAR **Shadow** is usually passive in this meaning.

shadow³ *adj* [only before noun] **1 Shadow Chancellor/Foreign Secretary etc** the politician in the main opposition party in the British parliament who would become CHANCELLOR etc if their party was in government, and who is responsible for speaking on the same subjects **2 Shadow Cabinet** the group of politicians in the British parliament who would become ministers if their party was in government

ˈshadow ˌboxing *n* [U] fighting with an imaginary opponent, especially as training for BOXING

ˌshadow eˈconomy *n* [C] *technical* business activities that are difficult for the authorities to find out about, for example because they are illegal

shad·ow·y /ˈʃædəʊi $ -doʊi/ *adj* **1** mysterious and difficult to know anything about: *the* ***shadowy figures*** *who control international terrorist organizations* **2** full of shadows, or difficult to see because of shadows: *a shadowy room*

shad·y /ˈʃeɪdi/ *adj* (*comparative* **shadier**, *superlative* **shadiest**) **1** protected from the sun or producing shade: *a shady street | It was nice and shady under the trees.* THESAURUS DARK **2** probably dishonest or illegal SYN **suspicious**: *a* ***shady character*** *| She's been involved in some* ***shady deals****.*

shaft¹ /ʃɑːft $ ʃæft/ *n* [C]
1 PASSAGE a passage which goes down through a building or down into the ground, so that someone or something can get in or out: **mine/elevator/ventilation etc shaft** *a 300-foot elevator shaft*
2 HANDLE a long handle on a tool, SPEAR etc
3 OF LIGHT a narrow beam of light: **shaft of light/sunlight**
4 ENGINE PART a long thin piece of metal in an engine or machine, that turns and passes on power or movement to another part of the machine: *a drive shaft*
5 FOR A HORSE [usually plural] one of a pair of poles between which a horse is tied to pull a vehicle
6 ARROW *literary* an ARROW
7 get the shaft *informal* to be treated very unfairly

shaft² *v* [T] *informal* to treat someone very unfairly, especially by dishonestly getting money from them: *I can't believe you paid that much. You* ***got shafted****.*

shag¹ /ʃæg/ (*also* **shag·pile** /ˈʃægpaɪl/) *adj* **shag carpet/rug** a CARPET or RUG with a rough surface made from long threads of wool

shag² *n* **1** [C] *BrE informal not polite* an act of having sex with someone **2** [C] a large black sea bird **3** [U] strong-tasting TOBACCO with thick leaves cut into small thin pieces

shag³ *v* (**shagged**, **shagging**) [I,T] *BrE informal not polite* to have sex with someone

shagged /ʃægd/ (*also* ˌ**shagged ˈout**) *adj BrE spoken not polite* very tired SYN **exhausted**: *I'm not going – I'm too shagged!*

shag·gy /ˈʃægi/ *adj* **1** shaggy hair or fur is long and untidy: *a shaggy black beard* **2** having shaggy hair: *a shaggy sheepskin coat* —**shagginess** *n* [U]

ˌshaggy ˈdog ˌstory *n* [C] *old-fashioned* a long joke that usually ends in a silly or disappointing way

shag·pile /ˈʃægpaɪl/ *adj* another word for SHAG¹

Shah /ʃɑː/ *n* [C] the title of the kings of Iran, used in the past

shake¹ /ʃeɪk/ ●●● S3 W2 *v* (*past tense* **shook** /ʃʊk/, *past participle* **shaken** /ˈʃeɪkən/)
1 MOVE [I,T] to move suddenly from side to side or up and down, usually with a lot of force, or to make something or someone do this: *She shook him to wake him up. | Shake the bottle before you open it. | The whole house started to shake. | The car shook as it went over a bump.* | **shake sth out of/off/from sth** *She shook the sand out of her shoes* (=removed it by shaking).
2 BODY [I] if someone shakes, or part of their body shakes, they make small sudden movements from side to side or up and down, especially because they are very frightened, cold, ill etc SYN **tremble** → **shiver**: *The little boy's hand was shaking.* | **shake with fear/laughter/anger etc** *I could see my neighbor shaking with laughter. | What's wrong with you? You're* ***shaking like a leaf*** (=shaking a lot because you are very nervous or frightened). | **be shaking in your shoes/boots** (=be very nervous) *I was shaking in my shoes – I thought he was going to fire me.*
3 shake your head to move your head from side to side as a way of saying no, or to show disapproval, surprise, or sadness: *When asked if he wanted anything else, he just shook his head. | Mark shook his head in disbelief.*
4 shake sb's hand/shake hands with sb to move someone's hand up and down with your own hand as a greeting or as a sign you have agreed something: *He shook my hand warmly. | Wilkins shook hands with him. | If we have a deal, let's* ***shake on it*** (=show that we have made an agreement by shaking hands).
5 SHOCK [T] to make someone feel very upset or shocked: *Kerrie was so shaken by the attack that she won't go out alone. | The murder shook the whole town.*
6 shake sb's confidence/beliefs etc to make someone feel less confident, less sure about their beliefs etc: *His confidence was badly shaken.*
7 sb's voice shakes if someone's voice is shaking, it is not steady and they sound very worried, angry, or frightened: *Her voice was shaking as she announced the news.* | **shake with rage/emotion etc** *Reg's voice shook with rage.*
8 shake your fist (at sb) to show that you are angry by holding up and shaking your tightly closed hand: *He shook his fist at the driver of the other car.*
9 shake a leg *spoken* used to tell someone to hurry, or quickly start doing something: *C'mon, shake a leg!*

shake down *phr v*
1 shake sb ↔ down *AmE informal* to get money from someone by using threats → **shakedown**: *Corrupt officials were shaking down local business owners.*
2 shake sb/sth ↔ down *AmE informal* to search a person or place thoroughly → **shakedown**
3 if a new situation or arrangement shakes down, people start to get used to it and it becomes more effective: *The restructure has shaken down, and staff are showing a new sense of purpose.*

shake sb/sth ↔ **off** *phr v*
1 to get rid of an illness, problem etc: *I can't seem to shake off this cold.* | **shake off your image/reputation as sth** *Outside investment has helped Sheridan to shake off its image as a depressed industrial town.*
2 to escape from someone who is chasing you: *I think we've shaken them off.*

S

shake out *phr v*
1 shake sth ↔ out to shake a cloth, a bag, a sheet etc so that any small pieces of dirt, dust etc come off: *He shook out the handkerchief and put it back in his pocket.*
2 if an organization or industry shakes out, it becomes calmer after a difficult period of time: *He'll look for bargains after the real estate market shakes out.*
3 shake sth ↔ out to change a situation by removing things from it that are not useful or that do not make a profit: *As the airline industry shakes out all but the very fittest, catering companies could face serious troubles.*
shake sb/sth **↔ up** *phr v*
1 to give someone a very unpleasant shock, so that they feel very upset and frightened: *She was badly shaken up by the accident.* → SHAKEN
2 to make changes to an organization in order to make it more effective SYN **overhaul**: *the government's plans to shake up the educational system* → SHAKEUP

shake² ●●○ *n*
1 [C] if you give something a shake, you move it up and down or from side to side: ***Give** the bottle a good **shake** before use.* | *He refused with a **shake of** the **head*** (=a movement of the head from side to side to mean 'no').
2 [C] a cold drink made from milk, ICE CREAM, and fruit or chocolate SYN **milk shake**: *a strawberry shake*
3 the shakes nervous shaking of your body caused by illness, fear, too much alcohol, not getting a drug you are dependent on etc: *If I don't smoke, I **get the shakes**.*
4 in a couple of shakes/two shakes *informal* very soon: *I'll be back in two shakes.*
5 no great shakes *spoken* not very skilful, or not very good: *He's no great shakes as a singer.*
6 get/give sb a fair shake *informal* to get or give someone fair treatment

shake·down /ˈʃeɪkdaʊn/ *n* [C] **1** *AmE informal* when someone gets money from another person by using threats: *a Mafia shakedown* **2** *AmE informal* a thorough search of a place or a person: *No weapons were found during the shakedown.* **3** a period of time when people start to get used to a new arrangement and it becomes more effective **4** a period of time when prices are falling on a financial market **5** a final test of a boat, plane etc before it is put into general use: *The new system is in its shakedown phase.* **6 the final shakedown** the final situation, after a lot of other things have happened

shak·en /ˈʃeɪkən/ (*also* ˌ**shaken ˈup**) *adj* [not usually before noun] upset, shocked, or frightened by something that has happened to you: *'How's Jacob?' 'Pretty shaken up, but he'll be all right.'* | *He was **badly shaken** after the attack.*
THESAURUS ▸ SHOCKED

shake·out /ˈʃeɪkaʊt/ *n* **1** [C usually singular] a situation in which several companies fail because they cannot compete with stronger companies in difficult economic conditions **2** [C] a SHAKEUP

shak·er /ˈʃeɪkə $ -ər/ *n* [C] **1** a container with holes in the lid, used to shake salt, sugar etc onto food: *a salt shaker* **2** (*also* **cocktail shaker**) a container in which drinks are mixed **3 Shaker** a member of a US religious group who lived together and had a simple way of life. Shaker furniture is made in the plain, simple, and attractive style that Shakers used to make things: *a Shaker chair* **4** a small container for shaking DICE → **movers and shakers** at **MOVER**(1) → see picture at **BOARD GAME**

Shakes·pea·re·an /ʃeɪkˈspɪəriən $ -ˈspɪr-/ *adj* [only before noun] **1** in the style of Shakespeare: *Shakespearean language* **2** relating to the work of Shakespeare: *a famous Shakespearean actor*

shake-up /ˈʃeɪkʌp/ *n* [C] a process by which an organization makes a lot of big changes in a short time to improve its effectiveness: **[+of]** *a big shakeup of the education system*

shak·y /ˈʃeɪki/ ●○○ *adj*
1 weak and unsteady because of old age, illness, or shock: *a shaky voice* | *Grandad was a little **shaky on** his **feet*** (=not able to walk very well). THESAURUS ▸ WEAK
2 not sure about the exact details of something, or not likely to be completely right: *My knowledge of history is a little shaky.* | *shaky evidence*
3 not firm or steady SYN **unstable**: *shaky foundations* —**shakily** *adv* —**shakiness** *n* [U]

shale /ʃeɪl/ *n* [U] a smooth soft rock which breaks easily into thin flat pieces

ˈ**shale gas** *n* [U] a type of natural gas that is in shale

shall /ʃəl; *strong* ʃæl/ ●●● S1 W1 *modal verb* (*negative short form* **shan't**)
1 shall I/we ... ? *spoken* used to make a suggestion, or ask a question that you want the other person to decide about: *Shall I open the window?* | *Shall we say 6 o'clock, then?* | *What shall I get for dinner?*
2 I/we shall *especially BrE formal* used to say what you will do in the future: *We shall be away next week.* | *I shall have to be careful.* | *I've never liked her and I never shall.* | *We shall have finished by Friday.*
3 *formal or old-fashioned* used to emphasize that something will definitely happen, or that you are determined that something should happen: *The truth shall make you free.* | *I said you could go, and so you shall.*
4 *formal* used in official documents to state an order, law, promise etc: *All payments shall be made in cash.*
GRAMMAR GUIDE ▸ VERBS

shal·lot /ʃəˈlɒt $ ʃəˈlɑːt/ *n* [C] a vegetable like a small onion

shal·low /ˈʃæləʊ $ -loʊ/ ●●● S3 *adj* (*comparative* **shallower**, *superlative* **shallowest**)
1 measuring only a short distance from the top to the bottom OPP **deep**: *a shallow river* | *The lake is quite shallow.* | ***the shallow end** of the pool* | *Place the meat in a shallow dish.*
2 not interested in or not showing any understanding of important or serious matters – used to show disapproval: *a shallow argument* | *If he's only interested in your looks, that shows how shallow he is.*
3 shallow breathing breathing that takes in only small amounts of air OPP **deep** —**shallowly** *adv*: *He lay there unconscious, **breathing shallowly**.* —**shallowness** *n* [U]

shal·lows /ˈʃæləʊz $ -loʊz/ *n* [plural] **the shallows** an area of shallow water

Sha·lom /ʃæˈlɒm $ ʃæˈloʊm/ *interjection* a Hebrew word used to say hello or goodbye

shalt /ʃəlt; *strong* ʃælt/ *v* **thou shalt** *old use* a phrase meaning 'you shall', used when talking to one person

shal·war ka·meez /ʃælwɑː kæˈmiːz $ -wɑːr-/ (*also* **salwar kameez**) *n* [C] loose trousers which are narrow at the bottom and a long loose shirt, worn by some South Asian women and, in some countries, men

sham¹ /ʃæm/ *n* **1** [singular] someone or something that is not what they are claimed to be – used to show disapproval: *The elections were a complete sham.* **2** [U] *literary* when someone tries to make something or someone seem better than they really are: *It all turned out to be sham and hypocrisy.* **3** [C] a cover for a PILLOW, especially one used for decoration

sham² *adj* [only before noun] made to appear real in order to deceive people SYN **false**: *a sham marriage*

sham³ *v* (**shammed**, **shamming**) [I,T] *especially BrE old-fashioned* to pretend to be upset, ill etc to gain sympathy or an advantage SYN **feign**: *She's not ill, she's only shamming.*

sha·man /ˈʃɑːmən, ˈʃeɪ-/ *n* [C] a person in some tribes who is a religious leader and is believed to be able to talk to SPIRITS and cure illnesses —**shamanism** *n* [U]

sham·ble /ˈʃæmbəl/ *v* [I always + adv/prep] to walk slowly and awkwardly, not lifting your feet much, for example because you are tired, weak, or lazy SYN **shuffle**: **[+over/past/along etc]** *The old man shambled out of the room muttering to himself.* | **shambling gait** (=a shambling way of walking)

sham·bles /ˈʃæmbəlz/ *n* **be (in) a shambles** *informal* **a)** if something is a shambles, it is very disorganized and there is a lot of confusion: *The meeting was a shambles* *from start to finish.* | *The economy is in a complete shambles.* **b)** if a place is a shambles, it is very untidy SYN **mess**: *My house is in an absolute shambles.*

sham·bol·ic /ʃæmˈbɒlɪk $ -ˈbɑː-/ *adj BrE* very disorganized: *the government's shambolic efforts to deal with the crisis*

shame¹ /ʃeɪm/ ●●● S2 *n*

1 it's a shame/what a shame etc *spoken* used when you wish a situation was different, and you feel sad or disappointed: *'She's failed her test again.' 'What a shame!'* | ***It's a shame that*** *you have to leave so soon.* | ***What a shame*** *we missed the wedding.* | ***It's a shame about*** *the weather.* | **it is a shame to do sth** *It's a shame to cover this beautiful table with a tablecloth.* | *I can't imagine why they canceled your show, Tracy.* ***That's such a shame.*** | **a crying/great/terrible shame** *It was a crying shame that they lost the game.*

> **REGISTER**
> In written English, people usually say something is **unfortunate** rather than **a shame**: ***It's unfortunate that*** *these warnings were not taken seriously.*

2 [U] the feeling you have when you feel guilty and embarrassed because you, or someone who is close to you, have done something wrong: *He felt a deep sense of shame.* | *Maria blushed with shame.* | ***To her shame*** (=it made her feel ashamed), *she gained back all the weight she'd lost.* | *He's* ***brought shame on*** *the whole family.* | **hang/bow your head in shame** (=look down, or feel like you should look down, because you feel so ashamed) *I bow my head in shame when I think of how I treated her.* | ***There's no shame in*** (=it should not make you feel ashamed) *saying 'I don't know.'*

3 [U] the ability to feel shame: *How could you do such a thing?* ***Have you no shame?***

4 shame on you/him/them etc *spoken* used to say that someone should feel guilty or embarrassed because of something they have done: *Shame on you, Fred. I thought you were my friend!*

5 put sb/sth to shame to be so much better than someone or something else that it makes the other thing seem very bad or ordinary: *His cooking puts mine to shame.*

> **THESAURUS**
>
> **shame** the feeling you have when you feel guilty and embarrassed because you, or someone who is close to you, have done something wrong: *She never overcame the shame of having abandoned her children.* | *Following the scandal, Garrison resigned in shame.*
>
> **humiliation** a feeling of shame and embarrassment because you have been made to look weak or stupid in front of other people: *What really upset me was the humiliation of having to ask her for money.* | *He suffered the humiliation of defeat in the first round of the competition.*
>
> **dishonour** *BrE*, **dishonor** *AmE formal* the loss of other people's respect because you have done something bad, or you have been unsuccessful: *His comments have* ***brought*** *shame and* ***dishonour on*** *him and his profession.* | *There is no dishonour in failure when you have done everything you possibly can to succeed.*
>
> **stigma** the feeling that other people in society disapprove of you because of something that has happened to you, or because you feel different from most other people in some way – used especially when this seems unfair and unreasonable: *Even when someone has been found innocent of a crime, the stigma often remains.* | *At first I found the stigma of being unemployed very difficult to cope with.*
>
> **GREAT SHAME**
>
> **disgrace** a complete loss of people's respect because you have done something very bad and shocking: *His actions* ***brought disgrace on*** *the family.* | *The players were sent home* ***in disgrace*** *after admitting taking drugs.*
>
> **ignominy** *formal* a feeling of great shame and embarrassment because you have been made to look weak or stupid – a very formal use: *The team suffered the ignominy of losing five games in a row.* | *She hoped to avoid the ignominy of having to appear in court.*

shame² *v* [T] **1** to make someone feel ashamed: *It shames me to say it, but I lied.* | *He felt shamed and humiliated by the treatment he had received.* **2 shame sb into doing sth** to force someone to do something by making them feel ashamed: *His wife shamed him into handing the money back.* **3** to be so much better than someone else that you make them seem bad or feel embarrassed: *Their training record shamed other companies.* **4** to make someone feel they have lost all honour and respect: *She had shamed her family name* (=done something that made her family lose honour).

shame·faced /ʃeɪmˈfeɪst◂/ *adj* if someone is shamefaced, they look and feel ashamed because they have done something wrong or they have behaved badly: *Conner looked a little shamefaced.* | **shamefaced smile/grin** THESAURUS ASHAMED —**shamefacedly** /-ˈfeɪsɪdli/ *adv*

shame·ful /ˈʃeɪmfəl/ *adj* shameful behaviour or actions are so bad that someone should feel ashamed: *It's shameful the way some people treat their pets.* | *a shameful family secret* —**shamefully** *adv* —**shamefulness** *n* [U]

shame·less /ˈʃeɪmləs/ *adj* not seeming to be ashamed of your bad behaviour although other people think you should be ashamed SYN **brazen**: *the shameless way he lied to us* —**shamelessly** *adv*: *She shamelessly took advantage of him.* —**shamelessness** *n* [U]

sham·my /ˈʃæmi/ (*also* **ˈshammy ˌleather**) *n* (*plural* **shammies**) [C,U] a piece of CHAMOIS leather, used for cleaning or polishing

sham·poo¹ /ʃæmˈpuː/ ●●● S3 *n*

1 [C,U] a liquid soap for washing your hair: *What kind of shampoo do you use?* | *a bottle of shampoo*

2 [C usually singular] when someone washes your hair using shampoo: *$21 for a shampoo, cut, and blow-dry* | **shampoo and set** (=when someone washes your hair and then dries it so that it has a particular style, especially using CURLERS)

3 [C,U] a liquid used for cleaning CARPETS

shampoo² *v* [T] to wash something with shampoo: *She showered and* ***shampooed*** *her short dark* ***hair***.

sham·rock /ˈʃæmrɒk $ -rɑːk/ *n* [C] a small plant with three green leaves on each stem, that is the national symbol of Ireland

SHAMROCK

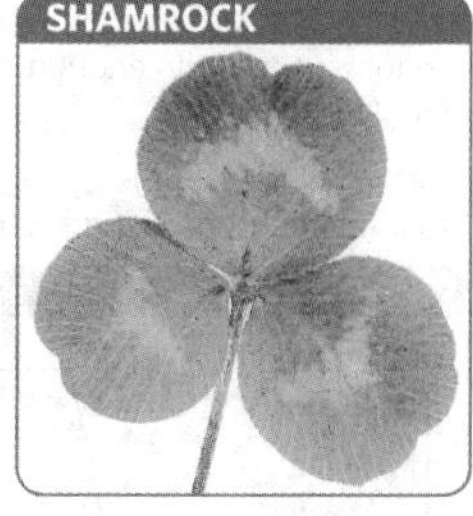

shan·dy /ˈʃændi/ *n* (*plural* **shandies**) [C,U] *BrE* a drink made of beer mixed with LEMONADE(2), or a glass of this drink

shang·hai /ʃæŋˈhaɪ/ *v* (**shanghaied**, **shanghaiing**, **shanghais**) [T] *old-fashioned* to trick or force someone into doing something unwillingly: **shanghai sb into doing sth** *I got shanghaied into organizing the kids' party.*

Shan·gri-La /ʃæŋgri ˈlɑː/ a distant beautiful imaginary place where everyone is happy. The name comes from the book *Lost Horizon* by James Hilton, about an imaginary valley in Tibet.

shank /ʃæŋk/ *n* **1** [C] a straight narrow part of a tool or object that connects the two ends: *a hammer shank* **2** [C,U] a piece of meat cut from the leg of an animal: *lamb shanks* **3** [C usually plural] the part of an animal's or a person's leg between the knee and ANKLE **4 (on) Shanks's pony** *BrE old-fashioned* walking, rather than using a vehicle

shan't /ʃɑːnt $ ʃænt/ *especially BrE* the short form of 'shall not': *I shan't see you again.*

shan·ty /ˈʃænti/ *n* (*plural* **shanties**) [C] **1** a small, roughly built hut made from thin sheets of wood, TIN, plastic etc that very poor people live in: *Workers were living in tents*

S

and shanties. **2** (*also* **sea shanty**) a song sung by sailors in the past, as they did their work

shan·ty·town /ˈʃæntiˌtaʊn/ *n* [C] a very poor area in or near a town where people live in small houses made from thin sheets of wood, TIN etc

shape¹ /ʃeɪp/ ●●● S2 W2 *n*

1 ROUND/SQUARE ETC [C,U] the form that something has, for example round, square, TRIANGULAR etc: *What shape is the table?* | *You can recognize a tree by the shape of its leaves.* | **round/square etc in shape** *The dining room was square in shape.* | *His battered old hat had completely lost its shape.* | **in the shape of sth** *a silver pin in the shape of a large bird* | *The plants grow in* **every shape and size**. | *The children cut out shapes* (=squares, triangles etc) *from the piece of cardboard.* | **out of shape** *The wheel had been bent out of shape.*

2 HEALTH/CONDITION **a) in good/bad/poor etc shape** in good, bad etc condition, or in good, bad etc health: *For an old car, it's in pretty good shape.* | *The economy is in worse shape now than it was last year.* | *Kaplan seemed to be in better shape than either of us.* **b) in shape/out of shape** in a good or bad state of health or physical FITNESS → **fit, unfit**: *I was feeling totally out of shape.* | *I've got to* **get into shape** *before summer.* | **keep/stay in shape** *She's bought an exercise bike to keep in shape.* **c) be in no shape to do sth** to be sick, tired, drunk etc, and not able to do something well: *Mel was in no shape to drive home after the party.*

3 knock/lick/get sb/sth into shape to make someone or something better so that they reach the necessary standard: *Some of them lack experience, but we'll soon knock them into shape.*

4 CHARACTER OF STH [singular] the way something looks, works, or is organized: **[+of]** *Computers have completely changed the shape of our industry.* | *This new technique is* **the shape of things to come** (=an example of the way things will develop in the future).

5 take shape to develop into a clear and definite form: *An idea was beginning to take shape in his mind.*

6 in the shape of sth used to explain what something consists of: *Help* **came in the shape of** *a $10,000 loan from his parents.*

7 not in any shape or form (*also* **not in any way, shape, or form**) used to say that you will not accept something for any reason: *We will not tolerate racism in any shape or form.*

8 THING NOT SEEN CLEARLY [C] a thing or person that you cannot see clearly enough to recognize: *A dark shape moved behind them.*

shape² ●●○ *v* [T]

1 to influence something such as a belief, opinion etc and make it develop in a particular way: *People's political beliefs are shaped by what they see in the papers.*

2 to make something have a particular shape, especially by pressing it: **shape sth into sth** *Shape the dough into small balls.* | **egg-shaped/V-shaped etc** *an L-shaped living room*

shape up *phr v informal*

1 to improve your behaviour or work: *You kids had better shape up, because I'm in no mood to fool around.*

2 to make progress in a particular way: *Ken's plans for the business are shaping up nicely.* | **[+as]** *Immigration is shaping up as a major issue in the campaign.* | **shape up to be sth** *It's shaping up to be a pretty big party.*

3 shape up or ship out *AmE spoken* used to tell someone that if they do not improve, they will be made to leave a place or their job

shape·less /ˈʃeɪpləs/ *adj* **1** not having a clear or definite shape: *a shapeless dress* **2** something such as a book or a plan that is shapeless does not seem to have a clear structure —**shapelessly** *adv*

shape·ly /ˈʃeɪpli/ *adj* having a body that has an attractive shape: *She had long shapely legs.*

shape·wear /ˈʃeɪpweə $ -wer/ *n* [U] underwear that is designed to hold your body firmly and make it appear to have a good shape

shard /ʃɑːd $ ʃɑːrd/ (*also* **sherd**) *n* [C] a sharp piece of broken glass, metal etc: **[+of]** *a shard of pottery*

share¹ /ʃeə $ ʃer/ ●●● S1 W1 *v*

1 USE TOGETHER [I,T] to have or use something with other people: *We don't have enough books, so you'll have to share.* | *The three of us shared a taxi.* | **share sth with sb** *I have an office that I share with some other teachers.*

2 LET SB USE STH [T] to let someone have or use something that belongs to you: *As a kid, he'd never share his toys.* | **share sth with sb** *Will you share your fries with me?*

3 DIVIDE [T] (*also* **share out**) to divide something between two or more people: **share sth between/among sb** *They shared the cake between them.* | *On his death, his property was shared out between his children.* THESAURUS GIVE

4 RESPONSIBILITY/BLAME [T] to have equal responsibility for doing something, paying for something etc: *We* **share** *the* **responsibility** *for the children.* | *I own the house, but we share the bills.* | *We all* **share** *some of* **the blame** *for the accident.*

5 SAME [T] to have the same opinion, quality, or experience as someone else: **share sb's view/concern/belief etc** *Other parents share her belief in the importance of reading.* | *I believe my view is* **widely shared**. | **share sth with sb** *Stubbornness was a characteristic he shared with his mother.*

6 TELL SB STH [I,T] to tell other people about an idea,

SHAPES

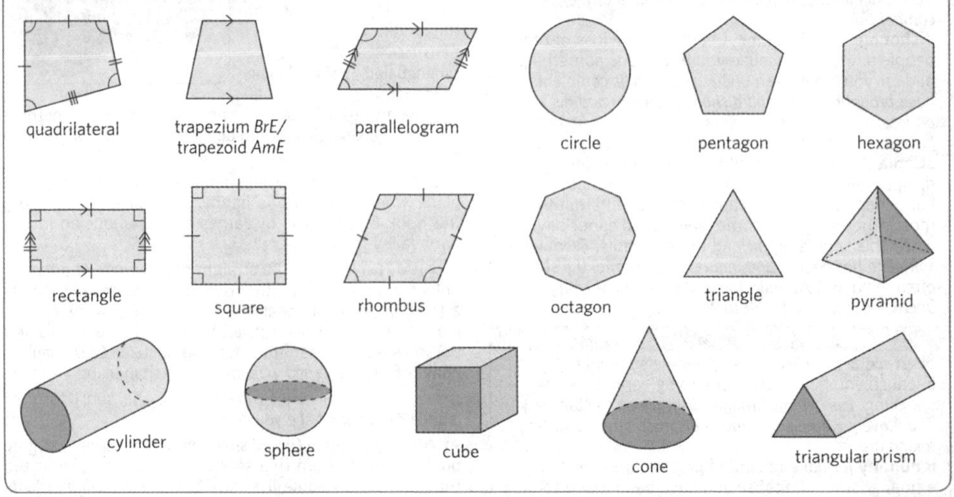

quadrilateral | trapezium *BrE*/ trapezoid *AmE* | parallelogram | circle | pentagon | hexagon

rectangle | square | rhombus | octagon | triangle | pyramid

cylinder | sphere | cube | cone | triangular prism

S

secret, problem etc: *Students were able to share their experiences.* | **share sth with sb** *Would you like to share your feelings with the group?*
7 share your life with sb if you share your life with someone, you spend your life together with them as their husband, wife etc: *I'm not ready to share my life with anyone.*
8 share and share alike *spoken* used to say that you should share things fairly and equally between everyone
share in sth *phr v* if you share in someone's success, happiness etc, you have it or enjoy it with them: *His daughters did not share in his happiness.*

share² ●●● S1 W1 *n*
1 IN A COMPANY [C] one of the equal parts into which the OWNERSHIP of a company is divided: **[+in]** *We've got shares in Allied Chemicals.* → STOCK¹(2)
2 PART OF STH [singular] the part of something that you own or are responsible for: **[+of/in]** *I gave them my share of the bill and left.* | *a share in the profits* | *I* ***do*** *my* ***share*** (=do my part) *of the housework.*
3 your (fair) share a) if you have had your share of something, for example problems, success, or adventure, a lot of it has happened to you: *You've sure* ***had*** *your* ***share*** *of problems, haven't you?* | *He'd had* ***more than*** *his* ***fair share of*** *adventure.* **b)** your share of something is the amount that you deserve to have: *Don't worry – you'll get your fair share.*
4 share in sth your part in an activity, event etc: *Employees are always given a share in decision-making.*
5 house/flat share *BrE* when people live together in the same house or flat and pay the rent together —**sharing** *n* [U] → **the lion's share** at LION(2), → TIMESHARE

COLLOCATIONS

VERBS

have/hold/own shares *A lot of the employees own shares in the company.*
buy/invest in shares *I bought some shares in British Gas five years ago.*
sell shares *This isn't a good time to sell shares.*
trade in/deal in shares (=buy and sell shares as a business) *They make their money by trading in stocks and shares.*
shares rise/go up (=their value increases) *The company's shares rose 5.5p to 103p.*
shares fall/go down (=their value decreases)

share + NOUN

share price *The company's share price has continued to go down.*
share ownership *The government tried to encourage wider share ownership.*
share dealing (=buying and selling shares as a business)

ˈshare-ˌcropper *n* [C] *especially AmE* a poor farmer who uses someone else's land, and gives the owner part of the crop in return

share·hold·er /ˈʃeəˌhəʊldə $ ˈʃerˌhoʊldər/ ●○○ *n* [C] someone who owns shares in a company or business SYN **stockholder**: *Shareholders have been told to expect an even lower result next year.*

share·hold·ing /ˈʃeəˌhəʊldɪŋ $ ˈʃerˌhoʊld-/ *n* [C] if you have a shareholding in a business, you own shares in it: **[+in]** *In 1992, United Distillers acquired a 75% shareholding in the company.*

ˈshare ˌindex *n* [C] *technical* an official and public list of SHARE prices

ˈshare-out *n* [C usually singular] *BrE* when something, especially money or property, is divided between two or more people, or the amount each person receives when it is divided

share·ware /ˈʃeəweə $ ˈʃerwer/ *n* [U] free or cheap computer SOFTWARE, usually produced by small companies, that you can use for a short time before you decide whether to buy it

sha·ri·a /ʃəˈriːə/ *n* [U] a system of religious laws followed by Muslims

shark /ʃɑːk $ ʃɑːrk/ ●●○ *n* [C]
1 a large sea fish with several rows of very sharp teeth that is considered to be dangerous to humans: *Sharks were circling around our boat.* | **shark-infested waters** (=waters where there are a lot of sharks) → see picture at FISH¹
2 *informal* someone who cheats other people out of money: **pool/card shark** (=someone who uses their skill at POOL or cards to cheat other players out of money) → LOAN SHARK

sharp¹ /ʃɑːp $ ʃɑːrp/ ●●● S3 W2 *adj* (*comparative* **sharper**, *superlative* **sharpest**)
1 ABLE TO CUT EASILY having a very thin edge or point that can cut things easily OPP **blunt**: *Make sure you use a good sharp knife.* | *Its teeth are* ***razor sharp*** (=very sharp).
2 TURN a sharp turn or bend changes direction suddenly: *We came to a sharp bend in the road.* | **sharp left/right** *Take a sharp left after the church.*
3 INCREASE/CHANGE a sharp increase, rise, fall etc happens suddenly and is great in amount SYN **steep**: *a sharp increase in prices* | *a sharp fall in unemployment*
4 DIFFERENCE sharp differences are very big and very noticeable: *sharp differences of opinion* | *There is a sharp distinction between domestic and international politics.* | *His honesty is* ***in sharp contrast to*** (=very different from) *some other politicians.*
5 PAIN/FEELINGS a sharp pain or feeling is sudden and severe OPP **dull**: *I felt a sharp pain in my back.* | *I was left with a sharp sense of disappointment.*
6 DISAPPROVING speaking in a way that shows you disapprove of something or are annoyed OPP **mild**: *a sharp rebuke* | *John's tone was sharp.* | *The boss can* ***be*** *very* ***sharp with*** *people when she's busy.* | **sb has a sharp tongue** (=they speak in a very disapproving way which often upsets people)
7 INTELLIGENT able to think and understand things very quickly, and not easily deceived OPP **dull, stupid**: *a journalist with an extremely sharp mind*
8 keep a sharp eye on sb to watch someone very carefully, especially because you do not trust them: *Keep a sharp eye on the kids at all times!*
9 PENCIL having a very thin point that can draw an exact line OPP **blunt**: *Make sure your pencils are sharp before we begin the test.*
10 SOUND a sharp sound or cry is loud, short, and sudden: *a sharp cry of pain* | *a sharp intake of breath*
11 TASTE having a slightly bitter taste OPP **mild**: *sharp cheddar cheese* | *Add mustard to give the dressing a sharper taste.*
12 CLOTHES attractive and fashionable SYN **smart** *BrE*: *Tod looked really sharp in his tux.* | *a sharp suit*
13 SHAPE not rounded or curved: *sharp features* | *Her mother had a sharp little nose.*
14 IMAGE/PICTURE if an image or picture is sharp, you can see all the details very clearly OPP **fuzzy**: *The outlines of the trees were sharp and clear.*
15 GOOD AT NOTICING THINGS able to see and notice details very well: **a sharp eye for detail** (=the ability to notice and deal with details)
16 MUSIC **a) F sharp/D sharp/C sharp etc** a musical note that is sharp has been raised by one SEMITONE from the note F, D, C etc **b)** if music or singing is sharp, it is played or sung at a slightly higher PITCH than it should be → FLAT¹(9), → NATURAL¹(10)
17 WEATHER **sharp wind/frost** a very cold wind or a severe FROST: *A sharp wind blew across the lake.*
18 sharp practice *BrE* behaviour, especially in business, that is dishonest but not illegal: *He's been guilty of sharp practice in the past.*
19 be on the sharp end (of sth) *BrE informal* to experience the worst effects of something: *We were always on the sharp end of clients' complaints.* —**sharpness** *n* [U] → SHARPLY

THESAURUS

sharp having a very thin edge or point that can cut things easily: *a sharp knife* | *The dog's teeth were very sharp.*

S

jagged having an irregular edge with a lot of sharp points: *a jagged rock | The floor was covered with jagged pieces of glass.*
spiky having a lot of thin sharp points: *a spiky cactus plant | The hedgehog uses its spiky fur for protection. | Some corals are quite smooth, others are sharp and spiky.*
prickly covered in a lot of small sharp points – used mainly about plants: *a prickly bush | prickly leaves*
serrated a serrated edge on a saw or knife has a lot of sharp points on it: *It's best to use a knife with a serrated edge.*
razor-sharp extremely sharp: *The cat had razor-sharp claws.*

sharp² *adv* **1 at ten thirty/2 o'clock etc sharp** at exactly 10.30, 2.00 etc: *We're meeting at one thirty sharp.* **2 sharp left/right** *BrE* if you turn sharp left or right, you make a sudden change of direction to the left or right: *You turn sharp right at the crossroads.* **3 look sharp** *BrE old-fashioned* used to tell someone to do something quickly: *If you look sharp, you might catch him before he leaves for London.* **4** played or sung at a slightly higher PITCH than is correct → **flat**

sharp³ *n* [C] **1** a musical note that has been raised one SEMITONE above the note written **2** the sign (#) in a line of written music, used to show that a musical note should be raised → **FLAT²(3)**

ˌsharp-ˈeared *adj* able to hear very well

sharp·en /ˈʃɑːpən $ ˈʃɑːr-/ ●○○ *v*
1 [I,T] to make something have a sharper edge or point, or to become sharper: *Anne sharpened her pencil and got out her homework.*
2 [T] to make a feeling stronger and more urgent: *A series of attacks have sharpened fears of more violence.*
3 [T] (*also* **sharpen sth ↔ up**) to improve something so that it is up to the necessary standard, quality etc: *The course will help students sharpen their writing skills.*

sharp·en·er /ˈʃɑːpənə, ˈʃɑːpnə $ ˈʃɑːrpənər, ˈʃɑːrpnər/ *n* [C] a tool or machine for sharpening pencils, knives etc

ˌsharp-ˈeyed *adj* able to see very well and notice small details: *My sharp-eyed mother had already spotted him.*

sharp·ish /ˈʃɑːpɪʃ $ ˈʃɑːr-/ *adv BrE spoken* quickly: *We'd better leave pretty sharpish if we want to catch that bus.*

sharp·ly /ˈʃɑːpli $ ˈʃɑːr-/ ●●○ W3 *adv*
1 suddenly and by a large amount: *Prices have risen sharply over the last few months. | His politics have moved sharply to the right.*
2 in a disapproving or unfriendly way: *'What do you mean by that?' Paul asked sharply. | a sharply critical report*
3 quickly and suddenly: *Graham looked up sharply, startled by a noise behind him. | Emily drew in her breath sharply.*
4 used when saying that two things are clearly and noticeably very different: *Opinion is* ***sharply divided****. | His beliefs and values* ***contrast sharply with*** (=are very different from) *his father's.*

ˈsharp ˌshooter *n* [C] someone who is very skilful at hitting what they aim at when shooting a gun

ˌsharp-ˈtongued *adj* [usually before noun] saying things in a disapproving or unfriendly way which often upsets people: *his sharp-tongued wife*

sharp-wit·ted /ʃɑːpˈwɪtɪd◂ $ ʃɑːrp-/ *adj* able to think and react very quickly SYN **quick-witted**

shat /ʃæt/ a past tense and past participle of SHIT³

shat·ter /ˈʃætə $ -ər/ ●●○ *v*
1 [I,T] to break suddenly into very small pieces, or to make something break in this way: **[+into]** *The plate hit the floor, and shattered into tiny bits. | The explosion shattered the building.* → see picture at **BREAK¹** THESAURUS **BREAK**
2 [T] to completely destroy or ruin something such as someone's beliefs or life: *A tragic accident* ***shattered*** *her* ***dreams*** *of Olympic glory. | A few weeks in a tiny damp room soon* ***shattered*** *his* ***illusions*** *about university life. | people whose* ***lives*** *have been* ***shattered*** *by war*
3 shatter the silence/peace if a loud noise shatters the silence or peace, it is suddenly heard: *The silence was shattered by a warning shout.*

shat·tered /ˈʃætəd $ -ərd/ *adj* [not before noun] **1** very shocked and upset: *I wasn't just disappointed, I was absolutely shattered.* **2** *BrE informal* very tired SYN **exhausted**: *By the time we got home we were both shattered.* THESAURUS **TIRED**

shat·ter·ing /ˈʃætərɪŋ/ *adj* **1** very shocking and upsetting: *His mother's death was a shattering blow.* **2** *BrE informal* making you very tired SYN **exhausting**: *I've had a shattering day.*

shat·ter·proof /ˈʃætəpruːf $ -tər-/ *adj* shatterproof glass is specially designed so that it will not form sharp dangerous pieces if it is broken

shave¹ /ʃeɪv/ ●●● S3 *v*
1 [I,T] to cut off hair very close to the skin, especially from the face, using a RAZOR: *He hadn't shaved for days. | Brian had* ***cut*** *himself* ***shaving****.* | **shave your head/legs/armpits etc** *She shaved her legs and underarms.*
2 [T] to remove very thin pieces from the surface of something: *Shave thin strips of cheese over the pasta.*

shave sth ↔ **off** *phr v*
1 to remove hair by shaving: *I've decided to shave off my beard.*
2 (*also* **shave sth off sth**) to remove very thin pieces from the surface of something, using a knife or other cutting tool: *I had to shave a few millimetres off the bottom of the door to make it shut.*
3 (*also* **shave sth off sth**) if you shave a small amount off something such as a price or a record, you make the price slightly smaller or the record time slightly shorter: *She shaved half a second off the world record.*

shave² *n* [C usually singular] **1** if a man has a shave, he cuts off the hair on his face close to his skin using a RAZOR: *He looked as if he needed a shave.* | **have a shave** *BrE*: *I'll just have a shave before we go.* **2 a close shave** a situation in which you only just avoid an accident or something bad SYN **narrow escape**: *Phew, that was a close shave.*

shav·en /ˈʃeɪvən/ *adj* with all the hair shaved off: *his shaven head* → **CLEAN-SHAVEN, UNSHAVEN**

shav·er /ˈʃeɪvə $ -ər/ *n* [C] a small piece of electrical equipment used for shaving: *He uses an electric shaver.* → **RAZOR(1)**

ˈshaving brush *n* [C] a brush used for spreading soap or shaving cream over your face when you shave → see picture at **BRUSH¹**

ˈshaving cream (*also* **ˈshaving foam** *BrE*) *n* [U] a special cream that you put on your face when you shave → see picture at **FOAM**

shav·ings /ˈʃeɪvɪŋz/ *n* [plural] very thin pieces, especially of wood, cut from a surface with a sharp blade: *a pile of wood shavings on the floor*

shawl /ʃɔːl $ ʃɒːl/ *n* [C] a piece of cloth, in a square or TRIANGULAR shape, that is worn around the shoulders or head, especially by women

she¹ /ʃi; *strong* ʃiː/ ●●● S1 W1 *pron* [used as the subject of a verb]
1 used to refer to a woman, girl, or female animal that has already been mentioned or is already known about: *You could always ask Beth – she's got plenty of money. | I saw you talking to that girl. Who is she? | What did she say when you told her?*
2 *old-fashioned* used to refer to a country, ship, or vehicle that has already been mentioned: *She was carrying over 1,500 passengers.*

she² /ʃiː/ *n* [singular] *informal* a female: *What a cute puppy! Is it a he or a she?*

she- /ʃiː/ *prefix* female: *a she-goat | a she-devil* (=evil woman)

s/he /ʃiː ɔː ˈhiː $ -ɔːr-/ *pron written* used in writing when the subject of the sentence can be either male or female: *If any student witnesses a crime, s/he should contact campus police immediately.*

shea but·ter /ʃiː bʌtə, ˈʃeɪ- $ -tər/ *n* [U] a type of oil from an African nut that is used in MOISTURIZERS to make your skin less dry

sheaf /ʃiːf/ *n* (*plural* **sheaves** /ʃiːvz/) [C] **1** several pieces of paper held or tied together: **[+of]** *He laid a sheaf of documents on the desk.* **2** a bunch of wheat, corn etc tied together after it has been cut

shear /ʃɪə $ ʃɪr/ *v* (*past tense* **sheared**, *past participle* **sheared** *or* **shorn** /ʃɔːn $ ʃɔːrn/) [T] **1** to cut the wool off a sheep **2** *literary* to cut off someone's hair: *Her long fair hair had been shorn.* **3 be shorn of sth** to have something valuable or important taken away from you: *Though shorn of some of its powers, the party remains in control.*

shear off *phr v* if part of something shears off, or is sheared off, it suddenly becomes separated, especially after being pulled or hit with a lot of force: **shear sth ↔ off** *The left wing had been almost completely sheared off.*

shear·er /ˈʃɪərə $ ˈʃɪrər/ (*also* **ˈsheep ˌshearer**) *n* [C] someone who cuts the wool off sheep

shears /ʃɪəz $ ʃɪrz/ *n* [plural] a heavy tool for cutting, like a big pair of scissors: *Sam was trimming the hedge with a **pair of** garden **shears**.* → see picture at **GARDEN**

sheath /ʃiːθ/ *n* (*plural* **sheaths**) [C] **1** a cover for the blade of a knife or sword: *His sword was back in its sheath.* → see picture at **KNIFE**[1] **2** *BrE old-fashioned* a CONDOM **3** a protective covering that fits closely around something: *The wire is covered by an outer plastic sheath.* **4** a simple close-fitting dress: *She was wearing a plain black sheath.*

sheathe /ʃiːð/ *v* [T] *literary* **1** to put a knife or sword into a sheath: *He sheathed his sword.* **2 be sheathed in/with sth** to be covered by something: *The grassy hills were sheathed in mist.*

sheath·ing /ˈʃiːðɪŋ/ *n* [C usually singular] a protective outer cover, for example for a building or a ship

ˈsheath knife *n* [C] a knife with a fixed blade that is carried in a sheath → see picture at **KNIFE**[1]

sheaves /ʃiːvz/ the plural of SHEAF

she·bang /ʃəˈbæŋ/ *n* **the whole shebang** *informal* the whole thing: *It's a big project, and she's in charge of the whole shebang.*

she·been /ʃəˈbiːn/ *n* [C] *informal* a place where alcoholic drinks are sold illegally – used especially in Ireland

shed[1] /ʃed/ ●●○ S3 *n* [C]

1 a small building, often made of wood, used especially for storing things: *a tool shed* | *a cattle shed*

2 a large industrial building where work is done, large vehicles are kept, machinery is stored etc

shed[2] ●●○ *v* (*past tense and past participle* **shed**, *present participle* **shedding**) [T]

1 GET RID OF to get rid of something that you no longer need or want: *The company is planning to shed about a quarter of its workforce.* | *The magazine is desperately trying to shed its old-fashioned image.* | *a diet to help you shed pounds*

> **REGISTER**
> **Shed** is used especially in journalism. In everyday English, people usually say that someone or something **gets rid of** something.

2 shed light a) to make something easier to understand, by providing new or better information: **[+on]** *Recent research has shed light on the causes of the disease.* | *Investigators hope to shed light on what started the fire.* **b)** if something sheds light, it lights the area around it: *The lamp shed a harsh yellow light.*

3 PLANTS/ANIMALS if a plant sheds its leaves or if an animal sheds skin or hair, they fall off as part of a natural process: *The trees were starting to **shed** their **leaves**.* | *As it grows, a snake will regularly **shed** its **skin**.*

4 DROP/FALL to drop something or allow it to fall: *He strode across the bathroom, shedding wet clothes as he went.* | **shed a load** *BrE*: *A lorry **shed** its **load** of steel bars on the M25.*

5 shed blood to kill or injure people, especially during a war or a fight: *Too much blood has already been shed in this conflict.* → **BLOODSHED**

6 shed tears *especially literary* to cry: *She had not shed a single tear during the funeral.*

7 WATER if something sheds water, the water flows off its surface, instead of sinking into it

she'd /ʃid; *strong* ʃiːd/ **1** the short form of 'she had': *She'd already gone when we got there.* **2** the short form of 'she would': *She'd like to come with us.*

shed·load /ˈʃedləʊd $ -loʊd/ *n* **shedloads of sth** *BrE informal* a lot of something: *They've got shedloads of stuff for sale.*

sheen /ʃiːn/ *n* [singular, U] a soft smooth shiny appearance: *Her hair had a lovely coppery sheen.*

sheep /ʃiːp/ ●●● S2 W3 *n* (*plural* **sheep**) [C]

1 a farm animal that is kept for its wool and its meat: *Sheep were grazing on the hillside.* | *a sheep farmer* | **flock of sheep** (=a group of sheep) → **LAMB**[1]

2 like sheep if people behave like sheep, they do not think independently, but follow what everyone else does or thinks: *Tourists were led around like sheep, from shrine to souvenir shop.*

3 make sheep's eyes at sb *old-fashioned* to look at someone in a way that shows you love them → **BLACK SHEEP**, → **count sheep** at **COUNT**[1](14), → **separate the sheep from the goats** at **SEPARATE**[2](9), → **a wolf in sheep's clothing** at **WOLF**[1](2)

ˈsheep-dip *n* [C,U] a chemical used to kill insects that live in sheep's wool, or a special bath in which this chemical is used

sheep·dog /ˈʃiːpdɒg $ -dɒːg/ *n* [C] **1** a dog that is trained to control sheep **2** a dog of a type that is often used for controlling sheep → **OLD ENGLISH SHEEPDOG**

sheep·ish /ˈʃiːpɪʃ/ *adj* slightly uncomfortable or embarrassed because you know that you have done something silly or wrong: *Sam **looked** a bit **sheepish**.* | *a **sheepish grin*** THESAURUS ▸ **EMBARRASSED** —**sheepishly** *adv*: *She **smiled sheepishly**.*

ˈsheep-pen *n* [C] a small area of ground with a fence around it, used for keeping sheep together for a short time

sheep·skin /ˈʃiːpˌskɪn/ *n* [C,U] the skin of a sheep with the wool still on it: *a **sheepskin coat***

sheer[1] /ʃɪə $ ʃɪr/ ●●○ *adj*

1 the sheer weight/size etc used to emphasize that something is very heavy, large etc: **[+of]** *The sheer size of the country makes communications difficult.*

2 sheer luck/happiness/stupidity etc luck, happiness etc with no other feeling or quality mixed with it SYN **pure**: *I'll never forget the look of sheer joy on her face.* | *sheer hypocrisy*

3 a sheer drop, cliff, slope etc is very steep and almost vertical

4 sheer NYLON, silk etc is very thin and fine, so that it is almost transparent: *sheer stockings*

sheer[2] *adv* straight up or down in an almost vertical line SYN **steeply**: *cliffs which rose sheer from the sea*

sheer[3] *v* [I always + adv/prep] to change direction suddenly, especially in order to avoid something SYN **swerve**: **[+off/away]** *The boat sheered away and headed out to sea.*

sheet /ʃiːt/ ●●● S1 W2 *n* [C]

1 FOR A BED a large piece of thin cloth that you put on a bed to lie on or lie under → **blanket**, **duvet**: *I'll go and find you some clean sheets and blankets.* | *white cotton sheets* | **change the sheets** (=put clean sheets on a bed)

2 PAPER a piece of paper for writing on, or containing information: **[+of]** *a **sheet of paper** with names and numbers on it* | **clean/blank sheet of paper** (=one with no writing on it) → see picture at **PIECE**[1]

3 THIN FLAT PIECE a thin flat piece of something such as metal or glass, that usually has four sides: **[+of]** *a **sheet** of glass* → **SHEET METAL** THESAURUS ▸ **PIECE**

4 LARGE FLAT AREA a large flat area of something such as ice or water spread over a surface: **[+of]** *A **sheet** of ice covered the lake.*

S

5 OF RAIN/FIRE a sheet of rain or fire is a very large moving mass of it: **[+of]** *Sheets of flame shot into the air.* | **in sheets** *The rain was coming down in sheets.*
6 ON A SHIP *technical* a rope or chain attached to a sail on a ship that controls the angle between a sail and the wind → BAKING SHEET, BALANCE SHEET, COOKIE SHEET, RAP SHEET, TIME SHEET, → **as white as a sheet** at WHITE[1](3), → **clean sheet** at CLEAN[1](9)

sheet·ing /ˈʃiːtɪŋ/ *n* [U] **1** material such as plastic or metal used to cover something and protect it: **plastic/rubber/metal etc sheeting** *The roof was covered in plastic sheeting.* **2** cloth used to make sheets for a bed

ˌsheet ˈlightning *n* [U] a type of LIGHTNING that appears as a sudden flash of brightness covering a large area of sky → FORKED LIGHTNING

ˈsheet ˌmetal *n* [U] metal in the form of thin sheets

ˈsheet ˌmusic *n* [U] music that is printed on single sheets and not fastened together inside a cover

sheikh, **sheik** /ʃeɪk $ ʃiːk/ *n* [C] **1** an Arab ruler or prince **2** a Muslim religious leader or teacher

sheikh·dom, **sheikdom** /ˈʃeɪkdəm $ ˈʃiːk-/ *n* [C] a place that is governed by an Arab prince or ruler

shei·la /ˈʃiːlə/ *n* [C] *informal* a young woman – used in Australia and New Zealand

shek·el /ˈʃekəl/ *n* [C] the standard unit of money in Israel

shelf /ʃelf/ ●●● S3 W3 *n* (*plural* **shelves** /ʃelvz/)
1 [C] a long flat narrow board attached to a wall or in a frame or cupboard, used for putting things on: **top/bottom/next etc shelf** *Put it back on the top shelf.* | *shelves of books* | *supermarket shelves* | *the amount of* **shelf space** *available*
2 [C] a narrow surface of rock shaped like a shelf, especially under water → CONTINENTAL SHELF
3 on the shelf a) if something is left on the shelf, it is not used or considered: *The album stayed on the shelf for several years, until it was finally released.* **b)** *BrE old-fashioned* too old to get married, used especially of women → OFF-THE-SHELF, SHELVE(3)

ˈshelf life *n* [singular] the length of time that a product, especially food, can be kept in a shop before it becomes too old to sell

shell[1] /ʃel/ ●●● S3 W3 *n* [C]
1 a) the hard outer part that covers and protects an egg, nut, or seed: *Never buy eggs with cracked shells.* | *peanuts roasted in their shells* **b)** the hard protective covering of an animal such as a SNAIL, MUSSEL, or CRAB: *a snail shell* | *The children were collecting shells on the beach.* → SEASHELL
2 a metal container, like a large bullet, which is full of an explosive substance and is fired from a large gun: *We ran for cover as shells dropped all around us.* | *an exploding* **mortar shell**
3 *especially AmE* a metal tube containing a bullet and an explosive substance SYN **cartridge**
4 the outside structure of something, especially the part of a building that remains when the rest of it has been destroyed: **[+of]** *the burnt-out shell of a nightclub*
5 out of your shell becoming less shy and more confident and willing to talk to people: *I had hoped that university would* **bring** *him* **out of** *his* **shell**. | *She's started to* **come out of** *her* **shell** *a little.*

shell[2] ●○○ *v* [T]
1 to fire shells from large guns at something: *The army has been shelling the town since yesterday.* THESAURUS ▸ SHOOT
2 to remove something such as beans or nuts from a shell or POD: *Josie was* **shelling peas** *in the kitchen.*

shell out (sth) *phr v informal* to pay a lot of money for something, especially unwillingly: *If you want the repairs done right, you'll have to shell out at least $800.* | **[+for]** *She ended up shelling out for two rooms.*

she'll /ʃɪl; *strong* ʃiːl/ the short form of 'she will'

shel·lac /ʃəˈlæk/ *n* [U] a type of transparent paint for protecting or hardening surfaces

shell·fire /ˈʃelfaɪə $ -faɪr/ *n* [U] an explosion caused by shells being fired from large guns: *a hospital badly damaged by shellfire*

SHELLFISH

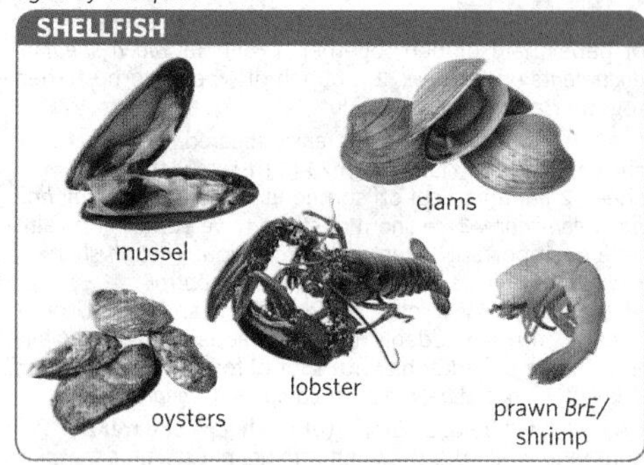

shell·fish /ˈʃelˌfɪʃ/ *n* (*plural* **shellfish**) [C,U] an animal that lives in water, has a shell, and can be eaten as food, for example CRABS, LOBSTERS, and OYSTERS

ˈshell game *n* [C] *AmE* a dishonest method of doing something, in which you pretend to be doing one thing when you are really doing another: *Critics called the proposal a shell game.*

shell·ing /ˈʃelɪŋ/ *n* [U] the firing of shells from large guns: **[+of]** *the shelling of villages* | *weeks of* **heavy shelling**

ˈshell shock *n* [U] *old-fashioned* a type of mental illness caused by the terrible experiences of fighting in a war or battle

ˈshell-shocked *adj* **1** *informal* feeling tired, confused, or anxious because of a recent difficult experience **2** *old-fashioned* mentally ill because of the terrible experiences of war

ˈshell suit *n* [C] *BrE* a light brightly coloured piece of clothing consisting of trousers and a jacket that fit tightly at the wrists and at the bottom of the legs

shel·ter[1] /ˈʃeltə $ -ər/ ●●○ W3 *n*
1 [U] a place to live, considered as one of the basic needs of life: *They are in need of food and shelter.*
2 [U] protection from danger or from wind, rain, hot sun etc: **[+of]** *We reached the shelter of the caves.* | **in/into/under etc the shelter of sth** *They were standing under the shelter of a huge tree.* | *The men* **took shelter** *in a bombed-out farmhouse.* | *All around me, people were* **running for shelter**. | **[+from]** *An old hut* **gave shelter** *from the storm.*
3 [C] a building where people or animals that have nowhere to live or that are in danger can stay and receive help: **[+for]** *a shelter for battered women* | *a* **homeless shelter** (=for people who have no homes) | *an* **animal shelter**
4 [C] a building or an area with a roof over it that protects you from the weather or from danger: **air-raid/bomb/fall-out shelter** (=a place to keep people safe from bombs dropped by planes) | **bus shelter** *BrE* (=a small structure with a roof where you wait for a bus) → TAX SHELTER

shelter[2] ●○○ *v*
1 [T] to provide a place where someone or something is protected, especially from the weather or from danger: *Collins was arrested for sheltering enemy soldiers.* | **shelter sb/sth from sb/sth** *Plant herbs next to a wall to shelter them from the wind.* THESAURUS ▸ PROTECT
2 [I] to stay in or under a place where you are protected from the weather or from danger: **[+from]** *We sat in the shade, sheltering from the sun.*

shel·tered /ˈʃeltəd $ -ərd/ *adj* **1 a sheltered life/childhood/upbringing etc** a life etc in which someone has been too protected by their parents from difficult or unpleasant experiences: *I had led a sheltered life and had never met prejudice before.* **2** a place that is sheltered is protected from extreme weather conditions: *a sheltered valley* **3 sheltered accommodation/housing** *BrE* a place for people to live who cannot look after themselves properly and where help is provided if they need it: *sheltered accommodation for the elderly*

shelve /ʃelv/ *v* **1** [T] to decide not to continue with a plan, idea etc, although you might continue with it at a later time: *Plans to reopen the school have been* ***shelved***. THESAURUS▶ CANCEL **2** [I always + adv/prep] land that shelves is at a slight angle: *The garden shelves gently towards the sea.* **3** [T] to put something on a shelf, especially books

shelves /ʃelvz/ the plural of SHELF

shelv·ing /ˈʃelvɪŋ/ *n* [U] **1** a set of shelves fixed to a wall **2** wood, metal etc used for shelves

she·nan·i·gans /ʃəˈnænɪɡənz/ *n* [plural] *informal* bad behaviour that is not very serious, or slightly dishonest activities: *She wouldn't put up with his shenanigans.* | *financial shenanigans*

shep·herd¹ /ˈʃepəd $ -ərd/ *n* [C] someone whose job is to take care of sheep

shepherd² *v* [T always + adv/prep] to lead or guide a group of people somewhere, making sure that they go where you want them to go: **shepherd sb into/out of/towards etc sth** *The tour guides shepherded the rest of the group onto the bus.* THESAURUS▶ LEAD

shep·herd·ess /ˈʃepədes $ -ərdɪs/ *n* [C] *old-fashioned* a woman whose job is to take care of sheep

ˌshepherd's ˈpie *n* [C,U] a traditional English dish made of small pieces of cooked meat, usually lamb, covered with cooked potato

sher·bet /ˈʃɜːbət $ ˈʃɜːr-/ *n* **1** [C,U] *AmE* a sweet frozen food made with water, fruit, sugar, and milk **2** [U] *BrE* a powder that is eaten as a sweet

sherd /ʃɜːd $ ʃɜːrd/ *n* [C] another spelling of SHARD

sher·iff /ˈʃerɪf/ ●●○ *n* [C]
1 an elected law officer of a COUNTY in the US
2 (*also* **High Sheriff**) the representative of the king or queen in a COUNTY of England and Wales, who has mostly ceremonial duties
3 the most important judge in a DISTRICT or COUNTY in Scotland

ˈsheriff ˌcourt (*also* **ˈsheriff's ˌcourt**) *n* [C] the lower court of law in Scotland, dealing with CIVIL and criminal cases

Sherlock Holmes → HOLMES, SHERLOCK

Sher·pa /ˈʃɜːpə $ ˈʃɜːr-/ *n* [C] a Himalayan person who is often employed to guide people through mountains and carry their equipment

sher·ry /ˈʃeri/ *n* (*plural* **sherries**) [C,U] a pale or dark brown strong wine, originally from Spain

she's /ʃiz; *strong* ʃiːz/ **1** the short form of 'she is': *She's not feeling well.* **2** the short form of 'she has': *She's got a new bike.*

Shet·land po·ny /ʃetlənd ˈpəʊni $ -ˈpoʊni/ *n* [C] a small strong horse with long rough hair

shew /ʃəʊ $ ʃoʊ/ *v* [I,T] an old spelling of SHOW

shh /ʃ/ *interjection* used to tell people to be quiet: *Shh! I can't hear what he's saying.*

Shi·a, **Shiah** /ˈʃiːə/ *n* **1 the Shia** the Shiite branch of the Muslim religion **2** [C] a Shiite

shi·a·tsu /ʃiˈætsuː $ ʃiˈɑː-/ *n* [U] a Japanese form of MASSAGE (=pressing and rubbing someone's body)

shib·bo·leth /ˈʃɪbəleθ $ -ləθ/ *n* [C] *formal* an old idea, custom, or principle that you think is no longer important or suitable for modern times

shield¹ /ʃiːld/ ●●○ *n* [C]
1 a) a large piece of metal or leather that soldiers used in the past to protect themselves when fighting **b)** a piece of equipment made of strong plastic, used by the police to protect themselves against angry crowds SYN **riot shield** → HUMAN SHIELD
2 a) something in the shape of a shield, wide at the top and curving to a point at the bottom, that is given as a prize for winning a competition, especially a sports competition **b)** a drawing or model of a shield, wide at the top and curving to a point at the bottom, that is used as a COAT OF ARMS
3 something that protects a person or thing from harm or damage: **[+against]** *The immune system is our body's shield against infection.*
4 *AmE* the small piece of metal that a police officer wears to show that they are a police officer SYN **badge**

shield² ●●○ *v* [T] to protect someone or something from being harmed or damaged: *Women will often lie to shield even the most abusive partner.* | **shield sb/sth from sb/sth** *He held up his hands, shielding his eyes from the sun.* | *import tariffs that shield firms from foreign competition* THESAURUS▶ PROTECT

> **REGISTER**
> **Shield** is used mostly in journalism or literature. In everyday English, people usually say **protect**: *He used his hands to* ***protect*** *his eyes from the sun.*

shift¹ /ʃɪft/ ●●○ S3 W3 AWL *v*
1 MOVE **a)** [I,T] to move from one place or position to another, or make something do this: *Joe listened, shifting uncomfortably from one foot to another.* | *She shifted her gaze from me to Bobby.* **b)** [T] *BrE informal* to move something, especially by picking it up and carrying it: *Give me a hand to shift these chairs.*
2 CHANGE ATTENTION [T] to change a situation, discussion etc by giving special attention to one idea or subject instead of to a previous one: **shift sth away/onto/from etc** *The White House hopes to shift the media's attention away from foreign policy issues.* | **attention/emphasis/focus shifts** *In this stage of a rape case, the focus often shifts onto the victim and her conduct.* | **shift gear** *AmE* (=change what you are doing) *It's hard to shift gear when you come home after a busy day at work.*
3 CHANGE OPINION [I,T] if someone's opinions, beliefs etc shift, they change: *Public opinion was beginning to shift to the right* (=become more right-wing). | *shifting attitudes towards marriage* | *He refused to* ***shift*** *his* ***ground*** (=change his opinion).
4 shift the blame/responsibility (onto sb) to make someone else responsible for something, especially for something bad that has happened: *It was a clear attempt to shift the responsibility for the crime onto the victim.*
5 COSTS/SPENDING [T always + adv/prep] to change the way that money is paid or spent SYN **direct**: *the need to shift more resources towards reducing poverty*
6 DIRT/MARKS [T] *BrE* to remove dirt or marks from a surface or piece of clothing: *a new washing powder that will* ***shift*** *any* ***stain***
7 IN A CAR [I,T] *especially AmE* to change the GEARS when you are driving SYN **change** *BrE*: *I shifted into second gear.*
8 SELL [T] *BrE informal* to sell a product, especially a lot of it: *The store shifted over 1,000 copies of the book last week.*

shift² ●●○ AWL *n* [C]
1 a change in the way people think about something, in the way something is done etc: **[+from/to]** *the shift from one type of economic system to another* | **[+in]** *an important shift in policy* | *a* ***marked shift*** (=noticeable change) *in attitudes towards women*
2 a) if workers in a factory, hospital etc work shifts, they work for a particular period of time during the day or night, and are then replaced by others, so that there are always people working: **do/work a (10-/12-/24- etc hour) shift** *Dave had to work a 12-hour shift yesterday.* | *I work shifts.* | **night/day etc shift** *The thought of working night shifts put her off becoming a nurse.* | **early/late shift** *I'm on the early shift tomorrow.* | **shift work/worker/working** *people who do shift work* | *A* ***shift system*** *has been introduced.* **b)** the workers who work during one of these periods: **night/day/early/late shift** *before the early shift goes off duty*
3 a SHIFT KEY: *To run the spell-checker, press SHIFT and F7.*
4 (*also* **shift dress**) a simple straight loose-fitting woman's dress

ˈshift key *n* [C] the KEY¹(3) on a KEYBOARD²(3) that you press to make a capital letter

shift·less /ˈʃɪftləs/ *adj* lazy and having no interest in working hard or trying to succeed —**shiftlessness** *n* [U]

S

shift·y /ˈʃɪfti/ *adj informal* looking dishonest: *He* ***looks*** *a bit* ***shifty*** *to me.* | *shifty eyes* —**shiftily** *adv*

Shih Tzu /ʃiːˈtzuː $ -ˈdzuː/ *n* [C] another spelling of SHITZU

Shi·ite /ˈʃiː-aɪt/ *n* [C] a member of one of the two main groups in the Muslim religion —**Shiite** *adj* [usually before noun] → SUNNI

shil·ling /ˈʃɪlɪŋ/ *n* [C] **1** an old British coin or unit of money. There were 20 shillings in one pound. **2** the standard unit of money in Kenya, Uganda, Tanzania, and Somalia

shil·ly-shal·ly /ˈʃɪli ˌʃæli/ *v* (**shilly-shallied, shilly-shallying, shilly-shallies**) [I] *informal* to waste time or take too long to make a decision SYN **dither**

shim·mer /ˈʃɪmə $ -ər/ *v* [I] to shine with a soft light that looks as if it shakes slightly: *The lake shimmered in the moonlight.* —**shimmer** *n* [singular, U]

shim·my /ˈʃɪmi/ *v* (**shimmied, shimmying, shimmies**) [I] to move forwards or backwards while also quickly moving slightly from side to side

shin[1] /ʃɪn/ *n* [C] the front part of your leg between your knee and your foot

shin[2] *v* (**shinned, shinning**) [I] *BrE* **shin up/down** to climb quickly up or down a tree, pole etc by using your hands and legs SYN **shinny** *AmE*: *He shinned up a tree.*

shin·bone /ˈʃɪnbəʊn $ -boʊn/ *n* [C] the front bone in your leg below your knee SYN **tibia**

shin·dig /ˈʃɪndɪg/ *n* [C] a noisy party - used especially in news reports

shine[1] /ʃaɪn/ ●●● S3 *v* (*past tense and past participle* **shone** /ʃɒn $ ʃoʊn/)
1 [I] to produce bright light: *The* ***sun*** *was* ***shining***. | *The* ***moon shone*** *brightly in the sky.* | **[+in/on]** *That lamp's shining in my eyes.*
2 [T] if you shine a light somewhere, you point it in that direction: **shine sth on/at/around etc sth** *Shine that torch over here, will you?*
3 [I] to look bright and smooth: *Marion polished the table until it shone.* | *She had* ***shining*** *black* ***hair***.
4 [T] (*past tense and past participle* **shined**) to make something bright by rubbing it SYN **polish**: *His shoes were shined to perfection.*
5 [I] if your eyes shine, or your face shines, you have an expression of happiness: **[+with]** *'It was wonderful!' Kate replied, her eyes shining with excitement.*
6 [I not in progressive] to be very good at something: *The concert will give young jazz musicians a chance to shine.* | **[+at/in]** *Peter didn't really shine at school.*
7 shining example something or someone that is an excellent example of a particular quality and should be admired: **[+of]** *The house is a shining example of Art Deco architecture.*

THESAURUS

TO PRODUCE LIGHT

shine to produce bright light: *The sun was shining.*
flash to shine brightly for a very short time, or to shine on and off very quickly many times: *Lightning flashed across the sky.* | *The police car's lights were flashing.*
glare to shine with a very strong light which hurts your eyes: *The sun glared in her eyes.*
flicker to shine with an unsteady light - used about a flame or light: *The candle flickered and went out.*
twinkle if stars or lights twinkle, they shine in the dark in a way that seems to change from bright to faint, especially because you are a long way away from them: *stars twinkling in the sky* | *The harbour lights twinkled in the distance.*
glow *especially literary* to shine with a warm soft light: *Lights glowed in the windows.*
blaze *literary* to shine very brightly: *The lights of the factory were still blazing.*

TO SHINE BY REFLECTING LIGHT

sparkle/glitter if something sparkles, it shines with many small bright points when light is on it: *The sea sparkled in the sunlight.* | *Jewels glittered around her neck.*
gleam to shine by reflecting the light - used especially about smooth clean surfaces, or about someone's eyes or teeth: *The sword's blade gleamed.* | *a gleaming sports car* | *His blue eyes gleamed with amusement.*
glint to shine with quick flashes of light: *The knife glinted in the sunlight.*
glisten *literary* to shine - used about wet or oily surfaces. Used especially when saying that someone's eyes are full of tears, or someone's skin is covered in sweat: *As they were leaving, her eyes glistened with tears.* | *His forehead was glistening with sweat.* | *The wet chairs glistened in the afternoon sun.*
catch the light if something catches the light, it shines because it is reflecting light: *Her diamond ring caught the light.*

shine through *phr v* if a quality that someone has shines through, you can easily see that they have it: *What shines through in all her work is her enthusiasm for life.*

shine[2] *n* **1** [singular, U] the brightness that something has when light shines on it: *Lucy's dark hair seemed to have lost its shine.* **2 take a shine to sb** *informal* to like someone very much when you have only just met them → **(come) rain or shine** at RAIN[1](4)

shin·gle /ˈʃɪŋgəl/ *n* **1** [C,U] one of many small thin pieces of wood or another building material, fastened in rows to cover a roof or wall **2** [U] small round pieces of stone on a beach: *the crash of waves on the shingle* | *a* ***shingle beach*** **3 hang out your shingle** *AmE informal* to start your own business, especially as a doctor or lawyer

shin·gled /ˈʃɪŋgəld/ *adj* a roof or wall that is shingled is covered with shingles

shin·gles /ˈʃɪŋgəlz/ *n* [U] a disease caused by an infection of the nerve endings, which produces painful red spots

GRAMMAR: Singular or plural verb?

Shingles is followed by a singular verb: ***Shingles is*** *caused by the same virus as chickenpox.*
GRAMMAR GUIDE ▶ NOUNS

shin·ny /ˈʃɪni/ *v* (**shinnied, shinnying, shinnies**) [I] *AmE* **shinny up/down** to climb quickly up or down a tree, pole etc by using your hands and legs SYN **shin** *BrE*

Shin·to /ˈʃɪntəʊ $ -toʊ/ (*also* **Shin·to·is·m** /ˈʃɪntəʊɪzəm $ -toʊ-/) *n* [U] the ancient traditional religion of Japan

shin·y /ˈʃaɪni/ ●●○ *adj* smooth and bright: *shiny black shoes* | *a shiny polished table* | *Her hair was thick and shiny.* —**shininess** *n* [U]

ship[1] /ʃɪp/ ●●● S2 W2 *n* [C]
1 a large boat used for carrying people or goods across the sea: *the ship's captain* | *a luxury cruise ship* | **by ship** *supplies that came by ship*
2 a large spacecraft → **jump ship** at JUMP[1](16), → **run a tight ship** at TIGHT[1](5)

ship[2] ●○○ *v* (**shipped, shipping**)
1 [T] to send goods somewhere by ship, plane, truck etc: **ship sth out/to/over etc** *A new engine was shipped over from the US.* THESAURUS ▶ TAKE
2 [I,T] *technical* to make a piece of computer equipment or software available for people to buy: *They're now shipping their long-awaited new anti-virus software.* | *Both products are due to ship at the beginning of June.*
3 [T] to order someone to go somewhere: **ship sb off/out etc** *He was shipped off to a juvenile detention center.*
→ SHIPPING, → **shape up or ship out** at SHAPE UP

-ship /ʃɪp/ *suffix* [in nouns] **1** a particular position or job, or the time during which you have it: *He was offered a professorship* (=the job of professor). | *in Mr Major's premiership* (=when he was prime minister) | *her application for British citizenship* **2** the state of having something: *Private car ownership has almost doubled in the past ten years.* | *Their friendship developed soon afterwards.* **3** a particular art or skill: *his superb musicianship* | *a work of great scholarship* → -MANSHIP **4** all the people in a particular group: *a magazine with a readership of 9,000* (=with 9,000 readers)

ship·board /ˈʃɪpbɔːd $ -bɔːrd/ *adj* [only before noun] happening on a ship: *a shipboard romance*

ship·build·er /ˈʃɪpˌbɪldə $ -ər/ *n* [C] a company that makes ships

ship·build·ing /ˈʃɪpˌbɪldɪŋ/ *n* [U] the industry of making ships: *a shipbuilding yard*

ship·load /ˈʃɪpləʊd $ -loʊd/ *n* [C] the amount of goods or people a ship can carry: **[+of]** *Several shiploads of grain arrived in the harbor that day.*

ship·mate /ˈʃɪpmeɪt/ *n* [C] a SAILOR's shipmate is another sailor who is working on the same ship

ship·ment /ˈʃɪpmənt/ ●○○ *n* [C,U] a load of goods sent by sea, road, or air, or the act of sending them: **[+of]** *a shipment of grain* | **arms/oil/drug etc shipment** *an illegal arms shipment* | *The goods are ready for shipment.*

ship·own·er /ˈʃɪpəʊnə $ -oʊnər/ *n* [C] someone who owns one or more ships

ship·per /ˈʃɪpə $ -ər/ *n* [C] a company that sends goods to places by ship

ship·ping /ˈʃɪpɪŋ/ *n* [U] **1** ships considered as a group: *The port is closed to all shipping.* **2** the delivery of goods, especially by ship: **shipping company/industry/agent etc** *a Danish shipping company* | *a shipping route* **3** *AmE* the amount of money you pay a company to deliver goods to you: *The jewelry can be yours for $15 plus **shipping and handling**.*

ˈshipping ˌforecast *n* [C] *BrE* a radio broadcast that says what the weather will be like at sea

ˈshipping ˌlane *n* [C] an officially approved path of travel that ships must follow

ˌship's ˈchandler *n* [C] someone who sells equipment for ships

ship·shape /ˈʃɪpʃeɪp/ *adj* [not before noun] neat and clean: *Let's get this house shipshape.* | **shipshape and Bristol fashion** *BrE* (=shipshape)

ˌship-to-ˈshore *adj* [only before noun] providing communication between a ship and people on land: *ship-to-shore radio*

ship·wreck[1] /ˈʃɪp-rek/ *n* **1** [C,U] the destruction of a ship in an accident: *survivors of the shipwreck* | *narrowly escaping shipwreck* **2** [C] a ship that has been destroyed in an accident SYN **wreck**

shipwreck[2] *v* **be shipwrecked** if someone is shipwrecked, they are in a boat or ship when it is destroyed in an accident: *Beatty was shipwrecked off the coast of Africa.*

ship·wright /ˈʃɪp-raɪt/ *n* [C] someone who builds or repairs ships

ship·yard /ˈʃɪp-jɑːd $ -jɑːrd/ *n* [C] a place where ships are built or repaired

shire /ʃaɪə $ ʃaɪr/ *n* [C] **1 the shires** (*also* **the shire counties**) COUNTIES in England that mostly consist of country areas **2** *BrE old use* a COUNTY

ˈshire horse *n* [C] a type of large powerful horse used for pulling large loads

shirk /ʃɜːk $ ʃɜːrk/ *v* [I,T] to deliberately avoid doing something you should do, because you are lazy: *He was fired for shirking.* | **shirk your responsibilities/duties/obligations** *parents who shirk their responsibilities towards their children* —**shirker** *n* [C]

shirt /ʃɜːt $ ʃɜːrt/ ●●● S2 W3 *n* [C]
1 a piece of clothing that covers the upper part of your body and your arms, usually has a collar, and is fastened at the front by buttons → **blouse**: *I have to wear **a shirt and tie** to work.* | *a check shirt*
2 keep your shirt on *spoken* used to tell someone who is becoming angry that they should stay calm
3 put/bet/stake your shirt on sth *BrE informal* to risk all your money on something → STUFFED SHIRT

shirt·front /ˈʃɜːtfrʌnt $ ˈʃɜːrt-/ *n* [C] the part of a shirt that covers your chest

ˈshirt-ˌlifter *n* [C] *taboo informal* a very offensive word for a man who is HOMOSEXUAL. Do not use this word.

shirt·sleeve /ˈʃɜːtsliːv $ ˈʃɜːrt-/ *n* **1 in (your) shirtsleeves** wearing a shirt but no JACKET **2** [C usually plural] the part of a shirt that covers your arm

ˈshirt tail *n* [C] the part of a shirt that is below your waist and is usually inside your trousers

shirt·y /ˈʃɜːti $ ˈʃɜːr-/ *adj BrE informal* bad-tempered, angry, and rude: *No need to **get shirty**!*

shish ke·bab /ˈʃɪʃ kəˌbæb $ -ˌbɑːb/ *n* [C] small pieces of meat that are put on a long thin stick and cooked

shit[1] /ʃɪt/ *interjection not polite* used to express anger, annoyance, fear, or disappointment SYN **damn**: *Shit! I've left my purse at home.*

shit[2] *n spoken not polite*
1 BODY WASTE **a)** [U] solid waste that comes out of your body from your BOWELS: *a car covered in bird shit* **b)** [singular] an act of getting rid of solid waste from your BOWELS: **take a shit** (*also* **have a shit** *BrE*)
2 STH BAD [U] something that you think is bad or of very bad quality, or a bad situation: *I'm not eating that shit!* | **piece/pile/load etc of shit**
3 STUPID/UNTRUE TALK [U] something that someone says that you think is stupid or untrue SYN **nonsense**: *You expect me to believe that shit?* | *You're **full of shit*** (=the things you say are stupid or untrue).
4 not give a shit (what/whether/about etc) to not care at all about something or someone SYN **not give a damn**: *I don't give a shit what you think!*
5 have/get the shits to have or get DIARRHOEA (=an illness in which solid waste comes out of your body in a much more liquid form than usual)
6 take/put up with shit (from sb) to allow someone to behave badly or treat you badly
7 PERSON [C] an insulting word for someone who is very unpleasant and treats other people badly. Do not use this word.
8 feel/look like shit to feel or look very ill, or to not look as neat and clean as you should
9 treat sb like shit to treat someone very badly
10 SB'S POSSESSIONS [U] *AmE* someone's possessions, especially the things they have with them: *Get your shit together, then come on over.*
11 shit happens used to say that sometimes bad things happen, and people cannot always prevent them from happening
12 ... and shit used to say that there are more details that you could mention, but it should be clear to someone else what you mean: *You said you had maps and shit.*
13 no shit *AmE* **a)** used to express surprise or to check whether what someone has just said is true: *'I can get you one for $50.' 'No shit?'* **b)** used to emphasize that what you are saying is true, or to agree that what someone else says is true: *They had like, no shit, 40 different kinds of beer.*
14 in deep shit (*also* **in the shit** *BrE*) in a lot of trouble SYN **in big trouble**
15 beat/kick etc the shit out of sb to beat, kick etc someone so violently that they are badly injured
16 give sb shit to insult someone or criticize them
17 the shit hits the fan used to say that there will be a lot of trouble when someone finds out about something → **be hot shit** at HOT[1](4), → **tough shit!** at TOUGH[1](8)

shit³ *v* (*past tense and past participle* **shit** *or* **shat** /ʃæt/, *present participle* **shitting**) *spoken not polite* **1 shit yourself** *BrE*, **shit (in) your pants** *AmE* to feel very worried or frightened **2** [I] to pass solid waste out of your body from your BOWELS **3** [T] *AmE* to tell someone something that is untrue: *Are you shitting me?* **4** [I] to treat someone very badly: **[+on]** *This will teach you not to shit on me.*

shit⁴ *adj BrE spoken not polite* very bad: *a really shit job* | **[+at]** *I'm shit at tennis.* → **up shit creek** at CREEK(3)

shite /ʃaɪt/ *interjection, n, adj BrE spoken not polite* another word for SHIT

shit·faced /ˈʃɪtfeɪst/ *adj BrE spoken informal not polite* very drunk

shit·head /ˈʃɪthed/ *n* [C] *taboo spoken* someone who you think is very stupid or who you are very angry with. Do not use this word.

shit·hole /ˈʃɪthəʊl $ -hoʊl/ *n* [C] *spoken not polite* a place that is very dirty and unpleasant

ˌshit-ˈhot *adj spoken not polite* extremely good

shit·less /ˈʃɪtləs/ *adj spoken not polite* **scare sb shitless** to make someone feel very frightened

ˌshit-ˈscared *adj* [not before noun] *BrE spoken not polite* very frightened

ˈshit-ˌstirrer *n* [C] *spoken not polite* someone who tries to cause or increase unfriendly feelings or arguments between people —**shit-stirring** *n* [U]

shit·ty /ˈʃɪti/ *adj spoken not polite* very bad, unpleasant, or nasty: *a shitty job*

shi·tzu, **Shih Tzu** /ʃiːˈtsuː $ -ˈdzuː/ *n* [C] a type of small dog with short legs, curly hair, long ears, and hair around its mouth that looks like a beard

S

shiv·er¹ /ˈʃɪvə $ -ər/ ●●○ *v* [I] to shake slightly because you are cold or frightened SYN **tremble**: *Jake stood shivering in the cold air.* | **shiver with cold/fear/delight etc** *She shivered with fear and anger.*

shiver² *n* [C] **1** a slight shaking movement of your body caused by cold or fear SYN **tremble**: *A* ***shiver ran through*** (=went through) *me.* | **[+of]** *She* ***felt*** *a* ***shiver*** *of apprehension.* **2 give you the shivers** *informal* to make you feel afraid → **send shivers/chills up (and down) your spine** at SEND(10)

shiv·er·y /ˈʃɪvəri/ *adj* [not before noun] trembling or shaking because of cold, fear, or illness: *He felt shivery and nauseous.* THESAURUS ▸ COLD

shoal /ʃəʊl $ ʃoʊl/ *n* [C] **1** a large group of fish swimming together SYN **school**: **[+of]** *a shoal of fish* THESAURUS ▸ GROUP **2** a small hill of sand just below the surface of water that makes it dangerous for boats

shock¹ /ʃɒk $ ʃɑːk/ ●●● S2 W2 *n*

1 UNEXPECTED EVENT/SITUATION [C usually singular] if something that happens is a shock, you did not expect it, and it makes you feel very surprised, and usually upset: **[+to]** *The news of his death came as a great shock to everyone.* | **it was a shock to find/discover etc that** *It was a real shock to hear that the factory would have to close.*

2 UNEXPECTED UNPLEASANT FEELING [singular, U] the feeling of surprise and disbelief you have when something very unexpected happens, especially something bad or frightening: *She was shaking with shock and humiliation.* | **the shock of (doing) sth** *Mom's never really gotten over the shock of Dad's death.*

3 MEDICAL [U] a medical condition in which someone looks pale and their heart and lungs are not working correctly, usually after a sudden very unpleasant experience: *He was bleeding from the head and* ***suffering from shock****.* | *He is clearly* ***in a state of shock****.* | *The tanker driver was* ***treated for shock*** *and released.*

4 ELECTRICITY [C] an ELECTRIC SHOCK

5 VEHICLE [C usually plural] a SHOCK ABSORBER

6 shock of hair a very thick mass of hair: *an energetic young man with a shock of red hair*

7 SUDDEN CHANGE [C] a sudden unexpected change which threatens the economic situation, way of life, or traditions of a group of people – used especially in news reports: *the oil shocks of the 1970s*

8 SHAKING [C,U] violent shaking caused for example by an explosion or EARTHQUAKE: *The shock was felt miles away.*

→ **SHOCK WAVE, CULTURE SHOCK, SHOCKED, SHELL SHOCK, TOXIC SHOCK SYNDROME**

COLLOCATIONS – MEANINGS 1 & 2

ADJECTIVES

a big/great shock *It was a great shock to find out he had been lying.*
a terrible/awful shock *Her death was a terrible shock to everyone.*
a complete/total shock *No one expected the factory to close – it was a complete shock.*
a nasty shock *especially BrE* (=one that is very unpleasant and upsetting)

VERBS

get/have a shock *I got a shock when I saw how thin he had become.*
give sb a shock *Oh, you gave me quite a shock.*
get over/recover from a shock *He hasn't got over the shock of losing his job yet.*

PHRASES

come as a shock (=be very unexpected) *The collapse of the company came as a shock to us all.*
be a bit of a shock *BrE especially spoken* (=be a shock, but not very serious or unpleasant) *I wasn't expecting to win, so it was a bit of a shock.*
be a shock to the system (=be strange because you are not used to something) *Having to work full-time again was quite a shock to the system.*
be in for a shock (=be likely to have a shock) *Anyone who thinks that bringing up children is easy is in for a shock.*
be in a state of shock (*also* **be in deep shock**) (=be very shocked and upset) | **get the shock of your life** (=get a very big shock)

shock² ●●● S2 *v*

1 [T] to make someone feel very surprised and upset, and unable to believe what has happened: *The hatred in her voice shocked him.* | **shock sb to hear/learn/discover etc that** *They had been shocked to hear that the hospital was closing down.* | **it shocks sb that/how/to do** *It shocked me to think how close we had come to being killed.* | **shock sb into (doing) sth** *She was* ***shocked into action*** *by the desperate situation in the orphanages.*

2 [I,T] to make someone feel very offended, by talking or behaving in an immoral or socially unacceptable way: *He seems to enjoy shocking people.* | *Just ignore the bad language – they only do it to shock.* → **SHOCKED, SHOCKING**

shock³ *adj* [only before noun] **1** very surprising – used especially in news reports: *England's shock defeat by Luxembourg* **2 shock tactics** methods of achieving what you want by deliberately shocking people: *Shock tactics are being used to stop drink drivers.*

ˈshock abˌsorber *n* [C] a piece of equipment connected to each wheel of a vehicle to make travelling on uneven ground more comfortable

ˌshock and ˈawe *n* [U] the very quick use of a very large amount of force by the military, in order to make the enemy no longer want to fight

shocked /ʃɒkt $ ʃɑːkt/ ●●● S3 *adj*

1 feeling surprised and upset by something very unexpected and unpleasant: **[+by]** *I was* ***deeply shocked*** *by Jo's death.* | **[+at]** *He is shocked at what happened to his son.* | **shocked look/expression/voice etc** *She gave him a shocked look.* | *For a few minutes she stood in* ***shocked silence****.* | *We were too shocked to talk.*

2 very offended because something seems immoral or socially unacceptable: **[+by]** *Many people were shocked by* the film when it first came out. | **[+at]** *They were* ***deeply shocked*** *at her behaviour.*

THESAURUS

shocked feeling surprised and upset by something very unexpected and unpleasant: *I was shocked when I heard what had happened.* | *We are all deeply shocked by his death.* | *They seemed shocked at the suggestion.*
shaken shocked because something very unpleasant or frightening has happened – used when the experience has made you feel weak or nervous: *He was badly shaken by the incident.* | *She looked shaken by the news.*
be in a state of shock to feel shocked and unable to do normal things: *He was uninjured but in a state of shock after the attack.*
horrified very shocked because something unpleasant or frightening has happened: *She was horrified to discover that her son had been taking drugs.* | *There was a horrified look on his face.*
appalled very shocked because you think something is very bad: *I was appalled by his behaviour.* | *Emma was appalled at how he'd treated his mother.*
traumatized so badly shocked that you are affected for a very long time: *The children were severely traumatized by years of civil war.*
outraged extremely shocked and angry: *The victim's family were outraged at the short jail sentence.*
devastated extremely shocked and sad – used when someone is extremely badly affected by something: *Petra was absolutely devastated by the death of her daughter.*
stunned so shocked that you are unable to do or say anything immediately: *He had been stunned by the news of his friend's sudden death.*
dazed very shocked and unable to think clearly: *He emerged from the wreck of the car, dazed but unhurt.*
aghast /əˈɡɑːst $ əˈɡæst/ [not before noun] *written* shocked: *She looked aghast at the suggestion.*

shock·er /ˈʃɒkə $ ˈʃɑːkər/ *n* [C] *informal* a film, news story, action etc that shocks you – used especially in news reports: *TV star in drugs shocker!*

shock·ing /ˈʃɒkɪŋ $ ˈʃɑːk-/ ●●● S3 *adj*
1 very surprising, upsetting, and difficult to believe: *the* ***shocking news*** *that Mark had hanged himself* | *a shocking discovery* | *The anger in his face was shocking.*
2 morally wrong: ***It's shocking that*** *hospitals can deny help to older people.* | *a* ***shocking waste*** *of money*
3 *BrE informal* very bad SYN **terrible**: *The path was in a shocking state.* | *I've got a shocking cold.* —**shockingly** *adv* → SHOCK²

ˌshocking ˈpink *n* [U] a very bright pink colour —**shocking pink** *adj*

ˈshock jock *n* [C] *especially AmE* someone on a radio show who plays music and talks about subjects that offend many people

shock·proof /ˈʃɒkpruːf $ ˈʃɑːk-/ *adj* a watch, machine etc that is shockproof is designed so that it is not easily damaged if it is dropped or hit

ˈshock ˌtreatment (*also* **ˈshock ˌtherapy**) *n* [U] **1** treatment of mental illness using powerful electric shocks **2** the use of extreme methods to change a system or solve a problem as quickly as possible – used especially in news reports: *the government's shock therapy economic programme*

ˈshock troops *n* [plural] soldiers who are specially trained to make sudden quick attacks

ˈshock wave *n* **1** [C,U] a very strong wave of air pressure or heat from an explosion, EARTHQUAKE etc: *The shock wave from the blast blew out 22 windows in the courthouse.* **2 shock waves** strong feelings of shock that people feel when something bad happens unexpectedly – used especially in news reports: *The child's murder* ***sent shock waves through*** *the neighborhood.* | *the shock waves caused by his resignation*

shod /ʃɒd $ ʃɑːd/ *adj especially literary* wearing shoes of the type mentioned: **well/elegantly/badly etc shod** *The children were well shod and happy.* | **[+in]** *His large feet were shod in trainers.* → SHOE²

shod·dy /ˈʃɒdi $ ˈʃɑːdi/ *adj* **1** made or done cheaply or carelessly: **shoddy goods/service/workmanship etc** *We're not paying good money for shoddy goods.* **2** unfair and dishonest: *shoddy journalism* —**shoddily** *adv* —**shoddiness** *n* [U]

shoe¹ /ʃuː/ ●●● S1 W3 *n* [C]
1 something that you wear to cover your feet, made of leather or some other strong material: *I sat down and took off my shoes and socks.* | *What size shoe do you take?* → BOOT¹(1), SANDAL, SLIPPER
2 in sb's shoes in someone else's situation, especially a bad one: *I wouldn't like to* ***be in*** *his* ***shoes*** *when his wife finds out what happened.* | *Anyone in her shoes would have done the same thing.* | *Don't be cross with them. Try to* ***put yourself in*** *their* ***shoes*** (=imagine what it would feel like to be in their situation).
3 step into/fill sb's shoes to do a job that someone else used to do, and do it as well as they did: *It'll be hard to find someone to fill Pete's shoes.*

SHOES

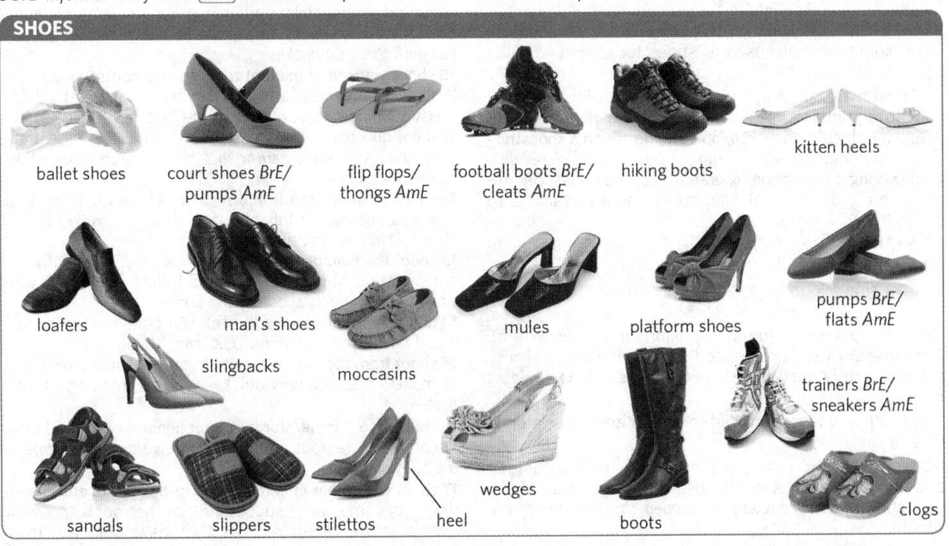

S

4 a curved piece of iron that is nailed onto a horse's foot SYN **horseshoe** → **if the shoe fits, (wear it)** at FIT¹(8)

COLLOCATIONS

VERBS

wear shoes *He was wearing smart black shoes.*
put your shoes on *Put your shoes on and get your coat.*
take your shoes off *They took off their shoes in the hallway.*
tie your shoes *He tied his shoes in a double knot.*
slip your shoes on/off (=put them on or take them off quickly or gently) | **kick your shoes off** (=take them off by moving your legs) | **clean/polish your shoes**

ADJECTIVES/NOUN + shoe

black/brown etc *Her shoes and handbag were brown.*
high-heeled shoes *You can't walk round town all day in high-heeled shoes!*
sensible shoes (=flat shoes that are not very fashionable) | **flat shoes** (=with no high heel) | **platform shoes** (=with a thick base) | **lace-up shoes** (=fastened with laces) | **leather/suede shoes** | **running/jogging/training etc shoes**

PHRASES

a pair of shoes *I need a new pair of shoes.*

shoe + NOUN

a shoe shop *BrE*, **a shoe store** *AmE* | **shoe polish** | **shoe laces**

COMMON ERRORS

⚠ Don't say 'put off your shoes'. Say **take off your shoes**.

S

shoe² *v* (*past tense and past participle* **shod** /ʃɒd $ ʃɑːd/, *present participle* **shoeing**) [T] to put a HORSESHOE on a horse: *We took the horses to be shod.* → SHOD

shoe·box /ˈʃuːbɒks $ -bɑːks/ *n* [C] **1** a CARDBOARD box that shoes are sold in **2** *BrE informal* a very small room, house etc: *I was living in a shoebox in Clapham.*

shoe·horn, **shoe-horn** /ˈʃuːhɔːn $ -hɔːrn/ *n* [C] a curved piece of metal or plastic that you put inside the back of a shoe when you put it on, to help your heel go in easily → see picture at SHOE¹

shoe·lace /ˈʃuːleɪs/ *n* [C] a thin piece of material, like string, that goes through holes in the front of your shoes and is used to fasten them SYN **lace**: **tie/untie a shoelace** *Roger bent to tie his shoelace.* | *Your shoelaces are undone.*

shoe·mak·er /ˈʃuːmeɪkə $ -ər/ *n* [C] someone who makes shoes and boots

shoe·shine /ˈʃuːʃaɪn/ *n* [C usually singular] an occasion when someone polishes your shoes for money: *a shoe-shine stand*

shoe·string /ˈʃuːˌstrɪŋ/ *n* [C] **1 on a shoestring** *informal* if you do something on a shoestring, you do it without spending much money: **run/operate/do sth on a shoestring** *The program was run on a shoestring.* **2 shoestring organization/operation etc** a business, organization etc that does not have much money available to spend **3** *AmE* a SHOELACE

sho·gun /ˈʃəʊgʌn $ ˈʃoʊ-/ *n* [C] a military leader in Japan until the middle of the 19th century

shone /ʃɒn $ ʃoʊn/ the past tense and past participle of SHINE

shon·ky /ˈʃɒŋki $ ˈʃɑːŋ-/ *adj informal especially AusE* **1** of poor quality: *Don't waste your money on this shonky product!* **2** dishonest: *I think there's some shonky business going on.*

shoo¹ /ʃuː/ *interjection* used to tell an animal or a child to go away

shoo² *v* [T always + adv/prep] *informal* to make an animal or a child go away, especially because they are annoying you: **shoo sb away/out etc** *He shooed the kids out of the kitchen.*

ˈshoo-in *n* [C] *especially AmE informal* someone who is expected to easily win a race, election etc: **[+for]** *He was far from a shoo-in for president.* | **shoo-in to do sth** *He looked like a shoo-in to win the Democratic nomination.*

shook /ʃʊk/ *v* the past tense of SHAKE

shoot¹ /ʃuːt/ ●●● S2 W2 *v* (*past tense and past participle* **shot** /ʃɒt $ ʃɑːt/)

1 KILL/INJURE [T] to deliberately kill or injure someone using a gun: *Police shot one suspect when he pulled a gun on them.* | *Smith killed his wife, and then shot himself.* | *A woman was* **shot dead** *in an attempted robbery.* | **shoot sb in the leg/head etc** *He had been shot in the back while trying to escape.* | *The guards have orders to* **shoot** *intruders* **on sight** (=shoot them as soon as they see them).

2 FIRE A GUN ETC [I,T] to make a bullet or ARROW come from a weapon: *Don't shoot! I'm coming out with my hands up.* | **[+at]** *Two guys walked in and started shooting at people.* | *The soldiers had orders to* **shoot to kill** (=shoot at someone with the intention of killing them). | **shoot bullets/arrows** *They shot arrows from behind the thick bushes.* | **shoot a gun/rifle etc** *Tod's grandfather taught him to shoot a rifle.*

3 BIRDS/ANIMALS [I,T] to shoot and kill animals or birds as a sport: *They spent the weekend in Scotland shooting grouse.*

4 MOVE QUICKLY [I,T always + adv/prep] to move quickly in a particular direction, or to make something move in this way: *She shot past me into the house.* | *The cat shot across the garden.* | *'Where does cotton come from?' Ron's hand shot up. 'America, Miss!'* | *The fountain shoots water 20 feet into the air.*

5 TRY TO SCORE [I,T] to kick or throw a ball in a sport such as football or BASKETBALL towards the place where you can get a point: *Giggs shot from the halfway line.* → see picture at FOOTBALL

6 LOOK AT SB **shoot sb a look/glance** (*also* **shoot a glance at sb**) to look at someone quickly, especially so that other people do not see, to show them how you feel: **shoot sb a quick/sharp/warning etc look/glance** *'You're welcome to stay as long as you like.' Michelle shot him a furious glance.* | *Jack shot an anxious look at his mother.*

7 PHOTOGRAPH/FILM [I,T] to take photographs or make a film of something SYN **film**: *The movie was shot in New Zealand.*

8 PAIN [I always + adv/prep] if pain shoots through your body, you feel it going quickly through it: **[+through/along]** *A sharp pain suddenly shot along his arm.* | **shooting pains** (=continuous short pains passing through your body)

9 shoot it out (with sb) if people shoot it out, they fight using guns, especially until one person or group is killed or defeated by the other: *a scene in which the cops shoot it out with the drug dealers*

10 shoot yourself in the foot to say or do something stupid that will cause you a lot of trouble: *If he keeps talking, pretty soon he'll shoot himself in the foot.*

11 shoot questions at sb to ask someone a lot of questions very quickly: *The prosecutor shot a series of rapid questions at Hendrickson.*

12 shoot your mouth off *informal* to talk about something that you should not talk about or that you know nothing about: *Don't go shooting your mouth off.*

13 shoot the bull/breeze *AmE informal* to have an informal conversation about unimportant things: *Cal and I were sitting on the porch, shooting the breeze.*

14 shoot *AmE spoken* used to tell someone to start speaking: *'I have a few questions.' 'OK, shoot.'*

15 shoot from the hip to say what you think in a direct way, or make a decision very quickly, without thinking about it first

16 shoot to fame/stardom/prominence to suddenly become very famous: *Brian, an air steward, shot to fame on the television show 'Big Brother'.*

17 shoot to number one/to the top of the charts etc to suddenly become very successful in the popular music CHARTS (=the list of records that have sold the most

copies that week): *Westlife's new album shot straight to the top of the charts.*
18 shoot hoops/baskets *informal* to practise throwing BASKETBALLS into the basket
19 shoot the rapids to sail a small boat along a river that is moving very fast over rocks, as a sport: *He was shooting the rapids when his canoe capsized.*
20 shoot pool *informal* to play the game of POOL
21 shoot craps *AmE informal* to play the game of CRAPS
22 PLANTS [I] if a plant shoots, a new part of it starts to grow, especially a new stem and leaves
23 LOCK ON A DOOR [T] to move the BOLT on a door so that it is in the locked or unlocked position
24 have shot your bolt *BrE*, **have shot your wad** *AmE informal* to have used all of your money, power, energy etc
25 shoot your load *informal* to EJACULATE → **blame/shoot the messenger** at MESSENGER[1](2)

THESAURUS

shoot *v* [I,T] to use a gun to fire bullets, or to kill or injure someone using a gun: *He ordered his men to stop shooting.* | *The guards shot the man as he was trying to escape.* | *President Kennedy was shot by a lone gunman.*
fire *v* [I,T] to shoot bullets from a gun, or send an explosive object towards someone or something: *Soldiers fired into the crowd.* | *Helicopters fired rockets at several buildings.*
launch *v* [T] to send a large rocket or MISSILE into the air: *American warships launched cruise missiles.*
open fire to start shooting: *Nineteen students were injured after a gunman opened fire.* | *Troops opened fire on a group of unarmed demonstrators.*
shell *v* [T] to fire shells (=metal containers filled with an explosive substance) at enemy soldiers, cities etc in a war, using large guns: *Border towns have been shelled by enemy aircraft for the past two months.*
bombard *v* [T] to attack a place for a long time with shells or bombs: *Allied forces bombarded the coast prior to the invasion.* | *Troops bombarded the area with shells.*
take a potshot at sb/sth to shoot at someone or something without aiming very carefully: *Someone tried to take a potshot at him, but hit the man behind instead.*

shoot sb/sth ↔ **down** *phr v*
1 to make an enemy plane crash to the ground, by firing weapons at it: *His plane was shot down over France in 1944.*
2 to kill or seriously injure someone by shooting them, especially someone who cannot defend themselves: *The army were accused of shooting down unarmed demonstrators.*
3 *informal* to say or show that someone's ideas or opinions are wrong or stupid: *I tried to help, but all my suggestions were **shot down in flames**, as usual.*

shoot for/at sth *phr v especially AmE informal* to try to achieve a particular aim, especially one that is very difficult SYN **aim for**: *We are shooting for a 50% increase in sales in the next financial year.*

shoot off *phr v BrE informal* to leave somewhere quickly or suddenly: *Sorry, but I'll have to shoot off before the end of the meeting.*

shoot through *phr v AusE informal* to leave a place quickly, especially in order to avoid someone or something → **be shot through with sth** at SHOT[2](3)

shoot up *phr v*
1 to increase very quickly and suddenly SYN **rocket**: *Demand for water has shot up by 70% over the last 30 years.*
2 if a child shoots up, he or she grows taller very quickly and suddenly: *I can't believe this is Joshua – he's shot up since we last saw him!*
3 shoot sb/sth ↔ up to cause serious injury or damage to someone or something by shooting them with bullets: *Then two men came in and shot up the entire lobby.*
4 shoot up (sth) *informal* to put illegal drugs into your blood, using a needle SYN **inject**: *Kids as young as ten are shooting up heroin.*

shoot² *n* [C] **1** the part of a plant that comes up above the ground when it is just beginning to grow, or a new part that grows on an existing plant: *Tender **green shoots** will appear in February.* **2** an occasion when someone takes photographs or makes a film: *a **photo shoot** sponsored by Kodak* | **on a shoot** *She's out on a **video shoot**.* **3** an occasion when people shoot birds or animals for sport, or the area of land where they do this: **on a shoot** *The royal party was on a shoot when the incident occurred.* **4 green shoots (of recovery)** *BrE* the first sign that a situation is improving, especially an economic situation

shoot³ *interjection AmE informal* used to show that you are annoyed or disappointed about something: *Oh, shoot! I forgot to buy milk.*

ˈshoot-ˈem-up *n* [C] a simple computer game in which you try to kill as many enemies as possible

shoot·er /ˈʃuːtə $ -ər/ *n* [C] **1** someone who shoots a gun **2** *informal* a gun **3** *AmE* a BASKETBALL player who is good at throwing the ball through the basket → PEASHOOTER, SIX-SHOOTER, TROUBLESHOOTER

shoot·ing /ˈʃuːtɪŋ/ ●●○ *n*
1 [C] a situation in which someone is injured or killed by a gun: *His brother was killed in a shooting incident last year.* | *the accidental shooting of a child*
2 [U] the sport of shooting animals and birds with guns: *the grouse **shooting season*** | *The **shooting party** set off shortly before dawn.*
3 [U] the process of taking photographs or making a film: *We had two weeks of rehearsals before shooting began.*

ˈshooting ˌgallery *n* [C] **1** a place where people shoot guns at objects to win prizes **2** *AmE informal* an empty building in a city, where people buy illegal drugs and INJECT them

ˈshooting match *n* **the whole shooting match** *BrE spoken* everything, or an event that is the most complete of its kind: *We're having a big church wedding with bridesmaids, a pageboy – the whole shooting match.*

ˌshooting ˈstar *n* [C] a piece of rock or metal from space, that burns brightly as it falls towards the Earth SYN **meteor**

ˈshooting stick *n* [C] *BrE* a pointed stick with a top that opens out to form a seat

ˈshoot-out *n* [C] a fight using guns: *a shoot-out with police* → PENALTY SHOOT-OUT

Frequencies of the nouns **shop** and **store** in British and American English.

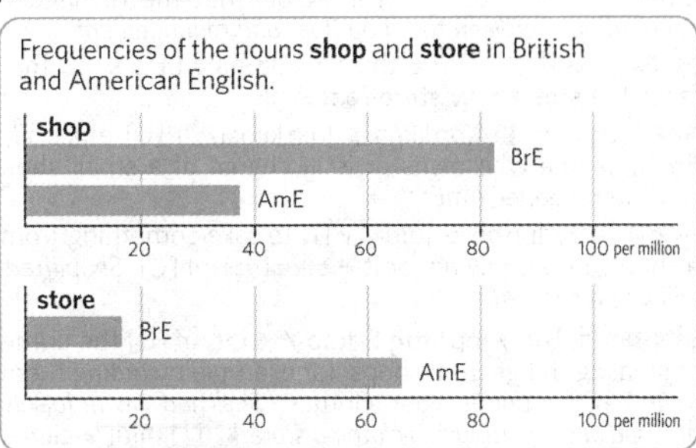

shop¹ /ʃɒp $ ʃɑːp/ ●●● S1 W1 *n*
1 PLACE WHERE YOU BUY THINGS [C] *especially BrE* a building or part of a building where you can buy things, food, or services SYN **store** *AmE*: **toy/pet/shoe/gift etc shop** *Her brother **runs** a record **shop** in Chester.* | *a barber's shop* | *a fish-and-chip shop* | *the local shops* | *Shirley saw her reflection in the shop window.* | **in the shops** *New potatoes are in the shops now.* | *I'm just **going** down **to the shops**.* | **wander/browse around the shops** *I spent a happy afternoon wandering around the shops.* → BUCKET SHOP, CORNER SHOP, COFFEE SHOP
2 PLACE THAT MAKES/REPAIRS THINGS [C] a place where something is made or repaired: *The generators are put*

together in the **machine shop**. | *a bicycle repair shop* → SHOP FLOOR, SHOP STEWARD

3 SCHOOL SUBJECT (*also* **shop class**) [U] *AmE* a subject taught in schools that shows students how to use tools and machinery to make or repair things: **in shop** *Doug made this table in shop.* | **wood/metal/print etc shop** *One auto shop class is run just for girls.*

4 set up shop *informal* to start a business

5 shut up shop *BrE*, **close up shop** *AmE informal* to close a shop or business, either temporarily or permanently

6 talk shop *informal* to talk about things that are related to your work, especially in a way that other people find boring: *I'm fed up with you two talking shop.* → SHOP TALK

7 all over the shop *BrE spoken* **a)** scattered around untidily: *There were bits of paper all over the shop.* **b)** confused and disorganized: *I'm all over the shop this morning.*

8 GO SHOPPING [singular] *BrE spoken* an occasion when you go shopping, especially for food and other things you need regularly: *She always* ***does*** *the weekly* ***shop*** *on a Friday.*

shop² ●●● S2 *v* (**shopped**, **shopping**)

1 [I] to go to one or more shops to buy things: **[+for]** *I usually shop for vegetables in the market.* | **[+at]** *She always shops at Tesco's.* → WINDOW-SHOPPING

2 go shopping (*also* **be out shopping**) to go to one or more shops to buy things, often for enjoyment: *The next day, Saturday, we went shopping.* | *Mum's out shopping with Granny.*

3 [T] *BrE informal* to tell the police about someone who has done something illegal: *He was shopped by his ex-wife.*

shop around *phr v* to compare the price and quality of different things before you decide which to buy: **[+for]** *Take time to shop around for the best deal.*

shop·a·hol·ic /ʃɒpəˈhɒlɪk $ ʃɑːpəˈhɒː-/ *n* [C] *informal* someone who loves to go shopping and buys lots of things they may not need

S

ˈshop asˌsistant ●●○ *n* [C] *BrE* someone whose job is to help customers in a shop SYN **sales clerk** *AmE*

ˈshop-bought *adj BrE* bought in a shop, rather than made at home SYN **store-bought** *AmE* OPP **homemade**: *Why buy shop-bought yoghurt when you can easily make your own?* | *Homemade marzipan has a better flavour than most shop-bought varieties.*

shop·fit·ting /ˈʃɒpˌfɪtɪŋ $ ˈʃɑːp-/ *n* [U] *BrE* the job of putting equipment in a shop, changing the way it looks etc —**shopfitter** *n* [C]

ˌshop ˈfloor *n* [singular] **1** the area in a factory where the ordinary workers do their work: **on the shop floor** *The chairwoman started her working life on the shop floor.* **2** the ordinary workers in a factory, not the managers: *negotiations between the shop floor and management*

ˈshop front *n* [C] *BrE* the outside part of a shop that faces the street SYN **storefront** *AmE*

shop·keep·er /ˈʃɒpˌkiːpə $ ˈʃɑːpˌkiːpər/ *n* [C] *especially BrE* someone who owns or is in charge of a small shop SYN **storekeeper** *AmE*

shop·lift /ˈʃɒpˌlɪft $ ˈʃɑːp-/ *v* [I] to take something from a shop without paying for it —**shoplifter** *n* [C]: *Shoplifters will be prosecuted.*

shop·lift·ing /ˈʃɒpˌlɪftɪŋ $ ˈʃɑːp-/ ●○○ *n* [U] the crime of stealing things from shops, for example by hiding them in a bag or under your clothes: *She had been falsely accused of shoplifting in a clothing store.* THESAURUS CRIME, STEAL

shop·per /ˈʃɒpə $ ˈʃɑːpər/ ●●○ *n* [C] someone who buys things in shops: *The streets were crowded with shoppers.* THESAURUS CUSTOMER

shop·ping /ˈʃɒpɪŋ $ ʃɑː-/ ●●● S2 W3 *n* [U]

1 the activity of going to shops and buying things: *Late-night shopping is becoming very popular.* | **shopping expedition/trip** *She's* ***gone on*** *a* ***shopping trip*** *to New York.* | *I* ***went on*** *a* ***shopping spree*** (=went shopping and bought a lot of things) *at the weekend and spent far too much money.* | *I've got to do some last-minute shopping.* | *the busy Christmas shopping season* → WINDOW-SHOPPING

2 do the shopping to go shopping to buy food and other things you need regularly: *I hate doing the shopping at weekends.*

3 *BrE* the things that you have just bought from a shop: *Can you help me carry the shopping, please?*

ˈshopping ˌbag *n* [C] a large bag that you use to carry things which you have bought → see picture at BAG¹

ˈshopping ˌbasket *n* [C] **1** a basket that you use to put things in as you walk around a shop **2** the part of a website, often represented by a picture of a basket, where you collect things to buy

ˈshopping ˌcart *n* [C] *AmE* a large metal basket on wheels that you push around when you are shopping in a SUPERMARKET SYN **cart** *AmE*, **shopping trolley** *BrE*

ˈshopping ˌcentre *BrE*, **shopping center** *AmE* ●●● S3 *n* [C] a group of shops together in one area, often in one large building

ˈshopping ˌlist *n* [C] a list of things you need to buy when you go shopping

ˈshopping mall (*also* **mall**) *n* [C] *especially AmE* a group of shops together in one large covered building

ˈshopping ˌprecinct *n* [C] *BrE* an area in a town where there are a lot of shops and where cars are not allowed

ˈshopping ˌtrolley *n* [C] *BrE* a large metal basket on wheels that you push around when you are shopping in a SUPERMARKET SYN **trolley** *BrE*, **shopping cart** *AmE*

ˈshop-soiled *adj BrE* **1** a product that is shop-soiled is slightly damaged or dirty because it has been in a shop for a long time SYN **shopworn** *AmE*: *shop-soiled goods* **2** an idea that is shop-soiled is no longer interesting because it has been discussed many times before SYN **shopworn** *AmE*: *the same old shop-soiled arguments*

ˌshop ˈsteward *n* [C] a worker who is elected by members of a TRADE UNION in a factory or other business to represent them in dealing with managers

ˈshop talk *n* [U] *AmE informal* conversation about your work, which other people may think is boring

shop·worn /ˈʃɒpwɔːn $ ˈʃɑːpwɔːrn/ *adj AmE* **1** a product that is shopworn is slightly damaged or dirty because it has been in a shop for a long time SYN **shop-soiled** *BrE* **2** an idea that is shopworn is no longer interesting because it has been discussed many times before SYN **shop-soiled** *BrE*: *shopworn management techniques*

shore¹ /ʃɔː $ ʃɔːr/ ●●● W3 *n*

1 [C,U] the land along the edge of a large area of water such as an ocean or lake: *We could see a boat about a mile from shore.* | *Only a few survivors reached the shore.* | *She began to swim to shore.* | **on the shores of sth** *a holiday resort on the shores of the Adriatic* | **on shore** *We had a couple of hours on shore* (=not on a ship). | **off shore** *The island is about three miles off shore* (=away from the coast). | **rocky/sandy shore**

2 these/British/our etc shores *written* a country that has a border on the sea: *Millions of immigrants flocked to these shores in the 19th century.* | *growing fears that English football players will be lured away to* ***foreign shores*** → ASHORE, OFFSHORE, ONSHORE

shore² *v*

shore sth ↔ **up** *phr v* **1** to support a wall or roof with large pieces of wood, metal etc to stop it from falling down: *The roof had been shored up with old timbers.* **2** to help or support something that is likely to fail or is not working well SYN **bolster**: *attempts to shore up the struggling economy*

shore·line /ˈʃɔːlaɪn $ ˈʃɔːr-/ *n* [C,U] the land along the edge of a large area of water such as an ocean or lake: *the bay's 13,000 km of shoreline*

shorn /ʃɔːn $ ʃɔːrn/ a past participle of SHEAR

short¹ /ʃɔːt $ ʃɔːrt/ ●●● S1 W1 *adj* (*comparative* **shorter**, *superlative* **shortest**)

1 TIME happening or continuing for only a little time or for less time than usual OPP **long**: *a short meeting* | *Morris gave a short laugh.* | *a short course on business English* | *Winter is coming and the days are getting shorter.* | *I've only been in Brisbane* ***a short time***. | *For* ***a short while*** (=a short time), *the city functioned as the region's capital.* | *I learned a* *lot during my* ***short period*** *as a junior reporter.* | *Germany achieved spectacular economic success in* ***a*** *relatively* ***short period of time.*** | *They met and married within* ***a short space of time.*** | *I promise to keep the meeting* ***short and sweet*** (=short in a way that is good, especially not talking for a long time). | *For a few short weeks* (=they seemed to pass very quickly), *the sun shone and the fields turned gold.*

2 LENGTH/DISTANCE measuring a small amount in length or distance OPP **long**: *a short skirt* | *Anita had her hair cut short.* | *They went by the shortest route, across the fields.* | *Carol's office was only a* ***short distance*** *away, and she decided that she would walk there.* | **a short walk/flight/drive** *It's a short drive to the airport.* | *The hotel is only a short walk from the beach.*

3 NOT TALL someone who is short is not as tall as most people OPP **tall**: *a short plump woman* | *Chris was short and stocky, with broad shoulders.* | *He's a bit shorter than me.*

4 BOOK/LETTER a book, letter etc that is short does not have many words or pages OPP **long**: *a short novel* | *I wrote a short note to explain.* → SHORT STORY

5 NOT ENOUGH **a)** if you are short of something, you do not have enough of it: **be short (of sth)** *Can you lend me a couple of dollars? I'm a little short.* | **be short of money/cash/funds** *Our libraries are short of funds.* | **be 5p/$10 etc short** *Have you all paid me? I'm about £9 short.* | **I'm a bit short** *BrE spoken* (=I haven't got much money at the moment) | **sb is not short of sth** *BrE* (=they have a lot of it) *Your little girl's not short of confidence, is she?* | *They're* ***not short of a few bob*** (=they are rich). **b)** if something is short, there is not enough of it: *Money was short in those days.* | *It's going to be difficult – time is short.* | *Gasoline* ***was in short supply*** (=not enough of it was available) *after the war.*

6 be short on sth to have less of something than you should have: *He's a nice guy, but a little short on brains.* | *The president's speech was* ***long on*** *colorful phrases but* ***short on*** *solutions.*

7 LESS THAN a little less than a number: **[+of]** *Her time was only two seconds short of the world record.* | **just/a little short of sth** *She was just short of six feet tall.*

8 short notice if something is short notice, you are told about it only a short time before it happens: *I can't make it Friday.* **It's** *very* **short notice**. | **at short notice** *BrE,* **on short notice** *AmE*: *The party was arranged at short notice.*

9 in the short term/run during the period of time that is not very far into the future → **short-term**: *These measures may save money in the short term, but we'll end up spending more later.*

10 have a short memory if someone has a short memory, they soon forget something that has happened: *Voters have very short memories.*

11 be short for sth to be a shorter way of saying a name: *Her name is Alex, short for Alexandra.*

12 be short of breath to be unable to breathe easily, especially because you are unhealthy: *He couldn't walk far without getting short of breath.*

13 be short with sb to speak to someone using very few words, in a way that seems rude or unfriendly: *Sorry I was short with you on the phone this morning.*

14 have a short temper/fuse to get angry very easily: *Mr Yanto, who had a very short fuse, told her to get out.*

15 get/be given short shrift if you or your idea, suggestion etc is given short shrift, you are told immediately that you are wrong and are not given any attention or sympathy: *McLaren got short shrift from all the record companies when he first presented his new band to them in 1976.*

16 be nothing/little short of sth used to emphasize that something is very good, very surprising etc: *Her recovery seemed nothing short of a miracle.* | *The results are little short of astonishing.*

17 draw/get the short straw to be given something difficult or unpleasant to do, especially when other people have been given something better: *Giles drew the short straw, and has to give us a talk this morning.*

18 make short work of (doing) sth to finish something quickly and easily, especially food or a job: *The kids made short work of the sandwiches.* | *Computers can make short work of complex calculations.*

19 have/get sb by the short and curlies (*also* **have/get sb by the short hairs**) *BrE informal not polite* to put someone in a situation in which they are forced to do or accept what you want: *I signed the contract – they've got me by the short and curlies.*

20 be one ... short of a ... *spoken* used humorously to say

THESAURUS: short

TIME

short not long: *I lived in Tokyo for a short time.* | *Smokers have a shorter life expectancy than non-smokers.*
brief *especially written* lasting only for a short time. **Brief** is more formal than **short**, and is used especially in written English: *The president will make a brief visit to Seattle today.* | *He coached Hingis for a brief period in the 1990s.*
quick [only before noun] taking a short time to do something: *I had a quick look at the map.* | *He had a quick shower and then went out.*
short-lived lasting only for a short time – used especially when someone wishes that a good situation had been able to last for longer: *short-lived success* | *The ceasefire was short-lived.* | *a short-lived romance* | *short-lived optimism about the economy*
fleeting lasting only for an extremely short time – used especially when someone wishes that something had been able to last for longer: *a fleeting visit* | *a fleeting smile* | *She caught a fleeting glimpse of him.* | *a fleeting moment of happiness*
momentary lasting for a very short time – used especially about feelings or pauses: *There was a momentary pause in the conversation.* | *The momentary panic ended when he found his two-year-old son waiting happily outside the store.*
passing [only before noun] lasting only for a short time – used especially when people are only interested in something or mention something for a short time: *passing fashions* | *He made only a passing reference to war.* | *It's just* ***a passing phase*** (=it will end soon).
ephemeral *formal* lasting only for a short time, and ending quickly like everything else in this world: *Beauty is ephemeral.* | *the ephemeral nature of our existence* | *His wealth proved to be ephemeral.*

PERSON

short someone who is short is not as tall as most people: *He was a short fat man.*
not very tall quite short. This phrase sounds more gentle than saying that someone is **short**: *She wasn't very tall – maybe about 1.60 m.*
small short and with a small body: *My mother was a small woman.* | *The girl was quite small for her age* (=smaller than other girls of the same age).
petite used about a woman who is attractively short and thin: *She was a petite woman with blonde hair.*
stocky used about a boy or man who is short, heavy, and strong: *Harry was stocky and middle-aged.*
dumpy short and fat: *a dumpy girl with red hair*
diminutive *formal or literary* very short or small – used especially in descriptions in novels: *a diminutive figure dressed in black*
stubby stubby fingers or toes are short and thick: *the baby's stubby little fingers*

that someone is a little crazy or stupid: *Lady, are you a few aces short of a deck?* | *He's* ***one sandwich short of a picnic****.*
21 short time *BrE* when workers work for fewer hours than usual, because the company cannot afford to pay them their full wage: *Most of the workers were put* ***on short time****.*
22 in short order *formal* in a short time and without delay
23 give sb short measure *BrE old-fashioned* to give someone less than the correct amount of something, especially in a shop
24 SOUND *technical* a short vowel is pronounced quickly without being emphasized, for example the sound of a in 'cat', e in 'bet', and i in 'bit' OPP **long** —**shortness** *n* [U]: *He was suffering from shortness of breath.* | *Shirley was very conscious of her shortness and always wore high heels.*
→ **life's too short** at LIFE(27)

GRAMMAR: Order of adjectives

If there is more than one adjective, the adjectives are usually used in a fixed order.
You say: *I bought a beautiful short dress.* ✗ Don't say: *I bought a short beautiful dress.*
You say: *She has short black hair.* ✗ Don't say: *She has black short hair.*
GRAMMAR GUIDE ▸ ADJECTIVES

short² ●●○ *n*
1 shorts [plural] **a)** short trousers ending at or above the knees: *a pair of shorts* | *tourists in shorts and T-shirts* → BERMUDA SHORTS, CYCLING SHORTS **b)** *especially AmE* men's underwear with short legs: *Craig was standing in the kitchen in his shorts.* → BOXER SHORTS, JOCKEY SHORTS
2 in short used when you want to give the main point of something: *Carter hoped for greater trust between the two nations, more trade, more cultural exchanges – in short, a genuine peace.*
3 for short used as a shorter way of saying a name: *His name's Maximilian, but we just call him Max for short.*
4 [C] *informal* a short film shown in the cinema
THESAURUS ▸ MOVIE
5 [C] *BrE informal* a strong alcoholic drink that is not beer or wine, drunk in a small glass SYN **shot** *AmE*: *Do you fancy a short?*
6 [C] *informal* a SHORT CIRCUIT: *a short in the system* → **the long and the short of it** at LONG¹(10)

short³ ●○○ *adv*
1 fall short of sth to be less than what you need, expected, or hoped for, or to fail to reach a satisfactory standard: *The Republicans increased their share of the vote, but still fell short of a majority.* | *Shares in the company dropped 26p yesterday, as profits* ***fell short of*** *City* ***expectations****.* | **fall short of a goal/target/ideal** *The economy fell short of the Treasury's target of 2% growth.* | **fall far/a long way/well short of sth** *Facilities in these schools fall far short of the standards required.* | *One or two songs on the album are interesting, but most* ***fall short of the mark*** (=are not good enough).
2 be running short (of/on sth) if you are running short of something, or if something is running short, it is being used up and there will soon not be enough left: *We're running short of coffee again.* | *Our supplies of petrol were running short.* | *Come on,* ***time's running short****!*
3 stop short of doing sth to almost do something but then decide not to do it: *They accused the president of incompetence, but stopped short of calling for his resignation.*
4 stop short to suddenly stop speaking or stop what you are doing, because something has surprised you or you have just thought of something: *Seeing her tears, he stopped short.*
5 be cut short if something is cut short, it is stopped before you expect or before it is finished: *His career was tragically cut short when, at the age of 42, he died of a heart attack.*
6 cut sb short to interrupt and stop someone when they are speaking: *I was halfway through my explanation when Walter cut me short.*
7 pull/bring sb up short to surprise or shock someone so that they stop what they are doing or saying to think for a moment: *The question brought her up short, but, after a moment's hesitation, she answered it.*
8 3 metres/5 miles etc short of sth without reaching a place you are trying to get to, because you are still a particular distance from it: *The plane touched down 200 metres short of the runway.*
9 two weeks/a month etc short of sth two weeks, a month etc before something: *He died two days short of his fifty-sixth birthday.*
10 short of (doing) sth without actually doing something: *Short of locking her in her room, he couldn't really stop her from seeing Jack.*
11 come up short to fail to win or achieve something: *We've been to the state tournament four times, but we've come up short every time.*
12 go short (of sth) *BrE* to have less of something than you need: *She made sure that her children never went short.*
13 be taken short/be caught short *BrE informal* to have a sudden strong need to go to the toilet when you are not near one

short⁴ (*also* **short out**) *v* [I,T] to SHORT-CIRCUIT, or make something do this: *The toaster shorted and caused a fire.*

short·age /ˈʃɔːtɪdʒ $ ˈʃɔːr-/ ●●○ *n* [C,U] a situation in which there is not enough of something that people need SYN **lack**: **[+of]** *a shortage of skilled labour* | ***There is no shortage of*** *funds.*

COLLOCATIONS

ADJECTIVES/NOUN + shortage

a severe/serious shortage *There is a serious shortage of food in some areas.*
an acute shortage (=very bad) *They were suffering because of an acute shortage of doctors and nurses.*
a desperate/dire shortage (=very serious and worrying) *There is a desperate shortage of fresh water in the disaster area.*
a chronic shortage (=very bad and existing for a long time) | **a growing shortage** (=one that is increasing) | **a general shortage** (=a shortage of lots of different kinds of things or people) | **a national/world shortage** | **a water/food/housing etc shortage**

VERBS

create/cause a shortage *Poor harvests could cause food shortages in the winter.*
lead to/result in a shortage *The strike led to serious shortages of fuel in some areas.*
face a shortage (=be likely to suffer a shortage) *The refugees face desperate shortages of food and water.*
ease a shortage (=make it less serious)

ˌshort back and ˈsides *n* [singular] *BrE* a way of cutting a man's hair so that it is very short at the back and sides of his head and slightly longer on top

short·bread /ˈʃɔːtbred $ ˈʃɔːrt-/ *n* [U] a hard sweet BISCUIT made with a lot of butter

short·cake /ˈʃɔːtkeɪk $ ˈʃɔːrt-/ *n* [U] **1** *BrE* shortbread **2** *AmE* cake over which a sweet fruit mixture is poured, especially STRAWBERRIES

ˌshort-ˈchange *v* [T] **1** to treat someone unfairly by not giving them what they deserve or hoped for: *When the band only played for 15 minutes, the fans felt they had been short-changed.* **2** to give back too little money to a customer who has bought something and paid more than the exact amount for it

ˌshort ˈcircuit *n* [C] a failure of an electrical system, caused by bad wires or a fault in a connection in the wires

short-ˈcircuit *v* **1** [I,T] to have a short circuit or cause a short circuit in something **2** [T] to get something done without going through the usual long methods SYN **bypass**: *I short-circuited the whole process by a simple telephone call.*

short·com·ing /ˈʃɔːtˌkʌmɪŋ $ ˈʃɔːrt-/ ●○○ *n* [C usually plural] a fault or weakness that makes someone or something less successful or effective than they should be:

Peter was painfully aware of his own shortcomings. | **[+of]** *the shortcomings of our local government system* | **[+in]** *The report suggested that there were severe shortcomings in police tactics.*

short·crust pas·try /ʃɔːtkrʌst ˈpeɪstri $ ʃɔːrt-/ *n* [U] *BrE* a type of PASTRY which breaks up easily and is used for making PIES

ˌshort ˈcut, **short-cut** / $ ˈ../ ●○○ *n* [C]
1 a quicker and more direct way of getting somewhere than the usual one: *Carlos decided to* ***take*** *a* ***short-cut*** *home.* | *We were late for the game, but found a short cut through the fields.*
2 a quicker way of doing something: **[+to]** *There aren't really any short cuts to learning English.*

short·en /ˈʃɔːtn $ ˈʃɔːrtn/ ●○○ *v* [I,T] to become shorter or make something shorter OPP **lengthen**: *The days are shortening.* | **[+to]** *His name is often shortened to Pat.*

short·en·ing /ˈʃɔːtnɪŋ $ ˈʃɔːrt-/ *n* [U] fat made from vegetable oil that you mix with flour when making PASTRY(1)

short·fall /ˈʃɔːtfɔːl $ ˈʃɔːrtfɒːl/ ●○○ *n* [C] the difference between the amount you have and the amount you need or expect → **deficit**: **[+in]** *Parents have been asked to pay £30 each to cover the shortfall in the budget.* | **[+of]** *an estimated shortfall of about £1 million*

short·hand /ˈʃɔːthænd $ ˈʃɔːrt-/ *n* [U] **1** a fast method of writing using special signs or shorter forms to represent letters, words, and phrases: **in shorthand** *The reporter took notes in shorthand.* | *a secretary who takes shorthand* (=writes in shorthand) → **LONGHAND** **2** a shorter but less clear way of saying something: **[+for]** *He's been 'relocated', which is shorthand for 'given a worse job a long way away'.*

short·hand·ed /ʃɔːtˈhændɪd◂ $ ʃɔːrt-/ *adj* having fewer helpers or workers than you need SYN **short-staffed**

ˌshorthand ˈtypist *n* [C] *BrE* someone whose job is to use shorthand to write down what someone else says and then TYPE a copy of it SYN **stenographer** *AmE*

ˈshort-haul *adj* a short-haul aircraft or flight travels a fairly short distance OPP **long-haul**: *short-haul routes within the UK*

ˈshort list, **short·list** /ˈʃɔːtlɪst $ ˈʃɔːrt-/ *n* [C] *BrE* a list of the most suitable people for a job or a prize, chosen from all the people who were first considered: **on the short list (for sth)** *Davies was on the shortlist for the Booker Prize.* | **draw up/compile a shortlist** *The panel will draw up a shortlist of candidates.*

short-list, **short·list** /ˈʃɔːtlɪst $ ˈʃɔːrt-/ *v* [T usually passive] *BrE* to put someone on a short list for a job or a prize: **short-list sb for sth** *She's been short-listed for the director's job.*

short-lived /ʃɔːt ˈlɪvd◂ $ ʃɔːrt ˈlaɪvd◂/ ●○○ *adj* existing or happening for only a short time: *Our happiness was short-lived.* **THESAURUS** ▸ SHORT

short·ly /ˈʃɔːtli $ ˈʃɔːrt-/ ●●● S3 W3 *adv*
1 soon: *Ms Jones will be back shortly.* | **shortly before/after sth** *The accident happened shortly before midday.* **THESAURUS** ▸ SOON
2 *written* speaking in an impatient and unfriendly way SYN **abruptly**: *'I've explained that already,' Rod said shortly.*

ˌshort-order ˈcook *n* [C] someone in a restaurant kitchen who cooks food that can be prepared easily or quickly

ˌshort-ˈrange *adj* **1** [only before noun] short-range weapons or MISSILES are designed to travel or be used over a short distance OPP **long-range**: *short-range nuclear weapons* **2 short-range plan/goal/forecast etc** concerned only with the period that is not very far into the future OPP **long-range**

ˈshort-sheet *v* [T] *AmE* to fold the top sheet on a bed so that no one can get into it, as a trick

ˌshort-ˈsighted *adj* **1** *especially BrE* unable to see objects clearly unless they are very close SYN **nearsighted** *AmE* OPP **long-sighted** **2** not considering the possible effects in the future of something that seems good now – used to show disapproval OPP **far-sighted**: *a short-sighted policy of reducing investment in training* —**short-sightedly** *adv* —**short-sightedness** *n* [U]: *Thanks to the government's short-sightedness, our hospitals are very short of cash.*

ˌshort-ˈstaffed *adj* having fewer than the usual or necessary number of workers SYN **short-handed**

ˈshort-stay *adj* [only before noun] *BrE* short-stay hotels, car parks etc are places that you can stay for only a short time OPP **long-stay**

short·stop /ˈʃɔːtstɒp $ ˈʃɔːrtstɑːp/ *n* [C] a player on a baseball team who tries to stop any balls that are hit between second and third BASE²(7)

ˌshort ˈstory *n* [C] a short written story about imaginary situations and characters

ˌshort-ˈtempered *adj* tending to become angry very quickly → **bad-tempered**: *She gets short-tempered when she's tired.* —**short temper** *n* [C]

ˌshort-ˈterm ●●○ *adj* [usually before noun] continuing for only a short time, or relating only to the period that is not very far into the future OPP **long-term**: *The treatment may bring short-term benefits to AIDS sufferers.* | *Most of the staff are on short-term contracts.* | *She's suffering from* ***short-term memory*** *loss.* → **in the short term** at TERM¹(6) —**short-term** *adv*

ˌshort-ˈtermism *n* [U] a way of planning or thinking that is concerned only with what gives you advantages now, rather than what might happen in the future: *plans to combat short-termism among investors in British industry*

ˈshort wave *n* [U] a range of short radio waves used for broadcasting around the world → **LONG WAVE**, **MEDIUM WAVE**

short·y /ˈʃɔːti $ ˈʃɔːrti/ *n* (*plural* **shorties**) **1** used as an insulting name for someone who is not very tall **2** [C] *informal* a woman – used especially by people who play or listen to HIP-HOP music **3** [C] *informal* a baby – used especially by people who play or listen to HIP-HOP music: *Shawna says she's gonna be having my shorty.*

shot¹ /ʃɒt $ ʃɑːt/ ●●● S2 W2 *n*
1 GUN [C] **a)** an act of firing a gun: *He pulled out his rifle and fired three shots.* | *She was killed by a single shot to the head.* **b)** the sound of a gun being fired: *Where were you when you heard the shot?* **c) a good/bad etc shot** someone who is good, bad etc at shooting: *Sergeant Cooper is an excellent shot.*
2 BULLETS [U] **a)** small metal balls that are shot, many at a time, from a SHOTGUN **b)** *old use* large metal balls that are shot from a CANNON
3 ATTEMPT TO SCORE [C] an attempt in sport to throw, kick, or hit the ball towards the place where you can get a point: *Shaw took a shot at the goal from the halfway line, but missed.* | ***Good shot!***
4 PHOTOGRAPH [C] a photograph SYN **picture**: **[+of]** *a close-up shot of a demonstrator being beaten by a policeman* | *I managed to* ***get*** *some* ***good shots*** *of the carnival.* | *We hired a photographer to* ***take*** *some publicity* ***shots***. | ***action shots*** *of football players* (=ones taken of people while they are moving) → **MUGSHOT**
5 FILM/TV [C] the view of something in a film or television programme that is produced by having the camera in a particular position: *In the opening shot, we see Travolta's feet walking down the sidewalk.*
6 ATTEMPT [C] *informal* an attempt to do something or achieve something, especially something difficult: **shot at (doing) sth** *This is her first shot at directing a play.* | *If Lewis won his next fight, he would be guaranteed a* ***shot at the title*** (=chance to win the title). | *I decided to* ***have a shot at*** *decorating the house myself.* | *I didn't think I had much chance of winning the race, but I thought I'd* ***give it a shot*** (=try to do it). | *The network finally* ***gave*** *Keaton* ***a shot at*** *presenting his own show.*
7 give sth your best shot to make as much effort as you can to achieve something difficult: *This case is going to be*

S

tough, but I promise I'll give it my best shot. | *Lydia didn't get the job, but at least she gave it her best shot.*
8 be a long shot a) used to say that a plan is worth trying, even though you think it is unlikely to succeed: *It's a long shot, but someone might recognise her from the photo and be able to tell us where she lives.* **b)** *AmE* if someone is a long shot, they are not likely to be chosen for a job or to win an election, competition etc: *Turner is a long shot to win next month's mayoral election.*
9 a 10 to 1 shot/50 to 1 shot etc a horse, dog etc in a race, whose chances of winning are expressed as numbers
10 a shot in the dark an attempt to guess something without having any facts or definite ideas: *My answer to the last question was a complete shot in the dark.*
11 CRITICAL REMARK [C] a remark that is intended to criticize or hurt someone: *I'm not going to sit here listening to you two* ***take shots at*** *each other all night.* | *She couldn't resist a* ***parting shot*** (=one that you make just before you leave) – *'And you were a lousy lover!'* | *That was a* ***cheap shot*** (=one that is unfair and unreasonable)*!*
12 like a shot if you do something like a shot, you do it very quickly and eagerly: *If he asked me to go to Africa with him, I'd go like a shot!*
13 a shot across the bows/a warning shot (across the bows) something you say or do to warn someone that you oppose what they are doing and will try to make them stop it – used especially in news reports: *The president's own supporters are* ***firing a warning shot across*** *his* ***bows****.*
14 big shot an important or powerful person, especially in business: *a big shot in the record business*
15 DRINK [C] a small amount of a strong alcoholic drink: **[+of]** *a shot of tequila* | *a* ***shot glass*** (=a small glass for strong alcoholic drinks) → see picture at GLASS[1]
16 DRUG [C] *especially AmE* an INJECTION of a drug (=when it is put into the body with a needle) SYN **jab** *BrE*: *Have you had your typhoid and cholera shots?*
17 a shot in the arm something that makes you more confident or more successful: *The new factory will give the local economy a much-needed shot in the arm.*
18 HEAVY BALL [C] a heavy metal ball that competitors try to throw as far as possible in the sport of SHOT PUT
→ **call the shots** at CALL[1](9), → **by a long chalk/shot** at LONG[1](21), → **long shot** at LONG[1](18), → **BUCKSHOT**, **GUNSHOT**, **SNAPSHOT**, **POT SHOT**

COLLOCATIONS

VERBS

fire a shot *The passenger in the car fired three shots.*
take a shot at sb (=fire a shot trying to hit someone) *Someone took a shot at her, but missed.*
a shot hits sb/sth *The shot hit the burglar in the chest and killed him instantly.*
a shot misses sb/sth (=doesn't hit them) *The first shot missed my head by inches.*
a shot rings out (=is heard)

ADJECTIVES/NOUN + shot

a pistol/rifle shot *A pistol shot rang out in the darkness.*
a single shot (=just one shot) *He died from a single shot to his heart.*
the fatal shot (=the shot that killed someone) *It wasn't clear who had fired the fatal shot.*
a warning shot (=one fired as a warning to someone)

PHRASES

a volley of shots (=a number of shots fired quickly)

shot² *adj* [not before noun] **1** *spoken* in bad condition because of being used too much or treated badly: *My back tires are shot.* | *My nerves were* ***shot to pieces*** *after my driving test.* **2 be/get/want shot of sb/sth** *BrE spoken* to get rid or want to get rid of someone or something: *I know the director wants shot of me.* **3 be shot through with sth a)** if a piece of cloth is shot through with a colour, it has very small threads of that colour woven into it: *a fine silk shot through with gold threads* **b)** to have a lot of a particular quality or feeling: *a charming collection of stories, shot through with a gentle humour*

shot³ the past tense and past participle of SHOOT

shot·gun /ˈʃɒtɡʌn $ ˈʃɑːt-/ *n* [C] a long gun fired from the shoulder, that shoots many small round balls at one time, used especially for killing birds or animals: *The robbers were armed with* ***sawn-off shotguns*** (=ones that have been made shorter, so the balls go in different directions).

ˌshotgun ˈwedding *n* [C] a wedding that has to take place immediately because the woman is going to have a baby

ˈshot put *n* [singular] a sport in which you throw a heavy metal ball as far as you can —**shot putter** *n* [C]: *an Olympic shot putter*

should /ʃəd; *strong* ʃʊd/ ●●● S1 W1 *modal verb* (*negative short form* **shouldn't**)
1 RIGHT THING **a)** used to say what is the right or sensible thing to do: *He shouldn't be so selfish.* | *Children shouldn't be allowed to play in the street.* | *'I don't care what people think.' 'Well, you should.'* | *Why shouldn't I smoke if I want to?* **b)** used to say what would have been right or sensible, but was not done: *They should have called the police.*
2 ADVICE used to give or ask for advice: *What should I do?* | *Should I trust him?* | *You should read his new book.* | ***I should*** *stay in bed* ***if I were you****.*
3 EXPECTED THING **a)** used to say that you expect something to happen or be true: *It should be a nice day tomorrow.* | *Try phoning Robert – he should be home by now.* | *Australia should win this match.* | *'Artistic people can be very difficult sometimes.' 'Well, you should know – you married one.'* **b)** used to say what was expected, but did not happen: *It was an easy test and he should have passed, but he didn't.*
4 CORRECT THING used to say what is the correct amount, the correct way of doing something etc: *Every sentence should start with a capital letter.* | *What do you mean, there are only ten tickets? There should be twelve.* | *White wine, not red, should be served with fish.*
5 ORDERS *formal* used in official orders and instructions: *Passengers should proceed to Gate 12.*
6 AFTER 'THAT' *BrE* used in a CLAUSE beginning with 'that' after particular adjectives and verbs: *It's strange that you should say that.* | *It is essential that he should have a fair trial.* | *The residents demanded that there should be an official inquiry.*
7 POSSIBILITY used to talk about something that may possibly happen or be true: *Naturally, he was nervous in case anything should go wrong.* | *What if I should fall sick and not be able to work?* | **should sb/sth do sth** *Should you need any help* (=if you need any help)*, you can always phone me at the office.*
8 IMAGINED SITUATIONS *especially BrE formal* used after 'I' or 'we' to say what you would do if something happened or was true: *If anyone treated me like that, I should complain to the manager.* | *I should be surprised if many people voted for him.*
9 REQUESTING/OFFERING *especially BrE formal* used to politely ask for something, offer to do something, or say that you want to do something: *I should be grateful if you could provide me with some information.* | *'What can I get you?' 'I should like a long cool drink.'* | *We should be delighted to help in any way we can.* | *I should like to thank you all for coming here tonight.*
10 PAST INTENTIONS/EXPECTATIONS used as the past tense of 'shall' after 'I' or 'we' to say what you intended or expected to do: *We knew that we should be leaving the next day.*
11 what should I see but sth/who should appear but sb etc used to show that you were surprised when you saw a particular thing, when a particular person appeared etc: *Just at that moment, who should walk in but old Jim himself.*
12 you should have seen/heard sth *spoken* used to emphasize how funny, strange, beautiful etc something was that you saw or heard: *You should have seen the look on her face when I told her I'd won first prize.*

13 how/why should ... ? used to express surprise that something has happened or that someone has asked you a particular question: *Why should anyone want to marry Tony?* | *Don't ask me. How should I know?*
14 I should think/imagine/hope *spoken* **a)** used to say that you think or hope something is true, when you are not certain: *I shouldn't think they've gone far.* | *'I suppose there'll be a lot of complaints?' 'I should imagine so.'* **b)** used to emphasize that you are not surprised by what someone has told you because you have moral reasons to expect it: *'She doesn't like to hear me swearing.' 'I should think not.'* | *'He did apologize.' 'I should hope so, after the way he behaved.'*
GRAMMAR GUIDE ▸ VERBS

shoul·der¹ /ˈʃəʊldə $ ˈʃoʊldər/ ●●● S2 W2 *n*
1 BODY PART [C] one of the two parts of the body at each side of the neck where the arm is connected: *She tapped the driver on the shoulder.* | *He put his arm around her shoulders.* | *His shoulders were broad and powerful.*
2 CLOTHES [C] the part of a piece of clothing that covers your shoulders: *a jacket with padded shoulders*
3 MEAT [C,U] the upper part of the front leg of an animal that is used for meat: **[+of]** *a shoulder of pork*
4 be looking over your shoulder to feel worried that something unpleasant is going to happen to you
5 a) a shoulder to cry on someone who gives you sympathy: *Ben is always there when I need a shoulder to cry on.* **b) cry on sb's shoulder** to get sympathy from someone when you tell them your problems
6 shoulder to shoulder a) having the same aims and wanting to achieve the same thing SYN **side by side**: **[+with]** *We are working shoulder to shoulder with local residents.* **b)** physically close together SYN **side by side**: *Blacks and whites* ***stood shoulder to shoulder*** *in the stands to applaud.*
7 on sb's shoulders if blame or a difficult job falls on someone's shoulders, they have to take responsibility for it: *The blame rests squarely on Jim's shoulders.*
8 put your shoulder to the wheel to start to work with great effort and determination
9 ROAD-SIDE [C] *AmE* an area of ground beside a road, where drivers can stop their cars if they are having trouble → HARD SHOULDER, SOFT SHOULDER
10 CURVED SHAPE [C] a rounded part just below the top of something → **give sb the cold shoulder** at COLD¹(7), → **have a chip on your shoulder** at CHIP¹(5), → **be/stand head and shoulders above the rest** at HEAD¹(29), → **rub shoulders with** at RUB¹(5), → **straight from the shoulder** at STRAIGHT¹(10)

COLLOCATIONS

VERBS
shrug your shoulders (=raise them to show that you do not know or care about something) *Susan just shrugged her shoulders and said nothing.*
hunch your shoulders (=raise your shoulders and bend them forwards slightly) *He hunched his shoulders against the rain.*
look/glance over your shoulder (=look behind you) *He glanced over his shoulder and grinned at me.*
sb's shoulders shake (=because they are crying or laughing) | **sb's shoulders slump/droop/sag** (=move downwards because they are sad or tired) | **sb's shoulders heave** (=move up and down because they are crying or breathing deeply)

ADJECTIVES
broad/wide *He was of medium height, with broad shoulders.*
strong/powerful *He had powerful shoulders and a thick neck.*
narrow/slim

shoulder² *v* **1 shoulder the responsibility/duty/cost/burden etc** to accept a difficult or unpleasant responsibility, duty etc: *The residents are being asked to shoulder the costs of the repairs.* **2** [T] to lift something onto your shoulder to carry it: *They shouldered the boat and took it down to the river.* **3 shoulder your way through/into etc** to move through a large crowd of people by pushing with your shoulder: *He ran after her, shouldering his way through the crowd.* **4 shoulder arms** an order given to soldiers telling them to hold their weapon against their shoulder

ˈshoulder bag *n* [C] a bag that hangs from your shoulder

ˈshoulder blade *n* [C] one of the two flat bones on each side of your back → see picture at SKELETON

ˌshoulder-ˈhigh *adj, adv* as high as your shoulder: *The grass was shoulder-high.*

ˈshoulder-ˌlength *adj* shoulder-length hair hangs down to your shoulders

ˈshoulder pad *n* [C] a small thick piece of material that is fixed inside the shoulders of a dress or jacket to make your shoulders look bigger

ˈshoulder strap *n* [C] **1** a long narrow piece of material on a dress or other piece of women's clothing that goes over the shoulder **2** a long narrow piece of material fixed to a bag etc so that you can carry it over your shoulder

ˈshoulder-ˌsurfing *n* [U] the act of looking over someone's shoulder when they are putting their PIN NUMBER into a machine, in order to use the number to steal money from their account

should·n't /ˈʃʊdnt/ the short form of 'should not'

shouldst /ʃədst; *strong* ʃʊdst/ *old use* the second person singular form of the verb SHOULD

shout¹ /ʃaʊt/ ●●● S2 W2 *v*
1 [I,T] to say something very loudly → **scream**, **yell**: *There's no need to shout! I can hear you!* | **[+at]** *I wish you'd stop shouting at the children.* | **[+for]** *We could hear them* ***shouting for help***. | *'Watch out!' she shouted, as the car started to move.* | **shout sth at sb** *He was shouting insults at the lorry driver.* | **shout sth to sb** *'He's down here!' she shouted to Alison.*
2 shout in pain/anger/frustration etc *BrE* to call out loudly SYN **scream** *AmE*: *Al shouted in pain.*
3 shout sth from the rooftops to tell everyone about something because you want everyone to know about it
4 [I] to write in capital letters in an email, which makes it look as if the writer is angry

GRAMMAR: Prepositions with shout
- You **shout at** someone when you are angry with them: *My teacher never shouts at us.*
- You **shout to** someone when you want them to hear you: *He shouted to me to throw down the rope.*
- You **shout for** something that you want: *They shouted for the driver to stop.*

THESAURUS
shout to say something very loudly: *The two men were shouting angrily at each other.* | *'Wait for me!' he shouted.*
yell (*also* **holler** *AmE*) to shout very loudly, especially because you are angry, excited, or in pain. **Yell** is more informal than **shout**: *The children were yelling at each other across the street.*
call (out) to shout in order to get someone's attention: *He called her name but she didn't hear him.* | *'Is anybody there?' he called out.*
cry (out) *written* to shout something loudly, especially because you are in pain, frightened, or very excited: *'I can't move,' Lesley cried.* | *He cried out in panic.* | *'Look what I've found!' she cried.*
scream to shout in a very loud high voice, because you are frightened, unhappy, angry etc: *The baby wouldn't stop screaming.* | *She screamed as she jumped into the cold water.* | *'It's my money!' she screamed at him.*
roar *written* to shout in a loud deep voice: *The crowd roared their appreciation.* | *'Stop this nonsense!' he roared.*
bellow *written* to shout in a loud deep voice, especially when you want a lot of people to hear you: *He was bellowing orders at the soldiers.*
bawl to shout in a loud and unpleasant way, because

you are angry or unhappy: *'What are you doing?' he bawled.* | *The kids were bawling in the back of the car.*
raise your voice to say something more loudly than normal, especially because you are angry: *I never heard my father raise his voice.*
cheer if a group of people cheer, they shout as a way of showing their approval: *The crowd cheered when the band came on stage.*

shout sb ↔ **down** *phr v* to shout so that someone who is speaking cannot be heard: *An older man tried to shout him down.*

shout sth ↔ **out** *phr v* to say something suddenly in a loud voice: *Don't shout out the answer in class, put up your hand.*

shout² ●●● W3 *n*
1 [C] a loud call expressing anger, pain, excitement etc → **scream, yell**: *a warning shout* | **[+of]** *Tom **gave** a **shout** of laughter when he saw them.* | *shouts of delight*
2 give sb a shout *BrE spoken* to go and find someone and tell them something: *Give me a shout when you're ready to go.*
3 a shout out to sb *informal* a message to someone that is broadcast on radio, put on a website etc: *I just want to give a quick shout out to my friend Dave, who's in hospital at the moment.*
4 sb's shout *BrE, AusE informal* someone's turn to buy drinks: *It's my shout. Same again?*
5 be in with a shout (of doing sth) *BrE informal* to have a chance of winning

shout·ing /ˈʃaʊtɪŋ/ *n* [U] **1** when people say things very loudly: *We heard a lot of shouting and went to investigate.* **2 be all over bar the shouting** *BrE spoken* used to say that something is almost finished and there is no doubt what the result will be

S

ˈshouting ˌmatch *n* [C] an angry argument in which people shout at each other

shout·y /ˈʃaʊti/ *adj informal* someone who is shouty shouts a lot: *The best way of dealing with a shouty boss is to stay quiet and calm.*

shove¹ /ʃʌv/ ●○○ *v*
1 [I,T] to push someone or something in a rough or careless way, using your hands or shoulders: *He shoved her towards the car.* | *Everyone was **pushing and shoving** to see the prince.* THESAURUS ▸ PUSH
2 [T always + adv/prep] to put something somewhere carelessly or without thinking much: *Tidying the room seems to mean shoving everything under the bed!* | *He shoved his hands into his pockets.* THESAURUS ▸ PUT
3 [T] *spoken* used to tell someone in a very impolite way that you do not want something: *They can take their three cents an hour raise and **shove it**.* → **when/if push comes to shove** at PUSH²(6)

shove off *phr v*
1 *BrE spoken* used to tell someone rudely or angrily to go away: *Shove off! I'm busy.*
2 to push a boat away from the land, usually with a pole

shove up/over *phr v BrE spoken* to move along on a seat to make space for someone else: *Shove up, mate, there's no room to sit down here.*

shove² *n* [C] a strong push: ***Give** the door a good **shove**.*

shov·el¹ /ˈʃʌvəl/ ●●○ *n* [C]
1 a tool with a rounded blade and a long handle used for moving earth, stones etc SYN **spade**
2 a part of a large vehicle or machine used for moving or digging earth

shovel² ●○○ *v* (**shovelled**, **shovelling** *BrE*, **shoveled**, **shoveling** *AmE*) [T]
1 to lift and move earth, stones etc with a shovel: *The workmen shovelled gravel onto the road.* | *They were out in freezing conditions shovelling snow off the pitch.* | **shovel the driveway/sidewalk etc** *AmE* (=shovel snow from a road or path) *Everyone was out shoveling their sidewalks.*
2 shovel sth into/onto sth to put something, usually food, somewhere quickly: *We shovelled food into our mouths as fast as we could.*

shov·el·ful /ˈʃʌvəlfʊl/ *n* [C] the amount of coal, snow, earth etc that you can carry on a shovel

ˈshovel-ˌready *adj* if a project, especially a building project, is shovel-ready, it is ready to start as soon as money is made available for it: *The government will provide money for shovel-ready projects in order to create jobs quickly.*

shov·el·ware /ˈʃʌvəlweə $ -wer/ *n* [U] information that first appears in printed form, for example in a book or newspaper, and then is put onto the Internet or CD-ROM without any new or interesting ways to look at or use the information: *Many of the educational software titles are nothing but shovelware.*

show¹ /ʃəʊ $ ʃoʊ/ ●●● S1 W1 *v* (*past tense* **showed**, *past participle* **shown** /ʃəʊn $ ʃoʊn/)
1 LET SB SEE [T] to let someone see something: **show sb sth** *The children proudly showed me their presents.* | **show sth to sb** *Show your ticket to the woman at the entrance.* | *The man grinned, showing bad teeth.*
2 PROVE STH [T] to provide facts or information that make it clear that something is true, that something exists, or that something has happened: *Figures showed a 9% rise in inflation.* | *Gary has shown his faith in the club's future by agreeing to stay on.* | **show (that)** *Mike needed a copy of the will to show that the books had been left to him.* | **show sb (that)** *We have shown our critics that we can succeed.* | **show how** *This document shows how to oppose bad decisions about new housing.* | **show what** *She just wants a chance to show what she can do.* | **show sb/sth to be sth** *Charles showed himself to be a fine leader.* | **be shown to be/do sth** *The campaign has been shown to be a waste of money.* | *The new treatment has been shown to reduce the number of deaths.* | **studies/evidence/research etc shows** *Several studies have shown that aggressive toys lead to bad behaviour.* | *The Polish economy began to **show signs of** recovery.* | *It just **goes to show** (=proves) how much people judge each other on how they look.*

REGISTER
In written English, people often prefer to use **indicate**, which sounds more formal than **show**: *The latest statistics **indicate** that the country is falling deeper into recession.*
In scientific contexts, they often prefer **prove** or **demonstrate**, which sound more definite: *This research **demonstrates** the need to treat cancer early.*

3 FEELINGS/ATTITUDES/QUALITIES [T] to let your feelings, attitudes, or personal qualities be clearly seen OPP **hide**: *Think positively and show some determination.* | *She had learned not to **show** her **emotions**.* | *It was the sound a man might make when in pain but trying not to show it.* | *Mary **showed** great **interest in** the children.*
4 EXPLAIN WITH ACTIONS [T] to explain to someone how to do something, by doing it yourself or using actions to help them learn: **show sb how** *Show me how the gun works.* | **show sb how to do sth** *Maureen showed Peter how to feed the young animals.* | **show sb sth** *Can you show Lucy the way to slice onions?* THESAURUS ▸ EXPLAIN
5 PICTURE/MAP ETC [T] if a picture, map etc shows something, you can see it on the picture, map etc: *I want a photograph that shows his face.* | *The map shows the main rivers of the region.*
6 GUIDE SB [T] to go with someone and guide them to a place: **show sb to/into sth** *Can you show Mrs Davies to the bathroom?* | **show sb out/in** *I can show myself out* (=out of the office or house). | **show sb sth** *Come on, I'll **show** you **the way**.* THESAURUS ▸ LEAD
7 POINT AT STH [T] to let someone see where a place or thing is, especially by pointing to it: **show sb where** *Can you show me exactly where he fell?*
8 FILM/TELEVISION [I,T] to make a film or television programme available on a screen for people to see, or to be on a screen: *The film was shown on television last night.* | *The match was shown live* (=could be seen on television while it was being played). | *It's now showing at cinemas across London.* → SHOWING(1)

9 BE EASY TO SEE [I] if something shows, it is easy to see: *His happiness showed in his face. | Her scar doesn't show, because her hair covers it. | Stephen was worried, and it showed.*

10 DIRT/MARK [T] if material shows the dirt or a mark, it is easy to see the dirt or mark on it: *Light-coloured clothes tend to show the dirt.*

11 INCREASE/DECREASE [T] to have an increase or decrease in something, or a profit or loss: *The price of players is the reason why many football clubs show big losses on their balance sheets. | Recent elections have shown significant gains by right-wing groups.*

12 ART/PICTURES [T] to put a group of paintings or other works of art in one place so that people can come and see them SYN **exhibit**: *Her recent sculptures are being shown at the Hayward Gallery. | The Whitney Museum was the first to show Mapplethorpe's photographs.*

13 I'll show him/them etc *spoken* used to say that you will prove to someone that you are better, more effective etc than they think you are

14 have sth to show for sth to have something as a result of what you have been doing: *If he fails, he'll have nothing to show for his time at school. | She had plenty of money to show for all her work.*

15 show your face if you will not show your face somewhere, you will not go there because you have a good reason to feel ashamed or embarrassed about being there: *She never shows her face around here.*

16 show your hand to make your true power or intentions clear, especially after you have been keeping them secret: *There were so many rumours that the company was forced to show its hand.*

17 ANIMAL [T] to put an animal into a competition with other animals: *Do you plan to show your dogs?*

18 ARRIVE [I] (*also* **show up**) *informal especially AmE* to arrive at the place where someone is waiting for you SYN **turn up**: *I went to meet Hank, but he never showed.*

19 show sb in a good/bad etc light if an action shows you in a good or bad light, it makes people have a good or bad opinion of you: *During an interview, you need to show yourself in the best possible light.*

20 show sb the door to make it clear that someone is not welcome and should leave

21 show (sb) who's boss *informal* to prove to someone who is threatening your authority that you are more powerful than they are: *You've got to show your dog who's boss. When you say 'Sit!', he should sit.*

22 show the way if you show the way for other people, you do something new that others then try to copy

23 show willing *BrE* to make it clear that you are willing to do something: *He hasn't done any cooking yet, but at least he's shown willing.*

24 show a leg! *BrE spoken* used to tell someone to get out of bed

25 show (sb) a clean pair of heels *BrE old-fashioned informal* to run away very fast

26 show me the money *AmE spoken informal* used to tell someone to give or pay you a lot of money, rather than just talk about the fact that they will give it to you

show sb **around** (sth) (*also* **show sb round (sth)** *BrE*) *phr v* to go around a place with someone when they first arrive there, to show them what is interesting, useful etc: *Harrison showed her around the house.*

show off *phr v*

1 to try to make people admire your abilities, achievements, or possessions – used to show disapproval → **show-off**: *He couldn't resist showing off on the tennis court.*

2 show sth ↔ off to show something to a lot of people because you are very proud of it: *a picture of the restaurant's owners showing off their award*

3 show sth ↔ off if one thing shows off something else, it makes the other thing look especially attractive SYN **complement**: *The white dress showed off her dark skin beautifully.*

show sb **over** sth *phr v especially BrE* to guide someone through an interesting building or a house that is for sale: *Ingrid has a job showing visitors over the castle.*

show up *phr v*

1 *informal* to arrive, especially at the place where someone is waiting for you SYN **turn up**: *Seth showed up, apologising for being late. | We had 200 people show up for our seminar.*

2 show sth ↔ up to make it possible to see or notice something that was not clear before: *The sunlight showed up the marks on the window.*

3 to be easy to see or notice: *Use a light colour which will show up on a dark background.*

4 show sb ↔ up to make someone feel embarrassed by behaving in a stupid or unacceptable way when you are with them SYN **embarrass**: *She says I showed her up in front of her friends when they came to the house.*

S

show² ●●● S1 W1 *n*

1 PERFORMANCE [C] a performance for the public, especially one that includes singing, dancing, or jokes: *I enjoyed the show immensely. | The show starts at 7:30 pm. | They've come to town to see a Broadway show. | Perry was the* ***star of the show***. → FLOOR SHOW, ROADSHOW

2 TV/RADIO [C] a programme on television or on the radio: *The senator appeared on the CBS show 'Face the Nation'. | a new television quiz show* → CHAT SHOW, GAME SHOW, TALK SHOW THESAURUS ▸ PROGRAMME

3 COLLECTION OF THINGS TO SEE [C] an occasion when a lot of similar things are brought together in one place so that people can come and look at them: *the Paris Boat Show | a* ***fashion show*** *for charity | Kelly has a show of her latest work opening shortly.*

4 on show being shown to the public: *Paintings by Matisse are on show at the New York Gallery. | The designer clothes*

THESAURUS: show

LET SOMEONE SEE

show to let someone see something, especially by holding it out in front of them: *Everyone has to show their identity cards at the entrance to the building.*

flash to show something to someone very quickly: *'We're police', he said, flashing his card at us. | Miranda flashed a surprised look into the mirror.*

let sb have a look/take a look *especially spoken* to show something to someone, especially so that they can examine it, repair it etc: *If the wound doesn't get better soon, you should let the doctor take a look at it.*

reveal *especially written* to let someone see or know about something that is usually hidden, or that you want to keep secret – often used about showing your feelings or private thoughts: *Suzy looked away quickly in order not to reveal her true feelings. | He lifted the lid of the box to reveal a small snake.*

expose *especially written* to let someone see something that could not be seen before: *The receding tide had exposed huge expanses of sand. | The bear opened its mouth, exposing rows of sharp teeth.*

SHOW SOMEONE HOW TO DO SOMETHING

show to explain to someone how to do something or how something works, especially by doing it yourself: *Laurie's been showing me how to snowboard. | Can I show you how the oven works?*

demonstrate to show how to do something or how something works – especially to a group of people: *A qualified instructor will demonstrate how to use the machines properly.*

guide/take sb through sth to show someone how to do something, or how a process happens, especially something difficult or complicated: *The book guides you through the different stages of starting your own business.*

will **go on show** *in Chicago next month.* | *Local antiques will be* **put on show** *in a new building especially built for the collection.*

5 a show of sth an occasion when someone deliberately shows a particular feeling, attitude, or quality: *I felt I should make a show of dignity.* | *The award will be seen as a show of support.* | **show of strength/force** *a strong and determined show of force by the police*

6 PRETENDED ACT [singular, U] when you pretend to do or feel something SYN **pretence**: **[+of]** *a show of gratitude* | *Susan* **put on a show of** *regret all day.* | *The waiter* **made a show of** *wiping the table.*

7 for show with the purpose of looking attractive or impressive rather than being useful: *He does actually play his guitar – it's not just for show.*

8 COLOURFUL SCENE [singular] an impressive scene, especially one that is very colourful SYN **display**: **[+of]** *a glorious show of colour in the rose garden* | *Maple trees put on their best show in the autumn.*

9 COMPETITION [C] a competition between similar things or animals to choose the best: *The dog show was being held in the Agricultural Hall.*

10 EVENT/SITUATION [singular] *informal* something which is being done or organized: *We need to find someone to* **run the show** (=be in charge).

11 put up a good/poor etc show *informal* to perform, play etc well or badly: *Our team put up a pretty good show, but we lost in the end.*

12 let's get this show on the road *spoken* used to tell people it is time to start working or start a journey

13 (jolly) good show *BrE old-fashioned spoken* used to express your approval of something → **steal the show** at STEAL[1](4)

S

COLLOCATIONS – MEANING 2

ADJECTIVES/NOUN + show

live (=broadcast on TV or radio as it is happening) *Tonight's show is live from Wembley Stadium.*

a TV/television/radio show *What's your favourite TV show?*

a quiz show (=in which people try to answer questions correctly) *It's the BBC's most popular quiz show.*

a game show (=in which people play games or answer questions to win prizes) | **a chat show** *BrE*, **a talk show** *AmE* (=in which famous or interesting people talk to someone about themselves) | **a family show** (=one that is suitable for families and children to watch)

VERBS

appear on/take part in a show (=to be a guest on a show) *They were trying to persuade Daniel Radcliffe to appear on the show.*

host a show (*also* **present a show** *BrE*) (=to be the person who introduces the different parts of a show, or who talks to guests) *He presents his own chat show on ITV.*

watch a show *People of all ages watch the show.*

ˌshow and ˈtell *n* [U] an activity for school children in which they bring an object to school and tell the other children about it: *Ramona brought in a fossil for show and tell.*

show·biz /ˈʃəʊbɪz $ ˈʃoʊ-/ *n* [U] *informal* SHOW BUSINESS

show·boat /ˈʃəʊbəʊt $ ˈʃoʊboʊt/ *v* [I] *informal* if someone playing a sport is showboating, they are trying to make people admire them by doing skilful tricks, but are not playing effectively for their team: *What did he ever do other than showboat around the pitch, beat five players, and end up losing the ball to the sixth?* —**showboating** *n* [U]

ˈshow ˌbusiness (*also* **showbiz** *informal*) *n* [U] the entertainment industry, for example television, films, popular theatre etc: **in show business** *Phyllis always wanted to be in show business.* | *The restaurant is always full of show business personalities.*

show·case /ˈʃəʊkeɪs $ ˈʃoʊ-/ *n* [C] **1** an event or situation that is designed to show the good qualities of a person, organization, product etc: **[+for]** *The new musical is a good showcase for her talents.* **2** a glass box containing objects for people to look at in a shop, at an art show etc —**showcase** *v* [T]: *She wants to showcase African-American literature.*

show·down /ˈʃəʊdaʊn $ ˈʃoʊ-/ *n* [C usually singular] a meeting, argument, fight etc that will settle a disagreement or competition that has continued for a long time: **[+with]** *a showdown with the striking workers* | *Britain has a World Cup showdown with Australia next month.*

show·er[1] /ˈʃaʊə $ ʃaʊr/ ●●● S2 *n* [C]

1 FOR WASHING IN a piece of equipment that you stand under to wash your whole body: *Why does the phone always ring when I'm in the shower?* | *I'd like to use the shower if that's all right.* | *The bathroom has a separate shower cubicle* (=a shower in a separate part of the room).

2 ACT OF WASHING an act of washing your body while standing under a shower: *I need a shower.* | **take a shower** *Nick rolled out of bed and took a shower.* | **have a shower** *especially BrE*: *Mary loves having a hot shower after she's been swimming.*

3 RAIN a short period of rain or snow: *More* **heavy showers** *are forecast for tonight.* | *a* **shower of rain** | *a snow shower* | *A few wintry showers are likely.* THESAURUS ▸ RAIN

4 LOTS OF THINGS a lot of small light things falling or going through the air together: **[+of]** *Peter kicked the fire and sent up a* **shower of sparks**. | *A shower of leaves fell towards the ground.*

5 PARTY *AmE* a party at which presents are given to a woman who is going to get married or have a baby: *We* **gave** *a* **shower** *for Beth.* | *a* **baby shower**

6 PEOPLE [usually singular] *BrE informal* a group of stupid or lazy people

shower[2] *v* **1** [I] to wash your whole body while standing under a shower: *Mike shaved and showered.* **2** [T] to give someone a lot of things: **shower sb with sth** *She showered him with kisses.* | *Tom showered Amy with presents.* | **shower sth on/upon sb** *She had no children and showered her love on her three nieces.* **3** [I always + adv/prep, T] to scatter a lot of things onto a person or place, or to be scattered in this way: **[+down/over/upon]** *The top shelf broke and books showered down.* | **shower sth with sth** *The ship was showered with hot ash from the volcano.* | **shower sth on/over sth** *Hundreds of leaflets were showered over the town.*

ˈshower cap *n* [C] a plastic hat that keeps your hair dry in a shower

ˈshower gel *n* [U] *BrE* a type of liquid soap that you use to wash yourself in a shower

show·er·proof /ˈʃaʊəpruːf $ ˈʃaʊr-/ *adj* showerproof clothes keep you dry in light rain but not in heavy rain

show·er·y /ˈʃaʊəri $ ˈʃaʊri/ *adj* raining frequently for short periods: *a showery day*

show·girl /ˈʃəʊɡɜːl $ ˈʃoʊɡɜːrl/ *n* [C] one of a group of women who sing or dance in a musical show

show·ground /ˈʃəʊɡraʊnd $ ˈʃoʊ-/ *n* [C] *BrE* a large area of land where an event such as a farming show or a FETE can be held

ˈshow house (*also* **ˈshow home**) *n* [C] *BrE* a house that has been built and filled with furniture to show buyers what similar new houses look like

show·ing /ˈʃəʊɪŋ $ ˈʃoʊ-/ *n* **1** [C] an occasion when a film, art show etc can be seen or looked at, especially a special occasion that people are invited to: *I saw a private showing of the film.* | *It was the comedy's first showing on TV.* **2** [singular] used to talk about a person's or thing's level of success: *Choose the candidate who* **makes** *the best* **showing** *in the interview.* | **strong/poor showing** *Women made a strong showing in the election.* | **on ... showing** *BrE*: *On present showing* (=judging by the way it is now), *there's a lot to do to get the newspaper's sales up.* | *On this showing* (=judging by this example), *she is becoming a very good writer indeed.*

ˈshow ˌjumping *n* [U] a sport in which horses with

riders have to jump a series of fences as quickly and skilfully as possible —**show jumper** *n* [C] → see picture at FENCE[1]

show·man /ˈʃəʊmən $ ˈʃoʊ-/ *n* (*plural* **showmen** /-mən/) [C] someone who is good at entertaining people and getting a lot of public attention: *He is the band's best showman.*

show·man·ship /ˈʃəʊmənʃɪp $ ˈʃoʊ-/ *n* [U] skill at entertaining people and getting public attention

shown /ʃəʊn $ ʃoʊn/ *v* the past participle of SHOW

ˈshow-off *n* [C] *informal* someone who always tries to show how clever or skilled they are so that other people will admire them - often used to show disapproval: *She's a bit of a show-off.*

ˌshow of ˈhands *n* [singular] a vote taken by counting the raised hands of the people at a meeting: *The dispute was settled with a show of hands.*

show·piece /ˈʃəʊpiːs $ ˈʃoʊ-/ *n* [C usually singular] something that an organization, government etc wants people to see, because it is a very good or successful example: *The new stadium is a showpiece for the Greeks.*

show·place /ˈʃəʊpleɪs $ ˈʃoʊ-/ *n* [C] a place which is open to the public because of its beauty, historical interest etc

ˌshow pony *n* (*plural* **show ponies**) [C] **1** a PONY (=small horse) that takes part in a competition which involves jumping fences or being judged on appearance **2** *informal* someone who is confident and enjoys being with other people, but who often tries to show how clever or skilled they are so that other people will admire them - used humorously SYN **show-off**

show·room /ˈʃəʊrʊm, -ruːm $ ˈʃoʊ-/ *n* [C] a large room where you can look at things that are for sale, such as cars or electrical goods: *a car showroom*

ˈshow-ˌstopping *adj* a show-stopping performance is extremely good or impressive: *a show-stopping dance routine* —**show-stopper** *n* [C]

show·time /ˈʃəʊtaɪm $ ˈʃoʊ-/ *n* [U] **1** the time that a play or film will begin in a theatre or cinema **2** *AmE informal* the time when an activity should begin

ˈshow ˌtrial *n* [C] an unfair TRIAL that is organized by a government for political reasons, not in order to find out whether someone is guilty: *Stalin staged a series of show trials.*

show·y /ˈʃəʊi $ ˈʃoʊi/ *adj* something that is showy is very colourful, big, expensive etc, especially in a way that attracts people's attention: *an attractive shrub with showy flowers* —**showily** *adv* —**showiness** *n* [U]

shrank /ʃræŋk/ *v* the past tense of SHRINK

shrap·nel /ˈʃræpnəl/ *n* [U] small pieces of metal from a bomb, bullet etc that are scattered when it explodes: *a soldier with **shrapnel wounds** in his chest*

shred[1] /ʃred/ *n* **1** [C] a small thin piece that is torn or cut roughly from something: **[+of]** *a shred of paper* | **tear/rip sth to shreds** *The clothes were ripped to shreds and covered in blood.* **2 tear/rip sth to shreds** to criticize something very severely: *Within a year, other researchers had torn the theory to shreds.* **3 in shreds a)** torn in many places: *Uncle Earl was exhausted and his shirt hung in shreds.* **b)** completely ruined: *His ambitious plan was in shreds.* | *If Myra gossips about this, my reputation will be in shreds.* **4 shred of sth** a very small amount of something: *There's **not a shred of doubt*** (=no doubt at all) *in my mind that we will win.* | *He does **not** have **a shred of evidence*** (=he has no evidence at all) *to prove his claim.* | *the last shred of hope*

shred[2] *v* (**shredded, shredding**) [T] **1** to cut or tear something into small thin pieces: *Coleslaw is made with shredded cabbage.* **THESAURUS** TEAR **2** to put a document into a shredder: *Carlson was collecting messages, reading them, then shredding them.*

shred·der /ˈʃredə $ -ər/ *n* [C] a machine that cuts documents into small pieces so that no one can read them

shrew /ʃruː/ *n* [C] **1** a very small animal like a mouse with a long pointed nose **2** *old-fashioned* an unpleasant woman who always argues and disagrees with people

shrewd /ʃruːd/ ●○○ *adj*
1 good at judging what people or situations are really like: *Malcolm is a shrewd businessman.* | *She was shrewd enough to guess who was responsible.* | *Capra looked at her with shrewd eyes.*
2 well judged and likely to be right: *a shrewd decision* | *Bridget has a shrewd idea of what will sell.* —**shrewdly** *adv*: *'Something tells me you've already decided,' he said shrewdly.* —**shrewdness** *n* [U]

shrew·ish /ˈʃruːɪʃ/ *adj old use* a shrewish woman is one who always argues and disagrees with people

shriek[1] /ʃriːk/ ●○○ *v*
1 [I] to make a very high loud sound, especially because you are afraid, angry, excited, or in pain SYN **scream**: *They were dragged from their homes, shrieking and weeping.* | *He shrieked in agony.* | **[+with]** *A group of students were shrieking with laughter.*
2 [T] to say something in a high loud voice because you are excited, afraid, or angry SYN **scream**: *'I'm pregnant!' she shrieked.* | **[+at]** *'I'll kill you!' Anne shrieked at him.*

shriek[2] *n* [C] a loud high sound made because you are frightened, excited, angry etc SYN **scream**: **[+of]** *a shriek of laughter* | **with a shriek** *With a shriek of delight, Jean hugged Maggie.* | **give/let out a shriek** *Ella let out a piercing shriek.*

shrift /ʃrɪft/ → **get/be given short shrift** at SHORT[1](15)

shrill[1] /ʃrɪl/ *adj* **1** a shrill sound is very high and unpleasant: *'That's not true,' she protested in a shrill voice.* | *a shrill whistle* | *Fran uttered a shrill scream.* **THESAURUS** HIGH **2** shrill complaints, criticism, demands etc are too loud or strong and seem unreasonable: *He hated the shrill demands of the children.* —**shrillness** *n* [U] —**shrilly** /ˈʃrɪl-li, ˈʃrɪli/ *adv*

shrill[2] *v* **1** [I] *written* to produce a very high and unpleasant sound: *The telephone shrilled twice.* **2** [T] to say something in a very high voice: *'I hate you!' she shrilled.*

shrimp /ʃrɪmp/ ●○○ *n* (*plural* **shrimp** *or* **shrimps**) [C]
1 a small sea creature that you can eat, which has ten legs and a soft shell SYN **prawn** *BrE* → see picture at SHELLFISH
2 someone who is very small - used humorously

ˌshrimp ˈcocktail *n* [C,U] *AmE* shrimps without their shells that are cooked and put in a pink sauce, and eaten cold before the main part of a meal SYN **prawn cocktail** *BrE*

shrimp·ing /ˈʃrɪmpɪŋ/ *n* [U] the activity of fishing for shrimps

shrine /ʃraɪn/ *n* [C] **1** a place that is connected with a holy event or holy person, and that people visit to pray: **[+of/to]** *his pilgrimage to the shrine of St John* **2** a place that people visit and respect because it is connected with a famous person or event: *Elvis' home has become a shrine for his fans.* | **[+to]** *The museum is a shrine to the great Spanish artist.*

shrink[1] /ʃrɪŋk/ ●●○ *v* (*past tense* **shrank** /ʃræŋk/, *past participle* **shrunk** /ʃrʌŋk/)
1 [I,T] to become smaller, or to make something smaller, through the effects of heat or water: *I'm worried about washing that shirt in case it shrinks.* → PRE-SHRUNK, SHRUNKEN
2 [I,T] to become or to make something smaller in amount, size, or value OPP **grow**: *The city continued to shrink.* | **[+to]** *The firm's staff had shrunk to only four people.* | *Treatment can shrink a tumour.* | *We want to expand the business, not shrink it.*
3 [I always + adv/prep] to move back and away from something, especially because you are frightened: *She listened, shrinking under the blankets, to their shouts.* | *Meredith was scared of him and shrank back.* | *His anger was enough to make the others shrink away from him.*

shrink from sth *phr v* to avoid doing something difficult or unpleasant: *The leadership too often shrinks from hard decisions.* | **shrink from doing sth** *We will not shrink from making the necessary changes in policy.*

S

shrink² *n* [C] *informal* a PSYCHOANALYST or PSYCHIATRIST – used humorously

shrink·age /ˈʃrɪŋkɪdʒ/ *n* [singular, U] the act of shrinking, or the amount that something shrinks: *Pollution led to a shrinkage of grasslands.*

ˌshrinking ˈviolet *n* [C] someone who is very shy – used humorously

ˌshrink-ˈwrapped *adj* goods that are shrink-wrapped are wrapped tightly in plastic —**ˈshrink-wrap** *n* [U]

shriv·el /ˈʃrɪvəl/ (*also* **shrivel up**) *v* (**shrivelled**, **shrivelling** *BrE*, **shriveled**, **shriveling** *AmE*) [I,T] if something shrivels, or if it is shrivelled, it becomes smaller and its surface becomes covered in lines because it is very dry or old: *The leaves change colour, then shrivel.* —**shrivelled** *BrE*, **shriveled** *AmE adj*: *a shrivelled apple*

shroud¹ /ʃraʊd/ *n* [C] **1** a cloth that is wrapped around a dead person's body before it is buried **2** *literary* something that hides or covers something: *The fog rolled in, and a grey shroud covered the city.* | **[+of]** *A shroud of silence surrounded the general's death.*

shroud² *v* [T] *literary* **1** to cover or hide something: *Joseph was shrouded under a dark blanket.* | **be shrouded in sth** *The cliff was shrouded in mist.* **2** to keep information secret so that people do not know what really happened: **be shrouded in sth** *The incident has always been* ***shrouded in mystery****.* | *The work is* ***shrouded in secrecy****.*

ˈshroud-ˌwaving *n* [U] *BrE* when people, especially doctors or politicians, publicly criticize the quality of medical care in the British National Health Service, in order to make the government provide more money for it

Shrove Tues·day /ʃrəʊv ˈtjuːzdi, -deɪ $ ʃroʊv ˈtuːz-/ *n* [C,U] the day before the first day of the Christian period of Lent, when people in Britain traditionally eat PANCAKES

S

shrub /ʃrʌb/ ●○○ *n* [C] a small bush with several woody stems

shrub·be·ry /ˈʃrʌbəri/ *n* (*plural* **shrubberies**) **1** [U] shrubs planted close together: *a tangled mass of overgrown shrubbery* **2** [C] a part of a garden where shrubs are planted close together

shrug¹ /ʃrʌg/ ●●○ W3 *v* (**shrugged**, **shrugging**) [I,T] to raise and then lower your shoulders in order to show that you do not know something or do not care about something: *I just* ***shrugged*** *my* ***shoulders*** *and ignored him.* | *Melanie shrugged and walked away.*

SHRUG

shrug sth ↔ **off** *phr v* to treat something as unimportant and not worry about it: *We can't just shrug these objections off.*

shrug² *n* [C] **1** [usually singular] a movement of your shoulders upwards and then downwards again that you make to show that you do not know something or do not care about something: **with a shrug** *'Suit yourself,' he said with a shrug.* **2** a very short CARDIGAN

shrunk /ʃrʌŋk/ *v* the past participle of SHRINK

shrunk·en /ˈʃrʌŋkən/ *adj* [usually before noun] having become smaller or been made smaller: *a shrunken old woman*

shtick, **schtick** /ʃtɪk/ *n* [U] *AmE* the style of humour that a particular actor or COMEDIAN is typically known for

shtum /ʃtʊm/ *adj* [not before noun] another spelling of SCHTUM

shuck /ʃʌk/ *v* [T] *AmE* to remove the outer cover of a vegetable such as corn, or the shell of OYSTERS

shuck sth ↔ **off** *phr v AmE informal* to take off a piece of clothing: *She shucked off her jacket.*

shucks /ʃʌks/ *interjection AmE old-fashioned* used to show you are a little disappointed about something

shud·der¹ /ˈʃʌdə $ -ər/ ●○○ *v* [I]
1 to shake for a short time because you are afraid or cold, or because you think something is very unpleasant: *Maria shuddered as she stepped outside.* | **[+with]** *I shudder with embarrassment whenever I think about it.* | **[+at]** *She shuddered at the thought that she could have been killed.*
2 if a vehicle or machine shudders, it shakes violently: *The car shuddered briefly as its engine died.* | *The train* ***shuddered to a halt****.*
3 I shudder to think *spoken* used to say that you do not want to think about something because it is too unpleasant: *I shudder to think what they'll say when they see the mess the house is in.*

shudder at sth *phr v* to think that something is very bad or unpleasant: *If you love skiing but shudder at the cost, take advantage of our superb family offer.* | *He* ***shuddered at the thought of*** *the conflict ahead.*

shudder² *n* [C usually singular] a shaking movement: *The building* ***gave*** *a sudden* ***shudder****.* | **a shudder ran/passed/went through sb** *A shudder ran through him at the touch of her fingers.*

shuf·fle¹ /ˈʃʌfəl/ ●○○ *v*
1 [I always + adv/prep] to walk very slowly and noisily, without lifting your feet off the ground: **[+forward/over/back etc]** *The official signaled to one of the waiters, who shuffled forward.* | *With sore legs and aching chest, he shuffled over to the bathroom.* THESAURUS ▸ WALK
2 shuffle your feet to move your feet slightly, especially because you are bored or embarrassed: *Monica shuffled her feet nervously and stared at the floor.*
3 [T] to move something such as papers into a different order or into different positions: *Jack sat nervously shuffling the papers around on his desk.* | **[+through]** *Frances shuffled through a pile of magazines.*
4 [I,T] to mix PLAYING CARDS into a different order before playing a game with them: *Is it my turn to shuffle?* | *Just* ***shuffle the cards****.* → RESHUFFLE

shuffle² *n* **1** [singular] a slow walk in which you do not lift your feet off the ground **2** [C] the act of mixing cards into a different order before playing a game **3 be/get lost in the shuffle** to not be noticed or considered because there are so many other things to deal with: *The information contained in the memo got lost in the shuffle once it reached headquarters.*

shun /ʃʌn/ *v* (**shunned**, **shunning**) [T] to deliberately avoid someone or something: *a shy woman who* ***shunned publicity*** | *Victims of the disease found themselves shunned by society.*

shunt¹ /ʃʌnt/ *v* [T] **1** to move someone or something to another place, especially in a way that seems unfair: **shunt sb off/around/aside etc** *Smith was shunted off to one of the company's smaller offices.* **2** to move a train or railway carriage onto a different track

shunt² *n* [C] **1** an act of moving a train or railway carriage to a different track **2** *especially BrE informal* a crash, especially in a car race: *His race ended after a shunt at the first corner.*

shush /ʃʊʃ/ *v* **1 shush!** *spoken* used to tell someone, especially a child, to be quiet SYN **shh**: *'Shush!' said Jerry. 'Not so loud.'* **2** [T] to tell someone to be very quiet, especially by putting your fingers against your lips or by saying 'shush': *He started to cry and Francesca shushed him.*

shut¹ /ʃʌt/ ●●● S1 W2 *v* (*past tense and past participle* **shut**, *present participle* **shutting**)
1 [I,T] to close something, or to become closed: *Shut the window, Ellen!* | *I heard his bedroom door shut.* | *She lay down on her bed and* ***shut*** *her* ***eyes****.* | **shut (sth) behind sb** *She walked quickly in and shut the door behind her.* | *He shut the drawer and turned the key.* THESAURUS ▸ CLOSE
2 shut your mouth/face/trap! (*also* **shut your gob!/shut it!** *BrE*) *spoken not polite* used to tell someone to stop talking
3 [I,T] *BrE* to stop being open to the public for a short time or permanently SYN **close**: *The post office shuts at 5 o'clock.* | *At midday we shut the shop for lunch.* | *He lost his job when they shut the factory.*
4 shut your eyes/ears to sth to deliberately refuse to notice or pay attention to something: *We ought not to shut our*

eyes to these facts. | *She heard the boys shouting to her to stop, but she shut her ears to them.*
5 shut sth in the door/drawer etc *BrE*, **shut the door/drawer etc on sth** *AmE* to shut a door etc against something so that it gets trapped there: *I shut my finger in the back door yesterday and it still hurts.*
shut sb/sth ↔ **away** *phr v*
1 to put someone or something in a place away from other people where they cannot be seen: *A lot of people are classed as mad and shut away unnecessarily.*
2 shut yourself away to deliberately avoid seeing people by staying at home or going to a quiet place, especially because you are very unhappy or want to study, write etc: *When news came of Robin's death, she shut herself away and saw no one.* | **[+in]** *She shut herself away in her room to work on her novel.*
shut down *phr v*
1 if a company, factory, large machine etc shuts down or is shut down, it stops operating, either permanently or for a short time: *Our local hardware shop has shut down.* | **shut sth ↔ down** *an accident which resulted in two of the plant's nuclear reactors being shut down* | *The way to shut the machine down is to type EXIT.*
2 shut sb ↔ down *informal* to prevent an opposing team or player from playing well or getting points: *We all knew that to win we'd have to shut down Bobby Mitchell.*
shut sb **in** (sth) *phr v*
1 if you shut someone in a room, you close the door and stop them from getting out: *Her parents shut her in an upstairs room.* | *He pushed the dogs into the breakfast room and shut them in.*
2 shut yourself in (sth) if you shut yourself in a room, you close the door and stay in there, and often stop other people from coming in: *Ellie darted back to her room and shut herself in.* | *He shut himself in his room and wrote letters.*
shut off *phr v*
1 if a machine, tool etc shuts off or if you shut it off, it stops operating SYN **turn off**: *The iron shuts off automatically if it gets too hot.* | **shut sth ↔ off** *I let the engine run for a minute and then shut it off.* | *Don't forget to shut off the water supply.*
2 shut sth ↔ off to prevent goods or supplies from being available or being delivered: *a strike that closed the mines and shut off coal supplies*
3 shut yourself off to avoid meeting and talking to other people: **[+from]** *He was cold and remote, shutting himself off from her completely.*
4 be shut off from sb/sth to be separated from other people or things, especially so that you are not influenced by them: *The valley is shut off from the modern world.*
shut out *phr v*
1 shut sb out to deliberately not let someone join you in an activity or share your thoughts and feelings: *How can I help you if you just keep shutting me out all the time?* | **[+from]** *I felt I was being shut out from all the family's affairs.*
2 shut sb/sth ↔ out to prevent someone or something from entering a place: *heavy curtains that shut out the sunlight* | **[+from]** *The door closed firmly, shutting me out from the warmth inside.*
3 shut sth ↔ out to stop yourself from thinking about or noticing something, so that you are not affected by it: *People close their windows at night in a vain attempt to shut out the sound of gunfire.* | *She shut out memories of James.* | *Jenny closed her eyes and tried to* ***shut everything out***.
4 shut out sb *AmE* to defeat an opposing sports team and prevent them from getting any points: *Colorado shut out Kansas City 3–0.*
shut up *phr v*
1 shut up! *spoken not polite* used to tell someone to stop talking SYN **be quiet!**: *Oh, shut up! I don't want to hear your excuses.* | *Just shut up and listen.* | **[+about]** *Shut up about your stupid dog, okay!*
2 shut (sb) up *informal* to stop talking or be quiet, or to make someone do this: *I can't stand that woman. She never shuts up.* | **[+about]** *I wish you'd shut up about Chris.* | *I only said that to shut her up.*
3 shut sb up to keep someone in a place away from other people, and prevent them from leaving: **[+in]** *I've had a terrible cold and been shut up in my room for a week.* | *Was there any need to keep us shut up here?*
4 shut sth ↔ up to close a shop, room etc so that people cannot get into it: *Bernadette cleaned the attic and then shut it up for another year.*
5 shut up shop *BrE informal* to close a business or stop working, at the end of the day or permanently

shut² ●●● S3 *adj* [not before noun]
1 not open SYN **closed**: *Is the* ***door shut*** *properly?* | *She* ***kept*** *the windows* ***shut***, *for fear of burglars.* | *He sat with his* ***eyes shut***. | *The windows were* ***tightly shut***. | **slam/bang/swing etc shut** *The door slammed shut behind him.* | **pull/kick/slam etc sth shut** *Jenny pulled the window shut.* → **keep your mouth shut** at KEEP¹(2)
2 *BrE* if a shop, bar etc is shut, it is not open for business SYN **closed**: *in the evening when the shops are shut* | *Sorry, but we're shut.* | **[+for]** *The first four hotels we tried were shut for the winter.*

shut·down /ˈʃʌtdaʊn/ ●○○ *n* [C] the closing of a factory, business, or piece of machinery, either permanently or for a short time: **[+of]** *Environmental groups had called for the permanent shutdown of the plant.* | *safety systems and automatic shutdown procedures*

ˈshut-eye *n* [U] *informal* sleep: *We'd better* ***get some shut-eye***.

ˈshut-in *n* [C] *AmE* someone who is ill or DISABLED and cannot leave their house very easily

ˈshut-out *n* [C] *AmE* a game in which one team is prevented by the other from getting any points

shut·ter¹ /ˈʃʌtə $ -ər/ *n* [C] **1** [usually plural] one of a pair of wooden or metal covers on the outside of a window that can be closed to keep light out or prevent thieves from coming in → see picture at BLIND³ **2** a part of a camera that opens for a very short time to let light onto the film

shutter² *v* [T] *AmE* to close a business, office etc for a short time or permanently: *The company shuttered its Hong Kong business a year ago.*

shut·ter·bug /ˈʃʌtəbʌg $ -ər-/ *n* [C] *AmE informal* someone who likes to take a lot of photographs

shut·tered /ˈʃʌtəd $ -ərd/ *adj* with closed shutters, or having shutters: *A gust of wind shook the shuttered windows.*

shut·tle¹ /ˈʃʌtl/ ●○○ *n* [C]
1 a SPACE SHUTTLE
2 a plane, bus, or train that makes regular short journeys between two places: *He took the Washington–New York shuttle.* | *A* ***shuttle bus*** *operates to and from the beach of San Benedetto.* | *There's a* ***shuttle service*** *from the city center to the airport.*
3 a pointed tool used in weaving, to pass a thread over and under the threads that form the cloth

shuttle² *v* **1** [I always + adv/prep] to travel frequently between two places SYN **commute**: **[+between/back and forth]** *Susan shuttles between Rotterdam and London for her job.* **2** [T] to move people from one place to another place that is fairly near SYN **transport**: *The passengers were shuttled to the hotel by bus.*

shut·tle·cock /ˈʃʌtlkɒk $ -kɑːk/ *n* [C] a small light object that you hit over the net in the game of BADMINTON SYN **birdie** *AmE* → see picture at SPORT¹

ˈshuttle diˌplomacy *n* [U] international talks in which someone travels between countries and talks to members of the governments, for example to make a peace agreement

shy¹ /ʃaɪ/ ●●○ *adj* (*comparative* **shyer**, *superlative* **shyest**)
1 nervous and embarrassed about meeting and speaking to other people, especially people you do not know: *He was a quiet shy man.* | **[+with]** *She was very shy with strangers.* | *a shy smile* | *As a teenager, I was* ***painfully shy*** (=extremely shy). | **shy to do sth** *He was* ***too shy*** *to come*

S

and sit by me in class. | **go all shy** *BrE* (=to suddenly become very shy) *Oh, have you gone all shy, Jenny?* THESAURUS CONFIDENT
2 sb is not shy about (doing) sth used to emphasize that someone is very willing to do something or get involved with something: *John has strong opinions and he's not shy about sharing them.*
3 unwilling to do something or get involved in something: **be shy about/of (doing) sth** *Employees are urged not to be shy about reporting incidents of sexual harassment.*
4 be shy (of sth) *especially AmE* to have less than a particular amount of something: *The Democrats are three votes shy of a majority.* | *Jessica died Monday. She was one week shy of her 13th birthday.*
5 used to say that someone does not like something and therefore tries to avoid it: *Although* ***publicity-shy****, he recently agreed to be interviewed.* → CAMERA-SHY, WORK-SHY
6 shy animals get frightened easily and are unwilling to come near people SYN **timid**: *Deer are* ***shy creatures****.*
—**shyly** *adv*: *He grinned shyly.* —**shyness** *n* [U]: *I* ***overcame*** *my* ***shyness****.* → **fight shy of (doing) sth** at FIGHT[1](22), → **once bitten, twice shy** at BITE[1](14)

THESAURUS

bashful shy and not willing to say very much
self-conscious worried and embarrassed about what you look like or what other people think of you
timid not brave or confident
reserved not liking to express your emotions or talk about your problems
introverted thinking a lot about your own interests, problems etc, and not liking to be with other people
withdrawn quiet and not wanting to talk to other people, especially because you are unhappy
antisocial not liking to meet people and talk to them
retiring *formal* not wanting to be with other people

S

shy[2] *v* (**shied, shying, shies**) [I] if a horse shies, it makes a sudden movement away from something because it is frightened: *The horse shied, throwing Darrel from his saddle.*
shy away from sth *phr v* to avoid doing or dealing with something because you are not confident enough or you are worried or nervous about it: *They criticized the leadership, but shied away from a direct challenge.*

shy[3] → COCONUT SHY

shys·ter /ˈʃaɪstə $ -ər/ *n* [C] *especially AmE informal* a dishonest person, especially a lawyer or BUSINESSMAN

Si·a·mese cat /ˌsaɪəmiːz ˈkæt/ *n* [C] a type of cat that has blue eyes, short grey or brown fur, and a dark face

ˌSiamese ˈtwin *n* [C usually plural] one of two people who are born joined to each other – sometimes considered offensive SYN **conjoined twin**

sib·i·lant[1] /ˈsɪbələnt/ *adj formal* making an 's' or 'sh' sound: *a sibilant whisper*

sibilant[2] *n* [C] *technical* a sibilant sound such as 's' or 'sh' in English

sib·ling /ˈsɪblɪŋ/ ●○○ *n* [C]
1 *formal* a brother or sister: *Most young smokers are influenced by their friends' and older siblings' smoking habits.*
2 sibling rivalry competition between brothers and sisters for their parents' attention or love

sic[1] /sɪk/ *adv written formal* used after a word that you have copied in order to show that you know it was not spelled or used correctly: *We had seen several signs that said 'ORANGE'S (sic) FOR SALE'.*

sic[2] *v* (**sicced, siccing**) [T] *AmE informal* **1** to tell a dog to attack someone: **sic sth on sb** *He* ***sicced*** *his* ***dog*** *on me.*
2 sic 'em! *spoken* used to tell a dog to attack someone
3 to tell someone in authority that someone has done something wrong, so that they are punished: **[+on]** *He sicced his lawyers on them.*

sick[1] /sɪk/ ●●● S1 W3 *adj*
1 ILL *especially AmE* suffering from a disease or illness: *His mother's very sick.* | *Maria can't come in today because she's sick.* | *a sick child* | *a sick animal* | **[+with]** *I have been sick with flu.* | **get sick** (=become ill) *AmE*: *At the last minute, I got sick and couldn't go.* | **be off sick** *BrE*, **be out sick** *AmE* (=be away from work or school because you are ill) *Two of his employees were out sick.* | *I was off sick for four days with the flu.* | **phone/ring/call in sick** (=phone to say you are not coming to work because you are ill) *He was upset because it was the first day of the sale and Astrid had called in sick.* | *What will happen to the business if you* ***fall sick*** (=become ill) *or die?* | *He* ***took sick*** (=became ill) *and died a week later.* | *Pete's at home in bed,* ***as sick as a dog*** (=very sick). THESAURUS ILL
2 be sick if you are sick, the food in your stomach comes up through your mouth SYN **vomit, throw up**: *I think I'm going to be sick.* | *He dashed to the bathroom and was sick again.* | *The cat's been sick on the carpet.* | *You'll be sick if you eat any more of that chocolate!* | *I was* ***violently sick*** (=suddenly and severely sick) *the last time I ate prawns.*
3 feel sick (*also* **be/feel sick to your stomach** *AmE*) to feel as if you are going to VOMIT: *As soon as the ship started moving I began to feel sick.* | **[+with]** *Mary felt sick with fear.* | *She began to shiver, feeling sick to her stomach.* | *Virginia had a* ***sick feeling*** *in her stomach.* → CARSICK, SEASICK, → **travel-sick** at TRAVEL SICKNESS
4 make me/you sick *spoken* **a)** to make you feel very angry: *People like you make me sick!* **b)** to make you feel jealous – used humorously: *You make me sick with your 'expenses paid' holidays!*
5 make sb/yourself sick *BrE* **a)** if something makes you sick, it makes you bring food up from your stomach through your mouth: *The smell of blood made him sick.* **b)** if you make yourself sick, you do something to bring food up from your stomach through your mouth: *I've never been able to make myself sick.* | *You'll make yourself sick if you eat any more!*
6 be sick (and tired) of (doing) sth (*also* **be sick to death of (doing) sth**) *spoken* to be angry or bored with something that has been happening for a long time: *I'm sick and tired of your excuses.* | *I am sick of working for other people.*
7 be worried sick/be sick with worry to be extremely worried: *Why didn't you tell me you were coming home late? I've been worried sick!*
8 STRANGE/CRUEL **a)** someone who is sick does things that are strange and cruel, and seems mentally ill: *I keep getting obscene phone calls from some sick pervert.* | *You're sick!* | *a* ***sick mind*** **b)** sick stories, jokes etc deal with death and suffering in a cruel or unpleasant way: *I don't want to hear any of your* ***sick jokes****, thank you.* | ***That's*** *really* ***sick****!*
9 sick at heart *literary* very unhappy, upset, or disappointed about something: *I was sick at heart to think that I would never see the place again.*
10 sick as a parrot *BrE spoken* extremely disappointed – used humorously
11 [not before noun] *BrE spoken* used by young people to say that something is very impressive and they admire it a lot

sick[2] *n* **1 the sick** [plural] people who are ill: *The sick and wounded were allowed to go free.* **2** [U] *BrE informal* VOMIT: *The phone box smelt of sick.*

sick[3] *v*
sick sth ↔ **up** *phr v BrE informal* to bring up food from your stomach – used especially of children SYN **vomit up** *AmE*: *Ruth had frequently sicked up her bottle milk.*

sick·bag /ˈsɪkbæg/ *n* [C] a special paper bag for people to use if they need to VOMIT, for example when they are travelling on a plane

sick·bay /ˈsɪkbeɪ/ *n* [C] a room on a ship, in a school etc where there are beds for people who are sick

sick·bed /ˈsɪkbed/ *n* [C usually singular] the bed where a sick person is lying: **from your sickbed** *The president carried on working from his sickbed.*

ˌsick ˈbuilding ˌsyndrome *n* [U] when chemicals and GERMS stay in an office building and make the people who work there feel ill: *A common household fungus can contribute to sick building syndrome.*

sick·en /ˈsɪkən/ *v* **1** [T] to make you feel shocked and angry, especially because you strongly disapprove of something SYN **disgust**: *The thought of such cruelty sickened her.* | *All decent people should be sickened by such a pointless waste of life.* **2** [I] *old-fashioned* to gradually become very ill: *The older people just sickened and died as food supplies ran low.*

be sickening for sth *phr v BrE* to be starting to have an illness: *Perhaps you're sickening for something.*

sicken of sth *phr v* to lose your desire for something or your interest in it: *He finally sickened of the endless round of parties and idle conversation.*

sick·en·ing /ˈsɪkənɪŋ, ˈsɪknɪŋ/ *adj* **1** very shocking, annoying, or upsetting SYN **disgusting**: *Police described it as a sickening racial attack.* | *their sickening hypocrisy* | **it is sickening that** *It is sickening that human beings have done this to two innocent young women.* **2 sickening thud/crash/sound etc** an unpleasant sound that makes you think someone has been injured or something has been broken: *His head hit the floor with a sickening thud.* | *There was a sickening sound of tearing metal.* **3** very unpleasant and making you feel as if you want to VOMIT: *The sickening stench of rotting rubbish rose into the air.* **4** *BrE spoken* making you feel jealous: *'Helen's just bought herself a huge house in the South of France.' 'God, how sickening!'* —**sickeningly** *adv*

sick·ie /ˈsɪki/ *n* [C] *informal* **1** *BrE* a day when you say that you are sick and do not go to work, even though you are not really sick: *Looks like he's* ***thrown*** *another* ***sickie*** (=pretended to be sick and not gone to work). **2** *AmE* a SICKO – used humorously

sick·le /ˈsɪkəl/ *n* [C] a tool with a blade in the shape of a hook, used for cutting wheat or long grass

ˈsick leave *n* [U] time that you are allowed to spend away from work because you are sick: **on sick leave** *He has been on sick leave for more than three months.*

ˌsickle-cell aˈnaemia *BrE*, **sickle-cell anemia** *AmE n* [U] a serious illness that mainly affects black people, in which the blood cells change shape, causing weakness and fever

sick·ly /ˈsɪkli/ *adj* **1** a sickly person or animal is weak, unhealthy, and often ill: *a* ***sickly child*** | *She looked pale and sickly.* THESAURUS ▸ ILL **2** *especially BrE* a sickly smell, taste etc is unpleasant and makes you feel sick: *A* ***sickly smell*** *clung to his clothes and hair.* THESAURUS ▸ SWEET **3** a sickly colour or light is unpleasantly pale or weak: *The walls were painted a sickly green.* | *a pale sickly moon* —**sickly** *adv*: *a* ***sickly sweet*** *perfume*

sick·ness /ˈsɪknəs/ ●●○ *n*

1 [U] the state of being ill SYN **illness**: *an insurance policy against long-term sickness and injury* | *working days lost due to sickness* THESAURUS ▸ ILLNESS

2 [U] the feeling that you are about to bring up food from your stomach, or the act of bringing food up SYN **nausea**: **travel/motion/car/sea etc sickness** (=sickness that some people get while travelling) | *Liam had suffered violent sickness and diarrhoea.* → MORNING SICKNESS, SLEEPING SICKNESS

3 [C] a particular illness: *war-related sicknesses*

4 [C,U] the serious problems and weaknesses of a social, political, or economic system: *He said the idea of 'success' was part of the sickness of Western cultures.*

ˈsickness ˌbenefit *n* [U] *BrE* money paid by the government to someone who is too ill to work

ˈsick note *n* [C] *BrE* a note written by your doctor or your parents saying that you were too ill to go to work or school SYN **excuse** *AmE*

sick·o /ˈsɪkəʊ $ -koʊ/ *n* (*plural* **sickos**) [C] *informal* someone who gets pleasure from things that most people find unpleasant or upsetting: *What kind of sicko would write something like that?*

ˈsick-out *n* [C] *AmE* a STRIKE (=protest about pay or working conditions) in which all the workers at a company say they are sick and stay home on the same day

ˈsick pay *n* [U] money paid by an employer to a worker who is too ill to work

sick·room /ˈsɪk-rʊm, -ruːm/ *n* [C] a room where someone who is ill can go to lie down

side¹ /saɪd/ ●●● S1 W1 *n* [C]

1 PART OF AN AREA one of the two areas that are on the left or the right of an imaginary line, or on the left or the right of a border, wall, river etc: **[+of]** *The south side of town is pretty run down.* | **on the ... side** *a scar on the right side of his face* | *Fuel is cheaper on the French side of the border.* | **to one/the side** *She tilted her head to one side, pretending to consider the question.* | *A man stood watching me from* ***the other side of*** *the road.* | *His friends and family were all on* ***the other side of*** *the world.* | *The restaurant was empty apart from another couple on* ***the far side of*** *the room* (=the area that is furthest away from you). | **the right-hand/left-hand side** (=the right side or the left side) *In Sri Lanka they drive on the left-hand side of the road.*

2 NEXT TO [usually singular] a position directly next to someone or something, on the right or the left: **on this/one side (of sb/sth)** *Stand on this side of me so Dad can get a photo.* | **at sb's side/at the side of sth** *A little girl was skipping along at her side.* | *There was a card tacked to the wall at the side of the photograph.* | **on either side (of sth)** *Two large screens stood on either side of the stage* (=one on the left and one on the right side of it). | **to sb's side** *Maggie hurried to his side.*

3 OF A BUILDING/OBJECT/VEHICLE ETC a surface of something that is not its front, back, top, or bottom: **[+of]** *He led the way round to the side of the building.* | *the side of her glass* | *Someone ran into the side of my car.* | **high-sided/straight-sided etc** *high-sided vehicles* | *a straight-sided dish*

4 EDGE the part of an object or area that is furthest from the middle, at or near the edge: **[+of]** *Jack sat down heavily on the side of the bed.* | *She pulled into the side of the road and stopped the car.* → FIRESIDE, LAKESIDE, RIVERSIDE, ROADSIDE, SEASIDE¹ THESAURUS ▸ EDGE

5 OF A THIN OBJECT one of the two surfaces of a thin flat object: **[+of]** *Write on only one side of the paper.* | *I'll paint the other side of the fence tomorrow.* | *There's a scratch on one side of the record.*

6 PART OF YOUR BODY the part of your body from the top of your arm to the top of your leg: *He had a scar running right the way down his side.* | *Betty was* ***lying on*** *her* ***side*** *on the bed.*

7 SHAPE one of the flat surfaces or edges of a shape: *A cube has six sides.* | **three-sided/four-sided etc** *a seven-sided coin*

8 MOUNTAIN/VALLEY one of the sloping areas of a hill, mountain etc: **[+of]** *Their house was on the side of the valley.* | **hillside/mountainside** *sheep grazing on the steep hillside* | **steep-sided/sheer-sided etc** *a steep-sided valley*

9 PAGE *BrE* a page of writing on one side of a piece of paper: *How many sides have we got to write?*

10 side by side a) next to each other: *We walked along the beach, side by side.* **b)** if people work side by side, they work together to achieve something: **[+with]** *Local citizens worked side by side with emergency crews to pull their neighbors out of the rubble.* **c)** if different things or groups exist side by side, they exist in the same place or at the same time, even though this may seem difficult or surprising: *a visit to see how modern agriculture and wildlife can exist side by side*

11 from side to side first to one side, then to the other, several times or continuously: *'Did you catch him?' Matthew shook his head from side to side.* | **swing/rock/sway from side to side** *The boat rocked violently from side to side.*

12 SUBJECT/SITUATION one part or feature of something, especially when compared with another part: **technical/financial/social etc side** *She takes care of the financial side of the business.* | **serious/funny/negative/positive etc side** *Can't you see the funny side of all this?* | *Environmental pollution gives great cause for concern, but,* ***on the positive side****, people are beginning to try and find solutions.* | ***Look on the bright side*** (=see the good side of a situation) *– at least you learned something from the experience.* | *It's a children's book about fairies and magic, but it does have a* ***dark side****.*

13 ARGUMENT/WAR one of the people, groups, or countries opposing each other in a quarrel, war etc: *He fought*

on the Republican side in the Spanish Civil War. | *a peace deal that is acceptable to both sides* | *During the war, he* ***changed sides*** *several times.* | **be on sb's side** (=support them) *Well, at least someone's on my side.* | **whose side are you on?** *spoken* (=used when someone is arguing against you when they should be supporting you) | *He always likes to be* ***on the winning side.***

14 OPINION one person's opinion or attitude in an argument or disagreement SYN **point of view**: *Try and* ***see*** *my* ***side of things*** *for a change!* | *Well, I can* ***see both sides.*** *They both have a point.* | **sb's side of the story** (=one person's opinion of what happened in a situation, especially someone who has been accused of doing something wrong) *We haven't heard Mike's side of the story yet.*

15 take sides to choose to support one person or group in an argument, and oppose the other one

16 SPORT *BrE* a sports team: *They're a good side, but I think we're a better one.*

17 PART OF SB'S CHARACTER [usually singular] one part of someone's character, especially when compared with another part: **[+of]** *It was a side of Shari that I hadn't seen before.* | ***There was a side to*** *him that worried her, that seemed cold and cruel.* | **sb's softer/feminine/emotional etc side** *These days men are not all afraid to show their softer side.*

18 OF A FAMILY a part of a family: *My* ***father's side of the family*** *are short, but my* ***mother's side*** *are tall.*

19 sb's side of a deal/bargain what someone agrees to do as part of an agreement: *The Russians* ***kept*** *their* ***side of the bargain****, and pulled out of East Germany.*

20 on the side a) used to say that someone does work in addition to their regular job: *Most consultants do private work on the side.* → SIDELINE[1](1) **b)** secretly, and dishonestly or illegally: *His wife discovered that he had a woman on the side.* → **a bit on the side** at BIT[3] **c)** food that is served on the side is ordered with the main dish in a restaurant, but is not usually part of that dish: *I'd like eggs with toast on the side.*

21 FOOD *AmE* a small amount of food that you order in a restaurant in addition to your main meal: **[+of]** *a hamburger with a side of fries*

22 on/from all sides (*also* **on/from every side**) **a)** in or from every direction: *Planes were attacking us from all sides.* | *The town is* ***surrounded on all sides*** *by vineyards.* **b)** by or from a lot of people with different opinions: *Clinton was praised on all sides for his warm manner and diplomatic approach.*

23 put/leave/set sth to one side to save something to be dealt with or used later: *Let's leave that question to one side for now.* | *Put a little money to one side each week.*

24 be at sb's side/stay by sb's side/not leave sb's side to be with someone, and take care of them or support them: *He faced the reporters with his wife at his side.* | *She nursed him through his illness, never leaving his side.*

25 take/draw sb to one side to take someone away from other people for a short time for a private talk: *Before they left, Colette took me to one side and warned me about Bernard.*

26 have sth on your side/sth is on your side used to say that you have an advantage that increases your chances of success: **have time/luck/God/right etc on your side** *Barnes didn't have much experience, but he had youth and enthusiasm on his side.*

27 get on the wrong side of sb to annoy someone or make them angry, especially someone who can cause serious problems for you: *Be careful not to get on the wrong side of her.*

28 keep on the right side of sb to be careful not to annoy someone, because you want them to help you and not cause problems for you: *We tried to keep on the right side of the housekeeper, so that she would let us bring beer in.*

29 on the right/wrong side of 30/40 etc *informal* younger or older than 30, 40 etc

30 on the small/high/heavy etc side *spoken* a little too small, too high, too heavy etc: *The trousers are a bit on the small side.*

31 this side of Christmas/midnight etc before a particular time – used to say that something will not happen before then: *I doubt we'll see him this side of Christmas.*

32 the best/biggest etc ... this side of sth used humorously to say that something is very good, big etc: *the best Chinese food this side of Peking*

33 on the wrong/right side of the law *informal* breaking or not breaking the law

34 be on the side of the angels to be doing what is morally right

35 let the side down *BrE* to behave badly or do something that embarrasses or disappoints your family, friends etc

36 criticize/nag/hassle sb up one side and down the other *AmE spoken* to criticize someone, complain to them in an annoying way etc without worrying about how they feel

37 MEAT **a side of beef/bacon etc** one half of an animal's body, used as food

38 TV STATION [usually singular] *BrE spoken* a television station SYN **channel**: *What's on the other side?*
→ **DOUBLE-SIDED, ONE-SIDED,** → **to be on the safe side** at SAFE[1](8), → **err on the side of caution** at ERR(1), → **FLIP SIDE,** → **split your sides** at SPLIT[1](10), → **the other side of the coin** at COIN[1](3), → **two sides of the same coin** at COIN[1](4)

side² ●●● S3 *adj* [only before noun]
1 in or on the side of something: *Hannah slipped out through a side exit.*
2 from the side of something: *Can you get a side view?*

side³ *v* [I] to support or argue against a person or group in a quarrel, fight etc: **[+with/against]** *Frank sided with David against their mother.*

side·arm /ˈsaɪd-ɑːm $ -ɑːrm/ *n* [C] a weapon carried or worn at someone's side, for example a gun or sword

side·bar /ˈsaɪdbɑː $ -bɑːr/ *n* [C] **1** a separate part of something such as a newspaper article where extra information is given **2** *AmE law* an occasion when the lawyers and the judge in a TRIAL discuss something without letting the JURY hear what they are saying

ˈside ˌbenefit *n* [C] an additional advantage or good result that comes from something, besides its main purpose: *A side benefit to filming close-up shots is that your microphone will pick up clearer sound.*

side·board /ˈsaɪdbɔːd $ -bɔːrd/ *n* **1** [C] a long low piece of furniture usually in a DINING ROOM, used for storing plates, glasses etc **2 sideboards** [plural] *BrE* sideburns

side·burns /ˈsaɪdbɜːnz $ -bɜːrnz/ *n* [plural] hair grown down the sides of a man's face in front of his ears

side·car /ˈsaɪdkɑː $ -kɑːr/ *n* [C] a small vehicle attached to the side of a MOTORCYCLE, in which a passenger can ride

ˈside dish *n* [C] a small amount of food such as a vegetable that you eat with a main meal

ˈside efˌfect ●○○ *n* [C]
1 an effect that a drug has on your body in addition to curing pain or illness: **harmful/serious/adverse etc side effect** *a natural remedy with no harmful side effects* | **[+of]** *the side effects of the medication*
2 an unexpected or unplanned result of a situation or event: *These policy changes could* ***have*** *beneficial* ***side effects*** *for the whole economy.*

ˈside ˌissue *n* [C] a subject or problem that is not as important as the main one, and may take people's attention away from the main subject: *The tax proposal is really a side issue with us.*

side·kick /ˈsaɪdˌkɪk/ *n* [C] *informal* someone who spends time with or helps another person, especially when that other person is more important than they are

side·light /ˈsaɪdlaɪt/ *n* [C] *BrE* one of the two small lights next to the main front lights on a car SYN **parking light** *AmE* → see picture at CAR

side·line¹ /ˈsaɪdlaɪn/ *n* **1** [C] an activity that you do as well as your main job or business, in order to earn more money: **as a sideline** *Zoë does a bit of freelance photography as a sideline.* **2 on the sidelines** not taking part in an activity even though you want to or should do: **stand/stay/remain etc on the sidelines** *You can't stay on the sidelines for ever; it's time you got involved.* **3 sidelines** [plural] the area just outside the lines that form the edge of a sports field: **on**

the sidelines *Wenger stood on the sidelines shouting instructions.* **4** [C] a line at the side of a sports field, which shows where the players are allowed to play

sideline² *v* [T] if you are sidelined, you are unable to play in a sports game because you are injured, or unable to take part in an activity because you are not as good as someone else: *Owen was once again sidelined through injury.* GRAMMAR **Sideline** is usually passive.

side·long /ˈsaɪdlɒŋ $ -lɒːŋ/ *adj* **sidelong look/glance** a way of looking at someone by moving your eyes to the side, especially so that it seems secret, dishonest, or disapproving: *He* ***gave*** *Oliver a* ***sidelong glance****.* —**sidelong** *adv*: *'You looked very well this morning,' she added,* ***glancing sidelong*** *at him.*

ˌside-ˈon *adj* coming from one side rather than from in front or behind: *a* ***side-on collision*** —**side-on** *adv*

ˈside ˌorder *n* [C] a small amount of food ordered in a restaurant to be eaten with a main meal but served on a separate dish: *a side order of onion rings*

ˈside road *n* [C] a road that is smaller than a main road, but is often connected to it

ˈside-ˌsaddle *adv* **ride/sit side-saddle** to ride or sit on a horse with both legs on the same side of the horse

side·show /ˈsaɪdʃəʊ $ -ʃoʊ/ *n* [C] **1** a separate small part of a FAIR or CIRCUS, where you pay to play games or watch a performance **2** an event that is much less important or serious than another one: *The initial conflict was a mere sideshow compared with the World War that followed.*

side·split·ting /ˈsaɪdˌsplɪtɪŋ/ *adj* extremely funny SYN **hilarious**: *He told some sidesplitting jokes.*

side·step /ˈsaɪdstep/ *v* (**sidestepped**, **sidestepping**) **1 sidestep a problem/issue/question** to avoid dealing with something difficult: *The report sidesteps the environmental issues.* **2** [I,T] to step quickly sideways to avoid being hit or walking into someone —**sidestep** *n* [C]

ˈside street *n* [C] a street that is smaller than a main street, but is often connected to it

side·swipe¹ /ˈsaɪdswaɪp/ *n* [C usually singular] if you take a sideswipe at someone or something, you criticize them while you are talking about something different: *Sir Kenneth concluded with a sideswipe at his critics.*

sideswipe² *v* [T] *AmE* to hit the side of a car with another car so that the two sides touch quickly: *She was going too fast and sideswiped a parked car.*

side·track /ˈsaɪdtræk/ *v* [T] **1** to make someone stop doing what they should be doing, or stop talking about what they started talking about, by making them interested in something else: *Don't* ***get sidetracked*** *by the audience's questions.* **2** *AmE* to delay or stop the progress of something: *An effort to improve security was sidetracked by budget problems.* GRAMMAR **Sidetrack** is usually passive.

ˌside-view ˈmirror *n* [C] *AmE* a mirror attached to the side of a car SYN **wing mirror** *BrE* → see picture at CAR

side·walk /ˈsaɪdwɔːk $ -wɒːk/ ●●● S3 *n* [C] *AmE* a hard surface or path at the side of a street for people to walk on SYN **pavement** *BrE*

side·ways /ˈsaɪdweɪz/ ●○○ *adv*
1 to or towards one side: *A strong gust of wind blew the car sideways into the ditch.*
2 with the side, rather than the front or back, facing forwards: *They brought the piano sideways through the front door.*
3 if you are moved sideways at work, you are given a job that is different from, but is at the same level as, your old job: *He would be moved sideways, rather than demoted.* —**sideways** *adj*: *a* ***sideways glance*** → **knock sb sideways** at KNOCK¹(13)

side·wheel·er /ˈsaɪdˌwiːlə $ -ər/ *n* [C] *AmE* an old-fashioned type of ship which is pushed forward by a pair of large wheels at the sides SYN **paddle steamer** *BrE*

sid·ing /ˈsaɪdɪŋ/ *n* **1** [C] a short railway track connected to a main track, where trains are kept when they are not being used **2** [U] *AmE* long narrow pieces of wood, metal, or plastic, used for covering the outside walls of houses

si·dle /ˈsaɪdl/ *v* [I always + adv/prep] to walk towards something or someone slowly and quietly, as if you do not want to be noticed: **[+up/towards/along]** *A woman sidled up to us and asked if we wanted to buy a watch.*

SIDS /sɪdz/ *n* [U] *medical* (***Sudden Infant Death Syndrome***) when a baby stops breathing and dies while it is sleeping, for no known reason → **cot death**, **crib death**

siege /siːdʒ/ ●●○ *n* [C,U]
1 a situation in which an army or the police surround a place and try to gain control of it or force someone to come out of it: *The siege lasted almost four months.* | *a three-day police siege at a remote country cottage* | **[+of]** *the siege of Leningrad* | **end/lift/raise a siege** (=end a siege)
2 lay siege to sb/sth a) if the army or police lay siege to a place, they start a siege against it: *In June 1176, King Richard laid siege to Limoges.* **b)** if you lay siege to someone, you do everything you can to try and get them to talk to you: *Then he set to work laying siege to her with letters.*
3 be under siege a) to be surrounded by an army in a siege **b)** to be being criticized, attacked, or threatened all the time: *The TV station has been under siege from irate viewers phoning in to complain.*
4 siege mentality the feeling among a group of people that they are surrounded by enemies and must do everything they can to protect themselves

si·en·na /siˈenə/ *n* [U] a yellowish-brown colour

si·er·ra /siˈerə/ *n* [C] a row or area of sharply pointed mountains

Siˈerra ˌClub, the *trademark* a US organization that tries to protect the environment, especially natural areas such as forests, mountains, and rivers. It is also a social club for people who like to HIKE.

si·es·ta /siˈestə/ *n* [C] a short sleep in the afternoon, especially in warm countries: **take/have a siesta** *The stores all close after lunch when everyone takes a siesta.*

sieve¹ /sɪv/ *n* [C] **1 a)** a round wire kitchen tool with a lot of small holes, used for separating solid food from liquid or small pieces of food from large pieces **b)** a round wire tool for separating small objects from large objects **2 have a memory like a sieve** *informal* to forget things easily

sieve² *v* [T] to put flour or other food through a sieve: *Sieve the flour and cocoa powder into a bowl.*

sift /sɪft/ *v* [T] **1** to put flour, sugar etc through a sieve or similar container in order to remove large pieces **2** (*also* **sift through**) to examine information, documents etc carefully in order to find something out or decide what is important and what is not: *Police are sifting through the evidence.*

sift sth ↔ **out** *phr v* to separate something from other things: **[+from]** *It's hard to sift out the truth from the lies in this case.*

sift·er /ˈsɪftə $ -ər/ *n* [C] **1** *BrE* a container with a lot of small holes in the top used for shaking flour, sugar etc onto things SYN **shaker** *AmE* **2** *AmE* a container with a handle and a lot of small holes on the bottom, used for removing large pieces from flour or for mixing flour and other dry things together in cooking

sigh¹ /saɪ/ ●●○ *v* [I]
1 to breathe in and out making a long sound, especially because you are bored, disappointed, tired etc: *'Well, there's nothing we can do about it now,' she sighed.* | **sigh heavily/deeply** *Frankie stared out of the window and sighed deeply.* | **[+with]** *He sighed with despair at the thought of all the opportunities he had missed.* THESAURUS ▸ BREATHE
2 *literary* if the wind sighs, it makes a long sound like someone sighing: *The wind sighed in the trees.*
3 sigh for sth to be sad because you are thinking about a pleasant time in the past: *Emilia sighed for her lost youth.*

sigh² ●●○ *n* [C] an act or sound of sighing: **[+of]** *She let out a sigh of impatience.* | **give/let out/heave a sigh** *Laura shrugged, and gave a heavy sigh.* | *We all breathed a* ***sigh of relief*** *when we heard they were safe.*

sight¹ /saɪt/ ●●● S2 W2 *n*
1 ABILITY TO SEE [U] the physical ability to see SYN **vision**: *Anne's sight is very good for someone of her age.* | *He began*

to **lose** his **sight** six years ago. | an emergency operation to save his sight | You will get a free sight test if you are under 16.

2 ACT OF SEEING [singular, U] the act of seeing something: **[+of]** *Just the sight of him made her go all weak.* | **at the sight of sth** *Marcie will faint at the sight of blood.* | *The house is **hidden from sight** behind trees.*

3 THING YOU SEE [C] **a)** something you can see: **familiar/common/rare etc sight** *Street dentists are a common sight in Pakistan.* | *As he reached the front door, he saw a strange sight.* | *the **sights and sounds** of the forest* → **not a pretty sight** at PRETTY²(3), → **sorry sight** at SORRY(8) **b) the sights** [plural] famous or interesting places that tourists visit: *In the afternoon, you'll have a chance to relax or **see the sights**.* | **[+of]** *So, Maria's **showing** you **the sights** of Copenhagen, is she?* → SIGHTSEEING

4 in/within sight a) inside the area that you can see: *I glanced around me quickly. There was **no one in sight**.* | *They burned **every** house **in sight**.* | *The boys get home and eat **everything in sight**.* | *Since my hotel was within sight, I told him he could go.* **b)** likely to happen soon: *Six months from the start of the strike, there is still **no end in sight**.* | *Peace is now in sight.*

5 within/in sight of sth a) in the area where you can see something: *We camped within sight of the lake.* | *At last they **came in sight of** the city.* **b)** in a position where you will soon be able to get something or achieve something: *Dan was now within sight of the championship.*

6 in your sights if you have someone or something in your sights, you intend to achieve it or get it for yourself, or to attack them: **have sb/sth in your sights** *Rogers had victory firmly in his sights.*

7 out of sight outside the area that you can see: *Karen waved until the car was out of sight.*

8 out of sight, out of mind used to say that people soon stop thinking about something or someone if they do not see them for a while

9 disappear/vanish from sight to disappear: *'Will she be all right?' asked Jen as the car disappeared from sight.*

10 come into sight to appear: *when the ship at last came into sight*

11 on sight as soon as you see someone: *The army has been ordered to **shoot** rebel soldiers **on sight**.* | *Jo disliked him on sight.*

12 not let sb out of your sight to make sure that someone stays near you: *Since the accident, Donna hasn't let the children out of her sight.*

13 be sick of/can't stand/hate the sight of sb/sth to dislike someone or something very much: *Alan and Sam can't stand the sight of each other.* | *Everybody hates the sight of you.*

14 a sight for sore eyes *spoken* **a)** someone or something that you feel very happy to see **b)** *BrE* someone or something that is very unattractive or very funny to look at

15 a (damn/darned/darn) sight more/better etc *informal* a lot more, a lot better etc: *I know the place a damn sight better than you do.* | *The old lady is a sight cleverer than Sarah.*

16 be a sight (*also* **look a sight**) to look very funny or stupid, or very untidy or unpleasant: *We'd had an all-night party, and the place looked a bit of a sight.*

17 sight unseen if you buy or choose something sight unseen, you do it without looking at the thing first: *I can't believe you would rent a place sight unseen.*

18 be a (beautiful/strange/frightening etc) sight to behold *formal* used to emphasize that something or someone looks very unusual, for example because they are very beautiful, strange, or frightening: *His garden was a sight to behold.* | *His face was not a pleasant sight to behold.*

19 GUN [C usually plural] the part of a gun or other weapon that guides your eye when you are aiming at something → **at first sight** at FIRST¹(6), → **know sb by sight** at KNOW¹(3), → **lose sight of sth** at LOSE(1), → **set your heart/mind/sights on (doing) sth** at SET¹(13)

THESAURUS

SOMETHING THAT YOU SEE

sight something that you see: *A herd of elephants is a magnificent sight.* | *Even Charles cheered up at the sight of the food.*

view the area you can see from a window or place, especially when it is beautiful: *The view from the top of the mountain is amazing.* | *The hotel has great views of Lake Windermere.* | *We had a good view of the firework display.*

panorama an impressive view of a very large area that stretches a long way across in front of you: *a panorama of snow-covered hills and mountains*

vista *written* a view of a large area of beautiful scenery - used in written descriptions: *The road around the island offers some spectacular vistas.*

scene what you see in a place, especially where people are moving around and doing things: *Reporters described the horrific scenes which followed the bombing.* | *His pictures are mainly of local scenes.*

spectacle something that you see that is very unusual, surprising, or strange: *It must have been an unusual spectacle.* | *I leaned over the balcony to get a look at the spectacle below.*

visuals [plural] pictures or parts of a film, video etc that people can see, as opposed to the parts you can hear: *Good visuals will help keep your audience's attention.*

sight² *v* [T] to see something from a long distance away, or see something you have been looking for: *The sailors gave a shout of joy when they **sighted land**.* | *Several rare birds have been sighted in the area.* THESAURUS SEE

sight·ed /ˈsaɪtɪd/ *adj* someone who is sighted can see, and is not blind → **visually impaired**: *Blind and sighted children are taught in the same classroom.* | *her **partially sighted** (=having limited ability to see) father* → CLEAR-SIGHTED, FAR-SIGHTED, LONG-SIGHTED, SHORT-SIGHTED

sight·ing /ˈsaɪtɪŋ/ *n* [C] an occasion on which something is seen, especially something rare or something that people are hoping to see: **[+of]** *There were two unconfirmed sightings of UFOs in the area.* | *Where was the latest sighting?*

sight·less /ˈsaɪtləs/ *adj literary* blind

sight-read /ˈsaɪtriːd/ *v* (*past tense and past participle* **sight-read** /-red/) [I,T] to play or sing written music when you look at it for the first time, without practising it first —**sight-reader** *n* [C] —**sight-reading** *n* [U]

sight·see·ing /ˈsaɪtˌsiːɪŋ/ ●●○ *n* [U] when you visit famous or interesting places, especially as tourists: *She swam and sunbathed, **went sightseeing**, and relaxed.*

sight·se·er /ˈsaɪtsiːə $ -ər/ *n* [C] someone, especially a tourist, who is visiting a famous or interesting place THESAURUS TOURIST

sign¹ /saɪn/ ●●● S1 W1 *n*

1 GIVES INFORMATION [C] a piece of paper, metal, or wood with words or a picture that gives people information, warnings, or instructions: *a sign on the door* | ***road signs*** | *a **no smoking sign*** | *Don't ignore the fog **warning signs**.*

2 SHOWS STH IS TRUE [C] an event, fact etc that shows that something is happening or that something is true or exists SYN **indication**: **[+of]** *A red morning sky is a sign of an impending storm.* | *Crying is seen as a sign of weakness.* | *A paw print in the dust was a **sign that** a tiger was close.* | *There are signs that the situation is improving.* | *There were no signs of forced entry into the house.*

3 MOVEMENT OR SOUND [C] a movement, sound etc that you make in order to tell someone something: *the thumbs-up sign* (=a sign that you make with your hand to show that something is successful) | **give/make a sign** *Wait until I give the sign.* | **sign that** *Bruce made a sign that he was ready to leave.* | **sign (for sb) to do sth** *Three short blasts on the whistle was the sign to begin.*

4 SYMBOL [C] a mark or shape that has a particular meaning SYN **symbol**: *the dollar sign* | *a minus sign*

SIGN

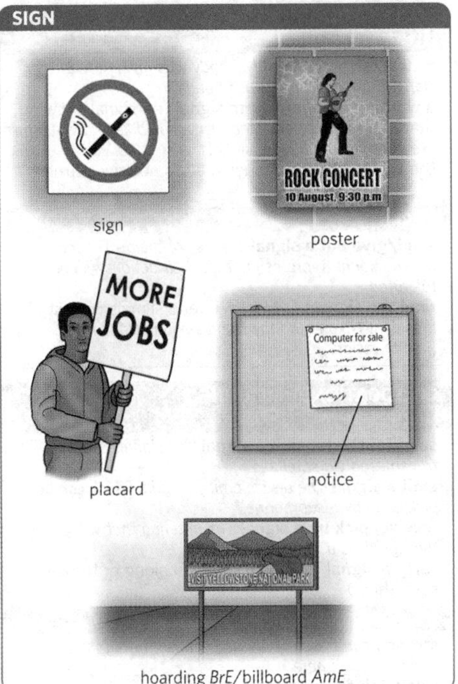

sign
poster
placard
notice
hoarding *BrE*/billboard *AmE*

5 STAR SIGN [C] (*also* **star sign**) a group of stars, representing one of 12 parts of the year, that some people believe influences your behaviour and your life: *What sign are you?*
6 LANGUAGE [U] a language that uses hand movements instead of spoken words, used by people who cannot hear SYN **sign language**
7 there is no sign of sb/sth used to say that someone or something is not in a place or cannot be found: *I waited for two hours but there was still no sign of her.*
8 sign of life a) a movement that shows that someone is alive, or something that shows that there are people in a particular place: *She listened intently for signs of life.* **b)** something that shows that a situation is becoming more active: *Commercial property markets are now* ***showing*** *definite* ***signs of life****.*
9 sign of the times something that shows how people live now: *It's just a sign of the times that many children have mobile phones.*
10 the sign of the Cross the hand movement that some Christians make in the shape of a cross, to show respect for God or to protect themselves from evil

COLLOCATIONS – MEANING 2

ADJECTIVES/NOUN + sign

a clear/obvious/unmistakable sign *There are clear signs of a slowdown in economic growth.*
a sure sign (=a very clear sign) *He was walking up and down, a sure sign that he was worried.*
a good/positive/encouraging/hopeful sign *If she can move her legs, that's a good sign.*
a bad/ominous sign *The jury was taking ages to make up its mind, which he felt was probably a bad sign.*
an outward/visible sign (=one that people can see clearly) | **a warning sign** (=one that shows something bad might be happening) | **a telltale/tell-tale sign** (=signs that clearly show something bad) | **the first sign of sth** (=the first thing that shows something is happening, or something exists)

VERBS

there are signs *There are now signs of an improvement in the economy.*
show signs of sth *Did she show any signs of distress?*
see/detect signs of sth *I could see some signs of improvement in her health.*

THESAURUS

sign [C] an event, fact etc that shows that something is happening or that something is true or exists: *The curtains were still drawn and there was no sign of activity.* | *A score of 80 or more is a sign that you are doing very well.*
indication [C] a sign. **Indication** is more formal than sign: *Recently there have been several indications of improving relations.*
evidence [U] facts or signs that show clearly that something exists or is true, especially something that you are trying to prove: *Scientists are hoping to find evidence that there was once life on Mars.* | *There was not enough evidence to convict him of the murder.*
symptom [C] a sign that someone has an illness or that a serious problem exists: *The first symptoms are tiredness and loss of weight.* | *Is this a symptom of the decay of Western civilization?*
indicator [C] a sign that shows you what is happening or what is true – used about a process, or about the state or level of something: *There are a number of indicators of economic slowdown.* | *The tests are considered a good indicator of intelligence.*
signal [C] a sign that shows that you should do something, or that you have a particular attitude: *Severe chest pain is a warning signal that cannot be ignored.*
mark [C] a sign, especially that you respect or honour someone: *People stood in silence as a mark of respect.*

sign² ●●● S1 W1 *v*
1 NAME [I,T] to write your SIGNATURE on something to show that you wrote it, agree with it, or were present: *Sign here, please.* | *The artist had* ***signed*** *his* ***name*** *in the corner of the painting.* | *You forgot to* ***sign*** *the* ***cheque****.* | *Over a hundred people have* ***signed*** *the* ***petition****.* | *Serena* ***signs*** *her* ***autograph*** *every time she's asked.* | *a signed photo of Paul McCartney* THESAURUS▸ WRITE
2 sign an agreement/contract/treaty etc to make a document, agreement etc official and legal by writing your SIGNATURE on it: *France has just signed a new trade deal with Japan.*
3 MUSIC/SPORT [I,T] if a football team or music company signs someone, or if someone signs for them, that person signs a contract in which they agree to work for them: *CBS Records had signed her back in 1988 on a three-album contract.* | **[+for/to/with]** *Miller worked in the shipyards before signing for Rangers.* | *Before long, they had signed with Virgin.*
4 sign on the dotted line *informal* to officially agree to something by signing a contract: *Make sure the repairs are done before you sign on the dotted line.*
5 sign a bill/legislation/agreement into law if someone in authority signs something into law, they make it part of the law by signing an official document
6 (all) signed and sealed (*also* **(all) signed, sealed, and delivered**) with all the necessary legal documents signed: *It'll all be signed and sealed by Friday, and you can move in then.*
7 USE MOVEMENTS [I] to try to tell someone something or ask them to do something by using signs and movements SYN **signal**: **sign to sb to do sth** *He signed to the maid to leave the room.* | **sign for sb to do sth** *She signed for us to go inside.*
8 LANGUAGE [I,T] to use, or translate something into, SIGN LANGUAGE —**signer** *n* [C]
sign sth ↔ **away** *phr v* to sign a document that gives your property or legal rights to someone else: *She had signed away all claims to the house.* | *I felt as if I was* ***signing away*** *my* ***life****.*
sign for sth *phr v* to sign a document to prove that you have received something: *This is a registered letter – someone will have to sign for it.*

S

sign in *phr v*
1 to write your name on a form, in a book etc when you enter a place such as a hotel, office, or club: *Remember to sign in at reception.*
2 sign sb ↔ in to write someone else's name in a book so that they are allowed to enter a club, an office etc
sign off *phr v*
1 *informal* to end a radio or television programme by saying goodbye
2 to write your final message at the end of an informal letter: *It's getting late, so I'll sign off now. Love, John.*
3 sign sb off *BrE* if a doctor signs someone off, he or she gives them a note saying that they are ill and not able to work: *For the last month, she has been* ***signed off sick*** *from work.*
4 sign sth ↔ off *BrE*, **sign off on sth** *AmE* to show that you approve of a plan or that something is finished by signing an official document: *Major repainting work now needs to be signed off by a qualified engineer.*
sign on *phr v*
1 *BrE* to state officially that you are unemployed by signing a form, so that you can get money from the government
2 to sign a document to show that you agree to work for someone: **[+as]** *He signed on as a soldier in the US army.* | **[+with]** *I'll probably have to sign on with a nursing agency.*
sign out *phr v*
1 to write your name in a book when you leave a place such as a hotel, an office, or a club
2 sign sth ↔ out to write your name on a form or in a book to show that you have taken or borrowed something: *Bernstein signed out a company car.*
3 sign sb ↔ out to write in a book that someone is allowed to leave somewhere such as a school, an office etc: *Parents must sign pupils out when collecting them for doctor's or dentist's appointments.*
sign sth ↔ **over** *phr v* to sign an official document that gives your property or legal rights to someone else: **[+to]** *When he became ill, he signed his property in France over to his son.*
sign up *phr v*
1 to put your name on a list for something because you want to take part in it: **[+for]** *I'm thinking of signing up for a yoga course.* | **sign up to do sth** *Over half the people who signed up to do engineering were women.*
2 sign sb ↔ up if someone is signed up by an organization, they sign a contract in which they agree to work for that organization: *Several well-known researchers have been signed up for the project.*

sign·age /ˈsaɪnɪdʒ/ *n* [U] *formal* the signs in or on a building, or in a public place: *The signage at the hospital is being made clearer.*

sig·nal[1] /ˈsɪɡnəl/ ●●● S2 W2 *n* [C]
1 a sound or an action that you make in order to give information to someone or tell them to do something: **signal (for sb) to do sth** *When she got up from the table, it was obviously the signal for us to leave.* | *At a prearranged signal the lights went out.* → SMOKE SIGNAL **THESAURUS** SIGN
2 an event or action that shows what someone feels, what exists, or what is likely to happen: **signal (that)** *These results are a signal that the child may need special help.* | **[+of]** *The opinion poll is a* ***clear signal*** *of people's dissatisfaction with the government.* | *the* ***danger signals*** *of a heart attack* | **send/give out a signal** *We don't want to give out the wrong signal to investors.*
3 a series of light waves, sound waves etc that carry an image, sound, or message, for example in radio or television: **send/transmit a signal** *This new pay-TV channel sends signals via satellite to cable companies.* | **receive/pick up/detect a signal** *a small antenna which can receive radio signals* | *The coastguard picked up a* ***distress signal*** *from a freighter 50 miles out at sea.*
4 a piece of equipment with coloured lights, used on a railway to tell train drivers whether they can continue or must stop: *a stop signal* | *a* ***signal failure*** (=when these lights do not work) → **busy signal** at BUSY[1](4)

COLLOCATIONS – MEANING 2

ADJECTIVES/NOUN + signal

a clear/strong signal *My body was giving me a clear signal that something was wrong.*
a warning/danger/alarm signal (=a signal showing that there is danger) *Managers should keep a watchful eye open for the danger signals.*
the wrong signals (=ones that do not give a true account of a situation)

VERBS

send/give out a signal *The use of the army sends out a clear signal to protesters that their actions will not be tolerated.*
read the signals (=to understand signals correctly) *President Nixon read the signals and decided it was time to resign.*

COLLOCATIONS – MEANING 3

VERBS

send (out)/transmit a signal *The signals are transmitted via satellites.*
emit a signal *The device emits a signal which can be picked up by a submarine.*
receive/pick up a signal *The antenna that will pick up the signals is a 12-metre dish.*
carry a signal (=allow it to travel along or through something)

ADJECTIVES/NOUN + signal

strong *I can't use my phone because the signal isn't strong enough here.*
weak/faint *The signals were too weak for the receiver to pick up.*
a radio/electrical/radar signal | **a digital signal**

signal[2] ●○○ *v* (**signalled**, **signalling** *BrE*, **signaled**, **signaling** *AmE*)
1 [I,T] to make a sound or an action in order to give information or tell someone to do something: *She signalled, and the waiter brought the bill.* | *The whistle signalled the end of the match.* | **[+at]** *Mary signalled wildly at them, but they didn't notice.* | **[+to]** *The judge signaled to a police officer and the man was led away.* | **[+for]** *He pushed his plate away and signalled for coffee.* | **signal (to) sb to do sth** *She signalled to the children to come inside.* | **signal that** *The bell signaled that school was over.*
2 [T] to make something clear by what you say or do – used in news reports: *Both sides have signaled their willingness to start negotiations.* | *British sources last night signalled their readiness to talk.* | **signal (that)** *The prime minister's speech today signals that there will be a shakeup in the cabinet.*
3 [T] to be a sign that something is going to happen: **signal the start/beginning/end of sth** *the lengthening days that signal the end of winter*
4 [I] to show the direction you intend to turn in a vehicle, using the lights SYN **indicate** *AmE*: *Signal before you pull out.*

signal[3] *adj* [only before noun] *formal* important: **signal achievement/success/failure etc** *The university has done me the signal honour of making me an Honorary Fellow.*

ˈsignal box *n* [C] *BrE* a small building near a railway, from which the signals and tracks are controlled

sig·nal·ler /ˈsɪɡnələ $ -ər/ *n* [C] *BrE* a SIGNALMAN(2)

sig·nal·ly /ˈsɪɡnəli/ *adv formal* very noticeably: *The government has* ***signally failed*** *to deal with the problem.*

sig·nal·man /ˈsɪɡnəlmən/ *n* (*plural* **signalmen** /-mən/) [C] **1** *especially BrE* someone whose job is to control railway signals **2** (*also* **signaller** *BrE*) a member of the army or navy who is trained to send and receive signals

sig·na·to·ry /ˈsɪɡnətəri $ -tɔːri/ *n* (*plural* **signatories**) [C] one of the people, organizations, or countries that signs an official agreement: **[+to/of]** *The UK is a signatory to the Berne Convention.* | *the signatories of the Helsinki Declaration*

S

sig·na·ture /ˈsɪɡnətʃə $ -ər/ ●●○ S3 *n*
1 [C] your name written in the way you usually write it, for example at the end of a letter, or on a cheque etc, to show that you have written it: *Her* ***signature*** *is totally* ***illegible*** (=cannot be read). | *The school collected 4,000 signatures for the petition.* | *The Ukrainians* ***put*** *their* ***signatures to*** *the Lisbon Protocol.* | *Someone's* ***forged*** *my* ***signature*** (=made an illegal copy of my name to deceive people) *on this letter.* | *Each child must* ***obtain*** *the* ***signature*** *of his or her parents.*
2 [U] *formal* the act of signing something: **for signature** *We will send you a copy of the agreement for signature.*
3 [C usually singular] something that is closely related to an event, person, or style: *Smith's signature singing style*
→ KEY SIGNATURE, TIME SIGNATURE

ˈsignature ˌtune *n* [C] *BrE* a short piece of music used at the beginning and end of a television or radio programme

sign·board /ˈsaɪnbɔːd $ -bɔːrd/ *n* [C] a flat piece of wood, CARDBOARD etc in a public place, with writing on it that gives people information

sig·net /ˈsɪɡnɪt/ *n* [C] a metal object used for printing a small pattern in WAX as an official SEAL[1](2)

ˈsignet ring *n* [C] a ring that has a signet on it

sig·nif·i·cance /sɪɡˈnɪfɪkəns/ ●●○ *n* [singular, U]
1 the importance of an event, action etc, especially because of the effects or influence it will have in the future OPP **insignificance**: *Stella didn't* ***attach*** *any* ***significance to*** *Doug's query.* | **[+of]** *the significance of climate change* | *The book* ***assesses*** *the* ***significance*** *of Stalin's policies between 1927 and 1939.* | **[+for]** *The results of the study have a* ***wider significance*** *for all the profession.* | **great/little significance (in/to/for sth)** *The crime problem has great significance to the general public.* | **grasp/appreciate the significance (of sth)** (=fully understand something) *The press were slow to grasp the significance of what happened.*
2 the meaning of a word, sign, action etc, especially when this is not immediately clear: **[+of]** *the significance of the words that refer to the bread Christ shares with his disciples* | **full/real/true significance** *Only later did we realize the true significance of his remark.*

sig·nif·i·cant /sɪɡˈnɪfɪkənt/ ●●● S2 W1 AWL *adj*
1 having an important effect or influence, especially on what will happen in the future OPP **insignificant**: *His most significant political achievement was the abolition of the death penalty.* | *Please inform us if there are any significant changes in your plans.* | **[+for]** *The result is* ***highly significant*** *for the future of the province.* | **it is significant that** *It is significant that the writers of the report were all men.*
THESAURUS ▸ IMPORTANT
2 large enough to be noticeable or have noticeable effects OPP **insignificant**: *A significant number of drivers fail to keep to speed limits.* | *A significant part of Japan's wealth is invested in the West.* | *There is a* ***significant difference*** *between the number of home births now and ten years ago.* | *The rise in temperature is not* ***statistically significant***.
3 a significant look, smile etc has a special meaning that is not known to everyone: *He gave me a significant look.*

sigˌnificant ˈfigure (*also* **sigˌnificant ˈdigit**) *n* [C] *technical* a figure that is part of a number and is known to be correct. Significant figures start with the first figure on the left that is not zero, and end with the last figure on the right that is not zero (unless the zero is known to be correct). So the number 0.0302 has three significant figures.

sig·nif·i·cant·ly /sɪɡˈnɪfɪkəntli/ ●●○ W2 AWL *adv*
1 in an important way or to an important degree: *Health problems can be significantly reduced by careful diet.* | *Methods used by younger teachers differ significantly from those used by older ones.* | **significantly better/greater/worse etc** *Delia's work has been significantly better this year.*
2 [sentence adverb] used to say that something is very important: *The Democrats, significantly, finished well behind the Green Party.*
3 in a way that seems to have a special meaning: *George paused, and glanced significantly in my direction.*

sigˌnificant ˈother *n* [C] your husband, wife, girlfriend, or boyfriend

sig·nif·i·ca·tion /ˌsɪɡnɪfɪˈkeɪʃən/ *n* [C,U] *formal* the intended meaning of a word

sig·ni·fy /ˈsɪɡnɪfaɪ/ ●○○ AWL *v* (**signified, signifying, signifies**) [not in progressive]
1 [T] to represent, mean, or be a sign of something: *Some tribes use special facial markings to signify status.* | *The image of the lion signified power and strength.* | **signify (that)** *The symbol used signifies that the frequency is measured in kHz.*
2 [T] *formal* if you signify a feeling, opinion etc, you do something that acts as a sign so that other people know your feeling or opinion SYN **indicate**: **signify that** *Hamilton waved his hand to signify that he didn't mind what they decided.* | **signify sth (to sb)** *He turned away from her slightly to signify his indifference.*
3 [I] to be important enough to have an effect on something: *These figures don't really signify in the overall results.*

sign·ing /ˈsaɪnɪŋ/ *n* **1** [U] the act of writing your name at the end of a document to show that you agree with it: *The formal signing will take place on April 9th.* | **[+of]** *the signing of the ceasefire agreement* **2 a)** [C] *BrE* someone who has just signed a contract to join a sports team or work with a record company: *New signing, Mark Brown, scored three goals in his first match.* **b)** [U] when a sports team or record company prepares a contract which someone then signs to say that they will join the team or work with the company: **[+of]** *Birmingham City have completed the signing of Doug Bell from Shrewsbury Town.* **3** [U] the use of sign language to communicate to or between people who cannot hear well

ˈsign ˌlanguage *n* [C,U] a language that uses hand movements instead of spoken words, used by people who cannot hear well

S

sign·post[1] /ˈsaɪnpəʊst $ -poʊst/ *n* [C] **1** *especially BrE* a sign at the side of a road showing directions and distances SYN **sign** *AmE*: *I'm sure that signpost is pointing the wrong way.* | *Just follow the signposts to the city centre.*
2 something that helps you understand how something is organized, where to go, or what will follow – used especially in news reports: *As yet, there are few* ***signposts pointing*** *to success.*

signpost[2] *v* [T] *BrE* **1 be well/clearly/badly signposted** to be clearly or unclearly shown by signposts: *The village isn't very well signposted.* **2** to show something clearly so that everyone will notice and understand it – used especially in news reports: *They have signposted their conclusions in the report.*

Sikh /siːk/ *n* [C] a member of an Indian religious group that developed from Hinduism in the 16th century —**Sikh** *adj*

Sikh·is·m /ˈsiːkɪzəm/ *n* [U] the religion of the Sikhs

si·lage /ˈsaɪlɪdʒ/ *n* [U] grass or other plants cut and stored so that they can be used as winter food for cattle

si·lence[1] /ˈsaɪləns/ ●●● W2 *n*
1 NO NOISE [U] complete absence of sound or noise SYN **quiet**: **[+of]** *Nothing disturbed the silence of the night.* | **silence falls/descends (on/upon sth)** *After the explosion, an eerie silence fell upon the scene.* | **break/shatter the silence** *A loud scream shattered the silence.*
2 NO TALKING [C,U] complete quiet because nobody is talking: *There was a* ***brief silence*** *before anyone answered.* | **in silence** *The four men sat in silence.* | **complete/total/dead silence** *'How long have you been here?' I asked. There was complete silence.* | *'Silence in court!' roared the judge.* | **embarrassed/awkward/stunned etc silence** *There was an awkward silence between them.* | *The accused exercised his* ***right to silence*** (=the legal right to choose to say nothing).
3 NO DISCUSSION/ANSWER [U] failure or refusal to discuss something or answer questions about something: **[+on]** *The government's silence on such an important issue seems very strange.* | *Once again the answer was a* ***deafening silence*** (=a very noticeable refusal to discuss something).
4 NO COMMUNICATION [U] failure to write a letter to

someone, telephone them etc: *After two years of silence, he suddenly got in touch with us again.*
5 one-minute/two-minute etc silence a period of time in which everyone stops talking as a sign of honour and respect towards someone who has died

silence² ●○○ *v* [T]
1 to make someone stop talking, or stop something making a noise: *She held up her hand to silence the children.*
2 to make someone stop expressing opposition or criticisms – used especially in news reports: *attempts to silence the rumours* | *Barnes has failed to silence his critics.*

si·lenc·er /ˈsaɪlənsə $ -sər/ *n* [C] **1** *BrE* a piece of equipment that is connected to the EXHAUST of a vehicle to make its engine quieter SYN **muffler** *AmE* **2** a thing that is put on the end of a gun so that it makes less noise when it is fired

si·lent /ˈsaɪlənt/ ●●● W3 *adj*
1 NOT SPEAKING **a)** not saying anything: *Alan was silent.* | **remain/stay/keep silent** *She kept silent, forcing Buchanan to continue.* | *The crowd* ***fell silent*** (=became silent) *when the president appeared.* **b)** [only before noun] not talking much to other people: **the strong silent type** (=a man who looks strong and does not talk very much)

REGISTER
Silent is used mainly in writing. In everyday English, people usually use **not say anything** rather than **be silent**: *She* ***didn't say anything****, so I carried on.* | *The article* ***doesn't say anything*** *about religion.*

2 NOT COMMUNICATING failing or refusing to talk about something or express an opinion: **[+on/about]** *The report was silent on the subject.*
3 QUIET without any sound, or not making any sound: *The large house was silent and lonely.* | *At last the guns* ***fell silent****.* | *Julie offered up a silent prayer that she would pass her exam.* | **as silent as the grave** (=completely silent in a mysterious or uncomfortable way) THESAURUS ▶ QUIET
4 FILMS [only before noun] a silent film has pictures but no sound
5 LETTER a silent letter in a word is not pronounced: *The 'w' in 'wreck' is silent.* —**silently** *adv*: *He sat silently by the bed.*

ˌsilent maˈjority *n* **the silent majority** the ordinary people in a country, who are not active politically and who do not make their opinions known

ˌsilent ˈpartner *n* [C] *AmE* someone who owns part of a business but is not actively involved in the way it operates SYN **sleeping partner** *BrE*

sil·hou·ette /ˌsɪluˈet/ *n*
1 [C,U] a dark image, shadow, or shape that you see against a light background: **[+of]** *a dark silhouette of domes and minarets* | **[+against]** *Soon the bombers would return, black silhouettes against a pale sky.* | **in silhouette** *The old windmill stood out in silhouette.*
2 [C,U] a drawing of something or someone, often from the side, showing a black shape against a light background: *silhouette pictures of snowmen and reindeer* | **in silhouette** *a picture of Mozart in silhouette* **3** [C] the particular shape certain clothes give you: *Fitted clothes often give the neatest silhouettes.* —**silhouetted** *adj*: *tall chimney stacks silhouetted against the orange flames*

SILHOUETTE
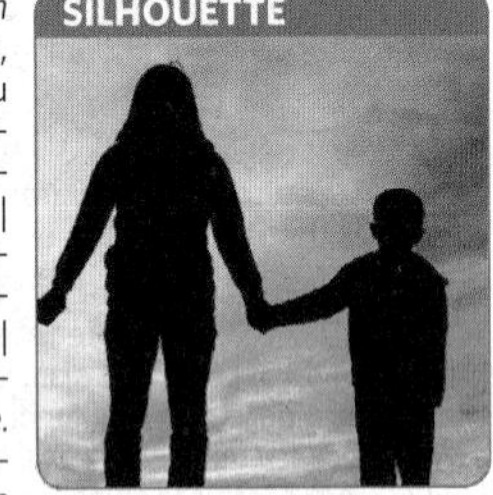

sil·i·ca /ˈsɪlɪkə/ *n* [U] a chemical COMPOUND that exists naturally as sand, QUARTZ, and FLINT, used in making glass

sil·i·cate /ˈsɪlɪkeɪt, -kət/ *n* [C,U] *technical* one of a group of common solid mineral substances that exist naturally in the earth

sil·i·con /ˈsɪlɪkən/ *n* [U] a chemical substance that exists as a solid or as a powder and is used to make glass, bricks, and parts for computers. It is a chemical ELEMENT: symbol Si

ˌsilicon ˈchip *n* [C] a computer CHIP

sil·i·cone /ˈsɪləkəʊn $ -koʊn/ *n* [U] a chemical that is not changed by heat or cold, does not let water through, and is used in making artificial body parts, paint, and rubber

ˌsilicone ˈimplant *n* [C] a piece of silicone that is put into the body, especially into a woman's breasts to make them larger

ˌSilicon ˈValley a part of California, in the area between San Francisco and San José, which is known as a centre of the computer industry. Many important inventions were discovered in this area, and many large and small companies producing computer SOFTWARE and HARDWARE are based there. It is called Silicon Valley because the computer industry is based on the SILICON CHIP.

silk /sɪlk/ ●●○ *n*
1 [U] a thin smooth soft cloth made from very thin thread which is produced by a silkworm: ***pure silk*** *stockings* | *a beautiful dress in* ***raw silk***
2 [C] *BrE law* a very important lawyer SYN **Queen's Counsel (QC)**: *His practice quickly grew and he* ***took silk*** (=became a QC) *in 1988.*
3 silks [plural] *technical* the coloured shirts worn by JOCKEYS (=people who ride horses in races)
4 make a silk purse out of a sow's ear to make something good out of something that is bad quality

silk·en /ˈsɪlkən/ *adj* [usually before noun] *literary*
1 soft, smooth, and shiny like silk SYN **silky**: *her silken hair*
2 made of silk SYN **silky**: *a silken handkerchief*

ˈsilk screen *adj* [only before noun] silk screen prints are made by forcing paint or ink onto a surface through a stretched piece of cloth —**silk screen** *n* [C]

silk·worm /ˈsɪlkwɜːm $ -wɜːrm/ *n* [C] a type of CATERPILLAR which produces silk thread

silk·y /ˈsɪlki/ *adj* **1** soft, smooth, and shiny like silk: *silky fur* **2** [only before noun] made of silk: *the silky fabric of her dress* **3** a silky voice is gentle, and is used especially when trying to persuade someone to do something —**silkily** *adv* —**silkiness** *n* [U]

sill /sɪl/ *n* [C] **1** the narrow shelf at the base of a window frame **2** the part of a car frame at the bottom of the doors

sil·la·bub /ˈsɪləbʌb/ *n* [C,U] *BrE* another spelling of SYLLABUB

sil·ly¹ /ˈsɪli/ ●●● S2 *adj* (*comparative* **sillier**, *superlative* **silliest**)
1 not sensible, or showing bad judgment: *Stop asking silly questions.* | *You made a lot of* ***silly mistakes****.* | *I left my keys at home, which was* ***a*** *pretty* ***silly thing to do****.* | *'Shall we go for a walk?'* ***'Don't be silly****, it's dark.'* THESAURUS ▶ STUPID
2 stupid in a CHILDISH or embarrassing way: *I feel so silly in this outfit.* | *a silly hat* | *I hate their parties – we always end up playing silly games.*
3 *spoken* not serious or practical: *They served us coffee in these silly little cups.*
4 bore sb silly *informal* to make someone extremely bored
5 drink/laugh/scare etc yourself silly *informal* to drink or laugh etc so much that you stop behaving sensibly —**silliness** *n* [U]

silly² *n spoken* used to tell someone that you think they are not behaving sensibly: *No, silly, I didn't mean that.*

ˈsilly ˌbilly *n* (*plural* **silly billies**) [C] *BrE spoken* used to tell someone, especially a child, that they are behaving in a silly way

ˈsilly ˌseason *n* **the silly season** *BrE informal* a period in the summer when newspapers print stories that are not very serious because there is not much political news

si·lo /ˈsaɪləʊ $ -loʊ/ *n* (*plural* **silos**) [C] **1** a tall structure like a tower that is used for storing grain, winter food for farm animals etc **2** a large structure under the ground from which a large MISSILE can be fired

silt¹ /sɪlt/ *n* [U] sand, mud, soil etc that is carried in water and then settles at a bend in a river, an entrance to a port etc

silt² *v*

silt up *phr v* if something silts up or is silted up, it becomes filled with silt: *The old harbour silted up years ago.*

sil·van /ˈsɪlvən/ *adj literary* SYLVAN

sil·ver¹ /ˈsɪlvə $ -ər/ ●●● W3 *n*

1 [U] a valuable shiny, light grey metal that is used to make jewellery, knives, coins etc. It is a chemical ELEMENT: symbol Ag: *a silver necklace* | *cups made of* ***solid silver***

2 [U] spoons, forks, dishes etc that are made of silver SYN **silverware**: *It was my job to polish the silver.*

3 [C,U] the colour of silver: *The lake sparkled with shades of blue and silver.* | *This season's colours are rich golds and elegant silvers.*

4 [C,U] *informal* a SILVER MEDAL: *He won a silver at the last Olympics.*

5 [U] *BrE* coins that contain silver or are the colour of silver: *He put his hand into his pocket and brought out a handful of silver.*

silver² ●●● W3 *adj*

1 made of silver: *a silver teapot* | *a silver coin* | *a* ***solid silver*** *brooch*

2 having the colour of silver: *an old man with silver hair*

3 on a silver platter if something is given to you on a silver platter, you do not have to make any effort to get it: *He had a scholarship handed to him on a silver platter.*

4 silver bullet *AmE* something that solves a difficult problem very quickly and easily: *There is no silver bullet for this problem.* → **be born with a silver spoon in your mouth** at BORN¹(8), → **every cloud has a silver lining** at CLOUD¹(6)

silver³ *v* [T] **1** *technical* to cover a surface with a thin shiny layer of silver or another metal in order to make a mirror **2** *literary* to make something shine and look the colour of silver: *The farmhouse appeared, silvered by the moon.*

ˌsilver anniˈversary *n* [C] SILVER WEDDING ANNIVERSARY

ˌsilver ˈbirch *n* [C,U] a type of tree that has a smooth silvery-white TRUNK and branches

ˌsilver ˈdollar *n* [C] a one-dollar coin that was used in the US in the past

sil·ver·fish /ˈsɪlvəfɪʃ $ -ər-/ *n* (*plural* **silverfish** *or* **silverfishes**) [C] a small silver-coloured insect that cannot fly and is found in houses

ˌsilver ˈfoil *n* [U] *BrE* FOIL

ˌsilver ˈjubilee *n* [C] *especially BrE* the date that is exactly 25 years after the date when something important happened, especially when someone became king or queen: *the Queen's Silver Jubilee*

ˌsilver ˈmedal *n* [C] a MEDAL made of silver that is given to the person who finishes second in a race or competition —**silver medallist** *n* [C]

ˌsilver ˈpaper *n* [U] *BrE* paper that is shiny like metal on one side, and is used for wrapping food → **foil**

ˌsilver ˈplate *n* [U] metal that is covered with a thin layer of silver —**silver-plated** *adj*: *a silver-plated candlestick*

ˌsilver ˈscreen *n* **the silver screen** *old-fashioned* the film industry, especially in Hollywood: *stars of the silver screen*

sil·ver·smith /ˈsɪlvəˌsmɪθ $ -ər-/ *n* [C] someone who makes jewellery and other things out of silver → **blacksmith**

ˌsilver ˈsurfer *n* [C] *informal* an old person who uses the Internet: *Many silver surfers use the Internet to keep in touch with their grandchildren.*

ˌsilver-ˈtongued *adj literary* good at talking to people and making them like you, or persuading them to do what you want SYN **charming**

sil·ver·ware /ˈsɪlvəweə $ -vərwer/ *n* [U] **1** *BrE* objects that are made of silver, for example dishes, plates, knives, forks etc **2** *AmE* knives, forks, and spoons that are made of silver or a similar metal **3** *BrE* a silver cup that a person or team wins in a sports competition: *The club has not yet given up hope of ending the season with some silverware.*

ˌsilver ˈwedding anniˌversary (*also* **silver anniversary**) *n* [C] the date that is exactly 25 years after the date of a wedding: *a party to celebrate their silver wedding anniversary*

sil·ver·y /ˈsɪlvəri/ *adj* **1** shiny and silver in colour: *her silvery hair* | *the silvery light of the moon* **2** *literary* a silvery voice or sound is light, pleasant, and musical: *Clara gave a small, silvery laugh.*

Sim card /ˈsɪm kɑːd $ -kɑːrd/ *n* [C] a plastic card in a MOBILE PHONE that stores your personal information and allows you to use the phone

sim·i·an /ˈsɪmiən/ *adj* **1** *literary* similar to a monkey: *his dark hair and simian features* **2** *technical* relating to monkeys: *simian diseases*

sim·i·lar /ˈsɪmələ, ˈsɪmɪlə $ -ər/ ●●● S1 W1 AWL *adj* almost the same OPP **different** → **alike**: *We have similar tastes in music.* | *Both approaches seem to achieve similar results.* | *A number of his friends had been affected* ***in a similar way.*** | *The two products* ***look*** *quite* ***similar.*** | **[+to]** *Her ideas are quite similar to mine.* | **[+in]** *The two cars are very similar in size and design.* | **broadly/roughly similar** *The two groups have broadly similar aims.* | **remarkably/strikingly similar** *The speech was strikingly similar to one given by the American president earlier this year.* → **SIMILARLY**

GRAMMAR: Prepositions with similar

- Someone or something is **similar to** another person or thing: *His surname is similar to mine.* ✗ Don't say: *His surname is similar with mine.*
- People or things are **similar in** size, appearance, shape, character etc: *My sister and I are similar in character.*

THESAURUS

similar *adj* almost the same: *Jo said she'd had a similar experience.* | *The colours are very similar, but I like this one best.*

like *prep* similar to something or someone else: *It tastes a little like chicken.* | *She still looks like a teenager.*

alike *adj* [not before noun] very similar – used especially about the way people look or behave: *She and her sister look alike.* | *Lawyers are all alike - I don't trust them.*

close *adj* very similar: *The film* ***bears a close resemblance*** *to real life* (=is very similar). | *The painting is remarkably* ***close to*** *the original.*

much the same very similar: *The glass is still made in much the same way as it was 100 years ago.* | *People are much the same, wherever you go.*

identical *adj* exactly the same: *The two computers were identical in design.* | *identical names*

matching *adj* having the same colour, style, pattern etc as something else – used about clothes or furniture that you wear or use together: *She wore matching silver shoes and handbag.* | *a dining table and matching chairs*

akin to sth *formal* fairly similar to something: *These dialects are akin to Arabic, though different in several respects.*

sim·i·lar·i·ty /ˌsɪməˈlærəti/ ●●○ AWL *n* (*plural* **similarities**) [C,U] if there is a similarity between two things or people, they are similar in some way OPP **difference** → **likeness**: **[+between]** *There are some* ***striking similarities*** *between the two plays.* | **[+to]** *the song's* ***close similarity*** *to traditional Jewish music* | *The present crisis* ***bears*** *some* ***similarity to*** *the oil crisis of the 1970s.* | **[+of]** *the similarity of their names* | **[+in]** *I was struck by the similarities in their early lives.* | **[+with]** *The police are checking for similarities with other recent attacks in the area.* | ***There are similarities*** *with German, though Yiddish is a distinct language.* | *They are both blonde, but* ***there the similarity ends.***

sim·i·lar·ly /ˈsɪmələli $ -ərli/ ●●○ W3 AWL *adv* in a similar way OPP **differently**: *The first letter she wrote me was less than a page long, and her second letter was similarly brief.* | [sentence adverb] *The cost of food and clothing has come down in recent years. Similarly, fuel prices have fallen quite considerably.*

sim·i·le /ˈsɪməli/ ●○○ *n* [C,U] an expression that

S

describes something by comparing it with something else, using the words 'as' or 'like', for example 'as white as snow' → **metaphor** THESAURUS LANGUAGE

sim·mer¹ /ˈsɪmə $ -ər/ *v* **1** [I,T] to boil gently, or to cook something slowly by boiling it gently: *Bring the soup to the boil and allow it to* ***simmer gently*** *for about half an hour.*
2 [I] if you are simmering with anger, or if anger is simmering in you, you feel very angry but do not show your feelings: **[+with]** *He was left simmering with rage.*
3 [I] if an argument is simmering, people feel angry with each other but only show it slightly: *The row has been simmering for some time.* | *Violent revolt was simmering in the country.*

simmer down *phr v* to become calm again after you have been very angry: *We decided she needed some time to simmer down.*

simmer² *n* [singular] when something is boiling gently: *Bring the vegetables to a simmer.*

sim·nel cake /ˈsɪmnəl ˌkeɪk/ *n* [C] *BrE* a cake made with dried fruit that is traditionally eaten at Easter

sim·pat·i·co /sɪmˈpætɪkəʊ $ -koʊ/ *adj AmE informal* **1** someone who is simpatico is pleasant and easy to like **2** in agreement: *We're simpatico about most things.*

sim·per /ˈsɪmpə $ -ər/ *v* [I] to smile in a silly annoying way: *Betsy simpered at him as she spoke.* | *a silly, simpering girl* —**simper** *n* [C]

sim·ple /ˈsɪmpəl/ ●●● S1 W1 *adj* (*comparative* **simpler**, *superlative* **simplest**)
1 EASY not difficult or complicated to do or understand: *a simple but effective solution to the problem* | *There is no simple answer to this question.* | *I'm sure there's a* ***perfectly simple*** *explanation.* | **simple to use/make/operate etc** *Modern cameras are very simple to use.* | **relatively/fairly/quite etc simple** *There are relatively simple exercises to build strength.* | *We want to* ***keep*** *the costumes as* ***simple*** *as possible.* | *We can't pay people any more money until the company is more profitable. I'm afraid* ***it's as simple as that.***
THESAURUS EASY
2 PLAIN made in a plain style, without a lot of decoration or unnecessary things added: *She dressed with simple elegance.* | *simple but delicious food* | *a building constructed in a simple classic style*
3 ONLY [usually before noun] used to emphasize that only one thing is involved: *Completing the race is not just a simple matter of physical fitness.* | ***The simple fact is,*** *he's not very good at his job.* | *Their motive was greed,* ***pure and simple.***
4 NOT HAVING MANY PARTS made or built of only a few parts, and not having a complicated structure: *It's a very simple machine.* | *They evolved from simple life forms that existed millions of years ago.*
5 ORDINARY honest and ordinary and not special in any way: *Joe was just a simple farmer.*
6 GRAMMAR *technical* simple tenses are not formed with an AUXILIARY such as 'have' or 'be'
7 the simple life life without too many possessions or modern machines, usually in the countryside
8 STUPID [not before noun] someone who is simple is not very intelligent: *I'm afraid Luke's a bit simple.*

ˌsimple ˈfracture *n* [C] *medical* an injury in which a bone in your body is broken but does not cut through the flesh that surrounds it → COMPOUND FRACTURE

ˌsimple ˈinterest *n* [U] INTEREST that is calculated on the sum of money that you first INVESTed, and does not include the interest it has already earned → COMPOUND INTEREST

ˌsimple-ˈminded *adj* not very intelligent, and unable to understand complicated things SYN **simple**

sim·ple·ton /ˈsɪmpəltən/ *n* [C] *old-fashioned* someone who has a very low level of intelligence

sim·pli·ci·ty /sɪmˈplɪsəti/ ●○○ *n* [U] the quality of being simple and not complicated, especially when this is attractive or useful: *Mona wrote with a beautiful simplicity of style.* | *For the sake of simplicity, the tax form is divided into three sections.* | *James' solution to this problem was* ***simplicity itself*** (=very simple).

sim·pli·fy /ˈsɪmplɪfaɪ/ ●○○ *v* (**simplified, simplifying, simplifies**) [T] to make something easier or less complicated: *an attempt to simplify the tax system* | *The law needs to be simplified.* | *a simplified version of the game* —**simplification** /ˌsɪmplɪfɪˈkeɪʃən/ *n* [C,U]: *These figures are a simplification. The real situation is much more complicated than this.* → OVERSIMPLIFY

sim·plis·tic /sɪmˈplɪstɪk/ ●○○ *adj* treating difficult subjects in a way that is too simple: *This is a very simplistic approach to the problem.* —**simplistically** /-kli/ *adv*

sim·ply /ˈsɪmpli/ ●●● S1 W1 *adv*
1 used to emphasize what you are saying: *This work is simply not good enough.* | *He simply won't accept the committee's decision.* | *That would be simply wonderful!* | *It is* ***quite simply*** *the most ridiculous idea I've ever heard.*
2 only SYN **just**: *Some students lose marks simply because they don't read the question properly.* | *It's not simply a question of money.* | *What we need is not simply a smaller organization, but a more efficient one.*
3 used to emphasize how easy it is to do something: *Simply fill in the coupon and take it to your local store.*
4 if you say or explain something simply, you say it in a way that is easy for people to understand: *Try to express yourself more simply.* | ***To put it simply,*** *the tax cuts mean the average person will be about 3% better off.*
5 if you live simply, you live in a plain and ordinary way, without spending much money: *We had to live very simply on my father's small salary.*

sim·u·la·crum /ˌsɪmjəˈleɪkrəm/ *n* (*plural* **simulacra** /-krə/) [C + of] *formal* something that is made to look like another thing

sim·u·late /ˈsɪmjəleɪt/ ●○○ AWL *v* [T]
1 to make or produce something that is not real but has the appearance or feeling of being real: *a machine that simulates conditions in space* | *Interviews can be simulated in the classroom.*
2 *formal* to pretend to have a feeling: *He found it impossible to simulate grief.*

sim·u·lat·ed /ˈsɪmjəleɪtɪd/ ●○○ AWL *adj* not real, but made to look, sound, or feel real: *a simulated nuclear explosion* | *She looked at the report with simulated interest.*
THESAURUS ARTIFICIAL

sim·u·la·tion /ˌsɪmjəˈleɪʃən/ ●○○ AWL *n* [C,U] the activity of producing conditions which are similar to real ones, especially in order to test something, or the conditions that are produced: *a* ***computer simulation*** *used to train airline pilots* | **[+of]** *a simulation of a rainforest environment*

sim·u·la·tor /ˈsɪmjəleɪtə $ -ər/ *n* [C] a machine that is used for training people by letting them feel what real conditions are like, for example in a plane: *a flight simulator*

sim·ul·cast /ˈsɪməlkɑːst $ ˈsaɪməlkæst/ *v* (*past tense and past participle* **simulcast**) [T] to broadcast something at the same time on two or more MEDIA such as television, radio, or Internet, or at the same time as it is happening: *Her keynote speech at the conference is going to be simulcast on the Web.* —**simulcast** *n* [C]

sim·ul·ta·ne·ous /ˌsɪməlˈteɪniəs◂ $ ˌsaɪ-/ ●○○ *adj* things that are simultaneous happen at exactly the same time: *They grabbed each other's hands in simultaneous panic.* | *Up to twenty users can have simultaneous access to the system.* | **[+with]** *The withdrawal of British troops should be simultaneous with that of US forces.* | *The speeches will be broadcast live, with* ***simultaneous translation*** (=immediate translation, as the person is speaking) *into English.* —**simultaneously** *adv*: *The opera will be broadcast simultaneously on television and radio.*

> **REGISTER**
> In everyday English, people often say that two things happen **at the same time**, rather than say that they are **simultaneous**: *Up to twenty people can use the system* ***at the same time.***

sin¹ /sɪn/ ●●○ *n*
1 [C,U] an action that is against religious rules and is considered to be an offence against God: **[+of]** *the sin of pride* | *She needed to* ***confess*** *her* ***sins*** *and ask for forgiveness.* | *He knew that he had* ***committed*** *a terrible* ***sin***. | **the seven deadly sins** (=seven bad feelings or desires, in the Christian religion)
2 a sin *informal* something that you think is very wrong: **it is a sin (to do sth)** *There's so much lovely food here, it would be a sin to waste it.*
3 live in sin *old-fashioned* if two people live in sin, they live together in a sexual relationship without being married
4 as miserable/ugly/guilty as sin *spoken* very unhappy, ugly, or guilty: *I saw Margaret this morning looking as miserable as sin.*
5 for my sins *BrE spoken* an expression used to suggest jokingly that you have to do something as a punishment: *I work at head office now, for my sins.* → **sinful** → **cover/hide a multitude of sins** at MULTITUDE(4), → **CARDINAL SIN, MORTAL SIN, ORIGINAL SIN**

sin² *v* (**sinned**, **sinning**) [I] **1** to do something that is against religious rules and is considered to be an offence against God: **[+against]** *You have sinned against God.*
2 be more sinned against than sinning *old-fashioned* used to say that someone should not be blamed for what they have done wrong, because they have been badly treated by other people

sin³ *technical* the written abbreviation of ***sine***

ˈsin bin *n* [singular] *BrE informal* a place away from the playing area where players in some sports, for example ICE HOCKEY, are sent if they break the rules

since /sɪns/ ●●● S1 W1 *prep, conjunction, adv*
1 from a particular time or event in the past until the present, or in that period of time: *We've been waiting here since two o'clock.* | *I haven't played rugby since I left university.* | *She left London ten years ago, and I haven't seen her since.* | *The factory has been here since the 1970s.* | *It was exactly five years since her father had died.* | *Since the end of the war, over five thousand prisoners have been released.* | *He lost his job five years ago, but has since found other work.* | *I left school in 1995, and* ***since then*** *I've lived in London.* | **ever since** (=all the time since) *We've been friends ever since we were at school together.* | *She's been terrified of the sound of aircraft ever since the crash.* | *We came to the UK in 1974 and have lived here ever since.*
2 used to give the reason for something: *Since you are unable to answer, perhaps we should ask someone else.* **THESAURUS** BECAUSE
3 since when? *spoken* used in questions to show that you are very surprised or angry: *Since when have you been interested in my feelings?*
4 long since if something has long since happened, it happened a long time ago: *I've long since forgiven her for what she did.*

GRAMMAR: Comparison

since
• You use **since** with a time, year, date, or other point in time: *He has been living in England* ***since 2008***. | *We've known about it* ***since May***.
• Don't use **since** with a period of time. ✗ Don't say: *He has been living in England since 12 years.*
• You use the present perfect before **since**: *I* ***have liked*** *him since we first met.* | *We****'ve been driving*** *since six this morning.* ✗ Don't say: *I like him since we first met.*
• You also use the past perfect before **since**: *She* ***had been waiting*** *since five o'clock.* ✗ Don't say: *She was waiting since five o'clock.*
• You use the simple past tense after **since**: *He has grown* ***since*** *I last* ***saw*** *him.*
for
• You use **for** with a period of time: *I've known him* ***for ten years***. | *We've been waiting* ***for hours***.

sin·cere /sɪnˈsɪə $ -ˈsɪr/ ●○○ *adj*
1 a feeling, belief, or statement that is sincere is honest and true, and based on what you really feel and believe SYN **genuine**: **sincere thanks/thank you/gratitude** *I would like to say a sincere thank you to everyone who has helped and supported me.* | *Please accept my* ***sincere apologies***. | *his sincere desire to find out the truth*
2 someone who is sincere is honest and says what they really feel or believe OPP **insincere**: *a warm-hearted, sincere man* | **[+in]** *They were obviously sincere in their beliefs.* | *I wasn't sure that he was sincere in what he was saying.*

sin·cere·ly /sɪnˈsɪəli $ -ˈsɪr-/ ●○○ *adv*
1 if you feel or believe something sincerely, you really feel or believe it and are not just pretending SYN **truly**: *I sincerely hope I'll see her again.* | *We are sincerely grateful for your help.*
2 (yours) sincerely an expression used to end a formal letter, especially one that you have begun by using someone's name

sin·cer·i·ty /sɪnˈserəti/ *n* [U] when someone is sincere and really means what they are saying OPP **insincerity**: *I don't doubt her sincerity, but I think she's got her facts wrong.* | *May I say* ***in all sincerity*** *that we could not have achieved this much without your help and support.*

sine /saɪn/ *n* [C] *technical* (*written abbreviation* **sin**) the FRACTION(2) calculated for an angle by dividing the length of the side opposite it in a TRIANGLE that has a RIGHT ANGLE, by the length of the side opposite the right angle → **COSINE, TANGENT**

si·ne·cure /ˈsaɪnɪkjʊə, ˈsɪn- $ -kjʊr/ *n* [C] *formal* a job which you get paid for even though you do not have to do very much work

si·ne qua non /ˌsɪni kwɑː ˈnəʊn $ -ˈnɑːn/ *n* [singular] *formal* something that you must have, or which must exist, before something else can happen SYN **prerequisite**: **[+for/of]** *The control of inflation is a sine qua non for economic stability.*

sin·ew /ˈsɪnjuː/ *n* [C,U] **1** a part of your body that connects a muscle to a bone: *The sinews on his neck stood out like knotted string.* **2 the sinews of sth** *literary* something that gives strength or support to a government, country, or system: *They have begun building the sinews of an independent nation.*

sin·ew·y /ˈsɪnjuːi/ *adj* a sinewy person has a thin body and strong muscles: *a big man with long, sinewy arms*

sin·ful /ˈsɪnfəl/ *adj* **1** against religious rules, or doing something that is against religious rules → **wicked**: *Dancing was believed to be sinful.* | *a wicked, sinful man*
2 very wrong or bad: *a sinful waste of taxpayers' money*
—**sinfully** *adv*

sing /sɪŋ/ ●●● S1 W2 *v* (*past tense* **sang** /sæŋ/, *past participle* **sung** /sʌŋ/)
1 WITH YOUR VOICE [I,T] to produce a musical sound with your voice: *She can sing beautifully.* | *Most children enjoy singing.* | *We had a great time* ***singing*** *some of the old* ***songs***. | **[+to]** *My mother used to sing to me when I was young.* | *He was singing to himself quietly.* | **sing sb sth** *Come on, sing us a song!* | *I've never been able to* ***sing in tune*** (=sing the correct notes). | *She patiently* ***sang*** *the baby* ***to sleep***. → **SINGING**
2 BIRDS [I] if birds sing, they produce high musical sounds: *I could hear the birds singing outside my window.*
3 HIGH NOISE [I always + adv/prep] to make a high whistling sound: *A kettle was singing on the stove.* | **[+past]** *A bullet sang past my ear.*
4 sing sb's praises to praise someone very much: *Mrs Edwards was singing your praises today.*
5 sing a different tune to say something different from what you said before: *You're singing a different tune now!*
6 be singing from the same hymn sheet/book used to say that a group of people all have the same aims or all express the same opinion on a particular subject: *Union representatives are all singing from the same hymn sheet on the issue of pay.*
7 GIVE INFORMATION [I] *informal* to tell people everything you know about a crime when they ask you questions about it – used especially by criminals and the police: *I think he'll sing.*

S

sing along *phr v* to sing with someone else who is already singing: *Sing along if you know the words.* | **[+to]** *Jess was singing along to the radio.*

sing out *phr v*

1 sing out (sth) to shout or sing some words clearly and loudly: *'Freeze!' a shrill voice sang out.*

2 *AmE* to sing loudly so that people can hear you easily

sing up *phr v BrE* to sing more loudly: *Sing up, boys, I can't hear you!*

sing·a·long /ˈsɪŋəlɒŋ $ -lɔːŋ/ *n* [C] an informal occasion when people sing songs together SYN **singsong** *BrE*

singe[1] /sɪndʒ/ *v* (**singed**, **singeing**) [I,T] to burn the surface of something slightly, or to be burned slightly: *The flames had singed her hair.* THESAURUS ▸ BURN

singe[2] *n* [C] a mark on the surface of something where it has been burned slightly

sing·er /ˈsɪŋə $ -ər/ ●●● S3 *n* [C] someone who sings: **pop/opera/folk etc singer** *her favourite pop singer* | *a famous Italian opera singer* | *the* ***lead singer*** (=main singer) *of Slade* | *Tina Turner's* ***backing singers*** (=people who sing with her)

ˌsinger-ˈsongwriter *n* [C] someone who writes songs and sings them

sing·ing /ˈsɪŋɪŋ/ *n* [U] the activity of producing musical sounds with your voice: *He entered the Royal College of Music to study singing.*

sin·gle[1] /ˈsɪŋɡəl/ ●●● S1 W1 *adj*

1 ONE [only before noun] only one: *A single tree gave shade from the sun.* | *They won the game by a single point.* | *the highest price ever paid for a single work of art* | *a* ***single-sex school*** (=one for only boys or girls)

2 every single used to emphasize that you are talking about every person or thing: *Don't write down every single word I say.* | *He works every single day.*

3 not a single no people or things at all: *The plane was brought down safely and not a single passenger was killed.* | *We didn't get a single reply to the advertisement.*

4 the single biggest/greatest etc used to emphasize that you are talking about the one thing that is the biggest, greatest etc: *Cigarette smoking is the single most important cause of lung cancer.* | *Tourism is the country's single biggest earner.*

5 NOT MARRIED not married, or not involved in a romantic relationship with anyone: *The changes in tax rates will benefit single people the most.* | *Is he single?* THESAURUS ▸ MARRIED

6 single bed/room etc a bed, room etc that is meant to be used by one person only: *You have to pay extra for a single room.* → DOUBLE[1](4)

7 TICKET *BrE* a single ticket etc is for a trip from one place to another but not back again SYN **one-way** → **return**, **round-trip**

single[2] ●●○ *n* [C]

1 MUSIC a CD that has only one song on it, not a number of songs, or a song which is sold in this way → **album**: *Have you heard their latest single?*

2 SPORT **a)** one RUN[2] in a game of CRICKET **b)** a hit that allows the person who is hitting the ball to reach first BASE in a game of baseball

3 TENNIS **singles** [U] a game, especially in tennis, in which one person plays on their own against another person: *I prefer* ***playing singles***. | *Who won the women's singles?* → **doubles** at DOUBLE[2](3)

4 NOT MARRIED **singles** [plural] people who are not married and are not involved in a romantic relationship with anyone: *The show is especially popular among young singles.* | *a singles night at the club*

5 TICKET *BrE* a ticket for a trip from one place to another but not back again SYN **one-way ticket** *AmE* → **return**: *A single to Oxford, please.*

6 MONEY *AmE* a piece of paper money worth one dollar: *Anybody have five singles?*

7 ROOM a room in a hotel for just one person → **double**: *I'm afraid we haven't got any singles available.*

single[3] *v*

single sb/sth ↔ **out** *phr v* to choose one person or thing from among a group because they are better, worse, more important etc than the others: **[+for]** *I don't see why he should be singled out for special treatment.* | **[+as]** *One programme was singled out as being particularly good.*

ˌsingle-ˈbreasted *adj* a single-breasted jacket or suit has only one set of buttons down the front → DOUBLE-BREASTED

ˌsingle ˈcombat *n* [U] when one person, usually a soldier, fights against one other person: *He had already defeated an enemy champion in single combat.*

ˌsingle ˈcream *n* [U] *BrE* thin cream that you can pour easily → DOUBLE CREAM, HEAVY CREAM

ˌsingle ˈcurrency *n* [singular] a unit of money that is shared by several different countries: *Europe is moving steadily towards a single currency.*

ˌsingle-ˈdecker, **single decker** *n* [C] *BrE* a bus with only one level → DOUBLE-DECKER(1) —**single-decker** *adj* [only before noun]: *a single-decker bus*

ˌsingle ˈfigures *n* [plural] a number below 10 → **double figures**: **in single figures** *Interest rates have stayed in single figures for over a year now.* | *The number of cases of the disease is now down to single figures.*

ˌsingle ˈfile *n* **in single file** moving in a line, with one person behind another: *We walked in single file across the bridge.* —**single file** *adv*

ˌsingle-ˈhandedly (*also* **ˌsingle-ˈhanded**) *adv* if one person does something single-handedly, they do it without help from anyone else SYN **alone**: *She brought up three children single-handedly.* —**single-handed** *adj* [only before noun]: *a single-handed voyage across the Atlantic*

ˌsingle ˈhonours *n* [U] a university degree course in Britain in which you study only one main subject → JOINT HONOURS

ˌsingle ˈmarket *n* **the single market** a group of countries in Europe that allow goods to be moved, bought, and sold between them with very few controls

ˌsingle-ˈminded *adj* someone who is single-minded has one clear aim and works very hard to achieve it: *a tough, single-minded lady* | *He worked with single-minded determination.* THESAURUS ▸ DETERMINED —**single-mindedly** *adv* —**single-mindedness** *n* [U]

sin·gle·ness /ˈsɪŋɡəlnəs/ *n* **singleness of purpose** *formal* great determination when you are working to achieve something

ˌsingle ˈparent *n* [C] a mother or father who looks after their children on their own, without a partner SYN **lone parent**

sin·glet /ˈsɪŋɡlɪt/ *n* [C] *BrE* a piece of clothing that you wear for sport which covers the top part of your body but not your arms

ˌsingle track ˈroad *n* [C] *BrE* a road that is only wide enough for one car to go along it

sin·gly /ˈsɪŋɡli/ *adv* alone, or one at a time: *Plant the trees singly or in small groups.*

ˈSing Sing a prison in New York State, known in the past for controlling prisoners very strictly

sing·song /ˈsɪŋsɒŋ $ -sɔːŋ/ *n* **1** [singular] a way of speaking in which your voice keeps rising and falling: *I recognized her soft singsong immediately.* **2** [C] *BrE* an informal occasion when people sing songs together SYN **singalong** *AmE*: *We had a bit of a singsong later.* —**singsong** *adj*: *a singsong voice*

sin·gu·lar[1] /ˈsɪŋɡjələ $ -ər/ ●●● *adj*

1 a singular noun, verb, form etc is used when writing or speaking about one person or thing → **plural**: *the* ***singular form*** *of the noun* | *If the subject is singular, use a singular verb.*

2 [usually before noun] *formal* very great or very noticeable: *He showed a* ***singular lack*** *of tact in the way he handled the situation.* | *a singular achievement*

3 *literary* very unusual or strange: *I wondered why she was behaving in so singular a fashion.*

singular[2] ●●● *n* **the singular** the form of a word used when writing or speaking about one person or thing

→ **plural**: *'Datum' is the singular of 'data'.* | **in the singular** *Should the verb be in the singular or the plural?*

sin·gu·lar·i·ty /ˌsɪŋgjəˈlærəti/ *n* (*plural* **singularities**) **1** [C] *technical* an extremely small point in space that contains an extremely large amount of material and which does not obey the usual laws of nature, for example a BLACK HOLE or the point at the beginning of the universe **2** [U] *old-fashioned* the quality of something that makes it unusual or strange: *He had an attractive singularity of viewpoint.*

sin·gu·lar·ly /ˈsɪŋgjələli $ -lərli/ *adv formal* in a way that is very noticeable or unusual: *a singularly foolish plan* | *He has singularly failed to live up to his promises.*

Sin·ha·lese /ˌsɪnhəˈliːz◂/ *n* (*plural* **Sinhalese**) **1** [C] someone who belongs to the race of people that forms the largest part of the population in Sri Lanka **2** [U] the language used by the Sinhalese —**Sinhalese** *adj*

sin·is·ter /ˈsɪnɪstə $ -ər/ ●○○ *adj* making you feel that something evil, dangerous, or illegal is happening or will happen: **there is something/nothing sinister about sb/sth** *There was something sinister about Mr Scott's death.* | *There is a sinister side to these events.* | *He was a handsome man, in a sinister sort of way.* | *a sinister atmosphere*

sink¹ /sɪŋk/ ●●● W3 *v* (*past tense* **sank** /sæŋk/ *or* **sunk** /sʌŋk/ *AmE*, *past participle* **sunk** /sʌŋk/)
1 IN WATER [I] to go down below the surface of water, mud etc OPP **float**: *Their motorboat struck a rock and began to sink.* | *The kids watched as the coin* ***sank to the bottom of*** *the pool.* | *The heavy guns sank up to their barrels in the mud.*
2 BOAT [T] to damage a ship so badly that it sinks: *A luxury yacht was sunk in a bomb attack yesterday.*
3 MOVE LOWER [I] to move downwards to a lower level: *The* ***sun*** *was* ***sinking*** *behind the coconut palms.* | *Her chin sank onto her chest, and she looked despairing.*
4 FALL/SIT DOWN [I] to fall down or sit down heavily, especially because you are very tired and weak: **[+into/to/down/back etc]** *She let out a groan and sank into a chair.* | *He let go of her shoulders and she sank at once to the floor.* | *Marion sank down on a rock, and wept.* | *The minister* ***sank to*** *his* ***knees*** (=he went down into a kneeling position) *and prayed.*
5 GET WORSE [I always + adv/prep] to gradually get into a worse condition: **[+into]** *They lost all their money and sank into desperate poverty.* | *The good mood left me and I sank into depression.* | *The doctor said that the boy was* ***sinking fast*** (=getting weaker and about to die).
6 your heart sinks (*also* **your spirits sink**) used to say that you lose hope or confidence: *His heart sank the way it always did when she left him.* | *She felt desperately tired, and her spirits sank.*
7 LOWER AMOUNT/VALUE [I] to go down in amount or value SYN **drop** OPP **rise**: *Shares in the company have sunk as low as 620p.* | **[+to]** *The population of the village sank to just a few families.*
8 VOICE [I] *written* if your voice sinks, it becomes very quiet: **[+to/into]** *Her voice sank to a whisper.*
9 sinking feeling *informal* the unpleasant feeling that you get when you suddenly realize that something bad is going to happen: *I* ***had*** *a* ***sinking feeling*** *inside as I realized I was going to fail yet again.*
10 be sunk *spoken* to be in a situation where you are certain to fail or have a lot of problems: *If I don't get paid by next week, I'll really be sunk.*
11 sink without trace *especially BrE* (*also* **sink like a stone** *especially AmE*) if something sinks without trace, it fails quickly or no one pays attention to it: *He made a few records, which all sank without trace.*
12 sink so low (*also* **sink to doing sth**) to be dishonest enough or SELFISH enough to do something very bad or unfair SYN **stoop**: *How could he have sunk so low?*
13 USE SOMETHING SHARP [T] to put your teeth or something sharp into someone's flesh, into food etc: **sink sth into sth** *The dog* ***sank*** *its* ***teeth*** *into my arm.* | *She sank her fork into the pie.*
14 DIG INTO GROUND [T] if you sink something such as a well or part of a building, you dig a hole to put it into the ground: *A* ***well*** *was* ***sunk*** *in the back garden, and water could be pumped up into the kitchen.*
15 sink or swim to succeed or fail without help from anyone else: *They don't give you a lot of guidance – you're just left to sink or swim, really.*
16 MONEY [T] to spend a lot of money on something: **sink sth in/into sth** *They sank their entire savings into their house.*
17 BALL [T] to put a ball into a hole or BASKET in games such as GOLF or BASKETBALL
18 sink your differences *BrE* to agree to stop arguing and forget about your disagreements, especially in order to unite and oppose someone else: *Nations must sink their differences to achieve greater security.*
19 DRINK [T] *BrE informal* to drink alcohol, especially in large quantities: *We sank a few pints at the pub first.*
sink in *phr v* if information, facts etc sink in, you gradually understand them or realize their full meaning: *He paused a moment for his words to sink in.* | *The implications of Labour's defeat were beginning to sink in.*

sink² ●●● S3 *n* [C] a large open container that you fill with water and use for washing yourself, washing dishes etc → **basin**: *Dirty plates were piled high in the sink.* → **everything but the kitchen sink** at EVERYTHING(7)

sink³ *adj* **sink estate/school** *BrE* an area where people live or a school that is in a very bad condition and seems unlikely to improve: *Go to almost any city and you find sink estates where you get the feeling that the council hates the place and the people too.*

sink·er /ˈsɪŋkə $ -ər/ → **hook, line, and sinker** at HOOK¹(9)

ˈsinking ˌfund *n* [C] *technical* money saved regularly by a business to pay for something in the future

sin·ner /ˈsɪnə $ -ər/ *n* [C] *especially biblical* someone who has sinned (SIN) by not obeying God's laws

Sino- /saɪnəʊ $ -noʊ/ *prefix* [in nouns and adjectives] **1** Chinese and something else: *Sino-Japanese trade* **2** relating to China: *a Sinologist* (=someone who studies Chinese culture, language, history etc)

sin·u·ous /ˈsɪnjuəs/ *adj* **1** moving with smooth twists and turns, like a snake: *the sinuous grace of a cat* **2** with many smooth twists and turns: *They followed the sinuous trail deep into the mountains.* —**sinuously** *adv*

si·nus /ˈsaɪnəs/ *n* [C] your sinuses are the spaces in the bones of your head that are connected to the inside of your nose: *blocked sinuses* | *a sinus infection*

si·nus·i·tis /ˌsaɪnəˈsaɪtɪs/ *n* [U] a condition in which your sinuses swell up and become painful

sip¹ /sɪp/ ●●○ *v* (**sipped**, **sipping**) [I,T] to drink something slowly, taking very small mouthfuls: *She was sitting at the table sipping her coffee.* | **[+at]** *He sipped at his wine with pleasure.* THESAURUS DRINK

sip² *n* [C] a very small amount of a drink: **[+of]** *a sip of water* | *She poured more wine and* ***took*** *a* ***sip***.

si·phon¹ (*also* **syphon** *BrE*) /ˈsaɪfən/ *n* [C] **1** a bent tube used for getting liquid out of a container, used by holding one end of the tube at a lower level than the end in the container **2** (*also* **soda siphon**) a type of bottle for holding SODA WATER, which is forced out of the bottle using gas pressure

siphon² (*also* **syphon** *BrE*) *v* [T always + adv/prep] **1** (*also* **siphon sth ↔ off/out**) to remove liquid from a container by using a siphon: *It took him only a few minutes to siphon off the petrol and drive away.* | **siphon sth out of/from sth** *Crews began siphoning oil from the leaking boat.* **2** (*also* **siphon sth ↔ off**) to dishonestly take money from a business, account etc to use it for a purpose for which it was not intended: *Emergency aid was siphoned off by foreign ministry officials for their own use.* | **siphon sth from sth** *I found she had siphoned thousands of dollars from our bank account.*

ˈsipping lid *n* [C] a plastic cover with a small hole in it that you put on a cup of coffee, tea etc, so that you can drink from the cup while walking, travelling etc

sir /sə; *strong* sɜː $ sər *strong* sɜːr/ ●●● S1 W3 *n*
1 *spoken* used when speaking to a man in order to be polite or show respect: *'Report back to me in an hour,*

S

sergeant.' 'Yes, sir.' | Can I help you, sir? | Sir! You dropped your wallet. → MADAM(1), MA'AM
2 Dear Sir/Sirs used at the beginning of a formal letter to a man or to people you do not know
3 Sir a title used before the first name of a KNIGHT or BARONET: *Sir Paul McCartney | Sir Jasper*
4 *BrE spoken* used by children at school when speaking to or talking about a male teacher: *Sir, I've forgotten my homework. | Look out – sir's coming back!* → MISS²(4)
5 no/yes sir! (*also* **no/yes siree!** *especially AmE*) *old-fashioned spoken* used to emphasize a statement or an answer to a question: *I will not have that man in my home, no sir!*

sire¹ /saɪə $ saɪr/ *n* **1** *old use* used when speaking to a king: *The people await you, sire.* **2** [C usually singular] the father of a four-legged animal, especially a horse

sire² *v* [T] **1** to be the father of an animal, especially a horse or dog: *a stallion that has sired several race winners* **2** *old-fashioned* to be the father of a child: *Sam sired eight children.*

si·ren /ˈsaɪərən $ ˈsaɪr-/ *n* [C] **1** a piece of equipment that makes very loud warning sounds, used on police cars, fire engines etc: *the wail of the ambulance sirens | I heard police sirens in the distance.* **2 siren voices/song/call** *literary* encouragement to do something that seems very good, especially when this could have bad results: *siren voices calling for the sale of weapons to the region* **3** a woman who is very attractive but also dangerous to men – used especially in newspapers: *a Hollywood siren* **4 the Sirens** a group of women in ancient Greek stories, whose beautiful singing made sailors sail towards them into dangerous water

Sir Hum·phrey /sə ˈhʌmfri $ sər-/ a name used, especially in newspapers, for a typical British CIVIL SERVANT (=someone who works for a government minister, but who is not a politician) of high rank. The name is based on a character called Sir Humphrey Appleby, in the humorous British television programme *Yes, Minister*, who uses clever and dishonest methods to make sure that his minister always does what Sir Humphrey wants.

sir·loin /ˈsɜːlɔɪn $ ˈsɜːr-/ (*also* ˌ**sirloin** ˈ**steak**) *n* [C,U] a good-quality piece of BEEF which is cut from the lower part of a cow's back

si·roc·co /səˈrɒkəʊ $ -ˈrɑːkoʊ/ *n* (*plural* **siroccos**) [C] a hot wind that blows from the desert of North Africa across to southern Europe

sis /sɪs/ *n spoken informal* a name used when speaking to your sister

si·sal /ˈsaɪsəl/ *n* [U] a Central American plant whose leaves produce strong FIBRES, also called sisal, which are used in making rope

sis·sy, cissy /ˈsɪsi/ *n* [C] *informal not polite* a boy that other boys dislike because he prefers doing things that girls enjoy: *He wanted to go to dance classes, but he was afraid the other boys would call him a sissy.* —**sissy** *adj*

sis·ter /ˈsɪstə $ -ər/ ●●● S1 W1 *n* [C]
1 a girl or woman who has the same parents as you → **brother**, **half-sister**, **step-sister**: *Janet and Abby are sisters. | He has two sisters and a brother.* | **older/big sister** *My older sister is a nurse.* | **younger/little sister** *Where's your little sister? | She's my* ***twin sister****.*
2 sister paper/publication/company etc a newspaper etc that belongs to the same group or organization: *the Daily Post's sister paper, the Liverpool Echo*
3 (*also* **Sister**) a NUN: *Good morning, Sister Mary.*
4 *BrE* (*also* **Sister**) a nurse in charge of a hospital WARD: *the* ***ward sister*** *| I'm feeling a bit better today, Sister.*
5 a word used by women to talk about other women and to show that they have feelings of friendship and support towards them: *We appeal to our sisters all over the world to stand by us.*
6 *AmE spoken* a way of talking to or about an African-American woman, used especially by African Americans

sis·ter·hood /ˈsɪstəhʊd $ -ər-/ *n* **1** [U] a special loyal relationship among women who share the same ideas and aims, especially among FEMINISTS: *the special bond of sisterhood that joins women together* **2** [C] a group of women who live a religious life together → **brotherhood**: *the Christian sisterhood*

ˈ**sister-in-ˌlaw** ●●○ *n* (*plural* **sisters-in-law**) [C]
1 the sister of your husband or wife
2 your brother's wife
3 the wife of the brother of your husband or wife

sis·ter·ly /ˈsɪstəli $ -ər-/ *adj* typical of a loving sister → **brotherly**: *She gave Lee a sisterly kiss. | Their friendship can best be described as sisterly.*

Sis·y·phus /ˈsɪsəfəs/ in ancient Greek stories, an evil king whose punishment after death was to roll a very large stone to the top of a steep hill. Each time he got near to the top of the hill, the stone rolled down to the bottom, and he had to start again, and he had to continue doing this forever. A very difficult job that seems impossible to finish is sometimes described as a 'Sisyphean task'.

sit /sɪt/ ●●● S1 W1 *v* (*past tense and past participle* **sat** /sæt/, *present participle* **sitting**)
1 IN A CHAIR ETC **a)** (*also* **be sitting down**) [I] to be on a chair or seat, or on the ground, with the top half of your body upright and your weight resting on your BUTTOCKS: **[+on/in/by etc]** *I sat on the shore and looked at the sea. | She was sitting in a chair by the fire. | She's the girl who sits next to me at school. | In the driving seat sat a man of average height.* | **sit at a desk/table etc** (=sit facing it) *Jean sat at the table writing a letter.* | **sit doing sth** *They sat sipping their drinks. | We used to* ***sit and*** *listen to her for hours.* **b)** (*also* **sit down**) [I always + adv/prep] to get into a sitting position somewhere after you have been standing up: *He came over and sat beside her. | Sam sat opposite her and accepted a cigarette.* **c)** (*also* **sit sb down**) [T always + adv/prep] to make someone sit, or help them to sit: **sit sb on/in etc sth** *I gently led her to the chair and sat her on it.*
2 OBJECTS/BUILDINGS ETC [I always + adv/prep] to be in a particular position or condition: **[+on/in etc]** *a little church sitting on a hillside | The parliament building sits in a large square. | He's got a computer sitting on his desk, but he doesn't use it. | My climbing boots were sitting unused in a cupboard. | The house has* ***sat empty*** *for two years.*
3 DO NOTHING [I always + adv/prep] to stay in one place for a long time, especially sitting down, doing nothing useful or helpful: *I spent half the morning sitting in a traffic jam. | Well, I can't* ***sit here*** *chatting all day. | Are you just going to* ***sit there*** *complaining?*
4 COMMITTEE/PARLIAMENT ETC [I] to be a member of a committee, parliament, or other official group: **[+in/on]** *They both sat on the management committee. | He was the first journalist to sit in parliament.*
5 MEETING [I] to have a meeting in order to carry out official business: *The council only sits once a month. | The court will sit until all the evidence has been heard.*
6 ANIMAL/BIRD [I always + adv/prep] **a)** to be in, or get into, a resting position, with the tail end of the body resting on a surface: *The cat likes to sit on the wall outside the kitchen.* **b) Sit!** used to tell a dog to sit with the tail end of its body resting on the ground or floor **c)** if a bird sits on its eggs, it covers them with its body to make the eggs HATCH
7 LOOK AFTER [I + for] to look after a baby or child while its parents are out SYN **babysit**
8 sit tight *spoken* **a)** to stay where you are and not move: *Just sit tight – I'll be there in five minutes.* **b)** to stay in the same situation, and not change your mind and do anything new: *We're advising all our investors to sit tight till the market improves.*
9 be sitting pretty to be in a very good or favourable position: *We've paid off the mortgage, so we're sitting pretty now.*
10 sit in judgment (on/over sb) to give your opinion about whether someone has done something wrong, especially when you have no right to do this: *How can you sit in judgment on somebody you hardly know?*
11 not sit well/easily/comfortably (with sb) if a situation, plan etc does not sit well with someone, they do not like

S

it: *He had never before been accused of stealing, and it did not sit well with him.*
12 sit on the fence to avoid saying which side of an argument you support or what your opinion is about a particular subject: *The weakness of the book is that it sits on the fence on important issues.*
13 sit on your hands to delay taking action when you should do something: *Workers are losing their jobs while the government sits on its hands and does nothing.*
14 EXAMS [I,T] *BrE* to take an examination: *Tracy's sitting her GCSEs this year.* | **[+for]** *They were preparing children to sit for the entry examination.*
15 PICTURE/PHOTO [I] to sit somewhere so that you can be painted or photographed: **[+for]** *She sat for* (=was painted by) *Holman Hunt and Millais.*

COLLOCATIONS

ADVERBS

sit still (=without moving) *Young children find it almost impossible to sit still.*
sit quietly (=without talking) *Mac sat quietly in the back of the car.*
be sitting comfortably *She was sitting comfortably on the sofa.*
sit up straight/sit upright (=with your back straight) | **sit bolt upright** (=suddenly sit up very straight, for example because you hear something) | **sit cross-legged** (=with your legs bent and crossed over in front of you)

THESAURUS

sit to be resting your weight on your bottom somewhere, or to move into this position: *He was sitting in front of the fire.* | *She sat on the bed and kicked off her shoes.*
sit down to sit on a chair, bed, floor etc after you have been standing: *I sat down on the sofa.* | *Come in and sit down.*
be seated *formal* to be sitting in a particular chair or place: *John was seated on my left.*
take a seat to sit – used especially when asking someone to sit down: *Please take a seat – she will be with you in a minute.* | *Would the audience please take their seats – the show will begin in five minutes.*
sink into sth to sit in a comfortable chair and let yourself fall back into it: *We switched on the TV and sank into our armchairs.*
lounge to sit in a very comfortable relaxed way: *They lounged around all day by the pool.*
perch to sit on the edge of something: *He perched on the arm of the sofa.* | *My sister was perched* (=was sitting) *on a high stool.*
be slumped to be sitting while leaning against something, especially because you are injured, drunk, or asleep: *They found him slumped against the steering wheel.*
squat to sit with your knees bent under you, your bottom just off the ground, balancing on your feet: *A little boy was squatting at the edge of the pool.*

sit around (*also* **sit about** *BrE*) *phr v* to spend a lot of time sitting and doing nothing very useful: *We sat around for a bit, chatting.*
sit back *phr v*
1 to get into a comfortable position, for example in a chair, and relax: ***Sit back and relax*** *– I'll open a bottle of wine.*
2 to relax and make no effort to get involved in something or influence what happens: *Don't just **sit back and** wait for new business to come to you.*
sit by *phr v* to allow something wrong or illegal to happen without doing anything about it: *I'm not going to sit by and watch a man go to prison for something I've done.*
sit down *phr v*
1 to be in a sitting position or get into a sitting position: *It was good to be sitting down eating dinner with my family.* | *Sit down, Amy – you look tired.* | **sit yourself down** *Sit yourself down and have a drink.*
2 sit sb down to make someone sit down or help them to sit down: **[+in/on]** *I helped her into the room and sat her down in an armchair.*
3 sit down and do sth to try to solve a problem or deal with something that needs to be done, by giving it all your attention: *The three of us need to sit down and have a talk.* | *Sit down and work out just what you spend.*
sit in *phr v* to be present at a meeting but not take an active part in it: **[+on]** *Would you like to sit in on some of my interviews?*
sit in for sb *phr v* to do a job, go to a meeting etc instead of the person who usually does it: *This is Alan James sitting in for Suzy Williams on the mid-morning show.*
sit on sth *phr v informal* to delay dealing with something: *I sent my application about six weeks ago and they've just been sitting on it.*
sit sth ↔ **out** *phr v*
1 to stay where you are and do nothing until something finishes, especially something boring or unpleasant: *She had two weeks to **sit it out** while she waited to hear if she had got the job.* | *She was prepared to sit out the years of Jack's jail sentence.*
2 to not take part in something, especially a game or dance, when you usually take part: *Johnson sat out the game with a shoulder injury.*
sit through sth *phr v* to attend a meeting, performance etc, and stay until the end, even if it is very long and boring: *I wasn't the least bit interested in all the speeches I had to sit through.*
sit up *phr v*
1 to be in a sitting position or get into a sitting position after you have been lying down: *He was sitting up in bed, reading his book.* | *She sat up and reached for her glass.*
2 sit sb up to help someone to sit after they have been lying down: **[+in/on etc]** *I'll sit you up on the pillows and you'll be nice and comfortable.*
3 to sit in a chair with your back straight: *Just **sit up straight** and stop slouching.*
4 to stay up very late: *Sometimes we just sit up and watch videos all night.*
5 sit up (and take notice) to suddenly start paying attention to someone, because they have done something surprising or impressive: *If Maria succeeded, then everyone would sit up and take notice.*

sit·ar /ˈsɪtɑː $ -ɑːr/ *n* [C] a very long musical instrument from India, similar to a GUITAR, with two sets of strings and a round body

sit·com /ˈsɪtkɒm $ -kɑːm/ *n* [C,U] (***situation comedy***) a funny television programme in which the same characters appear in different situations each week THESAURUS ➤ PROGRAMME

ˈsit-down[1] *adj* **1** a sit-down meal or restaurant is one in which you sit at a table and eat a formal meal: *a sit-down meal for 20 people* **2 sit-down strike/protest** a protest in which people sit down, especially to block a road or other public place, until their demands are considered or agreed to → **sit-in**

sit-down[2] *n* [singular] *BrE* if you have a sit-down, you sit and rest for a short while: *You look as if you need a sit-down.*

site[1] /saɪt/ ●●● S1 W2 AWL *n* [C]
1 a place where something important or interesting happened: *an archaeological site* | **[+of]** *The house is built on the site of a medieval prison.* | *the site of the air crash* THESAURUS ➤ PLACE
2 an area of ground where something is being built or will be built: **[+of/for]** *the site of a proposed missile base* | *a site for a new airport* | **building/construction site** *He managed to get himself a job on a building site.*
3 a place that is used for a particular purpose: *a **camping site*** | **[+of/for]** *a nesting site for birds*
4 a WEBSITE
5 on site at the place where people work, study, or stay: *There's a bar, restaurant, and gym on site.*

site[2] ●○○ *v* [T] to place or build something in a

S

particular place: **be sited in/on/at/near etc sth** *Some of this new housing has been sited in inner city areas.*

ˌsite-speˈcific *adj* designed and made to be used in a particular place, or relating to a particular place: *a site-specific policy*

ˈsit-in *n* [C] a type of protest in which people refuse to leave the place where they work or study until their demands are considered or agreed to: **hold/stage a sit-in** *Several thousand students staged sit-ins and protest marches.*

sit·ter /ˈsɪtə $ -ər/ *n* [C] **1** *especially AmE* a BABYSITTER **2** someone who sits or stands while someone else paints them or takes photographs of them SYN **model**

sit·ting /ˈsɪtɪŋ/ *n* [C] **1** one of the times when a meal is served in a place where there is not enough space for everyone to eat at the same time: *School dinners are served in three sittings.* **2 at/in one sitting** during one continuous period when you are sitting in a chair: *I sat down and read the whole book in one sitting.* **3** an occasion when you have yourself painted or photographed **4** a meeting of a law court or parliament

ˌsitting ˈduck (*also* **ˌsitting ˈtarget**) *n* [C] someone who is easy to attack or easy to cheat: *Out in the open, the soldiers were sitting ducks for enemy fire.*

ˌsitting ˈmember *n* [C] *BrE* someone who is a member of a parliament at the present time: *the sitting member for Newbury*

ˈsitting room *n* [C] *especially BrE* the room in a house where you sit, relax, watch television etc SYN **living room**

ˌsitting ˈtenant *n* [C] *BrE* someone who lives in a rented house or FLAT, especially when this gives them legal rights to stay there

sit·u /ˈsɪtjuː $ ˈsaɪtuː/ → **IN SITU**

sit·u·ate /ˈsɪtʃueɪt/ *v* [T] *formal* to describe or consider something as being part of something else or related to something else: **situate sth in sth** *The women have the opportunity to situate their own struggles in a wider historical context.*

sit·u·at·ed /ˈsɪtʃueɪtɪd/ ●●○ *adj* **be situated** to be in a particular place or position SYN **located**: **[+in/near/at etc]** *The house is situated near the college.* | *a farm situated in the valley* | **conveniently/ideally/beautifully etc situated** *The hotel is ideally situated near the seafront.*

sit·u·a·tion /ˌsɪtʃuˈeɪʃən/ ●●● S1 W1 *n* [C]
1 a combination of all the things that are happening and all the conditions that exist at a particular time in a particular place: *I explained the situation to everyone.* | **in a ... situation** *She coped well in a very difficult situation.*
2 the type of area where a building is situated – used especially by people who sell or advertise buildings SYN **location**: *The house is in a charming situation, on a wooded hillside.*
3 *old-fashioned* a job: *She managed to get a situation as a parlour maid.*

COLLOCATIONS

VERBS

create a situation (=cause it to happen) *Tom's arrival created an awkward situation.*
assess/review a situation *Ballater was trying to assess the situation objectively.*
monitor a situation (=watch to see how it develops) *The bank is monitoring the situation closely.*
deal with a situation *He had no idea how to deal with the situation.*
improve/remedy a situation *They are doing what they can to improve the situation.*
defuse the situation (=make people less angry) | **a situation arises** *formal* (=it happens) | **a situation comes about** (=it happens) | **a situation changes** | **a situation improves** | **a situation worsens/deteriorates/gets worse**

ADJECTIVES/NOUN + situation

difficult/tricky *This book will show you how to deal with difficult situations.*
impossible (=very difficult) *I was in an impossible situation.*
dangerous *The situation was becoming increasingly dangerous.*
the present/current situation *The present situation in Afghanistan is very worrying.*
the economic/political situation *The country's economic situation continued to deteriorate.*
the security situation (=how safe a place is) | **sb's financial situation** (=how much money someone has) | **a social situation** (=a situation in which someone is with other people) | **a work situation** (=a situation at work) | **a no-win situation** (=one in which there will be a bad result whatever happens) | **a win-win situation** (=one in which everyone gets what they want)

ˌsituation ˈcomedy *n* [C,U] *formal* a SITCOM

ˈsit-up *BrE*, **sit·up** *AmE* /ˈsɪtʌp/ *n* [C] an exercise to make your stomach muscles strong, in which you sit up from a lying position, while keeping your feet on the floor → **crunch**: *Jerry says he* ***does*** *two hundred* ***sit-ups*** *a day.* → see picture at **GYM**

SI unit /es ˈaɪ ˌjuːnɪt/ *n* [C] *technical* a standard unit of measurement in an international system used especially by scientists. SI units include the metre, kilogram, second, AMPERE, and KELVIN.

six /sɪks/ ●●● S2 W2 *number*
1 the number 6: *six months ago* | *She arrived just after six* (=six o'clock). | *He learnt to play the violin when he was six* (=six years old).
2 six figures/digits used to talk about a number that is between 100,000 and 1,000,000: *The final cost of the project will easily* ***run into six figures*** (=be over £100,000 or $100,000).
3 at sixes and sevens *informal* disorganized and confused: *When the visitors arrived, we were still at sixes and sevens.*
4 it's six of one and half a dozen of the other *spoken* used to say that both people or groups who are involved in a situation are equally responsible for something bad that happens: *In any family quarrel, it's usually six of one and half a dozen of the other.*
5 knock/hit sb for six *BrE spoken* to affect someone strongly in a bad way: *Losing his job really knocked him for six.*
6 [C] a hit in CRICKET that scores six RUNS because the ball crosses the edge of the playing area before touching the ground

ˌsix-ˈfigure *adj* [only before noun] used to describe a number that is 100,000 or more, especially an amount of money: *a six-figure sum* | *a six-figure salary*

six·fold /ˈsɪksfəʊld $ -foʊld/ *adv formal* by six times as much or as many: *Burglaries have* ***increased sixfold***. —**sixfold** *adj*: *a sixfold increase in teenage pregnancies*

ˌSix ˌNations ˈChampionship, the a Rugby Union competition that takes place every year between teams from England, Ireland, Scotland, Wales, France, and Italy

ˈsix-pack *n* [C] **1** six cans or bottles of a drink, especially beer, sold together as a set: *There's a six-pack in the fridge.* | **[+of]** *a six-pack of beer* **2** well-developed muscles that you can see on a man's stomach – used humorously

six·pence /ˈsɪkspəns/ *n* [C,U] a small silver-coloured coin worth six old PENNIES, used in Britain in the past

ˈsix-ˌshooter *n* [C] *especially AmE old-fashioned* a small gun that holds six bullets

six·teen /ˌsɪkˈstiːn◂/ ●●● S3 W3 *number* the number 16: *sixteen years later* | *He moved to London when he was sixteen* (=16 years old). —**sixteenth** *adj, pron*: *her sixteenth birthday* | *the sixteenth century* | *Let's have dinner on* ***the 16th*** (=the 16th day of the month).

six·teenth /ˌsɪkˈstiːnθ◂/ *n* [C] one of 16 equal parts of something

ˈsixteenth ˌnote *n* [C] *AmE* a musical note which continues for a sixteenth of the length of a WHOLE NOTE SYN **semiquaver** *BrE*

S

sixth¹ /sɪksθ/ ●●● S3 W3 *adj* coming after five other things in a series: *her sixth birthday | the sixth century* —**sixth** *pron*: *Let's have dinner on* ***the sixth*** (=the sixth day of the month).

sixth² *n* [C] one of six equal parts of something: *About one sixth of the children admitted to taking drugs.*

ˈsixth form *n* [C] the highest level in the British school system. Children aged between 16 and 18 stay in the sixth form for two years while they prepare to take A LEVELS (=the highest level of school exams). —**sixth former** *n* [C]

ˈsixth form ˌcollege *n* [C] a type of school in Britain for students who are preparing to take A LEVELs (=the highest level of school exams)

ˌsixth ˈsense *n* [singular] a special ability to know things without using any of your five ordinary senses such as your hearing or sight: *He seemed to* ***have a sixth sense*** *for knowing when his brother was in trouble.*

six·ty /ˈsɪksti/ ●●● W3 *number*
1 the number 60: *sixty years ago*
2 the sixties [plural] (*also* **the '60s, the 1960s**) the years from 1960 to 1969: *The book was written in the sixties.* | **the early/late sixties** *the student riots in Paris in the late sixties*
3 be in your sixties to be aged between 60 and 69: **early/mid/late sixties** *I'd say she was in her late sixties.*
4 in the sixties if the temperature is in the sixties, it is between 60 degrees and 69 degrees: **in the low/mid/high sixties** *a fine spring day, with the temperatures in the low sixties* —**sixtieth** *adj, pron*: *her sixtieth birthday*

siz·a·ble /ˈsaɪzəbəl/ *adj* another spelling of SIZEABLE

size¹ /saɪz/ ●●● S1 W1 *n*
1 HOW BIG [C,U] how big or small something is: *He's a small boy, about John's size. | The Jensens' house is about* ***the same size as*** *ours.* | **[+of]** *The firm underestimated the size of the market for their new product. | I saw a spider* ***the size of*** (=the same size as) *my hand in the backyard. | He's quite a big dog, but he's still not* ***full size*** *yet.* | **in size** *The apartment is roughly 360 square feet in size.* | **(of) that/this size** (=as big as that or this) *In a class this size, there are bound to be a few troublemakers. | We can't give loans of that size to just anyone.* | **in all/different/various (shapes and) sizes** *These phones come in all shapes and sizes.* | **good/fair/nice size** (=fairly big) *The breakfast room is a good size.*
2 VERY BIG [U] used to say that something is very big: **[+of]** *I can't believe the size of her car! | The* ***sheer size*** *of the classes makes learning difficult for students.*
3 CLOTHES/GOODS [C] one of a set of standard measures according to which clothes and other goods are produced and sold: *These shoes are one size too big. | The shirts come in three sizes: small, medium, and large. | Do you have these pants in a size 12?*
4 large-sized/medium-sized/pocket-size etc of a particular size, or about the same size and shape as something: *a medium-sized car | a pocket-size mirror* | **good-sized/fair-sized/decent-sized** (=big enough for a particular purpose)
5 do sth to size if you cut, make, or prepare something to size, you make it the right size for a particular use: *The materials will be provided, and everything is already cut to size.*
6 that's about the size of it *spoken* used to agree that someone's description of a situation is correct
7 PASTE [U] (*also* **sizing**) a thick sticky liquid used for giving stiffness and a shiny surface to cloth, paper etc, or used to prepare walls for WALLPAPER → **cut sb down to size** at **CUT DOWN**, → **try sth on for size** at **TRY¹(2)**

THESAURUS

size *n* [C,U] how big someone or something is: *What size is that shirt? | The price will depend on the size and quality of the carpet.*
dimensions *n* [plural] the length, width, and height of an object, room, building etc: *What are the dimensions of the table?*
measurements *n* [plural] the length, width, or height of something, or of someone's body: *I need to check the measurements of the window. | Your waist measurement is 31 inches.*
proportions *n* [plural] the relative sizes of the different parts of an object, room, building etc: *The proportions don't look right to me.*
area *n* [C,U] the amount of space that a flat surface such as a floor or field covers: *To measure the area of a room, you need to multiply the length by the width.*
extent *n* [U] the size of a large area: *The extent of the ranch is enormous. | The island measured about 1,600 kilometres in extent.*
bulk *n* [U] the very large size of something: *The statue's massive bulk made it difficult to move. | his enormous bulk*
capacity *n* [singular] the amount that a container will hold: *The capacity of the tank is around 500 gallons. | All the storage units were filled to capacity.*
volume *n* [singular] the amount of space that a substance fills, or that an object contains: *The average domestic swimming pool has a volume of 45,000 litres. | This instrument measures the volume of air in your lungs.*

size² *v* [T] **1** to sort things according to their size: *Shrimp are sized and selected for canning.* **2** to make something into a particular size or sizes: *Most costume patterns are sized for children.* **3** to put SIZE¹(7) on a wall before decorating

size sb/sth ↔ **up** *phr v* to look at or consider a person or situation and make a judgment about them SYN **assess**: *It only took a few seconds for her to size up the situation.*

size·a·ble, **sizable** /ˈsaɪzəbəl/ *adj* fairly large: **sizeable amount/number** *a sizeable amount of money* | **sizeable proportion/portion/minority (of sth)** *Part-time students make up a sizeable proportion of the college population.*

ˌsize ˈzero *n* **1** [U] the smallest size of women's clothing in the US **2** [C] a woman who is very thin: *These clothes only look good on size zeroes.* —**size zero** *adj*: *size zero models*

siz·zle /ˈsɪzəl/ *v* [I] to make a sound like water falling on hot metal: *The bacon began to sizzle in the pan.*

siz·zling /ˈsɪzəlɪŋ/ *adj especially AmE* **1** very hot SYN **boiling**: *a sizzling afternoon* **2** very exciting, especially in a sexual way: *a sizzling scandalous affair*

ska /skɑː/ *n* [U] a kind of popular music from the West Indies with a fast regular beat, similar to REGGAE

skag, **scag** /skæg/ *n* [U] *informal* HEROIN

skank /skæŋk/ *n* [U] *informal* HEROIN

skan·ky /ˈskæŋki/ *adj informal* **1** very unpleasant or dirty: *The toilets there are really skanky.* **2** *AmE* a skanky woman is or looks very willing to have sex - used to show disapproval

SKATES

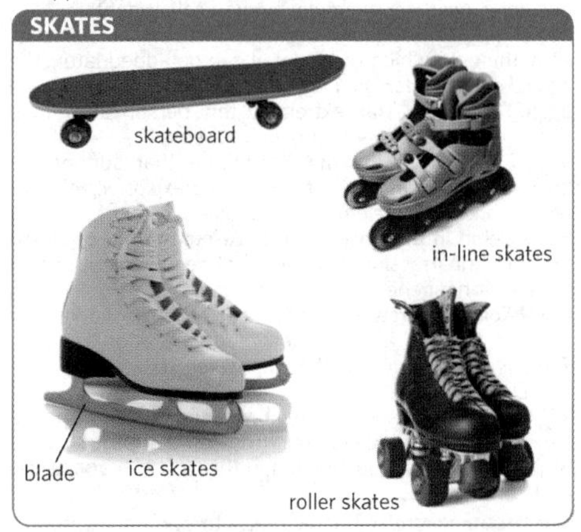

skate¹ /skeɪt/ ●●○ *n*
1 [C] one of a pair of boots with metal blades on the bottom, for moving quickly on ice SYN **ice skate**

S

2 [C] one of a pair of boots or frames with small wheels on the bottom, for moving quickly on flat smooth surfaces SYN **roller skate**
3 [C,U] (*plural* **skate** *or* **skates**) a large flat sea fish that can be eaten
4 get/put your skates on *BrE spoken* used to tell someone to hurry: *Put your skates on, or you'll be late for school.*

skate² ●●○ *v* [I]
1 to move on skates: *The children skated on the frozen pond.*
2 be skating on thin ice *informal* to be doing something that may get you into trouble —**skater** *n* [C]
skate over/around sth *phr v* to avoid mentioning a problem or subject, or not give it enough attention: *The president was accused of skating over the issue of the homeless.*

skate·board /ˈskeɪtbɔːd $ -bɔːrd/ ●●○ *n* [C] a short board with two small wheels at each end, which you can stand on and ride for fun or as a sport —**skateboarding** *n* [U] —**skateboarder** *n* [C] → see picture at SKATE¹

skate·park /ˈskeɪtpɑːk $ -pɑːrk/ *n* [C] an area for skateboarders to use, which has special slopes or other structures

skat·ing /ˈskeɪtɪŋ/ ●●● S3 *n* [U] the activity or sport of moving around on skates for fun or as a sport: *We* ***went skating*** *in Central Park.*

ˈskating ˌrink *n* [C] a place or building where you can skate SYN **ice rink**

ske·dad·dle /skɪˈdædl/ *v* [I] *spoken* to leave a place quickly, especially because you do not want to be caught - used humorously

skeet shoot·ing /ˈskiːt ʃuːtɪŋ/ *n* [U] *AmE* the sport of shooting at clay objects that have been thrown into the air SYN **clay pigeon shooting** *BrE*

skeeve /skiːv/ *v*
skeeve sb **out** *phr v AmE informal* to make someone feel sick or upset because they think something is unpleasant: *I hate touching raw meat. I just* ***get skeeved out****.*

skein /skeɪn/ *n* [C] **1** a long loosely wound piece of thread, wool, or YARN **2** *literary* a complicated series of things that are related to each other SYN **web**: *a skein of lies*

skel·e·tal /ˈskelətəl/ *adj* **1** like a skeleton or relating to a skeleton: *Police discovered the* ***skeletal remains*** *of a corpse buried near the river.* **2** someone who is skeletal is so thin that you can see their bones through their skin SYN **emaciated**: *prisoners whose clothes hung loosely on their skeletal bodies* THESAURUS ▸ THIN

skel·e·ton /ˈskelətən/ ●○○ *n*
1 BONES [C] **a)** the structure consisting of all the bones in a human or animal body: *the human skeleton* **b)** a set of these bones or a model of them, fastened in their usual positions, used, for example, by medical students
2 BASIC PARTS [singular] the most important parts of something, to which more detail can be added later: *We agreed on a skeleton outline of the proposal.*
3 THIN PERSON [C] an extremely thin person or animal: *The disease had reduced Harry to a skeleton.*
4 STRUCTURE [C] the main structure that supports a building, bridge etc: *Minutes after the explosion, all that remained was the skeleton of the bridge.*
5 a skeleton in the closet (*also* **a skeleton in the cupboard** *BrE*) an embarrassing or unpleasant secret about something that happened to you in the past
6 skeleton staff/crew/service etc only enough workers or services to keep an operation or organization running: *The bus company is operating a skeleton service on Christmas Day.*
7 SPORT **a)** [U] a sport in which you slide down a special ice track while lying on your front on a type of SLEDGE **b)** [C] the vehicle you slide on in this sport → BOBSLEIGH, LUGE

ˈskeleton key *n* [C] a key made to open a number of different locks

skep·tic /ˈskeptɪk/ *n* [C] the American spelling of SCEPTIC

SKELETON

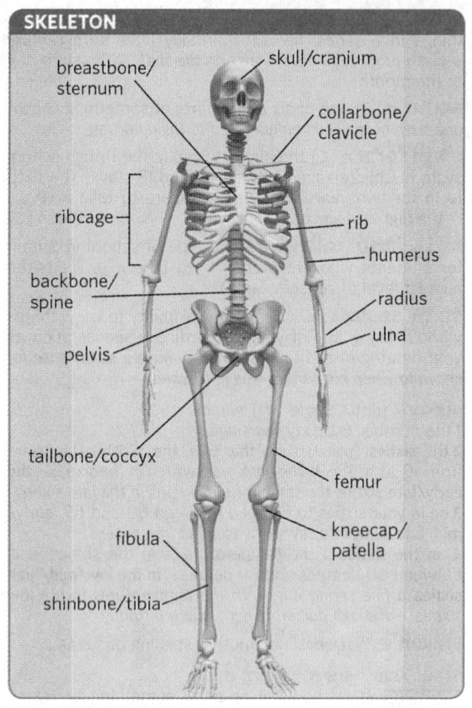

skep·ti·cal /ˈskeptɪkəl/ *adj* the American spelling of SCEPTICAL

skep·ti·ci·sm /ˈskeptɪsɪzəm/ *n* [C,U] the American spelling of SCEPTICISM

sketch¹ /sketʃ/ ●●○ *n* [C]
1 a simple, quickly made drawing that does not show much detail: **[+of]** *Cantor drew a* ***rough sketch*** *of his apartment on a napkin.*
2 a short humorous scene on a television programme, in a theatre etc, that is part of a larger show: *Her TV programme is made up of a series of comic sketches.*
3 a short written or spoken description: **[+of]** *a brief sketch of the main weaknesses of the British economy | a* ***thumbnail sketch*** (=very brief description) *of topics treated in depth elsewhere*

sketch² ●●○ *v*
1 [I,T] to draw a sketch of something THESAURUS ▸ DRAW
2 (*also* **sketch out**) [T] to describe something in a general way, giving the basic ideas: *Holford sketched a 10-year programme for rebuilding the city.*
sketch in ↔ sth *phr v* to add more information about something: *I'd like to sketch in a few details for you.*

sketch·pad /ˈsketʃpæd/ (*also* **sketch·book** /ˈsketʃbʊk/) *n* [C] a number of sheets of paper fastened together and used for drawing

sketch·y /ˈsketʃi/ *adj* not thorough or complete, and not having enough details to be useful SYN **vague**: ***Details*** *of the accident are still* ***sketchy****.*

skew /skjuː/ *v* [T] **1** if something skews the results of a test etc, it affects them, making them incorrect: *All the people we questioned lived in the same area, which had the effect of skewing the figures.* **2** to affect or influence someone's ideas, actions, or judgment, especially in a way that makes the ideas etc not correct or fair: *These assumptions about Communism skewed American foreign policy for decades.*

skewed /skjuːd/ *adj* **1** an opinion, piece of information, result etc that is skewed is incorrect, especially because it has been affected by a particular thing or because you do not know all the facts: *The media's coverage of the election has been skewed from the very beginning.* **2** something that is skewed is not straight and is higher on one side than the other SYN **crooked**: *The picture on the wall was slightly skewed.*

skew·er¹ /ˈskjuːə $ -ər/ *n* [C] a long metal or wooden stick that is put through pieces of meat to hold them together while they are cooked

skewer² *v* [T] **1** to make a hole through a piece of food, an object etc with a skewer or with some other pointed object **2** to criticize someone very strongly, often in a way that other people find humorous: *Du Bois skewered Washington's policies in his book, 'The Souls of Black Folks'.*

ˌskew-ˈwhiff *adj* [not before noun] *BrE spoken informal* not straight SYN **crooked**: *The top of the bookcase is skew-whiff.*

ski¹ /skiː/ ●●○ *n* (*plural* **skis**) [C]
1 one of a pair of long thin narrow pieces of wood or plastic that you fasten to your boots and use for moving on snow or on water: *ski slopes* | *a ski resort* (=where people can go skiing)
2 a long thin narrow piece of strong material, fastened under a small vehicle so that it can travel on snow

ski² ●●○ *v* (**skied**, **skiing**, **skis**) [I] to move on skis for sport or in order to travel on snow or water → **skiing**: *I'm learning to ski.* | *We skied down to the village of Argentière.*

ˈski boot *n* [C] a specially made boot that fastens onto a ski

skid¹ /skɪd/ *v* (**skidded**, **skidding**) [I] if a vehicle or a wheel on a vehicle skids, it suddenly slides sideways and you cannot control it: *The car skidded as she turned onto the highway.* | **[+on/into/across etc]** *The bus skidded off the road and into a ditch.* → see picture at SLIP¹

skid² *n* [C]
1 SLIDING MOVEMENT a sudden sliding movement of a vehicle that you cannot control: *Turn the car towards the skid if you lose control of it.* | *He slammed on the brakes and we* ***went into*** *a long* ***skid*** (=started to skid).
2 on the skids *informal* in a situation that is bad and getting worse: *He's been on the skids since losing his job.*
3 put the skids under sth *BrE informal* to make it likely or certain that something will fail: *The recession put the skids under his plans for starting a new business.*
4 SPORT [usually singular] *AmE* a period of time during which a person or team is not successful - used in news reports: *The Red Sox victory ended a six-game skid.*
5 AIRCRAFT a flat narrow part that is under some aircraft such as HELICOPTERS, and is used in addition to wheels for landing
6 USED TO LIFT/MOVE [usually plural] a piece of wood that is put under a heavy object to lift or move it

ˈskid mark *n* [C usually plural] **1** a long mark that is left on the ground when a vehicle skids: *There were skid marks on the road where the crash occurred.* **2** *informal* a dirty mark inside someone's underwear

Ski-Doo, **ski·doo** /skɪˈduː/ *n* [C] *trademark* a small motor vehicle for travelling fast over snow

skid row, **Skid Row** /ˌskɪd ˈrəʊ $ -ˈroʊ/ *n* **1 be on skid row** *informal* if someone is on skid row, they drink too much alcohol and have no job, nowhere to live etc **2** [U] used to talk about a part of a city with a lot of old buildings in bad condition, where poor people who drink too much alcohol spend their time

ski·er /ˈskiːə $ -ər/ *n* [C] someone who SKIS

skies /skaɪz/ the plural of SKY

skiff /skɪf/ *n* [C] a small light boat for one person

skif·fle /ˈskɪfəl/ *n* [U] *especially BrE* a type of popular music played in the 1950s and often using instruments made by the musicians themselves

ski·ing /ˈskiːɪŋ/ ●●● S3 *n* [U] the sport of moving down hills, across land in the snow, or on water wearing SKIS: *We're going to* ***go skiing*** *in Colorado this winter.* | **cross-country/downhill skiing** → WATER SKIING

ski·jor·ing /ˈskiːˌdʒɔːrɪŋ/ *n* [U] a sport in which a SKIER is pulled over snow or ice by one or more dogs —**skijor** *v* [I]

ˈski jump *n* [C] a long steep sloping PLATFORM which people go down on SKIS and jump off to see how far they can go through the air in sports competitions —**ski jumping** *n* [U]

skil·ful *BrE*, **skillful** *AmE* /ˈskɪlfəl/ ●●● W2 *adj*
1 good at doing something, especially something that needs special ability or training: *a skilful footballer* | **skilful at (doing) sth** *After a few years, he became very skilful at drawing.*
2 made or done very well, showing a lot of ability: *the skilful use of sound effects* | *sensitive and skillful leadership* —**skilfully** *adv*: *She had used make-up skilfully to mask the bruise.*

THESAURUS

skilful *BrE*, **skillful** *AmE* good at doing something, especially something that needs special ability or training: *a skilful player* | *the artist's skillful use of color*
good at sth able to do something well: *Maria is extremely good at her job.* | *He was very good at swimming.* | *I'm not very good at Maths.*
skilled having a lot of training and experience, and able to do a job well: *There is a demand for carpenters and other skilled craftsmen.* | *The country needs* ***highly skilled*** *foreign workers.* | *Our advisors are skilled at dealing with financial problems.*
talented having a natural ability to do something well: *a talented artist* | *She's an exceptionally talented student.*
gifted having a great natural ability, which few people have: *a gifted writer* | *a gifted player* | *a special school for gifted children*

VERY SKILFUL

accomplished very skilful because you have had a lot of experience of doing something - used especially about musicians, artists, performers etc: *a* ***highly accomplished*** *pianist* | *She is one of the most accomplished theatre performers.*
expert extremely skilful and having a lot of knowledge about doing something: *He was an expert skier.* | *Students learn to cook French food with the help of expert chefs.* | *Politicians are expert at deflecting criticism.*
virtuoso [only before noun] extremely skilful and impressive - used especially about musicians, performers, or performances: *a virtuoso violinist* | *The team gave a virtuoso performance in the final.*

ˈski lift *n* [C] a piece of equipment that carries SKIERS up to the top of a slope

skill /skɪl/ ●●● S2 W1 *n* [C,U] an ability to do something well, especially because you have learned and practised it → **talent**: *Reading and writing are two different skills.* | *Many jobs today require computer skills.* | **[+in/at]** *He was valued for his skill in raising money for the company.* | **with skill** *The whole team played with great skill and determination.*

COLLOCATIONS

VERBS

have a skill *He didn't have the right skills for the job.*
learn a skill (*also* **acquire a skill** *formal*) *People can acquire new skills while they are unemployed.*
develop a skill *We will give you the opportunity to develop your skills.*
use a skill *I am sure you can use your communication skills to get your message across.*
require/take skill (=to need skill) *It's a difficult task, which requires skill and experience.*

ADJECTIVES/NOUN + skill

great/considerable skill (=a lot of skill) *He played with great skill.*
good skills *He's got good management skills.*
basic skills *The basic skills can be acquired very quickly.*
practical skills *Students will have the opportunity to learn a lot of practical skills.*

S

technical skills | **management skills** | **computer/IT skills** | **reading/writing skills** | **communication skills** (=the ability to communicate well with people) | **social skills** (=the ability to get on well with people) | **people/interpersonal skills** (=the ability to deal with people) | **language skills** (=the ability to use a language)

THESAURUS

skill [C,U] an ability to do something well, especially because you have learned and practised it: *He plays the piano with great skill.* | *communication/language/computer etc skills*
talent [C,U] a natural ability to do something well which can be developed with practice: *She was a young artist with a lot of talent.* | *She showed a talent for acting from an early age.* | *He is* ***a man of many talents****.*
genius [U] very great ability, which only a few people have: *The opera shows Mozart's genius as a composer.* | *Picasso was a painter* ***of genius****.*
gift [C] a natural ability to do something very well, which you were born with: *You can see that he has a gift for the game.* | *Winterson has great gifts as a writer.*
flair [singular, U] skill for doing something, especially something that needs imagination and creativity: *The job does require some creative flair.* | *She has a flair for languages.*
expertise [U] specialized knowledge of a technical subject, which you get from experience of doing that type of work: *The technical expertise for building the dam is being provided by a US company.*
a/the knack /næk/ [singular] *informal* a special skill for doing a particular thing, especially a simple everyday thing: *Breadmaking is easy once you get the knack.* | *He has a knack for making people feel relaxed.*

S

skilled /skɪld/ ●●○ *adj*
1 someone who is skilled has the training and experience that is needed to do something well OPP **unskilled**: ***Skilled craftsmen****, such as carpenters, are in great demand.* | *The company is fortunate to have such* ***highly skilled*** *workers.* | **[+at/in]** *She's very skilled at dealing with the public.* | *The school offers a program for students who are skilled in metalwork.* THESAURUS ▸ SKILFUL
2 [usually before noun] skilled work needs people with special abilities or training to do it OPP **unskilled**: *Bricklaying is very skilled work.*

skil·let /ˈskɪlɪt/ *n* [C] a flat heavy cooking pan with a long handle SYN **frying pan**

skill·ful /ˈskɪlfəl/ *adj* the American spelling of SKILFUL

skim /skɪm/ *v* (**skimmed**, **skimming**) **1** [T] to remove something from the surface of a liquid, especially floating fat, solids, or oil: **skim sth off/from sth** *After simmering the meat, skim the fat from the surface.* **2** [I,T] to read something quickly to find the main facts or ideas in it SYN **scan**: *Julie skimmed the sports page.* | **[+through/over]** *Just skim through the second section to save time.* **3** [I,T] to move along quickly over a surface, never touching it or not touching it often: *seagulls skimming the waves* | **[+over/along/across]** *The ball skimmed across the grass and stopped against the wall.* **4 skim stones/pebbles etc** *BrE* to throw smooth flat stones into a lake, river etc in a way that makes them jump across the surface SYN **skip** *AmE* **5** [T] to secretly record the details of someone's CREDIT CARD electronically in order to use them illegally

skim sb/sth ↔ **off** *phr v* **1** to take the best people or the best part of something for yourself: *Professional sport skims off all the best players.* **2** to take money illegally or dishonestly: *For years his business partner had been skimming off the profits.*

ˌskimmed ˈmilk *BrE*, **ˈskim milk** *AmE n* [U] milk that has had all the fat and cream removed from it

skim·ming /ˈskɪmɪŋ/ *n* [U] the crime of using a CARD READER (=machine that checks the details on a credit card or debit card) to get private information about someone's CREDIT CARD in order to steal money from them

skimp /skɪmp/ *v* [I,T] to not spend enough money or time on something, or not use enough of something, so that what you do is unsuccessful or of bad quality: **[+on]** *It's vital not to skimp on staff training.*

skimp·y /ˈskɪmpi/ *adj* **1** a skimpy dress or skirt etc is very short and does not cover very much of a woman's body **2** not enough of something: *a skimpy meal*

skin[1] /skɪn/ ●●● S2 W2 *n*
1 BODY [C,U] the natural outer layer of a person's or animal's body: *She had thick black hair and smooth dark skin.* | *The skin on his hands was dry and rough.* → SKINCARE
2 FROM AN ANIMAL [C,U] the skin of an animal, sometimes including its fur, used to make leather, clothes etc: *a leopard skin*
3 FOOD [C,U] **a)** the natural outer cover of some fruits and vegetables SYN **peel**: *banana skins* **b)** the outer cover of a SAUSAGE
4 ON A LIQUID [C,U] a thin solid layer that forms on the top of a liquid, especially when it gets cold: *Cover the soup to stop a skin from forming.*
5 PART OF AN OBJECT [C] a layer that is part of a vehicle, building, object etc, especially on the outside: *The outer skin of the aircraft was not punctured.* | *The lampshade has a double skin so that it remains cool.*
6 COMPUTER [C,U] the way particular information appears on a computer screen, especially when this can be changed quickly and easily
7 have (a) thin/thick skin to be easily upset or not easily upset by criticism: *This is not a job for someone with thin skin.*
8 get under sb's skin *informal* if someone gets under your skin, they annoy you, especially by the way they behave: *What really gets under my skin is people who push straight to the front of the line.*
9 by the skin of your teeth *informal* if you do something by the skin of your teeth, you only just succeed in doing it, and very nearly failed to do it: *Two others made it by the skin of their teeth.*
10 make sb's skin crawl *informal* to make someone feel very uncomfortable or slightly afraid: *Her singing makes my skin crawl.*
11 be skin and bone *BrE*, **be skin and bones** *AmE informal* to be extremely thin in a way that is unattractive and unhealthy
12 it's no skin off sb's nose *spoken* used to say that someone does not care what another person thinks or does, because it does not affect them: *If she doesn't want me to help, it's no skin off my nose!*
13 sth is only skin deep used to say that something may seem to be important or effective, but it really is not because it only affects the way things appear: *Beauty is only skin deep.*
14 skins [plural] *BrE informal* papers for rolling a cigarette, especially one with MARIJUANA in it → **save sb's skin** at SAVE[1](11), → **jump out of your skin** at JUMP[1](4)

COLLOCATIONS

ADJECTIVES

fair/pale/white *I have fair skin that burns very easily.*
dark/brown/black *a girl with beautiful dark skin*
olive (=the colour typical of people from Greece, Italy etc)
tanned *His skin was slightly tanned.*
smooth/soft *Her skin was smooth and pale.*
good/healthy/clear (=smooth and without any red spots) *Vitamin E helps keep your skin healthy.*
bad/terrible (=with many spots or marks) *I had terrible skin when I was a teenager.*
flawless (=perfect, with no spots or marks) | **dry** | **oily** | **sensitive** (=becoming red or sore easily) | **itchy** (=making you want to scratch) | **rough** (=not smooth or soft) | **leathery** (=thick and dry) | **wrinkled** (=covered in lines because of age) | **scaly** (=hard and dry, like the skin on animals such as lizards)

VERBS

burn/damage your skin *Strong sunlight can damage your skin.*
break the skin (=make a hole in it) *Luckily the skin wasn't broken.*
protect your skin *It's important to use suntan lotion to protect your skin.*
irritate your skin (=make it red or sore) *Some types of make-up can irritate your skin.*
soothe your skin (=to stop it feeling painful or uncomfortable)
your skin glows/shines (=it looks healthy) *beauty products that will make your skin glow*
your skin peels (=the top layer comes off after you have had a sun tan) | **your skin sags** (=it hangs down in loose folds, because you are old)

skin + NOUN

skin colour (*also* **the colour of your skin**) *There is still discrimination on the basis of skin colour.*
skin tone (=how light or dark someone's skin is) *Do the colours of your clothes enhance your skin tone?*
a skin condition/complaint/disease *She suffers from a nasty skin condition.*
skin irritation | **a skin rash** | **skin cancer**

skin² *v* (**skinned**, **skinning**) [T] **1** to remove the skin from an animal, fruit, or vegetable → **peel**: *Add the tomatoes, skinned and sliced.* **2** to hurt yourself by rubbing off some skin SYN **graze**: *She fell and skinned her knee.* **3 skin sb alive** to punish someone very severely – used humorously: *Dad will skin you alive when he sees this place!* **4** *informal* to completely defeat someone SYN **hammer**: *The football team really skinned Watertown last year.* **5 there's more than one way to skin a cat** used to say that there are several ways of achieving something

skin up *phr v BrE informal* to make a cigarette with MARIJUANA in it

skin·care /ˈskɪnkeə $ -ker/ *n* [U] things that you do in order to improve the condition of your skin, especially the skin on your face: *expensive* ***skincare products***

ˈskin-ˌdiving, **skin diving** *n* [U] the sport of swimming under water with light breathing equipment but without a protective suit —**skin diver** *n* [C]

skin·flint /ˈskɪnˌflɪnt/ *n* [C] *informal* someone who hates spending money or giving it away – used to show disapproval SYN **miser**

skin·ful /ˈskɪnfʊl/ *n* **have a skinful** *BrE spoken* to drink a lot of alcohol and become drunk

ˈskin graft *n* [C] a medical operation in which healthy skin is removed from one part of your body and used on another part to replace burned or damaged skin

skin·head /ˈskɪnhed/ *n* [C] a young white person who has hair that is cut very short, especially one who behaves violently towards people of other races

skin·ny /ˈskɪni/ ●○○ *adj* (*comparative* **skinnier**, *superlative* **skinniest**)
1 very thin, especially in a way that is unattractive: *Some supermodels are far too skinny.* THESAURUS ▸ THIN
2 skinny trousers fit tightly all the way down the legs: *skinny jeans*
3 made with SKIMMED MILK (=milk with all the fat and cream removed from it): *a skinny latte*

ˈskinny-ˌdipping *n* [U] *informal* swimming with no clothes on: *As soon as it got dark, we all* ***went skinny-dipping***.

skint /skɪnt/ *adj* [not before noun] *BrE informal* having no money, especially for a short time SYN **broke**: *I'm skint at the moment.*

ˌskin-ˈtight *adj* skin-tight clothes fit tightly against your body OPP **baggy**: *skin-tight jeans*

skip¹ /skɪp/ ●●○ *v* (**skipped**, **skipping**)
1 NOT DO STH [T] *informal* to not do something that you usually do or that you should do SYN **miss**: *She skipped lunch in order to go shopping.* | *Williams skipped the game to be with his wife in the hospital.* | **skip school/class** *especially AmE: He skipped chemistry class three times last month.*
2 NOT DEAL WITH STH [I,T] to not read, mention, or deal with something that would normally come or happen next: *I decided to skip the first chapter.* | **[+to]** *Let's skip to the last item on the agenda.* | **[+over]** *I suggest we skip over the details and get to the point.*
3 CHANGE SUBJECTS [I always + adv/prep] to go from one subject to another in no fixed order: **[+about/around/from]** *It's difficult to have a conversation with her because she skips from one topic to another.*
4 MOVEMENT [I] to move forward with quick steps and jumps: **[+across/along etc]** *He turned and skipped away, singing happily to himself.* THESAURUS ▸ JUMP
5 JUMP OVER A ROPE [I] to jump over a rope as you swing it over your head and under your feet, as a game or for exercise SYN **jump rope** *AmE* → see picture at JUMP¹
6 skip town/skip the country *informal* to leave a place suddenly and secretly, especially to avoid being punished or paying debts: *Then they found that Zaffuto had already skipped town.*
7 skip it! *informal especially AmE* used to say angrily and rudely that you do not want to talk about something: *'Sorry, what were you saying?' 'Oh, skip it!'*
8 skip rocks/stones *AmE* to throw smooth flat stones into a lake, river etc in a way that makes them jump across the surface SYN **skim** *BrE*
9 BALL [I always + adv/prep] if a ball or something similar skips off a surface, it quickly moves away from that surface after hitting it – used especially in news reports: **[+off/along/across etc]** *The ball skipped off Bond's glove and bounced toward the fence.*
10 skip a year/grade to start a new school year in a class that is one year ahead of the class you would normally enter → **sb's heart skips a beat** at HEART¹

skip off *BrE*, **skip out** *AmE phr v* to leave suddenly and secretly, especially in order to avoid being punished or paying money: *He skipped off without paying.* | **[+on]** *AmE: Tenants who skip out on utility bills are the focus of a new law.* | *Joel skipped out on his wife when she was 8 months pregnant.*

skip² *n* [C] **1** a skipping movement **2** *BrE* a large container for bricks, wood, and similar heavy waste SYN **dumpster** *AmE*

ˈski pants *n* [plural] **1** thick trousers with long thin pieces of cloth that fasten over your shoulders, worn while SKIing: *a pair of ski pants* **2** tight trousers with a band of cloth that goes under your foot, worn by women

ˈski plane *n* [C] an aircraft that has long thin narrow parts on the bottom instead of wheels, for landing on snow

ˈski pole *n* [C] one of two pointed short poles that you hold to help you balance and push off the snow when SKIing

skip·per¹ /ˈskɪpə $ -ər/ *n* [C] *informal* **1** the person in charge of a ship SYN **captain** **2** the leader of a sports team SYN **captain**

skipper² *v* [T] *informal* to be in charge of a ship, sports team etc – used especially in news reports SYN **captain**

ˈskipping ˌrope *n* [C] *BrE* a long piece of rope with handles that children use for jumping over SYN **jump rope** *AmE*

skir·mish /ˈskɜːmɪʃ $ ˈskɜːr-/ *n* [C] **1** a fight between small groups of soldiers, ships etc, especially one that happens away from the main part of a battle – used in news reports: **[+with/between/over]** *The young soldier was killed in a skirmish with government troops.* THESAURUS ▸ WAR **2** a short argument, especially between political or sports opponents: **[+with/between/over]** *Bates was sent off after a skirmish with the referee.* | *a budget skirmish between the president and Congress* —**skirmish** *v* [I]: *They skirmished briefly with soldiers from Fort Benton.*

skirt¹ /skɜːt $ skɜːrt/ ●●● S3 *n* [C]
1 a piece of outer clothing worn by women and girls, which hangs down from the waist like the bottom part of

S

a dress: *She wore a white blouse and a plain black skirt.* | **leather/pleated/cotton etc skirt** *a green velvet skirt* | **short/long skirt** *a short skirt and high heels*
2 (*also* **skirts** [plural]) *old-fashioned* the part of a dress or coat that hangs down from the waist
3 the skirts of a forest/hill/village etc *BrE* the outside edge of a forest etc SYN **outskirts**
4 a bit of skirt *BrE informal not polite* an offensive expression meaning an attractive woman

skirt² (*also* **skirt around/round**) *v* [T] **1** to go around the outside edge of a place or area: *The old footpath skirts around the village.* **2** to avoid talking about an important subject, especially because it is difficult or embarrassing - used to show disapproval: *a disappointing speech that **skirted around** all the main **issues***

'skirt-ˌchasing *adj* [only before noun] *informal* trying to have sexual relationships with many different women - used to show disapproval: *She finally left her skirt-chasing husband.* —**skirt-chasing** *n* [U] —**skirt-chaser** *n* [C]

'skirting board (*also* **skirt·ing** /'skɜːtɪŋ $ 'skɜːr-/) *n* [C,U] *BrE* a long narrow piece of wood that is fastened along the bottom of the walls in a room SYN **baseboard** *AmE*

'ski run *n* [C] a track that has been marked on a slope so that people can SKI on it

'ski slope *n* [C] a snow-covered part of a mountain which has been prepared for people to SKI down

skit /skɪt/ *n* [C] a short humorous performance or piece of writing SYN **sketch**

skit·ter /'skɪtə $ -ər/ *v* [I always + adv/prep] to move very quickly and lightly, like a small animal SYN **scurry**: **[+across/down/along etc]** *Something skittered across the alley.*

S

skit·tish /'skɪtɪʃ/ *adj* **1** an animal, especially a horse, that is skittish gets excited or frightened very easily **2** a person who is skittish is not very serious, and their feelings, behaviour, and opinions keep changing **3** if people who buy SHARES are skittish, they are nervous and worried about them dropping in value, and might sell the shares that they own because of this SYN **jittery**: *Some skittish Wall Street investors are staying away from the market.* —**skittishly** *adv*

skit·tle /'skɪtl/ *n* **1 skittles** [U] a British game in which a player tries to knock down objects shaped like bottles by rolling a ball at them **2** [C] one of the objects you roll the ball at in the game of skittles

skive /skaɪv/ (*also* **skive off**) *v* [I] *BrE informal* to avoid work or school by staying away or leaving without permission → **play truant** —**skiver** *n* [C]

skiv·vy¹ /'skɪvi/ *n* (*plural* **skivvies**) **1** [C] *BrE* a servant who does only the dirty unpleasant jobs in a house: *You iron your shirt - I'm not your skivvy.* **2 skivvies** [plural] *informal* a man's underwear

skivvy² *v* (**skivvied, skivvying, skivvies**) [I] *BrE* to do all the dirty unpleasant jobs in a house, as if you were a servant

skul·dug·ge·ry, skullduggery /ˌskʌl'dʌgəri/ *n* [U] *old-fashioned* secretly dishonest or illegal activity - also used humorously

skulk /skʌlk/ *v* [I always + adv/prep] to hide or move about secretly, trying not to be noticed, especially when you are intending to do something bad SYN **lurk**: **[+about/around/in etc]** *He was still skulking around outside when they left the building.*

skull /skʌl/ ●●○ *n* [C]
1 the bones of a person's or animal's head → see picture at SKELETON
2 sb can't get it into their (thick) skull *spoken* someone is unable to understand something very simple: *He can't seem to get it into his skull that I'm just not interested in him.*

ˌskull and 'crossbones *n* [singular] **1** a picture of a human skull with two bones crossed below it, used in past times on the flags of PIRATE ships **2** a picture of a human skull with two bones crossed below it, used on containers to show that what is inside is poison or very dangerous

'skull cap *n* [C] a small round close-fitting hat for the top of the head, worn sometimes by Christian priests or Jewish men

skull·dug·ge·ry /ˌskʌl'dʌgəri/ *n* [U] *old-fashioned* another spelling of SKULDUGGERY

skunk /skʌŋk/ *n* **1** [C] a small black and white North American animal that produces a strong unpleasant smell if it is attacked or afraid **2** [U] a very strong type of MARIJUANA

skunk·works /'skʌŋkwɜːks $ -wɜːrks/ *n* [C] a place where a large company gives a small group of workers the job of trying to develop new products within a shorter period of time than usual

sky /skaɪ/ ●●● S2 W2 *n* (*plural* **skies**)
1 [singular, U] the space above the Earth where clouds and the Sun and stars appear: *The sky grew dark, and a cold rain began to fall.* | *A shooting star sped across the night sky.* | **in the sky** *There wasn't a cloud in the sky.*
2 skies [plural] a word meaning 'sky', used especially when describing the weather or what the sky looks like in a place: *a land of blue skies and warm sunshine* | *The skies were overcast, and it was chilly and damp.*
3 the sky's the limit *spoken* used to say that there is no limit to what someone can achieve, spend, win etc: *Francis believes the sky's the limit for the young goalkeeper.* → **pie in the sky** at PIE(4), → **praise sb/sth to the skies** at PRAISE¹(1)

COLLOCATIONS - MEANINGS 1 & 2

ADJECTIVES/NOUN + sky
blue *The sky was blue and the sun was shining.*
grey *BrE*, **gray** *AmE*: *Rain was starting to fall from the grey sky.*
dark/black *Fireworks burst up into the dark sky.*
cloudy/dull/overcast (=with clouds) *Cloudy skies were forecast.*
bright/clear/cloudless (=without clouds) *The sun rose higher in the cloudless sky.*
azure *literary* (=bright blue) | **a starry sky** (=with a lot of stars) | **the darkening sky** (=becoming darker) | **the night/evening/morning sky** | **the summer/winter sky** | **the open sky** (=a large area of sky)

VERBS
the sky darkens *The sky darkened and thunder rolled in from the west.*
the sky clouds over (=clouds appear) *The sky was beginning to cloud over.*
the sky clears (=the clouds disappear)

ˌsky-'blue *adj* bright blue, like the colour of the sky when there are no clouds —**sky blue** *n* [U]

sky·cap /'skaɪkæp/ *n* [C] *AmE* someone whose job is to carry passengers' bags at an airport

sky·div·ing /'skaɪˌdaɪvɪŋ/ *n* [U] the sport of jumping from a plane and falling through the sky before opening a PARACHUTE —**skydive** *v* [I] —**skydiver** *n* [C]

ˌsky-'high *adj, adv* **1** extremely high: *sky-high prices* | *Her confidence is sky-high.* **2 blow sth sky-high** to destroy something completely with an explosion

sky·lark /'skaɪlɑːk $ -lɑːrk/ *n* [C] a small bird that sings while flying high in the sky SYN **lark**

sky·light /'skaɪlaɪt/ *n* [C] a window in the roof of a building → see picture at WINDOW

sky·line /'skaɪlaɪn/ *n* [C] the shape made by hills or buildings against the sky: *the famous New York skyline*

'sky marshal *n* [C] a specially trained person who carries a gun and whose job is to travel on a passenger plane and protect it from attacks by TERRORISTS SYN **air marshal**

Skype /skaɪp/ *n* [U] *trademark* software that can be used to make telephone calls over the Internet **THESAURUS** PHONE —**Skype** *v* [T]: *I'll Skype you later.*

sky·rock·et /'skaɪˌrɒkɪt $ -ˌrɑː-/ *v* [I] *informal* if a price or an amount skyrockets, it greatly increases very quickly: *The trade deficit has skyrocketed.* | *skyrocketing inflation*

sky·scrap·er /ˈskaɪˌskreɪpə $ -ər/ *n* [C] a very tall modern city building

sky·wards /ˈskaɪwədz $ -wərdz/ (*also* **sky·ward** /-wəd $ wərd/) *adv literary* up into the sky or towards the sky: *The bird soared skywards.* —**skyward** *adj*

slab /slæb/ ●○○ *n* [C]
1 a thick flat piece of a hard material such as stone: *a concrete slab* | *paving slabs* | **[+of]** *They used a slab of concrete as a lid.* → see picture at PIECE[1] THESAURUS PIECE
2 slab of cake/chocolate/meat etc a large flat piece of cake etc
3 on the slab *informal* lying dead in a hospital or MORTUARY

slack[1] /slæk/ *adj* **1** hanging loosely, or not pulled tight OPP **taut**: *Keep the rope slack until I tell you to pull it.* **2** with less business activity than usual SYN **slow**: *Business remained slack throughout the day.* **3** not taking enough care or making enough effort to do things correctly – used to show disapproval SYN **careless**: *Slack defending by Real Madrid allowed Manchester United to score.* —**slackly** *adv* —**slackness** *n* [U]

slack[2] *n* **1 take up/pick up the slack a)** to make a system or organization as EFFICIENT as possible by making sure that money, space, or people are fully used: *Without another contract to help pick up the slack, employees may face job losses.* **b)** to do something that needs to be done because someone else is no longer doing it **c)** to make a rope tighter **2** [U] part of a rope that is not stretched tight **3** [U] money, space, people, or time that an organization or person has available, but is not using fully: *There is still some slack in the budget.* **4 cut/give sb some slack** *spoken* to allow someone to do something without criticizing them or making it more difficult: *Hey, cut me some slack, man. I'm only a few bucks short.* **5 slacks** [plural] trousers: *a* ***pair of slacks*** | *dress slacks* (=for more formal occasions) **6** [U] *BrE* very small pieces of coal

slack[3] (*also* **slack off**) *v* [I] to make less effort than usual, or to be lazy in your work: *He was accused of slacking and taking too many holidays.*

slack·en /ˈslækən/ *v* [I,T] *written* **1** (*also* **slacken off**) to gradually become slower, weaker, less active etc, or to make something do this: *The heavy rain showed no signs of slackening off.* | **slacken your pace/speed** (=go or walk more slowly) *Guy slackened his pace as he approached the gate.* **2** to make something looser, or to become looser OPP **tighten**: *He did not let her go, but his grip on her slackened.*

slack·er /ˈslækə $ -ər/ *n* [C] *informal* someone who is lazy and does not do all the work they should – used to show disapproval

ˌ**slack-jawed** *adj* having your mouth slightly open, especially because you are surprised or stupid SYN **open-mouthed**: *They looked at him, slack-jawed with disbelief.*

slag[1] /slæg/ *n* **1** [C] *BrE taboo informal* a very offensive word for a woman who has sex with a lot of different people. Do not use this word. **2** [U] a waste material similar to glass, which remains after metal has been obtained from rock

slag[2] *v* (**slagged**, **slagging**)
slag sb ↔ **off** *phr v BrE informal* to criticize someone in an unpleasant way, especially when this is unfair: *He's always slagging her off behind her back.*

ˈ**slag heap** *n* [C] *especially BrE* a pile of waste material at a mine or factory

slain /sleɪn/ *v* the past participle of SLAY

slake /sleɪk/ *v* [T] *literary* **1 slake your thirst** to drink so that you are not thirsty anymore **2 slake a desire/craving etc** to satisfy a desire etc

sla·lom /ˈslɑːləm/ *n* [C,U] a race for people on SKIs or in CANOEs down a curving course marked by flags

slam[1] /slæm/ ●●○ *v* (**slammed**, **slamming**)
1 DOOR ETC [I,T] if a door, gate etc slams, or if someone slams it, it shuts with a loud noise SYN **bang**: *We heard a car door slam.* | *He* ***slammed*** *the door* ***shut***. THESAURUS CLOSE
2 PUT STH SOMEWHERE [T always + adv/prep] to put something on or against a surface with a fast violent movement: **slam sth down/against/onto** *Henry slammed the phone down angrily.*
3 HIT WITH FORCE [I always + adv/prep] to hit or attack someone or something with a lot of force: **[+into/against etc]** *All 155 passengers died instantly when the plane slammed into the mountain.*
4 CRITICIZE [T] to criticize someone or something strongly – used especially in newspapers SYN **slate**: *Local media slammed plans to build a prison in the area.* | **slam sb for sth** *The council was slammed for its unfair selection procedure.*
5 slam on the brakes to make a car stop very suddenly by pressing the BRAKEs very hard
6 slam the door in sb's face a) to close a door hard when someone is trying to come in **b)** to rudely refuse to meet someone or talk to them

slam[2] *n* [C usually singular] the noise or action of a door, window etc slamming

ˈ**slam dunk** *n* [C] **1** when a BASKETBALL player jumps high above the net and throws the ball down through it **2** *AmE informal* a very impressive act: *The biggest legal slam dunk came when a judge sentenced four men to 505 years in prison.*

ˈ**slam-dunk** *v* [I,T] to put a ball through the net in BASKETBALL, by jumping very high and throwing the ball down through the net

slam·mer /ˈslæmə $ -ər/ *n* **the slammer** *informal* prison: **in the slammer** *He had to spend his twentieth birthday in the slammer.*

slan·der[1] /ˈslɑːndə $ ˈslændər/ *n* **1** [C,U] a false spoken statement about someone, intended to damage the good opinion that people have of that person → **libel 2** [U] the crime of making false spoken statements about someone → **libel**: *He is being* ***sued for slander***.

slander[2] *v* [T] to say false things about someone in order to damage other people's good opinion of them → **libel**

slan·der·ous /ˈslɑːndərəs $ ˈslæn-/ *adj* a slanderous statement about someone is not true, and is intended to damage other people's good opinion of them → **libellous**: *slanderous remarks*

slang /slæŋ/ *n* [U] very informal, sometimes offensive language that is used especially by people who belong to a particular group, such as young people or criminals: *schoolboy slang* | **slang word/expression/term** THESAURUS WORD —**slangy** *adj*

ˈ**slanging** ˌ**match** *n* [C] *BrE informal* an angry argument in which people insult each other

slant[1] /slɑːnt $ slænt/ *v* **1** [I,T] to slope or make something slope in a particular direction: *The sun's rays slanted through the trees.* | *slanting eyes* **2** [T] to provide information in a way that unfairly supports one opinion, gives an advantage to one group etc: *The researchers were accused of slanting their findings in favour of their own beliefs.*

slant[2] *n* [singular] **1** a way of writing about or thinking about a subject that is based on a particular opinion or set of ideas: *The article* ***had*** *an anti-union* ***slant***. | **new/different/fresh etc slant** *Each article has a slightly different slant on the situation.* | *Recent events have* ***put*** *a new* ***slant on*** *the president's earlier comments.* **2** a sloping position or angle SYN **slope**: **at/on a slant** *The house seems to be built on a steep slant.*

slant·ed /ˈslɑːntɪd $ ˈslæn-/ *adj* **1** providing facts or information in a way that unfairly supports only one side of an argument or one opinion – used to show disapproval SYN **biased**: **[+towards]** *The report was heavily slanted towards the city council's version of events.* **2** sloping: *her slightly slanted eyes*

slap¹ /slæp/ ●●○ *v* (**slapped**, **slapping**)
1 [T] to hit someone with the flat part of your hand → **punch**: *Sarah slapped Aaron across the face.* THESAURUS HIT
2 [T always + adv/prep] to put something down on a surface with force, especially when you are angry: *Giles slapped his cards down on the table.*
3 slap sb on the back to hit someone on the back in a friendly way, often as a way of praising them
4 [I always + adv/prep] to hit a surface with a lot of force, making a loud sharp sound: **[+against]** *Small waves slapped against the side of the boat.*
slap sb **down** *phr v BrE* to rudely tell someone that their suggestions, questions, ideas etc are stupid
slap sth ↔ **on** *phr v informal*
1 to put or spread something quickly or carelessly onto a surface: *She ran upstairs and slapped on some make-up.* | **slap sth on sth** *We could slap some paint on it.*
2 to suddenly announce a new charge, tax etc or say that something is not allowed – used especially when you think this is unfair: *Many tour operators slap on supplements for single people.* | **slap sth on sth** *In 1977, the president slapped a ban on the commercial reprocessing of nuclear fuel.*

slap² *n* **1** [C] a quick hit with the flat part of your hand → **punch**: *Julia **gave** Roy a **slap** on the cheek.* **2 a slap in the face** an action that seems to be deliberately intended to offend or upset someone, especially someone who has tried very hard to do something **3 a slap on the wrist** a punishment that you think is not severe enough **4 a slap on the back** an action of hitting someone on the back in a friendly way, especially as a way of praising them **5** [U] *informal* MAKE-UP

ˌslap ˈbang (*also* **slap**) *adv informal* **1** if you run, drive etc slap bang into something, you hit it with a lot of force: **[+into]** *I ran slap bang into a lamp-post.* **2** exactly in a particular place or at a particular time: **[+next to]** *Anne's house is slap bang next to the station.*

slap·dash /ˈslæpdæʃ/ *adj* careless and done too quickly OPP **painstaking**: *a very slapdash piece of work*

slap·hap·py /ˈslæpˌhæpi/ *adj* careless, silly, and likely to make mistakes

slap·head /ˈslæphed/ *n* [C] *BrE informal not polite* someone who is BALD (=has little or no hair on their head)

slap·per /ˈslæpə $ -ər/ *n* [C] *BrE informal* an offensive word for a woman who has sex with lots of people

slap·stick /ˈslæpˌstɪk/ *n* [U] humorous acting in which the performers fall over, throw things at each other etc: *a slapstick comedy*

ˈslap-up *adj* **slap-up meal/dinner etc** *BrE informal* a very large enjoyable meal

slash¹ /slæʃ/ ●●○ *v*
1 [I,T always + adv/prep] to cut or try to cut something violently with a knife, sword etc: *Someone had slashed the tires.* | **[+at/through]** *The leopard's claws slashed through the soft flesh.* THESAURUS CUT
2 [T] to greatly reduce an amount, price etc – used especially in newspapers and advertising SYN **cut**: *The workforce has been slashed by 50%.* THESAURUS REDUCE
3 slash your wrists to cut the VEINS in your wrists with the intention of killing yourself

slash² ●●○ *n* [C]
1 a quick movement that you make with a knife, sword etc in order to cut someone or something
2 (*also* **slash mark**) a line (/) used in writing to separate words, numbers, or letters
3 a long narrow cut in something → **gash**: *Cut several slashes across the top of the loaf before baking.*
4 have/take a slash *BrE spoken not polite* to URINATE

slash·er /ˈslæʃə $ -ər/ *n* **slasher film/movie etc** *informal* a very violent film

slat /slæt/ *n* [C] a thin flat piece of wood, plastic etc, used especially in furniture → see picture at BLIND³ —**slatted** *adj*

slate¹ /sleɪt/ *n*
1 ROCK [U] a dark grey rock that can easily be split into flat thin pieces
2 ON A ROOF [C] *especially BrE* a small piece of slate or similar material that is used for covering roofs SYN **tile**: *There were several slates missing from the roof.*
3 slate blue/grey a dark blue or grey colour
4 POLITICS [C] a list of people that voters can choose in an election, or who are being considered for an important job
5 FOR WRITING ON [C] a small black board or a flat piece of slate in a wooden frame, used for writing on in the past
6 put sth on the slate *BrE old-fashioned* to arrange to pay for something later, especially food or drink → **a clean slate** at CLEAN¹(9)

slate² *v* [T] **1** *BrE informal* to criticize a book, film etc severely, especially in a newspaper SYN **slam**: *Doherty's most recent novel has been slated by the critics.* **2 be slated to do sth/be slated for sth** *especially AmE* if something is slated to happen, it is planned to happen in the future, especially at a particular time: *He is slated to appear at the Cambridge Jazz Festival next year.* | *Every house on this block is slated for demolition.* GRAMMAR **Slate** is usually passive.

slath·er /ˈslæðə $ -ər/ *v* [T always + adv/prep] *AmE* to cover something with a thick layer of a soft substance SYN **smother**: **slather sth in/with/on sth** *a slice of home-made bread, slathered with jam*

slat·tern /ˈslætən $ -ərn/ *n* [C] *old-fashioned* a dirty untidy woman – used to show disapproval —**slatternly** *adj*

slaugh·ter¹ /ˈslɔːtə $ ˈslɒːtər/ ●○○ *v* [T]
1 to kill an animal, especially for its meat
2 to kill a lot of people in a cruel or violent way SYN **butcher**: *Hundreds of innocent civilians had been slaughtered by government troops.* THESAURUS KILL
3 *informal* to defeat an opponent in a sport or game by a large number of points SYN **hammer**: *We got slaughtered, 110-54.*

slaughter² ●○○ *n* [U]
1 when people kill animals, especially for their meat: *the export of live animals for slaughter*
2 when large numbers of people are killed in a cruel or violent way: *the slaughter of defenceless women and children*

slaugh·tered /ˈslɔːtəd $ ˈslɒːtərd/ *adj* [not before noun] *BrE informal* very drunk SYN **plastered**: *We all **got** completely **slaughtered** last night.*

slaugh·ter·house /ˈslɔːtəhaʊs $ ˈslɒːtər-/ *n* [C] a building where animals such as cows or pigs are killed for their meat SYN **abattoir**

Slav /slɑːv $ slɑːv, slæv/ *n* [C] someone who belongs to any of the races of Eastern and Central Europe who speak Slavic languages such as Russian, Bulgarian, Polish etc

slave¹ /sleɪv/ ●●○ *n* [C]
1 someone who is owned by another person and works for them for no money: **the slave trade** (=the buying and selling of slaves, especially Africans who were taken to America)
2 be a slave to/of sth to be so strongly influenced by something that you cannot make your own decisions – used to show disapproval: *a **slave to fashion***

slave² *v* [I always + adv/prep] to work very hard with little time to rest: **slave away (at sth)** *I've been slaving away at this report.* | **[+over]** *He's been slaving over his history essay.* | **slave (away) over a hot stove** (=cook – used humorously)

ˈslave ˌdriver *n* [C] someone who makes people work very hard – used in a disapproving or humorous way

ˌslave ˈlabour *BrE*, **slave labor** *AmE n* [U] **1** work done by slaves, or the people who do this work **2** *informal* work for which you are paid an unfairly small amount of money

slav·er¹ /ˈslævə $ -ər/ *v* [I] *literary* to let SALIVA (=liquid produced inside your mouth) come out of your mouth, especially because you are hungry SYN **drool**

slav·er² /ˈsleɪvə $ -ər/ *n* [C] *old use* **1** someone who sells slaves **2** a ship for moving slaves from one place to another

slav·e·ry /ˈsleɪvəri/ ●○○ *n* [U]
1 the system of having slaves: *attempts to* ***abolish slavery*** (=officially end it)
2 the state of being a slave: **sell sb into slavery** (=sell someone as a slave)

Slav·ic /ˈslɑːvɪk $ ˈslɑː-, ˈslæ-/ (*also* **Slavonic**) *adj* relating to the Slavs or their languages

slav·ish /ˈsleɪvɪʃ/ *adj* obeying, supporting, or copying someone completely – used to show disapproval: *a* ***slavish adherence*** *to the rules* —**slavishly** *adv*: *not a rule to be* ***slavishly followed*** *in every instance* —**slavishness** *n* [U]

Sla·von·ic /sləˈvɒnɪk $ -ˈvɑː-/ *adj* SLAVIC

slaw /slɔː $ slɒː/ *n* [U] *AmE* COLESLAW

slay /sleɪ/ *v* (*past tense* **slew** /sluː/, *past participle* **slain** /sleɪn/) [T] **1** *literary* to kill someone – used especially in newspapers THESAURUS▸ KILL **2** *AmE spoken informal* to amuse someone a lot —**slayer** *n* [C]

slay·ing /ˈsleɪ-ɪŋ/ *n* [C] an act of killing someone – used especially in newspapers: *gang-related slayings*

sleaze /sliːz/ *n* **1** [U] immoral behaviour, especially involving sex or lies: *Many people are tired of all the sleaze on TV.* | *sleaze and corruption in politics* **2** (*also* **sleazebag**, **sleazebucket**) [C] *AmE informal* someone who behaves in an immoral or dishonest way

slea·zy /ˈsliːzi/ *adj* (*comparative* **sleazier**, *superlative* **sleaziest**) **1** a sleazy place is dirty, cheap, or in bad condition: *a sleazy bar* **2** relating to sex or dishonest behaviour – used to show disapproval: *a sleazy lawyer* —**sleaziness** *n* [U]

sleb /sleb/ *n* [C] *BrE informal* a CELEBRITY – used especially in magazines SYN **celeb**: *We've got gossip on all the top slebs.*

sledge¹ /sledʒ/ *BrE*, **sled** /sled/ *AmE n* [C] a small vehicle used for sliding over snow, often used by children or in some sports → **sleigh**

sledge² *BrE*, **sled** *AmE v* [I] to travel on a sledge

sledge·ham·mer /ˈsledʒˌhæmə $ -ər/ *n* [C] a large heavy hammer

sleek¹ /sliːk/ *adj* **1** a vehicle or other object that is sleek has a smooth attractive shape: *the* ***sleek lines*** *of the new Mercedes* **2** sleek hair or fur is straight, shiny, and healthy-looking **3** someone who is sleek looks rich and is well dressed —**sleekly** *adv* —**sleekness** *n* [U]

sleek² *v* [T always + adv/prep] to make hair or fur smooth and shiny by putting water or oil on it: **sleek sth back/down etc** *His hair was sleeked back with oil.*

sleep¹ /sliːp/ ●●● S1 W2 *v* (*past tense and past participle* **slept** /slept/) [I]
1 to rest your mind and body, usually at night when you are lying in bed with your eyes closed → **asleep**: *I usually sleep on my back.* | *Did you sleep well?* | *He's lucky because at least he has somewhere to sleep.*
2 sleep rough *BrE* to sleep outdoors in uncomfortable conditions, especially because you have no money
3 sleep on it *spoken* to not make a decision about something important until the next day
4 sleep tight *spoken* said especially to children before they go to bed to say that you hope they sleep well: *Good night, Jenny. Sleep tight!*
5 sb can sleep easy used to say that someone no longer has to worry about something: *Unlike some other Internet sites, when you buy from us, you can sleep easy.*
6 sleep two/four/six etc to have enough beds for a particular number of people: *The villa sleeps four.*
7 let sleeping dogs lie to deliberately avoid mentioning a subject, so that you do not cause any trouble or argument
8 *literary* if a village, house etc sleeps, it is very quiet during the night

COLLOCATIONS

ADVERBS

sleep well *I haven't been sleeping well lately.*
sleep badly *Eleanor slept badly that night.*
sleep soundly/deeply (=in a way that means you are not likely to wake) *Within seconds, Maggie was sleeping soundly.*
sleep peacefully *Celia slept peacefully beside him.*
sleep fitfully *literary* (=sleep badly, waking up after short periods, especially because you are worried) |
sleep late (=not wake up until late in the morning)

THESAURUS

sleep to rest your mind and body with your eyes closed. Sleep is usually used when talking about how long, how deeply, or where someone sleeps. When saying that someone is not awake, you use **be asleep**: *Most people sleep for about eight hours.* | *He slept downstairs.* | *Did you sleep well?*
be asleep to be sleeping: *The baby's asleep – don't wake her.* | *He was* ***fast asleep*** (=completely asleep) *by the time I got home.*
oversleep to sleep for longer than you intended so that you wake up late in the morning: *I overslept and was late for work.*
take a nap (*also* **have a nap** *especially BrE*) (*also* **have forty winks** *informal*) to sleep for a short time during the day: *I think I'll have a nap.* | *She had been awake all night and was looking forward to taking a nap.*
have/take a snooze *informal* to sleep for a short time, especially in a chair, not in a bed: *I think I'll have a quick snooze.*
doze to sleep lightly, for example in a chair, and be easily woken: *I wasn't really asleep – I was just dozing.* | *I must have* ***dozed off*** (=started sleeping) *halfway through the film.*

sleep around *phr v informal* to have sex with a lot of different people without having a serious relationship with any of them – used to show disapproval

sleep in *phr v informal* to let yourself sleep later than usual in the morning: *We usually sleep in on Sunday mornings.*

sleep sth ↔ **off** *phr v informal* to sleep until you do not feel ill anymore, especially after drinking too much alcohol: *He went to his room to* ***sleep it off.***

sleep over *phr v* to sleep at someone's house for a night – used especially by children

sleep through *phr v*
1 sleep through sth to sleep while something is happening and not be woken by it: *How did you manage to sleep through that thunderstorm?*
2 sleep through (sth) to sleep continuously for a long time: *I slept right through till lunchtime.* | *The baby slept peacefully through the night.*

sleep together *phr v* if people sleep together, they have sex with each other

sleep with sb *phr v* to have sex with someone, especially someone you are not married to: *Everybody in the office knows he's been sleeping with Kathy.*

sleep² ●●● S2 W3 *n*
1 BEING ASLEEP [U] the natural state of resting your mind and body, usually at night → **beauty sleep**: *I didn't get much sleep last night.* | *Her eyes were red through lack of sleep.* | **in your sleep** (=while sleeping) *Ed often talks in his sleep.* | *She died peacefully in her sleep.*
2 PERIOD OF SLEEPING [singular] a period when you are sleeping: *I had a little sleep in the afternoon.* | *She was woken from a deep sleep by a ring at the door.*
3 go to sleep a) to start sleeping: *I went to sleep at 9 o'clock and woke up at 6.* **b)** *informal* if a part of your body goes to sleep, you cannot feel it for a short time because it has not been getting enough blood
4 lose sleep over sth to worry about something: *It's a practice game – I wouldn't lose any sleep over it.*
5 put sb/sth to sleep a) to give drugs to a sick animal so that it dies without too much pain – used to avoid saying the word 'kill' **b)** *informal* to make someone unconscious before a medical operation by giving them drugs
6 sb can do sth in their sleep *informal* used to say that someone is able to do something very easily, especially

S

because they have done it many times before: *She knew the music so well she could play it in her sleep.*
7 send sb to sleep a) to make someone go to sleep: *The combination of warmth and music sent him to sleep.* **b)** if something sends someone to sleep, it is extremely boring
8 IN YOUR EYES [U] *informal* a substance that forms in the corners of your eyes while you are sleeping: *She rubbed the sleep from her eyes.*
9 3/5/8 etc sleeps until/till sth *informal* used to say how many nights there are until something: *Only five more sleeps till Christmas!*

COLLOCATIONS – MEANINGS 1 & 2

VERBS

go to sleep (=start sleeping) *He turned over and went to sleep.*
drift/drop off to sleep (=start sleeping, especially without meaning to) *She'd drifted off to sleep on the sofa.*
get to sleep (=succeed in starting to sleep) *Last night I couldn't get to sleep.*
go back/get back to sleep (=sleep again after waking up) *He shut his eyes and went back to sleep.*
send sb to sleep (=make someone start sleeping) *She hoped the music would send her to sleep.*
get some sleep (=sleep for a while) *You'd better get some sleep.*
have a sleep *BrE* (=sleep for a short while) *Are you going to have a sleep after lunch today?*
catch up on some sleep (=sleep after not having enough sleep) | **sing/rock/lull sb to sleep** (=make someone sleep by singing etc)

ADJECTIVES

a long sleep *He needed a decent meal and a long sleep.*
a little/short sleep *I always have a little sleep in the afternoon.*
a deep/sound/heavy sleep (=a sleep from which you cannot easily be woken) *The noise woke him from a deep sleep.*
a light sleep (=a sleep from which you can easily be woken) *I fell into a light sleep.*
an exhausted sleep (=because you were very tired) | **a fitful/restless/uneasy sleep** (=in which you keep moving or waking)

PHRASES

a good night's sleep (=when you sleep well) *I woke up refreshed after a good night's sleep.*
five/eight etc hours' sleep *After eight hours' sleep, I woke up in pitch blackness.*
cry yourself to sleep (=cry until you fall asleep)

COMMON ERRORS

⚠ Don't say 'go sleep'. Say **go to sleep**.

sleep·er /ˈsliːpə $ -ər/ *n* [C] **1** someone who sleeps in a particular way: **light sleeper** (=someone who wakes easily) | **heavy sleeper** (=someone who does not wake easily) **2** someone who is asleep **3** *BrE* a heavy piece of wood or CONCRETE that supports a railway track SYN **tie** *AmE* **4 a)** a night train with carriages that have beds for passengers to sleep in **b)** a SLEEPING CAR **c)** *AmE* a bed on a train for a passenger to sleep in **5** *especially AmE* a film, book etc which is successful, even though people did not expect it to be **6** *AmE* a piece of clothing for a baby that covers its whole body including its feet **7** a SPY who is sent to a particular place and who lives an ordinary life there until a later time, when they begin their spying activities

ˈsleeping bag *n* [C] a large warm bag that you sleep in, especially when camping

ˌSleeping ˈBeauty the main character in a FAIRY TALE called *Sleeping Beauty*, who is a princess who lives in a castle. An evil FAIRY makes the princess and everyone else in the castle fall asleep forever. A thick forest grows around the castle and hides it until, after a hundred years, a prince finds Sleeping Beauty and kisses her, and then she and everyone else in the castle wakes up. Someone who seems to be sleeping peacefully is sometimes described as 'Sleeping Beauty': *Just look at Sleeping Beauty there!*

ˈsleeping car *n* [C] a railway carriage with beds for passengers to sleep in SYN **sleeper**

ˌsleeping ˈpartner *n* [C] *BrE* someone who owns part of a business but is not actively involved in running it SYN **silent partner** *AmE*

ˈsleeping pill *n* [C] a PILL which helps you to sleep

ˌsleeping poˈliceman *n* [C] *BrE* a narrow raised part in a road which makes traffic go slowly SYN **speed bump**

ˈsleeping ˌsickness *n* [U] a serious TROPICAL disease that is carried by the TSETSE FLY (=a type of insect). It causes extreme tiredness and fever, and makes you lose weight.

sleep·less /ˈsliːpləs/ *adj* **1 a sleepless night** a night when you are unable to sleep: *Adrian spent a sleepless night wondering what to do.* **2** unable to sleep: *She lay sleepless for hours, worrying.* —**sleeplessly** *adv* —**sleeplessness** *n* [U]

sleep·o·ver /ˈsliːpəʊvə $ -oʊvər/ *n* [C] a party for children in which they stay the night at someone's house

sleep·walk /ˈsliːpwɔːk $ -wɒːk/ *v* [I] **1** to walk while you are sleeping **2** [always + adv/prep] to get into a bad situation without intending to, because you are not paying attention to what is happening: **[+into]** *The government is sleepwalking into a crisis.* —**sleepwalking** *n* [U]

sleep·walk·er /ˈsliːpˌwɔːkə $ -ˌwɒːkər/ *n* [C] someone who walks while they are sleeping

sleep·y /ˈsliːpi/ ●●● S3 *adj* (*comparative* **sleepier**, *superlative* **sleepiest**)
1 tired and ready to sleep: *The warmth from the fire made her feel sleepy.*
2 a sleepy town or area is very quiet, and not much happens there OPP **lively** THESAURUS QUIET —**sleepily** *adv* —**sleepiness** *n* [U]

sleep·y·head /ˈsliːpihed/ *n* [C] *spoken* someone, especially a child, who looks as if they want to go to sleep: *It's time for bed, sleepyhead.*

sleet /sliːt/ *n* [U] half-frozen rain that falls when it is very cold: *scattered sleet and snow showers* THESAURUS RAIN —**sleet** *v* [I]: ***It was sleeting*** *so hard we could barely see for 30 yards.* —**sleety** *adj*

sleeve /sliːv/ ●●○ *n* [C]
1 the part of a piece of clothing that covers all or part of your arm: *a dress with long sleeves* | **long-sleeved/short-sleeved etc** *a short-sleeved shirt*
2 have something up your sleeve *informal* to have a secret plan or idea that you are going to use later: *Don't worry. He still has a few tricks up his sleeve.*
3 a stiff paper cover that a record is stored in SYN **jacket**

sleeve·less /ˈsliːvləs/ *adj* a sleeveless jacket, dress etc has no sleeves

sleigh /sleɪ/ *n* [C] a large open vehicle with no wheels that is used for travelling over snow and is pulled along by animals → **sledge**

sleight of hand /ˌslaɪt əv ˈhænd/ *n* [U] **1** the use of quick and skilful movements with your hands when doing a magic trick, so that people cannot understand how you did the trick **2** the use of skilful tricks and lies in order to deceive someone

slen·der /ˈslendə $ -ər/ ●○○ *adj*
1 thin in an attractive or graceful way SYN **slim**: *She is slender and stylish.* | *Laura's tall,* ***slender figure*** | **slender legs/arms/fingers etc** THESAURUS THIN
2 small or very limited in amount or size SYN **slim**: *The company only has a slender hope of survival.* | *The Republicans won the election by a slender majority.* | *We had to make the most of our rather slender resources.* —**slenderness** *n* [U]

REGISTER

Slender sounds rather literary. In everyday English, people usually say **slim** or **thin**: *I don't know how she stays so slim.*

slept /slept/ the past tense and past participle of SLEEP

sleuth /slu:θ/ *n* [C] *old-fashioned* someone who tries to find out information about a crime SYN **detective** —**sleuthing** *n* [U]

slew¹ /slu:/ *v* [I,T always + adv/prep] to turn or slide in a different direction suddenly and violently, or to make a vehicle do this SYN **skid**: **[+around/sideways]** *I lost control of the car and it slewed sideways into the ditch.*

slew² *v* the past tense of SLAY

slew³ *n* **a slew of sth** *informal* a large number of things: *a whole slew of cheap motels*

slice¹ /slaɪs/ ●●● S3 *n* [C]
1 a thin flat piece of food cut from a larger piece: **[+of]** *a* ***slice of bread*** | *pizza slices* | **thin/thick slice** *a thin slice of ham* | ***Cut** the tomatoes* ***into slices***. → see pictures at FRUIT¹, PIECE¹ THESAURUS ▸ PIECE
2 a part or share of something: **[+of]** *Everybody wants a slice of the profits.*
3 fish slice *BrE* a kitchen tool used for lifting and serving pieces of food SYN **spatula** *AmE*
4 a way of hitting the ball in sports such as tennis or golf, that makes the ball go to one side with a spinning movement, rather than straight ahead
5 a slice of life a film, play, or book which shows life as it really is

slice² ●●○ *v*
1 [T] (*also* **slice up**) to cut meat, bread, vegetables etc into thin flat pieces → **chop**: ***Thinly slice*** *the cucumbers.* | *Slice up the onions and add them to the meat.* | *sliced ham* THESAURUS ▸ CUT
2 [I,T always + adv/prep] to cut something easily with one movement of a sharp knife or edge: **[+into/through]** *The blade's so sharp it could slice through your finger.* | **slice sth in two/half** *Slice the eggs in two and arrange them on a serving dish.*
3 [I always + adv/prep] to move quickly and easily through something such as water or air: **[+through/into]** *The boat was slicing through the sparkling waves.*
4 [T] to hit a ball, for example in tennis or golf, so that it spins sideways instead of moving straight forward: *With an open goal in front of him, Wiltord* ***sliced*** *his* ***shot*** *wide of the left post.*
5 any way you slice it *AmE spoken* whatever way you choose to consider the situation: *It's the truth, any way you slice it.*

slice sth ↔ **off** *phr v*
1 to remove part of something by cutting it with one movement of a sharp knife or edge SYN **cut off**: *His knife had slipped and sliced off the top of his finger.*
2 to reduce a cost or total by a particular amount quickly and easily: **slice sth off sth** *By using volunteers, we were able to slice £10,000 off the cost of the project.*

ˌsliced ˈbread *n* [U] **1** bread that is sold already cut into slices **2 the best/greatest thing since sliced bread** *informal* used humorously to say that something new is very helpful, useful etc: *He reckons his new mobile phone is the best thing since sliced bread.*

slick¹ /slɪk/ *adj* **1** if something is slick, it is done in a skilful and attractive way and seems expensive, but it often contains no important or interesting ideas: *a slick Hollywood production* | *slick advertising* | *The presentation was very slick.* **2** if someone is slick, they are good at persuading people, often in a way that does not seem honest: *a slick used-car salesman* **3** done smoothly and quickly: *He got round the defender using some slick footwork.* **4** smooth and slippery: **[+with]** *Cars were sliding off roads that were slick with rain.* **5** *AmE old-fashioned* very good or attractive —**slickly** *adv* —**slickness** *n* [U]

slick² *n* [C] **1** (*also* **oil slick**) an area of oil on the surface of water or on a road **2** *AmE* a magazine printed on good-quality paper with a shiny surface, usually with a lot of colour pictures SYN **glossy magazine 3** *technical* a smooth car tyre used for racing

slick³ *v*
slick sth ↔ **down/back** *phr v* to make hair smooth and shiny by putting oil, water etc on it: *His hair had been combed back and slicked down with something to make it neat.*

slick·er /ˈslɪkə $ -ər/ *n* [C] *AmE* a coat made of smooth shiny material that keeps out the rain

slide¹ /slaɪd/ ●●● S3 W3 *v* (*past tense and past participle* **slid** /slɪd/)
1 [I,T] to move smoothly over a surface while continuing to touch it, or to make something move in this way: **[+along/across/down etc]** *Francesca slid across the ice.* | **slide sth across/along etc** *He opened the oven door and slid the pan of cookies in.* | *He* ***slid open*** *the door of the glass cabinet.* → see picture at SLIP¹
2 [I,T always + adv/prep] to move somewhere quietly and smoothly, or to move something in this way: **[+into/out of etc]** *Daniel slid out of the room when no one was looking.* | *She slid into the driver's seat.* | **slide sth into/out of etc sth** *He slid the gun into his pocket.*
3 [I] if prices, amounts, rates etc slide, they become lower SYN **drop** OPP **rise**: *Stocks slid a further 3% on the major markets today.* THESAURUS ▸ DECREASE
4 [I] to gradually become worse, or to begin to have a problem: *Students' test scores started to slide in the mid-1990s.* | **[+into]** *Murphy gradually slid into a pattern of drug abuse.*
5 let sth slide a) to let a situation get gradually worse: *Management has let safety standards slide at the factory.* **b)** *spoken* to ignore a mistake, problem, remark etc, without becoming angry or trying to punish it: *Well, I guess we can* ***let it slide*** *this time.*

slide² ●●○ S3 *n* [C]
1 FOR CHILDREN a large structure with steps leading to the top of a long sloping surface that children can slide down
2 DECREASE [usually singular] a decrease in prices, amounts etc OPP **rise**: **[+in]** *the current slide in house prices* | **on the slide** *The company's shares were on the slide again yesterday, down 7p at 339p.*
3 PICTURE a small piece of film in a frame that you shine a light through to show a picture on a SCREEN or wall: *a* ***slide show***
4 GETTING WORSE [usually singular] a situation in which something gradually gets worse, or someone develops a problem: **[+in]** *School administrators were unable to explain the slide in student performance.* | **[+into]** *a slide into economic chaos*
5 SCIENCE a small piece of thin glass used for holding something that you want to look at under a MICROSCOPE → see picture at MICROSCOPE
6 MUSIC/MACHINE a sliding part of a machine or musical instrument, such as the U-shaped tube of a TROMBONE
7 MOVEMENT [usually singular] a sliding movement across a surface: *The car* ***went into a slide***.
8 EARTH/SNOW a sudden fall of earth, stones, snow etc down a slope: *a rock slide*
9 FOR HAIR *BrE* a small metal or plastic object that holds your hair in place

ˈslide proˌjector *n* [C] a piece of equipment that shines a light through SLIDES so that pictures appear on a screen or wall

ˈslide rule *n* [C] an old-fashioned instrument used for calculating numbers, that looks like a ruler and has a middle part that slides across

ˌsliding ˈdoor *n* [C] a door that opens by sliding to one side

ˌsliding ˈscale *n* [C usually singular] a system for calculating how much you pay for taxes, medical treatment etc, in which the amount that you pay changes according to different conditions: **on a sliding scale** *Fees are calculated on a sliding scale.*

slight¹ /slaɪt/ ●●● S2 W3 *adj* (*comparative* **slighter**, *superlative* **slightest**)
1 [usually before noun] small in degree OPP **big**: *a slight improvement* | *a slight increase* | *a slight change of plan* | *a slight pause* | *a slight problem* THESAURUS ▸ SMALL
2 not the slightest chance/doubt/difference etc no chance,

S

doubt etc at all: *I didn't have the slightest idea who that man was.*
3 someone who is slight is thin and delicate OPP **stocky** THESAURUS ▸ THIN
4 not in the slightest *BrE spoken* not at all: *'Did he mind lending you the car?' 'Not in the slightest.'*

slight² *v* [T] to offend someone by treating them rudely or without respect: *Derek* ***felt slighted*** *when no one phoned him back.* —**slight** *n* [C]: *She may take it as a* ***slight on*** *her ability as a mother.* | *a* ***slight to*** *his authority*

slight·ly /ˈslaɪtli/ ●●● S1 W2 *adv*
1 a little: *a* ***slightly different*** *color* | *a* ***slightly more*** *powerful engine* | **slightly higher/lower/better/larger etc** *January's sales were slightly better than average.* | *He was someone I already knew slightly.* | *a slightly tart flavor* | *He leaned forward* ***ever so slightly****.*
2 slightly-built having a thin and delicate body

slim¹ /slɪm/ ●●○ S3 *adj* (*comparative* **slimmer**, *superlative* **slimmest**)
1 someone who is slim is attractively thin SYN **slender**: *a slim young woman* | *a slim waist* THESAURUS ▸ THIN
2 very small in amount or number SYN **slender**: *There's only a* ***slim chance*** *that anyone survived the crash.* | *The Republicans held a slim majority in the Senate.*
3 not wide or thick SYN **thin**: *a* ***slim volume*** *of poetry* → see picture at THIN¹

slim² *v* (**slimmed**, **slimming**) [I] *BrE* to make yourself thinner by eating less, taking a lot of exercise etc → **diet** —**slimmer** *n* [C]

slim down *phr v* **1** to reduce the size or number of something, or to become reduced in size or number: **slim sth ↔ down** *The company is trying to slim down its workforce.* | **[+to]** *The Cabinet has been slimmed down to 16 members.* **2** to make your body thinner, or to become thinner, especially in order to be healthier or more attractive: **slim sth ↔ down** *How can I slim down my hips?* | **[+to]** *She slimmed down to a healthy 61 kilos.* —**slimmed-down** *adj*

S

slime /slaɪm/ *n* [U] an unpleasant thick slippery substance: *a pond full of green slime* | *the trails of slime left by snails*

slime·ball /ˈslaɪmbɔːl $ -bɒːl/ *n* [C] *informal* someone who is immoral, extremely unpleasant, and cannot be trusted – used to show disapproval

slim·line /ˈslɪmlaɪn/ *adj BrE* **1** a slimline drink has fewer CALORIES than the normal type → **diet** **2** a slimline piece of equipment is smaller or thinner than others of the same type: *a slimline dishwasher*

slim·ming¹ /ˈslɪmɪŋ/ *n* [U] *BrE* the activity of trying to make yourself thinner by eating less, taking exercise etc

slimming² *adj* making you look thinner: *Solid colors are more slimming than patterns.*

slim·y /ˈslaɪmi/ *adj* **1** covered with SLIME, or wet and slippery like slime: *slimy mud* **2** *informal* friendly in an unpleasant way that does not seem sincere – used to show disapproval: *a slimy politician* —**sliminess** *n* [U]

sling¹ /slɪŋ/ *v* (*past tense and past participle* **slung** /slʌŋ/) [T] **1** to throw or put something somewhere with a careless movement and some force SYN **chuck**: *Lou slung his suitcase onto the bed.* | **sling sb sth** *Sling me the keys.* | *Pete* ***slung*** *his bag* ***over*** *his* ***shoulder****.* **2** [always + adv/prep] *informal* to make someone leave or go to a place: **sling sb into/out of sth** *Sam was slung into jail for punching a cop.* **3** to hang something loosely: **be slung around/over/across sth** *Dave wore a tool belt slung around his waist.* **4 sling your hook** *BrE informal* used to tell someone to go away

sling² *n* [C] **1** a piece of cloth tied around your neck to support an injured arm or hand: **in a sling** *She had her arm in a sling.* **2** a set of ropes or strong pieces of cloth that are used to lift and carry heavy objects **3** a special type of bag that fastens over your shoulders, in which you can carry a baby close to your body **4** a piece of rope with a piece of leather in the middle, used in past times as a weapon for throwing stones **5 slings and arrows** *written* problems or criticisms: *We've all* ***suffered the slings and arrows*** *of day-to-day living.*

sling·back /ˈslɪŋbæk/ *n* [C] a woman's shoe that is open at the back and has a narrow band going around the heel → see picture at SHOE¹

sling·shot /ˈslɪŋʃɒt $ -ʃɑːt/ *n* [C] *AmE* a small Y-shaped stick with a thin band of rubber across the top, used to throw stones SYN **catapult** *BrE*

slink /slɪŋk/ *v* (*past tense and past participle* **slunk** /slʌŋk/) [I always + adv/prep] to move somewhere quietly and secretly, especially because you are afraid or ashamed SYN **creep**: *Edward was hoping to slink past unnoticed.*

slink·y /ˈslɪŋki/ *adj* **1** a slinky dress, skirt etc is smooth and tight and shows the shape of a woman's body in a way that looks sexually attractive: *a slinky black dress* **2** slinky movements, music, or voices are slow in a way that is sexually attractive: *a song with slinky bass lines*

slip¹ /slɪp/ ●●● S3 W2 *v* (**slipped**, **slipping**)
1 FALL OR SLIDE [I] to slide a short distance accidentally, and fall or lose your balance slightly: *Wright slipped but managed to keep hold of the ball.* | **[+on]** *He slipped on the ice.* THESAURUS ▸ FALL
2 GO SOMEWHERE [I always + adv/prep] to go somewhere, without attracting other people's attention SYN **slide**: *Ben slipped quietly out of the room.* | *One man managed to slip from the club as police arrived.*
3 PUT STH SOMEWHERE [T always + adv/prep] to put something somewhere quietly or smoothly SYN **slide**: *Ann slipped the book into her bag.* | *A letter had been slipped under his door.* | *Carrie slipped her arm through her brother's.* THESAURUS ▸ PUT
4 GIVE STH TO SB [T] to give someone something secretly or without attracting much attention: **slip sb sth** *I slipped him a ten-dollar bill to keep quiet.* | **slip sth to sb** *Carr slips the ball to King who scores easily.*
5 MOVE [I] to move smoothly, especially off or from something: *As he bent over, the towel round his waist slipped.* | **[+off/down/from etc]** *He watched the sun slip down behind the mountains.* | *The ring had slipped off Julia's finger.* | *Cally* ***slipped from*** *his* ***grasp*** *and fled.*
6 KNIFE [I] if a knife or other tool slips, it moves so that it accidentally cuts the wrong thing: *The knife slipped and cut his finger.*
7 GET WORSE [I] to become worse or lower than before: *Standards have slipped in many parts of the industry.* | *His popularity slipped further after a series of scandals.* | *You're slipping, Doyle! You need a holiday.*
8 CHANGE CONDITION [I always + adv/prep] to gradually start being in a particular condition SYN **fall**: **[+into]** *He had begun to slip into debt.* | *She slipped into unconsciousness and died the next day.* | *The project has slipped behind schedule.*
9 CLOTHES [I,T always + adv/prep] to put a piece of clothing on your body, or take it off your body, quickly and smoothly: **slip sth off/on** *Peter was already at the door slipping on his shoes.* | **[+into/out of]** *She slipped out of her clothes and stepped into the shower.*

10 TIME [I always + adv/prep] if time slips away, past etc, it passes quickly: **[+away/past/by]** *The search for the missing child continued, but time was slipping away.* | *The hours slipped past almost unnoticed.*
11 slip your mind/memory if something slips your mind, you forget it: *I meant to buy some milk, but it completely slipped my mind.*
12 let sth slip to say something without meaning to, when you had wanted it to be a secret: *He **let it slip that** they were planning to get married.*
13 GET FREE [T] to get free from something that was holding you: *The dog slipped his collar and ran away.*
14 slip through the net *BrE*, **slip through the cracks** *AmE* if someone or something slips through the net, they are not caught or dealt with by the system that is supposed to catch them or deal with them: *In a class of 30 children, it is easy for one to slip through the net and learn nothing.*
15 let sth slip (through your fingers) to not take an opportunity, offer etc: *Don't let a chance like that slip through your fingers!*
16 slip one over on sb *especially AmE informal* to deceive or play a trick on someone
17 slip a disc to suffer an injury when one of the connecting parts between the bones in your back moves out of place
slip away *phr v*
1 to leave a place secretly or without anyone noticing: *He slipped away into the crowd.*
2 if something such as an opportunity slips away, it is no longer available: *This time, Radford did not let her chance slip away.*
slip sth ↔ **in** *phr v* to use a word or say something without attracting too much attention: *He had slipped in a few jokes to liven the speech up.*
slip out *phr v* if something slips out, you say it without really intending to: *I didn't mean to say it. The words slipped out.*
slip up *phr v* to make a mistake → **slip-up**: *The company apologized for slipping up so badly.* | **[+on]** *Someone had slipped up on the order.*

slip² ●●○ S3 *n*
1 PAPER [C] a small or narrow piece of paper: *a **slip of paper** | an order slip | a betting slip* → **PAYSLIP**
2 MISTAKE [C] a small mistake: *Molly knew she could not afford to **make** a single **slip**.*
3 slip of the tongue/pen a small mistake you make when you are speaking or writing, especially by using the wrong word: *It was just a slip of the tongue.* → **FREUDIAN SLIP**
4 give sb the slip *informal* to escape from someone who is chasing you: *Somehow she'd given them the slip.*
5 CLOTHING [C] a piece of underwear, similar to a thin dress or skirt, that a woman wears under a dress or skirt: *a white silk slip*
6 GETTING WORSE [C usually singular] an occasion when something becomes worse or lower SYN **drop**: **[+in]** *a slip in house prices*
7 SLIDE [C] an act of sliding a short distance or of falling by sliding
8 a slip of a girl/boy etc *old-fashioned* a small thin young person – often used humorously
9 CRICKET [C usually plural] a part of the field where players stand, trying to catch the ball in CRICKET
10 CLAY [U] *technical* a mixture of clay and water that is used for decorating pots

ˈslip case *n* [C] *AmE* a plastic container for a CD or a DVD

slip·case /ˈslɪpkeɪs/ *n* [C] a hard cover, like a box, for putting a book in

slip·co·ver /ˈslɪpˌkʌvə $ -ər/ *n* [C] a loose cloth cover for furniture

slip·knot /ˈslɪpnɒt $ -nɑːt/ *n* [C] a knot that you can make tighter by pulling one of its ends

ˈslip-ons *n* [plural] shoes that do not have a fastening —**slip-on** *adj*: *slip-on shoes*

slip·page /ˈslɪpɪdʒ/ *n* [C,U] *formal* **1** failure to do something at the planned time, at the planned cost etc: *Slippage on any job will entail slippage on the overall project.* **2** when something becomes worse or lower: **[+in/of]** *slippage in sales* **3** when something slips: *snow slippage*

ˌslipped ˈdisc (*also* **slipped disk** *AmE*) *n* [C usually singular] a painful injury caused when one of the connecting parts between the bones in your back moves out of place

slip·per /ˈslɪpə $ -ər/ *n* [C] a light soft shoe that you wear at home → see picture at SHOE¹

slip·per·y /ˈslɪpəri/ ●●○ *adj*
1 something that is slippery is difficult to hold, walk on etc because it is wet or GREASY: *In places, the path can be wet and slippery.* | *Harry's palms were slippery with sweat.*
2 *informal* someone who is slippery cannot be trusted: *Martin is a **slippery customer*** (=someone you should not trust) *so be careful what you say to him.*
3 not having one clear meaning and able to be understood in different ways: *the slippery notion of 'standards'*
4 (be on) a/the slippery slope *BrE informal* used to talk about a process or habit that is difficult to stop and which will develop into something extremely bad: **[+to/towards]** *He is on the slippery slope to a life of crime.* —**slipperiness** *n* [U]

slip·py /ˈslɪpi/ *adj BrE informal* a slippy surface or object is slippery

ˈslip road *n* [C] *BrE* a road for driving onto or off a MOTORWAY SYN **ramp** *AmE*

slip·shod /ˈslɪpʃɒd $ -ʃɑːd/ *adj* done too quickly and carelessly – used to show disapproval SYN **slapdash**: *a slipshod piece of work*

slip·stream /ˈslɪpstriːm/ *n* [singular] the area of low air pressure just behind a vehicle that is moving quickly

ˈslip-up *n* [C] a careless mistake: *We cannot afford another slip-up.* THESAURUS ▸ MISTAKE

slip·way /ˈslɪpweɪ/ *n* [C] a sloping track that is used for moving boats into or out of the water

slit¹ /slɪt/ *v* (*past tense and past participle* **slit**, *present participle* **slitting**) [T] to make a straight narrow cut in cloth, paper, skin etc: *Guy **slit open** the envelope.* | **slit sb's throat** (=kill someone by cutting their throat) | **slit your wrists** (=try to kill yourself by cutting your wrists) THESAURUS ▸ CUT

slit² *n* [C] a long straight narrow cut or hole: *light shining through a slit in the door* | *a skirt with a slit up the side*

SLITHER

A snake slithered across the grass.

slith·er /ˈslɪðə $ -ər/ *v* [I always + adv/prep] to slide somewhere over a surface, twisting or moving from side to side: *A snake slithered across the grass.* | *He slithered down the muddy bank.*

slith·er·y /ˈslɪðəri/ *adj* unpleasantly slippery

sliv·er /ˈslɪvə $ -ər/ *n* [C] a small pointed or thin piece that has been cut or broken off something: **[+of]** *a sliver of glass* | *a sliver of cake*

slob¹ /slɒb $ slɑːb/ *n* [C] *informal* someone who is lazy and untidy: *a lazy slob*

slob² *v* (**slobbed**, **slobbing**)
slob around/out *phr v BrE informal* to spend time doing nothing and being lazy

slob·ber /ˈslɒbə $ ˈslɑːbər/ *v* [I] to let SALIVA (=the liquid produced by your mouth) come out of your mouth and run down SYN **drool**: *I hate dogs that slobber everywhere.*
slobber over sb/sth *phr v* to show how much you want, like, or love someone or something, without controlling yourself: *I caught Rick slobbering over the models in a magazine.*

slob·ber·y /ˈslɒbəri $ ˈslɑː-/ *adj* a slobbery kiss or mouth is unpleasantly wet

sloe /sləʊ $ sloʊ/ *n* [C] a small bitter fruit like a PLUM

S

ˌsloe ˈgin *n* [U] an alcoholic drink made with sloes, GIN, and sugar

slog¹ /slɒg $ slɑːg/ *v* (**slogged**, **slogging**) [I,T] *informal* **1** to work hard at something without stopping, especially when the work is difficult, tiring, or boring: *Mother slogged all her life for us.* | **[+away]** *After a day slogging away at work, I need to relax.* | **[+through]** *You just have to sit down and slog through long lists of new vocabulary.* **2** [always + adv/prep] to make a long hard journey somewhere, especially on foot: *He's been slogging round the streets delivering catalogues.* | **slog your way through/round etc sth** *He started to slog his way up the hill.* **3 slog it out** *BrE* to fight, compete, or argue about something until one side wins: *The teams will be slogging it out on Saturday.*

slog² *n* **1** [singular, U] *BrE informal* a piece of work that takes a lot of time and effort and is usually boring: *It'll be a slog, but I know we can do it.* | *months of* ***hard slog*** **2** [singular] a long period of tiring walking: *a long* ***hard slog*** *uphill*

slo·gan /ˈsləʊgən $ ˈsloʊ-/ ●●○ *n* [C] a short phrase that is easy to remember and is used in advertisements, or by politicians, organizations etc → **catchphrase**: *an* ***advertising slogan*** | *demonstrators shouting* ***political slogans*** | *the Democrats'* ***campaign slogan*** THESAURUS PHRASE

slo·gan·eer·ing /ˌsləʊgəˈnɪərɪŋ $ ˌsloʊgəˈnɪr-/ *n* [U] the use of slogans in advertisements or by politicians, organizations etc – used to show disapproval: *political sloganeering*

slo-mo /ˈsləʊ məʊ $ ˈsloʊ moʊ/ *adj* [only before noun] *informal* used to describe action that appears to happen more slowly than it really happens, in computer games, on film etc → **slow-motion**: *slo-mo mode* —**slo-mo** *n* [U]

sloop /sluːp/ *n* [C] a small ship with one central MAST (=pole for sails)

slop¹ /slɒp $ slɑːp/ *v* (**slopped**, **slopping**) **1** [I always + adv/prep] if liquid slops somewhere, it moves around or over the edge of a container in an uncontrolled way SYN **splash**: *Coffee slopped over the rim of her cup.* | *With each wave, more water slopped into the cabin.* **2** [T always + adv/prep] to put a liquid somewhere in a careless way: *She put the glass down, slopping beer onto the table.* **3** [T] *AmE* to feed slop to pigs

slop around/about *phr v BrE informal* to relax, wearing clothes that are untidy or old: *Jan would never slop around in old jeans.*

slop out *phr v BrE* if prisoners slop out, they empty their toilet buckets —**slopping-out** *n* [U]

slop² *n* [U] (*also* **slops** [plural]) **1** waste food that can be used to feed animals **2** *BrE* dirty water or URINE: *Prisoners had to use slop buckets at night.* **3** *informal* food that is too soft and tastes bad: *Do you actually expect us to eat this slop?*

slope¹ /sləʊp $ sloʊp/ ●●○ W3 *n*

1 [C] a piece of ground or a surface that slopes: *a* ***steep slope*** | *a* ***gentle*** (=not steep) ***slope*** | *She looked back up the grassy slope.*

2 an area of steep ground covered with snow that people SKI down: *We got to Tahoe on Friday, and* ***hit the slopes*** (=skied on them) *the next day.*

3 [singular] the angle at which something slopes in relation to a flat surface: *a slope of 30 degrees*

slope² *v* [I] if the ground or a surface slopes, it is higher at one end than the other: **[+up/down/away etc]** *a pleasant garden that slopes down to the river*

slope off *phr v BrE informal* to leave somewhere quietly and secretly, especially when you are avoiding work: *Mike sloped off early today.*

slop·py /ˈslɒpi $ ˈslɑːpi/ *adj* **1** not done carefully or thoroughly SYN **careless**: *sloppy work* | *His written reports are incredibly sloppy.* THESAURUS CARELESS **2** sloppy clothes are loose-fitting, untidy, or dirty: *Ann was dressed in a sloppy brown sweater.* **3** expressing feelings of love too strongly and in a silly way SYN **slushy**: *The film is a sloppy romance.* **4** not solid enough: *sloppy jelly* —**sloppily** *adv* —**sloppiness** *n* [U]

ˌsloppy ˈjoe *n* [C] *AmE* a type of sandwich, made with BEEF with spices added and served on a BUN

slosh /slɒʃ $ slɑːʃ/ *v* **1** [I,T always + adv/prep] if a liquid sloshes somewhere, or if you slosh it, it moves or is moved about in an uncontrolled way SYN **slop**: **[+around/about]** *Water was sloshing about in the bottom of the boat.* | *He put the glass down hard and beer sloshed over the edge.* **2** [T always + adv/prep] to put a liquid in a container or on a surface in a careless way SYN **slop**: *Jo sloshed more wine into her glass.* | *Slosh a bit of paint on.* **3** [I always + adv/prep] to walk through water or mud in a noisy way SYN **splash**: *People were sloshing around in the mud.*

sloshed /slɒʃt $ slɑːʃt/ *adj* [not before noun] *informal* drunk: *Most of them were too sloshed to notice.*

slot¹ /slɒt $ slɑːt/ ●●● S3 *n* [C]

1 a long narrow hole in a surface, that you can put something into: *Alan dropped another quarter into the slot on the pay phone.* → see picture at HOLE¹ THESAURUS HOLE

2 a short period of time allowed for one particular event on a programme or TIMETABLE: *a ten-minute slot on the breakfast show* | *landing slots at Heathrow Airport* | *A new comedy is scheduled for the 9 pm* ***time slot***.

slot² *v* (**slotted**, **slotting**) [I,T always + adv/prep] to go into a slot, or to put something in a slot: **slot sth into sth** *Mary slotted the key into the lock.* | **[+into]** *Each length of board slots easily into the next.* | *All the wood parts come pre-cut so that they can be* ***slotted together*** (=put together using slots).

slot in *phr v BrE informal* to fit something or someone into a plan, organization etc, or to fit in: *Stewart has slotted in well.* | **slot sb/sth ↔ in** *We should be able to slot the meeting in before lunch.*

sloth /sləʊθ $ sloʊθ/ *n* **1** [C] an animal in Central and South America that moves very slowly, has grey fur, and lives in trees **2** [U] *formal* laziness

sloth·ful /ˈsləʊθfəl $ ˈsloʊθ-/ *adj formal* lazy or not active SYN **idle** —**slothfulness** *n* [U]

ˈslot maˌchine *n* [C] **1** a machine used for playing a game, that starts when you put money into it **2** *BrE* a machine that you buy cigarettes, food, or drink from SYN **vending machine**

ˌslotted ˈspoon *n* [C] a large spoon with holes in it

slouch¹ /slaʊtʃ/ *v* [I] to stand, sit, or walk with a slouch: **[+back/against/in etc]** *Jimmy slouched back in his chair.* | *She slouched across the living room.*

slouch² *n* **1 be no slouch (at sth)** *informal* to be very good at something: *Horowitz was no slouch at languages.* **2** [singular] a way of standing, sitting, or walking with your shoulders bent forward that makes you look tired or lazy

slough¹ /slʌf/ *v*

slough sth ↔ **off** *phr v* **1** *technical* to get rid of a dead layer of skin **2** *literary* to get rid of something, especially something that is damaging you: *The president wanted to slough off the country's bad image.*

slough² /slaʊ $ sluː, slaʊ/ *n* **1** [singular] *literary* a bad situation or a state of sadness that you cannot get out of easily: **[+of]** *Harry was in a slough of despondency for weeks.* **2** [C] an area of land covered in deep dirty water or mud

slov·en·ly /ˈslʌvənli/ *adj* lazy, untidy, and careless: *slovenly habits* | *a large slovenly woman* | *a slovenly way of speaking* —**slovenliness** *n* [U]

slow¹ /sləʊ $ sloʊ/ ●●● S2 W2 *adj* (*comparative* **slower**, *superlative* **slowest**)

1 NOT QUICK not moving, being done, or happening quickly OPP **quick**, **fast** → **slowly**: *The car was travelling at a very slow speed.* | *a slow walker* | *The economy faces a year of slower growth.* | *Take a few deep, slow breaths.*

2 TAKING TOO LONG taking too long OPP **fast**: *Taylor was concerned at the slow progress of the investigations.* | *The legal system can be* ***painfully slow*** (=much too slow). | **slow to do sth** *The wound was slow to heal.*

3 WITH DELAY [not before noun] if you are slow to do something, you do not do it as soon as you can or should:

slow to do sth *Farmers have been slow to exploit this market.* | *Their attitude was slow to change.* | **slow in doing sth** *He has been slow in announcing the name of his successor.* | *New ideas have been slow in coming.*
4 LONGER TIME taking a longer time than something similar OPP **fast**: *We got on the slow train* (=one that stops at more stations) *by mistake.*
5 BUSINESS if business or trade is slow, there are not many customers or not much is sold: *Business is often slow in the afternoon.* | *The company is experiencing slow sales.*
6 CLOCK [not before noun] if a clock or watch is slow, it is showing a time earlier than the correct time OPP **fast**: **ten minutes/five minutes etc slow** *The clock is about five minutes slow.*
7 NOT CLEVER not good or quick at understanding things: *Teaching assistants have time to help the slower pupils.*
8 slow on the uptake not quick to understand something new: *Sometimes Tim's a little slow on the uptake.*
9 slow off the mark not quick enough at reacting to something
10 do a slow burn *AmE informal* to slowly get angry: *Tony fumbled the ball and I could see the coach doing a slow burn.*
11 slow handclap *BrE* if a group of people give someone a slow handclap, they CLAP their hands slowly to show their disapproval
12 a slow oven an OVEN that is at a low temperature
13 PHOTOGRAPHY a slow film does not react to light very easily —**slowness** *n* [U]

THESAURUS
slow not moving quickly or not doing something quickly: *I was always one of the slowest runners in my class.* | *My computer's really slow compared to the ones at school.*
gradual happening, developing, or changing slowly over a long period of time: *a gradual rise in the Earth's temperature* | *I've noticed a gradual improvement in his work.*
leisurely *especially written* moving or doing something slowly, especially because you are enjoying what you are doing and do not have to hurry: *a leisurely breakfast* | *They walked at a leisurely pace.*
unhurried *especially written* moving or doing something in a slow and calm way, without rushing at all: *She continued to listen, seeming relaxed and unhurried.* | *the doctor's calm unhurried manner*
sluggish moving or reacting more slowly than usual, especially because of a loss of power or energy. Also used when business, sales, or the economy seem very slow: *The car seems rather sluggish going uphill.* | *The drink was making her sluggish.* | *the company's sluggish performance this year*
lethargic moving slowly, because you feel as if you have no energy and no interest in doing anything: *She woke up feeling heavy and lethargic.* | *His son seemed depressed and lethargic.*
languid *literary* slow and with very little energy or activity - used about people, actions, or periods of time: *She lifted her hand in a languid wave.* | *a long languid afternoon in the middle of summer*

slow² ●●● S3 W2 (*also* **slow down/up**) *v* [I,T] to become slower or to make something slower: *Her breathing slowed and she fell asleep.* | *Ian slowed up as he approached the traffic lights.*
slow down *phr v*
1 to become slower or to make something slower: *Growth in sales has slowed down.* | **slow sb/sth ↔ down** *The ice on the road slowed us down.*
2 to become less active or busy than you usually are: *It is important to slow down, rest, and eat sensibly.*

slow³ *adv* (*comparative* **slower**, *superlative* **slowest**) *informal* slowly: *If you go slower, you'll see much more.* → GO-SLOW

slow·coach /ˈsləʊkəʊtʃ $ ˈsloʊkoʊtʃ/ *n* [C] *BrE informal* someone who moves or does things too slowly

slow·down /ˈsləʊdaʊn $ ˈsloʊ-/ *n* **1** [C usually singular] a reduction in activity or speed: **[+in]** *a slowdown in the US economy* **2** [C] *AmE* a period when people deliberately work slowly in order to protest about something

ˈslow lane *n* [C] **1** the part of a large road where vehicles drive more slowly than the other vehicles on the road → **fast lane 2 in the slow lane** if a company, organization etc is in the slow lane, it is less successful than others: *The country is expected to remain in the slow lane of economic recovery.*

slow·ly /ˈsləʊli $ ˈsloʊ-/ ●●● S3 W2 *adv*
1 at a slow speed OPP **quickly**: *He shook his head slowly.* | *'That's true,' said Joe slowly.*
2 slowly but surely used to emphasize that a change is happening, although it is happening slowly: *We are slowly but surely gaining the support of the public.*

THESAURUS
slowly at a slow speed: *Large white clouds drifted slowly across the sky.* | *The situation is slowly improving.*
gradually happening slowly over a period of time: *I practised every day, and gradually got better.* | *Many of our forests are gradually disappearing.*
little by little/bit by bit slowly, in a series of small amounts or stages: *Add the olive oil, little by little.* | *It's best to do the work bit by bit.*
at a snail's pace extremely slowly, especially when this is annoying: *Traffic was moving at a snail's pace.*

ˌslow ˈmotion *n* [U] movement on film or television shown at a slower speed than it really happened: **in slow motion** *Let's see that goal again in slow motion.*

ˈslow-pitch *n* [U] *AmE* a game like SOFTBALL, usually played by mixed teams of men and women

slow·poke /ˈsləʊpəʊk $ ˈsloʊpoʊk/ *n* [C] *AmE informal* someone who moves or does things too slowly

ˌslow-ˈwitted *adj* not good at understanding things SYN **stupid**

sludge /slʌdʒ/ *n* [U] **1** soft thick mud, especially at the bottom of a liquid **2** the solid substance that is left when industrial waste or SEWAGE (=the liquid waste from toilets) has been cleaned **3** thick dirty oil in an engine —**sludgy** *adj*

slug¹ /slʌg/ *n* [C] **1** a small creature with a soft body, that moves very slowly and eats garden plants **2** *AmE informal* a bullet: *Perez still has a slug lodged in his left shoulder.* **3** *informal* a small amount of a strong alcoholic drink: **[+of]** *a slug of brandy* **4** *AmE informal* a piece of metal shaped like a coin, used to illegally get a drink, ticket etc from a machine **5** *AmE* someone who gets to work by standing in a particular place until a driver stops and lets them go with them in their car

slug² *v* (**slugged**, **slugging**) [T] **1 slug it out** if two people slug it out, they fight or compete until one of them has won **2** *informal* to hit someone hard with your closed hand SYN **punch 3** to hit a ball hard **4** (*also* **slug back**) to drink an alcoholic drink, especially by swallowing large amounts at the same time

slug·fest /ˈslʌgfest/ *n* [C] *especially AmE informal* a situation in which people are arguing or fighting in a rude or angry way

slug·ger /ˈslʌgə $ -ər/ *n* [C] *AmE informal* a baseball player who hits the ball a very long way

slug·ging /ˈslʌgɪŋ/ *n* [U] *AmE* a system, used in some American cities, of sharing car rides to work with people you do not know, in which people wait in a particular place for a driver to pick them up

slug·gish /ˈslʌgɪʃ/ *adj* moving or reacting more slowly than normal: *Alex woke late, feeling tired and sluggish.* | *Economic recovery has so far been sluggish.* THESAURUS SLOW —**sluggishly** *adv* —**sluggishness** *n* [U]

sluice¹ /sluːs/ *n* [C] a passage for water to flow through, with a special gate which can be opened or closed to control it

sluice² *v* **1** [T] to wash something with a lot of water: **sluice sth out/down** *He was sluicing down the table and the*

S

floor. **2** [I always + adv/prep] if water sluices somewhere, a large amount of it suddenly flows there

slum¹ /slʌm/ ●○○ *n*
1 [C] a house or an area of a city that is in very bad condition, where very poor people live: *a slum area | slum housing | the slums of London* **THESAURUS** AREA
2 [singular] *BrE informal* a very untidy place

slum² *v* **slum it/be slumming** *informal* to spend time in conditions that are much worse than you are used to – often used humorously: *Jeremy doesn't slum it when he goes away.*

slum·ber¹ /ˈslʌmbə $ -ər/ *v* [I] *literary* to sleep

slumber² *n* [singular, U] (*also* **slumbers** [plural]) *literary* sleep: *He passed into a deep slumber.*

ˈslumber ˌparty *n* [C] *AmE* a children's party when a group of children sleep at one child's house

slum·lord /ˈslʌmlɔːd $ -lɔːrd/ *n* [C] *AmE* someone who owns houses in a very poor area and charges high rents for buildings that are in bad condition

ˌslummy ˈmummy *n* [C] *BrE informal* an unattractive, badly dressed young mother – used mainly in newspapers and magazines → **yummy mummy**

slump¹ /slʌmp/ ●○○ *v*
1 [I] to fall or lean against something because you are not strong enough to stand: **[+against/over/back etc]** *She slumped against the wall. | Carol slumped back in her chair, defeated. | Ben staggered and slumped onto the floor.*
2 [I] to suddenly go down in price, value, or number OPP **soar**: *Sales slumped by 20% last year.* | **[+to]** *The currency slumped to a record low.*
3 [I,T] (*also* **be slumped**) if your shoulders or head slump or are slumped, they bend forward because you are unhappy, tired, or unconscious: *Her shoulders slumped and her eyes filled with tears.*

S

slump² ●○○ *n* [C usually singular]
1 a sudden decrease in prices, sales, profits etc: **[+in]** *a slump in car sales*
2 a period when there is a reduction in business and many people lose their jobs OPP **boom**: *The war was followed by an economic slump. | a worldwide slump*
3 *especially AmE* a period when a player or team does not play well: **in a slump** *The Dodgers have been in a slump for the last three weeks.*

slung /slʌŋ/ the past tense and past participle of SLING

slunk /slʌŋk/ the past tense and past participle of SLINK

slur¹ /slɜː $ slɜːr/ *v* (**slurred**, **slurring**) **1** [I,T] to speak unclearly without separating your words or sounds correctly: **slur your words/speech** *She was slurring her words as if she was drunk. | His voice sounded slurred.* **2** [T] to criticize someone or something unfairly **3** [T] to play a group of musical notes smoothly together

slur² *n* [C] **1** an unfair criticism that is intended to make people dislike someone or something: **[+on/against]** *Milton regarded her comment as a slur on his country. | How dare she* ***cast*** *a* ***slur on*** (=criticize) *my character? | a racist slur* **2** *technical* a curved line written over musical notes to show they must be played together smoothly

slurp /slɜːp $ slɜːrp/ *v* [I,T] to drink a liquid while making a noisy sucking sound **THESAURUS** DRINK, EAT —**slurp** *n* [C usually singular]

slur·ry /ˈslʌri $ ˈslɜːri/ *n* [U] a mixture of water and mud, coal, or animal waste

slush /slʌʃ/ *n* **1** [U] partly melted snow: *Children were sliding around in the snow and slush.* **2** [U] *informal* feelings or stories that seem silly because they are too romantic: *sentimental slush* **3** [C,U] *especially AmE* a drink made with crushed ice and a sweet liquid: *cherry slush* —**slushy** *adj*

ˈslush fund *n* [C] an amount of money kept for dishonest purposes, especially in politics

slut /slʌt/ *n* [C] *taboo informal* a very offensive word for a woman who has sex with a lot of different people. Do not use this word. —**slutty** *adj* —**sluttish** *adj*

sly /slaɪ/ *adj* **1** someone who is sly cleverly deceives people in order to get what they want SYN **cunning** **THESAURUS** DISHONEST **2 sly smile/glance/wink etc** a smile, look etc that shows you know something secret: *He leaned forward with a sly smile.* **3 on the sly** *informal* secretly, especially when you are doing something that you should not do: *They'd been seeing each other on the sly for months.* —**slyly** *adv* —**slyness** *n* [U]

smack¹ /smæk/ *v* [T] **1** to hit someone, especially a child, with your open hand in order to punish them → **slap**: *the debate about whether parents should smack their children* **THESAURUS** HIT **2** [always + adv/prep] to hit something hard against something else so that it makes a short loud noise: *He smacked the money down on the table and walked out.* **3 smack your lips** to make a short loud noise with your lips before or after you eat or drink something to show that it is good: *He drained his glass and smacked his lips appreciatively.* **4** *BrE informal* to hit someone hard with your closed hand SYN **punch**

smack of sth *phr v* if a situation smacks of something unpleasant, it seems to involve that thing: *To me, the whole thing smacks of a cover-up.*

smack sb **up** *phr v informal* to hit someone hard many times with your hand: *Don't make me come over there and smack you up.*

smack² *n* **1** [C] **a)** a hit with your open hand, especially to punish a child → **slap**: *You're going to* ***get*** *a* ***smack*** *in a minute!* **b)** *BrE informal* a hard hit with your closed hand SYN **punch**: **smack in the mouth/face/gob** *Talk like that and I'll give you a smack in the mouth.* **2** [C usually singular] a short loud noise caused when something hits something else: *The book landed with a smack.* **3** [U] *informal* HEROIN **4 give sb a smack on the lips/cheek** *informal* to kiss someone loudly **5** [C] a small fishing boat

smack³ *adv informal* **1** exactly or directly in the middle of something, in front of something etc: **smack in the middle/in front of sth etc** *There was a hole smack in the middle of the floor.* | **smack bang** *BrE*, **smack dab** *AmE*: *It's smack dab in the middle of an earthquake zone.* **2** if something goes smack into something, it hits it with a lot of force: *The car ran smack into the side of the bus.*

smack·er /ˈsmækə $ -ər/ *n* [C] *informal* **1** a pound or a dollar **2** (*also* **smack·e·roo** /ˌsmækəˈruː/) a loud kiss

smack·head /ˈsmækhed/ *n* [C] *informal* someone who uses the drug HEROIN

small¹ /smɔːl $ smɒːl/ ●●● S1 W1 *adj* (*comparative* **smaller**, *superlative* **smallest**)
1 SIZE not large in size or amount: *a small piece of paper | a small car | a small town | a small dark woman | The T-shirt was too small for him. | The sweater comes in three sizes – small, medium, and large. | Only a relatively* ***small number*** *of people were affected. | a* ***small amount*** *of money | A much* ***smaller proportion*** *of women are employed in senior positions.* **THESAURUS** SHORT
2 NOT IMPORTANT a small problem, job, mistake etc is not important or does not have a large effect SYN **minor**: *We may have to make a few small changes. | There's been a small problem. | There's only a small difference between them. | It was good to feel we had helped in some small way.*
3 no small degree/achievement/task etc a large degree, achievement etc: *The success of the project is due in no small measure to the work of Dr Peterson. | That is no small achievement in the circumstances.*
4 YOUNG a small child is young: *She has three small children. | I've known him since he was a small boy.* **THESAURUS** YOUNG
5 small business/firm/farmer etc a business that does not involve large amounts of money or does not employ a large number of people: *grants for small businesses*
6 LETTER small letters are letters in the form a, b, c etc rather than A, B, C etc SYN **lower case** OPP **capital**
7 conservative with a small 'c'/democrat with a small 'd' etc *informal* someone who believes in the principles you have mentioned, but does not belong to an organized group or political party

8 VOICE a small voice is quiet and soft: *'What about me?' she asked in a small voice.*
9 look/feel small to seem or feel stupid, unimportant, or ashamed: *She jumped at any opportunity to* ***make*** *me* ***look small****.*
10 (it's a) small world *especially spoken* used to express surprise when you unexpectedly meet someone you know or find out that someone has an unexpected connection to you: *Did you know David went to school with my brother? It's a small world, isn't it?*
11 a small fortune a large amount of money: **cost/spend/pay a small fortune** *It must have cost him a small fortune.*
12 small change coins of low value: *I didn't have any small change for the parking meter.*
13 be thankful/grateful for small mercies/favours to be pleased that a bad situation is not even worse: *She wasn't too badly hurt, so we should be thankful for small mercies.*
14 the small hours (*also* **the wee small hours** *BrE*) the early morning hours, between about one and four o'clock: **in/into the small hours** *He finally fell exhausted into bed in the small hours.* | *The party continued into the wee small hours.*
15 small arms guns that you hold with one or both hands when firing them
16 sth is small potatoes (*also* **sth is small beer** *BrE*) *informal* used to say that someone or something is not important, especially when compared to other people or things: *Even with £10,000 to invest, you are still small beer for most investment managers.* —**small** *adv*: *He writes so small I can't read it.* —**smallness** *n* [U]

GRAMMAR: Order of adjectives

If there is more than one adjective, the adjectives are usually used in a fixed order.
You say: *They live in a nice small town.* ✗ Don't say: *They live in a small nice town.*
You say: *She had a small white dog.* ✗ Don't say: *She had a white small dog.*
GRAMMAR GUIDE ▶ ADJECTIVES

small[2] *n* **1 the small of your back** the lower part of your back where it curves **2 smalls** [plural] *BrE old-fashioned informal* underwear

ˈsmall ad *n* [C] *BrE* an advertisement put in a newspaper by someone who wants to buy or sell something SYN **want ad** *AmE*

ˌsmall ˈclaims court *n* [C] a court where people can make legal claims involving small amounts of money

ˈsmall fry *n* [U] people or things that are not important when compared to other people or things: *There's no point in arresting the small fry.*

small·hold·er /ˈsmɔːlˌhəʊldə $ ˈsmɒːlˌhoʊldər/ *n* [C] *BrE* someone who has a smallholding

small·hold·ing /ˈsmɔːlˌhəʊldɪŋ $ ˈsmɒːlˌhoʊld-/ *n* [C] *BrE* a piece of land used for farming, that is smaller than an ordinary farm

ˌsmall inˈtestine *n* [C] the long tube that food goes through after it has gone through your stomach → **large intestine** → see picture at HUMAN[1]

small·ish /ˈsmɔːlɪʃ $ ˈsmɒːl-/ *adj especially BrE* fairly small: *She's smallish with red hair.*

ˌsmall-ˈminded *adj* thinking too much about your own life and problems and not about important things – used to show disapproval → **narrow-minded**: *People around here are so small-minded.* —**small-mindedness** *n* [U]

ˌsmall office/ˈhome office *n* [C] (*abbreviation* **SOHO**) a room in someone's home, with electronic equipment such as a computer and a FAX machine, that is used as a place in which to work

small·pox /ˈsmɔːlpɒks $ ˈsmɒːlpɑːks/ *n* [U] a serious disease that causes spots which leave marks on your skin

ˈsmall ˌprint *n* [U] *especially BrE* all the rules and details relating to a contract or agreement SYN **fine print** *AmE*: **read/check the small print** *Always read the small print before you sign anything.*

ˌsmall-ˈscale *adj* involving only a small number of things or a small area OPP **large-scale**: *a small-scale study*

ˈsmall ˌscreen *n* **the small screen** television – used especially when comparing television to the cinema → **big screen**: *a film made for the small screen*

ˈsmall talk *n* [U] polite friendly conversation about unimportant subjects: *We stood around* ***making small talk****.*

ˈsmall-time *adj* **small-time crook/gangster etc** a criminal who is not involved in large or serious crimes —**small-timer** *n* [C]

ˈsmall-town *adj* [only before noun] **1** from, or relating to, a small town: *a small-town newspaper* **2** *AmE* (*also* **small·ville** /ˈsmɔːlvɪl $ ˈsmɒːl-/) relating to ideas, qualities etc that people in small towns are supposed to have, which sometimes include a lack of interest in anything new or different → **parochial**: *small-town attitudes*

smarm·y /ˈsmɑːmi $ -ɑːr-/ *adj* polite in an insincere way – used to show disapproval: *smarmy comments* | *a smarmy car salesman*

THESAURUS: small

small not large in size, amount, or effect: *a small boat* | *small businesses* | *a small amount of money* | *small changes*
little [usually before noun] small – used about objects, places, and living things. Used especially with other adjectives to show how you feel about someone or something: *It's a very pretty little town.* | *The poor little dog has hurt its leg.* | *The cake was decorated with little flowers.*
low used about prices, rents, levels, or standards: *People on low incomes are finding it difficult to pay fuel bills.* | *The crime rate in the area is relatively low.*
slight [usually before noun] small and not very important or not very noticeable: *a slight problem* | *There's been a slight improvement in his health.* | *a slight increase in sales*
minor small and not important or not serious: *minor injuries* | *We've made some minor changes to the program.*
compact small – used about places, buildings etc in which space is used effectively, or about phones, cameras, cars etc which are designed to be much smaller than usual: *The apartments are very compact.* | *a compact camera*
poky *especially BrE* used about a room, house etc that is too small: *a poky bedroom* | *a poky flat*
cramped used about a space, room, or vehicle that is too small because people do not have enough room to move around: *They all lived together in a cramped apartment.* | *The car feels cramped with four adults in it.*

VERY SMALL

tiny very small – used about objects, numbers, or amounts: *a tiny island* | *Dairy foods provide your body with a tiny amount of vitamin D.*
teeny *informal* very small – used for emphasis: *I'll just have a teeny bit of cream.* | *There's just one teeny little problem.*
minute /maɪˈnjuːt $ -ˈnuːt/ extremely small and extremely difficult to see or notice: *They found minute traces of poison in his body.* | *The differences are minute.* | *minute creatures*
miniature a miniature camera, watch, railway etc is made in a very small size. A miniature horse, dog etc is bred to be a very small size: *The spy used a miniature camera.* | *the fashion for miniature pets*
microscopic extremely small and impossible to see without special equipment: *microscopic organisms* | *microscopic particles of dust*
minuscule /ˈmɪnəskjuːl/ extremely small in a surprising way: *She was wearing a minuscule bikini.* | *The threat from terrorism is minuscule compared to other risks in our lives.*

S

smart¹ /smɑːt $ smɑːrt/ ●●● S2 W2 *adj* (*comparative* **smarter**, *superlative* **smartest**)
1 INTELLIGENT *especially AmE* intelligent or sensible SYN **clever** OPP **stupid**: *The smart kids get good grades and go off to college.* | *I was smart enough to wait for a week.* | *His decision to become a director was a* ***smart move*** (=sensible thing to do).
2 DISRESPECTFUL trying to seem clever in a disrespectful way: *Don't* ***get smart with*** *me, young man.* | *He made some smart remark.*
3 NEAT *BrE* **a)** a smart person is wearing neat attractive clothes and has a generally tidy appearance SYN **sharp** *AmE* OPP **scruffy**: *You're* ***looking*** *very* ***smart***. **b)** smart clothes, buildings etc are clean, tidy, and attractive SYN **sharp** *AmE*: *a smart black suit* | *smart new offices*
4 FASHIONABLE *BrE* fashionable or used by fashionable people: *one of Bonn's smartest restaurants*
5 TECHNOLOGY smart machines, weapons, materials etc are controlled by computers and are designed to react in a suitable way depending on the situation → **smart bomb**: *smart weapons*
6 the smart money is on sb/sth used to say that a particular person or thing is likely to do something or be successful
7 QUICK *BrE* a smart movement is done quickly, especially with force: *a smart blow on the head* | *She set off* ***at a smart pace*** (=fairly fast). —**smartly** *adv*: *a smartly dressed young man* | *He turned smartly and walked away.* —**smartness** *n* [U]

smart² *v* [I] **1** to be upset because someone has hurt your feelings or offended you: **[+from]** *She was still smarting from the insult.* **2** if a part of your body smarts, it hurts with a stinging pain: *My eyes were smarting with the smoke.*
smart off *phr v AmE informal* to make funny rude remarks THESAURUS HURT

ˈsmart ˌalec, smart aleck *n* [C] *informal* someone who always says clever things or always has the right answer, in a way that is annoying

ˈsmart arse *BrE*, **ˈsmart ass** *AmE n* [C] *informal not polite* a smart alec —**smart-arse** *BrE*, **smart-ass** *AmE adj*: *smart-arse remarks*

ˈsmart bomb *n* [C] a bomb that is fired from an aircraft and uses a computer to hit a particular place

smart·book /ˈsmɑːtbʊk $ ˈsmɑːrt-/ *n* [C] a piece of equipment which works as a SMARTPHONE but is slightly larger and has a KEYBOARD

ˈsmart card *n* [C] a small plastic card with an electronic part that records and remembers information

ˈsmart drug *n* [C] a drug that is intended to improve your memory and ability to think

smart·en /ˈsmɑːtn $ ˈsmɑːr-/ *v*
smarten sth ↔ **up** *phr v especially BrE* **1 smarten yourself up** to make yourself look neat and tidy: *You'd better smarten yourself up.* **2** to make something look neater: *We need to smarten the place up a bit.* **3 smarten up your act/ideas** to improve the way you behave or do something: *The company needs to smarten up their act if they are to keep customers.*

smart·phone /ˈsmɑːtfəʊn $ ˈsmɑːrtfoʊn/ *n* [C] a MOBILE PHONE that is also a small computer and can connect to the Internet

smarts /smɑːts $ smɑːrts/ *n* [U] *AmE informal* intelligence: *If she had any smarts, she'd get rid of the guy.*

smart·y·pants /ˈsmɑːti ˌpænts $ ˈsmɑːr-/ *n* [C] *informal* someone who always says clever things or always has the right answer, in a slightly annoying way SYN **clever clogs** *BrE*

smash¹ /smæʃ/ ●●○ *v*
1 [I,T] to break into pieces violently or noisily, or to make something do this by dropping, throwing, or hitting it: *Vandals had smashed all the windows.* | *Firemen had to smash the lock to get in.* | *Several cups fell to the floor and* ***smashed to pieces***. → see picture at BREAK¹ THESAURUS BREAK
2 [I,T always + adv/prep] to hit an object or surface violently, or to make something do this: *A stolen car smashed into the bus.* | *He smashed his fist down on the table.*
3 smash a record to do something much faster, better etc than anyone has done before: *The film smashed all box office records.*
4 [T] to destroy something such as a political system or criminal organization: *Police say they have smashed a major crime ring.*
5 [T] to hit a high ball with a strong downward action, in tennis or similar games → see picture at TENNIS
smash sth ↔ **down** *phr v* to hit a door, wall etc violently so that it falls to the ground
smash sth ↔ **in** *phr v* to hit something so violently that you break it and make a hole in it: *The door had been smashed in.* | **smash sb's face/head in** (=hit someone hard in the face or head) *I'll smash his head in if he comes here again!*
smash sth ↔ **up** *phr v* to deliberately destroy something by hitting it: *Hooligans started smashing the place up.*

smash² *n* **1** [C] *BrE* a serious road or railway accident - used especially in newspapers SYN **crash**: *Young boy hurt in car smash.* **2** [C] (*also* **smash hit**) a new film, song etc which is very successful: *a box-office smash* (=a film which many people go to see at the cinema) **3** [C] a hard downward shot in tennis or similar games → see picture at TENNIS **4** [singular] the loud sound of something breaking: **[+of]** *He heard the smash of glass.*

ˌsmash-and-ˈgrab *adj BrE* **smash-and-grab raid/attack etc** a crime in which someone robs a shop by breaking the window and stealing things quickly —**smash and grab** *n* [C]

smashed /smæʃt/ *adj* [not before noun] *informal* very drunk or affected by a drug → **stoned**: *It's just an excuse to go out and* ***get smashed***.

smash·er /ˈsmæʃə $ -ər/ *n* [C] *BrE old-fashioned* someone who you think is very attractive, or something that is very good

ˈsmash hit *n* [C] a very successful new play, book, film etc: *They had a smash hit with their first single.*

smash·ing /ˈsmæʃɪŋ/ *adj BrE old-fashioned* very good SYN **brilliant**: *We had a smashing holiday.*

smat·ter·ing /ˈsmætərɪŋ/ *n* [singular] **1** a small number or amount of something: **[+of]** *a smattering of applause* **2 have a smattering of sth** to have a small amount of knowledge about a subject, especially a foreign language

SME /ˌes em ˈiː/ *n* [C] *especially BrE* (***small or medium enterprise***) a company whose TURNOVER and number of people working in it are lower than a particular amount

smear¹ /smɪə $ smɪr/ *n* [C] **1** a dirty mark made by a small amount of something spread across a surface: **[+of]** *a smear of paint* | *It left a black smear on his arm.* THESAURUS MARK **2** *BrE* a SMEAR TEST **3** an untrue story about a politician or other important person that is told in order to make people lose respect for them - used especially in newspapers —**smeary** *adj*: *a smeary glass*

smear² *v*
1 SPREAD [T always + adv/prep] to spread a liquid or soft substance over a surface, especially in a careless or untidy way: **smear sth with sth** *His face was smeared with mud.* | **smear sth on/over etc sth** *Elaine smeared suntan lotion on her shoulders.*
2 TELL LIES [T] to tell an untrue story about someone important in order to make people lose respect for them - used especially in newspapers: *an attempt to smear the party leadership*
3 DIRTY [T] to put dirty or oily marks on something: *smeared windows*
4 INK/PAINT [I,T] if writing, a picture, or paint smears or is smeared, the ink or paint is accidentally touched and spread across the surface SYN **smudge**: *Several words were smeared.*

ˈsmear camˌpaign *n* [C] a deliberate plan to tell untrue stories about an important person in order to make people lose respect for them - used especially in newspapers

ˈsmear test *n* [C] *BrE* a medical test in which some cells are removed from the entrance to a woman's WOMB (=the place where a baby grows) and examined under a microscope

smell¹ /smel/ ●●● S2 W3 *n*
1 [C] the quality that people and animals recognize by using their nose: **[+of]** *The air was filled with the smell of flowers.* | *What's that horrible smell?*
2 [C] an unpleasant smell: *I think the smell's getting worse.*
3 [U] the ability to notice or recognize smells: *loss of taste and smell* | *Dogs have a very good* ***sense of smell****.*
4 [C usually singular] an act of smelling something: ***Have a smell of*** *this cheese; does it seem all right?*

COLLOCATIONS

ADJECTIVES

strong *There was a strong smell of burning in the air.*
faint (=not strong) *I noticed a faint smell of perfume.*
overpowering (=very strong) *The smell of disinfectant was overpowering.*
nice/pleasant/lovely *There was a lovely smell of fresh coffee.*
bad/unpleasant/horrible etc *The smell in the shed was awful.*
a strange/funny/odd smell *What's that funny smell?*
a sweet smell | **a delicious smell** (=a pleasant smell of food) | **a sickly smell** (=sweet and unpleasant) | **a pungent smell** *formal* (=strong and unpleasant) | **an acrid smell** (=strong and bitter) | **a musty/stale/sour smell** (=old and not fresh)

VERBS

have a strong/sweet etc smell *The flowers had a lovely sweet smell.*
give off a smell (=produce a smell) *Rubber gives off a strong smell when it is burned.*
notice/smell a smell (*also* **detect a smell** *formal*) *He detected a faint smell of blood.*
a smell comes from somewhere (*also* **a smell emanates from somewhere** *formal*) *A delicious smell of baking came from the kitchen.*
a smell wafts somewhere (=moves there through the air)

COMMON ERRORS

⚠ Don't say 'feel the smell of sth'. Say **smell sth**.

THESAURUS

smell something that you can recognize by breathing in through your nose: *the smell from the kitchen* | *What's that awful smell?* | *the sweet smell of roses*
whiff something that you smell for a short time: *He caught a whiff of her perfume.* | *a whiff of apple blossom*
scent a smell – used especially about the pleasant smell from flowers, plants, or fruit. Also used about the smell left by an animal: *The rose had a beautiful scent.* | *Cats use their scent to mark their territory.*
fragrance/perfume a pleasant smell, especially from flowers, plants, or fruit. **Fragrance** and **perfume** are more formal than **scent**: *the sweet perfume of the orange blossoms* | *Each mango has its own special fragrance.*
aroma *formal* a pleasant smell from food or coffee: *the aroma of fresh coffee* | *The kitchen was filled with the aroma of mince pies.*
odour *BrE*, **odor** *AmE formal* an unpleasant smell: *An unpleasant odour was coming from the dustbins.* | *the odor of stale tobacco smoke*
pong *BrE informal* an unpleasant smell: *What's that horrible pong?*
stink/stench a very strong and unpleasant smell: *I couldn't get rid of the stink of sweat.* | *The toilet gave off a terrible stench.*

smell² ●●● S2 W3 *v* (*past tense and past participle* **smelled** *especially AmE or* **smelt** /smelt/ *BrE*)
1 NOTICE A SMELL [T] to notice or recognize a particular smell: **can smell sth** *I can smell burning.* | *Can you smell something?*
2 HAVE A SMELL [linking verb] to have a particular smell: **smell good/sweet/delicious/fresh etc** *The stew smelled delicious.* | *Mm! Something smells good!* | **smell bad/funny/awful etc** *The water smells funny.* | **smell of/like sth** *My clothes smelt of smoke.* | *It smells like rotten eggs.* | **sweet-smelling/foul-smelling etc** *sweet-smelling flowers*

GRAMMAR: Linking verbs

Smell is a linking verb in this meaning. It links the subject of the sentence with an adjective: *The cream smells funny* (=it has a strange smell).

3 HAVE A BAD SMELL [I] to have an unpleasant smell: *Your feet smell!* | *The room* ***smelled to high heaven*** (=had a very bad smell).
4 PUT YOUR NOSE NEAR STH [T] to put your nose near something in order to discover what kind of smell it has SYN **sniff**: *She bent down and smelt the flowers.*
5 HAVE ABILITY [I] to have the ability to notice and recognize smells: *I've got a cold and I can't smell.*
6 smell trouble/danger etc to feel that something is going to happen, especially something bad: *Miller had smelled trouble the moment she said who she was.*
7 smell a rat *informal* to guess that something wrong or dishonest is happening
8 smell wrong/fishy/odd etc *informal* to seem dishonest or untrue: *The whole thing is beginning to smell fishy to me.*
→ **come up/out smelling of roses** at ROSE¹(6)

GRAMMAR: Using the progressive

• The verb **smell** is not usually used in the progressive. You say: *I smell gas.* | *That smells nice.*
✗ Don't say: *I am smelling gas.* | *That is smelling nice.*
• You often say someone **can smell** something when describing what they smell: *I can smell gas.* | *I could smell her perfume.*
• The present participle **smelling** is used to form adjectives such as **sweet-smelling** and **foul-smelling**.
GRAMMAR GUIDE ▸ VERBS

smell sth ↔ **out** *phr v*
1 to find something by smelling SYN **sniff out**: *They use dogs trained to smell out explosives.*
2 *informal* to find or recognize something because you have a natural ability to do this SYN **sniff out**: *They'll be able to smell out any corruption.*

smel·lies /ˈsmeliz/ *n* [plural] *informal* PERFUME and bath products that have a nice smell: *I usually give my mum smellies for Christmas.*

ˈsmelling salts *n* [plural] a strong-smelling chemical that you hold under someone's nose to make them conscious again when they have FAINTED

smell·y /ˈsmeli/ *adj* (*comparative* **smellier**, *superlative* **smelliest**) having a strong unpleasant smell SYN **stinky**: *smelly feet* —**smelliness** *n* [U]

smelt¹ /smelt/ *BrE* a past tense and past participle of SMELL

smelt² *v* [T] to melt a rock that contains metal in order to remove the metal

smid·gin, **smidgen** /ˈsmɪdʒɪn/ (*also* **smidge** /smɪdʒ/) *n* [singular] *informal* a very small amount of something SYN **touch**: **[+of]** *I added just a smidgin of chilli sauce.*

smile¹ /smaɪl/ ●●● S3 W1 *v*
1 [I] to make your mouth curve upwards, in order to be friendly or because you are happy or amused: **[+at]** *Susan smiled at him and waved.* | *She had to smile at his enthusiasm* (=she was amused by it). | *her smiling face* | **[+about]** *I haven't had much to smile about lately.* | **smile to yourself** *Mark read the message and smiled to himself.*

GRAMMAR

You **smile at** someone: *They all smiled at me.* ✗ Don't say: *They all smiled to me.*

2 [T] to say or express something with a smile: *'It's good to have you back,' she smiled.*

S

3 fortune/the gods etc smile on sb *especially literary* if FORTUNE, the gods etc smile on you, you have good luck

THESAURUS

smile to make your mouth curve upwards, in order to be friendly or because you are happy or amused: *She smiled when she read his email.* | *'I'm delighted to meet you,' George said, smiling at the girl.*
grin to give a big smile: *The two boys were grinning at each other.* | *The coach was* ***grinning from ear to ear*** (=was grinning a lot) *when the team scored.*
beam to give a big happy smile for a long time, because you are very pleased or proud: *She beamed with pride as her son collected the award.* | *The wedding couple were outside beaming at the camera.*
smirk to smile in an unpleasant way, for example because you are pleased about someone else's bad luck or because you know something that someone else does not know: *The children smirked when the teacher dropped all the books on the floor.* | *What are you smirking about?*
simper *disapproving written* to smile in a silly and annoying way: *a group of simpering schoolgirls* | *I hated the way she simpered every time a man spoke to her.*

smile² ●●● S2 W2 *n* [C] an expression in which your mouth curves upwards, when you are being friendly or are happy or amused: *He had a big smile on his face.* | **with a smile** *'Oh, I'm fine,' Anna replied with a smile.* → **wipe the smile/grin off sb's face** at WIPE¹(7)

COLLOCATIONS

VERBS

give (sb) a smile *The boy gave a friendly smile.*
flash (sb) a smile (=give a quick smile) *She flashed him a smile.*
have a smile on your face/lips *They all had broad smiles on their faces.*
be all smiles (=be happy or friendly and smile a lot) *One moment he's all smiles, the next moment he shouts at me.*
force/manage a smile (=smile when you do not really feel happy or friendly) | **wear a smile** (=have a smile on your face) | **return sb's smile** (=smile back at someone) | **sb breaks into a smile/sb's face breaks into a smile** (=they suddenly smile) | **a smile spreads across sb's face** (=they smile) | **sb's smile broadens** (=it gets bigger) | **sb's smile fades/vanishes** (=they stop smiling)

ADJECTIVES

a big/broad/wide smile (=when you are very happy) *She had a big smile on her face.*
a warm/friendly smile *Peter Leary welcomed Rachel with a warm smile.*
a little/faint/slight smile *She gave him an apologetic little smile.*
a quick smile *She gave him a quick smile.*
a slow smile *A slow smile spread across his face.*
a dazzling smile (=a big smile which shows someone's white teeth) | **a beaming/radiant smile** (=when you are very happy) | **a bright smile** *written* (=when you look very happy, but you may not feel happy) | **a tight smile** *written* (=when you are not really happy or friendly) | **a wry smile** *written* (=when a situation is bad but also amusing) | **a rueful smile** *written* (=when you feel slightly sad) | **a knowing smile** (=when you know something secret)

S

smile·y /ˈsmaɪli/ *n* [C] a sign that looks like a face when you look at it sideways, for example :-), used in email messages to show that you are happy or pleased about something

smil·ing·ly /ˈsmaɪlɪŋli/ *adv* done or said with a smile: *'Of course,' she replied smilingly.*

smirk /smɜːk $ smɜːrk/ *v* [I] to smile in an unpleasant way that shows that you are pleased by someone else's bad luck or think you are better than other people: *The boys tried not to smirk.* | **[+at]** *What are you smirking at?* —**smirk** *n* [C]: *He had a self-satisfied smirk on his face.*

smite /smaɪt/ *v* (*past tense* **smote** /sməʊt $ smoʊt/, *past participle* **smitten** /ˈsmɪtn/) [T] **1** *old use* to hit something with a lot of force **2** *biblical* to destroy, attack, or punish someone

smith /smɪθ/ *n* [C] someone who makes and repairs things made of iron SYN **blacksmith**

-smith /smɪθ/ *suffix* [in nouns] a maker of something: *a gunsmith* (=someone who makes guns) | *a wordsmith* (=someone who works with words, for example a journalist)

smith·e·reens /ˌsmɪðəˈriːnz/ *n* [plural] **smash/blow etc sth to smithereens** *informal* to destroy something by breaking it into very small pieces, or with an explosion: *The shop was blown to smithereens by the explosion.*

smith·y /ˈsmɪði $ -θi, -ði/ *n* (*plural* **smithies**) [C] a place where iron objects such as HORSESHOES were made and repaired in the past

smitten¹ /ˈsmɪtn/ *v* the past participle of SMITE

smit·ten² *adj* [not before noun] **1** suddenly feeling that you love someone very much: *As soon as he saw her, he was smitten.* | **[+by/with]** *She was totally smitten with Steve.* **2 smitten with/by sth** suddenly affected by an illness or a feeling: *Dan was smitten with remorse.* | *The whole family were smitten with flu.*

smock /smɒk $ smɑːk/ *n* [C] **1** a long loose shirt or a loose dress **2** a loose piece of clothing worn by artists or other workers to protect their other clothing

smock·ing /ˈsmɒkɪŋ $ ˈsmɑː-/ *n* [U] a type of decoration made on cloth by pulling the cloth into small regular folds held tightly with stitches

smog /smɒg $ smɑːg, smɒːg/ ●○○ *n* [C,U] dirty air that looks like a mixture of smoke and FOG, caused by smoke from cars and factories in cities —**smoggy** *adj*

smoke¹ /sməʊk $ smoʊk/ ●●● S1 W2 *n*
1 [U] white, grey, or black gas that is produced by something burning: ***clouds of*** *black* ***smoke*** | *cigarette smoke* | *Smoke from burning fields drifted across nearby roads.* | *the* ***pall of smoke*** (=thick cloud of smoke) *that hung over the city* | **wisp/puff of smoke** (=a small amount of smoke) *Rangers watched from their fire towers for any wisps of smoke.*
2 [C usually singular] an act of smoking a cigarette etc: *He went outside for a quiet smoke.*
3 go up in smoke a) if something goes up in smoke, it burns so that it is completely destroyed: *The whole factory went up in smoke.* **b)** *informal* if a plan or some work goes up in smoke, it fails or you cannot continue with it: *We haven't worked this long just to see everything go up in smoke.*
4 [C] *spoken* a cigarette or drugs that are smoked: *Where are the smokes, Jeff?*
5 there's no smoke without fire (*also* **where there's smoke there's fire**) *spoken* used to say that if something bad is being said about someone, it is probably partly true
6 when the smoke clears when things have stopped happening and the results can be clearly seen: *When the smoke clears, I think you'll find the company is in a stronger position.*
7 the Smoke *BrE old-fashioned informal* London or any large town or city

smoke² ●●● S2 W2 *v*
1 [I,T] to suck or breathe in smoke from a cigarette, pipe etc or to do this regularly as a habit: *I don't smoke and I don't drink much.* | *Do you mind if I smoke?* | *He sat on the grass smoking a cigarette.* | *He admitted that he had smoked marijuana when he was a student.*
2 [I] if something smokes, it has smoke coming from it: *a smoking chimney*
3 [T] to give fish or meat a special taste by hanging it in smoke

smoke sb/sth ↔ **out** *phr v*
1 to fill a place with smoke in order to force someone or something to come out: *He smoked the bees out of their nest.*
2 to discover who is causing a particular problem and force them to make themselves known: *an operation to smoke out double agents*

ˈ**smoke aˌlarm** (*also* **smoke detector**) *n* [C] a piece of electronic equipment which warns you when there is smoke or fire in a building: *The smoke alarm went off.*

ˈ**smoke bomb** *n* [C] something that lets out clouds of smoke when it is thrown, used especially by police to control crowds

smoked /sməʊkt $ smoʊkt/ *adj* **smoked salmon/bacon/sausage etc** fish, meat etc that has been left in smoke to give it a special taste

ˈ**smoke deˌtector** *n* [C] a SMOKE ALARM

ˌ**smoked ˈglass** *n* [U] glass that is a dark grey colour

ˌ**smoke-filled ˈroom** *n* [C] used to talk about a place where plans or decisions are made secretly by a small group of powerful people rather than in an open way – used especially in newspapers

ˌ**smoke-ˈfree** *adj* **smoke-free environment/zone etc** a place where people are not allowed to smoke SYN **non-smoking**: *new laws to create a smoke-free environment at work*

smoke·less /ˈsməʊkləs $ ˈsmoʊk-/ *adj* **1 smokeless coal/fuel** FUEL that burns without producing smoke **2 smokeless tobacco** tobacco that you chew rather than smoke

smok·er /ˈsməʊkə $ ˈsmoʊkər/ ●●○ *n* [C] someone who smokes cigarettes, CIGARS etc OPP **non-smoker**: *My grandad was a* ***heavy smoker*** (=someone who smokes a lot). | *He had a* ***smoker's cough*** (=a cough caused by smoking cigarettes regularly).

smoke·screen /ˈsməʊkskriːn $ ˈsmoʊk-/ *n* [C] **1** something that you do or say to hide your real plans or actions: *a government that rules behind a smokescreen of democracy* **2** a cloud of smoke produced so that it hides soldiers, ships etc during a battle

ˈ**smoke ˌsignal** *n* [C] a message sent out to people who are far away, using the smoke from a fire, used especially by Native Americans in past times

smoke·stack /ˈsməʊkstæk $ ˈsmoʊk-/ *n* [C] a tall CHIMNEY at a factory or on a ship

ˈ**smokestack ˌindustry** *n* [C usually plural] a big traditional industry such as car making

smok·ing /ˈsməʊkɪŋ $ ˈsmoʊk-/ ●●● S2 *n* [U] the activity of breathing in tobacco smoke from a cigarette, pipe etc: **stop/quit/give up smoking** *I gave up smoking nearly ten years ago.* | *The sign says 'No Smoking'.* | *a no smoking area* | *the risks of* ***passive smoking*** (=breathing in smoke from other people's cigarettes)

ˌ**smoking ˈgun** *n* [C] something that shows who is responsible for something bad or how something really happened

ˈ**smoking ˌjacket** *n* [C] a formal jacket that men wore after dinner in the past

ˈ**smoking room** (*also* ˈ**smoking lounge** *AmE*) *n* [C] a room where smoking is allowed in a public building

smok·y /ˈsməʊki $ ˈsmoʊ-/ *adj* **1** filled with smoke: *a smoky room* **2** producing too much smoke: *a smoky engine* **3** having the taste, smell, or appearance of smoke: *smoky green eyes* | *a smoky flavour* —**smokiness** *n* [U]

smol·der /ˈsməʊldə $ ˈsmoʊldər/ *v* [I] the American spelling of SMOULDER

smooch /smuːtʃ/ *v* [I + with] *informal* if two people smooch, they kiss and hold each other in a romantic way, especially while dancing

smooch·y /ˈsmuːtʃi/ *adj BrE informal* a smoochy song is slow and romantic

smooth¹ /smuːð/ ●●● W3 *adj* (*comparative* **smoother**, *superlative* **smoothest**)

1 SURFACE a smooth surface has no rough parts, lumps, or holes, especially in a way that is pleasant and attractive to touch OPP **rough**: *Her skin felt smooth and cool.* | *a smooth pebble* | *The stone steps had been* ***worn smooth***. THESAURUS ▸ FLAT

2 HAPPENING WITHOUT PROBLEMS happening or operating successfully, without any problems: **smooth running/operation** *Sarah is responsible for the smooth running of the sales department.* | *The new government has promised a smooth transition of power.* → **go smoothly** at SMOOTHLY(2)

3 MOVEMENT [only before noun] with no sudden movements or changes of direction, especially in a way that is graceful or comfortable: *Swing the tennis racket in one smooth motion.* | *The jet made a smooth landing.* | **smooth flight/ride** (=a comfortable trip in an airplane or car) *It wasn't a very smooth ride.* THESAURUS ▸ COMFORTABLE

4 PERSON someone who is smooth is polite, confident, and relaxed, but is often not sincere: *a smooth salesman* | *He was a* ***smooth talker***. | *George is a* ***smooth operator*** (=someone who does things in a smooth way).

5 LIQUID MIXTURE a liquid mixture that is smooth has no big pieces in it OPP **lumpy**: *Beat the eggs and flour until they are smooth.*

6 SOUND a voice or music that is smooth is soft and pleasant to listen to: *smooth jazz* | *He has one of those* ***silky smooth*** (=very smooth) *voices.*

7 TASTE a drink such as wine, coffee, WHISKY, or beer that is smooth is not bitter but tastes pleasant: *a smooth full-bodied wine* —**smoothness** *n* [U]: *the smoothness of his skin* → SMOOTH-TALKING

smooth² ●●○ *v* [T]

1 to make something such as cloth or hair flat by moving your hands across it: *Liz smoothed her skirt and sat down.* | **smooth sth back/down** *She smoothed back her hair.*

2 (*also* **smooth down**) to make a rough surface flat and even: *The wood was smoothed and trimmed to size.* | *Smooth down all the surfaces before you start painting.*

3 [always + adv/prep] to rub a liquid, cream etc gently over a surface or into a surface: **smooth sth into/over sth** *She smoothed suntan lotion over her legs.*

4 smooth the way/path for sth to make it easier for something to happen, by dealing with any problems first: *Staff helped smooth the way for the new administration.*

smooth sth ↔ **away** *phr v* to get rid of problems or difficulties: *A few objections have to be smoothed away before we can start the project.*

smooth sth ↔ **out** *phr v*

1 to make something such as paper or cloth flat by moving your hands across it: *They smoothed out the map on the table.* | *Smooth out all the wrinkles.*

2 to make something happen in an even regular way: *Sometimes central banks intervene to smooth out price fluctuations.*

3 to get rid of problems or difficulties

smooth sth ↔ **over** *phr v* if you smooth over problems, difficulties etc, you make them seem less serious and easier to control, especially by talking to the people who are involved in the problem: *Sally managed to smooth over the bad feelings between them.*

smooth·ie /ˈsmuːði/ *n* [C] **1** *informal* someone who is confident and attractive, but is often not sincere: *Kyle's a* ***real smoothie***. **2** a thick drink made of fruit and fruit juices mixed together, sometimes with ice, milk, or YOGHURT: *a strawberry-banana smoothie*

smooth·ly /ˈsmuːðli/ ●○○ *adv*

1 in a steady way, without stopping and starting again: *Traffic flowed smoothly.*

2 if a planned event, piece of work etc goes smoothly, there are no problems to spoil it: *It'll take about three hours if everything* ***goes smoothly***. | *Donna keeps the office* ***running smoothly***.

3 if you say something smoothly, you say it in a calm and confident way: *'All taken care of,' he said smoothly.*

4 in a way that produces a smooth surface: *The jacket fit smoothly over her hips.*

ˈ**smooth-ˌtalking** *adj* a smooth-talking person is good at persuading people and saying nice things, but you do not trust them: *a smooth-talking salesman*

smor·gas·bord /ˈsmɔːgəsbɔːd $ ˈsmɔːrgəsbɔːrd/ *n* **1 a smorgasbord of sth** a large variety of different things: *a smorgasbord of art from around the world* **2** [C,U] a meal in which people serve themselves from a large number of different dishes SYN **buffet**

smote /sməʊt $ smoʊt/ *v* the past tense of SMITE

S

smoth·er /ˈsmʌðə $ -ər/ *v* [T] **1** to completely cover the whole surface of something with something else, often in a way that seems unnecessary or unpleasant: **smother sth with/in sth** *noodles smothered in garlic sauce* **2** to kill someone by putting something over their face to stop them breathing → **suffocate**: *A teenage mother was accused of smothering her 3-month-old daughter.* **3** to stop yourself from showing your feelings or from doing an action SYN **stifle**: *The girls tried to smother their giggles.* **4** to give someone so much love and attention that they feel as if they are not free and become unhappy: *I don't want him to feel smothered.* **5 smother sb with kisses** to kiss someone a lot **6** to make a fire stop burning by preventing air from reaching it: *We used a wet towel to smother the fire.* **7** to get rid of anyone who opposes you – used to show disapproval: *They ruthlessly smother all opposition.*

smoul·der *BrE*, **smolder** *AmE* /ˈsməʊldə $ ˈsmoʊldər/ *v* [I] **1** if something such as wood smoulders, it burns slowly without a flame THESAURUS ▸ BURN **2** *literary* if someone smoulders, or if their feelings smoulder, they have strong feelings that they do not fully express: *He sensed a smouldering hostility towards him.* | **[+with]** *She had spent the evening smouldering with resentment.*

SMS /ˌes em ˈes/ *n* [U] (***short messaging system*** or ***short message service***) a feature on a MOBILE PHONE that allows a user to send or receive written messages

smudge¹ /smʌdʒ/ *n* [C] a dirty mark SYN **smear**: **[+of]** *a smudge of lipstick on the cup* THESAURUS ▸ MARK —**smudgy** *adj*

smudge² *v* **1** [I,T] if ink, writing etc smudges, or if you smudge it, it becomes dirty and unclear because it has been touched or rubbed: *Don't touch it! You'll smudge the ink.* **2** [T] to make a dirty mark on a surface: *Someone had smudged the paper with their greasy hands.*

smug /smʌg/ *adj* showing too much satisfaction with your own cleverness or success – used to show disapproval SYN **self-satisfied**: **[+about]** *What are you looking so smug about?* | **smug expression/look/face/smile etc** *'I knew I'd win,' she said with a smug smile.* THESAURUS ▸ PROUD —**smugly** *adv* —**smugness** *n* [U]

smug·gle /ˈsmʌgəl/ ●○○ *v* [T]
1 to take something or someone illegally from one country to another: **smuggle sth across sth** *The guns were smuggled across the border.* | **smuggle sth into/out of/from sth** *Illegal immigrants are smuggled into the country by boat.*
2 *informal* to take something or someone secretly to a place where they are not allowed to be: **smuggle sth into sth** *He smuggled his notes into the exam.*

smug·gler /ˈsmʌgələ $ -ər/ *n* [C] someone who takes something illegally from one country to another: *a drug smuggler*

smug·gling /ˈsmʌgəlɪŋ/ *n* [U] the crime of taking something illegally from one country to another: *He was arrested in connection with drug smuggling.*

smut /smʌt/ *n* **1** [U] books, stories, talk etc that offend some people because they are about sex: *I won't have smut like that in my house!* **2** [C,U] dirt or SOOT (=black powder produced by burning), or a piece of dirt or soot

smut·ty /ˈsmʌti/ *adj* **1** books, stories etc that are smutty offend some people because they are about sex SYN **dirty**: *smutty jokes* **2** marked with small pieces of dirt or SOOT

snack¹ /snæk/ ●●● S2 *n* [C] a small amount of food that is eaten between main meals or instead of a meal: *I grabbed a quick snack.* | *Drinks and* ***light snacks*** *are served at the bar.* | ***snack foods*** *like crisps and peanuts*

snack² /snæk/ *v* [I] to eat small amounts of food between main meals or instead of a meal: *I'm trying not to snack between meals.*

ˈsnack bar *n* [C] a place where you can buy snacks or small meals

snaf·fle /ˈsnæfəl/ *v* [T] *BrE informal* to take something quickly, especially before anyone else has had the time or the chance to do this SYN **grab**: *I managed to snaffle a couple of biscuits.*

sna·fu /snæˈfuː/ *n* [C] *AmE informal* a situation in which a plan does not happen in the way it should: *There were no major snafus.*

snag¹ /snæg/ *n* [C] **1** a problem or disadvantage, especially one that is not very serious, which you had not expected: *It's an interesting job.* ***The*** *only* ***snag is that*** *it's not very well paid.* | **hit/run into a snag** *The grand opening hit a snag when no one could find the key.* THESAURUS ▸ PROBLEM

> **REGISTER**
> **Snag** is slightly informal. In written English, people usually prefer to use **problem** or **disadvantage** instead: *The only* ***disadvantage*** *is that it takes a little longer.*

2 a part of a dead tree that sticks out, especially one that is under water and can be dangerous **3** a sharp part of something that sticks out and holds or cuts things that touch it

snag² *v* (**snagged**, **snagging**) [T] **1** to damage something by getting it stuck on something sharp: *Oh no! I've snagged my stockings.* **2** *AmE informal* to succeed in getting something, especially something difficult to get: *I snagged a parking space in the last row.*

ˈsnagging list *n* [C] a list of small but important jobs that remain to be done on a new building, and which have to be done before the building is considered to be completely finished

snag·gle-toothed /ˈsnægəl tuːθt/ *adj* a snaggle-toothed person has uneven or broken teeth

snail /sneɪl/ ●○○ *n* [C]
1 a small soft creature that moves very slowly and has a hard shell on its back
2 at a snail's pace extremely slowly: *Traffic was moving at a snail's pace.*

ˈsnail mail *n* [U] the system of sending letters by post, as opposed to using email – used humorously

snake¹ /sneɪk/ ●●● W3 *n* [C]
1 an animal with a long thin body and no legs, that often has a poisonous bite: *A snake slithered across our path.* | **a poisonous/venomous snake** → see picture at REPTILE
2 (*also* **snake in the grass**) *informal* someone who cannot be trusted

snake² *v* [I,T always + adv/prep] if a river, road, train, or line snakes somewhere, it moves in long twisting curves SYN **wind**: **[+along/past/down etc]** *The road snaked along the valley far below.* | *The train was* ***snaking its way*** *through the mountains.*

snake·bite /ˈsneɪkbaɪt/ *n* [C,U] the bite of a poisonous snake

ˈsnake ˌcharmer *n* [C] someone who controls snakes by playing music to them, in order to entertain people

ˈsnake eyes *n* [plural] *informal* a situation in a game in which a pair of DICE both show one spot

ˈsnake oil *n* [U] *especially AmE informal* **1** something that is claimed to be a solution to a problem, but is not effective **2 snake oil salesman/peddler** someone who deceives people by persuading them to accept false information, solutions that are not effective etc

snake·skin /ˈsneɪkˌskɪn/ *n* [U] the skin of a snake used to make shoes, bags etc: *snakeskin shoes*

snap¹ /snæp/ ●●● W3 *v* (**snapped**, **snapping**)
1 BREAK [I,T] to break with a sudden sharp noise, or to make something do this: *A twig snapped under my feet.* | *The wind snapped branches and power lines.* | **snap (sth) off (sth)** *I snapped the ends off the beans and dropped them into a bowl.* | **snap (sth) in two/in half** (=break into two pieces) *The teacher snapped the chalk in two and gave me a piece.* → see picture at BREAK¹ THESAURUS ▸ BREAK

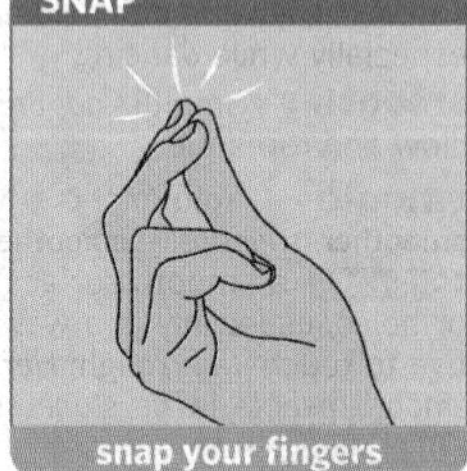

2 MOVE INTO POSITION [I,T always + adv/prep] to move into a particular position suddenly, making a short sharp noise, or to make something move like this: **[+together/back etc]** *The pieces just snap together like this.* | *The policeman snapped the handcuffs around her wrist.* | **snap (sth) open/shut** *She snapped her briefcase shut.*
3 SAY STH ANGRILY [I,T] to say something quickly in an angry way: *'What do you want?' Mike snapped.* | **[+at]** *He snapped at Walter for no reason.*
4 BECOME ANGRY/ANXIOUS ETC [I] to suddenly stop being able to control your anger, anxiety, or other feelings in a difficult situation: *The stress began to get to her, and one morning she just snapped.* | ***Something*** *inside him* ***snapped****, and he hit her.*
5 ANIMAL [I] if an animal such as a dog snaps, it tries to bite you: **[+at]** *The dog started snapping at my heels.*
6 PHOTOGRAPH [I,T] *informal* to take a photograph: *Dave snapped a picture of me and Sonia.*
7 snap your fingers to make a short sharp noise by moving one of your fingers quickly against your thumb, for example in order to get someone's attention or to mark the beat of music
8 snap to it *spoken* used to tell someone to hurry and do something immediately: *Come on, snap to it – get that room cleaned up!*
9 STOP [T] *AmE* to end a series of events – used especially in newspapers: *The Rockets snapped a seven-game losing streak by beating Portland.*
10 snap to attention if soldiers snap to attention, they suddenly stand very straight → SNAP-ON
snap on/off *phr v* to switch something on or off, or to switch on or off: *A light snapped on in one of the huts.* | **snap sth ↔ on/off** *Kathy snapped off the light.*
snap out of sth *phr v* to stop being sad or upset and make yourself feel better: *Chantal's been depressed for days. I wish she'd* ***snap out of it****.*
snap sb/sth ↔ **up** *phr v*
1 to buy something immediately, especially because it is very cheap: *People were snapping up bargains.*
2 to eagerly take an opportunity to have someone as part of your company, team etc: *Owen was snapped up by Liverpool before he'd even left school.*

snap² *n*
1 SOUND [singular] a sudden loud sound, especially made by something breaking or closing: *He shut the book with a snap.*
2 PHOTOGRAPH [C] *especially BrE informal* a photograph taken quickly and often not very skilfully SYN **snapshot**: *holiday snaps*
3 be a snap *AmE informal* to be very easy to do: *The test was a snap.*
4 CLOTHING [C] *AmE* a small metal fastener on clothes that works when you press its two parts together SYN **press stud** *BrE*: *baby clothing with snaps*
5 a snap of sb's fingers a sudden sound made by quickly moving one of your fingers against your thumb: *At a snap of his owner's fingers, the dog came running.*
6 GAME [U] a card game in which players put down one card after another and try to be the first to shout 'Snap!' when there are two cards that are the same → COLD SNAP

snap³ *adj* **1 snap judgment/decision** a judgment or decision made quickly, without careful thought or discussion **2 snap election** *BrE* an election that is announced suddenly and unexpectedly

snap⁴ *interjection* **1** *BrE* used when you see two things that are exactly the same: *Hey, snap! My hat's the same as yours.* **2** said in the game of snap when two cards that are the same are put down

snap·drag·on /ˈsnæpˌdræɡən/ *n* [C] a garden plant with white, red, or yellow flowers

ˈ**snap-on** *adj* [only before noun] a snap-on part of something can be fastened on and removed easily

snap·per /ˈsnæpə $ -ər/ *n* [C] a type of fish that lives in warm seas, often used as food

snap·py /ˈsnæpi/ *adj* **1** a snappy title or phrase is short, clear, and often funny: *We need a snappy title for the book.* | *Keep your answer* ***short and snappy****.* **2** *especially BrE* quick to react in an angry way SYN **irritable**: *She seemed snappy and impatient.* | **[+with]** *There's no need to be so snappy with the children.* **3 make it snappy** (*also* **look snappy** *BrE*) *informal* used to tell someone to hurry: *Get me a drink, and make it snappy.* **4** *BrE informal* snappy clothes, objects etc are attractive and fashionable: *a snappy suit* | **snappy dresser** (=someone who wears fashionable clothes) —**snappily** *adv*

snap·shot /ˈsnæpʃɒt $ -ʃɑːt/ *n* [C] **1** a photograph taken quickly and often not very skilfully SYN **snap**: **[+of]** *a snapshot of his girlfriend* **2** a piece of information that quickly gives you an idea of what the situation is like at a particular time: **[+of]** *The book* ***gives*** *us a* ***snapshot*** *of life in the Middle Ages.*

snare¹ /sneə $ sner/ *n* [C] **1** a trap for catching an animal, especially one that uses a wire or rope to catch the animal by its foot: *A rabbit was caught in the snare.* **2** *literary* something that is intended to trick someone and get them into a difficult situation SYN **trap**: *I didn't want to* ***fall into*** *the same* ***snare*** *again.*

snare² *v* [T] **1** to catch an animal by using a snare **2** to get something or someone you want in a clever way, often by deceiving other people: *She's hoping to snare a wealthy husband.*

ˈ**snare drum** *n* [C] a small flat drum that makes a hard continuous sound when you hit it

snarf /snɑːf $ snɑːrf/ (*also* **snarf down**) *v* [T] *AmE informal* to eat something quickly, especially in an untidy or noisy way: *workers snarfing lunch at their desks*

snar·ky /ˈsnɑːki $ ˈsnɑːr-/ *adj especially AmE informal* annoyed, or saying rude things in an annoyed or SARCASTIC way —**snark** *n* [U]: *His TV reviews are full of snark in a highly amusing way.*

snarl /snɑːl $ snɑːrl/ *v* **1** [I] if an animal snarls, it makes a low angry sound and shows its teeth → **growl**: **[+at]** *The dog growled and snarled at me.* **2** [I,T] to speak or say something in a nasty, angry way: *'Shut up,' he snarled.* **THESAURUS** SAY **3** [T] (*also* **snarl up** *BrE*) to prevent traffic from moving: *The traffic was snarled up on both sides of the road.* —**snarl** *n* [C]: *an angry snarl*

ˈ**snarl-up** *n* [C] *BrE* **1** a confused situation that prevents work from continuing **2** a situation in which traffic is prevented from moving → **congestion**: *There was a big snarl-up on the M1.*

snatch¹ /snætʃ/ ●○○ *v* [T]
1 to take something away from someone with a quick, often violent, movement SYN **grab**: *The thief snatched her purse and ran.* | **snatch sth away/back from sb** *Keith snatches toys away from the other children.*
2 to take someone away from a person or place, especially by force: *Vargas was snatched from his home by two armed men.*
3 to quickly get something, especially sleep or rest, because you do not have very much time SYN **grab**: *I managed to snatch an hour's sleep on the train.*
snatch at sth *phr v* to quickly put out your hand to try to take or hold something: *Jessie snatched at the bag but I pulled it away.*

snatch² *n* [C] **1 a snatch of conversation/music/song etc** a short part of a conversation, song etc that you hear: *I could hear snatches of the conversation from across the room.* **2 in snatches** for short periods: *I only slept in snatches during the night.* **3** when someone quickly takes or steals something: *reports of a bag snatch* **4** *taboo informal* a very offensive word for a woman's sex organ. Do not use this word.

ˈ**snatch squad** *n* [C] a group of police officers or soldiers who go quickly into a crowd in order to catch people who are causing trouble

snaz·zy /ˈsnæzi/ *adj informal* bright, fashionable, and attractive: *a snazzy red jacket* —**snazzily** *adv* —**snazziness** *n* [U]

S

sneak¹ /sniːk/ ●○○ *v* (*past tense and past participle* **sneaked** *or* **snuck** /snʌk/ *AmE*)
1 GO SECRETLY [I always + adv/prep] to go somewhere secretly and quietly in order to avoid being seen or heard SYN **creep**: **[+in/out/away etc]** *They sneaked off without paying!* | *She snuck out of the house once her parents were asleep.* THESAURUS ➤ WALK
2 TAKE/GIVE SECRETLY [T] to hide something and take it somewhere or give it to someone secretly: *I snuck her a note.* | **sneak sth through/past etc sb/sth** *Douglas had sneaked his camera into the show.*
3 sneak a look/glance/peek to look at something quickly and secretly, especially something that you are not supposed to see: *He sneaked a look at her.*
4 STEAL [T] *informal* to quickly and secretly steal something unimportant or of little value: **sneak sth from sb** *We used to sneak cigarettes from Dad.*
sneak on sb *phr v BrE old-fashioned informal* to tell someone such as a parent or teacher about something that another person has done wrong, because you want to cause trouble for that person: *A little brat named Oliver sneaked on me.*
sneak up *phr v* to come near someone very quietly, so that they do not see you until you reach them: **[+on/behind etc]** *I wish you wouldn't sneak up on me like that!*

sneak² *n* [C] **1** *BrE informal* a child who other children dislike, because they tell adults about bad things that the other children have done: *You little sneak!* **2** *AmE informal* someone who is not liked because they do things secretly and cannot be trusted

sneak³ *adj* [only before noun] doing things very secretly and quickly, so that people do not notice you or cannot stop you: *a sneak attack* | *a sneak thief*

sneak·er /ˈsniːkə $ -ər/ ●●○ *n* [C] *especially AmE* a type of light soft shoe with a rubber SOLE (=bottom), used for sports → **plimsoll**: *a pair of white sneakers* → see picture at SHOE¹

S

sneak·ing /ˈsniːkɪŋ/ *adj* **have a sneaking feeling/suspicion/admiration** to have a feeling about something or someone, but to not say anything about it because you are not sure or you might be embarrassed: *I always had a sneaking admiration for him.* | *She had a sneaking suspicion that he was lying.*

ˌsneak ˈpreview *n* [C] an occasion when you can see a film, play, product etc before it is shown to people in general: *In this week's show, we'll be giving you a sneak preview of Steven Spielberg's latest film.*

sneak·y /ˈsniːki/ ●○○ *adj* doing things in a secret and often dishonest or unfair way SYN **underhand**: *a sneaky little trick* THESAURUS ➤ DISHONEST —**sneakily** *adv* —**sneakiness** *n* [U]

sneer¹ /snɪə $ snɪr/ *v* [I,T] to smile or speak in a very unkind way that shows you have no respect for someone or something: *'Is that your best outfit?' he sneered.* | **[+at]** *She sneered at Tom's musical tastes.* —**sneering** *adj*: *a sneering tone* —**sneeringly** *adv*

sneer² *n* [C] an unkind smile or remark that shows you have no respect for something or someone: *'You probably wouldn't understand,' he said with a sneer.*

sneeze¹ /sniːz/ ●●● S3 *v* [I]
1 if you sneeze, air suddenly comes from your nose, making a noise, for example when you have a cold: *She started coughing and sneezing.* | *The dust was* **making** *him* **sneeze**.
2 not to be sneezed at *BrE*, **nothing to sneeze at** *AmE spoken* used about an offer, especially of money, that is very good, and which you should consider carefully: *In those days, £5 an hour was not to be sneezed at.*

sneeze² *n* [C] the act or sound of sneezing: *There was a loud sneeze from someone in the back of the audience.*

snick·er /ˈsnɪkə $ -ər/ *v* [I] *AmE* to laugh quietly and in a way that is not nice at something which is not supposed to be funny SYN **snigger** *BrE*: **[+at]** *The other students snickered at Steve.* —**snicker** *n* [C]: *a barely hidden snicker*

snide /snaɪd/ *adj informal* if you say something snide, you say something unkind, often in a clever indirect way: **snide remarks/comments** *a snide remark about her clothes* —**snidely** *adv*

sniff¹ /snɪf/ ●●○ *v*
1 [I] to breathe air into your nose noisily, for example when you are crying or have a cold: *Margaret sniffed miserably and nodded.* | *Stop sniffing and blow your nose.*
2 [I,T] to breathe air in through your nose in order to smell something: *He opened the milk and sniffed it.* | **[+at]** *The dog was sniffing at the carpet.*
3 [T] to say something in a way that shows you think something is not good enough: *'Is that all?' she sniffed.*
4 [T] to take a harmful drug by breathing it up your nose → **snort**: *kids who sniff glue*
sniff at sth *phr v*
1 sth is not to be sniffed at *spoken* used to say that something is good enough to be accepted or considered seriously: *An 8% salary increase is not to be sniffed at.*
2 to refuse something in a proud way, or behave as if something is not good enough for you: *He sniffed at my choice of restaurants and suggested his own favorite.*
sniff sth ↔ **out** *phr v*
1 to discover or find something by its smell: *A customs officer came round with a dog to sniff out drugs.*
2 *informal* to find out or discover something: *Vic's been trying to sniff out where you went last night.*

sniff² *n* [C] **1** when you breathe in air noisily through your nose, for example in order to smell something, because you have a cold, or in order to show your disapproval: *a sniff of disapproval* | *She* **gave** *a loud* **sniff**. **2** *BrE informal* a small amount or sign of something SYN **hint**: **[+of]** *He got us into this mess, and then left* **at** *the first* **sniff of trouble**! **3 have a sniff around/round** *BrE informal* to examine a place carefully **4 not get a sniff of sth** *BrE informal* to not have any chance of getting something or being successful: *He never even got a sniff of the target.*

ˈsniffer dog *n* [C] *BrE* a dog that has been trained to find drugs or explosives by using its sense of smell

snif·fle¹ /ˈsnɪfəl/ *v* [I] *spoken* to keep sniffing in order to stop liquid from running out of your nose, especially when you are crying or you have a cold: *For goodness' sake, stop sniffling!*

sniffle² *n* **have the sniffles** *spoken* if you have the sniffles, you keep sniffing, especially because you have a cold

sniff·y /ˈsnɪfi/ *adj BrE informal* having a disapproving attitude towards something or someone, especially because you think they are not good enough for you: **[+about]** *Well, don't* **get sniffy** *about it!*

snif·ter /ˈsnɪftə $ -ər/ *n* [C] **1** *AmE* a special large glass for drinking BRANDY **2** *BrE old-fashioned* a small amount of an alcoholic drink

snig·ger /ˈsnɪgə $ -ər/ *v* [I] *BrE* to laugh quietly in a way that is not nice at something which is not supposed to be funny SYN **snicker** *AmE*: **[+at]** *What are you sniggering at? This is a serious poem.* THESAURUS ➤ LAUGH —**snigger** *n* [C]

snip¹ /snɪp/ *v* (**snipped**, **snipping**) [I,T] to cut something by making quick cuts with scissors: *I snipped the string and untied the parcel.* | **snip sth off** (=remove it by snipping) *Snip the ends of the beans off before you cook them.* THESAURUS ➤ CUT

snip² *n* [C] **1** a quick small cut with scissors **2 be a snip** *BrE informal* to be surprisingly cheap: *At £20 for a dozen, they're a snip.*

snipe¹ /snaɪp/ *v* [I] **1** to shoot from a hidden position at people who are not protected: **[+at]** *soldiers sniping at civilians* **2** to criticize someone in a nasty way: **[+at]** *His former associates have been sniping at him in the press.* —**sniping** *n* [U]

snipe² *n* [C] a bird with a very long thin beak that lives in wet areas

snip·er /ˈsnaɪpə $ -ər/ *n* [C] someone who shoots at people from a hidden position

snip·pet /ˈsnɪpɪt/ *n* [C] a small piece of news, information, or conversation SYN **bit**: **[+of]** *snippets of information*

snip·py /ˈsnɪpi/ *adj AmE informal* quick to show that you are angry or offended, or that you will not obey someone

snit /snɪt/ *n* **be in a snit** *AmE informal* to be very annoyed about something, especially in a way that other people think is unreasonable: *She's been in a snit ever since the party.*

snitch¹ /snɪtʃ/ *v informal* **1** [I] to tell someone in authority about something that another person has done wrong, because you want to cause trouble for that person: **[+on]** *Somebody snitched on me.* **2** [T] to quickly steal something unimportant or of little value SYN **nick** *BrE*

snitch² *n* [C] *informal* someone who is not liked because they tell people in authority when other people do things that are wrong or against the rules SYN **sneak**: *He didn't want to be a snitch, and besides, Kevin was his friend.*

snit·ty /ˈsnɪti/ *adj especially AmE informal* annoyed, or rude to someone because you are annoyed: *I get snitty about bad service in restaurants.*

sniv·el /ˈsnɪvəl/ *v* (**snivelled**, **snivelling** *BrE*, **sniveled**, **sniveling** *AmE*) [I usually progressive] to behave or speak in a weak complaining way, especially when you are crying: *A small boy was sniveling on a chair.* | *a snivelling coward*

snob /snɒb $ snɑːb/ ●○○ *n* [C]
1 someone who thinks they are better than people from a lower social class – used to show disapproval: *Stop being such a snob.* | *I don't want to sound like a snob, but I thought she was vulgar.*
2 someone who thinks they are better than other people because they know more about something – used to show disapproval: *a bunch of* ***intellectual snobs*** | **music/wine snob**
3 snob value/appeal *BrE* something that has snob value is liked by people who think they are better than other people: *That kind of car* ***has*** *real* ***snob appeal***.

snob·be·ry /ˈsnɒbəri $ ˈsnɑː-/ *n* [U] behaviour or attitudes which show that you think you are better than other people, because you belong to a higher social class or know much more than they do – used to show disapproval: ***intellectual snobbery*** → INVERTED SNOBBERY

snob·bish /ˈsnɒbɪʃ $ ˈsnɑː-/ (*also* **snob·by** /ˈsnɒbi $ ˈsnɑː-/) *adj* behaving in a way that shows you think you are better than other people because you are from a higher social class or know more than they do: *Her family seems snobbish.* —**snobbishly** *adv* —**snobbishness** *n* [U]

snog /snɒg $ snɑːg/ *v* (**snogged**, **snogging**) [I,T] *BrE informal* if two people snog, they kiss each other, especially for a long time: *I saw them snogging in the corner.* —**snog** *n* [C usually singular]

snook /snuːk $ snʊk, snuːk/ → **cock a snook** at COCK²(5)

snoo·ker¹ /ˈsnuːkə $ ˈsnʊkər/ *n* [U] a game played especially in Britain on a special table covered in green cloth, in which two people use long sticks to hit coloured balls into holes at the sides and corners of the table → **billiards**: **snooker table/room/hall** | *They meet up every Friday to* ***play snooker***.

snooker² *v* [T] *BrE informal* to make it impossible for someone to do what they want to do: *If the council refuses our planning application, we're snookered.*

snoop /snuːp/ *v* [I] to try to find out about someone's private affairs by secretly looking in their house, examining their possessions etc: **[+around/about]** *I caught him snooping around in my office.* | **[+on]** *reporters snooping on celebrities* —**snoop** *n* [singular] —**snooper** *n* [C]

snoot·y /ˈsnuːti/ *adj informal* rude and unfriendly, because you think you are better than other people SYN **snotty**: *snooty neighbours* —**snootily** *adv* —**snootiness** *n* [U]

snooze /snuːz/ *v* [I] *informal* to sleep lightly for a short time SYN **doze**: *Dad was snoozing in his armchair.* —**snooze** *n* [C]

ˈsnooze ˌbutton (*also* **ˈsnooze ˌalarm**) *n* [C usually singular] part of an ALARM CLOCK that you press to turn off the ALARM for a short period of time, so that you can sleep a little longer

snooze·fest /ˈsnuːzfest/ *n* [C] *informal* something that is very boring SYN **borefest**

snore /snɔː $ snɔːr/ ●○○ *v* [I] to breathe in a noisy way through your mouth and nose while you are asleep: *He could hear the old man snoring.* **THESAURUS** BREATHE —**snore** *n* [C]: *I heard a snore and knew he'd fallen asleep.* —**snorer** *n* [C]

snor·kel /ˈsnɔːkəl $ ˈsnɔːr-/ *n* [C] a tube that allows someone who is swimming to breathe air under water: *This is the best snorkel at that price.* → see picture at SPORT¹

snor·kel·ling *BrE*, **snorkeling** *AmE* /ˈsnɔːkəlɪŋ $ ˈsnɔːr-/ *n* [U] when you swim under water using a snorkel: *We* ***went snorkeling*** *in Hawaii.* —**snorkel** *v* [I]

snort¹ /snɔːt $ snɔːrt/ ●○○ *v*
1 [I,T] to breathe air in a noisy way out through your nose, especially to show that you are annoyed or amused: *'Certainly not,' he snorted.* | **[+with]** *She* ***snorted with laughter***. | *The horse snorted and stamped its hoof impatiently.*
2 [T] to take drugs by breathing them in through your nose → **sniff**: *snorting cocaine*

snort² *n* [C] **1** a loud sound made by breathing out through your nose, especially to show that you are annoyed or amused: *He* ***gave*** *a loud* ***snort***. | *There were* ***snorts of laughter*** *from the audience.* **2** a small amount of a drug that is breathed in through the nose: *a snort of cocaine*

snot /snɒt $ snɑːt/ *n informal* **1** [U] an impolite word for the thick MUCUS (=liquid) produced in your nose **2** [singular] someone who is SNOTTY: *the little snot*

snot·ty /ˈsnɒti $ ˈsnɑːti/ *adj informal* **1** someone who is snotty is rude and annoying, especially because they think that they are more important than other people – used to show disapproval SYN **snooty**: *some snotty little clerk* **2** wet and dirty with MUCUS

ˈsnotty-nosed *BrE*, **ˈsnot-nosed** *AmE adj informal* used about an annoying child: *a snotty-nosed little kid*

snout /snaʊt/ *n* **1** [C] the long nose of some kinds of animals, such as pigs **2** [C] *BrE informal* a criminal who gives information about other criminals to the police

snow¹ /snəʊ $ snoʊ/ ●●● S2 W3 *n*
1 [U] soft white pieces of frozen water that fall from the sky in cold weather and cover the ground → **sleet**: *Snow was falling heavily as we entered the village.* | *I could see footprints in the snow.* | *The town was buried under three feet of snow.*
2 [C] a period of time in which snow falls: *one of the* ***heaviest snows*** *this winter*
3 snows [plural] a large amount of snow that has fallen at different times during the winter: *the melting of the winter snows*
4 [U] small white spots on a television picture, caused by bad weather conditions, weak television signals etc
5 [U] *informal* COCAINE

COLLOCATIONS

VERBS

snow falls *Outside in the dark, snow was falling silently.*
snow settles (=stays on the ground) *The snow was beginning to settle.*
snow drifts (=is blown into deep piles) *The snow had drifted up against the hedge.*
snow covers/blankets sth *The ground was covered with snow.*
snow melts (=turns to water)

ADJECTIVES

deep *The snow was quite deep in places.*
heavy (=when a lot of snow falls) *France has been expecting heavy snow all week.*
fresh *I had watched the tracks I'd made disappear under fresh snow.*
powdery *The powdery snow flies up as I walk through it.*

S

wet snow *He cleared the wet snow from the car windscreen.*
light snow (=when only a small amount falls) | **driving snow** (=falling fast) | **swirling snow** (=blowing around as it falls)

PHRASES

several inches/feet of snow *More than eight inches of snow fell in 48 hours.*
a blanket/carpet of snow *Within an hour, Bucharest was buried under a blanket of snow.*
flakes of snow (=individual pieces of snow) *A few flakes of snow started to fall.*
a flurry of snow/a snow flurry (=when a small amount of snow blows around in the wind)
a fall of snow (=an occasion when it snows) *We had our first fall of snow in mid-November.*

snow² ●●● S2 *v*
1 it snows if it snows, snow falls from the sky: *It snowed all night.* | *It* ***started snowing*** *around five.*
2 be snowed in to be unable to travel from a place because so much snow has fallen there: *We were snowed in for three days last winter.*
3 be snowed under a) *informal* to have more work than you can deal with: **[+with]** *I found myself snowed under with work.* **b)** if an area is snowed under, a lot of snow has fallen there so that people are not able to travel
4 [T] *AmE informal* to persuade someone to believe or support something, especially by lying to them: **snow sb into doing sth** *Millions of readers were snowed into believing it was a true story.*

snow·ball¹ /ˈsnəʊbɔːl $ ˈsnoʊbɒːl/ *n* [C] **1** a ball of snow that children make and throw at each other: *We* ***had*** *a massive* ***snowball fight***. **2 snowball effect** if something has a snowball effect, it starts a series of events or changes that all happen because of each other **3 not have a snowball's chance in hell** *informal* to have no chance at all

snowball² *v* [I] if a plan, problem, business etc snowballs, it grows bigger at a faster and faster rate: *Interest in the sport is snowballing.*

snow·bird /ˈsnəʊbɜːd $ ˈsnoʊbɜːrd/ *n* [C] *AmE informal* someone, especially an old person, who every year leaves their home in a cold part of the US to go and live in a warm part of the US for the winter

snow·blade /ˈsnəʊbleɪd $ ˈsnoʊ-/ *n* [C] a type of short SKI that people use without the poles that are usually used with longer skis

snow·blad·ing /ˈsnəʊbleɪdɪŋ $ ˈsnoʊ-/ *n* [U] the sport of SKIING on snow, using snowblades —**snowblader** *n* [C]

ˈsnow ˌblindness *n* [U] eye pain and difficulty in seeing things, caused by looking at snow in bright light from the sun —**snow blind** *adj*

snow·blow·er /ˈsnəʊbləʊə $ ˈsnoʊbloʊər/ *n* [C] a machine that clears snow from roads, paths etc by sucking it up and blowing it away

snow·board /ˈsnəʊbɔːd $ ˈsnoʊbɔːrd/ *n* [C] a long wide board made of plastic, which people stand on to go down snow-covered hills as a sport

snow·board·ing /ˈsnəʊbɔːdɪŋ $ ˈsnoʊbɔːrd-/ *n* [U] the sport of going down snow-covered hills on a snowboard —**snowboarder** *n* [C]: *a group of skiers and snowboarders*

snow·bound /ˈsnəʊbaʊnd $ ˈsnoʊ-/ *adj* blocked or prevented from leaving a place by large amounts of snow: *travelers who are snowbound at the airport*

ˈsnow-capped *adj literary* snow-capped mountains are covered in snow at the top

ˈsnow chains *n* [plural] a set of chains that are fastened around the wheels of a car so that it can drive over snow without slipping

ˈsnow cone *n* [C] *AmE* crushed ice with a coloured sweet liquid poured over it, served in a CONE-shaped paper cup

ˈsnow day *n* [C] *AmE* a day when schools and businesses are closed because there is too much snow for people to travel

snow·drift /ˈsnəʊˌdrɪft $ ˈsnoʊ-/ *n* [C] a deep mass of snow formed by the wind

snow·drop /ˈsnəʊdrɒp $ ˈsnoʊdrɑːp/ *n* [C] a European plant with a small white flower which appears in early spring

snow·fall /ˈsnəʊfɔːl $ ˈsnoʊfɒːl/ *n* [C,U] an occasion when snow falls from the sky, or the amount that falls in a particular period of time: ***Heavy snowfalls*** *are forecast.* | *an average snowfall of eight inches a year*

snow·field /ˈsnəʊfiːld $ ˈsnoʊ-/ *n* [C] an area of land that is covered in snow

snow·flake /ˈsnəʊfleɪk $ ˈsnoʊ-/ *n* [C] a small soft flat piece of frozen water that falls as snow

ˈsnow globe *n* [C] a round glass object containing water, small models of people, animals etc, and very small white pieces. When you shake it, the white pieces move about and then fall like snow.

ˈsnow job *n* [singular] *AmE informal* an act of making someone believe something that is not true

ˈsnow line *n* **the snow line** the level above which snow on a mountain never melts

snow·man /ˈsnəʊmæn $ ˈsnoʊ-/ ●○○ *n* (*plural* **snowmen** /-men/) [C] a simple figure of a person made of snow, made especially by children

snow·mo·bile /ˈsnəʊməbiːl $ ˈsnoʊmoʊ-/ *n* [C] a small vehicle with a motor that moves over snow or ice easily

ˈsnow pea *n* [C] *AmE* a type of PEA whose outer part is eaten as well as its seeds SYN **mangetout** *BrE* → see picture at VEGETABLE¹

ˈsnow plough *BrE*, **snow plow** *AmE n* [C] **1** a vehicle, or piece of equipment on the front of a vehicle, that is used to push snow off roads, railways etc **2** *BrE* a position in SKIING in which you have the fronts of your SKIS together and the backs of your skis apart. It is used to slow down and to turn: *a snow plough turn*

ˈsnow route *n* [C] *AmE* an important road in a city that cars must be removed from when it snows, so that the snow can be cleared away from it

snow·shoe /ˈsnəʊʃuː $ ˈsnoʊ-/ *n* [C] a special wide flat frame that you attach to your shoe so that you can walk on deep snow without sinking

snow·storm /ˈsnəʊstɔːm $ ˈsnoʊstɔːrm/ ●●○ *n* [C]
1 a storm with strong winds and a lot of snow **THESAURUS** ▸ STORM
2 *BrE* a SNOW GLOBE

ˈsnow tire *n* [C] *AmE* a special car tyre with a pattern of deep lines, used when driving on snow or ice

ˌsnow-ˈwhite *adj* pure white

snow·y /ˈsnəʊi $ ˈsnoʊi/ ●●● S3 *adj*
1 with a lot of snow: *the snowy fields* | *one snowy January day*
2 *literary* pure white, like snow: *snowy hair*

Snr *BrE* the written abbreviation of ***senior***, used after someone's name → **Jnr**: *James Taylor, Snr*

snub¹ /snʌb/ *v* (**snubbed**, **snubbing**) [T] to treat someone rudely, especially by ignoring them when you meet: *the boys who had snubbed her in high school*

snub² *n* [C] an act of snubbing someone: *Eisenhower saw the action as a deliberate snub.*

ˌsnub ˈnose *n* [C] a snub nose is short and flat and points slightly upwards

ˌsnub-ˈnosed *adj* **1** having a snub nose **2 snub-nosed pistol/revolver etc** a small gun with a very short BARREL (=tube where the bullets come out)

snuck /snʌk/ *AmE* a past tense and past participle of SNEAK

snuff¹ /snʌf/ *v* **1** (*also* **snuff out**) [T] to stop a CANDLE burning by pressing the burning part with your fingers or by covering it **2 snuff it** *BrE informal* to die **3** [I,T] if an animal snuffs, it breathes air into its nose in a noisy way, especially in order to smell something SYN **sniff**

snuff sth/sb ↔ **out** *phr v* **1** to stop a CANDLE burning by pressing the burning part with your fingers or by covering it **2** to stop or end something in a sudden way: *a rebellion* *that will snuff out democracy* **3** *informal* to kill someone: *a young woman snuffed out by an unknown killer*

snuff² *n* [U] **1** a type of tobacco in powder form, which people breathe in through their noses: *He took a* ***pinch of snuff***. | *a* ***snuff box*** (=a small box used to keep snuff in) **2 up to snuff** *AmE informal* good enough for a particular purpose: *A lot of money was spent to* ***bring*** *the building* ***up to snuff***.

snuf·fle /ˈsnʌfəl/ *v* [I] to breathe noisily through your nose, sometimes because you are crying: *The little boys snuffled in their sleep.*

snug¹ /snʌɡ/ *adj* **1** a room, building, or space that is snug is small, warm, and comfortable, and makes you feel protected SYN **cosy**: *She wished she was back in her snug little house.* THESAURUS ▸ COMFORTABLE **2** someone who is snug feels comfortable, happy, and warm: *The kids were* ***warm and snug*** *in their beds.* **3** clothes that are snug fit closely SYN **tight**: *snug jeans* —**snugly** *adv* —**snugness** *n* [U]

snug² *n* [C] *BrE* a small comfortable room in a PUB

snug·gle /ˈsnʌɡəl/ *v* [I always + adv/prep] *informal* to settle into a warm comfortable position: **[+up/down/against etc]** *She snuggled up in Lea's lap to listen to the story.*

so¹ /səʊ $ soʊ/ ●●● S1 W1 *adv*

1 a) [+adj/adv] used to emphasize how great a feeling or quality is, or how large an amount is: *It was so embarrassing!* | *Why didn't you call? We were so worried.* | *I love her so much.* | **ever so** *BrE*: *They're being ever so quiet.* **b)** [+adj/adv] as great, nice, many etc as this: *Why are you being so horrible to me?* | *I've never seen so many people here before!* | *How had they achieved it in so short a time?* **c)** [+adj/adv] used when emphasizing the degree or amount of something by saying what the result is: **so ... (that)** *He was so weak that he could hardly stand up.* | *There was so much smoke that they couldn't see across the hallway.* | *Everything happened so quickly I hadn't time to think.* | **so ... as to be** *The particles are so small as to be almost invisible.* **d)** *spoken old-fashioned* used before or after a verb to emphasize that someone does something a lot or to a great degree: *I wish you wouldn't fuss so* (=as much as you do). *It makes me nervous.* | *He does so enjoy reading your letters.* **e)** *spoken informal* used before a noun phrase to emphasize what you are saying – used especially by young people: *He is just* ***so not*** *the right person for her.*

REGISTER

In written English, people often prefer to use **extremely** rather than **so** to emphasize an adjective or adverb, because it sounds more formal: *These schools are* ***extremely*** *difficult to get into.*

GRAMMAR

• You use **such (a)** before an adjective and noun: *There is not* ***such a*** *big difference.* | *How can* ***such*** *awful things happen?*

• Don't use 'so' before an adjective and noun. Don't say: *a so big difference* | *so awful things*

2 not so big/good/bad etc not very big, good etc: *I'm afraid the news is not so good.* | *Of course I'd like to help, but things aren't so simple.*

3 [not used with negative verbs] used to add that what has just been said is also true about someone or something else: **so do I/so is he/so would Peter etc** *Joe was a little upset, and so was I.* | *He's been ill, and so has his wife.* | *As the demand rises, so do prices.*

4 used to refer back to an idea, action, quality, situation etc that has just been mentioned: **hope so/think so/say so etc** *'Will I need my umbrella?' 'I don't think so.'* | *If you want to go home, just say so.* | **be more so/less so/too much so** *The band is popular and likely to become more so.* | *Jerry is very honest, perhaps too much so.* | *The troops will not advance until ordered to* ***do so***. | *Did Luke sell them? And,* ***if so***, *what happened to the money?* | *'Has he lost a fortune?' '****So they say***.' | *'Look – I've even cleaned the windows.' '****So I see***.' | *Parents can withdraw their child from school* ***if*** *they* ***so wish***.

5 be so to be true or correct: *'It belongs to my father.' '****Is that so****?'* | *Morton says his parents kicked him out, but his brothers say this* ***isn't so***.

6 ... or so used when you cannot be exact about a number, amount, or period of time and you think it may be a little more than the figure you are mentioning: *We have to leave in five minutes or so.* | *I stopped reading after thirty or so pages.*

7 *spoken* used to get someone's attention, especially in order to ask them a question: *So, how was school today?*

8 *spoken* used to check that you have understood something: *So this is just a copy?*

9 *spoken* used when asking a question about what has just been said: *'He's going to Paris on business.' 'So when is he coming back?'*

10 be not so much ... as ... used to say that one description of someone or something is less suitable or correct than another: *The details are not so much wrong as they are incomplete.*

11 not/without so much as sth used when you are surprised or annoyed that someone did not do something: *He left without so much as a goodbye.*

12 so long! *AmE spoken* used to say goodbye

13 not so ... as ... *formal* used in comparisons to say that something or someone has less of a particular quality than another person or thing: *The bed was not so comfortable as his own.*

GRAMMAR

In comparisons without 'not', you say **as ... as**: *Your writing is* ***as*** *bad* ***as*** *mine.* ✗ Don't say: *Your writing is so bad as mine.*

14 so much for sb/sth *spoken* used to say that a particular action, idea, statement etc was not useful or did not produce the result that was hoped for: *He's late again. So much for good intentions!*

15 only so many/much used to say that there is only a limited quantity of something: *There's only so much that anybody's brain can handle at any one time.* | *There are only so many hours in the working day.*

16 *spoken* used with a movement of your hand to show how big, high etc something or someone is: *Oh, he's about so tall, with brown hair and eyes.*

17 *spoken* used to show that you have found something out about someone: *So! You've got a new girlfriend?*

18 like so *spoken* used when you are showing someone how to do something: *Then turn the paper over and fold it, like so.*

19 and so on/forth used at the end of a list to show that you could continue it in a similar way: *You can do things for your health in the way of diet, exercise, good lifestyle, not smoking and so on.*

20 *literary or formal* in the way that is described: *Dorothy and Sarah continued to write to each other, and so began a lifelong friendship.* | **so ... that** *The furniture is so arranged that the interviewee and the interviewer are not physically separated by a desk.*

21 and so and therefore: *Madeira has an ideal climate, and so it is not surprising that it has become a tourist paradise.* | *This was considered to be a religious issue and so to be a matter for the church courts.*

22 so she is/so there are etc *BrE spoken* used to show that you agree with something that has just been mentioned, especially something that you had not noticed or had forgotten: *'Look! She's wearing a hat just like yours.' 'So she is.'*

23 be just/exactly so to be arranged tidily, with everything in the right place: *Everything had to be just so, or Edna would make us do it again.*

24 so be it *spoken* used to show you do not like or agree with something, but you will accept it: *If that means delaying the trip, so be it.*

25 *spoken* **a)** used to say that a person's behaviour or action is typical of that person: *'He was about half an hour late.' 'That is just so Chris.'* **b)** used to say that something suits someone or is the type of thing they like: *You must buy that jacket – it's so you!*

26 I do so/it is so etc *AmE spoken* used especially by children to say that something is true, can be done etc when someone else says that it is not, cannot etc: *'You can't swim.' 'I can so.'*

27 *spoken* used to introduce the next part of a story you are telling someone: *So anyway, he goes in and his boots get stuck in the mud.*

28 so? (*also* **so what?**) *spoken not polite* used to tell someone that something does not matter: *So what if we're a little late?* | *'She might tell someone.' 'So? No one will believe her.'* → SO-SO, → **even so** at EVEN[1](4), → **so far** at FAR[1](7), → **so far as I'm concerned** at FAR[1](14), → **so far as sth is concerned** at FAR[1](15), → **so far as I know/I can remember/I can tell etc** at FAR[1](16), → **as/so long as** at LONG[2](5), → **so much the better** at BETTER[3](4), → **so to speak** at SPEAK(6)

so² ●●● S1 W3 *conjunction*

1 used to say that someone does something because of the reason just stated: *I was feeling hungry, so I made myself a sandwich.* **THESAURUS** THEREFORE

> **REGISTER**
> In written English, people often prefer to use **therefore** or **consequently** rather than **so**, because they sound more formal: *She had previous experience, **therefore** she seemed the best candidate.*

2 so (that) a) in order to make something happen, make something possible etc: *He lowered his voice so Doris couldn't hear.* | *Why don't you start out early so that you don't have to hurry?* **b)** used to say that something happens or is true as a result of the situation you have just stated: *There are no buses, so you'll have to walk.* | *The gravestones were covered with moss, so that it was impossible to read the names on them.*

3 so as to do sth *formal* in order to do something: *I drove at a steady 50 mph so as to save fuel.* | *We went along silently on tiptoe **so as not to** disturb anyone.*

4 (just) as ..., so ... *formal* used to compare two people or things, when they are similar: *Just as the French love their wine, so the English love their beer.*

so³ *n* [singular] the fifth note in a musical SCALE according to the SOL-FA system

soak¹ /səʊk $ soʊk/ ●●○ *v*

1 [I,T] if you soak something, or if you let it soak, you keep it covered with a liquid for a period of time, especially in order to make it softer or easier to clean: *Soak the clothes in cold water.* | *Let the pans soak; I'll wash them later.* | **soak sth off/out** (=remove it by soaking) *Put the bottle in soapy water to soak the label off.*

2 [I always + adv/prep, T] to make something completely wet: *Police aimed water hoses at the marchers, soaking them.* | **[+through/into etc]** *The blood soaked through the bandage.* | **soak sth in/with sth** *a rag soaked with oil*

3 [I] to spend a long time taking a bath: *Soak in a warm bath to relax.*

4 [T] *informal* to make someone pay too much money in prices or taxes: *taxes that soak the middle classes*

soak sth ↔ **up** *phr v*

1 if something soaks up a liquid, it takes the liquid into itself: *He used a towel to soak up the blood.*

2 soak up the sun/rays/sunshine etc to sit outside for a long time enjoying the sun

3 to enjoy a place by watching it or becoming involved in it: *Go to a sidewalk café, order coffee, and **soak up the atmosphere**.*

4 to learn something quickly and easily: *Children soak up language incredibly quickly.*

soak² *n* [singular] **1** a long and enjoyable time spent taking a bath: *I **had** a good long **soak** in the bath.* **2** *BrE* when you soak something: ***Give** the towels a good **soak**, they're very dirty.* **3 an old soak** someone who is often drunk – used humorously

soaked /səʊkt $ soʊkt/ *adj* **1** very wet or wearing very wet clothes SYN **drenched**: *I was soaked and very cold.* | *It was raining so hard we were quickly **soaked through*** (=completely wet). | *He came in from the barn, **soaked to the skin**.* | *Her shoes **got soaked** as she walked through the wet grass.* | **blood-soaked/oil-soaked etc** *his blood-soaked clothes* **THESAURUS** WET **2 be soaked in/with sth** to be full of a particular quality SYN **be steeped in sth**: *a city soaked in history*

soak·ing¹ /ˈsəʊkɪŋ $ ˈsoʊ-/ (*also* ˌ**soaking** ˈ**wet**) *adj* very wet: *a soaking wet towel*

soaking² *n* [C] if someone or something gets a soaking, they get very wet

ˈso-and-so *n* **1** [U] used to refer to a particular person or thing when you do not give a specific name → **such and such**: *I'd find myself thinking, 'I wonder what so-and-so is doing?'* **2** [C] a very unpleasant or unreasonable person – used when you want to avoid using a swear word: *Peter can be a real so-and-so at times.*

soap¹ /səʊp $ soʊp/ ●●● S3 *n*

1 [C,U] the substance that you use to wash your body → **detergent**: *Wash thoroughly with **soap and water**.* | *a **bar of soap*** → see pictures at BAR[1], PIECE

2 [C] *informal* a SOAP OPERA

soap² *v* [T] to rub soap on or over someone or something

soap·box /ˈsəʊpbɒks $ ˈsoʊpbɑːks/ *n* [C usually singular] *informal* if someone is on their soapbox, they are telling people their opinions about something in a loud and forceful way: **on your soapbox** *Environmental activists have climbed on their soapboxes to protest the president's action.*

soap·flakes /ˈsəʊpfleɪks $ ˈsoʊp-/ *n* [plural] *BrE* small thin pieces of soap used for washing delicate clothes

ˈsoap ˌopera ●○○ *n* [C] a television or radio story about the daily lives and relationships of the same group of people, which is broadcast regularly

ˈsoap ˌpowder *n* [C,U] *BrE* a powder that is made from soap and other chemicals, used for washing clothes SYN **detergent**

soap·stone /ˈsəʊpstəʊn $ ˈsoʊpstoʊn/ *n* [U] a soft stone that feels like soap

soap·suds, **ˈsoap suds** /ˈsəʊpsʌdz $ ˈsoʊp-/ *n* [plural] the mass of small bubbles that form on top of water with soap in it

soap·y /ˈsəʊpi $ ˈsoʊpi/ *adj* **1** containing soap: *hot **soapy water*** **2** like soap: *a rock with a soapy feel*

soar /sɔː $ sɔːr/ ●○○ *v* [I]

1 AMOUNTS/PRICES ETC to increase quickly to a high level OPP **plummet**: *Her temperature soared.* | *The price of petrol has soared in recent weeks.* | *soaring unemployment* **THESAURUS** INCREASE

2 IN THE SKY **a)** to fly, especially very high up in the sky, floating on air currents: *She watched the dove soar above the chestnut trees.* **b)** to go quickly upwards to a great height: *The ball soared to left field.*

3 SPIRITS/HOPES if your SPIRITS (=the way you are feeling, for example happy, sad etc) or hopes soar, you begin to feel very happy or hopeful OPP **sink**: *Adam's smile **sent** her **spirits soaring**.*

4 LOOK TALL [not in progressive] if buildings, trees, towers etc soar, they look very tall and impressive SYN **tower**: *Here the cliffs soar a hundred feet above the sea.* | *a soaring skyscraper*

sob /sɒb $ sɑːb/ ●●○ *v* (**sobbed**, **sobbing**)

1 [I] to cry noisily while breathing in short sudden bursts: *He began **sobbing uncontrollably**.* **THESAURUS** CRY

2 [T] (*also* **sob out**) to say something while you are sobbing: *'It's too late,' she sobbed.* —**sob** *n* [C]: *loud sobs*

SOB, **S.O.B.** /ˌes əʊ ˈbiː $ -oʊ-/ *n* [C] *AmE not polite* the abbreviation of ***son of a bitch***

so·ber¹ /ˈsəʊbə $ ˈsoʊbər/ ●○○ *adj*

1 not drunk: *He's a nice guy when he's sober.*

2 serious, and thinking or making you think carefully

about things: *a sober hard-working young man | a sober reminder of the difficulties we face*
3 plain and not at all brightly coloured: *a sober grey suit* —**soberly** *adv*

sober² (*also* **sober down**) *v* [I,T] to become more serious in behaviour or attitude, or to make someone become more serious: *His expression sobered instantly.*

sober up *phr v* to gradually become less drunk, or to make someone become less drunk: *I had sobered up by now and felt terrible.* | **sober sb ↔ up** *Some coffee should sober you up.*

so·ber·ing /ˈsəʊbərɪŋ $ ˈsoʊ-/ *adj* making you feel very serious: *It was a* ***sobering thought****.* | *The news had a sobering effect.*

so·bri·e·ty /səˈbraɪəti/ *n* [U] *formal* **1** when someone is not drunk: *John had periods of sobriety, but always went back to drinking.* **2** behaviour that shows a serious attitude to life

soˈbriety ˌcheckpoint *n* [C] *AmE* a place in the road where the police stop vehicles so they can test drivers to see if they have drunk too much alcohol or used illegal drugs

so·bri·quet /ˈsəʊbrɪkeɪ $ ˈsoʊ-/ (*also* **sou·bri·quet** /ˈsuː-/) *n* [C] *formal* an unofficial title or name SYN **nickname**

ˈsob ˌstory *n* [C] *informal* a story, especially one that is not true, that someone tells you in order to make you feel sorry for them: *a sob story about how she lost all her money*

Soc. the written abbreviation of ***society***

soc·a /ˈsəʊkə $ ˈsoʊ-/ *n* [U] a style of Caribbean music that is a mixture of SOUL and CALYPSO

ˈso-called ●●○ W3 *adj* [only before noun]
1 used to describe someone or something that has been given a name that you think is wrong: *The so-called experts couldn't tell us what was wrong.*
2 used to show that something or someone is usually called a particular name: *the health threats posed by so-called 'mad cow disease'*

soc·cer /ˈsɒkə $ ˈsɑːkər/ ●●● S2 *n* [U] a sport played by two teams of 11 players, who try to kick a round ball into their opponents' GOAL SYN **football** *BrE*

ˈsoccer mom *n* [C] *AmE* a mother who spends a lot of time driving her children to sports practice, music lessons etc, considered as a typical example of women from the middle to upper classes in US society

so·cia·ble /ˈsəʊʃəbəl $ ˈsoʊ-/ *adj* someone who is sociable is friendly and enjoys being with other people OPP **unsociable**: *a pleasant, sociable couple* —**sociably** *adv* —**sociability** /ˌsəʊʃəˈbɪləti $ ˌsoʊ-/ *n* [U]

so·cial¹ /ˈsəʊʃəl $ ˈsoʊ-/ ●●● S1 W1 *adj*
1 SOCIETY relating to human society and its organization, or the quality of people's lives: *social issues, such as unemployment and education | the country's serious social problems | a challenge to* ***the social order*** (=how a particular society is organized)
2 RANK relating to your position in society, according to your job, family, wealth etc: *The students come from a variety of* ***social classes*** (=groups of people that have the same social position). | *the social status of her family*
3 MEETING PEOPLE relating to meeting people, forming relationships with them, and spending time with them: *social interaction | a club with lots of social events | Exercise classes are a good way to keep fit and improve your* ***social life****.* | *Group play helps children develop* ***social skills*** (=ability to deal with people easily). | *He lacked* ***social graces*** (=good and polite behaviour towards other people).
4 someone who is social enjoys meeting and talking to other people SYN **sociable**
5 ANIMALS forming groups or living together in their natural state OPP **solitary**: *Elephants are* ***social animals****.*
→ ANTISOCIAL, SOCIABLE, UNSOCIAL

social² *n* **1** [C] a party for the members of a group, club, or church **2 the social** *BrE informal old-fashioned* SOCIAL SECURITY

ˌsocial ˈaudit (*also* **ethical audit**) *n* [C] an official examination of how well a company behaves, for example how it treats its workers, the environment etc: *a social audit of Ben & Jerry's Ice Cream*

ˌsocial ˈclimber *n* [C] someone who tries to get accepted into a higher social class by becoming friendly with people who belong to that class – used to show disapproval

ˈsocial ˌclub *n* [C] a club where its members can go to spend time, talk, drink etc with other members

ˌsocial ˈconscience *n* [singular, U] if someone has a social conscience, they know about and want to help people who have problems in society, for example people who are poor or have family problems

ˌsocial ˈcontract *n* [singular] an arrangement by which people in a society accept that they all have rights and duties, and give up some freedoms so that they are protected by the state

ˌsocial deˈmocracy *n* **1** [U] a political and economic system based on some ideas of SOCIALISM combined with DEMOCRATIC principles, such as personal freedom and government by elected representatives **2** [C] a country with a government based on social democracy —**ˌsocial ˈdemocrat** *n* [C]

ˌsocial engiˈneering *n* [U] the practice of making changes to laws in order to change society according to a political idea

ˌsocial exˈclusion *n* [U] *BrE* the situation that results when people suffer the effects of a combination of problems such as unemployment, crime, and bad HOUSING, and have very little chance of being able to improve their lives: *efforts to combat poverty and social exclusion*

ˈsocial ˌfund *n* [C usually singular] *BrE* money that is used to help people with social problems, such as family problems or money problems

ˌsocial ˈgaming *n* [U] the activity of playing computer games that involve many players

ˌsocial ˈhousing *n* [U] *BrE* houses or apartments that the local government provides, which can be rented for a small amount of money

so·cial·is·m /ˈsəʊʃəl-ɪzəm $ ˈsoʊ-/ ●○○ *n* [U] an economic and political system in which large industries are owned by the government, and taxes are used to take some wealth away from richer citizens and give it to poorer citizens → **capitalism**, **communism**

so·cial·ist¹ /ˈsəʊʃəl-ɪst $ ˈsoʊ-/ ●○○ *adj*
1 based on socialism or relating to a political party that supports socialism: *socialist principles*
2 a socialist country or government has a political system based on socialism

socialist² *n* [C] someone who believes in socialism, or who is a member of a political party that supports socialism

so·cia·lis·tic /ˌsəʊʃəˈlɪstɪk◂ $ ˌsoʊ-/ *adj* based on socialism – usually used to show disapproval: *socialistic ideas*

so·cial·ite /ˈsəʊʃəl-aɪt $ ˈsoʊ-/ *n* [C] someone who is well known for going to many fashionable parties, and who is often rich: *a Washington socialite*

so·cial·i·za·tion (*also* **-isation** *BrE*) /ˌsəʊʃəl-aɪˈzeɪʃən $ ˌsoʊʃələ-/ *n* [U] **1** the process by which people, especially children, are made to behave in a way that is acceptable in their society: *Schools play an important part in the socialization of our children.* **2** the process of making something work according to SOCIALIST ideas: *the socialization of medicine*

so·cial·ize (*also* **-ise** *BrE*) /ˈsəʊʃəl-aɪz $ ˈsoʊ-/ *v* **1** [I] to spend time with other people in a friendly way: **[+with]** *People don't socialize with their neighbours as much as they used to.* **2** [T] to train someone to behave in a way that is acceptable in the society they are living in: **be socialized into sth** *Girls are socialized into 'feminine' behavior.*

ˌsocialized ˈmedicine *n* [U] *especially AmE* medical care provided by a government and paid for through taxes

S

so·cial·ly /ˈsəʊʃəli $ ˈsoʊ-/ ●●○ *adv*
1 in a way that relates to human society and its organization, or the quality of people's lives: ***socially responsible** companies* | *She wanted to do a socially useful job.*
2 in a way that relates to your position in society, according to your job, the amount of money you have etc: *socially disadvantaged families*
3 in situations that involve meeting people, forming relationships with them, and spending time with them: *She found him shy and socially awkward.*
4 in a way that relates to society's rules about polite behaviour: **socially acceptable/unacceptable** | *Being drunk in public is seen as socially unacceptable in many countries.*

ˌsocial ˈmedia *n* [plural] ways of sharing information, opinions, images, videos etc using the Internet, especially SOCIAL NETWORKING SITES

ˌsocial ˈnetworking ●●○ *n* [U] the use of the Internet to make information about yourself available to other people, especially people you share an interest or connection with, and to send messages to them

ˌsocial ˈnetworking site (*also* **ˌsocial ˈnetworking ˌwebsite**) *n* [C] a website where people put information about themselves and can send messages to other people

ˌsocial ˈscience *n* **1** [U] the study of people in society **2** [C] a particular subject relating to the study of people in society, such as history, politics, SOCIOLOGY, or ANTHROPOLOGY —**social scientist** *n* [C] → **natural science**

ˌsocial seˈcurity *n* [U] **1** *BrE* government money that is paid to people who are unemployed, old, ill etc SYN **welfare** *AmE*: *social security benefits* | **be/live on social security** (=be receiving money from the government) **2 Social Security** a US government programme into which workers must make regular payments, and which pays money regularly to old people and people who are unable to work → **National Insurance**

ˌsocial ˈservice *n* **1 social services** [plural] *BrE* the government department that helps people with problems, for example family or money problems, or the services it provides: *Contact social services for help.* | *social service workers* | *the provision of social services* **2** [C] a service that helps society work properly: *The country railways provided a vital social service.*

ˈsocial ˌstudies *n* [plural] the study of people in society SYN **social science**

ˈsocial work *n* [U] work done by government or private organizations to improve bad social conditions and help people who are poor, have family problems, are unable to find a job etc

ˈsocial ˌworker *n* [C] someone who is trained to help people who are poor, have family problems etc

so·ci·e·tal /səˈsaɪətl/ *adj* relating to a particular society: *societal attitudes*

so·ci·e·ty /səˈsaɪəti/ ●●● S1 W1 *n* (*plural* **societies**)
1 PEOPLE IN GENERAL [U] people in general, considered in relation to the laws, organizations etc that make it possible for them to live together: *technology and its effects on modern society* | *Children are the most vulnerable **members of society**.*
2 A PARTICULAR GROUP [C,U] a particular large group of people who share laws, organizations, customs etc: *Britain is now a multiracial society.* | *the capitalist societies of the West* | *the conservative **segment of** American **society***
3 CLUB [C] an organization or club with members who share similar interests, aims etc: *the university film society* | *the American Cancer Society* | **[+of]** *the Society of Black Lawyers* THESAURUS ORGANIZATION
4 UPPER CLASS [U] the fashionable group of people who are rich and powerful: *a society wedding* | **high society** (=the richest, most fashionable etc people)
5 BEING WITH PEOPLE [U] *formal* when you are together with other people: **[+of]** *Holidays are a time to enjoy the society of your family.*
6 polite society middle- or upper-class people who behave correctly in social situations: **in polite society** (=among middle- or upper-class people) *The subject was rarely mentioned in polite society.* → BUILDING SOCIETY, FRIENDLY SOCIETY

socio- /səʊsiəʊ, -siə, səʊʃiəʊ, -ʃiə $ soʊsioʊ, -siə, soʊʃioʊ, -ʃiə/ *prefix technical* **1** relating to society: *sociology* (=the study of society) **2** social and something else: *sociopolitical* | *sociolinguistics*

so·ci·o·ec·o·nom·ic /ˌsəʊsiəʊekəˈnɒmɪk, ˌsəʊʃiəʊ-, -iːkə- $ ˌsoʊsioʊekəˈnɑː-, ˌsoʊʃioʊ-, -iːkə-/ *adj* based on a combination of social and economic conditions —**socioeconomically** /-kli/ *adv*

so·ci·ol·o·gy /ˌsəʊsiˈɒlədʒi, ˌsəʊʃi- $ ˌsoʊsiˈɑːl-/ ●○○ *n* [U] the scientific study of societies and the behaviour of people in groups —**sociologist** *n* [C] —**sociological** /ˌsəʊsiəˈlɒdʒɪkəl, ˌsəʊʃi- $ ˌsoʊsiəˈlɑː-, ˌsoʊʃi-/ *adj*: *a sociological study* —**sociologically** /-kli/ *adv* → **anthropology**, **ethnology**, **social science**

so·ci·o·path /ˈsəʊsiəˌpæθ, ˈsəʊʃiə- $ ˈsoʊ-/ *n* [C] someone whose behaviour towards other people is considered unacceptable, strange, and possibly dangerous —**sociopathic** /ˌsəʊsiəˈpæθɪk◂, ˌsəʊʃiə- $ ˌsoʊ-/ *adj* → **psychopath**

sock[1] /sɒk $ sɑːk/ ●●● S3 *n* [C]
1 a piece of clothing made of soft material that you wear on your foot inside your shoe: ***a pair of socks*** | *white ankle socks* → see picture at UNDERWEAR
2 knock/blow sb's socks off *informal* to surprise and excite someone very much: *a new band that will knock your socks off*
3 pull your socks up *especially BrE informal* to make an effort to improve your behaviour or your work: *If they want promotion, United have got to pull their socks up.*
4 put a sock in it *informal* used to tell someone in a joking way to stop talking or making a noise
5 *informal* a hard hit, especially with your hand closed: *Larry **gave** him a **sock** on the arm.*

sock[2] *v* [T] **1** *informal* to hit someone very hard, especially with your hand closed SYN **thump**: *He socked her in the face.* **2** *informal* if someone is socked with something bad, they are suddenly affected by it: **be/get socked with sth** *I got socked with a big car repair bill.* **3 be socked in** *AmE* if an airport, road, or area is socked in, it is very difficult to see far and no one can travel because of bad FOG, snow, or rain **4 sock it to sb** *old-fashioned* to tell someone to do something in a direct and forceful way

sock sth ↔ **away** *phr v AmE* to save money by putting it in a safe place: *Roger socked away more than $1 million a year.*

sock·et /ˈsɒkɪt $ ˈsɑː-/ ●○○ *n* [C]
1 a place in a wall where you can connect electrical equipment to the supply of electricity SYN **power point** *BrE*, **outlet** *AmE* → see picture at PLUG[1]
2 the place on a piece of electrical equipment that you put a PLUG or a LIGHT BULB into: *a headphone socket*
3 a hollow part of a structure into which something fits: *the eye sockets*

ˈsock ˌpuppet *n* [C] **1** a simple PUPPET worn on the hand, which consists of a sock with eyes and sometimes other features attached to it **2** a false name and description that someone uses on the Internet, especially so that they can say good things about themselves or bad things about other people without their real name being known

sod[1] /sɒd $ sɑːd/ *n* **1** [C] *BrE informal not polite* a very offensive word for someone, especially a man, who you think is stupid or annoying: *Get up, you lazy sod!* **2 be a sod** *BrE informal not polite* to be very difficult to do or deal with: *That door's a sod to open.* **3** [C usually singular] *BrE informal not polite* used to refer to a person: *The **poor sod**'s wife left him.* | *You lucky sod!* **4 not give/care a sod** *BrE spoken not polite* to not care at all about something: *I don't give a sod who it is!* **5** [C,U] a piece of earth or the layer of earth with grass and roots growing in it

sod[2] *v BrE spoken not polite* **1 sod it/that** used to rudely express anger or annoyance at something or someone: *Sod it, I've missed the train.* **2** [T only in imperative or infinitive] used to say rudely that something is not important: *Sod the job, I'm going home.* **3 sod off** an offensive way of telling someone to go away

so·da /ˈsəʊdə $ ˈsoʊ-/ ●●● S3 *n*
1 [C,U] (*also* **soda water**) water that contains bubbles and is often added to alcoholic drinks: *a Scotch and soda*
2 [C,U] (*also* **soda pop**) *AmE* a sweet drink containing bubbles, or a can or bottle of this drink SYN **pop**: *a can of orange soda | a cooler full of sodas*
3 [C] *AmE* an ICE-CREAM SODA: *a strawberry soda*
4 [U] a substance in the form of a powder containing SODIUM, that is used for cooking or cleaning SYN **bicarbonate of soda**: *baking soda*

ˈsoda ˌfountain *n* [C] *AmE* a place in a shop at which drinks, ice cream etc were served in the past

sod ˈall *n* [U] *BrE informal not polite* nothing at all: *I got sod all from the deal.*

ˈsoda pop *n* [C,U] *AmE* a sweet drink containing bubbles

ˈsoda ˌsiphon *n* [C] *BrE* a special type of bottle from which SODA WATER is forced out in a fast stream

ˈsoda ˌwater *n* [U] water that contains bubbles and is often added to alcoholic drinks

sod·den /ˈsɒdn $ ˈsɑːdn/ *adj* very wet and heavy: *sodden clothes | The earth was sodden.* | **rain-sodden/water-sodden** *rain-sodden hair* THESAURUS ▸ WET

sod·ding /ˈsɒdɪŋ $ ˈsɑː-/ *adj BrE spoken not polite* said when someone is angry or annoyed, or to emphasize what they are saying: *The sodding computer's crashed!*

so·di·um /ˈsəʊdiəm $ ˈsoʊ-/ *n* [U] a common silver-white metal that usually exists in combination with other substances, for example in salt. It is a chemical ELEMENT: symbol Na

ˌsodium biˈcarbonate (*also* **bicarbonate of soda**) *n* [U] a white powder used in baking to make cakes, BISCUITS etc lighter, or for cleaning things SYN **baking soda**

ˌsodium ˈchloride *n* [U] *technical* the type of salt that is used in cooking

Sod·om and Go·mor·rah /ˌsɒdəm ənd gəˈmɒrə $ ˌsɑː- -ˈmɔː-/ a place or situation where people's sexual behaviour is regarded as very shocking. These are the names of two ancient cities in the Middle East which, according to the Bible, were destroyed by God as a punishment for the immoral sexual behaviour of their people.

sod·o·mite /ˈsɒdəmaɪt $ ˈsɑː-/ *n* [C] *old use* someone who practises sodomy

sod·o·my /ˈsɒdəmi $ ˈsɑː-/ *n* [U] *formal or law* a sexual act in which a man puts his sex organ into someone's ANUS, especially that of another man SYN **buggery** —**sodomize** *v* [T]

ˌSod's ˈlaw *n* [U] *BrE* the natural tendency for things to go wrong whenever possible – used humorously SYN **Murphy's Law** *AmE*: *It's Sod's law that the car breaks down when you need it most.*

so·fa /ˈsəʊfə $ ˈsoʊ-/ ●●● S3 *n* [C] a comfortable seat with raised arms and a back, that is wide enough for two or three people to sit on SYN **couch**, **settee** *BrE*

ˈsofa bed *n* [C] a sofa that has a bed inside that can be folded out

ˈsofa ˌsurfing *n* [U] another word for COUCH SURFING

soft /sɒft $ sɔːft/ ●●● S2 W2 *adj* (*comparative* **softer**, *superlative* **softest**)
1 NOT HARD **a)** not hard, firm, or stiff, but easy to press OPP **hard**: *My feet sank into the soft ground. | the softest sofa and pillows | Cook the onions until they* ***go soft***. **b)** less hard than average OPP **hard**: *a soft lead pencil | soft cheese*
2 NOT ROUGH having a surface that is smooth and pleasant to touch OPP **rough**: *a baby's soft skin | The fur was soft to the touch.*
3 NOT LOUD a soft sound or voice, or soft music, is quiet and pleasant to listen to OPP **loud**, **harsh**: *soft music | His voice was softer now.* THESAURUS ▸ QUIET
4 COLOUR/LIGHT [only before noun] soft colours or lights are pleasant and relaxing because they are not too bright OPP **bright**: *All the stores will be re-fitted with softer lighting. | a soft shade of peach* THESAURUS ▸ COLOUR
5 NO HARD EDGES not having any hard edges or sharp angles: *soft curves*
6 RAIN/WIND gentle and without much force: *a soft breeze | soft rain*
7 NOT STRICT someone who is soft seems weak because they are not strict enough with other people OPP **strict**, **tough**: *If you appear to be soft, people take advantage of you.* | **[+on]** *No politician wants to seem* ***soft on crime***. | *Courts have been* ***taking a soft line*** (=not being strict enough) *with young offenders.*
8 SENSITIVE kind, gentle, and sympathetic to other people OPP **hard**: *He has a* ***soft heart*** *beneath that cold exterior. | a soft kiss*
9 WEAK CHARACTER not very brave and not having a strong character OPP **hard**: *Don't be soft – just jump!*
10 SALES/MARKETS decreasing in price, value, or the amount sold: *soft oil prices*
11 soft loan/credit money that is lent at a lower interest rate than usual, because it will be used to help people in some way
12 soft money money that people, companies, or organizations give to political parties, rather than to a particular CANDIDATE
13 TOO EASY *informal* a soft job, life etc is too easy and does not involve much work or hard physical work: *Mike's found himself a soft job in the stores.* | **soft option** *BrE* (=a choice that allows you to avoid difficulties or hard work) ***Taking the soft option*** *won't help your career to develop.*
14 WEAK BODY *informal* having a body that is not in a strong physical condition, because you do not do enough exercise: *He'd* ***got soft*** *after all those years in a desk job.*
15 WATER soft water does not contain many minerals, so that it forms bubbles from soap easily
16 have a soft spot for sb to continue to like someone even when they do not behave well: *She's always had a soft spot for Grant.*
17 a soft touch *informal* someone from whom you can easily get what you want, because they are kind or easy to deceive
18 soft in the head *old-fashioned* very stupid or crazy
19 STUPID *BrE* stupid or silly: *You must be soft if you think I'll give you fifty quid!*
20 be soft on sb *old-fashioned* to be sexually attracted to someone
21 CONSONANTS *technical* not sounding hard: *a soft g* —**softly** *adv*: *She stroked his head softly. | Music played softly in the background.* —**softness** *n* [U]

THESAURUS

soft not hard, firm, or stiff, but easy to press: *a soft mattress | Her skin was lovely and soft. | soft ground*
tender used about meat or vegetables that are soft and easy to cut, especially because they have been well cooked: *The beef was very tender. | Cook the carrots until tender.*
soggy very wet and too soft, in a way that seems unpleasant – used about bread, vegetables, and the ground: *soggy cabbage | a piece of soggy bread | The ground was too soggy to walk on.*
squishy soft and easy to press – used especially about fruit that is too soft, and about soft wet ground which makes a noise when you walk on it: *squishy tomatoes | The leaves were squishy under our feet.*
squashy *BrE* soft and easy to press – used especially about fruit that is too soft, and about chairs that are soft and comfortable: *The peaches have gone all squashy. | a big squashy sofa*
mushy used about fruit or vegetables that are very soft, wet, and unpleasant, because they are not fresh or have been cooked for too long: *mushy pieces of banana | a few mushy carrots*
spongy soft and full of holes that contain air or liquid like a sponge: *a spongy foam | a spongy loaf | His boots sank into the spongy soil.*

COLLOCATIONS CHECK
tender meat/vegetables
soggy ground/bread/vegetables/paper
squishy fruit/ground
squashy fruit/chair
mushy fruit/vegetables
spongy ground/texture/foam/loaf

soft·ball /ˈsɒftbɔːl $ ˈsɒːftbɒːl/ *n* **1** [U] a game similar to baseball but played on a smaller field with a slightly larger and softer ball **2** [C] the special ball used to play this game

ˌsoft-ˈboiled *adj* an egg that is soft-boiled is boiled long enough for the white part to become solid, but the yellow part in the centre is still liquid → **hard-boiled**

ˈsoft ˌcopy *n* [U] *technical* information stored in a computer's memory or shown on a screen rather than printed on paper → **hard copy**

ˌsoft ˈcurrency *n* [C,U] money of a particular country that may fall in value and is difficult to exchange for the money of a country that is economically stronger → **hard currency**

ˈsoft drink ●●○ *n* [C] a cold drink that does not contain alcohol

ˌsoft ˈdrug *n* [C] an illegal drug, such as MARIJUANA, that is not considered to be very harmful → **hard drug**

soft·en /ˈsɒfən $ ˈsɒː-/ ●●○ *v*
1 [I,T] (*also* **soften up**) to become less hard or rough, or make something less hard or rough OPP **harden**: *Use moisturizer to soften your skin.* | *Cook until the onion softens.*
2 [I,T] if your attitude softens, or if something softens it, it becomes less strict and more sympathetic OPP **harden**: *The government has softened its stance on public spending.* | **[+towards]** *I felt that he was beginning to soften towards me.*
3 [I,T] to make the effect of something seem less unpleasant or severe, or to become less unpleasant or severe: **soften the blow/impact** *The impact of the tax was softened by large tax-free allowances.*
4 [I,T] if your expression or voice softens, or if something softens it, you look or sound kinder and more gentle OPP **harden**: *His voice softened as he spoke to her.*
5 [T] to make the shape or colour of something look less severe: *Climbing plants soften the outline of a fence.*

soften sb/sth ↔ **up** *phr v*
1 *informal* to be nice to someone before you ask them to do something, so that they will agree to help you: *She was just softening me up.*
2 to make an enemy weaker so that they are easier to attack: *Use artillery to soften up the enemy forces.*
3 to make something less hard or rough

soft·en·er /ˈsɒfənə $ ˈsɒːfənər/ *n* [C,U] a substance that you add to water to make clothes feel soft after washing: *fabric softener* → **WATER SOFTENER**

ˌsoft ˈfocus *n* [U] a way of photographing or filming things so that the edges of the objects in the photograph are not sharp or clear

ˌsoft ˈfruit *n* [C,U] *especially BrE* small fruits, such as STRAWBERRIES, that you can eat that do not have a hard skin or large seed

ˌsoft ˈfurnishings *n* [plural] *BrE* things such as curtains, chair covers etc that are made of cloth and are used in decorating a room

soft-heart·ed /ˌsɒft ˈhɑːtɪd◂ $ ˌsɒːft ˈhɑːr-/ *adj* easily affected by feelings of pity or sympathy for other people OPP **hard-hearted**: *a soft-hearted woman*

soft·ie, **softy** /ˈsɒfti $ ˈsɒːf-/ *n* [C] someone who is easily affected by feelings of pity or sympathy, or who is easily persuaded: *He's a real softie.*

ˌsoft ˈlanding *n* [C] **1** a situation in which a SPACECRAFT comes down onto the ground gently and without any damage OPP **crash landing 2** if the ECONOMY of a country has a soft landing, it does not experience bad effects after an attempt to control increases in the COST OF LIVING: *Hopes for a soft landing have faded.*

ˌsoftly-ˈsoftly *adj BrE* **softly-softly approach** a way of dealing with something or someone which involves being very patient and careful: *We need to adopt a softly-softly approach with Mike.*

ˌsoftly-ˈspoken *adj* another form of the word SOFT-SPOKEN

ˌsoft ˈpalate *n* [C] the soft part at the back of the top of your mouth

ˌsoft-ˈpedal *v* (**soft-pedalled**, **soft-pedalling** *BrE*, **soft-pedaled**, **soft-pedaling** *AmE*) [T] *informal* to make something seem less important or less urgent than it really is

ˌsoft ˈporn *n* [U] magazines, pictures etc that show people wearing no clothes, or sexual activity, but that do not show sexual activity completely clearly or in a violent way → **hard porn**

ˌsoft ˈsell *n* [singular] a way of advertising or selling things that involves gently persuading people to buy something → **hard sell**

ˌsoft ˈshoulder *n* [C] the edge of a road, when this edge is made of dirt rather than a hard material → **hard shoulder**

ˈsoft-soap *v* [T] *BrE informal* to say nice things to someone in order to persuade them to do something: *Don't think you can soft-soap me!* —**soft soap** *n* [U]

ˌsoft-ˈspoken, **softly-spoken** *adj* having a pleasant quiet voice: *a soft-spoken man*

ˌsoft ˈtarget *n* [C] a person or thing that is easy to attack or criticize

ˈsoft-top *n* [C] a car with a cloth roof that you can fold back or remove SYN **convertible** → **hardtop**

ˌsoft ˈtoy *n* [C] *BrE* a toy for young children that is made of cloth and filled with soft material

soft·ware /ˈsɒftweə $ ˈsɒːftwer/ ●●● S3 W1 *n* [U] the sets of programs that tell a computer how to do a particular job → **hardware**: *She **loaded** the new **software**.* | **design/anti-virus/database etc software** *word-processing software* | *a software company*

soft·wood /ˈsɒftwʊd $ ˈsɒːft-/ *n* [C,U] wood from trees such as PINE and FIR that is cheap and easy to cut, or a tree with this type of wood → **hardwood**

soft·y /ˈsɒfti $ ˈsɒːf-/ *n* [C] another spelling of SOFTIE

sog·gy /ˈsɒgi $ ˈsɑːgi/ *adj* unpleasantly wet and soft: *The ground was soggy from the rain.* | *The sandwiches have **gone** all **soggy**.* **THESAURUS** SOFT, WET

soh /səʊ $ soʊ/ *n* [singular] another spelling of SO^3 (=a musical note)

So·ho /ˈsəʊhəʊ/ an area in central London famous for its SEX SHOPS and GAY bars, and also as a place where there are many shops and restaurants selling foreign food, especially Chinese and Italian food

So·Ho /ˈsʊhʊ/ an area of Manhattan, New York City, south of Houston Street, where there are many art galleries (GALLERY), restaurants, and small fashionable shops

SOHO the abbreviation of SMALL OFFICE/HOME OFFICE

soi·gné, **soignée** /ˈswɑːnjeɪ $ swɑːnˈjeɪ/ *adj formal* dressed fashionably and with care: *a soignée woman politician*

soil^1 /sɔɪl/ ●●● W2 *n*
1 [C,U] the top layer of the earth in which plants grow SYN **earth**: ***fertile soil*** (=good for growing crops) | *The **soil** here is very **poor*** (=not good for growing crops). | *Roses grow well in a clay soil.* → see picture at **PLUG^1** **THESAURUS** GROUND
2 on British/French/foreign etc soil *formal* in Britain, France etc: *The crime was committed on American soil.*
3 [U] a place or situation where something can develop: *Eastern Europe provided **fertile soil** for political activists.*
4 sb's native soil *literary* your own country
5 the soil *literary* farming as a job or way of life: *They make their living from the soil.*

soil^2 *v* [T] **1** *formal* to make something dirty, especially with waste from your body **2 not soil your hands** to not do something because you consider it too unpleasant or dishonest: *Keep your money – I wouldn't soil my hands with it.* —**soiled** *adj*: *soiled diapers*

soi·ree, **soirée** /ˈswɑːreɪ $ swɑːˈreɪ/ *n* [C] a formal or fashionable evening party

soj·ourn /ˈsɒdʒɜːn $ ˈsoʊdʒɜːrn/ *n* [C] *formal* a short period of time that you stay in a place that is not your home SYN **stay**: *a brief sojourn in Europe* —**sojourn** *v* [I]

sol /sɒl $ soʊl/ *n* [singular] SO³ (=a musical note)

sol·ace /ˈsɒlɪs $ ˈsɑː-/ *n formal* **1** [U] a feeling of emotional comfort at a time of great sadness or disappointment: **seek/find solace in sth** *After the death of her son, Val found solace in the church.* **2 be a solace to sb** to bring a feeling of comfort and calmness to someone, when they are sad or disappointed: *Mary was a great solace to me after Arthur died.* —**solace** *v* [T] *literary*

so·lar /ˈsəʊlə $ ˈsoʊlər/ ●●○ *adj* [only before noun]
1 relating to the sun → **lunar**: *a solar eclipse*
2 using the power of the sun's light and heat: *solar energy*

ˌsolar ˈcell *n* [C] a piece of equipment for producing electric power from sunlight

ˈsolar farm *n* [C] a large area of solar panels

so·lar·i·um /səʊˈleəriəm $ soʊˈler-/ *n* [C] **1** a place with SUNBEDS (=beds with special lamps), where you can get a SUNTAN **2** a room, usually enclosed by glass, where you can sit in bright sunlight

ˌsolar ˈpanel *n* [C] a piece of equipment, usually kept on a roof, that collects and uses the sun's energy to heat water or make electricity

solar plex·us /ˌsəʊlə ˈpleksəs $ ˌsoʊlər-/ *n* [singular] the front part of your body just below your RIBS: *a blow to the solar plexus*

ˈsolar ˌsystem ●○○ *n*
1 the solar system the Sun and the PLANETS that go around it
2 [C] this kind of system around another star

ˌsolar ˈyear *n* [C] the period of time in which the Earth travels once around the Sun, equal to just over 365 days

sold /səʊld $ soʊld/ the past tense and past participle of SELL

sol·der¹ /ˈsɒldə, ˈsəʊl- $ ˈsɑːdər/ *n* [U] a soft metal, usually a mixture of LEAD and TIN, which can be melted and used to join two metal surfaces, wires etc

solder² *v* [T + onto/together] to join or repair metal surfaces with solder

ˈsoldering ˌiron *n* [C] a tool which is heated, usually by electricity, and used for melting solder and putting it on surfaces

sol·dier¹ /ˈsəʊldʒə $ ˈsoʊldʒər/ ●●● S3 W2 *n* [C] a member of the army of a country, especially someone who is not an officer → **troop**: *A British soldier was wounded in the fighting.* | *an enemy soldier*

soldier² *v*
soldier on *phr v especially BrE* to continue working in spite of difficulties: *We'll just have to soldier on without him.*

sol·dier·ing /ˈsəʊldʒərɪŋ $ ˈsoʊl-/ *n* [U] the life or job of a soldier

sol·dier·ly /ˈsəʊldʒəli $ ˈsoʊldʒərli/ *adj formal* typical of a good soldier

ˌsoldier of ˈfortune *n* (*plural* **soldiers of fortune**) [C] someone who works as a soldier for anyone who will pay them SYN **mercenary**

sol·dier·y /ˈsəʊldʒəri $ ˈsoʊl-/ *n* [singular, U] *old-fashioned* soldiers

ˌsold ˈout, **ˈsold-out** ●●○ *adj*
1 if a concert, performance etc is sold out, all the tickets for that show have been sold: *The group will play three sold-out shows at Wembley Stadium.*
2 if a shop or store is sold out of a particular product, it has sold all of that product: **[+of]** *The store was completely sold out of tuna fish.*

sole¹ /səʊl $ soʊl/ ●●○ W3 AWL *adj* [only before noun]
1 the sole person, thing etc is the only one SYN **only**: *the sole American in the room* | *Griffiths is the **sole survivor** of the crash.* | *The story was published **with the sole purpose of** selling newspapers.*
2 not shared with anyone else: *Derek **has sole responsibility** for sales in Dublin.* | *The company has the **sole rights** to market Elton John's records.*

sole² ●○○ *n*
1 [C] the bottom surface of your foot, especially the part you walk or stand on: *The **soles of** his **feet** were caked in mud.*
2 [C] the flat bottom part of a shoe, not including the heel: *the **soles of** her **shoes***
3 [C,U] (*plural* **sole** *or* **soles**) a flat fish that is often used for food → **lemon sole**: *Dover sole*

sole³ *v* [T] to put a SOLE on a shoe: **thick-soled/leather-soled etc** (=having soles that are thick, made of leather etc) GRAMMAR **Sole** is usually passive.

so·le·cis·m /ˈsɒlɪsɪzəm $ ˈsɑː-/ *n* [C] *formal* **1** a mistake in the use of written or spoken language **2** something that is not considered polite behaviour: *a social solecism*

sole·ly /ˈsəʊl-li $ ˈsoʊl-/ ●●○ AWL *adv* not involving anything or anyone else SYN **only**: *Scholarships are given solely on the basis of financial need.* | *I shall hold you **solely responsible** for anything that goes wrong.*

sol·emn /ˈsɒləm $ ˈsɑː-/ ●○○ *adj*
1 very serious and not happy, for example because something bad has happened or because you are at an important occasion: *a solemn expression* | *Their faces suddenly grew solemn.* | *a solemn procession of mourners*
THESAURUS ▸ SERIOUS
2 a solemn promise is one that is made very seriously and with no intention of breaking it: *a **solemn vow*** | *I'll never be unfaithful again. I give you my **solemn word**.*
3 performed in a very serious way: **solemn ritual/ceremony** —**solemnly** *adv*

so·lem·ni·ty /səˈlemnəti/ *n* **1** [U] the quality of being serious in behaviour or manner: *the solemnity of a great religious occasion* **2 solemnities** [plural] the ceremonies of an important and serious occasion

sol·em·nize (*also* **-ise** *BrE*) /ˈsɒləmnaɪz $ ˈsɑː-/ *v* **solemnize a marriage** *formal* to perform a wedding ceremony in a church

sol-fa /ˌsɒl ˈfɑː $ ˌsoʊl-/ *n* [U] the system in which the notes of the musical SCALE are represented by seven short words, DO, RE, MI, FA, SO, LA, TI, which are used especially in singing

so·li·cit /səˈlɪsɪt/ *v* **1** [I usually progressive] to offer to have sex with someone in exchange for money: *She was arrested for soliciting.* **2** [I,T] *formal* to ask someone for money, help, or information: *Morgan is accused of illegally soliciting campaign contributions.* | **solicit sth from sb** *The governor sent two officials to Mexico City to solicit aid from the president.* **3** [I,T] *AmE* to try to sell a product or service by taking it to homes or businesses and showing it to the people there: *No soliciting on company premises is allowed.*

so·li·ci·ta·tion /səˌlɪsɪˈteɪʃən/ *n* [C,U] the act of asking someone for money, help, or information

so·lic·i·tor /səˈlɪsɪtə $ -ər/ ●●○ S3 W2 *n* [C]
1 a type of lawyer in Britain who gives legal advice, prepares the necessary documents when property is bought or sold, and defends people, especially in the lower courts of law → **lawyer**, **advocate**, **barrister**: *You need to see a solicitor.* | *a small firm of solicitors*
2 *AmE* someone who goes from place to place trying to sell goods or services: *A sign on the door read, 'No Solicitors'.*

soˌlicitor ˈgeneral *n* [C] the government law officer next in rank below the ATTORNEY GENERAL

so·lic·i·tous /səˈlɪsɪtəs/ *adj formal* very concerned about someone's safety, health, or comfort —**solicitously** *adv* —**solicitousness** *n* [U]

so·lic·i·tude /səˈlɪsɪtjuːd $ -tuːd/ *n* [U] *formal* care and concern for someone's health, safety etc: *She was grateful to him for his solicitude.*

sol·id¹ /ˈsɒlɪd $ ˈsɑː-/ ●●● S3 W3 *adj*
1 FIRM/HARD hard or firm, with a fixed shape, and not a liquid or gas: *The lake was* ***frozen solid****.* | *It was good to be back on* ***solid ground*** *again.* | *Is the baby eating* ***solid food*** (=bread, meat etc) *yet?* | *The ship's sonar can detect the presence of* ***solid objects*** *in the water.* THESAURUS ▸ HARD
2 ONLY ONE MATERIAL consisting completely of one type of material: **solid gold/silver etc** *a solid gold cup* | **solid wood/pine/oak etc** *a chest made of solid oak*
3 NOT HOLLOW having no holes or spaces inside OPP **hollow**: *a solid rubber ball* | *a shrine carved out of solid rock*
4 WITHOUT SPACES continuous, without any spaces or breaks: *It's not safe to pass when the lines in the middle of the road are solid.*
5 STRONGLY MADE strong and well made OPP **flimsy**: *a solid piece of furniture* | *The frame is as* ***solid as a rock*** (=extremely solid).
6 GOOD AND LONG-LASTING a solid achievement or solid work is of real, practical, and continuing value: *five years of solid achievement* | *The first two years provide a* ***solid foundation*** *in the basics of computing.*
7 DEPENDABLE someone or something that is solid can be depended on or trusted SYN **sound**: *a* ***solid reputation*** | *The prosecution in this case has no* ***solid evidence****.* | *You can rely on Wylie for good solid advice.* | *a solid Labour stronghold* (=where people always vote for this party)
8 CONTINUING WITHOUT INTERRUPTION *informal* used to emphasize that something continues for a long time without any pauses: *The lecture lasted two solid hours.* | **five hours/two weeks etc solid** *On Saturday I went to bed and slept fourteen hours solid.*
9 packed solid *informal* if shops, trains, buses etc are packed solid, they are full of people
10 on solid ground confident because you are dealing with a subject you are sure about, or because you are in a safe situation: *To make sure that he was on solid ground, he confirmed his findings with others.*
11 GOOD *BrE informal* good
12 DIFFICULT *BrE informal* very difficult: *I couldn't do any of the maths last night – it was solid.*
13 SHAPE *technical* having length, width, and height SYN **three-dimensional**: *A sphere is a solid figure.*
14 IN AGREEMENT **be solid** *BrE* to be in complete agreement: *The workers are 100% solid on this issue.* —**solidly** *adv*: *solidly built* —**solidness** *n* [U]

solid² ●○○ *n*
1 [C] a firm object or substance that has a fixed shape, not a gas or liquid: *the properties of liquids and solids*
2 solids [plural] foods that are not liquid: *He's still too ill to eat solids.*
3 [C] *technical* the part of a liquid which has the qualities of a solid when it is separated from the SOLVENT (=watery part)
4 [C] *technical* a shape which has length, width, and height, such as a SPHERE or CYLINDER → **plane**

sol·i·dar·i·ty /ˌsɒləˈdærəti $ ˌsɑː-/ ●○○ *n* [U] loyalty and general agreement between all the people in a group, or between different groups, because they all have a shared aim: *a gesture of solidarity* | *an appeal for worker solidarity* | **show/express/demonstrate your solidarity (with sb)** *I come before you today to express my solidarity with the people of New York.*

ˌsolid ˈfuel *n* [C] a solid substance such as coal that is burnt to produce heat or power

so·lid·i·fy /səˈlɪdɪfaɪ/ *v* (**solidified, solidifying, solidifies**) **1** [I,T] to become solid or make something solid: *The volcanic lava solidifies as it cools.* | *solidified cream* **2** [T] to make an agreement, plan, attitude etc more definite and less likely to change SYN **strengthen**: *The two countries signed a treaty to solidify their alliance.* —**solidification** /səˌlɪdɪfɪˈkeɪʃən/ *n* [U]

so·lid·i·ty /səˈlɪdəti/ *n* [U] **1** the strength or hardness of something: *the solidity of the stone walls* **2** the quality of something that is permanent and can be depended on: *the solidity of middle-class institutions*

ˌsolid-ˈstate *adj* **1** solid-state electrical equipment contains electronic parts, such as SILICON CHIPS, rather than moving MECHANICAL parts **2** solid-state PHYSICS is concerned with the qualities of solid substances, especially the way in which they CONDUCT electricity

sol·i·dus /ˈsɒlɪdəs $ ˈsɑː-/ *n* (*plural* **solidi** /-daɪ/) [C] an OBLIQUE²

so·lil·o·quy /səˈlɪləkwi/ *n* (*plural* **soliloquies**) [C,U] a speech in a play in which a character, usually alone on the stage, talks to himself or herself so that the AUDIENCE knows their thoughts → **monologue** —**soliloquize** /-kwaɪz/ *v* [I]

sol·ip·sis·m /ˈsɒləpsɪzəm $ ˈsɑː-, ˈsoʊ-/ *n* [U] *technical* the idea in PHILOSOPHY that only the SELF exists or can be known

sol·ip·sis·tic /ˌsɒləpˈsɪstɪk◂ $ ˌsɑːl-, ˌsoʊ-/ *adj* **1** interested only in yourself and the things that affect you **2** *technical* relating to the view in PHILOSOPHY that only the SELF exists or can be known

sol·i·taire /ˌsɒləˈteə $ ˌsɑːləˈter/ *n* **1** [U] a game played by one person with small wooden or plastic pieces on a board **2** [C] a single jewel, or a piece of jewellery with a single jewel in it, especially a large diamond: *a diamond solitaire* → see picture at **JEWELLERY** **3** [U] *AmE* a game of cards for one person SYN **patience** *BrE*

sol·i·ta·ry¹ /ˈsɒlətəri $ ˈsɑːləteri/ ●○○ *adj*
1 [only before noun] used to emphasize that there is only one of something SYN **single**: *the solitary goal of the match* | *The benches were empty except for a single solitary figure.*
2 doing something without anyone else with you: *a long, solitary walk*
3 spending a lot of time alone, usually because you like being alone OPP **sociable**: *a solitary man* | *Pandas are solitary creatures.* | *He led a rather solitary existence.*
4 not a solitary word/thing etc used to emphasize that there is not even one: *He followed her round without a solitary word.* —**solitarily** *adv* —**solitariness** *n* [U]

solitary² *n* (*plural* **solitaries**) **1** [U] *informal* solitary confinement: *He spent two weeks in solitary.* **2** [C] *BrE literary* someone who lives completely alone SYN **hermit**

ˌsolitary conˈfinement *n* [U] a punishment in which a prisoner is kept alone and is not allowed to see anyone else: **in solitary confinement** *He spent more than half his time in prison in solitary confinement.*

sol·i·tude /ˈsɒlɪtjuːd $ ˈsɑːlɪtuːd/ *n* [U] when you are alone, especially when this is what you enjoy → **loneliness**: **in solitude** *Carl spent the morning in solitude.* | *the solitude of her house on the lake*

so·lo¹ /ˈsəʊləʊ $ ˈsoʊloʊ/ ●●○ *n* (*plural* **solos**) [C]
1 a piece of music for one performer → **duet**, **trio**: *a gorgeous piano solo*
2 when someone flies or does an activity alone: *his first solo*

solo² *adj* [only before noun] **1** done alone without anyone else helping you: **solo flight/voyage/ascent** *Ridgeway's solo voyage across the Atlantic* | *the first solo ascent of Everest* | *a* ***solo effort*** **2** relating to a record or piece of music that is performed by a single musician, not a group: *a solo album* | *a solo passage for viola* —**solo** *adv*: *When did you first fly solo?* | *Amos quit the company, determined to* ***go solo*** (=work for himself).

solo³ *v* [I] **1** to perform a solo in a piece of music: *Brokaw solos brilliantly on this album.* **2** to fly an aircraft alone

so·lo·ist /ˈsəʊləʊɪst $ ˈsoʊloʊ-/ *n* [C] a musician who performs alone or plays an instrument alone: *cello soloist Yo Yo Ma*

Sol·o·mon /ˈsɒləmən $ ˈsɑːl-/ (10th century BC) a king of Israel, the son of King David, who built the temple in Jerusalem, and is known for being extremely wise. Someone with 'the wisdom of Solomon' has a very special ability to make the right decision in situations where it is extremely difficult to know what to do: *The chairman of the peace talks is going to need the wisdom of Solomon.*

sol·stice /ˈsɒlstɪs $ ˈsɑːl-/ *n* [C] the time when the sun is furthest north or south of the EQUATOR: **the summer/winter solstice** (=the longest or shortest day of the year) → **equinox**

sol·u·ble /ˈsɒljəbəl $ ˈsɑː-/ *adj* **1** a soluble substance can be DISSOLVEd in a liquid: *soluble aspirin* | **water-soluble** (=that can be dissolved in water) **2** *formal* a problem that is soluble can be solved OPP **insoluble** —**solubility** /ˌsɒljəˈbɪləti $ ˌsɑː-/ *n* [U]

so·lu·tion /səˈluːʃən/ ●●● S2 W1 *n*
1 [C] a way of solving a problem or dealing with a difficult situation → **solve**: *The best solution would be for them to separate.* | **[+to/for]** *There are no simple solutions to the problem of overpopulation.*
2 [C] the correct answer to a problem in an exercise or competition SYN **answer** → **solve**: **[+to]** *The solution to last week's puzzle is on page 12.*
3 [C,U] a liquid in which a solid or gas has been mixed: *a weak sugar solution* | *saline solution*

COLLOCATIONS

ADJECTIVES

a good solution *A good solution is to harvest the crop early in September.*
the best/perfect/ideal solution *Locking people in prison is not necessarily the ideal solution.*
an effective solution *The government has failed to come up with an effective solution.*
a satisfactory solution (=good enough) *We will not rest until a satisfactory solution is found.*
the only solution *The only solution is to greatly reduce our use of water.*
the real solution (=the only good solution) *The real solution to the waste problem is to produce much less waste.*
a possible solution *There are three possible solutions to this problem.*
an alternative solution | **a simple/easy solution** | **a quick/speedy solution** | **a practical/workable solution** (=one that is really possible) | **a long-term solution** (=one that will be effective for a long time) | **a quick-fix solution** (=one that solves a problem for a short time only) | **a peaceful/political solution** (=one that does not involve fighting)

VERBS

find/come up with a solution *We are working together to find the best solution we can.*
seek/look for a solution *The company is still seeking a solution to its financial problems.*
provide/offer a solution *I don't think that tourism will provide a long-term solution to rural employment problems.*
suggest/put forward a solution

solve /sɒlv $ sɑːlv/ ●●● S2 W3 *v* [T]
1 to find or provide a way of dealing with a problem → **solution**: *Charlie thinks money will solve all his problems.* | *the best way of solving our dilemma*
2 to find the correct answer to a problem or the explanation for something that is difficult to understand → **solution**: **solve a crime/mystery/case etc** *More than 70% of murder cases were solved last year.* | *attempts to* ***solve*** *a mathematical* ***equation*** | **solve a puzzle/riddle** —**solvable** *adj*

sol·vent¹ /ˈsɒlvənt $ ˈsɑːl-/ *adj* [not usually before noun] having enough money to pay your debts OPP **insolvent**: **stay/remain/keep solvent** *I don't know how we managed to remain solvent.* —**solvency** *n* [U]

solvent² *n* [C,U] a chemical that is used to DISSOLVE another substance

ˈsolvent aˌbuse *n* [U] *BrE formal* when someone breathes in gases from glues or similar substances in order to get a pleasant feeling, especially when they become dependent on doing this SYN **glue-sniffing**

som·bre *BrE*, **somber** *AmE* /ˈsɒmbə $ ˈsɑːmbər/ *adj* **1** sad and serious SYN **grave**: *They sat in sombre silence.* | *We were all in a* ***somber mood*** *that night.* | *a sombre expression* | *on the sombre occasion of his mother's funeral* **THESAURUS** SERIOUS **2** dark and without any bright colours: *a sombre grey suit* —**sombrely** *adv* —**sombreness** *n* [U]

som·bre·ro /sɒmˈbreərəʊ $ sɑːmˈbreroʊ/ *n* (*plural* **sombreros**) [C] a Mexican hat for men that is tall with a wide round BRIM¹ turned up at the edges → see picture at HAT

some¹ /səm; strong sʌm/ ●●● S1 W1 *determiner*
1 a number of people or things, or an amount of something, when the exact number or amount is not stated: *I need some apples for this recipe.* | *My mother has inherited some land.* | *They're looking for someone with some experience.* | *The doctor gave her some medicine for her cough.*
2 a number of people or things or an amount of something, but not all: *Some people believe in life after death.* | *She's been so depressed that some days she can't get out of bed.*
3 *formal* a fairly large number of people or things or a fairly large amount of something: *It was* ***some time*** *before they managed to turn the alarm off.* | *The donation went* ***some way*** *toward paying for the damage.*
4 used to mean a person or thing, when you do not know or say exactly which: *There must be some reason for her behaviour.* | *Can you give me some idea of the cost?* | **some kind/type/form/sort of sth** *We can hopefully reach some kind of agreement.*
5 *informal* used when you are talking about a person or thing that you do not know, remember, or understand, or when you think it does not matter: *Some guy called for you while you were gone.* | **some sth or other/another** *Just give him some excuse or other.*
6 used to say that something was very good or very impressive: *That was some party last night!*
7 some friend you are/some help she was etc *spoken* used, especially when you are annoyed, to mean someone or something has disappointed you by not behaving in the way you think they should: *You won't lend me the money? Some friend you are!*

some² /sʌm/ ●●● S1 W1 *pron*
1 a number of people or things or an amount of something, when the exact number or amount is not stated: *I've just made a pot of coffee. Would you like some?* | *'Do you know where the screws are?' 'There are some in the garage.'*
2 a number of people or things or an amount of something, but not all: *Many local businesses are having difficulties, and some have even gone bankrupt.* | *Some say it was an accident, but I don't believe it.* | *Many of the exhibits were damaged in the fire, and some were totally destroyed.* | **[+of]** *Some of his jokes were very rude.* | *Can I have some of your cake?*
3 and then some *spoken informal* used to say that the actual amount is probably a lot more than what someone has just said: *'They say he earns $2.5 million a season.' 'And then some.'*

some³ /səm; strong sʌm/ ●●● S1 W1 *adv*
1 some more an additional number or amount of something: *Would you like some more cake?*
2 *AmE spoken* a little: *'Are you feeling better today?' 'Some, I guess.'*
3 some 500 people/50%/£100 etc an expression meaning about 500 people, 50%, £100 etc – used especially when this seems a large number or amount: *She gained some 25 pounds in weight during pregnancy.*
4 some little/few sth *literary* a fairly large number or amount of something: *We travelled some little way before noticing that Bradley wasn't with us.*

-some /səm/ *suffix* **1** [in adjectives] tending to behave in a particular way, or having a particular quality: *a troublesome boy* (=who causes trouble) | *a bothersome back injury* (=that bothers you) **2** [in nouns] a group of a particular number, for example in a game: *a golf foursome* (=four people playing golf together)

some·bod·y¹ /ˈsʌmbɒdi, -bədi $ -bɑːdi, -bədi/ ●●● S1 W3 *pron* used to mean a person, when you do not know or do not say who the person is SYN **someone**

S

→ **anybody**, **everybody**, **nobody**: *There's somebody waiting to see you.* | *Somebody's car alarm kept me awake all night.* | **somebody new/different/good etc** *We need somebody neutral to sort this out.* | *If you can't make it Friday, we can invite* ***somebody else*** (=a different person). | *'Who can we get to babysit?' 'I'll call Suzie* ***or somebody****.'*

somebody² *n* **be somebody** to be or feel important: *She was the first teacher who'd made Paul feel like he was somebody.*

some·day, ˈ**some day** /ˈsʌmdeɪ/ ●●○ *adv* at an unknown time in the future, especially a long time in the future: *I'd like to visit Japan someday.* | *He hopes, someday, to have his own business.*

some·how /ˈsʌmhaʊ/ ●●● S2 W2 *adv*
1 in some way, or by some means, although you do not know how: *Don't worry, we'll get the money back somehow.* | *Somehow, I managed to lose my keys.* | *Maybe we could glue it together* ***somehow or other****.*
2 for some reason that is not clear to you or that you do not understand: *Somehow, I just don't think it'll work.*

some·one¹ /ˈsʌmwʌn/ ●●● S1 W1 *pron* used to mean a person, when you do not know or do not say who the person is SYN **somebody** → **anyone**, **everyone**, **no one**: *What would you do if someone tried to rob you in the street?* | *Will someone please explain what's going on?* | **someone new/different etc** *'When are you planning to hire someone?' 'As soon as we find someone suitable.'* | *Can you ask* ***someone else*** (=a different person) *to help you? I'm really busy.* | *Have Brooks* ***or someone*** *fax this to New York right away.*

someone² *n* **be someone** to be or feel important: *Gerber was determined to be someone.*

S

some·place /ˈsʌmpleɪs/ *adv* [not usually in questions or negatives] *AmE spoken* somewhere: *I must have left my jacket someplace.*

som·er·sault /ˈsʌməsɔːlt $ -ərsɒːlt/ *n* [C] **1** *BrE* a movement in which someone rolls or jumps forwards or backwards so that their feet go over their head before they stand up again: **do/turn a somersault** *Lana turned a somersault in midair.* **2** *AmE* a FORWARD ROLL —**somersault** *v* [I]: *He crashed into the table,* ***somersaulted over*** *it and landed on the carpet.*

some·thing /ˈsʌmθɪŋ/ ●●● S1 W1 *pron*
1 used to mean a particular thing when you do not know its name or do not know exactly what it is → **anything**, **everything**, **nothing**: *There's something in my eye.* | *Sarah said something about coming over later.* | **something new/old/good etc** *It's a good car, but I'm looking for something newer.* | *The house was too small, so they decided to look for* ***something else*** (=a different one). | *I think there's* ***something wrong*** (=a problem) *with the phone.* | *I don't know what he does exactly, but I know it* ***has something to do with*** *computers* (=is related to them in some way). THESAURUS THING
2 something to eat/drink/read/do etc some food, a drink, a book, an activity etc: *Would you like something to drink?* | *I should take something to read on the plane.*
3 do something to do something in order to deal with a problem or difficult situation: *Don't just stand there – do something!* | **[+about]** *Can you do something about that noise?*
4 something about sb/sth used to say that a person, situation etc has a quality or feature that you recognize but you cannot say exactly what it is: **(there is) something different/odd/unusual about sb/sth** *There was something rather odd about him.* | ***There's something about*** *her voice that I find really sexy.*
5 ... or something *spoken* used when you cannot remember, or do not think it is necessary to give, another example of something you are mentioning: *Her name was Judith, or Julie, or something.* | *Here's some money. Get yourself a sandwich or something.*
6 something like 100/2,000 etc close to but not exactly a large amount such as 100, 2,000 etc: *Something like 50,000 homes are without power.*
7 be thirty-something/forty-something etc used to say that someone is aged between 30 and 39, between 40 and 49 etc when you do not know exactly
8 be (really/quite) something *spoken* used to say that something is very good and impressive: *Running your own company at 21 is really something.* | *That was really something, wasn't it?*
9 be something else *spoken* to be unusual or funny to other people: *You really are something else!*
10 there's something in/to sth used to admit that someone's words are true or their ideas are successful etc: *They had to concede that there was something in his teaching methods.* | *Do you think there's something to the rumours about Larry and Sue?*
11 have something of sth to have a few of the same features or qualities that someone else has: *It was clear that Jenkins had something of his father's brilliance.*
12 be something of a gardener/an expert etc to know a lot about something or to be very good at something: *Charlie's always been something of an expert on architecture.*
13 something of a shock/surprise etc *formal* used to say that something is a shock, surprise etc, but not completely or not in a strong or severe way: *The news* ***came as something of*** *a surprise.*
14 a little something used when you are telling someone that you have bought them a present: *I got you a little something for your birthday.*
15 sixty something/John something etc *spoken* used when you cannot remember the rest of a number or name: *'How much did you spend on groceries?' 'A hundred and twenty something.'*
16 make something of yourself to become successful
17 that's something used to say that there is one thing that you should be glad about: *At least we have some money left. That's something, isn't it?*

some·time¹, ˈ**some time** /ˈsʌmtaɪm/ ●●● S2 *adv* at a time in the future or in the past, although you do not know exactly when: **[+around/in/during etc]** *We'll take a vacation sometime in September.* | *Our house was built sometime around 1900.*

sometime² *adj* [only before noun] **1** *formal* former: *Sir Richard Marsh, the sometime chairman of British Rail* **2** *AmE* used to say that someone does or has a particular job part of the time: *Grimm, a sometime delivery driver, lives with his elderly mother.*

some·times /ˈsʌmtaɪmz/ ●●● S1 W1 *adv* on some occasions but not always → **occasionally**: *I sometimes have to work late.* | *Sometimes, Grandma would tell us stories about her childhood in Italy.* | *'Do you ever wish you were back in Japan?' 'Sometimes. Not very often.'* | *The journey takes an hour, sometimes even longer.*

GRAMMAR: Word order

- **Sometimes** usually comes before a verb: *I sometimes see him at the supermarket.*
- **Sometimes** can also come after the object of the verb: *I see him sometimes at the supermarket.*
- **Sometimes** usually comes after the verb 'be': *She is sometimes late.*
- **Sometimes** usually comes after an auxiliary verb such as 'do' or 'have': *The government has sometimes tried to prevent newspapers from publishing stories.*
- You can also use **sometimes** at the beginning or end of a sentence: *Sometimes I see him at the supermarket.* | *I see him at the supermarket sometimes.*

GRAMMAR GUIDE ADVERBS

THESAURUS

sometimes on some occasions but not always: *Sometimes, I wish I was still living in Tokyo.* | *He sometimes plays football with my brother.*
occasionally (*also* **on occasion** *written*) used about something that only happens a few times. Occasionally is used when something happens more rarely than **sometimes**: *I prefer trousers but I do wear skirts occasionally.* | *Occasionally, operations have to be*

cancelled. | On occasion, prisoners were allowed visits from their families.
(every) now and then/again (*also* **from time to time**) sometimes but not often or regularly: *We still call each other every now and then. | Every now and again, an invention comes along which changes people's lives completely. | Even experienced doctors make mistakes from time to time.*
every so often sometimes at fairly regular periods: *He looked up from his book every so often. | Every so often, a train whizzed past.*
at times if something happens at times, it happens sometimes but is not what usually happens: *The job can be frustrating at times. | At times I've wondered whether I made the right decision in moving here.*
(every) once in a while sometimes but very rarely: *We only see each other every once in a while.*

some·way /ˈsʌmweɪ/ *adv AmE informal* SOMEHOW(1)

some·what /ˈsʌmwɒt $ -wɑːt/ ●●● S3 W2 AWL *adv* more than a little but not very: **somewhat larger/higher/newer etc** *The price is somewhat higher than I expected. | Things have changed somewhat since then. |* **[+of]** *To say that I was surprised is somewhat of an understatement.*

some·where /ˈsʌmweə $ -wer/ ●●● S1 W2 *adv*
1 in or to a place, but you do not say or know exactly where: *My wallet must be around here somewhere. |* **somewhere to do sth** *There must be somewhere to eat cheaply in this town. |* **somewhere safe/different etc** *Is there somewhere safe where I can leave my bike? | Go and play* ***somewhere else*** (=in a different place) *– I'm trying to work. | We could meet for dinner at Giorgio's* ***or somewhere*** (=or a similar place).
2 somewhere around/between etc a little more or a little less than a particular number or amount, especially a large one SYN **approximately**: *We have* ***somewhere in the region of*** *500 firefighters in this area.*
3 be getting somewhere to be making progress: *At last I feel we're getting somewhere.*

som·nam·bu·list /sɒmˈnæmbjələst $ sɑːm-/ *n* [C] *formal* someone who walks while they are asleep SYN **sleepwalker** —**somnambulism** *n* [U]

som·no·lent /ˈsɒmnələnt $ ˈsɑːm-/ *adj literary*
1 almost starting to sleep SYN **sleepy**: *He lay quiet, somnolent after the day's exertions.* **2** making you want to sleep SYN **soporific**: *a somnolent summer's afternoon* —**somnolence** *n* [U]

son /sʌn/ ●●● S1 W1 *n*
1 [C] someone's male child → **daughter**: *Her son Sean was born in 1983. | They have three sons and a daughter. | In those days, the property went to the eldest son. | their youngest son, George |* **[+of]** *the son of a poor farmer* → **like father like son** at FATHER[1](7)
2 [singular] *spoken* used by an older person as a way to address a boy or young man: *What's your name, son?*
3 the Son Jesus Christ, the second member of the group from the Christian religion that also includes the Father and the Holy Spirit
4 [C] *written* a man, especially a famous man, from a particular place or country: *Frank Sinatra, New Jersey's most famous son*
5 my son used by a priest to address a man or boy → **favourite son** at FAVOURITE[1](2)

so·nar /ˈsəʊnɑː, -nə $ ˈsoʊnɑːr, -nər/ *n* [U] equipment on a ship or SUBMARINE that uses SOUND WAVES to find out the position of objects under the water

so·na·ta /səˈnɑːtə/ *n* [C] a piece of music with three or four parts that is written for a piano, or for a piano and another instrument: *a piano sonata*

son et lu·mi·ère /ˌsɒn eɪ ˈluːmieə $ ˌsɑːn eɪ luːmˈjer/ *n* [singular, U] *BrE* a performance that tells the story of a historical place or event using lights and recorded sound

song /sɒŋ $ sɔːŋ/ ●●● S1 W2 *n*
1 MUSIC WITH WORDS **a)** [C] a short piece of music with words that you sing: *We used to listen to pop songs on the radio. | They sat round with guitars, singing songs.* **b)** [U] songs in general: *The bravery of past warriors was celebrated in song.*
2 BIRDS [C,U] the musical sounds made by birds and some other animals such as WHALES: *the song of the lark*
3 for a song very cheaply: *He bought the house for a song five years ago.*
4 a song and dance (about sth) *informal* **a)** *BrE* if you make a song and dance about something, you behave as if it was worse, more important, more difficult etc than it really is: *Suzy was there,* ***making a song and dance*** *about her aching feet.* **b)** *AmE* an explanation or excuse that is too long and complicated: *She* ***gave us a long song and dance*** *about why she was late.* → SWANSONG

COLLOCATIONS

VERBS
sing a song *He started singing a little song.*
play a song (=with singing and musical instruments) *The band played a lot of their old songs.*
perform a song (=in public) *He doesn't like performing his songs live.*
write/compose a song *Do they write their own songs?*
record a song (=onto a CD so that it can be sold)

ADJECTIVES/NOUN + song
good/great *That's a great song!*
new *Are any of the songs on the album new?*
old *People always want to hear their old songs.*
a pop/folk song | a popular song (=used mainly of songs written before the 1960s) **| a love song | a protest song | a Beatles/REM etc song**

PHRASES
burst/break into song (=start singing) *The crowd spontaneously burst into song.*

song·bird /ˈsɒŋbɜːd $ ˈsɔːŋbɜːrd/ *n* [C] a bird that can make musical sounds

song·book /ˈsɒŋbʊk $ ˈsɔːŋ-/ *n* [C] a book with the words and music of many songs

song·ster /ˈsɒŋstə $ ˈsɔːŋstər/ *n* [C] **1** a singer – used in newspapers **2** *literary* a songbird

song·stress /ˈsɒŋstrɪs $ ˈsɔːŋ-/ *n* [C] a female singer – used in newspapers

song·writ·er /ˈsɒŋˌraɪtə $ ˈsɔːŋˌraɪtər/ ●●○ *n* [C] someone who writes the words and usually the music of songs

song·writ·ing /ˈsɒŋˌraɪtɪŋ $ ˈsɔːŋ-/ *n* [U] the process of writing songs: *There's some excellent songwriting on this album.*

son·ic /ˈsɒnɪk $ ˈsɑː-/ *adj* [only before noun] *technical* relating to sound, SOUND WAVES, or the speed of sound

ˌsonic ˈboom *n* [C] the loud sound like an explosion that an aircraft makes when it starts to travel faster than the speed of sound

ˈson-in-ˌlaw ●●○ *n* (*plural* **sons-in-law**) [C] the husband of your daughter → **daughter-in-law**

son·net /ˈsɒnɪt $ ˈsɑː-/ *n* [C] a poem with 14 lines which RHYME with each other in a fixed pattern: *Shakespeare's sonnets*

son·ny /ˈsʌni/ *n old-fashioned spoken* used when speaking to a boy or young man who is much younger than you: *Now you listen to me, sonny.*

ˌSonny ˈJim *n BrE old-fashioned spoken* used when speaking to a man or boy, especially when you are telling him that he has done something wrong

ˌson of a ˈbitch *n* (*plural* **sons of bitches**) *spoken not polite especially AmE* **1** [C] an offensive expression for a man that you are very angry with: *He's a filthy lying son of a bitch.* **2 son of a bitch!** used when you are annoyed or surprised: *Son of a bitch! You did it!* **3 be a son of a bitch** to be very difficult: *Getting the new tire on was a real son of a bitch.*

ˌson of a ˈgun *n* [singular] *AmE spoken* **1** a man you like or admire – used humorously: *Duke, you old son of a gun,* *how are you?* **2** a man that you are annoyed with: *Somebody go tell that son of a gun we're all waiting here.* **3** an object that is difficult to deal with – used humorously **4 son of a gun!** used to express surprise

ˌSon of ˈGod *n* **the Son of God** used by Christians to mean Jesus Christ

son·o·gram /ˈsɒnəgræm $ ˈsɑː-/ *n* [C] *AmE technical* an image, for example of an unborn baby inside its mother's body, that is produced by a special machine SYN **ultrasound** *BrE*

so·nor·ous /ˈsɒnərəs, səˈnɔːrəs $ səˈnɔːrəs, ˈsɑːnərəs/ *adj literary* having a pleasantly deep loud sound: *a sonorous voice* —**sonorously** *adv*

soon /suːn/ ●●● S1 W1 *adv* (*comparative* **sooner**, *superlative* **soonest**)

1 in a short time from now, or a short time after something else happens: *It will be dark soon.* | *David arrived sooner than I expected.* | **soon after** *Paula became pregnant soon after they were married.* | *'Who?' 'You'll find out* ***soon enough*** (=fairly soon).'

2 quickly: ***How soon*** *can you finish the report?* | *Try and get the car fixed* ***as soon as possible***.

3 as soon as immediately after something happens, without delay: *As soon as she entered the room, she knew there was something wrong.* | *I'll come over to your place as soon as I can.*

4 the sooner (...) the better used to say that it is important that something should happen very soon: *The sooner we get this job finished the better.* | *Let's get out of here! The sooner the better!*

5 the sooner ... the sooner used to say that you want something to happen soon, so that something else can then happen: *The sooner I get this work done, the sooner I can go home.*

6 no sooner had/did ... than used to say that something happened almost immediately after something else: *No sooner had he sat down than the phone rang.*

7 sooner or later used to say that something is certain to happen at some time in the future, though you cannot be sure exactly when: *His wife's bound to find out sooner or later.*

8 too soon too early: **too soon to do sth** *It's still too soon to say whether the operation was a success.* | *The holidays were over* ***all too soon*** (=much earlier than you would like).

9 no sooner said than done used to say that you will do something immediately

10 not a moment too soon/none too soon almost too late: *'The doctor's here!' 'And not a moment too soon!'*

11 sb would sooner do sth (than) if you would sooner do something, you would much prefer to do it, especially instead of something that seems unpleasant: *I'd sooner die than marry you!*

12 sb would (just) as soon *formal* used to say that someone would prefer to do something or would prefer something to happen: *I'd just as soon you didn't drive the car while I'm gone.*

GRAMMAR GUIDE ▸ VERBS

THESAURUS

soon in a short time from now, or a short time after something else happens: *See you soon!* | *It seemed difficult at first, but I soon got used to it.*

in the near future in the next few weeks or months. In the near future is more formal than **soon**: *The book will be on sale in the near future.*

in no time (at all) very soon – used to talk about something good happening: *You'll be feeling better in no time at all.* | *In no time at all, her son was starting to speak Japanese.*

in a minute *spoken* used to say that you will do something or something will happen within a few minutes: *I'll be ready in a minute.* | *The film's going to start in a minute.*

any minute now *spoken* used to say that something will or may happen very soon, but you do not know exactly when: *They should be here any minute now.*

any day now *spoken* used to say that something will or may happen in the next few days, but you do not know exactly when: *I'm hoping to hear from her any day now.*

shortly *formal* a short time from now: *They will be with us shortly.* | *the new laws that will shortly be coming into effect*

before long *especially literary* soon – used especially when something happens which you expected to happen: *They got married, and before long Anna was expecting a baby.*

it will not be long used when saying that something will happen soon: *It won't be long before everything is back to normal.*

soot /sʊt/ *n* [U] black powder that is produced when something is burned —**sooty** *adj*

soothe /suːð/ ●○○ *v* [T]

1 to make someone feel calmer and less anxious, upset, or angry: *Lucy soothed the baby by rocking it in her arms.* | *She made a cup of tea to soothe her nerves.*

2 (*also* **soothe sth ↔ away**) to make a pain become less severe, or slowly disappear: *I bought some lozenges to soothe my sore throat.* | *Massage can gently soothe away your aches and pains.* —**soothing** *adj*: *gentle, soothing music* —**soothingly** *adv*

sooth·say·er /ˈsuːθˌseɪə $ -ər/ *n* [C] *old use* someone who is believed to be able to say what will happen in the future SYN **clairvoyant**

sop[1] /sɒp $ sɑːp/ *n* [C usually singular] something not very important or valuable that a government or someone in authority offers to people to stop them from complaining or protesting – used to show disapproval: **[+to]** *The company agreed to inspect the river regularly, as a sop to the environmental lobby.*

sop[2] *v* (**sopped**, **sopping**)

sop sth **↔ up** *phr v* to remove liquid from a surface by using a piece of cloth that takes the liquid into itself

so·phis·ti·cate /səˈfɪstɪkeɪt/ *n* [C] *formal* someone who is sophisticated

so·phis·ti·cat·ed /səˈfɪstɪkeɪtɪd/ ●●○ *adj*

1 having a lot of experience of life, and good judgment about socially important things such as art, fashion etc: *a sophisticated, witty American* | *Clarissa's hair was swept up into a sophisticated style.*

2 a sophisticated machine, system, method etc is very well designed and very advanced, and often works in a complicated way: *sophisticated software* | *a* ***highly sophisticated*** *weapons system*

3 having a lot of knowledge and experience of difficult or complicated subjects and therefore able to understand them well: *British voters have become much more sophisticated.* THESAURUS ▸ ADVANCED —**sophistication** /səˌfɪstɪˈkeɪʃən/ *n* [U]: *a New York nightclub that was* ***the height of sophistication*** (=very fashionable and expensive)

soph·ist·ry /ˈsɒfəstri $ ˈsɑː-/ *n* (*plural* **sophistries**) [C,U] *formal* the clever use of reasons or explanations that seem correct but are really false, in order to deceive people

soph·o·more /ˈsɒfəmɔː $ ˈsɑːfəmɔːr/ *n* [C] *AmE* a student who is in their second year of study at a college or HIGH SCHOOL → **freshman**, **junior**, **senior**

soph·o·mor·ic /ˌsɒfəˈmɒrɪk◂ $ ˌsɑːfəˈmɔːrɪk◂, -ˈmɑː-/ *adj AmE formal* silly, and behaving in a way that is typical of someone much younger: *sophomoric humor*

sop·o·rif·ic /ˌsɒpəˈrɪfɪk◂ $ ˌsɑː-/ *adj formal* making you feel ready to sleep: *His voice had an almost soporific effect.*

sop·ping /ˈsɒpɪŋ $ ˈsɑː-/ (*also* **ˌsopping ˈwet**) *adj* very wet SYN **soaking**: *My clothes were absolutely sopping!*

sop·py /ˈsɒpi $ ˈsɑːpi/ ●○○ *adj* (*comparative* **soppier**, *superlative* **soppiest**) *BrE informal*

1 expressing love or emotions in a way that seems silly SYN **sappy** *AmE*: *a soppy film*

2 be soppy about sb/sth to be very fond of someone or something, in a way that seems silly to other people: *She's soppy about dogs.*

S

so·pra·no¹ /sə'prɑːnəʊ $ -'prænoʊ/ *n* (*plural* **sopranos**)
1 [C] a very high singing voice belonging to a woman or a boy, or a singer with a voice like this → MEZZO-SOPRANO
2 [singular] the part of a musical work that is written for a soprano voice or instrument: *She **sings soprano**.* → **alto**, **baritone**, **bass**, **tenor**

soprano² *adj* [only before noun] a soprano voice or instrument has the highest range of notes

sor·bet /'sɔːbeɪ $ 'sɔːrbɪt/ *n* [C,U] a frozen sweet food made of fruit juice, sugar, and water → **ice cream**

sor·cer·er /'sɔːsərə $ 'sɔːrsərər/ *n* [C] a man in stories who uses magic and receives help from evil forces → **wizard**

sor·cer·ess /'sɔːsərɪs $ 'sɔːr-/ *n* [C] a woman in stories who uses magic and receives help from evil forces → **witch**

sor·cer·y /'sɔːsəri $ 'sɔːr-/ *n* [U] magic that uses the power of evil forces → **black magic**

sor·did /'sɔːdɪd $ 'sɔːr-/ *adj* **1** involving immoral or dishonest behaviour: **sordid business/affair/story etc** *The whole sordid affair came out in the press.* | *She discovered the truth about his sordid past.* | *I want to hear all **the sordid details**!* **2** very dirty and unpleasant SYN **squalid**: *a sordid little room*

sore¹ /sɔː $ sɔːr/ ●●● S3 *adj*
1 a part of your body that is sore is painful, because of infection or because you have used a muscle too much: *I had a **sore throat** and aching limbs.* | **[+from]** *My arms are sore from all the lifting.* THESAURUS ▸ PAINFUL
2 sore point/spot/subject (with sb) something that is likely to make someone upset or angry when you talk about it: *Just don't mention it – it's always been a sore point with him.*
3 [not before noun] *especially AmE informal* upset, angry, and annoyed, especially because you have not been treated fairly: *Mac's still sore because I didn't invite him.* | **[+at]** *Don't be sore at me – I just forgot to tell you.*
4 [only before noun] *BrE* used to emphasize how serious, difficult etc something is: *Inner city schools are **in sore need of** extra funds.*
5 sore loser someone who gets angry or upset when they lose a game or competition: *Nobody likes a sore loser.*
6 stick/stand out like a sore thumb *informal* if someone or something sticks out like a sore thumb, they are very noticeable because they are different from everyone or everything else: *You stick out like a sore thumb in that uniform.* → **be like a bear with a sore head** at BEAR²(3), → **a sight for sore eyes** at SIGHT¹(14)

sore² *n* [C] a painful, often red, place on your body caused by a wound or infection: *They were starving and covered with sores.* → COLD SORE, BEDSORE, → **running sore** at RUNNING²(5)

sore·head /'sɔːhed $ 'sɔːr-/ *n* [C] *AmE informal* someone who is unpleasant or angry in an unreasonable way

sore·ly /'sɔːli $ 'sɔːrli/ *adv* very much or very seriously SYN **greatly**: *Jim will be **sorely missed**.* | *Sabine was **sorely tempted** to throw her drink in his face.* | *Your help is **sorely needed**.* | *Courage is a quality that is **sorely lacking** in world leaders today.*

sor·ghum /'sɔːgəm $ 'sɔːr-/ *n* [U] a type of grain that is grown in tropical areas

so·ror·i·ty /sə'rɒrəti $ sə'rɔː-/ *n* (*plural* **sororities**) [C] a club for women students at some American colleges and universities → **fraternity**

sor·rel /'sɒrəl $ 'sɔː-, 'sɑː-/ *n* [U] a plant with leaves that taste bitter, sometimes used in cooking

sor·row¹ /'sɒrəʊ $ 'sɑːroʊ, 'sɔː-/ ●○○ *n*
1 [U] a feeling of great sadness, usually because someone has died or because something terrible has happened to you → **grief**: **great/deep sorrow** *a time of great sorrow* | **[+at]** *He expressed his sorrow at my father's death.* | **[+for]** *Claudia felt a deep pang of sorrow for the woman.*

> **REGISTER**
> In everyday English, people usually say **sadness** rather than **sorrow**: *She talked about her **sadness** after his death.*

2 [C] an event or situation that makes you feel great sadness: *the family's joys and sorrows*
3 more in sorrow than in anger in a way that shows you are sad or disappointed rather than angry about a particular situation: *He said that his decision to resign was made more in sorrow than in anger.* → **drown your sorrows** at DROWN(5)

sorrow² *v* [I] *literary* to feel or express sorrow: **[+over]** *Her friend was sorrowing over the loss of a child.* | *sorrowing parents*

sor·row·ful /'sɒrəʊfəl $ 'sɑːroʊ-, 'sɔː-/ *adj literary* very sad: *a sorrowful expression* —**sorrowfully** *adv*: *'A lot of damage has already been done,' he said sorrowfully.*

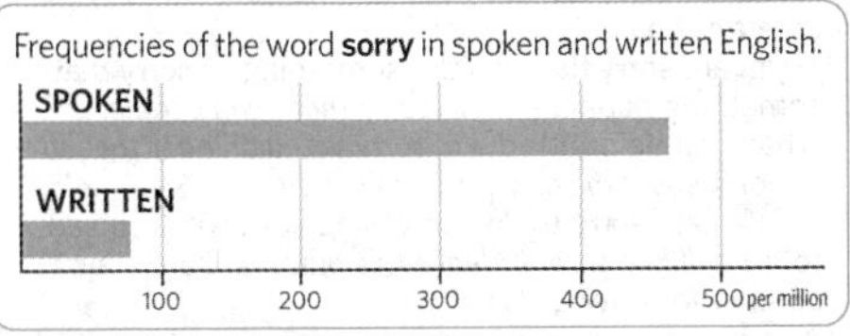

sor·ry /'sɒri $ 'sɑːri, 'sɔːri/ ●●● S1 W2 *adj* (*comparative* **sorrier**, *superlative* **sorriest**)
1 sorry/I'm sorry *spoken* **a)** used to tell someone that you wish you had not done something that has affected them badly, hurt them etc: *I'm really sorry. I didn't mean to hurt your feelings.* | *'Matt, stop doing that!' 'Sorry!'* | *I'm sorry, did I step on your foot?* | **sorry (that)** *I'm sorry I'm late – the traffic was terrible.* | **sorry about sth** *Sorry about the mess – I'll clean it up.* | **sorry for (doing) sth** *I'm sorry for making such a fuss.* | ***Sorry to bother you**, but what was the address again?* **b)** used as a polite way of introducing disappointing information or a piece of bad news: *I'm sorry, but all the flights to Athens are fully booked.* **c)** used when you have said something that is not correct, and want to say something that is correct: *Turn right – sorry left – at the traffic lights.* **d)** used when you refuse an offer or request: *'Are you coming to lunch?' 'Sorry, no. I've got to finish this work.'* | *'I'll give you $50 for it.' 'Sorry, no deal.'* **e)** used when you disagree with someone, or tell someone that they have done something wrong: *I'm sorry, but I find that very hard to believe, Miss Brannigan.*
2 ASHAMED [not before noun] feeling ashamed or unhappy about something bad you have done: **sorry for sth** *She was genuinely sorry for what she had done.* | **sorry (that)** *Casey was sorry he'd gotten so angry.* | **say (you are) sorry** (=tell someone that you feel bad about hurting them, causing problems etc) *It was probably too late to say sorry, but she would try anyway.*
3 sorry? *spoken* used to ask someone to repeat something that you have not heard properly SYN **pardon**: *Sorry? What was that again?* | *'Want a drink?' 'Sorry?' 'I said, would you like a drink?'*
4 FEELING PITY **be/feel sorry for sb** to feel pity or sympathy for someone because something bad has happened to them or because they are in a bad situation: *I've got no sympathy for him, but I feel sorry for his wife.* | *Tina was sorry for her. She seemed so lonely.* | **feel sorry for yourself** (=feel unhappy and pity yourself) *It's no good feeling sorry for yourself. It's all your own fault.*
5 SAD/DISAPPOINTED [not before noun] feeling sad about a situation, and wishing it were different: **sorry (that)** *Brigid was always sorry she hadn't kept up her piano lessons.* | **sorry to do sth** *We were sorry to miss your concert.* | *I won't be sorry to leave this place.* | **sorry to hear/see/learn** *I was sorry to hear about your accident.* | **[+about]** *I'm so sorry about your father* (=sorry something bad has happened to him).
6 you'll be sorry *spoken* used to tell someone that they will soon wish they had not done something, especially because someone will be angry or punish them: *You'll be sorry when your dad hears about this.*
7 I'm sorry to say (that) *spoken* used to say that you are disappointed that something has happened: *I wrote several times but they never replied, I'm sorry to say.*
8 VERY BAD [only before noun] very bad, especially in a way that makes you feel pity or disapproval: *the **sorry state** of the environment* | *It's a **sorry state of affairs** when an*

S

old lady has to wait 12 hours to see a doctor. | *the* ***sorry sight*** *of so many dead animals* | *This whole* ***sorry episode*** (=bad thing that happened) *shows just how incompetent the government has become.* → **better safe than sorry** at SAFE¹(10)

GRAMMAR: Patterns with sorry

• You are **sorry about** something bad that has happened: *I'm sorry about what I said.* | *I'm sorry about your car* (=sorry that your car has been damaged).
• You are **sorry for** the delay, the inconvenience, or the trouble: *The next train will arrive in 12 minutes. We are sorry for the delay.*
• You are **sorry for doing** something bad: *I'm sorry for upsetting you.*
• You are **sorry that** you did something or **sorry that** something happened: *I'm sorry that I can't come.* 'That' can be omitted: *I'm sorry you didn't get the job.* ✗ Don't say: *I'm sorry for I can't come.*
• If you are **sorry to do** something, it makes you sad to do it: *I'll be sorry to leave this place.* ✗ Don't say: *I'll be sorry for leaving this place.*

Frequencies of the noun **sort** in spoken and written English.

SPOKEN

WRITTEN

500 1000 per million

sort¹ /sɔːt $ sɔːrt/ ●●● S1 W1 *n*
1 TYPE/KIND [C] a group or class of people, things etc that have similar qualities or features SYN **type**, **kind**: **[+of]** *What sort of shampoo do you use?* | **all sorts (of sth)** (=a lot of different types of things) *I like all sorts of food – I'm not fussy.* | **of this/that sort** *On expeditions of this sort, you have to be prepared for trouble.* | **of some sort/some sort of sth** (=used when you do not know exactly what type) *He wondered if Rosa was in some sort of trouble.* | *There was a game of some sort going on inside.* | *Most of the victims developed psychological problems* ***of one sort or another*** (=of various different types). | *They do burgers, pizzas,* ***that sort of thing.***
2 sort of *spoken* **a)** used to say that something is partly true but does not describe the exact situation: *I sort of like him, but I don't know why.* | *'Do you know what I mean?' 'Sort of.'* **b)** used when you are trying to describe something but it is difficult to find the right word or to be exact: *Then they started sort of chanting.* | *The walls are a sort of greeny-blue colour.* | **sort of like** (=used very informally when searching for the right words) *It was sort of like really strange and mysterious, walking round this empty building.* **c)** used to make what you are saying sound less strong or direct: *Well, I sort of thought we could go out together sometime.* | *It was sort of a shock when I found out.* **d) sort of price/time/speed etc** *especially BrE* a price etc that is not very exact, but could be slightly more or less: *That's the sort of price I was hoping to pay.* | *What sort of time were you thinking of starting?*
3 of sorts (*also* **of a sort**) used when something is not a good or typical example of its kind of thing: *I had a conversation of sorts with a very drunk man at the bus stop.*
4 sort of thing *BrE spoken* used when you are mentioning or describing something in a way that is not definite or exact: *We could just stay here and pass the time, sort of thing.* | *She uses a wheelchair sort of thing.*
5 what sort of ... ? *BrE spoken* used when you are angry about what someone has said or done: *What sort of time do you call this to come in?*
6 nothing of the sort *BrE spoken* used to say angrily that something is not true or that someone should not do something: *'I'm going to watch TV.' 'You'll do nothing of the sort!'*
7 PERSON [singular] *BrE* someone who has a particular type of character, and is therefore likely to behave in a particular way SYN **type**: *Iain's never even looked at another woman. He's not* ***the sort.***
8 it takes all sorts (to make a world) *BrE* used to say that you think someone is behaving in a strange or crazy way: *He goes climbing up cliffs without ropes or anything? Oh well, it takes all sorts.*
9 COMPUTER [singular] if a computer does a sort, it puts things in a particular order
10 ILL/UPSET **out of sorts** feeling a little ill or upset: *Louise went back to work feeling rather out of sorts.*

sort² ●●● S1 W3 *v* [T]
1 to put things in a particular order or arrange them in groups according to size, type etc: *The eggs are sorted according to size.* | **sort sth into sth** *Let's sort all the clothes into piles.* | *All the names on the list have been sorted into alphabetical order.*
2 *BrE spoken* to deal with a situation so that all the problems are solved and everything is organized → **sorted**: *Right, I'll leave this for Roger and Terry to sort, then.*

sort sth/sb ↔ **out** *phr v*
1 to arrange or organize something that is mixed up or untidy, so that it is ready to be used: *We need to sort out our camping gear before we go away.*
2 to separate one type of thing from another: *I've sorted out the papers that can be thrown away.* | **[+from]** *First, sort the white things out from the other clothes.*
3 *especially BrE* to successfully deal with a problem or difficult situation: *She went to a psychiatrist to try to* ***sort out*** *her* ***problems.*** | *I'll be glad to* ***get*** *this misunderstanding* ***sorted out.*** | **sort yourself out/get yourself sorted out** (=deal with all your problems) *I'm staying with a friend until I manage to sort myself out.*
4 *especially BrE* to succeed in making arrangements for something: *Have you sorted out where you're going to live yet?* | *She is trying to sort out childcare.*
5 sort itself out *BrE* if something sorts itself out, it stops being a problem without you having to do anything: *Our financial problems should sort themselves out in a week or two.*
6 *BrE informal* to stop someone from causing problems or annoying you, especially by attacking or punishing them: *If he bothers you again, I'll sort him out.*

sort through sth *phr v* to look for something among a lot of similar things, especially when you are arranging these things into an order: *Vicky sat down and sorted through the files.*

sort·ed /ˈsɔːtɪd $ ˈsɔːr-/ *adj* [not before noun] *BrE spoken informal* **1** properly arranged or planned: *Good, that's the accommodation sorted.* | *Calm down.* ***It's all sorted.*** | *I just want to* ***get*** *everything* ***sorted*** *before I go away.* **2** provided with the things that you want: *'Can I get you anything?' 'We're sorted, thanks.'* | **[+for]** *Are we sorted for alcohol for tonight?*

sor·tie¹ /ˈsɔːti $ ˈsɔːrti/ *n* [C] **1** a short flight made by a plane over enemy land, in order to bomb a city, military defences etc: *The US and its allies carried out 44,000 sorties during this period.* **2** a short trip, especially to an unfamiliar place: *We* ***made*** *a* ***sortie*** *from our hotel to the open-air market.* **3** *BrE* an attempt to do or take part in something new: **[+into]** *Australia's first sortie into the wine trade* **4** *BrE* an attack in which an army leaves its position for a short time to attack the enemy

sortie² *v* [I] to make a short attack on an enemy position or a flight over enemy land: *It was five months since the battleship had last sortied from home waters.*

ˈsorting ˌoffice *n* [C] *BrE* a place where letters and packages are put into groups according to where they have to be delivered

ˈsort-out *n* [singular] *BrE informal* an occasion when you tidy a room, desk etc and get rid of the things you do not need: *These cupboards need a good sort-out.*

SOS /ˌes əʊ ˈes $ -oʊ-/ *n* [singular] **1** a signal or message that a ship or plane sends when it is in danger and needs help → **mayday** **2** an urgent message that someone is in trouble and needs help: *This is an SOS for a Mr Tucker, whose mother is seriously ill.*

ˈ**so-so** ●●○ *adj, adv spoken* neither very good nor very bad SYN **average**: *'How was the party?' 'Oh, so-so.'*

sot /sɒt $ sɑːt/ *n* [C] *old-fashioned* someone who is drunk all the time SYN **drunkard**

sot·to vo·ce /ˌsɒtəʊ ˈvəʊtʃi $ ˌsɑːtoʊ ˈvoʊ-/ *adv formal* in a very quiet voice, so that other people cannot easily hear: *'No, it was Daniel,' she continued, sotto voce.*

sou /suː/ *n* [singular] *BrE old-fashioned* a very small amount of money: *He didn't have a sou.*

sou·bri·quet /ˈsuːbrɪkeɪ/ *n* [C] *formal* another spelling of SOBRIQUET

souf·flé /ˈsuːfleɪ $ suːˈfleɪ/ *n* [C,U] a baked food made with eggs, flour, milk, and often cheese or fruit all mixed together until it is light and full of air

sought /sɔːt $ sɒːt/ the past tense and past participle of SEEK

ˈ**sought-ˌafter** *adj* wanted by a lot of people but rare or difficult to get: **much/highly sought-after** *a much sought-after defense lawyer | By the mid-1920s, she had become one of Broadway's most sought-after actresses.*

souk /suːk/ *n* [C] a market in an Arab country

soul /səʊl $ soʊl/ ●●○ S3 W3 *n*

1 SB'S SPIRIT [C] the part of a person that is not physical, and that contains their character, thoughts, and feelings. Many people believe that a person's soul continues to exist after they have died. → **spirit**: *the immortality of the soul | It was as if those grey eyes could see into the very* ***depths of*** *her* ***soul***. | **in sb's soul** *the restlessness deep in his soul | the souls of the dead*

2 PERSON [C] used in particular phrases to mean a person: **happy/sensitive/brave/simple etc soul** *He is really quite a sensitive soul.* | **not a (living) soul** (=no one) *I promise I* ***won't tell a soul***. | **not a soul in sight/not a soul to be seen** *The night was dark and still, and there was not a soul in sight.* | **poor (old) soul** (=used to show pity for someone) *The poor old soul had fallen and broken her hip.*

3 MUSIC (*also* **soul music**) [U] a type of popular music that often expresses deep emotions, usually performed by black singers and musicians: *He listens to a lot of soul. | a soul band*

4 SENSE OF BEAUTY [U] **a)** the ability to be emotionally affected by art, music, literature etc: *My brother thinks that anyone who doesn't like poetry has no soul.* **b)** the quality that affects people emotionally, that a painting, piece of music etc can have: *Her performance was technically perfect, but it lacked soul.*

5 SPECIAL QUALITY [U] the special quality or part that gives something its true character: **[+of]** *Basho's poems capture the true soul of old Japan.*

6 be the soul of discretion to always be extremely careful to keep secrets: *Leon is the very soul of discretion.*

7 be good for the soul if something is good for the soul, it is good for you and you should do it, even though it may seem unpleasant - often used humorously: *They say that hardship is good for the soul.*

8 God rest his/her soul used when you mention the name of someone who is dead: *My father, God rest his soul, died here at Vernison Hall.*

9 PEOPLE IN A PLACE **souls** [plural] *literary* the number of souls in a place is the number of people who live there: *a village of two or three hundred souls*

10 bless my soul/upon my soul *old-fashioned spoken* used to express surprise → **bare your soul** at BARE²(2), → **be the life and soul of the party** at LIFE(16), → **keep body and soul together** at BODY(11), → **heart and soul** at HEART¹(2), → **sell your soul (to the devil)** at SELL¹

ˈ**soul-desˌtroying** *adj* something that is soul-destroying is extremely boring or makes you feel very unhappy: *a soul-destroying experience*

ˈ**soul food** *n* [U] traditional foods that are cooked and eaten by African-Americans in the southern US

soul·ful /ˈsəʊlfəl $ ˈsoʊl-/ *adj* expressing deep, usually sad, emotions: *He looked up with those great* ***soulful eyes***. | **soulful voice/vocals/melody etc** *his powerful, soulful voice* —**soulfully** *adv* —**soulfulness** *n* [U]

ˈ**soul jazz** *n* [U] a type of music that combines features of SOUL MUSIC and JAZZ

soul·less /ˈsəʊl-ləs $ ˈsoʊl-/ *adj* lacking the attractive qualities that make people happy: *a soulless city of grey concrete* —**soullessly** *adv* —**soullessness** *n* [U]

ˈ**soul mate** *n* [C] someone you have a very close relationship with because you share or understand the same emotions and interests

ˈ**soul ˌmusic** *n* [U] SOUL(3)

ˈ**soul patch** *n* [C] a small area of hair under a man's lower lip

ˈ**soul-ˌsearching** *n* [U] careful examination of your thoughts and feelings because you are very worried about whether or not it is right to do something: *After much soul-searching, I decided to resign.*

sound¹ /saʊnd/ ●●● S1 W1 *n*

1 [C,U] something that you hear, or what can be heard SYN **noise**: *There were strange sounds coming from the next room.* | **[+of]** *She could hear the sound of voices. | a vowel sound* → see Thesaurus box on p. 1750

2 [U] **a)** the sound produced by a television or radio programme, a film etc: *We apologize for the loss of sound during that report. | a sound engineer* **b)** the loudness of a television, radio, film etc SYN **volume**: **turn the sound down/up** *Turn the sound down a little, will you?*

3 [C usually singular, U] the particular quality that a singer's or group's music has: *We're trying to develop a harder, funkier sound.*

4 by/from the sound of it/things judging from what you have heard or read about something: *By the sound of it, things are worse than we thought.*

5 not like the sound of sth to feel worried by something that you have heard or read: *'There's been a slight change in our plans.' 'I don't like the sound of that.'*

6 sounds [plural] *BrE informal* songs or music that are on a record, CD, or tape: *I need to buy some new sounds.*

7 [C usually singular] a narrow area of water that connects two larger areas of water

COLLOCATIONS

ADJECTIVES

loud *There was a loud creaking sound and the branch snapped.*
faint/soft (=not loud) *The sound was so faint I wasn't sure what it was at first.*
deafening (=very loud) *The sound of the waterfall was deafening.*
distinctive/unmistakable *Suddenly from below came the unmistakable sound of gunfire.*
a strange sound *I heard a strange sound coming from outside.*
a familiar sound | **a distant sound** (=a long way away) | **a muffled sound** (=not clear) | **a banging/tearing/hissing etc sound**

VERBS

hear a sound *She heard the sound of a car starting.*
make a sound *The machine made a strange hissing sound.*
not make a sound (=be completely quiet) *He lay still and didn't make a sound.*
a sound comes from somewhere *The sounds seemed to be coming from the study below.*
sound travels | **sound carries** (=can be heard some distance away) | **a sound stops** | **a sound dies away** (=stops gradually)

COMMON ERRORS

⚠ Don't say 'a strong sound'. Say **a loud sound**.

sound² ●●● S1 W2 *v*

1 SEEM [linking verb] if something or someone sounds good, bad, strange etc, that is how they seem to you when you hear about them or read about them: **[+adj]** *Istanbul sounds really exciting. | The whole story sounded very odd. | $80 sounds about right for a decent hotel*

S

room. | **[+noun]** *BrE*: *That sounds a good idea.* | **[+like]** *Nick sounds like a nice guy.* | **it sounds as if/as though** *It sounds to me as if he needs professional help.* | **it sounds like** *informal*: *It sounds like you had a good time on your trip.* | *I'll come over to Richmond and take you out for dinner.* ***How does that sound*** (=used to ask someone what they think of your suggestion)? | *faraway places with strange-sounding names*

2 NOISE [linking verb] if a noise sounds like a particular thing, that is how it seems to you when you hear it: **[+like]** *To Thomas, her laugh sounded horribly like a growl.* | *I heard* ***what sounded like*** *fireworks.* | **[+adj]** *Her breathing sounded very loud.* | **(it) sounds as if/as though** *The banging sounded as if it was coming from next door.* | **(it) sounds like** *informal*: *It sounds like the dog wants to be let out.*

3 VOICE [linking verb] if someone sounds tired, happy, sad etc, that is how they seem to you when you hear their voice: **[+adj]** *Are you okay? You sound tired.* | *Josie didn't sound very keen when I spoke to her.* | *Her voice sounded very young.* | **sound as if/as though** *You sound as if you've got a cold.* | **sound like** *informal*: *She sounded like she'd been crying.* | **[+like]** *You sound just like my mother* (=the things you say, opinions you express etc are just like the things my mother says).

4 WARNING [T] to publicly give a warning or tell people to be careful: *Several earlier studies had* ***sounded*** *similar* ***warnings***. | **sound a note of caution/warning** *I would, however, sound a note of caution.* | *Now it is an American economist who is* ***sounding the alarm***.

5 MAKE A NOISE [I,T] if something such as a horn or bell sounds, or if you sound it, it makes a noise: *The bell sounded for dinner.* | *Sound your horn to warn other drivers.* | *She was unable to* ***sound the alarm***.

6 PRONOUNCE [T] *technical* to make the sound of a letter in a word: *The 's' in 'island' is not sounded.* GRAMMAR **Sound** is usually passive in this meaning.

7 MEASURE DEPTH [T] *technical* to measure the depth of the sea, a lake etc → **soundings**

THESAURUS: sound

A HIGH SOUND

squeak a very short high sound or cry: *I heard the squeak of his shoes on the tiled floor.* | *Annie gave a squeak of surprise.*

creak a long high sound that something makes when someone opens it, walks on it, sits on it etc – used especially about a door, wooden floor, bed, or stairs: *the creak of floorboards* | *The door opened with a creak.*

screech a loud, long, unpleasantly high sound – used especially about someone's voice, or about brakes, tyres etc: *There was a screech of tyres followed by a bang.* | *She let out a screech of horror.*

beep (*also* **bleep** *BrE*) a high electronic sound that a machine sends out, especially in order to attract someone's attention: *You'll hear a bleep when the photocopier's finished printing.*

A QUIET SOUND

hum a quiet low continuous sound, especially from electrical equipment, traffic, an engine, or people's conversation: *The only sound was the faint hum of the air-conditioning unit.* | *He could hear the hum of distant traffic.*

rustle a continuous quiet sound from papers, leaves, or clothes when they rub together: *She heard the rustle of dried leaves behind her.* | *the rustle of silk dresses*

murmur a quiet low continuous sound, especially from people's voices that are far away: *The murmur of voices died away.* | *They spoke in a low murmur.*

rumble a series of long low sounds, especially from big guns, traffic, or THUNDER: *I heard a rumble of thunder.* | *the low rumble of a train approaching*

MADE BY A LIQUID

splash the sound that a liquid makes when something hits it, or when it hits against another thing: *She jumped into the pool with a big splash.* | *the splash of the waves against the rocks*

gurgle the low sound that water makes when it flows gently over or through something: *the gurgle of a stream* | *She listened to the gurgle as the water drained out of the bath.*

plop the sudden short sound when something is dropped into a liquid: *Kate dropped the ice into her glass with a plop.*

MADE BY AIR OR GAS

hiss a continuous high sound when air or gas comes out of something: *There was a hiss of steam from the coffee machine.* | *Workers reported hearing a loud hiss moments before the explosion.*

MADE BY AN EXPLOSION, GUN ETC

bang a short sudden loud noise made by a gun, bomb etc: *There was a loud bang as the bomb exploded.* | *The firework went off with a bang.*

boom a very loud sound from an explosion, which you can hear for several seconds after it begins: *The building exploded into rubble with a loud boom.* | *The boom of artillery fire echoed in the distance.*

roar a continuous very loud noise that gets louder and continues for a long time: *The light was followed by the deafening roar of explosions.* | *the roar of the ship's guns*

MADE BY THINGS HITTING OTHER THINGS

bang a loud sound caused especially when something hard or heavy hits something else: *I heard a loud bang and rushed out to see what had happened.* | *He slammed the door shut with a bang.*

crash a very loud sound caused when something hits something else, especially when damage is caused: *The tray of dishes fell to the floor with a crash.* | *I heard an enormous crash outside our house, and I went to see what had happened.*

thud a quiet low sound made when a heavy object falls down onto surface: *There was a dull thud as the box hit the floor.* | *His head hit the ground with a sickening thud.*

thump a dull loud sound made when a heavy object hits something else: *There was a loud thump as Eddie threw Luther back against the wall.*

clink a short ringing sound made when two glass, metal, or china objects hit each other: *the clink of champagne glasses* | *The clink of cutlery could be heard in the restaurant.*

tinkle the pleasant sound that is made by light pieces of glass or metal hitting each other repeatedly: *He listened to the faint tinkle of cow bells in the distance.*

jingle the sound of small metal objects being shaken together: *the jingle of her bracelets* | *the jingle of keys*

rattle a short repeated sound made when things hit against each other – used especially when part of something is loose and is hitting against something: *There was a strange rattle coming from the engine.* | *the rattle of the trolley*

GRAMMAR: Linking verbs

Sound is a linking verb. This type of verb links the subject of the sentence with an adjective or noun: *That sounds ridiculous.* | *It sounds a good idea.*

sound off *phr v*
1 *informal* to express strong opinions about something, especially when you complain angrily in a way that other people find rude or boring: **[+about]** *She's always sounding off about too much sex in the media.* | *He should check his facts before sounding off.*
2 *AmE* if soldiers sound off, they shout out numbers or their names to show that they are there

sound sb/sth ↔ **out** *phr v* to talk to someone in order to find out what they think about a plan or idea: *He sounded people out and found the responses favourable.* | *They want to sound out his opinion before they approach him formally.* | **[+about]** *I wanted to sound her out about a job that I'm thinking of applying for.*

sound³ ●●○ W3 *adj*
1 WELL-JUDGED sensible or good, and likely to produce the right results OPP **poor**: *The book is full of sound advice.* | *a man of great integrity and sound judgement* | **ecologically/ideologically/theoretically etc sound** *environmentally sound farming practices* | *a sound investment*
2 PERSON *BrE* **a)** someone who is sound can be depended on to make good decisions and give good advice: **[+on]** *He's very sound on matters of law.* **b)** *informal* someone who is sound is a good person and can be trusted – used especially by young people: *My mum's sound. She'd never throw me out.*
3 THOROUGH [only before noun] complete and thorough: *a sound understanding of money and banking systems* | *a sound knowledge of English* | *He has a sound grasp of European history.*
4 IN GOOD CONDITION in good condition and not damaged in any way OPP **unsound**: *The floor was completely sound.* | *Is the building* ***structurally sound****?* | **sound as a bell** *BrE spoken* (=in perfect condition)
5 HEALTHY physically or mentally healthy OPP **unsound**: **of sound mind** *law* (=not mentally ill) | **sound as a bell** *BrE spoken* (=in perfect health)
6 SLEEP sound sleep is deep and peaceful: **sound sleeper** (=someone who always sleeps well) —**soundness** *n* [U]

sound⁴ *adv* **sound asleep** deeply asleep: *The baby was sound asleep.*

sound·bar /ˈsaʊndbɑː $ -bɑːr/ *n* [C] a long object containing SPEAKERS, for sound from a television

ˈsound ˌbarrier *n* **the sound barrier** the sudden increase in air pressure against a vehicle, especially an aircraft, when it is travelling near the speed of sound: **break the sound barrier** (=travel faster than the speed of sound)

ˈsound bite *n* [C] a very short part of a speech or statement, especially one made by a politician, that is broadcast on a radio or television news programme

sound·card, **ˈsound card** /ˈsaʊndkɑːd $ -kɑːrd/ *n* [C] a CIRCUIT BOARD that can be added to a computer so that it is able to produce sound

ˈsound check *n* [C] the process of checking that all the equipment needed for broadcasting or recording is working properly

ˈsound efˌfects *n* [plural] sounds produced artificially for a radio or television programme, a film etc

ˈsounding board *n* [C usually singular] someone you discuss your ideas with in order to see if they think your ideas are good: **[+for]** *John always used her as a sounding board for new ideas.*

sound·ings /ˈsaʊndɪŋz/ *n* [plural] **1** careful or secret questions that you ask someone to find out what they think about something: *We're* ***taking soundings*** *to find out how people feel about the changes.* **2** measurements you make to find out how deep water is

sound·less /ˈsaʊndləs/ *adj literary* without any sound SYN **silent** —**soundlessly** *adv*: *Theo crept soundlessly into the room.* —**soundlessness** *n* [U]

sound·ly /ˈsaʊndli/ *adv* **1** if you sleep soundly, you sleep deeply and peacefully: *The baby slept soundly all night.* **2 soundly defeated/beaten/thrashed** completely defeated or severely punished: *The Republicans were soundly defeated.*

sound·proof¹ /ˈsaʊndpruːf/ *adj* a soundproof wall, room etc is one that sound cannot pass through or into

soundproof² *v* [T] to make something soundproof

sound·smith /ˈsaʊndsmɪθ/ *n* [C] *AmE informal* someone who makes new music by electronically mixing the sounds from different musical instruments, songs etc: *the ever-innovating soundsmiths known as Matmos*

sound·stage /ˈsaʊndsteɪdʒ/ *n* [C] a large room that has been specially made so that no sounds from outside the room can be heard, used for making films and television programmes

ˈsound ˌsystem *n* [C] equipment for playing music, especially to people in a large space, for example at a rock concert or a club

sound·track /ˈsaʊndtræk/ *n* [C] the recorded music from a film: **[+to]** *the soundtrack to 'Top Gun'*

ˈsound wave *n* [C usually plural] the form that sound takes when it travels

soup¹ /suːp/ ●●● S3 *n* [C,U]
1 cooked liquid food, often containing small pieces of meat, fish, or vegetables: *homemade tomato soup*
2 be in the soup *informal* to be in trouble

soup² *v*
soup sth ↔ **up** *phr v informal* to improve something, especially a car, by making it more powerful

soup·çon /ˈsuːpsɒn $ -sɑːn/ *n* [singular + of] *formal* a very small amount of something – often used humorously

ˌsouped-ˈup *adj* a souped-up car has been made more powerful

ˈsoup ˌkitchen *n* [C] a place where people with no money and no homes can get free food

ˈsoup spoon *n* [C] a round spoon that is used for eating soup

soup·y /ˈsuːpi/ *adj* having a thick liquid quality like soup

sour¹ /saʊə $ saʊr/ ●●● S3 *adj*
1 having a sharp acid taste, like the taste of a LEMON or a fruit that is not ready to be eaten OPP **sweet** → **bitter**: *Rachel sampled the wine. It was sour.* | *sour cherries*
→ **SWEET-AND-SOUR** THESAURUS TASTE
2 milk or other food that is sour is not fresh and has a bad taste: **turn/go sour** (=become sour)

REGISTER

In everyday English, people usually say milk **goes bad** or, in British English, **goes off**, rather than **goes sour**.

3 unfriendly or looking bad-tempered: **sour look/face/smile etc** *Eliza was tall and thin, with a rather sour face.* | *a* ***sour-faced*** *old man*
4 *informal* if a relationship or plan turns or goes sour, it becomes less enjoyable, pleasant, or satisfactory: *As time went by, their marriage* ***turned sour****.* | *The meeting ended on a* ***sour note****, with neither side able to reach agreement.*
5 sour grapes used to say that someone is pretending that they dislike something because they want it but cannot have it – used to show disapproval —**sourly** *adv* —**sourness** *n* [U]

sour² *v* [I,T] **1** if a relationship or someone's attitude sours, or if something sours it, it becomes unfriendly or unfavourable: *An unhappy childhood has soured her view of life.* THESAURUS SPOIL **2** if milk sours, or if something sours it, it begins to have an unpleasant sharp taste

source¹ /sɔːs $ sɔːrs/ ●●● S2 W1 AWL *n* [C]
1 a thing, place, activity etc that you get something from: *They get their money from various sources.* | **[+of]** *Beans are a very good source of protein.* | *For me, music is a great source of enjoyment.* | **at source** *BrE*: *Is your pension taxed at source* (=before it is paid to you)?
2 the cause of something, especially a problem, or the place where it starts: **[+of]** *We've found the source of the*

S

trouble. | *The recent name change has been the source of some confusion.*
3 a person, book, or document that supplies you with information: *List all your sources at the end of your essay.* | *I've heard from* **reliable sources** *that the company is in trouble.*
4 the place where a stream or river starts → **mouth**
5 *technical* source code

COLLOCATIONS

ADJECTIVES/NOUN + source

a good/excellent/rich source (=a source that provides a lot of something) *Milk is a good source of calcium.*
a useful source *People said television was their most useful source of local information.*
a major/important source *The lead mines were once a major source of employment for the islanders.*
a great source *In times of stress, food can be a great source of comfort.*
the main/primary source *It started as a hobby, but now it is his main source of income.*
an alternative source *The university is exploring alternative funding sources.*
an energy source *We hope to see increased usage of renewable energy sources.*
a food source | **a power source** (=something that produces power) | **a light source** (=something that produces light)

source² AWL *v* [T] *technical* **1** if goods are sourced from a particular place, they are obtained from that place: **[+from]** *Fish for the restaurant is sourced daily from British ports.* | *locally sourced milk* **2** to find out where something can be obtained: *We might be able to source the parts.*

ˈsource code *n* [U] *technical* the original form in which a computer program is written before it is changed into a form that a particular type of computer can read → **machine code**

ˌsour ˈcream (*also* **ˌsoured ˈcream** *BrE*) *n* [U] cream which has been made thicker by adding BACTERIA

sour·dough /ˈsaʊədəʊ $ ˈsaʊrdoʊ/ *n* [U] uncooked DOUGH (=bread mixture) that is left to FERMENT before being used to make bread

sour·puss /ˈsaʊəpʊs $ ˈsaʊr-/ *n* [C] *old-fashioned* someone who complains a lot and is never happy or satisfied

south¹, **South** /saʊθ/ ●●● S1 W1 *n* [singular, U] (*written abbreviation* **S**)
1 the direction that is at the bottom of a map of the world, below the Equator. It is on the right if you are facing the rising sun: *Which way is south?* | **from/towards the south** *By now, the army was approaching from the south.* | **to the south (of sth)** *Gatwick airport is a few miles to the south of London.*
2 the south the southern part of a country or area: **in the south** *They lived in a small town in the south.* | **[+of]** *the south of India*

south², **South** ●●● S2 W2 *adj* [only before noun] (*written abbreviation* **S**)
1 in the south, or facing the south: *a village on the south coast* | *I am currently teaching in south Texas.*
2 a south wind comes from the south

south³ ●●● S3 W3 *adv* (*written abbreviation* **S**)
1 towards the south: *Most of the birds had already flown south.* | **[+of]** *a seaside town 99 km south of London* | *a south-facing garden*
2 down south a) *BrE informal* in or to the southern part of England: *We moved down south about five years ago.* **b)** *AmE* (*also* **down South**) in or to the southern US states: *His sister lives down south.*
3 go south *AmE informal* if a situation, organization, or set of standards goes south, it becomes very bad although it was once very good: *It seems like all our moral standards have just gone south.*

south·bound /ˈsaʊθbaʊnd/ *adj, adv* travelling or leading towards the south: *southbound traffic* | *The southbound lanes are closed.* | *The car was last seen traveling southbound on I-35.*

south·east¹, **Southeast** /ˌsaʊθˈiːst◂/ ●●○ *n* [U] (*written abbreviation* **SE**)
1 the direction that is exactly between south and east
2 the southeast the southeastern part of a country —**southeast** *adv*: *We continued southeast to Kells.*

southeast², **Southeast** ●●○ *adj* (*written abbreviation* **SE**)
1 a southeast wind comes from the southeast
2 in the southeast of a place: *the southeast quarter of the city*

south·east·er /ˌsaʊθˈiːstə $ -ər/ *n* [C] a strong wind or storm coming from the southeast

south·east·er·ly /ˌsaʊθˈiːstəli $ -ər-/ *adj* **1** towards or in the southeast: *Snow will spread to southeasterly regions tonight.* **2** a southeasterly wind comes from the southeast

south·east·ern /ˌsaʊθˈiːstən $ -ərn/ *adj* (*written abbreviation* **SE**) in or from the southeast part of a country or area: *southeastern Europe*

south·east·wards /saʊθˈiːstwədz $ -wərdz/ *adv* (*also* **south·east·ward** /-wəd $ -wərd/) towards the southeast —**southeastward** *adj*

south·er·ly /ˈsʌðəli $ -ər-/ *adj* **1** towards or in the south: *Tara walked* **in a southerly direction**. **2** a southerly wind comes from the south

south·ern, **Southern** /ˈsʌðən $ -ərn/ ●●● S2 W2 *adj* (*written abbreviation* **S**) in or from the south of a country or area: *a southern accent* | *Southern Italy*

ˌSouthern ˈbelle *n* [C] an attractive young woman from the South of the US, who comes from an upper-class family. The expression is mostly used when talking about the past, and a typical example of a Southern belle is Scarlet O'Hara, the main character in the book and film *Gone with the Wind*.

south·ern·er, **Southerner** /ˈsʌðənə $ -ərnər/ *n* [C] someone from the southern part of a country

ˌsouthern ˈhemisphere, **Southern Hemisphere** *n* **the southern hemisphere** the half of the world that is south of the Equator

ˌSouthern ˈLights *n* **the Southern Lights** bands of coloured light that are seen in the night sky in the most southern parts of the world SYN **aurora australis**

south·ern·most /ˈsʌðənməʊst $ -ərnmoʊst/ *adj* furthest south: *the southernmost tip of India*

south·paw /ˈsaʊθpɔː $ -pɒː/ *n* [C] *informal* someone who uses their left hand more than their right hand, especially a PITCHER in baseball or a BOXER

ˌSouth ˈPole *n* **the South Pole** the most southern point on the surface of the Earth → **magnetic pole**, **north pole** → see picture at **EARTH¹**

south·wards /ˈsaʊθwədz $ -wərdz/ (*also* **south·ward** /-wəd $ -wərd/) *adv* towards the south: *We followed the coast southwards.* —**southward** *adj*: *the southward route to Charlestown*

south·west¹, **Southwest** /ˌsaʊθˈwest◂/ ●●○ *n* [U] (*written abbreviation* **SW**)
1 the direction that is exactly between south and west
2 the southwest the southwestern part of a country —**southwest** *adv*: *The plane flew southwest toward Egypt.*

southwest², **Southwest** ●●○ *adj* (*written abbreviation* **SW**)
1 a southwest wind comes from the southwest
2 in the southwest of a place: *the southwest corner of France*

south·west·er·ly /ˌsaʊθˈwestəli $ -ərli/ *adj* **1** towards or in the southwest: *The plane was flying in a southwesterly direction.* **2** a southwesterly wind comes from the southwest

south·west·ern /ˌsaʊθˈwestən $ -ərn/ *adj* (*written abbreviation* **SW**) in or from the southwest part of a country or area: *southwestern Colorado*

south·west·wards /saʊθˈwestwədz $ -wərdz/ (*also*

south·west·ward /-wəd $ -wərd/) *adv* towards the south-west —**southwestward** *adj*

sou·ve·nir /ˌsuːvəˈnɪə,ˈsuːvənɪə $ -nɪr/ ●●○ *n* [C] an object that you buy or keep to remind yourself of a special occasion or a place you have visited SYN **memento**: **[+of]** *I bought a model of the Eiffel Tower* ***as a souvenir of*** *Paris.* | *a* ***souvenir shop*** | **[+from]** *a souvenir programme from the Gala Concert*

sou'west·er /saʊˈwestə $ -ər/ *n* [C] a hat made of shiny material that keeps the rain off, with a wide piece at the back that covers your neck

sove·reign[1] /ˈsɒvrɪn $ ˈsɑːv-/ ●○○ *n* [C]
1 *formal* a king or queen
2 a British gold coin used in the past that was worth £1

sovereign[2] ●○○ *adj*
1 having the highest power in a country: **sovereign power/control**
2 a sovereign country or state is independent and governs itself

sove·reign·ty /ˈsɒvrənti $ ˈsɑːv-/ *n* [U] **1** complete freedom and power to govern: *the sovereignty of Parliament* | **[+over]** *Spain's claim of sovereignty over the territory* **2** the power that an independent country has to govern itself: *the defence of our national sovereignty*

so·vi·et /ˈsəʊviət,ˈsɒ- $ ˈsoʊ-, ˈsɑː-/ *n* [C] an elected council in a Communist country

Soviet *adj* relating to the former USSR (Soviet Union) or its people

sow[1] /səʊ $ soʊ/ ●●○ *v* (*past tense* **sowed**, *past participle* **sown** /səʊn $ soʊn/ *or* **sowed**)
1 [I,T] to plant or scatter seeds on a piece of ground: *Sow the seeds in late March.* | **sow sth with sth** *These fields used to be sown with oats.*
2 [T] to do something that will cause a bad situation in the future: *repressive laws that are* ***sowing the seeds of*** *future conflicts* | **sow doubt/confusion/dissatisfaction etc** *an attempt to sow doubt among the jury members*
3 sow your wild oats if a man sows his wild oats, he has sex with many different women, especially when he is young —**sower** *n* [C]

sow[2] /saʊ/ *n* [C] a fully grown female pig → **boar**

sown /səʊn $ soʊn/ a past participle of SOW[1]

sox /sɒks $ sɑːks/ *n* [plural] an American spelling of 'socks', used especially in advertising

soy·a /ˈsɔɪə/ *BrE*, **soy** /sɔɪ/ *AmE n* [U] soya beans

ˈsoya bean *BrE*, **soy·bean** /ˈsɔɪbiːn/ *AmE n* [C] the bean of an Asian plant from which oil and food containing a lot of PROTEIN are produced

soy sauce /ˌsɔɪ ˈsɔːs $ ˈ../ (*also* ˌ**soya ˈsauce** *BrE*) *n* [U] a dark brown liquid made from soya beans that is used especially in Japanese and Chinese cooking

soz /sɒs $ sɑːz, sɔːz/ *interjection informal* sorry – used mainly by young people

soz·zled /ˈsɒzəld $ ˈsɑː-/ *adj BrE informal* drunk

spa /spɑː/ ●○○ *n* [C]
1 a) a place where the water has special minerals in it, and where people go to improve their health by drinking the water or swimming in it: *a historic spa town* **b)** (*also* **health spa**) a place where people go to improve their health and beauty, especially through swimming, exercise, beauty treatments etc
2 (*also* **spa bath**) *AmE* a bath or pool that sends currents of hot water around you SYN **Jacuzzi**

space[1] /speɪs/ ●●● S1 W1 *n*
1 EMPTY AREA [U] the amount of an area, room, container etc that is empty or available to be used: **[+for]** *There's space for a table and two chairs.* | ***How much space*** *is there on each disk?* | **more/less/enough space** *Now that we've got three kids, it'd be nice to have a bit more space.* | **space to do sth** *He had* ***plenty of space*** *to study.* | *The hedge* ***takes up*** *too much* ***space***. | **sense/feeling of space** (=the feeling that a place is large and empty, so you can move around easily) *In small homes, a single colour scheme can create a sense of space.*
2 AREA FOR PARTICULAR PURPOSE [C,U] an area, especially one used for a particular purpose: *a supermarket with 700 free* ***parking spaces*** | **storage/cupboard/shelf space** *We really do need more storage space.* | *the factory's* ***floor space*** (=the size of the available floor area)
3 BETWEEN THINGS [C] an empty place between two things, or between two parts of something SYN **gap**: **[+between]** *the space between the house and the garage* | *There was an empty space where the flowers had been.*
THESAURUS ▸ HOLE
4 OUTSIDE THE EARTH [U] the area beyond the Earth where the stars and PLANETS are: **in/into space** *Who was the first American in space?* | *creatures from* ***outer space*** (=far away in space) | **space travel/research/programme/exploration** *the history of space travel*

> **GRAMMAR**
> Don't say 'the space' in this meaning. You say: *One day people will live in space.* ✗ Don't say: *One day people will live in the space.*
> GRAMMAR GUIDE ▸ NOUNS

5 WHERE THINGS EXIST [U] all of the area in which everything exists, and in which everything has a position or direction: *the exact* ***point in space*** *where two lines meet* | *how people of other cultures think about* ***time and space***
6 TIME a) in/within the space of sth within a particular period of time: *Mandy had four children in the space of four years.* **b) a short space of time** a short period of time: *They achieved a lot in a short space of time.*
7 EMPTY LAND [C,U] land, or an area of land that has not been built on: *a pleasant town centre with plenty of* ***open space*** | *the* ***wide open spaces*** *of the prairies* | *the loss of* ***green space*** *in cities*
8 FREEDOM [U] the freedom to do what you want or do things on your own, especially in a relationship with someone else: *We* ***give*** *each other* ***space*** *in our marriage.* | *She* ***needed*** *time and* ***space*** *to sort out her life.*
9 IN WRITING [C] **a)** an empty area between written or printed words, lines etc: *Leave a space after each number.* **b)** the width of a TYPED letter of the alphabet: *The word 'the' takes up three spaces.* **c)** a place provided for you to write your name or other information on a document, piece of paper etc: *Please write any comments in the space provided.*
10 IN A REPORT/BOOK [U] the amount of space in a newspaper, magazine, or book that is used for a particular subject: *The story* ***got*** *very little* ***space*** *in the national newspapers.*
11 look/stare/gaze into space to look straight in front of you without looking at anything in particular, usually because you are thinking → BREATHING SPACE, PERSONAL SPACE, → **waste of space** at WASTE[1](5), → **watch this space** at WATCH[1](11)

> **COLLOCATIONS – MEANING 3**
> **ADJECTIVES**
> **small** *There was only a small space between the car and the wall.*
> **narrow** *Nathan stood in the doorway, filling the narrow space.*
> **a confined/enclosed space** (=small and enclosed) *It was difficult being together in such a confined space.*
> **an empty space** | **a blank space** (=on a page, wall etc)
> **VERBS**
> **clear/make a space** *Jack cleared a space for his newspaper on the table.*
> **leave a space** *Leave a space for the title at the top.*
> **fit in/into a space** *Decide what kind of table and chairs will fit best into the space.*

space[2] ●●○ (*also* **space out**) *v*
1 [T always + adv/prep] to arrange objects or events so that they have equal spaces or periods of time between them: *They used three microphones* ***spaced*** *several yards* ***apart***. | *Try to space out your classes and study in between.* | **be**

S

evenly spaced (=with equal spaces) *For security, use three evenly spaced bolts per post.*
2 [I] *informal* to stop paying attention and just look in front of you without thinking, especially because you are bored or have taken drugs: *I completely spaced out during the lecture.* → SPACED OUT

ˈspace-age *adj* very modern: *space-age technology*

ˈspace bar *n* [C] the wide key at the bottom of a computer KEYBOARD or TYPEWRITER that you press to make a space

ˈspace caˌdet *n* [C] *informal* someone who forgets things, does not pay attention, and often behaves strangely

ˈspace ˌcapsule *n* [C] the part of a spacecraft that carries people into space to obtain information and then comes back to Earth

space·craft /ˈspeɪs-krɑːft $ -kræft/ *n* (*plural* **spacecraft**) [C] a vehicle that is able to travel in space

ˌspaced ˈout *adj informal* not fully conscious of what is happening around you, especially because you are extremely tired or have taken drugs

space·man /ˈspeɪsmæn/ *n* (*plural* **spacemen** /-men/) [C] **1** *informal* a man who travels into space SYN **astronaut 2** someone in stories who visits the Earth from another world → **alien**

ˈspace probe *n* [C] a spacecraft without people in it, that is sent into space to collect information about the conditions there and send the information back to Earth

space·ship /ˈspeɪsˌʃɪp/ *n* [C] a vehicle for carrying people through space

ˈspace ˌshuttle *n* [C] a vehicle that is designed to go into space and return to Earth several times

ˈspace ˌstation *n* [C] a large spacecraft that stays above the Earth and is a base for people travelling in space or for scientific tests

space·suit /ˈspeɪs-suːt, -sjuːt $ -suːt/ *n* [C] a special protective suit that people wear in space, that covers the whole body and provides a supply of air

ˈspace ˌtourist *n* [C] someone who pays to go on a journey into space on a spacecraft

space·walk /ˈspeɪswɔːk $ -wɒːk/ *n* [C] the act of moving around outside a spacecraft while in space, or the time spent outside it

space·y /ˈspeɪsi/ *adj informal* behaving as though you are not fully conscious of what is happening around you: *I felt tired and kind of spacey.*

spac·ing /ˈspeɪsɪŋ/ *n* [U] the amount of space between the printed letters, words, or lines on a page: **single spacing** (=lines with no empty lines between them) | **double spacing** (=lines with one empty line after each one)

spa·cious /ˈspeɪʃəs/ ●●○ *adj* a spacious house, room etc is large and has plenty of space to move around in OPP **cramped**: *a spacious living area* —**spaciously** *adv* —**spaciousness** *n* [U]

spade /speɪd/ ●●○ *n* [C]
1 a tool for digging that has a long handle and a broad metal blade that you push into the ground → **shovel** → see picture at **GARDEN**
2 (*also* **spades** [plural]) a PLAYING CARD belonging to the set of cards that have one or more black shapes that look like pointed leaves printed on them: *the queen of spades*
3 call a spade a spade to speak about things in a direct and honest way, even though it may be impolite to do this
4 in spades to a great degree, or in large amounts: *Beauty, intelligence, wealth – my mother **had** all of them **in spades**.*
5 [C] *taboo old-fashioned* a very offensive word for a black person. Do not use this word.

spade·work /ˈspeɪd-wɜːk $ -wɜːrk/ *n* [U] hard work that has to be done in preparation before something can happen SYN **legwork**: *Most of **the spadework** had been **done** by 1981.*

spa·ghet·ti /spəˈgeti/ ●●● S3 *n* [U] a type of PASTA in very long thin pieces, that is cooked in boiling water: **spaghetti bolognaise** *BrE* (=cooked spaghetti served with a meat and tomato sauce) → **macaroni, tagliatelle**

Spaˌghetti ˈJunction *n* [C] **1** a place in Birmingham in central England where a lot of roads meet and cross over each other **2** *AmE informal* a place where a lot of roads cross over each other

spaˌghetti ˈwestern *n* [C] a film about American COWBOYS in the Wild West, especially one made in Europe by an Italian director

spake /speɪk/ *biblical or literary* a past tense of SPEAK

spam¹ /spæm/ *v* (**spammed, spamming**) [I,T] to send the same message to many different people using email or the Internet, usually as a way of advertising something – used to show disapproval —**spamming** *n* [U] —**spammer** *n* [C]

spam² *n* [U] email messages that a computer user has not asked for and does not want to read, for example from someone who is advertising something: *You can filter out spam with special software.* THESAURUS ADVERTISEMENT

Spam *n* [U] *trademark* a type of cheap CANNED meat made mainly from PORK

spam·block·ing /ˈspæmˌblɒkɪŋ $ -ˌblɑːk-/ *n* [U] ways of stopping unwanted emails from being sent to you, for example by having a list of addresses from which you will not accept emails → **munging**

spam·dex·ing /ˈspæmˌdeksɪŋ/ *n* [U] the practice of repeating certain popular words on a WEBPAGE many times, so that the website appears near the top of a list produced when you type the word into a SEARCH ENGINE

span¹ /spæn/ a past tense of SPIN¹

span² *n* [C] **1** a period of time between two dates or events: **over/within/in a span of sth** *Over a span of ten years, the company has made great progress.* | *It'll be difficult to hire that many new staff in such a short **time span**.*
2 the length of time over which someone's life, ability to pay attention to something etc continues: **attention/concentration span** *Most two-year-olds have a very **short attention span**.* | *Captivity vastly reduces the **life span** of whales.*
3 the part of a bridge, ARCH etc that goes across from one support to another **4** the distance from one side of something to the other: *a bird with a large wing span*

span³ *v* (**spanned, spanning**) [T] **1** to include all of a period of time: *a **career** which **spanned** nearly 60 years*
2 to include all of a particular space or area: *The Mongol Empire spanned much of Central Asia.* **3** if a bridge spans an area of water, especially a river, it goes from one side to the other

Span·dex /ˈspændeks/ *n* [U] *trademark* a material that stretches, used especially for making tight-fitting sports clothes

span·gle¹ /ˈspæŋgəl/ *v* [T] to cover something with shiny points of light: **be spangled with sth** *The city skyline was spangled with lights.* —**spangled, spangly** *adj*: *acrobats in spangled tights*

spangle² *n* [C] a small piece of shiny metal or plastic sewn onto clothes to give them a shining effect SYN **sequin**

Span·glish /ˈspæŋglɪʃ/ *n* [U] a mixture of Spanish and English, spoken especially in the US

Span·iard /ˈspænjəd $ -ərd/ *n* [C] *old-fashioned* someone from Spain

span·iel /ˈspænjəl/ *n* [C] a type of dog with long ears that hang down

Span·ish¹ /ˈspænɪʃ/ *adj* relating to Spain, its people, or its language

Spanish² *n* **1** [U] the language used in Spain and parts of Latin America **2 the Spanish** [plural] people from Spain

spank /spæŋk/ *v* [T] to hit a child on their bottom with your open hand, as a punishment SYN **smack** THESAURUS HIT —**spank** *n* [C]: *a spank on the bottom*

spank·ing¹ /ˈspæŋkɪŋ/ *n* [C,U] the act of hitting a child on their bottom with your open hand, as a punishment: *If you don't stop that noise, you'll **get** a **spanking**!*

spanking² *adv informal* **1 spanking new** very new and impressive: *a spanking new shopping centre* **2 spanking clean** very clean

spanking³ *adj BrE* **at a spanking pace/rate** *old-fashioned* very fast: *They started walking at a spanking rate.*

span·ner /ˈspænə $ -ər/ *n* [C] *BrE* **1** a metal tool that fits over a NUT, used for turning the nut to make it tight or to undo it SYN **wrench** *AmE* → see picture at TOOL¹ **2 put/throw a spanner in the works** *informal* to unexpectedly do something that prevents a plan or process from succeeding

spar¹ /spɑː $ spɑːr/ *v* (**sparred**, **sparring**) [I] **1** to practise BOXING with someone: **[+with]** *He broke his nose while sparring with Vega.* **2** to argue with someone but not in an unpleasant way: **[+over]** *Senators are sparring over the health bill.* | **[+with]** *He's been sparring with the security guards.* → SPARRING PARTNER

spar² *n* [C] a thick pole, especially one used on a ship to support sails or ropes → **mast**

spare¹ /speə $ sper/ ●●○ *adj*
1 EXTRA **spare key/battery/clothes etc** a key etc that you keep in addition to the one you usually use, so that it is available if the one you usually use breaks, gets lost etc: *a spare key* | *Bring a towel and some spare clothes.* | *a supply of spare batteries* | *a spare tyre*
2 NOT USED/NEEDED [usually before noun] not being used or not needed at the present time: *Have you got any spare boxes?* | *You could sleep in the spare bedroom.* | *Do you have any spare cash?* | *I'll go and see if there are any spare seats.* | *A decline in beer sales had left the industry with* ***spare capacity*** (=the ability to produce more than can be sold).
3 TIME **spare time/moment/hour etc** time when you are not working: *What do you do in your spare time?* | *Eric spent every spare moment he had in the library.*
4 MONEY **spare change** coins of little value that you do not need and can give to other people: *There are beggars on every corner asking for spare change.*
5 be going spare *BrE spoken* if something is going spare, it is available for you to have or use: *I'll have some of that cake if it's going spare.*
6 go spare *BrE informal* to become very angry or worried: *Dad would go spare if he found out.*
7 PLAIN a spare style of writing, painting etc is plain or basic and uses nothing unnecessary
8 THIN *literary* someone who is spare is tall and thin

spare² ●○○ *v* [T]
1 GIVE to make something such as time, money, or workers available for someone, especially when this is difficult for you to do: *Sorry, I* ***can't spare*** *the* ***time***. | *I'd like you to come over when you can spare a couple of hours.* | *Can you spare £5?* | **spare sb/sth to do sth** *We're too busy to spare anyone to help you right now.* | **spare sb ten minutes/an hour etc** *Could you possibly spare me a few moments in private* (=used to ask someone if they have time to quickly talk to you)? | *It's very kind of you to spare me so much of your time.*
2 money/time etc to spare if you have money, time etc to spare, you have some left in addition to what you have used or need: *Anyone who has time to spare and would like to help can contact Moira.* | **with sth to spare** *They got to the airport with seconds to spare.* | *They still have some money to spare.*
3 spare sb the trouble/difficulty/pain etc (of doing sth) to prevent someone from having to experience something difficult or unpleasant: *I wanted to spare them the trouble of buying me a present.* | *Thankfully, she had been spared the ordeal of surgery.*
4 NOT DAMAGE OR HARM to not damage or harm someone or something, even though other people or things are being damaged, killed, or destroyed: *I could not understand why I had been spared and they had not.* | *the soldier who had* ***spared*** *his* ***life*** | **spare sb/sth from sth** *Today we will hear whether the school is to be spared from closure.*
5 spare a thought for sb to think about another person who is in a worse situation than you are: *Spare a thought for Nick, who's doing his exams right now.*
6 spare no expense/effort to spend as much money or do everything necessary to make something really good or successful: **spare no expense/effort to do sth** *No expense was spared in developing the necessary technology.* | *No effort will be spared to bring the people responsible to justice.*
7 spare sb (the details) to not tell someone all the details about something, because it is unpleasant or boring: *He spared us the details, saying only that he had been injured in the war.* | *'They own three houses. One in the country, one in ...' 'Spare me.'*
8 spare sb's feelings to avoid doing something that would upset someone: *Just tell me the truth. Don't worry about sparing my feelings.*
9 spare a glance *BrE written* to look quickly at someone or something: **[+at]** *Before leaving the old town, spare another glance at the tower.* | **spare sb/sth a glance** *a bored waitress who scarcely spared them a glance*
10 spare sb's blushes *BrE* to avoid doing something that would embarrass someone

spare³ *n* **1** [C] an additional thing, for example a key, that you keep so that it is available: *If you forget the key, Mrs Jones over the road has a spare.* | *The batteries are dead. Have you got any spares?* **2** [C] a SPARE TYRE **3 spares** [plural] *BrE* SPARE PARTS: **motor/car/aircraft etc spares** *a shortage of aircraft spares*

ˌspare ˈpart *n* [C usually plural] a new part for a vehicle or machine, that is used to replace a part that is damaged or broken

ˌspare ˈribs / $ ˈ../ *n* [plural] the RIBS of a pig and the meat on them, eaten as food

ˌspare ˈroom *n* [C] a bedroom in your house for guests SYN **guest room**

ˌspare ˈtyre *BrE*, **spare tire** *AmE n* [C] **1** an additional wheel with a tyre on it, that you keep in a car to use if another tyre gets damaged **2** the fat around someone's waist – used humorously

spar·ing·ly /ˈspeərɪŋli $ ˈsper-/ *adv* using or doing only a little of something: ***Use*** *the spices* ***sparingly***. —**sparing** *adj*: *We must be sparing with our resources.*

spark¹ /spɑːk $ spɑːrk/ ●○○ *n*
1 FIRE [C] a very small piece of burning material produced by a fire or by hitting or rubbing two hard objects together: *sparks from the fire* | *The scrape of metal on metal sent up a* ***shower of sparks***.
2 ELECTRICITY [C] a flash of light caused by electricity passing across a space: *electric sparks from a broken wire*
3 spark of interest/excitement/anger etc a small amount of a feeling or quality: *Rachel looked at her and felt a spark of hope.*
4 CAUSE [C] a small action or event that causes something to happen, especially trouble or violence: *The judge's verdict provided the spark for the riots.* | *Interest rate cuts were the spark the market needed.*
5 INTELLIGENCE/ENERGY [U] a quality of intelligence or energy that makes someone successful or fun to be with: *She was tired, and lacked her usual spark.* | *McKellen's performance gives the play its* ***spark of life*** (=quality of energy).
6 sparks [plural] anger or angry arguments: *The* ***sparks*** *were really* ***flying*** (=people were arguing angrily) *at the meeting!* → **bright spark** at BRIGHT(11)

spark² ●○○ *v*
1 [T] (*also* **spark sth ↔ off**) to be the cause of something, especially trouble or violence SYN **provoke**: *The police response sparked outrage in the community.* | *A discarded cigarette sparked a small brush fire.*
2 spark sb's interest/hope/curiosity etc to make someone feel interested, hopeful etc: *topics that spark children's imaginations*
3 [I] to produce sparks of fire or electricity

ˈsparking plug *n* [C] *BrE* a SPARK PLUG

spar·kle¹ /ˈspɑːkəl $ ˈspɑːr-/ ●●○ *v* [I]
1 to shine in small bright flashes → **sparkling**: *The sea sparkled in the sun.* | *The crystal chandelier sparkled.*
THESAURUS SHINE

S

2 if someone's eyes sparkle, they seem to shine brightly, especially because the person is happy or excited → **sparkling**: **[+with]** *Ron's eyes sparkled with excitement.*

sparkle² *n* [C,U] **1** a bright shiny appearance, with small points of flashing light: *the sparkle of the diamonds* **2** a quality that makes something or someone seem interesting and full of life: *the sparkle and zest of a live performance* **3** if someone has a sparkle in their eyes, their eyes seem to shine, and you can see a feeling in them, especially happiness or excitement: *There was a sparkle of fun in her brown eyes.*

spar·kler /ˈspɑːklə $ ˈspɑːrklər/ *n* [C] a type of FIREWORK that you can hold in your hand, consisting of a thin stick that gives off sparks of fire

spark·ling /ˈspɑːklɪŋ $ ˈspɑːr-/ *adj* **1** shining brightly with points of flashing light: *a sparkling blue lake* **2** very clean, and seeming to shine brightly: *a sparkling white beach* | *a* ***sparkling clean*** *kitchen* **3** a sparkling drink has bubbles of gas in it SYN **fizzy**: *a glass of sparkling wine* **4** full of life and intelligence: *Claire's sparkling personality*

ˈspark plug (*also* **sparking plug** *BrE*) *n* [C] a part in a car engine that produces an electric SPARK to make the petrol mixture start burning

spark·y /ˈspɑːki $ ˈspɑːr-/ *adj BrE* full of life and energy SYN **lively**: *Why would a sparky girl like Nicola want to marry him?*

ˈsparring ˌpartner *n* [C] **1** someone you practise BOXING with **2** someone you regularly have friendly arguments with

spar·row /ˈspærəʊ $ -roʊ/ *n* [C] a small brown bird, very common in many parts of the world

sparse /spɑːs $ spɑːrs/ *adj* existing only in small amounts: *his sparse brown hair* | *rural areas with sparse populations* —**sparsely** *adv*: *a* ***sparsely populated*** *area* —**sparseness** *n* [U]

spar·tan /ˈspɑːtn $ -ɑːr-/ *adj* spartan conditions or ways of living are simple and without any comfort: *spartan accommodation* | *a spartan existence*

spas·m /ˈspæzəm/ *n* **1** [C,U] an occasion when your muscles suddenly become tight, causing you pain: *Maggie felt a muscle spasm in her back.* | *Tom's jaw muscles had* ***gone into spasm.*** | **back/shoulder/throat etc spasm** **2** **spasm of grief/laughter/coughing etc** a sudden strong feeling or reaction that you have for a short period of time: *I felt a spasm of fear.*

spas·mod·ic /spæzˈmɒdɪk $ -ˈmɑː-/ *adj* **1** happening for short irregular periods, not continuously: *spasmodic machine gun fire* **2** *formal or medical* of or relating to a muscle spasm: *a spasmodic cough* —**spasmodically** /-kli/ *adv*

spas·tic /ˈspæstɪk/ *adj* **1** *old-fashioned* having CEREBRAL PALSY, a disease that prevents control of the muscles **2** *informal not polite* an insulting way of describing someone who drops things, falls easily, and is stupid – used especially by children —**spastic** *n* [C]

spat¹ /spæt/ the past tense and past participle of SPIT¹

spat² *n* [C] **1** *informal* a short unimportant quarrel: *a marital spat* **2** **spats** [plural] special pieces of cloth that fasten with buttons on top of a man's shoes, worn in the past

spate /speɪt/ *n* **1** **spate of sth** a large number of similar things that happen in a short period of time, especially bad things: *a spate of burglaries* **2** **in spate** *BrE* a river, stream etc that is in spate is very full and flowing very fast

spa·tial /ˈspeɪʃəl/ *adj* relating to the position, size, shape etc of things —**spatially** *adv*

spat·ter /ˈspætə $ -ər/ *v* [I,T] if a liquid spatters, or if something spatters it, drops of it fall or are thrown all over a surface SYN **splatter**: **spatter sb/sth with sth** *The walls were spattered with blood.* | **spatter sth on/over etc sth** *a sweatshirt with paint spattered over it* | **[+on/across/over etc]** *The first drops of rain spattered on the stones.* —**spatter** *n* [C]

spat·u·la /ˈspætjələ $ -tʃələ/ *n* [C] **1** a kitchen tool with a wide flat blade, used for spreading, mixing, or lifting soft substances **2** *BrE* a small instrument with a flat surface, used by doctors to hold your tongue down so that they can examine your throat

spawn¹ /spɔːn $ spɒːn/ *v* **1** [T] to make a series of things happen or start to exist: *New technology has spawned new business opportunities.* **2** [I,T] if a fish or FROG spawns, it produces eggs in large quantities at the same time

spawn² *n* [U] the eggs of a fish or FROG laid together in a soft mass

spay /speɪ/ *v* [T] to remove part of the sex organs of a female animal so that it is not able to have babies → **neuter**

speak /spiːk/ ●●● S1 W1 *v* (*past tense* **spoke** /spəʊk $ spoʊk/, *past participle* **spoken** /ˈspəʊkən $ ˈspoʊ-/)

1 IN CONVERSATION [I always + adv/prep] to talk to someone about something: **speak to sb** *I spoke to her last Wednesday.* | *'Hello, may I speak to Jim Smith?' 'Yes, speaking* (=used on the telephone)*'.* | *I know her by sight, but* ***not to speak to*** (=not well enough to talk to her). | **speak to sb about sth** *I haven't spoken to Steve about all this.* | **speak with sb** *especially AmE*: *They did not want to speak with reporters.* | **speak of sth** *It was the first time she had ever spoken of marriage.* THESAURUS ▸ TALK

2 SAY WORDS [I] to use your voice to produce words: *I was so shocked I couldn't speak.* | *He spoke very softly* (=quietly).

3 LANGUAGE [T not in progressive] to be able to talk in a particular language: *Do you speak English?* | *I* ***don't speak a word of*** *French* (=do not speak any French at all). | **can/can't speak sth** *Several children in the class can't speak English.* | **French-speaking/Italian-speaking etc** *a German-speaking secretary*

4 FORMAL SPEECH [I] to make a formal speech: **[+at]** *Jones spoke at the teachers' annual convention.* | **[+to]** *She asked me to speak to her students about my work in marketing.* | **[+in favour of/against]** *Only one MP spoke against the bill.* → SPEAKER(1)

5 EXPRESS IDEAS/OPINIONS [I always + adv/prep] to say something that expresses your ideas or opinions: **speak as a parent/teacher/democrat etc** *He emphasized that he was speaking as a private citizen, not in any official capacity.* | **speak well/highly/ill of sb** (=say good or bad things about someone) *Her co-workers spoke highly of her.* | *It's wrong to speak ill of the dead.* | **strictly/generally/roughly speaking** (=used when expressing an idea that you think is exactly true, generally true etc) *Strictly speaking, it's my money, not yours. I earned it.*

6 **so to speak** used when you are saying something in words that do not have their usual meaning: *We have to pull down the barriers, so to speak, of poverty.*

7 **speak your mind** to tell people exactly what you think, even if it offends them: *He was a tough politician who wasn't afraid to speak his mind.*

8 **be not speaking/not be on speaking terms** if two people are not speaking, they do not talk to each other, usually because they have argued: *He was not on speaking terms with his brother or sisters.*

9 **speak volumes (about/for sth)** if something speaks volumes, it clearly shows the nature of something or the feelings of a person: *What you wear speaks volumes about you.*

10 **speak with one voice** if a group of people speak with one voice, they all express the same opinion: *On this issue, the 12 organizations spoke with one voice.*

11 **speak the same language** if two people or groups speak the same language, they have similar attitudes and opinions

12 **speak out of turn** to say something when you do not have the right or authority to say it → **actions speak louder than words** at ACTION¹(13), → **the facts speak for themselves** at FACT(8), → **in a manner of speaking** at MANNER(5)

THESAURUS

TO SPEAK A LANGUAGE

speak to be able to talk in a foreign language: *Do you speak German?* | *I learnt Spanish for years, but I still don't speak it very well.*

be fluent in sth to be very good at speaking and understanding a foreign language, so that you can speak it almost as well as your own language: *Applicants should be fluent in Cantonese.*
get by to speak enough of a language to be able to buy things, ask for help etc: *'What's your Italian like?' 'Not great, but I can get by.'* | *I've just bought a book called 'Get by in Portuguese'.*
have/pick up a smattering of sth to speak or learn to speak a small but useful amount of a language: *While I was in Bali, I picked up a smattering of Indonesian.*

speak for *phr v*
1 speak for sb/sth to express the feelings, thoughts, or beliefs of a person or group of people: *Dan, speaking for the students, started the meeting.*
2 speak for yourself *spoken* used to tell someone that you do not have the same opinion as they do, or that something that is true for them is not true for you: *'We don't want to go.' 'Speak for yourself!'*
3 be spoken for if something or someone is spoken for, they have already been promised to someone else: *They're all either married or spoken for.*
4 speak for itself/themselves to show something very clearly: *The results speak for themselves.*

speak of sth *phr v*
1 *literary* to show clearly that something happened or exists: *Her skin spoke of warm summer days spent in the sun.*
2 no ... to speak of (*also* **none/nothing to speak of**) very little of something or a very small thing: *There's been no rain to speak of for several months.* | *The house had no garden to speak of.*

speak out *phr v* to publicly speak in protest about something, especially when protesting could be dangerous: **[+about/against]** *Five students who had spoken out against the regime were arrested.*

speak to sb/sth *phr v*
1 to talk to someone who has done something wrong and tell them not to do it again: *Joe was late again today. You'll have to speak to him.*
2 if something such as a poem, painting, or piece of music speaks to you, you like it because it expresses a particular meaning, quality, or feeling to you: *Modern art just doesn't speak to me.*
3 to show that a situation exists or something is true: *This situation speaks to a need for a better tax system.* | *The party's success speaks to the fact that many people in the US want change.*
4 to talk or write about something, especially something that needs discussing or dealing with: *I am qualified to speak to this issue.*

speak up *phr v*
1 used to ask someone to speak louder: *Could you speak up, please?*
2 to say something, especially to express your opinion: *There was a brief silence, then Gerald spoke up.*
3 speak up for sb to speak in support of someone: *He is willing to speak up for the rights of women.*

-speak /spiːk/ *suffix* [in nouns] the special language or difficult words that are used in a particular business or activity: *computerspeak*

speak·eas·y /ˈspiːkˌiːzi/ *n* (*plural* **speakeasies**) [C] a place in the US in the 1920s and 1930s where you could buy alcohol illegally

speak·er /ˈspiːkə $ -ər/ ●●● S2 W2 *n* [C]
1 someone who makes a formal speech to a group of people: **[+at]** *the* ***guest speaker*** *at the conference* | *The* ***keynote speaker*** (=main or most important speaker) *was Robert Venturi, the architect.* | **after-dinner speaker** (=someone who makes a speech after a formal meal)
2 someone who speaks a particular language: **French-speaker/Spanish-speaker etc** | **[+of]** *Some English words are difficult for speakers of other languages.* | *a* ***native speaker*** *of Chinese*
3 the part of a radio, SOUND SYSTEM etc where the sound comes out
4 *formal* someone who says something: *Pay attention to the body language of the speaker.*
5 the Speaker an official who controls discussions in a parliament
6 the Speaker of the House the politician who controls discussions in the House of Representatives in the US Congress

speak·er·phone /ˈspiːkəfəʊn $ -kərfoʊn/ *n* [C] *especially AmE* a telephone that contains a MICROPHONE and a LOUDSPEAKER, so that you can use it without holding it. Speakerphones are especially used in business meetings when groups of people in different places want to talk to each other.

spear¹ /spɪə $ spɪr/ *n* [C] **1** a pole with a sharp pointed blade at one end, used as a weapon in the past **2** a thin pointed stem of a plant: *asparagus spears*

spear² *v* [T] **1** to push or throw a spear into something, especially in order to kill it **2** to push a pointed object, usually a fork, into something, so that you can pick it up → **stab**

spear·head¹ /ˈspɪəhed $ ˈspɪr-/ *v* [T] to lead an attack or organized action: *the troops who spearheaded the rescue mission*

spearhead² *n* [C usually singular] a person or group of people who lead an attack or organized action: **[+of]** *The group became the spearhead of the labor union movement.*

spear·mint /ˈspɪəˌmɪnt $ ˈspɪr-/ *n* [U] **1** a fresh MINT taste, often used in sweets **2** a type of MINT plant

spec /spek/ *n informal* **1** [C usually plural] a detailed instruction about how a building, car, piece of equipment etc should be made SYN **specification**: *the specs for the company's new video games console* **2 on spec** if you do something on spec, you do it without being sure that you will get what you are hoping for: *I sent in an application on spec.* **3 specs** [plural] glasses that help you see

S

spe·cial¹ /ˈspeʃəl/ ●●● S1 W1 *adj*
1 not ordinary or usual, but different in some way and often better or more important: *a special place in the classroom for reading* | *No one receives special treatment.* | *Maria's special recipe for apple pie* | *The good china was used only on* ***special occasions***. | *Each village has its* ***own special*** *charm.* | **anything/something/nothing special** *Are you doing anything special for Christmas?*
2 particularly important to someone and deserving attention, love etc: *a party with a few special friends* | *a teacher who made every child* ***feel special*** | *Her second son* ***had a special place in*** *her* ***heart***.
3 [only before noun] a special position or job has a particular purpose or aim, and continues only until that purpose or aim is achieved: *Mitchell acted as a special envoy in the Northern Ireland peace talks.*
4 [only before noun] more than usual SYN **particular**: *Pay special attention to how you clean the wound.*

special² *n* [C usually singular] **1** something that is not usual or ordinary, and is made or done for a special purpose: *a TV special on the election* **2** *especially AmE* a lower price than usual for a particular product for a short period of time SYN **special offer**: *a lunch special for $4.99* | **be on special** *Breyer's ice cream is on special this week.*

ˌspecial ˈagent *n* [C] *AmE* someone who works for the FBI

ˈSpecial ˌBranch *n* a department of the British police force that deals with political crimes or crimes affecting the safety of the government, for example TERRORISM

ˌspecial ˈconstable *n* [C] someone in Britain who sometimes works as a police officer without being paid, and who also has another main job

ˌspecial deˈlivery *n* [C,U] a service that delivers a letter or package very quickly

ˌspecial eduˈcation *n* [U] the education of children who have physical problems or learning problems

ˌspecial efˈfect *n* [C usually plural] an unusual image or sound that has been produced artificially to be used in a film or television programme

ˌspecial ˈforces *n* [plural] soldiers who have been specially trained to fight against GUERRILLA or TERRORIST groups

ˌspecial ˈinterest ˌgroup *n* [C] a group of people who share the same political or business aims, and who try to influence the government to help them with those aims

ˌspecial ˈinterests *n* [plural] special interest groups in general: *Special interests donate millions of dollars to political campaigns.*

spe·cial·is·m /ˈspeʃəlɪzəm/ *n BrE* **1** [C] a particular activity or subject that you know a lot about (SYN) **specialization** *AmE*: **[+in]** *graduates with a specialism in Tourism and Leisure* **2** [U] the practice of limiting your interests or activities to particular subjects (SYN) **specialization** *AmE*

spe·cial·ist /ˈspeʃəlɪst/ ●●○ (S3) (W3) *n* [C]
1 someone who knows a lot about a particular subject, or is very skilled at it (SYN) **expert**: **[+in]** *an attorney who is a specialist in banking law* **THESAURUS** EXPERT
2 a doctor who knows more about one particular type of illness or treatment than other doctors: *a heart specialist* **THESAURUS** DOCTOR

spe·ci·al·i·ty /ˌspeʃiˈæləti/ ●○○ *n* (*plural* **specialities**) [C] *BrE*
1 a type of food that a person, restaurant, or area is well known for (SYN) **specialty** *AmE*: *The restaurant offers a wide variety of local specialities.* | *the region's speciality cheese* **THESAURUS** FOOD
2 a subject or job that you know a lot about or have a lot of experience of (SYN) **specialty** *AmE*: *Preston's speciality was night photography.*

spe·cial·i·za·tion (*also* **-isation** *BrE*) /ˌspeʃəlaɪˈzeɪʃən $ -lə-/ *n* [C,U] **1** an activity or subject that you know a lot about **2** the practice of limiting your interests or activities to one particular subject: *industrial specialization*

spe·cial·ize (*also* **-ise** *BrE*) /ˈspeʃəlaɪz/ ●○○ *v* [I] to limit all or most of your study, business etc to a particular subject or activity: **[+in]** *Simmons specialized in contract law.*

spe·cial·ized (*also* **-ised** *BrE*) /ˈspeʃəlaɪzd/ ●○○ *adj* trained, designed, or developed for a particular purpose, type of work, place etc: *specialized training for specific jobs* | *the* ***highly specialized*** *plants that live in desert areas*

ˌspecial ˈlicence *n* [C,U] *BrE* special permission given by the Church of England for a marriage to take place at a time or place not usually allowed

spe·cial·ly /ˈspeʃəli/ ●●○ *adv*
1 for one particular purpose, and only for that purpose: *specially trained police dogs* | **specially designed/built/made etc** *The boats are specially built for the disabled.*
2 *spoken* much more than usual, or much more than other people or things (SYN) **especially**: *He specially liked the pie.*

ˌspecial ˈmeasures *n* [plural] if a school in England is in special measures, it has been officially told to make improvements and is regularly checked until the improvements have been made

ˌspecial ˈneeds ●○○ *n* [plural] needs that someone has because they have mental or physical problems: *children with special needs*

ˌspecial ˈoffer *n* [C] a low price charged for a product for a short time: *The hotel has a special offer of five nights for the price of three.* | **[+on]** *special offers on dishwashers* | **be on special offer** *BrE*: *The wine is currently on special offer at £2.69.* —**special offer** *adj* [only before noun]: *Our special offer price is £25.95.*

ˌspecial ˈpleading *n* [U] when someone tries to persuade you to do something by giving you only those facts that support their argument

ˌspecial ˈprosecutor *n* [C] in the US, an independent lawyer who is chosen to examine the actions of a government official and find out if they have done anything wrong or illegal

ˈspecial ˌschool *n* [C] *especially BrE* a school for children with physical problems or learning problems

spe·cial·ty /ˈspeʃəlti/ *n* (*plural* **specialties**) [C] *AmE*
1 a type of food that a person, restaurant, or area is well known for (SYN) **speciality** *BrE*: *Our specialty is clam chowder.* **2** a subject or job that you know a lot about or have a lot of experience of (SYN) **speciality** *BrE*: *Johnson's specialty is medieval European history.* **3** a particular product or business that has one purpose or sells one type of thing: *an area with clothes retailers and specialty shops*

spe·cies /ˈspiːʃiːz/ ●●○ (W3) *n* (*plural* **species**) [C] a group of animals or plants whose members are similar and can breed together to produce young animals or plants → **genus**: *Seven species of birds of prey have been observed.* | *pandas and other* ***endangered species*** (=ones that may soon no longer exist) **THESAURUS** ANIMAL

spe·cif·ic[1] /spəˈsɪfɪk/ ●●● (S1) (W1) (AWL) *adj*
1 [only before noun] a specific thing, person, or group is one particular thing, person, or group (OPP) **non-specific**: *games suitable for specific age groups* | *a specific example of alcohol's effect on the body*
2 detailed and exact (OPP) **non-specific**: *Mr Howarth gave us very specific instructions.* | **[+about]** *Could you be more specific about what you're looking for?*
3 **specific to sth** *formal* limited to or affecting only one particular thing: *a disease specific to horses*

specific[2] (AWL) *n* **1 specifics** [plural] particular details: **[+of]** *the specifics of the lawsuit* | **give/go into/provide etc specifics** *Thurman was reluctant to go into specifics about the deal.* **2** [C] *medical* a drug that has an effect only on one particular disease

spe·cif·ic·ally /spəˈsɪfɪkli/ ●●○ (S3) (W3) (AWL) *adv*
1 relating to or intended for one particular type of person or thing only: *advertising that specifically targets children*
2 in a detailed or exact way: *I specifically asked you not to do that!*
3 [sentence adverb] used when you are adding more exact information: *Specifically, the department wanted answers to the following questions.*

spe·ci·fi·ca·tion /ˌspesɪfɪˈkeɪʃən/ ●○○ (AWL) *n* [C]
1 [usually plural] a detailed instruction about how a car, building, piece of equipment etc should be made: **build/manufacture/produce sth to ... specifications** *The airport building had been constructed to FAA specifications.* | *The bolts* ***met*** *all the engineering* ***specifications****.*
2 *especially BrE* a clear statement of what is needed or wanted: *a specification of what role each member will play* | **job specification** (=a detailed description of what a job involves)

speˌcific ˈgravity *n* [C,U] *technical* the weight of a substance divided by the weight of the amount of water that would fill the same space

spe·ci·fy /ˈspesɪfaɪ/ ●●○ (W3) (AWL) *v* (**specified**, **specifying**, **specifies**) [T] to state something in an exact and detailed way: *Payments will be made for a specified number of months.* | **specify who/what/how etc** *Regulations specify how long maintenance crews can work.* | **specify that** *The rules clearly specify that competitors must not accept payment.*

spe·ci·men /ˈspesɪmɪn/ ●○○ *n* [C]
1 a small amount or piece that is taken from something, so that it can be tested or examined: *a blood specimen* | **[+of]** *a specimen of rock*
2 a single example of something, often an animal or plant: **[+of]** *a very fine specimen of 12th-century glass*
3 a person you are describing in a particular way – used humorously: *Her boyfriend is an impressive physical specimen.*

spe·cious /ˈspiːʃəs/ *adj formal* seeming to be true or correct, but actually false (SYN) **misleading**: *a specious argument*

speck /spek/ *n* [C] a very small mark, spot, or piece of something: **[+of]** *a speck of dust* → see picture at PIECE[1] **THESAURUS** PIECE

speck·led /ˈspekəld/ *adj* covered with many small marks or spots: *speckled eggs*

speck·les /ˈspekəlz/ *n* [plural] small marks or spots covering a background of a different colour

spec·ta·cle /ˈspektəkəl/ ●○○ *n* [C]
1 a very impressive show or scene: *a multimedia dance and opera spectacle*
2 [usually singular] an unusual or interesting thing or situation that you see or notice – used especially in order to show disapproval: *The trial was turned into a* ***public spectacle***. | **[+of]** *the spectacle of drunken young men on the streets* THESAURUS ▸ SIGHT
3 spectacles [plural] *formal or old-fashioned* glasses that help you see
4 make a spectacle of yourself to behave in an embarrassing way that is likely to make other people notice you and laugh at you

spec·tac·u·lar[1] /spekˈtækjələ $ -ər/ ●●○ *adj*
1 very impressive: *a mountainous area with spectacular scenery* | *a spectacular success*
2 very sudden, unexpected, or extreme: *The news caused a spectacular fall in the stock market.* —**spectacularly** *adv*

spectacular[2] *n* [C] an event or performance that is very large and impressive: *a television spectacular*

spec·tate /spekˈteɪt $ ˈspekteɪt/ *v* [I] to watch a sports event

spec·ta·tor /spekˈteɪtə $ ˈspekteɪtər/ ●●○ *n* [C] someone who is watching an event or game → **audience**: *The match attracted over 40,000 spectators.*

specˈtator ˌsport / $ ˈ... ˌ./ *n* [C] **1** a sport that people go and watch **2** something that you watch rather than take part in – usually used humorously: *Life is not a spectator sport.*

spec·ter /ˈspektə $ -ər/ *n* [C] the American spelling of SPECTRE

spec·tra /ˈspektrə/ the plural of SPECTRUM

spec·tral /ˈspektrəl/ *adj* **1** *literary* relating to or like a spectre **2** *technical* relating to or made by a spectrum

spec·tre *BrE*, **specter** *AmE* /ˈspektə $ -ər/ *n* **1 the spectre of sth** something that people are afraid of because it may affect them badly: *The recession is again* ***raising the spectre of*** *unemployment.* **2** [C] *literary* a GHOST

spec·tro·scope /ˈspektrəskəʊp $ -skoʊp/ *n* [C] an instrument used for forming and looking at spectra —**spectroscopy** /spekˈtrɒskəpi $ -ˈtrɑː-/ *n* [U] —**spectroscopic** /ˌspektrəˈskɒpɪk◂ $ -ˈskɑː-/ *adj*

spec·trum /ˈspektrəm/ ●○○ *n* (*plural* **spectra** /-trə/) [C]
1 a complete range of opinions, people, situations etc, going from one extreme to its opposite: **[+of]** *the ethnic spectrum of America* | **across the spectrum** *The bill drew support from across the political spectrum.* | **broad/wide/full etc spectrum** *a broad spectrum of environmental groups* | *The two articles here represent* ***opposite ends of the spectrum***.
2 the set of bands of coloured light into which a beam of light separates when it is passed through a PRISM
3 a complete range of radio, sound etc waves: *the electromagnetic spectrum*

spec·u·late /ˈspekjəleɪt/ ●○○ *v*
1 [I,T] to guess about the possible causes or effects of something, without knowing all the facts or details: *She refused to speculate.* | **speculate on/about (why/what etc)** *Jones refused to speculate about what might happen.* | **speculate that** *Some analysts speculated that jobs will be lost.*
2 [I] to buy goods, property, SHARES in a company etc, hoping that you will make a large profit when you sell them: **[+in/on]** *He speculated in stocks.*

spec·u·la·tion /ˌspekjəˈleɪʃən/ ●○○ *n* [C,U]
1 when you guess about the possible causes or effects of something without knowing all the facts, or the guesses that you make: **speculation that** *There is speculation that the president is ill.* | **[+about/on]** *speculation about the future* | *The witness's statement was* ***pure speculation*** (=not based on any knowledge). | **wild/idle speculation** (=speculation that is unlikely to be true)
2 when you try to make a large profit by buying goods, property, SHARES etc and then selling them: *property speculation*

spec·u·la·tive /ˈspekjələtɪv $ -leɪ-/ *adj* **1** based on guessing, not on information or facts: **highly/purely/largely speculative** *a purely speculative theory about life on other planets* **2** bought or done in the hope of making a profit later: *speculative investments* **3** if you give someone a speculative look, you look at them while trying to guess something about them —**speculatively** *adv*: *Delaney eyed her speculatively.*

spec·u·la·tor /ˈspekjəleɪtə $ -ər/ *n* [C] someone who buys goods, property, SHARES in a company etc, hoping that they will make a large profit when they sell them: *a New York property speculator*

sped /sped/ a past tense and past participle of SPEED[2]

speech /spiːtʃ/ ●●● S2 W2 *n*
1 [C] a talk, especially a formal one about a particular subject, given to a group of people: **make/give/deliver a speech** *Each child had to give a short speech to the rest of the class.* | *He has to make a lot of* ***after-dinner speeches***. | **[+on/about]** *a major speech on relations with China* | *Collins gave the* ***keynote speech*** (=most important speech).
2 [U] the ability to speak: *Only humans are capable of speech.*
3 [U] spoken language rather than written language: *In speech we use a smaller vocabulary than in writing.*
4 [U] the particular way in which someone speaks: *Bob's speech was slurred, and he sounded drunk.*
5 [C] a set of lines that an actor must say in a play: *Hamlet's longest speech* → DIRECT SPEECH, FIGURE OF SPEECH, INDIRECT SPEECH, PART OF SPEECH, REPORTED SPEECH, → **speech bubble** at BUBBLE[1](4), → **freedom of speech** at FREEDOM(1)

THESAURUS

speech a talk, especially a formal one about a particular subject, given to a group of people: *The bridegroom usually makes a speech after the wedding.* | *In her speech, she proposed major changes to the welfare system.*
address *formal* a speech that a very important person gives to a large group of people: *the president's address to the nation*
talk an occasion when someone speaks to a group of people giving them information about a particular subject or about their experiences: *I went to an interesting talk on the wildlife of Antarctica.* | *He's been asked to give a talk about his trip to India.*
lecture a talk, especially on an ACADEMIC subject and given to students in a university: *a lecture on 17th-century French literature* | *Professor Black is giving the lecture.*
presentation a talk in which you describe or explain a new product or idea, especially one you give for your company: *I had to give a presentation to the board of directors.*
sermon a talk given by a priest or a religious leader: *The vicar preached a sermon about the need for forgiveness.*
statement a spoken or written announcement that someone makes in public, often to JOURNALISTS: *The minister issued a short statement in which he said he had no plans to resign.*

ˈspeech day *n* [C] an occasion held once a year in some British schools, when prizes are given to children and people give speeches

spee·chi·fy /ˈspiːtʃɪfaɪ/ *v* (**speechified**, **speechifying**, **speechifies**) [I] *informal* to make speeches in a way that makes you seem important – used to show disapproval

ˈspeech imˌpediment *n* [C] a physical or nervous problem that affects your speech

speech·less /ˈspiːtʃləs/ *adj* unable to speak because you feel very angry, upset etc: **[+with]** *His comments* ***left me speechless*** *with rage.* THESAURUS ▸ SURPRISED —**speechlessly** *adv* —**speechlessness** *n* [U]

ˈspeech marks *n* [plural] *BrE* the marks (' ') or (" "), that show when someone starts speaking and when they stop SYN **quotation marks**

S

ˈspeech ˌsynthesizer (*also* **speech synthesiser** *BrE*) *n* [C] a computer system that produces sounds like human speech

ˈspeech ˌtherapy *n* [U] treatment that helps people who have difficulty in speaking properly —**speech therapist** *n* [C]

speech·writ·er /ˈspiːtʃˌraɪtə $ -ər/ *n* [C] someone whose job is to write speeches for other people

speed¹ /spiːd/ ●●● S2 W1 *n*

1 OF MOVEMENT [C,U] the rate at which something moves or travels: *The truck was travelling* ***at a speed of*** *50 mph.* | *particles that travel at the speed of light.*

> **REGISTER**
> In everyday English, people usually talk about how **fast** something or someone is rather than using the noun **speed**: ***What speed*** *was he going?* → ***How fast*** *was he going?*

2 OF ACTION [C,U] the rate at which something happens or is done: **[+of]** *the speed of change within the industry* | *a* ***high-speed*** *computer* | *The population was growing at great speed.*

3 FAST [U] the quality of being fast: *The women's basketball team has talent, speed, and power.* | **with speed** *She acted with speed and efficiency.* | **at speed** *BrE*: *a van travelling at speed*

4 PHOTOGRAPHY [C] **a)** the degree to which photographic film is sensitive to light **b)** the time it takes for a camera SHUTTER to open and close: *a shutter speed of 1/250 second*

5 DRUG [U] *informal* an illegal drug that makes you very active SYN **amphetamine**

6 five-speed/ten-speed etc having five, ten etc GEARS: *a ten-speed bike*

7 up to speed having the latest information or knowledge about something: *Some school officials are only now* ***getting up to speed*** *regarding computers.* | *John will* ***bring*** *you* ***up to speed*** (=tell you the latest information). → **full speed/steam ahead** at FULL¹(18)

COLLOCATIONS – MEANINGS 1 & 2

VERBS

increase your speed *He increased his speed until he was running flat out.*
gain/gather/pick up speed (=go faster) *The Mercedes was gradually picking up speed.*
reach a speed *The trains will reach speeds of 140 mph.*
maintain a speed (=keep the same speed) *The aircraft is designed to maintain a steady speed.*
reduce speed (=slow down deliberately) *She reduced speed as she approached the village.*
lose speed (=slow down without wanting to)

ADJECTIVES/NOUN + speed

an average speed *Our average speed was 88 mph.*
a constant/steady speed *The disc revolves at a constant speed.*
a top/maximum speed (=the highest possible) *The car has a top speed of 132 mph.*
wind speed (=the speed of the wind) | **air speed** (=the speed of a plane in relation to the air around it)

PHRASES

at high/great speed *The train was travelling at high speed.*
at low/slow speed *Even at low speed, an accident could mean serious injury for a child.*
at full speed (=running, driving etc as fast as possible) *He ran past us at full speed.*
at/with lightning speed (=very quickly) | **at breakneck speed** (=very quickly)

speed + NOUN

a speed limit *The speed limit is 40 mph here.*
a speed restriction *New speed restrictions have been introduced.*
a speed camera (=designed to photograph vehicles going too fast)

speed² ●○○ *v* (*past tense and past participle* **sped** /sped/ *or* **speeded**)

1 [I always + adv/prep] to go quickly: *The car sped along the dusty highway.*

2 [T always + adv/prep] to take someone or something somewhere very quickly: *An ambulance sped her to the hospital.*

3 be speeding to be driving faster than the legal limit: *I got* ***caught speeding*** *on the A40 yesterday.*

4 (*also* **speed sth ↔ up**) [T] to make something happen faster OPP **slow down**: *This news should speed his recovery.*

speed by *phr v* if time speeds by, it seems to pass very quickly: *The weeks sped by and soon it was time to go back to school.*

speed up *phr v* to move or happen faster, or to make something move or happen faster OPP **slow down**: *The truck speeded up going down the hill.* | **speed sth ↔ up** *The new system will speed up the registration process.*

speed·boat /ˈspiːdbəʊt $ -boʊt/ *n* [C] a small boat with a powerful engine, designed to go fast

ˈspeed bump (*also* **ˈspeed hump** *BrE*) *n* [C] a narrow raised area put across a road to force traffic to go slowly SYN **sleeping policeman**

ˈspeed ˌcamera *n* [C] *BrE* a special camera that takes photographs of cars that are travelling faster than the legal speed limit. The photographs are used as proof that drivers have broken the law.

ˈspeed ˌdating *n* [U] an event at which you meet and talk to a lot of different people for only a few minutes at a time. People do this in order to try to meet someone and have a romantic relationship.

ˈspeed ˌdial (*also* **ˈspeed ˌdialling** *BrE*, **speed dialing** *AmE*) *n* [U] a special feature on a telephone that lets you DIAL someone's telephone number very quickly by pressing one button —**speed-dial** *v* [I,T]

speed·ing /ˈspiːdɪŋ/ *n* [U] the offence of driving faster than the legal limit: *a speeding ticket* | *She got stopped for speeding.*

ˈspeed ˌlimit *n* [C] the fastest speed allowed by law on a particular piece of road: *a 30 mph speed limit* | **exceed/break the speed limit**

speed·om·e·ter /spɪˈdɒmətə, spiː- $ -ˈdɑːmɪtər/ (*also* **speed·o** /ˈspiːdəʊ $ -doʊ/ *informal*) *n* [C] an instrument in a vehicle that shows how fast it is going → see picture at CAR

ˈspeed ˌreading *n* [U] the skill of reading very quickly

ˈspeed ˌskating *n* [U] the sport of racing on ice wearing ICE SKATES

ˈspeed trap *n* [C] a place on a road where police wait to catch drivers who are going too fast

speed·up, **ˈspeed-up** /ˈspiːdʌp/ *n* [C usually singular] an increase in the speed of something or in the rate at which a process happens: **[+in]** *a speedup in population growth*

speed·way /ˈspiːdweɪ/ *n* **1** [U] the sport of racing MOTORCYCLES or cars on a special track **2** [C] a special track for the sport of speedway

speed·y /ˈspiːdi/ *adj* (*comparative* **speedier**, *superlative* **speediest**) **1** happening or done quickly or without delay SYN **quick**: *a speedy recovery from injury* **THESAURUS** FAST **2** a speedy car, boat etc goes fast SYN **fast** —**speedily** *adv*: *The matter was speedily resolved.*

spe·le·ol·o·gy /ˌspiːliˈɒlədʒi $ -ˈɑːl-/ *n* [U] *technical* **1** *BrE* the sport of walking and climbing in CAVES SYN **spelunking** *AmE* **2** the scientific study of CAVES —**speleologist** *n* [C]

spell¹ /spel/ ●●● S2 *v* (*past tense and past participle* **spelt** /spelt/ *especially BrE or* **spelled** *especially AmE*)

1 [I,T] to form a word by writing or naming the letters in order: ***How do you spell*** *'juice'?* | *Pupils should know how to spell commonly used words.* | **spell sth wrong/wrongly** *You've spelled my name wrong.*

S

2 [T] if letters spell a word, they form it: *B-O-O-K spells 'book'.* | *'Love' is spelled L-O-V-E.*
3 spell trouble/disaster/danger etc if a situation or action spells trouble etc, it makes you expect trouble etc: *The lack of rain could spell disaster for farmers.*
4 [T] *AmE* to do someone else's work for them for a short period so that they can rest: *I can spell you if you get tired.*
spell sth ↔ **out** *phr v*
1 to explain something clearly and in detail: **spell out how/what etc** *The report spelled out in detail what the implications were for teacher training.*
2 to show how a word is spelled by writing or saying the letters separately in order: *'W-E-I-R,' she said, spelling it out.*
3 to write a word in its complete form instead of using an ABBREVIATION

spell² ●○○ *n* [C]
1 a piece of magic that someone does, or the special words or ceremonies used in doing it: *a* ***magic spell*** | **put/cast a spell on sb** (=do a piece of magic to change someone) | *The kiss of the prince* ***broke*** *the* ***spell*** (=stopped the magic from working). | **be under a spell** *The whole town seemed to be under a spell.*
2 a period of a particular kind of activity, weather, illness etc, usually a short period: **brief/short spell** *After a brief spell in the army, I returned to teaching.* | **[+of]** *a spell of bad luck* | **cold/wet/dry spell** *Water the young plants carefully during dry spells.* | *a day of* ***sunny spells*** *and scattered showers* | *He began to suffer from* ***dizzy spells***.
3 a power that attracts, interests, and influences you very strongly: **fall/come/be under a spell** *I fell under the spell of her charm.* | *an ancient city that still* ***casts*** *its* ***spell over*** *travellers*
4 break the spell to make someone stop paying all their attention to something, or to make a time stop feeling special: *He lay still, not wanting to break the spell.*

spell·bind·ing /ˈspelbaɪndɪŋ/ *adj* extremely interesting and holding your attention completely SYN **riveting**: *a spellbinding tale* THESAURUS ▸ INTERESTING

spell·bound /ˈspelbaʊnd/ *adj* extremely interested in something you are listening to: *'King Lear' still* ***holds*** *audiences* ***spellbound***.

ˈspell-ˌchecker *n* [C] a computer program that tells you when you have spelled a word wrongly —**spell-check** *v* [I,T]

spel·ler /ˈspelə $ -ər/ *n* **good/bad/poor etc speller** someone who is good or bad at spelling words correctly: *words that confuse even good spellers*

spell·ing /ˈspelɪŋ/ ●●● S2 *n*
1 [U] the act of spelling words correctly, or the ability to do this: *Her spelling has improved.* | *an essay full of* ***spelling mistakes***
2 [C] the way in which a word is spelled: *She quickly gave the correct spelling.*

ˈspelling bee *n* [C] *AmE* a competition in which the winner is the person who spells the most words correctly

spelt /spelt/ *especially BrE* a past tense and past participle of SPELL¹

spe·lunk·ing /spəˈlʌŋkɪŋ/ *n* [U] *AmE* the sport of walking and climbing in CAVES —**spelunker** *n* [C]

spend /spend/ ●●● S1 W1 *v* (*past tense and past participle* **spent** /spent/)
1 MONEY [I,T] to use your money to pay for goods or services: *I can't afford to* ***spend*** *any more* ***money*** *this week.* | **spend £5/$10 etc** *I only want to spend about $20.* | **spend sth on sth** *More money should be spent on education.* | **spend sth on sb** *Mum never spends any money on herself.* | *The repairs cost a lot, but it's* ***money well spent*** (=a sensible way of spending money).

GRAMMAR
You **spend** money **on** something: *I don't spend much on clothes.* ✗ Don't say: *I don't spend much for clothes.*

2 TIME [T] to use time doing a particular thing or pass time in a particular place: **spend time etc with sb** *I want to spend more time with my family.* | **spend time etc in/at sth** *We'll have to spend the night in a hotel.* | *His childhood was spent in Brazil.* | **spend time etc doing sth** *Stacey spends all her free time painting.*
3 a) spend the night with sb to stay for the night and have sex with someone **b) spend the night (at sth)** if someone spends the night at someone's house, they sleep at that person's house for a night: *She spent the night at a friend's house.*
4 FORCE/EFFORT [T] to use effort or energy to do something: *I love to cook, but I don't feel like spending the energy every evening.*
5 spend a penny *BrE spoken old-fashioned* to URINATE – used when you want to avoid saying this directly

THESAURUS
spend to use money to buy things: *I bought two skirts and a T-shirt and I only spent $50.* | *How much do you spend a week on food?*
go through sth (*also* **get through sth** *BrE*) to spend all of an amount of money over a period of time – used especially when saying that someone spends a lot of money: *I got through all my money in less than a month, and had to get my parents to send me more.*
go to great expense to spend a lot of money in order to do something, because you think it is important or special: *The party was wonderful – they had obviously gone to great expense.* | *There's no need to go to great expense.*
squander /ˈskwɒndə $ ˈskwɑːndər/ to waste money on unnecessary things, instead of saving it or using it carefully: *His son had squandered the family fortune on gambling and women.*
splash out *BrE informal* to spend a lot of money on something you really want or will enjoy: *Let's splash out on a bottle of champagne.* | *People often splash out for Christmas and then regret it later.*
blow *informal* to spend a lot of money on something, especially on something that you do not really need: *Her husband blew all their savings on a new sports car.*

spend·er /ˈspendə $ -ər/ *n* [C] someone who spends money → **saver**: *The new casino hopes to attract* ***big spenders*** (=people who spend a lot of money).

spend·ing /ˈspendɪŋ/ ●●○ *n* [U] the amount of money spent, especially by a government or organization SYN **expenditure**: **government/public/defence etc spending** *a plan to increase military spending*

ˈspending ˌmoney *n* [U] money that you have available to spend on the things you want rather than need

spend·thrift /ˈspendˌθrɪft/ *n* [C] someone who spends money carelessly, even when they do not have a lot of it

spend·y /ˈspendi/ *adj especially AmE informal* expensive

spent¹ /spent/ the past tense and past participle of SPEND

spent² *adj* **1** already used, and now empty or useless: *He tried to eject the spent cartridge and reload.* | *spent matches* **2 a spent force** if a political idea or organization is a spent force, it no longer has any power or influence: *Socialism had become a spent political force.* **3** *literary* extremely tired

sperm /spɜːm $ spɜːrm/ *n* (*plural* **sperm** *or* **sperms**) **1** [C] (*also* ˈ**sperm cell**) a cell produced by the sex organs of a male person or animal, which is able to join with the female egg to produce a new life **2** [U] the liquid from the male sex organs that these cells swim in SYN **semen** **3 sperm count** a medical measurement of the number of sperm a man has, which shows if he is able to make a woman PREGNANT

sper·ma·to·zo·on /ˌspɜːmətəˈzəʊɒn $ ˌspɜːrmətəˈzoʊɑːn/ *n* (*plural* **spermatozoa** /-ˈzəʊə $ -ˈzoʊə/) [C] *technical* a sperm

ˈsperm bank *n* [C] a place where SEMEN is kept to be used in medical operations that help women become PREGNANT

sper·mi·cide /ˈspɜːmɪsaɪd $ ˈspɜːr-/ *n* [C,U] a cream or liquid that kills SPERM, used while having sex to prevent the woman from becoming PREGNANT —**spermicidal** /ˌspɜːməˈsaɪdl◂ $ ˌspɜːr-/ *adj* [only before noun]: *spermicidal cream*

ˈsperm whale *n* [C] a large WHALE sometimes hunted for its oil and fat

spew /spjuː/ *v* **1** [I always + adv/prep, T] (*also* **spew out/forth**) to flow out of something quickly in large quantities, or to make something flow out in this way: *Factory chimneys spewed fumes out into the sky.* | **[+from/into/over etc]** *Brown water spewed from the tap.* **2** [I always + adv/prep, T] (*also* **spew out/forth**) to say a lot of bad or negative things very quickly: *Groups like these use the Internet to spew racial hatred.* **3** [I,T] (*also* **spew up**) *informal* to VOMIT

SPF /ˌes piː ˈef/ *n* [singular, U] (***Sun Protection Factor***) a number that shows you how much protection a special cream gives you from the sun: *an SPF 25 cream*

sphag·num /ˈsfægnəm/ (*also* **ˈsphagnum ˌmoss**) *n* [U] a type of MOSS (=simple plant) that grows in wet places

sphere /sfɪə $ sfɪr/ ●●○ AWL *n* [C]
1 a ball shape → see picture at **SHAPE¹**
2 a particular area of activity, work, knowledge etc: **in the ... sphere** *television's increasing role in the political sphere* | **public/private sphere** *Women have often been excluded from positions of power in the public sphere.*
3 **sb's/sth's sphere of influence** a person's, country's, organization's etc sphere of influence is the area where they have power to change things

-sphere /sfɪə $ sfɪr/ *suffix* [in nouns] *technical* relating to the air or gases surrounding the Earth: *the atmosphere*

spher·i·cal /ˈsferɪkəl/ AWL *adj* having the shape of a sphere SYN **round**

sphe·roid /ˈsfɪərɔɪd $ ˈsfɪr-/ *n* [C] *technical* a shape that is similar to a ball, but not perfectly round

sphinc·ter /ˈsfɪŋktə $ -ər/ *n* [C] *medical* a muscle that surrounds an opening in your body, and can become tight in order to close the opening

sphinx, **Sphinx** /sfɪŋks/ *n* [C] an ancient Egyptian image of a lion with a human head, lying down

spic, **spik** /spɪk/ *n* [C] *AmE taboo* a very offensive word for a Spanish-speaking person. Do not use this word.

spice¹ /spaɪs/ ●●○ *n*
1 [C,U] a type of powder or seed, taken from plants, that you put into food you are cooking to give it a special taste → **spicy**: *herbs and spices*
2 [singular, U] interest or excitement that is added to something: *Travel* ***adds spice*** *to your life.* → **variety is the spice of life** at **VARIETY**(5)

spice² (*also* **spice up**) *v* [T] **1** to add interest or excitement to something: *Millions have bought the book to spice up their sex lives.* **2** to add spice to food: **[+with]** *baked apples spiced with cinnamon*

spick and span, **spic and span** /ˌspɪk ən ˈspæn/ *adj* [not before noun] *informal* a room, house etc that is spick and span is completely clean and tidy SYN **immaculate**

spic·y /ˈspaɪsi/ ●●● S3 *adj*
1 food that is spicy has a pleasantly strong taste, and gives you a pleasant burning feeling in your mouth SYN **hot** → **spice**: *a spicy tomato sauce* **THESAURUS** ▸ **TASTE**
2 a story or picture that is spicy is slightly shocking or rude because it tells about or shows something relating to sex

spi·der /ˈspaɪdə $ -ər/ ●●● S3 *n* [C]
1 a small creature with eight legs, which catches insects using a fine network of sticky threads
2 *technical* a computer program that searches the Internet for the best websites with the information you want, so that you can find it quickly SYN **crawler, bot** → **crawl the Net/web**

spi·der·web /ˈspaɪdəweb $ -dər-/ (*also* **web**) *n* [C] *AmE* a very fine network of sticky threads made by a spider to catch insects → **cobweb**

spi·der·y /ˈspaɪdəri/ *adj* covered with or made of lots of long thin uneven lines: *spidery handwriting*

spiel /ʃpiːl, spiːl/ *n* [C,U] *informal* a quick speech that the speaker has used many times before, especially one that is intended to persuade people to buy something: *A salesman started* ***giving*** *us a* ***spiel*** *about life insurance.*

spif·fy /ˈspɪfi/ *adj especially AmE old-fashioned informal* very neat, attractive, and fashionable: *a spiffy blue suit*

spig·ot /ˈspɪgət/ *n* [C] **1** a TAP in a large container that controls the flow of liquid from it **2** *especially AmE* an outdoor TAP

spik /spɪk/ *n* [C] *AmE taboo* another spelling of SPIC

spike¹ /spaɪk/ ●○○ *n* [C]
1 something long and thin with a sharp point, especially a pointed piece of metal
2 [usually singular] a sudden large increase in the number or rate of something: **[+in]** *a spike in interest rates*
3 **spikes** [plural] shoes with metal points on the bottom, worn by people who run races, play golf etc
4 **spike heels** [plural] a pair of women's shoes with very high thin heels

spike² *v* **1** [T] to secretly add strong alcohol or a drug to someone's drink or food: **spike sth with sth** *The orange juice had been spiked with gin.* **2** [I] if the number or rate of something spikes, it increases quickly and by a large amount: *New telephone orders have spiked in the last two years.* **3** [T] to push a sharp tool or object into something **4** [T] to prevent someone from saying something or printing something in a newspaper: *a clumsy attempt to spike rumours of a cabinet split* **5** **a) spike the ball** *AmE* to powerfully throw an American football down on the ground to celebrate a TOUCHDOWN **b)** [I,T] to powerfully hit a VOLLEYBALL down over the net **6** **spike sb's guns** *BrE* to spoil an opponent's plans

spik·y /ˈspaɪki/ *adj* **1** hair that is spiky is stiff and stands up on top of your head: *short black spiky hair* **2** having long sharp points: *a spiky cactus* **THESAURUS** ▸ **SHARP** **3** *BrE informal* easily offended or annoyed

spill¹ /spɪl/ ●●● S3 *v* (*past tense and past participle* **spilt** /spɪlt/ *especially BrE or* **spilled** *especially AmE*)
1 [I,T] if you spill a liquid, or if it spills, it accidentally flows over the edge of a container → **pour**: *Katie almost spilled her milk.* | **spill sth down/on/over sth** *Oh no! I've spilt coffee all down my shirt!* | **[+on/over etc]** *He slipped and the wine spilled all over the carpet.*
2 [I always + adv/prep] if people or things spill out of somewhere, they move or fall out in large numbers SYN **pour**: **[+out/into/onto etc]** *Crowds from the theatre were spilling onto the street.*
3 **spill the beans** *informal* to tell something that someone else wanted you to keep a secret
4 **spill your guts** *AmE informal* to tell someone all about your private life, or about a personal secret
5 **spill blood** *literary* to kill or wound people → **cry over spilt milk** at **CRY¹**(3)

spill into/onto sth *phr v literary* if light spills onto or into something, it shines through a window, door, hole etc onto something else: *The morning light spilled into the room.*

spill over *phr v* if a problem or bad situation spills over, it spreads and begins to affect other places, people etc: **[+into]** *The conflict might spill over into neighbouring towns.*

spill² *n* **1** [C,U] when you spill something, or an amount of something that is spilled: *the enormous oil spill off the southern tip of the Shetland Islands* **2** [C] a fall from a horse, bicycle etc: *Tyson broke a rib when he* ***took*** *a* ***spill*** *on his motorcycle.*

spil·lage /ˈspɪlɪdʒ/ *n* [C,U] a SPILL²(1)

spill·o·ver /ˈspɪləʊvə $ -oʊvər/ *n* [C,U] the effect that one situation or problem has on another situation: *Not all of the violence in Miami was spillover from the trial.* | **spillover effect/benefit/cost** *The weak European economy will have a spillover effect on the US dollar.*

spilt /spɪlt/ *especially BrE* a past tense and past participle of SPILL¹

spim /spɪm/ *n* [U] email messages that someone has

not asked for and does not want to read, which have been sent to a computer that has INSTANT MESSAGING → **spam**

spin¹ /spɪn/ ●●● S3 *v* (*past tense and past participle* **spun** /spʌn/, *present participle* **spinning**)
1 TURN AROUND [I,T] to turn around and around very quickly, or to make something do this: *The plane's propellers were spinning.* | **spin (sth/sb) around** *She grabbed Norm's arm and spun him around to face her.*
2 sb's head is spinning (*also* **the room is spinning**) if your head or the room is spinning, you feel as if you might FAINT (=become unconscious) because you are shocked, excited, or drunk: *I was pouring with sweat, and my head was spinning.* | *The room started to spin.*
3 SITUATION/INFORMATION [T] to describe a situation or information in a way that is intended to influence the way people think about it - used especially about what politicians or business people do: *Supporters attempted to spin the bill's defeat to their advantage.*
4 spin a tale/story/yarn to tell a story, especially using a lot of imagination: *She spun a story about a trip to Athens to meet one of the authors.*
5 WOOL/COTTON [I,T] to make cotton, wool etc into thread by twisting it
6 DRIVE [I always + adv/prep] *written* to drive or travel quickly SYN **speed**: **[+past/along etc]** *Barbara spun past in her new sports car.*
7 spin your wheels *AmE* to continue trying to do something without having any success: *I felt like I was just spinning my wheels trying to make him understand.*
8 WET CLOTHES [T] *BrE* to get water out of clothes using a machine after you have washed them
9 INSECT [T] if a SPIDER or insect spins a WEB or COCOON, it produces thread to make it
spin off *phr v* to make part of a company into a separate and partly independent company, or to become a separate company: **spin sth ↔ off** *At the time of the merger, Loral spun off its space divisions into a separate firm.* | **[+from]** *Lucent spun off from AT&T several years ago.* → SPIN-OFF(2)
spin out *phr v*
1 spin sth ↔ out *BrE* to make something continue for longer than is necessary SYN **drag out**: *I'm paid by the hour, so I spin the work out as long as I can.*
2 spin sth ↔ out *BrE* to use money, food etc as carefully and slowly as possible, because you do not have very much of it: **[+over]** *I've only got £10 left, so we'll have to spin it out over the whole week.*
3 *AmE* if a car spins out, the driver loses control of it and the car spins around

spin² *n*
1 TURNING [C] an act of turning around quickly: *the Earth's spin* | *The Russian skater finished her routine with a series of spins.*
2 CAR [singular] *informal* a short trip in a car for pleasure SYN **drive**: *Let's* ***go for a spin*** *in the country.* | *Do you want to* ***take*** *my car* ***for a spin****?*
3 BALL [U] if you put spin on a ball in a game such as tennis or CRICKET, you deliberately make the ball turn very quickly so that it is difficult for your opponent to hit
4 INFORMATION [singular, U] the way someone, especially a politician or business person, talks about information or a situation, especially in order to influence the way people think about it: *They tried to* ***put a*** *positive* ***spin on*** *the sales figures.* → **SPIN DOCTOR**
5 AIRCRAFT [singular] if an aircraft goes into a spin, it falls suddenly, turning around and around
6 in/into a (flat) spin if you are in a spin, you are very confused and anxious: *The sudden fall on the stock market sent brokers into a spin.*
7 WET CLOTHES **give sth a spin** *BrE* to turn clothes around very fast in a machine to remove water from them

spi·na bif·i·da /ˌspaɪnə ˈbɪfədə/ *n* [U] a serious condition in which a person's SPINE does not develop correctly before they are born, so that their SPINAL CORD is not protected

spin·ach /ˈspɪnɪdʒ, -ɪtʃ/ *n* [U] a vegetable with large dark green leaves

spin·al /ˈspaɪnl/ *adj* belonging to or affecting your SPINE: *spinal injuries*

ˈspinal ˌcolumn *n* [C] *technical* your SPINE

ˈspinal cord *n* [C] the thick string of nerves enclosed in your SPINE, by which messages are sent to and from your brain

spin·dle /ˈspɪndl/ *n* [C] **1** a part of a machine shaped like a stick, around which something turns **2** a round pointed stick used for twisting the thread when you are spinning wool

spin·dly /ˈspɪndli/ *adj* long and thin in a way that looks weak: *spindly legs*

ˈspin ˌdoctor *n* [C] *informal* someone whose job is to give information to the public in a way that gives the best possible advantage to a politician or organization: *White House spin doctors*

ˌspin-ˈdryer *n* [C] *BrE* a machine that removes most of the water from washed clothes by spinning them around and around very fast —**spin-dry** *v* [T]

spine /spaɪn/ ●●○ *n*
1 [C] the row of bones down the centre of your back that supports your body and protects your SPINAL CORD SYN **backbone** → **spinal** → see picture at **SKELETON**
2 [C] a stiff sharp point on an animal or plant → **spiny**: *cactus spines*
3 [C] the part of a book that the pages are fastened onto
4 [U] courage or determination

ˈspine-ˌchilling *adj* a spine-chilling story or film is very frightening in a way that people enjoy THESAURUS FRIGHTENING —**spine-chiller** *n* [C]

spine·less /ˈspaɪnləs/ *adj* **1** lacking courage and determination - used to show disapproval: *a bunch of spineless politicians* **2** without a spine

spi·net /spɪˈnet $ ˈspɪnɪt/ *n* [C] **1** a musical instrument of the 16th and 17th centuries, which is played like a piano **2** *AmE* a small UPRIGHT PIANO

ˈspine-ˌtingling *adj* making you feel very excited or frightened, in an enjoyable way: *The festival opened with Nic Roeg's latest spine-tingling film.*

spin·na·ker /ˈspɪnəkə $ -kər/ *n* [C] a sail with three points at the front of a boat, used when the wind is directly behind

spin·ner /ˈspɪnə $ -ər/ *n* [C] **1** someone whose job is to make thread by twisting cotton, wool etc **2** a BOWLER in a game of CRICKET who throws the ball with a spinning action **3** a thing used for catching fish that spins when pulled through the water → **MONEY-SPINNER**

spin·ney /ˈspɪni/ *n* [C] *BrE* a small area of trees and bushes SYN **copse**

spin·ning /ˈspɪnɪŋ/ *n* [U] *trademark* the activity of doing AEROBICS exercises on an EXERCISE BICYCLE

ˈspinning wheel *n* [C] a simple machine consisting of a wheel on a frame that people used in their homes in the past for making cotton, wool etc into thread

ˈspin-off, **spin·off** /ˈspɪnɒf $ -ɒːf/ *n* [C] **1** a television programme involving characters that were previously in another programme or film **2** a separate and partly independent company that is formed from parts of an existing company, or the action of forming a company in this way **3** an unexpected but useful result of something, that happens in addition to the intended result: *Laser research has had important spin-offs for eye surgery.*

spin·ster /ˈspɪnstə $ -ər/ *n* [C] *old-fashioned* an unmarried woman, usually one who is no longer young and seems unlikely to marry → **bachelor** THESAURUS MARRIED

spin·y /ˈspaɪni/ *adj* a spiny animal or plant has lots of stiff sharp points → **spine**: *spiny sea urchins* | *spiny bushes*

spi·ral¹ /ˈspaɪərəl $ ˈspaɪr-/ ●○○ *n* [C]
1 a line in the form of a curve that winds around a central point, moving further away from the centre all the time
2 a process, usually a harmful one, in which something gradually but continuously gets worse or better: **in/into a**

S

spiral *Unemployment rose and the city went into a spiral of decline.* | **downward/upward spiral** *The company is in a downward spiral.*
3 inflationary spiral a situation in which wages and prices rise continuously because the level of INFLATION is high —**spiral** *adj*

spiral² *v* (**spiralled**, **spiralling** *BrE*, **spiraled**, **spiraling** *AmE*) [I] **1** [always + adv/prep] to move in a continuous curve that gets nearer to or further from its central point as it goes round: **[+to/around etc]** *The damaged plane spiralled to the ground.* **2** if a situation spirals, it gets worse, more violent etc in a way that cannot be controlled: *Crime has* ***spiraled out of control****.* **3** if debt or the cost of something spirals, it increases quickly in a way that cannot be controlled SYN **escalate** —**spiralling** *BrE*, **spiraling** *AmE* *adj*: *the spiralling cost of legal services*

ˈspiral-bound *adj* a spiral-bound book or NOTEBOOK has pages that are attached together by a long wire that is twisted around and put through small holes in the sides of the pages

ˌspiral ˈnotebook *n* [C] a book in which you write notes, made of pieces of paper that are attached to a wire spiral

ˌspiral ˈstaircase *n* [C] a set of stairs arranged in a circular pattern so that they go around a central point as they get higher

spire /spaɪə $ spaɪr/ *n* [C] a roof that rises steeply to a point on top of a tower, especially on a church → **steeple**

spir·it¹ /ˈspɪrɪt/ ●●● S2 W2 *n*
1 CHARACTER [singular, U] the qualities that make someone live the way they do, and make them different from other people: **in spirit** *I'm 85, but I still feel young in spirit.* | **independent/proud/free etc spirit** (=a person with a particular type of character) *She is a strong and independent spirit.* → **kindred spirit** at KINDRED²(1)
2 HAPPY/SAD spirits [plural] the way someone feels at a particular time, for example if they are happy or sad → **mood**: **be in good/high spirits** (=be excited and happy) *Cooper was still in high spirits after winning the race.* | *His* ***spirits*** *were so* ***low*** (=he was so sad) *that he refused to answer his phone.* | **raise/lift sb's spirits** (=make someone happier) *The warm morning sun lifted our spirits.* | *She wrote poetry while she was in the hospital to* ***keep*** *her* ***spirits up*** (=keep happy). | **sb's spirits rise/lift/sink** (=they become more or less happy) *My spirits sank when I saw the mess they'd left.*
3 SOUL [C] the part of someone that you cannot see, that consists of the qualities that make up their character, which many people believe continues to live after the person has died → **soul**: *Although Laurie is dead, I can feel his spirit with me.*
4 NO BODY [C] a creature without a physical body that some people believe exists, such as an ANGEL or a dead person, who has returned to this world and has strange or magical powers → **ghost**: *an evil spirit*
5 DETERMINATION [U] courage, energy, and determination - used to show approval: *Sandra is small, but she makes up for it with great spirit.* | *a young team with strong* ***fighting spirit*** | *When they took away his freedom, they* ***broke*** *his* ***spirit*** (=made him lose his courage).
6 ATTITUDE [singular, U] the attitude that you have towards something or while you are doing something: *You've got to approach this meeting in the right spirit.* | **[+of]** *the spirit of cooperation between the two sides*
7 team/community/public etc spirit a strong feeling of belonging to a particular group and wanting to help them
8 TYPICAL QUALITIES [C usually singular] the set of ideas, beliefs, feelings etc that are typical of a particular period in history, a place, or a group of people: **[+of]** *Tourism has not destroyed the spirit of Bali.* | **the spirit of the age/times** *His beliefs conflicted with the spirit of the age.*
9 in spirit if you say you will be somewhere in spirit or with someone in spirit, you will not be with them but will be thinking about them: *I can't come to your wedding, but I'll be there in spirit.*
10 get/enter into the spirit (of sth) to start to feel as happy, excited etc as the people around you: *Judith couldn't really enter into the spirit of the occasion.*
11 INTENTION [U] the meaning or qualities that someone intended something to have, especially the meaning that a law or rule was intended to have: *Thoreau believed that his actions were in the spirit of American institutions.* | *Miller's actions may not be actually illegal, but they have violated* ***the spirit of the law****.* → **the letter of the law** at LETTER¹(4)
12 the Spirit the HOLY SPIRIT
13 DRINK [C usually plural] **a)** *especially BrE* a strong alcoholic drink such as WHISKY or BRANDY **b)** *BrE* liquid such as alcohol, used for cleaning
14 that's the spirit *spoken* used to express approval of someone's behaviour or attitude
15 when/as the spirit moves you when you feel that you want to do something
16 the spirit is willing (but the flesh is weak) used when saying that you want to do something, but you are too tired or do not feel strong enough - often used humorously

spirit² *v*
spirit sb/sth **away/off** *phr v written* to take someone or something away quickly and secretly: *After his speech, Jackson was spirited away through a back door.*

spir·it·ed /ˈspɪrɪtɪd/ *adj* **1** having energy and determination - used to show approval: *a spirited and energetic girl* | **spirited defence/debate/discussion etc**
2 sweet-spirited/tough-spirited/rebellious-spirited etc having a particular type of character → **HIGH-SPIRITED, LOW-SPIRITED, MEAN-SPIRITED, PUBLIC-SPIRITED**

spir·it·less /ˈspɪrətləs/ *adj* **1** having no energy or determination **2** not cheerful

ˈspirit ˌlevel *n* [C] *especially BrE* a tool used for testing whether a surface is level

spir·i·tu·al¹ /ˈspɪrətʃuəl/ ●●○ W3 *adj*
1 relating to your spirit rather than to your body or mind: *Painting helps fill a spiritual need for beauty.* | *spiritual values*
THESAURUS ▸ RELIGIOUS
2 relating to religion SYN **religious**: *Islam was inspired by the teachings of the spiritual leader Mohammed.*
3 sb's spiritual home a place where you feel you belong because you share the ideas and attitudes of that society —**spiritually** *adv*

spiritual² *n* [C] a religious song of the type sung originally by African-Americans

spir·i·tual·is·m /ˈspɪrətʃʊlɪzəm/ *n* [U] the belief that dead people are able to send messages to living people —**spiritualist** *n* [C]

spir·i·tu·al·i·ty /ˌspɪrətʃuˈæləti/ *n* [U] the quality of being interested in religion or religious matters

spit¹ /spɪt/ ●●○ *v* (*past tense and past participle* **spat** /spæt/ *or* **spit** *AmE*, *present participle* **spitting**)
1 LIQUID FROM YOUR MOUTH [I] to force a small amount of SALIVA (=the liquid in your mouth) out of your mouth: *Nick rolled down his window and spat.* | **[+at/on/into]** *A group of fans spat on the players as they left the field.*
2 FOOD/DRINK ETC [T] to force something out of your mouth: *Billy stood up slowly, rubbed his jaw, and spat blood.* | **spit sth out** *Diana tasted her martini and quickly spat it out.*
3 RAIN be spitting *BrE* to be raining very lightly SYN **drizzle**: *You don't need an umbrella - it's only spitting.*
4 SAY STH (*also* **spit out**) [T] to say something quickly in a very angry way: *'Shut up!', spat Maria furiously.*
5 spit it out *spoken* used to ask someone to tell you something that they seem too frightened or embarrassed to say: *Come on, Jean. Spit it out!*
6 SMALL PIECES [I,T] to send out small bits of something, for example fire or hot oil, into the air: *A log fire was crackling and spitting in the hearth.*
7 CAT [I] if a cat spits, it makes short angry sounds
8 be within spitting distance (of sth) *spoken* to be very close to someone or something
9 spit the dummy *informal* to react to something in a very angry way - used when suggesting that the person is

behaving like a child and not reacting like an adult should

spit up *phr v AmE* if someone, especially a baby, spits up, they bring a small amount of food or drink up from their stomach out through their mouth: **spit sth ↔ up** *I was a difficult child, always crying and spitting up my food.* | *On one occasion, our daughter spat up all over him.*

spit² *n* **1** [U] *informal* the watery liquid that is produced in your mouth SYN **saliva** **2** [C] a long thin stick that you put through meat so that you can turn it when cooking it over a fire **3** [C] a long narrow piece of land that sticks out into the sea, into a river etc **4 be the (dead) spit of sb** *BrE spoken* to look exactly like someone else: *Sam is the dead spit of his dad.* **5 spit and polish** *informal* when something is thoroughly cleaned and polished: *It was Christmas, so Ellen gave the dining room a little extra spit and polish.*

spit·ball /ˈspɪtbɔːl $ -bɒːl/ *n* [C] *AmE* a small piece of paper that children roll into a ball and then spit or throw at each other

spite¹ /spaɪt/ ●●○ W3 *n* [U]

1 in spite of sth without being affected or prevented by something SYN **despite**: *We went out in spite of the rain.* | *Kelly loved her husband* ***in spite of the fact that*** *he drank too much.*

2 a feeling of wanting to hurt or upset people, for example because you are JEALOUS or think you have been unfairly treated: **out of spite** (=because of spite) *She broke it just out of spite.* | **pure/sheer spite** (=spite and nothing else)

3 in spite of yourself if you do something in spite of yourself, you do it although you did not expect or intend to do it: *The picture made her laugh in spite of herself.*

spite² *v* [T only in infinitive] to deliberately annoy or upset someone: *The neighbours throw things over the garden wall* ***just to spite*** *us.* → **cut off your nose to spite your face** at CUT

spite·ful /ˈspaɪtfəl/ *adj* deliberately nasty to someone in order to hurt or upset them SYN **vicious**: *She was spiteful and unkind, both to Isabel and to her son.* | *a spiteful remark* **THESAURUS** UNKIND —**spitefully** *adv*

ˌspitting ˈimage *n* **be the spitting image of sb** to look exactly like someone else

spit·tle /ˈspɪtl/ *n* [U] the liquid in your mouth SYN **spit**

spit·toon /spɪˈtuːn/ *n* [C] a container that people SPIT into

spiv /spɪv/ *n* [C] *BrE old-fashioned* a man who gets money from small dishonest business deals

splash¹ /splæʃ/ ●●● W3 *v*

1 [I] if a liquid splashes, it hits or falls on something and makes a noise: **[+against/on/over]** *The ocean splashed against the pier.*

2 [T always + adv/prep] to make someone or something wet with a lot of small drops of water or other liquid: **splash sth on/over/with etc sth** *He splashed cold water on his face.*

3 [I] (*also* **splash about/around**) to make water fly up in the air with a loud noise by hitting it or by moving around in it: *The children were splashing about in the pool.* | **[+through]** *She ran up the drive, splashing through the puddles.*

4 [T] *informal* if a newspaper or television programme splashes a story or picture on the page or screen, it makes it large and easy to notice: **[+across/over]** *The gunman's picture was splashed across the front page.*

splash out (sth) *phr v BrE informal* to spend a lot of money on something: **[+on]** *We splashed out on a new kitchen.* | *Last year Roberts splashed out more than £1 million to buy a new home.*

splash² ●●○ *n*

1 [C] the sound of a liquid hitting something or being moved around quickly: *Rachel fell into the river with a loud splash.* **THESAURUS** SOUND

2 [C] a mark made by a liquid splashing onto something else: **[+of]** *There were splashes of paint all over my clothes.*

3 splash of colour a small area of bright colour

4 make a splash *informal* to do something that gets a lot of public attention: *Russell's new show made a big splash in New York.*

5 [singular] a small amount of liquid added to a drink: **[+of]** *a cup of coffee with a splash of brandy*

splash·back /ˈsplæʃbæk/ *n* [C] *BrE* the area of a bathroom or kitchen wall that is behind the TAPS and covered in TILES

splash·down /ˈsplæʃdaʊn/ *n* [C,U] a landing by a spacecraft in the sea

ˈsplash guard *n* [C] *AmE* a flat piece of rubber hanging behind the wheel of a vehicle to prevent mud being thrown up

splash·y /ˈsplæʃi/ *adj* big, bright, or very easy to notice SYN **flashy**: *a splashy orange shirt*

splat¹ /splæt/ *n* [singular] *informal* a noise like something wet hitting a surface hard

splat² *v* (**splatted**, **splatting**) [I,T] to make a noise like something wet hitting a surface, or to make something make this noise: *Big raindrops splatted against the windscreen.*

splat·ter /ˈsplætə $ -ər/ *v* [I always + adv/prep, T] if liquid splatters somewhere, or if someone splatters it, it falls or is thrown onto a surface SYN **spatter**: **splatter sth with sth** *The room was splattered with blood.* | **[+over/across]** *Paint splattered all over the carpet.*

splay /spleɪ/ (*also* **splay out**) *v* [I,T] to spread apart widely, or to make things do this, especially parts of the body: *He sat with his legs splayed out in front of him.*

spleen /spliːn/ *n* **1** [C] an organ near your stomach that controls the quality of your blood **2** [U] *formal* anger, especially unreasonable or unfair anger: *Obviously you're annoyed, but that doesn't give you the right to* **vent** *your* ***spleen*** *on me* (=get angry with me).

splen·did /ˈsplendɪd/ ●●○ *adj*

1 *old-fashioned* very good SYN **excellent**: *a splendid idea* | *a splendid opportunity* | *The staff are doing a splendid job.*

2 beautiful and impressive SYN **magnificent**: *All the rooms have splendid views.* | *a splendid cathedral*

3 *BrE spoken old-fashioned* used to show that you approve of or are pleased by something SYN **great**: *'I'll see you tomorrow then.' 'Splendid!'*

4 in splendid isolation used to emphasize that something is not with other things: *The house sits in splendid isolation on top of a steep hill.* —**splendidly** *adv*: *a splendidly equipped new sports centre* | *The team played splendidly.*

splen·dour *BrE*, **splendor** *AmE* /ˈsplendə $ -ər/ *n* **1** [U] impressive beauty, especially of a large building or large place: **[+of]** *We marvelled at the splendour of the scenery.* | *The palace has now been restored to its original splendour.* **2 splendours** [plural] impressive beautiful features, especially of a large building or place: **[+of]** *the splendours of the imperial court*

sple·net·ic /spləˈnetɪk/ *adj formal* bad-tempered and often angry

splice¹ /splaɪs/ *v* [T] **1** to join the ends of two pieces of rope, film etc so that they form one continuous piece **2 get spliced** *BrE informal* to get married

splice² *n* [C] the act of joining the ends of two things together, or the place where this join has been made

splic·er /ˈsplaɪsə $ -ər/ *n* [C] a machine for joining pieces of film or recording tape neatly together

spliff /splɪf/ *n* [C] *BrE informal* a cigarette containing CANNABIS SYN **joint**

splint /splɪnt/ *n* [C] a flat piece of wood, metal etc used for keeping a broken bone in position while it mends

splin·ter¹ /ˈsplɪntə $ -ər/ *n* [C] a small sharp piece of wood, glass, or metal, that has broken off a larger piece: *I've got a splinter in my finger.* | **[+of]** *splinters of glass* —**splintery** *adj*

splinter² *v* [I,T] **1** if something such as wood splinters, or if you splinter it, it breaks into thin sharp pieces **2** to separate into smaller groups or parts, or to make a group or organization do this, especially because of a disagreement: **[+into]** *The once-powerful Communist Party has splintered into hundreds of pieces.*

ˈsplinter group *n* [C] a group of people that have separated from a political or religious organization because they have different ideas

split[1] /splɪt/ ●●● S2 W3 *v* (*past tense and past participle* **split**, *present participle* **splitting**)

1 DISAGREE [I,T] if a group of people splits, or if it is split, people in the group disagree strongly with each other and the group sometimes divides into separate smaller groups: *It was feared that the issue would split the church.* | **be split on/over sth** *The party is split over the issue of immigration.* | *The government appears* ***deeply split*** *on this issue.* | **[+from]** *The Pan-Africanist Congress split from the ANC in 1959.* | **split sth in two/down the middle** *The war has split the nation in two.* THESAURUS ▸ BREAK, SEPARATE, TEAR

2 SEPARATE INTO PARTS (*also* **split up**) [I,T] to divide or separate something into different parts or groups, or to be divided into different parts or groups: **[+into]** *Can you split into groups of three now?* | **split sth into sth** *The book is split into six sections.*

3 BREAK OR TEAR [I,T] if something splits, or if you split it, it tears or breaks along a straight line: *The branch split under their weight.* | *One of the boxes had* ***split open***. | **split (sth) in two/half** *The board had split in two.* | ***Split*** *the pineapple* ***down the middle***. → see picture at BREAK[1]

4 SHARE [T] to divide something into separate parts and share it between two or more people: **split sth between sb/sth** *Profits will be split between three major charities.* | **split sth with sb** *He agreed to sell the car and split the proceeds with his brother.* | **split sth three/four etc ways** (=share something between three, four etc people or groups) *The money will have to be split three ways.* | *We agreed to* ***split the cost***.

5 INJURE [T] to make someone's head or lip have a cut in it, as a result of a fall or hit: *She fell against a table and* ***split*** *her* ***lip***. | *The force of the blow nearly* ***split*** *his* ***head open***.

6 END RELATIONSHIP (*also* **split up**) [I] *informal* if people split, they end a marriage or relationship with each other: **[+with/from]** *He split from his wife last year.* | *The band split two years ago.*

7 LEAVE [I] *old-fashioned informal* to leave a place quickly: *Come on – let's split.*

8 split hairs to argue that there is a difference between two things, when the difference is really too small to be important: *This is just splitting hairs.*

9 split the difference to agree on an amount that is exactly between two amounts that have been mentioned: *OK, let's split the difference, and I'll give you £20.*

10 split your sides *informal* to laugh a great deal

split off *phr v*

1 (*also* **split away**) if one part of something splits off from the rest, it becomes completely separate from it: **[+from]** *A huge lump of rock had split off from the cliff face.*

2 (*also* **split away**) if a small group of people split off from a larger group, they become separate from it: **[+from]** *The group split away from the Green Party and formed the Environmental Alliance.*

3 split sth ↔ off to separate one part of something and make it completely separate from the rest: **[+from]** *This part of the business has now been split off from the main company.*

split on sb *phr v BrE informal* to tell someone in authority about something wrong that someone else has done: *Don't you dare split on us!*

split up *phr v*

1 if people split up, or if someone splits them up, they end a marriage or relationship with each other: *Steve's parents split up when he was four.* | **[+with]** *I thought she'd split up with her boyfriend.* | **split sb ↔ up** *Why would she try to split us up?*

2 to divide people into different groups, or to be divided into groups: *Please don't split up when we get to the museum.* | **split sth/sb ↔ up** *The teacher split up the class into three groups.*

3 split sth ↔ up to divide something into different parts: **[+into]** *The house has now been split up into individual flats.*

GRAMMAR: Reciprocal verbs

Split up is a reciprocal verb. This type of verb is used when saying that two or more people or things do something that involves both or all of them: *Her mum and dad split up.* You can also say: *Her mum split up with her dad.* | *Her mum and dad split up with each other.*

GRAMMAR GUIDE ▸ VERBS

split[2] ●○○ *n* [C]

1 TEAR a tear or crack in something made of cloth, wood etc: **[+in]** *a long split in the sleeve of his coat*

2 DISAGREEMENT a serious disagreement that divides an organization or group of people into smaller groups SYN **rift**: **[+in/within]** *The argument could lead to a damaging split in the party.* | *a deep split within the government* | **[+between]** *a split between the radicals and the moderates within the group* | **[+over]** *The union is desperate to avoid a split over this issue.*

3 END OF RELATIONSHIP *informal* the end of a marriage or relationship – used especially in newspapers and magazines: *rumours of a* ***marriage split*** | **[+with]** *She seems to be getting over her recent split with her fiancé.*

4 DIVIDING STH the way in which something, especially money, is shared between several people: *In a publishing deal, the average split used to be 50:50 between writer and publisher.* | **three-way/four-way etc split** (=when something is shared equally between three, four etc people) *a three-way split in the profits*

5 SEPARATION *informal* a clear separation or difference between two things: **[+between]** *the traditional split between the state and church*

6 do the splits to spread your legs wide apart so that your legs touch the floor along their whole length

ˌsplit ˈends *n* [plural] a condition of someone's hair in which the ends have split into several parts

ˌsplit inˈfinitive *n* [C] a phrase in which you put an adverb or other word between 'to' and a verb, as in 'to easily win'. Some people think this is incorrect English.

ˌsplit-ˈlevel *adj* a split-level house, room, or building has floors at different heights in different parts

ˌsplit personˈality *n* [C] a condition in which someone has two very different ways of behaving

ˌsplit ˈscreen *n* [C] a method of showing different scenes or pieces of information at the same time on a film, television, or computer screen: *a split-screen movie*

ˌsplit ˈsecond *n* **a split second** an extremely short period of time: **for a split second** *For a split second the two men hesitated.* | **in a split second** *In that split second Graham knew he had won.* —**split-second** *adj*: *It was a technique which required split-second timing.*

ˌsplit ˈshift *n* [C] a period of work that is divided into two or more parts on the same day

ˌsplit ˈticket *n* [C] a vote in US elections in which the voter has voted for some CANDIDATES of one party and some of the other party —**split-ticket** *adj*: *split-ticket voting*

split·ting /ˈsplɪtɪŋ/ *adj* **splitting headache** a very bad HEADACHE

splodge /splɒdʒ $ splɑːdʒ/ *n* [C] *BrE informal* a large mark of mud, paint etc with an irregular shape SYN **blotch**: **[+of]** *splodges of colour* —**splodgy** *adj*

splosh /splɒʃ $ splɑːʃ/ *v* [I always + adv/prep] *BrE informal* to make a noise by falling into or moving through water SYN **splash**: *a sploshing sound* —**splosh** *n* [C]

splotch /splɒtʃ $ splɑːtʃ/ *n* [C] a SPLODGE

splurge /splɜːdʒ $ splɜːrdʒ/ *v* [I,T] *informal* to spend more money than you can usually afford SYN **splash out**: **splurge (sth) on sth** *Within a couple of months, I'd splurged about £2,500 on clothes.* THESAURUS ▸ BUY —**splurge** *n* [C]

splut·ter /ˈsplʌtə $ -ər/ *v* **1** [I,T] to talk quickly in short confused phrases, especially because you are angry or surprised: *'But ... but ... I can't believe ... how could you?' she spluttered.* | **[+with]** *Katie was spluttering with rage.* **2** [I] to make a series of short sharp noises: *Bill started* ***coughing and spluttering****.* | *The engine spluttered into life.* —**splutter** *n* [C]

spod /spɒd $ spɑːd/ *n* [C] *BrE informal* someone who spends too much time studying - used to show disapproval SYN **swot** —**spoddy** *adj*

spoil¹ /spɔɪl/ ●●● S3 *v* (*past tense and past participle* **spoiled** *or* **spoilt** /spɔɪlt/ *BrE*)

1 DAMAGE [T] to have a bad effect on something so that it is no longer attractive, enjoyable, useful etc SYN **ruin**: *The whole park is spoiled by litter.* | *We didn't let the incident spoil our day.* | *I don't want to spoil your fun.* | *Why do you always have to* ***spoil everything****?* → **spoil/ruin your appetite** at APPETITE(1) THESAURUS DAMAGE

2 TREAT TOO KINDLY [T] to give a child everything they want, or let them do whatever they want, often with the result that they behave badly: *She's an only child, but they didn't really spoil her.* | *His mother and sisters* ***spoil*** *him* ***rotten*** (=spoil him very much).

3 TREAT KINDLY [T] to look after someone in a way that is very kind or too kind: *You'll have to let me spoil you on your birthday.* | **spoil yourself** *Go on, spoil yourself. Have another piece of cake.*

4 DECAY [I] to start to decay: *Food will spoil if the temperature in your freezer rises above 8°C.*

5 VOTING [T] *BrE* to mark a BALLOT PAPER wrongly so that your vote is not included

6 be spoiling for a fight/argument to be very eager to fight or argue with someone

THESAURUS

spoil to have a bad effect on something so that it is much less attractive, enjoyable etc: *New housing developments are spoiling the countryside.* | *The bad weather completely spoiled our holiday.*

ruin to spoil something completely and permanently: *Using harsh soap to wash your face can ruin your skin.* | *The argument ruined the evening for me.*

mar *written* to spoil something by making it less attractive or enjoyable: *His handsome Arab features were marred by a long scar across his face.* | *Outbreaks of fighting marred the New Year celebrations.*

detract from sth to slightly spoil something that is generally very good, beautiful, or impressive: *The huge number of tourists rather detracts from the city's appeal.* | *There were a few minor irritations, but this did not detract from our enjoyment of the holiday.*

undermine to spoil something that you have been trying to achieve: *The bombings undermined several months of careful negotiations.*

sour to spoil a friendly relationship between people or countries: *The affair has soured relations between the UK and Russia.*

poison to spoil a close relationship completely, so that people can no longer trust each other: *Their marriage was poisoned by a terrible dark secret.*

mess sth up *informal* to spoil something important or something that has been carefully planned: *If there's any delay, it will mess up our whole schedule.*

spoil² *n* **1 spoils** [plural] *formal* **a)** the things that someone gets by being successful: *They tried to take more than a fair share of the spoils.* **b)** things taken by an army from a defeated enemy, or things taken by thieves: **the spoils of war/victory etc 2** [U] waste material such as earth and stones from a mine or hole in the ground: *spoil heaps*

spoil·age /ˈspɔɪlɪdʒ/ *n* [U] *technical* waste resulting from something being spoiled

spoiled /spɔɪld/ (*also* **spoilt** *BrE*) *adj* **1** a spoiled person, especially a child, is rude and behaves badly because they have always been given what they want and allowed to do what they want: *Ben was a* ***spoilt brat*** (=a spoiled and unpleasant child). | *Their children were* ***spoiled rotten*** (=very spoiled). **2 be spoilt/spoiled for choice** *BrE* to have so many good things to choose from that you cannot decide which one to choose

spoil·er /ˈspɔɪlə $ -ər/ *n* [C]

1 CAR a raised part on a racing car that prevents the car from lifting off the road at high speeds

2 PLANE part of an aircraft wing that can be lifted up to slow the plane down

3 PREVENT SUCCESS someone or something that prevents another person or thing from being successful

4 TEAM *AmE* a person or team that spoils another's winning record

5 SURPRISE a message or report that is intended to ruin the surprising part of a popular film, book etc by telling people about the surprise before they see or read it

spoil·sport /ˈspɔɪlspɔːt $ -spɔːrt/ *n* [C] *informal* someone who spoils other people's fun: *Don't be such a spoilsport.*

spoilt¹ /spɔɪlt/ *adj* a British form of the word SPOILED

spoilt² *BrE* a past tense and past participle of SPOIL¹

spoke¹ /spəʊk $ spoʊk/ *v* the past tense of SPEAK

spoke² *n* [C] **1** one of the thin metal bars which connect the outer ring of a wheel to the centre, especially on a bicycle → see picture at **BICYCLE 2 put a spoke in sb's wheel** *BrE* to prevent someone from doing something they have planned

spok·en¹ /ˈspəʊkən $ ˈspoʊ-/ *v* the past participle of SPEAK

spoken² ●●○ *adj*

1 spoken English/language etc the form of language that you speak rather than write → **written**

2 the spoken word spoken language rather than written language or music: *pupils' understanding of the spoken word* | *a spoken-word CD*

3 quietly/softly-spoken *BrE* speaking in a quiet way: *a softly-spoken young man*

4 be spoken for a) if someone is spoken for, they are married or already have a serious relationship with someone **b)** if something is spoken for, you cannot buy it because it is being kept for someone else → **WELL-SPOKEN**

spokes·man /ˈspəʊksmən $ ˈspoʊks-/ ●●○ W3 *n* (*plural* **spokesmen** /-mən/) [C] a man who has been chosen to speak officially for a group, organization, or government → **spokesperson**: *a White House spokesman* | **[+for]** *a spokesman for the victims' families*

spokes·per·son /ˈspəʊksˌpɜːsən $ ˈspoʊksˌpɜːr-/ ●●○ *n* (*plural* **spokespeople** /-ˌpiːpəl/) [C] a spokesman or spokeswoman

spokes·wom·an /ˈspəʊksˌwʊmən $ ˈspoʊks-/ ●●○ *n* (*plural* **spokeswomen** /-ˌwɪmɪn/) [C] a woman who has been chosen to speak officially for a group, organization, or government → **spokesperson**

sponge¹ /spʌndʒ/ ●●○ *n*

1 [C,U] a piece of a soft natural or artificial substance full of small holes, which can suck up liquid and is used for washing

2 [C] a simple sea creature from which natural sponge is produced

3 [singular] *BrE* an act of washing something with a sponge

4 [C,U] *BrE* a light cake made from flour, sugar, butter, and eggs: *a Victoria sponge*

5 [C] a SPONGER

sponge² *v* **1** (*also* **sponge down**) [T] to wash something with a wet cloth or sponge: *Clean the rug by sponging it gently.* | *She stood on the bath mat and sponged herself down.* **2** [I] *informal* to get money, free meals etc from other people, without doing anything for them - used to show disapproval: **[+off/on]** *These people are just sponging off the taxpayers.* **3** [T always + adv/prep] to remove liquid or a mark with a wet cloth or sponge: **sponge sth off (sth)** *I'll go and sponge this juice off my dress.* **4** [T] to put paint on a surface using a sponge: **sponge sth on (sth)** *Just sponge the paint on, like this.*

ˈsponge bag *n* [C] *BrE* a small bag for carrying the things that you need to wash with SYN **toilet bag** → see picture at **BAG¹**

S

ˈsponge cake *n* [C,U] a light cake made from flour, sugar, butter, and eggs

ˌsponge ˈpudding *n* [C] *BrE* a British food made from flour, sugar, eggs, and butter, that is eaten hot

spon·ger /ˈspʌndʒə $ -ər/ *n* [C] someone who gets money, free meals etc from other people and does nothing for them – used to show disapproval

spong·y /ˈspʌndʒi/ *adj* soft and full of holes that contain air or liquid like a SPONGE¹(1): *The earth was soft and spongy underfoot.* **THESAURUS** SOFT —**sponginess** *n* [U]

spon·sor¹ /ˈspɒnsə $ ˈspɑːnsər/ ●○○ *n* [C]
1 a) a person or company that pays for a show, broadcast, sports event etc, especially in exchange for the right to advertise at that event: **[+of]** *Eastman Kodak is a major sponsor of the Olympics.* | *corporate sponsors* **b)** a person or company that supports someone by paying for their training, education, living costs etc
2 someone who agrees to give someone else money for a CHARITY if they walk, run etc a particular distance
3 someone who officially introduces or supports a proposal for a new law
4 someone who officially agrees to help someone else, or to be responsible for what they do: *You cannot get a work visa without an American sponsor.*
5 a GODPARENT

sponsor² ●○○ *v* [T]
1 a) to give money to a sports event, theatre, institution etc, especially in exchange for the right to advertise: *The competition was sponsored by British Airways.* | *government-sponsored projects* **b)** to support someone by paying for their training, education, living costs etc: *The bank had offered to sponsor him at university.*
2 to officially support a proposal for a new law
3 to agree to help someone or be responsible for what they do
4 to agree to give someone money for CHARITY if they walk, run etc a particular distance
5 sponsored walk/swim etc *BrE* an event in which many people walk, swim etc a particular distance so that people will give them money for a CHARITY
6 UN-sponsored/US-sponsored/government-sponsored etc supported and encouraged by the UN, the US etc: *US-sponsored peace talks*

spon·sor·ship /ˈspɒnsəʃɪp $ ˈspɑːnsər-/ ●○○ *n*
1 [plural, U] financial support for an activity or event: **[+from]** *The expedition is looking for sponsorship from one of the major banks.* | *a $5 million sponsorship deal* | *commercial sponsorships*
2 [U] the act of sponsoring someone or something, or of being sponsored: **[+of]** *private sector sponsorship of sport*

spon·ta·ne·ous /spɒnˈteɪniəs $ spɑːn-/ ●○○ *adj*
1 something that is spontaneous has not been planned or organized, but happens by itself, or because you suddenly feel you want to do it: *The crowd gave a spontaneous cheer.* | *My spontaneous reaction was to run away.*
2 someone who is spontaneous does things without planning them first – used to show approval —**spontaneously** *adv*: *She laughed spontaneously.* —**spontaneity** /ˌspɒntˈniːəti, -ˈneɪəti $ ˌspɑːn-/ *n* [U]

sponˌtaneous comˈbustion *n* [U] burning caused by chemical changes inside something rather than by heat from outside

spoof /spuːf/ *n* [C] a funny book, play, or film that copies something serious or important and makes it seem silly → **take-off**: **[+of/on]** *The play is a spoof on Shakespeare's tragedy 'Julius Caesar'.* | *a spoof documentary* —**spoof** *v* [T]

spook¹ /spuːk/ *n* [C] *informal* **1** a GHOST **2** *especially AmE* a SPY

spook² *v* [T] *informal* to frighten someone: *I'm not easily spooked.*

spook·y /ˈspuːki/ *adj informal* strange or frightening in a way that makes you think of GHOSTS: *a spooky old house* | *spooky stories* | *The candlelight created a rather spooky atmosphere.* **THESAURUS** FRIGHTENING

spool /spuːl/ *n* [C] an object shaped like a wheel that you wind thread, wire etc around

spoon¹ /spuːn/ ●●● S3 *n* [C]
1 an object that you use for eating, cooking, or serving food. It has a small bowl-shaped part and a long handle
2 a SPOONFUL: **[+of]** *two spoons of sugar* → **be born with a silver spoon in your mouth** at BORN¹(8), → **DESSERTSPOON, GREASY SPOON, SOUP SPOON, WOODEN SPOON**

spoon² *v* [T always + adv/prep] to move food with a spoon: **spoon sth into/over/onto sth** *Spoon the mixture carefully into the bowls.*

spoo·ner·is·m /ˈspuːnərɪzəm/ *n* [C] a phrase in which the speaker accidentally exchanges the first sounds of two words, with a funny result, for example 'sew you to a sheet' instead of 'show you to a seat'

ˈspoon-feed *v* (*past tense and past participle* **spoon-fed**) [T] **1** to give too much information and help to someone – used to show disapproval: *I don't believe in spoon-feeding students.* **2** to feed someone, especially a baby, with a spoon

spoon·ful /ˈspuːnfʊl/ *n* [C] the amount that a spoon will hold: **[+of]** *Two spoonfuls of sugar, please.*

spoor /spɔː, spʊə $ spɔːr, spʊr/ *n* [singular, U] *technical* the track of footmarks or solid waste that a wild animal leaves as it moves along

spo·rad·ic /spəˈrædɪk/ *adj* happening fairly often, but not regularly SYN **intermittent**: *There has been sporadic violence downtown.* —**sporadically** /-kli/ *adv*: *The fighting continued sporadically for several days.*

spore /spɔː $ spɔːr/ *n* [C] a cell like a seed that is produced by some plants such as MUSHROOMS and can develop into a new plant

spor·ran /ˈspɒrən $ ˈspɔː-, ˈspɑː-/ *n* [C] a special bag made of leather or fur, that a Scotsman wears in front of a KILT

sport¹ /spɔːt $ spɔːrt/ ●●● S2 W2 *n*
1 GAMES **a)** [C] a physical activity in which people compete against each other: *My favourite sports are tennis and swimming.* | *a sports team* | *All students are encouraged to take part in a sport.* | *He picked up the newspaper and turned to the sports pages.* **b)** [U] *BrE* sports in general: *Why is there so much sport on TV?* | *I always hated sport at school.*

GRAMMAR: Countable or uncountable?
- In British English, you say: *I like watching sport on TV.* **Sport** is an uncountable noun in this meaning.
- In American English, you say: *I like watching sports on TV.* **Sports** is a plural noun in this meaning.

2 HUNTING [C] an activity that people do in the countryside, especially hunting or fishing: *the sport of falconry* | *a demonstration by people opposed to* ***blood sports*** (=sports that involve killing animals)
3 HELPFUL PERSON [C usually singular] (*also* **good sport**) *old-fashioned* a helpful cheerful person who lets you enjoy yourself: **be a sport** (=used when asking someone to help you) *Be a sport and lend me your bike.*
4 a good sport someone who does not get angry when they lose at a game or sport
5 a bad/poor sport someone who gets angry very easily when they lose at a game or sport
6 MAN/BOY *spoken* **a)** *AusE* used when speaking to someone, especially a man, in a friendly way: *See you later, sport.* **b)** *AmE old-fashioned* used when speaking to a boy in a friendly way
7 FUN [U] *old-fashioned* fun or amusement: *Did she torment him merely for sport?*
8 make sport of sb *old-fashioned* to joke about someone in a way that makes them seem stupid → **FIELD SPORTS, WATER SPORTS, WINTER SPORTS**

COLLOCATIONS

VERBS

play (a) sport *My ambition was to play sport at the highest level.*

take part in (a) sport *Students are encouraged to take part in a sport of some kind.*
do sport *BrE*, **do sports** *AmE* *I did a lot of sport at school.*
take up a sport (=start doing it) *I took up the sport six years ago.*
compete in a sport (=do that sport in competitions)

ADJECTIVES/NOUN + sport

a team sport *I liked playing team sports such as football and rugby.*
an individual sport *You have to be mentally tough to compete in individual sports.*
a spectator sport (=one that people enjoy watching) *Football is the most popular spectator sport.*
competitive sport(s) (=in which people compete and try to win) | **a contact sport** (=one in which players have physical contact with each other) | **a winter sport** (=skiing, ice skating etc) | **an extreme sport** (=one that is dangerous) | **professional sport(s)** (=which people are paid to do)

sports + NOUN

a sports team *A lot of schools have their own sports teams.*
a sports club *She joined her local sports club.*
a sports field/ground | **a sports event** | **a sports fan** (=someone who enjoys watching sport) | **a sports personality** (=someone who is famous for playing sport) | **sports facilities** | **sports equipment** | **a sports injury**

COMMON ERRORS

⚠ Don't say 'make (a) sport'. Say **do (a) sport** or **play (a) sport**.

sport² *v* **1 be sporting sth** to be wearing something or have something on your body and show it to people in a proud way: *Eric was sporting a new camelhair coat.* **2** [I] *literary* to play together happily: *the sight of dolphins sporting amidst the waves*

ˈsport coat *n* [C] *AmE* a SPORTS JACKET

sport·ing /ˈspɔːtɪŋ $ ˈspɔːr-/ *adj* **1** [only before noun] relating to sports: *The college offers a wide range of sporting activities.* | *one of the major* ***sporting events*** *of the year* | *a great sporting achievement* | *Britain's sporting heroes* | **sporting goods** *AmE*: *a sporting goods store* **2** *BrE* someone who is sporting behaves in a fair and generous way during a game or competition and does not try to win in an unfair way OPP **unsporting**: *It was very sporting of them to wait until the rest of our team had arrived.* **3 sporting chance (of doing sth)** a fairly good chance of succeeding or winning: *I think we've got a sporting chance of winning.* —**sportingly** *adv BrE*: *They sportingly agreed to postpone the race until our boat was repaired.*

ˈsport ˌjacket *n* [C] *AmE* a SPORTS JACKET

ˈsports bra *n* [C] a special type of BRA (=a piece of underwear that supports a woman's breasts) that is designed for women to wear while playing sports

ˈsports car ●●○ *n* [C] a low fast car, often with a roof that can be folded back or removed

sports·cast /ˈspɔːtskɑːst $ ˈspɔːrtskæst/ *n* [C] *AmE* a television broadcast of a sports game

sports·cast·er /ˈspɔːtsˌkɑːstə $ ˈspɔːrtsˌkæstər/ *n* [C] *AmE* someone who describes a sports game as it is being broadcast on television → **commentator**

ˈsports ˌcentre *BrE*, **sports center** *AmE* ●●○ *n* [C] a building where people can go to play many different types of indoor sports

ˈsports coat *n* [C] a SPORTS JACKET

ˈsports day *n* [C] *BrE* a day on which the children at a school have sports competitions SYN **field day** *AmE*

ˈsport shirt *n* [C] *AmE* a SPORTS SHIRT

ˈsports ˌjacket *n* [C] a man's jacket that is not part of a suit

sports·man /ˈspɔːtsmən $ ˈspɔːrts-/ *n* (*plural* **sportsmen** /-mən/) [C] **1** a man who plays several different sports → **sportswoman**: *He's a very* ***keen sportsman***. | *a talented all-round sportsman* **2** *AmE* a man who enjoys outdoor activities such as hunting and fishing

sports·man·like /ˈspɔːtsmənlaɪk $ ˈspɔːrts-/ *adj* behaving in a fair, honest, and polite way when competing in sports OPP **unsportsmanlike**: *As a club, we try to encourage* ***sportsmanlike behaviour***.

sports·man·ship /ˈspɔːtsmənʃɪp $ ˈspɔːrts-/ *n* [U] behaviour that is fair, honest, and polite in a game or sports competition: *His sportsmanship and style of play are refreshing.* | **good/bad/poor sportsmanship** (=good or bad behaviour in a sport) *We try to teach the kids good sportsmanship.*

sports·per·son /ˈspɔːtsˌpɜːsən $ ˈspɔːrtsˌpɜːr-/ *n* (*plural* **sportspeople** /-ˌpiːpəl/) [C] *BrE* someone who takes part in sports or a sport

S

SPORTS EQUIPMENT

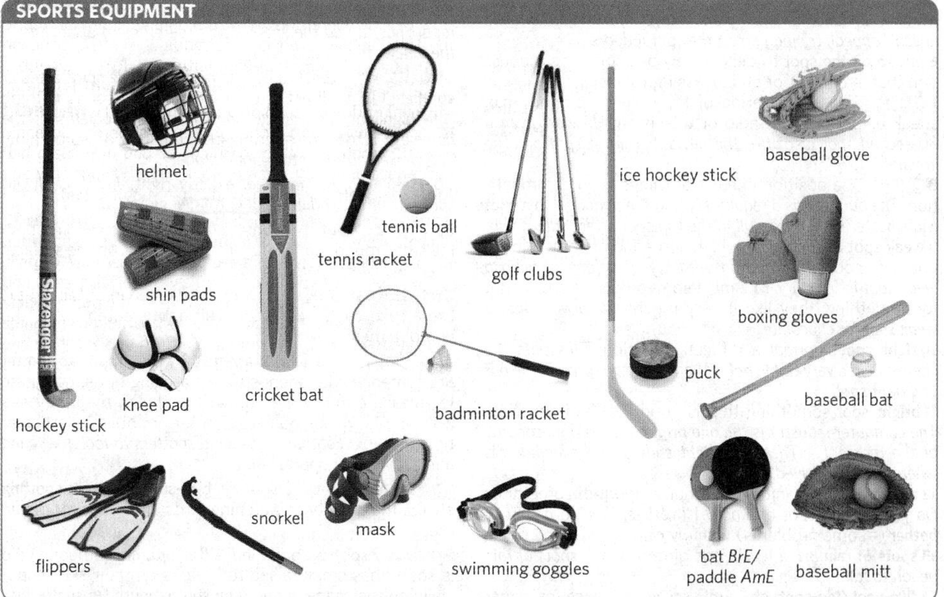

ˌsports shirt *n* [C] a shirt for men that is worn on informal occasions

sports·wear /ˈspɔːtsweə $ ˈspɔːrtswer/ *n* [U] **1** clothes that you wear to play sports or when you are relaxing **2** *AmE* clothes that are suitable for informal occasions SYN **casual clothes**

sports·wom·an /ˈspɔːtsˌwʊmən $ ˈspɔːrts-/ *n* (*plural* **sportswomen** /-ˌwɪmɪn/) [C] a woman who plays many different sports → **sportsman**: *a great all-round sportswoman*

sports·writ·er /ˈspɔːtsˌraɪtə $ ˈspɔːrtsˌraɪtər/ *n* [C] someone whose job is to write about sports for a newspaper or magazine

ˌsport-uˈtility ˌvehicle *n* [C] *AmE* an SUV

sport·y /ˈspɔːti $ ˈspɔːrti/ *adj informal* **1** *especially BrE* someone who is sporty likes sport and is good at it SYN **athletic 2** sporty clothes are designed to look attractive in a bright informal way: *a sporty jacket and skirt* **3** a sporty car is designed to look attractive and go fast: *The new model is slightly more sporty.*

spot¹ /spɒt $ spɑːt/ ●●● S2 W2 *n* [C]

1 PLACE a particular place or area, especially a pleasant place where you spend time: *a nice quiet spot on the beach* | *I chose a spot well away from the road.* | **in a spot** *a small cottage in an idyllic spot* | **on a spot** *Why do they want to build a house on this particular spot?* | **the exact/same/very spot** *the exact spot where the king was executed* | **[+for]** *an ideal spot for a picnic* THESAURUS PLACE

2 AREA a usually round area on a surface that is a different colour or is rougher, smoother etc than the rest SYN **patch**: *a white cat with brown spots* | **[+of]** *Two spots of colour appeared in Jill's cheeks.*

3 MARK a small mark on something, especially one that is made by a liquid: *There was a big damp spot on the wall.* | **[+of]** *a few spots of blood*

4 ON SKIN **a)** a small round red area on someone's skin that shows that they are ill: *He had a high fever and was covered in spots.* **b)** *BrE* a small raised red mark on someone's skin, especially on their face SYN **pimple**: *Becka was very self-conscious about her spots.*

5 on the spot a) if you do something on the spot, you do it immediately, often without thinking about it very carefully → **on-the-spot**: *He had to make a decision on the spot.* **b)** if you are on the spot, you are in the place where something is happening: *We ought to find out the views of the people on the spot.* **c)** *BrE* if you walk, run, or jump on the spot, you do it staying in the same place, without moving around SYN **in place** *AmE*: *If running outside doesn't appeal, try jogging on the spot indoors.*

6 put sb on the spot to deliberately ask someone a question that is difficult or embarrassing to answer

7 TV/RADIO a short period of time when someone can speak or perform on radio or television: *He was given a 30-second spot just after the news.* | *a* **guest spot** *on 'The Tonight Show'*

8 POSITION a position in a list of things or in a competition: *The budget has a regular spot on the agenda.* | **in a spot** *Manchester United are still in the top spot after today's win.*

9 weak spot a) a point at which someone or something is not very good: *I carried on with my questions, sensing a weak spot in his story.* **b)** *AmE* if someone has a weak spot for something, they like it very much: *I've always* **had a weak spot for** *chocolate.*

10 tight spot *informal* a difficult situation: *This* **puts** *the chairman* **in** *a very* **tight spot**. | *I hope you can help* **get** *me* **out of a tight spot**.

11 bright spot something that is good in a bad situation: *The computer industry is the* **one bright spot** *in the economy at the moment.* | *The* **only bright spot** *of the evening was when the food arrived.*

12 a spot of sth *BrE informal* a small amount of something: *Do you fancy a spot of lunch?* | *I've been having* **a spot of bother** (=some problems) *with my car.*

13 spots of rain *BrE* a few drops of rain: *A few spots of rain began to fall.*

14 five-spot/ten-spot etc *AmE spoken* a piece of paper money worth five dollars, ten dollars etc → BEAUTY SPOT, BLACKSPOT, BLIND SPOT, → **change your spots** at CHANGE¹(16), → G-SPOT, → **high point/spot** at HIGH¹(12), → **hit the spot** at HIT¹(28), → HOT SPOT, → **knock spots off** at KNOCK¹(19), → **be rooted to the spot** at ROOT²(5), → **have a soft spot for sb** at SOFT(16), → TROUBLE SPOT

spot² ●●○ S3 *v* (**spotted**, **spotting**) [T]

1 to notice someone or something, especially when they are difficult to see or recognize: *I spotted a police car behind us.* | *It can be hard for even a trained doctor to spot the symptoms of lung cancer.* | **spot sb doing sth** *Meg spotted someone coming out of the building.* | **difficult/easy to spot** *Drug addicts are fairly easy to spot.* | **spot that** *One of the station staff spotted that I was in difficulty, and came to help.* THESAURUS NOTICE, SEE

2 be spotted with sth to have small round marks or small pieces of something on the surface: *The windscreen was spotted with rain.*

3 *AmE* to give the other player in a game an advantage: **spot sb sth** *He spotted me six points and he still won.*

spot³ *adj* [only before noun] for buying or paying immediately, not at some future time: *They won't take credit; they want* **spot cash**. | *He quoted us a* **spot price** *for the goods.*

ˌspot ˈcheck *n* [C] an examination of a few things or people from a group, to check whether everything is correct or satisfactory: **[+on]** *spot checks on quality* | **make/do/carry out etc spot checks** *We* **carry out spot checks** *on the vehicles before they leave the depot.* —**ˈspot check** *v* [T]: *We spot check everyone's work.*

spot·less /ˈspɒtləs $ ˈspɑːt-/ *adj* **1** completely clean → **pristine**: *a spotless white handkerchief* | *By the time she had finished the house was* **absolutely spotless**. THESAURUS CLEAN **2** if someone has a spotless REPUTATION or record, people know or think they have never done anything bad: *a company whose reputation was spotless until this scandal broke* —**spotlessly** *adv*: *The whole house was* **spotlessly clean**.

spot·light¹ /ˈspɒtlaɪt $ ˈspɑːt-/ ●○○ *n*

1 [C] a light with a very bright beam which can be directed at someone or something. Spotlights are often used to light a stage when actors or singers are performing: *The yard was lit by three huge spotlights.* | **under the spotlights** *I was sweating under the spotlights.* | **in/into the spotlight** *She stepped into the spotlight and began to sing.* → see picture at LAMP

2 the spotlight a lot of attention in newspapers, on television etc: **in/under the spotlight** *Education is once again under the spotlight.* | **put/turn the spotlight on sth** *A new report has turned the spotlight on the problem of poverty in the inner cities.*

spotlight² *v* (*past tense and past participle* **spotlighted** *or* **spotlit**) [T] **1** to direct attention to someone or something SYN **highlight**: *The article spotlights the problems of the homeless.* **2** to shine a strong beam of light on something: *She walked out onto the spotlit stage.*

ˌspot-ˈon *adj BrE informal* exactly right: *Judith is always spot-on with her advice.* THESAURUS RIGHT

spot·ted /ˈspɒtɪd $ ˈspɑː-/ *adj* [usually before noun] having small round marks of a different colour on the surface: *a red and white spotted blouse*

ˌspotted ˈdick *n* [U] a sweet food eaten in Britain that is like a cake containing dried fruit and is eaten hot at the end of a meal

spot·ter /ˈspɒtə $ ˈspɑːtər/ *n* [C] **1 bird/train etc spotter** *BrE* someone who spends time watching birds, trains etc for pleasure and writes down the things that they see **2** someone whose job is to look for or notice a particular type of thing: *Football clubs send spotters to look for young talent.* | **weather spotter** *AmE*

spot·ting /ˈspɒtɪŋ $ ˈspɑː-/ *n* **bird-spotting/train-spotting etc** *BrE* the activity of watching birds, trains etc for pleasure

spot·ty /ˈspɒti $ ˈspɑːti/ *adj* **1** *BrE informal* someone who is spotty has small raised red marks on their skin, especially on their face: *a tall, thin, spotty youth* | *a spotty face*

2 *AmE* good only in some parts, but not in other parts SYN **patchy** *BrE*

spouse /spaʊs, spaʊz/ ●○○ *n* [C] *formal* a husband or wife: *Spouses were invited to the company picnic.* THESAURUS MARRIED —**spousal** /ˈspaʊzəl/ *adj*: *spousal abuse*

spout¹ /spaʊt/ *n* [C] **1** a small pipe on the side of a container that you pour liquid out through **2 spout of water/blood etc** a sudden strong stream of liquid which comes out of somewhere very fast → WATERSPOUT(1) **3 up the spout** *BrE informal* if something is up the spout, it is completely wrong or has failed completely: *The computer's up the spout!* | *My plans for the weekend seem to have* ***gone up the spout***.

spout² *v* **1 a)** [I always + adv/prep] if liquid or fire spouts from somewhere, it comes out very quickly in a powerful stream SYN **spurt**: **[+from]** *Blood was spouting from the wound in her arm.* **b)** [T] to send out liquid or flames very quickly in a powerful stream: *a volcano spouting lava* **2** (*also* **spout off**) [I,T] *informal* to talk a lot about something in a boring or annoying way: *My father was spouting his usual nonsense!* | *I hate it when he spouts off like that!* | **[+about]** *I'm tired of listening to Jim spouting about politics.* **3** [I] if a WHALE spouts, it sends out a stream of water from a hole in its head

sprain /spreɪn/ ●○○ *v* [T] to damage a joint in your body by suddenly twisting it SYN **twist**: *I fell down the steps and* ***sprained*** *my* ***ankle***. THESAURUS HURT, INJURY —**sprain** *n* [C]: *I thought my wrist might be broken, but it was just a bad sprain.*

sprang /spræŋ/ *v* the past tense of SPRING²

sprat /spræt/ *n* [C] a small fish that is cooked and eaten whole

sprawl¹ /sprɔːl $ sprɒːl/ ●○○ (*also* **sprawl out**) *v* [I always + adv/prep] **1** to lie or sit with your arms or legs stretched out in a lazy or careless way: *He sprawled out on the sofa.* | *I tripped on a stone and* ***went sprawling*** *on the pavement.* | *a blow which* ***sent*** *him* ***sprawling*** **2** if buildings sprawl, they spread out over a wide area in an untidy and unattractive way: *The town seemed to sprawl for miles.*

SPRAWL

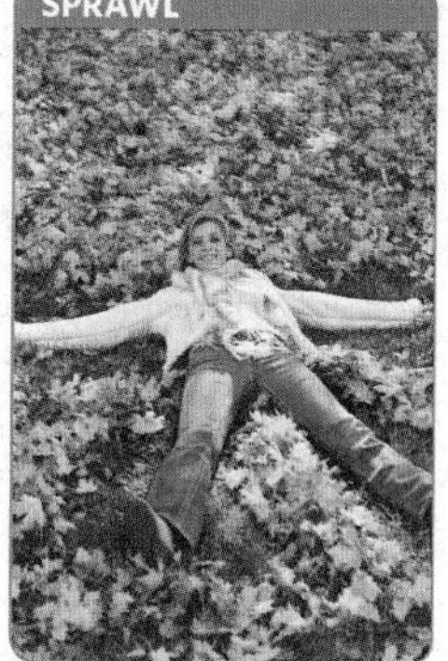

sprawl² *n* [singular, U] a large area of buildings that are spread out in an untidy and unattractive way: *We drove through miles of* ***urban sprawl*** *before we finally got out into the countryside.*

sprawled /sprɔːld $ sprɒːld/ *adj* **be/lie/sit sprawled (out)** to be lying or sitting with your arms or legs stretched out in a lazy or careless way: *He was sprawled in an armchair in front of the TV.* | *A girl lay sprawled across the bed.*

spraw·ling /ˈsprɔːlɪŋ $ ˈsprɒːl-/ *adj* spreading over a wide area in an untidy or unattractive way: *a vast, sprawling city*

spray¹ /spreɪ/ ●●● S3 *v* **1** [T] to force liquid out of a container so that it comes out in a stream of very small drops and covers an area → **squirt**: **spray sb/sth with sth** *She sprayed herself with perfume.* | **spray sth on/onto/over sth** *Someone had sprayed blue paint over his car.* | *Vandals had sprayed graffiti on the walls.* | **spray crops/plants etc** (=cover them with liquid to protect them from insects or disease) *The fruit is sprayed every four weeks.* → see picture at SQUIRT **2** [I always + adv/prep] if liquids or small bits spray somewhere, they are quickly scattered through the air: **[+from]** *Champagne sprayed from the bottle.* **3 spray sb/sth with bullets** to shoot a lot of bullets towards a person or place very quickly: *Gunmen sprayed the crowd with bullets.*

spray² ●●● S3 *n* **1** LIQUID FROM A CONTAINER [C,U] liquid which is forced out of a special container in a stream of very small drops: *a new hair styling spray* | *Most farmers use pesticide sprays.* **2** CONTAINER [C] a container which forces liquid out in a stream of small drops: *Mary took a perfume spray from her handbag.* **3** MOVING LIQUID **a)** [U] water in very small drops that is blown from the sea etc or sent up by vehicles on a wet road: *spray from the waves* | *My face was stinging from the salt spray.* **b)** [C] liquid that comes quickly from somewhere in very small drops: **[+of]** *A spray of blood came from his mouth.* **4** BRANCH [C] a small branch or stem with leaves or flowers on it, used for decoration SYN **sprig**: **[+of]** *a spray of holly* **5** FLOWERS [C] an attractive arrangement of flowers or leaves: **[+of]** *a spray of violets and primroses* **6 a spray of bullets/gravel etc** a lot of bullets or very small objects moving quickly through the air

ˈspray can *n* [C] a can from which you can spray paint onto things

spray·er /ˈspreɪə $ -ər/ *n* [C] a piece of equipment that is used for spraying large amounts of liquid, especially over crops

ˈspray gun *n* [C] a piece of equipment that you hold in your hand and use to spray liquid in very small drops

ˈspray-on *adj* [only before noun] a spray-on substance can be sprayed from a container onto a surface: *a spray-on water repellent for clothing*

ˈspray paint *n* [U] paint that you spray from a can —**spray-paint** *v* [I,T]

ˈspray tan *n* [C,U] a process in which someone is SPRAYed with a coloured substance so that their skin looks as if it has been turned brown by the sun

spread¹ /spred/ ●●● S2 W2 *v* (*past tense and past participle* **spread**) **1** AFFECT MORE PEOPLE/PLACES [I,T] if something spreads or is spread, it becomes larger or moves so that it affects more people or a larger area: **[+through]** *Fire quickly spread through the building.* | **[+over]** *He watched the dark stain spread over the gray carpet.* | **[+among]** *The disease* ***spread rapidly*** *amongst the poor.* | **spread (from sth) to sth** *The cancer had spread to her liver.* | *Revolution quickly spread from France to Italy.* **2** INFORMATION/IDEAS **a)** [I] to become known about or used by more and more people: *News of the explosion spread swiftly.* | **[+to/through/over etc]** *Buddhism spread to China from India.* | *The news* ***spread like wildfire*** (=very quickly). | ***Word spread*** *quickly that she was leaving.* **b)** [T] to tell a lot of people about something: *Andy loves spreading rumours about his colleagues.* | *They are* ***spreading the word*** *about the benefits of immunization.* **3** OPEN/ARRANGE (*also* **spread out**) [T] to open something out or arrange a group of things so that they cover a flat surface: **spread sth over/across/on sth** *Papers and photos were spread across the floor.* | *He spread the map out on the desk.* | *a table spread with a white cloth* **4** THROUGHOUT AN AREA [I] (*also* **be spread**, **spread out**) to cover or exist across a large area: **[+over]** *the forest that spread over the whole of that region* | **[+throughout]** *The company has more than 2,500 shops spread throughout the UK.* **5** SOFT SUBSTANCE [I,T] to put a soft substance over a surface, or to be soft enough to be put over a surface: **spread sth on/over sth** *He spread plaster on the walls.* | **spread sth with sth** *Spread the toast thinly with jam.* | *If you warm up the butter, it'll spread more easily.* | ***Spread*** *the nut mixture* ***evenly*** *over the bottom.* **6** ARMS/FINGERS ETC [T] if you spread your arms, fingers, or legs, you move them far apart: *He shrugged and spread his hands.* **7** OVER TIME [T] (*also* **spread out**) to do something over a period of time, rather than at one time: **spread sth over sth**

S

Could I spread the repayments over a longer period? | *There will be 12 concerts spread throughout the summer.*
8 SHARE [T] to share or divide something among several people or things: **spread the load/burden** *The bills are sent out on different dates to spread the workload on council staff.* | *They want the country's wealth to be more* ***evenly spread****.*
9 SMILE/LOOK [I always + adv/prep] if an expression spreads over someone's face, it slowly appears on their face: **[+over/across]** *A slow smile spread over her face.*
10 spread your wings a) to start to have an independent life and experience new things: *A year spent studying abroad should allow him to spread his wings a bit.* **b)** if a bird or insect spreads its wings, it stretches them wide
11 a) be spread (too) thin/thinly if money, effort etc is spread thin, it is being used for many things so there is not enough for each thing: *They complained that resources were spread too thinly.* **b) spread yourself too thin** to try to do too many things at the same time so that you do not do any of them effectively
12 spread seeds/manure/fertilizer to scatter seeds, MANURE etc on the ground → **spread your net wide** at **NET¹(8)**
spread out *phr v*
1 if a group of people spread out, they move apart from each other so that they cover a wider area: *The search party spread out to search the surrounding fields.*
2 spread sth ↔ out to open something out or arrange a group of things on a flat surface: *Sue spread out her notes on the kitchen table and began to write.*
3 (*also* **be spread out**) to cover a large area: *The city spread out below her looked so calm.*
4 spread sth ↔ out to do something over a period of time, rather than at one time: **[+over]** *The course is spread out over four days.*

S

spread² ●●○ *n*
1 INCREASE [singular] when something affects or is known about by more people or involves a larger area → **increase**: **[+of]** *an attempt to stop the spread of nuclear weapons* | *the* ***rapid spread*** *of cholera in Latin America*
2 SOFT FOOD [C,U] **a)** a soft substance made from vegetable oil that is used like butter: *one slice of toast with a low-fat spread* **b)** a soft food which you spread on bread: **cheese/chocolate etc spread**
3 RANGE [singular] a range of people or things: **wide/broad/good spread of sth** *We have a good spread of ages in the department.* | *a broad spread of investments*
4 AREA [singular] the total area in which something exists: *the* ***geographical spread*** *of the company's hotels*
5 double-page spread/centre spread a special article or advertisement in a newspaper or magazine, which covers two pages or covers the centre pages: *There's a double-page spread in Sunday's paper.*
6 LARGE MEAL [singular] *informal* a large meal for several guests on a special occasion: *Tom's mum laid on a huge spread.*
7 HAND/WINGS [U] the area covered when the fingers of a hand, or a bird's wings, are fully stretched
8 BED COVER [C] a BEDSPREAD
9 MONEY [C] *technical* the difference between the prices at which something is bought and sold, or the INTEREST rates for lending and borrowing money: **[+between]** *the spread between the city banks' loan rates and deposit rates*
10 SPORT [singular] *AmE* the number of points between the scores of two opposing teams: *a four-point spread*
11 spread of land/water an area of land or water
12 FARM [C] *AmE* a large farm or RANCH → **middle-aged spread** at **MIDDLE-AGED(3)**

ˈspread ˌbetting *n* [U] **1** a type of BETTING on sports events in which someone says what they think the final score will be **2** a way of buying and selling SHARES in which someone BETS money on whether shares in a particular company will go up or down in value —**spread bet** *n* [C]

spread·ea·gled /spredˈiːɡəld $ ˈsprediːɡəld/ *adj* lying with arms and legs stretched out SYN **sprawled**: *He lay spreadeagled on the bed.*

spread·sheet /ˈspredʃiːt/ ●○○ *n* [C]
1 a computer program that can show and calculate financial information
2 a document that contains rows and COLUMNs of numbers that can be used to calculate something

spree /spriː/ *n* [C] a short period of time when you do a lot of one activity, especially spending money or drinking alcohol: **on a spree** *They* ***went on*** *a drinking* ***spree****.* | *a* ***shopping spree***

sprig /sprɪɡ/ *n* [C] a small stem or part of a branch with leaves or flowers on it: **[+of]** *a sprig of parsley*

sprigged /sprɪɡd/ *adj* sprigged cloth or a sprigged pattern is decorated with leaves or flowers on stems

spright·ly /ˈspraɪtli/ *adj* an old person who is sprightly is still active and full of energy – used to show approval —**sprightliness** *n* [U]

spring¹ /sprɪŋ/ ●●● S2 W2 *n*
1 SEASON [C,U] the season between winter and summer when leaves and flowers appear: **[+of]** *the spring of 1933* | **in/during the spring** *It's due to open in the spring.* | **late/early spring** *It was a cold, sunny day in early spring.* | *spring flowers*
2 CURVED METAL **a)** [C usually plural] something, usually a twisted piece of metal, that will return to its previous shape after it has been pressed down: *an old armchair with broken springs* **b)** [U] the ability of a chair, bed etc to return to its normal shape after being pressed down
3 WATER [C] a place where water comes up naturally from the ground: *spring water* | *There are several* ***hot springs*** *in the area.*
4 spring in your step if you walk with a spring in your step, you move quickly and happily: *As he walked into the office that morning, there was a spring in his step.*
5 full of the joys of spring happy and full of energy – used humorously
6 SUDDEN JUMP [singular] a sudden quick movement or jump in a particular direction SYN **leap**

GRAMMAR: Patterns with spring

in spring/in the spring
• You use **in spring** or **in the spring** when saying that something happens at this time: *In spring the days get longer.* | *She's coming to visit us in the spring.*

last spring/this spring etc
Don't use **in** with these words:
• You say **last spring**: *They moved here last spring.*
✗ Don't say: *They moved here in last spring.*
• You say **this spring**: *The flowers are beautiful this spring.* ✗ Don't say: *The flowers are beautiful in this spring.*
• You say **next spring**: *They're getting married next spring.* ✗ Don't say: *They're getting married in next spring.*
• You say **that spring**: *It rained a lot that spring.*
✗ Don't say: *It rained a lot in that spring.*

spring² ●●○ *v* (*past tense* **sprang** /spræŋ/ *or* **sprung** /sprʌŋ/ *AmE, past participle* **sprung**)
1 MOVE SUDDENLY [I always + adv/prep] to move suddenly and quickly in a particular direction, especially by jumping SYN **leap**: **[+out of/from]** *Tom sprung out of bed and ran downstairs.* | **spring out at sb** *Two men sprang out at me as I was walking through the park.* | *He* ***sprang to his feet*** (=stood up suddenly) *and rushed after her.* | **spring to sb's aid/assistance** (=move quickly to help someone) *One of the young policemen sprang to her assistance.*

REGISTER
Spring is used mostly in literature. In everyday English, people usually say **jump**: *He* ***jumped*** *out of bed.*

2 MOVE BACK [I always + adv/prep] if something springs back, open etc, it moves quickly, suddenly, and with force, especially after being pushed down or sideways: **[+back/up]** *The branch sprang back and hit him in the face.* | **spring open/shut** *The gate sprang shut behind them.*
3 spring to (sb's) mind if someone or something springs to

mind, you immediately think of them: *Two questions spring to mind.*
4 spring into action (*also* **spring to/into life**) to suddenly become active, start moving, or start working: *They were prepared and ready to spring into action. | Finally, the engine sprang to life.*
5 spring a surprise to do something surprising: *Roy is unlikely to spring any surprises.*
6 tears spring to/into sb's eyes *written* used to say that someone starts to cry
7 spring into existence/being to suddenly begin to exist: *A lot of small businesses sprang into existence during the 1980s.*
8 spring a trap a) if an animal springs a trap, it is caught by the trap **b)** to make someone say or do something by tricking them
9 spring a leak if a boat or a container springs a leak, it begins to let liquid in or out through a crack or hole
10 spring to sb's defence to quickly defend someone who is being criticized: *Charlene sprang immediately to her son's defence.*
11 spring to attention if soldiers spring to attention, they stand suddenly upright
12 HELP SB ESCAPE [T + from] *informal* to help someone escape from prison
spring for sth *phr v AmE informal* to pay for something: *I'll spring for the beer tonight.*
spring from sth *phr v spoken* to be caused by something or start from something: *behaviour which springs from prejudices*
spring sth **on** sb *phr v* to tell someone something or ask them to do something when they do not expect it and are not ready for it: *It's not fair to spring this on her without any warning.*
spring up *phr v* to suddenly appear or start to exist: *Fast-food restaurants are springing up all over town.*

spring·board /ˈsprɪŋbɔːd $ -bɔːrd/ *n* [C] **1** something that helps you to start doing something: **[+for]** *The TV soap has been a springboard for a lot of careers.* **2** a strong board for jumping on or off, used when diving (DIVE¹(1)) or doing GYMNASTICS

spring·bok /ˈsprɪŋbɒk $ -bɑːk/ *n* [C] a small DEER that can run fast and lives in South Africa

ˌspring ˈbreak *n* [C] *AmE* a holiday from college or university in the spring, usually two weeks long

ˌspring ˈchicken *n* [C] **sb is no spring chicken** used to say that someone is no longer young - used humorously

ˌspring-ˈcleaning *n* [U] when you clean a house thoroughly, usually once a year: *Judith's busy* ***doing the spring-cleaning****.* —**spring-clean** *n* [singular] *BrE* —**spring-clean** *v* [I,T]

ˌspring ˈfever *n* [U] a sudden feeling of energy that you have in the spring

ˌspring-ˈloaded *adj* containing a metal SPRING that presses one part against another

ˌspring ˈonion *n* [C] *BrE* a strong tasting onion with a small white round part and a long green stem, usually eaten raw SYN **scallion**, **green onion** *AmE* → see picture at **VEGETABLE¹**

ˌspring ˈroll / $ ˈ../ *n* [C] a type of Chinese food consisting of a piece of thin rolled PASTRY filled with vegetables and sometimes meat and cooked in oil SYN **egg roll** *AmE*

ˌspring ˈtide *n* [C] a large rise and fall in the level of the sea at the time of the NEW MOON and the FULL MOON → **neap tide**

spring·time /ˈsprɪŋtaɪm/ *n* [U] the time of the year when it is spring: **in (the) springtime** *when the snow melts in the springtime*

ˌspring ˈtraining *n* [U] *AmE* the period when a BASEBALL team gets ready for competition

spring·y /ˈsprɪŋi/ *adj* **1** something that is springy is soft and comes back to its normal shape after being pressed or walked on: *The grass was soft and springy.* **2 springy step/walk** a way of walking which is quick and full of energy —**springily** *adv* —**springiness** *n* [U]

sprin·kle¹ /ˈsprɪŋkəl/ ●○○ *v*
1 [T] to scatter small drops of liquid or small pieces of something: **sprinkle sth with sth** *Sprinkle the top with cheese.* | **sprinkle sth on/over sth** *I sprinkled cocoa over my latte.*
2 be sprinkled with jokes/quotations etc to be full of jokes etc: *The book is* ***liberally sprinkled*** *with clichés.*
3 it is sprinkling *AmE* if it is sprinkling, it is raining lightly

SPRINKLE

sprinkle² *n* [singular] **1** a small amount of something, especially scattered on top of something SYN **sprinkling**: **[+of]** *Add a sprinkle of salt.* **2** *AmE* a light rain SYN **drizzle**

sprin·kler /ˈsprɪŋklə $ -ər/ *n* [C] **1** a piece of equipment used for scattering water on grass or soil → see picture at **GARDEN 2** a piece of equipment on a ceiling that scatters water if there is a fire

sprin·kling /ˈsprɪŋklɪŋ/ *n* [singular] a small amount of something, especially scattered over an area: **[+of]** *The hilltops were covered with a sprinkling of snow.*

sprint¹ /sprɪnt/ *v* [I] **1** to run very fast for a short distance → **jog**: **[+along/across/up etc]** *Bill sprinted up the steps.* THESAURUS **RUN 2** to ride, swim etc very fast for a short distance

sprint² *n* **1** [C] a short race in which the runners, riders, swimmers etc move very fast over a short distance: *the 100-metre sprint* **2** [singular] a short period of running or moving very fast: *He made a desperate sprint for the train.*

sprint·er /ˈsprɪntə $ -ər/ *n* [C] someone who runs in fast races over short distances

sprite /spraɪt/ *n* [C] a FAIRY(1)

spritz /sprɪts/ *v* [T] *AmE* to SPRAY small amounts of a liquid on something —**spritz** *n* [C]

spritz·er /ˈsprɪtsə $ -ər/ *n* [C] a drink made with SODA WATER and white wine

sprock·et /ˈsprɒkɪt $ ˈsprɑː-/ *n* [C] **1** (*also* **sprocket wheel**) a wheel with TEETH (=parts along the edge) that fit into and turn a bicycle chain, a photographic film with holes etc **2** one of the teeth on a sprocket wheel

sprog /sprɒg $ sprɑːg/ *n* [C] *BrE informal* a child or baby - used humorously

sprout¹ /spraʊt/ *v* **1** [I,T] if vegetables, seeds, or plants sprout, they start to grow, producing SHOOTS, BUDS, or leaves: *Move the pots outside when the seeds begin to sprout. | Trees were starting to sprout new leaves.* **2** [I] (*also* **sprout up**) to appear suddenly in large numbers: *Office blocks are sprouting up everywhere.* **3** [I,T] if something such as hair sprouts or if you sprout it, it starts to grow: *Jim seemed to have sprouted a beard.*

sprout² *n* [C] **1** *especially BrE* a small green vegetable like a very small CABBAGE SYN **brussels sprout** → see picture at **VEGETABLE 2** a new growth on a plant SYN **shoot 3** [usually plural] *AmE* an ALFALFA seed which has grown a stem and is eaten **4** [usually plural] *AmE* a BEANSPROUT

spruce¹ /spruːs/ *n* [C,U] a tree that grows in northern countries and has short leaves shaped like needles

spruce² *v*
spruce up *phr v informal* to make yourself or something look neater and tidier: *Paul went upstairs to spruce up before dinner.* | **spruce sb/sth ↔ up** *The cottage had been spruced up a bit since her last visit.*

spruce³ *adj BrE* neat and clean: *Mr Bailey was looking very spruce in a white linen suit.* —**sprucely** *adv*

sprung¹ /sprʌŋ/ *v* a past tense and the past participle of SPRING²

S

sprung² *adj* supported or kept in shape by SPRINGS: *a sprung mattress*

spry /spraɪ/ *adj* a spry old person has energy and is active SYN **sprightly**: *He's still remarkably spry.* —**spryly** *adv*

spud /spʌd/ *n* [C] *informal* a POTATO

spume /spjuːm/ *n* [U] *literary* the mass of bubbles that forms on the top of waves when the sea is rough SYN **foam**

spun /spʌn/ the past tense and past participle of SPIN¹

spunk /spʌŋk/ *n* [U] *informal* **1** *especially AmE* courage: *She had a lot of spunk.* **2** *BrE not polite* SEMEN

spunk·y /ˈspʌŋki/ *adj informal* having a lot of courage, energy, or determination: *a spunky performance* | *a spunky heroine*

spur¹ /spɜː $ spɜːr/ *n* [C] **1 on the spur of the moment** suddenly, without any previous planning or thought: *We would often decide what to play on the spur of the moment.* → SPUR-OF-THE-MOMENT **2** a fact or event that makes you try harder to do something: **[+to]** *It provided the spur to further research.* | *The crowd's reaction only acted as a spur.* **3** a sharp pointed object on the heel of a rider's boot which is used to encourage a horse to go faster **4 earn/win your spurs** to show that you deserve to succeed because you have the right skills **5** a piece of high ground which sticks out from the side of a hill or mountain **6** a railway track or road that goes away from a main line or road

spur² *v* (**spurred**, **spurring**) **1** [T] (*also* **spur sb on**) to encourage someone or make them want to do something: *The band were spurred on by the success of their last two singles.* | **spur sb (on) to do sth** *His misfortunes spurred him to write.* | **spur sb (on) to sth** *the coach who spurred him on to Olympic success* | *It was an article in the local newspaper which finally* ***spurred*** *him* ***into action***. **2** [T] to make an improvement or change happen faster SYN **encourage**: *Lower taxes would spur investment and help economic growth.* **3** [I,T] to encourage a horse to go faster, especially by pushing it with special points on the heels of your boots

spu·ri·ous /ˈspjʊəriəs $ ˈspjʊr-/ *adj* **1** a spurious statement, argument etc is not based on facts or good thinking and is likely to be incorrect: *He demolished the Opposition's spurious arguments.* THESAURUS FALSE **2** insincere: *spurious sympathy* —**spuriously** *adv* —**spuriousness** *n* [U]

spurn /spɜːn $ spɜːrn/ *v* [T] *literary* to refuse to accept something or someone, especially because you are too proud SYN **reject**: *She spurned all offers of help.* | *a spurned lover*

ˌspur-of-the-ˈmoment *adj* [only before noun] a spur-of-the-moment decision or action is made or done suddenly without planning SYN **spontaneous**

spurt¹ /spɜːt $ spɜːrt/ *v* **1 a)** [I] if liquid or flames spurt from something, they come out of it quickly and suddenly: **[+from/out of]** *Blood spurted from his nose.* | *Flames spurted through the roof.* **b)** [T] to send out liquid or flames quickly or suddenly: *It boiled over, spurting hot water everywhere.* **2** [I always + adv/prep] to suddenly start moving more quickly, especially for a short time: *He suddenly spurted ahead of the others.*

spurt² *n* [C] **1** when an amount of liquid or flame suddenly comes quickly out of something: **[+of]** *a sudden spurt of flame* | **in spurts** *The water came out of the tap in short spurts* (=a small amount at a time). **2** a short sudden increase of activity, effort, speed, or emotion: **[+of]** *In a sudden spurt of anger, Ellen slammed the door shut.* | **growth spurt** (=when a child suddenly grows quickly) | **in spurts** *We weren't consistent – we played in spurts.*

sput·ter /ˈspʌtə $ -ər/ *v* **1** [I] if something such as an engine or a fire sputters, it makes short soft uneven noises like very small explosions SYN **splutter**: *Suddenly the engine sputtered and stopped.* **2** [I,T] to talk quickly in short confused phrases, especially because you are angry or shocked SYN **splutter**: *'What do you mean?' sputtered Annabelle.* —**sputter** *n* [C,U]

spu·tum /ˈspjuːtəm/ *n* [U] *medical* liquid in your mouth which you have coughed up from your lungs → **phlegm**

spy¹ /spaɪ/ ●●○ *n* (*plural* **spies**) [C] someone whose job is to find out secret information about another country, organization, or group SYN **secret agent**: *She worked as a spy for the American government.* | **spy ring/network** (=an organized group of spies) | **spy plane/satellite**

spy² ●●○ *v* (**spied**, **spying**, **spies**)
1 [I] to secretly collect information about an enemy country or an organization you are competing against: **[+on]** *He was charged with spying on British military bases.* | **[+for]** *He confessed to spying for North Korea.*
2 [T] *literary* to suddenly see someone or something, especially after searching for them SYN **spot**: *Ellen suddenly spied her friend in the crowd.* —**spying** *n* [U]
spy on sb *phr v* to watch someone secretly in order to find out what they are doing: *She sent you to spy on me, didn't she?*
spy sth ↔ **out** *phr v*
1 to secretly find out information about something
2 spy out the land *BrE* to secretly find out more information about a situation before deciding what to do

spy·glass /ˈspaɪɡlɑːs $ -ɡlæs/ *n* [C] a small TELESCOPE used by sailors in the past

spy·hole /ˈspaɪhəʊl $ -hoʊl/ *n* [C] *BrE* a hole in a door, wall etc, through which you can look at someone secretly

spy·ware /ˈspaɪweə $ -wer/ *n* [U] computer software that secretly records information about which websites you visit. This information is then used by advertising companies, who try to sell you products.

sq. (*also* **sq** *BrE*) the written abbreviation of ***square***: *30 cm sq floor tiles* | *40 Merrion Sq., Dublin*

squab·ble /ˈskwɒbəl $ ˈskwɑː-/ *v* [I] to argue about something unimportant SYN **quarrel**: **[+over/about]** *They're always squabbling over money.* | **[+with]** *He's squabbling with the referee.* THESAURUS ARGUE, ARGUMENT —**squabble** *n* [C]: *a petty squabble* | *bitter squabbles between employers and unions*

squad /skwɒd $ skwɑːd/ ●●○ W3 *n* [C]
1 a group of players from which a team will be chosen for a particular sports event: *the Italian World Cup squad*
2 the police department responsible for dealing with a particular kind of crime: **drugs/fraud/vice etc squad** *A controlled explosion was carried out by bomb squad officers.*
3 a small group of soldiers working together as a unit: *a drill squad*
4 *AmE* a group of CHEERLEADERS → **DEATH SQUAD, FIRING SQUAD, FLYING SQUAD**

ˈsquad car *n* [C] a car used by police on duty SYN **patrol car**

squad·dy, **squaddie** /ˈskwɒdi $ ˈskwɑː-/ *n* (*plural* **squaddies**) [C] *BrE informal* a soldier who is not an officer

squad·ron /ˈskwɒdrən $ ˈskwɑː-/ *n* [C] a military force consisting of a group of aircraft or ships

ˈsquadron ˌleader *n* [C] an officer in the British air force below a WING COMMANDER

squal·id /ˈskwɒlɪd $ ˈskwɑː-/ *adj* **1** very dirty and unpleasant because of a lack of care or money → **squalor**: *How can anyone live in such squalid conditions?* | *a tiny squalid apartment* THESAURUS DIRTY **2** *especially BrE* immoral or dishonest: *squalid behaviour* | *a squalid affair*

squall¹ /skwɔːl $ skwɒːl/ *n* [C] a sudden strong wind, especially one that brings rain or snow: *snow squalls*

squall² *v* [I] if a baby or child squalls, it cries noisily SYN **bawl**

squal·ly /ˈskwɔːli $ ˈskwɒːli/ *adj BrE* squally rain or snow comes with sudden strong winds: *squally showers*

squal·or /ˈskwɒlə $ ˈskwɑːlər, ˈskwɒː-/ *n* [U] the condition of being dirty and unpleasant because of a lack of care or money → **squalid**: *We lived in squalor for a year and a half.*

squan·der /ˈskwɒndə $ ˈskwɑːndər/ *v* [T] to carelessly waste money, time, opportunities etc: *The home team squandered a number of chances in the first half.* | **squander sth on sth** *They squandered the profits on expensive cars.* THESAURUS ➤ SPEND

square¹ /skweə $ skwer/ ●●● S2 W3 *adj*
1 SHAPE having four straight equal sides and 90° angles at the corners: *a large square room*
2 ANGLE forming a 90° angle, or being close to or similar to a 90° angle: *square corners*
3 square metre/mile etc an area of measurement equal to a square with sides a metre long, a mile long etc: *about four square metres of ground*
4 five feet/two metres etc square having the shape of a square with sides that are five feet, two metres etc long: *The room is six metres square.*
5 LEVEL [not before noun] parallel with a straight line: **[+with]** *I don't think the shelf is square with the floor.*
6 square meal a good satisfying meal: *Children should have three square meals a day.*
7 BODY if someone's body or a part of their body is square, it looks broad and strong: *a square jaw*
8 all square *BrE* to have the same number of points as your opponent in a competition: *The teams were all square at the end of the first half.*
9 (all) square *informal* if two people are square, they do not owe each other any money: *Here's your £10 back, so that* ***makes us square***.
10 square deal honest and fair treatment from someone, especially in business: *I'm not* ***getting*** *a* ***square deal*** *here.*
11 BORING *informal* someone who is square is boring and old-fashioned
12 a square peg in a round hole *informal* someone who is in a job or situation that is not suitable for them —**squareness** *n* [U] → **win (sth)/beat sb fair and square** at FAIR³(1)

square² ●●● S2 W3 *n* [C]
1 SHAPE a shape with four straight equal sides with 90° angles at the corners → **rectangle**: *First of all, draw a square.* | **[+of]** *a small square of cloth*
2 IN A TOWN a large open area in the centre of a town or city, usually in the shape of a square, or the buildings surrounding it: **main/market/town square** *The hotel is just off the main square of Sorrento.* | *She lives in Hanover Square.*
3 square one the situation from which you started to do something: **be back to/at square one** *The police are now back at square one in their investigation.* | **go back to square one** (=used when you start something again because you were not successful the first time) *Okay, let's go back to square one and try again.* | **from square one** *I've had to relearn the game from square one.*
4 NUMBER the result of multiplying a number by itself → **square root**: **[+of]** *The square of 4 is 16.*
5 IN A GAME a space on a board used for playing a game such as CHESS
6 PERSON *informal* someone who is considered boring and unfashionable SYN **nerd**
7 TOOL (*also* **set square**) a flat object with a straight edge, often shaped like an L, used for drawing or measuring 90° angles

square³ *v* [T]
1 MULTIPLY to multiply a number by itself
2 IN A COMPETITION *BrE* to win a point or game so that you have now won the same number of points or games as the other team or player: *India won the second match to square the series at one each.*
3 square your shoulders to stand straight and push your shoulders back, usually to show your determination
4 MAKE STH STRAIGHT to make something straight or parallel
5 square the circle to attempt something impossible
square sth ↔ **away** *phr v AmE* to finish something, especially by putting the last details in order: ***Get*** *your work* ***squared away*** *before you leave.* GRAMMAR **Square away** is usually passive.
square off *phr v*
1 square sth ↔ off to make something have neat corners
2 *AmE* to get ready to fight someone
square up *phr v*
1 to pay money that you owe: *I'll pay for the drinks and you can square up later.*
2 *BrE* to get ready to fight someone: **[+to]** *The two lads squared up to each other.*
3 square up to sb/sth to deal with a difficult situation or person in a determined way
square with *phr v*
1 square (sth) with sth if you square two ideas, statements etc with each other or if they square with each other, they are considered to be in agreement: *His story simply does not square with the facts.* | *How do you square that with your religious beliefs?* | **square sth with your conscience** (=make yourself believe that what you are doing is morally right)
2 square sth with sb *BrE* to persuade someone to agree to something: *I'll take the day off if I can square it with my boss.*

square⁴ *adv* **1** directly and firmly SYN **squarely**: ***Look*** *him* ***square in the eye*** *and say no.* **2** at 90° to a line SYN **squarely**: **[+to]** *Wright passed the ball square to Brown.*

ˌ**square ˈbracket** *n* [C] *BrE* one of the pair of signs [ ] that are used for enclosing information SYN **bracket** *AmE*: **in square brackets** *The words in square brackets should be deleted.*

squared /skweəd $ skwerd/ *adj* **1** *BrE* divided into squares or marked with squares: *squared paper* **2 3/9/10 etc squared** the number three, nine etc multiplied by itself: *Three squared equals nine.*

ˈ**square dance** *n* [C] a type of traditional country dance in which four pairs of dancers face each other in a square, and someone calls out the movements they should do

ˈ**square knot** *n* [C] *AmE* a type of knot that will not come undone easily

square·ly /ˈskweəli $ ˈskwer-/ *adv* **1** directly and firmly: *He turned and faced her squarely.* | *She hit him squarely on the nose.* **2** completely and with no doubt: *The blame lies squarely on the shoulders of the police.* **3** straight on something and centrally SYN **square**: *Dr Soames jammed his hat squarely on his head.* **4** at 90° to a line SYN **square**

ˌ**square ˈroot** *n* [C] the square root of a number is the number which, when multiplied by itself, equals that number: **[+of]** *The square root of nine is three.*

squar·ish /ˈskweərɪʃ $ ˈskwer-/ *adj* shaped almost like a square

SQUASH

squash¹ /skwɒʃ $ skwɑːʃ, skwɒːʃ/ ●●○ *v*
1 PRESS [T] to press something into a flatter shape, often breaking or damaging it SYN **flatten**: *The cake* ***got*** *a bit* ***squashed*** *on the way here.* | **squash sth down** *Her hair had been squashed down by her hat.* | *Move over – you're squashing me.*
2 SMALL SPACE [I,T always + adv/prep] to push yourself or

S

something else into a space that is too small SYN squeeze: **[+into]** *Seven of us squashed into the car.* | **squash sth in** *We can probably squash another couple of things in.*
3 STOP STH [T] *informal* to use your power or authority to stop something SYN **quash**: *Her suggestions were always squashed.* | **squash rumours/hopes/reports etc** (=say that a rumour etc is not true) *The government was quick to squash any hopes of reform.*
4 CONTROL EMOTION [T] to control or ignore an emotion SYN **suppress**: *She felt anger rising but quickly squashed it.*
squash up *phr v BrE* to move closer together or closer to something, especially in order to make room for someone or something else: **[+against]** *The others squashed up against Jo.*

squash² ●○○ *n*
1 SPORT [U] a game played by two people who use RACKETS to hit a small rubber ball against the walls of a square court: *a squash court*
2 it's a squash *BrE spoken* used to say that there is not enough space for everyone to fit in comfortably
3 VEGETABLE [C,U] one of a group of large vegetables with solid flesh and hard skins, such as PUMPKINS → see picture at VEGETABLE¹
4 DRINK [U] *BrE* a drink made from fruit juice, sugar, and water: *a glass of orange squash*

squashed /skwɒʃt $ skwɑːʃt, skwɒːʃt/ *adj* **1** broken or made flat by being pressed hard: *squashed tomatoes* **2** [not before noun] in a space that is too small: *I was squashed between Jan and Dave in the back seat.*

squash·y /ˈskwɒʃi $ ˈskwɑːʃi, ˈskwɒːʃi/ *adj BrE informal* soft and easy to press THESAURUS SOFT

squat¹ /skwɒt $ skwɑːt/ ●○○ *v* (**squatted**, **squatting**) [I]
1 to sit with your knees bent under you and your bottom just off the ground, balancing on your feet: **[+down]** *He squatted down beside the little girl.* → see picture at CROUCH THESAURUS SIT
2 to live in a building or on a piece of land without permission and without paying rent

squat² *adj* short and thick or low and wide, especially in a way which is not attractive: *squat stone cottages* | *a squat little old man*

squat³ *n* **1** [C] a squatting position **2** [C] *BrE* a house that people are living in without permission and without paying rent: *She lives in a squat in Camden.* **3** [U] *AmE informal* nothing, or nearly nothing. Squat is often used in negative sentences for emphasis: *He had a job that paid him squat.* | *You don't know squat about it.*

squat·ter /ˈskwɒtə $ ˈskwɑːtər/ *n* [C] someone who lives in an empty building or on a piece of land without permission and without paying rent

squaw /skwɔː $ skwɒː/ *n* [C] *old use* a word for a Native American woman, now usually considered offensive

squawk /skwɔːk $ skwɒːk/ *v* [I,T] **1** if a bird squawks, it makes a loud sharp angry sound **2** *informal* to complain loudly and angrily —**squawk** *n* [C]

squeak¹ /skwiːk/ ●●○ *v*
1 [I] to make a short high noise or cry that is not loud: *A rat squeaked and ran into the bushes.* | *The door squeaked open.*
2 [I,T] to say something in a very high voice, especially because you are nervous or excited: *'Too late!' she squeaked.*
3 [I always + adv/prep] *informal* to succeed, win, or pass a test by a very small amount so that you only just avoid failure SYN **scrape**: **[+through/by/past/in]** *She just squeaked through her math test.*

squeak² *n* [C] **1** a very short high noise or cry SYN **squeal**: **[+of]** *a squeak of alarm* | *the high-pitched squeak of a bat* THESAURUS SOUND **2 not a squeak** if there is not a squeak from someone, they do not say anything or communicate at all: *We didn't hear a squeak from him in months.*

squeak·y /ˈskwiːki/ *adj* **1** making very high noises that are not loud: *a squeaky voice* | *squeaky floorboards* THESAURUS HIGH **2 squeaky clean** *informal* **a)** never having done anything morally wrong: *politicians who are less than squeaky clean* **b)** completely clean: *squeaky clean hair* —**squeakily** *adv* —**squeakiness** *n* [U]

squeal¹ /skwiːl/ ●○○ *v*
1 [I,T] to make a long loud high sound or cry → **scream**: **[+with/in]** *The children squealed with delight.* | *They drove off, tyres squealing.* | *'Let me go!' she squealed.*
2 [I + on] *informal* to tell the police or someone in authority about someone you know who has done something wrong SYN **inform**

squeal² *n* [C] a long loud high sound or cry → **scream**: **[+of]** *She gave a squeal of laughter.* | *There was a squeal of brakes.*

squeam·ish /ˈskwiːmɪʃ/ *adj* **1** easily shocked or upset, or easily made to feel sick by seeing unpleasant things **2 the squeamish** [plural] people who are squeamish: *His new novel is* **not for the squeamish**. —**squeamishness** *n* [U]

squee·gee /ˈskwiːdʒiː/ *n* [C] a tool with a thin rubber blade and a short handle, used for removing or spreading a liquid on a surface

squeeze¹ /skwiːz/ ●●● S3 *v*
1 PRESS [T] to press something firmly together with your fingers or hand: *She smiled as he squeezed her hand.* | *He squeezed the trigger, but nothing happened.*
2 PRESS OUT LIQUID [T] to get liquid from something by pressing it: *Squeeze the oranges.* | **squeeze sth out** *Try to squeeze a bit more out.* | **squeeze sth on/onto sth** *Squeeze a bit of lemon juice onto the fish.* → see picture at SQUASH¹
3 SMALL SPACE [I,T always + adv/prep] to try to make something fit into a space that is too small, or to try to get into such a space SYN **squash**: **[+into]** *Five of us squeezed into the back seat.* | **[+through/past]** *He had squeezed through a gap in the fence.* | **squeeze sb/sth in** *We could probably squeeze in a few more people.*
4 squeeze your eyes shut to close your eyes very tightly
5 JUST SUCCEED [I always + adv/prep] to succeed, win, or pass a test by a very small amount so that you only just avoid failure: *Greece just squeezed through into the next round.*
6 LIMIT MONEY [T] to strictly limit the amount of money that is available to a company or organization: *The government is squeezing the railways' investment budget.*
squeeze sb/sth ↔ **in** (*also* **squeeze sth into sth**) *phr v* to manage to meet someone or do something although you are very busy: *How do you manage to squeeze so much into one day?* | *I can squeeze you in at four o'clock.*
squeeze sth ↔ **out** *phr v*
1 to do something so that someone or something is no longer included or able to continue: *If budgets are cut, vital research may be squeezed out.*
2 to squeeze something wet in order to remove the liquid from it: *Squeeze the cloth out first.*
3 squeeze sth out of sb to force someone to tell you something: *See if you can squeeze more information out of them.*
squeeze up *phr v BrE* to move close to the person next to you to make space for someone else

squeeze² *n* [C] **1 a (tight) squeeze** a situation in which there is only just enough room for things or people to fit somewhere: *It'll be a squeeze with six people in the car.* **2** an act of pressing something firmly with your fingers or hand: *Marty* **gave** *her hand a little* **squeeze**. **3 squeeze of lemon/lime etc** a small amount of juice obtained by squeezing a piece of fruit **4** a situation in which wages, prices, borrowing money etc are strictly controlled or reduced: **[+on]** *cuts due to the squeeze on public sector spending* | *a credit squeeze* | *All manufacturers are* **feeling the squeeze** (=noticing the effects of a difficult financial situation). **5 put the squeeze on sb** *informal* to try to persuade someone to do something **6 sb's (main) squeeze** *especially AmE informal* someone's BOYFRIEND or GIRLFRIEND

squeeze-box /ˈskwiːzbɒks $ -bɑːks/ *n* [C] *informal* an ACCORDION

ˌsqueezed ˈmiddle *n* **the squeezed middle** *BrE* the people who are most badly affected when the economy is bad, because they are not rich but are not poor enough to receive money from the government

squeez·er /ˈskwiːzə $ -ər/ *n* [C] an object used for squeezing juice from fruit such as LEMONS

squelch /skweltʃ/ *v* **1** [I] to make a sucking sound by walking or moving in something soft and wet: *My hair was dripping and my shoes squelched as I walked.* | **[+through/along/up]** *We squelched across the field.* **2** [T] *AmE* to stop something from continuing to develop or spread SYN **squash**: *Her creativity had been squelched.* —**squelch** *n* [C]

squelch·y /ˈskweltʃi/ *adj BrE* squelchy mud or ground is soft and wet and makes a sucking noise when you walk on it

squib /skwɪb/ *n* [C] **1** a small exploding FIREWORK **2** *literary* a short amusing piece of writing that attacks someone → **damp squib** at **DAMP**[1](2)

squid /skwɪd/ *n* (*plural* **squid** *or* **squids**) [C] a sea creature with a long soft body and ten arms around its mouth

squidg·y /ˈskwɪdʒi/ *adj BrE* soft and easy to press: *We don't want soft squidgy sandwiches.*

squif·fy /ˈskwɪfi/ *adj BrE old-fashioned* slightly drunk SYN **tipsy**

squig·gle /ˈskwɪɡəl/ *n* [C] a line with irregular curves: *Shorthand just looks like a series of funny squiggles to me.* —**squiggly** *adj*: *squiggly lines*

squil·lion /ˈskwɪljən/ *n* [C] *informal humorous* a very large number of things, especially pounds or dollars: *Restoring the house to its former glory will cost squillions.*

squint[1] /skwɪnt/ *v* [I] **1** to look at something with your eyes partly closed in order to see better: *Anna squinted in the sudden bright sunlight.* | **[+at]** *Stop squinting at the screen - put your glasses on.* **2** [not in progressive] *BrE* to have each eye looking in a slightly different direction

squint[2] *n* [singular] **1** *especially BrE* a condition of your eye muscles that makes each eye look in a slightly different direction **2 have/take a squint at sth** *BrE informal* to look at something

squire /skwaɪə $ skwaɪr/ *n* **1** [C] the man who in the past owned most of the land around a country village in England **2** [C] a young man in the Middle Ages who learned how to be a KNIGHT by serving one **3** *BrE old-fashioned spoken* used by some men to address a man when they do not know his name

squirm /skwɜːm $ skwɜːrm/ *v* [I] **1** to twist your body from side to side because you are uncomfortable or nervous, or to get free from something which is holding you SYN **wriggle**: *Christine squirmed uncomfortably in her chair.* | *The boy tried to squirm free.* THESAURUS MOVE **2** to feel very embarrassed or ashamed: **[+with]** *He made me squirm with embarrassment.* —**squirm** *n* [singular]

squir·rel[1] /ˈskwɪrəl $ ˈskwɜːrəl/ ●●○ *n* [C] a small animal with a long furry tail that climbs trees and eats nuts

squirrel[2] *v* (**squirrelled**, **squirrelling** *BrE*, **squirreled**, **squirreling** *AmE*)

squirrel sth ↔ **away** *phr v* to keep something in a safe place to use later SYN **stash away**: *By December I had $300 squirreled away.*

squir·rel·ly, **squirrely** /ˈskwɪrəli $ ˈskwɜː-/ *adj AmE informal* not able to stay still SYN **restless**: *squirrely kids*

SQUIRT

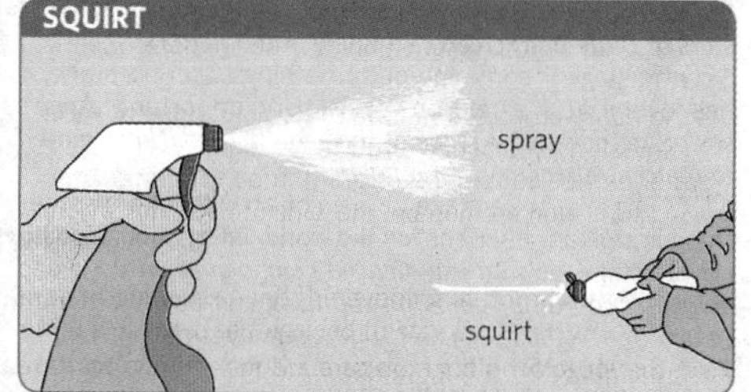

squirt[1] /skwɜːt $ skwɜːrt/ *v* **1** [I,T] if you squirt liquid or if it squirts somewhere, it is forced out in a thin fast stream → **spray**: **[+out/from/into]** *Water suddenly squirted out from a hole in the pipe.* | **squirt sth into/through sth** *Squirt some oil in the lock.* **2** [T] to hit or cover someone or something with a thin fast stream of liquid → **spray**: **squirt sb/sth with sth** *Mom! Chad's squirting me with the hose!* | *Some kids squirted a water pistol in her face.*

squirt[2] *n* [C] **1** a fast thin stream of liquid: **[+of]** *a squirt of water* **2** *spoken* an insulting word for a short person, especially someone who is annoying you

ˈsquirt gun *n* [C] *AmE* a WATER PISTOL

squish /skwɪʃ/ *v* **1** [I always + adv/prep] to make a soft sucking sound by moving in or through something soft and wet **2** [I,T] *informal* to SQUASH something, especially something soft and wet, or to become squashed

squish·y /ˈskwɪʃi/ *adj* soft and easy to press: *squishy mud* THESAURUS SOFT

Sr *BrE*, **Sr.** *AmE* **1** the written abbreviation of ***Senior***: *Douglas Fairbanks, Sr.* **2** the written abbreviation of ***Señor***: *Sr Lopez* **3** the written abbreviation of ***Sister***, used in front of the name of a NUN: *Sr Bernadette*

SS *BrE*, **S.S.** *AmE* /ˈes es/ **1** the abbreviation of ***steamship***: *aboard the SS Great Britain* **2** *BrE* the written abbreviation of ***saints***: *statues of SS Augustine and Thomas*

ssh /ʃ/ *interjection* used to ask people to be quiet SYN **shush**: *Ssh! You'll wake everybody up.*

st *BrE*, **st.** *AmE* the written abbreviation of ***stone*** or ***stones***: *She weighs 9 st 8 lb.*

-st /st/ *suffix* **1** forms written ORDINAL numbers with 1: *the 1st (=first) prize* | *my 21st birthday* **2** *old use or biblical* another form of the suffix -EST(2): *thou dost (=you do)*

St *BrE*, **St.** *AmE* **1** the written abbreviation of ***Street***, used in addresses: *Wall St.* **2** the written abbreviation of ***saint***: *St Luke's Gospel*

S

stab[1] /stæb/ ●●○ *v* (**stabbed**, **stabbing**)
1 [T] to push a knife into someone or something → **stabbing**: *He was* ***stabbed to death*** *in a fight.* | **stab sb in the heart/arm etc** *She had been stabbed in the chest repeatedly.* THESAURUS ATTACK
2 [I,T] to make quick pushing movements with your finger or something pointed SYN **jab**: *He raised his voice and stabbed the air with his pen.*
3 stab sb in the back to do something that harms someone who likes and trusts you SYN **betray**

stab[2] *n* [C] **1** an act of stabbing or trying to stab someone with a knife: *severe stab wounds* | *a stab victim* | *He killed him with a stab to the heart.* **2 stab of pain/disappointment/fear etc** a sudden sharp feeling of pain or a strong emotion: *He felt a stab of guilt.* **3 stab at (doing) sth** *informal* an attempt to do something, often not successfully: **have/make/take a stab at (doing) sth** *I'll have one more stab at it.* **4 stab in the back** when someone you thought was a friend tries to harm you

stab·bing[1] /ˈstæbɪŋ/ *adj* [only before noun] a stabbing pain is sharp and sudden

stabbing[2] *n* [C] a crime in which someone is stabbed: *a fatal stabbing*

sta·bil·i·ty /stəˈbɪləti/ ●○○ AWL *n* [U]
1 the condition of being steady and not changing OPP **instability** → **stable**: *a period of relative stability* | **[+of]** *It could threaten the peace and stability of the region.*
2 *technical* the ability of a substance to stay in the same state

sta·bil·ize (*also* **-ise** *BrE*) /ˈsteɪbəlaɪz/ ●○○ AWL *v* [I,T] to become firm, steady, or unchanging, or to make something firm or steady → **stable**: *The patient's condition has now stabilized.* | *an attempt to stabilize the economy* —**stabilization** /ˌsteɪbəlaɪˈzeɪʃən $ -lə-/ *n* [U]

sta·bil·iz·er (*also* **-iser** *BrE*) /ˈsteɪbəlaɪzə $ -ər/ *n* [C] **1** a chemical that helps something such as a food to stay in the same state, for example to prevent it from separating into different liquids **2** a piece of equipment that helps make something such as a plane or ship steady → see picture at **PLANE**[1] **3** [usually plural] *BrE* one of a pair of small wheels that are fastened to the back wheel of a child's bicycle to prevent it from falling over

sta·ble¹ /ˈsteɪbəl/ ●●○ W3 AWL *adj*
1 steady and not likely to move or change OPP **unstable** → **stability**: *A wide base will make the structure much more stable.* | **in a stable condition** *BrE*, **in stable condition** *AmE*: *He is said to be in a stable condition in hospital.* | *Children like a stable environment.*
2 calm, reasonable, and not easy to upset OPP **unstable** → **stability**: *He was clearly not a very stable person.*
3 *technical* a stable substance tends to stay in the same chemical or ATOMIC state OPP **unstable** —**stably** *adv*

stable² ●●○ *n* [C]
1 a building where horses are kept → see picture at **HOME¹**
2 stables [plural] a place where horses are kept and that often gives riding lessons
3 a group of racing horses that has one owner or trainer
4 a group of people working for the same company or with the same trainer: *actors from the same Hollywood stable*
5 shut/close the stable door after the horse has bolted *BrE* to try to prevent something when it is too late and harm has already been done

stable³ *v* [T] to put or keep a horse in a stable

ˈstable boy *BrE*, **sta·ble·man** *AmE* /ˈsteɪbəlmæn/ *n* [C] a man or boy who works in a stable

ˈstable girl *n* [C] a girl or woman who works in a stable

sta·ble·mate /ˈsteɪbəlmeɪt/ *n* [C] **sb's/sth's stablemate** something produced by the same company, or someone who works for the same company: *the Daily Mirror's Scottish stablemate, the Daily Record*

sta·bling /ˈsteɪblɪŋ/ *n* [U] space in a building where horses can be kept

S

stac·cat·o /stəˈkɑːtəʊ $ -toʊ/ *adv* if music is played staccato, the notes are cut short —**staccato** *adj*

stack¹ /stæk/ ●○○ *n*
1 [C] a neat pile of things → **heap**: **[+of]** *a stack of papers* | *stacks of dirty dishes* → see picture at **PILE¹**
2 a stack of sth/stacks of sth *especially BrE informal* a large amount of something: *He's got stacks of money.*
3 [C] a chimney
4 the stacks [plural] the rows of shelves in a library where the books are kept → **blow your top/stack** at **BLOW¹(16)**

stack² ●○○ *v*
1 (*also* **stack up**) [I,T] to make things into a neat pile, or to form a neat pile: *The assistants price the items and stack them on the shelves.* | *a stacking hi-fi system*
2 [T] to put neat piles of things on something: *He went back to stacking the shelves.* | **be stacked with sth** *The floor was stacked with boxes.*
3 the odds/cards are stacked against sb used to say that someone is unlikely to be successful
4 stack the cards *BrE*, **stack the deck** *AmE informal* to arrange cards dishonestly in a game

stack up *phr v*
1 stack sth ↔ up to make things into a neat pile
2 *informal* used to talk about how good something is compared with something else: **[+against]** *Parents want to know how their kids' schools stack up against others.*
3 if a number of things stack up, they gradually collect or get stuck in one place: *Traffic stacked up behind the bus.*

stacked /stækt/ *adj not polite* used to describe a woman with large breasts

sta·di·um /ˈsteɪdiəm/ ●●● W3 *n* (*plural* **stadiums** *or* **stadia** /-diə/) [C] a building for public events, especially sports and large rock music concerts, consisting of a playing field surrounded by rows of seats: *the new Olympic Stadium*

staff¹ /stɑːf $ stæf/ ●●● S2 W2 *n*
1 WORKERS [C,U] the people who work for an organization: **staff of 10/50 etc** *Our department has a staff of seven.* | *The entire staff has done an outstanding job this year.* | *They employ a total of 150 staff.* | *The staff were very helpful.* | **medical/academic/library etc staff** *a strike by ambulance staff* | *one of our longest-serving* ***staff members*** | **member of staff** *BrE*: *I'd like to welcome a new member of staff.* | **on the staff (of sth)** *We were both on the staff of the British Film Institute at the time.* | **on staff** *AmE*: *Joan is the only lawyer we have on staff.* | *a* ***staff meeting*** | **staff room** *BrE* (=a room for teachers in a school)

GRAMMAR: Singular or plural verb?
- In British English, **staff** is usually followed by a plural verb: *The staff* ***are*** *against the idea.*
- In American English, **staff** is usually followed by a singular verb: *The museum's staff* ***is*** *composed of volunteers.*
- You say a **staff member** (or a **member of staff** in British English) or an **employee**, when talking about one person on the staff. ✗ Don't use *a staff* to refer to one person.
- When talking about different groups of people, the plural form **staffs** is sometimes used, but it is much less common than **staff**: *head teachers and their staffs*

GRAMMAR GUIDE ▸ NOUNS

2 STICK [C] (*plural* **staves** /steɪvz/) **a)** *old use* a long thick stick to help you walk **b)** a long thick stick that an official holds in some ceremonies
3 MUSIC [C] *especially AmE* the set of five lines that music is written on SYN **stave**
4 the staff of life *literary* bread → **GENERAL STAFF**, **GROUND STAFF**

staff² *v* [T] to be or provide the workers for an organization → **overstaffed**, **understaffed**: *The centre is staffed mainly by volunteers.* GRAMMAR **Staff** is usually passive. —**staffing** *n* [U]: *staffing levels*

staff·er /ˈstɑːfə $ ˈstæfər/ *n* [C] *AmE* someone who is paid to work for an organization

ˈstaff ˌnurse *n* [C] *BrE* a British hospital nurse whose rank is just below a SISTER(2) or CHARGE NURSE

ˈstaff ˌofficer *n* [C] a military officer whose job is to help an officer of a higher rank

ˈstaff ˌsergeant *n* [C,U] a lower rank in the army or the US Air Force or MARINES, or someone who has this rank

stag /stæg/ *n* [C] **1** a fully grown male DEER SYN **buck** *AmE* **2 go stag** *AmE informal* if a man goes stag, he goes to a party without a woman → **STAG NIGHT**, **STAG PARTY**

stage¹ /steɪdʒ/ ●●● S1 W1 *n*
1 TIME/STATE [C] a particular time or state that something reaches as it grows or develops → **phase**, **step**: **[+of/in]** *the early stages of a child's development* | *It's a good move at this stage in his career.* | *We're getting to the stage where we hardly ever go out together.*
2 PART OF PROCESS [C] one of the parts which something such as a competition or process is divided into: **[+of]** *The team reached the semi-final stage of the competition.* | **stage two/six etc** *We're now reaching the end of stage three of the construction.* | *The* ***next stage*** *is to complete an application form.* | **in stages** *The rest of the money will be paid in stages* (=a small amount at a time).
3 THEATRE [C] the raised area in a theatre which actors or singers stand on when they perform → **backstage**: **on stage** *She is on stage for most of the play.* | *She* ***appeared on stage*** *with George Michael.* → see picture at **THEATRE**
4 ACTING **the stage** acting as a profession, especially in theatres: *I wanted to* ***go on the stage*** (=become an actor). | *stars of* ***stage and screen*** (=theatre and cinema)
5 centre stage if someone or something is centre stage, it has everyone's attention, or is very important: *Anne's sculpture* ***took centre stage*** *at the show.* | *The UN has* ***moved to the centre stage*** *of world politics.*
6 PLACE [singular] a place or area of activity where something important happens: **on the world/international/political etc stage** *He's an experienced campaigner on the world stage.* | *important figures on the European political stage* | **[+for]** *Geneva has been the stage for many such conferences.*
7 set the stage for sth to prepare for something or make something possible: *Will this agreement merely set the stage for another war?* → **LANDING STAGE**

COLLOCATIONS

ADJECTIVES

the early/initial stages *Sometimes there are problems in the early stages of a project.*
the later/final/closing stages *She was well cared for during the final stages of her life.*
the halfway stage *He was in the lead at the halfway stage.*
an advanced stage *Negotiations are at an advanced stage.*
a new stage *It marked the beginning of a new stage in my life.*
a critical/crucial stage (=very important because it affects the future success of something) | **a formative stage** (=when someone or something is developing)

VERBS

reach/get to a stage *We have reached the stage where no-one is safe to walk our streets at night.*
enter a stage *He is entering a new stage of his career.*
go through a stage *Most young people go through a rebellious stage.*
mark a stage *The election marks an important stage in the rebuilding of the country.*
take sth a stage further *We then took the experiment a stage further.*

PHRASES

a stage of development *We have several ideas in various stages of development.*
at one stage (=at a time in the past) *At one stage I had to tell him to calm down.*
at some stage *Four out of ten people are likely to contract cancer at some stage in their lives.*
at this/that stage *At this stage his wife did not realise he was missing.*
at an early/late stage *I can't change my plans at this late stage.*
at a later stage

stage² ●●○ *v* [T]
1 to organize a public event: **stage a strike/demonstration/sit-in etc** *Activists staged a protest outside the parliament.* | *exhibitions staged in Paris* | *The candidates' public appearances were **carefully staged*** (=not natural).
2 stage a comeback/recovery etc to start doing something again or being successful, after you had stopped or not been successful for some time: *He staged an amazing comeback.*

stage·coach /ˈsteɪdʒkəʊtʃ $ -koʊtʃ/ *n* [C] a vehicle pulled by horses that was used in past times for carrying passengers and letters

stage·craft /ˈsteɪdʒkrɑːft $ -kræft/ *n* [U] skill and experience in writing, or organizing the performance of, a play

ˈstage diˌrection *n* [C] a written instruction to an actor to do something in a play

ˌstage ˈdoor *n* [C usually singular] the side or back entrance to a theatre, used by actors and theatre workers

ˈstage fright *n* [U] nervousness felt by someone who is going to perform in front of a lot of people: *Den **suffered** terribly **from stage fright**.* | *an attack of stage fright*

stage·hand /ˈsteɪdʒhænd/ *n* [C] someone who works on a theatre stage, getting it ready for a play or for the next part of a play

ˌstage ˈleft *adv* on the left side of a theatre stage from the view of an actor facing the people in the AUDIENCE: *He entered stage left.*

ˌstage-ˈmanage *v* [T] to organize a public event, such as a meeting, in a way that will give you the result that you want - often used to show disapproval: *The press conference was cleverly stage-managed.*

ˈstage ˌmanager *n* [C] someone who is in charge of the technical parts of organizing a performance of a play, such as the LIGHTING, SCENERY etc

ˈstage ˌname *n* [C] a name used by an actor instead of his or her real name

ˌstage ˈright *adv* on the right side of a theatre stage from the view of an actor facing the people in the AUDIENCE: *She had to exit stage right.*

stage-struck /ˈsteɪdʒstrʌk/ *adj* loving to see plays, or wanting very much to become an actor

ˌstage ˈwhisper *n* [C] **1** a loud WHISPER used by an actor in a play, which the other actors on the stage seem not to hear **2** a loud WHISPER that is intended to be heard by everyone

stage·y /ˈsteɪdʒi/ *adj* another spelling of STAGY

stag·fla·tion /stægˈfleɪʃən/ *n* [U] an economic situation in which there is INFLATION (=a continuing rise in prices) but many people do not have jobs and businesses are not doing well

stag·ger¹ /ˈstægə $ -ər/ ●●○ *v*
1 [I always + adv/prep] to walk or move unsteadily, almost falling over SYN **stumble**: *He managed to stagger home.* | *She staggered back a step.* | *The old man staggered drunkenly to his feet.* **THESAURUS** ▸ WALK
2 [T] to make someone feel very surprised or shocked SYN **amaze**: *What staggered us was the sheer size of her salary.*
3 [I] (*also* **stagger on**) to continue doing something when you seem to be going to fail and you do not know what will happen: *He staggered on for another two years.* | **stagger from sth to sth** *The company staggered from one crisis to the next.*
4 [T] to arrange people's working hours, holidays etc so that they do not all begin and end at the same time: *Jim and his wife stagger their work hours so one of them can be at home with the kids.*
5 [T] to start a race with each runner at a different place on a curved track

stagger² *n* [C usually singular] an unsteady movement of someone who is having difficulty in walking

stag·gered /ˈstægəd $ -ərd/ *adj* [not before noun] extremely surprised SYN **amazed**: *I was absolutely staggered when I saw the bill.* | **[+at/by]** *She was staggered by the directness of his question.* **THESAURUS** ▸ SURPRISED

stag·ger·ing /ˈstægərɪŋ/ *adj* extremely great or surprising SYN **amazing**: *The cost was a staggering $10 million.* | *The financial impact on the town was staggering.* **THESAURUS** ▸ SURPRISING —**staggeringly** *adv*: *a staggeringly beautiful landscape*

stag·ing /ˈsteɪdʒɪŋ/ *n* **1** [C,U] when a play is performed on stage: *a modern-dress staging of 'Hamlet'* **2** [U] a flat raised surface that is put up for a short time for people to stand and work on

ˈstaging ˌarea *n* [C] a place where soldiers meet and where military equipment is gathered before it is moved to another place

ˈstaging post *n* [C] a place where people, planes, ships etc stop on a long journey, for example to rest or get supplies: *a staging post on the flight from Australia*

stag·nant /ˈstægnənt/ *adj* **1** stagnant water or air does not move or flow and often smells bad: *a stagnant pond* **2** not changing or making progress, and continuing to be in a bad condition: *a government plan to revive the stagnant economy*

stag·nate /stægˈneɪt $ ˈstægneɪt/ *v* [I] to stop developing or making progress: *Growth is expected to stagnate next year.* | *His career had stagnated.* —**stagnation** /stægˈneɪʃən/ *n* [U]: *economic stagnation*

ˈstag night *n* [C] *BrE* a night before a man's wedding, which he spends with his male friends, drinking or having a party

ˈstag ˌparty *n* [C] a party for men only, especially on a night before a man's wedding → **hen party**

stag·y, stagey /ˈsteɪdʒi/ *adj* behaviour that is stagy is not natural and is like the way an actor behaves on a stage: *a very stagy manner* —**stagily** *adv*

staid /steɪd/ *adj* serious, old-fashioned, and boring: *a staid old bachelor*

S

stain¹ /steɪn/ ●○○ *v*
1 [I,T] to accidentally make a mark on something, especially one that cannot be removed, or to be marked in this way: *Be careful you don't stain the carpet.* | *This tablecloth stains very easily.* | *Her fingers were stained yellow from years of smoking.* | **[+with]** *a cowboy hat stained with dust and sweat*
2 [T] to change the colour of something, especially something made of wood, by using a special liquid → **dye**: *We've decided to stain the shelves blue.*
3 stain sb's name/honour/reputation etc *literary* to damage the good opinion that people have about someone

stain² ●○○ *n*
1 [C] a mark that is difficult to remove, especially one made by a liquid such as blood, coffee, or ink: **[+on]** *There was a dark red stain on the carpet.* | **remove/get rid of a stain** *White vinegar is great for removing stains.* | **wine/coffee/blood etc stain** *How do you get wine stains out of a tablecloth?* | **stubborn stains** (=ones that are very difficult to remove) THESAURUS MARK
2 [C,U] a special liquid that you use to change the colour of something, especially wood → **dye**
3 stain on sb's character/name/reputation etc something that damages the good opinion that people have about someone

ˌstained ˈglass *n* [U] glass of different colours, used for making pictures and patterns in windows, especially in a church: *stained glass windows*

ˌstainless ˈsteel *n* [U] a type of steel that does not RUST: *stainless steel cutlery*

stair /steə $ ster/ ●●● S2 W3 *n*
1 stairs [plural] a set of steps built for going from one level of a building to another → **upstairs**, **downstairs**: **up/down the stairs** *Jerry ran up the stairs.* | **the top/head of the stairs** *I left my briefcase at the top of the stairs.* | **the bottom/foot of the stairs** *'Lisa,' he cried from the foot of the stairs.* | *We walked up four* ***flights of stairs*** (=sets of stairs).
2 [C] one of the steps in a set of stairs: *Lucy sat down on the bottom stair.*
3 [singular] *literary* a STAIRCASE
4 below stairs *BrE old-fashioned* in the servants' part of a large house, in the past

stair·case /ˈsteəkeɪs $ ˈster-/ ●●○ *n* [C] a set of stairs inside a building with its supports and the side parts that you hold on to

STAIRCASE

stair·way /ˈsteəweɪ $ ˈster-/ *n* [C] a staircase, especially a large or impressive one

stair·well /ˈsteəwel $ ˈster-/ *n* [C] the space going up through all the floors of a building, where the stairs go up

stake¹ /steɪk/ ●○○ *n*
1 at stake if something that you value very much is at stake, you will lose it if a plan or action is not successful: *They have to win the contract – thousands of jobs are at stake.* | *National pride is at stake in next week's game against England.*
2 COMPANY/BUSINESS [C] if you have a stake in a business, you have INVESTed money in it: **hold/have a stake in sth** *He holds a 51% stake in the firm.*
3 have a stake in sth if you have a stake in something, you will get advantages if it is successful, and you feel that you have an important connection with it: *Young people don't feel they have a stake in the country's future.*
4 MONEY RISKED [C] money that you risk as the result of a horse race, card game etc: *For a dollar stake, you can win up to $1,000,000.*
5 high stakes a) if the stakes are high when you are trying to do something, you risk losing a lot or it will be dangerous if you fail: *Climbing is a dangerous sport and* ***the stakes are high***. **b)** if the stakes are high when you are doing something such as playing a card game, you risk losing a lot of money: *We're* ***playing for high stakes*** *here.*
6 POINTED STICK [C] a pointed piece of wood, metal etc, especially one that is pushed into the ground to support something or mark a particular place: *tent stakes* | ***Drive*** *two* ***stakes into the ground*** *about three feet apart.*
7 the stake a post to which a person was tied in former times before being killed by burning: *Suspected witches were* ***burnt at the stake***.
8 in the popularity/fashion etc stakes used when saying how popular, fashionable etc someone or something is: *Ben wouldn't score very highly in the popularity stakes.*
9 (be prepared to) go to the stake for/over sth *BrE* to be willing to do anything to protect or defend an idea or belief: *That's my opinion, but I wouldn't go to the stake for it.*
10 pull up stakes (*also* **up stakes** *BrE*) *informal* to leave your job or home: *We're going to pull up stakes and move to Montana.*

stake² *v* [T] **1** to risk losing something that is valuable or important to you on the result of something: **stake sth on sb/sth** *Kevin is staking his reputation on the success of the project.* | *Jim staked his whole fortune on one card game.* **2 I'd stake my life on it** *spoken* used when saying that you are completely sure that something is true, or that something will happen: *I'm sure that's Jesse – I'd stake my life on it.* **3** (*also* **stake up**) to support something with stakes: *Young trees have to be staked.* **4** (*also* **stake off**) to mark or enclose an area of ground with stakes: *A corner of the field has been staked off.* **5 stake (out) a claim** to say publicly that you think you have a right to have or own something: **[+to]** *Both countries staked a claim to the islands.*

stake sth ↔ **out** *phr v informal* **1** to watch a place secretly and continuously → **stakeout**: *Police officers have been staking out the warehouse for weeks.* **2** to mark or control a particular area so that you can have it or use it: *We went to the show early to stake out a good spot.* **3** to state your opinions about something in a way that shows how your ideas are clearly separate from other people's ideas: *Johnson staked out the differences between himself and the other candidates.*

stake·hold·er /ˈsteɪkˌhəʊldə $ -ˌhoʊldər/ *n* [C] **1** someone who has INVESTed money into something, or who has some important connection with it, and therefore is affected by its success or failure: **[+in]** *Citizens should be stakeholders in the society they live in.* **2** *law* someone, usually a lawyer, who takes charge of a property during a quarrel or a sale **3** someone chosen to hold the money that is risked by people on a race, competition etc and to give all of it to the winner

ˌstakeholder eˈconomy *n* [C] *BrE* an economic system in a society that citizens feel they receive advantages from and have responsibilities to

stake·out /ˈsteɪkaʊt/ *n* [C] when the police watch a place secretly and continuously in order to catch someone who is doing something illegal

stal·ac·tite /ˈstæləktaɪt $ stəˈlæktaɪt/ *n* [C] a sharp pointed object hanging down from the roof of a CAVE, which is formed gradually by water that contains minerals as it drops slowly from the roof → **stalagmite**

stal·ag·mite /ˈstæləgmaɪt $ stəˈlægmaɪt/ *n* [C] a sharp pointed object coming up from the floor of a CAVE, formed by drops from a stalactite

stale /steɪl/ ●●○ *adj*
1 bread or cake that is stale is no longer fresh or good to eat OPP **fresh**: *French bread* ***goes stale*** (=becomes stale) *very quickly.* | *stale cake*
2 air that is stale is not fresh or pleasant OPP **fresh**: *the smell of stale smoke*
3 not interesting or exciting anymore: *stale jokes* | *Other marriages might* ***go stale***, *but not theirs.*
4 if you get stale, you have no new ideas, interest, or energy, because you have been doing the same thing for too long: *If you stay in the job for more than ten years, you* ***get stale***. | *He was becoming stale and running out of ideas.*
—**staleness** *n* [U]

stale·mate /ˈsteɪlmeɪt/ *n* [C,U] **1** a situation in which it seems impossible to settle an argument or disagreement, and neither side can get an advantage SYN **deadlock**: *an attempt to* ***break the stalemate*** | *The discussions with the miners' union* ***ended in stalemate***. THESAURUS PROGRESS **2** a position in CHESS in which neither player can win —**stalemate** *v* [T]

stalk[1] /stɔːk $ stɒːk/ *n* [C] **1** a long narrow part of a plant that supports leaves, fruits, or flowers: *celery stalks* **2** a thin upright object **3 sb's eyes are out on stalks** *BrE informal* if your eyes are out on stalks, you are very surprised or shocked

stalk[2] *v* **1** [T] to follow a person or animal quietly in order to catch and attack or kill them → **shadow**: *a tiger stalking its prey* | *We know the rapist stalks his victims at night.* THESAURUS FOLLOW **2** [T] to follow and watch someone over a long period of time in a way that is very annoying or threatening, and that is considered a crime in some places: *She was stalked by an obsessed fan.* **3** [I always + adv/prep] to walk in a proud or angry way, with long steps: **[+out/off/away]** *Yvonne turned and stalked out of the room in disgust.* **4** [T] *literary* if something bad stalks a place, you see or feel it everywhere in that place: *Fear stalks every dark stairwell and walkway.*

stalk·er /ˈstɔːkə $ ˈstɒːkər/ *n* [C] someone who follows and watches another person over a period of time in a way that is very annoying or threatening

stalk·ing /ˈstɔːkɪŋ $ ˈstɒː-/ *n* [U] the crime of following and watching someone over a period of time in a way that is very annoying or threatening

ˈstalking ˌhorse *n* [C] someone or something that hides someone's true purpose, especially a politician who says they want their leader's job when the real plan is that another, more important politician should get it

stall[1] /stɔːl $ stɒːl/ ●●○ S3 *n*
1 [C] a table or a small shop with an open front, especially outdoors, where goods are sold: *a market stall*
2 [C] an enclosed area in a building for an animal such as a horse or cow
3 [C usually singular] if a plane goes into a stall, its engine stops working
4 [C usually plural] a seat in a row of fixed seats for priests and singers in some larger churches: *choir stalls*
5 bathroom/toilet/shower stall a small enclosed private area for washing or using the toilet
6 the stalls *BrE* the seats on the main level of a theatre or cinema: *a good seat in the front row of the stalls* → see picture at THEATRE

stall[2] *v* **1** [I,T] if an engine or vehicle stalls, or if you stall it, it stops because there is not enough power or speed to keep it going: *The car kept stalling.* | *An inexperienced pilot may easily stall a plane.* **2** [I] *informal* to deliberately delay because you are not ready to do something, answer questions etc: ***Quit stalling*** *and answer my question!* | *He was just* ***stalling for time***. **3** [T] *informal* to make someone wait or stop something from happening until you are ready: *Maybe we can stall the sale until the prices go up.* | *We've got to stall him somehow.* **4** [I] to stop making progress or developing: *While his career has stalled, hers has taken off.*

stall·hold·er /ˈstɔːlˌhəʊldə $ ˈstɒːlˌhoʊldər/ *n* [C] *BrE* someone who rents and keeps a market stall

stal·lion /ˈstæljən/ *n* [C] a male horse that is fully grown, especially one that is used for breeding → **mare**

stal·wart[1] /ˈstɔːlwət $ ˈstɒːlwərt/ *n* [C] someone who is very loyal to a particular organization or set of ideas, and works hard for them: *old party stalwarts* | **[+of]** *Rob's a stalwart of the school's chess club.*

stalwart[2] *adj* **1 stalwart supporter/ally etc** a very loyal and strong supporter etc **2** *formal* strong in appearance —**stalwartly** *adv*

sta·men /ˈsteɪmən/ *n* [C] *technical* the male part of a flower that produces POLLEN

stam·i·na /ˈstæmənə/ ●○○ *n* [U] physical or mental strength that lets you continue doing something for a long time without getting tired: *You need stamina to be a long-distance runner.* | *Elaine has the stamina and the determination to succeed.*

stam·mer[1] /ˈstæmə $ -ər/ *v* [I,T] to speak with a lot of pauses and repeated sounds, either because you have a speech problem, or because you are nervous, excited etc SYN **stutter**: *Whenever he was angry, he would begin to stammer slightly.* | *Ben stammered out an apology.* THESAURUS SAY —**stammerer** *n* [C]

stammer[2] *n* [C usually singular] a speech problem which makes someone speak with a lot of pauses and repeated sounds SYN **stutter**: *Jeff spoke with a slight stammer.*

stamp[1] /stæmp/ ●●● S2 *n* [C]
1 MAIL (*also* **postage stamp** *formal*) a small piece of paper that you buy and stick onto an envelope or package before posting it: *a 29-cent stamp* | *Richard collects stamps.* | *a second-class stamp*
2 PRINTED MARK a tool for pressing or printing a mark or pattern onto a surface, or the mark made by this tool: *a date stamp* | *a passport stamp*
3 the stamp of sth if something has the stamp of a particular quality, it clearly has that quality: *The speech* ***bore*** (=had) ***the stamp of*** *authority.*
4 PAYMENT *BrE* a small piece of paper that is worth a particular amount of money and is bought and collected for something over a period of time: *television licence stamps*
5 TAX *BrE* a piece of paper for sticking to some official papers to show that British tax has been paid
6 of ... stamp *formal* someone with a particular kind of character: *He's clearly of a very different stamp.*
7 WITH FOOT an act of stamping, especially with your foot: *an angry stamp* → FOOD STAMP

stamp[2] ●●○ *v*
1 PUT FOOT DOWN [I,T] to put your foot down onto the ground loudly and with a lot of force: *The audience stamped and shouted.* | *'I will not!' Bert yelled and* ***stamped*** *his* ***foot*** (=because he was angry). | *She stood at the bus stop* ***stamping*** *her* ***feet*** (=because she was cold). | **stamp on sb/sth** (=try to hurt or kill someone or something, by putting your foot down onto them) *Marta shrieked and started stamping on the cockroach.*
2 WALK NOISILY [I always + adv/prep] to walk somewhere in a noisy way by putting your feet down hard onto the ground because you are angry SYN **stomp**: **[+around/out of/off etc]** *My mother stamped off down the stairs.*
3 MAKE A MARK [T] to put a pattern, sign, or letters on something, using a special tool: *The woman at the desk stamped my passport.* | *Among the papers was a brown folder stamped 'SECRET'.* | **stamp sth on sth** *Stamp the date on all the letters.*
4 AFFECT SB/STH [T] to have an important or permanent effect on someone or something: *The experience remained* ***stamped on*** *her* ***memory*** *for many years.* | **stamp sb with sth** *His army years had stamped him with an air of brisk authority.*
5 MAIL [T] to stick a stamp onto a letter, PARCEL etc

stamp sb **as** sth *phr v* to show that someone has a particular type of character: *It was his manners that stamped him as a real gentleman.*

stamp on sb/sth *phr v* to use force or your authority to stop someone from doing something, or stop something from happening, especially in an unfair way: *Officers were given orders to stamp on any hint of trouble.*

stamp sth ↔ **out** *phr v*
1 to prevent something bad from continuing: *We aim to stamp out poverty in our lifetimes.*
2 to stop a fire from burning by stepping hard on the flames
3 to make a shape or object by pressing hard on something using a machine or tool

ˈstamp colˌlecting *n* [U] the practice of collecting stamps from interest or because of their financial value SYN **philately** —**stamp collector** *n* [C]

ˈstamp ˌduty *n* [U] a tax that must be paid in Britain on particular legal documents that have to be officially checked, especially when buying a house

ˌstamped adˌdressed ˈenvelope *n* [C] *BrE* (abbreviation **sae**) an envelope with your name, your address, and a stamp on it, which you send to a person or organization so that they can send you information

stam·pede¹ /stæmˈpiːd/ *n* [C] **1** when a group of people all want to do the same thing at the same time: *a stampede to buy shares in high-tech companies* **2** when a group of large animals or people suddenly start running in the same direction because they are frightened or excited: *a cattle stampede*

stampede² *v* **1** [I,T] if a group of large animals or people stampede, they suddenly start running together in the same direction because they are frightened or excited: *a herd of stampeding buffalo* | *Children came stampeding out of the school doors.* **2 be/get stampeded** to be made frightened or worried so that you do something too quickly, without thinking enough about it: **[+into]** *Don't get stampeded into any rash decisions.*

ˈstamping ground *n* [C] *especially BrE* **sb's stamping ground** a favourite place where someone often goes

stance /stɑːns $ stæns/ ●○○ *n* [C usually singular]
1 an opinion that is stated publicly SYN **stand**: **[+on]** *What is your stance on environmental issues?* | **[+against]** *a* ***strong stance*** *against abortion* | **take/adopt a stance** *The president has adopted a* ***tough stance*** *on terrorism.*
2 a position in which you stand, especially when playing a sport: *a fighting stance*

stanch /stɑːntʃ $ stɒːntʃ, stɑːntʃ/ *v* [T] an American spelling of STAUNCH²

stan·chion /ˈstæntʃən, ˈstɑːn- $ ˈstæn-/ *n* [C] a strong upright bar used to support something

S

stand¹ /stænd/ ●●● S1 W1 *v* (*past tense and past participle* **stood** /stʊd/)
1 BE ON FEET (*also* **be standing up**) [I] to support yourself on your feet or be in an upright position: *It looks like we'll have to stand – there are no seats left.* | *She stood in the doorway.* | ***Stand still*** (=do not move) *and listen to me.* | *Don't just* ***stand there*** (=stand and not do anything) *– help me!* | **stand on tiptoe/stand on your toes** (=support yourself on your toes) *If he stood on tiptoe, he could reach the shelf.* | **stand (somewhere) doing sth** *They just stood there laughing.* | *We stood watching the rain fall.*
2 RISE (*also* **stand up**) [I] to rise to an upright position: *Smiling, she stood and closed the blinds.*
3 STEP [I always + adv/prep] **a)** to step a short distance: **[+back/aside]** *She stood back to let him in.* | **stand clear of sth** *BrE* (=step away from something in order to be safe) *Stand clear of the doors, please.* **b)** *BrE* to accidentally step on or in something: **[+on/in]** *Don't stand in that puddle!*
4 IN A PARTICULAR POSITION [I,T usually + adv/prep] to be upright in a particular position, or to put something or someone somewhere in an upright position: *A lamp stood on the table.* | *Near the railway station stood a hotel.* | *Some remains of the original house still stand.* | **stand sth on/in etc sth** *Can you stand that pole in the corner for now?* | *I closed the lid and stood the case against the wall.* | **stand sb (up) on sth** *Stand Molly up on a chair so she can see.*
5 IN A STATE/CONDITION [linking verb] to be or stay in a particular state or condition: *The kitchen door* ***stood open*** *so she went in.* | **stand empty/idle** (=not being used) *scores of derelict houses standing empty* | *I'm not too thrilled with* ***the way things stand*** (=the state that the situation is in) *at the moment.* | *The evidence,* ***as it stands*** (=as it is now), *cannot be conclusive.* | **where/how do things stand?** (=used to ask what is happening in a situation) *Where do things stand in terms of the budget?* | *I will know within the next month or two how I stand* (=what my situation is). | **stand united/divided** (=agree or disagree completely) *He urged the whole community to stand united and to reject terrorism.* | **stand prepared/ready to do sth** (=be prepared to do something whenever it is necessary) *We should stand ready to do what is necessary to guarantee the peace.* | *countries that have* ***stood together*** (=stayed united) *in times of crisis* | **stand in awe of sb** (=admire them, be afraid of them, or both)
6 NOT LIKE **can't stand** *spoken* used to say that you do not like someone or something at all, or that you think that something is extremely unpleasant SYN **can't bear**: *I can't stand bad manners.* | *I know he* ***can't stand the sight of*** *me.* | **can't stand (sb/sth) doing sth** *Lily can't stand working in an office.* | *I can't stand people smoking around me when I'm eating.* | **can't stand to do sth** *She can't stand to hear them arguing.*
7 ACCEPT A SITUATION [T usually in questions and negatives] to be able to accept or deal well with a difficult situation SYN **tolerate**: **can/could stand sth** *I couldn't stand the thought of leaving Danielle.* | *I've had about as much as I can stand of your arguing!* | *I don't know if I can stand the waiting any longer.* | **can stand sb doing sth** *How can you stand Marty coming home late all the time?* | *She's a strong woman who* ***stands no nonsense*** *from anyone.*
8 BE GOOD ENOUGH [T] to be good or strong enough to last a long time or to experience a particular situation without being harmed, damaged etc: *Linen can stand very high temperatures.* | *His poetry will* ***stand the test of time*** (=stay popular).
9 stand to do sth to be likely to do or have something: **stand to gain/lose/win/make** *What do firms think they stand to gain by merging?* | *After the oil spill, thousands of fishermen stand to lose their livelihoods.*
10 NOT MOVE [I] to stay in a particular place without moving → **standstill**: *The car's been standing in the garage for weeks.* | *The mixture was left to stand at room temperature for 15 minutes.* | *The train was already standing at the platform.*
11 HEIGHT [linking verb] *formal* to be a particular height: *The trophy* ***stands*** *five feet* ***high***. | *John* ***stood*** *six feet* ***tall***.
12 LEVEL/AMOUNT [linking verb] to be at a particular level or amount: **[+at]** *His former workforce of 1,300 now stands at 220.* | *Illiteracy rates are still thought to stand above 50 percent.*
13 RANK/POSITION [I always + adv/prep] to have a particular rank or position when compared with similar things or people SYN **rank**: *The president stands high in the public opinion polls.* | *How do their sales stand in relation to those of similar firms?* | *His book could stand alongside the best.*
14 ELECTION [I] *BrE* to try to become elected to a council, parliament etc SYN **run** *AmE*: **[+for]** *She announced her intention to stand for parliament.*
15 DECISION/OFFER [I not in progressive] if a decision, offer etc stands, it continues to exist, be correct, or be VALID: *Despite protests, the official decision stood.* | *My offer of help still stands.*
16 if you can't stand the heat, get out of the kitchen used to tell someone that they should leave a job or situation if they cannot deal with its difficulties
17 sb/sth could stand sth used to say very directly that it would be a good idea for someone to do something or for something to happen: *His smile exposed teeth that could stand a good scrubbing.* | **sb could stand to do sth** *My doctor told me I could stand to lose a few pounds.*
18 I stand corrected *spoken formal* used to admit that your opinion or something that you just said was wrong
19 where sb stands someone's opinion about something: **[+on]** *We still do not know where he stands on the matter.* | *You must decide where you stand.*
20 from where I stand *spoken* according to what I know or feel: *I knew from where I stood that the stocks were practically worthless.*
21 know where you stand (with sb) to know how someone feels about you, or what you are allowed to do in a particular situation: *At least we know where we stand with Steven now.* | *I'd like to know where I stand.* | *It helps to know where you stand legally.*
22 stand to attention *BrE*, **stand at attention** *AmE* if soldiers stand to attention, they stand very straight and stiff to show respect
23 stand on your head/hands to support yourself on your head or hands, with your feet in the air
24 stand in line *AmE* to wait in a line of people until it is

your turn to do something SYN **queue** *BrE*: *Customers stood in line for 20 minutes at the cash register.*
25 stand firm/stand fast a) to refuse to be forced to move backwards: *She stood firm, blocking the entrance.* **b)** to refuse to change your opinions, intentions, or behaviour: *The government continued to stand firm and no concessions were made.* | **[+on/against]** *He stands firm on his convictions.*
26 stand pat *AmE* to refuse to change a decision, plan etc: **[+on]** *Harry's standing pat on his decision to fire Janice.*
27 stand alone a) to continue to do something alone, without help from anyone else: *Some of the Pacific islands are too small to stand alone as independent states.* **b)** to be much better than anything or anyone else: *For sheer entertainment value, Kelly stood alone.*
28 stand still to not change or progress at all, even though time has passed: *No industry can stand still.* | ***Time** seems to have **stood still** in this lovely hotel.*
29 stand a chance/hope (of doing sth) to be likely to be able to do something or to succeed: *You'll stand a better chance of getting a job with a degree.* | *Maybe their relationship had never really stood a chance.*
30 stand in sb's way (*also* **stand in the way**) to prevent someone from doing something: *I always encouraged Brian. I didn't want to stand in his way.* | *You can't stand in the way of progress!*
31 stand on your own (two) feet to be able to do what you need to do, earn your own money, etc without help from others: *She's never learned to stand on her own feet.*
32 it stands to reason (that) used to say that something should be completely clear to anyone who is sensible: *It stands to reason that you cannot find the right person to do a job unless you know exactly what that job is.*
33 stand or fall by/on sth to depend on something for success: *The case against him will stand or fall on its own merits.*
34 LIQUID [I] a liquid that stands does not flow or is not made to move: *standing pools of marsh water*
35 stand guard (over sb/sth) to watch someone or something so that they do not do anything wrong or so that nothing bad happens to them: *Soldiers stand guard on street corners.* | *You must stand guard over him at all times.*
36 stand bail *BrE* to promise to pay money if someone does not return to a court of law to be judged
37 stand trial to be brought to a court of law to have your case examined and judged: **[+for/on]** *Gresham will stand trial for murder.* | *The accused was ordered to stand trial on a number of charges.*
38 stand accused (of sth) a) to be the person in a court of law who is being judged for a crime: *The former president stands accused of lying to the nation's parliament.* **b)** if you stand accused of doing something bad or wrong, other people say that you have done it: *The radio station stands accused of racism.*
39 stand tall a) to stand with your back straight and your head raised: *Stand tall with your feet comfortably apart.* **b)** *AmE* to be proud and feel ready to deal with anything: *We will stand tall and fight for issues of concern to our community.*
40 sb can do sth standing on their head *informal* used to say that someone is able to do something easily: *This is basic stuff. I can do it standing on my head.*
41 be stood on its head if something is stood on its head, it becomes the opposite of what it was before: *One area of the business which has been stood on its head is internal communications.*
42 not stand on ceremony *BrE* to not worry about the formal rules of polite behaviour: *Come on, Mal. Don't stand on ceremony here at home.*
43 stand sb a drink/meal etc *BrE* to pay for something as a gift to someone: *Come on, Jack. I'll stand you a drink if you like.* → **make sb's hair stand on end** at HAIR(8), → **leave sb/sth standing** at LEAVE[1](15), → **not have a leg to stand on** at LEG[1](7), → **stand/serve/hold sb in good stead** at STEAD(2), → **stand your ground** at GROUND[1](7)

THESAURUS

stand to be on your feet in an upright position: *There were no seats, so we had to stand.* | *When we entered, Stephen was standing by his desk.*
be on your feet to be standing, especially for a long time: *If you have young kids, you're on your feet all day.*
get up to stand after you have been sitting or lying down: *He got up and turned off the TV.* | *Mum fell in her flat and was unable to get up.*
stand up to stand after you have been sitting, or to be in a standing position: *I stood up when she came in and shook her hand.* | *It's generally better to do this exercise standing up.*
get to your feet *written* to stand up, especially slowly or when it is difficult for you: *My attorney got slowly to his feet, breathing heavily.*
rise *formal* to stand after you have been sitting, especially at a formal event: *As the bride entered the cathedral, the congregation rose.* | *Audience members rose to their feet, cheering and clapping.*

stand against sb/sth *phr v* to oppose a person, organization, plan, decision etc: *She hadn't the strength to stand against her aunt's demands.* | *There are only a hundred of them standing against an army of 42,000 troops.*
stand around *phr v* to stand somewhere and not do anything: *We stood around saying goodbye for a while.*
stand by *phr v*
1 to not do anything to help someone or prevent something from happening → **bystander**: *I'm not going to stand by and see her hurt.*
2 stand by sth to keep a promise, agreement etc, or to say that something is still true: *I stand by what I said earlier.* | *He stood by his convictions.*
3 stand by sb to stay loyal to someone and support them, especially in a difficult situation: *His wife stood by him during his years in prison.*
4 to be ready to do something if necessary → **standby**: *Rescue crews were standing by in case of a breakdown.* | **[+for]** *Stand by for our Christmas competition.* | **stand by to do sth** *Police stood by to arrest any violent fans.*
stand down *phr v BrE*
1 to agree to leave your position or to stop trying to be elected, so that someone else can have a chance SYN **step down** *AmE*: **[+as]** *He was obliged to stand down as a parliamentary candidate.*
2 to leave the WITNESS BOX in a court of law
3 stand (sb) down if a soldier stands down or is stood down, he stops working for the day
stand for sth *phr v*
1 if a letter or symbol stands for something, it represents a word or idea, especially as a short form: *What does ATM stand for?*
2 to support a particular set of ideas, values, or principles: *It's hard to tell what the party stands for these days.*
3 not stand for sth *BrE* to not allow something to continue to happen or someone to do something: *She's been lying about me, and I won't stand for it.*
stand in *phr v* to temporarily do someone else's job or take their place → **stand-in**: **[+for]** *Would you mind standing in for me for a while?*
stand out *phr v*
1 to be very easy to see or notice: *The outlines of rooftops and chimneys stood out against the pale sky.* | *She always **stood out in a crowd**.* | *I am sure illnesses stand out in all childhood memories.*
2 to be much better than other similar people or things → **standout**: **[+as]** *That day still stands out as the greatest day in my life.* | **[+from/among/above]** *Three of the cars we tested stood out among the rest.*
3 to rise up from a surface: *The veins stood out on his throat and temples.*
stand out against sth *phr v BrE* to be strongly opposed to an idea, plan etc: *We must stand out against bigotry.*
stand over sb *phr v* to stand very close behind someone and watch as they work to make sure they do nothing wrong: *I can't concentrate with him standing over me like that.*
stand to *phr v BrE* to order a soldier to move into a position so that they are ready for action, or to move into this position: **stand sb to** *The men have been stood to.*

S

stand up *phr v*
1 to be on your feet, or to rise to your feet → **stand-up**: *I've been standing up all day.* | ***Stand up straight*** *and don't slouch!* | *Jim stood up stiffly.*
2 [always + adv/prep] to stay healthy or in good condition in a difficult environment or after a lot of hard use: **[+to]** *Most of the plants stood up well to the heat.*
3 to be proved to be true, correct, useful etc when tested: **[+to/under]** *The memoirs stand up well to cross-checking with other records.* | *Without a witness, the charges will never* ***stand up in court*** (=be successfully proved in a court of law).
4 stand sb up *informal* to not meet someone who you have arranged to meet: *I was supposed to go to a concert with Kyle on Friday, but he stood me up.*
5 stand up and be counted to make it very clear what you think about something when this is dangerous or might cause trouble for you

stand up for sb/sth *phr v* to support or defend a person or idea when they are being attacked: *It's time we stood up for our rights.* | *Silvia is capable of standing up for herself.*

stand up to sb/sth *phr v* to refuse to accept unfair treatment from a person or organization: *He'll respect you more if you stand up to him.* | *Cliff couldn't stand up to bullying.*

STANDS

stand² ●●● S2 W2 *n* [C]
1 FOR SUPPORT a piece of furniture or equipment used to hold or support something: *a music stand* | *a cake stand* | *He adjusted the microphone stand.* | **coat stand/hat stand** (=for hanging coats or hats on)
2 FOR SELLING a table or small structure used for selling or showing things SYN **stall** *BrE*: *a hotdog stand* | *an exhibition stand* | *The shop was crowded with display stands and boxes.* | *One week, three magazines* ***hit the stands*** (=became available to buy) *with Peace Corps stories.* → NEWSSTAND
3 OPINION/ATTITUDE [usually singular] a position or opinion that you state firmly and publicly: **[+on]** *the Republicans' conservative stand on social and environmental issues* | *She was accused of not* ***taking a stand on*** *feminism or civil rights.*
4 OPPOSE/DEFEND a strong effort to defend yourself or to oppose something: **take/make/mount a stand (against sth)** *We have to take a stand against racism.*
5 the stands [plural] (*also* **the stand** *BrE*) a building where people stand or sit to watch the game at a sports ground → **grandstand**: *In the stands, fifty of Jill's friends and family have come to watch her last game.*
6 the stand a WITNESS BOX: *Will the next witness please* ***take the stand*** (=go into the witness box)?
7 CRICKET the period of time in which two BATSMEN are playing together in a game of CRICKET, or the points that they get during this time
8 TAXIS/BUSES a place where taxis or buses stop and wait for passengers: *There's a taxi stand on Glen Road.*
9 TREES a group of trees of one type growing close together: **[+of]** *a stand of eucalyptus trees*

stand·a·lone /ˈstændələʊn $ -loʊn/ *adj* [only before noun] **1** a standalone computer works on its own without being part of a network **2** a standalone company is one that is not part of a larger company —**standalone** *n* [C]

stan·dard¹ /ˈstændəd $ -ərd/ ●●● S2 W2 *n*
1 LEVEL OF QUALITY/ACHIEVEMENT [C,U] the level that is considered to be acceptable, or the level that someone or something has achieved: *Students have to reach a certain standard or they won't pass.* | *The airline has rigorous safety standards.* | **[+of]** *The committee is assessing the standard of care in local hospitals.*
2 MORAL PRINCIPLES **standards** [plural] moral principles about what kind of behaviour or attitudes are acceptable: *the recent decline in* ***moral standards*** | **standards fall/slip/go down** *Standards have slipped since I was a boy.*
3 MEASUREMENT [C] a fixed official rule for measuring weight, PURITY, value etc: *an official government standard for the purity of silver*
4 SONG [C] a popular song that has been sung by many different singers: *popular jazz standards*
5 FLAG [C] *old-fashioned* a flag used in ceremonies: *the royal standard* → DOUBLE STANDARD, LIVING STANDARD

COLLOCATIONS

VERBS

meet/reach a standard *Many food businesses fail to meet basic standards of hygiene.*
set/lay down a standard *The government sets standards that all hospitals must reach.*
raise/improve standards *We are determined to raise standards in our schools.*
lower standards *He refused to lower his standards.*
maintain standards (=keep them at a good level) | **standards improve** | **standards fall/slip/decline**

ADJECTIVES/NOUN + standard

high/good *The standard of their work was generally very high.*
low/poor *The report says the standard of children's diet in Britain is poor.*
acceptable *All too often their behaviour has fallen below acceptable standards.*
stringent/strict/rigorous/tough standards (=high standards that are difficult to reach) | **international standards** | **safety/hygiene/quality etc standards** | **academic/educational standards** | **living standards** (*also* **standard of living**) (=the level of comfort and the amount of money people have)

PHRASES

an improvement/rise in standards *There has been an improvement in living standards.*
a decline/drop in standards
be/come up to standard (=be good enough) *Her work was not up to standard.*
be below standard (=not be good enough) *His performance yesterday was below standard.*
by modern standards/today's standards *The technology was crude by modern standards.*
by our standards (=judging by what we are used to) | **by British/African etc standards**

standard² ●●● S2 W2 *adj*
1 accepted as normal or usual: *We paid them the standard rate.* | **standard practice/procedure** (=the usual way of doing things) *Searching luggage at airports is now standard practice.* | *The format is fairly standard.* THESAURUS NORMAL
2 regular and usual in shape, size, quality etc OPP **non-standard**: *We make shoes in standard and wide sizes.* | *All these vans are made to a standard design.*

3 a standard book, work etc is read by everyone studying a particular subject
4 the standard form of a language is the one considered to be correct and is used by most people OPP **non-standard**: *the standard spelling | standard English pronunciation*

ˈstandard-ˌbearer *n* [C] *formal* **1** an important leader in a moral argument or political group **2** a soldier in past times who carried the STANDARD (=flag) at the front of an army

ˌstandard deviˈation *n* [C] *technical* a number in STATISTICS that shows by how much members of a mathematical set can be different from the average set

ˈStandard ˌGrade *n* [C] a school examination in one of a range of subjects that is taken by students in Scotland, usually at the age of 16

ˌstandard-ˈissue *adj* **1** a standard-issue thing is the common or usual type of that thing **2** included as an ordinary part of military equipment

stan·dard·ize (*also* **-ise** *BrE*) /ˈstændədaɪz $ -ər-/ ●○○ *v* [T] to make all the things of one particular type the same as each other: *Attempts to standardize English spelling have never been successful.* | *standardized tests* —**standardization** /ˌstændədaɪˈzeɪʃən $ -dərdə-/ *n* [U]

ˈstandard lamp *n* [C] *BrE* a tall lamp that stands on the floor SYN **floor lamp** *AmE* → see picture at LAMP

ˌstandard of ˈliving ●○○ *n* [C usually singular] the amount of wealth, comfort, and other things that a particular person, group, country etc has SYN **living standard**: **high/low standard of living** *a nation with a high standard of living*

ˌstandard ˈtime *n* [U] the time to which all clocks in a particular area of the world are set

stand·by[1], **ˈstand-by** /ˈstændbaɪ/ *n* (*plural* **standbys**) **1 on standby a)** ready to help immediately if you are needed: *A special team of police were* ***kept on standby***. **b)** if you are on standby to do something, for example to travel by plane, you are on a list of people who may be allowed to do it if places become available: *We can* ***put*** *you* ***on standby***. → STAND BY **2** [C] something that is kept ready so that it can be used when needed: *Powdered milk is a good standby in an emergency.*

standby[2] *adj* [only before noun] a standby ticket is one that you can get only if places become available, for example if other people cannot use their tickets

ˈstandby time *n* [U] **1** the time during which a person or a machine is available to work but is not able to work because they are waiting to be given a specific job to do **2** the period of time that passes while you wait for a computer to do what you have asked it to do

ˈstand-in *n* [C] **1** someone who does the job or takes the place of someone else for a short time: *Gilbert failed to find a stand-in and so could not go to the party.* **2** someone who takes the place of an actor for some scenes in a film: **[+for]** *a stand-in for Tom Cruise* → **stand in** at STAND[1]

stand·ing[1] /ˈstændɪŋ/ *adj* [only before noun] **1** permanently agreed or arranged: *You have to pay* ***standing charges*** *whether or not you use the service.* | **standing invitation** (=permission to visit someone whenever you like) | **a standing army** (=a professional permanent army) | *A* ***standing committee*** *was established to coordinate the army and navy.* **2** done from a standing position: *The runners set off from a* ***standing start***. | **standing ovation** (=when people stand up to clap after a performance) **3 standing joke** something that happens often and that people make jokes about: *The whole incident became a standing joke between us.*

standing[2] *n* [U] **1** someone's rank or position in a system, organization, society etc, based on what other people think of them: *Barb's work helped to improve her standing with her colleagues.* | **[+in]** *The scandal damaged the governor's standing in the polls.* | **of high/low standing** *a lawyer of high standing* THESAURUS ▸ REPUTATION **2 sth of five/many etc years' standing** used to show the time during which something such as an agreement has existed: *an arrangement of several years' standing*

ˌstanding ˈorder *n* [C,U] *BrE* an arrangement by which a bank pays a fixed amount of money from your account every month, year etc → **direct debit**

ˈstanding room *n* [U] space for standing in a theatre, sports ground etc: *There was* ***standing room only*** (=no seats were left) *in the courthouse.*

stand-off /ˈstændɒf $ -ɒːf/ *n* [C] a situation in which neither side in a fight or battle can gain an advantage

stand-of·fish, **standoffish** /ˌstænd ˈɒfɪʃ $ -ˈɒːf-/ *adj informal* rather unfriendly and formal SYN **aloof**: *She was cold and stand-offish.* —**stand-offishly** *adv* —**stand-offishness** *n* [U]

stand·out /ˈstændaʊt/ *adj* [only before noun] *AmE* used about a person or thing in a group that is much better than all the rest: *the standout track on the album* —**standout** *n* [singular]: *He was the standout in last Saturday's game.*

stand·pipe /ˈstændpaɪp/ *n* [C] a pipe that provides water in a public place in the street

stand·point /ˈstændpɔɪnt/ ●○○ *n* [C usually singular] a way of thinking about people, situations, ideas etc SYN **point of view**: **from a theoretical/political/economic etc standpoint** *Let's look at the questions from an economic standpoint.* | *a discussion of marriage* ***from the standpoint of*** *women*

stand·still /ˈstændˌstɪl/ *n* [singular] a situation in which there is no movement or activity at all: **come to a standstill/bring sth to a standstill** *Strikers brought production to a standstill.* | **at a standstill** *Traffic was at a standstill.*

ˈstand-up[1], **stand·up** /ˈstændʌp/ *adj* [only before noun] **1** stand-up COMEDY involves one person telling jokes alone as a performance: *a stand-up comedian* **2** a stand-up meeting, meal etc is one in which people stand up: *We had a stand-up buffet.* **3** a stand-up fight, argument etc is one in which people shout loudly at each other or are violent: *If it came to a stand-up fight, I wouldn't have a chance.* **4** able to stay upright: *a photo in a stand-up frame* | *a stand-up collar* → **stand up** at STAND[1]

stand-up[2], **standup** *n* [U] **1** stand-up COMEDY: *Mark used to* ***do stand-up*** *at Roxy's Bar.* **2** a COMEDIAN who does stand-up COMEDY

stank /stæŋk/ *v* the past tense of STINK[1]

ˌStanley ˈCup, the a prize given to the winner of the National Hockey League, which is made up of the highest level of professional ICE HOCKEY teams from Canada and the US

Stan·ley knife /ˈstænli ˌnaɪf/ *n* [C] *trademark BrE* a very sharp knife with a small TRIANGULAR blade, that you use in activities such as decorating and WOODWORK SYN **Exacto knife** *AmE*

stan·za /ˈstænzə/ *n* [C] a group of lines in a repeated pattern forming part of a poem SYN **verse**

sta·ple[1] /ˈsteɪpəl/ ●●○ *n* [C]
1 a small piece of thin wire that is pushed into sheets of paper and bent over to hold them together
2 a small U-shaped piece of metal with pointed ends, used to hold something in place
3 a food that is needed and used all the time: *staples like flour and rice*
4 the main product that is produced in a country: *Bananas and sugar are the staples of Jamaica.*

staple[2] *v* [T] to fasten two or more things together with a staple: **staple sth together** *The handouts are all stapled together.* | **staple sth to sth** *I stapled the order form to the invoice.*

staple[3] *adj* [only before noun] **1** forming the greatest or most important part of something: *Oil is Nigeria's staple export.* | *a staple ingredient of comedy* **2 staple diet a)** the food that you normally eat: **[+of]** *They live on a staple diet of rice and vegetables.* **b)** something that is always being produced, seen, bought etc: **[+of]** *television's staple diet of soap operas and quiz shows* **3** used all the time: *Marty's* ***staple excuses***

S

ˈstaple gun *n* [C] a tool used for putting strong staples into walls

sta·pler /ˈsteɪplə $ -ər/ *n* [C] a tool used for putting staples into paper → see picture at STATIONERY

star¹ /stɑː $ stɑːr/ ●●● S2 W2 *n* [C]

1 IN THE SKY a large ball of burning gas in space that can be seen at night as a point of light in the sky → **constellation**, **galaxy**, **supernova**: *I lay on my back and looked up at the stars.* | *The sky was filled with stars.* | *The* ***stars*** *were* ***shining****.* | *The* ***stars*** *were all* ***out*** (=they were shining). | *The* ***stars*** *were* ***twinkling*** *overhead* (=shining and quickly changing from bright to faint). | **under the stars** (=outdoors at night) *sitting around a campfire under the stars* → FALLING STAR, MORNING STAR, SHOOTING STAR

2 FAMOUS PERFORMER/PLAYER a famous and successful actor, musician, or sports player: *By the age of 20, she was already a* ***big star*** (=a very famous and successful performer). | **a pop/movie/TV/football etc star** | *He is a* ***rising star*** (=someone who is becoming famous and successful) *in the music world.* | *She's a good actress but she lacks* ***star quality*** (=a special quality that could make someone a star). THESAURUS ACTOR

3 MAIN PERSON IN A FILM/PLAY ETC the person who has the main part, or one of them, in a film, play, show etc: **[+of]** *Ray Grimes, the star of the television series 'Brother John'*

4 BEST/MOST SUCCESSFUL PERSON **a)** the person who gives the best performance in a film, play, show etc: *Laporte, as Ebenezer Scrooge, is undoubtedly* ***the star of the show****.* | *Shamu, the killer whale, is the show's* ***star attraction*** (=best and most popular person or thing). **b)** the best or most successful person in a group of players, workers, students etc: **star player/performer/salesman etc** *the team's star player* | *the school's star pupil* | *the star columnist of 'The Sunday Times'*

5 SHAPE **a)** a shape with four or more points, which represents the way a star looks in the sky **b)** a mark in the shape of a star, used to draw attention to something written SYN **asterisk**: *I put a star next to the items that we still need to buy.* **c)** a piece of cloth or metal in the shape of a star, worn to show someone's rank or position – used especially on military uniforms: *a four-star general*

6 HOTELS/RESTAURANTS a mark used in a system for judging the quality of hotels and restaurants: **three-star/four-star/five-star etc** *a two-star hotel*

7 the stars *BrE informal* a description, usually printed in newspapers and magazines, of what will happen to you in the future, based on the position of the stars and PLANETS at the time of your birth SYN **horoscope**: **sb's stars** *I never* ***read*** *my* ***stars****.* → STAR SIGN

8 sth is written in the stars used to say that what happens to a person is controlled by FATE (=a power that is believed to influence what happens in people's lives): *Their marriage was surely written in the stars.*

9 see stars to see flashes of light, especially because you have been hit on the head: *I felt a little dizzy and could see stars.*

10 have stars in your eyes to imagine that something you want to do is much more exciting or attractive than it really is → STARRY-EYED

11 you're a star!/what a star! *BrE spoken* said when you are very grateful or pleased because of what someone has done: *Thanks, Mel. You're a real star!* → **guiding star** at GUIDING(2), → **born under a lucky/unlucky star** at BORN¹(7), → **reach for the stars** at REACH¹(12), → **thank your lucky stars** at THANK(3)

THESAURUS – MEANING 2

A FAMOUS PERSON

star a famous and successful actor, musician, or sportsperson: *She dreamed of becoming a movie star.* | *a talent show to find the stars of the future*

celebrity someone who often appears in newspapers, on television etc and is well-known to the public. **Celebrities** are often famous for being famous, not because they have any great TALENT: *The magazine is full of gossip about celebrities.*

name a famous person whose name is known by many people – used especially in the following expressions: *All the* ***big names*** *in football were at the awards dinner.* | *Giorgio Armani is one of the most* ***famous names*** *in fashion.* | *He is yet to become a* ***household name*** (=someone who everyone has heard of).

personality an entertainer or sports player who is famous and often appears in the newspapers, on television etc – used especially in the following phrases: *Many advertisers use* ***TV personalities*** *to promote their products.* | *He was chosen as* ***sports personality*** *of the year.*

A VERY FAMOUS PERSON

superstar an extremely famous performer, especially a musician or film actor: *The film made Tom Cruise an international superstar.*

legend someone who is famous and admired for being extremely good at doing something – used especially about people who are at the end of a long career or who have died: *blues legend John Lee Hooker*

great [usually plural] someone who was one of the best players or performers that there have ever been: *He was one of the all-time soccer greats.*

star² ●●○ *v* (**starred**, **starring**)

1 [I] if someone stars in a film, television show etc, they are one of the main characters in it: **[+in]** *Eastwood starred in 'The Good, the Bad, and the Ugly'.* | **[+with/opposite]** *DeVito stars opposite Dreyfuss in the movie.* | **[+as]** *Hugh Grant stars as the romantic hero.* | *'The Freshman' was Brando's first* ***starring role*** (=the most important part in a film) *in ten years.*

2 [T] if a film, television show, or play stars someone, that person is one of the main characters in it SYN **feature**: *a film starring Meryl Streep* | **star sb as ...** *The movie starred Orson Welles as Harry Lime.*

3 [T] to put an ASTERISK (=a star-shaped mark) next to something written: *The starred items are available.* GRAMMAR **Star** is usually passive in this meaning.

ˌstar ˈanise *n* [U] a small dried star-shaped fruit that is used as a spice, especially in Chinese cooking

star·board /ˈstɑːbəd $ ˈstɑːrbərd/ *n* [U] the side of a ship or aircraft that is on your right when you are facing forwards → **port** —**starboard** *adj*

starch¹ /stɑːtʃ $ stɑːrtʃ/ *n* **1** [C,U] a substance which provides your body with energy and is found in foods such as grain, rice, and potatoes, or a food that contains this substance SYN **carbohydrate**: *He eats a lot of starch.* | *Avoid fatty foods and starches.* **2** [U] a substance that is mixed with water and is used to make cloth stiff

starch² *v* [T] to make cloth stiff, using starch: *a starched tablecloth*

ˌstar ˈchamber *n* [C] *BrE* a group of people that meets secretly and makes important decisions

starch·y /ˈstɑːtʃi $ ˈstɑːr-/ *adj* **1** containing a lot of STARCH¹(1): ***starchy foods*** **2** *BrE* very formal and correct in your behaviour – used to show disapproval: *She spoke in a rather starchy manner.* —**starchily** *adv* —**starchiness** *n* [U]

ˈstar-crossed *adj literary* being in a situation that prevents something happy or good happening: ***star-crossed lovers*** (=people who love each other but cannot be together)

star·dom /ˈstɑːdəm $ ˈstɑːr-/ *n* [U] the state of being a famous performer → **fame**: *his rapid rise to stardom* | **shoot/rise/zoom to stardom** (=become famous very quickly) *Ellen shot to stardom as a model last year.*

star·dust /ˈstɑːdʌst $ ˈstɑːr-/ *n* [U] *literary* an imaginary magic substance

stare¹ /steə $ ster/ ●●● S3 W2 *v* [I]

1 to look at something or someone for a long time without moving your eyes, for example because you are surprised, angry, or bored: **[+at]** *What are you staring at?* | **stare (at sb) in disbelief/amazement/horror etc** *She stared*

at me in disbelief. | *She sat there* ***staring into space*** (=looking for a long time at nothing). THESAURUS▸ LOOK
2 be staring sb in the face a) *informal* if something is staring you in the face, it is very clear or easy to notice but you have not noticed it: *The solution was staring me right in the face all along.* **b)** to seem impossible to avoid: *Defeat was staring us in the face.* → **stark staring mad** at STARK²(2)
stare sb **out** *BrE*, **stare sb down** *AmE phr v* to look at someone for so long that they start to feel uncomfortable and look away

stare² ●●○ *n* [C] when you look at something or someone for a long time in a steady way: *She* ***gave*** *him a long hard* ***stare***. | *She laughed, ignoring the stares of everyone around her.* | *His pleas were met by a* ***blank stare*** (=a stare with no expression, understanding, or interest).

star·fish /ˈstɑːˌfɪʃ $ ˈstɑːr-/ *n* (*plural* **starfish**) [C] a flat sea animal that has five arms forming the shape of a star

star·fruit /ˈstɑːˌfruːt $ ˈstɑːr-/ *n* (*plural* **starfruit**) [C] a pale green tropical fruit that you can cut into pieces that have the shape of stars → see picture at FRUIT¹

star·gaz·er /ˈstɑːˌɡeɪzə $ ˈstɑːrˌɡeɪzər/ *n* [C] *informal* someone who studies ASTRONOMY or ASTROLOGY —**stargazing** *n* [U]

ˈstar jump *n* [C usually plural] *BrE* one of a series of exercise jumps that you do from a standing position with your arms and legs pointing out at each side SYN **jumping jack**

stark¹ /stɑːk $ stɑːrk/ *adj* **1** very plain in appearance, with little or no colour or decoration: *In the cold dawn light, the castle looked stark and forbidding.* | *the stark beauty of New Mexico* **2** unpleasantly clear and impossible to avoid SYN **harsh**: *The movie shows the stark realities of life in the ghetto.* | *The extreme poverty of the local people is in* ***stark contrast*** *to the wealth of the tourists.* | *We are faced with a* ***stark choice***. | *a* ***stark reminder*** *of life under Communist rule* —**starkly** *adv* —**starkness** *n* [U]

stark² *adv* **1 stark naked** not wearing any clothes at all: *Ben was standing there stark naked.* **2 stark raving mad/bonkers** (*also* **stark staring mad** *BrE*) completely crazy: *He's gone stark raving mad.*

stark·ers /ˈstɑːkəz $ ˈstɑːrkərz/ *adj* [not before noun] *BrE informal* not wearing any clothes SYN **naked**

star·less /ˈstɑːləs $ ˈstɑːr-/ *adj literary* with no stars showing in the sky: *a starless night*

star·let /ˈstɑːlɪt $ ˈstɑːr-/ *n* [C] a young actress who plays small parts in films and hopes to become famous

star·light /ˈstɑːlaɪt $ ˈstɑːr-/ *n* [U] the light that comes from the stars in the night sky

star·ling /ˈstɑːlɪŋ $ ˈstɑːr-/ *n* [C] a common bird with shiny black feathers that lives especially in cities

star·lit /ˈstɑːˌlɪt $ ˈstɑːr-/ *adj literary* made brighter by light from the stars: *a starlit night*

Star of Da·vid /ˌstɑːr əv ˈdeɪvɪd/ *n* [C usually singular] a star with six points that represents the Jewish religion or Israel

star·ry /ˈstɑːri/ *adj* **1** having many stars: *a starry winter sky* **2** starry eyes shine brightly **3** bright like a star or shaped like a star: *white starry flowers*

ˌstarry-ˈeyed *adj informal* happy and hopeful about things in a way that is silly or UNREALISTIC

ˌStars and ˈStripes, the the national flag of the US

ˈstar sign (*also* **sign**) *n* [C] one of the 12 signs of the ZODIAC (=the system that uses people's birth dates to say what will happen to them in the future)

ˌStar-Spangled ˈBanner, the 1 the NATIONAL ANTHEM (=national song) of the US **2** the national flag of the US

ˈstar-ˌstudded *adj* [only before noun] including many famous performers: *a star-studded cast*

This graph shows how common the different grammar patterns of the verb **start** are.

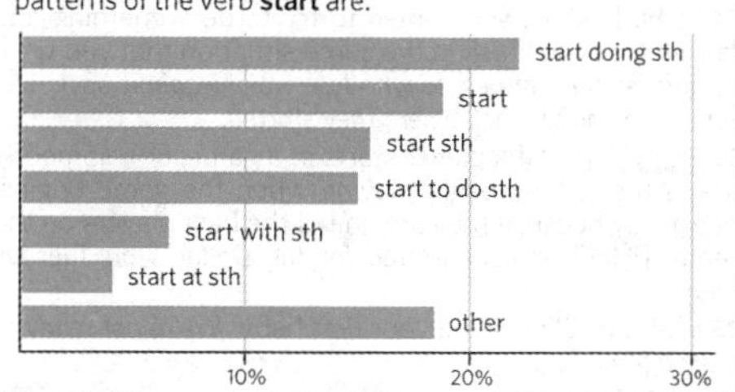

start¹ /stɑːt $ stɑːrt/ ●●● S1 W1 *v*

1 BEGIN DOING STH [I,T] to do something that you were not doing before, and continue doing it SYN **begin**: *There's so much to do I don't know where to start.* | *Have you started your homework?* | **start doing sth** *Then the baby started crying.* | **start to do sth** *It's starting to rain.* | *He got up and* ***started*** *running* ***again***. | *I'd better* ***get started*** (=start doing something) *soon.* | **start sb doing sth** *What Kerry said started me thinking* (=made me start thinking).

2 BEGIN HAPPENING [I,T] (*also* **start off**) to begin happening, or to make something begin happening: *What time does the film start?* | *Lightning started a fire that burned 500 acres.* | *The party was just* ***getting started*** *when Sara arrived.* | **starting (from) now/tomorrow/next week etc** *You have two hours to complete the test, starting now.*

3 BEGIN IN A PARTICULAR WAY [I always + adv/prep, T] (*also* **start off**) to begin something in a particular way, or to begin in a particular way: *A healthy breakfast is a good way to start the day.* | **[+with]** *The festivities started with a huge fireworks display.* | **[+as]** *The restaurant started as a small take-out place.* | **start badly/well/slowly etc** *Any new exercise program should start slowly.* | **start (sth) by doing sth** *Chao starts by explaining some basic legal concepts.*

4 BUSINESS/ORGANIZATION [T] (*also* **start up**) to make something begin to exist: **start a business/company/firm etc** *She wanted to start her own catering business.*

5 JOB/SCHOOL [I,T] to begin a new job, or to begin going to school, college etc: *When can you start?* | **start school/college/work** *I started college last week.*

6 CAR/ENGINE ETC [I,T] (*also* **start up**) if you start a car or engine, or if it starts, it begins to work: *The car wouldn't start this morning.* | **get the car/engine etc started** *He couldn't get his motorbike started.*

7 BEGIN GOING SOMEWHERE [I] (*also* **start off/out**) to begin travelling or moving in a particular direction SYN **set out**: *We'll have to start early to get there by lunchtime.*

8 LIFE/PROFESSION [I always + adv/prep, T] (*also* **start off/out**) to begin your life or profession in a particular way or place: **[+as/in]** *She started as a dancer in the 1950s.* | *It's difficult for new lawyers to* ***get started*** *in private practice.*

9 ROAD/RIVER/PATH ETC [I always + adv/prep] if a river, road, path etc starts somewhere, it begins in that place: *The trail starts immediately behind the hotel.* | **[+in/at]** *The race will start at the town hall.*

10 PRICES/AMOUNTS [I always + adv/prep] if prices, amounts, or rates start at or from a particular number, that is the lowest number at which you can get or buy something: **[+at/from]** *Room prices start from £25 a night.*

11 start from scratch/zero to begin doing a job or activity completely from the beginning: *There were no textbooks, so the teachers had to start from scratch.*

12 DELIBERATELY BEGIN STH [T] to deliberately make something start happening, especially something bad: *I* ***started*** *a* ***fire*** *to warm the place up.* | **start a fight/argument** *Oh, don't go trying to start an argument.* | *Other girls were* ***starting rumours*** *about me.*

13 to start with *spoken* **a)** said when talking about the beginning of a situation, especially when it changes later: *I was pretty nervous to start with, but after a while I was fine.* **b)** said to emphasize the first of a list of facts or opinions

S

you are stating: *There are problems. To start with, neither of us likes housework.*

14 be back where you started to try to do something and fail, so that you finish in the same situation that you were in before: *A lot of people who lose weight gain it back over time, and end up back where they started.*

15 SPORTS [I,T] if a player starts in a game, or if someone starts them, they begin playing when the game begins, especially because they are one of the best players on the team: **[+for]** *Astacio started for the Dodgers on Tuesday night.*

16 start a family to have your first baby: *We're not ready to start a family yet.*

17 start afresh/anew to stop doing what you are doing and begin doing it again in a better or different way: *She saw her new job as a chance to start afresh.*

18 sb started it! *spoken* used to say that someone else has caused an argument or problem: *'Don't hit her!' 'But she started it!'*

19 start something/anything to begin causing trouble: *It looks like Jess is trying to start something.*

20 MOVE SUDDENLY [I] to move your body suddenly, especially because you are surprised or afraid SYN **jump**: *A loud knock at the door made her start.* | **[+from]** *Emma started from her chair and rushed to the window.*

21 start young to begin doing something when you are young, especially when it is unusual to do it: *Woods started young, and was coached by his father.*

22 don't (you) start! *BrE spoken* used to tell someone to stop complaining, arguing, or annoying you: *'Mum, I don't like this ice cream.' 'Oh, don't you start!'*

GRAMMAR

Start belongs to a group of verbs where the same noun can be the subject of the verb or its object.

- You can say: *We'll start the show at 7.30.* In this sentence, 'the show' is the object of **start**.
- You can say: *The show will start at 7.30.* In this sentence, 'the show' is the subject of **start**.

GRAMMAR GUIDE ▸ VERBS

start back *phr v* to begin returning to the place you came from: **[+to/down/up etc]** *I started back down the mountain to camp.*

start in *phr v AmE*

1 to begin doing something, especially with a lot of effort: *I decided to just start in and see what I could do.* | **[+on]** *Lilly started in on her burger.*

2 to begin criticizing someone or complaining to them about something: **[+on]** *Mom turned away from Rose and started in on me.*

start off *phr v*

1 to begin something in a particular way, or to begin in a particular way: **start sth ↔ off with sth/by doing sth** *The theater company started off their new season with a Shakespeare play.* | **start off with sth/by doing sth** *I started off by drawing the flowers I had collected.*

2 to be a particular thing or have a particular quality at the beginning of something, especially when this changes later: *The puppies start off white, and get their black spots later.* | **[+as]** *The games start off as a social event, but players soon become competitive.* | *I started off as a drummer.*

3 start sth ↔ off to make something begin happening: *We're not sure what starts the process off.*

4 start sb ↔ off to help someone begin an activity: **[+with]** *He started me off with some stretching exercises.*

5 to begin going somewhere: *I sat in the car for a few minutes before starting off.* | **[+to/towards/back etc]** *She started off to school in her new uniform.*

6 start sb off *BrE informal* to make someone get angry or start laughing, by saying something: *Don't say that; that'll just start him off.* | **start sb off doing sth** *He made her jump, and that started her off giggling.*

start on sb/sth *phr v*

1 to begin doing something or using something: *You'd better start on your homework.*

2 start sb on sth to make someone start doing something regularly, especially because it will be good for them: *Try starting your baby on solid foods at four months old.*

3 *BrE informal* to begin criticizing someone or complaining to them about something: **[+at]** *Ray's wife started on at him about spending too much time in the pub.*

start out *phr v*

1 to begin happening or existing in a particular way, especially when this changes later: **[+as]** *'The Star' started out as a small weekly newspaper.* | *The leaves start out a pale green, and later get darker.*

THESAURUS: start

TO START DOING SOMETHING

start to begin doing something: *I'm starting a new job next week.* | *It's time we started.*

begin to start doing something. **Begin** is more formal than **start**, and is used especially in written English: *He began to speak.* | *The orchestra began playing.* | *Shall we begin?*

commence *formal* to start doing something: *The company will commence drilling next week.* | *Work was commenced on the next power station.*

get down to sth to finally start doing something, especially your work: *Come on, Sam – it's time you got down to some homework.* | *We'd better* ***get down to business***.

set off to start a journey: *What time do you have to set off in the morning?* | *I usually set off for work at about 8.30.*

set out to start a long journey: *The ship set out from Portsmouth on July 12th.*

embark on sth *especially written* to start something, especially something new, difficult, or exciting: *The Law Society has embarked on a major programme of reform.*

resume *formal* to start doing something again after stopping it or being interrupted: *Normal train services will be resumed on April 5th.*

get cracking *informal* to start doing something or going somewhere: *I think we should get cracking straightaway.*

TO START HAPPENING

start/begin to begin: *What time does the film start?*

begin to start. Begin is more formal than **start** and is used especially in written English: | *The trial began in March.* | *Work on the new bridge will begin early next year.*

open to start being shown to the public – used about a play, show, or exhibition: *A major exhibition of her work will open in New York in November.*

commence *formal* to start happening: *The voting has already commenced.* | *The work is scheduled to commence in April.*

get under way to start happening or being done – used especially about something that is likely to last a long time: *Construction work is getting under way on a new train network.* | *Discussions concerning the plan got under way on April 2.*

break out to start happening – used especially about a fire, a fight, war, or a disease: *Police were called in when fighting broke out in the crowd.* | *The blaze broke out on the third floor of the hotel.*

kick off *informal* to start – used especially about a football game or a meeting: *The match is due to kick off this afternoon at Wembley Stadium.*

2 to begin your life or profession, or an important period of time: *When the band first started out, they played at small clubs.* | **[+as]** *She started out as a model.* | **[+on]** *young couples starting out on their life together*
3 to begin going somewhere: *Oliver started out at five, when it was still dark.*
start over *phr v AmE* to start doing something again from the beginning, especially because you want to do it better: *If you make a mistake, just erase it and start over.*
start up *phr v*
1 if you start up a business, company etc, or it starts up, it begins to exist: *Tax breaks help new companies start up.* | **start sth ↔ up** *Jordan started up a band of his own.*
2 if an engine, car etc starts up, or you start it up, it begins working: *The driver got back into the car and started up.* | **start sth ↔ up** *Rory started up the engine and got the vehicle moving.*
3 if a sound, activity, or event starts up, it begins to exist or happen: *The crickets had started up now that it was evening.*

start² ●●● S1 W2 *n*
1 OF AN ACTIVITY/EVENT [C usually singular] the first part of an activity or event, or the point at which it begins to develop: **[+of]** *We arrived late and missed the start of the film.* | **(right) from the start** *We've had problems with this project right from the start.* | *She read the letter* ***from start to finish*** *without looking up.* | **get off to a good/bad etc start** (=begin well or badly) *a free bottle of wine to get your holiday off to a great start* | **a rocky/shaky/slow etc start** (=a bad beginning) *After a rocky start, the show is now very popular.* | *He wanted an* ***early start*** *on his election campaign.*
THESAURUS ▸ BEGINNING
2 OF A PERIOD OF TIME [C usually singular] the first part of a particular period of time SYN **beginning**: **[+of]** *Since the start of 1992, the company has doubled in size.* | **the start of the year/day/season** *the start of an election year*
3 make a start (on sth) to begin doing something: *I'll make a start on the washing-up.*
4 SUDDEN MOVEMENT [singular] a sudden movement of your body, usually caused by fear or surprise: **with a start** *Ted woke up with a start and felt for the light switch.* | *She said his name, and Tom* ***gave a start*** (=made a sudden movement).
5 good/better/healthy etc start (in life) if you have a good etc start, you have all the advantages or opportunities that your situation, your parents etc could provide to help you succeed: *Good health care for the mother before birth* ***gives*** *babies a healthy* ***start***. | *Naturally we want to give our kids the best possible* ***start in life***.
6 WHERE RACE BEGINS **the start** the place where a race begins: *The horses were all lined up at the start.*
7 BEING AHEAD [C usually singular] the amount of time or distance by which one person is ahead of another, especially in a race or competition: **[+on]** *The prisoners had a three-hour start on their pursuers.* → HEAD START(2)
8 for a start *BrE informal* used to emphasize the first of a list of facts or opinions you are stating: *Well, for a start, the weather was horrible.*
9 be a start *spoken* used to say that something you have achieved may not be impressive, but it will help with a bigger achievement: *One exercise class a week isn't enough, but* ***it's a start***.
10 JOB a) [C usually singular] the beginning of someone's job, which they will develop in the future, especially a job that involves acting, writing, painting etc: *Pacino* ***got*** *his* ***start*** *on the stage, before his success in films.* | *I* ***gave*** *you your* ***start***, *so remember me when you win the Pulitzer Prize.* **b)** [C usually plural] a job that has just started, a business that has just been started, or someone who has just started a new job: *The number of business starts plummeted 10.5% during the second half of the year.* | *a training course for* ***new starts***
11 starts (*also* **housing starts**) [plural] *technical* when people begin to build a number of new houses
12 SPORT [C usually plural] **a)** a race or competition that someone has taken part in: *The horse Exotic Wood was unbeaten in five starts.* **b)** an occasion when a player plays when a sports match begins: *Jackson played in 353 games, with 314 starts.* → FALSE START, → **fresh start** at FRESH¹(4), → **in/by fits and starts** at FIT³(7)

start·er /ˈstɑːtə $ ˈstɑːrtər/ ●●○ *n* [C]
1 *BrE* a small amount of food eaten at the start of a meal before the main part SYN **appetizer** *AmE*: *We had soup* ***as a starter***, *followed by steak.*
2 a person, horse, car etc that is in a race when it starts: *Of the seven starters, only three finished the race.*
3 someone who gives the signal for a race to begin: *The starter fired his gun.* | **under starter's orders** (=about to begin the race)
4 late starter *BrE* someone who begins doing something, especially a job, later in life than people generally do
5 for starters *spoken informal* used to emphasize the first of a series of facts, opinions, questions etc: *Well, for starters, you'll need to fill out an application form.*
6 a STARTER MOTOR → **NONSTARTER**, **SELF-STARTER**

ˈstarter home *n* [C] a small house or apartment bought by people who are buying their first home

ˈstarter ˌmotor *n* [C] an electric motor for starting an engine

ˈstarter pack (*also* **ˈstarter kit**) *n* [C] the basic equipment and instructions that you need to start doing something

ˈstarting ˌblocks *n* [plural] the pair of blocks fastened to the ground that a runner pushes their feet against at the start of a race

ˈstarting gate *n* [C] a gate or pair of gates that open to allow a horse or dog to start running in a race

ˈstarting line *n* [C] the line where a race begins

ˈstarting ˌpoint *n* [C usually singular] **1** an idea or situation from which a discussion, process etc can develop: **[+for]** *The article provides a starting point for discussion.* **2** a place from where a journey starts

ˈstarting price *n* [C usually singular] **1** the lowest possible price for a particular type of thing such as a car or house without any special features, or the lowest price you are willing to accept for something you are selling **2** *BrE* the final ODDS that are offered just before a horse or dog race begins

start·le /ˈstɑːtl $ ˈstɑːrtl/ ●○○ *v* [T] to make someone suddenly surprised or slightly shocked: *Sorry, I didn't mean to startle you.* | **be startled to do sth** *I was startled to see Amanda.* —**startled** *adj*: *a startled expression*

start·ling /ˈstɑːtlɪŋ $ ˈstɑːrt-/ *adj* very unusual or surprising: *Paddy's words had a startling effect on the children.* | *a startling discovery* | **it is startling to do sth** *It is startling to read that his father never visited him in hospital.* —**startlingly** *adv*

ˈstart-up¹ *adj* [only before noun] connected with starting a new business: *start-up costs*

start-up² *n* [C] a new small company or business, especially one whose work involves computers or the Internet: *an Internet start-up*

ˌstar ˈturn *n* [C] *BrE* the most successful person in a group of people of the same type, especially the most successful actor, musician, or sports player

starv·a·tion /stɑːˈveɪʃən $ stɑːr-/ *n* **1** [U] suffering or death caused by lack of food → **hunger**: *people dying of starvation* **2 starvation diet** *informal* when you eat very little food, especially to become thinner **3 starvation wages** extremely low wages

starve /stɑːv $ stɑːrv/ ●●○ S3 *v*
1 [I] to suffer or die because you do not have enough to eat: *Thousands of people will starve if food doesn't reach the city.* | *pictures of starving children* | *They'll either die from the cold or* ***starve to death*** (=die from lack of food).
2 [T] to prevent someone from having enough food to live: *The poor dog looked like it had been starved.*
3 be starving (*also* **be starved** *AmE*) to be very hungry: *You must be starving!*
starve sb/sth **of** sth (*also* **starve sb/sth for sth** *AmE*) *phr v* to not give something that is needed: **be starved of sth**

S

The schools are starved of funding. | **be starved for sth** *The poor kid's just starved for attention.*

starve sb ↔ **out** *phr v* to force someone to leave a place by preventing them from getting food: *If we can't blast them out, we'll starve them out!*

stash¹ /stæʃ/ *v* [T always + adv/prep] *informal* to store something secretly or safely somewhere: **stash sth away** *He* **has** *money* **stashed away** *in the Bahamas.* | **[+in/under]** *You can stash your gear in here.*

stash² *n* [C] an amount of something that is kept in a secret place, especially money, weapons, or drugs SYN **hoard**: *Mike went into the bedroom to check on his stash.* | **[+of]** *a stash of drugs*

sta·sis /ˈsteɪsɪs $ ˈsteɪ-, ˈstæ-/ *n* [U] *technical or formal* a state or period in which there is no change or development

state¹ /steɪt/ ●●● S1 W2 *n*

1 CONDITION [C] the physical or mental condition that someone or something is in: **[+of]** *There are fears for the state of the country's economy.* | **in a bad/terrible etc state** *When we bought the house, it was in a terrible state.* | **sb's mental/physical/emotional state** *Frankly, I wouldn't trust his emotional state right now.* | *She was in an extremely confused* **state of mind**. | **in no fit state to do sth** (=should not do something because you are not in a suitable condition) *David's in no fit state to drive.* | *She can't go home now.* **Look at the state of** *her!* | **be in a good/bad state of repair** (=be in good condition and not need repairing, or be in bad condition) *The boat was in a good state of repair.* | *The country was* **in a state of war** (=officially fighting a war). | *Water exists in three states: liquid, gaseous, and solid.* → STATE OF EMERGENCY

2 GOVERNMENT [singular, U] (*also* **the State**) *especially BrE* the government or political organization of a country: *The state has allocated special funds for the emergency.* | **state employees/property/regulations etc** *limits on salary increases for state workers* | **state-owned/state-funded/state-subsidized etc** (=owned, paid for etc by the government) *a state-funded community housing project* | **matters/affairs of state** (=the business of the government) → WELFARE STATE

3 COUNTRY [C] a country considered as a political organization: *a NATO* **member state** (=a country belonging to NATO) | **democratic/one-party/totalitarian etc state** → POLICE STATE THESAURUS COUNTRY

4 PART OF A COUNTRY [C] (*also* **State** *BrE*) one of the areas with limited law-making powers that together make up a country controlled by a central government, such as the US and Australia → **province**, **county**, **region**: *Queensland is one of the states of Australia.* | *the state of Iowa* | **state employees/property/regulations etc** *the state government* | *state and federal taxes*

5 the States *spoken* a word meaning the US, used especially by someone when they are outside the US: *Which part of the States would you suggest I visit?*

6 be in a state/get into a state *BrE spoken* to be or become very nervous, anxious, or excited: *Mum and Dad were in a right state when I got in.*

7 OFFICIAL CEREMONY [U] the official ceremonies and events connected with government or rulers: *the Queen's first* **state visit** *here in 17 years* | *music for* **state occasions** (=special public events)

8 state of affairs *formal* a situation: **unsatisfactory/sad/sorry etc state of affairs** *I must say this is a very unsatisfactory state of affairs.*

9 the state of play *especially BrE* **a)** the position reached in an activity or process that has not finished yet: *What is the state of play in the current negotiations?* **b)** the score in a sports game

10 lie in state if the body of an important person who has just died lies in state, it is put in a public place so that people can go and show their respect

state² ●●○ S3 W2 *v* [T]

1 to formally say or write a piece of information or your opinion: *Please state your name and address.* | *Rembert again stated his intention to resign from Parliament.* | *The government needs to clearly state its policy on UN intervention.* | **state (that)** *The witness stated that he had not seen the woman before.* | *Fine, but aren't you just* **stating the obvious** *here?* THESAURUS SAY

2 if a document, newspaper, ticket etc states information, it contains the information written clearly: *The price of the tickets is stated on the back.*

ˌstate atˈtorney *n* [C] *AmE* a lawyer who represents a US state in court cases

ˌstate ˈbenefit *n* [C,U] *BrE* money given by the government in Britain to people who are poor, without a job, ill etc

ˈstate court *n* [C] a court in the US which deals with legal cases that are concerned with state laws or a state's CONSTITUTION

ˈState Deˌpartment *n* **the State Department** the US government department that deals with anything connected with foreign countries

state·hood /ˈsteɪthʊd/ *n* [U] **1** the condition of being an independent nation **2** the condition of being one of the states that make up a nation such as the US: **achieve/obtain/gain statehood** *Utah obtained statehood in 1896.*

State·house /ˈsteɪthaʊs/ *n* [C usually singular] the building where people who make laws in a US state do their work

state·less /ˈsteɪtləs/ *adj formal* not officially being a citizen of any country: *Millions of refugees remain stateless.* —**statelessness** *n* [U]

ˌstate ˈline *n* [C] the border between two states in the US: *We crossed the state line into Missouri.*

state·ly /ˈsteɪtli/ *adj* **1** done slowly and with a lot of ceremony: *the stately progress of the procession* **2** impressive in style and size: *stately buildings* —**stateliness** *n* [U]

ˌstately ˈhome *n* [C] *BrE* a large house in the countryside in Britain which has historical interest, especially one open to the public

state·ment¹ /ˈsteɪtmənt/ ●●● S2 W1 *n*

1 [C] something you say or write, especially publicly or officially, to let people know your intentions or opinions, or to record facts: *In an official statement, she formally announced her resignation.* | **[+on/about]** *the prime minister's recent statements on Europe* THESAURUS SPEECH

2 [C] a record showing amounts of money paid, received, owed etc: *the company's annual financial statements* | *I haven't received my* **bank statement** *for last month yet.*

3 [C] something you do, make, wear etc that causes people to have a certain opinion about you: *The type of car you drive* **makes a statement** *about you.* | *a fashion statement*

4 [U] *formal* the act of expressing something in words: *presentation and clarity of statement*

COLLOCATIONS

VERBS

make a statement (=say something, especially in public) *The minister will make a statement on the matter tomorrow.*

give a statement (=make a statement, especially to the police) *He gave a statement to the police.*

issue/release/put out a statement (=give a written statement to newspapers, TV etc) | **take/get a statement from sb** | **withdraw your statement** (=say that a statement you gave is not true)

ADJECTIVES/NOUN + statement

a short/brief statement *Police last night issued a brief statement about the incident.*

a clear statement (=giving an opinion clearly) *The article was a clear statement of his beliefs.*

a sweeping statement (=one that is too general) *Researchers do not want to make any sweeping statements at this stage.*

a false/misleading statement (=one that is not true) | **an official statement** | **a formal statement** (=one you must sign to show that it is true) | **a public statement** (=one made in public) | **a written statement** | **a prepared statement** (=one that is prepared and then read out) | **a sworn statement** (=one that you officially promise is true) | **a policy statement** (=one that explains a government policy) | **a mission statement** (=one in which an organization states its aims)

statement[2] *v* [T] *BrE* if an education authority statements a child who has special educational needs, they give a school additional money to help teach that child

statement[3] *adj* [only before noun] statement pieces of jewellery, shoes etc are very noticeable and impressive – used especially in magazines

ˌstate of eˈmergency *n* (*plural* **states of emergency**) [C] when a government gives itself special powers in order to try to control an unusually difficult or dangerous situation, especially when this involves limiting people's freedom: *After* ***declaring*** *a* ***state of emergency****, the government arrested all opposition leaders.*

ˌstate-of-the-ˈart *adj* using the most modern and recently developed methods, materials, or knowledge: *state-of-the-art technology | His new laptop is state-of-the-art.* **THESAURUS** ADVANCED, MODERN

ˌstate ˈpark *n* [C] a large park owned and managed by a US state, often in an area of natural beauty

state·room /ˈsteɪtrʊm, -ruːm/ *n* [C] **1** a private room or place for sleeping on a ship **2** one of the large rooms in a palace

ˈstate ˌschool *n* [C] **1** *BrE* a British school which receives money from the government and provides free education → **public school 2** *AmE informal* a college or university that receives money from the US state it is in, to help pay its costs

ˌState's ˈevidence *n AmE* **turn State's evidence** if a criminal turns State's evidence, they give information in a court of law about other criminals

states·man /ˈsteɪtsmən/ ●○○ *n* (*plural* **statesmen** /-mən/) [C] a political or government leader, especially one who is respected as being wise and fair: *a respected* ***elder statesman*** —**statesmanship** *n* [U]

states·man·like /ˈsteɪtsmənlaɪk/ *adj* showing the qualities of a statesman – used to show approval: *his statesmanlike handling of the crisis*

ˌstate ˈtrooper *n* [C] a member of a police force that is controlled by one of the US state governments, who works anywhere in that state

ˌstate uniˈversity *n* (*plural* **state universities**) [C] a university in the US which receives money from a state to help pay its costs

state·wide /ˈsteɪtwaɪd/ *adj, adv* affecting or involving the whole of a US state: *a statewide poll | a model that could be used in towns statewide*

stat·ic[1] /ˈstætɪk/ ●○○ *adj* not moving, changing, or developing OPP **dynamic**: *Economists predict that house prices will remain static for a long period.*

static[2] *n* [U] **1** noise caused by electricity in the air that blocks or spoils the sound from radio or TV **2** static electricity **3** *especially AmE informal* complaints or opposition to a plan, situation, or action: *His promotion has caused a lot of static.* —**statically** /-kli/ *adv*

ˌstatic elecˈtricity *n* [U] electricity that is not flowing in a current, but collects on the surface of an object and gives you a small ELECTRIC SHOCK

stat·ics /ˈstætɪks/ *n* [U] the science dealing with the forces that produce balance in objects that are not moving → **dynamics**

stat·in /ˈstætɪn $ ˈstætn/ *n* [C,U] a drug that is used to lower CHOLESTEROL and reduce the risk of getting heart disease

sta·tion[1] /ˈsteɪʃən/ ●●● S1 W1 *n*

1 TRAIN/BUS [C] a place where trains or buses regularly stop so that passengers can get on and off, goods can be loaded etc, or the buildings at such a place → **terminus**: *I want to get off at the next station. | Grand Central Station | Is there a waiting room in the station?* | **train station/railway station** *BrE* | *the city bus station*

2 CENTRE FOR A SERVICE OR ACTIVITY [C] a building or place that is a centre for a particular kind of service or activity: *a police station | a fire station* | **petrol station** *BrE*, **gas station** *AmE* (=where petrol is sold) | **polling station** (=where you vote in an election) | *an Antarctic* ***research station*** → ACTION STATIONS

3 RADIO/TV [C] an organization which makes television or radio broadcasts, or the building where this is done: *New York jazz station WBGO | a local TV station*

4 SOCIAL RANK [C] *old-fashioned* your position in society: *Karen was definitely getting* ***ideas above her station*** (=higher than her social rank).

5 POSITION [C] *formal* a place where someone stands or sits in order to be ready to do something quickly if needed: *You're not to leave your station unless told.*

6 FARM [C] a large sheep or cattle farm in Australia or New Zealand

7 ARMY/NAVY [C] a small military establishment: *an isolated naval station*

station[2] *v* [T] **1** to send someone in the military to a particular place for a period of time as part of their military duty SYN **post**: *I was stationed overseas at the time.* **2** *formal* to move to a particular place and stand or sit there, especially in order to be able to do something quickly, or to cause someone to do this: *A security guard was stationed near the door.* GRAMMAR **Station** is usually passive.

sta·tion·a·ry /ˈsteɪʃənəri $ -neri/ ●○○ *adj* standing still instead of moving: *How did you manage to drive into a stationary vehicle?* ⚠ Do not confuse with the noun **stationery** (=writing materials such as paper).

ˈstation break *n* [C] a pause during a radio or television broadcast in the US, so that local stations can give their names or broadcast advertisements

sta·tion·er /ˈsteɪʃənə $ -ər/ *n* [C] *BrE* **1 stationer's** a shop that sells stationery **2** someone in charge of a shop that sells stationery

sta·tion·e·ry /ˈsteɪʃənəri $ -neri/ *n* [U] **1** paper for writing letters, usually with matching envelopes: *a letter on hotel stationery* **2** materials that you use for writing, such as paper, pens, pencils etc → see picture on *p. 1792*

ˈstation ˌhouse *n* [C] *AmE old-fashioned* the local office of the police in a town, part of a city etc SYN **police station**

ˈstation ˌmaster *n* [C] someone who is in charge of a railway station

ˈstation ˌwagon *n* [C] *AmE* a large car with extra space at the back, with a door there for loading and unloading SYN **estate car** *BrE*

sta·tis·tic /stəˈtɪstɪk/ ●●○ W3 AWL *n*

1 statistics a) [plural] a set of numbers which represent facts or measurements: *the* ***official*** *crime* ***statistics*** | **[+for]** *statistics for injuries at work |* ***Statistics show*** *that 50% of new businesses fail in their first year.* **b)** [U] the science of collecting and examining such numbers: *Statistics is a branch of mathematics.*

2 [singular] a single number which represents a fact or measurement: *The statistic comes from a study recently conducted by the British government.*

3 a statistic *informal* if someone is just a statistic, they are just another example of someone who has died because of a particular type of accident or disease: *We can't let these boys become just another statistic.* → **VITAL STATISTICS**

sta·tis·ti·cal /stəˈtɪstɪkəl/ ●●○ *adj* relating to statistics: ***statistical analysis*** | *statistical evidence* —**statistically** /-kli/ *adv*: *The variation is not statistically significant.*

stat·is·ti·cian /ˌstætəˈstɪʃən/ AWL *n* [C] someone who works with statistics

sta·tive /ˈsteɪtɪv/ *adj technical* a stative verb describes a state rather than an action or event, and is not usually used in PROGRESSIVE[1](3) forms, for example 'belong' in the sentence 'this book belongs to me'

stats /stæts/ *n* [plural] *informal* STATISTICS

stat·u·a·ry /ˈstætʃuəri $ -tʃueri/ *n* [U] *formal* statues: *a fine collection of Greek statuary*

S

STATIONERY

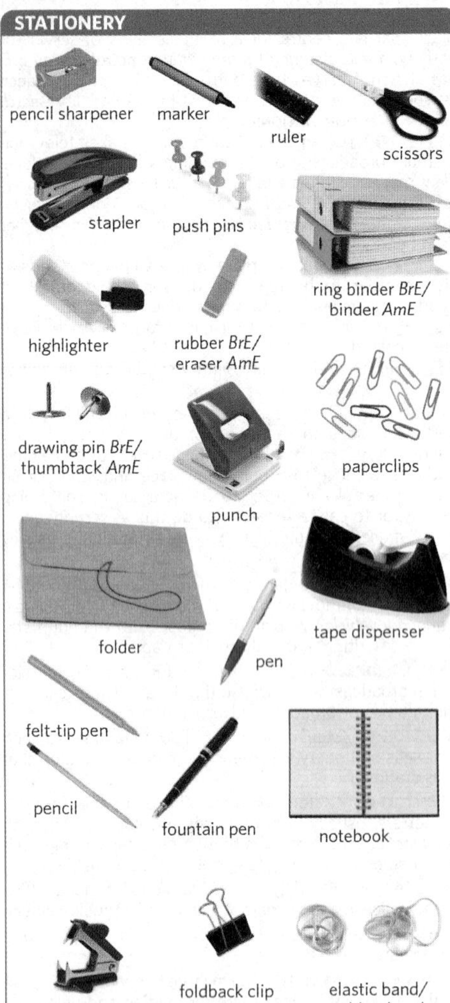

stat·ue /ˈstætʃuː/ ●●○ *n* [C] an image of a person or animal that is made in solid material such as stone or metal and is usually large → **sculpture**: *Churchill's **statue stands** outside the parliament building.* | *A bronze **statue** was **erected** in his honour.* | **[+of]** *Statues of Lenin were torn down all across Eastern Europe.*

ˌStatue of ˈLiberty, the a statue of a woman on Liberty Island, in New York Harbor, given to the US by France in 1884 to celebrate the American and French REVOLUTIONS. The woman is holding up a TORCH in her right hand and she represents freedom.

stat·u·esque /ˌstætʃuˈesk◂/ *adj* large and beautiful in an impressive way, like a statue: *a statuesque woman*

stat·u·ette /ˌstætʃuˈet/ *n* [C] a very small statue that can be put on a table or shelf

stat·ure /ˈstætʃə $ -ər/ *n* [U] *written* **1** the degree to which someone is admired or regarded as important: **of world/international/national stature** *Armstrong was a musician of world stature.* | *He **grew in stature*** (=became more admired or popular) *during the campaign.* | **[+as]** *his growing stature as an artist* **THESAURUS** REPUTATION
2 someone's height or size: *Bernard was short in stature, with a large head.*

sta·tus /ˈsteɪtəs $ ˈsteɪtəs, ˈstæ-/ ●●○ S3 W2 AWL *n*
1 [C,U] the official legal position or condition of a person, group, country etc → **standing**: *These documents have no **legal status** in Britain.* | *What is your **marital status*** (=are you married or not)?
2 [U] your social or professional rank or position, considered in relation to other people: **high/low status** *low-status jobs* | *Doctors have traditionally enjoyed high **social status**.*
3 [U] respect and importance that someone or something is given SYN **prestige**: *the status given to education* | *Mandela's status as a world leader*
4 the status of sth a situation at a particular time, especially in an argument, discussion etc: *What's the status of the trade talks?*

status quo /ˌsteɪtəs ˈkwəʊ $ ˌsteɪtəs ˈkwoʊ, ˌstæ-/ *n* **the status quo** the state of a situation as it is: **maintain/preserve/defend the status quo** (=not make any changes) *Will the West use its influence to maintain the status quo and not disrupt the flow of oil?*

ˈstatus ˌsymbol *n* [C] something that you have or own that you think shows high social rank or position: *A Rolls Royce is seen as a status symbol.*

stat·ute /ˈstætʃuːt/ ●○○ *n* [C]
1 a law passed by a parliament, council etc and formally written down: *Protection for the consumer is **laid down by statute*** (=established by law). **THESAURUS** RULE
2 a formal rule of an institution or organization: *College statutes forbid drinking on campus.*

ˈstatute book *n* **on the statute book** officially part of the law: *The government would like to see this new law on the statute book as soon as possible.*

ˈstatute law *n* [U] the whole group of written laws established by a parliament, council etc → **common law**

ˌstatute of limiˈtations *n* (*plural* **statutes of limitations**) [C] *law* a law which gives the period of time within which action may be taken on a legal question or crime

stat·u·to·ry /ˈstætʃətəri $ -tɔːri/ ●○○ *adj* fixed or controlled by law SYN **mandatory**: *statutory employment rights* | *She's below the **statutory age** for school attendance.* —**statutorily** *adv*

ˌstatutory ofˈfence *n* [C] *law* a crime that is described by a law and can be punished by a court

ˌstatutory ˈrape *n* [C] *law* the crime of having sex with someone who is younger than a particular age

staunch¹ /stɔːntʃ $ stɒːntʃ, stɑːntʃ/ *adj* [only before noun] giving strong loyal support to another person, organization, belief etc SYN **steadfast**: *a staunch conservative* | **staunch supporter/ally/advocate** *one of Bush's staunchest supporters* —**staunchly** *adv* —**staunchness** *n* [U]

staunch² (*also* **stanch** *AmE*) *v* [T] to stop the flow of liquid, especially of blood from a wound SYN **stem**: *He used a rag to staunch the flow of blood.*

stave¹ /steɪv/ *n* [C] **1** the set of five lines on which music is written **2** one of the thin curved pieces of wood fitted close together to form the sides of a BARREL

stave² *v*
stave sth ↔ **in** *phr v* (*past tense and past participle* **staved** *or* **stove** /stəʊv $ stoʊv/) to break something inwards: *The ship's side was stove in when it went onto the rocks.*
stave sth ↔ **off** *phr v* (*past tense and past participle* **staved**) to keep someone or something from reaching you or affecting you for a period of time: *She brought some fruit on the journey to **stave off hunger**.*

staves /steɪvz/ the plural of STAFF¹(2)

stay¹ /steɪ/ ●●● S1 W1 *v*
1 IN A PLACE [I] to remain in a place rather than leave: *They stayed all afternoon chatting.* | **stay (at) home** *I decided to stay home.* | **stay for a year/ten minutes/a week etc** *Isabel stayed for a year in Paris to study.* | **[+in]** *Stay in bed and drink plenty of liquids.* | *She **stayed late** to finish the report.* | **stay here/there** *Stay right there! I'll be back in a minute.* | **stay to dinner/stay for lunch etc** *Why don't you stay for supper?* | **[+behind/after]** *Some of the students stayed after class* (=remained after others had gone) *to talk.* | **stay and do sth** *I should stay and help.*
2 IN A CONDITION [I always + adv/prep, linking verb] to continue to be in a particular position, place, or state, without changing SYN **remain**: *Rollings will stay as chairman this*

year. | **[+adj]** *Eat right to stay healthy.* | *It was hard to stay awake.* | *Nine women gained weight, and four* ***stayed the same****.* | **[+away/in/on etc]** *Stay away from my daughter!* | *You stay on this road for a mile before turning off.* | **[+around]** *Most of her boyfriends don't stay around* (=stay with her) *very long.*

GRAMMAR: Linking verbs

Stay is a linking verb in this meaning. This type of verb links the subject of the sentence with an adjective or noun: *They're just trying to stay alive.* | *I hope we can stay friends.*

3 LIVE SOMEWHERE [I] to live in a place for a short time as a visitor or guest: *How long are they going to stay?* | **[+at/with]** *My mother is staying with us this week.* | **[+in]** *They're staying in the same hotel.* | **stay the night/stay overnight/stay over** (=stay from one evening to the next day) *Did you stay the night at Carolyn's?*

4 stay put *spoken* to remain in one place and not move: *Stay put until I get back.*

5 be here to stay to become accepted and used by most people: *Professional women's basketball is here to stay.*

6 stay after (school) to remain at school after the day's classes are finished, often as a punishment

7 stay the course *informal* to finish something in spite of difficulties: *Dieters should try hard to stay the course.*

8 stay tuned a) to continue watching or listening to the same television CHANNEL or radio station **b)** used to say that you should look or listen for more information about a particular subject at a later time: *The project is still under discussion, so stay tuned.*

9 stay! used to tell a dog not to move

10 stay sb's hand *literary* to stop someone from doing something

11 stay an order/ruling/execution etc *law* if a judge stays an order, ruling etc, they stop a particular decision from being used or a particular action from happening → **stay in touch** at TOUCH[2](4)

THESAURUS

stay to not leave a place, or to be in a place for a particular period of time: *Stay where you are and don't move.* | *John only stayed at the party for a couple of hours.*

remain *formal* to stay somewhere. In written English, people often prefer to use **remain** rather than **stay**, because it sounds more formal: *Some 2,000 protesters remained outside the building and refused to leave.* | *The judge recommended that he remain in jail for the rest of his life.*

linger to stay in a place a little longer than you need to, because you are enjoying yourself, or because you hope to see someone or something: *He lingered outside the lecture hall, hoping for a chance to talk to her.* | *There are plenty of small cafés where you can linger over a cappuccino.*

loiter to stay in a place not doing anything – used when you think someone is waiting for the chance to do something bad or illegal: *The two men had been seen loitering in the area on the day that the car was stolen.*

hang around *informal* to stay somewhere not doing anything: *There are gangs of boys hanging around on street corners.* | *I don't mind hanging around for a few minutes.*

stick around *informal* to stay in the same place or situation for a period of time, especially while you are waiting for something to happen or someone to arrive: *I decided to stick around and see how it all turned out.*

stay in *phr v* to spend the evening at home rather than go out: *I was tired, so I decided to stay in.*

stay on *phr v* to continue to do a job or to study after the usual or expected time for leaving: *He resigned as chairman, but stayed on as an instructor.*

stay out *phr v*

1 to remain away from home during the evening or night: *He started* ***staying out late****, drinking.*

2 stay out of sth *spoken* to not get involved in an argument or fight: *You* ***stay out of it****. It's none of your business.*

stay up *phr v* to not go to bed at the time you would normally go to bed: *We stayed up all night talking.* | *I let the kids* ***stay up late*** *on Fridays.*

stay² ●●○ S3 *n*

1 [C usually singular] a limited time of living in a place: **[+in/at]** *I met her towards the end of my stay in Los Angeles.* | **long/short/overnight etc stay** *a short stay in the hospital*

2 [C,U] *law* the stopping or delay of an action because a judge has ordered it: **stay of execution** (=a delay in punishing someone by killing them)

3 [C] a strong wire or rope used for supporting a ship's MAST

4 [C] a short piece of plastic or wire used to keep a shirt COLLAR stiff

ˈstay-at-ˌhome *adj* [only before noun] staying at home, rather than working somewhere else, usually in order to take care of children: *a stay-at-home mom*

stay·ca·tion /steɪˈkeɪʃən/ *n* [C] a holiday that you spend relaxing at or near your home rather than travelling somewhere else – used especially in newspapers and magazines: *You can save money by having a staycation rather than a vacation.*

stay·er /ˈsteɪə $ -ər/ *n* [C] *BrE* a horse or person that is able to continue to the end of a long race, job etc

ˈstaying ˌpower *n* [U] the ability or energy to continue doing something difficult until it is finished → **stamina**: *a team with staying power*

St Ber·nard /sənt ˈbɜːnəd $ ˌseɪnt bərˈnɑːrd/ *n* [C] a large strong dog that in the past was trained to help find people who were lost in the snow

STD /ˌes tiː ˈdiː/ *n* [C,U] *medical* (***sexually transmitted disease***) a disease that one person passes to another through having sex, such as AIDS or HERPES

stead /sted/ *n* **1 do sth in sb's stead** *formal* to do something that someone else usually does or was going to do: *Pearson was appointed to go in Harrison's stead.* **2 stand/serve/hold sb in good stead** to be very useful to someone when needed: *His years of training were standing him in good stead.*

stead·fast /ˈstedfɑːst $ -fæst/ *adj literary* **1** faithful and very loyal: *her father's steadfast love for her* **2** being certain that you are right about something and refusing to change your opinion in any way: **[+in]** *Dr Faraday* ***remained steadfast*** *in his plea of innocence.* —**steadfastly** *adv* —**steadfastness** *n* [U]

stead·i·ly /ˈstedəli/ ●●○ *adv*

1 gradually and continually: *The company's exports have* ***grown steadily****.* | *Debt was* ***increasing steadily****.* | *The track climbs steadily.*

2 in a calm way, without stopping: *He looked steadily at his uncle.*

stead·y¹ /ˈstedi/ ●●○ W3 *adj*

1 CONTINUOUS continuing or developing gradually or without stopping, and not likely to change: *Paul is making steady progress.* | *a steady rain* | **hold/remain steady** *Employment is holding steady at 96%.* | **steady stream/flow/trickle etc** *a steady stream of traffic*

2 NOT MOVING firmly held in a particular position and not moving or shaking → **stable**: **hold/keep sth steady** *Keep the camera steady while you take a picture.* | *It takes* ***a steady hand*** *to perform surgery.*

3 steady job/work/income a job or work that will definitely continue over a long period of time: *It's hard to find a steady, well-paying job.*

4 VOICE/LOOK if someone's voice is steady, or they look at you in a steady way, they seem calm and do not stop speaking or looking at you: *There were tears in her eyes, but her voice was steady.* | *He could not meet Connor's steady gaze.*

S

5 PERSON someone who is steady is sensible and you can depend on them: *a steady worker*
6 steady boyfriend/girlfriend someone that you have been having a romantic relationship with for a long time
7 steady relationship a serious and strong relationship that continues for a long time —**steadiness** *n* [U]

steady² *v* (**steadied**, **steadying**, **steadies**) **1** [I,T] to hold someone or something so they become more balanced or controlled, or to become more balanced or controlled: **steady yourself** *He reached the chair and steadied himself.* | *The plane steadied, and the passengers relaxed.* **2** [I] to stop increasing or decreasing and remain about the same SYN **stabilize**: *The dollar has steadied after early losses on the money markets.* **3** [I,T] to become calmer, or to make someone do this: *Tamar took a deep breath to* ***steady*** *her* ***nerves***. | *Jess is a steadying influence on the rest of the team.*

steady³ *adv* **go steady (with sb)** to have a long regular romantic relationship with someone

steady⁴ *n* (*plural* **steadies**) [C] *AmE old-fashioned informal* a BOYFRIEND or GIRLFRIEND that someone has been having a romantic relationship with

steady⁵ *interjection* **1** used when you want to tell someone to be careful or not to cause an accident: *Steady! You nearly knocked me over.* **2 steady on!** *BrE informal* used when you think that what someone is saying or doing is too extreme: *Steady on! That bottle's got to last all night.*

ˌsteady ˈstate ˌtheory *n* [singular] *technical* the idea that things in space have always existed and have always been moving away from each other as new atoms begin to exist → **big bang theory**

steak /steɪk/ ●●● S3 *n*
1 [C,U] good quality BEEF, or a large thick piece of any good quality red meat
2 cod/salmon/tuna etc steak a large thick piece of fish
3 [U] *BrE* BEEF that is not of very good quality and is used in making CASSEROLES etc

steak·house /ˈsteɪkhaʊs/ *n* [C] a restaurant that serves steak

ˌsteak tarˈtare *n* [U] steak that is cut into very small pieces and eaten raw, usually with a raw egg

steal¹ /stiːl/ ●●● S3 W3 *v* (*past tense* **stole** /stəʊl $ stoʊl/, *past participle* **stolen** /ˈstəʊlən $ ˈstoʊ-/)
1 TAKE STH [I,T] to take something that belongs to someone else: *Boys broke into a shop and stole £45 in cash.* | **[+from]** *He stole money from his parents.* | **steal sth from sb/sth** *He'd stolen the flowers from our garden.*
2 USE IDEAS [I,T] to use someone else's ideas without getting permission or without admitting that they are not your own ideas SYN **pinch**: *Inventors know that someone is always going to try to steal their designs.* | **steal sth from sb** *A well-known scientist was accused of stealing ideas from his former student.*
3 MOVE SOMEWHERE [I always + adv/prep] to move quietly without anyone noticing you SYN **creep**: **[+into/across etc]** *He dressed quietly and stole out of the house.*
4 steal the show/limelight/scene to do something, especially when you are acting in a play, that makes people pay more attention to you than to other people: *Elwood stole the show with a marvellous performance.*
5 steal a look/glance etc to look at someone or something quickly and secretly
6 SPORT **a)** [I,T] to run to the next BASE before someone hits the ball in the sport of baseball **b)** [T] to suddenly take control of the ball, PUCK etc when the other team had previously had control of it, for example in BASKETBALL or ICE HOCKEY: *Roy* ***steals the ball*** *four times in the first half.*
7 steal a kiss to kiss someone quickly when they are not expecting it
8 steal a march on sb to gain an advantage over someone by doing something that they had planned to do before them: *He was afraid another scholar was going to steal a march on him and publish first.*
9 steal sb's thunder to get the success and praise someone else should have got, by doing what they had intended to do
10 steal sb's heart *literary* to make someone fall in love with you → **beg, borrow, or steal** at BEG(8)

THESAURUS

steal to illegally take something that belongs to someone else: *The thieves stole over £10,000 worth of computer equipment.* | *Thousands of cars get stolen every year.*
take to steal something – used when it is clear from the situation that you mean that someone takes something dishonestly: *The boys broke into her house and took all her money.* | *They didn't take much – just a few items of jewellery.*
burgle *BrE*, **burglarize** *AmE* [usually passive] to go into someone's home and steal things, especially when the owners are not there: *Their house was burgled while they were away.* | *If you leave windows open, you are asking to be burgled.*
rob to steal money or other things from a bank, shop, or person: *The gang were convicted of robbing a bank in Essex.* | *An elderly woman was robbed at gunpoint in her own home.*
mug to attack someone in the street and steal something from them: *People in this area are frightened of being mugged when they go out.* | *Someone tried to mug me outside the station.*
nick/pinch *BrE informal* to steal something: *Someone's nicked my wallet!* | *When I came back, my car had been pinched.*
embezzle to steal money from the organization you work for, especially money that you are responsible for: *Government officials embezzled more than $2.5 million from the department.*
shoplifting stealing things from a shop by taking them when you think no one is looking: *Shoplifting costs stores millions of pounds every year.*
phishing the activity of dishonestly persuading people to give you their credit card details over the Internet, so that you can steal money from their bank account: *Phishing is becoming very popular with computer criminals.*

steal² *n* [C] **1 be a steal** *informal* to be very cheap: *an excellent seafood dish that is a steal at $8.25* **2** the act of suddenly taking control of the ball when the other team had previously had control of it, especially in BASKETBALL: *Johnson had ten points and a steal in the first half.* **3** the act of running to the next BASE before someone hits the ball in the sport of baseball

stealth /stelθ/ *n* [U] **1** when you do something very quietly, slowly, or secretly, so that no one notices you: *Cats rely on stealth to catch their prey.* **2** (*also* **Stealth**) a system of making military aircraft that cannot be discovered by RADAR instruments: **stealth bomber/aircraft/fighter etc** (=a plane made using this system)

ˈstealth tax *n* [C] *BrE* an extra tax or charge that a government introduces in such a way that people do not realize that they are paying more money – used to show disapproval

stealth·y /ˈstelθi/ *adj* moving or doing something quietly and secretly: *the stealthy approach of the soldiers* —**stealthily** *adv*

steam¹ /stiːm/ ●●○ W3 *n* [U]
1 GAS the hot mist that water produces when it is boiled: ***Steam rose*** *from the hot tub.*
2 MIST ON SURFACE the mist that forms on windows, mirrors etc when warm wet air suddenly becomes cold
3 POWER power that is produced by boiling water to make steam, in order to make things work or move: *The engines are driven by steam.* | **steam engine/train/hammer etc** (=an engine etc that works by steam power)
4 let/blow off steam to get rid of your anger, excitement, or energy in a way that does not harm anyone by doing something active
5 get/pick/build up steam (*also* **gather/gain steam**) **a)** if an engine picks up steam, it gradually starts to go faster **b)** if plans, beliefs etc pick up steam, they gradually become

more important and more people become interested in them: *The election campaign is picking up steam.*
6 run out of steam (*also* **lose steam**) to no longer have the energy or the desire to continue doing something, especially because you are tired: *I usually just let her yell until she runs out of steam.*
7 under your own steam if you go somewhere under your own steam, you get there without help from anyone else: *I'll get to the restaurant under my own steam.*
8 RAILWAY a railway system in which the trains use steam for power: *the age of steam* → **full steam ahead** at FULL[1](18)

steam² ●●○ *v*
1 [I] if something steams, steam rises from it, especially because it is hot: *A pot was* ***steaming*** *on top of the cooker.*
2 [T] to cook something in steam → **boil**: *Steam the vegetables lightly.* | *steamed broccoli* THESAURUS▶ COOK
3 [I always + adv/prep] to travel somewhere in a boat or train that uses steam to produce power: **[+into/from etc]** *We steamed from port to port.*
4 [I] *especially BrE* to go somewhere very quickly: **[+in/down]** *Geoff steamed in, ten minutes late.*
5 be steaming (mad) (*also* **be steamed (up)**) *AmE spoken* to be very angry

steam ahead *phr v* to start doing something very quickly: *The company is steaming ahead with its investment programme.*

steam sth ↔ **open/off** *phr v* to use steam to open an envelope or to remove a stamp from an envelope

steam up *phr v* to cover something with steam, or to become covered with steam: *My glasses are all steamed up.* | **steam sth ↔ up** *A pan was boiling on the stove, steaming up the windows.* → STEAMED-UP

steam·boat /ˈstiːmbəʊt $ -boʊt/ *n* [C] a boat that uses steam for power and is sailed along rivers and coasts

ˈsteam clean *v* [T] to clean something by using a machine that produces steam

ˌsteamed-ˈup *adj* [not before noun] *informal* excited and angry or worried: *Don't get so steamed-up about it – it's not really important.*

steam·er /ˈstiːmə $ -ər/ *n* [C] **1** a STEAMSHIP **2** a container used to cook food in steam **3** a member of a large group of young people who go into a public place, surprise and frighten the people there, and then rob them

steam·ing¹ /ˈstiːmɪŋ/ *adj* **1** (*also* **steaming hot**) very hot: *It was a steaming hot day.* **2** very drunk – used in Scotland and northern England

steaming² *n* [U] a method of stealing in which a large group of young people go into a public place, surprise and frighten the people there, and then rob them

ˈsteam iron *n* [C] an electric IRON that produces steam in order to make clothes easier to press smooth

steam·punk /ˈstiːmpʌŋk/ *n* [U] a type of SCIENCE FICTION or FANTASY in which some things are like they were in the 19th century, and there are machines such as spacecraft or ROBOTS that are made in an old-fashioned way and do not use electricity

steam·roll /ˈstiːmrəʊl $ -roʊl/ *v* [T] *AmE* to steamroller

steam·roll·er¹ /ˈstiːmˌrəʊlə $ -ˌroʊlər/ *n* [C] **1** a heavy vehicle with very wide wheels that is driven over road surfaces to make them flat **2** someone who uses their power and influence to make sure that something happens the way they want it to

steamroller² *v* [T] *informal* to make sure something happens by using all your power and influence, or to defeat your opponents badly: *He steamrollered the bill through Parliament against fierce opposition.*

ˈsteam room *n* [C] a room filled with steam that people sit in to relax → **sauna**

steam·ship /ˈstiːmʃɪp/ *n* [C] a large ship that uses steam to produce power

ˈsteam ˌshovel *n* [C] *AmE* a large machine that digs and moves earth

steam·y /ˈstiːmi/ *adj* **1** full of steam or covered in steam: *steamy windows* **2** sexually exciting and slightly shocking: *a steamy love scene* **3** a steamy day or steamy weather feels hot and HUMID

steed /stiːd/ *n* [C] *literary* a strong fast horse

steel¹ /stiːl/ ●●○ S3 W3 *n*
1 [U] strong metal that can be shaped easily, consisting of iron and CARBON: *a steel bridge* | ***stainless steel*** (=steel that does not change colour) *knives*
2 [U] the industry that makes steel: *Sheffield is a major steel town.*
3 nerves of steel the ability to be brave and calm in a dangerous or difficult situation
4 [C] a thin bar of steel used for making knives sharp

steel² *v* [T] **steel yourself** to prepare yourself to do something that you know will be unpleasant or upsetting: **steel yourself to do sth** *He steeled himself not to look away.*

ˌsteel ˈband *n* [C] a group of people who play music on steel drums

ˌsteel ˈdrum *n* [C] a type of drum from the West Indies, made from oil BARRELS, which you hit in different areas to produce different musical sounds

ˌsteel guiˈtar (*also* **pedal steel guitar**) *n* [C] a musical instrument with ten strings that is played using a steel bar and a PEDAL (=a bar you press with your foot)

steel·mak·er /ˈstiːlmeɪkə $ -ər/ *n* [C] a company that makes steel —**steelmaking** *n* [U]

ˈsteel mill *n* [C] a factory where steel is made

ˌsteel ˈwool *n* [U] a rough material made of fine steel threads, that is used to make surfaces smooth, remove paint etc → **wire wool**

steel·work·er /ˈstiːlˌwɜːkə $ -ˌwɜːrkər/ *n* [C] someone who works in a factory where steel is made

steel·works /ˈstiːlwɜːks $ -wɜːrks/ *n* (*plural* **steelworks**) [C] a factory where steel is made

steel·y /ˈstiːli/ *adj* **1** extremely determined and very strong: *a look of* ***steely determination*** **2** if someone has steely eyes or is steely-eyed, they look very determined **3** having a grey colour like steel: *a steely sky*

steep¹ /stiːp/ ●●○ S3 *adj* (*comparative* **steeper**, *superlative* **steepest**)
1 a road, hill etc that is steep slopes at a high angle: *The road became rocky and steep.* | *a steep climb to the top*
2 steep prices, charges etc are unusually expensive OPP **low**: *steep rents*
3 involving a big increase or decrease SYN **sharp**: *steep cuts in benefits* | **steep increase/rise** *a steep increase in house prices* | **steep decrease/drop** *a steep drop in orders* —**steeply** *adv* —**steepness** *n* [U]

steep² *v* [I,T] **1 be steeped in history/tradition/politics etc** to have a lot of a particular quality: *a town steeped in history* **2** to put food in a liquid and leave it there, so that it becomes soft or has the same taste as the liquid, or so that it gives the liquid its taste: *Leave the tea bag to steep.*

steep·en /ˈstiːpən/ *v* [I,T] if a slope, road etc steepens, or if something steepens it, it becomes steeper

stee·ple /ˈstiːpəl/ *n* [C] a tall pointed tower on the roof of a church

stee·ple·chase /ˈstiːpəlˌtʃeɪs/ *n* [C] **1** a long race in which horses jump over gates, water etc **2** a long race in which people run and jump over fences, water etc

stee·ple·jack /ˈstiːpəlˌdʒæk/ *n* [C] someone whose work is repairing towers, tall CHIMNEYS etc

steer¹ /stɪə $ stɪr/ ●●○ *v*
1 CAR/BOAT ETC [I,T] to control the direction a vehicle is going, for example by turning a wheel: *He was steering with only one hand.* | **[+for/towards etc]** *Steer towards the left.*
2 CHANGE SB/STH [T] to guide someone's behaviour or the way a situation develops: **steer sb towards/away from/through etc sth** *Teachers try to steer pupils away from drugs.* | *Helen tried to* ***steer the conversation*** *away from herself.*
3 BE IN CHARGE OF [T always + adv/prep] to be in charge of an organization, team etc and make decisions that help it to be successful, especially during a difficult time: **steer**

sth through/to etc sth *McKinney steered the company through the recession.*
4 GUIDE SB TO A PLACE [T] to guide someone to a place, especially while touching them: **steer sb towards/to etc sth** *Joel steered Don and Louise towards the backyard.*
5 steer clear (of sb/sth) *informal* to avoid someone or something unpleasant or difficult: *Jo tried to steer clear of political issues.*
6 steer a course to choose a particular way of doing something: *Managers were allowed to steer their own course.* | *The government chose to* ***steer a middle course*** *between the two strategies* (=chose a strategy that was not extreme).

steer² *n* [C] a young male cow whose sex organs have been removed → **bullock**, **heifer**

steer·age /ˈstɪərɪdʒ $ ˈstɪr-/ *n* [U] the part of a passenger ship where people who had the cheapest tickets used to travel in the past

steer·ing /ˈstɪərɪŋ $ ˈstɪr-/ *n* [U] the parts of a car, boat etc that allow you to control its direction: *power steering*

ˈsteering comˌmittee *n* [C] a committee that guides or directs a particular activity

ˈsteering wheel ●●○ *n* [C] a wheel that you turn to control the direction of a car → see picture at CAR

steers·man /ˈstɪəzmən $ ˈstɪrz-/ *n* (*plural* **steersmen** /-mən/) [C] someone who steers a ship

stein /staɪn/ *n* [C] a tall cup for drinking beer, often decorated and with a lid

stel·lar /ˈstelə $ -ər/ *adj* [only before noun] **1** relating to the stars → INTERSTELLAR **2** *especially AmE* extremely good: *the company's stellar growth* | *McKellen gave a* ***stellar performance***. **3 go stellar** *BrE informal* if a POP band, actor etc goes stellar, they become very popular and famous: *There's a stand-up comedian, and my sources tell me he is about to go stellar.*

S

stem¹ /stem/ ●●○ *n* [C]
1 the long thin part of a plant, from which leaves, flowers, or fruit grow SYN **stalk**
2 the long thin part of a wine glass, VASE etc, between the base and the wide top
3 the narrow tube of a pipe used to smoke tobacco
4 long-stemmed/short-stemmed etc having a long stem, a short stem etc: *long-stemmed wine glasses*
5 the part of a word that stays the same when different endings are added to it, for example 'driv-' in 'driving'

stem² *v* (**stemmed**, **stemming**) [T] **1** to stop something from happening, spreading, or developing: **stem the tide/flow/flood of sth** *The measures are meant to stem the tide of illegal immigration.* | **stem the growth/rise/decline etc** *an attempt to stem the decline in profits* **2** *formal* to stop the flow of a liquid: *A tight bandage should stem the bleeding.*
stem from sth *phr v* to develop as a result of something else: *His headaches stemmed from vision problems.*

STEM /stem/ the abbreviation of ***science, technology, engineering, and mathematics***, used especially when talking about education

ˈstem cell *n* [C] *technical* a special type of cell in the body, that can divide in order to form other types of cells that have particular qualities or purposes

stench /stentʃ/ *n* [C usually singular] **1** a very strong bad smell SYN **stink**: *the stench of urine* THESAURUS ▸ SMELL **2** something unpleasant that makes you believe that something very bad and dishonest is happening: **[+of]** *a government filled with the stench of corruption*

sten·cil¹ /ˈstensəl/ *n* [C] **1** a piece of plastic, metal, or paper in which designs or letters have been cut out, that you put over a surface and paint over, so that the design is left on the surface **2** a design made on something using a stencil

stencil² *v* (**stencilled**, **stencilling** *BrE*, **stenciled**, **stenciling** *AmE*) [T] to make a design, letters etc using a stencil

Sten gun /ˈsten ɡʌn/ *n* [C] a small British SUBMACHINE GUN

sten·o /ˈstenəʊ $ -noʊ/ *n* (*plural* **stenos**) *informal* **1** [C] a short form of STENOGRAPHER **2** [U] a short form of STENOGRAPHY

ste·nog·ra·pher /stəˈnɒɡrəfə $ -ˈnɑːɡrəfər/ *n* [C] *AmE or BrE old-fashioned* someone whose job is to write down what someone else is saying, using stenography, and then type a copy of it

ste·nog·ra·phy /stəˈnɒɡrəfi $ -ˈnɑː-/ *n* [U] *AmE or BrE old-fashioned* a fast way of writing in which you use special signs or short forms of words, used especially to record what someone is saying SYN **shorthand**

sten·to·ri·an /stenˈtɔːriən/ *adj literary* a stentorian voice is very loud and powerful

step¹ /step/ ●●● S2 W1 *n*
1 MOVEMENT [C] the movement you make when you put one foot in front of or behind the other when walking: *a video of baby's first steps* | *He* ***took*** *one* ***step*** *and fell.* | **[+back/forwards/towards etc]** *Tom took a step back and held the door open.* | *I had to* ***retrace my steps*** (=go back the way I came) *several times before I found the shop.*
2 ACTION [C] one of a series of things that you do in order to deal with a problem or to succeed: **step in (doing) sth** *This is the first step in reforming the welfare system.* | **step to do sth** *The president took immediate steps to stop the fighting.* | **[+towards]** *an important step towards peace*
3 IN A PROCESS [C] a stage in a process, or a position on a scale: *Each book goes up one step in difficulty.* | *Record your result, and go on to step 3.* | **[+in]** *the next step in the process* | *Drug companies influence the scientific process* ***every step of the way*** (=during every stage). | *Describe* ***step by step*** (=describing each stage) *how you went about achieving your goal.* | *Moving to Cottage Grove represented a definite* ***step up*** (=something that is better than you had before) *for my parents.* | *He saw the job as a* ***step down*** (=something that is worse than he had before).
4 STAIR [C] a flat narrow piece of wood or stone, especially one in a series, that you put your foot on when you are going up or down, especially outside a building: *Jenny sat on the step in front of the house, waiting.* | *He* ***climbed*** *the wooden* ***steps*** *and rang the bell.* | *a* ***flight of*** (=set of) *broad stone* ***steps*** → DOORSTEP¹(1), see picture at STAIRCASE
5 DISTANCE [C] the short distance you move when you take a step while walking SYN **pace**: *Roy was standing only a few steps away.*
6 SOUND [C] the sound you make when you put your foot down while walking SYN **footstep**: *I heard a step in the corridor.*
7 DANCING [C] a movement of your feet in dancing: *the steps for the Charleston*
8 in step a) having ideas or actions that are like those of other people: **[+with]** *He isn't in step with ordinary voters.* **b)** moving your feet so that your right foot goes forward at the same time as people you are walking with
9 out of step a) having ideas or actions that are different from those of other people: **[+with]** *This type of training is out of step with changes in the industry.* **b)** moving your feet in a different way from people you are walking with
10 watch your step (*also* **mind your step** *BrE*) **a)** to be careful about what you say or how you behave: *You'd better watch your step – he's the boss here.* **b)** to be careful when you are walking: *Mind your step – the railing's loose.*
11 fall into step (with sb) a) to start walking beside someone at the same speed as them: *Maggie fell into step beside her.* **b)** to start thinking or doing the same as other people: *The administration has fallen into step with its European allies on this issue.*
12 be/keep/stay one step ahead (of sb) a) to be better prepared for something or know more about something than someone else: *A good teacher is always at least one step ahead of his students.* **b)** to manage not to be caught by someone who is trying to find or catch you
13 WAY SB WALKS [C usually singular] the way someone walks, which often tells you how they are feeling: *Gianni's usual bouncy step*
14 steps [plural] *BrE* a STEPLADDER
15 EXERCISE [U] a type of exercise you do by walking

onto and off a flat piece of equipment around 15-30 CENTIMETRES high: *a step class*

16 MUSIC [C] *AmE* the difference in PITCH between two musical notes that are separated by one KEY on the piano SYN **tone** *BrE*

COLLOCATIONS - MEANING 2

VERBS

take a step *The authority will take steps to reunite the child and his family.*

ADJECTIVES

an important/major/big step *The move is seen as a major step forward for UK firms.*
the first step *The first step in resolving conflict is to understand what the other person wants.*
the next step *He met in Washington with his campaign advisers to plan his next step.*
a small step *This is a small step in the right direction.*
a positive step (=an action that will have a good effect) *This is a positive step which gives cause for some optimism.*
an unusual/unprecedented step (=something that is not usually done/has never been done before) *Police last night took the unusual step of releasing photographs of him.*
immediate steps *We believe immediate steps could be taken to generate jobs.*
reasonable steps | **necessary steps**

PHRASES

a step forward (=an action that makes things better) *The declaration which we have just signed is a big step forward for both of our nations.*
a step backwards/a backward step (=an action that makes things worse) *A rationing system would be a major step backwards.*
a step in the right direction (=an action that helps to improve things) *Environmentalists said the law was a step in the right direction.*

step² ●●● S3 W3 *v* (**stepped**, **stepping**) [I always + adv/prep]

1 to raise one foot and put it down in front of or behind the other one in order to walk or move: **[+forward/back/down/into etc]** *He stepped back to let me through.* | *I stepped outside and closed the door.* | *Mr Ives? Please* ***step this way*** (=walk in the direction I am showing you).

2 to bring your foot down on something SYN **tread** *BrE*: **[+in/on etc]** *I accidentally stepped in a puddle.* | *You're stepping on my foot.*

3 step on sb's toes to offend or upset someone, especially by trying to do their work: *I'm not worried about stepping on anybody's toes.*

4 step out of line to behave badly by breaking rules or disobeying orders

5 step on it (*also* **step on the gas** *AmE*) *spoken* to drive faster → **step into the breach** at BREACH¹(7)

step down (*also* **step aside**) *phr v* to leave your job or official position, because you want to or because you think you should: *Morris should step aside until the investigation is completed.* | **[+as]** *Eve Johnson has stepped down as chairperson.* | **[+from]** *He was forced to step down from his post.*

step forward *phr v* to come and offer help, information etc: *Police are appealing for witnesses to step forward.*

step in *phr v* to become involved in an activity, discussion, or disagreement, sometimes in order to stop trouble SYN **intervene**: *The military may step in if the crisis continues.* | *Parents have stepped in to provide homework help in the afternoon program.*

step into sth *phr v* to start doing something, or become involved in a situation: *Sally stepped into the role of team leader.*

step out *phr v* to leave your home or office for a short time SYN **pop out** *BrE*: *She's just stepped out for a few minutes.*

step up *phr v*

1 step sth ↔ up to increase the amount of an activity or the speed of a process in order to improve a situation: *The health department is stepping up efforts to reduce teenage smoking.* | *stepped-up security at airports*

2 (*also* **step up to the plate**) *especially AmE* to agree to help someone or to be responsible for doing something: *Residents will have to step up if they want to rid this area of crime.*

step- /step/ *prefix* used to show that someone is related to you not by birth but because a parent has married again: *her stepdad* | *the problems of stepfamilies*

ˌstep aeˈrobics *n* [U] a type of physical exercise in which you step on and off a small raised PLATFORM while doing movements with the upper part of your body

step·broth·er /ˈstepbrʌðə $ -ər/ *n* [C] the son of your stepmother or stepfather

ˌstep-by-ˈstep *adj* [only before noun] a step-by-step plan, method etc explains or does something carefully and in a particular order: **step-by-step guide/approach/instructions etc** *a step-by-step guide to making it in the music business* —**step by step** *adv*: *Take each lesson* ***step by step.***

ˈstep change *n* [singular] *BrE* a big and important change in an organization or in society: **[+in]** *The new law marks a step change in our programme for reforming public services.*

step·child /ˈsteptʃaɪld/ *n* (*plural* **stepchildren** /-ˌtʃɪldrən/) [C] a stepdaughter or stepson

step·daugh·ter /ˈstepdɔːtə $ -dɒːtər/ *n* [C] a daughter that your husband or wife has from a relationship before your marriage

step·fa·ther /ˈstepfɑːðə $ -ər/ ●●○ *n* [C] a man who is married to your mother but who is not your father

Step·ford Wives, The /ˌstepfəd ˈwaɪvz $ -fərd-/ a HORROR FILM, based on a book by Ira Levin, about a group of married women in a US village whose husbands secretly replace them with ROBOTS. The robots look exactly like the women, but they are designed to be interested only in cooking, cleaning their houses, and pleasing their husbands in every way. The phrase is sometimes used to describe women who behave in this way.

step·lad·der /ˈstepˌlædə $ -ər/ *n* [C] a LADDER which has two sloping parts that are joined at the top so that it can stand without support, and which can be folded flat → see picture at **LADDER¹**

step·moth·er /ˈstepmʌðə $ -ər/ ●●○ *n* [C] a woman who is married to your father but who is not your mother

step·par·ent /ˈstepˌpeərənt $ -ˌper-/ *n* [C] a stepfather or stepmother

steppe /step/ *n* [C,U] (*also* **the steppes** [plural]) a large area of land without trees, especially in Russia, Asia, and eastern Europe

ˈstepping-ˌstone *n* [C] **1** something that helps you to progress towards achieving something: **[+to/toward(s)]** *The course will be a stepping stone to another career.* **2 stepping stones** [plural] a row of large flat stones that you walk on to get across a stream

step·sis·ter /ˈstepsɪstə $ -ər/ *n* [C] the daughter of your stepmother or stepfather

step·son /ˈstepsʌn/ *n* [C] a son that your husband or wife has from a relationship before your marriage

ster·e·o¹ /ˈsteriəʊ, ˈstɪər- $ ˈsterioʊ, ˈstɪr-/ *n* (*plural* **stereos**) **1** (*also* **ˈstereo ˌsystem**) [C] a machine for playing records, CDs etc that produces sound from two SPEAKERS: *a stereo with good speakers* | **on a stereo** *He was listening to the Beatles on the car stereo.* **2 in stereo** if sound is played or broadcast in stereo, it is directed through two speakers → **PERSONAL STEREO**

stereo² (*also* **ster·e·o·phon·ic**) /ˌsteriəˈfɒnɪk◂, ˌstɪər- $ ˌsteriəˈfɑːnɪk◂, ˌstɪr-/ *adj* using a recording or broadcasting system in which the sound is directed through two SPEAKERS → **mono**, **quadraphonic**: *stereo equipment*

S

ster·e·o·scop·ic /ˌsteriəˈskɒpɪk◂, ˌstɪər- $ ˌsteriəˈskɑː-, ˌstɪr-/ *adj* **1** a stereoscopic picture, photograph etc appears solid when you look at it through a special machine **2** *technical* able to see the length, width, and depth of objects: ***stereoscopic vision***

ster·e·o·type¹ /ˈsteriətaɪp, ˈstɪər- $ ˈster-, ˈstɪr-/ ●●○ *n* [C] a belief or idea of what a particular type of person or thing is like. Stereotypes are often unfair or untrue: **racial/sexual/cultural etc stereotype** *racist stereotypes in the media* | **[+of]** *women who don't* ***fit the stereotype*** *of the good mother* | **[+about]** *stereotypes about the elderly* —**stereotypical** /ˌsteriəˈtɪpɪkəl, ˌstɪər- $ ˌster-, ˌstɪr-/ *adj*: *the stereotypical Californian – tall, fit, and tanned* —**stereotypically** /-kli/ *adv*

stereotype² *v* [T] to decide unfairly that a type of person has particular qualities or abilities because they belong to a particular race, sex, or social class: **be stereotyped as sth** *Homeless people are stereotyped as alcoholics or addicts.* GRAMMAR **Stereotype** is often used in the passive. —**stereotyping** *n* [U] —**stereotyped** *adj*

ster·ile /ˈsteraɪl $ -rəl/ *adj* **1** a person or animal that is sterile cannot produce babies SYN **infertile** OPP **fertile**: **make/render/leave sb sterile** *Radiotherapy has left her permanently sterile.* **2** completely clean and not containing any BACTERIA that might cause infection: **sterile equipment/water/bandages etc** *Rinse the eye with sterile water.* THESAURUS ▸ CLEAN **3** lacking new ideas, interest, or imagination OPP **productive**: **sterile argument/debate etc** *the increasingly sterile debate on political reform* **4** a sterile building, room etc is not interesting or attractive and is often very plain: *The classrooms are sterile, with no artwork on the walls.* **5** sterile land cannot be used to grow crops SYN **barren** —**sterility** /stəˈrɪləti/ *n* [U]

S

ster·il·ize (*also* **-ise** *BrE*) /ˈsterəlaɪz/ *v* [T] **1** to make something completely clean by killing any BACTERIA in it: *Sterilize the bottles with boiling water.* | *sterilized milk* | *sterilizing solution* **2** if a person or animal is sterilized, they have an operation to stop them producing babies —**sterilizer** *n* [C]: *an electric sterilizer* —**sterilization** /ˌsterəlaɪˈzeɪʃən $ -lə-/ *n* [C,U]

ster·ling¹ /ˈstɜːlɪŋ $ ˈstɜːr-/ *n* [U] **1** (*also* **Sterling**) the standard unit of money in the United Kingdom, based on the pound **2** (*also* ˌ**sterling** ˈ**silver**) silver that is at least 92% pure

sterling² *adj* [only before noun] very good: *Ella has done some sterling work.* | *He has sterling qualities.*

stern¹ /stɜːn $ stɜːrn/ ●○○ *adj*
1 serious and strict, and showing strong disapproval of someone's behaviour: *sterner penalties for drug offences* | **stern look/voice/expression etc** *'Wait!' I shouted in my sternest voice.* | **stern warning/rebuke** *His actions have earned him stern rebukes from human rights organizations.* THESAURUS ▸ STRICT
2 be made of sterner stuff to have a strong character and be more determined than other people to succeed in a difficult situation: *Ann, made of sterner stuff than I, refused all offers of help.* —**sternly** *adv* —**sternness** *n* [U]

stern² *n* [C usually singular] the back of a ship → **bow**

ster·num /ˈstɜːnəm $ ˈstɜːr-/ *n* (*plural* **sternums** *or* **sterna** /-nə/) [C] *technical* a BREASTBONE

ste·roid /ˈstɪərɔɪd, ˈste- $ ˈstɪr-/ *n* [C] **1** a chemical that the body produces naturally or that can be made as a drug to treat illness and injuries. Steroids are sometimes used illegally by people doing sports to improve their performance: **on steroids** *a body builder on steroids* **2 sth on steroids** *AmE informal* used to say that something is much bigger, stronger, more impressive etc than something else that is similar to it – used humorously: *They sell cinnamon rolls on steroids.*

steth·o·scope /ˈsteθəskəʊp $ -skoʊp/ *n* [C] an instrument that a doctor uses to listen to your heart or breathing

Stet·son /ˈstetsən/ *n* [C] *trademark* a tall hat with a wide BRIM (=edge), worn especially in the American West

ste·ve·dore /ˈstiːvədɔː $ -dɔːr/ *n* [C] someone whose job is loading and unloading ships

stew¹ /stjuː $ stuː/ ●●○ *n*
1 [C,U] a hot meal made by cooking meat and vegetables slowly in liquid for a long time SYN **casserole**: *a pot of stew* | *beef stew*
2 in a stew *informal* confused or worried about a difficult situation you are in

stew² *v* **1** [T] to cook something slowly in liquid: *stewed apples* **2 let sb stew** *informal* (*also* **let sb stew in their own juice**) to leave someone to suffer the unpleasant results of their own actions instead of helping them: *Let him stew – I'm not going to help him.*

stew·ard /ˈstjuːəd $ ˈstuːərd/ *n* [C] **1** a man whose job is to serve food and drinks to passengers on a plane or ship → **flight attendant** **2** someone who is in charge of a horse race, meeting, or other public event: *race stewards* **3** someone who protects something or is responsible for it, especially something such as nature, public property, or money: **[+of]** *Kissinger was now chief steward of US foreign policy.* **4** a man whose job is to manage a large property, such as a farm → SHOP STEWARD

stew·ard·ess /ˈstjuːədɪs $ ˈstuːərd-/ *n* [C] a woman whose job is to serve food and drinks to passengers on a plane or ship → **flight attendant**

stew·ard·ship /ˈstjuːədʃɪp $ ˈstuːərd-/ *n* [U] someone's stewardship of something is the way that they control or protect it: **[+of]** *Some critics have doubts about his stewardship of the nation.* | **under sb's stewardship** *The farm was quite a different place under Mom's stewardship.*

stewed /stjuːd $ stuːd/ *adj* **1** [not before noun] *informal old-fashioned* drunk **2** *BrE* tea that is stewed tastes unpleasantly strong because it has been left in the pot too long

stick¹ /stɪk/ ●●● S1 W3 *v* (*past tense and past participle* **stuck** /stʌk/)
1 ATTACH [I,T] to attach something to something else using a substance, or to become attached to a surface: **stick sth on/to/in etc sth** *Someone had stuck posters all over the walls.* | **[+to/together]** *I could feel my shirt sticking to my back.* | *The oil keeps the pasta from sticking together.* | *This stamp won't stick properly.*
2 PUSH IN [I,T always + adv/prep] if a pointed object sticks into something, or if you stick it there, it is pushed into it: **stick (sth) in/into/through sth** *pins stuck in a notice board* | *The boy stuck his finger up his nose.*
3 PUT [T always + adv/prep] *informal* to put something somewhere quickly and without much care SYN **bung**: *Just stick it in the microwave for a few minutes.* | *The cards had been stuck through the letterbox.* THESAURUS ▸ PUT
4 MOVE PART OF BODY [T always + adv/prep] if you stick a part of your body somewhere, you put it in a position where other people can see it SYN **put**: *Clara stuck her head around the door to see who was there.* | *The baby stuck his legs in the air.* | *Don't* ***stick*** *your* ***tongue out****. It's rude!*
5 DIFFICULT TO MOVE [I] if something sticks, it becomes fixed in one position and is difficult to move: *This door keeps sticking.* | *The wheels* ***stuck fast*** (=stuck completely) *in the mud.*
6 stick in sb's mind if something sticks in your mind, you remember it well because it is unusual or interesting: *It's the kind of name that sticks in your mind.*
7 make sth stick *informal* **a)** to prove that something is true: *Is there enough evidence to* ***make*** *the* ***charges stick****?* **b)** to make a change become permanent: *The government has succeeded in making this policy stick.*
8 NAME [I] if a name that someone has invented sticks, people continue using it: *One newspaper dubbed him 'Eddie the Eagle', and the name stuck.*
9 sb can stick sth *spoken* used to say angrily that you do not want what someone is offering you: *I told them they could stick their job.*
10 STAY IN BAD SITUATION [T] *BrE spoken* to continue to accept a situation or person, even though you do not like them SYN **stand**: *I* ***can't stick*** *mum's new boyfriend.* | **can't**

stick doing sth *Gerry can't stick working for Featherstone's any longer.* | *I don't know how you **stick it**.*
11 stick in sb's throat/gullet *BrE*, **stick in sb's craw** *AmE* if a situation or someone's behaviour sticks in your throat, it is so annoying that you cannot accept it: *Her criticism really stuck in my craw.*
12 stick in sb's throat if words stick in your throat, you are unable to say them because you are afraid or upset
13 stick to sb's ribs *informal* food that sticks to your ribs is very satisfying, so you are not hungry after you have eaten → STUCK[1], → **stick/poke your nose into sth** at NOSE[1](3)
stick around *phr v informal* to stay in a place a little longer, waiting for something to happen: *Perhaps you'd like to stick around and watch?* | *Tom will be sticking around for a while.*
stick at sth *phr v BrE*
1 to continue doing something in a determined way in order to achieve something: *Revising with your friends may help you **stick at it**.*
2 stick at nothing *informal* to be willing to do anything, even if it is illegal, in order to achieve something: **stick at nothing to do sth** *He will stick at nothing to make money.*
stick by sb/sth *phr v*
1 to remain loyal to a friend when they have done something wrong or have problems: *I love him and, whatever happens, I'll stick by him.* | *Jean has **stuck by** her husband **through thick and thin**.*
2 to do what you promised or decided to do: **stick by a decision/promise etc** *He has stuck by his radical plans for economic reform.*
stick out *phr v*
1 if something sticks out, you notice it because part of it comes out further than the rest of a surface: *The children were so thin their ribs stuck out.* | **[+of/from/through etc]** *Paul's legs were sticking out from under the car.*
2 stick it out to continue doing something that is difficult, painful, or boring: *It wasn't a happy period of his life, but he stuck it out.*
3 stick your neck out *informal* to risk giving your opinion about something, even though you may be wrong or other people may disagree with you: *I'm going to stick my neck out with some predictions for the next two years.*
4 stick out to sb/stick out in sb's mind to seem more important to someone than other people or things: *The thing that sticks out to me is that they need more help than they're getting.* → **stick/stand out a mile** at MILE(5), → **stick out like a sore thumb** at SORE[1](6)
stick out for sth *phr v BrE informal* to refuse to accept less than what you asked for SYN **hold out for**: *They offered him £250 but Vic stuck out for £500.*
stick to sth *phr v*
1 to do or keep doing what you said you would do or what you believe in, even when it is difficult SYN **keep to**: *Have you been sticking to your diet?* | **stick to your decision/principles etc** *Miguel was determined to stick to his decision.* | *It looks as if Nick will **stick to** his **word** this time.*
2 to keep using or doing one particular thing and not change to anything else: *If you're driving, stick to soft drinks.* | **stick to doing sth** *Reporters should stick to investigating the facts.*
3 stick to your guns *informal* to refuse to change your mind about something, even though other people are trying to persuade you that you are wrong: *Having made up his mind, he stuck to his guns.*
4 stick to the point/subject/facts to talk only about what you are supposed to be talking about or what is certain: *Never mind whose fault it was. Just stick to the facts.*
5 stick to the rules *informal* to do something exactly according to the rules
6 stick to the path/road etc to stay on a marked path or road so that you do not get lost
7 stick to the/your story *spoken* to continue to say that what you have told someone is true, even though they do not believe you: *You intend to stick to this story that she knew nothing of your financial prospects?*
8 stick to the/your knitting *AmE informal* to continue paying attention to your own work and not to get involved with what other people are doing: *I wish Mrs Reese would stick to her knitting.*
9 stick it to sb *AmE informal* to make someone suffer, pay a high price etc: *The politicians stick it to the tourists because the tourists don't vote.*
stick together *phr v informal* if people stick together, they continue to support each other when they have problems: *We're a family, and we stick together no matter what.*
stick up *phr v*
1 if a part of something sticks up, it is raised up or points upwards above a surface: **[+from/out of/through etc]** *Part of the boat was sticking up out of the water.*
2 stick 'em up *spoken informal* used to tell someone to raise their hands when threatening them with a gun – used in films, stories etc
stick up for sb *phr v informal* to defend someone who is being criticized, especially when no one else will defend them: *You're supposed to be sticking up for me!* | **stick up for yourself** *She's always known how to stick up for herself.*
stick with sth/sb *phr v informal*
1 to continue doing something the way you did or planned to do before: *Let's stick with the original plans.*
2 to stay close to someone: *You just stick with me. I'll explain everything as we go along.*
3 to continue doing something, especially something difficult: *If you **stick with it**, your playing will gradually get better.*
4 be stuck with sth/sb to be made to accept something, do something, spend time with someone etc, when you do not want to: *Bill left and I was stuck with the bill.*
5 to remain in someone's memory: *Those words will stick with me for the rest of my life.*

stick² ●●● S3 *n* [C]
1 PART OF TREE a long thin piece of wood from a tree, which is no longer attached to the tree → **branch**, **twig**: *They collected sticks to start the fire.*
2 TOOL a long thin piece of wood, plastic etc that you use for a particular purpose: *a pair of drum sticks* | *a measuring stick* | *Aunt Lou **walks with a stick*** (=uses a stick to help her walk).
3 PIECE a long thin or round piece of something: *carrot sticks with dip* | *a glue stick* | **[+of]** *a stick of chewing gum*
4 SPORTS a long, specially shaped piece of wood, plastic etc that you use in some sports to hit a ball: *a hockey stick* → see picture at SPORT[1]
5 (out) in the sticks a long way from a town or city: *They live out in the sticks.*
6 get (hold of) the wrong end of the stick *BrE informal* to understand a situation in completely the wrong way: *People who think the song is about drugs have got the wrong end of the stick.*
7 a stick to beat sb with something that can be used as a reason for criticizing someone: *These tests will just give politicians yet another stick to beat the teachers with.*
8 PLANE the handle you use to control a plane → JOYSTICK
9 CAR *AmE informal* a STICK SHIFT
10 get on the stick *AmE spoken* to start doing something you should be doing
11 give sb/get (some) stick *BrE spoken* if you give someone stick, you criticize them for something they have done: *He's going to get some stick for this!*
12 up sticks *BrE informal* if you up sticks, you move to a different area → **carrot and stick** at CARROT(3)

stick·a·bil·i·ty /ˌstɪkəˈbɪləti/ *n* [U] *BrE informal* the ability to continue doing something that is difficult or tiring SYN **stick-to-it-iveness** *AmE*

stick·er /ˈstɪkə $ -ər/ ●●● S3 *n* [C] a small piece of paper or plastic with a picture or writing on it that you can stick on to something → **label**: *Children get stickers for good work.* | **bumper sticker** (=a sticker on the back of a car)

ˈsticker ˌprice *n* [C usually singular] *AmE* the price of something, especially a car, that is written on it or given in advertisements, but that may be reduced by the person selling it

ˈstick ˌfigure *n* [C] a very simple drawing of a person

S

ˈsticking ˌpoint *n* [singular] something that a group of people cannot agree on and that stops them from making progress: *North Korea's refusal had long been a sticking point.*

ˈstick ˌinsect *n* [C] *BrE* a long thin insect that looks like a small stick: *young models who look like stick insects* (=are very thin)

ˈstick-in-the-ˌmud *n* [C] someone who refuses to try anything new – used to show disapproval

stick·ler /ˈstɪklə $ -ər/ *n* **be a stickler for detail/rules/accuracy etc** to think that rules etc are very important and that other people should think so too

ˈstick man *n* [C] a STICK FIGURE

ˈstick-on *adj* [only before noun] stick-on things have a sticky back so that you can attach them to something: *stick-on sequins*

stick·pin /ˈstɪkˌpɪn/ *n* [C] *AmE* a decorated pin worn as jewellery

ˈstick shift *n* [C] *AmE* **1** a metal bar in a car that you move to control the GEARS SYN **gear stick** *BrE* **2** a car that uses a stick shift system to control the GEARS → **automatic**

stick-to-it-ive·ness /stɪk ˈtuː ɪtəvnəs/ *n* [U] *AmE informal* the ability to continue doing something that is difficult or tiring SYN **stickability** *BrE*

ˈstick-up *n* [C] *informal* a HOLD-UP

stick·y /ˈstɪki/ ●●○ *adj* (*comparative* **stickier**, *superlative* **stickiest**)

1 made of or covered with a substance that sticks to surfaces: *There's some **sticky stuff** in your hair.* | *a sticky floor* | **sticky tape/label etc** *BrE* (=tape etc that is made so it will stick to surfaces)

2 weather that is sticky makes you feel uncomfortably hot, wet, and dirty SYN **humid**: *It was **hot and sticky** and there was nowhere to sit.*

3 a sticky situation, question, or problem is difficult or dangerous: *a sticky political issue* | **sticky patch** *BrE*: *The business hit a sticky patch and lost £4.8 million.*

4 a website that is sticky is interesting to the people looking at it and makes them want to look at it for a long period of time

5 have sticky fingers *informal* to be likely to steal something

6 come to/meet a sticky end *BrE informal* to die in a violent way

7 be on a sticky wicket *BrE informal* to be in a situation that will cause problems for you —**stickiness** *n* [U]

ˈsticky ˌnote (*also* **yellow sticky**) *n* [C] a small piece of paper, often yellow in colour, that you can stick to things. Stickies are often used for leaving messages SYN **Post-it Note™**

stiff¹ /stɪf/ ●●○ S3 *adj* (*comparative* **stiffer**, *superlative* **stiffest**)

1 BODY if someone or a part of their body is stiff, their muscles hurt and it is difficult for them to move: **stiff from doing sth** *Her legs were stiff from kneeling.* | **[+with]** *Her fingers were stiff with cold.* | **stiff neck/back/joint etc** *Alastair woke with a stiff neck.* | *I never **felt stiff** after training until I was in my thirties.* | *The next morning I was **as stiff as a board*** (=very stiff). THESAURUS ▸ PAINFUL

2 MATERIAL/SUBSTANCE firm, hard, or difficult to bend: *a shirt with a stiff collar* THESAURUS ▸ HARD

3 MIXTURE a stiff mixture is thick and almost solid, so that it is not easy to mix: *Beat the egg whites until stiff.* | *a stiff dough*

4 DIFFICULT difficult to do or deal with: *a **stiff test*** | **stiff competition/opposition** *Graduates face stiff competition in getting jobs.*

5 SEVERE a stiff punishment is great or severe: **stiff sentence/penalty/fine** *calls for stiffer penalties for rapists*

6 DOOR/DRAWER ETC *BrE* difficult to move, turn, or open: *Pull hard – that drawer's very stiff.*

7 UNFRIENDLY if someone's behaviour is stiff, they behave in a very formal or unfriendly way: *Their goodbyes were **stiff and formal**.* | *Parsons gave a stiff performance in the main role.*

8 PRICE a stiff price etc is high, especially higher than the price etc of similar things: *a stiff tax on cigarettes*

9 stiff wind/breeze a fairly strong wind etc

10 stiff drink/whisky etc a very strong alcoholic drink

11 stiff upper lip the ability to stay calm and not show your feelings in a difficult or upsetting situation: *Men were taught to **keep a stiff upper lip**.* —**stiffly** *adv* —**stiffness** *n* [U]

stiff² *adv* **1 bored/scared/worried stiff** *informal* extremely bored, frightened, or worried: *As a child, I was scared stiff of going down to the cellar.* **2 frozen stiff a)** extremely cold: *Goodness, your hands are frozen stiff!* **b)** cloth that is frozen stiff is hard because the water in it has frozen

stiff³ *n* [C] *informal* **1** the body of a dead person **2 working stiff** *AmE* an ordinary person who works to earn enough money to live **3** someone who you think is old-fashioned and too formal: *His business tactics outraged the stiffs of the UK establishment.*

stiff⁴ *v informal* **1** [T] *AmE* to cheat someone by not paying them, especially by not leaving a TIP in a restaurant: *I can't believe that couple stiffed me!* **2** [I] if a new product, film, show etc stiffs, it does not sell well or fails completely SYN **bomb**: *They had a hit in the 1990s, but their subsequent releases stiffed.*

stiff·en /ˈstɪfən/ *v* **1** [I] if you stiffen, your body suddenly becomes firm, straight, or still because you feel angry or anxious OPP **relax**: *He touched her, and she stiffened.* **2** [I,T] to become stronger, more severe, or more determined, or to make something do this: *a campaign to stiffen rules against drink-driving* | *Their opposition only **stiffened** my **resolve**.* **3** [I] (*also* **stiffen up**) to become painful and difficult to move: *His **joints** had **stiffened**.* | *My back had stiffened up.* **4** [T] to make material stiff so that it will not bend easily

ˌstiff-ˈnecked *adj* too proud, and refusing to change or obey SYN **stubborn**

stiff·y /ˈstɪfi/ *n* (*plural* **stiffies**) [C] *informal not polite* an ERECTION

sti·fle /ˈstaɪfəl/ *v* **1** [T] to stop something from happening or developing OPP **encourage**: *rules and regulations that stifle innovation* | *How can this party stifle debate on such a crucial issue?* **2** [T] to stop a feeling from being expressed: *He **stifled** an **urge** to hit her.* | **stifle a yawn/smile/grin etc** *I tried to stifle my laughter.* **3** [I,T] if you are stifled by something, it stops you breathing comfortably → **suffocate**: *He was almost stifled by the fumes.* | *I felt like I was stifling in the humid air.* GRAMMAR **Stifle** is usually passive in this meaning, when used as a transitive verb.

sti·fling /ˈstaɪflɪŋ/ *adj* **1** a room or weather that is stifling is very hot and uncomfortable, so that it seems difficult to breathe: *a stifling, crowded train* | *the **stifling heat** of the tropics* **2** a situation that is stifling stops you from developing your own ideas and character: *an emotionally stifling relationship*

stig·ma /ˈstɪɡmə/ ●○○ *n*

1 [C usually singular, U] a strong feeling in society that being in a particular situation or having a particular illness is something to be ashamed of: **the stigma of alcoholism/mental illness etc** *The stigma of alcoholism makes it difficult to treat.* | *There is a social **stigma attached to** single parenthood.* | *In the US, smoking **carries** a **stigma**.* THESAURUS ▸ SHAME

2 [C] *technical* the top of the centre part of a flower that receives the POLLEN which allows it to form new seeds

stig·ma·ta /ˈstɪɡmətə, stɪɡˈmɑːtə/ *n* [plural] marks that appear on the hands and feet of some holy people, and which look like the wounds made by nails on the body of Christ

stig·ma·tize (*also* **-ise** *BrE*) /ˈstɪɡmətaɪz/ *v* **be stigmatized** to be treated by society as if you should feel ashamed of your situation or behaviour: *Single mothers often feel that they are stigmatized by society.* —**stigmatization** /ˌstɪɡmətaɪˈzeɪʃən $ -tə-/ *n* [U]

stile /staɪl/ *n* [C] a set of steps that helps people climb over a fence in the countryside

sti·let·to /stəˈletəʊ $ -toʊ/ *n* (*plural* **stilettos** *or* **stilettoes**) [C] **1** (*also* **stiletto heel**) a woman's shoe that has a very high thin heel → see picture at **SHOE**[1] **2** the heel of a stiletto shoe **3** a small knife with a thin blade

still[1] /stɪl/ ●●● S1 W1 *adv*
1 used when saying that something continues to be the same as before, or has not happened yet: *He still lives with his parents.* | *Do you still have Julie's phone number?* | *I still haven't finished painting the spare room.*

GRAMMAR: Word order

- **Still** comes before a main verb: *The system* ***still*** *works.* | *I* ***still*** *love you.*
- **Still** comes after 'am',' is', 'was' etc: *I'm* ***still*** *angry.* | *It was* ***still*** *dark outside.* | *She is* ***still*** *not ready.*
- **Still** can come before the verb 'be' when it is part of a contraction such as 'isn't' or 'wasn't': *She* ***still*** *isn't ready.*
- **Still** comes after the first auxiliary verb in positive sentences: *I can* ***still*** *remember them.* | *The marks can* ***still*** *be seen.*
- **Still** comes before the first auxiliary verb in negative sentences: *I* ***still*** *can't remember his name.* | *We* ***still*** *do not know exactly what happened.*

2 in spite of what has just been said or done: *Clare didn't do much work, but she still passed the exam.* | [sentence adverb] *The hotel was terrible. Still, we were lucky with the weather.*
3 **still more/further/another/other** used to emphasize that something increases more, there is more of something etc: *Kevin grew still more depressed.*
4 **better/harder/worse etc still** (*also* **still better/harder/worse etc**) even better, harder etc than something else: *Dan found biology difficult, and physics harder still.*

still[2] ●●● S3 *adj*
1 not moving: *We* ***stood still*** *and watched as the deer came closer.* | ***Keep still*** *while I tie your shoe.* | *the* ***still waters*** *of the lake*
2 quiet and calm: *The house was completely still.*
3 not windy: *a hot* ***still day***
4 *BrE* a still drink does not contain gas: *still or sparkling mineral water*
5 **still waters run deep** used to say that someone who is quiet may have very strong feelings or a lot of knowledge —**stillness** *n* [U]: *Somewhere in the* ***stillness of the night****, an owl hooted.*

STILL

still water fizzy/sparkling water

still[3] *n* [C] **1** a photograph of a scene from a film **2** a piece of equipment for making alcoholic drinks from grain or potatoes **3** **the still of the night/evening etc** *literary* the calm and quiet of the night etc

still[4] *v literary* **1** [I,T] to stop moving, or make something stop moving: *The ground beneath them trembled, then stilled.* **2** [I,T] if a noise stills or is stilled, it stops: *The murmurs stilled.* | *He stilled their protests with a wave of his hands.* **3** [T] if a doubt or fear is stilled, it becomes weaker or goes away

still·birth /ˈstɪlbɜːθ, ˌstɪlˈbɜːθ $ -ɜːrθ/ *n* [C,U] a birth in which the baby is born dead

still·born /ˈstɪlbɔːn, ˌstɪlˈbɔːn $ -ɔːrn/ *adj* **1** born dead: *a stillborn baby* **2** *written* completely unsuccessful from the beginning and not developing at all: *a stillborn romance*

ˌstill ˈlife *n* (*plural* **still lifes**) [C,U] a picture of an arrangement of objects, for example flowers or fruit → see picture at **PAINTING**

stilt /stɪlt/ *n* [C usually plural] **1** one of a set of poles that support a building above the ground or above water: **on stilts** *a house built on stilts* **2** one of two poles which you can stand on and walk high above the ground

stilt·ed /ˈstɪltɪd/ *adj* a stilted style of writing or speaking is formal and unnatural: *a* ***stilted conversation*** —**stiltedly** *adv*

Stil·ton /ˈstɪltən/ *n* [U] a type of English cheese that is white with grey-blue marks and has a strong taste

stim·u·lant /ˈstɪmjələnt/ *n* [C] **1** a drug or substance that makes you feel more active and full of energy: *artificial stimulants* **2** something that encourages more of a particular activity SYN **stimulus**: *economic stimulants* | **[+to]** *Increases in new construction would be a stimulant to the economy.* —**stimulant** *adj*: *a drug with stimulant properties*

stim·u·late /ˈstɪmjəleɪt/ ●○○ *v* [T]
1 to encourage or help an activity to begin or develop further OPP **suppress**: **stimulate growth/demand/the economy etc** *the president's plan to stimulate economic growth*
2 to encourage someone by making them excited about and interested in something: *Her* ***interest*** *in art was* ***stimulated*** *by her father.* | **stimulate sb to do sth** *An inspiring teacher can stimulate students to succeed.*
3 to make a plant or part of the body become active or stronger OPP **suppress**: *Light stimulates plant growth.* —**stimulative** /-lətɪv $ -leɪtɪv/ *adj* —**stimulation** /ˌstɪmjəˈleɪʃən/ *n* [U]: *Children need variety and stimulation.*

stim·u·lat·ing /ˈstɪmjəleɪtɪŋ/ ●○○ *adj*
1 exciting or full of new ideas OPP **boring**: *a stimulating discussion of world politics* THESAURUS ▸ INTERESTING
2 making you feel more active: *the* ***stimulating effects*** *of coffee and tea*

stim·u·lus /ˈstɪmjələs/ ●○○ *n* (*plural* **stimuli** /-laɪ/)
1 [C usually singular, U] something that helps a process to develop more quickly or more strongly: *Tax cuts provided the stimulus which the slow economy needed.* | **[+to]** *The discovery of oil acted as a stimulus to industrial development.*
2 [C] something that makes someone or something move or react: *At this age, the infant begins to react more to visual stimuli.*

sting[1] /stɪŋ/ ●●○ *v* (*past tense and past participle* **stung** /stʌŋ/)
1 [I,T] if an insect or a plant stings you, it makes a very small hole in your skin and you feel a sharp pain because of a poisonous substance: *He was stung by a bee.* ⚠ A bee, wasp, scorpion, or plant can **sting** you. For a mosquito or snake, use **bite**. THESAURUS ▸ BITE
2 [I,T] to make something hurt with a sudden sharp pain, or to hurt like this: *Antiseptic stings a little.* | *Chopping onions makes my eyes sting.* THESAURUS ▸ HURT
3 [I,T] if you are stung by a remark, it makes you feel upset: *Their criticism really stung.* | **be stung into (doing) sth** *Her harsh words stung him into action.*

sting sb **for** sth *phr v BrE informal*
1 to charge someone too much for something: *The garage stung him for £300.*
2 to borrow money from someone: *Can I sting you for a fiver?*

sting[2] ●●○ *n*
1 WOUND [C] a wound or mark made when an insect or plant stings you: *a* ***bee sting***
2 INSECT [C] *BrE* the sharp needle-shaped part of an insect's or animal's body, with which it stings you SYN **stinger** *AmE*
3 PAIN [singular] a sharp pain in your eyes or skin, caused by being hit, by smoke etc: *She felt the sting of tears in her eyes.*
4 **a sting in the tail** if a story, event, or announcement has a sting in its tail, there is an unpleasant part at the end of it
5 [singular] the upsetting or bad effect of a situation: *the sting of rejection* | **take the sting out of sth** (=make something less unpleasant or painful) *She smiled to take the sting out of her words.*
6 CRIME [C] a clever way of catching criminals in which the police secretly pretend to be criminals themselves

S

sting·er /ˈstɪŋə $ -ər/ *n* [C] *AmE* the sharp needle-shaped part of an insect's or animal's body, with which it stings you SYN **sting** *BrE*

sting·ing /ˈstɪŋɪŋ/ *adj* **stinging attack/report/letter etc** an attack, report, letter etc that very strongly criticizes someone or something: *Dr Forwell made a stinging attack on government policy.*

ˈstinging ˌnettle *n* [C] a wild plant with leaves that sting and leave red marks on your skin

sting·ray /ˈstɪŋreɪ/ *n* [C] a large flat fish that has a long tail with sharp poisonous points on it

stin·gy /ˈstɪndʒi/ *adj* **1** *informal* not generous, especially with money SYN **mean**: *She's too stingy to give money to charity.* **2** a stingy amount of something, especially food, is too small: *a stingy portion of vegetables* —**stingily** *adv* —**stinginess** *n* [U]

stink¹ /stɪŋk/ ●●○ *v* (*past tense* **stank** /stæŋk/, *past participle* **stunk** /stʌŋk/) [I]

1 to have a strong and very unpleasant smell: *It stinks in here!* | **[+of]** *His breath stank of alcohol.* | *The toilets* ***stank to high heaven*** (=stank very much).

2 *spoken* used to say that something is bad, unfair, dishonest etc: *Don't eat there – the food stinks!* | *The whole justice system stinks.*

stink sth ↔ **out** *BrE*, **stink sth** ↔ **up** *AmE phr v* to fill a place with a very unpleasant smell: *Those onions are stinking the whole house out.*

stink² *n* [C usually singular] **1** a very bad smell SYN **stench**: **[+of]** *the stink of burning rubber* THESAURUS SMELL **2 cause/kick up/make etc a stink** to complain very strongly: *Activists have raised a stink about the shipments of nuclear waste.* **3 work/run/go like stink** *BrE old-fashioned* to work etc as fast and as well as you can: *We had to work like stink to meet the deadline.*

ˈstink bomb *n* [C] a small container that produces an extremely bad smell when it is broken

stink·er /ˈstɪŋkə $ -ər/ *n* [C] *informal* **1** someone or something that is very unpleasant or difficult: *This cold I've got is a* ***real stinker***. | *You really are a stinker.* **2** a film, book, performance etc that is very bad: **have a stinker** *BrE* (=play badly) *In the last game he had a stinker.*

stink·ing¹ /ˈstɪŋkɪŋ/ *adj* **1** having a very strong unpleasant smell SYN **smelly**: *stinking garbage cans* **2** [only before noun] *spoken* used to emphasize what you are saying when you are angry: *I hate this stinking boring job!* **3** [only before noun] *especially BrE informal* very unpleasant: *I've got a* ***stinking cold***. **4 stinking letter** *BrE informal* an angry letter in which you complain very strongly about something

stinking² *adv informal* **1 stinking rich** extremely rich – used especially when you think this is unfair **2 stinking drunk** extremely drunk

stink·y /ˈstɪŋki/ *adj* (*comparative* **stinkier**, *superlative* **stinkiest**) *informal* smelling unpleasant SYN **smelly**: *stinky socks*

stint¹ /stɪnt/ *n* [C usually singular] a period of time spent doing a particular job or activity: **[+in/at]** *Mark* ***did*** *a two-year* ***stint*** *in the army.* | **[+as]** *his stint as chairman*

stint² *v* [I,T usually in negatives] to provide or use too little of something: **[+on]** *They didn't stint on food and drink at their wedding.* | **stint yourself** *In order to avoid stinting yourself, make sure you have enough money to cover all your expenses.*

sti·pend /ˈstaɪpend/ *n* [C] *formal* an amount of money paid regularly to someone, especially a priest, as a salary or as money to live on

sti·pen·di·a·ry ma·gis·trate /staɪˌpendiəri ˈmædʒəstreɪt, -strət $ -dieri-/ (*also* **stipendiary**) *n* [C] a MAGISTRATE in Britain who is paid by the state

stip·ple /ˈstɪpəl/ *v* [T] to draw or paint a picture or pattern using short STROKES or spots instead of lines —**stippled** *adj* —**stippling** *n* [U]

stip·u·late /ˈstɪpjəleɪt/ ●○○ *v* [T] *formal* if an agreement, law, or rule stipulates something, it must be done SYN **state**: *Laws stipulate the maximum interest rate that banks can charge.* | **stipulate that** *The regulations stipulate that everything has to comply to the relevant safety standards.*

stip·u·la·tion /ˌstɪpjəˈleɪʃən/ *n* [C,U] *formal* something that must be done, and which is stated as part of an agreement, law, or rule: **stipulation that** *The agreement included a stipulation that half of the money had to be spent on housing for lower-income families.*

stir¹ /stɜː $ stɜːr/ ●●● S3 W3 *v* (**stirred**, **stirring**)

1 MIX [T] to move a liquid or substance around with a spoon or stick in order to mix it together: *Stir the paint to make sure it is smooth.* | **stir sth with sth** *She stirred her coffee with a plastic spoon.* | **stir sth in/into sth** *Stir a cup of cooked brown rice into the mixture.* THESAURUS MIX

2 MOVE SLIGHTLY [I,T] to move slightly, or to make something move slightly: *The crowd began to stir as they waited for the band to start.* | *A gentle breeze stirred the curtains.* THESAURUS MOVE

3 LEAVE A PLACE [I] to leave or move from a place: *He hadn't stirred from his chair all morning.*

4 FEELINGS **a)** [T] to make someone have a strong feeling or reaction: **stir memories/emotions etc** *Looking at the photographs stirred childhood memories of the long hot summers.* | *The poem succeeds in* ***stirring the imagination***. **b)** [I] if a feeling stirs in you, you begin to feel it: *Excitement stirred inside her.*

5 DO STH [T] to make someone start doing something: **stir sb to do sth** *The incident stirred students to protest.*

6 CAUSE TROUBLE **be stirring (it)** *BrE informal* to cause trouble between people by spreading false or secret information: *Ben's always stirring!*

stir sb/sth ↔ **up** *phr v*

1 to deliberately try to cause arguments or bad feelings between people: *John was always* ***stirring up trouble*** *in class.* | *Dave's just trying to* ***stir things up*** *because he's jealous.*

2 to make small pieces of something move around in the air or in water: *The wind had stirred up a powdery red dust.*

stir² *n* **1** [C usually singular] a feeling of excitement or annoyance: **create/cause a stir** *Plans for the motorway caused quite a stir among locals.* **2** [C usually singular] an act of stirring something: ***Give*** *that pan a* ***stir***, *will you?* **3** [C,U] *AmE old-fashioned informal* a prison

ˌstir-ˈcrazy *adj informal* extremely nervous and upset, especially because you feel trapped in a place: *I'm going to* ***go stir-crazy*** *if I don't get out of this house.*

ˈstir-fry¹ *v* (**stir-fried**, **stir-frying**, **stir-fries**) [T] to cook small pieces of food quickly by moving them around continuously in very hot oil: *stir-fried vegetables* THESAURUS COOK

stir-fry² *n* (*plural* **stir-fries**) [C] a dish made by stir-frying small pieces of food

stir·rer /ˈstɜːrə $ -ər/ *n* [C] **1** *BrE informal* someone who likes to cause trouble between people by spreading false or secret information – used to show disapproval **2** an object shaped like a stick, that is used to mix liquids

stir·ring¹ /ˈstɜːrɪŋ/ *adj* producing strong feelings or excitement in someone SYN **rousing**: *a stirring speech* | *stirring music* —**stirringly** *adv*

stirring² *n* [C] an early sign that something is starting to happen: **[+of]** *the first stirrings of spring*

stir·rup /ˈstɪrəp $ ˈstɜː-/ *n* [C] one of the rings of metal in which someone riding a horse rests their feet

ˈstirrup ˌpants *n* [plural] *AmE* stretchy women's trousers that have bands at the bottom of the legs which fit under your feet

stitch¹ /stɪtʃ/ ●○○ *n*

1 SEWING [C] a short piece of thread that has been sewn into a piece of cloth, or the action of the thread going into and out of the cloth

2 FOR WOUND [C] a piece of special thread which has been used to sew the edges of a wound together: *He had to have ten stitches in his head.*

3 PAIN [C usually singular] a sharp pain in the side of your body, which you can get by running or laughing a lot

4 WITH WOOL [C] a small circle of wool that is formed around a needle when you are KNITTING: **drop a stitch** (=lose a stitch because the wool has come off the needle)
5 STYLE [C,U] a particular way of sewing or KNITTING that makes a particular pattern: *Purl and plain are the two main stitches in knitting.*
6 not have a stitch on *informal* to be wearing no clothes
7 in stitches laughing a lot in an uncontrollable way: **have/keep sb in stitches** (=make someone laugh) *Her jokes had us all in stitches.*
8 a stitch in time (saves nine) *spoken* used to say that it is better to deal with problems early than to wait until they get worse

stitch² *v* [T] to sew two pieces of cloth together, or to sew a decoration onto a piece of cloth: *Mary is stitching a bedspread.* | **stitch sth onto/across sth** *The jersey has his name stitched across the back.*
stitch sth ↔ **together** *phr v AmE* **1** to put different things or parts of something together to make one larger thing: *In ten years, they have been able to stitch together a national network of banks.* **2** to get a deal or agreement arranged
stitch sb/sth ↔ **up** *phr v* **1** to put stitches in cloth or a wound in order to fasten parts of it together: *She stitched up the cut and left it to heal.* **2** to get a deal or agreement completed satisfactorily so that it cannot be changed: *The deal was stitched up in minutes.* **3** *BrE informal* to deceive someone, especially in order to gain money from them **4** *BrE informal* to make someone seem guilty of a crime by providing false information SYN **frame**

stitch·ing /ˈstɪtʃɪŋ/ *n* [U] a line of stitches in a piece of material

ˈstitch-up, **stitch up** *n* [C] *BrE* a situation in which someone is deliberately deceived

St ˌJohn ˈAmbulance (*also* **St John's Ambulance**) a British organization whose unpaid members are trained to give FIRST AID to anyone who is hurt or becomes ill. They often attend sports and other public events.

stoat /stəʊt $ stoʊt/ *n* [C] a small wild animal, similar to a WEASEL, that has a long thin body and brown fur

stock¹ /stɒk $ stɑːk/ ●●● S2 W2 *n*
1 IN A SHOP [C,U] a supply of a particular type of thing that a shop has available to sell: *We have a huge stock of quality carpets on sale.* | *Buy now while stocks last!* | **out of stock/in stock** (=unavailable or available in a particular shop) *I'm sorry, that swimsuit is completely out of stock in your size.*
2 FINANCE **a)** [C] *especially AmE* a SHARE in a company: *the trading of stocks and shares* **b)** [U] the total value of all of a company's SHARES
3 AMOUNT AVAILABLE [C] the total amount of something that is available to be used in a particular area: *Cod stocks in the North Atlantic have dropped radically.* | *the stock of housing in rural areas*
4 SUPPLIES [C] a supply of something that you keep and can use when you need to: **[+of]** *He keeps a stock of medicines in the cupboard.* | *The country has been* ***building up*** *its* ***stock*** *of weapons.*
5 take stock (of sth) to think carefully about the things that have happened in a situation in order to decide what to do next: *While in hospital, Jeremy took stock of his life.*
6 COOKING [C,U] a liquid made by boiling meat or bones and vegetables, which is used to make soups or to add FLAVOUR to other dishes: *chicken stock* | *vegetable stock*
7 GUN [C] the part of a gun that you hold or put against your shoulder, usually made of wood
8 ANIMALS [U] farm animals, especially cattle SYN **livestock**
9 the stocks a) a wooden structure in a public place to which criminals were fastened by their feet or hands in the past **b)** a wooden structure in which a ship is held while it is being built
10 sb's stock is high/low if someone's stock is high or low, they are very popular or very unpopular: *Simon's stock is high in the network news business.*
11 stock of jokes/knowledge/courage etc the jokes, knowledge etc that someone knows or has: *John seems to have an inexhaustible stock of funny stories.*
12 be of Scottish/Protestant/good etc stock to belong to a family that in the past lived in Scotland, were Protestants, were respected etc
13 FLOWER [C] a plant with pink, white, or light purple flowers and a sweet smell
14 PLANT [C] a thick part of a stem onto which another plant can be added so that the two plants grow together
15 ACTORS [C] *AmE* a STOCK COMPANY(2)

stock² ●●○ *v* [T]
1 if a shop stocks a particular product, it keeps a supply of it to sell: *We stock a wide range of kitchen equipment.*
2 to fill something with a supply of something: **stock sth with sth** *Our refrigerator at college was always stocked with beer.*
stock up *phr v* to buy a lot of something in order to keep it for when you need to use it later: **[+on]** *I have to stock up on snacks for the party.*

stock³ *adj* **1 stock excuse/question/remark etc** an excuse etc that people often say or use, especially when they cannot think of anything more interesting or original – used to show disapproval **2** [only before noun] **stock item/size** something that is available in a shop and does not have to be ordered

stock·ade /stɒˈkeɪd $ stɑː-/ *n* [C usually singular] a fence built from long thick pieces of wood pushed into the ground, used to defend a place

stock·breed·er /ˈstɒkbriːdə $ ˈstɑːkˌbriːdər/ *n* [C] a farmer who breeds cattle

stock·brok·er /ˈstɒkˌbrəʊkə $ ˈstɑːkˌbroʊkər/ *n* [C] a person or organization whose job is to buy and sell SHARES, BONDS etc for people —**stockbroking** *n* [U]

ˈstock car *n* [C] **1** a car that has been made stronger so that it can compete in a race where cars often crash into each other: *stock car racing* **2** *AmE* a railway carriage for cattle

ˈstock cerˌtificate *n* [C] *AmE* an official document that shows that you own SHARES in a company

ˈstock ˌcompany *n* [C] *AmE* **1** a company whose money is divided into SHARES so that many people own a small part of it SYN **joint-stock company 2** (*also* **stock**) a group of actors who work together doing several different plays

ˈstock cube *n* [C] a small solid CUBE made from the dried juices of meat or vegetables that is mixed with boiling water to make STOCK

ˈstock exˌchange *n* [C usually singular] **1** the business of buying and selling STOCKS and SHARES **2** a place where STOCKS and SHARES are bought and sold SYN **stock market**

stock·hold·er /ˈstɒkˌhəʊldə $ ˈstɑːkˌhoʊldər/ *n* [C] *especially AmE* someone who owns STOCKS in a business SYN **shareholder** *BrE*

ˈstock ˌindex *n* [C] an official and public list of STOCK prices

stock·i·nette /ˌstɒkɪˈnet $ ˌstɑː-/ *n* [U] *especially BrE* a soft cotton material that stretches, used especially for BANDAGES

stock·ing /ˈstɒkɪŋ $ ˈstɑː-/ *n* [C usually plural] **1** a thin close-fitting piece of clothing that covers a woman's leg and foot → **tights 2** *old-fashioned* a man's sock **3 in your stockinged/stocking feet** not wearing any shoes

ˈstocking ˌfiller *BrE*, **ˈstocking ˌstuffer** *AmE n* [C] a small present that you put in a CHRISTMAS STOCKING

ˈstocking ˌmask *n* [C] a stocking that someone wears over their face when they are doing something illegal such as robbing a bank

ˌstock-in-ˈtrade *n* [U] **1** something that is typical of a particular person or thing, especially what they say or do: *Stewart's stock-in-trade was the face-to-face interview.* **2** *literary* the things you need to do your job: *Vanessa's looks have been her stock-in-trade as an actress.*

stock·ist /ˈstɒkɪst $ ˈstɑː-/ *n* [C] *BrE* a person, shop, or company that keeps a particular product to sell: *Call us to order or to get details of **local stockists**.*

stock·man /ˈstɒkmən $ ˈstɑːk-/ *n* (*plural* **stockmen** /-mən/) [C] a man whose job is to take care of farm animals

ˈstock ˌmarket ●○○ *n* [C usually singular]
1 the business of buying and selling STOCKS and SHARES
2 a place where STOCKS and SHARES are bought and sold SYN **stock exchange**

ˈstock ˌoption *n* [C usually plural] *AmE* STOCK that a company offers to sell to an EMPLOYEE at a price that is lower than the usual price

stock·pile¹ /ˈstɒkpaɪl $ ˈstɑːk-/ *n* [C] a large supply of things that is kept ready for use in the future SYN **store**: **[+of]** *a stockpile of nuclear weapons*

stockpile² *v* [T] to keep adding to a supply of goods, weapons etc that you are keeping ready to use if you need them in the future: *An enormous volume of explosives was stockpiled inside one of the buildings.*

stock·pot /ˈstɒkpɒt $ ˈstɑːkpɑːt/ *n* [C] a pot in which you make STOCK

stock·room /ˈstɒkrʊm, -ruːm $ ˈstɑːk-/ *n* [C] a room for storing things in a shop or office

ˌstock-ˈstill *adv* not moving at all: *Oscar stood stock-still and listened.*

stock·tak·ing /ˈstɒkˌteɪkɪŋ $ ˈstɑːk-/ *n* [U] *BrE* when a company or shop checks the quantities of materials and goods that it has a supply of SYN **inventory** *AmE*

stock·y /ˈstɒki $ ˈstɑː-/ *adj* (*comparative* **stockier**, *superlative* **stockiest**) a stocky person is short and heavy and looks strong: *a **stocky build*** THESAURUS ▸ SHORT —**stockily** *adv* —**stockiness** *n* [U]

stock·yard /ˈstɒkjɑːd $ ˈstɑːkjɑːrd/ *n* [C] a place where cattle, sheep etc are kept before being taken to a market and sold

stodge /stɒdʒ $ stɑːdʒ/ *n* [U] *BrE informal* heavy food that makes you feel full very quickly

stodg·y /ˈstɒdʒi $ ˈstɑː-/ *adj* **1** if someone or something is stodgy, they are boring and formal or old-fashioned – used to show disapproval: *a stodgy play* **2** *BrE* stodgy food is heavy and makes you feel full very quickly – used to show disapproval OPP **light** —**stodginess** *n* [U]

sto·gie /ˈstəʊgi $ ˈstoʊ-/ *n* [C] *AmE informal* a CIGAR, especially a thick cheap one

sto·ic /ˈstəʊɪk $ ˈstoʊ-/ *n* [C] someone who does not show their emotions and does not complain when bad things happen to them

sto·ic·al /ˈstəʊɪkəl $ ˈstoʊ-/ (*also* **stoic**) *adj* not showing emotion or not complaining when bad things happen to you —**stoically** /-kli/ *adv*: *She bore the pain stoically.*

sto·i·cis·m /ˈstəʊɪsɪzəm $ ˈstoʊ-/ *n* [U] patience and calmness when bad things happen to you

stoke /stəʊk $ stoʊk/ (*also* **stoke up**) *v* [T] **1** to add more coal or wood to a fire: *I stoked the furnace for the night.* **2** to cause something to increase: *Rising oil prices stoked inflation.* | **stoke fear/anger/envy etc** *The scandal has stoked public outrage.*

stoke up *phr v* **1 stoke sth ↔ up** to add more coal or wood to a fire: *We kept the fire stoked up high on cold nights.* **2 stoke up sth** if something stokes up fear, anger etc, it makes a lot of people feel frightened etc: *The leaflets stoked up fears of an invasion.* **3 stoke up on/with sth** to eat a lot of food, for example because you will not eat again for a long time: *We stoked up on hot soup before going out in the snow.*

stoked /stəʊkt $ stoʊkt/ *adj* [not before noun] *AmE spoken* very pleased and excited

stok·er /ˈstəʊkə $ ˈstoʊkər/ *n* [C] someone whose job is to put coal or other FUEL on a fire or into a FURNACE, for example on a STEAMSHIP or a steam train

stole¹ /stəʊl $ stoʊl/ *v* the past tense of STEAL¹

stole² *n* [C] a long straight piece of cloth or fur that a woman wears across her shoulders

sto·len¹ /ˈstəʊlən $ ˈstoʊ-/ *v* the past participle of STEAL¹

stolen² ●●○ *adj* having been taken illegally: *stolen cars*

stol·id /ˈstɒlɪd $ ˈstɑː-/ *adj* someone who is stolid does not react to situations or seem excited by them when most people would react – used to show disapproval SYN **impassive** —**stolidly** *adv*

stom·ach¹ /ˈstʌmək/ ●●● S3 W3 *n* [C]
1 the organ inside your body where food begins to be DIGESTED: *I was so hungry my stomach hurt.* | *His stomach was full of food.* → see picture at **HUMAN¹**
2 the front part of your body, below your chest: *He turned round and punched Carlos in the stomach.*
3 do sth on an empty stomach to do something when you have not eaten: *You shouldn't take the pills on an empty stomach.*
4 turn your stomach to make you feel sick or upset: *The sight of the slaughtered cow turned my stomach.*
5 have no stomach for a fight/task etc to have no desire to do something difficult, upsetting, or frightening
6 have a strong stomach to be able to see or do things that are unpleasant without feeling sick or upset: *Don't go and see this film unless you have a strong stomach.*

COLLOCATIONS

ADJECTIVES

full (=full of food) *A lot of these children don't know what it is like to have a full stomach.*
empty (=with no food in) *It was 11 o'clock, and my stomach was empty.*
an upset stomach (=a stomach affected by illness) *Debbie was at home because she had an upset stomach.*

stomach + NOUN

(a) stomach ache *I had terrible stomach ache last night.*
stomach pains/cramps *He complained of acute stomach pains.*
a stomach bug (=an illness you have caught that affects your stomach) | **a stomach upset** (=when your stomach is affected by illness) | **a stomach ulcer** | **stomach cancer**

VERBS

sb's stomach rumbles (=it makes a noise because they are hungry) *She felt her stomach rumble.*
sb's stomach churns (=they feel sick because they are nervous or frightened) | **sb's stomach lurches/tightens** (=it suddenly feels tight because they are frightened)

stomach² *v* [T usually in negatives] **1** to be able to accept something, especially something unpleasant SYN **endure**: *A 26% water rate increase is more than most residents **can stomach**.* | **hard/difficult to stomach** *Rob found Cathy's attitude hard to stomach.* **2** to eat something without becoming ill: *I've never been able to stomach seafood.*

stom·ach·ache, **stomach ache** /ˈstʌmək-eɪk/ ●●● S3 *n* [C,U] pain in your stomach or near your stomach

ˈstomach-ˌchurning *adj* if something is stomach-churning, it is extremely unpleasant and makes you feel sick: *the stomach-churning extremes of physical torture*

ˈstomach pump *n* [C] a machine with a tube that doctors use to suck out food or liquid from someone's stomach, especially after they have swallowed something harmful

stomp /stɒmp $ stɑːmp/ *v* [I always + adv/prep] to walk with heavy steps or to put your foot down very hard, especially because you are angry SYN **stamp**: *Alex stomped angrily out of the meeting.* | **[+on]** *Rogers was injured after being stomped on by another player.* THESAURUS ▸ WALK

ˈstomping ˌground *n AmE* **sb's stomping ground** a favourite place where someone often goes SYN **stamping ground** *BrE*

stone¹ /stəʊn $ stoʊn/ ●●● S2 W1 *n*
1 ROCK [U] a hard solid mineral substance: *a **stone wall*** | *stone steps* | *The floors are made of stone.*

STONES

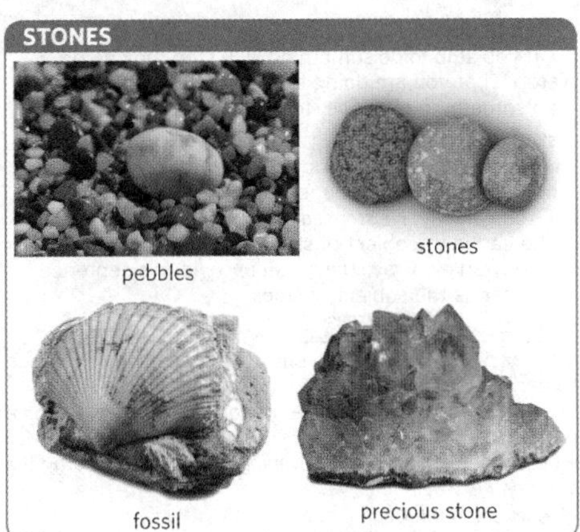

2 PIECE OF ROCK [C] a small piece of rock of any shape, found on the ground SYN **rock** *AmE*: *A handful of protesters began throwing stones at the police.*
3 JEWELLERY [C] a jewel SYN **precious stone**
4 FRUIT [C] *BrE* the large hard part at the centre of some fruits, such as a PEACH or CHERRY, which contains the seed SYN **pit** *AmE* → see picture at **FRUIT**[1]
5 MEDICAL [C] a ball of hard material that can form in organs such as your BLADDER or KIDNEYS
6 WEIGHT (*plural* **stone**) [C] (*written abbreviation* **st**) a British unit for measuring weight, equal to 14 pounds or 6.35 kilograms
7 a stone's throw from sth/away (from sth) very close to something: *The hotel is only a stone's throw from the beach.*
8 be made of stone (*also* **have a heart of stone**) to not show any emotions or pity for someone
9 not be carved/etched in stone used to say an idea or plan could change: *John has several new ideas for the show, but nothing is etched in stone yet.*
10 leave no stone unturned to do everything you can in order to find something or to solve a problem: *Jarvis left no stone unturned in his search to find the ring.*

stone[2] *v* [T] **1** to throw stones at someone or something: *Rioters blocked roads and stoned vehicles.* **2 stone sb to death** to kill someone by throwing stones at them, used as a punishment **3** *BrE* to take the stone out of fruit SYN **pit** *AmE*: *stoned dates* **4 stone the crows!** (*also* **stone me!**) *BrE old-fashioned* used to express surprise or shock

'Stone Age *n* **the Stone Age** a very early time in human history, when only stone was used for making tools, weapons etc: *Stone Age weapons* | *a Stone Age settlement*

,stone 'circle *n* [C] a circle of big tall stones, built thousands of years ago

,stone-'cold *adj, adv* **1** if something is stone-cold, it is completely cold even though it should be warm or hot: *Dinner was stone-cold by the time I got home.* **2 stone-cold sober** having drunk no alcohol at all **3** *AmE* if a player or sports team is stone-cold, they are not able to get any points

stoned /stəʊnd $ stoʊnd/ *adj* **1** *informal* feeling very excited or relaxed because you have taken an illegal drug such as MARIJUANA **2** *old-fashioned* very drunk

,stone 'dead *adj* **1** used to emphasize that a person or animal is dead **2 kill sth stone dead** to completely destroy something or prevent it from being successful: *The wrong music can kill a commercial stone dead.*

,stone 'deaf *adj* completely unable to hear

,stone-'faced (*also* **stony-faced**) *adj* showing no emotion or friendliness

'stone-ground *adj* stone-ground flour is made by crushing grain between two MILLSTONES

Stone·henge /ˌstəʊnˈhendʒ◂ $ ˈstəʊnhendʒ/ a group of very large tall stones that are arranged in a large circle with a smaller circle inside it, which stand on Salisbury Plain in Wiltshire, southern England. It is believed they were put there about 4,000 years ago and were used for studying the movements of the sun, moon, and stars. Some people also believe that they were used by the Druids (=ancient priests before the Christian period) in religious ceremonies.

stone·ma·son /ˈstəʊnmeɪsən $ ˈstoʊn-/ *n* [C] someone whose job is cutting stone into pieces to be used in buildings

Stone of Scone, the /ˌstəʊn əv ˈskuːn $ ˌstoʊn-/ a stone seat that was traditionally used in the ceremony for officially making someone king or queen of Scotland. It is also called the Stone of Destiny. The stone was taken from Scotland in 1296 and kept in Westminster Abbey in London, but Scottish Nationalists, who believed that the stone belonged in Scotland, tried to steal it. In 1996 it was officially returned to Scotland.

ston·er /ˈstəʊnə $ ˈstoʊnər/ *n* [C] *informal* someone who often smokes MARIJUANA

stone·wall /ˌstəʊnˈwɔːl $ ˌstoʊnˈwɒːl/ *v* [I] to delay a discussion, decision etc by talking a lot and refusing to answer questions

stone·ware /ˈstəʊnweə $ ˈstoʊnwer/ *n* [U] pots, bowls etc that are made from a special hard clay

,stone-'washed *adj* stone-washed JEANS etc have been washed with small stones so that they look older and paler

stone·work /ˈstəʊnwɜːk $ ˈstoʊnwɜːrk/ *n* [U] the parts of a building that are made of stone

stonk·er /ˈstɒŋkə $ ˈstɑːŋkər/ *n* [C] *BrE informal* something that is very good SYN **corker**: *Stephen Carr scored **a stonker** of a goal.*

stonk·ing[1] /ˈstɒŋkɪŋ $ ˈstɑːŋ-/ *adj BrE informal* extremely good: *a stonking performance*

stonking[2] *adv BrE informal* extremely: *a stonking good time*

ston·y /ˈstəʊni $ ˈstoʊ-/ *adj* **1** covered by stones or containing stones: *stony soil* **2** not showing any friendliness or pity: *stony faces* | *a **stony silence*** **3 fall on stony ground** if a request, suggestion, joke etc falls on stony ground, it is ignored or people do not like it —**stonily** *adv*: *Camilla stared stonily ahead.*

,stony-'faced (*also* **stone-faced**) *adj* showing no emotion or friendliness: *Tony stared at me in **stony-faced silence**.*

stood /stʊd/ the past tense and past participle of STAND[1]

stooge /stuːdʒ/ *n* [C] **1** *informal* someone who is used by someone else to do something unpleasant, dishonest, or illegal - used to show disapproval **2** one of two performers in a COMEDY show, who the other performer makes jokes about and makes look stupid

stool /stuːl/ ●●● S3 *n* [C]
1 a seat that has three or four legs, but no back or arms: *a **bar stool*** → see picture at **CHAIR**[1]
2 *medical* a piece of solid waste from your BOWELS

stool·pi·geon /ˈstuːlˌpɪdʒɪn/ *n* [C] *AmE informal* someone, especially a criminal, who helps the police to catch another criminal, usually by giving them information SYN **informer**

stoop[1] /stuːp/ *v* [I] **1** (*also* **stoop down**) to bend your body forward and down: *We had to stoop to pass through the low entrance.* | *Dave stooped down to tie his shoes.* **2** to stand with your back and shoulders bent forwards

stoop to sth *phr v* to do something bad or morally wrong, which you do not normally do: **stoop to doing sth** *I didn't expect you to stoop to lying.* | **stoop to sb's/that level** *Don't stoop to her level.*

stoop[2] *n* **1** [singular] if you have a stoop, your shoulders are bent forward: *Mr Hamilton was an odd, quiet man who walked with a stoop.* **2** [C] *AmE* a raised area at the door of a house, usually big enough to sit on

stooped /stuːpt/ (*also* **stoop·ing** /ˈstuːpɪŋ/) *adj* bent forwards and down: *a thin man with stooped shoulders*

This graph shows how common the different grammar patterns of the verb **stop** are.

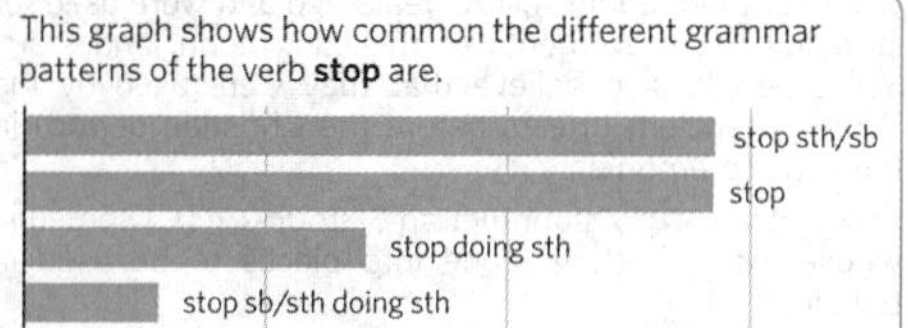

stop¹ /stɒp $ stɑːp/ ●●● S1 W1 *v* (**stopped, stopping**)
1 NOT CONTINUE **a)** [I,T] to not continue, or to make someone or something not continue: *By midday the rain had stopped.* | *This is where the path stops.* | *The referee stopped the fight.* | *The doctor advised me to stop the medication.* | *People are fighting to stop the destruction of the rain forests.* | **stop sb doing sth** *I couldn't stop her crying.* **b)** [I,T] if you stop doing something, you do not continue to do it: **stop doing sth** *I stopped digging and looked at him.* | *What time do you stop work?* | *I've been smoking for over ten years, and I can't stop.* | **stop it/that** (=stop doing something annoying) *Come on, you two! Stop it!* | *Right,* ***stop what you're doing*** *and come over here.*
2 PREVENT [T] to prevent someone from doing something or something from happening: *The government tried to stop publication of the book.* | *I'm leaving now, and you can't stop me.* | **stop sb/sth (from) doing sth** *Lay the carpet on paper to stop it sticking to the floor.* | *The rain didn't stop us from enjoying the trip.* | **stop yourself (from) doing sth** *I couldn't stop myself laughing.* | *She grabbed the rail to stop herself from falling.* | **there's nothing to stop sb (from) doing sth** *There's nothing to stop you applying for the job yourself.*
3 NOT MOVE [I,T] to not walk, move, or travel anymore, or to make someone or something do this: *He stopped suddenly when he saw Ruth.* | *Stop! Come back!* | *He stopped the car and got out.* | *I was worried that the security guards would stop us at the gate.* | **[+at/outside/in etc]** *She stopped outside the post office.* | *A car stopped behind us.* | **stop to do sth** *Sam stopped to give me a lift.* | **stop and do sth** *He stopped and looked into her face.* | **[+for]** *I need to stop for a rest.* | **stop dead/short/in your tracks** (=stop walking suddenly) *Sally saw the ambulance and stopped short.* | **stop on a dime** *AmE* (=stop very quickly – used about cars) *This truck can stop on a dime!*
4 PAUSE [I] to pause in an activity, journey etc in order to do something before you continue: **[+for]** *We stopped for a drink on the way home.* | **stop to do sth** *I stopped to tie my shoe.* | **stop to think/consider etc** *It's time we stopped to think about our next move.*
5 STAY [I] *BrE informal* to stay somewhere for a short time, especially at someone's house: *I won't sit down – I'm not stopping.* | **[+for]** *Will you stop for a cup of tea?*
6 will/would stop at nothing (to do sth) to be ready to do anything to achieve something that you want to achieve: *We will stop at nothing to save our child.*
7 stop short of (doing) sth to decide that you are not willing to do something wrong or dangerous, though you will do something similar that is less dangerous: *The US government supported sanctions but stopped short of military action.*
8 MONEY [T] if you stop an amount of money, you prevent it from being paid to someone: *Dad threatened to stop my pocket money.* | **stop sth from sth** *£200 will be stopped from your wages next month to pay for the damage.* | *I phoned the bank and asked them to* ***stop*** *the* ***cheque*** (=not pay a cheque that I had written). | *My mother called the bank to* ***stop payment*** *on the check.*
9 BLOCK [T] (*also* **stop up**) to block a hole or pipe so that water, smoke etc cannot go through it

GRAMMAR: Patterns with stop

stop doing sth
• If you **stop doing** something, you do not continue doing it: *Stop writing and put your pens down.* ✗ Don't say: *Stop to write and put your pens down.*

stop to do sth
• If you **stop to do** something, you stop moving or stop what you are doing for a short time, in order to do something else: *She stopped to look at the map.*

stop sth/sth stops
• **Stop** belongs to a group of verbs where the same noun can be the subject of the verb or its object.
• You can say: *He stopped the car.* In this sentence, 'the car' is the object of **stop**.
• You can also say: *The car stopped.* In this sentence, 'the car' is the subject of **stop**.
GRAMMAR GUIDE ▸ VERBS

stop back *phr v AmE* to go back to a place you have been to earlier: *Can you stop back later? I'm busy right now.*
stop by (sth) *phr v* to make a short visit to a place or a person's home, especially while you are going somewhere else: *I'll stop by this evening.* | *Daniel stopped by the store on his way home.*
stop in *phr v informal*
1 to make a short visit to a place or person, especially while you are going somewhere else: *I'll stop in and see you on my way home.* | **[+at]** *I need to stop in at the library.*
2 *BrE* to stay at home: *I'm stopping in to wash my hair tonight.*
stop off *phr v* to make a short visit to a place during a journey, especially to rest or to see someone: *We can stop off and see you on our way back.* | **[+in/at etc]** *We stopped off in Santa Rosa for a day.*
stop out *phr v BrE informal* to stay out later than usual: *It was a real treat being allowed to stop out late.*
stop over *phr v* to stop somewhere and stay a short time before continuing a long journey, especially when travelling by plane: *The plane stops over in Dubai on the way to India.* → STOPOVER
stop up *phr v*
1 stop sth ↔ up to block a hole or pipe so that water, smoke etc cannot go through it
2 *BrE informal* to stay up late: *Joe stopped up till 3 o'clock to watch the boxing.*

stop² ●●● S2 W3 *n* [C]
1 come/roll/jerk/skid etc to a stop if a vehicle comes to a stop, it stops moving: *The bus came to a stop outside the school.* | *The car skidded to a stop.*
2 come to a stop if an activity comes to a stop, it stops happening: *Work on the project has come to a stop because of lack of funding.*
3 bring sth to a stop to stop something moving or happening: *David brought the truck to a shuddering stop.* | *The UN is trying to bring the war to a stop.*
4 DURING JOURNEY a time or place when you stop during a journey for a short time: *Our first stop was Paris.* | *We'll* ***make*** *a* ***stop*** *at the foot of the hill.* | *The trip includes an* ***overnight stop*** *in London.*
5 BUS/TRAIN a place where a bus or train regularly stops for people to get on and off: *Our next stop will be York.* | *This is your stop, isn't it?*
6 put a stop to sth to prevent something from continuing or happening: *The government is determined to put a stop to the demonstrations.*
7 pull out all the stops to do everything you possibly can to make something happen and succeed: *The hospital staff pulled out all the stops to make sure the children had a wonderful day.*
8 MONEY the action or fact of telling your bank not to pay an amount of money to someone: *I* ***put a stop on*** *that check to the store.*
9 MUSIC a handle that you push in or out on an ORGAN to control the amount of sound it produces
10 CONSONANT a consonant sound, like /p/ or /k/, that you make by stopping the flow of air completely and then suddenly letting it out of your mouth → FULL STOP¹

stop·cock /ˈstɒpkɒk $ ˈstɑːpkɑːk/ *n* [C] a TAP that controls the flow of a liquid or gas through a pipe

stop·gap /ˈstɒpgæp $ ˈstɑːp-/ *n* [C] something or someone that you use for a short time until you can replace them with something better: *It's only a* ***stopgap measure****, not a long-term solution.*

ˌstop-ˈgo *adj* **stop-go approach/policies etc** *BrE* a way of controlling the ECONOMY by restricting government spending for a period of time and then not restricting it so severely for a time

stop·light /ˈstɒplaɪt $ ˈstɑːp-/ (*also* **stoplights** [plural]) *n* [C] *AmE* a set of coloured lights used to control and direct traffic SYN **traffic lights**

ˌstop-ˈloss ˌorder *n* [C] *technical* an arrangement in which the person who buys and sells STOCKS for you agrees to buy or sell them when they reach a particular price

stop·o·ver /ˈstɒpˌəʊvə $ ˈstɑːpˌoʊvər/ *n* [C] a short stay somewhere between parts of a journey, especially on a long plane journey: *a two-day stopover in Hong Kong*

stop·page /ˈstɒpɪdʒ $ ˈstɑːp-/ *n* **1** [C] a situation in which workers stop working for a short time as a protest: *time lost in disputes and stoppages* | *a* ***work stoppage*** *by government employees* **2** [C,U] *especially BrE* when something stops moving or happening: *We had five minutes of* ***stoppage time*** (=extra time played in a sports match because of pauses) *at the end of the first half.* **3** [C] something that blocks a tube or container: *an intestinal stoppage*

stop·per /ˈstɒpə $ ˈstɑːpər/ *n* [C] the thing that you put in the top part of a bottle to close it → **cork** —**stopper** *v* [T]: *a small, stoppered jar*

ˈstopping ˌdistance *n* [C,U] the distance that a driver is supposed to leave between their car and the one in front in order to be able to stop safely

ˈstopping ˌtrain *n* [C] *BrE* a train that stops at all stations, not just the main ones

ˌstop ˈpress *n* [singular] late news added to a newspaper after the main part has been printed

stop·watch /ˈstɒpwɒtʃ $ ˈstɑːpwɑːtʃ, -wɒːtʃ/ *n* [C] a watch used for measuring the exact time it takes to do something, especially to finish a race → see picture at MEASURE[1]

stor·age /ˈstɔːrɪdʒ/ ●●○ W3 *n* [U]
1 the process of keeping or putting something in a special place while it is not being used: *the storage of radioactive material* | **storage space/capacity** (=space etc for keeping things in) *They moved to a house with lots of storage space.*
2 when you pay to keep furniture or other goods in a special place until you need to use them: **in storage** *I put some of my things in storage.* | *storage costs*
3 the way that information is kept on a computer: *data storage*

ˈstorage ˌheater *n* [C] *BrE* a HEATER that stores heat at times when electricity is cheaper, for example at night

store[1] /stɔː $ stɔːr/ ●●● S1 W1 *n* [C]
1 SHOP a place where goods are sold to the public. In British English, a store is large and sells many different things, but in American English, a store can be large or small, and sell many things or only one type of thing. → **shop**: *At Christmas the stores stay open late.* | **shoe/clothing/grocery etc store** *AmE* (=one that sells one type of goods) *She worked in a grocery store before going to college.* | **go to the store** *AmE* (=go to a store that sells food) *I need to go to the store for some milk.* → CHAIN STORE, DEPARTMENT STORE, GENERAL STORE
2 SUPPLY a supply of something that you keep to use later: **[+of]** *a store of wood* | *fat stores in the body* (=that your body keeps)
3 PLACE TO KEEP THINGS a large building in which goods are kept so they can be used or sold later: *a grain store*
4 in store (for sb) if something unexpected such as a surprise or problem is in store for someone, it is about to happen to them: *There's a real treat in store for you this*

S

THESAURUS: stop

TO STOP DOING SOMETHING

stop to not do something any longer: *I wish she would stop talking.* | *He waited for them to stop.*
quit *especially AmE informal* to stop doing something: *She needs to quit complaining about her life.* | *It's too late for him to quit now.*
give sth up to stop doing something, especially something that you have been doing for a long time: *It's so hard to give up smoking.* | *She wants to give up her job.*
pack sth in *informal* to stop doing something, especially because you feel tired or annoyed: *Sometimes I feel like packing in my job and starting again somewhere else.* | *Pack it in, will you!* (=used when telling someone to stop doing something, because they are annoying you)
pull out of sth to stop taking part in something that you have agreed to take part in: *The unions have pulled out of the negotiations.* | *The US decided to pull out of the competition.*
cease *formal* to stop doing something: *The company has decided to cease production of its film cameras.* | *The US government ceased talks with North Korea.*

TO STOP FOR A SHORT TIME

stop to stop for a short time: *Shall we stop for coffee now?* | *I stopped to have a look at the map.*
pause to stop speaking or doing something for a short time before starting again: *He paused for a moment to consider the question.*
have/take a break to stop working, studying, or driving for a short time in order to rest: *Okay, everyone. Take a ten-minute break.* | *If you're feeling tired, you should have a break.*

TO STOP HAPPENING

stop to stop happening: *The noise suddenly stopped.* | *We waited for the rain to stop.*
come to an end to stop – used about something that has continued for a long time: *The war finally came to an end in 1918.*
wear off to gradually stop – used about a pain, a feeling, or the effects of something: *The pain will soon wear off.* | *The excitement was beginning to wear off.* | *The anaesthetic took a long time to wear off.*
peter out to gradually stop happening or existing: *The campaign petered out after only a few weeks.*
cease *formal* to stop: *The fighting has ceased.* | *Production at the factory has ceased.*

TO STOP MOVING

stop to stop moving: *Can we stop soon? I'm tired.* | *The bus stops right in front of the hotel.*
come to a halt *especially written* to move more slowly and then stop – used about a vehicle: *The train slowly came to a halt just outside the station.*
pull over to move to the side of the road and stop – used about a vehicle or its driver: *The bus pulled over to the side of the road, with smoke coming out of its engine.* | *The police officer was waving at him to pull over.*
pull up to stop close to something – used about a vehicle or its driver: *The taxi pulled up outside her house.* | *He pulled up next to our car.*
come to a standstill to go slower and then stop moving completely: *The road was blocked by an accident, and the traffic quickly came to a standstill.*

*Christmas! | As we left, I wondered what the future **held in store**.*
5 MILITARY **stores** [plural] **a)** supplies of food and equipment that are used by an army, navy etc: *medical stores* **b)** the building or room in an army camp, ship etc where these are kept
6 set great/considerable etc store by sth to consider something to be important: *Patrick has never set much store by material things.*

store² ●●● S3 W3 *v* [T]
1 to put things away and keep them until you need them: **store sth away/up** *Squirrels are storing up nuts for the winter. | Store the beans in an airtight jar.*
2 to keep facts or information in your brain or a computer: *Standard letters can be stored on floppy discs.*
3 store up trouble/problems etc to behave in a way that will cause trouble for you later: *Smokers may be storing up disease for their unborn children.*

ˈstore brand *n* [C] *especially AmE* a type of product that is made for a particular shop and has the shop's name on it: *Store brands are cheaper than name brands.*

ˈstore card *n* [C] *BrE* a card provided by a particular shop, that you can use to buy goods at that shop and pay for them at a later date SYN **charge card**

ˈstore deˌtective *n* [C] someone who is employed in a large shop to watch the customers and to stop them stealing

store·front /ˈstɔːfrʌnt $ ˈstɔːr-/ *n* [C] *AmE* **1** the part of a store that faces the street **2 storefront church/law office/school etc** a small church etc in a shopping area

store·house /ˈstɔːhaʊs $ ˈstɔːr-/ *n* [C] **1 storehouse of information/memories etc** something that contains a lot of information etc: *The local archives service offers a storehouse of material.* **2** *old-fashioned* a building where things are stored SYN **warehouse**

store·keep·er /ˈstɔːˌkiːpə $ ˈstɔːrˌkiːpər/ *n* [C] *AmE* someone who owns or manages a shop SYN **shopkeeper** *BrE*

store·room /ˈstɔːrʊm, -ruːm/ *n* [C] a room where goods are stored

sto·rey *BrE*, **story** *AmE* /ˈstɔːri/ ●○○ *n* [C] a floor or level of a building: *a staircase leads to the **upper storey** |* **two-storey/five-storey etc** (=having two etc storeys) THESAURUS ▸ FLOOR

stor·ied /ˈstɔːrid/ *adj* **1 two-storied/five storied etc** *AmE* having two etc storeys **2** [only before noun] *literary* being the subject of many stories SYN **famous**: *Sun Tzu, the storied Chinese leader and philosopher*

stork /stɔːk $ stɔːrk/ *n* [C] a tall white bird with long legs and a long beak

storm¹ /stɔːm $ stɔːrm/ ●●● W3 *n*
1 [C] a period of very bad weather when there is a lot of rain or snow, strong winds, and often LIGHTNING: *The weather forecast is for severe storms tonight. | Twenty people were killed when the storm struck the Midwest.*
2 [C usually singular] a situation in which people suddenly express very strong feelings about something that someone has said or done: *The governor found himself at the center of a **political storm**.* | **storm of protest/criticism etc** *Government plans for hospital closures provoked a storm of protest.*
3 take somewhere by storm a) to be very successful in a particular place: *The new show took London by storm.* **b)** to attack a place using large numbers of soldiers, and succeed in getting possession of it
4 weather the storm to experience a difficult period and reach the end of it without being harmed or damaged too much: *I'll stay and weather the storm.*
5 a storm in a teacup *BrE* an unnecessary expression of strong feelings about something that is very unimportant
6 dance/sing/cook etc up a storm to do something with all your energy: *They were dancing up a storm.*

COLLOCATIONS

ADJECTIVES/NOUN + storm

a big storm *The tree had come down on the day of the big storm.*
a bad/terrible storm *This was the worst storm for 50 years.*
a severe/violent/fierce storm *He set out in a violent storm for Fort William.*
a great storm *literary: the great storm of 1987*
a tropical storm *The tropical storm smashed through the Bahamas.*
a rain/snow storm | an electrical storm (=one with lightning) **| a winter/summer storm | a freak storm** (=an unexpected and unusually violent one)

VERBS

a storm blows up (=starts) *That night, a storm blew up.*
a storm breaks (=suddenly starts, after clouds have been increasing) *The storm broke at five o'clock.*
a storm is brewing (=is likely to start soon) *He could feel that a storm was brewing.*
a storm rages (=is active and violent) *By the time we reached the airfield, a tropical storm was raging.*
a storm hits/strikes (a place) *We should try to get home before the storm hits.*
a storm lashes/batters a place *literary* **| a storm abates/passes | a storm blows itself out** (=ends)

storm + NOUN

storm clouds *We could see storm clouds in the distance.*
storm damage *A lot of buildings suffered storm damage.*

COMMON ERRORS

⚠ Don't say 'a strong storm' or 'a hard storm'. Say **a big storm, a bad storm**, or **a violent storm**.

THESAURUS

storm a period of very bad weather when there is a lot of rain or snow, strong winds, and often lightning: *The ship sank in a violent storm. | They got caught in a storm on top of the mountain.*
thunderstorm a storm in which there is a lot of THUNDER (=loud noise in the sky) and LIGHTNING (=flashes of light in the sky): *When I was young I was terrified of thunderstorms.*
hurricane a storm that has very strong fast winds and that moves over water – used about storms in the North Atlantic Ocean: *Hurricane Katrina battered the US Gulf Coast. | the hurricane season*
typhoon a very violent tropical storm – used about storms in the Western Pacific Ocean: *A powerful typhoon hit southern China today.*
cyclone a severe storm affecting a large area, in which the wind moves around in a big circle: *Thousands of people died when a tropical cyclone hit Bangladesh.*
tornado (*also* **twister** *AmE informal*) an extremely violent storm that consists of air that spins very quickly and causes a lot of damage: *The tornado ripped the roof off his house.*
snowstorm a storm with strong winds and a lot of snow: *A major snowstorm blew across Colorado.*
blizzard a severe snowstorm in which the snow is blown around by strong winds, making it difficult to see anything: *We got stuck in a blizzard. | Denver is bracing itself for **blizzard conditions**.*

storm² ●○○ *v*
1 [T] to suddenly attack and enter a place using a lot of force: *An angry crowd stormed the embassy.* THESAURUS ▸ ATTACK
2 [I always + adv/prep] to go somewhere in a noisy fast way that shows you are extremely angry: **[+out of/into/off etc]** *Alan stormed out of the room.*

3 [I,T] *literary* to shout something in an angry way: *'What difference does it make?' she stormed.*

ˈstorm ˌcellar *n* [C] *AmE* a place under a house where you can go to be safe during violent storms

ˈstorm cloud *n* [C] **1** a dark cloud which you see before a storm **2** [usually plural] a sign that something very bad is going to happen: ***Storm clouds are gathering*** *over the trade negotiations.*

ˈstorm door *n* [C] a second door that is fitted to the outside of a door in winter in the US to give protection against rain, snow etc

ˈstorm drain *n* [C] an opening at the side of a street that carries away rainwater during a storm

ˈstorm ˌlantern *n* [C] a lamp which has a cover to protect the flame against the wind, used in the past

storm·troop·er /ˈstɔːmˌtruːpə $ ˈstɔːrmˌtruːpər/ *n* [C] a member of a special group of German soldiers in the Second World War

ˈstorm ˌwindow *n* [C] a second window fitted to the outside of a window in winter in the US to give more protection against rain, snow etc

storm·y /ˈstɔːmi $ ˈstɔːr-/ ●●● S3 *adj*
1 with strong winds, heavy rain, and dark clouds: *The sky was starting to look stormy.* | *a dark and stormy night*
2 a stormy relationship, meeting etc is full of strong and often angry feelings: *a stormy affair*
3 stormy seas are very rough, with big waves that are caused by strong winds: *hostile, stormy seas*

sto·ry /ˈstɔːri/ ●●● S1 W1 *n* (*plural* **stories**) [C]
1 FOR ENTERTAINMENT a description of how something happened, that is intended to entertain people, and may be true or imaginary → **tale**: **[+about/of]** *a story about a princess* | **fairy/ghost/love etc story** *a detective story* | **tell/read sb a story** *Mommy, will you read me a story?* | *a book of* ***short stories*** | *We cuddled together over a* ***bedtime story***. | *The film was based on a* ***true story***. | *Don't be frightened – it's only a story* (=it is imaginary).
2 NEWS a report in a newspaper or news broadcast about a recent event, or something that is reported on: *a front-page story* | *'The Observer'* ***ran a story*** *about the scandal* (=printed it). | **cover story** (=the main story in a magazine, which is about the picture on the cover)
3 EVENTS an account of something that has happened, usually one that people tell each other, and which may not be true: *The* ***full story*** *of what happened has never been reported.* | *Her parents did not believe her story.* | *First, he wanted to hear Matthew's* ***side of the story*** (=his description of what happened). | *He was having an affair with Julie, or* ***so the story goes*** (=people are saying this).
4 EXCUSE an excuse or explanation, especially one that you have invented: *Where were you? And don't give me some story about working late!* | *Well, that's my story* (=that is what I say happened)*, and I'm sticking to it.*
5 HISTORY a description of the most important events in someone's life or in the development of something: *the Charlie Parker Story* | *He wanted to have his* ***life story*** *told on film.*
6 BUILDING *AmE* a floor or level of a building SYN **storey** *BrE*: *a 50-story building*
7 OF A FILM/PLAY ETC what happens in a film, play, or book SYN **plot**: *The story is similar in all her books.*
8 it's the same story here/there/in ... used to say the same thing is happening in another place: *Unemployment is falling in the US, and it's the same story in Europe.*

SPOKEN PHRASES
9 it's the same old story used to say that the present bad situation has often happened before: *It's the same old story – too much work and not enough time.*
10 it's a long story used to tell someone that you do not want to give them all the details that a full answer to their question would need
11 to cut a long story short (*also* **to make a long story short** *AmE*) used when you only give the main point of something you are talking about, and not all the other details
12 but that's another story used when you have mentioned something that you are not going to talk about on this occasion
13 that's not the whole story used to say that there are more details which people need to know in order to understand the situation
14 that's the story of my life used after a disappointing experience to mean that similar disappointing things always seem to happen to you
15 end of story used to say that there is nothing more to say about a particular subject: *As far as I'm concerned, Terry is still a friend – end of story.*

16 it's a different story used to say that something is not what you expect it to be: *It looks like a big house, but inside it's a different story.*
17 LIE a lie – used by children or when speaking to children SYN **tale**: *You shouldn't* ***tell stories***. → SHORT STORY, → **cock and bull story** at COCK¹(4), → HARD-LUCK STORY, SOB STORY, → **success story** at SUCCESS(5)

THESAURUS

story a description of how something happened that is intended to entertain people, and may be true or imaginary: *a ghost story* | *a love story* | *It's a story about a man who loses his memory.*
tale a story about strange imaginary events, or exciting events that happened in the past: *a fairy tale by Hans Christian Andersen* | *I loved hearing tales of his travels.*
myth *n* [C,U] a very old imaginary story about gods and magical creatures: *an ancient myth* | *Greek and Roman myths*
legend *n* [C,U] an old story about brave people or magical events that are probably not true: *popular legends of the creation of the world* | *According to legend, King Arthur was buried there.*
fable a traditional imaginary short story that teaches a moral lesson, especially a story about animals: *the fable of the tortoise and the hare* | *a Chinese fable*
epic a story told in a long book, film, or poem which is about great or exciting events, especially in history: *an epic about 13th-century Scottish hero William Wallace*
saga a story about a series of events that take place over a long period of time, especially events involving one family: *a family saga beginning in the 1880s*
yarn *informal* a long exciting story that is not completely true: *The movie's a rattling good yarn and full of action.*

sto·ry·board /ˈstɔːriˌbɔːd $ -ˌbɔːrd/ *n* [C] a set of drawings that are done before a film is made in order to show what will happen in it —**storyboarding** *n* [U]: *I can't do any storyboarding until I get the script.*

sto·ry·book¹ /ˈstɔːribʊk/ *n* [C] a book of stories for children: *colourful storybooks*

storybook² *adj* **storybook ending/romance etc** an ending etc that is so happy or perfect that it is like one in a children's story SYN **fairytale**: *It would have been storybook stuff if he had won the competition.*

ˈstory line, sto·ry·line /ˈstɔːrilaɪn/ ●○○ *n* [C] the main set of related events in a story SYN **plot**: *The play had a strong story line.*

sto·ry·tell·er /ˈstɔːriˌtelə $ -ər/ *n* [C] someone who tells stories, especially to children

stoup /stuːp/ *n* [C] a container for holy water near the entrance to a church

stout¹ /staʊt/ *adj* **1** fairly fat and heavy, or having a thick body: *a short, stout man* **2** *literary* strong and thick SYN **sturdy**: *a stout pair of shoes* **3** *formal* brave and determined: **stout defence/support/resistance** *He put up a stout defence in court.* —**stoutly** *adv*: *She stoutly denied the rumours.* —**stoutness** *n* [U]

stout² *n* [U] strong dark beer

stout·heart·ed /ˌstaʊtˈhɑːtɪd◂ $ -ɑːr-/ *adj literary* brave and determined

S

stove¹ /stəʊv $ stoʊv/ ●●○ *n* [C]
1 a piece of kitchen equipment on which you cook food in pots and pans, and that contains an OVEN SYN **cooker** *BrE*: **on the stove** *a pot of soup simmering on the stove*
2 a thing used for heating a room or for cooking, which works by burning wood, coal, oil, or gas: *a wood-burning stove*

stove² a past tense and past participle of STAVE²

stow /stəʊ $ stoʊ/ (*also* **stow away**) *v* [T always + adv/prep] to put or pack something tidily away in a space until you need it again SYN **stash**: *I stowed my bag under the seat.* | *equipment stowed away in a closet*

stow away *phr v* to hide on a vehicle in order to travel secretly or without paying: *A boy was caught trying to stow away on a plane.* → **STOWAWAY**

stow·age /ˈstəʊɪdʒ $ ˈstoʊ-/ *n* [C] space available in a vehicle, especially a boat, for storing things

stow·a·way /ˈstəʊəweɪ $ ˈstoʊ-/ *n* [C] someone who hides on a vehicle in order to travel secretly or to avoid paying

strad·dle /ˈstrædl/ *v* [T] **1** to sit or stand with your legs on either side of someone or something: *The photo shows him dressed in leather, straddling a motorbike.* **2** if something straddles a line, road, or river, part of it is on one side and part on the other side: **straddle sth between sth** *Mount Elgon straddles the border between Kenya and Uganda.* **3** to include different areas of activity, groups, time etc: *Her research straddles mathematics and social sciences.* | *immigrants straddling two cultures*

strafe /streɪf, strɑːf $ streɪf/ *v* [T] to attack a place from an aircraft by flying low and firing a lot of bullets

strag·gle /ˈstræɡəl/ *v* [I] **1** if the people in a group straggle somewhere, they go there fairly slowly and with large spaces between them: **[+in/into/through etc]** *The children were beginning to straggle in from the playground.* | **[+behind]** *Ali straggled behind, carrying the shopping.* **2** to move, grow, or spread out untidily in different directions: *thin, black, straggling hair* | **[+along/across/down etc]** *Unpainted wooden buildings straggle along the main road out of town.*

strag·gler /ˈstræɡlə $ -ər/ *n* [C] a person or animal that is behind the others in a group, because they are moving more slowly: *Wait for the stragglers to catch up.*

strag·gly /ˈstræɡəli/ *adj* growing untidily and spreading out in different directions: *straggly hair*

S

straight¹ /streɪt/ ●●● S1 W2 *adv*
1 IN A STRAIGHT LINE in a line or direction that is not curved or bent: **[+ahead/at/down/in front of etc]** *The book is on the table straight in front of you.* | *She was looking straight at me.* | *Terry was so tired he couldn't walk straight.* | *He was sitting with his legs stretched straight out in front of him.*
2 POSITION in a level or correct position: *Sit up straight, don't slouch.*
3 IMMEDIATELY immediately, without delay, or without doing anything else first: **[+to/up/down/back etc]** *I went straight up to bed.* | *Go* ***straight home*** *and tell your mother.* | **[+after]** *I've got a meeting straight after lunch.* | *I think I should* ***get straight to the point***.
4 ONE AFTER THE OTHER happening one after the other in a series: *He's been without sleep now for three days straight.*
5 HONEST (*also* **straight out**) if you say or ask something straight, you say it in an honest direct way, without trying to hide your meaning: *I just told him straight that I wouldn't do it.* | *She* ***came straight out with it*** *and said she was leaving.* | *I hope, for your sake, you're* ***playing it straight*** (=being honest). | *I told him* ***straight to his face*** (=speaking directly to him) *what I thought of him.*
6 think/see straight if you cannot think or see straight, you cannot think or see clearly: *Turn the radio down – I can't think straight.*
7 straight away (*also* **straight off**) *BrE spoken* immediately or without delay: *I phoned my mum straight away.*
8 go straight *informal* to stop being a criminal and live an honest life: *Tony's been trying to go straight for about six months.*
9 straight up *spoken* **a)** used to ask someone if they are telling the truth: *Straight up? Did you really pay that much for it?* **b)** used to emphasize that what you are saying is true: *No, straight up, I've never seen him before.*
10 straight from the shoulder *BrE informal* if someone speaks straight from the shoulder, they say things in a very direct way, without trying to be polite

STRAIGHT

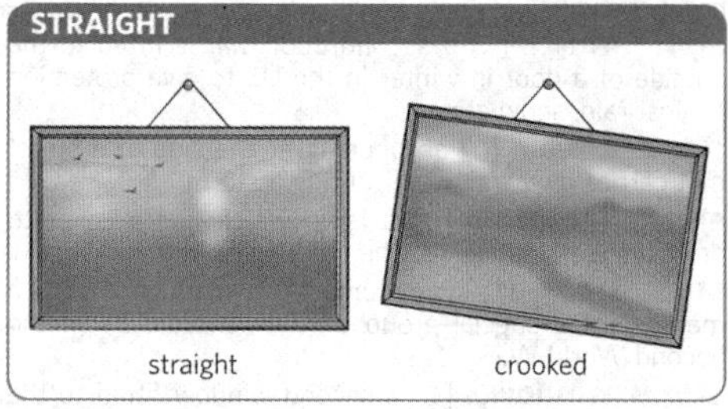
straight crooked

straight² ●●● S2 W3 *adj* (*comparative* **straighter**, *superlative* **straightest**)
1 NOT BENDING OR CURVING something that is straight does not bend or curve: *a long, straight road* | *Try to keep your legs straight.* | *Always lift with a straight back.* | *her long, straight black hair* | *They sat down* ***in a straight line***. | *The road was* ***dead straight*** (=completely straight). → see picture at **HAIRSTYLE**
2 LEVEL/UPRIGHT level or upright, and not leaning to one side: *Is my tie straight?* | *straight white teeth*
3 TRUTHFUL honest and truthful: *I'd like a* ***straight answer*** *please.* | *Just give me a straight yes or no.* | *I think it's time for some* ***straight talk*** *now.* | **be straight with sb** *I wish you'd just be straight with me.* THESAURUS HONEST
4 ONE AFTER ANOTHER [only before noun] happening immediately one after another in a series: *The team now has an amazing record of 43 straight wins.*
5 TIDY [not before noun] a room that is straight is clean and tidy and everything is in its proper place: *It took me two hours to* ***get*** *the house* ***straight***.
6 get sth straight *spoken* to understand the facts of a situation and be able to tell them correctly: *I wanted to get the facts straight.* | *Let me get this straight – Tom sold the car and gave you the money?*
7 set/put sb straight to make someone understand the true facts about a situation: *Tell him to ask Ruth – she'll put him straight.*
8 straight face if you have a straight face, you are not laughing or smiling even though you would like to: *I found it very difficult to* ***keep a straight face***.
9 SEXUAL CHOICE *informal* someone who is straight is attracted to people of the opposite sex SYN **heterosexual**
10 ALCOHOLIC DRINK a straight alcoholic drink has no water or any other drink added to it: *a straight whisky*
11 NOT OWING MONEY [not before noun] *spoken* if two people are straight, they no longer owe money to each other: *If you give me £10, then we're straight.*
12 CHOICE/EXCHANGE [only before noun] a straight choice or exchange is between only two possible choices or things: *It was a* ***straight choice*** *between my career or my family.* | *We did a straight swap – one of my cards for one of his.*
13 FIGHT/COMPETITION [only before noun] a straight fight or competition is between only two people: *The election is now a straight fight between Labour and the Conservatives.*
14 NORMAL *informal* someone who is straight behaves in a way that is accepted as normal by many people but which you think is boring
15 NOT FUNNY a straight actor or character does not try to make people laugh
16 ONLY ONE TYPE completely one particular type of something: *It's not a straight historical novel.*
17 DRUGS *informal* someone who is straight does not take illegal drugs → **set/put the record straight** at **RECORD¹**

straight³ *n* **1** [singular] *especially BrE* the straight part of a RACETRACK **2 the straight and narrow** *old-fashioned* an honest and morally good way of life **3** [C] *informal* someone who is attracted to people of the opposite sex OPP **gay**

ˌstraight ˈarrow *n* [C] *AmE informal* someone who is very honest and moral and who never does anything exciting or unusual

straight·a·way¹ /ˌstreɪtəˈweɪ/ *adv* at once SYN **immediately**: *We need to start work straightaway.*

straight·a·way² /ˈstreɪtəweɪ/ *n* [singular] *AmE* the straight part of a RACETRACK SYN **straight**

straight·en /ˈstreɪtn/ ●○○ *v*

1 [I,T] (*also* **straighten out**) to become straight, or to make something straight: *Can you straighten your leg?*

2 [I] (*also* **straighten up**) to make your back straight, or to stand up straight after bending down

3 [T] (*also* **straighten up**) to make something tidy: *Mum told me to straighten my room.*

straighten out *phr v*

1 straighten sth ↔ out to deal with problems or a confused situation and make it better, especially by organizing things SYN **sort out**: *There are several financial problems that need to be straightened out quickly.*

2 to become straight, or to make something straight: *The path soon bends to the right, then straightens out.* | **straighten sth ↔ out** *She straightened out her legs.*

3 to improve your bad behaviour or deal with personal problems, or to help someone do this: *He straightened out when he joined the army.* | **straighten sb ↔ out** *Her parents changed her school, hoping it would straighten her out.*

straighten up *phr v*

1 to make your back straight, or to stand up straight after bending down: *He remained bent over for several seconds before slowly straightening up.*

2 straighten sth ↔ up to make something tidy

3 *AmE* to begin to behave well after behaving badly: *You'd better straighten up, young lady!*

straight·faced /ˌstreɪtˈfeɪst◂/ *adj* without smiling or laughing, even though you are joking or saying something untrue: *'No, I really do love you,' said Kim, straightfaced.* —**straightfacedly** /-ˈfeɪsɪdli◂/ *adv*

straight·for·ward /ˌstreɪtˈfɔːwəd◂ $ -ˈfɔːrwərd◂/ ●●○ S3 AWL *adj*

1 simple and easy to understand OPP **complicated**: **relatively/quite/fairly straightforward** *Installing the program is relatively straightforward.* | *This area of law is* ***far from straightforward*** (=complicated). | **straightforward matter/task/process etc** *For someone who can't read, shopping is by no means a straightforward matter.* THESAURUS ▸ EASY

2 honest about your feelings or opinions and not hiding anything: *Jack is tough, but always straightforward and fair.* —**straightforwardly** *adv* —**straightforwardness** *n* [U]

straight·jack·et /ˈstreɪtˌdʒækɪt/ *n* [C] another spelling of STRAITJACKET

ˈstraight man *n* [C] an entertainer who works with a COMEDIAN, providing him or her with opportunities to make jokes

ˈstraight ˌshooter *n* [C] *AmE informal* an honest person who you can trust

ˌstraight ˈticket *n* [C] a vote in which someone chooses all the CANDIDATES from a particular political party in the US → **split ticket**

ˌstraight-to-ˈvideo *n* [C] a film that is never shown in a cinema but is only available on a DVD

straight·way /ˈstreɪt-weɪ/ *adv old use* STRAIGHTAWAY

strain¹ /streɪn/ ●●○ W3 *n*

1 WORRY [C,U] worry that is caused by having to deal with a problem or work too hard over a long period of time → **stress**: *I couldn't look after him anymore; the strain was too much for me.* | *Did you* ***find*** *the job a* ***strain***? | *the* ***stresses and strains*** *of police life* | **[+for]** *The trial has been a terrible strain for both of us.* | **[+on]** *It's quite a strain on me when he's drinking heavily.* | **put/place a strain on sb** *The long working hours put a severe strain on employees.* | **under (a) strain** *I know you've been under a lot of strain lately.* | **crack/collapse/buckle etc under the strain** (=become unable to deal with a problem or work) *I could see that she was beginning to crack under the strain.*

2 DIFFICULTY [C,U] a difficulty or problem that is caused when a person, relationship, organization, or system has too much to do or too many problems to deal with: **[+on]** *The dry summer has further increased the strain on water resources.* | **put/place (a) strain on sth** *The flu epidemic has put a huge strain on the health service.* | **[+in]** *The attack has led to strains in the relationship between the two countries.* | **under (a) strain** *His marriage was under strain.* | **break/crack/collapse etc under the strain** *The party split under the strain.*

3 FORCE [U] a situation in which something is being pulled or pushed, or is holding weight, and so might break or become damaged: **[+on]** *The strain on the cables supporting the bridge is enormous.* | **put/place (a) strain on sth** *Some of these exercises put too much strain on the back muscles.* | *These four posts* ***take the strain*** *of the whole structure.* | **break/snap/collapse etc under the strain** *The rope snapped under the strain.*

4 INJURY [C,U] an injury to a muscle or part of your body that is caused by using it too much: *Long hours working at a computer can cause eye strain.* | *The goalkeeper is still out of action with a knee strain.* THESAURUS ▸ INJURY

5 PLANT/ANIMAL [C] a type of animal, plant, or disease: **[+of]** *different strains of wheat* | *a new strain of the flu virus*

6 QUALITY [singular] a particular quality which people have, especially one that is passed from parents to children: **[+of]** *There's a strain of madness in his family.*

7 WAY OF SAYING STH [singular] *formal* an amount of a feeling that you can see in the way someone speaks, writes, paints etc: *a strain of bitterness in Young's later work*

8 strains of sth *literary* the sound of music being played: *We sipped wine to the strains of Beethoven.*

strain² ●●○ *v*

1 INJURE [T] to injure a muscle or part of your body by using it too much or making it work too hard: *I've strained a muscle in my leg.* | *You'll strain your eyes trying to read in this light.* THESAURUS ▸ HURT

2 EFFORT [I,T] to try very hard to do something using all your strength or ability: **strain (sth) to do sth** *She was straining to keep her head above the water.* | **[+for]** *Bill choked and gasped, straining for air.* | **strain your ears/eyes** (=try very hard to hear or see) *I strained my ears, listening for any sound in the silence of the cave.*

3 LIQUID [T] to separate solid things from a liquid by pouring the mixture through something with very small holes in it → **sieve**: *She strained the pasta.*

4 DIFFICULTY [T] to cause difficulties for something by making too much work or too many problems which it cannot deal with easily: *The increased costs will certainly strain our finances.* | *The incident has strained relations between the two countries.* | *I felt that my patience was being* ***strained to the limit***.

5 PULL/PUSH [I] to pull hard at something or push hard against something: **[+against]** *Buddy's huge gut strained against the buttons on his shirt.* | **[+at]** *a dog straining at its lead*

6 strain every nerve to try as hard as possible to do something: *He was straining every nerve to impress the judges.*

7 be straining at the leash to be eager to be allowed to do something: *There are 30,000 troops in the area, all straining at the leash.*

8 not strain yourself to not work too hard or do too much physical activity – often used in an IRONIC way: *Don't strain yourself.*

strained /streɪnd/ *adj* **1** a strained situation or behaviour is not relaxed, natural, or friendly SYN **tense**: *I couldn't stand the* ***strained atmosphere*** *at dinner anymore.* | *the increasingly* ***strained relations*** *between the French and German governments* **2** showing the effects of worry or too much work: *Nina's voice sounded strained.* | *Alex's pale, strained face*

strain·er /ˈstreɪnə $ -ər/ *n* [C] a kitchen tool with lots of small holes in it, that is used for separating solids from liquids → **sieve**: *a tea strainer*

S

strait /streɪt/ ●○○ *n* [C]
1 (*also* **straits** [plural]) a narrow passage of water between two areas of land, usually connecting two seas: *the Bering Strait*
2 be in dire straits to be in a very difficult situation, especially a financial one: *After the war, the country's economy was in dire straits.* | *The firm is now* ***in dire financial straits***.

strait·ened /ˈstreɪtnd/ *adj formal* if you are living in straitened circumstances, you do not have enough money, especially not as much as you had before: *the* ***straitened circumstances*** *of post-war Japan*

strait·jack·et, **straightjacket** /ˈstreɪtˌdʒækɪt/ *n* [C]
1 a special piece of clothing that prevents someone from moving their arms, used to control someone who is being violent or, in the past, someone who was mentally ill
2 something such as a law or set of ideas that puts very strict or unfair limits on someone: *the straitjacket of censorship*

strait·laced /ˌstreɪtˈleɪst◂/ *adj* having strict old-fashioned ideas about moral behaviour: *straitlaced Victorian society*

strand /strænd/ ●○○ *n* [C]
1 a single thin piece of thread, wire, hair etc: **[+of]** *He reached out and brushed a* ***strand of hair*** *away from her face.*
2 one of the parts of a story, idea, plan etc: **strand of thought/opinion/argument** *Plato draws all the strands of the argument together.*

strand·ed /ˈstrændɪd/ *adj* a person or vehicle that is stranded is unable to move from the place where they are SYN **stuck**: *Air travellers were* ***left stranded*** *because of icy conditions.* | **[+in/on/at]** *There I was, stranded in Rome with no money.*

strange[1] /streɪndʒ/ ●●● S2 W2 *adj* (*comparative* **stranger**, *superlative* **strangest**)
1 unusual or surprising, especially in a way that is difficult to explain or understand SYN **odd**: *strange noises* | *Does Geoff's behaviour seem strange to you?* | *She felt there was* ***something strange about*** Dexter's voice. | ***Isn't it strange how*** *animals seem to sense danger?* | ***It's strange that*** *we've never met before.* | ***For some strange reason***, *I slept like a baby despite the noise.* | ***Strange as it may seem***, *I actually prefer cold weather.* | ***That's strange***. *I was sure Jude was right here a second ago.* | ***The strange thing is*** *all four victims had red hair.* | **strange to say** *BrE* (=strangely) *Strange to say, I was just thinking that myself.*
2 someone or something that is strange is not familiar because you have not seen or met them before: *As a child, she'd been taught never to speak to strange men.* | *I was just 20, a young girl in a strange city.* | **[+to]** *It was all strange to him, but he'd soon learn his way around.*
3 feel strange to feel as if something is slightly wrong or unusual, either physically or emotionally: *Can you get me a glass of water? I feel a bit strange.* | *It felt strange to be back in Dublin.* —**strangeness** *n* [U]

strange[2] *adv* [only after verb] *AmE* in a way that is unusual or surprising SYN **strangely**: *The cat's been acting really strange – I wonder if it's sick.*

strange·ly /ˈstreɪndʒli/ ●●○ *adv* in an unusual or surprising way SYN **oddly**: *Mick's been acting very strangely lately.* | *strangely shaped hills* | *The crowd fell strangely silent.* | ***Strangely enough***, *I wasn't that disappointed.*

strang·er /ˈstreɪndʒə $ -ər/ ●●○ W2 *n* [C]
1 someone that you do not know: *Children must not talk to strangers.* | **perfect/complete/total stranger** (=used to emphasize that you do not know them) *Julie finds it easy to speak to complete strangers.* ⚠ Do not use **stranger** to mean 'a person from another country'. Use **foreigner** or, more politely, say that someone is **from abroad/overseas**.
2 be no stranger to sth to have had a lot of a particular kind of experience: *a politician who is no stranger to controversy*
3 someone in a new and unfamiliar place: *'Where's the station?' 'Sorry, I'm a stranger here myself.'*
4 hello, stranger! *spoken* used to greet someone who you have not seen for a long time
5 don't be a stranger! *spoken* used when someone is leaving to invite them back to see you soon

stran·gle /ˈstræŋɡəl/ *v* [T] **1** to kill someone by pressing their throat with your hands, a rope etc → **choke**: **[+with]** *The victim had been strangled with a belt.* **2** to limit or prevent the growth or development of something: *Mills argues that high taxation strangles the economy.* —**strangler** *n* [C]

stran·gled /ˈstræŋɡəld/ *adj* **strangled cry/gasp/voice etc** a cry or other sound that is suddenly stopped before it is finished: *Ed gave a strangled cry.*

stran·gle·hold /ˈstræŋɡəlhəʊld $ -hoʊld/ *n* [C]
1 [usually singular] complete control over a situation, organization etc: **[+on]** *Just a few firms* ***have a stranglehold*** *on the market for this software.* | **break/loosen the stranglehold of sb** (=stop someone having complete control)
2 a strong hold around someone's neck that stops them from breathing

stran·gu·lat·ed /ˈstræŋɡjəleɪtɪd/ *adj* **1** *medical* if a part of your BOWEL is strangulated, it becomes tightly pressed or twisted so that the flow of blood stops: *a strangulated hernia* **2** *written* if someone's voice sounds strangulated, they sound as though their throat is being pressed: *Clearly terrified, he let out a strangulated whimper.*

stran·gu·la·tion /ˌstræŋɡjəˈleɪʃən/ *n* [U] the act of killing someone by pressing on their throat, or the fact of being killed in this way

THESAURUS: strange

strange unusual or surprising, especially in a way that is difficult to understand, or that is a little frightening: *What's that strange noise downstairs?* | *That's strange – I'm sure I left my keys on the table.* | *a strange old man*
funny/odd *especially spoken* a little strange and making you feel slightly surprised or worried: *There's a funny smell in the kitchen.* | *It's odd that you can't remember him at all.*
curious *especially written* strange, especially in an interesting way. **Curious** is a little more formal than **strange**: *a curious fact* | *There's something rather curious about small-town America.* | *She remembered curious little details.*
mysterious strange – used about something that people know little about and are unable to explain or understand: *He had disappeared in mysterious circumstances.* | *There were reports of mysterious lights in the sky.*
eccentric strange in a way that seems slightly crazy and amusing – used about people and their behaviour: *He lived completely alone and had some slightly eccentric habits.* | *an eccentric old lady*
peculiar slightly strange, and different from what you would normally expect – used especially when this is either amusing or worrying: *She sometimes wears rather peculiar clothes.* | *He had a peculiar expression on his face.*

VERY STRANGE

weird very strange or very different from what you are used to: *I had a weird dream last night.* | *It's a weird and wonderful place.*
bizarre extremely strange and different from what is usually considered normal: *It was a bizarre situation.* | *Mark's behaviour was really bizarre.*
surreal extremely strange and unconnected with real life or normal experiences, like something out of a dream: *His paintings are full of surreal images.* | *There is something surreal about the climate change talks in Bali.*
uncanny very strange – used especially about someone having an unusual ability to do something, or looking surprisingly similar to someone: *She had an uncanny knack* (=ability) *of putting her finger right on a problem.* | *Alice had an uncanny resemblance to Josie.*

strap[1] /stræp/ ●●○ *n* [C] a narrow band of strong material that is used to fasten, hang, or hold onto something: *a bra strap* | *The strap of my bag is broken.* → CHINSTRAP, SHOULDER STRAP → see picture at BAG[1]

strap[2] *v* (**strapped**, **strapping**) [T] **1** [always + adv/prep] to fasten something or someone in place with one or more straps: **strap sth on/down etc** *He was only ten when he strapped on a guitar for the first time.* | *soldiers with grenades strapped to their belts* | **be strapped in** (=have a belt fastened around you in a car) *Are the kids strapped in?* **2** *BrE* (*also* **strap up**) to tie BANDAGES firmly round a part of your body that has been hurt

strap·less /ˈstræpləs/ *adj* **strapless dress/gown/bra** one that does not have straps over the shoulders

strapped /stræpt/ *adj* **strapped (for cash)** *informal* having little or no money at the moment: *Can you lend me ten dollars? I'm a little strapped for cash.*

strap·ping /ˈstræpɪŋ/ *adj* [only before noun] a strapping young man or woman is strong, tall, and looks healthy and active: *a strapping young lad*

stra·ta /ˈstrɑːtə $ ˈstreɪtə/ *n* **1** the plural of STRATUM **2** a plural form sometimes used instead of STRATUM

strat·a·gem /ˈstrætədʒəm/ *n* [C] *formal* a trick or plan to deceive an enemy or gain an advantage SYN **ploy**

stra·te·gic /strəˈtiːdʒɪk/ ●●○ W3 AWL (*also* **stra·te·gic·al** /-dʒɪkəl/) *adj*
1 done as part of a plan, especially in a military, business, or political situation: *UN forces made a strategic withdrawal.* | ***strategic planning** meetings* | *a strategic decision to move production to Hungary*
2 useful or right for a particular purpose: *Marksmen were placed at strategic points along the president's route.*
3 relating to fighting wars → **tactical**: *Marseilles was of great **strategic importance**.* | **strategic arms/weapons** (=weapons designed to reach an enemy country from your own) *strategic nuclear missiles* —**strategically** /-kli/ *adv*: ***Strategically placed** video cameras can alert police to any trouble.*

strat·e·gist /ˈstrætɪdʒɪst/ AWL *n* [C] someone who is good at planning things, especially military or political actions

strat·e·gy /ˈstrætɪdʒi/ ●●○ W3 AWL *n* (*plural* **strategies**)
1 [C] a planned series of actions for achieving something: *the government's long-term **economic strategy*** | *a company's **business strategy*** | **strategy for doing sth** *a strategy for dealing with crime* | **strategy to do sth** *a strategy to attract younger audiences to jazz* **THESAURUS** METHOD, PLAN, WAY
2 [C,U] the skill of planning the movements of armies in a war, or an example of this: *military strategies* | *It is the general's role to develop **overall strategy**.*
3 [U] skilful planning in general: *The company must first resolve questions of strategy.*

strat·i·fi·ca·tion /ˌstrætɪfɪˈkeɪʃən/ *n* [C,U] **1** when society is divided into separate social classes: *The Indian caste system is an example of **social stratification**.* **2** the way in which earth, rocks etc form layers over time —**stratify** /ˈstrætɪfaɪ/ *v* [I,T]

strat·i·fied /ˈstrætɪfaɪd/ *adj* **1** having different social classes: *a stratified society* **2** having several layers of earth, rock etc: *stratified rock*

strat·os·phere /ˈstrætəsfɪə $ -sfɪr/ *n* **1 the stratosphere** the outer part of the air surrounding the Earth, from 10 to 50 kilometres above the Earth → **atmosphere**
2 [singular] *informal* a very high position, level, or amount: *Oil prices soared **into the stratosphere**.* | *He's now at the top of the political stratosphere.*

strat·o·spher·ic /ˌstrætəˈsferɪk◂ $ -ˈsfɪr-, -ˈsfer-/ *adj* **1** [only before noun] relating to the outer part of the air surrounding the Earth **2** *informal* a stratospheric price, amount, level etc is extremely high or great: *stratospheric house prices*

stra·tum /ˈstrɑːtəm $ ˈstreɪ-/ *n* (*plural* **strata** /-tə/) [C] **1** a layer of rock or earth **2** a social class in a society: *people of different social strata*

straw /strɔː $ strɒː/ ●●○ S3 *n*
1 a) [U] the dried stems of wheat or similar plants that animals sleep on, and that are used for making things such as baskets, hats etc → **hay**: *a straw hat* **b)** [C] a single dried stem of straw
2 [C] a thin tube of paper or plastic for sucking up liquid from a bottle or a cup: *She sipped her lemonade through a straw.*
3 the last straw (*also* **the straw that breaks the camel's back**) the last problem in a series of problems that finally makes you give up, get angry etc: *Making me work late on Friday was the last straw.*
4 be clutching/grasping at straws to be trying everything you can to succeed, even though the things you are doing are not likely to help or work
5 straw in the wind *BrE* a sign of what might happen in the future: *There have been a few straws in the wind suggesting things might be getting a little better.*
6 straw man *AmE* a weak opponent or imaginary argument that can easily be defeated → **draw the short straw** at DRAW[1](29)

straw·ber·ry /ˈstrɔːbəri $ ˈstrɒːberi, -bəri/ ●●● S3 *n* (*plural* **strawberries**) [C] a soft red juicy fruit with small seeds on its surface, or the plant that grows this fruit → see picture at FRUIT[1]

ˌstrawberry ˈblonde *n* [C] someone, especially a girl or woman, with light reddish-yellow hair —**strawberry blonde** *adj*

ˈstraw-ˌcoloured *adj* light yellow

ˌstraw ˈpoll *n* [C] an informal test of several people's opinions to see what the general feeling about something is

straw·weight /ˈstrɔːˌweɪt $ ˈstrɒː-/ *n* [C] a BOXER who weighs less than 47.63 kilograms, and who belongs to the lightest weight class of boxers

stray[1] /streɪ/ ●○○ *v* [I]
1 to move away from the place you should be: **[+into/onto/from]** *Three of the soldiers strayed into enemy territory.*
2 to begin to deal with or think about a different subject from the main one, without intending to: **[+into/onto/from]** *We're straying into ethnic issues here.* | *This meeting is beginning to **stray from the point**.*
3 if your eyes stray, you begin to look at something else, usually without intending to: **[+to/back/over etc]** *Her eyes strayed to the clock.*
4 to start doing something that is wrong or immoral, when usually you do not do this

stray[2] ●○○ *adj* [only before noun]
1 a stray animal, such as a dog or cat, is lost or has no home
2 accidentally separated from other things of the same kind: *One man was hit by a stray bullet and taken to hospital.*

stray[3] *n* [C] **1** an animal that is lost or has no home **2** *informal* someone or something that has become separated from others of the same kind → **waifs and strays** at WAIF(2)

streak[1] /striːk/ ●●○ *n* [C]
1 a coloured line, especially one that is not straight or has been made accidentally: *Sue has blonde streaks in her hair.*
2 a part of someone's character that is different from the rest of their character: *a mean streak* | **[+of]** *His serious nature was lightened by a streak of mischief.*
3 a period of time during which you continue to be successful or to fail: **be on a winning/losing streak** *Celtic are on a six-game winning streak.*
4 streak of lightning/fire/light etc a long straight flash of LIGHTNING, fire etc

streak[2] *v* **1** [I always + adv/prep] to run or fly somewhere so fast you can hardly be seen: **[+across/along/down etc]** *Two jets streaked across the sky.* **2** [T] to cover something with lines of colour, liquid etc: *The sky was streaked yellow and purple.* | **be streaked with** *His hands and arms were streaked with paint.* GRAMMAR **Streak** is usually passive in this meaning. **3** [I] to run across a public place with no clothes on as a joke or in order to shock people

S

streak·er /ˈstriːkə $ -ər/ *n* [C] someone who runs across a public place with no clothes on as a joke or in order to shock people

streak·y /ˈstriːki/ *adj* marked with streaks: *streaky grayish marks*

ˌstreaky ˈbacon *n* [U] *BrE* smoked or salted meat from a pig that has lines of fat going through it

stream¹ /striːm/ ●●● W3 *n* [C]

1 SMALL RIVER a natural flow of water that moves across the land and is narrower than a river → DOWNSTREAM, UPSTREAM

2 CONTINUOUS SERIES a long and almost continuous series of events, people, objects etc: **[+of]** *a stream of traffic* | *a stream of abuse* | **steady/constant/endless etc stream** *A steady stream of visitors came to the house.*

3 AIR/WATER a flow of water, air, smoke etc, or the direction in which it is flowing: *A stream of cold air rushed through the open door.* → GULF STREAM, JET STREAM

4 come on stream *especially BrE* to start working or producing something: *The new factory will come on stream at the end of the year.*

5 SCHOOL *BrE* a level of ability within a group of students of the same age: *Kim's in the top stream.* → BLOODSTREAM, MAINSTREAM¹, STREAM OF CONSCIOUSNESS

stream² ●○○ *v*

1 POUR [I always + adv/prep] to flow quickly and in great amounts SYN **pour**: **[+out/from/onto etc]** *Water came streaming out of the burst pipe.* | *Tears streamed down her cheeks.*

2 FLOW [I always + adv/prep] to move in a continuous flow in the same direction: **[+out/across/past etc]** *People streamed past us on all sides.*

3 GIVE OUT LIQUID [I,T] to produce a continuous flow of liquid: **[+with]** *When I got up, my face was streaming with blood.* | **streaming cold** *BrE* (=an illness in which a lot of liquid comes out of your nose)

4 LIGHT [I always + adv/prep] if light streams somewhere, it shines through an opening into a place or onto a surface SYN **flood**: **[+in/through/from etc]** *The first rays of morning sunlight streamed through the open doorway.*

5 MOVE FREELY [I always + adv/prep, usually in progressive] to move freely in a current of wind or water: **[+in/out/behind etc]** *Elise ran, her hair streaming out behind her.*

6 COMPUTER [T] if you stream sound or video, you play it on your computer while it is being DOWNLOADed from the Internet, rather than saving it as a FILE and then playing it

7 SCHOOL [T] *BrE* to put school children in groups according to their ability SYN **track** *AmE* —**streaming** *n* [U]

stream·er /ˈstriːmə $ -ər/ *n* [C] **1** a long narrow piece of coloured paper, used for decoration on special occasions **2** a long narrow flag

stream·ing /ˈstriːmɪŋ/ *n* [U] when you play sound or video on your computer while it is being broadcast over the Internet, instead of DOWNLOADing it and saving it into a FILE so that you can listen to it or watch it later

ˈstreaming ˌmedia *n* [U] *technical* sound and video that are sent over the Internet in a continuous way

stream·line /ˈstriːmlaɪn/ *v* [T] **1** to make something such as a business, organization etc work more simply and effectively: *efforts to streamline the production process* **2** to form something into a smooth shape, so that it moves easily through the air or water: *All these new cars have been streamlined.* —**streamlined** *adj*

ˌstream of ˈconsciousness *n* [U] the expression of thoughts and feelings in writing exactly as they pass through your mind, without the usual structure they have in formal writing

street /striːt/ ●●● S1 W1 *n* [C]

1 a public road in a city or town that has houses, shops etc on one or both sides: *We moved to Center Street when I was young.* | *She lives just a few streets away.* | *I walked on further* ***down the street***. | *Someone just moved in* ***across the street***. | *a car parked* ***on the other side of the street***

2 the streets [plural] (*also* **the street**) the busy public parts of a city where there is a lot of activity, excitement, and crime, or where people without homes live: **on the streets** *young people living on the streets* | *She felt quite safe* ***walking the streets*** *after dark.* | *Children as young as five are left to* ***roam the streets*** (=walk around the streets) *at night.* | ***street musicians*** (=ones who play on the street) | *She has written about the realities of* ***street life*** (=living on the streets).

3 the man/woman in the street (*also* **the man/woman on the street**) the average person, who represents the general opinion about things: *The man on the street assumes that all politicians are corrupt.*

4 (right) up your street *BrE* exactly right for you

5 streets ahead (of sb/sth) *BrE informal* much better than someone or something else: *James is streets ahead of the rest of the class at reading.* → BACKSTREET¹, → **be (living) on easy street** at EASY¹(13), → **one-way street** at ONE-WAY(1), HIGH STREET, TWO-WAY STREET, → **walk the streets** at WALK¹(8)

COLLOCATIONS

ADJECTIVES

busy (=with a lot of traffic or people) *The house faces onto a busy street.*
crowded (=with a lot of people) *The streets get very crowded at weekends.*
quiet (=with very few people) *It was late and the streets were quiet.*
empty/deserted (=with no people) *As he walked home, the street was deserted.*
narrow *an old city with quaint narrow streets*
the main street (=the biggest street in a town or village) *They drove slowly along the main street.*
the high street *BrE* (=the main street with shops) | **a shopping street** *BrE* (=with a lot of shops) | **a residential street** (=with houses, not shops) | **a one-way street** (=in which you can only drive in one direction) | **a side/back street** (=a small quiet street near the main street) | **winding streets** (=streets that turn in many directions) | **cobbled streets** (=with a surface made from round stones)

VERBS

cross the street (=walk to the other side) *She crossed the street and walked into the bank.*

street + NOUN

a street corner (=a place where streets meet) *Youths were standing around on street corners.*
a street light/lamp *It was getting dark, and the street lamps were already on.*
street crime/violence (=when people are attacked in the street)

street·car /ˈstriːtkɑː $ -kɑːr/ *n* [C] *AmE* a type of bus that runs on electricity along metal tracks in the road SYN **tram** *BrE*

ˈstreet ˌchildren *n* [plural] children who live or work on the streets

ˈstreet cred (*also* **ˈstreet crediˌbility**) *n* [U] the qualities in a young person that other young people admire, especially because of their knowledge and experience of real life: *It'll wreck your street cred if you're seen helping the police.* —**street-credible** *adj*

street·light /ˈstriːtlaɪt/ (*also* **street·lamp** /-læmp/) *n* [C] a light at the top of a tall post in the street

ˈstreet ˌpeople *n* [plural] people who have no home and live on the streets SYN **the homeless**

ˈstreet-smart *adj especially AmE informal* STREETWISE —**street smarts** *n* [U]

ˈstreet ˌvalue *n* [C,U] the price for which something, especially drugs, can be sold illegally: *Detectives seized drugs with a street value of almost £300,000.*

street·walk·er /ˈstriːtwɔːkə $ -wɔːkər/ *n* [C] *old-fashioned* a PROSTITUTE

street·wise /ˈstriːtwaɪz/ *adj* able to deal with the dangerous situations and people that are common in some cities and towns

strength /streŋθ, strenθ/ ●●● S2 W2 *n*
1 PHYSICAL [U] the physical power and energy that makes someone strong OPP **weakness**: **have/find the strength to do sth** *She didn't even have the strength to stand up.* | *I'm trying to* ***build up*** *my* ***strength***. | *Jo hit him* ***with all her strength***. | *He never ceased to be amazed by her* ***physical strength***.
2 DETERMINATION [U] the quality of being brave or determined in dealing with difficult or unpleasant situations: **have/find the strength to do sth** *Jenny didn't have the strength to end the relationship.* | *She had enormous* ***strength of character*** (=strong ability to deal with difficult situations). | **strength of mind/purpose** *The sea was very cold and it required great strength of mind to get in.* | *I think you have to find an* ***inner strength*** *in order to feel good about yourself.* → **tower of strength** at TOWER[1](3)
3 FEELING/BELIEF [U] how strong a feeling, belief, or relationship is SYN **depth**: **[+of]** *Governments cannot ignore the strength of public opinion.* | *We understand the* ***strength of feeling*** *against the proposal.*
4 ORGANIZATION/COUNTRY ETC [U] the political, military, or economic power of an organization, country, or system: **[+of]** *the strength of the US economy* | *The socialists organized a* ***show of strength*** (=when a country or organization shows how strong it is).
5 USEFUL QUALITY OR ABILITY [C] a particular quality or ability that gives someone or something an advantage OPP **weakness**: *Her main strength is her critical thinking ability.* | **[+of]** *The great strength of our plan lies in its simplicity.* | *Be aware of your own* ***strengths and weaknesses***.
6 OBJECT [U] how strong an object or structure is, especially its ability to last for a long time without breaking OPP **weakness**: **[+of]** *a device for testing the strength of concrete structures*
7 SUBSTANCE/MIXTURE [C,U] how strong a substance or mixture is: *Add water to dilute the solution to the required strength.* | **full-strength/half-strength/double-strength etc** *Young plants can be fed with half-strength liquid fertilizer.*
8 NUMBER OF PEOPLE [U] the number of people in a team, army etc: *The Edinburgh team are now at* ***full strength***. | **below strength** *The police force is below strength at the moment* (=there are fewer police than there should be). | **in strength** *Security forces were out in strength* (=in large numbers) *but did not intervene.*
9 MONEY [U] the value of a country's money when compared to other countries' money: **[+of]** *the strength of the dollar on the international money markets*
10 on the strength of sth because of something: *I bought the book on the strength of your recommendation.*
11 position of strength a position where you have an advantage over someone, especially in a discussion: *We must negotiate from a position of strength.*
12 go from strength to strength to become more and more successful: *For several years, the business went from strength to strength.*
13 NATURAL FORCE [U] how strong a natural force is: *the strength of the sunlight*
14 COLOUR/LIGHT/FLAVOUR/SMELL ETC [U] how strong a colour, taste etc is
15 give me strength! *spoken* used when you are annoyed or angry about something
16 not know your own strength to not realize how strong you are

strength·en /ˈstreŋθən, ˈstrenθən/ ●●○ W3 *v*
1 FEELING/BELIEF/RELATIONSHIP [I,T] to become stronger or make something stronger OPP **weaken**: *Our friendship has steadily strengthened over the years.* | *Steve's opposition only* ***strengthened her resolve*** *to go ahead.* | **strengthen sth's ties/bonds/links etc** *The university hopes to strengthen its ties with the local community.* | *The company plans to* ***strengthen*** *its* ***hand*** (=make itself more powerful) *in Europe by opening an office in Spain.*
2 TEAM/ARMY ETC [T] to make an organization, army etc more powerful, especially by increasing the number or quality of the people in it OPP **weaken**: *The team has been strengthened by the arrival of two new players.*
3 FINANCIAL SITUATION [I,T] if the financial situation of a country or company strengthens or is strengthened, it improves or is made to improve OPP **weaken**: *measures to strengthen the economy*
4 MONEY [I,T] to increase in value, or to increase the value of money OPP **weaken**: *The pound has strengthened against other currencies.*
5 BODY/STRUCTURE [T] to make something such as your body or a building stronger OPP **weaken**: *Metal supports were added to strengthen the outer walls.*
6 PROOF/REASON [T] to help prove something: *Fresh evidence has greatly strengthened the case against him.*
7 WIND/CURRENT [I] to increase in force: *The wind had strengthened during the night.*

stren·u·ous /ˈstrenjuəs/ *adj* **1** needing a lot of effort or strength: *a strenuous climb* | *The doctor advised Ken to avoid strenuous exercise.* **2** active and determined: *Sherry's been making a* ***strenuous effort*** *to lose weight.* —**strenuously** *adv*: *Barrett strenuously denied rumors that he would resign.*

strep throat /ˌstrep ˈθrəʊt $ -ˈθroʊt/ *n* [U] *AmE* an illness in which your throat is very painful

strep·to·coc·cus /ˌstreptəˈkɒkəs $ -ˈkɑː-/ *n* (*plural* **streptococci** /-kaɪ/) [C] a group of BACTERIA that causes infections, especially in the throat

stress[1] /stres/ ●●● S3 W3 AWL *n*
1 WORRY [C,U] continuous feelings of worry about your work or personal life, that prevent you from relaxing → **strain**: *Your headaches are due to stress.* | *Janet's been under a lot of stress since her mother's illness.* | *all the stresses of public life* | *A lot of illnesses are stress-related.*
2 FORCE [C,U] the physical force or pressure on an object: *Shoes with high heels* ***put*** *a great deal of* ***stress on*** *knees and ankles.*
3 IMPORTANCE [U] the special attention or importance given to a particular idea, fact, or activity SYN **emphasis**: **put/lay stress on sth** *Pugh laid particular stress on the need for discipline.*
4 WORD/MUSIC [C,U] the degree of force or loudness with which a part of a word is pronounced or a note in music is played, which makes it sound stronger than other parts or notes

COLLOCATIONS

VERBS

suffer from stress *If you are suffering from stress, you may be more likely to become ill.*
cause stress *Moving house often causes stress.*
cope with/deal with stress *People find different ways of dealing with stress.*
reduce/relieve stress

ADJECTIVES

great/considerable/enormous *Staff experienced considerable stress as a result of the changes.*
mental/emotional stress *It was a time of great emotional stress for me.*

PHRASES

be under stress *She's been under a lot of stress lately.*
a cause of stress *Balancing work and family is the main cause of stress for many people.*
signs/symptoms/effects of stress
sb's stress level (*also* **sb's level of stress**) *Exercise reduces stress levels.*
stresses and strains (=a lot of different worries that are caused by something) *the stresses and strains of everyday life*

stress[2] ●●● S3 W3 AWL *v*
1 [T] to emphasize a statement, fact, or idea: **stress that** *The report stressed that student math skills need to improve.* | *Crawford* ***stressed the need for*** *more housing downtown.* | *She* ***stressed the importance of*** *a balanced diet.*
THESAURUS EMPHASIZE
2 [T] to pronounce a word or part of a word so that it sounds louder or more forceful: *The word 'machine' is stressed on the second syllable.*
3 [I] *informal* to feel very worried about something: *She's stressing about her exams.*

S

stress sb **out** *phr v informal* to make someone so worried or nervous that they cannot relax: *Studying for exams always stresses me out.*

stressed /strest/ AWL *adj* **1** [not before noun] (*also* **stressed out**) *informal* so worried and tired that you cannot relax: *I always eat when I'm feeling stressed.* **2** *technical* an object, especially a metal object, that is stressed has had a lot of pressure or force put on it

stress·ful /ˈstresfəl/ ●○○ AWL *adj* a job, experience, or situation that is stressful makes you worry a lot: *Moving to a new house is a very stressful experience.*

ˈstress mark *n* [C] a mark (ˈ) that shows which part of a word you emphasize when you pronounce it

stress·y /ˈstresi/ *adj informal* **1** feeling so worried or tired that you cannot relax SYN **stressed**: *I kept yelling at the kids because I was feeling so stressy.* **2** making you worry a lot SYN **stressful**: *At the end of a stressy day, I just want to sit and watch TV.*

stretch¹ /stretʃ/ ●●● S3 W3 *v*
1 MAKE STH BIGGER/LOOSER **a)** [I,T] to make something bigger or looser by pulling it, or to become bigger or looser as a result of being pulled: *A spider's web can stretch considerably without weakening.* | *Where can I buy those things that stretch your shoes?* **b)** [I not in progressive] if a material stretches, it can become bigger or longer when you pull it and then return to its original shape when you stop
2 BODY [I,T] to straighten your arms, legs, or body to full length: *Carl sat up in bed, yawned, and stretched.* | *Always stretch before exercising.* → see picture at GYM
3 REACH [I always +adv/prep] to reach a long way for something: **[+across/over]** *Ann stretched across the couch and grabbed the phone.*
4 MAKE STH TIGHT [T] to pull something so that it is tight: *The canvas is stretched over a wooden frame.*
5 TIME/SERIES [I,T always + adv/prep] to continue over a period of time or in a series, or to make something do this: **[+into/on/over etc]** *Berg's career as a government official stretched over 20 years.* | *With a goal in the second half, Spurs stretched their lead to 3–0.*
6 IN SPACE [I always + adv/prep] to spread out or cover a large area of land: **[+to/into/away etc]** *Row after row of orange trees stretched to the horizon.* | *a line stretching around the block*
7 stretch your legs *informal* to go for a walk, especially after sitting for a long time
8 stretch (sb's) patience/credulity to be almost beyond the limits of what someone can accept or believe: *The kids stretch my patience to the limit.*
9 RULE/LIMIT [T] *BrE* to allow something that would not normally be allowed by a rule or limit: *This once, I'll* ***stretch the rules*** *and let you leave work early.* | *We'll* ***stretch a point*** (=allow a rule to be broken) *and let the baby travel free this time.* → **stretch the rules** at RULE¹(1)
10 stretch the truth/facts to say or write something that is not completely true: *Reporters sometimes stretch the facts to make a point.*
11 be stretching it *informal* to make something seem more important, bigger etc than it really is: *He's a good player, but 'world-class' is stretching it.*
12 FOOD/MONEY [I,T] if you make an amount of money, food etc stretch or it stretches, you use less of it than you usually would so that you have it for a longer time: *I'm going to have to stretch this $20 until payday.*
13 be stretched (to the limit) to have hardly enough money, supplies, time etc for your needs: *We're stretched at the moment, otherwise we'd go.*
14 not stretch to sth *BrE* if someone's money will not stretch to something, they cannot afford it: *The budget won't stretch to a new car this year.*
15 ABILITIES [T] to make someone use all of their skill, abilities, or intelligence: *The work's too easy. The students aren't being stretched enough.*

stretch out *phr v*
1 *informal* to lie down, usually in order to sleep or rest: *I'm just going to stretch out on the couch for ten minutes.*
2 stretch sth ↔ out to put out your hand, foot etc in order to reach something: *Jimmy stretched out his hand to take the candy.*

stretch² ●○○ *n*
1 LENGTH OF LAND/WATER [C] an area of land or water, especially one that is long and narrow: **[+of]** *a beautiful stretch of countryside*
2 TIME [C] a continuous period of time: **[+of]** *a stretch of three weeks without sunshine* | *She doesn't leave the house for* ***long stretches of time***. | *She rarely sleeps for eight hours* ***at a stretch*** (=without stopping).
3 BODY [C] the action of stretching a part of your body out to its full length, or a particular way of doing this: *The ski instructor showed us some special stretches.*
4 by any stretch (of the imagination) *spoken* used to emphasize that a negative statement is true: *My family wasn't wealthy by any stretch of the imagination.*
5 the home/final stretch a) the last part of a track before the end of a race **b)** the last part of an activity, trip, or process: *As they* ***enter the home stretch*** *of the campaign, the president's lead has grown.*
6 MATERIAL [U] the ability a material has to increase in length or width without tearing → **stretchy**
7 at full stretch *BrE* **a)** using everything that is available: *With staff shortages and appalling weather conditions, the emergency services were at full stretch.* **b)** with your body or part of your body stretched as far as possible: *He dived and caught the ball at full stretch.*
8 JAIL [C usually singular] *informal* a period of time spent in prison

stretch³ *adj* [only before noun] stretch clothes or material stretch if you pull them, and then return to their original shape: *stretch Levis*

stretch·er¹ /ˈstretʃə $ -ər/ *n* [C] a type of bed used for carrying someone who is too injured or ill to walk

STRETCHER

stretcher² *v* [T always + adv/prep] *BrE* to carry someone on a stretcher: **be stretchered off/into etc** *Ward was stretchered off early in the game.*

ˈstretcher-ˌbearer *n* [C] someone, usually a soldier, who carries one end of a stretcher

ˈstretch ˌlimo *n* [C] a very large comfortable car that has been made longer than usual

ˈstretch mark *n* [C usually plural] a mark left on your skin as a result of it stretching too much, especially during PREGNANCY

stretch·y /ˈstretʃi/ *adj informal* material that is stretchy can stretch when you pull it and then return to its original shape: *stretchy cotton leggings*

strew /struː/ *v* (*past tense* **strewed**, *past participle* **strewn** /struːn/ *or* **strewed**) [T] **1** to scatter things around a large area: **be strewn with sth** *The street was strewn with broken glass.* | **be strewn around/about/over etc sth** *clothes strewn across the floor* **2 strewn with sth** *written* containing a lot of something: *conversation liberally strewn with swear words* **3** *literary* to lie scattered over something: *Flowers strewed the path.*

strewth /struːθ/ *interjection BrE, AusE old-fashioned* used to express surprise, annoyance etc

stri·at·ed /straɪˈeɪtɪd $ ˈstraɪeɪtɪd/ *adj technical* having narrow lines or bands of colour SYN **striped** —**striation** /straɪˈeɪʃən/ *n* [C usually plural]

strick·en /ˈstrɪkən/ *adj formal* very badly affected by trouble, illness, unhappiness etc: *Fire broke out on the stricken ship.* | **[+by/with]** *a country stricken by severe economic problems* | **drought-stricken/cancer-stricken/tragedy-stricken etc** *drought-stricken farmers* → GRIEF-STRICKEN, PANIC-STRICKEN, POVERTY-STRICKEN

strict /strɪkt/ ●●○ S3 *adj* (*comparative* **stricter**, *superlative* **strictest**)
1 expecting people to obey rules or to do what you say OPP **lenient**: *a strict teacher* | **[+about]** *This company is very strict about punctuality.* | **[+with]** *The Stuarts are very strict with their children.*
2 a strict order or rule is one that must be obeyed: *You had strict instructions not to tell anybody.* | *There are* ***strict limits*** *on presidential campaign contributions.* | *He's under* ***strict orders*** *from his doctor to quit smoking.* | *I'm telling you this* ***in the strictest confidence*** (=it must be kept completely secret).
3 [usually before noun] exact and correct, often in a way that seems unreasonable: *Amy was attractive, although not beautiful* ***in the strictest sense of the word****.*
4 obeying all the rules of a religion or set of principles: *He was raised a strict Catholic.* | *a strict vegetarian* —**strictness** *n* [U]

THESAURUS

strict expecting people to obey rules or to do what you say – used especially about parents, teachers, or organizations: *Our teachers were very strict.* | *Most schools are quite strict about the way students dress.*
firm showing that you are in control of the situation and will not change your opinion, especially when you are telling someone what to do: *You have to be firm with young children.* | *I'll be firm with him and tell him he can't have any more money.*
tough determined that your orders or decisions will be obeyed, especially in order to make sure that a situation improves – used especially when you think that someone is right to be strict: *We need a government that is tough on crime.* | *She can be quite tough with her students, but they respect her for it.*
stern strict in a serious, disapproving, and rather unfriendly way: *Her grandfather was a stern man who rarely smiled.*
harsh punishing or criticizing someone in a way that seems very severe, often too severe: *Don't be too harsh on her – she's only a child.*
authoritarian *disapproving* very strict about forcing people to obey rules or laws, and punishing them very severely if they fail to do this – used about people and governments: *Her father was very authoritarian and insisted on total obedience.* | *an authoritarian government*

strict·ly /ˈstrɪktli/ ●●○ *adv*
1 in a way that must be obeyed: *Alcohol is* ***strictly forbidden*** *on school premises.* | *The ban on hunting is not* ***strictly enforced****.*
2 exactly and completely: *That isn't strictly true.*
3 strictly speaking used to say that something is true if you are going to be very exact and correct about it: *Strictly speaking, spiders are not insects.*
4 only for a particular person, thing, or purpose and no one else: *This is strictly between us. Nobody else must know.*

stric·ture /ˈstrɪktʃə $ -ər/ *n* [C often plural] *formal* **1** a rule that strictly limits what you can do: **[+on/against]** *religious strictures on marriage* **2** a severe criticism

stride¹ /straɪd/ ●○○ *n*
1 STEP [C] a long step you make while you are walking → **pace**: *Paco reached the door in only three strides.*
2 IMPROVEMENT [C] an improvement in a situation or in the development of something: **make great/major/giant etc strides** *The government has made great strides in reducing poverty.*
3 take sth in your stride *BrE*, **take sth in stride** *AmE* to not allow something to annoy, embarrass, or upset you: *When the boss asked Judy to stay late, she took it in stride.*
4 get into your stride *BrE*, **hit your stride** *AmE* to start doing something confidently and well: *Once I get into my stride, I can finish an essay in a few hours.*
5 WAY OF WALKING [singular] the way you walk or run: *the runner's long, loping stride*
6 break (your) stride *especially AmE* **a)** to begin moving more slowly or to stop when you are running or walking **b)** if you break your stride, or if someone or something breaks it, you are prevented from continuing in what you are doing: *Collins dealt with the reporters' questions* ***without breaking stride****.*
7 put sb off their stride *especially BrE*, **knock/throw/keep sb off stride** *AmE* to make someone unable to do something effectively, by not allowing them to give all their attention to it: *Shea's testimony threw the defense off stride.*
8 (match sb) stride for stride to manage to be just as fast, strong, skilled etc as someone else, even if they keep making it harder for you

stride² ●○○ *v* (*past tense* **strode** /strəʊd $ stroʊd/, *past participle* **stridden** /ˈstrɪdn/) [I always + adv/prep] *written* to walk quickly with long steps → **march**: **[+across/into/down etc]** *He strode toward her.* THESAURUS ▸ WALK

stri·dent /ˈstraɪdənt/ *adj* **1** forceful and determined, especially in a way that is offensive or annoying: *strident criticism* **2** a strident sound or voice is loud and unpleasant: *the strident calls of seagulls* —**stridently** *adv* —**stridency** *n* [U]

strife /straɪf/ *n* [U] *formal* trouble between two or more people or groups SYN **conflict**: **ethnic/religious/civil etc strife** *a time of political strife*

strike¹ /straɪk/ ●●● S3 W3 *v* (*past tense and past participle* **struck** /strʌk/)
1 HIT [T] *written* to hit or fall against the surface of something: *She fell heavily, striking her head against the side of the boat.* | *A snowball struck him on the back of the head.* | *Several cars were struck by falling trees.* | *The last rays of the setting sun struck the windows.*

REGISTER
In everyday English, people usually say **hit** rather than **strike**: *I* ***hit*** *my head on the shelf.* | *He was* ***hit*** *by a rock.*

2 HIT WITH HAND/WEAPON ETC [T] *formal* to deliberately hit someone or something with your hand or a weapon: *She struck him hard across the face.* | **strike sth with sth** *The victim had been struck with some kind of wooden implement.* | *Paul* ***struck*** *him* ***a blow*** *to the head.* | *The assassin's bullet* ***struck home*** (=hit exactly where it should). THESAURUS ▸ HIT
3 THOUGHT/IDEA [T] if something strikes you, you think of it, notice it, or realize that it is important, interesting, true etc: *A rather worrying thought struck me.* | *The first thing that struck me was the fact that there were no other women present.* | **it strikes sb (that)** *It struck her that losing the company might be the least of her worries.* | **be struck by sth** *You can't help being struck by her kindness.*

GRAMMAR: Using the progressive
Strike is not used in the progressive in this meaning. You say: *It strikes me that they are similar.* ✗ Don't say: *It is striking me that they are similar.*
GRAMMAR GUIDE ▸ VERBS

4 strike sb as (being) sth to seem to have a particular quality or feature: *His jokes didn't strike Jack as being very funny.* | **it strikes sb as strange/odd etc that** *It struck me as odd that the man didn't introduce himself before he spoke.*
5 STOP WORK [I] if a group of workers strike, they stop working as a protest against something relating to their work, for example how much they are paid, bad working conditions etc: *In many countries, the police are forbidden to strike.* | **[+for]** *They're striking for the right to have their trade union recognized in law.*
6 ATTACK [I,T] to attack someone, especially suddenly: *The killer might strike again.* | *Guerrillas struck a UN camp, killing 75.* | *Opponents of the war say that civilian villages have been struck several times.*
7 HARM [I,T] to damage or harm someone or something: **[+at]** *The law would strike at the most basic of civil rights.* | *Such prejudices* ***strike*** *right* ***at the heart of*** *any notions of a civilized society.* | **strike a blow at/against/to sth** *The scandal*

seemed to have struck a mortal blow to the government's chances of re-election.
8 STH BAD HAPPENS [I,T] if something bad strikes, it suddenly happens or suddenly begins to affect someone: *The plague struck again for the third time that century.* | *Everything seemed to be going fine when suddenly* ***disaster struck.*** → STRICKEN THESAURUS HAPPEN
9 strike a balance (between sth) to give the correct amount of importance or attention to two separate things: *He was finding it difficult to strike a balance between his family and his work.* | *It isn't always easy to* ***strike the right balance.***
10 strike a bargain/deal to agree to do something for someone if they do something for you: *There are rumors that the president struck a private deal with the corporation's chairman.*
11 strike a happy/cheerful/cautious etc note to express a particular feeling or attitude: *The article struck a conciliatory note.* | *Moderate Republicanism appeared to* ***strike*** *exactly* ***the right note*** *with the voters* (=be what the people wanted).
12 strike a chord to say or do something that other people agree with or have sympathy with: **[+with]** *Their story is bound to strike a chord with all parents.*
13 strike a match to produce a flame from a match by rubbing it hard across a rough surface
14 strike gold/oil etc to find a supply of gold, oil etc in the ground or under the sea: *If they strike oil, drilling will begin early next year.*
15 strike gold *informal* to do something that makes you a lot of money: *Jackie eventually struck gold with her third novel.*
16 LIGHTNING [I,T] if LIGHTNING strikes something, it hits and damages it: *The temple burned down after it was* ***struck by lightning*** *last year.* → **lightning never strikes twice** at LIGHTNING[1]
17 strike a blow for sb/sth to do something to help achieve a principle or aim: *It's time we struck a blow for women's rights.*
18 be within striking distance a) to be close enough to reach a place easily: *By now, they were within striking distance of the shore.* **b)** to be very close to achieving something: *The French team are within striking distance of the world record.*
19 strike it rich to suddenly make a lot of money
20 strike it lucky *BrE* to be very lucky, especially when you were not expecting to: *We struck it lucky in Bangkok, where we were told there were some extra seats on the plane that night.*
21 CLOCK [I,T] if a clock strikes one, two, six etc, its bell makes a sound once, twice, six etc times according to what time it is: *The church clock began to strike twelve.* | **strike the hour** (=strike when it is exactly one o'clock, two o'clock etc)
22 GAIN ADVANTAGE [I] to do something that gives you an advantage over your opponent in a fight, competition etc: *Brazil struck first with a goal in the third minute.*
23 strike home if something that you say strikes home, it has exactly the effect on someone that you intended: *She saw the emotion in her father's face and knew her words had struck home.*
24 strike terror/fear into sb's heart to make someone feel very frightened: *The word 'cancer' still strikes terror into many hearts.*
25 strike a pose/attitude to stand or sit with your body in a particular position: *Malcolm struck his usual pose: hands in pockets, shoulders hunched.*
26 be struck dumb to suddenly be unable to talk, usually because you are very surprised or shocked → DUMBSTRUCK
27 be struck with horror/terror/awe etc to suddenly feel very afraid, shocked etc: *As she began to speak to him, she was struck with shyness.*
28 strike while the iron is hot to do something immediately rather than waiting until a later time when you are less likely to succeed
29 strike sb dead to kill someone: *May God strike me dead if I'm telling a lie!*

strike back *phr v* to attack or criticize someone who attacked or criticized you first: *We instruct our staff never to strike back, however angry they feel.* | **[+at]** *The prime minister immediately struck back at his critics.*
strike sb ↔ **down** *phr v*
1 to kill someone or make them extremely ill: *Over 50 nurses at the clinic have been struck down with a mystery virus.* | *They would rob the bodies of those struck down in battle.* GRAMMAR **Strike down** is usually passive in this meaning.
2 *formal* to hit someone so hard that they fall down
3 *law* to say that a law, decision etc is illegal and officially end it
strike sb/sth ↔ **off** *phr v*
1 be struck off *BrE* if a doctor, lawyer etc is struck off, their name is removed from the official list of people who are allowed to work as doctors, lawyers etc
2 to remove someone or something from a list: *Terri was told to strike off the names of every person older than 30.*
strike on/upon sth *phr v formal* to discover something or have a good idea about something → **be struck on sb/sth** at STRUCK[2]
strike out *phr v*
1 to attack or criticize someone suddenly or violently: **[+at]** *Unhappy young people will often strike out at the people closest to them.*
2 strike sth ↔ out to draw a line through something written on a piece of paper
3 [always + adv/prep] to start walking or swimming in a particular direction, especially in a determined way: *She struck out for the side of the pool.*
4 strike out on your own to start doing something or living independently
5 to not hit the ball in baseball three times, so that you are not allowed to continue trying, or to make someone do this: **strike sb ↔ out** *He struck out the first batter he faced.* → STRIKEOUT
6 *AmE informal* to not be successful at something: *'Did she say she'd go out with you?' 'No, I struck out.'*
7 strike sth ↔ out *law* to say officially that something cannot be considered as proof in a court of law
strike up *phr v*
1 strike up a friendship/relationship/conversation etc to start to become friendly with someone, to start talking to them, etc: *I struck up a conversation with the girl sitting next to me.*
2 strike up (sth) to begin playing a piece of music: *The band struck up a tango.*

strike[2] ●●● S3 W2 *n*
1 NOT WORKING [C,U] a period of time when a group of workers deliberately stop working because of a disagreement about pay, working conditions etc: *The government has promised that the army will be called in to help if there is a firemen's strike.* | **[+by]** *a six-week strike by railway workers* | **[+over]** *a strike over pay cuts* | **[+against]** *a national strike against mine closures*
2 ATTACK [C] a military attack, especially by planes dropping bombs: **[+against/on]** *a surprise* ***air strike*** *on military targets* | *American aircraft carriers have* ***launched*** *several* ***strikes.*** → FIRST STRIKE
3 DISCOVERY [C usually singular] the discovery of something valuable under the ground: *an oil strike*
4 two/three strikes against sb/sth *AmE* a condition or situation that makes it extremely difficult for someone or something to be successful: *Children from poor backgrounds have two strikes against them by the time they begin school.*
5 BASEBALL [C] an attempt to hit the ball in baseball that fails, or a ball that is thrown to the BATTER in the correct area but is not hit
6 BOWLING [C] a situation in BOWLING in which you knock down all the PINS (=bottle-shaped objects) with a ball on your first attempt → HUNGER STRIKE, LIGHTNING STRIKE

COLLOCATIONS

VERBS

be (out) on strike *Teachers are on strike again this week.*
go on strike/come out on strike (=start a strike) *An estimated 70,000 public sector workers went on strike.*
begin a strike *Dock workers began a 24-hour strike last night.*
call a strike (=tell people to strike) *The union threatened to call a strike.*
stage a strike (=organize a short strike) *Health workers will stage a two-day strike next week.*
end/call off a strike (=decide not to continue with it) | **break a strike** (=force workers to end it)

ADJECTIVES/NOUN + strike

a one-day/two-week etc strike *A three-day strike is planned for next week.*
an indefinite strike (=with no end planned) *Workers at the processing plant have begun an indefinite strike.*
a general strike (=when workers from most industries strike) *They threatened to call a general strike.*
a national/nationwide strike (=all over the country) | **a rail/coal/postal etc strike** (=affecting the rail/coal etc industry) | **a miners'/teachers'/pilots' etc strike** (=by miners, teachers etc) | **an unofficial strike** (=not organized by a trade union) | **a wildcat strike** (=without any warning)

strike + NOUN

strike action (=a strike) *Hospital workers have voted in favour of strike action.*
a strike call (=when a group asks people to strike) | **a strike ballot** *BrE* (=when workers vote on whether to strike)

COMMON ERRORS

⚠ Don't say 'go on a strike'. Say **go on strike**.

strike·break·er /ˈstraɪkˌbreɪkə $ -ər/ *n* [C] someone who continues working during a strike – used to show disapproval → BLACKLEG, SCAB(2)

strike·out /ˈstraɪkaʊt/ *n* [C] in baseball, an occasion when the BATTER is not allowed to try to hit the ball anymore, because he has three strikes

ˈ**strike pay** *n* [U] money paid by a union to workers who are on STRIKE

strik·er /ˈstraɪkə $ -ər/ *n* [C] **1** someone who is not working because they are on STRIKE **2** a player in football whose main job is to score GOALS

strik·ing /ˈstraɪkɪŋ/ ●○○ *adj*
1 unusual or interesting enough to be easily noticed: **striking contrast/similarity/parallel etc** *a striking contrast between wealth and poverty*
2 attractive in an unusual way that is easy to notice: *a dark man with striking features*
3 [only before noun] not working because of being on STRIKE: *striking auto workers* → **be within striking distance** at STRIKE[1](18)

strik·ing·ly /ˈstraɪkɪŋli/ *adv* **1** in a way that is very easy to notice: **strikingly similar/different** *The two experiments produced strikingly different results.* **2** used to emphasize that someone or something is beautiful in a way that is easy to notice: *one of the most strikingly attractive regions in Britain*

string[1] /strɪŋ/ ●●● S3 W2 *n*
1 THREAD [C,U] a strong thread made of several threads twisted together, used for tying or fastening things → **rope**: *Her key hung on a string around her neck.* | *a ball of string* | *I need a* **piece of string** *to tie this package.* → see picture at ROPE[1]
2 GROUP/SERIES [C] **a)** a number of similar things or events coming one after another SYN **series**: **[+of]** *a string of hit albums* **b)** a group of similar things: **[+of]** *She owns a string of health clubs.* **c)** *technical* a group of letters, words, or numbers, especially in a computer program
3 no strings (attached) having no special conditions or limits on an agreement, relationship etc: *The policy offers 15% interest, with no strings attached.*
4 string of pearls/lights/beads etc several objects of the same type connected with a thread, chain etc
5 MUSIC **a)** [C] one of the long thin pieces of wire, NYLON etc that are stretched across a musical instrument and produce sound **b) the strings/the string section** the people in an ORCHESTRA or band who play musical instruments that have strings, such as VIOLINS → see picture at PIANO[1]
6 first-string/second-string etc relating to or being a member of a team or group with the highest, second highest etc level of skill: *a first-string quarterback*
7 have sb on a string *informal* to be able to make someone do whatever you want: *Susie has her mother on a string.*
8 have more than one string to your bow *BrE* to have more than one skill, idea, plan etc that you can use if you need to → G-STRING, → **how long is a piece of string?** at LONG[1](9), → **pull strings** at PULL[1](8), → **pull the/sb's strings** at PULL[1](9), → **the purse strings** at PURSE[1](5)

string[2] *v* (*past tense and past participle* **strung** /strʌŋ/) [T] **1** to put things together onto a thread, chain etc: *beads strung on a silver chain* **2** [always + adv/prep] to hang things in a line, usually high in the air, especially for decoration: **string sth along/across etc sth** *Christmas lights were strung from one end of Main Street to the other.* **3 be strung (out) along/across etc sth** *written* to be spread out in a line: *the houses and shops were strung out along the bay* **4** to put a string or a set of strings onto a musical instrument → **highly-strung** at HIGHLY

string along *phr v informal* **1 string sb along** to deceive someone for a long time by making them believe that you will help them, that you love them etc: *He's just stringing you along.* **2** *BrE* to go somewhere with someone for a short time, especially because you do not have anything else to do: **[+with]** *If you're going into town, I'll string along with you.*

string sth ↔ **out** *phr v informal* to make something continue longer than it should: *Rebel leaders attempted to string out negotiations to avoid reaching a settlement.*

string sth ↔ **together** *phr v* **1 string words/a sentence together** to manage to say or write something that other people can understand: *He was so drunk he could hardly string two words together.* **2** to combine things in order to make something that is complete, good, useful etc: *They string together image after image until the documentary is completed.*

string sb ↔ **up** *phr v informal* to kill someone by hanging them → STRUNG-UP

ˌ**string ˈbean** *n* [C] a type of long thin green bean

ˌ**stringed ˈinstrument** *n* [C] a musical instrument such as a VIOLIN, that produces sound from a set of STRINGS → see picture on *p. 1820*

strin·gent /ˈstrɪndʒənt/ *adj* **1** a stringent law, rule, standard etc is very strict and must be obeyed: *stringent anti-noise regulations* **2** stringent economic conditions exist when there is a severe lack of money and strict controls on the supply of money —**stringently** *adv* —**stringency** *n* [U]

string·er /ˈstrɪŋə $ -ər/ *n* [C] someone who regularly sends in news stories to a newspaper, but who is not employed by that newspaper

ˈ**string ˌtheory** *n* [U] *technical* the idea that the smallest pieces of matter are shaped like strings with one DIMENSION, rather than points

ˌ**string ˈtie** *n* [C] a thick string worn around your neck and held in place by a decorative object, worn especially by men in the western US

string·y /ˈstrɪŋi/ *adj* **1** stringy meat, fruit, or vegetables are full of long thin pieces that are difficult to eat → **tough**: *Scoop out the pumpkin's stringy fibres.* **2** stringy hair is very thin and looks like string, especially because it is dirty **3** tall and thin

STRINGED INSTRUMENTS

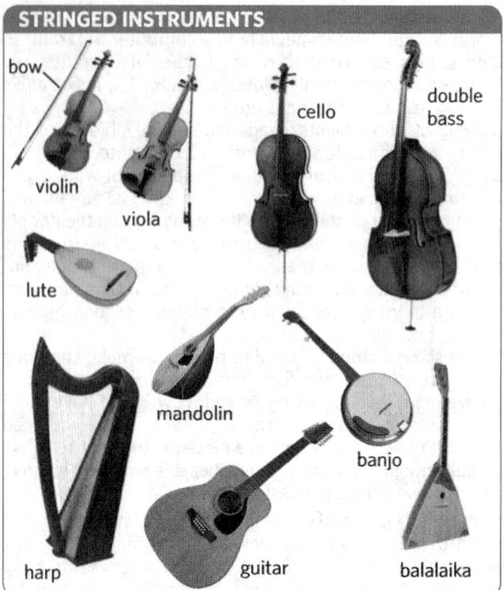

strip¹ /strɪp/ ●●● W3 *n* [C]
1 a long narrow piece of paper, cloth etc: *a strip of paper* **THESAURUS** PIECE
2 a long narrow area of land: *A strip of sand between the cliffs and the sea.*
3 do a strip to take your clothes off, especially in a sexually exciting way as a form of entertainment
4 *AmE* a road with a lot of shops, restaurants etc along it: *the Las Vegas strip*
5 [usually singular] *BrE* the clothes worn by a sports team: *Liverpool's famous red strip*
6 a STRIP CARTOON → **COMIC STRIP**, **LANDING STRIP**, → **tear sb off a strip** at **TEAR²**(8)

strip² ●●○ *v* (**stripped**, **stripping**)
1 TAKE OFF CLOTHES a) [I,T] (*also* **strip off**) to take off your clothes or take off someone else's clothes → **undress**: *Jack stripped and jumped into the shower.* | *The prisoner was stripped and beaten.* | **strip off sth** *He stripped off his sweater and threw it onto the couch.* | *Eric stood in the hot sun,* ***stripped to the waist*** (=not wearing any clothes on the top half of his body). | *Terry* ***stripped down to*** *her bra and pants* (=removed all her clothes except her bra and pants) *and tried on the dress.* | *The boys* ***stripped naked*** *and jumped in the pond.* **b)** [I] to take off your clothes in a sexually exciting way as entertainment for someone else
2 REMOVE [T] to remove something that is covering the surface of something else: *Strip the beds and wash the sheets.* | **strip sth off/from sth** *We need to strip the wallpaper off the walls first.* | **strip sth of sth** *tall windows stripped of curtains*
3 ENGINES/EQUIPMENT [T] (*also* **strip down**) to separate an engine or piece of equipment into pieces in order to clean or repair it SYN **dismantle**
4 BUILDING/SHIP ETC [T] to remove everything that is inside a building, all the equipment from a car etc so that it is completely empty: *The apartment had been* ***stripped bare****.*
5 DAMAGE [T] to damage or break the GEARS of something or the THREAD (=raised line) on a screw so that it does not work correctly anymore → **ASSET STRIPPING**

strip sth ↔ **away** *phr v* to remove something, especially something that hides or protects someone or something: *His book aims to strip away the lies and show the world as it really is.*

strip sb **of** sth *phr v* to take away something important from someone as a punishment, for example their title, property, or power: *Captain Evans was found guilty and stripped of his rank.*

ˌstrip carˈtoon *n* [C] *BrE* a series of drawings inside a row of small boxes that tells a short story SYN **comic strip** → **cartoon**

ˈstrip club *n* [C] *informal* a place where people go to see performers who take off their clothes in a sexually exciting way

stripe /straɪp/ ●●○ *n* [C]
1 a line of colour, especially one of several lines of colour all close together: *a shirt with black and white stripes* | **vertical/horizontal stripes**
2 of all stripes/of every stripe of all different types: *Politicians of all stripes complained about the plan.*
3 a narrow piece of material worn on the arm of a uniform as a sign of rank → **earn your stripes** at **EARN**

striped /straɪpt/ ●●○ *adj* having lines or bands of colour SYN **stripy**: *a blue and white striped shirt* → see picture at **PATTERN¹**

stripe·y /ˈstraɪpi/ *adj BrE* another spelling of STRIPY

ˈstrip joint *n* [C] *informal* a STRIP CLUB

ˈstrip light *n* [C] *BrE* an electric light that consists of a long white FLUORESCENT tube

ˈstrip ˌlighting *n* [U] *BrE* lighting provided by long white FLUORESCENT tubes

strip·ling /ˈstrɪplɪŋ/ *n* [C] *old-fashioned* a boy who is almost a young man - sometimes used humorously about a man who is quite old SYN **youth**

ˈstrip mall *n* [C] *AmE* a row of shops built together, with a large area for parking cars in front of it

ˈstrip mine *n* [C] *AmE* a very large hole that is made in the ground to remove metal, coal etc from the earth SYN **opencast** *BrE* —**strip-mine** *v* [I,T] —**strip mining** *n* [U]

strip·per /ˈstrɪpə $ -ər/ *n* **1** [C] someone whose job is to take off their clothes in a sexually exciting way in order to entertain people **2** [C,U] a tool or liquid chemical used to remove something from a surface: *paint stripper*

ˌstrip ˈpoker *n* [C] a game of POKER (=card game) in which players that lose must take off pieces of their clothing

ˈstrip search *n* [C] a process in which you have to remove your clothes so that your body can be checked, usually for hidden drugs —**strip search** *v* [T]

ˈstrip show *n* [C] a form of entertainment where people take off their clothes in a sexually exciting way

strip·tease /ˈstrɪptiːz, ˌstrɪpˈtiːz/ *n* [C,U] a performance in which someone takes off their clothes in a sexually exciting way

strip·y, **stripey** /ˈstraɪpi/ *adj BrE* STRIPED: *He was wearing jeans and a stripy T-shirt.*

strive /straɪv/ ●○○ *v* (*past tense* **strove** /strəʊv $ stroʊv/, *past participle* **striven** /ˈstrɪvən/) [I] *formal* to make a great effort to achieve something: **strive to do sth** *I was still striving to be successful.* | **[+for/after]** *We must continue to strive for greater efficiency.* **THESAURUS** TRY —**striving** *n* [C,U]

strobe light /ˈstrəʊb ˌlaɪt $ ˈstroʊb-/ (*also* **strobe**) *n* [C] a light that flashes on and off very quickly, often used in places where you can dance

strode /strəʊd $ stroʊd/ *v* the past tense of STRIDE²

stroke¹ /strəʊk $ stroʊk/ ●●○ S3 *n* [C]
1 ILLNESS if someone has a stroke, an ARTERY (=tube carrying blood) in their brain suddenly bursts or becomes blocked, so that they may die or be unable to use some muscles: *She died following a massive stroke.* | **have/suffer a stroke** *I looked after my father after he had a stroke.* | *a stroke patient*
2 SWIMMING/ROWING a) one of a set of movements in swimming or rowing in which you move your arms or the OAR forward and then back: *She swam with strong steady strokes.* **b)** a style of swimming or rowing: *the breast stroke*
3 SPORT the action of hitting the ball in games such as tennis, GOLF, and CRICKET: *a backhand stroke*
4 PEN/BRUSH a) a single movement of a pen or brush when you are writing or painting: *A few strokes of her pen*

brought out his features clearly. **b)** a line made by a pen or brush: *the thick downward strokes of the characters*
5 at a/one stroke with a single sudden action: *At one stroke, the country lost two outstanding leaders.*
6 on the stroke of seven/nine etc at exactly seven o'clock etc: *She arrived home on the stroke of midnight.* | *The only goal of the match came on the stroke of half time.*
7 stroke of luck/fortune something lucky that happens to you unexpectedly: *In a stroke of luck, a suitable organ donor became available.*
8 stroke of genius/inspiration etc a very good idea about what to do to solve a problem: *It was a stroke of genius to film the movie in Toronto.*
9 HIT an action of hitting someone with something such as a whip or thin stick: *He cried out at each stroke of the whip.*
10 A MOVEMENT OF YOUR HAND a gentle movement of your hand over something: *I* ***gave*** *her hair a gentle* ***stroke***.
11 with/at a stroke of the pen if someone in authority does something with a stroke of the pen, they sign an official document to make a decision with important and serious results: *He had the power to order troops home with a stroke of his pen.*
12 not do a stroke (of work) *BrE informal* to not do any work at all
13 stroke of lightning a bright flash of lightning, especially one that hits something
14 CLOCK/BELL a single sound made by a clock giving the hours, or by a bell, GONG etc
15 put sb off their stroke *BrE informal* to make someone stop giving all their attention to what they are doing: *Seeing Frank watching me put me off my stroke.*
16 IN NUMBERS *BrE* used when you are saying a number written with the mark (/) in it SYN **slash**: *The serial number is seventeen stroke one* (=17/1).

stroke² ●●○ *v* [T]
1 to move your hand gently over something: *He reached out and stroked her cheek tenderly.* THESAURUS ▸ TOUCH
2 [always + adv/prep] to move something somewhere with gentle movements of your hand: *He lifted her face and stroked her hair from her eyes.*
3 [always + adv/prep] to hit or kick a ball with a smooth movement in games such as tennis, golf, and CRICKET: *He stroked the ball into an empty net, with a minute to go.*
4 stroke sb's ego to say nice things to someone to make them feel good, especially because you want something from them

stroll /strəʊl $ stroʊl/ ●○○ *v* [I] to walk somewhere in a slow relaxed way: **[+down/over/along]** *We were strolling along, laughing and joking.* THESAURUS ▸ WALK —**stroll** *n* [C]: *They* ***went for a stroll*** *in the park.*

stroll·er /ˈstrəʊlə $ ˈstroʊlər/ *n* [C] **1** *AmE* a small chair on wheels, in which a small child sits and is pushed along SYN **buggy**, **pushchair** *BrE* **2** someone who is strolling: *evening strollers on the promenade*

stroll·ing /ˈstrəʊlɪŋ $ ˈstroʊ-/ *adj* [only before noun] **1** a strolling entertainer travels around the country giving performances in different places SYN **travelling 2** a strolling musician plays music while walking among people who are listening to them

strong /strɒŋ $ strɔːŋ/ ●●● S1 W1 *adj* (*comparative* **stronger**, *superlative* **strongest**)
1 ABLE TO LIFT HEAVY THINGS/DO HARD WORK having a lot of physical power so that you can lift heavy things, do hard physical work etc: *He was a big strong man.* | *Jack was tall and strong.* | **strong hands/arms/muscles etc** *He picked her up in his big strong arms.* | *I'm not strong enough to fight him.* → see Thesaurus box on *p. 1822*
2 NOT EASILY BROKEN OR DAMAGED not easily broken or damaged: *good strong shoes* | *The locks on the doors were solid and strong.*
3 ABLE TO DEAL WITH DIFFICULTY determined and able to deal with a difficult or upsetting situation: *I'm not strong enough to take insults and hatred.* | *Laura had a strong character.*
4 POWERFUL having a lot of power or influence: *The Fifth French Republic was established with a strong president in 1958.* | *a strong national army* | *Our party is the strongest as we come up to the election.* THESAURUS ▸ POWERFUL
5 FEELINGS/OPINIONS strong emotions, opinions, beliefs etc are ones that you feel or believe a lot and are very serious about: *He had* ***a strong sense of*** *responsibility to his vocation of preaching.* | *There has been* ***strong support*** *for the strike.* | *The proposal has met with* ***strong opposition*** *from local people.* | **strong feelings/views/opinions** *Many people have strong feelings about the issue.*
6 AFFECT/INFLUENCE a strong desire, influence etc affects you very much: *He had a* ***strong desire*** *for power.* | *Such feelings may* ***have a strong influence*** *over your decisions.* | *The temptation is very strong.*
7 RELATIONSHIP a strong relationship, friendship etc is very loyal and likely to last a long time: *He maintained* ***strong links*** *with the world of the deaf.* | *She still has a* ***strong relationship*** *with her mother.* | *I have a* ***strong commitment*** *to the quality of teaching.*
8 ARGUMENT/REASON ETC likely to persuade other people that something is true or the correct thing to do: *There is* ***a strong case*** *for an energy conservation programme.* | *They need* ***strong evidence*** *to secure a conviction.* | *a* ***strong argument***
9 LIKELY likely to succeed or happen: *She's a strong candidate for the party leadership.* | **strong possibility/chance/probability** *A year ago, there was a strong possibility that he wouldn't live.*
10 HEALTHY healthy, especially after you have been ill: *I don't think her heart is very strong.* | *You've been blessed with a* ***strong constitution*** (=you are healthy and do not easily become ill).
11 be in a strong position (*also* **gain a strong position**) to be in a situation where you have power over other people or are likely to get what you want: *The company have gained a strong position in the cheese market.*
12 strong wind/current/tide wind, water etc that moves with great force: *A strong wind was blowing across the lake.*
13 GOOD AT STH very good at something: *His writing* ***was strong on*** *description.* | *We beat a team that was much stronger than ourselves.* | **be sb's strong point/suit** (=the thing that someone is especially good at) *Tact never was my strong point.*
14 TASTE/SMELL having a taste or smell that you notice easily: *strong coffee* | *This cheese has a very strong flavour.* | *a strong smell of petrol*
15 ALCOHOL/DRUGS ETC having a lot of a substance, such as alcohol, that gives something its effect: ***extra strong*** *beer* | *strong painkillers* | *I haven't touched* ***strong drink*** (=alcoholic drinks) *for years.*
16 LIGHT/COLOUR bright and easy to see: *The light was not very strong.* THESAURUS ▸ BRIGHT
17 strong language speech or writing that contains a lot of swearing: *This film is not suitable for children under 12 as it contains strong language.*
18 strong accent the way that someone pronounces words that shows clearly that they come from a particular area or country: *a strong German accent*
19 strong nose/chin/features a nose etc that is large and noticeable, especially in an attractive way: *She has the same strong features as her mother.*
20 MONEY a strong CURRENCY (=the type of money used in a country) does not easily lose its value compared with other currencies
21 600/10,000 etc strong [only after number] used to give the number of people in a crowd or organization: *the company's 2,200 strong workforce* | *The crowd was 10,000 strong.*
22 be going strong to continue to be active or successful, even after a long time: *He celebrated his ninetieth birthday this month, and he's* ***still going strong***. → **come on strong** at COME ON

ˈstrong-arm *adj* [only before noun] **strong-arm tactics/methods etc** the use of force or violence, especially when this is not necessary —**strong-arm** *v* [T]

strong·box /ˈstrɒŋbɒks $ ˈstrɔːŋbɑːks/ *n* [C] a box,

S

usually made of metal, that can be locked and that valuable things are kept in SYN **safe**

strong·hold /ˈstrɒŋhəʊld $ ˈstrɒːŋhoʊld/ *n* [C] **1** an area where there is a lot of support for a particular way of life, political party etc: *The area is a Republican stronghold.* **2** an area that is strongly defended by a military group: *The fighters moved south to their mountain stronghold.* **3** an area where there are large numbers of a rare animal: *one of the last strongholds of the European wolf*

strong·ly /ˈstrɒŋli $ ˈstrɒːŋ-/ ●●○ S3 *adv*
1 if you feel or believe in something strongly, you are very sure and serious about it: *I'm* ***strongly opposed to*** *capital punishment. | We strongly believe that she is innocent. | I'm strongly in favour of marriage.*
2 in a way that is meant to persuade someone to do something: **strongly suggest/advise/recommend sth** *Before taking action, you are strongly recommended to consult an accountant.*
3 in a way that is easy to notice: *The house smelt strongly of food.* ⚠ Don't say 'hold/grip something strongly'. Use **firmly** or **tightly**: *He gripped my arm tightly.*

strong·man /ˈstrɒŋmæn $ ˈstrɒːŋ-/ *n* (*plural* **strongmen** /-men/) [C] **1** a politician or leader who uses violence or threats to get what they want **2** a very strong man who performs in a CIRCUS

ˌstrong-ˈminded *adj* not easily influenced by other people to change what you believe or want SYN **determined**: *They were both strong-minded women.*

strong·room /ˈstrɒŋruːm, -rʊm $ ˈstrɒːŋ-/ *n* [C] a special room in a bank, shop etc where valuable objects can be kept safely

ˌstrong-ˈwilled *adj* knowing exactly what you want to do and being determined to achieve it, even if other people advise you against it OPP **weak-willed**

stron·ti·um /ˈstrɒntiəm $ ˈstrɑːn-/ *n* [U] a soft silver-white metal that is used to make FIREWORKS. It is a chemical ELEMENT: symbol Sr

strop /strɒp $ strɑːp/ *n* [C] **1** a narrow piece of leather used for making a RAZOR sharp **2 in a strop** *BrE informal* annoyed about something: *She's a nice person but she just* ***gets in a strop*** *so easily.*

strop·py /ˈstrɒpi $ ˈstrɑːpi/ *adj BrE informal* bad-tempered and easily offended or annoyed: *I try not to get stroppy, but sometimes I just can't help it.* —**stroppiness** *n* [U]

strove /strəʊv $ stroʊv/ *v* the past tense of STRIVE

struck¹ /strʌk/ the past tense and past participle of STRIKE¹

struck² *adj* **be struck on sb/sth** *BrE informal* to think that someone or something is very good: *She seemed rather struck on Vincent.*

struc·tur·al /ˈstrʌktʃərəl/ ●○○ AWL *adj* connected with the structure of something: *structural changes in the computer industry | The earthquake caused minor structural damage.* —**structurally** *adv*: *Is the building* ***structurally sound*** (=in good condition)?

ˌstructural engiˈneer *n* [C] an engineer skilled in planning the building of large structures such as bridges —**structural engineering** *n* [U]

struc·tur·al·is·m /ˈstrʌktʃərəlɪzəm/ *n* [U] a method of studying language, literature, society etc in which you examine the relationships of the different parts or ideas in order to determine their meaning —**structuralist** *adj, n*

struc·ture¹ /ˈstrʌktʃə $ -ər/ ●●● S3 W2 AWL *n*
1 [C,U] the way in which the parts of something are connected with each other and form a whole, or the thing that these parts make up → **structural**: **social/political/economic etc structure** *the social structure of organizations | challenges to the existing* ***power structure*** *| A new* ***management structure*** *has been introduced.* | **[+of]** *the structure of the brain | molecular structures*
2 [C] something that has been built, especially something large such as a building or a bridge: *a high wooden structure with a curved roof*
3 [C,U] a situation where activities are carefully organized and planned: *These kids require a lot of structure and stability.* → **career structure** at CAREER¹(1)

structure² ●○○ AWL *v* [T] to arrange the different parts of something into a pattern or system in which each part is connected to the others SYN **organize**: *The exhibition is structured around three topics. | software that helps users structure their work and their data*

struc·tured /ˈstrʌktʃəd $ -ərd/ AWL *adj* carefully organized, planned, or arranged: *The interviews were* ***highly structured****. | a structured approach to teaching*

ˌstructured reˈality *n* [U] television programmes in which people who are not actors are filmed in situations that look like their real lives but have often been arranged by the programme's producers

stru·del /ˈstruːdl/ *n* [C,U] a type of Austrian or German cake, made of PASTRY with fruit inside

THESAURUS: strong

HAVING A STRONG BODY

strong having a lot of physical strength: *It took four strong men to lift the piano. | You open it – you're stronger than I am.*
powerful very strong – used about someone's body, arms, muscles etc: *his big powerful shoulders | He was a tall man with a powerful physique.*
muscular having big muscles and looking strong: *She liked men who were big and muscular. | He had a firm muscular body.*
well-built a well-built man is strong and tall and has a big body: *Police say the man they are looking for is 36 years old, 6 feet tall, and well-built.*
hunky *informal* strong and attractive: *She married hunky Hollywood star Brad Pitt. | He looks hunky, but he's not really my type.*

NOT EASILY BROKEN OR DAMAGED

strong not easily broken or damaged: *The bags are made of strong black plastic. | We need a strong rope for this job.*
tough strong – used especially about something that can be used a lot without damaging it or making it weaker: *a pair of tough leather boots | Kitchen floors need to be tough enough to withstand heavy use.*
heavy-duty [only before noun] extremely strong – used about materials, tools, machines etc that are made especially to be used a lot without being easily damaged: *heavy-duty rubber gloves | a heavy-duty carpet for the hallway*
sturdy strong and often thick, and not likely to fall over or get broken: *a fence made with sturdy wooden posts | The furniture is simple but sturdy.*
unbreakable extremely strong and impossible to break: *Babies need to have unbreakable dishes and cups.*
indestructible impossible to break, damage, or destroy, and lasting forever: *Gold is virtually indestructible. | The pyramids were built as indestructible tombs for the Pharaohs.*
durable *especially written* used about materials and products that will remain in good condition for a long time – often used on product labels: *The jacket has a durable nylon lining. | Varnish is more durable than paint.*
robust *especially written* strongly made – used especially about the structure of something, for example a vehicle or machine: *a mountain bike with a robust frame*

strug·gle[1] /ˈstrʌɡəl/ ●●○ W3 *v* [I]
1 to try extremely hard to achieve something, even though it is very difficult: **struggle to do sth** *She's struggling to bring up a family alone.* | **[+with]** *The airline is struggling with high costs.* | **[+for]** *Millions of people are struggling for survival.* | **[+against]** *Firms are struggling against a prolonged recession.* **THESAURUS** ▸ TRY
2 a) to fight someone who is attacking you or holding you, especially so that you can escape: **[+with]** *James was hit in the mouth as he struggled with the burglars.* | **struggle to do sth** *She struggled to free herself.* **b)** if two people struggle, they fight each other for something, especially something one of them is holding: **[+for]** *They struggled for possession of the gun.*
3 to move somewhere with great difficulty: **[+up/out of/into etc]** *Walkers were struggling up the dusty track.*
4 to be likely to fail, even though you are trying very hard: *The team has been struggling all season.* | **a struggling artist/writer/business**
struggle on *phr v* to continue doing something that you find very difficult or tiring: *He struggled on despite his condition.*

struggle[2] ●●○ W3 *n* [C]
1 a long hard fight to get freedom, political rights etc: **[+for]** *a struggle for survival* | *a* ***power struggle*** *between forces favoring and opposing change*
2 a long period of time in which you try to deal with a difficult problem: **[+with/against]** *She spoke of her struggles with shyness.*
3 a fight between two people for something, or an attempt by one person to escape from the other: *Police said there were no signs of a struggle.*
4 be a struggle (for sb) if something is a struggle, you find it very difficult to do

strum /strʌm/ *v* (**strummed, strumming**) [I,T] to play an instrument such as a GUITAR by moving your fingers up and down across its strings

strum·pet /ˈstrʌmpɪt/ *n* [C] *old-fashioned* an insulting word meaning a woman who has sex for money SYN **prostitute**

strung /strʌŋ/ the past tense and past participle of STRING[2]

ˌstrung-ˈout *adj* [not before noun] *informal*
1 strongly affected by a drug, so that you cannot react normally SYN **high**: **[+on]** *strung-out on drugs*
2 extremely tired and worried

ˌstrung-ˈup *adj BrE informal* very nervous, worried, or excited

strut[1] /strʌt/ *v* (**strutted, strutting**) [I] **1** to walk proudly with your head high and your chest pushed forwards, showing that you think you are important: **[+around/about/across etc]** *I strutted around Chicago as if I were really somebody.* **2 strut your stuff** *informal* to show your skill at doing something, especially dancing or performing: *The band strutted their stuff in a free concert.*

strut[2] *n* **1** [C] a long thin piece of metal or wood used to support a part of a building, the wing of an aircraft etc **2** [singular] a proud way of walking, with your head high and your chest pushed forwards

strych·nine /ˈstrɪkniːn $ -naɪn, -niːn/ *n* [U] a very poisonous substance sometimes used in small amounts as a medicine

stub[1] /stʌb/ *n* [C] **1** the short part of something long and thin, such as a cigarette or pencil, that is left when the rest has been used: *a pencil stub* **2** the part of a ticket that is given back to you after it has been torn, as proof that you have paid: *a ticket stub* **3** a piece of a cheque left in a cheque book as a record after the main part has been torn out: *a check stub*

stub[2] *v* (**stubbed, stubbing**) **stub your toe** to hurt your toe by hitting it against something **THESAURUS** ▸ HIT
stub sth ↔ **out** *phr v* to stop a cigarette from burning by pressing the end of it against something

stub·ble /ˈstʌbəl/ *n* [U] **1** short stiff hairs that grow on a man's face if he does not SHAVE **2** short stiff pieces left in the fields after wheat, corn etc has been cut —**stubbly** *adj*

stub·born /ˈstʌbən $ -ərn/ ●●○ *adj*
1 determined not to change your mind, even when people think you are being unreasonable: *Why are you so stubborn?* | *I've got a very* ***stubborn streak*** (=a tendency to be stubborn). | *Paul can be* ***as stubborn as a mule*** (=very stubborn). **THESAURUS** ▸ DETERMINED
2 stubborn resistance/refusal/determination etc a very strong and determined refusal etc: *a stubborn refusal to face reality*
3 difficult to remove, deal with, or use SYN **tough**: *stubborn stains* —**stubbornly** *adv*: *'I don't care,' she said stubbornly.* —**stubbornness** *n* [U]

stub·by /ˈstʌbi/ *adj* short and thick or fat: *stubby fingers* **THESAURUS** ▸ SHORT

stuc·co /ˈstʌkəʊ $ -koʊ/ *n* [U] a type of PLASTER that is used especially to cover the outside walls of buildings

stuck[1] /stʌk/ the past tense and past participle of STICK[1]

stuck[2] ●●○ *adj* [not before noun]
1 impossible or unable to move from a particular position: *Sara tried to open the window but it was stuck.* | *They* ***got stuck*** *in a traffic jam.* | **[+in]** *The boat was stuck in the mud.* | *I've* ***got*** *something* ***stuck*** *in my throat.*
2 *informal* unable to escape from a bad or boring situation: **[+in/at]** *Mum resented being stuck at home with two young kids.* | *We could be stuck in this place for days.*
3 *informal* unable to do any more of something that you are working on because it is too difficult: *Can you help me with my homework, Dad? I'm stuck.* | **[+on]** *If you* ***get stuck*** *on a difficult word, just ask for help.*
4 be stuck with sth *informal* to have something you do not want because you cannot get rid of it: *We are, unfortunately, stuck with this huge, ugly building.*
5 be stuck with sb to have to spend time with someone or have a relationship with them, even though you do not want to: *They are stuck with each other with no end in sight.*
6 be stuck for sth to be unable to think what to say or do: *For once Anthony was* ***stuck for words*** (=did not know what to say).
7 get stuck in/get stuck into sth *BrE spoken* to start doing something eagerly and with a lot of energy: *Take your jacket off and get stuck in!*
8 be stuck on sb *informal* to be attracted to someone: *He says he's stuck on me.*

ˌstuck-ˈup *adj informal* proud and unfriendly because you think you are better and more important than other people – used to show disapproval SYN **snooty**: *His wife was a bit stuck-up.*

stud /stʌd/ *n*
1 ANIMAL [C,U] the use of animals, especially horses, for breeding, an animal that is used in this way, or a place where this is done: *a stud dog*
2 MAN [C] *informal* a man who has a lot of sexual partners and who is very proud of his sexual ability
3 ON SHOES [C] *BrE* one of a set of small pointed pieces of metal or plastic that are attached to the bottom of a running shoe, football boot etc to stop you from slipping
4 IN YOUR EAR [C] a small round EARRING
5 FOR DECORATION [C] a round piece of metal that is stuck into a surface for decoration
6 FOR A SHIRT [C] a small thing for fastening a shirt or collar, that consists of two round flat pieces of metal joined together by a bar
7 BOARD [C] *AmE* a board that is used to make the frame of a house

stud·ded /ˈstʌdɪd/ *adj* **1** decorated with a lot of studs or small jewels etc: *studded leather jackets* | *a diamond-studded watch* | **[+with]** *a belt studded with jewels* **2** covered or filled with a lot of something: **[+with]** *The sky was clear and studded with stars.* → **STAR-STUDDED**

stu·dent /ˈstjuːdənt $ ˈstuː-/ ●●● S1 W1 *n* [C]
1 someone who is studying at a university, school etc → **pupil**: **[+at]** *a first-year student at the University of Oslo* | **law/science/medical etc student** *There are plenty of job opportunities for engineering students.* | **student teacher/nurse etc** (=someone who is studying to be a teacher,

S

nurse etc) | **A/B/C student** (=a student who always gets A's, B's etc for their work) → MATURE STUDENT
2 be a student of sth to be very interested in a particular subject: *He's obviously an excellent student of human nature.*

THESAURUS

student someone who is studying at a university or school. In British English, **student** is not usually used to refer to a child at primary school: *a student at Moscow University | How many students are there in your class?*
pupil *especially BrE* someone who is being taught in a particular school or by a particular teacher: *The school has 300 pupils. | He received a letter from one of his former pupils.*
schoolchild a child who goes to school: *The play was performed by a group of local schoolchildren.*
schoolboy/schoolgirl *especially BrE* a boy or girl who goes to school – used especially when talking about how they behave, or that time in someone's life: *They were behaving like naughty schoolgirls. | When he was a schoolboy, no one had heard of computers.*
learner someone who is learning a foreign language: *Learners often have problems with pronunciation. | a book for foreign learners of English*

ˌstudent ˈbody *n* [C] *AmE* all of the students in a HIGH SCHOOL, college, or university, considered as a group
ˌstudent ˈgovernment (*also* **ˌstudent ˈcouncil**) *n* [C] *AmE* an elected group of students in a HIGH SCHOOL, college, or university who represent the students in meetings and who organize school activities
ˌstudent ˈloan *n* [C] an amount of money that you borrow from the government or a bank to pay for your education at a college or university
ˌstudent ˈteaching *n* [U] *AmE* the period of time during which students who are learning to be teachers practise teaching in a school SYN **teaching practice** *BrE*
ˌstudent ˈunion (*also* **ˌstudents' ˈunion** *BrE*) *n* [C] **1** a building where students go to meet socially **2** *BrE* an association of students in a particular college or university
stud·ied /ˈstʌdid/ *adj* a studied way of behaving is deliberate and often not sincere, because it has been planned carefully: *She spoke with studied politeness.*
stu·di·o /ˈstjuːdiəʊ $ ˈstuːdioʊ/ ●●● S3 W2 *n* (*plural* **studios**) [C]
1 a room where television and radio programmes are made and broadcast or where music is recorded: *a TV studio | a* ***recording studio*** *in Nashville*
2 (*also* **studios** [plural]) a film company or the buildings it owns and uses to make its films: *Depardieu is making a film with one of the big Hollywood studios.*
3 a room where a painter or photographer regularly works: *a photographer's studio*
4 a room where dancing lessons are given or that dancers use to practise in
5 (*also* **studio apartment** *AmE*, **studio flat** *BrE*) a small apartment with one main room: *a tiny studio*
ˌstudio ˈaudience *n* [C] a group of people who watch and are sometimes involved in a radio or television programme while it is being made
stu·di·ous /ˈstjuːdiəs $ ˈstuː-/ *adj* spending a lot of time studying and reading: *a quiet, studious young man* —**studiously** *adv* —**studiousness** *n* [U]
ˈstud ˌmuffin *n* [C] *informal* an attractive man who is very good at sex and who has sex with a lot of people
stud·y¹ /ˈstʌdi/ ●●● S1 W1 *n* (*plural* **studies**)
1 RESEARCH [C] a piece of work that is done to find out more about a particular subject or problem, and usually includes a written report: *Recent studies show that women still get paid a lot less than men.* | **[+of/into/on]** *a study of Australian wild birds | The study was carried out between January and May 2008.* → CASE STUDY
2 LEARNING [U] when you spend time learning, especially at home or by yourself rather than during school: *Set aside a period of time specifically for study. | ways to improve* ***study skills*** (=skills that help you study efficiently and be successful in school)
3 SUBJECT [U] (*also* **studies** [plural]) a subject that people study at a college or university: **[+of]** *Linguistics is the study of language. | Environmental Studies* | **literary/historical/scientific etc study** *the scientific study of earthquakes*
4 sb's studies the work that someone does in order to learn about a particular subject, especially the courses they take at a college or university: *How are your studies coming along?* | **begin/continue/stop etc your studies** *I gave up my studies when I had the baby.*
5 CAREFUL CONSIDERATION [U] when you examine or consider something very carefully and in detail: *a report that deserves careful study*
6 ROOM [C] a room in a house that is used for work or study → **office**
7 ART [C] a small detailed drawing, especially one that is done to prepare for a large painting: *Renoir's studies of small plants and flowers*
8 MUSIC [C] a piece of music, usually for piano, that is often intended for practice
9 make a study of sth to try to find out more about a subject
10 be a study in sth *literary* to be a perfect example of something: *His face was a study in fear.*
11 a quick study *AmE* someone who learns things quickly

COLLOCATIONS

VERBS

do a study/carry out a study (*also* **conduct a study** *formal*) *The scientists are carrying out a study into the effects of global warming.*
a study finds sth *The study found that men were more likely to take risks.*
a study shows sth *Studies have shown that the drug works.*
a study suggests/indicates sth *A British study suggests that older drivers are safer drivers.*
a study reveals sth (=shows something, especially something surprising) | **a study confirms sth** (=shows that something is true) | **a study aims to do sth** | **publish a study** | **fund a study** (=pay for it) | **commission a study** (=ask someone to carry out a study)

ADJECTIVES/NOUN + study

a research study *Research studies have found that young people are drinking no more than they were 20 years ago.*
a detailed study (*also* **an in-depth study**) *They carried out a detailed study into the effects of the disease on mice.*
a two-year/three-month etc study *They are engaged in a five-year study into the effects of calcium on bone health.*
a huge/massive study *The journal published the results of a massive study of 87,000 women.*
a previous/earlier study | **a pilot study** (=one done to find out if something will be successful) | **a feasibility study** (=one done to find out if something is possible or practical)

PHRASES

the aims of a study *The aims of this study are to examine the reliability of current techniques.*
the results/findings of a study *The results of this study suggest that the drug is effective in over 80% of cases.*

study² ●●● S1 W1 *v* (**studied**, **studying**, **studies**)
1 [I,T] to learn about a subject at school, university etc: *I've been studying English for six years. | I can't study with that music playing all the time.* | **study law/business/history etc** (=study a subject at a school or university) *Anna is studying French literature.* | **study at a university/school etc**

Stephen is currently studying at Exeter University. | **study to be a doctor/lawyer etc** *My brother's studying to be an accountant.* | **study for an exam/diploma etc** *I've only got three weeks left to study for my exams.* | **study under sb** (=be trained by a famous teacher) *a psychologist who studied under Jung in Zurich* THESAURUS ▸ LEARN
2 [T] to try to find out more about a subject or problem, using scientific methods: *Goodall was studying the behavior of chimpanzees in the wild.* | *The scientists were studying the action of a protein called ubiquitin.* | **study how/what/why etc** *They're studying how stress affects body chemistry.* THESAURUS ▸ EXAMINE
3 [T] to look at something carefully SYN **look at**: *She studied his face.* | *They got out of the car and studied the map.* | *I haven't had time to study the proposals yet.*

THESAURUS

study *v* [I,T] to learn about a subject at school, university etc: *If you study hard, you'll get a good job.* | *He studied law at Harvard University.*
take *v* [T] to study a subject that you have chosen at school, college etc: *What classes are you taking next semester?* | *In my final year, I decided to take English and economics.*
do *v* [T] *BrE informal* to study a particular subject at school or university: *I can't decide whether to do German or Spanish next year.* | *Did you do computing at school?*
major in sth *phr v AmE* to study something as your main subject at a college or university: *Diane majored in psychology at the University of Washington.*
revise *v* [I] *BrE* to study to prepare for an examination: *It's best to start revising early.* | *He's revising for his final exams.*
cram *v* [I] *informal* to study very hard and try to learn a lot of information just before an examination: *Everyone's cramming for their final exams.*
do research to study something in a very detailed way, especially in order to discover new information about it: *He does research at Oxford University.* | *I'm doing research into second language learning.* | *It's difficult to do research on humans.*

ˈstudy hall *n* [U] *AmE* a period of time during the school day when students must go to a room to study, instead of going to a lesson

stuff¹ /stʌf/ ●●● S1 W3 *n* [U]
1 THINGS *informal* used when you are talking about things such as substances, materials, or groups of objects when you do not know what they are called, or it is not important to say exactly what they are: *I've got some sticky stuff on my shoe.* | *How do you think you're going to fit all that stuff into the car?* | *I felt sorry for the ones who had to eat the awful stuff.* | *Where's all the camping stuff?*
2 sb's stuff *informal* the things that belong to someone: *Did you get the rest of your stuff?*
3 ACTIVITIES/IDEAS *informal* used when talking about different activities, subjects, or ideas, when you do not say exactly what these are: *What kind of stuff do you like to read?* | *I've got so much stuff to do this weekend.* | *There's a lot of interesting stuff in this book.* | *He's talked to me about* ***all that stuff*** *too.* | *He does mountain biking and skiing, and* ***stuff like that.***
4 WORK/ART *informal* used when you are talking about what someone has done or made, for example writing, music, or art: *I don't like his stuff.* | *John Lee was getting ready to play his stuff.* | *He did some great stuff in his early films.* | **good stuff** *BrE* (=used to tell someone that their work is good) *This is good stuff.*
5 ... and stuff *spoken informal* used to say that there are other things similar to what you have just mentioned, but you are not going to say what they are: *There's some very good music there, CD systems and stuff, and laser disks.*
6 the (very) stuff of dreams/life/politics exactly the kind of thing that dreams etc consist of: *an enchanting place – the very stuff of dreams*
7 CHARACTER the qualities of someone's character: *Does he have* ***the right stuff*** (=qualities that make you able to deal with difficulties)? | *Surely you're not going to give up? I thought you* ***were made of sterner stuff*** (=were more determined).
8 do/show your stuff *informal* to do what you are good at when everyone wants you to do it: *Come on Gina, get on the dance floor and do your stuff!* → **bit of stuff** at BIT¹(14), → **kid's stuff** at KID¹(4), → **know your stuff** at KNOW¹(5), → **strut your stuff** at STRUT¹(2)

GRAMMAR: Comparison

stuff
• **Stuff** is an uncountable noun and is not used in the plural. You say: *The shop sells all kinds of stuff.* ✗ Don't say: *The shop sells all kind of stuffs.*

foodstuff
• **Foodstuff** is a countable noun and is often used in the plural: *The country has to import basic foodstuffs such as rice.*

stuff² ●●○ *v* [T]
1 PUSH [always + adv/prep] to push or put something into a small space, especially in a quick careless way SYN **shove**: **stuff sth into/in/up sth** *She stuffed two more sweaters into her bag.* THESAURUS ▸ PUSH
2 FILL to fill something until it is full: *Volunteers were busy stuffing envelopes.* | **be stuffed with sth** *a pillow stuffed with feathers* | *boxes* ***stuffed full*** *of papers* THESAURUS ▸ FILL
3 FOOD to fill a chicken, pepper etc with a mixture of bread or rice, onion etc before cooking it
4 DEAD ANIMAL to fill the skin of a dead animal in order to make the animal look still alive: *a stuffed owl*
5 stuff yourself (*also* **stuff your face**) *informal* to eat so much food that you cannot eat anything else: **[+with]** *The kids have been stuffing themselves with candy.*
6 get stuffed *BrE spoken* used to tell someone very rudely and angrily that you do not want to talk to them or accept their offer: *He only offered me £10 for it, so I told him to get stuffed.*
7 sb can stuff sth *spoken* used to say very angrily or rudely that you do not want what someone is offering: *'All right. You can stuff your money!' Reynolds exploded.*
8 stuff it *spoken* used to say angrily or rudely that you do not care about something or do not want something: *I thought, stuff it, I'll do what I want.*

stuffed /stʌft/ ●○○ *adj* [not before noun] *informal* completely full, so that you cannot eat any more: *No, no dessert – I'm stuffed.*

ˌstuffed ˈanimal (*also* **ˌstuffed ˈtoy**) *n* [C] *AmE* a toy animal covered and filled with soft material SYN **soft toy** *BrE*

ˌstuffed ˈshirt *n* [C] *informal* someone who behaves in a very formal way and thinks that they are important

ˌstuffed-ˈup *adj* unable to breathe properly through your nose because you have a cold SYN **bunged up**

stuff·ing /ˈstʌfɪŋ/ *n* [U] **1** a mixture of bread or rice, onion etc that you put inside a chicken, pepper etc before cooking it: *sage and onion stuffing* **2** soft material that is used to fill something such as a CUSHION → **knock the stuffing out of sb** at KNOCK¹(12)

stuff·y /ˈstʌfi/ *adj* **1** a room or building that is stuffy does not have enough fresh air in it: *It's getting stuffy in here – do you mind if I open the window?* **2** people, occasions, or places that are stuffy are too formal and old-fashioned – used to show disapproval: *Their wedding was stuffy and formal.* | *a stuffy old family* —**stuffiness** *n* [U]: *the stuffiness of the room*

stul·ti·fy·ing /ˈstʌltəfaɪ-ɪŋ/ *adj formal* so boring that you feel as though you are losing your ability to think: *a stultifying office environment* —**stultify** *v* [T]

stum·ble /ˈstʌmbəl/ ●○○ *v* [I]
1 to hit your foot against something or put your foot down awkwardly while you are walking or running, so that you almost fall SYN **trip**: *In her hurry, she stumbled and spilled the milk all over the floor.* | **[+over/on]** *Vic stumbled over the step as he came in.* THESAURUS ▸ FALL

S

2 to walk in an unsteady way and often almost fall SYN **stagger**: **[+in/out/across etc]** *He stumbled upstairs and into bed.*
3 to stop or make a mistake when you are reading to people or speaking: **[+over/at/through]** *I hope I don't stumble over any of the long words.* —**stumble** *n* [C]

stumble on/across/upon sth *phr v* to find or discover something by chance and unexpectedly SYN **come across**: *Researchers have stumbled across a drug that may help patients with Parkinson's disease.*

ˈstumbling ˌblock *n* [C] a problem or difficulty that stops you from achieving something: **[+to]** *The main stumbling block to starting new research is that we lack qualified people.*

stump¹ /stʌmp/ *n* [C] **1** the bottom part of a tree that is left in the ground after the rest of it has been cut down: *an old* ***tree stump*** **2** the short part of someone's leg, arm etc that remains after the rest of it has been cut off **3** the small useless part of something that remains after most of it has broken off or worn away: *There was only a stump of the candle left.* **4** one of the three upright sticks in CRICKET that you throw the ball at **5 stump speech/speaker** *AmE* a speech made by a politician who is travelling around in order to gain political support, or the politician who gives this speech **6 be on the stump** *BrE* to be travelling around an area, making speeches in order to gain political support

stump² *v* **1** [T] if you are stumped by a question or problem, you are unable to find an answer to it: *a case that has stumped the police | The doctors were stumped and had to call in a specialist.* **2** [I] to walk with heavy steps SYN **stomp**: **[+up/along/across etc]** *He stumped down the hall.* **3** [T] to put a BATSMAN out of the game in CRICKET by touching the stumps with the ball when he is out of the hitting area **4** [I,T] *AmE* to travel around an area, meeting people and making speeches in order to gain political support: *Alexander has been stumping in New Hampshire.*

stump up (sth) *phr v BrE informal* to pay money, even if it is difficult or when you do not want to: *We stumped up eight quid each.*

stumped /stʌmpt/ *adj* unable to find an answer or think of a reply: *The question had me completely stumped.* | **stumped for words/an answer/a reply** *Travis seemed absolutely stumped for words.*

stump·y /ˈstʌmpi/ *adj* stumpy legs, fingers etc are short and thick in an unattractive way SYN **stubby**

stun /stʌn/ *v* (**stunned**, **stunning**) [T not in progressive] **1** to surprise or upset someone so much that they do not react immediately → **stagger**: *Redfern stunned the crowd with a last-minute goal.* **2** to make someone unconscious for a short time: *The impact of the ball had stunned her.* → STUNNED, STUNNING

stung /stʌŋ/ the past tense and past participle of STING¹

ˈstun gun *n* [C] a weapon that produces a very strong electric current and can be used to make animals or people unconscious

stunk /stʌŋk/ *v* the past participle of STINK¹

stunned /stʌnd/ ●○○ *adj* too surprised or shocked to speak: *He looked completely stunned.* | *The audience sat in* ***stunned silence.*** **THESAURUS** ▸ SHOCKED, SURPRISED

stun·ner /ˈstʌnə $ -ər/ *n* [C] *informal* **1** someone or something that is very attractive, especially a woman: *Lucy was a real stunner.* **2** a situation or event that surprises you

stun·ning /ˈstʌnɪŋ/ ●○○ *adj*
1 extremely attractive or beautiful: *You look absolutely stunning in that dress.* | *a stunning view* **THESAURUS** ▸ BEAUTIFUL
2 very surprising or shocking SYN **staggering**: *stunning news* —**stunningly** *adv*: *a stunningly beautiful woman*

stunt¹ /stʌnt/ *n* [C] **1** a dangerous action that is done to entertain people, especially in a film: *Not many actors* ***do*** *their own* ***stunts.*** | *a stunt flying show* **2** something that is done to attract people's attention, especially in advertising or politics: *Todd flew over the city in a hot-air balloon as a* ***publicity stunt.*** **3 pull a stunt** to do something that is silly or that is slightly dangerous: *Next time you pull a stunt like that don't expect me to get you out of trouble.*

stunt² *v* [T] to stop something or someone from growing to their full size or developing properly: *Lack of sunlight will stunt the plant's growth.*

stunt·ed /ˈstʌntɪd/ *adj* not developing properly or to full size: *He's emotionally stunted.*

ˈstunt man *n* [C] a man who is employed to take the place of an actor when something dangerous has to be done in a film

ˈstunt ˌwoman *n* [C] a woman who is employed to take the place of an actress when something dangerous has to be done in a film

stu·pe·fied /ˈstjuːpɪfaɪd $ ˈstuː-/ *adj* so surprised, tired, or bored that you cannot think clearly: *I stared up at Keith in stupefied amazement.* | *We sat there stupefied.* —**stupefaction** /ˌstjuːpəˈfækʃən $ ˌstuː-/ *n* [U]

stu·pe·fy·ing /ˈstjuːpəfaɪ-ɪŋ $ ˈstuː-/ *adj* making you feel extremely surprised, tired, or bored: *a stupefying amount of money* —**stupefy** *v* [T]

stu·pen·dous /stjuːˈpendəs $ stuː-/ *adj* surprisingly large or impressive SYN **magnificent**: *a stupendous achievement* —**stupendously** *adv*

stu·pid¹ /ˈstjuːpɪd $ ˈstuː-/ ●●● S1 W3 *adj*
1 showing a lack of good sense or good judgment SYN **silly**: *stupid mistakes | That was a stupid thing to say. | I can't believe Kate was stupid enough to get involved in this.* | **stupid idea/question** *Whose stupid idea was this?* | ***It was stupid of me*** *to lose my temper.*
2 having a low level of intelligence, so that you have difficulty learning or understanding things: *He understands - he's not stupid. | I couldn't do it, and it made me feel stupid.*
3 *spoken* used when you are talking about something or someone that makes you annoyed or impatient: *I can't get this stupid radio to work. | What is that stupid idiot doing?*
4 stupid with cold/sleep/shock etc unable to think clearly because you are extremely cold, tired etc —**stupidly** *adv*: *I stupidly agreed to organize the party.*

THESAURUS

stupid showing a total lack of good sense or good judgment. Stupid sounds very strong and is often used when you are annoyed or strongly criticizing someone's behaviour: *I wish you'd stop asking stupid questions. | It was stupid of me to leave the door unlocked.*
silly doing or saying things that are not sensible or serious, and that may make you feel embarrassed later. Silly sounds much gentler than **stupid**: *a silly mistake | Don't be so silly! There's nothing wrong with you.*
daft *informal* not sensible, often in a way that is also amusing: *Is this another of your daft ideas? | Don't be daft! Of course you're not too old to go clubbing.*
dumb *informal especially AmE* stupid: *a dumb question | He was dumb enough to believe her.*
foolish stupid. Foolish sounds rather formal and is used mainly in written English. The usual words to use in everyday English are **silly** or **stupid**: *It was a foolish thing to say. | They did not want to look foolish.*
unwise *formal* done without thinking carefully enough about the possible disadvantages that may result: *She knew the marriage was unwise. | an unwise choice of words*

VERY STUPID

crazy not at all sensible or reasonable - used when you are very surprised by someone's behaviour or what they have said: *Ian's got some crazy plan to drive across Africa. | She looked at me as if I was crazy!*
ridiculous extremely stupid: *You look ridiculous in that hat. | Some people spend a ridiculous amount of money on cars.*

absurd/ludicrous extremely stupid – used especially when an idea or situation seems strange or illogical: *How can a return ticket cost less than a single? It's totally absurd!* | *It was a ludicrous idea.*
laughable so stupid that you cannot believe someone is telling the truth or being serious: *The accusations were almost laughable.* | *a laughable suggestion*

stupid² *n spoken not polite* an insulting way of talking to someone who you think is being stupid: *No, stupid, don't do it like that!*

stu·pid·i·ty /stjuːˈpɪdəti $ stuː-/ *n* (*plural* **stupidities**) **1** [C,U] behaviour or actions that show a lack of good sense or good judgment: *all the horrors and stupidities of war* **2** [U] the quality of being stupid

stu·por /ˈstjuːpə $ ˈstuːpər/ *n* [C,U] a state in which you cannot think, speak, see, or hear clearly, usually because you have drunk too much alcohol or taken drugs: *We found him lying at the bottom of the stairs* ***in a drunken stupor***.

stur·dy /ˈstɜːdi $ ˈstɜːr-/ ●○○ *adj* (*comparative* **sturdier**, *superlative* **sturdiest**)
1 an object that is sturdy is strong, well-made, and not easily broken → **solid**: *That chair doesn't look very sturdy.* | *sturdy comfortable shoes* **THESAURUS** STRONG
2 someone who is sturdy is strong, short, and healthy looking → **stocky**: *a sturdy young man* | *sturdy legs*
3 determined and not easily persuaded to change your opinions: *They kept up a sturdy opposition to the plan.* —**sturdily** *adv* —**sturdiness** *n* [U]

stur·geon /ˈstɜːdʒən $ ˈstɜːr-/ *n* [C,U] a large fish, from which CAVIAR is obtained, or the meat of this fish

stut·ter¹ /ˈstʌtə $ -ər/ *v* **1** [I,T] to speak with difficulty because you cannot stop yourself from repeating the first CONSONANT of some words → **stammer**: *'I'm D-d-david,' he stuttered.* **THESAURUS** SAY **2** [I] if a machine stutters, it keeps making little noises and does not work smoothly: *a refrigerator which stuttered and hummed*

stutter² *n* [singular] an inability to speak normally because you stutter SYN **stammer**: *a nervous stutter*

sty /staɪ/ *n* (*plural* **sties**) [C] **1** a place where pigs are kept SYN **pigsty 2** (*also* **stye**) an infected place on the edge of your EYELID, which becomes red and swollen

Sty·gi·an /ˈstɪdʒiən/ *adj* [usually before noun] *literary* unpleasantly dark, and making you feel nervous or afraid: *the Stygian gloom*

style¹ /staɪl/ ●●● S2 W1 AWL *n*
1 WAY OF DOING STH [C,U] a particular way of doing, designing, or producing something, especially one that is typical of a particular place, period of time, or group of people: *an attempt to use Japanese management style in a European business* | **[+of]** *different styles of handwriting* | **Baroque-/Swedish-/country- etc style** *Cuban-style black beans and rice* | *a Colonial-style house* | *The dinner will be served buffet-style.*
2 SB'S WAY OF BEHAVING [C] the particular way that someone behaves, works, or deals with other people: *Children have different styles of learning: some learn by seeing, some by hearing, some by doing.* | **be more sb's style** (=used to say that you prefer something) *I don't think the parachuting weekend is for me – the art class is more my style.* | *I* ***like your style*** (=approve of the way you do things)*, Simpson.* | *I can't ask a man out –* ***it's not my style*** (=it is not the way I usually behave).
3 ART/LITERATURE/MUSIC [C,U] a typical way of writing, painting etc that is used by a particular person or during a particular period of time: *The paintings are in an expressionistic style.* | *Hemingway's direct style* | **in the style of sb/sth** *a play in the style of classical Greek tragedy*
4 FASHION/DESIGN **a)** [C] a particular design or fashion for something such as clothes, hair, furniture etc SYN **fashion**: *Car styles have changed radically in the past 20 years.* | **traditional/modern style** *The rooms are furnished in a modern style.* **b)** [U] the quality of being fashionable: *young women interested in style rather than comfort* | **in/out of style** *Long skirts are back in style.*
5 ATTRACTIVE QUALITY [U] a confident and attractive quality that makes people admire you, and that is shown in your appearance, or the way you do things → **stylish**: *You may not like her, but she certainly* ***has style***. | *The team played* ***with style***. → STYLISH
6 CORRECT WRITING [U] a way of using words or spelling that is considered correct: *It's not good style to use abbreviations in an essay.*
7 in style done in a way that people admire, especially because it is unusual, shows great determination, or involves spending a lot of money: **in great/grand/fine etc style** *Nadal won the match in fine style, not losing a single game.* → **cramp sb's style** at CRAMP², LIFESTYLE

style² AWL *v* [T] **1** to design clothing, furniture, or the shape of someone's hair in a particular way: *These shoes have been styled for maximum comfort.* | *She has her hair styled by Giorgio.* **2 style yourself sth** *formal* to give yourself a particular title or name: *They style themselves 'the terrible twins'.* **3 style it out** *BrE informal* to make an effort to appear relaxed and confident, especially when you have done something embarrassing → SELF-STYLED

ˈstyle sheet *n* [C] a set of instructions that states what the TYPEFACE and colours of an electronic document should be

styl·ing /ˈstaɪlɪŋ/ AWL *n* [U] **1** the design and appearance of an object, especially a car: *I like the new Audi in terms of styling.* **2 styling products/mousse/spray etc** substances you use to make your hair look attractive

styl·ish /ˈstaɪlɪʃ/ ●○○ AWL *adj* attractive in a fashionable way: *a stylish woman in her forties* | *Jack is quite stylish.* | *a stylish restaurant in the West End* **THESAURUS** FASHIONABLE —**stylishly** *adv* —**stylishness** *n* [U]

styl·ist /ˈstaɪlɪst/ *n* [C] **1** someone who cuts or arranges people's hair as their job: *Renee was the top stylist at the salon.* **2** someone who has carefully developed a good style of writing **3** someone who has their own typical way of singing or playing music: *Billie Holiday, one of jazz's most distinctive stylists*

styl·is·tic /staɪˈlɪstɪk/ *adj* relating to the particular way an artist, writer, musician etc makes or performs something, especially the technical features or methods they use: *the sculptor's stylistic development* | **stylistic feature/device** *stylistic features of the story* —**stylistically** /-kli/ *adv*

styl·is·tics /staɪˈlɪstɪks/ *n* [U] the study of style in written or spoken language

sty·lized (*also* **-ised** *BrE*) /ˈstaɪlaɪzd/ AWL *adj* drawn, written, or performed in an artificial style that does not look natural or real, but that is still pleasant to look at: *a stylized picture of the sun* —**stylization** /ˌstaɪlaɪˈzeɪʃən $ -lə-/ *n* [U]

sty·lus /ˈstaɪləs/ *n* [C] **1** the small pointed part of a RECORD PLAYER, that touches the record **2** a thing shaped like a pen, used for writing on WAX, making marks on metal, writing on a special computer screen etc

sty·mie /ˈstaɪmi/ *v* [T] *informal* to prevent someone from doing what they have planned or want to do SYN **thwart**: *Investigators have been stymied by uncooperative witnesses.*

Sty·ro·foam /ˈstaɪərəfəʊm $ ˈstaɪrəfoʊm/ *n* [U] *trademark* a soft light plastic material that prevents heat or cold from passing through it, used especially to make containers: *a Styrofoam cup*

suave /swɑːv/ *adj* someone who is suave is polite, confident, and relaxed, sometimes in an insincere way SYN **smooth**: *a suave and sophisticated gentleman* —**suavely** *adv* —**suavity, suaveness** *n* [U]

sub¹ /sʌb/ *n* [C] *informal* **1** a SUBMARINE **2** a SUBSTITUTE in sports such as football **3** a SUBSCRIPTION **4** *BrE* part of your wages that you receive earlier than usual because you need money SYN **advance 5** *AmE* a long bread roll, split open and filled with meat, cheese etc **6** *AmE* a SUBSTITUTE TEACHER **7** *BrE* a SUB-EDITOR

S

sub² *v* (**subbed**, **subbing**) *informal* **1** [I] to act as a SUBSTITUTE for someone: **[+for]** *Roy's subbing for Chris in tonight's game.* **2** [T] *BrE* to give someone part of their wages earlier than usual or lend them money: *I subbed Fenella a tenner to get a decent bunch of flowers.* **3** [T] *BrE* to SUBEDIT something

sub- /sʌb/ *prefix* **1** under or below a particular level or thing: *sub-zero temperatures* | *subsoil* (=beneath the surface) **2** less important or powerful than someone or something, or of lower rank than someone: *a sublieutenant* **3** part of a bigger whole: *a subsection* | *a subcommittee* **4** not as good as other people or things: *substandard housing* | *subnormal intelligence* **5** *technical* almost: *subtropical heat*

sub·al·tern /ˈsʌbəltən $ səˈbɒːltərn/ *n* [C] a middle rank in the British army, or someone who has this rank

sub-aq·ua /sʌb ˈækwə/ *adj* [only before noun] *BrE* relating to sports that take place under water: *sub-aqua diving*

sub·a·tom·ic /ˌsʌbəˈtɒmɪk◂ $ -ˈtɑː-/ *adj* smaller than an atom or existing within an atom: *subatomic particles*

sub·com·mit·tee /ˈsʌbkəˌmɪti/ *n* [C] a small group formed from a committee to deal with a particular subject in more detail

sub·com·pact /sʌbˈkɒmpækt $ -ˈkɑːm-/ *n* [C] *AmE* a type of very small and inexpensive car

sub·con·scious¹ /sʌbˈkɒnʃəs $ -ˈkɑːn-/ *adj* subconscious feelings, desires etc are hidden in your mind and affect your behaviour, but you do not know that you have them: *a subconscious fear of failure* —**subconsciously** *adv*: *Subconsciously, he blames himself for the accident.*

subconscious² *n* [singular] the part of your mind that has thoughts and feelings you do not know about SYN **unconscious**: *anger buried deep in the subconscious*

S

sub·con·ti·nent /ˌsʌbˈkɒntɪnənt $ -ˈkɑːn-/ *n* [C] **1** a very large area of land that is part of a CONTINENT **2 the subcontinent** the area of land that includes India, Pakistan, and Bangladesh

sub·con·tract /ˌsʌbkənˈtrækt $ -ˈkɑːntrækt/ (*also* **subcontract out**) *v* [T] if a company subcontracts work, they pay other people to do part of their work for them: *We will be subcontracting most of the electrical work.* | **subcontract sth to sb** *Some of the work will be subcontracted to another company.* —**subcontract** /sʌbˈkɒntrækt $ -ˈkɑːn-/ *n* [C]

sub·con·trac·tor /ˌsʌbkənˈtræktə $ -ˈkɑːntræktər/ *n* [C] someone who does part of the work of another person or company

sub·cul·ture /ˈsʌbˌkʌltʃə $ -ər/ *n* [C] a particular group of people within a society and their behaviour, beliefs, and activities - often used to show disapproval: *the drug subculture of the inner city*

sub·cu·ta·ne·ous /ˌsʌbkjuːˈteɪniəs◂/ *adj technical* beneath your skin: *subcutaneous fat* —**subcutaneously** *adv*

sub·di·rect·o·ry /ˈsʌbdaɪrektəri, -də-/ *n* (*plural* **subdirectories**) [C] an area in a computer where FILES are stored inside another directory, in order to keep the files organized

sub·di·vide /ˌsʌbdəˈvaɪd/ *v* [T] to divide into smaller parts something that is already divided: *Over time, developers subdivided the land.* | **subdivide sth into sth** *The house was subdivided into apartments.*

sub·di·vi·sion /ˌsʌbdəˈvɪʒən/ *n* **1** [C,U] when something is subdivided, or the parts that result from doing this **2** [C] *AmE* an area of land that has been subdivided for building houses on

sub·due /səbˈdjuː $ -ˈduː/ *v* [T] **1** to defeat or control a person or group, especially using force: *Police managed to subdue the angry crowd.* | *Napoleon subdued much of Europe.* **2** *formal* to prevent your emotions from showing or being too strong SYN **control**: *an excitement she could not subdue*

sub·dued /səbˈdjuːd $ -ˈduːd/ *adj* **1** subdued lighting, colours etc are less bright than usual SYN **gentle 2** a person that is subdued is unusually quiet and possibly unhappy: *Richard seems very subdued tonight.* | *a subdued manner* | *'Oh,' she said in a subdued voice.* **3** an activity that is subdued does not have as much excitement as you would expect OPP **lively**: *The housing market is fairly subdued.* **4** a sound that is subdued is quieter than usual

sub·ed·it /ˌsʌbˈedɪt/ *v* [T] *BrE* to examine other people's writing for mistakes and correct them SYN **copyedit**

ˌsub-ˈeditor *n* [C] *BrE* someone whose job is to examine other people's writing, such as a newspaper article, and to correct mistakes

sub·group /ˈsʌbgruːp/ *n* [C] a separate, smaller, and sometimes less important part of a group

sub·head·ing /ˈsʌbˌhedɪŋ/ *n* [C] a short phrase used as a title for a small part within a longer piece of writing

sub·hu·man /sʌbˈhjuːmən $ -ˈhjuː-, -ˈjuː-/ *adj* **1** not having all the qualities a normal human being has: *The enemy was regarded as subhuman.* **2** subhuman conditions are very bad or cruel → **inhuman**: *The refugees were living a subhuman existence.*

sub·ject¹ /ˈsʌbdʒɪkt/ ●●● S2 W1 *n* [C]

1 THING TALKED ABOUT the thing you are talking about or considering in a conversation, discussion, book, film etc: *Paul has strong opinions on most subjects.* | *The subjects covered in this chapter are exercise and nutrition.* | **[+of]** *Truffaut's childhood memories were the subject of his first film.* | *While we're* **on the subject of** *money, do you have the $10 you owe me?* ⚠ Don't say 'the subject is about ... ': *The subject of the poem is war.* | *The poem is about war.* → SUBJECT MATTER

2 AT SCHOOL an area of knowledge that you study at a school or university: *My favorite subject is math.*

3 IN ART the thing or person that you show when you paint a picture, take a photograph etc: *Monet loved to use gardens as his subjects.*

4 IN A TEST a person or animal that is used in a test or EXPERIMENT: *The subjects of this experiment were all men aged 18–35.*

5 GRAMMAR a noun, noun phrase, or PRONOUN that usually comes before a main verb and represents the person or thing that performs the action of the verb, or about which something is stated, for example 'she' in 'She hit John' or 'elephants' in 'Elephants are big' → OBJECT¹(6)

6 CITIZEN *formal* someone who was born in a country that has a king or queen, or someone who has a right to live there: *a British subject* → CITIZEN(2), NATIONAL²

COLLOCATIONS

VERBS

discuss/talk about a subject *Have you discussed the subject with your husband?*
change the subject (=start talking about something different) *She tried to change the subject.*
mention a subject *The subject was not mentioned again.*
deal with/cover a subject (=speak or write about it) *The subject is dealt with in great detail in his previous book.*
touch on a subject (=say or write a little about it) | **bring up/raise a subject** (=deliberately start talking about it) | **get onto a subject** (=happen to start talking about it) | **broach a subject** (=start talking about a sensitive subject) | **get back to a subject** | **drop a subject** (=stop talking about it) | **avoid/keep off/stay off a subject** (=not talk about it) | **a subject comes up** (=people start talking about it)

ADJECTIVES

an interesting/fascinating subject *Fame is a fascinating subject.*
a difficult/complex subject (=very complicated) *Immigration is a complex subject.*
a controversial subject *The content of the curriculum has become a controversial subject.*
a sensitive/touchy subject (=one that people may get upset about) | **a taboo subject** (=one that it is not acceptable to mention)

PHRASES

a subject of/for discussion *TV is a favourite subject for discussion.*
a subject of conversation *She searched for a new subject of conversation.*
a subject of/for debate (=a subject people discuss and disagree about) | **a subject of controversy** (=a subject people disagree about strongly)

subject² ●○○ *adj*
1 be subject to sth a) if someone or something is subject to something, especially something bad, it is possible or likely that they will be affected by it: *All flights are subject to delay.* | *Prices are* ***subject to change****.* **b)** if something is subject to something such as approval, it depends on that thing happening before it can happen: *The funding is subject to approval by the Board of Education.*
2 be subject to a rule/law/penalty/tax etc if you are subject to a rule, law, penalty etc, you must obey the rule or pay an amount of money: *Violators are subject to a $100 fine.*
3 [only before noun] *formal* a subject country, state, people etc are strictly governed by another country: *subject peoples*

sub·ject³ /səbˈdʒekt/ ●○○ *v* [T] *formal* to force a country or group of people to be ruled by you, and control them very strictly
subject sb/sth **to** sth *phr v* to force someone or something to experience something very unpleasant, especially over a long time: *Police subjected him to hours of questioning.* | **subject sb to an ordeal/abuse/harassment** *Barker subjected his victim to awful abuse.*

sub·jec·tion /səbˈdʒekʃən/ *n* [U] *formal* when a person or a group of people are controlled by a government or by another person: **in subjection** *The government used brute force to keep people in subjection.* | **[+to]** *a period of subjection to Assyrian rulers* | *the subjection of women*

sub·jec·tive /səbˈdʒektɪv/ ●○○ *adj*
1 a statement, report, attitude etc that is subjective is influenced by personal opinion and can therefore be unfair OPP **objective**: *As a critic, he is far too subjective.* | *a* ***highly subjective*** *point of view* | **subjective judgment/opinion etc** *The ratings were based on the subjective judgement of one person.*
2 [no comparative] existing only in your mind or imagination OPP **objective**: *our subjective perception of colours*
3 *technical* relating to the subject in grammar —**subjectively** *adv*: *His work was judged objectively as well as subjectively.* —**subjectivity** /ˌsʌbdʒekˈtɪvəti/ *n* [U]

ˈsubject ˌmatter *n* [U] what is being talked about in speech or writing, or represented in art: *The movie has been rated 'R' due to adult subject matter.*

sub ju·di·ce /ˌsʌbˈdʒuːdɪsi $ -ˈdʒuːdɪsi, -ˈjuːdɪkeɪ/ *adv* [only after verb] *law* a legal case being considered sub judice is now being dealt with by a court, and therefore is not allowed to be publicly discussed, for example in a newspaper

sub·ju·gate /ˈsʌbdʒəgeɪt/ *v* [T] *formal* to defeat a person or group and make them obey you: *The native population was subjugated and exploited.* | **a subjugated people/nation/country** | **be subjugated to sb/sth** *Her own needs had been subjugated to* (=not considered as important as) *the needs of her family.* —**subjugation** /ˌsʌbdʒəˈgeɪʃən/ *n* [U]

sub·junc·tive /səbˈdʒʌŋktɪv/ *n* [C] a verb form or a set of verb forms in grammar, used in some languages to express doubt, wishes etc. For example, in 'if I were you', the verb 'to be' is in the subjunctive. → **imperative**, **indicative** —**subjunctive** *adj*

sub·let /sʌbˈlet/ *v* (*past tense and past participle* **sublet**, *present participle* **subletting**) [I,T] to rent to someone else a property that you rent from its owner: **sublet sth to sb** *I sublet my apartment to my sister, packed my van, and headed west.* —**sublet** /ˈsʌblet/ *n* [C]

sub·lieu·ten·ant /ˌsʌblefˈtenənt, -lə- $ -luː-/ *n* [C] a middle rank in the Royal Navy, or someone who has this rank

sub·li·mate /ˈsʌblɪmeɪt/ *v* [I,T] *technical* to use the energy that comes from sexual feelings to do something, such as work or art, that is more acceptable to your society —**sublimation** /ˌsʌbləˈmeɪʃən/ *n* [U]

sub·lime¹ /səˈblaɪm/ ●○○ *adj*
1 something that is sublime is so good or beautiful that it affects you deeply: *The view was sublime.* | *Her songs are a sublime fusion of pop and Brazilian music.*
2 used to describe feelings or behaviour that are very great or extreme, especially when someone seems not to notice what is happening around them: *an air of sublime contentment* —**sublimely** *adv* —**sublimeness** *n* [U] —**sublimity** /səˈblɪməti/ *n* [U]

sublime² *n* **1 the sublime** something that is so good or beautiful that you are deeply affected by it: *The works on display range from the mainstream to the sublime.*
2 from the sublime to the ridiculous used to say that a serious and important thing or event is being followed by something very silly, unimportant, or bad

sub·lim·i·nal /sʌbˈlɪmɪnəl/ *adj* affecting your mind in a way that you are not conscious of: *a* ***subliminal message*** | ***subliminal advertising*** (=with hidden messages and pictures in it)

sub·ma·chine gun /ˌsʌbməˈʃiːn gʌn/ *n* [C] a type of MACHINE GUN that is light and easily moved

sub·ma·rine¹ /ˈsʌbməriːn, ˌsʌbməˈriːn/ ●●○ (*also* **sub**) *n* [C] a ship, especially a military one, that can stay under water: *a nuclear submarine*

submarine² *adj* [only before noun] growing or used under the sea: *submarine plant life*

sub·mar·i·ner /sʌbˈmærɪnə $ ˈsʌbməriːnər/ *n* [C] a sailor living and working in a submarine

ˌsubmarine ˈsandwich *n* [C] *AmE* a long bread roll which is split open and filled with meat, cheese etc SYN **sub**

sub·merge /səbˈmɜːdʒ $ -ˈmɜːrdʒ/ *v* **1 a)** [T] to cover something completely with water or another liquid: *The tunnel entrance was submerged by rising sea water.* **b)** [I] to go under the surface of the water and be completely covered by it: *The submarine submerged.* **2** [T] to hide feelings, ideas, or opinions and make yourself stop thinking about them SYN **suppress**: *Feelings she thought she'd submerged were surfacing again.* **3 submerge yourself in sth** to make yourself very busy doing something, especially in order to forget about something else: *Alice submerged herself in work to try and forget about Tom.* —**submerged** *adj*: *submerged rocks* —**submergence** *n* [U]

sub·mer·si·ble /səbˈmɜːsəbəl $ -ˈmɜːr-/ *n* [C] a small vehicle that can travel under water, especially one that travels to very great depths in the ocean for scientific purposes —**submersible** *adj*

sub·mer·sion /səbˈmɜːʃən $ -ˈmɜːrʒən/ *n* [U] the action of going under water, or the state of being completely covered in liquid

sub·mis·sion /səbˈmɪʃən/ ●○○ AWL *n*
1 [U] the state of being completely controlled by a person or group, and accepting that you have to obey them: **force/frighten/beat etc sb into submission** *Napoleon threatened to starve the country into submission.* | **in submission** *His head was bowed in submission.*
2 [C,U] when you give or show something to someone in authority, for them to consider or approve: *The deadline for the submission of proposals is May 1st.* | *Plans were drawn up* ***for submission to*** *the housing council.* | *Submissions will not be accepted after May.*
3 [U] *formal* an opinion or thought that you state SYN **view**: *It is important,* ***in my submission****, that a wider view of the matter be taken.*
4 [C] *law* a request or suggestion that is given to a judge for them to consider

sub·mis·sive /səbˈmɪsɪv/ *adj* always willing to obey someone and never disagreeing with them, even if they are unkind to you OPP **assertive**: *In those days, women*

S

were expected to be quiet and submissive. —**submissively** *adv* —**submissiveness** *n* [U]

sub·mit /səbˈmɪt/ ●●○ S3 W3 AWL *v* (**submitted, submitting**)
1 [T] to give a plan, piece of writing etc to someone in authority for them to consider or approve: **submit an application/claim/proposal etc** *All applications must be submitted by Monday.*
2 [I,T] *formal* to agree to obey someone or something or to go through a process, especially when you have no choice SYN **give in**: **[+to]** *Derek has agreed to submit to questioning.*
3 [T] *formal law* to suggest or say something: **submit (that)** *I submit that the jury has been influenced by the publicity in this case.*

sub·nor·mal /ˌsʌbˈnɔːməl◂ $ -ˈnɔːr-/ *adj technical* less or lower than normal: *subnormal temperatures*

sub·or·di·nate[1] /səˈbɔːdənət $ -ˈbɔːr-/ ●○○ AWL *adj*
1 in a less important position than someone else: *a subordinate officer* | **[+to]** *Women were subordinate to men.*
2 less important than something else SYN **secondary**: **[+to]** *These aims were subordinate to the main aims of the mission.*

subordinate[2] ●○○ AWL *n* [C] someone who has a lower position and less authority than someone else in an organization

sub·or·di·nate[3] /səˈbɔːdəneɪt $ -ˈbɔːr-/ AWL *v* [T] to put someone or something in a less important position: **subordinate sb/sth to sb/sth** *Why subordinate your wishes to those of your family?* —**subordination** /səˌbɔːdəˈneɪʃən $ -ˌbɔːr-/ *n* [U]

suˌbordinate ˈclause *n* [C] a DEPENDENT CLAUSE

sub·orn /səˈbɔːn $ -ˈbɔːrn/ *v* [T] *law* to persuade someone to tell lies in a court of law or to do something else that is illegal, especially for money: *an attempt to suborn a witness* —**subornation** /ˌsʌbɔːˈneɪʃən $ -bɔːr-/ *n* [U]

sub·plot /ˈsʌbplɒt $ -plɑːt/ *n* [C] a PLOT (=set of events) that is connected with but less important than the main plot in a story, play etc: *the novel's romantic subplot*

sub·poe·na[1] /səˈpiːnə, səb-/ *n* [C] *law* a written order to come to a court of law and be a WITNESS

subpoena[2] *v* (*past tense and past participle* **subpoenaed**) [T] *law* to order someone to come to a court of law and be a WITNESS: *James was subpoenaed as a witness.* THESAURUS ORDER

ˌsub-ˈpost office *n* [C] a small British post office that has fewer services than a main post office

sub·prime /sʌbˈpraɪm/ *adj* [only before noun] a subprime LOAN is an amount of money that is lent to someone who may not be able to pay it back, usually at a higher than normal rate of interest: ***Subprime mortgages*** (=loans to buy a home) *are granted to individuals who would not qualify for a conventional mortgage.*

sub·scribe /səbˈskraɪb/ ●○○ *v*
1 [I] to pay money, usually once a year, to have copies of a newspaper or magazine sent to you, or to have some other service: **[+to]** *You can subscribe to the magazine for as little as $32 a year.*
2 [I] *BrE* to pay money regularly to be a member of an organization or to help its work: **[+to]** *She subscribes to an environmental action group.*
3 [I] to agree to buy or pay for SHARES: **[+for]** *Each employee may subscribe for up to £2,000 worth of shares.*
subscribe to sth *phr v formal* if you subscribe to an idea, you agree with it or support it: **subscribe to the view/belief/theory etc** *I have never subscribed to the view that schooldays are the happiest days of your life.*

sub·scrib·er /səbˈskraɪbə $ -ər/ *n* [C] **1** someone who pays money, usually once a year, to receive copies of a newspaper or magazine, or to have a service: *cable television subscribers* **2** *BrE* someone who pays money to be part of an organization or to help its work

sub·scrip·tion /səbˈskrɪpʃən/ ●○○ *n*
1 [C,U] an amount of money you pay, usually once a year, to receive copies of a newspaper or magazine, or receive a service, or the act of paying money for this: **[+to]** *Are you interested in **taking out** a **subscription** to 'Newsweek'* (=arranging to buy it on a regular basis)? | *You may **cancel** your **subscription** at any time.* | *I've decided not to **renew** my **subscription**.*
2 [C,U] *BrE* an amount of money you pay regularly to be a member of an organization or to help its work, or the act of paying money for this: **[+to]** *a subscription to Amnesty International*
3 [U] when people in a country or place give money in order to pay for something to be done: *The church's 120-foot Gothic spire was paid for* **by public subscription** *in 1939.*

sub·sec·tion /ˈsʌbsekʃən/ ●○○ *n* [C] a part of a SECTION, especially in a legal document

sub·se·quent /ˈsʌbsəkwənt/ ●●○ W2 AWL *adj formal* happening or coming after something else → **consequent**: *These skills were passed on to subsequent generations.* | *subsequent pages of the book* | **subsequent to sth** *events that happened subsequent to the accident*

sub·se·quent·ly /ˈsʌbsəkwəntli/ ●●○ W3 AWL *adv formal* after an event in the past OPP **previously**: *The book was subsequently translated into 15 languages.* | *Subsequently, the company filed for bankruptcy.* THESAURUS AFTER

sub·ser·vi·ent /səbˈsɜːviənt $ -ˈsɜːr-/ *adj* **1** always obeying another person and doing everything they want you to do – used when someone seems too weak and powerless: **[+to]** *Don remained entirely subservient to his father.* | **subservient role/position** *His wife refused to accept a traditional subservient role.* **2** *formal* less important than something else SYN **subordinate**: **[+to]** *the rights of the individual are made subservient to the interests of the state* —**subserviently** *adv* —**subservience** *n* [U]

sub·set /ˈsʌbset/ *n* [C] a group of people or things that is part of a larger group of people or things: **[+of]** *a small subset of the city's immigrant population*

sub·side /səbˈsaɪd/ ●○○ *v* [I]
1 if a feeling, pain, sound etc subsides, it gradually becomes less and then stops SYN **die down**: *Simon waited until the laughter subsided.* | *The pains in his head had subsided, but he still felt dizzy and sick.*
2 *formal* if a building or an area of land subsides, it gradually sinks to a lower level: *After the heavy rains, part of the road subsided.*
3 if bad weather conditions subside, they gradually return to a normal state: *The wind gradually subsided, and all was quiet.*
4 if water, especially flood water, subsides, it gradually goes underground or back to a normal level: *When the floods subsided, the streets were littered with bodies.*

sub·si·dence /səbˈsaɪdəns, ˈsʌbsɪdəns/ *n* [C,U] the process by which an area of land sinks to a lower level than the land surrounding it, or a building begins to sink into the ground: *Is your house insured against subsidence?*

sub·sid·i·ar·i·ty /səbˌsɪdiˈærəti/ *n* [U] a word meaning a political POLICY(1) in which power to make decisions is given to a smaller group – used especially about the European Union giving power to its member countries

sub·sid·i·a·ry[1] /səbˈsɪdiəri $ -dieri/ ●○○ *n* (*plural* **subsidiaries**) [C] a company that is owned or controlled by another larger company: *a subsidiary of a US company* | *one of our Japanese subsidiaries* THESAURUS COMPANY

subsidiary[2] ●○○ AWL *adj formal* connected with, but less important than, something else SYN **secondary**: *a subsidiary hypothesis* | **[+to]** *All other issues are subsidiary to this one.*

sub·si·dize (*also* **-ise** *BrE*) /ˈsʌbsədaɪz/ ●○○ AWL *v* [T] if a government or organization subsidizes a company, activity etc, it pays part of its costs: *Farming is* ***heavily subsidized*** (=subsidized a lot) *by the government.* GRAMMAR **Subsidize** is often used in the passive.

—**subsidized** *adj* [only before noun]: *heavily subsidized agricultural exports* —**subsidization** /ˌsʌbsədaɪˈzeɪʃən $ -də-/ *n* [U]

sub·si·dy /ˈsʌbsədi/ ●○○ AWL *n* (*plural* **subsidies**) [C] money that is paid by a government or organization to make prices lower, reduce the cost of producing goods etc: **trade/agricultural etc subsidies** *international disagreement over trade subsidies*

sub·sist /səbˈsɪst/ *v* [I] **1** to stay alive when you only have small amounts of food or money SYN **survive**: **[+on]** *We had to subsist on bread and water.* | *Old people often have to subsist on very low incomes.* **2** *especially law* to continue to exist SYN **survive**

sub·sis·tence /səbˈsɪstəns/ *n* [U] **1** the condition of only just having enough money or food to stay alive: *Many of the families are forced to live at the subsistence level.* | *The land provided subsistence and little more.*
2 subsistence farming/agriculture etc farming that produces just enough food for the farmer to live on, but does not produce enough food to sell to other people
3 subsistence allowance/payment etc money that is paid to someone so that they can buy meals, pay for a place to stay etc

sub·soil /ˈsʌbsɔɪl/ *n* [U] the layer of soil between the ground's surface and the lower layer of hard rock

sub·son·ic /ˌsʌbˈsɒnɪk◂ $ -ˈsɑː-/ *adj* slower than the speed of sound → **supersonic**

sub·spe·cies /ˈsʌbˌspiːʃiːz/ *n* (*plural* **subspecies**) [C] a group of similar plants or animals that is smaller than a SPECIES

sub·stance /ˈsʌbstəns/ ●●● W3 *n*
1 MATERIAL [C] a particular type of solid, liquid, or gas: *The leaves were covered with a strange sticky substance.* | **dangerous/toxic/hazardous/poisonous etc substance** *harmful substances in the atmosphere* | *Plutonium 238 is one of the most toxic substances known to man.* | **illegal/banned/prohibited/controlled substance** (=used especially about illegal drugs) *Police found an illegal substance in his car.*
2 TRUTH [U usually in questions and negatives] *formal* if something has substance, it is true: ***There is no substance to** the rumours* (=they are untrue). | **without substance** (=untrue) *O'Connell's remarks are completely without substance.*
3 IDEAS [singular, U] the most important ideas contained in an argument or piece of writing SYN **essence**: ***The substance of his argument** was that people on welfare should work.* | **in substance** *What she said, in substance, was that the mayor should resign.*
4 IMPORTANCE [U] *formal* importance SYN **significance**: *It was an entertaining speech, but it **lacked substance*** (=there was no important information in it). | **matters/issues of substance** *We should be discussing matters of substance.*
5 man/woman of substance *BrE literary* a rich man or woman

ˈsubstance aˌbuse *n* [U] the habit of taking too many illegal drugs, in a way that harms your health SYN **drug abuse**

sub·stan·dard /ˌsʌbˈstændəd◂ $ -ərd◂/ *adj* not as good as the average, and not acceptable → **non-standard, standard**: *substandard housing*

sub·stan·tial /səbˈstænʃəl/ ●●○ *adj*
1 large in amount or number SYN **considerable** OPP **insubstantial**: *We have the support of a substantial number of parents.* | *a substantial salary* | *a substantial breakfast* | *The document requires substantial changes.*
THESAURUS ▶ BIG
2 [only before noun] large and strongly made OPP **insubstantial**: *a substantial piece of furniture*

sub·stan·tial·ly /səbˈstænʃəli/ ●○○ *adv*
1 very much or a lot SYN **considerably**: *substantially higher prices* | *The deer population has increased substantially in recent years.*
2 used to say that in many ways something is true, the same, different etc SYN **essentially**: *There are one or two minor differences, but they're substantially the same text.*

sub·stan·ti·ate /səbˈstænʃieɪt/ *v* [T] *formal* to prove the truth of something that someone has said, claimed etc: *Katzen offered little evidence to **substantiate** his **claims**.* —**substantiation** /səbˌstænʃiˈeɪʃən/ *n* [U]

sub·stan·tive¹ /səbˈstæntɪv, ˈsʌbstəntɪv/ ●○○ *adj formal* dealing with things that are important or real: **substantive matters/issues** *The State Department reported that substantive discussions had taken place with Beijing.* —**substantively** *adv*

sub·stan·tive² /ˈsʌbstəntɪv/ *n* [C] *technical* a noun

sub·sta·tion /ˈsʌbˌsteɪʃən/ *n* [C] a place where electricity is passed on from the place that produces it into the main system

sub·sti·tute¹ /ˈsʌbstɪtjuːt $ -tuːt/ ●●○ AWL *n* [C]
1 (*also* **sub** *informal*) someone who does someone else's job for a limited period of time, especially in a sports team or school: *Germany brought on a substitute at half time.* | *substitute goalkeeper* | **[+for]** *The coach has to find a substitute for Tim.*
2 a person or thing that you use instead of the one that you usually have, because the usual one is not available: *a sugar substitute* | *a father substitute*
3 be no substitute for sth used to emphasize that something is not as good as another thing: *Vitamin pills are no substitute for a healthy diet.*

substitute² ●●○ AWL *v*
1 [T] to use something new or different instead of something else: **substitute sth for sth** *The recipe says you can substitute yoghurt for the sour cream.*
2 [I] to do someone's job until the person who usually does it is able to do it again SYN **stand in**: **[+for]** *Bill substituted for Larry, who was off sick.*
3 [T] to replace someone with another person, especially another player: *Michael Owen had to be substituted after 20 minutes on the field.*

ˌsubstitute ˈteacher (*also* **substitute**, **sub** *informal*) *n* [C] *AmE* a teacher who teaches a class when the usual teacher is ill SYN **supply teacher** *BrE*

sub·sti·tu·tion /ˌsʌbstɪˈtjuːʃən $ -ˈtuː-/ AWL *n* [C,U] when someone or something is replaced by someone or something else, or the person or thing being replaced: *Coach Ross made two substitutions in the second half.* | **substitution of sth for sth** *the substitution of English for French as the world's common language*

sub·stra·tum /ˌsʌbˈstrɑːtəm $ -ˈstreɪ-/ *n* (*plural* **substrata** /-tə/) [C] *technical* a layer that lies beneath another layer, especially in the earth: *a substratum of rock* | *a social substratum*

sub·struc·ture /ˈsʌbˌstrʌktʃə $ -ər/ *n* [C] **1** one of the structures (STRUCTURE¹(3)) within a society or organization that combines with others to form a whole **2** a solid base under the ground, that supports a building above the ground → **superstructure**

sub·sume /səbˈsjuːm $ -ˈsuːm/ *v* [T] *formal* to include someone or something as a member of a group or type, rather than considering it separately: **subsume sb/sth under sth** *A wide range of offences are usually subsumed under the category of robbery.*

sub·ten·ant /ˌsʌbˈtenənt/ *n* [C] someone who pays rent for an apartment, office etc to the person who is renting it from the owner —**subtenancy** *n* [C,U]

sub·ter·fuge /ˈsʌbtəfjuːdʒ $ -ər-/ *n* [C,U] *formal* a secret trick or slightly dishonest way of doing something, or the use of this: **by subterfuge** *Sereni was lured to Moscow by subterfuge.*

sub·ter·ra·ne·an /ˌsʌbtəˈreɪniən◂/ *adj* [usually before noun] beneath the surface of the Earth SYN **underground**: *subterranean passage*

sub·text /ˈsʌbtekst/ *n* [C usually singular] a hidden or second meaning behind someone's words or actions: *What's the subtext here? What's the writer really saying?*

sub·ti·tle /ˈsʌbˌtaɪtl/ ●○○ *n*
1 subtitles [plural] the words printed over a film in a foreign language to translate what is being said by the actors: *a French film with English subtitles*

S

2 [singular] a second title below the main title in a book, which gives more information about what is in the book, show etc: *The opera's subtitle is 'The School for Lovers'.* | *The book is subtitled 'A Psychology of Masculinity'.* —**subtitle** *v* [I,T] —**subtitled** *adj*: *a subtitled version of the film*

sub·tle /ˈsʌtl/ ●●○ *adj* (*comparative* **subtler** *or* **more subtle**, *superlative* **subtlest**)
1 not easy to notice or understand unless you pay careful attention OPP **obvious**: *The pictures are similar, but there are subtle differences between them.* | *The warning signs of the disease are so subtle that they are often ignored.* | *a **subtle form** of racism* | **subtle taste/flavour/smell etc** *The flavour of the dried berries is more subtle.* | *The dish had a **subtle hint** of ginger.*
2 behaving in a skilful and clever way, especially using indirect methods or language to hide what you are trying to do: *I think we need a more subtle approach.* | *a subtle plan* | **[+about]** *She wasn't very subtle about it. She just said she didn't love him anymore.*
3 very clever in noticing and understanding things → **sensitive**: *a subtle mind* —**subtly** *adv*: *a subtly different colour*

sub·tle·ty /ˈsʌtlti/ *n* (*plural* **subtleties**) **1** [U] the quality that something has when it has been done in a clever or skilful way, with careful attention to small details: *The play lacks subtlety.* | *She argued her case with considerable subtlety.* **2** [C usually plural] a thought, idea, or detail that is important but difficult to notice or understand: **[+of]** *Some of the subtleties of the language are lost in translation.*

sub·to·tal /ˈsʌbˌtəʊtl $ -ˌtoʊtl/ *n* [C] the total of a set of numbers, especially on a bill, that is added to other numbers, such as a tax, to form a complete total

sub·tract /səbˈtrækt/ *v* [T] to take a number or an amount from a larger number or amount → **add**, **deduct**, **minus**: **subtract sth from sth** *If you subtract 30 from 45, you get 15.*

S

sub·trac·tion /səbˈtrækʃən/ *n* [C] the process of taking a number or amount from a larger number or amount → **addition**

sub·trop·i·cal /ˌsʌbˈtrɒpɪkəl◂ $ -ˈtrɑː-/ (*also* **semi-tropical**) *adj* relating to or typical of an area that is near a tropical area: *subtropical vegetation*

sub·urb /ˈsʌbɜːb $ -ɜːrb/ ●●○ *n* [C] an area where people live which is away from the centre of a town or city: *a London suburb* | **[+of]** *a suburb of Los Angeles* | *a kid from **the suburbs*** | **in a suburb** *Don't you get bored living out here in the suburbs?* THESAURUS ▸ AREA, CITY

sub·ur·ban /səˈbɜːbən $ -ˈbɜːr-/ *adj* **1** related to a suburb, or in a suburb: *a quiet, suburban street* **2** boring and typical of people who live in the suburbs: *narrow-minded, suburban attitudes*

sub·ur·ban·ite /səˈbɜːbənaɪt $ -ˈbɜːr-/ *n* [C] someone who lives in a suburb - often used to show disapproval: *Patsy's father is a typical suburbanite.*

sub·ur·bi·a /səˈbɜːbiə $ -ˈbɜːr-/ *n* [U] suburbs in general, and the behaviour, opinions, and ways of living that are typical of people who live there - often used to show disapproval: *middle-class suburbia*

sub·ven·tion /səbˈvenʃən/ *n* [C] *formal* a gift of money, usually from a government, for a special use

sub·ver·sion /səbˈvɜːʃən $ -ˈvɜːrʒən/ *n* [U] secret activities that are intended to damage or destroy the power or influence of a government or established system: *Murray was jailed for subversion.*

sub·ver·sive¹ /səbˈvɜːsɪv $ -ˈvɜːr-/ *adj* subversive ideas, activities etc are secret and intended to damage or destroy a government or an established system: *He was engaged in **subversive activities**.* | **subversive propaganda/literature** —**subversively** *adv*

subversive² *n* [C] someone who secretly tries to damage or destroy the government or an established system: *a known subversive* —**subversiveness** *n* [U]

sub·vert /səbˈvɜːt $ -ˈvɜːrt/ *v* [T] *formal* **1** to try to destroy the power and influence of a government or the established system: *an attempt to subvert the democratic process* **2** to destroy someone's beliefs or loyalty

sub·way /ˈsʌbweɪ/ ●●○ *n* [C]
1 *AmE* a railway system that runs under the ground below a big city SYN **underground** *BrE*: *the New York City subway* | *a crowded subway station* | *Boston has the oldest **subway system** in the US.*
2 *BrE* a path for people to walk under a road or railway SYN **underpass**

ˌsub-ˈzero *adj* [usually before noun] below zero in temperature: **sub-zero weather/temperatures**

suc·ceed /səkˈsiːd/ ●●● S3 W2 *v*
1 [I] to do what you tried or wanted to do: *She wanted to be the first woman to climb Mount Everest, and she almost succeeded.* | **succeed in doing sth** *Scientists claim they have succeeded in finding a cure for cancer.* | *Very few people succeed in losing weight and keeping it off.*

GRAMMAR

- You **succeed in doing** something: *She succeeded in persuading him.* ✗ Don't say: *She succeeded to persuade him.*
- You can also use **succeed** on its own: *I hope you succeed.*
- **Succeed** is not used transitively in this meaning. ✗ Don't say: *I hope you succeed it.*

GRAMMAR GUIDE ▸ VERBS

2 [I] to have the result or effect something was intended to have: *Unfortunately his plan did not succeed.*

REGISTER

In everyday English, people often say that a method or treatment **works** rather than **succeeds**: *We tried rebooting the computer, but that didn't **work**.*

3 [I] to do well in your job, especially because you have worked hard at it for a long time: **[+as]** *I'm not sure he has the determination to succeed as an actor.* | **[+in]** *a woman who succeeded in politics*
4 [I,T] to be the next person to take a position or job after someone else: **succeed sb as sth** *Reeves will succeed Segal as Speaker of the House.* | **succeed sb to the throne** (=to be the next king or queen after someone else) *Who will succeed him to the throne?*
5 [T] to come after or replace something else, especially another product: *This car is intended to succeed the popular Fiesta.*
6 nothing succeeds like success used to say that success often leads to even greater success
7 only succeed in doing sth used when someone does the opposite of what they intended to do: *It seems I've only succeeded in upsetting you.*

THESAURUS

SUCCEED IN DOING STH

succeed *v* [I] to do something you tried or wanted to do: *Will they **succeed in** winning the election?* | *He wanted to make her jealous, and he succeeded.*

manage *v* [I] to succeed in doing something difficult, after trying hard. **Manage to do sth** is very commonly used instead of **succeed in doing sth** in everyday English: *He finally managed to find an apartment near his office.* | *Don't worry – I'm sure we'll manage somehow.*

achieve *v* [T] to succeed in doing something good or important: *She's achieved a lot in the short time she's been with the company.* | *If we are to **achieve** our **goals**, we have to plan properly.*

accomplish *v* [T] *formal* to achieve something: *The government **accomplished** its **objective** of reducing violent crime.* | *What do you hope to accomplish this year?*

make it to be successful in your career, or to succeed in reaching a place or part of a competition: *Only a few people make it to the top and become professional singers.* | *We finally made it to Chicago.* | *Which two teams will make it to the final?*

pull off *phrasal verb* to succeed in doing something, especially when you could easily have not succeeded. **Pull off** sounds rather informal: *Italy pulled off a great victory over Germany.* | *I'd never performed on my own before, and wasn't sure if I could pull it off.*

suc·ceed·ing /sək'siːdɪŋ/ *adj* [only before noun] coming after something else OPP **preceding**: *Over the succeeding weeks things went from bad to worse.* | *succeeding generations*

suc·cess /sək'ses/ ●●● S1 W1 *n* [C,U]
1 when you achieve what you want or intend OPP **failure**: *The experiment was a big success.* | **without success** *I tried to contact him, but without success.* | **success in doing sth** *Did you* ***have*** *any* ***success*** *in persuading Alan to come?*
2 when a lot of people like something, buy something, go to see something etc OPP **failure**: **be a big/huge/great etc success** *The film was a great success.* | *Her book has* ***enjoyed*** *a lot of* ***success*** (=it has been very successful). | *The play was a* ***box-office success*** (=many people went to see it). | *The show was an* ***overnight success*** (=it was immediately successful).
3 when someone achieves a high position in their job, on a course, in a sport, in society etc OPP **failure**: *Success isn't everything, you know.* | **[+in]** *He has already had a lot of success in his career.* | **be a success as a ...** (=be successful in a particular job) *She wasn't much of a success as a lawyer.* | *She's determined to* ***make a success of*** (=be successful in) *her career.*
4 when a business makes a lot of money OPP **failure**: *the success of his latest business venture* | **be a big/huge/great etc success** *The firm wasn't a great success.*
5 success story someone or something that is successful: *The company has been a major success story.*

COLLOCATIONS

ADJECTIVES

a great success *Everyone agreed the picnic was a great success.*
a big/huge/major success *The government claimed the policy was a major success.*
a resounding/outstanding/spectacular success (=very great success) *Financially, the event was a resounding success.*
great/considerable success *This plant can be grown by the absolute beginner with great success.*
some success *The group is already achieving some success.*
little/no success | **limited success** (=not very much success) | **commercial/economic/financial success** | **academic success** (=success in education) | **electoral success** (=success in elections) | **military success**

VERBS

have/achieve success *China has had considerable success in conserving water since 1983.*
meet with success (=be successful)

PHRASES

sb's chance of success *They have a good chance of success.*
the secret of sb's success (=what makes them successful) *A visitor asked Connie the secret of her success with growing roses.*
the success rate (=what percentage of actions are successful)

COMMON ERRORS

⚠ Don't say 'make success' or 'make a success'. Say **have success** or **achieve success**.

suc·cess·ful /sək'sesfəl/ ●●● S2 W1 *adj*
1 achieving what you wanted, or having the effect or result you intended: *The operation was successful.* | *a* ***highly successful*** (=very successful) *meeting* | **successful in (doing) sth** *Were you successful in persuading him to change his mind?*
2 a successful business, film, product etc makes a lot of money: *The show's had a pretty successful run.* | *a* ***highly successful*** (=very successful) *product*
3 a successful person earns a lot of money or is very well known and respected: *Arthur was a* ***highly successful*** (=very successful) *businessman.* | **[+in]** *He later became successful in politics.* | **[+as]** *I think she'll be successful as a photographer.* —**successfully** *adv*: *He successfully completed a master's degree.*

THESAURUS

successful achieving what you wanted, or having the effect or result you intended: *He applied for a visa three times and in the end he was successful.* | *The treatment was successful.* | *It was a highly successful campaign.*
effective having the effect or result that was wanted - used especially about treatments, drugs, or methods: *The drug is effective against a range of diseases.* | *We still haven't found an effective way to solve the problem.*
victorious successful as a result of winning in a game, election, war etc: *the captain of the victorious team* | *She emerged victorious in the second round of voting.*
promising likely to be very successful in the future, used especially about someone who is good at a job, sport, art etc: *a promising young athlete* | *He gave up a promising career in banking.*
thriving very successful - used about a company, industry, or organization that is doing well at a particular time: *The area has a thriving tourist industry.* | *The school is thriving academically.*
booming extremely successful - used about an economy, or when business or trade is increasing: *the booming economy in China* | *Business is booming.*

suc·ces·sion /sək'seʃən/ ●○○ AWL *n*
1 in succession happening one after the other without anything different happening in between: *She won the championship four times in succession.* | **in quick/rapid/close succession** (=quickly one after the other) *He fired two shots in quick succession.*
2 a succession of sth a number of people or things of the same kind, following, coming, or happening one after the other SYN **stream**: *A succession of visitors came to the door.*
3 [U] the act of taking over an official job or position, or the right to be the next to take it → **accession**: *If the prince dies, the succession passes to his son.* | **[+to]** *the queen's succession to the throne*

suc·ces·sive /sək'sesɪv/ ●○○ AWL *adj* [only before noun] coming or following one after the other: *The team has had five successive victories.* | *Successive governments have tried to deal with this issue.* —**successively** *adv*

suc·ces·sor /sək'sesə $ -ər/ ●○○ AWL *n* [C]
1 someone who takes a job or position previously held by someone else → **predecessor**: *His successor died after only 15 months in office.* | *I'm sure she will be a* ***worthy successor*** (=someone who is very good and deserves to be someone's successor). | **[+to]** *her successor to the post* | **[+as]** *Sloan will be Barrett's successor as treasurer.*
2 *formal* a machine, system etc that exists after another one in a process of development: *the transistor's successor, the microchip*

suc·cinct /sək'sɪŋkt/ *adj* clearly expressed in a few words - use this to show approval SYN **concise**: *a succinct explanation* —**succinctly** *adv*: *Anderson put the same point more succinctly.* —**succinctness** *n* [U]

suc·co·tash /'sʌkətæʃ/ *n* [U] *AmE* a dish made from corn, beans, and TOMATOes cooked together

suc·cour[1] *BrE*, **succor** *AmE* /'sʌkə $ -ər/ *n* [U] *literary* help and sympathy that is given to someone: *They give succour to the victims of war.*

succour[2] *BrE*, **succor** *AmE* *v* [T] *literary* to give help and sympathy to someone: *succouring the needy*

S

suc·cu·bus /ˈsʌkjəbəs/ *n* (*plural* **succubi** /-baɪ/) [C] a female devil that in the past was believed to have sex with a sleeping man

suc·cu·lent¹ /ˈsʌkjələnt/ *adj* juicy and good to eat: *a succulent steak* —**succulence** *n* [U]

succulent² *n* [C] *technical* a plant such as a CACTUS, that has thick soft leaves or stems that can hold a lot of liquid

suc·cumb /səˈkʌm/ *v* [I] *formal* **1** to stop opposing someone or something that is stronger than you, and allow them to take control SYN **give in**: **[+to]** ***Succumbing to pressure*** *from the chemical industry, Governor Blakely amended the regulations.* | *Gina* ***succumbed to temptation*** *and had a second serving of cake.* **2** if you succumb to an illness, you become very ill or die of it: **[+to]** *About 400,000 Americans succumb each year to smoking-related illnesses.*

such /sʌtʃ/ ●●● S1 W1 *determiner, predeterminer, pron*
1 of the same kind as the thing or person which has already been mentioned: *Such behavior is just not acceptable in this school.* | *The rules make it quite clear what should be done in such a situation.* | *A victory for Brazil had been predicted, and such indeed was the result.* | *She needs to see a psychiatrist* ***or some such*** *person.* | *'You said you'd be finished by today.' 'I said* ***no such*** *thing!'* | **such as this/these** *There is now a greater awareness of problems such as these.* | **treated/recognized/accepted etc as such** *Birth is a natural process, and should be treated as such.*
2 such as used when giving an example of something: *Cartoon characters such as Mickey Mouse and Snoopy are still popular.* | *large electrical goods such as television sets and washing machines* | **such as?** (=used to ask someone to give an example) *'There are lots of useful things you could do.' 'Such as?'*
3 used to emphasize your description of something or someone: *They're such nice people.* | *It's such a long way from here.* | *I felt such an idiot.*
4 a) used to mention the result of a quality that something or someone has: *It's such a tiny kitchen that I don't have to do much to keep it clean.* | *He came to such a sudden stop that we almost hit him.* **b)** *formal* used to say that something is so great, so bad etc that something else happens: **be such that/as to do sth** *The force of the explosion was such that windows were blown out.* | *His manner was such as to offend nearly everyone he met.* | **in such a way/manner that/as to do sth** *He lectured in such a way that many in the audience found him impossible to understand.* | **to such an extent/degree that** *Her condition deteriorated to such an extent that a blood transfusion was considered necessary.*
5 used to show that you think that something is not good enough or that there is not enough of it: **such as it is/such as they are etc** *We will look at the evidence, such as it is, for each of these theories.* | **such ... as** *formal*: *Such food as they gave us was scarcely fit to eat.*
6 *formal* used to refer only to people or things of a particular group or kind: **such ... as/who/that** *Such individuals who take up this role often find life frustrating.* | **such of sb/sth as** *Such of you as wish to leave may do so now.*
7 there's no such person/thing etc as sb/sth used to say that a particular person or thing does not exist: *There's no such thing as magic.*
8 not (...) as such a) *spoken* used to say that the word you are using to describe something is not exactly correct: *There isn't a garden as such, just a little vegetable patch.* **b)** used to say that something does not include or is not related to all things or people of a particular type: *We have nothing against men as such.*
9 and such *spoken* used to say that other people or things like the ones you have just mentioned are included: *It won't be anything special – just a few cakes and sandwiches and such.*

GRAMMAR: Word order

You use **such a** before an adjective and a noun, or before a singular noun: *I'm lucky to have such a wonderful teacher.* | *He gave me such a fright.* ✗ Don't say: *a such wonderful teacher* | *a such fright*

ˈsuch and ˌsuch *pron, predeterminer spoken* used to talk about a particular thing, time, amount etc without saying exactly what it is: *They will ask you to come on such and such a day, at such and such a time.*

such·like /ˈsʌtʃlaɪk/ *pron spoken* **and suchlike** and things of that kind: *money for food, clothes, and suchlike* —**suchlike** *adj* [only before noun]

suck¹ /sʌk/ ●●○ S3 *v*
1 [I,T] to take air, liquid etc into your mouth by making your lips form a small hole and using the muscles of your mouth to pull it in: **suck sth in** *Michael put the cigarette to his lips and sucked in the smoke.* | **[+at]** *a baby sucking at its mother's breast* | **suck sth up** *Jennie sucked up the last bit of milk shake with her straw.*
2 [I,T] to hold something in your mouth and pull on it with your tongue and lips: *Don't suck your thumb, dear.* | **[+on]** *a picture of Lara sucking on a lollipop*
3 [T] to pull someone or something with great power and force into or out of a particular place: **suck sth into sth** *A bird was sucked into one of the jet's engines.* | **suck sb/sth under/down** *The river sucked him under.* | **suck sth out of/from sth** *The fluid was sucked from his lungs.*
4 sth sucks *spoken not polite* used when you dislike something very much or think something is very bad: *If you ask me, the whole thing sucks.*
5 suck it and see *BrE informal* to use something or do something for a short time, to find out if it works, if you like it etc

be sucked in (*also* **be sucked into sth**) *phr v* to become involved in a situation, especially a bad situation, when you do not want to: *The US has no intention of getting sucked into another war in Europe.*

suck up *phr v informal*
1 to say or do a lot of nice things in order to make someone like you or to get what you want – used to show disapproval: **[+to]** *He's always sucking up to the boss.*
2 suck it up *AmE* to accept an unpleasant situation without complaining

suck² *n* [C usually singular] an act of sucking

suck·er¹ /ˈsʌkə $ -ər/ *n* [C]
1 PERSON *informal* someone who is easily tricked or persuaded to do something: *You fell for that old line? Sucker!*
2 be a sucker for sb/sth *informal* to like someone or something very much, especially so that you cannot refuse them: *I'm a total sucker for seafood.*
3 PART OF AN ANIMAL a part of an insect or of an animal's body that it uses to hold on to a surface
4 SWEET *AmE* a LOLLIPOP
5 PLANT a part of a plant that grows from the root or lower stem to become a new plant
6 RUBBER a flat round piece of rubber that sticks to a surface by SUCTION

sucker² *v*

sucker sb **into** sth *phr v AmE* to persuade someone to do something they do not want to do, especially by tricking them or lying to them

ˈsucker punch *v* [T] *informal* to hit someone very quickly when they do not expect to be hit —**sucker punch** *n* [singular]

suck·le /ˈsʌkəl/ *v* **1** [T] to feed a baby or young animal with milk from the breast: *a sheep suckling her lamb* **2** [I] if a baby or young animal suckles, it sucks milk from a breast → **breast-feed**, **nurse**

suck·ling /ˈsʌklɪŋ/ *n* [C] *literary* a young human or animal still taking milk from its mother

su·crose /ˈsuːkrəʊz, ˈsjuː- $ ˈsuːkroʊz/ *n* [U] *technical* the most common form of sugar → **fructose**, **lactose**

suc·tion /ˈsʌkʃən/ *n* [U] **1** the process of removing air or liquid from an enclosed space so that another substance is sucked in, or so that two surfaces stick together: *My vacuum cleaner has very good suction.* | *a* ***suction pump*** **2** the force that causes a substance to be sucked into a closed space when the air or liquid already present is removed

sud·den /ˈsʌdn/ ●●● S2 W3 *adj*
1 happening, coming, or done quickly or when you do not expect it: *a* **sudden change** *in the weather | Life is cruel, she thought, with a* **sudden rush of** *anger. | a* **sudden movement** *| Her death was sudden.*
2 all of a sudden suddenly: *All of a sudden the lights went out.* —**suddenness** *n* [U]

ˌsudden ˈdeath *n* [U] a way of deciding the winner of a game when the scores are equal at the end. The game goes on until one player or team gains the lead: *a sudden death play-off*

ˌSudden ˌInfant ˈDeath ˌSyndrome *n* [U] *technical* (*abbreviation* **SIDS**) when a baby stops breathing and dies while it is sleeping, for no known reason SYN **crib death** *AmE*, **cot death** *BrE*

sud·den·ly /ˈsʌdnli/ ●●● S1 W1 *adv* quickly and unexpectedly: *I* **suddenly realized** *that there was someone following me. | George died very suddenly. |* [sentence adverb] *Suddenly, the eagle opened its wings.*

THESAURUS

suddenly used when something happens very quickly and unexpectedly: *Suddenly, there was a loud bang. | I suddenly realized what had happened. | Her husband* **died suddenly** *at the age of 64.*
all of a sudden suddenly – used especially in stories or descriptions of past events: *All of a sudden, he takes a gun out of his pocket and shoots. | He just all of a sudden decided to leave.*
without warning suddenly and with no signs that it was going to happen – used about bad or dangerous things: *One day, he collapsed without warning. | Then, without warning, her husband left her.*
out of the blue suddenly and unexpectedly – used especially when you hear from someone you have not seen for a long time or when someone tells you something that surprises you: *She turned up on my doorstep, out of the blue. | The offer had come completely out of the blue.*
at short notice *BrE*, **on short notice** *AmE* suddenly, so that there is not much time to prepare or change arrangements: *He came into the side at short notice, when another player was injured. | Occasionally, tours may have to be cancelled at short notice.*
on the spur of the moment used when talking about things you decide to do suddenly, without planning them beforehand: *We all buy things on the spur of the moment. | On the spur of the moment, I decided to go and talk to her about it.*

su·do·ku /suːˈdəʊkuː $ -ˈdoʊ-/ *n* [C,U] a game in which you have to write numbers in a large square which is made up of 81 smaller squares. Each line of squares across and down, and each of the nine groups of nine squares, must contain the numbers 1 to 9 once only.

suds /sʌdz/ *n* [plural] the mass of bubbles formed on the top of water with soap in it —**sudsy** *adj*

sue /sjuː $ suː/ ●○○ *v* [I,T]
1 to make a legal claim against someone, especially for money, because they have harmed you in some way: *If the builders don't fulfil their side of the contract, we'll sue. | The company is suing a former employee. |* **sue (sb) for libel/defamation/negligence/slander etc** *Miss James could not afford to sue for libel. | She was suing doctors for negligence over the loss of her child. | The railway may* **sue for damages** (=in order to get money) *because of loss of revenue. | He is being* **sued for divorce** (=in order to end a marriage) *by his wife.*
2 sue for peace *formal* if a country or army sues for peace, they ask for peace, especially because there is no other good choice: *They had hoped to force the North to sue for peace.*

suede /sweɪd/ *n* [U] soft leather with a slightly rough surface: *suede shoes | a suede jacket*

su·et /ˈsuːɪt, ˈsjuːɪt $ ˈsuː-/ *n* [U] hard fat from around an animal's KIDNEYS, used in cooking in Britain

suf·fer /ˈsʌfə $ -ər/ ●●● S1 W1 *v*
1 PAIN [I,T] to experience physical or mental pain: *At least he died suddenly and didn't suffer. | She's suffering a lot of pain.*
2 DISEASE/MEDICAL CONDITION [I] to have a particular disease or medical condition, especially for a long time: **[+from]** *Craig suffers from a rare bone disease. | The writer suffered from ill health for most of his life.*

REGISTER
In everyday English, people usually say that someone **has** a medical condition, rather than **suffers from** it: *Both her children* **have** *asthma.*

3 BAD EXPERIENCE/SITUATION [I,T] if someone suffers an unpleasant or difficult experience, or is in a difficult situation, it happens to them or they experience it: **[+from]** *London employers were suffering from a desperate shortage of school-leavers. | Most of us have* **suffered the consequences** *of stupid decisions taken by others. | In June 1667, England* **suffered** *a humiliating* **defeat** *by the Dutch. |* **suffer loss/damage/injury** *They are unlikely to suffer any further loss of business. | He suffered head injuries in the crash. | Small businesses have suffered financially during the recession.*
4 BECOME WORSE [I] to become worse in quality because a bad situation is affecting something or because nobody is taking care of it OPP **benefit**: *Safety might suffer if costs are cut. | I'm worried and my work is beginning to suffer.*
5 not suffer fools gladly to not be patient with people you think are stupid: *He was a perfectionist who didn't suffer fools gladly.*

suf·fer·ance /ˈsʌfərəns/ *n* **on sufferance** *formal* if you live or work somewhere on sufferance, you are allowed to do it by someone who would prefer you did not do it: *He was never going to let her forget she was only here on sufferance.*

suf·fer·er /ˈsʌfərə $ -ər/ *n* [C] someone who suffers, especially from a particular illness → **victim**: **[+from]** *sufferers from headaches |* **AIDS/cancer/asthma/arthritis etc sufferers** *a support group for cancer sufferers*

suf·fer·ing /ˈsʌfərɪŋ/ ●○○ *n* [C,U] serious physical or mental pain: *the suffering of the refugees after the war | the* **pain and suffering** *caused by road accidents* THESAURUS PAIN

suf·fice /səˈfaɪs/ ●○○ *v* [I]
1 *formal* to be enough: *A light lunch* **will suffice**. | **[+for]** *A few brief observations will suffice for present purposes. |* **suffice to do sth** *A few more statistics will suffice to show the trends of the time.*
2 suffice (it) to say (that) used to say that the statement that follows is enough to explain what you mean, even though you could say more: *Suffice it to say that they're having marital problems.*

suf·fi·cien·cy /səˈfɪʃənsi/ AWL *n formal* **1** [U] the state of being or having enough: *The war has affected the country's economic sufficiency.* **2 a sufficiency of sth** a supply that is enough: *a sufficiency of raw materials*

suf·fi·cient /səˈfɪʃənt/ ●●○ W2 AWL *adj formal* as much as is needed for a particular purpose SYN **enough** OPP **insufficient**: *We can only prosecute if there is sufficient evidence. | Unauthorized absence is sufficient reason for dismissal. | We need sufficient time to deal with the problem. |* **sufficient to do sth** *The money is not sufficient to cover everything that needs doing. |* **[+for]** *The recipe is sufficient for six people.* THESAURUS ENOUGH —**sufficiently** *adv*: *Students must reach a sufficiently high standard to pass.*

suf·fix /ˈsʌfɪks/ *n* [C] a letter or letters added to the end of a word to form a new word, such as 'ness' in 'kindness' or 'ly' in 'suddenly' → **affix**, **prefix**

suf·fo·cate /ˈsʌfəkeɪt/ *v* **1** [I,T] to die or make someone die by preventing them from breathing: *The animal seizes its prey by the throat and suffocates it to death. | One of the puppies suffocated inside the plastic bag.* **2 be suffocating** to

S

feel uncomfortable because there is not enough fresh air: *Can you open a window? I'm suffocating.* **3** [T] to prevent a relationship, plan, business etc from developing well or being successful: *Jealousy can suffocate any relationship.* —**suffocation** /ˌsʌfəˈkeɪʃən/ *n* [U]

suf·fo·cat·ed /ˈsʌfəkeɪtɪd/ *adj* **feel suffocated** to feel as if you are not free or do not have enough space: *He feels suffocated by London and longs to escape to the country.*

suf·fra·gan /ˈsʌfrəgən/ *adj* [only before noun] a suffragan BISHOP helps another bishop of higher rank in their work —**suffragan** *n* [C]

suf·frage /ˈsʌfrɪdʒ/ *n* [U] the right to vote in national elections

suf·fra·gette /ˌsʌfrəˈdʒet/ *n* [C] a woman who tried to gain the right to vote for women, especially as a member of a group in Britain or the US in the early 20th century

suf·fuse /səˈfjuːz/ *v* [T] *literary* **1** if warmth, colour, liquid etc suffuses something or someone, it covers or spreads through them: *The light of the setting sun suffused the clouds.* | *Hot colour suffused her cheeks.* **2 be suffused with sth** if someone is suffused with a feeling, they are full of that feeling: *She was suffused with happiness.*

sug·ar¹ /ˈʃʊgə $ -ər/ ●●● S2 W3 *n*
1 [U] a sweet white or brown substance that is obtained from plants and used to make food and drinks sweet: *Do you take sugar in your coffee?*
2 [C] *BrE* the amount of sugar that a small spoon can hold: *How many sugars do you want in your tea?*
3 [C] *technical* one of several sweet substances formed in plants
4 *spoken* used to address someone you like very much

sugar² *v* [T] to add sugar or cover something with sugar SYN **sweeten**: *Did you sugar my coffee?* —**sugared** *adj*: *sugared almonds*

ˈ**sugar beet** *n* [U] a vegetable that grows under the ground, from which sugar is obtained

sug·ar·cane /ˈʃʊgəkeɪn $ -ər-/ *n* [U] a tall tropical plant from whose stems sugar is obtained

ˌ**sugar-ˈcoated** *adj* **1** covered with sugar: *sugar-coated cereals* **2** used to describe something that is made to seem better than it really is

ˈ**sugar cube** *n* [C] a sugar lump

ˈ**sugar ˌdaddy** *n* [C] *informal* an older man who gives a young person presents and money in return for their company and often for sex

sug·ar·ing /ˈʃʊgərɪŋ/ *n* [U] a way of removing hair in which a sticky substance containing sugar is spread on the skin and then quickly removed

ˈ**sugar lump** *n* [C] *BrE* a square piece of solid sugar

sug·ar·y /ˈʃʊgəri/ *adj* **1** containing sugar, or tasting like sugar: *sugary foods* THESAURUS▸ SWEET **2** language, emotions etc that are sugary are too nice and seem insincere: *She said goodbye in a sickeningly sugary tone.*

sug·gest /səˈdʒest $ səgˈdʒest/ ●●● S1 W1 *v* [T]
1 to tell someone your ideas about what they should do, where they should go etc → **propose**: *The zoo asked its visitors to suggest a name for the new baby panda.* | **suggest (that)** *Her mother suggested that she should go and see the doctor.* | *I suggest you call him first.* | ***It has been suggested that*** *the manager will resign if any more players are sold.* | **suggest sth to sb** *Johnson suggested to Boswell that they should buy the island.* | **suggest doing sth** *Tracey suggested meeting for a drink after work.* | **suggest how/where/what etc** *Can you suggest what kind of tool I should use?* | **can/may I suggest** (=used to politely suggest a different idea) *May I suggest that you think carefully before rushing into this?* THESAURUS▸ ADVISE
2 to make someone think that a particular thing is true SYN **indicate**: *Trends in spending and investment suggest a gradual economic recovery.* | **suggest (that)** *Opinion polls suggest that only 10% of the population trust the government.* | **evidence/results/data/studies etc suggest(s) that** *The evidence suggests that single fathers are more likely to work than single mothers.*
3 to tell someone about someone or something that is suitable for a particular job or activity SYN **recommend**: **suggest sb/sth for sth** *John Roberts has been suggested for the post of manager.*
4 to state something in an indirect way SYN **imply**: *Are you suggesting my husband's been drinking?*
5 to remind someone of something or help them to imagine it: *The stage was bare, with only the lighting to suggest a prison.*
6 sth suggests itself if an idea suggests itself, you think of it: *I'll look at my cookbooks and see if anything suggests itself.*
7 I'm not suggesting *spoken* used to say that what you have said is not exactly what you intended to say: *I'm not suggesting for one moment that these changes will be easy.*

GRAMMAR: Patterns with suggest

- You **suggest** something **to** someone: *He suggested a solution to us.* ✗ Don't say: *He suggested us a solution.*
- You **suggest doing** something: *I suggested going for a walk in the park.* ✗ Don't say: *I suggested to go for a walk in the park.*
- In everyday English, you **suggest that** someone **does** something: *I suggest that she waits a few weeks.* ✗ Don't say: *I suggest her to wait a few weeks.*
- In more formal English, you **suggest that** someone **do** something, using the base form of the verb (=the infinitive without 'to'): *I suggest that she wait a few weeks.*
- You can also use the base form of the verb when talking about the past: *I suggested that she wait a few weeks.*
- You **suggest that** someone **should do** something: *The doctor suggested that she should sit down.*
- In more formal English, you can say **it has been suggested that** something is true: *It has been suggested that the substance can cause cancer.*

GRAMMAR GUIDE▸ VERBS

THESAURUS

suggest to tell someone your ideas about what they should do: *'Why don't you come with us?', Alan suggested.* | *It was a sunny afternoon and so I suggested going to the beach.*
recommend to suggest that someone goes somewhere, tries something etc because you know that it is good and you think they will like it: *Can you recommend a good restaurant near here?* | *It's a brilliant book - I'd recommend it to anyone.*
propose *formal* to formally suggest a plan or course of action, especially at a meeting: *The government has proposed building a new town just north of the city.*
put forward to suggest an idea, plan, reason etc: *The party has put forward new proposals to reduce the number of cars in the town centre.* | *The idea was first put forward by Aristotle.* | *A number of reasons have been put forward to explain these negative results.*
nominate to officially suggest someone for an important job or position, or a person, film etc for a prize, especially when people will vote to make a decision: *He's been nominated for the Nobel Prize in Literature several times.*

sug·gest·i·ble /səˈdʒestəbəl $ səg-/ *adj* easily influenced by other people or by things you see and hear: **very/highly/extremely suggestible** *At that age, kids are highly suggestible.*

sug·ges·tion /səˈdʒestʃən $ səg-/ ●●● S1 W2 *n*
1 [C] an idea, plan, or possibility that someone mentions, or the act of mentioning it: *Any suggestions would be welcome.* | **suggestion that** *The committee rejected the suggestion that houses should be built on this site.* | **[+for]** *Here are some suggestions for further activities.* | **[+about]** *My suggestion about menus was ignored.* | **at sb's suggestion** *She took a seat at his suggestion.*
2 [singular, U] a sign or possibility of something: **[+of]** *There was never any suggestion of criminal involvement.* |

The government have denied any suggestion of involvement in her death. | **suggestion that** *There's some suggestion that the intruder was the same person that killed Angie.*
3 a suggestion of sth a slight amount of something: *There was just a suggestion of a smile on her face.*
4 [U] an indirect way of making you accept an idea, for example by HYPNOTISM: *the power of suggestion*

COLLOCATIONS

VERBS

make a suggestion *Can I make a suggestion?*
offer/put forward a suggestion *A few suggestions were put forward.*
have a suggestion *I have a suggestion for you.*
come up with a suggestion (=think of something to suggest) *We've come up with five suggestions.*
accept/adopt a suggestion (=do what is suggested) | **reject a suggestion** (=not do what is suggested) | **be open to suggestions** (=be willing to listen to suggestions) | **welcome suggestions** (=be keen to listen to suggestions)

ADJECTIVES

a good/excellent suggestion *I think that's an excellent suggestion.*
a helpful/useful/valuable suggestion *He made various helpful suggestions.*
a sensible suggestion

sugˈgestion ˌengine *n* [C] a piece of software that makes suggestions about products or services that you may like, based on things you have chosen before or things chosen by people who like the same things as you SYN **recommendation engine**

sug·ges·tive /səˈdʒestɪv $ səɡ-/ *adj* **1** similar to something: **[+of]** *Her symptoms are suggestive of a panic disorder.* | *It was a huge sound, suggestive of whales calling each other.* **2** a remark, behaviour etc that is suggestive makes you think of sex: *He kept giving me suggestive looks.* —**suggestively** *adv* —**suggestiveness** *n* [U]

su·i·cid·al /ˌsuːəˈsaɪdl◂, ˌsjuː- $ ˌsuː-/ *adj* **1** wanting to kill yourself: *She was depressed and almost suicidal.* | *For many years before treatment, Clare had* ***suicidal tendencies*** (=behaviour that showed she wanted to kill herself). **2** likely to lead to death: *It was suicidal trying to put out that fire.* **3** likely to lead to a lot of damage or trouble: *Her economic policies would prove suicidal for our economy.*

su·i·cide /ˈsuːəsaɪd, ˈsjuː- $ ˈsuː-/ ●○○ *n* [C,U]
1 the act of killing yourself: *More people* ***commit suicide*** *at Christmas than at any other time.* | *My mother* ***attempted suicide*** *on many occasions.* | *He apparently left a* ***suicide note*** *on his desk* (=letter explaining his reasons for killing himself).
2 political/economic suicide something you do that ruins your good position in politics or the ECONOMY: *He said a vote for Labour would be a vote for economic suicide.*
3 suicide attack/mission/bombing etc an attack etc in which the person who carries out the attack deliberately kills himself or herself in the process of killing other people
4 suicide by cop *AmE* an occasion when someone deliberately threatens a police officer in order to make the police officer shoot, as a way of committing suicide

ˈsuicide ˌbomber *n* [C] someone who hides a bomb on their body and explodes it in a public place, killing himself or herself and other people, usually for political reasons

ˈsuicide ˌpact *n* [C] an arrangement between two or more people to kill themselves at the same time

suit¹ /suːt, sjuːt $ suːt/ ●●● S2 W3 *n* [C]
1 CLOTHES a set of clothes made of the same material, usually including a jacket with trousers or a skirt: *a grey lightweight suit* | *a business suit* | *a tweed suit* | *She was wearing a black trouser suit.* → MORNING SUIT
2 bathing/jogging etc suit a piece of clothing or a set of clothes used for swimming, running etc → BOILER SUIT, SHELL SUIT, SWEAT SUIT, TRACKSUIT, WET SUIT
3 LAW a problem or complaint that a person or company brings to a court of law to be settled SYN **lawsuit**: *Johnson has* ***filed suit*** *against her.* | *a* ***civil suit***
4 OFFICE WORKER *informal* a man, especially a manager, who works in an office and who has to wear a suit when he is at work: *I bought myself a mobile phone and joined the other suits on the train to the City.*
5 CARDS one of the four types of cards in a set of playing cards
6 sb's strong suit something that you are good at: *Sympathy is not Jack's strong suit.* → **in your birthday suit** at BIRTHDAY(3), → **follow suit** at FOLLOW(14)

suit² ●●● S3 W3 *v* [T]
1 to be acceptable, suitable, or CONVENIENT for a particular person or in a particular situation: *Whatever your reason for borrowing, we have the loan that* ***suits*** *your* ***needs***. | *There's a range of restaurants to* ***suit all tastes***. | *There are countryside walks to* ***suit everyone***. | *We have gifts to* ***suit every pocket*** (=of all prices). | *Either steak or chicken would* ***suit*** *me* ***fine***. | *The climate there will* ***suit*** *you* ***down to the ground*** (=suit you very well). | **suit sth to sth** *She had the ability to suit her performances to the audience.*
2 clothes, colours etc that suit you make you look attractive: *That coat really suits Paul.* | *Red suits you.* | *Jill's new hairstyle doesn't really suit her.* GRAMMAR **Suit** is never passive in this meaning.
3 best/well/ideally/perfectly etc suited to/for sth to have the right qualities to do something: *The activity holidays on offer are really best suited to groups.* | *land well suited for agriculture* | *the candidate most ideally suited to doing the job*
4 suit yourself *spoken* used to tell someone they can do whatever they want to, even though it annoys you or you think they are not doing the right thing: *'Mind if I sit here?' he said gently. 'Suit yourself.'*
5 suit sb's book *BrE informal* to fit well into someone's plans

suit·a·bil·i·ty /ˌsuːtəˈbɪləti, ˌsjuː- $ ˌsuː-/ *n* [U] the degree to which something or someone has the right qualities for a particular purpose: **[+for]** *There's no doubt about Christine's suitability for the job.* | **[+as]** *his suitability as a father*

suit·a·ble /ˈsuːtəbəl, ˈsjuː- $ ˈsuː-/ ●●● S3 W2 *adj* having the right qualities for a particular person, purpose, or situation OPP **unsuitable**: *We are hoping to find a suitable school.* | **suitable for sb/sth** *The house is not really suitable for a large family.* | **suitable place/time etc to do sth** *a suitable place to rear young children* | **suitable to use/be shown etc** *These crayons are not suitable to use in very hot weather.*

REGISTER

In everyday English, people usually say that someone or something is **the right** person or thing for them, instead of using **suitable**: *We think this is* ***the right*** *school for our child.*

THESAURUS

suitable having the right qualities for a particular purpose or person: *a suitable place for a picnic* | *They don't consider him a suitable husband for their daughter.*
right completely suitable in every way: *It's a nice house, but it isn't right for us.* | *We'll tell her when the time is right.*
appropriate suitable for a particular purpose. **Appropriate** is more formal than **suitable**: *She filled out all the appropriate forms.* | *It may not be an appropriate time to ask him about it.*
proper the proper tool, piece of equipment, or way of doing something is the one that most people think is most suitable: *You can't change a wheel without the proper tools.* | *the proper procedure for hiring staff*
suited to sth if someone is suited to something, he or she has the right qualities to do it: *He'd be well suited to the job.*

S

suit·a·bly /ˈsuːtəbli, ˈsjuː- $ ˈsuː-/ ●○○ *adv*
1 suitably dressed/prepared/equipped etc wearing the right clothes, having the right information, equipment etc for a particular situation: *We were relieved that Gordon had arrived at the wedding suitably dressed.*
2 [+adj/adv] having the amount of a feeling or quality you would hope for in a particular situation: *'He owns three hotels.' The others looked* ***suitably impressed****.*

suit·case /ˈsuːtkeɪs, ˈsjuːt- $ ˈsuːt-/ ●●● S3 *n* [C] a large case with a handle, used for carrying clothes and possessions when you travel → see picture at CASE[1]

suite /swiːt/ ●○○ *n* [C]
1 ROOMS a set of rooms, especially expensive ones in a hotel: *a honeymoon suite | a* ***suite of rooms*** *for palace guests*
2 FURNITURE *especially BrE* a set of matching furniture for a room: *a pink* ***bathroom suite*** | **three-piece suite** (=a large seat and two chairs)
3 COMPUTERS *technical* a group of related computer PROGRAMS
4 MUSIC a piece of music made up of several short parts: *the Nutcracker Suite*
5 POLITICS *formal* the people who work for or help an important person SYN **retinue**

suit·ing /ˈsuːtɪŋ, ˈsjuː- $ ˈsuː-/ *n* [U] *technical* material used for making suits, especially woven wool

sui·tor /ˈsuːtə, ˈsjuː- $ ˈsuːtər/ *n* [C] *old use* a man who wants to marry a particular woman

sul·fate /ˈsʌlfeɪt/ *n* [C,U] the American spelling of SULPHATE

sul·fide /ˈsʌlfaɪd/ *n* [C,U] the American spelling of SULPHIDE

sul·fur /ˈsʌlfə $ -ər/ *n* [U] the American spelling of SULPHUR

S

ˌsulfur diˈoxide *n* [U] the American spelling of SULPHUR DIOXIDE

sul·fu·ric a·cid /sʌlˌfjʊərɪk ˈæsɪd $ -ˌfjʊr-/ *n* [U] the American spelling of SULPHURIC ACID

sul·fu·rous /ˈsʌlfərəs/ *adj* the American spelling of SULPHUROUS

sulk[1] /sʌlk/ *v* [I] to be silently angry and refuse to be friendly or discuss what is annoying or upsetting you – used to show disapproval: *Nicola sulked all morning.*

sulk[2] *n* [C] a time when someone is sulking: **in/into a sulk** *Mike could go into a sulk that would last for days. | She's* ***having a sulk****.* | **the sulks** *a fit of the sulks*

sulk·y /ˈsʌlki/ *adj* sulking, or tending to sulk → **moody**: *a sulky child | He put on a sulky expression. | Katherine sat in a sulky silence.* —**sulkily** *adv* —**sulkiness** *n* [U]

sul·len /ˈsʌlən/ *adj* **1** angry and silent, especially because you feel life has been unfair to you → **morose**: *Bill sat in sullen silence and refused to eat his lunch. | a look of sullen resentment* **2** *literary* a sullen sky or sea is dark and looks as if bad weather is coming SYN **overcast** —**sullenly** *adv* —**sullenness** *n* [U]

sul·ly /ˈsʌli/ *v* (**sullied**, **sullying**, **sullies**) [T] *formal or literary* to spoil or reduce the value of something that was perfect: *a scandal that sullied his reputation*

sul·phate *BrE*, **sulfate** *AmE* /ˈsʌlfeɪt/ *n* [C,U] a SALT formed from SULPHURIC ACID: *copper sulphate*

sul·phide *BrE*, **sulfide** *AmE* /ˈsʌlfaɪd/ *n* [C,U] a mixture of sulphur with another substance

sul·phur *BrE*, **sulfur** *AmE* /ˈsʌlfə $ -fər/ *n* [U] a common light yellow chemical substance that burns with a very strong unpleasant smell, and is used in drugs, explosives, and industry. It is a chemical ELEMENT: symbol S

ˌsulphur diˈoxide *BrE*, **sulfur dioxide** *AmE* *n* [U] a poisonous gas that is a cause of air POLLUTION in industrial areas

sul·phu·ric ac·id *BrE*, **sulfuric acid** *AmE* /sʌlˌfjʊərɪk ˈæsɪd $ -ˌfjʊr-/ *n* [U] a powerful acid

sul·phu·rous *BrE*, **sulfurous** *AmE* /ˈsʌlfərəs/ *adj* relating to, full of, or used with sulphur

sul·tan /ˈsʌltən/ *n* [C] a ruler in some Muslim countries

sul·ta·na /sʌlˈtɑːnə $ -ˈtænə/ *n* [C] **1** *BrE* a small pale RAISIN (=dried fruit) without seeds, used in baking SYN **golden raisin** *AmE* **2** the wife, mother, or daughter of a sultan

sul·tan·ate /ˈsʌltəneɪt, -nət/ *n* [C] **1** a country ruled by a sultan: *the sultanate of Oman* **2** the position of a sultan, or the period of time during which he rules

sul·try /ˈsʌltri/ *adj* **1** weather that is sultry is hot with air that feels wet SYN **humid**: *a hot and sultry day | Since the rain, the air had become heavy and still and sultry.* **2** a woman who is sultry makes other people feel strong sexual attraction to her: *She threw Carlo a sultry glance. | a sultry film star* —**sultriness** *n* [U]

sum[1] /sʌm/ ●●○ W2 AWL *n* [C]
1 MONEY an amount of money: *He owes me a large* ***sum of money****.* | **[+of]** *the sum of £4,000* | **large/substantial/considerable etc sum** *Bill wants to spend a large sum on modernizing the farm.* | **small/modest/trifling etc sum** *We should be happy to buy it for a modest sum.* → LUMP SUM, → **princely sum** at PRINCELY(1)
2 the sum of sth the total produced when you add two or more numbers or amounts together: *You will have to pay the sum of the two sets of costs.*
3 greater/more/better etc than the sum of its parts having a quality or effectiveness as a group that you would not expect from the quality of each member: *The team is greater than the sum of its parts.*
4 CALCULATION a simple calculation by adding, multiplying, dividing etc, especially one done by children at school
5 do your sums *BrE informal* to calculate whether you have enough money to do something: *Do your sums first before you decide how much to spend.*
6 in sum *formal* used before a statement that gives the main information about something in a few simple words: *In sum, soul music is important to the record industry.* → SUM TOTAL

sum[2] ●○○ AWL *v* (**summed**, **summing**)
sum up *phr v*
1 to give the main information in a report, speech etc in a short statement at the end SYN **summarize**: *Gerald will open the debate and I will sum up.* | **to sum up** *To sum up, for a healthy heart you must take regular exercise and stop smoking.* | **sum sth ↔ up** *In your final paragraph, sum up your argument.*
2 when a judge sums up or sums up the case at the end of a TRIAL, he or she explains the main facts of the case → SUMMING-UP
3 sum sth ↔ up to describe something using only a few words SYN **summarize**: *The city's problem can be summed up in three words: too many people.*
4 sum sth ↔ up to show the most typical qualities of someone or something: *That image sums up the whole film.*
5 sum sb/sth ↔ up to form a judgment or opinion about someone or something SYN **assess**: *Pat summed up the situation at a glance.*
6 that (about) sums it up *spoken* used to say that a description of a situation is correct: *'So you want us to help you change but you don't believe change is possible?' 'That about sums it up.'*

sum·bitch /ˈsʌmbɪtʃ/ *n* [C] *AmE informal not polite* SON OF A BITCH

sum·ma cum lau·de /ˌsʊmə kʊm ˈlaʊdeɪ, ˌsʌmə kʌm ˈlɔːdi $ ˌsʊmə kʊm ˈlaʊdi/ *adv AmE* having achieved the highest level in your college or university degree → **cum laude**: *He graduated summa cum laude in 1968.*

sum·ma·ri·ly /ˈsʌmərəli/ *adv* immediately, and without following the normal process: *He was summarily dismissed.*

sum·mar·ize (*also* **-ise** *BrE*) /ˈsʌməraɪz/ ●○○ AWL *v* [I,T] to make a short statement giving only the main information and not the details of a plan, event, report etc SYN **sum up**: *The authors summarize their views in the introduction.* | **to summarize** *To summarize, in most cases the schools were achieving the standards set.*

sum·ma·ry[1] /ˈsʌməri/ ●●○ AWL *n* (*plural* **summaries**) [C] a short statement that gives the main information about something, without giving all the details: *A brief summary is given on a separate sheet.* | **[+of]** *The group produces a monthly summary of their research.* | **in summary** *In summary, do not sell your shares.*

summary² AWL *adj* [only before noun] **1** *formal* done immediately, and not following the normal process: *a summary execution* **2** a summary report, statement etc gives the main facts in a report etc without any of the details or explanations

sum·mat /ˈsʌmət/ *pron spoken* something – used in northern England

sum·ma·tion /səˈmeɪʃən/ AWL *n* [C] *formal* **1** a SUMMARY or SUMMING-UP **2** the total amount or number when two or more things are added together

sum·mer¹ /ˈsʌmə $ -ər/ ●●● S1 W1 *n* [C,U]
1 the time of the year when the sun is hottest and the days are longest, between spring and autumn → **summery**: *the long hot summer of 1976* | *The children play on the beach during the summer.* | **in (the) summer** *Miriam likes to relax in her garden in summer.* | **this/next/last summer** *We're going to Italy next summer.* | *a hot summer's day* | *a sunny summer afternoon* | *a three-week summer vacation* | **early/late summer** *The tourist season lasts through late summer.* | *Parts of Spain are extremely hot in* ***high summer*** (=the hottest part of summer).
2 20/50 etc summers *literary* 20, 50 etc years of age: *a child of 11 summers* → INDIAN SUMMER

GRAMMAR: Patterns with summer

in summer/in the summer
• You use **in summer** or **in the summer** when saying that something happens at that time: *In summer we get six weeks' vacation.* | *He worked as a lifeguard in the summer.*

last summer/this summer etc
Don't use **in** with these words:
• You say **last summer**: *We went to Italy last summer.*
✗ Don't say: *We went to Italy in last summer.*
• You say **this summer**: *Do you plan to travel this summer?* ✗ Don't say: *Do you plan to travel in this summer?*
• You say **next summer**: *We will graduate next summer.*
✗ Don't say: *We will graduate in next summer.*
• You say **that summer**: *That summer she met Jeff.*
✗ Don't say: *In that summer she met Jeff.*

summer² *v* [I] to spend the summer in a particular place → **winter**

ˈsummer ˌcamp *n* [C,U] a place where children in the US can stay during the summer, and take part in various activities

ˌsummer ˈholidays *n* [plural] *BrE* the period of time during the summer when schools and universities are closed SYN **summer vacation** *AmE*

sum·mer·house /ˈsʌməhaʊs $ -ər-/ *n* [C] a small building in your garden, where you can sit in warm weather

ˌsummer ˈpudding *n* [C,U] a British sweet dish made from pieces of bread and fruit such as berries

ˈsummer school *n* [C,U] courses you can take in the summer at a school, university, or college

ˌsummer ˈsolstice *n* [singular] the longest day in the northern HEMISPHERE (=top half of the Earth), around June 22nd

sum·mer·time /ˈsʌmətaɪm $ -ər-/ *n* [U] the season when it is summer: **in (the) summertime** *It doesn't rain much in the summertime.* → BRITISH SUMMER TIME

ˌsummer vaˈcation *n* [U] *AmE* the period of time during the summer when schools and universities are closed SYN **summer holidays** *BrE*

sum·mer·y /ˈsʌməri/ *adj* suitable for or reminding you of the summer: *a light summery dress* | *a summery breeze*

ˌsumming-ˈup *n* (*plural* **summings-up**) [C] a statement giving the main facts but not the details of something, especially made by a judge at the end of a TRIAL: *In his summing-up, the judge said that it was dangerous to convict on this evidence alone.* → SUM UP

sum·mit /ˈsʌmɪt/ ●○○ *n* [C]
1 an important meeting or set of meetings between the leaders of several governments: *the European summit* | *The two presidents agreed to* ***hold a summit*** *in the spring.* | *a five-nation* ***summit meeting*** THESAURUS MEETING
2 the top of a mountain → **peak**: **[+of]** *Many people have now reached the summit of Mount Everest.*
3 the summit of sth *formal* the greatest amount or highest level of something SYN **peak**: *His election as president represented the summit of his career.*

sum·mon /ˈsʌmən/ ●○○ *v* [T] *formal*
1 to order someone to come to a place: *Robert summoned the waiter for the bill.* | **summon sb to sth** *The president summoned Taylor to Washington.* | **summon sb to do sth** *He was summoned to attend an emergency meeting.*
2 to officially order someone to come to a court of law: *Hugh was* ***summoned to appear*** *before the magistrate.*
3 (*also* **summon sth up**) to try very hard to have enough of something such as courage, energy, or strength, because you need it: *He had to summon the energy to finish the race.*
4 summon a meeting/conference etc to arrange for a meeting to take place and order people to come to it SYN **convene**: *He summoned a meeting of business leaders.*

summon up ↔ sth *phr v*
1 if something summons up a memory, thought, or image, it makes you remember it or think of it SYN **conjure up**: *The smell summoned up memories of family holidays by the sea.*
2 to try very hard to have enough courage, energy, or strength, because you need it: *Ruth took a deep breath, summoned up her courage, and told him the truth.*

sum·mons¹ /ˈsʌmənz/ *n* (*plural* **summonses**) [C] an official order to appear in a court of law: *The judge must* ***issue*** *a* ***summons***. | *He had been accused of a drug offence but police had been unable to* ***serve*** *a* ***summons*** *on him* (=officially order him to appear in court).

summons² *v* [T] to order someone to appear in a court of law: *She has been* ***summonsed to appear*** *in court.* | *Basil was summonsed for wounding a police officer.*

su·mo /ˈsuːməʊ $ -moʊ/ (*also* **ˈsumo ˌwrestling**) *n* [U] a Japanese form of WRESTLING, done by men who are very large —**sumo wrestler** *n* [C]

sump /sʌmp/ *n* [C] **1** the lowest part of a DRAINAGE system, where liquids or wastes remain **2** *BrE* the part of an engine that contains the supply of oil SYN **oil pan** *AmE*

sump·tu·ous /ˈsʌmptʃuəs/ *adj* very impressive and expensive: *a sumptuous feast* | *a sumptuous palace* —**sumptuously** *adv* —**sumptuousness** *n* [U]

ˌsum ˈtotal *n* **the sum total** the whole of an amount: **[+of]** *That's the sum total of my knowledge about it.*

sun¹ /sʌn/ ●●● S2 W1 *n*
1 the sun/the Sun the large bright object in the sky that gives us light and heat, and around which the Earth moves → **solar**: *The sky was blue and the sun was shining.*
2 [U] the heat and light that come from the sun → **sunny**: *Too much sun is bad for you.* | **in the sun** *We sat in the sun, eating ice cream.* | *the warmth of the afternoon sun*
3 [C] any star around which PLANETs move
4 everything/anything etc under the sun used to emphasize that you are talking about a large range of things: *You can buy jeans in every colour under the sun.*
5 catch the sun *BrE*, **get some sun** *AmE* if someone catches or gets the sun, they become slightly red or brown because they have been outside in the sun → **make hay while the sun shines** at HAY(2)

COLLOCATIONS – MEANINGS 1 & 2

VERBS

the sun shines *When I woke, the sun was shining.*
the sun beats down/blazes down (=shines with a lot of light and heat) *The sun beats down on us as we work.*

S

the sun comes out (=appears when cloud moves away) *The rain stopped and the sun came out.*
the sun rises/comes up (=appears at the beginning of the day) *As the sun rises, the birds take flight.*
the sun sets/goes down (=disappears at the end of the day) *It is a good place to sit and watch the sun go down.*
the sun sinks (=gradually disappears at the end of the day)

ADJECTIVES/NOUN + sun

the hot/warm sun *The hot sun beat down on the men working.*
the blazing/burning sun *Tourists trudge around in the blazing sun.*
a bright sun *It was a warm day with a bright sun overhead.*
the morning/afternoon/evening sun | the midday/noonday sun | the rising/setting sun (=the sun as it appears/disappears)

PHRASES

the sun is high/low in the sky *They walked until the sun was low in the sky.*

sun² *v* (**sunned, sunning**) **sun yourself** to sit or lie outside when the sun is shining → **sunbathe**: *The beaches were full of families sunning themselves.*

Sun. (*also* **Sun** *BrE*) the written abbreviation of ***Sunday***

'sun-baked *adj* made very hard and dry by the sun: *the sun-baked ground*

sun·bathe /'sʌnbeɪð/ *v* [I] to sit or lie outside in the sun, especially in order to become brown: *Her mother was sunbathing in the back garden.* ⚠ There is no noun 'sunbath': *Let's go and sunbathe/do some sunbathing (NOT have a sunbath).*

sun·beam /'sʌnbiːm/ *n* [C] a beam of light from the sun

sun·bed /'sʌnbed/ *n* [C] **1** a metal structure the size of a bed that you lie on to make your skin brown using light from special lamps **2** a SUN LOUNGER → **SUNLAMP**

Sun·belt, the /'sʌnbelt/ the southern and southwestern parts of the US, from Virginia to South California. The name comes from the hot sunny climate in this area.

sun·block /'sʌnblɒk $ -blɑːk/ *n* [C,U] cream or oil that you rub into your skin, in order to completely stop the sun's light from burning you → **sunscreen**

sun·burn /'sʌnbɜːn $ -bɜːrn/ *n* [U] red and painful skin that you can get from spending too much time in the sun

sun·burned /'sʌnbɜːnd $ -bɜːrnd/ (*also* **sun·burnt** /-bɜːnt $ -bɜːrnt/) *adj* **1** having a red and painful skin as a result of spending too much time in the sun **2** having skin that is attractively brown as a result of spending time in the sun

'sun cream *n* [C,U] *BrE* a cream that you rub into your skin to stop the sun from burning you too much SYN **suntan lotion**

sun·dae /'sʌndeɪ $ -di/ *n* [C] a dish made from ICE CREAM, fruit, sweet sauce, nuts etc: *a chocolate sundae*

Sun·day /'sʌndi, -deɪ/ ●●● S2 W2 *n* [C,U]
1 (*written abbreviation* **Sun.**) the day between Saturday and Monday: **on Sunday** *We're going to a match on Sunday.* | *What are you doing Sunday? AmE* | **Sunday morning/afternoon etc** *Sunday nights are usually pretty quiet.* | **last Sunday** *It was our wedding anniversary last Sunday.* | **this Sunday** *There's another antiques market this Sunday.* | **next Sunday** (=Sunday of next week) *We'll announce the winners next Sunday.* | **a Sunday** (=one of the Sundays in the year) *Finding a dentist on a Sunday can be very difficult.*
2 your Sunday best your best clothes, worn only for special occasions or for church
3 Sunday driver an insulting expression meaning someone who annoys other people by driving too slowly → **never in a month of Sundays** at MONTH(6)

'Sunday school *n* [C,U] a place where children are taught about Christianity on Sundays

sun·deck /'sʌndek/ *n* [C] a part of a ship where people can sit in the sun

sun·der /'sʌndə $ -ər/ *v* [T] *literary* to break something into parts, especially violently SYN **split**

sun·dial /'sʌndaɪəl/ *n* [C] an object used in the past for telling the time. The shadow of a pointed piece of metal shows the time and moves round as the sun moves. → see picture at CLOCK¹

sun·down /'sʌndaʊn/ *n* [U] *old-fashioned* SUNSET(1)

sun·down·er /'sʌnˌdaʊnə $ -ər/ *n* [C] *informal especially BrE* an alcoholic drink drunk in the evening

'sun-drenched *adj* a sun-drenched place is one where the sun shines most of the time - used especially in advertisements, magazines etc: *sun-drenched tropical islands*

sun·dress /'sʌndres/ *n* [C] a dress that you wear in hot weather, which does not cover your arms or shoulders

'sun-dried *adj* [only before noun] sun-dried food has been left in the sun to dry in order to give it a particular taste: *sun-dried tomatoes*

sun·dries /'sʌndriz/ *n* [plural] *formal* small objects that are not important enough to be named separately → **SUNDRY**

sun·dry /'sʌndri/ *adj* [only before noun] **1 all and sundry** everyone, not just a few carefully chosen people: *I don't want you telling our private business to all and sundry.* **2** *formal* not similar enough to form a group SYN **various**: *He makes films about animals, plants and sundry other subjects.*

sun·fish /'sʌnfɪʃ/ *n* (*plural* **sunfish**) [C] a fish that lives in the sea and has a large round body

sun·flow·er /'sʌnˌflaʊə $ -ˌflaʊər/ *n* [C] a very tall plant with a large yellow flower, and seeds that can be eaten → see picture at FLOWER¹

sung /sʌŋ/ *v* the past participle of SING

sun·glass·es /'sʌnˌglɑːsɪz $ -ˌglæ-/ ●●● S3 *n* [plural] dark glasses that you wear to protect your eyes when the sun is very bright SYN **shades**

'sun god *n* [C] a god in some ancient religions who represents the sun or has power over it

'sun hat *n* [C] a hat that you wear to protect your head from the sun → see picture at HAT

sunk /sʌŋk/ the past tense and past participle of SINK¹

sunk·en /'sʌŋkən/ *adj* **1** [only before noun] having fallen to the bottom of the sea, a lake, or a river: *the wrecks of sunken ships* | *sunken treasure* **2 sunken cheeks/eyes etc** cheeks or eyes that have fallen inwards, especially because of age or illness SYN **hollow**: *Her eyes looked dull and sunken.* **3** [only before noun] built or placed at a lower level than the surrounding floor or ground: *Steps led down to a sunken garden.* | *a sunken bath*

'sun-kissed *adj literary* **1** sunny: *the famous sun-kissed resort of Acapulco* **2** sun-kissed skin or hair has been made an attractive colour by the sun

sun·lamp /'sʌnlæmp/ *n* [C] a lamp that produces a special light used for making your skin brown

sun·less /'sʌnləs/ *adj* having no light from the sun SYN **dark**: *the sunless depths of the ocean*

sun·light /'sʌnlaɪt/ ●●○ *n* [U] natural light that comes from the sun: *The water sparkled in the bright sunlight.* | **morning/afternoon/evening sunlight** *The garden looked lovely in the evening sunlight.* | ***Sunlight streamed*** (=came in large amounts) *through the windows.* | *a* ***shaft of sunlight*** (=beam of sunlight)

sun·lit /'sʌnlɪt/ *adj* made brighter by light from the sun: *a sunlit garden*

'sun lounge *n* [C] *BrE* a room with large windows and often a glass roof, designed to let in a lot of light SYN **sun porch** *AmE*

'sun ˌlounger *n* [C] a light chair like a folding bed, which you can sit or lie on outside → see picture at CHAIR¹

Sun·ni /'sʊni, 'sʌni/ *n* [C] a Muslim who follows one of the two main branches of the Muslim religion → **Shiite**

sun·nies /ˈsʌniz/ *n* [plural] *informal* SUNGLASSES

sun·ny /ˈsʌni/ ●●● S3 *adj*
1 having a lot of light from the sun SYN **bright**: *a warm sunny day | a sunny morning | a nice sunny room | I hope **it's sunny** tomorrow. | **sunny periods/spells/intervals*** (=periods when it is sunny) | *Tuesday will be dry with sunny spells.*
2 *informal* happy and friendly: *a sunny smile*

ˌsunny-side ˈup *adj* [not before noun] *AmE* an egg that is cooked sunny-side up is cooked in hot fat on one side only, and not turned over in the pan

ˈsun porch *n* [C] *AmE* a room with large windows and often a glass roof, designed to let in lots of light SYN **sun lounge** *BrE*

sun·rise /ˈsʌnraɪz/ ●●○ *n*
1 [U] the time when the sun first appears in the morning → **daybreak**: **at sunrise** *A farmer's day begins at sunrise.*
2 [C,U] the coloured part of the sky where the sun is appearing in the morning: *a picture of sunrise over Mount Fuji*

ˈsunrise ˌindustry *n* [C] an industry, such as ELECTRONICS or making computers, that uses modern processes and takes the place of older industries → **sunset industry**

sun·roof /ˈsʌnruːf/ *n* [C] a part of the roof of a car that you can open to let in air and light → see picture at CAR

sun·screen /ˈsʌnskriːn/ *n* [C,U] a cream or oil that you rub into your skin to stop the sun from burning you → **sunblock**

sun·set /ˈsʌnset/ ●●○ *n*
1 [U] the time of day when the sun disappears and night begins: **at sunset** *We take the flag down at sunset.*
2 [C,U] the coloured part of the sky where the sun is disappearing at the end of the day → **dusk**: *a glorious sunset*

ˈsunset ˌindustry *n* [C] an industry that uses old equipment and methods, usually in an area that once had many industries like it, and that is becoming less successful → **sunrise industry**: *sunset industries such as steel*

sun·shade /ˈsʌnʃeɪd/ *n* [C] an object shaped like an UMBRELLA, used especially in the past as protection from the sun SYN **parasol**

sun·shine /ˈsʌnʃaɪn/ ●●○ *n* [U]
1 the light and heat that come from the sun when there is no cloud: *We had three days of spring sunshine.* | **afternoon/morning/evening sunshine** *Couples strolled in the afternoon sunshine.*
2 *informal* happiness: *She brought sunshine into our lives.* | **ray of sunshine** (=a person or thing that makes you happy) *He was the only ray of sunshine in her life.*
3 *spoken informal* used when speaking to someone you are annoyed with: *Look, sunshine, I've had just about enough of you!*

sun·spot /ˈsʌnspɒt $ -spɑːt/ *n* [C] *technical* a small dark area on the sun's surface

sun·stroke /ˈsʌnstrəʊk $ -stroʊk/ *n* [U] fever, weakness etc caused by being outside in the sun for too long

sun·tan /ˈsʌntæn/ ●●○ *n* [C] brown skin that someone with pale skin gets after they have spent time in the sun SYN **tan** → **sunburn** —**suntanned** *adj*

ˈsuntan ˌlotion (*also* **ˈsuntan ˌoil**) *n* [C,U] a cream or oil that you rub into your skin to stop the sun from burning you too much

sun·trap /ˈsʌntræp/ *n* [C] a place that is sheltered and gets a lot of heat and light from the sun

ˈsun-up *n* [U] *old-fashioned* SUNRISE

ˈsun-ˌworshipper *n* [C] *informal* someone who likes to lie in the sun to get a SUNTAN

sup /sʌp/ *v* (**supped**, **supping**) **1** [T] to drink something **2** [I] *old-fashioned* to eat supper —**sup** *n* [C]

su·per¹ /ˈsuːpə $ -pər/ ●●● S2 *adj informal* extremely good SYN **wonderful**: *an old car in super condition | That sounds super. | What a super idea!*

super² *n* [C] *AmE informal* a SUPERINTENDENT(4)

super³ *adv AmE spoken* extremely: *Sorry, I'm super tired, I have to turn in.*

super- /suːpə $ -pər/ *prefix* more, larger, greater, or more powerful: *the super-rich | super-efficient | super-fit*

su·per·a·bun·dance /ˌsuːpərəˈbʌndəns/ *n* [singular] *formal* more than enough of something: **[+of]** *a superabundance of cars in our streets* —**superabundant** *adj*

su·per·an·nu·at·ed /ˌsuːpərˈænjueɪtɪd/ *adj formal* old and no longer useful or no longer able to do things: *superannuated sportsmen | superannuated computing equipment*

su·per·an·nu·a·tion /ˌsuːpərænjuˈeɪʃən/ *n* [U] *especially BrE technical* money paid as a PENSION¹, especially from your former employer

ˌsuperannuˈation ˌscheme *n* [C] *BrE* a type of PENSION PLAN that is paid for by your employer

su·perb /sjuːˈpɜːb, suː- $ sʊˈpɜːrb/ ●●○ *adj* [no comparative] extremely good SYN **excellent**: *The food was superb. | superb weather* THESAURUS GOOD —**superbly** *adv*

ˈSuper Bowl, the a football game played in the US each year, usually in late January on a Sunday, known as Super Bowl Sunday. The game decides which team is the winning team of the year in the NFL (=the American National Football League).

su·per·bug /ˈsuːpəbʌg $ -ər-/ *n* [C] a type of BACTERIA that cannot be killed by traditional drugs

su·per·charged /ˈsuːpəˌtʃɑːdʒd $ -pərˌtʃɑːrdʒd/ *adj* a supercharged engine is very powerful because air or FUEL is supplied to it at a higher pressure than normal

su·per·cil·i·ous /ˌsuːpəˈsɪliəs◂ $ -pər-/ *adj formal* behaving as if you think that other people are less important than you – used to show disapproval SYN **self-important**: *supercilious wine waiters* —**superciliously** *adv* —**superciliousness** *n* [U]

su·per·com·put·er /ˈsuːpəkəmˌpjuːtə $ -pərkəmˌpjuːtər/ *n* [C] a computer that is more powerful than almost all other computers

su·per·con·duc·tiv·i·ty /ˌsuːpəkɒndəkˈtɪvəti $ -pərkɑːn-/ *n* [U] the ability of some substances to allow electricity to flow through them very easily, especially at very low temperatures

su·per·con·duc·tor /ˌsuːpəkənˈdʌktə $ -pərkənˈdʌktər/ *n* [C] a substance that allows electricity to flow through it very easily, especially at very low temperatures

su·per·du·per /ˌsuːpəˈduːpə◂ $ -pərˈduːpər◂/ *adj spoken informal* extremely good

su·per·e·go /ˌsuːpərˈiːgəʊ, -ˈegəʊ $ -pərˈiːgoʊ/ *n* (*plural* **superegos**) [C] *technical* used in Freudian PSYCHOLOGY to refer to the part of your mind that tells you whether what you are doing is morally right or wrong SYN **conscience** → **ego**, **id**

su·per·fi·cial /ˌsuːpəˈfɪʃəl◂ $ -pər-/ ●○○ *adj*
1 NOT LOOKING/STUDYING CAREFULLY not studying or looking at something carefully and only seeing the most noticeable things: **superficial examination/study etc** *Even a superficial inspection revealed serious flaws. | Naturally, such visits can allow only the most superficial understanding of prison life.*
2 APPEARANCE seeming to have a particular quality, although this is not true or real: **superficial resemblance/similarity** *Despite their superficial similarities, the two novels are, in fact, very different. | Beneath his refined manners and superficial elegance lay something treacherous.* | **at/on a superficial level** *At a superficial level, things seem to have remained the same.*
3 WOUND/DAMAGE affecting only the surface of your skin or the outside part of something, and therefore not serious: *She escaped with only superficial cuts and bruises. | superficial damage*
4 PERSON someone who is superficial does not think about things that are serious or important – used to show disapproval SYN **shallow**: *All the other girls seemed silly and superficial to Darlene.*

S

5 NOT IMPORTANT superficial changes, difficulties etc are not important and do not have a big effect SYN **minor**: *superficial changes in government policies*
6 TOP LAYER existing in or relating to the top layer of something, especially soil, rock etc —**superficially** *adv* —**superficiality** /ˌsuːpəfɪʃiˈæləti $ -pər-/ *n* [U]

su·per·flu·i·ty /ˌsuːpəˈfluːəti $ -pər-/ *n formal* **a superfluity of sth** a larger amount of something than is necessary

su·per·flu·ous /suːˈpɜːfluəs $ -ˈpɜːr-/ *adj formal* more than is needed or wanted SYN **unnecessary**: *a modern building with no superfluous decoration* —**superfluously** *adv*

su·per·food /ˈsuːpəfuːd $ -pər-/ *n* [C] a food that is believed to contain a lot of substances that make you healthy: *These berries are considered a superfood because they are rich in vitamin C.* THESAURUS ▸ FOOD

super-G /ˈsuːpə dʒiː $ -pər-/ *n* [singular] (***super giant slalom***) a race in which competitors SKI as fast as possible down a course with turns in it

Su·per·glue /ˈsuːpəgluː $ -pər-/ *n* [U] *trademark* a very strong glue that sticks very quickly and is difficult to remove —**superglue** *v* [T]

su·per·grass /ˈsuːpəgrɑːs $ -pərgræs/ *n* [C] *BrE informal* a criminal who gives the police information about many other criminals, in order to get a less severe punishment

su·per·he·ro /ˈsuːpəˌhɪərəʊ $ -pərˌhɪroʊ/ *n* (*plural* **superheroes**) [C] a character in stories who uses special powers, such as great strength or the ability to fly, to help people

su·per·high·way /ˈsuːpəˌhaɪweɪ $ -pər-/ *n* [C] *AmE* a very large road on which you can drive fast for long distances → INFORMATION SUPERHIGHWAY

su·per·hu·man /ˌsuːpəˈhjuːmən◂ $ -pərˈhjuː-, -ˈjuː-/ *adj* much greater than ordinary human powers or abilities: **superhuman power/strength/effort etc** *It will require a superhuman effort to get the job done on time.*

su·per·im·pose /ˌsuːpərɪmˈpəʊz $ -ˈpoʊz/ *v* [T] **1** to put one picture, image, or photograph on top of another so that both can be partly seen: **superimpose sth on/onto sth** *A photo of a cup of cappuccino had been superimposed on a picture of Venice.* **2** to combine two systems, ideas, opinions etc so that one influences the other: **superimpose sth on/onto sth** *Eastern themes superimposed onto Western architecture* —**superimposition** /ˌsuːpərɪmpəˈzɪʃən/ *n* [U]

su·per·in·junc·tion /ˈsuːpərɪnˌdʒʌŋkʃən/ *n* [C] *BrE* an order given by a court which says that an event, fact, or claim cannot be publicly reported, and also says that the order itself cannot be reported

su·per·in·tend /ˌsuːpərɪnˈtend/ *v* [T] *formal* to be in charge of something, and control how it is done SYN **supervise** —**superintendence** *n* [U]

su·per·in·tend·ent /ˌsuːpərɪnˈtendənt/ *n* [C] **1** a high rank in the British police, or someone who has this rank **2** (*also* **superintendent of schools**) someone who is in charge of all the schools in a particular area in the US **3** someone who is officially in charge of a place, job, activity etc: *a young park superintendent* | *the superintendent of the Methodist Church in Hawaii* **4** *AmE* someone who is in charge of an apartment building and is responsible for making repairs in it SYN **caretaker** *BrE*

su·pe·ri·or¹ /suːˈpɪəriə $ sʊˈpɪriər/ ●●○ *adj*
1 better, more powerful, more effective etc than a similar person or thing, especially one that you are competing against OPP **inferior**: *Fletcher's superior technique brought him victory.* | **[+to]** *Your computer is far superior to mine.* | *He loves making fun of women. It makes him* ***feel superior***. | *a* ***vastly superior*** (=very much better, stronger etc) *army* THESAURUS ▸ BETTER
2 thinking that you are better than other people – used to show disapproval: *She had that superior tone of voice.*
3 [only before noun] having a higher position or rank than someone else OPP **inferior**: *Don't you usually salute a* ***superior officer***? | *a* ***superior court***
4 [only before noun] of very good quality – used especially in advertising: *a superior wine* → MOTHER SUPERIOR

GRAMMAR
• Something or someone is **superior to** another thing or person: *We can't say one language is superior to another.* ✗ Don't say: *superior than*
• **Superior** already has 'more' as part of its meaning. ✗ Don't say: *more superior*

superior² ●○○ *n* [C] someone who has a higher rank or position than you, especially in a job: *He had a good working relationship with his* ***immediate superior*** (=the person directly above him).

su·per·i·or·i·ty /suːˌpɪəriˈɒrəti $ sʊˌpɪriˈɔː-, -ˈɑː-/ ●○○ *n* [U]
1 the quality of being better, more skilful, more powerful etc than other people or things OPP **inferiority**: **[+of]** *the supposed superiority of the male sex* | **[+over]** *the intellectual superiority of humans over other animals* | **[+in]** *US superiority in air power*
2 an attitude that shows you think you are better than other people – used to show disapproval: *Janet always spoke with an air of superiority.* | *his* ***sense of superiority***

su·per·la·tive¹ /suːˈpɜːlətɪv, sjuː- $ sʊˈpɜːr-/ *adj* **1** excellent: *a superlative performance* **2** a superlative adjective or adverb expresses the highest degree of a particular quality. For example, the superlative form of 'tall' is 'tallest'. → **comparative**

superlative² *n* **1 the superlative** the superlative form of an adjective or adverb. For example, 'biggest' is the superlative of 'big'. → **comparative 2** [C] a word that shows that you think someone or something is very good: *an actress who deserves superlatives*

su·per·la·tive·ly /suːˈpɜːlətɪvli, sjuː- $ sʊˈpɜːr-/ *adv* extremely: *superlatively happy*

su·per·mall /ˈsuːpəmɔːl $ -pərmɒːl/ *n* [C] *AmE* a very big indoor shopping and entertainment centre, built outside a city centre

su·per·man /ˈsuːpəmæn $ -pər-/ *n* (*plural* **supermen** /-men/) [C] a man of unusually great ability or strength

su·per·mar·ket /ˈsuːpəˌmɑːkɪt $ -pərˌmɑːr-/ ●●● S3 *n* [C] a very large shop that sells food, drinks, and things that people need regularly in their homes

su·per·mod·el /ˈsuːpəˌmɒdl $ -pərˌmɑːdl/ *n* [C] a very famous fashion model

su·per·mom /ˈsuːpəmɒm $ -pərmɑːm/ *n* [C usually singular] *AmE informal* a mother who takes care of her children, cooks, cleans the house etc, in addition to having a job outside the house, and is admired because of this

su·per·nat·u·ral¹ /ˌsuːpəˈnætʃərəl◂ $ -pər-/ *adj* impossible to explain by natural causes, and therefore seeming to involve the powers of gods or magic: *supernatural powers* —**supernaturally** *adv*

supernatural² *n* **the supernatural** events, powers, and creatures that cannot be explained, and seem to involve gods or magic: *belief in the supernatural*

su·per·no·va /ˌsuːpəˈnəʊvə $ -pərˈnoʊ-/ *n* (*plural* **supernovae** *or* **supernovas**) [C] a very large exploding star

ˈsuper ˌpower *n* [C] a special power, such as the ability to fly, that a SUPERHERO has

su·per·pow·er /ˈsuːpəˌpaʊə $ -pərˌpaʊr/ *n* [C] a nation that has very great military and political power THESAURUS ▸ COUNTRY

su·per·script /ˈsuːpəskrɪpt $ -pər-/ *adj* written or printed above a number, letter etc —**superscript** *n* [C,U]

su·per·sede /ˌsuːpəˈsiːd $ -pər-/ *v* [T] if a new idea, product, or method supersedes another one, it becomes used instead because it is more modern or effective SYN **replace**: *Their map has since been superseded by photographic atlases.*

su·per·size¹ /ˈsuːpəsaɪz $ -pər-/ *adj* [only before noun] *AmE* a supersize drink or meal in a FAST FOOD restaurant is the largest size that the restaurant serves: *Could I get a supersize fries with that?*

S

supersize² *v* [T] *AmE* to give someone a larger meal or drink in a FAST FOOD restaurant

su·per·son·ic /ˌsuːpəˈsɒnɪk◂ $ -pərˈsɑː-/ *adj* faster than the speed of sound: *supersonic aircraft*

su·per·star /ˈsuːpəstɑː $ -pərstɑːr/ *n* [C] an extremely famous performer, especially a musician or film actor THESAURUS ▸ STAR

su·per·state /ˈsuːpəsteɪt $ -pər-/ *n* [C] a group of countries that are connected very closely politically, and who often act as if they were one country: *He was totally against the idea of a European superstate.*

su·per·sti·tion /ˌsuːpəˈstɪʃən $ -pər-/ ●○○ *n* [C,U] a belief that some objects or actions are lucky or unlucky, or that they cause events to happen, based on old ideas of magic: *the old superstition that walking under a ladder is unlucky*

su·per·sti·tious /ˌsuːpəˈstɪʃəs◂ $ -pər-/ ●○○ *adj* influenced by superstitions: *a superstitious woman* —**superstitiously** *adv*

su·per·store /ˈsuːpəstɔː $ -pərstɔːr/ ●●○ *n* [C] a very large shop that sells a large variety of or one type of product: *a DIY superstore*

su·per·struc·ture /ˈsuːpəˌstrʌktʃə $ -pərˌstrʌktʃər/ *n* [singular, U] **1** a structure that is built on top of the main part of something such as a ship or building **2** *formal* a political or social system that has developed from a simpler system: *the whole superstructure of capitalism*

su·per·tank·er /ˈsuːpəˌtæŋkə $ -pərˌtæŋkər/ *n* [C] an extremely large ship that can carry large quantities of oil or other liquids

su·per·vene /ˌsuːpəˈviːn $ -pər-/ *v* [I] *formal* to happen unexpectedly, especially in a way that stops or interrupts an event or situation

su·per·vise /ˈsuːpəvaɪz $ -pər-/ ●○○ *v* [I,T] to be in charge of an activity or person, and make sure that things are done in the correct way: *Griffiths closely supervised the research.* THESAURUS ▸ CONTROL

su·per·vi·sion /ˌsuːpəˈvɪʒən $ -pər-/ ●○○ *n* [U] when you supervise someone or something: *The baby needs constant supervision.* | **under sb's supervision** *Costumes and sets were also made under his supervision.*

su·per·vi·sor /ˈsuːpəvaɪzə $ -pərvaɪzər/ ●○○ *n* [C]
1 someone who supervises a person or activity
2 *AmE* someone who is a member of the city, COUNTY etc government in some parts of the US —**supervisory** /ˈsuːpəvaɪzəri $ ˌsuːpərˈvaɪzəri/ *adj*: *I had a supervisory role.*

su·per·wom·an /ˈsuːpəˌwʊmən $ -pər-/ *n* (*plural* **superwomen** /-ˌwɪmɪn/) [C] a woman who is successful in her job and also takes care of her children and home

su·pine /ˈsuːpaɪn, ˈsjuː- $ suːˈpaɪn/ *adj formal* **1** lying on your back OPP **prone**: *in a supine position* **2** allowing other people to make decisions instead of you, in a way that seems very weak: *a supine and cowardly press*

sup·per /ˈsʌpə $ -ər/ ●●● S3 *n* [C,U]
1 the meal that you have in the early evening SYN **dinner**: *Why don't you come over for supper on Friday?* | *We* ***had supper*** *in a small Italian place.* | *Have you* ***eaten supper****?* | *For supper we had spaghetti.*
2 *BrE* a very light meal, for example a drink and a piece of cake, that you have just before you go to bed

sup·plant /səˈplɑːnt $ səˈplænt/ *v* [T] to take the place of a person or thing so that they are no longer used, no longer in a position of power etc SYN **replace**: *Barker was soon supplanted as party leader.*

sup·ple /ˈsʌpəl/ *adj* **1** someone who is supple bends and moves easily and gracefully OPP **stiff**: *She exercises every day to keep herself supple.* **2** leather, skin, wood etc that is supple is soft and bends easily —**suppleness** *n* [U]

sup·ple·ment¹ /ˈsʌpləmənt/ ●○○ AWL *n* [C]
1 something that you add to something else to improve it or make it complete: *vitamins and other* ***dietary supplements*** | **[+to]** *The payments are a supplement to his usual salary.*
2 an additional part at the end of a book, or a separate part of a newspaper, magazine etc: *the Sunday supplements*
3 an amount of money that is added to the price of a service, hotel room etc: *Single rooms are available at a supplement.*

sup·ple·ment² /ˈsʌpləment/ ●○○ AWL *v* [T] to add something, especially to what you earn or eat, in order to increase it to an acceptable level: **supplement sth by/with sth** *Kia supplements her regular salary by tutoring in the evenings.* —**supplementation** /ˌsʌpləmenˈteɪʃən/ *n* [U]

sup·ple·men·ta·ry /ˌsʌpləˈmentəri◂/ ●○○ AWL *adj* provided in addition to what already exists SYN **additional**: *supplementary information* THESAURUS ▸ MORE

sup·pli·ant /ˈsʌpliənt/ *n* [C] *literary* a supplicant —**suppliant** *adj*

sup·pli·cant /ˈsʌplɪkənt/ (*also* **suppliant**) *n* [C] *literary* someone who asks for something, especially from someone in a position of power or from God

sup·pli·ca·tion /ˌsʌplɪˈkeɪʃən/ *n* [U] *literary* when someone asks for help from someone in power or from God: **in supplication** *Paolo knelt and bowed his head in supplication.*

sup·pli·er /səˈplaɪə $ -ər/ *n* [C] (*also* **suppliers** [plural]) a company or person that provides a particular product: **[+of]** *the UK's largest supplier of office equipment*

sup·ply¹ /səˈplaɪ/ ●●● S2 W2 *n* (*plural* **supplies**)
1 AMOUNT AVAILABLE [C] an amount of something that is available to be used: **[+of]** *I've only got a week's supply of tablets left.* | **plentiful/abundant/adequate etc supply** *There was a plentiful supply of cheap labour.* | *The nation's fuel supplies will not last forever.* | *To protect the* ***food supply****, the government ordered the slaughter of affected cattle.* → MONEY SUPPLY
2 NECESSARY THINGS **supplies** [plural] food, clothes, and things necessary for daily life or for a particular purpose, especially for a group of people over a period of time: *Supplies were brought in by air.* | **vital/essential/emergency supplies** *trucks loaded with emergency supplies* | **medical/school/cleaning etc supplies** *foreign aid used to buy medical supplies*
3 **gas/electricity/water etc supply** a system that is used to supply gas etc: *the public water supply* | *If you fail to pay your bill, you run the risk of having your electricity* ***supply cut off*** (=stopped).
4 ACT OF SUPPLYING [U] when you supply something: **[+of/to]** *The military government is trying to stop the supply of guns to the rebels.*
5 **supply ship/convoy/route etc** a ship etc used for bringing or storing supplies → **in short supply** at SHORT¹

supply² ●●● S3 W2 *v* (**supplied, supplying, supplies**) [T]
1 to provide people with something that they need or want, especially regularly over a long period of time: *Paint for the project was supplied by the city.* | **supply sb with sth** *An informer supplied the police with the names of those involved in the crime.* | **supply sth to sb** *They were arrested for supplying drugs to street dealers.*
2 **be well/poorly/generously supplied with sth** to have a lot of something, a little of something etc: *The lounge was well supplied with ashtrays.*

supˌply and deˈmand *n* [U] the relationship between the quantity of goods for sale and the quantity of goods that people want to buy, especially the way it influences prices: *the* ***law of supply and demand***

ˈsupply line *n* [C usually plural] the different ways, places etc that an army uses to send food and equipment to its soldiers during a war: *the threat to supply lines*

supˌply-side ecoˈnomics *n* [U] *technical* the idea that if the government reduces taxes, people will be able to make more goods and this will improve a country's economic situation

supˈply ˌteacher *n* [C] *BrE* a teacher who works at different schools doing the work of other teachers who are ill, on courses etc SYN **substitute teacher** *AmE*

S

sup·port¹ /səˈpɔːt $ -ɔːrt/ ●●● (S2) (W1) *v* [T]
1 AGREE AND HELP to say that you agree with an idea, group, or person, and usually to help them because you want them to succeed: *The bill was supported by a large majority in the Senate.* | **support sb in (doing) sth** *We need to support our teachers in their efforts to raise standards.* | *We* ***strongly support*** *the peace process.*
2 BE KIND TO SB to help someone by being sympathetic and kind to them during a difficult time in their life: *My wife supported me enormously.*
3 PROVIDE MONEY TO LIVE to provide enough money for someone to pay for all the things they need: *I* ***have*** *a wife and two children* ***to support****.* | **support sb by (doing) sth** *She supports her family by teaching evening classes.* | **support yourself** *I have no idea how I am going to support myself.*
4 GIVE MONEY TO STH to give money to a group, organization, or event etc to encourage it or pay for its costs: *There are a handful of charities which I support regularly.*
5 HOLD STH UP to hold the weight of something, keep it in place, or prevent it from falling: *The middle part of the bridge is supported by two huge towers.* | *During sleep, our spine no longer needs to* ***support*** *the* ***weight*** *of our body.* | **support yourself (on sth)** *I got to my feet, supporting myself on the side of the table.*
6 PROVE STH if results, facts, studies etc support an idea or statement, they show or prove that it is correct: *The results support our original theory.* | *There is little evidence to support such explanations.*
7 SPORTS TEAM *BrE* to like a particular sports team and go to watch the games they play: *Which* ***team*** *do you* ***support****?* | *I've supported Liverpool all my life.*
8 COMPUTERS to provide information and material to improve a computer program or system, or to make it keep working: *I don't think they support that version of the program anymore.*
9 LAND if land can support people or animals, it is of good enough quality to grow enough food for them to live: *This land can't support many cattle.*
10 WATER/AIR/EARTH if water, air, or earth can support life, it is clean enough, has enough oxygen etc to keep animals or plants alive: *Because of pollution, this lake is now too acid to support fish.* | *healthy soil that can support plant life*
11 support a habit to get money in order to pay for a bad habit, especially taking drugs: *He turned to crime to support his habit.*

THESAURUS

TO AGREE WITH AND HELP SB/STH

support to say that you agree with a person or idea, and usually help them because you want them to succeed: *We will support your decision.* | *Thanks to everyone who supported us throughout the trial.*
back to support a person or plan by providing money or practical help – used about governments or other powerful groups: *The £100 million scheme is backed by the British government.*
endorse to formally and officially say that you support a person, plan, or idea: *Agriculture ministers refused to endorse the Commission's proposals.*
get behind sb/sth to support a person or plan and help them be successful – used especially about a group of people: *The England fans really got behind the team.*
stand up for sb/sth to say that you support someone or something when they are being attacked: *You were the only person who stood up for me at the meeting.* | *He stood up for what he believed in.*
side with sb to support one of the people or groups involved in an argument – used especially when you disapprove of this or think it is unfair: *I felt she was siding with her mother rather than standing up for me.* | *The jury often side with the defendant in these situations.*

support² ●●● (S2) (W1) *n*
1 APPROVAL [U] approval, encouragement, and perhaps help for a person, idea, plan etc: *Local people have given us a lot of support in our campaign.* | **[+for]** *There was widespread support for the war.* | **in support** *They signed a petition in support of the pay claim.* | **[+of]** *He had the full support of the general committee.*
2 SYMPATHY/HELP [U] sympathy and help that you give to someone who is in a difficult situation or who is very unhappy: *I couldn't have made it through those times without the support of my boyfriend Rob.*
3 MONEY [U] money that you give a person, group, organization etc to help pay for their costs: *The European Union is considering whether to provide* ***financial support*** *for the expedition.* | **with sb's support** *With your support, we can help these youngsters.*
4 HOLDING STH UP [C,U] something that presses on something else to hold it up or in position: *The roof may need extra support.* | *the wooden supports of the bridge* | **for support** *She grabbed at his shoulders for support.*
5 PROOF [U] facts that show that an idea or statement is correct: **[+for]** *My own research provides some support for this view.*
6 COMPUTERS [U] the help or information that you receive to improve a computer system, make it continue working, or use it correctly: *our* ***technical support*** *team*
7 CONCERT/PERFORMANCE [U] a band, singer, or performer that performs for a short time at the same concert as a more famous and popular band etc: *We* ***played support to*** *a band called Shallow.* | *the* ***support band*** | *the* ***support act*** (=the support band)
8 SOLDIERS [U] help or protection that is given by one group of soldiers to another group who are fighting in a battle: *logistical support* | **air/ground support** (=help or protection that comes from people in aircraft or people on the ground)
9 FOR PART OF BODY [C] something that you wear to hold a weak or damaged part of your body in the right place: **back/neck/knee etc support** → CHILD SUPPORT, INCOME SUPPORT, LIFE SUPPORT SYSTEM, → **moral support** at MORAL¹(3)

COLLOCATIONS

VERBS

have support *The extreme right-wing parties don't have much popular support.*
give (your) support (*also* **lend (your) support** *formal*) *The American people gave him their enthusiastic support.*
pledge/offer (your) support (=say that you will support someone or something) *Both the opposition parties pledged full support for the new administration.*
get/draw support *The plan drew wide support from parents.*
win/gain/attract support *Try to win the support of local shopkeepers.*
enjoy/command support *formal* (=have support) *His views were too extreme to command general support.*
drum up/rally support (=get people's support by making an effort) | **enlist sb's support** *formal* (=ask for and get their support) | **mobilize support** (=get people to support something in an active way) | **build (up) support** (=increase it)
withdraw support (=no longer support) *He's decided to withdraw his support for the project.*

ADJECTIVES

public/popular support *There seemed to be no popular support for war.*
widespread/wide/general support *There is widespread support for the Government's proposal.*
strong support *A survey found strong support for the project among hospital staff.*
massive support *We have massive public support.*
sb's full support *That view deserves the full support of all farmers.*
whole-hearted/enthusiastic support *I want you to know that you have my whole-hearted support.*
active support (=approval and help) | **unanimous support** (=when all members of a group support something)

S

sup·port·er /sə'pɔːtə $ -ɔːrtər/ ●●● S3 W2 *n* [C]
1 someone who supports a particular person, group, or plan → **fan**: **strong/firm/staunch supporter** *one of Bush's staunchest supporters* | **[+of]** *supporters of animal rights legislation*
2 *BrE* someone who likes a particular sports team, and often goes to watch them play SYN **fan**: *Manchester United supporters*

sup'port group *n* [C] a group of people who meet to help each other with a particular problem, for example ALCOHOLISM

sup·port·ing /sə'pɔːtɪŋ $ -ɔːr-/ *adj* **1 supporting part/role/actor etc** a small part in a play or film, or the actor who plays such a part **2 supporting wall/beam etc** a wall etc that supports the weight of something

sup·por·tive /sə'pɔːtɪv $ -ɔːr-/ ●○○ *adj* giving help or encouragement, especially to someone who is in a difficult situation – used to show approval: *My family were very supportive throughout the divorce.*

sup·pose /sə'pəʊz $ -'poʊz/ ●●● S1 W1 *v* [T]

SPOKEN PHRASES

1 I suppose a) used to say you think something is true, although you are uncertain about it SYN **I guess**: **I suppose (that)** *I suppose you're right.* | *So things worked out for the best, I suppose.* | *'Aren't you pleased?' 'Yes, **I suppose so**.'* **b)** used when agreeing to let someone do something, especially when you do not really want to SYN **I guess**: *'Can we come with you?' 'Oh, **I suppose so**.'* **c)** used when saying in an angry way that you expect something is true SYN **I guess**: **I suppose (that)** *I suppose you thought you were being clever!* **d)** used to say that you think that something is probably true, although you wish it was not and hope someone will tell you it is not SYN **I guess**: **I suppose (that)** *I suppose it's too late to apply for that job now.* **e)** used when guessing that something is true SYN **I guess**: *She looked about 50, I suppose.*
2 I don't suppose (that) a) used to ask a question in an indirect way, especially if you think the answer will be 'no': *I don't suppose you have any idea where my address book is, do you?* **b)** used to ask for something in a very polite way: *I don't suppose you'd give me a lift to the station?* **c)** used to say that you think it is unlikely something will happen: *I don't suppose I'll ever see her again.*
3 do you suppose (that) ... ? used to ask someone their opinion about something, although you know that it is unlikely that they have any more information about the situation than you do: *Do you suppose this is the exact spot?* | **who/what/why etc do you suppose ... ?** *Who on earth do you suppose could have done this?* | *How do you suppose he got here?*
4 what's that supposed to mean? used when you are annoyed by what someone has just said: *'It sounds like things aren't going too well for you lately.' 'What's that supposed to mean?'*
5 suppose/supposing (that) used when talking about a possible condition or situation, and then imagining the result: *Look, suppose you lost your job tomorrow, what would you do?* | *Supposing it really is a fire!*

6 be supposed to do/be sth a) used to say what someone should or should not do, especially because of rules or what someone in authority has said: *We're supposed to check out of the hotel by 11 o'clock.* | *I'm not supposed to tell anyone.* | *What time are you supposed to be there?* **b)** used to say what was or is expected or intended to happen, especially when it did not happen: *No one was supposed to know about it.* | *The meeting was supposed to take place on Tuesday, but we've had to postpone it.* | *The new laws are supposed to prevent crime.* **c)** used to say that something is believed to be true by many people, although it might not be true or you might disagree: *The castle is supposed to be haunted.* | *'Dirty Harry' is supposed to be one of Eastwood's best films.* | *Mrs Carver is supposed to have a lot of money.*
7 to think that something is probably true, based on what you know SYN **presume**: *There were many more deaths than was first supposed.* | **suppose (that)** *What makes you suppose we're going to sell the house?* | ***There's no reason to suppose*** (=it is unlikely that) *he's lying.*

GRAMMAR
In more formal English, you can say **it is supposed that** something is true: *It is usually supposed that girls are less aggressive than boys.*
GRAMMAR GUIDE ▸ **VERBS**

8 *formal* to expect that something will happen or be true, and to base your plans on it: *The company's plan supposes a steady increase in orders.*

sup·posed /sə'pəʊzd, sə'pəʊzɪd $ -'poʊzd, -'poʊzɪd/ ●○○ *adj* [only before noun] claimed by other people to be true or real, although you do not think they are right: *gossip about Emma's supposed affair with Peter*

sup·pos·ed·ly /sə'pəʊzɪdli $ -'poʊ-/ ●○○ *adv* used when saying what many people say or believe is true, especially when you disagree with them: *How could a supposedly intelligent person be so stupid?* | [sentence adverb] *Anne is coming for a visit in March, supposedly.*

sup·po·si·tion /ˌsʌpə'zɪʃən/ *n* [C,U] something that you think is true, even though you are not certain and cannot prove it: *His version of events is **pure supposition**.* | **supposition (that)** *The police are acting on the supposition that she took the money.*

sup·pos·i·to·ry /sə'pɒzətəri $ sə'pɑːzətɔːri/ *n* (*plural* **suppositories**) [C] a small piece of solid medicine that is placed in someone's RECTUM or VAGINA

sup·press /sə'pres/ ●○○ *v* [T]
1 to stop people from opposing the government, especially by using force: *The uprising was ruthlessly suppressed.*
2 if important information or opinions are suppressed, people are prevented from knowing about them, even if they have a right to know: *The police were accused of suppressing evidence.*
3 to stop yourself from showing your feelings: *Harry could scarcely suppress a smile.* | *suppressed anger*
4 to prevent something from growing or developing, or from working effectively: *The virus suppresses the body's immune system.* —**suppressible** *adj* —**suppression** /sə'preʃən/ *n* [U]: *the suppression of opposition parties*

sup·press·ant /sə'presənt/ *n* [C] **appetite/cough/pain etc suppressant** a drug or medicine that makes you less hungry, cough less etc

su·pra·na·tion·al /ˌsuːprə'næʃənəl◂/ *adj* involving more than one country: *a supranational organization*

su·prem·a·cist /sʊ'preməsəst, sjuː- $ sʊ-, suː-/ *n* [C] someone who believes that their own particular race or group is better than any other → WHITE SUPREMACIST

su·prem·a·cy /sʊ'preməsi, sjuː- $ sʊ-, suː-/ *n* [U] the position in which you are more powerful or advanced than anyone else: *Japan's unchallenged supremacy in the field of electronics* → WHITE SUPREMACIST

su·preme /sʊ'priːm, sjuː- $ sʊ-, suː-/ ●○○ *adj*
1 having the highest position of power, importance, or influence: *the Supreme Allied Commander in Europe* | *a country where the car **reigns supreme*** (=is the most important thing)
2 [only before noun] the greatest possible: *supreme courage in the face of terrible danger* | *It required a supreme effort to stay awake.* | *a matter of supreme importance*
3 make the supreme sacrifice to die for your country, for a principle etc

Suˌpreme 'Being *n* [singular] *literary* God

Suˌpreme 'Court *n* [singular] the most important court of law in some countries or some states of the US

su·preme·ly /sʊ'priːmli, sjuː- $ sʊ-, suː-/ ●○○ *adv* [+adj/adv] extremely or to the greatest possible degree: *a supremely talented player*

su·prem·o /sʊ'priːməʊ, sjuː- $ sʊ'priːmoʊ, suː-/ *n* (*plural* **supremos**) [C] *BrE informal* someone who controls a particular activity, organization, or industry, and has unlimited powers

Supt. the written abbreviation of ***superintendent***

S

sur·charge¹ /ˈsɜːtʃɑːdʒ $ ˈsɜːrtʃɑːrdʒ/ *n* [C] money that you have to pay in addition to the basic price of something: **[+on]** *a 10% surcharge on airline tickets*

surcharge² *v* [T] to make someone pay an additional amount of money

sure¹ /ʃɔː $ ʃʊr/ ●●● S1 W1 *adj*

1 CERTAIN YOU KNOW STH [not before noun] confident that you know something or that something is true or correct SYN **certain**: *'That's Sarah's cousin.' 'Are you sure?' | 'What time does the show start?' 'I'm not sure.'* | **sure (that)** *I'm sure there's a logical explanation for all this. | Are you sure that you know how to get there? | My mother, I* **felt sure**, *had not met him before.* | **not sure how/where/when etc** *Henry wasn't sure how to answer this.* | **not sure if/whether** *I'm not sure if I'm pronouncing this correctly.* | **[+of]** *He wasn't even sure of his mother's name. | They were talking about her, she was* **sure of that**. | **[+about]** *'That's the man I saw in the building last night.' 'Are you* **quite sure** (=completely sure) *about that?'*

2 make sure a) to find out if something is true or to check that something has been done: *'Did you lock the front door?' 'I think so, but I'd better make sure.'* | **make sure (that)** *I wanted to make sure you were all right. | First, make sure the printer has enough paper in it.* **b)** to do something so that you can be certain of the result: **make sure (that)** *I'll walk you home, just to make sure no one bothers you.* | **make sure of (doing) sth** *Spain made sure of their place by holding Japan to a 1-1 draw. | Thomas would be sorry – she would* **make sure of that**.

3 CERTAIN ABOUT YOUR FEELINGS [not before noun] certain about what you feel, want, like etc: **sure (that)** *Are you sure you really want a divorce?* | **[+of]** *Carla says she is very sure of her love for Tony.*

4 CERTAIN TO BE TRUE certain to be true: **one thing is (for) sure** *One thing's for sure, we'll never be able to move this furniture on our own.* | **sure sign/indication** *Those black clouds are a sure sign of rain.*

5 CERTAIN TO HAPPEN/SUCCEED certain to happen, succeed, or have a particular result: **sure to do sth** *He's sure to get nervous and say something stupid.* | **sure way to do sth/of doing sth** *There was only one sure way of finding out – and that was to visit him.* | **sure thing/bet** *AmE* (=something that will definitely happen, win, succeed etc)

6 be sure of (doing) sth to be certain to get something or be certain that something will happen: *United must beat Liverpool to be sure of winning the championship. | You* **can be sure of** *one thing – there'll be a lot of laughs.*

7 sure of yourself confident in your own abilities and opinions, sometimes in a way that annoys other people: *Kids nowadays seem very sure of themselves.*

8 be sure to do sth *spoken* used to tell someone to remember to do something: *Be sure to ring and let us know you've got back safely.*

9 for sure a) *informal* certainly or definitely: *No one knows for sure what really happened.* **b)** *spoken* used to emphasize that something is true: *We'll always need teachers,* **that's for sure**. **c)** *AmE informal spoken* used to agree with someone

10 sure thing *spoken informal* used to agree to something: *'Can you pick me up later?' 'Sure thing.'*

11 to be sure *spoken formal* used to admit that something is true, before saying something that is the opposite: *It was difficult, to be sure, but somehow we managed to finish the job.*

12 (as) sure as hell *spoken informal* used to emphasize a statement: *If I could get you out of there, I sure as hell would.*

13 have a sure hold/footing if you have a sure hold or footing, your hands or feet are placed firmly so they cannot slip —**sureness** *n* [U]

THESAURUS

sure *adj* believing that something is definitely true or correct: *I'm sure that you're right. | 'The car was a BMW.' 'Are you sure?' | I'm not sure what the best thing to do is.*

certain *adj* completely sure. **Certain** is more formal than **sure**, and it is very commonly used in writing: *The police were certain that they had found the killer. | I think he's married, but I'm not certain about it.*

convinced *adj* sure that something is true, even though you cannot prove it: *She became convinced that her boyfriend was seeing someone else. | Brown's wife was convinced of his innocence.*

positive *adj especially spoken* completely sure that something is true, especially when other people are not sure: *She said she was positive that the exam was next Tuesday. | I'm absolutely positive I haven't made a mistake.*

satisfied *adj* sure that you know the truth about something that has happened, because you have enough information: *The authorities are now satisfied that her death was an accident.*

confident *adj* sure that something good will happen or that you will achieve something: *Doctors are confident that he'll make a full recovery. | A spokesman said the government was confident of winning the vote.*

have no doubt (*also* **be in no doubt**) *v phrase* to have no doubts in your mind about something: *I have no doubt that his story is true. | He was in no doubt about what he should do next.*

know *v* to have a strong feeling that something is true or correct: *I just know that she will love this necklace. | When the phone rang, we knew something terrible must have happened.*

sure² ●●● S1 *adv*

1 sure enough used to say that something did actually happen in the way that you said it would: *Sure enough, Mike managed to get lost.*

2 YES *spoken* used to say 'yes' to someone: *'Can you give me a ride to work tomorrow?' 'Sure.'*

3 ACCEPT THANKS *AmE spoken* used as a reply when you accept thanks from someone: *'Thanks for your help, Karen.' 'Sure.'*

4 EMPHASIZE *AmE informal* used to emphasize a statement: *It sure is hot out here. | I sure hope they get there all right.*

5 BEFORE STATEMENT *spoken* used at the beginning of a statement admitting that something is true, especially before adding something very different: *Sure Joey's happy now, but will it last?*

sure·fire /ˈʃɔːfaɪə $ ˈʃʊrfaɪr/ *adj* [only before noun] *informal* certain to succeed: *Children soon learn that bad behaviour is a* **surefire way** *of getting attention. | a* **surefire recipe** *for success*

ˌsure-ˈfooted *adj* **1** able to walk without sliding or falling, in a place where it is not easy to do this: *The hill ponies are very sure-footed.* **2** skilful and confident and not making any mistakes: *We need a sure-footed government which understands the nature of the economic challenges we face.*

sure·ly /ˈʃɔːli $ ˈʃʊrli/ ●●● S1 W2 *adv*

1 [sentence adverb] used to show that you think something must be true, especially when people seem to be disagreeing with you: *You must have heard about the riots, surely? | There must surely be some explanation. | Surely we can't just stand back and let this happen?*

2 surely not *spoken* used to show you cannot believe that something is true: *'The chairman's just handed in his resignation.' 'Surely not.'*

3 *formal* certainly: *Such sinners will surely be punished.*

4 *AmE old-fashioned* used to say 'yes' to someone or to express agreement with them → **slowly but surely** at SLOWLY(2)

sur·e·ty /ˈʃɔːrəti $ ˈʃʊr-/ *n* (*plural* **sureties**) [C,U] *law* **1** someone who will pay a debt, appear in court etc if someone else fails to do so **2 stand surety (for sb)** to be responsible for paying a debt, appearing in court etc if someone else fails to do so **3** money someone gives to make sure that someone will appear in court

surf¹ /sɜːf $ sɜːrf/ ●○○ *v* [I,T]

1 to ride on waves while standing on a special board

2 surf the Net/Internet to look quickly through information on the Internet for anything that interests you → SURFER, SURFING

surf² *n* [U] the white substance that forms on top of waves as they move towards the shore

sur·face¹ /ˈsɜːfɪs $ ˈsɜːr-/ ●●● S3 W1 *n* [C]
1 WATER/LAND the top layer of an area of water or land: **[+of]** *Dead leaves floated on the surface of the water.* | *Nearly 10% of the Earth's surface is covered by ice.* | *Gas bubbles in any liquid tend to* ***rise to the surface****.* | **beneath/under/below the surface** *The tunnel was some 300 feet below the surface.*
2 OUTSIDE/TOP LAYER the outside or top layer of something: **[+of]** *the surface of the vase* | *The road surfaces tend to be worse in the towns than in the country.* | *a frying pan with a non-stick surface* | **on sth's surface** *mold growing on the cheese's surface*
3 PERSON/SITUATION ETC **the surface** the qualities, emotions etc of someone or something that are easy to notice, but which are not the only or not the real qualities, emotions etc: **on the surface** *On the surface, it seems a simple story.* | *Half an hour later, Enid had calmed down,* ***at least on the surface****.* | **beneath the surface** *I sensed a lot of tension and jealousy beneath the surface.* | *Prejudice is* ***never far beneath the surface*** (=often appears) *in the region.* | **rise/be brought/come to the surface** *Violence has risen to the surface in the inner city.*
4 FOR WORKING ON a flat area on the top of a cupboard, table, desk etc, that you use for cooking or working on: **work/kitchen surface** *Keep kitchen surfaces clean and tidy.* | *Work on a clean, flat surface.*
5 SIDE OF AN OBJECT one of the sides of an object: *How many surfaces does a cube have?* → **scratch the surface** at SCRATCH¹(8)

surface² *v* **1** [I] if information, feelings, or problems surface, they become known about or easy to notice: **[+in]** *Rumors about the killings have* ***begun to surface*** *in the press.* | *the jealousy that had surfaced in her* **2** [I] if someone or something surfaces, they suddenly appear somewhere, especially after being gone or hidden for a long time SYN **pop up**: *Last year Toole surfaced again in Cuba.* **3** [I] to rise to the surface of water: *divers surfacing near the boat* **4** [I] *BrE informal* to get out of bed, especially late: *Joe never surfaces before midday on Sunday.* **5** [T] to put a surface on a road

surface³ *adj* [only before noun] **1** relating to the part of the army, navy etc that travels by land or on the sea, rather than by air or under the sea: *the Navy's* ***surface forces*** **2** appearing to be true or real, but not representing what someone really feels or what something is really like SYN **superficial**: *Beneath the surface calm, she felt very insecure.*

ˈsurface ˌarea *n* [C] the area of the outside of an object that can be measured

ˈsurface ˌmail *n* [U] the system of sending letters or packages by land or sea, rather than by air

ˌsurface ˈtension *n* [U] the way the MOLECULES in the surface of a liquid stick together so that the surface is held together

ˌsurface-to-air ˈmissile *n* [C] a MISSILE that is fired at planes from the land or from a ship

ˌsurface-to-surface ˌmissile *n* [C] a MISSILE that is fired from land or a ship at another point on land or at another ship

surf·board /ˈsɜːfbɔːd $ ˈsɜːrfbɔːrd/ *n* [C] a long piece of plastic, wood etc that you stand on when you go surfing

sur·feit /ˈsɜːfɪt $ ˈsɜːr-/ *n formal* **a surfeit of sth** an amount of something that is too large or that is more than you need SYN **excess**: *a surfeit of food and drink*

surf·er /ˈsɜːfə $ ˈsɜːrfər/ *n* [C] **1** someone who rides on waves while standing on a special board **2 Net/Internet/Web surfer** someone who looks quickly through information on the Internet to find information that interests them

surf·ing /ˈsɜːfɪŋ $ ˈsɜːr-/ ●●○ *n* [U]
1 the activity or sport of riding over the waves on a special board: *When we were in Hawaii, we* ***went surfing*** *every day.*
2 the activity of looking quickly through information on the Internet to find something that interests you → CHANNEL SURFING

surf 'n' turf /ˌsɜːf ən ˈtɜːf $ ˌsɜːrf ən ˈtɜːrf/ *n* [U] a meal that includes SEAFOOD and meat, usually STEAK, on the same plate

surge¹ /sɜːdʒ $ sɜːrdʒ/ ●○○ *v* [I]
1 [always + adv/prep] to suddenly move very quickly in a particular direction: **[+forward/through etc]** *The taxi surged forward.* | *The crowd surged through the gates.*
2 (*also* **surge up**) if a feeling surges or surges up, you begin to feel it very strongly: *She could feel anger surging inside her.*
3 [usually + adv/prep] if a large amount of a liquid, electricity, chemical etc surges, it moves very quickly and suddenly: *A wave surged up towards them.* | *Adrenalin surged through her veins.*
4 to suddenly increase SYN **shoot up**: *Oil prices surged.*

surge² ●○○ *n* [C usually singular]
1 **a surge of sth** a sudden large increase in a feeling: *a surge of excitement*
2 a sudden increase in amount or number: **[+in/of]** *a surge in food costs* | *a surge of reporters' interest in his finances*
3 a sudden movement of a lot of people: **[+of]** *a surge of refugees into the country*
4 a sudden quick movement of a liquid, electricity, chemical etc through something: *a device that protects your computer against electrical surges*

sur·geon /ˈsɜːdʒən $ ˈsɜːr-/ ●●○ *n* [C] a doctor who does operations in a hospital THESAURUS DOCTOR → DENTAL SURGEON

sur·ge·ry /ˈsɜːdʒəri $ ˈsɜːr-/ ●●○ S3 W2 *n* (*plural* surgeries)
1 [U] medical treatment in which a surgeon cuts open your body to repair or remove something inside → **operation**: **[+on]** *She required surgery on her right knee.* | **[+for]** *He underwent surgery for lung cancer.* | **in surgery** *She was in surgery for two hours Thursday.* → COSMETIC SURGERY, PLASTIC SURGERY
2 [U] *especially AmE* the place where operations are done in a hospital SYN **operating room** *AmE*, **theatre** *BrE*: *Dr. Hanson is in surgery.*
3 [C] *BrE* a place where a doctor or DENTIST gives treatment SYN **office** *AmE*
4 [U] *BrE* a regular period each day when people can see a doctor or DENTIST SYN **office hours** *AmE*: *Surgery is from 9 am to 1 pm on weekdays.*
5 [C] *BrE* a special period of time when people can see a MEMBER OF PARLIAMENT to discuss problems

COLLOCATIONS

VERBS

have surgery *Leslie had surgery on her toe last year.*
undergo surgery *formal* (=have surgery) *He underwent surgery to remove a bullet from his chest.*
do/carry out surgery (*also* **perform surgery** *formal*) *A San Antonio doctor has volunteered to perform the surgery at no cost.*
need surgery (*also* **require surgery** *formal*) *He is likely to need surgery in the near future.*

ADJECTIVES/NOUN + surgery

successful *The surgery was successful and he's recovering well.*
major/minor surgery *He will require major surgery to remove the lump.*
heart/knee/brain etc surgery *She is now fit again after knee surgery.*
emergency surgery (=done quickly, in an emergency) | **cosmetic/plastic surgery** (=surgery to improve someone's appearance) | **laser surgery** (=surgery done using a laser) | **keyhole surgery** (=surgery done through a very small hole in the skin)

S

COMMON ERRORS

⚠ Don't say 'make surgery'. For a doctor, say **perform surgery** or **carry out surgery**. For the patient, say **have surgery** or **undergo surgery**.

sur·gi·cal /ˈsɜːdʒɪkəl $ ˈsɜːr-/ ●○○ *adj* [only before noun]
1 relating to or used for medical operations: *surgical techniques* | **surgical equipment/instruments/treatment** *scalpels and other surgical instruments* → see picture at MASK[1]
2 surgical stocking/collar etc *BrE* a STOCKING etc that someone wears to support a part of their body that is injured or weak
3 done very carefully and in exactly the right place: ***With surgical precision** he cut four inches off the legs of the jeans.* —**surgically** /-kli/ *adv*: *The lump was **surgically removed**.*

ˌsurgical ˈspirit *n* [U] *BrE* a type of alcohol used for cleaning wounds or skin SYN **rubbing alcohol** *AmE*

ˌsurgical ˈstrike *n* [C] a carefully planned quick military attack intended to destroy something in a particular place without damaging the surrounding area

sur·ly /ˈsɜːli $ ˈsɜːrli/ *adj* bad-tempered and unfriendly SYN **sullen**: *a surly teenager* —**surliness** *n* [U]

sur·mise /səˈmaɪz $ sər-/ *v* [T] *formal* to guess that something is true, using the information you know already: **surmise that** *When she came in, he didn't look up, so she surmised that he was in a bad mood.* —**surmise** *n* [C,U]: *Charles was glad to have his surmise confirmed.*

sur·mount /səˈmaʊnt $ sər-/ *v* [T] *formal* **1** to succeed in dealing with a problem or difficulty SYN **overcome**: *He has had to surmount immense physical disabilities.* **2** to be above or on top of something: *a tower surmounted by a dome* GRAMMAR **Surmount** is usually passive in this meaning. —**surmountable** *adj*

sur·name /ˈsɜːneɪm $ ˈsɜːr-/ ●●● S3 *n* [C] the name that you share with your parents, or often with your husband if you are a married woman, and which in English comes at the end of your full name SYN **last name, family name** → **forename**

sur·pass /səˈpɑːs $ sərˈpæs/ ●○○ *v* [T] to be even better or greater than someone or something else: *He had **surpassed** all our **expectations**.* | *The number of multiple births has surpassed 100,000 for the first time.* | **surpass yourself** (=do something better than you have ever done before) *With this painting he has surpassed himself.*

sur·pass·ing /səˈpɑːsɪŋ $ sərˈpæ-/ *adj* [only before noun] *literary* much better than that of other people or things SYN **outstanding**: *a picture of surpassing beauty*

sur·plice /ˈsɜːplɪs $ ˈsɜːr-/ *n* [C] a piece of clothing made of white material, worn over other clothes by priests or singers in church

sur·plus[1] /ˈsɜːpləs $ ˈsɜːr-/ ●○○ *n* [C,U]
1 an amount of something that is more than what is needed or used SYN **excess**: *Any surplus can be trimmed away.* | **[+of]** *a surplus of crude oil*
2 the amount of money that a country or company has left after it has paid for all the things it needs: *a huge **budget surplus** of over £16 billion* → TRADE SURPLUS

surplus[2] ●○○ *adj*
1 more than what is needed or used: *Ethiopia has no surplus food.* | **surplus cash/funds/revenues** *Surplus cash can be invested.*
2 be surplus to requirements *BrE formal* to be no longer necessary: *He found out he was surplus to requirements in London and left.*

sur·prise[1] /səˈpraɪz $ sər-/ ●●● S3 W2 *n*
1 EVENT [C] an unexpected or unusual event → **shock**: *What a surprise to find you here!* | *We had a big surprise when we found out the truth.*
2 FEELING [C,U] the feeling you have when something unexpected or unusual happens → **shock**: *The man had a look of surprise on his face.* | **in/with surprise** *Bill looked at him in surprise.* | **to sb's surprise** (=in a way that surprises someone) *Much to his surprise, she gave him her phone number.*

GRAMMAR

You say: *To my surprise, the whole family was there.*
✗ Don't say: *for my surprise*

3 take/catch sb by surprise to happen unexpectedly: *The question took her by surprise.*
4 take sb/sth by surprise to suddenly attack a place or an opponent when they are not ready: *The guerrillas were killed when army troops took them by surprise.*
5 GIFT/PARTY ETC [C usually singular] an unexpected present, trip etc which you give to someone or organize for them, often on a special occasion: **[+for]** *'I've got a surprise for you,' she said.*
6 surprise guest/visitor etc someone who arrives somewhere unexpectedly
7 surprise! *spoken* used when you are just about to show someone something that you know will surprise them
8 a) surprise, surprise used when saying in a joking way that you expected something to happen or be true: *The American TV networks are, surprise, surprise, full of stories about the election.* **b)** *BrE spoken* used when you suddenly appear in front of someone who you know is not expecting to see you
9 METHOD [U] the use of methods which are intended to cause surprise: *An **element of surprise** is important to any attack.*

COLLOCATIONS

VERBS

be a surprise *His decision to marry was a complete surprise.*
come as a surprise (=be surprising) *The announcement came as a surprise to most people.*
get/have a surprise *We got a surprise when we got home and found him waiting for us.*
give sb a surprise *She wanted to give him a surprise.*
have a surprise for sb (=be planning to give someone a surprise)

ADJECTIVES

a big/great surprise *The results were a big surprise.*
a complete/total surprise *The news came as a complete surprise.*
a nice/pleasant/lovely surprise *It's a lovely surprise to see you.*
an unpleasant/nasty surprise

PHRASES

come as no surprise (=not be surprising) *It came as no surprise when Lester got the job.*
be in for a surprise (=be going to have a surprise) | **there's a surprise in store (for sb)** (=something unexpected is going to happen)

surprise + NOUN

a surprise visit *Environmental health inspectors made a surprise visit to the restaurant.*
a surprise party *His friends had planned a surprise party for him.*
a surprise announcement | **a surprise victory** | **a surprise attack** | **a surprise move** (=an unexpected action)

COMMON ERRORS

⚠ Don't say 'a bad surprise'. Say **an unpleasant surprise** or **a nasty surprise**.

surprise[2] ●●● S3 W2 *v* [T]
1 to make someone feel surprised → **shock**: *His strange question surprised her.* | **it surprises sb to see/find/know etc** *It had surprised me to find how fussy he was about some things.* | *I didn't know you two knew each other. Mind you, **it doesn't surprise me**.* | ***What surprised** me **most** was that she didn't seem to care.* | **it surprises sb that/how/what** *Looking back, does it surprise you that she left?* | ***It wouldn't surprise** me **if** he married Jo.*
2 to find, catch, or attack someone when they are not expecting it, especially when they are doing something

they should not be doing: *A security guard surprised the burglars in the storeroom.*

sur·prised /səˈpraɪzd $ sər-/ ●●● S2 W2 *adj* having a feeling of surprise: *He* ***looked surprised*** *to see Cassie standing by the front door.* | **[+at/by]** *We were greatly surprised at the news.* | **surprised (that)** *She was surprised that no one was there to greet her.* | **surprised to see/hear/learn etc** *I bet she'll be really surprised to see me.* | *He had a* ***surprised look*** *on his face.* | ***Don't be surprised if*** *the interviewer is rather direct.* | ***I wouldn't be surprised*** *if she married that fellow.*

THESAURUS

surprised having the feeling you get when something happens that you did not expect: *I was surprised to see her again so soon.* | *I'm really surprised that he remembered my birthday.* | *Nobody was surprised when they split up.* | *a surprised expression*
amazed [not before noun] extremely surprised, especially by something good or by something that seems hard to believe: *I'm amazed that he survived.* | *You'll be amazed when you see the difference.*
astonished extremely surprised: *He was astonished by how much she had changed.* | *an astonished look*
astounded extremely surprised or shocked. Astounded sounds a little more formal and a little stronger than **astonished**: *She was astounded by how much it cost.*
staggered/flabbergasted/dumbfounded [not before noun] extremely surprised or shocked: *'What?' I said, utterly staggered by his answer.* | *She just sat there looking flabbergasted.*
stunned so surprised that you do not know what to do or say: *I was too stunned to protest.* | *Everyone seemed stunned by his outburst.* | *They listened in stunned silence.*
speechless so surprised that you cannot speak: *I was speechless when I heard that I'd won.*
taken aback [not before noun] surprised by what someone says or does, so that you are not sure how to react: *I was a little taken aback by her question.*
nonplussed /nɒnˈplʌst $ nɑːn-/ *formal* surprised and a little confused: *She was nonplussed by such an odd question.*

sur·pris·ing /səˈpraɪzɪŋ $ sər-/ ●●● S3 W3 *adj* unusual or unexpected: *She told me a surprising thing.* | *A surprising number of his paintings have survived.* | **it is surprising (that)** *It is not surprising that most parents experience occasional difficulties.* | **it is surprising how/what etc** *It's surprising how quickly you get used to things.* | *It is* ***hardly surprising*** *that new mothers often suffer from depression.*

THESAURUS

surprising making you feel surprised: *It's surprising how quickly you get used to it.* | *We got some very surprising results.*
astonishing/astounding very surprising. Astounding sounds a little more formal and a little stronger than **astonishing**: *The results of the tests were astounding.* | *Things are changing* ***at an astonishing speed***.
extraordinary very unusual and surprising: *It is extraordinary that such a young boy should be so good at maths.*
amazing very surprising – used especially about good or impressive things: *an amazing achievement* | *It's amazing what you can do when you really try.*
staggering very surprising, especially by being so large: *The project cost a staggering $8 million.*
unbelievable (*also* **incredible**) so surprising that you can hardly believe it: *It is unbelievable that she is only the same age as me.* | *The incredible thing is that he thinks he is ugly.*

sur·pris·ing·ly /səˈpraɪzɪŋli $ sər-/ ●●○ W3 *adv* unusually or unexpectedly: *The exam was surprisingly easy.* | ***Not surprisingly***, *with youth unemployment so high, some school-leavers with qualifications fail to find jobs.*

sur·real /səˈrɪəl/ *adj* a situation or experience that is surreal is very strange and difficult to understand, like something from a dream: *The house was a surreal mixture of opulence and decay.* THESAURUS ▸ STRANGE

sur·real·is·m /səˈrɪəlɪzəm/ *n* [U] a style of 20th-century art or literature in which the artist or writer connects unrelated images and objects in a strange way —**surrealist** *adj*: *a surrealist painting* —**surrealist** *n* [C]

sur·real·is·tic /səˌrɪəˈlɪstɪk◂/ *adj* **1** seeming very strange because of a combination of many unusual unrelated events, images etc **2** *literary* relating to surrealism SYN **surrealist** —**surrealistically** /-kli/ *adv*

sur·ren·der[1] /səˈrendə $ -ər/ ●●○ *v*
1 [I] to say officially that you want to stop fighting, because you realize that you cannot win: *Germany surrendered on May 7th, 1945.* | *The terrorists were given ten minutes to surrender.*
2 [I,T] to go to the police or the authorities, and say that you want to stop trying to escape from them: **surrender (yourself) to sb** *He immediately surrendered himself to the authorities.*
3 [T] to give up something or someone, especially because you are forced to: *They agreed to surrender their weapons.* | *She was reluctant to surrender her independence.* | *Marchers who had cameras were forced to surrender their film.*
4 surrender to sth to allow yourself to be controlled or influenced by something: *Colette surrendered to temptation and took out a cigarette.*
5 [T] *formal* to give something such as a ticket or a PASSPORT to an official: **surrender sth to sb** *Steir voluntarily surrendered his license to the State.*

surrender[2] ●○○ *n* [singular, U]
1 when you say officially that you want to stop fighting because you realize that you cannot win: *the humiliation of* ***unconditional surrender*** (=accepting total defeat) | **surrender to sb/sth** *the Nazis' surrender to the Allied forces*
2 when you give away something or someone, usually because you are forced to: **[+of]** *a surrender of power* | *the surrender of all illegal weapons*
3 when you allow yourself to be controlled or influenced by something: *total surrender to drug addiction*

sur·rep·ti·tious /ˌsʌrəpˈtɪʃəs◂ $ ˌsɜː-/ *adj* done secretly or quickly because you do not want other people to notice: *Rory tried to sneak a* ***surreptitious glance*** *at Adam's wristwatch.* —**surreptitiously** *adv* —**surreptitiousness** *n* [U]

sur·rey /ˈsʌri $ ˈsɜː-/ *n* [C] *AmE* a light carriage with two seats, which was pulled by a horse and was used in the past

sur·ro·gate[1] /ˈsʌrəgeɪt, -gət $ ˈsɜːr-/ *adj* [only before noun] a surrogate person or thing is one that takes the place of someone or something else: *William was acting as a* ***surrogate father*** *for his brother's son.*

surrogate[2] *n* [C] **1** a person or thing that takes the place of someone or something else: **[+for]** *Bright-light therapy is used as a surrogate for sunshine.* **2** a surrogate mother

ˌsurrogate ˈmother (*also* **surrogate**) *n* [C] a woman who has a baby for another woman who cannot have one, and then gives her the baby after it is born

sur·round[1] /səˈraʊnd/ ●●● W2 *v* [T]
1 to be all around someone or something on every side: **be surrounded by sth** *The field was surrounded by trees.* | *He glared at the people who surrounded the tent.* GRAMMAR **Surround** is often passive in this meaning.
2 be surrounded by sb/sth to have a lot of a particular type of people or things near you: *He's always been surrounded by people who adore him.*
3 if police or soldiers surround a place, they arrange themselves in positions all the way around it: *Armed police surrounded a house in the High Street.*
4 to be closely related to a situation or event: *Some of the issues surrounding alcohol abuse are very complex.* | *Silence and secrecy surround the murder.*

S

5 surround yourself with sb/sth to choose to have certain people or things near you all the time: *The designer surrounded himself with exquisite objects.*

surround² *n* [C] an area around the edge of something, especially one that is decorated or made of a different material: *a solid mahogany fire surround*

sur·round·ing /səˈraʊndɪŋ/ ●●○ *adj* [only before noun] near or around a particular place SYN **nearby**: *Troops sealed off the* ***surrounding area****.* | *We decided to explore the* ***surrounding countryside****.*

sur·round·ings /səˈraʊndɪŋz/ ●●○ *n* [plural] the objects, buildings, natural things etc that are around a person or thing at a particular time: **sb's surroundings** *He switched on the light and examined his surroundings.* | *I need to work in pleasant surroundings.*

surˈround-ˌsound, **surround sound** *n* [U] a system of four or more SPEAKERS (=pieces of equipment that sound comes out of) used so that sounds from a film or television programme come from all directions —**surround-sound** *adj* [only before noun]: *surround-sound speakers*

sur·tax /ˈsɜːtæks $ ˈsɜːr-/ *n* [U] an additional tax on money you earn if it is higher than a particular amount

sur·veil·lance /səˈveɪləns $ sər-/ *n* [U] **1** when the police, army etc watch a person or place carefully because they may be connected with criminal activities: **[+of]** *24-hour surveillance of the building* | **under surveillance** *They were under constant close surveillance day and night.* | *The suspects were* ***kept under surveillance****.* | *electronic surveillance equipment* **2** when one country watches the military activities of another country to see what they are planning to do: *a surveillance mission* | *surveillance aircraft* **3** when doctors, health departments etc watch an ill person or watch the development of a disease in a population: **under surveillance** *Diane was placed under psychiatric surveillance.*

S

sur·vey¹ /ˈsɜːveɪ $ ˈsɜːr-/ ●●○ W2 AWL *n* [C]
1 a set of questions that you ask a large number of people in order to find out about their opinions or behaviour → **poll**: **carry out/conduct a survey** (=do a survey) *We conducted a survey of parents in the village.* | **[+of]** *a survey of US businesses* | **survey shows/reveals (that)** *The survey showed that Britain's trees are in good health.*
2 an examination of an area of land in order to make a map of it → **surveyor**
3 *BrE* an examination of a house or other building done especially for someone who wants to buy it → **surveyor**
4 a general description or report about a particular subject or situation: *a survey of modern English literature*

sur·vey² /səˈveɪ $ sər-/ ●○○ AWL *v* [T]
1 to ask a large number of people questions in order to find out their attitudes or opinions: *Of the 100 companies surveyed, 10% had a turnover of £50m to £99m.* GRAMMAR **Survey** is often passive in this meaning.
2 to look at or consider someone or something carefully, especially in order to form an opinion about them: *She turned to survey her daughter's pale face.* | *They got out of the car to survey the damage.*
3 *BrE* to examine the condition of a house or other building and make a report on it, especially for people who want to buy it
4 to examine and measure an area of land and record the details on a map: *There were many voyages to survey the ocean depths in the nineteenth century.*

ˈsurvey ˌcourse *n* [C] *AmE* a university course that gives an introduction to a subject for people who have not studied it before

sur·vey·or /səˈveɪə $ sərˈveɪər/ *n* [C] someone whose job is to examine the condition of a building, or to measure and record the details of an area of land → QUANTITY SURVEYOR

sur·viv·al /səˈvaɪvəl $ sər-/ ●●○ W3 AWL *n*
1 [U] the state of continuing to live or exist: **[+of]** *Illegal hunting is threatening the survival of the species.* | *The doctors gave him a one in ten* ***chance of survival****.* | *A lot of small companies are having to* ***fight for survival*** (=work hard in order to continue to exist).
2 survival of the fittest a situation in which only the strongest and most successful people or things continue to exist
3 a survival from sth *especially BrE* something that has continued to exist from a much earlier period, especially when similar things have disappeared SYN **relic**: *The cult is a survival from the old Zoroastrian religion.*

sur·viv·al·ist /səˈvaɪvəlɪst $ sər-/ *n* [C] someone who makes preparations so that they will be able to survive if something very bad happens that affects a lot of people, for example a NUCLEAR war

surˈvival kit *n* [C] a set of things in a special container that you need to help you stay alive if you get hurt or lost

sur·vive /səˈvaɪv $ sər-/ ●●● S2 W2 AWL *v*
1 [I,T] to continue to live after an accident, war, or illness: *Only 12 of the 140 passengers survived.* | *She survived the attack.* | *people who survive cancer*
2 [I,T] to continue to live normally in spite of many problems: *I'm sure she will survive this crisis.* | *I've had a tough few months, but I'll survive.*
3 [I] to manage to live a normal life even though you have very little money: **[+on]** *I don't know how you all manage to survive on Jeremy's salary.* | *the amount that a family needs each week just to survive*
4 [I] to continue to exist after a long time: *A few pages of the original manuscript still survive.* | **[+from]** *Several buildings in the town have survived from medieval times.* | **[+into]** *an old custom which has survived into the twenty-first century* | **[+as]** *The main building was demolished, but the library still survives as a museum.*
5 [I,T] to continue to be successful: *The car industry cannot survive without government help.* | *A lot of smaller firms did not survive the recession.*
6 [T] to live longer than someone else, usually someone closely related to you: *He is survived by his wife Sue.*

sur·vi·vor /səˈvaɪvə $ sərˈvaɪvər/ ●●○ AWL *n* [C]
1 someone who continues to live after an accident, war, or illness: **[+of]** *Emergency help is needed for survivors of the earthquake.* | *She was the* ***sole survivor*** (=only survivor) *of the massacre.*
2 someone who manages to live normally in spite of many problems: *Don't worry about Kurt; he's a survivor.*
3 someone who continues to live after other members of their family have died: *She was the last survivor of the family.*
4 a company that continues to be successful in spite of many problems: *The company hopes to be one of the survivors of this recession.*

sus·cep·ti·bil·i·ty /səˌseptəˈbɪləti/ *n* (*plural* **susceptibilities**) **1** [C,U] how easily someone or something is affected by something: **[+to]** *One of the side effects of the drug is an increased susceptibility to infections.* **2 sb's susceptibilities** *formal* someone's feelings, especially when they are easily offended or upset: *I knew I would have to be careful not to* ***offend*** *their* ***susceptibilities****.*

sus·cep·ti·ble /səˈseptəbəl/ ●○○ *adj*
1 likely to suffer from a particular illness or be affected by a particular problem → **immune**: **[+to]** *Older people are more susceptible to infections.* | *Soil on the mountain slopes is very susceptible to erosion.*
2 a susceptible person is easily influenced or attracted by someone or something SYN **impressionable**: *A lot of TV advertising is aimed at susceptible young children.* | **[+to]** *She was very susceptible to flattery.*
3 susceptible of sth *formal* if something is susceptible of an action, that action can be done to it: *Working conditions are susceptible of improvement by legislation.*

su·shi /ˈsuːʃi/ *n* [U] a Japanese dish that consists of small cakes of cooked rice served with raw fish

sus·pect¹ /səˈspekt/ ●●○ W3 *v* [T]
1 to think that something is probably true, especially something bad: **suspect (that)** *I suspected that there was something wrong with the engine.* | *She* ***strongly suspected*** *he*

*was lying to her. | She's not going to be very happy about this, **I suspect**.*
2 to think that something bad has happened or is happening: *The doctors suspected pneumonia.* | **suspect murder/foul play** *The position of the body led the police to suspect murder.* | **suspect something/nothing/anything** *He never suspected anything.*
3 to think that someone is probably guilty of a crime: *Who do you suspect?* | **suspect sb of (doing) sth** *He's suspected of murder.* | *Pilcher was suspected of giving away government secrets to the enemy.*
4 to think that something is not honest or true: *I began to suspect his motives in inviting me.*

GRAMMAR

Patterns with suspect

- You **suspect** that someone **does**, **did**, or **has done** something: *I suspect she knows.* | *I suspect he took the money.* | *I suspect they have met before.*
- You **suspect** that something **may** or **might** be true: *We suspect that he may know something about the robbery.* | *The police suspect that he might be a terrorist.*
- You **suspect** that someone **may** or **might have** done something: *Police suspect Foster may have been involved in a fraud.* | *I suspect he might have exaggerated a lot of the things in the book.*
- You **suspected** that something **would** happen: *He suspected that the problem would only get worse.* | *I suspected that I would not enjoy the meeting.*
- In all the above patterns, 'that' is optional. You can say **I suspect that** or just **I suspect**.

Using the progressive

Suspect is not used in the progressive. You say: *I suspect he's lying.* ✗ Don't say: *I am suspecting he's lying.*

sus·pect² /ˈsʌspekt/ ●○○ *n* [C]
1 someone who is thought to be guilty of a crime: *Two suspects were arrested today in connection with the robbery.* | *Police have issued a description of the murder suspect.* | **[+for]** *the two suspects for the robbery* | **[+in]** *a suspect in a burglary case* | **main/prime/chief suspect** *Davies is still the chief suspect.*
2 the usual suspects the people or things that are usually involved in or responsible for a particular activity: *a wine shop stocking all the usual suspects: wines from California, France, Australia*

suspect³ *adj* **1** not likely to be completely honest SYN **dodgy**: *I've always thought he was a bit of a suspect character.* | *The company was involved in some **highly suspect** business dealings.* **2** not likely to be completely true: *The two men were convicted on the basis of some **highly suspect** evidence.* **3** likely to have problems and not work well: *The engine sounded a bit suspect.* **4** [only before noun] likely to contain a bomb or something illegal or dangerous: *Police were called in to check out a suspect van.*

sus·pect·ed /səˈspektɪd/ *adj* [only before noun]
1 suspected burglar/terrorist/spy etc someone who is thought to be guilty of a crime: *a suspected child-killer*
2 if you have a suspected illness or injury, doctors think that you might have it but do not know for certain: *He was taken to hospital after a suspected heart attack.*

sus·pend /səˈspend/ ●○○ AWL *v* [T]
1 STOP to officially stop something from continuing, especially for a short time → **suspension**: *Sales of the drug will be suspended until more tests are completed.* | *Talks between the two countries have now been suspended.*
2 LEAVE A SCHOOL/JOB to make someone leave their school or job for a short time, especially because they have broken the rules → **suspension**: *The two police officers have been suspended until an enquiry is carried out.* | **suspend sb from sth** *Dave was suspended from school for a week.*
3 HANG *formal* to attach something to a high place so that it hangs down: **suspend sth from sth** *A large light was suspended from the ceiling.* | **suspend sth by sth** *He was suspended by his feet and beaten with metal bars.*
4 suspend judgment to decide not to make a firm decision or judgment about something until you know more about it
5 suspend disbelief to try to believe that something is true, for example when you are watching a film or play
6 be suspended in sth *technical* if something is suspended in a liquid or in air, it floats in it without moving

susˌpended aniˈmation *n* [U] **1** a state in which a person or creature is unconscious and their body works very slowly, but from which they can wake up when the situation is right **2** a feeling that you cannot do anything because you are waiting for something to happen

susˌpended ˈsentence *n* [C] a punishment given by a court, in which a criminal is told they will be sent to prison if they do anything else illegal within the time mentioned: *a two-year suspended sentence*

sus·pend·er /səˈspendə $ -ər/ *n* **1** [C usually plural] *BrE* a part of a piece of women's underwear that hangs down and can be attached to STOCKINGS to hold them up SYN **garter** *AmE* **2 suspenders** [plural] *AmE* two bands of cloth that go over your shoulders and fasten to your trousers to hold them up SYN **braces** *BrE*

susˈpender ˌbelt *n* [C] *BrE* a piece of women's underwear with suspenders joined to it SYN **garter belt** *AmE*

sus·pense /səˈspens/ *n* [U] a feeling of excitement or anxiety when you do not know what will happen next → **tension**: **in suspense** *They **kept** us **in suspense** for over two hours.* | *Come on then, tell me what happened; **the suspense is killing me*** (=I feel very excited or anxious because I do not know what will happen next). | *She couldn't **bear the suspense** a moment longer.* | **suspense novel/story/movie etc** (=one which is exciting because you do not know what will happen next)

S

sus·pen·sion /səˈspenʃən/ ●○○ AWL *n*
1 STOPPING STH [U] when something is officially stopped for a period of time: **[+of]** *Both sides are now working towards a suspension of hostilities.*
2 MAKING SB LEAVE [C] when someone is not allowed to go to school, do their job, or take part in an activity for a period of time as a punishment: *He received a six-month suspension for unprofessional behaviour.* | **[+from]** *The fight led to his suspension from school.*
3 PART OF A VEHICLE [U] a part attached to the wheels of a vehicle that makes it more comfortable on roads that are not smooth: *a car with an excellent suspension system*
4 LIQUID [C] *technical* a liquid mixture in which very small pieces of solid material are contained but have not combined with it

susˈpension ˌbridge *n* [C] a bridge that has no supports under it, but is hung from strong steel ropes fixed to towers → see picture at BRIDGE¹

sus·pi·cion /səˈspɪʃən/ ●●○ *n*
1 [C,U] a feeling you have that someone is probably guilty of doing something wrong or dishonest: *I can't say for definite who did it, but I certainly **have** my **suspicions**.* | *Police **suspicions** were **confirmed** when the stolen property was found in his flat.* | *I wondered how I could leave early without **arousing** anyone's **suspicions**.* | **on suspicion of (doing) sth** *She was arrested on suspicion of murder.* | **under suspicion** *He felt he was still under suspicion.* | *Mitchell later **came under suspicion** of assaulting two young girls.* | **above/beyond suspicion** *She felt that she ought to be above suspicion* (=so honest that no one could think that she had done anything wrong).
2 [C,U] a feeling that you do not trust someone: *She always **treated** us **with suspicion**.* | *People moving into the area are often **regarded with suspicion**.*
3 [C] a feeling you have that something is true, especially something bad: **suspicion (that)** *I **have** a **suspicion** that the local authority may be planning to close the school.* | *She was left with a **sneaking suspicion*** (=a small suspicion) *that Steven was not telling the truth.*

4 a suspicion of sth *formal* a very small amount of something that you can only just see, hear, or taste: *I could see the faintest suspicion of a tear in her eyes.*

sus·pi·cious /səˈspɪʃəs/ ●●○ *adj*
1 thinking that someone might be guilty of doing something wrong or dishonest: **[+of]** *Some of his colleagues at work became suspicious of his behaviour.* | **[+about]** *They were suspicious about my past.* | *His reluctance to answer my questions **made** me **suspicious**.* | *She gave him a suspicious glance.* | *You've got a very suspicious mind!*
2 making you think that something bad or illegal is happening: *They found a suspicious package under the seat.* | *a suspicious death* | *He was behaving in a **highly suspicious** manner.* | *a suspicious-looking character* | **something/anything/nothing suspicious** *Call the police if you see anything suspicious.* | *Her mother had died **in suspicious circumstances**.*
3 feeling that you do not trust someone or something SYN **wary**: **[+of]** *She was always suspicious of strangers.* | *He was **deeply suspicious** of the legal system.*

sus·pi·cious·ly /səˈspɪʃəsli/ *adv* **1** in a way that shows you think someone has done something wrong or dishonest: *Meg looked at me suspiciously.* | *'What do you want it for?' he asked suspiciously.* **2** in a way that makes people think that something bad or illegal is happening: *He saw two youths **acting suspiciously**.* | *He seemed to be taking a suspiciously long time.* | *This sounded **suspiciously like** an attempt to get rid of me.* **3** in a way that shows you do not trust something or someone: *They eyed the food suspiciously.*

suss /sʌs/ *v* (*also* **suss sb/sth ↔ out**) [T] *BrE informal* to realize or discover something, or to find out the things that you need to know about someone or something: *He finally sussed out the truth.* | **suss (that)** *I soon sussed that she wasn't telling the truth.*

sussed /sʌst/ *adj BrE informal* knowing all about someone or something: *These boys are sussed and streetwise.* | **have/get sb/sth sussed** *Don't worry, I've got him sussed.*

sus·tain /səˈsteɪn/ ●●○ W3 AWL *v* [T]
1 MAKE STH CONTINUE to make something continue to exist or happen for a period of time SYN **maintain**: *She found it difficult to sustain the children's interest.* | *He was incapable of sustaining close relationships with women.* | *the policies necessary to sustain economic growth* → SUSTAINED
2 SUFFER *formal* to suffer damage, an injury, or loss of money: *Two of the firefighters sustained serious injuries.* | *Some nearby buildings sustained minor damage.* | *The company has sustained heavy financial losses this year.*
3 FOOD/DRINK *formal* if food or drink sustains a person, animal, or plant, it makes them able to continue living → **sustenance**: *They gave me barely enough food to sustain me.*
4 GIVE STRENGTH *formal* to make someone feel strong and hopeful: *The thought of seeing her again was all that sustained me.*
5 WEIGHT *formal* to hold up the weight of something SYN **support**: *He leant against her so heavily that she could barely sustain his weight.*
6 IDEA *formal* to support an idea or argument, or prove that it is right: *This argument is difficult to sustain.*

sus·tain·a·ble /səˈsteɪnəbəl/ ●○○ AWL *adj*
1 able to continue without causing damage to the environment: *The government should do more to promote sustainable agriculture.* | *the sustainable use of rainforest resources* | *Cycling is a totally sustainable form of transport.* | ***environmentally sustainable** development* THESAURUS ENVIRONMENTALLY FRIENDLY
2 able to continue for a long time: *The party is promising low inflation and sustainable economic growth.* —**sustainability** /səˌsteɪnəˈbɪləti/ *n* [U]

sus·tained /səˈsteɪnd/ AWL *adj* [only before noun] continuing for a long time: *a period of sustained economic development* | *a sustained attack on the government*

sus·te·nance /ˈsʌstənəns/ AWL *n* [U] *formal*
1 food that people or animals need in order to live: *Without sustenance, the animals will soon die.* | *Potatoes were their only means of sustenance.* **2** when something is made to continue: *Elections are necessary for the sustenance of democracy.*

sut·tee /ˈsʌtiː $ sʌˈtiː, ˈsʌtiː/ *n* [U] the ancient custom in the Hindu religion of burning a wife with her husband when he dies

su·ture /ˈsuːtʃə $ -ər/ *n* [C] *medical* a stitch that is used to sew a wound together —**suture** *v* [T]

SUV /ˌes juː ˈviː/ *n* [C] *AmE* (**sport-utility vehicle**) a type of vehicle that is bigger than a car and is made for travelling over rough ground → **four-by-four**

su·ze·rainty /ˈsuːzəreɪnti $ -rənti, -reɪnti/ *n* [U] *formal* the right of a country or leader to rule over another country

svelte /svelt/ *adj literary* thin and graceful SYN **lithe**: *She was slim, svelte, and sophisticated.*

Sven·ga·li /svenˈgɑːli/ *n* [C] a man who has the power to control people's minds and make them do bad or immoral things

SW the written abbreviation of ***southwest*** or ***southwestern***

swab[1] /swɒb $ swɑːb/ *n* [C] **1** a small piece of material used to clean a wound or take a small amount of a substance from someone's body in order to test it: *a cotton swab* **2** a small amount of a substance that is taken from someone's body with a swab in order to test it: *The doctor took a throat swab to check for infection.*

swab[2] *v* (**swabbed**, **swabbing**) [T] **1** (*also* **swab sth ↔ down**) to clean something using a large amount of water: *a girl who was swabbing the tiled floor with a mop* **2** to clean a wound with a small piece of special material

swad·dle /ˈswɒdl $ ˈswɑːdl/ *v* [T] *old-fashioned* to wrap a baby tightly to keep it warm and protect it

ˈswaddling ˌclothes *n* [plural] *old use* large pieces of cloth that people used to wrap around babies to keep them warm and protect them

swag /swæg/ *n* **1** [U] *old-fashioned informal* goods that someone has stolen SYN **loot 2** [C] **a)** a large piece of material that is hung above a window as decoration **b)** a rope covered with flowers or fruit that is hung somewhere as decoration, or CARVED or painted on something **3** [U] *AusE old-fashioned* clothes and possessions that someone who is travelling on foot carries wrapped in a cloth

swag·ger[1] /ˈswægə $ -ər/ *v* [I always + adv/prep] to walk proudly, swinging your shoulders in a way that shows you are very confident – used to show disapproval: *He swaggered over towards me.*

swagger[2] *n* [singular, U] a way of walking, talking, or behaving that shows you are very confident – used to show disapproval: *He walked in with a swagger.*

swain /sweɪn/ *n* [C] *old use* a young man from the country who loves a woman

swal·low[1] /ˈswɒləʊ $ ˈswɑːloʊ/ ●●○ *v*
1 FOOD [I,T] to make food or drink go down your throat and towards your stomach: *He swallowed the last of his coffee and asked for the bill.* | *Most snakes **swallow** their prey **whole**.*
2 NERVOUSLY [I] to make some of the liquid in your mouth go down your throat because you are frightened or nervous: *Leo **swallowed hard** and walked into the room.* | *She **swallowed nervously** before beginning.*
3 BELIEVE/ACCEPT [T] *informal* to believe a story, explanation etc that is not actually true: *Do they really think we are stupid enough to swallow that?* | *I found his story a bit **hard to swallow*** (=difficult to believe). THESAURUS BELIEVE
4 FEELINGS [T] to stop yourself from showing a feeling, especially anger: *She swallowed her anger and turned to face him.*
5 swallow your pride to do something even though it is embarrassing for you, because you have no choice: *I swallowed my pride and phoned him.* → **a bitter pill (to swallow)** at BITTER[1](7)

swallow sb/sth ↔ **up** *phr v*
1 if a company or country is swallowed up by a larger one,

it becomes part of it and no longer exists on its own: *Hundreds of small companies have been swallowed up by these huge multinationals.*
2 *written* if something is swallowed up, it disappears because something covers it or hides it: *Jane was soon swallowed up in the crowd.* | *The countryside is gradually being swallowed up by new developments.*
3 if an amount of money is swallowed up, you have to spend it to pay for things: *The extra cash was soon swallowed up.*

swallow² *n* [C] **1** a small black and white bird that comes to northern countries in the summer **2** an action in which you make food or drink go down your throat: *He downed his whisky in one swallow.*

swam /swæm/ *v* the past tense of SWIM¹

swa·mi /ˈswɑːmi/ *n* [C] a Hindu religious teacher

swamp¹ /swɒmp $ swɑːmp/ ●○○ *n* [C,U] land that is always very wet or covered with a layer of water —**swampy** *adj*: *the soft, swampy ground*

swamp² *v* [T] **1** to suddenly give someone a lot of work, problems etc to deal with SYN **inundate**: **be swamped by/with sth** *We've been swamped with phone calls since the advert appeared.* **2** to go somewhere or surround something in large numbers, especially in a short period of time: **be swamped by/with sth** *In the summer the village is swamped by visitors.* GRAMMAR **Swamp** is usually passive in meanings 1 and 2. **3** to suddenly cover an area with a lot of water SYN **flood**: *Huge waves swamped the vessel.*

swan¹ /swɒn $ swɑːn/ *n* [C] a large white bird with a long neck that lives on rivers and lakes

swan² *v* (**swanned, swanning**) [I always + adv/prep] *BrE informal* to enjoy yourself and behave in a relaxed way that is annoying to other people: **[+off/around]** *He's gone swanning off to Rome for the weekend!*

Swa·nee, the /ˈswɒni $ ˈswɑː-/ **1** the Suwannee, a river in the south of the US, flowing through Georgia and Florida to the Gulf of Mexico **2 go down the Swanee** *BrE informal* if a plan goes down the Swanee, it fails or does not happen in the way you intended

swank¹ /swæŋk/ *v* [I] *BrE old-fashioned* to speak or behave in a way that shows you think you are better than other people: *I wish you'd stop swanking!*

swank² *n BrE old-fashioned* [U] proud confident behaviour that shows you think you are better than other people

swank·y /ˈswæŋki/ *adj informal* very fashionable and expensive: *eating meals at swanky hotels*

swan·song /ˈswɒnsɒŋ $ ˈswɑːnsɔːŋ/ *n* [C] the last piece of work that an artist or writer produces, or the last time someone gives a performance: *This concert will be her swansong.*

swap¹ (*also* **swop** *BrE*) /swɒp $ swɑːp/ ●●○ S3 *v* (**swapped, swapping**)
1 [I,T] to give something to someone and get something in return SYN **exchange**: *Do you want to swap umbrellas?* | **swap sth for sth** *He swapped his watch for a box of cigars.* | **swap sth with sb** *The girls chatted and swapped clothes with each other.*
2 [T] to tell information to someone and be given information in return SYN **exchange**: *We need to get together to swap ideas and information.* | *They sat in a corner and swapped gossip.*
3 (*also* **swap over**) [I,T] to do the thing that someone else has been doing, and let them do the thing that you have been doing SYN **change**: *They decided to swap roles for the day.* | *You start on the windows and I'll do the walls, then we can swap over after an hour or so.* | **swap sth with sb** *She ended up swapping jobs with her secretary.*
4 [T] to stop using or get rid of one thing and put or get another thing in its place: *The driver announced that we would have to swap buses.* | **swap sth for sth** *She had swapped her long skirts for jeans and T-shirts.* | *He swapped his London home for a cottage in Scotland.*
5 [T] (*also* **swap sth around**) to move one thing and put another in its place: *Someone had gone into the nursery and swapped all the babies around.* | **swap sth with sth** *Why don't we swap the TV with the bookcase?*
6 swap places *BrE* to let someone sit or stand in your place, so that you can have their place SYN **change places**: *Can we swap places, please?*

swap² (*also* **swop** *BrE*) *n* [C] *informal* **1** [usually singular] a situation in which you give something to someone and get another thing in return SYN **exchange**: *a fair swap* | *We can* ***do a swap*** *if you like.* **2** a situation in which people each do the job that the other usually does

ˈswap ˌmeet *n* [C] *AmE* an occasion when people meet to buy and sell used goods, or to exchange them

sward /swɔːd $ swɔːrd/ *n* [C] *literary* an area of land covered with grass

swarm¹ /swɔːm $ swɔːrm/ *n* [C] **1** a large group of insects, especially BEES, moving together **2** a crowd of people who are moving quickly: **[+of]** *Swarms of tourists jostled through the square.*

swarm² *v* [I] **1** [always + adv/prep] if people swarm somewhere, they go there as a large uncontrolled crowd: *Photographers were swarming around the princess.* **2** if BEES swarm, they leave a HIVE (=place where they live) in a large group to look for another home

swarm with sb/sth *phr v* to be full of a moving crowd of people or animals: *The museum was swarming with tourists.*

swar·thy /ˈswɔːði $ -ɔːr-/ *adj* someone who is swarthy has dark skin: *a small, swarthy man* | *a swarthy complexion*

swash·buck·ling /ˈswɒʃˌbʌkəlɪŋ $ ˈswɑːʃ-, ˈswɒːʃ-/ *adj* relating to adventures in which people do brave exciting things and fight against their enemies with swords: *a swashbuckling hero* | *a swashbuckling tale of pirates* —**swashbuckler** *n* [C]

swas·ti·ka /ˈswɒstɪkə $ ˈswɑː-/ *n* [C] a sign consisting of a cross with each end bent at 90°, used as a sign for the Nazi Party in Germany

swat /swɒt $ swɑːt/ *v* (**swatted, swatting**) [T] to hit an insect in order to kill it: *He calmly swatted a couple of flies.* —**swat** *n* [C]

swatch /swɒtʃ $ swɑːtʃ/ *n* [C] a small piece of cloth that people can look at when they are choosing cloth for clothes or for their home

swathe¹ /sweɪð $ swɑːð, swɒːð, sweɪð/ (*also* **swath** /swɒθ $ swɑːθ/) *n* [C] **1** a long thin area of something, especially land: **[+of]** *The bomb had left a swathe of the town centre in ruins.* | *A swathe of sunlight lay across the floor.* **2** a long thin area of grass or plants that has been cut down: *We* ***cut a swathe through*** *the dense undergrowth.* **3 cut a swathe through sth** to destroy a large amount or part of something

swathe² *v* [T] *literary* to wrap or cover something in something: *women swathed in expensive furs* | *The moon was swathed in mist.*

SWAT team /ˈswɒt tiːm $ ˈswɑːt-/ *n* [C] *especially AmE* (***Special Weapons and Tactics team***) a specially trained group of police who deal with the most dangerous and violent situations

sway¹ /sweɪ/ ●●○ *v*
1 [I] to move slowly from one side to another: *The trees swayed gently in the breeze.* THESAURUS ▸ MOVE
2 [T] to influence someone so that they change their opinion: *Don't allow yourself to be swayed by his promises.*

sway² *n* [U] **1** *literary* power to rule or influence people: *These old attitudes still* ***hold sway*** *in the church.* | **under sb's sway** *She was now completely under his sway.* **2** a swinging movement from side to side: *the sway of the ship*

sway·backed /ˈsweɪbækt/ *adj AmE* curved downwards or inwards in the middle

swear /sweə $ swer/ ●●○ S3 *v* (*past tense* **swore** /swɔː $ swɔːr/, *past participle* **sworn** /swɔːn $ swɔːrn/)
1 OFFENSIVE LANGUAGE [I] to use rude and offensive language: *Don't swear in front of the children.* | **[+at]** *He turned round and swore at me.*
2 PROMISE [T] to promise that you will do something: **swear (that)** *Victor swore he would get his revenge.* | **swear**

S

to do sth *Mona swore never to return home.* | *Do you* ***swear on your honour*** (=promise very strongly) *that you will never tell anyone?* **THESAURUS** ▸ PROMISE
3 STATE THE TRUTH [I,T] *informal* to say very strongly that what you are saying is true: *I never touched your purse, I swear!* | **swear (that)** *He says he was there all the time, but I swear I never saw him.* | **swear blind** *BrE* (=say very strongly) *She swore blind that she had never seen him before.* | *I never touched her, I* ***swear to God.*** | *I think it was about ten o'clock when we left, but I* ***couldn't swear to it*** (=I am not certain).
4 sb could have sworn (that) ... used to say that someone was sure about something but now they think they were wrong: *I could have sworn I had my keys.*
5 PUBLIC PROMISE [I,T] to make a public official promise, especially in a court of law: **[+on]** *Witnesses have to swear on the Bible.* | *Remember that you have* ***sworn an oath*** *and so must tell the truth.* | *Presidents must* ***swear allegiance*** *to the US constitution.*
6 swear sb to secrecy/silence to make someone promise not to tell anyone what you have told them —**swearing** *n* [U]: *He was cautioned for swearing.* | *lots of shouting and swearing*
swear by sth *phr v informal* to have great confidence in how good or effective something is: *He swears by vitamin C pills.*
swear sb ↔ **in** *phr v* if someone with a new public job or position is sworn in, they make an official promise to do their duty well: *The new governor will be sworn in next week.* | *The jury have not yet been sworn in.*
ˌswearing-ˈin *n* [singular] a ceremony in which someone with a new public job or position officially promises to do their duty well
ˈswear word ●○○ *n* [C] a word that is considered to be rude, offensive, and shocking by most people
swear·y /ˈsweəri $ ˈsweri/ *adj informal* using or containing a lot of rude or offensive words: *Some of the songs are a bit sweary.*
sweat[1] /swet/ ●●○ *v*
1 LIQUID FROM SKIN [I,T] to have drops of salty liquid coming out through your skin because you are hot, ill, frightened, or doing exercise SYN **perspire**: *I was sweating a lot despite the air conditioning.* | **sweat heavily/profusely** (=sweat a lot) *Within minutes she was sweating profusely.* | **sweat like a pig/sweat buckets** *informal* (=sweat a lot) *basketball players sweating buckets*
2 WORK [I,T] *informal* to work hard: *They sweated and saved for ten years to buy a house.* | **[+over]** *He'd sweated over the plans for six months.* | **sweat blood/sweat your guts out** (=work very hard) *I sweated blood to get that report finished.* | *We've been sweating our guts out here!*
3 WORRY [I,T] *informal* to be anxious, nervous, or worried about something: *Let them sweat a bit before you tell them.* | **sweat bullets** *AmE* (=be very anxious) *Workers are sweating bullets over the possibility of job losses.*
4 don't sweat it *AmE spoken* used to tell someone not to worry about something: *Don't sweat it, I'll lend you the money.*
5 don't sweat the small stuff *AmE spoken* used to tell someone not to worry about unimportant things
6 PRODUCE LIQUID [I] if something such as cheese sweats, fat from inside appears on its surface
7 COOK [T] *BrE* to heat food gently in a little water or fat: *Sweat the vegetables until the juices run out.*
sweat sth ↔ **off** *phr v* to lose weight by sweating a lot
sweat sth ↔ **out** *phr v*
1 to wait anxiously for news that is very important to you: *Charles is* ***sweating it out*** *while the coach decides which players he's taking to the Olympics.*
2 *AmE* to work very hard on something, especially something difficult: *kids sweating out a test*
3 to do hard physical exercise: *They were* ***sweating it out*** *in the gym.*
4 to get rid of an illness by making yourself sweat a lot
sweat[2] ●●○ *n*
1 LIQUID ON SKIN [singular, U] drops of salty liquid that come out through your skin when you are hot, frightened, ill, or doing exercise SYN **perspiration**: *Ian came off the squash court* ***dripping with sweat.*** | ***Beads of sweat*** *appeared on his forehead.* | ***Sweat poured*** *down his face.*
2 [C] the condition of sweating: *Symptoms include fatigue and night sweats.* | **work up a sweat** (=do physical exercise or hard work that makes you sweat)
3 a (cold) sweat a state of nervousness or fear, especially one in which you are sweating: **in/into a (cold) sweat** *I woke up from the nightmare in a cold sweat.* | *Don't get into such a sweat about it! It's only a test.*
4 break into a sweat/break out in a sweat a) to start sweating **b)** to become very nervous or frightened: *Drops in stock market prices have investors breaking out into a sweat.*
5 break sweat *BrE*, **break a sweat** *AmE* to start sweating because you are making an effort: *Karen was on the exercise bikes, just beginning to break a sweat.*
6 no sweat *spoken* used to say that you can do something easily: *'Are you sure you can do it on time?' 'Yeah, no sweat!'*
7 sweats [plural] *AmE informal* **a)** clothes made of thick soft cotton, worn especially for sport SYN **sweatsuit b)** trousers of this type SYN **sweat pants**
8 WORK [singular] *old-fashioned* hard work, especially when it is boring or unpleasant
9 the sweat of sb's brow *literary* the hard effort that someone has made in their work
sweat·band /ˈswetbænd/ *n* [C] **1** a narrow band of cloth that you wear around your head or wrist to stop sweat running down when you are doing sport **2** a narrow piece of cloth that is sewn on the inside of a hat
ˌsweated ˈlabour *BrE*, **sweated labor** *AmE n* [U] **1** hard work done for very low wages, especially in a factory **2** the people who do this work
sweat·er /ˈswetə $ -ər/ ●●● S2 *n* [C] a piece of warm wool or cotton clothing with long sleeves, which covers the top half of your body SYN **jumper** *BrE*
ˈsweat gland *n* [C] a small organ under your skin that produces sweat
sweat·pants /ˈswetpænts/ *n* [plural] *AmE* loose warm trousers, worn especially for sport or relaxation
sweat·shirt /ˈswet-ʃɜːt $ -ʃɜːrt/ ●●● S3 *n* [C] a loose warm piece of clothing which covers the top part of your body and arms and is worn especially for sport or relaxation
sweat·shop /ˈswet-ʃɒp $ -ʃɑːp/ *n* [C] a small business, factory etc where people work hard in bad conditions for very little money - used to show disapproval
ˈsweat suit, **sweat·suit** /ˈswetsuːt, -sjuːt $ -suːt/ *n* [C] *AmE* a set of loose warm clothes, worn especially for sport or relaxation
sweat·y /ˈsweti/ *adj* (*comparative* **sweatier**, *superlative* **sweatiest**) **1** covered or wet with SWEAT: *We came home hot and sweaty after the day's work.* | *sweaty palms*
2 [usually before noun] unpleasantly hot or difficult, so that you SWEAT: *a sweaty August day* | *a sweaty job*
swede /swiːd/ *n* [C,U] *BrE* a round yellow vegetable that grows under the ground SYN **rutabaga** *AmE* → see picture at **VEGETABLE**[1]
Swede *n* [C] someone from Sweden
Swe·dish[1] /ˈswiːdɪʃ/ *adj* relating to Sweden, its people, or its language
Swedish[2] *n* **1 the Swedish** [plural] people from Sweden
2 [U] the language used in Sweden
sweep[1] /swiːp/ ●●● W3 *v* (*past tense and past participle* **swept** /swept/)
1 CLEAN STH [T] to clean the dust, dirt etc from the floor or ground, using a brush with a long handle SYN **brush**: *Bert swept the path in front of the house.* | **sweep sth off/out/up etc** *Will you sweep the leaves off the patio?* → see picture at **CLEAN**[2]
2 PUSH STH SOMEWHERE [T always + adv/prep] to move things from a surface with a brushing movement: *I swept the papers quickly into the drawer.*
3 PUSH SB/STH WITH FORCE [T always + adv/prep] to force someone or something to move in a particular direction:

The windsurfer was swept out to sea. | *Jessie was swept along by the angry crowd.*
4 GROUP MOVES [I always + adv/prep] if a group of people or animals sweep somewhere, they quickly move there together: **[+through/along etc]** *The crowd swept through the gates of the stadium.*
5 WIND/WAVES ETC [I,T always + adv/prep] if winds, waves, fire etc sweep a place or sweep through, across etc a place, they move quickly and with a lot of force: *Thunderstorms swept the country.* | **[+across/through etc]** *Ninety-mile per hour winds swept across the plains.*
6 BECOME POPULAR [I,T always + adv/prep] *written* if an idea, feeling, or activity sweeps a group of people or a place, it quickly becomes very popular or common: **sweep the country/nation/state etc** *a wave of nationalism sweeping the country* | **[+across/through etc]** *the latest craze sweeping through the teenage population*
7 FEELING [I always + adv/prep] if a feeling sweeps over you, you are suddenly affected by it: **[+over]** *A feeling of isolation swept over me.*
8 PERSON [I always + adv/prep] if someone sweeps somewhere, they move quickly and confidently, especially because they are impatient or like to seem important: **[+into/through etc]** *Eva swept into the meeting and demanded to know what was going on.*
9 POLITICS [I,T] to win an election easily and in an impressive way: **sweep to power/victory** *Nixon and Agnew swept to victory with 47 million votes.* | *Herrera was* ***swept into office*** *on the promise of major reforms.*
10 SPORTS [T] *AmE* to win all of the games in a series of games against a particular team: *Houston swept Orlando to become NBA champions.*
11 sweep the board *BrE* to win everything that can be won, especially very easily
12 FORM A CURVE [I always + adv/prep] to form a long curved shape: **[+down/along etc]** *The hills swept down to the sea.*
13 LOOK [I,T always + adv/prep] to look quickly at all of something: *The general's eyes swept the horizon.* | **[+over/across/around etc]** *the beam from the lighthouse sweeping across the sea*
14 sweep sb off their feet to make someone feel suddenly and strongly attracted to you in a romantic way: *Jill's been swept off her feet by an older man.*
15 sweep/brush sth under the carpet (*also* **sweep sth under the rug** *AmE*) to try to keep something a secret, especially something you have done wrong
16 HAIR [T always + adv/prep] to pull your hair back from your face: **sweep sth back/up** *Kerry swept her hair back into a ponytail.*
sweep sb **along** *phr v* to SWEEP someone AWAY
sweep sth ↔ **aside** *phr v* to refuse to pay attention to something someone says: *Branson swept all the objections aside.*
sweep sb/sth **away** *phr v*
1 sweep sth ↔ away to completely destroy something or make something disappear: *houses swept away by the floods* | *A sudden feeling of grief swept all my anger away.*
2 sweep sb away (*also* **sweep sb along**) if you are swept away or swept along by something, you are so excited that you do not think clearly or you forget about other things: *We couldn't help being swept away by Bette's enthusiasm.* | *Nineteenth-century scientists were swept along on the tide of Darwin's theories.*
sweep up *phr v*
1 to clean the dust, dirt etc from the floor or ground using a brush with a long handle: *The janitor was just sweeping up as I left the building.* | **sweep sth ↔ up** *Jan was sweeping up the bits of paper and broken glass.*
2 sweep sb ↔ up to pick someone up in one quick movement: *Harriet swept the child up in her arms and hugged her.*

sweep² *n* [C] **1** a long swinging movement of your arm, a weapon etc: *With a single sweep of his sword, he cut through the rope.* **2** [usually singular] *BrE* the act of cleaning a room with a long-handled brush: *The kitchen needs a good sweep.* **3 the sweep of sth a)** a long curved line or area of land: *the* ***wide sweep*** *of lawn* **b)** the many different and important ideas, events, or qualities of something: *the* ***broad sweep*** *of history* **4** [usually singular] a search or attack that moves over a large area: *He watched the helicopter* ***make a sweep*** *over the beach.* **5 the sweeps** (*also* **sweeps month/period**) *AmE* a period of time during the year when television stations try to find out which shows are the most popular **6** *AmE* a series of several games that one team wins against another team **7** a CHIMNEY SWEEP → **clean sweep** at CLEAN¹(14)

sweep·er /ˈswiːpə $ -ər/ *n* [C] **1** someone or something that sweeps: *a road sweeper* **2** *BrE* a football player who plays in a position behind other defending players

sweep·ing /ˈswiːpɪŋ/ ●○○ *adj*
1 affecting many things, or making an important difference to something: **sweeping changes/cuts/reforms etc** *They want to make sweeping changes to education policies.*
2 [only before noun] including a lot of information about something: *a sweeping look at European history*
3 sweeping statement/generalization a statement etc that is too general and that does not consider all the facts – used to show disapproval: *sweeping generalizations about women drivers*
4 forming a curved shape: *the sweeping curve of the driveway* | *a sweeping gesture*
5 sweeping victory the winning of an election by a large number of votes: *a sweeping victory for Labour*

sweep·ings /ˈswiːpɪŋz/ *n* [plural] dirt, dust etc that is left to be swept up

sweep·stake /ˈswiːpsteɪk/ *BrE*, **sweepstakes** *AmE n* [C] **1** a type of BETTING in which the winner receives all the money risked by everyone else **2** *AmE* a type of competition in which you have the chance to win a prize if your name is chosen **3** *AmE* a competition, election etc in which no one knows who will be the winner: *the presidential sweepstakes*

sweet¹ /swiːt/ ●●● S2 W3 *adj* (*comparative* **sweeter**, *superlative* **sweetest**)
1 TASTE containing or having a taste like sugar → **sour**, **bitter**, **dry**: *This tea is too sweet.* | *sweet juicy peaches* | *sweet wine* THESAURUS ▸ TASTE
2 CHARACTER kind, gentle, and friendly: *a sweet smile* | *How* ***sweet of you*** *to remember my birthday!* → SWEET-TEMPERED THESAURUS ▸ KIND, NICE
3 CHILDREN/SMALL THINGS *especially BrE* looking pretty and attractive SYN **cute**: *Your little boy looks very sweet in his new coat.*
4 THOUGHTS/EMOTIONS making you feel pleased, happy, and satisfied: *Revenge is sweet.* | *the* ***sweet smell of success*** | *the* ***sweet taste of victory*** | *Goodnight, Becky.* ***Sweet dreams.***
5 SMELLS having a pleasant smell SYN **fragrant**: *sweet-smelling flowers* | *the* ***sickly sweet*** (=unpleasantly sweet) *smell of rotting fruit*
6 SOUNDS pleasant to listen to OPP **harsh**: *She has a very sweet singing voice.*
7 have a sweet tooth to like things that taste of sugar
8 WATER/AIR if you describe water or air as sweet, you mean that it is fresh and clean OPP **stale**: *She hurried to the door and took great gulps of the sweet air.*
9 keep sb sweet *informal* to behave in a pleasant friendly way towards someone, because you want them to help you later: *I'm trying to keep Mum sweet so that she'll lend me the car.*
10 in your own sweet way/time if you do something in your own sweet way or time, you do it in exactly the way that you want to or when you want to, without considering what other people say or think: *You can't just go on in your own sweet way; we have to do this together.*
11 a sweet deal *AmE* a business or financial deal in which you get an advantage, pay a low price etc: *I got a sweet deal on the car.*
12 sweet FA (*also* **sweet Fanny Adams**) *BrE informal* nothing at all – used when someone wants to avoid saying a swear word directly: *'How much did they pay you for that job?' 'Sweet FA!'*
13 sweet nothings things that lovers say to each other: *a couple* ***whispering sweet nothings*** *to each other*

14 be sweet on sb *old-fashioned* to be very attracted to or in love with someone
15 sweet! *spoken informal* used to say that you think that something is very good: *'I got four tickets to the concert.' 'Sweet!'* —**sweetly** *adv* → **home sweet home** at HOME[1](13), → **short and sweet** at SHORT[1](1), **SWEETNESS**

THESAURUS

sweet sweet food or drink has had sugar added or contains natural sugars: *Italian oranges are very sweet.* | *a cup of hot sweet tea*
sugary sweet because a lot of sugar has been added: *Sugary foods are bad for your teeth.*
sickly *BrE* tasting unpleasantly sweet: *The dessert was rather sweet and sickly.* | *a* ***sickly sweet*** *fruit drink*
cloying tasting or smelling unpleasantly sweet: *I find strawberry and peach drinks too cloying.* | *the cloying smell of fish oil*

sweet² ●●● S2 *n*
1 [C] *BrE* a small piece of sweet food made of sugar or chocolate SYN **candy** *AmE*: *Eating sweets is bad for your teeth.* | *a sweet shop* | *a packet of* ***boiled sweets*** (=hard sweets that taste of fruit) **THESAURUS** TASTE
2 [C,U] *BrE* sweet food served after the meat and vegetables part of a meal SYN **dessert**: *Would you like a sweet, or some cheese and biscuits?*
3 (my) sweet *old-fashioned* used when speaking to someone you love: *Don't cry, my sweet.*

ˌsweet-and-ˈsour *adj* [only before noun] a sweet-and-sour dish in Chinese cooking has both sweet and sour tastes together: *sweet-and-sour pork*

sweet·bread /ˈswiːtbred/ *n* [C usually plural] meat from the PANCREAS of a young sheep or cow

sweet·corn /ˈswiːtkɔːn $ -kɔːrn/ *n* [U] *BrE* the soft yellow seeds from MAIZE that are cooked and eaten SYN **corn** *AmE*

sweet·en /ˈswiːtn/ *v* **1** [I,T] to make something sweeter, or become sweeter: *Sweeten the mixture with a little honey.* **2** [T] (*also* **sweeten sb ↔ up**) *informal* to try to persuade someone to do what you want, by giving them presents or money or promising them something: *a cash bonus to sweeten the deal* → SWEETENER(2) **3** [T] *literary* to make someone kinder, gentler etc: *Old age had not sweetened her.* → **sweeten the pill** at PILL[1](4)

ˌsweetened conˈdensed milk *n* [U] *especially AmE* CONDENSED MILK

sweet·ener /ˈswiːtnə $ -ər/ *n* **1** [C,U] a substance used to make food or drink taste sweeter: *No artificial sweeteners are used in this product.* **2** [C] *informal* something that you give to someone to persuade them to do something, especially to accept a business deal: *These tax cuts are just a pre-election sweetener.*

ˌsweet ˈgum / $ ˈ../ *n* [C] a tree with hard wood and groups of seeds like PRICKLY balls, common in North America

sweet·heart /ˈswiːthɑːt $ -hɑːrt/ ●●○ *n*
1 *spoken* a way of speaking to someone you love SYN **darling**: *Come here, sweetheart.*
2 *spoken* an informal way of speaking to a woman you do not know, which some women find offensive
3 sweetheart deal *AmE* an agreement that is unfair because it gives an advantage to people who know each other well or to people who have a lot of influence: *Members of the council had arranged a sweetheart deal with CTS.*
4 [C] *old-fashioned* the person that you love: *They were* ***childhood sweethearts***.

sweet·ie /ˈswiːti/ *n* [C] *spoken* **1** *BrE* a SWEET – used by children or when speaking to children **2** someone who is kind and easy to love: *Guy's father is such a sweetie.* **3** a way of speaking to someone you love

ˈsweetie pie *n* [C] *AmE spoken* a way of speaking to someone you love

sweet·meat /ˈswiːtmiːt/ *n* [C] *BrE old-fashioned* a SWEET, or any food made of or preserved in sugar

sweet·ness /ˈswiːtnəs/ *n* [U] **1** how sweet something tastes or smells: *the sweetness of the wild rose* **2** how pleasant something is: *a smile of great sweetness* **3 be all sweetness and light a)** to behave in a way that is very pleasant and friendly, especially when you do not normally behave like this: *She's all sweetness and light when Paul's around.* **b)** to be enjoyable and without problems: *Life is not all sweetness and light.*

ˌsweet ˈpea / $ ˈ../ *n* [C] a climbing plant with sweet-smelling flowers in pale colours

ˌsweet ˈpepper *n* [C] a green, red, or yellow vegetable that is hollow with many seeds

ˌsweet poˈtato *n* [C] a vegetable that looks like a red potato, is yellow inside, and tastes sweet → **yam** → see picture at **VEGETABLE[1]**

ˈsweet roll *n* [C] *AmE* a small sweet PASTRY

ˈsweet-talk *v* [T] *informal* to persuade someone to do something by talking to them nicely and making them feel good: **sweet-talk sb into doing sth** *I managed to sweet-talk her into driving me home.* —**sweet talk** *n* [U]

ˌsweet-ˈtempered *adj* having a character that is kind and gentle

sweet wil·liam /ˌswiːt ˈwɪljəm/ *n* [C,U] a plant with sweet-smelling flowers

swell¹ /swel/ ●○○ *v* (*past tense* **swelled**, *past participle* **swollen** /ˈswəʊlən $ ˈswoʊ-/)
1 SIZE [I] (*also* **swell up**) to become larger and rounder than normal – used especially about parts of the body → **swollen**: *Her ankle was already starting to swell.* | *The window frame had swollen shut.*
2 AMOUNT/NUMBER [I,T] to increase in amount or number: **[+to]** *The crowd swelled to around 10,000.* | *The river was swollen with melted snow.* | **swell the ranks/numbers of sth** (=increase the number of people in a particular situation) *Large numbers of refugees have swollen the ranks of the unemployed.*
3 swell with pride/anger etc to feel very proud, angry etc: *His heart swelled with pride as he watched his daughter collect her prize.*
4 SHAPE [I,T] (*also* **swell out**) to curve or make something curve: *The wind swelled the sails.*
5 SOUND [I] *literary* to become louder: *Music swelled around us.*
6 SEA [I] to move suddenly and powerfully upwards → **GROUNDSWELL**

swell² *n* **1** [singular] the way the sea moves up and down: *The sea wasn't rough, but there was a* ***heavy swell*** (=large movements of the water). **2** [singular] a situation in which something increases in number or amount: **[+of]** *the growing swell of anti-government feeling* | *a swell of pride* **3** [singular] an increase in sound level, especially in music SYN **crescendo** **4** [singular] the roundness or curved shape of something: *the firm swell of her breasts* **5** [C] *old-fashioned* a fashionable or important person

swell³ *adj AmE old-fashioned* very good SYN **great**: *You look swell!*

ˌswell-ˈheaded *adj AmE informal* thinking that you are more important or clever than you really are SYN **big-headed**

swell·ing /ˈswelɪŋ/ *n* **1** [C] an area of your body that has become larger than normal, because of illness or injury: **[+in/on]** *a painless swelling in his neck* **2** [U] the condition of having swelled: *The spider's bite can cause pain and swelling.* | *These tablets should* ***reduce*** *the* ***swelling***.

swel·ter /ˈsweltə $ -ər/ *v* [I] to feel extremely hot and uncomfortable: *Crowds of shoppers sweltered in the summer heat.*

swel·ter·ing /ˈsweltərɪŋ/ *adj* extremely hot and uncomfortable: *sweltering August days*

swept /swept/ the past tense and past participle of SWEEP[1]

ˌswept-ˈback *adj* **1** hair that is swept-back is brushed backwards from your face **2** swept-back wings on an aircraft look like the letter v

SWERVE

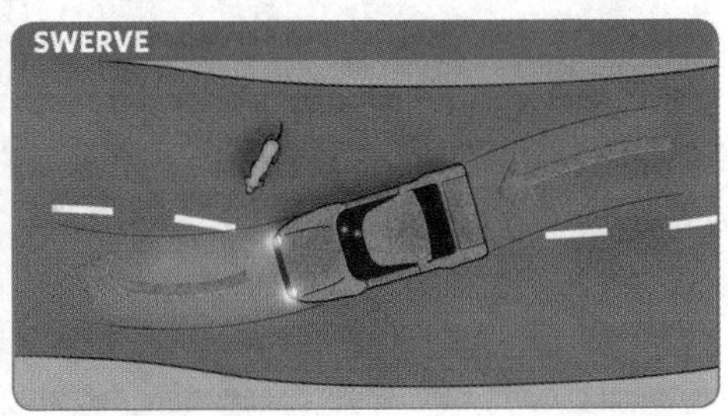

swerve /swɜːv $ swɜːrv/ *v* [I] **1** to make a sudden sideways movement while moving forwards, usually in order to avoid hitting something: **swerve violently/sharply** *The car swerved sharply to avoid the dog.* | **[+across/off/into etc]** *The bus swerved off the road.* **2** [usually in negatives] *formal* to change from an idea, course of action, purpose etc: **[+from]** *He would never swerve from the truth.* —**swerve** *n* [C]

swift¹ /swɪft/ ●○○ *adj*
1 happening or done quickly and immediately: *My letter received a swift reply.* | *She shot a swift glance at Paul.* | **swift to do sth** *They were swift to deny the accusations.*
2 [only before noun] moving, or able to move, very fast: *a swift runner* | *She wiped her tears away in one swift movement.* THESAURUS ▸ FAST
3 sb is not too swift *AmE spoken* used to say that someone is not very intelligent —**swiftly** *adv*: *Alice dressed swiftly.* —**swiftness** *n* [U]

swift² *n* [C] a small brown bird that has pointed wings, flies very fast, and is similar to a SWALLOW

swig /swɪɡ/ *v* (**swigged**, **swigging**) [T] *informal* to drink something in large mouthfuls, especially from a bottle SYN **gulp**: *He sat swigging beer and smoking.* THESAURUS ▸ DRINK —**swig** *n* [C]: *She* ***took*** *a long* ***swig*** *of Coke.*

swill¹ /swɪl/ *v* **1** [T] *BrE* to wash something by pouring a lot of water over it or into it: **swill sth away/down/out** *Get a bucket to swill the yard down.* **2** [I,T] if a liquid swills around or you swill it around, it moves around something: **[+around/round]** *He swilled his brandy gently round his glass.* **3** [T] (*also* **swill down**) *informal* to drink something in large amounts: *He does nothing but swill beer all day.*

swill² *n* **1** [U] food for pigs, mostly made of unwanted bits of human food → PIGSWILL **2** [C] *BrE* the act of washing something by pouring a lot of water over it

swim¹ /swɪm/ ●●● S3 *v* (*past tense* **swam** /swæm/, *past participle* **swum** /swʌm/, *present participle* **swimming**)
1 MOVE THROUGH WATER [I,T] to move yourself through water using your arms and legs: **[+in]** *We swam in the chilly water.* | **[+around/across etc]** *She could swim across the lake.* | *kids learning to swim the backstroke* | *She was the first woman to swim the Channel.*
2 WATER ANIMALS [I always + adv/prep] when fish, ducks etc swim, they move around the water using their tails and FINS, their feet etc: *Tropical fish swam slowly around in the tank.*
3 NOT THINKING/SEEING PROPERLY [I] **a)** if your head swims, you start to feel confused or that everything is spinning around: *My head was swimming after looking at that screen all day.* **b)** if something you are looking at swims, it seems to be moving around, usually because you are ill, tired, or drunk: *The numbers swam before my eyes.*
4 be swimming in sth to be covered by a lot of liquid: *potatoes swimming in thick gravy*
5 swim against the tide/current etc to do or say things which are different from what most people do or say, because you do not mind being different OPP **swim with the tide** → **sink or swim** at SINK¹(15)

swim² ●●○ *n* [C]
1 a period of time that you spend swimming: *Let's* ***go for*** *a swim.*
2 in the swim (of things) *informal* knowing about and involved in what is happening in a particular situation

swim·mer /ˈswɪmə $ -ər/ *n* [C] **1** someone who swims well, often as a competitor: **good/strong swimmer** *Peter's a very strong swimmer.* **2** someone who is swimming: *We watched the swimmers heading out across the lake.*

SWIM

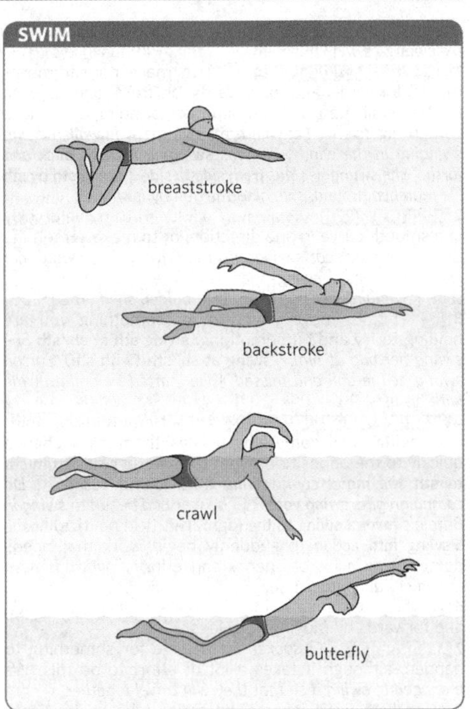

swim·ming /ˈswɪmɪŋ/ ●●● S2 *n* [U] the sport of moving yourself through water using your arms and legs: *Swimming is great exercise.* | *a swimming club* | *We* ***went swimming*** *on Saturday.*

ˈswimming bath *n* [C] *BrE old-fashioned* a public swimming pool, usually indoors

ˈswimming cap *n* [C] a tight-fitting rubber hat that you wear when you are swimming to keep your hair dry

ˈswimming ˌcostume ●●● S3 *n* [C] *BrE* a piece of clothing worn for swimming, especially the type worn by women SYN **swimsuit**

swim·ming·ly /ˈswɪmɪŋli/ *adv old-fashioned* **go swimmingly** if something you plan goes swimmingly, it happens without problems

ˈswimming pool ●●● S3 *n* [C] a structure that has been built and filled with water for people to swim in SYN **pool**

ˈswimming suit *n* [C] *AmE* SWIMSUIT

ˈswimming trunks ●●● S3 *n* [plural] a piece of clothing like SHORTS, worn by men and boys for swimming

swim·suit /ˈswɪmsuːt, -sjuːt $ -suːt/ ●●○ *n* [C] a piece of clothing worn for swimming

swim·wear /ˈswɪmweə $ -wer/ *n* [U] clothing used for swimming

swin·dle¹ /ˈswɪndl/ *v* [T] to get money from someone by deceiving them SYN **cheat**: **swindle sb out of sth** *a businessman who swindled investors out of millions of pounds* —**swindler** *n* [C]

swindle² *n* [C] a situation in which someone gets money by deceiving someone else: *a big tax swindle*

swine /swaɪn/ *n* [C] **1** (*plural* **swine** or **swines**) *informal* someone who behaves very rudely or unpleasantly: *Leave her alone, you filthy swine!* **2** (*plural* **swine**) *old use* a pig

ˈswine flu *n* [U] a type of INFLUENZA which is caused by a VIRUS that originally infected pigs

swine·herd /ˈswaɪnhɜːd $ -hɜːrd/ *n* [C] *old use* someone who looks after pigs

S

swing¹ /swɪŋ/ ●●● W3 *v (past tense and past participle* **swung** /swʌŋ/)
1 MOVE FROM A FIXED POINT [I,T] to make regular movements forwards and backwards or from one side to another while hanging from a particular point, or to make something do this: *Let your arms swing as you walk.* | *a sign swinging in the wind* | *He was* ***swinging*** *his bag* ***back and forth****.* | *She* ***swung*** *her legs* ***from side to side****.* | **swing sth by sth** *He marched around, swinging the gun by its handle.*
2 MOVE IN A CURVE [I,T always + adv/prep] to move quickly in a smooth curve in one direction, or to make something do this: *A black car swung into the drive.* | *Kate swung her legs out of bed.* | **swing open/shut** *The heavy door swung shut.* | *Swinging her bag over her shoulder, she hurried on.*
3 HIT [I,T] to move your arm or something you are holding to try and hit something: **swing sth at sb/sth** *She swung her bag at him.* | **swing at sb/sth (with sth)** *Garson swung at the ball and missed.* | *He started swinging at me with his fists.*
4 CHANGE OPINIONS/EMOTIONS [I,T] if emotions or opinions swing, or if something swings them, they change quickly to the opposite of what they were: **swing from sth to sth** *His* ***mood*** *could* ***swing*** *from joy to despair.* | *Do campaign gifts* ***swing votes****?* | *The war had begun to* ***swing in*** *Britain's* ***favor****.* | **swing to the Right/Left** (=in politics)
5 swing into action to suddenly begin work that needs doing, using a lot of energy and effort: *Politicians have already swung into action.*
6 PLAY [I] to sit on a swing and make it move backwards and forwards by moving your legs
7 ARRANGE STH [T] *spoken* to arrange for something to happen, although it takes a lot of effort to do this: *We managed to* ***swing it*** *so that they will travel together.*
8 swing both ways *informal* someone who swings both ways is BISEXUAL
9 swing the lead *BrE* to avoid work by pretending to be ill
→ **there's not enough room to swing a cat** at ROOM¹(5)
swing around/round *phr v* to turn around quickly, or to make something do this: *She swung around to face him.* | **swing sth/sb ↔ around/round** *He swung the boat around and headed for the shore.*
swing by (sth) *phr v AmE informal* to visit a place or person for a short time: *I'll swing by the grocery store on my way.*

swing² ●●○ *n*
1 SEAT WITH ROPES [C] a seat hanging from ropes or chains, usually used by children to play on by moving it forwards and backwards using their legs: *kids* ***playing on the swings*** | *a porch swing*
2 MOVEMENT [C] a curved movement made with your arm, leg etc: *He* ***took a swing at*** (=tried to hit) *my head and missed.* | *the swing of her hips as she walked*
3 CHANGE [C] a noticeable change in opinions or emotions: **[+to/towards/between etc]** *a big swing towards right-wing ideology* | *She suffers from* ***mood swings****.*
4 SPORTS [singular] the movement you make when you hit the ball in GOLF, baseball, or some other sports: *I spent months correcting my swing.*
5 MUSIC [U] a type of dance music played by a big band in the 1930s and 1940s that is similar to JAZZ
6 get into the swing of it/things to become fully involved in an activity: *Once we got into the swing of it, it took no time at all.*
7 be in full swing if an event or process is in full swing, it has reached its highest level of activity: *By midnight, the end-of-course party was in full swing.*
8 go with a swing *BrE* if a party or activity goes with a swing, it is enjoyable and successful: *everything you need to* ***make*** *your party* ***go with a swing***
9 swings and roundabouts *BrE* used to say that two choices have an equal number of gains and losses, so there is little difference between them

ˌswing ˈbridge *n* [C] *BrE* a bridge that can be pulled up for tall ships to go under it

ˌswing ˈdoor *n* [C] *BrE* a door that you can push open from either side, which swings shut afterwards SYN **swinging door** *AmE*

swinge·ing /ˈswɪndʒɪŋ/ *adj* **swingeing cuts** *BrE* very severe reductions in spending, especially by a government or organization SYN **sweeping**: *swingeing cuts in public spending*

swing·er /ˈswɪŋə $ -ər/ *n* [C] *old-fashioned informal*
1 someone who is fashionable and goes to a lot of parties
2 someone who has sexual relationships with many people, especially someone who exchanges sexual partners with other people

swing·ing /ˈswɪŋɪŋ/ *adj old-fashioned informal* exciting and enjoyable: *a swinging social life*

ˌswinging ˈdoor *n* [C] *AmE* a door that you can push open from either side, which swings shut afterwards SYN **swing door** *BrE*

swinging ˈsixties *n* **the swinging sixties** the 1960s, a time when social and sexual freedom increased: *Dad grew up in the swinging sixties.*

swing·om·e·ter /swɪŋˈɒmɪtə $ -ˈɑːmɪtər/ *n* [C] *BrE informal* a piece of equipment used in television programmes to show how many votes each political party is getting during an election

ˈswing set *n* [C] *AmE* a tall metal frame with SWINGS hanging from it, for children to play on

ˈswing shift *n* [singular] *AmE informal* workers who work from three or four o'clock in the afternoon until 11 or 12 o'clock at night, or the system of working these times

swin·ish /ˈswaɪnɪʃ/ *adj BrE old-fashioned* extremely unpleasant or difficult to deal with

swipe¹ /swaɪp/ *v*
1 [I,T] to hit or to try to hit someone or something by swinging your arm or an object very quickly: *She swiped me across the face.* | **[+at]** *He jumped forward, intending to swipe at her.*
2 [T] *informal* to steal something SYN **pinch** *BrE*: *The photos were probably swiped by an employee.*
3 [T] to pull a plastic card through a machine that can read the electronic information on it: *Swipe your card to open the door.*

SWIPE

swipe² *n* [C] **1** a criticism of someone or something SYN **dig**: **[+at]** *His comments were a sarcastic swipe at the police.* | *In her latest article, she* ***takes a swipe at*** (=criticizes) *her critics.* **2** when you hit or try to hit someone or something by swinging your arm very quickly: *She* ***took a swipe at*** *the ball.*

ˈswipe card *n* [C] a special plastic card that you slide through a machine in order to get into a building or open a door

swirl¹ /swɜːl $ swɜːrl/ ●○○ *v*
1 [I,T] to move around quickly in a twisting circular movement, or to make something do this: **[+around/round]** *Smoke swirled around her.* | **swirl sth around/round** *He swirled the brandy around in his glass.* | *The river had become a swirling torrent.*
2 [I] if stories or ideas swirl around a place, a lot of people start to talk about them – used especially in news reports SYN **circulate**: **[+around]** *Rumours of a takeover began to swirl around the stock markets.*

swirl² *n* [C] **1** a swirling movement or amount of something: **[+of]** *a swirl of dust* **2** a twisting circular pattern

swish¹ /swɪʃ/ *v* [I,T] to move or make something move quickly through the air with a quiet sound: *Her skirt swished as she walked.* —**swish** *n* [singular]

swish² *adj BrE* fashionable and expensive: *a swish new apartment block*

swish·ing /ˈswɪʃɪŋ/ *n* [U] the activity of taking part in a social event at which people exchange clothes or other things they no longer want

S

Swiss[1] /swɪs/ *adj* relating to Switzerland or its people

Swiss[2] *n* **the Swiss** [plural] people from Switzerland

ˌSwiss ˈball *n* [C] *trademark* a large plastic ball that you sit on or lie against in order to do special exercises

ˌSwiss ˈchard *n* [U] a vegetable with large green leaves

ˌSwiss ˈroll *n* [C,U] *BrE* a long thin cake that is rolled up with JAM or cream inside

ˌSwiss ˈsteak *n* [C,U] *AmE* a thick flat piece of BEEF covered in flour and cooked in a sauce

switch[1] /swɪtʃ/ ●●● S2 W3 *v*

1 [I,T] to change from doing or using one thing to doing or using another: **[+to]** *She worked as a librarian before switching to journalism.* | **switch from sth to sth** *Duval could switch easily from French to English.* | **switch between sth and sth** *He switches between TV and theatre work.* | *The terrorists will* ***switch tactics.*** | **switch sides/allegiance** (=start supporting a different person, party etc) *He switched sides just days before the election.* | **switch attention/focus/emphasis** *We want to switch focus away from criticism.*

2 [T] to replace one thing with another, or exchange things SYN **change**: **switch sth for sth** *Tim may switch his BMW for something else.* | **switch sth from sth to sth** *We've switched the meeting from Tuesday to Thursday.* | **switch sth around** *It's not easy to switch clerical workers around.*

3 [I,T] *AmE* if you switch with someone who does the same job as you, you exchange your working times with theirs for a short time SYN **swap**: **[+with]** *Tom said he'd switch with me on Saturday.* | *He asked if we could switch shifts.*

4 [T always + adv/prep] to change the way a machine operates, using a switch: **switch sth to sth** *Switch the freezer to 'defrost'.*

switch off *phr v*

1 to turn off a machine, light, radio etc using a switch: **switch sth ↔ off** *The burglar alarm was switched off.* | *Don't forget to switch off before you go.*

2 *informal* to stop listening to someone: *He just switches off and ignores me.*

3 to relax for a short time: *Switch off by listening to music.*

switch on *phr v* to turn on a machine, light, radio etc using a switch: **switch sth ↔ on** *He switched the torch on.* | *The lights* ***switch on automatically*** *when it gets dark.*

switch over *phr v*

1 to change from one method, product etc to another: **[+to]** *We've switched over to telephone banking.*

2 to change the television CHANNEL you are watching or the radio station you are listening to: **[+to]** *Switch over to BBC 2.*

switch[2] ●●● S3 *n* [C]

1 ON/OFF a piece of equipment that starts or stops the flow of electricity to a machine, light etc when you push it: *Where's the* ***light switch?*** | *an* ***on-off switch*** | **press/flick/throw etc a switch** *Tom flicked the switch, but nothing happened.* | *She claims she is willing to throw the switch of the electric chair.* | **at the flick of a switch** (=very quickly and easily, by pressing a switch) *Petrol can be chosen at the flick of a switch.* → see picture at PLUG[1]

2 CHANGE [usually singular] a complete change from one thing to another: *an important policy switch* | **[+from/to]** *the switch from agriculture to dairy production* | **[+in]** *a switch in emphasis* | *More shoppers are* ***making the switch*** *to organic food.* | **that's a switch** *AmE spoken informal* (=used to say that someone's behaviour is different from usual) *'Ed's the only one who's not eating.' 'That's a switch!'*

3 RAILWAY *AmE* a piece of railway track that can be moved to allow a train to cross over from one track to another

4 STICK *old-fashioned* a thin stick that bends easily

switch·back /ˈswɪtʃbæk/ *n* [C] a road or track that goes up and down steep slopes and around sharp bends

switch·blade /ˈswɪtʃbleɪd/ *n* [C] a knife with a blade inside the handle which springs out when you press a button → see picture at KNIFE[1]

switch·board /ˈswɪtʃbɔːd $ -bɔːrd/ *n* [C] a system used to connect telephone calls in an office building, hotel etc, or the people who operate the system: *switchboard operators* | *Hundreds of callers* ***jammed the switchboard*** *trying to win the tickets* (=there were too many calls for the switchboard to deal with).

ˈSwitch card *n* [C] *trademark BrE* a plastic card from your bank that you use to pay for things and that allows the money to be taken straight from your account

ˌswitched-ˈon *adj informal* quick to notice new ideas and fashions

swiv·el[1] /ˈswɪvəl/ (*also* **swivel around/round**) *v* (**swivelled**, **swivelling** *BrE*, **swiveled**, **swiveling** *AmE*) [I,T] to turn around quickly and face a different direction, or to make something do this → **spin**: *Anna swivelled round to face him.* | *She swivelled her head round to watch what was happening.* | *Danny swiveled his chair away from me.*

swivel[2] *n* [C] an object that joins two parts of something and helps it to turn around

ˈswivel chair *n* [C] a chair whose seat part can be turned while the legs remain in the same position → see picture at CHAIR[1]

swizz /swɪz/ *n BrE spoken* **a swizz** something that makes you feel disappointed and as though you have been deceived: *The packet's half empty – what a swizz!*

swiz·zle stick /ˈswɪzəl ˌstɪk/ *n* [C] a small stick for mixing drinks

swol·len[1] /ˈswəʊlən $ ˈswoʊ-/ *v* the past participle of SWELL[1]

swollen[2] *adj* **1** a part of your body that is swollen is bigger than usual, especially because you are ill or injured: *swollen glands* | *a badly swollen ankle* | *His eyes were swollen from crying.* **2** a river that is swollen has more water in it than usual **3 have a swollen head/be swollen-headed** *BrE* to be too proud and think you are very clever or important

swoon /swuːn/ *v* [I] **1** to be extremely excited and unable to control yourself because you admire someone so much: **[+over]** *crowds of teenage girls swooning over pop stars* **2** *old-fashioned* to fall to the ground because you have been affected by an emotion or shock SYN **faint** —**swoon** *n* [singular]

swoop[1] /swuːp/ *v* [I] **1** if a bird or aircraft swoops, it moves suddenly down through the air, especially in order to attack something: *The eagle hovered, ready to swoop at any moment.* | **[+down/over/across etc]** *A helicopter suddenly swooped down.* **2** *written* if the police, army etc swoop on a place, they go there without any warning in order to look for someone or something: **[+on]** *Drug officers swooped on several addresses in London last night.*

swoop[2] *n* [C] **1** a sudden surprise attack on a place in order to get something or take people away – used especially in news reports: **[+on]** *Police arrested a man in a swoop on his house last night.* **2** a swooping movement or action → **at/in one fell swoop** at FELL[4]

swoosh /swuːʃ/ *v* [I] to make a sound by moving quickly through the air —**swoosh** *n* [C]

swop /swɒp $ swɑːp/ *v, n* a British spelling of SWAP

sword /sɔːd $ sɔːrd/ ●●○ *n* [C]

1 a weapon with a long pointed blade and a handle

2 a/the sword of Damocles *literary* a bad thing that might happen at any time: *The treaty* ***hung like a sword of Damocles over*** *French politics.*

3 put sb to the sword *literary* to kill someone with a sword

4 turn/beat swords into ploughshares *literary* to start using money, equipment, and skills for peaceful purposes rather than for fighting → **cross swords (with sb)** at CROSS[1](16), → **double-edged sword** at DOUBLE-EDGED(1)

ˈsword dance *n* [C] a dance in which people dance over swords or using swords

sword·fish /ˈsɔːdˌfɪʃ $ ˈsɔːrd-/ *n* (*plural* **swordfish**) [C] a large fish with a very long pointed upper jaw → see picture at FISH[1]

swords·man /ˈsɔːdzmən $ ˈsɔːrdz-/ *n* (*plural* **swordsmen** /-mən/) [C] **1** someone who is good at fighting with a sword **2** *informal* a man who has sex very often and with a lot of different women

S

swords·man·ship /ˈsɔːdzmənʃɪp $ ˈsɔːrdz-/ *n* [U] skill in fighting with a sword

swore /swɔː $ swɔːr/ *v* the past tense of SWEAR

sworn[1] /swɔːn $ swɔːrn/ *v* the past participle of SWEAR

sworn[2] *adj* **1 sworn enemies** two people or groups of people who will always hate each other **2 sworn statement/evidence/testimony etc** a statement etc that someone makes after officially promising to tell the truth

swot[1] /swɒt $ swɑːt/ *n* [C] *BrE informal* someone who spends too much time studying and seems to have no other interests – used to show disapproval —**swotty** *adj*

swot[2] *v* (**swotted**, **swotting**) [I] *BrE informal* to study a lot in a short time, especially for an examination SYN **revise**: **[+for]** *students swotting for exams*

swot up *phr v BrE* to learn as much as you can about a subject, especially in order to prepare for an examination: **[+on]** *It's worth swotting up on all the different types of computer before you buy one.* | **swot sth ↔ up** *I spent all last night swotting up German verbs.*

SWOT /swɒt $ swɑːt/ *n* [U] (***strengths, weaknesses, opportunities, threats***) a system for examining the way a company is run or the way someone works, in order to see what the good and bad features are: *a* ***SWOT analysis***

swum /swʌm/ *v* the past participle of SWIM[1]

swung /swʌŋ/ the past tense and past participle of SWING[1]

syb·a·rit·ic /ˌsɪbəˈrɪtɪk◂/ *adj literary* wanting or enjoying expensive pleasures and comforts

syc·a·more /ˈsɪkəmɔː $ -mɔːr/ *n* [C,U] **1** a European tree that has leaves with five points and seeds with two parts like wings, or the wood of this tree **2** a North American tree with broad leaves, or the wood of this tree

S

syc·o·phant /ˈsɪkəfənt/ *n* [C] *formal* someone who praises powerful people too much because they want to get something from them – used to show disapproval: *a dictator surrounded by sycophants*

syc·o·phan·tic /ˌsɪkəˈfæntɪk◂/ *adj formal* praising important or powerful people too much because you want to get something from them – used to show disapproval: *sycophantic journalists* | *a sycophantic letter* —**sycophancy** /ˈsɪkəfənsi/ *n* [U]

syl·lab·ic /səˈlæbɪk/ *adj* **1** based on or relating to SYLLABLES: *syllabic stress* **2** *technical* a syllabic consonant forms a whole SYLLABLE, for example the /l/ in 'battle'

syl·la·ble /ˈsɪləbəl/ ●●○ *n* [C] a word or part of a word which contains a single vowel sound → **in words of one syllable** at WORD[1](19)

syl·la·bub, **sillabub** /ˈsɪləbʌb/ *n* [C,U] *BrE* a sweet food made by mixing cream with sugar and wine or fruit juice

syl·la·bus /ˈsɪləbəs/ *n* [C] a plan that states exactly what students at a school or college should learn in a particular subject → **curriculum**: **on a syllabus** *Two Shakespeare plays are on this year's English syllabus.*

syl·lo·gis·m /ˈsɪlədʒɪzəm/ *n* [C] *technical* a statement with three parts, the first two of which prove that the third part is true, for example 'all men will die, Socrates is a man, therefore Socrates will die' —**syllogistic** /ˌsɪləˈdʒɪstɪk◂/ *adj*

sylph /sɪlf/ *n* [C] **1** *literary* an attractively thin woman **2** an imaginary female creature who lived in the air, according to ancient stories

sylph·like /ˈsɪlf-laɪk/ *adj literary* a sylphlike woman is attractively thin and graceful

syl·van, **silvan** /ˈsɪlvən/ *adj literary* relating to a forest or trees

sym- /sɪm/ *prefix* the form used for SYN- before the letters b, m, or p

sym·bi·o·sis /ˌsɪmbaɪˈəʊsɪs $ -ˈoʊ-/ *n* [singular, U] **1** *formal* a relationship between people or organizations that depend on each other equally **2** *technical* the relationship between different living things that depend on each other

sym·bi·ot·ic /ˌsɪmbaɪˈɒtɪk $ -ˈɑː-/ *adj formal* a symbiotic relationship is one in which the people, organizations, or living things involved depend on each other

sym·bol /ˈsɪmbəl/ ●●● W3 AWL *n* [C]
1 a picture or shape that has a particular meaning or represents a particular organization or idea → **sign**: *The symbol on the packet is a guarantee that the food has been produced organically.* | **[+of]** *The dove is a symbol of peace.*
2 a letter, number, or sign that represents a sound, an amount, a chemical substance etc: **[+for]** *Fe is the chemical symbol for iron.*
3 someone or something that represents a particular quality or idea: **[+of]** *Space exploration provides a symbol of national pride.* → SEX SYMBOL

sym·bol·ic /sɪmˈbɒlɪk $ -ˈbɑː-/ ●○○ AWL *adj*
1 a symbolic action is important because of what it represents but may not have any real effect: **symbolic gesture/act** *The protest was a symbolic gesture of anger at official policy.* | **symbolic significance/importance** *a meeting of symbolic importance* | **purely/largely symbolic** *It was a largely symbolic gesture from a government trying to win support.*
2 representing a particular idea or quality: *Each element of the ceremony has a* ***symbolic meaning****.* | **[+of]** *Today's fighting is symbolic of the chaos which the country is facing.*
3 using or involving symbols: *A map is a form of symbolic representation.* —**symbolically** /-kli/ *adv*

sym·bol·is·m /ˈsɪmbəlɪzəm/ ●○○ AWL *n* [U] the use of symbols to represent ideas or qualities: *religious symbolism*

sym·bol·ize (*also* **-ise** *BrE*) /ˈsɪmbəlaɪz/ ●○○ AWL *v* [T] if something symbolizes a quality, feeling etc, it represents it: *Crime often symbolizes a wider social problem.* | *Growing discontent has been symbolized by the protests.*

sym·met·ri·cal /sɪˈmetrɪkəl/ ●○○ (*also* **sym·met·ric** /sɪˈmetrɪk/) *adj* an object or design that is symmetrical has two halves that are exactly the same shape and size OPP **asymmetrical**: *The pattern was perfectly symmetrical.* —**symmetrically** /-kli/ *adv*

sym·me·try /ˈsɪmətri/ ●○○ *n* [U]
1 the quality of being symmetrical OPP **asymmetry**: **[+of]** *the symmetry of the design*
2 the quality that a situation has when two events or actions seem to be balanced or equal in some way OPP **asymmetry**: *There was a certain symmetry to coming back to New York, where I started my artistic life all those years ago.*

sym·pa·thet·ic /ˌsɪmpəˈθetɪk◂/ ●●○ *adj*
1 caring and feeling sorry about someone's problems: *a sympathetic friend* | *a sympathetic attitude* | **[+to/towards]** *I'm sympathetic to parents who are worried about what their children see on television.* | *We hope always to provide a friendly* ***sympathetic ear*** (=someone willing to listen to someone else's problems). THESAURUS ▸ KIND
2 [not before noun] willing to give approval and support to an aim or plan: **[+to/towards]** *Senator Capp is very sympathetic to environmental issues.*
3 sympathetic figure/character *literary* someone in a book, play etc who most people like
4 providing the right conditions for someone OPP **hostile**: *a sympathetic environment* —**sympathetically** /-kli/ *adv*: *Jill smiled sympathetically.*

THESAURUS

sympathetic kind to someone who is having problems: *My friends were very sympathetic when I lost my job.* | *Jill was a very sympathetic listener.* | *a sympathetic attitude*

compassionate wanting to help people who are suffering or having problems: *The doctor was a compassionate man who always acted in his patients' best interests.*

understanding not getting angry with someone or criticizing them, because you can see that they have problems: *I have had a lot of time off work, but my boss is very understanding.* | *an understanding look*

caring caring about other people's feelings and wanting to help them: *I have very caring parents.* | *Most of the nurses are very caring.*

sym·pa·thize (*also* **-ise** *BrE*) /ˈsɪmpəθaɪz/ *v* [I] **1** to feel sorry for someone because you understand their problems: *I sympathize, but I don't know how to help.* | **[+with]** *I can sympathize with those who have lost loved ones.* **2** to support someone's ideas or actions: **[+with]** *The public sympathized with the miners' strike.*

sym·pa·thiz·er (*also* **-iser** *BrE*) /ˈsɪmpəθaɪzə $ -ər/ *n* [C] someone who supports the aims of an organization or political party SYN **supporter**: *The anti-abortion rally attracted many sympathizers.*

sym·pa·thy /ˈsɪmpəθi/ ●●○ W3 *n* (*plural* **sympathies**)

1 [plural, U] the feeling of being sorry for someone who is in a bad situation: **[+for]** *I have a lot of sympathy for her; she had to bring up the children on her own.* | *I have absolutely no sympathy for students who get caught cheating in exams.* | *Our sympathies are with the families of the victims.*

2 [plural, U] belief in or support for a plan, idea, or action, especially a political one: **in sympathy with sth** *Willard is in sympathy with many Green Party issues.* | *Her* ***sympathies lie*** *firmly* ***with*** *the Conservative Party.* | **Communist/Republican/left-wing etc sympathies** *Matheson is known for his pro-socialist sympathies.* | **[+with/for]** *Sullivan expressed sympathy for the striking federal workers.*

3 [U] a feeling that you understand someone because you are similar to them: *There was no personal sympathy between them.*

COLLOCATIONS

VERBS

have/feel sympathy for sb *It's hard not to feel sympathy for the losing team.*
express/offer (your) sympathy *Everyone there expressed their sympathy.*
get sympathy from sb *I thought at least I'd get some sympathy from you.*
deserve sympathy *He doesn't deserve any sympathy - it's his own fault.*
play on sb's sympathy (=make someone feel sorry for you in order to get an advantage for yourself) | **expect sympathy**

ADJECTIVES

deep/deepest sympathy (=used when someone is upset after a death) *We'd like to offer our deepest sympathy to Hilda and her family.*
great sympathy *I have great sympathy for the people affected by the housing crisis.*

PHRASES

a message/letter of sympathy *We are grateful for all the messages of sympathy we have received.*
have every sympathy for sb (=feel very sorry for someone - often used when you have had a similar experience yourself) *I have every sympathy for people who find it hard to give up smoking.*
you have my sympathy (=used when saying that you feel sorry for someone) *It must be difficult – you have my sympathy.*
extend your sympathy to sb *formal* (=express sympathy) *I'd like to extend my deepest sympathy to the victim's family.*
my/our sympathy goes out to sb *formal* (=used to formally express sympathy)

sym·pho·ny /ˈsɪmfəni/ ●○○ *n* (*plural* **symphonies**) [C]

1 a long piece of music usually in four parts, written for an ORCHESTRA: *Bruckner's Fifth Symphony*

2 (*also* **symphony orchestra**) a large group of CLASSICAL musicians led by a CONDUCTOR —**symphonic** /sɪmˈfɒnɪk $ -ˈfɑː-/ *adj*

sym·po·si·um /sɪmˈpəʊziəm $ -ˈpoʊ-/ *n* (*plural* **symposiums** *or* **symposia** /-ziə/) [C] **1** a formal meeting in which people who know a lot about a particular subject have discussions about it → **conference**: **[+on]** *a symposium on women's health* **2** a group of articles on a particular subject collected together in a book

symp·tom /ˈsɪmptəm/ ●○○ *n* [C]

1 something wrong with your body or mind which shows that you have a particular illness: **[+of]** *Common symptoms of diabetes are weight loss and fatigue.* THESAURUS SIGN

2 a sign that a serious problem exists: **[+of]** *The disappearance of jobs is a symptom of a deeper socioeconomic change.*

symp·to·mat·ic /ˌsɪmptəˈmætɪk◂/ *adj* **1** *formal* if a situation or type of behaviour is symptomatic of something, it shows that a serious problem exists: **[+of]** *The rise in unemployment is symptomatic of a general decline in the economy.* **2** *medical* showing that someone has a particular illness —**symptomatically** /-kli/ *adv*

syn- /sɪn/ *prefix* together: *a synthesis* (=combining of separate things)

syn·aes·the·si·a /ˌsɪnəsˈθiːziə $ -ʒə-/ *n* [U] a medical condition which makes people experience a mixture of feelings from two of their five senses at the same time, for example seeing numbers as colours or experiencing colours as a smell

syn·a·gogue /ˈsɪnəgɒg $ -gɒːg/ *n* [C] a building where Jewish people meet for religious worship

syn·apse /ˈsaɪnæps, ˈsɪn- $ ˈsɪnæps, sɪˈnæps/ *n* [C] the place where nerve cells meet, especially in the brain —**synaptic** /sɪˈnæptɪk/ *adj*

sync[1], **synch** /sɪŋk/ *n* **1 in sync (with sth/sb) a)** if things are in sync, they are working well together at exactly the same time and speed: **be/move/work in sync** *The two mechanisms have to work in sync.* | *The soundtrack is not quite in sync with the picture.* **b)** matching or in agreement: *a celebrity who is in sync with young people's lifestyles* | *The president is in sync with Thompson's views on many issues.* **2 out of sync (with sth/sb) a)** if things are out of sync, they are not working well together at exactly the same time and speed **b)** not matching or not in agreement

sync[2], **synch** (*also* **sync sth ↔ up**) *v* [I,T] to arrange for two or more things to happen at exactly the same time, or to happen at the same time or in the same way as something else SYN **synchronize**: *The hardest part was syncing the music to the video.* | *Wait for the computer to synch up with your command.*

syn·chro·ni·city /ˌsɪŋkrəˈnɪsəti/ *n* [U] when two or more events happen at the same time or place and seem to be connected in some way

syn·chro·nize (*also* **-ise** *BrE*) /ˈsɪŋkrənaɪz/ *v* **1** [I,T] to happen at exactly the same time, or to arrange for two or more actions to happen at exactly the same time: **synchronize sth with sth** *Businesses must synchronize their production choices with consumer choices.* **2 synchronize your watches** to make two or more watches show exactly the same time —**synchronization** /ˌsɪŋkrənaɪˈzeɪʃən $ -nə-/ *n* [U]

ˌsynchronized ˈswimming *n* [U] a sport in which swimmers move in patterns in the water to music

syn·chro·nous /ˈsɪŋkrənəs/ *adj formal* if two or more things are synchronous, they happen at the same time or work at the same speed

syn·co·pat·ed /ˈsɪŋkəpeɪtɪd/ *adj* syncopated music has a RHYTHM in which the beats that are usually weak are emphasized

syn·co·pa·tion /ˌsɪŋkəˈpeɪʃən/ *n* [U] a RHYTHM in a line of music in which the beats that are usually weak are emphasized

syn·di·cal·is·m /ˈsɪndɪkəlɪzəm/ *n* [U] a political system in which workers control industry, or a belief in this type of system —**syndicalist** *n* [C] —**syndicalist** *adj*

syn·di·cate[1] /ˈsɪndəkət/ *n* [C] a group of people or

companies who join together in order to achieve a particular aim: **[+of]** *a syndicate of banks*

syn·di·cate² /'sɪndɪkeɪt/ *v* [T] to arrange for written work, photographs etc to be sold to a number of different newspapers, magazines etc: *His column is syndicated throughout America.* —**syndication** /ˌsɪndɪ'keɪʃən/ *n* [U]

syn·drome /'sɪndrəʊm $ -droʊm/ ●○○ *n* [C]
1 *medical* an illness which consists of a set of physical or mental problems - often used in the name of illnesses: *people who suffer from irritable bowel syndrome*
2 a set of qualities, events, or types of behaviour that is typical of a particular kind of problem: *'The underdog syndrome' is a belief that things are beyond your control.*

syn·er·gy /'sɪnədʒi $ -ər-/ *n* [U] *technical* the additional effectiveness when two or more companies or people combine and work together

syn·od /'sɪnəd, -nɒd $ -nəd/ *n* [C] an important meeting of church members

syn·o·nym /'sɪnənɪm/ ●○○ *n* [C] *technical* a word with the same meaning as another word in the same language → **antonym**: **[+for/of]** *'Shut' is a synonym of 'closed'.*

sy·non·y·mous /sɪ'nɒnɪməs $ -'nɑː-/ ●○○ *adj*
1 something that is synonymous with something else is considered to be very closely connected with it: **[+with]** *Nixon's name has become synonymous with political scandal.*
2 two words that are synonymous have the same meaning —**synonymously** *adv*

sy·nop·sis /sɪ'nɒpsɪs $ -'nɑːp-/ *n* (*plural* **synopses** /-siːz/) [C] a short description of the main events or ideas in a book, film etc SYN **summary**: **[+of]** *a synopsis of the play*

S

syn·tac·tic /sɪn'tæktɪk/ *adj technical* relating to syntax: *syntactic structure* —**syntactically** /-kli/ *adv*

syn·tax /'sɪntæks/ ●○○ *n* [U] *technical*
1 the way words are arranged to form sentences or phrases, or the rules of grammar which control this
2 the rules that describe how words and phrases are used in a computer language

synth /sɪnθ/ *n* [C] *informal* a synthesizer

syn·the·sis /'sɪnθɪsɪs/ ●○○ *n* (*plural* **syntheses** /-siːz/)
1 [C,U] something that has been made by combining different things, or the process of combining things SYN **combination**: **[+of]** *a synthesis of Eastern and Western philosophical ideas* THESAURUS MIXTURE
2 [U] the act of making a chemical or biological substance: **[+of]** *the synthesis of proteins*
3 [U] the production of sounds, speech, or music electronically: *speech synthesis software*

syn·the·size (*also* **-ise** *BrE*) /'sɪnθɪsaɪz/ *v* [T] **1** to make something by combining different things or substances: *DDT is a pesticide that was first synthesized in 1874.* **2** to combine separate things into a complete whole **3** to produce sounds, speech, or music electronically

syn·the·siz·er (*also* **-iser** *BrE*) /'sɪnθəsaɪzə $ -ər/ *n* [C] an electronic instrument that produces the sounds of various musical instruments

syn·thes·pi·an /sɪn'θespiən/ *n* [C] an actor who seems like a real person, but who is an image made using a computer SYN **VActor**

syn·thet·ic /sɪn'θetɪk/ ●○○ *adj* produced by combining different artificial substances, rather than being naturally produced OPP **natural**: *synthetic chemicals* | **synthetic fibres/materials/fabrics** THESAURUS ARTIFICIAL —**synthetically** /-kli/ *adv*

syn·thet·ics /sɪn'θetɪks/ *n* [plural] substances or materials, especially cloth, that are made using a chemical process

syph·i·lis /'sɪfəlɪs/ *n* [U] a very serious disease that is passed from one person to another during sexual activity —**syphilitic** /ˌsɪfə'lɪtɪk◂/ *adj*

sy·phon /'saɪfən/ *n* [C] a British spelling of SIPHON

sy·ringe¹ /sə'rɪndʒ/ *n* [C] an instrument for taking blood from someone's body or putting liquid, drugs etc into it, consisting of a hollow plastic tube and a needle SYN **hypodermic** → see picture at FIRST AID KIT

syringe² *v* [T] to clean something with a syringe, for example your ears

syr·up /'sɪrəp $ 'sɜː-, 'sɪ-/ *n* [U] **1** a thick sticky sweet liquid, eaten on top of or mixed with other foods: *ice cream and maple syrup* **2** sweet liquid made from sugar and water, used in cans of fruit → **cough syrup** at COUGH MIXTURE

syr·up·y /'sɪrəpi $ 'sɜː-, 'sɪ-/ *adj* **1** thick and sticky like syrup, or containing syrup: *a syrupy liquid* **2** too nice or kind in a way that seems insincere - used to show disapproval: *a syrupy speech*

sys·ad·min /'sɪsˌædmɪn/ *n* [C] *technical* a SYSTEM ADMINISTRATOR

sys·tem /'sɪstɪm/ ●●● S1 W1 *n*
1 RELATED PARTS [C] a group of related parts that work together as a whole for a particular purpose: *an alarm system* | *a well-designed heating system* | *the digestive system* | *the railway system*
2 METHOD [C] an organized set of ideas, methods, or ways of working: **system of/for doing sth** *We've got a good system for dealing with complaints from customers.* | *I don't understand your filing system.* | **under a system** *Under the present system, we do not have any flexibility.*
3 COMPUTERS [C] a group of computers that are connected to each other: *The system has crashed* (=stopped working).
4 sb's system someone's body - used when you are talking about its medical or physical condition: *All this overeating is not good for my system.*
5 all systems go used, sometimes humorously, to say that you are ready to do something or that something is ready to happen
6 the system the official rules and powerful organizations that restrict what you can do: *You can't* ***beat the system***.
7 get sth out of your system *informal* to do something that helps you get rid of unpleasant strong feelings: *I was furious, so I went for a run to get it out of my system.*
8 ORDER [U] the use of sensible and organized methods: *We need a bit more system in the way we organize our files.*

COLLOCATIONS – MEANING 2

ADJECTIVES/NOUN + system

effective/efficient *It was a highly effective system of communication.*
inefficient *He described the tax system as inefficient and unfair.*
complex/complicated *The Australian health care system is extremely complex.*
the current/existing system | **the political/legal/educational etc system** | **the economic/banking system** | **the health care system**

VERBS

develop a system (=create a new one) *The Environment Agency has developed a new national flood warning system.*
introduce a system (=start to use it) *The government has introduced a system of student loans.*
adopt a system (=decide to use it) *They decided to adopt the electoral system used in Britain.*
use/run/operate a system *They use a system of grades to evaluate each hospital's performance.*
a system operates/works (=exists and is used) *He tried to explain how the planning system operates.*
a system works (=is successful) | **a system breaks down/fails** | **modernize/reform a system**

PHRASES

a system of government/education/justice etc *Why was Britain so slow to develop a national system of education?*

'system adˌministrator *n* [C] *technical* someone

whose job is to look after a computer system which has many users, for example a LAN

sys·te·mat·ic /ˌsɪstəˈmætɪk◂/ ●○○ *adj* organized carefully and done thoroughly: **a systematic approach/way/method** *a systematic approach to solving the problem* | *a systematic way of organizing your work* THESAURUS CAREFUL —**systematically** /-kli/ *adv*

sys·te·ma·tize (*also* **-ise** *BrE*) /ˈsɪstəmətaɪz/ *v* [T] to put facts, numbers, ideas etc into a particular order —**systematization** /ˌsɪstəmətaɪˈzeɪʃən $ -mətə-/ *n* [U]

sys·te·mic /sɪˈstemɪk, -ˈstiː- $ sɪˈstemɪk/ *adj technical or formal* affecting the whole of something: *a systemic disease* | *a systemic insecticide* | *Corruption in the police force is systemic.*

ˈsystems ˌanalyst *n* [C] someone whose job is to study a company's computer needs and provide them with suitable software and equipment —**ˌsystems aˈnalysis** *n* [U]

ˈsystem tray *n* [C] the place where the clock and some ICONS (=small pictures that are used to start a particular operation) are shown on a computer screen

S

Tt

T, **t** /tiː/ (*plural* **T's, t's**) *n* **1** [C,U] the 20th letter of the English alphabet **2 to a T/tee** *informal* perfectly or exactly: *That dress* ***suits*** *you* ***to a T***. → T-BONE STEAK, T-JUNCTION, T-SHIRT, T-SQUARE

t **1** the written abbreviation of ***tonne*** or ***tonnes*** **2** the written abbreviation of ***ton*** or ***tons***

ta /tɑː/ *interjection BrE informal spoken* thank you

TA /ˌtiː ˈeɪ/ *n* **1** [singular] *BrE* the abbreviation of TERRITORIAL ARMY **2** [C] the abbreviation of TEACHING ASSISTANT

tab¹ /tæb/ *n* [C]

1 IN TYPING **a)** a TAB KEY **b)** a set position in a line of writing that you get to by pressing the tab key

2 MONEY THAT YOU OWE an amount of money that you owe, or a record of an amount of money that you owe: *The tab for the campaign was nearly $500 million.* | *I'll* ***put it on*** *your* ***tab*** *and you can pay tomorrow.* | *He* ***ran up a*** *$4,000* ***tab*** *in long-distance calls.* THESAURUS ▸ BILL

3 pick up the tab to pay for something, especially when it is not your responsibility to pay: *Taxpayers will pick up the tab for the stadium.*

4 TO OPEN **a)** *especially AmE* a small piece of metal that you pull to open a can of drink SYN **ring pull** *BrE* **b)** a small piece of metal, plastic, or paper that you pull to open something

5 SMALL PIECE OF PAPER/PLASTIC ETC a small piece of paper, cloth, plastic etc that sticks out from the edge of something, so that you can find it more easily: *an index tab labeled 'Expenses'*

6 (*also* **license tab**) a small piece of sticky plastic with a date on it that you put on your car's LICENSE PLATE in the US to show that the car is legally allowed on the road

7 keep (close) tabs on sb/sth *informal* to watch someone or something carefully to check what they are doing: *The police have been keeping tabs on Rogers since he got out of prison.*

8 DRUG *informal* a form of the illegal drug LSD or ECSTASY: *a tab of acid*

9 CIGARETTE *BrE informal* a cigarette

10 INTERNET one of a number of WEB PAGES you have open at the same time: *Do you want to close all tabs or the current tab?*

tab² *v* (**tabbed**, **tabbing**) [I] to press the TAB KEY on a computer or TYPEWRITER

tab·ard /ˈtæbɑːd $ -bərd/ *n* [C] *BrE* a piece of clothing that covers your chest and back and has no sleeves, worn over a shirt or jacket

Ta·bas·co /təˈbæskəʊ $ -koʊ/ (*also* **Taˌbasco ˈsauce**) *n* [U] *trademark* a very spicy red sauce made from CHILLI peppers

tab·by /ˈtæbi/ *n* (*plural* **tabbies**) [C] a cat with light and dark lines on its fur —**tabby** *adj*

tab·er·nac·le /ˈtæbənækəl $ -bər-/ *n* [C] **1** a church or other building used by some Christian groups as a place of WORSHIP **2** a box in which holy bread and wine are kept in Catholic churches **3 the Tabernacle** the small tent in which the ancient Jews kept their most holy objects

ˈtab key (*also* **ˈtab stop**) *n* [C] a button on a computer or TYPEWRITER that you press in order to move forward to a particular place on a line of writing SYN **tab**

tab·la /ˈtæblə $ ˈtɑː-/ *n* [C] a pair of small drums that are played with the hands, and that are used especially in Indian music

ta·ble¹ /ˈteɪbəl/ ●●● S1 W1 *n* [C]

1 FURNITURE a piece of furniture with a flat top supported by legs: *The food was served on long tables.* → COFFEE TABLE, DRESSING TABLE

2 RESTAURANT a table for people to eat at in a restaurant: *I've booked a table for two.*

TABLES

3 SPORT/GAME **snooker/billiard/ping-pong etc table** a special table for playing a particular indoor sport or game on

4 LIST a list of numbers, facts, or information arranged in rows across and down a page: **[+of]** *a* ***table of results*** | *the* ***table of contents***

5 on the table an offer, idea etc that is on the table has been officially suggested and someone is considering it: *The offer on the table is a 10% wage increase.*

6 turn the tables (on sb) to change a situation completely, so that someone loses an advantage and you gain one: *The tables were turned in the second half, when Leeds United scored from the penalty spot.*

7 under the table *informal* money that is paid under the table is paid secretly and illegally: *Payments were made under the table to local officials.*

8 MATHS **times table** a list that young children learn, in which all the numbers between 1 and 12 are multiplied by each other SYN **multiplication table**: **three/four etc times table** *He's 12 years old and still doesn't know his three times table.*

9 GROUP the group of people sitting around a table: *His stories kept the whole table amused.*

COLLOCATIONS

VERBS

set/lay the table (=put knives, forks etc on a table before a meal) *The table was set for fourteen.*

clear the table (=take plates etc off) *Do you want me to clear the table?*
sit at a table *He was sitting at a corner table.*
sit around a table | get up from/leave the table | book/reserve a table (=in a restaurant)

NOUN + table

dinner/breakfast table *Will you clear the breakfast table?*
bedside/kitchen/dining-room table

table² *v* [T] **1 table a proposal/question/motion etc** *BrE* to formally present a proposal etc for other people to discuss: *Dr Clark tabled a motion for debate at next month's committee meeting.* **2 table a bill/measure/proposal etc** *AmE* to leave a bill etc to be discussed or dealt with in the future

tab·leau /ˈtæbləʊ $ ˈtæbloʊ, tæˈbloʊ/ *n* (*plural* **tableaux** /-ləʊz $ -loʊz/) [C] **1** a group of people shown in a work of art **2** a group of people arranged on stage like a picture **3** something you see that looks like a picture, especially a group of people who are not moving or speaking

ta·ble·cloth /ˈteɪbəlklɒθ $ -klɒːθ/ *n* [C] a cloth used for covering a table

ˈtable ˌdancing *n* [U] dancing with sexy movements that is performed close to a customer's table in a restaurant or NIGHTCLUB

ta·ble d'hôte /ˌtɑːbəl ˈdəʊt $ -ˈdoʊt/ *n* [U] *BrE* a meal served in a restaurant at a fixed price, with a limited number of dishes you can choose from → **à la carte**

ˈtable ˌfootball *n* [U] *BrE* a game played on a special table by two players or teams. You score goals by moving rows of model football players from side to side so that they can kick the ball, using handles attached to the players. → **foosball**

ˈtable ˌlamp *n* [C] a small electric lamp that you put on a table or other piece of furniture

ta·ble·land /ˈteɪbəl-lænd/ (*also* **tablelands**) *n* [C] *technical* a large area of high flat land

ˈtable ˌlinen *n* [U] all the cloths used during a meal, such as NAPKINS and tablecloths

ˈtable ˌmanners *n* [plural] the way in which someone eats their food - used when considering how socially acceptable it is: *Their children have very good table manners.*

ˈtable mat *n* [C] *BrE* a small board or piece of cloth that you put under a hot dish or plate to protect the table

ta·ble·spoon /ˈteɪbəlspuːn/ ●●○ *n* [C]
1 a large spoon used for serving food
2 (*also* **ta·ble·spoon·ful** /-spuːnfʊl/) (*written abbreviation* **tbsp** *or* **tbs**) the amount that a tablespoon can hold, used as a unit for measuring food or liquid in cooking: **[+of]** *two tablespoons of flour*

tab·let /ˈtæblɪt/ ●●● S3 *n* [C]
1 a small round hard piece of medicine which you swallow SYN **pill**: *She **took** a couple of headache **tablets**.* | **vitamin/sleeping/indigestion etc tablet**
2 a small hard piece of a substance, especially one that DISSOLVES in water: *water purification tablets*
3 a flat piece of stone or clay with words cut into it, for example above someone's GRAVE
4 be written/set/cast in tablets of stone *BrE* used to say that something does not change: *The programme should not be set in tablets of stone, but improved continuously.*
5 *AmE* a set of pieces of paper for writing on that are glued together at the top SYN **pad** *BrE*
6 (*also* **tablet computer**) a computer that you can carry with you which has a TOUCH SCREEN and does not have a separate KEYBOARD

ˈtable ˌtennis *n* [U] an indoor game played on a table by two or four players who hit a small plastic ball to each other across a net SYN **ping-pong**

ˈtable-top exˌperiment *n* [C] a small EXPERIMENT which helps scientists to guess what might happen on a much larger scale

ta·ble·top sale /ˈteɪbəltɒp ˌseɪl $ -tɑːp-/ *n* [C] an event at which people sell things they no longer want on tables, especially in order to get money for a CHARITY

ta·ble·ware /ˈteɪbəlweə $ -wer/ *n* [U] *formal* the plates, glasses, knives etc used when eating a meal

ˈtable ˌwine *n* [C,U] a fairly cheap wine

tab·loid /ˈtæblɔɪd/ (*also* ˌ**tabloid** ˈ**newspaper**) *n* [C] a newspaper that has small pages, a lot of photographs, and stories mainly about sex, famous people etc rather than serious news → **broadsheet** THESAURUS NEWSPAPER —**tabloid** *adj* [only before noun]: *tabloid journalists*

ta·boo¹ /təˈbuː, tæ-/ *adj* **1** a taboo subject, word, activity etc is one that people avoid because it is extremely offensive or embarrassing: *Rape is a **taboo subject**.* **2** not accepted as socially correct: *It's taboo to date a man a lot younger than you.* **3** too holy or evil to be touched or used

taboo² *n* (*plural* **taboos**) [C] a custom that says you must avoid a particular activity or subject, either because it is considered offensive or because your religion does not allow it: **[+about/on/against]** *There are taboos against appearing naked in public places.*

ta·bor /ˈteɪbə $ -ər/ *n* [C] a small DRUM, played with one hand, used especially in the MIDDLE AGES

tab·u·lar /ˈtæbjələ $ -ər/ *adj* arranged in rows across and down a page, in the form of a TABLE

tab·u·la ra·sa /ˌtæbjələ ˈrɑːzə/ *n* [singular] *literary* your mind in its original state, before you have learned anything

tab·u·late /ˈtæbjəleɪt/ *v* [T] to arrange figures or information together in a set or a list, so that they can be easily compared —**tabulation** /ˌtæbjəˈleɪʃən/ *n* [C,U]

tach·o·graph /ˈtækəgrɑːf $ -græf/ *n* [C] *technical* a piece of equipment for recording the speed of a vehicle, the distance it has travelled etc

ta·chom·e·ter /tæˈkɒmɪtə $ -ˈkɑːmɪtər/ *n* [C] *technical* a piece of equipment used to measure the speed at which the engine of a vehicle turns

ta·cit /ˈtæsɪt/ *adj* tacit agreement, approval, support etc is given without anything actually being said SYN **unspoken**: *a **tacit agreement** between the three big companies* —**tacitly** *adv*

ta·ci·turn /ˈtæsətɜːn $ -ɜːrn/ *adj formal* speaking very little, so that you seem unfriendly → **monosyllabic** THESAURUS QUIET —**taciturnity** /ˌtæsəˈtɜːnəti $ -ɜːr-/ *n* [U]

tack¹ /tæk/ *n*
1 NAIL [C] a small nail with a sharp point and a flat top → see picture at SCREW¹
2 PIN [C] *AmE* a short pin with a large round flat top, for attaching notices to boards, walls etc SYN **thumbtack**, **drawing pin** *BrE*
3 WAY OF DOING STH [C,U] the way you deal with a particular situation or a method that you use to achieve something: *If that doesn't work, we'll try **a different tack**.* | *Rudy **changed tack**, his tone suddenly becoming friendly.*
4 SHIP **a)** [C,U] the direction that a sailing boat moves, depending on the direction of the wind and the position of its sails **b)** [C] the action of changing the direction of a sailing boat, or the distance it travels between these changes: *a long tack into the bay*
5 HORSES [U] *technical* the equipment you need for riding a horse, such as a SADDLE etc
6 SEWING [C] a long loose stitch used for fastening pieces of cloth together before sewing them
7 UGLY OBJECTS [U] *BrE* ugly cheap objects sold as decorations: *souvenir shops full of tack*

tack² *v* **1** [T always + adv/prep] to attach something to a wall, board etc, using a tack: **tack sth to sth** *A handwritten note was tacked to the wall.* **2** [I] to change the course of a sailing ship so that the wind blows against its sails from the opposite direction **3** [T] to fasten pieces of cloth together with long loose stitches, before sewing them
tack sth ↔ **on** *phr v* to add something new to something that is already complete, especially in a way that looks

wrong or spoils the original thing: *a beautiful old house with a hideous modern extension tacked on at the back*

tack·le¹ /ˈtækəl/ ●●○ S3 W3 *v*
1 [T] to try to deal with a difficult problem: *There is more than one way to tackle the problem.* | *It took twelve fire engines to **tackle** the **blaze**.* THESAURUS ▸ DEAL
2 [I,T] **a)** to try to take the ball away from an opponent in a game such as football or HOCKEY **b)** to force someone to the ground so that they stop running, in a game such as American football or RUGBY → see picture at **FOOTBALL**
3 [T] *BrE* to talk to someone in order to deal with a difficult problem: **tackle sb about sth** *When I tackled Susan about it, she admitted she'd made a mistake.*
4 [T] to start fighting someone, especially a criminal: *I certainly couldn't tackle both of them on my own.* —**tackler** *n* [C]

tackle² *n* **1** [C] **a)** an attempt to take the ball from an opponent in a game such as football **b)** an attempt to stop an opponent by forcing them to the ground, especially in American football or RUGBY → see picture at **AMERICAN FOOTBALL** **2** [C] a player in American football who stops other players by tackling them or preventing them from moving forward **3** [U] the equipment used in some sports and activities, especially fishing **4** [C,U] ropes and PULLEYS (=wheels) used for lifting heavy things **5** [U] *BrE informal* a man's sexual organs

tack·y /ˈtæki/ *adj* **1** if something is tacky, it looks cheap or badly made, and shows poor taste: *tacky ornaments* **2** *especially AmE* showing that you do not have good judgment about what is socially acceptable: *It's kind of tacky to give her a present that someone else gave you.* **3** slightly sticky: *The paint's still slightly tacky.* —**tackily** *adv* —**tackiness** *n* [U]

tac·o /ˈtækəʊ, ˈtɑː- $ ˈtɑːkoʊ/ *n* (*plural* **tacos**) [C] a type of Mexican food made from a corn TORTILLA that is folded in half and filled with meat, beans etc

tact /tækt/ ●○○ *n* [U] the ability to be careful about what you say or do, so that you do not upset or embarrass other people → **tactful**, **tactless**: *With great tact, Clive persuaded her to apologize.*

tact·ful /ˈtæktfəl/ *adj* not likely to upset or embarrass other people OPP **tactless**: *There was no tactful way of phrasing what he wanted to say.* | *a tactful man* —**tactfully** *adv*

tac·tic /ˈtæktɪk/ ●●○ *n* [C]
1 a method that you use to achieve something: *a **tactic employed** to speed up the peace process* | *Republicans accuse Democrats of using **delaying tactics*** (=something you do in order to give yourself more time) *to prevent a final vote on the bill.* | ***Shock tactics** are being used in an attempt to stop drink drivers.*
2 **tactics** [plural] the science of arranging and moving military forces in a battle → **strong-arm tactics** at **STRONG-ARM**

tac·tic·al /ˈtæktɪkəl/ ●○○ *adj*
1 relating to what you do to achieve what you want, especially as part of a game or large plan: *Two players were substituted for **tactical reasons**.* | **tactical move/decision/ploy** *a tactical decision to send in troops* | **tactical error/mistake/blunder** (=a mistake that will harm your plans later)
2 **tactical weapon/missile** a MISSILE that is sent a short distance in military battle
3 relating to the way military forces are arranged in a battle —**tactically** /-kli/ *adv*

ˌtactical ˈvoting *n* [U] *BrE* the practice of voting for a political party that you do not support in order to prevent another party from winning an election

tac·ti·cian /tækˈtɪʃən/ *n* [C] someone who is very good at TACTICS

tac·tile /ˈtæktaɪl $ ˈtæktl/ *adj* **1** relating to your sense of touch: *tactile sensations* **2** a tactile person likes to touch people, for example when talking to them

tact·less /ˈtæktləs/ *adj* likely to upset or embarrass someone without intending to OPP **tactful**: *I thought it would be tactless to ask about her divorce.* | *She's one of the most tactless people I've ever met.* | *a **tactless remark*** THESAURUS ▸ CARELESS, RUDE, UNKIND —**tactlessly** *adv* —**tactlessness** *n* [U]

tad /tæd/ *n spoken* **a tad a)** a small amount: *'Would you like some milk?' 'Just a tad.'* **b)** slightly: *It's a tad expensive.*

tad·pole /ˈtædpəʊl $ -poʊl/ *n* [C] a small creature that has a long tail, lives in water, and grows into a FROG or TOAD

tae·kwon·do /taɪˈkwɒndəʊ $ -ˈkwɑːndoʊ/ *n* [U] a style of fighting from Korea, and also a sport, in which you kick and hit but do not use weapons → **karate**

taf·fe·ta /ˈtæfɪtə/ *n* [U] a shiny stiff cloth made from silk or NYLON

taffy *n* (*plural* **taffies**) [C,U] *AmE* a type of soft CHEWY sweet

Taf·fy /ˈtæfi/ *n* [C] *BrE taboo* an offensive word for someone from Wales. Do not use this word.

tag¹ /tæg/ ●●● S3 *n*
1 SMALL PIECE OF PAPER ETC [C] a small piece of paper, plastic etc attached to something to show what it is, who owns it, what it costs etc: **name/identity/price tag** *All the staff wore name tags.* → **DOG TAG**
2 GAME [U] a children's game in which one player chases and tries to touch the others
3 ELECTRONIC OBJECT (*also* **electronic tag**) [C] *BrE* a piece of equipment that you attach to an animal or person, especially someone who has just left prison, so that you always know where they are
4 COMPUTER [C] a computer CODE attached to a word or phrase in a computer document in order to arrange the DATA in a particular way
5 NAME [C] a word or phrase which is used to describe a person, group, or thing, but which is often unfair or not correct: *His speed earned him the tag of 'the runner'.*
6 GRAMMAR [C] *technical* a TAG QUESTION
7 NAME PAINTED ON WALL [C] *especially AmE informal* someone's name that they paint illegally on a wall, vehicle etc
8 CAR *AmE* **a) tags** [plural] *informal* the LICENSE PLATES on a car **b)** [C] a small piece of sticky plastic with a date on it that you put on your car's LICENSE PLATE to show that the car is legally allowed on the road in that year

tag² *v* (**tagged**, **tagging**) [T] **1** to attach a tag to something: *Each bird was tagged and released into the wild.* **2** to give someone or something a name or title, or describe them in a particular way: **be tagged (as) sth** *The country no longer wants to be tagged as a Third World nation.* **3** to attach a tag in a computer program or document: *All the words are tagged with their part of speech.* **4** *informal* to illegally paint your name on a wall, vehicle etc **5** *AmE* to touch someone you are chasing in a game, especially to touch someone with the ball in baseball → see picture at **BASEBALL**

tag along *phr v* to go somewhere with someone, especially when they have not asked you to go with them SYN **tag on** *BrE*: **[+with]** | *Kate tagged along with Mum and Vicky.*

tag on *phr v* **1 tag sth ↔ on** to add something, especially something that was thought of later **2** *BrE* to tag along

tag·a·long /ˈtægəlɒŋ $ -lɒːŋ/ *n* [C] **1** *BrE* something that is attached to and pulled behind something else: *The tagalong attaches to an adult's bicycle.* **2** someone who goes somewhere with someone else: *We were tagalongs on my parents' vacations.*

ˈtag cloud *n* [C] a drawing of the TAGS or words used on a website, with the more frequent words shown larger and the less frequent words shown smaller → **word cloud**

tag·ging /ˈtægɪŋ/ *n* [U] when someone illegally paints their name or symbol on a wall, vehicle etc —**tagger** *n* [C]

ta·gine, **tajine** /təˈʒiːn/ *n* [C] **1** a North African dish that consists of pieces of meat and vegetables cooked slowly in a closed container with spices **2** a round clay dish with a tall lid shaped like a CONE, in which tagines are cooked and served → see Thesaurus box on *p. 1872*

ta·glia·tel·le /ˌtæljəˈteli $ ˌtɑː-/ *n* [U] a type of PASTA that is cut into very long thin flat pieces

ˈtag ˌquestion *n* [C] *technical* a question that is formed by adding a phrase such as 'can't we?', 'wouldn't he?', or 'is it?' to a sentence

T'ai Chi /ˌtaɪ ˈtʃiː, -ˈdʒiː/ *n* [U] a Chinese form of exercise that involves extremely slow movements, and that trains your mind and body

tai·ko·naut /ˈtaɪkənɔːt $ -nɒːt/ *n* [C] an ASTRONAUT from China

tail¹ /teɪl/ ●●● S2 W3 *n* [C]
1 ANIMAL the part that sticks out at the back of an animal's body, and that it can move: *The dog* ***wagged*** *its* ***tail***. | **white-tailed/long-tailed etc** *a white-tailed eagle* → see pictures at BIG CAT, HORSE¹
2 AIRCRAFT the back part of an aircraft → see picture at PLANE¹
3 SHIRT the bottom part of your shirt at the back, that you put inside your trousers
4 BACK PART [usually singular] the back or last part of something, especially something that is moving away from you: *We saw the tail of the procession disappearing round the corner.*
5 tails a) [plural] a man's jacket which is short at the front and divides into two long pieces at the back, worn to very formal events SYN **tailcoat b)** [U] *spoken* said when you are TOSSing a coin (=throwing it up in the air to decide which of two things you will do or choose) OPP **heads**
6 the tail end of sth the last part of an event, situation, or period of time
7 be on sb's tail *informal* to be following someone closely
8 FOLLOW *informal* someone who is employed to watch and follow someone, especially a criminal: **put a tail on sb** (=order someone to follow another person)
9 turn tail *informal* to run away because you are too frightened to fight or attack
10 with your tail between your legs embarrassed or unhappy because you have failed or been defeated
11 it's (a case of) the tail wagging the dog *informal* used to say that an unimportant thing is wrongly controlling a situation
12 chase tail *AmE informal* to try to get a woman to have sex with you

tail² *v* [T] *informal* to follow someone and watch what they do, where they go etc: *The police have been tailing him for several months.* THESAURUS FOLLOW

tail away *phr v BrE* to TAIL OFF

tail back *phr v BrE* if traffic tails back, a long line of cars forms, for example because the road is blocked

tail off (*also* **tail away** *BrE*) *phr v* **1** to become gradually less, smaller etc, and often stop or disappear completely: *Profits tailed off towards the end of the year.* **2** *written* if someone's voice tails off, it becomes quieter and then stops: *'I didn't mean ...' Her voice tailed off in embarrassment.*

tail·back /ˈteɪlbæk/ *n* [C] **1** *BrE* a line of traffic that is moving very slowly or not moving at all: *a five-mile tailback on the M25* **2** *AmE* the player who is the furthest back from the front line in American football

tail·board /ˈteɪlbɔːd $ -bɔːrd/ *n* [C] a TAILGATE

tail·bone /ˈteɪlbəʊn $ -boʊn/ *n* [C] the small bone at the bottom of your SPINE SYN **coccyx**

tail·coat /ˈteɪlkəʊt $ -koʊt/ *n* [C] a man's jacket which is short at the front and divided into two long pieces at the back, worn to very formal events SYN **tails**

tail·gate¹ /ˈteɪlgeɪt/ *n* [C] *AmE* **1** a door at the back of a truck or car that opens out and down **2** a tailgate party

tailgate² *v* [I,T] to drive too closely to the vehicle in front of you

ˈtailgate ˌparty (*also* **tailgate**) *n* [C] *AmE* a party before an American football game, where people eat and drink near their cars in the CAR PARK of the place where the game is played

ˈtail light *n* [C] one of the two red lights at the back of a vehicle

tai·lor¹ /ˈteɪlə $ -ər/ ●○○ *v* [T] to make something so that it is exactly right for someone's particular needs or for a particular purpose: **tailor sth to sth** *Treatment is tailored to the needs of each patient.* | **tailor sth to meet/suit sb's needs/requirements** *The classes are tailored to suit learners' needs.* | **tailor sth for sb** *We tailored the part specifically for her.*

tailor² *n* [C] someone whose job is to make men's clothes, that are measured to fit each customer perfectly → **dressmaker**

tai·lored /ˈteɪləd $ -ərd/ *adj* **1** a piece of clothing that is tailored is made to fit very well: *a tailored suit* **2** made or done specially for someone's particular need or situation: *tailored financial advice*

tai·lor·ing /ˈteɪlərɪŋ/ *n* [U] the work of making men's clothes, or the style in which they are made

ˌtailor-ˈmade *adj* exactly right or suitable for someone or something: **[+for]** *The job's tailor-made for you.* | **[+to]** *insurance tailor-made to each client's requirements*

tail·piece /ˈteɪlpiːs/ *n* [C] *BrE* a part that forms or is added to the end of something, especially a piece of writing

tail·pipe /ˈteɪlpaɪp/ *n* [C] *AmE* a pipe on a vehicle or machine through which gas or steam passes

tail·spin /ˈteɪlˌspɪn/ *n* [C usually singular] **1 in/into a tailspin** in or into a bad situation that keeps getting worse in a way that you cannot control: *Raising interest rates could* ***send*** *the economy* ***into a tailspin***. **2** when a plane falls through the air, with the front pointing downwards and the back spinning in a circle

tail·wind /ˈteɪlˌwɪnd/ *n* [C] a wind blowing in the same direction that something or someone is travelling → **headwind**

taint¹ /teɪnt/ *v* [T] **1** if a situation or person is tainted by something, it damages them by making them seem bad: *Baker argues that his trial was tainted by negative publicity.* **2** to damage something by adding an unwanted substance to it: **be tainted with sth** *The water had been tainted with a deadly toxin.*

taint² *n* [singular] the appearance of being related to something bad or morally wrong: **[+of]** *The city has suffered for many years under the taint of corruption.*

taint·ed /ˈteɪntɪd/ *adj especially AmE* **1** a tainted substance, especially food or drink, is not safe because it is spoiled or contains a harmful substance or poison: *a tainted blood supply* **2** affected or influenced by something illegal, dishonest, or morally wrong: *a tainted witness*

take¹ /teɪk/ ●●● *v* (*past tense* **took** /tʊk/, *past participle* **taken** /ˈteɪkən/) S1 W1
1 MOVE [T] to move or go with someone or something from one place to another OPP **bring**: **take sb/sth to/into etc sth** *Barney took us to the airport.* | *Would you mind* ***taking*** *Susie* ***home***? | *When he refused to give his name, he was taken into custody.* | *My job has taken me all over the world.* | **take sb/sth with you** *His wife went to Australia, taking the children with her.* | **take sb sth** *I have to take Steve the money tonight.* | **take sb to do sth** *He took me to meet his parents.* THESAURUS BRING, LEAD
2 ACTION [T] used with a noun instead of using a verb to describe an action. For example, if you take a walk, you walk somewhere: *Would you like to take a look?* | *Mike's just taking a shower.* | *Sara took a deep breath.* | *I waved, but he* ***didn't take any notice*** (=pretended not to notice). *BrE* | *Please* ***take a seat*** (=sit down). | **take a picture/photograph/photo** *Would you mind taking a photo of us together?*
3 REMOVE [T] to remove something from a place: **take sth off/from etc sth** *Take your feet off the seats.* | *Someone's taken a pen from my desk.* | *Police say money and jewellery were taken in the raid.* → TAKE THESAURUS STEAL
4 TIME/MONEY/EFFORT ETC [T] if something takes a particular amount of time, money, effort etc, that amount of time etc is needed for it to happen or succeed: *How* ***long*** *is this going to* ***take***? | *Organizing a successful street party takes a lot of energy.* | **take (sb) sth (to do sth)** *Repairs take time to carry out.* | ***It took*** *a few minutes for his eyes to adjust*

T

to the dark. | **take (sb) ages/forever** *informal*: *It took me ages to find a present for Dad.* | **take some doing** *BrE informal* (=need a lot of time or effort) *Catching up four goals will take some doing.* | **take courage/guts** *It **takes** courage to admit you are wrong.* | **have what it takes** *informal* (=to have the qualities that are needed for success) *Neil's got what it takes to be a great footballer.*

5 ACCEPT [T] to accept or choose something that is offered, suggested, or given to you: *Will you take the job?* | *Do you take American Express?* | *If you **take** my **advice**, you'll see a doctor.* | *Our helpline **takes** 3.5 million **calls*** (=telephone calls) *a year.* | *Some doctors are unwilling to take new patients without a referral.* | *Liz found his criticisms **hard to take**.* | *I just **can't take any more*** (=can't deal with a bad situation any longer). | *Staff have agreed to take a 2% pay cut.* | **take a hammering/beating** (=be forced to accept defeat or a bad situation) *Small businesses took a hammering in the last recession.* | **I take your point/point taken** (=used to say that you accept someone's opinion) | **take sb's word for it/take it from sb** (=accept that what someone says is true) *That's the truth – **take it from me**.* | **take the credit/blame/responsibility** *He's the kind of man who makes things happen but lets others take the credit.* | **take it as read/given** (=ASSUME that something is correct or certain, because you are sure that this is the case) *It isn't official yet, but you can take it as read that you've got the contract.*

6 HOLD STH [T] to get hold of something in your hands: *Let me take your coat.* | *Can you take this package while I get my wallet?* | **take sb/sth in/by sth** *I just wanted to take him in my arms.*

7 TRAVEL [T] to use a particular form of transport or a particular road in order to go somewhere: *Let's take a cab.* | *I took the first plane out.* | *Take the M6 to Junction 19.*

8 STUDY [T] to study a particular subject in school or college for an examination: *Are you taking French next year?* **THESAURUS** STUDY

9 TEST [T] to do an examination or test SYN **sit** *BrE*: *Applicants are asked to take a written test.*

10 SUITABLE [T] to be the correct or suitable size, type etc for a particular person or thing: *a car that takes low sulphur fuel* | *What size shoe do you take?* | *The elevator takes a maximum of 32 people.*

GRAMMAR: Using the progressive

In this meaning, **take** is not used in the progressive. You say: *I take size 12.* ✗ Don't say: *I'm taking size 12.*

GRAMMAR GUIDE VERBS

11 COLLECT [T] to collect or gather something for a particular purpose: *Investigators will **take samples** of the wreckage to identify the cause.* | **take sth from sth** *The police **took** a **statement** from both witnesses.*

12 CONSIDER [I,T always + adv/prep] to react to someone or something or consider them in a particular way: **take sb/sth seriously/badly/personally etc** *I was joking, but he took me seriously.* | *Ben took the news very badly.* | *She does **not take kindly to** criticism* (=reacts badly to criticism). | **take sth as sth** *I'll take that remark as a compliment.* | **take sth as evidence/proof (of sth)** *The presence of dust clouds has been taken as evidence of recent star formation.* | **take sb/sth to be sth** *I took her to be his daughter.* | **take sb/sth for sth** *Of course I won't tell anyone! **What do you take me for**?* (=what sort of person do you think I am?) | ***I take it*** (=I ASSUME) *you've heard that Rick's resigned.*

13 FEELINGS [T usually + adv] to have or experience a particular feeling: **take delight/pleasure/pride etc in (doing) sth** *You should take pride in your work.* | *At first, he **took** no **interest in** the baby.* | **take pity on sb** *She stood feeling lost until an elderly man took pity on her.* | **take offence** (=feel offended) *Don't take offence. Roger says things like that to everybody.* | **take comfort from/in (doing) sth** *Investors can **take comfort from the fact that** the World Bank is underwriting the shares.*

14 CONTROL [T] to get possession or control of something: *Enemy forces have taken the airport.* | *Both boys were **taken prisoner**.* | **take control/charge/power** *The communists took power in 1948.* | *Youngsters need to take control of their own lives.* | **take the lead** (=in a race, competition etc)

15 MEDICINE/DRUGS [T] to swallow, breathe in, INJECT etc a drug or medicine: *The doctor will ask whether you are taking any medication.* | *Take two tablets before bedtime.* | **take drugs** (=take illegal drugs) *Most teenagers start taking drugs through boredom.* | *She **took** an **overdose** after a row with her boyfriend.*

16 do you take sugar/milk? *BrE spoken* used to ask someone whether they like to have sugar or milk in a drink such as tea or coffee

17 LEVEL [T always + adv/prep] to make someone or something go to a higher level or position: **take sth to/into sth** *The latest raise takes his salary into six figures.* | *Even if you have the talent to **take** you **to the top**, there's no guarantee you'll get there.* | *If you want to **take** it **further**, you should consult an attorney.*

18 MEASURE [T] to measure the amount, level, rate etc of something: *Take the patient's pulse first.*

19 NUMBERS [T] to make a number smaller by a particular amount SYN **subtract**: **take sth away/take sth (away) from sth** *'Take four from nine and what do you get?' 'Five.'* | *Ten take away nine equals one.*

20 MONEY [T] *BrE* if a shop, business etc takes a particular amount of money, it receives that amount of money from its customers SYN **take in** *AmE*: *The stall took £25 on Saturday.*

21 sb can take it or leave it a) to neither like nor dislike something: *To some people, smoking is addictive. Others can take it or leave it.* **b)** used to say that you do not care whether someone accepts your offer or not

22 take sb/sth (for example) used to give an example of something you have just been talking about: *People love British cars. Take the Mini. In Japan, it still sells more than all the other British cars put together.* **THESAURUS** EXAMPLE

23 TEACH [T] *BrE* to teach a particular group of students in a school or college: **take sb for sth** *Who takes you for English?*

24 WRITE [T] to write down information: *Let me take your email address.* | *Sue offered to **take notes**.*

25 take sb out of themselves *BrE* to make someone forget their problems and feel more confident: *Alf said joining the club would take me out of myself.*

26 take a lot out of you/take it out of you to make you very tired: *Looking after a baby really takes it out of you.*

27 take it upon/on yourself to do sth *formal* to decide to do something without getting someone's permission or approval first: *Reg took it upon himself to hand the press a list of names.*

28 take sth to bits/pieces *BrE* to separate something into its different parts: *how to take an engine to bits*

29 be taken with/by sth to be attracted by a particular idea, plan, or person: *I'm quite taken by the idea of Christmas in Berlin.*

30 be taken ill/sick *formal* to suddenly become ill

31 SEX [T] *literary* if a man takes someone, he has sex with them

32 take a bend/fence/corner etc to try to get over or around something in a particular way: *He took the bend at over 60 and lost control.*

33 HAVE AN EFFECT [I] if a treatment, DYE, drug etc takes, it begins to work successfully

THESAURUS

take to move or go with someone or something from one place to another: *Don't forget to take your keys.* | *Shall I take you home?* | *I took Alice a cup of tea.*

bring to take someone or something to the place where you are now: *We've brought someone to see you!* | *Will you bring your photos with you when you come?*

transport to take large quantities of goods from one place to another in a plane, train, ship etc: *The plane is used for transporting military equipment.* | *The coal was transported by rail.*

deliver to take goods, letters, newspapers etc to someone's home or office: *Unfortunately, the package was delivered to the wrong address.*

fly to take someone or something somewhere by plane: *The bread is specially flown in from Paris.*

ship to take goods from one place to another – this can be by ship, truck, plane, or train: *Half the whisky is shipped to Japan and the US.*
carry to take people or goods somewhere – used especially when saying how many people or things, or what kind: *The new plane can carry up to 600 passengers.* | *The ship was carrying a full cargo of oil.*
lead to take someone to a place by going in front of them: *He led Julia through the house to his study.* | *Roland **led the way** back to the car in silence.*
guide to take someone to a place and show them the way: *Emily guided him through a side gate into a large garden.*
escort to take someone to a place and protect or guard them: *The prisoner was escorted into the room by two police officers.* | *The singer was escorted by her assistant and her bodyguard.*

be taken aback *phr v* to be very surprised about something: *Emma was somewhat taken aback by his directness.*
take after sb *phr v* to look or behave like an older relative: *Jenni really takes after her mother.*

GRAMMAR: Using the progressive

Take after is not used in the progressive. You say: *He takes after you.* ✗ Don't say: *He is taking after you.*
GRAMMAR GUIDE ▸ **VERBS**

take sb/sth **apart** *phr v*
1 to separate something into all its different parts (OPP) **put together**: *Tom was always taking things apart in the garage.*
2 to search a place very thoroughly: *The police took the house apart looking for clues.*
3 to beat someone very easily in a game, sport, fight etc
4 to show that someone is wrong or something is not true: *Tariq takes several gay myths apart in his book.*
take against sb/sth *phr v BrE* to begin to dislike someone or something, especially without a good reason: *Voters took against the relationship between the government and the unions in the 1970s.*
take sb/sth ↔ **away** *phr v*
1 to remove someone or something, or make something disappear: *She whisked the tray off the table and took it away.* | *He was taken away to begin a prison sentence.* | *This should take some of the pain away.*
2 to take away *BrE* if you buy food to take away, you buy cooked food from a restaurant and take it outside to eat it somewhere else → **takeaway**: *Fish and chips to take away, please.*
3 take your breath away to be very beautiful, exciting, or surprising
take away from sth *phr v* to spoil the good effect or success that something has: *The disagreement between the two men should not take away from their accomplishments.*
take sb/sth ↔ **back** *phr v*
1 take sth ↔ back to admit that you were wrong to say something: *You'd better take back that remark!*
2 take sth ↔ back to take something you have bought back to a shop because it is not suitable: *If the shirt doesn't fit, take it back.*
3 take sb back to make you remember a time in the past: *Having the grandchildren around takes me back to the days when my own children were small.*
take sth ↔ **down** *phr v*
1 to move something that is fixed in a high position to a lower position: *She made us take down all the posters.*
2 to write down information: *Can I just take some details down?*
3 to pull a piece of clothing such as trousers part of the way down your legs
take sb/sth ↔ **in** *phr v*
1 be taken in to be completely deceived by someone who lies to you: *Don't be taken in by products claiming to help you lose weight in a week.*
2 take sb ↔ in to let someone stay in your house because they have nowhere else to stay: *Brett's always taking in stray animals.*
3 take sth ↔ in to understand and remember new facts and information (SYN) **absorb**: *He watches the older kids, just taking it all in.* | *His eyes quickly took in the elegance of her dress.*
4 take sth ↔ in *AmE* to collect or earn a particular amount of money (SYN) **take** *BrE*
5 to visit a place while you are in the area: *They continued a few miles further to take in Hinton House.*
6 *AmE old-fashioned* if you take in a show, play etc, you go to see it
7 take sb ↔ in *BrE old-fashioned* if the police take someone in, they take them to a police station to ask them questions about a crime: *All five teenagers were arrested and **taken in for questioning**.*
8 take sth ↔ in to make a piece of clothing fit you by making it narrower (OPP) **let out**
take off *phr v*
1 take sth ↔ off to remove a piece of clothing (OPP) **put on**: *He sat on the bed to take his boots off.* | *Charlie was taking off his shirt when the phone rang.*
2 if an aircraft takes off, it rises into the air from the ground (SYN) **lift off** → **takeoff**: *I felt quite excited as the plane took off from Heathrow.*
3 to suddenly start being successful: *Mimi became jealous when Jack's **career** started **taking off**.*
4 take sth off (sth) to have a holiday from work on a particular day, or for a particular length of time: **take time off (work/school)** *I rang my boss and arranged to take some time off.* | **take a day/the afternoon etc off** *Dad took the day off to come with me.*
5 take sb ↔ off *BrE informal* to copy the way someone speaks or behaves, in order to entertain people
take sb/sth ↔ **on** *phr v*
1 take sb ↔ on to start to employ someone → **hire**: *We're taking on 50 new staff this year.*
2 take sth ↔ on to agree to do some work or be responsible for something: *Don't take on too much work – the extra cash isn't worth it.*
3 take sth ↔ on to begin to have a particular quality or appearance: *Her face took on a fierce expression.* | *His life had taken on a new dimension.*
4 take sb ↔ on to compete against someone or start a fight with someone, especially someone bigger or better than you: *Nigeria will take on Argentina in the first round of the World Cup on Saturday.* | *He was prepared to take on anyone who laid a finger on us.*
5 take sth ↔ on if a plane or ship takes on people or things, they come onto it: *We stopped to take on fuel.*
take sb/sth ↔ **out** *phr v*
1 take sb ↔ out to take someone as your guest to a restaurant, cinema, club etc: **[+for]** *We're taking my folks out for a meal next week.*
2 take sth ↔ out to make a financial or legal arrangement with a bank, company, law court etc: **take out a policy/injunction/loan etc** *Before taking a loan out, calculate your monthly outgoings.*
3 take sth ↔ out to get money from your bank account (SYN) **withdraw**: *How much would you like to take out?*
4 take sth ↔ out to borrow books from a library: *You can take out six books at a time.*
5 take sb/sth ↔ out *informal* to kill someone or destroy something: *The building was taken out by a bomb.*
take sth **out on** sb *phr v* to treat someone badly when you are angry or upset, even though it is not their fault: *Don't **take it out on** me just because you've had a bad day.* | **take your anger/frustration etc out on sb** *Irritated with herself, she took her annoyance out on Bridget.*
take over *phr v* to take control of something → **takeover**: **take sth ↔ over** *His only reason for investing in the company was to take it over.* | *Ruth moved into our apartment and promptly took over.*
take to sb/sth *phr v*
1 to start to like someone or something: *Sandra **took to** it **straight away**.* | *Charles was an odd character whom Kelly had never really taken to.*

2 to start doing something regularly: **take to doing sth** *Dee's taken to getting up at 6 and going jogging.*
3 take to your bed to get into your bed and stay there: *He was so depressed, he took to his bed for a week.*
take up *phr v*
1 take sth ↔ up to become interested in a new activity and to spend time doing it: *Roger took painting up for a while, but soon lost interest.*
2 take sth up to start a new job or have a new responsibility: *Peter will take up the management of the finance department.* | **take up a post/a position/duties etc** *The headteacher takes up her duties in August.*
3 take sth ↔ up if you take up a suggestion, problem, complaint etc, you start to do something about it: *Now the papers have taken up the story.* | **[+with]** *The hospital manager has promised to **take the matter up** with the member of staff involved.* | *I am still very angry and will be taking it up with the authorities.*
4 take up sth to fill a particular amount of time or space: **be taken up with sth** *The little **time** I had outside of school was **taken up** with work.* | **take up space/room** *old books that were taking up space in the office*
5 take sth ↔ up to accept a suggestion, offer, or idea: *Rob **took up the invitation** to visit.* | **take up the challenge/gauntlet** *Rick took up the challenge and cycled the 250-mile route alone.*
6 take up sth to move to the exact place where you should be, so that you are ready to do something: *The runners are **taking up** their **positions** on the starting line.*
7 take sth ↔ up to make a piece of clothing shorter OPP **let down**
8 take sth ↔ up to continue a story or activity that you or someone else had begun, after a short break: *I'll take up the story where you left off.*
take sb **up on** sth *phr v* to accept an invitation or suggestion: **take sb up on an offer/promise/suggestion etc** *I'll take you up on that offer of a drink, if it still stands.*
take up with sb/sth *phr v old-fashioned* to become friendly with someone, especially someone who may influence you badly

take² *n* **1** [C] an occasion when a film scene, song, action etc is recorded: *We had to do six takes for this particular scene.* THESAURUS ▸ EXAMPLE **2 sb's take (on sth)** someone's opinion about a situation or idea: *What's your take on this issue?* **3 be on the take** *informal* to be willing to do something wrong in return for money: *Is it true that some of the generals are on the take?* **4** [usually singular] *AmE informal* the amount of money earned by a shop or business in a particular period of time

take·a·way /ˈteɪkəweɪ/ *n* [C] *BrE* **1** a meal that you buy at a shop or restaurant to eat at home SYN **takeout** *AmE*: *Let's have a takeaway tonight.* **2** a shop or restaurant that sells meals to be eaten somewhere else

ˈtake-home ˌpay *n* [U] the amount of money that you receive from your job after taxes etc have been taken out

tak·en /ˈteɪkən/ *v* the past participle of TAKE

ˈtake-off *n* **1** [C,U] the time when a plane leaves the ground and begins to fly **2** [C] a humorous performance that copies the way someone behaves **3** [C] the time when your feet leave the ground when you are jumping

take·out, **ˈtake-out** /ˈteɪk-aʊt/ *n* [C,U] *AmE* a meal that you buy at a restaurant to eat at home SYN **takeaway** *BrE* —**takeout** *adj*: *takeout food*

take·o·ver /ˈteɪkˌəʊvə $ -ˌoʊvər/ ●○○ *n* [C]
1 when one company takes control of another by buying more than half its SHARES: *Thornbury has announced a **takeover bid** of a regional TV company.* | *He prevented a **hostile takeover*** (=when the takeover is not wanted by the company being bought) *of the company.*
2 an act of getting control of a country or political organization, using force: *a communist takeover*

ta·ker /ˈteɪkə $ -ər/ *n* [C] **1 be no/few/not many takers** if there are no takers for something, no one accepts or wants what is being offered **2** someone who accepts support and help from other people, but who is not willing to give them support or help

-taker /teɪkə $ -ər/ *suffix* used with nouns to describe people who take or collect things: *senior decision-takers* | *I'm just a message-taker.* | *a ticket-taker at the recreation hall* | *the policy of not doing deals with hostage takers* | *treatment for **drug takers***

ˈtake-up *n* [U] *BrE* the rate at which people accept something that is offered to them: *Take-up for college places has been slow.*

tak·ings /ˈteɪkɪŋz/ *n* [plural] the money that a business, shop etc gets from selling its goods over a particular period of time: **the day's/week's etc takings** *He counted the night's takings.* | **bar/box-office etc takings** *Cinema box-office takings in 2001 were £600m.* THESAURUS ▸ PROFIT

talc /tælk/ *n* [U] talcum powder

tal·cum pow·der /ˈtælkəm ˌpaʊdə $ -dər/ *n* [U] a powder with a nice smell which you put on your skin after washing

tale /teɪl/ ●●● W3 *n* [C]
1 a story about exciting imaginary events: **[+of]** *tales of adventure* | *a book of old Japanese **folk tales*** (=traditional stories) | *a **fairy tale** by Hans Christian Andersen* | *a **cautionary tale*** (=one that is told to warn people about the dangers of something) THESAURUS ▸ STORY
2 a description of interesting or exciting things that happened to someone, often one which is not completely true about every detail: **[+of/about]** *tales of her life in post-war Berlin* | **tale of/about how** *He was in the middle of **telling** me a long **tale** about how he once met Bob Dylan.*
3 tell tales *BrE* to tell someone in authority about something wrong that someone else has done SYN **tattle** *AmE*: **[+to]** *Don't go telling tales to the teacher!*
4 tale of woe a) a description of events that made you unhappy **b)** a series of bad things that happened to someone: *The England team's tale of woe continued, and they lost the next three games.* → FAIRY TALE, → **old wives' tale** at OLD(24)

tal·ent /ˈtælənt/ ●●● W3 *n*
1 [C,U] a natural ability to do something well: *He **has** a lot of **talent**, and his work is fresh and interesting.* | **[+for]** *She **showed** a **talent** for acting at an early age.* | *a persuasive speaker with **a natural talent** for leadership* | *His latest book reveals **hidden talents**.* | *Sadly, she inherited none of her father's **musical talent**.* | *Your brother is **a man of many talents**.* | *There's a **wealth of talent** in English football.* THESAURUS ▸ SKILL
2 [U] a person or people with a natural ability or skill: *Britain's footballing talent*
3 [U] *BrE informal* sexually attractive people

tal·ent·ed /ˈtæləntɪd/ ●●○ *adj* having a natural ability to do something well → **gifted**: *a talented actor* THESAURUS ▸ SKILFUL

tal·ent·less /ˈtæləntləs/ *adj* not having any special abilities or skills: *a noisy, talentless band*

ˈtalent scout (*also* **ˈtalent-ˌspotter**) *n* [C] someone whose job is to find young people who are very good at sport, music etc

ˈtalent-ˌspotting *n* [U] the work of finding young people who are good at sport, music etc

tal·is·man /ˈtæləzmən/ *n* (*plural* **talismans**) [C] an object that is believed to have magic powers to protect the person who owns it

talk¹ /tɔːk $ tɒːk/ ●●● S1 W1 *v*
1 CONVERSATION [I] to say things to someone as part of a conversation: *I could hear Sarah and Andy talking in the next room.* | **[+about]** *English people love to talk about the weather.* | *All through the afternoon, they sat and talked about their trip.* | **[+to]** *She spent a long time talking to him.* | *She's very easy to talk to.* | **[+with]** *I got the truth from talking with Elena.* | **[+together]** *They were talking together in the hall.* | *Sue and Bob still **aren't talking*** (=are refusing to talk to each other). | **talk in a low voice/a whisper etc** *They were talking in low voices, and I couldn't catch what they were saying.* | **[+of]** (=used especially in formal or literary contexts) *We talked of old times.* → see Thesaurus box on p. 1872

2 SERIOUS SUBJECT [I,T] to discuss something serious or important with someone: *Joe, we need to talk.* | *Is there somewhere we can talk in private?* | **[+to]** *You should talk to a lawyer.* | **[+about]** *We've been talking about getting married.* | **[+with]** *Parents should talk with their children about drug abuse.* | **talk sport/politics/business etc** *'Let's not talk politics now,' said Hugh impatiently.*

REGISTER
In written English, people usually say that they are going to **discuss**, **deal with**, or **address** a subject rather than **talk about** it: *In this essay I will **discuss** the problem of over-population.*

3 SAY WORDS [I] to produce words and express thoughts, opinions, ideas etc: *She was talking so fast I could hardly understand her.* | *How do babies **learn to talk**?* | *Some residents were frightened to talk publicly.* | **talk (in) French/German etc** *They started talking in Spanish.* | *Don't let Dad hear you **talking like that*** (=expressing things in a particular way).

4 A SPEECH [I] to give a speech: **[+on/about]** *Professor Davis will talk about 'Trends in Network Computing'.*

5 SECRET INFORMATION [I] if someone who has secret information talks, they tell someone else about it: *Even under torture, Maskell **refused to talk**.* | *He tried to stop his ex-wife from talking on live TV.* | *We should stop meeting like this. People will talk.*

6 talk sense/rubbish/nonsense etc *spoken* used to say that you think someone is saying something sensible, something stupid etc: *You do talk rubbish sometimes, Jules.*

7 talk (some) sense into sb to persuade someone to behave sensibly: *She hoped Father McCormack would be able to talk some sense into her son.*

8 talk to yourself to say your thoughts out loud: *'What did you say?' 'Sorry, I was just talking to myself.'*

9 know what you are talking about *spoken* to know a lot about a particular subject: *I worked in hotels for years, so I know what I'm talking about.*

10 talk the hind leg(s) off a donkey *informal* to talk a lot, especially about unimportant things

11 talk about lazy/cheap/hungry etc *spoken* used to emphasize that someone or something is very lazy, cheap, hungry etc: *Talk about lucky. That's the second time he's won this week!*

12 talking of/about sth *spoken* used to say more about a subject that someone has just mentioned: *Talking of Venice, have you seen the masks I bought there last year?*

13 what are you talking about? *spoken* used when you think what someone has said is stupid or wrong: *What are you talking about? We got there in plenty of time.*

14 I'm talking to you! *spoken* used when you are angry that the person you are talking to is not paying attention: *Rob! I'm talking to you!*

15 be like talking to a brick wall *spoken* used to say that it is annoying to speak to someone because they do not pay attention to you

16 talk sb's ear off *AmE spoken* to talk too much to someone

17 talk trash *AmE informal* to say rude or offensive things to or about someone, especially to opponents in a sports competition: *Both teams were talking trash on the court.*

18 talk the talk *AmE informal* to say the things that people expect or think are necessary in a particular situation: *She didn't talk the talk of feminism, but her career was the most important thing in her life.* → **walk the walk** at WALK[1](12)

19 I'm/we're/you're talking (about) sth *spoken* used in conversation to emphasize a fact or remind someone of it: *I'm not talking about ancient history, I'm talking about last season's performance.*

20 now you're talking *spoken* used to say that you think someone's suggestion is a good idea: *'Fancy an ice cream?' 'Now you're talking.'*

21 look who's talking, (*also* **you're a fine one to talk**, **you can talk**) *spoken* used to tell someone they should not criticize someone else's behaviour because their own behaviour is just as bad: *'Peggy shouldn't smoke so much.' 'Look who's talking!'*

22 we're/you're talking £500/three days etc *spoken* used to tell someone how much something will cost, how long something will take to do etc: *To do a proper job, you're talking £750 minimum.*

23 talk your way out of sth *informal* to escape from a bad or embarrassing situation by giving explanations, excuses etc: *She's good at talking her way out of trouble.*

24 talk nineteen to the dozen *BrE informal*, **talk a blue streak** *AmE informal* to talk very quickly without stopping

25 talk in riddles to deliberately talk in a strange and confusing way: *Stop talking in riddles and explain what's going on.*

26 talk tough (on sth) *informal* to give people your opinions very strongly: *The president is talking tough on crime.*

27 talk shop if people talk shop, they talk about their work when there are people present who are not interested or involved in it - used to show disapproval: *Are you two going to talk shop all night?*

28 talk dirty (to sb) *informal* to talk in a sexual way to someone in order to make them feel sexually excited

29 be talking through your hat *BrE informal* if someone is talking through their hat, they say stupid things about something that they do not understand

30 talk smack *AmE informal* to criticize someone or something in an unpleasant way

31 talk to the hand *spoken informal* used to tell someone rudely that you do not want to listen to anything he or she is going to say to you. When people use this expression, they also usually turn their face away from the other person and hold the PALM of their hand out towards them.

GRAMMAR: Patterns with talk

- Two people **talk**: *We'll talk later.*
- You **talk to** someone: *I'll talk to you later.* ✗ Don't say: *I'll talk you later.*
- You **talk with** someone: *I've talked with her teacher.*
- You **talk about** something or **talk about doing** something: *He talked about his feelings.* | *We talked about changing the system.* ✗ Don't say: *He talked his feelings.*
- In formal or literary English, you **talk of** something or **of doing** something: *She's talking of leaving.*
- You **talk in** a particular type of voice: *She was talking in a really loud voice.*

talk around/round *phr v BrE*

1 talk sb around/round to persuade someone to change their opinion about something: *Leave Betty to me. I'll soon talk her round.*

2 talk around/round sth to discuss a problem without really dealing with the important parts of it: *They had spent half the night talking round the subject.*

talk back *phr v* to answer someone in authority such as a teacher or parent in a rude or impolite way

talk sb/sth ↔ **down** *phr v*

1 *BrE* to make something seem less successful, interesting, good etc than it really is: *the pessimists who are talking down Britain*

2 to help a PILOT land an aircraft by giving them instructions from the ground by radio

talk down to sb *phr v* to talk to someone as if they are stupid, although they are not SYN **patronize**: *The students felt that they were talked down to as though they were children.*

talk sb **into** sth *phr v* to persuade someone to do something: **talk sb into doing sth** *My husband talked me into going skiing.*

talk sth ↔ **out** *phr v informal*

1 to discuss a problem thoroughly in order to solve it: *We need to spend a little time talking this out.* | **[+with]** *It might help if you talked it out with Dad.*

2 *BrE* if politicians talk out a proposal, they talk about it for a long time deliberately so that there will not be enough time to vote on it SYN **filibuster**: *The Land Protection Bill was talked out by MPs from rural areas.*

talk sb **out of** sth *phr v* to persuade someone not to do

T

something: **talk sb out of doing sth** *Can't you talk them out of selling the house?*

talk sth ↔ **over** *phr v* to discuss a problem with someone before deciding what to do: **[+with]** *Talk over any worries with your GP.*

talk through sth *phr v*

1 talk sth ↔ through to discuss something thoroughly so that you are sure you understand it: *Allow time to talk through any areas of difficulty.*

2 talk sb through sth to help someone understand a process, method etc by explaining it to them carefully before they use it: *Trevor talked me through loading the software.*

talk to sth *phr v* to tell people about or explain something that you have some knowledge of: *I can't talk to the technical aspects of the proposal, but it sounds in general like a good idea.*

talk sth ↔ **up** *phr v* to make something appear more important, interesting, successful etc than it really is: *Jones talked up the idea at the meeting.*

talk² ●●● S1 W1 *n*

1 CONVERSATION [C] a conversation: *After a* ***long talk***, *we decided on divorce.* | *John, I'd like to* ***have a talk with*** *you.* | **[+about]** *We must have a talk about money.*

2 DISCUSSION **talks** [plural] formal discussions between governments, organizations etc: **peace/trade etc talks** *The peace talks look promising.* | *The president* ***held talks*** *with Chinese officials.* | **[+with]** *Talks with the rebels have failed.*

3 SPEECH [C] a speech: *an entertaining talk* | **[+on/about]** *a talk on local history* | **give/do/deliver a talk** *Dr Howard will give a talk on herbal medicine.* **THESAURUS** ▸ SPEECH

4 NEWS [U] information or news that people talk about and hear about a lot, but that is not official: **[+of]** *Tickets sold so quickly there's talk of a second concert.* | **talk of doing sth** *the administration's talk of reducing weapons* | **talk that** *There's talk that she's difficult to work with.* | **just/only talk** *It's just talk. He'll never do it.*

5 TYPE OF CONVERSATION [U] type of conversation: *That's enough of that kind of talk.* | *persuasive* ***sales talk*** | *That's* ***fighting talk*** (=brave and confident words) *from Italy's manager.*

6 be all talk *spoken* someone who is all talk talks a lot about what they intend to do, but never actually does it

7 be the talk of the town/Paris etc someone who is the talk of the town has done something bad, shocking, exciting etc and everyone is talking about them: *She's the talk of London's theatre-goers since her last performance.*

8 talk is cheap used to say that you do not believe someone will do what they say → PEP TALK, SMALL TALK, → **idle talk** at IDLE¹(2), → **pillow talk** at PILLOW¹(3)

talk·a·tive /ˈtɔːkətɪv $ ˈtɒːk-/ ●●○ *adj* someone who is talkative talks a lot OPP **quiet**

talk·back /ˈtɔːkbæk $ ˈtɒːk-/ *n* [U] an electronic system used in a film or television STUDIO, so that someone can talk to someone else without other people hearing them

talk·board /ˈtɔːkbɔːd $ ˈtɒːkbɔːrd/ *n* [C] a website, or part of a website, where people can write their opinions, ask questions etc

talk·er /ˈtɔːkə $ ˈtɒːkər/ *n* [C] *informal* someone who talks a lot or talks in a particular way: *Media people need to be good talkers and skilled negotiators.* | *Mom thinks he's a* ***smooth talker*** (=someone who is polite and pleasant but who you do not trust).

talk·fest /ˈtɔːkfest $ ˈtɒːk-/ *n* [C] *informal* an occasion when people have long conversations or discussions: *His radio show has always been an enjoyable talkfest.*

talk·ie /ˈtɔːki $ ˈtɒːki/ *n* [C] *old-fashioned* a film made using sound

ˌtalking ˈbook *n* [C] a book that has been recorded onto DVD for blind people

ˌtalking ˈhead *n* [C] *informal* someone on television who talks directly to the camera, especially to give their opinions

ˈtalking point *n* [C] *BrE* a subject that a lot of people want to talk about

ˈtalking shop *n* [singular] *BrE* a committee, group etc whose job is to discuss and solve problems, but who do not achieve any action

ˈtalking-to *n* [C usually singular] *informal* an occasion when you talk to someone angrily, especially a child or someone who is below you in rank

ˌtalk ˈradio *n* [U] *AmE* a type of radio programme in which people call the radio station to give their opinions or discuss a subject

ˈtalk show *n* [C] a television show in which famous people answer questions about themselves SYN **chat show** *BrE*: *a talk show host*

ˈtalk time *n* [U] the amount of time a MOBILE PHONE can be used to make or receive calls or messages: *The battery allows approximately 135 minutes of talk time.*

THESAURUS: talk

talk to use words to communicate with someone about something: *I need to talk to you about your work.* | *She always enjoyed talking to Jim.* | *Can we talk?*

speak to talk. **Speak** is a little more formal than **talk**. You often use it when saying that someone **speaks** in a particular way, or that you will **speak** to someone in order to try to get something done. You only use **speak** when saying that someone **speaks** a language: *He spoke with confidence and authority.* | *I'd like to speak to the manager.* | *Do you speak German?*

go on/drone on/ramble to talk too much or for too long about something, in a way that makes people bored: *He went on about how great the team was.* | *I'd better stop rambling and let you get on with your work.*

waffle /ˈwɒfəl/ *BrE disapproving informal* to talk using a lot of words but without saying anything important: *I wish he would stop waffling and get to the point!*

prattle on *disapproving informal* to talk continuously about silly and unimportant things: *She prattled on about her boyfriend for the entire journey.*

TO TALK ABOUT EVERYDAY THINGS

have a conversation to talk to someone for a long time about everyday things: *She was having a conversation with one of her friends.* | *When I arrived, Joe and Jane* ***were deep in conversation*** (=very involved in a conversation).

chat/have a chat *informal* to have a friendly informal conversation about things that are not very important: *The girls were chatting outside the house.* | *It's been nice having a chat with you.*

gossip to talk about other people's private lives when they are not there, especially about things that you have heard, which are not completely true: *What are you two gossiping about?*

visit with sb *AmE informal* to have a conversation with someone: *I visited with him last week.*

converse *formal* to have a conversation with someone: *We met once and conversed briefly.*

TO TALK SERIOUSLY

discuss to talk seriously about problems, ideas, or plans: *They met to discuss how the building should be designed.* | *She refuses to discuss the matter.*

talk sth over to discuss something with someone because it will affect them, especially someone close to you: *Before you accept the job, talk it over with your family.* | *You two need to sit down and talk things over.*

debate to discuss a subject formally when you are trying to make a decision or solve a problem: *The issue will be debated on Tuesday.* | *The UN Security Council debated whether to impose sanctions.*

tall /tɔːl $ tɒːl/ ●●● S2 W2 *adj* (*comparative* **taller**, *superlative* **tallest**)
1 a person, building, tree etc that is tall is a greater height than normal: *He was young and tall.* | *a house surrounded by tall trees* | *This bush* ***grows tall*** *very quickly.* THESAURUS ▸ HIGH
2 you use 'tall' to say or ask what the height of something or someone is: **6ft/2m/12 inches etc tall** *He's only 5 feet tall.* | ***How tall*** *is that building?* | *She's a little taller than her sister.*
3 *AmE* a tall drink contains a small amount of alcohol mixed with a large amount of a non-alcoholic drink
4 a tall order *informal* a request or piece of work that is almost impossible: *Finding a replacement is going to be a tall order.*
5 tall story/tale a story that is so unlikely that it is difficult to believe —**tallness** *n* [U] → **stand tall** at STAND[1](39), → **walk tall** at WALK[1](10)

tall·boy /ˈtɔːlbɔɪ $ ˈtɒːl-/ *n* [C] *BrE* a tall piece of wooden furniture with several drawers

tal·low /ˈtæləʊ $ -loʊ/ *n* [U] hard animal fat used to make CANDLES

ˌtall ˈpoppy ˌsyndrome *n* [U] *BrE* the practice of criticizing people who are very successful

ˌtall ˈship *n* [C] a type of ship with square sails and very tall MASTS, used especially in the past

tal·ly[1] /ˈtæli/ *n* (*plural* **tallies**) [C] a record of how much you have spent, won etc by a particular point in time: *The* ***final tally*** *was $465,000.* | *the two goals that* ***took*** *his* ***tally*** *for Scotland to 15* | ***Keep a tally of*** (=write down) *the number of cars that pass.*

tally[2] *v* (**tallied, tallying, tallies**) **1** [I] (*also* **tally up**) if numbers or statements tally, they match exactly: *Some of the records held by the accounts departments did not tally.* | **[+with]** *The number of ballot papers did not tally with the number of voters.* **2** [T] to calculate a total number

Tal·mud /ˈtælmʊd $ ˈtɑːl-, ˈtæl-/ *n* **the Talmud** the writings that make up Jewish law about religious and non-religious life —**Talmudic** /tælˈmʊdɪk $ tɑːlˈmuːdɪk. tæl-/ *adj*

tal·on /ˈtælən/ *n* [C usually plural] a sharp powerful curved nail on the feet of some birds that catch animals for food → see picture at BIRD OF PREY

tam·a·rind /ˈtæmərɪnd/ *n* [C] a tropical tree, or the fruit of this tree

tam·bou·rine /ˌtæmbəˈriːn/ *n* [C] a circular musical instrument consisting of a frame covered with skin or plastic and small pieces of metal that hang around the edge. You shake it or hit it with your hand.

tame[1] /teɪm/ *adj* **1** a tame animal or bird is not wild any longer, because it has been trained to live with people OPP **wild**: *tame elephants* **2** *informal* dull and disappointing: *Most of the criticism has been pretty tame.* | *I decided that teaching was too tame for me.* **3** [only before noun] *BrE* used to describe a person who is willing to do what other people ask, even if it is slightly dishonest: *If you have a tame doctor, he might give you a sick note.* —**tamely** *adv* —**tameness** *n* [U]

tame[2] *v* [T] **1** to reduce the power or strength of something and prevent it from causing trouble: *The prime minister managed to tame the trade unions.* **2** to train a wild animal to obey you and not to attack people SYN **domesticate**: *The Asian elephant can be tamed and trained.*

ta·mox·i·fen /təˈmɒksəfen $ -ˈmɑːk-/ *n* [U] a drug that is used to treat breast CANCER

tamp /tæmp/ (*also* **tamp down**) *v* [T always + adv/prep] to press or push something down by lightly hitting it several times: *The old man tamped down the tobacco with his thumb.*

Tam·pax /ˈtæmpæks/ *n* (*plural* **Tampax**) [C] *trademark* the name of a very common type of TAMPON

tam·per /ˈtæmpə $ -ər/ *v*
tamper with sth *phr v* to touch something or make changes to it without permission, especially in order to deliberately damage it: *He noticed that the instruments had been tampered with.* | *I don't see the point in tampering with a system that's worked fine so far.*

ˈtamper-ˌevident *adj BrE* a package or container that is tamper-evident is made so that you can see if someone has opened it before it is sold in the shops SYN **tamper-resistant** *AmE*

ˈtamper-proof *adj* a package or container that is tamper-proof is made in a way that prevents someone from opening it before it is sold

ˈtamper-reˌsistant *adj AmE* TAMPER-EVIDENT

tam·pon /ˈtæmpɒn $ -pɑːn/ *n* [C] a tube-shaped mass of cotton or similar material that a woman puts inside her VAGINA during her PERIOD (=monthly flow of blood)

tan[1] /tæn/ *v* (**tanned, tanning**) **1** [I,T] if you tan, or if the sun tans you, your skin becomes darker because you spend time in the sun: *She has a pale skin which doesn't tan easily.* **2** [T] to make animal skin into leather by treating it with TANNIN (=a kind of acid)

tan[2] *n* **1** [C] the attractive brown colour that someone with pale skin gets after they have been in the sun SYN **suntan**: *I wish I could* ***get*** *a* ***tan*** *like that.* **2** [U] a light yellowish-brown colour

tan[3] *adj* **1** having a light yellowish-brown colour: *tan shoes* **2** *AmE* having darker skin after spending time in the sun SYN **tanned**: *She arrived home tan and rested.*

tan·dem /ˈtændəm/ *n* [C] **1** a bicycle built for two riders sitting one behind the other **2 in tandem** doing something together or at the same time as someone or something else: *The two companies often work in tandem.* | **[+with]** *The group operated in tandem with local criminals.*

tan·doo·ri /tænˈdʊəri $ -ˈdʊri/ *adj* [only before noun] tandoori dishes are Indian meat dishes cooked in a clay OVEN: *a tandoori restaurant* | *tandoori chicken*

tang /tæŋ/ *n* [singular] a taste or smell that is pleasantly strong or sharp: *The beer had a sharp, bitter tang.* | **[+of]** *the salty tang of the sea* | *the tang of fresh lemons* —**tangy** *adj*: *tangy orange cake*

tan·gent /ˈtændʒənt/ *n* [C] **1 go off at a tangent** *BrE*, **go off on a tangent** *AmE informal* to suddenly start thinking or talking about a subject that is only slightly related, or not related at all, to the original subject: *Let's stay with the topic and not go off at a tangent.* **2** *technical* a straight line that touches the outside of a curve but does not cut across it

tan·gen·tial /tænˈdʒenʃəl/ *adj formal* tangential information, remarks etc are only related to a particular subject in an indirect way: **[+to]** *The matter you raise is rather tangential to this discussion.* —**tangentially** *adv*

tan·ge·rine /ˌtændʒəˈriːn/ *n* **1** [C] a small sweet fruit like an orange with a skin that comes off easily **2** [U] a bright orange colour —**tangerine** *adj*

tan·gi·ble /ˈtændʒəbəl/ ●○○ *adj*
1 clear enough or definite enough to be easily seen or noticed OPP **intangible**: *The scheme must have* ***tangible benefits*** *for the unemployed.* | **tangible evidence/proof** *He has no tangible evidence of John's guilt.*
2 tangible assets/property property such as buildings, equipment etc
3 *technical* if something is tangible, you can touch or feel it: *The silence of the countryside was* ***almost tangible***. —**tangibly** *adv* —**tangibility** /ˌtændʒəˈbɪləti/ *n* [U]

tan·gle[1] /ˈtæŋgəl/ *v* **1** [I,T] (*also* **tangle up**) to become twisted together, or make something become twisted together, in an untidy mass: *My hair tangles easily.* | *His parachute became tangled in the wheels of the plane.* **2** [I] to argue or fight with someone: **[+with]** *It was not an animal you'd care to tangle with.*

tangle[2] *n* [C] **1** a twisted mass of something such as hair or thread: *Her hair was full of tangles after being out in the wind.* | **[+of]** *John was sitting on the floor in a tangle of blankets.* | **tangle of bushes/branches/vegetation etc** *She followed him, pushing through the dense tangle of bushes and branches.* **2** a confused state or situation: **[+of]** *Her brain was teeming with a whole* ***tangle of emotions***.

T

3 *informal* a quarrel or fight: **[+with]** *She got into a tangle with the staff.*

tan·gled /ˈtæŋɡəld/ (*also* ˌ**tangled** ˈ**up**) *adj* **1** twisted together in an untidy mass: *Your bedclothes are all tangled up.* | *He had hair like tangled string.* **2** complicated or not easy to understand: *the* ***tangled web*** *of local politics* | *tangled emotions*

tan·go¹ /ˈtæŋɡəʊ $ -ɡoʊ/ *n* (*plural* **tangos**) [C] a fast dance from South America, or a piece of music for this dance

tango² *v* [I] **1** to dance the tango **2 it takes two to tango** *spoken* used to say that if a problem involves two people, then both people are equally responsible

tank¹ /tæŋk/ ●●● S2 W2 *n* [C]
1 a large container for storing liquid or gas: *The* ***water tank*** *is leaking.* | *Somehow the chemical got from a* ***storage tank*** *into water supplies.* | **fish/marine/breeding tank** (=for keeping or breeding fish in) | *the plane's* ***fuel tank*** | **petrol tank** *BrE*, **gas tank** *AmE*
2 (*also* **tankful**) the amount of liquid or gas held in a tank: *We set off next day on a full tank.* | **[+of]** *a tankful of petrol*
3 a heavy military vehicle that has a large gun and runs on two metal belts fitted over its wheels
4 a large artificial pool for storing water
5 in the tank *AmE informal* failing and losing money: **be/go in the tank** *Sales can't keep going up, but that doesn't mean the industry is going in the tank.* → THINK TANK, SEPTIC TANK, DRUNK TANK

tank² *v* **1** [I] to decrease quickly or be very unsuccessful: *Not long after the chairman resigned, shares in the company tanked.* **2** [I] *BrE informal* to travel very fast in a car or vehicle **3** [I] *informal* to fail badly and be very unsuccessful SYN **flop**: *His last film tanked in the States, but did well in the UK.* **4** (*also* **tank it**) [T] to deliberately lose a sports game that you could have won

tank up *phr v especially AmE* to put petrol in your car so that the tank is full SYN **fill up**

tan·kard /ˈtæŋkəd $ -ərd/ *n* [C] a large metal cup, usually with a handle, which you can drink beer from

ˌ**tanked** ˈ**up** *BrE*, **tanked** *AmE* /tæŋkt/ *adj* [not before noun] *informal* drunk: *He went down the pub and got tanked up.*

tank·er /ˈtæŋkə $ -ər/ *n* [C] a vehicle or ship specially built to carry large quantities of gas or liquid, especially oil → OIL TANKER

tan·ki·ni /tæŋˈkiːni/ *n* [C] a set of clothes worn by women for swimming. The top piece of clothing covers the body but not the arms. → **bikini**

ˈ**tank top** *n* [C] **1** *BrE* a piece of clothing like a SWEATER, but with no SLEEVES **2** *AmE* a piece of clothing like a T-SHIRT but with no SLEEVES

tanned /tænd/ *adj* having a darker skin colour because you have been in the sun: *He had a tough tanned face and clear eyes.*

tan·ner /ˈtænə $ -ər/ *n* [C] someone whose job is to TAN animal skins (=make them into leather by treating them with a special acid)

tan·ne·ry /ˈtænəri/ *n* (*plural* **tanneries**) [C] a place where animal skins are TANNED (=made into leather by treating them with a special acid)

tan·nin /ˈtænɪn/ (*also* **tan·nic acid** /ˌtænɪk ˈæsɪd/) *n* [U] a reddish acid used in preparing leather, making ink etc

Tan·noy, **tannoy** /ˈtænɔɪ/ *n* [C] *trademark BrE* a system for giving out information in public places using LOUDSPEAKERS: **over the tannoy** *The train's approach was announced over the tannoy.*

tan·o·rex·ic /ˌtænəˈreksɪk/ *adj* someone who is tanorexic likes spending a lot of time in the sun or using SUNBEDS so that their skin becomes brown, even though they know it is bad for the health of their skin —**tanorexia** *n* [U]

tan·ta·lize (*also* **-ise** *BrE*) /ˈtæntəl-aɪz/ *v* [I,T] to show or promise something that someone really wants, but then not allow them to have it

tan·ta·liz·ing (*also* **-ising** *BrE*) /ˈtæntəl-aɪzɪŋ/ *adj* making you feel a desire to have or do something SYN **tempting**: *the tantalizing smell of fried bacon* —**tantalizingly** *adv*: *She was tantalizingly out of reach.*

tan·ta·mount /ˈtæntəmaʊnt/ *adj* **be tantamount to sth** if an action, suggestion, plan etc is tantamount to something bad, it has the same effect or is almost as bad: *To leave a dog home alone is tantamount to cruelty.*

tan·trum /ˈtæntrəm/ *n* [C] a sudden short period when someone, especially a child, behaves very angrily and unreasonably: **have/throw a tantrum** *She throws a tantrum when she can't have the toy she wants.* | *children's* ***temper tantrums***

Tao /taʊ, daʊ/ *n* [U] the natural force that unites all things in the universe, according to Taoism

Tao·is·m /ˈtaʊɪzəm, ˈdaʊ-/ *n* [U] a way of thought developed in ancient China, based on the writings of Lao Tzu, emphasizing a natural and simple way of life

tap¹ /tæp/ ●●○ S3 *n*
1 WATER/GAS [C] *especially BrE* a piece of equipment for controlling the flow of water, gas etc from a pipe or container SYN **faucet** *AmE*: ***Tap water*** (=water that comes out of a tap) *is usually heavily treated with chemicals.* | *She went into the bathroom and* ***turned on the taps***. | **kitchen/bath/garden tap** *I washed my hands under the kitchen tap.* | **cold/hot tap** (=the tap that cold or hot water comes from)
2 A LIGHT HIT [C] an act of hitting something lightly, especially to get someone's attention: **[+at/on]** *She felt a tap on her shoulder.* | *There was a tap at the door.*
3 on tap a) beer that is on tap comes from a BARREL **b)** *informal* something that is on tap is ready to use when you need it: *We've got all the information on tap.*
4 DANCING [U] (*also* **tap dancing**) dancing in which you wear special shoes with pieces of metal on the bottom which make a loud sharp sound on the floor
5 TELEPHONE [C] an act of secretly listening to someone's telephone, using electronic equipment: *The police had put a tap on his phone line.*
6 BARREL [C] a specially shaped object used for letting liquid out of a BARREL, especially beer
7 TUNE **taps** [plural] a song or tune played on the BUGLE at night in an army camp, and at military funerals

tap² ●●○ *v* (**tapped**, **tapping**)
1 HIT LIGHTLY [I,T] to hit your fingers lightly on something, for example to get someone's attention: **tap sb on the shoulder/arm/chest etc** *He turned as someone tapped him on the shoulder.* | **[+on]** *I went up and tapped on the window.* | **tap sth on/against/from etc sth** *Mark tapped his fingers on the tabletop impatiently.* | *She tapped ash from her cigarette.* THESAURUS ▶ HIT
2 MUSIC [T] to make a regular pattern of sounds with your fingers or feet, especially when you are listening to music: *She tapped her feet in time to the music.* | *a toe-tapping tune*
3 ENERGY/MONEY [T] (*also* **tap into**) to use or take what is needed from something such as an energy supply or an amount of money: *People are tapping into the power supply illegally.* | *We hope that additional sources of funding can be tapped.*
4 IDEAS [T] (*also* **tap into**) to make as much use as possible of the ideas, experience, knowledge etc that a group of people has: *Your adviser's experience is there to be tapped.* | *helping people tap into training opportunities*
5 TELEPHONE [T] to listen secretly to someone's telephone by using a special piece of electronic equipment: *Murray's* ***phone*** *calls to Australia were* ***tapped***.
6 TREE [T] to get liquid from the TRUNK of a tree by making a hole in it
7 PLAYER [T] (*also* **tap up**) *BrE informal* if a football club taps a player from another team, it illegally tries to persuade that player to join its team

tap sth ↔ **in** (*also* **tap sth into sth**) *phr v BrE* to put information, numbers etc into a computer, telephone etc by pressing buttons or keys: *Tap in your password before you log on.*

tap sth ↔ **out** *phr v*
1 to hit something lightly, especially with your fingers or foot, in order to make a pattern of sounds: *He whistled the tune and tapped out the rhythm.*
2 to write something with a computer: *Brian tapped out a name on his small electronic organizer.*

tap·as /ˈtæpəs $ ˈtɑː-/ *n* [U] small dishes of food eaten as part of the first course of a Spanish meal

ˈtap ˌdancing *n* [U] dancing in which you wear shoes with pieces of metal on the bottom, which make a sound as you move —**tap dance** *v* [I,T] —**tap dancer** *n* [C]

tape[1] /teɪp/ ●●● S3 W3 AWL *n*
1 FOR RECORDING **a)** [U] narrow plastic material covered with a special MAGNETIC substance, on which you can record sounds, pictures, or computer information: **on tape** (=recorded on tape) *We've got the film on tape.* | *I hate hearing my voice on tape.* **b)** [C] a special plastic box containing a length of tape that you can record sound on SYN **cassette**: *I'll listen to the tape tomorrow.* | *William lent me some of his Beatles tapes.* | **[+of]** *We played a tape of African music and began dancing.* | *Bring me a* ***blank tape*** *and I'll record it for you.* **c)** [C] a special plastic box containing a length of tape that you can record sound and pictures on SYN **videotape**
2 STICKY MATERIAL [U] a narrow length of plastic that is sticky on one side and is used to stick things together SYN **Sellotape** *BrE*, **Scotch tape** *AmE*: *a photo stuck to the wall with tape*
3 THIN PIECE OF MATERIAL [C,U] a long thin piece of plastic or cloth used for purposes such as marking out an area of ground or tying things together: *Crime-scene tape marked out the position of the murdered man.*
4 the tape a string stretched out across the finishing line in a race and broken by the winner
5 FOR MEASURING [C] a TAPE MEASURE → **RED TAPE**

tape[2] ●●○ AWL *v*
1 RECORD STH [I,T] (*also* **tape record**) to record sound or pictures onto a tape: *Would you mind if I taped this conversation?* | *Quiet – the machine's still taping.*
2 STICK STH [T] to stick something onto something else using tape: **tape sth to sth** *There were two pictures taped to the side of the fridge.*
3 FASTEN STH [T] (*also* **tape up**) to fasten a package, box etc with sticky tape
4 INJURY [T] (*also* **tape up**) *especially AmE* to tie a BANDAGE firmly around an injured part of someone's body SYN **strap** *BrE*: *His ankle had been taped.*
5 have (got) sth/sb taped *BrE informal* to understand someone or something completely and know how to deal with them: *You can't fool Liz – she's got you taped.*

ˈtape deck *n* [C] the part of a TAPE RECORDER that winds the tape, and records and plays back sound

ˈtape ˌmeasure *n* [C] a long narrow band of cloth or steel, marked with centimetres, feet etc, used for measuring something → see picture at **MEASURE[1]**

ta·per[1] /ˈteɪpə $ -ər/ *v* [I,T] to become gradually narrower towards one end, or to make something become narrower at one end: **[+to]** *His wide chest tapers to a small waist.* —**tapering** *adj*: *long tapering fingers*

taper off *phr v* to decrease gradually: *Profits may be tapering off in the near future.*

taper[2] *n* [C] **1** a very thin CANDLE: *small boys holding lighted tapers* **2** a piece of string covered in WAX, used for lighting lamps, CANDLES etc: *The box contained a taper to light each firework.*

ˈtape reˌcord *v* [T] to record sound using a tape recorder

ˈtape reˌcorder *n* [C] a piece of electrical equipment that can record sound on tape and play it back

ˈtape reˌcording *n* [C] something that has been recorded with a tape recorder: **[+of]** *The court heard tape recordings of the meeting.*

ta·pered /ˈteɪpəd $ -ərd/ *adj* having a shape that gets narrower towards one end: *tapered trousers*

tap·es·try /ˈtæpəstri/ *n* (*plural* **tapestries**) [C,U] **1** a large piece of heavy cloth on which coloured threads are woven to produce a picture, pattern etc: *a colourful tapestry depicting a hunting scene* **2** something that is made up of many different people and things: *This was all new to her – part of* ***life's rich tapestry***.

tape·worm /ˈteɪpwɜːm $ -wɜːrm/ *n* [C] a long flat WORM that lives in the BOWELS of humans and other animals and can make them ill

tap·i·o·ca /ˌtæpiˈəʊkə $ -ˈoʊ-/ *n* [U] small hard white grains made from the crushed dried roots of CASSAVA, or a DESSERT made from cooking this

ta·pir /ˈteɪpə, -pɪə $ -pər, teɪˈpɪr/ *n* [C] an animal like a pig with thick legs, a short tail, and a long nose, that lives in tropical America and Southeast Asia

tap·root /ˈtæpruːt/ *n* [C] the large main root of a plant, from which smaller roots grow

ˈtap ˌwater *n* [U] water that comes out of a TAP rather than a bottle

tar[1] /tɑː $ tɑːr/ *n* [U] **1** a black substance, thick and sticky when hot but hard when cold, used especially for making road surfaces → **COAL TAR 2** a sticky substance that forms when tobacco burns, and that gets into the lungs of people who smoke: *high tar cigarettes*

tar[2] *v* (**tarred, tarring**) [T] **1** to cover a surface with tar: *a tarred roof* **2 be/get tarred with the same brush** if someone is tarred with the same brush as someone else, people think they have the same faults or have committed the same crimes, even if they have not: *You've made it very clear that you think I'm tarred with the same brush as William.* **3 tar and feather** to cover someone in tar and feathers as a cruel unofficial punishment

ta·ra·ma·sa·la·ta /ˌtærəməsəˈlɑːtə $ ˌtɑː-/ *n* [U] a Greek food consisting of a pink creamy mixture made from fish eggs

tar·an·tel·la /ˌtærənˈtelə/ *n* [C] a fast Italian dance, or the music for this dance

ta·ran·tu·la /təˈræntjələ $ -tʃələ/ *n* [C] a large poisonous SPIDER from Southern Europe and tropical America

tar·dy /ˈtɑːdi $ ˈtɑːrdi/ *adj formal* **1** arriving or done late: *Do please forgive this tardy reply.* | *He's been tardy three times this semester.* THESAURUS ▸ LATE **2** doing something too slowly or late: **[+in]** *people who are tardy in paying their bills* —**tardily** *adv* —**tardiness** *n* [U]

tare /teə $ ter/ *n* [usually singular] *technical* **1** the weight of the materials in which goods are packed **2** the weight of an unloaded vehicle, used to calculate the actual weight of the goods in it

tar·get[1] /ˈtɑːgɪt $ ˈtɑːr-/ ●●● S2 W2 AWL *n* [C]
1 AIM something that you are trying to achieve, such as a total, an amount, or a time SYN **goal**: **sales/attainment/growth etc targets** *demanding financial targets* | **[+of]** *the target of a one-third reduction in road accidents* | **[+for]** *Higher degrees in English are a target for foreign students.* | *There is no* ***target date*** *for completion of the new project.* | *The government may fail to* ***meet*** *(=achieve) its* ***target*** *of recycling 25% of domestic waste.* | *Jiang* ***set*** *annual growth* ***targets*** *of 8–9%.* | **on target** (=likely to achieve a target) *The company says that growth of 10% is on target.* THESAURUS ▸ AIM
2 OBJECT OF ATTACK an object, person, or place that is deliberately chosen to be attacked: **[+for/of]** *Railway stations are* ***prime targets*** (=very likely targets) *for bombs.* | **easy/soft target** *Cars without security devices are an easy target for the thief.*
3 OBJECT OF AN ACTION the person or place that is most directly affected by an action, especially a bad one: **[+for/of]** *The area has become a* ***prime target*** *for supermarket development.* | *The country is a target of criticism for its human rights record.*
4 SHOOTING something that you practise shooting at, especially a round board with circles on it: *The area is used by the army for* ***target practice***.
5 target audience/group/area etc a limited group, area etc that a plan, idea etc is aimed at: *Our target audience is men aged between 18 and 35.*

T

6 target language the language that you are learning or that you are translating into

target² ●○○ AWL *v* [T]

1 to make something have an effect on a particular limited group or area: *The advertisement was designed to target a mass audience.* | **target sth on/at sb/sth** *a new benefit targeted on low-income families* | *The programme is targeted at improving the health of women of all ages.*

2 to aim something at a target: **target sth on/at sb/sth** *The missiles are targeted at several key military sites.*

3 to choose a particular person or place to do something to, especially to attack them or criticize them: *It's clear that smaller, more vulnerable banks have been targeted.* | *He was targeted by terrorists for a second time last night.*

tar·iff /ˈtærɪf/ ●○○ *n* [C]

1 a tax on goods coming into a country or going out of a country: **[+on]** *The government may **impose tariffs** on imports.*

2 *BrE* a list of fixed prices charged by a hotel or restaurant, for example for the cost of meals or rooms

3 *BrE* a list or system of prices which MOBILE PHONE companies charge for the services they provide

tar·mac¹ /ˈtɑːmæk $ ˈtɑːr-/ *n trademark* **1** (*also* **tar·ma·cad·am** *BrE* /ˌtɑːməˈkædəm $ ˌtɑːr- $ ˌtɑːr-/) [U] a mixture of TAR and very small stones, used for making the surface of roads SYN **asphalt 2 the tarmac** an area covered with tarmac outside airport buildings: **on the tarmac** *Journalists waited on the tarmac to question him.*

tarmac² *v* (**tarmacked**, **tarmacking**) [T] to cover a road's surface with tarmac

tarn /tɑːn $ tɑːrn/ *n* [C] a small lake among mountains

tar·nish¹ /ˈtɑːnɪʃ $ ˈtɑːr-/ *v* **1** [T] if an event or fact tarnishes someone's REPUTATION, record, image etc, it makes it worse: *His regime was tarnished by human rights abuses.* **2** [I,T] if metals such as silver, COPPER, or BRASS tarnish, or if something tarnishes them, they become dull and lose their colour: *Gold does not tarnish easily.* | *tarnished silver spoons*

tarnish² *n* [singular, U] dullness of colour, or loss of brightness

T

ta·ro /ˈtɑːrəʊ $ -roʊ/ *n* (*plural* **taros**) [C,U] a tropical plant grown for its thick root, which is boiled and eaten

tar·ot /ˈtærəʊ $ -roʊ/ *n* [singular, U] a set of 78 cards, used for telling what will happen to someone in the future

tar·pau·lin /tɑːˈpɔːlɪn $ tɑːrˈpɒː-/ *especially BrE*, **tarp** /tɑːp $ tɑːrp/ *AmE n* [C,U] a large heavy cloth or piece of thick plastic that water will not pass through, used to keep rain off things

tar·ra·gon /ˈtærəgən/ *n* [U] the leaves of a small European plant, used in cooking to give food a special taste: *chicken with tarragon*

tar·ry¹ /ˈtæri/ *v* (**tarried**, **tarrying**, **tarries**) [I] *literary* **1** to stay in a place, especially when you should leave SYN **linger 2** to delay or be slow in going somewhere

tar·ry² /ˈtɑːri/ *adj* covered with TAR (=a thick black liquid)

ˈtar sands *n* [plural] sand or SANDSTONE that contains BITUMEN (=a thick form of oil) which can be taken and used, for example as FUEL

tar·sus /ˈtɑːsəs $ ˈtɑːr-/ *n* (*plural* **tarsi**) /-saɪ/ [C] *technical* your ANKLE, or one of the seven small bones in your ankle —**tarsal** *adj*

tart¹ /tɑːt $ tɑːrt/ *n* **1** [C,U] a PIE without a top on it, containing something sweet: **apple/treacle/jam etc tart** → see picture at DESSERT THESAURUS TASTE **2** [C] *informal* an insulting word for a woman who you think is too willing to have sex **3** [C] *informal* a PROSTITUTE

tart² *adj* **1** food that is tart has a sharp sour taste: *a tart apple* THESAURUS TASTE **2 tart reply/remark etc** a reply, remark etc that is sharp and unkind —**tartly** *adv*: *'I don't think so!' she replied tartly.* —**tartness** *n* [U]

tart³ *v*

tart sth ↔ **up** *phr v BrE informal* **1** to try to make something more attractive by decorating it, often in a way that other people think is cheap or ugly: *We'll need to tart the place up a bit.* **2 tart yourself up/get tarted up** if a woman tarts herself up or gets tarted up, she tries to make herself look attractive by putting on nice clothes, MAKE-UP etc – often used humorously: *She got all tarted up for the party.*

tar·tan /ˈtɑːtn $ ˈtɑːrtn/ *n* [C,U] a traditional Scottish pattern of coloured squares and crossed lines, or cloth, especially wool cloth, with this pattern SYN **plaid** *AmE*: *the MacGregor tartan* (=the special pattern worn by the MacGregor family) —**tartan** *adj*: *a tartan scarf* → see picture at PATTERN¹

tar·tar /ˈtɑːtə $ ˈtɑːrtər/ *n* **1** [U] a hard substance that forms on your teeth **2** [C] *BrE informal* someone who has a violent temper: *She's a real tartar.*

tar·tare sauce /ˌtɑːtə ˈsɔːs $ ˌtɑːrtər ˈsɒːs/ *n* [U] a cold white sauce often eaten with fish, made from egg, oil, GHERKINS, and CAPERS

tar·tar·ic ac·id /tɑːˌtærɪk ˈæsɪd $ tɑːr-/ *n* [U] a strong acid that comes from a plant and is used in preparing some foods and medicines

tart·y /ˈtɑːti $ ˈtɑːrti/ *adj BrE informal* a woman who looks tarty looks like she is too willing for sex: *Do you think this dress looks too tarty?*

Tar·zan /ˈtɑːzən $ ˈtɑːr-/ the main character in books by Edgar Rice Burroughs, which were later made into many films, about a baby who is left in the African forest and is cared for by APEs until he becomes a man

Ta·ser /ˈteɪzə $ -ər/ *n* [C] *trademark* a type of gun that produces a strong electric current and that is used by the police in some countries —**tase** *v* [T]

task¹ /tɑːsk $ tæsk/ ●●● S2 W1 *n*

1 [C] a piece of work that must be done, especially one that is difficult or unpleasant or that must be done regularly SYN **job**: **[+of]** *The task of the union representative is to fight on behalf of the members.* | *Sara **had the task of** preparing the agenda for meetings.* | *I was **given the task** of building a fire.* | *the skills required to **carry out** these **tasks*** | *He soon realized the scale of the **task** he had **undertaken**.* | *Our **first task** is to gather information.* | *Monkeys can be taught to do **simple tasks**.* | *They have the **unenviable task** of supervising the most dangerous prison in the country.* | *Volunteers had the **thankless task** of distributing campaign leaflets.* | *Trying to bring up a small daughter on your own is **no easy task**.*

> **REGISTER**
> In everyday English, people usually say **job** rather than **task**: *I was given the **job** of building the fire.*

2 take someone to task to strongly criticize somebody for something they have done: **[+for]** *He was taken to task for not reporting the problem earlier.*

task² AWL *v* [T] to give someone the responsibility for doing something: **be tasked with (doing) sth** *We were tasked with completing the job by the end of 2006.* GRAMMAR **Task** is usually passive.

task·bar /ˈtɑːskbɑː $ ˈtæskbɑːr/ *n* [C] a narrow area across the bottom of a computer screen, that shows which documents or programs are open

ˈtask force *n* [C] **1** a group formed for a short time to deal with a particular problem: **[+on]** *a task force on health care reform* **2** a military force sent to a place for a special purpose

task·mas·ter /ˈtɑːskˌmɑːstə $ ˈtæskˌmæstər/ *n* **be a hard/stern/tough taskmaster** to force people to work very hard

tas·sel /ˈtæsəl/ *n* [C] threads tied together at one end and hung as a decoration on clothes, curtains etc —**tasselled** *BrE*, **tasseled** *AmE adj*

taste¹ /teɪst/ ●●● S2 W2 *n*

1 FOOD **a)** [C,U] the feeling that is produced by a particular food or drink when you put it in your mouth SYN **flavour**: *The medicine had a slightly bitter taste.* | **[+of]** *I don't really like the taste of meat anymore.* **b)** [U] the sense by which you know one food from another: *Some* *birds have a highly developed* ***sense of taste****.* **c) have a taste (of sth)** if you have a taste of some food or drink, you put a small amount in your mouth to try it: *You must have a taste of the fruitcake.*

2 WHAT YOU LIKE [C,U] the kind of things that someone likes: **[+in]** *He asked about my taste in music.* | **[+for]** *While she was in France she developed a taste for fine wines.*

3 JUDGMENT [U] someone's judgment when they choose clothes, decorations etc: **have good/bad etc taste** *She has such good taste.* | **[+in]** *Some people have really bad taste in clothes.*

4 WHAT IS ACCEPTABLE/NOT OFFENSIVE [U] the quality of being acceptable and not offensive: *All television companies accept the need to maintain standards of* ***taste and decency****.* | **be in bad/poor etc taste** (=likely to offend people) *She acknowledged her remark had been in bad taste.*

5 EXPERIENCE [usually singular] a short experience of something that shows you what it is like: **[+of]** *Schoolchildren can* ***get a taste of*** *the countryside first-hand.* | *It* ***gave*** *him his first* ***taste*** *of acting for the big screen.* | *The autumn storms gave us a taste of what was to come* (=showed what would happen later).

6 FEELING [singular] the feeling that you have after an experience, especially a bad experience: *The way he spoke to those children* ***left a nasty taste in my mouth****.* | *the bitter taste of failure* | *the sweet taste of victory*

7 ... to taste if you add salt, spices etc to taste, you add as much as you think makes it taste right – used in instructions in cook books: *Add salt to taste.* → **give sb a taste of their own medicine** at MEDICINE(4)

COLLOCATIONS – MEANING 2

ADJECTIVES

similar/the same *We have similar musical tastes.*
same/similar/different *Their tastes in movies were very different.*
expensive/sophisticated *He was a man of expensive tastes.* (=he liked expensive things)
simple (=liking simple things) | **eclectic** (=liking a wide variety of different things) | **musical/literary/artistic taste** | **your personal taste** | **public/popular taste** | **an acquired taste** (=something that people do not like at first)

VERBS

have ... tastes *Josh and I have the same tastes.*
have a taste for sth (=like something) *She certainly has a taste for adventure.*
get/develop a taste for sth (*also* **acquire a taste for sth** *formal*) (=to start to like something) *At university she developed a taste for performing.*
share a taste (=have the same taste as someone else) | **suit/satisfy/appeal to sb's tastes** (=provide what someone likes)

PHRASES

be to sb's taste (=be something that someone likes) *If her books are not to your taste, there are plenty of books by other writers.*
be too bright/modern etc for sb's taste *The building was too modern for my taste.*
sth is a matter of taste (=different people have different opinions about what is good or right) | **there's no accounting for taste** (=used humorously to say that you do not understand why someone likes something)

THESAURUS

DESCRIBING THE TASTE OF SOMETHING

delicious having a very good taste: *This cake is delicious!* | *a delicious meal*
disgusting/revolting having a very bad taste: *The medicine tasted disgusting.* | *They had to eat revolting things, like fish eyes.*
sweet tasting full of sugar: *The oranges were very sweet.*
tasty *especially spoken* tasting good and with plenty of flavour: *She cooked us a simple but tasty meal.* | *That was really tasty!*
sour/tart having a taste that stings your tongue slightly, like lemon does – used especially when this is rather unpleasant: *The apples were a little sour.* | *The wine has rather a tart taste, which not everyone will like.*
tangy having a taste that stings your tongue slightly, like lemon does, in a way that seems good: *The dressing was nice and tangy.*
bitter having a strong taste which is not sweet and is sometimes rather unpleasant – used for example about black coffee, or chocolate without sugar: *bitter chocolate* | *The medicine had rather a bitter taste.*
salty containing a lot of salt: *Danish salami has a salty flavour.*
hot/spicy having a burning taste because it contains strong spices: *I love hot curries.* | *a spicy tomato sauce*
piquant /ˈpiːkənt/ *formal* a little spicy – used especially by people who write about food. This word can sound rather PRETENTIOUS in everyday conversation: *cooked vegetables in a piquant sauce*
mild not having a strong or hot taste – usually used about foods that can sometimes be spicy: *a mild curry*
bland not having an interesting taste: *I found the sauce rather bland.*

taste² ●●● S2 *v*

1 [linking verb] to have a particular kind of taste: **taste good/delicious/sweet/fresh etc** *Mmm! This tastes good!* | *The food tasted better than it looked.* | **taste awful/disgusting etc** *The coffee tasted awful.* | **taste of sth** *This yoghurt tastes of strawberries.* | *It didn't taste much of ginger.* | **taste like sth** *It tastes just like champagne to me.* | *What does pumpkin taste like* (=how would you describe its taste)? | **sweet-tasting/bitter-tasting etc** *a sweet-tasting soup*

GRAMMAR

Linking verbs

Taste is a linking verb in this meaning. It links the subject of the sentence with an adjective: *The soup tastes salty.* | *Fresh strawberries always taste delicious.*

Using the progressive

- The verb **taste** is not usually used in the progressive. You say: *I tasted blood.* | *It tastes sour.*
✗ Don't say: *I was tasting blood.* | *It is tasting sour.*
- You often say someone **can taste** something when describing what they taste: *I could taste blood.*
- The present participle **tasting** is used to form adjectives such as **sweet-tasting** and **foul-tasting**.

GRAMMAR GUIDE ▸ VERBS

2 [T] to experience or recognize the taste of food or drink: *She* ***could taste*** *blood.* | *Can you taste the difference?* | *It was like nothing I'd ever tasted before.*

3 [T] to eat or drink a small amount of something to see what it is like: *It's always best to keep tasting the food while you're cooking it.*

4 taste success/freedom/victory etc to have a short experience of something that you want more of: *There was a lot of hard work before we first tasted success.*

ˈtaste bud *n* [C usually plural] one of the small parts of the surface of your tongue with which you can taste things

taste·ful /ˈteɪstfəl/ *adj* made, decorated, or chosen with good taste: *tasteful furnishings* ⚠ Do not confuse with **tasty**. Use **tasty** to describe food that tastes good: *This food is really tasty.* —**tastefully** *adv*: *tastefully decorated* —**tastefulness** *n* [U]

taste·less /ˈteɪstləs/ *adj* **1** food or drink that is tasteless is unpleasant because it has no particular taste **2** slightly offensive: *a tasteless remark* **3** made, decorated,

T

or chosen with bad taste: *a tasteless outfit* | *ugly and tasteless housing*

tast·er /'teɪstə $ -ər/ *n* [C] **1** someone whose job is to test the quality of foods, teas, wines etc by tasting them: *a wine taster* **2** *informal* a small example of something that is provided so that you can see if you like it: **[+of]** *Here's a taster of what will be in print next month.* | **[+from]** *a taster from her next album*

-tastic /tæstɪk/ *suffix* [in adjectives] *informal* used after a noun to describe something as being or involving something very good: *You can win tickets for this rocktastic show* (=show with very good rock songs).

tast·ing /'teɪstɪŋ/ *n* [C] an event that is organized so that you can try different foods or drinks to see if you like them: *a wine and cheese tasting*

tast·y /'teɪsti/ ●●○ *adj* (*comparative* **tastier**, *superlative* **tastiest**)
1 food that is tasty has a good taste, but is not sweet: *a simple but tasty meal* → **TASTEFUL** **THESAURUS** **TASTE**
2 *informal* tasty news, GOSSIP etc is especially interesting and often connected with sex or surprising behaviour
3 *BrE informal* sexually attractive

tat /tæt/ *n* **1** [U] *BrE informal* things that are cheap and badly made **2** [C] *AmE informal* an informal American word for TATTOO → **TIT FOR TAT**

ta-ta /tæ 'tɑː $ tɑː 'tɑː/ *BrE informal* goodbye

ta·ter /'teɪtə $ -ər/ *n* [C] *informal* a potato

tatt /tæt/ *n* [C] *informal* another word for TATTOO

tat·tered /'tætəd $ -ərd/ *adj* clothes, books etc that are tattered are old and torn: *He produced a tattered envelope from his pocket.*

tat·ters /'tætəz $ -ərz/ *n* [plural] **1 in tatters a)** if a plan or someone's REPUTATION is in tatters, it is ruined: *Tonight, the peace agreement lies in tatters.* | *His credibility is in tatters after a series of defeats and failures.* **b)** clothes that are in tatters are old and torn **2** clothing that is old and torn SYN **rags**

tat·tie /'tæti/ *n* [C] a potato - used in Scotland

tat·ting /'tætɪŋ/ *n* [U] a kind of LACE that you make by hand, or the process of making it

tat·tle /'tætl/ *v* [I] **1** *old-fashioned* to talk about other people's private lives SYN **gossip 2** *especially AmE* if a child tattles, they tell a parent or teacher that another child has done something bad: **[+on]** *Robert is always tattling on me for things I didn't do.* → **TITTLE-TATTLE** —**tattle** *n* [U] —**tattler** *n* [C]

tat·tle·tale /'tætlteɪl/ *n* [C] *AmE informal* a word meaning someone who tattles - used by or to children SYN **telltale** *BrE*

tat·too[1] /tə'tuː, tæ'tuː/ *n* (*plural* **tattoos**) **1** [C] a picture or writing that is permanently marked on your skin using a needle and ink: *He has a tattoo of a snake on his left arm.* **2** [C] an outdoor military show with music, usually at night **3** [singular] a fast continuous beating of a drum, or a sound like this

tattoo[2] *v* [T] to mark a permanent picture or writing on someone's skin with a needle and ink: *She's got a heart tattooed on her right shoulder.* —**tattooed** *adj*: *heavily tattooed arms*

tat·too·ist /tə'tuːəst, tæ-/ (*also* **tat'too ˌartist**) *n* [C] someone whose job is tattooing

tat'too ˌparlour *BrE*, **tattoo parlor** *AmE* *n* [C] a place where you can go to get a tattoo

tat·ty /'tæti/ *adj* (*comparative* **tattier**, *superlative* **tattiest**) *informal* in bad condition SYN **shabby**: *tatty jeans* | *a few tatty old chairs* —**tattily** *adv* —**tattiness** *n* [C]

taught /tɔːt $ tɒːt/ the past tense and past participle of TEACH

taunt[1] /tɔːnt $ tɒːnt/ *v* [T] to try to make someone angry or upset by saying unkind things to them → **tease**: **taunt sb about sth** *The other children taunted him about his weight.* | **taunt sb with sth** *They taunted him with the nickname 'Fatso'.* | *'And he'll believe you, will he?' Maria taunted.* —**tauntingly** *adv*

taunt[2] *n* [C often plural] a remark or joke intended to make someone angry or upset: *racist taunts* **THESAURUS** **COMMENT**

taupe /təʊp $ toʊp/ *n* [U] a brownish-grey colour —**taupe** *adj*

Tau·rus /'tɔːrəs/ *n* **1** [U] the second sign of the ZODIAC, represented by a BULL, which some people believe affects the character and life of people born between April 21 and May 21 **2** [C] (*also* **Taurean**) someone who was born between April 21 and May 21 —**Taurean** *adj*

taut /tɔːt $ tɒːt/ *adj* **1** stretched tight OPP **slack**: *The rope was stretched taut.* **2** showing signs of worry, anger etc and not relaxed SYN **tense**: *a taut smile* | *Catherine looked upset, her face taut.* **3** having firm muscles: *her taut brown body* **4** a taut book, film, or play is exciting and does not have any unnecessary parts: *a taut thriller*

taut·en /'tɔːtn $ 'tɒːtn/ *v* [I,T] to make something stretch tight, or to become stretched tight

tau·tol·o·gy /tɔː'tɒlədʒi $ tɒː'tɑː-/ *n* (*plural* **tautologies**) [C,U] *technical* a statement in which you say the same thing twice using different words in a way which is not necessary, for example, 'He sat alone by himself.' → **redundant** —**tautological** /ˌtɔːtə'lɒdʒɪkəl◂ $ ˌtɒːtə'lɑː-/ (*also* **tautologous** /tɔː'tɒləgəs $ tɒː'tɑː-/) *adj*

tav·ern /'tævən $ -ərn/ *n* [C] **1** *BrE old use* a PUB where you can also stay the night **2** a word for a bar, often used in the name of a bar: *Murphy's Tavern*

taw·dry /'tɔːdri $ 'tɒː-/ *adj* **1** cheaply and badly made: *tawdry jewellery and fake furs* **2** showing low moral standards: *a tawdry tale of lies and deception* —**tawdriness** *n* [U]

taw·ny /'tɔːni $ 'tɒː-/ *adj* brownish-yellow in colour: *a lion's tawny fur*

tax[1] /tæks/ ●●● S1 W1 *n* [C,U] an amount of money that you must pay to the government according to your income, property, goods etc and that is used to pay for public services: **[+on]** *a tax on fuel* | *He already pays 40% tax on his income.* | **before/after tax** *profits before tax of £85.9m* → **CAPITAL GAINS TAX**, → **corporation tax** at **CORPORATION(1)**, **COUNCIL TAX**, **INCOME TAX**, **SALES TAX**, **STEALTH TAX**, **VAT**, **PAYE**

COLLOCATIONS

VERBS

pay tax *Many people feel they are paying too much tax.*
raise/increase taxes (*also* **put up taxes** *BrE*) *He claimed the Labour Party would put up taxes.*
lower/cut/reduce taxes

ADJECTIVES/NOUN + tax

high *Higher taxes will slow down consumer spending.*
low *Republican voters say they want lower taxes and sensible spending cuts.*
income tax (=tax paid on money that you earn) | **sales tax** (=a tax on things you buy) | **inheritance tax** (=tax paid on money, property etc that you receive from someone when they die)

tax + NOUN

the tax rate/the rate of tax *The government reduced the basic rate of tax to 25p in the pound.*
tax cuts *He believes that big tax cuts will encourage economic growth.*
tax increases *He accused the president of planning the biggest tax increases in US history.*
tax incentives (=lower taxes that encourage people to do something) | **a tax allowance** (=an amount you can earn without paying tax on it)

tax[2] ●○○ *v* [T]
1 to charge a tax on something: **tax sth at 10%/a higher rate etc** *They may be taxed at a higher rate.* | **tax sb on sth** *The individual is taxed on the amount of dividend received.* | *Cigarettes are* ***heavily taxed*** *in Britain.*
2 *BrE* to pay the sum of money charged each year for using a vehicle on British roads → **CAR TAX**, **ROAD TAX**
3 to make someone have to work hard or make an effort:

tax sb's patience/strength etc *The kids are really taxing my patience today.* | *It shouldn't tax your brain too much.* → TAXING

tax sb **with** sth *phr v formal* to complain to someone they have done something wrong

tax·a·ble /ˈtæksəbəl/ *adj* if money that you receive is taxable, you have to pay tax on it OPP **non-taxable**: **taxable income/profits/earnings etc**

tax·a·tion /tækˈseɪʃən/ ●○○ *n* [U] *formal*
1 the system of charging taxes: *the government's economic and* ***taxation policy*** | **direct taxation** (=tax on income) | **indirect taxation** (=tax on things you buy)
2 money collected from taxes: *higher levels of taxation*

ˈtax aˌvoidance *n* [U] the practice of trying to pay less tax in legal ways → **tax evasion**

ˈtax ˌbracket *n* [C] a particular range of income levels on which the same rate of tax is paid: *It may put you in a higher tax bracket.*

ˈtax break *n* [C] a special reduction in taxes: *tax breaks for small businesses*

ˈtax colˌlector *n* [C] someone who works for the government and makes sure that people pay their taxes

ˌtax-deˈductible *adj* tax-deductible costs can be taken off your total income before it is taxed: *If you're self-employed, your travel expenses are tax-deductible.*

ˌtax-deˈferred *adj AmE* not taxed until a later time: *tax-deferred savings*

ˈtax disc *n* [C] a small round piece of paper on a car WINDSCREEN in Britain that shows the driver has paid ROAD TAX

ˈtax dodge *n* [C] *informal* a way of paying less tax

ˈtax eˌvasion *n* [U] the crime of paying too little tax → **tax avoidance**

ˌtax exˈempt *adj* if SAVINGS, income etc are tax exempt, you do not have to pay tax on them

ˈtax ˌexile *n* [C] someone who lives abroad in order to avoid paying high taxes in their own country

ˌtax-ˈfree *adj* not taxed: *He was paid a tax-free cash sum as compensation.* —**tax-free** *adv*: *You can earn up to £65 per week tax-free.*

ˈtax ˌhaven *n* [C] a place where people go to live to avoid paying high taxes in their own country

tax·i[1] /ˈtæksi/ ●●● S3 *n* [C] a car and driver that you pay to take you somewhere SYN **cab**: *They sent me home in a taxi.*

GRAMMAR: Patterns with taxi

- You say **get in a taxi**: *He got in a taxi and left.* ✗ Don't say: *get on a taxi*
- You say **get out of a taxi**: *Two women got out of the taxi.* ✗ Don't say: *get off a taxi*
- You say that someone is **in a taxi**: *I read my notes while I was in the taxi.*
- You go somewhere **by taxi**: *She goes everywhere by taxi.*

COLLOCATIONS

VERBS

take/get a taxi *We took a taxi to the hotel.*
go/come/arrive by taxi *I went back home by taxi.*
hail a taxi (=wave or call to a taxi to stop for you to get in) | **phone for/call a taxi** (=telephone for a taxi to come) | **call sb a taxi** (=telephone for a taxi to come for someone else)

taxi + NOUN

a taxi ride *The centre of town is a five minute taxi ride away.*
a taxi fare *She couldn't afford the £18 taxi fare.*
a taxi driver | **a taxi service** | **a taxi rank** *BrE*, **a taxi stand** *AmE* (=a place where taxis wait for customers)

taxi[2] *v* (*past tense and past participle* **taxied**, *present participle* **taxiing**, *third person singular* **taxis** *or* **taxies**) [I] if a plane taxis, it moves along the ground before taking off or after landing: *The plane taxied to a halt.*

tax·i·cab /ˈtæksikæb/ *n* [C] a taxi

tax·i·der·mist /ˈtæksɪdɜːmɪst $ -ɜːr-/ *n* [C] someone whose job is taxidermy

tax·i·der·my /ˈtæksədɜːmi $ -ɜːr-/ *n* [U] the art of filling the skins of dead animals, birds, or fish with a special material so that they look as though they are alive

tax·ing /ˈtæksɪŋ/ *adj* needing a lot of effort SYN **demanding**: *The job turned out to be more taxing than I'd expected.*

ˈtax inˌspector *n* [C] someone who works for the government, deciding how much tax a person or company should pay

ˈtaxi rank (*also* **ˈtaxi stand** *AmE*) *n* [C] a place where taxis wait for customers SYN **cabstand** *AmE*

tax·i·way /ˈtæksiweɪ/ *n* [C] the surface which an aircraft drives on to get to and from the RUNWAY

tax·man /ˈtæksmæn/ *n* (*plural* **taxmen** /-men/) [C]
1 the taxman *informal* the government department that collects taxes: *A lot of the money will go straight to the taxman.* **2** someone whose job is collecting taxes

tax·on·o·my /tækˈsɒnəmi $ -ˈsɑː-/ *n* (*plural* **taxonomies**) [C,U] the process or a system of organizing things into different groups that show their natural relationships, especially plants or animals —**taxonomist** *n* [C]

tax·pay·er /ˈtæksˌpeɪə $ -ər/ ●○○ *n* [C] a person that pays tax: *The proposal could cost* ***the taxpayer*** (=all ordinary people who pay tax) *another £18m a year.*

ˈtax reˌlief *n* [U] *BrE* when you do not have to pay tax on part of what you earn, especially because you use the money for a particular purpose: **[+on]** *You can get tax relief on private health insurance premiums.*

ˈtax reˌturn *n* [C] the form on which you have to give information so that your tax can be calculated

ˈtax ˌshelter *n* [C] a plan or method that allows you to legally avoid paying tax

ˈtax year *n* [C] the period of 12 months in which income is calculated for paying taxes. The tax year begins on April 6th in Britain, and January 1st in the US.

TB /ˌtiː ˈbiː/ *n* [U] (***tuberculosis***) a serious infectious disease that affects the lungs and other body parts

tba (***to be announced***) used in writing to show that a time, place etc will be given or decided later

T-ball /ˈtiː bɔːl $ -bɒːl/ *n* [U] *trademark* an easy form of BASEBALL for young children SYN **tee-ball**

tbc (***to be confirmed***) *BrE* used in writing to show that the time, place etc of a future event is not yet definite: *The concert will be in Harrogate (venue tbc) on the 29th.*

T-bone steak /ˌtiː bəʊn ˈsteɪk $ -boʊn-/ *n* [C] a thinly cut piece of BEEF that has a T-shaped bone in it

tbsp (*also* **tbs**) (*plural* **tbsp** *or* **tbsps**) the written abbreviation of ***tablespoon*** or tablespoons: *1 tbsp sugar*

T cell /ˈtiː sel/ *n* [C] *BrE medical* a type of WHITE BLOOD CELL that helps the body fight disease

tea /tiː/ ●●● S1 W2 *n*
1 DRINK/LEAVES **a)** [C,U] a hot brown drink made by pouring boiling water onto the dried leaves from a particular Asian bush, or a cup of this drink: *Would you like a cup of tea or coffee?* | *Do you take milk and sugar in your tea?* | *I'd like two teas and a piece of chocolate cake, please.* **b)** [U] dried, finely cut leaves that are used to make tea **c)** [U] bushes whose leaves are used to make tea: *tea plantations*
2 mint/camomile etc tea a hot drink made by pouring boiling water onto leaves or flowers, sometimes used as a medicine
3 MEAL [C,U] *BrE* **a)** a small meal of cake or BISCUITS eaten in the afternoon with a cup of tea: *We serve lunch and* ***afternoon tea***. | *We stopped for a* ***cream tea*** *on the way home* (=tea and cream cakes). **b)** used in some parts of Britain to mean a large meal that is eaten early in the evening: *We had baked beans on toast for tea.* → **HIGH TEA**
4 tea and sympathy *BrE* kindness and attention that you give

someone when they are upset → **not be your cup of tea** at CUP[1]

tea·bag /ˈtiːbæg/ *n* [C] a small paper bag with tea leaves inside, used for making tea

ˈtea break *n* [C] *BrE* a short pause from work in the middle of the morning or afternoon for a drink, a rest etc SYN **coffee break**

ˈtea ˌcaddy *n* [C] a small metal box that you keep tea in

tea·cake /ˈtiːkeɪk/ *n* [C] *BrE* a small flat round amount of bread with RAISINS or CURRANTS in it

teach /tiːtʃ/ ●●● S1 W2 *v* (*past tense and past participle* **taught** /tɔːt $ tɒːt/)

1 SCHOOL/COLLEGE ETC [I,T] to give lessons in a school, college, or university, or to help someone learn about something by giving them information → **learn**: **[+at]** *Neil teaches at the Guildhall School of Music in London.* | **teach (sb) English/mathematics/history etc** *He taught geography at the local secondary school.* | **teach sb (sth) about sth** *We were never taught anything about other religions.* | **teach sth to sb** *I'm teaching English to Italian students.* | **teach school/college etc** *AmE* (=teach in a school etc)

2 SHOW SB HOW [T] to show someone how to do something: **teach sb (how) to do sth** *My father taught me to swim.* | *different methods of teaching children how to read* | **teach sb sth** *Can you teach me one of your card tricks?*

3 CHANGE SB'S IDEAS [T] to show or tell someone how they should behave or what they should think: **teach sb to do sth** *When I was young, we were taught to treat older people with respect.* | **teach sb sth** *No one ever taught him the difference between right and wrong.* | **teach sb that** *He taught me that the easy option isn't always the best one.*

4 EXPERIENCE SHOWS STH [T] if an experience or situation teaches you something, it helps you to understand something about life: **teach sb to do sth** *Experience has taught me to avoid certain areas of the city.* | **teach sb that** *It's certainly taught me that work and money aren't the most important things in life.*

5 that'll teach you (to do sth) *spoken* used when something unpleasant has just happened to someone because they acted stupidly: *That'll teach you to be late!*

6 teach sb a lesson *informal* if someone or something teaches you a lesson, you are punished for something you have done, so that you will not want to do it again

7 you can't teach an old dog new tricks used to say that older people often do not want to change the way they do things

8 teach your grandmother (to suck eggs) *BrE* to give someone advice about something that they already know

THESAURUS

teach to give lessons in a school, college, or university: *I taught for a year in France.* | *He teaches physics at York University.*
lecture to teach in a college or university by giving talks to groups of students on a subject: *He lectures in engineering at a local college.*
instruct *formal* to teach someone how to do something, especially a particular practical skill: *He was instructing them how to use the computer system.* | *Staff are instructed in how to respond in the event of a fire.*
tutor to teach one student or a small group: *I found work tutoring Mexican students in English.*
coach *especially BrE* to give private lessons, especially so that someone can pass an important test: *He coaches students for their university entrance exams.*
train to teach a person or group of people in the particular skills or knowledge they need to do a job: *It will take at least a month to train the new assistant.*
educate to teach someone over a long period, usually at school or university: *He was educated in England.* | *Her parents want to educate her at home.*
show sb the ropes *informal* to show someone how to do a job or task that they have just started doing: *Miss McGinley will show you the ropes and answer any questions you may have.*

teach·er /ˈtiːtʃə $ -ər/ ●●● S1 W1 *n* [C] someone whose job is to teach, especially in a school: *a primary school teacher* | **language/history/science etc teacher** | **teacher training/education** (=professional training to become a teacher)

THESAURUS

teacher someone who teaches as their job, especially in a school: *a high school teacher*
principal (*also* **headteacher** *BrE*) the teacher who is in charge of a school or college: *The teacher sent him to the principal's office.*
tutor someone who gives private lessons to one student or a small group of students. In Britain, a tutor is also a teacher in a university: *They hired a tutor to help him with his English.* | *Your tutor will help you find a subject for your essay.*
lecturer someone who teaches in a university or college: *University lecturers aren't very well paid.*
professor a teacher in a college or university. In Britain, a **professor** is a high-ranking university teacher, especially one who is head of a department: *She was professor of linguistics at Cambridge University.*
instructor someone who teaches a sport or a practical skill such as swimming or driving: *He works as a ski instructor in the winter.* | *a driving instructor*
coach someone who helps a person or team improve in a sport: *a professional tennis coach*
educator *especially AmE formal* someone whose job involves teaching people, or someone who is an expert on education: *Most educators agree that class sizes are still too big.*
trainer someone who teaches people particular skills, especially the skills they need to do a job: *a teacher trainer* | *Many companies pay outside trainers to teach management skills to their staff.*
governess a woman who lived with a family and taught their children in past times: *As a governess, Charlotte Brontë received twenty pounds a year.*

ˌteacher's ˈpet *n* [singular] *informal* a child who everyone thinks is the teacher's favourite student and is therefore disliked by the other students

ˈtea chest *n* [C] a large wooden box that used to have tea in it, often used afterwards for moving and storing things

ˈteach-in *n* [C] an informal meeting of people who are interested in a particular subject, where they have the opportunity to learn more about it

teach·ing /ˈtiːtʃɪŋ/ ●●● S2 W2 *n* [U]

1 the work or profession of a teacher: *Mrs Ward had many years of experience in teaching.* | *She's thinking of going into teaching* (=becoming a teacher). | **language/science etc teaching** *extra funding for English teaching in schools* | **the teaching profession** | **teaching methods/materials etc** | **teaching practice** *BrE*, **student teaching** *AmE* (=a period of teaching done by someone who is training to be a teacher)

2 (*also* **teachings** [plural]) the moral, religious, or political ideas of a particular person or group which are taught to other people: **[+of]** *the teachings of Gandhi* | **religious/Christian/Buddhist etc teachings**

ˈteaching asˌsistant *n* [C] **1** *BrE* a person who is not a trained teacher who helps a school teacher in classes **2** *AmE* a GRADUATE student at a university who teaches classes

ˈteaching ˌhospital *n* [C] a hospital where medical students receive practical training from experienced doctors

ˈtea cloth *n* [C] *BrE* a TEA TOWEL

ˈtea ˌcosy *n* [C] *BrE* a thick cover that you put over a TEAPOT to keep the tea hot

tea·cup[1] /ˈtiːkʌp/ *n* [C] a cup that you serve tea in → **storm in a teacup** at STORM[1](5)

teacup[2] *adj* **teacup dog/pig/cat etc** a very small dog, pig, cat etc that is kept as a pet and often carried around

ˈtea ˌgarden *n* [C] a large area of land used for growing tea SYN **tea plantation**

tea·house /ˈtiːhaʊs/ *n* [C] a special house in China or Japan where tea is served, often as part of a ceremony

teak /tiːk/ *n* [U] a hard yellowish-brown wood that is used for making ships and good quality furniture

teal /tiːl/ *n* **1** [C] a small wild duck **2** [U] a greenish-blue colour

'tea leaves *n* [plural] the small pieces of leaves used to make tea. People sometimes look at the leaves left at the bottom of a cup to find out what will happen in the future.

tea·light /'tiːˌlaɪt/ *n* [C] a small short CANDLE in a metal container

team¹ /tiːm/ ●●● S1 W1 AWL *n* [C]
1 a group of people who play a game or sport together against another group: *Which team do you support?* | **in a team** *BrE*, **on a team** *AmE*: *Bobby Charlton was in the team that won the World Cup.* THESAURUS ▸ GROUP
2 a group of people who have been chosen to work together to do a particular job: **[+of]** *a team of experts* | **management/research/sales etc team** *a senior member of the design team* | *Our success lies in* ***working*** *together* ***as a team***. | *It was a tremendous* ***team effort***. | *You need to choose a* ***team leader***.
3 two or more animals that are used to pull a vehicle

GRAMMAR: Singular or plural verb?

- **Team** is usually followed by a singular verb: *Our team* ***is*** *winning.* | *A team of doctors* ***works*** *at the clinic.*
- In British English, you can also use a plural verb: *Our team* ***are*** *winning.* | *A team of doctors* ***work*** *at the clinic.*

GRAMMAR GUIDE ▸ NOUNS

COLLOCATIONS

ADJECTIVES/NOUN + team

a football/basketball etc team *China's football team failed to qualify for the World Cup.*
the school team *I played for my school cricket team.*
the national team *He coached the Italian national team.*
the home team (=the team whose sports field a game is being played on) | **the visiting team** (=the team who have travelled to their opponents' sports field) | **the opposing team** | **the first team** *BrE* (=the team with the best players in a school, club etc) | **the winning/losing team**

VERBS

play for a team *He wants to play for a better team.*
support a team *'Which team do you support?' 'Chelsea.'*
captain a team (=be the captain of a team) | **make the team** (=be chosen as a member of a team) | **drop sb from a team** (=decide that someone should not play for a team)

team + NOUN

the team captain *The cup was presented to the team captain.*
a team member/a member of a team *He's the eldest team member.*
the team manager/coach *Who do you think will be the next England team manager?*
a team game/sport (=one that is played by teams)

PHRASES

play as a team *One reason for the 49ers' success is that they play as a team.*

team² ●●○ AWL *v* [T] to put two things or people together, because they will look good or work well together: **team sth with sth** *black trousers teamed with a bright shirt*

team up *phr v* to join with someone in order to work on something: **[+with]** *You can team up with one other class member if you want.*

'team-mate *BrE*, **team·mate** /'tiːm-meɪt/ ●○○ *n* [C] someone who belongs to the same team as you: *He finished just ahead of his Ferrari team-mate.*

'team ˌplayer *n* [C] someone who works well as a member of a team, especially in business: *He was a good businessman, but never a team player.*

ˌteam 'spirit *n* [U] willingness to work as part of a team

team·ster /'tiːmstə $ -ər/ *n* [C] *AmE* someone whose job is to drive a truck

team·work /'tiːmwɜːk $ -wɜːrk/ ●○○ *n* [U] when a group of people work effectively together: *We want to encourage good teamwork and communication.*

'tea ˌparty *n* [C] **1** a small party in the afternoon at which tea, cake etc is served **2 be no tea party** *AmE informal* to be very difficult or unpleasant to do

tea·pot /'tiːpɒt $ -pɑːt/ ●●○ *n* [C] a container for making and serving tea, which has a handle and a SPOUT¹(1) → see picture at POT¹

tear¹ /tɪə $ tɪr/ ●●● S2 W3 *n*
1 [C usually plural] a drop of salty liquid that comes out of your eye when you are crying: *The children were all* ***in tears***. | *She came home* ***in floods of tears***. | *I could see that Sam was* ***close to tears***. | *Bridget suddenly* ***burst into tears*** *and ran out.* | *He was* ***fighting back tears*** *as he spoke.* | *A lot of people were* ***moved to tears*** *by his story.* | *He kissed her cheek, a gesture that* ***brought tears to*** *her* ***eyes***. | *I must admit I* ***shed*** *a few* ***tears*** *when the school closed.* | *I saw grown men* ***reduced to tears*** *that day.* | *'Please don't talk like that,' Ellen implored him, her* ***eyes filling with tears***. | *By this time,* ***tears*** *were* ***streaming down*** *my face.* | *The tears he shed were* ***tears of joy***.
2 it'll (all) end in tears *BrE spoken* used to warn someone that something they are doing will cause problems or arguments between people → **bore sb to tears** at BORE²(1), → **crocodile tears** at CROCODILE(4)

tear² /teə $ ter/ ●●● S2 W3 *v* (*past tense* **tore** /tɔː $ tɔːr/, *past participle* **torn** /tɔːn $ tɔːrn/)
1 PAPER/CLOTH **a)** [T] to damage something such as paper or cloth by pulling it hard or letting it touch something sharp SYN **rip**: *Be careful not to tear the paper.* | *His clothes were old and torn.* | **tear sth on sth** *She realized she had torn her jacket on a nail.* | **tear sth off** *Tear off the slip at the bottom of this page and send it back to us.* | **tear sth out (of sth)** *He tore a page out of his notebook and handed it to her.* | *The dog had* ***torn a*** *huge* ***hole in*** *the tent.* | *He picked up the envelope and* ***tore*** *it* ***open***. | *She* ***tore*** *the letter* ***to pieces*** *and threw it in the bin.* | *Most of her clothes had been* ***torn to shreds***. **b)** [I] if paper or cloth tears, it splits and a hole appears, because it has been pulled too hard or has touched something sharp: *The paper is old and tears easily.*
THESAURUS ▸ BREAK
2 MOVE QUICKLY [I always + adv/prep] to run or drive somewhere very quickly, especially in a dangerous or careless way: *She tore back into the house.* | *We tore down to the hospital.* | *He tore off into town.* THESAURUS ▸ RUN
3 REMOVE STH [T always + adv/prep] to pull something violently from a person or place: **tear sth from sb/sth** *He tore the letter from my hand.* | *A bridge was torn from the bank by the floodwaters.* | **tear sth off sth** *High winds nearly tore the roof off the house.*
4 be torn a) if you are torn, you are unable to decide what to do because you have different feelings or different things that you want: **[+between]** *She was torn between her love of dancing and her fear of performing in public.* | *He was torn two ways.* | *Jess was torn by anger and worry.* **b)** if a country or group is torn, it is divided because people in it have very different ideas and are arguing or fighting with each other: *The country was torn by civil war.* | *She spent two months in the* ***war-torn*** *city.*
5 MUSCLE [T] to damage a muscle or LIGAMENT: *She had torn a muscle in her leg.*
6 tear loose to move violently and no longer be attached to something: *One end had torn loose.*
7 tear sb/sth to shreds/pieces *informal* to criticize someone or something very severely: *He tore her arguments to shreds.*
8 tear sb off a strip/tear a strip off sb *BrE informal* to talk to someone very angrily because they have done something wrong
9 tear sb limb from limb *literary* to attack someone in a very violent way
10 be tearing your hair out *BrE informal* to feel anxious and upset because you are worried, or because you have to deal with something that is very difficult: *I've been tearing my hair out trying to get done in time.*

T

11 be in a tearing hurry *BrE* to be doing something very quickly because you are late
12 tear sb's heart (out)/tear at sb's heart to make someone feel extremely upset: *The thought of her out there alone tore at my heart.*
13 that's torn it! *BrE spoken old-fashioned* used when something bad has happened that stops you from doing what you intended to do: *Oh, no, that's torn it! I've left my keys in the car!*

THESAURUS

tear to damage paper or cloth by pulling it too hard, or letting it touch something sharp: *She unwrapped the present carefully, trying not to tear the paper.* | *I tore a hole in my jacket, climbing over the fence.*
rip to tear something quickly or violently: *Beth excitedly ripped open the package.* | *Stop pulling my dress! You'll rip it!*
split to tear your trousers or shirt when you put them on, because they are too tight for you: *He bent down and split his trousers.*
ladder *BrE* if a woman ladders her TIGHTS or STOCKINGS, she tears them so that a long thin line appears in them: *Damn! I've laddered my tights!*
shred to deliberately destroy letters, documents etc by cutting them into thin pieces, often by using a special machine: *In order to prevent fraud, it's best to shred your bank statements.*
frayed torn a little along the edges – used about clothes, carpets etc that have been used a lot: *He was wearing an old pair of frayed jeans.* | *The rug was a little frayed around the edges.*

tear sb/sth **apart** *phr v*
1 tear sth ↔ apart to cause serious arguments in a group of people SYN **rip apart**: *Scandal is tearing the government apart.* | *a row that tore the family apart*
2 *literary* to separate people who are in a close relationship with each other: *Nothing can tear us apart!*
3 to make someone feel extremely unhappy or upset: *Seeing her so upset really tore him apart.*
4 tear sth ↔ apart to break something violently into a lot of small pieces SYN **rip apart**: *Her body had been torn apart by wolves.*
tear at sb/sth *phr v* to pull violently at someone or something: *The children were screaming and tearing at each other's hair.*
tear sb **away** *phr v* to make yourself or someone else leave a place when you or they do not want to leave: *He was enjoying the fun and couldn't tear himself away.* | **[+from]** *We finally managed to tear him away from the TV.*
tear sth ↔ **down** *phr v* to destroy a building deliberately: *A lot of the old tower blocks have been torn down to make way for new housing.*
tear into sb/sth *phr v*
1 to attack someone by hitting them very hard: *The two boys tore into each other.*
2 to criticize someone very strongly and angrily: *From time to time she would really tear into her staff.*
3 to start doing something quickly, with a lot of energy: *I was amazed at the way she tore into her work.*
tear sth ↔ **off** *phr v* to remove your clothes as quickly as you can: *He tore off his clothes and dived into the water.*
tear sth ↔ **up** *phr v*
1 to tear a piece of paper or cloth into small pieces SYN **rip up**: *She tore up his letter and threw it away.*
2 to remove something from the ground by pulling or pushing it violently: *the remains of trees that had been torn up by the storm*
3 tear up an agreement/contract etc to say that you no longer accept an agreement or contract: *threats to tear up the peace agreement*
4 tear it up *informal* **a)** to have fun in an extreme way **b)** to do something, for example play music or dance, very well on a particular occasion

tear³ /teə $ ter/ *n* [C] a hole in a piece of cloth or paper where it has been torn: **[+in]** *There was a huge tear in his shirt.* → **wear and tear** at WEAR²(2)

tear⁴ /tɪə $ tɪr/ *v* [I] *especially AmE* if your eyes tear, they produce salty liquid, for example because of cold air or smoke SYN **water**: *Why does cutting up onions make my eyes tear?*
tear up *phr v* if you are tearing up, you are starting to have tears in your eyes because you feel very sad, happy etc: *As she waved her mother goodbye, she found herself tearing up.*

tear·a·way /ˈteərəweɪ $ ˈter-/ *n* [C] *informal* a young person who behaves badly and often gets into trouble: *His car was wrecked by a couple of young tearaways.*

tear·drop /ˈtɪədrɒp $ ˈtɪrdrɑːp/ *n* [C] *literary* a single drop of salty liquid that comes out of your eye when you are crying: *A large teardrop ran down her cheek.*

tear·ful /ˈtɪəfəl $ ˈtɪr-/ (*also* **teary** *informal*) *adj* someone who is tearful is crying a little, or almost crying: *a tearful farewell* —**tearfully** *adv*: *She looked at me tearfully.*

tear gas /ˈtɪə gæs $ ˈtɪr-/ *n* [U] a gas that stings your eyes, used by the police to control crowds: *The police used tear gas to break up the demonstration.*

tear·jerk·er /ˈtɪəˌdʒɜːkə $ ˈtɪrˌdʒɜːrkər/ *n* [C] *informal* a film, book, or story that is very sad and makes you cry

tea·room /ˈtiːruːm, -rʊm/ (*also* **tea shop**) *n* [C] a restaurant where tea and small meals are served

tear·y /ˈtɪəri $ ˈtɪri/ *adj informal* TEARFUL

tease¹ /tiːz/ ●●○ *v*
1 LAUGH [I,T] to laugh at someone and make jokes in order to have fun by embarrassing them, either in a friendly way or in an unkind way: *Don't get upset. I was **only teasing**.* | *He used to **tease** her **mercilessly**.* | **tease sb about sth** *She used to tease me about my hair.*

REGISTER
In everyday English, people often say **make fun of** rather than **tease**: *Stop **making fun of** me!*

2 ANNOY AN ANIMAL [T] to deliberately annoy an animal: *Stop teasing the cat!*
3 SEX [I,T] to deliberately make someone sexually excited without intending to have sex with them, in a way that seems unkind
4 HAIR [T] *AmE* to comb your hair in the opposite direction to which it grows, so that it looks thicker SYN **backcomb** *BrE*
tease sth ↔ **out** *phr v*
1 to succeed in learning information that is hidden, or that someone does not want to tell you: **[+of]** *I finally managed to tease the truth out of her.*
2 to gently move hairs or threads that are stuck together so that they become loose or straight again: *She combed her hair, gently teasing out the knots.*

tease² *n* [C] *informal* **1** someone who enjoys making jokes at people, and embarrassing them, especially in a friendly way: *Don't take any notice of Joe – he's a big tease.* **2** something that you say or do as a joke, to tease someone: *I'm sorry, it was only a tease.* **3** someone who deliberately makes you sexually excited, but has no intention of having sex with you

tea·sel /ˈtiːzəl/ *n* [C] a plant with leaves and flowers that feel sharp when you touch them

teas·er /ˈtiːzə $ -ər/ *n* [C] *informal* **1** a very difficult question that you have to answer as part of a game or competition **2** a short advertisement which appears a few days or weeks before a full advertisement for a product

ˈteaser ad *n* [C] an advertisement that is used to make people interested in a product, but that does not give very much information about the product, so that people will pay attention to more advertisements later

ˈtea ˌservice *n* [C] a matching set with a teapot, cups, and plates, which you use for serving tea

ˈtea shop *n* [C] a TEAROOM

teas·ing·ly /ˈtiːzɪŋli/ *adv* in a way that shows you are joking and trying to have fun by embarrassing someone in a friendly way

tea·spoon /ˈtiːspuːn/ ●●○ *n* [C]
1 a small spoon that you use for mixing sugar into tea and coffee
2 (*also* **teaspoonful** /ˈtiːspuːnfʊl/) (*written abbreviation* **tsp**) the amount that a teaspoon can hold, used as a unit for measuring food or liquid in cooking: **[+of]** *Add a teaspoon of salt.*

teat /tiːt/ *n* [C] **1** *BrE* the rubber part on a baby's bottle that the baby sucks milk from SYN **nipple** *AmE* **2** one of the small parts on a female animal's body that her babies suck milk from

tea·time /ˈtiːtaɪm/ *n* [U] *BrE* a time in the late afternoon or early evening when people have a meal: *John won't be back until teatime.*

ˈtea ˌtowel *n* [C] *BrE* a small cloth that you use for drying cups, plates etc after you have washed them SYN **dish towel** *AmE*

ˈtea tree ˌoil *n* [U] oil from an Australian tree, that is used to treat skin problems

ˈtea urn *n* [C] *BrE* a large metal container that you use for heating water to make a lot of cups of tea

tea·zel, **teazle** /ˈtiːzəl/ *n* [C] another spelling of TEASEL

tech /tek/ *n* [C] *BrE old-fashioned informal* a TECHNICAL COLLEGE

tech·ie /ˈteki/ *n* [C] *informal* someone who knows a lot about computers and electronic equipment

tech·ni·cal /ˈteknɪkəl/ ●●● S2 W2 AWL *adj*
1 MACHINES connected with knowledge of how machines work: *Our staff will be available to give you* ***technical support****.* | *I have no* ***technical knowledge*** *at all.* | ***technical training***
2 **technical problem/hitch** a problem involving the way a machine or system works: *We've been having some technical problems with the new hardware.*
3 LANGUAGE technical language is language that is difficult for most people to understand because it is connected with one particular subject or used in one particular job: *I didn't understand all the* ***technical terms****.*
4 DETAILS/RULES relating to small exact details or rules that say how a system should work: *He called for the legislation to be delayed on a technical point.* | *This is a technical violation of the treaty.*
5 SKILLS technical ability is the ability to do the difficult things that you have to do in order to play music, do a sport etc: *a young player with a lot of technical ability*

ˈtechnical ˌcollege *n* [C] a college in Britain where, in the past, students could study to take examinations in practical subjects

tech·ni·cal·i·ty /ˌteknəˈkæləti/ *n* (*plural* **technicalities**)
1 **technicalities** [plural] the small details of how to do something or how a system or process works: **[+of]** *I don't really want to get into discussing the technicalities of laser printing.*
2 [C] a small detail in a law or a set of rules, especially one that forces you to make a decision that seems unfair: *The case against him had to be dropped because of a legal technicality.* | **on a technicality** *The proposal was rejected on a technicality* (=because of a technicality).

tech·ni·cally /ˈteknɪkli/ ●○○ AWL *adv*
1 according to the exact details of a rule or law: [sentence adverb] *Technically, the two countries are still at war, as a peace treaty was never signed.* | [+adj/adv] *What you have done is technically illegal.*
2 [+adj/adv] concerning the special skills that are needed to play music, do a sport etc: *a technically brilliant pianist* | *The dance looks simple, but is technically very difficult.*
3 concerning the way machines are used to do work: *Agriculture is becoming more and more* ***technically advanced****.*
4 **technically possible/difficult/feasible etc** possible, difficult etc using the scientific knowledge that is available now: *It could soon be technically possible to produce a human being by cloning.*

ˌtechnical supˈport (*also* **ˌtech supˈport**) *n* [U]
1 help or information that you receive to improve a computer program or system, make it continue working, or use it correctly **2** the department of a company that provides help with using computers: *Maybe you'd better try calling tech support.*

tech·ni·cian /tekˈnɪʃən/ ●●○ *n* [C]
1 someone whose job is to check equipment or machines and make sure that they are working properly: *a laboratory technician* | *a hospital technician*
2 someone who is very good at the skills of a particular sport, music, art etc: *Whether he was a great artist or not, Dali was a superb technician.*

Tech·ni·col·or /ˈteknɪkʌlə $ -ər/ *n* [U] *trademark* a way of producing the colour in films, used for the cinema

tech·ni·col·our *BrE*, **technicolor** *AmE* /ˈteknɪkʌlə $ -ər/ *n* **in full/glorious technicolour** if you see something in glorious technicolour, you see it clearly on a screen, with lots of bright colours

tech·nique /tekˈniːk/ ●●● S3 W1 AWL *n*
1 [C] a special way of doing something → **method**: **[+for]** *There are various techniques for dealing with industrial pollution.* | **[+of]** *In mathematics, we use many techniques of problem-solving.* THESAURUS ▸ METHOD, WAY
2 [U] the special way in which you move your body when you are playing music, doing a sport etc, which is difficult to learn and needs a lot of skill → **technical**: *He's a great player, with brilliant technique.*

tech·no /ˈteknəʊ $ -noʊ/ *n* [U] a type of popular electronic dance music with a fast strong beat

techno- /teknə, -noʊ $ -nə, noʊ/ *prefix* concerning machines and electronic equipment such as computers: *technophobia* (=dislike of computers, machines etc) | *techno-literacy* (=skill in using computers)

tech·noc·racy /tekˈnɒkrəsi $ -ˈnɑː-/ *n* (*plural* **technocracies**) [C,U] a social system in which people with a lot of knowledge about science, machines, and computers have a lot of power

tech·no·crat /ˈteknəkræt/ *n* [C] a skilled scientist who has a lot of power in industry or government

tech·no·fix /ˈteknəʊfɪks $ -noʊ-/ *n* [C] *informal* a technological solution to a problem

ˈtechno-ˌgeek *n* [C] *informal* someone whose main interest is electronic equipment, especially equipment connected with computers and the Internet, and who spends too much time buying this equipment and using it – often used to show disapproval: *techno-geeks on the hunt for new tools*

tech·no·lo·gi·cal /ˌteknəˈlɒdʒɪkəl◂ $ -ˈlɑː-/ ●●○ AWL *adj* relating to technology: *The steam engine was the greatest technological advance of the 19th century* —**technologically** /-kli/ *adv*: *the most technologically advanced factory in Europe.*

tech·nol·o·gist /tekˈnɒlədʒɪst $ -ˈnɑː-/ *n* [C] someone who has special knowledge of technology

tech·nol·o·gy /tekˈnɒlədʒi $ -ˈnɑː-/ ●●● S2 W1 AWL *n* (*plural* **technologies**) [C,U] new machines, equipment, and ways of doing things that are based on modern knowledge about science and computers: *Modern technology makes moving money around much easier than it used to be.* | *Advances in technology have improved crop yields by over 30%.* | *There have been major new developments in satellite technology.* | *Many people are unwilling to embrace new technologies.*

tech·no·phobe /ˈteknəfəʊb $ -foʊb/ *n* [C] someone who does not like modern machines, such as computers, and would prefer to live without them —**technophobia** /ˌteknəˈfəʊbiə $ -ˈfoʊ-/ *n* [U]

ˈtech-ˌsavvy *adj informal* knowing a lot about modern technology and how to use it: *tech-savvy teenagers*

tech·y /ˈteki/ *adj informal* **1** relating to or involving new technology: *I usually buy him something techy for Christmas – he loves gadgets.* **2** knowing a lot about modern technology and how to use it SYN **tech-savvy**

tec·ton·ic /tekˈtɒnɪk $ -ˈtɑːn-/ *adj* [only before noun] *technical* relating to PLATE TECTONICS: *tectonic movements*

ted·dy bear /ˈtedi beə $ -ber/ (*also* **teddy**) *n* [C] a soft toy in the shape of a bear

T

ˈteddy boy *n* [C] a member of a group of young men in Britain in the 1950s who had their own special style of clothes and music

te·di·ous /ˈtiːdiəs/ ●○○ *adj* something that is tedious continues for a long time and is not interesting SYN **boring**: *The work was tiring and tedious.* THESAURUS BORING —**tediously** *adv*: *a tediously long film*

te·di·um /ˈtiːdiəm/ *n* [U] the feeling of being bored because the things you are doing are not interesting and continue for a long time without changing SYN **boredom**: *We sang while we worked, to* ***relieve the tedium***. | **[+of]** *the tedium of everyday life*

tee[1] /tiː/ *n* [C] **1** a small object that you use in a game of GOLF to hold the ball above the ground before you hit it → see picture at **GOLF** **2** the place where you first hit the ball towards each hole in a game of GOLF **3** another word for T-SHIRT

tee[2] *v* (*past tense and past participle* **teed**)

tee off *phr v* **1** to hit the ball towards a hole for the first time in a game of GOLF → see picture at **GOLF** **2 tee sb off** *AmE informal* to make someone angry: *His attitude really tees me off.*

ˈTee-ball *n* [U] another spelling of T-BALL

teed off /ˌtiːd ˈɒf $ -ˈɒːf/ *adj AmE informal* annoyed or angry

teem /tiːm/ *v*

teem down *phr v BrE* to rain very heavily SYN **pour**: *It's been teeming down all day.*

teem with sb/sth *phr v* **1** to be very full of people or animals, all moving about: *The island was teeming with tourists.* **2** *BrE* if it is teeming with rain, it is raining very heavily SYN **pour**

teem·ing /ˈtiːmɪŋ/ *adj* **1** full of people, animals etc that are all moving around: *the teeming streets of the city* **2** *BrE* teeming rain is very heavy rain: *She walked home through the teeming rain.*

teen[1] /tiːn/ ●●○ *n* [C]
1 *AmE informal* a teenager
2 teens [plural] your teens is the period of your life when you are between 13 and 19 years old: **be in your teens** *She was in her teens when she met him.* | **early/late teens** *We moved to York when I was in my early teens.*

teen[2] *adj* [only before noun] *informal* relating to teenagers or used by teenagers SYN **teenage**: *a rock star and teen idol* | *a teen magazine*

teen·age /ˈtiːneɪdʒ/ ●●○ (*also* **teen·aged** /ˈtiːneɪdʒd/) *adj* [only before noun]
1 aged between 13 and 19: *a teenage boy* | *my teenage daughter* THESAURUS YOUNG
2 relating to or affecting people aged between 13 and 19: *the teenage years* | *teenage rebellion* | *the problem of teenage pregnancy*

teen·ag·er /ˈtiːneɪdʒə $ -ər/ ●●● S3 (*also* **teen** *informal*) *n* [C] someone who is between 13 and 19 years old: *a TV sex education series aimed at teenagers* THESAURUS CHILD

tee·ny /ˈtiːni/ *adj informal* very small SYN **tiny**: *I was just a teeny bit disappointed.*

tee·ny·bop·per /ˈtiːniˌbɒpə $ -ˌbɑːpər/ *n* [C] *old-fashioned* a girl between the ages of about 9 and 14, who is very interested in popular music, teenage fashions etc

tee·ny wee·ny /ˌtiːni ˈwiːni◂/ (*also* **teen·sy ween·sy** /ˌtiːnzi ˈwiːnzi◂/) *adj informal* a word meaning very small – used especially by children or when speaking to children

tee·pee /ˈtiːpiː/ *n* [C] another spelling of TEPEE

ˈtee ˌshirt *n* [C] another spelling of T-SHIRT

tee·ter /ˈtiːtə $ -ər/ *v* [I] **1** to stand or walk moving from side to side, as if you are going to fall: *She teetered along in her high-heeled shoes.* **2 be teetering on the brink/edge of sth** to be very close to being in an unpleasant or dangerous situation: *The country teetered on the brink of war.*

ˈteeter-ˌtotter *n* [C] *AmE* a large toy like a board on which two children sit, one at each end SYN **seesaw** *BrE*

teeth /tiːθ/ the plural of TOOTH

teethe /tiːð/ *v* [I] **be teething** if a baby is teething, its first teeth are growing

ˈteething ˌtroubles (*also* **ˈteething ˌproblems**) *n* [plural] small problems that you have when you first start doing a new job or using a new system

tee·to·tal /ˌtiːˈtəʊtl◂ $ -ˈtoʊ-/ *adj* someone who is teetotal never drinks alcohol —**teetotalism** *n* [U]

tee·to·tal·ler *BrE*, **teetotaler** *AmE* /tiːˈtəʊtələ $ -ˈtoʊtələr/ *n* [C] someone who never drinks alcohol

TEFL /ˈtefəl/ *n* [U] *BrE* the teaching of English as a foreign language

Tef·lon /ˈteflɒn $ -lɑːn/ *n* [U] *trademark* a plastic that stops things from sticking to it, used on the inside of pans to stop food sticking to the pan

tel the written abbreviation of ***telephone number***

tele- /teli, telə/ *prefix* **1** at or over a long distance: *a telescope* (=for seeing a long way) | *telecommunications* (=communicating with people a long way away) | *teleshopping* (=using a computer in your home to order goods) **2** for television or broadcast on television: *a teleplay* **3** using a telephone: **telesales** (=selling products to people by telephone)

tel·e·care /ˈtelikeə $ -ker/ *n* [U] the use of communications technology in providing support and care for people who are ill or old, for example by having equipment in their home that sends a message if they need help

tel·e·cast /ˈtelikɑːst $ -kæst/ *n* [C] something that is broadcast on television —**telecast** *v* [T]: *The game will be telecast live.*

tel·e·com·mu·ni·ca·tions /ˌtelikəmjuːnəˈkeɪʃənz/ ●○○ *n* [plural] the sending and receiving of messages by telephone, radio, television etc: *a new telecommunications system* | *the telecommunications industry*

tele·com·mut·er /ˈtelikəˌmjuːtə $ -tər/ *n* [C] someone who works at home using a computer connected to a company's main office —**telecommuting** *n* [U]

tel·e·con·fe·rence[1] /ˈteliˌkɒnfərəns $ -ˌkɑːn-/ *n* [C] a discussion in which people in different places talk to each other using telephones or video equipment

teleconference[2] *v* [I] to have a meeting in which people in different places talk to each other using telephones or video equipment —**teleconferencing** *n* [U]

tel·e·gen·ic /ˌteləˈdʒenɪk◂/ *adj* someone who is telegenic looks nice on television

tel·e·gram /ˈteləgræm/ *n* [C] a message sent by telegraph

tel·e·graph[1] /ˈteləgrɑːf $ -græf/ *n* **1** [U] an old-fashioned method of sending messages using radio or electrical signals **2** [C] a piece of equipment that receives or sends messages in this way —**telegraphic** /ˌteləˈgræfɪk◂/ *adj*

telegraph[2] *v* **1** [I,T] to send a message by telegraph: *Once he knew where we were, Lewis telegraphed every few hours.* **2** [T] *informal* to let people know what you intend to do without saying anything: *A slight movement of the hand telegraphed his intention to shoot.*

te·leg·ra·pher /təˈlegrəfə $ -ər/ *n* [C] a telegraphist

te·leg·ra·phist /tɪˈlegrəfɪst/ *n* [C] someone in the past whose job was to send and receive messages by telegraph

ˈtelegraph ˌpole *n* [C] *BrE* a tall wooden pole for supporting telephone wires SYN **telephone pole** *AmE*

tel·e·mar·ket·ing /ˌteliˈmɑːkətɪŋ $ -ˈmɑːr-/ *n* [U] a way of selling products to people in which you telephone people to see if they want to buy something

tel·e·med·icine /ˈteliˌmedsən $ -ˌmedəsən / *n* [U] the use of communications technology, especially the telephone and Internet, to provide health care

tel·e·path·ic /ˌteləˈpæθɪk◂/ *adj* **1** someone who is telepathic has a mysterious ability to know what other people are thinking **2** a telepathic message is sent from one person to another by using thoughts, not by talking or writing

te·lep·a·thy /təˈlepəθi/ *n* [U] a way of communicating

in which thoughts are sent from one person's mind to another person's mind

tel·e·phone¹ /ˈteləfəʊn $ -foʊn/ ●●● S1 W2 *n*
1 the telephone the system of communication that you use to have a conversation with someone in another place SYN **phone**: **by telephone** *Reservations can be made by telephone.* | **on the telephone** *I've never met him, but I've spoken to him on the telephone.* | **over the telephone** *I read the names out to him over the telephone.* | **down the telephone** *BrE*: *He shouted at me down the telephone.*

REGISTER
In everyday English, people usually say **phone** rather than **telephone**: *She's been on the **phone** all evening.*

2 [C] the piece of equipment that you use when you are talking to someone by telephone SYN **phone**: *The **telephone rang** just as I was leaving.* | *She **picked up the telephone** and dialled a number.* | *I said goodbye and **put down the telephone**.*
3 be on the telephone a) to be talking to someone, using the telephone: *I was on the telephone when he came in.* **b)** to have a telephone in your home, office etc

COLLOCATIONS – MEANINGS 1 & 2

VERBS
a telephone rings *The telephone rang, but Tom didn't answer it.*
answer the telephone *When I called the house, Mike answered the telephone.*
talk on the telephone *He was talking on the telephone when the doorbell rang.*
use the telephone *May I use your telephone?*
pick up the telephone | put down the telephone | call sb on the telephone

telephone + NOUN
a telephone call *She got a telephone call from Joe last night.*
a telephone conversation *We had a long telephone conversation.*
a telephone line

COMMON ERRORS
⚠ Don't say 'get/have a telephone from sb'. Say **get/have a telephone call from sb**.

telephone² ●●○ *v* [I,T] *BrE formal* to talk to someone by telephone SYN **phone**, **call**: *Sammy telephoned to say that he would be late.* | *I'll telephone you later.* THESAURUS PHONE

ˌtelephone ˈbanking *n* [U] a service provided by banks so that people can find out information about their bank account, pay bills etc by telephone rather than by going to a bank

ˈtelephone ˌbook *n* [C] a TELEPHONE DIRECTORY

ˈtelephone ˌbooth *n* [C] *AmE* a small structure that is partly or completely enclosed, containing a public telephone SYN **phone booth**

ˈtelephone ˌbox *BrE*, **telephone booth** *AmE n* [C] a very small building in a street where there is a telephone that the public can use

TELEPHONE BOX

telephone box *BrE*/ telephone booth *AmE*

ˈtelephone ˌcall *n* [C] when you speak to someone by telephone: *There's a telephone call for you, Mr Baron.* | **have/get/receive a telephone call** *I had a telephone call from George this morning.* | *Can I **make** a quick **telephone call**?*

ˈtelephone diˌrectory *n* [C] a book containing a list of the names, addresses, and telephone numbers of all the people in a particular area SYN **phone book**

ˈtelephone exˌchange *n* [C] an office where telephone calls are connected

ˈtelephone ˌnumber *n* [C] the number that you use to telephone a person: *What's your telephone number?* | *He gave me his address and telephone number.*

ˈtelephone ˌpole *n* [C] *AmE* a tall wooden pole for supporting telephone wires SYN **telegraph pole** *BrE*

te·leph·o·nist /tɪˈlefənɪst/ *n* [C] *BrE* someone whose job is to connect telephone calls to people in a large organization

te·leph·o·ny /təˈlefəni/ *n* [U] telephone services, systems, or communication

te·le·pho·to lens /ˌteləfəʊtəʊ ˈlenz $ -foʊtoʊ-/ *n* [C] a long LENS that you put on a camera so that you can take clear photographs of things that are a long way away

tel·e·port /ˈteləpɔːt $ -pɔːrt/ *v* [I,T] in SCIENCE FICTION, to send a person or thing from one place to another in the form of energy or a copy, or to travel in this way: *They are teleported from the ship down to the planet's surface.* —**teleportation** /ˌteləpɔːˈteɪʃən $ -pɔːr-/ *n* [U]

tel·e·print·er /ˈteləˌprɪntə $ -ər/ *n* [C] a machine that prints messages that have been written on a machine somewhere else and sent along telephone lines SYN **teletypewriter** *AmE*

tel·e·sales /ˈteliseɪlz/ *n* [U] a way of selling products to people by telephone

tel·e·scope¹ /ˈteləskəʊp $ -skoʊp/ ●●○ *n* [C] a piece of equipment shaped like a tube, used for making distant objects look larger and closer: **through a telescope** *Details on the Moon's surface can only be seen through a telescope.* → RADIO TELESCOPE → see picture at OPTICAL

telescope² *v* **1** [T] to make a process or set of events happen in a shorter time: **be telescoped into sth** *The whole legal process was telescoped into a few weeks.* **2** [I] if something telescopes, the parts of it press together or slide over each other, and it becomes smaller: *The front of the car telescoped when it hit the wall.*

tel·e·scop·ic /ˌteləˈskɒpɪk◂ $ -ˈskɑː-/ *adj* **1** made of parts that slide over each other so that the whole thing can be made longer or shorter: *a tripod with telescopic legs* **2** making distant things look bigger, like a telescope does: *a telescopic lens* | *a rifle with a telescopic sight* **3** done using a telescope: *his telescopic observations of the Moon*

tel·e·thon /ˈteləθɒn $ -θɑːn/ *n* [C] a long television show in which famous people provide entertainment and ask people watching to give money to help people

tel·e·type·writ·er /ˌteliˈtaɪpraɪtə $ -ər/ *n* [C] *AmE* a TELEPRINTER

tel·e·van·ge·list /ˌtelɪˈvændʒəlɪst/ *n* [C] someone who appears regularly on television to try to persuade people to become Christians, and often also asks people to give them money —**televangelism** *n* [U]

tel·e·vise /ˈteləvaɪz/ ●○○ *v* [T] to broadcast something on television SYN **show**: *The game was **televised live** on ABC.*

tel·e·vi·sion /ˈteləˌvɪʒən, ˌteləˈvɪʒən/ ●●● S1 W1 *n*
1 [C] (*also* **television set** *formal*) a piece of electronic equipment shaped like a box with a screen, on which you can watch programmes SYN **TV**: *Lucy turned on the television to watch the evening news.* | *They have a television in every room.*

REGISTER
In everyday English, people usually say **TV** rather than **television**: *What's on **TV** tonight?*

2 [U] the programmes broadcast in this way SYN **TV**: *In the evenings I like to relax and watch television.*
3 on (the) television broadcast or being broadcast on television: *What's on television tonight?*
4 [U] the business of making and broadcasting programmes on television SYN **TV**: **in television** *Jean works in television.* | *a television film crew*

GRAMMAR: Patterns with television

on (the) television

• You watch or see something **on television** or **on the television**: *We saw the game on television.*

• You say that someone or something is **on television** or **on the television**: *My friend was on television last night.* | *There are a lot of quiz shows on the television.*

✗ Don't say: *We saw the game in television.* | *My friend was in the television.*

in television

You say that someone works **in television**, when they work for a television company: *I've always wanted to work in television.*

COLLOCATIONS

VERBS

watch television *Mum was in the lounge watching television.*

see/watch sth on television *She saw the race on television.*

turn/switch the television on/off | **turn the television up/down** (=make it louder or quieter)

television + NOUN

a television show/programme *Her favourite television programme was just starting.*

a television series (=a set of programmes with the same characters or subject, broadcast every day or every week) *He starred in the popular television series, 'Friends'.*

a television film/movie (=a film that has been made to be shown on television, not in a cinema) | **a television documentary** | **the television news** | **a television screen** | **a television presenter** *BrE* | **a television reporter/journalist**

ADJECTIVES/NOUN + television

live television *The accident was shown on live television.*

national television *The president went on national television to appeal for calm.*

satellite/cable television | **digital television** | **high definition/HD television** | **a widescreen television** | **a plasma/LCD television** | **a flat screen television**

T

'television ˌlicence *n* [C] an official piece of paper that you need to buy in Britain in order to legally use a television in your home

tel·e·vi·sual /ˌteləˈvɪʒuəl◂/ *adj* [only before noun] *BrE* relating to television: *a major televisual event like the Olympics*

tel·e·work·er /ˈteliwɜːkə $ -wɜːrkər/ *n* [C] someone who works from home, and communicates with their employer, customers etc using a computer, telephone etc —**teleworking** *n* [U]

tel·ex /ˈteleks/ *n* **1** [U] a method of communication, in which messages are written on a special machine and then sent using the telephone network **2** [C] a message sent in this way —**telex** *v* [I,T]

tell /tel/ ●●● *v* (*past tense and past participle* **told**) /təʊld $ toʊld/ (S1) (W1)

1 COMMUNICATE STH [T] if someone tells you something, they communicate information, a story, their feelings etc to you: **tell sb (that)** *I wish someone had told me the meeting was canceled.* | *The Chief of Police told reporters that two people were killed in the blast.* | **tell sb what/how/where/who etc** *Jack had to go, but he didn't tell me why.* | *I think you'd better* **tell** *me* **exactly** *what's been going on around here.* | **tell sb about sth** *No one had told them about the drug's side effects.* | *I'll* **tell** *you* **all about** *it when I get back.* | **tell sb sth** *Tell me your phone number again.* | **tell (sb) a story/joke/secret/lie** *She told us some funny stories about her sister.* | *Sheppard was* **telling the truth**. | **tell sb straight** (=tell someone the truth, even though it might upset them) *Tell me straight, Adam. Just answer yes or no.* THESAURUS ▸ EXPLAIN, REVEAL → see Thesaurus box on p. 1887

REGISTER

In written English, people often prefer to say that another writer **describes** something, rather than using **tell**: *His book* **describes** *how the human brain has developed.*

2 SHOW STH [T] to give information in ways other than talking: **tell sb how/what/where/who etc** *The light tells you when the machine is ready.* | *The bear's sense of smell tells it where prey is hiding.* | **tell sb about sth** *What do these fossils tell us about climate change?*

3 WHAT SB SHOULD DO [T] to say that someone must do something: **tell sb (not) to do sth** *The teacher told the children to sit down quietly.* | *I thought I told you not to touch anything!* | **tell sb (that)** *Bernice was told she had to work late this evening.* | **tell sb what/how etc** *Stop trying to tell me what to do all the time.* | ***Do as you are told*** (=obey me) *and don't ask questions.* THESAURUS ▸ ADVISE, ORDER, RECOMMEND

4 KNOW [I,T not in progressive] to know something or be able to recognize something because of certain signs that show this: **can/can't tell** *She might have been lying. Benjy couldn't tell.* | **tell (that)** *The moment Kramer walked in, I could tell that things were not going well.* | **tell (sth) a mile off** (=know easily) *You could tell a mile off that he was lying.* | **tell when/how/whether/if etc** *It's* **hard to tell** *how long the job will take.* | **tell sth by sth/from sth** *I could tell from his tone of voice that Ken was disappointed.*

5 RECOGNIZE DIFFERENCE [T not in progressive] to be able to see how one person or thing is different from another: **tell sth from sth** *How can you tell a fake Vuitton handbag from the real thing?* | *Can you* **tell the difference between** *sparkling wine and champagne?* → TELL

6 tell yourself sth to persuade yourself that something is true: *I keep telling myself there is nothing I could have done to save him.*

7 WARN [T usually in past tense] to warn someone that something bad might happen: **tell sb (that)** *I told you it was a waste of time talking to him.* | **tell sb (not) to do sth** *My mother told me not to trust Robert.*

8 TELL SB ABOUT BAD BEHAVIOUR [I] *informal* to tell someone in authority about something wrong that someone you know has done – used especially by children (SYN) **tell on sb**: *If you hit me, I'll tell.* → KISS-AND-TELL

9 tell tales *BrE* to say something that is not true about someone else, in order to cause trouble for them – used especially about children: *an unpopular boy, who was always telling tales on the other children* → TELLTALE[2]

10 all told altogether, when everyone or everything has been counted: *There must have been eight cars in the accident, all told.*

11 AFFECT [I not in progressive] to have an effect on someone, especially a harmful one: **tell on sb** *These late nights are really beginning to tell on him.*

12 tell the time *BrE*, **tell time** *AmE* to be able to know what time it is by looking at a clock

SPOKEN PHRASES

13 I/I'll tell you what (*also* **tell you what**) **a)** used when you are suggesting or offering something: *I tell you what – let's have a picnic in the park.* **b)** *AmE* used in order to emphasize what you are really saying: *I tell you what, I'm not looking forward to standing up in court tomorrow.*

14 to tell (you) the truth used to emphasize that you are being very honest: *I don't really want to go out, to tell the truth.*

15 I can tell you/I'm telling you used to emphasize that what you are saying is true even though it may be difficult to believe: *I'm telling you, Sheila, I've never seen anything like it in my life.*

16 tell me used before asking a question: *Tell me, do you think this dress goes with these shoes?* | *So tell me, how was it in Argentina?*

17 I told you so used when you have warned someone about a possible danger that has now happened and they

have ignored your warning: *I suppose you've come to say 'I told you so.'*
18 I'll tell you something/one thing/another thing (*also* **let me tell you something/one thing/another thing**) used to emphasize what you are saying: *I'll tell you one thing – you'll never get me to vote for him.* | *Let me tell you something – if I catch you kids smoking again, you'll be grounded for a month at least.*
19 you can tell him/her etc from me used to ask someone to tell another person something, when you are annoyed or determined: *Well, you can tell him from me that I'm going to make a complaint.*
20 I couldn't tell you used to tell someone that you do not know the answer to their question: *'How much would a rail ticket cost?' 'I couldn't tell you; I always drive.'*
21 I can't tell you a) used to say that you cannot tell someone something because it is a secret: *'Where are you taking me?' 'I can't tell you; it would spoil the surprise.'* **b)** used to say that you cannot express your feelings or describe something properly: **[+how/why/what etc]** *I can't tell you how worried I've been.*
22 don't tell me used to interrupt someone because you know what they are going to say or because you want to guess – used especially when you are annoyed: *'I'm sorry I'm late but ...' 'Don't tell me – the car broke down again?'*
23 sb tells me (that) used to say what someone has told you: *Mike tells me you've got a new job.*
24 you're telling me used to emphasize that you already know and agree with something that someone has just said: *'He's such a pain to live with.' 'You're telling me!'*
25 tell me about it used to say that you already know how bad something is, especially because you have experienced it yourself: *'I've been so tired lately.' 'Yeah, tell me about it!'*
26 you never can tell/you can never tell used to say that you cannot be certain about what will happen in the future: *The boy might turn out to be a genius. You never can tell.*
27 there's no telling what/how etc used to say that it is impossible to know what has happened or what will happen next: *There's no telling what she'll try next.*
28 that would be telling used to say that you cannot tell someone something because it is a secret
29 tell sb where to go/where to get off used to tell someone angrily that what they have said is insulting or unfair: *'Andy started criticizing the way I was dressed.' 'I hope you told him where to get off!'*
30 tell it like it is *AmE* to say exactly what you think or what is true, without hiding anything that might upset or offend people: *Don always tells it like it is.*
31 I'm not telling (you) used to say that you refuse to tell someone something: *'Mum, what are you getting me for my birthday?' 'I'm not telling you – you'll have to wait and see.'*
32 tell me another (one) used when you do not believe what someone has told you

GRAMMAR: Patterns with tell

- In meaning 1, **tell** is transitive and must be followed by an object.
- You **tell** someone something: *He told her the news.*
- You **tell** something **to** someone: *He told the news to his mother.* ✗ Don't say: *He told to his mother the news.*
- You **tell** someone **about** something: *He told me about his feelings.* ✗ Don't say: *He told about his feelings.*
- You **tell** someone **to do** something: *He told me to sit down.*
- You use **tell** someone **(that)** when reporting what someone said: *He told them that he was sorry.* | *She told me I could go.* ✗ Don't say: *He told that he was sorry.*

GRAMMAR GUIDE ▶ VERBS

tell against sb *phr v BrE formal* to make someone less likely to succeed in achieving or winning something: *I badly wanted the job, but knew that my age would probably tell against me.*
tell sb/sth **apart** *phr v* if you can tell two people or things apart, you can see the difference between them, so that you do not confuse them SYN **distinguish**: *It's almost impossible to tell the twins apart.*
tell of sb/sth *phr v literary* to describe an event or person: *The poem tells of the deeds of a famous warrior.*

REGISTER
In everyday English, people usually say that a poem, story etc **is about** something rather than **tells of** something: ***What's** his latest poem **about**?*

tell sb ↔ **off** *phr v* if someone in authority tells you off, they speak to you angrily about something wrong that you have done: **be/get told off** *Shelley was one of those kids who was always getting told off at school.* | **tell sb off for doing sth** *My dad told me off for swearing.*
tell on sb *phr v informal* to tell someone in authority about something wrong that someone you know has done – used especially by children: *Please don't tell on me – my parents will kill me if they find out!*

THESAURUS: tell

tell to give someone information by speaking or writing to them: *She wrote to tell me she was getting married.* | *Can you tell us where the nearest garage is?*
let sb know *especially spoken* to tell someone something when you know more about it: *Let me know your new address as soon as you can.* | *Let us know what happens at the interview.*
pass a message on to sb (*also* **pass it on** *informal*) to tell another person the information that has been told to you: *She's with a client at the moment, but I'll pass the message on to her.* | *If I get any news, I'll pass it on.*
brief to give someone all the necessary information about a situation, so that they can do their work: *Police officers were briefed before going out to arrest the suspects.*
relate *formal* to tell someone about something that happened to you or to someone else: *One girl related a story about a friend who had accidentally become pregnant.*
recount *formal* to tell someone about a series of events: *The guide recounted the history of the castle, from the 1300s onwards.*
bring sth to sb's attention to tell someone about something that they did not know about, but which they need to know about: *I wanted to bring the matter to your attention.* | *She was the first person to study the effects of pesticides, and to bring them to people's attention.*
fill sb in *informal* to tell someone about things that have happened recently, especially at work: *Can you fill Robert in on the progress we've made while he's been on holiday?*

TO OFFICIALLY TELL SOMEONE

inform to officially tell someone about something: *Do you think we ought to inform the police?* | *Doctors should inform patients about the possible side effects of any drugs they prescribe.*
announce to tell people publicly and officially about something: *The university chancellor announced his resignation on Friday.* | *It was announced that the company had made a profit of $6 billion.*
report to officially tell someone about something that has happened: *She was able to report that the project was nearly finished.*
notify *formal* to tell someone officially about something that has happened or that is planned to happen: *Staff were notified several months in advance that they would be losing their jobs.*

tell·er /ˈtelə $ -ər/ *n* [C] **1** someone whose job is to receive and pay out money in a bank **2** someone who counts votes

tell·ing[1] /ˈtelɪŋ/ *adj* **1** having a great or important effect SYN **significant**: *a telling argument* **2** showing the true character or nature of someone or something, often without being intended SYN **revealing**: **telling comment/example/detail etc** —**tellingly** *adv*

telling[2] *n* **1** [C,U] when you tell a story: *The story gets better with each telling.* **2 there is no telling** used to say that there is no way to know what will happen in a certain situation: *There's no telling who is going to show up tonight.*

ˌtelling-ˈoff *n* (*plural* **tellings-off**) [C usually singular] *BrE* the act of telling someone that they have done something wrong: *I've already had one telling-off from Dad this week.* → **tell off** at TELL

tell·tale[1] /ˈtelteɪl/ *adj* **telltale signs/marks etc** signs etc that clearly show something has happened or exists, often something that is a secret: *They examined the child carefully, looking for telltale signs of abuse.*

telltale[2] *n* [C] *BrE* a child who tells adults about other children's secrets or bad behaviour – used by children to show disapproval SYN **tattletale** *AmE*

tel·ly /ˈteli/ ●○○ *n* (*plural* **tellies**) [C,U] *BrE informal* television: **on telly** *Is there anything good on telly tonight?*

tem·blor /ˈtemblə, -blɔː $ -blər, -blɔːr/ *n* [C] *formal* an EARTHQUAKE

te·mer·i·ty /təˈmerəti/ *n* [U] *formal* when someone says or does something in a way that shows a lack of respect for other people and is likely to offend them → **audacity**: *He actually* ***had the temerity to*** *tell her to lose weight.*

temp[1] /temp/ *n* [C] an office worker who is only employed temporarily

temp[2] *v* [I] to work as a temp: *Carol's temping until she can find another job.*

tem·per[1] /ˈtempə $ -ər/ ●●○ *n*

1 [C,U] a tendency to become angry suddenly or easily: *That temper of hers will get her into trouble one of these days.* | *According to Nathan, Robin* ***has*** *quite* ***a temper****.* | *Theo needs to learn to* ***control*** *his* ***temper****.* | **quick/bad/fiery etc temper** *Be careful, he's got a pretty violent temper.* | **tempers flare** (*also* **tempers become frayed** *BrE*) (=people become angry) *Mason's temper flared when he spotted his girlfriend kissing another man.*

2 lose your temper to suddenly become very angry so that you cannot control yourself: *I've never seen Vic lose his temper.*

3 [singular, U] the way you are feeling at a particular time, especially when you are feeling angry for a short time: **in a temper** *It's no use talking to him when he's in a temper.* | *Pete hit his brother in a* ***fit of temper****.* | **be in a bad/foul temper** (=to be angry) *Watch out – she's been in a foul temper all day.* | **fly into a temper** *Her boss would fly into a temper if a project wasn't done on time.*

4 keep your temper to stay calm when it would be easy to get angry: *I was finding it increasingly difficult to keep my temper.*

5 good-tempered/foul-tempered/quick-tempered etc having a good, bad temper etc: *Minnie was always good-tempered and agreeable.*

6 [singular] *formal* the general attitude that people have in a particular place at one time: **[+of]** *the temper of life in Renaissance Italy* → BAD-TEMPERED, EVEN-TEMPERED, ILL-TEMPERED

temper[2] *v* [T] **1** *formal* to make something less severe or extreme: **temper sth with/by sth** *The heat in this coastal town is tempered by cool sea breezes.* **2** to make metal as hard as is needed by heating it and then putting it in cold water: *tempered steel*

tem·pe·ra /ˈtempərə/ *n* [U] a type of paint in which the colour is mixed with a thick liquid

tem·pe·ra·ment /ˈtempərəmənt/ ●○○ *n* [C,U] the emotional part of someone's character, especially how likely they are to be happy, angry etc: **artistic/nervous/good etc temperament** *Jill has such a lovely relaxed temperament.* | **by temperament** *Tolkien was, by temperament, a very different man from Lewis.*

tem·pe·ra·men·tal /ˌtempərəˈmentl◂/ *adj* **1** likely to suddenly become upset, excited, or angry – used to show disapproval: *Preston is particularly good at handling temperamental people.* **2** a machine, system etc that is temperamental does not always work properly: *Sorry if the heater's a bit temperamental.* **3** relating to the emotional part of someone's character: *serious temperamental differences between the couple* —**temperamentally** *adv*

tem·pe·rance /ˈtempərəns/ *n* [U] **1** *old-fashioned* when someone never drinks alcohol because of their moral or religious beliefs **2** *formal* sensible control of the things you say and do, especially the amount of alcohol you drink SYN **moderation**

tem·pe·rate /ˈtempərət/ *adj* **1 temperate climate/zone/region etc** a type of weather or a part of the world that is never very hot or very cold **2** *formal* behaviour that is temperate is calm and sensible OPP **intemperate**

ˈtemperate ˌzone *n* [C] one of the two parts of the Earth that are north and south of the TROPICS

tem·pera·ture /ˈtemprətʃə $ -ər/ ●●● S2 W2 *n*

1 [C,U] a measure of how hot or cold a place or thing is: *The temperature of the water was just right for swimming.* | *Water boils at a temperature of 100°C.*

2 sb's temperature the temperature of your body, especially used as a measure of whether you are sick or not: *The nurse* ***took*** (=measured) *my* ***temperature****.*

3 have a temperature (*also* **be running a temperature**) to have a body temperature that is higher than normal, especially because you are sick: *Susie has a temperature and has gone to bed.*

4 [C] the temperature of a situation is the way people are reacting, for example whether they are behaving angrily or calmly: *The referee's decision to give a penalty* ***raised the temperature*** *of the match.*

COLLOCATIONS

ADJECTIVES/NOUN + temperature

high *At high temperatures water is not able to hold as much oxygen.*
low *Temperatures were so low most plants could not survive.*
constant *The temperature of the room is kept constant.*
extreme temperatures | **sub-zero temperatures** | **the air/water temperature** | **sb's body temperature**

PHRASES

a rise in temperature/a temperature rise *The result was a rise in the Earth's temperature.*
a drop/fall in temperature *At night there is a dramatic drop in temperature.*
a change in temperature *The oil is affected by changes in temperature.*
at room temperature *Store the wine at room temperature.*

VERBS

the temperature rises *The temperature rose steadily throughout the morning.*
the temperature soars (=rises quickly to a high level) | **the temperature falls/drops** | **raise the temperature** | **lower the temperature**

tem·pest /ˈtempɪst/ *n* [C] **1** *literary* a violent storm **2 a tempest in a teapot** *AmE* an unimportant matter that someone has become upset about: *Haley dismissed the lawsuit as a tempest in a teapot.*

tem·pes·tu·ous /temˈpestʃuəs/ *adj* **1** a tempestuous relationship or period of time involves a lot of difficulty and strong emotions: *a tempestuous marriage* **2** *literary* a tempestuous sea or wind is very rough and violent SYN **stormy**

tem·plate /ˈtempleɪt, -plət/ *n* [C] **1** a thin sheet of plastic or metal in a special shape or pattern, used to help cut other materials in a similar shape **2** *technical* a computer document containing some basic information that you use as a model for writing other documents, such as business letters, envelopes etc **3** *written* something that is used as a model for another thing: **[+for]** *Her childhood became a template for how she brought up her own children.*

tem·ple /ˈtempəl/ ●●○ *n* [C]
1 a building where people go to WORSHIP, in the Jewish, Hindu, Buddhist, Sikh, and Mormon religions
2 [usually plural] one of the two fairly flat areas on each side of your FOREHEAD

tem·po /ˈtempəʊ $ -poʊ/ *n* (*plural* **tempos**) [C]
1 the speed at which music is played or should be played
2 the speed at which something happens: *the easy tempo of island life*

tem·po·ral /ˈtempərəl/ *adj formal* **1** relating to or limited by time: *the temporal character of human existence* **2** relating to practical instead of religious affairs: *Edgar ruled over the Church as well as his temporal kingdom.*

tem·po·ra·ry /ˈtempərəri, -pəri $ -pəreri/ ●●● S3 W3 AWL *adj*
1 continuing for only a limited period of time OPP **permanent**: *temporary pain relief | I'm living with my parents, but it's only temporary. | You might want to consider* ***temporary work*** *until you decide what you want to do. | She was employed* ***on a temporary basis****.*
2 intended to be used for only a limited period of time OPP **permanent**: ***temporary accommodation*** *| The bridge was erected as a* ***temporary measure****.* —**temporarily** /ˈtempərərəli $ ˌtempəˈrerəli/ *adv*: *Due to a small fire, the office will be closed temporarily.*

tem·po·rize (*also* **-ise** *BrE*) /ˈtempəraɪz/ *v* [I] *formal* to delay or avoid making a decision in order to gain time → **procrastinate**

tempt /tempt/ ●●○ *v* [T]
1 to try to persuade someone to do something by making it seem attractive: **tempt sb into doing sth** *The new program is designed to tempt young people into studying engineering.* | **tempt sb to do sth** *It would take a lot of money to tempt me to quit this job.*
2 to make someone want to have or do something, even though they know they really should not: *If you leave valuables in your car it will tempt thieves.* | **be tempted to do sth** *I'm tempted to buy that dress.*
3 tempt fate (*also* **tempt providence** *BrE*) **a)** to do something that involves unnecessary risk and may cause serious problems: *Fire officials said developers are tempting fate by building deep into the scenic canyons.* **b)** to say too confidently that something will have a good result, that there will be no problems etc, when it is likely there will be problems

temp·ta·tion /tempˈteɪʃən/ ●●○ *n* [C,U]
1 a strong desire to have or do something even though you know you should not: **temptation to do sth** *There might be a temptation to cheat if students sit too close together. |* ***Resist*** *the* ***temptation*** *to buy the item until you're certain you need it. | I finally* ***gave in to*** *the* ***temptation*** *and had a cigarette.*
2 something that makes you want to have or do something, even though you know you should not: *Selling alcohol at truck stops is an unnecessary temptation for drivers.*

temp·ting /ˈtemptɪŋ/ ●●○ *adj* something that is tempting seems very good and you would like to have it or do it: *a tempting job offer | That pie looks tempting.* | **be tempting to do sth** *It's tempting to believe her story.*

temp·tress /ˈtemptrɪs/ *n* [C] *old-fashioned* a woman who makes a man want to have sex with her

tem·pu·ra /ˈtempʊrə/ *n* [U] a type of Japanese food that consists of fish or vegetables fried in BATTER

ten /ten/ ●●● S1 W2 *number, n*
1 the number 10: *Snow had been falling steadily for ten days. | I need to be home by ten* (=ten o'clock). *| At the time, she was about ten* (=ten years old).
2 ten to one *informal* used to say that something is very likely: *Ten to one he'll have forgotten all about it tomorrow.*
3 be ten a penny *BrE informal* to be very common and therefore not special or unusual → **be a dime a dozen** at DIME(2)
4 (get) ten out of ten (for sth) *BrE* used in schools to give a perfect mark, or humorously to praise someone: *You get ten out of ten for effort, Simon.*
5 [C] a piece of paper money that is worth ten dollars or ten pounds: *I reached inside my purse and handed him a ten.*

ten·a·ble /ˈtenəbəl/ *adj* a belief, argument etc that is tenable is reasonable and can be defended successfully: *an idea which is no longer tenable*

te·na·cious /təˈneɪʃəs/ *adj* **1** determined to do something and unwilling to stop trying even when the situation becomes difficult: *a tenacious negotiator* THESAURUS DETERMINED **2** tenacious beliefs, ideas etc continue to have a lot of influence for a long time: *a tenacious religious tradition that is still practised in Shinto temples* —**tenaciously** *adv* —**tenacity** /təˈnæsəti/ *n* [U]

ten·an·cy /ˈtenənsi/ *n* (*plural* **tenancies**) *formal* **1** [C] the period of time that someone rents a house, land etc → **tenant**: *a six-month tenancy | a tenancy agreement*
2 [C,U] the right to use a house, land etc that is rented

ten·ant /ˈtenənt/ ●●○ *n* [C] someone who lives in a house, room etc and pays rent to the person who owns it → **landlord**: *The desk was left by the previous tenant.*

ˌtenant ˈfarmer *n* [C] someone who farms land that is rented from someone else

ˌTen Comˈmandments, the according to the Old Testament of the Bible, the set of rules that God gave to Moses on Mount Sinai, in order to tell people how they should behave. They are supposed to have been written on two stone TABLETS (=flat pieces of stone) and they appear in the Christian, Jewish, and Islamic religions. The ten rules include 'Thou shalt not kill' and 'Thou shalt not steal'. A set of basic rules is sometimes called the 'Ten Commandments': *The 'Ten Commandments of Good Communication' are designed to help people to communicate better within an organization.*

tend /tend/ ●●● S1 W1 *v*
1 tend to do sth if something tends to happen, it happens often and is likely to happen again: *People tend to need less sleep as they get older. | My car tends to overheat in the summer.*
2 (*also* **tend to sb/sth**) [T] *old-fashioned* to look after someone or something: *Sofia was in the bedroom tending to her son.*
3 tend towards sth to have one particular quality or feature more than others: *Charles tends towards obesity.*
4 tend bar *especially AmE* to work as a BARTENDER
5 [I always + adv/prep] *formal* to move or develop in a particular direction: **[+upwards/downwards]** *Interest rates are tending upwards.*

ten·den·cy /ˈtendənsi/ ●●○ S3 W3 *n* (*plural* **tendencies**) [C]
1 if someone or something has a tendency to do or become a particular thing, they are likely to do or become it: **a tendency to do sth** *Greg's tendency to be critical made him unpopular with his co-workers. | The drug is effective but* ***has a tendency to*** *cause headaches.* | **[+to/towards]** *Some people may inherit a tendency to alcoholism.* | **[+for]** *Researchers believe that the tendency for diabetes is present at birth.*
2 a general change or development in a particular direction: **there is a tendency (for sb) to do sth** *There is an increasing tendency for women to have children later in life.* | **[+to/towards]** *a general tendency towards conservation and recycling* | **[+among]** *a tendency among Americans to get married at a later age*
3 aggressive/suicidal/criminal/artistic etc tendencies a part of someone's character that makes them likely to behave in a certain way or become an artist, criminal etc: *children with aggressive or anti-social tendencies*
4 a group within a larger political group that supports ideas that are usually more extreme than those of the main group: *the growing fascist tendency*

T

GRAMMAR: Singular or plural verb?

- In this meaning, **tendency** is usually followed by a singular verb: *The extremist tendency* ***is*** *becoming more powerful.*
- In British English, you can also use a plural verb: *The extremist tendency* ***are*** *becoming more powerful.*

GRAMMAR GUIDE ▸ NOUNS

ten·den·tious /tenˈdenʃəs/ *adj formal* a tendentious speech, remark, book etc expresses a strong opinion that is intended to influence people

ten·der¹ /ˈtendə $ -ər/ ●○○ *adj*
1 FOOD tender food is easy to cut and eat, especially because it has been well cooked OPP **tough**: *Continue cooking until the meat is tender.* THESAURUS ▸ SOFT
2 PART OF YOUR BODY a part of your body that is tender is painful if someone touches it: *My arm is still tender where I bruised it.* THESAURUS ▸ PAINFUL
3 GENTLE gentle and careful in a way that shows love: *Her voice was tender and soft.* | *a slow, tender kiss*
4 EASILY DAMAGED easily damaged – used especially about plants or flowers: *tender plants that were killed by the harsh winter*
5 tender loving care *usually spoken* sympathetic treatment and a lot of attention SYN **TLC**
6 tender age the time when you are young or do not have much experience: **at the tender age of four/five/six etc** *Nicholas was sent to boarding school at the tender age of seven.* —**tenderly** *adv* —**tenderness** *n* [U]

tender² *v* **1** [T] *formal* to formally offer or show something to someone: *As company secretary, you must tender the proposal.* | **tender sth to sb** *The seller has the right to keep the goods until payment is tendered to him.* | *Minton* ***tendered*** *her* ***resignation*** *on Friday.* **2** [I] *BrE* to make a formal offer to do a job or provide goods or services for a particular price SYN **bid** *AmE*: **[+for]** *We are unable to tender competitively for the contract.*

tender³ *n* [C] **1** *especially BrE* a formal statement of the price you would charge for doing a job or providing goods or services SYN **bid** *AmE*: *Our bid was the lowest tender.* | **put sth out to tender** *BrE* (=to ask different companies to say how much they will charge for doing a particular job) *The contract for building the houses will be put out to tender.* **2** a small boat that takes people or supplies between the shore and a larger boat **3** part of a steam train used for carrying coal and water for the train → BARTENDER, LEGAL TENDER

tender·heart·ed /ˌtendə ˈhɑːtɪd◂ $ -dər ˈhɑːr-/ *adj* very kind and gentle

ten·der·ize (*also* **-ise** *BrE*) /ˈtendəraɪz/ *v* [T] to make meat softer and easier to eat by preparing it in a special way

ten·der·iz·er (*also* **-iser** *BrE*) /ˈtendəraɪzə $ -ər/ *n* [C,U] a substance that is put onto raw meat to make it softer and easier to eat after it has been cooked

ten·der·loin /ˈtendəlɔɪn $ -ər-/ *n* [U] meat that is soft and easy to eat, cut from each side of the BACKBONE of cows or pigs

ten·don /ˈtendən/ *n* [C] a thick strong string-like part of your body that connects a muscle to a bone

ten·dril /ˈtendrəl/ *n* [C] **1** a thin leafless curling stem by which a climbing plant fastens itself to a support **2** *literary* a thin curling piece of hair

ten·e·ment /ˈtenəmənt/ *n* [C] a large building divided into apartments, especially in the poorer areas of a city: **tenement building/house/block**

ten·et /ˈtenɪt/ *n* [C] a principle or belief, especially one that is part of a larger system of beliefs: **central/basic/fundamental etc tenet** *one of the basic tenets of democracy* | **[+of]** *the main tenet of his philosophy*

ten·fold /ˈtenfəʊld $ -foʊld/ *adj, adv* ten times as much or as many of something: *Business has* ***increased tenfold*** *in the past two years.*

ˌten-gallon ˈhat *n* [C] a tall hat made of soft material with a wide BRIM, worn especially by COWBOYS

ten·ner /ˈtenə $ -ər/ *n* [C] *BrE informal* £10 or a ten-pound note: *Can you lend me a tenner?*

ten·nis /ˈtenɪs/ ●●● S3 W3 *n* [U] a game for two people or two pairs of people who use RACKETS to hit a small soft ball backwards and forwards over a net

ˈtennis court *n* [C] the four-sided area that you play tennis on

ˌtennis ˈelbow *n* [U] a medical problem in which your elbow is very painful

ˈtennis shoe *n* [C] a light shoe used for playing sports, with a rubber surface on the bottom

ten·on /ˈtenən/ *n* [C] *technical* an end of a piece of wood, that has been cut to fit exactly into a MORTISE in order to form a strong joint

ten·or¹ /ˈtenə $ -ər/ *n* **1** [C] a male singing voice that can reach the range of notes below the lowest woman's voice, or a man with a voice like this **2** [singular, U] the part of a musical work that is written for a tenor voice → **alto**, **baritone**, **bass**, **soprano**: *Arthur Davies sings the tenor solo.* **3 the tenor of sth** *formal* **a)** the general way in which an event or process takes place SYN **tone**: *Many voters admitted being disturbed by the tenor of the election campaign.* **b)** the general meaning of something written

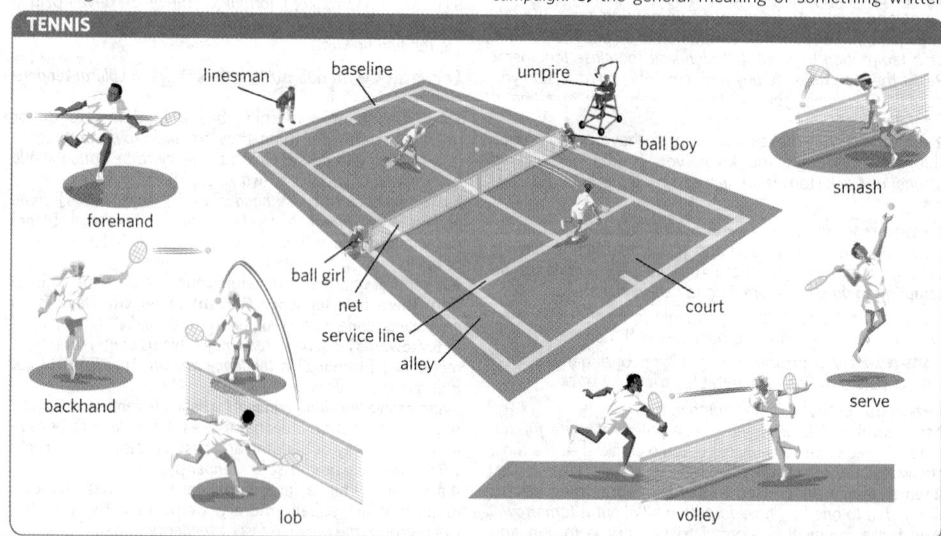

or spoken, or the general attitude expressed in it SYN **tone**: *the **general tenor** of her speech*

tenor² *adj* a tenor voice or instrument has a range of notes that is lower than an ALTO voice or instrument: *a tenor saxophone*

ten·pin /ˈtenˌpɪn/ *n* [C] *BrE* one of the ten bottle-shaped wooden objects that you try to knock down in BOWLING

ˌtenpin ˈbowling *n* [U] *BrE* an indoor sport in which you roll a heavy ball along a floor to knock down bottle-shaped wooden objects SYN **bowling** *AmE*

tense¹ /tens/ ●●○ AWL *adj*

1 a tense situation is one in which you feel very anxious and worried because of something bad that might happen → **tension**: **tense situation/atmosphere/moment etc** *Marion spoke, eager to break the tense silence.* THESAURUS NERVOUS

2 feeling worried, uncomfortable, and unable to relax OPP **relaxed**: *Is anything wrong? You look a little tense.*

3 unable to relax your body or part of your body because your muscles feel tight → **tension**: *Massage is great if your neck and back are tense. | She tried to relax her tense muscles.* —**tensely** *adv* —**tenseness** *n* [U]

tense² ●●○ *n* [C,U] any of the forms of a verb that show the time, continuance, or completion of an action or state that is expressed by the verb. 'I am' is in the present tense, 'I was' is past tense, and 'I will be' is future tense.

tense³ (*also* **tense up**) *v* [I,T] to make your muscles tight and stiff, or to become tight and stiff: *Relax, and try not to tense up so much. | Every time the phone rang, she tensed.*

ˌtensed ˈup *adj* [not before noun] *informal* feeling so nervous or worried that you cannot relax: *Brian got so tensed up he could hardly speak.*

ten·sile /ˈtensaɪl $ ˈtensəl/ *adj* [only before noun] *technical* able to be stretched without breaking: *tensile rubber*

ˌtensile ˈstrength *n* [U] *technical* the ability of steel or CONCRETE etc to bear pressure or weight without breaking

ten·sion /ˈtenʃən/ ●●○ W3 AWL *n*

1 NERVOUS FEELING [U] a nervous worried feeling that makes it impossible for you to relax → **tense**: *The tension was becoming unbearable, and I wanted to scream.* | **reduce/relieve/ease etc tension** *Exercise is the ideal way to relieve tension after a hard day.*

2 NO TRUST [C usually plural, U] the feeling that exists when people or countries do not trust each other and may suddenly attack each other or start arguing: **political/racial/social etc tension** *In those days, there was a great deal of racial tension on campus.* | **[+between]** *The obvious tension between Warren and Anne made everyone else uncomfortable.*

3 DIFFERENT INFLUENCES [C,U] if there is tension between two things, there is a difference between the needs or influences of each, and that causes problems: **[+between]** *In business, there's always a tension between the needs of customers and shareholders.*

4 TIGHTNESS [U] tightness or stiffness in a wire, rope, muscle etc: *Tension in the neck muscles can cause headaches. | **Muscle tension** can be a sign of stress.*

5 FORCE [U] the amount of force that stretches something: *This wire will take 50 pounds tension.* | **[+on]** *There was a lot of tension on the wire before it snapped.*

TENT

dome tent

ridge tent *BrE*/ A-frame tent *AmE*

tent /tent/ ●●○ S3 *n* [C] a shelter consisting of a sheet of cloth supported by poles and ropes, used especially for camping: *We looked for a flat spot where we could **pitch** our **tent*** (=put up our tent). → OXYGEN TENT

ten·ta·cle /ˈtentɪkəl/ *n* [C] **1** one of the long thin parts of a sea creature such as an OCTOPUS which it uses for holding things **2 tentacles** [plural] the influence or effect that something has on other people or things - used to show disapproval: *The company's tentacles spread from car manufacturing to railways.*

ten·ta·tive /ˈtentətɪv/ ●○○ *adj*

1 not definite or certain, because you may want to change things SYN **provisional** OPP **definite**: *I passed on my **tentative conclusions** to the police. | The government is taking **tentative steps** towards tackling the country's economic problems.*

2 done without confidence SYN **hesitant**: *a tentative smile* —**tentatively** *adv*: *Albi knocked tentatively and entered.* —**tentativeness** *n* [U]

ˌtent ˈcity *n* [C] a group of tents or other similar structures that are temporary homes for people

ten·ter·hooks /ˈtentəhʊks $ -ər-/ *n especially BrE* **be on tenterhooks** to feel nervous and excited because you are waiting to find out something or for something to happen SYN **be on edge**: *She had been on tenterhooks all night, expecting Joe to return at any moment.*

tenth¹ /tenθ/ ●●● S3 W3 *adj* coming after nine other things in a series: *in the tenth century | her tenth birthday* —**tenth** *pron*: *I'm planning to leave on **the tenth*** (=the tenth day of the month).

tenth² *n* [C] one of ten equal parts of something

ten·u·ous /ˈtenjuəs/ *adj* **1** a situation or relationship that is tenuous is uncertain, weak, or likely to change: *For now, the band's travel plans are tenuous.* | **tenuous link/connection etc** *The United Peace Alliance had only a tenuous connection with the organized Labour movement. | The link between her family and the King's is rather tenuous.* **2** *literary* very thin and easily broken —**tenuously** *adv*

ten·ure /ˈtenjə, -jʊə $ -jər/ *n* [U] **1** the right to stay permanently in a teaching job: *It's becoming increasingly difficult to acquire **academic tenure**.* **2** *formal* the period of time when someone has an important job: *The company has doubled in value during his tenure.* **3** *law* the legal right to live in a house or use a piece of land for a period of time —**tenured** *adj*: *a tenured professor | a tenured position*

te·pee /ˈtiːpiː/ *n* [C] a round tent with a pointed top, used by some Native Americans

tep·id /ˈtepɪd/ *adj* **1** a feeling, reaction etc that is tepid shows a lack of excitement or interest SYN **lukewarm**: *a tepid response from the audience* **2** tepid liquid is slightly warm, especially in a way that seems unpleasant SYN **lukewarm**: *tepid coffee*

te·qui·la /təˈkiːlə/ *n* [C,U] a strong alcoholic drink made in Mexico

tera- /terə/ *prefix* [in nouns] a TRILLION - used with units of measurement

ter·a·byte /ˈterəbaɪt/ *n* [C] (*written abbreviation* **TB** *or* **Tb**) a unit for measuring computer information, equal to 1,024 GIGABYTES, and used less exactly to mean one TRILLION BYTES

ter·a·flop /ˈterəflɒp $ -flɑːp/ *n* [C usually plural] a unit that measures how fast a computer works. One teraflop is one TRILLION operations every second. → **megaflop**

ter·cen·te·na·ry /ˌtɜːsenˈtiːnəri $ ˌtɜːrsenˈtenəri, tɜːrˈsentəneri/ *n* (*plural* **tercentenaries**) [C] *BrE* the day or year exactly 300 years after a particular event

term¹ /tɜːm $ tɜːrm/ ●●● S1 W1 *n*

1 in terms of sth if you explain or describe something in terms of a particular fact or event, you are explaining or describing it only in relation to that fact or event: **describe/measure/evaluate etc sth in terms of sth** *Femininity is still **defined in terms of** beauty. | It's a mistake to **think of** Florida only **in terms of** its tourist attractions. | It's too early to start **talking in terms of** casualties.* | **in terms of what/how/who etc** *Did the experiment find any differences in terms of what children learned?*

2 in general/practical/financial etc terms used to show that you are describing or considering a subject in a particular way or from a particular point of view: **in general/broad/**

T

simple etc terms *We explain in simple terms what the treatment involves.* | *It would be wrong to describe society* ***purely in*** *economic* ***terms****.* | *The war, although successful* ***in military terms****, left the economy in ruins.* | *What do these statistics mean* ***in human terms****?* | **in sb's terms** *In our terms, the scheme has not been a success.* | **in real/absolute terms** (=accurate, true, or including any related changes) *Rail fares have fallen 17 per cent in real terms.* | **in relative terms** (=compared with other, similar things) *Students have less money in relative terms, but spend more on books.*

3 WORD [C] a word or expression with a particular meaning, especially one that is used for a specific subject or type of language: **[+for]** *'Multimedia' is the term for any technique combining sounds and images.* | **in no uncertain terms** (=in very clear and angry language) *Journalists were told in no uncertain terms that they were not welcome.* → **a contradiction in terms** at CONTRADICTION(3) THESAURUS WORD

4 PERIOD OF TIME [C] a fixed period of time during which someone does something or something happens: **term of/in office** (=the time someone spends doing an important job in government) *The mayor was coming to the end of his term in office.* | **[+of]** *the maximum term of imprisonment* | *The lease runs for a term of 99 years.* | **prison/jail term** *The men each received a 30-year prison term.* → FIXED-TERM

5 SCHOOL/UNIVERSITY [C,U] *especially BrE* one of the periods of time that the school or university year is divided into. In Britain, there are usually three terms in a year. → **half-term**, **semester**, **quarter**: **summer/autumn/spring term** *The exams are at the end of the summer term.* | *Teachers often feel overworked* ***in term time*** (=during the term). | **first/last day of term** *that all-important first day of term*

6 in the long/short/medium term used to say what will happen or what happens generally over a long, short, or MEDIUM period of time: *The cost of living will go up in the short term.* | *In the long term, alcohol causes high blood pressure.* → LONG-TERM, SHORT-TERM

7 END [singular, U] *technical* the end of a particular period of time: *The agreement* ***reaches its term*** *next year.* | *a child born two months before* ***full term*** (=of pregnancy) | *We can prolong life beyond its* ***natural term****.*

8 come to terms with sth to accept an unpleasant or sad situation and no longer feel upset or angry about it: *George and Elizabeth have* ***come to terms with the fact that*** *they will never have children.* | *Counselling helped her come to terms with her grief.*

9 CONDITIONS **terms** [plural] **a)** the conditions that are set for an agreement, contract, arrangement etc: ***Under the terms of*** *the agreement, the debt would be repaid over 20 years.* | *your* ***terms and conditions*** *of employment* | *Delivery is* ***within the terms of*** *this contract.* | **equal/unequal/the same etc terms** (=conditions that are equal, unequal etc) *Small businesses have to* ***compete on equal terms with*** *large organisations.* | *Men and women should be able to work* ***on level terms****.* | **on sb's (own) terms** (=according to the conditions that someone wants) *He wanted our relationship to be only on his terms.* **b)** the arrangements for payment that you agree to when you buy or sell something: **reasonable/favourable/cheaper etc terms** *Some insurance companies offer very reasonable terms.* | *This allowed tenant farmers to buy land* ***on easy terms*** (=by paying small sums of money over a long period).

10 RELATIONSHIP **terms** [plural] if you are on good, bad etc terms with someone, you have a good, bad etc relationship with them: **be on good/bad/friendly etc terms (with sb)** *By now, Usha and I were on* ***familiar terms****.* | *He is barely on* ***speaking terms*** *with his father* (=they are angry and almost never speak to each other). | *We were soon on* ***first-name terms*** (=using each other's first names, as a sign of friendship).

11 terms of reference *formal* the subjects that a person or group of people agree to consider: *the committee's terms of reference*

12 NUMBER/SIGN [C] *technical* one of the numbers or signs used in a mathematical calculation

COLLOCATIONS - MEANING 3

ADJECTIVES/NOUN + term

a legal/medical term *The site provides a glossary of legal terms.*
a technical term *'Gender' is a technical term in grammar.*
a slang term *'The Old Bill' is a slang term for the police.*
a derogatory/pejorative term (=one that is insulting or disapproving)

VERBS

use a term *a term used by psychiatrists*
coin a term (=invent it) *Funk coined the term 'vitamin' in 1912.*

PHRASES

a term of abuse (=a word that is offensive or deliberately rude) *'Geek' is used as a term of abuse.*
a term of endearment (=a word that expresses your love for someone) *terms of endearment like 'love', 'dear', and 'honey'*
in strong terms *The pope condemned both Nazism and Communism in strong terms.*
in glowing terms (=praising someone or something highly) | **in layman's terms** (=using ordinary words, not technical words)

term² ●○○ *v* [T] to use a particular word or expression to name or describe something: **be termed sth** *This condition is sometimes termed RSI, or repetitive strain injury.* | *These developments are* ***loosely termed*** *'advanced manufacturing techniques'.* | **term yourself sth** *Roosevelt termed himself and his policies 'liberal'.* GRAMMAR **Term** is often used in the passive.

terminal¹ /ˈtɜːmɪnəl $ ˈtɜːr-/ ●●○ AWL *n* [C]
1 a big building where people wait to get onto planes, buses, or ships, or where goods are loaded: *the airport's passenger terminal* | **ferry/bus terminal**
2 a piece of computer equipment consisting of at least a KEYBOARD and a screen, that you use for putting in or taking out information from a large computer
3 one of the points at which you can connect wires in an electrical CIRCUIT: **positive/negative terminal**

ter·mi·nal² ●●○ AWL *adj*
1 a terminal illness cannot be cured, and causes death → **fatal**: *terminal cancer*
2 (in) terminal decline *BrE* in a state of becoming worse and worse and never getting better: *The once great industry is now in terminal decline.* —**terminally** *adv*: *terminally ill patients*

ter·mi·nate /ˈtɜːməneɪt $ ˈtɜːr-/ ●●○ AWL *v*
1 [I,T] *formal* if something terminates, or if you terminate it, it ends SYN **end**: *The court ruled that the contract must be terminated.* | *a woman's decision on whether or not to terminate the pregnancy*
2 [I] if a train, bus, or ship terminates at a particular place, its journey ends there: *The train from Paris terminates at St Pancras International.*

ter·mi·na·tion /ˌtɜːməˈneɪʃən $ ˌtɜːr-/ AWL *n*
1 [C] *formal* the act of ending something, or the end of something: **[+of]** *You may face a reduction or termination of benefits.* **2** [C,U] *technical* a medical operation to end the life of a developing child before it is born SYN **abortion**

ˈterminator ˌgene *n* [C] a GENE that is put into a plant to make it unable to produce more plants

ˈterminator ˌseed *n* [C] a STERILE seed from a GENETICALLY MODIFIED plant, that cannot be used to produce future crops

ter·mi·nol·o·gy /ˌtɜːməˈnɒlədʒi $ ˌtɜːrməˈnɑː-/ ●○○ *n* (*plural* **terminologies**) [C,U] the technical words or expressions that are used in a particular subject: *computer terminology* —**terminological** /ˌtɜːmənəˈlɒdʒɪkəl◂ $ ˌtɜːmənəˈlɑː-/ *adj*

ter·mi·nus /ˈtɜːmɪnəs $ ˈtɜːr-/ *n* (*plural* **termini** /-naɪ/) [C] the station or stop at the end of a railway or bus line

ter·mite /ˈtɜːmaɪt $ ˈtɜːr-/ *n* [C] an insect that eats and destroys wood from trees and buildings

ˈterm ˌlimit *n* [C] *AmE* a particular number of years that the law allows someone to stay in a particular political position

term·ly /ˈtɜːmli $ ˈtɜːr-/ *adj BrE* happening each TERM (=one of the three periods in the school or university year): *Students can pay fees in termly instalments.*

ˈterm ˌpaper *n* [C] *AmE* a long piece of written work done by college students in the US, that is the most important piece of work in their course

ˈterm-time *n* [U] *BrE* the part of the year when classes are given at a school, college, or university

tern /tɜːn $ tɜːrn/ *n* [C] a black and white sea bird that has long wings and a tail with two points

ter·race /ˈterɪs/ ●●○ *n* [C]
1 HOUSES *BrE* a row of houses that are joined to each other, or a street with one of these rows in it
2 PLACE YOU CAN SIT a flat outdoor area next to a building or on a roof, where you can sit outside to eat, relax etc
3 FOOTBALL **the terraces** [plural] *BrE* the wide steps that the people watching a football match can stand on
4 FLAT LAND one of a series of flat areas cut out of a hill like steps, and used to grow crops —**terracing** *n* [U]: *football terracing*

ter·raced /ˈterɪst/ *adj* [only before noun] a terraced field, slope, garden etc has been cut into a series of flat areas along the side of the slope: *terraced rice fields*

ˌterraced ˈhouse *n* [C] *BrE* a house which is part of a row of houses that are joined together SYN **row house** *AmE*

ter·ra·cot·ta, **terra cotta** /ˌterəˈkɒtə◂ $ -ˈkɑː-/ *n* [U]
1 hard reddish-brown baked CLAY: *a terracotta pot*
2 a brownish red colour —**terracotta** *adj*

ter·ra fir·ma /ˌterə ˈfɜːmə $ -ˈfɜːr-/ *n* [U] land, rather than sea or air - used humorously: *We were glad to be back on terra firma.*

ter·ra·form /ˈterəfɔːm $ -fɔːrm/ *v* [T] to change the conditions on a PLANET so that people can live on it: *Would it be possible to terraform Mars?*

ter·rain /teˈreɪn, tə-/ ●○○ *n* [C,U] a particular type of land: *rocky terrain* THESAURUS ▸ GROUND

ter·ra·pin /ˈterəpɪn/ *n* [C] a small TURTLE that lives in water

ter·ra·ri·um /təˈreəriəm $ -ˈrer-/ *n* [C] a large glass container that you grow plants in as a decoration

ter·res·tri·al /təˈrestriəl/ *adj* [usually before noun] *technical* **1** relating to the Earth rather than to the Moon or other PLANETS → EXTRATERRESTRIAL[2] **2** living on or relating to land rather than water **3 terrestrial TV/broadcasting/channels etc** *BrE* TV etc that is broadcast from the Earth rather than from a SATELLITE

ter·ri·ble /ˈterəbəl/ ●●● S1 W3 *adj*
1 extremely severe in a way that causes harm or damage SYN **horrible**, **awful**: *Their son had been injured in a terrible accident.* | *We're worried that something terrible might have happened to Greg.* | *a terrible storm* THESAURUS ▸ HORRIBLE
2 very bad SYN **awful**: *The hotel was absolutely terrible.* | *I'd better write this down; I have a terrible memory.* THESAURUS ▸ BAD
3 making you feel afraid or shocked: *There was a terrible noise and the roof caved in.* | *She wept when she heard the terrible news.*
4 to a very great degree SYN **grave**: *You're making a terrible mistake.*

GRAMMAR

Terrible is not used with 'very'. You say: *I feel absolutely terrible today.* ✗ Don't say: *I feel very terrible today.*

GRAMMAR GUIDE ▸ ADJECTIVES

ter·ri·bly /ˈterəbli/ ●●○ *adv*
1 [+adj/adv] *especially BrE* very SYN **extremely**: *I'm* ***terribly sorry*** *to have kept you waiting.* | *The coach was* ***not terribly*** *worried about his team's poor performance.*
2 very badly SYN **severely**: *The little boy missed his mother terribly.*

ter·ri·er /ˈteriə $ -ər/ *n* [C] a small active type of dog that was originally used for hunting

ter·rif·ic /təˈrɪfɪk/ ●●○ *adj*
1 *informal* very good, especially in a way that makes you feel happy and excited SYN **great**: *That's a terrific idea!* | *The actress who played the lawyer was terrific.* THESAURUS ▸ GOOD
2 very large in size or degree: *a terrific bang* | *He drank a terrific amount of beer.*

ter·rif·i·cally /təˈrɪfɪkli/ *adv* [+adj/adv] very SYN **extremely**: *She had been so terrifically busy that she barely had time to sleep.*

ter·ri·fied /ˈterɪfaɪd/ ●●○ *adj* very frightened: *a terrified little girl* | **[+of]** *Sid is terrified of heights.* | *She was terrified of being caught.* | **terrified (that)** *We were terrified that the bridge would collapse.* | **[+at]** *He was terrified at the thought of being stranded in the woods.* | **terrified to do sth** *He was terrified to stay home alone.* THESAURUS ▸ FRIGHTENED

ter·ri·fy /ˈterɪfaɪ/ ●●○ *v* (**terrified**, **terrifying**, **terrifies**) [T] to make someone extremely afraid: *Her husband's violence terrified her.*

ter·ri·fy·ing /ˈterəfaɪ-ɪŋ/ ●●○ *adj* extremely frightening: **terrifying experience/ordeal** *He told her of his terrifying experience.* | *terrifying screams* | ***It was*** *absolutely* ***terrifying.*** THESAURUS ▸ FRIGHTENING —**terrifyingly** *adv*

ter·rine /teˈriːn, tə-/ *n* [C,U] a food made of cooked meat, fish, or fruit formed into a LOAF shape and served cold, or the dish this is served in

ter·ri·to·ri·al /ˌterəˈtɔːriəl◂/ ●○○ *adj*
1 relating to land that is owned or controlled by a particular country: *a territorial dispute* | *territorial claims*
2 animals or people that are territorial are careful to guard the area of land that they consider to be their own, and prevent others from using it

ˌTerritorial ˈArmy, the a military force of people in Britain who train as soldiers in their free time SYN **TA** → NATIONAL GUARD

ˌterritorial ˈwaters *n* [plural] the sea near a country's coast, which that country has legal control over

ter·ri·to·ry /ˈterətəri $ -tɔːri/ ●●○ W3 *n* (*plural* **territories**)
1 GOVERNMENT/MILITARY [C,U] land that is owned or controlled by a particular country, ruler, or military force: *Hong Kong became Chinese territory in 1997.* | **occupied/enemy/disputed/hostile territory** *The plane was flying over enemy territory.* THESAURUS ▸ LAND
2 TYPE OF LAND [U] land of a particular type: **uncharted/unexplored territory** *an expedition through previously unexplored territory*
3 ANIMAL [C,U] the area that an animal, bird etc regards as its own and will defend against other animals: *A tiger has a large territory to defend.* | *A dog uses urine to* ***mark*** *its* ***territory.***
4 NEW OR FAMILIAR EXPERIENCE [U] a particular area of experience or knowledge: **new/unfamiliar/uncharted territory** *The company is moving into unfamiliar territory with this new software.* | *Actor Patrick Bergin returns to more* ***familiar territory*** *to play a menacing killer.*
5 BUSINESS [C,U] an area in a town, country etc that someone is responsible for as part of their job, especially someone whose job is to sell products: *a sales territory*
6 come/go with the territory to be a natural and accepted part of a particular job, situation, place etc: *I'm a cop - getting shot at goes with the territory.*
7 LAND THAT IS NOT A STATE [C] land that belongs to the United States, Canada etc but that is not a state: *the US territory of Guam*

ter·ror /ˈterə $ -ər/ ●●○ W3 *n*
1 FEAR [U] a feeling of extreme fear: **in terror** *People* ***fled in terror*** *as fire tore through the building.* | *Shots rang out, and I*

screamed in terror. | *We* ***lived in terror of*** *our father when he was drinking.* | *There was a look of* ***sheer terror*** (=complete terror) *on his face.* | **strike terror into sb/sb's heart** *The sound of enemy planes struck terror into our hearts.* **THESAURUS** ▸ **FEAR**

2 FRIGHTENING SITUATION [C] an event or situation that makes people feel extremely frightened, especially because they think they may die: **[+of]** *the terrors of war* | *Death* ***holds no terrors for*** (=does not frighten) *me.*

3 VIOLENT ACTION [U] violent action for political purposes SYN **terrorism**: *The resistance movement started a* ***campaign of terror***. | *The Red Army Faction tried to undermine the state by* ***terror tactics***. | *Pol Pot's* ***reign of terror*** *in Cambodia*

4 PERSON [C] *informal* a child who is difficult to control: *That Johnson kid's a real little terror!* → **reign of terror** at REIGN[1](4), → **a holy terror** at HOLY(4)

ter·ror·is·m /ˈterərɪzəm/ ●●○ *n* [U] the use of violence such as bombing, shooting, or KIDNAPPING to obtain political demands such as making a government do something: *The government is doing everything possible to* ***combat terrorism***. | *a despicable* ***act of terrorism*** | *their involvement in* ***international terrorism***

ter·ror·ist /ˈterərɪst/ ●●○ W3 *n* [C] someone who uses violence such as bombing, shooting etc to obtain political demands: *We refuse to talk to terrorists.* | **terrorist attack/activity/offence** *Twenty people were killed in the latest terrorist attack.* | **terrorist group/organization** | *A* ***terrorist bomb*** *that left 168 people dead.* → **GUERRILLA**

ter·ror·ize (*also* **-ise** *BrE*) /ˈterəraɪz/ *v* [T] to deliberately frighten people by threatening to harm them, especially so they will do what you want: **be terrorized into doing sth** *Many people have been terrorized into leaving.* | *gangs who terrorize the neighbourhood*

ter·ry·cloth /ˈteriklɒθ $ -klɒːθ/ (*also* **ter·ry** /ˈteri/) *n* [U] a type of thick cotton cloth with uncut threads on both sides, that can take liquid into itself, and is used to make TOWELS

terse /tɜːs $ tɜːrs/ *adj* a terse reply, message etc uses very few words and often shows that you are annoyed SYN **abrupt**: *Derek's terse reply ended the conversation.* —**tersely** *adv*: *'Continue!' he said tersely.* —**terseness** *n* [U]

ter·tia·ry /ˈtɜːʃəri $ ˈtɜːrʃieri, -ʃəri/ *adj technical* third in place, degree, or order

ˌtertiary eduˈcation *n* [U] *formal* education at a college, university etc SYN **higher education**

Te·ry·lene /ˈterəliːn/ *n* [U] *trademark BrE* a light strong artificial cloth

TESL /ˈtesəl/ *n* [U] the teaching of English as a second language

TESOL /ˈtiːsɒl $ -sɑːl/ *n* [U] *especially AmE* the teaching of English to speakers of other languages

tes·sel·la·ted /ˈtesɪleɪtɪd/ *adj technical* made of small flat pieces in various shapes and colours that fit together to form a pattern

test[1] /test/ ●●● S1 W1 *n* [C]

1 EXAM a set of questions, exercises, or practical activities to measure someone's skill, ability, or knowledge: **[+on]** *We have a test on irregular verbs tomorrow.* | *Did you get a good mark in the test?* ⚠ You **take** or **do** a test. Don't say 'make a test'. To **pass** a test means to succeed in it, not simply to take it.

2 MEDICAL **a)** a medical examination on a part of your body, or a substance taken from your body, to check your health or to discover what is wrong with you: *The doctor said I needed to have a* ***blood test***. | *an* ***eye test*** | *a* ***hearing test*** | *I'm still waiting for my* ***test results*** *from the hospital.* | **do/run a test** *They don't know what's wrong with her yet – they're doing tests.* | **a test is positive/negative** (=it shows that someone has/does not have a condition, a substance in their blood etc) *The tests were negative and the doctor said that she was in perfect health.* | **[+for]** *a test for HIV* **b)** an examination of someone's blood, breath etc carried out by the police, to discover if they have done something illegal: *a* ***drugs test*** | *The results of the DNA test proved that Simmons was the rapist.* | **breath test** (=to find out if someone has been drinking alcohol before driving a car) **c)** a piece of equipment used for carrying out a medical examination: *a pregnancy test*

3 MACHINE/PRODUCT a process used to discover whether equipment or a product works correctly, or to discover more about it: *nuclear weapons tests* | **[+for]** *a test for chemicals in the water* | ***Laboratory tests*** *show that the new drug is very effective.* | *We went to the* ***test site*** *in Nevada.*

4 DIFFICULT SITUATION a difficult situation in which the qualities of someone or something are clearly shown: *Chess player Nigel Short faces Anatoly Karpov in the toughest test of his career so far.* | **test of character/strength/courage/endurance etc** *The problems she faced were a real test of character.*

5 put sb/sth to the test to force someone or something into a difficult situation in order to discover what the limits of their strength, skills etc are: *Living together will soon put their relationship to the test.* | *Paul soon found himself in an emergency situation that put all his training to the test.*

6 SPORT *BrE* a TEST MATCH → **SMEAR TEST, MEANS TEST,** → **stand the test of time** at STAND[1](8), → **the acid test** at ACID[2](3)

COLLOCATIONS

VERBS

take a test (*also* **do/sit a test** *BrE*) *All candidates have to take a test.*

pass a test (=succeed in it) *She passed her driving test first time.*

fail a test (*also* **flunk a test** *AmE informal*) *He failed the test and had to take it again.*

do well/badly in a test *BrE*, **do well/badly on a test** *AmE* *I didn't do very well in the first part of the test.*

give sb a test | **grade a test** (*also* **mark a test** *BrE*)

ADJECTIVES/NOUN + test

a biology/history etc test *On Monday we had a French test.*

a spelling/reading/listening test *I didn't do very well in the listening test.*

a driving test | **a written test** | **a multiple choice test** (=in which each question has a list of answers to choose from) | **an aptitude test** (=a test that measures your natural abilities)

test + NOUN

a test paper *The teacher began handing out the test papers.*

a test result/score *The test results are out on Friday.*

a test question

COMMON ERRORS

⚠ Don't say 'make a test'. Say **take a test** or **do a test**.

THESAURUS

test a set of questions or practical activities, which are intended to find out how much someone knows about a subject or skill: *I have a chemistry test tomorrow.* | *Did Lauren pass her driving test?*

exam (*also* **examination** *formal*) an important test that you do at the end of a course of study or class or at the end of the school year: *He's upstairs, revising for an exam.* | *When do you get your exam results?* | *There's a written examination at the end of the course.*

quiz *AmE* a quick test that a teacher gives to a class, usually to check that students are learning the things they should be learning: *We have a math quiz every Monday.* | *a* ***pop quiz*** (=a quiz given by a teacher without any warning)

finals *BrE* the last exams that you take at the end of a British university course

final *AmE* an important test that you take at the end of a particular class in high school or college

midterm *AmE* an important test that you take in the middle of a term, covering what you have learned in a particular class in high school or college
oral exam (*also* **oral** *BrE*) an exam in which you answer questions by speaking, instead of writing, for example to test how good you are at speaking a foreign language
practical *BrE* an exam that tests your ability to do or make things, rather than your ability to write about them
mocks/mock exams *BrE informal* tests that you take as practice before the official examinations
paper *BrE* a set of printed questions used as an examination in a particular subject, or the answers people write: *The history paper was really difficult.* | *The papers are marked by the other teachers.*

test[2] ●●● S3 W2 *v*
1 MEDICAL [T] to examine someone's blood, body etc in order to find out what is wrong with them, or to see if they have taken an illegal drug: *I must have my eyes tested.* | **test sb for sth** *They tested her for diabetes.* | **test positive/negative (for sth)** *Athletes who test positive for steroids are immediately banned.*
2 SUBSTANCE [I,T] to examine a substance or thing in order to find out its qualities or what it contains: **test (sth) for sth** *The water should be tested for lead.*
3 KNOWLEDGE/ABILITY [T] to ask someone spoken or written questions, or make them do a practical activity, to discover what they know about a subject: *This task is designed to test your reading skills* | **test sb on sth** *We're being tested on grammar tomorrow.*
4 MACHINE/PRODUCT [T] (*also* **test out**) to use something for a short time to see if it works in the correct way: *The Ferrari team wanted to test their new car out on the racetrack.* | **test sth on sb/sth** *None of this range of cosmetics has been tested on animals.* THESAURUS ▸ CHECK
5 SHOW HOW GOOD/STRONG [T] to show how good or strong someone or something is, especially by putting them in a difficult situation: *a game that will test the contestants' strength and skill* | *The next six months will test your powers of leadership.* | *I felt that she was testing me, leaving all that cash lying around.* → TESTING
6 IDEA/PLAN [T] (*also* **test out**) to start to use an idea or plan to find out if it is correct or effective: *Dr Lee set up a series of experiments to test out this hypothesis.* | **test sth against sth** *The theory was then tested against the results of the study.*
7 test the water/waters to check people's reaction to a plan before you decide to use it: *The government is clearly testing the water, to gauge the country's reactions to their proposals.* → **tried and tested** at TRIED[2]

test·a·ble /ˈtestəbəl/ *adj* testable things can be tested: *I don't think this theory is testable.*

tes·ta·ment /ˈtestəmənt/ *n* [C] *formal* **1 be a testament to sth** to prove or show very clearly that something exists or is true: *The aircraft's safety record is a testament to its designers' skill.* **2** a WILL[2](2) —**testamentary** /ˌtestəˈmentəri◂/ *adj* → NEW TESTAMENT, OLD TESTAMENT

ˈtest ban *n* [C] an agreement between countries to stop testing NUCLEAR weapons: *the test ban treaty*

ˈtest card *n* [C] *BrE* a pattern or picture that is shown on television when there are no programmes

ˈtest case *n* [C] a legal case that establishes a particular principle, that is then used as a standard which other similar cases can be judged against

ˈtest cerˌtificate *n* [C] *BrE* the official paper that proves that a car is legally safe enough to drive → MOT

ˈtest drive *n* [C] an occasion when you drive a car so that you can decide if you want to buy it —**test-drive** *v* [T]

test·er /ˈtestə $ -ər/ *n* [C] **1** a person or piece of equipment that tests something **2** a small bottle of PERFUME[1](1) etc, in a shop, for customers to try

tes·tes /ˈtestiːz/ *n* the plural of TESTIS

tes·ti·cle /ˈtestɪkəl/ *n* [C] one of the two round organs that produce SPERM in a male, that are enclosed in a bag of skin behind and below the PENIS —**testicular** /teˈstɪkjələ $ -ər/ *adj*

tes·ti·fy /ˈtestɪfaɪ/ ●○○ *v* (**testified, testifying, testifies**)
1 [I,T] to make a formal statement of what is true, especially in a court of law: *Mr Molto has agreed to testify at the trial.* | **[+against]** *Later, the witness who had testified against Muawad withdrew his allegation.*
2 [I,T] *written* to show clearly that something is the case: **[+to]** *The empty shops in the high street testify to the depth of the recession.* | **testify that** *The full ashtrays testify that smoking hasn't been stubbed out.* | *Can you testify that you saw the defendant at the scene of the crime?*
3 [I] *AmE* to stand up and tell people about how God has helped you in your life SYN **witness**

tes·ti·mo·ni·al /ˌtestəˈməʊniəl $ -ˈmoʊ-/ *n* [C] **1** a formal written statement describing someone's character and abilities → **reference 2** something that is given or done to someone to thank or praise them, or show admiration for them: *a testimonial dinner in honour of Senator Frank Flint*

tes·ti·mo·ny /ˈtestəməni $ -moʊni/ ●○○ *n* (*plural* **testimonies**) [C,U]
1 a formal statement saying that something is true, especially one a WITNESS makes in a court of law: *Barker's testimony is crucial to the prosecution's case.* | *In his testimony, he denied that the company had ignored safety procedures.*
2 a fact or situation that shows or proves very clearly that something exists or is true: **be a testimony to/of sth** *These results are a testimony to the coach's skill and hard work.*

test·ing /ˈtestɪŋ/ *adj* a testing situation, experience etc is difficult to deal with: *It's been a* ***testing time***.

ˈtesting ground *n* [C] **1** a place where machines, cars etc are tested to see if they work properly **2** a situation or problem in which you can try new ideas and methods to see if they work: *Eastern Europe has become a testing ground for high-speed privatization.*

tes·tis /ˈtestɪs/ *n* (*plural* **testes** /-tiːz/) [C] *technical* a TESTICLE

ˈtest match *n* [C] a CRICKET or RUGBY match that is played between the teams of different countries

tes·tos·ter·one /teˈstɒstərəʊn $ -ˈstɑːstəroʊn/ *n* [U] the HORMONE (=chemical produced by the body) in males that gives them their male qualities

ˈtest ˌpilot *n* [C] a pilot who flies new aircraft in order to test them

ˈtest run *n* [C] an occasion when you try doing something or using something before you really need to use it, to make sure everything works properly

ˈtest tube *n* [C] a small glass container that is shaped like a tube and is used in chemistry → LABORATORY

TEST TUBE

ˈtest-tube ˌbaby *n* [C] a baby that develops from an egg removed from a woman's body, that is then put back inside the woman to continue developing

tes·ty /ˈtesti/ *adj* impatient and easily annoyed SYN **irritable**: *testy remarks* | *It had been a long day, and Sarah was getting a little testy.* —**testily** *adv* —**testiness** *n* [U]

tet·a·nus /ˈtetənəs/ *n* [U] a serious illness caused by BACTERIA that enter your body through cuts and wounds and make your muscles, especially your jaw, go stiff SYN **lockjaw**

tetch·y /ˈtetʃi/ *adj BrE informal* likely to get angry or upset easily SYN **irritable**: *Jane's a bit tetchy this morning.* —**tetchily** *adv* —**tetchiness** *n* [U]

tête-à-tête /ˌteɪt ɑː ˈteɪt, ˌteɪt e-/ *n* [C] a private

T

conversation between two people: *friends having a cosy tête-à-tête*

teth·er¹ /ˈteðə $ -ər/ *n* [C] **1 be at the end of your tether** to be so worried, tired etc that you feel you can no longer deal with a difficult or upsetting situation **2** a rope or chain that an animal is tied to so that it can only move around within a limited area

tether² *v* [T] **1** to tie an animal to a post so that it can only move around within a limited area **2** *technical* to use a MOBILE PHONE to make a computer able to connect with the Internet

tetra- /tetrə/ *prefix* having four of something: *a tetrahedron* (=solid shape with four sides)

tet·ra·kai·dec·a·he·dron /ˌtetrəˌkaɪdekəˈhiːdrən/ *n* (*plural* **tetrakaidecahedra** /-drə/) [C] *technical* a solid shape with fourteen sides

Teu·ton·ic /tjuːˈtɒnɪk $ tuːˈtɑː-/ *adj* **1** having qualities that are thought to be typical of German people: *Teutonic efficiency* **2** relating to the ancient German peoples of northwest Europe: *Teutonic mythology*

Tex-Mex /ˈteks meks/ *adj* [only before noun] *informal* relating to the music, cooking etc of Mexican-American people: *a Tex-Mex restaurant*

text¹ /tekst/ ●●● S2 W1 AWL *n*

1 [U] any written material: *One disk can store the equivalent of 500 pages of text.*

2 [U] the writing that forms the main part of a book, magazine etc, rather than the pictures or notes → **textual**: *There should not be too much text in children's books.*

3 [C] a book or other piece of writing that is connected with learning or intended for study: *Some of the original text has survived.* | ***Literary texts****, like all other works of art, have a historical context.* | *'Hamlet' is a* **set text** (=one that must be studied for an examination) *this year. BrE*

4 [C] *AmE* a textbook: *a chemistry text*

5 the text of sth the exact words of a speech, article etc: *Only 'The Times' printed the full text of the president's speech.*

6 [C] a TEXT MESSAGE: *He sent me a text saying he would be late.*

7 [C] a short piece from the Bible that someone reads and talks about during a religious service

text² ●●● S2 *v* [I,T] to send someone a written message on a MOBILE PHONE —**texting** *n* [U]

text·book¹ /ˈtekstbʊk/ ●●● *n* [C] a book that contains information about a subject that people study, especially at school or college: *a biology textbook*
THESAURUS BOOK → COURSEBOOK

textbook² *adj* [only before noun] used to describe something that is done exactly as it should be done, or happens exactly as it should happen: **textbook case/example** *The advertising campaign was a textbook example of how to sell a product.*

tex·tile /ˈtekstaɪl/ ●●○ *n* [C]

1 any type of woven cloth that is made in large quantities - used especially by people in the business of making clothes etc: *Their main exports are textiles, especially silk and cotton.* | **textile industry/design/manufacture etc** *textile design and technology* | *a textile mill*

2 textiles [plural] the industry involved in making cloth

ˈtext ˌmessage¹ *n* [C] a written message that is sent or received on a MOBILE PHONE or PAGER

text ˌmessage² (*also* **text**) *v* [T] to send someone a written message on a MOBILE PHONE or PAGER: *She's always text messaging her friends.* —**text-messaging** *n* [U]

text·speak /ˈtekstˌspiːk/ *n* [U] the abbreviations used in text messages: *'NP' is textspeak for 'No problem'.*

tex·tu·al /ˈtekstʃuəl/ AWL *adj formal* relating to the way that a book, magazine etc is written → **textual**: *a detailed textual analysis of the Bible*

tex·ture /ˈtekstʃə $ -ər/ ●●○ *n* [C,U]

1 the way a surface or material feels when you touch it, especially how smooth or rough it is: **smooth/silky/rough etc texture** *the smooth texture of silk* | *a designer who experiments with different colours and textures*

2 the way that a particular type of food feels in your mouth: **creamy/crunchy/meaty etc texture** *This soup has a lovely creamy texture.*

3 *formal* the way the different parts of a piece of writing, music, art etc are combined in order to produce a final effect: *the rich texture of Shakespeare's English* —**textural** *adj* —**texturally** *adv*

tex·tured /ˈtekstʃəd $ -ərd/ *adj* **1** having a surface that is not smooth: *textured wallpaper* **2 smooth-textured/coarse-textured/fine-textured etc** having a texture that is smooth etc: *smooth-textured skin* **3** used to describe a work of art, literature, music etc that has many different parts that are combined to produce a final effect: *a richly textured novel*

ˌtextured ˌvegetable ˈprotein *n* [U] (*abbreviation* **TVP**) a substance made from beans, used instead of meat

-th /θ/ *suffix* **1** forms ORDINAL numbers, except with 1, 2, or 3: *the 17th of June* | *a fifth of the total* → **-ND**, **-RD**, **-ST**
2 *old use or biblical* another form of -ETH: **he doth** (=does)

Tha·lid·o·mide /θəˈlɪdəmaɪd/ *n* [U] *trademark* a drug given to people to make them calm, until it was discovered that it harmed the development of the arms and legs of unborn babies

thal·li·um /ˈθæliəm/ *n* [U] a soft blue-white metal that is poisonous, used in PHOTOELECTRIC CELLS and to kill rats, mice, and insects. It is a chemical ELEMENT: symbol Tl

than /ðən; *strong* ðæn/ ●●● S1 W1 *conjunction, prep*

1 used when comparing two things, people, situations etc: *Natalie was prettier than her sister.* | *You need that money more than I do.* | *There were more people there than I expected.* | *If it costs more than $60, I won't buy it.* | *She had woken even earlier than usual.* | *Divorce is more common than it was a generation ago.*

2 other than except for a particular person or thing: *We never go to church other than for funerals and weddings.* | *We know he lived in Fleet Road, but other than that we don't know much about him.*

3 would rather/would sooner ... than used to say that you prefer one thing to another: *I'd rather drive than go by train.* | *She said she'd rather die than live in the city.*

4 no sooner/hardly had ... than used to say that one thing happens immediately after another thing: *No sooner had I got into the house than the phone rang.* | *Hardly had they reached Edinburgh than they were ordered to return to London.*

thane /θeɪn/ *n* [C] a man who fought for the King but was below the rank of a KNIGHT in early English history

thank /θæŋk/ ●●● S1 W2 *v* [T]

1 to tell someone that you are pleased and grateful for something they have done, or to be polite about it: *I haven't had a chance to thank him yet.* | **thank sb for (doing) sth** *Did you thank Uncle Ron for the present?* | *Madeleine thanked everyone for coming.*

2 thank God/goodness/heavens used to show that you are very glad about something: *Thank God that's over! I've never been so nervous in my life!* | **[+for]** *'Only ten miles to go.' 'Thank heavens for that!'*

3 thank your lucky stars *spoken* used to tell someone that they are very lucky, especially because they have avoided an unpleasant or dangerous situation: *You should thank your lucky stars I got here when I did!*

4 only have yourself to thank (for sth) *spoken* used to say that you are responsible for something bad that has happened to you: *She has only herself to thank if she doesn't have any friends.*

5 you'll thank me *spoken* used to tell someone not to be annoyed with you for doing or saying something, because it will be helpful to them later: *You'll thank me for this one day, Laura.*

6 sb won't thank you (for doing sth) used to tell someone that another person will be annoyed because of what they have done: *I know you're just trying to help, but he won't thank you for telling him how to do it.*

7 I'll thank you to do sth *spoken formal* used to tell someone in an angry way not to do something because it is annoying you: *I'll thank you to mind your own business.*
8 have sb to thank for (doing) sth to say that you are grateful to someone who is responsible for something good happening. This expression is sometimes used humorously to mean that you are not grateful for what someone has done: *I have Phil to thank for getting me my first job.* | *And who do I have to thank for that mess on my desk?* → THANK YOU

thank·ful /ˈθæŋkfəl/ *adj* [not before noun] grateful and glad about something that has happened, especially because without it the situation would be much worse: **[+for]** *I'll be thankful for a good night's sleep after the week I've had.* | **thankful (that)** *She was thankful that Chantal was there.* | **thankful to do sth** *I was thankful to make any sort of progress at all.* —**thankfulness** *n* [U] → **be thankful for small mercies/favours** at SMALL[1](13)

thank·ful·ly /ˈθæŋkfəli/ ●○○ *adv*
1 [sentence adverb] used to say that you are glad that something has happened, especially because a difficult situation has ended or been avoided: *Thankfully, I managed to pay off all my debts before we got married.*
2 feeling grateful and glad about something, especially because a difficult situation has ended or been avoided: *We came in and collapsed thankfully onto our beds.*

thank·less /ˈθæŋkləs/ *adj* **1** a thankless job is difficult and you do not get any praise for doing it: **thankless task/job/chore etc** *Cooking every day is a thankless task.* **2** *literary* a thankless person is not grateful

thanks¹ /θæŋks/ ●●● S1 *interjection informal*
1 used to tell someone that you are grateful for something they have given you or done for you SYN **thank you**: *'Pass the salt, please ... thanks.'* | **[+for]** ***Thanks a lot*** *for the drink.* | ***Thanks very much*** *for your help.* | ***Many thanks*** *for the lovely flowers.* | **thanks for doing sth** *I'd love to go to the party. Thanks for asking me.*
2 used as a polite way of accepting something that someone has offered you: *'Do you want another cup of coffee?' 'Oh, thanks.'*
3 *spoken* used when politely answering someone's question: *'Hi, Bill, how are you?' 'Fine, thanks.'*
4 no thanks used to say politely that you do not want something: *'How about some cake?' 'Oh, no thanks, I'm on a diet.'*
5 thanks a lot (*also* **thanks a bunch** *AmE spoken*) used when really you are annoyed about something and you do not mean 'thank you' at all

thanks² ●●○ W3 *n* [plural]
1 the things you say or do to show that you are grateful to someone: *Joe got up and left without* ***a word of thanks***. | **[+to]** *My thanks to all of you for your help.*
2 thanks to sb/sth *informal* because of someone or something: *We've reached our goal of $50,000, thanks to the generosity of the public.* | *Some ski resorts opened early, thanks to a late-October snowstorm.* ⚠ Don't say 'thank to someone/something'.
3 no thanks to sb/sth *spoken* an expression meaning 'in spite of', used when someone should have helped you but did not: *It was no thanks to you that we managed to win the game.* → VOTE OF THANKS

thanks·giv·ing /ˌθæŋksˈɡɪvɪŋ◂/ *n* [C,U] *formal* an expression of thanks to God

Thanksgiving ●●● S2 *n* [U] a public holiday in the US and in Canada when families have a large meal together to celebrate and be thankful for food, health, families etc

ˈthank you ●●● S1 *interjection*
1 used to tell someone that you are grateful for something they have given you or done for you SYN **thanks**: *Margaret handed him the butter. 'Thank you,' said Samuel.* | ***Thank you very much****, Brian.* | **thank you for (doing) sth** *It's good to see you, Mr Mathias. Thank you for coming.* | *Dear Grandma, thank you for the lovely shirt you sent me for Christmas.* ⚠ Don't say 'I thank you'.
2 used as a polite way of accepting something that someone has offered: *'Can I give you a lift into town?' 'Oh, thank you.'*
3 used when politely answering someone's question: *'How was your trip to Paris?' 'Very nice, thank you.'*
4 no, thank you used to say politely that you do not want something: *'Would you like some more coffee?' 'No, thank you, I'm fine.'*
5 used at the end of a sentence when telling someone firmly that you do not want their help or advice and are slightly annoyed by it: *I can manage quite well on my own, thank you!*

ˈthank-you *n* [C] **1** something you say or do in order to thank someone: *This present's a thank-you for helping me last week.* | *I just want to say a big thank-you to everyone who supported us.* **2 thank-you letter/note/card** a short letter etc in which you thank someone

that¹ /ðæt/ ●●● S1 W1 *determiner, pron*
1 (*plural* **those** /ðəʊz $ ðoʊz/) used to refer to a person, thing, idea etc that has already been mentioned or is already known about: *'You never cared about me.' 'That's not true.'* | *I wish you wouldn't say things like that.* | *What did you do with those sandwiches?* | *Victoria Street? That's where my sister lives.* | *Do you remember that nice Mr Hoskins who came to dinner?* | *I've got that pain in my back again.* | *He killed a man once and that's why he had to leave Ireland.* | *'We've been cheated,' she said. Those were her exact words.* | *'I have to go,' she said, and* ***with that*** (=after saying that) *she hung up the phone.*
2 /ðət/ used after a noun as a RELATIVE PRONOUN like 'who', 'whom', or 'which' to introduce a CLAUSE: *There are lots of things that I need to buy before the trip.* | *the people that live next door* | *They've got a machine that prints names on badges.* | *the greatest boxer that ever lived* | *Who was it that said 'The Law's an Ass'?* | *The day that my father died, I was on holiday in Greece.*

GRAMMAR
- In everyday English, **that** is often omitted when it is the object of the relative clause: *I like the clothes that she wears.* | *I like the clothes she wears.*
- You do not omit **that** when it is the subject of the clause: *The family that lives downstairs is Polish.*
✗ Don't say: *The family lives downstairs is Polish.*

3 (*plural* **those** /ðəʊz $ ðoʊz/) *formal* used to refer to a particular person or thing of the general type that has just been mentioned: *In my opinion, the finest wines are those from France.* | **[+of]** *His own experience was different from that of his friends.*
4 those who people who: *There are those who disapprove of all forms of gambling.* | *Those who saw the performance thought it memorable.*
5 at that used after adding a piece of information which emphasizes and increases what you have just said: *You should be able to answer the question in a single sentence, and a short one at that.*
6 that is (to say) used to give more exact information about something or to correct a statement: *One solution would be to change the shape of the screen, that is, to make it wider.* | *Languages are taught by the direct method, that is to say, without using the student's own language.* | *I loved him – that is, I thought I did.*

SPOKEN PHRASES
7 (*plural* **those**) used to refer to a person or thing that is not near you: *Is that my pen you've got there?* | *That's Eileen's house across the road.* | *Look at those men in that car. What on earth are they doing?* | *Our tomatoes never get as big as that.*
8 that's life/men/politics etc (for you) used to say that something is typical of a particular group of people, situation etc: *I don't think I was fairly treated, but then that's life, isn't it?* | *We go out for a romantic meal and all he wants to do is talk about football. That's men for you.*
9 that's it a) used to say that something is completely finished or that a situation cannot be changed: *That's it,*

then. There's nothing more we can do. **b)** used to tell someone that they are doing something correctly: *Slowly ... slowly. Yeah, that's it.* **c)** (*also* **that does it**) used when you are angry about a situation and you do not want it to continue: *That's it. I'm leaving.*
10 that's that used to emphasize that a situation or a decision cannot be changed: *I refuse to go and that's that! | There's no money left, so that's that.*
11 used when you are not sure who is answering the telephone: *Hello, is that Joan Murphy?*
12 and (all) that *BrE* and similar things: *I knew he was interested in computers and all that.*
13 that's a good girl/that's a clever dog etc used to praise a child or animal
14 that is not an option used when you want to emphasize that something that has just been suggested is not acceptable to you

USAGE: That, who, which

- You use **that** as a relative pronoun when saying which person or thing you are talking about: *This is the friend that I told you about. | They didn't have the book that I wanted.*
- **That** can be omitted: *This is the friend I told you about. | They didn't have the book I wanted.*
- You use **who** or **which** when adding extra information about the person or thing: *She looked after her husband, who was ill. | I did it myself, which was difficult.*
- In clauses like this, **who** or **which** can not be omitted. ✗ Don't say: *She looked after her husband, that was ill.*
- You use **who** when talking about a person: *There's the man who I saw yesterday.* Don't use **which** about people. ✗ Don't say: *She looked after her husband, which was ill.*
- You can also use **that** when talking about a person. **That** is used about both people and things: *There's the man that I saw yesterday.*
- In clauses like this, both **that** and **who** can be omitted: *There's the man I saw yesterday.*

that² /ðət/ ●●● S1 W1 *conjunction*
1 used after verbs, nouns, and adjectives to introduce a CLAUSE which shows what someone says or thinks, or states a fact or reason: *If she said that she'd come, she'll come. | I can't believe that he's only 17. | Are you sure that they live in Park Lane? | allegations that he is guilty of war crimes | The fact that he is your brother-in-law should not affect your decision. | He might have left the money for the simple reason that he didn't know it was there.*

GRAMMAR

- In everyday English, **that** is often omitted. Instead of saying *I'm not surprised* ***that*** *you were upset*, you say *I'm not surprised you were upset.*
- In formal English, **that** is used more often in this situation.

2 used after a phrase with 'so' or 'such' to introduce a CLAUSE that shows the result of something: *I was so tired that I fell asleep. | The school was so badly damaged that it had to be pulled down. | We had been away for such a long time that I had forgotten her name.*
3 used to introduce a CLAUSE that refers to a fact, when describing it: *It's odd that I haven't heard of you. | That anyone should want to kill her was unthinkable. | The problem is that no-one knows what will happen.*
4 *formal* in order that something may happen or someone may do something: *Give us strength that we may stand against them.*
5 *literary* used to express a wish for something to happen or be true, especially when this is not possible: *Oh, that she were alive to see this!* → **so (that)** at **so²**(2)

that³ /ðæt/ ●●● S1 W2 *adv* [+adj/adv]
1 *spoken* used to say how big, how much etc, especially when you are showing the size, amount etc with your hands: *It was quite a large fish – about that long. | He missed hitting the car in front by that much.*
2 [usually in negatives] *spoken* as much as in the present situation or as much as has been stated: *I'm sorry, I hadn't realized the situation was that bad. | No one expected it to cost that much. | The advanced exam is more difficult, but not many students progress that far.*
3 not (all) that long/many etc *spoken* used to mean fairly short, only a few etc: *Will's not that tall, considering he's 16. | The film wasn't all that good.*
4 *BrE spoken informal* used to emphasize how big, bad, much etc something is: *I was that embarrassed I didn't know what to say.*

thatch /θætʃ/ *n* **1** [C,U] STRAW, REEDS, leaves etc used to make a roof, or the roof made of them **2** [singular] a thick untidy pile of hair on someone's head

thatched /θætʃt/ *adj* a thatched roof is made with dried STRAW, REEDS, leaves etc: *a thatched cottage* (=one with a thatched roof) —**thatch** *v* [I,T]

thatch·er /ˈθætʃə $ -ər/ *n* [C] someone whose job is making roofs from dried STRAW, REEDS, leaves etc

thaw¹ /θɔː $ θɒː/ *v* **1** [I,T] (*also* **thaw out**) if ice or snow thaws, or if the sun thaws it, it turns into water OPP **freeze**: *The lake thawed in March.* **2 it thaws** if it thaws, the weather becomes warmer, so that ice and snow melt: *It thawed overnight.* **3** [I,T] (*also* **thaw out**) to let frozen food become warmer until it is ready to cook OPP **freeze**: *Thaw frozen meat in its packet and then cook as soon as possible.* **4** [I] to become friendlier and less formal: *After a few glasses of wine Robert began to thaw a little.*
thaw out *phr v* if your body thaws out, or if you thaw it out, it gets warmer until it is a normal temperature again: **thaw sth ↔ out** *He held his hands in front of the fire to thaw them out.*

thaw² *n* **1** [singular] a period of warm weather during which snow and ice melt: *The thaw begins in March.* **2** [C] an improvement in relations between two countries, after a period of unfriendliness

the¹ /ðə; *before vowels* ði; *strong* ðiː/ ●●● S1 W1 *definite article, determiner*
1 used to show that you are talking about a particular thing or person that has already been mentioned, is already known about, or is the only one: *The audience clapped and cheered. | I ordered a pizza and salad. The pizza was nice but the salad was disgusting. | the tallest building in the world | sailing across the Pacific | The prime minister has intervened personally. | Elections will be held later in the year* (=this year). *| How are all the family* (=your family)?
2 used before nouns referring to actions and changes when they are followed by 'of': *the growth of the steel industry | the arrival of our guests*
3 used when you are about to make it clear which person or thing you mean: *That's the school that Terry went to. | She laughed at the birthday card from Myra.*
4 used before the name of a family in the plural to refer to all the members of that family: *The Johnsons had lived in this house for many years.*
5 used to refer to something that everyone knows because it is part of our natural environment or part of daily life: *What was the weather like? | I looked out into the darkness. | Sometimes the traffic kept her awake at night. | The shops open at 9 o'clock.*
6 used before a singular noun to refer to a type of institution, shop, system etc: *You used to buy them from the chemist. | I heard it on the radio. | I'll put it in the mail for you today.*
7 used to refer to a part of someone's body: *Lieutenant Taylor was wounded in the knee. | How's the ankle? Is it still hurting?*
8 used before an adjective to make it into a plural noun when you are referring to all the people that the adjective describes: *She devoted her life to helping the poor. | a school for the deaf | wars between the English and the French*
9 used before an adjective to make it into a noun when you are referring to the particular kind of situation or

T

thing that the adjective describes: *Come on now, that's asking for the impossible.* | *fantasy movies that make the unreal seem real*

10 used before a singular noun when you are referring to a particular type of thing or person in a general way: *The tiger is without doubt the most magnificent of the big cats.* | *The computer has changed everyone's lives in so many ways.* | *complicated dances like the tango*

11 a) used to refer to a period of time, especially a period of 10 or 100 years: *fashions of the 60s* | *the great novelists of the 1900s* | *She remembers the war years.* | *In the thirties unemployment was widespread.* **b)** used to mention a date: *the 3rd of November* | *The battle took place on March the 21st, 1940.* | *Shall we meet on the twelfth?*

12 enough of something for a particular purpose: *I haven't the time to talk just now.* | *Eric didn't even have the common sense to send for a doctor.*

13 used to say which type of musical instrument someone plays: *Fiona's learning the flute.* | *He plays the violin.*

14 used to refer to a type of sport or a sports event, especially in ATHLETICS or swimming: *Who won the long jump?* | *She swam up and down, practising the crawl.*

15 *spoken* used before a word or phrase that describes someone or something when you are angry, JEALOUS, surprised etc: *He's stolen my parking space, the bastard!* | *I can't get this carton open, the stupid thing.* | *'Jamie's won a holiday in Hawaii.' 'The lucky devil!'*

16 used to emphasize that the person, place, or thing you are mentioning is the famous one, or the best or most fashionable one. 'The' is pronounced strongly or written in a special way: *'Elizabeth Taylor was there.' 'Not the Elizabeth Taylor, surely?'* | *Miami is THE place for girls who like to live life to the full.*

17 used before the names of certain common illnesses: *If one of the children got the measles, we all got the measles.*

the² ●●● S3 *adv*

1 used before two COMPARATIVE adjectives or adverbs to show that the degree of one event or situation is related to the degree of another one: *The more he eats the fatter he gets.* | *'When do you want it?' 'The sooner the better.'*

2 used before an adjective or adverb to emphasize that something is bigger, better etc than all others, or as big, good etc as it is possible for it to be: *He likes you the best.* | *I had the worst headache last night.*

the- /θi/ *prefix* another form of THEO-

THEATRE

1 stage
2 orchestra pit
3 curtains
4 row
5 seat
6 circle *BrE*/balcony *AmE*
7 stalls *BrE*/orchestra *AmE*
8 boxes

thea·tre *BrE*, **theater** *AmE* /ˈθɪətə $ -ər/ ●●● S2 W2 *n*

1 BUILDING [C] a building or place with a stage where plays and shows are performed: *an open-air theatre* (=a theatre that is outside) | *the Mercury Theater*

2 PLAYS [U] **a)** plays as a form of entertainment: *I enjoy theater and swimming.* | **the theatre** *He's really interested in literature and the theatre.* | *Yeats' plays are great poetry but they are not* ***good theatre*** (=good entertainment). **b)** the work of acting in, writing, or organizing plays: *classes in theater and music* | **in the theatre** *She's been working in the theatre over thirty years.*

3 PLACE TO SEE A FILM [C] *AmE* a building where films are shown SYN **movie theater** *AmE*, **cinema** *BrE*: *'Bambi' was the first movie I ever saw in the theater.*

4 HOSPITAL [C,U] *BrE* a special room in a hospital where medical operations are done SYN **operating room** *AmE*: **in theatre** *Marilyn is still in theatre.*

5 WAR [C] *formal* a large area where a war is being fought: *the Pacific theater during World War II*

thea·tre·go·er *BrE*, **theatergoer** *AmE* /ˈθɪətəˌɡəʊə $ -tərˌɡoʊər/ *n* [C] someone who regularly watches plays at the theatre

ˌtheatre-in-the-ˈround *n* [U] the performance of a play on a central stage with the people watching sitting in a circle around it

the·at·ri·cal /θiˈætrɪkəl/ ●○○ *adj*

1 relating to the performing of plays: *a Polish theatrical company*

2 behaving in a loud or very noticeable way that is intended to get people's attention: *She gave a theatrical sigh.* —**theatrically** /-kli/ *adv*

the·at·ri·cals /θiˈætrɪkəlz/ *n* [plural] **1** performances of plays: *amateur theatricals* **2** *BrE informal* behaviour that is very loud and noticeable, and is intended to get people's attention SYN **theatrics**: *We can do without all these theatricals, Andrew!*

the·at·rics /θiˈætrɪks/ *n* [plural] *especially AmE* behaviour that is very loud and noticeable, and is intended to get people's attention

thee /ðiː/ *pron old use* a word meaning 'you', used as the OBJECT of a sentence

theft /θeft/ ●●○ *n*

1 [U] the crime of stealing → **thief**, **burglary**, **robbery**: *Car theft is on the increase.* | *an arrest for* ***petty theft*** (=stealing small things) | *Three men were charged with* ***attempted theft***. THESAURUS➤ CRIME

2 [C] an act of stealing something: *There have been a number of thefts in the area.* | **[+of]** *the theft of £150 from the office*

their /ðə; strong ðeə $ ðər strong ðer/ ●●● S1 W1 *determiner* [possessive form of 'they']

1 belonging to or connected with people or things that have already been mentioned: *They washed their faces and went to bed.* | *The twins spend all their time together.* | *People had moved back into* ***their own*** *homes.*

2 used when talking about someone who may be male or female, to avoid saying 'his or her': *Everyone is free to express their own opinion.* | *Each student will have their own course-work folder.* → HIS(2)

theirs /ðeəz $ ðerz/ ●●● S3 *pron* [possessive form of 'they']

1 used to refer to something that belongs to or is connected with people that have already been mentioned: *When our washing machine broke, our neighbours let us use theirs.* | *Our house is number 25, and theirs is just opposite.* | *We compared scores and found that theirs were higher than ours.* | **of theirs** *They shared the prize money with a* ***friend of theirs***.

2 used when talking about someone who may be male or female, to avoid saying 'his or hers': *Everyone wants what is theirs by right.* → HIS(2)

the·is·m /ˈθiːɪzəm/ *n* [U] the belief in the existence of God or gods OPP **atheism** → **deism**

them¹ /ðəm; strong ðem/ ●●● S1 W1 *pron* [object form of 'they']

1 used to refer to two or more people or things that have already been mentioned or are already known about: *Has anyone seen my keys? I can't find them anywhere.* | *The*

police were very helpful when I spoke to them. | I lent him several books, but he hasn't read any of them.
2 used when talking about someone who may be male or female, to avoid saying 'him or her': *If anyone phones, tell them I'll be back later.*

them² /ðem/ *determiner spoken* used to mean 'those'. Many people think this use is incorrect: *I couldn't understand all them long words.*

the·mat·ic /θɪˈmætɪk/ (AWL) *adj* relating to a particular THEME, or organized according to a theme: *the thematic organization of paintings in the exhibit* —**thematically** /-kli/ *adv*

theme /θiːm/ ●●● (S2) (W2) (AWL) *n* [C]
1 SUBJECT the main subject or idea in a piece of writing, speech, film etc: *The book's theme is the conflict between love and duty.* | **main/central/major etc theme** *Campbell has made health care a central theme in his campaign.* | *Nature is a* ***recurrent theme*** (=a theme that appears repeatedly) *in Frost's poetry.* | *Most of Kurt's other pictures were* ***variations on*** *the same* ***theme***.
2 theme music/song/tune music or a song that is often played during a film or musical play, or at the beginning and end of a television or radio programme: *the theme song from 'The Brady Bunch'*
3 REPEATED TUNE a short simple tune that is repeated and developed in a piece of music: *Freia's theme in Wagner's opera*
4 STYLE a particular style: *Her bedroom is decorated in a Victorian theme.*
5 PIECE OF WRITING *AmE old-fashioned* a short piece of writing on a particular subject that you do for school (SYN) **essay**: **[+on]** *Your homework is to write a two-page theme on pollution.*

themed /θiːmd/ (*also* **theme**) *adj* [usually before noun] a themed place or event has been designed to make people who go there feel like they are in a particular place or historical period: *themed restaurants such as the Rainforest Café*

ˈtheme park *n* [C] a type of park where you can have fun riding on big machines such as a ROLLER COASTER, and where the whole park is based on one subject such as water or space travel

ˈtheme ˌparty *n* [C] *BrE* a party where everyone has to dress in a particular way connected with a particular subject: *a Wild West theme party*

them·self /ðəmˈself/ *pron spoken* used when you are talking about one person, but you want to avoid saying 'himself' or 'herself' because you do not know the sex of the person. Many people think this use is incorrect: *It makes me happy to help someone help themself.*

them·selves /ðəmˈselvz/ ●●● (S1) (W1) *pron*
1 used to show that the people who do something are affected by their own action: *Teachers have no choice but to take measures to protect themselves.* | *Our neighbours have just bought themselves a jacuzzi.* | *The kids seem very pleased with themselves.*
2 used to emphasize the pronoun 'they', a plural noun etc: *Doctors themselves are the first to admit the treatment has side effects.*
3 used after words like 'everyone', 'anyone', 'no one' etc when you talk about someone already mentioned and you do not know what sex they are or it is not important. Many teachers think this is not correct English: *Someone told me they'd actually seen the accident happen themselves.*
4 in themselves (*also* **in and of themselves**) considered without other related ideas or situations: *The carvings are works of art in themselves, even disregarding their religious significance.*
5 (all) by themselves a) alone: *older people who are living all by themselves* **b)** without help from anyone else: *Did the children make the model all by themselves?*
6 (all) to themselves if people have something to themselves, they do not have to share it with anyone: *They had the whole beach to themselves.*
7 not be/feel themselves if people are not themselves, they do not feel or behave in the way they usually do because they are nervous, upset, or ill

then¹ /ðen/ ●●● (S1) (W1) *adv*
1 at a particular time in the past or future: *I wish I had known then what I know now.* | *It was then that I realised she'd tricked me.* | *He started his career in St Petersburg – or Leningrad as it then was.* | **by/until/since then** *They're sending out the results next week, so we won't know anything until then.* | *It was late evening when the doctor arrived, and by then it was too late.* | *That was in 1970. Since then the place has changed a lot.* | *They met in 1942 and* **from then on** (=starting at that time) *they were firm friends.* | *Silently she closed the door.* ***Just then*** *she heard a noise.* | *I was paid £1,000, which was a lot of money* ***back then*** (=a long time ago when things were different) *in the 1950s.*
2 used to say what happens next or what you do next: *Mix the flour and butter, then add the eggs.* | *Byron travelled to Italy and then to Greece.*
3 a) used when saying what the result of a situation or action will be: ***If*** *you won't tell him,* ***then*** *I will.* | *Start off early, then you won't have to rush.* **b)** *spoken* used when you think that something is probably true because of what you know about the situation: *Still in your pyjamas? Have you just got out of bed then?*
4 but then (again) used to say that although something is true, something else is also true which makes the first thing seem less important: *William didn't succeed first time, but then very few people do.* | *Elaine's father might lend them the money, but then again he might not.*
5 *spoken* **a)** used at the beginning of a conversation or activity: *Now then, what would you like to do today?* | *Right then, shall we start?* **b)** used at the end of a conversation, especially to show that something has been agreed: *Good, that's settled then. We'll all meet here next Wednesday.* | *Okay then, I'll see you at work.* **c)** used to show that you are saying something because of what someone has just said: *'We're late.' 'We'd better hurry, then.'* | *'Friday's no good.' 'Then how about Saturday?'*
6 used to add something to what you have just mentioned: *We have to invite your parents and my parents, and then there's your brother.*
7 used to refer back to what you have just been talking about: *This then was the situation facing the government at the end of the war.*
8 then and there (*also* **there and then**) immediately: *He wasn't prepared to wait – he wanted the money then and there.* → **(every) now and then** at NOW¹(5)

then² *adj* [only before noun] used when mentioning the person who had a particular job, title, or position at a time in the past: *a visit to China by the then US President, Richard Nixon*

thence /ðens/ *adv formal* from there or following that: *We went to Trieste, and thence by train to Prague.*

thence·forth /ðensˈfɔːθ $ ˈðensfɔːrθ/ (*also* **thence·forward** /ðensˈfɔːwəd $ -ˈfɔːrwərd/) *adv formal* starting from that time → **henceforth**

theo- /θiːə/ (*also* **the-**) *prefix* relating to God or gods: *theology* (=study of religion)

the·oc·ra·cy /θiˈɒkrəsi $ -ˈɑː-/ *n* (*plural* **theocracies**) [C] a social system or state controlled by religious leaders —**theocratic** /ˌθiːəˈkrætɪk◂/ *adj: a theocratic state*

the·od·o·lite /θiˈɒdəlaɪt $ θiˈɑː-/ *n* [C] a piece of equipment used by a land SURVEYOR for measuring angles

the·o·lo·gian /ˌθiːəˈləʊdʒən $ -ˈloʊ-/ *n* [C] someone who has studied theology

theoˈlogical ˌcollege *BrE*, **theoˈlogical ˌseminary** *AmE* *n* [C] a college for training people to become priests or church ministers

the·ol·o·gy /θiˈɒlədʒi $ θiˈɑː-/ *n* (*plural* **theologies**)
1 [U] the study of religion and religious ideas and beliefs: *He studied theology at college.* **2** [C,U] a particular system of religious beliefs and ideas: *According to Muslim theology there is only one God.* | *a comparison of Eastern and Western theologies* —**theological** /ˌθiːəˈlɒdʒɪkəl◂ $ -ˈlɑː-/ *adj: theological debate* —**theologically** /-kli/ *adv*

the·o·rem /ˈθɪərəm $ ˈθiːə-/ *n* [C] *technical* a statement, especially in mathematics, that you can prove by showing that it has been correctly developed from facts → **proof**

theo·ret·i·cal /θɪəˈretɪkəl $ ˌθiːə-/ ●●○ W3 AWL (*also* **theo·ret·ic** /θɪəˈretɪk $ ˌθiːə-/) *adj*
1 relating to the study of ideas, especially scientific ideas, rather than to practical uses of the ideas or practical experience → **theory**, **practical**, **applied**: *theoretical physics | Aristotle's theoretical model of the universe | She has theoretical knowledge of teaching, but no practical experience.*
2 a theoretical situation or condition could exist but does not really exist SYN **hypothetical**: *Equality between men and women in our society is still only theoretical. | a theoretical risk of an explosion*

theo·ret·i·cally /θɪəˈretɪkli $ ˌθiːə-/ ●○○ AWL *adv* [sentence adverb]
1 used to say what is supposed to be true in a particular situation, especially when the opposite is true OPP **in practice**: *Theoretically, Damian's the boss, but I coordinate the team on a day-to-day basis.*
2 according to a scientific idea that has not been proven to be true in a practical way SYN **hypothetically**: *It is theoretically possible for computers to be programmed to think like humans.*

theo·rist /ˈθɪərɪst $ ˈθiːə-/ ●○○ AWL (*also* **theo·re·ti·cian** /ˌθɪərəˈtɪʃən $ ˌθiːə-/) *n* [C] someone who develops ideas within a particular subject that explain why particular things happen or are true: *a leading economic theorist*

theo·rize (*also* **-ise** *BrE*) /ˈθɪəraɪz $ ˈθiːə-/ *v* [I,T] to think of a possible explanation for an event or fact SYN **hypothesize**: **theorize that** *Researchers theorize that there was once a common language for all humanity.* | **[+about]** *They have been theorizing about what may have caused the fire.*

theo·ry /ˈθɪəri $ ˈθiːəri/ ●●● S2 W1 AWL *n* (*plural* **theories**)
1 [C] an idea or set of ideas that is intended to explain something about life or the world, especially an idea that has not yet been proved to be true → **theoretical**: **[+about/on]** *different theories about how the brain works* | **[+of]** *Darwin's theory of evolution* | **theory that** *the theory that light is made up of waves*
2 [U] general principles and ideas about a subject: *Freudian theory has had a great influence on psychology.* | **political/economic/literary etc theory** *I'm taking a course on political theory.*
3 in theory something that is true in theory is supposed to be true, but might not really be true or might not be what will really happen OPP **in practice**: *In theory, everyone will have to pay the new tax.*
4 [C] an idea or opinion that someone thinks is true but for which they have no proof: **theory that** *Detectives are working on a theory that he knew his murderer.*

COLLOCATIONS

VERBS

come up with/develop a theory *These birds helped Darwin develop his theory of natural selection.*
test a theory *Researchers gave workers a questionnaire to test that theory.*
prove a theory *No evidence emerged to prove either theory.*
support a theory *Modern research strongly supports this theory.*
disprove a theory (*also* **refute a theory** *formal*) (=show that it is wrong) | **discredit a theory** (=make people stop believing in it)

ADJECTIVES/NOUN + theory

a scientific theory *Scientific theories can be tested experimentally.*
an economic theory *His economic theory assumes that both labour and capital are perfectly mobile.*
a conspiracy theory (=a theory that an event was the result of secret plan made by two or more people) | **a pet theory** (=a personal theory that you strongly believe)

PHRASES

the theory of evolution/relativity etc *According to the theory of relativity, nothing can travel faster than light.*

ther·a·peu·tic /ˌθerəˈpjuːtɪk◂/ ●○○ *adj*
1 making you feel calm and relaxed: *I find swimming very therapeutic. | the therapeutic effect of gardening*
2 [usually before noun] relating to the treatment or cure of an illness → **therapy**: *Some claim that the herb has therapeutic value for treating pain.* —**therapeutically** /-kli/ *adv*

ther·a·peu·tics /ˌθerəˈpjuːtɪks/ *n* [U] *technical* the part of medical science relating to the treatment and cure of illness

ther·a·pist /ˈθerəpɪst/ ●●○ *n* [C] someone who has been trained to give a particular form of treatment for physical or mental illness: *a speech therapist* THESAURUS ▸ DOCTOR

ther·a·py /ˈθerəpi/ ●●○ *n* (*plural* **therapies**)
1 [C,U] the treatment of an illness or injury over a fairly long period of time: *new drug therapies | radiation therapy for cancer treatment*
2 [U] the treatment or examination of someone's mental problems by talking to them for a long time about their feelings SYN **psychotherapy**: **in therapy** *Rob was in therapy for several years.* | *a therapy group* → CHEMOTHERAPY, OCCUPATIONAL, PHYSIOTHERAPY, SPEECH THERAPY, HORMONE REPLACEMENT THERAPY

there[1] /ðeə, ðə $ ðer, ðər/ ●●● S1 W1 *pron* **there is/exists/remains etc** used to say that something exists or happens: *Is there any milk left? | There are a few things we need to discuss. | There must be easier ways of doing this. | There seems to be a lack of communication. | There remain several questions still to be answered. | Suddenly there was a loud explosion. | They were all laughing when there came a knock at the door.*

GRAMMAR

• You use **there are** before a plural noun: *There are a lot of problems.* ✗ Don't say: *There is a lot of problems.* You will sometimes hear native speakers say this is in informal conversation, but it is grammatically incorrect.
• Instead of saying **there is**, you often say **there's**: *There's one small problem.*
• **There** cannot be omitted. ✗ Don't say: *Is one small problem.*

USAGE: Spelling

Don't confuse **there** and **their**. You write: *They love their jobs.* ✗ Don't write: *They love there jobs.*

there[2] /ðeə $ ðer/ ●●● S1 W1 *adv*
1 in or to a particular place that is not where you are → **here**: *We could go back to my cottage and have lunch there. | Scotland? I've always wanted to go there. | Hold it right there and don't move. | Can you pass me that wine glass there? | Look, there's that bookshop I was telling you about. | Who's that man* ***over there****? | It's too far to drive* ***there and back*** *in one day. | Are we going to* ***get there*** (=arrive) *before the banks close?* | **out/in/under etc there** *I know there's a mouse under there somewhere. | We flew to Miami and from there to La Paz.* ⚠ Don't say 'to there': *We went there (NOT went to there) by car.*
2 if something is there, it exists: *The chance was there, but I didn't take it. | The countryside is there for everyone to enjoy. | Three months after the operation, the pain was still there.*
3 at or to a particular point in time, in a process, or in a story: *Let's stop there and I'll tell you the rest of the story tomorrow. | She got a divorce, but her troubles didn't end there. | There's still a lot of work to do, but we're* ***getting there*** (=coming to the end of the process) *slowly.*

T

4 there and then (*also* **then and there**) immediately: *I thought I'd have to wait, but they offered me the job there and then.*

SPOKEN PHRASES

5 used to refer to something that someone has said when you are answering them: *That's true. I agree with you there.* | *'Why did the system fail?' 'Well, there you've got me – I really don't know.'*
6 used when greeting someone or calling to them: *Hi there, you must be Laura.* | *Hey, you there! Watch out!*
7 there it is/there they are etc used when you have found something or someone that you are looking for: *Have you seen my keys anywhere? Ah, there they are.* | *There you are. I've been looking for you.*
8 used when you want to speak to someone on the telephone and someone else answers: *Hello, Georgie, is your mother there?*
9 be there (for sb) to be always ready to help someone when they need help: *That's what I loved about my father – he was always there for me.*
10 there I was/there they were etc used to describe what situation someone was in at a particular point in the story you are telling: *So there I was, stranded in London with no money.*
11 be not all there *informal* someone who is not all there seems stupid or slightly crazy
12 there's a good boy/clever dog etc used to praise a child or animal
13 there it is/there you are/there you go used to say that nothing can be done to change an unsatisfactory situation: *It's all very sad, but there it is. There's absolutely nothing any of us can do about it.*
14 there you go/she goes etc (again) used when someone does something annoying that they often do: *There you go, blaming everything on me, as usual.* | *There she goes again, complaining about the weather.*
15 there you are/there you go a) used when giving something to someone or when you have done something for someone: *There you are. I'll just wrap it up for you.* **b)** used when you think you have proved to someone that what you are telling them is right: *There you are, then. There's nothing to worry about.*
16 there's sth for you a) used to say that an action or situation is a good example of a particular quality: *There's intelligence for you! She's solved the problem already.* **b)** used when you are annoyed or disappointed to say that someone's behaviour is the opposite of the quality you are naming: *Well, there's gratitude for you. She didn't even say thank you.*
17 there goes sth/sb a) used when you see someone or something going past or away from you: *There goes a very worried man.* **b)** used to say that you can hear something such as a bell ringing: *There goes the phone. I'll answer it.* **c)** used when you are losing something, for example an opportunity or money, as a result of something that has just happened: *There go our chances of winning the championship.* | *There goes my career.*

there³ /ðeə $ ðer/ ●●○ *interjection*
1 *spoken* used to express satisfaction that you have been proved right or that you have done what you intended to do: *There! I've done it! I've resigned.* | *There, what did I tell you? I knew it wouldn't work.*
2 there, there! *spoken* used to comfort someone who is crying, especially a child: *There, there, don't get so upset!*
3 so there! *spoken* used to show someone that you do not care what they think and you are not going to change your mind – used by children: *I'm going to Elly's party, and you can't stop me, so there!*

there·a·bouts /ˌðeərəˈbaʊts $ ˌðer-/ (*also* **thereabout** /-ˈbaʊt/) *adv* near a particular time, place, number etc, but not exactly: *These houses were built in 1930* ***or thereabouts***.

there·af·ter /ðeərˈɑːftə $ ðerˈæftər/ ●○○ *adv formal* after a particular event or time SYN **afterwards**: *10,000 men had volunteered by the end of September; thereafter, approximately 1,000 men enlisted each month.* | *Sophie was born in France, but* ***shortly thereafter*** *her family moved to the United States.*

there·by /ðeəˈbaɪ, ˈðeəbaɪ $ ðerˈbaɪ, ˈðer-/ ●○○ AWL *adv formal* with the result that something else happens: **thereby doing sth** *He became a citizen in 1978, thereby gaining the right to vote.*

there·fore /ˈðeəfɔː $ ˈðerfɔːr/ ●●● S3 W1 *adv formal* as a result of something that has just been mentioned: *Their car was bigger and therefore more comfortable.* | *Progress so far has been very good. We are, therefore, confident that the work will be completed on time.*

THESAURUS

therefore for this reason: *She already had a lot of experience and therefore seemed the best candidate for the job.*
so therefore. So is less formal than **therefore**, and is more common in everyday English: *They had not eaten all day, so they were very hungry.*
thus *formal* as a result of what you have just mentioned: *The program is very simple and thus easy to run.*
hence *formal* for this reason: *This material is highly poisonous, hence the importance of careful handling.*
as a result used when saying that because of a particular situation, something else happens or is true: *Some people suffer from stress at work and become ill as a result.* | *Economic growth slowed down as a result of inflation.*
consequently/as a consequence used when saying that because of a particular situation, something else happens or is true. **Consequently** and **as a consequence** are more formal than **as a result**: *The disease attacks the plant, the flower does not open, and consequently no seeds are produced.*
this means that used when saying what the result of something is: *If students arrive late, this means that lesson time is wasted.*
for this reason used when explaining the reason for something: *Spell check programs do not recognize when you have used the wrong word. For this reason, you must still read over your work carefully.*

there·in /ðeərˈɪn $ ðer-/ *adv formal* **1** in that place, or in that piece of writing: *See Thompson, 1983, and the references cited therein.* **2 therein lies sth** used to say that something is caused by or comes from a particular situation: *The treaty was imposed by force, and therein lay the cause of its ineffectiveness.* → HEREIN

there·in·af·ter /ˌðeərɪnˈɑːftə $ ˌðerɪnˈæftər/ *adv law* later in the same official paper, statement etc

there·of /ðeərˈɒv $ ðerˈɑːv/ *adv formal* relating to something that has just been mentioned: *States differ in standards for products and the labelling thereof.* | *Money, or the* ***lack thereof***, *played a major role in their marital problems.*

there·on /ðeərˈɒn $ ðerˈɒːn, -ˈɑːn/ *adv formal* **1** on the thing that has just been mentioned **2** THEREUPON

there·to /ðeəˈtuː $ ðerˈtuː/ *adv formal* relating to an agreement, piece of writing, or thing that has just been mentioned: *the treaty and any conditions attaching thereto*

there·un·der /ðeərˈʌndə $ ðerˈʌndər/ *adv formal* **1** under something that has just been mentioned **2** according to a document, law, or part of an agreement that has just been mentioned

there·up·on /ˌðeərəˈpɒn, ˈðeərəpɒn $ ˌðerəˈpɒːn, -ˈpɑːn, ˈðerə-/ *adv formal* **1** immediately after something else has happened, and usually as a result of it SYN **then**: *Thereupon the whole audience began cheering.* **2** relating to a subject that has just been mentioned: *I read your article, and wish to comment thereupon.*

therm /θɜːm $ θɜːrm/ *n* [C] a unit for measuring heat, especially when calculating amounts of gas used: *UK gas was selling for as little as 6p a therm.*

therm- /θɜːm $ θɜːrm/ *prefix* another form of THERMO-

ther·mal¹ /ˈθɜːməl $ ˈθɜːr-/ *adj* [only before noun] **1** relating to or caused by heat: *thermal energy* **2** thermal clothing is made from special material to keep you warm in very cold weather: *thermal underwear* **3** thermal water is heated naturally under the earth: *thermal springs*

thermal² *n* **1** [C] a rising current of warm air used by birds **2 thermals** [plural] *BrE informal* special warm clothing, especially underwear, worn under your other clothes

thermo- /θɜːməʊ, -mə $ θɜːrmoʊ, -mə/ (*also* **therm-**) *prefix technical* relating to heat: *a **thermostat*** (=for controlling temperature) | ***thermostable*** (=not changing when heated)

ther·mo·dy·nam·ics /ˌθɜːməʊdaɪˈnæmɪks $ ˌθɜːrmoʊ-/ *n* [U] the science that deals with the relationship between heat and other forms of energy —**thermodynamic** *adj*

ther·mom·e·ter /θəˈmɒmɪtə $ θərˈmɑːmɪtər/ ●●○ *n* [C] a piece of equipment that measures the temperature of the air, of your body etc: *The thermometer registered over 100° C.* | **a candy/meat thermometer** (=used in cooking) → see picture at MEASURE¹

ther·mo·nu·cle·ar /ˌθɜːməʊˈnjuːkliə◂ $ ˌθɜːrmoʊˈnuːkliər◂/ *adj* thermonuclear weapons use a NUCLEAR reaction, involving the splitting of atoms, to produce very high temperatures and a very powerful explosion: *a thermonuclear device*

ther·mo·plas·tic /ˌθɜːməʊˈplæstɪk◂ $ ˌθɜːrmə-/ *n* [C,U] *technical* a plastic that is soft and bendable when heated but hard when cold

Ther·mos /ˈθɜːməs $ ˈθɜːr-/ (*also* **ˈThermos ˌflask** *BrE*) *n* [C] *trademark* a special container like a bottle, that keeps drinks hot or cold SYN **flask** *BrE* → see picture at FLASK

ther·mo·set·ting /ˈθɜːməʊˌsetɪŋ $ ˈθɜːrmoʊ-/ *adj technical* thermosetting plastic becomes hard and unbendable after it has been heated

ther·mo·stat /ˈθɜːməstæt $ ˈθɜːr-/ *n* [C] an instrument used for keeping a room or a machine at a particular temperature

the·sau·rus /θɪˈsɔːrəs/ *n* (*plural* **thesauruses** *or* **thesauri** /-raɪ/) [C] a book in which words are put into groups with other words that have similar meanings

these /ðiːz/ the plural of THIS

the·sis /ˈθiːsɪs/ ●○○ AWL *n* (*plural* **theses** /-siːz/) [C]
1 a long piece of writing about a particular subject that you do as part of an advanced university degree such as an MA or a PhD: *Cynthia's still working on her thesis.* | **graduate/master's/doctoral thesis** *He wrote his doctoral thesis on contemporary French literature.*
2 *formal* an idea or opinion about something, that you discuss in a formal way and give examples for: *Their **main thesis** was that the rise in earnings was due to improvements in education.*
3 *AmE* in writing, the thesis is the sentence or group of sentences which state what the main idea of an ESSAY is: *a paragraph introducing your **thesis statement***

thes·pi·an /ˈθespiən/ *n* [C] *formal* an actor - sometimes used humorously: *a distinguished thespian* —**thespian** *adj*

they /ðeɪ/ ●●● S1 W1 *pron* [used as the subject of a verb]
1 used to refer to two or more people or things that have already been mentioned or are already known about: *Bob and Sue said they wouldn't be able to come.* | *Ken gave me some flowers. Aren't they beautiful?* | *They all want to come to the wedding.*
2 they say/think etc used to state what people in general say or think: *They say it's bad luck to spill salt.*
3 *spoken* used to refer to a particular organization or group of people: *Where are they going to build the new highway?* | *They're going to take an X-ray.*
4 used when talking about someone who may be male or female, to avoid saying 'he or she': *If anyone has any information related to the crime, will they please contact the police.* | *Every child, whoever they are, deserves to have a mum and a dad.*

USAGE: They, them, their

- If you want to talk in general about someone, and you do not want to say if the person is male or female, you often use **they**, **them**, or **their**: *If **anyone** doesn't like it, **they** can leave.* | *When **a friend** upsets you, do you tell **them**?* | ***Someone** has left **their** coat behind.*
- People do this in order to avoid suggesting that the person can only be male, or to avoid using longer expressions such as 'he or she', 'him or her'.
- This use is acceptable and very common in spoken English, and is becoming more acceptable in writing as well.
- However, some people consider this use to be incorrect. You can sometimes avoid the problem by making the subject plural: *If **people** don't like it, **they** can leave.* | *When **friends** upset you, do you tell **them**?*
- In the past, people used to use 'he' to refer to men or women, but most people now avoid doing this.

they'd /ðeɪd/ **1** the short form of 'they had': *If only they'd been there.* **2** the short form of 'they would': *It's a pity my parents didn't come – they'd have enjoyed it.*

they'll /ðeɪl/ the short form of 'they will': *They'll be tired after the long journey.*

they're /ðə; *strong* ðeə, ðeɪə $ ðər *strong* ðer, ðeɪər/ the short form of 'they are': *They're going to Crete next week.*

they've /ðeɪv/ the short form of 'they have': *They've had a lot of trouble with their car.*

thi·am·in, **thi·a·mine** /ˈθaɪəmiːn, -mɪn/ *n* [U] a natural chemical in some foods, that you need in order to prevent particular illnesses

THICK

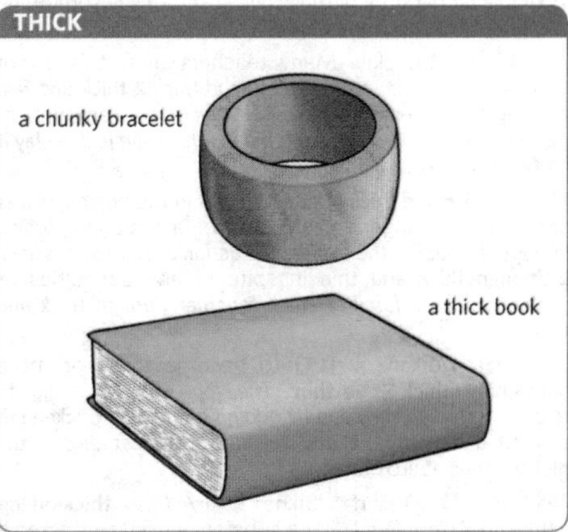

thick¹ /θɪk/ ●●● S2 W2 *adj* (*comparative* **thicker**, *superlative* **thickest**)
1 NOT THIN if something is thick, there is a large distance or a larger distance than usual between its two opposite surfaces or sides OPP **thin**: *a thick oak door* | *a thick slice of homemade bread* | *He was wearing thick glasses.* | *short thick fingers* | *thick wool socks* (=socks that are heavy and warm) | *If you want a thicker blanket, there are more here in the closet.* | *The meat is done when the thickest part turns from pink to white.* | **[+with]** *The furniture was **thick with dust*** (=there was thick dust on the furniture).
2 MEASUREMENT measuring a particular distance between two opposite sides or surfaces of something: **3 feet/1 cm/two inches etc thick** *The walls are about two meters thick.* | *How thick should the glass in the tank be?* | *This layer of brain tissue is no thicker than 2 mm.*
3 TREES/BUSHES ETC growing very close together or having a lot of leaves SYN **dense**: *birds hiding in the thick undergrowth* | **[+with]** *The walls were thick with ivy.*
4 SMOKE/CLOUD ETC filling the air, and difficult to see through or breathe in SYN **dense**: *thick fog* | **[+with]** *The air was **thick with** cigarette **smoke**.*
5 LIQUID almost solid, and therefore flowing very slowly,

or not flowing at all: *For a thicker gravy, add more flour.* | *The paint is too thick.*
6 HAIR/FUR having a lot of hair or fur: *She ran her fingers through her thick brown hair.*
7 STUPID *BrE informal* a thick person is stupid: *He's a nice guy, but he's a bit thick.* | **(as) thick as two short planks** (=very stupid)
8 VOICE **a)** if someone has a thick ACCENT, the way they speak shows clearly which particular place or part of a country they come from: **a thick German/Yorkshire etc accent** *Olga speaks English with a thick Russian accent.* **b)** if someone's voice is thick, it is not as clear or high as usual, for example because they are upset: *Bill's voice was thick and gruff.* | **[+with]** *Her voice was thick with emotion.*
9 LARGE AMOUNT *especially written* containing a lot of people or things: *The cod were so thick in the water that they caught thousands very quickly.* | **[+with]** *The roads were thick with holiday traffic.*
10 be thick on the ground *BrE* to be present or available in large amounts or numbers OPP **thin on the ground**: *Cheap houses aren't as thick on the ground as they used to be.*
11 have a thick skin to not care if people criticize you or do not like you → THICK-SKINNED
12 FRIENDLY **be (as) thick as thieves** if two people are as thick as thieves, they are very friendly with each other and seem to share a lot of secrets, making other people think they are hiding or planning something: *Lately Nick and Lou have been as thick as thieves.*
13 give sb a thick ear/get a thick ear *BrE spoken* to hit someone or be hit on the head, as a punishment: *Any more cheek from you and you'll get a thick ear.*
14 be thick with sb *old-fashioned* to be very friendly with someone
15 (it's) a bit thick *BrE old-fashioned* used to say something is a little unfair or annoying

thick² *adv* **1** thickly. Many teachers think this is not correct English: *peanut butter spread thick* **2 thick and fast** arriving or happening very frequently, in large amounts or numbers: *Entries have been coming in thick and fast.* → **lay it on (a bit thick)** at LAY

thick³ *n* **1 in the thick of sth** involved in the busiest, most active, most dangerous etc part of a situation: *Brown hopes to be back in the thick of the action as soon as possible.* **2 through thick and thin** in spite of any difficulties or problems: *Then, families **stuck together through thick and thin**.*

thick·en /ˈθɪkən/ *v* [I,T] to become thick, or make something thick OPP **thin**: *The fog was beginning to thicken.* | *Thicken the soup by adding potatoes.* | **thicken sth with sth** *a stew thickened with lentils and vegetables* → **the plot thickens** at PLOT¹(3)

thick·en·er /ˈθɪkənə, ˈθɪknə $ -ər/ (*also* **thick·en·ing** /ˈθɪkənɪŋ,ˈθɪknɪŋ/) *n* [C,U] a substance used to thicken a liquid

thick·et /ˈθɪkɪt/ *n* [C] a group of bushes and small trees SYN **copse** THESAURUS ▸ FOREST

ˌthick-ˈheaded *adj informal* extremely stupid: *He's so thick-headed he can't understand simple instructions.*

thick·ly /ˈθɪkli/ *adv* **1** in a way that makes a thick piece or layer of something OPP **thinly**: *The cheese was sliced thickly.* | *a thickly carpeted hallway* **2 thickly populated/wooded etc** if an area is thickly populated, wooded etc, there are a lot of people, trees etc there close together SYN **densely**: *The eastern part of the country is more thickly populated.*

thick·ness /ˈθɪknəs/ ●○○ *n*
1 [C,U] how thick something is: *The thickness of the walls is 5 feet.*
2 [C] a layer of something: **[+of]** *Wrap the cake in a double thickness of foil.*

thick·o /ˈθɪkəʊ $ -koʊ/ *n* (*plural* **thickos**) [C] *BrE spoken* someone who is very stupid

thick·set /ˌθɪkˈset◂/ *adj* having a wide strong body SYN **stocky**: *a short thickset man*

ˌthick-ˈskinned *adj* not easily offended by other people's criticism or insults OPP **thin-skinned**: *a thick-skinned insurance salesman*

thief /θiːf/ ●●○ *n* (*plural* **thieves** /θiːvz/) [C] someone who steals things from another person or place → **theft**, **burglar**, **robber**: *Thieves broke into the offices and stole some computer equipment.* | **a car/jewel etc thief** | *They were nothing but **petty thieves*** (=thieves who steal small things). → **be (as) thick as thieves** at THICK¹(12)

THESAURUS

thief someone who steals things from a person or place: *The thief grabbed her handbag and ran off down the street.* | *Car thieves are operating in this area.*
burglar someone who goes into houses, offices etc to steal things: *Burglars broke into the house and took a computer worth £1,000.*
robber someone who steals from banks, offices, houses etc, especially using threats or violence: *a gang of bank robbers* | *an armed robber* (=a robber with a gun)
shoplifter someone who takes things from shops without paying for them, especially by hiding them in their clothes or in a bag: *The store has installed hidden cameras to catch shoplifters.*
pickpocket someone who steals from people's pockets, especially in a crowded public place: *Look out for pickpockets in busy tourist areas.*
mugger a thief who violently attacks someone in the street and robs them: *The mugger punched him in the face and tried to steal his wallet.*
joyrider someone who steals a car and drives it very fast for fun: *Police pursued the teenage joyriders across three counties.*
looter someone who breaks into shops or homes and steals things, after there has been a natural disaster, a war, or a violent protest: *Police chiefs have warned that looters will be shot.*
bandit a member of an armed group of thieves who travel around attacking people in country areas: *The village was attacked by a gang of bandits.*
poacher someone who hunts animals, birds etc illegally on other people's land: *Their job is to prevent poachers from killing the elephants.*

thiev·e·ry /ˈθiːvəri/ *n* [U] *formal* thieving

thiev·ing /ˈθiːvɪŋ/ *n* [U] *BrE informal* the act of stealing things —**thieving** *adj*: *thieving pirates*

thiev·ish /ˈθiːvɪʃ/ *adj literary* like a thief

thigh /θaɪ/ ●●○ *n* [C]
1 the top part of your leg, between your knee and your HIP
2 the top part of a bird's leg, used as food: *chicken thighs*

thigh·bone /ˈθaɪbəʊn $ -boʊn/ *n* [C] the bone in the top part of a leg

thim·ble /ˈθɪmbəl/ *n* [C] a small metal or plastic cap used to protect your finger when you are sewing

thim·ble·ful /ˈθɪmbəlfʊl/ *n* [C + of] *informal* a very small quantity of liquid

thin¹ /θɪn/ ●●● S2 W2 *adj* (*comparative* **thinner**, *superlative* **thinnest**)
1 NOT THICK if something is thin, there is only a small distance between its two opposite sides or surfaces OPP **thick**: *a thin gold chain* | *She's only wearing a thin summer jacket* (=a jacket made of light material). | *two thin slices of bread* | *The road was covered with a thin layer of ice.* | *The skin on the eyelids is the thinnest on the body.* | **paper/wafer thin** (=very thin) *Keep your voice down - the walls are paper thin.*
2 NOT FAT having little fat on your body OPP **fat**: *He was tall and thin, with short brown hair.* | **thin arms/legs/lips etc** *He has long thin hands.* | *Most high school girls say they want to be thinner.* | **as thin as a rake/rail/whippet** (=very thin)
3 HAIR if someone has thin hair, they do not have a lot of hair: *a thin straggly beard* | *His hair is quite thin on top.*

THIN

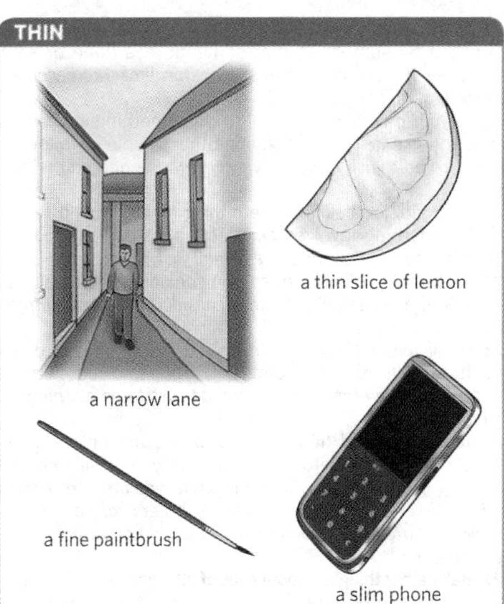

4 LIQUID a liquid that is thin flows very easily because it has a lot of water in it OPP **thick**: *thin paint*
5 SMOKE/MIST smoke or mist that is thin is easy to see through OPP **thick**: *The fog is quite thin in places.*
6 AIR air that is thin is more difficult to breathe than usual because it has less OXYGEN in it: *the thinner air high in the mountains*
7 EXCUSE/ARGUMENT/EVIDENCE ETC a thin excuse, argument, or evidence is not good or detailed enough to be useful or effective: *Evidence that capital punishment deters crime is pretty thin.*
8 a thin margin/majority etc a very small number or amount of something: *Engle beat Blanchard by a razor-thin margin* (=a very small number of votes) *in the race for governor.*
9 SMILE a thin smile does not seem very happy or sincere: *Charlie gave her a thin smile.*
10 VOICE/SOUND a thin voice or sound is high and unpleasant to listen to: *His thin voice trailed off.*
11 the thin end of the wedge *BrE spoken* an expression meaning something that you think is the beginning of a harmful development: *Workers believe the job cuts are just the thin end of the wedge.*
12 be thin on the ground if a particular type of person or thing is thin on the ground, there are very few available: *Taxis seem to be thin on the ground.*
13 be having a thin time (of it) *BrE spoken* to be in a difficult situation, especially one in which you do not have enough money
14 be (walking/treading/skating) on thin ice to be in a situation in which you are likely to upset someone or cause trouble: *I was on thin ice, and I knew it.*
15 disappear/vanish into thin air to disappear completely in a mysterious way: *Victor and his kidnappers had vanished into thin air.*
16 out of thin air out of nowhere, as if by magic: *It seems like researchers have just pulled the numbers out of thin air.*
→ WEAR[1](6) —**thinness** *n* [U]

THESAURUS

PERSON

thin having little fat on your body: *a tall, thin man*
slim thin in an attractive way: *her slim figure | a slim woman in her fifties | Magazines are always full of advice about how to stay slim.*
slender *written* thin in an attractive and graceful way - used especially about parts of the body, and used especially about women: *her long, slender legs | She is slender, with very fair hair.*
lean thin and looking healthy and fit: *his lean body | He was lean and looked like a runner.*
skinny very thin in a way that is not attractive: *a skinny teenager | Your arms are so skinny!*
slight *written* thin and delicate: *a small, slight girl with big eyes*
scrawny /ˈskrɔːni $ ˈskrɒː-/ very thin, small, and weak-looking: *a scrawny kid in blue jeans*
underweight below the usual weight for someone of your height, and therefore too thin: *He had no appetite and remained underweight.*
gaunt /gɔːnt $ gɒːnt/ *written* very thin and pale, especially because of illness or continued worry: *He looked gaunt and had not shaved for days.*
emaciated /ɪˈmeɪʃieɪtəd, -si-/ *written* extremely thin and weak, because you are ill or not getting enough to eat: *The tents were filled with emaciated refugees.*
skeletal *written* used about someone who is so thin that you can see the shape of their bones: *The soldiers were shocked by the skeletal figures of the camp's prisoners.*
anorexic used about someone who is extremely thin because they have a mental illness that makes them stop eating: *Her daughter is anorexic. | anorexic teenagers*

OBJECT/MATERIAL

thin not wide: *a thin slice of cake | a thin layer of ice | The gold was very thin.*
slim thin, especially in a way that looks attractive: *a slim volume of poetry | a slim mobile phone | a slim wooden box*
slender *written* tall or long and thin, in a way that looks attractive, but is often not very strong: *the slender columns that supported the roof | The spider was hanging by a slender thread.*
paper-thin/wafer-thin extremely thin, like paper: *The walls of the apartment were paper-thin. | wafer-thin slices of pastry*

thin[2] ●●○ *v* (**thinned, thinning**)
1 [I,T] (*also* **thin out**) to become fewer in number, especially when there were many before, or to remove people, plants, or things so that fewer remain: *The crowd had thinned out and only a few people were left. | The trees thinned as we got closer to the top of the mountain. | Traffic was finally thinning. | Thin the carrots to two inches apart. | Her hair had been thinned and cut shorter.*
2 [I,T] to make something thinner or to become thinner OPP **thicken**: *The clouds had begun to thin. | A narrow smile thinned his lips.*
3 [T] (*also* **thin down**) to make a liquid weaker by adding water or another liquid: *Thin the sauce by adding milk.* | **thin sth with sth** *The pastels can be thinned with water.*
4 [I] if someone's hair is thinning, they have less hair than they used to: *a tall man with thinning hair*
5 thin the ranks if something thins the ranks of a group of people, there are fewer of them as a result of it: *Illness had thinned our ranks.*

thin[3] *adv* thinly. Many teachers think this is not correct English: *Don't cut the bread so thin.*

thine[1] /ðaɪn/ *possessive pron old use* yours

thine[2] *possessive adj old use* a word meaning your, used before a word beginning with a vowel or 'h'

thing /θɪŋ/ ●●● S1 W1 *n*
1 IDEA/ACTION/FEELING/FACT [C] an idea, action, feeling, or fact that someone thinks, does, says, or talks about, or that happens: *People say things they don't mean when they are angry. | It was a horrible thing to happen. | I plan to* **do** *all the* **things** *I've been meaning to do for ages. | The first* **thing to do** *is to give them food and shelter. | That's a terrible* **thing to say**. | **do the right/decent/honourable etc thing** *I kept wondering if I was doing the right thing.* | **this/that/what sort of thing** *A priest has to arrange funerals, marriages, that sort of thing. | Getting more American ideas into British business would be* **a good thing**. | *'I did* **no such thing**,' *he protested. | I know* **a thing or two** (=a lot) *about dogs. | In a democracy,* **it is no bad thing to** *be able to compromise* (=it is good, even though it may not seem good).

2 OBJECT [C] an object that you are talking about without saying its name, or whose name you do not know: *What's that red thing?* | *I'll just switch this thing off.* | *There was a round metal thing on the path.* | **... and things** (=and other similar things) *The shed is where we keep our tools and things.*

3 CLOTHES/POSSESSIONS **things** [plural] *especially BrE* clothes and possessions SYN **stuff** *AmE*: **sb's things** *Jim began to unpack his things.* | *I want to sell some of my things, but they aren't worth much.*

4 EQUIPMENT **things** [plural] *especially BrE* the tools, equipment, clothes etc that you need for a particular job, sport etc SYN **stuff** *AmE*: **sb's writing/school/Christmas etc things** *I left my swimming things at home.* | *the shed where he kept his gardening things*

5 SITUATION **things** [plural] life in general and the way it is affecting people: *By the end of 1942, things were starting to change.* | *Things could be worse.* | *As things turned out, we didn't have much time.* | ***How are things** with you, Sarah?* | **make things easy/difficult/hard** *She would get angry quickly, which made things difficult for me.* | *We can't change **the way things are**.*

6 NOTHING [singular, U] used as part of a negative statement to mean 'anything': **not a thing** *I couldn't find a thing that I wanted to buy.* | *He took his glasses off and couldn't see a thing.* | *Don't worry about a thing.* | *There's **no such thing as** ghosts* (=they do not exist).

7 PERSON/ANIMAL [C] used to talk to or about a person or animal, when you are describing what they are like or showing sympathy for them: *The baby is a nice **little thing** when he's not screaming.* | *She was terribly upset, **poor thing**.*

8 MAKE A COMMENT [C usually singular] used to say something about a particular part of a situation, person etc: **[+about]** *The thing about teaching is that it takes more time to prepare than most people realize.* | **the funny/strange/best etc thing** *The funny thing is, I really enjoyed it, even though I hadn't expected to.* | ***It's a** good **thing** you saw her before she saw you.*

9 the thing is *spoken* used when you are going to explain something, give the reason for something, or give an opinion: *'It sounds like a good idea. Why don't you invest?' 'Well, the thing is, I can't afford to.'* | **the thing is that** *The thing is that you can't always judge your own work.*

10 the last thing sb wants/expects/needs etc something that someone does not want, expect etc at all: *The last thing I want is to upset him.* | *The last thing I should have done was let her move into my house.*

11 last thing *BrE* at the end of a day, afternoon, evening etc: *She likes a hot bath **last thing at night**.*

12 first thing at the beginning of a day, morning, afternoon etc: *Jean liked to go for a swim **first thing in the morning**.*

13 among other things used when you are giving one fact, reason, effect etc but want to suggest that there are many others: *The substance is used in the manufacture of cosmetics and drugs, among other things.*

14 for one thing used to give one reason for something: *Well, for one thing, it's too big.* | *He's not that wonderful. He's bad-tempered for one thing.*

15 be a thing of the past to no longer exist or happen: *Before AIDS, many health care experts believed that large-scale infectious diseases were a thing of the past.*

16 it's a good thing (that) *spoken* used to say that it is lucky or good that something has happened: *It's a good thing we brought some food with us.*

17 sth is just one of those things used to say that something unpleasant or unlucky cannot be prevented: *It wasn't really the driver's fault; it was just one of those things.*

18 the thing about/with sb/sth used to say what the problem with someone or something is: *The thing about talk shows is that you never know how they will turn out.*

19 all (other) things being equal used to say that something is true in general, but that other things may cause the situation to change: *All things being equal, smaller animals need smaller brains.*

20 just the thing/the very thing exactly the thing that you want or that is necessary: *A holiday is probably just the thing for you.*

21 of all things used to show that you are surprised or shocked by something that someone has done or said: *She gave up a promising career as a stockbroker to become a weaver, of all things.*

22 do your own thing *informal* to do something in the way that you like instead of copying other people or following strict rules: *I just want to live my own life and do my own thing.*

23 it's a girl/football/music etc thing *informal* used to say that something involves or affects a particular group of people only: *Computer games aren't just a guy thing.*

24 all things considered when you consider all the parts or events of a situation: *All things considered, we had surprisingly few injuries.*

25 be all things to all men/people to try to please or be useful to all of many different groups, often without succeeding: *In order to get votes, he tries to be all things to all men.*

26 be onto a good thing *informal* if you are onto a good thing, you are in a situation that is very helpful, comfortable, or profitable for you: **think/know you are onto a good thing** *Directors who take dividends instead of salary may think they are onto a good thing but could have problems on retirement.*

27 make a big thing of/about/out of sth to make something seem more important than it really is: *You can apologise without making a big thing out of it.*

28 the done thing *BrE old-fashioned informal* the way of behaving or doing something that is socially acceptable: ***It is not the done thing** for teachers to hit children.*

29 it's one thing to ..., (it's) another thing to ..., used to say that doing one thing is very different from doing another thing, especially where the second thing is more difficult, important, or serious: *It's one thing being able to run fast, but quite another to win a marathon.*

30 what with one thing and another *BrE spoken* used to explain that you have had a lot of work, problems, or jobs that you had to do: *I've been so busy these last few days, what with one thing and another.*

31 have a thing about sb/sth *informal* to like or dislike someone or something very much, often without a good reason: *She's always had a thing about Peter.*

32 one thing leads to another used to explain how a series of events caused something to happen without giving any details: *One thing led to another and, before I knew it, I had invited her family to stay.*

33 the (latest) thing *informal* something that is popular or fashionable at the moment: *When Amelia bought a new car it had to be the latest thing.*

34 (do/try) the ... thing *AmE spoken* used to talk about an activity and everything that is involved with it: *Jody tried the college thing but finally dropped out.*

35 there's only one thing for it *BrE spoken* used to say that there is only one action that you can take: *There's only one thing for it. We'll have to call the police.*

36 one (damn/damned) thing after another used to say that a lot of unpleasant or unlucky things keep happening to you

37 taking one thing with another *BrE* considering all the facts

38 do things to sb to have a strong effect on someone → **amount/come to the same thing** at SAME[1](4), → **the best thing since sliced bread** at SLICE[2](4), → **first things first** at FIRST[1](7), → **living things** at LIVING[1](1), → **be hearing things** at HEAR(10), → **be seeing things** at SEE[1](27)

THESAURUS

thing used when you do not need to say the name, or when you do not know the name: *What's that thing on the kitchen table?* | *Have you got all your things?*

something a thing – used when you are not sure what the thing is: *There's something on your shirt.*

object *especially written* a solid thing: *a sharp metal object*

item *formal* a particular kind of thing, or one of a group of things: *household items* | *a luxury item* | *an*

item of equipment | *The items included pieces of old pottery.*
article *formal* a particular kind of thing, or one of a group of things. **Article** is very formal, and is used especially in the phrase **an article of clothing**: *They found several articles of clothing in the bushes.* | *suspicious articles*
artifact (*also* **artefact**) *formal* an object that someone has made, especially one that is very old and has historical value: *The museum has a collection of early Roman artifacts.*
thingy (*also* **thingamajig/thingamabob**) *spoken informal* a thing – used especially when you cannot remember the name of the thing, but often the other person knows what you are talking about: *Can you pass me the thingy?*

thing·a·ma·jig /ˈθɪŋəmədʒɪɡ/ (*also* **thing·a·ma·bob** /ˈθɪŋəməbɒb $ -bɑːb/), **thing·y** /ˈθɪŋi/ *n* [C] *spoken* **1** used when you cannot remember or do not know the name of the thing you want to mention: *What do you call that thingamajig? You know – the circle with the line through it.* **2** *BrE* used when you cannot remember or do not know the name of the person you want to mention: *Is thingy going?*

think[1] /θɪŋk/ ●●● S1 W1 *v* (*past tense and past participle* **thought** /θɔːt $ θɒːt/)
1 OPINION/BELIEF [T] to have a particular opinion or to believe that something is true: **think (that)** *I think that you're being unfair.* | *I thought I heard something.* | *He didn't think anyone would believe him.* | *Do you think I should call him?* | *For some reason, I keep thinking it's Friday today.* | *The recession lasted longer than anyone thought it would.* | ***Am I right in thinking that** you have a brother?* | ***I can't help thinking** that he's made a mistake.* | *Do you **honestly think** I would do something so stupid?* | **what do you think of/about sb/sth?** (=used to ask someone for their opinion) *What do you think of your new school?* | **think it necessary/possible/best etc** (=believe it is necessary, possible etc) *I thought it best to call first.* | *I thought it appropriate to invite her to speak at the meeting.* | *We must start **thinking in terms of** reducing costs.* | **be thought to be (doing) sth** (=be believed to be (doing) something) *Fraud is thought to be costing software companies millions of dollars a year.* → see Thesaurus box on *p. 1908*
2 USE YOUR MIND [I,T] to use your mind to decide about something, form an opinion, imagine something etc: *She thought very carefully before answering.* | *Wait a minute – I'm thinking.* | **[+about/of]** *She lay awake thinking about the money.* | **think what/how/when etc** *I can't think what else we could have done.* | **think (long and) hard** (=think for a long time) *She thought very hard before deciding to leave her job.* | *Holmes sat **thinking deeply*** (=thinking in a serious and careful way). | **I dread/shudder/hate to think** (=I do not want to think about something because it will be unpleasant) *I dread to think how much this call is going to cost.*
3 HAVE AN IDEA [T] to have words or ideas in your mind without telling them to anyone: *'How strange!' he thought.* | *'I don't care!' she **thought to herself**.* | *It was impossible to know what he was thinking.* | **think what/how/when etc** *I was just thinking what a lovely time we had yesterday.*
4 REMEMBER [T] to remember something: **think where/what etc** *He was trying to think where he'd seen her before.* | *I couldn't think where I'd left my keys.*
5 CONSIDER SB/STH [I,T] to consider that someone or something is a particular thing or has a particular quality: **think of sb/sth as sth** *Peter had always thought of Kate as someone to be avoided.* | *I want you to think of this as your home.* | **think of yourself as sth** *I've always thought of myself as a sensible person.* | **think sb (to be) sth** *My parents never thought me capable of doing a degree.* | *We have good reason to **think kindly of*** (=consider in an approving way) *a school that has provided all our children with an excellent education.*
6 think of/about doing sth to consider the possibility of doing something: *I had never thought of becoming an actor.* | *We did think about moving to Tokyo.* | ***Don't even think about** calling him* (=used to tell someone strongly not to do something).
7 think twice to think very carefully before deciding to do something, because you know about the dangers or problems: *A visible alarm makes burglars think twice.* | **[+about]** *A previous divorce can make you think twice about getting married again.* | **think twice before doing sth/before you do sth** *I'd think twice before taking out such a large loan.*
8 think again to think carefully about a plan, decision, idea etc, especially with the result that you change your mind or do something differently: *If you think car crime can't happen to you, think again.* | **[+about]** *Universities may be forced to think again about the courses they provide.*

SPOKEN PHRASES
9 I think used when you are saying that you believe something is true, although you are not sure: *Mary is in the garden, I think.* | *I don't think Ray will mind.* | *'Do you understand what I mean?' 'Yes, **I think so**.'* | *'Haven't we met before?' '**I don't think so**.'* | *I thought he was honest, but I was wrong.*
10 I think I'll ... used to say what you will probably do: *I think I'll go to bed early tonight.*
11 I thought (that) used when you are politely suggesting something to do: *I thought we'd go swimming tomorrow.* | *I thought we could meet for lunch.*
12 I would think (*also* **I would have thought**, **I should think/I should have thought** *BrE*) used when you are saying that you believe something is probably true: *We'll need about 10 bottles of wine, I should think.* | *I would have thought it would be better to wait a while.*
13 you would have thought (that) (*also* **you would think (that)**) used to say that you expect something to be true, although it is not: *You would have thought the school would do more to help a child like Craig.*
14 do you think (that) ... ? a) used when you are asking someone politely to do something for you: *Do you think you could help me move these boxes?* **b)** used to ask someone's opinion: *Do you think I need to bring a jacket?*
15 who/what etc do you think? a) used to ask someone's opinion: *Who do you think will win?* **b)** used when asking someone angrily about something: *Where do you think you're going?*
16 I think not *formal* used to say that you strongly believe something is not true or that you disagree with someone: *This could be a coincidence, but I think not.*
17 (just) think used to ask someone to imagine or consider something: *Just think – we could be millionaires!* | **[+of]** *It would be lovely, but think of the expense!* | **just think what/how etc** *Just think what could have happened.*
18 (now I) come to think of it used to mention something you have just realized or remembered: *'Were there any letters for me?' 'Yes there were, come to think of it.'*
19 I wasn't thinking (*also* **I didn't think**) used as a way of saying you are sorry because you have upset someone: *Sorry, I shouldn't have said that. I wasn't thinking.*
20 to think (that) ... ! used to show that you are very surprised about something: *To think we lived next door to him and never knew what he was doing!*
21 if you think ..., you've got another think coming! used to tell someone that if they think someone is going to do something, they are wrong: *If you think I'm going to wait for you, you've got another think coming!*
22 that's what you/they etc think! used to say that you strongly disagree with someone
23 who would have thought? used to say that something is very surprising: *Who would have thought she'd end up dancing for a living?*
24 I thought as much used to say that you are not surprised by something someone tells you: *'Andy failed his driving test.' 'I thought as much when I saw his face.'*
25 I should have thought ... *BrE* used as a polite or joking way of showing that you disagree with what someone has said or think it is silly: *'Why isn't it working?' 'I should have thought it was obvious.'*

T

26 think better of it to not do something that you had planned to do, because you realize that it is not a good idea: *He started to say something, then thought better of it.*
27 think nothing of doing sth to think that a particular activity is normal or easy, even though other people think it is unusual or difficult: *He thinks nothing of staying up all night in casinos.*
28 think nothing of sth to think that something is not important and then realize later that it is important: *I had a pain in my back but **thought nothing of it** at the time.*
29 not think to do sth to not consider doing something, especially when you later wish you had done it: *I didn't think to question the treatment I was given.* | *I never thought to ask him for his address.*
30 think for yourself to have ideas and thoughts of your own rather than believing what other people say: *Parents have to teach their children to think for themselves.*
31 think aloud (*also* **think out loud**) to say what you are thinking, without talking to anyone in particular: *Oh, sorry. I was thinking aloud.*
32 think straight [usually in negatives] to think clearly: *I'm so nervous I can't think straight.* | *How can I think straight with you talking all the time?*
33 not think much of sb/sth to not like someone or something very much: *I didn't think much of his new girlfriend.*
34 think highly of sb/sth (*also* **think a lot of sb/sth**) to admire or respect someone or something: *Your boss must think highly of you if she gives you so much responsibility.*
35 think the world of sb *informal* to like or love someone very much: *The children think the world of her.*
36 think badly of sb (*also* **think less of sb**) *formal* to disapprove of someone or what they have done: *Please don't think badly of me.* | **[+for]** *Do you think less of me for agreeing to do it?*
37 think the best/worst of sb to consider someone's behaviour in a way that makes them seem as good as possible or as bad as possible: *He's determined to think the worst of me.*
38 think big *informal* to plan to do things that are difficult, but will be very impressive, make a lot of profit etc: *The company is thinking big.*
39 think outside the box to think of new, different, or unusual ways of doing something, especially in business
40 think positive/positively to believe that you are going to be successful or that good things are going to happen: *You have to think positive if you're going to be successful in this game.*
41 think on your feet to think of ideas and make decisions very quickly: *In this job you need to be able to think on your feet.*
42 think to do sth *literary* to try to do something: *They had thought to deceive me.*
43 anyone would think (that) used to say that someone behaves as if a particular thing were true, although it is not: *Anyone would think he owns the place, the way he talks!*
→ **can't hear yourself think** at **HEAR(12)**

GRAMMAR

Using the progressive

• When **think** means 'believe', it is not normally used in the progressive. You say: *I think you look nice.* ✗ Don't say: *I am thinking you look nice.*
• In spoken English, people sometimes say **I'm thinking** to describe their present thoughts about something that is happening right now: *I'm thinking we should leave.*

Using the passive

In more formal English, you can say **it is thought that** something is true: *It is thought that as many as a billion people are learning English.*
GRAMMAR GUIDE ▸ **VERBS**

think back *phr v* to think about things that happened in the past: *Thinking back, it amazes me how we survived on so little sleep.* | **[+to/over/on]** *He thought back to the day he'd first met Sophie.*
think of sb/sth *phr v*
1 to produce an idea, name, suggestion etc by thinking: *They're still trying to think of a name for the baby.* | *Can you think of any other way to do it?*
2 to remember something: *I can't think of the name of the hotel we stayed in.*
3 to behave in a way that shows that you want to treat other people well: *It was very good of you to think of me.* | *He's always thinking of other people.*
4 think only of yourself to only do things that are good for you and not think about what other people want – used

THESAURUS: think

TO HAVE A PARTICULAR OPINION

think: *I think you're right.* | *She didn't think that the film was very good.*
believe to have an opinion that you are sure is right, especially about an important subject such as politics or religion: *The protestors believe that it is wrong to experiment on animals.* | *Do you really believe that the only solution to violence is more violence?*
feel to have a particular opinion, especially one that is based on your feelings, not on facts: *She feels that there is no alternative.* | *I just felt that it was the right thing to do.*
take the view that *formal* to have a particular opinion: *The court took the view that the company had acted unreasonably.* | *The college takes the view that smoking in the workplace is a fire risk.*

TO THINK ABOUT SOMETHING

think to use your mind to decide about something, form an opinion, imagine something etc: *I've been thinking about what you said – maybe you're right.* | *I need some time to think.*
consider to think about something carefully before deciding what to do: *Have you considered working for a year before going to college?*
weigh (*also* **weigh up** *BrE*) to carefully think about a plan or choice by comparing all the advantages and disadvantages involved: *You need to **weigh up the pros and cons*** (=the advantages and disadvantages)*, and decide which investment is the best one for you.* | *The committee are still weighing the alternatives.*
give sth some/a lot of thought to think carefully about something, before you make a final decision about it: *Why don't you give it some thought and then get back to me?* | *He had obviously given the matter a lot of thought.*
mull sth over to think about a problem, plan etc before making a decision: *Can you give me a bit of time to mull it over?*
ponder to spend time thinking carefully and seriously about something, especially a problem or something complicated: *She is still pondering what to do.* | *Officials are pondering ways to remove the oil from the beaches.*
contemplate to think about something you might do in the future: *Did you ever contemplate resigning?*
reflect *formal* to think carefully about something, especially something that happened in the past: *It was a good time to reflect upon the changes that had happened in my life.*

TO KEEP THINKING ABOUT SOMETHING

brood to keep thinking for a long time about something that worries you or that makes you angry or upset: *There's no point brooding over things you can't change.*
dwell on sth to spend too much time thinking about something sad or unpleasant: *I try to enjoy my life today and not dwell on the past.*

to show disapproval: *She's a spoiled child who thinks only of herself.*
5 be thinking of sb used to say that you care about and feel sympathy for someone who is in a difficult situation: *Take care! I'll be thinking of you.*
think sth ↔ **out** *phr v* to think about all the parts of something carefully before deciding or planning exactly what to do: *He went for a walk to* ***think things out***. | *The proposal needs to be carefully thought out.* | **think out what/how/whether etc** *She had thought out what she was going to say.*
think sth ↔ **over** *phr v* to consider something carefully before making a decision: *I've been thinking over your suggestion.* | *Why don't you* ***think it over*** *and give me a call in a couple of days?* | *I want some more time to* ***think things over***.
think sth ↔ **through** *phr v* to think carefully about the possible results of something: *The policy has not been thought through properly.* | *It's my fault. I didn't* ***think it through***. | *I need time to* ***think things through***. | **think through what/how** *People need time to think through what the changes will mean for them.*
think sth ↔ **up** *phr v* to produce a new idea, name etc by thinking: *She was trying to think up an excuse.* | *Did you think that up yourself?* | *Who thinks up names for new products?*
think² *n* **have a think** *BrE* to think about a problem or question: *I'll have a think and let you know.*
think·a·ble /ˈθɪŋkəbəl/ *adj* [not before noun] able to be thought about or considered SYN **possible**: *At that time, it would not have been thinkable to openly criticize the government.*
think·er /ˈθɪŋkə $ -ər/ ●○○ *n* [C]
1 someone who thinks carefully about important subjects such as science or PHILOSOPHY, especially someone who is famous for thinking of new ideas: *great thinkers such as Kant and Schopenhauer*
2 an independent/positive/free etc thinker a person who thinks in a particular way
think·ing¹ /ˈθɪŋkɪŋ/ ●●○ *n* [U]
1 your opinion or ideas about something, or your attitude towards it: *The Administration's thinking changed as the war progressed.* | *Well,* ***to my way of thinking*** (=in my opinion), *they should have done that years ago.* | *He laughed and accused me of* ***wishful thinking*** (=falsely believing that something will happen just because I want it to). | *the rich countries'* ***current thinking*** *on aid* | **[+behind]** *the thinking behind the company's new public relations campaign*
2 when you think about something: *If it weren't for Jeff's* ***quick thinking****, Tillie could have been badly hurt.* | *I really needed to* ***do*** *some* ***thinking***. | **clear/critical/analytical etc thinking** (=a particular way of thinking about things)
3 put on your thinking cap *informal* to try to think seriously about a problem in order to solve it → LATERAL THINKING
thinking² *adj* [only before noun] **1** a thinking person is intelligent and tries to think carefully about important subjects **2 the thinking man's/woman's etc sth** used to say that someone or something is liked by intelligent people: *the thinking man's pop band*
ˈthink tank *n* [C] a group of people with experience or knowledge of a particular subject, who work to produce ideas and give advice: **right-wing/liberal/economic etc think tank** *a leading member of a Tory think tank*

GRAMMAR: Singular or plural verb?
• **Think tank** is usually followed by a singular verb: *The think tank* ***has*** *suggested some major reforms.*
• In British English, you can also use a plural verb: *The think tank* ***have*** *suggested some major reforms.*
GRAMMAR GUIDE ▸ NOUNS

thin·ly /ˈθɪnli/ ●●○ *adv*
1 in a way that has a very small distance between two sides or two flat surfaces OPP **thickly**: *thinly sliced bread*
2 scattered or spread over a large area, with a lot of space in between: *Sow the radish seeds thinly.* | *The mountain regions are more* ***thinly populated*** *than the lowlands.*
3 thinly disguised/veiled if something is thinly disguised etc, someone is pretending it is something else, but you can easily see what it really is: *He looked at Frank's new car with thinly veiled envy.*
thin·ner /ˈθɪnə $ -ər/ *n* [U] a liquid such as TURPENTINE that you add to paint to make it less thick
thin·ning /ˈθɪnɪŋ/ *adj* someone with thinning hair is losing their hair
ˌthin-ˈskinned *adj* too easily offended or upset by criticism OPP **thick-skinned**
third¹ /θɜːd $ θɜːrd/ ●●● W2 S2 *adj*
1 coming after two other things in a series: *in the third century* | *her third birthday*
2 third time lucky *BrE*, **(the) third time's the charm** *AmE spoken* used when you have failed to do something twice and hope to be successful the third time —**third** *pron*: *I'm planning to leave on* ***the third*** (=the third day of the month). —**thirdly** *adv*
third² ●●● W3 *n* [C]
1 one of three equal parts of something: *Divide it into thirds.* | **[+of]** ***A third*** *of these jobs are held by women.* | **one-third/two-thirds** *Two-thirds of the profits are given to charities.*
2 the lowest type of degree that is given by a British university
ˌthird ˈclass *n* [U] **1** a cheap class of mail in the US, usually used for sending advertisements **2** the lowest type of degree that is given by a British university **3** *old-fashioned* the cheapest and least comfortable part of a train or ship —**third-class** *adj, adv*: *We travelled third-class.* → FIRST CLASS, SECOND CLASS
ˌthird deˈgree *n* **give sb the third degree** *informal* to ask someone a lot of questions in order to get information from them: *I got home after midnight and Dad gave me the third degree.*
ˈthird-degree *adj* [always before noun] **1 third-degree burn** [usually plural] the most serious kind of burn, that goes right through your skin **2 third-degree murder/burglary/assault etc** *AmE* murder etc that is considered by a court to be the least serious of three different kinds
ˌthird ˈparty¹ *n* [C] *law* someone who is not one of the two main people involved in an agreement or legal case, but who is affected by it or involved in it in some way
ˌthird ˈparty² *adj* **third party insurance/cover/policy** insurance that pays money to someone who is hurt or whose property is damaged by something that you have done: *Does third party insurance cover (=pay for) this type of damage?* → COMPREHENSIVE
ˌthird ˈperson *n* **1 the third person** a form of a verb or PRONOUN that is used for showing the person, thing or group that is being mentioned. 'He', 'she', 'it', and 'they' are third person pronouns. **2 in the third person** a story written in the third person is told as the experience of someone else, using the pronouns 'he', 'she', or 'they' → FIRST PERSON, SECOND PERSON
ˌthird-ˈrate *adj* of very bad quality: *a third-rate hotel*
ˌthird ˈsector *n* **the third sector** organizations such as CHARITIES and VOLUNTARY organizations which do not have making a profit as their aim → **private sector**, **public sector**
ˌThird ˈWorld *noun* **the Third World** countries that are poor and have little industrial development. This phrase can cause offence and people now usually say 'developing countries'. —**Third World** *adj*: *Third World debt*
thirst¹ /θɜːst $ θɜːrst/ ●●○ *n*
1 [singular] the feeling of wanting or needing a drink → **thirsty**, **hunger**: *Ice water is the only thing that really* ***quenches*** *my* ***thirst*** (=gets rid of it). | *We had* ***worked up a thirst*** (=done something that made us thirsty), *and so we decided to stop for a beer.* | *Maggie woke up with a* ***raging thirst*** (=an extremely strong thirst).
2 [U] the state of not having enough to drink: *Many of the animals had* ***died of thirst***.
3 a thirst for knowledge/education/information etc *literary* a

strong desire for knowledge etc: *the thirst for knowledge in Renaissance Italy*

thirst² *v* [I] *old use* to be thirsty

thirst for/after sth *phr v literary* to want something very much: *young men thirsting for adventure*

thirst·y /ˈθɜːsti $ ˈθɜːr-/ ●●● S3 *adj* (*comparative* **thirstier**, *superlative* **thirstiest**)
1 feeling that you want or need a drink → **thirst**, **hungry**: *Can I have a glass of water? I'm really thirsty.* | *He'd been working in the garden and was very hot and thirsty.* | *All this digging is* **thirsty work** (=work that makes you want a drink).
2 *literary* having a strong desire for something: **[+for]** *a generation thirsty for change*
3 fields or plants that are thirsty need water —**thirstily** *adv*

thir·teen /ˌθɜːˈtiːn◂ $ ˌθɜːr-/ ●●● S3 W3 *number* the number 13: *They've only sold thirteen tickets so far.* | *When it happened, I was thirteen* (=13 years old). —**thirteenth** *adj, pron*: *It's Roberto's thirteenth birthday.* | *the thirteenth century*

thir·ty /ˈθɜːti $ ˈθɜːrti/ ●●● S3 W3 *number*
1 the number 30
2 the thirties (*also* **the '30s, the 1930s**) [plural] the years from 1930 to 1939: *In the thirties, air travel really began to take off.* | **the early/mid/late thirties** *The family sold the house in the early thirties.*
3 be in your thirties to be aged between 30 and 39: **early/mid/late thirties** *She must be in her early thirties by now.*
4 in the thirties if the temperature is in the thirties, it is between 30 degrees and 39 degrees: **in the low/mid/high thirties** *a hot day, with temperatures in the low thirties* —**thirtieth** *adj, pron*: *her thirtieth birthday*

thir·ty·some·thing /ˈθɜːtiˌsʌmθɪŋ $ ˈθɜːr-/ *n* [C] *informal* someone between the age of 30 and 39: *a new magazine aimed at thirtysomethings* —**thirtysomething** *adj*

this¹ /ðɪs/ ●●● S1 W1 *determiner, pron* (*plural* **these** /ðiːz/)
1 used to refer to a person, thing, idea etc that has just been mentioned or to something that has just happened: *We must make sure this doesn't happen again.* | *Is there any way of solving these problems?* | *If young Daly continues to improve at this rate, he'll soon be in the A Team.* | *This will be discussed in the next chapter.* | *This boyfriend of yours - how old is he?*
2 used to talk about the present time or a time that is close to the present: *There will be another meeting later this week.* | *This has been the worst year of my life.* | *I thought he would have been back before this.* | *We'll be seeing Malcolm this Friday* (=on Friday of the present week). | *I'm sorry I was late this morning* (=today in the morning). | *Everyone seems to be in a hurry* **these days** (=at the present period). | *I want to see you in my office* **this minute** (=immediately).
3 used to talk about the present situation: *I hate this cold damp weather.* | *Things have never been as bad as this before.*

SPOKEN PHRASES
4 used to talk about a thing or person that is near you, the thing you are holding, or the place where you are: *These are your gloves, aren't they?* | *You have to park on this side of the road.* | *I can't bear the atmosphere in this house much longer.*
5 used to refer to something that you are going to say or that is just about to happen: *Now, listen to this.* | *Wait till you hear this joke.* | *This is going to surprise you.*
6 used in stories, jokes etc when you mention a person or thing for the first time: *I met this really weird guy last night.* | *Suddenly, there was this tremendous bang.*
7 a) used to introduce someone to someone else: *Sam, this is my sister, Liz.* **b)** used to give your name when you are speaking on the telephone: *'Can I speak to Joan, please?' 'This is Joan speaking.'*
8 this, that, and the other (*also* **this and that**) various different things, subjects etc: *'What have you two been gossiping about all evening?' 'Oh this, that, and the other.'*
9 what's (all) this? used to ask what is happening, what people are saying, what someone's problem is etc: *What's this? Crying again?* | *What's all this about a ghost?*
10 this is it used to say that something you expected to happen is actually going to happen: *This is it, boys, the moment we've been waiting for.*

this² ●●● S1 *adv* [+adj/adv]
1 *spoken* used to say how big, how much etc, when you are showing the size, amount etc with your hands: *The table's about this high and this wide.* | *You need to cut about this much off the end of the pipe.*
2 [usually in questions and negatives] *spoken* as good, bad, much etc as in the present situation: *I hadn't realised that things had got this bad.* | *I've never had this much money before.*

this·tle /ˈθɪsəl/ *n* [C,U] a wild plant which has leaves with sharp points and purple or white furry flowers → see picture at FLOWER¹

this·tle·down /ˈθɪsəldaʊn/ *n* [U] the soft feathery substance fastened to thistle seeds that helps them to float in the air

thith·er /ˈðɪðə $ ˈθɪðər/ *adv old use* in that direction

tho' /ðəʊ $ ðoʊ/ *adv informal* a short form of 'though'

thong /θɒŋ $ θɒːŋ/ *n* [C] **1** a long thin piece of leather used to fasten something or as part of a whip **2** [usually plural] *AmE* a type of shoe that covers the bottom of your foot, with a STRAP that goes between your toes to hold it on your foot as you walk SYN **flip-flops** → see picture at SHOE¹ **3** a piece of underwear or the bottom half of a BIKINI that has a single string instead of the back part

tho·rax /ˈθɔːræks/ *n* (*plural* **thoraxes** *or* **thoraces** /-rəsiːz/) [C] **1** *technical* the part of your body between your neck and DIAPHRAGM (=area just above your stomach) **2** the part of an insect's body between its head and its ABDOMEN —**thoracic** /θɔːˈræsɪk/ *adj* → see picture at INSECT

thorn /θɔːn $ θɔːrn/ ●○○ *n*
1 [C] a sharp point that grows on the stem of a plant such as a rose
2 [C,U] a bush or tree that has thorns: *a long, low hedge of thorns*
3 a thorn in sb's side someone or something that annoys you or causes problems for a long period of time: *He's been a thorn in the side of the party leadership for years.*

thorn·y /ˈθɔːni $ ˈθɔːrni/ *adj* **1 a thorny question/problem/issue etc** a question etc that is complicated and difficult: *the thorny question of immigration policy* **2** a thorny bush, plant etc has thorns —**thorniness** *n* [U]

thor·ough /ˈθʌrə $ ˈθʌroʊ, ˈθʌrə/ ●●○ *adj*
1 including every possible detail → **thoroughly**: *The doctor gave him a thorough check-up.* | *a thorough and detailed biography* | *The police investigation was very thorough.* | *thorough notes of the meeting*
2 [not usually before noun] careful to do things properly so that you avoid mistakes: *The screening of applicants must be thorough.* **THESAURUS** CAREFUL
3 a thorough pest/nuisance/mess *BrE* used to emphasize the bad qualities of someone or something —**thoroughness** *n* [U]

thor·ough·bred /ˈθʌrəbred $ ˈθʌroʊ-, ˈθʌrə-/ *n* [C] **1** a horse that has parents of the same very good breed: *a thoroughbred stallion* **2** *especially BrE* someone who seems to do something naturally to a very high standard: *football thoroughbred Mick Jones* —**thoroughbred** *adj*

thor·ough·fare /ˈθʌrəfeə $ ˈθʌroʊfer, ˈθʌrə-/ *n* **1** [C] the main road through a place such as a city or village: *The motel was off the* **main thoroughfare**. **2 no thoroughfare** *BrE* a written sign used to tell people that they cannot go on a particular road or path

thor·ough·go·ing /ˌθʌrəˈgəʊɪŋ◂ $ -ˈgoʊ-/ *adj formal* **1** very thorough and careful: *a thoroughgoing analysis of the data* **2** [only before noun] a thoroughgoing action or quality is complete: *The programme has been a thoroughgoing success.*

thor·ough·ly /ˈθʌrəli $ ˈθʌroʊli,ˈθʌrə-/ ●●○ *adv*
1 completely: *She sat feeling thoroughly miserable.* | *thoroughly cooked meat*
2 carefully, so that nothing is forgotten: *The room had been thoroughly cleaned.*

those /ðəʊz $ ðoʊz/ the plural of THAT

thou¹ /θaʊ/ *number spoken* a thousand or a thousandth: *They paid about sixty-nine thou for it.*

thou² /ðaʊ/ *pron old use* a word meaning 'you', used as the subject of a sentence → **HOLIER-THAN-THOU**

though¹ /ðəʊ $ ðoʊ/ ●●● S1 W1 *conjunction*
1 used to introduce a statement that makes the main statement coming after it seem surprising, unlikely, or unexpected SYN **although**: *Though she's almost 40, she still plans to compete.* | *Pascal went ahead with the experiment* ***even though*** *he knew it was dangerous.* | **though old/tired etc** *The rooms, though small, were pleasant and airy.* | **old though it is/tired though he was etc** *Strange though it may seem, I like housework.*
2 used like 'but' to add a fact or opinion that makes what you have just said seem less definite, less important etc: *I thought he'd been drinking, though I wasn't completely sure.* | *The offenders were dealt with firmly though fairly.*
3 as though a) in a way that makes you think something is true SYN **as if**: *It looks as though everyone else has gone home.* **b)** in a way that might make you think something was true, although you know it is not true SYN **as if**: *She stared at me as though I were a complete stranger.*

though² ●●● S1 *adv spoken* used after adding a fact, opinion, or question which seems surprising after what you have just said, or which makes what you have just said seem less true: *Two heart attacks in a year. It hasn't stopped him smoking, though.* | *It sounds like a lot of fun. Isn't it rather risky though?*

thought¹ /θɔːt $ θɒːt/ the past tense and past participle of THINK¹

thought² ●●● S1 W1 *n*
1 STH YOU THINK ABOUT [C] something that you think of, remember, or realize SYN **idea**: *It's an interesting thought.* | ***The thought that*** *I might not have a job next year is a bit troubling.* THESAURUS ▸ **IDEA**
2 IDEAS/OPINIONS **thoughts** [plural] a person's ideas or opinions about something: *What are your thoughts, Michael?* | **[+on]** *Any thoughts on how we should spend the money?*
3 CAREFUL CONSIDERATION [U] careful and serious consideration: *With more thought and care this would have been a first-class essay.* | **give sth thought/give thought to sth** (=think carefully about something) *I've been giving your proposal a lot of thought.* | *Have you given any more thought to going back to school?*
4 ACT OF THINKING [U] the act or process of thinking: **lost/deep in thought** (=thinking so much that you do not notice what is happening around you) *Derek was staring out of the window, lost in thought.* | *Piaget's research focused on children's* ***thought processes*** (=the way their minds work).
5 CARING ABOUT STH [C,U] a feeling of worrying or caring about something: **[+for]** *He went back into the burning building with no thought for his own safety.* | *Have you no thought for anyone but yourself?* | *You are always* ***in my thoughts*** (=used to tell someone that you think and care about them a lot).
6 INTENTION [C,U] intention or hope of doing something: **thought of doing sth** *I had no thought of gaining any personal advantage.* | *Lucy* ***gave up all thought of*** *finishing the essay that day.*
7 WAY OF THINKING [U] a way of thinking that is typical of a particular group, period of history etc: **ancient Greek/feminist/18th-century etc thought** *Kant's ideas had a strong influence on political thought.*
8 spare a thought for sb *BrE* used to tell someone that they should think about someone who is in a worse situation than they are: *Spare a thought for those who don't have enough to eat.*
9 it's just a thought *spoken* used to say that what you have just said is only a suggestion and you have not thought about it very much: *It was just a thought, Duncan. I didn't mean any offence.*
10 it's/that's a thought! *spoken* used to say that someone has made a good suggestion: *'Why don't you ask Walter?' 'That's a thought! I'll phone him right away.'*
11 don't give it another thought *spoken* used to tell someone not to worry after they have told you they are sorry
12 it's the thought that counts *spoken* used to say that you are grateful for a gift from someone even though it is small or unimportant → **perish the thought!** at PERISH(3), → **on second thoughts** at SECOND¹(8), → **school of thought** at SCHOOL¹(8)

COLLOCATIONS

VERBS

have a thought *I just had a funny thought.*
express your thoughts (=say what they are or tell other people about them) *He was finding it difficult to express his thoughts.*
a thought occurs to/comes to/strikes sb (=someone suddenly has a thought) *The thought occurred to him that she might be lying.*
a thought crosses sb's mind (=someone has a thought) *The thought never crossed my mind that I could be wrong.*
can't bear the thought of sth *I can't bear the thought of you being hurt.*
sb's thoughts turn to sth (=they start thinking about something) *As summer approaches, people's thoughts turn to holidays.*

ADJECTIVES

sb's first thought *My first thought was that a bomb had gone off.*
a passing thought (=a quick, not very serious thought) *He never gives his appearance more than a passing thought.*
a sobering thought (=one that makes you feel serious) *We have the power to destroy the world, which is a sobering thought.*
a comforting thought | **a sudden thought**

PHRASES

the very thought (=even the idea of doing something) *The very thought of going on stage made her feel ill.*

thought·ful /ˈθɔːtfəl $ ˈθɒːt-/ ●○○ *adj*
1 always thinking of the things you can do to make people happy or comfortable OPP **thoughtless**: *Paul is very thoughtful.* | **it is thoughtful of sb to do sth** *It was really thoughtful of you to remember my birthday.* THESAURUS ▸ **KIND**
2 serious and quiet because you are thinking a lot: *a* ***thoughtful look*** | *a* ***thoughtful silence***
3 well planned and carefully thought about: *a thoughtful analysis* —**thoughtfully** *adv* —**thoughtfulness** *n* [U]

thought·less /ˈθɔːtləs $ ˈθɒːt-/ ●○○ *adj* not thinking about the needs and feelings of other people, especially because you are thinking about what you want OPP **thoughtful**: *a selfish and thoughtless man* | **it is thoughtless of sb to do sth** *It was thoughtless of her not to tell you where she was going.* THESAURUS ▸ **UNKIND** —**thoughtlessly** *adv* —**thoughtlessness** *n* [U]

ˌthought-ˈout *adj* **carefully/well/badly thought-out** planned and organized carefully, well etc: *a carefully thought-out speech*

ˈThought Poˌlice, the the police organization in George Orwell's novel *Nineteen Eighty-Four* whose job is to control what people think and the way that they think. The expression 'thought police' is sometimes used for describing any group that tries to tell other people what opinions they should have or what words they should use.

T

ˈthought-proˌvoking *adj* making people think seriously about a particular subject SYN **stimulating**: *a thought-provoking article*

thou·sand /ˈθaʊzənd/ ●●● W3 *number* (*plural* **thousand** *or* **thousands**)
1 the number 1,000: *a journey of almost a thousand miles* | **two/three/four etc thousand** *five thousand dollars* | *The company employs thirty thousand people.*
2 an extremely large number of things or people: **a thousand** *I've been this route a thousand times before.* | **thousands of** *There are thousands of things I want to do.* —**thousandth** *adj*: *the thousandth anniversary of the founding of the city* —**thousandth** *n* [C]

thral·dom *BrE*, **thralldom** *AmE* /ˈθrɔːldəm $ ˈθrɒːl-/ *n* [U] *literary* the state of being a slave SYN **slavery**

thrall /θrɔːl $ θrɒːl/ *n* **in sb's/sth's thrall** (*also* **in thrall to sb/sth**) *literary* controlled or strongly influenced by someone or something: *We have a congress that is in thrall to special interest groups.*

thrash[1] /θræʃ/ *v* **1** [I always + adv/prep, T] to move or make something move from side to side in a violent or uncontrolled way: **[+about/around]** *The girl was thrashing about in the water.* | *Salmon thrash their tails and leap from the water.* **2** [T] to beat someone violently, especially in order to punish them: *My poor brother used to get thrashed for all kinds of minor offences.* **3** [T] *informal* to defeat someone very easily in a game: *Brazil thrashed Italy 5-0.*
THESAURUS ▸ BEAT

thrash sth ↔ **out** *phr v* to discuss something thoroughly with someone until you find an answer, reach an agreement, or decide on something: *We still have to get together and thrash out the details.*

thrash[2] *n* **1** [singular] a violent movement from side to side **2** [U] *informal* a type of loud fast ROCK music **3** [C] *BrE old-fashioned* a loud noisy party

thrash·ing /ˈθræʃɪŋ/ *n* [C] *especially BrE* **1** an occasion when you beat someone or are beaten violently as a punishment: *If you speak to your mother like that again, you'll* ***get*** *a* ***thrashing***. | *I'll* ***give*** *you the* ***thrashing*** *you deserve.* **2** *informal* an occasion when you defeat someone or are defeated very easily in a game: *The manager resigned after his team's 14-0 thrashing.*

T

thread[1] /θred/ ●●○ *n*
1 FOR SEWING [C,U] a long thin string of cotton, silk etc used to sew or weave cloth: *I'm looking for a needle and thread.* | *hand-sewn with gold and silver thread* | *a spool of thread* (=small object that thread is wound around) → see picture at ROPE[1]
2 IDEAS [singular] an idea, feeling, or feature that connects the different parts of an explanation, story etc: *a* ***common thread*** *running within his work* | *His mind wandered, and he* ***lost the thread*** *of what she was saying* (=was no longer able to understand it). | *a* ***thread running through*** *the film* | **[+of]** *a thread of spirituality in her work*
3 pick up the thread(s) to begin something again after a long period, especially a relationship or way of life: *They had known each other as children, and were picking up the threads of their friendship.*
4 INTERNET [C] a series of messages concerning the same subject, written by members of an Internet discussion group: *I'd like to refer to something that was posted in an earlier thread.*
5 LINE [C] *literary* a long thin line of something, such as light, smoke etc: **[+of]** *The Colorado River was just a thread of silver, 4,000 feet below.*
6 ON A SCREW [C] a continuous raised line of metal that winds around the curved surface of a screw
7 threads [plural] *AmE old-fashioned* clothes → **hang by a thread** at HANG[1](9)

thread[2] *v* [T usually + adv/prep] **1** to put a thread, string, rope etc through a hole: *Will you* ***thread*** *the* ***needle*** *for me?* | **thread sth through sth** *Tom threaded the rope through the safety harness.* **2** to put a film, tape etc correctly through parts of a camera, PROJECTOR, or TAPE RECORDER **3** to connect two or more objects by pushing something such as string through a hole in them: *Sue threaded the glass beads onto a piece of heavy string.* **4 thread your way through/into etc sth** to move through a place by carefully going around things that are blocking your way: *She came towards me, threading her way through the crowd.*

thread·bare /ˈθredbeə $ -ber/ *adj* **1** clothes, CARPETS etc that are threadbare are very thin and in bad condition because they have been used a lot: *a threadbare old sofa* **2 threadbare excuse/argument/joke etc** an excuse etc that is no longer effective because it has been used too much

threading /ˈθredɪŋ/ *n* [U] a way of removing hair from the face in which hairs are pulled out with a thread

threat /θret/ ●●● S3 W2 *n*
1 [C,U] a statement in which you tell someone that you will cause them harm or trouble if they do not do what you want: *Your threats don't scare me.* | **[+of]** *the threat of military invasion* | **[+from]** *He says his family received phone threats from the group.* | ***threats made against*** *his wife and children* | *Nichols never* ***carried out*** *his* ***threat*** *to resign.* | *The government will not* ***give in to*** *terrorist* ***threats***. | *She dismissed the statement as an* ***empty threat***. | *They warned him with* ***veiled threats*** *not to mention anything he had witnessed.* | *The police are investigating* ***death threats*** *made against the two men.* | *Officials at the school say they received a* ***bomb threat*** *at approximately 11:30 a.m. today.*
2 [C usually singular] the possibility that something very bad will happen: **[+of]** *the threat of famine* | **[+from]** *According to the Secretary of State, the Russians face no threat from an expanded NATO.* | **under threat** *The area remains under threat from commercial developers.* | **be under threat of closure/attack etc** (=be likely to be closed, attacked etc) *The program is under threat of closure due to lack of funding.*
3 [C usually singular] someone or something that is regarded as a possible danger: **[+to]** *The fighting is a major threat to stability in the region.* | **present/pose a threat (to sb/sth)** *Pollution poses a threat to fish.*

threat·en /ˈθretn/ ●●● S3 W2 *v*
1 [T] to say that you will cause someone harm or trouble if they do not do what you want: *Postal workers are threatening a strike if they don't receive a pay increase.* | **threaten to do sth** *He threatened to take them to court.* | **threaten sb with sth** *Doctors are sometimes threatened with violence if they don't do what patients want.* | **threaten (that)** *Then he became angry and threatened that he would go to the police.*
2 [T] to be likely to harm or destroy something: *Poaching threatens the survival of the rhino.* | **threaten to do sth** *The incident threatens to ruin his chances in the election.* | **be threatened with sth** *Large areas of the jungle are now threatened with destruction.*
3 [I,T] to be likely to happen or be in a bad situation: *Britain's fishing industry remains threatened.* | *Dark clouds threatened rain.*

threat·en·ing /ˈθretn-ɪŋ/ *adj* **1** if someone's behaviour is threatening, you believe they intend to harm you: *His voice sounded threatening.* | *a threatening gesture* **2** if the sky or clouds are threatening, bad weather is likely: *a threatening thundercloud* —**threateningly** *adv*

three /θriː/ ●●● S1 W2 *number*
1 the number 3: *They've won their last three games.* | *We'd better go. It's almost three* (=three o'clock). | *My little sister's only three* (=three years old).
2 in threes in groups of three people or things: *Teachers taking part will be asked to work in threes.* → THREESOME, THIRD[1]

ˌthree-ˈcornered *adj* [usually before noun] **1** having three corners **2 three-cornered contest/fight** *especially BrE* a competition which involves three people or groups

ˌthree-day eˈvent *n* [C] *BrE* a horse-riding competition that takes place for three days

ˌthree-diˈmensional ●○○ *adj*
1 having, or seeming to have, length, depth, and height → **two-dimensional**: *a three-dimensional structure* | *objects that are three-dimensional*

2 a three-dimensional character in a book, film etc seems like a real person → **one-dimensional**

three·fold /ˈθriːfəʊld $ -foʊld/ *adj* three times as much or as many: *a threefold increase in production* —**threefold** *adv*

three-leg·ged race /ˌθriː ˈlegəd reɪs/ *n* [C] a race in which two people run together, with one person's right leg tied to the other person's left leg

ˌthree-line ˈwhip *n* [C] *BrE* **1** an order from a leader of a British political party telling MPs in that party that they must vote in a particular way **2** *informal* a very firm instruction that people must come to a meeting or take part in an event

ˌThree Mile ˈIsland a place in Pennsylvania in the US, where there was a serious accident in 1979 in a NUCLEAR POWER station (=a place where electricity is produced using nuclear energy). The people in charge managed to prevent a MELTDOWN (= when the nuclear material melts and burns through its containers), but the accident increased opposition to nuclear power in the US and prevented new power stations from being built.

three·pence /ˈθrepəns, ˈθrʌ-/ *n* [U] *BrE old use* three old pence

three·pen·ny bit /ˌθrepəni ˈbɪt, ˌθrʌ-/ *n* [C] a small coin used in Britain before 1971 that was worth three old pence

ˌthree-piece ˈsuit *n* [C] a suit that consists of a JACKET, WAISTCOAT, and trousers made from the same material

ˌthree-piece ˈsuite *n* [C] *BrE* two chairs and a SOFA covered in the same material

ˈthree-ply *adj* three-ply wood, wool, TISSUE etc consists of three layers or threads

ˌthree-point ˈturn *n* [C] a way of turning your car so that it faces the opposite way, by driving forwards, backwards, and then forwards again while turning

three-ˈquarter *adj* [only before noun] three quarters of the full size, length etc of something: *a three-quarter violin* | *a* ***three-quarter length*** *coat*

three-ˈquarters *n* [plural] an amount equal to three of the four equal parts that make up a whole: **[+of]** *three-quarters of an hour*

three·quel /ˈθriːkwəl/ *n* [C] a film or book that continues the story of two previous films or books - used humorously → **sequel**, **prequel**: *The first two films were huge hits, but the threequel flopped.*

ˌthree-ring ˈcircus *n* **1** [singular] *AmE informal* a place or situation that is confusing because there is too much activity: *I don't know how you can work in that office - it's like a three-ring circus.* **2** [C usually singular] a CIRCUS that has three areas in which people or animals perform at the same time

three Rs /ˌθriː ˈɑːz $ -ˈɑːrz/ *n* **the three Rs** reading, writing, and ARITHMETIC, considered as the basic things that children must learn in school

three·score /ˈθriːskɔː $ -skɔːr/ *number old use* 60 → SCORE³(1)

three·some /ˈθriːsəm/ *n* [C usually singular] *informal* a group of three people or things

ˈthree-star *adj* [only before noun] a three-star hotel, restaurant etc has been judged to be of a high standard

ˌthree-ˈwheeler *n* [C] **1** *BrE* a car that has three wheels **2** *AmE* a vehicle that has three wheels, especially a MOTORCYCLE, TRICYCLE, or special WHEELCHAIR

ˌThree Wise ˈMen, the (*also* **the Three Kings**, **the Magi**) in the New Testament of the Bible, three kings or wise men who came from the East, guided by a star, and brought gifts of gold, FRANKINCENSE, and MYRRH for the baby Jesus. The expression 'three wise men' is sometimes used, especially in newspapers, to describe three men who work together as a group: *MPs are debating the report provided by the three wise men.*

thren·o·dy /ˈθrenədi/ *n* (*plural* **threnodies**) [C] *literary* a funeral song or poem for someone who has died

thresh /θreʃ/ *v* [I,T] to separate grains of corn, wheat etc from the rest of the plant by beating it with a special tool or machine —**thresher** *n* [C]

ˈthreshing maˌchine *n* [C] a machine used for separating grains of corn, wheat etc from the rest of the plant

thresh·old /ˈθreʃhəʊld, -ʃəʊld $ -oʊld/ ●○○ *n* [C]
1 the entrance to a room or building, or the area of floor or ground at the entrance: *She opened the door and stepped across the threshold.*
2 the level at which something starts to happen or have an effect: *Eighty percent of the vote was the threshold for approval of the plan.* | **a high/low pain/boredom etc threshold** (=the ability or inability to suffer a lot of pain or boredom before you react to it)
3 at the beginning of a new and important event or development SYN **brink**: **be on the threshold of sth** *The creature is on the threshold of extinction.*

threw /θruː/ *v* the past tense of THROW¹

thrice /θraɪs/ *adv old use* three times

thrift /θrɪft/ *n* [U] *old-fashioned* wise and careful use of money, so that none is wasted → SPENDTHRIFT

ˈthrift shop *n* [C] *AmE* a shop that sells used goods, especially clothes, often in order to get money for a CHARITY

thrift·y /ˈθrɪfti/ *adj* using money carefully and wisely SYN **economical**: *hard-working, thrifty people* —**thriftily** *adv* —**thriftiness** *n* [U]

thrill¹ /θrɪl/ ●●○ *n*
1 [C] a sudden strong feeling of excitement and pleasure, or the thing that makes you feel this: *Winning first place must have been quite a thrill.* | **the thrill of (doing) sth** (=the excitement you get from something) *the thrill of travelling at high speeds* | *Even though I've been acting for years, I still* ***get a thrill out of*** *going on stage.* | *It* ***gave*** *Pat* ***a thrill*** *to finally see the group perform live.* | **a thrill of excitement/anticipation/fear etc** *She felt a thrill of pride as her son stepped forward.* | **do sth for the thrill of it** (=do something for excitement and not for any serious reason)
2 thrills and spills (*also* **thrills and chills**) *informal* the excitement and danger involved in an activity, especially a sport
3 the thrill of the chase/hunt the excitement you feel when you are trying to get something that is difficult to get, especially when you are trying to get a romantic relationship with someone → **cheap thrill** at CHEAP¹(6)

thrill² ●●○ *v* [T] to make someone feel excited and happy → **thrilling**: *His music continues to thrill audiences.*

thrill to sth (*also* **thrill at sth**) *phr v formal* to feel excited and happy about something: *In the 1960s, the public thrilled to the idea of space exploration.*

thrilled /θrɪld/ ●●○ *adj* [not before noun] very excited, happy, and pleased: **be thrilled to see/hear/learn etc sth** *We were so thrilled to hear about the baby.* | **thrilled (that)** *I'm absolutely thrilled that you are coming.* | **[+about]** *He was thrilled about being asked to play.* | **thrilled to bits/pieces** (=very thrilled) THESAURUS ▸ EXCITED, HAPPY

thrill·er /ˈθrɪlə $ -ər/ ●●○ *n* [C] a book or film that tells an exciting story about murder or crime THESAURUS ▸ MOVIE

thrill·ing /ˈθrɪlɪŋ/ ●●○ *adj* interesting and exciting: *a thrilling 3-2 victory* THESAURUS ▸ EXCITING —**thrillingly** *adv*

ˈthrill-ˌseeker *n* [C] someone who does things that are dangerous because they like the feeling of excitement it gives them: *a roller coaster that will please thrill-seekers*

thrive /θraɪv/ ●○○ *v* (*past tense* **thrived** *or* **throve** /θrəʊv $ θroʊv/, *past participle* **thrived**) [I] *formal* to become very successful or very strong and healthy: *plants that thrive in tropical rain forests* | *a business which managed to thrive during a recession*

> **REGISTER**
> In everyday English, people usually say **do well** rather than **thrive**: *The whole family seems to be* ***doing well***.

thrive on sth *phr v* to enjoy or be successful in a particular situation, especially one that other people find difficult

T

or unpleasant: *I wouldn't want that much pressure, but she seems to thrive on it.*

thri·ving /'θraɪvɪŋ/ *adj* a thriving company, business etc is very successful SYN **flourishing**: *a thriving tourist industry* THESAURUS ▸ SUCCESSFUL

throat /θrəʊt $ θroʊt/ ●●● S3 W3 *n* [C]
1 the passage from the back of your mouth to the top of the tubes that go down to your lungs and stomach: *The singer complained of a* **sore throat** *after Wednesday's show.* → see picture at HUMAN[1]
2 the front of your neck: *She fingered the pearls at her throat.*
3 clear your throat to make a noise in your throat, especially before you speak, or in order to get someone's attention
4 force/ram/shove sth down sb's throat *informal* to force someone to accept or listen to your ideas and opinions
5 be at each other's throats if two people are at each other's throats, they are fighting or arguing
6 cut your own throat to behave in a way that is certain to harm you, especially because you are proud or angry → **a lump in/to sb's throat** at LUMP[1](4), → **have a frog in your throat** at FROG(2), → **jump down sb's throat** at JUMP[1](13), → **stick in sb's throat** at STICK[1](12)

throat·y /'θrəʊti $ 'θroʊ-/ *adj* a throaty laugh, cough, voice etc sounds low and rough —**throatily** *adv* —**throatiness** *n* [C,U]

throb[1] /θrɒb $ θrɑːb/ *v* (**throbbed**, **throbbing**) [I] **1** if a part of your body throbs, you have a feeling of pain in it that regularly starts and stops: *The back of my neck throbbed painfully.* | **[+with]** *Her foot was throbbing with pain.* | *I woke up with a* **throbbing headache**. THESAURUS ▸ HURT **2** if music or a machine throbs, it makes a low sound or VIBRATION with a strong regular beat: *a throbbing bass line* **3** if your heart throbs, it beats faster or more strongly than usual **4** if a place throbs with life, energy etc, it has a lot of life etc: *The river is throbbing with life.*

throb[2] (*also* **throb·bing**) /'θrɒbɪŋ $ 'θrɑː-/ *n* [C] a low strong regular beat or sensation: **[+of]** *the throb of the engines* | *a steady throb of pain* → HEARTTHROB

throes /θrəʊz $ θroʊz/ *n* [plural] **in the throes of sth** *formal* in the middle of a very difficult situation: *a country in the throes of a profound economic crisis* → DEATH THROES

throm·bo·sis /θrɒm'bəʊsɪs $ θrɑːm'boʊ-/ *n* (*plural* **thromboses**) [C,U] *technical* a serious medical problem caused by a CLOT forming in your blood that prevents the blood from flowing normally

throne /θrəʊn $ θroʊn/ ●●○ *n*
1 [C] a special chair used by a king or queen at important ceremonies
2 the throne the position and power of being a king or queen: *He is* **next in line to the throne** (=will become king when the present ruler dies). | *In 1913, George V was* **on the throne** (=was ruling).

throng[1] /θrɒŋ $ θrɒːŋ/ *n* [C] *written* a large group of people in one place SYN **crowd**: *She got lost in the throng.* | **[+of]** *a throng of excited spectators*

throng[2] *v* **1** [I always + adv/prep, T] if people throng a place, they go there in large numbers: *Tourists thronged the bars and restaurants.* **2 be thronged with sb/sth** if a place is thronged with people or things, there are a lot of them there: *The streets were thronged with Christmas shoppers.*

throt·tle[1] /'θrɒtl $ 'θrɑːtl/ *v* [T] **1** to kill or injure someone by holding their throat very tightly so that they cannot breathe SYN **strangle**: *He grabbed her by the throat and began throttling her.* **2** to make it difficult or impossible for something to succeed: *policies which are throttling many Asian economies* **3** to slow down the speed of an Internet connection

throttle back *phr v* to reduce the amount of FUEL flowing into an engine, in order to reduce its speed

throttle[2] *n* [C] **1** *technical* a piece of equipment that controls the amount of FUEL going into a vehicle's engine: **at/on full throttle** *The engines were at full throttle* (=the throttle was open so the engines could go very fast). → see picture at MOTORBIKE **2 full throttle** as fast or as much as possible: *The team's offense ran full throttle.* | **at/on full throttle** *a political campaign on full throttle*

through[1] /θruː/ ●●● S1 W1 *prep, adv*
1 DOOR/PASSAGE ETC into one side or end of an entrance, passage, hole etc and out of the other side or end: *She smiled at him as he walked through the door.* | *Water will be pumped through a pipe.* | *I managed to squeeze through a gap in the hedge.* | *They were suddenly plunged into darkness as the train went through a tunnel.* | *There were people standing in the doorway and I couldn't get through.* | **[+to]** *I went through to the kitchen to see who was there.*
2 CUTTING/BREAKING cutting or breaking something, or making a hole from one side of it to the other: *A football came crashing through the window.* | **straight/right/clean through** *The bullet passed straight through his skull.*
3 ACROSS AN AREA from one side of an area to the other or between a group of things: *We passed through France on our way to Italy.* | *We made our way through the village to the farm.* | *The wind howled through the trees.* | *He had to push his way through the crowd to get to her.* | *Let me through – I'm a doctor.* | **get through/make it through** (=reach a place after a difficult journey) *You'll never get through – the snow's two metres deep.* | *Rescue teams have finally made it through to the survivors.* | *We drove* **right through** *the town centre.* | *Carry on* **straight through** *the village.*
4 SEE THROUGH STH if you see something through glass, a window etc, you are on one side of the glass etc and it is on the other: *I could see her through the window.* | *I could* **see right through** *the thin curtains.*
5 PAST A PLACE past a place where you are supposed to stop: *It took us ages to get through passport control.* | *He drove* **straight through** *a red light.*
6 TIME during and to the end of a period of time: *The cold weather continued through the spring.* | *He slept* **right through** *the day.* | *The fighting went on* **all through** *the night.*
7 PROCESS/EXPERIENCE from the beginning to the end of a process or experience: *The book guides you through the whole procedure of buying a house.* | *When you have been through a terrible experience like that, it takes a long time to recover.* | *It's a miracle that these buildings came through the war undamaged.*
8 COMPETITIONS past one stage in a competition to the next stage: **[+to]** *This is the first time they've ever made it through to the final.* | *They didn't even* **get through** *the first round of the contest.*
9 BECAUSE OF STH because of something: *How many working days were lost through sickness last year?*
10 BY MEANS OF STH/SB by means of a particular method, service, person etc: *She got her first job through an employment agency.* | *a success that was achieved through co-operative effort and wise leadership* | *I heard about it through a friend.* THESAURUS ▸ BECAUSE
11 PARLIAMENT/CONGRESS if a proposal passes through a parliament, it is agreed and accepted as a law: *A special bill was rushed through Congress to deal with the emergency.*
12 UNTIL **May through June/Wednesday through Friday etc** *AmE* from May until June, from Wednesday until Friday etc: *The store is open Monday through Saturday.*
13 halfway through (sth) in the middle of an event or period of time: *I left halfway through the film.*
14 TELEPHONE *BrE* connected to someone by telephone: *I tried phoning you, but I couldn't* **get through**. | *Please hold the line and I'll* **put** *you* **through**. | **[+to]** *Did you manage to get through to her?*
15 COMPLETELY **wet through/cooked through etc** *informal* completely wet, cooked etc: *You're wet through. What on earth have you been doing?* | *It should only take a few minutes to heat this through.*
16 through and through if someone is a particular type of person through and through, they are completely that type of person: *I'll say one thing for Sandra – she's a professional through and through.*
17 ALL THE WAY **through to London/Paris etc** as far as London, Paris etc: *Does this train go through to Glasgow?*

18 USE QUICKLY **get/go/run through sth** to use a lot of something quickly: *George Ward started smoking at the age of nine, and at one time he was getting through 80 a day.* | *By the end of the year he had run through all the money inherited from his father.*

through² *adj* **1 be through (with sb/sth)** *informal* **a)** to have finished doing something or using something: *I'm not through just yet – I should be finished in an hour.* | *Are you through with the computer yet?* **b)** to no longer be having a relationship with someone: *That's it! Simon and I are through.* | *I'm through with you!* **2 through train** a train by which you can reach a place, without having to use other trains **3 through road** a road that joins cities, towns, or villages together

through·out /θruːˈaʊt/ ●●● S2 W1 *prep, adv*
1 in every part of a particular area, place etc: *a large organization with offices throughout the world* | *The disease spread rapidly throughout Europe.* | *The house is in excellent condition, with fitted carpets throughout.*
2 during all of a particular period, from the beginning to the end: *We are open every weekend throughout the year.* | *He was involved in politics throughout his life.* | *The debate continued, but Meredith remained silent throughout.*

through·put /ˈθruːpʊt/ *n* [U] the amount of work, goods, or people that are dealt with in a particular period of time: **[+of]** *an airport with a weekly throughput of 100,000 passengers* | **high/low throughput** *a large store with a high throughput of goods*

through·way /ˈθruːweɪ/ *n* [C] *AmE* a THRUWAY

throve /θrəʊv $ θroʊv/ *v old-fashioned* the past tense of THRIVE

throw¹ /θrəʊ $ θroʊ/ ●●● S1 W1 *v* (*past tense* **threw** /θruː/, *past participle* **thrown** /θrəʊn $ θroʊn/)
1 THROW A BALL/STONE ETC [I,T] to make an object such as a ball move quickly through the air by pushing your hand forward quickly and letting the object go: **throw sth to sb** *He threw his shirt to someone in the crowd.* | **throw sth at sb/sth** *Someone threw a stone at the car.* | *a crowd of boys throwing snowballs at each other* | **throw sb sth** *Throw me that towel, would you.* ⚠ You throw something **to** someone when you want them to catch it. You throw something **at** someone when you want to hit them. → see picture at BASEBALL
2 PUT STH CARELESSLY [T always + adv/prep] to put something somewhere quickly and carelessly: *He threw a handful of money onto the table.* | *Don't just throw your clothes on the floor – pick them up!*
3 PUSH ROUGHLY/VIOLENTLY [T always + adv/prep] to push someone or something roughly and violently: *The bus stopped suddenly and we were all thrown forwards.* | *The guards* ***threw*** *Biko* ***to the ground*** *and started kicking him.* | *The bomb exploded,* ***throwing*** *bricks and debris* ***into the air***. | *She drew the curtains and* ***threw open*** *the windows.*
4 MAKE SB FALL [T] **a)** to make your opponent fall to the ground in a sport in which you fight **b)** if a horse throws its rider, it makes them fall onto the ground
5 MOVE HANDS/HEAD ETC [T always + adv/prep] to suddenly and quickly move your hands, arms, head etc into a new position: *I threw my arms around her and kissed her.* | *He threw his head back and laughed.*
6 CONFUSE SB [T] to make someone feel very confused: *It* ***threw*** *me* ***completely*** *when she said she was coming to stay with us.*
7 throw yourself at/on/into/down etc to move or jump somewhere suddenly and with a lot of force: *He threw himself down onto the bed.* | *She committed suicide by throwing herself out of a tenth-floor window.*
8 throw sb in/into prison/jail to put someone in prison: *Anyone who opposes the regime is thrown in jail.*
9 throw sb out of work/office etc to suddenly take away someone's job or position of authority: *Hundreds of men were thrown out of work when the mine closed down.* | *Elections were held, and the government was thrown out of office.*
10 throw sb/sth into confusion/chaos/disarray etc to make people feel very confused and not certain about what they should do: *Everyone was thrown into confusion by this news.* | *The transport industry has been thrown into chaos by the strike.*
11 throw doubt on sth to make people think that something is probably not true: *Fresh evidence has thrown doubt on her story.*
12 throw suspicion on sb to make people think that someone is probably guilty: *This latest document throws suspicion on the company chairman.*
13 throw sb a look/glance/smile etc to quickly look at someone with a particular expression that shows how you are feeling: *He threw Anna a big smile.* | *He threw a glance at Connor.*
14 throw a fit/tantrum to react in a very angry way: *I can't tell my parents – they'd throw a fit!*
15 throw a question/remark etc (at sb) to say something to someone or ask them something roughly: *They threw a few awkward questions at me.* | *'You're early!' she threw at him accusingly.*
16 throw sth open a) to allow people to go into a place that is usually kept private: **[+to]** *Plans have been announced to throw the Palace open to the public.* **b)** to allow anyone to take part in a competition or a discussion: **[+to]** *I would now like to throw the debate open to our audience.*
17 throw a switch/handle/lever to make something start or stop working by moving a control: *He threw a switch and the lights all went out.*
18 throw a party to organize a party and invite people
19 throw money at sth *informal* to try to solve a problem by spending a lot of money but without really thinking about the problem: *The problem cannot be solved by throwing money at it.*
20 be thrown back on sth to be forced to have to depend on your own skills, knowledge etc: *Once again, we were thrown back on our own resources.*
21 throw yourself into sth to start doing an activity with a lot of effort and energy: *Since her husband died, she's thrown herself into her work.*
22 throw your weight around to use your position of authority to tell people what to do in an unreasonable way: *He's the sort of insensitive bully who enjoys throwing his weight around.*
23 throw your weight behind sb/sth to support a plan, person etc and use your power to make sure they succeed: *The party leadership is throwing its weight behind the campaign.*
24 throw light on sth to make something easier to understand by providing new information: *Recent investigations have thrown new light on how the two men died.*
25 throw a light/shadow to make light or shadow fall on a particular place: *The trees threw long, dark shadows across the cornfield.*
26 throw the book at sb *informal* to punish someone as severely as possible or charge them with as many offences as possible: *If you get caught they'll throw the book at you!*
27 throw sth (back) in sb's face to be unkind to someone after they have been kind to you or helped you: *I felt that everything I'd done for them was thrown back in my face.*
28 throw up your hands (in horror/dismay etc) to do something that shows you think something is not good but feel you cannot do anything to change it: *Ted threw up his hands in disgust. 'Can't you make her change her mind?' he asked.*
29 throw in your hand to stop trying to do something SYN **give up**
30 throw yourself at sb *informal* to try very hard to attract someone's attention because you want to have a sexual relationship with them
31 throw a punch to try to hit someone with your hand in a fight: *We need to sort this out before people start throwing punches.*
32 throw a match/game/fight to deliberately lose a fight or sports game that you could have won: *He was allegedly offered £20,000 to throw the match.*
33 throw dice/a six/a four etc to roll DICE or to get a

particular number by rolling dice: *You have to throw a six to start.*
34 throw a pot to make a pot by shaping clay as it turns round on a special wheel
35 throw your voice to use a special trick to make your voice seem to be coming from a different place from the place you are standing
36 throw caution to the wind(s) to ignore the risks and deliberately behave in a way that may cause trouble or problems: *I threw caution to the winds and followed him.*
37 throw the baby out with the bath water to get rid of good useful parts of a system, organization etc when you are changing it in order to try and make it better
38 throw shapes *informal* to dance to popular music, for example in a NIGHTCLUB, making shapes with your arms
→ **throw in/cast your lot with sb** at LOT²(8)

THESAURUS

throw to make something such as a ball or stone move quickly through the air using your hand: *I threw the ball back to him.* | *Protestors began throwing stones at the police.* | *I just threw the letter in the bin.*
toss (*also* **chuck**) *informal* to throw something, especially in a careless way without using much effort: *She tossed her coat onto the bed.* | *Can you chuck me the remote control?*
hurl to throw something with a lot of force: *Someone hurled a brick through his window.*
fling to angrily throw something somewhere with a lot of force, or to carelessly throw something somewhere because you have very little time: *He flung her keys into the river.* | *I flung a few things into a suitcase.*
heave /hiːv/ to throw something heavy using a lot of effort: *They heaved the log into the river.*
lob to throw something high into the air over someone or something: *The police lobbed tear gas canisters over the heads of the demonstrators.*

TO THROW A BALL IN A SPORT

pass to throw the ball to another member of your team: *He passed the ball to Wilkinson, who kicked the ball over the goalposts.*
pitch to throw the ball to the batter in a game of baseball: *Stoddard pitched for the Chicago White Sox.*
bowl to throw the ball towards the person who is batting in a game of cricket: *Harmison bowled superbly and took 5 wickets.*

throw sth ↔ **away** *phr v*
1 to get rid of something that you do not want or need: *I never throw clothes away.* | *I shouldn't have thrown away the receipt.*
2 to spend money in a way that is not sensible: *I can't afford to throw money away.*
3 to waste something good that you have, for example a skill or an opportunity: *This could be the best chance you'll ever have. Don't throw it away!*
throw sth ↔ **in** *phr v*
1 to add something to what you are selling, without increasing the price: *We paid $2,000 for the boat, with the trailer and spares thrown in.*
2 if you throw in a remark, you say it suddenly without thinking carefully: *She threw in a couple of odd remarks about men.*
3 throw in the sponge/towel *informal* to admit that you have been defeated
throw sb/sth ↔ **off** *phr v*
1 to take off a piece of clothing in a quick careless way: *They threw off their clothes and dived in.*
2 to get free from something that has been limiting your freedom: *In 1845, they finally threw off the yoke of foreign rule.*
3 if you throw off an illness, you get better from it: *It's taken me ages to throw off this cold.*
4 to escape from someone or something that is chasing you: *We ran flat out for about half a mile before we could throw them off.*
5 to produce large amounts of heat or light: *The engine was throwing off so much heat that the air above it shimmered with haze.*
throw sth ↔ **on** *phr v* to put on a piece of clothing quickly and carelessly: *I threw on a pair of jeans and a T-shirt.*
throw sb/sth ↔ **out** *phr v*
1 to get rid of something that you do not want or need: *We usually throw out all our old magazines.*
2 to make someone leave a place, school, or organization, especially because they have done something that is against the rules: *Nick got thrown out of college in the second year for taking drugs.* | *I knew he would never* ***throw*** *us* ***out on the street*** (=make us leave our home when we have nowhere else to live).
3 if people throw out a plan or suggestion, they refuse to accept it: *The idea was thrown out by the committee.* | *The bill was thrown out by the Senate.*
4 if something throws out smoke, heat, dust etc, it produces a lot of it and fills the air with it: *huge trucks throwing out noxious fumes from their exhausts*
throw sb ↔ **over** *phr v* *old-fashioned* to end a romantic relationship with someone
throw sb/sth ↔ **together** *phr v*
1 to make something such as a meal quickly and not very carefully: *There's lots of food in the fridge – I'm sure I can throw something together.*
2 if a situation throws people together, it makes them meet and know each other: *It was the war that had thrown them together.*
throw up *phr v*
1 to bring food or drink up from your stomach out through your mouth because you are ill SYN **vomit**: *Georgia was bent over the basin, throwing up.*
2 throw sth ↔ up *BrE* to produce problems, ideas, results etc: *The arrangement may throw up problems in other areas.*
3 throw sth ↔ up if a vehicle, runner etc throws up dust, water etc as they move along, they make it rise into the air
4 throw sth ↔ up *BrE informal* to suddenly leave your job, your home etc: *I can't just throw everything up and come and live with you.*
5 throw sth ↔ up *BrE* to build something quickly: *new houses hastily thrown up by developers*

throw² ●●○ *n* [C]
1 an action in which someone throws something: *That was a great throw!* | *a throw of over 80 metres*
2 an action in which someone rolls a DICE in a game: *It's your throw.*
3 a large piece of cloth that you put loosely over a chair to cover it and make it look attractive: *a brightly-coloured cotton throw*

throw·a·way /ˈθrəʊəweɪ $ ˈθroʊ-/ *adj* [only before noun]
1 throwaway remark/line/comment etc something that someone says or writes quickly, without thinking carefully about it: *It was only a throwaway comment.* | *He claims people overreacted to a few throwaway lines in the article.* **2** throwaway products have been produced cheaply so that you can throw them away after you have used them SYN **disposable**: *a throwaway cigarette lighter*
3 throwaway society used to show disapproval when talking about modern societies in which products are not made to last a long time

throw·back /ˈθrəʊbæk $ ˈθroʊ-/ *n* [C usually singular] something that is similar to something that existed in the past, or belongs to the past: **[+to]** *Her whole outfit was a throwback to the 1970s.* | *a social event which is a throwback to a different age*

ˈthrow-in *n* [C] an action in which someone throws the ball back onto the field in a game of football: *Beckham will* ***take*** *the* ***throw-in****.* → see picture at FOOTBALL

ˈthrow ˌpillow *n* [C] *AmE* a small CUSHION that you put on SOFAs and chairs for decoration SYN **scatter cushion** *BrE*

thru /θruː/ *adj, adv, prep AmE informal* a short form of THROUGH

thrum /θrʌm/ *v* (**thrummed**, **thrumming**) [I] to make a low sound like the sound of an engine: *The engine thrummed into life.* —**thrum** *n* [singular]: *the thrum of passing cars*

thrush /θrʌʃ/ *n* **1** [C] a brown bird with spots on its front **2** [U] an infectious disease that can affect a person's VAGINA or mouth

thrust¹ /θrʌst/ ●●○ *v* (*past tense and past participle* **thrust**)
1 [T always + adv/prep] to push something somewhere roughly: *She thrust a letter into my hand.* | *He thrust me roughly towards the door.* THESAURUS ▸ PUT
2 [I] to make a sudden movement forward with a sword or knife: **[+at]** *He skipped aside as his opponent thrust at him.*
thrust sth ↔ **aside** *phr v* to refuse to think about something: *Our complaints were thrust aside and ignored.*
thrust sth **upon/on** sb *phr v* if something is thrust upon you, you are forced to accept it even if you do not want it: *She never enjoyed the fame that was thrust upon her.* | *He* ***had*** *marriage* ***thrust upon*** *him.*

thrust² ●○○ *n*
1 [C] a sudden strong movement in which you push something forward: *He jumped back to avoid another thrust of the knife.*
2 [singular] the main meaning or aim of what someone is saying or doing: **[+of]** *the* ***main thrust*** *of the government's education policy*
3 [U] *technical* the force of an engine that makes a car, train, or plane move forward

thrust·er /ˈθrʌstə $ -ər/ *n* [C] *technical* a small engine on a spacecraft that controls its height and direction by pushing out gas

thru·way, **throughway** /ˈθruːweɪ/ *n* [C] *AmE* a wide road for fast traffic that you pay to use

thud¹ /θʌd/ *n* [C] the low sound made by a heavy object hitting something else: **a dull/hard/heavy thud** *There was a dull thud as the box hit the floor.* | *His head hit the floor with* ***a sickening thud.*** THESAURUS ▸ SOUND

thud² *v* (**thudded, thudding**) [I] **1** [always + adv/prep] to hit something with a low sound: *The stone thudded to the ground.* | *waves thudding against the side of the ship* **2** [always + adv/prep] to walk or run with your feet making a heavy sound as they touch the ground: *A horse thudded over the frozen grass.* **3** if your heart thuds, it beats strongly because you are excited or frightened: *Peter was aware of his heart thudding in his chest.*

thug /θʌg/ ●○○ *n* [C] a violent man: *He was beaten up by a gang of young thugs.*

thug·ge·ry /ˈθʌgəri/ *n* [U] violent behaviour in which people fight and attack others: *the problem of football thuggery*

thug·gish /ˈθʌgɪʃ/ *adj* thuggish behaviour is violent behaviour in which people fight and attack others

thumb¹ /θʌm/ ●●● S3 *n* [C]
1 the part of your hand that is shaped like a thick short finger and helps you to hold things: *a baby sucking its thumb* | *She held the coin carefully between finger and thumb.* → see picture at HAND¹
2 the part of a GLOVE that fits over your thumb
3 be all fingers and thumbs *BrE*, **be all thumbs** *AmE informal* to be unable to do something in which you have to make small careful movements with your fingers: *Would you do up these buttons for me? I seem to be all thumbs today.*
4 the thumbs up/down *informal* when an idea or plan is officially accepted or not accepted: *The project was finally* ***given the thumbs up.*** | *Her performance* ***got the thumbs down*** *from the critics.*
5 be under sb's thumb to be so strongly influenced by someone that they control you completely: *He was still under his father's thumb.* → **rule of thumb** at RULE¹(8), → **stand/stick out like a sore thumb** at SORE¹(6)

thumb² *v* **1 thumb a lift** *BrE*, **thumb a ride** *AmE informal* to persuade a driver of a passing car to stop and take you somewhere, by putting your hand out with your thumb raised: *I thumbed a lift into town.* **2 thumb your nose at sb/sth** to show that you do not respect rules, laws etc or you do not care what someone thinks of you: *a chance to thumb his nose at the college authorities*
thumb through sth *phr v* to look through a book, magazine etc quickly: *I began thumbing through the pages of a gardening catalogue.*

ˈthumb drive *n* [C] a small piece of electronic equipment that uses FLASH MEMORY to store information and can be fitted into a computer SYN **flash drive, USB drive**

ˈthumb ˌindex *n* [C] a line of round cuts in the edge of a large book which have the letters of the alphabet on them and help you find the part of the book you want

thumb·nail¹ /ˈθʌmneɪl/ *adj* **thumbnail sketch/portrait** a short description that gives only the main facts about a person, thing, or event: *a thumbnail sketch of recent political events in America*

thumbnail² *n* [C] **1** the nail on your thumb **2** a small picture of a document on a computer screen, showing you what it will look like when you print it: *Click on the thumbnails to view a larger version of each image.*

thumb·screw /ˈθʌmskruː/ *n* [C] an object that was used in the past to punish people by crushing their thumbs

thumb·tack /ˈθʌmtæk/ *n* [C] *AmE* a short pin with a flat top that is used for fixing notices on walls SYN **drawing pin** *BrE* → see picture at STATIONERY

thump¹ /θʌmp/ ●○○ *v*
1 [T] *informal* to hit someone very hard with your hand closed: *If you don't shut up, I'm going to thump you!* | *She thumped the table with her fist.* THESAURUS ▸ HIT
2 [I,T always + adv/prep] to hit against something loudly: *His feet thumped loudly on the bare boards.* | *He thumped his cup down on the table.*
3 [I always + adv/prep] to walk or run with your feet making a loud heavy sound as they touch the ground: *Stella came thumping down the stairs.*
4 [I] if your heart thumps, it beats very strongly and quickly because you are frightened or excited: *My heart was thumping inside my chest.*

thump² *n* [C] **1** the dull sound that is made when something hits a surface: *The box fell to the floor with a thump.* THESAURUS ▸ SOUND **2** [usually singular] *especially BrE* an action in which you hit someone or something: *If he does that again, I'll give him a good thump.* | *a thump on the jaw*

thump·ing /ˈθʌmpɪŋ/ *adj* [only before noun] **1** *BrE informal* (*also* **thumping great**) very big or great: *Mulroney swept to power with a thumping majority.* | *He told us some thumping great lies!* **2** thumping music has a strong loud beat **3 thumping headache** a very bad headache

thun·der¹ /ˈθʌndə $ -ər/ ●●○ *n*
1 [U] the loud noise that you hear during a storm, usually after a flash of lightning: *We were woken in the night by thunder.*
2 [singular] a loud deep noise: *She heard the thunder of hooves behind her.*
3 a face like thunder if someone has a face like thunder, they look very angry → BLOOD-AND-THUNDER, → **steal sb's thunder** at STEAL¹(9)

thunder² *v* **1** [I] **it thunders** if it thunders, there is a loud noise in the sky, usually after a flash of lightning **2** [I always + adv/prep] to run or move along quickly, in a way that makes a very loud noise: *The children came thundering downstairs.* | *Huge lorries thundered past us.* **3** [I] to make a very loud deep noise: *Guns roared and thundered all around us.* **4** [T] to shout loudly and angrily: *'You must be mad!' he thundered.*

thun·der·bolt /ˈθʌndəbəʊlt $ -dərboʊlt/ *n* [C] **1** a flash of LIGHTNING which hits a person or thing and kills or destroys them **2** a sudden event or piece of news that shocks you: *The idea hit her like a thunderbolt.*

thun·der·clap /ˈθʌndəklæp $ -ər-/ *n* [C] a single loud noise of thunder: *A thunderclap exploded above us.*

T

thun·der·cloud /ˈθʌndəklaʊd $ -ər-/ *n* [C] a large dark cloud that you see before or during a storm

thun·der·ous /ˈθʌndərəs/ *adj* **1** extremely loud: *His speech was greeted with* ***thunderous applause****.* THESAURUS▶ LOUD **2** looking or sounding very angry: *a thunderous voice* —**thunderously** *adv*

thun·der·storm /ˈθʌndəstɔːm $ -dərstɔːrm/ ●●○ *n* [C] a storm with thunder and lightning THESAURUS▶ STORM

thun·der·struck /ˈθʌndəstrʌk $ -ər-/ *adj* [not before noun] extremely surprised or shocked: *Jeff looked thunderstruck when he saw me.*

thun·der·y /ˈθʌndəri/ *adj* thundery weather is the type of weather that comes before a thunderstorm

Thurs·day /ˈθɜːzdi, -deɪ $ ˈθɜːrz-/ ●●● S2 W2 *n* [C,U] (*written abbreviation* **Thurs.** *or* **Thur.**) the day between Wednesday and Friday: **on Thursday** *I went to Edinburgh on Thursday.* | *She was working Thursday. AmE* | **Thursday morning/afternoon etc** *There's a meeting on Thursday night.* | **last Thursday** *He was arrested last Thursday.* | **this Thursday** *Mark and I are driving south this Thursday.* | **next Thursday** (=Thursday of next week) *I'll see you next Thursday.* | **a Thursday** (=one of the Thursdays in the year) *Christmas Day is on a Thursday this year.*

thus /ðʌs/ ●●○ W3 *adv formal*
1 [sentence adverb] as a result of something that you have just mentioned: *Most of the evidence was destroyed in the fire. Thus it would be almost impossible to prove him guilty.* THESAURUS▶ THEREFORE
2 in this manner or way: *They diluted the drug, thus reducing its effectiveness.*
3 thus far until now: *Her political career thus far had remained unblemished.*

> REGISTER
> **Thus** is formal or literary. In everyday English, people usually say **so**: ***So*** *it was decided that he should be chairman.* | *We haven't had any problems* ***so far****.*

thwack /θwæk/ *n* [C] a short loud sound like something hitting a hard surface —**thwack** *v* [T]

thwart /θwɔːt $ θwɔːrt/ ●○○ *v* [T] *formal* to prevent someone from doing what they are trying to do: *Fierce opposition thwarted the government's plans.* | *thwarted ambition*

THX a written abbreviation of 'thanks', used in email or TEXT MESSAGES on MOBILE PHONES

thy /ðaɪ/ *determiner old use* your: *We praise thy name, O Lord.*

thyme /taɪm/ *n* [U] a plant used for giving food a special taste

thy·roid /ˈθaɪrɔɪd/ (*also* **ˈthyroid ˌgland**) *n* [C] an organ in your neck that produces substances that affect the way your body grows and the way you behave

thy·self /ðaɪˈself/ *pron old use* yourself

ti /tiː/ *n* [singular] the seventh note in a musical SCALE according to the SOL-FA system

ti·a·ra /tiˈɑːrə/ *n* [C] a piece of jewellery like a small CROWN, that a woman sometimes wears on very formal or important occasions: *a diamond tiara* → see picture at JEWELLERY

tib·i·a /ˈtɪbiə/ *n* (*plural* **tibiae** /-bi-iː/ *or* **tibias**) [C] *technical* a bone in the front of your leg → see picture at SKELETON

tic /tɪk/ *n* [C] a sudden movement of a muscle in your face, that you cannot control

tick¹ /tɪk/ ●●○ *v*
1 [I] (*also* **tick away**) if a clock or watch ticks, it makes a short repeated sound: *The old clock ticked noisily.*
2 [T] *BrE* to mark a test, list of questions etc with a tick, in order to show that something is correct, to choose something etc SYN **check** *AmE*: *Tick the description that best fits you.* | *Just* ***tick*** *the* ***box*** *on your order form.*
3 what makes sb tick *informal* the thoughts, feelings, opinions etc that give someone their character or make them behave in a particular way: *I've never really understood what makes her tick.*
4 tick all the right boxes *informal* if something ticks all the right boxes, it does everything that you wanted it to do or is everything you wanted it to be

tick away/by/past *phr v* if time ticks away, by, or past, it passes, especially when you are waiting for something to happen: *We need a decision – time's ticking away.* | *The minutes ticked past and still she didn't call.*

tick sb/sth ↔ **off** *phr v*
1 *BrE informal* to tell someone angrily that you are annoyed with them or disapprove of them: *Mrs Watts will tick you off if you're late again.*
2 *BrE* to mark the things on a list with a tick to show that they have been dealt with, chosen etc SYN **check off** *AmE*: *As you finish each task, tick it off.* | *Have you ticked off Kate's name on the list?*
3 *AmE informal* to annoy someone: *Her attitude is really ticking me off.*
4 *AmE* to tell someone a list of things, especially when you touch a different finger as you say each thing on the list: *Carville began ticking off points on his fingers.*

tick over *phr v BrE*
1 if an engine ticks over, it works while the vehicle is not moving: *Mark left the engine ticking over and went back inside.*
2 if a system, business etc ticks over, it continues working but without producing very much or without much happening: *The business is just about ticking over.* | *Jane will* ***keep things ticking over*** *while I'm away.*

tick² *n* **1** [C] *BrE* a mark (✔) written next to an answer, something on a list etc, to show that it is correct or has been dealt with SYN **check** *AmE*: ***Put*** *a* ***tick*** *in the box if you agree with this statement.* → CROSS² **2** [C] a very small animal like an insect that lives under the skin of other animals and sucks their blood **3** [singular] the short repeated sound that a clock or watch makes every second **4** [C] *BrE spoken* a very short time SYN **moment**: *I'll be with you* ***in a tick*** (=soon). | *It'll only take two ticks.* **5 on tick** *BrE old-fashioned informal* if you buy something on tick, you arrange to take it now and pay later SYN **credit**

tick·box /ˈtɪkbɒks $ -bɑːks/ *n* [C] *BrE* a small square space on a document or computer screen where you can put a mark to choose something SYN **checkbox**

ˌticked ˈoff *adj* [not before noun] *AmE informal* angry or annoyed: *Mark's ticked off with me for some reason.*

tick·er /ˈtɪkə $ -ər/ *n* [C] **1** *informal* your heart **2** *AmE* a special machine that prints or shows the price of company STOCKS as they go up and down

ˈticker tape *n* **1** [U] long narrow paper on which information, for example the price of company STOCKS, is printed by a special machine **2 ticker tape parade** *AmE* an occasion when someone important or famous walks or drives through an American city and pieces of paper are thrown from high buildings to welcome them

tick·et¹ /ˈtɪkɪt/ ●●● S1 W2 *n* [C]
1 CINEMA/BUS/TRAIN ETC a printed piece of paper which shows that you have paid to enter a cinema, travel on a bus, plane etc: **[+for]** *How much are tickets for the concert?* | **[+to]** *I'd like two tickets to Berlin.* | **a ticket to do sth** *a ticket to watch the US Open* → SEASON TICKET
2 FOR A PRIZE a printed piece of paper with a number on it that you buy because you will get a prize if that number is chosen: **raffle/lottery ticket**
3 DRIVING OFFENCE a printed note ordering you to pay money because you have done something illegal while driving or parking your car: **parking/speeding ticket**
4 IN SHOPS a piece of paper fastened to something in a shop that shows its price, size etc SYN **tag** *AmE*: *How much does it say on the* ***price ticket****?*
5 ELECTION [usually singular] *especially AmE* a list of the people supported by a particular political party in an election: *He ran for governor on the Republican ticket.*
6 ticket to success/fame/stardom etc *especially AmE* a way

of becoming successful, famous etc: *Michael thought an MBA would be a ticket to success.*
7 be (just) the ticket *old-fashioned* to be exactly what is needed → DREAM TICKET, MEAL TICKET

COLLOCATIONS

ADJECTIVES/NOUN + ticket

a train/bus/coach ticket *I've lost my train ticket.*
an airline/plane/air ticket | **a theatre/concert ticket** | **a one-way ticket** (*also* **a single ticket** *BrE*) (=a ticket to a place but not back again) | **a return ticket** *BrE*, **a round-trip ticket** *AmE* (=a ticket to a place and back) | **a season ticket** (=one that allows you to make a journey or go to a sports stadium, theatre etc as often as you like during a fixed time period) | **a valid ticket** (=one that is legally or officially acceptable)

VERBS

book/reserve a ticket *We booked our tickets well in advance.*
buy a ticket

ticket + NOUN

a ticket office/booth/counter (=a place where you can buy tickets) *There was a long queue at the ticket office.*
a ticket machine | **the ticket barrier** *BrE* (=a gate or other barrier at a station that you need a ticket to get through) | **a ticket agency** (=a company that sells tickets for concerts, sporting events etc)

ticket² *v* [T] **1** to produce and sell tickets for an event, journey etc: *air travel sold and ticketed in the UK* | *ticketed events such as concerts* **2** *especially AmE* to give someone a ticket for parking their car in the wrong place, driving too fast etc: *Drivers stopping here will be ticketed and have their cars towed.* **3 be ticketed for sth** *especially AmE* to be intended for a particular use, purpose, job etc: *Three of the army bases have been ticketed for closure.*

tick·et·ing /ˈtɪkətɪŋ/ *n* [U] the process or system of selling or printing tickets for planes, trains, concerts etc: *Most airlines are using electronic ticketing now.*

ˈticket ˌtout *n* [C] *BrE* someone who sells tickets outside a theatre or sports ground at a high price because there are not many available SYN **scalper** *AmE*

tick·ing /ˈtɪkɪŋ/ *n* [U] a thick strong cotton cloth used for making MATTRESS and PILLOW covers

ˌticking ˈoff *n* **give sb a ticking off** *BrE informal* to tell someone angrily that you are annoyed with them or disapprove of something they have done SYN **tick off**

tick·le¹ /ˈtɪkəl/ ●●○ *v*
1 [T] to move your fingers gently over someone's body in order to make them laugh: *Stop tickling me!* THESAURUS TOUCH
2 [I,T] if something touching your body tickles you, it makes you want to rub your body because it is slightly uncomfortable: *Mommy, this blanket tickles.* | *Mazie's fur collar was tickling her neck.*
3 [T] if a situation, remark etc tickles you, it amuses or pleases you: **be tickled pink** (=be very pleased or amused) *The kids were tickled pink to see you on TV!*
4 tickle sb's fancy *informal* if something tickles your fancy, you want to have it or to try doing it: *If I see something that tickles my fancy, I'm going to buy it.*

tickle² *n* [singular] **1** a feeling in your throat that makes you want to cough: *I've got a tickle in my throat.* **2 give sb a tickle** to move your fingers gently over someone's body in order to make them laugh

tick·lish /ˈtɪklɪʃ/ *adj* **1** someone who is ticklish laughs a lot when you tickle them **2** [usually before noun] *informal* a ticklish situation or problem is difficult and must be dealt with carefully, especially because you may upset people: *Handling awkward neighbours can be **a ticklish business**.* **3** (*also* **tick·ly** /ˈtɪkli/) [usually before noun] a ticklish cough is in your throat rather than in your chest

tick-tock /ˌtɪk ˈtɒk $ -ˈtɑːk/ *n* [singular] the regular sound that a large clock makes every second

tick·y-tack·y /ˈtɪki ˌtæki/ (*also* **ticky-tack** /-ˌtæk/) *adj AmE informal* ticky-tacky houses, buildings etc are made of material that is cheap and of low quality —**ticky-tacky** *n* [U]

tic-tac-toe, **tick-tack-toe** /ˌtɪk tæk ˈtəʊ $ -ˈtoʊ/ *n* [U] *AmE* a children's game in which two players draw X's or O's in a pattern of nine squares, trying to get three in a row SYN **noughts and crosses** *BrE*

tid·al /ˈtaɪdl/ *adj* relating to the regular rising and falling of the sea → **tide**: *tidal currents*

ˈtidal wave *n* [C] **1** a very large ocean wave that flows over the land and destroys things **2** a very large amount of a particular kind of feeling or activity happening at one time: **[+of]** *a tidal wave of crime* | *Voters were swept away on a tidal wave of enthusiasm.*

tid·bit /ˈtɪdˌbɪt/ *n* [C] *AmE* **1** a small piece of food that tastes good SYN **titbit** *BrE* **2** a small but interesting piece of information, news etc SYN **titbit** *BrE*: **[+of]** *juicy **tidbits of** hot **news***

tid·dler /ˈtɪdlə $ -ər/ *n* [C] *BrE informal* a very small fish

tid·dly /ˈtɪdli/ *adj BrE informal* **1** slightly drunk **2** very small: *a tiddly little insect*

tid·dly·winks /ˈtɪdliwɪŋks/ *n* [U] a children's game in which you try to make small round pieces of plastic jump into a cup by pressing their edge with a larger piece

tide¹ /taɪd/ ●●○ *n*
1 the tide the regular rising and falling of the level of the sea: **the tide is in/out** (=the sea is at a high/low level) | *Is the tide **going out** or **coming in**?* | *We went for a walk and **got cut off by the tide**.* → HIGH TIDE(1), LOW TIDE
2 [C] a current of water caused by the tide: *Strong tides make swimming dangerous.*
3 [C usually singular] the way in which events or people's opinions are developing: **[+of]** *With the tide of public opinion against him, the president may lose.* | *It was their first major victory. **The tide** had **turned** (=changed).* | *The **tide** of battle **turned against** the Mexican army.* | **swim with/against the tide** (=support or oppose what most people think)
4 [C usually singular] a large amount of something that is increasing and is difficult to control: **tide of violence/crime etc** *The crisis prompted a **rising tide** of protest.* | *She swallowed back a tide of emotion.* | *efforts to **stem** the **tide** of hysteria caused by the shootings* (=prevent it from getting worse)
5 [singular] a large number of people or things moving along together: **[+of]** *the tide of refugees flowing over the border*
6 Christmastide/eveningtide/morningtide etc *old use* a particular time of the year or day

COLLOCATIONS

ADJECTIVES

the tide is in (=the sea covers the shore) *You can't walk on the beach when the tide is in.*
the tide is out | **high tide** | **low tide** | **the incoming tide** | **the rising tide**

VERBS

the tide comes in (=the sea comes nearer) *Once the tide comes in, the cove is cut off.*
the tide goes out | **the tide turns** (=starts coming in or going out) | **be cut off by the tide** (=become trapped as the sea rises)

tide² *v*
tide sb **over** (sth) *phr v* to help someone through a difficult period, especially by lending them money: *Could you lend me £10 to tide me over till next week?*

ˈtide-mark *n* [C] **1** a mark left on the beach by the sea, that shows how high the sea reached **2** *BrE informal* a dirty mark left around the inside of a bath by the water

ˈtide pool *n* [C] *AmE* a small area of water left among rocks by the sea when the tide goes out SYN **rock pool** *BrE*

T

tide·wa·ter /ˈtaɪdˌwɔːtə $ -ˌwɒːtər, -ˌwɑː-/ *n* **1** [U] water that flows onto the land or into rivers when the tide rises **2** [C] *AmE* an area of land at or near the coast

tid·ings /ˈtaɪdɪŋz/ *n* [plural] *old use* news: **good/glad tidings** (=good news)

TIDY

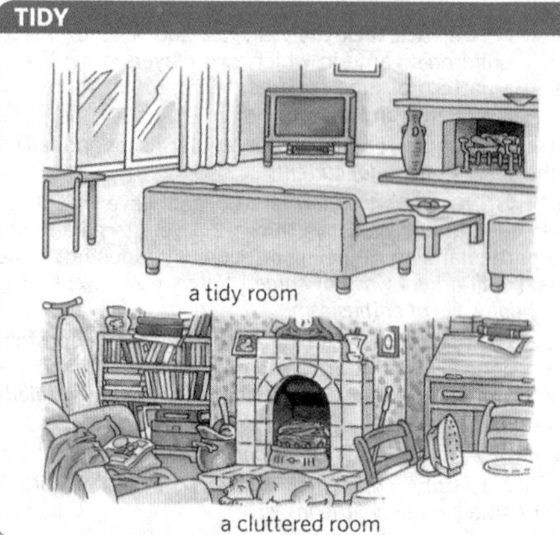

a tidy room

a cluttered room

ti·dy¹ /ˈtaɪdi/ ●●● S3 *adj* (*comparative* **tidier**, *superlative* **tidiest**) *especially BrE*

1 a room, house, desk etc that is tidy is neatly arranged with everything in the right place SYN **neat** OPP **untidy**, **messy**: *a tidy desk* | *I try to* ***keep*** *the garden* ***tidy***. | *Ellen's room is always* ***neat and tidy***.

2 someone who is tidy keeps their house, clothes etc neat and clean: *Chris is a naturally tidy person.*

3 a tidy sum/profit *informal* a large amount of money: *We sold the house for a tidy sum and moved south.*

4 a tidy mind *BrE* if someone has a tidy mind, the way they think is very organized and clear —**tidily** *adv* —**tidiness** *n* [U]

THESAURUS

tidy *BrE* a place, room etc that is tidy looks nice because everything has been arranged and put in the right place: *a tidy desk* | *I want to leave the place clean and tidy before we go.*

neat use this about things that are carefully arranged in a way that is nice to look at: *a neat pile of towels* | *The room was neat and tidy.*

immaculate /ɪˈmækjələt/ a place or thing that is immaculate is perfectly clean and neat - use this to emphasize how clean something looks: *Our house was always immaculate.*

well-kept a well-kept building or garden is very well cared for and looks neat and clean: *a large house on well-kept grounds*

orderly arranged or organized in a sensible or neat way: *The room was orderly and uncluttered.*

tidy² ●●○ (*also* **tidy up**) *v* (**tidied**, **tidying**, **tidies**) [I,T] to make a place look tidy: *Tidy your room!* | *It's time we tidied up the office.* | **tidy up after sb** *I'm tired of tidying up after you boys* (=tidying somewhere that someone else has made untidy).

tidy sth ↔ **away** *phr v BrE* to put something back in the place where it should be, especially in a cupboard, drawer etc: *Let's tidy these toys away.*

tidy³ *n* (*plural* **tidies**) [C] *BrE* **desk/car/sink tidy** a container for putting small objects in, used to keep your desk, car etc tidy

tie¹ /taɪ/ ●●● S2 W3 *v* (**tied**, **tying**, **ties**)

1 STRING/ROPE **a)** [T] to fasten things together or hold them in a particular position using a piece of string, rope etc OPP **untie**: **tie sth to/behind/onto etc sth** *Tie this label to your suitcase.* | **tie sb to sth** *They tied him to a tree and beat him up.* | **tie sth together (with sth)** *I kept all his letters tied together with a ribbon.* | **tie sb's hands/arms/legs/feet** *One of them tied her hands behind her back.* | *I* ***tie*** *my hair* ***back*** *when I'm jogging.* **b)** [T] to fasten something around, over etc something else and tie the ends together OPP **untie**: **tie sth around/over/under etc sth** *He had only a towel tied around his waist.* | *She tied a scarf over her head.* **c)** [T] to make a knot in a piece of string, rope etc, for example to fasten shoes or other clothes: *Can you* ***tie*** *your* ***shoelaces*** *by yourself?* | **tie a knot/bow** *She pulled the ribbon tightly and tied a bow.* **d)** [I] if a piece of clothing ties in a particular place, you fasten it there using a belt, BOW etc: *This dress ties at the back.*

2 GAME/COMPETITION [I] (*also* **be tied**) if two players, teams etc tie or are tied in a game or competition, they finish it with an equal number of points: **[+with]** *At the end of the season, we were tied with the Tigers.* | **tie for first/second etc place** *Woosnam and Lyle tied for fourth place on 264.*

3 be tied to sth to be related to something and dependent on it: *The flat is tied to the job.* | *Interest rates are tied to the rate of inflation.*

4 be tied to/by sth to be restricted by a particular situation, job etc, so that you cannot do exactly what you want: *Many women felt tied to the house.* | **be tied to doing sth** *I didn't want to be tied to commuting to London.* | *With children, you're tied by school holidays.*

5 tie the knot *informal* to get married

6 tie yourself (up) in knots *informal* to become very upset because you are confused, nervous, or worried

7 tie one on *AmE informal* to get drunk → **sb's hands are tied** at HAND¹(44)

tie sb **down** *phr v* to restrict someone's freedom to do what they want to do: *She didn't want to be tied down by a full-time job.* | **[+to]** *Are you ready to be tied down to a wife and children?*

tie in with sth *phr v*

1 to be similar to another idea, statement etc, so that they seem to be true SYN **match**: *Her description tied in with that of the other witness.*

2 (*also* **be tied in with sth**) to be related in some way to something else: *How does all this tie in with their long-term aims?*

3 to happen at the same time as something else: *The book was published to tie in with the TV series.*

tie up *phr v*

1 PERSON **tie sb ↔ up** to tie someone's arms, legs etc so that they cannot move SYN **bind**: *The intruders tied Kurt up and left him.*

2 OBJECT **tie sth ↔ up** to fasten something together, using string, rope etc: *He tied up all the old newspapers.*

3 BUSY **be tied up** to be very busy, so that you cannot do anything else: *I can't see you tomorrow - I'll be tied up all day.*

4 TRAFFIC/PHONE/COURT ETC **tie sth ↔ up** *especially AmE* to block a system or use it so much that other people cannot use it or it does not work effectively → **tie-up**: *Don't tie up the phone lines making personal calls.* | *Protesters tied up the traffic for three hours today.*

5 MONEY **be tied up** if your money is tied up in something, it is all being used for that thing and is not available for anything else: **[+in]** *My money's all tied up in the house.*

6 ARRANGEMENTS **tie sth ↔ up** to finish arranging all the details of something such as an agreement or a plan SYN **finalize**: *We'd better tie up the details with a solicitor.*

7 be tied up with sth to be very closely related to something SYN **be linked to**: *The shortage of teachers is tied up with the issue of pay.*

8 tie up loose ends to do the things that are necessary in order to finish a piece of work: *I need to tie up a few loose ends before I go on vacation.*

9 ANIMAL **tie sth ↔ up** to tie an animal to something with a rope, chain etc SYN **tether**: **[+to]** *She left the dog tied up to a tree.*

10 BOAT to tie a boat to something with a rope, chain etc SYN **moor**: *We tied up alongside a barge.* | **tie sth ↔ up** *There was a boat tied up at the jetty.*

tie² ●●● S3 W3 *n* [C]

1 MEN'S CLOTHES a long narrow piece of cloth tied in a

knot around the neck, worn by men: *I wear a shirt and tie at work.* → **BLACK-TIE, BOW TIE**
2 CONNECTION/RELATIONSHIP [usually plural] a strong relationship between people, groups, or countries: **close/strong ties** *the importance of strong* ***family ties*** | **[+between/with]** *close ties between the two countries* | **economic/diplomatic/personal etc ties** *Japan's strong economic ties with Taiwan* | **the ties of marriage/friendship/love etc** → **OLD SCHOOL TIE**
3 RESULT [usually singular] the result of a game, competition, or election when two or more people or teams get the same number of points, votes etc SYN **draw** *BrE*: *The match ended in a tie.*
4 FOR CLOSING STH a piece of string, wire etc used to fasten or close something such as a bag
5 GAME *BrE* one game, especially of football, that is part of a larger competition: **[+against]** *England's World Cup tie against Argentina* | **first round/second round etc tie** | **home/away tie**
6 PREVENT YOU FROM DOING STH something that means you must stay in one place, job etc or prevents you from being free to do what you want: *If you enjoy travelling, young children can be a tie.*
7 RAILWAY *AmE* a heavy piece of wood or metal supporting a railway track SYN **sleeper** *BrE*

tie·break·er /ˈtaɪbreɪkə $ -ər/ *n* [C] **1** an extra question in a game or QUIZ, used to decide who will win when two people have the same number of points **2** (*also* **tie·break** /ˈtaɪbreɪk/) the final game of a SET in tennis, played when each player has won six games

ˌtied ˈcottage *n* [C] *BrE* a house that a farm worker rents from a farmer while he is working on that farm

ˌtied ˈhouse *n* [C] *BrE* a PUB that can only sell the beer made by a particular company → **FREE HOUSE**

ˈtie-dye *v* [T] to make a pattern on a piece of material by tying string around it and colouring it with DYE (=coloured liquid)

ˈtie-in *n* [C] a product such as a record, book, or toy that is related to a new film, TV show etc

ˈtie-pin *n* [C] *BrE* a thing used for keeping a man's TIE fastened to his shirt or as a decoration

tier /tɪə $ tɪr/ ●○○ *n* [C]
1 one of several levels or layers that rise up one above the other: *The lower tier has 10,000 seats.* | **in tiers** *Terraces of olive trees rose in tiers.* | **two-tiered/three-tiered etc** (=having two, three etc levels or layers) *a three-tiered wedding cake* → see picture at **LAYER**[1]
2 one of several levels in an organization or system: **[+of]** *the most senior tier of management* | **the first/second etc tier** *The second tier of the programme is in-house training.* | *a* ***two-tier*** *system of government*

ˈtie-up *n* [C] *informal* **1** an agreement to become business partners: **[+with]** *IBM's tie-up with Auspex System Inc* **2** *BrE* a strong connection between two or more things: **[+between]** *the tie-up between class interests and politics* **3** *AmE* a situation in which traffic is prevented from moving or there is a problem which prevents a system or plan from working → **tie up** at **TIE**[1]

tiff /tɪf/ *n* [C] a slight argument between friends or people who are in love: **[+with]** *Dave's* ***had*** *a* ***tiff*** *with his girlfriend.* THESAURUS ▸ **ARGUMENT**

ti·ger /ˈtaɪɡə $ -ər/ ●●● W3 *n* [C] a large wild animal that has yellow and black lines on its body and is a member of the cat family → **PAPER TIGER** → see picture at **BIG CAT**

ˈtiger ˌmother *n* [C] a mother who is extremely strict with her children so that they will behave very well and achieve a lot

tight[1] /taɪt/ ●●● S2 W3 *adj* (*comparative* **tighter**, *superlative* **tightest**)
1 CLOTHES tight clothes fit your body very closely, especially in a way that is uncomfortable OPP **loose**: *tight jeans* | *My shoes were so tight that I could hardly walk.* | *The jacket is rather* ***a tight fit*** (=it fits too tightly). → see picture at **LOOSE**[1]
2 PULLED/STRETCHED FIRMLY string, wire, cloth etc that is tight has been pulled or stretched firmly so that it is straight or cannot move: *The bandage must be tight enough to stop the bleeding.* | *She tied the rope around the post and* ***pulled*** *it* ***tight***.
3 ATTACHED FIRMLY a screw, lid etc that is tight is firmly attached and difficult to move: *Check that the screws are tight.*
4 HOLDING STH FIRMLY **a tight hold/grip** if you keep or have a tight hold on something, you hold it firmly: *His mother* ***kept a tight hold on*** *his hand.*
5 STRICT controlling something very strictly or firmly: *The government is* ***keeping tight control on*** *immigration.* | **keep a tight grip/hold/rein on sth** (=control it very firmly) *The former dictator still keeps a tight grip on power.* | *Anna was determined to keep a tight hold on her feelings.* | ***Security*** *is always* ***tight*** *for the opening day of parliament.* | **run/keep a tight ship** (=manage a company, organization etc strictly and effectively)
6 LITTLE MONEY if money is tight, you do not have enough of it: **money is tight/things are tight** *Money was tight and he needed a job badly.* | *As you know, I run the magazine on a pretty* ***tight budget***.
7 LITTLE TIME if time is tight, it is difficult for you to do everything you need to do in the time available: ***Time is tight****, and she has another meeting to go to this afternoon.* | *We should arrive on time, but it'll be tight.* | *As usual, his* ***schedule*** *on Saturday was* ***tight*** (=he had arranged to do several things in a short time). | *I'm working to a very* ***tight deadline*** (=I have to finish a piece of work very quickly).
8 LITTLE SPACE if space is tight, there is only just enough space to fit something into a place: **be a tight squeeze/fit** *Six in the car will be a tight squeeze.*
9 NOT GENEROUS *informal* not generous, or trying hard to avoid spending money: *Don't be so tight!*
10 CLOSE TOGETHER placed or standing closely together: *The animal's body was curled up in a tight little ball.* | *She wore her hair in a tight bun.*
11 CLOSE RELATIONSHIP a tight group of people, countries etc have a close relationship with each other SYN **tight-knit**: *Together, the young film-makers formed a tight group.* | *the tight bonds that had grown between them*
12 BEND/TURN a tight bend or turn is very curved and turns quickly in another direction: *Danny lost control on a tight bend, and the car ran off the road.*
13 CHEST/STOMACH/THROAT if your chest, stomach, or throat feels tight, it feels painful and uncomfortable, because you are ill or worried: *Before she went on stage her chest felt tight and her throat hurt.*
14 EXPRESSION/SMILE/VOICE a tight expression, smile, or voice shows that you are annoyed or worried SYN **tight-lipped**: *'Look, I'm sorry ...,' she said, forcing a tight smile.*
15 DIFFICULT SITUATION **in a tight corner/spot** *informal* in a difficult situation: *He's a good man to have around if ever you're in a tight corner.* | *'Did something go wrong?' 'Let's just say I got into a bit of a tight spot.'*
16 PLAY/PERFORMANCE playing a piece of music or giving a performance very exactly and well, without any pauses or mistakes: *The band gave a really tight performance.* | *a tight, well-rehearsed production*
17 GAME/COMPETITION a tight game, competition etc is one in which the teams, players etc play equally well, and it is not easy to win: *The opening quarter of the game was very tight.*
18 DRUNK [not before noun] *old-fashioned informal* drunk
—**tightness** *n* [U] → **AIRTIGHT, WATERTIGHT**

tight[2] ●●● S2 *adv* very firmly or closely SYN **tightly**: ***Hold tight*** *to the handrail!* | *I kept my eyes* ***tight shut***. → **sit tight** at **SIT**(8), → **sleep tight** at **SLEEP**[1](4)

tight·en /ˈtaɪtn/ ●●○ (*also* **tighten up**) *v*
1 [T] to close or fasten something firmly by turning it OPP **loosen**: *Tighten the screws firmly.* | *I'd put the new tyre on, but I hadn't tightened up the wheel.*
2 [I,T] if you tighten a rope, wire etc, or if it tightens, it is stretched or pulled so that it becomes tight: *When you*

T

tighten guitar strings, the note gets higher. | *The rope tightened around his body.*
3 [I,T] to become stiff or make a part of your body become stiff OPP **relax**: *His mouth tightened into a thin, angry line.* | *Tighten up the muscles of both arms.*
4 tighten your grip/hold on sth a) to control a place or situation more strictly: *Rebel forces have tightened their hold on the capital.* **b)** to hold someone or something more firmly: *Sarah tightened her grip on my arm.*
5 [T] to make a rule, law, or system more strict OPP **relax**: *Efforts to tighten the rules have failed.* | **tighten up on sth** *a range of measures to tighten up on illegal share dealing*
6 tighten your belt *informal* to try to spend less money than you used to: *Businesses were tightening their belts and cutting jobs.*
7 tighten the screws (on sb) *informal* to try to force someone to do something, by threatening them or making things difficult for them - used in news reports: *Closing the border would tighten the screws on the terrorists.*
8 [I] *AmE* if a race or competition tightens, the distance between the competitors becomes smaller: *He expects the presidential race to tighten.*
tighten up *phr v* if a team or group tightens up, they start working together more effectively: **tighten sth ↔ up** *We have tightened up the defence and are winning matches as a result.*

tight-fist·ed /ˌtaɪt ˈfɪstɪd◂/ *adj informal* not generous with money SYN **stingy** —**tight-fistedness** *n* [U]

ˌtight-ˈfitting *adj* fitting very closely or tightly: *a tight-fitting skirt*

ˌtight-ˈknit *adj* [usually before noun] a tight-knit group of people are closely connected with each other: *a tight-knit island community*

tight-lipped /ˌtaɪt ˈlɪpt◂/ *adj* **1** unwilling to talk about something: *Diplomats are remaining tight-lipped about the negotiations.* **2** with your lips tightly pressed together because you are angry

tight·ly /ˈtaɪtli/ ●●○ *adv*
1 very firmly or closely: *He gripped the steering wheel more tightly.* | *Marie held the baby tightly in her arms.* | *Her eyes were tightly shut.*
2 in a strict way: *The media is* ***tightly controlled*** *in some countries.* | *tightly guarded government buildings*
3 in a way that shows you are annoyed or worried: *Caroline smiled tightly.*
4 with not much space between people or things: *The houses were tightly packed together.*

ˌtightly-ˈknit *adj* TIGHT-KNIT

tight·rope /ˈtaɪt-rəʊp $ -roʊp/ *n* [C] **1** a rope or wire high above the ground that someone walks along in a CIRCUS **2 walk a tightrope** to be in a difficult situation in which something bad could happen if you make a mistake: *I feel as though I'm walking a tightrope between success and failure.*

tights /taɪts/ *n* [plural] **1** *BrE* a piece of women's clothing made of very thin material that fits tightly over the feet and legs and goes up to the waist SYN **pantyhose** *AmE* **2** a piece of clothing similar to women's tights but too thick to see through, worn especially by dancers

tight·wad /ˈtaɪtwɒd $ -wɑːd/ *n* [C] *AmE informal* someone who hates to spend or give money

ti·gress /ˈtaɪgrɪs/ *n* [C] a female tiger

tik·ka /ˈtiːkə/ *n* [U] a type of Indian food that consists of small pieces of meat covered in spices, and cooked: *chicken tikka*

til, 'til /tɪl,tl/ a short form of TILL[1]

til·de /ˈtɪldə/ *n* [C] a mark (~) placed over the letter 'n' in Spanish to show that it is pronounced /nj/

tile¹ /taɪl/ ●●○ S3 *n*
1 [C] a flat square piece of baked clay or other material, used for covering walls, floors etc: *bathroom tiles*
2 [C] a thin curved piece of baked clay used for covering roofs → see picture at ROOF[1]
3 on the tiles *BrE informal* out drinking, dancing etc for enjoyment until late at night

tile² *v* [T] to cover a roof, floor etc with tiles —**tiled** *adj*: *a tiled floor* —**tiler** *n* [C]

til·ing /ˈtaɪlɪŋ/ *n* [U] an area or surface covered with tiles, or the work of covering a surface with tiles

till¹ /tɪl, tl/ ●●● S1 *prep, conjunction spoken* until: *I didn't have a boyfriend till I was 17.* | *The shop's open till nine o'clock on Fridays.*

till² /tɪl/ *n* [C] **1** *BrE* a machine used in shops, restaurants etc for calculating the amount you have to pay, and for storing the money SYN **cash register** *AmE* **2 in the till** *AmE* money in the till is money that a company or organization has: *You keep as much money as you need in the till to run your operations.* **3 have your hands/fingers in the till** to steal money from the place where you work: **be caught with your hands/fingers in the till** (=to be caught stealing from your employer)

till³ *v* [T] to prepare land for growing crops SYN **cultivate**: **till the soil/land/fields etc**

till·age /ˈtɪlɪdʒ/ *n* [U] the activity of preparing land for growing crops

til·ler /ˈtɪlə $ -ər/ *n* [C] a long handle fastened to the RUDDER (=part that controls the direction) of a boat

tilt¹ /tɪlt/ ●○○ *v* [I,T]
1 to move a part of your body, especially your head or chin, upwards or to the side SYN **tip**: *My mother tilted her head and smiled.* | *Ned's mouth tilted upwards slightly at the corners.*
2 to move or make something move into a position where one side is higher than the other SYN **tip**: *As it came in to land, the plane tilted sideways.* | *The man was tilting his chair back.*
3 if an opinion or situation tilts, or if something tilts it, it changes so that people start to prefer one person, belief, or action to others: *Crisis situations tend to* ***tilt the balance*** *of power in favour of the president.* | **[+toward/towards]** *Government tax policy has tilted toward industrial development.*
tilt at sb/sth *phr v*
1 to attack someone in what you say or write
2 tilt at windmills to waste time and energy attacking an enemy that is not real

tilt² *n* **1 (at) full tilt** as fast as possible: *He charged full tilt down the slope.* **2** [C,U] a movement or position in which one side of something is higher than the other: *a slight* ***tilt of the head*** **3** [C] a preference for one person, belief, or action over others: **[+toward/towards]** *the recent tilt toward the Democrats* **4** [C] *BrE* an attempt to win something: **[+at]** *The team is preparing for another tilt at the European Cup.* **5** [C] a spoken or written attack on someone or something

tim·ber /ˈtɪmbə $ -ər/ ●●○ *n*
1 [U] *BrE* wood used for building or making things SYN **lumber** *AmE*: *a bench made of timber*
2 [U] trees that produce wood used for building or making things: *the timber trade*
3 [C] a wooden beam, especially one that forms part of the main structure of a house
4 timber! *spoken* used to warn people that a tree being cut down is about to fall

tim·bered /ˈtɪmbəd $ -ərd/ *adj* timbered buildings have a frame made of wooden beams, or have wooden beams showing on the outside: **timbered houses/cottages** → HALF-TIMBERED

tim·ber·land /ˈtɪmbəlænd $ -ər-/ *n* [C,U] *AmE* an area of land that is covered by trees, especially ones that will be used for wood

tim·ber·line /ˈtɪmbəlaɪn $ -ər-/ *n* [singular] *technical* **1** the height above the level of the sea beyond which trees will not grow **2** the northern or southern limit in the world beyond which trees will not grow

tim·bre /ˈtæmbə, ˈtɪm- $ -ər/ *n* [C,U] *formal* the quality of the sound made by a particular instrument or voice

tim·brel /ˈtɪmbrəl/ *n* [C] *old use* a TAMBOURINE

Tim·buk·tu /ˌtɪmbʌkˈtuː/ a city on the edge of the Sahara Desert in Mali, West Africa, whose correct name is Tombouctou. People sometimes mention Timbuktu as an example of a place that is very far away: *There were enough cars to stretch from here to Timbuktu.*

time[1] /taɪm/ ●●● S1 W1 *n*

1 MINUTES/HOURS ETC [U] the thing that is measured in minutes, hours, days, years etc using clocks: *Einstein changed the way we think about space and time.* | *close relationships established over a long* ***period of time*** | *Customers have only a limited* ***amount of time*** *to examine the goods.* | **time passes/goes by** *Their marriage got better as time went by.* THESAURUS▸ PERIOD

2 ON A CLOCK [singular] a particular point in time shown on a clock in hours and minutes: *'What time is it?' 'It's about two thirty.'* | *What time are you going out tonight?* | **what time do you make it?** *BrE*, **what time do you have?** *AmE* (=used to ask someone with a watch what time it is) | **have you got the time?** *BrE*, **do you have the time?** *AmE* (=used to ask someone if they know what time it is) | **tell the time** *BrE*, **tell time** *AmE* (=be able to understand a clock) *Robin's just learning to tell the time.* | **look at the time** (=used when you realize that it is later than you thought it was) *Oh no. Look at the time. I'll be late.* | **is that the time?** (=used when you suddenly realize what the time is) *Is that the time? I must go.* | **this time tomorrow/last week etc** *By this time tomorrow I'll know whether I've got the job.*

3 OCCASION [C] an occasion when something happens or someone does something: *That was the only time we disagreed.* | *Do you remember the time I hit Tom Benson?* | *Mary had seen the film many times.* | **(for) the first/second/last etc time** *It was the first time that he had lost a game.* | *Gerry had just had back surgery for the third time in two years.* | **(the) next time/(the) last time/this time** *Why don't you drop in for a drink next time you're over this way?* | *The last time* (=the most recent time) *I saw Jonathan was Thursday evening.* | *The freezing weather did not return until February but this time we were prepared.* | **the first/second/next/last etc time round** (=the first, second etc time something happens) *I missed their concert the first time round so I'm going next week.* | **every/each time** *I meet up with Julie every time I go to Washington.* | **how many times ... ?** *How many times did you take your driving test?* | *How many times have I told you not to wander off like that?* (=I have told you many times) | ***One time*** (=once) *I went to a garage sale and bought fifteen books.*

GRAMMAR

You say: *The first time I saw it, I loved it.* ✗ Don't say: *At the first time I saw it, I loved it.*

4 POINT WHEN STH HAPPENS [C,U] the particular minute, hour, day etc when something happens or should happen: **at the time of sth** *She was three months pregnant at the time of Stephen's death.* | **at some/any/that time** *He is performing as well as at any time in his career.* | *The UK has 500,000 stray dogs on its streets* ***at any one time*** (=at any particular time). | **at a/the time when ...** *At the time when this scheme was introduced, it was recognised that there might be problems.* | **by the time ...** *The phone was ringing but by the time she got indoors, it had stopped.* | **it's time to do sth** *Rosie – it's time to get up.* | **it's time for sth** *Come on, it's time for bed.* | *He glanced at his watch. 'It's time for me to go.'* | **it's time sb did sth** *It's time I fed the dog.* | *Now is* ***the right time*** *for us to move to London.* | **a good/bad time** *This might be a good time to start planning the new garden.* | **not the time/hardly the time** *Now is not the time to annoy Peter.* | **there's no time like the present** (=used to say that now is a good time to do something) *'When do you want to meet?' 'Well, there's no time like the present.'* | **dinner/lunch/tea etc time** *It's nearly dinner time.* | **opening/closing time** (=the time when a shop, bar etc opens or closes) *We empty the till each night at closing time.* | **arrival/departure time** (=the time when a train, plane etc arrives or leaves) *Our estimated arrival time is 2:30 pm.* | **time of day/year** *England is so lovely at this time of year.* | *We'll sort that out* ***when the time comes*** (=when it becomes necessary).

5 PERIOD OF TIME [singular, U] a period of time during which something happens or someone does something: *Dustin wanted to* ***spend*** *as much* ***time*** *as possible with his family.* | **a long/short/limited time** *I first met Jennifer a long time ago.* | *They stopped for a short time to rest the horses.* | *Andy and Tom talked* ***for some time*** (=for a fairly short period). | *Alison was married,* ***for a time*** (=for a fairly short period), *to a comedian.* | *Martin disliked being away from his family* ***for any length of time*** (=for more than just a short period). | *It* ***took*** *her a long* ***time*** *to make a decision.* | *Learning a language isn't easy – it* ***takes time*** (=takes a long period of time). | **take time to do sth** (=deliberately spend time doing something) *While in New York he took time to visit some friends.* | **travel time** *I wanted to make better use of my travel time.*

6 AVAILABLE TIME [U] an amount of time that is available for you to do something: *I'll visit him if I* ***have time.*** | *Molly would like to do some diving if* ***there is time.*** | **have time for sth** *She realized she would have time for a coffee before her train left.* | *We don't have to rush. We* ***have all the time in the world*** (=have plenty of time). | *June had little* ***time to spare*** (=available time) *for making her own clothes.* | **free/spare time** (=time when you are not working) *He writes poetry in his spare time.* | *Being prepared for meetings will* ***save time.*** | *I don't want to* ***waste time*** *arguing.* | *She spent* ***precious time*** (=valuable and important time) *looking for a telephone.* | *I seem to* ***spend*** *most of my* ***time*** *on the phone.* | *McDuff* ***passed the time*** *writing letters* (=wrote letters because he had nothing else to do). | **have time on your hands/time to kill** (=not have enough to do) *Now the children have left home, she has too much time on her hands.* | **make/find time (for sth/to do sth)** (=plan so that you have time available for something) *Make time to talk to your children.* | *Book your ticket soon, as* ***time is running out.*** | **time's up** (=used to say that it is the end of the time allowed for something such as a competition or examination) | **we're out of time** (=used on radio and television programmes to say that there is no more time available on the programme)

7 all the time (*also* **the whole time**) continuously or very often: *I keep practising and I'm improving all the time.* | *He worries about her the whole time.*

8 most of the time very often or almost always: *I can speak German but we speak English most of the time.*

9 half the time if something happens half the time, especially something annoying, it happens quite often: *Half the time you don't even notice what I'm wearing.*

10 at times sometimes: *Life is hard at times.*

11 from time to time sometimes, but not regularly or very often: *These food safety scares happen from time to time.*

12 time after time/time and time again often, over a long period: *The police were catching the same kids stealing time after time.*

13 at all times always – used especially in official rules and statements: *Children must be supervised at all times while in the park.* | *Parents are welcome at all times.*

14 nine times out of ten/99 times out of 100 etc used to say that something is almost always true or almost always happens: *Nine times out of ten she's right.*

15 at the time at a particular moment or period in the past when something happened, especially when the situation is very different now: *I was about ten or eleven at the time.*

16 at one time at a time in the past but not now: *At one time she wanted to be a nurse, but the thought of working at night put her off.*

17 at this time *AmE* at this particular moment: *The president said his actions were 'the right ones at this time'.*

18 at no time used to say strongly that something never happened or should never happen: **at no time did/was etc** *At no time did anyone involved speak to the press.* | *At no time was the company informed.*

19 for the time being for a short period of time from now, but not permanently: *Now, for the time being, she is living with her father in Tijuana.*

20 in 10 days'/five years'/a few minutes' etc time ten days, five years etc from now: *He has an appointment with the doctor in two days' time.*

21 in time a) before the time by which it is necessary for something to be done: *Will you be able to finish it in time?* | **in time to do sth** *They ran all the way to the corner* ***just in time*** *to see the bus disappearing up the street.* | **[+for]** *The*

T

painting was successfully repaired in time for the opening of the exhibition. | **in good time/in plenty of time** (=a long time before the necessary time) *We arrived at the concert hall in good time.* **b)** after a certain period of time, especially after a gradual process of change and development: *He wants to see changes in the company and I am sure he will, in time.*

22 with time to spare sooner than expected or necessary: *We should arrive in New York with time to spare.*

23 over time if something happens over time, it happens gradually during a long period: *The research project will be assessed over time.* | *Students are encouraged to consider the way language* ***changes over time****.*

24 with time/given time after a period of time: *These symptoms will start to get better with time.* | *I would have thought of the answer, given time.*

25 take your time a) to do something slowly or carefully without hurrying: **take your time doing sth** *Marie took her time cutting my hair and did it really well.* | **[+over]** *He had planned to take his time over the journey.* **b)** to do something more slowly than seems reasonable: *You're taking your time with the lab tests. We need the results now.*

26 five/ten/many etc times ... used to say how much greater, more etc one thing is than another: *Sound travels four times faster in water than in air.* | *There were three times as many girls as boys.*

27 ... at a time a) if someone deals with things one, three, ten etc at a time, they deal with them separately or in groups of three, ten etc: *If you raise your hands, I'll answer questions one at a time.* | *Frank took the stairs two at a time.* **b)** if something happens for hours, days, months etc at a time, it continues for several hours, months etc: *Because of his work, he's often away for weeks at a time.*

28 on time at the correct time or the time that was arranged: *Jack was worried about whether he'd be able to get there on time.* | **right/bang/dead on time** (=at exactly the right time) *The plane arrived right on time.*

USAGE: On time, in time

- **On time** means 'at the correct or agreed time': *Please arrive on time.* ✗ Don't say: *Please arrive in time.*
- **In time** means 'early enough for something or to do something': *He arrived in time for supper.*

29 ahead of/behind time earlier or later than the time when something happens, should be done etc: *Prepare what you plan to say in the meeting ahead of time* (=before the meeting). | *The train left twenty minutes behind time* (=after it should have left).

30 it's about time (*also* **it's high time**) *spoken* used to say strongly that you think something should happen soon or should already have happened: *It's about time our team won.* | *It's high time we had a party.*

31 not before time/and about time (too) *spoken* used to say that something should have happened sooner: *Philip is going to be punished and not before time.*

32 the best/biggest etc ... of all time the best, biggest etc of a particular kind of person or thing that has ever existed: *He is the greatest athlete of all time, in my opinion.*

33 in no time (at all)/in next to no time very quickly or soon: *We'll be there in no time.*

34 any time (now) very soon: *'When is she due back?' 'Any time now.'*

35 it's (only/just) a matter/question of time used to say that something will definitely happen at some time in the future, but you do not know when: *I'll find the key eventually. It's just a question of time.* | *It's only a matter of time before we catch the person who killed her.*

36 (only) time will tell used to say that at some time in the future it will become clear whether or not something is true, right etc: *Only time will tell if the treatment has been successful.*

37 PERIOD IN HISTORY [C] (*also* **times** [plural]) a particular period in history: *Mankind has used the horse since* ***ancient times****.* | *In earlier times, servants would use the bare wooden stairs at the back of the house.* | **at/in/during etc the time of sth** *He lived at the time of the Napoleonic wars.* | **our time(s)** (=the present period in history) *Air pollution has become one of the most significant health problems of our time.*

38 behind the times old-fashioned: *Our equipment is a bit behind the times.*

39 move/change/keep up with the times to change when other things in society, business etc change: *We've got to move with the times.*

40 ahead of your/its time having or using the most advanced ideas, methods, designs, technology etc: *Coleridge was far ahead of his time in his understanding of the unconscious.*

41 PLEASANT/UNPLEASANT [C] a good time, bad time, difficult time etc is a period or occasion when you have good, bad, difficult etc experiences: *This was the happiest time of her life.* | **good/bad/hard etc times** *They had their happy times, but they had their hard times too.* | **have a good/great/lovely etc time** (=enjoy yourself) *Did you have a good time at the party?* | *Julie went to a wedding at the weekend and* ***had the time of*** *her* ***life*** (=enjoyed herself very much).

42 sb's time in/at/as sth the period of time when you were living in a particular place, working for a particular company etc: *In her time at the United Nations she was considered a tough negotiator.*

43 before your time a) before you were born or before you started working or living somewhere: *They say he was a great actor but that was before my time.* **b)** if you do something, especially get old, before your time, you do it before the time when most people usually do it in their lives: *He seemed to grow into an old man before his time.*

44 IN PART OF THE WORLD [U] the way of referring to points in time in one particular part of the world: *Eastern Standard Time* | *British Summer Time* | *The flight to Boston arrives at 1.15 pm* ***local time****.*

45 TIME TAKEN [C] **a)** the amount of time taken by a competitor in a race: *The Olympic medallist's time in the 200 metres final was 19.21 seconds.* **b) journey time** the amount of time a journey takes: *The journey time to London is approximately four hours.*

46 SPORTS [U] *BrE* the end of the normal period of playing time in a sports game, especially football SYN **full time**: *Mason's goal 13 minutes from time earned his team a place in the finals.*

47 MUSIC [U] the number of beats in each BAR in a piece of music: *Waltzes are usually in three-four time.*

48 in time to/with sth if you do something in time to a piece of music, you do it using the same RHYTHM and speed as the music: *Gloria was tapping her feet in time to the music.*

49 keep/beat time to show the RHYTHM and speed that a piece of music should be played at to a group of musicians, using your hands

50 keep perfect/good etc time if a clock keeps good time, it always shows the correct time

51 PRISON **do time** to spend a period of time in prison: *Paul was doing time for burglary.*

52 pass the time of day (with sb) to say hello to someone and have a short talk with them: *People like to pass the time of day with neighbours.*

53 time was (when) used to say that there was a time when you used to be able to do something, when something used to happen etc: *Time was when no one had television.*

54 there's no time to lose used to say that you must do something quickly because there is very little time

55 make good time if you make good time on a journey, you travel quickly, especially more quickly than you expected: *We made good time and were at the hotel by lunchtime.*

56 race/work/battle against time to try to finish or achieve something even though you have very little time: *Mark was racing against time to complete the work by Friday.*

57 time is money used to say that wasting time or delaying something costs money

58 time is on your side used to say that someone is young enough to be able to wait before doing something or until something happens

59 time is a great healer/heals all wounds used to say that someone will become less upset as time passes
60 time flies used to say that time seems to pass very quickly: *Time flies when you're having fun.*
61 in your own time if you study or do work in your own time, you do it outside normal school or work hours: *Nurses in training study in their own time.*
62 in your own (good) time *informal* when you are ready: *Bobby will tell them about it in his own good time.*
63 all in good time used to tell someone to be patient because something they are waiting for will certainly happen after a period of time, and probably quite soon: *'I'd love to see it.' 'All in good time.'*
64 have a lot of/no time for sb/sth *informal* if you have a lot of time for someone or something, you like or admire them, and if you have no time for them, you do not like or admire them: *He has no time for* (=does not like) *people who talk too much.*
65 time of life used to refer to someone's age: *At my time of life, you can't take too many shocks like that.*
66 your time used in certain expressions to refer to the period when you are alive: **in your time** *I've met some rude women in my time but she's the worst.* | *He was many things in his time – musician, pilot, cattle-rancher, industrialist, journalist.* | *If I* ***had*** *my* ***time over again*** (=lived my life again), *I'd probably do exactly the same things.*
67 time of the month the time when a woman has her PERIOD: *It's that time of the month.*
68 time out of mind *literary* a very long time, or a very long time ago → BIG TIME[1], FULL-TIME, HALF-TIME, PART-TIME, REAL-TIME, → **at the best of times** at BEST[3](11), → **time is of the essence** at ESSENCE(4), → **bide your time** at BIDE(1), → **in the fullness of time** at FULLNESS(1), → **give sb/sth time** at GIVE[1](21), → **kill time** at KILL[1](8), → **lose time** at LOSE(8), → **mark time** at MARK[1](11), → **move with the times** at MOVE[1](17), → **in the nick of time** at NICK[1](1), → **for old times' sake** at OLD(19), → **once upon a time** at ONCE[1](14), → **play for time** at PLAY[1](18), → **the time is ripe** at RIPE(3), → **at the same time** at SAME[1](3), → **sign of the times** at SIGN[1](9), → **a stitch in time (saves nine)** at STITCH[1](8), → **have a whale of a time** at WHALE[1](2)

THESAURUS

A TIME WHEN SOMETHING HAPPENS

time a time when something happens or when you should do something: *The last time I saw her she was in high school.* | *It's time for you to go to bed.*
occasion a time when something happens. **Occasion** is more formal than **time**: *They have been seen together on several occasions.*
moment a particular point in time when something happens: *At that moment* (=at exactly that time), *the door bell rang.* | *The next moment she was gone.*
point a particular time during a longer period of time: *At one point during the play she completely forgot her lines.* | *the lowest point of the holiday*

A LONG TIME

a long time a long period of time, especially many months or years: *They've been married a long time – nearly 30 years.*
hours/weeks/months/years many hours, weeks, months, or years – used to emphasize that it is a long time, or much longer than it should be: *It's years since I rode a bike.*
ages *especially BrE informal* a very long time: *I've been standing here for ages.*
a while (*also* **some time**) a fairly long time: *I hadn't seen Paul for a while, and he'd completely changed.*
the longest time *AmE* a very long time: *For the longest time, my daughter wasn't reading at all.*

A SHORT TIME

a minute/moment a short time: *I'll call you back in a minute.* | *Can I show you something? It will only take a moment.*
a second a very short time: *I'll be ready in a second.* | *Just a second – I can't find my wallet.*
an instant *written* a very short time: *In an instant, they were gone.* | *He paused for an instant.*
a little while/a short while a short period of time, especially a few hours, days, or weeks: *I've been to Tokyo, but I was only there for a short while.*

time[2] ●●● S1 W2 *v* [T]
1 to arrange that something should happen at a particular time: *I saw from the station clock that I had timed my arrival perfectly.* | **be timed to do sth** *The tour has been timed to allow visitors to attend the opening night of the Verona opera season.* | *Her book was* ***timed to coincide with*** (=arranged to be at the same time as) *an exhibition of Goya's paintings at the National Gallery.* | **be timed for sth** *The meeting has been timed for three o'clock.* GRAMMAR **Time** is often passive in this meaning.
2 to measure how fast someone or something is going, how long it takes to do something etc: *We had to run up the stairs while the Sergeant timed us.* | **time sb/sth at sth** *They timed the winner at 2 minutes and 14.05 seconds.*
3 to hit a ball or make a shot at a particular moment → **mistime**: **time sth well/badly etc** *Keith timed the pass well.* | *a beautifully timed shot* → ILL-TIMED, WELL-TIMED

ˌtime and a ˈhalf *n* [U] one and a half times the normal rate of pay: *We get time and a half for working on Sunday.*
ˌtime and ˈmotion ˌstudy *n* [C] a study of working methods to find out how effective they are
ˈtime bomb *n* [C] **1** a bomb that is set to explode at a particular time **2** a situation that is likely to become a very serious problem: *Cutting down the rainforest is an environmental time bomb.*
ˈtime ˌcapsule *n* [C] a container that is filled with objects from a particular time, so that people in the future will know what life was like then
ˈtime card *n* [C] a piece of card on which the hours you have worked are recorded by a special machine
ˈtime clock *n* [C] a special clock that records the exact time when someone arrives at and leaves work
ˈtime-conˌsuming ●○○ *adj* taking a long time to do: *a complex and time-consuming process*
ˈtime-crunched *adj AmE informal* short of time: *It's hard for a time-crunched mom to fit exercise into her day.*
ˈtime deˌlay *n* [singular] a short period of time between one thing happening and another thing happening, especially in broadcasting or communications: *The programme will be broadcast with a time delay so that rude words can be edited out.*
ˈtime frame *n* [C] the period of time during which you expect or agree that something will happen or be done: *There is a ten year time frame for the implementation of the new policies.*
ˈtime-ˌhonoured *BrE*, **time-honored** *AmE adj* [only before noun] a time-honoured method or custom is one that has existed for a long time: *Sharon became involved with music* ***in the time-honoured fashion*** *– through her family.*
time·keep·er /ˈtaɪmˌkiːpə $ -ər/ *n* [C] **1** someone who officially records the times taken to do something, especially at a sports event **2 good/bad timekeeper** *BrE* **a)** someone who is good or bad at arriving at work at the right time **b)** a watch or clock that is good or bad at showing the right time —**timekeeping** *n* [U]
ˈtime lag (*also* **ˈtime lapse**) *n* [C] the period of time between two connected events: *There is generally a two-year time lag in the information being made available.*
ˈtime-lapse *adj* [only before noun] time-lapse photography involves taking many pictures of something over a period of time and then showing them together, so that a very slow process seems to happen much faster

time·less /ˈtaɪmləs/ ●○○ *adj*
1 remaining attractive and not becoming old-fashioned: *the timeless beauty of Venice*
2 *literary* continuing for ever: *the timeless universe* —**timelessly** *adv* —**timelessness** *n* [U]
ˈtime ˌlimit *n* [C] the longest time that you are allowed

T

in which to do something: **[+for/on sth]** *The time limit for applications is three weeks.*

time·line /ˈtaɪmlaɪn/ *n* [C] **1** a plan for when things will happen or how long you think something will take: *The timeline for the project is optimistic.* **2** a line showing the order in which events happened

time·ly /ˈtaɪmli/ ●○○ *adj* done or happening at exactly the right time: *The fight ended only with the timely arrival of the police.* | **in a timely manner/fashion** (=as quickly as is reasonable in a particular situation) *We aim to settle all valid claims in a timely manner.* | **a timely reminder (of sth)** *BrE* (=one that makes you remember something important) *The crash served as a timely reminder of the dangers of drinking and driving.*

ˈtime maˌchine *n* [C] in stories, a machine in which people can travel backwards or forwards in time

ˌtime ˈoff *n* [U] time when you are officially allowed not to be at work or studying: **take/have/get etc time off** *Have you ever had to take time off for health reasons?*

ˌtime ˈout *n* **1 take time out (to do sth)** *informal* to rest or do something different from your usual job or activities: *In between jobs, Liz always took time out to return to her first love – travelling.* **2** [C,U] a short break during a sports match when the teams can rest, get instructions from their manager etc: *With 15.7 seconds left, Washington State **called time out**.* **3** [C] an occasion when a computer stops using a particular program because the user has not done any work for a period of time

time·piece /ˈtaɪmpiːs/ *n* [C] *old use* a clock or watch

ˌtime-ˈpoor *adj BrE* someone who is time-poor does not have very much free time because they work all day and often work in the evenings too

tim·er /ˈtaɪmə $ -ər/ *n* [C] **1** an instrument that you use to measure time, when you are doing something such as cooking: *Set the timer on the cooker for three minutes.* → EGG-TIMER, see picture at MEASURE[1] **2 part-timer/full-timer** someone who works part or all of a normal working week

times[1] /taɪmz/ *prep* multiplied by: *two times two equals four (2 x 2 = 4)*

times[2] *v* [T] *spoken* to multiply a number: *Then you times that by 1,000.*

ˈtime-ˌsaving *adj* designed to reduce the time usually needed to do something: *a time-saving device* —**time-saver** *n* [C]

time·scale, **ˈtime scale** /ˈtaɪmskeɪl/ ●○○ *n* [C] *especially BrE* the period of time it takes for something to happen or be completed: *The timescale for completing the work would be fairly tight.*

time·serv·er /ˈtaɪmˌsɜːvə $ -ˌsɜːrvər/ *n* [C] *informal* someone who does the least amount of work possible in their job —**timeserving** *adj, n* [U]

time·share /ˈtaɪmʃeə $ -ʃer/ *n* [C,U] a holiday home that you buy with other people so that you can each spend a period of time there every year, or when you arrange to do this —**timeshare** *adj*: *timeshare flats*

ˈtime-ˌsharing *n* [U] **1** *technical* a situation in which one computer is used by many different people at different TERMINALS at the same time **2** the practice of owning a timeshare

ˈtime sheet *n* [C] a piece of paper on which the hours you have worked are written or printed

ˈtime ˌsignal *n* [C] a sound on the radio that shows the exact time

ˈtime ˌsignature *n* [C] two numbers at the beginning of a line of music that tell you how many BEATS there are in a BAR

time·sink /ˈtaɪmˌsɪŋk/ *n* [C] *informal* an activity that takes a lot of time – used to show disapproval SYN **timesuck**: *Looking for things to buy on the Internet is a real timesink.*

ˌtime span, **time·span** /ˈtaɪmspæn/ *n* [C] a period of time: *It's difficult to imagine a time span of a million years.*

ˌTimes ˈSquare a large SQUARE (=a broad open area with buildings on all sides) in New York City, close to many theatres. Each year there is a big New Year's Eve celebration in Times Square, and at midnight a large red ball is lowered down a building to show that the New Year has begun.

ˌtimes ˈtable *n* [C] a list, used especially by children in school, that shows the results when each number between one and twelve is multiplied by each number between one and twelve: *Do you know the eleven times table?*

time·suck /ˈtaɪmˌsʌk/ *n* [C] *informal* another word for TIMESINK

ˈtime switch *n* [C] an electronic control that can be set to start or stop a machine at a particular time

time·ta·ble[1] /ˈtaɪmˌteɪbəl/ ●●● W3 *n* [C]
1 *BrE* a list of the times at which buses, trains, planes etc arrive and leave SYN **schedule** *AmE*: **a railway/train/bus timetable**
2 a list of the times of classes in a school, college etc SYN **schedule** *AmE*
3 a plan of events and activities, with their dates and times SYN **schedule**: **[+for]** *The Council has set out a timetable for returning to civilian rule.*

timetable[2] *v BrE* **1** [T] to plan that something will happen at a particular time in the future SYN **schedule**: *The carnival parade is timetabled for 12.00 on both days.* **2** [I,T] to arrange the times at which classes will take place in a school or college SYN **schedule** *AmE*: *The course is timetabled for one period each week.* | *Art students have very few timetabled hours.* GRAMMAR **Timetable** is usually passive. —**timetabling** *n* [U]

ˈtime ˌtravel *n* [U] in SCIENCE FICTION, the action of going to a time in the past or the future —**time traveller** *n* [C]

ˈtime warp *n* [C] **1 be (caught/locked/stuck) in a time warp** to have not changed even though everyone or everything else has: *The house seemed to be stuck in a 19th-century time warp.* **2** an imaginary situation in which the past or future becomes the present

ˈtime-ˌworn *adj* **1** time-worn objects are old and have been used a lot: *time-worn steps* **2** time-worn ideas and beliefs are no longer sensible or useful SYN **outdated**: *time-worn prejudices*

ˈtime zone *n* [C] one of the 24 areas that the world is divided into, each of which has its own time

tim·id /ˈtɪmɪd/ *adj* not having courage or confidence SYN **shy** OPP **confident**: *I was a timid child.* | *a policy that is both timid and inadequate* **THESAURUS** SHY —**timidly** *adv* —**timidity** /təˈmɪdəti/ *n* [U]

REGISTER
In everyday English, people usually say that someone is **shy** rather than **timid**.

tim·ing /ˈtaɪmɪŋ/ ●●○ *n*
1 [U] the skill of doing something at exactly the right time: **perfect/good/bad etc timing** *He was just walking into the restaurant when we got there. Perfect timing.* | *He told jokes with an exquisite **sense of timing**.*
2 [C,U] the time when someone does something or when something happens, especially when you are considering how suitable this is: **[+of]** *The president and I did not discuss the timing of my departure.* | *Ferry schedules and precise timings are subject to weather conditions on the day of departure.*
3 [U] the way in which electricity is sent to the SPARK PLUGS in a car engine

tim·o·rous /ˈtɪmərəs/ *adj formal* lacking confidence and easily frightened SYN **fearful** OPP **bold**: *She was no helpless, timorous female.* —**timorously** *adv* —**timorousness** *n* [U]

tim·pa·ni /ˈtɪmpəni/ *n* [U] a set of large drums that are played in an ORCHESTRA

tin[1] /tɪn/ ●●○ *n*
1 [U] a soft silver-white metal that is often used to cover and protect iron and steel. It is a chemical ELEMENT: symbol Sn: *an old tin bath*

2 [C] *BrE* (*also* **tin can**) a small metal container in which food or drink is sold SYN **can** *AmE*: *a sardine tin* | **[+of]** *a tin of baked beans* → see pictures at CONTAINER, CAN[2]
3 [C] a metal container with a lid in which food can be stored: *a biscuit tin* → see picture at BOX[1]
4 [C] *BrE* a metal container in which food is cooked SYN **pan** *AmE*: *a 7-inch cake tin* | *a roasting tin*
5 [C] *BrE* a metal container with a lid, in which paint, glue etc is sold: **[+of]** *a tin of brown paint*

tin² *adj* made of TIN: *a tin roof* | *a tin mug*

tinc·ture /ˈtɪŋktʃə $ -ər/ *n* [C,U + of] *technical* a medical substance mixed with alcohol

tin·der /ˈtɪndə $ -ər/ *n* [U] dry material that burns easily and can be used for lighting fires

tin·der·box /ˈtɪndəbɒks $ -dərbɑːks/ *n* **1** [C usually singular] a place or situation that is dangerous and where there could suddenly be a lot of fighting or problems: *The area is a tinderbox that could again plunge the country into civil war.* **2** [C] a box containing things needed to make a flame, used in the past

ˈtinder-dry *adj* extremely dry and likely to burn very easily: *The whole forest is tinder-dry.*

tine /taɪn/ *n* [C] a pointed part of something that has several points, for example a fork

tin·foil /ˈtɪnfɔɪl/ *n* [U] thin shiny metal that bends like paper and is used for covering food

ting /tɪŋ/ *n* [C] a high clear ringing sound —**ting** *v* [I,T]

ˌting-a-ˈling *n* [C] *informal* the high clear ringing sound that is made by a small bell

tinge¹ /tɪndʒ/ *n* [C] a very small amount of a colour, emotion, or quality: **[+of]** *There was a tinge of sadness in her voice.* | *This glass has a greenish tinge.*

tinge² *v* (*present participle* **tinging** *or* **tingeing**) [T] *literary* to give something a small amount of a particular colour, emotion, or quality: **tinge sth with sth** *The light of the setting sun tinges the buildings with delicate colours.* | *Pink tinged her cheeks.*

tinged /tɪndʒd/ *adj* showing a small amount of a colour, emotion or quality: **[+with]** *His voice was* ***tinged with sadness*** *and regret.* | *white blossom tinged with pink* | **pink-tinged/jazz-tinged/romantically-tinged etc**

tin·gle /ˈtɪŋgəl/ *v* [I] **1** if a part of your body tingles, you feel a slight stinging feeling, especially on your skin: *My body tingled all over and I had a terrible headache.* | **tingling feeling/sensation** *Graham felt a tingling sensation in his hand.* **2 tingle with excitement/fear/anticipation etc** to feel excitement, fear etc very strongly: *She tingled with excitement. Soon she would be able to tell Martha everything.* —**tingle** *n* [C]

tin·ker¹ /ˈtɪŋkə $ -ər/ *v* [I] to make small changes to something in order to repair it or make it work better: **[+with]** *Congress has been tinkering with the legislation.* | **tinker around with sth** *Dad was always tinkering around with engines.*

tinker² *n* [C] **1** in the past, a tinker was someone who travelled from place to place selling things or repairing metal pots, pans etc **2** *BrE old-fashioned* a disobedient or annoying young child

tin·kle¹ /ˈtɪŋkəl/ *n* [C usually singular] **1** a light ringing sound: **[+of]** *the distant tinkle of a cow-bell* THESAURUS SOUND **2 give sb a tinkle** *BrE old-fashioned informal* to call someone on the telephone: *I'll give you a tinkle tomorrow.* **3 have a tinkle** *BrE spoken* to URINATE (=pass water from your body) - used especially by children or when talking to children

tinkle² *v* **1** [I,T] to make light ringing sounds, or to make something do this: *a tinkling bell* **2** [I] *spoken* to URINATE (=pass water from your body) - used especially by children or when talking to children: *Do you have to* ***go tinkle****?*

tinned /tɪnd/ *adj* [usually before noun] *BrE* tinned food is food that is sold in small metal containers which can be kept for a long time before they are opened SYN **canned** *AmE*: *tinned tomatoes*

tin·ni·tus /ˈtɪnɪtəs/ *n* [U] *medical* an illness in which you hear noises, especially ringing, in your ears

tin·ny /ˈtɪni/ *adj* a tinny sound is high, weak, and unpleasant, and sounds like it is coming out of something made of metal: *tinny music*

ˈtin ˌopener *n* [C] *BrE* a tool for opening TINS of food SYN **can opener**

ˌTin Pan ˈAlley *n* [U] *informal old-fashioned* the people who produce popular music or the part of the city where they work

tin·plate /ˈtɪnpleɪt/ *n* [U] very thin sheets of iron or steel covered with TIN

ˈtin-pot *adj* [only before noun] a tin-pot person, organization etc is not very important, although they think that they are - used to show disapproval: *a tin-pot dictator*

tin·sel /ˈtɪnsəl/ *n* [U] **1** thin strings of shiny paper used as decorations, especially at Christmas **2** something that seems attractive but is not valuable or important: *the tinsel and glamour of Hollywood*

Tin·sel·town /ˈtɪnsəltaʊn/ a humorous informal name for Hollywood, which is used to give the idea that people in Hollywood care only about GLAMOUR and the way things look, and not about anything serious

tint¹ /tɪnt/ *n* [C] **1** a small amount of a particular colour SYN **shade, hue**: *paper with a yellowish tint* THESAURUS COLOUR **2** an artificial colour that is used to slightly change the colour of your hair: *red tints in her hair*

tint² *v* [T] to slightly change the colour of something, especially hair → **dye**

tint·ed /ˈtɪntɪd/ *adj* [only before noun] tinted glass is coloured, rather than completely transparent

ˌtin ˈwhistle *n* [C] a musical instrument like a small pipe with six holes, that you play by blowing

ti·ny /ˈtaɪni/ ●●● S2 W2 *adj* (*comparative* **tinier**, *superlative* **tiniest**) extremely small: *a tiny community in the Midwest* | *The earrings were tiny.* | *a* ***tiny little*** *baby* | *She always felt a* ***tiny bit*** *sad.* | *Bad teachers are a* ***tiny minority****.* | ***tiny pieces*** *of paper* THESAURUS SMALL

-tion /ʃən/ *suffix* [in nouns] another form of the suffix -ION

tip¹ /tɪp/ ●●● S2 W3 *n*
1 END [C] the end of something, especially something pointed: **[+of]** *He kissed the tip of her nose.* | *the southern tip of South America* | *lights on the wing tips of aeroplanes* → FINGERTIP(1)
2 MONEY [C] a small amount of additional money that you give to someone such as a WAITER or a taxi driver: *Did you* ***leave a tip****?* | **large/generous/big tip** *I* ***gave*** *the guy* ***a big tip****.* | *a $5 tip*
3 ADVICE [C] a helpful piece of advice: *Perhaps she could* ***give*** *us a few* ***tips****.* | **[+on/for]** *This week's magazine has some tips on healthy eating.* | **handy tip** (=useful tip) *handy tips for decorating a small flat* | *gardening tips*
4 the tip of the iceberg a small sign of a problem that is much larger: *The reported cases of food poisoning are only the tip of the iceberg.*
5 on the tip of your tongue a) if something is on the tip of your tongue, you really want to say it, but then you decide not to: *It was on the tip of my tongue to say, 'I'd rather have dinner with a snake.'* **b)** if a word, name etc is on the tip of your tongue, you know it but cannot remember it: *What is her name? It's on the tip of my tongue. Joan. Joan Simpson. That's it!*
6 WASTE [C] *BrE* an area where unwanted waste is taken and left SYN **dump**: *a* ***rubbish tip*** | *I'll take this lot to the tip.*
7 UNTIDY [singular] *BrE informal* an extremely dirty or untidy place: *The house was an absolute tip.*
8 HORSE RACE [C] *informal* special information about which horse will win a race
9 WARNING [C] a secret warning or piece of information, especially to police about illegal activities: *Acting on a tip, the police were able to find and arrest Upton.*

COLLOCATIONS – MEANING 3

VERBS

give sb a tip *He gave me some tips on how to improve my game.*

pass on a tip *The writer passes on many tips that she has learned over the years.*
follow a tip *To keep your bike in good condition, follow these simple tips.*
pick up a tip

ADJECTIVES/NOUN + tip

a good/useful/helpful/handy tip *Go to their website to find useful tips on buying and selling a home.*
a simple tip *He has some simple tips for saving money when you're at the supermarket.*
cooking tips | gardening tips | beauty tips | safety tips

tip² ●●○ S3 *v* (**tipped, tipping**)
1 LEAN [I,T] to move into a sloping position, so that one end or side is higher than the other, or to make something do this SYN **tilt**: **[+forward/back/to etc]** *His helmet had tipped forward and the boy pushed it back.* | *Eric fell asleep, his head gently tipping to one side.* | **tip sth forward/back etc** *'So what?' asked Brian, tipping his chair back on its rear legs.*
2 POUR [T always + adv/prep] to pour something from one place or container into another: **tip sth onto/into sth** *Tip the onions and oil into a large ovenproof dish.* | *Ben tipped the contents of the drawer onto the table.* | **tip sth out** *Shall I tip the water out?*
3 GIVE MONEY [I,T] to give an additional amount of money to someone such as a WAITER or taxi driver: *Did you tip the waiter?* | **tip sb sth** *I tipped him $5.*
4 BE LIKELY TO SUCCEED [T] if someone or something is tipped to do something, people think that they are most likely to succeed in doing it: **be tipped to do sth** *the man tipped to become the next president* | **be tipped for/as sth** *He's tipped as a future world champion.* | **widely/strongly/hotly tipped** *He had been widely tipped to get the new post of deputy director.* GRAMMAR **Tip** is usually passive in this meaning.
5 gold-tipped/steel-tipped/rubber-tipped etc having a tip that is made of or covered with gold, steel etc: *a silver-tipped walking stick*
6 tip the balance/scales to give a slight advantage to someone or something: *Three factors helped to* ***tip the balance in favour of*** *the Labour leadership.*
7 tip the scales at sth to weigh a particular amount, used especially of someone who will be taking part in a sports competition: *At today's weigh-in he tipped the scales at just over 15 stone.*
8 it's tipping (it) down *BrE spoken* said when it is raining very heavily: *It was absolutely tipping it down.*
9 be tipped with sth to have one end covered in something: *arrows tipped with poison* | *red petals tipped with white*
10 tip your hat/cap (to sb) a) to touch or raise your hat as a greeting to someone **b)** *AmE* to say or do something that shows you admire what someone has done
11 tip sb the wink *BrE informal* to give someone secret information
tip sb ↔ **off** *phr v* to give someone such as the police a secret warning or piece of information, especially about illegal activities: *The police must have been tipped off.* | **tip sb off that** *His contact had tipped him off that drugs were on the premises.* | **[+about]** *Did you tip him off about Bernard?*
tip over *phr v* if you tip something over, or if it tips over, it falls or turns over: *The candle tipped over and the hay caught fire.* | **tip sth ↔ over** *The current was starting to tip the canoe over and I began to panic.*
tip up *phr v* if you tip something up, or if it tips up, it moves into a sloping position, so that one end or side is higher than the other: **tip sth ↔ up** *He tipped the bottle up so that the last of the liquid flowed into his glass.* | *Ken tipped up the wheelbarrow, then stood back to rest.*

ˈtip-off *n* [C] **1** *informal* a secret warning or piece of information, especially one given to the police about illegal activities: *The arrests came after a tip-off from a member of the public.* **2** *AmE informal* something that shows you that something is true, even though you did not expect it to be true: *The fact that he hasn't called should be a tip-off that he's not interested.* **3** the beginning of a BASKETBALL game, when the ball is thrown into the air and two players jump up to try to gain control of it

tipp·ex /ˈtɪpeks/ *v* [T + out] *BrE* to use a white liquid in order to cover over mistakes in writing, TYPING etc

Tipp-Ex /ˈtɪp eks/ *n* [U] *trademark BrE* white liquid that is used to cover over mistakes in writing, TYPING etc

ˈtipping point *n* [C] the moment when one particular result of a process becomes the most likely one, after a period when the result is not sure

tip·ple /ˈtɪpəl/ *n informal* **sb's favourite tipple** someone's favourite alcoholic drink

tip·pler /ˈtɪplə $ -ər/ *n* [C] *especially BrE informal* someone who drinks alcohol

tip·py·toes /ˈtɪpitəʊz $ -toʊz/ *n* [plural] *AmE* **on (my) tippytoes** on TIPTOE – used especially by children or when talking to children

ˈtip sheet *n* [C] *informal* a newspaper that gives advice and information about which SHARES should be bought and sold: *a tip sheet for private investors*

tip·ster /ˈtɪpstə $ -ər/ *n* [C] someone who gives information about which horse is likely to win a race

tip·sy /ˈtɪpsi/ *adj informal* slightly drunk —**tipsily** *adv* —**tipsiness** *n* [U]

tip·toe¹ /ˈtɪptəʊ $ -toʊ/ ●○○ *n* **on tiptoe/on (your) tiptoes** if you stand or walk on tiptoe, you stand or walk on your toes, in order to make yourself taller or in order to walk very quietly: *She* ***stood on tiptoe*** *to kiss him.*

tiptoe² ●○○ *v* (**tiptoed, tiptoeing**) [I always + adv/prep] to walk quietly and carefully on your toes, so that nobody hears you: *His mother tiptoed into the room.* | *I tiptoed along the corridor.* THESAURUS ▸ WALK
tiptoe around (sth) *phr v* to try to avoid dealing with a difficult or embarrassing subject or problem: *They were tiptoeing around the delicate subject of money.*

ˌtip-ˈtop *adj informal* excellent: *The car's* ***in tip-top condition.***

ti·rade /taɪˈreɪd, tə- $ ˈtaɪreɪd, təˈreɪd/ *n* [C] a long angry speech criticizing someone or something: **[+against]** *He* ***launched into a tirade*** *against the church.* | **[+of]** *a* ***tirade of abuse***

tire¹ /taɪə $ taɪr/ ●○○ *v* [I,T] to start to feel tired, or make someone feel tired: *As we neared the summit, we were tiring fast.*

REGISTER
In everyday English, people usually say **get tired** rather than **tire**: *The climbers were starting to* ***get tired.***

tire of sb/sth *phr v*
1 to become bored with someone or something: *Sooner or later he'll tire of politics.*
2 never tire of doing sth to enjoy doing something again and again, especially in a way that annoys other people: *He never tires of talking about the good old days.*
tire sb ↔ **out** *phr v* to make someone very tired SYN **exhaust**: *All that walking tired me out.*

tire² *n* [C] the American spelling of TYRE → see picture at CAR

tired /taɪəd $ taɪrd/ ●●● S1 W2 *adj*
1 feeling that you want to sleep or rest: **so tired (that)** *I'm so tired I could sleep for a week.* | **too tired to do sth** *He was too tired to argue.* | *He looks* ***tired out*** (=very tired). | *'No,' Frank said in a tired voice.*
2 tired of (doing) sth bored with something, because it is no longer interesting, or has become annoying: *I'm tired of watching television; let's go for a walk.* | *I was getting tired of all her negative remarks.*
3 familiar and boring OPP **fresh**: ***tired old*** *speeches* —**tiredness** *n* [U] —**tiredly** *adv* → DOG-TIRED, → **be sick (and tired) of sth** at SICK¹(6)

GRAMMAR: Prepositions with tired

• If you are **tired of** doing something, you do not want to do it anymore because it has started to annoy or bore you: *I'm tired of explaining it.* ✗ Don't say: *I'm tired from explaining it.*

• If you are **tired from** doing something, you feel tired because you have used a lot of effort: *He was tired from walking all day.* ✗ Don't say: *He was tired of walking all day.*

THESAURUS

tired feeling that you want to sleep or rest: *I was really tired the next day.* | *the tired faces of the children*
exhausted extremely tired: *I was exhausted after the long trip home.*
worn out [not before noun] very tired because you have been working hard: *With three small children to care for, she was always worn out.*
weary /ˈwɪəri $ ˈwɪr-/ *written* tired because you have been travelling, worrying, or doing something for a long time: *weary travellers* | *a weary sigh* | *He looks tired and weary after 20 years in office.*
drained [not before noun] very tired and feeling as if all your energy has gone: *Afterwards, he felt drained, both physically and mentally.*
bushed/beat [not before noun] *informal* very tired: *I'm bushed. I think I'll go to bed early.* | *I'm beat. I don't think I'll go for a run tonight.*
shattered [not before noun] *BrE informal* extremely tired: *When I first started teaching, I came home shattered every night.*
dead *spoken* extremely tired, so that you cannot do anything but sleep: *I was absolutely dead by the time I got home.*

tire·less /ˈtaɪələs $ ˈtaɪr-/ *adj* working very hard in a determined way without stopping: *the tireless efforts of the rescue workers* THESAURUS ENERGETIC —**tirelessly** *adv*

tire·some /ˈtaɪəsəm $ ˈtaɪr-/ ●○○ *adj* making you feel annoyed or impatient: *the whole tiresome business of filling out the forms* ⚠ Do not confuse with **tiring** (=making you feel tired): *It was a long, tiring day.*

tir·ing /ˈtaɪərɪŋ $ ˈtaɪr-/ ●●● S3 *adj* making you feel that you want to sleep or rest: *We've all had a long tiring day.*

THESAURUS

tiring making you feel that you want to sleep or rest: *The journey was really tiring.* | *I've had such a tiring day.* | *It was tiring work.*
exhausting extremely tiring: *I had to drive nine hours without a break - it was exhausting.* | *an exhausting week of singing, acting, and dancing*
hard very tiring and difficult - used about days, journeys etc: *a hard day at work* | *The last part of the journey was very hard.*
wearing /ˈweərɪŋ $ ˈwer-/ tiring because you have to use a lot of your mental energy, and often become bored - used about people, situations etc: *I find her constant questions rather wearing.* | *Kids of that age can be very wearing.*
gruelling *BrE*, **grueling** *AmE* (*also* **punishing**) very tiring physically or mentally - used when you have to keep doing something for a long time: *a gruelling journey across the desert* | *a gruelling race* | *a punishing schedule*
backbreaking backbreaking work is extremely tiring and needs a lot of physical effort: *Clearing the land was slow backbreaking work.*

'tis /tɪz/ *literary* it is - used especially in poetry

tis·sue /ˈtɪʃuː, -sjuː $ -ʃuː/ ●●● S2 *n*
1 [C] a piece of soft thin paper, used especially for blowing your nose on: *a box of tissues*
2 [U] (*also* **tissue paper**) light thin paper used for wrapping, packing etc
3 [U] the material forming animal or plant cells: **lung/brain etc tissue**
4 a tissue of lies *BrE* a story or account that is completely untrue

tit /tɪt/ *n* [C] **1** *informal not polite* a woman's breast **2 get on sb's tits** *BrE spoken not polite* to annoy someone a lot **3** a type of small European bird

ti·tan, **Titan** /ˈtaɪtn/ *n* [C] a very strong or important person SYN **giant**

ti·tan·ic /taɪˈtænɪk/ *adj* very big, strong, impressive etc: *a titanic struggle*

Titanic, the a large British passenger ship which was considered impossible to sink, but which hit an ICEBERG in the Atlantic Ocean, and as a result sank, killing more than 1,500 of its passengers. According to one story, the band continued playing while the ship was sinking. People sometimes use the phrase 'like re-arranging the deck chairs on the Titanic' to describe the actions of a person or organization which makes small and useless changes to a situation, when the situation is already hopeless and certain to fail.

ti·ta·ni·um /taɪˈteɪniəm/ *n* [U] a strong light silver-white metal that is used to make aircraft and spacecraft, and is often combined with other metals. It is a chemical ELEMENT: symbol Ti

Ti·tans, the /ˈtaɪtnz/ in Greek MYTHOLOGY, the first gods who ruled the universe, before Zeus became the most powerful god. They were thought of as GIANTS (=like humans, but extremely large and tall). → TITAN

tit·bit /ˈtɪtˌbɪt/ *n* [C] *BrE* **1** a small piece of food SYN **tidbit** *AmE* **2 titbit of information/gossip/news etc** a small but interesting piece of information etc

titch /tɪtʃ/ *n* [singular] *BrE* a humorous or insulting way of talking to or about a small person

titch·y /ˈtɪtʃi/ *adj BrE informal* extremely small

ˌtit for ˈtat *n* [U] *informal* something bad that you do to someone because they have done something bad to you

tithe /taɪð/ *n* [C] **1** a particular amount that some Christians give to their church **2** a tax paid to the church in the past —**tithe** *v* [I,T]

tit·il·late /ˈtɪtəleɪt/ *v* [T] if a picture or a story titillates someone, it makes them feel sexually interested —**titillating** *adj* —**titillation** /ˌtɪtəˈleɪʃən/ *n* [U]

ti·tle /ˈtaɪtl/ ●●● S3 W1 *n*
1 [C] the name given to a particular book, painting, play etc: **[+of]** *The title of this play is 'Othello'.*

REGISTER
In everyday English, people usually say that something **is called ...**, rather than saying **its title is ...**: *The play's* ***title is*** *'Blasted'.* → *The play* ***is called*** *'Blasted'.*

2 [C] a book: *the UK's 20 best-selling titles*
3 [C] **a)** a name such as 'Sir' or 'Professor', or abbreviations such as 'Mrs' or 'Dr', that are used before someone's name to show their rank or profession, whether they are married etc **b)** a name that describes someone's job or position: *Her official title is editor.*
4 [C] the position of being the winner of an important sports competition: *Tyson won the WBA title in 1987.*
5 [singular, U] *law* the legal right to have or own something: **[+to]** *He* ***has title*** *to the land.*

ˈtitle bar *n* [C] the coloured bar at the top of a computer window that shows the name of the program and whether it is being used at that time

ti·tled /ˈtaɪtld/ ●○○ *adj* having a title in the ARISTOCRACY, such as 'lord', DUKE, EARL etc

ˈtitle deed *n* [C] a piece of paper giving legal proof that someone owns a particular property

ˈtitle ˌholder *n* [C] **1** the person or team that is the winner of an important sports competition **2** someone who owns a title deed

ˈtitle page *n* [C] the page at the front of a book which shows the book's name, the writer etc

ˈtitle role *n* [C] the main acting part in a play or film, which is the same as the name of the play or film

ˈtitle track *n* [C] the song or piece of music on an ALBUM (=collection of songs or pieces of music) that has the same name as the whole album

T

ti·tlist /ˈtaɪtlɪst/ *n* [C] *AmE* someone who has won an important sports competition

tit·ter /ˈtɪtə $ -ər/ *v* [I] to laugh quietly in a high voice, especially because you are nervous: *At the word 'breast', some of the class tittered.* —**titter** *n* [C]

tit·tle-tat·tle /ˈtɪtl ˌtætl/ *n* [U] unimportant conversation about other people and what they are doing SYN **gossip**

tit·ty /ˈtɪti/ *n* (*plural* **titties**) [C] *informal not polite* a woman's breast

tit·u·lar /ˈtɪtʃələ $ -ər/ *adj* [only before noun] **titular head/leader/monarch etc** someone who is the official leader or ruler of a country but who does not have real power or authority

TiVo /ˈtiːvəʊ $ -voʊ/ *n* [U] *trademark* a system that allows you to record television programmes DIGITALLY —**TiVo** *v* [T]

tiz·zy /ˈtɪzi/ (*also* **tizz** /tɪz/) *n* [singular] *informal* **in a tizzy** feeling worried, nervous, and confused

T-junc·tion /ˈtiː ˌdʒʌŋkʃən/ *n* [C] *BrE* a place where two roads meet and form the shape of the letter T

TLA /ˌtiː el ˈeɪ/ *n* [C] (***three-letter acronym***) the first letters of the words in a three-word phrase, for example BTW ('by the way') or IMO ('in my opinion'), used as a short form, especially on the Internet and in emails

TLC /ˌtiː el ˈsiː/ *n* [U] *informal* (***tender loving care***) kindness and love that you show someone to make them feel better and happier

TM /ˌtiː ˈem/ **1** a written abbreviation of TRADEMARK **2** an abbreviation of TRANSCENDENTAL MEDITATION

TNT /ˌtiː en ˈtiː/ *n* [U] a powerful explosive SYN **dynamite**

to[1] /tə; *before vowels* tʊ; *strong* tuː/ ●●● S1 W1 [used before the basic form of a verb to show that it is in the infinitive]

1 a) used after a verb, noun, or adjective when an INFINITIVE completes its meaning: *We tried to explain.* | *It was starting to rain.* | *The manager asked them to leave.* | *an attempt to escape* | *Have you got permission to stay here?* | *Our team's certain to win.* | *Are you ready to start?* | *This delicious dessert is easy to make* (=you can make it easily). **b)** used by itself instead of an INFINITIVE in order to avoid repeating the same verb: *You can drive today if you want to* (=if you want to drive). | *I could have helped, but nobody asked me to.*

2 used after a word such as 'how', 'where', 'who', 'what', or 'whether' to refer to an action about which someone is not certain: *I know where to go but I don't know how to get there.* | *She wondered whether or not to trust him.*

3 used to show a purpose or intention: *They left early to catch the 7.30 train.* | *To find out more about university courses, write to this address.* | *We need more money to improve transport in London.*

> **REGISTER**
> In written English, people often use **in order to** rather than just **to** when expressing a purpose or intention, because it sounds more formal: *Investment has been increased **in order to** improve the transport system.*

4 used to refer to an action or state, when describing it: *It's nice to be wanted.* | *He's finding it hard to cope.* | *To say I am disappointed is an understatement.* | *The simplest solution would be to increase the price.*

5 used to say what can or cannot be done, or what should be done: *You'll soon be old enough to vote in elections.* | *He did not have the energy to resist.* | *I'm too tired to go out tonight.*

6 used after the verb 'be' to give an order or to state arrangements for the future: *You are to wait here until I return.* | *They are to be married on May 25th.*

7 used to say what someone discovers or experiences when they do something: *He arrived there to find that the last train had already left.* | *The princess stepped ashore to be greeted by an enthusiastic crowd of admirers.* | *She woke to see Ben standing by the window.*

8 used to say what your attitude or purpose is in saying something: *I've never heard of him, to be quite honest.* | *To begin with, let's look at Chapter 3.*

to[2] ●●● S1 W1 *prep*

1 used to say where someone or something goes: *She stood up and walked to the window.* | *the road to London* | *our weekly trip to the supermarket* | *sending a spaceship to Mars* | *These people go from house to house selling goods* (=visit many different houses).

2 used to say who receives something or is told or shown something: *He sent presents to the children.* | *She whispered something to the girl beside her.* | *Give my best wishes to your parents when you see them.* | *Don't show these letters to anyone else.* | *a message from the Emperor to his people*

3 used to show in which direction something is in relation to something else: *Knutsford is about 16 miles to the south of Manchester.* | *There was a table to the left of the doorway.*

4 used to show the purpose, event, or activity for which you go somewhere: *Sophie goes to gymnastics every Friday.* | *Did you get an invitation to their wedding?* | *Don't forget, we're going to a party tomorrow night.* | *If he needed help, Mother came rushing to the rescue.*

5 used to say what state someone or something is in as a result of an action or change: *She sang the baby to sleep.* | *Wait until the lights change to green.* | *a return to a traditional way of life*

6 used to say that one thing is touching another: *He held a knife to her throat.* | *They danced cheek to cheek.*

7 used to say where something is fastened or connected: *He tied the rope to a tree.* | *Attach a recent photograph to your application form.* | *Cash machines are linked up to a central computer.*

8 facing something or in front of it: *I sat with my back to the window.* | *We were standing face to face.*

9 used to show a relationship with someone or something: *George's sister was married to an Italian.* | *He was first cousin to King Philip VI.* | *The robbery may be linked to other crimes of violence.*

10 a) as far as a particular point or limit: *She can already count from one to twenty.* | *The water came right up to our knees.* | *Temperatures dropped to 25 degrees below zero.* | *It's ten kilometres from here to the coast.* | *She read the novel from beginning to end.* | *Does your interest in nuclear physics extend to nuclear weaponry?* **b)** until and including a particular time or date: *They stayed from Friday night to Sunday morning.* | *I'll be on duty from 8 am to 10 pm.*

11 used to say what or who an action, attitude, situation etc affects or is related to: *The factory clearly represents a danger to health.* | *She's always been kind to animals.* | *his attitude to life* | *What have you done to the radio? It's not working.*

12 used to say who someone works for: *Jane is secretary to the managing director.*

13 used to say what something is needed for: *I'm still waiting for an answer to my question.* | *Have you seen the key to the back door?*

14 used when comparing two things, numbers etc: *England beat Scotland by two goals to one.* | *Yes, she was punished, but it was nothing to what she deserved.*

15 used to say who has a particular attitude or opinion about something: *The whole thing sounds very suspicious to me.* | *Tickets cost £10 each and to some people that's a lot of money.* | *To my mind, age does not matter; love is what matters.*

16 used to say what someone's reaction is when something happens: *Much to everyone's surprise she passed the exam with distinction.* | *I discovered to my horror that my passport was missing.*

17 used when saying how much time there is before a particular event or time: *It's only two weeks to Christmas.* | *How long is it to dinner?* | **ten to five/twenty to one etc** (=ten minutes, twenty minutes etc before a particular hour)

18 a) used when talking about a rate or quantity to say how many smaller units equal a larger unit: *We're only getting 130 yen to the dollar at the moment.* | *There are just over four and a half litres to a gallon.* **b)** used to show the relationship between two different measurements or

quantities: *The car will do over 40 miles to the gallon.* | *The scale of your map is one inch to the mile.*
19 used to say that a particular sound is heard at the same time as something happens: *I woke to the sound of torrential rain.* | *The royal couple arrived to a fanfare of trumpets.* | *I like to exercise to music.*
20 used between two numbers when you do not know exactly what the real number or amount is: *There must have been eighteen to twenty thousand people at the concert.* | *He drowned in 10 to 12 feet of water.*
21 **(all) to yourself** if you have something or someone to yourself, you do not have to share them with other people: *It was the first time I'd had a room to myself.*
22 used to say what the chances of something happening are: *I'll bet you ten to one he'll forget all about it.*

to³ /tuː/ ●●○ *adv BrE* if a door is pushed to, it closes or almost closes: *The wind blew the door to.* → COME TO

toad /təʊd $ toʊd/ *n* [C] a small animal that looks like a large FROG and lives mostly on land

ˌtoad-in-the-ˈhole *n* [U] a British dish made of SAUSAGES cooked in a mixture of eggs, milk, and flour

toad·stool /ˈtəʊdstuːl $ ˈtoʊd-/ *n* [C] a wild plant like a MUSHROOM, that can be poisonous

toad·y¹ /ˈtəʊdi $ ˈtoʊ-/ *n* (*plural* **toadies**) [C] *informal* someone who pretends to like an important person and does things for them, so that that person will help them – used to show disapproval

toady² *v* (**toadied**, **toadying**, **toadies**) [I] to pretend to like an important person and do things for them, so that they will help you – used to show disapproval: **[+to]** *toadying to the boss*

to and fro¹ /ˌtuː ən ˈfrəʊ $ -ˈfroʊ/ *adv* if someone or something moves to and fro, they move in one direction and then back again SYN **backwards and forwards** —**to-and-fro** *adj*

to and fro² *n* [U] *informal* continuous movement of people or things from place to place → TOING AND FROING(1)

toast¹ /təʊst $ toʊst/ ●●○ S3 *n*
1 [U] bread that has been heated so that it is brown on both sides and no longer soft: *I had a* ***piece of toast*** *for breakfast.* → see picture at BREAD
2 [C] if you drink a toast to someone, you drink something in order to thank them, wish them luck etc: *I'd like to* ***propose a toast*** (=ask people to drink a toast) *to the bride and groom.* THESAURUS DRINK
3 **be the toast of Broadway/Hollywood etc** to be very popular and praised by many people for something you have done in a particular field of work
4 **warm as toast** *BrE* very warm and comfortable: *They sat near the fire, warm as toast.*
5 **be toast** *informal* to be in trouble because of something you have done: *If you challenge her, you're toast.* → FRENCH TOAST

toast² *v* [T] **1** to drink a glass of wine etc to thank someone, wish someone luck, or celebrate something: **toast sb/sth with sth** *They toasted the birth of their new baby with champagne.* **2** to make bread or other food brown by placing it close to heat: *I toasted the cheese sandwiches.* THESAURUS COOK **3** to sit near a fire to make yourself warm: *Tom was toasting his feet by the fire.*

toast·er /ˈtəʊstə $ ˈtoʊstər/ ●●○ *n* [C] a machine you use for toasting bread

ˈtoasting fork *n* [C] a long fork used to hold bread over a fire to toast it

toast·mas·ter /ˈtəʊstˌmɑːstə $ ˈtoʊstˌmæstər/ *n* [C] someone who introduces the speakers at a formal occasion such as a BANQUET (=large formal meal)

toast·y /ˈtəʊsti $ ˈtoʊs-/ *adj informal* warm and comfortable: *our nice toasty bed*

to·bac·co /təˈbækəʊ $ -koʊ/ ●●○ *n* [U]
1 the dried brown leaves that are smoked in cigarettes, pipes etc
2 the plant that produces these leaves

to·bac·co·nist /təˈbækənɪst/ *n* [C] **1** someone who has a shop that sells tobacco, cigarettes etc **2** **tobacconist's** *BrE* a shop that sells tobacco, cigarettes etc

-to-ˈbe *suffix* **bride-/husband-/parent- etc to-be** someone who will soon be married, soon be a parent etc: *a magazine aimed at young mums-to-be*

to·bog·gan¹ /təˈbɒgən $ -ˈbɑː-/ *n* [C] a light wooden board with a curved front, used for sliding down hills covered in snow → **sledge**

toboggan² *v* [I] to slide down a hill on a toboggan —**tobogganing** *n* [U]

toc·ca·ta /təˈkɑːtə/ *n* [C] a piece of music, usually for piano or organ, that is played very quickly

toc·sin /ˈtɒksɪn $ ˈtɑːk-/ *n* [C] a loud warning bell, used in the past

tod /tɒd $ tɑːd/ *n BrE spoken informal* **on your tod** by yourself

to·day¹ /təˈdeɪ/ ●●● S1 W1 *adv*
1 on the day that is happening now → **yesterday**, **tomorrow**: *I couldn't go shopping yesterday so I'll have to go today.* | *Ed has his music lesson today.* | **a week from today** (*also* **today week/a week today** *BrE*): *We're going on holiday today week.*
2 at the present time: *Students today seem to know very little about geography.*

today² *n* [U] **1** the day that is happening now → **yesterday**, **tomorrow**: *Today is my birthday!* | *Have you seen today's paper?* **2** the present period of time: *Today's computers are becoming much smaller and lighter.* | *young people of today*

tod·dle /ˈtɒdl $ ˈtɑːdl/ *v* [I] **1** if a small child toddles, it walks with short unsteady steps **2** [always + adv/prep] *especially BrE* to walk somewhere, especially in a slow and relaxed way SYN **stroll**: *Every afternoon, Marge would toddle down to the library.*

tod·dler /ˈtɒdlə $ ˈtɑːdlər/ ●○○ *n* [C] a very young child who is just learning to walk THESAURUS BABY

tod·dy /ˈtɒdi $ ˈtɑːdi/ *n* (*plural* **toddies**) [C] a hot drink made with WHISKY, sugar, and hot water

to-ˈdie-for *adj informal* extremely good or desirable – used humorously: *Betty's strawberry cheesecake is simply to-die-for.*

to-ˈdo *n* [singular] *informal* a lot of unnecessary excitement or angry feelings about something SYN **fuss**: *There was such a to-do when I said I didn't want to be married in a church!*

to-ˈdo list *n* [C] a list of jobs you have to do: *Painting the bedroom is at the top of my to-do list.*

toe¹ /təʊ $ toʊ/ ●●● S3 *n* [C]
1 one of the five movable parts at the end of your foot → **finger**: *He* ***stubbed*** *his* ***toe*** (=hurt it by kicking it against something) *on a rock.* | **big toe** (=the largest of your toes)
2 the part of a shoe or sock that covers the front part of your foot → see picture at SHOE¹
3 **tread on sb's toes** *BrE*, **step on sb's toes** *AmE* to offend someone, especially by becoming involved in something that they are responsible for
4 **keep sb on their toes** to make sure that someone is ready for anything that might happen: *They do random checks to keep workers on their toes.*
5 **make sb's toes curl** to make someone feel very embarrassed or uncomfortable
6 **touch your toes** to bend downwards so that your hands touch your toes, without bending your knees
7 **put/dip a toe in the water** to try a little of something or try an activity for a short time to see if you like it → **from head to toe** at HEAD¹(1), → **from top to toe** at TOP¹(23)

toe² *v* (**toed**, **toeing**) **toe the line** to do what other people in a job or organization say you should do, whether you agree with them or not: *You toe the line or you don't stay on the team!*

toe·cap /ˈtəʊkæp $ ˈtoʊ-/ *n* [C] a piece of metal or leather that covers the front part of a shoe

T

ˈtoe-curling *adj informal* making you feel very embarrassed: *There's a toe-curling scene in the film where he keeps accidentally offending his girlfriend's parents.* —**toe-curlingly** *adv*: *It was toe-curlingly embarrassing.*

toe·hold /ˈtəʊhəʊld $ ˈtoʊhoʊld/ *n* **1** [singular] your first involvement in a particular activity, from which you can develop and become stronger: **[+in]** *The company has* ***gained a toehold*** *in the competitive computer market.* **2** [C] a place on a rock where you can put your foot when you are climbing

TOEIC /ˈtəʊɪk/ *trademark* (***Test of English for International Communication***) a test for people whose first language is not English that measures how well they can use and understand English at work or in business

toe·nail /ˈtəʊneɪl $ ˈtoʊ-/ ●○○ *n* [C] the hard part that covers the top of each of your toes

toe·rag /ˈtəʊræg $ ˈtoʊ-/ *n* [C] *BrE spoken not polite* someone you dislike

toff /tɒf $ tɑːf/ *n* [C] *BrE old-fashioned* someone who is rich or has a high social position – used to show disapproval

tof·fee /ˈtɒfi $ ˈtɑːfi/ *n* [C,U] **1** a sticky sweet brown substance that you can eat, made by boiling sugar, water, and butter together, or a piece of this substance **2 can't do sth for toffee** *BrE informal* to be very bad at doing something: *He can't sing for toffee!*

ˈtoffee ˌapple *n* [C] *BrE* an apple covered with toffee and put on a stick

ˈtoffee-ˌnosed *adj BrE informal* a toffee-nosed person thinks that they are better than other people because of their social position – used to show disapproval

to·fu /ˈtəʊfuː $ ˈtoʊ-/ *n* [U] a soft white food made from SOYA BEANS, used in cooking instead of meat

tog[1] /tɒg $ tɑːg, tɒːg/ *n* [C] **1 togs** [plural] *informal* clothes **2** a unit for measuring the warmth of DUVETS, SLEEPING BAGS, jackets etc

tog[2] *v BrE informal* **be/get togged up/out** to be or get dressed for a particular occasion or activity

to·ga /ˈtəʊgə $ ˈtoʊ-/ *n* [C] a long loose piece of clothing worn by people in ancient Rome

to·geth·er[1] /təˈgeðə $ -ər/ ●●● S1 W1 *adv*

1 WITH EACH OTHER if two or more people do something together, they do it with each other OPP **alone, separately**: *We've very much enjoyed* ***working together****. | They've decided to spend more time together. | He and my father were at school together. | Together they went back inside the villa.*

2 MAKE ONE THING if you put two or more things together, you join them so that they touch or form one whole thing or group OPP **apart**: *He'd tried to glue the broken pieces together. | Mix the butter and sugar together. | She clasped her hands together. | He took the engine apart and then put it* ***back together*** *again. | The model was held together with string.*

3 BE A COUPLE if two people are together, they are married, or are having a romantic or sexual relationship: *Mark and I have been together eight years now. | Are those two together? | A lot of people* ***live together*** *before getting married. | Sometimes I don't know what* ***keeps us together****.*

4 IN ONE PLACE if you keep, collect etc things together, you keep or collect them all in one place: *She keeps all the important documents together in one file. | Embarrassed, she gathered her things together and left. | Goods of a similar kind should be stored together.*

5 close/packed/crowded etc together if people or objects are close together, packed together etc, they are placed very near to each other: *The trees had been planted a little too close together. | The climbers were sitting huddled together for warmth.*

6 AGAINST EACH OTHER if you rub or hit things together, you rub or hit them against each other: *Max was rubbing his hands together with glee. | Knock the brushes together to clean them.*

7 IN AGREEMENT if people are together, come together etc, they are or become united, especially in order to try and achieve something: *Together we can win. | The Conference called on all good men to* ***come together*** *to resist socialism. | He said that the main purpose of the Baha'i faith was to* ***bring people together****.*

8 AT THE SAME TIME at the same time: *Both letters should have arrived. I mailed them together. | 'Oh!' they said together.* | **all together (now)** (=used to tell a group of people to all say or do something at the same time) *Right men. All together now ... push!*

9 COMBINE AMOUNTS when two amounts or quantities are added together, they are combined: *Add these numbers together and then divide the total by 7. | Together they won only 21% of the votes. | The table and chairs are together worth about £200.*

10 together with sth/sb a) in addition to something else: *Just bring it back to the store, together with your receipt. | Becoming self-employed meant giving up a secure salary, together with sick leave and long vacation time.* **b)** used to mention someone else who is also involved in an activity or situation: *He, together with Bill Dunn, decided to climb out of the canyon.* → **bring together** at BRING, → **get together** at GET, → **get your act together** at ACT[1](4), → **hold together** at HOLD[1], → **piece sth together** at PIECE[2], → **pull together** at PULL[1]

together[2] *adj spoken* someone who is together is confident, thinks clearly, and does things in a sensible organized way – used to show approval: *Jane is such a together person.*

to·geth·er·ing /təˈgeðərɪŋ/ *n* [U] the practice of taking a holiday with many people from your family, such as grandparents, aunts, etc, or with many of your friends

to·geth·er·ness /təˈgeðənəs $ -ðər-/ *n* [U] the pleasant feeling you have when you are part of a group of people who have a close relationship with each other: *the togetherness we felt at college*

tog·gle /ˈtɒgəl $ ˈtɑː-/ *n* [C] **1** a small piece of wood or plastic that is used as a button on coats, bags etc **2** something on a computer that lets you change from one operation to another —**toggle** *v* [I,T]

ˈtoggle switch *n* [C] *technical* a small part on a machine that is used to turn electricity on and off by moving it up or down

toil[1] /tɔɪl/ *v* [I always + adv/prep] **1** (*also* **toil away**) to work very hard for a long period of time: **[+at]** *I've been toiling away at this essay all weekend.* **2** *literary* to move slowly and with great effort: **[+up/through/along etc]** *They toiled slowly up the hill.*

toil[2] *n* [U] *formal* **1** hard unpleasant work done over a long period: *a life of toil* **2 the toils of sth** *literary* if you are caught in the toils of an unpleasant feeling or situation, you are trapped by it

toi·let /ˈtɔɪlɪt/ ●●● S2 *n*

1 [C] a large bowl that you sit on to get rid of waste liquid or waste matter from your body: *He* ***flushed the toilet*** (=pulled the handle so that water ran into the toilet to clean it).

2 [C] *BrE* a room or building containing a toilet SYN **bathroom, restroom** *AmE*: *public toilets*

3 go to the toilet *especially BrE* to pass waste liquid or waste matter from your body: *Mummy, I need to go to the toilet!*

4 [U] *old-fashioned* the act of washing and dressing yourself: *She finished her toilet.*

ˈtoilet bag *n* [C] a bag in which you keep things such as soap, TOOTHPASTE etc when travelling SYN **sponge bag** *BrE* → see picture at BAG[1]

ˈtoilet ˌpaper ●●○ *n* [U] soft thin paper used for cleaning yourself after you have used the toilet

toi·let·ries /ˈtɔɪlətriz/ *n* [plural] things such as soap and TOOTHPASTE that are used for cleaning yourself

ˈtoilet roll *n* [C] *BrE* toilet paper that is wound around a small tube

ˈtoilet-ˌtraining *n* [U] when you teach a child to use a toilet —**toilet-train** *v* [T] —**toilet-trained** *adj*

ˈtoilet ˌwater *n* [U] a kind of PERFUME (=pleasant-smelling liquid) that does not have a very strong smell

to·ing and fro·ing /ˌtuːɪŋ ən ˈfrəʊɪŋ $ -ˈfroʊ-/ *n* [U] **1** movement backwards and forwards many times between two or more places **2** a lot of activity that does not help you to do something: *After much toing and froing, they finally reached a decision.*

toke /təʊk $ toʊk/ *v* [I,T] *informal* to breathe in the smoke from a MARIJUANA cigarette —**toke** *n* [C]

to·ken¹ /ˈtəʊkən $ ˈtoʊ-/ ●○○ *n* [C]
1 a round piece of metal that you use instead of money in some machines
2 *formal* something that represents a feeling, fact, event etc: **a token of your gratitude/respect/appreciation etc** *Please accept this gift as a small token of our appreciation.*
→ **by the same token** at SAME¹(8)
3 book/record/gift token *BrE* a special piece of paper that you can exchange for a book, record etc in a shop SYN **gift certificate** *AmE*: *a £10 book token*

token² ●○○ *adj* [only before noun]
1 a token action, change etc is small and not very important, and is usually only done so that someone can pretend that they are dealing with a problem: *The government thinks it can get away with token gestures on environmental issues.*
2 token woman/black etc someone who is included in a group to make everyone think that the group has all types of people in it, when this is not really true
3 done as a first sign that an agreement, promise etc will be kept and that more will be done later: *A small token payment will keep the bank happy.*

to·ken·ism /ˈtəʊkənɪzəm $ ˈtoʊ-/ *n* [U] actions that are intended to make people think that an organization deals fairly with people or problems, when in fact it does not

told /təʊld $ toʊld/ the past tense and past participle of TELL

tol·e·ra·ble /ˈtɒlərəbəl $ ˈtɑː-/ *adj* **1** a situation that is tolerable is not very good, but you are able to accept it OPP **intolerable** → **tolerate**: *The apartment is really too small, but it's tolerable for the time being.* **2** unpleasant or painful and only just able to be accepted OPP **intolerable** → **tolerate**: *The heat in this room is barely tolerable.*

tol·e·ra·bly /ˈtɒlərəbli $ ˈtɑː-/ *adv* [+adj/adv] fairly, but not very much SYN **reasonably**: *We were tolerably happy at first.*

tol·e·rance /ˈtɒlərəns $ ˈtɑː-/ ●●○ *n*
1 [U] willingness to allow people to do, say, or believe what they want without criticizing or punishing them OPP **intolerance** → **tolerate**: **[+of/towards/for]** *tolerance towards religious minorities*
2 [C,U] the degree to which someone can suffer pain, difficulty etc without being harmed or damaged → **tolerate**: **[+to]** *Many old people have a very limited tolerance to cold.*

ˈtolerance ˌzone *n* [C] an area of a town or city where PROSTITUTES are allowed to work legally

tol·e·rant /ˈtɒlərənt $ ˈtɑː-/ ●●○ *adj*
1 allowing people to do, say, or believe what they want without criticizing or punishing them OPP **intolerant** → **tolerate**: **[+of/towards]** *Luckily, my parents were tolerant of my choice of music.* | *a tolerant society*
2 plants that are tolerant of particular weather or soil conditions can exist in those conditions: **[+of]** *trees that are tolerant of salt sea winds*

tol·e·rate /ˈtɒləreɪt $ ˈtɑː-/ ●●○ *v* [T]
1 to allow people to do, say, or believe something without criticizing or punishing them → **tolerant**, **tolerance**: *We simply will not tolerate vigilante groups on our streets.*
2 to be able to accept something unpleasant or difficult, even though you do not like it → **tolerant**, **tolerance** SYN **stand**, **bear**: *I couldn't tolerate the long hours.*

> **REGISTER**
> In everyday English, people usually say **stand** rather than **tolerate**: *I don't know how she can* ***stand*** *working there.*

3 if a plant tolerates particular weather or soil conditions, it can exist in them: *plants that tolerate drought*
4 if a person or their body can tolerate a food or other substance, it can use it without becoming ill: *Women's bodies can tolerate less alcohol than men's.*

tol·e·ra·tion /ˌtɒləˈreɪʃən $ ˌtɑː-/ *n* [U] willingness to allow people to believe what they want without being criticized or punished: *religious toleration*

toll¹ /təʊl $ toʊl/ ●○○ *n* [C]
1 [usually singular] the number of people killed or injured in a particular accident, by a particular illness etc: *The* ***death toll*** *has risen to 83.* | *The bombings* ***took*** *a heavy* ***toll****, killing hundreds of Londoners.*
2 a very bad effect that something has on something or someone over a long period of time: **[+on]** *Years of smoking have* ***taken*** *their* ***toll*** *on his health.* | *a heavy toll on the environment*
3 the money you have to pay to use a particular road, bridge etc THESAURUS COST
4 the sound of a large bell ringing slowly

toll² *v* [I,T] if a large bell tolls, or if you toll it, it keeps ringing slowly, especially to show that someone has died

toll·booth /ˈtəʊlbuːθ $ ˈtoʊl-/ *n* [C] a place where you pay to drive on a road, bridge etc

ˈtoll bridge *n* [C] a bridge that you pay to drive across

ˌtoll-ˈfree *adv AmE* if you telephone a particular number toll-free, you do not have to pay for the call —**toll-free** *adj*: *a toll-free number*

toll·gate /ˈtəʊlgeɪt $ ˈtoʊl-/ *n* [C] a gate across a road, at which you have to pay money before you can drive any further

ˈtoll ˌplaza *n* [C] *AmE* a row of TOLLBOOTHS on a toll road

ˈtoll road *n* [C] a road that you pay to use

toll·way /ˈtəʊlweɪ $ ˈtoʊl-/ *n* [C] *AmE* a large long road that you pay to use

tom /tɒm $ tɑːm/ *n* [C] *informal* a TOMCAT

tom·a·hawk /ˈtɒməhɔːk $ ˈtɑːməhɒːk/ *n* [C] a light AXE used by Native Americans

to·ma·to /təˈmɑːtəʊ $ -ˈmeɪtoʊ/ ●●● S2 *n* (*plural* **tomatoes**) [C] a round soft red fruit eaten raw or cooked as a vegetable → see picture at **VEGETABLE¹**

tomb /tuːm/ ●○○ *n* [C] a stone structure above or below the ground where a dead person is buried: *the family tomb*

tom·bo·la /tɒmˈbəʊlə $ tɑːmˈboʊ-/ *n* [U] *BrE* a game in which you buy a ticket with a number on it in order to try and win a prize that has the same number on it → **raffle**

tom·boy /ˈtɒmbɔɪ $ ˈtɑːm-/ *n* [C] a girl who likes playing the same games as boys

tomb·stone /ˈtuːmstəʊn $ -stoʊn/ *n* [C] a stone that is put on a GRAVE and shows the dead person's name, dates of birth and death etc SYN **gravestone**

tomb·ston·ing /ˈtuːmstəʊnɪŋ $ -stoʊn-/ *n* [U] *BrE* the activity of jumping from a high cliff or PIER into water for fun

tom·cat /ˈtɒmkæt $ ˈtɑːm-/ *n* [C] a male cat

tome /təʊm $ toʊm/ *n* [C] *literary* a large heavy book

tom·fool·e·ry /tɒmˈfuːləri $ tɑːm-/ *n* [U] *old-fashioned* silly behaviour

tom·my gun /ˈtɒmi gʌn $ ˈtɑː-/ *n* [C] *old-fashioned informal* a gun that can fire many bullets very quickly

to·mor·row¹ /təˈmɒrəʊ $ -ˈmɔːroʊ, -ˈmɑː-/ ●●● S1 W2 *adv* on or during the day after today → **yesterday**, **today**: *Our class is going to London tomorrow.* | **a week from tomorrow** (*also* **a week tomorrow/tomorrow week** *BrE*): *Terry's new job starts a week tomorrow.* | **tomorrow morning/night etc** *We're meeting tomorrow evening.*

tomorrow² *n* [U] **1** the day after today → **yesterday**, **today**: *I'll see you at tomorrow's meeting.* **2** the future, especially the near future: *The computers of tomorrow will be smaller and more powerful.* **3 do sth like there's no tomorrow** do something very quickly and carelessly, without worrying about the future: *Rita's spending money like there's no tomorrow.*

ˌTom ˈThumb a character in a FAIRY TALE (=a story for children in which magical things happen) who was only as big as a person's thumb

ˈtom-tom *n* [C] a tall narrow drum that you play with your hands

ton /tʌn/ ●●○ S3 *n* [C]
1 (*plural* **tons** *or* **ton**) (*written abbreviation* **t**) a unit for measuring weight, equal to 2,240 pounds or 1,016 kilograms in Britain, and 2,000 pounds or 907.2 kilograms in the US → TONNE
2 tons of sth *informal* a lot of something: *I've got tons of work to do.*
3 weigh a ton *informal* to be very heavy: *Your bag weighs a ton!*
4 come down on sb like a ton of bricks *informal* to get very angry with someone about something they have done
5 hit sb like a ton of bricks *AmE informal* to have a strong emotional effect on someone

ton·al /ˈtəʊnl $ ˈtoʊ-/ *adj* **1** relating to tones of colour or sound: *The tonal range she uses is wide and varied.* **2** *technical* a piece of music that is tonal is based on a particular KEY OPP **atonal**

ton·al·i·ty /təʊˈnæləti $ toʊ-/ *n* (*plural* **tonalities**) [C,U] *technical* the character of a piece of music that depends on the KEY of the music and the way in which the tunes and HARMONIES are combined

tone¹ /təʊn $ toʊn/ ●●○ S3 W2 *n*
1 VOICE [C] the way your voice sounds, which shows how you are feeling or what you mean: **in a ... tone** *'You must be Annie,' he said in a friendly tone.* | **in sb's tone** *There was urgency in his tone.* | *Her tone was sharp with anger.* | *It was obvious from her* ***tone of voice*** *that she didn't like me.* | **don't take that tone with me** (=do not speak to me in that rude or unpleasant way)
2 SOUND [C,U] the quality of a sound, especially the sound of a musical instrument or someone's voice → **pitch**, **timbre**: *the guitar's clean tone* | **in ... tones** *They talked in hushed tones.* | *'No I didn't,' he said in a* ***low tone*** (=quietly). | **deep-toned/even-toned/shrill-toned etc** (=having a low, calm etc tone) *an even-toned voice*
3 GENERAL FEELING/ATTITUDE [singular, U] the general feeling or attitude expressed in a piece of writing, a speech, an activity etc: **[+of]** *The tone of the report was radical.* | *The meetings were noted for their deeply religious tone.* | **in tone** *The article was moderate in tone.* | **set the tone (for/of sth)** (=establish the general attitude or feeling of an event, activity etc) *Opening remarks are important since they set the tone for the rest of the interview.*
4 COLOUR [C,U] one of the many types of a particular colour, each slightly darker, lighter, brighter etc than the next SYN **shade** → **tonal**: **[+of]** *different tones of green* | *Perhaps a darker tone would be better.* | *your* ***skin tone*** (=the colour of your skin) | **in tone** *The dried colour is slightly deeper in tone than it appears when first applied.*
→ TWO-TONE THESAURUS▸ COLOUR
5 ELECTRONIC SOUND [C] a sound made by electronic equipment, such as a telephone: *Please leave a message after the tone.* | **dialling tone** *BrE*, **dial tone** *AmE* (=the sound you hear when you pick up the telephone that lets you know that you can make a call) | **engaged tone** *BrE*, **busy tone** *AmE* (=the sound you hear when you telephone someone but they are already talking to someone else)
6 raise/lower the tone (of sth) to make a place or event more or less socially acceptable, attractive etc: *That horrible building lowers the whole tone of the neighborhood.* | *Trust you to lower the tone of the conversation* (=by making rude remarks etc).
7 BODY [U] *technical* how firm and strong your muscles or skin are: *A regular brisk walk will improve* ***muscle tone***.
8 MUSIC [C] *technical* the difference in PITCH between two musical notes that are separated by one KEY on the piano SYN **step** *AmE*
9 VOICE LEVEL [C] *technical* how high or low your voice is when you produce different sounds: *There is a* ***falling tone*** *on the first syllable and a* ***rising tone*** *on the other.*

tone² (*also* **tone up**) *v* [T] to improve the strength and firmness of your muscles, skin etc: *Exercise can strengthen and tone muscles.* | *He began to use weights in order to tone up his body.* | *a well-toned body*

tone sth ↔ **down** *phr v* **1** to reduce the effect of something such as a speech or piece of writing, so that people will not be offended: *His advisers told him to tone down his speech.* **2** to make a colour less bright: *Blue can be used to tone down very sunny rooms.*

tone in *phr v BrE* if one colour or pattern tones in with another, they are similar and look good together SYN **complement**: **[+with]** *Choose candles that will tone in with your tablecloth and china.*

ˌtone-ˈdeaf *adj* unable to hear the difference between different musical notes

ˈtone ˌlanguage *n* [C] a language such as Chinese in which the way a sound goes up or down affects the meaning of the word

tone·less /ˈtəʊnləs $ ˈtoʊn-/ *adj* a toneless voice does not express any feelings SYN **expressionless**: *'I'm sorry,' he said, in a flat toneless voice.*

ˈtone ˌpoem *n* [C] a piece of music that has been written to represent an idea, place, or story

ton·er /ˈtəʊnə $ ˈtoʊnər/ *n* [U] **1** a type of ink that is used in machines that print or copy documents **2** a liquid that you put on your face to make your skin feel soft and smooth

tongs /tɒŋz $ tɑːŋz, tɒːŋz/ *n* [plural] a tool that you use to lift up small objects. It has two bars joined at one end, that you press together to lift objects.

tongue¹ /tʌŋ/ ●●● S3 W3 *n*
1 MOUTH [C] the soft part inside your mouth that you can move about and use for eating and speaking: *Joe ran his tongue over his dry lips.* | *The taste of the chocolate was still on her tongue.* | *The girl scowled at me, then* ***stuck out*** *her* ***tongue***.
2 click your tongue to make a sharp noise with your tongue to show that you are annoyed or disappointed: *She clicked her tongue and shook her head.*
3 sharp tongue if you have a sharp tongue, you often talk in a way that shows you are angry: *Gina's sharp tongue will get her into trouble one day.*
4 silver tongue *literary* if you have a silver tongue, you can talk in a way that makes people like you or persuades them that you are right
5 sharp-tongued/silver-tongued etc able to talk in a very angry or pleasant way: *a sharp-tongued young teacher*
6 with (your) tongue in (your) cheek if you say something with your tongue in your cheek, you say it as a joke, not seriously → TONGUE-IN-CHEEK
7 slip of the tongue a small mistake in something you say: *Did I say $100? It must have been a slip of the tongue.*
8 bite your tongue to stop yourself saying something because you know it would not be sensible to say it: *I wanted to argue, but I had to bite my tongue.*
9 Cat got your tongue? (*also* **Lost your tongue?**) *spoken* used to ask someone why they are not talking
10 get your tongue around sth *informal* to be able to say a difficult word or phrase: *I couldn't get my tongue around the names of the villages we'd visited.*
11 trip/roll off the tongue *informal* if a name or phrase trips or rolls off your tongue, it is easy or pleasant to say: *Their names trip off the tongue very easily.*
12 loosen sb's tongue *informal* if something such as alcohol loosens your tongue, it makes you talk a lot: *The wine had certainly loosened her tongue.*
13 find your tongue *informal* to say something after you have been silent for a time because you were afraid or shy: *Polly found her tongue at last and told them about the attack.*
14 set tongues wagging to do something that people will talk about in an unkind way: *Angela's divorce will certainly set tongues wagging.*
15 keep a civil tongue in your head *old-fashioned spoken* used to tell someone that they should talk politely to people

T

16 speak with forked tongue to say things that are not true – used humorously
17 speak in tongues to talk using strange words as part of a religious experience
18 LANGUAGE *literary* a language: *Anton lapsed into his own tongue when he was excited.* | **mother/native tongue** (=the language you learn as a child) *She felt more comfortable talking in her native tongue.*
19 FOOD [U] the tongue of a cow or sheep, cooked and eaten cold
20 SHAPE [C] something that has a long thin shape: **[+of]** *Huge tongues of fire were licking the side of the building.*
21 SHOE [C] the part of a shoe that lies on top of your foot, under the part where you tie it → **on the tip of your tongue** at TIP[1](5), → **hold your tongue** at HOLD[1](29)

tongue[2] *v* **1** [I,T] to use your tongue to make separate sounds when playing a musical instrument **2** [T] to touch something with your tongue

ˌtongue and ˈgroove *adj* tongue and groove boards fit together by pushing a piece that sticks out along the edge of one board into a hollow area along the edge of another board: *tongue and groove floorboards*

ˈtongue deˌpressor *n* [C] *AmE* a small flat piece of wood that a doctor uses to hold down your tongue while examining your throat SYN **spatula** *BrE*

ˌtongue-in-ˈcheek *adj* a tongue-in-cheek remark is said as a joke, not seriously: *I love that kind of tongue-in-cheek wit.* —**tongue-in-cheek** *adv*: *I think he was talking tongue-in-cheek.*

ˈtongue-tied *adj* unable to talk in a relaxed way because you feel nervous or embarrassed: *When adults spoke to her, she became tongue-tied and shy.*

ˈtongue ˌtwister *n* [C] a word or phrase that is difficult to say quickly

ton·ic /ˈtɒnɪk $ ˈtɑː-/ *n* **1** [C,U] (*also* **ˈtonic ˌwater**) a clear bitter-tasting drink that you can mix with alcoholic drinks such as GIN or VODKA: *She sat and sipped a gin and tonic.* **2** [C] a drink that you have as a medicine to give you more energy or strength when you feel tired: *A lot of people need a tonic at the end of the winter.* **3** [C usually singular] *BrE* something that makes you feel happy and full of energy: *A weekend by the sea was the perfect tonic.* **4** [C] a liquid that you put on your hair or skin to improve it and make it more healthy: *a herbal skin tonic* **5** [C usually singular] *technical* the first note in a musical SCALE of eight notes

to·night[1] /təˈnaɪt/ ●●● S1 W2 *adv* during the night of this day: *I think I'll go to bed early tonight.* | *We're meeting him at 9 o'clock tonight.*

tonight[2] *n* [U] the night of this day: *I'm really looking forward to tonight.* | *Tonight should be fun.* | *Here is tonight's news bulletin.*

ˈtoning ˌtables *n* [plural] a piece of equipment that you lie on and that moves your arms and legs up and down, which is supposed to make your muscles firmer

ton·nage /ˈtʌnɪdʒ/ *n* [C,U] **1** the size of a ship or the amount of goods it can carry, shown in TONNES **2** the total number of TONNES that something weighs: *A huge tonnage of bombs has already been dropped on the area.*

tonne /tʌn/ *n* (*plural* **tonnes** *or* **tonne**) [C] (*written abbreviation* **t**) a unit for measuring weight, equal to 1,000 kilograms → **TON**(1)

tons /tʌnz/ *adv informal* very much or very many: *I feel tons better after a rest.* THESAURUS ▶ MANY

ton·sil /ˈtɒnsəl $ ˈtɑːn-/ *n* [C] your tonsils are the two small round pieces of flesh at the sides of your throat: *If you keep getting throat infections you might have to* ***have your tonsils out*** (=have them removed).

ton·sil·li·tis /ˌtɒnsɪˈlaɪtɪs $ ˌtɑːn-/ *n* [U] an infection of the tonsils: *Sam's* ***got tonsillitis.***

ton·sure /ˈtɒnʃə $ ˈtɑːnʃər/ *n* [C] a small round area on the top of someone's head where their hair has been removed because they are a priest or a MONK —**tonsured** *adj*: *his tonsured head*

to·ny /ˈtəʊni $ ˈtoʊ-/ *adj AmE informal* fashionable and expensive: *We met in a tony restaurant uptown.*

ˈTony Aˌward (*also* **Tony**) *n* [C] a prize given to the best theatre actor, best actress, best play etc, shown in New York in a particular year

too /tuː/ ●●● S1 W1 *adv*
1 [+adj/adv] more than is acceptable or possible: *Do you think the music's too loud?* | *You've put too much salt in the soup.* | *There are too many cars on the road.* | **much/far too** *Amanda is far too young to get married.* | **too ... for sth/sb** *I was getting too old for romantic relationships.* | *My boots were three sizes too big for me.* | **too ... to do sth** *He was too ill to travel.* | **too ... for sb to do sth** *The box was too heavy for me to lift.*

GRAMMAR
Word order
The correct word order is **too** + adjective + **a** + noun: *It is too high a price to pay.* | *It's too big a risk.*
✗ Don't say: *It is a too high price to pay.* | *It's a too big risk.*
Comparison
too
• You use **too** before an adjective. You say: *The house is too expensive.*
too much
• You use **too much** before a noun. You say: *The house costs too much money.*
• Don't use **too much** before an adjective. ✗ Don't say: *The house is too much expensive.*

2 also: *There were people from all over Europe, and America too.* | *Can I come too?* | *'I'm feeling hungry.' 'Me too.'* | *It's a more efficient system and it's cheaper too.*

GRAMMAR: Word order
• **Too** is usually used at the end of a sentence or clause: *He was a teacher too.*
• In more formal English, **too** is also used near the beginning of a sentence, after the subject, or after an adverb or phrase: *We too must play our part.* | *Here, too, there are problems with the economy.*

3 [+adj/adv] *spoken* used with a negative to mean 'not very': *She doesn't seem too upset about it.* | *'What was the weather like?' 'Oh, not too bad.'* | *She was* ***none too*** *pleased* (=not at all pleased) *when I told her.*
4 all too/only too used to emphasize that a particular situation exists when you wish it did not exist: *Beggars are becoming an all too familiar sight in our cities.* | *I regret to say that these rumours are only too true.*
5 used to emphasize a remark that you are adding: *'He's been banned from driving.' 'A good thing too!'* | *'A woman farmer?' asked Gabriel. 'Yes, and a rich one too.'*
6 I am/he is/you are etc too! *especially AmE informal* used to emphasize that you disagree with what someone has said about someone or something: *'You're not smart enough to use a computer.' 'I am too!'*
7 be too much for sb used to say that something is so difficult, tiring, upsetting etc that someone cannot do it or bear it: *Working full-time was too much for her.* | *The shock was too much for him.*
8 [+adj/adv] *spoken formal* very: *Thank you. You are too kind.*
9 be only too glad/pleased to do sth to be very willing to do something: *I'd be only too pleased to assist you.*
10 too little, too late used to complain that not enough is being done to solve a problem and that the action did not start early enough: *Doctors have criticized the government's response to the crisis as too little, too late.*

took /tʊk/ *v* the past tense of TAKE

tool[1] /tuːl/ ●●● S2 W2 *n* [C]
1 something that you hold in your hand and use to do a particular job: *I don't have the right tools to start fiddling around with the engine.* | *a shop selling garden tools* → see picture on p. 1936
2 a piece of equipment or a skill that is useful for doing your job: *Television is an important tool for the modern*

T

teacher. | *These books are* **the tools of** *my* **trade** (=the things I need to do my job).

3 someone who is used unfairly by another person and who has to do things they do not really want to do - used to show disapproval: **[+of]** *The king was merely a tool of the military government.*

4 *informal not polite* a man's PENIS (=sex organ) → **down tools** at DOWN²(3)

tool² *v* [I always + adv/prep] *AmE informal* to drive along a street, especially for fun: *He spent the afternoon tooling around town.*

tool up *phr v* to prepare a factory for producing goods by providing the necessary tools and machinery: **tool sth ↔ up** *The factory was tooled up to produce light weapons.*

tool·bar /ˈtuːlbɑː $ -bɑːr/ *n* [C] a row of small pictures at the top of a computer screen that allow you to do particular things in a document

tool·box, **tool box** /ˈtuːlbɒks $ -bɑːks/ *n* [C] **1** a box for keeping tools in → see picture at BOX¹ **2** a set of COMMANDS or FUNCTIONS which do various things in a computer program: *The default toolbox contains tools for drawing lots of different shapes.*

tooled /tuːld/ *adj* tooled leather has been decorated by having patterns cut into its surface

ˌ**tooled ˈup** *adj BrE informal* having or carrying a weapon SYN **armed**

ˈ**tool kit** *n* [C] a set of tools: *I realized I'd left my tool kit at home.*

ˈ**tool shed** *n* [C] a small building in a garden, where you keep tools

toot¹ /tuːt/ *v* [I,T] if you toot your car horn, or if it toots, it makes a short high sound: *The taxi driver was angrily tooting his horn.* | *A car tooted at us.*

toot² *n* [C] a short high sound made by a car horn

tooth /tuːθ/ ●●● S2 W2 *n* (*plural* **teeth** /tiːθ/) [C]

1 IN MOUTH one of the hard white objects in your mouth that you use to bite and eat food: *Sugar is bad for your teeth.* → BABY TOOTH, → **canine tooth** at CANINE²(1), EYE TOOTH(2), MILK TOOTH, WISDOM TOOTH, BUCK TEETH, FALSE TEETH, GAP-TOOTHED

2 ON A TOOL ETC one of the sharp or pointed parts that sticks out from the edge of a comb or SAW

3 POWER **have teeth** if a law or an organization has teeth, it has the power to force people to obey it: *We need an Environment Agency that really has teeth.*

4 fight tooth and nail to try with a lot of effort or determination to do something: *We fought tooth and nail to get these plans accepted.*

5 get your teeth into sth *informal* to start to do something with a lot of energy and determination: *I can't wait to get my teeth into the new course.*

6 in the teeth of sth in spite of opposition or danger from something: *Permission for the development was granted in the teeth of opposition from local shopkeepers.*

7 set sb's teeth on edge if a sound or taste sets your teeth on edge, it gives you an uncomfortable feeling in your mouth: *a horrible scraping sound that set my teeth on edge* → **armed to the teeth** at ARMED(1), → **cut your teeth on sth** at CUT¹(23), → **by the skin of your teeth** at SKIN¹(9), → **a kick in the teeth** at KICK²(5), → **lie through your teeth** at LIE²(1), → **have a sweet tooth** at SWEET¹(7), → **take the bit between your teeth** at BIT²(9)

COLLOCATIONS

VERBS

brush your teeth (*also* **clean your teeth** *BrE*) *I brush my teeth twice a day.*

have a tooth out *BrE*, **have a tooth pulled** *AmE* (=have a tooth removed) *He's gone to the dentist to have a tooth out.*

lose a tooth (=no longer have it) *Many of the men had lost all their teeth by the age of 40.*

bare your teeth (=show them, especially in an angry or threatening way) *The dog bared its teeth and snarled.*

grit/clench your teeth (=put them firmly together) | **grind your teeth** (*also* **gnash your teeth** *literary*) (=move them against each other because you are angry) | **sink your teeth into sth** (=put your teeth into someone's flesh, into food etc) | **sb's teeth chatter** (=hit together quickly because someone is cold or afraid)

ADJECTIVES

sb's front/back teeth *Some of his front teeth were missing.*

white/yellow *His teeth were white and even.*

sharp *The fish has small but very sharp teeth.*

good/perfect | **bad/rotten** | **even** (=all of the same height) | **crooked** | **loose**

tooth + NOUN

tooth decay *Brushing regularly helps prevent tooth decay.*

COMMON ERRORS

⚠ Don't say 'wash your teeth'. Say **brush your teeth** or **clean your teeth**.

tooth·ache /ˈtuːθ-eɪk/ ●●● S3 *n* [C,U] a pain in a tooth: *I've* **got toothache**. | *I had* **terrible toothache** *all last night.*

TOOLS

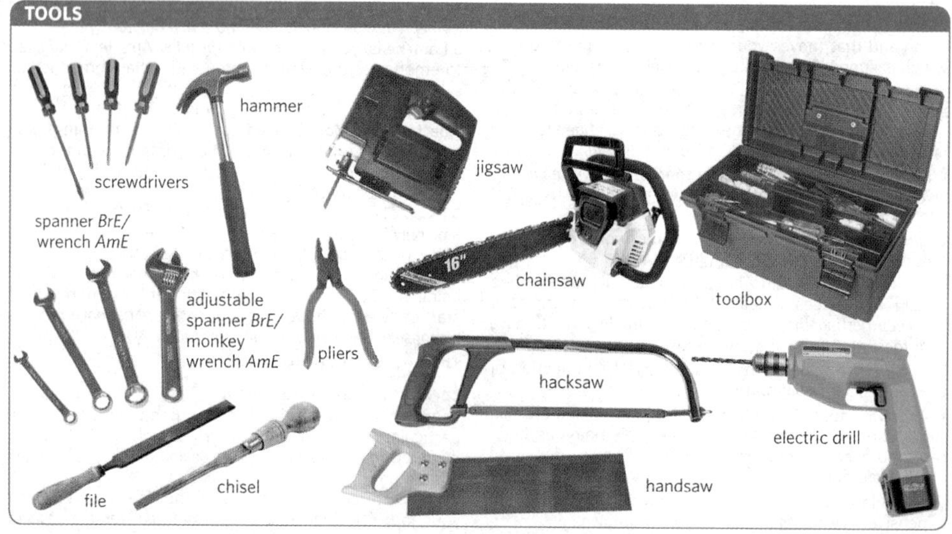

T

tooth·brush /ˈtuːθbrʌʃ/ ●●● S3 *n* [C] a small brush that you use for cleaning your teeth → see picture at BRUSH[1]

ˈtooth ˌfairy *n* **the tooth fairy** an imaginary person who children believe comes into their BEDROOM and leaves them money for teeth which have fallen out

tooth·ing /ˈtuːθɪŋ/ *n* [U] when someone uses a MOBILE PHONE with a BLUETOOTH connection to send a message to another person near them who also has a Bluetooth mobile phone, arranging to have sex with them

tooth·less /ˈtuːθləs/ *adj* **1** someone who is toothless has no teeth: *a toothless old woman* | **a toothless smile/grin** *He gave us a toothless grin.* **2** an organization that is toothless has no power to make people obey its rules: *Does the agency have the power to prosecute companies, or is it a toothless organization?*

tooth·paste /ˈtuːθpeɪst/ ●●● S3 *n* [U] a thick substance that you use to clean your teeth → see picture at CONTAINER

tooth·pick /ˈtuːθˌpɪk/ *n* [C] a very small pointed stick that you can use for removing bits of food that are stuck between your teeth

ˈtooth ˌpowder *n* [U] a special powder you can use to clean your teeth

tooth·some /ˈtuːθsəm/ *adj old-fashioned* tasting very good: *an attractive and toothsome dish*

tooth·y /ˈtuːθi/ *adj* **toothy smile/grin** a smile in which you show a lot of teeth: *He grinned a wide, toothy grin.*

toot·le /ˈtuːtl/ *v* [I] *BrE informal* **1** [always + adv/prep] *old-fashioned* to move slowly in a car: *We spent the afternoon tootling along the coast.* **2** to play an instrument that you blow: *tootling away on a flute*

toots /tʊts/ *n* [C] *AmE old-fashioned* a way of talking to a woman, sometimes considered offensive: *Hey, toots! How're you doing?*

toot·sies /ˈtʊtsiz/ *n* [plural] *informal* toes – used especially by children or when you are talking to a child

top¹ /tɒp $ tɑːp/ ●●● S1 W1 *n* [C]

1 HIGHEST PART the highest part of something OPP bottom: **[+of]** *The tops of the mountains were still covered with snow.* | *She could only just see over the tops of their heads.* | **at the top (of sth)** *He was standing at the top of the stairs.* | *We'll sit down once we're at the top.* | *Write your name at the top of the page.* | **to the top (of sth)** *Stop and wait for us when you get to the top of the slope.* | *I filled the glass* **right to the top**. | *The book I wanted was at the* **very top** *of the pile.* | **cliff top/mountaintop/hilltop/treetop** *We could just see the white cliff tops in the distance.*

2 UPPER SURFACE the flat upper surface of an object: *a low wooden table with a glass top* | **[+of]** *We walked along the top of the ancient city walls.* | **on (the) top of sth** *She put the papers down on the top of the piano.* | *Her fingers drummed on the* **table top**.

3 BEST POSITION **the top** the best, most successful, or most important position in an organization, company, or profession OPP bottom: **[+of]** *He has reached the top of his profession.* | **at the top (of sth)** *It's the people at the top who make the decisions.* | **to the top (of sth)** *All young footballers dream of making it to the top.* | *the groups that are currently at* **the top** *of* **the tree** (=the highest position in a profession) *in the pop world*

4 COVER something that you put on or over an object to cover it, protect it, or prevent liquid coming out of it: *I can't get the top off the jar.* | *You've left the top off the toothpaste again!* | *Can you put the top back on the bottle when you've finished with it?* | **bottle top/pen top etc** *Has anyone seen my pen top?*

5 CLOTHES a piece of clothing that you wear on the upper part of your body: *She was wearing a stripy knitted top.* | *a skirt with a matching top* | *a bikini top* | *I can't find my pyjama top.*

6 be (at the) top of the list/agenda something that is at the top of a list will be dealt with or discussed first: *Europe is once again at the top of the political agenda.*

7 on top a) on the highest part or surface of something: *The cake was a bit burnt on top.* | *a high roof with a chimney on top* **b)** on the highest part of your head: *Can you cut it quite short on top, please.* **c)** winning in a game or competition: *After the first set, the Australian was comfortably on top.*

8 on top of sth a) on the highest surface of something: *There should be an envelope on top of the fridge.* **b)** in complete control of a situation: *Don't worry; I'm back on top of things now.* | *I should be more on top of my work next week.* **c)** if something bad happens to you on top of something else, it happens when you have other problems: *On top of everything else, I now have to go to work next Saturday!*

9 one on top of the other (*also* **on top of one another**) in a pile: *We stacked the crates one on top of the other.*

10 on top of sb if something dangerous or threatening is on top of you, it is very near you: *The truck was almost on top of us.*

11 get on top of sb if your work or a problem gets on top of you, it begins to make you feel unhappy and upset: *Things are starting to get on top of him.*

12 come out on top to win a difficult struggle or argument, especially one that has continued for a long time: *It's difficult to predict who will come out on top.*

13 on top of the world *informal* extremely happy: *When I heard she'd been released I felt on top of the world!*

14 PLANT the part of a fruit or vegetable where it was attached to the plant, or the leaves of a plant whose root you can eat: *Cut the tops off the tomatoes.* | *I've found a recipe for beetroot tops.*

15 STREET/FIELD ETC the part of the street or of a piece of land that is the furthest away from you: *I waited at the top of East Street.*

16 the top of the milk *BrE* the cream that rises to the top of a bottle of milk

17 the top of the table the part of a long dinner table where the most important people sit

18 off the top of your head *informal* if you say something off the top of your head, you say it immediately, without thinking carefully about it or checking the facts: *Just off the top of my head, I'd say there were about 50.*

19 sing/shout at the top of your voice to sing or shout as loudly as you can: *Angela ran out of the house, shouting at the top of her voice.*

20 be at the top of your game (*also* **be on top of your game**) to be doing your job, especially playing a sport, very well

21 from the top *spoken* an expression meaning from the beginning, used especially in the theatre: *Right, let's take it from the top once more.*

22 from top to bottom if you clean or search somewhere from top to bottom, you do it very thoroughly: *The whole house needs cleaning from top to bottom.*

23 from top to toe if a person is dressed or covered in something from top to toe, they are completely dressed or covered in it: *They were covered in mud from top to toe.*

24 the top and bottom of it *BrE spoken* the general result or meaning of a situation, expressed in a few words: *He's trying to embarrass you, that's the top and bottom of it.*

25 not have much up top *BrE spoken* to be not very intelligent: *Poor Nigel, he doesn't have very much up top.*

26 TOY a child's toy that spins around on its point when you twist it

27 spin like a top to spin or turn round very quickly: *The impact of the blow sent me spinning like a top.* → TOPS

top² ●●● S1 W1 *adj*

1 HIGHEST [only before noun] nearest to the top of something OPP bottom: *We have a flat on the* **top floor** *of the building.* | *the top button of his shirt* | *I managed to scrape off the top layer of paint.* | *I found the letter in the top drawer of his desk.*

2 BEST [usually before noun] best or most successful: *our top tennis players* | *a top New York salon* | *one of the world's top engineering companies* | *people in top jobs* | *She got top marks.* | *The top score was 72.*

3 WINNING winning in a game or competition: **[+of]** *Barcelona remain top of the league after beating Real Madrid.* |

T

Despite losing last night, Manchester United are still top (=the highest in a list of clubs in a competition).
4 top left/right/centre expressions meaning the picture at the top of a page on the left or right or in the centre, used in magazines and newspapers: *Top right: silk blouse £195 from Harrods.*
5 top speed the fastest speed a vehicle can move at: *We tore down the motorway at top speed. | a sports car with a top speed of 140 miles per hour*
6 top priority the thing that you think is most important: *Education is this government's top priority.*
7 GOOD *BrE spoken informal* very good: *Clive's a top bloke.*
8 top copy *BrE* a letter or document from which copies can be made

top³ ●○○ *v* (**topped, topping**) [T]
1 BE HIGHER to be higher than a particular amount: *Their profits have reportedly topped £1,000,000 this year.*
2 BE MOST SUCCESSFUL to be in the highest position in a list because you are the most successful: *The Tower of London tops the list of London's most popular tourist attractions. | the team that has topped the Premiership for the last three seasons | In 1998 the group* ***topped*** *the* ***charts*** *with the song 'Don't Stop Loving Me'.*
3 DO BETTER if you top something, you do something that is better than it: *He topped his previous best performance, coming second in the 100 metres.*
4 top an offer/a bid etc to offer more money than someone else: *A rival company topped our offer by $5 million.*
5 be topped by sth to have something on top: *The roof was topped by a chimney. | a hill topped by pine trees*
6 be topped (off) with sth if food is topped with something, it has that thing on it or over the top of it: *a strawberry tart topped with whipped cream | The cake can be topped off with fresh fruit.*
7 to top it all *spoken* in addition to other bad things that have happened to you: *To top it all I lost my job.*
8 top that *spoken* used when you are asking someone if they have done something more exciting or successful than you: *Well, I've been asked to appear on a TV show later this year, so top that!*
9 top and tail *BrE* to cut the top and bottom off a piece of fruit or a vegetable
10 top yourself *BrE informal* to kill yourself deliberately
11 REACH THE TOP *literary* if you top a hill, you reach the top of it: *We topped the hill and looked down towards the valley below us.*

top sth ↔ **off** *phr v* to complete something successfully by doing one last thing: *Let's top off the evening with a drink.*

top out *phr v* if something such as a price that is increasing tops out, it reaches its highest point and stops rising: *Do you think interest rates have topped out now?*

top sth/sb ↔ **up** *phr v especially BrE*
1 to add more liquid to a container that is partly full: *I'll just top up the coffee pot.*
2 to put more drink in someone's glass or cup after they have drunk some: *Can I top you up?*
3 to increase the level of something slightly so as to bring it back to the level you want: *He had to do extra jobs at the weekend to top up his income.* → TOP-UP

to·paz /ˈtəʊpæz $ ˈtoʊ-/ *n* [C,U] a transparent yellow stone that is used as a jewel

ˌtop baˈnana *n* **be top banana** *especially AmE informal* to be the most powerful person in an organization or group

ˌtop ˈbrass *n* [singular] *informal* people in positions of high rank in a company, or in the army, navy etc: *The top brass are coming in from Washington to see how we do things here. | The meeting was attended by top diplomats and military top brass.*

ˌtop-ˈclass *adj* of very good quality or a very high standard: *a top-class athlete | a top-class restaurant*

top·coat /ˈtɒpkəʊt $ ˈtɑːpkoʊt/ *n* **1** [C,U] the last layer of paint that you put on a surface **2** [C] *old-fashioned* a warm long coat SYN **overcoat**

ˌtop ˈdog *n* [C] the person who has the most power in a group, especially after a struggle: *He always wanted to be the one in control, the top dog.*

ˌtop ˈdollar *n* [U] if you pay top dollar for something, you pay a lot of money for it: *Computer customers are willing to pay top dollar for fast repair.*

ˌtop-ˈdown *adj* [only before noun] *BrE* **1** a top-down way of organizing a business is one in which the most important people make decisions and tell the people below them what they should do: *The company has a top-down management system. | a top-down approach to decision-making* **2** a top-down way of understanding or explaining something starts with a general idea and adds details later

ˌtop-ˈdrawer *adj* [only before noun] *informal* of the highest quality: *England need to produce a top-drawer performance if they want to win this match.*

top·dress·ing /ˌtɒpˈdresɪŋ $ ˈtɑːpˌdresɪŋ/ *n* [C,U] *technical* a layer of FERTILIZER that is spread over land so that it will produce better crops

to·pee, topi /ˈtəʊpiː $ toʊˈpiː/ *n* [C] a light hard hat that you wear to protect your head from the sun in hot countries

ˌtop-ˈflight *adj* [only before noun] very successful or skilful: *They've hired a really top-flight sales team.*

ˌtop ˈgear *n* [U] *BrE* **1** the highest GEAR of a car, bus etc: **in top gear** *The car will cruise at 80 mph in top gear.* **2 move/get into top gear** to begin to work with as much effort as possible: *The party's election campaign is now moving into top gear.*

ˈtop-ˌgrossing *adj* [only before noun] a top-grossing film earns more money than any other film at a particular time

ˌtop ˈhat *n* [C] a man's tall black or grey hat, now worn only on formal occasions → see picture at **HAT**

ˌtop-ˈheavy *adj* **1** too heavy at the top and therefore likely to fall over **2** an organization that is top-heavy has too many managers compared to the number of ordinary workers: *The company was burdened by a top-heavy bureaucracy.*

to·pi /ˈtəʊpiː $ toʊˈpiː/ *n* another spelling of TOPEE

to·pi·a·ry /ˈtəʊpiəri $ ˈtoʊpieri/ *n* [U] trees and bushes cut into the shapes of birds, animals etc, or the art of cutting them in this way

top·ic /ˈtɒpɪk $ ˈtɑː-/ ●●● S3 W2 AWL *n* [C] a subject that people talk or write about: *The environment is a popular topic these days. |* **[+of]** *We shall return to the topic of education in Chapter 7. |* **topic of conversation/debate etc** *The wedding has been the only topic of conversation for weeks. | The main* ***topic for discussion*** *will be the proposed new supermarket. | a wide* ***range of topics***

top·ic·al /ˈtɒpɪkəl $ ˈtɑː-/ AWL *adj* a subject that is topical is interesting because it is important at the present time: **topical subject/issue/theme etc** *a new TV comedy dealing with topical issues | topical jokes* (=jokes about topical subjects) —**topically** /-kli/ *adv* —**topicality** /ˌtɒpɪˈkæləti $ ˌtɑː-/ *n* [U]

top·knot /ˈtɒpnɒt $ ˈtɑːpnɑːt/ *n* [C] hair that is tied together on top of your head

top·less /ˈtɒpləs $ ˈtɑːp-/ *adj* if a woman is topless, she is not wearing any clothes on the upper part of her body, so that her breasts are not covered: *topless sunbathing |* **topless bar/show** (=one in which the women serving or performing are topless)

ˌtop-ˈlevel *adj* [only before noun] involving the most powerful people in a country, organization etc: *top-level meetings between EU leaders*

top·most /ˈtɒpməʊst $ ˈtɑːpmoʊst/ *adj* [only before noun] the topmost part of something is its highest part SYN **top**: *The topmost branches were still bathed in sunlight.*

ˌtop-ˈnotch *adj informal* something that is top-notch is of the highest quality or standard: *I was lucky and got myself a job with a top-notch company.*

ˌtop-of-the-ˈrange *BrE*, **ˌtop-of-the-ˈline** *AmE adj* a product that is top-of-the-range is the best of its kind: *a top-of-the-range electric guitar*

to·pog·ra·phy /tə'pɒgrəfi $ -'pɑː-/ *n* [U] *technical* **1** the science of describing an area of land, or making maps of it **2** [+of] the shape of an area of land, including its hills, valleys etc —**topographer** *n* [C] —**topographical** /ˌtɒpə'græfɪkəl◂ $ ˌtɑː-,ˌtoʊ-/ *adj*

top·per /'tɒpə $ 'tɑːpər/ *n* [C] *informal* a TOP HAT

top·ping /'tɒpɪŋ $ 'tɑː-/ *n* [C,U] something you put on top of food to make it look nicer or taste better: *a pizza with extra toppings*

top·ple /'tɒpəl $ 'tɑː-/ ●○○ *v*
1 [I,T] to become unsteady and then fall over, or to make something do this: **[+over]** *A stack of plates swayed, and began to topple over.*
2 [T] to take power away from a leader or government, especially by force SYN **overthrow**: *This scandal could topple the government.*

ˌtop-'ranking *adj* [only before noun] most powerful and important within an organization: *top-ranking diplomats*

ˌtop-'rated *adj* [only before noun] *informal* very popular with the public: *a top-rated TV show*

'top round *n* [U] *AmE* high-quality BEEF cut from the upper leg of the cow SYN **topside** *BrE*

tops /tɒps $ tɑːps/ *adv spoken informal* **1** at the most: *It should take two hours tops.* **2** the best or most popular: *The store was voted tops for its outstanding facilities for children.*

ˌtop-'secret *adj* top-secret documents or information must be kept completely secret: *a top-secret code*

top·side¹ /'tɒpsaɪd $ 'tɑːp-/ *n* [U] *BrE* high quality BEEF cut from the upper leg of the cow SYN **top round** *AmE*

topside² (*also* **top·sides** /-saɪdz/) *adv* towards or onto the DECK (=upper surface) of a boat or ship

'top-slice *v* [T] to take part of an amount of money that has been collected or received and use it for another purpose: *One proposal is to top-slice the BBC licence fee and spread the proceeds to other broadcasters.* —**top-slicing** *n* [U]

top·soil /'tɒpsɔɪl $ 'tɑːp-/ *n* [U] the upper level of soil in which most plants have their roots

top·spin /'tɒpˌspɪn $ 'tɑːp-/ *n* [U] the turning movement of a ball that has been hit or thrown in such a way that it spins forward

top·sy-tur·vy /ˌtɒpsi 'tɜːvi◂ $ ˌtɑːpsi 'tɜːrvi◂/ *adj informal* in a state of complete disorder or confusion: *He left his room all topsy-turvy.*

ˌtop 'table *n* [C] *BrE* the table at a formal meal, for example at a wedding, where the most important people sit SYN **head table** *AmE*

'top-up *n* [C] *BrE* **1** an amount of liquid that you add to a glass, cup etc in order to make it full again: *Would you like a top-up?* **2** an extra payment that brings an amount to the desired level: *top-up loans for students*

'top-up ˌcard *n* [C] a card that you buy in order to be able to continue using a PAY-AS-YOU-GO mobile phone

tor /tɔː $ tɔːr/ *n* [C] *BrE* a rocky hill

torch¹ /tɔːtʃ $ tɔːrtʃ/ ●●○ *n* [C]
1 *BrE* a small electric lamp that you carry in your hand SYN **flashlight** *AmE*: *We shone our torches around the cavern.* → see picture at **LAMP**
2 a long stick with burning material at one end that produces light: *the Olympic torch*
3 carry a torch for sb *old-fashioned* to secretly love and admire someone

torch² *v* [T] *informal* to deliberately make a building, vehicle etc start to burn: *Rioters torched several abandoned cars.*

torch·light /'tɔːtʃlaɪt $ 'tɔːr-/ *n* [U] **1** *BrE* the light produced by an electric torch **2** the light produced by burning torches: *a torchlight procession*

'torch song *n* [C] a sad song about love —**torch singer** *n* [C]

tore /tɔː $ tɔːr/ *v* the past tense of TEAR²

to·re·a·dor /'tɒriədɔː $ 'tɔːriədɔːr, 'tɑː-/ *n* [C] a person who fights BULLS to entertain people in Spain SYN **bullfighter**

tor·ment¹ /'tɔːment $ 'tɔːr-/ *n* **1** [U] severe mental or physical suffering: **in torment** *She lay awake all night in torment.* **2** [C] someone or something that makes you suffer a lot: *The journey must have been a torment for them.*

tor·ment² /tɔː'ment $ tɔːr-/ *v* [T] **1** to make someone suffer a lot, especially mentally: *Seth was tormented by feelings of guilt.* **2** to deliberately treat someone cruelly by annoying them or hurting them SYN **torture**: *The older boys would torment him whenever they had the chance.* —**tormentor** *n* [C]

torn /tɔːn $ tɔːrn/ *v* the past participle of TEAR²

tor·na·do /tɔː'neɪdəʊ $ tɔːr'neɪdoʊ/ *n* (*plural* **tornadoes** *or* **tornados**) [C] an extremely violent storm consisting of air that spins very quickly and causes a lot of damage → **hurricane**, **cyclone** **THESAURUS** STORM, WIND

tor·pe·do¹ /tɔː'piːdəʊ $ tɔːr'piːdoʊ/ *n* (*plural* **torpedoes**) [C] a long narrow weapon that is fired under the surface of the sea and explodes when it hits something

torpedo² *v* [T] **1** to attack or destroy a ship with a torpedo **2** to stop something such as a plan from succeeding SYN **destroy**: *New threats of violence have effectively torpedoed the peace talks.*

tor·pid /'tɔːpɪd $ 'tɔːr-/ *adj formal* not active because you are lazy or sleepy: *a torpid mind*

tor·por /'tɔːpə $ 'tɔːrpər/ *n* [singular, U] *formal* a state of being not active because you are lazy or sleepy: *She tried to rouse him from the torpor into which he had sunk.*

torque /tɔːk $ tɔːrk/ *n* [U] *technical* the force or power that makes something turn around a central point, especially in an engine

tor·rent /'tɒrənt $ 'tɔː-, 'tɑː-/ *n* [C] **1** a large amount of water moving very quickly and strongly in a particular direction → **flood**: *After five days of heavy rain the Telle river was a* ***raging torrent*** (=a very violent torrent). | **in torrents** *The rain came down in torrents.* **2 a torrent of sth** a lot of words spoken quickly, especially in order to insult or criticize someone SYN **stream**: *When I asked him to move, he unleashed a* ***torrent of abuse***. | **a torrent of Greek/Italian etc** *The woman poured out a torrent of Italian.*

tor·ren·tial /tə'renʃəl, tɒ- $ tɔː-/ *adj* **torrential rain** very heavy rain

tor·rid /'tɒrɪd $ 'tɔː-, 'tɑː-/ *adj* **1** involving strong emotions, especially of sexual love: *a torrid love affair* **2** *literary* torrid weather is very hot: *the torrid desert sun* **3** *BrE* a torrid time is a very difficult one: *He had a torrid time out there on the racetrack.*

tor·sion /'tɔːʃən $ 'tɔːr-/ *n* [U] *technical* the twisting of a piece of metal

tor·so /'tɔːsəʊ $ 'tɔːrsoʊ/ *n* (*plural* **torsos**) [C] **1** your body, not including your head, arms, or legs: *the torso of a woman* **2** a STATUE of a torso

tort /tɔːt $ tɔːrt/ *n* [C,U] *law* an action that is wrong but not criminal and can be dealt with in a CIVIL court of law

tor·til·la /tɔː'tiːjə $ tɔːr-/ *n* [C] a type of thin flat Mexican bread made from corn or wheat flour

tor'tilla ˌchip *n* [C] a small hard flat piece of food made from corn, similar to a CRISP

tor·toise /'tɔːtəs $ 'tɔːr-/ *n* [C] a slow-moving land animal that can pull its head and legs into the hard round shell that covers its body → **turtle** → see picture at **REPTILE**

tor·toise·shell /'tɔːtəsʃel, 'tɔːtəʃel $ 'tɔːr-/ *n* **1** [U] a hard shiny brown and white material made from the shell of a tortoise **2** [C] a cat that has yellow, brown, and black marks on its fur **3** [C] a BUTTERFLY that has brown and orange wings

tor·tu·ous /'tɔːtʃuəs $ 'tɔːr-/ *adj* **1** a tortuous path, stream, road etc has a lot of bends in it and is therefore difficult to travel along: *a tortuous path over the mountains to Kandahar* **2** complicated and long and therefore confusing: *The book begins with a long, tortuous introduction.* —**tortuously** *adv*

T

tor·ture¹ /ˈtɔːtʃə $ ˈtɔːrtʃər/ ●○○ *n* [C,U]
1 an act of deliberately hurting someone in order to force them to tell you something, to punish them, or to be cruel: *He died after five days of excruciating torture.*
2 severe physical or mental suffering: *The waiting must be torture for you.*

torture² ●○○ *v* [T]
1 to deliberately hurt someone in order to force them to give you information, to punish them, or to be cruel: *Political opponents of the regime may be tortured.*
2 if a feeling or knowledge tortures you, it makes you suffer a lot mentally SYN **torment**: *Rachel sat alone for hours at home, tortured by jealousy.* —**torturer** *n* [C]

tor·tur·ous /ˈtɔːtʃərəs $ ˈtɔːr-/ *adj* very painful or unpleasant to experience: *a torturous five days of fitness testing*

To·ry /ˈtɔːri/ *n* (*plural* **Tories**) [C] a member of the British Conservative Party: *a lifelong Tory* —**Tory** *adj* [only before noun]: *Tory principles*

tosh /tɒʃ $ tɑːʃ/ *n* [U] *BrE informal* nonsense: *What a load of old tosh!*

toss¹ /tɒs $ tɒːs/ ●●○ *v*
1 [T] to throw something, especially something light, with a quick gentle movement of your hand: **toss sth into/onto etc sth** *She crumpled the letter and tossed it into the fire.* | **toss sth aside/over etc** *Toss that book over, will you?* | **toss sth to sb** *'Catch!' said Sandra, tossing her bag to him.* | **toss sb sth** *Frank tossed her the newspaper.* THESAURUS ▸ THROW
2 [I,T] to move about continuously in a violent or uncontrolled way, or to make something do this: **toss sth around/about** *The small boat was tossed about like a cork.*
3 toss and turn to keep changing your position in bed because you cannot sleep: *I've been tossing and turning all night.*
4 [I,T] (*also* **toss up**) *especially BrE* to throw a coin in the air, so that a decision will be made according to the side that faces upwards when it comes down SYN **flip** *AmE*: *They* ***tossed*** *a* ***coin*** *to decide who would go first.* | **toss (sb) for it** *We couldn't make up our minds, so we decided to toss for it.*
5 [T] to throw something up into the air and let it fall to the ground: *The crowd cheered, banging pots and tossing confetti into the air.*
6 toss a pancake *BrE* to throw a PANCAKE upwards so that it turns over in the air and lands on the side that you want to cook SYN **flip** *AmE*
7 [T] to move pieces of food about in a small amount of liquid so that they become covered with the liquid: *Toss the carrots in some butter before serving.*
8 toss your head/hair *written* to move your head or hair back suddenly, often with a shaking movement showing anger: *He tossed his head angrily and left the room.*

toss off *phr v*
1 toss sth ↔ off to produce something quickly and without much effort: *one of those painters who can toss off a couple of pictures before breakfast*
2 toss sth ↔ off *written* to drink something quickly: *He tossed off a few whiskies.*
3 toss (sb) off *BrE informal not polite* to MASTURBATE

toss sth/sb **↔ out** *phr v AmE informal*
1 to get rid of something that you do not want SYN **throw out**: *I tossed most of that stuff out when we moved.*
2 to make someone leave a place, especially because of bad behaviour SYN **throw out**: **[+of]** *Kurt was tossed out of the club for trying to start a fight.*

toss² *n* [C] **1** the act of throwing a coin in the air to decide something, especially who will do something first in a game: ***The toss of a coin*** *decided who would go first.* | **win/lose the toss** *Malory won the toss and will serve.* **2** a sudden backwards movement of your head, so that your hair moves, often showing anger: *'I'll see,' the nurse said, with an officious* ***toss of*** *her* ***head.*** **3** a gentle throw **4 not give a toss** *BrE spoken* to not care about something at all: *I really couldn't give a toss what Sam thinks.* → **argue the toss** at ARGUE(5)

toss·er /ˈtɒsə $ ˈtɒːsər/ *n* [C] *BrE spoken not polite* an offensive word for someone who you think is stupid or unpleasant

ˈtoss-up *n* **1 it's a toss-up** *spoken* used when you do not know which of two things will happen, or which of two things to choose: *I don't know who'll get the job – it's a toss-up between Carl and Steve.* **2** [C usually singular] *BrE* an act of tossing a coin in order to decide something

tot¹ /tɒt $ tɑːt/ *n* [C] **1** *informal* a very small child **2** *especially BrE* a small amount of a strong alcoholic drink: **[+of]** *a tot of rum*

tot² *v* (**totted**, **totting**) *BrE*
tot sth **↔ up** *phr v informal* to add together numbers or amounts of money in order to find the total SYN **total up**: *The waiter quickly totted up the bill.*

to·tal¹ /ˈtəʊtl $ ˈtoʊ-/ ●●● S1 W1 *adj*
1 [usually before noun] complete, or as great as is possible: **total failure/disaster** *The sales campaign was a total disaster.* | *a* ***total ban*** *on cigarette advertising* | *He looked at her with a* ***total lack*** *of comprehension.* | *a sport that demands* ***total commitment***
2 total number/amount/cost etc the number, amount etc that is the total: *total sales of 200,000 per year* | *Her total income was £10,000 a year.*

total² ●●● S2 W2 *n* [C]
1 the final number or amount of things, people etc when everything has been counted: *That's £7 and £3.50, so the total is £10.50.* | **a total of 20/100 etc** *A total of thirteen meetings were held to discuss the issue.* | **in total** *There were probably about 40 people there in total.* | **the sum total** (=the whole of an amount when everything is considered together)
2 grand total a) the final total, including all the totals added together → **subtotal b)** used humorously when you think the final total is small: *I earned a grand total of $4.15.*

total³ ●●○ *v* (**totalled**, **totalling** *BrE*, **totaled**, **totaling** *AmE*)
1 [linking verb, T] to reach a particular total: *The group had losses totalling $3 million this year.*

> **REGISTER**
> **Total** is used especially in journalism. In everyday English, people usually say that something **makes** or **adds up to** a particular total: *Three and six* ***make*** *nine.*

2 [T] *especially AmE informal* to damage a car so badly that it cannot be repaired: *Chuck totaled his dad's new Toyota.*
total sth **↔ up** *phr v* to find the total number or total amount of something by adding: *At the end of the game, total up everyone's score to see who has won.*

to·tal·i·tar·i·an /təʊˌtæləˈteəriən $ toʊˌtæləˈter-/ *adj* based on a political system in which ordinary people have no power and are completely controlled by the government: **a totalitarian state/regime** THESAURUS ▸ GOVERNMENT —**totalitarianism** *n* [U]

to·tal·i·ty /təʊˈtæləti $ toʊ-/ *n* [U] *formal* **1** the whole of something: **in sth's totality** *It's essential that we look at the problem in its totality.* **2** a total amount

tot·al·ly /ˈtəʊtl-i $ ˈtoʊ-/ ●●● S1 W2 *adv* [+adj/adv] completely: *That's a* ***totally different*** *matter.* | *It's like learning a* ***totally new*** *language.* | **totally unacceptable/unnecessary/unsuitable etc** *Terrorism is totally unacceptable in a civilised world.* | *I totally agree.*

tote /təʊt $ toʊt/ (*also* **tote around**) *v* [T] *especially AmE informal* to carry something, especially regularly: *Kids have to tote heavy textbooks around.*

Tote *n* **the Tote** a system in Britain in which a machine adds together the amounts of money BET on a horse race and divides the total among the people who bet on the winner

ˈtote bag *n* [C] *AmE* a large bag for carrying things

to·tem /ˈtəʊtəm $ ˈtoʊ-/ *n* [C] an animal, plant etc that is thought to have a special SPIRITUAL connection with a particular tribe, especially in North America, or a figure made to look like the animal etc —**totemic** /təʊˈtemɪk $ toʊ-/ *adj*

ˈtotem pole *n* [C] **1** a tall wooden pole with one or more totems cut or painted on it, made by the Native Americans of northwest North America **2 low man on the totem pole** *AmE* someone of low rank in an organization or business

totes /təʊts $ toʊts/ *adverb informal* totally – used mainly by young people: *Her hair is totes amazing!*

to·to /ˈtəʊtəʊ $ ˈtoʊtoʊ/ → IN TOTO

tot·ter /ˈtɒtə $ ˈtɑːtər/ *v* [I] **1** to walk or move unsteadily from side to side as if you are going to fall over: *Lorrimer swayed a little, tottered, and fell.* **2** if a political system or organization totters, it becomes less strong and is likely to stop working

tot·ty /ˈtɒti $ ˈtɑːti/ *n* [U] *BrE informal not polite* an offensive word used by men to refer to women who they think are sexually attractive

tou·can /ˈtuːkən, -kæn/ *n* [C] a tropical American bird with bright feathers and a very large beak

touch[1] /tʌtʃ/ ●●● S2 W2 *v*

1 FEEL [T] to put your hand, finger etc on someone or something: *She reached out to touch his arm.* | *If your house has been burgled, you shouldn't touch anything until the police arrive.* | *'Don't touch me!' she yelled.* | **touch sb on the arm/leg etc** *A hand touched her on the shoulder.*

2 NO SPACE BETWEEN [I,T] if two things touch, or one thing touches another thing, they reach each other so that there is no space between them: *As our glasses touched, he said 'Cheers!'* | *Her dress was so long that it was touching the ground.*

GRAMMAR: Reciprocal verbs

Touch is a reciprocal verb. This type of verb is used when saying that two or more people or things do something that involves both or all of them. It does not need to have an object: *Their hands touched.* In this sentence, **touch** is intransitive and does not have an object.
You can also say: *Their hands touched each other.* | *His hand touched hers.* In these sentences, **touch** is transitive.
GRAMMAR GUIDE ▸ VERBS

3 touch sth to sth *literary* to move something so that it reaches something else with no space between the two things: *She touched the handkerchief to her nose.* | *He touched his lips to her hair.*

4 AFFECT SB'S FEELINGS [T] to affect someone's emotions, especially by making them feel sympathy or sadness: *Her plight has* ***touched the hearts*** *of people around the world.* | *She could sense his concern and it touched her.* → TOUCHED, TOUCHING[1]

5 HAVE AN EFFECT [T] to have an effect on someone or something, especially by changing or influencing them: *He has touched the lives of many people.* | *Unemployment remains an evil that touches the whole community.* | *He* ***was*** *often* ***touched by*** *doubt* (=doubt affected him).

6 USE [T usually in negatives] to use or handle something: *The law doesn't allow him to touch any of the money.* | *It's a long time since I've touched a piano.*

7 not touch sth a) to not eat or drink something: *What's wrong? You've hardly touched your food.* | *My grandfather was an alcoholic but I* ***never touch the stuff*** (=never drink alcohol). **b)** to not deal with something that you should deal with: *I brought home loads of work, but I haven't touched any of it yet.*

8 not touch sb/sth to not hurt someone or not damage something: *The older boys swore they hadn't touched the child.* | *Parma had not been touched.*

9 DEAL WITH SB/STH [T] to become involved with or deal with a particular problem, situation, or person: *He was the only lawyer who would touch the case.* | *Everything he touches turns to disaster.* | *No school would touch a teacher who had been convicted of assault.*

10 REACH AN AMOUNT [T] *especially BrE* to reach a particular amount or level: *At the time, the unemployment rate was touching 10 percent and rising.*

11 HIT/KICK [T] *BrE* to gently hit or kick a ball – used especially in reports of sports games: *Evans was just able to touch the ball away from Wilkinson.*

12 not touch sth/sb (with a bargepole) *BrE*, **not touch sth/sb with a ten-foot pole** *AmE* used to say that you think someone or something is bad and people should not be involved with them: *I wouldn't touch him with a bargepole.* | *Financial analysts have warned investors not to touch these offers with a ten-foot pole.*

13 be touched with sth *literary* to have a small amount of a particular quality: *His voice was touched with the faintest of Italian accents.* | *Her nails had been manicured and lightly touched with colour.*

14 EXPRESSION [T] if an expression such as a smile touches your face, your face has that expression for a short time: *A smile touched her lips.*

15 RELATE TO STH [T] to be about or to deal with a particular subject, situation, or problem: *Though the question touched a new vein, Nelson answered promptly.* | *The discourse touches many of the issues which are currently popular.*

16 LIGHT [T] *literary* if light touches something, it shines on it: *The sun was just touching the tops of the mountains.*

17 nothing/no one can touch sb/sth used for saying that nothing or no one is as good as a particular person or thing: *He describes the events with a passion that no other writer can touch.*

18 touch base (with sb) to talk to someone in order to find out how they are or what is happening: *I just wanted to touch base and make sure you hadn't changed your mind about seeing me.*

19 touch bottom a) to reach the ground at the bottom of a sea, river etc: *He swam down but could not touch bottom.* **b)** to reach the lowest level or worst condition: *The housing market has touched bottom.* → **touch a (raw) nerve** at NERVE[1](6), → **touch wood** at WOOD(3)

THESAURUS

touch to put your fingers or hand onto someone or something for a very short time: *Don't touch the iron – it's hot!*

feel to touch something with your fingers in order to find out about it: *Feel how soft this material is.* | *I felt his forehead. It was cold.*

handle to touch something and pick it up and hold it in your hands: *Children should always wash their hands before handling food.* | *The glass was very fragile, and she handled it with great care.*

finger to touch or handle something with your fingers, especially while you are thinking of other things: *She fingered the heavy necklace around her neck.*

rub to move your hand over a surface while pressing it: *Bob rubbed his eyes and yawned.*

scratch to rub part of your body with your nails, often because it ITCHES: *The dog kept scratching its ear.* | *Bob scratched his head thoughtfully.*

tickle to move your fingers lightly over someone's body in order to make them laugh: *The baby giggled as I tickled him.*

TOUCH SB GENTLY OR LOVINGLY

stroke to move your hand gently over something, especially in a loving way: *She stroked the child's hair.* | *Our cat won't let people stroke him.*

pat to touch an animal or child lightly several times, with your hand flat: *He knelt down to pat the dog.* | *She patted the little boy's head.*

pet to touch and move your hand gently over someone, especially an animal or child: *The goats, pigs, sheep, and cows here allow you to pet them.*

caress /kəˈres/ to gently touch a part of someone's body in a loving way: *a mother caressing her child* | *She caressed his cheek.*

fondle to touch a part of someone's body in a loving or sexual way – use this especially about touching someone in a sexual way that is not wanted: *He tried to fondle her and she immediately pulled away from him.*

touch down *phr v*
1 when an aircraft touches down, it lands on the ground: *The plane finally touched down at Heathrow airport around midday.*
2 in the sport of RUGBY, to score by putting the ball on the ground behind the other team's GOAL LINE

touch sb **for** sth *phr v BrE informal* to persuade someone to give or lend you something, especially money: *He tried to touch me for the taxi fare home.*

touch sth ↔ **off** *phr v* to cause a difficult situation or violent events to begin: *It was these national rivalries that eventually touched off the First World War.*

touch on/upon sth *phr v* to mention a particular subject when talking or writing: *The report touches on the relationship between poverty and poor health.* | *These issues were touched on in Chapter 2.*

touch sb/sth ↔ **up** *phr v*
1 to improve something by changing it slightly or adding a little more to it: *She quickly touched up her lipstick.* | *The photograph had obviously been touched up.* | *The speech he finally gave had been touched up by his staff.*
2 *BrE informal* to touch someone in a sexual way when they do not want you to: *He was accused of touching up one of his students.*

touch² ●●● S2 W2 *n*
1 TOUCHING SB/STH [C usually singular] the action of putting your hand, finger, or another part of your body on something or someone: *She felt a gentle touch on her shoulder.* | **[+of]** *He remembered the touch of her fingers on his face.*
2 ABILITY TO FEEL THINGS [U] the sense that you use to discover what something feels like, by putting your hand or fingers on it: *the* ***sense of touch*** | **by touch** *Visually impaired people orient themselves by touch.* | *Bake the cake for 30 minutes until risen and firm* ***to the touch***.
3 in touch (with sb) talking or writing to someone: *We'll* ***get in touch*** (=start talking or writing to you) *as soon as we know the results of the test.* | *Can I have your phone number in case I need to* ***get in touch with*** *you?* | *Bye. I'll* ***be in touch***. | ***Are*** *you still* ***in touch with*** *John* (=are you talking to him regularly)? | *I'm* ***in close touch*** *with Anna.* | **stay/keep in touch** (=keep writing or talking, even though you do not see each other often) *Anyway, we must stay in touch.* | *I met him when I worked in Madrid, and I've kept in touch with him ever since.* | *I* ***lost touch with*** (=stopped writing or talking to) *Julie after we moved.* | *I can* ***put*** *you* ***in touch with*** *a local photography club* (=give you their address or phone number so you can talk to them).

USAGE: In touch, in contact
• If you **stay/keep in touch** or **keep in contact** with someone, you keep writing to them or calling them: *I hope you'll keep in touch while you're away.*
• If two things are **in contact** or **come into contact**, they touch each other: *Make sure that the two wires don't come into contact.* ✗ Don't say *in touch* in this meaning.

4 be/keep/stay etc in touch (with sth) to have the latest information or knowledge about something: *A regular newsletter keeps people in touch with local events.* | *The speech was good and you felt he was in touch with people's needs.* | *Rescuers were kept in touch through radio links.* | *A head-teacher needs to remain* ***in close touch with*** *teachers' everyday concerns.*
5 be out of touch a) (*also* **lose touch (with sth)**) to not have the latest knowledge about a subject, situation, or the way people feel: **[+with]** *I'm out of touch with modern medicine.* | *The party cannot afford to lose touch with political reality.* **b)** to not know much about modern life: *Judges are often accused of being out of touch.*
6 get in touch with sth *especially AmE* to realize and understand something such as your feelings and attitudes: *The first stage is to get in touch with your perceptions and accept responsibility for your relationships.*
7 DETAIL/ADDITION [C] a small detail that improves or completes something: **put the final/finishing touches to sth** *Emma was putting the finishing touches to the cake.* | *There was a vase of flowers in the room, which was* ***a nice touch***. | *Brass pans added a decorative touch to the plain brick wall.*
8 WAY OF DOING STH [C] a particular way of doing something, or the ability to do it in a particular way: *The room was decorated with a very artistic touch.* | *Our staff combine efficient service with a* ***personal touch*** (=they do things in a friendly way). | *The* ***feminine touch*** *was evident throughout the house.* | *His* ***sure touch*** (=confident way of doing things) *and attention to detail are just as evident now.* | *Barbara has a* ***magic touch*** *in the garden* (=she grows things very well). | *King obviously hasn't* ***lost*** *his* ***touch*** (=lost his ability) *– his latest book sold in the millions.*
9 a touch of sth a small amount of something: *Our furniture is guaranteed to add a touch of class to your bedroom.* | *Add a lace top for a touch of glamour.* | *'What?' asked Hazel, with a touch of irritation.*
10 a touch disappointed/faster/impatient etc slightly disappointed, faster etc: *He sounded a touch upset when I spoke to him on the phone.*
11 with/at the touch of a button/key used to emphasize that something can be done very easily by pressing a button: *This card allows you to access your money at the touch of a button.* | *You can get all the latest information with the touch of a button.*
12 a soft/easy touch *informal* if someone is a soft or an easy touch, you can easily persuade them to do what you want, especially give you money
13 WAY STH FEELS [C usually singular] the way that something feels and the effect it has on your skin: *the warm touch of his lips*
14 SOCCER/RUGBY [U] the area outside the lines that mark the playing area: **into touch** *The ball rolled into touch.*
→ **common touch** at COMMON¹(13), → **a/the human touch** at HUMAN¹(5), → **kick sth into touch** at KICK¹(11), → **lose your touch** at LOSE(1), → **magic touch** at MAGIC²(5), → MIDAS TOUCH, → **a soft touch** at SOFT(17)

ˌtouch-and-ˈgo *adj informal* **it's touch-and-go** used about a situation in which there is a serious risk that something bad could happen: *It was touch-and-go whether the doctor would get there on time.*

touch·down /ˈtʌtʃdaʊn/ ●○○ *n* [C]
1 the moment at which a plane or spacecraft lands
2 an act of putting the ball down on the ground behind the opposing team's GOAL LINE in RUGBY
3 an act of moving the ball across the opposing team's GOAL LINE in American football

tou·ché /ˈtuːʃeɪ $ tuːˈʃeɪ/ *interjection* used to emphasize in a humorous way that someone has made a very good point during an argument

touched /tʌtʃt/ *adj* [not before noun] **1** feeling happy and grateful because of what someone has done: **[+by]** *We were* ***deeply touched*** *by their present.* | **touched that** *Cathryn was touched that Sarah had come to see her off.* → TOUCH¹(4)
2 *informal* slightly crazy

ˈtouch ˌfootball *n* [U] *AmE* a type of American football in which you touch the person with the ball instead of TACKLING them

touch·ing¹ /ˈtʌtʃɪŋ/ ●○○ *adj* making you feel pity, sympathy, sadness etc: *a touching reunion of father and son* —**touchingly** *adv* → TOUCH¹(4)

touching² *prep formal* concerning: *matters touching the conduct of diplomacy*

touch·less /ˈtʌtʃləs/ *adj* a touchless piece of equipment can be operated without touching it, especially by moving your hand near it: *a touchless soap dispenser*

touch·line /ˈtʌtʃlaɪn/ *n* [C] one of the two lines that mark the longer sides of a sports playing area, especially in football

touch·pad /ˈtʌtʃpæd/ *n* [C] a small flat part on a computer which you touch with your finger in order to move the CURSOR on the screen

touch·pa·per /ˈtʌtʃˌpeɪpə $ -ər/ *n* [C] *BrE* a piece of special paper that burns slowly, used in order to start a FIREWORK burning: *Light the blue touchpaper, then move to a safe distance.*

ˈtouch screen *n* [C] a type of computer screen that you touch in order to tell the computer what to do or to get information

touch·stone /ˈtʌtʃstəʊn $ -stoʊn/ *n* [C] something used as a test or standard: **[+of]** *Pupil behaviour was seen as 'the touchstone of quality' of the school system.*

ˈTouch-Tone ˌphone *n* [C] *trademark* a telephone that produces different sounds when different buttons are pushed

ˈtouch-type *v* [I] to use a TYPEWRITER or a computer KEYBOARD without having to look at the letters while you are using it

touch·y /ˈtʌtʃi/ *adj* **1** easily becoming offended or annoyed SYN **sensitive**: **[+about]** *She is very touchy about her past.* **2 touchy subject/question etc** a subject etc that needs to be dealt with very carefully, especially because it may offend people SYN **sensitive**: *Asking about a reporter's sources can be a touchy business.* —**touchiness** *n* [U]

ˌtouchy-ˈfeely *adj* too concerned with feelings and emotions, rather than with facts or actions: *a touchy-feely drama*

tough¹ /tʌf/ ●●● S2 W2 *adj* (*comparative* **tougher**, *superlative* **toughest**)

1 DIFFICULT difficult to do or deal with: *It was a tough race.* | *She's had a tough life.* | *The company admitted that it had been a tough year.* | *Tough decisions will have to be made.* | *The reporters were asking a lot of* ***tough questions****.* | **have a tough time (of it)** (=face a lot of difficult problems) *The family has had a tough time of it these last few months.* | **it's tough doing sth** *It's tough being married to a cop.* | **be tough on sb** (=cause problems for someone or make their life difficult) *Having to stay indoors all day is tough on a kid.* | ***It was a tough call*** (=a difficult decision), *but we had to cancel the game because of the weather.* | *I find his books pretty* ***tough going*** (=difficult to read). | *Gage predicted the president's proposal would be a* ***tough sell*** (=something that is difficult to persuade someone about) *before Congress. AmE* | **when the going gets tough (the tough get going)** *informal* (=used to say that when a situation becomes difficult, strong people take the necessary action to deal with it) THESAURUS ▸ DIFFICULT

2 STRONG PERSON physically or emotionally strong and able to deal with difficult situations: *The men who work on the oil rigs are a tough bunch.* | **tough cookie/customer** *informal* (=someone who is very determined to do what they want and not what other people want) | **as tough as nails/as tough as old boots** (=very tough) *He's as tough as nails – a good man to have on the team.* THESAURUS ▸ DETERMINED

3 STRONG MATERIAL not easily broken or made weaker: *tough, durable plastic* | *a very tough, hard-wearing cloth* THESAURUS ▸ STRONG

4 STRICT/FIRM very strict or firm: **[+on/with]** *My mother was very tough on my sister.* | *It's time to* ***get tough*** *with drunk drivers.* | *The EU is* ***taking a tough line*** *with the UK over this issue.* THESAURUS ▸ STRICT

5 VIOLENT AREA a tough part of a town has a lot of crime or violence: **tough neighborhood/area/part of town etc** *a tough area of Chicago*

6 tough!/that's tough! *spoken* used when you do not have any sympathy with someone: *'I'm getting wet.' 'Tough! You should've brought your umbrella.'* | *She didn't tell us she was coming, so if this screws up her plans that's just tough.*

7 tough luck! *spoken* **a)** used when you do not have any sympathy for someone's problems: *Well, that's just their tough luck! It was their mistake.* **b)** *BrE* used when you feel sympathy about something bad that has happened to someone: *You didn't get the job? Oh, tough luck!*

8 tough shit! *spoken not polite* used when you do not have any sympathy for someone's problems

9 VIOLENT PERSON likely to behave violently and having no gentle qualities: *one of football's most notorious* ***tough guys*** | *tough young thugs looking for trouble*

10 FOOD difficult to cut or eat OPP **tender**: *The meat was tough and hard to chew.* | *the tough outer leaves of the cabbage* THESAURUS ▸ HARD

11 tough love a way of helping someone to change their behaviour by treating them in a kind but strict way
—**toughly** *adv* —**toughness** *n* [U]

tough² *v*

tough sth ↔ **out** *phr v* to deal with a difficult situation by being determined, rather than leaving or changing your decision: *She told herself to be brave and* ***tough it out****.*

tough³ *n* [C] *old-fashioned* someone who often behaves in a violent way

tough⁴ *adv* in a way that shows you are very determined: *Washington played tough in the second half of the game.* | *You're talking tough now but you wait until you get into the interview.*

tough·en /ˈtʌfən/ (*also* **toughen up**) *v* [I,T] to become tougher, or to make someone or something tougher: *toughened glass* | *Three years in the army toughened him up.*

tou·pée /ˈtuːpeɪ $ tuːˈpeɪ/ *n* [C] a small artificial piece of hair that some men wear over a place on their heads where the hair no longer grows

tour¹ /tʊə $ tʊr/ ●●● S3 W2 *n* [C]

1 a journey for pleasure, during which you visit several different towns, areas etc: **[+of/around/round]** *a 10-day tour of China* | **a walking/cycling/sightseeing etc tour** *a cycling tour of Cornwall* | *We met on a coach tour in Italy.* → PACKAGE TOUR THESAURUS ▸ JOURNEY

2 a short trip through a place to see it: **[+of/around/round]** *a* ***guided tour*** *around the Kennedy Space Center* | *Kim worked as a* ***tour guide*** *in Cambridge last summer.*

3 a planned journey made by musicians, a sports team etc in order to perform or play in several places: **[+of]** *the England cricket team's tour of India* | **on tour** *The Moscow Symphony Orchestra is here on tour.* | *the first* ***leg of*** *the band's European* ***tour*** (=the first part of it)

4 a period during which you go to live somewhere, usually abroad, to do your job, especially military work: *his third tour in Northern Ireland*

5 tour of inspection an official visit to a place, institution, group etc in order to check its quality or performance

tour² ●●○ *v*

1 [I,T] to visit several parts of a country or area: *We're touring the Greek islands this summer.* THESAURUS ▸ TRAVEL

2 [T] to go round or be shown round a place: *The minister had been invited to tour the new factory.*

tour de force /ˌtʊə də ˈfɔːs $ ˌtʊr də ˈfɔːrs/ *n* [singular] *written* something that is done very skilfully and successfully, and is very impressive: *His speech to the Democratic Convention was a tour de force.*

Tou·rette's syn·drome /tʊˈrets ˌsɪndrəʊm $ -droʊm/ (*also* **Tourette's**) *n* [U] *medical* a medical condition that causes someone to make sudden movements and sounds, sometimes including rude words

tour·is·m /ˈtʊərɪzəm $ ˈtʊr-/ ●●○ *n* [U]

1 the business of providing things for people to do, places for them to stay etc while they are on holiday: *The country depends on tourism for much of its income.*

2 medical/sex/libel etc tourism travel to a foreign country in order to do a particular thing, especially because you cannot do it in your own country or it is more expensive or less easy there

tour·ist /ˈtʊərɪst $ ˈtʊr-/ ●●● W3 *n* [C]

1 someone who is visiting a place for pleasure on holiday: *Cambridge is always full of tourists in the summer.* | *The Statue of Liberty is a major* ***tourist attraction****.* | *What effect will this have on the local* ***tourist industry****?* | **tourist centre/destination/resort etc** *Durham, with its cathedral and castle, is a popular tourist centre.* THESAURUS ▸ TRAVEL

2 medical/sex/libel etc tourist someone who travels to a foreign country in order to do a particular thing, especially because they cannot do it in their own country or it is more expensive or less easy there

T

THESAURUS

tourist someone who is visiting a place for pleasure on holiday: *The hotel is very popular with tourists.* | *a major tourist destination*
traveller *BrE*, **traveler** *AmE* someone who travels somewhere: *a weary traveller returning home after a long journey* | *The building's luxurious interior will appeal to business travellers.* | *The strike will affect air travellers.*
visitor someone who comes to visit a particular country, area, museum etc: *Times Square attracts more than 30 million visitors annually.*
holiday-maker *BrE*, **vacationer** *AmE* someone who is on holiday somewhere: *The beach was packed with holiday-makers.*
sightseer a tourist who is visiting a famous or interesting place: *Crowds of sightseers come to London every year.*
backpacker someone who is travelling for pleasure, staying in cheap accommodation and carrying a BACKPACK: *a cheap hotel which is used mainly by backpackers*

ˈtourist class *n* [U] the cheapest standard of travelling conditions on a plane, ship etc —**tourist class** *adv*

ˈtourist ˌoffice (*also* **ˌtourist inforˈmation ˌoffice**) *n* [C] an office that gives information to tourists in an area

ˈtourist ˌtrap *n* [C] a place that many tourists visit, but where drinks, hotels etc are more expensive - used to show disapproval

tour·ist·y /ˈtʊərəsti $ ˈtʊr-/ *adj informal* **1** a place that is touristy is full of tourists and the things that attract tourists - used to show disapproval: *Benidorm is too touristy for me.* **2** a touristy activity is typical of the things that tourists do - used to show disapproval: *We did all the usual touristy things.*

tour·na·ment /ˈtʊənəmənt, ˈtɔː- $ ˈtɜːr-, ˈtʊr-/ ●●○ *n* [C]
1 a competition in which players compete against each other in a series of games until there is one winner: *I feel I can win this tournament.* | **tennis/chess/badminton etc tournament**
2 a competition to show courage and fighting skill between soldiers in the Middle Ages

tour·ney /ˈtʊəni, ˈtɔː- $ ˈtɜːr-, ˈtɔːr-/ *n* [C] *AmE informal* a TOURNAMENT

tour·ni·quet /ˈtʊənɪkeɪ, ˈtɔː- $ ˈtɜːrnɪkət, ˈtʊr-/ *n* [C] a band of cloth that is twisted tightly around an injured arm or leg to stop it bleeding

ˌtour of ˈduty *n* (*plural* **tours of duty**) [C] a period of time when you are working in a particular place or job, especially abroad while you are in the army etc

ˈtour ˌoperator *n* [C] *BrE* a company that arranges travel tours

tou·sle /ˈtaʊzəl/ *v* [T] to make someone's hair look untidy

tou·sled /ˈtaʊzəld/ *adj* tousled hair or a tousled appearance looks untidy: *She had just awakened, her eyes sleepy and her* **hair tousled**. | *A small tousled head appeared in the doorway.*

tout¹ /taʊt/ ●○○ *v*
1 [T] to praise something or someone in order to persuade people that they are important or worth a lot: *his much touted musical* | **be touted as sth** *Nell is being touted as the next big thing in Hollywood.*
2 [I,T] *especially BrE* to try to persuade people to buy goods or services you are offering: **tout for business/custom** *BrE* (=look for customers) *Minicab drivers are not allowed to tout for business.*
3 [I,T] *AmE* to give someone information about a horse in a race

tout² (*also* **ticket tout**) *n* [C] *BrE* someone who buys tickets for a concert, sports match etc and sells them at a higher price, usually on the street near a sports ground, theatre etc SYN **scalper** *AmE*

tow¹ /təʊ $ toʊ/ ●○○ *v* [T] to pull a vehicle or ship along behind another vehicle, using a rope or chain: *The ship had to be towed into the harbor.* | **tow sth away** *Our car had been towed away.* → see picture at TRUCK **THESAURUS** PULL

tow² *n* **1** [C] an act of pulling a vehicle behind another vehicle, using a rope or chain: *Can you give us a tow to the garage?* → see picture at TRUCK **2 in tow** *informal* following closely behind someone or something: *Hannah arrived with her four kids in tow.* | *He turned up at my office with two lawyers in tow.* **3 take sth in tow** to connect a rope or a chain to a vehicle or ship so that it can be towed **4 under/on tow** *BrE* if a ship is under tow or a car is on tow, it is being pulled along by another vehicle

to·wards /təˈwɔːdz $ tɔːrdz, twɔːrdz/ ●●● S1 W1 *especially BrE*, **to·ward** /təˈwɔːd $ tɔːrd, twɔːrd/ *especially AmE prep*
1 DIRECTION used to say that someone or something moves, looks, faces etc in the direction of someone or something: *He noticed two policemen coming towards him.* | *All the windows face toward the river.* | *He was standing with his back towards me.*
2 PRODUCING A RESULT in a process that will produce a particular result: *These negotiations are the first step toward reaching an agreement.* | *The crisis continued as Britain drifted towards war.*
3 FEELING/ATTITUDE your feeling, attitude, or behaviour towards someone or something is how you feel or think about them or how you treat them: *Brian's attitude towards his work has always been very positive.* | *Her parents had been more sympathetic towards her.*
4 HELP PAY FOR money put, saved, or given towards something is used to pay for it: *The money collected will be put towards repairing the church roof.*
5 BEFORE just before a particular time: *Toward the end of the afternoon it began to rain.*
6 NEAR near a particular place: *Uncle Dick and Aunt Mavis live at High Burnton out towards the coast.*

tow-a-way zone /ˈtəʊəweɪ ˌzəʊn $ ˈtoʊəweɪ ˌzoʊn/ *n* [C] *AmE* an area where cars are not allowed to park, and from which they can be taken away by the police

tow·bar /ˈtəʊbɑː $ ˈtoʊbɑːr/ *n* [C] *BrE* a metal bar on the back of a car for TOWING a CARAVAN or boat

tow·el¹ /ˈtaʊəl/ ●●● S3 *n* [C] a piece of cloth that you use for drying your skin or for drying things such as dishes: *Have you got a clean towel I could use?* | **bath/beach/kitchen towel** *She dried her hands on the kitchen towel.* → PAPER TOWEL, SANITARY PAD, TEA TOWEL, → **throw in the towel** at THROW

towel² (*also* **towel down/off**) *v* (**towelled, towelling** *BrE*, **toweled, toweling** *AmE*) [T] to dry yourself using a towel: *He stood in the doorway, towelling his hair dry.* → TOWELLING

tow·el·ling *BrE* /ˈtaʊəlɪŋ/ *n* [U] thick soft cloth, used especially for making towels or BATHROBES SYN **terrycloth** *AmE*: *a towelling robe*

ˈtowel rail (*also* **ˈtowel rack** *AmE*) *n* [C] a bar or frame on which towels can be hung, especially in a bathroom → see picture at RAIL¹

tow·er¹ /ˈtaʊə $ -ər/ ●●○ S3 W3 *n* [C]
1 a tall narrow building either built on its own or forming part of a castle, church etc: *the Eiffel Tower* | *a castle with tall towers* | **bell/clock tower** *The bell tower was added to the church in 1848.* | **[+of]** *the leaning tower of Pisa*
2 a tall structure, often made of metal, used for signalling, broadcasting etc: *an air traffic control tower*
3 tower of strength someone who gives you a lot of help, sympathy, and support when you are in trouble: *Her father was a tower of strength to her when her marriage broke up.*
4 a tall piece of furniture that you use to store things: *a CD tower* → COOLING TOWER, IVORY TOWER, WATER TOWER

tower² *v* [I] **1** to be much taller than the people or things around you: **[+above/over]** *He towered over his mother.* **2** to be much better than any other person or organization that does the same thing as you: **[+above/over]** *Mozart towers over all other composers.*

ˈ**tower block** *n* [C] *BrE* a tall building containing apartments or offices SYN **high-rise** *AmE*

tow·er·ing /ˈtaʊərɪŋ/ *adj* [only before noun] **1** very tall: *great towering cliffs* THESAURUS ▸ HIGH **2** much better than other people of the same kind SYN **outstanding**: *a towering genius of his time* **3 in a towering rage** very angry

tow·line /ˈtəʊlaɪn $ ˈtoʊ-/ *n* [C] a TOWROPE

town /taʊn/ ●●● S1 W1 *n*

1 PLACE [C] a large area with houses, shops, offices etc where people live and work, that is smaller than a city and larger than a village: *an industrial town in the Midlands* | **[+of]** *the town of Norwalk, Connecticut* | *I walked to the nearest town.* THESAURUS ▸ CITY

2 MAIN CENTRE [U] the business or shopping centre of a town: *We're **going into town** tonight to see a film.* | *They have a small apartment in town.*

3 PEOPLE [singular] all the people who live in a particular town: *The whole town turned out to watch the procession.*

4 WHERE YOU LIVE [U] the town or city where you live: *Cam **left town** about an hour ago, so he should be out at the farm by now.* | *I'll be **out of town** for about a week.* | *Guess who's **in town**? Jodie's sister!* | *Do you know of a good place to eat? I'm **from out of town*** (=from a different town). | *We're moving to another part of town.*

5 VILLAGE [C] *AmE* several houses forming a small group around a church, shops etc SYN **village** *BrE*: *Rowayton is a small town of around 4,000 people.*

6 NOT COUNTRY **the town** life in towns and cities in general: *Which do you prefer, the town or the country?*

7 go to town (on sth) *informal* to do something in a very eager or thorough way: *Angela really went to town on buying things for her new house.*

8 (out) on the town *informal* going to restaurants, bars, theatres etc for entertainment in the evening: *Frank is taking me out for **a night on the town**.*

9 town and gown used to describe the situation in which the people living in a town and the students in a town seem to be separate and opposing groups → GHOST TOWN, HOME TOWN, → **paint the town (red)** at PAINT²(5)

COLLOCATIONS

ADJECTIVES/NOUN + town

small/big *I grew up in a small town in Iowa.*
a little town *a pretty little town in the French Alps*
a major town *It is one of the UK's biggest retailers with shops in every major town.*
busy/bustling *The town was busy even in November.*
quiet *The town is quiet in the summer.*
sleepy (=very quiet, with not much happening) | **a historic/ancient town** | **an industrial town** | **a seaside town** | **a provincial town** (=one that is not near the capital) | **a market town** (=a town in Britain where there is a regular outdoor market) | **sb's home town** (=the town where someone was born)

PHRASES

the centre of town/the town centre *BrE*, **the center of town/the town center** *AmE* *The hotel was right in the center of town.*
the outskirts/edge of a town

ˌ**town ˈcentre** *BrE n* [C] the main business area in the centre of a town SYN **downtown** *AmE*

ˌ**town ˈclerk** *n* [C] an official who keeps the records of a town

ˌ**town ˈcouncil** *n* [C] *especially BrE* an elected group of people who are responsible for public areas and services, such as roads, parks etc, in a particular town —**town councillor** *n* [C]

ˌ**town ˈcrier** *n* [C] someone employed in the past to walk around the streets of a town, shouting news, warnings etc

ˌ**town ˈhall** ●●○ *n* [C] a public building used for a town's local government

town·house /ˈtaʊnhaʊs/ *n* [C] **1** a house in a town or city, especially a fashionable one in a central area **2** *BrE* a house in a town that belongs to someone who also owns a house in the countryside: *the Duke's townhouse in Mayfair* **3** *AmE* a house in a group of houses that share one or more walls

town·ie /ˈtaʊni/ *n* [C] *informal* someone who lives in a town or city and does not know anything about life in the countryside

ˌ**town ˈmeeting** *n* [C] *AmE* a meeting at which the people who live in a town discuss subjects or problems that affect their town

ˌ**town ˈplanning** *n* [U] the study of the way towns work, so that roads, houses, services etc can be provided as effectively as possible —**town planner** *n* [C]

town·scape /ˈtaʊnskeɪp/ *n* [C] the way a town or large parts of a town look → **landscape**: *industrial townscapes* | *Edinburgh's historic townscape*

town·ship /ˈtaʊnʃɪp/ *n* [C] a town in Canada or the US that has some local government

towns·peo·ple /ˈtaʊnzpiːpəl/ (*also* **towns·folk** /-fəʊk $ -foʊk/) *n* [plural] all the people who live in a particular town: *the proud townspeople of Semer Water*

tow·path /ˈtəʊpɑːθ $ ˈtoʊpæθ/ *n* [C] a path along the side of a CANAL or river, used especially in the past by horses pulling boats

tow·rope /ˈtəʊrəʊp $ ˈtoʊroʊp/ (*also* **towline**) *n* [C] a rope or chain used for pulling vehicles along

tow·truck /ˈtəʊtrʌk $ ˈtoʊ-/ *n* [C] *AmE* a strong vehicle that can pull cars behind it SYN **breakdown truck** *BrE* → see picture at TRUCK¹

tox·ae·mi·a *BrE*, **toxemia** *AmE* /tɒkˈsiːmiə $ tɑːk-/ *n* [U] *medical* a medical condition in which your blood contains poisons

tox·ic /ˈtɒksɪk $ ˈtɑːk-/ ●●○ *adj*

1 containing poison, or caused by poisonous substances → **toxin**: *fumes from a **toxic** waste dump* | **toxic chemicals/substances/fumes/gases** *Toxic chemicals were spilled into the river.* | *a **highly toxic** pesticide* THESAURUS ▸ HARMFUL

2 toxic debt/loan/asset money that has been lent to someone that is unlikely to be paid back or bring the lender any profit

3 *informal* very unpleasant and causing a lot of harm or unhappiness: *You are clearly in a toxic relationship and you need to get out of it.* —**toxicity** /tɒkˈsɪsəti $ tɑːk-/ *n* [C,U]: *The metal has a relatively low toxicity to humans.*

tox·i·col·o·gy /ˌtɒksɪˈkɒlədʒi $ ˌtɑːksɪˈkɑː-/ *n* [U] the science and medical study of poisons and their effects —**toxicologist** *n* [C] —**toxicological** /ˌtɒksɪkəˈlɒdʒɪkəl $ ˌtɑːksɪkəˈlɑː-/ *adj*

ˌ**toxic ˈshock ˌsyndrome** *n* [U] a serious illness that causes a high temperature and is thought to be connected with the use of TAMPONS

ˌ**toxic ˈwaste** *n* [C,U] waste products from industry that are harmful to people, animals, or the environment: *a toxic waste dump* | *international agreements about the disposal of toxic waste*

tox·in /ˈtɒksɪn $ ˈtɑːk-/ *n* [C] a poisonous substance, especially one that is produced by BACTERIA and causes a particular disease → **toxic**

toy¹ /tɔɪ/ ●●● S3 *n* [C]

1 an object for children to play with: *some toys for the baby* | **toy car/soldier/gun etc** | **soft/cuddly toy** *BrE* (=a toy that looks like an animal and is covered in fur) | *Annie was **playing** happily **with** her **toys**.*

2 an object that you buy because it gives you pleasure and enjoyment, especially one that you don't really need: *The food mixer is her latest toy.*

3 sex toy an object that adults use to obtain sexual pleasure

toy² ●○○ *v*

toy with sb/sth *phr v*

1 to think about an idea or possibility, usually for a short time and not very seriously: **toy with the idea of doing sth** *I've been toying with the idea of going to Japan to visit them.*

2 to keep moving and touching an object or food: *He*

spoke casually and toyed with his pen. | Laura was **toying with** her **food** and looking increasingly bored.
3 to lie to someone or trick them, for example saying that you love them when you do not

toy³ *adj* [only before noun] a toy animal or dog is a type of dog that is specially bred to be very small: *a toy poodle*

ˈtoy boy *n* [C] *informal* a young man who is having a sexual relationship with an older woman – used humorously

trace¹ /treɪs/ ●●○ AWL *v* [T]
1 FIND SB/STH to find someone or something that has disappeared by searching for them carefully: *She had given up all hope of tracing her missing daughter. | Police are trying to trace a young woman who was seen near the accident.* THESAURUS ▸ FIND
2 ORIGINS to find the origins of when something began or where it came from: **trace sth (back) to sth** *They've traced their ancestry to Scotland. | The style of these paintings can be traced back to early medieval influences.*
3 HISTORY/DEVELOPMENT to study or describe the history, development, or progress of something: *Sondheim's book traces the changing nature of the relationship between men and women.*
4 COPY to copy a drawing, map etc by putting a piece of transparent paper over it and then drawing the lines you can see through the paper THESAURUS ▸ DRAW
5 WITH YOUR FINGER to draw real or imaginary lines on the surface of something, usually with your finger or toe: **trace sth on/in/across sth** *Rosie's fingers traced a delicate pattern in the sand.*
6 trace a call to find out where a telephone call is coming from by using special electronic equipment: *His call was traced and half an hour later police arrested him.* —**traceable** *adj*

trace² ●●○ AWL *n*
1 SIGN OF STH [C,U] a small sign that shows that someone or something was present or existed: *There was* **no trace** *of anyone having entered the room since then. | Petra's lost* **all trace** *of her German accent. | Officers were unable to find* **any trace** *of drugs.* | **disappear/vanish/sink without (a) trace** (=disappear completely, without leaving any sign of what happened) *The plane vanished without a trace.*
2 SMALL AMOUNT [C] a very small amount of a quality, emotion, substance etc that is difficult to see or notice: **[+of]** *I saw the faintest trace of a smile cross Sandra's face. | traces of poison*
3 TELEPHONE [C] *technical* a search to find out where a telephone call came from, using special electronic equipment: *The police put a trace on the call.*
4 INFORMATION RECORDED [C] *technical* the mark or pattern made on a SCREEN or on paper by a machine that is recording an electrical signal: *This trace shows the heartbeat.*
5 CART/CARRIAGE [C] one of the two pieces of leather, rope etc by which a CART or carriage is fastened to an animal pulling it → **kick over the traces** at KICK¹(19)

ˈtrace ˌelement *n* [C] *technical* **1** a chemical ELEMENT that your body needs a very small amount of to live **2** a chemical ELEMENT that only exists in small amounts on Earth

trac·er /ˈtreɪsə $ -ər/ *n* [C,U] a bullet that leaves a line of smoke or flame behind it

trac·e·ry /ˈtreɪsəri/ *n* (*plural* **traceries**) [C,U] **1** *technical* the curving and crossing lines of stone in the upper parts of some church windows **2** *literary* an attractive pattern of lines that cross each other: *the delicate tracery of the bare branches against the sky*

tra·che·a /trəˈkiːə $ ˈtreɪkiə/ *n* (*plural* **tracheas** *or* **tracheae** /-ˈkiː-i $ -ki-iː/) [C] *technical* the tube that takes air from your throat to your lungs

trach·e·ot·o·my /ˌtrækiˈɒtəmi $ ˌtreɪkiˈɑːt-/ *n* (*plural* **tracheotomies**) [C] *technical* an operation to cut a hole in someone's throat so that they can breathe

trac·ing /ˈtreɪsɪŋ/ AWL *n* [C] a copy of a map, drawing etc made by TRACING it

ˈtracing ˌpaper *n* [U] strong transparent paper used for TRACING

TRACKS

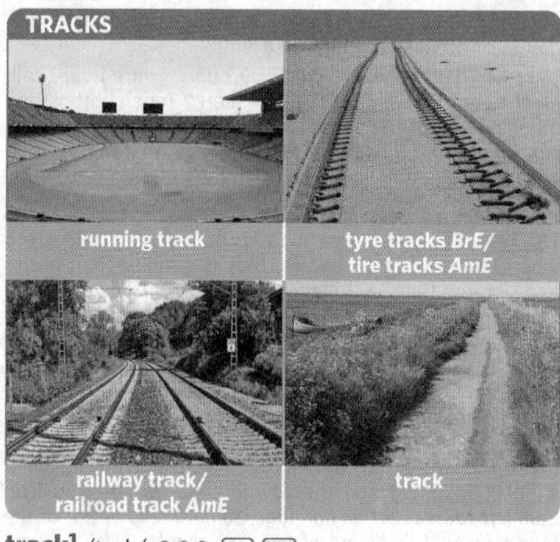

track¹ /træk/ ●●● S2 W2 *n*
1 PATH/ROAD [C] a narrow path or road with a rough uneven surface, especially one made by people or animals frequently moving through the same place: *The road leading to the farm was little more than a* **dirt track**. | *The track led through dense forest. | a steep mountain track*
2 MARKS ON GROUND **tracks** [plural] a line of marks left on the ground by a moving person, animal, or vehicle: *We followed the tyre tracks across a muddy field. | The tracks, which looked like a fox's, led into the woods.*
3 FOR RACING [C] a circular course around which runners, cars etc race, which often has a specially prepared surface: *To run a mile, you have to run four circuits of the track.* → DIRT TRACK(2)
4 TRAIN **a)** [C,U] the two metal lines along which trains travel SYN **railway line**: *The track was damaged in several places. | That particular section of track was laid last year.* **b)** [C] *AmE* the particular track that a train leaves from or arrives at: *The train for Boston is leaving from track 2.*
5 be on the right/wrong track to think in a way that is likely to lead to a correct or incorrect result: *We've had the initial test results and it looks as though we're on the right track.*
6 keep/lose track of sb/sth to pay attention to someone or something, so that you know where they are or what is happening to them, or to fail to do this: *It's difficult to keep track of all the new discoveries in genetics. | I just* **lost** *all* **track of time**.
7 MUSIC/SONG [C] one of the songs or pieces of music on an ALBUM (=collection of songs or pieces of music): *There's a great Miles Davis track on side two.* THESAURUS ▸ MUSIC
8 stop/halt (dead) in your tracks to suddenly stop, especially because something has frightened or surprised you
9 cover your tracks to be careful not to leave any signs that could let people know where you have been or what you have done because you want to keep it a secret, usually because it is illegal: *He tried to cover his tracks by burning all the documents.*
10 SPORT [U] *AmE* **a)** sport that involves running on a track: *The next year he didn't* **run track** *or play football.* **b)** all the sports in an ATHLETICS competition such as running, jumping, or throwing the JAVELIN: *a famous track star | She went out for track in the spring* (=she joined the school's track team).
11 be on track *spoken* to be likely to achieve the result you want: *We're still on track for 10% growth.*
12 get off the track *spoken* to begin to deal with a new subject rather than the main one which was being discussed: *Don't get off the track, we're looking at this year's figures not last year's.*
13 be on the track of sb/sth to hunt or search for someone or something: *Police are on the track of the bank robbers.*
14 make tracks *spoken* used to say you must leave a place: *It's time we started making tracks.*
15 DIRECTION [C] the direction or line taken by something

as it moves: **[+of]** *islands that lie in the track of North Atlantic storms*
16 ON A VEHICLE [C] a continuous metal band that goes over the wheels of a vehicle such as a BULLDOZER, allowing it to move over uneven ground → **off the beaten track** at BEATEN(1), → ONE-TRACK MIND, → **be from the wrong side of the tracks** at WRONG[1](18)

track² ●○○ *v*
1 SEARCH [T] to search for a person or animal by following the marks they leave behind them on the ground, their smell etc: *Police have been tracking the four criminals all over Central America.* | **track sb to sth** *The dogs tracked the wolf to its lair.* THESAURUS FOLLOW
2 DEVELOPMENT [T] to record or study the behaviour or development of someone or something over time: *The progress of each student is tracked by computer.*
3 AIRCRAFT/SHIP [T] to follow the movements of an aircraft or ship by using RADAR: *a tracking station*
4 CAMERA [I + in/out] to move a film or television camera away from or towards a scene in order to follow the action that you are recording
5 SCHOOL [T] *AmE* to put schoolchildren in groups according to their ability SYN **stream** *BrE*
6 MARK [T] *AmE* to leave behind a track of something such as mud or dirt when you walk: *Which of you boys tracked mud all over the kitchen floor?*
track sb/sth ↔ **down** *phr v* to find someone or something that is difficult to find by searching or looking for information in several different places: *I finally managed to track down the book you wanted in a shop near the station.* | *Detectives had tracked her down in California.*

ˌtrack and ˈfield *n* [U] sports such as running and jumping SYN **athletics** *BrE*

track·ball /ˈtrækbɔːl $ -bɒːl/ *n* [C] a small ball connected to a computer, that you turn in order to move the CURSOR

track·er /ˈtrækə $ -ər/ *n* [C] someone who follows and finds other people, especially by following the marks that they have left on the ground

ˈtracker dog *n* [C] a dog that has been specially trained to follow and find people

ˈtrack eˌvent *n* [C] *AmE* a running race

track·ie /ˈtræki/ *n* [C usually plural] *BrE informal* a TRACKSUIT: *trackie bottoms* | *I can't find my trackies.*

track·ing /ˈtrækɪŋ/ *n* [U] the system on a video recorder that keeps the picture from a VIDEOTAPE clear on the screen

ˈtracking ˌstation *n* [C] a place from which objects moving in space, such as SATELLITES and ROCKETS, can be recognized and followed

ˈtrack meet *n* [C] *AmE* a sports event consisting of competitions in running, jumping etc

ˈtrack ˌrecord *n* [singular] all of a person's or organization's past achievements, successes, or failures, which show how well they have done something in the past and how well they are likely to do in the future: **[+in]** *We're looking for someone with a* ***proven track record*** *in selling advertising.* | **[+of]** *The fund has a* ***good track record*** *of investing in the equity market.*

track·suit /ˈtræksuːt, -sjuːt $ -suːt/ *n* [C] *BrE* loose clothes consisting of trousers and a JACKET, worn especially for sport

tract /trækt/ ●○○ *n* [C]
1 the digestive/reproductive/urinary etc tract a system of connected organs that have one main purpose in a part of your body
2 a large area of land: *vast tracts of woodland*
3 *formal* a short piece of writing, especially about a moral or religious subject: *a tract on the dangers of drink*

trac·ta·ble /ˈtræktəbəl/ *adj formal* easy to control or deal with OPP **intractable**: *The issues have proved to be less tractable than expected.* —**tractability** /ˌtræktəˈbɪləti/ *n* [U]

trac·tion /ˈtrækʃən/ *n* [U] **1** the process of treating a broken bone with special medical equipment that pulls it: **in traction** *He was in traction* (=receiving this kind of treatment) *for weeks after the accident.* **2** the force that prevents something such as a wheel sliding on a surface: *The tires were bald* (=completely worn) *and lost traction on the wet road.* **3** the type of power needed to make a vehicle move, or to pull a heavy load **4** if a new idea or thing gains traction, it becomes accepted by or popular with more and more people: *The idea of changing the structure of the school year is* ***gaining traction.***

trac·tor /ˈtræktə $ -ər/ ●○○ *n* [C] a strong vehicle with large wheels, used for pulling farm machinery

ˈtractor-ˌtrailer *n* [C] *AmE* a large truck that has two parts, one small part in the front where the driver sits and a large part at the back where goods are carried

trad /træd/ (*also* **ˌtrad ˈjazz**) *n* [U] a style of JAZZ that was popular in the 1920s. One instrument plays complicated RHYTHMS and notes, and the rest of the instruments play regular rhythms.

trade¹ /treɪd/ ●●● S3 W1 *n*
1 BUYING/SELLING [U] the activity of buying, selling, or exchanging goods within a country or between countries SYN **commerce**: **[+between]** *There has been a marked increase in trade between East and West.* | ***international trade*** *agreements* | *unfair* ***trade practices*** | **[+in]** *Trade in ivory has been banned since 1990.* | **the arms/drug/slave etc trade** (=the buying and selling of weapons, drugs etc) → BALANCE OF TRADE, FREE TRADE, → **trade war** at WAR(3)
2 the hotel/tourist etc trade the business done by companies, hotels etc → **industry**: *Working on Saturdays is usual in the retail trade.*
3 AMOUNT OF BUSINESS [U] *BrE* business activity, especially the amount of goods or products that are sold SYN **business**: *A lot of pubs nowadays do most of their trade at lunchtimes.* | **passing trade** (=customers who go into a shop when they are passing it, not regular customers) *Souvenir shops rely mainly on passing trade.* → **do a roaring trade** at ROARING(3)
4 AN EXCHANGE OF THINGS [singular] *AmE* **a)** when you exchange something you have for something that someone else has: *Let's* ***make a trade*** *– my frisbee for your baseball.* **b)** when a player on a sports team is exchanged for a player from another team: *The Celtics star demanded a trade after talks with management broke down.*
5 the trade a particular kind of business, and the people who are involved in it: *I could get Ron to look at your car for you; he works in the trade.*
6 JOB/WORK [C,U] a particular job, especially one needing special skill with your hands: *Brian insisted that his sons* ***learn a trade.*** | *My grandfather was a plumber* ***by trade*** (=that was his job). | **tools of your trade** (=the things that you need to do your job) → STOCK-IN-TRADE, JACK-OF-ALL-TRADES, → **ply your trade** at PLY[1](1), → **tricks of the trade** at TRICK[1](7)

trade² ●●○ S3 W3 *v*
1 [I,T] to buy and sell goods, services etc as your job or business: **[+with]** *India began trading with Europe in the 15th and 16th centuries.* | **[+in]** *The company trades in silk, tea, and other items.* | *They had to travel into town to trade the produce from their farm.*
2 [I] *BrE* to exist and operate as a business: *The firm now* ***trades under*** *the* ***name*** *Lanski and Weber.* | **cease trading** (=stop being a business because you are bankrupt)
3 [T] to buy or sell something on the STOCK EXCHANGE: *Over a million shares were traded today.* GRAMMAR **Trade** is usually passive in this meaning.
4 trade insults/blows etc to insult or hit each other during an argument or fight
5 [I,T] *especially AmE* to exchange something you have for something someone else has SYN **swap** *BrE*: *We traded necklaces.* | **trade sth with sb** *I wouldn't mind trading jobs with her.* | **trade (sb) sth for sth** *I'll trade you my camera for your drill.*
trade at sth *phr v* if shares etc trade at a particular price, they cost that amount to buy
trade down *phr v* to replace something you own with something cheaper, or buy a cheaper type of thing than before: **[+to]** *Many of their customers are trading down to cheaper cigarettes.*

T

trade sth ↔ **in** *phr v* to give something such as a car to the person you are buying a new one from, as part of the payment: **[+for]** *He traded his old car in for a new model.* → TRADE-IN

trade sth ↔ **off** *phr v* to balance one situation or quality against another, in order to produce an acceptable result: **[+for/against]** *Companies are under pressure to trade off price stability for short-term gains.* → TRADE-OFF

trade on/upon sth *phr v* to use a situation or someone's kindness in order to get an advantage for yourself: *If you ask me, they're just trading on Sam's good nature.*

trade up *phr v* to replace something you own with something better, or buy a better type of thing than before: **[+to/from]** *It also encourages existing home owners to trade up to larger accommodation.*

ˈtrade ˌbalance *n* [C] BALANCE OF TRADE

ˈtrade ˌdeficit (*also* **trade gap**) *n* [C] the amount by which the value of what a country buys from abroad is more than the value of what it sells

ˈtrade ˌdiscount *n* [C] a special reduction in the price of goods sold to people who are going to sell the goods in their own shop or business

ˈtrade fair *n* [C] a large event when several companies show their goods or services in one place, to try to sell them SYN **trade show**

ˈtrade gap *n* [C] TRADE DEFICIT

ˈtrade-in *n* [C] *AmE* a used car, piece of equipment etc that you give to a seller of a new one that you are buying as part of the payment SYN **part exchange** *BrE*: *Are you going to give your Ford as a trade-in?* | **trade-in price/value** *The trade-in value is roughly $3,000.*

trade·mark /ˈtreɪdmɑːk $ -mɑːrk/ *n* [C] **1** a special name, sign, or word that is marked on a product to show that it is made by a particular company, that cannot be used by any other company **2** a particular way of behaving, dressing etc by which someone or something can be easily recognized: *The striped T-shirt became the comedian's trademark.*

ˈtrade name *n* [C] a name given to a particular product, that helps you recognize it from other similar products SYN **brand name**

ˈtrade-off *n* [C] a balance between two opposing things, that you are willing to accept in order to achieve something: **a trade-off between sth and sth** *There has to be a trade-off between quality and quantity if we want to keep prices low.*

ˈtrade price *n* [C] the price at which goods are sold to shops by the companies that produce them

trad·er /ˈtreɪdə $ -ər/ ●○○ *n* [C] someone who buys and sells goods or STOCKS → **retailer**: **small/local trader** *a small trader who sells hats in Oxford* | **bond/currency/commodity etc trader** *To the surprise of many Wall Street traders, the dollar rose yesterday.*

ˈtrade route *n* [C] a way across land or sea used by traders in the past: *ancient trade routes between Europe and Asia*

ˈtrade ˌschool *n* [C] *especially AmE* a school where people go in order to learn a particular TRADE

ˌtrade ˈsecret *n* [C] **1** a piece of secret information about a particular business, that is only known by the people who work there: *The Coca-Cola formula is a well-kept trade secret.* **2** *informal* a piece of information about how to do or make something, that you do not want other people to know: *Could you give me the recipe for that 'coq au vin' or is it a trade secret?*

ˈtrade show *n* [C] a TRADE FAIR

trades·man /ˈtreɪdzmən/ *n* (*plural* **tradesmen** /-mən/) [C] **1** *BrE* someone who buys and sells goods or services, especially in a shop **2** *especially AmE* someone who works at a job or TRADE that involves skill with your hands **3** *BrE* someone who goes to people's houses to sell or deliver goods

trades·peo·ple /ˈtreɪdzˌpiːpəl/ *n* [plural] **1** *BrE old-fashioned* people who buy and sell goods or services **2** *especially AmE* people who work at a job or TRADE that involves skill with their hands

ˌtrade ˈsurplus *n* [C] *technical* the amount by which the value of the goods that a country sells to other countries is more than the value of the goods it buys from them

ˌtrade ˈunion (*also* **ˌtrades ˈunion**) *n* [C] *BrE* an organization, usually in a particular trade or profession, that represents workers, especially in meetings with employers SYN **labor union** *AmE* —**trade unionist** *n* [C] —**trade unionism** *n* [U]

ˈtrade wind *n* [C] a tropical wind that blows towards the EQUATOR from either the northeast or the southeast

trad·ing /ˈtreɪdɪŋ/ ●○○ *n* [U]
1 the activity of buying and selling goods or services: **Sunday trading** *BrE* (=shops being open on Sunday)
2 the activity of buying and selling STOCKS etc: **heavy/light trading** (=a lot of trading or a little trading) *Shares dropped 10% in heavy trading.*

ˈtrading esˌtate *n* [C] *BrE* an area of land, often at the edge of a city, where there are small factories and businesses

ˈtrading ˌpartner *n* [C] a country that buys your goods and sells their goods to you

ˈtrading post *n* [C] a place where people can buy and exchange goods in a country area, especially in the US or Canada in the past: *a remote trading post in the Yukon*

tra·di·tion /trəˈdɪʃən/ ●●● S2 W2 *n*
1 [C,U] a belief, custom, or way of doing something that has existed for a long time, or these beliefs, customs etc in general: *the traditions of South East Asia* | *the* ***tradition that*** *the eldest son inherits the property* | ***By tradition****, it's the bride's parents who pay for the wedding.* THESAURUS ▶ HABIT
2 (be) in the tradition of sb/sth to have the same features as something that has been made or done in the past: *His paintings are very much in the tradition of Picasso and Matisse.*

COLLOCATIONS

ADJECTIVES/NOUN + tradition

a long tradition *This country has a long tradition of accepting political refugees.*
a time-honoured/long-standing tradition (=a long tradition) *In time-honoured tradition, they have a drink in every pub along the high street.*
a strong tradition *There is a strong tradition of sport at the school.*
an old/ancient tradition | **a family tradition** | **a cultural/religious tradition** | **a local tradition**

VERBS

follow a tradition (=do what has been done before) *He followed the family tradition and became a doctor.*
maintain/carry on/continue/uphold a tradition (=make a tradition continue in the same way or at the same standard as before) *We maintain a tradition of cider making dating from Norman times.*
break with tradition (=not follow a tradition) | **establish a tradition** | **be steeped in tradition** (=have many traditions)

tra·di·tion·al /trəˈdɪʃənəl/ ●●● S3 W1 AWL *adj*
1 being part of the traditions of a country or group of people: *traditional Italian cooking* | *a traditional Irish folk song* | *a traditional method of brewing beer* | **it is traditional (for sb) to do sth** *It is traditional not to eat meat on Good Friday.*
2 following ideas and methods that have existed for a long time, rather than doing anything new or different SYN **conventional**: *He has a* ***traditional view*** *of women.* | *I went to a very traditional school.* | ***traditional*** *family* ***values*** | *a traditional way of life*

tra·di·tion·al·is·m /trəˈdɪʃənəlɪzəm/ *n* [U] belief in the importance of TRADITIONS and customs

tra·di·tion·al·ist /trəˈdɪʃənəlɪst/ AWL *n* [C] someone who respects TRADITION and does not like change —**traditionalist** *adj*

tra·di·tion·al·ly /trəˈdɪʃənəli/ ●●○ AWL *adv* according to tradition: *More women are entering traditionally male jobs.* | *The color black is traditionally associated with mourning.* | [sentence adverb] *Traditionally, everything is carried in baskets on the head or shoulders.*

tra·duce /trəˈdjuːs $ -ˈduːs/ *v* [T] *formal* to deliberately say things that are untrue or unpleasant

traf·fic¹ /ˈtræfɪk/ ●●● S1 W2 *n* [U]
1 the vehicles moving along a road or street: *There wasn't much traffic on the roads.* | *The sound of the traffic kept me awake.*
2 the movement of aircraft, ships, or trains from one place to another: *air traffic control* | *the problems of **air traffic** congestion in Europe*
3 *formal* the movement of people or goods by aircraft, ships, or trains: **[+of]** *Most long-distance traffic of heavy goods is done by ships.*
4 the secret buying and selling of illegal goods: *drugs traffic* | **[+in]** *traffic in firearms*

COLLOCATIONS

VERBS
be stuck/caught/held up in traffic *Sorry I'm late – I was stuck in traffic.*
avoid/miss the traffic *I left early, hoping to miss the traffic.*
cut/reduce traffic | **traffic moves/flows** | **traffic is diverted** (=made to go in another direction)

ADJECTIVES/NOUN + traffic
heavy *We ran into heavy traffic near the airport.*
light *The traffic is fairly light at this time of day.*
bad/terrible | **slow/slow-moving** | **rush-hour traffic** | **local traffic** | **oncoming traffic** (=traffic coming towards you)

traffic + NOUN
a traffic jam (=a line of cars that have stopped, or are moving very slowly) *She spent two hours sitting in a traffic jam.*
traffic congestion (=when the roads are full of traffic) *efforts to cut traffic congestion*
traffic flow (=the steady movement of traffic) | **a traffic accident**

PHRASES
the volume of traffic *The new ring road will reduce the volume of traffic through the village.*
a stream of traffic (=a long continuous series of cars, trucks etc)

traffic² ●○○ *v* (**trafficked**, **trafficking**) [T] to take someone to another country and force them to work, for example as a PROSTITUTE: *He had made a fortune by trafficking young women.*

traffic in sth *phr v* to buy and sell illegal goods: *Lewis was found guilty of trafficking in drugs.*

ˈtraffic ˌcalming *n* [U] *BrE* changes made to a road to stop people driving too fast: ***Traffic calming measures** have been introduced.*

ˈtraffic ˌcircle *n* [C] *AmE* a circular place where two or more roads join, which all traffic must drive around SYN **roundabout** *BrE*

ˈtraffic ˌcone *n* [C] a plastic object in the shape of a CONE that is put on the road to show where repairs are being done

ˈtraffic cop *n* [C] *informal* **1** a police officer who stands in the road and directs traffic **2** a police officer who stops people who are driving in an illegal way

ˈtraffic ˌcourt *n* [C] a US court of law that deals with people who have done something illegal while driving

ˈtraffic ˌisland *n* [C] a raised area in the middle of a road where people can wait until it is safe to cross

ˈtraffic ˌjam ●●○ *n* [C] a long line of vehicles on a road that cannot move or can only move very slowly: *We were **stuck in a traffic jam** for two hours.*

traf·fick·er /ˈtræfɪkə $ -ər/ *n* [C] **1** someone who buys and sells illegal goods, especially drugs **2** someone who takes people to another country and forces them to work

TRAFFIC CONE

traffic cone/pylon *AmE* | bollard *BrE*

traf·fick·ing /ˈtræfɪkɪŋ/ *n* [U] **1** the buying and selling of illegal goods, especially drugs: *drug trafficking* **2** the activity of taking people to another country and forcing them to work: *human trafficking*

ˈtraffic ˌlights ●●● S3 *n* [plural] a set of red, yellow, and green lights that control traffic

ˈtraffic ˌschool *n* [C] *AmE* a class that teaches you about driving laws, that you can go to instead of paying money for something you have done wrong while driving

ˈtraffic-ˌstopper *n* [C] *informal* someone or something that is extremely attractive, surprising, or interesting to look at, so they attract everyone's attention: *This yellow and purple dress is a real traffic-stopper.*

ˈtraffic ˌwarden *n* [C] *BrE* someone whose job is to check that people have not parked their cars illegally

tra·ge·di·an /trəˈdʒiːdiən/ *n* [C] *formal* an actor or writer of tragedy → **comedian**

tra·ge·dy /ˈtrædʒədi/ ●●○ *n* (*plural* **tragedies**)
1 [C,U] a very sad event, that shocks people because it involves death: *The tragedy happened as they were returning home from a night out.* | ***Tragedy struck** the family when their two-year-old son was killed in an accident.*
2 [C] *informal* something that seems very sad and unnecessary because something will be wasted, lost, or harmed: *It's a tragedy to see so much talent going to waste.*
3 a) [C] a serious play or book that ends sadly, especially with the death of the main character → **comedy**: *'Hamlet' is one of Shakespeare's best known tragedies.* **b)** [U] this type of play or book: *an actor specializing in tragedy*

tra·gic /ˈtrædʒɪk/ ●●○ *adj*
1 a tragic event or situation makes you feel very sad, especially because it involves death or suffering → **comic**: *The parents were not to blame for the **tragic death** of their son.* | *Lillian Board's death at 22 was a **tragic loss** for British athletics.*
2 [only before noun] relating to tragedy in books or plays OPP **comic**: *a great tragic actor* | **tragic hero** (=the main person in a tragedy)

tra·gic·ally /ˈtrædʒɪkli/ *adv* in a way that makes you feel sad, especially because someone has died: *She was tragically killed in a car accident.* | [sentence adverb] *Tragically, her dancing career ended only six months later.* | [+adj/adv] *He died when a parachute jump went tragically wrong.*

tra·gi·com·e·dy /ˌtrædʒɪˈkɒmədi $ -ˈkɑː-/ *n* (*plural* **tragicomedies**) [C,U] a play or a story that is both sad and funny —**tragicomic** /ˌtrædʒɪˈkɒmɪk◂ $ -ˈkɑː-/ *adj*

trail¹ /treɪl/ ●●○ *v*
1 PULL [I,T] to pull something behind you, especially along the ground, or to be pulled in this way: *A plane trailing a banner was circling overhead.* | **[+in/on/over etc]** *She walked slowly along the path, her skirt trailing in the mud.* | **trail sth in/across/through etc sth** *Rees was leaning out of the boat trailing his hand through the water.*
2 WALK SLOWLY [I always + adv/prep] to walk slowly, especially behind other people because you are tired or bored: **[+behind/around]** *Susie trailed along behind her parents.* | *We spent the afternoon trailing around the shops.*
3 LOSE A COMPETITION [I,T usually in progressive] to be losing in a game, competition, or election: *The Democratic candidate is still trailing in the opinion polls.* | **trail (sb) by sth**

Manchester United were trailing by two goals to one. | **trail in/home** (=finish in a bad position) *He trailed in last after a disastrous race.*
4 FOLLOW SB [T] to follow someone by looking for signs that they have gone in a particular direction: *Police trailed the gang for several days.*
trail away/off *phr v* if someone's voice trails away or trails off, it becomes gradually quieter and then stops: *She trailed off, silenced by the look Kris gave her.*

trail² ●●○ *n* [C]
1 a rough path across countryside or through a forest: *The trail led over Boulder Pass before descending to a lake.* → NATURE TRAIL
2 a long line or a series of marks that have been left by someone or something: **[+of]** *a trail of wet footprints* | *The bus* ***left a trail*** *of black smoke behind it.* | *The typhoon left* ***a trail of devastation.***
3 a series of unpleasant situations or feelings that have been left by someone or something: **[+of]** *He left a trail of broken hearts and broken promises.*
4 a sign that a person or animal has been in a place, used for finding or catching them: *The hunters lost the tiger's trail in the middle of the jungle.* | *Police tracked him to Valencia and there the* ***trail went cold*** (=they could not find any signs of him).
5 be on the trail of sb/sth to be trying to find someone or something by getting information about them: *industrial spies on the trail of technological secrets* | *Police believe they are* ***hot on the trail of*** *a drug-smuggling gang* (=they are close to finding them).
6 all the places that a particular group of people visit for a particular purpose: *a town on the tourist trail* | **campaign/election trail** *politicians on the campaign trail*
7 the set of things that someone does to achieve something: *New players should put the team back* ***on the winning trail.*** → **blaze a trail** at BLAZE²(5), → **hit the trail/road** at HIT¹(17)

trail·blaz·er /ˈtreɪlˌbleɪzə $ -ər/ *n* [C] someone who is the first to discover or develop new methods of doing something: *a trailblazer in the field of medical research* —**trailblazing** *adj*

trail·er /ˈtreɪlə $ -ər/ ●●○ S3 *n* [C]
1 a vehicle that can be pulled behind another vehicle, used for carrying something heavy THESAURUS ADVERTISEMENT
2 *AmE* a vehicle that can be pulled behind a car, used for living and sleeping in during a holiday SYN **caravan** *BrE*
3 an advertisement for a new film or television show THESAURUS MOVIE

ˈtrailer park (*also* **ˈtrailer court**) *n* [C] *AmE* an area where trailers are parked and used as people's homes

ˈtrailer trash *n* [U] *AmE informal* an offensive expression for poor people who live in trailer parks

trail·ing /ˈtreɪlɪŋ/ *adj* a trailing plant grows along the ground or hangs down

train¹ /treɪn/ ●●● S1 W2 *n* [C]
1 RAILWAY a set of several carriages that are connected to each other and pulled along a railway line by an engine: **[+to]** *the train to Munich* | **by train** *We went all the way to Inverness by train.* → BOAT TRAIN
2 SERIES **a train of sth** a series of events or actions that are related: *The decision set off a* ***train of events*** *which led to his resignation.*
3 train of thought a related series of thoughts that are developing in your mind: *The phone interrupted my train of thought.* | *I've lost my train of thought.*
4 bring sth in its train *formal* if an action or event brings something in its train, that thing happens as a result of it: *a decision that brought disaster in its train*
5 set sth in train *BrE formal* to make a process start happening: *Plans to modernize have been set in train.*
6 PEOPLE/ANIMALS a long line of moving people, animals, or vehicles: *a camel train*
7 DRESS a part of a long dress that spreads out over the ground behind the person wearing it: *a wedding dress with a long train*
8 SERVANTS a group of servants or officers following an important person, especially in the past

GRAMMAR: Patterns with train

- You usually say **get on a train**: *I got on the train at Bristol.*
- You usually say **get off a train**: *She got off the train in Geneva.*
- You say that someone is **on a train**: *There were a lot of tourists on the train.*
- You go somewhere **by train**: *He travels to work by train.* ✗ Don't say: *go by the train* | *travel by the train*
- You often talk about **the train**: *It's easier if you take the train.*

COLLOCATIONS

VERBS

take/get a train *I took the first train home.*
catch a train *He was in a hurry to catch a train.*
go by/travel by train *We decided to go by train.*
get on/board a train *At Stoke, another passenger boarded the train.*
get off a train | **wait for a train** | **miss a train** (=be too late to get on a train) | **trains run** (=take people from one place to another at fixed times) | **a train arrives** | **a train leaves/departs** | **a train pulls into/out of a station**

ADJECTIVES/NOUN + train

a freight/goods train *a freight train carrying hazardous chemicals*
a passenger train *a passenger train bound for Geneva*
a commuter train (=a train that people going to work use) | **an express train/a fast train** (=one that does not stop at many places) | **a slow train** (*also* **a stopping train** *BrE*) (=one that stops at a lot of places)

train + NOUN

a train journey *BrE*, **a train trip** *AmE They were not looking forward to the long train journey.*
a train fare *How much is the train fare to Derby?*
a train driver | **a train crash** (*also* **a train wreck** *AmE*)

train² ●●● S1 W2 *v*
1 TEACH SB [I,T] to teach someone the skills of a particular job or activity, or to be taught these skills → **training**: **train sb in sth** *All staff will be trained in customer service skills.* | **train to do sth** *She's training to be a doctor.* | **train sb to do sth** *Employees are trained to deal with emergency situations.* | **[+as]** *Nadia trained as a singer.* | *a* ***highly trained*** *workforce* | *Trained staff will be available to deal with your queries.* THESAURUS LEARN, TEACH
2 TEACH AN ANIMAL [T] to teach an animal to do something or to behave correctly: *a well-trained puppy* | **train sth to do sth** *These dogs are trained to detect drugs.*
3 PREPARE FOR SPORT [I,T] to prepare for a sports event or tell someone how to prepare for it, especially by exercising → **training**: **[+for]** *Brenda spends two hours a day training for the marathon.* THESAURUS PRACTISE
4 AIM STH [T] to aim something such as a gun or camera at someone or something: **train sth on/at sb/sth** *She trained her binoculars on the bird.*
5 DEVELOP STH [T] to develop and improve a natural ability or quality: *You can train your mind to relax.* | *To the* ***trained eye*** *the difference between these flowers is obvious* (=the difference is clear to someone who has developed skills to notice something).
6 PLANT [T] to make a plant grow in a particular direction by bending, cutting, or tying it

train·ee /ˌtreɪˈniː◂/ ●●○ *n* [C] someone who is being trained for a job: *The trainees start next week.* | **trainee manager/solicitor/teacher etc** *a trainee hairdresser*

train·er /ˈtreɪnə $ -ər/ ●●○ *n* [C]
1 someone who trains people or animals for sport or work → **coach**: *a racehorse trainer* THESAURUS TEACHER
2 *BrE* a type of strong shoe that you wear for sport SYN **tennis shoe** *AmE* → see picture at SHOE¹

T

train·ing /ˈtreɪnɪŋ/ ●●● S2 W1 *n*
1 [singular, U] the process of teaching or being taught the skills for a particular job or activity → **train**: **[+in]** *On the course we* **received training** *in every aspect of the job.* | *Police drivers have to* **undergo** *intensive* **training**. | *a rigorous* **training session** | **On-the job training** *will be supplemented by classroom lectures.* | *The shop opens late on Fridays because of* **staff training**.
2 [U] physical exercises that you do to stay healthy or prepare for a competition → **train**: *Lesley does weight training twice a week.* | **be in training for sth** *She's in training for the Olympics.* → SPRING TRAINING

ˈtraining ˌcollege *n* [C,U] *BrE* a college for adults that gives training for a particular profession: *a teacher training college* | *a training college for pilots*

ˈtraining wheel *n* [C usually plural] *AmE* a small wheel that is fastened to the back of a young child's bicycle to make it more steady SYN **stabilizer** *BrE*

ˈtrain set *n* [C] a toy train with railway tracks

ˈtrain ˌspotter *n* [C] *BrE* **1** someone who collects the numbers of railway engines for fun **2** someone who you think is boring and only interested in unimportant details —**trainspotting** *n* [U]

ˈtrain ˌstation *n* [C] a place where trains stop for passengers to get on and off SYN **railway station** *BrE*

train·wreck /ˈtreɪnrek/ *n* [C] *informal* someone or something that is a complete failure or very bad: *My life is a trainwreck.*

traipse /treɪps/ *v* [I always + adv/prep] *informal* to walk somewhere in a slow or unwilling way because you are tired or bored SYN **trail**: **[+around/through/across etc]** *I've been traipsing around the shops all morning.*

trait /treɪ, treɪt $ treɪt/ ●●○ *n* [C] *formal* a particular quality in someone's character: **personality/character traits** *a mental illness associated with particular personality traits* | **genetic/inherited traits**

trai·tor /ˈtreɪtə $ -ər/ ●○○ *n* [C,U] someone who is not loyal to their country, friends, or beliefs → **treason**: **[+to]** *a traitor to the cause of women's rights* | *a politician who* **turned traitor** (=became a traitor) *to the government*

trai·tor·ous /ˈtreɪtərəs/ *adj especially literary* not loyal to your country, friends, or beliefs —**traitorously** *adv*

tra·jec·to·ry /trəˈdʒektəri/ *n* (*plural* **trajectories**) [C] **1** *technical* the curved path of an object that has been fired or thrown through the air **2** *formal* the events that happen during a period of time, which often lead to a particular aim or result: *The decision was certain to affect the trajectory of French politics for some time to come.*

TRAJECTORY

trajectory

tram /træm/ ●○○ (*also* **tram·car** /ˈtræmkɑː $ -kɑːr/) *n* [C] *especially BrE* a vehicle for passengers, which travels along metal tracks in the street SYN **streetcar** *AmE*

tram·lines /ˈtræmlaɪnz/ *n* [plural] *BrE* **1** the metal tracks in the road, used by trams **2** *informal* the two parallel lines at the edge of a tennis court

tram·mel /ˈtræməl/ *v* (*past tense and past participle* **trammelled**, *present participle* **trammelling** *BrE*, **trammeled**, **trammeling** *AmE*) [T] *formal* to limit or prevent someone's freedom or development → UNTRAMMELLED

tramp¹ /træmp/ *n* [C] **1** someone who has no home or job and moves from place to place, often asking for food or money **2** a long or difficult walk: *a long tramp through the snow* **3** *especially AmE old-fashioned* a woman who has too many sexual partners – used to show disapproval **4 the tramp of feet/boots** the sound of heavy walking: *the steady tramp of soldiers' feet*

tramp² *v* [I always + adv/prep, T] to walk somewhere slowly and with heavy steps: *He tramped the streets looking for work.* | **[+through/across/around etc]** *The walk involved tramping through mud.*

tram·ple /ˈtræmpəl/ *v* [I always + adv/prep, T] **1** to step heavily on something, so that you crush it with your feet: **[+on/over/through etc]** *There was a small fence to stop people trampling on the flowers.* | **trample sb/sth underfoot** *The children were in danger of being trampled underfoot in the crowd.* | **trample sb to death** (=kill someone by stepping heavily on them) *Several people were nearly trampled to death in the rush to get out.* **2** to behave in a way that shows that you do not care about someone's rights or feelings: **trample on/over sb/sth** *Don't let people trample all over you.* | *Their interests and rights had been* **trampled underfoot**.

tram·po·line /ˈtræmpəliːn/ *n* [C] a piece of equipment that you jump up and down on as a sport. It consists of a metal frame with a piece of strong cloth stretched tightly over it.

tram·po·lin·ing /ˈtræmpəliːnɪŋ/ *n* [U] the sport or activity of jumping up and down on a trampoline

trance /trɑːns $ træns/ *n* **1** [C] a state in which you behave as if you were asleep but are still able to hear and understand what is said to you: **go/fall into a trance** *She went into a deep hypnotic trance.* **2** [C] a state in which you are thinking about something so much that you do not notice what is happening around you: **in a trance** *What's the matter with you? You've been in a trance all day.* **3** [U] a type of popular electronic dance music with a fast beat and long continuous notes played on a SYNTHESIZER

tranche /trɑːnʃ/ *n* [C] *technical* part of a larger sum of money or group of shares: *The second tranche of the loan would be repaid over three years.*

tran·ny /ˈtræni/ *n* (*plural* **trannies**) [C] *informal* **1** someone who has the physical features of both sexes, usually as the result of medical treatment → **transsexual** **2** a TRANSVESTITE —**tranny** *adj*

tran·quil /ˈtræŋkwəl/ *adj* pleasantly calm, quiet, and peaceful: *a small tranquil village* THESAURUS QUIET —**tranquilly** *adv* —**tranquillity** *BrE*, **tranquility** *AmE* /træŋˈkwɪləti/ *n* [U]: *the tranquillity of the Tuscan countryside*

tran·quil·lize (*also* **-ise**) *BrE*, **tranquilize** *AmE* /ˈtræŋkwəlaɪz/ *v* [T] to make a person or animal calm or unconscious by using a drug

tran·quil·lizer (*also* **-iser**) *BrE*, **tranquilizer** *AmE* /ˈtræŋkwəlaɪzə $ -ər/ *n* [C] a drug used for making someone feel less anxious

trans- /træns, trænz/ *prefix* **1** on or to the far side of something SYN **across**: *transatlantic flights* | *the trans-Siberian railway* **2** between two things or groups SYN **inter-**: *trans-racial fostering* **3** shows a change: *He's been transformed by the experience.*

trans·act /trænˈzækt/ *v* [I,T] *formal* to do business with someone: *Most deals are transacted over the phone.*

trans·ac·tion /trænˈzækʃən/ ●○○ *n formal*
1 [C] a business deal or action, such as buying or selling something: *The bank charges a fixed rate for each transaction.* | *financial transactions*
2 [U] the process of doing business: *the transaction of his public duties*
3 transactions [plural] discussions that take place at the meetings of an organization, or a written record of these

trans·at·lan·tic /ˌtrænzətˈlæntɪk◂/ *adj* [only before noun] **1** crossing the Atlantic Ocean: *transatlantic flights* **2** involving countries on both sides of the Atlantic Ocean: *a transatlantic agreement* **3** on the other side of the Atlantic Ocean: *one of America's transatlantic military bases*

trans·cei·ver /trænˈsiːvə $ -ər/ *n* [C] a radio that can send and receive messages

tran·scend /trænˈsend/ ●○○ *v* [T] *formal* to go beyond the usual limits of something: *The desire for peace transcended political differences.*

tran·scen·dent /trænˈsendənt/ *adj formal* going far

T

beyond ordinary limits: *the transcendent genius of Mozart* —**transcendently** *adv*

tran·scen·den·tal /ˌtrænsenˈdentl◂/ *adj* transcendental experiences or ideas are beyond normal human understanding and experience

tran·scen·den·tal·is·m /ˌtrænsenˈdentəl-ɪzəm/ *n* [U] the belief that knowledge can be obtained by studying thought rather than by practical experience

ˌtranscendental mediˈtation *n* [U] a method of becoming calm by repeating particular words in your mind

trans·con·ti·nen·tal /ˌtrænzkɒntəˈnentl, ˌtræns- $ -kɑːn-/ *adj* crossing a CONTINENT: *a transcontinental railway*

tran·scribe /trænˈskraɪb/ *v* [T] **1** to write down something exactly as it was said: *A secretary transcribed the witnesses' statements.* **2** to write an exact copy of something: *He had been asked to transcribe an ancient manuscript.* **3** *technical* to represent speech sounds with PHONETIC symbols **4** *formal* to change a piece of writing into the alphabet of another language: **transcribe sth into sth** *The book has been transcribed into braille.* **5** to arrange a piece of music for a different instrument or voice: **transcribe sth for sth** *a piece transcribed for piano* **6** *technical* to copy recorded music, speech etc from one system to another, for example from TAPE to CD

tran·script /ˈtrænskrɪpt/ ●○○ *n* [C]
1 a written or printed copy of a speech, conversation etc: **[+of]** *A transcript of the tapes was presented in court.*
2 *AmE* an official college document that shows a list of a student's classes and the results they received

tran·scrip·tion /trænˈskrɪpʃən/ *n* **1** [U] when you transcribe something: *Pronunciation is shown by a system of phonetic transcription.* **2** [C] an exact written or printed copy of something SYN **transcript**

tran·sept /ˈtrænsept/ *n* [C] one of the two parts of a church that are built out from the main area of the church to form a cross shape

trans·fer¹ /trænsˈfɜː $ -ˈfɜːr/ ●●○ S3 W3 AWL *v* (**transferred**, **transferring**)
1 MOVE TO DIFFERENT PLACE ETC [I,T] to move from one place, school, job etc to another, or to make someone do this, especially within the same organization: **transfer (from sth) to sth** *Swod transferred from MI6 to the Security Service.* | **transfer sb (from sth) to sth** *They're transferring him to a special unit at Great Ormond Street Hospital.* | *You'll be transferred to the Birmingham office.*
2 PUT STH IN DIFFERENT PLACE [I,T] *formal* to move from one place to another, or to move something from one place to another: **transfer (from sth) to sth** *The exhibition transfers to York City Art Gallery on 23rd January.* | **transfer sth (from sth) to sth** *Transfer the meat to warm plates.*
3 SPORTS PERSON [T] to sell a sports player to another team: *He was transferred for a fee of £8 million.*
4 MONEY [T] to move money from one account or institution to another: **transfer sth (from sth) to sth** *I'd like to transfer $500 to my checking account.*
5 transfer your affections/loyalty/allegiance etc to change from loving or supporting one person to loving or supporting a different one
6 SKILL/IDEA/QUALITY [I,T] if a skill, idea, or quality transfers from one situation to another, or if you transfer it, it can be used in the new situation: *Ideas that work well in one school often don't transfer well to another.*
7 transfer power/responsibility/control (to sb) to officially give power etc to another person or organization: *The ageing president is preparing to transfer power to his son.*
8 PHONE [T] to connect the call of someone who has telephoned you to someone else's telephone so that that person can speak to them: *Hold on one moment while I transfer your call.*
9 PROPERTY [T] *law* to officially give property or land to someone else
10 TRAVEL [I,T] to change from one bus, plane etc to another while you are travelling, or arrange for someone to do this: *You will be met on arrival at the airport and transferred to your hotel.*
11 INFORMATION/MUSIC [T] to copy recorded information, music etc from one system to another: *Transfer the files onto a memory stick.*
12 DISEASE [T] if a disease is transferred from one person or animal to another, the second person or animal begins to have the disease SYN **pass**: **transfer sth (from sb/sth) to sb/sth** *It is unlikely that the disease will be transferred from animals to humans.* —**transferable** *adj*: *transferable skills* —**transferability** /trænsˌfɜːrəˈbɪləti/ *n* [U]

trans·fer² /ˈtrænsfɜː $ -fɜːr/ ●●○ W3 AWL *n*
1 a) [C,U] the process by which someone or something moves or is moved from one place, job etc to another: **[+of]** *the transfer of assets within a group of companies* | **[+to]** *Penny's applied for a transfer to head office.* | *electronic data transfer* **b)** [C] someone or something that has been moved in this way
2 transfer of power a process by which the control of a country is taken from one person or group and given to another: *the transfer of power to a civilian government*
3 [C] the act of changing from one bus, aircraft etc to another while travelling: *Getting there often means a couple of transfers on a bus line.*
4 [C] *especially BrE* a drawing, pattern etc that can be stuck or printed onto a surface SYN **decal** *AmE*
5 [C] *especially AmE* a ticket that allows a passenger to change from one bus, train etc to another without paying more money

trans·fer·ence /ˈtrænsfərəns $ trænsˈfɜːr-/ AWL *n* [U]
1 *formal* the process of moving someone or something from one place, position, job etc to another: **[+of]** *the transference of skills acquired at school to the workplace*
2 *technical* the process of beginning to have the same unconscious feelings about someone in the present that you had for someone such as your parents in the past

ˈtransfer fee *n* [C] *BrE* the money that one football club pays another for the transfer of a player

ˈtransfer list *n* [C] *BrE* a list of the football players in one team who can be sold to another team

trans·fig·ure /trænsˈfɪɡə $ -ɡjər/ *v* [T] *literary* to change the way someone or something looks, especially so that they become more beautiful: *Her face was transfigured with joy.* —**transfiguration** /trænsˌfɪɡəˈreɪʃən $ -ɡjə-/ *n* [C,U]

trans·fix /trænsˈfɪks/ *v* [T] **1** to surprise, interest, frighten etc someone so much that they do not move **2** *literary* to make a hole through something or someone with a sharp pointed weapon

trans·fixed /trænsˈfɪkst/ *adj* [not before noun] unable to move because you are very surprised, shocked, frightened, interested etc: *For a moment she stood transfixed in the doorway.*

trans·form /trænsˈfɔːm $ -ˈfɔːrm/ ●●○ W3 AWL *v* [T] to completely change the appearance, form, or character of something or someone, especially in a way that improves it: *Increased population has transformed the landscape.* | **transform sb/sth (from sth) into sth** *The movie transformed her almost overnight from an unknown schoolgirl into a megastar.*

trans·for·ma·tion /ˌtrænsfəˈmeɪʃən $ -fər-/ ●○○ AWL *n* [C,U] a complete change in someone or something: *In recent years, the movie industry has* ***undergone*** *a dramatic* ***transformation****.* | **transformation from sth to/into sth** *the gradual transformation from woodland to farmland* | **[+of]** *What leads to the transformation of one economic system to another?*

trans·form·er /trænsˈfɔːmə $ -ˈfɔːrmər/ *n* [C] a piece of equipment for changing electricity from one VOLTAGE to another

trans·fu·sion /trænsˈfjuːʒən/ *n* [C,U] **1** the process of putting blood from one person's body into the body of someone else as a medical treatment: *A* ***blood transfusion*** *saved his life.* **2** the process of giving something important or necessary, such as money, to a group or organization that needs it: **[+of]** *The mayor has promised a transfusion of $8 million in redevelopment funds.*

trans·gen·der /trænzˈdʒendə $ trænsˈdʒendər/ *n* [U] a

general word for people who feel that they belong to the other sex, and not the sex they were born with, and who express this in their sexual behaviour → **transsexual**: *the transgender community | transgender issues* —**transgendered** *adj* —**transgenderism** *n* [U]

trans·gen·ic /trænz'dʒenɪk $ træns-/ *adj technical* having one or more GENES from a different type of animal or plant: *transgenic mice*

trans·gress /trænz'gres $ træns-/ *v* [I,T] *formal* to do something that is against the rules of social behaviour or against a moral principle: *Orton's plays transgress accepted social norms.* —**transgressor** *n* [C] —**transgression** /-'greʃən/ *n* [C,U]

tran·si·ent[1] /'trænziənt $ 'trænʃənt/ *adj formal* **1** continuing only for a short time: *transient fashions* **2** working or staying somewhere for only a short time: *a transient population* —**transience** *n* [U]

transient[2] *n* [C] *AmE* someone who has no home and moves around from place to place

tran·sis·tor /træn'zɪstə $ -ər/ *n* [C] **1** a small piece of electronic equipment in radios, televisions etc that controls the flow of electricity **2** a transistor radio

tran,sistor 'radio *n* [C] *old-fashioned* a small radio that you can carry around with you

tran·sit /'trænsɪt, -zɪt/ ●○○ AWL *n* [U]
1 the process of moving goods or people from one place to another: *baggage that is lost or damaged* ***in transit*** (=while it is being moved) | *transit by air or sea*
2 a system for moving people from place to place SYN **transport** *BrE*, **transportation** *AmE*: ***rapid transit*** *networks* | **public transit** *AmE* (=buses, trains etc) *promises to improve public transit* —**transit** *v* [I]

'transit ,camp *n* [C] a place where REFUGEES stay before moving to somewhere more permanent

tran·si·tion[1] /træn'zɪʃən,-'sɪ-/ ●●○ W3 AWL *n* [C,U] *formal* when something changes from one form or state to another: **transition from sth to sth** *the* ***smooth transition*** *from full-time work to full retirement* | ***Making*** *the* ***transition*** *from youth to adulthood can be very painful.* | *a society that is* ***in transition*** (=changing) | *the* ***period of transition*** *to full democracy*

transition[2] *v* [I] to change to a new state or start using something new: **[+to/into]** *He will transition to his new role next month.*

tran·si·tion·al /træn'zɪʃənəl, -'sɪ-/ ●○○ AWL *adj*
1 relating to a period during which something is changing from one state or form into another: **transitional period/stage etc** *a transitional period during the switch to the euro*
2 transitional government a temporary government, usually one that governs until official elections can take place in a country —**transitionally** *adv*

tran·si·tive /'trænsətɪv, -zə-/ *adj technical* a transitive verb must have an object, for example the verb 'break' in the sentence 'I broke the cup'. Transitive verbs are marked [T] in this dictionary. → **ditransitive**, **intransitive** —**transitively** *adv* —**transitivity** /,trænsə'tɪvəti, -zə-/ *n* [U]

'transit ,lounge *n* [C] an area in an airport where passengers can wait

tran·si·to·ry /'trænzətəri $ -tɔːri/ AWL *adj* continuing or existing for only a short time

'transit ,visa *n* [C] a VISA (=special document) that allows someone to pass through one country on their way to another

trans·late /træns'leɪt, trænz-/ ●●● S3 *v*
1 CHANGE LANGUAGES [I,T] to change written or spoken words into another language → **interpret**: **translate sth (from sth) into sth** *Translate the text from Italian into English.* | *Poetry doesn't usually translate well.* | **[+as]** *Dagda, an ancient Irish deity, literally translates as 'the good god'.*
2 HAPPEN AS RESULT [I,T] if one thing translates into another, the second thing happens as a result of the first: **translate (sth) into sth** *A small increase in local spending will translate into a big rise in property tax.*
3 HAVE SAME MEANING [I] to mean the same as something else: **translate into/to sth** *These rates translate into a return of 8.5% for dollar investors.*
4 CHANGE FORMS [I,T] to change something, or be changed, from one form into another: **translate (sth) into sth** *the danger of translating your emotions into actions* | *Jokes often don't translate well into print.*
5 USE IN NEW SITUATION [I,T] to be used in a new situation, or to make something do this SYN **adapt**: **translate sth to sth** *It's amazing how well the play has been translated to film.* —**translatable** *adj*

trans·la·tion /træns'leɪʃən, trænz-/ ●●● S3 *n*
1 [C,U] when you translate something, or something that has been translated: **[+of]** *a new translation of the Bible* | **[+from]** *a* ***literal translation*** *from Arabic* | *She read the letter and gave us a* ***rough translation*** (=she did not translate everything exactly). | *I've only read 'Madame Bovary'* ***in translation*** (=not in its original language). | *Much of the book's humour has been lost in translation* (=is no longer effective when translated).
2 [U] *formal* the process of changing something into a different form

trans·la·tor /træns'leɪtə, trænz- $ -ər/ ●●○ *n* [C] someone who changes writing into a different language → **interpreter**

trans·lit·e·rate /trænz'lɪtəreɪt $ træns-/ *v* [T] to write a word, sentence etc in the alphabet of a different language or writing system —**transliteration** /trænz,lɪtə'reɪʃən $ træns-/ *n* [C,U]

trans·lu·cent /trænz'luːsənt $ træns-/ *adj* not transparent, but clear enough to allow light to pass through: *Blue veins showed through her translucent skin.* —**translucence** *n* [U]

trans·mi·gra·tion /,trænzmaɪ'greɪʃən $,træns-/ *n* [U] *technical* the time when the soul passes into another body after death, according to some religions

trans·mis·sion /trænz'mɪʃən $ træns-/ ●○○ AWL *n*
1 [U] the process of sending out electronic signals, messages etc, using radio, television, or other similar equipment: *worldwide* ***data transmission***
2 [U] *formal* the process of sending or passing something from one person, place, or thing to another: **[+of]** *the transmission of disease*
3 [C] *formal* something that is broadcast on television, radio etc SYN **broadcast**: *a* ***live transmission*** *of the tennis championship*
4 [C,U] the parts of a vehicle that take power from the engine to the wheels

trans·mit /trænz'mɪt $ træns-/ ●○○ AWL *v* (**transmitted**, **transmitting**)
1 [I,T usually + adv/prep] to send out electronic signals, messages etc using radio, television, or other similar equipment: *The US Open will be* ***transmitted live*** *via satellite.* | *The system transmits information over digital phone lines.*
2 [T] *formal* to send or pass something from one person, place or thing to another SYN **pass**: **transmit sth (from sb/sth) to sb/sth** *Mathematical knowledge is transmitted from teacher to student.* → SEXUALLY TRANSMITTED DISEASE
3 [T] *technical* if an object or substance transmits sound or light, it allows sound or light to travel through or along it

trans·mit·ter /trænz'mɪtə $ træns'mɪtər/ *n* [C] **1** equipment that sends out radio or television signals **2** *formal* someone or something that passes something on to another person or thing: **[+of]** *What is the main transmitter of the virus?*

trans·mog·ri·fy /trænz'mɒgrɪfaɪ $ træns'mɑː-/ *v* (**transmogrified**, **transmogrifying**, **transmogrifies**) [T] to change the shape of something completely, as if by magic – used humorously SYN **transform** —**transmogrification** /trænz,mɒgrɪfɪ'keɪʃən $ træns,mɑː-/ *n* [U]

trans·mute /trænz'mjuːt $ træns-/ *v* [T + into] *formal* to change one substance or type of thing into another —**transmutation** /,trænzmjuː'teɪʃən $,træns-/ *n* [C,U]

T

trans·na·tion·al /trænzˈnæʃənəl/ *adj* involving more than one country or existing in more than one country: *transnational corporations*

tran·som /ˈtrænsəm/ *n* [C] **1** a bar of wood that forms the top of the back part of a boat **2** a bar of wood or stone which separates a door from a window above it, or which divides a window into two parts **3** *AmE* a small window over a door or over a larger window SYN **fanlight** *BrE*

trans·par·en·cy /trænˈspærənsi, -ˈspeər- $ -ˈspær-,ˈsper-/ *n* (*plural* **transparencies**) **1** [C] a sheet of plastic or a piece of photographic film through which light can be shone to show a picture on a large screen **2** [U] the quality of glass, plastic etc that makes it possible for you to see through it → **opacity 3** [U] the quality of being easy to understand or know about → **obscurity**

trans·par·ent /trænˈspærənt, -ˈspeər- $ -ˈspær-, -ˈsper-/ ●●○ *adj*

1 if something is transparent, you can see through it SYN **clear** → **opaque, translucent**: *a transparent plastic container*

2 *formal* language or information that is transparent is clear and easy to understand: *The way the system works will be transparent to the user.*

3 a lie, excuse etc that is transparent does not deceive people —**transparently** *adv*

ˈtrans ˌperson *n* (*plural* **trans people**) [C usually plural] *AmE* someone who feels that they do not belong to only the male or only the female sex, and who expresses this in their sexual behaviour, sometimes having medical treatment to change their bodies → **transsexual**

trans·pho·bic /ˌtrænzˈfəʊbɪk $ ˌtrænsˈfoʊ-/ *adj* feeling or expressing hatred or fear of TRANSGENDERED people

tran·spi·ra·tion /ˌtrænspəˈreɪʃən/ *n* [U] *technical* the process of passing water through the surface of a plant's leaves → **respiration**

tran·spire /trænˈspaɪə $ -ˈspaɪr/ *v* **1 it transpires that** *formal* if it transpires that something is true, you discover that it is true: *It now transpires that he kept all the money for himself.* **2** [I] *formal* to happen: *Exactly what transpired remains unknown.* **3** [I,T] *technical* when a plant transpires, water passes through the surface of its leaves

trans·plant¹ /ˈtrænsplɑːnt $ -plænt/ ●○○ *n*

1 [C,U] the operation of transplanting an organ, piece of skin etc → **implant**: *heart transplant surgery* | *a bone marrow transplant*

2 [C] the organ, piece of skin etc that is moved in a transplant operation → **implant**

trans·plant² /trænsˈplɑːnt $ -ˈplænt/ *v* [T] **1** to move an organ, piece of skin etc from one person's body and put it into another as a form of medical treatment **2** to move a plant from one place and plant it in another place **3** *formal* to move something or someone from one place to another —**transplantation** /ˌtrænsplɑːnˈteɪʃən $ -plæn-/ *n* [U]

trans·pond·er /trænˈspɒndə $ -ˈspɑːndər/ *n* [C] *technical* a piece of radio or RADAR equipment that sends out a signal when it receives a signal telling it to do this

trans·port¹ /ˈtrænspɔːt $ -ɔːrt/ ●●● S2 W2 AWL *n*

1 [U] *BrE* a system or method for carrying passengers or goods from one place to another SYN **transportation** *AmE*: **air/rail/road transport** *Improved rail transport is essential for business.* | *commuters who travel on* ***public transport*** (=buses, trains etc) | *It's easier to get to the college if you have your* ***own transport*** (=a car, bicycle etc). | **means/mode/form of transport** *Horses were the only means of transport.*

> **GRAMMAR: Countable or uncountable?**
> In this meaning, **transport** is an uncountable noun and has no plural form. You say: *Public transport is very cheap.* ✗ Don't say: *public transports*
> GRAMMAR GUIDE ▸ NOUNS

2 [U] the process or business of taking goods from one place to another SYN **transportation** *AmE*: **[+of]** *Canals were used for the transport of goods.*

3 [C] a ship or aircraft for carrying soldiers or supplies

4 be in a transport of delight/joy etc *literary* to be feeling very strong emotions of pleasure, happiness etc

trans·port² /trænˈspɔːt $ -ɔːrt/ ●●○ AWL *v* [T usually + adv/prep]

1 to take goods, people etc from one place to another in a vehicle: *trucks used for transporting oil* | **transport sb/sth to sth** *The statue was transported to London.* THESAURUS ▸ TAKE

2 be transported back to/into sth to imagine that you are in another place or time because of something that you see or hear: *One look, and I was transported back to childhood.*

3 be transported with delight/joy etc *literary* to feel very strong emotions of pleasure, happiness etc

4 to send a criminal to a distant country such as Australia as a punishment in the past —**transportable** *adj*

trans·por·ta·tion /ˌtrænspɔːˈteɪʃən $ -spər-/ ●●● W3 AWL *n* [U]

1 *AmE* a system or method for carrying passengers or goods from one place to another SYN **transport** *BrE*: *The city needs to improve its* ***public transportation*** (=buses, trains etc). | **means/mode/form of transportation** *People need to get out of their cars and use other modes of transportation.*

2 *AmE* the process or business of taking goods from one place to another SYN **transport** *BrE*: **[+of]** *the transportation of dangerous chemicals by road*

3 the punishment of sending a criminal to a distant country, especially Australia, in the past

ˈtransport ˌcafe / $ ˈ...ˌ./ *n* [C] *BrE* a cheap restaurant beside a main road, used mainly by truck drivers

trans·port·er /trænˈspɔːtə $ -ˈspɔːrtər/ AWL *n* [C] a long vehicle that can carry one or more other vehicles

ˈtransport ˌplane *n* [C] a plane that is used especially for carrying military equipment or soldiers

ˈtransport ˌship *n* [C] a ship used especially for carrying soldiers

trans·pose /trænˈspəʊz $ -ˈspoʊz/ *v* [T + into/to] *technical* **1** *formal* to change the order or position of two or more things **2** to use a system or method in a different situation from the one you used it in originally **3** to write or perform a piece of music in a musical KEY that is different from the one that it was first written in —**transposition** /ˌtrænspəˈzɪʃən/ *n* [C,U]

trans·put·er /trænzˈpjuːtə $ trænsˈpjuːtər/ *n* [C] *technical* a powerful computer MICROCHIP that can deal with very large amounts of information very fast

trans·sex·u·al /trænˈsekʃuəl $ trænsˈsek-/ *n* [C] a man who wants to be a woman and has medical treatment to make him into one, or a woman who wants to be a man and has medical treatment to make her into one → **transvestite** —**transsexual** *adj* —**transsexualism** *n* [U]

tran·sub·stan·ti·a·tion /ˌtrænsəbstænʃiˈeɪʃən/ *n* [U] the belief of some Christians that the bread and wine taken in Holy Communion become the actual body and blood of Christ

trans·verse /trænzˈvɜːs $ trænsˈvɜːrs/ *adj* [no comparative] lying or placed across something: *a transverse beam*

trans·ves·tite /trænzˈvestaɪt $ træns-/ *n* [C] someone, especially a man, who enjoys dressing like a person of the opposite sex → **transsexual** —**transvestite** *adj* —**transvestism** *n* [U]

trap¹ /træp/ ●●○ *n* [C]

1 FOR ANIMALS a piece of equipment for catching animals: *The only way to catch mice is to* ***set a trap***. | *He stepped into a bear trap covered in snow.* → MOUSETRAP

2 CLEVER TRICK a clever trick that is used to catch someone or to make them do or say something that they did not intend to: **lay/set a trap (for sb)** *Police had set a trap for hooligans at the match.* | **fall/walk into a trap** *Mr Smith has walked straight into a trap laid by the Tories.*

3 BAD SITUATION an unpleasant or difficult situation that is difficult to escape from: *Amanda felt that marriage was a*

trap. | **debt/unemployment etc trap** *people caught in the unemployment trap*
4 fall into/avoid the trap of doing sth to do something that seems good at the time but is not sensible or wise, or to avoid doing this: *Don't fall into the trap of investing all your money in one place.*
5 keep your trap shut *spoken* a rude way of telling someone to not say anything about things that are secret: *Just keep your trap shut.*
6 shut your trap! *spoken* a rude way of telling someone to stop talking
7 VEHICLE a vehicle with two wheels, pulled by a horse
8 SPORT *AmE* SANDTRAP SYN **bunker** *BrE*
9 DOG RACE a special gate from which a GREYHOUND is set free at the beginning of a race → **BOOBY TRAP, DEATH TRAP**, → **poverty trap** at **POVERTY**(3), → **SPEED TRAP, TOURIST TRAP**

trap² ●●○ *v* (**trapped, trapping**) [T]
1 IN A DANGEROUS PLACE to prevent someone from escaping from somewhere, especially a dangerous place: *Twenty miners were trapped underground.* | *The building collapsed, trapping dozens of people in the rubble.* | *There's no way out! We're trapped!* GRAMMAR **Trap** is often passive in this meaning.
2 IN A BAD SITUATION **be/feel trapped** to be in a bad situation from which you cannot escape: **[+in]** *Julia felt trapped in her role of wife and mother.*
3 ANIMAL to catch an animal or bird using a trap
4 CATCH SB to catch someone by forcing them into a place from which they cannot escape: *The police trapped the terrorists at a roadblock.* THESAURUS CATCH
5 TRICK to trick someone so that you make them do or say something that they did not intend to: **trap sb into (doing) sth** *I was trapped into signing a confession.*
6 CRUSH *BrE* to get a part of your body crushed between two objects SYN **pinch** *AmE*: *Mind you don't trap your fingers in the door.* | *pain from a* ***trapped nerve***
7 GAS/WATER ETC to prevent something such as gas or water from getting away: *solar panels that trap the sun's heat*

trap·door /ˈtræpdɔː $ -dɔːr/ *n* [C] a small door that covers an opening in a roof or floor

tra·peze /trəˈpiːz $ træ-/ *n* [C] a short bar hanging from two ropes high above the ground, used by ACROBATS

tra·pe·zi·um /trəˈpiːziəm/ *n* [C] *technical* **1** *BrE* a shape with four sides, only two of which are parallel → see picture at **SHAPE¹** **2** *AmE* a shape with four sides, none of which are parallel

trap·e·zoid /ˈtræpəzɔɪd/ *n* [C] *technical* **1** *BrE* a shape with four sides, none of which are parallel **2** *AmE* a shape with four sides, only two of which are parallel

trap·per /ˈtræpə $ -ər/ *n* [C] someone who traps wild animals, especially for their fur

trap·pings /ˈtræpɪŋz/ *n* [plural] things such as money, influence, possessions etc that are related to a particular type of person, job, or way of life: **[+of]** *the trappings of power*

Trap·pist /ˈtræpɪst/ *n* [C] a member of a Catholic religious group who live together, follow strict rules, and do not speak

trap·shoot·ing /ˈtræpʃuːtɪŋ/ *n* [U] the sport of shooting special clay objects fired into the air

trash¹ /træʃ/ ●●● S3 *n* [U]
1 *AmE* things that you throw away, such as empty bottles, used papers, food that has gone bad etc SYN **rubbish** *BrE*: *Will someone* ***take out the trash*** (=take it outside the house)? | *Just put it* ***in the trash***.
2 *informal* something that is of very poor quality: *How can you read that trash?*
3 *AmE informal not polite* someone from a low social class who you do not respect because you think they are lazy or immoral → **WHITE TRASH**

trash² *v* [T] **1** *informal* to destroy something completely, either deliberately or by using it too much: *The place got trashed last time we had a party.* THESAURUS DESTROY
2 *especially AmE* to criticize someone or something very severely: *The researchers are angry that attempts have been made to trash their work.*

ˈtrash can *n* [C] *AmE* a large container with a lid into which you put empty bottles, used papers, food that has gone bad etc SYN **dustbin** *BrE* → see picture at **BIN¹**

ˈtrash comˌpactor *n* [C] *AmE* a machine that presses waste material together into a very small mass

trashed /træʃt/ *adj AmE spoken* **1** very drunk: *We got trashed last night.* **2** completely destroyed: *We need a new map – this one's trashed.*

trash-talk /ˈtræʃtɔːk $ -tɔːk/ *n* [U] *AmE informal* unpleasant things that you say about someone

ˈtrash ˌtalking, trash-talking *n* [U] *AmE* when a sports player or sports FAN says rude or unpleasant things to or about a sports player: *Coaches say they want to take trash talking out of high school football.*

trash·y /ˈtræʃi/ *adj* of extremely bad quality: *trashy novels* —**trashiness** *n* [U]

trau·ma /ˈtrɔːmə, ˈtraʊmə $ ˈtraʊmə, ˈtrɒː-/ ●○○ *n*
1 [C] an unpleasant and upsetting experience that affects you for a long time: *traumas such as death or divorce*
2 [U] a mental state of extreme shock caused by a very frightening or unpleasant experience: **[+of]** *the trauma of being a young refugee* | *the* ***emotional trauma*** *of rape*
3 [C,U] *technical* an injury: *the hospital's trauma unit*

trau·mat·ic /trɔːˈmætɪk $ trɒː-/ ●○○ *adj* a traumatic experience is so shocking and upsetting that it affects you for a long time: *His son's death was the most traumatic event in Stan's life.* —**traumatically** /-kli/ *adv*

trau·ma·tize (*also* **-ise** *BrE*) /ˈtrɔːmətaɪz, ˈtraʊ- $ ˈtraʊ-, ˈtrɒː-/ *v* [T usually passive] to shock someone so badly that they are affected by it for a very long time: *He was traumatized by his war experiences.* —**traumatized** *adj*

trav·ail /ˈtræveɪl/ *n* [U] *written* (*also* **travails** [plural]) a difficult or unpleasant situation, or very tiring work: **[+of]** *the travails of last year's water shortage*

trav·el¹ /ˈtrævəl/ ●●● S2 W2 *v* (**travelled, travelling** *BrE*, **traveled, traveling** *AmE*)
1 JOURNEY **a)** [I] to go from one place to another, or to several places, especially ones that are far away: *Someday I'd like to* ***travel abroad***. | **[+to/across/through/around etc]** *We're planning to travel across America this summer.* | **travel widely/extensively** *He has travelled extensively in China.* | **travel by train/car/air etc** *We travelled by train across Eastern Europe.* | *He'd travelled far, but he'd* ***travelled light*** (=without taking many possessions). **b) travel the world/country** to go to most parts of the world or of a particular country
2 DISTANCE [I,T] to go a particular distance or at a particular speed: **[+at]** *The train was travelling at 100 mph.* | *They travelled 200 miles on the first day.*
3 well-travelled a) (*also* **widely-travelled**) having travelled to many different countries: *a well-travelled businesswoman* **b)** having been travelled on by many people: *a well-travelled road*
4 NEWS [I] to be passed quickly from one person or place to another: *News travels fast.*
5 travel well to remain in good condition or be equally successful when taken to another country: *Exporters have to find wines that travel well.* | *Many British television programmes don't travel well.*
6 EYES [I always + adv/prep] *written* if your eyes travel over something, you look at different parts of it: *His gaze travelled over her face.*
7 LIGHT/SOUND [I] to move at a particular speed or in a particular direction: *Light travels faster than sound.*
8 SPORT [I] to take more than three steps while you are holding the ball in BASKETBALL

travel² ●●● S2 W2 *n*
1 [U] the activity of travelling: *The new job involves a fair amount of travel.* THESAURUS JOURNEY → see Thesaurus box on *p. 1955*
2 travels [plural] journeys to places that are far away, usually for pleasure: **on sb's travels** *We met some very interesting people on our travels in Thailand.*

GRAMMAR: Comparison

travel

• You use **travel** to talk in general about the activity of travelling: *Long-distance travel has become much cheaper.* | *My interests are travel and photography.*

• **Travel** is only used as an uncountable noun. ✗ Don't say: *a travel* | *the travel*

travels

• Someone's **travels** are their journeys to many different places: *On her travels, she visited Egypt, Jordan, and South Africa.* | *I'll call you when I get back from my travels.*

• **Travels** is always used as a plural noun in this meaning. ✗ Don't say: *her travel* | *my travel*

trip

• You use **trip** to talk about an occasion when someone travels somewhere: *He has gone to New York on a business trip.* | *They have made several trips to Europe.*

• **Trip** is a countable noun and can be used in the singular with 'a' or in the plural. Don't use **travel** in this meaning. You say: *Have a nice trip!* ✗ Don't say: *Have a nice travel!*

COLLOCATIONS

ADJECTIVES/NOUN + travel

air travel *There has been a major increase in air travel during the last twenty years.*
rail travel *The measures were introduced to make rail travel safer.*
bus/coach/car etc travel | **foreign/international/overseas travel** | **long-distance travel** | **business travel** | **space travel**

travel + NOUN

the travel industry *The storms have had a huge effect on the country's travel industry.*
travel arrangements *I still have to make all the travel arrangements.*
travel expenses/costs | **travel insurance** | **a travel book/guide** | **a travel writer**

PHRASES

a form/mode/method/means of travel *I find the train a more comfortable mode of travel.*

ˈtravel ˌagency *n* [C] a company that arranges hotel rooms, plane tickets etc for people who want to travel

ˈtravel ˌagent *n* [C] someone who owns or works in a travel agency

trav·el·a·tor /ˈtrævəleɪtə $ -ər/ *n* [C] another spelling of TRAVOLATOR

ˈtravel ˌbureau *n* [C] a TRAVEL AGENCY

trav·el·ler *BrE*, **traveler** *AmE* /ˈtrævələ $ -ər/ ●●○ *n* [C]
1 someone who is on a journey or someone who travels often: *frequent travellers to France* **THESAURUS** ▸ **TOURIST, TRAVEL**
2 *BrE* someone who travels around from place to place living in a CARAVAN → **gipsy**

ˈtraveller's ˌcheque *BrE*, **traveler's check** *AmE* *n* [C] a special cheque for a fixed amount that can be exchanged for the money of a foreign country

trav·el·ling[1] *BrE*, **traveling** *AmE* /ˈtrævəlɪŋ/ ●○○ *adj* [only before noun]
1 travelling expenses money that is used to pay for the cost of travelling while someone is on a trip for their company
2 travelling companion someone you are on a journey with
3 travelling musician/circus/exhibition etc someone or something that goes from place to place
4 travelling rug/clock etc *BrE* a clock etc designed to be used when you are travelling
5 travelling people/folk *BrE* TRAVELLERS

travelling[2] *BrE*, **traveling** *AmE* *n* [U] **1** the act or activity of going from one place to another, especially places that are far away: *After retiring, we'll do some travelling.* **2** taking more than three steps while holding the ball in BASKETBALL

ˌtravelling ˈsalesman *BrE*, **traveling salesman** *AmE* *n* [C] someone who goes from place to place selling their company's products

trav·el·ogue (*also* **travelog** *AmE*) /ˈtrævəlɒg $ -lɑːg, -lɒːg/ *n* [C] a film or piece of writing that describes travel in a particular country, or a particular person's travels

ˈtravel ˌsickness *n* [U] when you feel ill because you are travelling in a vehicle —**travel-sick** *adj*

tra·verse[1] /ˈtrævɜːs $ trəˈvɜːrs/ *v* [T] *formal* to move across, over, or through something, especially an area of land or water: *two minutes to traverse the park*

trav·erse[2] /ˈtrævɜːs $ -vɜːrs/ *n* [C] *technical* a sideways movement across a very steep slope in mountain-climbing

trav·es·ty /ˈtrævəsti/ *n* (*plural* **travesties**) [C usually singular] used in order to say that something is extremely bad and is not what it is claimed to be: *Their marriage was*

THESAURUS: travel

TO TRAVEL

travel to go from one place to another, especially places that are far apart: *We travelled to Russia by train.* | *I love to travel.*
go to go somewhere - often used instead of **travel**: *We're going to Greece for our holidays this year.* | *He's gone to London on business.* | *It's quicker to go by plane.*
commute to travel to work or school: *She commutes to work by bicycle.*
cross to travel across a very large area, for example a desert or ocean: *The slaves crossed the Atlantic in the holds of the ships.*
tour to travel in order to visit many different places, especially as part of a holiday: *They're touring Europe by coach.*
go trekking to do a long and difficult walk in a place far from towns and cities: *They went trekking in the mountains.*
roam *especially written* to travel or move around an area with no clear purpose or direction, usually for a long time: *When he was young, he roamed from one country to another.* | *The tribes used to roam around freely, without any fixed territory.*
journey *literary* to travel, especially a long distance: *He journeyed on horseback through Palestine.*

PEOPLE WHO TRAVEL

traveller *BrE*, **traveler** *AmE* someone who is travelling a long distance: *Weary travellers waited at the airport.* | *My aunt was a great traveller* (=she travelled a lot).
tourist someone who is travelling somewhere for a holiday: *During the summer, over a million tourists visit the island each year.*
passenger someone who is travelling in a vehicle, plane, ship etc but not driving it or working on it: *The driver and two passengers were killed in the crash.*
commuter someone who travels to work every day: *commuters on the train to London*
backpacker someone who travels to a lot of different places, carrying their clothes etc in a RUCKSACK: *The hostels are great for backpackers.*
explorer someone who travels to places that people have not visited before: *Potatoes were brought to England by explorers such as Sir Francis Drake and Sir Walter Raleigh.*

T

a complete travesty. | **[+of]** *O'Brien described his trial as a* ***travesty of justice***.

trav·o·la·tor /ˈtrævəleɪtə $ -ər/ *n* [C] *BrE* a moving band that you stand on, which moves you along a floor, especially at an airport

trawl[1] /trɔːl $ trɒːl/ *v* [I,T] **1** to search through a lot of documents, lists etc in order to find out information: **[+through]** *I'll have to trawl through all my lecture notes again.* | **[+for]** *She spent the morning in the library, trawling for information for her project.* **2** to fish by pulling a special wide net behind a boat

trawl[2] *n* [C] **1** an act of searching through a lot of documents, lists etc in order to find something **2** (*also* **trawl net**) a wide net that is pulled along the bottom of the sea to catch fish

trawl·er /ˈtrɔːlə $ ˈtrɒːlər/ *n* [C] a fishing boat that uses a trawl net

TRAYS

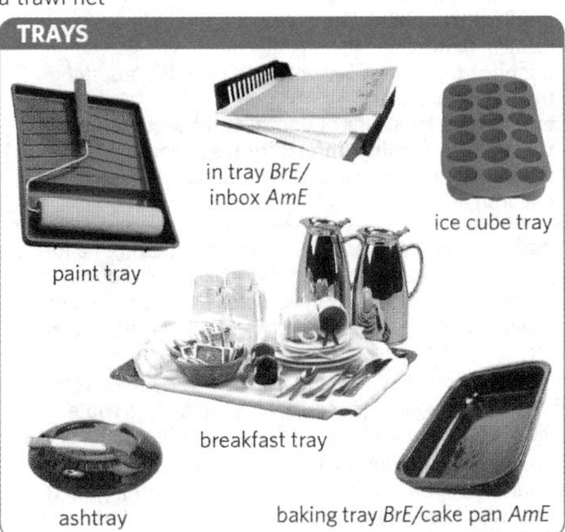

tray /treɪ/ ●●○ S3 *n* [C]

1 a flat piece of plastic, metal, or wood, with raised edges, used for carrying things such as plates, food etc: *The waiter brought drinks on a tray.*

2 a flat open container with three sides used for holding papers, documents etc on a desk: **in tray** (=for holding documents you still have to deal with) | **out tray** (=for holding documents you have dealt with)

3 *especially BrE* a flat open container with four sides used for holding certain things: *a cat litter tray* | **seed tray** (=a tray in which you plant seeds) → BAKING TRAY, SYSTEM TRAY

ˈtray bake *n* [C] a cake or sweet food that is baked in a square or RECTANGULAR metal pan and then cut into pieces

treach·e·rous /ˈtretʃərəs/ *adj* **1** someone who is treacherous cannot be trusted because they are not loyal and secretly intend to harm you: *a sly and treacherous woman* | *a treacherous plot to overthrow the leader* **2** ground, roads, weather conditions etc that are treacherous are particularly dangerous because you cannot see the dangers very easily: *treacherous mountain roads* | *Strong winds and loose rocks made climbing treacherous.* THESAURUS DANGEROUS —**treacherously** *adv*

treach·e·ry /ˈtretʃəri/ *n* (*plural* **treacheries**) **1** [U] behaviour in which someone is not loyal to a person who trusts them, especially when this behaviour helps that person's enemies: *the treachery of those who plotted against the king* **2** [C usually plural] a disloyal action against someone who trusts you

trea·cle /ˈtriːkəl/ *n* [U] **1** *BrE* a thick sweet black sticky liquid that is obtained from raw sugar and used in cooking SYN **molasses** *AmE* **2** a way of expressing love and emotions that seems silly or insincere: *a film that does not turn into treacle* **3** GOLDEN SYRUP: *a treacle tart* —**treacly** *adj*

tread[1] /tred/ ●○○ *v* (*past tense* **trod** /trɒd $ trɑːd/, *past participle* **trodden** /ˈtrɒdn $ ˈtrɑːdn/)

1 STEP IN/ON [I always + adv/prep] *BrE* to put your foot on or in something while you are walking SYN **step**: **[+in/on]** *Sorry, did I tread on your foot?* | *She trod barefoot on the soft grass.*

2 tread carefully/warily/cautiously etc to be very careful about what you say or do in a difficult situation: *If I wanted to keep my job, I knew I'd have to tread lightly.*

3 CRUSH **a)** [T] *BrE* to press or crush something into the floor or ground with your feet SYN **track** *AmE*: **tread sth into/onto/over sth** *Stop treading mud all over my clean kitchen floor!* | *Bits of the broken vase got trodden into the carpet.* **b) tread grapes** to crush GRAPES with your feet in order to produce juice for making wine

4 tread a path *BrE written* to take a particular action or series of actions: *Getting the right balance between home and work is a difficult path to tread.*

5 tread water (*past tense and past participle* **treaded**) **a)** to stay floating upright in deep water by moving your legs as if you are riding a bicycle **b)** to make no progress in a particular situation, especially because you are waiting for something to happen: *All I could do was tread water until the contracts arrived.*

6 WALK [I,T always + adv/prep] *literary* to walk: *David trod wearily along behind the others.*

7 tread the boards *humorous* to work as an actor → **tread on sb's toes** at TOE[1](3)

tread[2] *n* **1** [C,U] the pattern of lines on the part of a tyre that touches the road **2** [C] the part of a stair that you put your foot on **3** [singular] *literary* the particular sound that someone makes when they walk: *I heard the back door bang, and Rex's tread in the hall.*

tread·le /ˈtredl/ *n* [C] a flat piece of metal or wood that you move with your foot to turn a wheel in a machine

tread·mill /ˈtredˌmɪl/ *n* **1** [C] a piece of exercise equipment that has a large belt around a set of wheels, that you can walk or run on while staying in the same place → see picture at GYM **2** [singular] work or a way of life that seems very boring because you always have to do the same things: *the treadmill of working in the office* **3** [C] a MILL worked in the past by prisoners treading on steps fixed to a very large wheel

trea·son /ˈtriːzən/ *n* [U] the crime of being disloyal to your country or its government, especially by helping its enemies or trying to remove the government using violence → **treachery**: **[+against]** *Richter is accused of* ***committing treason*** *against the state.* | *The defendant was convicted of* ***high treason*** (=treason of the worst kind) *and sentenced to death.* —**treasonable, treasonous** *adj*: *a treasonable act against the head of state*

trea·sure[1] /ˈtreʒə $ -ər/ ●●○ *n*

1 [U] a group of valuable things such as gold, silver, jewels etc: **buried/hidden/sunken treasure**

2 [C] a very valuable and important object such as a painting or ancient document: *The Book of Kells is Trinity College's greatest treasure.*

3 [singular] *informal* someone who is very useful or important to you: *Our housekeeper is a real treasure.*

treasure[2] *v* [T] to keep and care for something that is very special, important, or valuable to you: *Jim treasured the gold pocket watch that his grandfather had given him.* —**treasured** *adj* [only before noun]: *A battered old guitar was his* ***most treasured possession***.

ˈtreasure ˌchest *n* [C] a box that holds treasure

ˈtreasure ˌhunt *n* [C] a game in which you have to find something that has been hidden by answering questions that are left in different places

trea·sur·er /ˈtreʒərə $ -ər/ *n* [C] someone who is officially responsible for the money for an organization, club, political party etc

treasure trove /ˈtreʒə trəʊv $ -ʒər troʊv/ *n* [U] **1** a group of valuable or interesting things or pieces of information, or the place where they are: **[+of]** *Our Science Shop is a treasure trove of curiosities and gadgets.* **2** *BrE law* valuable objects, coins etc that are found where they have been hidden or buried, which are not claimed by anyone

trea·su·ry /ˈtreʒəri/ *n* (*plural* **treasuries**) **1 the Treasury (Department)** a government department that controls the

T

money that the country collects and spends **2** [C] a place in a castle, church, PALACE etc where money or valuable objects are kept

treat[1] /triːt/ ●●● (S2) (W1) *v* [T]
1 BEHAVE TOWARDS SB/STH [always + adv/prep] to behave towards someone or something in a particular way → **treatment**: **treat sb like/as sth** *She treats me like one of the family.* | *Penny doesn't think her co-workers treat her as an equal.* | *He treated his automobiles almost as tenderly as he did his wife.* | **badly treated/well treated** *The prisoners were well treated by their guards.* | **treat sb with respect/contempt/courtesy etc** *Despite her seniority, Margot was never treated with much respect.* | **treat sb like dirt/a dog** (=treat someone unkindly and without respect) *I don't know why he stays with her – she treats him like dirt.*
2 DEAL WITH STH [always + adv/prep] to deal with, regard, or consider something in a particular way → **treatment**: **treat sth as sth** *Please treat this information as completely confidential.* | *She treats everything I say as a joke.* | **treat sth favourably/seriously/carefully etc** *Any complaint about safety standards must be treated very seriously.*
3 ILLNESS/INJURY to try to cure an illness or injury by using drugs, hospital care, operations etc → **treatment**: *It was difficult to treat patients because of a shortage of medicine.* | **treat sb/sth with sth** *Nowadays, malaria can be treated with drugs.*
4 BUY STH FOR SB to buy or do something special for someone that you know they will enjoy: **treat sb to sth** *We treated Mom to lunch at the Savoy.* | *I **treated myself** to a new dress.*
5 PROTECT/CLEAN to put a special substance on something or use a chemical process in order to protect, clean, or preserve it → **treatment**: *sewage treated so that it can be used as fertilizer* → TRICK OR TREAT

treat[2] ●●● (S3) *n*
1 [C] something special that you give someone or do for them because you know they will enjoy it: **as a treat** *Steven took his son to a cricket match as a birthday treat.*
2 [singular] an event that gives you a lot of pleasure and is usually unexpected: *When we were kids, a trip to the beach was a **real treat**.*
3 [C] a special food that tastes good, especially one that you do not eat very often: *The cafe serves an assortment of gourmet treats.*
4 my treat *spoken* used to tell someone that you will pay for something such as a meal for them: *Let's go out to lunch – my treat.*
5 go down a treat *BrE informal* if something goes down a treat, people like it very much: *That new vegetarian restaurant seems to be going down a treat.*
6 look/work a treat *BrE informal* to look very good or work very well: *The sports ground looked a treat, with all the flags flying.*

treat·a·ble /ˈtriːtəbəl/ *adj* a treatable illness or injury can be helped with drugs or an operation: *Certain forms of cancer are treatable with drugs.*

trea·tise /ˈtriːtɪs, -tɪz/ *n* [C] a serious book or article about a particular subject: **[+on]** *a treatise on medical ethics*

treat·ment /ˈtriːtmənt/ ●●● (S2) (W1) *n*
1 MEDICAL [C,U] something that is done to cure someone who is injured or ill → **treat**: **[+of/for]** *There have been great advances in the treatment of cancer.* | *The best treatment for a cold is to rest and drink lots of fluids.*
2 BEHAVIOUR TOWARDS SB [U] a particular way of behaving towards someone or of dealing with them → **treat**: **[+of]** *Civil rights groups have complained about the harsh treatment of prisoners.* | **special/preferential treatment** (=when one person is treated better than another) *The two young princes were not singled out for special treatment at school.* | *Just lately, Kyra has been giving me **the silent treatment*** (=refusing to speak to me because she is angry with me).
3 OF A SUBJECT [C,U] a particular way of dealing with or talking about a subject → **treat**: *I didn't think the film gave the issue serious treatment.*
4 CLEAN/PROTECT [C,U] a process by which something is cleaned, protected etc → **treat**: **[+of]** *the treatment of polluted rivers*

COLLOCATIONS

VERBS

give sb treatment *He was given treatment at a local hospital.*
get/have/receive treatment *Two boys received treatment for gunshot wounds.*
undergo treatment (=have it) *A few years earlier she'd undergone fertility treatment.*
need/require treatment | **respond to treatment** (=become better when given treatment)

ADJECTIVES/NOUN + treatment

effective *The drug may prove to be an effective treatment for brain tumours.*
medical treatment *Every patient has a right to refuse medical treatment.*
hospital treatment *Several people needed hospital treatment for burns.*
emergency treatment | **dental treatment** | **cancer treatment** | **fertility/infertility treatment** (=treatment to help someone who is unable to have children)

treat·y /ˈtriːti/ ●●○ (W3) *n* (*plural* **treaties**) [C] a formal written agreement between two or more countries or governments: *Both sides have agreed to **sign the treaty**.* | *The **peace treaty** ends nearly four years of violence.* | **[+on]** *a treaty on political union*

treb·le[1] /ˈtrebəl/ *predeterminer BrE* three times as big, as much, or as many as something else (SYN) **triple** *AmE*: *They sold the house for treble the amount they paid for it.*

treble[2] *v* [I,T] *BrE* to become three times as big in amount, size, or number, or to make something increase in this way (SYN) **triple** *AmE*: *Their profits have trebled in the last two years.*

treble[3] *n* **1** [U] the upper half of the whole range of musical notes → BASS[1](3) **2** [C] a boy's high singing voice, or a boy with a voice like this **3** [C] the part of a musical work that is written for a treble voice or instrument

treble[4] *adj* [only before noun] a treble voice or instrument produces high notes

ˌtreble ˈclef *n* [C] *technical* a sign (𝄞) at the beginning of a line of written music which shows that the note written on the bottom line of the STAVE is an E above MIDDLE C

tree /triː/ ●●● (S1) (W1) *n* [C]
1 a very tall plant that has branches and leaves, and lives for many years: *As a kid, I loved to climb trees.* | **a cherry/peach/apple etc tree** *We **planted** a peach **tree** in the backyard.* | *the trunk of an old oak tree* (=the main central part, from which the branches grow)
2 a drawing that connects things with lines to show how they are related to each other → FAMILY TREE → **top of the tree** at TOP[1](3), → **it doesn't grow on trees** at GROW(7), → **be up a gum tree** at GUM TREE(2)

tree·house /ˈtriːhaʊs/ *n* [C] a wooden structure built in the branches of a tree for children to play in

ˈtree-ˌhugger *n* [C] *informal* someone who wants to protect the environment, and who takes part in protests which some people think are silly – used to show disapproval

tree·less /ˈtriːləs/ *adj* a treeless area has no trees in it: *a treeless landscape*

ˈtree line *n* [singular] the TIMBERLINE

ˈtree-lined *adj* a tree-lined road has trees on both sides

ˈtree ˌsurgery *n* [U] the treatment of damaged trees, especially by cutting off branches

tree·top /ˈtriːtɒp $ -tɑːp/ *n* [C usually plural] the branches at the top of a tree

tre·foil /ˈtriːfɔɪl, ˈtrefɔɪl/ *n* [C] *technical* **1** a type of small plant that has leaves which divide into three parts **2** a pattern in the shape of these leaves

treg·gings /ˈtregɪŋz/ *n* [plural] tight trousers which are stretchy like LEGGINGS, but are made of thicker material → **jeggings**

trek¹ /trek/ ●○○ *n* [C]
1 a long and difficult journey, made especially on foot as an adventure SYN **hike**: *a lonely trek through the forest* THESAURUS▸ JOURNEY
2 *informal* a distance that seems long when you walk it: *I'm afraid it's a bit of a trek to the station.*

trek² *v* (**trekked**, **trekking**) [I always + adv/prep] **1** *informal* to make a long and difficult journey, especially on foot SYN **hike**: **[+up/down etc]** *The elevator was broken, so we had to trek up six flights of stairs.* **2** to walk a long way, especially in the mountains, as an adventure SYN **hike**: **[+in/across etc]** *For five days he trekked across the mountains of central China.* THESAURUS▸ WALK

trel·lis /ˈtrelɪs/ *n* [C] a frame made of long narrow pieces of wood that cross each other, used to support climbing plants

trem·ble /ˈtrembəl/ ●●○ *v* [I]
1 to shake slightly in a way that you cannot control, especially because you are upset or frightened: *His lip started to tremble and then he started to cry.* | **tremble with anger/fear etc** *Greene was on his feet now, his body trembling with rage.*
2 to shake slightly: *The whole house trembled as the train went by.*
3 if your voice trembles, it sounds nervous and unsteady
4 to be worried or frightened about something: *I* ***tremble to think*** *what will happen when she finds out.* —**tremble** *n* [C]

tre·men·dous /trɪˈmendəs/ ●●○ *adj*
1 very big, fast, powerful etc: *Suddenly, there was a tremendous bang, and the whole station shook.* | *She was making a* ***tremendous effort*** *to appear calm.* | *She praised her husband for the* ***tremendous support*** *he had given her.* | *Sales have been tremendous so far this year.* | *This plan could save us* ***a tremendous amount of*** *money.* THESAURUS▸ BIG
2 excellent: *She's got a tremendous voice, hasn't she?* —**tremendously** *adv*: *tremendously wealthy*

trem·o·lo /ˈtreməlǝʊ $ -loʊ/ *n* (*plural* **tremolos**) [C] musical notes which are repeated very quickly

trem·or /ˈtremə $ -ər/ *n* [C] **1** a small EARTHQUAKE in which the ground shakes slightly: *an earth tremor* **2** a slight shaking movement in your body that you cannot control, especially because you are ill, weak, or upset

trem·u·lous /ˈtremjələs/ *adj literary* shaking slightly, especially because you are nervous: *a tremulous voice* —**tremulously** *adv*

trench /trentʃ/ ●○○ *n* [C]
1 a long narrow hole dug into the surface of the ground: *Workers* ***dug*** *a* ***trench*** *for gas lines.*
2 *technical* a long narrow valley in the ground beneath the sea
3 [usually plural] a deep trench dug in the ground as a protection for soldiers: *the trenches of World War I*
4 the trenches the place or situation where most of the work or action in an activity takes place: *Lane left teaching after 30 years in the trenches.*

tren·chant /ˈtrentʃənt/ *adj written* expressed very strongly, effectively, and directly without worrying about offending people: *Stockman became one of the president's most trenchant critics.* —**trenchantly** *adv*

ˈtrench coat *n* [C] a long RAINCOAT with a belt

trench·er /ˈtrentʃə $ -ər/ *n* [C] *BrE* a plate used in the past for serving food

ˌtrench ˈwarfare *n* [U] a method of fighting in which soldiers from opposing armies are in TRENCHes facing each other

TREE

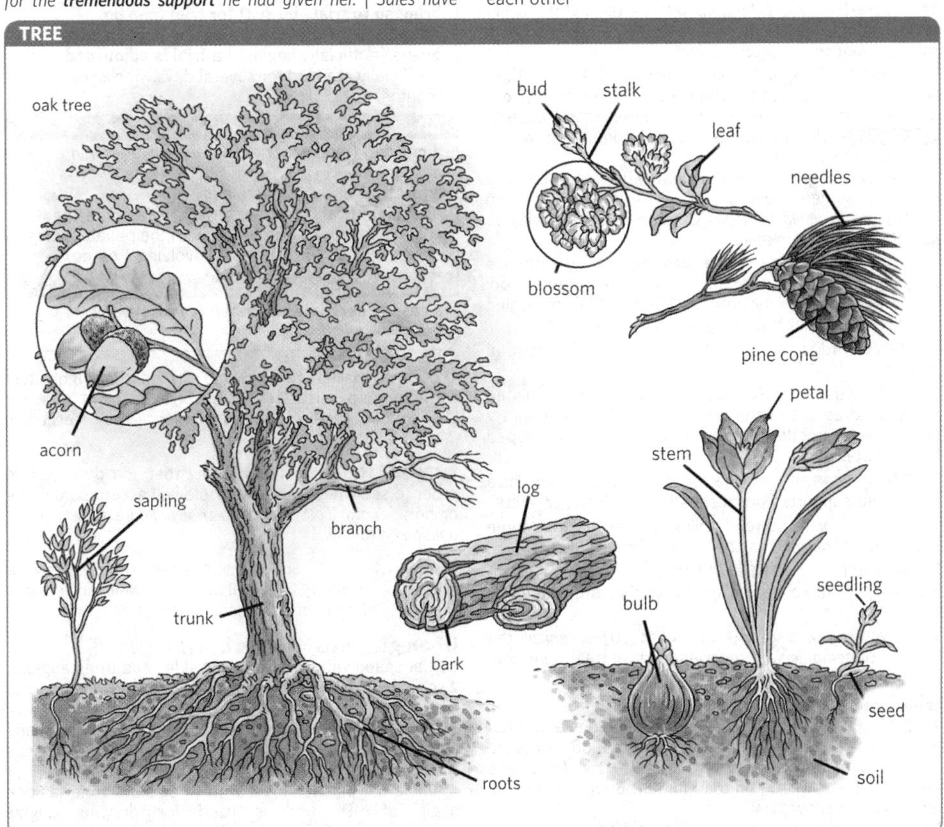

T

trend /trend/ ●●○ S3 W2 *n* [C]
1 a general tendency in the way a situation is changing or developing: **[+towards]** *Lately there has been a trend towards hiring younger, cheaper employees.* | **[+in]** ***recent trends*** *in education* | *The* ***current trend*** *is towards more part-time employment.* | *the* ***general trend*** *towards the centralization of political power* | *A* ***disturbing trend*** *is that victims of violence are getting younger.* | *The* ***growing trend*** *is for single mothers to bring up children by themselves.* | *Even so, the* ***underlying trend*** *is positive.* | *national and international* **economic trends** | *the* **downward trend** *in the price of gold* | *Successive presidents have tried to* ***reverse this trend****, but without success.*
2 set the trend to start doing something that other people copy: *Larger corporations are setting the trend for better maternity benefits.*
3 on trend fashionable - used especially in magazines: *This striped dress is bang on trend.*

ˈtrending ˌtopic *n* [C] one of the most popular subjects in recent messages sent using the SOCIAL NETWORKING service Twitter

trend·set·ter /ˈtrendˌsetə $ -ər/ *n* [C] someone who starts a new fashion or makes it popular —**trendsetting** *adj* [only before noun]

trend·spot·ter /ˈtrendˌspɒtə $ -ˌspɑːtər/ *n* [C] someone who notices and reports on new fashions, activities that people are starting to do, or the way a situation is developing —**trendspotting** *n* [U]

trend·y¹ /ˈtrendi/ *adj* (*comparative* **trendier**, *superlative* **trendiest**) influenced by the most fashionable styles and ideas: *a trendy Bay Area restaurant* THESAURUS FASHIONABLE —**trendiness** *n* [U]

trendy² *n* (*plural* **trendies**) [C] *BrE informal* someone who tries hard to be fashionable and follows all the latest styles - used to show disapproval: *young trendies from art college*

trep·i·da·tion /ˌtrepəˈdeɪʃən/ *n* [U] a feeling of anxiety or fear about something that is going to happen: ***With some trepidation****, I opened the door.*

tres·pass¹ /ˈtrespəs $ -pəs, -pæs/ *v* [I] **1** to go onto someone's private land without their permission: **[+on]** *She was arrested for trespassing on government property.* THESAURUS ENTER **2** *old use* to do something wrong SYN **sin** —**trespasser** *n* [C]
trespass on sth *phr v formal* to unfairly use more than you should of someone else's time, help etc for your own advantage: *It would be trespassing on their hospitality to accept any more from them.*

trespass² *n* **1** [C,U] (*also* **trespassing** *AmE*) the offence of going onto someone's land without their permission: *He will be prosecuted for trespass.* **2** [C] *biblical* something you have done that is morally wrong SYN **sin**

tress·es /ˈtresɪz/ *n* [plural] *literary* a woman's beautiful long hair

tres·tle /ˈtresəl/ *n* [C] *especially BrE* **1** an A-shaped frame used as one of the two supports for a temporary table **2** (*also* **trestle bridge**) a bridge with an A-shaped frame supporting it

ˈtrestle ˌtable *n* [C] *BrE* a temporary table made of a long board supported on trestles → see picture at TABLE¹

tri- /traɪ/ *prefix* three: **trilingual** (=speaking three languages) | **triangle** (=a shape with three sides)

tri·ad /ˈtraɪæd/ *n* [C] **1** a Chinese secret criminal group **2** a group of three people or things that are related or similar to each other

tri·age /ˈtriːɑːʒ $ triˈɑːʒ, ˈtriːɑːʒ/ *n* [U] *technical* the method of deciding who receives medical treatment first, according to how seriously someone is injured

tri·al¹ /ˈtraɪəl/ ●●● S3 W2 *n*
1 COURT [C,U] a legal process in which a judge and often a JURY in a court of law examine information to decide whether someone is guilty of a crime → **try**: *The trial is due to start next week.* | **on trial (for sth)** *Brady was on trial for assault.* → SHOW TRIAL
2 TEST [C,U] a process of testing to find out whether something works effectively and is safe: *a new drug that is undergoing* ***clinical trials***
3 TRY SB/STH [C,U] a short period during which you use or do something or employ someone to find out whether they are satisfactory for a particular purpose or job → **try**: **on trial** *They let me have the computer on trial for thirty days.* | *The security system will be reviewed after a three-month* ***trial period****.* | *Smith was hired* ***on a six-month trial basis****.* | **trial separation** (=a period of time in which a husband and wife do not live together, to find out whether they want to stay married)
4 by/through trial and error if you do something by trial and error, you test many different methods of doing something in order to find the best: *I learned most of what I know about gardening through trial and error.*
5 DIFFICULTY [C usually plural] something that is difficult to deal with, and that is worrying or annoying → **trying**: *the daily trials of living in a poor country* | **be a trial (to/for sb)** *My brothers and I were always a real trial to my parents.* | *the* ***trials and tribulations*** *of running a business*
6 SPORTS **trials** [plural] *BrE* a special sports competition in which people who want to be on a team are tested, so that the best can be chosen SYN **tryout** *AmE*: **horse/sheepdog trials** (=a sporting competition in which horses or dogs compete)

COLLOCATIONS

VERBS

be on trial (=be being judged in a court of law) *Her son is on trial charged with murder.*
stand/face trial (=be judged in a court of law) *Doctors said he was unfit to stand trial.*
go on trial *Taylor went on trial accused of fraud.*
be awaiting/facing trial *Its managing director is awaiting trial on corruption charges.*
put sb on trial *They should never have been put on trial, let alone convicted.*
bring sb to trial | **be sent for trial** (*also* **be committed for trial** *BrE*) | **a trial is held** | **a trial opens** (=officially begins) | **a trial is adjourned** (=it is officially stopped for several days, weeks, or months)

ADJECTIVES/NOUN + trial

a murder/fraud etc trial *She was a witness in a murder trial.*
a fair trial *He is entitled to a fair trial.*
a criminal trial (=for cases involving a crime) | **a civil trial** (=for cases dealing with the private affairs of citizens, rather than cases involving a crime)

PHRASES

a case goes/comes to trial *If the case ever went to trial, he would probably lose.*

trial² *v* (**trialled**, **trialling**) [T] *BrE* to thoroughly test something to see if it works correctly or is effective SYN **try out**: *These techniques were trialled by teachers in 300 schools.*

ˈtrial balˌloon *n* [C] something that you do or say in order to see whether other people will accept something or not: *Senator Lott is floating trial balloons to test public opinion on the bill.*

ˌtrial ˈrun *n* [C] an occasion when you test a new method or system to see if it works well: *This year is something of a trial run for the new service.*

tri·an·gle /ˈtraɪæŋɡəl/ ●●● *n* [C]
1 a flat shape with three straight sides and three angles
2 something that is shaped like a triangle: *a triangle of land*
3 a musical instrument made of metal bent into the shape of a triangle. You hit it with a metal stick to make a ringing sound.
4 *AmE* a flat plastic object with three sides that has one angle of 90° and is used for drawing angles SYN **set-square** *BrE*

TRIANGLES

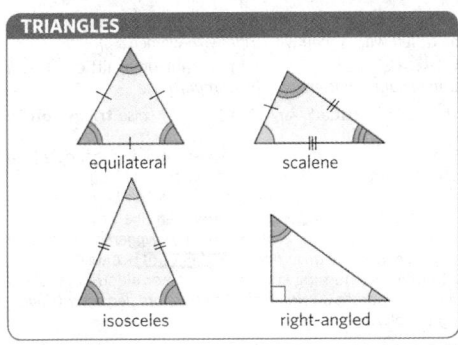

equilateral
scalene
isosceles
right-angled

tri·an·gu·lar /traɪˈæŋgjələ $ -ər/ ●○○ *adj*
1 shaped like a triangle
2 involving three people or teams: *a triangular sporting competition*

tri·an·gu·la·tion /traɪˌæŋgjəˈleɪʃən/ *n* [U] a method of finding your position by measuring the lines and angles of a triangle on a map

Tri·as·sic /traɪˈæsɪk/ *adj* belonging or relating to the period between about 245 million and 202 million years ago, when life in the sea and on land changed and spread a lot, and DINOSAURS first appeared

tri·ath·lon /traɪˈæθlən/ *n* [C] a sports competition in which competitors run, swim, and cycle long distances

trib·al /ˈtraɪbəl/ ●○○ *adj* [usually before noun] relating to a tribe or tribes: *a tribal dance* | *tribal cultures*

trib·al·is·m /ˈtraɪbəl-ɪzəm/ *n* [U] **1** behaviour and attitudes that are based on strong loyalty to your tribe **2** the state of being organized into tribes

tribe /traɪb/ ●●○ *n* [C]
1 a social group consisting of people of the same RACE who have the same beliefs, customs, language etc, and usually live in one particular area ruled by their leader: *a tribe of Aborigines known as the Dolphin People*
2 a group of people with the same interests – used especially to show disapproval: *tribes of journalists*
3 a group of related animals or plants: *the cat tribe*
4 *humorous* a large family: *We were only expecting Jack and his wife, but the whole tribe turned up.*

tribes·man /ˈtraɪbzmən/ *n* (*plural* **tribesmen** /-mən/) [C] a man who is a member of a tribe

tribes·wom·an /ˈtraɪbzˌwʊmən/ *n* (*plural* **tribeswomen** /-ˌwɪmɪn/) [C] a woman who is a member of a tribe

trib·u·la·tion /ˌtrɪbjəˈleɪʃən/ *n* [C,U] *formal* serious trouble or a serious problem: *Even close friends were unaware of the tribulations she faced.* → **trials and tribulations** at TRIAL[1](5)

tri·bu·nal /traɪˈbjuːnl/ ●○○ *n* [C] a type of court that is given official authority to deal with a particular situation or problem: *The case of your redundancy will be heard by an independent tribunal.* → INDUSTRIAL TRIBUNAL

trib·une /ˈtrɪbjuːn/ *n* [C] an official in ancient Rome who was elected by the ordinary people to protect their rights

trib·u·ta·ry /ˈtrɪbjətəri $ -teri/ *n* (*plural* **tributaries**) [C] a stream or river that flows into a larger river

trib·ute /ˈtrɪbjuːt/ ●●○ *n* [C,U]
1 something that you say, do, or give in order to express your respect or admiration for someone: *The players wore black armbands as a tribute to their late teammate.* | *I'd like to* ***pay tribute to*** (=praise and admire publicly) *the party workers for all their hard work.*
2 be a tribute to sb/sth to be a clear sign of the good qualities that someone or something has: *It was a tribute to her teaching methods that so many children passed the test.*
3 a payment of goods or money by one ruler or country to another more powerful one, especially in order to be protected
4 floral tribute *BrE* flowers sent to a funeral

ˈtribute band *n* [C] a group of musicians who play and sing the songs of a famous group, trying to sound and look like them

trice /traɪs/ *n* **in a trice** *BrE old-fashioned* very quickly or soon: *He should be here in a trice.*

tri·ceps /ˈtraɪseps/ *n* [C] the large muscle at the back of your upper arm

tri·chol·o·gist /trɪˈkɒlədʒɪst $ -ˈkɑː-/ *n* [C] someone who deals with problems affecting people's hair or the skin on their heads

trick[1] /trɪk/ ●●● S3 *n* [C]
1 STH THAT DECEIVES SB something you do in order to deceive someone: *Pretending he doesn't remember is an old trick of his.* | *He didn't really lose his wallet – that's just a trick.*
2 JOKE something you do to surprise someone and to make other people laugh: *I'm getting tired of your silly tricks.* | *The girls were* ***playing tricks*** *on their teacher.*
3 STH THAT MAKES THINGS APPEAR DIFFERENT something that makes things appear to be different from the way they really are: *After walking for hours in the hot sun, his mind began* ***playing tricks on*** *him.* | *At first he thought someone was coming towards him, but it was just* ***a trick of the light****.*
4 a dirty/rotten/mean trick an unkind or unfair thing to do: *He didn't turn up? What a dirty trick!*
5 do the trick *spoken* if something does the trick, it solves a problem or provides what is needed to get a good result: *A bit more flour should do the trick.*
6 MAGIC a skilful set of actions that seem like magic, done to entertain people: *My uncle was always showing me* ***card tricks*** *when I was a kid.* | *a* ***magic trick***
7 CLEVER METHOD a way of doing something that works very well but may not be easy to notice: *The trick is to bend your knees as you catch the ball.* | *a salesman who knew all* ***the tricks of the trade*** (=clever methods used in a particular job)
8 use/try every trick in the book to use every method that you know, even dishonest ones, to achieve what you want
9 teach/show sb a trick or two *informal* used to say that someone knows more than someone else or can do something better than them: *Experienced teachers can show new teachers a trick or two.*
10 sb is up to their (old) tricks *informal* to be doing the same dishonest things that you have often done before
11 CARDS the cards played or won in one part of a game of cards: *He won the first three tricks easily.*
12 HABIT **have a trick of doing sth** *BrE* to have a habit of using a particular expression or of moving your face or body in a particular way: *She had this trick of raising her eyebrows at the end of a question.*
13 never miss a trick *spoken* to always know exactly what is happening even if it does not concern you: *Dave's found out. He never misses a trick, does he?*
14 how's tricks? *old-fashioned spoken* used to greet someone in a friendly way: *Hello, Bill! How's tricks?*
15 SEX *AmE old-fashioned informal* someone who pays a PROSTITUTE to have sex: **turn a trick** (=to have sex with someone for money) → CONFIDENCE TRICK, → **dirty trick** at DIRTY[1](6), → **you can't teach an old dog new tricks** at TEACH(7), → HAT TRICK

trick[2] ●●● S3 *v* [T]
1 to deceive someone in order to get something from them or to make them do something: *She knew she'd been tricked, but it was too late.* | **trick sb into doing sth** *He claimed he was tricked into carrying drugs.* | **trick sb out of sth** *The corporation was tricked out of $20 million.* | **trick your way into/past/onto etc sth** *He tricked his way into her home by pretending to be a policeman.*
2 be tricked out with/in sth *BrE literary* to be decorated with something: *a hat tricked out with ribbons*

trick[3] *adj* **1 trick photography** when a photograph or picture has been changed so that it looks different from what was really there **2 a trick question** a question which seems easy to answer but has a hidden difficulty **3 a trick knee/ankle/shoulder etc** *AmE* a joint that is weak and can suddenly cause you problems

T

trick·e·ry /ˈtrɪkəri/ *n* [U] the use of tricks to deceive or cheat people

trick·le¹ /ˈtrɪkəl/ *v* [I always + adv/prep] **1** if liquid trickles somewhere, it flows slowly in drops or in a thin stream: **[+down/into/out]** *The tears trickled down her cheeks.* **2** if people, vehicles, goods etc trickle somewhere, they move there slowly in small groups or amounts: **[+in/into/away]** *The first few fans started to trickle into the stadium.*

trickle down *phr v* if money trickles down, it moves slowly from the richest people to the poorest people in a society, or from the richest countries to the poorest countries

trickle up *phr v* if money trickles up, it moves slowly from the poorest people to the richest people in a society, or from the poorest countries to the richest countries

trickle² *n* **1** [C] a thin slow flow of liquid: *The water in the stream had been reduced to a trickle.* **2** [singular] a movement of people, vehicles, goods etc into a place in very small numbers or amounts: *Recent legislation has reduced immigration to a trickle.* | **[+of]** *a trickle of cars on the highway*

ˈtrickle-down efˌfect *n* [singular] a belief that additional wealth gained by the richest people in society will have a good economic effect on the lives of everyone because the rich people will put the extra money into businesses, INVESTMENTS etc

ˌtrick or ˈtreat *v* **1 go trick or treating** if children go trick or treating, they dress in COSTUMES and go from house to house on HALLOWEEN saying 'trick or treat' in order to get sweets **2** the words that children say when they go trick or treating, to say that they will play a trick on someone if they are not given a TREAT (=sweet)

trick·ster /ˈtrɪkstə $ -ər/ *n* [C] someone who deceives or cheats people: **confidence trickster** *BrE*: *a slick, fast-talking confidence trickster*

trick·y /ˈtrɪki/ ●●○ S3 *adj* (*comparative* **trickier**, *superlative* **trickiest**)
1 something that is tricky is difficult to deal with or do because it is complicated and full of problems: *I can get you tickets for the show but it'll be tricky.* THESAURUS ➤ DIFFICULT
2 a tricky person is clever and likely to deceive you SYN **crafty**

tri·col·our *BrE*, **tricolor** *AmE* /ˈtrɪkələ $ ˈtraɪˌkʌlər/ *n* [C] a flag with three equal bands of different colours, especially the national flags of France or Ireland

tri·cy·cle /ˈtraɪsɪkəl/ *n* [C] a bicycle with three wheels, especially for young children

tri·dent /ˈtraɪdənt/ *n* [C] **1** a weapon with three points that looks like a large fork **2 Trident missile/submarine** a type of NUCLEAR weapon, or the SUBMARINE that shoots it

tried¹ /traɪd/ the past tense and past participle of TRY

tried² *adj* **tried and tested/trusted/true** a tried and tested method has been used successfully many times: *tried and tested safety procedures*

tri·en·ni·al /traɪˈeniəl/ *adj* happening every three years → **annual**

tri·er /ˈtraɪə $ -ər/ *n* [C] *especially BrE informal* someone who always makes a great effort, even if they do not often succeed

tri·fle¹ /ˈtraɪfəl/ *n* **1 a trifle** *formal* slightly: **a trifle eccentric/odd/unexpected etc** **2** [C] *old-fashioned* something unimportant or not valuable: *There's no point in arguing over trifles.* **3** [C,U] a cold British sweet dish made of layers of cake, fruit, JELLY, CUSTARD, and cream

trifle² *v*

trifle with sb/sth *phr v* to treat someone or something without respect or not in a serious way: *He's not a man to be trifled with.* | *men who trifle with women's affections*

tri·fling /ˈtraɪflɪŋ/ *adj* unimportant or of little value: *a trifling sum* | *matters of trifling importance*

trig·ger¹ /ˈtrɪgə $ -ər/ ●●○ AWL (*also* **trigger off**) *v* [T]
1 to make something happen very quickly, especially a series of events: *The assassination triggered off a wave of rioting.* | *Certain forms of mental illness can be triggered by food allergies.* | **trigger a memory** (=make you suddenly remember something) | *His action **triggered** a massive **response** from the government.* THESAURUS ➤ CAUSE
2 to make something such as a bomb or electrical system start to operate SYN **set off**: *The burglars fled after **triggering** the **alarm**.*

trigger² ●○○ AWL *n* [C]
1 the part of a gun that you pull with your finger to fire it: **pull/squeeze the trigger** *He took aim and squeezed the trigger.*
2 be the trigger (point) (for sth) to be the thing that quickly causes a serious problem: *The hijacking became a trigger point for military action.*

trigger-ˌhappy (*also* **ˈtrigger-ˌready**) *adj informal* someone who is trigger-happy is much too willing to use weapons, especially guns: *a trigger-happy cop*

ˈtrigger ˌman *n* [C] *AmE informal* a person who shoots another person, especially when they do this for someone else: *Even if the trigger men are caught, those who ordered the killing escape punishment.*

trig·o·nom·e·try /ˌtrɪgəˈnɒmətri $ -ˈnɑː-/ *n* [U] the part of mathematics concerned with the relationship between the angles and sides of TRIANGLES

trike /traɪk/ *n* [C] *informal* a TRICYCLE

tri·lat·e·ral /traɪˈlætərəl/ *adj* [only before noun] involving three groups, countries etc → **bilateral**: *trilateral peace talks*

tril·by /ˈtrɪlbi/ (*also* **ˌtrilby ˈhat**) *n* (*plural* **trilbies**) [C] *especially BrE* a man's soft FELT hat

tri·lin·gual /ˌtraɪˈlɪŋgwəl◂/ *adj* **1** able to speak three languages **2** using three languages: *a trilingual medieval inscription*

trill¹ /trɪl/ *v* [I,T] **1** to make a short repeated high sound: *birds trilling in the trees* | *The phone trilled sharply.* **2** to say something in a high happy voice that sounds slightly false: *'Have a nice time, darling,' she trilled.*

trill² *n* [C] **1** *technical* a musical sound made by quickly moving between two notes **2** a short repeated high sound: *the trill of blackbirds*

tril·lion /ˈtrɪljən/ ●○○ *number* (*plural* **trillion** *or* **trillions**)
1 the number 1,000,000,000,000: *In a short time the number of cells is more than a trillion.* | **two/three/four etc trillion** *$5.3 trillion* | *Japan's exports were worth $43 trillion last year.* | **trillions of pounds/dollars etc** *the trillions of dollars in the bond markets*
2 *informal* an extremely large number of people or things: **a trillion** *a shirt with a trillion holes in it* | **trillions of** *We've made this mistake trillions of times before.*
3 *BrE old use* the number 1,000,000,000,000,000,000 —**trillionth** *adj* —**trillionth** *n* [C]

tri·lo·bite /ˈtraɪləbaɪt/ *n* [C] a type of FOSSIL of a small sea creature

tril·o·gy /ˈtrɪlədʒi/ *n* (*plural* **trilogies**) [C] a series of three plays, books etc that are about the same people or subject: *part 2 of a trilogy*

trim¹ /trɪm/ ●●○ *v* (**trimmed, trimming**) [T]
1 CUT to make something look neater by cutting small pieces off it: *Pete was trimming the lawn around the roses.* | *I have my hair trimmed every six weeks.* | **trim sth away/off** *Trim away any excess glue with a knife.* THESAURUS ➤ CUT
2 REDUCE to reduce a number, amount, or the size of something: *We need to **trim costs** by £500m.* | *The bill would trim the number of immigrants to the US.* | **trim sth**

from/off sth *The company trimmed £46,000 from its advertising budget.*
3 DECORATE to decorate something, especially clothes, by adding things that look pretty: **be trimmed with sth** *a dress trimmed with lace | At Christmas, the whole family helps trim the tree.* GRAMMAR **Trim** is often passive in this meaning.
4 SAIL to move the sails of a boat in order to go faster
trim sth ↔ **back** *phr v* to make something shorter or smaller: *Trim the stems back carefully. | Most airlines have trimmed back their operations.*
trim down *phr v* to lose weight deliberately: *Anne has trimmed down from 22 stone to 18.*

trim² *adj* **1** a person who is trim is thin in an attractive healthy way SYN **slim**: *I play tennis to keep trim. | a* ***trim figure*** **2** neat and well cared for: *trim suburban gardens*

trim³ *n* **1** [singular] when something is cut to make it look neater: *My beard needs a trim.* **2 in (good) trim** *informal* in good condition: **keep/get (sth) in trim** *If you want to get in trim for summer, try aerobics. | My job was to keep the garden in trim.* **3** [singular, U] additional decoration on a car, piece of clothing etc: *suede sandals with gold trim*

tri·ma·ran /ˈtraɪməræn/ *n* [C] a type of sailing boat with three HULLS

tri·mes·ter /trɪˈmestə $ traɪˈmestər/ *n* [C] **1** *AmE* one of three periods of equal length that the school year is divided into SYN **term** *BrE* **2** one of the three-month periods of PREGNANCY

trim·mer /ˈtrɪmə $ -ər/ *n* [C] a machine for cutting the sides of HEDGES, LAWNS etc

trim·mings /ˈtrɪmɪŋz/ *n* [plural] **1 with all the trimmings** food that is served with all the trimmings is enjoyable because it is served with lots of extra types of food: *a roast chicken platter with all the trimmings* **2** small pieces that are left after you have cut something larger: *hedge trimmings* **3** pieces of material used to decorate clothes: *a hat with fur trimmings*

trin·i·ty /ˈtrɪnəti/ *n* **the Trinity** (*also* **the Holy Trinity**) in the Christian religion, the union of Father, Son, and Holy Spirit in one God

trin·ket /ˈtrɪŋkɪt/ *n* [C] a piece of jewellery or a small pretty object that is not valuable

tri·o /ˈtriːəʊ $ ˈtriːoʊ/ *n* (*plural* **trios**) [C] **1** a group of three people or things: **[+of]** *He was met by a trio of smiling executives. | a classical guitar trio* (=three musicians playing together) **2** a piece of music for three performers → **DUET¹**, **QUARTET**

trip¹ /trɪp/ ●●● S2 W2 *n*
1 [C] a visit to a place that involves a journey, for pleasure or a particular purpose: **[+to]** *Did you enjoy your trip to Disneyland?* | **[+from]** *The Palace is only a short trip from here.* | **business/school/shopping etc trip** *a business trip to Japan | Two lucky employees won a round-the-world trip.* | **coach/boat/bus trip** *a boat trip up the Thames* | **day trip** (=a pleasure trip done in one day) | *It's an 80-mile* ***round trip*** (=a journey to a place and back again) *to Exeter.* | **return trip** (=when you are travelling back to where you started) | *I'm afraid you've had a* ***wasted trip*** (=a trip in which you do not achieve your purpose), *Mr Burgess has already left.* | **go on/take a trip** *We're thinking of taking a trip to the mountains. | He was unable to* ***make*** *the* ***trip*** *to accept the award.* THESAURUS ▸ JOURNEY
2 [C] *informal* the strange mental experiences someone has when they take a drug such as LSD: *a bad trip*
3 [singular] *AmE informal* a person or experience that is amusing and unusual: *Julie's such a trip!*
4 [C] an act of falling as a result of hitting something with your foot: *accidents caused by trips or falls* → **EGO TRIP**, → **guilt trip** at **GUILT¹**(4), → **ROUND-TRIP¹**

GRAMMAR: Comparison

trip
• You **go on a trip** somewhere: *We went on a trip to Morocco.* ✗ Don't say: *go for a trip somewhere*

walk
• You **go for a walk** somewhere: *Miranda went for a long walk on the beach.*

drive
• You **go for a drive** somewhere: *We went for a drive in the mountains.*

trip² ●●○ *v* (**tripped**, **tripping**)
1 FALL (*also* **trip up**) [I] to hit something with your foot by accident so that you fall or almost fall SYN **stumble**: *He* ***tripped and fell.*** | **[+over]** *Clary tripped over a cable and broke his foot.* | **[+on]** *He tripped on the bottom step.*
2 MAKE SB FALL (*also* **trip up**) [T] to make someone fall by putting your foot in front of them when they are moving: *Baggio was tripped inside the penalty area.*
3 SWITCH ON [T] to switch on a piece of electrical equipment by accident: *An intruder had tripped the alarm.*
4 WALK/DANCE [I always + adv/prep] *literary* to walk, run, or dance with quick light steps: *a little girl tripping down the lane*
5 trip off the tongue to be easy to say or pronounce: *Monofluorophosphate! It doesn't exactly trip off the tongue, does it?*
6 DRUG (*also* **trip out**) [I] *informal* to experience the mental effects of a drug such as LSD: *They must have been tripping.*
7 trip the light fantastic to dance – used humorously
trip up *phr v*
1 to make a mistake, or to force someone to make a mistake by tricking them: *On his latest album, Kowalski trips up attempting more modern songs.* | **trip sb ↔ up** *an attempt to trip up the prime minister on policy issues*
2 to hit something with your foot so that you fall, or to make someone do this: **trip sb ↔ up** *He chased the thief, tripped him up, and grabbed the camera.*

tri·par·tite /traɪˈpɑːtaɪt $ -ˈpɑːr-/ *adj* [only before noun] *formal* involving three parts, groups etc: **tripartite agreement/talks etc** *a tripartite agreement between France, Britain, and Germany*

tripe /traɪp/ *n* [U] **1** the stomach of a cow or pig, used as food: *tripe and onions* **2** *especially BrE informal* something someone says or writes that is stupid or untrue: *What Charles was saying was utter tripe.*

ˈtrip hop *n* [U] a type of dance music played with electronic instruments that has a slow beat

trip·le¹ /ˈtrɪpəl/ ●●○ *adj* [only before noun], *predeterminer*
1 having three parts or involving three groups, people, events etc → **double**: *a triple murder investigation | a triple bill of horror movies | the triple world champion | a triple bypass heart operation*
2 three times more than a particular number → **double**: *The rail system has triple the average number of accidents.*

triple² ●●○ *v* [I,T] to increase by three times as much, or to make something do this → **double**: *The company has* ***tripled in size.*** | *We expect to triple our profits next year.*
THESAURUS ▸ INCREASE

triple³ *n* [C] **1** a hit of the ball in baseball that allows the BATTER to get to the third BASE **2** three turns of your body in a sport such as ICE SKATING or GYMNASTICS

ˌTriple ˈCrown, the 1 a title for winning all three of a set of important events in various sports **a)** in British horse-racing, the title for winning the St Leger, the Derby, and the Two Thousand Guineas **b)** in American horse-racing, the title for winning the Kentucky Derby, the Preakness, and the Belmont Stakes **c)** in Rugby Union, the title for beating all three of the other home countries **2** a title given to the baseball player who is the best hitter in his LEAGUE in three different categories (CATEGORY)

ˌtriple-dip reˈcession *n* [C] a situation in which an economy goes into RECESSION, and then twice begins to get better but goes back into recession again

ˈtriple jump *n* [singular] an ATHLETICS event in which you jump with one foot, then with your other foot, and finally

T

with both feet —**triple jumper** *n* [C]: *Triple jumper Edwards set a new world record.*

trip·let /ˈtrɪplɪt/ *n* [C] one of three children born at the same time to the same mother → **twin**

trip·lex /ˈtrɪpleks $ ˈtrɪ-, ˈtraɪ-/ *n* [C] *AmE* a house containing three separate apartments → **duplex**

trip·li·cate /ˈtrɪplɪkət/ *n* **in triplicate** if a document is in triplicate, there are three copies of it → **duplicate**: *Is it really necessary to complete the forms in triplicate?*

tri·pod /ˈtraɪpɒd $ -pɑːd/ *n* [C] a support with three legs, used for a piece of equipment, camera etc → see picture at STAND[2]

trip·per /ˈtrɪpə $ -ər/ *n* [C] a DAY TRIPPER

trip·py /ˈtrɪpi/ *adj informal* strange, like something that someone experiences when they take a drug such as LSD: *trippy lighting effects*

trip·tan /ˈtrɪptæn/ *n* [C] a type of drug used to treat MIGRAINES (=very bad pain in your head)

trip·tych /ˈtrɪptɪk/ *n* [C] *technical* a religious picture painted on three pieces of wood that are joined together

trip·wire /ˈtrɪpˌwaɪə $ -waɪr/ *n* [C] a wire stretched across the ground as part of a trap

tri·state /ˈtraɪsteɪt/ *adj* [only before noun] *AmE* relating to a group of three states in the US: *It's one of the best restaurants in the tristate area.*

trite /traɪt/ *adj* a trite remark, idea etc is boring, not new, and insincere: *Her remarks sounded trite and ill-informed.* —**triteness** *n* [U] —**tritely** *adv*: *tritely familiar replies*

tri·umph[1] /ˈtraɪəmf/ ●●○ *n*
1 [C] an important victory or success after a difficult struggle: *Winning the championship is a great* ***personal triumph***. | **[+for]** *a tremendous* ***diplomatic triumph*** *for France* | **[+over]** *the triumph over hardship* THESAURUS ▸ VICTORY
2 [U] a feeling of pleasure and satisfaction that you get from victory or success: *a shout of triumph* | **in triumph** *He rode in triumph to the Tsar.*
3 [singular] a very successful example of something: **[+of]** *The gallery is a triumph of design.*

T

triumph[2] *v* [I] *formal* to gain a victory or success after a difficult struggle: **[+over]** *In the end, good shall triumph over evil.* THESAURUS ▸ WIN

tri·um·phal /traɪˈʌmfəl/ *adj* [only before noun] done or made to celebrate a victory: *a triumphal procession* | *a triumphal arch*

tri·um·phal·is·m /traɪˈʌmfəlɪzəm/ *n* [U] behaviour which shows that someone is too proud of their success and too pleased about the defeat of their opponents – used to show disapproval: *charges of triumphalism*

tri·um·phant /traɪˈʌmfənt/ ●○○ *adj*
1 showing pleasure and pride because of a victory or success: *I feel exhausted, but also triumphant.* | **triumphant look/smile/expression etc** *a triumphant grin*
2 having gained a victory or success: *the triumphant army* | *The Nationalists* ***emerged triumphant*** *from the political crisis.* —**triumphantly** *adv*: *'I've got a job,' she announced triumphantly.*

tri·um·vir·ate /traɪˈʌmvərət/ *n* [C] *formal* a group of three very powerful people

triv·et /ˈtrɪvɪt/ *n* [C] a metal support used to hold a hot dish

triv·i·a /ˈtrɪviə/ *n* [plural] **1** detailed facts about history, sport, famous people etc: *a selection of golfing trivia* | *a trivia quiz* **2** unimportant or useless details: *meaningless trivia*

triv·i·al /ˈtrɪviəl/ ●●○ *adj* not serious, important, or valuable: **trivial problem/matter/complaint etc** *We were punished for the most trivial offences.* | *a trivial sum* | *Her feelings for Simon seemed* ***trivial by comparison***. THESAURUS ▸ UNIMPORTANT

triv·i·al·i·ty /ˌtrɪviˈæləti/ *n* (*plural* **trivialities**) **1** [C] something that is not important at all: *Don't waste time on trivialities.* **2** [U] the fact of not being at all important or serious: *the triviality of daytime TV*

triv·i·al·ize (*also* **-ise** *BrE*) /ˈtrɪviəlaɪz/ *v* [T] to make something seem less important or serious than it really is – used to show disapproval: *The article trivializes the whole issue of equal rights.* | *The debate has been trivialized by the media.* —**trivialization** /ˌtrɪviəlaɪˈzeɪʃən $ -lə-/ *n* [U]

trod /trɒd $ trɑːd/ *v* the past tense of TREAD[1]

trod·den /ˈtrɒdn $ ˈtrɑːdn/ *v* the past participle of TREAD[1]

trog·lo·dyte /ˈtrɒglədaɪt $ ˈtrɑːg-/ *n* [C] someone who lived in a CAVE in PREHISTORIC times

troi·ka /ˈtrɔɪkə/ *n* [C] *formal* a group of three people, countries etc: *the ruling troika*

Tro·jan /ˈtrəʊdʒən $ ˈtroʊ-/ *n old-fashioned* **work like a Trojan** to work very hard

troll[1] /trəʊl, trɒl $ troʊl/ *n* [C] **1** an imaginary creature in stories that looks like an ugly person **2** someone who leaves offensive or upsetting messages on the Internet, just in order to get a reaction

troll[2] *v* [I,T] **1** *AmE* to try to remove something from a river, ocean etc by pulling a rope, line etc through the water: *Ships towing huge magnets trolled the ocean floor.* | **[+for]** *I would troll for fish from the rowboat.* **2** *AmE* to try to obtain something by searching, asking people etc SYN **trawl** *BrE*: **troll (sth) for sth** *Stewart spent hours trolling the Web for information.* **3** to leave offensive or upsetting messages on the Internet, just in order to get a reaction

trol·ley /ˈtrɒli $ ˈtrɑːli/ ●○○ *n* [C]
1 *BrE* a large basket on wheels that you use for carrying bags, shopping etc SYN **cart** *AmE*: *a supermarket trolley*
2 *BrE* a small table on wheels used for serving food SYN **cart** *AmE*: *a drinks trolley* | *the sweet trolley* (=one for serving sweet dishes, cakes etc in a restaurant)
3 *AmE* an electric vehicle for carrying passengers which moves along the street on metal tracks SYN **tram** *BrE*
4 a TROLLEYBUS
5 be off your trolley *BrE informal humorous* to be crazy

TROLLEY

supermarket trolley *BrE*/ shopping cart *AmE*

trol·ley·bus /ˈtrɒlibʌs $ ˈtrɑː-/ *n* [C] a bus that uses power from electric wires above the street

trol·leyed /ˈtrɒlid $ -ˈtrɑː-/ *adj* [not before noun] *BrE informal* extremely drunk

trol·lop /ˈtrɒləp $ ˈtrɑː-/ *n* [C] *old-fashioned not polite* an offensive word for a sexually immoral woman

trom·bone /trɒmˈbəʊn $ trɑːmˈboʊn/ *n* [C] a large metal musical instrument that you play by blowing into it and sliding a long tube in and out to change the notes → see picture at BRASS —**trombonist** *n* [C]

troop[1] /truːp/ ●●● W2 *n*
1 troops [plural] soldiers in an organized group: *Both countries agreed to* ***withdraw*** *their* ***troops***. | **French/UN/government etc troops** *Johnson took the popular step of* ***sending in*** *American* ***troops***. | ***troops stationed in*** *Hawaii*
2 troop movement/withdrawal etc movements etc of troops: *increased* ***troop deployment*** (=when troops are moved to places where they are needed)
3 [C] a group of soldiers, especially on horses or in TANKS: *the troop commander*
4 [C] a group of people or animals that do something together: *a troop of monkeys* | *a Scout troop* → **TROUPE**

troop[2] *v* [I always + adv/prep] *informal* if a group of people troop somewhere, they walk there together in a way that shows they are tired or bored: **[+off/along/out etc]** *After rehearsals, we'd all troop off to the cafeteria.*

ˈtroop ˌcarrier *n* [C] a ship, aircraft, or vehicle used for moving soldiers

troop·er /ˈtruːpə $ -ər/ *n* **1** [C] a soldier of the lowest

rank in the part of the army that uses TANKS or horses
2 [C] a member of a state police force in the US
3 swear like a trooper *old-fashioned* to swear a lot

ˌTrooping the ˈColour a traditional British ceremony held every year in London on the official birthday of the queen or king. Many soldiers on horses or on foot march across Horse Guards Parade carrying their 'colours' (=flags), and they SALUTE the queen or king as they march past. It is a very colourful ceremony and is popular especially with tourists.

troop·ship /ˈtruːpˌʃɪp/ *n* [C] a ship used for moving soldiers

trope /trəʊp $ troʊp/ *n* [C] *technical* words, phrases, images etc that are used for an unusual or interesting effect: *cinematic tropes*

tro·phy /ˈtrəʊfi $ ˈtroʊ-/ ●●○ *n* (*plural* **trophies**) [C]
1 a large object such as a silver cup or plate that someone receives as a prize for winning a competition: *walls lined with banners and athletic trophies* | **Football League/Masters/Heisman etc Trophy** (=the name given to a particular competition for which the prize is a trophy) → see picture at CUP[1]
2 something that you keep to prove your success in something, especially in war or hunting: *A lion's head was among the trophies of his African trip.*
3 trophy wife *informal* a young beautiful woman who is married to a rich successful man who is much older than her – used to show disapproval
4 trophy property/artwork/client etc *informal* a property, piece of art, CLIENT etc that is very desirable and gives a lot of STATUS to the person who has it: *a rare opportunity to acquire a trophy property in this prestigious location*

trop·ic /ˈtrɒpɪk $ ˈtrɑː-/ *n* **1** [C] one of the two imaginary lines around the world, either the Tropic of Cancer which is 23½° north of the EQUATOR, or the Tropic of Capricorn which is 23½° south of the equator **2 the tropics** the hottest part of the world, which is around the EQUATOR: *plant species found in the tropics*

trop·i·cal /ˈtrɒpɪkəl $ ˈtrɑː-/ ●●○ *adj*
1 coming from or existing in the hottest parts of the world: *the* ***tropical rain forests*** | *tropical fruit* | **tropical diseases/medicine** (=diseases that are common in hot countries or the study of these diseases)
2 weather that is tropical is very hot and wet: *a steamy tropical night*

trot[1] /trɒt $ trɑːt/ ●○○ *v* (**trotted**, **trotting**)
1 [I] if a horse trots, it moves fairly quickly with each front leg moving at the same time as the opposite back leg → **canter**, **gallop**
2 [I always + adv/prep] if a person or animal trots, they run fairly slowly, taking short regular steps: *She came trotting down the steps from the library.* THESAURUS ▸ RUN
3 [I always + adv/prep] *informal* to walk or go somewhere, especially fairly quickly: *He trotted off and came back a couple of minutes later, holding a parcel.*

trot sth ↔ **out** *phr v informal* to give opinions, excuses, reasons etc that you have used too many times and that do not seem sincere: *Steve trotted out the same old excuses.*

trot[2] *n*
1 HORSE **a)** [singular] the movement of a horse at trotting speed: *Our horses slowed to a trot.* **b)** [C] a ride on a horse at trotting speed
2 on the trot *BrE informal* **a)** one directly following another: *The class has been cancelled three weeks on the trot now.* **b)** busy doing something SYN **on the go**: *I've been on the trot all day.*
3 SLOW RUN [singular] a fairly slow way of running in which you take short regular steps: *She* ***broke into a trot*** *(=started running slowly) and hurried on ahead of us.*
4 STUDENTS' ANSWERS [C] *AmE* a book of notes or answers used by students, especially to cheat in tests SYN **crib**
5 the trots *informal* DIARRHOEA

troth /trəʊθ $ trɒːθ, trɑːθ, troʊθ/ *n* → **plight your troth** at PLIGHT[2]

Trot·sky·ite /ˈtrɒtskiaɪt $ ˈtrɑːt-/ (*also* **Trot·sky·ist** /-skiɪst/) *n* [C] someone who believes in the political ideas of Leon Trotsky, especially that the working class should take control of the state —**Trotskyite** *adj*

trot·ter /ˈtrɒtə $ ˈtrɑːtər/ *n* [C] a pig's foot, especially when cooked and used as food

trou·ba·dour /ˈtruːbədɔː, -dʊə $ -dɔːr, -dʊr/ *n* [C] a type of singer and poet who travelled around the PALACES and castles of Southern Europe in the 12th and 13th centuries

troub·le[1] /ˈtrʌbəl/ ●●● S1 W2 *n*
1 PROBLEMS [U] (*also* **troubles** [plural]) problems or difficulties: **[+with]** *We're having a lot of trouble with the new computer system.* | *Recent stock market losses point to trouble ahead.* THESAURUS ▸ PROBLEM
2 BAD POINT [singular] used when saying what is bad about a person or situation or what causes problems: ***The trouble with*** *you* ***is that*** *you don't listen.* | ***The trouble is*** *there are too many people and not enough places.* | *But no one ever remembers –* ***that's the trouble****.* | *You never think,* ***that's*** *your* ***trouble****.*
3 BAD SITUATION **in/into/out of trouble a)** if someone or something is in trouble, they are in a situation with a lot of problems: *He admitted that their marriage was in trouble.* | **get/run into trouble** *The company ran into trouble when it tried to expand too quickly.* | **in serious/deep trouble** *The economy was in serious trouble.* | *the dangers of trying to borrow your way out of trouble* **b)** if someone is in trouble, they have done something which someone will punish them for or be angry about: **in deep/big trouble** *We'll be in big trouble if Mr Elliott finds out.* | **in trouble with sb** *I think I'm in trouble with Dad.* | *I didn't say anything because I didn't want to* ***get into trouble****.* | **keep/stay out of trouble** *I hope Tim stays out of trouble this year.*
4 FIGHTING [U] fighting, violence, or violent behaviour: *If the kids start to* ***cause trouble****, ask them to move on.* | *A handful of people came* ***looking for trouble****.* | *If you* ***start*** *any* ***trouble****, you'll regret it.* | *There was* ***crowd trouble*** *before the match.*
5 WORRIES [U] (*also* **troubles** [plural]) problems in your life which you are worried about: *He* ***poured out*** *all his* ***troubles*** *to me* (=told me all about his problems).
6 EFFORT [U] an amount of effort and time that is needed to do something: **take the trouble to do sth** (=make a special effort to do something) *The teacher* ***took the trouble*** *to learn all our names on the first day.* | *They've obviously* ***gone to*** *a lot of* ***trouble*** *to arrange everything.* | **save sb the trouble (of doing sth)** *If you'd asked me first, I could have saved you the trouble.* | *I find that making my own clothes is* ***more trouble than it's worth*** (=takes too much time and effort).
7 no trouble used to say politely that you are happy to do something for someone: *'Are you sure you don't mind?' 'It's no trouble.'* | *The kids were no trouble* (=used to say you were happy to look after them because they were well-behaved).
8 HEALTH [U] a problem that you have with your health: *He* ***has trouble with*** *his breathing.* | **heart/stomach/skin etc trouble** *He suffers from back trouble.* THESAURUS ▸ ILLNESS
9 MACHINE/SYSTEM [U] when something is wrong with a machine, vehicle, or system: *engine trouble* | **[+with]** *He had to retire from the race because of trouble with the gearbox.*

GRAMMAR: Countable or uncountable?

- **Trouble** is usually used as an uncountable noun: *Are you having trouble with your car?* ✗ Don't say: *Are you having a trouble with your car?* **Trouble** is not used with 'a'.
- The plural form **troubles** is used when talking about worries or bad experiences that someone has: *Tell me about all your troubles.*

COLLOCATIONS

VERBS

have trouble *He is having trouble getting his message across to the voters.*

have no trouble *We had no trouble finding her house.*
cause trouble *I hope the delay hasn't caused you any trouble.*
there is trouble *There was some trouble at her office, but she didn't say what it was.*
mean/spell trouble (=mean there will be trouble) | **be asking for trouble** (=be silly or dangerous) | **avoid trouble**

ADJECTIVES

big/great trouble *High interest rates spell big trouble for homeowners.*
terrible trouble *I've been having terrible trouble sleeping.*
endless trouble (=a lot of trouble) *They had endless trouble with the water supply.*
serious trouble | **teething troubles** *BrE* (=small problems that you have when you first start doing a new job or using a new system)

PHRASES

what the trouble is *A couple of nurses rushed into the room to see what the trouble was.*
without any/much trouble (=easily)

trouble² ●●○ *v* [T]
1 WORRY if a problem troubles you, it makes you feel worried or upset: *There is one thing that's been troubling me.* | *They have been* ***deeply troubled*** *by the allegations.* | *His conscience troubled him.*
2 INCONVENIENCE *formal* to say something or ask someone to do something which may use or waste their time or upset them SYN **bother**: *I promise not to trouble you again.* | **trouble sb with sth** *I don't want to trouble the doctor with it.* | *I won't trouble you with the details.*
3 may I trouble you?/sorry to trouble you *spoken formal* used when politely asking someone to do something for you or give you something: *Sorry to trouble you, but could you tell me the way to the station, please?* | *May I trouble you for the salt?*
4 don't trouble yourself *spoken* used to politely tell someone not to help you: *Please don't trouble yourself. I can manage.*
5 not trouble to do sth to not do something because it needs too much effort: *They never troubled to ask me what I would like.* | *Luke didn't trouble to hide his disgust.*

REGISTER
In everyday English, people usually say **not bother to do sth** rather than **not trouble to do sth**: *They didn't* ***bother to*** *ask me what I thought.*

6 HEALTH PROBLEM if a medical problem troubles you, it causes you pain or problems: *He is still being troubled by an ankle injury.*
7 CAUSE PROBLEMS to cause someone problems or difficulties: *They look good enough to trouble most teams in the competition.*

troub·led /ˈtrʌbəld/ ●○○ *adj*
1 worried or anxious: **troubled face/eyes/look** | *Benson* ***looked troubled*** *when he heard the news.* THESAURUS ▸ WORRIED
2 having many problems: *These are* ***troubled times*** *for the coal industry.* | *the troubled electronics company* | **troubled marriage/relationship**
3 troubled waters a difficult situation, especially where there is a lot of disagreement and problems: *We don't want to enter the troubled waters of race and religion.* | **pour oil on troubled waters** (=try to make an angry situation calmer)

ˌtrouble-ˈfree *adj* without any problems: *We ensure that you have a trouble-free and enjoyable holiday.*

troub·le·mak·er /ˈtrʌbəlˌmeɪkə $ -ər/ *n* [C] someone who deliberately causes problems or arguments: *a handful of troublemakers who are damaging the club's reputation*

troub·le·shoot·er /ˈtrʌbəlʃuːtə $ -ər/ *n* [C] **1** an independent person who is employed to come into an organization to deal with serious problems **2** computer software which asks you a series of questions to try to find the cause of a computer problem, and suggests possible solutions —**troubleshooting** *n* [U]

troub·le·some /ˈtrʌbəlsəm/ ●○○ *adj* causing problems, in an annoying way: *a troublesome child* | *troublesome itching*

ˈtrouble ˌspot *n* [C] a place where trouble often happens, especially war or violence: *She's reported from many of the world's trouble spots.*

troub·ling /ˈtrʌblɪŋ/ *adj* worrying: *This incident raises troubling questions.*

trough /trɒf $ trɒːf/ *n* [C]
1 CONTAINER a long narrow open container that holds water or food for animals: *a horse trough*
2 LOW POINT a short period of low activity, low prices etc OPP **peak**: **[+of]** *The graph showed peaks and troughs of activity.*
3 WAVES the hollow area between two waves
4 WEATHER *technical* a long area of fairly low pressure between two areas of high pressure
5 have your nose/snout in the trough *BrE* if people have their noses in the trough, they are involved in something which they hope will get them a lot of money or political power – used to show disapproval

trounce /traʊns/ *v* [T] to defeat someone completely: *We were trounced 13–0.* THESAURUS ▸ BEAT

troupe /truːp/ *n* [C] a group of singers, actors, dancers etc who work together

troup·er /ˈtruːpə $ -ər/ *n* [C] *informal* **1** someone who has a lot of experience of work in the entertainment business **2** someone who works hard and keeps trying, even when the situation is difficult

trou·ser /ˈtraʊzə $ -ər/ *v* [T] *BrE informal* to get a large amount of money – used to show disapproval: *Even though he has in effect been sacked, he will trouser a £150,000 bonus.*

ˈtrouser press *n* [C] *BrE* a piece of equipment that you can keep your trousers in to keep them flat and smooth, often found in hotel rooms

This graph shows how common the nouns **trousers** and **pants** are in British and American English.

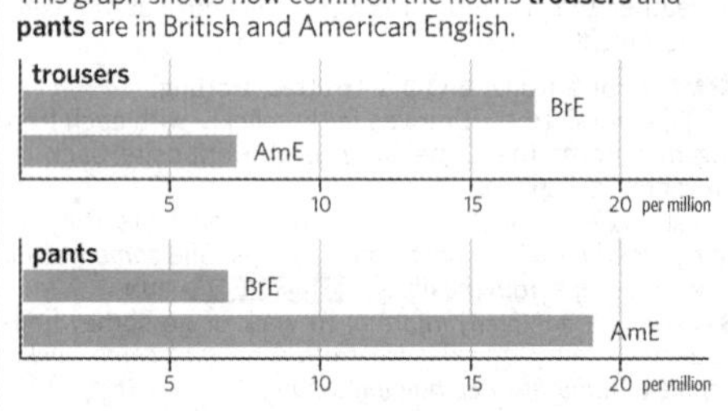

In British English **trousers** is used to mean 'a piece of clothing that covers the lower half of your body, with a separate part fitting over each leg'. In American English **pants** is generally used for this meaning. **Pants** is commonly used in British English to mean 'underwear', but Americans use the word **underwear**.

trou·sers /ˈtraʊzəz $ -ərz/ ●●● S2 *n* [plural] *especially BrE* a piece of clothing that covers the lower half of your body, with a separate part fitting over each leg SYN **pants** *AmE*: *His trousers were slightly too short.* | *I need a new* ***pair of trousers*** *for work.* —**trouser** *adj* [only before noun]: *The tickets are in my trouser pocket.* → **wear the trousers** at WEAR¹(7), → **catch sb with their trousers down** at CATCH¹(6)

ˈtrouser suit *n* [C] *BrE* a woman's suit consisting of a jacket and matching trousers SYN **pant suit** *AmE*

trous·seau /ˈtruːsəʊ, truːˈsəʊ $ -soʊ/ *n* (*plural* **trousseaus** *or* **trousseaux** /-səʊz $ -soʊz/) [C] *old-fashioned* the clothes etc that a woman brings with her when she marries

trout /traʊt/ ●○○ *n*
1 (*plural* **trout**) [C,U] a common river-fish, often used for food, or the flesh of this fish
2 old trout *BrE spoken* an unpleasant or annoying old person, especially a woman

trove /trəʊv $ troʊv/ *n* → TREASURE TROVE

trow·el /ˈtraʊəl/ *n* [C] **1** a garden tool like a very small SPADE → see picture at GARDEN **2** a small tool with a flat blade, used for spreading CEMENT on bricks etc **3 lay it on with a trowel** *BrE informal* to say things that make something seem much better, worse etc than it really is SYN **exaggerate**: *'I really don't feel too good,' I croaked, laying it on with a trowel.*

troy weight /ˈtrɔɪ weɪt/ *n* [U] a system of measuring weights in Britain and the US, used especially for weighing gold, silver etc

tru·an·cy /ˈtruːənsi/ *n* [U] when students deliberately stay away from school without permission: *the school's truancy rate*

tru·ant /ˈtruːənt/ *n* [C] **1** a student who stays away from school without permission: *persistent truants* **2 play truant** *BrE* to stay away from school without permission SYN **skive** *BrE*, **play hooky** *AmE* —**truant** *v* [I] —**truant** *adj AmE: Nick was truant seven days this month.*

truce /truːs/ ●○○ *n* [C] an agreement between enemies to stop fighting or arguing for a short time, or the period for which this is arranged → **ceasefire**: *They agreed to* ***call a truce***. | **[+with/between]** *There was an* ***uneasy truce*** *between Alex and Dave over dinner.*

TRUCKS

breakdown truck *BrE*/ towtruck *AmE*

fire engine/fire truck *AmE*

fork-lift truck

pick-up truck *AmE*

truck/lorry *BrE*

truck¹ /trʌk/ ●●● S2 W3 *n* [C]
1 a large road vehicle used to carry goods SYN **lorry** *BrE*: *a* ***truck driver*** | **pick-up/fork-lift/delivery etc truck** (=large vehicles used for particular purposes) *His car was taken away on the back of a breakdown truck.*
2 *BrE* a railway vehicle that is part of a train and carries goods SYN **car** *AmE*: *coal trucks*
3 a simple piece of equipment on wheels used to move heavy objects
4 have/hold/want no truck with sb/sth to refuse to be involved with someone or to accept an idea

truck² *v AmE* **1** [T] (*also* **truck in**) to take something somewhere by truck: *They ordered sand to be trucked in from the desert.* **2** [I always + adv/prep] *spoken* to go, move, or travel quickly: *We were trucking on down to Jack's place.* **3 get trucking** *spoken* to leave **4 keep on trucking** *spoken* used to encourage someone to continue what they are doing, especially in the 1970s

truck·er /ˈtrʌkə $ -ər/ *n* [C] *AmE* a truck driver

ˈtruck farm *n* [C] *AmE* an area for growing vegetables and fruit for sale SYN **market garden** *BrE*

truck·ing /ˈtrʌkɪŋ/ *n* [U] *AmE* the business of taking goods from place to place by road

truck·load /ˈtrʌkləʊd $ -loʊd/ *n* [C] the amount that fills a truck: **[+of]** *a truckload of oranges*

ˈtruck stop *n* [C] *AmE* a cheap place to eat on a main road, used mainly by truck drivers

truc·u·lent /ˈtrʌkjələnt/ *adj literary* bad-tempered and always willing to argue with people SYN **awkward**: *a truculent attitude* —**truculently** *adv* —**truculence** *n* [U]

trudge /trʌdʒ/ *v* [I always + adv/prep] to walk with slow heavy steps, especially because you are tired or it is difficult to walk: *We trudged home through the snow.* THESAURUS ▸ WALK —**trudge** *n* [singular]: *the long trudge back up the hill*

true¹ /truː/ ●●● S1 W1 *adj*
1 NOT FALSE based on facts and not imagined or invented OPP **false** → **truly**, **truth**: **it is true (that)** *It's not true that I'm going to marry him.* | *No, honestly, it's a* ***true story***. | *Students decide if statements are* ***true or false***. | **[+of]** *The same is true of all political parties.* | **[+for]** *This is especially true for old people.* | ***It's*** *generally* ***true to say that*** *fewer people are needed nowadays.* | *The results appear to* ***hold true*** (=still be correct) *for other countries.* → **too good to be true** at GOOD¹(24), → **not ring true** at RING²(5)
2 REAL [only before noun] the true nature of something is its real nature, which may be hidden or not known SYN **real**: **true value/cost etc (of sth)** *The house was sold for only a fraction of its true value.* | *We need to understand the* ***true extent*** *of the problem.* | **true nature/meaning/identity etc (of sth)** *She wasn't aware of the true nature of their relationship.* | *She managed to conceal her* ***true feelings***. | *After a couple of days she showed her* ***true self*** (=real character).
3 ADMITTING STH *especially spoken* used when you are admitting that something is correct, but saying that something else, often opposite, is also correct: *'He's very hard-working.' 'True, but I still don't think he's the right man for the job.'* | **it is true (that)** *It is true that there have been improvements in some areas.*
4 PROPER [only before noun] having all the qualities which a type of thing or person should have: *The heroine finally finds* ***true love***. | *She's been a* ***true friend*** *to me.* | *It's an amateur sport* ***in the true sense of the word*** (=with the exact meaning of this word). THESAURUS ▸ GENUINE
5 come true if wishes, dreams etc come true, they happen in the way that someone has said or hoped that they would: *The prediction seems to have come true.* → **be a dream come true** at DREAM¹(5)
6 LOYAL faithful and loyal to someone, whatever happens: **[+to]** *Throughout the whole ordeal, she remained true to her husband.*
7 true to form/type used to say that someone is behaving in the bad way that you expect them to: *True to form, Henry turned up late.*
8 true to your word/principles etc behaving in the way you said you would or according to principles which you believe in: *He was true to his word and said nothing about it to Lisa.*
9 true to life/true-to-life a book, play, description etc that is true to life seems very real and natural SYN **realistic**: *The film is frighteningly true-to-life and very funny.*
10 (all/only) too true used to say that you know something is true, when you do not like it: *'It's not as easy as it looks.' 'Too true!'* | *It is only too true that people are judged by their accents.*
11 STRAIGHT/LEVEL [not before noun] *technical* fitted, placed, or formed in a way that is perfectly flat, straight, correct etc: *If the door's not true, it won't close properly.*
12 sb's aim is true if your aim is true, you hit the thing that you were throwing or shooting at
13 your true colours if you show your true colours, you do something which shows what your real attitudes and qualities are, especially when they are bad: **show/reveal**

your true colours *He was forced to reveal his true colours when asked how he would vote.*
14 (there's) many a true word spoken in jest *old-fashioned* used to say that when people are joking they sometimes say things that are true and important

THESAURUS

true based on real facts, and not imagined or invented: *The film was based on a true story.* | *Do you think the rumours are true?*
accurate based on facts and not containing any mistakes – used about descriptions, information, and numbers: *The measurements are accurate.* | *His assessment of the current economic situation is accurate.*
undeniable/indisputable definitely true, so that no one can argue or disagree about it: *It is indisputable that the situation has got worse.*
factual based on facts, or involving facts: *The court makes its decision based on factual evidence.* | *There is very little factual information about the incident.*
verifiable *formal* able to be proven to be true or correct: *The data was verifiable.*
it is a fact used when saying that something is definitely true: *It is a fact that women live longer than men.*
be the truth to be true – used when saying that someone is not lying: *What I told you was the truth.*
be the case if a situation is the case, that is the way the situation truly is: *It is certainly the case that crime rates are lower in Europe than in the US.*

true² *adv* **1** in an exact straight line: *The arrow flew straight and true to its target.* **2** *technical* if a type of animal breeds true, the young animals are exactly like their parents

true³ *n* **out of true** *BrE* not completely straight, level, or balanced: *The walls are slightly out of true.*

ˌtrue-ˈblue *adj* **1** *BrE informal* believing completely in the ideas of the British CONSERVATIVE PARTY: *a true-blue Tory* **2** *AmE* completely loyal to a person or idea: *a true-blue friend*

T

true-heart·ed /ˌtruː ˈhɑːtɪd◂ $ -ɑːr-/ *adj literary* faithful SYN **loyal**

ˌtrue-ˈlife *adj* [only before noun] based on real facts and not invented: *a true-life adventure*

ˌtrue ˈlove *n* [C] *literary* the person that you love

ˌtrue ˈnorth *n* [U] north as it appears on maps, calculated as a line through the centre of the Earth rather than by using the MAGNETIC POLE

truf·fle /ˈtrʌfəl/ *n* [C] **1** a black or light brown FUNGUS that grows underground, and is a very expensive food **2** a soft creamy sweet made with chocolate: *a rum truffle*

trug /trʌg/ *n* [C] *BrE* an open wooden container with a handle, used by gardeners for carrying flowers, fruit, vegetables etc

tru·is·m /ˈtruːɪzəm/ *n* [C] a statement that is clearly true, so that there is no need to say it: *His speech was just a collection of clichés and truisms.*

tru·ly /ˈtruːli/ ●●○ W3 *adv*
1 [+adj/adv] used to emphasize that the way you are describing something is really true SYN **really**: *His work is truly original.* | *Fawcett was a* ***truly remarkable*** *man.* | *a* ***truly great*** *work of medieval literature*
2 sincerely: *I am truly sorry.* | *She truly believed he was innocent.* | ***I can truly say*** *I've never enjoyed myself so much.*
3 in an exact or correct way: *Is it a truly representative sample?*
4 well and truly *especially spoken* completely: *We were well and truly beaten.* | *The party was well and truly over.*
5 really and truly *BrE spoken* used to emphasize that something is definitely or completely true: *I couldn't believe we were really and truly going at last.*
6 yours truly a) used at the end of a letter, before the signature **b)** *informal* used humorously to mean yourself: *So, yours truly was left to clean up.*

trump¹ /trʌmp/ *n* **1 trumps** [plural] (*also* **trump** *AmE*) the SUIT (=one of the four types of cards in a set) chosen to have a higher value than the other suits in a particular card game: *Hearts are trumps.* **2** [C] (*also* **trump card**) a card from the SUIT that has been chosen to have a higher value than the other suits in a particular game **3 trump card** something that you can do or use in a situation, which gives you an advantage: *But then he decided to* ***play*** *his* ***trump card*** (=use his advantage). | *They hold all the trump cards* (=have things which could give them an advantage). **4 come/turn up trumps** to provide what is needed, especially unexpectedly and at the last moment: *Paul came up trumps and managed to borrow a car for us.*

trump² *v* [T] **1** to play a trump that beats someone else's card in a game **2** to do better than someone else in a situation when people are competing with each other: *By wearing a simple but stunning dress, she had trumped them all.*

trump sth ↔ **up** *phr v* to use false information to make someone seem guilty of doing something wrong: *They had trumped the whole thing up to get rid of him.* —**trumped-up** *adj*: *Dissidents were routinely arrested on* ***trumped-up charges.***

trum·pet¹ /ˈtrʌmpɪt/ ●●○ *n* [C] a musical instrument that you blow into, which consists of a curved metal tube that is wide at the end, and three buttons you press to change the notes → **blow your own trumpet** at BLOW¹(19) → see picture at BRASS

trumpet² *v* **1** [T] to tell everyone about something that you are proud of, especially in an annoying way: *They are proudly trumpeting the fact that they are creating more jobs.* **2** [I] if an ELEPHANT trumpets, it makes a loud noise

trum·pet·er /ˈtrʌmpɪtə $ -ər/ *n* [C] someone who plays a trumpet

trun·cate /trʌŋˈkeɪt $ ˈtrʌŋkeɪt/ *v* [T] *formal* to make something shorter SYN **shorten**: *If the list is too long, it will be truncated by the computer.* | *The report is also available in a truncated version.* —**truncation** /trʌŋˈkeɪʃən/ *n* [U]

trun·cheon /ˈtrʌnʃən/ *n* [C] *especially BrE* a short thick stick that police officers carry as a weapon SYN **nightstick** *AmE*

trun·dle /ˈtrʌndl/ *v* [I always + adv/prep, T] to move slowly along on wheels, or to make something do this by pushing or pulling it: *Two large wagons trundled by.*

trunk /trʌŋk/ ●●● S3 *n* [C]
1 TREE the thick central woody stem of a tree: *He left his bicycle leaning against a* ***tree trunk.*** | **[+of]** *the trunk of an old oak tree* → see picture at TREE
2 CAR *AmE* the part at the back of a car where you can put bags, tools etc SYN **boot** *BrE*: *Put your suitcase in the trunk.*
3 ELEPHANT the very long nose of an ELEPHANT
4 CLOTHES **swim trunks** *AmE*, **swimming trunks** *BrE* [plural] a piece of clothing like very short trousers, worn by men for swimming
5 BOX a very large box made of wood or metal, in which clothes, books etc are stored or packed for travel → see picture at BOX¹
6 BODY *technical* the main part of your body, not including your head, arms, or legs SYN **torso** → SUITCASE

ˈtrunk call *n* [C] *BrE old-fashioned* a telephone call between places that are a long distance apart

ˈtrunk road *n* [C] *BrE* a main road used for travelling long distances

truss¹ /trʌs/ *v* [T] **1** (*also* **truss up**) to tie someone's arms, legs etc very firmly with rope so that they cannot move: *They trussed up their victim and left him for dead.* **2** to prepare a chicken, duck etc for cooking by tying its legs and wings into position

truss² *n* [C] **1** a special belt worn to support a HERNIA (=medical problem that affects the muscles below your stomach) **2** a frame supporting a roof or bridge

trust¹ /trʌst/ ●●● S1 W2 *n*
1 BELIEF [U] a strong belief in the honesty, goodness etc

of someone or something: *At first there was a* ***lack of trust*** *between them.* | *an agreement made on the basis of* ***mutual trust*** (=when people trust each other) | **put/place your trust in sb/sth** *You shouldn't put your trust in a man like that.* | *You* ***betrayed*** *your father's* ***trust*** (=did something bad even though he trusted you). → **breach of trust** at BREACH[1](3)
2 ORGANIZATION [C usually singular] an organization or group that has control over money that will be used to help someone else: *a charitable trust*
3 FINANCIAL ARRANGEMENT [C,U] an arrangement by which someone has legal control of your money or property, either until you are old enough to use it or to INVEST it for you: *The money your father left you will be* ***held in trust*** *until you are 21.* → TRUST FUND, UNIT TRUST
4 take sth on trust to believe that something is true without having any proof: *I just had to take it on trust that he would deliver the money.*
5 position of trust a job or position in which you have been given the responsibility of making important decisions
6 COMPANIES [C] *especially AmE* a group of companies that illegally work together to reduce competition and control prices: *anti-trust laws*

trust² ●●● S2 W3 *v* [T]
1 PEOPLE to believe that someone is honest or will not do anything bad or wrong OPP **distrust, mistrust**: *I just don't trust him.* | **trust sb to do sth** *Can they be trusted to look after the house?* | *I didn't trust myself not to say something rude, so I just kept quiet.* | **trust sb completely/implicitly** *He was a good driver and I trusted him implicitly.* | **not trust sb an inch/not trust sb as far as you can throw them** (=not trust someone at all)
2 FACTS/JUDGMENT to be sure that something is correct or right SYN **believe in, rely on**: *Can we trust these statistics?* | *I* ***trust*** *his* ***judgement*** *completely.* | ***Trust*** *your* ***instincts*** (=do what you feel is the right thing)!
3 THINGS to be sure that something will work properly SYN **rely on**: *Not trusting her voice, she shook her head.* | **trust sth to do sth** *You can't trust the trains to run on time.* | *He sat down suddenly, as if he didn't trust his legs to support him.*
4 trust you/him/them etc (to do sth)! *spoken* used to say that someone has behaved in a bad or stupid way that is typical of them: *Trust you to write down the wrong number!*
5 I trust (that) *spoken formal* used to say politely that you hope something is true: *I trust that from now on you will take greater precautions.* → TRUSTING, → **tried and trusted** at TRIED²

trust in sth/sb *phr v formal* to believe in someone or something: *We trust in God.*

trust to sth *phr v* to hope that what you want to happen will happen, because there is nothing you can do about it: *I'll just have to* ***trust to luck*** *that it works out okay.* | *I hope I may trust to your discretion.*

trust sb **with** sth *phr v* to let someone have something or have control over something, believing that they will be careful with it: *I wouldn't trust him with the keys.* | *I'd trust her with my life.*

trust·a·fa·ri·an /ˌtrʌstəˈfeəriən $ -ˈfer-/ *n* [C] *BrE informal* a young person from a rich family who does not need to work, but likes to pretend they are poor in order to be fashionable - often used to show disapproval

trust·ee /ˌtrʌˈstiː/ ●○○ *n* [C]
1 someone who has control of money or property that is in a TRUST for someone else
2 a member of a group that controls the money of a company, college, or other organization

trust·ee·ship /trʌsˈtiːʃɪp/ *n* **1** [C,U] the job of being a trustee **2** [U] the responsibility for governing an area, which is given to a country or countries by the United Nations

ˈtrust fund *n* [C] money belonging to someone that is controlled for them by a trustee

trust·ing /ˈtrʌstɪŋ/ *adj* **1** willing to believe that other people are good and honest: *a shy and trusting child* | **[+of]** *She's so trusting of people.* **2** involving trust: *a loving and* ***trusting relationship***

trust·wor·thy /ˈtrʌstˌwɜːði $ -ɜːr-/ ●○○ *adj* able to be trusted and depended on —**trustworthiness** *n* [U]

trust·y¹ /ˈtrʌsti/ *adj* [only before noun] *old-fashioned* a trusty weapon, vehicle, animal etc is one that you have had for a long time and can depend on - often used humorously SYN **reliable**: *He had his* ***trusty old*** *penknife with him.*

trusty² *n* (*plural* **trusties**) [C] *BrE* a prisoner who is given special jobs or rights, because they behave in a way that can be trusted

truth /truːθ/ ●●● S1 W2 *n*
1 TRUE FACTS **the truth** the true facts about something, rather than what is untrue, imagined, or guessed OPP **lie, falsehood, untruth**: *How do we know you're telling us the truth?* | **[+about]** *She hoped to find out the truth about her family.* | **[+behind]** *We'll never know the truth behind what happened.*
2 BEING TRUE [U] the state or quality of being true: **[+in]** *There was some truth in the accusations.* | **grain/element of truth** (=small amount of truth) *There wasn't a grain of truth in what he said.* | *There was an element of truth* (=a small amount of truth) *in what he said.* | *There is no truth in the rumour.*
3 IMPORTANT IDEAS [C usually plural] *formal* an important fact or idea that is accepted as being true: *The experience has taught us some* ***basic truths.*** | **an unhappy/unpleasant/unwelcome truth** (=an unpleasant or disappointing fact) *It is in his interest to hide unhappy truths about his agency's performance.*
4 in truth in fact SYN **really**: *Early independence leaders were in truth little better than rebels.*
5 if (the) truth be known/told used when telling someone the real facts about a situation, or your real opinion: *If the truth be known, I felt a little left out at school.*
6 to tell (you) the truth *spoken* used when giving your personal opinion or admitting something: *To tell the truth, I was frightened to death.*
7 nothing could be further from the truth used to say that something is definitely not true
8 the truth will out *old-fashioned* used to say that even if you try to stop people from knowing something, they will find out in the end → HALF-TRUTH, HOME TRUTH, → **the moment of truth** at MOMENT(16)

COLLOCATIONS

VERBS

tell the truth *It's better to tell the truth.*
speak the truth *He always spoke the truth, whether it was popular or not.*
know the truth *At last I knew the truth about my father's death.*
find out/discover/uncover the truth *She was determined to find out the truth.*
learn the truth *When she learns the truth, she may decide to help us.*
get at/to the truth *informal* (=discover the truth) | **reveal the truth** | **accept/admit the truth** | **be/come close to the truth** | **get the truth out of sb** (=make someone tell you the truth)

ADJECTIVES/NOUN + truth

the whole/full truth *Investors should have been told the whole truth.*
the simple/plain/naked truth (=the truth, with nothing added, left out, or hidden) *The simple truth is that there isn't enough money to pay for it.*
the sad/painful truth (=something that is true but that you regret) *She still misses him, and that's the sad truth.*
the awful/terrible/dreadful etc truth | **the honest truth** (=used to emphasize that you are telling the truth) | **the gospel truth** (=the complete truth)

PHRASES

the truth of the matter *The truth of the matter is that we don't know what really happened.*

COMMON ERRORS

⚠ Don't say 'say the truth'. Say **tell the truth**.

ˈtruth ˌdrug *BrE*, **ˈtruth ˌserum** *AmE n* [C,U] a drug that is supposed to make people tell the truth

truth·ful /ˈtruːθfəl/ *adj* **1** someone who is truthful does not usually tell lies SYN **honest**: *a truthful child | You and I must be truthful with each other.* **2** a truthful statement gives the true facts about something SYN **honest**: *I have only one question to ask you, and I want a truthful answer.* —**truthfully** *adv*: *Answer this question truthfully.* —**truthfulness** *n* [U]

try¹ /traɪ/ ●●● S1 W1 *v* (*past tense and past participle* **tried**, *present participle* **trying**, *third person singular* **tries**)

1 ATTEMPT [I,T] to take action in order to do something that you may not be able to do: *Let's have a rest and then we'll try again.* | **try to do sth** *He tried to control his voice.* | *She was trying not to cry.* | **try and do sth** *Try and take some form of daily exercise.* | **try hard/desperately (to do sth)** (=make a lot of effort to do something) *She dabbed at her face and tried hard not to sniff.* | *I* ***tried everything*** *to lose weight with no success.* | **try your best/hardest (to do sth)** (=make as much effort as possible to do something) *I tried my best to comfort her.* | *I* ***tried and tried*** (=kept making an effort) *and eventually I was offered a job.* | ***Try as he might*** (=as hard as he could), *he could not get the incident out of his mind.* | **it wasn't for lack/want of trying** (=used to say that if someone does not achieve something it is not because they have not tried) *They didn't get any goals, but it wasn't for lack of trying.* | **you couldn't do sth if you tried** (=used to say that someone does not have the skill or ability to do something) *She couldn't speak French if she tried.*

2 TEST/USE [T] to do or use something for a short while to discover if it is suitable, successful, enjoyable etc: *It works really well – you should try it.* | **try doing sth** *They decided they would try living in America for a while.* | *Try logging off and logging on again.* | **try sth new/different** (=do or use something that is different from what you usually do or use) *If I'm going out for a meal, I prefer to try something different.* | **try sth on sb/sth** *We tried the machine on hardwood and soft wood.* | **try sb on sth** *Petra's trying the baby on solid foods.* | **try sth for size** (=put on a piece of clothing or test something to find out if it is the correct size or suitable) *Always try a sleeping bag for size before you buy it.*

3 FOOD/DRINK [T] to taste food or drink to find out if you like it SYN **taste**: *Would you like to try some crisps?*

4 TRY TO FIND SB/STH [I,T] to go to a place or person, or call them, in order to find something or someone: *Sorry, he's not in. Would you like to try again later?* | *Let's try Mouncy Street. He could be there.*

5 DOOR/WINDOW [T] to attempt to open a door, window etc in order to see if it is locked: *She tried the door and it opened.* | *He* ***tried*** *the* ***handle*** *but the door was locked.*

6 LAW [T] to examine and judge a legal case, or someone who is thought to be guilty of a crime in a court → **trial**: **be tried for sth** *He was tried for attempting to murder his wife.* | *The defence argued that a regional court was not competent to try their case.* GRAMMAR **Try** is often passive in this meaning.

7 try sb's patience to make someone feel impatient → **trying**: *The programs take too long to load and try the patience of young pupils.*

8 try your hand at sth to try a new activity in order to see whether it interests you or whether you are good at it: *I tried my hand at water-skiing for the first time.*

9 try your luck to try to achieve something or get something you want, usually by taking a risk: *After the war my father went to Canada to try his luck at farming.*

10 try it on (with sb) *BrE spoken* **a)** to behave badly in order to find out how bad you can be before people become angry: *She is naughty, that one. She tries it on with me sometimes!* **b)** to attempt to start a sexual relationship with someone: *When I came back in, one of the men was trying it on with my wife!*

GRAMMAR: Comparison

try to do sth

• If you **try to do something**, you attempt to do it: *We must try to prevent this from happening again.*

try doing sth

• If you **try doing something**, you do it in order to find out if it is enjoyable or produces the result you want: *I've never tried bungee jumping.* | *Try using margarine instead of butter.*

GRAMMAR GUIDE ▸ VERBS

THESAURUS

try to take action in order to do something that you may not be able to do: *I tried to explain what was wrong.* | *He* ***tries hard*** *in class, but he's finding the work difficult.*

attempt to try to do something, especially something difficult. **Attempt** is more formal than **try** and is used especially in written English: *Any prisoner who attempts to escape will be shot.* | *He was attempting to climb one of the world's highest mountains.*

do your best to try as hard as you can to do something: *We will do our best to help them.*

make an effort to do sth to try to do something, when you find this difficult: *It is worth making an effort to master these skills.* | *She made a big effort to be nice to him.*

struggle to try very hard to do something that is very difficult, especially for a long time: *She's still struggling to give up smoking.* | *Many of these families are struggling to survive.*

strive *formal* to try very hard to achieve something: *The company must constantly strive for greater efficiency.*

endeavour *BrE*, **endeavor** *AmE* /ɪnˈdevə $ -ər/ *formal* to try hard to do something: *Each employee shall endeavour to provide customers with the best service possible.*

have a go/try *informal* to try to do something, especially when you are not sure that you will succeed: *I'm not very good at fixing taps, but I'll have a go.* | *Do you want to have another try?*

see if you can do sth *spoken* to try to do something – used when offering to do something, or suggesting that someone should do something: *I'll see if I can get you a ticket.* | *See if you can persuade her to come.*

try for sth *phr v BrE* to try and get something you really want, such as a job, a prize, or a chance to study somewhere: *I decided I must try for some paid work.* | *We have been* ***trying for a baby*** (=trying to have a baby) *for nine years.*

try sth ↔ **on** *phr v* to put on a piece of clothing to see if it fits you or if it suits you, especially in a shop: *Meg was trying on some red sandals.*

try sth ↔ **out** *phr v*

1 to test something such as a method or a piece of equipment to see if it is effective or works properly → **try-out**: *I'm trying out a new computer.*

2 to practise a skill in order to improve it: **[+on]** *She enjoyed trying her French out on Jean-Pierre.*

try out for sth *phr v AmE* to try to be chosen as a member of a team, for a part in a play etc SYN **audition for** → **tryout**: *In high school, I tried out for all the female leads.*

try² ●●● S3 *n* (*plural* **tries**) [C]

1 an attempt to do something: *She didn't manage to break the record, but it was a good try.* | *'You really think you can do that?' 'I'm going to* ***have a try****.'* | *'What are the chances for getting tickets now?' 'I guess I could* ***give it a try****.'* | *It might sound a ludicrous excuse but he thought it was* ***worth a try****.* | **on the first/second etc try** *Only half the students passed the test on their first try.*

2 a test of something to see if it is suitable or successful or to find out if you like it: *I decided to* ***give*** *modelling* ***a try****.* | *Wines from Apulia's ancient vineyards are well* ***worth a try****.*

T

3 four points won by putting the ball on the ground behind the opponents' GOAL LINE in RUGBY

try·ing /ˈtraɪ-ɪŋ/ ●○○ *adj* annoying or difficult in a way that makes you feel worried, tired etc: *That child is very trying.* | *The beginning of the show is often a* ***trying time*** *because of latecomers.* | *They do the best they can in* ***trying circumstances****.*

try·out /ˈtraɪaʊt/ *n* [C] *AmE* **1** a time when people who want to be in a sports team, activity etc are tested, so that the best can be chosen: *baseball tryouts* **2** a period of time during which a play, television show etc is shown to find out if people like it

ˈtry-out *n* [C] *BrE* a period of time spent trying a new method, tool, machine etc to see if it is useful

tryst /trɪst, traɪst/ *n* [C] *literary* a meeting between lovers in a secret place or at a secret time – often used humorously

tsar, **tzar, czar** /zɑː, tsɑː $ zɑːr, tsɑːr/ *n* [C] a male ruler of Russia before 1917

tsa·ri·na, **tzarina, czarina** /zɑːˈriːnə, tsɑː-/ *n* [C] a female ruler of Russia before 1917, or the wife of a tsar

tsar·ism, **tzarism, czarism** /ˈzɑːrɪzəm, ˈtsɑː-/ *n* [U] a system of government controlled by a tsar, especially the system in Russia before 1917 —**tsarist** *n* [C] —**tsarist** *adj*

tset·se fly, **tzetze fly** /ˈtetsi flaɪ, ˈtsetsi-, ˈsetsi-/ *n* [C] an African fly that sucks the blood of people and animals and spreads serious diseases

T-shirt, **tee-shirt** /ˈtiː ʃɜːt $ -ʃɜːrt/ ●●● S2 *n* [C] a soft shirt with short SLEEVES and no collar: *She was wearing jeans and a T-shirt.*

tsk tsk *interjection* a way of writing a sound that is made to show disapproval

tsp (*plural* **tsp** *or* **tsps**) the written abbreviation of ***teaspoon*** or teaspoons: *Add 2 tsp salt.*

T-square /ˈtiː skweə $ -skwer/ *n* [C] a large T-shaped piece of wood or plastic used to draw exact plans or pictures

tsu·na·mi /tsʊˈnɑːmi/ *n* [C] *technical* a very large wave, caused by extreme conditions such as an EARTHQUAKE, which can cause a lot of damage when it reaches land

tub /tʌb/ ●○○ *n* [C]

1 CONTAINER **a)** a small container made of paper or plastic with a lid, in which food is bought or stored: **[+of]** *a tub of ice cream* | *a margarine tub* **b)** an open container that is usually round, used for washing, storing things in etc: *trees growing in tubs* → see picture at **CONTAINER**

2 AMOUNT (*also* **tubful**) the amount of liquid, food etc that a tub can contain: **[+of]** *We ate a tub of ice cream.*

3 BATH *AmE* a large container in which you sit to wash yourself SYN **bathtub**: *I had a long soak in the tub.*

4 BOAT *BrE informal* an old boat that travels slowly

5 PERSON **tub of lard** *informal not polite* someone who is short and fat

tu·ba /ˈtjuːbə $ ˈtuːbə/ *n* [C] a large metal musical instrument that consists of a curved tube with a wide opening that points straight up. It produces very low sounds when you blow into it. → see picture at **BRASS**

tub·by /ˈtʌbi/ *adj informal* short and slightly fat, with a round stomach SYN **plump**: *a tubby little man*

tube¹ /tjuːb $ tuːb/ ●●● S3 W3 *n*

1 PIPE FOR LIQUID [C] a round pipe made of metal, glass, rubber etc, especially for liquids or gases to go through → **INNER TUBE, TEST TUBE**

2 [C] a long hollow object that is usually round: *pasta tubes* | *a toilet roll tube*

3 CONTAINER [C] a narrow container made of plastic or soft metal and closed at one end, that you press between your fingers in order to push out the soft substance that is inside: *a tube of toothpaste* → see picture at **CONTAINER**

4 IN YOUR BODY [C] a tube-shaped part inside your body: *the bronchial tubes*

5 TRAINS **the tube** *BrE* the system of trains that run under the ground in London SYN **subway** *AmE*: **take/catch the tube** *Take the tube to Acton.* | *a tube station* | **by tube** *It's best to travel by tube.*

6 go down the tubes *informal* if a situation goes down the tubes, it quickly becomes ruined or spoiled: *When Moira turned up, Tess could see all her good work going down the tubes.*

7 TELEVISION **the tube** *AmE spoken* the television: *What's on the tube tonight?*

8 ELECTRICAL EQUIPMENT [C] *technical* the part of a television that produces the picture on the screen SYN **cathode ray tube**

tube² *v* [I] to float on a river on a large INNER TUBE for fun

tu·ber /ˈtjuːbə $ ˈtuːbər/ *n* [C] a round swollen part on the stem of some plants, such as the potato, that grows below the ground and from which new plants grow —**tuberous** *adj*

tu·ber·cu·lo·sis /tjuːˌbɜːkjəˈləʊsɪs $ tuːˌbɜːrkjəˈloʊ-/ *n* [U] a serious infectious disease that affects many parts of your body, especially your lungs SYN **TB** —**tubercular** /tjuːˈbɜːkjələ $ tuːˈbɜːrkjələr/ *adj*

ˈtube sock *n* [C] *AmE* a sock that is long and straight and has no special place for your heel

ˈtube top *n* [C] *AmE informal* a piece of women's clothing that goes around your chest and back to cover your breasts but does not cover your shoulders or stomach

tub·ing /ˈtjuːbɪŋ $ ˈtuː-/ *n* [U] **1** tubes in general, especially when connected together into a system: *rubber tubing* **2** the activity of floating on a river on a large INNER TUBE for fun

ˈtub-ˌthumping *adj* [only before noun] *BrE informal* trying to persuade people about your opinions in a loud and forceful way: *He is still addressing rallies in his usual tub-thumping, arrogant way.* —**tub-thumping** *n* [U] —**tub-thumper** *n* [C]

tu·bu·lar /ˈtjuːbjələ $ ˈtuːbjələr/ *adj* made of tubes or in the form of a tube: *tubular metal furniture*

tuck¹ /tʌk/ ●●○ *v*

1 [T always + adv/prep] to push something, especially the edge of a piece of cloth or paper, into or behind something so that it looks tidier or stays in place: **tuck sth in** *Jack tucked his shirt in.* | **tuck sth into/under/behind etc sth** | *She tucked an unruly lock of hair behind her ear.*

2 [T always + adv/prep] to put something into a small space, especially in order to protect, hide, carry, or hold it: **tuck sth behind/under/into etc sth** *Giles was tucking his pile of books under his arm.* | *He took the glasses off and tucked them in his pocket.*

3 [T] to put a TUCK (=special fold) in a piece of clothing

tuck sth ↔ **away** *phr v*

1 be tucked away a) if a place is tucked away, it is in a quiet area: *The village of Eyam is tucked away behind the hills.* **b)** if someone or something is tucked away, they are hidden or difficult to find: *The envelope was tucked away in her jewel box.*

2 *informal* to store something, especially money, in a safe place: *Every member of the family can now tuck away either £9 or £18 a month in one of these savings plans.*

3 *BrE informal* to eat a lot of food, usually quickly and with enjoyment

tuck in *phr v*

1 tuck sb in to make a child comfortable in bed by arranging the sheets around them

2 tuck sth ↔ in to move a part of your body inwards so that it does not stick out so much: *Stand up straight and tuck in your tummy.*

3 (*also* **tuck into sth**) *informal* to eat something eagerly: *The ice creams came and we tucked in.* | *They tucked into a hearty breakfast of eggs.*

tuck sb ↔ **up** *phr v*

1 to make someone comfortable in bed by arranging the sheets around them: *Dad tucked me up in his and Carrie's bed.*

2 be tucked up in bed *informal* to be lying or sitting in bed: *I ought to be tucked up in bed now.*

tuck² *n* **1** [C] a narrow flat fold of cloth sewn into a piece of clothing for decoration or to give it a special shape

2 [C] a small medical operation done to make your face or stomach look flatter and younger: *a tummy tuck*
3 [U] *BrE old-fashioned* cakes, sweets etc – used especially by schoolchildren: *the school tuck shop*

tuck·er¹ /ˈtʌkə $ -ər/ *v*
tucker sb **out** *phr v AmE informal* to make someone very tired: *By the end of the day, we were all tuckered out.*

tucker² *n* [U] *AusE informal* food → **your best bib and tucker** at BIB(3)

ˈtude /tjuːd $ tuːd/ *n* [C,U] *spoken* a style, type of behaviour etc that shows that you have the confidence to do unusual and exciting things without caring what other people think – used humorously SYN **attitude**: *the trend of restaurants serving nasty 'tude with their food*

Tu·dor /ˈtjuːdə $ ˈtuːdər/ *adj* relating to the period in British history between 1485 and 1603: **Tudor house/buildings/architecture etc** (=built in the style used in the Tudor period)

Tues·day /ˈtjuːzdi, -deɪ $ ˈtuːz-/ ●●● S2 W2 *n* [C,U] (*written abbreviation* **Tues.** *or* **Tue.**) the day between Monday and Wednesday: **on Tuesday** *The sale starts on Tuesday.* | *I'll see you Tuesday. AmE* | **Tuesday morning/afternoon etc** *He first heard the news on Tuesday evening.* | **last Tuesday** *It was my birthday last Tuesday.* | **this Tuesday** *I'm sorry I can't make it this Tuesday.* | **next Tuesday** (=Tuesday of next week) *Shall we meet next Tuesday?* | **a Tuesday** (=one of the Tuesdays in the year) *We left Miami on a Tuesday.*

tuft /tʌft/ *n* [C] a bunch of hair, feathers, grass etc growing or held closely together at their base: **[+of]** *tufts of grass*

tuft·ed /ˈtʌftɪd/ *adj* with a tuft or tufts: *a tufted duck*

tug¹ /tʌg/ ●●○ *v* (**tugged**, **tugging**)
1 [I,T] to pull with one or more short, quick pulls: *The woman gently tugged his arm.* | **[+at/on sth]** *Joe was tugging at her sleeve.* THESAURUS ▸ PULL
2 [T always + adv/prep] *BrE* to pull a piece of clothing quickly onto your body: **tug sth on** *Alice was tugging on a sweater.*
3 **tug at sb's heart/heartstrings** *written* to make someone feel sympathy for someone or something

T

tug² *n* [C] **1** (*also* **ˈtug boat**) a small strong boat used for pulling or guiding ships into a port, up a river etc **2** [usually singular] a sudden strong pull: *She removed the bandage with a sharp tug.* **3** [usually singular] a strong and sudden feeling: **[+of]** *Kate felt a tug of jealousy.*

ˌtug of ˈlove *n* [singular] *BrE* a situation in which parents who have separated from each other fight over who is going to have the children – used especially in newspaper reports

ˌtug-of-ˈwar *n* [singular] **1** a test of strength in which two teams pull opposite ends of a rope against each other **2** a situation in which two people or groups try very hard to get or keep the same thing: *There was a constant tug-of-war between the military and the president.*

tu·i·tion /tjuˈɪʃən $ tu-/ ●●○ *n* [U]
1 teaching, especially in small groups: *I had to have extra tuition in maths.*
2 *AmE*, **tuition fees** *BrE* the money you pay for being taught: *When I started college, tuition was $350 a quarter.*

tuk-tuk /ˈtʊk tʊk/ *n* [C] a motor vehicle with three wheels that is used as a taxi in Thailand

tu·lip /ˈtjuːlɪp $ ˈtuː-/ *n* [C] a brightly coloured flower that is shaped like a cup and grows from a BULB in spring → see picture at **FLOWER¹**

tulle /tjuːl $ tuːl/ *n* [U] a thin soft silk or NYLON material like a net

tum /tʌm/ *n* [C] *BrE informal* stomach SYN **tummy**: *I've lost another two inches from my tum.*

tum·ble¹ /ˈtʌmbəl/ ●○○ *v* [I]
1 [always + adv/prep] to fall down quickly and suddenly, especially with a rolling movement: **[+over/backwards/down]** *She lost her balance and tumbled backwards.* | *A few stones came tumbling down the cliff.*
2 [always + adv/prep] to move in an uncontrolled way: **[+into/through/out etc]** *We tumbled out into the street.*
3 if prices or figures tumble, they go down suddenly and by a large amount: *Oil prices have tumbled.* | **[+to]** *Mortgage rates tumbled to their lowest level for 25 years.*
4 [always + adv/prep] *literary* if someone's hair tumbles down, it is long, thick, and curly: *Her long dark hair tumbled over her shoulders.*
5 *literary* if words tumble out of someone's mouth, they speak very quickly because they are excited or upset: **[+out/over]** *The words tumbled out as if he hardly knew what to say first.*
6 [always + adv/prep] if water tumbles somewhere, it flows there quickly: *A narrow stream tumbled over the rocks.*
7 **come tumbling down a)** if something comes tumbling down, it falls suddenly to the ground: *Removing the debris could cause the rest of the building to come tumbling down.* **b)** if a system, problem etc comes tumbling down, it suddenly stops working or existing: *In the last year, barriers have come tumbling down.*
8 *AmE* to do TUMBLING

tumble² *n* [C] a fall, especially from a high place or level: *It's possible that stocks could* ***take a tumble*** *next year.* → ROUGH AND TUMBLE

tum·ble·down /ˈtʌmbəldaʊn/ *adj* [only before noun] a tumbledown building is old and beginning to fall down: *a tumbledown cottage*

ˌtumble ˈdryer, **tumble-drier** *n* [C] *BrE* a machine that uses hot air to dry clothes after they have been washed SYN **dryer**

tum·bler /ˈtʌmblə $ -ər/ *n* [C] **1** a glass with a flat bottom and no handle → see picture at **GLASS¹** **2** (*also* **tumblerful** /-fʊl/ *BrE*) the amount of liquid that this type of glass can contain **3** *old-fashioned* someone who performs special movements such as doing SOMERSAULTS (=a jump in which you turn over completely in the air) SYN **acrobat**

tum·ble·weed /ˈtʌmbəlwiːd/ *n* [C,U] a plant that grows in the desert areas of North America and is blown from place to place by the wind

tum·bling /ˈtʌmblɪŋ/ *n* [U] a sport similar to GYMNASTICS but with all the exercises done on the floor

tu·mes·cent /tjuːˈmesənt $ tuː-/ *adj technical* swollen or swelling —**tumescence** *n* [U]

tum·my /ˈtʌmi/ ●●○ *n* (*plural* **tummies**) [C] STOMACH – used especially by or to children: *He was up all night with* ***tummy ache***. | **tummy bug/upset** *BrE* (=an illness of the stomach that makes you vomit)

tu·mour *BrE*, **tumor** *AmE* /ˈtjuːmə $ ˈtuːmər/ ●○○ *n* [C] a mass of diseased cells in your body that have divided and increased too quickly: *a* ***brain tumour*** | **malignant/benign tumour** (=caused by or not caused by CANCER)

tu·mult /ˈtjuːmʌlt $ ˈtuː-/ *n* [C,U] *formal* **1** a confused, noisy, and excited situation, often caused by a large crowd SYN **turmoil**: *I could simply not be heard in the tumult.* | **in tumult** *The whole country is in tumult.* **2** a state of mental confusion caused by strong emotions such as anger, sadness etc SYN **turmoil**

tu·mul·tu·ous /tjuːˈmʌltʃuəs $ tuː-/ *adj* **1** full of activity, confusion, or violence: *the tumultuous years of the Civil War* **2** very loud because people are happy and excited: *He received a tumultuous welcome.* | *tumultuous applause*

tu·mu·lus /ˈtjuːmjələs $ ˈtuː-/ *n* (*plural* **tumuli** /-laɪ, -li/) [C] a very large pile of earth put over a GRAVE by people in the past

tu·na /ˈtjuːnə $ ˈtuːnə/ ●○○ *n* (*plural* **tuna**)
1 [C] a large sea fish caught for food
2 [U] (*also* **tuna fish**) the flesh of this fish, usually sold cooked in TINS

tun·dra /ˈtʌndrə/ *n* [C,U] the large flat areas of land in the north of Russia, Canada etc, where it is very cold and there are no trees

tune¹ /tjuːn $ tuːn/ ●●● S3 *n*
1 [C] a series of musical notes that are played or sung and are nice to listen to SYN **melody**: *That's a nice tune.* | *She*

sang some old classics and a few new tunes. | **to the tune of sth** (=using the same tune as another song) *The song was sung to the tune of 'Amazing Grace'.* **THESAURUS** ➔ MUSIC
2 in tune playing or singing the correct musical note: *They sang perfectly in tune.*
3 out of tune playing or singing higher or lower than the correct musical note: *Greg's bass guitar was out of tune.*
4 in tune with sb/sth, out of tune with sb/sth able or unable to realize, understand, or agree with what someone else thinks or wants: *The industry is changing in tune with changing demand.*
5 to the tune of $1,000/£2 million etc *informal* used to emphasize how large an amount or number is: *Canada is funding the programme to the tune of $30 million.* → **call the tune** at CALL[1](9), → **change your tune** at CHANGE[1](14), → **dance to sb's tune** at DANCE[2](4), → **FINE-TUNE, SIGNATURE TUNE**

COLLOCATIONS

VERBS

play a tune *He played a tune on the piano.*
hum/whistle a tune *She was humming a little tune to herself.*
write/compose a tune

ADJECTIVES/NOUN + tune

catchy/memorable (=one that is easy to remember) *His songs have simple words and catchy tunes.*
the theme tune/signature tune (=the tune at the beginning or end of a television programme etc) *the theme tune from the movie 'Titanic'*
a show tune (=a tune from a musical) | **a dance tune** | **a hymn tune**

tune² ●○○ *v* [T]
1 to make a musical instrument play at the right PITCH: *Someone's coming tomorrow to tune the piano.*
2 (*also* **tune up**) to make small changes to an engine so that it works as well as possible
3 to make a radio or television receive broadcasts from a particular place: **tune sth to sth** *The radio was tuned to a classical station.* → **stay tuned** at STAY[1](8)
4 finely/highly tuned finely tuned feelings, senses, or systems are extremely sensitive and able to react quickly: **be tuned to sth** *a species finely tuned to life in the desert*
tune in *phr v*
1 to watch or listen to a broadcast on radio or television: **[+to]** *People get their information by tuning in to foreign radio stations.* | *More than 150 million Americans tuned in to watch the final episode.*
2 (*also* **be tuned in**) to realize or understand what is happening or what other people are thinking: **[+to]** *Try to tune in to your partner's needs.* | *The company aims to be more tuned in to customer needs.*
tune out *phr v informal* to ignore or stop listening to someone or something: *A bored child may simply tune out.* | **tune sb/sth ↔ out** *I learned to tune out the background noise.*
tune up *phr v*
1 when musicians tune up, they prepare their instruments to play at the right PITCH: **tune sth ↔ up** *The band were tuning up their guitars.*
2 tune sth ↔ up to make small changes to an engine so that it works as well as possible

tune·ful /ˈtjuːnfəl $ ˈtuːn-/ *adj* pleasant to listen to: *tuneful melodies* —**tunefully** *adv* —**tunefulness** *n* [U]

tune·less /ˈtjuːnləs $ ˈtuːn-/ *adj* not having a pleasant tune: *tuneless humming* —**tunelessly** *adv*

tun·er /ˈtjuːnə $ ˈtuːnər/ *n* [C] **1** the part of a radio or television that you can change to receive different TV or radio stations **2** a person who tunes pianos **3** an electronic machine that helps you to tune a musical instrument such as a GUITAR

ˈtune-up *n* [singular] **1** the process of making small changes to an engine so that it works as well as possible **2** an occasion that someone uses as preparation for a more important occasion: *He is treating the semi-finals as a tune-up.*

tung·sten /ˈtʌŋstən/ *n* [U] a hard metal that is used to make steel and in the thin wires in electric light BULBS. It is a chemical ELEMENT: symbol W

tu·nic /ˈtjuːnɪk $ ˈtuː-/ *n* [C] **1** a long loose piece of clothing, usually without sleeves, worn in the past **2** a long loose women's shirt, usually worn with trousers **3** *BrE* a specially shaped short coat worn by soldiers, police officers etc as part of a uniform

ˈtuning fork *n* [C] a small U-shaped steel instrument that makes a particular musical note when you hit it → see picture at FORK[1]

ˈtuning peg *n* [C] a screw used for making the strings on a GUITAR etc tighter or looser

tun·nel¹ /ˈtʌnl/ ●●● W3 *n* [C]
1 a passage that has been dug under the ground for cars, trains etc to go through: *a railway tunnel* | *the Channel Tunnel* (=between England and France)
2 a passage under the ground that animals have dug to live in

tunnel² *v* (**tunnelled, tunnelling** *BrE*, **tunneled, tunneling** *AmE*) [I always + adv/prep, T] **1** to dig a long passage under the ground: **[+into/through/under]** *They were tunnelling into the mountainside.* | **tunnel your way under/through etc** *The prisoners tunneled their way under the fence.* **2** if insects tunnel into something, they make holes in it: **[+into]** *The grubs tunnel into the wood.*

ˌtunnel ˈvision *n* [U] **1** the tendency to only think about one part of something such as a problem or plan, instead of considering all the parts of it: *I've got tunnel vision when it comes to what I want to do.* **2** a condition in which someone's eyes are damaged so that they can only see things that are straight ahead

tun·ny /ˈtʌni/ *n* (*plural* **tunny**) [C,U] a British word for TUNA

tup·pence /ˈtʌpəns/ *n* [U] *BrE* **1** an amount of money worth two pence **2 not care/give tuppence** to not care at all about someone or something

tup·peny, **tuppenny** /ˈtʌpəni/ *adj BrE* costing two pence

Tup·per·ware /ˈtʌpəweə $ -pərwer/ *n* [U] *trademark* a type of plastic container that closes very tightly and is used to store food

ˈTupperware ˌparty *n* [C] an occasion on which people get together at someone's house in order to buy Tupperware

tur·ban /ˈtɜːbən $ ˈtɜːr-/ *n* [C] a long piece of cloth that you wind tightly round your head, worn by men in parts of North Africa and Southern Asia and sometimes by women as a fashion

tur·bid /ˈtɜːbɪd $ ˈtɜːr-/ *adj formal* turbid water or liquid is dirty and muddy —**turbidity** /tɜːˈbɪdəti $ tɜːr-/ *n* [U]

tur·bine /ˈtɜːbaɪn $ ˈtɜːrbən, -baɪn/ *n* [C] an engine or motor in which the pressure of a liquid or gas moves a special wheel around → **GAS TURBINE, WIND TURBINE**

tur·bo /ˈtɜːbəʊ $ ˈtɜːrboʊ/ *n* (*plural* **turbos**) [C] a car with a turbocharged engine: *an Audi turbo diesel*

tur·bo·charged /ˈtɜːbəʊˌtʃɑːdʒd $ ˈtɜːrboʊ-ˌtʃɑːrdʒd/ *adj* a turbocharged engine or vehicle has a turbocharger

tur·bo·charg·er /ˈtɜːbəʊˌtʃɑːdʒə $ ˈtɜːrboʊˌtʃɑːrdʒər/ *n* [C] a system that makes a vehicle more powerful by using a turbine to force air and petrol into the engine under increased pressure

tur·bo·jet /ˈtɜːbəʊdʒet $ ˈtɜːrboʊ-/ *n* [C] **1** a powerful engine that makes something, especially an aircraft, move forwards, by forcing out hot air and gases at the back **2** an aircraft that gets power from this type of engine

tur·bo·prop /ˈtɜːbəʊprɒp $ ˈtɜːrboʊprɑːp/ *n* [C] **1** a TURBINE engine that drives a PROPELLER **2** an aircraft that gets power from this type of engine

tur·bot /ˈtɜːbɒt, -bət $ ˈtɜːrbət/ *n* (*plural* **turbot** or **turbots**) [C,U] a large flat European fish

T

tur·bu·lence /ˈtɜːbjələns $ ˈtɜːr-/ ●○○ *n* [U]
1 irregular and violent movements of air or water that are caused by the wind
2 a political or emotional situation that is very confused SYN **turmoil**: *A period of political turbulence followed the civil war.*

tur·bu·lent /ˈtɜːbjələnt $ ˈtɜːr-/ ●○○ *adj*
1 a turbulent situation or period of time is one in which there are a lot of sudden changes: *the turbulent times of the French Revolution | He has had a turbulent political career.*
2 turbulent air or water moves around a lot: *the dark turbulent waters of the river*

turd /tɜːd $ tɜːrd/ *n* [C] *informal* **1** *not polite* a piece of the solid brown waste material you pass from your body **2** *taboo* an offensive word for an unpleasant person. Do not use this word: *You stupid little turd!*

tu·reen /tjʊˈriːn $ təˈriːn/ *n* [C] a large dish with a lid, used for serving soup or vegetables

turf¹ /tɜːf $ tɜːrf/ ●○○ *n* (*plural* **turfs** *or* **turves**) /tɜːvz $ tɜːrvz/
1 [U] *especially BrE* a surface that consists of soil with grass on top, or an artificial surface that looks like this: *soft green turf*
2 [C] *BrE* a square piece of turf cut out of the ground
3 the turf the sport of horse racing, or the track on which horses race
4 [U] *informal* an area that you think of as being your own: *How vigorously will the local companies defend their turf?* | **sb's own/home turf** (=the place that someone comes from or lives in) *We beat Canada on their home turf.* | **turf war/battle** (=a fight or argument over the areas or things you think belong to you) *turf wars among government bureaucracies*

turf² *v* [T] to cover an area of land with turf

turf sb ↔ **out** (*also* **turf sb off (sth)**) *phr v BrE informal* to make someone leave a place or organization, usually suddenly or roughly SYN **kick sb out**: **[+of]** *The families claim they are being turfed out of their homes.*

ˈ**turf acˌcountant** *n* [C] *BrE* someone who has a business where people can BET on the results of horse races, football games etc SYN **bookmaker**

tur·gid /ˈtɜːdʒɪd $ ˈtɜːr-/ *adj formal* **1** turgid writing or speech is boring and difficult to understand SYN **dull**: *a turgid Social Science textbook* **2** full and swollen with liquid or air —**turgidity** /tɜːˈdʒɪdəti $ tɜːr-/ *n* [U]

Turk /tɜːk $ tɜːrk/ *n* [C] someone from Turkey

tur·key /ˈtɜːki $ ˈtɜːrki/ ●●● S3 *n*
1 [C] a bird that looks like a large chicken and is often eaten at Christmas and at Thanksgiving
2 [U] the meat from a turkey eaten as food: *roast turkey*
3 [C] *AmE informal* an unsuccessful film or play
4 talk turkey *especially AmE informal* to talk seriously about details, especially in business → COLD TURKEY

Turk·ish¹ /ˈtɜːkɪʃ $ ˈtɜːr-/ *adj* relating to Turkey, its people, or its language

Turkish² *n* [U] the language used in Turkey

ˌ**Turkish ˈbath** *n* [C] a type of bath in which you sit in a very hot steamy room, have a MASSAGE, then take a cold SHOWER or bath

ˌ**Turkish ˈcoffee** *n* [C,U] very strong black coffee that you drink in small cups with sugar

ˌ**Turkish deˈlight** *n* [U] *BrE* a type of sweet made from firm JELLY that is cut into pieces and covered in sugar or chocolate

tur·me·ric /ˈtɜːmərɪk $ ˈtɜːr-/ *n* [U] a yellow powder used to give a special colour or taste to food, especially CURRY

tur·moil /ˈtɜːmɔɪl $ ˈtɜːr-/ ●○○ *n* [singular, U] a state of confusion, excitement, or anxiety: **political/emotional/economic/religious etc turmoil** *the prospect of another week of political turmoil* | **in (a) turmoil** *Ashley gazed at him, her thoughts in turmoil.*

turn¹ /tɜːn $ tɜːrn/ ●●● S1 W1 *v*
1 YOUR BODY [I,T] to move your body so that you are looking in a different direction → **twist**: *Ricky turned and walked away. | She turned her head in surprise.* | **[+around/round/away]** *Dan turned away, hiding the fear in his eyes.* | **turn (your head/face) to do sth** *He turned around to look at Kim.* | *'No,' she said, turning her head to see David's reaction.* | *Brigitte glared at him,* **turned on her heel** (=turned away suddenly because of anger), *and stomped out of the room.*
2 OBJECT [T usually + adv/prep] to move something so that it is pointing or aiming in a different direction: **turn sth around/over/upside down etc** *You may turn over your exam papers now.* | **turn sth on sth/sb** *The firemen turned their hoses on the blaze.* | **turn sth to face sth/sb** *Could you* **turn** *your chairs* **to face this way**? | **turn a/the page** (=move a page in a book over so that you can read the next page) | **turn sth down/up** *He turned down the corner of the sheet to peep at the baby.*
3 DIRECTION a) [I,T] to go in a new direction when you are walking, driving etc, or to make the vehicle you are using do this: *I watched until he* **turned the corner**. | **turn left/right** *Turn left at the church.* | **[+into/onto/down etc]** *She cycled up the street and turned into Long Road.* | **Turning the car around**, *we headed home.* **b)** [I] if a road, river etc turns, it curves and starts to go in a new direction: *Further on, the river turns east.* | *The road* **turns sharply** *at the top of the hill.*
4 MOVE AROUND CENTRAL POINT [I,T] to move around a central or fixed point, or to make something move in this way: *The wheels turned slowly, then picked up speed.* | *For some reason, the key wouldn't turn.* | **turn the handle/knob/key/tap etc** *She gently turned the handle of the bedroom door.*
5 CHANGE [linking verb, T] to start to have a different quality, or to make something do this: **turn (sth) red/blue/white etc** *Rose's hair was already turning grey.* | *In October the leaves turn orange and yellow.* | *The sun had turned the sky a glowing pink.* | **the weather turns cold/nasty etc** (*also* **it turns cold/nasty etc**) *Then it turned cold and started to rain.* | **turn nasty/mean/violent etc** (=suddenly become angry, violent etc) *The police are worried that the situation could turn violent.* THESAURUS ▸ BECOME

GRAMMAR: Linking verbs

Turn is a linking verb in this meaning. It links the subject of the sentence with an adjective: *His face turned pale.* | *Their relationship turned sour.*

6 ATTENTION/THOUGHTS [I,T] to start to think about, deal with, look at etc a particular person, thing, or subject, instead of what you were thinking about etc before: **turn your attention/thoughts/efforts etc to sth/sb** *Many investors have turned their attention to opportunities abroad.* | *Phil turned his gaze towards the older man.* | **turn to/towards etc sth** *As usual, the conversation turned back to her children.* | *Now is the time of year when thoughts turn in the direction of summer holidays.* | *Next the Senator turned to education.*
7 turn your back (on sb/sth) a) to refuse to help, support, or be involved with someone or something: *How can you turn your back on your own mother?* | *In his twenties he turned his back on his Catholic faith.* **b)** to turn so that your back is pointing towards someone or something, and you are not looking at them: *Angrily, she turned her back on him.*
8 AGE/TIME [T] to become a particular age, or to reach a particular time: **sb turns 15/20/40 etc** *My son's just turned 18.* | **it's turned 2 o'clock/5/midday etc** *It's just turned three.*
9 turn sth inside out a) to pull a piece of clothing, bag etc so that the inside is facing out: *Turn the sweater inside out before you wash it.* **b)** (*also* **turn sth upside down**) to search everywhere for something, in a way that makes a place very untidy: *Thieves had turned the house upside down.* **c)** (*also* **turn sth upside down/turn sth on its head**) to completely change the way that something is done, organized, thought about etc: *New approaches to marketing turn old practices upside down.* | *Her opinion of him had been turned on its head.*

10 have turned the corner to start to improve after going through a difficult period or experience: *The manager of the hotel chain claims that they have turned the corner.*
11 MAKE/LET GO OUT [T] to make or let someone or something go out from where they are: **turn sb/sth out/outside/into etc (sth)** *Turn the dough out onto a lightly floured board.* | *There are some criminals who cannot be* ***turned loose*** *onto the streets.*
12 TIDE [I] if the TIDE turns, the sea starts to come in or go out again
13 CHANGE DEVELOPMENT [I,T] if something such as a war, situation, game of sport etc turns, or someone turns it, something happens to change the way it is developing: *Mills turned the game by scoring twice.* | *The victory* ***turned the tide*** *of the war in North Africa.*
14 turn traitor to be disloyal to a person, group, or idea that you have strongly supported before
15 turn your ankle to twist your ANKLE in a way that injures it SYN **sprain**: *Wright turned his ankle in the first minutes of the game.*
16 an actor turned politician/a housewife turned author etc someone who has done one job and then does something completely different → **poacher turned gamekeeper** at POACHER
17 turn sb's head to be attractive in a romantic or sexual way: *She turned heads whenever she walked into a room.*
18 turn (people's) heads if something turns people's heads, they are surprised by it: *It did turn some heads when he moved back to the village.*
19 turn a profit *AmE* to make a profit
20 turn a phrase to say something in a particular way: *Cohen knows how to turn a phrase in his lyrics.*
21 LAND [T] to break up soil so that it is ready for growing crops: *a distant tractor turning the soil*
22 WOOD/METAL [T] to shape a wooden or metal object using a special tool
23 MILK [I] *BrE* if milk turns, it becomes sour → **turn a blind eye (to sth)** at BLIND[1](3), → **turn the other cheek** at CHEEK[1](4), → **turn full circle** at CIRCLE[1](6), → **sb would turn in their grave** at GRAVE[1](3), → **not turn a hair** at HAIR(11), → **turn your hand to (doing) sth** at HAND[1](26), → **turn over a new leaf** at LEAF[1](3), → **turn your nose up (at sth)** at NOSE[1](5), → **turn your stomach** at STOMACH[1](4), → **turn the tables (on sb)** at TABLE[1](6), → **turn tail** at TAIL[1](9)

turn (sb) **against** sb/sth *phr v* to stop liking or supporting someone or something, or to make someone do this: *Many people had turned against the war.* | *Dave felt she was deliberately turning the kids against him.*

turn around (*also* **turn round** *BrE*) *phr v*
1 if a business, department etc that is not successful turns around, or if someone turns it around, it starts to be successful: *The company turned around from losses of £1.4 million last year to profits of £26,800.* | **turn sth ↔ around** *At Rockwell International he had turned around a badly performing division.* → TURNAROUND
2 if a situation, game etc turns around, or if someone turns it around, it changes and starts to develop in the way you want: *After I met him, my whole life turned around.* | **turn sth ↔ around** *Fender's batting could turn matches around in half an hour.*
3 turn around and say/do etc sth *spoken* to say or do something that is unexpected or that seems unfair or unreasonable: *You can't just turn around and say that it was all my fault.*
4 turn sth ↔ around to consider an idea, question etc in a different way, or change the words of something so that it has a different meaning: *Let's turn the whole idea around and look at it from another angle.*
5 turn sth ↔ around to complete the process of making a product or providing a service: *We can turn around 500 units by next week.*
6 every time sb turns around *spoken* very often or all the time: *Every time I turn around he seems to be checking up on me.*

turn away *phr v*
1 turn sb ↔ away to refuse to let someone enter a place or join an organization, for example because it is full: *The show was so popular police had to turn people away.* | *Thousands of applicants are turned away each year.*
2 turn sb ↔ away to refuse to give someone sympathy, help, or support: *Anyone who comes to us will not be turned away.* | *The insurance company has promised not to turn away its existing customers.*
3 turn (sb) away from sb/sth to stop supporting someone, or stop using or being interested in something, or to make someone do this: *Consumers are turning away from credit cards.* | *events that turned Henry away from his family*

turn back *phr v*
1 to go back in the direction you came from, or to make someone or something do this: *It's getting late – maybe we should turn back.* | **turn sb/sth ↔ back** *The UN convoy was turned back at the border.*
2 to return to doing something in the way it was done before: **[+to]** *The people are turning back to natural resources to survive.* | *We've promised to help, and* ***there's no turning back*** (=you cannot change this)*!* → **turn back the clock** at CLOCK[1](3)

turn sb/sth ↔ **down** *phr v*
1 to turn the switch on a machine such as an OVEN, radio etc so that it produces less heat, sound etc OPP **turn up**: *Can you turn the TV down? I'm trying to work.*
2 to refuse an offer, request, or invitation: *They offered her the job but she turned it down.* | *I'm not going to turn down an invitation to go to New York!* | *Josie's already* ***turned him down*** (=refused his offer of marriage).

turn in *phr v*
1 turn sth ↔ in to give something to a person in authority, especially an illegal weapon or something lost or stolen: *The rebels were told to turn in their weapons and ammunition.* | **[+to]** *My wallet was turned in to the police two days later.*
2 turn sth ↔ in *AmE* to give back something you have borrowed or rented SYN **return**: *When do the library books have to be turned in?*
3 turn in sth to produce a particular profit, result etc: *Bimec turned in net profits of £2.4 million.* | *Last night the team turned in another dazzling performance.*
4 turn sb ↔ in to tell the police who or where a criminal is: *Margrove's wife finally turned him in.*
5 to go to bed: *I think I'll turn in early tonight.*
6 turn sth ↔ in *AmE* to give a piece of work you have done to a teacher, your employer etc SYN **hand in** *BrE*: *Have you all turned in your homework assignments?*

turn (sb/sth) **into** sth *phr v*
1 to become something different, or to make someone or something do this: *The sofa turns into a bed.* | *A few weeks later, winter had turned into spring.* | *Hollywood discovered her and turned her into a star.*
2 to change by magic from one thing into another, or to make something do this: *In a flash, the prince turned into a frog.* | *The witch had turned them all into stone.*
3 days turned into weeks/months turned into years etc used to say that time passed slowly while you waited for something to happen: *Weeks turned into months, and still there was no letter.*

turn off *phr v*
1 turn sth ↔ off to make a machine or piece of electrical equipment such as a television, engine, light etc stop operating by pushing a button, turning a key etc SYN **switch off** OPP **turn on**: *Don't forget to turn the lights off when you leave.*
2 turn sth ↔ off to stop the supply of water, gas etc from flowing by turning a handle OPP **turn on**: *They've turned the gas off for a couple of hours.*
3 turn off (sth) to leave the road you are travelling on and start travelling on another road: **[+at/near etc]** *I think we should have turned off at the last exit.* | **turn off the road/motorway etc** *Mark turned off the highway and into Provincetown.* → TURN-OFF
4 turn sb ↔ off to make someone decide they do not like something: *Any prospective buyer will be turned off by the sight of rotting wood.* → TURN-OFF

T

5 turn sb ↔ off to make someone feel that they are not attracted to you in a sexual way OPP **turn on**: *Men who stink of beer really turn me off.* → TURN-OFF

turn on *phr v*

1 turn sth ↔ on to make a machine or piece of electrical equipment such as a television, engine, light etc start operating by pushing a button, turning a key etc SYN **switch on** OPP **turn off**: *Jake turned on his computer and checked his mail.*

2 turn sth ↔ on to make the supply of water, gas etc start flowing from something by turning a handle OPP **turn off**: *He turned on the gas and lit the stove.* | *'I'm thirsty,' she said,* ***turning on the tap****.*

3 turn on sb *also* **turn upon sb** to suddenly attack someone, using physical violence or unpleasant words: *Peter turned on Rae and screamed, 'Get out of my sight!'*

4 turn on sth *also* **turn upon sth** if a situation, event, argument etc turns on a particular thing or idea, it depends on that thing: *As usual, everything turned on how much money was available.*

5 turn sb on to make someone feel sexually excited: *The way he looked at her really turned her on.* → TURN-ON

6 turn sb on to interest someone, or to make someone become interested in something: *Science fiction just doesn't turn me on.* | **[+to]** *It was Walter who turned me on to vegetarian food.*

7 turn on the charm *also* **turn it on** to suddenly start to be very nice, amusing, and interesting, especially in a way that is not sincere: *Simon was good at turning on the charm at parties.*

turn out *phr v*

1 to happen in a particular way, or to have a particular result, especially one that you did not expect: **turn out well/badly/fine etc** *It was a difficult time, but eventually things turned out all right.* | **it turns out (that)** *It turned out that I was wrong.* | ***As it turned out*** (=used to say what happened in the end)*, he passed the exam quite easily.* | **turn out to be sth** *That guy turned out to be Maria's second cousin.*

2 turn the light out to stop the flow of electricity to a light by pressing a switch, pulling a string etc: *Don't forget to turn out the lights when you go!*

3 if a lot of people turn out for an event, they go to watch it or take part in it: **[+for]** *About 70% of the population turned out for the election.* | **turn out to do sth** *Thousands turned out to watch yesterday's match against Ireland.* → TURNOUT

4 turn sb ↔ out to force someone to leave a place permanently, especially their home: *If you can't pay the rent, they turn you out.*

5 turn sth ↔ out to produce or make something: *The factory turns out 300 units a day.*

6 well/beautifully/badly etc turned out dressed in good, beautiful etc clothes: *elegantly turned-out young ladies*

7 turn sth ↔ out a) to empty something completely by taking out the contents: *The policeman made him turn out his pockets.* **b)** *BrE* to take out everything in a room, drawer etc and clean the room etc thoroughly: *Lea decided to turn out the attic.*

turn over *phr v*

1 turn sth over to sb to give someone the right to own something, or to make someone responsible for dealing with something: *He'll turn the shop over to his son when he retires.* | **turn the matter/problem/responsibility etc over to sb** *I'm turning the project over to you.*

2 turn sth over to sth to use land, a building etc for a different purpose: *There is a new plan to turn the land over to wind farming.*

3 turn sb over to sb to take a criminal to the police or another official organization: *Suspected terrorists are immediately turned over to the law.*

4 turn over sth if a business turns over a particular amount of money, it earns that amount in a particular period of time: *Within ten years the theme park was turning over £20 million.* → TURNOVER

5 if an engine turns over, or if someone turns it over, it starts to work: *The engine turned over twice and then stopped.*

6 *BrE* to turn a page in a book or a sheet of paper to the opposite side: *Turn over and look at the next page.*

7 *BrE* to change to another CHANNEL on a television: *Can we turn over? There's a film I want to see.*

8 turn sth over *BrE* to search a place thoroughly or steal things from it, making it very untidy: *Burglars had been in and turned the whole house over.* → **turn over a new leaf** at LEAF¹(3), → **turn sth over in your mind** at MIND¹(17)

turn round *phr v BrE* → TURN AROUND

turn to sb/sth *phr v*

1 to try to get help, advice, or sympathy from someone: *I don't know who to turn to.* | *The Namibian government turned to South Africa for help.*

2 to start to do or use something new, especially as a way of solving a problem: *Many people here are turning to solar power.* | **turn to drink/crime/drugs etc** *addicts who turn to crime to finance their habit*

3 turn (sth) to sth to become a different quality, attitude, form of a substance etc, or to make something do this: *Our laughter turned to horror as we realized that Jody was really hurt.* | *When water turns to steam, it expands.* | *A sudden storm turned the earth to mud.*

4 to look at a particular page in a book: *Turn to page 655 for more information.*

turn up *phr v*

1 turn sth ↔ up to turn a switch on a machine such as an OVEN, radio etc so that it produces more heat, sound etc OPP **turn down**: *Turn the oven up to 220.* | *Turn up the radio!*

2 to be found, especially by chance, after having been lost or searched for: *Eventually my watch turned up in a coat pocket.*

3 to arrive at a place, especially in a way that is unexpected: *You can't just turn up and expect a meal.* | **turn up late/early/on time etc** *Steve turned up late, as usual.*

4 if an opportunity or situation turns up, it happens, especially when you are not expecting it: *Don't worry, I'm sure a job will turn up soon.*

5 turn sth ↔ up to find something by searching for it thoroughly: *The police investigation hasn't turned up any new evidence.*

6 turn sth ↔ up *BrE* to shorten a skirt, trousers etc by folding up the bottom and sewing it → **turn up trumps** at TRUMP¹(4)

turn upon sb/sth *phr v formal*

1 to suddenly attack someone, using physical violence or unpleasant words SYN **turn on**

2 if a situation, event, argument etc turns upon a particular thing or idea, it depends on that thing SYN **turn on**: *The court case turned upon a technicality of company law.*

turn² ●●● S1 W1 *n*

1 CHANCE TO DO STH [C] the time when it is your chance, duty, or right to do something that each person in a group is doing one after the other SYN **go** *BrE*: **turn to do sth** *Whose turn is it to set the table?* | ***It's*** *your* ***turn****. Roll the dice.* | *I think* ***it's*** *our* ***turn to*** *drive the kids to school this week.*

> **REGISTER**
> In everyday English, people often say that it is someone's **go** in a game rather than **turn**: *Whose* ***go*** *is it now?* | *Wait until it's your* ***go****.*

2 take turns (*also* **take it in turns**) *BrE* if two or more people take turns doing work, using something etc, they do it one after the other, for example in order to share the work or play fairly: *You'll have to take turns on the swing.* | **take turns doing sth** *The students were taking turns reading aloud.* | **take turns in doing sth** *BrE*: *We took turns in pushing the bike along.* | **take turns to do sth** *Dan and I usually take turns to cook.*

3 in turn a) as a result of something: *Interest rates were cut and, in turn, share prices rose.* **b)** one after the other, especially in a particular order: *Each of us in turn had to describe how alcohol had affected our lives.*

4 ROAD [C] **a)** *AmE* a place where one road goes in a different direction from the one you are on SYN **turning**

BrE: According to the map we missed our turn back there. | **take the first/a wrong etc turn** (=go along the first etc road) *I think we took a wrong turn coming out of town.* | *Take the second turn on the left.* **b)** a curve in a road, path etc: *There's a* ***sharp turn*** *coming up ahead.*

5 CHANGE DIRECTION [C] a change in the direction you are moving: **make a left/right turn** *Make a left turn at the station.*

6 CHANGE IN EVENTS [C] a sudden or unexpected change that makes a situation develop in a different way: **take a dramatic/fresh/different etc turn** *From then on, our fortunes took a downward turn.* | *My career had already taken a new turn.* | *The president was stunned by the sudden* ***turn of events.*** | **take a turn for the worse/better** *Two days after the operation, Dad took a turn for the worse.*

7 the turn of the century/year the beginning of a new century or year: *the short period from the turn of the century until World War One*

8 at every turn happening again and again, especially in an annoying way: *problems that presented themselves at every turn*

9 ACT OF TURNING STH [C] the act of turning something completely around a fixed point: *I gave the screw another two or three turns.*

10 by turns changing from one quality, feeling etc to another: *By turns, a 14 year old is affectionate then aggressive, silent then outspoken.*

11 turn of phrase a) the ability to say things in a clever or funny way: *Kate has a colourful turn of phrase.* **b)** a particular way of saying something SYN **expression**: *What a strange turn of phrase!*

12 speak/talk out of turn to say something you should not say in a particular situation, especially because you do not have enough authority to say it: *I'm sorry if I spoke out of turn, Major Karr.*

13 do sb a good/bad turn to do something that is helpful or unhelpful for someone: *You did me a good turn by driving Max home last night.*

14 one good turn deserves another used to say that if someone does something nice for you, you should do something nice for them

15 turn of mind the particular way that someone usually thinks or feels: **an academic/practical etc turn of mind** *youngsters with an independent turn of mind*

16 on the turn *BrE* **a)** if the TIDE is on the turn, the sea is starting to come in or go out **b)** starting to change, or in the process of changing: *Hopefully my luck was on the turn.* **c)** if milk, fish, or other food is on the turn, it is no longer fresh

17 turn of speed *BrE* a sudden increase in your speed, or the ability to increase your speed suddenly: *He's a top goalkicker with a surprising turn of speed.*

18 be done to a turn *BrE* to be perfectly cooked

19 take a turn in/on etc sth *old-fashioned* to walk somewhere for pleasure

20 give sb a turn *old-fashioned* to frighten someone

21 have a turn *BrE old-fashioned* to feel slightly ill

turn·a·bout /ˈtɜːnəbaʊt $ ˈtɜːrn-/ *n* **1** [C usually singular] *BrE* a complete change in someone's opinions, ideas, or methods: *an extraordinarily rapid turnabout in attitudes* **2 turnabout is fair play** *AmE* used to say that because someone else has done something to you, you can do it to them too

turn·a·round /ˈtɜːnəraʊnd $ ˈtɜːrn-/ (*also* **turnround** *BrE*) *n* [singular] **1** the time it takes to receive something, deal with it and send it back, especially on a plane, ship etc: *The average turnaround for a passport application is six working days.* | *We must reduce costs and shorten* ***turnaround times.*** **2** a complete change from a bad situation to a good one: **[+in]** *the remarkable turnaround in our economy* → **turn around** at TURN[1] **3** a TURNABOUT

turn·coat /ˈtɜːnkəʊt $ ˈtɜːrnkoʊt/ *n* [C] someone who stops supporting a political party or group and joins the opposing side: *Casson was publicly criticized as a turncoat and a traitor.*

turn·er /ˈtɜːnə $ ˈtɜːrnər/ *n* [C] *especially BrE* someone who uses a LATHE (=special tool) to make shapes out of wood or metal

turn·ing /ˈtɜːnɪŋ $ ˈtɜːr-/ *n* [C] *BrE* a road that connects with the one you are on SYN **turn** *AmE*: *He must have* ***taken*** *a* ***wrong turning*** *in the dark.* | *Take* ***the*** *first* ***turning on the left.***

ˈturning ˌcircle (*also* **ˈturning ˌradius**) *n* [C] the smallest space in which a vehicle can drive around in a circle

ˈturning point *n* [C] the time when an important change starts, especially one that improves the situation: **[+in]** *Meeting her was the turning point in my life.*

tur·nip /ˈtɜːnɪp $ ˈtɜːr-/ *n* [C,U] a large round pale yellow vegetable that grows under the ground, or the plant that produces it → see picture at VEGETABLE[1]

turn·key /ˈtɜːnkiː $ ˈtɜːrn-/ *adj* [only before noun] ready to be used immediately: *the development and sale of* ***turnkey systems*** *for telecommunications customers*

ˈturn-off *n* **1** [C] a smaller road that leads off a main road: *I missed the turn-off to the farm.* **2** [singular] *informal* something that makes you lose interest in something, especially sex: *Pornographic pictures are a real turn-off to most women.* → **turn off** at TURN[1]

ˌturn-of-the-ˈcentury *adj* [only before noun] existing or happening around the beginning of a century, especially the beginning of the 20th century → **fin de siècle**: *narrow turn-of-the-century streets*

ˈturn-on *n* [singular] *informal* something that makes you feel excited, especially sexually: *It was a turn-on to be the centre of attention.* → TURN ON

turn·out, **ˈturn-out** /ˈtɜːnaʊt $ ˈtɜːrn-/ ●○○ *n*
1 [singular] the number of people who vote in an election: **high/low turnout** *the low turn-out of 54 percent in the March elections* → TURN OUT
2 [singular] the number of people who go to a party, meeting, or other organized event: *I was disappointed by the turn-out for our home match.*
3 [C] *AmE* a place at the side of a narrow road where cars can wait to let others pass

turn·o·ver /ˈtɜːnˌəʊvə $ ˈtɜːrnˌoʊvər/ ●○○ *n*
1 [singular, U] *BrE* the amount of business done during a particular period: **[+of]** *The illicit drugs industry has an* ***annual turnover*** *of some £200 billion.* | **turnover rose/fell** *Turnover rose 9%.* THESAURUS ▸ PROFIT
2 [singular, U] the rate at which a particular kind of goods is sold: **[+of]** *Tri-Star's fast turnover of stock*
3 [singular, U] the rate at which people leave an organization and are replaced by others: **[+of]** *Low pay accounts for the* ***high turnover.*** | **staff/labour turnover** *a high degree of labour turnover among women*
4 [C] a small fruit PIE: *an apple turnover*

turn·pike /ˈtɜːnpaɪk $ ˈtɜːrn-/ *n* [C] *AmE* a large road for fast traffic that drivers have to pay to use: *the New Jersey Turnpike*

turn·round /ˈtɜːnraʊnd $ ˈtɜːrn-/ *n* [C usually singular] *BrE* a TURNAROUND

ˈturn ˌsignal *n* [C] *AmE* one of the lights on a car that flash to show which way the car is turning SYN **indicator** *BrE* → see picture at CAR

turn·stile /ˈtɜːnstaɪl $ ˈtɜːrn-/ *n* [C] a small gate that spins around and only lets one person at a time go through an entrance → **revolving door**: *We've had 600,000 admissions through the turnstiles.*

turn·ta·ble /ˈtɜːnˌteɪbəl $ ˈtɜːrn-/ *n* [C] **1** the part of a STEREO on which the record turns round **2** a large flat round surface on which railway engines are turned around

turn·ta·blist /ˈtɜːnteɪblɪst $ ˈtɜːrn-/ *n* [C] *informal* a DJ who plays recorded music at parties or dances, and who mixes together parts of different records to form new music

ˈturn-up *n* [C] *BrE* **1** the bottom of a trouser leg that is folded up for decoration or to make it shorter SYN **cuff** *AmE* **2 a turn-up for the book(s)** *informal* an unexpected and surprising event: *Fancy you being in New York too. What a turn-up for the books!*

tur·pen·tine /ˈtɜːpəntaɪn $ ˈtɜːr-/ *n* [U] a type of oil used for making paint more liquid or removing it from clothes, brushes etc

tur·pi·tude /ˈtɜːpɪtjuːd $ ˈtɜːrpɪtuːd/ *n* [U] *formal* very immoral behaviour: *laziness and* ***moral turpitude***

turps /tɜːps $ tɜːrps/ *n* [U] *BrE informal* turpentine

tur·quoise /ˈtɜːkwɔɪz, -kwɑːz $ ˈtɜːrkwɔɪz/ *n* **1** [C,U] a valuable greenish-blue stone or a jewel that is made from this: *turquoise earrings* **2** [U] a greenish-blue colour: *The room was painted in turquoise.* —**turquoise** *adj*: *a clear turquoise sea*

tur·ret /ˈtʌrɪt/ *n* [C] **1** a small tower on a large building, especially a CASTLE **2** the place on a TANK from which guns are fired —**turreted** *adj*

tur·tle /ˈtɜːtl $ ˈtɜːrtl/ ●○○ *n* [C]
1 a REPTILE that lives mainly in water and has a soft body covered by a hard shell → see picture at **REPTILE**
2 *AmE* any REPTILE that has a hard shell covering its body, for example a TORTOISE
3 turn turtle a ship or boat that turns turtle turns upside down

tur·tle·dove /ˈtɜːtldʌv $ ˈtɜːr-/ *n* [C] a type of bird that makes a pleasant soft sound and is sometimes used to represent love

tur·tle·neck /ˈtɜːtlnek $ ˈtɜːr-/ *n* [C] a type of SWEATER with a high, close-fitting collar that covers most of your neck → **polo neck**, **v-neck** → see picture at **NECK**[1]

turves /tɜːvz $ tɜːrvz/ the plural of TURF[1](2)

tush /tʊʃ/ *n* [C] *AmE informal* the part of your body that you sit on

tusk /tʌsk/ *n* [C] one of a pair of very long pointed teeth, that stick out of the mouth of animals such as ELEPHANTS

tus·sle[1] /ˈtʌsəl/ *n* [C] **1** a fight using a lot of energy, in which two people get hold of each other and struggle SYN **struggle**: *After quite a tussle, I finally wrenched the letter from him.* **2** a struggle or argument in which people try to beat each other to get something SYN **contest**: *his defeat in the leadership tussle*

T

tussle[2] *v* [I] **1** to fight or struggle without using any weapons, by pulling or pushing someone rather than hitting them: **[+with]** *He was tussling with the other boys.* **2** to try to beat someone in order to get something SYN **wrestle**: **[+for]** *They tussled for first place in the race.*

tus·sock /ˈtʌsək/ *n* [C] *literary* a small thick mass of grass

tut[1] /tʌt/ (*also* **tut-ˈtut**) *interjection* the sound that you make by touching the top of your mouth with your tongue in order to show disapproval

tut[2] (*also* **tut-ˈtut**) *v* (**tutted**, **tutting**) [I] to express disapproval by making a tut sound: *The nurse rushed in, tutting with irritation.*

tu·te·lage /ˈtjuːtəlɪdʒ $ ˈtuː-/ *n* [U] *formal* **1** when you are taught or looked after by someone: **under sb's tutelage** *You can attend embroidery classes under the tutelage of Jocelyn James.* **2** responsibility for someone's education, actions, or property: *parental tutelage*

tu·tor[1] /ˈtjuːtə $ ˈtuːtər/ ●●○ *n* [C]
1 someone who gives private lessons to one student or a small group, and is paid directly by them: *The children were educated at home by a succession of tutors.* **THESAURUS** TEACHER
2 a teacher in a British university or college → **tutorial**: *She was my tutor at Durham.*

tutor[2] *v* [T] to teach someone as a tutor: *He was privately tutored.* | **tutor sb in sth** *Young men were tutored in the art of handling horses.* **THESAURUS** TEACH

tu·to·ri·al[1] /tjuːˈtɔːriəl $ tuː-/ ●○○ *n* [C]
1 a period of teaching and discussion with a tutor, especially in a British university: *the tutorial system*
2 a computer program that is designed to teach you how to use another program

tutorial[2] *adj* relating to a tutor or their work: *tutorial staff* | *tutorial supervision*

tut·ti frut·ti /ˌtuːti ˈfruːti/ *n* [U] a type of ICE CREAM that has very small pieces of fruit and nuts in it

tu·tu /ˈtuːtuː/ *n* [C] a short skirt made of many folds of stiff material, worn by BALLET dancers

tux·e·do /tʌkˈsiːdəʊ $ -doʊ/ (*also* **tux** /tʌks/ *informal*) *n* (*plural* **tuxedos**) [C] **1** a man's JACKET that is usually black, worn on formal occasions **2** a man's suit that includes this type of JACKET

TV /ˌtiː ˈviː◂/ ●●● S2 W2 *n* [C,U] television: **on TV** *I watched the film on TV.* | **TV series/programme/show/station/channel etc** *a TV series based on the novel* | **cable/satellite TV** | *a new* ***TV set*** | *He's the top* ***TV presenter*** *for children's programmes.*

GRAMMAR: Patterns with TV

- You watch or see something **on TV** or **on the TV**: *We saw the game on TV.* ✗ Don't say: *We saw the game in TV.*
- You say that a programme, person etc is **on TV** or **on the TV**: *The news is on TV right now.* ✗ Don't say: *The news is in TV right now.*

ˌTV ˈdinner *n* [C] a meal that is sold already prepared, so that you just need to heat it before eating

TVP /ˌtiː viː ˈpiː/ *n* [U] the abbreviation of ***textured vegetable protein***

twad·dle /ˈtwɒdl $ ˈtwɑːdl/ *n* [U] *informal* something that someone has said or written that you think is stupid SYN **nonsense**: *I don't believe in all that twaddle about fate.*

twain /tweɪn/ *number old use* **1** two **2 never the twain shall meet** used to say that two things are so different that they can never exist together

twang[1] /twæŋ/ *n* [C usually singular] **1** a quality in the way someone speaks, produced when the air used to speak passes through their nose as well as their mouth: *a* ***nasal twang*** | *Her voice had a slight Australian twang.* **2** a quick ringing sound like the one made by pulling a very tight wire and then suddenly letting it go

twang[2] *v* [I,T] if you twang something or if it twangs, it makes a quick ringing sound by being pulled and then suddenly let go: *She twanged the guitar strings.*

twas /twɒz $ twɑːz/ *literary* it was

twat /twɒt, twæt $ twɑːt/ *n* [C] *taboo informal* **1** an offensive word for a stupid or unpleasant person. Do not use this word. **2** a very offensive word for a woman's VAGINA (=sex organ). Do not use this word.

tweak /twiːk/ *v* [T] **1** to suddenly pull or twist something: *She leant forward and tweaked both ends of his moustache.* **2** to make small changes to a machine, vehicle, or system in order to improve the way it works: *Maybe you should tweak a few sentences before you send in the report.* —**tweak** *n* [C usually singular]

twee /twiː/ *adj BrE* very pretty or perfect, in a way that you find silly or unpleasant: *She produced twee little flower paintings.*

tweed /twiːd/ *n* **1** [U] rough WOOLLEN cloth woven from threads of different colours, used mostly to make JACKETS, suits, and coats: *a thick tweed suit* **2 tweeds** [plural] a suit of clothes made from this type of cloth: *He wore casual country tweeds.*

Twee·dle·dum and Twee·dle·dee /twiːdlˌdʌm ənd twiːdlˈdiː/ two people or groups who are almost exactly the same as each other, especially when they both seem to be bad. The names come from two characters in the book *Through The Looking-Glass* by Lewis Carroll. They are fat little men, who are both dressed in school uniform and look exactly like each other: *Some voters felt there was little real difference between the two party leaders – a case of choosing between Tweedledum and Tweedledee.*

tweed·y /ˈtwiːdi/ *adj* **1** *BrE* wearing tweed clothes in a way that is thought to be typical of the British upper class **2** made of tweed or like tweed

tween /twiːn/ *prep literary* between

tweet /twiːt/ *v* **1** [I] to make the short high sound of a small bird **2** [I,T] to send a short message using the SOCIAL NETWORKING service Twitter —**tweet** *n* [C]

tweet·a·ble /ˈtwiːtəbəl/ *adj* worth tweeting about or able to be sent as a message on Twitter: *His speech contained a lot of tweetable quotes.*

tweet·er /ˈtwiːtə $ -ər/ *n* [C] **1** a SPEAKER (=piece of equipment) through which the high sounds from a STEREO etc are made louder → **woofer 2** someone who sends short messages using the SOCIAL NETWORKING service Twitter

twee·zers /ˈtwiːzəz $ -ərz/ *n* [plural] a small tool that has two narrow pieces of metal joined at one end, used to pull or move very small objects: *She was plucking her eyebrows with a* ***pair of tweezers****.*

twelfth /twelfθ/ *n* [C] one of twelve equal parts of something

twelve /twelv/ ●●● S3 W2 *number* the number 12 → **dozen**: *He received a twelve-month jail sentence.* | *Come at twelve* (=12 o'clock). | *Their son Dylan is twelve* (=12 years old). —**twelfth** *adj, pron*: *her twelfth birthday* | *in the twelfth century* | *I'm planning to leave on* ***the twelfth*** (=the 12th day of the month).

twen·ty /ˈtwenti/ ●●● S2 W2 *number, n*

1 the number 20: *a small village twenty miles from Nairobi* | *I'm nearly twenty* (=20 years old).

2 the twenties [plural] (*also* **the 20s, the 1920s**) the years from 1920 to 1929: *In the twenties the business expanded.* | **the early/mid/late twenties** *The photograph was taken in the late twenties.*

3 be in your twenties to be aged between 20 and 29: **early/mid/late twenties** *She was in her early twenties when I met her.*

4 in the twenties if the temperature is in the twenties, it is between 20 degrees and 29 degrees: **in the low/mid/high twenties** *a warm day, with temperatures in the low twenties*

5 [C] a piece of paper money that is worth £20 or $20: *I offered the driver a twenty.* —**twentieth** *adj, pron*: *in the twentieth century* | *her twentieth birthday* | *I'm planning to leave on* ***the twentieth*** (=the 20th day of the month).

ˌtwenty-ˈfirst *n* [C usually singular] your twenty-first BIRTHDAY or the celebration you have for it

ˌtwenty-four ˈseven, 24-7 *adv* if something happens twenty-four seven, it happens all the time, every day

ˌtwenty-ˈone *n* [U] *AmE* a card game, usually played for money SYN **pontoon** *BrE*

ˌtwenty ˈquestions (*also* **Animal, Vegetable or Mineral** *BrE*) a game in which one person thinks of an object and others have to guess what it is by asking questions about it which can only be answered with 'Yes' or 'No'. You sometimes mention the game when you think that someone is asking or making you ask too many questions: *Just tell me straight, don't make me play twenty questions.*

twen·ty·some·thing /ˈtwentiˌsʌmθɪŋ/ *n* [C] *informal* someone who is between the ages of 20 and 29 → **thirty-something**: *A crowd of twentysomethings were gathered outside the club.* —**twentysomething** *adj*

ˌtwenty-ˈtwenty, 20/20 *n* [U] **1 twenty-twenty vision** the ability to see things normally, without needing glasses: *A pilot must have twenty-twenty vision.* **2 twenty-twenty hindsight** used to say that it is easy to know what you should have done in a situation after it has happened, but you did not know what to do earlier

Twen·ty20 /ˌtwenti ˈtwenti/ *n* [U] a type of CRICKET competition in which teams play against each other in short matches of only twenty OVERS for each side. Twenty20 was introduced in England in 2003 and has since become popular in many parts of the world.

twerp /twɜːp $ twɜːrp/ *n* [C] *informal* a person who you think is stupid or annoying

twice /twaɪs/ ●●● S2 W2 *adv, predeterminer*

1 two times: *He was questioned by police twice yesterday.* | **twice a day/week/year etc** (=two times in the same day, week etc) *Letters were delivered twice a week only.* | *None of our dinner menus are exactly the same* ***twice over****.*

2 two times more, bigger, better etc than something else: **twice as many/much (as sth)** *They employ 90 people, twice as many as last year.* | **twice as high/big/large etc (as sth)** *Interest rates are twice as high as those of our competitors.* | **twice the size/number/rate/amount etc** *an area twice the size of Britain* → **once bitten, twice shy** at ONCE[1](19), → **once or twice** at ONCE[1](12), → **think twice** at THINK[1](8)

twid·dle /ˈtwɪdl/ *v* **1 twiddle your thumbs** *informal* to do nothing while you are waiting for something to happen: *Let's go – there's no point in sitting here twiddling our thumbs.* **2** [I,T] to move or turn something around with your fingers many times, especially because you are nervous or bored: **[+with]** *She was twiddling with her earrings.* —**twiddle** *n* [C]

twig¹ /twɪg/ ●●○ *n* [C] a small very thin stem of wood that grows from a branch on a tree —**twiggy** *adj*

twig² *v* (**twigged, twigging**) [I,T] *BrE informal* to suddenly realize something about a situation: *It took ages before he twigged.*

twi·light /ˈtwaɪlaɪt/ ●○○ *n*

1 [U] the small amount of light in the sky as the day ends: **in the twilight** *The end of the cigarette glowed in the twilight.*

2 [U] the time when day is just starting to become night SYN **dusk**: **at twilight** *romantic walks along the beach at twilight*

3 [singular] the period just before the end of the most active part of someone's life: **[+of]** *in the twilight of her acting career* | *Depression in the* ***twilight years*** (=the last years of your life) *is usually related to illness.*

4 twilight world *literary* a strange situation involving mystery, dishonesty etc: **[+of]** *the twilight world of espionage*

twi·lit /ˈtwaɪlɪt/ *adj literary* lit by twilight

twill /twɪl/ *n* [U] strong cloth woven to produce parallel sloping lines across its surface: *grey twill trousers*

twin¹ /twɪn/ ●●● S3 *n* [C] one of two children born at the same time to the same mother: *The twins are now eight months old.* → IDENTICAL TWIN, SIAMESE TWIN

twin² ●●○ *adj* [only before noun]

1 used to describe one of two children who are twins: **twin sister/brother** *Meet my twin sister.*

2 used to describe two things that happen at the same time and are related to each other: *the twin problems of poverty and unemployment*

3 twin room/bedroom a room that contains two single beds: *All the twin rooms have private bathrooms.* → TWINSET, TWIN TOWN

twin³ *v* (**twinned, twinning**) [T] **1** *BrE* to form a relationship between two similar towns in different countries in order to encourage visits between them: **be twinned with sth** *Chichester in England is twinned with Chartres in France.* **2** to form a relationship between two places, people, or ideas: **be twinned with sth** *Dole has been twinned in the history books with his old rival Bush.* GRAMMAR **Twin** is usually passive. → TWIN TOWN

ˌtwin ˈbed *n* [C] **1** [usually plural] one of a pair of single beds in a room for two people **2** *AmE* a bed that is just big enough for one person → **double bed** —**twin-bedded** *adj BrE*: *twin-bedded rooms*

twine¹ /twaɪn/ *n* [U] strong string made by twisting together two or more threads or strings: *a bundle of papers tied up with twine*

twine² *v* [I,T] *written* to wind or twist around something else, or to make something do this: **twine sth round/around sth** *She twined her arms round him and kissed his cheek.* | **[+round/around]** *A dark green ivy plant twined around the pole.*

twin-en·gined /ˌtwɪn ˈendʒɪnd◂/ *adj* a twin-engined aircraft has two engines

twinge /twɪndʒ/ *n* [C] **1** a sudden feeling of slight pain: *I felt a twinge of pain in my back.* THESAURUS PAIN **2 a twinge of guilt/envy/sadness/jealousy etc** a sudden slight feeling of guilt etc: *He felt a sharp twinge of guilt for not taking the trouble to visit her.*

twin·kle¹ /ˈtwɪŋkəl/ *v* [I] **1** if a star or light twinkles, it shines in the dark with an unsteady light: *stars twinkling in* *the sky* | *I saw lights twinkling in the little town below us.* THESAURUS SHINE **2** if someone's eyes twinkle, they have a happy expression: **[+with]** *Her eyes twinkled with amusement.*

twinkle² *n* [C usually singular] **1 a twinkle in your eye** an expression in your eyes that shows you are happy or amused: *a kindly, white-haired old gentleman with a twinkle in his eye* **2** a small bright shining light that becomes brighter and then fainter

twin·kling /ˈtwɪŋklɪŋ/ *n* **in the twinkling of an eye** (*also* **in a twinkling**) very quickly

twin·set /ˈtwɪnset/ *n* [C] *BrE* a woman's SWEATER and CARDIGAN that are meant to be worn together

ˌtwin ˈtown *n* [C] *BrE* a town that has formed a relationship with a similar town in another country in order to encourage visits between them: *Oxford's twin town is Bonn.* → TWIN³(1)

twirl /twɜːl $ twɜːrl/ *v* [I,T] to turn around and around or make something do this: **[+around/round]** *Couples were twirling around the dance floor.* | **twirl sth around/round** *She twirled the liquid around in her glass.* —**twirl** *n* [C] —**twirly** *adj*

twist¹ /twɪst/ ●●○ S3 *v*

1 MOVE [I,T] **a)** to turn a part of your body around or change your position by turning: *He* ***twisted*** *his* ***head*** *slightly, and looked up at her.* | **[+round/around]** *She twisted round, so that she could see the dog better.* **b)** if you twist your mouth or features, you smile in an unpleasant way or look angry, disapproving etc: *His* ***mouth twisted*** *in a humourless smile.*

2 BEND [T] to bend or turn something, such as wire, hair, or cloth, into a particular shape: **twist sth into sth** *She twisted her handkerchief into a knot.* | **twist sth together** *Twist the two ends of the wire together.*

3 WIND [T always + adv/prep] to wind something around or through an object: **twist sth round/around/through etc sth** *She twisted a silk scarf round her neck.* | *Ann twisted some daisies through Katherine's thick brown hair.*

4 TURN [T] to turn something in a circle using your hand: **twist sth off (sth)** *Jack twisted the cap off the bottle.*

5 ROAD/RIVER [I] if a road, river etc twists, it changes direction in a series of curves: *The road twisted between spectacular mountains.*

6 WORDS [T] to change the true or intended meaning of a statement, especially in order to get some advantage for yourself: *He's always trying to* ***twist*** *my* ***words*** *and make me look bad.*

7 twist your ankle/wrist/knee to hurt your wrist etc by pulling or turning it too suddenly while you are moving: *Harriet slipped on the stairs and twisted her ankle.* THESAURUS HURT

8 twist and turn a) if a path, road, stream etc twists and turns, it has a lot of bends in it: *The river twists and turns through the green fields.* **b)** if a person or animal twists and turns, they make twisting movements

9 twist sb's arm a) *informal* to persuade someone to do something they do not want to do: *No one twisted my arm about coming to see you.* **b)** to bend someone's arm upwards behind their back in order to hurt them: *The policeman twisted my arm behind me and arrested me.* → **twist/wrap sb around your little finger** at FINGER¹(8), → **twist the knife (in the wound)** at KNIFE¹(3)

twist² ●○○ *n* [C]

1 an unexpected feature or change in a situation or series of events: **a new/cruel/unexpected/strange etc twist** *The robbery took a deadly new twist as the robber pulled out a gun.* | *an unexpected twist in the plot* | *By an amazing* ***twist of fate****, we met again in Madrid five years later.*

2 a twisting action or movement: *He smiled, a slow cynical twist of his lips.*

3 a bend in a river or road

4 a small piece of something that is twisted into a particular shape: **[+of]** *a twist of lemon*

5 the twist a popular fast dance from the 1960s in which you twist your body from side to side

6 round the twist *BrE spoken* **a)** crazy: *'The woman's mad,' she told herself. 'She's round the twist.'* **b)** very angry —**twisty** *adj*: *a twisty road* → **(don't) get your knickers in a twist** at KNICKERS(3)

twist·ed /ˈtwɪstɪd/ ●●○ (*also* **ˌtwisted ˈup**) *adj*

1 something twisted has been bent in many directions or turned many times, so that it has lost its original shape: *the plane's twisted wreckage* → see picture at CURVED

2 seeming to enjoy things that are cruel or shocking, in a way that is not normal SYN **sick**: *Whoever sent those letters has a twisted mind.*

twist·er /ˈtwɪstə $ -ər/ *n* [C] **1** *BrE informal* someone who cheats other people **2** *AmE informal* a TORNADO

twit /twɪt/ *n* [C] *informal* a person who you think is stupid or silly

twitch¹ /twɪtʃ/ *v* **1** [I,T] if a part of someone's body twitches, or if they twitch it, it makes a small sudden movement: *His* ***mouth twitched*** *slightly, and then he smiled.* | *He twitched his eyebrows.* THESAURUS MOVE **2** [T] to move something quickly and suddenly: *Sarah twitched the reins, and we moved off.*

twitch² *n* [C] **1** a quick movement of a muscle, especially one that you cannot control: *a nervous twitch* **2** a sudden quick movement: *There was no movement in the house, not even a twitch of the curtains.*

twitch·er /ˈtwɪtʃə $ -ər/ *n* [C] *BrE informal* a keen BIRD-WATCHER

twitch·y /ˈtwɪtʃi/ *adj* behaving in a nervous way because you are anxious about something: *I was very twitchy about the way things would turn out.*

twit·ter¹ /ˈtwɪtə $ -ər/ *v* [I] **1** if a bird twitters, it makes a lot of short high sounds **2** to talk about unimportant and silly things, usually very quickly and nervously in a high voice **3** to send a short message using the SOCIAL NETWORKING service Twitter

twitter² *n* **1** [singular] the short high sounds that birds make **2 be all of a twitter** (*also* **be in a twitter**) *BrE* to be excited and nervous: *She's been all of a twitter since her daughter's engagement.*

Twitter *trademark* a SOCIAL NETWORKING service on the Internet which allows MINI-BLOGGING (=sending short text messages to other users)

ˈTwitter storm, Twitterstorm *n* [C] a sudden large number of messages about someone or something on the SOCIAL NETWORKING service Twitter: *His controversial comments caused a Twitter storm.*

twixt /twɪkst/ *prep old use* between

two /tuː/ ●●● S2 W1 *number*

1 the number 2: *I'll be away for almost two weeks.* | *We have to be there by two* (=two o'clock). | *His family moved to Australia when he was two* (=two years old).

2 in twos in groups of two people or things: *I'd like you to line up in twos, please.* → TWOSOME

3 put two and two together to guess the meaning of something you have heard or seen: *I saw him leaving her house and I put two and two together.*

4 that makes two of us *spoken* used to tell someone that you are in the same situation and feel the same way: *'But I don't know anything about children!' 'Well, that makes two of us.'*

5 two can play at that game *spoken* used to tell someone that they will not have an advantage over you by doing something because you can do it too

6 a year/a week/a moment/an hour etc or two *spoken* one or a few years, weeks etc

7 two sides of the same coin used to talk about two ways of looking at the same situation

8 two heads are better than one used to say that two people are more likely to solve a problem or think of an idea than one person working alone

9 be in two minds (about sth) *BrE*, **be of two minds (about sth)** *AmE* to be unable to decide what to do, or what you think about something: *I was in two minds about whether to go with him.*

10 two cents (worth) *AmE informal* your opinion or what you want to say about a subject: *Everyone had to put in their two cents worth.*

11 two's company, three's a crowd used to say that it is better to leave two people alone to spend time with each other → **don't care two hoots** at HOOT[1](5), → **two/three etc of a kind** at KIND[1](6), → **be two/ten a penny** at PENNY(11), → **in ones and twos** at ONE[1](3), → **it takes two to tango** at TANGO[2](2), → **kill two birds with one stone** at KILL[1](13), → **no two ways about it** at WAY[1](54), → **fall between two stools** at FALL[1](32)

ˈtwo-bit *adj especially AmE informal* not at all good or important SYN **second-rate**: *She's just a two-bit movie star.*

ˌtwo-diˈmensional ●○○ *adj*
1 flat: *a two-dimensional shape*
2 a two-dimensional character in a book, play etc does not seem like a real person

ˌtwo-ˈedged *adj* **1** having two effects or meanings, one good and one bad: *a two-edged comment* | **a two-edged sword** (=something that has as many bad results as good ones) *Strong leadership is a two-edged sword.* **2** having two edges that can cut: *a two-edged blade*

ˌtwo-ˈfaced *adj informal* changing what you say according to who you are talking to, in a way that is insincere and unpleasant - used to show disapproval: *He's a two-faced liar.*

two·fold /ˈtuːfəʊld $ -foʊld/ *adj* **1** two times as much or as many of something: *a **twofold increase** in cases of TB* **2** having two important parts: *The benefits of the scheme are twofold.* —**twofold** *adv*: *Student numbers have expanded twofold in ten years.*

ˌtwo-ˈhanded *adj* **1** using or needing both hands to do something: *a two-handed catch* | *a two-handed sword* **2** a two-handed tool is used by two people together

ˈtwo-man *adj* designed to be used by two people SYN **two-person**: *a two-man tent*

two·pence /ˈtʌpəns/ *n* [C,U] *BrE* another word for TUPPENCE

two·pen·ny /ˈtʌpəni $ ˈtʌpəni, ˈtuːpeni/ *adj BrE old-fashioned* **1** [only before noun] costing two pence SYN **tuppenny** **2** **twopenny-halfpenny** worth almost nothing

ˌtwo-percent ˈmilk *n* [U] *AmE* milk that has had about half the fat removed

ˌtwo-ˈperson *adj* [only before noun] **1** consisting of two people: *a two-person household* **2** designed to be used by two people SYN **two-man**

ˈtwo-piece *adj* [only before noun] a two-piece suit consists of a matching JACKET and trousers

ˌtwo-ˈseater *n* [C] a vehicle or a piece of furniture with seats for two people: *a two-seater sofa*

ˌtwo-ˈsided *adj* having two different parts: *a two-sided problem* → ONE-SIDED, MANY-SIDED

two·some /ˈtuːsəm/ *n* [C usually singular] two people who work together or spend a lot of time together: *a well-known comedy twosome*

ˈtwo-star *adj* [only before noun] a two-star hotel, restaurant etc has been judged to be of a MEDIUM standard

ˈtwo-step *n* [singular] a dance with long sliding steps, or the music for this type of dance

ˈtwo-stroke *adj* a two-stroke engine is one in which there is a single up-and-down movement of a PISTON

ˈtwo-time *v* [T] *informal* to have a secret relationship with someone who is not your regular partner SYN **cheat**: *He doesn't know Claire's been two-timing him.* —**two-timer** *n* [C]

ˈtwo-tone *adj* having two different colours or sounds: *two-tone shoes* | *a two-tone alarm*

ˌtwo-ˈtwo, 2:2 *n* [C] the lower of two levels of a SECOND-CLASS university degree in Britain

ˌtwo-ˈup, ˌtwo-ˈdown *n* [C] *BrE* a small house with two rooms upstairs and two rooms downstairs

ˌtwo-ˈway *adj* **1** moving or allowing movement in both directions: *two-way traffic* | *two-way trade* **2** used to describe a relationship which needs effort from both the people or groups involved: *Corruption is a two-way process.* **3** a two-way radio both sends and receives messages

ˌtwo-way ˈmirror *n* [C] glass that is a mirror from one side, but that you can see through from the other

ˌtwo-way ˈstreet *n informal* **sth is a two-way street** used to say that a situation depends on two people working well together: *Marriage has to be a two-way street.*

-ty /ti/ *suffix* [in nouns] another form of -ITY: *certainty* (=being certain)

ty·coon /taɪˈkuːn/ *n* [C] someone who is successful in business or industry and has a lot of money and power: **media/property/business/newspaper tycoon** *a multi-millionaire property tycoon*

ty·ing /ˈtaɪ-ɪŋ/ the present participle of TIE

tyke /taɪk/ *n* [C] **1** *BrE spoken* a child who is behaving badly **2** *AmE informal* a small child **3** *BrE informal* someone from Yorkshire

tym·pa·num /ˈtɪmpənəm/ *n* (*plural* **tympanums** *or* **tympana** /-nə/) [C] *technical* an EARDRUM

type¹ /taɪp/ ●●● S1 W1 *n*
1 [C] one member of a group of people or things that have similar features or qualities: **of this/that/each etc type** *I've already seen a few movies of this type.* | **[+of]** *What type of music do you like?* | *There are two main types of sleep.*

GRAMMAR: Countable or uncountable?

Type is a countable noun and should be plural after words such as 'these', 'those', and 'many': *this type of building* | *these types of building* ✗ Don't say: *these type of building*

2 [singular] a person who has, or seems to have, a particular character: *Jo's not really the sporty type.* | *Beth **is not the type to** make a fuss.*
3 be sb's type *especially spoken* to be the kind of person someone is sexually attracted to: *He wasn't my type really.*
4 [U] printed letters: *italic type*
5 [C,U] a small block with a raised letter on it that is used to print with, or a set of these

COLLOCATIONS

ADJECTIVES/NOUN + type

this/that type *He is not suited to this type of work.*
a particular type *Have you flown this particular type of aircraft before?*
the same type *They use the same type of axe as a tool and a weapon.*
a different type *I've learned to work with different types of people.*
a new type *These architects felt the time had come for a new type of public building.*
the main type *Methane is the main type of gas produced.*
skin/hair type *The best cleanser for you depends on your skin type.*
blood type *AmE* (=one of the classes into which human blood can be separated) *Mother and child had the same blood type.*
personality type (=with a particular type of character) *Find out your personality type by answering our simple questionnaire.*
soil type (=for example, sandy soil or clay soil)

type² ●●● S2 W3 *v*
1 [I,T] to write something using a computer or a TYPEWRITER: *He types with two fingers.* | *Type your password, then press 'Return'.* | **type sth up** (=type a copy of something written by hand, in note form, or recorded) *I went home to type up the report.* | **type sth in** (=write information on a computer) *Please wait while I type in your details.*
2 [T] *technical* to find out what group something such as blood, cells, or a disease belong to: *DNA typing*

type·cast /ˈtaɪpkɑːst $ -kæst/ *v* (*past tense and past participle* **typecast**) [T] **1** to always give an actor the same type of character to play: *He always gets typecast as the villain.* **2** to give someone a particular type of job, activity etc to do, because you think it suits their character —**typecasting** *n* [U]

type·face /ˈtaɪpfeɪs/ *n* [C] a group of letters, numbers etc of the same style and size, used in printing SYN **font**: *The new logo features a more modern typeface.*

T

type·script /ˈtaɪpˌskrɪpt/ *n* [C] a copy of a document that has been typed

type·set·ting /ˈtaɪpˌsetɪŋ/ *n* [U] the job or activity of arranging TYPE[1](5) for printing: *computerized typesetting* —**typesetter** *n* [C] —**typeset** *v* [T]

type·writ·er /ˈtaɪpˌraɪtə $ -ər/ *n* [C] a machine with keys that you press in order to print letters of the alphabet onto paper

type·writ·ten /ˈtaɪpˌrɪtn/ *adj* written using a computer or a TYPEWRITER: *typewritten notes*

ty·phoid /ˈtaɪfɔɪd/ (*also* ˌ**typhoid** ˈ**fever**) *n* [U] a serious infectious disease that is caused by dirty food or drink: *a sudden outbreak of typhoid*

ty·phoon /ˌtaɪˈfuːn◂/ *n* [C] a very violent tropical storm **THESAURUS** ▸ STORM, WIND

ty·phus /ˈtaɪfəs/ *n* [U] a serious infectious disease carried by insects that live on the bodies of people and animals: *a typhus epidemic*

typ·i·cal /ˈtɪpɪkəl/ ●●● S2 W2 *adj*
1 having the usual features or qualities of a particular group or thing: *typical British weather* | **[+of]** *This painting is typical of his work.* | *This advertisement is a* ***typical example*** *of their marketing strategy.*
2 happening in the usual way: *On a* ***typical day****, our students go to classes from 7.30 am to 1 pm.* | *Try calculating your budget for a typical week.*
3 behaving in the way that you expect: *Bennett accepted the award with typical modesty.* | **it is typical of sb to do sth** *It's not typical of Gill to be so critical.* | *Mr Stevens' appointment was a* ***typical case*** *of promoting a man beyond his level of competence.*
4 typical! *spoken* used to show that you are annoyed when something bad happens again, or when someone does something bad again

THESAURUS

typical a typical person or thing is a good example of that type of person or thing: *With his camera around his neck, he looked like a typical tourist.* | *The windows are typical of houses built during this period.*
classic used to describe a very typical and very good example of something: *It was a classic case of the cure being worse than the disease.* | *a classic mistake*
archetypal the archetypal person or thing is the most typical example of that kind of person or thing, and has all their most important qualities: *the archetypal English village* | *Indiana Jones is the archetypal adventure hero.*
quintessential used when you want to emphasize that someone or something is the very best example of something – used especially when you admire them very much: *the quintessential guide to New York* | *Robert Plant is the quintessential rock 'n' roll singer.*
stereotypical having the characteristics that many people believe a particular type of person or thing has – used when you think these beliefs are not true: *Hollywood films are full of stereotypical images of women as wives and mothers.* | *He challenges stereotypical ideas about people with disabilities.*
representative containing the most common types of people or things that are found in something, and showing what it is usually like: *a representative sample of college students*
characteristic very typical of a particular type of thing, or of someone's character or usual behaviour: *Each species of bird has its own characteristic song.* | *What gives Paris its characteristic charm?*
be the epitome of sth to be the best possible example of a particular type of person or thing or of a particular quality: *His house was thought to be the epitome of good taste.*

typ·i·cally /ˈtɪpɪkli/ ●●○ *adv*
1 in a way that a person or group is generally believed to behave: *Typically, he didn't even bother to tell anyone he was going.* | *Al was his typically cheerful self again.*
2 in a way that shows the usual or expected features of someone or something: *a delightful, typically Dutch hotel* | *The male of the species is typically smaller than the female.*
3 in the way that a particular type of thing usually happens SYN **generally**: *Women in developing countries typically have their first child when they are very young.* | *I typically get around 30 emails a day.*

typ·i·fy /ˈtɪpɪfaɪ/ *v* (**typified**, **typifying**, **typifies**) [T] **1** to be a typical example of something: *the features which typify a Scottish Highland landscape* | *non-violent protest,* ***typified by*** *Gandhi* **2** to be a typical part or feature of something: *the long complicated sentences that typify legal documents*

typ·ing /ˈtaɪpɪŋ/ *n* [U] the activity of using a computer or a TYPEWRITER to write something: *typing errors* | *I'm no good at typing.*

ˈ**typing pool** *n* [C] a group of typists in a large office who type letters for other people

typ·ist /ˈtaɪpɪst/ *n* [C] **1** a secretary whose main job is to TYPE letters **2** someone who uses a computer KEYBOARD or a TYPEWRITER: *I'm a slow typist.*

ty·po /ˈtaɪpəʊ $ -poʊ/ *n* (*plural* **typos**) [C] a small mistake in the way something has been TYPEd or printed **THESAURUS** ▸ MISTAKE

ty·pog·ra·pher /taɪˈpɒɡrəfə $ -ˈpɑːɡrəfər/ *n* [C] **1** someone who designs TYPEFACES **2** a COMPOSITOR

ty·pog·ra·phy /taɪˈpɒɡrəfi $ -ˈpɑː-/ *n* [U] **1** the work of preparing written material for printing **2** the arrangement, style, and appearance of printed words —**typographic** /ˌtaɪpəˈɡræfɪk◂/, **typographical** *adj*: *typographic errors* —**typographically** /-kli/ *adv*

ty·pol·o·gy /taɪˈpɒlədʒi $ -pɑː-/ *n* (*plural* **typologies**) [C,U] a system or the study of dividing a group of things into smaller groups according to the similar qualities they have —**typological** /ˌtaɪpəˈlɒdʒɪkəl◂ $ -ˈlɑː-/ *adj*

ty·ran·ni·cal /təˈrænɪkəl/ *adj* behaving in a cruel and unfair way towards someone you have power over → **tyrant**: *a tyrannical parent* | *tyrannical laws*

tyr·an·nize (*also* **-ise** *BrE*) /ˈtɪrənaɪz/ *v* [I,T] to use power over someone cruelly or unfairly: *The children were tyrannized by their father.* | **[+over]** *armed groups tyrannizing over civilians*

ty·ran·no·sau·rus /təˌrænəˈsɔːrəs◂/ (*also* **ty**ˌ**rannosaurus** ˈ**rex**) *n* [C] a very large flesh-eating DINOSAUR

tyr·an·nous /ˈtɪrənəs/ *adj old-fashioned* TYRANNICAL

tyr·an·ny /ˈtɪrəni/ *n* (*plural* **tyrannies**) [C,U] **1** cruel or unfair control over other people: *Gorky was often the victim of his grandfather's tyranny.* | *the fight against tyranny* **2** cruel and unfair government: *organizations which have criticized the tyrannies of the government* **3 tyranny of the majority** the idea that if everyone has the right to vote, they will make decisions which will harm the country **4** something in your life that limits your freedom to do things the way you want to: **[+of]** *the tyranny of the nine-to-five working day*

ty·rant /ˈtaɪərənt $ ˈtaɪr-/ ●○○ *n* [C]
1 a ruler who has complete power and uses it in a cruel and unfair way: *The country had long been ruled by tyrants.*
2 someone who has power over other people, and uses it cruelly or unfairly: *My headmaster was a real tyrant.*

tyre *BrE*, **tire** *AmE* /taɪə $ taɪr/ ●●● S3 *n* [C] a thick rubber ring that fits around the wheel of a car, bicycle etc: *I had a* ***flat tyre*** (=all the air went out of it) *on the way home.* | *The* ***spare tyre****'s in the boot.* | **front/rear/back tyre** *a punctured front tyre* → **SPARE TYRE**, see pictures at **BICYCLE, CAR**

tzar /zɑː, tsɑː $ zɑːr, tsɑːr/ *n* [C] another spelling of TSAR

tza·ri·na /zɑːˈriːnə, tsɑː-/ *n* [C] another spelling of TSARINA

tzar·is·m /ˈzɑːrɪzəm,ˈtsɑː-/ *n* [U] another spelling of TSARISM

tze·tze fly /ˈtetsi flaɪ, ˈtsetsi-, ˈsetsi-/ *n* [C] another spelling of TSETSE FLY

Uu

U¹, **u** /juː/ (*plural* **U's, u's**) *n* **1** [C,U] the 21st letter of the English alphabet **2** [singular, U] *BrE* used to describe a film that has been officially approved as suitable for people of any age → **PG** SYN **G** *AmE* **3** [C] *BrE* a mark given to a student's work to show that it is extremely bad → **U-BOAT**, **U-TURN**

U² *pron written informal* a way of writing 'you', used especially in emails and TEXT MESSAGES: *I love U!*

U., **U** /juː/ *AmE informal* an abbreviation of ***university***: *Indiana U*

UAV /ˌjuː eɪ ˈviː/ *n* [C] *AmE* (***unmanned aerial vehicle***) a type of plane that has no pilot, used especially for gathering information and taking photographs

uber- /uːbə, juːbə $ -ər/ *prefix informal* better, larger, or greater SYN **super**: *uberbabe Pamela Lee* | *I want to do something uber-cool with my webpage.*

u·biq·ui·tous /juːˈbɪkwɪtəs/ ●○○ *adj formal* seeming to be everywhere – sometimes used humorously: *Coffee shops are ubiquitous these days.* | *a French film, starring the ubiquitous Gérard Depardieu* **THESAURUS** **COMMON** —**ubiquitously** *adv* —**ubiquity** *n* [U]

U-boat /ˈjuː bəʊt $ -boʊt/ *n* [C] a German SUBMARINE, especially one that was used in the Second World War

ud·der /ˈʌdə $ -ər/ *n* [C] the part of a cow, female goat etc that hangs down between its back legs and that produces milk

UFO /ˈjuːfəʊ, ˌjuː ef ˈəʊ $ -foʊ, -ˈoʊ/ *n* [C] (***unidentified flying object***) a strange object in the sky, that some people believe is a SPACESHIP from another world SYN **flying saucer**

ugh /ʊx, ʌg/ *interjection* the sound that people make when something is extremely unpleasant: *Ugh! That's disgusting!*

ug·ly /ˈʌgli/ ●●● S3 *adj* (*comparative* **uglier**, *superlative* **ugliest**)

1 extremely unattractive and unpleasant to look at SYN **hideous** OPP **beautiful**: *a very ugly man* | *the ugliest building in town* | *Nick's dog is* ***as ugly as sin*** (=very ugly).

2 used to describe a situation which is very bad or violent, and which makes you feel frightened or threatened: *There were* ***ugly scenes*** *as rival gangs started attacking each other.* | *an* ***ugly incident***

3 ugly ideas, feelings, remarks etc are unpleasant: *Jealousy is an ugly emotion.* | *ugly rumors*

4 ugly duckling someone who is less attractive, successful etc than other people, but who becomes beautiful and successful later —**ugliness** *n* [U]

THESAURUS

ugly very unpleasant to look at – used about people, objects, and buildings: *She thinks she's ugly but she's not.* | *an ugly block of flats* | *cheap ugly furniture*

unattractive not pleasant to look at. Unattractive sounds more formal and less strong than **ugly**: *an unattractive modern town which was built during the 1960s* | *Women found him unattractive.*

unsightly *formal* not pleasant to look at, and spoiling the appearance of something: *Unsightly red spots started to appear on her face.* | *The windows have been blocked off with unsightly metal bars.*

EXTREMELY UGLY

hideous extremely ugly: *His hideous face twisted into a smile.* | *a hideous concrete shopping centre*

repulsive extremely ugly, especially in a way that makes you want to look away: *His appearance was so repulsive he had to wear a mask.*

grotesque extremely ugly in a strange or unnatural way: *A grotesque figure appeared out of the darkness.*

an eyesore (*also* **a blot on the landscape**) *n* [singular] something that is so ugly that it spoils the appearance of an area: *Local residents regard the new office building as an eyesore.*

ˌUgly Aˈmerican, the *AmE* an American travelling abroad who behaves in a way that people find offensive, especially by showing a lack of understanding of, or lack of interest in, the CULTURE and way of life of other countries

ˌUgly ˈSisters, the two characters in the FAIRY TALE about Cinderella. They are Cinderella's sisters, and are ugly and treat her very badly. In the UK, the story is often performed as a PANTOMIME (=a humorous play for children), and the Ugly Sisters are almost always played by male actors.

UHF /ˌjuː eɪtʃ ˈef/ *n* [U] (***ultra-high frequency***) a range of radio waves that produces a very good quality of sound

uh huh /ʌ ˈhʌ,ˈʌ hʌ/ *interjection informal* a sound that you make to say 'yes', or when you want someone to continue what they are saying: *'Can I sit here?' 'Uh huh.'*

uh-oh /ˈʌ əʊ $ -oʊ/ *interjection informal* a sound that you make when you have made a mistake, or when something bad is going to happen: *Uh-oh, I think I just deleted all my work.* | *Uh-oh! Here she comes.*

UHT milk /ˌjuː eɪtʃ tiː ˈmɪlk/ *n* [U] *BrE* milk that has been heated to a very high temperature to preserve it

uh-uh /ˈʌ ʌ/ *interjection informal* a sound that you make to say 'no': *'Is Paul here yet?' 'Uh-uh.'*

UK, the, **the U.K.** /ˌjuː ˈkeɪ◂/ the abbreviation of ***the United Kingdom***

u·ku·le·le, **ukelele** /ˌjuːkəˈleɪli/ *n* [C] a musical instrument with four strings, like a small GUITAR

-ular /jələ $ -ər/ *suffix* [in adjectives] of or relating to something: *glandular fever* | *tubular steel*

ul·cer /ˈʌlsə $ -ər/ ●○○ *n* [C] a sore area on your skin or inside your body that may BLEED or produce poisonous substances: *stomach ulcers* —**ulcerous** *adj*

ul·cer·ate /ˈʌlsəreɪt/ *v* [I,T] to form an ulcer, or become covered with ulcers —**ulcerated** *adj* —**ulceration** /ˌʌlsəˈreɪʃən/ *n* [U]

ul·na /ˈʌlnə/ *n* (*plural* **ulnae** /-niː/) [C] *medical* the inner bone of your lower arm, on the side opposite to your thumb → see picture at **SKELETON**

ul·te·ri·or /ʌlˈtɪəriə $ -ˈtɪriər/ *adj* **ulterior motive/purpose etc** a reason for doing something that you deliberately hide in order to get an advantage for yourself: *He's just being nice. I don't think he* ***has*** *any* ***ulterior motives***.

ul·ti·mate¹ /ˈʌltəmət/ ●●○ W3 AWL *adj* [only before noun]

1 someone's ultimate aim is their main and most important aim, that they hope to achieve in the future SYN **final**: **ultimate goal/aim/objective etc** *Complete disarmament was the ultimate goal of the conference.* | *Our ultimate objective is to have as many female members of parliament as there are male.*

2 the ultimate result of a long process is what happens at the end of it: *The* ***ultimate outcome*** *of the experiment cannot be predicted.* | *The* ***ultimate fate*** *of the tribe was even sadder.* | *the ultimate failure of the project*

3 if you have ultimate responsibility for something, you are the person who must make the important final decisions about it: *The ultimate responsibility for policy lies with the president.* | *The* ***ultimate decision*** *rests with the Public Health Service.*

4 better, bigger, worse etc than all other things or people of the same kind: *The Rolling Stones are the ultimate rock and roll band.* | *The female nude is surely the ultimate test of artistic skill.*

ultimate² *n* **the ultimate in sth** the best or most modern example of something: *The plane was the ultimate in air technology in the '60s.* | *Guy's home is* ***the ultimate in luxury***.

ˌultimate ˈfighting (*also* **extreme fighting**) *n* [U] a competition, similar to BOXING, in which two people hit or kick each other and in which there are almost no rules

ul·ti·mate·ly /ˈʌltəmətli/ ●●○ W3 AWL *adv* finally, after everything else has been done or considered: [sentence adverb] *Ultimately, the decision rests with the child's parents.* | *a long but ultimately successful campaign*

ul·ti·ma·tum /ˌʌltəˈmeɪtəm/ ●○○ *n* (*plural* **ultimatums** *or* **ultimata** /-tə/) [C] a threat saying that if someone does not do what you want by a particular time, you will do something to punish them: *The club* ***gave*** *him* ***an ultimatum*** *- either he apologized, or he would be expelled from the team.* | *The army* ***issued an ultimatum*** *for all weapons in the city to be surrendered by October 26th.*

ultra- /ʌltrə/ *prefix* **1** extremely: *an ultra-modern building* | *He remained ultra-cautious.* | *an ultra-light jacket* **2** *technical* above and beyond something in a range: *ultrasound* (=sound that is too high for humans to hear) → INFRA-

Ul·tra·book /ˈʌltrəbʊk/ *n* [C] *trademark* a very thin fast light LAPTOP computer

ul·tra·ma·rine /ˌʌltrəməˈriːn◂/ *n* [U] a very bright blue colour —**ultramarine** *adj*

ul·tra·port·a·ble /ˌʌltrəˈpɔːtəbəl $ -ˈpɔːr-/ *adj* ultraportable computers are very small and easy to carry: *Which are the best ultraportable laptops?*

ul·tra·son·ic /ˌʌltrəˈsɒnɪk◂ $ -ˈsɑː-/ *adj* ultrasonic sound waves are too high for humans to hear

ul·tra·sound /ˈʌltrəsaʊnd/ *n* **1** [U] sound that is too high for humans to hear **2** [C,U] a medical process using this type of sound, that produces an image of something inside your body: *investigation of the liver by ultrasound* | *An* ***ultrasound scan*** *revealed that the baby was a boy.*

ul·tra·vi·o·let /ˌʌltrəˈvaɪəlɪt◂/ *adj* (*abbreviation* **UV**) ultraviolet light cannot be seen by people, but is responsible for making your skin darker when you are in the sun: **ultraviolet radiation/rays** *ultraviolet radiation from the sun*

u·lu·late /ˈjuːljəleɪt, ˈʌl- $ ˈʌl-, ˈjuː-/ *v* [I] *literary* to cry out with a long high sound, especially because you are very sad or in pain SYN **wail** —**ululation** /ˌjuːljəˈleɪʃən, ˌʌl- $ ˌʌl-, ˌjuː-/ *n* [C,U]

um /ʌm, əm/ *interjection* used when you cannot immediately decide what to say next: *Um, yeah, I guess so.*

u·ma·mi /uːˈmɑːmi/ *adj* having a strong pleasant taste that is not sweet, sour, salty, or bitter, especially like the tastes found in meat, strong cheeses, tomatoes etc —**umami** *n* [U]

ˌum and ˈah *v* [I] *informal* to think for some time before making a decision: *He ummed and ahed a bit but eventually agreed to help us.*

um·ber /ˈʌmbə $ -ər/ *n* [U] a brown colour like earth

um·bil·i·cal cord /ʌmˈbɪlɪkəl ˌkɔːd $ -ˌkɔːrd/ *n* [C] **1** a long narrow tube of flesh that joins an unborn baby to its mother **2** a strong feeling of belonging to or a strong feeling of relationship with a particular place, person, organization etc: *All modern popular music has an umbilical cord linking back to blues and R and B.* | *Teenage boys especially feel a need to* ***cut the umbilical cord*** *tying them to their mothers.*

um·brage /ˈʌmbrɪdʒ/ *n* **take umbrage (at sth)** to be offended by something that someone has done or said, often without good reason

um·brel·la /ʌmˈbrelə/ ●●● S3 *n* [C]

1 an object that you use to protect yourself against rain or hot sun. It consists of a circular folding frame covered in cloth → **parasol**: *It started to rain, so Tricia stopped to* ***put up*** *her* ***umbrella***. | *I spent the day on the beach, lying under a* ***beach umbrella***, *reading.*

2 umbrella organization/group/agency etc an organization that includes many smaller groups

3 umbrella term/word/title etc a word whose meaning includes many different types of a particular thing: *District nurses, health visitors, and school nurses will come under the umbrella term 'community nursing'.*

4 (come/work etc) under the umbrella of sth to be part of a larger organization or involved in the work done by it: *The international education program came under the umbrella of the State Department.*

5 the protection given by a powerful country, army, a weapons system etc: *the American nuclear umbrella over western Europe*

um·laut /ˈʊmlaʊt/ *n* [C] a sign (¨) written over a German vowel to show how it is pronounced

ump /ʌmp/ *n* [C] *AmE spoken* an umpire

UMPIRE

um·pire¹ /ˈʌmpaɪə $ -paɪr/ ●○○ *n* [C] the person who makes sure that the players obey the rules in sports such as tennis, baseball, and CRICKET → **referee** → see picture at TENNIS

umpire² *v* [I,T] to be the umpire in a game or competition

ump·teen /ˌʌmpˈtiːn◂/ *number informal* very many - used especially when you are annoyed there are so many: *There seemed to be umpteen rules and regulations to learn.* | *She'd called the apartment umpteen times, but never got an answer.*

ump·teenth /ˌʌmpˈtiːnθ◂/ *adj* [only before noun] if something happens for the umpteenth time, it happens again after having happened many times before - used when you are annoyed that it has happened so often: *'This is crazy,' she told herself* ***for the umpteenth time***.

un- /ʌn/ *prefix* **1** [in adjectives, adverbs, and nouns] used to show a negative, a lack, or an opposite SYN **not**: *unfair* | *unhappy* | *unfortunately* | *uncertainty* **2** [in verbs] used to show an opposite of a particular action: *to undress* (=to take your clothes off) | *Have you unpacked yet* (=taken your things out of your suitcase)? | *I heard Lila unlock the front door.*

'un /ən/ *pron BrE spoken* **good 'un/bad 'un/little 'un etc** a short form of 'one', used to say that someone or something is good, bad etc. Teachers and careful speakers of English do not use this expression: *He's a bad 'un.* | *I ought to collect the little 'uns* (=young children) *from school.*

U.N., **UN** /ˌjuː ˈen/ *n* **the UN** (*the* ***United Nations***) an international organization that tries to find peaceful solutions to world problems

un·a·bashed /ˌʌnəˈbæʃt◂/ *adj written* not ashamed or embarrassed, especially when doing something unusual or rude: *She stared at him with unabashed curiosity.*

un·a·bat·ed /ˌʌnəˈbeɪtɪd◂/ *adj, adv* continuing without becoming any weaker or less violent: *The storm* ***continued unabated*** *throughout the night.* | *his unabated ambition*

un·a·ble /ʌnˈeɪbəl/ ●●● W2 *adj* [not before noun] not able to do something → **inability**: **unable to do sth** *Lucy was unable to find out what had happened.* | *Unable to sleep, I got up and made myself a drink.*

> **REGISTER**
> In everyday English, people usually say that they **can't/couldn't do sth** rather than **are/were unable to do sth**: *She* ***couldn't*** *find out what had happened.*

U

un·a·bridged /ˌʌnəˈbrɪdʒd◂/ *adj* a piece of writing, speech etc that is unabridged is in its full form and has not been made shorter: *the complete and unabridged works of Dickens*

un·ac·cept·a·ble /ˌʌnəkˈseptəbəl◂/ ●●○ *adj* something that is unacceptable is so wrong or bad that you think it should not be allowed: *I found her attitude totally unacceptable.* | *unacceptable levels of pollution* | **[+to]** *The recommendations from this report are unacceptable to many black people.* | **unacceptable to do sth** *It was socially unacceptable to discuss sex then.* —**unacceptably** *adv*: *Unemployment is unacceptably high.*

un·ac·com·pa·nied /ˌʌnəˈkʌmpənid◂/ AWL *adj* **1** someone or something that is unaccompanied has no one with them → **accompany**: ***Unaccompanied children*** *are not allowed on the premises.* | **unaccompanied bag/luggage etc** *The airport X-rays all unaccompanied baggage.* **2 unaccompanied by sth** *formal* without something: *Many large Third World cities have arisen unaccompanied by national industrial growth.* **3** an unaccompanied singer or musician sings or plays alone → **accompaniment**, **accompanist**: *Lizzie* ***sang unaccompanied***. | *works for unaccompanied violin*

un·ac·count·a·ble /ˌʌnəˈkaʊntəbəl◂/ *adj formal* **1** very surprising and difficult to explain: *the unaccountable shyness she always felt in Louise's presence* | ***For some unaccountable reason****, he arrived a day early.* **2** not having to explain your actions or decisions to anyone else OPP **accountable**: **[+to]** *Doctors still remain largely unaccountable to the public.*

un·ac·count·a·bly /ˌʌnəˈkaʊntəbli/ *adv* [sentence adverb] used to say that something is very surprising and difficult to explain: *Unaccountably, the woman had refused.* | *The planned military assault on the city yesterday was unaccountably delayed.*

un·ac·count·ed for /ʌnəˈkaʊntəd fɔː $ -fɔːr/ *adj* something or someone that is unaccounted for cannot be found or their absence cannot be explained: *Two people are still unaccounted for after the floods.*

un·ac·cus·tomed /ˌʌnəˈkʌstəmd◂/ *adj formal* **1 unaccustomed to (doing) sth** not used to something: *a country boy, unaccustomed to city ways* **2** [only before noun] not usual, typical, or familiar: *She was completely exhausted by the unaccustomed heat.*

> **REGISTER**
> In everyday English, people usually say that they are **not used to** something rather than **unaccustomed to** it: *She* ***wasn't used to*** *living on her own.*

un·ac·knowl·edged /ˌʌnəkˈnɒlɪdʒd◂ $ -ˈnɑː-/ *adj* **1** ignored or not noticed: *Unacknowledged anger can often cause problems in later life.* **2** not receiving the public thanks, praise, or reward that something deserves: *Women's work in the home tends to be both unpaid and unacknowledged.* **3 the unacknowledged leader/authority etc** someone who is a leader etc but who has not publicly or officially been given that position

un·a·dorned /ˌʌnəˈdɔːnd◂ $ -ˈdɔːrnd◂/ *adj written* without unnecessary or special features or decorations: *They liked their churches to be unadorned.*

un·a·dul·te·rat·ed /ˌʌnəˈdʌltəreɪtɪd◂/ *adj* **1** [only before noun] complete or total: *a feeling of pure unadulterated pleasure* **2** not mixed with other less pure substances

un·af·fect·ed /ˌʌnəˈfektɪd◂/ ●○○ AWL *adj* **1** not changed or influenced by something: **[+by]** *The north* ***remained*** *largely* ***unaffected*** *by the drought.* **2** natural in the way you behave - use this to show approval: *her easy unaffected manner* —**unaffectedly** *adv*

un·a·fraid /ˌʌnəˈfreɪd/ *adj* [not before noun] *written* **1** not frightened: *She was exhausted but unafraid.* | **[+of]** *The rats were huge and completely unafraid of human beings.* **2** confident that you can do something or deal with something: **unafraid of (doing) sth** *a gifted writer who is unafraid of trying new things* | **unafraid to do sth** *an independent woman unafraid to say what she believes*

un·aid·ed /ʌnˈeɪdɪd/ AWL *adj* without help: *She can no longer walk unaided.*

un·al·loyed /ˌʌnəˈlɔɪd◂/ *adj literary* complete, pure, or total: *unalloyed joy*

un·al·ter·a·ble /ʌnˈɔːltərəbəl $ -ˈɒːl-/ AWL *adj formal* not possible to change: *an unalterable fact* —**unalterably** *adv*

un·am·big·u·ous /ˌʌnæmˈbɪgjuəs◂/ ●○○ AWL *adj* a statement, instruction etc that is unambiguous is clear and easy to understand because it can only mean one thing —**unambiguously** *adv*

un-A'merican *adj* not loyal to generally accepted American customs and ways of thinking: *This kind of censorship is un-American.* | **un-American activities** (=political activity believed to be harmful to the US)

u·na·nim·i·ty /ˌjuːnəˈnɪməti/ *n* [U] *formal* a state or situation of complete agreement among a group of people

u·nan·i·mous /juːˈnænɪməs/ ●○○ *adj* **1** a unanimous decision, vote, agreement etc is one in which all the people involved agree: *It was decided by a unanimous vote that the school should close.* | **almost/virtually unanimous** *The decision to appoint Matt was almost unanimous.*
2 agreeing completely about something: **unanimous in (doing) sth** *The banks were unanimous in welcoming the news.* —**unanimously** *adv*

un·an·nounced /ˌʌnəˈnaʊnst◂/ *adj, adv* happening without anyone expecting or knowing about it: *We arrived unannounced.*

un·an·swer·a·ble /ʌnˈɑːnsərəbəl $ ʌnˈæn-/ *adj* **1** an unanswerable question is one that cannot be answered **2** definitely true and therefore impossible to argue against: *The* ***case*** (=reasons for doing something) *for better public transport is* ***unanswerable***.

un·an·swered /ʌnˈɑːnsəd $ -ˈænsərd/ *adj* **1** an unanswered question has not been answered: *Many other* ***questions remain unanswered***. **2** an unanswered letter, telephone call, or request for help has not been replied to: *The children's cries for help* ***went unanswered***.

un·an·tic·i·pat·ed /ˌʌnænˈtɪsɪpeɪtɪd/ AWL *adj* an unanticipated event or result is one that you did not expect SYN **unforeseen**: *an unanticipated increase in inflation*

un·a·pol·o·get·ic /ˌʌnəpɒləˈdʒetɪk◂ $ -pɑː-/ *adj* not feeling or saying you are sorry for something you have done, especially when other people would expect you to feel or say sorry: **[+about]** *He is entirely unapologetic about the violence in his movies.*

un·ap·peal·ing /ˌʌnəˈpiːlɪŋ◂/ *adj* not pleasant or attractive: *an unappealing shade of grey*

un·ap·pe·tiz·ing (*also* **-ising** *BrE*) /ʌnˈæpətaɪzɪŋ/ *adj* food that is unappetizing has an unattractive appearance that makes you think that it will not taste good: *a rather unappetizing egg sandwich*

un·ap·proach·a·ble /ˌʌnəˈprəʊtʃəbəl◂ $ -ˈproʊ-/ AWL *adj* seeming unfriendly and therefore difficult to talk to

un·ar·gu·a·ble /ʌnˈɑːgjuəbəl $ -ˈɑːr-/ *adj* something that is unarguable is definitely true or correct: *unarguable proof* —**unarguably** *adv*

un·armed /ˌʌnˈɑːmd◂ $ -ˈɑːrmd◂/ *adj* not carrying any weapons: *the killing of unarmed civilians* | **unarmed combat** (=fighting without weapons)

un·a·shamed /ˌʌnəˈʃeɪmd◂/ *adj* not feeling embarrassed or ashamed about something that people might disapprove of: *his unashamed love of money* —**unashamedly** /-mɪdli/ *adv*

un·asked /ʌnˈɑːskt $ -ˈæskt/ *adj* **1** if a question remains unasked, no one asks it, often because they are embarrassed **2** *BrE* if you do something unasked, you do it without anyone asking or inviting you to: *George sat down unasked.*

un'asked-for *adj* not asked for, and often not wanted: *unasked-for advice*

U

un·as·sail·able /ˌʌnəˈseɪləbəl◂/ *adj formal* not able to be criticized, made weaker, or beaten: *an unassailable argument | The party's **position** looked **unassailable**. | The result gave the team an **unassailable lead**.*

un·as·sum·ing /ˌʌnəˈsjuːmɪŋ◂, -ˈsuː- $ -ˈsuː-/ *adj* showing no desire to be noticed or given special treatment SYN **modest**

un·at·tached /ˌʌnəˈtætʃt◂/ AWL *adj* **1** not married or involved in a romantic relationship SYN **single**: *According to Jo, Mark was still unattached.* **2** not connected or fastened to anything

un·at·tain·a·ble /ˌʌnəˈteɪnəbəl◂/ AWL *adj* impossible to achieve: *A military victory is unattainable.* | **unattainable ideal/dream/goal etc** THESAURUS ▸ IMPOSSIBLE

un·at·tend·ed /ˌʌnəˈtendɪd◂/ *adj* left alone without anyone in charge: *an unattended vehicle | Children should not be **left unattended** in the playground.*

un·at·trac·tive /ˌʌnəˈtræktɪv◂/ *adj* **1** not attractive, pretty, or pleasant to look at: *an unattractive man* **2** not good or desirable: *the unattractive aspects of nationalism* —**unattractively** *adv*

un·au·tho·rized (*also* **-ised** *BrE*) /ʌnˈɔːθəraɪzd $ -ˈɒː-/ ●○○ *adj* without official approval or permission: *the unauthorized use of government funds | Unauthorized personnel are not allowed on the premises.*

un·a·vail·a·ble /ˌʌnəˈveɪləbəl/ ●○○ AWL *adj* [not before noun]
1 not able to be obtained: *Funding for the new school is unavailable.* | **[+to]** *materials that were unavailable to researchers in the past*
2 not able or willing to meet someone: **[+for]** *Officials were **unavailable for comment*** (=not able or willing to talk to reporters).

un·a·vail·ing /ˌʌnəˈveɪlɪŋ◂/ *adj literary* not successful or effective SYN **unsuccessful**: *unavailing efforts to make her happy*

un·a·void·a·ble /ˌʌnəˈvɔɪdəbəl/ ●○○ *adj* impossible to prevent: *There are now fears that war is unavoidable.* —**unavoidably** *adv*: *Molly was unavoidably delayed.*

un·a·ware /ˌʌnəˈweə $ -ˈwer/ ●●○ AWL *adj* [not before noun] not noticing or realizing what is happening: **[+of]** *Mike seems unaware of the trouble he's causing.* | **unaware (that)** *She was **totally unaware** that she was being watched.*

un·a·wares /ˌʌnəˈweəz $ -ˈwerz/ *adv* **1 take/catch sb unawares** if something takes you unawares, it happens when you are not expecting it and are not prepared: *The question caught me completely unawares.* **2** *formal* without noticing: *We had walked unawares over the border.*

un·bal·ance /ʌnˈbæləns/ *v* [T] **1** to make a situation, relationship, or work of art not as good as it used to be or could be, especially by adding too much of one thing: *Having children can often unbalance even the closest of relationships.* **2** to make someone or something unsteady, so that they are likely to fall down: *He banged against the cupboard, unbalancing a pile a books.* **3** to make someone slightly crazy

un·bal·anced /ʌnˈbælənst/ *adj* **1** someone who is unbalanced is slightly crazy **2** a report, argument etc that is unbalanced is unfair because it emphasizes one opinion too much **3** a relationship that is unbalanced is not equal because one person has more influence, power etc

un·bear·a·ble /ʌnˈbeərəbəl $ -ˈber-/ *adj* too unpleasant, painful, or annoying to deal with SYN **intolerable**: *The **pain** was almost **unbearable**. | He was making life unbearable for his parents.* —**unbearably** *adv*: *an unbearably hot day*

un·beat·a·ble /ʌnˈbiːtəbəl/ *adj* **1** something that is unbeatable is the best of its kind: *carpets at unbeatable prices* **2** a team, player etc that is unbeatable cannot be defeated

un·beat·en /ˌʌnˈbiːtn◂/ *adj* a team, player etc that is unbeaten has not been defeated

un·be·com·ing /ˌʌnbɪˈkʌmɪŋ◂/ *adj old-fashioned* **1** clothes that are unbecoming make you look unattractive SYN **unflattering** **2** behaviour that is unbecoming is shocking or unsuitable: **[+to]** ***conduct unbecoming** to a teacher*

un·be·known /ˌʌnbɪˈnəʊn $ -ˈnoʊn/ (*also* **un·be·knownst** /-ˈnəʊnst $ -ˈnoʊnst/ *written*) *adv* [sentence adverb] **unbeknown to sb** without that person knowing about it: *Unbeknown to him, his wife had been trying to phone him all morning.*

un·be·lief /ˌʌnbəˈliːf/ *n* [U] *literary* a lack of religious belief, or a refusal to believe in a religious faith → **disbelief**

un·be·liev·a·ble /ˌʌnbəˈliːvəbəl◂/ ●○○ *adj*
1 very good, successful, or impressive SYN **amazing**: *The opportunities are unbelievable. | an unbelievable talent*
2 very bad or shocking SYN **terrible**: *The pain was unbelievable. | acts of unbelievable cruelty | **It was unbelievable that** we were expected to pay twice.*
3 so extreme that it hardly seems possible: *He's so lazy it's unbelievable. | an unbelievable speed* THESAURUS ▸ SURPRISING
4 very difficult to believe and therefore probably untrue: *Yvonne's excuse for being late was totally unbelievable.* —**unbelievably** *adv*: *an unbelievably bad movie*

un·be·liev·er /ˌʌnbəˈliːvə $ -ər/ *n* [C] someone who does not believe in God or a particular religion

un·bend /ʌnˈbend/ *v* (*past tense and past participle* **unbent** /-ˈbent/) [I] to relax and start behaving in a less formal way

un·bend·ing /ʌnˈbendɪŋ/ *adj* unwilling to change your opinions, decisions etc OPP **flexible**

un·bi·ased /ʌnˈbaɪəst/ AWL *adj* unbiased information, advice etc is fair because the person giving it is not influenced by their own or other people's opinions SYN **impartial**: *We aim to provide a service that is balanced and unbiased. | an unbiased observer*

un·bid·den /ʌnˈbɪdn/ *adj, adv literary* without being asked for, expected, or invited

un·blem·ished /ʌnˈblemɪʃt/ *adj* **1** not spoiled by any mistake or bad behaviour SYN **spotless**: *a law firm with an unblemished reputation* **2** without marks or damage SYN **flawless**: *her smooth unblemished skin*

un·blink·ing /ʌnˈblɪŋkɪŋ/ *adj literary* if you look at something or someone with unblinking eyes, you look continuously at them without BLINKing (=quickly closing and opening your eyes): **unblinking stare/gaze** *His father's unblinking gaze was fixed on the fire.*

un·block /ʌnˈblɒk $ -ˈblɑːk/ *v* [T] if you unblock a pipe, you remove something that is blocking it: **unblock a toilet/drain/chimney etc**

un·born /ˌʌnˈbɔːn◂ $ -ɔːrn◂/ *adj* [only before noun] not yet born: *an unborn child*

un·bound·ed /ʌnˈbaʊndɪd/ *adj formal* extreme or without any limit SYN **boundless**: *the child's unbounded energy*

un·bowed /ʌnˈbaʊd/ *adj* [not before noun] not willing to give up or accept defeat – used especially in news reports: *After the fight, Ali was **bloody but unbowed**.*

un·break·a·ble /ʌnˈbreɪkəbəl/ *adj* not able to be broken: *unbreakable glass* THESAURUS ▸ STRONG

un·bridge·a·ble /ʌnˈbrɪdʒəbəl/ *adj* unbridgeable differences between two people, groups, or ideas are so big that no one will ever agree about them or be satisfied with them: **unbridgeable gulf/gap/chasm etc (between sb/sth and sb/sth)** *the unbridgeable gulf between the rich and the poor*

un·bri·dled /ʌnˈbraɪdld/ *adj literary* not controlled and too extreme or violent: *unbridled greed*

un·bro·ken /ʌnˈbrəʊkən $ -ˈbroʊ-/ *adj* continuing without being interrupted or broken: *their unbroken record of success | a time of unbroken peace*

un·buck·le /ʌnˈbʌkəl/ *v* [T] to unfasten the BUCKLE on a belt, a shoe etc

un·bur·den /ˌʌnˈbɜːdn $ -ɜːr-/ *v* [T] **unburden yourself (to sb)** to tell someone your problems, secrets etc so that you feel better

U

un·but·ton /ʌnˈbʌtn/ *v* [T] to undo the buttons on a piece of clothing OPP **button up**: *He took off his sweater and unbuttoned his shirt.* → see picture at UNDO

un·called for /ʌnˈkɔːld fɔː $ -ˈkɒːld fɔːr/ *adj* behaviour or remarks that are uncalled for are not fair or suitable

un·can·ny /ʌnˈkæni/ *adj* very strange and difficult to explain: *an uncanny coincidence* THESAURUS STRANGE —**uncannily** *adv*

un·cared for /ʌnˈkeəd fɔː $ -ˈkerd fɔːr/ *adj* [not before noun] not looked after or not looked after properly: *The dogs looked hungry and uncared for.*

un·ceas·ing /ʌnˈsiːsɪŋ/ *adj* never stopping: *his unceasing efforts to help the poor* —**unceasingly** *adv*

un·cer·e·mo·ni·ous·ly /ˌʌnserəˈməʊniəsli $ -ˈmoʊ-/ *adv* in a rough or sudden way, without showing any respect or politeness: *He grabbed her arms and hauled her unceremoniously to her feet.* —**unceremonious** *adj*

un·cer·tain /ʌnˈsɜːtn $ -ɜːr-/ ●●○ *adj*
1 [not before noun] feeling doubt about something SYN **unsure**: **uncertain whether/how/what etc** *He was uncertain how much further he could walk.* | **[+about/of]** *I was uncertain about what to do next.*
2 not clear, definite, or decided SYN **unclear**: **it is uncertain whether/how/what etc** *It is uncertain how likely this is to occur.* | *My whole* ***future*** *now seemed* ***uncertain***.
3 in no uncertain terms if you tell someone something in no uncertain terms, you tell them very clearly without trying to be polite: *I told Colin in no uncertain terms what I thought of him.*
4 if someone walks in an uncertain way, they seem as though they might fall SYN **unsteady**: *She took a few* ***uncertain steps*** *forward.* —**uncertainly** *adv*

un·cer·tain·ty /ʌnˈsɜːtnti $ -ˈsɜːr-/ ●●○ *n* (*plural* **uncertainties**)
1 [U] when you feel doubt about what will happen: *Times of great change are also times of uncertainty.* | **[+about/as to]** *There is a great deal of* ***uncertainty*** *about* ***the*** *company's* ***future***.
2 [C usually plural] a situation which you are not sure about because you do not know what will happen: *life's uncertainties* | **[+of]** *the uncertainties of old age*

un·chal·lenge·a·ble /ʌnˈtʃæləndʒəbəl/ *adj* **1** a belief, idea etc that is unchallengeable is definitely true and cannot be questioned or argued with: *unchallengeable evidence* **2** if someone's power or authority is unchallengeable, it cannot be taken from them

un·chal·lenged /ʌnˈtʃæləndʒd/ *adj* **1** accepted and believed by everyone and not doubted: *She couldn't let a statement like that* ***go unchallenged***. **2** someone who goes somewhere unchallenged is not stopped and asked who they are or what they are doing

un·chang·ing /ʌnˈtʃeɪndʒɪŋ/ ●●○ (*also* **un·changed** /ʌnˈtʃeɪndʒd/) *adj* always staying the same

un·char·ac·ter·is·tic /ʌnˌkærətəˈrɪstɪk◂/ *adj* not typical of someone or something and therefore surprising: **[+of]** ***It's uncharacteristic*** *of her to be late.* —**uncharacteristically** /-kli/ *adv*: *He was uncharacteristically quiet.*

un·char·it·a·ble /ʌnˈtʃærətəbəl/ *adj* unkind or unfair in the way you judge people: *uncharitable remarks*

un·chart·ed /ʌnˈtʃɑːtɪd $ -ɑːr-/ AWL *adj*
1 uncharted waters/territory/area etc a situation or activity that you have never experienced or tried before: *This new project will take us into uncharted territory.* **2** not marked on any maps: *an uncharted island*

un·checked /ˌʌnˈtʃekt◂/ *adj* if something bad or harmful goes unchecked, it is not controlled or stopped and develops into something worse: **continue/grow/go unchecked** *We cannot allow such behaviour to continue unchecked.* | *This habit, if* ***left unchecked***, *may cause serious problems later.*

un·civ·i·lized (*also* **-ised** *BrE*) /ʌnˈsɪvəlaɪzd/ *adj*
1 behaviour that is uncivilized is rude or socially unacceptable **2** *old-fashioned* societies that are uncivilized have a very simple way of life, and have not developed social, legal, economic etc systems SYN **primitive**

un·cle /ˈʌŋkəl/ ●●● S2 W3 *n* [C]
1 the brother of your mother or father, or the husband of your aunt → **aunt**: *I went to stay with my uncle and aunt for a few days.* | *Uncle Philip* | *I was very excited about* ***becoming an uncle*** (=your sister or your brother's wife has a child).
2 used by children, in front of a first name, to address or refer to a man who is a close friend of their parents
3 say uncle *AmE spoken* used by children to tell someone to admit they have been defeated

un·clean /ˌʌnˈkliːn◂/ *adj* **1** *biblical* morally or SPIRITUALLY bad: *an unclean spirit* **2** unclean food, animals etc are those that a particular religion says must not be eaten, touched etc **3** dirty: *unclean drinking water* —**uncleanness** *n* [U]

un·clear /ˌʌnˈklɪə◂ $ -ˈklɪr◂/ ●●○ *adj*
1 difficult to understand or be sure about, so that there is doubt or confusion: *The terms of the contract are very unclear.*
2 be unclear about sth to not understand something clearly: *I'm rather unclear about what I'm supposed to be doing here.*

Uncle Sam /ˌʌŋkəl ˈsæm/ *n informal* the US, or the US government, sometimes represented by the figure of a man with a white BEARD and tall hat

Uncle Tom /ˌʌŋkəl ˈtɒm $ -ˈtɑːm/ *n* [C] *AmE* a black person who is too respectful to white people – used to show disapproval

un·clothed /ʌnˈkləʊðd $ -ˈkloʊðd/ *adj formal* not wearing clothes SYN **naked**

un·coil /ʌnˈkɔɪl/ *v* [I,T] if you uncoil something, or if it uncoils, it stretches out straight after being wound around in a circle SYN **unwind**: *Slowly, the snake uncoiled.*

un·com·fort·a·ble /ʌnˈkʌmftəbəl, -ˈkʌmfət- $ -ˈkʌmfərt-, -ˈkʌmft-/ ●●● W3 *adj*
1 not feeling physically comfortable, or not making you feel comfortable: *This sofa is so uncomfortable.*
2 unable to relax because you are embarrassed: *She always felt slightly uncomfortable in a hat.* | *an uncomfortable silence* THESAURUS EMBARRASSED —**uncomfortably** *adv*

un·com·mit·ted /ˌʌnkəˈmɪtɪd◂/ *adj* not having decided or promised to support a particular group, political belief etc: *uncommitted voters* | *So far, they are uncommitted to his plan.*

un·com·mon /ʌnˈkɒmən $ -ˈkɑː-/ ●○○ *adj* rare or unusual: *Violent crimes against the elderly are fortunately very uncommon.* | **it is not uncommon for sb to do sth** *It is not uncommon for students to have bank loans.*

un·com·mon·ly /ʌnˈkɒmənli $ -ˈkɑː-/ *adv* [+adj/adv] *old-fashioned* very SYN **unusually**: *an uncommonly cold morning*

un·com·plain·ing /ˌʌnkəmˈpleɪnɪŋ◂/ *adj* willing to accept a difficult or unpleasant situation without complaining —**uncomplainingly** *adv*

un·com·pre·hend·ing /ˌʌnkɒmprɪˈhendɪŋ $ -kɑːm-/ *adj* not understanding what is happening —**uncomprehendingly** *adv*

un·com·pro·mis·ing /ʌnˈkɒmprəmaɪzɪŋ $ -ˈkɑːm-/ *adj* unwilling to change your opinions or intentions: *an uncompromising opponent of democratic reform* —**uncompromisingly** *adv*

un·con·cern /ˌʌnkənˈsɜːn $ -ɜːrn/ *n* [U] when you do not care about something that other people worry about: **[+about/for/over]** *the government's apparent unconcern about high inflation*

un·con·cerned /ˌʌnkənˈsɜːnd $ -ɜːrnd/ *adj* **1** not worried about something because you think it does not affect you: **[+about]** *Many large companies seem totally unconcerned about the environment.* **2** not interested in a particular aim or activity: **[+with]** *unconcerned with making a profit* —**unconcernedly** /-nɪdli/ *adv*

un·con·di·tion·al /ˌʌnkənˈdɪʃənəl◂/ ●○○ *adj* not limited by or depending on any conditions: *the unconditional*

U

release of all political prisoners | unconditional surrender —**unconditionally** *adv*

un·con·firmed /ˌʌnkənˈfɜːmd◂ $ -ˈfɜːrmd◂/ *adj* **unconfirmed report/story/rumour etc** a report etc that has not been proved or supported by official information: *We've received unconfirmed reports of an explosion in central London.*

un·con·nect·ed /ˌʌnkəˈnektɪd◂/ *adj* if two events, facts, or situations are unconnected, they are not related to each other in any way: *The murders are probably unconnected.* | **[+with/to]** *Wolf's work is completely unconnected to the current study.*

un·con·scion·a·ble /ʌnˈkɒnʃənəbəl $ -ˈkɑːn-/ *adj formal* much more than is reasonable or acceptable: *The war caused an unconscionable amount of suffering.* —**unconscionably** *adv*

un·con·scious[1] /ʌnˈkɒnʃəs $ -ˈkɑːn-/ ●●○ *adj*
1 unable to see, move, feel etc in the normal way because you are not conscious: *She was found alive but unconscious.* | **knock/beat sb unconscious** *Levin was knocked unconscious by the impact.*
2 a feeling or thought that is unconscious is one that you have without realizing it → **subconscious**: **unconscious feeling/desire/need etc** *an unconscious need to be loved*
3 be unconscious of sth to not realize the effect of something you have said or done: *Doreen appeared to be unconscious of the amusement she had caused.*
4 an action that is unconscious is not deliberate —**unconsciously** *adv* —**unconsciousness** *n* [U]

unconscious[2] *n* **the/sb's unconscious** the part of your mind in which there are thoughts and feelings that you do not realize you have → **subconscious**

un·con·sid·ered /ˌʌnkənˈsɪdəd◂ $ -ərd◂/ *adj written* unconsidered remarks or actions are made without care or thinking about the possible results

un·con·sti·tu·tion·al /ˌʌnkɒnstəˈtjuːʃənəl $ -kɑːnstɪˈtuː-/ ●○○ AWL *adj* not allowed by the CONSTITUTION (=set of rules or principles by which a country or organization is governed): *claims that the president's action was unconstitutional* —**unconstitutionally** *adv*

un·con·test·ed /ˌʌnkənˈtestɪd◂/ *adj* **1** an uncontested action or statement is one that no one opposes or disagrees with: *After an uncontested divorce, Peggy married Charlie.* **2** an uncontested election is one in which only one person wants to be elected

U

un·con·trol·lable /ˌʌnkənˈtrəʊləbəl◂ $ -ˈtroʊl-/ *adj* **1** if an emotion, desire, or physical action is uncontrollable, you cannot control it or stop yourself from feeling it or doing it: *I felt an uncontrollable urge to scream.* | *Mother burst into uncontrollable sobs.* **2** someone who is uncontrollable behaves badly and will not obey anyone: *The presence of some uncontrollable children spoilt the evening.* **3** if a situation is uncontrollable, nothing can be done to control it or stop it getting worse: *uncontrollable bleeding* | *uncontrollable inflation*

un·con·trolled /ˌʌnkənˈtrəʊld◂ $ -ˈtroʊld◂/ *adj* uncontrolled emotions or behaviour continue because you are not trying to stop them: *uncontrolled weeping*

un·con·ven·tion·al /ˌʌnkənˈvenʃənəl◂/ AWL *adj* very different from the way people usually behave, think, dress etc: *unconventional political views* **THESAURUS** ▸ **UNUSUAL**

un·con·vinc·ed /ˌʌnkənˈvɪnst/ *adj* not persuaded that something is true or good: *I remain unconvinced that the idea will work.*

un·con·vinc·ing /ˌʌnkənˈvɪnsɪŋ◂/ *adj* failing to make you believe that something is true or real: *an unconvincing smile* | *an unconvincing explanation* | *Some readers will find the arguments unconvincing.* —**unconvincingly** *adv*

un·cooked /ˌʌnˈkʊkt◂/ *adj* food that is uncooked has not been cooked SYN **raw**: *Always wash your hands after handling uncooked meat.*

un·cool /ˌʌnˈkuːl◂/ *adj informal* not fashionable or acceptable – used especially by young people: *Have you seen his shorts? They are just so uncool!* | *It was uncool to get on well with teachers.*

un·co·op·er·a·tive /ˌʌnkəʊˈɒpərətɪv◂ $ -koʊˈɑːp-/ *adj* not willing to work with or help someone

un·co·or·di·nat·ed /ˌʌnkəʊˈɔːdɪneɪtɪd◂ $ -koʊˈɔːr-/ *adj* **1** someone who is uncoordinated is not good at physical activities because they cannot control their movements effectively **2** a plan or operation that is uncoordinated is not well organized, with the result that the different parts of it do not work together effectively

un·cork /ʌnˈkɔːk $ -ˈkɔːrk/ *v* [T] to open a bottle by removing its CORK

un·cor·rob·o·rat·ed /ˌʌnkəˈrɒbəreɪtɪd $ -ˈrɑː-/ *adj* an uncorroborated claim or statement is one which is not supported by any proof: *He was convicted on the* ***uncorroborated evidence*** *of the alleged victim.*

un·count·a·ble /ʌnˈkaʊntəbəl/ *adj* an uncountable noun has no plural form and refers to something which cannot be counted or regarded as either singular or plural, for example 'money' or 'happiness'. In this dictionary uncountable nouns are marked [U] OPP **countable**

un·coup·le /ʌnˈkʌpəl/ *v* [T] to separate one piece of machinery, one part of a train etc from another that it is connected to: *Evidence suggests that the wagon was deliberately uncoupled.*

un·couth /ʌnˈkuːθ/ *adj* behaving and speaking in a way that is rude or socially unacceptable —**uncouthly** *adv* —**uncouthness** *n* [U]

un·cov·er /ʌnˈkʌvə $ -ər/ ●●○ *v* [T]
1 to find out about something that has been kept secret → **discover**: *Customs officials uncovered a plot to smuggle weapons into the country.*
2 to remove the cover from something

un·crit·i·cal /ʌnˈkrɪtɪkəl/ *adj* unable or unwilling to see faults in something or someone – used to show disapproval: **[+of]** *John's mother is totally uncritical of his behaviour.* —**uncritically** /-kli/ *adv*

un·crowned /ˌʌnˈkraʊnd◂/ *adj* **the uncrowned king/queen of sth** the person who is thought to be the best or most famous in a particular activity: *the uncrowned king of jazz*

un·crush·a·ble /ʌnˈkrʌʃəbəl/ *adj* very determined and not easily persuaded not to do something: *her uncrushable will to survive*

unc·tu·ous /ˈʌŋktʃuəs/ *adj formal* too friendly and praising people too much in a way that seems very insincere SYN **ingratiating** —**unctuously** *adv* —**unctuousness** *n* [U]

un·curl /ʌnˈkɜːl $ -ˈkɜːrl/ *v* [I,T] to stretch out straight from a curled position, or to make something do this

un·cut /ˌʌnˈkʌt◂/ *adj* **1** a film, book etc that is uncut has not been made shorter, for example by having violent or sexual scenes removed: *the uncut version of 'Lady Chatterley's Lover'* **2** an uncut jewel that is still in its natural form has not been cut into a particular shape: *uncut diamonds*

un·dat·ed /ʌnˈdeɪtɪd/ *adj* a letter, article, painting etc that is undated does not have a date written on it

un·daunt·ed /ʌnˈdɔːntɪd $ -ˈdɒːn-/ *adj* not afraid of continuing to try to do something in spite of difficulties or danger SYN **undeterred**: **[+by]** *Undaunted by the enormity of the task, they began rebuilding the village.*

un·de·cid·ed /ˌʌndɪˈsaɪdɪd◂/ *adj* **1** [not before noun] not having made a decision about something important SYN **unsure**, **uncertain**: **[+about]** *I'm* ***still undecided*** *about how I'll vote.* | **undecided what/which/whether etc** *Nadine was undecided whether or not to go to college.* **2** a game or competition that is undecided has no definite winner —**undecidedly** *adv*

un·de·clared /ˌʌndɪˈkleəd◂ $ -ˈklerd◂/ *adj* not officially announced or called something: *a scandal involving undeclared payments to politicians* | *an undeclared civil war*

un·de·lete /ˌʌndɪˈliːt/ *v* [I,T] to bring back something that you DELETEd on a computer

un·de·mon·stra·tive /ˌʌndɪˈmɒnstrətɪv $ -ˈmɑːn-/ *adj* not showing your feelings of love or friendliness

un·de·ni·a·ble /ˌʌndɪˈnaɪəbəl◂/ AWL *adj* definitely true or certain: *undeniable proof* THESAURUS TRUE —**undeniably** *adv*

un·der /ˈʌndə $ -ər/ ●●● S1 W1 *prep, adv*
1 BELOW below or at a lower level than something, or covered by something OPP **over**: *Wendy had hidden the box under her bed.* | *We sailed under the Golden Gate Bridge.* | *Write your name under your picture.* | *I could see something glittering under the water.* | *He was wearing a jacket under his coat.* | *Under her arm, she carried a large portfolio.* | *In summer, we often slept under the stars.* | *I'd scare my mom by diving in and staying under* (=staying under the water) *for as long as I could.* | *The bench collapsed* ***under the weight of*** (=unable to support the weight of) *so many people.*
2 LESS THAN less than a particular number, amount, age, or price OPP **over**: *These toys are not suitable for children under five.* | *Most of the events listed cost under £60.* | *I spend* ***just under*** *four hours a day seeing customers.* | **and/or under** *Children aged 12 or under must be accompanied by an adult.* | **be under age** (=be too young to legally drink, have sex etc)
3 HAVING STH DONE TO IT used to say what is being done to something or how it is being dealt with: **under discussion/consideration/review etc** *The possibility of employing more staff is still under discussion* (=being discussed, considered etc). | *All categories of expenditure are under review.* | *Four new power stations are currently under construction.* | *The port was coming under attack from enemy warships.*
4 AFFECTED BY STH affected by a particular condition, influence, or situation: *She's been* ***under*** *a lot of* ***pressure*** *at work.* | **under the influence of alcohol/drink/drugs etc** *He was accused of driving while under the influence of alcohol.* | *The operation was carried out while she was under general anaesthetic.* | *I'm glad to see that you have everything* ***under control****.* | *Two of our national parks are currently* ***under threat*** *from road schemes.* | *The doctor injected something into my arm and I immediately felt myself* ***going under*** (=becoming unconscious).
5 under ... conditions/circumstances if something happens under particular conditions, it happens when those conditions exist: *I wish I'd met him under different circumstances.* | *The system operates well under normal conditions.*
6 LAW/AGREEMENT according to a particular agreement, law etc: *the question of whether the trade is illegal under international law* | *Under the terms of the agreement, the debt will be repaid over a 20-year period.*
7 IN POWER if something happens under a particular leader, government etc, it happens when they are in power: *a program initiated under President Clinton and continued under President Bush* | *Under her leadership, the magazine's circulation doubled in less than a year.* | *Would it have been different under a Labour government?*
8 POSITION AT WORK if you work under someone, they have a higher position in the company, organization etc than you, and they help to direct your work: *She had a total staff of ten working under her.* | *From 1847 to 1851 he served under Captain John Randolph Stokes.* | *At Cambridge he studied under* (=was a student of) *F. R. Leavis.*
9 WHERE INFORMATION IS used to say in which part of a book, list, or system particular information can be found: **be/be filed/be listed etc under** *The baby's records are filed under the mother's last name.*
10 DIFFERENT NAME if you write or do something under a particular name, you do it using that name instead of your real name: *He made a few records* ***under the name of*** *Joe Ritchie.*

THESAURUS

under something that is under something else has that thing directly above it or covering it: *The pen was under the desk.* | *She had a T-shirt on under her sweater.*
below in a lower position than something else, though not always directly under it: *From the cliffs we could barely see the people on the beach below us.* | *His apartment is below ours on the left.*
underneath under – used especially to emphasize that something covers, touches, or hides something: *The girls wear shorts underneath their cheerleading skirts.* | *I found the book underneath the sofa.*
beneath *formal* under or at a lower level: *They strolled hand in hand beneath the summer moon.* | *The water lies just beneath the surface of the earth.*

under- /ʌndə $ -dər/ *prefix* **1** less of an action or quality than is correct, needed, or desired: *underdevelopment* | *undercooked cabbage* **2** going under something: *an underpass* (=a road or path that goes under another road) **3** inside or beneath other things: *undergarments* **4** less important or lower in rank: *a head gardener and three under-gardeners*

un·der·a·chiev·er /ˌʌndərəˈtʃiːvə $ -ər/ *n* [C] someone who does not do as well at school or at work as they could do if they worked harder —**underachieve** *v* [I] —**underachievement** *n* [U]

un·der·age /ˌʌndərˈeɪdʒ◂/ *adj* too young to legally buy alcohol, drive a car, vote etc: *underage drinking*

un·der·arm[1] /ˈʌndərɑːm $ -ɑːrm/ *adv BrE* if you throw a ball underarm, you throw it without moving your arm above your shoulder OPP **overarm** SYN **underhand** *AmE*

underarm[2] *adj* **1** [only before noun] relating to or used on your ARMPITS: *underarm hair* | *underarm deodorants* **2** an underarm throw is one where you throw a ball without moving your arm above your shoulder OPP **overarm**: *underarm bowling*

underarm[3] *n* [C] the hollow area under your arm, where it joins your body SYN **armpit**

un·der·bel·ly /ˈʌndəˌbeli $ -ər-/ *n* [singular] *literary* **1** the unpleasant parts of a place or society that are normally hidden: **[+of]** *photographs that capture the underbelly of the United States – its poverty, its injustice, and its alienated underclass* **2** the weakest part of an organization or a person's character, that is most easily attacked or criticized: **[+of]** *They needed to find the* ***soft underbelly*** *of their opponents.* **3** the lower part of an animal's body, including the stomach

un·der·brush /ˈʌndəbrʌʃ $ -ər-/ *n* [U] *especially AmE* bushes, small trees etc growing under and around larger trees in a forest SYN **undergrowth**

un·der·cap·i·tal·ized (*also* **-ised** *BrE*) /ˌʌndəˈkæpətl-aɪzd $ -dər-/ *adj* if a business is undercapitalized, it has not been given enough money to operate effectively

un·der·car·riage /ˈʌndəˌkærɪdʒ $ -ər-/ *n* [C] the wheels of an aircraft, train etc and the structure that holds them → see picture at PLANE[1]

und·er·charge /ˌʌndəˈtʃɑːdʒ $ ˌʌndərˈtʃɑːrdʒ/ *v* [I,T] to charge too little or less than the correct amount of money for something OPP **overcharge**: *The city is grossly undercharging* (=charging far too little) *companies to use the land.* | **undercharge sb by £1/$2 etc** *They undercharged me by about $2.*

un·der·class /ˈʌndəklɑːs $ -dərklæs/ *n* [singular] the lowest social class, consisting of people who are very poor and who are not likely to be able to improve their situation: *an urban underclass, who have limited access to health care* → SOCIAL EXCLUSION

un·der·class·man /ˌʌndəˈklɑːsmən $ -dərˈklæs-/ *n* (*plural* **underclassmen** /-mən/) [C] *AmE* a student in the first two years of school or college

un·der·clothes /ˈʌndəkləʊðz -kləʊz $ -dərkloʊðz, -kloʊz/ *n* [plural] (*also* **ˈunder-ˌclothing** [U]) clothes that you wear next to your body under your other clothes SYN **underwear**

un·der·coat /ˈʌndəkəʊt $ -dərkoʊt/ *n* [C] a layer of paint that you put onto a surface before you put the final layer on → **topcoat**

un·der·cov·er /ˌʌndəˈkʌvə◂ $ -dərˈkʌvər◂/ *adj* [only before noun] undercover work is done secretly by the police in order to catch criminals or find out information:

an **undercover investigation** | **undercover policeman/cop/agent etc** *undercover detectives* **THESAURUS** SECRET —**undercover** *adv*: *a cop who* **goes undercover** *to catch drug dealers* | *He* **worked undercover** *in Germany and Northern Ireland.*

un·der·cur·rent /ˈʌndəˌkʌrənt $ -dərˌkɜːr-/ *n* [C] **1** a feeling, especially of anger or dissatisfaction, that people do not express openly: **[+of]** *He sensed an undercurrent of resentment among the crowd.* **2** a hidden and often dangerous current of water that flows under the surface of the sea or a river

un·der·cut /ˌʌndəˈkʌt $ -ər-/ *v* (*past tense and past participle* **undercut**, *present participle* **undercutting**) [T] **1** to sell goods or a service at a lower price than another company SYN **undersell**: *Online bookstores can undercut retailers by up to 30%.* **2** to make something weaker or less effective SYN **undermine**: *Is a lack of self-confidence undercutting your performance at work?*

un·der·de·vel·oped /ˌʌndədɪˈveləpt◂ $ -dər-/ *adj* **1 underdeveloped country/region etc** a country, area etc that is poor and where there is not much modern industry → **developing country 2** not having grown or developed as much as is usual or necessary: *a baby born with underdeveloped kidneys* —**underdevelopment** *n* [U]

un·der·dog /ˈʌndədɒg $ ˈʌndərdɒːg/ *n* [C] a person, team etc that is weaker than the others, is always expected to be unsuccessful, and that is often treated badly: *Crowds often feel sympathy for* **the underdog**.

un·der·done /ˌʌndəˈdʌn◂ $ -ər-/ *adj* not completely cooked OPP **overdone**

un·der·dressed /ˌʌndəˈdrest◂ $ -ər-/ *adj* wearing clothes that are too informal for a particular occasion OPP **overdressed**

un·der·em·ployed /ˌʌndərɪmˈplɔɪd◂/ *adj* working in a job where you cannot use all your skills or where there is not enough work for you to do → **unemployed**

un·der·es·ti·mate¹ /ˌʌndərˈestɪmeɪt/ ●●○ AWL *v* **1** [I,T] to think or guess that something is smaller, cheaper, easier etc than it really is OPP **overestimate**: **underestimate how/what** *We underestimated how long it would take to get there.* | **underestimate the importance/extent/effect/power etc of sth** *Never underestimate the power of the press.*
2 [T] to think that someone is not as good, clever, or skilful, as they really are

U

un·der·es·ti·mate² /ˌʌndərˈestəmət/ AWL *n* [C] a guessed amount or number that is too low OPP **overestimate**: *Fourteen percent may be an underestimate.*

un·der·ex·pose /ˌʌndərɪkˈspəʊz $ -ˈspoʊz/ *v* [T] to not let enough light reach the film when you are taking a photograph OPP **overexpose** —**underexposed** *adj*

un·der·fed /ˌʌndəˈfed $ -ər-/ *adj* not given enough food to eat OPP **overfed**

un·der·felt /ˈʌndəfelt $ -ər-/ *n* [U] *BrE* soft material that you put between a CARPET and the floor

un·der·floor heat·ing /ˌʌndəflɔː ˈhiːtɪŋ $ ˌʌndərflɔːr-/ *n* [U] a heating system that is designed to go under the floor in a building

un·der·foot /ˌʌndəˈfʊt $ -ər-/ *adv* **1** under your feet where you are walking: **wet/firm/soft etc underfoot** *The wet wood is very slippery underfoot.* **2 trample sb/sth underfoot a)** to crush someone or something on the ground by stepping heavily on them **b)** to completely destroy someone or something

un·der·fund·ed /ˌʌndəˈfʌndɪd $ -dər-/ *adj* a project, organization etc that is underfunded has not been given enough money to be effective: **seriously/chronically/badly etc underfunded** *Our education system is seriously underfunded.* —**underfunding** *n* [U]: *underfunding in the National Health Service*

un·der·gar·ment /ˈʌndəˌgɑːmənt $ ˈʌndərˌgɑːr-/ *n* [C] *old-fashioned* a piece of underwear

un·der·go /ˌʌndəˈgəʊ $ ˌʌndərˈgoʊ/ ●●○ AWL *v* (*past tense* **underwent** /-ˈwent/, *past participle* **undergone** /-ˈgɒn $ -ˈgɒːn/) [T] if you undergo a change, an unpleasant experience etc, it happens to you or is done to you: *The country has* **undergone** *massive* **changes** *recently.* | *He has been released from prison to* **undergo** *medical* **treatment** *in the United States.* | *She has been* **undergoing tests** *since Monday.* | *Teachers should be expected to* **undergo** *mid-career* **training** *and development.*

un·der·grad·u·ate /ˌʌndəˈgrædʒuət◂ $ -ər-/ ●●○ *n* [C] a student at college or university, who is working for their first degree → **graduate**, **postgraduate**: *second-year undergraduates* | **undergraduate student/course/degree etc**

un·der·ground¹ /ˈʌndəgraʊnd $ -ər-/ ●●○ *adj* **1** below the surface of the earth: *an underground passage* | *The car park is underground.*
2 [only before noun] an underground group, organization etc is secret and illegal: *an underground terrorist organization* **THESAURUS** SECRET
3 [only before noun] underground literature, newspapers etc are read by a small number of people, and would seem slightly strange or shocking to most people: *the underground press*

un·der·ground² /ˌʌndəˈgraʊnd $ -ər-/ *adv* **1** under the earth's surface: *This animal spends most of its life underground.* | *nuclear waste buried* **deep underground 2 go underground** to start doing something secretly, or hide in a secret place: *The ANC was forced to go underground when its leaders were arrested.*

un·der·ground³ /ˈʌndəgraʊnd $ -ər-/ *n* **the Underground a)** *BrE* a railway system under the ground SYN **subway** *AmE* **b)** an illegal group working in secret against the rulers of a country

un·der·growth /ˈʌndəgrəʊθ $ -dərgroʊθ-/ *n* [U] bushes, small trees, and other plants growing around and under bigger trees

un·der·hand¹ /ˌʌndəˈhænd◂ $ ˈʌndərhænd/ (*also* **un·der·hand·ed** /ˌʌndəˈhændɪd $ ˌʌndər-/) *adj* dishonest and done secretly: *They did it all in such an underhand way.* | *He's been involved in some underhand dealings.* **THESAURUS** DISHONEST → OVERHAND

underhand² *adv AmE* if you throw a ball underhand, you throw it without moving your arm above your shoulder SYN **underarm** *BrE*

un·der·lay /ˈʌndəleɪ $ -ər-/ *n* [C,U] thick material that is put between a CARPET and the floor

un·der·lie /ˌʌndəˈlaɪ $ -ər-/ AWL *v* (*past tense* **underlay** /-ˈleɪ/, *past participle* **underlain** /-ˈleɪn/, *present participle* **underlying**, *third person singular* **underlies**) [T] *formal* to be the cause of something, or be the basic thing from which something develops: *the one basic principle that underlies all of the party's policies* → UNDERLYING

un·der·line /ˌʌndəˈlaɪn $ -ər-/ ●●○ *v* [T]
1 to draw a line under a word to show that it is important
2 to show that something is important SYN **highlight**: *This tragic incident underlines the need for immediate action.* **THESAURUS** EMPHASIZE

un·der·ling /ˈʌndəlɪŋ $ -ər-/ *n* [C] an insulting word for someone who has a low rank – often used humorously

un·der·ly·ing /ˌʌndəˈlaɪ-ɪŋ◂ $ -ər-/ ●●○ AWL *adj* **underlying cause/principle/problem etc** the cause, idea etc that is the most important, although it is not easily noticed: *the underlying causes of her depression* | *There is an* **underlying assumption** *that younger workers are easier to train.*

un·der·manned /ˌʌndəˈmænd◂ $ -ər-/ *adj* a ship, office etc that is undermanned does not have enough workers to operate effectively SYN **understaffed**

un·der·mine /ˌʌndəˈmaɪn $ -ər-/ ●●○ *v* [T] to gradually make someone or something less strong or effective: *economic policies that threaten to undermine the health care system* | **undermine sb's confidence/authority/position/credibility etc** *The constant criticism was beginning to undermine her confidence.* **THESAURUS** SPOIL

un·der·neath¹ /ˌʌndəˈniːθ $ -ər-/ ●●● S2 *prep, adv* **1** directly under another object or covered by it: *He got out*

of the car and looked underneath. | *It's near where the railway goes underneath the road.* | *She was wearing a smart jacket with a T-shirt underneath.* | *Her blonde hair was hidden underneath a baseball cap.* THESAURUS UNDER
2 on the lower surface of something: *The car was rusty underneath.* | *A number had been painted underneath the table.*
3 used to say what someone's character is really like when their behaviour shows a different character: *She seems confident, but she's really quite shy underneath.* | *I think he's a genuinely nice guy* ***underneath it all****.*

underneath[2] *n BrE* **the underneath** the bottom surface of something, or the part of something that is below or under something else SYN **the underside**: *We need to paint the underneath with a rust preventer.*

un·der·nour·ished /ˌʌndəˈnʌrɪʃt◂ $ ˌʌndərˈnɜː-, -ˈnʌ-/ *adj* unhealthy and weak because you have not had enough food or the right type of food SYN **malnourished** —**undernourishment** *n* [U]

un·der·paid /ˌʌndəˈpeɪd◂ $ -ər-/ *adj* earning less money than you deserve for your work: *Teachers are* ***overworked and underpaid****.*

un·der·pants /ˈʌndəpænts $ -ər-/ ●●○ *n* [plural]
1 *BrE* a short piece of underwear worn by men under their trousers → see picture at UNDERWEAR
2 *AmE* a short piece of underwear worn under trousers by men or women

un·der·pass /ˈʌndəpɑːs $ ˈʌndərpæs/ *n* [C] *BrE* a road or path that goes under another road or a railway

un·der·pay /ˌʌndəˈpeɪ $ -ər-/ *v* (*past tense and past participle* **underpaid**) [T] to pay someone too little for their work

un·der·per·form /ˌʌndəpəˈfɔːm $ ˌʌndərpərˈfɔːrm/ *v* [I] if a business underperforms, it does not make as much profit as it expected to make

un·der·pin /ˌʌndəˈpɪn $ -ər-/ ●○○ *v* (**underpinned, underpinning**) [T]
1 to give strength or support to something and to help it succeed: *the theories that underpin his teaching method* | *America's wealth is underpinned by a global system which exploits the world's poor.*
2 *technical* to put a solid piece of metal under a wall or house in order to make it stronger —**underpinning** *n* [C,U]

un·der·play /ˌʌndəˈpleɪ $ -ər-/ *v* [T] to make something seem less important or less serious than it really is SYN **play down** OPP **overplay**: *She underplays her achievements.*

un·der·priv·i·leged /ˌʌndəˈprɪvəlɪdʒd◂ $ -dər-/ *adj* very poor, with worse living conditions, educational opportunities etc than most people in society: *underprivileged children*

un·der·ra·ted /ˌʌndəˈreɪtɪd◂/ *adj* better than people think or say OPP **overrated**: *a much underrated novel*

un·der·re·sourced /ˌʌndərɪˈzɔːst, -ˈsɔːst $ -ɔːr-/ *adj* not provided with enough money, equipment etc

un·der·score /ˌʌndəˈskɔː $ -dərˈskɔːr/ ●○○ *v* [T] *especially AmE*
1 to emphasize the fact that something is important or true SYN **underline** THESAURUS EMPHASIZE
2 to draw a line under a word or phrase to show that it is important SYN **underline**

un·der·sea /ˈʌndəsiː $ -ər-/ *adj* [only before noun] happening or existing below the surface of the sea → **submarine**: *undersea exploration*

un·der·sec·re·ta·ry /ˌʌndəˈsekrətəri $ ˈʌndərˌsekrəteri/ *n* (*plural* **undersecretaries**) [C] **1** a very important official in a US government department who is one position in rank below the SECRETARY **2** a minister in a British government department, who is one position in rank below the minister who is in charge of that department **3** a government official who is in charge of the daily work of a British government department

un·der·sell /ˌʌndəˈsel $ -ər-/ *v* (*past tense and past participle* **undersold** /-ˈsəʊld $ -ˈsoʊld/) [T] **1** to sell goods at a lower price than someone else **2** to make other people think that someone or something is less good, effective, skilful etc than they really are: *I think he undersold himself at the interview.*

ˌunder-ˈserved *adj* not getting enough care and help from the government: *The area is under-served for medical care.*

un·der·sexed /ˌʌndəˈsekst◂ $ -ər-/ *adj* having less desire to have sex than is normal OPP **oversexed**

un·der·shirt /ˈʌndəʃɜːt $ ˈʌndərʃɜːrt/ *n* [C] *AmE* a piece of underwear with or without arms, worn under a shirt → see picture at UNDERWEAR

un·der·shorts /ˈʌndəʃɔːts $ ˈʌndərʃɔːrts/ *n* [plural] UNDERPANTS for men or boys

un·der·side /ˈʌndəsaɪd $ -ər-/ *n* [singular] **the underside (of sth)** the bottom side or surface of something: *The leaves are green on top and silvery on the underside.*

un·der·signed /ˈʌndəsaɪnd $ -ər-/ *n formal* **the undersigned** the person or people who have signed a document

un·der·sized /ˌʌndəˈsaɪzd◂ $ -ər-/ (*also* **un·der·size** /-ˈsaɪz◂/) *adj* too small

un·der·staffed /ˌʌndəˈstɑːft◂ $ ˌʌndərˈstæft◂/ *adj* not having enough workers, or fewer workers than usual

This graph shows how common the different grammar patterns of the verb **understand** are.

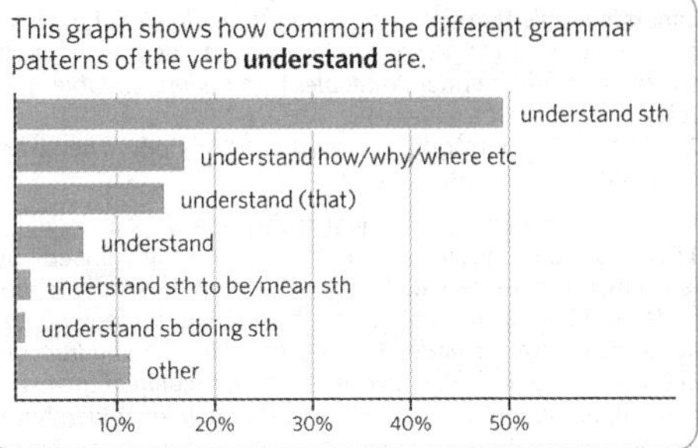

un·der·stand /ˌʌndəˈstænd $ -ər-/ ●●● S1 W1 *v* (*past tense and past participle* **understood** /-ˈstʊd/)
1 MEANING [I,T] to know the meaning of what someone is telling you, or the language that they speak → **misunderstood**: *She doesn't understand English.* | *I'm sorry, I don't understand. Can you explain that again?* | *The woman had a strong accent, and I couldn't understand what she was saying.* | **make yourself understood** (=make what you say clear to other people, especially when speaking a foreign language) *I'm not very good at German, but I can make myself understood.* → see Thesaurus box on *p. 1992*
2 FACT/IDEA [I,T] to know or realize how a fact, process, situation etc works, especially through learning or experience: *I don't really understand the political situation in Egypt.* | **understand how/why/where etc** *You don't need to understand how computers work to be able to use them.* | *How the drug works isn't* ***fully understood****.* | **understand (that)** *I understand that this treatment may not work.*
3 PERSON/FEELINGS [I,T] to realize how someone feels and why they behave the way they do, and to be sympathetic: *My parents just don't understand me.* | *Just tell him how you feel – I'm sure he'll understand.* | **understand how/what etc** *I understand how you feel, but I think you're overreacting.* | **(can) understand sb doing sth** *I can understand her wanting to live alone and be independent.*
4 BELIEVE/THINK [T] to believe or think that something is true because you have heard it or read it: **understand (that)** *'I understand that he was 62 when he died,' McLeish said.* | **it is understood (that)** *It is understood that the Queen approves of her nephew's romance.* | **be understood to be (doing) sth** *Dillons is understood to be reorganising the company's management structure.*

GRAMMAR

In more formal English, you say **it is understood that** when saying what people in general believe is true: *It is understood that an agreement will be signed today.*

5 give sb to understand (that) *formal* to make someone

U

believe that something is true, going to happen etc, without telling them this directly: *I was given to understand that the property was in good condition.*
6 be understood (that) *formal* if something is understood, everyone knows it, or has agreed to it, and there is no need to discuss it: *From childhood it was understood that your parents would choose your husband.*
7 understand sth to be/mean sth to accept something as having a particular meaning: *In this document, 'children' is understood to mean people under 14.*
8 do you understand? *spoken* used when you are telling someone what they should or should not do, especially when you are angry with them: *Never speak to me like that again! Do you understand?*

GRAMMAR: Using the progressive

Understand is not used in the progressive. You say: *I understand what you're saying.* ✗ Don't say: *I'm understanding what you're saying.*
GRAMMAR GUIDE ▸ VERBS

un·der·stand·a·ble /ˌʌndəˈstændəbəl $ -dər-/ ●○○ *adj*
1 understandable behaviour, reactions etc seem normal and reasonable because of the situation you are in: ***It is understandable that*** *parents are angry, and looking for someone to blame.* | *He just can't face anyone at the moment, which is* ***perfectly understandable****.* | *an understandable mistake*
2 able to be understood —**understandably** *adv*: *They were understandably upset.*

un·der·stand·ing¹ /ˌʌndəˈstændɪŋ $ -ər-/ ●●○ W3 *n*
1 [singular, U] knowledge about something, based on learning or experience: **[+of]** *How does this add to our understanding of the problem?* | *If you know the neighbourhood, you* ***have an understanding of*** *what the children are like.* | *Linguists currently* ***have little understanding of*** *the exact cause of language change.* | *How can we* ***gain an understanding of*** *other cultures?* | *Over time, you will get* ***a*** *far* ***better understanding of*** *the job.* | *Success depends on* ***a clear understanding of*** *the problem.* | ***a basic understanding of*** *AIDS prevention*
2 [C usually singular] an unofficial or informal agreement: **come to/reach an understanding** (=stop arguing and agree) *My father was furious at first, but eventually we came to an understanding.* | *We* ***had an understanding*** *that Jean-Claude should never be mentioned.*
3 [singular, U] the ability to understand people's behaviour and to forgive them when they do something wrong: *The principal listened to the boy's story with sympathy and understanding.*
4 sb's understanding (of sth) the way in which someone judges the meaning of something: *According to my understanding of the letter, it means something quite different.*
5 on the understanding that if you agree to something on the understanding that something else will be done, you agree to it, believing that it will be done: *Jack lent Sarah the money on the understanding that she would pay it back next month.*

understanding² *adj* sympathetic and kind about other people's problems: *Luckily, I have a very understanding boss.* THESAURUS ▸ SYMPATHETIC

un·der·state /ˌʌndəˈsteɪt $ -ər-/ *v* [T] to describe something in a way that makes it seem less important or serious than it really is OPP **overstate**: *The press have tended to understate the extent of the problem.*

un·der·stat·ed /ˌʌndəˈsteɪtɪd◂ $ -ər-/ *adj* an understated style is one that is attractive because it is simple and does not have too many decorations SYN **subtle**: *the understated elegance of the Hotel Traiano*

un·der·state·ment /ˌʌndəˈsteɪtmənt $ -dər-/ ●○○ *n*
1 [C] a statement that is not strong enough to express how good, bad, impressive etc something really is: *To say the movie was bad* ***is an understatement****.* | *'It wasn't very easy to find the house.' 'That's got to be* ***the understatement of the year****!'*
2 [U] the practice of making something seem to have less of a particular quality than it really has: **with understatement** *'We have not done quite well enough,' Macmillan said, with characteristic understatement.*

un·der·stood /ˌʌndəˈstʊd $ -ər-/ the past tense and past participle of UNDERSTAND

un·der·stud·y¹ /ˈʌndəˌstʌdi $ -ər-/ *n* (*plural* **understudies**) [C] an actor who learns a part in a play so that they can act the part if the usual actor is ill THESAURUS ▸ ACTOR

understudy² *v* (**understudied**, **understudying**, **understudies**) [T] to be an understudy for a particular actor in a play

un·der·sub·scribed /ˌʌndəsəbˈskraɪbd $ -dər-/ *adj* an activity, sale, service etc that is undersubscribed is not bought or used by enough people OPP **oversubscribed**

un·der·take /ˌʌndəˈteɪk $ -dər-/ ●●○ W3 AWL *v* (*past tense* **undertook** /-ˈtʊk/, *past participle* **undertaken** /-ˈteɪkən/) [T] *formal*
1 to accept that you are responsible for a piece of work, and start to do it: **undertake a task/a project/research/a study etc** *Dr Johnson undertook the task of writing a comprehensive English dictionary.*
2 undertake to do sth to promise or agree to do something: *He undertook to pay the money back in six months.* THESAURUS ▸ PROMISE

un·der·tak·er /ˈʌndəteɪkə $ -dərteɪkər/ *n* [C] *BrE* someone whose job is to arrange funerals SYN **funeral director** *AmE*

un·der·tak·ing /ˌʌndəˈteɪkɪŋ $ ˈʌndərteɪ-/ ●●○ AWL *n*
1 [C usually singular] an important job, piece of work, or

THESAURUS: understand

understand to know the meaning of something, or the reasons for something: *I understand what you're saying.* | *Doctors are beginning to understand what causes the disease.*
see *especially spoken* to understand something, especially the truth about a situation or the reasons for something: *I can see why you don't like him.* | *Do you see what I mean?* | *Oh, I see!*
get *informal* to understand a joke, what someone says, the reasons why something is true etc: *She didn't seem to get the joke.* | *Do you get me?* | *He explained the math homework twice, but I still* ***don't get it****.*
comprehend *formal* to understand something, or understand why something is important: *The dream was easy to describe, but difficult to comprehend.* | *They had failed to comprehend the significance of the problem.*
know what sb means *spoken* to understand what someone is telling you, or what a situation is like, especially because you have some experience or knowledge about this: *'It can be really hard to give up smoking.' 'I know exactly what you mean.'*
follow to understand something such as an explanation or story as you hear it, read it etc: *The plot is hard to follow.* | *His instructions were easy to follow.*

TO UNDERSTAND SOMETHING DIFFICULT

grasp to completely understand an idea or a fact, especially a complicated one: *Some of his theories can be rather difficult for the ordinary reader to grasp.* | *I don't think Stuart really grasped the point I was making.*
fathom /ˈfæðəm/ *formal* to understand what something means or the reasons for something, after thinking carefully about it: *She looked at him, puzzled, trying to fathom the reasons for his actions.*
make sense of sth to understand something that is not easy to understand, especially by thinking about it: *People are still trying to make sense of the news.*

activity that you are responsible for: *Starting a new business can be a risky undertaking.*
2 [C] *formal* a promise to do something: *Both organizations* ***gave*** *an* ***undertaking*** *to curb violence among their members.*
3 [U] the business of an undertaker

ˌunder-the-ˈcounter *adj informal* under-the-counter goods are bought or sold secretly, especially because they are illegal

un·der·tone /ˈʌndətəʊn $ -dərtoʊn/ *n* [C] **1** a feeling or quality that is not directly expressed but can still be recognized → **overtone**: **[+of]** *There was an undertone of sadness in her letter.* | *Opponents claim the policy has racist undertones.* **2** *literary* if you speak in an undertone, you speak quietly: **in an undertone** *'Don't be too upset if he doesn't come,' said Drew in an undertone.*

un·der·tow /ˈʌndətəʊ $ -dərtoʊ/ *n* [singular] **1** the water current under the surface of the sea, that pulls away from the land when a wave comes onto the shore: *The dangerous undertow means that swimming is not allowed.* **2** a tendency or feeling that seems weak, but in fact has a strong effect: **[+of]** *The humour of the novel cannot hide an undertow of sadness.*

un·der·used /ˌʌndəˈjuːzd◂ $ -ər-/ *adj* something that is underused is not used as much as it could be OPP **overused**

un·der·val·ue /ˌʌndəˈvæljuː $ -ər-/ *v* [T] to think that someone or something is less important or valuable than they really are: *Society undervalues staying at home and looking after children.* | *Analysts claim that the firm's assets were undervalued by £300 million.*

un·der·wa·ter /ˌʌndəˈwɔːtə◂ $ ˌʌndərˈwɒːtər◂, -ˈwɑː-/ ●●○ *adj* [only before noun] below the surface of an area of water, or able to be used there: *an underwater camera* —**underwater** *adv*: *He dived underwater and swam away.*

un·der·way /ˌʌndəˈweɪ $ -ər-/ ●○○ *adj* [not before noun]
1 happening now: *The project is already* ***well underway***. | *Your peace will be shattered when the tourist season* ***gets underway*** (=starts).
2 something such as a boat or train that is underway is moving → **be under way** at WAY¹(10)

UNDERWEAR

un·der·wear /ˈʌndəweə $ -dərwer/ ●●● S3 *n* [U] clothes that you wear next to your body under your other clothes: *You just need to take a change of underwear.*

un·der·weight /ˌʌndəˈweɪt◂ $ -ər-/ *adj* weighing less than is expected or usual OPP **overweight**: *Women who smoke risk giving birth to underweight babies.* THESAURUS THIN

un·der·went /ˌʌndəˈwent $ -ər-/ *v* AWL the past tense of UNDERGO

un·der·whelm /ˌʌndəˈwelm $ -ər-/ *v* [T] if you are underwhelmed by something, you do not think it is impressive – used humorously OPP **overwhelm**: *We were underwhelmed by the latest version of the software.*

un·der·world /ˈʌndəwɜːld $ ˈʌndərwɜːrld/ *n* [singular] **1** the criminals in a particular place and the criminal activities they are involved in: *New York's criminal underworld* **2 the Underworld** the place where the spirits of the dead are believed to live, for example in ancient Greek stories

un·der·write /ˌʌndəˈraɪt $ -ər-/ *v* (*past tense* **underwrote** /-ˈrəʊt $ -ˈroʊt/, *past participle* **underwritten** /-ˈrɪtn/) [T] **1** *formal* to support an activity, business plan etc with money, and to take financial responsibility if it fails: *The government has agreed to underwrite the project with a grant of £5 million.* **2** *technical* if an insurance company underwrites an insurance contract, it agrees to pay for any damage or loss that happens **3** *technical* to arrange to sell SHARES to INVESTORS, and to agree to buy any which are not bought by them

un·der·writ·er /ˈʌndəˌraɪtə $ -tər/ *n* [C] someone who makes insurance contracts

un·de·served /ˌʌndɪˈzɜːvd◂ $ -ˈzɜːrvd◂/ *adj* undeserved criticism, praise etc is unfair because you do not deserve it: *She had an undeserved reputation for rudeness.*

un·de·sir·a·ble¹ /ˌʌndɪˈzaɪərəbəl◂ $ -ˈzaɪr-/ ●○○ *adj formal* something or someone that is undesirable is not welcome or wanted because they may affect a situation or person in a bad way: **undesirable effects/consequences etc** *The drug may have other undesirable effects.* | *punishment of undesirable behaviour* THESAURUS BAD

undesirable² *n* [C usually plural] someone who is considered to be immoral, criminal, or socially unacceptable: *security measures to keep out undesirables*

un·de·tect·ed /ˌʌndɪˈtektɪd◂/ *adj* if something, especially something bad, goes undetected, no one notices it: **go/remain undetected** *Doctors can make mistakes and diseases can remain undetected.* | *The thieves escaped undetected through a basement window.*

un·de·terred /ˌʌndɪˈtɜːd $ -ˈtɜːrd/ *adj* if you are undeterred by something, you do not allow it to stop you doing what you want: **[+by]** *Undeterred by his early failures, he decided to keep writing.*

un·de·vel·oped /ˌʌndɪˈveləpt◂/ *adj* **1** used in order to describe land which has not yet been used for building, farming etc: *an undeveloped stretch of coastline* **2** used in order to describe a country or area that does not have modern industry, and usually has a low standard of living → **underdeveloped**: *the undeveloped regions of the world* **3** not fully grown: *a child's undeveloped mind*

un·did /ʌnˈdɪd/ *v* the past tense of UNDO

un·dies /ˈʌndiːz/ *n* [plural] *informal* underwear

un·dif·fer·en·ti·at·ed /ˌʌndɪfəˈrenʃieɪtɪd/ *adj* something which is undifferentiated is not split into parts, or has different parts but you cannot tell the difference between them: *shows aimed at large undifferentiated groups of people* | *Colonial officials tended to see Indian society as an undifferentiated whole.*

un·dig·ni·fied /ʌnˈdɪɡnɪfaɪd/ *adj* behaving in a way that is embarrassing or makes you look silly: *There was an undignified scramble for the free drinks.*

un·di·lut·ed /ˌʌndaɪˈluːtɪd◂/ *adj* **1** *literary* an undiluted feeling is very strong and not mixed with any other feelings: *undiluted joy* **2** an undiluted liquid has not been made weaker by adding water: *undiluted fruit juice*

un·di·min·ished /ˌʌndɪˈmɪnɪʃt◂/ AWL *adj* not weaker or less important than before: *Neil continued with undiminished enthusiasm.* | *Forty years on, the book's power to shock is undiminished.*

un·dis·charged /ˌʌndɪsˈtʃɑːdʒd◂ $ -ɑːr-/ *adj law* **1** an undischarged debt is one that has not been paid **2 an undischarged bankrupt** someone who still owes money and is not legally allowed to stop repaying their debt

un·dis·closed /ˌʌndɪsˈkləʊzd◂ $ -ˈkloʊzd◂/ *adj* used to describe information which is not given to the public: *Developers have agreed to buy the site for an undisclosed sum.*

un·dis·crim·i·nat·ing /ˌʌndɪˈskrɪməneɪtɪŋ/ *adj* not having the ability to see a difference between two people or things, and therefore unable to make judgments about them

un·dis·guised /ˌʌndɪsˈgaɪzd◂/ *adj* [usually before noun] an undisguised feeling is clearly shown and not hidden: *There was undisguised contempt in his voice.*

un·dis·mayed /ˌʌndɪsˈmeɪd◂/ *adj formal* not worried or frightened by something unpleasant or unexpected

un·dis·put·ed /ˌʌndɪˈspjuːtɪd◂/ *adj* **1** known to be definitely true: *Doctors found undisputed evidence of nerve damage.* **2** accepted by everyone: **undisputed leader/champion/master etc** *the undisputed world heavyweight champion*

un·dis·turbed /ˌʌndɪˈstɜːbd◂ $ -ɜːr-/ *adj* **1** not interrupted or moved: *At last I was able to work undisturbed.* | **be left/remain undisturbed** *The land is to be left undisturbed as a nature reserve.* **2 be undisturbed by sth** not upset or worried by something: *Mark seemed undisturbed by her threats.*

un·di·vid·ed /ˌʌndɪˈvaɪdɪd◂/ *adj* **1** [usually before noun] complete: *I'll give the matter my* ***undivided attention.*** **2** not separated into smaller parts: *an undivided country*

un·do /ʌnˈduː/ ●●○ *v* (*past tense* **undid** /-ˈdɪd/, *past participle* **undone** /-ˈdʌn/, *third person singular* **undoes** /-ˈdʌz/) [T]
1 to open something that is tied, fastened, or wrapped: *The screws can be undone by hand.* | *I undid the package carefully.* | **undo your jacket/shirt/bra etc** *He undid his coat.* THESAURUS ▸ OPEN
2 to try to remove the bad effects of something you have done: *We cannot* ***undo the damage*** *of a lifetime in only 30 days.* | *If a medicine is taken again too soon, it may undo all the good that has been done.*
3 *technical* to remove the effect of your previous action on a computer

un·do·ing /ʌnˈduːɪŋ/ *n* **be sb's undoing** to cause someone's shame, failure etc: *In the end, drink was his undoing.*

un·done /ˌʌnˈdʌn◂/ ●●○ *adj* [not before noun]
1 not fastened: *Your zip's undone.* | *One of these buttons has* ***come undone.***
2 not finished: *The washing-up had been* ***left undone.***
3 *old use* destroyed and without hope: *In the end, Othello is undone by his jealousy.*

un·doubt·ed /ʌnˈdaʊtɪd/ *adj* definitely true or known to exist: *her undoubted talent* | *The film was an undoubted success.*

un·doubt·ed·ly /ʌnˈdaʊtɪdli/ ●●○ *adv* used for saying that something is definitely true: *That is undoubtedly true.* | [sentence adverb] *Undoubtedly, public interest in folk music has declined.*

un·dreamed-of /ʌnˈdriːmd- ɒv $ -ɑːv/ (*also* **undreamt-of** /ʌnˈdremt-/) *adj* much more or much better than you thought was possible: *undreamt-of success* | *Men were becoming interested in fashion on a scale undreamed-of in the 1960s.*

un·dress[1] /ʌnˈdres/ ●●○ *v* [I,T] to take your clothes off, or take someone else's clothes off: *Matt undressed and got into bed.* | *Joe still needs an adult to undress him.*

> **REGISTER**
> In everyday English, people usually say **get undressed** rather than **undress**: *You can* ***get undressed*** *in here.*

undress[2] *n* [U] *formal* when you are wearing few or no clothes: *Cindy was wandering about her room* ***in a state of undress.***

un·dressed /ˌʌnˈdrest◂/ *adj* **1** [not before noun] not wearing any clothes: *He started to* ***get undressed*** (=to take his clothes off). **2** an undressed wound has not been covered to protect it

un·due /ˌʌnˈdjuː◂ $ -ˈduː◂/ *adj* [only before noun] *formal* more than is reasonable, suitable, or necessary: *De Gaulle felt that America had* ***undue influence*** *in Europe.* | **undue pressure/stress/strain etc** *Exercise gently and avoid putting yourself under undue strain.* | *The kick should be taken without* ***undue delay.***

un·du·late /ˈʌndjəleɪt $ -dʒə-/ *v* [I] *formal* to move or be shaped like waves that are rising and falling: *undulating hills* —**undulation** /ˌʌndjəˈleɪʃən $ -dʒə-/ *n* [C,U]

un·du·ly /ʌnˈdjuːli $ -ˈduː-/ *adv formal* more than is normal or reasonable: **unduly worried/concerned/anxious etc** *She doesn't seem unduly concerned about her exams.* | *It didn't trouble me unduly.*

un·dy·ing /ʌnˈdaɪ-ɪŋ/ *adj* [only before noun] continuing for ever: **undying love/devotion/support etc** *They declared their undying love for each other.*

un·earned /ˌʌnˈɜːnd◂ $ -ˈɜːrnd◂/ *adj* **unearned income** money that you receive but did not earn by working

un·earth /ʌnˈɜːθ $ -ˈɜːrθ/ *v* [T] **1** to find something after searching for it, especially something that has been buried in the ground or lost for a long time: *Farmers still sometimes unearth human bones here.* | *In one shop, I unearthed a wonderful collection of 1920s toys.* THESAURUS ▸ FIND **2** to find information or the truth about something or someone SYN **dig up**: *The inquiry unearthed some disturbing evidence.*

un·earth·ly /ʌnˈɜːθli $ -ˈɜːr-/ *adj* **1** very strange and unnatural, and probably frightening: *His eyes shone with an unearthly light.* **2 unearthly hour/time etc** *informal* very early or very late and therefore extremely inconvenient: *He suggested a meeting at some unearthly hour of the morning.*

un·ease /ʌnˈiːz/ *n* [U] a feeling of worry or slight fear about something: **sense/feeling of unease** *As she neared the door, Amy felt a growing sense of unease.* | *public unease about defence policy*

un·eas·y /ʌnˈiːzi/ ●○○ *adj*
1 worried or slightly afraid because you think that something bad might happen: **[+about]** *Ninety percent of those questioned* ***felt uneasy*** *about nuclear power.* THESAURUS ▸ NERVOUS, WORRIED
2 used to describe a period of time when people have agreed to stop fighting or arguing, but which is not really calm: **uneasy peace/truce/alliance/compromise** *The treaty restored an uneasy peace to the country.*
3 not comfortable, peaceful, or relaxed: *She eventually fell into an uneasy sleep.* —**uneasily** *adv*: *Bill shifted uneasily in his chair.* | *Charles' concern for the environment* ***sits uneasily*** *with* (=does not fit well with) *his collection of powerful cars.* —**uneasiness** *n* [U]

un·eat·able /ʌnˈiːtəbəl/ *adj* a word meaning unpleasant or unsuitable to eat, that some people think is incorrect SYN **inedible**

un·eat·en /ˌʌnˈiːtn◂/ *adj* not eaten: *I had to throw away the uneaten food.*

un·e·co·nom·ic /ˌʌniːkəˈnɒmɪk◂, ˌʌnekə- $ -ˈnɑː-/ *adj* **1** not making enough money or profit: *the closure of uneconomic industries* **2** uneconomical

un·e·co·nom·i·cal /ˌʌniːkəˈnɒmɪkəl, ˌʌnekə- $ -ˈnɑː-/ AWL *adj* using too much effort, money, or materials to make a profit: *Old vehicles are often uneconomical.* —**uneconomically** /-kli/ *adv*

un·ed·i·fy·ing /ʌnˈedəfaɪ-ɪŋ/ *adj formal* unpleasant and embarrassing: **unedifying spectacle/sight/scene etc** *the unedifying spectacle of players attacking the referee*

un·ed·u·cat·ed /ʌnˈedjəkeɪtɪd $ -dʒə-/ *adj* not educated to the usual level, or showing that someone is not well educated: *a largely uneducated workforce*

un·e·lect·ed /ˌʌnɪˈlektɪd◂/ *adj* someone who is unelected has a position of power although they were not elected – often used to show disapproval

un·e·mo·tion·al /ˌʌnɪˈməʊʃənəl◂ $ -ˈmoʊ-/ *adj* not showing your feelings: *His voice was unemotional.* | *Zoe is normally an unemotional person.*

un·em·ploy·able /ˌʌnɪmˈplɔɪəbəl◂/ *adj* not having the skills or qualities needed to get a job

un·em·ployed¹ /ˌʌnɪmˈplɔɪd◂/ ●●● S2 W3 *adj* without a job SYN **out of work**: *an unemployed actor* | *I've only been unemployed for a few weeks.*

THESAURUS

unemployed someone who is unemployed does not have a job: *Fifty percent of the men in this town are unemployed.*
out of work unemployed, especially for a long period of time, when you had a job before: *I've been out of work for two years.*
redundant *BrE* if someone is redundant, they have been told that they no longer have a job: *He was made redundant earlier this year.* | *redundant miners*
be on the dole *BrE*, **be on welfare/on unemployment** *AmE* to be receiving money from the government because you do not have a job: *I didn't want to go back on the dole.* | *Many people on welfare don't have anyone to take care of the kids while they train for a job.*
be looking for work if someone is looking for work, they do not have a job and are trying to find one: *How long have you been looking for work?*
jobless people who are jobless do not have jobs – used especially in news reports: *The jobless totals have risen by 6% in the last year.* | *jobless youths*

unemployed² *n* **the unemployed** [plural] people who have no job: **the long-term unemployed** (=people who have not had a job for a long time) *a retraining scheme for the long-term unemployed*

un·em·ploy·ment /ˌʌnɪmˈplɔɪmənt/ ●●● S2 W2 *n* [U]
1 the number of people in a particular country or area who cannot get a job: *a town where there is high unemployment*
2 when someone does not have a job: *Closure of the plant means 80 workers are facing unemployment.*
3 *AmE* money paid regularly by the government to people who have no job: **on unemployment** *He's been on unemployment for two months.*

COLLOCATIONS

ADJECTIVES

high *They live in an area where unemployment is high.*
low *The area has the lowest unemployment in Europe.*
rising/falling unemployment *Rising unemployment led to more crime.*
mass unemployment (=when very large numbers of people are unemployed) *the mass unemployment of the 1930s*
long-term unemployment (=when people are unemployed for a long period of time) | **serious/severe unemployment** | **widespread unemployment** (=in many places)

VERBS

reduce/cut/bring down unemployment *The government is spending more on projects to cut unemployment.*
cause unemployment *People blamed immigrants for causing unemployment.*
unemployment increases/rises | **unemployment soars** (=increases quickly to a high level)

PHRASES

a rise/increase in unemployment *The crisis meant a sharp rise in unemployment.*
a fall/reduction in unemployment

unemployment + NOUN

the unemployment rate *The unemployment rate was 17 percent.*
the unemployment level *The unemployment level among young people is rising.*
unemployment figures/statistics | **an unemployment blackspot** *BrE* (=an area where there is higher unemployment than in other places)

COMMON ERRORS

⚠ Don't say 'big unemployment'. Say **high unemployment**.

unemˈployment ˌbenefit *BrE*, **unemˈployment ˌbenefits/compenˌsation** *AmE n* [U] money paid regularly by the government to people who have no job: **on unemployment benefit** (=be getting unemployment benefit) *people on unemployment benefit*

un·end·ing /ʌnˈendɪŋ/ *adj* something, especially something bad, that is unending seems as if it will continue for ever: *an unending stream of people*

un·en·dur·a·ble /ˌʌnɪnˈdjʊərəbəl◂ $ -ˈdʊr-/ *adj formal* too unpleasant, painful etc to bear SYN **unbearable**: *The pain was unendurable.*

un·en·vi·a·ble /ʌnˈenviəbəl/ *adj* difficult and unpleasant: **unenviable task/job etc (of doing sth)** *the unenviable task of informing the victim's relations* | *Edward III was in a delicate and* ***unenviable position.***

un·e·qual /ʌnˈiːkwəl/ ●○○ *adj*
1 used to describe a situation or a social system which is unfair because some groups or people have more power than others → **inequality**: *an unequal contest* | *the unequal distribution of wealth*
2 not equal in number, amount, or level: **of unequal size/length etc** *two rooms of unequal size* | **be unequal in size/weight etc** *The pieces were unequal in length.*
3 be unequal to the task/job etc to not have enough strength, ability etc to do something —**unequally** *adv*

un·e·qualled *BrE*, **unequaled** *AmE* /ʌnˈiːkwəld/ *adj* better than any other: *The hotel has a range of facilities unequalled in the city.*

un·e·quiv·o·cal /ˌʌnɪˈkwɪvəkəl◂/ *adj formal* completely clear and without any possibility of doubt: *His answer was an unequivocal 'No'.* —**unequivocally** /-kli/ *adv*

un·er·ring /ʌnˈɜːrɪŋ/ *adj* always right: *He passes the ball with* ***unerring accuracy.*** —**unerringly** *adv*

un·eth·i·cal /ʌnˈeθɪkəl/ AWL *adj* morally unacceptable → **ethics**: *unethical medical practices* —**unethically** /-kli/ *adv*

un·e·ven /ʌnˈiːvən/ ●○○ *adj*
1 not smooth, flat, or level: *She walked back carefully over the uneven ground.* THESAURUS ROUGH
2 not regular: *His breathing had become uneven.* | *uneven rates of development*
3 not equal or equally balanced: *an uneven distribution of resources*
4 good in some parts and bad in others: *an uneven performance* —**unevenly** *adv* —**unevenness** *n* [U]

un·e·vent·ful /ˌʌnɪˈventfəl◂/ *adj* with nothing exciting or unusual happening: *Annie led a quiet uneventful*

U

life. | *The journey was uneventful.* —**uneventfully** *adv* —**uneventfulness** *n* [U]

un·ex·ci·ting /ˌʌnɪkˈsaɪtɪŋ◂/ *adj* ordinary and slightly boring: *After Tokyo, Okinawa seemed unexciting at first.*

un·ex·pect·ed /ˌʌnɪkˈspektɪd◂/ ●●○ *adj* used to describe something that is surprising because you were not expecting it: *The experiment produced some unexpected results.* | *Her death was* ***totally unexpected****.* | *Hague's announcement was* ***not entirely unexpected****.* —**unexpectedly** *adv*: *His father died unexpectedly.*

un·ex·plained /ˌʌnɪkˈspleɪnd◂/ *adj* something that is unexplained is something you cannot understand because you do not know the reason for it: *patients with unexplained symptoms* | *For some unexplained reason, he wants to move to Ipswich.*

un·ex·plod·ed /ˌʌnɪkˈspləʊdɪd◂ $ -ˈsploʊ-/ *adj* [only before noun] used to describe something such as a bomb which has not yet exploded

un·ex·plored /ˌʌnɪkˈsplɔːd◂ $ -ˈsplɔːrd◂/ *adj* **1** an unexplored place has not been examined or put on a map: *unexplored planets* **2** an unexplored idea has not been thought about or discussed: *The study looks at a relatively unexplored area of human relationships.*

un·ex·pur·gat·ed /ʌnˈekspəgeɪtɪd $ -pər-/ *adj* an unexpurgated book, play etc is complete and has not had parts that might offend people removed

un·fail·ing /ʌnˈfeɪlɪŋ/ *adj* always there, even in times of difficulty or trouble: **unfailing help/support etc** *I'd like to thank you all for your unfailing support.* | *She battled against cancer with* ***unfailing good humour****.* —**unfailingly** *adv*: *The staff are unfailingly polite.*

un·fair /ˌʌnˈfeə◂ $ -ˈfer◂/ ●●● S3 *adj* not right or fair, especially because not everyone has an equal opportunity SYN **unjust**: *an* ***unfair advantage*** | *laws aimed at preventing* ***unfair competition*** | *Many employers have recognized that age discrimination is unfair.* | *She won £20,000 for* ***unfair dismissal*** (=being illegally made to leave your job). —**unfairly** *adv*: *Mrs Taylor believes her son has been* ***unfairly treated****.* | *The tribunal decided that Mr Matthews had been* ***unfairly dismissed****.* —**unfairness** *n* [U]

un·faith·ful /ʌnˈfeɪθfəl/ ●○○ *adj* someone who is unfaithful has sex with someone who is not their wife, husband, or usual partner → **infidelity**: **[+to]** *Geoff had been unfaithful to her on many occasions.* —**unfaithfully** *adv* —**unfaithfulness** *n* [U]

un·fal·ter·ing /ʌnˈfɔːltərɪŋ $ -ˈfɒːl-/ *adj formal* strong, determined, and not becoming weaker: *unfaltering confidence*

un·fa·mil·i·ar /ˌʌnfəˈmɪliə◂ $ -ər◂/ ●○○ *adj*
1 not known to you: **unfamiliar surroundings/place/environment etc** *She stood on deck to gaze at the unfamiliar surroundings.* | *a crowd of unfamiliar faces* | **[+to]** *Some of the technical vocabulary may be unfamiliar to you.*
2 be unfamiliar with sth to not have any experience of something: *We were unfamiliar with the neighbourhood.* —**unfamiliarity** /ˌʌnfəmɪliˈærəti/ *n* [U]

un·fash·ion·a·ble /ʌnˈfæʃənəbəl/ ●●○ *adj* not popular or fashionable at the present time: *unfashionable clothes* THESAURUS➤ OLD-FASHIONED

un·fas·ten /ʌnˈfɑːsən $ -ˈfæsən/ *v* [T] to undo something such as a button, belt, rope etc: *He unfastened the top button of his shirt.* THESAURUS➤ OPEN

un·fath·om·a·ble /ʌnˈfæðəməbəl/ *adj literary* too strange or mysterious to be understood

un·fa·vour·a·ble *BrE*, **unfavorable** *AmE* /ʌnˈfeɪvərəbəl/ *adj* **1** unfavourable conditions, situations etc are not good: *unfavourable circumstances* THESAURUS➤ BAD **2** if someone's reaction or attitude to something is unfavourable, they do not like it: *unfavourable reviews* | ***unfavourable publicity*** | *Careless spelling mistakes in a letter can create an* ***unfavourable impression****.* —**unfavourably** *adv*

un·fazed /ʌnˈfeɪzd/ *adj* not confused or shocked by a difficult situation or by something bad that has happened: **[+by]** *The prime minister appeared to be totally unfazed by the protesters.*

un·feel·ing /ʌnˈfiːlɪŋ/ *adj* not sympathetic towards other people's feelings: *Dave had been quite wrong to call Michelle* ***cold and unfeeling****.*

un·fet·tered /ʌnˈfetəd $ -ərd/ *adj formal* not restricted by laws or rules: *unfettered economic activity*

un·filled /ˌʌnˈfɪld◂/ *adj* **1** an unfilled job, position etc is available but no one has been found for it yet: *unfilled vacancies* **2 an unfilled order** a request by a customer for a product that has not been sent

un·fin·ished /ʌnˈfɪnɪʃt/ ●●○ *adj*
1 not completed: *Rachael left her meal unfinished.*
2 unfinished business something that you have not yet dealt with

un·fit /ʌnˈfɪt/ *adj* **1** not in a good physical condition SYN **out of shape**: *She never gets any exercise – she must be really unfit.* **2** not good enough to do something or to be used for a particular purpose: **[+for]** *Jenkins is unfit for public office.* | *The meat was declared* ***unfit for human consumption*** (=not suitable to eat). | *The house was* ***unfit for human habitation*** (=not good enough to live in). | **unfit to do sth** *Hubbard was declared* ***mentally unfit*** *to stand trial.*

un·flag·ging /ʌnˈflægɪŋ/ *adj* continuing strongly and never becoming tired or weak: *his unflagging energy*

un·flap·pa·ble /ʌnˈflæpəbəl/ *adj informal* having the ability to stay calm and not become upset, even in difficult situations

un·flat·ter·ing /ʌnˈflætərɪŋ/ *adj* making someone look or seem bad or unattractive: *an unflattering portrait*

un·flinch·ing /ʌnˈflɪntʃɪŋ/ *adj* not changing or becoming weaker, even in a very difficult or dangerous situation: *unflinching courage* —**unflinchingly** *adv*

un·fo·cused, **unfocussed** /ʌnˈfəʊkəst $ -ˈfoʊ-/ *adj* **1** not dealing with or paying attention to the most important ideas, causes etc: *The discussion was becoming unfocused.* **2** eyes that are unfocused are open, but are not looking at anything specific: *He gave her an unfocused look.*

un·fold /ʌnˈfəʊld $ -ˈfoʊld/ ●●○ *v*
1 [I,T] if a story unfolds, or if someone unfolds it, it is told: *As the story unfolds, we learn more about Max's childhood.*
2 [I] if a series of events unfolds, they happen: *He had watched* ***the drama unfold*** *from a nearby ship.*
3 [I,T] if you unfold something that was folded, or if it unfolds, it opens out: *He unfolded the map.*

un·fol·low /ˌʌnˈfɒləʊ $ -ˈfɑːloʊ/ *v* [T] to stop looking at the messages sent by a particular person using the SOCIAL NETWORKING service Twitter

un·fore·see·a·ble /ˌʌnfɔːˈsiːəbəl◂ $ -fɔːr-/ *adj* an unforeseeable event, situation etc could not have been expected: *unforeseeable danger*

un·fore·seen /ˌʌnfɔːˈsiːn◂ $ -fɔːr-/ *adj* an unforeseen situation is one that you did not expect to happen: **unforeseen circumstances/events/changes etc** *Due to* ***unforeseen circumstances****, the play has been cancelled.* | **unforeseen problems/difficulties/delays** *unforeseen delays in supplying the equipment*

un·for·get·ta·ble /ˌʌnfəˈgetəbəl◂ $ -fər-/ *adj* an unforgettable experience, sight etc affects you so strongly that you will never forget it, especially because it is particularly good or beautiful → **memorable**: *A visit to Morocco is a truly unforgettable experience.* —**unforgettably** *adv*

un·for·giv·a·ble /ˌʌnfəˈgɪvəbəl◂ $ -fər-/ *adj* an unforgivable action is so bad or cruel that you cannot forgive the person who did it: *Patrick had deceived her, and that was unforgivable.* | *the* ***unforgivable sin*** *of informing on your friends* —**unforgivably** *adv*

un·for·giv·ing /ˌʌnfəˈgɪvɪŋ◂ $ -fər-/ *adj* **1** someone who is unforgiving does not forgive people easily **2** an unforgiving place is very difficult to live in, for example because it is extremely hot or cold

un·formed /ˌʌnˈfɔːmd◂ $ -ɔːr-/ *adj* not yet developed: *the unformed mind of a child*

un·for·tu·nate¹ /ʌnˈfɔːtʃənət $ -ˈfɔːr-/ ●●○ S3 *adj*
1 someone who is unfortunate has something bad happen to them: *When we entered the room, the teacher was yelling at some unfortunate student.*
2 an unfortunate situation, condition, quality etc is one that you wish was different: *an unfortunate turn of events* | *He has an* ***unfortunate habit*** *of repeating himself.* | **it is unfortunate (that)** *It's unfortunate that so few people seem willing to help.* | *It's* ***most unfortunate*** (=very unfortunate) *that your father can't come to the wedding.*
3 happening because of bad luck: *an* ***unfortunate accident***
4 *formal* unfortunate behaviour, remarks etc make people feel embarrassed or offended: *an unfortunate choice of words*

unfortunate² *n* [C] *literary* someone who has no money, home, job etc

un·for·tu·nate·ly /ʌnˈfɔːtʃənətli $ -ˈfɔːr-/ ●●● S1 W3 *adv* [sentence adverb] used when you are mentioning a fact that you wish was not true: *Unfortunately, you were out when we called.*

un·found·ed /ʌnˈfaʊndɪd/ ●○○ AWL *adj* unfounded statements, feelings, opinions etc are wrong because they are not based on facts: **unfounded rumours/claims/allegations etc** *Unfounded rumours began circulating that Ian and Susan were having an affair.* | **prove (to be) unfounded** *Sadly, my optimism proved unfounded.*

un·fre·quent·ed /ˌʌnfrɪˈkwentɪd◂ $ ʌnˈfriːkwəntəd, ˌʌnfrɪˈkwen-/ *adj formal* not often visited by many people: *an unfrequented spot*

un·friend /ʌnˈfrend/ *v* [T] *informal* to remove someone from your list of friends on a SOCIAL NETWORKING SITE SYN **defriend**: *I don't know why he unfriended me.*

un·friend·ly /ʌnˈfrendli/ ●●○ *adj* (*comparative* **unfriendlier**, *superlative* **unfriendliest**)
1 not kind or friendly: *The old man looked cross and unfriendly.* | *a lonely unfriendly place* | **[+to/towards]** *The villagers were really quite unfriendly towards us.*
2 not helping or wanting a type of person or thing: **[+to]** *We have created cities that are unfriendly to pedestrians.*
3 an unfriendly government or nation is one that opposes yours

THESAURUS

PERSON/VOICE/BEHAVIOUR

unfriendly/not friendly behaving towards someone in a way that shows you are not interested in them or are not ready to talk to them or help them: *The hotel staff were unfriendly and unhelpful.* | *an unfriendly tone of voice*
hostile very unfriendly, and ready to argue or fight: *He was openly hostile towards me when I arrived.* | *A hostile crowd gathered outside the US embassy.*
cold behaving towards other people as if you do not like them or care about them: *He gave her a cold stare.* | *a cold voice*
frosty unfriendly, especially because you are angry with someone: *When she spoke, her tone was frosty.* | *He got* ***a frosty reception*** *from his wife when he finally returned home* (=she was not very friendly towards him).
aloof [not before noun] not wanting to talk to other people or spend time with them, especially because you think you are better than them: *Some politicians are criticized for being too aloof.*
antagonistic unfriendly and always trying to start arguments with someone: *Why are Kate and John so antagonistic towards each other?*
antisocial not interested in meeting other people or forming friendly relationships with them: *Sorry if I'm being antisocial, but I need to get my work done.* | *He was an antisocial loner with no friends.*

PLACE/ORGANIZATION

unfriendly making you feel as though you are not wanted: *The report found that the church can seem unfriendly to outsiders.*
unwelcoming unfriendly – used especially about the physical characteristics or appearance of something: *The entrance to the factory is cold, bare, and unwelcoming.*
impersonal lacking the normal friendly relations between people who work or do business together: *I had no desire to work for a large impersonal organization.*
forbidding unfriendly, uncomfortable, and a little frightening, so that you do not want to go there: *The school was a rather forbidding building surrounded by a high steel fence.*

un·frock /ʌnˈfrɒk $ -ˈfrɑːk/ *v* [T] to remove someone from their position as a priest as a punishment for behaviour or beliefs that the Church does not approve of GRAMMAR **Unfrock** is usually passive.

un·ful·filled /ˌʌnfʊlˈfɪld◂/ *adj* **1** an unfulfilled hope, desire, dream etc has not been achieved: *His dream of competing in the Olympics* ***remained unfulfilled.*** **2** someone who is unfulfilled feels they could be achieving more in their job, relationship etc: *Her job left her feeling unfulfilled and unappreciated.*

un·fun·ny /ʌnˈfʌni/ *adj informal* an unfunny joke or action is not amusing, although it is intended to be – used to show disapproval

un·furl /ʌnˈfɜːl $ -ɜːrl/ *v* [I,T] if a flag, sail etc unfurls, or if someone unfurls it, it unrolls and opens

un·fur·nished /ʌnˈfɜːnɪʃt $ -ɜːr-/ *adj* an unfurnished room, house etc has no furniture in it

un·gain·ly /ʌnˈgeɪnli/ *adj* moving in a way that does not look graceful: *a tall ungainly teenager* —**ungainliness** *n* [U]

un·glued /ʌnˈgluːd/ *adj* **1 come unglued** *AmE informal* **a)** if a plan, situation etc comes unglued, it stops working well: *When his parents got divorced, his whole world came unglued.* **b)** to become extremely upset or angry about something: *If someone talked to me like that, I would just come unglued.* **2** no longer glued together

un·god·ly /ʌnˈgɒdli $ -ˈgɑːd-/ *adj* **1** [only before noun] unreasonable and annoying: **at an ungodly hour** (=very early in the morning or very late at night) *Why did you wake me up at such an ungodly hour?* **2** *literary* showing a lack of respect for God

un·gov·ern·a·ble /ʌnˈgʌvənəbəl $ -vər-/ *adj* **1** a country or area that is ungovernable is one in which the people cannot be controlled by the government, the police etc **2** *formal* feelings or types of behaviour that are ungovernable are impossible to control: *ungovernable rage*

un·gra·cious /ʌnˈgreɪʃəs/ *adj* not polite or friendly: *After Anna's kindness to me, I don't want to seem ungracious.* —**ungraciously** *adv*

un·grate·ful /ʌnˈgreɪtfəl/ *adj* not expressing thanks for something that someone has given to you or done for you: *Don't be so ungrateful!*

un·guard·ed /ʌnˈgɑːdɪd $ -ɑːr-/ *adj* **1 an unguarded moment** a time when you are not paying attention to what you are doing or saying: *In an unguarded moment, he admitted that he wanted to quit his job.* **2** an unguarded remark, statement etc is one that you make carelessly without thinking of the possible effects **3** not guarded or protected by anyone

un·guent /ˈʌŋgwənt/ *n* [C] an oily substance used on your skin SYN **ointment**

un·hap·pi·ly /ʌnˈhæpəli/ *adv* **1** in a way that shows you are not happy: *'I'm not sure what to do,' Seb admitted unhappily.* **2** [sentence adverb] *old-fashioned* used when you are mentioning a fact that you wish were not true SYN **unfortunately**: *Unhappily, she was not able to complete the course.*

un·hap·py /ʌnˈhæpi/ ●●● S3 *adj* (*comparative* **unhappier**, *superlative* **unhappiest**)
1 not happy → **sad**: *If you're so unhappy, why don't you*

U

change jobs? | Leslie had an unhappy childhood. | an unhappy marriage | I was ***desperately unhappy****.* **THESAURUS** SAD

REGISTER
In everyday English, people often say they feel **down** or **fed up** rather than **unhappy**: *The situation at home was making her feel very* ***down****.*

2 feeling worried or annoyed because you do not like what is happening in a particular situation: **unhappy about/at (doing) sth** *Dennis is unhappy about having to work on a Saturday.* | **[+with]** *We were all unhappy with the quality of the service.*
3 *formal* an unhappy remark, situation etc is not suitable, lucky, or desirable SYN **unfortunate**: *an unhappy coincidence* —**unhappiness** *n* [U]

un·harmed /ʌnˈhɑːmd $ -ɑːr-/ *adj* [not before noun] not hurt or harmed: *The hostages were* ***released unharmed****. | The girl managed to* ***escape unharmed****.*

un·health·y /ʌnˈhelθi/ ●●○ *adj* (*comparative* **unhealthier**, *superlative* **unhealthiest**)
1 likely to make you ill: *unhealthy living conditions*
2 not normal or natural and likely to be harmful: *an unhealthy relationship* | **unhealthy interest/obsession/fear etc** *Gareth had an unhealthy interest in death.*
3 not physically healthy SYN **ill**, **sick**: *an unhealthy baby*
4 unhealthy skin, hair etc shows that you are ill or not healthy: *an unhealthy pale complexion* —**unhealthily** *adv*

un·heard /ʌnˈhɜːd $ -ɜːrd/ *adj* not heard or listened to: *Her cries for help* ***went unheard****.*

unˈheard of, **unheard-of** *adj* something that is unheard of is so unusual that it has not happened or been known before: *Travel for pleasure was almost unheard of until the 19th century.*

un·heed·ed /ʌnˈhiːdɪd/ *adj literary* noticed but not listened to, accepted, or believed: *Her warnings* ***went unheeded****.*

un·help·ful /ʌnˈhelpfəl/ *adj* not helping in a situation and sometimes making it worse: *The authorities are being particularly unhelpful.* —**unhelpfully** *adv* —**unhelpfulness** *n* [U]

un·her·ald·ed /ʌnˈherəldɪd/ *adj formal* **1** if an event is unheralded, there is no warning that it is going to happen: *an unheralded visit from his aunt* **2** not known about or recognized as good SYN **unsung**: *the unheralded members of the team*

un·hinge /ʌnˈhɪndʒ/ *v* [T] to make someone become very upset or mentally ill: *The terrible experience seemed to have unhinged him slightly.* —**unhinged** *adj*

un·hip /ʌnˈhɪp/ *adj informal* unfashionable

un·hitch /ʌnˈhɪtʃ/ *v* [T] to unfasten something that is joined to something else

un·ho·ly /ʌnˈhəʊli $ -ˈhoʊ-/ *adj* [no comparative] **1 an unholy alliance** an agreement between two people or organizations who would not normally work together, usually for a bad purpose **2** [only before noun] *informal* bad and extreme: *An* ***unholy row*** *broke out between two of the men drinking in the bar. | an* ***unholy mess*** **3** not holy, or not respecting what is holy **4 unholy amusement/delight/pleasure** pleasure etc that you get from someone else's suffering: *He was taking an unholy delight in humiliating Sarah.*

un·hook /ʌnˈhʊk/ *v* [T] to unfasten or remove something from a hook

un·hoped-for /ʌnˈhəʊpt fɔː $ -ˈhoʊpt fɔːr/ *adj* much better than had been expected: *unhoped-for success*

un·hur·ried /ʌnˈhʌrid $ -ˈhɜː-/ *adj* slow and calm: *the unhurried pace of a small town* **THESAURUS** SLOW —**unhurriedly** *adv*

un·hurt /ʌnˈhɜːt $ -ɜːrt/ ●●○ *adj* [not before noun] not hurt: *The driver* ***escaped unhurt*** *from the accident.*

un·hy·gie·nic /ˌʌnhaɪˈdʒiːnɪk◂ $ -ˈdʒe-, -ˈdʒiː-/ *adj* dirty and likely to make people ill: *unhygienic conditions* **THESAURUS** DIRTY —**unhygienically** /-kli/ *adv*

u·ni /ˈjuːni/ *n* [singular, U] *BrE, AusE spoken* university

uni- /juːnə/ *prefix* one SYN **single**: *unidirectional* (=going in only one direction)

u·ni·cel·lu·lar /ˌjuːnɪˈseljələ $ -ər/ *adj technical* consisting of only one cell: *unicellular organisms such as amoebas*

u·ni·corn /ˈjuːnəkɔːn $ -ɔːrn/ *n* [C] an imaginary animal like a white horse with a long straight horn growing on its head

u·ni·cy·cle /ˈjuːniˌsaɪkəl/ *n* [C] a vehicle that is like a bicycle but has only one wheel

un·i·den·ti·fied /ˌʌnaɪˈdentɪfaɪd◂/ *adj* an unidentified person or thing is one that you do not know the name of: *An unidentified man was spotted near the scene of the crime.*

u·ni·fi·ca·tion /ˌjuːnɪfɪˈkeɪʃən/ ●○○ AWL *n* [U] the act of combining two or more groups, countries etc to make a single group or country: **[+of]** *the unification of Germany*

u·ni·fied /ˈjuːnɪfaɪd/ AWL *adj* created from more than one part, group etc: *a unified approach | a unified EU import market*

u·ni·form[1] /ˈjuːnəfɔːm $ -ɔːrm/ ●●● S3 *n* [C,U]
1 a particular type of clothing worn by all the members of a group or organization such as the police, the army etc: **school/army/police etc uniform** *He was still* ***wearing*** *his* ***school uniform****.*
2 in uniform a) wearing a uniform: *He was on duty and in uniform.* **b)** in the Army, Navy etc: *my 33 years in uniform*

uniform[2] ●○○ AWL *adj* being the same in all its parts or among all its members: *Grade A eggs must be of uniform size.* —**uniformly** *adv*

u·ni·formed /ˈjuːnəfɔːmd $ -ɔːr-/ *adj* wearing a uniform: *uniformed police officers*

u·ni·form·i·ty /ˌjuːnəˈfɔːməti $ -ɔːr-/ ●○○ AWL *n* [U] the quality of being or looking the same as all other members of a group: *There seems to be no uniformity among the various systems.*

u·ni·fy /ˈjuːnɪfaɪ/ ●○○ AWL *v* (**unified**, **unifying**, **unifies**) [I,T] if you unify two or more parts or things, or if they unify, they are combined to make a single unit SYN **unite** OPP **divide** → **unification**: *Strong support for the war has unified the nation. | His music unifies traditional and modern themes.*

u·ni·lat·e·ral /ˌjuːnəˈlætərəl◂/ ●○○ *adj formal* a unilateral action or decision is done by only one of the groups involved in a situation → **bilateral**, **multilateral**: *a unilateral declaration of independence* | **unilateral disarmament** (=when one country gets rid of its own NUCLEAR weapons without waiting for other countries to do the same) —**unilateralism** *n* [U] —**unilaterally** *adv*

un·i·ma·gin·a·ble /ˌʌnɪˈmædʒənəbəl◂/ *adj* not possible to imagine: *unimaginable wealth* —**unimaginably** *adv*

un·i·ma·gin·a·tive /ˌʌnɪˈmædʒənətɪv◂/ *adj* **1** lacking the ability to think of new or unusual ideas **2** ordinary and boring, and not using any new ideas: *unimaginative architecture | unimaginative housing policies*

un·i·ma·gined /ˌʌnɪˈmædʒɪnd◂/ *adj* [usually before noun] *literary* so good, large, great etc that it is hard to imagine

un·im·paired /ˌʌnɪmˈpeəd◂ $ -ˈperd◂/ *adj* not damaged or made weak

un·im·peach·a·ble /ˌʌnɪmˈpiːtʃəbəl◂/ *adj formal* so good or definite that criticism or doubt is impossible: *unimpeachable morals* —**unimpeachably** *adv*

un·im·ped·ed /ˌʌnɪmˈpiːdɪd◂/ *adj* happening or moving without being stopped or having difficulty: *unimpeded progress*

un·im·por·tant /ˌʌnɪmˈpɔːtənt◂ $ -ɔːr-/ *adj* not important SYN **trivial**: *unimportant details*

THESAURUS
unimportant not important: *The exact details are unimportant. | Girls' education was seen as unimportant.*
of no/little importance not important, or not very important. These phrases sound a little more formal

than **unimportant**: *If you're capable of doing the job, your age is of no importance. | It's of little importance whether or not this story is true.*
minor small and not very likely to have an important effect - used especially about changes, problems, injuries, damage, or differences: *I've made a few minor changes. | The driver suffered minor injuries. | These are just minor problems.*
trivial very unimportant and not worth worrying about or spending time on: *They had a disagreement about some trivial matter. | She tends to get upset about trivial things.*
insignificant very small and unimportant, especially when compared to other things: *Her own problems seemed insignificant. | The amount of carbon they produce is relatively insignificant.*
negligible extremely small and not important - used especially about effects, amounts, differences, or risks: *So far, the program has had a negligible effect. | The difference in price is negligible.*
secondary not as important as something else: *These issues are of secondary importance. | For many women, a career is secondary to being a mother.*

un·im·pressed /ˌʌnɪmˈprest/ *adj* not thinking that someone or something is good, interesting etc: **[+with/by]** *Board members were unimpressed with the plan.*

un·im·pres·sive /ˌʌnɪmˈpresɪv◂/ *adj* not as good, large etc as expected or necessary: *unimpressive test results*

un·in·formed /ˌʌnɪnˈfɔːmd◂ $ -ɔːr-/ *adj* not having enough knowledge or information: *Parents were left anxious, uninformed, and isolated. | uninformed criticism from uninformed journalists |* **[+about]** *Many immigrants are uninformed about US tax laws.*

un·in·hab·it·a·ble /ˌʌnɪnˈhæbətəbəl◂/ *adj* if a place is uninhabitable, it is impossible to live in: *Much of the country is uninhabitable because it is desert. | Many houses were so badly damaged in the war that they were made permanently uninhabitable.*

un·in·hab·it·ed /ˌʌnɪnˈhæbɪtɪd◂/ *adj* an uninhabited place does not have anyone living there SYN **deserted**: *an* ***uninhabited island*** THESAURUS ▸ EMPTY

un·in·hib·it·ed /ˌʌnɪnˈhɪbɪtɪd◂/ *adj* confident or relaxed enough to do or say what you want to: *uninhibited laughter* —**uninhibitedly** *adv*

un·i·ni·ti·at·ed /ˌʌnɪˈnɪʃieɪtɪd◂/ *n* **the uninitiated** [plural] people who do not have special knowledge or experience of something: *To the uninitiated, this will make little sense.* —**uninitiated** *adj*

un·in·spired /ˌʌnɪnˈspaɪəd◂ $ -ˈspaɪrd◂/ *adj* not showing any imagination: *an uninspired performance*

un·in·spir·ing /ˌʌnɪnˈspaɪərɪŋ◂ $ -ˈspaɪr-/ *adj* not at all interesting or exciting: *No one deserved to win this uninspiring game.*

un·in·stall /ˌʌnɪnˈstɔːl $ -ˈstɒːl/ *v* [T] to completely remove a program from a computer

un·in·tel·li·gi·ble /ˌʌnɪnˈtelədʒəbəl◂/ *adj* impossible to understand OPP **clear**: *Eva muttered* ***something unintelligible****. |* **[+to]** *technical jargon that is unintelligible to outsiders* —**unintelligibly** *adv*

un·in·ten·tion·al /ˌʌnɪnˈtenʃənəl◂/ *adj* not done deliberately OPP **deliberate**: *I know she upset you, but I'm sure it was unintentional.* —**unintentionally** *adv*

un·in·terest·ed /ʌnˈɪntrɪstɪd/ *adj* not interested → **disinterested**: **[+in]** *He was uninterested in politics.*

un·in·ter·rupt·ed /ˌʌnɪntəˈrʌptɪd◂/ *adj* **1** continuous: *uninterrupted sleep* **2 uninterrupted view** if you have an uninterrupted view of something, there is nothing between you and that thing to stop you from seeing it clearly: *an uninterrupted view of the mountains* —**uninterruptedly** *adv*

un·in·vit·ed /ˌʌnɪnˈvaɪtɪd◂/ *adj* not invited and expected: *uninvited guests | Helen turned up uninvited.*

un·in·vit·ing /ˌʌnɪnˈvaɪtɪŋ◂/ *adj* **1** an uninviting place seems unattractive or unpleasant: *The building was cold, dark, and uninviting.* **2 uninviting prospect** something unpleasant that you will have to do: *He faced the uninviting prospect of a two-hour wait for the next train.*

u·nion /ˈjuːnjən/ ●●○ S3 W3 *n*
1 [C] (*also* **trade union** *BrE*, **labor union** *AmE*) an organization formed by workers to protect their rights: **[+of]** *the National Union of Teachers | Are you planning to* ***join*** *the* ***union****? |* ***union members*** THESAURUS ▸ ORGANIZATION
2 [C] used in the names of some clubs or organizations: *the British Golf Union*
3 [singular] *formal* the act of joining two or more things together, or the state of being joined together: **[+of]** *The artist's work shows the perfect union of craftsmanship and imagination. |* **[+with]** *Some militants favour independence for Kashmir or union with Pakistan.*
4 [singular] a group of countries or states with the same central government: *the former Soviet Union*
5 the Union used in the past to talk about the United States, especially the northern states during the Civil War
6 [C,U] *formal* marriage
7 [C,U] *formal* the activity of having sex, or an occasion when this happens

u·nion·is·m /ˈjuːnjənɪzəm/ *n* [U] belief in the principles of TRADE UNIONS —**unionist** *n* [C]

U·nion·ist /ˈjuːnjənɪst/ *n* [C] a member of a political party that wants Northern Ireland to remain part of the United Kingdom —**Unionism** *n* [U]

u·nion·ize (*also* **-ise** *BrE*) /ˈjuːnjənaɪz/ *v* [I,T] if workers unionize or are unionized, they become members of a TRADE UNION —**unionized** *adj* —**unionization** /ˌjuːnjənaɪˈzeɪʃən $ -jənə-/ *n* [U]

ˌUnion ˈJack *n* [C] the national flag of the United Kingdom

ˈunion ˌsuit *n* [C] *AmE* a piece of underwear that covers the whole body, with long legs and long sleeves

u·nique /juːˈniːk/ ●●● S3 W2 AWL *adj* [no comparative]
1 *informal* unusually good and special: *This is a unique opportunity to study these rare creatures.*

GRAMMAR
People sometimes use 'very' with **unique** in this meaning, but this use is often considered to be incorrect.
GRAMMAR GUIDE ▸ ADJECTIVES

2 being the only one of its kind: *Each person's fingerprints are unique.* THESAURUS ▸ DIFFERENT
3 unique to sb/sth existing only in a particular place or in relation to a particular person or people: *The issues being discussed here are not unique to the US.* —**uniqueness** *n* [U]

u·nique·ly /juːˈniːkli/ ●○○ AWL *adv*
1 something that is uniquely good, difficult etc is very good, difficult etc in a way that few other things are: *his uniquely busy lifestyle | an actor uniquely suited to the part*
2 in a way that is typical of a particular place or group of people, and that does not exist anywhere else: **uniquely British/Japanese/American etc** *It is not a uniquely American problem.*
3 in a way that is different from anything or anyone else: *There are 45 uniquely designed buildings.*

u·ni·sex /ˈjuːnɪseks/ *adj* intended for both men and women: *a unisex hairdressing salon*

u·ni·son /ˈjuːnəsən, -zən/ *n* **in unison a)** if people speak or do something in unison, they say the same words at the same time or do the same thing at the same time: *'Good morning!' the kids replied in unison.* **b)** if two groups, governments etc do something in unison, they do it together because they agree with each other: *Management and workers must act in unison to compete with foreign business.*

u·nit /ˈjuːnɪt/ ●●● S2 W2 *n* [C]
1 GROUP a group of people working together as part of a larger group: *The man is in the hospital's* ***intensive care unit****.*

U

2 MEASURING an amount of something used as a standard of measurement: **[+of]** *The watt is a unit of electrical power.*
3 PART a thing, person, or group that is regarded as one single whole part of something larger: *a Russian* ***army unit*** | **[+of]** *The family is the basic social unit of modern society.*
4 PART OF A BOOK one of the numbered parts into which a TEXTBOOK (=a book used in schools) is divided
5 PRODUCT *technical* a single complete product made by a company: *The factory's output is now up to 150,000 units each month.*
6 PART OF A MACHINE a piece of equipment which is part of a larger machine: **control/display/filter etc unit**
7 FURNITURE a piece of furniture, especially one that can be attached to others of the same type: *fitted* ***kitchen units*** *BrE* | ***storage units***
8 APARTMENT *AmE* a single apartment in a larger building
9 SCHOOL/UNIVERSITY *AmE* an amount of work that a student needs to do in order to complete a particular course
10 NUMBER *BrE technical* any whole number less than ten: *hundreds, tens, and units*

U·ni·ta·ri·an /ˌjuːnəˈteəriən $ -ˈter-/ *n* [C] a member of a Christian group that does not believe in the Trinity —**Unitarian** *adj*

u·ni·ta·ry /ˈjuːnətəri $ -teri/ *adj formal* relating to or existing as a single unit: *a single unitary authority for the whole region*

u·nite /juːˈnaɪt/ ●●○ *v* [I,T] if different people or organizations unite, or if something unites them, they join together in order to achieve something → **union**: *Our goal is to unite the opposition parties and defeat the president.* | **[+against/behind]** *Party members united behind their leader.* | **unite to do sth** *In 1960, the regions united to form the Somali Republic.*

Unite the largest TRADE UNION in the United Kingdom, with over two million members in the public and private SECTORS. It was formed in 2007 by the MERGER (=joining together) of two trade unions (Amicus and the Transport and General Workers' Union).

u·nit·ed /juːˈnaɪtɪd/ ●●○ *adj*
1 joined or closely connected by feelings, aims etc: *a united Europe* | *The two countries were united against a common enemy.*
2 involving or done by everyone: *a united effort to clean up the environment*
3 used in the names of some football teams and companies: *Manchester United* | *United Airlines*

Uˌnited ˈNations *n* **the United Nations** (*abbreviation* **the UN**) an international organization that tries to find peaceful solutions to world problems

ˈunit ˌprice *n* [C] *technical* the price that is charged for each single thing or quantity that is sold

ˈunit ˌtrust *n* [C] *BrE* a company through which you can buy shares in many different businesses SYN **mutual fund** *AmE*

u·ni·ty /ˈjuːnəti/ ●●○ W3 *n* (*plural* **unities**)
1 [U] when a group of people or countries agree or are joined together: *economic unity* | *European unity*
2 [U] the quality of having matching parts: *His essays often lack unity.*
3 [C] *technical* one of the three related principles that say a play should be about a single set of related events which happen in one place on one day

Univ. (*also* **Univ** *BrE*) a written abbreviation of ***university***

u·ni·ver·sal /ˌjuːnəˈvɜːsəl◂ $ -ɜːr-/ ●●○ W3 *adj*
1 involving everyone in the world or in a particular group: *free universal health care* | *These stories have* ***universal appeal.*** | *a topic of* ***universal interest*** | *a democracy based on* ***universal suffrage*** (=when every adult has the right to vote)
2 true or suitable in every situation: *a* ***universal truth*** —**universality** /ˌjuːnəvɜːˈsæləti $ -ɜːr-/ *n* [U]

ˌuniversal ˈjoint *n* [C] a part in a machine, at the point where two other parts join together, that can turn in all directions

u·ni·ver·sal·ly /ˌjuːnəˈvɜːsəli $ -ɜːr-/ ●○○ *adv*
1 by everyone in the world or everyone in a particular group: *These arguments were not* ***universally accepted.*** | *In Edinburgh he is universally known as 'Big Tam'.*
2 in every situation: *Is that a model which should be applied universally?*

ˌUniversal ˈProduct Code *n* [C] *AmE* (*abbreviation* **UPC**) a BAR CODE

u·ni·verse /ˈjuːnəvɜːs $ -ɜːrs/ ●●○ W3 *n*
1 the universe all space, including all the stars and PLANETS: **in the universe** *everything in the universe*
2 [C] a world or an area of space that is different from the one we are in: **a parallel/an alternative universe**
3 be the centre of sb's universe to be the most important person or thing to someone
4 sb's universe a person's life, including all of the people, places, and ideas which affect them

u·ni·ver·si·ty /ˌjuːnəˈvɜːsəti◂ $ -ɜːr-/ ●●● S2 W1 *n* (*plural* **universities**) [C,U] an educational institution at the highest level, where you study for a DEGREE: **at a university** *She's at Cambridge University.* | **[+of]** *the University of Texas*

COLLOCATIONS

VERBS

go to university *Her daughter was about to go to university.*
be at university *BrE We were at university together.*
study (sth) at a university *She studied law at Edinburgh University.*
apply for university | **start university** (*also* **enter university** *formal*) | **leave university** | **graduate from university** (=leave after getting a degree) | **drop out of university** (=leave before finishing your course)

university + NOUN

a university course *He studied history at school and was now planning to take a university course.*
a university student *Thirty years ago 33% of university students were female.*
a university graduate (=someone who has completed a university course) | **a university lecturer/professor** | **a university degree** | **a university education** | **the university campus** (=the area of land containing the main buildings of a university)

un·just /ʌnˈdʒʌst◂/ ●○○ *adj formal* not fair or reasonable SYN **unfair**: *unjust laws* —**unjustly** *adv*

un·just·i·fi·a·ble /ʌnˈdʒʌstəfaɪəbəl/ *adj* completely wrong and unacceptable: *Poisoning the Earth's atmosphere is ecologically and morally unjustifiable.* —**unjustifiably** *adv*

un·just·i·fied /ʌnˈdʒʌstɪfaɪd/ AWL *adj* done without an acceptable reason: *unjustified price increases*

un·kempt /ˌʌnˈkempt◂/ *adj* unkempt hair or plants have not been cut and kept neat

un·kind /ˌʌnˈkaɪnd◂/ ●●○ *adj* nasty, unpleasant, or cruel: *A lot of unkind things were said.* | **[+to]** *Her husband is very unkind to her.* —**unkindly** *adv* —**unkindness** *n* [U] → see Thesaurus box on *p. 2001*

REGISTER
In everyday English, people usually say **mean**, **nasty**, or **horrible** rather than **unkind**: *The other kids were really* ***mean*** *to me.*

un·know·ing /ʌnˈnəʊɪŋ $ -ˈnoʊ-/ *adj* [only before noun] *formal* not realizing what you are doing or what is happening SYN **unaware** —**unknowingly** *adv*: *She became ill after unknowingly taking an illegal drug.*

un·known[1] /ˌʌnˈnəʊn◂ $ -ˈnoʊn◂/ ●●● W2 *adj, adv*
1 not known about: *The murderer's identity* ***remains unknown.*** | ***For some unknown reason,*** *Mark quit his job and moved to Greece.* | *a voyage through unknown territory* | ***An unknown number of*** *people were killed.*
2 not famous: *an unknown artist*

3 unknown to sb without someone knowing: *Unknown to his wife, Ron had been having an affair.*
4 be an unknown quantity if someone or something is an unknown quantity, you do not know what their abilities are or how they are likely to behave

unknown² *n* [C] **1** someone who is not famous: *At that point in her career she was still an unknown.* **2** something that is not known: *The long-term effects of the drug are still an unknown.* **3 the unknown a)** a place that is not known about or that has not been visited by humans: *The astronauts began their journey into the unknown.* **b)** things that you do not know or understand: *a fear of the unknown*

un·law·ful /ʌnˈlɔːfəl $ -ˈlɒː-/ ●○○ *adj law* not legal SYN **illegal**: *The jury returned a verdict of unlawful killing.* —**unlawfully** *adv*

un·lead·ed /ʌnˈledɪd/ *adj* unleaded petrol does not contain any LEAD —**unleaded** *n* [U]: *Ben's car only takes unleaded.*

un·learn /ʌnˈlɜːn $ -ɜːrn/ *v* (*past tense and past participle* **unlearned** *or* **unlearnt** /-ˈlɜːnt $ -ˈlɜːrnt/) [T] *informal* to deliberately forget something you have learned, in order to change the way you do something: *It's difficult to unlearn bad driving habits.*

un·leash /ʌnˈliːʃ/ ●○○ *v* [T]
1 to suddenly let a strong force, feeling etc have its full effect: *Lefèvre's comments unleashed a wave of protest.*
2 to let a dog run free after it has been held on a LEASH

un·leav·ened /ʌnˈlevənd/ *adj* unleavened bread is flat because it is not made with YEAST

un·less /ʌnˈles, ən-/ ●●● S1 W1 *conjunction*
1 used to say that something will happen or be true if something else does not happen or is not true: *Unless some extra money is found, the theatre will close.* | *I think you should complain – unless, of course, you are happy with the situation.* | *He won't go to sleep unless you tell him a story.* | *I can't leave her unless I know she's all right.* **THESAURUS** IF
2 not unless only if: *'Will you go with her?' 'Not unless she wants me to.'*

GRAMMAR: Choosing the right tense

• You use the simple present tense with **unless**: *Unless the government changes its policy, the economic situation will get worse.*
• Don't use 'will' in the clause after **unless**. ✗ Don't say: *Unless the government will change its policy ...*
• You can also use the present perfect tense with **unless**: *I won't change anything unless someone has asked me to.* ✗ Don't say: *unless someone will have asked me to* | *unless someone will ask me to*
• To talk about the past, use the simple past with **unless**: *Unless the company got a loan, it would go bankrupt.* | *They threatened to kill him unless he gave them the money.* ✗ Don't say: *Unless the company would get a loan ...*

USAGE: Unless, in case, or else

• You use **unless** when saying that if something does not happen, something else will happen: *Unless I hear from you* (=if I don't hear from you), *I'll assume everything's OK.*
• You use **in case** when saying that you do something in order to be prepared if something happens: *Take a sweater in case you get cold.*
• You use **or else** when saying that something bad will happen if you do not do something: *You'd better go now, or else you'll miss the train.*

un·let·tered /ʌnˈletəd $ -ərd/ *adj formal* unable to read, or uneducated SYN **illiterate**

un·li·censed /ʌnˈlaɪsənst/ AWL *adj* without a LICENCE (=official document that gives you permission to do or have something): *unlicensed guns*

un·like¹ /ʌnˈlaɪk/ ●●● W3 *prep*
1 completely different from a particular person or thing: *Tammy was unlike any other woman I have ever known.*
2 not typical of someone at all: *It's unlike Greg to be late.*
3 used when saying how one person or thing is different from another: *Unlike most people in the office, I don't come to work by car.*
4 not unlike similar to: *In appearance John is not unlike his brother.* | *The landscape is **not unlike that of** Scotland.*

unlike² *adj literary* not alike SYN **different** **THESAURUS** DIFFERENT

THESAURUS: unkind

unkind treating people in a way that makes them unhappy or upset. **Unkind** sounds rather formal. In everyday English, people usually say **mean** or **nasty**: *Children can be very unkind to each other.* | *a rather unkind remark*
mean *especially spoken* unkind: *Don't be mean to your sister!* | *It was a mean thing to do.*
nasty deliberately unkind, and seeming to enjoy making people unhappy: *He said some really nasty things before he left.* | *a nasty man*
hurtful unkind – used about remarks and actions: *Joe couldn't forget the hurtful things she had said.*
spiteful deliberately unkind to someone because you are jealous of them or angry with them: *The other women were spiteful to her, and gave her the hardest work to do.* | *She watched them with spiteful glee* (=pleasure).
malicious deliberately behaving in a way that is likely to upset, hurt, or cause problems for someone: *Someone had been spreading malicious rumours about him.* | *There was a malicious smile on her face.*
unsympathetic not seeming to care about someone's problems, and not trying to help them or make them feel better: *Her parents were very unsympathetic, and told her that she deserved to fail her exam.* | *an unsympathetic boss*
hard-hearted very unsympathetic and not caring at all about other people's feelings: *Was he hard-hearted enough to leave his son in jail overnight?* | *a hard-hearted businessman*

VERY UNKIND

horrible *especially spoken* very unkind: *Why is Jack always so horrible to me?*
cruel very unkind and deliberately making people feel unhappy or making them suffer physically: *Her father was very cruel to her.* | *a selfish, cruel woman*
wicked /ˈwɪkəd/ extremely unkind and behaving in a very immoral way: *a wicked thing to do* | *the wicked stepmother in Cinderella*
sadistic extremely unkind and enjoying making other people suffer: *Their father was a sadistic bully who beat them regularly.* | *He took a certain sadistic pleasure in his job.*

UNINTENTIONALLY UNKIND

thoughtless/inconsiderate not thinking about the effects of your actions on other people: *It was inconsiderate of him not to say that he would be late.* | *a thoughtless disregard for other people's feelings*
tactless someone who is tactless carelessly says or does things that are likely to upset someone, without realizing what they are doing: *How could you be so tactless?* | *a tactless question*
insensitive behaving in a way that is likely to upset someone, or not seeming to care about someone's feelings. **Insensitive** is rather a formal word: *The article is insensitive to the family and friends of the victim.*

unlike[3] *v* [T] to show on Facebook that you no longer like or agree with something, after showing that you liked it

un·like·ly /ʌnˈlaɪkli/ ●●● S3 W2 *adj*
1 not likely to happen: *Donna might be able to come tomorrow, but* ***it's*** *very* ***unlikely***. | **unlikely to do sth** *The weather is unlikely to improve over the next few days.* | **it is unlikely (that)** *It's unlikely that the thieves will be caught.* | **in the unlikely event of sth** (=if something which is unlikely happens) *In the unlikely event of a fire, passengers should move to the top deck.*
2 an unlikely place, person, or thing is strange and not what you would expect: *The birds had nested in some* ***unlikely places***. | *The quiet village of Brockhampton was an* ***unlikely setting*** *for such a crime.*
3 not likely to be true: *an unlikely story*

un·lim·i·ted /ʌnˈlɪmɪtɪd/ ●●○ *adj*
1 without any limit: *The system can support an* ***unlimited number*** *of users.* | *unlimited access to information* | *The ticket offers unlimited travel on the London underground for seven days.*
2 very large in amount: *an unlimited variety of cookies*

un·list·ed /ʌnˈlɪstɪd/ *adj* **1** not shown on an official STOCK EXCHANGE list **2** *AmE* not in the list of numbers in the telephone DIRECTORY SYN **ex-directory** *BrE*

un·lit /ˌʌnˈlɪt◂/ *adj* dark because there are no lights: *an unlit stairway*

un·load /ʌnˈləʊd $ -ˈloʊd/ ●○○ *v*
1 VEHICLE/SHIP **a)** [T] to remove a load from a vehicle, ship etc: **unload sth from sth** *The driver unloaded some boxes from the back of the truck.* **b)** [I] if a ship unloads, the goods that it carries are removed from it
2 GET RID OF STH [T] *informal* **a)** to get rid of something illegal or not very good by selling it quickly: *Investors continued to unload technology stocks on Thursday.* | **unload sth on/onto sth** *Hundreds of cheap videos were unloaded on the British market.* **b)** to get rid of work or responsibility by giving it to someone else: **unload sth on/onto sb** *Don't let him unload his problems onto you.*
3 FEELINGS [I,T] *AmE* to express strong feelings, especially anger, to someone when you are extremely upset: *Koch unloaded his concerns over dinner one night.* | **unload (sth) on sb** *When he got back to the office, Green unloaded on his staff.*
4 CAMERA [T] to remove the film from a camera
5 GUN [I,T] to remove the bullets from a gun

un·lock /ʌnˈlɒk $ -ˈlɑːk/ ●●○ *v* [T]
1 to unfasten the lock on a door, box etc THESAURUS ▸ OPEN
2 unlock the secrets/mysteries of sth to discover important facts about something

un·looked-for /ʌnˈlʊkt fɔː $ -fɔːr/ *adj* not expected: *unlooked-for success*

un·loose /ʌnˈluːs/ *v* [T] *literary* to untie or unfasten something

un·loved /ʌnˈlʌvd/ *adj* not loved by anyone

un·love·ly /ʌnˈlʌvli/ *adj literary* ugly

un·luck·y /ʌnˈlʌki/ *adj* (*comparative* **unluckier**, *superlative* **unluckiest**) **1** having bad luck → **misfortune**: **unlucky to do sth** *Inter Milan were unlucky to lose the match.* | **[+with]** *We were unlucky with the weather this weekend. It rained constantly.* | *Thierry Henry was* ***desperately unlucky*** *not to score when his shot hit the post.* **2** causing bad luck: *Some people think black cats are unlucky.* **3** happening as a result of bad luck SYN **unfortunate**: *an unlucky accident* | ***It was unlucky*** *for Stephen* ***that*** *the boss happened to walk in just at that moment.* —**unluckily** *adv*

un·made /ˌʌnˈmeɪd◂/ *adj* **1** an unmade bed has not been made tidy after someone has slept in it **2** an unmade road is one whose surface has not been covered with a special hard material

un·man·age·a·ble /ʌnˈmænɪdʒəbəl/ *adj* difficult to control or deal with

un·man·ly /ʌnˈmænli/ *adj* not thought to be suitable for or typical of a man

un·manned /ˌʌnˈmænd◂/ *adj* **1** an unmanned spacecraft does not have a person inside it **2** if a place is unmanned, nobody is working there: *an unmanned railway crossing*

un·marked /ˌʌnˈmɑːkt◂ $ -ˈmɑːrkt◂/ *adj* something that is unmarked has no words or signs on it to show where or what it is: *an* ***unmarked grave*** | *an* ***unmarked police car***

un·mar·ried /ˌʌnˈmærid◂/ ●○○ *adj* not married SYN **single**: *unmarried mothers*

un·mask /ʌnˈmɑːsk $ -ˈmæsk/ *v* [T] to make known the hidden truth about someone: *He was one of the most high-ranking spies ever unmasked by the CIA.*

un·matched /ˌʌnˈmætʃt◂/ *adj literary* better than any other SYN **unequalled**: *a woman of unmatched beauty*

un·men·tion·a·ble /ʌnˈmenʃənəbəl/ *adj* too shocking or embarrassing to talk about: *unmentionable scandals*

un·men·tion·a·bles /ʌnˈmenʃənəbəlz/ *n* [plural] *old-fashioned* underwear – used humorously

un·met /ˌʌnˈmet◂/ *adj* unmet needs, demands etc have not been dealt with

un·mis·tak·a·ble, **unmistakeable** /ˌʌnməˈsteɪkəbəl◂/ ●○○ *adj* easy to recognize: *the unmistakable sound of gunfire* THESAURUS ▸ OBVIOUS —**unmistakably** *adv*

un·mit·i·gat·ed /ʌnˈmɪtɪgeɪtɪd/ *adj* **an unmitigated disaster/failure/pleasure etc** something that is completely bad or good

un·moved /ʌnˈmuːvd/ *adj* [not before noun] feeling no pity, sympathy, or sadness: **[+by]** *Richard seemed unmoved by the tragedy.*

un·named /ˌʌnˈneɪmd◂/ *adj* an unnamed person, place, or thing has been mentioned but not referred to by name

un·nat·u·ral /ʌnˈnætʃərəl/ ●○○ *adj*
1 different from what you would normally expect: *It was very cold, which seemed unnatural for late spring.*
2 seeming false, or not real or natural SYN **fake**: *Julia's laugh seemed forced and unnatural.*
3 different from normal human behaviour in a way that seems morally wrong: *unnatural sexual practices*
4 different from anything produced by nature SYN **artificial**, **fake**: *Her hair was an unnatural orange.* —**unnaturally** *adv*

un·ne·ces·sa·ry /ʌnˈnesəsəri $ -seri/ ●●○ *adj* not needed, or more than is needed: **unnecessary expense/cost/extravagance etc** *an unnecessary expense* | *There's no point in taking unnecessary risks.* | *We can't afford any unnecessary delays.* | *Williams was found guilty of causing* ***unnecessary suffering*** *to animals* —**unnecessarily** /ʌnˈnesəsərəli $ ˌʌn-nesəˈserəli/ *adv*: *I don't want to worry you unnecessarily.*

un·nerve /ʌnˈnɜːv $ -ɜːrv/ *v* [T] to upset or frighten someone so that they lose their confidence or their ability to think clearly: *He was unnerved by the way Sylvia kept staring at him.* —**unnerving** *adj*: *an* ***unnerving experience***

un·no·ticed /ʌnˈnəʊtɪst $ -ˈnoʊ-/ *adj, adv* without being noticed: *Elsa stood unnoticed at the edge of the crowd.* | **go/pass unnoticed** *His remark went unnoticed by everyone except me.*

un·num·bered /ˌʌnˈnʌmbəd◂ $ -ərd◂/ *adj* **1** not having a number: *an unnumbered Swiss bank account* **2** *literary* too many to be counted

un·ob·served /ˌʌnəbˈzɜːvd $ -ɜːrvd/ *adj, adv* not noticed: *Frank slipped out of the meeting unobserved.*

un·ob·struct·ed /ˌʌnəbˈstrʌktɪd◂/ *adj* not blocked by anything SYN **clear**: *an* ***unobstructed view*** *of the lake*

un·ob·tain·a·ble /ˌʌnəbˈteɪnəbəl◂/ AWL *adj* impossible to get: *Fresh fruit was unobtainable in the winter.*

un·ob·tru·sive /ˌʌnəbˈtruːsɪv◂/ *adj* not easily noticed: *The staff are trained to be unobtrusive.* —**unobtrusively** *adv*

un·oc·cu·pied /ʌnˈɒkjəpaɪd $ -ˈɑːk-/ *adj* **1** a seat, house, room etc that is unoccupied has no one in it THESAURUS ▸ EMPTY **2** an unoccupied country or area is not controlled by the enemy during a war

un·of·fi·cial /ˌʌnəˈfɪʃəl◂/ ●○○ *adj*
1 done or produced without formal approval or permission: *Hodges wrote an unofficial biography of the artist.*
2 not done as part of your job: *The president made an unofficial visit to the Senator's house.* —**unofficially** *adv*

un·o·pened /ʌnˈəʊpənd $ -ˈoʊ-/ *adj* an unopened package, letter etc has not been opened yet: *The letter was returned to us unopened.*

un·op·posed /ˌʌnəˈpəʊzd◂ $ -ˈpoʊzd◂/ *adj* without any opponent or opposition, especially in an election: *Roberts was* ***elected unopposed*** *as president.*

un·or·ga·nized (*also* **-ised** *BrE*) /ʌnˈɔːgənaɪzd $ -ˈɔːr-/ *adj* **1** DISORGANIZED **2** people who are unorganized do not have an organization, union, group etc to help or support them

un·or·tho·dox /ʌnˈɔːθədɒks $ ʌnˈɔːrθədɑːks/ ●○○ *adj* unorthodox opinions or methods are different from what is usual or accepted by most people: **unorthodox view/approach/theory etc** *Her unorthodox views tend to attract controversy.* THESAURUS ▸ UNUSUAL

un·pack /ʌnˈpæk/ ●○○ *v*
1 [I,T] to take everything out of a box, bag, SUITCASE etc: *I haven't had a chance to unpack yet.* | *She unpacked her suitcase and headed for the beach.* | *Maggie carefully unpacked the gifts she had bought.*
2 [T] to make an idea or problem easier to understand by considering all the parts of it separately: *Some of the issues surrounding mental illness have been unpacked in Chapter 3.*

un·paid /ʌnˈpeɪd◂/ ●○○ *adj*
1 an unpaid bill or debt has not been paid
2 done without receiving payment: *unpaid work* | *unpaid leave*

un·pal·at·a·ble /ʌnˈpælətəbəl/ *adj* **1** an unpalatable fact or idea is very unpleasant and difficult to accept: *The* ***unpalatable truth*** *is that the team isn't getting any better.* | **[+to]** *an idea that's unpalatable to most people* **2** unpalatable food tastes unpleasant

un·par·al·leled /ʌnˈpærəleld/ AWL *adj formal* bigger, better, or worse than anything else: *an achievement unparalleled in sporting history*

un·par·don·a·ble /ʌnˈpɑːdnəbəl $ -ˈpɑːr-/ *adj formal* unpardonable behaviour is completely unacceptable SYN **unforgivable**: *an unpardonable offence* —**unpardonably** *adv*

un·pat·ri·ot·ic /ˌʌnpætriˈɒtɪk, -peɪ- $ -peɪtriˈɑː-/ *adj* not supporting your country

un·paved /ʌnˈpeɪvd◂/ *adj* an unpaved road does not have a smooth hard surface

un·peeled /ʌnˈpiːld◂/ *adj* unpeeled fruit or vegetables still have their skin on them

un·per·turbed /ˌʌnpəˈtɜːbd◂ $ -pərˈtɜːrbd◂/ *adj* not worried or annoyed by something that has happened: *John seemed unperturbed by the news.*

un·pick /ʌnˈpɪk/ *v* [T] **1** to take out stitches from a piece of cloth or KNITTING **2** to examine the different parts of a subject, deal etc, especially in order to find faults: *I didn't want to unpick the past.* | *There are fears that the president might unpick the treaty.*

un·placed /ʌnˈpleɪst◂/ *adj BrE* not one of the first three to finish in a race or competition

un·planned /ʌnˈplænd◂/ *adj* not planned or expected: *an unplanned pregnancy*

un·play·a·ble /ʌnˈpleɪəbəl/ *adj* **1** in sport, a ball that is unplayable is difficult to hit because of its position or speed **2** a sports field that is unplayable is in too bad a condition to play on

un·pleas·ant /ʌnˈplezənt/ ●●○ *adj*
1 not pleasant or enjoyable: *an unpleasant experience* | *an extremely unpleasant smell* | *an unpleasant surprise*
2 not kind or friendly OPP **nice**: *He said some very unpleasant things.* | *a thoroughly unpleasant man* —**unpleasantly** *adv*

un·pleas·ant·ness /ʌnˈplezəntnəs/ *n* [U] *especially BrE* trouble or arguments between people

un·plug /ʌnˈplʌg/ ●○○ *v* (**unplugged**, **unplugging**) [T] to disconnect a piece of electrical equipment by pulling its PLUG out of a SOCKET: *Unplug the TV before you go to bed.*

un·plugged /ʌnˈplʌgd/ *adj, adv* if a group of musicians perform unplugged, they perform without electric instruments

un·pop·u·lar /ʌnˈpɒpjələ $ -ˈpɑːpjələr/ ●●○ *adj* not liked by most people: *an unpopular choice* | *an unpopular teacher* | **[+with/among]** *a decision that was* ***deeply unpopular*** *with students* —**unpopularity** /ʌnˌpɒpjəˈlærəti $ -ˌpɑːp-/ *n* [U]

un·pre·ce·dent·ed /ʌnˈpresɪdentɪd/ ●○○ AWL *adj* never having happened before, or never having happened so much: *He* ***took*** *the* ***unprecedented step*** *of stating that the rumours were false.* | *Crime has increased* ***on an unprecedented scale***. | **[+in]** *an event that is unprecedented in recent history* THESAURUS ▸ UNUSUAL —**unprecedentedly** *adv*

un·pre·dict·a·ble /ˌʌnprɪˈdɪktəbəl◂/ ●○○ AWL *adj*
1 changing a lot so it is impossible to know what will happen: *unpredictable weather* | *the unpredictable nature of language*
2 someone who is unpredictable tends to change their behaviour or ideas suddenly, so that you never know what they are going to do or think —**unpredictably** *adv* —**unpredictability** /ˌʌnprɪdɪktəˈbɪləti/ *n* [U]

un·pre·pared /ˌʌnprɪˈpeəd◂ $ -ˈperd◂/ *adj* **1** not ready to deal with something: **[+for]** *I was* ***totally unprepared*** *for the challenge which faced me.* **2 unprepared to do sth** *formal* not willing to do something: *They were unprepared to accept the conditions of the contract.*

un·pre·pos·sess·ing /ˌʌnpriːpəˈzesɪŋ/ *adj formal* not very attractive or noticeable: *Despite his unprepossessing appearance, he was very popular with women.*

un·pre·ten·tious /ˌʌnprɪˈtenʃəs◂/ *adj* not trying to seem better, more important etc than you really are – use this to show approval: *an unpretentious hotel* | *an unpretentious woman*

un·prin·ci·pled /ʌnˈprɪnsəpəld/ AWL *adj formal* not caring whether what you do is morally right SYN **unscrupulous**

un·print·a·ble /ʌnˈprɪntəbəl/ *adj* words or remarks that are unprintable are so rude or shocking that you do not want to say what they are

un·pro·duct·ive /ˌʌnprəˈdʌktɪv◂/ *adj* not achieving very much: *an unproductive meeting*

un·pro·fes·sion·al /ˌʌnprəˈfeʃənəl◂/ *adj* behaving in a way that is not acceptable in a particular profession: *Johnson was fired for unprofessional conduct.* —**unprofessionally** *adv*

un·prof·it·a·ble /ʌnˈprɒfətəbəl $ -ˈprɑː-/ *adj* **1** making no profit: *unprofitable businesses* **2** *formal* producing no advantages: *It would be unprofitable to pursue this argument any further.*

un·prom·is·ing /ʌnˈprɒməsɪŋ $ -ˈprɑː-/ *adj* not likely to be good or successful: *Sales improved after an* ***unpromising start***. | *an unpromising place for a picnic*

un·prompt·ed /ʌnˈprɒmptɪd $ ʌnˈprɑːmp-/ *adj formal* said or done without anyone asking you to: *Quite unprompted, he offered to help.*

un·pro·nounce·a·ble /ˌʌnprəˈnaʊnsəbəl◂/ *adj* an unpronounceable word or name is very difficult to say

un·pro·tect·ed /ˌʌnprəˈtektɪd◂/ *adj* **1** not protected against possible harm or damage: *Thieves often target unprotected vehicles.* | *Part-time workers are unprotected by this law.* **2** unprotected machines are not covered and could injure someone: *Machinery was often unprotected and accidents were frequent.* **3 unprotected sex** sex without using a CONDOM

un·pro·ven /ʌnˈpruːvən, -ˈprəʊ- $ -ˈpruː-/ *adj* not proved or tested: *unproven allegations* | *unproven medical treatments*

U

un·pro·voked /ˌʌnprəˈvəʊkt◂ $ -ˈvoʊkt◂/ *adj* unprovoked anger, attacks etc are directed at someone who has not done anything to deserve them: *It was a totally unprovoked attack on an innocent man.*

un·pub·lished /ʌnˈpʌblɪʃt/ AWL *adj* unpublished writing, information etc has never been PUBLISHed

un·pun·ished /ʌnˈpʌnɪʃt/ *adj* **go unpunished** if someone or something bad they have done goes unpunished, they are not punished: *An attack like that cannot go unpunished.*

un·put·down·a·ble /ˌʌnpʊtˈdaʊnəbəl/ *adj BrE* an unputdownable book is very interesting and exciting

un·qual·i·fied /ʌnˈkwɒlɪfaɪd $ -ˈkwɑː-/ *adj* **1** not having the right knowledge, experience, or education to do something: *unqualified staff* | **[+for]** *He was unqualified for the job.* | **unqualified to do sth** *I feel unqualified to advise you.* ⚠ Do not confuse with **disqualified** (=officially not allowed to do something): *She was disqualified from driving.* **2** [usually before noun] used for emphasizing that a quality is complete and total: *The experiment had not been* ***an unqualified success****.* | *He gave her his* ***unqualified support****.*

un·quench·a·ble /ʌnˈkwentʃəbəl/ *adj* an unquenchable desire is one that is impossible to satisfy: *the seemingly* ***unquenchable thirst*** (=desire) *for Western art*

un·ques·tion·a·bly /ʌnˈkwestʃənəbli/ *adv* used to emphasize that something is certainly true: *The Eiffel Tower is unquestionably one of Paris's most familiar landmarks.* —**unquestionable** *adj*: *a man of unquestionable integrity*

un·ques·tioned /ʌnˈkwestʃənd/ *adj* something that is unquestioned is accepted or believed by everyone: *The whole approach is based on unquestioned assumptions.* | *an unquestioned right*

un·ques·tion·ing /ʌnˈkwestʃənɪŋ/ *adj* an unquestioning faith, attitude etc is very certain and without doubts: *an unquestioning belief in God* —**unquestioningly** *adv*

un·qui·et /ˌʌnˈkwaɪɪt◂/ *adj literary* making you feel anxious

un·quote /ˌʌnˈkwəʊt $ -ˈkwoʊt/ → **quote ... unquote** at QUOTE¹(7)

un·rav·el /ʌnˈrævəl/ ●○○ *v* (**unravelled**, **unravelling** *BrE*, **unraveled**, **unraveling** *AmE*)

1 [T] to understand or explain something that is mysterious or complicated: *Detectives are still trying to unravel the mystery surrounding his death.*

2 [I,T] if you unravel threads, string etc, or if they unravel, they stop being twisted together

3 [I] if a system, plan, organization etc unravels, it starts to fail SYN **fall apart**: *The company started to unravel when two of the directors were arrested.*

un·read /ˌʌnˈred◂/ *adj* unread books, papers etc have not been read

un·read·a·ble /ʌnˈriːdəbəl/ *adj* **1** if someone's expression or face is unreadable, you cannot tell what they are thinking **2** an unreadable book or piece of writing is difficult to read because it is boring or complicated **3** unreadable writing is so untidy that you cannot read it SYN **illegible**

un·real /ˌʌnˈrɪəl◂/ ●○○ *adj*

1 [not before noun] an experience, situation etc that is unreal seems so strange that you think you must be imagining it: *It seemed unreal to be sitting and talking to someone so famous.*

2 not related to real things that happen: *Many people go into marriage with unreal expectations.*

3 *spoken* very exciting SYN **excellent**: *Our trip to Disneyland was unreal.* —**unreality** /ˌʌnriˈæləti/ *n* [U]

un·rea·lis·tic /ˌʌnrɪəˈlɪstɪk◂/ ●○○ *adj* unrealistic ideas or hopes are not reasonable or sensible: **it is unrealistic to do sth** *It is unrealistic to expect these changes to happen overnight.* | *Some parents have totally* ***unrealistic expectations*** *of teachers.* —**unrealistically** /-kli/ *adv*

un·real·ized (*also* **-ised** *BrE*) /ʌnˈrɪəlaɪzd/ *adj* **1** not achieved: *unrealized potential* **2** *technical* unrealized profits, losses etc have not been changed into a form that can be used as money

un·rea·son·a·ble /ʌnˈriːzənəbəl/ ●●○ *adj*

1 not fair or sensible: *I think he's being unreasonable.* | *Don't let your boss make* ***unreasonable demands*** *on you.* | **it is unreasonable to do sth** *It's unreasonable to expect you to work seven days a week.* | *It's not unreasonable to ask him to help you.*

2 unreasonable prices, costs etc are too high —**unreasonably** *adv*: *unreasonably high prices*

un·rea·son·ing /ʌnˈriːzənɪŋ/ *adj literary* an unreasoning feeling is not based on facts or good reasons

un·rec·og·niz·a·ble (*also* **-isable** *BrE*) /ʌnˈrekəgnaɪzəbəl, -ˈrekə-/ *adj* someone or something that is unrecognizable has changed or been damaged so much that you do not recognize them: *I hadn't been to the city for 20 years and it was almost unrecognizable.*

un·rec·og·nized (*also* **-ised** *BrE*) /ʌnˈrekəgnaɪzd, -ˈrekə-/ *adj* **1** not having received praise or respect for something good you have achieved: *one of the great unrecognized jazzmen of the 1930s* **2** not noticed or not thought to be important: *an illness that can* ***go unrecognized*** *for years* **3** an unrecognized group, meeting, agreement etc is not considered to be legal or acceptable by someone in authority **4** doing something without people recognizing who you are: *He was able to walk down the street totally unrecognized.*

un·re·con·struct·ed /ˌʌnriːkənˈstrʌktɪd/ *adj* not changing your ideas even though many people think they are old-fashioned

un·re·cord·ed /ˌʌnrɪˈkɔːdɪd◂ $ -ɔːr-/ *adj* not written down or recorded: *Many of the complaints have* ***gone unrecorded****.*

un·re·fined /ˌʌnrɪˈfaɪnd◂/ *adj* **1** an unrefined substance is in its natural form: *unrefined sugar* **2** *formal* not polite or educated

un·re·gis·tered /ʌnˈredʒəstəd $ -ərd/ *adj* not included on an official list: *unregistered land*

un·reg·u·lat·ed /ʌnˈregjəleɪtɪd/ AWL *adj* not controlled by a government or law: *an unregulated banking system*

un·re·lat·ed /ˌʌnrɪˈleɪtɪd◂/ ●○○ *adj*

1 two things that are unrelated are not connected to each other in any way: *The police think that the two incidents are unrelated.* | **[+to]** *His illness is unrelated to the accident.*

2 people who are unrelated are not from the same family

un·re·lent·ing /ˌʌnrɪˈlentɪŋ◂/ *adj formal* **1** an unpleasant situation that is unrelenting continues for a long time without stopping SYN **relentless**: *the unrelenting pressures of the job* **2** continuing to do something in a determined way without thinking about anyone else's feelings SYN **relentless**: *an unrelenting opponent*

un·re·li·a·ble /ˌʌnrɪˈlaɪəbəl◂/ ●●○ AWL *adj* unable to be trusted or depended on: *The car's becoming very unreliable.* | *an unreliable witness*

un·re·lieved /ˌʌnrɪˈliːvd◂/ *adj* an unpleasant situation that is unrelieved continues for a long time because nothing happens to change it: *unrelieved pain*

un·re·mark·a·ble /ˌʌnrɪˈmɑːkəbəl◂ $ -ɑːr-/ *adj formal* not very unusual or interesting SYN **ordinary**: *He led a busy but otherwise unremarkable life.*

un·re·mit·ting /ˌʌnrɪˈmɪtɪŋ◂/ *adj formal* continuing for a long time and not likely to stop: *unremitting poverty* —**unremittingly** *adv*

un·re·peat·a·ble /ˌʌnrɪˈpiːtəbəl◂/ *adj* **1** too rude or offensive to repeat: *He said something unrepeatable.* **2** unable to be done again

un·re·pent·ant /ˌʌnrɪˈpentənt◂/ *adj* not ashamed of your behaviour or beliefs, even though other people disapprove: *He remains unrepentant about his comments.* —**unrepentantly** *adv*

un·re·port·ed /ˌʌnrɪˈpɔːtɪd◂ $ -ˈpɔːr-/ *adj* not told to the public or to someone in authority: *Rape is a crime that often* ***goes unreported****.*

un·rep·re·sen·ta·tive /ˌʌnreprɪˈzentətɪv/ *adj* not typical of a particular group of things or people: **[+of]** *opinions that are unrepresentative of the population*

un·re·quit·ed /ˌʌnrɪˈkwaɪtɪd◂/ *adj* unrequited love or other strong feeling is love etc that you feel for someone but that they do not feel for you

un·re·served /ʌnriˈzɜːvd $ -ɜːr-/ *adj* **1** completed and without any doubts: *unreserved support for the prime minister* **2** not booked: *We found some unreserved seats on the train.*

un·re·serv·ed·ly /ˌʌnrɪˈzɜːvɪdli $ -ɜːr-/ *adv* if you express a feeling or opinion unreservedly, you do it completely and without any doubts: *He* ***apologized unreservedly****.*

un·re·solved /ˌʌnrɪˈzɒlvd◂ $ -ˈzɑːlvd◂, -ˈzɒːlvd◂/ AWL *adj* an unresolved problem or question has not been answered or solved: *the unresolved issue of who will pay for the project | an unresolved conflict*

un·res·pon·sive /ˌʌnrɪˈspɒnsɪv $ -rɪˈspɑːn-/ AWL *adj* not reacting to something or not affected by it: **[+to]** *The disease is totally unresponsive to conventional treatment. | His warning* ***fell on unresponsive ears*** (=was not listened to).

un·rest /ʌnˈrest/ ●○○ *n* [U] a political situation in which people protest or behave violently: *There is* ***growing unrest*** *throughout the country.* | **political/social/industrial etc unrest** *The protests were the biggest show of social unrest since the government came to power.*

un·re·strained /ˌʌnrɪˈstreɪnd◂/ AWL *adj* not controlled or limited: *unrestrained power*

un·res·trict·ed /ˌʌnrɪˈstrɪktɪd◂/ AWL *adj* not limited by anyone or anything: ***unrestricted access*** *to information*

un·re·ward·ed /ˌʌnrɪˈwɔːdɪd◂ $ -ˈwɔːr-/ *adj* not achieving what you want to achieve: *His efforts have not* ***gone unrewarded****.*

un·ripe /ˌʌnˈraɪp◂/ *adj* unripe fruit, grain etc is not fully developed or ready to be eaten

un·ri·valled *BrE*, **unrivaled** *AmE* /ʌnˈraɪvəld/ *adj formal* better than any other: *an unrivalled collection of Chinese art*

un·roll /ʌnˈrəʊl $ -ˈroʊl/ *v* [I,T] to open something that was in the shape of a ball or tube, and make it flat, or to become open in this way OPP **roll up**: *He unrolled the carpet.*

un·ruf·fled /ʌnˈrʌfəld/ *adj* calm and not upset by a difficult situation – use this to show approval: *Emily remained completely unruffled by the chaos.*

un·ru·ly /ʌnˈruːli/ *adj* **1** violent or difficult to control SYN **wild**: *unruly children | unruly behaviour* **2** unruly hair is difficult to keep tidy —**unruliness** *n* [U]

un·sad·dle /ʌnˈsædl/ *v* [T] to remove the SADDLE (=leather seat) from a horse

un·safe /ˌʌnˈseɪf◂/ ●○○ *adj*
1 dangerous or likely to cause harm: *The building is unsafe. | water that's unsafe to drink* THESAURUS DANGEROUS
2 likely to be harmed: *Many people feel unsafe walking alone at night.*
3 *BrE* an unsafe judgment in a court of law is based on facts that may be wrong: *an unsafe conviction*
4 unsafe sex sex without using a CONDOM

un·said /ʌnˈsed/ *adj* **be left unsaid** if something is left unsaid, you do not say it although you might be thinking it: *Some things* ***are better left unsaid*** (=it is better not to mention them).

un·san·i·ta·ry /ʌnˈsænətəri $ -teri/ *adj* dirty and likely to cause disease SYN **insanitary** OPP **hygienic**: *unsanitary conditions*

un·sat·is·fac·to·ry /ʌnˌsætəsˈfæktəri/ ●○○ *adj* not good enough or not acceptable: *an unsatisfactory situation*

un·sat·is·fied /ʌnˈsætəsfaɪd/ *adj* **1** an unsatisfied demand, request etc has not been dealt with: *an unsatisfied demand for graduates* **2** not pleased because you want something to be better: *unsatisfied consumers* → DISSATISFIED

un·sa·tu·rat·ed /ʌnˈsætʃəreɪtɪd/ *adj* unsaturated fats or oils usually come from plants rather than animals and are better for your health

un·sa·vour·y *BrE*, **unsavory** *AmE* /ʌnˈseɪvəri/ *adj* unpleasant or morally unacceptable: *The club has an unsavoury reputation. | There were a lot of* ***unsavoury characters*** *(=unpleasant people) around the station.*

un·scathed /ʌnˈskeɪðd/ *adj* [not before noun] not injured or harmed by something: **escape/emerge unscathed** *He escaped unscathed from the accident. | The government was* ***relatively unscathed*** *by the scandal.*

un·sched·uled /ʌnˈʃedjuːld $ ʌnˈskedʒəld/ AWL *adj* not planned or expected: *The plane made an unscheduled stop in New York.*

un·sci·en·tif·ic /ˌʌnsaɪənˈtɪfɪk/ *adj* not based on facts or the usual scientific methods of doing something: *unscientific ideas*

un·scram·ble /ʌnˈskræmbəl/ *v* [T] **1** to change a television SIGNAL or a message that has been sent in CODE (=a deliberately confusing way) so that it can be seen or read **2** to make a confusing situation or confusing feelings easier to understand

un·screw /ʌnˈskruː/ *v* [T] **1** to open something by twisting it THESAURUS OPEN **2** to take the screws out of something

un·script·ed /ʌnˈskrɪptɪd◂/ *adj* an unscripted broadcast, speech etc is not written or planned before it is made

un·scru·pu·lous /ʌnˈskruːpjələs/ ●○○ *adj* behaving in an unfair or dishonest way: *unscrupulous employers* THESAURUS DISHONEST —**unscrupulously** *adv*

un·sea·son·a·bly /ʌnˈsiːzənəbli/ *adv* **unseasonably warm/cold/hot etc** used for saying that the weather is warmer, colder etc than usual at a particular time of year —**unseasonable** *adj*

un·seat /ʌnˈsiːt/ *v* [T] **1** to remove someone from a powerful job or position: *an attempt to unseat the party leader* **2** if a horse unseats someone, it throws them off its back

un·se·cured /ˌʌnsɪˈkjʊəd◂ $ -ˈkjʊrd◂/ *adj* an unsecured debt or LOAN is one that does not make you promise to give the bank something you own if you cannot pay it back

un·seed·ed /ˌʌnˈsiːdɪd◂/ *adj* not chosen as a SEED (=someone with a numbered rank in a competition), especially in a tennis competition

un·see·ing /ˌʌnˈsiːɪŋ◂/ *adj literary* not noticing anything even though your eyes are open: *Jack gazed unseeing out of the window.* —**unseeingly** *adv*

un·seem·ly /ʌnˈsiːmli/ *adj formal* unseemly behaviour is not polite or not suitable for a particular occasion: *Ann thought it unseemly to kiss her husband in public.*

un·seen[1] /ˌʌnˈsiːn◂/ ●○○ *adj formal* not noticed or seen: *Raj crept out of the house unseen. | unseen dangers* → **sight unseen** at SIGHT[1](17)

un·seen[2] /ʌnˈsiːn/ *n* [C] *BrE* a piece of writing that you must translate into your own language in an examination

un·self·ish /ʌnˈselfɪʃ/ *adj* caring about other people and thinking about their needs and wishes before your own SYN **selfless**, **generous** —**unselfishly** *adv* —**unselfishness** *n* [U]

un·set·tle /ʌnˈsetl/ *v* [T] to make someone feel slightly nervous, worried, or upset: *The sudden changes unsettled Judy.*

un·set·tled /ʌnˈsetld/ *adj*
1 SITUATION making people feel uncertain about what will happen: *difficult and unsettled times*
2 FEELING slightly worried, upset, or nervous: *Children often feel unsettled if their parents divorce.*
3 ARGUMENT OR DISAGREEMENT still continuing without reaching any agreement: *The dispute remains unsettled.*
4 WEATHER changing a lot in a short period of time SYN **changeable**
5 LAND unsettled land has never had people living on it → **settler**
6 DEBT an unsettled debt or bill has not been paid
7 STOMACH feeling slightly sick SYN **upset**: *My stomach's a bit unsettled after all that rich food.*

un·set·tling /ʌnˈsetlɪŋ/ *adj* making you feel nervous or worried: *an unsettling experience*

U

un·shake·a·ble, **unshakable** /ʌn'ʃeɪkəbəl/ *adj* an unshakeable faith, belief etc is very strong and cannot be changed or destroyed

un·shak·en /ʌn'ʃeɪkən/ *adj formal* not having changed your attitude or belief: **[+in]** *He remained unshaken in his belief that she was wrong.*

un·shav·en /ʌn'ʃeɪvən/ *adj* a man who is unshaven has very short hairs growing on his face because he has not SHAVEd

un·sight·ly /ʌn'saɪtli/ *adj* ugly or unpleasant to look at: *unsightly buildings | unsightly marks*

un·signed /ˌʌn'saɪnd◂/ *adj* **1** an unsigned letter or document has not been signed with someone's name **2** an unsigned sports player or musician has not yet signed a contract to play for a sports team or record music for a company

un·skilled /ˌʌn'skɪld◂/ ●○○ *adj*
1 an unskilled worker has not been trained for a particular type of job: *companies employing* ***unskilled labour*** (=people who have no special training)
2 unskilled work, jobs etc do not need people with special skills

un·smil·ing /ʌn'smaɪlɪŋ/ *adj literary* looking serious and unfriendly: *an unsmiling face*

un·so·cia·ble /ʌn'səʊʃəbəl $ -'soʊ-/ *adj* not wanting to be with people or to go to social events SYN **anti-social** → UNSOCIAL

un·so·cial /ˌʌn'səʊʃəl◂ $ -'soʊ-/ (*also* **unsociable**) *adj* **work unsocial hours** to work during the night or early in the morning when most people do not have to work

un·so·lic·it·ed /ˌʌnsə'lɪsɪtɪd◂/ *adj* not asked for and often not wanted: *unsolicited calls | unsolicited advice*

un·solved /ˌʌn'sɒlvd◂ $ -'sɑːlvd◂, -'sɒːlvd◂/ *adj* a problem, mystery, or crime that is unsolved has never been solved: *The murder still remains unsolved.*

un·so·phis·ti·cat·ed /ˌʌnsə'fɪstɪkeɪtɪd◂/ *adj* **1** not having much knowledge or experience of modern and fashionable things: *an unsophisticated audience* **2** unsophisticated tools, methods, or processes are simple and do not have all the features of more modern ones SYN **crude**

un·sound /ˌʌn'saʊnd◂/ *adj* **1** not based on facts or good reasons: **ideologically/scientifically/ecologically etc unsound** *a test that's scientifically unsound* **2** an unsound building or structure is in bad condition: *The houses are* ***structurally unsound.*** **3** *formal* physically or mentally ill: *people* ***of unsound mind*** (=people who are mentally ill)

un·speak·a·ble /ʌn'spiːkəbəl/ *adj* **1** used for emphasizing how bad someone or something is: *an unspeakable tragedy* **2** *literary* unspeakable feelings are so extreme that it is impossible to describe them: *unspeakable joy* —**unspeakably** *adv*

un·spe·ci·fied /ʌn'spesɪfaɪd/ ●○○ AWL *adj* not known or not stated: *The meeting will take place at an unspecified date in the future.*

un·spoiled /ˌʌn'spɔɪld◂/ ●○○ (*also* **un·spoilt** /ˌʌn'spɔɪlt◂/ *BrE*) *adj*
1 an unspoiled place is beautiful because it has not changed for a long time and does not have a lot of new buildings: *unspoiled countryside*
2 someone who is unspoiled has not changed in spite of the good or bad things that have happened to them: *She remained unspoilt by her success.*

un·spok·en /ʌn'spəʊkən $ -'spoʊ-/ *adj* **1** an unspoken agreement, rule etc has not been discussed but is understood by everyone in a group: *an unspoken assumption* **2** not said for other people to hear: *unspoken questions*

un·sport·ing /ʌn'spɔːtɪŋ $ -'spɔːr-/ *adj* behaving in an unfair way, especially towards an opponent in a game or competition

un·sta·ble /ʌn'steɪbəl/ ●○○ AWL *adj*
1 likely to change suddenly and become worse → **instability**: *The political situation is still very unstable. | an unstable relationship*
2 something that is unstable is likely to move or fall
3 someone who is unstable changes very suddenly so that you do not know how they will react or behave: *a mentally unstable man*
4 an unstable chemical is likely to separate into simpler substances

un·stat·ed /ʌn'steɪtɪd/ *adj* not expressed in words: *unstated assumptions*

un·stead·y /ʌn'stedi/ *adj* **1** shaking or moving in a way you cannot control: *He poured the coffee with a very unsteady hand. | a baby's first unsteady steps | She was quite* ***unsteady on her feet*** (=she might fall over). **2** showing that you are nervous: *Her* ***voice was unsteady.*** *| She took a deep unsteady breath.* **3** an unsteady object is not balanced very well and could fall SYN **unstable**: *an unsteady ladder* **4** an unsteady situation, relationship etc could change or end at any time SYN **fragile**: *an unsteady peace* —**unsteadily** *adv* —**unsteadiness** *n* [U]

un·stint·ing /ʌn'stɪntɪŋ/ *adj formal* unstinting support, help, praise etc is complete and given willingly —**unstintingly** *adv*

un·stop·pa·ble /ʌn'stɒpəbəl $ -'stɑːp-/ *adj* unable to be stopped: *Once Janet gets an idea, she's unstoppable.*

un·stressed /ˌʌn'strest◂/ AWL *adj* an unstressed word or part of a word is pronounced with less force than other ones

un·struc·tured /ʌn'strʌktʃəd $ -ərd/ AWL *adj* not organized in a detailed way, and allowing people freedom to do what they want: *unstructured interviews*

un·stuck /ˌʌn'stʌk◂/ *adj* **come unstuck a)** *BrE informal* if a person, plan, or system comes unstuck, they fail at what they were trying to achieve: *a dangerous area of rock where many climbers come unstuck* **b)** if something comes unstuck, it becomes separated from the thing that it was stuck to

un·sub·scribe /ˌʌnsəb'skraɪb/ *v* [I] to tell a company to remove your email address from the list of people who are regularly sent information: **[+from]** *To unsubscribe from our mailing list, follow the instructions below.*

un·sub·stan·ti·at·ed /ˌʌnsəb'stænʃieɪtɪd/ *adj* not proved to be true: *unsubstantiated allegations of child abuse*

un·suc·cess·ful /ˌʌnsək'sesfəl◂/ ●●○ *adj* not having a successful result or not achieving what you wanted to achieve: *an* ***unsuccessful attempt*** *to climb Everest |* **unsuccessful in (doing) sth** *We have been unsuccessful in finding a new manager.* —**unsuccessfully** *adv*: *He tried unsuccessfully to make them change their decision.*

un·suit·a·ble /ʌn'suːtəbəl, -'sjuː- $ -'suː-/ ●○○ *adj* not having the right qualities for a particular person, purpose, or situation SYN **inappropriate**: *unsuitable housing |* **[+for]** *The book is* ***unsuitable for children.***

un·suit·ed /ʌn'suːtəd, -'sjuː- $ -'suː-/ *adj* [not before noun]
1 not having the right qualities for a particular job or purpose: **[+to/for]** *He was unsuited for the job. | old school buildings unsuited to modern education* **2** *BrE* two people who are unsuited are unlikely to have a successful romantic relationship because they have very different characters and interests SYN **mismatched**: *I now realize that Tom and I were* ***totally unsuited.***

un·sul·lied /ʌn'sʌlid/ *adj literary* not spoiled by anything

un·sung /ˌʌn'sʌŋ◂/ *adj* not praised or famous for something you have done, although you deserve to be: *one of the* ***unsung heroes*** *of French politics*

un·sure /ˌʌn'ʃɔː◂ $ -'ʃʊr◂/ ●○○ *adj*
1 not certain about something or about what you have to do: **[+of/about]** *I was unsure of the reaction I would get. | If you are unsure about anything, just ask.* | **unsure whether/what etc** *Peter was unsure what to do next.*
2 unsure of yourself not having enough confidence: *Chris seemed nervous and unsure of herself.*

un·sur·passed /ˌʌnsə'pɑːst◂ $ -sər'pæst◂/ *adj* better or greater than anyone or anything else: *an unsurpassed knowledge of Greek history*

un·sur·pris·ing /ˌʌnsə'praɪzɪŋ◂ $ -sər-/ *adj* not making you feel surprised: ***It's unsurprising that*** *the project failed.* | *an enjoyable but unsurprising album* —**unsurprisingly** *adv*

un·sus·pect·ing /ˌʌnsəˈspektɪŋ◂/ *adj* [usually before noun] not knowing that something bad is happening or going to happen: *unsuspecting victims* | *Fake designer clothes are being sold to an unsuspecting public.*

un·sus·tain·a·ble /ˌʌnsəˈsteɪnəbəl/ AWL *adj* unable to continue at the same rate or in the same way: *unsustainable economic growth*

un·sweet·ened /ʌnˈswiːtnd/ *adj* unsweetened food or drink has not had sugar added to it

un·swerv·ing /ʌnˈswɜːvɪŋ $ -ɜːr-/ *adj* an unswerving belief or attitude is one that is very strong and never changes: **unswerving loyalty/commitment/support etc** *a politician with unswerving loyalty to the president*

un·sym·pa·thet·ic /ˌʌnsɪmpəˈθetɪk/ *adj* **1** not kind or helpful to someone who is having problems THESAURUS UNKIND **2** not willing to support an idea, aim etc: **[+to/towards]** *a government that's unsympathetic to public opinion* **3** an unsympathetic person in a book or play is unpleasant and difficult to like: *an **unsympathetic character*** —**unsympathetically** /-kli/ *adv*

un·taint·ed /ʌnˈteɪntɪd/ *adj formal* not affected or influenced by something bad: **[+by]** *a politician untainted by corruption*

un·tamed /ˌʌnˈteɪmd◂/ *adj* **1** untamed land is still in its natural state and has not been developed by people **2** an untamed animal has not been trained to live or work with people SYN **wild**

un·tan·gle /ˌʌnˈtæŋgəl/ *v* [T] **1** to separate pieces of string, wire etc that are twisted together **2** to make something less complicated: *The research attempts to untangle some of these issues.*

un·tapped /ˌʌnˈtæpt◂/ *adj* an untapped supply, market, or TALENT is available but has not yet been used: *Older people are an untapped resource in the employment market.* | *We believe there is untapped potential.*

un·ten·a·ble /ʌnˈtenəbəl/ *adj formal* **1** an untenable situation has become so difficult that it is impossible to continue: *The scandal put the president in **an untenable position**.* **2** an untenable argument, suggestion etc is impossible to defend

un·tested /ʌnˈtestɪd/ *adj* **1** untested ideas, methods, or people have not been used in a particular situation so you do not know what they are like: *an argument based on untested assumptions* **2** an untested drug, medical treatment etc has not been given any scientific tests to discover if it is safe to use

un·think·a·ble /ʌnˈθɪŋkəbəl/ *adj* **1** impossible to accept or imagine: ***It is unthinkable that*** *a mistake like this could have happened.* | **it would be unthinkable for sb to do sth** *It would be unthinkable for me to stay anywhere but with the family.* THESAURUS IMPOSSIBLE **2 the unthinkable** something that is impossible to accept or imagine: *Then **the unthinkable happened** and the boat started to sink.* | *It was the job of the committee to **think the unthinkable*** (=plan for unexpected events or situations).

un·think·ing /ʌnˈθɪŋkɪŋ/ *adj* not thinking about the effects of something you say or do —**unthinkingly** *adv*

un·ti·dy /ʌnˈtaɪdi/ *adj especially BrE* **1** not neat SYN **messy**: *an untidy desk* | *untidy hair* | *Her clothes were in an untidy heap on the floor.*

> **REGISTER**
> In American English and in everyday British English, people usually say **messy** rather than **untidy**: *His room is always so **messy**.*

2 someone who is untidy does not keep their house, possessions etc neat SYN **messy** —**untidily** *adv* —**untidiness** *n* [U]

un·tie /ʌnˈtaɪ/ *v* (**untied**, **untying**, **unties**) [T] to take the knots out of something, or unfasten something that has been tied OPP **tie up**: *Peter untied his shoelaces.* → see picture at UNDO

un·til /ʌnˈtɪl, ən-/ ●●● S1 W1 *prep, conjunction*
1 if something happens until a particular time, it continues and then stops at that time: *The ticket is valid until March.* | *He waited until she had finished speaking.* | *Until recently, Anna worked as a teacher in Japan.* | ***Up until*** *last year, they didn't even own a car.*
2 not until used to emphasize that something does not happen before a certain point in time or before something else has happened: *'Can I go out and play now?' 'Not until you've done your homework.'* | *It was not until 1972 that the war finally came to an end.*

> **GRAMMAR: Choosing the right tense**
> • You use the simple present tense with **until**: *I will wait until I hear from you.*
> • Don't use 'will' in the clause after **until**. ✗ Don't say: *I will wait until I will hear from you.*
> • You can also use the present perfect tense with **until**: *I will wait until I have heard from you.* | *Stir until the sugar has dissolved.* ✗ Don't say: *until I will have heard from you* | *until the sugar will have dissolved*
> • You can also use the past perfect tense with **until**: *I waited until the train had left the station.*
> GRAMMAR GUIDE VERBS

> **USAGE: Until now, so far**
> • You usually use **until now** when a situation has just ended or changed: *I have never thought about it until now* (=but now I have thought about it).
> • You use **so far** when a situation has not changed: *We don't have any news about him so far.* ✗ Don't say: *We don't have any news about him until now.*

un·time·ly /ʌnˈtaɪmli/ *adj* **1** happening too soon or sooner than you expected: *the **untimely death** of a popular local man* | *The announcement brought the meeting to an **untimely end**.* **2** not suitable for a particular occasion or time: *an untimely interruption*

un·tir·ing /ʌnˈtaɪərɪŋ $ -ˈtaɪr-/ *adj* working very hard for a long period of time in order to do something – used to show approval SYN **tireless**: *untiring efforts to help the homeless*

un·ti·tled /ʌnˈtaɪtld/ *adj* an untitled song, painting etc has not been given a title

un·to /ˈʌntuː/ *prep old use* to: *Thanks be unto God.*

un·told /ˌʌnˈtəʊld◂ $ -ˈtoʊld◂/ *adj* [only before noun] **1** used to emphasize how bad something is: *The rumours will do **untold damage** to his reputation.* | *The floods have caused **untold misery** to hundreds of homeowners.* **2** used to emphasize that an amount or quantity is very large: **untold riches/wealth** *a game that offers untold wealth to the most talented players*

un·touch·a·ble /ʌnˈtʌtʃəbəl/ *adj* **1** someone who is untouchable is in such a strong position that they cannot be defeated, affected, or punished: *He was the boss's husband and therefore untouchable.* **2** belonging to the lowest social group, especially in the Hindu CASTE system —**untouchable** *n* [C]

un·touched /ˌʌnˈtʌtʃt◂/ ●○○ *adj*
1 not changed, damaged, or affected in any way: **[+by]** *an island that has been untouched by time*
2 not touched, moved, or eaten: *Several papers lay untouched on the desk.*

un·to·ward /ˌʌntəˈwɔːd $ ˌʌnˈtɔːrd/ *adj formal* unexpected, unusual, or not wanted: **anything/nothing untoward** *I walked past but didn't notice anything untoward.*

un·trained /ˌʌnˈtreɪnd◂/ ●○○ *adj*
1 not trained to do something: *untrained staff*
2 to the untrained eye/ear when someone who does not have special knowledge of a subject looks at something or listens to it: *To the untrained eye, the two flowers look remarkably similar.*

un·tram·melled *BrE*, **untrammeled** *AmE* /ʌnˈtræməld/ *adj formal* not limited by anyone or anything: **[+by]** *an organization untrammelled by legal restraints*

un·treat·ed /ʌnˈtriːtɪd/ *adj* **1** an untreated illness or

U

injury has not had medical treatment **2** harmful substances that are untreated have not been made safe: *untreated sewage* **3** untreated wood has not had any substances put on it to preserve it

un·tried /ˌʌn'traɪd◂/ *adj* **1** not having any experience of doing a particular job: *a young and untried minister* **2** something that is untried has not been tested to see whether it is successful: *untried and untested ways to make money*

un·true /ʌn'tru:/ *adj* **1** not based on facts that are correct SYN **false**: *allegations that are totally untrue* | ***It's untrue to say** that the situation has not changed.* THESAURUS WRONG

> REGISTER
> In everyday English, people usually say something is **not true** rather than **untrue**: *It's **not true** to say nothing has changed.*

2 *literary* someone who is untrue to their husband, wife etc is not faithful to them SYN **unfaithful**

un·trust·wor·thy /ʌn'trʌstˌwɜ:ði $ -ˌwɜ:r-/ *adj* someone who is untrustworthy cannot be trusted

un·truth /ʌn'tru:θ, 'ʌntru:θ/ *n* [C] *formal* a lie - used when you want to avoid saying the word 'lie'

un·truth·ful /ʌn'tru:θfəl/ *adj* dishonest or not true —**untruthfully** *adv*

un·tu·tored /ʌn'tju:təd $ -'tu:tərd/ *adj formal* not having been taught to do something SYN **untrained**: **to the untutored eye/ear/mind** *To the untutored ear, this music sounds as if it might have been written by Beethoven.*

un·typ·i·cal /ʌn'tɪpɪkəl/ *adj* not having the usual features or qualities that you would expect → **atypical**: **[+of]** *a building that is quite untypical of the period in which it was built* | *These problems are **not untypical*** (=they are normal). —**untypically** /-kli/ *adv*

un·us·a·ble /ʌn'ju:zəbəl/ *adj* something that is unusable is in such a bad condition that you cannot use it

un·used[1] /ˌʌn'ju:zd◂/ ●○○ *adj* not being used, or never used: *unused land*

un·used[2] /ˌʌn'ju:st◂/ *adj* **unused to (doing) sth** not experienced in dealing with something SYN **unaccustomed**: *a sensitive man unused to publicity* | *Maggie was unused to being told what to do.*

un·u·su·al /ʌn'ju:ʒuəl, -ʒəl/ ●●● S2 W3 *adj* different from what is usual or normal: *an unusual feature* | *unusual circumstances* | ***It's unusual for** Dave to be late.* | ***It's not unusual*** (=it is quite common) *to feel very angry in a situation like this.*

> **THESAURUS**
> **EVENTS/SITUATIONS**
> **unusual** different from what usually happens: *We had snow in May, which is very unusual.*
> **rare** not happening very often, or existing only in small numbers: *Violent crimes are rare.* | *Hatton gathered many rare plants from all over the world.*
> **exceptional** /ɪk'sepʃənəl/ very unusual and happening very rarely: *Ninety-day visas can be extended only in exceptional circumstances.* | *The presence of a jury in a civil trial is now quite exceptional.*
> **out of the ordinary** unusual and surprising or special: *It was a small village where nothing out of the ordinary ever seemed to happen.*
> **freak** extremely unusual and unexpected - used about an accident, storm etc: *A freak wave wrecked most of the seafront.*
> **unprecedented** /ʌn'presədentəd/ if something is unprecedented, it has never happened before - often used about successes and achievements: *An unprecedented number of students have received top grades.* | *This kind of deal is unprecedented.*
> **unheard of** if something is unheard of, it has never happened or been done before - used especially when something seems very surprising to people at that time: *In our small town, this kind of crime was almost unheard of.*
>
> **PEOPLE/BEHAVIOUR/METHODS ETC**
> **eccentric** behaving in a way that seems rather strange but not frightening: *The house was owned by an eccentric millionaire.* | *eccentric behaviour*
> **unconventional** very different from the way people usually behave, think, dress etc, often in a way that seems interesting: *His parents had a rather unconventional lifestyle, and let their children do whatever they pleased.*
> **unorthodox** unorthodox ideas or methods are different from the usual ones, and therefore seem surprising to many people: *He is known for his unorthodox political views.* | *unorthodox teaching methods*

un·u·su·al·ly /ʌn'ju:ʒuəli, -ʒəli/ ●●○ *adv* **1 unusually high/large/quiet etc** higher, larger etc than usual: *unusually high levels of pollution* **2** used to say that something is not what usually happens: *Unusually for me, I fell asleep very quickly.*

un·ut·ter·a·ble /ʌn'ʌtərəbəl/ *adj literary* an unutterable feeling is too extreme to be expressed in words —**unutterably** *adv*

un·var·nished /ʌn'vɑ:nɪʃt $ -ɑ:r-/ *adj* **1** [only before noun] simple and without any additional descriptions or details: *an unvarnished account of events* **2** not covered with VARNISH (=a transparent substance like paint, used to protect the surface of wood)

un·veil /ʌn'veɪl/ ●○○ *v* [T] **1** to show or tell people about a new product or plan for the first time: *The club has unveiled plans to build a new stadium.* **2** to remove the cover from something, especially as part of a formal ceremony: *The statue was unveiled by the Queen.* —**unveiling** *n* [C,U]

un·voiced /ˌʌn'vɔɪst◂/ *adj* **1** not expressed in words: *unvoiced fears* **2** *technical* unvoiced CONSONANTS are produced without moving your VOCAL CORDS. /d/ and /g/ are voiced consonants, and /t/ and /k/ are unvoiced.

un·waged /ˌʌn'weɪdʒd◂/ *adj BrE* not having a job that you get paid for SYN **unpaid**

un·want·ed /ʌn'wɒntɪd $ -'wɒ:nt-, -'wɑ:nt-/ ●○○ *adj* not wanted or needed: *an unwanted pregnancy*

un·war·rant·ed /ʌn'wɒrəntɪd $ -'wɔ:-, -'wɑ:-/ *adj* done without good reason, and therefore annoying: *unwarranted interference*

un·wa·ry /ʌn'weəri $ -'weri/ *adj formal* **1** not knowing about possible problems or dangers, and therefore easily harmed or deceived: *unwary travellers* **2 the unwary** people who are unwary: *pitfalls that can trap the unwary*

un·washed /ˌʌn'wɒʃt◂ $ -'wɒ:ʃt◂, -'wɑ:ʃt◂/ *adj* **1** dirty and needing to be washed: *unwashed cups* **2 the great unwashed** *humorous* people who are poor and have not been educated

un·wa·ver·ing /ʌn'weɪvərɪŋ/ *adj* an unwavering attitude, belief, expression etc does not change: *an unwavering stare* | *unwavering support* —**unwaveringly** *adv*

un·wel·come /ʌn'welkəm/ *adj* **1** something that is unwelcome is not wanted, especially because it might cause embarrassment or problems: *unwelcome publicity* | *unwelcome news* **2** unwelcome guests, visitors etc are people who you do not want in your home

un·well /ʌn'wel/ ●○○ *adj* [not before noun] *formal* ill, especially for a short time: *She had been feeling unwell.* THESAURUS ILL

> REGISTER
> In everyday English, people usually say that someone is **not well** rather than **unwell**: *He didn't come to school because he **wasn't well**.*

un·wield·y /ʌn'wi:ldi/ *adj* **1** an unwieldy object is big, heavy, and difficult to carry or use **2** an unwieldy system, argument, or organization is difficult to control or manage because it is too complicated: *unwieldy bureaucracy* —**unwieldiness** *n* [U]

U

un·will·ing /ʌnˈwɪlɪŋ/ ●●○ *adj*
1 [not before noun] not wanting to do something and refusing to do it: **unwilling to do sth** *He was unwilling or unable to pay the fine.*
2 [only before noun] not wanting to do something but doing it: *an unwilling helper* —**unwillingly** *adv* —**unwillingness** *n* [U]

un·wind /ʌnˈwaɪnd/ *v* (*past tense and past participle* **unwound** /-ˈwaʊnd/) **1** [I] to relax and stop feeling anxious: *a beautiful country hotel that is the perfect place to unwind* THESAURUS ▸ RELAX **2** [I,T] to undo something that has been wrapped around something else, or to become undone after being wrapped around something: *She started to unwind her scarf.*

un·wise /ˌʌnˈwaɪz◂/ ●○○ *adj* not based on good judgment: **(it is) unwise to do sth** *It's unwise to keep medicines in a place that can be reached by children.* THESAURUS ▸ STUPID —**unwisely** *adv*

un·wit·ting·ly /ʌnˈwɪtɪŋli/ *adv* in a way that shows you do not know or realize something SYN **unknowingly**: *Friedmann had unwittingly broken the law.* —**unwitting** *adj* [only before noun]: *an unwitting accomplice*

un·wont·ed /ʌnˈwəʊntɪd $ -ˈwoʊn-/ *adj* [only before noun] *formal* unusual and not what you expect to happen SYN **unaccustomed**: *unwonted freedom*

un·work·a·ble /ʌnˈwɜːkəbəl $ -ɜːr-/ *adj* an unworkable plan, system, law etc is not likely to be successful

un·world·ly /ʌnˈwɜːldli $ -ɜːr-/ *adj* **1** not interested in money or possessions **2** not having a lot of experience of life SYN **naive 3** unusual and having qualities that do not seem to belong to this world: *unworldly beauty*

un·wor·thy /ʌnˈwɜːði $ -ɜːr-/ *adj formal* **1** not deserving respect, attention etc: **[+of]** *an idea that's unworthy of serious consideration* **2** unworthy behaviour, attitudes etc are not acceptable from someone who is respected or who has an important job: **[+of]** *a suggestion that's unworthy of someone who hopes to become president* —**unworthiness** *n* [U]

un·wound /ʌnˈwaʊnd/ the past tense and past participle of UNWIND

un·wrap /ʌnˈræp/ ●●○ *v* (**unwrapped, unwrapping**) [T] to remove the paper, plastic etc that is around something OPP **wrap up**: *Brigitte was unwrapping her birthday presents.* THESAURUS ▸ OPEN

un·writ·ten /ʌnˈrɪtn/ *adj* an unwritten rule, law, agreement etc is one that everyone knows about although it is not official: *unwritten rules of social behaviour*

un·yield·ing /ʌnˈjiːldɪŋ/ *adj* **1** *formal* not willing to change your ideas or beliefs: *an unyielding resistance to change* **2** *literary* very hard and not changing in shape or form: *a harsh unyielding landscape*

un·zip /ʌnˈzɪp/ ●●○ *v* (**unzipped, unzipping**) [T]
1 to unfasten the ZIP on a bag, piece of clothing etc
2 to make a computer FILE its normal size again so that you can use it, after it has been made to use less space → see picture at **UNDO**

up¹ /ʌp/ ●●● S1 W1 *adv, prep, adj*
1 TO A HIGHER POSITION towards a higher place or position OPP **down**: *We walked slowly up the hill.* | *She picked her jacket up off the floor.* | *paths leading up into the mountains* | *Tim had climbed up a tree to get a better view.* | *Put up your hand if you know the answer.* | *The water was getting up my nose.* | *Karen lay on her back, staring up at the ceiling.*
2 IN A HIGHER POSITION in a higher place or position OPP **down**: *John's up in his bedroom.* | *a plane flying 30,000 feet up* | *Her office is just up those stairs.* | *The doctor's assistant was up a ladder in the stockroom.*
3 TO BE UPRIGHT into an upright or raised position: *Everyone stood up for the national anthem.* | *Mick turned his collar up against the biting winds.*
4 ALONG in or to a place that is further along something such as a road or path SYN **down**: *She lives just up the street.* | *We walked up the road towards the church.*
5 NORTH in or towards the north: *They live up north.* | *We're driving up to Chicago for the conference.* | *a stormy voyage up the east coast from Miami to Boston*
6 CLOSE very close to someone or something: *A man came up and offered to buy him a drink.* | **[+to]** *She drove right up to the front door.* | **[+against]** *The bed was up against the wall.*
7 TO MORE IMPORTANT PLACE used to show that the place someone goes to is more important than the place they start from: *Have you been up to London recently?*
8 RIVER towards the place where a river starts OPP **down**: *sailing up the Thames* | *The river steamers only went up as far as Mandalay.*
9 MORE at or towards a higher level or a greater amount OPP **down**: *Turn up the radio.* | *Violent crime went up by 9% last year.* | *Inflation is up by 2%.* | **[+on]** *Profits are up on last year.*

> **REGISTER**
> In written English, people often prefer to use **rise** rather than **be/go up**, because it sounds more formal: *Violent crime* **rose** *by 9% last year.*

10 WINNING *BrE* beating your opponent by a certain number of points OPP **down**: **two goals up/three points up etc** *United were a goal up at half time.*
11 NOT IN BED not in bed: *Are the kids still up?* | *They stayed up all night to watch the game.* | *It's time to* **get up** (=get out of bed). | *It's good to see you* **up and about** *again* (=out of bed after an illness and moving around normally).
12 FINISHING used after certain verbs to show that something is completely finished, used, or removed: *We've used up all our savings.* | *The children had to eat up all their food.* | *After a month, the wound had almost healed up.*
13 CUTTING/DIVIDING used after certain verbs to show that something is cut, broken etc into pieces or divided into parts: *Why did you tear up that letter?* | *We still haven't decided how to divide up the money.*
14 COLLECTING used after certain verbs to show that things are collected together: *Let's just add up these figures quickly.* | *Could you collect up the papers?*
15 PART ON TOP used to say which surface or part of an object should be on top: *Put the playing cards right side up.* | *Isn't that painting the wrong way up?*
16 ABOVE A LEVEL above and including a certain level, age, or amount: *All the women were naked from the waist up.* | *Children aged 12* **and up** *must pay the full fare.*
17 up and down a) backwards and forwards: *Ralph paced up and down the room, looking worried.* **b)** if someone is up and down, they sometimes feel well or happy and sometimes do not: *Jason's been very up and down since his girlfriend left him.* **c)** to a higher position and then a lower position, several times: *They were all jumping up and down and screaming excitedly.* | *Shivers ran up and down my body.* | **look sb up and down** (=look at someone in order to judge their appearance or character) *Maisie looked her rival up and down with a critical eye.*
18 up to sth a) as much or as many as a certain amount or number but not more: *The Olympic Stadium will hold up to 80,000 spectators.* | *a process that can take* **anything up to** *ten days* **b)** (*also* **up till**) for the whole of a period until a certain time or date: *She continued to care for her father up to the time of his death.* | *We've kept our meetings secret up to now.* **c)** [in questions and negatives] clever, good, or well enough to do something: *I'm afraid Tim just isn't up to the job* (=he does not have the necessary ability). | *You don't need to go back to school if you don't feel up to it.* | **up to doing sth** *He's not really up to seeing any visitors.* **d)** if something is up to a particular standard, it is good enough to reach that standard: *I didn't think last night's performance was up to her usual standard.* **e)** *spoken* doing something secret or something that you should not be doing: *The children are very quiet. I wonder what they're up to.* | *He knew Bailey was up to something. But what?* | *I always suspected that he was* **up to no good** (=doing something bad).
19 be up to sb a) used to say that someone can decide about something: *You can pay weekly or monthly – it's up to*

you. **b)** used to say that someone is responsible for a particular duty: *It's up to the travel companies to warn customers of any possible dangers.*
20 FINISHED TIME if a period of time is up, it is finished: *I'm sorry, we'll have to stop there. Our time is up.*
21 ROAD REPAIRS if a road is up, its surface is being repaired
22 COMPUTER if a computer system is up, it is working OPP **down**: *There could well be a few problems before your new computer is* ***up and running*** *properly.*
23 up against sth/sb having to deal with a difficult situation or opponent: *He came up against a lot of problems with his boss.* | *Murphy will be really* ***up against it*** *when he faces the champion this afternoon.*
24 up for sth a) available for a particular process: *The house is up for sale.* | *This week 14 of Campbell's paintings were put up for auction.* | *Even the most taboo subjects were up for discussion.* **b)** being considered for election or for a job: *Senator Frank Church was coming up for re-election that year.* | *She is one of five candidates up for the chief executive's job.* **c)** appearing in a court of law because you have been ACCUSED of a crime: *Ron's up for drinking and driving next week.* **d)** *spoken* willing to do something or interested in doing something: *We're going to the pub later – are you up for it?*
25 something is up *spoken* if something is up, someone is feeling unhappy because they have problems, or there is something wrong in a situation: *I could tell by the look on his face that something was up.* | **[+with]** *Is something up with Julie? She looks really miserable.* | **what's up?** *What's up? Why are you crying?*
26 be well up in/on sth (*also* **be up on sth** *AmE*) *informal* to know a lot about something: *I'm not all that well up in musical matters.* | *Conrad's really up on his geography, isn't he?*
27 be up before sth/sb *informal* to appear in a court of law because you have been ACCUSED of a crime: *He was up before the magistrates' court charged with dangerous driving.*
28 be up to here *BrE* (*also* **have had it up to here**) *spoken* to be very upset and angry because of a particular situation or person: **[+with]** *I'm up to here with this job; I'm resigning!*
29 up the workers!/up the reds! etc *BrE spoken* used to express support and encouragement for a particular group of people or for a sports team
30 up yours! *spoken not polite* used as a very rude and offensive reply to someone who has said something that annoys you: *'You're not allowed to park here.' 'Up yours, mate!'*
31 sb is (so) up himself/herself etc *informal* if you say that someone is up himself or up herself, you mean that they pay too much attention to themselves and what they do or what they look like – used to show disapproval → **not be up to much** at MUCH²(8)

up² *n* **1 ups and downs** *informal* the mixture of good and bad experiences that happen in any situation or relationship: *We have our ups and downs like all couples.* **2 be on the up** *BrE spoken* to be improving or increasing: *Business confidence is on the up.* **3 be on the up and up a)** *BrE informal* to be becoming more successful: *a brilliant young player who is on the up and up* **b)** *AmE spoken* if a person or business is on the up and up, they are honest and do things legally

up³ *v* (**upped**, **upping**) **1** [T] to increase the amount or level of something: *They've upped their offer by 5%.* **2 up and do sth** to suddenly do something different or surprising: *Without saying another word, he upped and left.* → **up the ante** at ANTE¹, → **up sticks** at STICK²(12)

up- /ʌp/ *prefix* **1** making something higher: *to upgrade a job* (=make it higher in importance) **2** [especially in adverbs and adjectives] at or towards the top or beginning of something: *uphill* | *upriver* (=nearer to where the river starts) **3** [especially in verbs] taking something from its place or turning it upside down: *an uprooted tree* | *She upended the bucket.* **4** [especially in adjectives and adverbs] at or towards the higher or better part of something: *upmarket* (=attracting richer people) → DOWN-

ˌup-and-ˈcoming *adj* [only before noun] likely to become successful or popular: *up-and-coming young artists*

up·beat /ˈʌpbiːt/ *adj* positive and making you feel that good things will happen OPP **downbeat**: *an upbeat message*

up·braid /ʌpˈbreɪd/ *v* [T] *formal* to tell someone angrily that they have done something wrong

up·bring·ing /ˈʌpˌbrɪŋɪŋ/ ●○○ *n* [singular, U] the way that your parents care for you and teach you to behave when you are growing up → **bring up**: *Mike had had a strict upbringing.*

UPC /ˌjuː piː ˈsiː/ *n* [C] *AmE* the abbreviation of ***Universal Product Code***

up·charge /ˈʌptʃɑːdʒ $ -ɑːr-/ *n* [C] *AmE* money that a customer pays for an extra feature or service: *You have to pay a $3 upcharge to watch a movie in 3D.*

up·chuck /ˈʌptʃʌk/ *v* [I] *AmE informal* to bring food or drink up from your stomach and out through your mouth because you are ill or drunk SYN **vomit**

up·com·ing /ˈʌpˌkʌmɪŋ/ ●●○ *adj* [only before noun] happening soon SYN **forthcoming**: *the upcoming elections*

ˌup-ˈcountry *adj old-fashioned* from a place without many people or towns, especially in the middle of a country —**up-country** *adv*

up·cycle /ˈʌpˌsaɪkəl/ *v* [T] to change something old in a way that makes it better or more valuable than it was before → **recycle**: *She upcycles old scarves into fabulous cushions.* —**upcycling** *n* [U]

up·date¹ /ʌpˈdeɪt/ ●●○ *v* [T]
1 to add the most recent information to something: *The files need updating.*
2 to make something more modern in the way it looks or operates: *plans to update manufacturing procedures*
3 *spoken* to tell someone the most recent information about a situation: **update sb on sth** *Can you update me on what's been happening?*

up·date² /ˈʌpdeɪt/ ●●○ *n* [C]
1 the most recent news or information about something: *a news update* | **[+on]** *The report provides a brief update on the progress of the project.*
2 a change or addition to a computer FILE so that it has the most recent information

updo /ˈʌpduː/ *n* [C] *informal* a hairstyle for women in which the hair is pinned up, so that it stays on top of the head rather than hangs down: *For her wedding, she wanted to wear her hair in an updo.*

up·end /ʌpˈend/ *v* [T] to turn something over so that it is upside down

up·front¹ /ˌʌpˈfrʌnt◂/ *adj* **1** [not before noun] behaving or talking in an honest way so that people know what you really think: *Mo's very upfront with him about their relationship.* THESAURUS ▸ HONEST **2** paid before any work has been done or before goods are supplied: *an upfront fee of $500*

upfront² *adv* **1** if you pay money upfront, you pay it before any work has been done or before any goods are supplied: *He requires you to pay him upfront.* **2** in football, if you play upfront, you play in a FORWARD position

up·grade /ʌpˈɡreɪd/ ●●○ *v*
1 [I,T] to make a computer, machine, or piece of software better and able to do more things: **upgrade (sth) to sth** *You'll need to upgrade your hard drive to 120Mb before running this software.*
2 [T] to improve something and make it more modern, especially in order to provide a better service: *The hotel has recently been refurbished and upgraded.*
3 [I,T] to give someone a better seat on a plane or a better room in a hotel than the one they paid for: **upgrade (sb) to sth** *We can upgrade you to business class.*
4 [T] to give someone a more important job
5 [T] to change the official description of something to make it seem better or more important OPP **downgrade**: **upgrade sth to sth** *Four of the regions were upgraded to the status of republic.*

6 upgrade your skills to learn new and more modern ways of doing a particular job —**upgrade** /ˈʌpgreɪd/ *n* [C]

up·heav·al /ʌpˈhiːvəl/ ●○○ *n* [C,U] a very big change that often causes problems: *political upheaval* | *Moving house is a **major upheaval**.*

up·hill¹ /ˌʌpˈhɪl◂/ *adj* **1** towards the top of a hill OPP **downhill**: *an uphill climb* **2 an uphill struggle/battle/task etc** something that is very difficult to do and needs a lot of effort and determination

uphill² *adv* towards the top of a hill OPP **downhill**: *The road twists uphill.*

up·hold /ʌpˈhəʊld $ -ˈhoʊld/ ●○○ *v* (*past tense and past participle* **upheld** /-ˈheld/) [T]
1 to defend or support a law, system, or principle so that it continues to exist: *a committee that aims to uphold educational standards*
2 if a court upholds a decision made by another court, it states that the decision was correct OPP **overrule**: *The conviction was upheld by the Court of Appeal.* —**upholder** *n* [C]

up·hol·ster /ʌpˈhəʊlstə $ -ˈhoʊlstər/ *v* [T] to cover a chair with material —**upholstered** *adj*

up·hol·ster·er /ʌpˈhəʊlstərə $ -ˈhoʊlstərər/ *n* [C] someone whose job is to cover chairs with material

up·hol·ster·y /ʌpˈhəʊlstəri $ -ˈhoʊl-/ *n* [U] **1** material used to cover chairs **2** the process of covering chairs with material

up·keep /ˈʌpkiːp/ *n* [U] **1** the process of keeping something in good condition SYN **maintenance**: **[+of]** *Most of the money is spent on the upkeep of the building.* **2** the cost or process of looking after a child or animal and giving them the things they need: *Poorer people find it hard to pay for their pet's upkeep.*

up·lands /ˈʌpləndz/ *n* [plural] the parts of a country that are away from the sea and are higher than other areas —**upland** *adj*

up·lift¹ /ˈʌplɪft/ *n* **1** [singular] an increase in something: **[+in]** *an uplift in sales* **2** [singular, U] a feeling of happiness and hope

up·lift² /ʌpˈlɪft/ *v* [T] *formal* **1** to make someone feel happier **2** to make something higher

up·lift·ed /ʌpˈlɪftɪd/ *adj* **1** feeling happier and more hopeful: *He felt uplifted by her presence.* **2** *literary* raised upwards

up·lift·ing /ʌpˈlɪftɪŋ/ *adj* making you feel happier and more hopeful: *an uplifting experience*

up·light·er /ˈʌpˌlaɪtə $ -ər/ *n* [C] an electric light that shines upwards → see picture at LAMP

up·load¹ /ʌpˈləʊd $ -ˈloʊd/ ●●○ *v* [I,T] if information, a computer program etc uploads, or if you upload it, you move it from a small computer to a computer network so that other people can see it or use it OPP **download**: *It might take a while for this to upload.*

up·load² /ˈʌpləʊd $ -loʊd/ *n* [C] information, computer programs etc that have been uploaded, or the process of uploading them OPP **download**: *tips on handling file uploads*

up·mar·ket /ˌʌpˈmɑːkɪt◂ $ -ɑːr-/ *adj, adv especially BrE* designed for or used by people who have a lot of money → **downmarket** OPP **downmarket**: *an upmarket restaurant* | **move/go upmarket** *a brand that's moved upmarket* (=it is trying to attract richer people)

up·on /əˈpɒn $ əˈpɑːn/ ●●● S3 W2 *prep formal*
1 used to mean 'on' or 'onto': *an honour bestowed upon the association* | *We are completely dependent upon your help.* | *Brandon threw him upon the ground.*
2 if a time or event is upon you, it is about to happen: *Winter is almost upon us.*
3 layer upon layer/mile upon mile etc used to emphasize that there are a lot of layers, miles etc: *mile upon mile of golden sand* → **once upon a time** at ONCE¹(14), → **take it upon yourself to do sth** at TAKE¹(27)

up·per¹ /ˈʌpə $ -er/ ●●● W2 *adj* [only before noun]
1 in a higher position than something else OPP **lower**: *the upper lip*
2 near or at the top of something OPP **lower**: *the upper floors of a building* | *There is an upper age limit for becoming a pilot.*
3 have/gain the upper hand to have more power than someone else, so that you are able to control a situation: *Police have gained the upper hand over the drug dealers in the area.*
4 more important than other parts or ranks in an organization, system etc: *the **upper echelons** (=the most important members) of corporate management*
5 further from the sea or further north than other parts of an area: *the **upper reaches** of the Nile* → **a stiff upper lip** at STIFF¹(11)

upper² *n* [C] **1** the top part of a shoe that covers your foot: *leather uppers* **2 uppers** [plural] *informal* illegal drugs that make you feel happy and give you a lot of energy SYN **amphetamines** **3 be on your uppers** *BrE old-fashioned* to have very little money

ˌupper ˈcase *n* [U] *technical* letters written in capitals (A, B, C) rather than in small form (a, b, c)

ˌupper ˈclass ●○○ *n* [singular] (*also* **upper classes** [plural]) the group of people who belong to the highest social class —**upper-class** *adj*: *upper-class families*

GRAMMAR: Singular or plural verb?
• **The upper class** is usually followed by a singular verb: *The upper class **doesn't** want the system to change.*
• In British English, you can also use a plural verb: *The upper class **don't** want the system to change.*
GRAMMAR GUIDE ▸ NOUNS

up·per·class·man /ˌʌpəˈklɑːsmən $ -pərˈklæs-/ *n* (*plural* **upperclassmen** /-mən/) [C] *AmE* a student in the last two years of a school or university

up·per·class·wom·an /ˌʌpəˈklɑːsˌwʊmən $ -pərˈklæs-/ *n* (*plural* **upperclasswomen** /-ˌwɪmɪn/) [C] *AmE* a female student in the last two years of school or university

ˌupper ˈcrust *n* [singular] *informal* the group of people who belong to the highest social class —**upper-crust** *adj*

up·per·cut /ˈʌpəkʌt $ -ər-/ *n* [C] a way of hitting someone in which you swing your hand up into their chin

ˌUpper ˈHouse *n* [C usually singular] a group of representatives in a country's parliament, that is smaller and less powerful than the country's LOWER HOUSE, for example the British House of Lords

up·per·most /ˈʌpəməʊst $ -pərmoʊst/ *adj* **1 be uppermost in your mind** if something is uppermost in your mind, you think about it a lot because it is very important to you: *A feeling of pity for David was uppermost in her mind.* **2** [not before noun] more important than anything else: *The one word which seems to be uppermost in every discussion is money.* **3** [usually before noun] higher than anything else SYN **topmost**: *the uppermost windows of the house* —**uppermost** *adv*: *She turned her hand over, palm uppermost.*

ˈupper school *n* [C] the classes of a school in Britain that are for older students, usually aged 14 to 18

up·pi·ty /ˈʌpɪti/ (*also* **uppish** *BrE* /ˈʌpɪʃ/) *adj informal* behaving as if you are more important than you really are, or not showing someone enough respect: *uppity kids*

up·raised /ˌʌpˈreɪzd◂/ *adj formal* raised or lifted up - used especially about someone's hand or arm

up·right¹ /ˈʌpraɪt/ ●○○ *adj, adv*
1 standing or sitting straight up: **sit/stand/walk upright** *The chimpanzee **stood upright** and grasped the bars of its cage.* | *Katie was still awake, **sitting bolt upright** (=sitting with her back very straight) staring at the television.* | **pull/push/draw etc yourself upright** *He pulled himself upright and faced me.*
2 placed in a vertical position (=pointing in a line that is at an angle of 90° to a flat surface): *Your seat should be in*

the **upright position** *when the plane is landing.* | *Keep the bottle upright.*
3 always behaving in an honest way: *He was a good honest upright man.* THESAURUS▸ HONEST —**uprightness** *n* [U]

upright² *n* [C] a long piece of wood or metal that stands straight up and supports something

ˌupright piˈano *n* [C] a piano with strings that are in a VERTICAL position → **grand piano** → see picture at PIANO¹

up·ris·ing /ˈʌpˌraɪzɪŋ/ ●○○ *n* [C] an attempt by a group of people to change the government, laws etc in an area or country SYN **rebellion**: *a* **popular uprising** (=by the ordinary people in a country) | *an* **armed uprising** THESAURUS▸ REVOLUTION

up·riv·er /ˌʌpˈrɪvə $ -ər/ *adv* away from the sea towards the place where a river begins OPP **downriver**

up·roar /ˈʌp-rɔː $ -rɔːr/ *n* [singular, U] a lot of noise or angry protest about something: **be in (an) uproar** *The house was in an uproar, with babies crying and people shouting.*

up·roar·i·ous /ʌpˈrɔːriəs/ *adj* very noisy, because a lot of people are laughing or shouting: *an uproarious party* —**uproariously** *adv*: *uproariously funny*

up·root /ʌpˈruːt/ *v* **1** [T] to pull a plant and its roots out of the ground **2** [I,T] to make someone leave their home for a new place, especially when this is difficult or upsetting: *He rejected the idea of uprooting himself and moving to America.*

up·scale /ˈʌpskeɪl/ *adj AmE* relating to people from a high social class who have a lot of money SYN **upmarket** *BrE*: *an affluent upscale audience*

up·sell /ˈʌpsel/ *v* [I,T] to persuade a customer to buy more or to buy something more expensive

up·set¹ /ˌʌpˈset◂/ ●●● S2 *adj*
1 [not before noun] unhappy and worried because something unpleasant or disappointing has happened: **[+by/about/at etc]** *She was* **deeply upset** *about the way her father treated her.* | **upset that** *Debbie was upset that he didn't spend more time with her.*
2 be upset with sb if you are upset with someone, you are angry and annoyed with them: *You're not still upset with me, are you?*
3 upset stomach an illness that affects the stomach and makes you feel sick

up·set² /ʌpˈset/ ●●● S2 *v* (*past tense and past participle* **upset**, *present participle* **upsetting**) [T]
1 MAKE SB UNHAPPY to make someone feel unhappy or worried: *Don't do anything that would upset him.* | **it upsets sb that/when/to do** *It upsets me to see you cry.*
2 CHANGE STH to change a plan or situation in a way that causes problems: *The chemicals* **upset the balance of** *the environment.*
3 MAKE STH FALL to push something over without intending to: *He upset a bowl of soup.*
4 DEFEAT to defeat an opponent who is considered to be much better than you: *Jones upset the 40th-ranked American, Cunningham.*
5 upset the apple cart *informal* to completely spoil someone's plans
6 upset your stomach to affect your stomach and make you feel sick: *The soup was revolting and upset my stomach.* —**upsetting** *adj*

up·set³ /ˈʌpset/ *n* **1** [C,U] worry and unhappiness caused by an unexpected problem: *If you are the victim of a burglary, the emotional upset can affect you for a long time.* **2** [C] when a person or team defeats an opponent who is considered to be much better than them: *There was a major upset when the young skater took the gold medal.* THESAURUS▸ VICTORY **3 stomach upset** an illness that affects the stomach and makes you feel sick

up·shot /ˈʌpʃɒt $ -ʃɑːt/ *n* **the upshot (of sth)** the final result of a situation: *The upshot was that after much argument they all agreed to help her.*

up·side¹ /ˈʌpsaɪd/ *n* [singular] *especially AmE* the positive part of a situation that is generally bad OPP **downside**: *The upside of the whole thing is that we got a free trip to Jamaica.*

upside² *prep* **upside the head/face etc** *AmE informal* on the side of someone's head etc

ˌupside ˈdown¹ ●●○ *adv*
1 with the top at the bottom and the bottom at the top: *To get the plant out of the pot, turn it upside down and give it a gentle knock.*
2 turn sth upside down a) to make a place very untidy when you are looking for something: *The burglars have turned our house upside down.* **b)** to cause a lot of change and confusion in a situation or in someone's life: *the story of a young girl whose life was turned upside down*

ˌupside ˈdown² *adj* in a position with the top at the bottom and the bottom at the top: *an upside down U shape*

up·size /ˈʌpsaɪz/ *v* [I,T] to become larger in size, amount etc, or to make something do this: *Do you want me to upsize your fries?*

up·skill·ing /ˈʌpˌskɪlɪŋ/ *n* [U] improving the skills of workers, usually through training, so that they will be better at their jobs

up·stage¹ /ʌpˈsteɪdʒ/ *v* [T] to do something that takes people's attention away from someone else who is more important: *All the big-name stars were upstaged by 12-year-old Katy Rochford.*

upstage² *adv* towards the back of the stage in a theatre OPP **downstage** —**upstage** *adj*

up·stairs¹ /ˌʌpˈsteəz◂ $ -ˈsterz◂/ ●●● S2 *adv* towards or on an upper floor in a building OPP **downstairs**: *I went upstairs and had a shower.* | *She's upstairs in bed feeling ill.* —**upstairs** *adj* [only before noun]: *an upstairs window* | *the upstairs rooms* → **kick sb upstairs** at KICK¹(16)

upstairs² *n* **the upstairs** one or all of the upper floors in a building OPP **the downstairs**: *Would you like to see the upstairs?*

up·stand·ing /ʌpˈstændɪŋ/ *adj formal* **1** honest and responsible: *upstanding young men and women* **2** standing upright or pointing upwards **3 be upstanding** *BrE spoken formal* used in a formal situation such as a law court to tell people to stand up as a sign of respect for an important person

up·start /ˈʌpstɑːt $ -ɑːrt/ *n* [C] someone who behaves as if they were more important than they really are and who shows a lack of respect towards people who are more experienced or older: *a cheeky young upstart* —**upstart** *adj*

up·state /ˈʌpsteɪt/ *adj* [only before noun] *AmE* in the northern part of a particular state OPP **downstate**: *upstate New York* —**upstate** *adv*

up·stream /ˌʌpˈstriːm◂/ *adv* along a river, in the opposite direction from the way the water is flowing OPP **downstream**: *Fish instinctively fight their way upstream against the current.* —**upstream** *adj*

up·surge /ˈʌpsɜːdʒ $ -sɜːrdʒ/ *n* [C] **1** a sudden increase: **[+in]** *There was an upsurge in violence during June and July.* **2** a sudden strong feeling: **[+of]** *There was a genuine upsurge of religious feeling.*

up·swing /ˈʌpswɪŋ/ *n* [C] an improvement or increase in the level of something: **[+in/of]** *an upswing in economic growth*

up·take /ˈʌpteɪk/ *n* **1 be slow/quick on the uptake** *informal* to be slow or fast at understanding something **2** [singular] the number of people who use a service or accept something that is offered: *The uptake of some vaccinations fell as the media stirred up fears of possible side effects.* **3** [C,U] the rate at which a substance is taken into the body, a system etc: *the uptake of sugars by the blood*

up-ˈtempo *adj* moving or happening at a fast rate: *music with an up-tempo beat*

up·tight /ˈʌptaɪt, ʌpˈtaɪt/ *adj informal* **1** behaving in an angry way because you are feeling nervous and worried: **[+about]** *You have to learn to laugh instead of* ***getting***

uptight about things. **2** having strict traditional attitudes and seeming unable to relax

up·time /ˈʌptaɪm/ *n* [U] the period of time when a computer is working normally and is able to be used OPP **downtime**: *Some customers need 99% or better uptime from their mainframe computers.*

ˌup-to-ˈdate, **up to date** ●●○ *adj*
1 including all the latest information OPP **out-of-date**: **up-to-date information/data/figures/news etc** *They have access to up-to-date information through a computer database.* | **keep/bring sb up to date** (=to give someone all the newest information about something) *Our magazine will keep you up to date with fashion.*
2 modern or fashionable OPP **out-of-date**: **up-to-date equipment/facilities/technology etc** *up-to-date kitchen equipment* | **keep/bring sth up to date** (=to make something more modern) *The old system should be brought up to date.* THESAURUS ▶ MODERN

ˌup-to-the-ˈminute *adj* **1** including all the latest information: *The general lacked* ***up-to-the-minute information*** *at the crucial moment.* **2** very modern or fashionable: *beach resorts packed with up-to-the-minute facilities and entertainment*

up·town /ˌʌpˈtaʊn◂/ *adv AmE* in or towards an area of a city that is away from the centre, especially one where the streets have larger numbers in their names and where people have more money OPP **downtown**: *He now lives in an apartment a little farther uptown.* —**uptown** *adj*: *uptown neighborhoods* —**uptown** *n* [U]

up·turn /ˈʌptɜːn $ -tɜːrn/ *n* [C] an increase in the level of something, especially in business activity OPP **downturn**: **[+in]** *an upturn in the housing market* | *an* ***economic upturn***

up·turned /ˌʌpˈtɜːnd◂ $ -ɜːr-/ *adj* [usually before noun]
1 pointing or turning upwards: *He smiled down into her* ***upturned face***. **2** turned upside down: *I sat on an upturned box.* | *an upturned boat*

UPVC, **uPVC** /ˌjuː piː viː ˈsiː/ *n* [U] (***unplasticized polyvinyl chloride***) a type of plastic, used especially to make window frames: *UPVC double-glazed windows*

up·ward /ˈʌpwəd $ -wərd/ ●○○ *adj* [only before noun]
1 increasing to a higher level OPP **downward**: **upward trend/movement** *an upward trend in sales* | *a sharp upward movement in property prices* | *upward pressure on bank interest rates*
2 moving or pointing towards a higher position OPP **downward**: *Stroke the cream onto your skin in an upward direction.*

ˌupwardly ˈmobile *adj* moving up through the social classes and becoming richer: *the upwardly mobile middle classes* —**ˌupward moˈbility** *n* [U]

up·wards /ˈʌpwədz $ -wərdz-/ ●●○ (*also* **upward** *especially AmE*) *adv*
1 moving or pointing towards a higher position OPP **downwards**: *Pointing upwards, he indicated a large nest high in the tree.* | *The path began to climb steeply upwards.*
2 increasing to a higher level OPP **downwards**: *The expected rate of inflation was revised upwards.* | *Prices are moving upwards again.*
3 more than a particular amount, time etc SYN **over**: *children of 14* ***and upwards*** | *The meeting was attended by* ***upwards of*** (=over) *500 people.*

up·wind /ʌpˈwɪnd/ *adv* in the opposite direction to the way the wind is blowing OPP **downwind**

u·ra·ni·um /jʊˈreɪniəm/ *n* [U] a heavy white metal that is RADIOACTIVE and is used to produce NUCLEAR power and nuclear weapons. It is a chemical ELEMENT: symbol U

U·ra·nus /ˈjʊərənəs, jʊˈreɪnəs $ ˈjʊr-, jʊˈreɪ-/ *n* the PLANET that is seventh in order from the Sun: *William Herschel discovered Uranus in 1781.*

ur·ban /ˈɜːbən $ ˈɜːr-/ ●●○ W2 *adj* [only before noun]
1 relating to towns and cities OPP **rural** → **suburban**: *unemployment in* ***urban areas*** | *the deprived sections of the urban population* THESAURUS ▶ CITY
2 relating to music such as RAP, R & B, REGGAE etc that is mainly played by black singers and musicians

ur·bane /ɜːˈbeɪn $ ɜːr-/ *adj* behaving in a relaxed and confident way in social situations: *Neil was urbane, witty, direct, and honest.* —**urbanely** *adv* —**urbanity** /ɜːˈbænəti $ ɜːr-/ *n* [U]

ur·ban·ized (*also* **-ised** *BrE*) /ˈɜːbənaɪzd $ ˈɜːr-/ *adj*
1 an urbanized country or area has a lot of houses, factories, shops, offices etc: *the most* ***heavily urbanized*** *regions* **2** in an urbanized society, there are a lot of people who live and work in towns and cities: *During the 19th century, Britain became the world's first modern urbanized society.* —**urbanization** /ˌɜːbənaɪˈzeɪʃən $ ˌɜːrbənə-/ *n* [U]: *the transformation of the social structure by urbanization*

ˌurban ˈmyth (*also* **ˌurban ˈlegend**) *n* [C] a story about an unusual event which happened recently that a lot of people believe, although it is probably not true

ˌurban reˈnewal (*also* **urban regeneration**) *n* [U] the process of improving poor city areas by building new houses, shops etc: *an urban renewal program*

ˌurban ˈsprawl *n* [U] the spread of city buildings and houses into an area that used to be countryside, or the area in which this has happened: *planning policies designed to limit the growth of urban sprawl*

ur·chin /ˈɜːtʃɪn $ ˈɜːr-/ *n* [C] *old-fashioned* a poor dirty untidy child → SEA URCHIN

Ur·du /ˈʊəduː, ˈɜːduː $ ˈɜːrduː/ *n* [U] the official language of Pakistan, also used in India

-ure /jə $ jər/ *suffix* [in nouns] used to make nouns that show actions or results: *the closure (=closing) of the factory* | *exposure* | *failure*

u·re·thra /jʊˈriːθrə/ *n* [C] *technical* the tube through which waste liquid flows out of the body from the BLADDER and also through which the SEMEN of males flows

urge[1] /ɜːdʒ $ ɜːrdʒ/ ●●○ W3 *v* [T]
1 to strongly suggest that someone does something: **urge sb to do sth** *I got a note from Moira urging me to get in touch.* | **urge that** *He urged that a referendum should be held by December.* | **urge sth on/upon sb** *I have urged upon him the need for extreme secrecy.* | *The charity urged quick action.* THESAURUS ▶ ADVISE, RECOMMEND
2 [always + adv/prep] *formal* to make someone or something move by shouting, pushing them etc: **urge sb/sth forward** *He urged her forward, his hand under her elbow.* | **urge sb into/towards sth** *She began urging him towards the front door.*

urge sb ↔ **on** *phr v* to encourage a person or animal to work harder, go faster etc: *Urged on by the crowd, the Italian team scored two more goals.*

urge[2] ●●○ *n* [C] a strong wish or need SYN **desire**: **urge to do sth** *He could no longer* ***resist*** *the* ***urge*** *to go and see Amanda.* | *Suddenly she had an overwhelming urge to be with her son.*

ur·gen·cy /ˈɜːdʒənsi $ ˈɜːr-/ ●○○ *n* [U]
1 the need to deal with something immediately because it is very important: *The issue should be discussed* ***as a matter of urgency***. | *Despite the crisis, there appeared to be no* ***sense of urgency***.
2 *formal* the feeling of wanting something immediately: *Emilia heard the urgency in his voice.*

ur·gent /ˈɜːdʒənt $ ˈɜːr-/ ●●○ S3 *adj*
1 very important and needing to be dealt with immediately: *He was* ***in urgent need of*** *medical attention.* | *The report called for* ***urgent action*** *to reduce lead in petrol.* | *an urgent message*
2 *formal* done or said in a way that shows that you want something to be dealt with immediately: *an urgent whisper* —**urgently** *adv*

urgh /ɜːg, ɜːx $ ɜːrg, ɜːrx/ *interjection* said when you have seen, heard, or tasted something that you think is extremely unpleasant SYN **ugh**

u·ric /ˈjʊərɪk $ ˈjʊr-/ *adj* relating to URINE

u·ri·nal /ˈjʊərənəl, jʊˈraɪ- $ ˈjʊrə-/ *n* [C] a type of toilet for men to urinate into, usually attached to a wall

U

u·ri·na·ry /ˈjʊərənəri $ ˈjʊrəneri/ *adj technical* relating to urine or the parts of your body through which urine passes: *the urinary tract*

u·ri·nate /ˈjʊərəneɪt $ ˈjʊr-/ *v* [I] *technical* to get rid of urine from your body —**urination** /ˌjʊərəˈneɪʃən $ ˌjʊr-/ *n* [U]

u·rine /ˈjʊərɪn $ ˈjʊr-/ *n* [U] the yellow liquid waste that comes out of the body from the BLADDER

URL /ˌjuː ɑːr ˈel/ *n* [C] *technical* (***uniform resource locator***) a website address

urn /ɜːn $ ɜːrn/ *n* [C] **1** a decorated container, especially one that is used for holding the ASHes of a dead body **2** a metal container that holds a large amount of tea or coffee

u·rol·o·gist /jʊˈrɒlədʒɪst $ -ˈrɑː-/ *n* [C] a doctor who treats conditions relating to the URINARY system and men's sexual organs —**urology** *n* [U] —**urological** /ˌjʊərəˈlɒdʒɪkəl◂ $ ˌjʊrəˈlɑː-/ *adj*

us /əs, s; *strong* ʌs/ ●●● S1 W1 *pron*

1 [the object form of 'we'] used by the person speaking or writing to refer to himself or herself and one or more other people: *Please help us.* | *He arranged for us all to have a drink.* | *She's invited us both.* | *My mother is coming to stay with us.* | *Send us a donation now.* | **us women/men/teachers etc** *Life is hard for us women.*

2 people in general: *Global warming will affect all of us.*

3 *BrE spoken* used instead of 'me'. Many people think this use is incorrect: *Give us a kiss.*

US, the (*also* **the U.S.**) /ˌjuː ˈes◂/ the United States —**US** *adj*: *the US Navy*

us·a·ble /ˈjuːzəbəl/ *adj* something that is usable can be used: *The computer language involved was readily usable.* | *usable information*

us·age /ˈjuːsɪdʒ, ˈjuːz-/ ●○○ *n*

1 [C,U] the way that words are used in a language: *a book on modern English usage*

2 [U] the way in which something is used, or the amount of it that is used: *Water usage is increasing.*

USB /ˌjuː es ˈbiː/ *n* [C] (***universal serial bus***) a system used to connect equipment such as a MOUSE or printer to a computer using wires so that all the equipment can work together: *Many USB devices come with their own built-in cable.*

USˈB drive *n* [C] a small piece of electronic equipment that uses FLASH MEMORY to store information and can be fitted into a computer SYN **flash drive**

use¹ /juːz/ ●●● S1 W1 *v*

1 USE STH [T] if you use a particular tool, method, service, ability etc, you do something with that tool, by means of that method etc, for a particular purpose: *Can I use your phone?* | *I'll show you which room you can use.* | *I always use the same shampoo.* | *Use your imagination when planning meals.* | *She booked the flight using a false name.* | **easy/difficult/simple etc to use** *Drop-down menus make the program very easy to use.* | **use sth for (doing) sth** *They were using animals for scientific experiments.* | *Bob uses the van for picking up groceries.* | **use sth as sth** *My parents use the house as a holiday home.* | **use sth to do sth** *Most people now use their cars to go shopping.* | **use force** (=use violent methods)

2 AMOUNT OF STH [T] to take an amount of something from a supply of food, gas, money etc: *We use about £40 worth of electricity a month.* | *Standard washing machines use about 40 gallons of water.*

3 TREAT SB UNFAIRLY [T] to make someone do something for you in order to get something you want: *Can't you see that Howard is just using you?* | *Gerald had been **using** her **for** his **own ends**.*

4 AN ADVANTAGE [T] to take advantage of a situation: **use sth to do sth** *She used her position as manager to get jobs for her friends.*

5 could use sth *spoken* if you say you could use something, you mean you would really like to have it: *I could use a drink.*

6 WORD [T] to say or write a particular word or phrase: *We use the word 'hardware' to describe the actual machine.* | *Don't **use** bad **language**.*

7 DRUGS [I,T] to regularly take illegal drugs → USED TO

THESAURUS

use to use something for a particular purpose: *Do you mind if I use your phone?* | *They rebuilt the church using local stone.* | *We use a range of different methods.*

make use of sth to use something that is available to you: *Staff can make use of a wide range of facilities.* | *She made full use of her contacts within the organization.*

employ *formal* to use a particular method or skill in order to achieve something: *The surgeons employed a new technique.* | *They employed every means at their disposal* (=every available method).

utilize *formal* to use something that is available to you, for a practical purpose: *The company has developed a new way to utilize solar energy.* | *a better way of utilizing the space*

exploit to use something as fully and effectively as possible, or to use something that will give you an advantage over your opponent: *The country's natural resources have not yet been fully exploited.* | *He was quick to exploit any weakness in his opponent's argument.*

apply to use something such as a method, idea, or system in a particular situation: *New technology is being applied to almost every industrial process.* | *I wanted to apply the things that I had learned on the course.*

draw on sth to use information, knowledge, or experience that you have learned in the past: *He was able to draw on his own experience as a diplomat when he was writing the book.*

resort to sth to use violence, force, threats etc as a way of achieving something: *Extremists on both sides resort to violence.* | *We are prepared to resort to force if necessary.*

use sth ↔ **up** *phr v* to use all of something: *She's used up all the hot water.*

use² /juːs/ ●●● S1 W1 *n*

1 [singular, U] the action or fact of using something: *an exit for use in emergencies* | **[+of]** *the increasing use of computers in education*

2 [C] a purpose for which something can be used: *Robots **have** many different **uses** in modern industry.* | **have/find a use for sth** *The cupboard is full of things I can never find a use for.*

3 make use of sth to use something that is available in order to achieve something or get an advantage for yourself: *We will make use of her vast experience.* | *There is an answering machine for you to make use of.* | *Try to **make good use of** your time.*

4 put sth to (good) use to use something such as knowledge or skills for a particular purpose: *a job where her management skills can be put to good use*

5 the use of sth the ability or right to use something: *Joe's given me the use of his office till he gets back.* | *He **lost the use of** both **legs** as a result of the accident.*

6 be (of) no use (to sb) to be completely useless: *You needed blankets to keep warm because the heating was no use.* | *Take this – it's of no use to me anymore.*

7 it's no use doing sth *spoken* used to tell someone not to do something because it will have no effect: *It's no use complaining.*

8 it's no use! *spoken* used to say that you are going to stop doing something because you do not think it will be successful: *Oh, it's no use! I can't fix it.*

9 what's the use (of sth) *spoken* used to say that something seems to be a waste of time: *What's the use of decorating the house if we are going to sell it?*

10 be in use a machine, place etc that is in use is being used: *Electric vehicles built in 1920 were still in use in the 1950s.*

11 for the use of sb provided for a particular person or group of people to use: *a bar for the use of the guests*

12 be of use (to sb/sth) to be useful: *He was charged with having information likely to be of use to terrorists.*
13 come into use (*also* **bring sth into use**) to start being used, or to start using something: *Computers first came into use in the early 1950s.*
14 go/be out of use a machine, place etc that goes out of use or is out of use is not being used: *Some 4,000 railway stations have gone out of use since the 1960s.*
15 have no use for sb/sth to have no respect for someone or something: *She has no use for people who are always complaining.*
16 sth/sb has their uses *spoken* used, often humorously, to say that something or someone can sometimes be useful, even though it may not seem that way: *Being stubborn can have its uses.*
17 [C] one of the meanings of a word, or the way that a particular word is used

used¹ /juːst/ ●●● S1 W2 *adj* **be/get used to (doing) sth** to have experienced something so that it no longer seems surprising, difficult, strange etc: *I do the dishes every day, so I'm used to it.* | *I can't get used to the idea that you're grown up now.*

used² /juːzd/ ●●○ *adj*
1 used cars/clothes etc cars, clothes etc that have already had an owner SYN **second-hand**: *a used car salesman*
2 dirty or not in good condition any longer, as a result of being used: *a used tissue*

used to /ˈjuːst tuː/ ●●● S1 W2 *modal verb*
1 if something used to happen, it happened regularly or all the time in the past, but does not happen now: *He used to go to our school.* | *We're eating out more often than we used to.* | **did not use to do sth** *You didn't use to eat chips when you were younger.* | **used not to do sth** *BrE*: *You used not to fuss like this.* | **never used to do sth** *spoken*: *It never used to bother me.* | **did sb use to do sth?** *Did you use to go to church regularly?*
2 if a particular situation used to exist, it existed for a period of time in the past, but does not exist now: *Jimmy used to be a friend of mine.* | *There used to be a large car park on this site.* | **did not use to be/do sth** *Why are you so bad-tempered? You didn't use to be like this.* | **did sb/sth use to be/do sth?** *Did this building use to be a hotel?* | *Where did you use to live before you came to Manchester?*

USAGE: Used to do sth, be used to sth
• Don't confuse **I used to do something** and **I am used to (doing) something**.
• You say *I used to live in Paris* when you lived in Paris in the past, but you do not live there now. In this meaning, **used to** is followed by the base form of the verb (=the infinitive without 'to').
• You say *I'm used to living in Paris* when you are accustomed to living in Paris because you have lived there for some time.
• **Be used to** is followed by an **-ing** form, not the infinitive. ✗ Don't say: *I'm used to live in Paris.*
GRAMMAR GUIDE ▶ VERBS

use·ful /ˈjuːsfəl/ ●●● S1 W1 *adj* helping you to do or get what you want OPP **useless**: *useful information* | *A little Japanese can be really useful.* | **[+for]** *The space under the desk is useful for storing CDs.* | **[+to]** *techniques that could be useful to teachers* | *Can you come and* ***make yourself useful*** (=help people to do something)? —**usefully** *adv*

THESAURUS
useful something that is useful makes it easier for you to do something: *He gave me some useful advice.* | *a useful thing to know*
handy *informal* useful – used especially about something that is convenient and easy to use: *a handy little booklet* | *The book is full of handy hints.* | *I always keep old jars – you never know when they might* ***come in handy*** (=be useful).
helpful useful because it helps you to do something: *This drug can be helpful in treating depression.* | *helpful advice* | *helpful suggestions*
of use [not before noun] if someone or something is of use, they are useful for you when you are doing something: *I hope you'll find the book of use.* | *He wants to be of use.*
worthwhile if doing something is worthwhile, it is useful for you and you benefit from doing it: *The training was certainly worthwhile.* | *a worthwhile experience*

VERY USEFUL
valuable very useful in helping you do something: *His information was very valuable to the police.* | *The course was a valuable experience for me.* | *a valuable contribution*
invaluable extremely useful in helping you do something: *His help was invaluable.* | *The drug could be invaluable for treating cancer patients.*
indispensable someone or something that is indispensable is so useful and important that you cannot do something without them: *For walkers, a good compass is indispensable.* | *He became an indispensable part of the team.*
be great for sth *informal* to be very useful for doing something: *The bag is great for taking on holiday.*

use·ful·ness /ˈjuːsfəlnəs/ ●○○ *n* [U] the state of being useful or the degree to which something is useful: **[+of]** *There are doubts as to the usefulness of this approach* (=it may not be useful). | *As a commuter service, the ferry has* ***outlived*** *its* ***usefulness*** (=is no longer useful).

use·less /ˈjuːsləs/ ●●○ *adj*
1 not useful or effective in any way OPP **useful**: *The doctor concluded that further treatment would be useless.* | *a website full of* ***useless information*** | **virtually/completely/totally etc useless** *Water had got into the radio, and now it was completely useless.* | **[+for]** *The land is useless for growing crops.* | **it is useless to do sth** *It was useless to complain.* | **worse than useless** (=not useful and in fact causing harm or problems) *The map was so out-of-date it was worse than useless.*
2 *informal* unable or unwilling to do anything properly: *Don't ask Tim to fix it. He's completely useless.* —**uselessly** *adv* —**uselessness** *n* [U]

us·er /ˈjuːzə $ -ər/ ●●● S3 W1 *n* [C]
1 someone or something that uses a product, service etc: *road users* | *a computer user* | *library users*
2 someone who takes illegal drugs: *Drug users were warned about the dangers of sharing needles.* → END USER

ˈuser fee *n* [C] *AmE* a tax on a service provided for the public

ˌuser-ˈfriendly ●○○ *adj* easy to use, understand, or operate: *a user-friendly guide to computing* THESAURUS ▶ EASY —**user-friendliness** *n* [U]

ˈuser ˌgroup *n* [C] **1** a group of people who have the same interests and use a particular product or service **2** a group of people who exchange information on the Internet about computers

ˌuser ˈinterface *n* [C] how a computer program looks on screen and how the user enters COMMANDS and information into the program

ˈuser name, **username** /ˈjuːzəneɪm/ ●●○ (*also* **ˈuser IˌD**) *n* [C] a name or special word that proves who you are and allows you to enter a computer system or use the Internet: *Please enter your user name and password and click 'OK'.*

ush·er¹ /ˈʌʃə $ -ər/ ●○○ *v* [T always + adv/prep] to help someone to get from one place to another, especially by showing them the way: **usher sb into/to sth** *He ushered her into the room.* | **usher sb in** *She stood back and ushered him in.* THESAURUS ▶ LEAD
usher sth ↔ **in** *phr v* to cause something new to start, or to be at the start of something new: *The discovery of oil ushered in an era of employment and prosperity.*

usher² *n* [C] **1** someone who shows people to their seats at a theatre, cinema, wedding etc **2** *BrE* someone

U

who works in a law court whose job is to guide people in and out of the courtrooms

ush·er·ette /ˌʌʃəˈret/ *n* [C] *especially BrE old-fashioned* a woman who works in a cinema, showing people to their seats

ˌUS ˈMasters ˌTournament, the an important US golf competition

USP /ˌjuː es ˈpiː/ *n* [C] (***unique selling proposition***) a feature of a product that makes it different from other similar products, and therefore more attractive to people who might buy it

u·su·al /ˈjuːʒuəl, ˈjuːʒəl/ ●●● S2 W2 *adj*
1 happening, done, or existing most of the time or in most situations: *Make a cheese sauce in the usual way.* | *I'll meet you at the usual time.* | **longer/higher/worse etc than usual** *It is taking longer than usual for orders to reach our customers.* | *She ate twice* ***as*** *much* ***as usual.*** | **it is usual (for sb) to do sth** *It's usual to keep records of all expenses.*
2 as usual in the way that happens or exists most of the time: *As usual, they'd left the children at home with Susan.* | *They didn't invite any women, as usual.*
3 as per usual *spoken* used to say that something bad that often happens has just happened again: *He just laughed at me, as per usual.*
4 the usual *spoken* **a)** used for talking about something that usually happens, is usually done etc: *'What was he going on about this time?' 'Oh, the usual.'* **b)** the drink that you usually have, especially in a particular bar: *A pint of the usual please, Paul.*
5 not your usual self behaving differently from the way you usually behave, especially by seeming worried or upset about something: *Keith doesn't seem his usual self these days.*

u·su·al·ly /ˈjuːʒuəli, ˈjuːʒəli/ ●●● S1 W1 *adv* used to talk about what happens on most occasions or in most situations SYN **generally**: *Women usually live longer than men.* | *Usually I wear black, grey, or brown.* | *The drive usually takes 15 or 20 minutes.*

GRAMMAR: Word order

• **Usually** can come before the verb or at the start of the sentence: *She usually takes the bus.* | *Usually she takes the bus.*
• **Usually** normally comes after 'be' or an auxiliary verb such as 'do' or 'have': *She is usually late.* | *I don't usually come here.* ✗ Don't say: *She usually is late.* | *I usually don't come here.*
GRAMMAR GUIDE ▸ ADVERBS

u·sur·er /ˈjuːʒərə $ -ər/ *n* [C] *formal old-fashioned* someone who lends money to people and makes them pay INTEREST[1](4)

u·su·ri·ous /juːˈzjuəriəs $ juːˈʒur-/ *adj formal* a usurious price or rate of INTEREST[1](4) is unfairly high

u·surp /juːˈzɜːp $ -ˈsɜːrp/ *v* [T] *formal* to take someone else's power, position, job etc when you do not have the right to: *There were a couple of attempts to usurp the young king.* —**usurper** *n* [C] —**usurpation** /ˌjuːzɜːˈpeɪʃən $ -sɜːr-/ *n* [U]

u·su·ry /ˈjuːʒəri/ *n* [U] *formal old-fashioned* the practice of lending money to people and making them pay INTEREST[1](4): *In medieval times, it was illegal for Christians to practise usury.*

u·ten·sil /juːˈtensəl/ ●○○ *n* [C] a thing such as a knife, spoon etc that you use when you are cooking: *kitchen utensils*

u·te·rus /ˈjuːtərəs/ *n* (*plural* **uteruses**) [C] the organ in a woman or female MAMMAL where babies develop SYN **womb** —**uterine** /-raɪn/ *adj*

u·til·i·tar·i·an /juːˌtɪləˈteəriən $ -ˈter-/ *adj*
1 *formal* intended to be useful and practical rather than attractive or comfortable: *ugly utilitarian buildings*
2 based on a belief in utilitarianism → MATERIALISTIC

u·til·i·tar·i·an·is·m /juːˌtɪləˈteəriənɪzəm $ -ˈter-/ *n* [U] the political belief that an action is good if it helps the largest number of people

u·til·i·ty /juːˈtɪləti/ ●○○ AWL *n* (*plural* **utilities**)
1 [C usually plural] a service such as gas or electricity provided for people to use: *Does your rent include utilities?*
2 [C] a piece of computer SOFTWARE that has a particular use: *It's a simple shareware utility that allows you to print signs and banners.*
3 [U] *formal* the quality of being useful, or the degree to which something is useful

uˈtility ˌpole *n* [C] *AmE* a tall wooden pole for supporting telephone and electric wires

uˈtility ˌroom *n* [C] a room in a house where washing machines, FREEZERS etc are kept

u·til·ize (*also* **-ise** *BrE*) /ˈjuːtəlaɪz/ ●○○ AWL *v* [T] *formal* to use something for a particular purpose: *We must consider how best to utilize what resources we have.* THESAURUS ▸ USE —**utilizable** *adj* —**utilization** /ˌjuːtəlaɪˈzeɪʃən $ -lə-/ *n* [U]

REGISTER
In everyday English, people usually say **use** rather than **utilize**: *The money will be* ***used*** *to build a new sports hall.*

ut·most¹ /ˈʌtməust $ -moust/ (*also* **uttermost**) *adj* **the utmost importance/respect/care etc** the greatest possible importance etc: *a matter of the utmost importance* | *I have the utmost respect for her accomplishments.* | *Baldwin treated the matter with the utmost seriousness.*

utmost² *n* [singular] the most that can be done: **to the utmost** *Both runners had pushed themselves to the utmost.* | *The medical staff* ***did*** *their* ***utmost*** (=tried as hard as they could) *to save the patient's life.*

u·to·pi·a, **Utopia** /juːˈtəupiə $ -ˈtou-/ *n* [C,U] an imaginary perfect world where everyone is happy → **dystopia** —**utopian** *adj*: *a utopian society* —**utopianism** *n* [U]

ut·ter¹ /ˈʌtə $ -ər/ ●○○ *adj* [only before noun] complete - used especially to emphasize that something is very bad, or that a feeling is very strong: *That's* ***utter nonsense!*** | *This company treats its employees with* ***utter contempt.*** | *I watched in* ***complete and utter*** *horror as he pulled out a gun.* | *fifteen years of utter confusion*

utter² ●○○ *v* [T] *formal*
1 to say something: *'You fool!' she uttered in disgust.* | *Cantor nodded without* ***uttering*** *a* ***word.***
2 to make a sound with your voice, especially with difficulty: *The wounded prisoner uttered a groan.*

ut·ter·ance /ˈʌtərəns/ *n formal* **1** [C] something you say: *Politicians are judged by their public utterances.* **2** [U] the action of saying something

ut·ter·ly /ˈʌtəli $ -ər-/ ●●○ *adv* [+adj/adv] completely - used especially to emphasize that something is very bad, or that a feeling is very strong: *You look utterly miserable.*

ut·ter·most /ˈʌtəməust $ -ərmoust/ *adj literary or formal* UTMOST

U-turn /ˈjuː tɜːn $ ˌjuː ˈtɜːrn/ *n* [C] **1** a turn that you make in a car, on a bicycle etc, so that you go back in the direction you came from: **make/do a U-turn** *He made a quick U-turn and sped away.* **2** a complete change of ideas, plans etc: **make/do a U-turn** *Critics accused the government of doing a U-turn on its promise to increase education spending.*

UV /ˌjuː ˈviː/ *adj* (***ultraviolet***) UV light cannot be seen by people, but is responsible for making your skin darker when you are in the sun: **UV light/radiation/rays etc** *the sun's harmful UV rays*

u·vu·la /ˈjuːvjələ/ *n* (*plural* **uvulae** /-liː/) [C] *technical* a small soft piece of flesh which hangs down from the top of your mouth at the back

Vv

V, v /viː/ (*plural* **V's, v's**) *n* **1** [C,U] the 22nd letter of the English alphabet **2** the number 5 in the system of ROMAN NUMERALS **3** [C usually singular] something that has a shape like the letter V: *She cut the material into a V.*

v. (*also* **v** *BrE*) **1 a** written abbreviation of ***verb*** **2** *BrE informal* the written abbreviation of ***very*** **3** a written abbreviation of ***versus*** (=against), used in the names of legal TRIALS, or in Britain when talking about games in which two teams or players play against each other: *the Roe v. Wade case | England v Australia* **4** the written abbreviation of ***volt*** or ***volts***

vac /væk/ *n* [C usually singular] *BrE informal* a university VACATION[1](3)

va·can·cy /ˈveɪkənsi/ ●○○ *n* (*plural* **vacancies**)
1 [C] a job that is available for someone to start doing: *There are still two vacancies on the school board.* | **[+for]** *We* ***have*** *no* ***vacancies*** *for photographers at the moment.* | *The council is making every effort to* ***fill*** *the* ***vacancies***. | *information about* ***job vacancies*** THESAURUS ▸ JOB
2 [C] a room in a hotel or building that is not being used and is available for someone to stay in: *Let me see if we* ***have*** *a* ***vacancy*** *for tonight.* | *'****No vacancies****', the sign read.*
3 [U] *written* lack of interest or thought: *His mouth fell open and the look of vacancy returned.*

va·cant /ˈveɪkənt/ ●●○ *adj*
1 a vacant seat, building, room, or piece of land is empty and available for someone to use: *Only a few apartments were still vacant.* | *There was only a* ***vacant lot*** (=empty unused area of land in a city) *where her house used to be.* THESAURUS ▸ EMPTY

> **REGISTER**
> In everyday English, people usually say that a seat or room is **free** rather than **vacant**: *Is this seat* ***free****?*

2 *formal* a job or position in an organization that is vacant is available for someone to start doing: **fall vacant** *BrE* (=become vacant) *He was offered the position of headmaster when it fell vacant.* | **situations vacant** *BrE* (=the part of a newspaper where jobs are advertised)
3 vacant expression/look/stare etc *written* an expression that shows that someone does not seem to be thinking about anything: *He gazed at me with vacant eyes.* —**vacantly** *adv*: *Cindy was staring vacantly into space.*

ˌvacant posˈsession *n* [U] *BrE technical* **house/flat with vacant possession** a home or other building whose previous owner has left, so that the new owner can move into it immediately

va·cate /vəˈkeɪt, veɪ- $ ˈveɪkeɪt/ *v* [T] *formal* **1** to leave a job or position so that it is available for someone else to do: *Clay will vacate the position on June 19.* **2** to leave a seat, room etc so that someone else can use it: *Guests must vacate their rooms by 11:00.*

va·ca·tion[1] /vəˈkeɪʃən $ veɪ-/ ●●● S2 W3 *n*
1 [C,U] *especially AmE* a holiday, or time spent not working: *We're planning a vacation in Europe.* | **on vacation** *He's on vacation this week.* | *We're planning to go on vacation soon.*
2 [U] *especially AmE* the number of days, weeks etc that you are allowed as paid holiday by your employer: *How much vacation do you get at your new job?* | *I think I have four* ***vacation days*** *left.* | *Employees are entitled to four weeks'* ***paid vacation*** *annually.*
3 a) [C] *BrE* one of the periods of time when a university is closed: **the Christmas/Easter/summer/long vacation** **b)** [C,U] *AmE* one of the periods of time when a school or university is closed: **Christmas/spring/summer vacation**

This graph shows how common the nouns **holiday** and **vacation** are in British and American English.

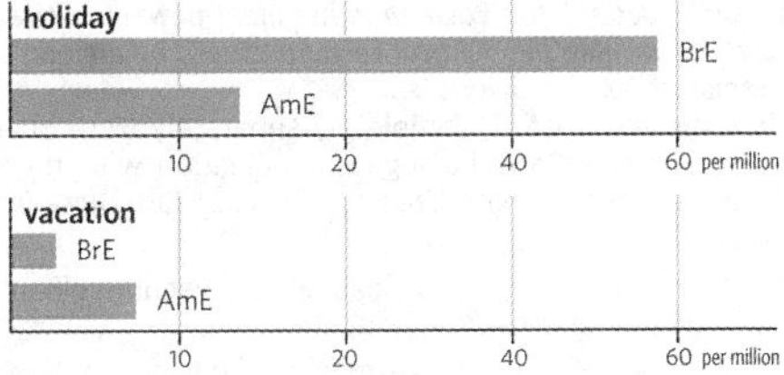

In British English the word **holiday** is used to mean a time of rest from work or school, or a period of time when you travel to another place for pleasure. Americans use **vacation** for this meaning, and to refer to a period when universities are closed. In both American and British English **holiday** is used to mean a day fixed by law on which people do not have to go to work or school. In British English **vacation** is used to refer to a period when universities are closed.

COLLOCATIONS

VERBS
take/have a vacation *We usually take a vacation once a year.*
go on vacation *I'm going on vacation next month.*
need a vacation *You're working too hard. You need a vacation.*

ADJECTIVES/NOUN + vacation
a summer vacation *What did you do on your summer vacation?*
a family vacation *We had to cancel the family vacation.*
a long vacation *She decided to take a long vacation.*
a two-week/three-day etc vacation

vacation + NOUN
a vacation spot (=a place for a vacation) *The island is my favorite vacation spot.*
a vacation day (=a day away from work on vacation)

COMMON ERRORS
⚠ Don't say 'have vacation'. Say **be on vacation**.

vacation[2] *v* [I] *AmE* to go somewhere for a holiday: **[+in/at]** *The Bernsteins are vacationing in Europe.*

va·ca·tion·er /vəˈkeɪʃənə $ veɪˈkeɪʃənər/ *n* [C] *AmE* someone who has gone somewhere for a holiday SYN **holidaymaker** *BrE*

vac·cin·ate /ˈvæksəneɪt/ *v* [T] to protect a person or animal from a disease by giving them a vaccine SYN **immunize**: **vaccinate sb against sth** *All children should be vaccinated against measles.* —**vaccination** /ˌvæksəˈneɪʃən/ *n* [C,U]: *a flu vaccination*

vac·cine /ˈvæksiːn $ vækˈsiːn/ ●○○ *n* [C,U] a substance which contains a weak form of the BACTERIA or VIRUS that causes a disease and is used to protect people from that disease: *a polio vaccine* | *Doctors worried that there would not be enough vaccine for everyone who needed it.*

vac·il·late /ˈvæsəleɪt/ *v* [I] *formal* to continue to change your opinions, decisions, ideas etc SYN **waver**: **[+between]** *Her parents vacillated between different approaches to discipline.* —**vacillation** /ˌvæsəˈleɪʃən/ *n* [C,U]

VActor /ˈvæktə $ -ər/ *n* [C] *trademark* (***virtual actor***) an actor who seems like a real person, but who is an image made using a computer SYN **synthespian**

va·cu·i·ty /vəˈkjuːəti, væ- $ væ-/ *n* [U] *formal* lack of intelligent, interesting, or serious thought

vac·u·ous /ˈvækjuəs/ *adj formal* showing no intelligence or having no useful purpose: *a vacuous expression* | *a vacuous romantic novel*

vac·u·um[1] /ˈvækjuəm, -kjʊm/ ●●○ *n*
1 [C] a space that is completely empty of all gas, especially one from which all the air has been taken away

2 [C] a vacuum cleaner
3 [singular] a situation in which someone or something is missing or lacking: **create/leave a vacuum (in sth)** *Her husband's death left a vacuum in her life.* | **power/political/moral etc vacuum** *the political vacuum caused by the ban on Communist Party activity*
4 in a vacuum existing completely separately from other people or things and having no connection with them: *The process of learning a language does not take place in a vacuum.*

vacuum² ●●○ *v* [I,T] to clean using a vacuum cleaner → see picture at CLEAN²

ˈvacuum ˌcleaner *n* [C] a machine that cleans floors by sucking up dirt SYN **Hoover** *BrE*

ˈvacuum ˌflask *n* [C] *BrE* a special container that keeps liquids hot or cold SYN **thermos**

ˈvacuum-ˌpacked / $ ˌ... ˈ.◂/ *adj* vacuum-packed food is in a container from which most of the air has been removed, so that the food will stay fresh for longer

ˈvacuum ˌtube *n* [C] *AmE* a VALVE(3)

vag·a·bond /ˈvægəbɒnd $ -bɑːnd/ *n* [C] *especially literary* someone who has no home and travels from place to place SYN **tramp**

va·ga·ries /ˈveɪgəriz/ *n* [plural] *formal* unexpected changes in a situation or someone's behaviour, that you cannot control but which have an effect on your life: **[+of]** *the vagaries of the English weather*

va·gi·na /vəˈdʒaɪnə/ *n* [C] the passage between a woman's outer sexual organs and her UTERUS —**vaginal** /vəˈdʒaɪnl $ ˈvædʒɪnəl/ *adj*

va·gran·cy /ˈveɪgrənsi/ *n* [U] the criminal offence of living on the street and begging (BEG) from people

va·grant /ˈveɪgrənt/ *n* [C] *formal* someone who has no home or work, especially someone who BEGS SYN **tramp**

vague /veɪg/ ●●○ S3 *adj*
1 unclear because someone does not give enough detailed information or does not say exactly what they mean: *The governor gave only a vague outline of his tax plan.* | **[+about]** *Julia was vague about where she had been and what she had been doing.*
2 have a vague idea/feeling/recollection etc (that) to think that something might be true or that you remember something, although you cannot be sure: *Larry had the vague feeling he'd done something embarrassing the night before.*
3 not having a clear shape or form SYN **indistinct**: *The vague shape of a figure loomed through the mist.* —**vagueness** *n* [U]

vague·ly /ˈveɪgli/ ●○○ *adv*
1 slightly OPP **clearly**: *I vaguely remember a woman in a red dress standing outside the door.* | *There was something vaguely familiar about him.* | *I was vaguely aware of another figure by the door.*
2 not clearly or exactly: *His statement was very vaguely worded.*
3 in a way that shows you are not thinking about what you are doing: *He smiled vaguely at the ceiling.*

vain /veɪn/ ●○○ *adj*
1 someone who is vain is too proud of their good looks, abilities, or position - used to show disapproval SYN **conceited**: *Men can be just as vain as women.* THESAURUS ▸ PROUD
2 in vain a) without success in spite of your efforts: *Police searched in vain for the missing gunman.* **b)** without purpose or without positive results: *Altman swore that his son's death would not be in vain.* → **take sb's name in vain** at NAME¹(12)
3 a vain attempt, hope, or search fails to achieve the result you wanted: **vain attempt/effort/bid** *The young mother died* ***in a vain attempt*** *to save her drowning son.*
4 vain threat/promise etc *literary* a threat, promise etc that is not worrying because the person cannot do what they say they will —**vainly** *adv*: *The instructor struggled vainly to open his parachute.*

vain·glo·ri·ous /veɪnˈglɔːriəs/ *adj literary* too proud of your own abilities, importance etc

val·ance, **valence** /ˈvæləns/ *n* [C] **1** a narrow piece of cloth that hangs from the edge of a shelf or from the frame of a bed to the floor **2** *especially AmE* a narrow piece of cloth above a window, covering the RAIL the curtains hang on SYN **pelmet** *BrE*

vale /veɪl/ *n* [C] *literary* **1** a broad low valley **2 a/the/this vale of tears** an expression used to mean the difficulties of life

val·e·dic·tion /ˌvæləˈdɪkʃən/ *n* [C,U] *formal* the act of saying goodbye, especially in a formal speech → **farewell**

val·e·dic·to·ri·an /ˌvælədɪkˈtɔːriən/ *n* [C] *AmE* the student who has received the best marks all the way through school, and who usually makes a speech at the GRADUATION ceremony

val·e·dic·to·ry /ˌvæləˈdɪktəri◂/ *n* (*plural* **valedictories**) [C] *formal* a speech or statement in which you say goodbye when you are leaving a school, job etc, especially on a formal occasion —**valedictory** *adj*: *a valedictory speech*

va·len·ce /ˈveɪləns/ (*also* **va·len·cy** /-lənsi/) *n* [C] *technical* **1** a measure of the power of atoms to combine together to form COMPOUNDS **2** another spelling of VALANCE

val·en·tine /ˈvæləntaɪn/ *n* [C] **1** someone you love or think is attractive, that you send a card to on St Valentine's Day: *Be my valentine.* **2** a card you send to someone on St Valentine's Day

val·et¹ /ˈvælət, ˈvæleɪ $ væˈleɪ/ *n* [C] **1** a male servant who looks after a man's clothes, serves his meals etc → **maid 2** (*also* **valet parker** *AmE*) someone who parks your car for you at a restaurant, hotel etc: *valet service*
3 *BrE* someone who cleans the clothes of people staying in a hotel

valet² *v* [T] *BrE* to clean someone's car: *a valeting service*

ˈvalet ˌparking (*also* **valet service**) *n* [U] *AmE* the service of having someone else park your car for you at a restaurant, hotel etc

val·i·ant /ˈvæliənt/ *adj* very brave, especially in a difficult situation SYN **courageous**: *Tarr threw himself in front of a train in a* ***valiant effort*** *to save the child.*

val·id /ˈvælɪd/ ●●○ AWL *adj*
1 a valid ticket, document, or agreement is legally or officially acceptable OPP **invalid**: *a valid credit card* | *Your return ticket is valid for three months.*
2 valid reason/argument/criticism etc a reason, argument etc that is based on what is reasonable or sensible: *Police officers must have a valid reason for stopping motorists.*
3 a valid PASSWORD, ID etc is one that will be accepted by a computer system OPP **invalid** —**validity** /vəˈlɪdəti/ *n* [U]: *I would question the validity of that statement.*

val·i·date /ˈvælədeɪt/ ●○○ AWL *v* [T]
1 *formal* to prove that something is true or correct, or to make a document or agreement officially and legally acceptable SYN **confirm**: *The Supreme Court has validated the lower court's interpretation of the law.* | *Many scientists plan to wait until the results of the study are validated by future research.*
2 to make someone feel that their ideas and feelings are respected and considered seriously: *Talking with people who think like you helps validate your feelings.*
3 *AmE* if a business validates a ticket from a PARKING GARAGE, it puts a special mark on it, showing that it will pay the parking costs —**validation** /ˌvæləˈdeɪʃən/ *n* [C,U]

va·lise /vəˈliːz $ vəˈliːs/ *n* [C] *old-fashioned* a small SUITCASE

Val·i·um /ˈvæliəm/ *n* [U] *trademark* a drug that makes people feel calmer and less anxious

val·ley /ˈvæli/ ●●● S3 W3 *n* [C] an area of lower land between two lines of hills or mountains, usually with a river flowing through it: *the San Fernando Valley*

val·our *BrE*, **valor** *AmE* /ˈvælə $ -ər/ *n* [U] *literary* great courage, especially in war: *medals awarded for valor* | *deeds of valour*

V

val·u·a·ble /ˈvæljuəbəl, -jəbəl $ ˈvæljəbəl/ ●●● W3 *adj*
1 worth a lot of money OPP **worthless**: *a valuable painting* | *Their most valuable belongings were locked in a safe in the bedroom.*
2 valuable help, advice, information etc is very useful because it helps you to do something: *Muriel has made a valuable contribution to our company's success.* | *a job that gave him valuable experience*
3 important because there is only a limited amount available SYN **precious**: *I won't waste any more of your valuable time.*

THESAURUS

WORTH A LOT OF MONEY

valuable worth a lot of money and expensive to buy: *a valuable piece of jewellery* | *The carpet is extremely valuable.*
priceless so valuable that it is impossible to calculate a price: *a priceless painting by Rembrandt* | *The statue is priceless.*
precious metal/stone precious metals such as gold, or stones such as diamonds are very rare and expensive : *Back in ancient times, coins contained precious metals.* | *The ring was set with dozens of precious stones.*
worth a lot/a fortune *informal* to be worth a very large amount of money: *Some rare baseball cards are worth a fortune.*

VERY SPECIAL AND IMPORTANT

precious very special and important to someone – used about people or things: *My family have always been precious to me.* | *His free time was very precious to him.* | *the place where I kept my most precious things*
prized very special and important to someone, so that they want very much to keep it or obtain it: *The book was one of his most **prized possessions**.* | *The shells are prized for their beauty* (=are considered to be very special).
treasured very special and important to someone, especially because it is connected with someone they love: *the case in which she kept her most **treasured possessions*** | *The holiday was now a treasured memory.* | *a treasured gift from her grandmother*
irreplaceable extremely special and important, especially because it is the only one of its kind: *The manuscripts are said to be irreplaceable.*

val·u·a·bles /ˈvæljuəbəlz, -jəbəlz $ -jəbəlz/ *n* [plural] things that you own that are worth a lot of money, such as jewellery, cameras etc: *Guests should leave their valuables in the hotel safe.*

val·u·a·tion /ˌvæljuˈeɪʃən/ *n* [C,U] **1** a professional judgment about how much something is worth: *The property has a valuation of $1.6 billion.* **2** a judgment about how effective or useful a particular idea or plan will be

val·ue¹ /ˈvælju:/ ●●● S2 W1 *n*
1 MONEY [C,U] the amount of money that something is worth: **[+of]** *The alterations doubled the value of the house.*
THESAURUS ▸ COST
2 WORTH THE MONEY PAID [C,U] used to say that something is worth what you pay for it, or not worth what you pay for it: **good/poor etc value (for money)** *BrE*, **a good/poor etc value** *AmE*: *The lunch special is really good value.* | *At only £45 a night, the hotel is great value for money.* | **value for money** *BrE* (=good value, or the quality of being good value) *Every customer is looking for value for money.*
3 IMPORTANCE/USEFULNESS [U] the importance or usefulness of something: **[+of]** *A group of athletes spoke to the students about the value of a college education.* | *the **nutritional value** of cereal* | **be of great/little value** *His research has been of little practical value.* | **place/put a high value on sth** *The Sioux Indians placed a high value on generosity.* | *The locket has great **sentimental value*** (=importance because it was a gift, it reminds you of someone etc).
4 of value a) worth a lot of money: *The thieves took nothing of value.* **b)** useful: *I hope this book will be of value to both teachers and students.*
5 INTERESTING QUALITY **shock/curiosity/novelty etc value** a good or interesting quality that something has because it is surprising, different, new etc: *After the initial curiosity value, the product's sales dropped considerably.*
6 IDEAS **values** [plural] your ideas about what is right and wrong, or what is important in life: *a return to **traditional values*** | *Your attitudes about sex are affected by your religious and **moral values**.* → FAMILY VALUES
7 AMOUNT [C] *technical* a mathematical quantity shown by a letter of the alphabet or sign: *Let x have the value 25.*

COLLOCATIONS

VERBS

increase/rise/go up in value *The dollar has been steadily increasing in value.*
fall/go down in value *There is a risk that the shares may fall in value.*
double in value *The house doubled in value over two years.*
put a value on sth (=say how much it is worth) *It's hard to put a value on something so unusual.*
the value of sth increases/rises *The value of the land had increased by $2m.*
the value of sth falls | **sth holds its value** (=its value does not fall over time)

ADJECTIVES/NOUN + value

high *You should insure any goods of high value.*
low *The low value of the dollar will benefit tourists.*
the market value (=the amount something can be sold for) *The mortgage is more than the house's current market value.*
the monetary/cash value (=the value of something in money) *They made an attempt to assess the cash value of the contract.*
the real value (=its value after considering inflation) | **the street value** (=the amount that users will pay for illegal drugs)

PHRASES

a fall/drop in value *There was a sudden drop in the value of oil.*
a rise/increase in value *We saw a rapid increase in the land's value.*

COMMON ERRORS

⚠ Don't say 'sth is value' or 'sth is very value'. Say **sth is good value** or **sth is very good value**.

value² ●●○ *v* [T]
1 to think that someone or something is important: *Shelley valued her privacy.* | **value sb/sth for sth** *Mr. Yeo valued Jan for her hard work.*
2 to decide how much money something is worth, by comparing it with similar things: *We decided to get the house valued.* | **be valued at sth** *Paintings valued at over $200,000 were stolen from her home.* GRAMMAR **Value** is usually passive in this meaning. —**valued** *adj*: *a valued friend*

ˌvalue-added ˈtax *n* [U] VAT

ˈvalue ˌjudgment *n* [C] a decision or judgment about how good something is, based on your personal opinions not facts

val·ue·less /ˈvælju:ləs/ *adj* **1** worth no money or very little money SYN **worthless**: *valueless currency* **2** having no worth, importance, or good qualities SYN **worthless**: *On most political issues my own opinion was pretty well valueless.*

val·u·er /ˈvæljuə $ -ər/ *n* [C] *BrE* someone whose job is to decide how much money something is worth

valve /vælv/ ●○○ *n* [C]
1 a part of a tube or pipe that opens and shuts like a door to control the flow of liquid, gas, air etc passing through it: *heart valves* → see picture at BICYCLE

V

2 the part on a TRUMPET or similar musical instrument that you press to change the sound of the note
3 *BrE* a closed glass tube used to control the flow of electricity in old radios, televisions etc SYN **vacuum tube** *AmE*

vamp /væmp/ *n* [C] *old-fashioned* a woman who uses her sexual attractiveness to make men do what she wants

vam·pire /ˈvæmpaɪə $ -paɪr/ *n* [C] in stories, a dead person that sucks people's blood by biting their necks

ˈvampire bat *n* [C] a South American BAT that sucks the blood of other animals

van /væn/ ●●● S2 W3 *n* [C]
1 a vehicle used especially for carrying goods, which is smaller than a TRUCK and has a roof and usually no windows at the sides: *a delivery van | a van driver*
2 *AmE* a large box-like car that can carry a lot of people
3 *especially BrE* a railway carriage with a roof and sides, used especially for carrying goods: *a luggage van*
4 be in the van (of sth) to be one of the people who are in front or who are leading a change: *She was in the van of the feminist movement.*

van·dal /ˈvændl/ *n* [C] someone who deliberately damages things, especially public property

van·dal·is·m /ˈvændəl-ɪzəm/ ●○○ *n* [U] the crime of deliberately damaging things, especially public property THESAURUS▸ CRIME

van·dal·ize (*also* **-ise** *BrE*) /ˈvændəl-aɪz/ ●○○ *v* [T] to damage or destroy things deliberately, especially public property: *The cemetery was vandalized during the night.* THESAURUS▸ DAMAGE

vane /veɪn/ *n* [C] a flat blade that is moved by wind or water to produce power to drive a machine

van·guard /ˈvæŋgɑːd $ -gɑːrd/ *n* **1 in/at the vanguard (of sth)** in the most advanced position of development: *The shop has always been in the vanguard of London fashion trends.* **2 the vanguard** the leading position at the front of an army or group of ships moving into battle, or the soldiers who are in this position

va·nil·la¹ /vəˈnɪlə/ ●●○ *n* [U] a substance used to give a special taste to ICE CREAM, cakes etc, made from the beans of a tropical plant

vanilla² ●●○ *adj*
1 having the taste of vanilla: *vanilla ice cream*
2 (*also* **plain-vanilla**) plain, ordinary, or uninteresting: *There are no plans for an inexpensive vanilla version of the software.*

V

van·ish /ˈvænɪʃ/ ●●○ *v* [I]
1 to disappear suddenly, especially in a way that cannot be easily explained: *My keys were here a minute ago but now they've vanished.* | **vanish without (a) trace/vanish off the face of the earth** (=disappear so that no sign remains) *The youngster vanished without a trace one day and has never been found.* | *The bird* ***vanished from sight***. | *She seemed to have just* ***vanished into thin air*** (=suddenly disappeared in a very mysterious way). THESAURUS▸ DISAPPEAR
2 to suddenly stop existing SYN **disappear**: **[+from]** *By the 1930s, the wolf had vanished from the American West.* | *Public support for the prime minister has now vanished.*

van·ish·ing·ly /ˈvænɪʃɪŋli/ *adv* **vanishingly small/improbable** extremely small or unlikely: *The chances of dying under anaesthetic are vanishingly small.*

ˈvanishing ˌpoint *n* [C usually singular] the point in the distance, especially on a picture, where parallel lines seem to meet

van·i·ty /ˈvænəti/ ●○○ *n* (*plural* **vanities**)
1 [U] too much PRIDE in yourself, so that you are always thinking about yourself and your appearance: *Sabrina had none of the vanity so often associated with beautiful women.*
2 [C] (*also* **vanity table**) a DRESSING TABLE
3 the vanity of sth *literary* the lack of importance of something compared to other things that are much more important

ˈvanity ˌcase *n* [C] a small bag used by a woman for carrying MAKE-UP etc

ˈvanity ˌplate *n* [C] a car NUMBER PLATE that has a combination of numbers or letters chosen by the owner, so that they spell a word that is connected with or describes the owner

ˈvanity ˌpress (*also* **ˈvanity ˌpublisher**) *n* [C usually singular] a company that writers pay to print their books

ˈvanity ˌtable *n* [C] *AmE* a DRESSING TABLE → see picture at TABLE¹

van·quish /ˈvæŋkwɪʃ/ *v* [T] *literary* to defeat someone or something completely

van·tage point /ˈvɑːntɪdʒ pɔɪnt $ ˈvæn-/ (*also* **vantage**) *n* [C] **1** a good position from which you can see something: *From my vantage point on the hill, I could see the whole procession.* **2** a way of thinking about things that comes from your own particular situation or experiences SYN **point of view**: *The whole dispute looked silly from my vantage point.*

vap·id /ˈvæpɪd/ *adj* lacking intelligence, interest, or imagination: *vapid conversation* —**vapidity** /væˈpɪdəti/ *n* [U]

va·por /ˈveɪpə $ -ər/ *n* [C,U] the American spelling of VAPOUR

va·por·ize (*also* **-ise** *BrE*) /ˈveɪpəraɪz/ *v* [I,T] to change into a vapour, or to make something, especially a liquid, do this

va·pour *BrE*, **vapor** *AmE* /ˈveɪpə $ -ər/ ●○○ *n* [C,U] a mass of very small drops of a liquid which float in the air, for example because the liquid has been heated → **evaporation**: *water vapour*

ˈvapour trail *BrE*, **vapor trail** *AmE* *n* [C] the white line that is left in the sky by a plane

var·i·a·ble¹ /ˈveəriəbəl $ ˈver-/ ●●○ AWL *adj*
1 likely to change often → **vary**: *Expect variable cloudiness and fog tomorrow.* | *Interest rates can be* ***highly variable***. | **variable in size/shape/colour etc** *These fish are highly variable in color and pattern.*
2 sometimes good and sometimes bad: *The quality of pork is often less variable than beef.*
3 able to be changed: *The heater has variable temperature settings.* —**variably** *adv* —**variability** /ˌveəriəˈbɪləti $ ˌver-/ *n* [U]

variable² ●○○ AWL *n* [C]
1 something that may be different in different situations, so that you cannot be sure what will happen OPP **constant**: *There are too many variables in the experiment to predict the result accurately.*
2 *technical* a mathematical quantity which can represent several different amounts OPP **constant**

var·i·ance /ˈveəriəns $ ˈver-/ AWL *n* **1 be at variance (with sb/sth)** *formal* if two people or things are at variance with each other, they do not agree or are very different: *Tradition and culture are often at variance with the needs of modern living.* **2** [C,U] *formal* the amount by which two or more things are different or by which they change → **differential**: *a price variance of 5%* **3** [C] *AmE law* the official permission to do something different from what is normally allowed: *The developer requested a variance to build a shopping center on the east side of town.*

var·i·ant /ˈveəriənt $ ˈver-/ ●○○ AWL *n* [C]
1 something that is slightly different from the usual form of something: **[+of/on]** *This game is a variant of netball.* | *a variant on the typical Hollywood hero*
2 *technical* a slightly different form of a word or phrase: *spelling variants in British and American English* —**variant** *adj*: *a variant form of the word*

var·i·a·tion /ˌveəriˈeɪʃən $ ˌver-/ ●●○ AWL *n*
1 [C,U] a difference between similar things, or a change from the usual amount or form of something: **[+of]** *White bread is really just a variation of French bread.* | **[+in]** *variations in the quality of the rugs* | **[+among]** *There is a great deal of* ***variation*** *among the responses.* | **[+between]**

The study concluded that the variation between the CD players was very small.
2 [C] something that is done in a way that is different from the way it is usually done: *Most of his poems are* ***variations on*** *the* ***theme*** *of love.*
3 [C] one of a set of short pieces of music, each based on the same simple tune: *Bach's Goldberg variations*

var·i·cose veins /ˌværəkəʊs ˈveɪnz $ -koʊs-/ *n* [plural] a medical condition in which the VEINS in your leg become swollen and painful

var·ied /ˈveərid $ ˈver-/ ●●○ AWL *adj* consisting of or including many different kinds of things or people, especially in a way that seems interesting: *a varied diet* | *The responsibilities of government are many, and they are varied.* | **richly/extremely/widely etc varied** *A good teacher is aware of the extremely varied needs of each student.*

var·ie·gat·ed /ˈveərɪgeɪtɪd $ ˈver-/ *adj* **1** a variegated plant, leaf etc has different coloured marks on it: *variegated grasses* **2** *formal* consisting of a lot of different types of thing

va·ri·e·ty /vəˈraɪəti/ ●●● S2 W1 *n* (*plural* **varieties**)
1 a variety of sth a lot of things of the same type that are different from each other in some way: *The girls come from a variety of different backgrounds.*
2 [U] the differences within a group, set of actions etc that make it interesting: *I really like the variety the store has to offer.* | **give/add/bring variety (to sth)** (=make something more interesting) *Occasionally working from home adds variety to a job.*
3 [C] a type of thing, such as a plant or animal, that is different from others in the same group: **[+of]** *The lake has more than 20 varieties of fish.*
4 [C usually singular] a particular type of person or thing – often used humorously: **of the ... variety** *Lon has no patience with anything of the child variety.*
5 variety is the spice of life used to say that doing a lot of different things, meeting different people etc is what makes life interesting

COLLOCATIONS

ADJECTIVES

a wide/great/large variety *They hold debates on a wide variety of topics.*
a huge/enormous variety *Fruit is eaten by a huge variety of animals and birds.*
an infinite/endless variety *There is a seemingly infinite variety of beers to choose from.*
a rich variety *A rich variety of plants grows here.*
a bewildering variety | **an amazing variety**

vaˈriety ˌshow *n* [C] a television or radio programme, or a performance that consists of many different shorter performances, especially musical and humorous ones

vaˈriety ˌstore *n* [C] *AmE* a shop that sells many different kinds of goods, often at low prices

var·i·fo·cals /ˈveəriˌfəʊkəlz $ ˈveriˌfoʊ-/ *n* [plural] glasses that help you to see things at many different distances → **bifocals** —**varifocal** *adj*

var·i·ous /ˈveəriəs $ ˈver-/ ●●● S1 W1 *adj* [usually before noun]
1 if there are various things, there are several different types of that thing: *The jacket is available in various colours.* | *There are various ways to answer your question.* | *He decided to leave school* ***for various reasons.***
2 many and various *BrE*, **various and sundry** *AmE* many different types of something: *The reasons why teenage girls get pregnant are many and various.*

var·i·ous·ly /ˈveəriəsli $ ˈver-/ ●○○ *adv* in many different ways: **variously described as/known as/called etc sth** *the phenomena variously known as 'mass culture', 'popular culture', or the 'public arts'* | *His fortune has been variously estimated at between $1 and $2 billion.*

var·nish[1] /ˈvɑːnɪʃ $ ˈvɑːr-/ *n* [C,U] a clear liquid that is painted onto things, especially things made of wood, to protect them, or the hard shiny surface produced by this

varnish[2] *v* [T] to cover something with varnish

var·si·ty /ˈvɑːsəti $ ˈvɑːr-/ *n* (*plural* **varsities**) [C,U]
1 *AmE* the main team that represents a university, college, or school in a sport: *the varsity football team*
2 *BrE old-fashioned* a university, especially Oxford or Cambridge

ˈVarsity ˌMatch, the a game of RUGBY between Oxford and Cambridge universities, played once a year at Twickenham in West London

var·y /ˈveəri $ ˈveri/ ●●● S3 W2 AWL *v* (**varied, varying, varies**)
1 [I] if several things of the same type vary, they are all different from each other SYN **differ**: *Test scores* ***vary from school to school.*** | *The heights of the plants* ***vary from*** *8 cm* ***to*** *20 cm.* | **[+in]** *flowers that vary in color and size* | *Medical treatment* ***varies greatly*** *from state to state.* | *Cooking times may* ***vary slightly****, depending on your oven.* | *Charges* ***vary according to*** *size.* | *She has tried different diets with* ***varying degrees of*** *success.* | *tests of* ***varying levels*** *of difficulty*
2 [I] if something varies, it changes depending on the situation: *Quentin's mood seems to* ***vary according to*** *the weather.* | *'What do you wear when you go out?' 'Well,* ***it varies.****'*
3 [T] to change something to make it different: *My doctor said I should vary my diet more.*

GRAMMAR

Vary belongs to a group of verbs where the same noun can be the subject of the verb or its object.
• You can say: *Banks can vary the interest rate.* In this sentence, 'the interest rate' is the object of **vary**.
• You can say: *The interest rate can vary.* In this sentence, 'the interest rate' is the subject of **vary**.
GRAMMAR GUIDE ▶ **VERBS**

vas·cu·lar /ˈvæskjələ $ -ər/ *adj medical* relating to the tubes through which liquids flow in the bodies of animals or in plants: *vascular disease*

vase /vɑːz $ veɪs, veɪz/ ●●○ *n* [C] a container used to put flowers in or for decoration

va·sec·to·my /vəˈsektəmi/ *n* (*plural* **vasectomies**) [C,U] a medical operation to cut the small tube through which a man's SPERM passes so that he is unable to produce children

Vas·e·line /ˈvæsəliːn/ *n* [U] *trademark* a soft clear substance used on the skin for various medical and other purposes

vas·sal /ˈvæsəl/ *n* [C] **1** a man in the Middle Ages who was given land to live on by a lord in return for promising to work or fight for him **2** *formal* a country that is controlled by another country: *a vassal state*

vast /vɑːst $ væst/ ●●○ W2 *adj*
1 extremely large SYN **huge**: **vast amounts/numbers/quantities/sums etc (of sth)** *The government will have to borrow vast amounts of money.* | *The refugees come across the border* ***in vast numbers.*** | **vast areas/expanses/tracts etc (of sth)** *vast areas of rainforest* | *In the past five years, there has been a vast improvement in graduation rates.* **THESAURUS** ▶ **BIG**
2 the vast majority (of sth) used when you want to emphasize that something is true about almost all of a group of people or things: *The vast majority of books on the subject are complete rubbish.* —**vastness** *n* [U]

vast·ly /ˈvɑːstli $ ˈvæstli/ ●○○ *adv* very much: *This book is vastly superior to his last one.* | *vastly different opinions*

vat /væt/ *n* [C] a very large container for storing liquids in

VAT /ˌviː eɪ ˈtiː, væt/ *n* [U] (***value-added tax***) a tax added to the price of goods and services in Britain and the EU

Vat·i·can /ˈvætɪkən/ *n* **the Vatican a)** the large PALACE in Rome where the Pope (=head of the Roman Catholic Church) lives and works **b)** the government of the Pope: *The Vatican is taking a hard line on birth control.*

vau·de·ville /ˈvɔːdəvɪl $ ˈvɒː-/ *n* [U] *AmE* a type of theatre entertainment, popular from the 1880s to the 1950s, in which there were many short performances of different kinds, including singing, dancing, jokes etc → **music hall**

vault¹ /vɔːlt $ vɒːlt/ ●○○ *n* [C]
1 a room with thick walls and a strong door where money, jewels etc are kept to prevent them from being stolen or damaged
2 a room where people from the same family are buried, often under the floor of a church
3 a jump over something
4 a roof or ceiling that consists of several ARCHes that are joined together, especially in a church

vault² *v* **1** [T] (*also* **vault over**) to jump over something in one movement, using your hands or a pole to help you: *The robber vaulted over the counter and took $200 in cash.* THESAURUS JUMP **2** [I] to move quickly from a lower rank or level to a higher one SYN **leap**: **[+from/to]** *On Sunday Michigan vaulted from No. 4 to the nation's top team.*

vault·ed /ˈvɔːltɪd $ ˈvɒːl-/ *adj* in the shape of or consisting of several ARCHes joined together: **vaulted ceiling/roof etc**

vault·ing¹ /ˈvɔːltɪŋ $ ˈvɒːl-/ *n* [U] ARCHes in a roof or ceiling: *Gothic vaulting*

vaulting² *adj* **vaulting ambition** *literary* the desire to achieve as much as possible: *a man of vaulting ambition with the talents to match*

vaunt·ed /ˈvɔːntɪd $ ˈvɒːn-, ˈvɑːn-/ *adj formal* a plan, system, achievement etc that is vaunted is praised or talked about too much and in a way that is too proud: *There's little sign that the* ***much-vaunted*** *IT investment is pulling France out of recession.*

va-va-voom /ˌvɑː vɑː ˈvuːm/ *n* [U] the quality of being exciting or sexually attractive: *There's a real feeling of va-va-voom in the club.*

V-chip /ˈviː tʃɪp/ *n* [C] an electronic CHIP in a television that allows parents to prevent their children from watching programmes that are violent or have sex in them

vCJD /ˌviː siː dʒeɪ ˈdiː/ *n* [U] *medical* (***new variant Creutzfeldt-Jakob Disease***) a human form of the serious brain disease BSE

VCR /ˌviː siː ˈɑː $ -ˈɑːr/ *n* [C] (***video cassette recorder***) a machine you use to record television programmes or play VIDEOTAPES SYN **video** *BrE*

VD /ˌviː ˈdiː/ *n* [C,U] *old-fashioned* (***venereal disease***) any disease that passes from one person to another during sex SYN **STD**

VDT /ˌviː diː ˈtiː/ *n* [C] *AmE technical* (***video display terminal***) a computer screen SYN **monitor**

VDU /ˌviː diː ˈjuː/ *n* [C] *BrE technical* (***visual display unit***) a computer screen SYN **monitor**: *VDU operators*

've /v, əv/ the short form of 'have': *We've finished.*

veal /viːl/ *n* [U] the meat of a CALF (=a young cow)

vec·tor /ˈvektə $ -ər/ *n* [C] *technical* **1** a quantity such as force that has a direction as well as size **2** an insect or animal that passes disease from one person to another SYN **carrier**: *Mosquitoes are feared as vectors of malaria.* **3** in biology, an animal or human cell that is used to carry DNA from one cell to another to produce a CLONE

vee·jay /ˌviːˈdʒeɪ/ *n* [C] a VIDEO JOCKEY

veep /viːp/ *n* [C] *AmE informal* VICE-PRESIDENT

veer /vɪə $ vɪr/ *v* [I always + adv/prep] **1** to change direction: **[+off]** *A tanker driver died when his lorry veered off the motorway.* | *The plane* ***veered off course***. | *Follow the path and veer left after 400m.* | *The wind was veering north.* **2** if opinions, ideas, attitudes etc veer in a particular direction, they gradually change and become quite different: *This latest proposal appears to veer in the direction of Democratic ideals.* | *The conversation veered back to politics.*

veg¹ /vedʒ/ *n* [C,U] *BrE informal* vegetables: *fruit and veg*

veg² *v* (**vegged**, **vegging**, **vegges**)
veg out *phr v spoken informal* to be very lazy and spend time doing very little: *Ralph vegged out in front of the TV all day again.*

ve·gan /ˈviːgən $ ˈviː-, ˈvedʒ-/ *n* [C] someone who does not eat any animal products at all, such as meat, fish, eggs, cheese, or milk → **vegetarian** —**vegan** *adj*: *a strict vegan diet*

Ve·ge·bur·ger /ˈvedʒiˌbɜːgə $ -ˌbɜːrgər/ *n* [C] *trademark BrE* a flat round cake made with vegetables and beans that looks like a BURGER but that does not contain meat

vege·ta·ble¹ /ˈvedʒtəbəl/ ●●● S3 W3 *n* [C]
1 a plant that is eaten raw or cooked, such as a CABBAGE, a CARROT, or PEAS: *fresh* ***fruit and vegetables*** | *organic methods of* ***growing vegetables*** | *vegetable soup* | *a neat* ***vegetable garden*** | *Vitamin A is found in liver and* ***green vegetables***. | **salad vegetables** (=vegetables such as LETTUCE or TOMATOes eaten raw)

GRAMMAR: Countable or uncountable?
- **Vegetable** is used as a countable noun: *Her son doesn't like eating vegetables.* ✗ Don't say: *Her son doesn't like eating vegetable.*
- **Vegetable** is used before nouns, for example **vegetable soup**, **vegetable oil**. ✗ Don't say: *vegetables soup*

2 *not polite* an offensive word for someone who is alive but who cannot talk or move because their brain is damaged

vegetable² *adj* [only before noun] *formal* relating to plants in general, rather than animals or things that are not living → **mineral**: *decomposing vegetable matter*

veg·e·tar·i·an /ˌvedʒəˈteəriən◂ $ -ˈter-/ ●●○ *n* [C] someone who does not eat meat or fish → **vegan**: *Our youngest daughter is a vegetarian.* | *dishes suitable for vegetarians* | *I'm thinking about* ***becoming a vegetarian***. —**vegetarian** *adj*: *a vegetarian restaurant*

veg·e·tar·i·an·is·m /ˌvedʒəˈteəriənɪzəm $ -ˈter-/ *n* [U] the practice of not eating meat or fish

veg·e·tate /ˈvedʒɪteɪt/ *v* [I] to live without doing much physical or mental activity and to feel bored as a result: *I was determined when I retired that I wasn't just going to vegetate.*

veg·e·ta·tion /ˌvedʒɪˈteɪʃən/ ●○○ *n* [U] *formal* plants in general: *Lefkas has an abundance of lush green vegetation.*

veg·e·ta·tive /ˈvedʒətətɪv $ -teɪtɪv/ *adj* [only before noun] **1** *technical* relating to plants, and particularly to the way they grow or make new plants: **vegetative reproduction/propagation** **2** **a vegetative state** a condition in which someone cannot think or move because their brain has been damaged

veg·gie¹ /ˈvedʒi/ *n* [C] **1** a VEGETARIAN **2** *AmE* a VEGETABLE: *fresh veggies*

veggie² *adj informal* veggie food is made using vegetables, nuts, beans etc rather than meat or fish: *veggie lasagne and chips*

ve·he·ment /ˈviːəmənt/ *adj* showing very strong feelings or opinions: **vehement opposition/criticism/hostility etc** *Despite vehement opposition, the Act became law.* | *Despite her vehement protests, he pulled her inside.* —**vehemently** *adv*: *Dan vehemently denies the charges.* —**vehemence** *n* [U]: *The vehemence of her answer surprised them both.*

ve·hi·cle /ˈviːɪkəl/ ●●● S2 W2 AWL *n* [C]
1 *formal* a machine with an engine that is used to take people or things from one place to another, such as a car, bus, or truck → **motor vehicle**: *a description of the stolen vehicle* | *Have you locked your vehicle?*
2 [usually singular] *formal* something you use to express and spread your ideas, opinions etc SYN **medium**: **[+for]** *The 1936 Olympics were used as a vehicle for Nazi propaganda.* | *'Eastern Eye' is an important vehicle for Black British opinion.*
3 [usually singular] a film, television programme etc that is made to gain public attention for one of the people in it: **[+for]** *This is the perfect vehicle for Fleming to make his triumphant return to the stage.* | *MGM made the film as a* ***star vehicle*** *for Brando.*

V

Vegetables

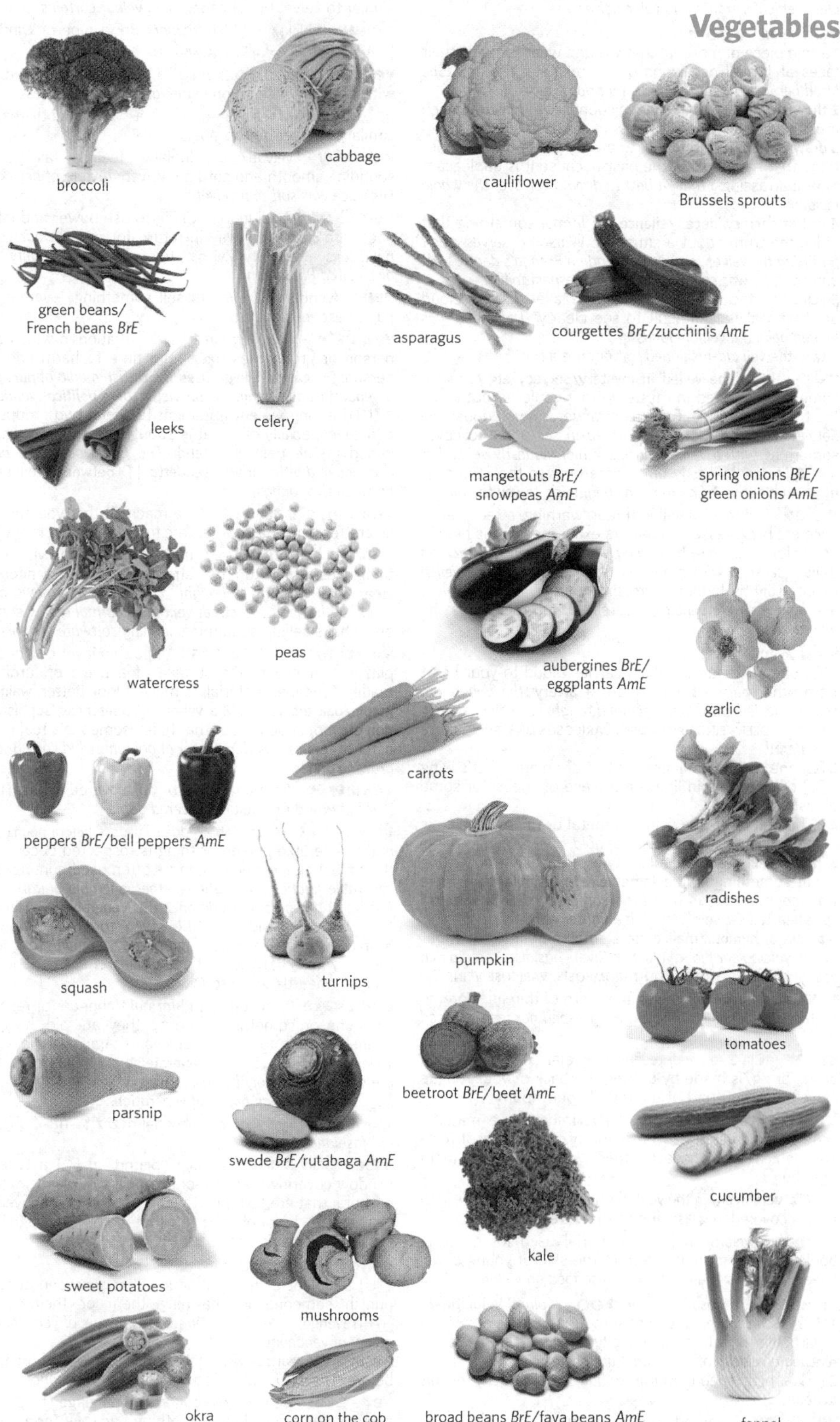
broccoli
cabbage
cauliflower
Brussels sprouts
green beans/
French beans *BrE*
asparagus
courgettes *BrE*/zucchinis *AmE*
leeks
celery
mangetouts *BrE*/
snowpeas *AmE*
spring onions *BrE*/
green onions *AmE*
watercress
peas
aubergines *BrE*/
eggplants *AmE*
garlic
carrots
peppers *BrE*/bell peppers *AmE*
radishes
pumpkin
squash
turnips
tomatoes
parsnip
beetroot *BrE*/beet *AmE*
swede *BrE*/rutabaga *AmE*
cucumber
kale
sweet potatoes
mushrooms
okra
corn on the cob
broad beans *BrE*/fava beans *AmE*
fennel

ve·hic·u·lar /viːˈhɪkjələ $ -ər/ *adj formal* relating to vehicles: *vehicular traffic | no vehicular access*

veil¹ /veɪl/ ●○○ *n* [C]
1 a thin piece of material that women wear to cover their faces at formal occasions or for religious reasons: *She lifted her veil with both hands. | a bridal veil*
2 the veil the system in Islamic countries in which women must cover their hair and faces in public
3 draw a veil over sth *formal* to avoid talking about something that happened in the past because it is unpleasant or embarrassing: *I think it best to draw a veil over the whole incident.*
4 veil of secrecy/deceit/silence etc *formal* something that hides the truth about a situation: *Watson deserves credit for* ***lifting the veil*** *of secrecy surrounding Brenda's death. | His pornography was covered by a veil of respectability.*
5 veil of mist/cloud/smoke etc a thin layer of mist, cloud etc that makes it difficult to see clearly: *The moon was hidden behind a veil of clouds.*
6 take the veil *old-fashioned* to become a NUN

veil² *v* [T] **1 be veiled in mystery/secrecy etc** *formal* if something is veiled in mystery etc, people do not know the truth about it so it seems strange or mysterious: *The details of the evacuation are veiled in secrecy.* **2** to cover something with a veil: *A black kerchief modestly veiled her hair.* **3** *literary* to partly hide something so that it cannot be seen clearly: *A fine rain was beginning to veil the hills.*

veiled /veɪld/ *adj* a veiled threat, warning, attack, reference etc is expressed so that its exact meaning is hidden or unclear: *His speech is being seen as a* ***veiled attack*** *on asylum-seekers. | 'I'm impressed,' said Greg, with* ***thinly veiled*** (=only slightly hidden) *sarcasm. | Jasper remained silent and his* ***eyes*** *were* ***veiled*** (=you could not guess what he was thinking).

vein /veɪn/ ●●○ *n*
1 [C] one of the tubes which carries blood to your heart from other parts of your body → **artery**: *the pulmonary vein | She felt the blood racing through her veins as they kissed.* → DEEP VEIN THROMBOSIS, VARICOSE VEINS, see picture at HUMAN¹
2 [C] one of the thin lines on a leaf or on an insect's wing
3 [C] one of the thin lines on a piece of cheese or some types of stone
4 [C] a thin layer of a valuable metal or mineral which is contained in rock: **[+of]** *veins of gold*
5 in a ... vein in a particular style of speaking or writing about something: **in the same vein/in a similar vein** *There was more humour, in much the same vein.* | **in a serious/light-hearted etc vein** *poems in a lighter vein*
6 a vein of humour/malice etc a small amount of humour etc: *In voicing our fear of old age, Rivers has discovered* ***a rich vein of*** *comedy.* → DEEP VEIN THROMBOSIS, VARICOSE VEINS

V

veined /veɪnd/ *adj* having a pattern of thin lines on the surface: *black-veined marble | He grasped her feeble veined hand.*

ve·lar /ˈviːlə $ -ər/ *adj technical* a velar CONSONANT such as /k/or /g/is made by putting the back of your tongue close to the soft part at the top of your mouth

Vel·cro /ˈvelkrəʊ $ -kroʊ/ *n* [U] *trademark* a material used to fasten clothes, consisting of two pieces of material which stick to each other when you press them together

veldt, **veld** /velt/ *n* **the veldt** high flat land in South Africa that is covered in grass and has few trees

vel·lum /ˈveləm/ *n* [U] a material used for covering books or writing on, made from the skin of young cows, sheep, or goats: *medieval maps inscribed on vellum*

ve·lo·ci·ty /vəˈlɒsəti $ -ˈlɑː-/ ●○○ *n* (*plural* **velocities**)
1 [C,U] *technical* the speed of something that is moving in a particular direction: *the velocity of light | The speedboat* ***reached*** *a* ***velocity*** *of 120 mph. | a* ***high velocity*** *bullet*
2 [U] a high speed: *Martinez had good velocity on his fastball.*

vel·o·drome /ˈvelədrəʊm $ -droʊm/ *n* [C] a circular track used for bicycle racing

ve·lour /vəˈlʊə $ -ˈlʊr/ *n* [U] a type of heavy cloth that is similar to velvet but cheaper: *gold velour curtains*

Ve·lux /ˈviːlʌks/ *n* [C] *trademark BrE* a type of window that is built into a sloping roof

vel·vet /ˈvelvɪt/ ●○○ *n* [U] a type of expensive cloth with a soft surface on one side: *green velvet drapes*

vel·ve·teen /ˌvelvəˈtiːn◂/ *n* [U] a type of cloth that is similar to velvet but cheaper

vel·vet·y /ˈvelvəti/ *adj* looking, feeling, tasting, or sounding smooth and soft: *the velvety texture of her skin | His voice was soft and velvety.*

ve·nal /ˈviːnl/ *adj formal* willing to use power and influence in a dishonest way in return for money: *our venal politicians* —**venality** /viːˈnæləti/ *n* [U]: *His venality has discredited Parliament.*

vend /vend/ *v* [T] *law* to sell something —**vending** *n* [U]: *street vending*

ven·det·ta /venˈdetə/ *n* **1** [C] a situation in which one person or group tries for a long time to harm another person: **[+against]** *He accused the British media of* ***pursuing a vendetta*** *against him. | the victim of a* ***political vendetta*** **2** [C,U] a long violent argument between two groups or people, especially one that is about something that happened in the past SYN **feud**: *The two sides have been engaged in a bitter* ***private vendetta***. | **[+between]** *vendettas between rival gangs*

ˈvending maˌchine *n* [C] a machine that you can get cigarettes, chocolate, drinks etc from by putting money in

vend·or /ˈvendə $ -ər/ *n* [C] **1** someone who sells things, especially on the street: **newspaper vendor/ice cream etc vendor** *He bought a copy from a newspaper vendor. | the shouts of* ***street vendors*** **2** *formal or law* someone who is selling something: *leading software vendors*

ve·neer /vəˈnɪə $ -ˈnɪr/ *n* **1** [C,U] a thin layer of wood or plastic that covers the surface of a piece of furniture made of cheaper material, to make it look better: **walnut/maple/oak etc veneer 2 a veneer of politeness/sophistication etc** *formal* behaviour that hides someone's real character or feelings: *A* ***thin veneer*** *of politeness hid Lady Bride's growing anger.*

ve·neered /vəˈnɪəd $ -ˈnɪrd/ *adj* covered with a thin layer of wood or plastic: *veneered doors*

ven·e·ra·ble /ˈvenərəbəl/ *adj* **1** [usually before noun] *formal* a venerable person or thing is respected because of their great age, experience etc – often used humorously: ***venerable*** *financial* ***institutions*** *| the venerable guitarist Pat Martino | a* ***venerable tradition*** **2 the Venerable ... a)** in the Church of England, the title given to an ARCHDEACON **b)** in the Roman Catholic religion, the title given to a dead person who is holy but not yet a SAINT **c)** in the Buddhist religion, the title given to a MONK

ven·e·rate /ˈvenəreɪt/ *v* [T] *formal* to honour or respect someone or something because they are old, holy, or connected with the past: *a symbol of Arab courage, to be venerated for generations* | **venerate sb as sth** *These children are venerated as holy beings.* —**veneration** /ˌvenəˈreɪʃən/ *n* [U]: *The sun was* ***an object of veneration***.

ve·ne·re·al dis·ease /vəˈnɪəriəl dɪˌziːz $ -ˈnɪr-/ *n* [C,U] *old-fashioned* VD

Ve·ne·tian blind /vəˌniːʃən ˈblaɪnd/ *n* [C] a type of window covering made of long flat bars of plastic, wood, or metal that are fastened together and can be moved to change the amount of light that comes through the window → see picture at BLIND³

ven·geance /ˈvendʒəns/ ●○○ *n*
1 [U] a violent or harmful action that someone does to punish someone for harming them or their family SYN **revenge**: *a desire for vengeance | a vow of vengeance | an act of vengeance*
2 with a vengeance with great force or more effort than before: *The music started up again with a vengeance.*

venge·ful /ˈvendʒfəl/ *adj literary* very eager to punish someone who has done something bad OPP **forgiving**: *a vengeful god*

ve·ni·al /ˈviːniəl/ *adj formal* a venial fault, mistake etc is not very serious and can be forgiven OPP **mortal**: *a **venial** sin*

ven·i·son /ˈvenəzən, -sən/ *n* [U] the meat of a DEER

Venn di·a·gram /ˈven ˌdaɪəgræm/ *n* [C] a picture showing the relationship between several things by using circles that partly cover each other

ven·om /ˈvenəm/ *n* [U] **1** great anger or hatred SYN **malice**: *There was real venom in her voice.* | *a look of pure venom* **2** a liquid poison that some snakes, insects etc produce when they bite or sting you: *The viper paralyses its prey by injecting it with venom.*

ven·om·ous /ˈvenəməs/ *adj* **1** full of hatred or anger: *Lisa shot him a venomous glance.* | *Reid reserved his most venomous attack for the Rail Authority.* **2** a venomous snake, insect etc produces poison SYN **poisonous** —**venomously** *adv*

ve·nous /ˈviːnəs/ *adj medical* relating to the VEINS (=tubes that carry blood) in your body

vent[1] /vent/ *n* [C] **1** a hole or pipe through which gases, liquid etc can enter or escape from an enclosed space or container: *a blocked **air vent*** | *a volcanic vent* **2 give vent to sth** *formal* to do something violent or harmful to express feelings of anger, hatred etc: *Children give vent to their anger in various ways.* | *He knew that if he gave **full vent** to his feelings, it would upset Joanna.* **3** a thin straight opening at the bottom of the back or side of a jacket or coat **4** *technical* the small hole through which small animals, birds, fish etc pass waste matter out of their bodies

vent[2] *v* [T] to express feelings of anger, hatred etc, especially by doing something violent or harmful: **vent sth on sb** *If he's had a bad day, Paul **vents** his **anger** on the family.* | **vent sth by doing sth** *I could hear mum **venting** her **frustration** by banging the pots noisily.* | *The meeting gave us a chance to **vent** our **spleen*** (=anger).

ven·ti·late /ˈventəleɪt $ -tl-eɪt/ *v* [T] **1** to let fresh air into a room, building etc: **well-ventilated/poorly ventilated etc** *a well-ventilated kitchen* **2** to pump air into and out of someone's lungs, using a special machine: *Both patients are sedated and ventilated.* **3** *formal* to express your opinions or feelings about something: *The important thing is to ventilate your anger.* —**ventilation** /ˌventəˈleɪʃən $ -tlˈeɪ-/ *n* [U]: *a ventilation system* | *artificial ventilation*

ven·ti·la·tor /ˈventəleɪtə $ -tl-eɪtər/ *n* [C] **1** a piece of equipment that puts fresh air into a room, building etc → **fan 2** a piece of equipment that pumps air into and out of someone's lungs: **on a ventilator** *He was **put on a ventilator** but died two hours later.*

ven·tral /ˈventrəl/ *adj* [only before noun] *technical* relating to the stomach area of an animal or fish → **dorsal**: *Its ventral fins are orange.*

ven·tri·cle /ˈventrɪkəl/ *n* [C] *technical* one of the two spaces in the bottom of your heart through which blood pumps out to your body → **auricle**

ven·tril·o·quist /venˈtrɪləkwɪst/ *n* [C] someone who entertains people by speaking without moving their lips and making it seem that the words are spoken by a model of a person called a DUMMY —**ventriloquism** *n* [U]

ven·ture[1] /ˈventʃə $ -ər/ ●○○ *n* [C] a new business activity that involves taking risks: **business/commercial venture** | **joint venture** (=when two companies do something together)

venture[2] ●○○ *v*

1 [I always + adv/prep] to go somewhere that could be dangerous: *When darkness fell, he would venture out.* | *She paused before venturing up the steps to the door.* | *children who lack the confidence to venture into libraries*

2 [T] to say or do something in an uncertain way because you are afraid it is wrong or will seem stupid: *'You're on holiday here?' he ventured.* | **venture to do sth** *I ventured to ask him what he was writing.* | **venture an opinion/question/word etc** *If we had more information, it would be easier to venture a firm opinion.* | *Roy ventured a tentative smile.* | **venture that** *I ventured that the experiment was not conclusive.*

3 nothing ventured, nothing gained used to say that you cannot achieve anything unless you take risks

venture into sth *phr v* to become involved in a new business activity: *Banks are venturing into insurance.*

venture on/upon sth *phr v* to do or try something that involves risks: *I thought I might venture on a new recipe.*

ˈventure ˌcapital *n* [U] money lent to someone so that they can start a new business —**venture capitalist** *n* [C]

ven·ture·some /ˈventʃəsəm $ -tʃər-/ *adj formal* willing to take risks SYN **daring**

ven·ue /ˈvenjuː/ ●●○ *n* [C] a place where an organized meeting, concert etc takes place: **sporting/conference/concert etc venue** | *The first thing to do is **book** a **venue**.* | *The band will **play** (=perform at) as many **venues** as possible.* | **[+for]** *the venue for the latest round of talks* THESAURUS ▸ PLACE

Ve·nus /ˈviːnəs/ *n* the PLANET that is second in order from the Sun: *the high surface temperatures of Venus*

ve·ra·ci·ty /vəˈræsəti/ *n* [U] *formal* the fact of being true or correct SYN **truth**: **[+of]** *Has anyone checked the veracity of these allegations?*

ve·ran·da, **verandah** /vəˈrændə/ *n* [C] an open area with a floor and a roof that is attached to the side of a house at ground level SYN **porch** *AmE*

verb /vɜːb $ vɜːrb/ ●●● *n* [C] a word or group of words that describes an action, experience, or state, such as 'come', 'see', and 'put on' → AUXILIARY VERB, LINKING VERB, MODAL VERB, PHRASAL VERB

verb·al[1] /ˈvɜːbəl $ ˈvɜːr-/ ●●○ *adj*

1 spoken rather than written: **verbal agreement/instructions etc**

2 relating to words or using words: *verbal skills* | ***verbal abuse*** (=cruel words) *from other kids on the street*

3 relating to a verb: *verbal nouns* —**verbally** *adv*: *Her boss failed to stop the other workers from verbally abusing her.*

verbal[2] *n* **1** [C] *technical* a word that has been formed from a verb, for example a GERUND, INFINITIVE, or PARTICIPLE **2** [U] relating to criticism, complaints, or an attack that you express in speech: *Maria was getting loads of verbal from her staff.*

verb·al·ize (*also* **-ise** *BrE*) /ˈvɜːbəlaɪz $ ˈvɜːr-/ *v* [I,T] *formal* to express something in words SYN **articulate**: *Urge your child to verbalize his feelings.*

ver·ba·tim /vɜːˈbeɪtɪm $ vɜːr-/ *adj, adv formal* repeating the actual words that were spoken or written SYN **word-for-word**: **verbatim account/quote/report etc** *a verbatim account of our conversation* | *Their stories were taped and transcribed verbatim.*

ver·bi·age /ˈvɜːbi-ɪdʒ $ ˈvɜːr-/ *n* [U] *formal* speech or writing that has many unnecessary words in it: *meaningless verbiage*

ver·bose /vɜːˈbəʊs $ vɜːrˈboʊs/ *adj* using or containing too many words: *For once, his usually verbose wife was content to listen.* | *Legal writing is often unclear and verbose.* —**verbosely** *adv* —**verbosity** /vɜːˈbɒsəti $ vɜːrˈbɑː-/ *n* [U]

ver·bo·ten /fəˈbəʊtn $ fərˈboʊ-/ *adj* not allowed: *Criticism of the organization's leader is verboten.*

ver·dant /ˈvɜːdənt $ ˈvɜːr-/ *adj literary* verdant land is thickly covered with fresh green plants SYN **lush**: *verdant fields*

ver·dict /ˈvɜːdɪkt $ ˈvɜːr-/ ●●○ *n* [C]

1 an official decision made in a court of law, especially about whether someone is guilty of a crime or how a death happened: *The verdict was 'not guilty'.*

2 an official decision made by a person or group with authority: *The players anxiously awaited the verdict of the umpire.*

3 someone's opinion about something: *The audience's **final verdict** was encouraging.* | **[+on]** *What's your verdict on the movie?* | **give (sb) your verdict (on sth)** *Trade unionists were quick to give their verdict on the proposals.*

COLLOCATIONS

VERBS

reach/arrive at a verdict (=agree on a decision) *The jury failed to reach a verdict.*
return/give/announce/deliver a verdict (=officially say what a verdict is) *The inquest jury returned a verdict of 'unlawful killing'.*
consider your verdict (=think about what it should be) *The jury retired to consider their verdict.*

ADJECTIVES/NOUN + verdict

a unanimous verdict (=when the whole jury agrees) *The jury found him guilty by a unanimous verdict.*
a majority verdict *BrE* (=when most of the jury agrees) | **a guilty/not guilty verdict** | **an open verdict** *BrE* (=stating that the facts about someone's death are not known)

PHRASES

a verdict of guilty/not guilty

ver·di·gris /ˈvɜːdəgriː, -griːs $ ˈvɜːr-/ *n* [U] a greenish-blue substance that sometimes appears on COPPER or BRASS

ver·dure /ˈvɜːdʒə $ ˈvɜːrdʒər/ *n* [U] *literary* green grass, plants etc

verge[1] /vɜːdʒ $ vɜːrdʒ/ ●○○ *n* [C]
1 be on the verge of sth to be at the point where something is about to happen: *Jess seemed* ***on the verge of tears***. | *an event which left her* ***on the verge of a nervous breakdown*** | *Mountain gorillas are on the verge of extinction.* | **be on the verge of doing sth** *The show was on the verge of being canceled due to low ratings.*
2 *BrE* the edge of a road, path etc: *The car skidded across the road and came to a stop on the grass verge.*

verge[2] *v*
verge on/upon sth *phr v* to be very close to a harmful or extreme state: *Many of Lewis's activities* ***verged on the*** *illegal.* | *Some of his ideas are* ***verging on the*** *dangerous.* | *His love of James Dean movies verged on fanaticism.*

ver·ger /ˈvɜːdʒə $ ˈvɜːrdʒər/ *n* [C] *BrE* someone whose job is to care for the inside of a church and help during services

ver·i·fy /ˈverɪfaɪ/ ●○○ *v* (**verified, verifying, verifies**) [T] *formal*
1 to discover whether something is correct or true: **verify that/whether** *A computer program verifies that the system is working.* | *American forces will remain to verify compliance with the treaty.*

REGISTER
In everyday English, people usually say **check** rather than **verify**: *Can I just* ***check*** *that I have spelt your name correctly.*

2 to state that something is true SYN **confirm**: *His statement was verified by several witnesses.* —**verifiable** *adj*: *a verifiable fact* —**verification** /ˌverɪfɪˈkeɪʃən/ *n* [C,U]: *automatic signature verification*

ver·i·ly /ˈverəli/ *adv biblical* a word used to emphasize a statement

ver·i·si·mil·i·tude /ˌverɪsɪˈmɪlɪtjuːd $ -tuːd/ *n* [U] *formal* the quality of being true or real: *questions about the verisimilitude of the document*

ver·i·ta·ble /ˈverətəbəl/ *adj* [only before noun] *formal* a word used to emphasize a description of someone or something SYN **real**: *The area is a veritable paradise for those who love walking and swimming.*

ver·i·ty /ˈverəti/ *n* (*plural* **verities**) [C usually plural] *formal* an important principle or fact that is always true SYN **truth**: *the* ***eternal verities*** *of life*

ver·mil·ion, **vermillion** /vəˈmɪljən $ vər-/ *n* [U] a very bright red colour —**vermilion** *adj*

ver·min /ˈvɜːmɪn $ ˈvɜːr-/ *n* [plural] **1** small animals, birds, and insects that are harmful because they destroy crops, spoil food, and spread disease: *The beds were filthy and full of vermin.* | *Foxes are considered vermin.* **2** unpleasant people who cause problems for society

ver·min·ous /ˈvɜːmɪnəs $ ˈvɜːr-/ *adj formal* covered with insects that bite: *a pair of verminous old cats*

ver·mouth /ˈvɜːməθ $ vərˈmuːθ/ *n* [U] an alcoholic drink made from wine with herbs and spices: *dry vermouth*

ver·nac·u·lar /vəˈnækjələ $ vərˈnækjələr/ *n* [C usually singular] **1** a form of a language that ordinary people use, especially one that is not the official language: **in the vernacular** *Galileo wrote in the vernacular to reach a larger audience.* | *He lapsed into the* ***local vernacular*** (=language spoken in a particular area). **2** a style of building, music, art etc that is suitable for ordinary people —**vernacular** *adj*: *vernacular American speech* | *vernacular architecture*

ver·nal /ˈvɜːnl $ ˈvɜːrnl/ *adj* [only before noun] *literary technical* relating to the spring → **autumnal**: *the vernal equinox*

ver·ru·ca /vəˈruːkə/ *n* [C] *BrE* a small hard infectious lump that grows on the bottom of your foot

versa → VICE VERSA

ver·sa·tile /ˈvɜːsətaɪl $ ˈvɜːrsətl/ ●○○ *adj*
1 someone who is versatile has many different skills: *a very versatile performer* | *a more versatile workforce*
2 having many different uses: *The potato is an extremely versatile vegetable.* —**versatility** /ˌvɜːsəˈtɪləti $ ˌvɜːr-/ *n* [U]: *Hegley's outstanding versatility as an all-round entertainer*

verse /vɜːs $ vɜːrs/ ●●○ *n*
1 [C] a set of lines that forms one part of a song, poem, or a book such as the Bible or the Quran (Koran): *Let's sing the last verse again.* | *Learn the first two verses of the poem by heart.* | *Genesis chapter 3, verse 13*
2 [U] words arranged in the form of poetry: *a book of comic verse* | **in verse** *Written in verse, the play was set in the Middle Ages.*

versed /vɜːst $ vɜːrst/ *adj formal* **be (well) versed in sth** to know a lot about a subject, method etc: *a woman well versed in the art of diplomacy*

ver·si·fi·ca·tion /ˌvɜːsɪfɪˈkeɪʃən $ ˌvɜːr-/ *n* [U] *technical* the particular pattern in which a poem is written

ver·sion /ˈvɜːʃən $ ˈvɜːrʒən/ ●●● S2 W2 AWL *n* [C]
1 a copy of something that has been changed so that it is slightly different: **[+of]** *a new version of the software* | **new/modern/final etc version** *the* ***original version*** *of the text* | **English/German/electronic/film etc version** (=presented in a different language or form) *a Japanese version of an English play* | *I think I preferred the television version.* | *the human version of mad cow disease*
2 someone's version of an event is their description of it, when this is different from the description given by another person: **[+of]** *according to the official* ***version of events*** | *Could Donna's version of what happened that night be correct?*
3 the ... version of sth a way of explaining or doing something that is typical of a particular group or period of time: **[+of]** *the Marxist version of economics* | *Is the coffee break the adult version of recess?* → **cover version** at COVER[2](10)

ver·so /ˈvɜːsəʊ $ ˈvɜːrsoʊ/ *n* [C] *technical* a page on the left-hand side of a book → **recto**

ver·sus /ˈvɜːsəs $ ˈvɜːr-/ ●●○ *prep*
1 (*written abbreviation* **v.** *BrE*, **vs.** *AmE*) used to show that two people or teams are competing against each other in a game or court case: *the New York Knicks versus the LA Lakers* | *the Supreme Court decision in Roe vs. Wade*
2 used when comparing the advantages of two different things, ideas etc SYN **against**: *The finance minister must weigh up the benefits of a tax cut versus those of increased public spending.*

ver·te·bra /ˈvɜːtəbrə $ ˈvɜːr-/ *n* (*plural* **vertebrae** /-briː, -breɪ/) [C] one of the small hollow bones down the centre of your back —**vertebral** *adj* [only before noun]

ver·te·brate /ˈvɜːtəbrət, -breɪt $ ˈvɜːr-/ *n* [C] a living creature that has a BACKBONE → **invertebrate** THESAURUS ANIMAL

V

ver·tex /ˈvɜːteks $ ˈvɜːr-/ *n* (*plural* **vertices** /-təsiːz/ *or* **vertexes**) [C] *technical* the point where two lines meet to form an angle, especially the point of a TRIANGLE

ver·ti·cal¹ /ˈvɜːtɪkəl $ ˈvɜːr-/ ●●○ *adj*
1 pointing up in a line that forms an angle of 90° with a flat surface OPP **horizontal** → **diagonal**: *a* ***vertical line*** | *the* ***vertical axis*** *of a graph* | *vertical window blinds* | **vertical cliff/climb/drop etc** (=one that is very high or steep) *a gorge lined with vertical cliffs*
2 having a structure in which there are top, middle, and bottom levels → **hierarchical**: *Formal communication channels are usually vertical.* —**vertically** /-kli/ *adv*

vertical² *n* **the vertical** the direction of something that is vertical: *The tower now leans about 15 degrees from the vertical.*

ˌvertical exˈpansion *n* [U] *technical* when a company starts to do or make some of the things that used to be done or made by companies it did business with

ˌvertical ˈportal (*also* **vortal**) *n* [C] an Internet PORTAL that limits its content and services so that they are attractive and interesting to one specific type of person

ver·tig·i·nous /vɜːˈtɪdʒɪnəs $ vɜːr-/ *adj formal* so high that you feel sick and DIZZY: *a vertiginous drop to the valley below*

ver·ti·go /ˈvɜːtɪgəʊ $ ˈvɜːrtɪgoʊ/ *n* [U] a feeling of sickness and DIZZINESS caused by looking down from a high place

vert ramp /ˈvɜːt ræmp $ ˈvɜːrt-/ *n* [C] a U-shaped RAMP used in activities such as SKATEBOARDING and SNOWBOARDING to perform special movements such as jumping high into the air

verve /vɜːv $ vɜːrv/ *n* [U] *literary* energy, excitement, or great pleasure: **with verve** *Cziffra played the Hungarian dances with great verve.*

ve·ry¹ /ˈveri/ ●●● S1 W1 *adv*
1 [+adj/adv] used to emphasize an adjective, adverb, or phrase: *It feels very cold today.* | *The fishing industry is very important to the area.* | *The traffic's moving very slowly this morning.* | *problems that are very similar to mine* | *I feel a lot better – thank you* ***very much***. | *I'm* ***very, very*** (=used for emphasis) *pleased you can come.* | *It's very kind of you to help.* | *My sister and I were married on* ***the very same*** (=exactly the same) *day.* | **the very best/latest/worst etc** *We only use the very best ingredients.*
2 not very good/happy/far etc not good etc at all: *I'm just not very good at spelling.* | *The garden's not very big, is it?* | *The assistant wasn't very helpful.* | *'Was the talk interesting?' 'Not very* (=only slightly).*'*
3 your very own used to emphasize the fact that something belongs to one particular person and to no one else: *She was thrilled at the idea of having her very own toys to play with.* | **of your very own** *At last, she had a home of her very own.*
4 *informal* used with adjectives to say that the quality something has is very noticeable or typical: *It was a very male reaction, I thought.* | *His films are always very French.*
5 very much so *spoken* used to emphasize your agreement or approval: *'Are you serious?' 'Very much so.'*
6 very well *old-fashioned spoken* used to agree to something

GRAMMAR: Comparison

very
• You use **very** with adjectives and adverbs: *She is very happy.* | *The train was moving very slowly.*

very much
• You use **very much** with the comparative form of adjectives: *She is very much happier now.* | *I feel very much better.*
• You use **very much** with verbs: *He very much regrets what happened.* | *Thank you very much.*
• You use **very much** with prepositional phrases: *The company's future is very much in doubt.*| *She was very much in demand as a speaker.*

very² ●●○ S3 W3 *adj* [only before noun] used to emphasize that you are talking exactly about one particular thing or person: *He died in* ***this very*** *room.* | *I'll start at the very beginning.* | *Those were his very words.* | *You'd better start doing some work this very minute* (=now, not later). | *That might provoke a riot,* ***the very thing*** *he was trying to avoid.* | ***The very fact that*** *you are reading this book suggests you want to improve your fitness.* | ***By its very nature****, capitalism involves exploitation of the worker.* | *His life's work was being destroyed* ***before*** *his* ***very eyes*** (=directly in front of him). | **the very thought/idea/mention (of sth)** (=just thinking about or suggesting something) *The very thought of food made me feel ill.*

ves·pers /ˈvespəz $ -ərz/ *n* [U] the evening service in some types of Christian church → **matins**

ves·sel /ˈvesəl/ ●○○ *n* [C]
1 *formal* a ship or large boat: *a fishing vessel*
2 *technical* a VEIN in your body: *a burst* ***blood vessel***
3 *old use* a container for holding liquids

vest¹ /vest/ ●●○ *n* [C]
1 *BrE* a piece of underwear without SLEEVES that you wear on the top half of your body SYN **undershirt** *AmE* → see picture at **UNDERWEAR**
2 a piece of special clothing without SLEEVES that you wear over your clothes to protect your body: *a bulletproof vest*
3 *AmE* a piece of clothing without SLEEVES and with buttons down the front that you wear as part of a suit SYN **waistcoat** *BrE*
4 a SWEATER without SLEEVES

vest² *v law*
vest sth **in** sb *phr v* to give someone the official right to do or own something: *Copyright is vested in the author for 50 years.*

vest·ed /ˈvestɪd/ *adj* **1 vested interest** a strong reason for wanting something to happen because you will gain from it: *Since he owns the strip of land, Cook* ***has*** *a* ***vested interest*** *in the project being approved.* **2 vested interests** the groups of people who will gain from a plan, project, proposal etc: *The proposal faces tough opposition from powerful vested interests.* **3** vested rights, powers, property etc belong to you and cannot be removed: *Shareholders* ***have a vested right to*** *10% per annum.* **4** *technical* having full rights to own or have something: **become/get vested (in sth)** *He only took the job to get vested in the pension fund.*

ves·ti·bule /ˈvestəbjuːl/ *n* [C] *formal* **1** a space inside the front door of a public building **2** *AmE* the space at each end of a railway carriage that connects it with the next carriage

ves·tige /ˈvestɪdʒ/ *n* [C] *formal* **1** a small part or amount of something that remains when most of it no longer exists SYN **trace**: **[+of]** *The new law removed* ***the last vestiges*** *of royal power.* **2** the smallest possible amount of a quality or feeling: **[+of]** *There's not a vestige of truth in the story.*

ves·ti·gi·al /veˈstɪdʒiəl, -dʒəl/ *adj* **1** *technical* a vestigial part of the body has never developed completely or has almost disappeared: *The legs of snakes are vestigial or absent altogether.* **2** *formal* remaining as a sign that something existed after most of it has gone: *his vestigial sense of pride*

vest·ment /ˈvestmənt/ *n* [C usually plural] a piece of clothing worn by priests during church services

ves·try /ˈvestri/ *n* (*plural* **vestries**) [C] a small room in a church where a priest puts on his or her vestments and where holy plates, cups etc are kept

vet¹ /vet/ ●●○ S3 *n* [C]
1 (*also* **veterinary surgeon** *BrE formal*) someone who is trained to give medical care and treatment to sick animals SYN **veterinarian** *AmE* THESAURUS **DOCTOR**
2 *AmE informal* a VETERAN(1): *a Vietnam vet*

vet² *v* (**vetted**, **vetting**) [T] **1** *BrE* to check someone's past activities, relationships etc in order to make sure that person is suitable for a particular job, especially an important one: *All candidates are carefully vetted by Central Office.* **2** to check a report, speech etc carefully to make

V

sure it is acceptable: *The author vets every script for the new TV series.*

vetch /vetʃ/ *n* [C] a plant with small flowers, often used to feed farm animals

vet·e·ran /ˈvetərən/ ●○○ *n* [C]
1 someone who has been a soldier, sailor etc in a war: **[+of]** *a veteran of the Second World War | a Vietnam veteran*
2 someone who has had a lot of experience of a particular activity: **[+of]** *a veteran of countless political campaigns* | **veteran politician/campaigner/leader etc** *the veteran leader of the socialist party* | **veteran journalist/actor/goalkeeper etc**

ˌveteran ˈcar *n* [C] *BrE* a car built before 1905

ˈVeterans Day *n* [C,U] a holiday in the US on 11 November when people show special respect to people who fought in wars as soldiers, SAILORS etc

vet·e·ri·na·ri·an /ˌvetərəˈneəriən $ -ˈner-/ ●○○ *n* [C] *AmE* someone who is trained to give medical care and treatment to sick animals SYN **vet** *BrE*

vet·e·ri·na·ry /ˈvetərənəri $ -neri/ *adj* [only before noun] relating to the medical care and treatment of sick animals: *veterinary medicine*

ˈveterinary ˌsurgeon *n* [C] *BrE formal* a VET[1](1)

ve·to[1] /ˈviːtəʊ $ -toʊ/ ●○○ *v* (**vetoed, vetoing, vetoes**) [T]
1 if someone in authority vetoes something, they refuse to allow it to happen, especially something that other people or organizations have agreed: **veto legislation/a measure/a proposal etc** *President Bush* ***vetoed*** *the* ***bill*** *on July 6.* THESAURUS ▸ **REFUSE, VOTE**
2 to refuse to accept a particular plan or suggestion: *Jenny wanted to invite all her friends, but I quickly* ***vetoed*** *that* ***idea***.

veto[2] ●○○ *n* (*plural* **vetoes**) [C,U] a refusal to give official permission for something, or the right to refuse to give such permission: **[+on]** *de Gaulle's veto on the British application to join the EEC* | **[+over]** *The head teacher has the* ***right of veto*** *over management-board decisions.* | **[+of]** *Washington's veto of Seoul's nuclear ambitions | The Senate had a sufficient majority to* ***override*** *the presidential* ***veto*** (=not accept his refusal). | **exercise/use your veto**

vex /veks/ *v* [T] *old-fashioned* to make someone feel annoyed or worried —**vexing** *adj*: *a vexing problem*

vex·a·tion /vekˈseɪʃən/ *n old-fashioned* **1** [U] when you feel worried or annoyed by something: **in vexation** *Erika stamped her foot in vexation.* **2** [C] something that worries or annoys you

vex·a·tious /vekˈseɪʃəs/ *adj old-fashioned* making you feel annoyed or worried —**vexatiously** *adv*

V

vexed /vekst/ *adj* **1 vexed question/issue/problem etc** a complicated problem that has caused a lot of discussion and argument and is difficult to solve: **[+of]** *the vexed question of sexism* **2** [+at/with] *old-fashioned* annoyed or worried

V-for·ma·tion /ˈviː fɔːˌmeɪʃən $ -fɔːr-/ *n* [C] if birds or planes fly in a V-formation, they form the shape of the letter V as they fly

VGA /ˌviː dʒiː ˈeɪ/ *n* [U] *technical* (***video graphics array***) a standard of GRAPHICS (=pictures and letters) on a computer screen that has many different colours and is of a high quality

VHF /ˌviː eɪtʃ ˈef/ *n* [U] *technical* (***very high frequency***) radio waves that move very quickly and produce good sound quality

vi·a /ˈvaɪə, ˈviːə/ ●●○ W2 AWL *prep*
1 travelling through a place on the way to another place: *We flew to Athens via Paris.*
2 using a particular person, machine etc to send something: *I sent a message to Kitty via her sister. | You can access our homepage via the Internet.*

vi·a·ble /ˈvaɪəbəl/ ●○○ *adj*
1 a viable idea, plan, or method can work successfully: **viable alternative/proposition/option etc** *The committee came forward with one viable solution.* | **economically/commercially/financially viable** *Will a hotel here be financially viable?* THESAURUS ▸ **POSSIBLE**
2 *technical* able to continue to live or to develop into a living thing OPP **non-viable**: *viable seeds* —**viably** *adv* —**viability** /ˌvaɪəˈbɪləti/ *n* [U]: *the long-term economic viability of the company*

vi·a·duct /ˈvaɪədʌkt/ *n* [C] a long high bridge, especially one with ARCHes, that crosses a valley and has a road or railway on it → see picture at **BRIDGE**

Vi·ag·ra /vaɪˈægrə/ *n* [U] *trademark* a drug that helps men to have an ERECTION

vi·al /ˈvaɪəl/ (*also* **phial** *BrE*) *n* [C] *formal* a very small bottle used for medicine, PERFUME etc

vi·ands /ˈvaɪəndz/ *n* [plural] *old use* food

vibes /vaɪbz/ *n* [plural] *informal* **1** the good or bad feelings that a particular person, place, or situation seems to produce and that you react to: **good/bad etc vibes** *I have good vibes about this contract.* **2** a VIBRAPHONE

vi·brant /ˈvaɪbrənt/ ●○○ *adj*
1 full of activity or energy in a way that is exciting and attractive SYN **lively**: *Hong Kong is a vibrant, fascinating city. | She was sixteen, young and vibrant.*
2 a vibrant colour is bright and strong: *a painting full of vibrant reds and blues* —**vibrancy** *n* [U] —**vibrantly** *adv*

vi·bra·phone /ˈvaɪbrəfəʊn $ -foʊn/ *n* [C] (*also* **vibes** [plural]) an electronic musical instrument that consists of metal bars that you hit with special sticks to produce a sound

vi·brate /vaɪˈbreɪt $ ˈvaɪbreɪt/ ●○○ *v* [I,T] if something vibrates, or if you vibrate it, it shakes quickly and continuously with very small movements: *The floor was vibrating to the beat of the music. | As air passes over our vocal cords, it makes them vibrate.*

vi·bra·tion /vaɪˈbreɪʃən/ ●○○ *n*
1 [C,U] a continuous slight shaking movement: *the vibrations from the earthquake | The microscope must be free from vibration.*
2 vibrations [plural] VIBES(1)

vi·bra·to /vɪˈbrɑːtəʊ $ -toʊ/ *n* [U] a way of singing or playing a musical note so that it goes up and down very slightly in PITCH

vi·braˌtor /vaɪˈbreɪtə $ ˈvaɪbreɪtər/ *n* [C] a piece of electrical equipment that produces a small shaking movement, used especially in MASSAGE or to get sexual pleasure

vic·ar /ˈvɪkə $ -ər/ *n* [C] a priest in the Church of England who is in charge of a church in a particular area

vic·ar·age /ˈvɪkərɪdʒ/ *n* [C] a house where a vicar lives

vi·car·i·ous /vɪˈkeəriəs $ vaɪˈker-/ *adj* [only before noun] experienced by watching or reading about someone else doing something, rather than by doing it yourself: **vicarious pleasure/satisfaction/excitement etc** *the vicarious pleasure that parents get from their children's success* —**vicariously** *adv*

vice /vaɪs/ *n* **1** [U] criminal activities that involve sex or drugs: *the fight against vice on the streets | The police have smashed a vice ring* (=a group of criminals involved in vice) *in Chicago.* **2** [C] a bad habit: *Smoking is my only vice.* **3** [C,U] a bad or immoral quality in a person, or bad or immoral behaviour OPP **virtue**: *Jealousy is a vice. | to reward virtue and punish vice* **4** [C] (*usually* **vise** *AmE*) a tool that holds an object very firmly so that you can work on it: *He held my arm* ***like a vice***. → **VICE-LIKE**

vice- /vaɪs/ *prefix* **vice-president/chairman etc** the person next in rank below someone in authority, who can represent them or act instead of them: **[+of]** *the vice-captain of the cricket team | vice-chairman Derek Edwards*

ˌvice-ˈadmiral *n* [C] a high rank in the British or US navy, or someone who has this rank

ˌvice-ˈchancellor *n* [C] **1** someone who is the head of a British university, and responsible for the way it is organized → **chancellor** **2** someone who is responsible for a particular part of some universities in the US: *the vice-chancellor for student affairs*

ˈ**vice-like**, **vice·like** *BrE*, **vise-like, viselike** *AmE* /ˈvaɪslaɪk/ *adj* **a vice-like grip** a very firm hold or a very strong pain: *He grabbed my neck in a vice-like grip.*

ˌ**vice-ˈpresident** *n* [C] **1** the person who is next in rank to the president of a country and who is responsible for the president's duties if he or she is unable to do them **2** *AmE* someone who is responsible for a particular part of a company: *our vice-president for marketing*

vice·roy /ˈvaɪsrɔɪ/ *n* [C] a man who was sent by a king or queen in the past to rule another country: **[+of]** *the viceroy of India*

vice ver·sa /ˌvaɪs ˈvɜːsə, ˌvaɪsi- $ -ɜːr-/ ●○○ *adv* used to say that the opposite of a situation you have just described is also true: *The boys may refuse to play with the girls, and vice versa.*

vi·cin·i·ty /vəˈsɪnəti/ ●○○ *n formal*
1 in the vicinity (of sth) in the area around a particular place: *The stolen car was found in the vicinity of the station.* | *There used to be a mill in the vicinity.*
2 in the vicinity of £3 million/$1,500/2 billion years etc close to a particular amount or measurement: *All meteorites are of the same age, somewhere in the vicinity of 4.5 billion years old.*

vi·cious /ˈvɪʃəs/ ●●○ *adj*
1 violent and cruel in a way that hurts someone physically: *a vicious murder* | *a vicious killer* | *Keep away from that dog, he can be vicious.* THESAURUS▸ CRUEL, VIOLENT
2 very unkind in a way that is intended to hurt someone's feelings or make their character seem bad SYN **malicious**: *Sarah can be quite vicious at times.* | *a vicious personal attack on the Duchess* | *She was shocked by the vicious tone in his voice.*
3 unpleasantly strong or severe SYN **violent**: *a vicious gust of wind* | *a vicious headache* —**viciously** *adv*: *He twisted her arm viciously.* —**viciousness** *n* [U]

ˌ**vicious ˈcircle** (*also* ˌ**vicious ˈcycle**) *n* [singular] a situation in which one problem causes another problem, that then causes the first problem again, so that the whole process continues to be repeated

vi·cis·si·tudes /vəˈsɪsətjuːdz $ -tuːdz/ *n* [plural] *formal* the continuous changes and problems that affect a situation or someone's life: **[+of]** *the vicissitudes of married life*

vic·tim /ˈvɪktɪm/ ●●● S3 W2 *n* [C]
1 someone who has been attacked, robbed, or murdered: *The victim received head injuries from which she died a week later.* | **rape/murder etc victim** *Most homicide victims are under 30.* | **[+of]** *victims of crime* | *a credit card fraud ring that stole millions of dollars from* ***unsuspecting victims***
2 someone who suffers because of something bad that happens or because of an illness: **[+of]** *victims of age discrimination* | *He* ***was the victim of*** *an administrative error.* | *a massive aid programme for the* ***famine victims*** | ***AIDS victims*** *and other patients who are terminally ill* | *All these people are* ***innocent victims***. | *He was used to being in charge, not being the* ***victim of circumstance***. | *Saying that the unemployed 'don't want to work' is a classic case of* ***blaming the victim***.
3 fall victim to sb/sth *written* **a)** to be attacked, killed etc by someone, or to get a particular illness, especially one that kills: *One theory is that the hostages fell victim to bandits.* **b)** to be badly affected or destroyed by a situation: *Many small businesses have fallen victim to the recession.*
4 be/become a victim of its own success to be badly affected by some unexpected results of being very successful: *There are now so many tourists that the area has become a victim of its own success.*
5 sacrificial victim a person or animal that is killed and offered as a SACRIFICE (=gift) to a god
6 fashion/style victim someone who always wears the most fashionable clothes even if they do not look good in them

vic·tim·hood /ˈvɪktəmhʊd/ *n* [U] the state of suffering because someone has treated you very badly: *She had therapy to help her overcome her sense of victimhood.*

vic·tim·ize (*also* **-ise** *BrE*) /ˈvɪktəmaɪz/ *v* [T] to treat someone unfairly because you do not like them, their beliefs, or the race they belong to SYN **pick on**: *The men claim they have been victimized because of their political activity.* GRAMMAR **Victimize** is often used in the passive. —**victimization** /ˌvɪktəmaɪˈzeɪʃən $ -mə-/ *n* [U]

vic·tor /ˈvɪktə $ -ər/ *n* [C] *formal* the winner of a battle, game, competition etc: *After the game the victors returned in triumph.*

Vic·to·ri·an¹ /vɪkˈtɔːriən/ *adj* **1** relating to or coming from the period from 1837-1901 when Victoria was Queen of England: *a big Victorian house* **2** morally strict in a way that was typical in the time of Queen Victoria: *Victorian values*

Victorian² *n* [C] an English person living in the period when Queen Victoria ruled

Vic·to·ri·a·na /vɪkˌtɔːriˈɑːnə $ -ˈænə/ *n* [U] objects made during the Victorian period

vic·to·ri·ous /vɪkˈtɔːriəs/ ●○○ *adj* having won a victory, or ending in a victory: *the victorious team* | *We were confident that the Allies would* ***emerge victorious*** (=finally win). THESAURUS▸ SUCCESSFUL —**victoriously** *adv*

vic·to·ry /ˈvɪktəri/ ●●● W2 *n* (*plural* **victories**) [C,U] a situation in which you win a battle, game, election, or DISPUTE OPP **defeat**: **[+over/against]** *the Raiders' 35-17 victory over St Louis* | **[+for]** *The court's decision represents a victory for all women.* → PYRRHIC VICTORY

COLLOCATIONS

ADJECTIVES/NOUN + victory

a great/major victory *He said the court's decision was a great victory.*
an easy victory *Arsenal expected an easy victory.*
a decisive victory *The battle was a decisive victory for the US.*
a landslide victory (=a win by a very large amount in an election) | **a narrow victory** (=a win by a small amount) | **an election/electoral victory** | **a military victory**

VERBS

win/score a victory *Today we have won an important victory.*
lead sb to victory *She led her team to victory in the finals.*
clinch victory (=finally win) *Adams scored a last-minute goal to clinch victory.*
pull off a victory (=win when it is difficult) | **sweep to victory** (=win easily)

victory + NOUN

victory celebrations *The victory celebrations went on all night.*
a victory parade

PHRASES

a string of victories (=a series of victories) *The team won a string of victories.*

COMMON ERRORS

⚠ Don't say 'get victory' or 'get the victory'. Say **win a victory** or **win victory**.

THESAURUS

victory *n* [C,U] a situation in which you win a battle, game, election, or DISPUTE: *The crowds celebrated Italy's victory against England.* | *The party won a comfortable victory in the general election.*
win *n* [C] a victory in a sports game or in a competition: *It was an important win for the Yankees.* | *A couple from London are celebrating a big lottery win.*
triumph *n* [C] *written* an important victory, especially in war or politics: *Thatcher's greatest triumph was becoming the UK's first female prime minister.*

V

conquest *n* [C] a situation in which one country wins a war against another country and takes control of it: *the Spanish conquest of Mexico*
landslide *n* [C] an election victory in which one party or CANDIDATE gets far more votes than their opponents: *In 1945, there was a Labour landslide.*
walkover *especially BrE*, **cakewalk** *AmE n* [C] *informal* a very easy victory: *The match was expected to be a walkover for Brazil.*
upset *n* [C] a situation in which the person, team, party etc that was expected to win is defeated: *Truman pulled off the greatest election upset in United States history.*

vict·ual /ˈvɪtl/ *v* [T] to supply a large number of people with food

vict·uals /ˈvɪtlz/ *n* [plural] *old use* food and drink

vi·cu·ña /vɪˈkjuːnə $ -ˈkuː-/ *n* [C,U] a large South American animal related to the LLAMA, or the cloth that is made from its wool: *a vicuña coat*

vi·de·li·cet /vəˈdiːləset, -ket $ -ˈde-/ *adv* VIZ

vid·e·o¹ /ˈvɪdiəʊ $ -dioʊ/ ●●● S1 W2 *n* (*plural* **videos**)
1 [C,U] a copy of a film or television programme, or a series of events, recorded on VIDEOTAPE: **hire a video** *BrE*, **rent a video** *AmE*: *How much does it cost to hire videos?* | *Let's stay at home and **watch** a **video**.* | ***Rewind** the **video** right to the beginning.* | *The school will be **making** a **video** of the play.* | **on video** *The movie has not yet been **released on video**.* | *coming soon to a **video store** near you*
2 [C] a plastic box containing special tape for recording programmes and films on television SYN **videotape**, **video cassette**: *Have we got a **blank video*** (=one with nothing recorded on it yet) *anywhere?*
3 [C] *BrE* a machine used to record television programmes or show videos SYN **VCR**, **video cassette recorder**: **programme/set the video** *Can you set the video to record the football match?*
4 [U] the process of recording or showing television programmes, films, real events etc on VIDEOTAPE: *The course aims to help children learn through video.*
5 [C] a short film that is made to go with a particular piece of popular music SYN **music video**
6 [C] a DIGITAL recording of an event, for example one made using a MOBILE PHONE: *a **video clip** shown on the Internet*

video² *v* (**videoed**, **videoing**) [T] *BrE* to record a television programme, film, or a real event on a video SYN **videotape**, **tape** *AmE*: *Could you video the movie at 8.00?* | *A friend videoed the wedding.*

video³ *adj* [only before noun] relating to or used in the process of recording and showing pictures on television → **audio**: *video production* | *video materials for language teaching*

ˈvideo arˌcade *n* [C] *AmE* a public place where there are a lot of VIDEO GAMES that you play by putting money in the machines

ˈvideo blogˌging *n* [U] the activity of making a BLOG using video

ˈvideo ˌcamera *n* [C] a special camera that can be used to film events on a video

vid·e·o·card /ˈvɪdiəʊˌkɑːd $ -oʊˌkɑːrd/ *n* [C] a CIRCUIT BOARD that can be added to a computer so that it is able to show moving pictures

ˌvideo casˈsette (*also* **videotape**) *n* [C] a VIDEO

ˌvideo casˈsette reˌcorder *n* [C] (*abbreviation* **VCR**) a machine used to record television programmes or show videos SYN **video**

ˈvideo ˌconferencing *n* [U] a system that makes it possible to have meetings with people in different parts of the world by sending pictures and sound electronically

ˈvideo ˌdiary *n* (*plural* **video diaries**) [C] a record on video of someone's activities during a day, or over a period of time: **make/keep a video diary** *The group decided to make a video diary of the cycling trip.*

ˈvideo ˌgame *n* [C] a computer game in which you move images on a screen using electronic controls

vid·e·og·ra·pher /ˌvɪdiˈɒɡrəfə $ -ˈɑːɡrəfər/ *n* [C] *AmE formal* someone who records events using a VIDEO CAMERA

ˈvideo ˌjockey *n* [C] *especially AmE* a VJ

ˌvideo ˈnasty *n* [C] *BrE informal* a video film that includes very violent and offensive scenes

vid·e·o·phone /ˈvɪdiəʊfəʊn $ -dioʊfoʊn/ *n* [C] a type of telephone that allows you to see the person you are talking to on a screen

ˈvideo reˌcorder *n* [C] a VIDEO CASSETTE RECORDER

ˈvideo ˌsnacking *n* [U] the activity of watching short videos on a computer, MOBILE PHONE etc

vid·e·o·tape¹ /ˈvɪdiəʊteɪp $ -dioʊ-/ *n* [C,U] a video: **[+of]** *a videotape of everyday life in Havana*

videotape² (*also* **video** *BrE*) *v* [T] to record a television programme, film, event etc on a video

Vid·e·o·tex /ˈvɪdiəʊˌteks $ -dioʊ-/ *n* [U] *trademark* a form of communication that allows information to be exchanged using a television system

vie /vaɪ/ *v* (**vied**, **vying**, **vies**) [I] to compete very hard with someone in order to get something: **[+for]** *Simon and Julian were vying for her attention all through dinner.* | **[+with]** *There are at least twenty restaurants **vying with each other** for custom.* | **vie to do sth** *All the photographers vied to get the best pictures.*

view¹ /vjuː/ ●●● S1 W1 *n*
1 OPINION [C] what you think or believe about something SYN **opinion**: **[+on/about]** *What's your view on the subject?* | **[+that]** *Their view is that competition is good for business.* | ***In my view**, the country needs a change of government.* → **POINT OF VIEW(2)**

REGISTER
In everyday English, people usually say **I think ...** rather than **In my view ...**, and **What do you think?** rather than **What is your view?**: ***What do you think** about her new boyfriend?*

2 WAY OF CONSIDERING [C usually singular] a way of thinking about or understanding something: **[+of]** *Mum's view of the situation was different to mine.* | **optimistic/pessimistic/balanced etc view** *a realistic view of human nature* | *traditional views of religion* | *You need to **have a clear view*** (=a definite idea) *of the kind of book you want to write.* | **take a dim/poor view of sth** (=disapprove) *She took a pretty dim view of his behaviour.* THESAURUS ▶ SIGHT
3 SIGHT [C,U] what you are able to see or whether you can see it: **[+of]** *We'd like a room with a view of the sea.* | **good/bad/wonderful etc view** *The house has wonderful views over the valley.* | **be in view/come into view** *Suddenly the pyramids came into view.* | **disappear/vanish/be hidden from view** *The gun was hidden from view behind the door.* | *Fran hit him **in full view of** all the guests* (=where they could see it clearly). | *During an eclipse, the Moon **blocks** our **view** of the Sun* (=stops us from seeing it).
4 SCENERY [C] the whole area that you can see from somewhere, especially when it is very beautiful or impressive: *From the top you get a **panoramic view** of the city.* | *A huge nuclear reactor now **spoils the view**.*
5 PICTURE [C] a photograph or picture showing a beautiful or interesting place: **[+of]** *The book contains over fifty scenic views of Cambridge.*
6 CHANCE TO SEE STH [C,U] an occasion or time when it is possible for people to see something such as an art show: **[+of]** *A **private view** of the Summer Exhibition will be held.* | **on view** (=being shown to the public) *The painting is currently on view at the Tate.*
7 in view of sth *formal* used to introduce the reason for a decision or action: *In view of his conduct, the club has decided to suspend him.*
8 with a view to (doing) sth because you are planning to do something in the future: *We bought the house with a view to retiring there.*
9 in view *formal* having something in your mind as an aim:

with this end/object/aim etc in view *Defence was all-important, and castles were designed with this end in view.* | *What sort of job did you* ***have in view****?*
10 take the long view (of sth) *BrE* to think about the effect that something will have in the future rather than what happens now

COLLOCATIONS

VERBS

have/hold a view (=have an opinion) *He has very left-wing views.*
take the view that ... (=have a particular view) *The Government took the view that the law did not need to be changed.*
express a view (=say what you think about something) *This is a chance for you to express your views.*
share a view (=agree with it) *This view is not shared by his colleagues.*
support a view (=believe or help to prove that it is right) *There are many people who would support his views.*
hear a view (*also* **listen to a view**) | **tell sb your view** (*also* **let sb have your view**)

ADJECTIVES

political views *His political views have not changed.*
sb's personal view *My own personal view is that they're being optimistic.*
the general view (=what most people think) *The general view was that he had done well.*
strong views *She has strong views on education.*
strongly held/deeply held views (=strong views that someone is unwilling to change) *He is known for his strongly held views on modern art.*
different views *Different people have different views about this subject.*
conflicting/opposing views (=completely different) *There are conflicting views about the best way to teach reading.*
extreme *a politician who has extreme views on immigration*
moderate | **traditional** | **old-fashioned** | **popular/unpopular**

PHRASES

be of the same view (=agree) *They were all of the same view.*
an exchange of views (=when people say what they think, especially when they disagree)

view[2] ●●○ *v* [T]
1 to think about something or someone in a particular way SYN **see**: **view sth as sth** *The law should be viewed as a way of meeting certain social goals.* | **view sth from a ... perspective/standpoint** *It's an issue that can be viewed from several perspectives.* | **view sth with caution/suspicion/scepticism etc** *The local people viewed newcomers with suspicion.*
2 *formal* to look at something, especially because it is beautiful or you are interested in it: **view sth from sth** *The mountain is best viewed from the north side.* | *Thousands of tourists come to view the gardens every year.* | **view a house/an apartment/a property** (=go to see a house etc that you are interested in buying)
3 *formal* to watch a television programme, film etc: *an opportunity to view the film before it goes on general release*

view·er /ˈvjuːə $ -ər/ ●●○ *n* [C]
1 someone who watches television: *The new series has gone down well with viewers.*
2 someone who looks at something: *In the painting, the woman has her back to the viewer.*
3 a small box with a light in it used to look at SLIDES (=colour photographs on special film)

view·find·er /ˈvjuːˌfaɪndə $ -ər/ *n* [C] the small square of glass on a camera that you look through to see exactly what you are photographing

view·point /ˈvjuːpɔɪnt/ ●●○ *n* [C]
1 a particular way of thinking about a problem or subject SYN **point of view**: **from sb's viewpoint/from the viewpoint of sb/sth** *Try and think of it from the child's viewpoint.* | *The islands were important from the viewpoint of American security.* | **[+on]** *the Church's viewpoint on divorce* | **political/scientific/feminist etc viewpoint** *From an ecological viewpoint, the motorway has been a disaster.*
2 a place from which you can see something: *Different viewpoints produce different images.*

vig·il /ˈvɪdʒəl/ *n* [C,U] **1** a period of time, especially during the night, when you stay awake in order to pray, remain with someone who is ill, or watch for danger: *Eva and Paul* ***kept*** *a constant* ***vigil*** *by their daughter's hospital bedside.* **2** a silent political protest in which people wait outside a building, especially during the night: **silent/candle-lit vigil** *Two thousand demonstrators* ***held*** *a candle-lit* ***vigil*** *outside the embassy.*

vig·i·lance /ˈvɪdʒələns/ *n* [U] careful attention that you give to what is happening, so that you will notice any danger or illegal activity: *the need for increased police vigilance*

vig·i·lant /ˈvɪdʒələnt/ *adj* giving careful attention to what is happening, so that you will notice any danger or illegal activity: *Please* ***remain vigilant*** *at all times and report anything suspicious.* —**vigilantly** *adv*

REGISTER
In everyday English, people usually use the expression **watch out** rather than **be vigilant**: *We were told to* ***watch out*** *for anything suspicious.*

vig·i·lan·te /ˌvɪdʒəˈlænti/ *n* [C] someone who illegally punishes criminals and tries to prevent crime, usually because they think the police are not doing this effectively —**vigilantism** *n* [U]

vi·gnette /vɪˈnjet/ *n* [C] *formal* **1** a short description in a book or play showing the typical features of a person or situation **2** a small picture or design at the beginning or end of a book or CHAPTER

vig·or /ˈvɪgə $ -ər/ *n* [U] the American spelling of VIGOUR

vig·o·rous /ˈvɪgərəs/ ●○○ *adj*
1 using a lot of energy and strength or determination: *Your dog needs at least 20 minutes of* ***vigorous exercise*** *every day.* | *Environmentalists have begun a vigorous campaign to oppose nuclear dumping in the area.* | *a vigorous debate* | *Vigorous efforts are being made to find a solution to the problem.* | *The measures provoked vigorous opposition in right-wing circles.*
2 strong and healthy: *a vigorous young man*

vig·o·rous·ly /ˈvɪgərəsli/ ●○○ *adv* in a way that uses a lot of energy and strength or determination: *She* ***campaigned vigorously*** *for women's rights.* | *Bailey* ***vigorously denied*** *the accusations.* | *He shook his head vigorously.*

vig·our *BrE*, **vigor** *AmE* /ˈvɪgə $ -ər/ *n* [U] physical or mental energy and determination: **with vigour** *He began working with* ***renewed vigour****.*

Vi·king /ˈvaɪkɪŋ/ *n* [C] a member of the group of Scandinavian people who sailed in ships to attack areas along the coasts of northern and western Europe from the 8th to 11th centuries

vile /vaɪl/ *adj* **1** *informal* extremely unpleasant or bad SYN **horrible**: *This coffee* ***tastes*** *really* ***vile****.* | *a* ***vile smell*** | *She has a* ***vile temper****.* **2** evil or immoral: *a vile act of betrayal* —**vilely** *adv* —**vileness** *n* [U]

vil·i·fy /ˈvɪlɪfaɪ/ *v* (**vilified, vilifying, vilifies**) [T] *formal* to say or write bad things about someone or something: **vilify sb/sth for (doing) sth** *Johnson was vilified in the press for refusing to resign.* —**vilification** /ˌvɪlɪfɪˈkeɪʃən/ *n* [U]

vil·la /ˈvɪlə/ *n* [C] **1** *BrE* a house that you use or rent while you are on holiday **2** a big house in the country with a large garden **3** a house in a town: *Victorian villas* **4** an ancient Roman house or farm with land surrounding it

V

vil·lage /ˈvɪlɪdʒ/ ●●● S1 W1 *n* [C]
1 a very small town in the countryside: *a little fishing village* | **village school/shop/church etc**
2 the village the people who live in a village: *The whole village came to the meeting.*

ˌvillage ˈgreen *n* [C] an area of grass in the middle of an English village

ˌvillage ˈidiot *n* [C] someone in the past who had mental difficulties and lived in a small village with the other people there

vil·lag·er /ˈvɪlɪdʒə $ -ər/ ●●○ *n* [C] someone who lives in a village

vil·lain /ˈvɪlən/ ●○○ *n* [C]
1 the main bad character in a film, play, or story
2 the villain of the piece the person or thing that has caused all the trouble in a particular situation
3 *informal* a bad person or criminal

vil·lain·ous /ˈvɪlənəs/ *adj literary* evil or criminal

vil·lain·y /ˈvɪləni/ *n* (*plural* **villainies**) [C,U] *literary* evil or criminal behaviour

-ville /vɪl/ *suffix* **1** used in the names of places, especially in the US, to mean city or town: *Jacksonville, Florida* **2** *informal* used humorously with adjectives or nouns followed by 's' to show that a person, place, or thing has a particular quality: *Her party was really dullsville.*

vil·lein /ˈvɪlən, ˈvɪleɪn/ *n* [C] a poor farm worker in the Middle Ages who was given a small piece of land in return for working on the land of a rich lord → **feudalism**

vim /vɪm/ *n* [U] *old-fashioned* energy: *She was full of* ***vim and vigour***.

vin·ai·grette /ˌvɪnəˈgret, ˌvɪneɪ-/ *n* [singular, U] a mixture of oil, VINEGAR, salt, and pepper that you put on a SALAD SYN **salad dressing**

vin·di·cate /ˈvɪndɪkeɪt/ *v* [T] *formal* **1** to prove that someone who was blamed for something is in fact not guilty: *The charges are false, and we are sure we will be vindicated in court.* **2** to prove that someone or something is right or true SYN **justify**: *The decision to advertise has been vindicated by the fact that sales have grown.* —**vindication** /ˌvɪndɪˈkeɪʃən/ *n* [singular, U]

vin·dic·tive /vɪnˈdɪktɪv/ *adj* unreasonably cruel and unfair towards someone who has harmed you: *a bitter and vindictive old man* —**vindictively** *adv* —**vindictiveness** *n* [U]

vine /vaɪn/ ●○○ *n* [C]
1 (*also* **grapevine**) a plant that produces GRAPES
2 a plant with long thin stems that attach themselves to other plants, trees, buildings etc

vin·e·gar /ˈvɪnɪgə $ -ər/ ●●○ *n* [U] a sour-tasting liquid made from MALT or wine that is used to improve the taste of food or to preserve it

vin·e·gar·y /ˈvɪnɪgəri/ *adj* tasting of vinegar

vine·yard /ˈvɪnjəd $ -jərd/ ●○○ *n* [C] a piece of land where GRAPEVINES are grown in order to produce wine

vi·no /ˈviːnəʊ $ -noʊ/ *n* [U] *informal* wine

vin·tage¹ /ˈvɪntɪdʒ/ ●○○ *adj* [only before noun]
1 vintage wine is good quality wine made in a particular year
2 old, but high quality: *vintage cars*
3 showing all the best or most typical qualities of something: *a vintage performance from Bruce Springsteen*
4 vintage year a) a year when a good quality wine was produced **b)** a year when something of very good quality was produced: **[+for]** *2001 was not a vintage year for movies.*

vintage² *n* **1** [C] a particular year or place in which a wine is made, or the wine itself **2 of recent vintage** having happened or started not very long ago: *There are some classic songs on the album, but most are of more recent vintage.*

ˌvintage ˈcar *n* [C] *BrE* a car made between 1919 and 1930

vint·ner /ˈvɪntnə $ -ər/ *n* [C] *formal* someone who buys and sells wines

vi·nyl /ˈvaɪnəl/ *n* [U] **1** a type of strong plastic **2** records that are played on a RECORD PLAYER – used especially when comparing them to CDS

vi·o·la /viˈəʊlə $ -ˈoʊ-/ *n* [C] **1** a wooden musical instrument that you play like a VIOLIN but that is larger and has a lower sound → see picture at **STRINGED INSTRUMENT**
2 a plant related to the VIOLET

vi·o·late /ˈvaɪəleɪt/ ●○○ AWL *v* [T]
1 to disobey or do something against an official agreement, law, principle etc: *Thirty-four protesters were arrested for violating criminal law.* | *regimes that violate human rights* **THESAURUS** ▸ **DISOBEY**
2 to do something that makes someone feel that they have been attacked or have suffered a great loss of respect: *Victims of burglaries often feel personally violated.* | *The media regularly* ***violates*** *people's* ***privacy***.
3 *formal* to break open a GRAVE, or force your way into a holy place without showing any respect: *Vandals had violated the graveyard.*
4 *literary* to force a woman to have sex SYN **rape**
—**violator** *n* [C]

vi·o·la·tion /ˌvaɪəˈleɪʃən/ ●○○ AWL *n* [C,U]
1 an action that breaks a law, agreement, principle etc: *human rights violations* | **[+of]** *a violation of international law* | **in violation of sth** *Troops crossed the border in violation of the agreement.*
2 an action that causes harm or damage by treating someone or their possessions without respect

vi·o·lence /ˈvaɪələns/ ●●● S2 W2 *n* [U]
1 behaviour that is intended to hurt other people physically: *There is too much sex and violence on TV these days.* | **[+against]** *violence against women*
2 extreme force: *the tremendous violence of a tornado*
3 do violence to sth *formal* to spoil something
4 *literary* an angry way of speaking or reacting: *She spoke with a violence that surprised them both.*

COLLOCATIONS

ADJECTIVES

physical violence *They were threatened with physical violence.*
domestic violence (=violence between a couple in their home) *Police said she was a victim of domestic violence.*
racial/ethnic violence (=between people of different racial/ethnic groups) *There were outbreaks of racial violence in some cities.*
gratuitous violence (=violence that there is no reason for) *These films are full of gratuitous violence.*
mindless violence (=stupid and without any purpose)

VERBS

resort to/use violence *They were willing to resort to violence to achieve their ends.*
violence erupts/breaks out/flares (=suddenly starts) *Violence erupted during the demonstration.*
the violence escalates (=becomes worse)

PHRASES

an act of violence *Police warned that acts of violence would not be tolerated.*
an outbreak of violence

vi·o·lent /ˈvaɪələnt/ ●●● S3 W3 *adj*
1 involving actions that are intended to injure or kill people, by hitting them, shooting them etc: *the increase in* ***violent crime*** | *violent clashes between the police and demonstrators* | *Thirty-one people have been injured in violent incidents throughout the day.* | *The riots ended in the violent deaths of three teenagers.*
2 someone who is violent is likely to attack, hurt, or kill other people SYN **aggressive**: *My father was a violent and dangerous man.* | *He had a reputation for* ***turning violent*** (=suddenly attacking people).
3 showing very strong angry emotions or opinions: **violent**

V

quarrel/argument/row etc *They had a violent quarrel and John stormed out.*
4 violent feelings are strong and very difficult to control: *They took a violent dislike to each other.* | *She has a violent temper.*
5 violent headache/fit etc a physical feeling or reaction that is very painful or difficult to control
6 violent film/play/drama a film etc that contains a lot of violence
7 a violent storm/earthquake/explosion etc a storm etc that happens with a lot of force
8 extremely bright: *Her cheeks turned a violent red colour.*

THESAURUS

violent /ˈvaɪələnt/ using force to hurt or kill people – used about people, crimes etc. Also used about films or books that contain a lot of violence: *a violent man who couldn't control his temper* | *the increase in violent crime* | *The film is too violent to be shown to children.*
vicious /ˈvɪʃəs/ violent and dangerous, and seeming to enjoy hurting people for no reason: *a vicious attack on an unarmed man* | *We were surrounded by a gang of vicious thugs, armed with knives.*
rough /rʌf/ using force or violence, but not causing serious injury: *Some of the boys were being a bit rough with the younger kids.* | *There were complaints about rough treatment by the police.*
brutal /ˈbruːtl/ behaving in a way that is very cruel and violent, and showing no pity: *Idi Amin was a brutal dictator.* | *a particularly brutal murder*
savage /ˈsævɪdʒ/ attacking people in a particularly cruel way – used about people and fighting, especially in news reports: *a savage killer* | *There was savage fighting in the capital Mogadishu.*
bloody a bloody battle or war is very violent and a lot of people are killed or injured: *a bloody civil war* | *The Russians were engaged in a bloody battle against the German army.*
ferocious /fəˈrəʊʃəs/ a ferocious attack or battle is extremely violent. Also used about animals that are likely to attack in a very violent way: *The two armies fought a ferocious battle.* | *a ferocious beast*
fierce a fierce animal or person looks frightening and likely to attack people: *A fierce dog stood growling at the gate.*
bloodthirsty a bloodthirsty person enjoys watching violence. A bloodthirsty story contains a lot of violent scenes: *In Mexico, humans were sacrificed to bloodthirsty gods.* | *a bloodthirsty tale of revenge*
gory showing or describing injuries, blood, death etc clearly and in detail: *a gory horror movie* | *The book was too gory for many readers.*

vi·o·lent·ly /ˈvaɪələntli/ ●○○ *adv*
1 with a lot of force in a way that is very difficult to control: **tremble/shiver/shake etc violently** *I was still trembling violently.* | **violently sick/ill** *He rushed to the bathroom, where he was violently sick.*
2 in a way that involves violence: *Several people have been violently attacked in the subway.*
3 with a lot of energy or emotion, especially anger: *Jenny protested violently.*

vi·o·let /ˈvaɪəlɪt/ *n* **1** [C] a plant with small dark purple flowers, or sometimes white or yellow ones → see picture at FLOWER[1] **2** [U] a bluish-purple colour —**violet** *adj*: *beautiful violet eyes*

vi·o·lin /ˌvaɪəˈlɪn/ ●●○ *n* [C] a small wooden musical instrument that you hold under your chin and play by pulling a BOW (=special stick) across the strings → see picture at **STRINGED INSTRUMENT**

vi·o·lin·ist /ˌvaɪəˈlɪnɪst/ *n* [C] someone who plays the violin

vi·o·lon·cel·lo /ˌvaɪələnˈtʃeləʊ $ -loʊ/ *n* (*plural* **violoncellos**) [C] *formal* a CELLO

VIP /ˌviː aɪ ˈpiː/ *n* [C] (***very important person***) someone who is very famous or powerful and is treated with special care and respect: *They treated us like VIPs.* | *We were given* ***VIP treatment***.

vi·per /ˈvaɪpə $ -ər/ *n* [C] **1** a small poisonous snake **2** *literary* someone who behaves in an unpleasant way and harms other people

vi·ra·go /vəˈrɑːgəʊ $ -goʊ/ *n* (*plural* **viragos**) [C] *formal* an offensive word for an angry woman who often argues with people

vi·ral[1] /ˈvaɪərəl $ ˈvaɪrəl/ ●○○ *adj*
1 relating to or caused by a VIRUS: *a* ***viral infection***
2 passed on to other people on the Internet or using MOBILE PHONES: *It is one of the most viewed viral videos on the web.*
3 go viral if a picture, video, joke etc goes viral, it spreads widely, especially on the Internet or MOBILE PHONES

viral[2] *n* [C] a viral video, advertisement etc: *They use humorous virals to promote their products.*

ˈviral ˌmarketing *n* [U] a type of advertising used by Internet companies in which computer users pass on advertising messages or images through email, sometimes without realizing that they are doing this: *You can reach more potential customers by using viral marketing techniques.*

vir·gin[1] /ˈvɜːdʒɪn $ ˈvɜːr-/ *n* [C] **1** someone who has never had sex **2 the Virgin Mary** (*also* **the (Blessed) Virgin**) Mary, the mother of Jesus Christ **3** someone who has never done a particular activity before: *a snowboarding virgin*

virgin[2] *adj* [only before noun] **1 virgin land/forest/soil/snow etc** land etc that is still in its natural state and has not been used or changed by people **2** without sexual experience: *a* ***virgin bride*** **3 virgin territory** something new that you are experiencing for the first time **4 (extra) virgin olive oil** the highest quality of OLIVE OIL, made from the first pressing of the olives

vir·gin·al /ˈvɜːdʒɪnəl $ ˈvɜːr-/ *adj* like a virgin

vir·gin·als /ˈvɜːdʒənəlz $ ˈvɜːr-/ *n* [plural] a small square musical instrument like a piano with no legs, popular in the 16th and 17th centuries

ˌvirgin ˈbirth *n* **the virgin birth** the birth of Jesus, which Christians believe was caused by God, not by sex between a man and a woman

vir·gin·i·a creep·er /vɜːˌdʒɪniə ˈkriːpə $ vɜːrˌdʒɪniə ˈkriːpər/ *n* [C,U] a garden plant that grows up walls and has large leaves that turn deep red in autumn

vir·gin·i·ty /vɜːˈdʒɪnəti $ vɜːr-/ *n* [U] the condition of never having had sex: **lose your virginity** (=have sex for the first time)

Vir·go /ˈvɜːgəʊ $ ˈvɜːrgoʊ/ *n* (*plural* **Virgos**) **1** [U] the sixth sign of the ZODIAC, represented by a young woman, which some people believe affects the character and life of people born between August 24 and September 23 **2** [C] someone who was born between August 24 and September 23

vir·ile /ˈvɪraɪl $ ˈvɪrəl/ *adj* having or showing traditionally male qualities such as strength, courage etc – use this to show approval → **macho**

vi·ril·i·ty /vəˈrɪləti/ *n* [U] **1** the typically male quality of being strong, brave, and full of energy – used to show approval **2** the ability of a man to have sex or make a woman PREGNANT

vi·rol·o·gy /vaɪəˈrɒlədʒi $ vaɪˈrɑː-/ *n* [U] the scientific study of VIRUSes or of the diseases caused by them —**virologist** *n* [C]

vir·tu·al /ˈvɜːtʃuəl $ ˈvɜːr-/ ●●○ AWL *adj* [only before noun]
1 very nearly a particular thing: *Car ownership is a virtual necessity when you live in the country.* | *Finding a cheap place to rent is a virtual impossibility in this area.*
2 made, done, seen etc on the Internet or on a computer, rather than in the real world: *The website allows you to take a virtual tour of the art gallery.* | *constructing virtual worlds*
THESAURUS ARTIFICIAL

vir·tu·al·ly /ˈvɜːtʃuəli $ ˈvɜːr-/ ●●● S2 W2 AWL *adv*
1 almost SYN **practically**: *Virtually all the children come to school by bus.* | *He was virtually unknown before running for office.* THESAURUS ALMOST
2 on a computer, rather than in the real world: *Professors can help students virtually by communicating over the Internet.*

ˌvirtual ˈmemory *n* [singular,U] *technical* space on a computer for storing instructions and programs until they are needed or being used → **RAM, ROM**

ˌvirtual ˈoffice *n* [C] a situation in which a company's workers do not go to an office to work, but instead use computers that are connected to the Internet to communicate with each other from different places: *Does the virtual office equal freedom or isolation?*

ˌvirtual reˈality *n* [U] an environment produced by a computer that looks and seems real to the person experiencing it

vir·tue /ˈvɜːtʃuː $ ˈvɜːr-/ ●●○ W3 *n*
1 [U] *formal* moral goodness of character and behaviour OPP **vice**: *Women have often been used as symbols of virtue.*
2 [C] a particular good quality in someone's character OPP **vice**: *Among her many virtues are loyalty, courage, and truthfulness.*
3 [C,U] an advantage that makes something better or more useful than something else: **[+of]** *Adam Smith believed in the virtues of free trade.* | *Wilkins is now* **extolling** (=praising very much) ***the virtues of*** *organic farming.* THESAURUS ADVANTAGE
4 by virtue of sth *formal* by means of, or as a result of something: *She became a British resident by virtue of her marriage.*
5 make a virtue of sth to get an advantage from a situation that you cannot change, usually a bad one: *She made a virtue of her acting limitations by joking about them.*
6 make a virtue of necessity to get an advantage from doing something that you have to do, or to pretend that you are doing it willingly
7 [U] *old use* the state of not having with someone, or not having sex with anyone except your husband

vir·tu·os·i·ty /ˌvɜːtʃuˈɒsəti $ ˌvɜːrtʃuˈɑː-/ *n* [U] *formal* a very high degree of skill in performing

vir·tu·o·so /ˌvɜːtʃuˈəʊsəʊ $ ˌvɜːrtʃuˈoʊsoʊ/ *n* (*plural* **virtuosos**) [C] someone who is a very skilful performer, especially in music: *violin virtuoso Vanessa Mae* THESAURUS EXPERT, SKILFUL —**virtuoso** *adj* [only before noun]: ***a virtuoso performance*** | *a virtuoso pianist*

vir·tu·ous /ˈvɜːtʃuəs $ ˈvɜːr-/ *adj* **1** *formal* behaving in a very honest and moral way OPP **wicked**: *a virtuous man* | *Sue considered herself very virtuous because she neither drank nor smoked.* **2** *old use* not willing to have sex, at least until you are married —**virtuously** *adv*

vir·u·lent /ˈvɪrələnt/ *adj* **1** a poison, disease etc that is virulent is very dangerous and affects people very quickly OPP **mild**: *a particularly* ***virulent form*** *of influenza* **2** *formal* full of hatred for something, or expressing this in a strong way - used to show disapproval: *virulent anti-Semitism* —**virulence** *n* [U] —**virulently** *adv*

vi·rus /ˈvaɪərəs $ ˈvaɪrəs/ ●●○ W3 *n*
1 [C,U] a very small living thing that causes infectious illnesses: *children* ***infected with*** *the Aids virus* | *a* ***virus infection***
2 [C] a set of instructions secretly put onto a computer or computer program, which can destroy information. When a computer that has a virus makes a connection with another computer, for example by EMAIL, the virus can make copies of itself and move to the other computer.
3 [C] a program that sends a large number of annoying messages to many people's MOBILE PHONES in an uncontrolled way

vi·sa /ˈviːzə/ ●●○ *n* [C] an official mark put on your PASSPORT that gives you permission to temporarily enter or leave a foreign country: *I was still in New York, trying to get a visa to visit Russia.* | **a work/student/tourist visa** *She applied for a three-month tourist visa.* | **an entry/exit visa**

vis·age /ˈvɪzɪdʒ/ *n* [C] *literary* a face

vis-à-vis /ˌviːz ɑː ˈviː, ˌviːz ə-/ *prep formal* in relation to or in comparison with something or someone: *the bargaining position of the UK vis-à-vis the rest of Europe*

vis·ce·ra /ˈvɪsərə/ *n* [plural] *medical* the large organs inside your body, such as your heart, lungs, and stomach

vis·ce·ral /ˈvɪsərəl/ *adj* **1** *literary* visceral beliefs and attitudes are the result of strong feelings rather than careful thought: *his visceral hatred of the ruling class* **2** *medical* relating to the viscera

vis·cid /ˈvɪsɪd/ *adj* VISCOUS

vis·count /ˈvaɪkaʊnt/ *n* [C] a British NOBLEMAN with a rank between that of an EARL and a BARON

vis·count·ess /ˈvaɪkaʊntɪs/ *n* [C] the wife of a viscount, or a woman who has the rank of a viscount

vis·cous /ˈvɪskəs/ *adj technical* a viscous liquid is thick and sticky and does not flow easily: *As the liquid cools, it becomes viscous.* —**viscosity** /vɪˈskɒsəti $ -ˈskɑː-/ *n* [U]

vise /vaɪs/ *n* [C] the American spelling of VICE

vis·i·bil·i·ty /ˌvɪzəˈbɪləti/ ●○○ AWL *n* [U]
1 the distance it is possible to see, especially when this is affected by weather conditions: *Visibility on the roads is down to 20 metres due to heavy fog.* | **good/poor visibility** *The search for survivors was abandoned because of poor visibility.*
2 the situation of being noticed by people in general: **[+of]** *The exhibition helped increase the visibility of women artists.*
3 the fact of being easy to see: ***high visibility*** *clothing*

vis·i·ble /ˈvɪzəbəl/ ●●○ W3 AWL *adj*
1 something that is visible can be seen OPP **invisible**: **clearly/highly/barely etc visible** *The outline of the mountains was clearly visible.* | **[+to]** *The sign was clearly visible to passing motorists.* | *The comet is* ***visible to the naked eye*** (=can be seen without using special equipment). | *Check the plant for any* ***visible signs*** *of disease.*
2 an effect that is visible is great enough to be noticed SYN **noticeable**: *There has been a* ***visible change*** *in his attitude.*
3 someone who is visible is in a situation in which a lot of people notice them: ***highly visible*** *politicians*

vis·i·bly /ˈvɪzəbli/ AWL *adv* in a way that is easy to see or notice: **visibly shaken/shocked/upset etc** *She was visibly shaken by the news.*

vi·sion /ˈvɪʒən/ ●●○ S3 W3 AWL *n*
1 [U] the ability to see SYN **sight** → **visual**: *She suffered temporary loss of vision after being struck on the head.* | *Tears* ***blurred*** *her* ***vision*** (=made it difficult for her to see). | **good/normal/poor etc vision** *children who are born with poor vision* | **twenty-twenty/20-20 vision** (=the ability to see perfectly) | **night vision** (=the ability to see when it is dark)
2 [U] the area that you can see: *a figure* ***at the edge of*** *her* ***vision*** | **sb's field/line of vision** (=the area someone is able to see without turning their head) *As the cars overtake you, they are temporarily outside your field of vision.*
3 [C] an idea of what you think something should be like: **[+of]** *He had a* ***clear vision*** *of how he hoped the company would develop.* | **[+for]** *The president outlined his vision for the future.* | **grand/powerful/original etc vision** *a grand vision for the country*
4 have visions of sth if you have visions of something happening, especially something bad, you imagine it happening: *I had visions of the kids getting lost and getting abducted by some weirdo.*
5 [C] something that you seem to see as part of a powerful religious experience: *She* ***had a vision*** *in which Jesus appeared before her.* | **in a vision** *He became a monk after seeing Saint Apollinaris in a vision.*
6 [U] the knowledge and imagination that are needed in planning for the future with a clear purpose: *We need a leader with vision and strong principles.* | *his enthusiasm and* ***breadth of vision***

V

7 a vision of beauty/loveliness etc *literary* someone who is very beautiful
8 [U] the quality of a picture that you can see on a television

vi·sion·a·ry[1] /ˈvɪʒənəri $ -neri/ *adj* **1** having clear ideas of what the world should be like in the future: *Under his visionary leadership, the city prospered.* **2** existing only in someone's mind and unlikely to ever exist in the real world

visionary[2] *n* (*plural* **visionaries**) [C] **1** someone who has clear ideas and strong feelings about the way something should be in the future **2** a holy person who has VISIONS

vis·it[1] /ˈvɪzɪt/ ●●● S2 W1 *v*
1 [I,T] to go and spend time in a place or with someone, especially for pleasure or interest: *Eric went to Seattle to visit his cousins.* | *I was really pleased that they* ***came to visit*** *me.* | *Which cities did you visit in Spain?* | *A recent trip to London gave me the opportunity to visit the Science Museum.* | *She doesn't visit very often.*

> **REGISTER**
> In everyday English, people often say that they **come/go to see** someone, rather than **visit** them: *He's gone to Scotland to* ***see*** *his family.*

2 [T] to go to a place as part of your official job, especially to examine it: *The building inspector is visiting the new housing project.* | **[+with]** *AmE*: *The president's first trip abroad will be to visit with troops in Bosnia.*
3 [T] *formal* to go to see a doctor, lawyer etc in order to get treatment or advice
4 [T] to look at a website on the Internet: *Over 1,000 people visit our site every week.*
5 [I] *AmE* to talk socially with someone: **[+with]** *Why don't you kids play outside while we visit with each other?*

> **THESAURUS**
> **A PLACE**
> **visit** to go and spend time in a place, for interest or pleasure: *You must visit Kyoto.* | *They visited all the usual places.*
> **go to** to visit a place. **Go to** is very commonly used in everyday English instead of **visit**: *Have you ever been to England?* | *They went to the Eiffel Tower and the Flea Market.*
> **go sightseeing** to visit places of interest in a country: *We went sightseeing in the old part of the city.*
> **A PERSON**
> **visit** to go and spend time with someone: *How often do you visit your grandparents?*
> **come around/by/over** (*also* **come round** *BrE*) to visit someone informally in their home, especially when you live near them: *A few friends came round last night.*
> **drop in/by** (*also* **call in/by** *BrE*) to visit someone in their home, especially on your way to another place: *Kate said she'd drop by later to give you the forms.*
> **look sb up** to visit someone who you do not see very often, when you are spending time in the area where they live: *Look me up if you're ever in Newark.*

visit sth **on** sb/sth *phr v biblical* to do something to punish someone or show them that you are angry: *God's wrath will be visited on sinners.*

visit[2] ●●● S3 W2 *n* [C]
1 an occasion when someone goes to spend time in a place or goes to see a person: **[+to]** *a visit to Chicago* | *We're just here* ***on a*** *short* ***visit****.* | *Why don't you come* ***for a visit*** *this summer?* | *I decided to* ***pay*** *him* ***a visit*** *at his office.* | *I've just* ***had*** *a* ***visit from*** *the police.* | *I'm only here for the weekend - just a* ***flying visit*** *this time.* | *his first* ***official visit*** *to Britain as Russian president* | *The town is* ***well worth a visit****.*
2 an occasion when you see a doctor, lawyer etc for treatment or advice
3 *AmE* an occasion when you talk socially with someone: *Barbara and I had a nice long visit.*

vis·i·ta·tion /ˌvɪzɪˈteɪʃən/ *n* **1** [C,U] *formal* an official visit to a place or person **2** [C,U] *law* an occasion when a parent is allowed to spend time with the children after a DIVORCE, or the right to do this: *visitation rights* **3** [C] an occasion when God or a spirit is believed to appear to someone on Earth **4** [C] *literary* an event that is believed to be God's punishment for something: *a visitation of plague* **5** [C] a long visit from someone that you do not want to see - used humorously

ˈvisiting card *n* [C] a small card with their name on it which people gave to someone they visited, in the past SYN **calling card** *AmE*

ˈvisiting hours *n* [plural] the times when you are allowed to visit people who are in a hospital

ˌvisiting proˈfessor *n* [C] a university teacher who has come from another university to teach for a period of time

vis·it·or /ˈvɪzɪtə $ -ər/ ●●● S3 W2 *n* [C] someone who comes to visit a place or a person: *Times Square attracts more than 30 million visitors annually.* | **[+to]** *Rina is a frequent visitor to the city.* | **[+from]** *visitors from overseas* THESAURUS TOURIST → HEALTH VISITOR

ˈvisitor ˌcentre *BrE*, **visitor center** *AmE* (*also* **visitors centre**) *n* [C] a place where tourists can find information about the place they are visiting

ˈvisitors' book *n* [C] a book, especially in a church or hotel, in which visitors write their names and addresses

vi·sor /ˈvaɪzə $ -ər/ *n* [C] **1** the part of a HELMET (=protective hard hat) that can be lowered to protect your face **2** *AmE* the curved part of a cap that sticks out in front above your eyes SYN **peak** *BrE* **3** a flat object fixed above the front window inside a car that can be moved down to keep the sun out of your eyes **4** a curved piece of plastic that you wear on your head so that it sticks out above your eyes and protects them from the sun

vis·ta /ˈvɪstə/ *n* [C] **1** *literary* a view of a large area of beautiful scenery: **[+of]** *stunning vistas of the Norfolk coast* THESAURUS SIGHT **2** the possibility of new experiences, ideas, events etc: *Exchange programs* ***open up new vistas*** *for students.*

vi·su·al[1] /ˈvɪʒuəl/ ●●○ W3 AWL *adj* [usually before noun] relating to seeing: *Artists translate their ideas into visual images.* | *The tall tower adds to the visual impact of the building.*

visual[2] *n* [usually plural] something such as a picture or the part of a film, video etc that you can see, as opposed to the parts that you hear: *the film's stunning visuals*

ˌvisual ˈaid *n* [C] something such as a map, picture, or film that helps people understand, learn, or remember information

ˌvisual ˈarts *n* [plural] art such as painting, SCULPTURE etc that you look at, as opposed to literature or music

ˌvisual diˈsplay ˌunit *n* [C] VDU

vi·su·al·ize (*also* **-ise** *BrE*) /ˈvɪʒuəlaɪz/ ●○○ AWL *v* [T] to form a picture of someone or something in your mind SYN **imagine**: *I tried to visualize the house while he was describing it.* | **visualize sb doing sth** *Somehow I can't visualize myself staying with this company for much longer.* | **visualize how/what etc** *It's hard to visualize how these tiles will look in our bathroom.* THESAURUS IMAGINE
—**visualization** /ˌvɪʒuəlaɪˈzeɪʃən $ -lə-/ *n* [U]

vi·su·al·ly /ˈvɪʒuəli/ ●○○ AWL *adv*
1 in appearance: *Chairs should be visually attractive as well as comfortable.*
2 visually impaired unable to see normally - used especially when you want to be polite about this condition → **blind**
3 in a way that involves the eyes: *The process is easy to understand when it is demonstrated visually.*

V

vi·tal /ˈvaɪtl/ ●●● W2 *adj*
1 extremely important and necessary for something to succeed or exist SYN **crucial**: *The work she does is **absolutely vital**.* | **[+to]** *These measures are vital to national security.* | **[+for]** *Regular exercise is vital for your health.* | **it is vital (that)** *It is vital that you keep accurate records.* | **it is vital to do sth** *It is vital to keep accurate records.* | *It is vital to be honest with your children.* | *The tourist industry is of **vital importance** to the national economy.* | *Richardson played a **vital role** in the team's success.* | *The samples could give scientists **vital information** about long-term changes in the Earth's atmosphere.* THESAURUS IMPORTANT, NECESSARY
2 full of energy in a way that is exciting and attractive: *Rodgers and Hart's music sounds as fresh and vital as the day it was written.*
3 [only before noun] necessary in order to keep you alive: *the body's vital processes* | ***vital organs*** (=heart, lungs etc)
4 vital signs *medical* the signs that show someone is alive, for example breathing and body temperature

vi·tal·i·ty /vaɪˈtæləti/ ●○○ *n* [U]
1 great energy and eagerness to do things: *Despite her eighty years, Elsie was full of vitality.*
2 the strength and ability of an organization, country etc to continue: *The process of restructuring has injected some much-needed vitality into the company.* | **[+of]** *The senator promised to restore the economic vitality of the region.*

vi·tal·ly /ˈvaɪtl-i/ *adv* in a very important or necessary way: *A sensible diet is **vitally important** if you want to remain in good health.*

ˌvital ˈorgan *n* [C usually plural] a part of your body that is necessary to keep you alive, for example your heart and lungs

vi·tals /ˈvaɪtlz/ *n* [plural] *old use* the parts of your body that are necessary to keep you alive, for example your heart and lungs

ˌvital staˈtistics *n* [plural] **1** figures giving information about the number of births, deaths, marriages etc within a population **2** *BrE informal* a woman's chest, waist, and HIP measurements **3** *informal* important facts about something, especially its size

vit·a·min /ˈvɪtəmən, ˈvaɪ- $ ˈvaɪ-/ ●●○ *n* [C]
1 a chemical substance in food that is necessary for good health: *Try to eat foods that are rich in vitamins and minerals.* | **vitamin A/B/C etc** (=a particular type of vitamin) | *Lack of vitamin E can cause skin diseases and tiredness.*
2 (*also* **vitamin pill**, **vitamin supplement**) a PILL containing vitamins: *Perhaps I ought to **take vitamins**.*

vi·ti·ate /ˈvɪʃieɪt/ *v* [T] *formal* to make something less effective or spoil it

vit·i·cul·ture /ˈvɪtəkʌltʃə $ -ər/ *n* [U] the science or practice of growing GRAPES for making wine

vit·re·ous /ˈvɪtriəs/ *adj technical* made of or looking like glass

vit·ri·fy /ˈvɪtrɪfaɪ/ *v* (**vitrified**, **vitrifying**, **vitrifies**) [I,T] *technical* if a substance vitrifies or is vitrified, it changes into glass —**vitrification** /ˌvɪtrɪfɪˈkeɪʃən/ *n* [U]

vit·ri·ol /ˈvɪtriəl/ *n* [U] **1** *formal* very cruel and angry remarks that are intended to hurt someone's feelings **2** *old use* SULPHURIC ACID

vit·ri·ol·ic /ˌvɪtriˈɒlɪk◂ $ -ˈɑːlɪk◂/ *adj formal* vitriolic language, writing etc is very cruel and angry towards someone: *vitriolic remarks*

vitro → IN VITRO FERTILIZATION

vi·tu·pe·ra·tion /vɪˌtjuːpəˈreɪʃən $ vaɪˌtuː-/ *n* [U] *formal* angry and cruel criticism SYN **invective**

vi·tu·pe·ra·tive /vɪˈtjuːpərətɪv $ vaɪˈtuː-/ *adj formal* full of angry and cruel criticism SYN **vicious**: *vituperative comments*

vi·va[1] /ˈvaɪvə/ (*also* **viva voce**) *n* [C] *BrE* a spoken examination taken at the end of a university course

vi·va[2] /ˈviːvə/ *interjection* used to show that you approve of someone and want them to continue to exist or be successful

vi·va·ce /vɪˈvɑːtʃi, -tʃeɪ/ *adj, adv* music that is vivace is played quickly and with a lot of energy

vi·va·cious /vəˈveɪʃəs $ və-, vaɪ-/ *adj* someone, especially a woman, who is vivacious has a lot of energy and a happy attractive manner – used to show approval SYN **lively**: *a vivacious personality* —**vivaciously** *adv* —**vivaciousness** *n* [U] —**vivacity** /vəˈvæsəti $ və-, vaɪ-/ *n* [U]

vi·var·i·um /vaɪˈveəriəm $ -ˈver-/ *n* [C] a place indoors where animals are kept in conditions that are as similar as possible to their natural environment

viv·a voc·e /ˌvaɪvə ˈvəʊtʃi, -ˈvəʊsi $ ˌvaɪvə ˈvoʊsi, ˌviːvə ˈvoʊtʃeɪ/ *n* [C] *BrE formal* a VIVA[1]

viv·id /ˈvɪvɪd/ ●●○ *adj*
1 vivid memories, dreams, descriptions etc are so clear that they seem real OPP **vague**: *I've got vivid memories of that summer.* | *He had a vivid picture of her in his mind.*
2 vivid imagination an ability to imagine unlikely situations very clearly
3 vivid colours or patterns are very bright: *his vivid blue eyes* THESAURUS COLOUR —**vividly** *adv*: *I can **vividly remember** the day we met.* —**vividness** *n* [U]

viv·i·sec·tion /ˌvɪvəˈsekʃən/ *n* [U] the practice of doing medical or scientific tests on live animals —**vivisectionist** *n* [C]

vivo → IN VIVO

vix·en /ˈvɪksən/ *n* [C] **1** a female FOX **2** *literary* an offensive word for a woman who is bad-tempered or who fights

viz /vɪz/ *adv formal written* used before naming things that you have just referred to in a general way: *three Greek cities viz Athens, Thessaloniki, and Patras*

vi·zier /vəˈzɪə $ -ˈzɪr/ *n* [C] an important government official in some Muslim countries in the past

VJ /ˌviː ˈdʒeɪ/ *n* [C] (***video jockey***) someone who introduces music videos on television

vlog /vlɒg $ vlɑːg/ *n* [C] (***video log***) a website that has VIDEOs recorded by a particular person, that include their ideas and opinions → **blog** —**vlogging** *n* [U] —**vlogger** *n* [C]

V-neck /ˈviː nek/ *n* [C] **1** an opening for the neck in a piece of clothing, shaped like the letter V: *a V-neck sweater* → see picture at NECK[1] **2** a piece of clothing with a V-neck —**V-necked** /-nekt/ *adj*

vo·cab /ˈvəʊkæb $ ˈvoʊ-/ *n* [U] VOCABULARY

vo·cab·u·la·ry /vəˈkæbjələri, vəʊ- $ -leri, voʊ-/ ●●● S3 *n* (*plural* **vocabularies**)
1 [C,U] all the words that someone knows or uses: *Teachers were impressed by his vocabulary.*
2 [C] all the words in a particular language: *English has the largest vocabulary of any language.*
3 [C,U] the words that are typically used when talking about a particular subject: *Most technical jobs use a specialized vocabulary.* | **[+of]** *the vocabulary of politics*
4 [C,U] the range of possible features, effects, actions etc, especially in a type of music or art: **[+of]** *Charlie Parker expanded the vocabulary of jazz.*
5 (the word) failure/guilt/compromise etc is not in sb's vocabulary used to say that someone never thinks of accepting failure etc
6 [C] *old-fashioned* a list of words with explanations of their meanings, especially in a book for learning a foreign language

COLLOCATIONS – MEANINGS 1 & 2

ADJECTIVES

large/wide/extensive *She has a very wide vocabulary.*
limited/small *He had just started learning English and his vocabulary was fairly limited.*
basic/essential vocabulary *The book teaches you the basic vocabulary that you need to know when you're on holiday.*
technical/specialized vocabulary *The instructions were full of technical vocabulary.*

sb's active vocabulary (=the words they can use) *Children of this age have an active vocabulary of about 1,000 words.*
sb's passive vocabulary (=the words they can understand but do not use)

VERBS

have a vocabulary *By eighteen months of age, the girl had a vocabulary of around 300 words.*
expand/improve your vocabulary (*also* **enrich your vocabulary** *formal*) *Reading helps to expand your vocabulary.*
learn vocabulary *What's the best way of learning new vocabulary?*

vocabulary + NOUN

a vocabulary test/exercise *The teacher gave us a vocabulary test.*
a vocabulary item *formal* (=a word, especially in a coursebook or a language class) *The difficult vocabulary items are explained at the bottom of the page.*

vo·cal[1] /ˈvəʊkəl $ ˈvoʊ-/ ●○○ *adj*
1 expressing strong opinions publicly, especially about things that you disagree with SYN **outspoken**: **[+in]** *Foley has been particularly vocal in his criticism of the government.* | **vocal opponent/critic/supporter etc** *She was a vocal opponent of the plan.*
2 [only before noun] relating to the voice or to singing: *vocal music* | *Allison's vocal style is influenced by country and blues music.* | *a female vocal group* —**vocally** *adv*

vocal[2] *n* [C usually plural] the part of a piece of music that is sung rather than played on an instrument: **on vocals** *The album features Jim Boquist on vocals.*

ˈvocal cords, **ˈvocal chords** *n* [plural] thin pieces of muscle in your throat that produce sounds when you speak

vo·cal·ist /ˈvəʊkəlɪst $ ˈvoʊ-/ *n* [C] someone who sings popular songs, especially with a band

vo·cal·ize (*also* **-ise** *BrE*) /ˈvəʊkəlaɪz $ ˈvoʊ-/ *v* [I,T] to make a sound or sounds with your voice —**vocalization** /ˌvəʊkəlaɪˈzeɪʃən $ ˌvoʊkələ-/ *n* [C,U]

vo·ca·tion /vəʊˈkeɪʃən $ voʊ-/ *n* [C,U] **1 a)** the feeling that the purpose of your life is to do a particular type of work, especially because it allows you to help other people: **[+for]** *Jan* ***has a vocation*** *for teaching.* | *a strong* ***sense of vocation*** | *You* ***missed*** *your* ***vocation*** (=you would have been good at a particular job). **b)** a particular type of work that you feel is right for you: *At 17 she* ***found*** *her* ***true vocation*** *as a writer.* **2** a strong belief that you have been chosen by God to be a priest or a NUN

vo·ca·tion·al /vəʊˈkeɪʃənəl $ voʊ-/ ●○○ *adj* teaching or relating to the skills you need to do a particular job → **academic**: *vocational qualifications*

voc·a·tive /ˈvɒkətɪv $ ˈvɑː-/ *n* [C] *technical* a word or particular form of a word used to show that you are speaking or writing directly to someone —**vocative** *adj*

vo·cif·er·ate /vəˈsɪfəreɪt, vəʊ- $ voʊ-/ *v* [I] *formal* to shout loudly, especially when you are complaining

vo·cif·er·ous /vəˈsɪfərəs, vəʊ- $ voʊ-/ *adj formal* expressing your opinions loudly and strongly: *a vociferous opponent of the plan* | **[+in]** *The minority population became more vociferous in its demands.* —**vociferously** *adv*

vod·cast /ˈvɒdkɑːst $ ˈvɑːdkæst/ *n* [C] a programme in the form of a video that can be DOWNLOADed from the Internet.

vod·ka /ˈvɒdkə $ ˈvɑːdkə/ *n* [C,U] a strong clear alcoholic drink originally from Russia, or a glass of this

vogue /vəʊg $ voʊg/ *n* [C usually singular, U] a popular and fashionable style, activity, method etc SYN **fashion**: **[+for]** *the vogue for large families in the pre-war years* | **be in vogue/be the vogue** *Short skirts are very much in vogue just now.* | *Suntanning first* ***came into vogue*** *in the mid-1930s.*

voice[1] /vɔɪs/ ●●● S2 W1 *n*
1 SPEAKING [C,U] the sounds that you make when you speak, or the ability to make these sounds: *He recognized her voice instantly.* | *I could hear angry voices.*
2 SINGING **a)** [C,U] the quality of sound you produce when you sing: *Sophie's got a lovely singing voice* **b)** [C] a person singing: *a piece written for six voices and piano*
3 OPINION **a)** [singular, U] the right or ability to express an opinion, to vote, or to influence decisions: *Parents should* ***have a voice*** *in deciding how their children are educated.* **b)** [C] an opinion or wish that is expressed: *The government needs to listen to the voice of middle-class Americans.* | *a fair, democratic society, in which individuals are able to* ***make*** *their* ***voice heard*** (=express their opinion so that people notice it) | *Since the new program was introduced, there have been some* ***dissenting voices*** (=people expressing disagreement). | *Senator Prior spoke out,* ***adding*** *her* ***voice to*** *the call for new laws to protect the environment.*
4 speak with one voice if a group of people speak with one voice, they all express the same opinion
5 REPRESENTATIVE [singular] a person, organization, newspaper etc that expresses the opinions or wishes of a group of people: **[+of]** *The senator is* ***the voice of*** *the religious right.*
6 the voice of reason/experience etc opinions or ideas that are reasonable, based on experience etc, or someone who has these ideas: *Ben, as ever, has been the voice of reason throughout the whole crisis.*
7 FEELINGS **give voice to sth** to express your feelings or thoughts: *Participants are encouraged to give voice to their personal hopes, fears and dreams.*
8 inner voice thoughts or feelings that you do not express but seem to warn, criticize, or advise you: *My inner voice told me to be cautious.*
9 GRAMMAR **active/passive voice** *technical* the form of a verb that shows whether the subject of a sentence does an action or has an action done to it

COLLOCATIONS

ADJECTIVES

loud *Her voice was loud and clear.*
quiet/low/soft (=not loud) *When he spoke, his voice was soft and gentle.*
a deep/low voice (=near the bottom of the range of sounds) *She heard the deep voice of her father downstairs.*
a high voice (=near the top of the range of sounds) *They used to repeat her words in silly high voices.*
a clear voice *Natalia's clear voice rang out.*
a small voice (=quiet and not strong or confident) *She answered in a small voice, 'I think I was afraid.'*
a trembling/shaking voice (=a voice that shakes because someone is very nervous or frightened) | **a squeaky voice** (=very high and not strong) | **a husky voice** (=low and slightly rough but in an attractive way) | **a gravelly voice** (=very deep and slightly rough) | **a sing-song voice** (=a voice that goes high and low in a pleasant musical way)

VERBS

raise your voice (=speak more loudly) *She did not raise her voice, or express any anger.*
lower your voice (=speak more quietly) *He lowered his voice to a whisper.*
keep your voice down (=not speak loudly) *Keep your voice down, they'll hear you!*
lose your voice (=lose the ability to speak, for example when you have a cold) *I'll have to whisper because I've lost my voice.*
sb's voice rises (=becomes louder or higher) *Her voice rose in panic.*
sb's voice drops (=becomes lower) | **sb's voice breaks/cracks** (=becomes higher or unsteady because they are upset) | **a boy's voice breaks** (=becomes deep as he becomes a man) | **sb's voice trembles/shakes** (=sounds unsteady) | **sb's voice trails off/away** (=becomes quieter until you cannot hear it)

PHRASES

in a loud/soft/deep etc voice *'Where is she?', Kate demanded in a shrill voice.*
sb's tone of voice *His tone of voice was aggressive.*
at the top of your voice (=in a very loud voice) *She shouted 'Help!' at the top of her voice.*

voice² ●●○ *v* [T]
1 to tell people your opinions or feelings about a particular subject: *The senator **voiced concern** at how minorities and immigrants are treated in California.* | *She angrily voiced her objections.*
2 *technical* to produce a sound with a movement of the VOCAL CORDS as well as the breath

'voice box *n* [C] the part of your throat that you use to produce sounds when you speak SYN **larynx**

voiced /vɔɪst/ *adj* **1 deep-voiced/squeaky-voiced/husky-voiced etc** having a voice that is deep, very high etc **2** *technical* voiced sounds are made using the VOCAL CORDS. For example, /d/and /g/are voiced CONSONANTS.

voice·less /'vɔɪsləs/ *adj* **1** unable to get your opinions or concerns noticed by people in power: *The vast majority of our people feel ignored and voiceless.* **2** *technical* voiceless sounds are made without using the VOCAL CORDS. For example, /p/and /k/are voiceless CONSONANTS.

voice·mail, **voice mail** /'vɔɪsmeɪl/ ●●○ *n* [U] a system which lets people leave recorded messages for you on your telephone when you are unable to answer it

,Voice of A'merica, the (*abbreviation* **VOA**) a US radio station which broadcasts news and other programmes to other countries

'voice-over *n* [C] information or remarks that are spoken on a television programme or film by someone who is not seen on the screen

'voice print *n* [C] someone's voice recorded on a machine, used to check who that person is

void¹ /vɔɪd/ ●○○ *n* [singular]
1 a feeling of great sadness that you have when someone you love dies or when something is taken from you: *Running the business helped to **fill the void** after his wife died.*
2 a situation in which something important or interesting is needed or wanted, but does not exist: *The amusement park will **fill** a **void** in this town, which has little entertainment for children.*
3 *literary* an empty area of space where nothing exists: *She looked over the cliff into the void.*

void² ●○○ *adj*
1 *technical* a contract or official agreement that is void is not legal and has no effect SYN **null and void**
2 void of sth *literary* completely lacking something SYN **devoid**: *Her eyes were void of all expression.*

void³ *v* [T] *law* to make a contract or agreement void so that it has no legal effect

voi·là /vwɑː'lɑː/ *interjection* used when you are showing or telling someone something surprising: *'Voilà!' she said, producing a pair of white shoes.*

voile /vɔɪl/ *n* [U] a very light almost transparent cloth made of cotton, wool, or silk

VoIP /ˌviː əʊ aɪ 'piː $ -oʊ-/ (*also* **IP telephony**) *n* [U] (***voice over Internet protocol***) the technology that allows people to use BROADBAND Internet connections to speak over the telephone. This is cheaper than using normal telephones.

vol. the written abbreviation of ***volume***

vol·a·tile /'vɒlətaɪl $ 'vɑːlətl/ ●○○ *adj*
1 a volatile situation is likely to change suddenly and without warning OPP **stable**: *an increasingly volatile political situation* | *the **highly volatile** stock and bond markets*
2 someone who is volatile can suddenly become angry or violent
3 *technical* a volatile liquid or substance changes easily into a gas OPP **stable** —**volatility** /ˌvɒlə'tɪləti $ ˌvɑː-/ *n* [U]

vol-au-vent /'vɒl əʊ ˌvɒn $ ˌvɔːl oʊ 'vɑːn/ *n* [C] *BrE* a small round piece of PASTRY that is filled with chicken, vegetables etc and eaten at parties

vol·can·ic /vɒl'kænɪk $ vɑːl-/ *adj* relating to or caused by a volcano: *black volcanic sand*

VOLCANO

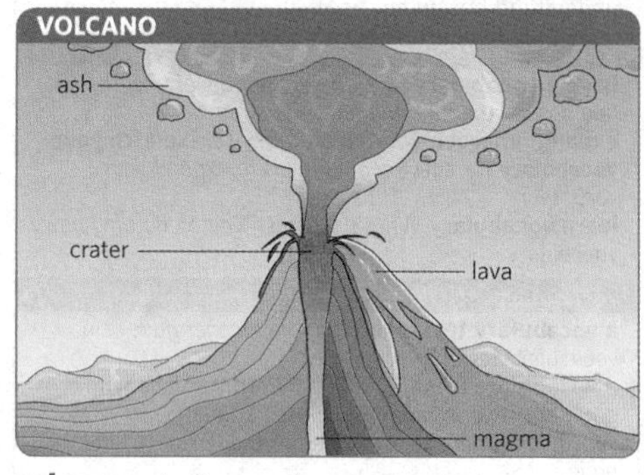

vol·ca·no /vɒl'keɪnəʊ $ vɑːl'keɪnoʊ/ ●○○ *n* (*plural* **volcanoes** *or* **volcanos**) [C] a mountain with a large hole at the top, through which LAVA (=very hot liquid rock) is sometimes forced out: *Pompei was destroyed when the **volcano erupted** in 79 AD.* | **active volcano** (=one that may explode at any time) | **dormant volcano** (=one that is not active at the moment) | **extinct volcano** (=one that is no longer active at all)

vole /vəʊl $ voʊl/ *n* [C] a small animal like a mouse with a short tail that lives in fields and woods and near rivers

vo·li·tion /və'lɪʃən $ voʊ-, və-/ *n* [U] **1 of your own volition** *formal* if you do something of your own volition, you do it because you want to, not because you are forced to: *Helena left the company of her own volition.* **2** *formal* the power to choose or decide something without being forced to do it: *She was without her own volition.*

vol·ley¹ /'vɒli $ 'vɑːli/ *n* [C] **1** a large number of bullets, rocks etc shot or thrown through the air at the same time: **[+of]** *a volley of bullets* **2** a lot of questions, insults, attacks etc that are all said or made at the same time: **[+of]** *a volley of abuse* **3** a hit in tennis, a kick in football etc when the player hits or kicks the ball before it touches the ground

volley² *v* **1** [I,T] to hit or kick a ball before it touches the ground, especially in tennis or football → see picture at **TENNIS** **2** [I] if a large number of guns volley, they are all fired at the same time

vol·ley·ball /'vɒlibɔːl $ 'vɑːlibɒːl/ ●●○ *n* [U] a game in which two teams use their hands to hit a ball over a high net

volt /vəʊlt $ voʊlt/ ●●○ *n* [C] (*written abbreviation* **V** *or* **v**) a unit for measuring the force of an electric current

volt·age /'vəʊltɪdʒ $ 'voʊl-/ ●○○ *n* [C,U] electrical force measured in volts: **high/low voltage**

volte-face /ˌvɒlt 'fæsˌ -'fɑːs $ ˌvɒːlt 'fɑːs/ *n* [C usually singular] *formal* a change to a completely opposite opinion or plan of action SYN **U-turn**

volt·me·ter /'vəʊltˌmiːtə $ 'voʊltˌmiːtər/ *n* [C] an instrument for measuring voltage

vol·u·ble /'vɒljəbəl $ 'vɑː-/ *adj formal* talking a lot or talking quickly: *Clarissa was extremely voluble on the subject of good manners.* —**volubly** *adv*

vol·ume /'vɒljuːm $ 'vɑːljəm/ ●●● S3 W2 AWL *n*
1 SOUND [U] the amount of sound produced by a television, radio etc: **turn the volume up/down** *Can you turn the volume up?*

REGISTER

In everyday English, people usually say **turn** something **up** or **turn** something **down** rather than use the noun **volume**: *Can you **turn** the TV **up** a bit?* | *She's always yelling at us to **turn** our music **down**.*

2 AMOUNT OF STH [C usually singular, U] the total amount of

something, especially when it is large or increasing: **[+of]** *The volume of traffic on the roads has increased dramatically in recent years.* | *the volume of trade* **THESAURUS** ▸ **AMOUNT**
3 SPACE FILLED [C usually singular] a measurement of the amount of space that a substance or object fills, or the amount of space in a container: **[+of]** *an instrument for measuring the volume of a gas* | *The volume of the container measures 10,000 cubic metres.* **THESAURUS** ▸ **SIZE**
4 BOOK [C] (*written abbreviation* **vol.**) **a)** a book that is part of a set, or one into which a very long book is divided: *The period from 1940-45 is in volume 9.* **b)** *formal* a book: **[+of]** *a volume of Keats's poetry* **c)** all the copies of a particular magazine printed in one particular year → **speak volumes** at SPEAK(9)

vo·lu·mi·nous /və'lu:mənəs, və'lju:- $ və'lu:-/ *adj formal* **1** a voluminous piece of clothing is very large and loose - often used humorously: *a voluminous cloak* **2** voluminous books, documents etc are very long and contain a lot of detail: *He took voluminous notes during the lecture.* **3** a voluminous container is very large and can hold a lot of things: *a voluminous suitcase*

vol·un·ta·ri·ly /'vɒləntərəli, ˌvɒlən'terəli $ ˌvɑ:lən'terəli/ ●○○ AWL *adv*
1 if you do something voluntarily, you do it willingly, without anyone telling you to do it: *She wasn't fired - she left voluntarily.*
2 if you do work voluntarily, you do it because you want to, and are not paid for it → **volunteer**: *Susan worked in the studios voluntarily, to gain experience.*

vol·un·ta·ry¹ /'vɒləntəri $ 'vɑ:lənteri/ ●●○ W3 AWL *adj*
1 a) voluntary organization/association/agency etc an organization etc that is organized or supported by people who give their money, services etc because they want to and who do not intend to make a profit → **volunteer**: *a voluntary organization providing help for the elderly* | *environmental work carried out by* **the voluntary sector** **b) voluntary work/service etc** work etc that is done by people who do it because they want to, and who are not paid: *She* **does** *a lot of* **voluntary work** *for the Red Cross.* | *a drop-in centre for homeless people, run* **on a voluntary basis**
2 done willingly and without being forced: *Workers are being encouraged to take voluntary redundancy.* → COMPULSORY
3 *technical* voluntary movements of your body are controlled by your conscious mind OPP **involuntary**

voluntary² *n* (*plural* **voluntaries**) [C] a piece of music played in church, usually by the ORGAN

vol·un·teer¹ /ˌvɒlən'tɪə $ ˌvɑ:lən'tɪr/ ●●○ AWL *n* [C]
1 someone who does a job willingly without being paid → **voluntary**: *Most of the relief work was done by volunteers.*
2 someone who is willing to offer help: *I need some volunteers to help with the washing-up.*
3 someone who joins the army, navy, or air force without being forced to → **conscript**

volunteer² ●●○ AWL *v*
1 [I,T] to offer to do something without expecting any reward, often something that other people do not want to do: **volunteer to do sth** *Helen volunteered to have Thanksgiving at her house this year.* | **[+for]** *Sidcup volunteered for guard duty.* | *I* **volunteered** *my* **services** *as a driver.*
2 [T] to tell someone something without being asked: *Michael volunteered the information before I had a chance to ask.*
3 [I] to offer to join the army, navy, or air force: *When war broke out, my father volunteered immediately.*
4 [T] to say that someone else will do a job even though they may not want to do it: **volunteer sb for sth** *Mum volunteered Dave for washing-up duties.*

vo·lup·tu·a·ry /və'lʌptʃuəri $ -tʃueri/ *n* (*plural* **voluptuaries**) [C] *literary* someone who enjoys physical pleasure and having expensive possessions

vo·lup·tu·ous /və'lʌptʃuəs/ *adj* **1** a woman who is voluptuous has large breasts and a soft curved body **2** expressing strong sexual feeling or sexual pleasure: *a voluptuous gesture* **3** *literary* something that is voluptuous gives you pleasure because it looks, smells, or tastes good: *the voluptuous fragrance of a summer garden* —**voluptuously** *adv* —**voluptuousness** *n* [U]

vom·it¹ /'vɒmɪt $ 'vɑ:-/ ●○○ *v* [I,T] to bring food or drink up from your stomach out through your mouth, because you are ill: *He had swallowed so much sea water he wanted to vomit.* | *I knew I was really in trouble when I began vomiting blood.* | **[+up]** *I vomited up most of my dinner.*

> **REGISTER**
> In everyday English, people usually say that someone **throws up**, **is sick**, or in American English **gets sick**: *He* ***threw up*** *his dinner.*

vomit² ●○○ *n* [U] food or other substances that come up from your stomach and through your mouth when you vomit

voo·doo /'vu:du:/ *n* [U] magical beliefs and practices used as a form of religion, especially by people in Haiti

ˌvoodoo ecoˈnomics *n* [U] *AmE* economic ideas that seem attractive but that do not work effectively over a period of time

vo·ra·cious /və'reɪʃəs, vɒ- $ vɔ:-, və-/ *adj* **1** eating or wanting large quantities of food: *Pigs are voracious feeders.* | *Kids can have* **voracious appetites**. **2** having an extremely strong desire to do or have a lot of something: *a* **voracious reader** | *Her* **appetite** *for information was* **voracious**. —**voraciously** *adv*: *Anne has always* **read voraciously**. —**voracity** /-'ræsəti/ *n* [U]

vor·tex /'vɔ:teks $ 'vɔ:r-/ *n* (*plural* **vortices** /-təsi:z/ *or* **vortexes**) [C] **1** a mass of wind or water that spins quickly and pulls things into its centre **2** [usually singular] *written* a situation that has a powerful effect on people's lives and that influences their behaviour, even if they do not want it to: **[+of]** *the vortex of emotions surrounding the case*

vo·ta·ry /'vəʊtəri $ 'voʊ-/ *n* (*plural* **votaries**) [C] *old-fashioned* someone who regularly practises a particular religion

vote¹ /vəʊt $ voʊt/ ●●● S2 W2 *v*
1 IN ELECTION/TO SUPPORT [I,T] to show which person or party you want, or whether you support a plan, by marking a piece of paper, raising your hand etc: *In 1918 British women got the right to vote.* | **[+for/against/in favour of]** *I voted for the Labour candidate in the last election.* | *53% of Danes voted in favour of the Maastricht treaty.* | **[+on]** *The people of Ulster had finally been given a chance to vote on the issue.* | **vote to do sth** *Congress voted to increase foreign aid by 10%.* | *Shareholders voted to reject the offer.* | **vote Democrat/Republican/Labour/Conservative etc** *I've voted Democrat all my life.* → **block voting** at BLOCK¹(5)
2 vote sb into/out of power/office/parliament etc to elect or dismiss someone by voting: *The chances are that the government will be voted out of office.*
3 CHOOSE FOR PRIZE [T] to choose someone or something for a particular prize by voting for them: **vote sb/sth sth** *In 1981 Henry Fonda was voted Best Actor for 'On Golden Pond'.*
4 MONEY [T] if a parliament, committee etc votes a sum of money for something, they decide by voting to provide money for that particular purpose: **vote sth for sth** *Parliament has voted £20 million extra funding for road improvements.*
5 vote sth a success/the best etc *BrE* if people vote something a success etc, they all agree that it is a success: *The evening was voted a great success.*
6 I vote ... *spoken* used to say that you prefer one particular choice or possible action: **vote (that)** *I vote we go to the movies.* | **[+for]** *'What do you want to eat?' 'I vote for Mexican.'*
7 vote with your wallet *BrE* **a)** (*also* **vote with your pocketbook** *AmE*) to vote for someone or something that you think will help you have the most money: *People generally vote with their pocketbooks against new taxes.* **b)** (*also* **vote with your dollars** *AmE*) to show you like something by choosing to buy it: *Readers vote with their wallets every day when they choose a newspaper.*

V

8 vote with your feet to show that you do not support a decision or action by leaving a place or organization

GRAMMAR: Comparison

vote

- You **vote for** someone or something: *Who are you going to vote for at the next election? | Most MPs voted for the bill.*
- You **vote against** someone or something: *The committee voted against the decision.*
- You **vote to** do something: *Congress voted to change the law.*

pass

- Parliament, Congress etc **passes** a bill or law: *Parliament passed a law against drug smuggling.*
- **Pass** is often used in the passive in this meaning: *The law was passed by a big majority.*

elect

- **Elect** is often used in the passive.
- You **elect** someone **as** something: *She was elected as MP for Corby.*
- You **elect** someone something: *Obama was elected president in 2008.*
- You **elect** someone **to** Parliament, Congress etc: *She was elected to the Senate.*

THESAURUS

vote [I,T] to show which person or party you want, or whether you support a plan, by marking a piece of paper, raising your hand etc: *I've voted Democrat all my life. | You can vote for your favourite singer.*
elect [T] to choose a leader, representative, or government by voting, so that they become the new leader, representative etc: *He was elected mayor of London. | the newly-elected government*
go to the polls if a country or voters go to the polls, they vote in an election – used especially in news reports: *The US goes to the polls in November.*
take a vote if a group of people at a meeting take a vote, they vote about something: *We should take a vote on whether or not to accept their offer.*
cast your vote *formal* to mark a piece of paper, call a telephone number etc in order to vote: *The first votes have been cast in the country's general election.*
ballot [T] to ask the members of an organization to vote on something in order to decide what to do: *The union will ballot its members on whether to go ahead with the strike action.*
veto [T] to vote against something that other people have agreed on, so that it cannot happen: *The president has the right to veto any piece of legislation.*

vote sth ↔ **down** *phr v* to defeat a plan, law etc by voting: *In 1999 the town had voted down a petition to close the school.*
vote sb ↔ **in** *phr v* to elect someone by voting: *A new chairman was voted in.*
vote sb ↔ **out** *phr v* to remove someone from a position of power by voting: *With policies like that, he'll be voted out in the next election.*
vote sth ↔ **through** *phr v BrE* to approve a plan, law etc by voting: *The proposals were voted through yesterday.*

vote² ●●● S2 W2 *n*
1 CHOICE BY VOTING [C] an act of voting in an election or meeting, or the choice that you make when you vote: *A vote for us is not a wasted vote. | The proposal was rejected* ***by** 19* ***votes to** 7.* | **[+for/in favour (of)/against]** *The House of Representatives approved the budget, with 52 votes in favor, 16 against and 12 abstentions.* | **cast your vote** (=vote in a political election) *Harkin won 74 percent of the votes cast. | policies designed to* ***win votes*** *in the South | It's the club secretary that* ***counts** the* ***votes**.* → CASTING VOTE
2 OCCASION OF VOTING [C usually singular] an occasion when a group of people vote in order to decide something or choose a representative SYN **ballot**: *The results of the vote were surprising – 80% of workers favoured strike action.* | **[+on]** *There will be a citywide vote* (=all the voters in a particular city) *on the matter.* | **take/have a vote (on sth)** *Unless anyone has anything to add, we'll take a vote. | Let's have a vote on it.* | **put sth to the/a vote** (=decide something by voting) *Let's put it to the vote. All those in favor raise your hands.* → FREE VOTE
3 the vote a) the total number of votes made in an election: *Davis won the election with 57% of the vote. | The Greens increased their* ***share of the vote*** *from 2.9% to 4.9%.* **b)** the right to vote in political elections: *In France women didn't* ***get the vote*** *until 1945. | At that time black people did not yet* ***have the vote**.*
4 the ... vote a) the black/Jewish/middle-class etc vote black, Jewish etc voters, or their votes: *The black vote is astonishingly loyal to the Democratic Party.* **b) the Labour/Conservative/Green etc vote** *BrE* the total number of votes the Labour Party, Conservative Party etc win in an election: *The Green vote looks likely to increase again.*
5 RESULT OF VOTING [singular] the result of a vote: *A close vote is expected. | The motion was passed* ***by a vote of*** *215* ***to*** *84.*
6 sb/sth gets my vote *spoken* used to say that you are ready to support someone or something, or that you think that someone or something is the best of their kind: *Anything that will mean a better deal for our children gets my vote.*

ˈvote-ˌgetter *n* [C] *AmE informal* someone who is voted for in an election: *Pfeifer was the top vote-getter in last year's election.*

ˌvote of ˈcensure *n* (*plural* **votes of censure**) [C] a process in which members of parliament vote in order to officially criticize the government for something

ˌvote of ˈconfidence *n* (*plural* **votes of confidence**) [C] **1** a formal process in which people vote in order to show that they support someone or something, especially the government: *On April 19 the new government* ***won** a* ***vote of confidence*** *by 339 votes to 207.* **2** something that you do or say that shows you support someone and approve of their actions: **[+in]** *The new investments are widely seen as a vote of confidence in the nation's economic future.*

ˌvote of no ˈconfidence *n* (*plural* **votes of no confidence**) [C] **1** a formal process in which people vote in order to show that they do not support someone or something, especially the government: **[+in]** *On April 22 the National Assembly* ***passed** a* ***vote of no confidence*** *in the government.* **2** something that you do or say that shows that you do not support someone

ˌvote of ˈthanks *n* **propose a vote of thanks (to sb)** to make a short formal speech in which you thank someone, especially at a public meeting or a formal dinner

vot·er /ˈvəʊtə $ ˈvoʊtər/ ●●○ *n*
1 [C] someone who has the right to vote in a political election, or who votes in a particular election: *Voters overwhelmingly rejected the Far Right in the May elections. | In Ireland 83% of voters favoured EC membership in 1972. | Tory voters*
2 voter apathy a situation in which a lot of people who have the right to vote do not vote: *Voter apathy is especially high among young people.* → FLOATING VOTER

ˈvoting booth *n* [C] an enclosed place where you can make your vote secretly SYN **polling booth** *BrE*

ˈvoting maˌchine *n* [C] a machine that records votes as they are made

vo·tive /ˈvəʊtɪv $ ˈvoʊ-/ *adj* [only before noun] *technical* given or done because of a promise made to God or to a SAINT: ***votive offerings***

vouch /vaʊtʃ/ *v*
vouch for sb/sth *phr v* **1** to say that you firmly believe that something is true or good because of your experience or knowledge of it: *I'll vouch for the quality of the report. I read it last night. | 'Where were you on the night of the murder?' 'In bed with flu. My wife can* ***vouch for that**.'*
2 to say that you believe that someone will behave well and that you will be responsible for their behaviour, actions etc: *Why don't you phone my office? They'll vouch for me.*

V

vouch·er /ˈvaʊtʃə $ -ər/ ●●○ *n* [C]
1 a ticket that can be used instead of money for a particular purpose: *The voucher can be used at most major supermarkets.* | *First prize is a £1,000 travel voucher.* → **gift voucher** at GIFT TOKEN, LUNCHEON VOUCHER
2 an official statement or RECEIPT that is given to someone to prove that their accounts are correct or that money has been paid

vouch·safe /vaʊtʃˈseɪf/ *v* [T] *old-fashioned formal* to promise or offer something, or tell someone something that they can be certain is the truth

vow¹ /vaʊ/ ●○○ *n* [C]
1 a serious promise → **oath**: *Jim made a vow that he would find his wife's killer.*
2 a religious promise that you will do something for God, the church etc: *a monk who had taken a vow of poverty*
3 vows [plural] **a)** (*also* **marriage/wedding vows**) the promises you make during your wedding **b)** the promises you make when you become a Catholic priest or NUN

COLLOCATIONS

VERBS

make a vow *I made a vow never to go near the place again.*
take a vow (=make a vow at a formal ceremony) *Priests have to take a vow of obedience to the Catholic Church.*
keep a vow (=do as you promised) *She kept her vow not to tell anyone about their affair.*
break a vow (=fail to do as you promised) *She accused him of breaking his marriage vows.*
exchange vows (=make promises to each other as part of a wedding ceremony) | **renew your vows** (=have a second wedding ceremony to repeat your promises)

ADJECTIVES/NOUN + vow

a solemn vow (=a very serious vow, which you must keep) *He made a solemn vow that he would do everything he could to help her.*
marriage/wedding vows *She wrote her own marriage vows.*
a holy/sacred vow

PHRASES

a vow of silence/poverty/celibacy etc *People close to him have finally broken their vow of silence.*

vow² ●○○ *v* [T]
1 to make a serious promise to yourself or someone else SYN **promise**: **vow to do sth** *Supporters have vowed to continue the protest until Adams is released.* | **vow (that)** *I vowed that I would never drink again.* THESAURUS ▸ PROMISE
2 *formal* to make a religious promise that you will do something for God, the church etc

vow·el /ˈvaʊəl/ ●●○ *n* [C]
1 one of the human speech sounds that you make by letting your breath flow out without closing any part of your mouth or throat
2 a letter of the alphabet used to represent a vowel. In English the vowels are a, e, i, o, u, and sometimes y.

vox pop /ˌvɒks ˈpɒp $ ˌvɑːks ˈpɑːp/ *n* [C,U] *BrE informal* opinions expressed by ordinary people when they are asked questions about a particular subject during a television, radio, or newspaper report

voy·age¹ /ˈvɔɪ-ɪdʒ/ ●●○ *n* [C]
1 a long journey in a ship or spacecraft: *The voyage from England to India used to take six months.* | *the Titanic's* ***maiden voyage*** (=first journey) | *I don't want to* ***make*** *the* ***voyage*** *single-handed.* | *These are the voyages of the starship Enterprise.* THESAURUS ▸ JOURNEY
2 voyage of discovery a situation in which you learn a lot of new things about something or someone: *Writing a biography is an absorbing voyage of discovery.* | *a voyage of self-discovery* (=when you learn more about yourself)

voyage² *v* [I always + adv/prep] *literary* to travel to a place, especially by ship

voy·ag·er /ˈvɔɪ-ɪdʒə $ -ər/ *n* [C] *literary* someone who makes long and often dangerous journeys, especially on the sea

voy·eur /vwɑːˈjɜː $ -ˈjɜːr/ *n* [C] **1** someone who gets sexual pleasure from secretly watching other people's sexual activities **2** someone who enjoys watching other people's private behaviour or suffering —**voyeurism** *n* [U] —**voyeuristic** /ˌvwɑːjəˈrɪstɪk◂/ *adj* —**voyeuristically** /-kli/ *adv*

VP, **V.P.** /ˌviː ˈpiː/ *n* [C] *informal* the abbreviation of ***vice-president***

vs. (*also* **vs** *BrE*) a written abbreviation of ***versus***

V sign /ˈviː saɪn/ *n* [C] **1** a sign meaning peace or victory, made by holding up the first two fingers of your hand with the front of the hand facing forwards **2** *BrE* a rude sign made by holding up the first two fingers of your hand with the back of your hand facing towards another person

VSO /ˌviː es ˈəʊ/ *trademark* (***Voluntary Service Overseas***) a British organization which sends people to developing countries for at least two years, to live and work there and to share their skills and knowledge with the local people

vul·can·ize (*also* **-ise** *BrE*) /ˈvʌlkənaɪz/ *v* [T] to make rubber stronger by using a special chemical treatment —**vulcanization** /ˌvʌlkənaɪˈzeɪʃən $ -nə-/ *n* [U]

vul·gar /ˈvʌlgə $ -ər/ ●○○ *adj*
1 remarks, jokes etc that are vulgar deal with sex in a very rude and offensive way
2 not behaving politely in social situations SYN **uncouth**: *vulgar behaviour*
3 not showing good judgment about what is beautiful or suitable: *a vulgar check suit* —**vulgarly** *adv*

ˌvulgar ˈfraction *n* [C] *BrE old-fashioned* a FRACTION that is written as one number above a line and one number below it, and not as a DECIMAL SYN **common fraction** *AmE*

vul·gar·i·ty /vʌlˈgærəti/ *n* **1** [U] the state or quality of being vulgar **2 vulgarities** [plural] vulgar remarks, jokes etc

vul·gar·ize (*also* **-ise** *BrE*) /ˈvʌlgəraɪz/ *v* [T] *formal* to spoil the quality or lower the standard of something that is good —**vulgarization** /ˌvʌlgəraɪˈzeɪʃən $ -rə-/ *n* [U]

Vul·gate, the /ˈvʌlgeɪt, -gət/ the Latin Bible commonly used in the Roman Catholic Church

vul·ne·ra·ble /ˈvʌlnərəbəl/ ●●○ W3 *adj*
1 someone who is vulnerable can be easily harmed or hurt OPP **invulnerable**: *He took advantage of me when I was at my most vulnerable.* | *We work mainly with the elderly and other vulnerable groups.* | **be vulnerable to sth** *Children are most vulnerable to abuse within their own home.*
2 a place, thing, or idea that is vulnerable is easy to attack or criticize OPP **invulnerable**: **[+to]** *The fort was vulnerable to attack from the north.* | *Their theories were badly thought out and very vulnerable to ridicule.* —**vulnerably** *adv* —**vulnerability** /ˌvʌlnərəˈbɪləti/ *n* [U]

vul·pine /ˈvʌlpaɪn/ *adj formal* relating to FOXes, or similar to a fox

vul·ture /ˈvʌltʃə $ -ər/ *n* [C] **1** a large bird that eats dead animals → see picture at **BIRD OF PREY** **2** someone who uses other people's problems and suffering for their own advantage – used to show disapproval: *He hadn't been dead five minutes before those vultures from the media were after his widow.*

vul·va /ˈvʌlvə/ *n* [C] the outer part of a woman's sexual organs

vu·vu·ze·la /ˌvuːvuːˈzeɪlə/ *n* [C] a long horn that football supporters blow at matches in South Africa to make a loud noise

vy·ing /ˈvaɪ-ɪŋ/ the present participle of VIE

Ww

W¹, **w** /ˈdʌbəljuː/ (*plural* **W's, w's**) *n* [C,U] the 23rd letter of the English alphabet

W², **w 1** the written abbreviation of ***west*** or ***western*** **2** the written abbreviation of ***watt*** or ***watts***

wack·o, **whacko** /ˈwækəʊ $ -oʊ/ *n* (*plural* **wackos**) [C] *informal* a crazy or strange person —**wacko** *adj*: *That guy's completely wacko.*

wack·y, **whacky** /ˈwæki/ *adj informal* silly in an exciting or amusing way SYN **crazy**: *a wonderfully wacky idea* —**wackiness** *n* [U]

wad¹ /wɒd $ wɑːd/ *n* [C] **1** a thick pile of pieces of paper or thin material: **[+of]** *a wad of dollar bills* → see picture at PILE¹ **2** a thick soft mass of material that has been pressed together: **[+of]** *a wad of cotton wool*

wad² *v* (**wadded**, **wadding**)

wad sth ↔ **up** *phr v AmE* to press something such as a piece of paper or cloth into a small tight ball

wad·ding /ˈwɒdɪŋ $ ˈwɑː-/ *n* [U] soft material used for packing or to protect a wound

wad·dle /ˈwɒdl $ ˈwɑːdl/ *v* [I] to walk with short steps, with your body moving from one side to the other - used especially about people or birds with fat bodies and short legs: **[+off/down/over etc]** *Half a dozen ducks waddled up the bank.* —**waddle** *n* [singular]

wade /weɪd/ ●○○ *v* [I always + adv/prep, T] to walk through water that is not deep **THESAURUS** WALK

wade in (*also* **wade into sth**) *phr v informal*

1 to enter a discussion, argument etc in a forceful and annoying way, often without thinking about the possible results: *I wish you wouldn't always wade in with your opinion.*

2 to move forward and attack someone: *The police waded into the crowd swinging sticks.*

wade through sth *phr v* to read or deal with a lot of boring papers or written work: *Each day Parkin wades through lengthy court reports.*

wad·er /ˈweɪdə $ -ər/ *n* [C] **1** (*also* ˈ**wading bird**) a bird that has long legs and a long neck, and that walks around in water to find its food **2 waders** [plural] high rubber boots that you wear for walking in deep water, usually when fishing

wa·di /ˈwɒdi $ ˈwɑː-/ *n* [C] a river bed in a desert which is usually dry but becomes full of water when there is a lot of rain

wad·ing pool /ˈweɪdɪŋ puːl/ *n* [C] *AmE* a small pool filled with water that is not very deep, for small children to play in SYN **paddling pool** *BrE*

W

wa·fer /ˈweɪfə $ -ər/ *n* [C] **1** a very thin BISCUIT **2** a thin round piece of bread eaten with wine in the Christian COMMUNION ceremony **3** a very thin flat piece of a hard substance: **[+of]** *wafers of silicon*

ˌ**wafer-ˈthin** *adj* extremely thin: *wafer-thin chocolates* **THESAURUS** THIN

waf·fle¹ /ˈwɒfəl $ ˈwɑː-/ *n* **1** [C] a flat cake, marked with a pattern of deep squares **2** [U] *BrE informal* talk or writing that uses a lot of words but says nothing important

waffle² *v* [I] *informal* **1** *BrE* (*also* **waffle on**) to talk or write using a lot of words but without saying anything important: *Stop waffling and get to the point.* **THESAURUS** TALK **2** *AmE informal* to be unable to decide what action to take: *He cannot continue to waffle on this issue.*

ˈ**waffle** ˌ**iron** *n* [C] a piece of kitchen equipment used to cook waffles

waft /wɑːft, wɒft $ wɑːft, wæft/ *v* **1** [I,T always + adv/prep] if a smell, smoke, or a light wind wafts somewhere, or if something wafts it somewhere, it moves gently through the air: **[+up/through/over etc]** *Cooking smells wafted up from downstairs.* **2** [I always + adv/prep] if sounds waft somewhere, you hear them there and they are pleasant but not very loud: **[+up/through/over etc]** *The sound of laughter wafted through the open window.* → **drift**

wag¹ /wæg/ ●○○ *v* (**wagged**, **wagging**)

1 [I,T] if a dog wags its tail, or if its tail wags, the dog moves its tail many times from one side to the other

2 [T] to move your finger or head from side to side, especially to show disapproval: *'You naughty girl!' Mom said,* ***wagging*** *her* ***finger*** *at me.* → **it's (a case of) the tail wagging the dog** at TAIL¹(11), → **set tongues wagging** at TONGUE¹(14)

wag² *n* **1** [C] *old-fashioned* someone who says or does something clever and amusing: *Some wag had drawn a face on the wall.* **2** [C usually singular] a wagging movement

WAG /wæg/ *n* [C] *BrE informal* (***wives and girlfriends***) the wife or girlfriend of a famous sports player: *Are WAGs good role models for girls?*

wage¹ /weɪdʒ/ ●●● S2 W2 *n*

1 [singular] (*also* **wages** [plural]) money you earn that is paid according to the number of hours, days, or weeks that you work → **salary**: *He* ***earns*** *a good* ***wage***. | **wage increase** (*also* **wage rise** *BrE*): *The wage increases will come into effect in June.* | **daily/weekly etc wage** *a weekly wage of $250* | **wage levels/rates** (=fixed amounts of money paid for particular jobs)

2 a living wage money you earn for work that is enough to pay for the basic things that you need to live: *The church no longer* ***paid a living wage***.

3 wage freeze an action taken by a company, government etc to stop wages increasing

4 wage claim the amount of money asked for by workers as an increase in wages

wage² *v* [T] to be involved in a war against someone, or a fight against something: **wage war (on sb/sth)** *The police are waging war on drug pushers in the city.* | **wage a campaign/struggle/battle etc** *The council has waged a vigorous campaign against the proposal.*

waged /weɪdʒd/ *adj* **1** waged work or employment is work for which you get paid OPP **unwaged** **2** someone who is waged has a job for which they earn money OPP **unwaged**

ˈ**wage-**ˌ**earner** *n* [C] **1** someone in a family who earns money for the rest of the family **2** someone who works for wages: *Both wage-earners and salaried officials were protected by the new regulations.*

ˈ**wage-**ˌ**packet** *n* [C] *BrE* an envelope that contains your wages

wa·ger¹ /ˈweɪdʒə $ -ər/ *n* [C] *old-fashioned* an agreement in which you win or lose money according to the result of something such as a race SYN **bet**

wager² *v* [T] *old-fashioned* **1** to agree to win or lose an amount of money on the result of something such as a race SYN **gamble**: **wager sth on sth** *Stipes wagered all his money on an unknown horse.* **2 I'll wager** used to say that you are confident that something is true

wag·gish /ˈwægɪʃ/ *adj BrE old-fashioned* a waggish person makes clever and amusing jokes, remarks etc —**waggishly** *adv* —**waggishness** *n* [U]

wag·gle /ˈwægəl/ *v* [I,T] to move something up and down or from side to side using short quick movements SYN **wiggle**: *Can you waggle your ears?* —**waggle** *n* [singular]

wag·on (*also* **waggon** *BrE*) /ˈwægən/ ●○○ *n* [C]

1 a strong vehicle with four wheels, used for carrying heavy loads and usually pulled by horses → **cart**

2 *BrE* a large open container pulled by a train, used for carrying goods SYN **freight car** *AmE*

3 be/go on the wagon *informal* to not drink alcohol anymore

4 fall off the wagon *informal* to start drinking alcohol again after you have stopped → PADDY WAGON

ˈ**wagon train** *n* [C] a long line of wagons and horses

used by the people who moved to the West of America in the 19th century

wag·tail /ˈwægteɪl/ *n* [C] a small European bird that moves its tail quickly up and down when it walks

waif /weɪf/ *n* [C] **1** someone, especially a child, who is pale and thin and looks as if they do not have a home **2 waifs and strays** *BrE* children or animals who do not have a home: *She loved cats, and would take any waifs and strays into her home.*

ˈwaif-like *adj* extremely pale and thin: *images of waif-like models in girls' magazines*

wail /weɪl/ *v* **1** [T] to say something in a loud, sad, and complaining way: *'But what shall I do?' Bernard wailed.* **2** [I] to cry out with a long high sound, especially because you are very sad or in pain: *Somewhere behind them a child began to wail.* **THESAURUS▶ CRY 3** [I] to make a long high sound: *The wind wailed in the chimney.* —**wail** *n* [C]: *the wail of police sirens*

wain·scot /ˈweɪnskət, -skɒt $ -skət, -skɑːt/ *n* [C] *BrE old-fashioned* a SKIRTING BOARD SYN **baseboard** *AmE*

waist /weɪst/ ●●● W3 *n* [C]
1 the narrow part in the middle of the human body: *The skirt was too big around the waist.* | **from the waist up/down** (=in the top or bottom half of your body) *Lota was paralysed from the waist down.* | **stripped to the waist** (=not wearing any clothes on the top half of your body) | **slim-waisted/narrow-waisted/thick-waisted** (=having a thin, thick etc waist)
2 [usually singular] the part of a piece of clothing that goes around this part of your body ⚠ Do not confuse with **waste**, which is used as a verb and a noun to talk about using too much of something, or not using it in a sensible way.

waist·band /ˈweɪstbænd/ *n* [C] the part of a skirt, trousers etc that fastens around your waist

waist·coat /ˈweɪskəʊt, ˈweskət $ ˈweskət/ *n* [C] *BrE* a piece of clothing without SLEEVES that has buttons down the front and is worn over a shirt, often under a JACKET as part of a man's suit SYN **vest** *AmE*

ˌwaist-ˈdeep *adj, adv* deep enough to reach your waist: *standing waist-deep in water*

ˌwaist-ˈhigh *adj, adv* high enough to reach your waist: *waist-high grass*

waist·line /ˈweɪstlaɪn/ *n* **1** [singular] the amount you measure around the waist, especially used to judge how fat or thin you are: *a trim waistline* **2** [C] the position of the waist of a piece of clothing

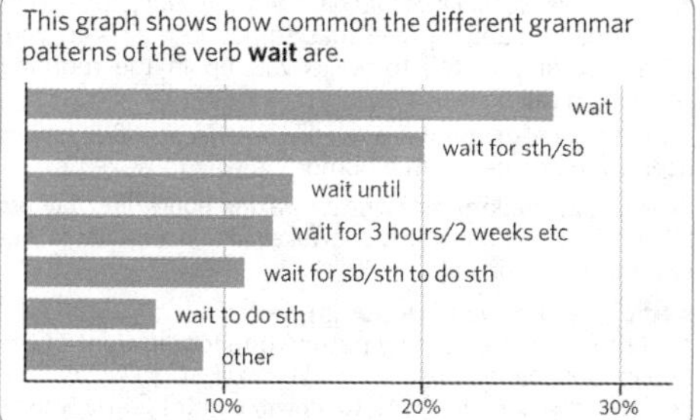

wait¹ /weɪt/ ●●● S1 W1 *v*
1 NOT GO/START STH [I] to stay somewhere or not do something until something else happens, someone arrives etc: *Hurry up! Everyone's waiting.* | *Would you mind waiting outside?* | **[+for]** *a queue of people waiting for a bus* | *Wait for me!* | **wait for sb/sth to do sth** *She paused, waiting for Myles to say something.* | *I sat waiting patiently for the wedding to end.* | **[+until/till]** *I'll wait till you come back.* | **wait (for) three hours/two weeks etc** *Can you wait for five minutes?* | *We've been* ***waiting ages.*** | **wait to do sth** *Are you waiting to use the phone?* | **keep sb waiting** (=make someone wait, especially by arriving late) *I'm sorry to have kept you waiting.*

GRAMMAR
- You **wait for** something or someone: *I waited for the next bus.* ✗ Don't say: *I waited the next bus.*
- You **wait for** someone to do something, or for something to happen: *She waited for him to finish speaking.* ✗ Don't say: *She waited him to finish speaking.*

2 STH HAS NOT HAPPENED [I] if you are waiting for something that you expect or hope will happen or arrive, it has not happened or arrived yet: *'Have you heard about the job?' 'No, I'm* ***still waiting.****'* | **[+for]** *I'm still waiting for my results.* | **wait for sb/sth to do sth** *I'm waiting for him to realize how stupid he's been.*
3 wait a minute/second/moment etc *spoken* **a)** used to ask someone not to leave or start doing something immediately: *Wait a second, I'll get my coat and come with you.* | *Wait a moment, just let me think.* **b)** used to interrupt someone, especially because you do not agree with what they are saying: *Wait a minute! That's not what we agreed!* **c)** used when you suddenly think of, remember, or notice something: *Wait a minute, I've got a better idea.*
4 sb can't wait/can hardly wait *spoken* **a)** used to emphasize that someone is very excited about something and is eager for it to happen: *We're going to Australia on Saturday – I can't wait!* | **can't wait to do sth** *I can't wait to tell Gloria the good news.* | *Laura could hardly wait to see the twins again.* | **[+for]** *I can't wait for the summer.* **b)** used humorously to say that something seems likely to be very boring: *A lecture on transformational grammar? I can hardly wait!*
5 sth can/can't wait if something can wait, it is not very urgent. If something can't wait, it is very urgent: *Go home. The report* ***can wait till*** *tomorrow.*
6 wait and see *spoken* used to say that someone should be patient because they will find out about something later: *'What's for dinner?' 'Wait and see.'* | *We* ***will just have to wait and see*** *how things develop.*
7 wait until/till ... *spoken* used when you are excited about telling or showing someone something: *Wait till you see Gaby's new house!*
8 be waiting (for sb) if something is waiting for you, it is ready for you to use, collect etc: *There'll be a rental car waiting for you at the airport.* | *Come round at eight and I'll* ***have*** *dinner* ***waiting.***
9 wait your turn to stay calm until it is your turn to do something, instead of trying to move ahead of other people: *I've got two hands and there are three of you. So you'll* ***have to wait your turn!***
10 sth is (well) worth waiting for *spoken* used to say that something is very good, even though it takes a long time to come: *Their new album was worth waiting for.*
11 (just) you wait *spoken* **a)** *BrE* used to warn or threaten someone: *I'll get you back for what you've done, just you wait.* **b)** used to tell someone you are sure something will happen: *It'll be a huge success. Just you wait.*
12 what are you waiting for? *spoken* used to tell someone to do something immediately: *Well, what are you waiting for? Go and apologize.*
13 what are we waiting for? *spoken* used to say in a cheerful way that you think everyone should start doing something immediately: *What are we waiting for? Let's go eat.*
14 wait for it *BrE spoken* **a)** used just before you tell someone something that is funny or surprising: *His name was – wait for it – Mr Bacon.* **b)** used to tell someone not to do something until the correct time because they seem very impatient to do it now
15 be waiting in the wings to be ready to do something if it is necessary or if a suitable time comes: *Other firms are waiting in the wings, ready to step in and make an offer should the current deal fall through.*
16 wait tables *AmE* to work in a restaurant serving food and drink to people at their tables: *I spent the summer waiting tables.*
17 (play) a/the waiting game if you play a waiting game, you try to gain an advantage for yourself in a particular situation by deliberately doing nothing until you have seen what other people do

THESAURUS

wait to stay somewhere or not do something until something else happens, someone arrives etc: *I'll wait here while you call him.* | *He said he was waiting for a friend.*
hang around (*also* **hang about** *BrE*) *informal* to wait in a place not doing anything, especially so that you are wasting time: *They kept us hanging around for hours at the hospital.*
hold on/hang on to wait because you are hoping that something will happen: *The captain decided it was best to hold on and wait for the other ship to arrive.* | *We hung on until the very last moment.*
can you hold on/hang on? *spoken* used when telling someone to wait: *Can you hang on a minute? I just want to finish this email.*
stand by/be on standby to wait and be ready to do something if needed – used especially about soldiers, police, medical teams etc: *The army are standing by.* | *Emergency services were on standby after someone called to say there was a bomb in the city centre.*
await *formal* to wait for something – used about something that you know will happen or arrive: *I will await your reply* (=in a formal letter). | *In February, nearly 200,000 prisoners were awaiting trial.*

wait around (*also* **wait about** *BrE*) *phr v* to stay in the same place and do nothing while you are waiting for something to happen, someone to arrive etc: *Movie-making involves acting for ten minutes and then waiting around for two hours.* | *We'd better be going. We can't wait about like this any longer.*
wait behind *phr v BrE* to stay somewhere after other people have left: *She waited behind to help Debbie with the clearing up.*
wait in *phr v BrE* to stay at home and wait there for someone to arrive: *I have to wait in for the repair man.*
wait on sb/sth *phr v*
1 to serve food and drink to someone at their table, especially in a restaurant
2 to wait for a particular event, piece of information etc, especially before doing something or making a decision: *We're waiting on the blood test results.*
3 wait on sb hand and foot to do everything for someone while they do nothing – used to show disapproval: *His wife waits on him hand and foot.*
wait sth ↔ **out** *phr v* if you wait out an event, period, or time, especially an unpleasant one, you wait for it to finish: *Let's find a place where we can wait out the storm.*
wait up *phr v*
1 to wait for someone to return before you go to bed: **[+for]** *Don't wait up for me; I may be late.*
2 Wait up! *AmE* used to tell someone to stop, so that you can talk to them or go with them: *'Wait up!' he called.*

wait² ●●○ *n* [singular] a period of time in which you wait for something to happen, someone to arrive etc: **[+for]** *The average wait for an appointment at the clinic was eight weeks.* | **long/three-hour/two-week etc wait** *There was an hour wait before the next train departed.* | *They'll* ***have a*** *long* ***wait***. → **lie in wait** at LIE¹(8)

wait·er /ˈweɪtə $ -ər/ ●●● S3 *n* [C] a man who serves food and drink at the tables in a restaurant

ˈ**waiting list** *n* [C] a list of people who have asked for something but who must wait before they can have it: **[+for]** *There is still a three-month waiting list for the cars.* | **on a waiting list** *I was then* ***put on a waiting list*** *to see a specialist at the local hospital.*

ˈ**waiting room** *n* [C] a room for people to wait in, for example before they see a doctor, until their train arrives etc

wait·list¹ /ˈweɪtlɪst/ *v* [T] *AmE* to put someone's name on a waiting list

waitlist² *n* [C] *AmE* a waiting list

wait·ress /ˈweɪtrɪs/ ●●● S3 *n* [C] a woman who serves food and drink at the tables in a restaurant

wait·ron /ˈweɪtrən/ *n* [C] a WAITER or WAITRESS – used humorously

waive /weɪv/ *v* [T] to state officially that a right, rule etc can be ignored: *She waived her right to a lawyer.*

waiv·er /ˈweɪvə $ -ər/ *n* [C] *technical* an official written statement saying that a right, legal process etc can be waived

wake¹ /weɪk/ ●●● S2 W3 (*also* **wake up**) *v* (*past tense* **woke** /wəʊk $ woʊk/, *past participle* **woken** /ˈwəʊkən $ ˈwoʊ-/) [I,T] to stop sleeping, or to make someone stop sleeping: *When she woke, the sun was streaming through the windows.* | *Try not to wake the baby.* | **[+to]** *Nancy woke to the sound of birds outside her window* (=she heard birds singing when she woke).
wake up *phr v*
1 to stop sleeping, or to make someone stop sleeping: *James usually wakes up early.* | **wake sb ↔ up** *I'll wake you up when it's time to leave.*
2 to start to listen or pay attention to something: ***Wake up*** (=give me your attention) *at the back there!*
3 wake up and smell the coffee *AmE spoken* used to tell someone to recognize the truth or reality of a situation
wake up to sth *phr v* to start to realize and understand a danger, an idea etc: *It's time you woke up to the fact that it's a tough world.*

wake² *n* [C] **1 in the wake of sth** if something, especially something bad, happens in the wake of an event, it happens afterwards and usually as a result of it: *Famine followed in the wake of the drought.* **2 in sb's/sth's wake** behind or after someone or something: *The car left clouds of dust in its wake.* **3** the time before or after a funeral when friends and relatives meet to remember the dead person **4** [usually singular] the track made behind a boat as it moves through the water

wake·board /ˈweɪkbɔːrd $ -bɔːrd/ *n* [C] a short wide board that you stand on while you are pulled behind a boat, usually done as a sport → **water skiing** —**wakeboarder** *n* [C] —**wakeboarding** *n* [U]

wake·ful /ˈweɪkfəl/ *adj literary* **a)** not sleeping or unable to sleep: *She lay wakeful in her room for most of the night.* **b)** a wakeful period of time is one when you cannot sleep —**wakefulness** *n* [U]

wak·en /ˈweɪkən/ (*also* **waken up**) *v* [I,T] *literary* to wake up, or to wake someone up: *She gently wakened the sleeping child.*

ˈ**wake-up** ˌ**call** *n* [C] **1** an experience or event that shocks you and makes you realize that you must do something to change a situation: *The success of extremist groups in the elections should be a wake-up call to all decent citizens.* **2** a telephone call that someone makes to you, especially at a hotel, to wake you up in the morning SYN **alarm call**

wak·ey-wak·ey /ˌweɪki ˈweɪki/ *interjection BrE spoken* used to tell someone in a humorous way to wake up

wak·ing /ˈweɪkɪŋ/ *adj written* **waking hours/life/day etc** all the time when you are awake: *His face haunted her every waking moment!*

walk¹ /wɔːk $ wɒːk/ ●●● S1 W1 *v*
1 [I,T] to move forward by putting one foot in front of the other: *'How did you get here?' 'We walked.'* | *Doctors said he'd never walk again.* | **[+into/down/up etc]** *Carrie walked into the room and sat down in her chair.* | *He loved walking in the hills.* | **walk a mile/200 metres/a short distance etc** *We must have walked ten miles today.* | *I walked all the way to San Rafael.* | **within (easy) walking distance (of sth)** (=near enough to be able to walk to) *There are plenty of bars and restaurants within walking distance of the hotel.* | **walking pace** (=the speed that you normally walk at)
2 [T] to walk somewhere with someone, especially in order to make sure that they are safe or to be polite: *It's late – I'll* ***walk*** *you* ***home***. | **walk sb to sth** *Schools are urging parents to walk their children to school.* | *She walked me to the front gate.*
3 [T] to take a dog for a walk for exercise: *Grandma's out* ***walking*** *the* ***dog***.

W

4 [I] *BrE informal* if something has walked, it has disappeared and you think someone may have taken it: *My pen seems to have walked.*
5 walk free (*also* **walk** *AmE*) to leave a court of law without being punished or sent to prison: *Ferguson walked free after the charges were dropped.* | *If more evidence isn't found, Harris will walk.*
6 walk it *BrE spoken* **a)** to make a journey by walking: *If the last bus has gone, we'll have to walk it.* **b)** to succeed or win something easily
7 be walking on air to be feeling extremely happy
8 walk the streets a) to walk around the streets in a town or city: *It was not safe to walk the streets at night.* **b)** *old-fashioned* to be a PROSTITUTE
9 walk the beat when a police officer walks the beat, they walk around an area of a town or city in order to make sure nobody is committing a crime
10 walk tall to be proud and confident because you know that you have not done anything wrong
11 walk sb off their feet *BrE*, **walk sb's legs off** *AmE informal* to make someone tired by making them walk too far
12 walk the walk to do the things that people expect or think are necessary in a particular situation: *People are motivated by leaders who actually walk the walk.* → **talk the talk** at TALK[1](18)
13 walk the plank to be forced to walk along a board laid over the side of a ship until you fall off into the sea, used as a punishment in the past
14 walk on eggshells (*also* **walk on eggs** *AmE*) to be very careful about how you behave with someone because they are easily upset or made angry

walk away *phr v*
1 to leave a bad or difficult situation, instead of trying to make it better: **[+from]** *You can't just walk away from 15 years of marriage!* | *When the business started to have problems, it was very tempting to walk away.*
2 to come out of an accident or very bad situation without being harmed: *Miraculously, both drivers walked away without a scratch.*

walk away with sth *phr v informal* to win something easily: *And the lucky winner will walk away with a prize of £10,000.*

walk in on sb *phr v* to go into a room and accidentally interrupt someone who is doing something private that they would not want you to see

walk into sth *phr v*
1 to hit an object accidentally as you are walking along: **walk straight/right/bang etc into sth** *Zeke wasn't looking and walked straight into a tree.*
2 if you walk into an unpleasant situation, you become involved in it without intending to: *He was fairly certain now that he was* ***walking into a trap****, and wished he'd come*

THESAURUS: walk

walk to move forward by putting one foot in front of the other: *I missed the bus so I decided to walk.* | *We've walked about eight miles today.*
wander to walk without any clear purpose or direction: *They wandered around the narrow streets of the old city.*
stride to walk with long steps in a determined, confident, or angry way: *A man in a suit came striding purposefully into the hall.* | *She strode onto the stage and began to address the audience.*
pace to walk first in one direction and then in another many times, especially because you are nervous: *Nick was pacing up and down, waiting for the phone to ring.*
march to walk quickly with firm regular steps - used especially about soldiers or someone who is angry: *The troops marched past with smart uniforms and good discipline.* | *Sheila marched into the office and demanded an apology.*
wade to walk through deep water: *We had to wade across the river.*
stomp to walk putting your feet down very hard, especially because you are angry: *She turned and stomped off without looking back.*

TO WALK QUIETLY

tiptoe to walk quietly and carefully on your toes because you do not want to make a noise: *I tiptoed out trying not to wake the baby.*
creep to walk quietly and slowly because you do not want anyone to see or hear you: *Stella crept up the stairs, hoping not to wake her parents.*
sneak to walk quietly so that no one notices you, especially because you are doing something you should not do: *They sneaked off without paying.* | *I quickly sneaked out to have a cigarette.*
pad to walk quietly without wearing shoes - also used about cats and dogs walking quietly: *Michelle got up and padded barefoot down to the kitchen.* | *The cat padded in, asking for her food.*

TO WALK SLOWLY

trudge /trʌdʒ/ to walk in a slow tired way because it is difficult to continue walking, or you do not want to go somewhere: *The men trudged along the road, heads bent against the wind.* | *I've spent hours trudging around the shops looking for a present.*
plod to walk slowly in a tired way - often used about a horse, donkey etc: *The donkey was plodding slowly along under its heavy load.* | *I plodded on growing thirstier and hungrier.*
shuffle to walk very slowly and noisily without lifting your feet off the ground: *The old man got up and shuffled to the door.*

TO WALK WITH DIFFICULTY

limp to walk with difficulty because one leg hurts, so that you put most of your weight on the other leg: *Jake was limping because of the injury to his knee.*
stagger to walk or move unsteadily, almost falling over, especially because you are drunk or have been injured: *They finally staggered back to the hotel at 4 o'clock in the morning.* | *He hit her and she staggered and fell.*
hobble to walk with difficulty in a slow and unsteady way because your legs or feet hurt or have been injured: *My new shoes were so painful I could only hobble along.* | *She hobbled out to the car on crutches.*

TO WALK FOR PLEASURE

take a walk (*also* **go for a walk**) to walk somewhere for pleasure: *We went for a walk in the park.*
stroll (*also* **go for a stroll**) to walk in a relaxed way, especially for pleasure: *People were strolling along beside the river.* | *On Sunday, they went for a stroll in the park.*
hike (*also* **go hiking**) to walk a long way in the mountains or countryside as an activity you enjoy: *We're going hiking in Scotland this summer.* | *They hiked around the Lake District.*
trek (*also* **go trekking**) to go for a walk lasting several days or weeks in a faraway place, carrying your clothes with you: *I've always wanted to go trekking in Nepal.* | *They trekked up to Everest Base Camp.*

armed. | **walk straight/right into sth** *I walked right into a mob of maybe 50 young white guys.*
3 *BrE* if you walk into a job, you get it very easily: *You can't expect to **walk** straight **into** a **job**.*
4 to make yourself look stupid when you could easily have avoided it if you had been more careful: **walk straight/right into sth** *You walked right into that one!*

walk off *phr v*
1 to leave someone by walking away from them, especially in a rude or angry way: *Don't just walk off when I'm trying to talk to you!*
2 walk sth ↔ off if you walk off an illness or unpleasant feeling, you go for a walk to make it go away: *Let's go out – maybe I can walk this headache off.* | **walk off dinner/a meal etc** (=go for a walk so that your stomach feels less full)
3 walk off (the/your etc job) *AmE* to stop working as a protest: *Without new contracts, mine workers will walk off their jobs Thursday.*

walk off with sth *phr v informal*
1 to win something easily: *Lottery winners can walk off with a cool £18 million.*
2 to steal something or take something that does not belong to you: *Thieves walked off with two million dollars' worth of jewellery.*

walk out *phr v*
1 to leave a place suddenly, especially because you disapprove of something: *The play was awful and we walked out after half an hour.* | **[+of]** *the issue that led to the US walking out of the trade talks this week*
2 to leave your husband, wife etc suddenly and go and live somewhere else: *Her husband walked out, leaving her with three children to look after.* | **[+on]** *Five years later she walked out on Matthew and their two boys.*
3 to leave your job suddenly because you no longer want to do it: *We're so short-staffed. I can't just walk out.* | **[+of]** *If you can afford to walk out of your job, why not?*
4 to stop working as a protest: *Workers are threatening to walk out if an agreement is not reached.*

walk out on sth *phr v* to stop doing something you have agreed to do or that you are responsible for: *'I never walk out on a deal,' Dee said.*

walk over sb *phr v* to treat someone badly by always making them do what you want them to do: *It's terrible – she **lets** her kids just **walk all over her**.*

walk² ●●● S2 W2 *n*
1 [C] a journey that you make by walking, especially for exercise or enjoyment: *It's a long walk. Maybe we should get the bus.* | **[+to/through/across etc]** *a walk through the castle grounds*
2 [C] a particular journey that you make by walking, especially one that goes through an interesting or attractive area: *He says he's **going on** a long **walk** tomorrow.* | *Have you ever **done** the Three Peaks **walk**?* | **coastal/hill etc walk** *There is a stunning 10-mile coastal walk from St Andrews to Crail.*
3 [C] an organized event when people walk for pleasure: *Let's all **go on** the beach **walk**.* | *The local tourist office organises a number of **guided walks**.*
4 [singular] the way someone walks SYN **gait**: *You can often recognize people by their walk.*
5 [singular] when you walk rather than run: *Breathless, she **slowed to a walk**.* → WALK OF LIFE, → **sponsored walk** at SPONSOR²(5)

COLLOCATIONS

VERBS

go for a walk *Let's go for a walk on the beach.*
take/have a walk *She took a walk through the town.*
take sb/a dog for a walk

ADJECTIVES/NOUN + walk

a long walk *We went for a long walk in the woods.*
a short walk *The house is only a short walk from local shops.*
a little walk *I just felt like a little walk.*
a five-mile/ten-kilometre etc walk | **a five-minute/two-hour etc walk**

COMMON ERRORS

⚠ Don't say 'go a walk' or 'make a walk'. Say **go for a walk**.

walk·a·bout /ˈwɔːkəbaʊt $ ˈwɒːk-/ *n* [C] *BrE*
1 *informal* an occasion when an important person walks through a crowd, talking informally to people: *The press conference was followed by a walkabout and a factory visit.*
2 go walkabout *spoken* to get lost – used humorously: *My watch has gone walkabout again.*

walk·a·way /ˈwɔːkəweɪ $ ˈwɒːk-/ *n* [C] *AmE informal* an easy victory SYN **walkover**

walk·er /ˈwɔːkə $ ˈwɒːkər/ ●○○ *n* [C]
1 *especially BrE* someone who walks for pleasure or exercise → **hiker**: *The area is popular with walkers.* | *climbers and **hill-walkers***
2 a fast/slow etc walker someone who walks fast, slowly etc
3 *especially AmE* a metal frame on wheels that old or sick people use to help them walk SYN **zimmer frame** *BrE*
4 a frame on wheels that a baby can sit in and move around using its legs, before it can walk SYN **baby walker** *BrE*

walk·ies /ˈwɔːkiz $ ˈwɒːk-/ *n* [plural] *BrE spoken* used to tell a dog that you are going to take it for a walk: *Come on, Shep! Walkies!*

walk·ie-talk·ie /ˌwɔːki ˈtɔːki $ ˌwɒːki ˈtɒːki/ *n* [C] one of a pair of radios that you can carry with you, and use to speak to the person who has the other radio

ˈwalk-in *adj* [only before noun] **1** big enough for a person to walk inside: *a walk-in closet* **2 walk-in business/clinic/centre etc** a business, doctor's office etc that you can use or go to without having previously arranged a time to do this

walk·ing¹ /ˈwɔːkɪŋ $ ˈwɒːk-/ *n* [U] **1** *especially BrE* the activity or sport of going for walks, especially in the countryside or mountains → **hiking**, **rambling**: *We **went walking** in the hills.* | **walking boots/shoes** | **walking holiday/tour etc** (=a holiday on which you walk a lot, especially in the countryside) **2** the sport of walking long distances as fast as you can without actually running

walking² *adj* [only before noun] **1 walking dictionary/encyclopedia** someone who knows a lot, and always has the information that you want – used humorously **2 walking disaster (area)** someone who always drops things, has accidents, makes mistakes etc – used humorously → **within walking distance** at DISTANCE¹(1)

ˈwalking ˌbus *n* [C] *BrE* a group of children who walk to or from school together, with other children and their parents joining the group at different places along the way

ˈwalking ˌpapers *n* [plural] **give sb their walking papers** *AmE* to tell someone that they must leave a place or a job → **be given/get your marching orders** at MARCH¹(5)

ˈwalking stick *n* [C] a stick that is used to support someone, especially an old person, while they walk SYN **cane**

ˌwalk of ˈlife *n* [C] the position in society someone has, especially the type of job they have: **from every walk of life/from all walks of life** *Our volunteers include people from all walks of life.*

ˈwalk-on *n* [C] **1** (*also* **walk-on part/role**) a small acting part with no words to say in a play or film, or an actor who has a part like this **2** *AmE* someone who plays for a college sports team without having been given a sports SCHOLARSHIP

walk·out, **ˈwalk-out** /ˈwɔːk-aʊt $ ˈwɒːk-/ *n* [C] an occasion when people stop working or leave a meeting as a protest: *Members of the Irish delegation **staged** a **walk-out**.* → **walk out** at WALK¹

walk·o·ver /ˈwɔːkˌəʊvə $ ˈwɒːkˌoʊvər/ *n* [C] *informal* a very easy victory THESAURUS▸ VICTORY → **walk over** at WALK¹

walk·through /ˈwɔːkθruː $ ˈwɒːk-/ *n* [C] *written* instructions that tell you all the details of how you should

W

play a VIDEO GAME: **[+for]** *the official walkthrough for 'Tomb Raider'*

ˈwalk-up *n* [C] *AmE informal* **1** a tall building with apartments in it that does not have an ELEVATOR **2** an apartment, office etc in a building like this

walk·way /ˈwɔːkweɪ $ ˈwɒːk-/ *n* [C] an outdoor path built for people to walk along, often above the ground: *The airport hotel will be linked to the terminal building by a covered walkway.*

wall¹ /wɔːl $ wɒːl/ ●●● S1 W1 *n* [C]

1 AROUND AN AREA an upright flat structure made of stone or brick, that divides one area from another or surrounds an area → **fence**: **stone/brick/concrete wall** *The estate is surrounded by high stone walls.* | **city/garden etc wall** *the ancient city walls* | *the Great Wall of China* | *We climbed over the wall into the orchard.*

2 IN A BUILDING one of the sides of a room or building: **on the wall** *I* **put** *some pictures up* **on** *the* **walls**. | *Bob leaned* **against the wall**. | **bedroom/kitchen etc wall** *We decided to paint the bathroom walls blue.*

3 BODY the side of something hollow, especially within the body: *The walls of the blood vessels had been damaged.* | *cell walls*

4 wall of fire/water etc a tall mass of something such as fire or water, that stops anything from getting past: *The boat was hit by a wall of water.*

5 wall of silence/secrecy a situation in which nobody will tell you what you want to know: *The police investigation was met with a wall of silence.*

6 INTERNET an area on a website such as Facebook where other people can leave messages and COMMENTS about you

7 up the wall *spoken* very angry or annoyed: *That noise is* **driving** *me* **up the wall** (=making me annoyed). | **go up the wall** *BrE*: *I've got to be on time or Sarah will go up the wall.*

8 off the wall *informal* very strange or unusual, often in an amusing way: *Some of Krista's ideas are a little off the wall.*

9 go to the wall *informal* if a company goes to the wall, it fails, especially because of financial difficulties: *Many small investors will go to the wall.*

10 these four walls *spoken* the room that you are in, especially considered as a private place: *I don't want anything repeated outside these four walls.*

11 be/come up against a (brick) wall to reach a point where you cannot make progress, especially because something or someone is stopping you: *We seem to have come up against a brick wall in this investigation.*

12 be climbing/crawling (up) the walls *informal* to be feeling extremely anxious, unhappy, or annoyed, especially because you are waiting for something or are in a situation which you cannot get away from: *The kids soon had him climbing the walls.*

13 walls have ears used to warn people to be careful what they say, because other people, especially enemies, could be listening

14 hit the wall *informal* to reach the point when you are most physically tired when doing a sport → **have your back to/against the wall** at BACK²(21), → **be (like) banging your head against a brick wall** at HEAD¹, → **like talking to a brick wall** at TALK¹(15), → **the writing is on the wall** at WRITING(8), → **OFF-THE-WALL**

wall² *v*

wall sth ↔ **in** *phr v* to surround an open area with walls

wall sth ↔ **off** *phr v* to keep one area or room separate from another, by building a wall: *The control room is walled off by soundproof glass.*

wall sb/sth ↔ **up** *phr v* **1 a)** to fill in an entrance, window etc with bricks or stone: *The entrance had long since been walled up.* **b)** to fill in all the entrances and windows of a place so that someone cannot get out **2** to keep someone as a prisoner in a building

wal·la·by /ˈwɒləbi $ ˈwɑː-/ *n* (*plural* **wallabies**) [C] an Australian animal like a small KANGAROO

wal·lah, **walla** /ˈwɒlə $ ˈwɑːlə/ *n* [C] someone who does a particular kind of job or duty – used in India and Pakistan

wall·chart /ˈwɔːltʃɑːt $ ˈwɒːltʃɑːrt/ *n* [C] a large piece of paper with information on it that is fastened to a wall

walled /wɔːld $ wɒːld/ *adj* [only before noun] **walled garden/city/town etc** a garden etc that has a wall around it

wal·let /ˈwɒlɪt $ ˈwɑː-/ ●●● S2 *n* [C]

1 a small flat case, often made of leather, that you carry in your pocket, for holding paper money, bank cards etc SYN **billfold** *AmE* → **purse**: **in your wallet** *I've only got about £10 in my wallet.* | *He took a credit card out of his wallet.* → see picture at **PURSE¹**

2 *BrE* a case for documents, often made of leather or plastic

ˌwall-ˈeyed *adj AmE* having one or both eyes that seem to point to the side, rather than straight forwards

wall·flow·er /ˈwɔːlˌflaʊə $ ˈwɒːlˌflaʊər/ *n* [C]

1 *informal* someone at a party, dance etc who is not asked to dance or take part in the activities **2** a sweet-smelling garden plant with yellow and red flowers

ˈwall-ˌmounted *adj* attached to a wall: **wall-mounted clock/heater/lights etc**

wal·lop /ˈwɒləp $ ˈwɑː-/ *v* [T] *informal* to hit someone or something very hard, especially with your hand —**wallop** *n* [singular]

wal·lop·ing¹ /ˈwɒləpɪŋ $ ˈwɑː-/ *n spoken* **give sb/get a walloping** to hit someone hard several times as a punishment, or to be hit in this way

walloping² *adj* [only before noun] *BrE spoken* very big: **walloping great/big** *a walloping great house*

wal·low /ˈwɒləʊ $ ˈwɑːloʊ/ *v* [I] **1 wallow in self-pity/despair/defeat etc** to seem to enjoy being sad etc, especially because you get sympathy from other people – used to show disapproval: *He'd been feeling sorry for himself, wallowing in self-pity.* **2** if an animal or person wallows, it rolls around in mud, water etc for pleasure or to keep cool: *hippos wallowing in the mud* **3** if a ship or boat wallows, it moves with difficulty through a rough sea —**wallow** *n* [C]

ˈwall ˌpainting *n* [C] a picture that has been painted directly onto a wall, especially a FRESCO SYN **mural**

wall·pa·per¹ /ˈwɔːlˌpeɪpə $ ˈwɒːlˌpeɪpər/ ●●○ *n* [C,U]

1 paper that you stick onto the walls of a room in order to decorate it

2 the colour, pattern, or picture which you have as the background on the screen of a computer → **desktop**

wallpaper² *v* [T] to put wallpaper onto the walls of a room SYN **paper**: *I haven't finished wallpapering the bedroom yet.*

ˈWall Street **1** a street in New York which is the most important financial centre in America **2** the American STOCK MARKET: **on Wall Street** *a drop in share prices on Wall Street*

ˌWall Street ˈCrash, the the sudden large fall in the value of company SHARES on the US Stock Exchange in October 1929. For about two years before this, the price of shares had risen very fast, and when people realized that companies were therefore worth more than their true value, they lost confidence. The severe fall that followed led directly to the Great Depression of the 1930s.

ˌwall-to-ˈwall *adj* **1** [only before noun] covering the whole floor: *wall-to-wall carpeting* **2** *informal* filling all the space or time available, especially in a way you do not like: *wall-to-wall advertising on TV*

wal·ly /ˈwɒli $ ˈwɑː-/ *n* (*plural* **wallies**) [C] *BrE informal* someone who behaves in a silly way: *Stop being such a wally!*

wal·nut /ˈwɔːlnʌt $ ˈwɒːl-/ *n* **1** [C] a nut that you can eat, shaped like a human brain: *coffee and walnut cake* → see picture at **NUT¹** **2** [C] (*also* **walnut tree**) a tree that produces this type of nut **3** [U] the wood from a walnut tree, often used to make furniture

wal·rus /ˈwɔːlrəs $ ˈwɒːl-, ˈwɑːl-/ *n* [C] a large sea animal with two long TUSKS (=things like teeth) coming down from the sides of its mouth → **seal**

W

Walter Mitty *adj* → MITTY, WALTER

waltz¹ /wɔːls $ wɒːlts/ *n* [C] **1** a fairly slow dance with a regular pattern of three beats **2** a piece of music intended for this type of dance: *a Strauss waltz*

waltz² *v* **1** [I] to dance a waltz: *They waltzed elegantly around the dance floor.* **2** [I always + adv/prep] *informal* to walk somewhere calmly and confidently – used to show disapproval: **[+in/into/up to]** *Jeff just waltzed up to the bar and helped himself to a drink.* | *She can't waltz in here and start making changes.*

waltz off with sth *phr v informal* to take something without permission or without realizing that you have done this: *Joe must have waltzed off with my jacket.*

waltz through sth *phr v informal* to pass an examination, win a game etc very well and without any difficulty SYN **sail through**

wam·pum /ˈwɒmpəm $ ˈwɑːm-/ *n* [U] shells put into strings, belts etc, used in the past as money by Native Americans

wan /wɒn $ wɑːn/ *adj literary* looking pale, weak, or tired: *She gave a wan smile.* —**wanly** *adv*

wand¹ /wɒnd $ wɑːnd/ *n* [C] **1** a thin stick that you hold in your hand to do magic tricks: **wave a (magic) wand** (=move a wand about to make something magical happen) *I can't just wave a magic wand and make it all better.* **2** a tool that looks like a thin stick: *a mascara wand*

wand² *v* [T] to move a small SCANNER over something or someone: *We were wanded by security guards before being allowed in.*

wan·der¹ /ˈwɒndə $ ˈwɑːndər/ ●●○ S3 *v*

1 WITHOUT DIRECTION [I,T] to walk slowly across or around an area, usually without a clear direction or purpose: **[+in/through/around etc]** *I'll wander around the mall for half an hour.* | *She* **wandered aimlessly** *about the house.* | *Ana wandered off to get a drink.* | *He was found* **wandering the streets** *of New York.* THESAURUS ▸ WALK

2 MOVE AWAY [I] (*also* **wander off**) to walk away from where you are supposed to stay: *Don't let any of the kids wander off.*

3 MIND/THOUGHTS [I] if your mind, thoughts etc wander, you no longer pay attention to something, especially because you are bored or worried: *Mrs Snell's mind wandered and the voices went on and on.*

4 CONVERSATION [I] to start to talk about something not related to the main subject that you were talking about before: **[+from/off]** *Pauline started to wander from the point.*

5 sb's mind is wandering used to say that someone has become unable to think clearly, especially because they are old

6 EYES [I] if your eyes or your GAZE wander, you look around slowly at different things or at all parts of something: *His gaze wandered round the room.*

7 ROAD/RIVER [I] if a road or a river wanders somewhere, it does not go straight but in curves SYN **meander**: **[+through/across/along]** *The Missouri River wanders across several states.*

8 HANDS [I] if a man's hands wander, he touches the body of a woman he is with, especially where she does not want him to: *Be careful, he's got* **wandering hands**.

wander² *n* [singular] *BrE* a short relaxed walk SYN **stroll**: **take/go for/have a wander** *I had a bit of a wander round the shops.*

wan·der·er /ˈwɒndərə $ ˈwɑːndərər/ *n* [C] a person who moves from place to place and has no permanent home

wan·der·ings /ˈwɒndərɪŋz $ ˈwɑːn-/ *n* [plural] *literary* journeys to places where you do not stay for very long: *his wanderings through the Australian outback*

wan·der·lust /ˈwɒndəlʌst $ ˈwɑːndər-/ *n* [singular, U] a strong desire to travel to different places

wane¹ /weɪn/ *v* [I] **1** if something such as power, influence, or a feeling wanes, it becomes gradually less strong or less important: *My enthusiasm for the project was waning.* | *The group's influence had begun to wane by this time.* **2** when the moon wanes, you gradually see less of it OPP **wax** → **wax and wane** at WAX²(4)

wane² *n* **on the wane** becoming smaller, weaker, or less important: *By the fifth century, the power of the Roman Empire was on the wane.*

wan·gle /ˈwæŋgəl/ *v* [T] *informal* to get something, or arrange for something to happen, by cleverly persuading or tricking someone: **wangle sth (out of sb)** *In the end she wangled an invitation.* | **wangle your way out of/into sth** *I wangled my way into art school.*

wank¹ /wæŋk/ *v* [I] *BrE informal not polite* to MASTURBATE

wank² *n BrE informal not polite* **1** [singular] an act of MASTURBATION **2** [U] something which you think is very stupid, useless, or of bad quality SYN **rubbish**: *This music's a load of wank.*

wank·er /ˈwæŋkə $ -ər/ *n* [C] *BrE taboo informal* a very offensive word for a boy or man who you think is stupid or unpleasant. Do not use this word.

wan·na /ˈwɒnə $ ˈwɑː-/ a short form of 'want to' or 'want a', used in writing to show how people sound when they speak

wan·na·be /ˈwɒnəbi $ ˈwɑː-/ *n* [C] *informal* someone who tries to look or behave like someone famous or like a particular type of successful person, because they want to be like them – usually used to show disapproval → **would-be**: *a load of Michael Schumacher wannabes trying to show what they can do on the track* | *wannabe pop stars*

want¹ /wɒnt $ wɒːnt, wɑːnt/ ●●● S1 W1 *v*

1 DESIRE [T] to have a desire for something: *I really want a drink.* | *What do you want for your birthday?* | *She'd always* **wanted to** *go to Thailand.* | *I don't* **want** *Linda* **to** *hear about this.* | *He didn't* **want** *the holiday* **to** *end.* | *You can order* **whatever you want**. | *This shampoo is mild enough to use every day* **if you want**. | *If she doesn't* **get what** *she* **wants**, *she's not happy.* | *He* **wanted** *that job so* **badly** *he was willing to kill for it.* | *They* **desperately wanted** *a son.* | ***What I want to*** *know is when we're going to get paid.* | ***All I want is*** *the chance to prove myself.* | *Oh thank you,* ***it's just what I've always wanted***.

2 NEED [T] used to say that you need something or to ask someone firmly to do something for you: *Do you still want these magazines, or can I throw them out?* | **want sth done** *I want that letter typed today.* | **want sb to do sth** *I want you to find out what they're planning.* | **make you want to cry/throw up etc** (=give you a strong feeling that you must do something) *It always makes me want to sneeze.* | ***What do you want with*** *a tool kit* (=what do you need it for)? | **want doing** *BrE informal* (=need to be done) *The carpet really wants cleaning.*

3 OFFER [T] used when offering or suggesting something to someone: ***Do you want*** *a drink?* | *Do you want me to come with you?* | ***Want*** *a game of chess?* | ***Who wants*** *a cup of coffee* (=used to offer something to a group of people)?

4 SHOULD [T] *spoken especially BrE* used to say that something is sensible or that someone should do it, especially when giving advice: **may/might want to do sth** *You might want to install anti-virus software.* | **wouldn't want to do sth** (=used to say something would not be a good idea) *I wouldn't want to come here at night.* | **want to do sth** *You want to see a doctor about that cough.* | *You don't want to leave that – it'll get wet.*

5 what do you want? used to ask, often in a slightly rude way, what someone wants you to give them, do for them etc: *What do you want now? I'm busy.* | *What do you want – chocolate or vanilla?*

6 ASK FOR SB [T] to ask for someone to come and talk to you, or to come to a particular place: *You're wanted on the phone.* | *Christine wants you in her office now.*

7 LACK [I,T] *formal* to suffer because you do not have something: *In many poorer countries, people still want basic food and shelter.*

8 if you want a) used to offer to do something: *I'll come with you if you want.* **b)** used to invite someone to do something or to give them permission: *Join in if you want.* | *You can stay* ***if you want to***. **c)** used when someone suggests doing something, to say that you will do it, although

you do not especially want to: *'Hey, shall we go to the beach?' 'If you want.'*
9 who wants ...? used to say that you do not like something or do not think that it is worth doing: *Who wants to go to a noisy disco anyway?*
10 I just wanted to say/know etc used to politely say something, ask about something etc: *I just wanted to check that the meeting is still on next week.*
11 I don't want to sound/be ..., but ... used to be polite when you are going to tell someone something that may upset them: *I don't want to sound rude, but I think you've had too much to drink.*
12 SEX [T] *informal* if you want someone, you want to have sex with them

GRAMMAR

Patterns with want

- You **want** something: *Do you want some more coffee?*
- You **want to** do something: *Do you want to have some more coffee?*
- You **want** someone **to** do something: *They want their son to go to a good university.*
- **Want** is not usually followed by a 'that' clause.

✗ Don't say: *They want that their son goes to a good university.*

- You say **I don't want** someone **doing** something, when this is annoying or causes problems: *I don't want other people telling me how to spend my money.* You can also say: *I don't want other people to tell me how to spend my money.*

Using the progressive

- **Want** is not usually used in the progressive. You say: *I want to sleep now.* | *I want some coffee.*

✗ Don't say: *I am wanting some coffee.*

- In spoken English, people sometimes say **I'm wanting** to describe their feelings about something that is happening right now or that they have just seen or heard about: *Suddenly I'm wanting to know more about this man.*

GRAMMAR GUIDE ▸ VERBS

want for sth *phr v* **not want for sth/want for nothing** to have something you need, or everything you need: *Say what you like, my kids never wanted for anything.*
want in *phr v informal*
1 *especially AmE* to want to be involved in something: *You want in, Mike?*
2 to want to go into a place: *The dog wants in.*
want out *phr v informal*
1 to want to stop being involved in something: *She was fed up and she wanted out.*
2 to want to leave a place: *I think the cat wants out.*

want² ●○○ *n*
1 for (the) want of sth used to say that you do not have or cannot find what you need in a particular situation: *The gallery closed down for want of funding.*
2 for want of a better word/phrase etc used to say that you cannot find an exact word or phrase to describe something: *They should behave, for want of a better word, decently.*
3 not for want of (doing) sth used to say that even though something did not happen or succeed, it was not because you did not try hard enough or have what you needed: *Well, if he doesn't get the job it **won't be for want of trying**!*
4 for want of anything better (to do) if you do something for want of anything better, you do it only because there is nothing else you want to do
5 LACK [C,U] *formal* something that you need but do not have: *a disgraceful want of proper care*
6 NO FOOD/MONEY ETC [U] a situation in which you do not have enough food, money, clothes etc: *the chronic want and deprivation in the townships*
7 be in want of sth *formal* to need something: *The house is sadly in want of repair.*

'want ad *n* [C] *AmE* CLASSIFIED AD

want·ed /ˈwɒntɪd $ ˈwɒːn-, ˈwɑːn-/ ●○○ *adj*
1 someone who is wanted is being looked for by the police: **[+for]** *He is wanted for the murder of a teenage girl.* | *one of the most **wanted men** in China*
2 someone, especially a child, who is wanted is loved and cared for

want·ing /ˈwɒntɪŋ $ ˈwɒːn-, ˈwɑːn-/ *adj* [not before noun] *formal* something that is wanting lacks or misses something that it needs or something that you expect it to have: *Their security procedures were **found wanting**.* | **[+in]** *They were skilled, but wanting in discipline.* | *A certain humanity is wanting in big cities.*

wan·ton /ˈwɒntən $ ˈwɒːn-, ˈwɑːn-/ *adj* **1** deliberately harming someone or damaging something for no reason: *an act of wanton aggression* | *a wanton disregard for life* **2** *old-fashioned* a wanton woman is considered immoral because she has sex with a lot of men **3** *formal* uncontrolled: *wanton growth* —**wantonly** *adv* —**wantonness** *n* [U]

WAP /wæp/ *n* [U] (***wireless application protocol***) a system that uses radio waves to allow electronic equipment that is not physically attached to a computer, for example a MOBILE PHONE, to use the Internet

wap·i·ti /ˈwɒpəti $ ˈwɑː-/ *n* [C] a large North American DEER

war /wɔː $ wɔːr/ ●●● S2 W1 *n*
1 [C,U] when there is fighting between two or more countries or between opposing groups within a country, involving large numbers of soldiers and weapons OPP **peace**: *the Vietnam War* | *He served as a pilot during the war.* | **[+against/with/between]** *the war with Spain*
2 [C,U] a struggle over a long period of time to control something harmful: **[+on/against]** *the State's war on drugs* | *the war against racism*
3 [C,U] a situation in which a person or group is fighting for power, influence, or control: *No one wants to start a **trade war** here.* | *a ratings war between the major TV networks* → PRICE WAR
4 be in the wars *BrE spoken* used, often humorously, to say that someone has lots of injuries or health problems: *You've really been in the wars lately, haven't you?*
5 this means war *spoken* used humorously to say that you are ready to fight or argue about something → COLD WAR, WAR OF ATTRITION, WAR OF NERVES, WAR OF WORDS, WARRING

COLLOCATIONS

VERBS

fight a war *The two countries fought a brief war in 1995.*
fight in a war (=take part as a soldier) *Her grandfather fought in the war.*
win/lose a war *The Allies had won the war.*
declare war *In 1941, Britain and the US declared war on Japan.*
wage/make war (=to start and continue a war) *Their aim was to destroy the country's capacity to wage war.*
go to war (=become involved in a war) | **war breaks out** (=it starts)

PHRASES

be at war *Russia was at war with Poland.*
be on the brink of war (=be about to be involved in a war) | **the outbreak of war** (=the time when a war starts) | **the horrors of war**

ADJECTIVES/NOUN + war

a world war *No one wants another world war.*
a civil war (=between opposing groups within a country) *the English Civil War*
a nuclear war (=involving nuclear weapons) | **a conventional war** (=not nuclear) | **a guerrilla war** (=involving a small unofficial military group) | **the Korean/Vietnam/Iraq etc War** | **World War I/ World War II** | **a just war** (=one that you believe is right) | **a religious war**

war + NOUN

the war years *The couple spent most of the war years apart.*
a war hero *At home he was hailed as a war hero.*
a war veteran (=someone who took part in a war) | **a war criminal** (=someone who behaves very cruelly in a war, in a way that is against international law) | **a war correspondent** (=a reporter sending reports from a war) | **a war zone** (=an area where a war is fought) | **a war crime** (=a cruel act in a war which is against international law)

COMMON ERRORS

⚠ Don't say 'do the war'. Say **go to war** or **make war**.

THESAURUS

war *n* [C,U] a situation in which there is fighting between countries or opposing groups within a country, with large numbers of soldiers and weapons: *He fought in World War II.* | *the horrors of war*
conflict *n* [C,U] a situation in which there is fighting or a war - used especially in news reports: *the conflict in the Middle East* | *There is increasing danger of armed conflict.*
fighting *n* [U] a situation in which people or groups fight each other and try to kill each other: *The fighting went on for months.* | *Fighting in the north has resulted in hundreds of deaths.*
hostilities *n* [plural] *formal* fighting in a war: *The agreement called on the guerrillas to* ***cease hostilities*** (=stop fighting) *and begin peace talks.*
warfare *n* [U] the activity of fighting in a war - used especially to talk about a method of fighting: *new and more advanced methods of warfare* | *chemical warfare*
battle *n* [C,U] an occasion when two armies, groups of ships etc fight each other in one place during a war: *the great naval battles of the Napoleonic Wars* | *the Battle of Trafalgar in 1805* | *He died in battle.*
skirmish /ˈskɜːmɪʃ/ *n* [C] a short fight between small groups of soldiers, ships etc, especially one that happens away from the main part of a war or battle: *There were minor skirmishes between Indian and Pakistani troops across the border.*
combat *n* [U] the act of fighting, especially during a war: *Few of them had any experience of combat.* | *hand-to-hand combat*
action *n* [U] military actions carried out by the army, navy etc of a country during a war - used especially in the following phrases: *He was* ***killed in action*** *in 1944.* | *Her son went* ***missing in action***. | *Her grandfather* ***saw action*** (=fought) *in two world wars.*

W

ˌWar and ˈPeace (1863-69) a novel by the Russian writer Leo Tolstoy, set during the Napoleonic Wars and considered by many people to be one of the greatest novels ever written. It is sometimes mentioned as being a very typical example of an extremely long book.

war·ble /ˈwɔːbəl $ ˈwɔːr-/ *v* **1** [I] to sing with a high continuous but quickly changing sound, the way a bird does **2** [I,T] to sing, especially not very well - used humorously: *Mills warbled a few notes.* —**warble** *n* [C]

war·bler /ˈwɔːblə $ ˈwɔːrblər/ *n* [C] **1** a bird that can make musical sounds **2** a singer, especially one who does not sing very well - used humorously

war·chalk·ing /ˈwɔːˌtʃɔːkɪŋ $ ˈwɔːrˌtʃɒːk-/ *n* [U] *technical* the activity of drawing symbols on the PAVEMENT to show the position of a WIRELESS Internet network which HACKERS can use to make a free connection to the Internet

ˈwar chest *n* [C] *informal* **1** the money that a government has available to spend on war **2** the money that a politician or organization has available to spend on achieving something: *The government's huge war chest could be used to improve transport.*

ˈwar crime *n* [C usually plural] a cruel act done during a war which is illegal under international law: *He was put on trial for war crimes.* | *an international* ***war crimes tribunal*** (=court judging war crimes) —**war criminal** *n* [C]

ˈwar cry *n* [C] a shout used by people fighting in a battle to show their courage and frighten the enemy SYN **battle cry**

ward¹ /wɔːd $ wɔːrd/ ●●○ W3 *n* [C]
1 a large room in a hospital where people who need medical treatment stay: **maternity/general/geriatric etc ward** (=a ward for people with a particular medical condition) | **on/in the ward** *a young nurse's first day on the wards* | *the other patients in the ward*
2 one of the small areas that a city has been divided into for the purpose of local elections → **constituency**
3 *law* someone, especially a child, who is under the legal protection of another person or of a law court: *She was made a* ***ward of court***.

ward² *v*
ward sth ↔ **off** *phr v* to do something to try to protect yourself from something bad, such as illness, danger, or attack: *Don't forget insect repellent to ward off the mosquitoes.* | *a spell to ward off evil spirits*

-ward /wəd $ wərd/ *suffix* [in adjectives] towards a particular direction or place: *our homeward journey* | *a downward movement*

ˈwar dance *n* [C] a dance performed by tribes in preparation for battle or to celebrate a victory

war·den /ˈwɔːdn $ ˈwɔːrdn/ *n* [C] **1** a person who is responsible for a particular place and whose job is to make sure its rules are obeyed: **[+of]** *the warden of the college* | **forest/park etc warden** → CHURCHWARDEN, GAME WARDEN, TRAFFIC WARDEN **2** *AmE* the person in charge of a prison SYN **governor** *BrE* **3** *BrE* someone who takes care of a building and the people in it, for example a place such as a home for old people

ward·er /ˈwɔːdə $ ˈwɔːrdər/ (*also* **prison warder**) *n* [C] *BrE* someone who works in a prison guarding the prisoners → **guard**

war·drobe /ˈwɔːdrəʊb $ ˈwɔːrdroʊb/ ●●● S3 *n*
1 [C] *BrE* a piece of furniture like a large cupboard that you hang clothes in → **closet**: *Can you hang these in the wardrobe, please?* | **fitted/built-in wardrobes** (=wardrobes built against a wall or fitted between two walls)
2 [C] the clothes that someone has: *You can win a complete new wardrobe.* | **winter/summer etc wardrobe** (=the clothes you have for a particular time of year)
THESAURUS ▸ CLOTHES
3 [singular] (*also* **wardrobe department**) a department in a theatre, television company etc that deals with the clothes worn by actors

ˈwardrobe malˌfunction *n* [C] an occasion when your clothing accidentally shows a part of your body that you want to be covered - used humorously

ward·room /ˈwɔːdrʊm, -ruːm $ ˈwɔːrd-/ *n* [C] the space in a WARSHIP where the officers live and eat, except for the captain

-wards /wədz $ wərdz/ (*also* **-ward** *especially AmE*) *suffix* [in adverbs] towards a particular direction or place: *We're travelling northwards.* | *look skywards*

-ware /weə $ wer/ *suffix* [in U nouns] **1** things made of a particular material, especially for use in the home: *glassware* (=glass bowls, glasses etc) | *silverware* (=silver spoons, knives etc) **2** things used in a particular place for the preparation or serving of food: *ovenware* (=dishes for use in the oven) | *tableware* (=plates, glasses, knives etc) **3** things used in operating a computer: *software* (=programs) | *shareware* (=programs which can be shared via the Internet)

ˈwar ˌeffort *n* [singular] things done by all the people in a country to help when that country is at war

ware·house /ˈweəhaʊs $ ˈwer-/ ●●○ *n* [C] a large building for storing large quantities of goods

ˈwarehouse ˌstore (*also* **ˈwarehouse ˌclub**) *n* [C] *AmE* a type of store that sells things in large amounts, so that you can buy them at a lower price than at normal stores

ware·hous·ing /ˈweəhaʊzɪŋ $ ˈwer-/ *n* [U] the business or practice of storing large quantities of goods, especially in warehouses: *warehousing costs | warehousing and distribution*

wares /weəz $ werz/ *n* [plural] *old-fashioned* things that are for sale, usually not in a shop: *craftspeople* ***selling*** *their* ***wares*** THESAURUS ➤ PRODUCT

war·fare /ˈwɔːfeə $ ˈwɔːrfer/ ●○○ *n* [U]
1 the activity of fighting in a war – used especially when talking about particular methods of fighting: *the realities of modern warfare* | **chemical/nuclear/germ etc warfare** | **trench/jungle/mountain etc warfare** | **guerrilla warfare** (=fighting by small groups of fighters in mountains, forests etc) THESAURUS ➤ WAR
2 a continuous and often violent struggle or argument between different groups: **class/gang/internecine etc warfare** *the problems of drugs and gang warfare* → **psychological warfare** at PSYCHOLOGICAL(3)

ˈwar ˌgame *n* [C] **1** an activity in which soldiers fight an imaginary battle in order to test military plans **2** a game played by adults in which models of soldiers, guns, horses etc are moved around a table, or a similar game played on a computer

war·head /ˈwɔːhed $ ˈwɔːr-/ *n* [C] the explosive part at the front of a MISSILE: **nuclear/chemical etc warhead**

war·horse /ˈwɔːhɔːs $ ˈwɔːrhɔːrs/ *n* [C] **1** *informal* a soldier or politician who has been in their job a long time, and enjoys dealing with all the difficulties involved in it **2** a horse used in battle

war·like /ˈwɔːlaɪk $ ˈwɔːr-/ *adj* **1** liking war and being skilful in it: *a warlike nation* **2** threatening war or attack: *a warlike stance*

war·lock /ˈwɔːlɒk $ ˈwɔːrlɑːk/ *n* [C] a man who has magical powers, especially evil powers SYN **sorcerer**, **wizard**

war·lord /ˈwɔːlɔːd $ ˈwɔːrlɔːrd/ *n* [C] the leader of an unofficial military group fighting against a government, king, or different group

warm¹ /wɔːm $ wɔːrm/ ●●● S2 W2 *adj*
1 BE WARM slightly hot, especially in a pleasant way OPP **cool** → **warmth**: *The house was lovely and warm. | I hope we get some warm weather soon. | I've put your dinner in the oven to* ***keep*** *it* ***warm****. | warm water* THESAURUS ➤ HOT
2 FEEL WARM if you are warm, your body is at a comfortable temperature: *Are you warm enough?* | **keep/stay warm** (=wear enough clothes not to feel cold) *Make sure you keep warm! | You'll be as* ***warm as toast*** *in that sleeping bag.*
3 CLOTHES/BUILDINGS clothes or buildings that are warm can keep in heat or keep out cold: *Here, put on your nice warm coat.*
4 FRIENDLY friendly or making someone feel comfortable and relaxed: *a warm, reassuring smile | Please give a* ***warm welcome*** *to our special guest. | a warm glow of satisfaction | The Hungarian people are* ***warm and friendly****.* THESAURUS ➤ FRIENDLY
5 COLOUR warm colours contain the colours red, yellow, and orange, which make you feel comfortable and happy OPP **cool**
6 CORRECT [not before noun] used especially in games to say that someone is near to guessing the correct answer or finding a hidden object OPP **cold**: *You're getting warmer.*
—**warmness** *n* [U]

warm² ●●○ (*also* **warm up**) *v* [I,T] to make someone or something warm or warmer, or to become warm or warmer: *They gathered round the fire to warm their hands.* | **warm yourself** *Warm yourself by the fire.*

warm to sb/sth (*also* **warm up to sb/sth** *AmE*) *phr v*
1 to begin to like someone you have just met: *Bruce didn't warm to him as he had to Casey.*
2 to become more eager, interested, or excited about something: **warm to a theme/subject/topic etc** *The more she spoke, the more she warmed to her subject. | Voters are starting to warm up to the idea.*

warm up *phr v*
1 MAKE WARM to become warm, or to make someone or something warm: *With the fire on, the room should soon warm up. | Once the weather warms up, you can move the plants outdoors.* | **warm sth ↔ up** *I turned on the grill to warm it up.* | **warm sb up** *Come inside and have a drink. It'll warm you up.*
2 FOOD to heat food, especially food that has already been cooked, so that it is hot enough to eat, or to become hot enough to eat: **warm sth ↔ up** *I'll put the lasagne in the oven to warm it up.*
3 DO EXERCISES to do gentle physical exercises to prepare your body for dancing, sport etc: *The runners began warming up.* → WARM-UP¹(1), WARM-UP²(2)
4 MACHINE/ENGINE if a machine or engine warms up, or if you warm it up, it becomes ready to work properly after being switched on: *He waited for the photocopier to warm up.* | **warm sth ↔ up** *He started to warm up the aircraft's engines.*
5 EVENT if a party, election etc warms up, it starts to become enjoyable or interesting, especially because more is happening: *The race for governor is beginning to warm up.*
6 PRACTISE if musicians, singers, or performers warm up, they practise just before a performance: *The band had little time to warm up before going on stage.*
7 PERFORM/SPEAK FIRST to perform or speak first at an event, so that the people listening are relaxed or excited before the main singer, speaker etc comes on: **warm sb ↔ up** *He warmed up the audience by telling them a few jokes.* | **[+for]** *They warmed up for U2 on one of their early tours.*
→ **look/feel like death warmed up/over** at DEATH(8)

warm³ *n* **the warm** *BrE* a place that is warm OPP **the cold**: *Come into the warm!*

warm⁴ *adv* **wrap up warm** to put on enough clothes so that you do not feel cold

ˌwarm-ˈblooded *adj* animals that are warm-blooded have a body temperature that remains fairly high whether the temperature around them is hot or cold OPP **cold-blooded**

ˈwarm-down *n* [C] exercises that you do to relax your body after playing a sport or dancing → **warm-up**: *A gentle walk can act as a warm-down after a race.*

ˌwarmed-ˈover *adj* [usually before noun] *AmE* **1** warmed-over food has been cooked before and then heated again for eating → **reheat** **2** warmed-over ideas or arguments have been used before and are not interesting or useful anymore → **look/feel like death warmed up/over** at DEATH(8)

ˌwarmed-ˈup *adj* if you are warmed-up, you have done a set of gentle exercises to prepare your body for playing a sport, dancing etc

ˈwar meˌmorial *n* [C] a MONUMENT in memory of the people who were killed in a war

warm·er /ˈwɔːmə $ ˈwɔːrmər/ *n* [C] something, especially a piece of equipment, that is used to make or keep things warm: *a plate warmer*

ˌwarm ˈfront *n* [C] an expression used especially in weather reports meaning the front edge of a mass of warm air OPP **cold front**

warm-heart·ed /ˌwɔːm ˈhɑːtɪd◂ $ ˌwɔːrm ˈhɑːr-/ *adj* friendly, kind, and always willing to help OPP **cold-hearted**: *a warm-hearted landlady* THESAURUS ➤ KIND —**warm-heartedness** *n* [U]

warm·ing¹ /ˈwɔːmɪŋ $ ˈwɔːr-/ *adj* making you feel pleasantly warm: *a warming cup of cocoa*

warming² *n* [singular] **1** an increase in the temperature of something: **[+of]** *the warming of the ocean currents in the Pacific* → GLOBAL WARMING **2** a situation in which a relationship becomes more friendly: **[+of]** *the warming of relations between Britain and Iran*

ˈwarming pan *n* [C] a metal container with a long handle, used in the past to hold hot coals for warming beds

warm·ly /ˈwɔːmli $ ˈwɔːrm-/ ●○○ *adv*
1 in a friendly way OPP **coldly**: *Terry* ***greeted*** *the visitor*

W

warmly. | *We were* ***warmly welcomed*** *by the villagers.* | *Jack* ***smiled warmly****.*
2 in a way that makes something or someone warm: *Pat* ***wrapped*** *the baby* ***up warmly****.* | *Make sure that the children are* ***dressed warmly****.*
3 in a way that shows that you like something very much: *His speech was warmly received.*

war·mon·ger /ˈwɔːˌmʌŋɡə $ ˈwɔːrˌmɑːŋɡər, -ˌmʌŋ-/ *n* [C] someone, especially a politician, who wants people to start fighting or start a war – used to show disapproval —**warmongering** *adj, n* [U]

warmth /wɔːmθ $ wɔːrmθ/ ●●○ *n* [U]
1 the heat something produces, or when you feel warm: **[+of]** *the warmth of the summer sun* | **for warmth** *The children huddled closely together for warmth.*
2 friendliness and happiness: **[+of]** *the warmth of her smile*

ˈwarm-up¹ *n* [C] **1** a set of gentle exercises you do to prepare your body for sport, dancing etc → **warm up** at WARM² **2 warm-ups** *AmE informal* clothes that you wear when you are doing exercises to prepare your body for playing a sport or dancing → **sweat suit**

warm-up² *adj* **1** a warm-up match, game, or race is held to give the sportsmen or players practice before a big event **2** warm-up exercises are done to prepare your body before playing a sport or dancing **3** a warm-up jacket is worn to keep you warm when you are doing exercises **4** a warm-up man or band prepares the people at an event for the main speaker, singer etc by singing, telling jokes etc

warn /wɔːn $ wɔːrn/ ●●● S3 W2 *v* [I,T]
1 to tell someone that something bad or dangerous may happen, so that they can avoid it or prevent it: *'Be careful, the rocks are slippery,' Alex warned.* | **warn sb about sth** *Travellers to Africa are being warned about the danger of HIV infection.* | **warn (sb) of sth** *Salmon farmers are warning of the severe crisis facing the industry.* | **warn sb (not) to do sth** *I warned you not to walk home alone.* | *Motorists are being warned to avoid the centre of London this weekend.* | **warn sb (that)** *We warned them that there was a bull in the field.*
2 to tell someone about something before it happens so that they are not worried or surprised by it: **warn sb (that)** *Warn her you're going to be back late.*

REGISTER
In everyday English, people often use the expression **let** someone **know** rather than **warn** someone: ***Let me know*** *if you're not going to finish on time.*

GRAMMAR: Patterns with warn
- You **warn** someone that something **will** happen (=you say it will definitely happen): *I must warn you that the treatment will have side effects.*
- In the past, you say that someone **warned** that something **would** happen (=they said that it would definitely happen): *Campaigners warned that the airport would harm the environment.*
- You **warn** that something **might** happen or **could** happen: *He warned that there might be another war.*
- **Warn** is also often used in the passive. You say that someone **was warned about** something: *We were warned about the dangers of global warming.*

GRAMMAR GUIDE ▶ VERBS

THESAURUS
warn to tell someone about something bad or dangerous that might happen, so that they can avoid it or prevent it: *I warned you about sitting out in the sun too long.* | *We were warned that there could be delays on the motorway, so we took another route.*
give sb a warning to tell someone that if they continue to behave in an unsatisfactory way, they will be punished: *He's already been given several warnings about handing in his essays late.*
alert to officially or publicly warn people of possible danger so that they can prevent it or be ready to deal with it: *a campaign to alert people to the dangers of smoking* | *An anonymous caller alerted the police that a bomb was due to go off.*
tip sb off *informal* to secretly warn someone about something that is going to happen – used especially about warning the police about a crime: *The police found the drugs after being tipped off by local residents.*
caution *formal* to warn someone to do or not to do something in order to avoid a dangerous or bad result: *People are being cautioned against using credit cards abroad, in case of fraud.*
forewarn /fɔːˈwɔːn $ fɔːrˈwɔːrn/ [usually passive] *formal* to warn someone about something that is going to happen, so that they are expecting it or ready for it: *We had been forewarned that the roads weren't very good.*

warn (sb) against sth *phr v* to advise someone not to do something because it may have dangerous or unpleasant results: *Her financial adviser warned her against such a risky investment.* | **warn (sb) against doing sth** *The police have warned tourists against leaving the main tourist centres.*

warn sb ↔ **away** *phr v* to tell someone that they should not go near something, especially because it may be dangerous: *The snake's markings are intended to warn away predators.*

warn off *phr v*
1 warn sb ↔ off to tell people that they should not go near something, especially because it might be dangerous: *Some animals mark their territory to warn off rivals.*
2 warn sb off (doing) sth *especially BrE* to tell someone that they should not do or use something because it might be dangerous: *Doctors should have warned people off using the drug much earlier than they did.*

warn·ing¹ /ˈwɔːnɪŋ $ ˈwɔːrn-/ ●●● S3 W2 *n*
1 [C,U] something, especially a statement, that tells you that something bad, dangerous, or annoying might happen so that you can be ready or avoid it: **[+of]** *a warning of floods* | **[+about]** *warnings about the dangers of smoking* | **[+against]** *This experience should serve as a warning against complacency.* | **[+to]** *a warning to pregnant women not to drink alcohol* | *a* ***warning that*** *grey squirrels are threatening the existence of red squirrels*
2 [C] a statement telling someone that if they continue to behave in an unsatisfactory way, they will be punished: *The Surrey team were* ***given*** *a* ***warning*** *last year for repeated offences.* | *I'm giving you a* ***final warning*** *– don't be late again.* | **written/verbal warning**

COLLOCATIONS

VERBS
give a warning *He slammed on the brakes without giving any warning.*
issue a warning (=officially warn people) *The government issued a warning about eating raw eggs.*
heed a warning (=take notice of it) | **ignore a warning**

ADJECTIVES/NOUN + warning
advance/prior warning *Workers were given no advance warning of the closure.*
a health warning (=a warning that something is bad for your health) *All tobacco products must carry a health warning.*
a flood/gale/tornado warning

PHRASES
without (any) warning *Police fired into the crowd without warning.*
a word of warning (=used before telling someone to be careful about something) *A word of warning: don't use too much glue.*

warning² *adj* [only before noun] **1** a warning action or thing tells you that something bad or dangerous might happen: *Red warning lights were flashing.* | *The government ignored all the* ***warning signs****.* | **a warning look/glance** *She said nothing but gave him a warning look.* **2 warning bell/**

W

bells used to say that something makes someone start to be worried or careful about something: **a warning bell rings/sounds** *As she read his letter, warning bells began to sound in her head.*

ˌwar of atˈtrition *n* (*plural* **wars of attrition**) [C] a struggle in which you harm your opponent in a lot of small ways, so that they become gradually weaker

ˌwar of ˈnerves *n* [singular] an attempt to make an enemy worried, and to destroy their courage by threatening them, spreading false information etc

ˌwar of ˈwords *n* [singular] a public argument between politicians etc

ˌWar on ˈTerrorism (*also* **ˌWar on ˈTerror**) *n* [singular] the name given to the actions and other measures taken by the US, Britain, and other countries to destroy international TERRORIST groups, especially al-Qaeda after the attacks on the World Trade Center and the Pentagon on September 11th, 2001. The actions taken include the wars in Afghanistan and Iraq.

warp[1] /wɔːp $ wɔːrp/ *v* **1** [I,T] if something warps, or if heat or cold warps it, it becomes bent or twisted, and loses its original shape: *The door must be warped. It won't close properly.* **2** [T] to influence someone in a way that has a harmful effect on how they think or behave: *You mustn't allow your dislike of her to* ***warp your judgment***.

warp[2] *n* **1 the warp** *technical* the threads used in weaving cloth that go from the top to the bottom of the machine → **weft 2** [singular] a part of something that has become bent or twisted from its original shape → TIME WARP

ˈwar paint *n* [U] **1** paint that some tribes put on their bodies and faces before going to war **2** MAKE-UP(1) – used humorously: *Josie's just putting on her war paint.*

war·path /ˈwɔːpɑːθ $ ˈwɔːrpæθ/ *n informal* **be on the warpath** to be angry and looking for someone to fight or punish

warped /wɔːpt $ wɔːrpt/ *adj* **1** someone who is warped has ideas or thoughts that most people think are unpleasant or not normal: *a warped mind | You really* ***have a warped sense of humour*** (=think strange and unpleasant things are funny). **2** something that is warped is bent or twisted so that it is not the correct shape

war·rant[1] /ˈwɒrənt $ ˈwɔː-, ˈwɑː-/ ●○○ *n*
1 [C] a legal document that is signed by a judge, allowing the police to take a particular action: **[+for]** *The magistrate* ***issued*** *a* ***warrant*** *for his arrest.* → **DEATH WARRANT, SEARCH WARRANT**
2 [C] an official document giving someone the right to do something, for example buy SHARES in a company: *The company* ***issued warrants*** *for 300,000 shares.*
3 no warrant for (doing) sth *formal* no good reason for doing something: *There is no warrant for copying other people's work.* → **UNWARRANTED**

warrant[2] ●○○ *v* [T]
1 to need or deserve: *This tiny crowd does not warrant such a large police presence.* | **warrant attention/consideration etc** *Another area that warrants attention is that of funding for universities.*
2 to promise that something is true: **warrant that** *The Author hereby warrants that the Publisher is the owner of the copyright.*
3 I'll warrant (you) *old-fashioned* used to tell someone that you are sure about something: **warrant (that)** *I'll warrant we won't see him again.*

ˈwarrant card *n* [C] an official card carried by British police officers to prove that they belong to the police

ˈwarrant ˌofficer *n* [C] a middle rank in the army, air force, or US Navy

war·ran·ty /ˈwɒrənti $ ˈwɔː-, ˈwɑː-/ ●○○ *n* (*plural* **warranties**) [C] a written agreement in which a company selling something promises to repair it if it breaks within a particular period of time: **under warranty** *The car is still under warranty. | a three-year warranty* → **guarantee**

war·ren /ˈwɒrən $ ˈwɔː-, ˈwɑː-/ *n* [C] **1** the underground home of rabbits **2** a place with so many streets, rooms etc that it is difficult to find the place that you want: *a warren of tiny streets*

war·ring /ˈwɔːrɪŋ/ *adj* [only before noun] at war or fighting each other: **warring factions/parties** (=groups of people fighting each other)

war·ri·or /ˈwɒriə $ ˈwɔːriər, ˈwɑː-/ ●○○ *n* [C] a soldier or fighter who is brave and experienced – used about people in the past: *a noble warrior*

war·ship /ˈwɔːˌʃɪp $ ˈwɔːr-/ *n* [C] a ship with guns that is used in a war → **battleship**

wart /wɔːt $ wɔːrt/ *n* [C] **1** a small hard raised part on someone's skin → **verruca 2 warts and all** *informal* including all the faults or unpleasant things: *Well, you married him – warts and all.* —**warty** *adj*: *warty skin*

wart·hog /ˈwɔːtˌhɒg $ ˈwɔːrtˌhɔːg, -ˌhɑːg/ *n* [C] an African wild pig with long front teeth that stick out of the side of its mouth

war·time /ˈwɔːtaɪm $ ˈwɔːr-/ ●○○ *n* [U] the period of time when a country is fighting a war OPP **peacetime**: **in/during wartime** *Even in wartime some people held concerts.* —**wartime** *adj* [only before noun]: *the hardships of wartime Britain | his wartime experiences*

ˈwar-torn *adj* [only before noun] a war-torn country, city etc is being destroyed by war

ˈwar ˌwidow *n* [C] a woman whose husband has been killed in a war

war·y /ˈweəri $ ˈweri/ ●○○ *adj* someone who is wary is careful because they think something might be dangerous or harmful: **be wary of (doing) sth** *I'm a bit wary of driving in this fog.* | **[+of]** *We must teach children to be wary of strangers.* | ***Keep a wary eye on*** *the weather before you set sail. | She had a wary expression on her face.* —**wariness** *n* [singular, U]: *a wariness in her voice* —**warily** *adv*: *She* ***eyed*** *him* ***warily***.

ˈwar zone *n* [C] an area where a war is being fought

was /wəz; *strong* wɒz $ wəz *strong* wɑːz/ *v* the first and third person singular of the past tense of BE

wa·sa·bi /wəˈsɑːbi/ *n* [U] a green strong-tasting Japanese food, which is added to SUSHI and other food in small amounts in order to make it taste hotter

wash[1] /wɒʃ $ wɒːʃ, wɑːʃ/ ●●● S1 W3 *v*
1 WASH STH [T] to clean something using water and a type of soap: *This shirt needs washing. | It's your turn to* ***wash the dishes***. → see picture at **CLEAN**[2] THESAURUS **CLEAN**
2 WASH YOURSELF [I,T] to clean your body with soap and water: *Amy washed and went to bed. | She had a hot bath and washed her hair. | I'm just going to wash my hands.* | **wash yourself** *When a cat has finished eating, it often washes itself.*

> **REGISTER**
> In everyday English, people usually say that someone **has a wash** (BrE) or **washes up** (AmE) rather than **washes**.

3 FLOW [I,T always + adv/prep] if a river, sea etc washes somewhere, or if something carried by the river or sea is washed somewhere, it flows or moves there: *The waves washed against the shore. | The sea washed over her. | The young man was* ***washed overboard*** (=pushed from a boat into the sea by the force of the water) *in the storm. | The body was* ***washed ashore*** (=brought to the shore by waves).
4 sth doesn't/won't wash (with sb) *spoken* used to say that you do not believe or accept someone's explanation, reason, attitude etc: *I'm sorry but all his charm just doesn't wash with me.*
5 wash your hands of sth to refuse to be responsible for something anymore: *I've washed my hands of the whole affair.*
6 wash your mouth out! *spoken old-fashioned* used to tell someone who has just sworn or said something rude that they should not have spoken that way
7 wash well to be easy to clean using soap and water: *Silk*

W

doesn't wash well. → **wash/air your dirty linen/laundry (in public)** at DIRTY[1](7)

wash sth ↔ **away** *phr v*
1 if water washes something away, it carries it away with great force: *Floods in Bangladesh have washed hundreds of homes away.*
2 to get rid of unhappy feelings, thoughts, or memories: *My anxiety was washed away.*

wash sth ↔ **down** *phr v*
1 to clean something large using a lot of water: *Can you wash down the driveway?*
2 to drink something with or after food or with medicine to help you swallow it: **[+with]** *steak and chips washed down with red wine*

wash off *phr v*
1 wash sth ↔ off to clean dirt, dust etc from the surface of something with water
2 if a substance washes off, you can remove it from the surface of something by washing: *Will this paint wash off?*

wash out *phr v*
1 wash sth ↔ out to wash the inside of something quickly: *I'll just wash out this vase for flowers.*
2 if a substance washes out, you can remove it from a material by washing it: *a dye that won't wash out*
3 be washed out if an event is washed out, it cannot continue because of rain: *The summer fair was washed out by the English weather.* → WASHED-OUT, WASHOUT

wash over sb *phr v*
1 if a feeling washes over you, you suddenly feel it very strongly: *A feeling of relief washed over her.*
2 if you let something wash over you, you do not pay close attention to it: *She was content to let the conversation wash over her.*

wash up *phr v*
1 *BrE* to wash plates, dishes, knives etc → WASHING-UP
2 *AmE* to wash your hands: *Go wash up before dinner.*
3 wash sth ↔ up if waves wash something up, they carry it to the shore: **[+on]** *His body was washed up on the beach the next morning.* → WASHED-UP

wash² ●●○ *n*
1 ACT OF CLEANING [C usually singular] an act of cleaning something using soap and water: *Those jeans need* ***a good wash*** (=a thorough wash). | *I'll just* ***have*** *a quick* ***wash*** *before we go out.*
2 CLOTHES [singular, U] clothes that are to be washed, are being washed, or have just been washed: *You'd better* ***put*** *that shirt* ***in the wash***. | *Do you need me to put another wash on?*
3 SKIN [C] a liquid used to clean your skin: *an anti-bacterial facial wash*
4 BOAT **the wash** the movement of water caused by a passing boat: *the wash of a large motorboat*
5 COLOUR [C] a very thin transparent layer of paint or colour
6 AREA OF LAND **the wash** an area of land that is sometimes covered by the sea
7 it will all come out in the wash *spoken* **a)** used to tell someone not to worry about a problem because it will be solved in the future **b)** used to say that the truth about something will be known in the end

wash·a·ble /ˈwɒʃəbəl $ ˈwɒːʃ-, ˈwɑːʃ-/ *adj* **1** something that is washable can be washed without being damaged: *washable cushion covers* | *The gloves are* ***machine washable***. **2** paint or ink that is washable will come out of cloth when you wash it

wash·ba·sin /ˈwɒʃˌbeɪsən $ ˈwɒːʃ-, ˈwɑːʃ-/ *n* [C] a container like a small SINK used for washing your hands and face

wash·board /ˈwɒʃbɔːd $ ˈwɒːʃbɔːrd, ˈwɑːʃ-/ *n* [C] **1** a piece of metal with a slightly rough surface, used in the past for rubbing clothes on when washing them **2 washboard stomach** a man's stomach that is not fat and has good muscles that can be clearly seen

wash·cloth /ˈwɒʃklɒθ $ ˈwɒːʃklɒːθ, ˈwɑːʃ-/ *n* [C] *AmE* a small square cloth used for washing your hands and face SYN **facecloth** *BrE*

wash·day /ˈwɒʃdeɪ $ ˈwɒːʃ-, ˈwɑːʃ-/ *n* [C,U] *old-fashioned* the day each week when you wash your clothes

ˌwashed-ˈout *adj* **1** not brightly coloured anymore, usually as a result of being washed many times: *a washed-out shade of blue* **2** [not before noun] feeling weak and looking unhealthy because you are very tired: *Debbie's looking a bit washed-out.* **3** *AmE* a washed-out road has been damaged by rain or FLOODS and cannot be driven on

ˌwashed-ˈup *adj* if a person or an organization is washed-up, they will never be successful again: *a washed-up movie star*

wash·er /ˈwɒʃə $ ˈwɒːʃər, ˈwɑː-/ *n* [C] **1** a thin flat ring of plastic, metal, rubber etc that is put over a BOLT before the NUT is put on, or between two pipes, to make a tighter joint **2** *informal* a WASHING MACHINE

ˌwasher-ˈdryer (*also* **washer-drier** *BrE*) *n* [C] a machine that both washes and dries clothes

wash·er·wom·an /ˈwɒʃəˌwʊmən $ ˈwɒːʃər-, ˈwɑː-/ *n* (*plural* **washerwomen** /-ˌwɪmɪn/) [C] a woman in the past whose job was to wash other people's clothes

wash·ing /ˈwɒʃɪŋ $ ˈwɒː-, ˈwɑː-/ ●●● S2 *n* [singular, U] *BrE* clothes that need to be washed, are being washed, or have just been washed SYN **wash** *AmE*: *I really must* ***do the washing*** (=wash the dirty clothes). | *Could you* ***put the washing out*** (=hang it on a washing line) *for me?*

ˈwashing day *n* [C] WASHDAY

ˈwashing line *n* [C,U] *BrE* a piece of string stretched between two poles that you hang wet clothes on so that they can dry outside SYN **clothesline**

ˈwashing maˌchine ●●● S3 *n* [C] a machine for washing clothes

ˈwashing ˌpowder ●●○ *n* [C,U] *BrE* soap in the form of a powder used for washing clothes

ˈwashing ˌsoda *n* [U] a chemical that is added to water to clean very dirty things

ˌwashing-ˈup ●●○ *n* [U] *BrE*
1 the washing of plates, dishes, knives etc: *It's your turn to* ***do the washing-up****, Sam.*
2 the dirty pans, plates, dishes, knives etc that have to be washed SYN **dishes** *AmE*: *a pile of washing-up*

ˌwashing-ˈup ˌliquid ●●○ *n* [U] *BrE* a liquid soap for washing plates, knives etc

wash·out /ˈwɒʃ-aʊt $ ˈwɒːʃ-, ˈwɑːʃ-/ *n* [C] *informal* **1** a failure: *The picnic was a total washout – nobody turned up!* **2** an occasion when heavy rain causes damage or stops an event from happening → **wash out** at **WASH¹**

wash·rag /ˈwɒʃræg $ ˈwɒːʃ-, ˈwɑːʃ-/ *n* [C] *AmE* a WASHCLOTH

wash·room /ˈwɒʃrʊm, -ruːm $ ˈwɒːʃ-, ˈwɑːʃ-/ *n* [C] *AmE* a room in a public building where you can wash and use the toilet

wash·stand /ˈwɒʃstænd $ ˈwɒːʃ-, ˈwɑːʃ-/ *n* [C] a table in a bedroom, used in the past for holding the things needed for washing your face

wash·tub /ˈwɒʃtʌb $ ˈwɒːʃ-, ˈwɑːʃ-/ *n* [C] a very large bowl used in the past for washing clothes in

was·n't /ˈwɒzənt $ ˈwɑː-/ the short form of 'was not': *Jason wasn't at the party.*

wasp /wɒsp $ wɑːsp, wɒːsp/ ●○○ *n* [C] a thin black and yellow flying insect that can sting you → see picture at **INSECT**

WASP /wɒsp $ wɑːsp, wɒːsp/ *n* [C] *AmE* (***White Anglo-Saxon Protestant***) an American whose family was originally from northern Europe and who is therefore considered to be part of the most powerful group in society

wasp·ish /ˈwɒspɪʃ $ ˈwɑː-, ˈwɒː-/ *adj* bad-tempered and cruel in the things that you say: *waspish remarks* —**waspishly** *adv*

W

was·sail /ˈwɒseɪl $ ˈwɑː-/ *v* [I] *old use* to enjoy yourself eating and drinking at Christmas

was·sup /wɒˈsʌp $ wɑː-/ *interjection* another spelling of WHASSUP

wast /wɒst $ wɑːst/ **thou wast** *old use* you were

wast·age /ˈweɪstɪdʒ/ *n* [U] *formal* **1** when something is lost or destroyed, especially in a way that is not useful or reasonable, or the amount that is lost or destroyed: *The system used to result in a great deal of food wastage.* | **[+of]** *wastage of ability among working class children* **2 natural wastage** *BrE* a reduction in the number of workers because of people leaving, RETIRING etc and not because they have lost their jobs

waste¹ /weɪst/ ●●● (S2) (W3) *n*

1 BAD USE [singular, U] when something such as money or skills are not used in a way that is effective, useful, or sensible: **[+of]** *Being unemployed is such a waste of your talents.* | *Many believe that state aid is a waste of taxpayers' money.* | ***What a waste** of all that good work!* | *excessive waste in state spending*

2 go to waste if something goes to waste, it is not used: *Don't let all this food go to waste.*

3 be a waste of time/money/effort etc to be not worth the time, money etc that you use because there is little or no result: *We should never have gone – it was a total waste of time.*

4 UNWANTED MATERIALS [U] unwanted materials or substances that are left after you have used something: *The emphasis now is on recycling waste.* → **NUCLEAR WASTE, TOXIC WASTE**

5 a waste of space *spoken* someone who has no good qualities

6 LAND **wastes** [plural] *literary* a large area of land where there are very few people, plants, or animals: **[+of]** *the icy wastes of Antarctica* | **icy/frozen/snowy etc wastes** → WASTE GROUND, WASTELAND

COLLOCATIONS – MEANING 4

VERBS

recycle waste *How much of our household waste is recycled?*
dispose of waste *environmentally friendly ways to dispose of waste*
dump waste

ADJECTIVES

household/domestic waste *Newspapers and magazines make up 10% of household waste.*
industrial/chemical waste *pollution caused by industrial waste*
hazardous/toxic waste | **radioactive/nuclear waste** | **human waste** (=from people going to the toilet)

waste + NOUN

a waste pipe *a washing machine waste pipe*

waste² ●●● (S2) (W3) *v* [T]

1 NOT USE SENSIBLY to use more money, time, energy etc than is useful or sensible: *Leaving the heating on all the time wastes electricity.* | **waste sth on sb/sth** *Don't waste your money on that junk!*

2 NOT USE FULLY to not make full use of someone or something: *Hannah is wasted in that clerical job.* | *His talents were being wasted as a lawyer.* (GRAMMAR) **Waste** is usually passive in this meaning.

3 be wasted on sb if something is wasted on someone, they do not understand how good or useful it is: *Her good advice was wasted on the children.*

4 waste your breath *spoken* to say something that has no effect: *Don't try to reason with Paul – you're wasting your breath.*

5 waste no time (in) doing sth to do something as quickly as you can because it will help you: *He wasted no time in introducing himself.*

6 waste not, want not *spoken* used to say that if you use what you have carefully, you will still have some of it if you need it later

7 HARM SB *AmE informal* to kill someone, severely injure them, or defeat them

waste away *phr v* to gradually become thinner and weaker, usually because you are ill

waste³ ●●○ (W3) *adj* [only before noun]

1 waste materials, substances etc are unwanted because the good part of them has been removed

2 waste land is empty or not looked after by anyone → **WASTELAND**, → **lay waste** at **LAY²(11)**

waste·bas·ket /ˈweɪstˌbɑːskɪt $ -ˌbæs-/ *n* [C] *AmE* a small container for holding paper, cans etc that are not wanted (SYN) **wastepaper basket** *BrE* → see picture at **BIN¹**

wast·ed /ˈweɪstɪd/ *adj* **1 wasted journey/trip/effort etc** a journey etc that does not achieve anything: *I'm sorry you've had a wasted trip. Mr Newton isn't here.* **2** very thin and weak because of illness, old age etc: *her thin, wasted body* **3** *informal* very drunk or affected by drugs

ˈwaste disˌposal *n* **1** [U] the process of getting rid of unwanted materials or substances: *the problem of radioactive waste disposal* **2** (*also* **waste disposal unit**) [C] *BrE* a small machine under the kitchen SINK that cuts food waste into small pieces so that it can be washed down the drain (SYN) **garbage disposal** *AmE*

waste·ful /ˈweɪstfəl/ ●○○ *adj* using more of something than you should, especially money, time, or effort (OPP) **economical**: *a wasteful use of resources* | **[+of]** *The software is very wasteful of memory.* —**wastefully** *adv*: *Lily had wastefully left the light on.* —**wastefulness** *n* [U]

ˈwaste ground *n* [U] an empty unattractive piece of land that is not used for anything: *a piece of waste ground*

waste·land /ˈweɪstlænd, -lənd/ *n* [C,U] **1** an unattractive area, often with old ruined buildings, factories etc on it: **urban/industrial wasteland** *the restoration of industrial wasteland* **2** a place, situation, or time that has no excitement or interest (SYN) **desert**: *The seventies were a cultural wasteland.*

ˌwaste ˈpaper *n* [U] paper that has been used and thrown away

waste·pa·per bas·ket /ˌweɪstˈpeɪpə ˌbɑːskət, ˈweɪstˌpeɪpə- $ ˈweɪstˌpeɪpər ˌbæ-/ ●●○ *n* [C] *BrE* a small container for holding paper, cans etc that are not wanted (SYN) **wastebasket** *AmE* → see picture at **BIN¹**

ˈwaste ˌproduct *n* [C] a useless material or substance that is produced during the process of making something else → **by-product**: *nuclear waste products*

wast·er /ˈweɪstə $ -ər/ *n* [C] **1** *BrE informal* someone who you think will never achieve any success in life: *All her friends are drunks or wasters.* **2 time/money/energy waster** someone or something that does not use time etc carefully or well

wast·ing /ˈweɪstɪŋ/ *adj* **1 wasting disease/illness** *formal* a disease that gradually makes you thinner and weaker **2 wasting asset** *technical* a property, business etc that is losing money: *The airline is a wasting asset.*

was·trel /ˈweɪstrəl/ *n* [C] *literary* a lazy person who does not try to achieve anything in life

watch¹ /wɒtʃ $ wɑːtʃ, wɒːtʃ/ ●●● (S1) (W1) *v*

1 LOOK [I,T] to look at someone or something for a period of time, paying attention to what is happening: *Do you mind if I watch?* | *We sat and watched the sunset.* | **watch carefully/closely/intently etc** *He watched helplessly as Paula fell into the icy water.* | *Watch carefully. You may learn something.* | **watch (sb/sth) with interest/amusement/delight etc** *Harriet watched him with interest.* | **watch sb/sth do/doing sth** *I watched him go, then went home.* | *Ruth could **not bear to watch** her parents arguing.* | **watch to do sth** *I watched to see how he'd react.* | **watch television/a film etc** *The debate was watched by 97 million viewers.* | *Most parents don't know what their kids are **watching on TV**.* | **watch what/how/when etc** *It's useful to watch how other pilots handle the glider.*

2 BE CAREFUL [T] to act carefully in order to avoid an accident or unwanted situation: **watch (that)** *Watch he doesn't run into the road.* | *She's a student and has to watch her budget closely.* | *Watch your head on the shelf.* | **watch**

W

what/how/where etc *Silly old fool! Why doesn't he **watch** where he's **going**?* | ***Watch what you're doing**! It's spilling everywhere!* | ***Watch yourself*** (=be careful) *in Madrid; there are some rough areas.* | **watch what you say/your tongue/your language/your mouth etc** (=be careful not to hurt or offend people by what you say) *Employees should watch what they say in personal emails.* | **watch your weight/watch what you eat** (=be careful not to get fat) *He may be a former athlete, but he still has to watch his weight.*

3 PAY ATTENTION [T] to pay attention to a situation that interests or worries you to see how it develops: **watch closely/carefully** *American companies are watching Japanese developments closely.* | *The government will watch the progress of these schemes with interest.*

4 CARE FOR [T] to stay with someone or something so that nothing bad happens to them: *She watches the kids for us occasionally.*

5 SECRETLY [T] to secretly watch a person or place: *I feel like I'm being watched.*

6 watch your step *informal* to be careful, especially about making someone angry: *He soon saw he'd have to watch his step with some of these guys.*

7 watch your back *informal* to be careful because other people may try to harm you

8 watch the clock *informal* to keep looking at the time because you are worried or bored: *anxious mums watching the clock*

9 watch the time to make sure you know what time it is to avoid being late

10 watch it *spoken* used to warn someone to be careful: *Watch it, there's a car.*

11 watch this space *informal* used to tell people to pay attention in the future because things are going to develop further – used especially in newspapers

12 one to watch someone or something that people should pay attention to because they are interesting or exciting: *In the tournament so far, Italy's Stefania Croce looks like the one to watch.*

13 watch the world go by to relax outside by just looking at the people around you: *lingering in a pavement café, watching the world go by*

14 you watch *informal* used to tell someone that you know what will happen: *He'll win this time, you watch.* → **watch sb like a hawk** at HAWK[1]

THESAURUS

watch to look at someone or something for a period of time and pay attention to what is happening: *They were all watching the game.* | *I watched him get out of his car.*

keep an eye on sb/sth to watch someone or something carefully so that you are prepared if anything bad happens: *The doctors are keeping a careful eye on her.* | *Can you keep an eye on my bag for me?*

observe to watch someone or something carefully in order to learn more about them: *A 24-hour camera is being used to observe the birds' behaviour.* | *During your teacher training you will be encouraged to observe lessons.*

monitor to watch a situation carefully to see how it changes over a period of time: *Class teachers are responsible for monitoring the progress of each student.*

spy on sb to watch someone secretly in order to find out what they are doing: *He hired a private detective to spy on her.*

watch (out) for sth *phr v* to pay close attention in a particular situation because you are expecting something to happen or you want to avoid something bad: *She stepped outside to watch for the cab.* | *What problems should I watch out for when buying an old house?*

watch out *phr v informal* used to tell someone to be careful: *You'll become an alcoholic **if you don't watch out**.*

watch over sb *phr v* to protect someone so that they are not harmed: *There must have been an angel watching over me that day.*

watch² ●●● S2 W3 *n*

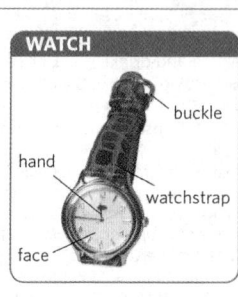

1 [C] a small clock that you wear on your wrist or keep in your pocket: *My **watch** has **stopped**.* | **look at/glance at/consult your watch** *She glanced nervously at her watch.* | *How do you keep track of time if you don't **wear** a **watch**?*

WATCH

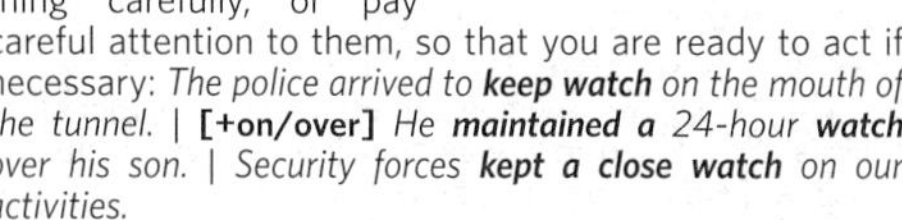

2 [singular, U] when you watch someone or something carefully, or pay careful attention to them, so that you are ready to act if necessary: *The police arrived to **keep watch** on the mouth of the tunnel.* | **[+on/over]** *He **maintained a** 24-hour **watch** over his son.* | *Security forces **kept a close watch** on our activities.*

3 keep a watch out for sb/sth (*also* **be on the watch for sb/sth**) to be looking and waiting for something that might happen or someone you might see, especially so that you can avoid danger, trouble etc: *Be on the watch for anything suspicious.*

4 [C] a group of people whose job is to guard or protect someone or something: *We were arrested and held until the arrival of the **night watch*** (=people responsible for keeping the streets safe at night, especially in past times). → NEIGHBOURHOOD WATCH

5 [C,U] a period of time when it is someone's duty to stay somewhere and look for signs of danger: *The first watch is from now until midnight.* | **on watch** *Who's on watch tonight?*

watch·a·ble /ˈwɒtʃəbəl $ ˈwɑːtʃ-, ˈwɒːtʃ-/ *adj informal* if a film, television programme etc is watchable, it is interesting and enjoyable: *a highly watchable film*

watch·band /ˈwɒtʃbænd $ ˈwɑːtʃ-, ˈwɒːtʃ-/ *n* [C] *AmE* a piece of leather or metal for fastening your watch on your wrist SYN **watchstrap** *BrE*

watch·dog /ˈwɒtʃdɒg $ ˈwɑːtʃdɒːg, ˈwɒːtʃ-/ *n* [C] **1** a person or group of people whose job is to protect the rights of people who buy things and to make sure companies do not do anything illegal or harmful: *a **consumer watchdog*** **2** *old-fashioned* a GUARD DOG

watch·er /ˈwɒtʃə $ ˈwɑːtʃər, ˈwɒː-/ *n* [C] someone who watches someone or something for pleasure or as part of their job: **bird/whale/royal etc watcher** *Fifteen thousand bird watchers visit annually.* | *Industry-watchers hailed the takeover as a triumph.*

watch·ful /ˈwɒtʃfəl $ ˈwɑːtʃ-, ˈwɒːtʃ-/ *adj* **1** very careful to notice what is happening, and to make sure that everything is all right: *The entrances are guarded by watchful security staff.* | *His **eyes** were **watchful**.* | ***Keep a watchful eye on** elderly residents.* **2 under sb's watchful eye** following someone's instructions or with someone's help: *Learn the basics under the watchful eye of a qualified instructor.* —**watchfully** *adv* —**watchfulness** *n* [U]

ˈwatching ˌbrief *n* [C] *BrE* instructions to someone to watch a situation carefully but not to become involved in it: *One of his responsibilities is to **keep a watching brief on** foreign broadcasts.*

watch·keep·er /ˈwɒtʃˌkiːpə $ ˈwɑːtʃˌkiːpər, ˈwɒːtʃ-/ *n* [C] someone whose job is to guard or protect something, especially a ship

ˈwatch list *n* [C] a list of people or things to keep your attention on because they may do something, especially a list of people who may be TERRORISTS

watch·mak·er /ˈwɒtʃˌmeɪkə $ ˈwɑːtʃˌmeɪkər, ˈwɒːtʃ-/ *n* [C] someone whose job is making and repairing clocks and watches

watch·man /ˈwɒtʃmən $ ˈwɑːtʃ-, ˈwɒːtʃ-/ *n* (*plural* **watchmen** /-mən/) [C] *old-fashioned* someone whose job is to guard a place SYN **security guard** → NIGHT WATCHMAN

watch·strap /ˈwɒtʃstræp $ ˈwɑːtʃ-, ˈwɒːtʃ-/ *n* [C] *BrE* a piece of leather or metal for fastening your watch on your wrist SYN **watchband** *AmE*

watch·tow·er /ˈwɒtʃˌtaʊə $ ˈwɑːtʃˌtaʊər, ˈwɒːtʃ-/ *n* [C] a high tower used for watching and guarding a place

watch·word /ˈwɒtʃwɜːd $ ˈwɑːtʃwɜːrd, ˈwɒːtʃ-/ *n* [singular] a word or phrase that expresses an attitude or belief: *Environmental quality will be the watchword for the 21st century.*

wa·ter¹ /ˈwɔːtə $ ˈwɒːtər, ˈwɑː-/ ●●● S1 W1 *n* [U]
1 LIQUID the clear liquid without colour, smell, or taste that falls as rain and that is used for drinking, washing etc: *There's water all over the bathroom floor.* | *Does anyone want a* ***drink of water****?* | *a glass of sparkling* ***mineral water*** | *All rooms have hot and cold* ***running water****.* | *Pour* ***boiling water*** *over the rice and let it soak.* | *a* ***fresh water*** *spring* | *When dealing with a burst pipe, always* ***turn off the water*** *first.* | *contamination of the local water supply*
2 AREA OF WATER **a)** an area of water such as the sea, a lake etc: **shallow/deep water** | *Rangoon is surrounded on three sides by water.* | *Denzil dived into the water.* | *He stepped down to the water's edge.* | **by water** (=by boat) *The temple can only be reached by water.* **b)** the surface of a lake, river etc → **underwater**: **on the water** *something floating on the water*
3 waters [plural] a large area of water, especially an ocean that is near or belongs to a particular country: *the* ***coastal waters*** *of Alaska* | **Korean/Mexican/Pacific etc waters** *The ship drifted into Turkish* ***territorial waters****.* | *a species found in* ***inland waters*** (=not the sea, but rivers, lakes etc)
4 high/low water the highest or lowest level of the sea and some rivers SYN **tide**
5 uncharted/troubled/murky waters *formal* a situation that is difficult, dangerous, or unfamiliar: *the uncharted waters of the 21st century*
6 be (all) water under the bridge *informal* used to say that what happened in the past should be forgotten
7 like water if you use something or spend money like water, you use or spend large amounts of it when you should try to save it – used to show disapproval: *Some of the companies were spending money like water.*
8 like water off a duck's back *informal* if criticism, warnings etc are like water off a duck's back, they have no effect on the person you are saying them to
9 sb's waters break when a PREGNANT woman's waters break, liquid comes from her body just before her baby is born
10 water on the brain/knee *old-fashioned informal* liquid around the brain or knee as the result of a disease
11 take the waters *old-fashioned* to wash yourself in or drink special water that is thought to make you healthy
12 make/pass water *formal* to URINATE → **SODA WATER**, **TOILET WATER**, → **in deep water** at DEEP¹(15), → **take to sth like a duck to water** at DUCK¹(4), → **of the first water** at FIRST¹(18), → **(be/feel) like a fish out of water** at FISH¹(3), → **not hold water** at HOLD¹(37), → **in hot water** at HOT¹(10), → **muddy the waters** at MUDDY²(2), → **pour cold water over/on sth** at POUR(6), → **still waters run deep** at STILL²(5), → **test the water** at TEST²(7), → **tread water** at TREAD¹(5), → **troubled waters** at TROUBLED(3)

water² ●●○ *v*
1 PLANT/LAND [T] if you water plants or the ground they are growing in, you pour water on them: *Will you water my houseplants while I'm away?* | *The garden needs watering daily.*
2 your eyes water if your eyes water, TEARS come out of them: *Chopping onions makes my eyes water.* → **MOUTH-WATERING**, → **make your mouth water** at MOUTH¹(11)
3 ANIMAL [T] to give an animal water to drink: *Have the horses been fed and watered?*
4 RIVER [T] *technical* if an area is watered by a river, the river flows through it and provides it with water: *Colombia is watered by several rivers.*
5 WEAKEN [T] (*also* **water down**) to add water to a drink to make it less strong

water sth ↔ **down** *phr v*
1 to make a statement, report etc less forceful by changing it or removing parts that may offend people – used to show disapproval: *The report of the investigation had been watered down.* → **WATERED-DOWN**
2 to add water to a drink to make it less strong SYN **dilute**

wa·ter·bed /ˈwɔːtəbed $ ˈwɒːtər-, ˈwɑː-/ *n* [C] a bed with a part inside that is made of rubber and filled with water

ˈwater bird *n* [C] a wild bird that swims and lives near water

ˈwater ˌbiscuit *n* [C] *BrE* a thin BISCUIT that is not sweet and is often eaten with cheese

wa·ter·board·ing /ˈwɔːtəˌbɔːdɪŋ $ ˈwɒːtərˌbɔːr-, ˈwɑː-/ *n* [U] the action of pouring water onto a prisoner's face so that they cannot breathe properly, in order to get information from them

wa·ter·borne /ˈwɔːtəbɔːn $ ˈwɒːtərbɔːrn, ˈwɑː-/ *adj* spread or carried by water → **airborne**: **waterborne disease/illness etc** *waterborne diseases such as cholera* | *waterborne traffic*

ˈwater ˌbottle *n* [C] a bottle used for carrying water to drink → see picture at BOTTLE¹

ˈwater ˌboy *n* [C] *AmE* **1** someone whose job is to give the members of a sports team water to drink **2** *informal* someone who has a very unimportant job

ˈwater ˌbuffalo *n* (*plural* **water buffaloes** *or* **water buffalo**) [C] a large animal like a cow with long horns, used to work on farms in Asia

ˈwater bug *n* [C] *AmE informal* a small insect that lives in water

ˈwater butt *n* [C] *BrE* a large container that is kept outside and used for collecting rainwater

ˈwater ˌcannon *n* [C,U] a machine that sends out a powerful stream of water, used by police to control violent crowds

ˈwater ˌchestnut *n* [C] the thick stem of a plant that grows in water, used in Chinese cooking

ˈwater ˌcloset *n* [C] *old-fashioned* a toilet

wa·ter·col·our *BrE*, **watercolor** *AmE* /ˈwɔːtəˌkʌlə $ ˈwɒːtərˌkʌlər, ˈwɑː-/ *n* **1** [C usually plural, U] a type of paint that you mix with water: *Margaret began experimenting with watercolor.* **2** [C] a picture painted using watercolours: *a watercolour of the castle*

ˈwater ˌcooler *n* [C] **1** a piece of equipment, used especially in offices, from which you can get a cup of cold water to drink **2 water cooler gossip** conversation about other people's behaviour or lives that happens in offices when people meet each other by the water cooler

wa·ter·course /ˈwɔːtəkɔːs $ ˈwɒːtərkɔːrs, ˈwɑː-/ *n* [C] **1** a place where water flows, for example a river or CANAL: *chemicals that pollute the local watercourse* **2** a long thin hole for water to flow through

wa·ter·cress /ˈwɔːtəkres $ ˈwɒːtər-, ˈwɑː-/ *n* [U] a small green plant with strong-tasting leaves that grows in water: *a bunch of watercress* → see picture at VEGETABLE¹

ˌwatered-ˈdown *adj* a watered-down plan, report etc has been changed so that it is less extreme or forceful than when it was first written – used to show disapproval → **water down**: *a* ***watered-down version*** *of the original*

ˌwatered ˈsilk *n* [U] a type of silk with a pattern of waves on it

wa·ter·fall /ˈwɔːtəfɔːl $ ˈwɒːtərfɒːl, ˈwɑː-/ ●○○ *n* [C] a place where water from a river or stream falls down over a cliff or rock

ˈwaterfall ˌcardigan *n* [C] a CARDIGAN which hangs in folds at the front. The front is often longer than the back.

ˈwater ˌfeature *n* [C] a small pool, stream, or other structure that has water in it or running through it, built in a garden to make it more interesting and attractive

ˈwater ˌfootprint *n* [C] the amount of water that something or someone uses

ˈwater ˌfountain *n* [C] **1** a DRINKING FOUNTAIN **2** a WATER COOLER

wa·ter·fowl /ˈwɔːtəfaʊl $ ˈwɒːtər-, ˈwɑː-/ *n* (*plural* **waterfowl**) [C,U] a wild bird that swims and lives near water: *the varied waterfowl of North America*

wa·ter·front /ˈwɔːtəfrʌnt $ ˈwɒːtər-, ˈwɑː-/ *n* [C usually singular] the part of a town or an area of land next to the sea, a river etc: *The hotel is down on the waterfront.*

W

wa·ter·hole /ˈwɔːtəhəʊl $ ˈwɒːtərhoʊl, ˈwɑː-/ *n* [C] a small area of water in a dry country where wild animals drink

ˈwater ice *n* [C,U] *BrE* SORBET

ˈwatering can *n* [C] a container used for pouring water on garden plants → see pictures at **CAN²**, **GARDEN**

ˈwatering hole *n* [C] **1** *informal* a bar or other place where people drink alcohol: *What's your favorite watering hole?* **2** a WATERHOLE

ˈwatering place *n* [C] **1** a WATERHOLE **2** a town which people visited in the past because they thought the water there was good for their health SYN **spa**

ˈwater jump *n* [C] an area of water that you have to jump over during a competition, race etc: *Her horse fell at the water jump.*

wa·ter·less /ˈwɔːtələs $ ˈwɒːtər-, ˈwɑː-/ *adj* a waterless place has no water for people or animals to drink: *a barren, waterless desert*

ˈwater ˌlily *n* (*plural* **water lilies**) [C] a plant that grows in water, with large white or pink flowers → see picture at **FLOWER**

wa·ter·line /ˈwɔːtəlaɪn $ ˈwɒːtər-, ˈwɑː-/ *n* **1 the waterline** the level that water reaches on the side of a ship etc: *Two torpedoes struck below the waterline.* **2** [singular] the edge of a large area of water, especially the sea, where it joins the land: *As the waterline advanced, the vegetation was swamped.*

wa·ter·logged /ˈwɔːtəlɒgd $ ˈwɒːtərlɒːgd, ˈwɑː-, -lɑːgd/ *adj* **1** a waterlogged area of land is flooded with water and cannot be used: **waterlogged ground/soil** *Heavy rain meant the pitch was waterlogged.* **THESAURUS** ▸ **WET** **2** a waterlogged boat is full of water and may sink —**waterlogging** *n* [U]: *The race was cancelled due to waterlogging.*

ˈwater main *n* [C] a large underground pipe that carries the public supply of water to buildings: *a burst water main*

wa·ter·mark /ˈwɔːtəmɑːk $ ˈwɒːtərmɑːrk, ˈwɑː-/ *n* [C] **1** a special design put onto paper, especially bank notes, that can only be seen when you hold it up to the light: **bear/carry a watermark** *The sheet bears the watermark '1836'.* **2** a special mark contained in electronic documents, pictures, music etc that is used to stop people from copying them: *The card has a **digital watermark** detectable only by electronic cash dispensers.* **3 high watermark** *especially AmE* the high watermark of a particular process is its most successful time or achievement SYN **high point**: **[+of]** *Reagan's presidency may prove to have been the high watermark of the US-Israeli alliance.* **4 high/low watermark** *AmE* a line showing the highest or lowest levels of the sea SYN **tide-mark** *BrE*

ˈwater ˌmeadow *n* [C] a field that is near a river and that is sometimes flooded

wa·ter·mel·on /ˈwɔːtəˌmelən $ ˈwɒːtər-, ˈwɑː-/ *n* [C,U] a large round fruit with hard green skin, red flesh, and black seeds → see picture at **FRUIT¹**

ˈwater ˌmeter *n* [C] a piece of equipment that measures how much water is used in a building

wa·ter·mill /ˈwɔːtəˌmɪl $ ˈwɒːtər-, ˈwɑː-/ *n* [C] a MILL that operates using water

ˈwater park *n* [C] a place where people can have fun in swimming pools, go down WATER SLIDES, have rides that involve water etc

ˈwater ˌpipe *n* [C] **1** an underground pipe used to carry the public water supply **2** a pipe used for smoking, consisting of a long tube and a container of water SYN **hookah**

ˈwater ˌpistol *n* [C] *BrE* a toy gun that shoots water

ˈwater ˌpolo *n* [U] a ball game played in water between two teams

ˈwater ˌpower *n* [U] power obtained from moving water, used to produce electricity or to make a machine work

wa·ter·proof¹ /ˈwɔːtəpruːf $ ˈwɒːtər-, ˈwɑː-/ *adj* not allowing water to enter: *a waterproof jacket | waterproof adhesive | Rub the wax in to **make** the shoe **waterproof**.* —**waterproof** *v* [T]: *Plastic sheeting was used to waterproof the shed.* —**waterproofed** *adj* [only before noun]: *a waterproofed sack*

waterproof² *n* [C usually plural] a jacket or coat that does not allow rain and water through it: **waterproofs** (=a waterproof jacket and trousers)

ˈwater rat *n* [C] an animal like a big mouse that can swim and lives near water

ˈwater-reˌpellent *adj* material that is water-repellent has been covered with a substance that makes water run off it, so that it does not become wet —**water-repellent** *n* [C]

ˈwater reˌsistant *adj* something that is water resistant does not allow water to enter easily: *Is this watch water resistant?*

wa·ter·shed /ˈwɔːtəʃed $ ˈwɒːtər-, ˈwɑː-/ *n* [singular] **1** an event or time when important changes happen in history or in your life SYN **turning point**: **[+in]** *The 1932 election represented a watershed in American politics.* | **watershed decision/case etc** *a watershed case on pension rights* **2 the (9 o'clock) watershed** *BrE* the time in the evening after which television programmes that are not considered suitable for children may be shown in Britain **3** *technical* the high land separating two river systems

wa·ter·side /ˈwɔːtəsaɪd $ ˈwɒːtər-, ˈwɑː-/ *n* [singular] the area at the edge of a lake, river etc —**waterside** *adj*: *a waterside restaurant*

ˈwater ˌskiing *n* [U] a sport in which you SKI over water while being pulled by a boat —**water ski** *v* [I] —**water skier** *n* [C]: *Tracy was a keen swimmer and water skier.*

ˈwater slide *n* [C] a SLIDE that goes down into a swimming pool, usually with water running down it

ˈwater ˌsoftener *n* **1** [U] a chemical used for removing unwanted minerals from water **2** [C] a piece of equipment used for removing unwanted minerals from water

ˈwater-ˌsoluble *adj* a water-soluble substance is solid but becomes liquid when mixed with water

ˈwater ˌsports *n* [plural] sports that you play in water

wa·ter·spout /ˈwɔːtəspaʊt $ ˈwɒːtər-, ˈwɑː-/ *n* [C] **1** a tall stream of water that the wind pulls up from the sea during a violent storm → **tornado** **2** *old-fashioned* a pipe that carries water

ˈwater stress *n* [U] a situation in which there is not enough water in a country or area for the people who live there

ˈwater ˌtable *n* [C] *technical* the level below the ground where there is water

wa·ter·tight /ˈwɔːtətaɪt $ ˈwɒːtər-, ˈwɑː-/ *adj* **1** a watertight container, roof, door etc does not allow water to get in or out → **airtight** **2** an argument, plan etc that is watertight is made very carefully so that people cannot find any mistakes in it: *Lucky for him, his alibi is watertight. | Unless the ban is watertight, EU laws will overturn it.*

ˈwater ˌtower *n* [C] a tall building supporting a large container of water that supplies the buildings near it

ˈwater ˌvapour *BrE*, **water vapor** *AmE* *n* [U] water in the form of small drops in the air

ˈwater vole *n* [C] *BrE* an animal like a big mouse that can swim and lives near water SYN **water rat**

wa·ter·way /ˈwɔːtəweɪ $ ˈwɒːtər-, ˈwɑː-/ *n* [C] a river or CANAL that boats travel on: ***inland waterways***

wa·ter·wheel /ˈwɔːtəwiːl $ ˈwɒːtər-, ˈwɑː-/ *n* [C] a large wheel that is turned by water and is used to drive machinery

wa·ter·wings /ˈwɔːtəˌwɪŋz $ ˈwɒːtər-, ˈwɑː-/ *n* [plural] two bags filled with air that you fasten on your arms when you are learning to swim

wa·ter·works /ˈwɔːtəwɜːks $ ˈwɒːtərwɜːrks, ˈwɑː-/ *n* [plural] **1** the system of pipes and water supplies in a town or city **2** a building in which water is cleaned and then pumped to houses, buildings etc **3 turn on the waterworks** *informal* to start crying in order to get sympathy: *'Don't turn on the waterworks,' he sighed.* **4** *informal* the organs in your body through which URINE (=liquid waste) is removed

wa·ter·y /ˈwɔːtəri $ ˈwɒː-, ˈwɑː-/ *adj* **1** full of water or relating to water: *Her* ***eyes*** *were red and* ***watery*** *from crying.* | *Snakes lay eggs in a watery environment.* **2** very weak or pale: *a watery sun* | *She gave him a* ***watery smile.*** **3** watery food or drink contains too much water and has little taste: *a bowl of watery stew* **4 a watery grave** *literary* if someone has a watery grave, they DROWN (=die by breathing in water)

Wat·ford /ˈwɒtfəd $ ˈwɑːtfərd/ **north of Watford** a humorous expression for the northern part of Britain, especially in its distance from London: *I don't know where that town is. It's north of Watford somewhere.*

watt /wɒt $ wɑːt/ ●○○ *n* [C] (*written abbreviation* **W** *or* **w**) a unit for measuring electrical power: *a 100-****watt bulb***

watt·age /ˈwɒtɪdʒ $ ˈwɑː-/ *n* [singular, U] the power of a piece of electrical equipment, measured in watts

wat·tle /ˈwɒtl $ ˈwɑːtl/ *n* **1** [U] a frame made from sticks woven together: *a wattle fence* | *walls made of* ***wattle and daub*** (=this frame covered with clay) **2** [C] the red flesh that grows on the head or neck of some birds, such as chickens

WAV /wæv/ *n* [U] *technical* (***waveform audio***) a type of computer FILE that contains sound

wave¹ /weɪv/ ●●● S3 W2 *n*

1 SEA [C] a line of raised water that moves across the surface of the sea: *Dee watched the* ***waves breaking*** *on the shore.* | *The ship tipped over, and finally vanished* ***beneath the waves.*** → TIDAL WAVE

2 INCREASE [C usually singular] a sudden increase in a particular type of behaviour, activity, or feeling: *There was a wave of public protest.*

3 PEOPLE AND THINGS [C] a sudden increase in the number of people or things arriving at the same time: **[+of]** *a new wave of immigrants* | *They faced* ***wave after wave*** *of fresh troops.*

4 LIGHT AND SOUND [C] the form in which some types of energy such as light and sound travel: **sound/light/radio wave** → LONG WAVE, MEDIUM WAVE, SHORT WAVE

5 SIGNAL [C usually singular] a movement in which you raise your arm and move your hand from side to side: *He dismissed her with* ***a wave of the hand.***

6 FEELING/ACTIVITY [C] a feeling or activity that happens again and again in a series: *The pain swept over him* ***in waves.*** | ***Wave after wave of*** *aircraft passed overhead.*

7 HAIR [C usually plural] a loose curl in your hair

8 make waves *informal* to cause problems, especially when you should not: *With so many jobs already cut, he didn't want to make waves.*

9 new wave a new style of music, art, film etc that is very different and unusual: *new wave music* | **[+of]** *the new wave of Black feminist theorists*

10 CROWD [C usually singular] *AmE* an occasion when many people who are watching an event stand up, move their arms up and down, and sit down again one after another in a continuous movement that looks like a wave moving on the sea SYN **Mexican wave** *BrE*

11 the waves *literary* the sea → AIRWAVES, SHOCK WAVE

COLLOCATIONS – MEANING 2

PHRASES

a wave of violence/attacks/bombings *The incident triggered a wave of violence.*

a wave of panic/relief/sympathy *A wave of relief washed over Harry.*

a wave of nausea/dizziness/tiredness

NOUN + wave

a crime wave (=a sudden increase in crime) *The city is experiencing a crime wave.*

a heat wave (=a period of unusually hot weather) *California is in the middle of a heat wave.*

VERBS

a wave hits sb/sth *He was hit by a wave of nausea every time he tried to stand up.*

a wave engulfs sb/sth (=it affects someone or something very strongly) *The city was engulfed by a fresh wave of violence.*

a wave sweeps/washes over sb (=someone suddenly experiences a feeling or emotion) *A sudden wave of joy swept over her.*

wave² ●●● S3 W3 *v*

1 HAND [I,T] to raise your arm and move your hand from side to side in order to make someone notice you: **[+to/at]** *She turned to wave to the approaching soldiers.* | *Enid waved at us and we waved back.* | **wave (sb) goodbye** (=say goodbye to someone by waving to them) *The nurses came out to wave Grandad goodbye.*

2 MOVE [I,T] if you wave something, or if it waves, it moves from side to side: *The starter* ***waved*** *a green* ***flag*** *to indicate that the race would begin.* | *a tree waving in the breeze* | *He* ***waved*** *a hand* ***in the air*** *to attract her attention.* | **wave sth under/at etc sb/sth** *Trudie waved a $50 bill under his nose.* | **wave sth around/about** *The stranger spoke rapidly, waving his arms around.*

3 SIGNAL [T always + adv/prep] to show someone which way to go by waving your hand in that direction: **wave sb through/on/away etc** *The border guards waved us through.* | *Peter waved them back to their seats.*

4 wave sth goodbye/wave goodbye to sth *informal* to be forced to accept that something you want will not happen: *If you're not careful, you can wave goodbye to any pay rise this year.*

5 wave a magic wand to make a bad situation better, even though this is impossible: *I can't wave a magic wand and change what happened.*

6 HAIR [I,T] if hair waves, or if it is waved, it forms loose curls

wave sth ↔ **aside** *phr v* to ignore someone's opinion or ideas because you do not think they are important: *He waved her protests aside.*

wave sb/sth ↔ **down** *phr v* to signal to the driver of a car to stop by waving at them: *People in passing cars tried waving him down.*

wave sb **off** *phr v* to wave goodbye to someone as they leave: *Are you coming to the station to wave me off?*

ˌwave and ˈpay *n* [U] a way of paying in which you put your CREDIT CARD, DEBIT CARD, or MOBILE PHONE near a machine

wave·band /ˈweɪvbænd/ *n* [C] a set of sound waves of a particular length, used to broadcast radio programmes

wave·length /ˈweɪvleŋθ/ ●○○ *n* [C]

1 the size of a radio wave used to broadcast a radio signal **2** *technical* the distance between two points on energy waves such as sound or light

3 be on the same/a different wavelength *informal* to have the same or different opinions and feelings as someone else: *Dad is just on a different wavelength from me.*

wa·ver /ˈweɪvə $ -ər/ *v* [I] **1** to become weaker or less certain: *Her* ***voice wavered*** *uncertainly.* | *The students'* ***attention*** *did not* ***waver.*** | **[+in]** *Harris never wavered in his loyalty.* | **[+from]** *We were determined not to waver from our goals.* **2** to not make a decision because you have doubts: *Shareholders who were wavering met the directors.* | **waver between sth and sth** *The party wavered between free trade and protectionism.* **3** to move gently in several different directions: *The candle flame wavered, throwing shadows on the wall.*

wa·ver·er /ˈweɪvərə $ -ər/ *n* [C] someone who cannot make a decision, especially in a vote: *a final push to win over the waverers*

wav·y /ˈweɪvi/ *adj* **1** wavy hair grows in waves → see picture at HAIRSTYLE **2** a wavy line is smoothly curved → see picture at CURVED

wax¹ /wæks/ ●●○ *n* [U]

1 a solid substance made of fat or oil and used to make CANDLES, POLISH etc: *wax crayons* → BEESWAX

2 a natural sticky substance in your ears

wax² *v* **1** [T] to rub a layer of wax into a floor, surface etc to protect it or make it shine **2 wax sentimental/eloquent/**

W

lyrical etc to talk with extreme feeling, liking, or pleasure about something – used humorously: **[+about]** *Journalists wax lyrical about the band.* **3** [I] when the moon waxes, it seems to get bigger each night OPP **wane** **4 wax and wane** to increase and decrease over time: *Interest in the show has waxed and waned.* **5** [T] if you wax your legs, arms etc, you remove the hair from them using wax

ˌwaxed ˈpaper (*also* **ˈwax paper**) *n* [U] *AmE* paper covered with a thin layer of wax, used to wrap food SYN **greaseproof paper** *BrE*

wax·en /ˈwæksən/ *adj literary* **1** pale and shiny like wax: *his waxen face* **2** made from wax: *waxen images*

wax·work /ˈwæksw3ːk $ -w3ːrk/ *n* [C] **1 waxworks** *BrE* a place where you can see models of famous people made of WAX SYN **wax museum** *AmE* **2** a WAX model of a person

wax·y /ˈwæksi/ *adj* like WAX, or made of wax: *the waxy blossoms of the water lily* | *young men with waxy faces*

way[1] /weɪ/ ●●● S1 W1 *n*

1 METHOD [C] a method that you use to do or achieve something: *There are several different ways we can tackle this problem.* | **way of doing sth** *Evening classes are one way of meeting new people.* | ***There's no way*** *of knowing if the treatment will work.* | **way to do sth** *What's the best way to learn a language?* | **in the same way/in various ways** *Make the drink with boiling water in the same way as tea.* | *Animals communicate in various ways.* | **(in) the right/wrong way** *I think you're* ***going about*** *this* ***the wrong way.*** | **ways and means** (=methods of doing something, especially ones that are secret or not yet decided) *There are ways and means of raising the money that we need.* | **[+out/out of/around]** *One way around the problem* (=method of dealing with it) *is recycling.* | *There seems to be no way out of the current economic crisis.* | **way into television/publishing/finance etc** (=a method of getting involved in a particular activity or type of work) *companies eager for a way into business in Europe* **THESAURUS** METHOD

2 MANNER [C] the manner or style in which someone does something or in which something happens: *Look at the way he's dressed!* | **in a ... way** *'Hello,' he said in a friendly way.* | *Maria got up and took a shower in a leisurely way.* | **(in) this/that way** *I find it easier to work in this way* (=like this). | *Sorry, I didn't know you felt that way* (=had that feeling or opinion). | *The drugs didn't seem to affect Anna* ***in the same way.*** | **that's no way to do sth** (=used to tell someone that they should not be doing something in a particular manner) *That's no way to speak to your father!* | **in more ways than one** (=in a number of ways) *The changes will benefit the company in more ways than one.* | **in sb's (own) way** (=in a personal way that other people may not recognize) *I'm sure he does love you, in his own way.*

3 DIRECTION/HOW TO GO SOMEWHERE [C] **a)** a road, path, direction etc that you take in order to get to a particular place: **the way to/from/out etc** *Which is* ***the quickest way*** *to the sea from here?* | *There are several ways through the woods.* | **ask/tell/show sb the way** *Could you tell me the way to the station?* | *Does anyone* ***know the way*** *from here?* | *I was afraid of* ***losing*** *my* ***way*** *in the dark.* | *Can you* ***find*** *your* ***way*** *back to the car park?* | **the way out** (=the door, path etc which you can use to leave a building or area) *Which is the way out?* | **the way in** (=the door, path etc which you can use to enter a building or area) *She looked all around, but she couldn't seem to find the way in.* | **on sb's way** (=in the same direction as someone is going) *Want a lift? It's on my way.* | **out of sb's way** (=not in the same direction as someone is going) *I live miles out of your way.* **b)** a particular direction from where you are now: ***Which way*** *is north?* | *Walk* ***this way.*** | *A big Mercedes was coming* ***the other way*** (=from the opposite direction). | *He left the house, looking carefully both ways.*

4 PART OF STH THAT IS TRUE [C] used to say that there is a fact or a feature of something that makes a statement or description true: **in a/one way** *In one way you're right, I suppose.* | **in some/many ways** *Working at home makes sense, in many ways.* | *Ben is a perfectly normal child* ***in every way.*** | *He never got mad at me. He was great* ***in that way.*** | **in no way** (=used to emphasize that something is not true) *This should in no way be seen as a defeat.*

5 DISTANCE/TIME [singular] a distance or a length of time, especially a long one: *I was still* ***a long way*** *from home.* | **some way/quite a way** (=quite a long distance) *She had to park some way from the restaurant.* | **a long way off/away/ahead etc** (=far away in distance or in time) *A peace settlement now seems a long way off.* | *I don't want to go* ***all that way*** *and not see him.* | **all the way down/across/through etc (sth)** (=the full distance or length of something) *Did you really swim all the way across?* | *I was awake all through the night.* | **a (long) ways** *AmE*: *That's quite a ways from here, isn't it?*

6 THE SPACE IN FRONT OF YOU [C usually singular] if someone or something is in the way, they are blocking the space in front of you, and you cannot move forward: **be in the way/be in sb's way** (=be blocking a road, someone's path etc so that they cannot move forward easily) *There was a big truck in the way.* | *Sorry, am I in your way?* | *A policeman yelled at the crowds to* ***get out of the way.*** | *The* ***way ahead*** *was blocked.*

7 make way (for sth/sb) a) to move to the side so that there is space for someone or something to pass: *The crowd stepped aside to make way for the procession.* **b)** to make it possible for something newer or better to be built, organized etc: *Several houses were demolished to make way for a new road.*

8 out of the way a) (*also* **out of sb's way**) if someone or something is out of the way, they are somewhere where they are not likely to cause a problem, need attention, be annoying etc: **move/put/push etc sth out of the way** *Why don't you tie your hair back, out of the way?* | *If Uncle Tom had been drinking, I* ***kept out of*** *his* ***way.*** | *When Mac was* ***safely out of the way,*** *Peter came round.* **b)** if a particular matter, job etc is out of the way, it has been done or dealt with: *I'd rather* ***get*** *the interview* ***out of the way*** *in the morning.* | *As soon as the contract's out of the way, we can start.* **c)** a place that is out of the way is far from any towns

9 on the/your/its way a) arriving or happening soon: *There's a letter on its way to you.* | *More changes are on the way.* **b)** travelling towards a particular place: *She should be on the way here by now.* | **[+to]** *The ships were already on their way to the gulf* **c)** while going from one place to another: **[+to/out/home etc]** *I ran out of gas on my way to the airport.* | *Guess who I bumped into on the way home.* **d)** (*also* **along the way**) while moving from one situation or part of your life to another: *Don's had to change jobs several times along the way.* **e)** if someone has a baby on the way, they are PREGNANT

10 be/get under way a) to have started to happen or be done: *Plans are* ***well under way*** *for a new shopping centre.* | *The tournament* ***got under way*** *on Friday.* **b)** to have started to move or travel somewhere: *Our train was already under way.*

11 make your way a) to go towards something, especially when this is difficult or takes a long time: **[+to/through/towards etc]** *The team slowly made their way back to base.* | **make your own way (home/to sth etc)** (=go somewhere without the help or company of other people) *Don't worry. I can make my own way to the beach.* **b)** to gradually become successful in a particular job, activity, profession etc: *young people who are making their way in industry*

12 push/grope/inch etc your way somewhere to get somewhere by using force or moving carefully: *She elbowed her way to the front of the queue.* | *He drank some water, then groped his way back to the bedroom.*

13 give way a) to be replaced by something else: **[+to]** *Stone has given way to glass and concrete.* | *My anger gave way to depression.* **b)** to agree to do what someone else wants, instead of what you want, especially after a lot of discussion or argument: *Despite growing pressure, the Minister of State refused to give way.* | **[+to]** *Maria seemed to despise him for giving way to her.* **c)** to break because of too much weight or pressure: *The floor's rotten and likely to give way.* **d)** *BrE* to stop or slow down when you are driving, in order to allow other vehicles to go first

SYN **yield** AmE: *In Britain, give way to cars coming from the right.*
14 clear/pave/open/prepare etc the way (for sth) to make it possible for something to happen or develop later: *a study that paved the way for further research* | *The Queen's death opened the way for him to return.*
15 a/the way forward an action, plan etc that seems a good idea because it is likely to lead to success: *A way forward lies in developing more economic links.* | **[+for]** *This treatment may be the way forward for many inherited disorders.*
16 STATE/CONDITION [singular] a particular state or condition: *My family was **in a bad way** financially.* | *The chicken's nice and crispy – just **the way I like it**.* | *It's worth thinking how you can improve **the way things are**.* | **sb was born/made that way** (=used to say that someone's character is not likely to change) *He'll always be mean – he was born that way.*
17 FACT/EVENT [singular] used to refer to something that happens: *I hate the way you always give in to him.*
18 BEHAVIOUR [C] someone's typical style of behaving, especially when it seems different or unusual: **be (just) sb's way** *Don't worry if she's quiet – that's just her way.* | *Esther quickly changed the subject, **as was** her **way**.* | **strange/funny/odd etc ways** *We all have our funny little ways.* | **change/mend your ways** (=stop behaving badly) → **see the error of your ways** at ERROR(6), → **be set in your ways** at SET[3](6)
19 DEVELOPMENT/PROGRESS [singular] used in expressions about developing and improving: *The team **has a long way to go*** (=needs to develop or improve a lot) *before it can match that performance.* | *Microwave ovens **have come a long way*** (=have developed or improved a lot) *since they first appeared in our kitchens.* | *Jen is now **well on the way to** recovery* (=she has improved and will be well soon).
20 go some way towards doing sth *also* **go a long way towards doing sth** to help a little or a lot to make something happen: *ideas that go some way towards reducing environmental problems*
21 CHOICES/POSSIBILITIES [C] used when talking about two choices someone could make, or two possibilities that could happen: *I'm not sure **which way** he'll decide.* | *The election **could go either way*** (=both results are equally possible). | *Make your mind up **one way or the other**.* | **either way** (=used to say that something will be the same, whichever of two things happens) *Either way, it's going to be expensive.*
22 within two feet/ten years etc either way no more than two feet etc more or less than a particular amount: *Your answer must be within a centimetre either way.*
23 (in) one way or another/one way or the other used to say that someone does or will do something somehow, although you are not sure how: *One way or the other he always seems to win.* | *We'll find the money, one way or another.*
24 way around/round/up a particular order or position that something should be in: *Which way around does this skirt go?* | **the other way around/round/up** (=in the opposite order or position) *The picture should be the other way up.* | *Art reflects life, or is it the other way around* (=is it 'life reflects art')? | **the right/wrong way around/round/up** *Are the batteries in the wrong way round?*
25 by way of sth a) (*also* **in the way of sth**) as a form or means of something: *I'd like to say something by way of introduction.* | **little in the way of sth** (*also* **not much/enough in the way of sth**) (=not much of something) *The town has little in the way of leisure facilities.* **b)** if you travel by way of a place, you go through it SYN **via**: *We went by way of London.*
26 get in the way of sth to prevent someone from doing something, or prevent something from happening: *Your social life must not get in the way of your studies.*
27 go out of your way to do sth to do something with more effort than is usual or expected: *She went out of her way to make me feel welcome.*
28 get/have your (own) way to do what you want to, even though someone else wants something different: *Don't let the children always get their own way.*
29 go your own way to do what you want, make your own decisions etc: *At 18, most young people are ready to go their own way.*
30 go sb's way a) if an event goes your way, it happens in the way you want: *The government are hopeful that the vote will go their way.* | **everything/nothing goes sb's way** (=used to talk about events in general) **b)** *literary* to continue a journey, or to leave and do what you want to do next: *She said goodbye and went her way.* **c)** to travel in the same direction as someone: *I can take you – I'm going your way.*
31 come sb's way if something comes your way, you get or experience it, especially by chance: *Luck had come her way at the very last moment.*
32 in a big/small way used to talk about the degree to which something happens, or how important it is: *The business was a success, in a small way.*
33 by a long way by a large amount: *He was the best in the group by a long way.*
34 talk/buy etc your way into/past etc sth/sb to get where you want or achieve something you want by saying or doing something: *Caroline managed to talk her way past the guard.*
35 work/munch/smoke etc your way through sth to deal with, eat, smoke etc a large amount of things: *He worked his way through the pile of documents.* | *She had munched her way through a packet of biscuits.*
36 be on the/your way out to be becoming less popular, important, powerful etc: *Is the royal family on the way out?*
37 across/over the way on the opposite side of the street: *They live across the way from us at number 23.*
38 have a way of doing sth used to say that something often or usually happens: *Cheer up – these problems have a way of working out.*
39 get into the way of doing sth *BrE* to start to do something regularly: *He'd got into the way of smoking first thing in the morning.*
40 not in any way, shape, or form used to emphasize that something is not true: *I am not responsible for his actions in any way, shape, or form.*
41 split sth two/three etc ways (*also* **divide sth two/three etc ways**) to divide something into two, three etc equal parts: *We'll split the cost between us five ways.*
42 have a way with sb/sth to be especially good at dealing with people or things of a particular type: *David seems to have a way with children.* | *She's always **had a way with words*** (=been good at using words effectively).
43 the way of the world how things always happen or are done, especially when this is not easy to change: *In those days these policies favoured men. That was the way of the world.*
44 every which way *informal* **a)** in all directions: *Bullets were flying every which way.* **b)** *BrE* every possible method: *I tried every which way to avoid it.*
45 Way used in the names of roads: *Church Way*

SPOKEN PHRASES

46 by the way used when saying something that is not related to the main subject you were talking about before: *By the way, have you seen my keys anywhere?*
47 no way! a) used to say that you will definitely not do or allow something: *'Can I borrow your car?' 'No way!'* | ***There's no way** I'll ever get married again.* | **No way José!** (=used to emphasize that you will not do something) **b)** *especially AmE* used to say that you do not believe something or are very surprised by it: *She's 45? No way!*
48 the way I see it (*also* **to my way of thinking**) used before telling someone your opinion: *The way I see it, it was a fair trade.*
49 that's the way used to tell someone that they are doing something correctly or well, especially when you are showing them how: *Now bring your foot gently off the clutch – that's the way.*
50 that's (just) the way sth/sb is/that's (just) the way sth goes used to say that a particular situation or person cannot be changed: *Don't try to fight it. That's just the way it is.* | *Sometimes Tim needs to be alone. That's the way he is.*
51 be with sb all the way to agree with someone completely: *I'm with you all the way on this salary issue, Joe.*

52 if I had my way used when telling someone what you think it would be best to do: *If I had my way, we'd leave this place tomorrow.*
53 have it your (own) way used to tell someone in an annoyed way that you will agree to what they want
54 (there are) no two ways about it used to say that something is definitely true, especially something unpleasant
55 you can't have it both ways used to say that you cannot have the advantages from both of two different possible decisions or actions: *It's a choice between the time and the money – you can't have it both ways!*
56 way to go! *AmE* used to tell someone that they have done something very well or achieved something special
57 (that's/it's) always the way! *BrE* used to say that things always happen in the way that is least convenient: *The train was late – always the way when you're in a hurry!*
58 down your/London etc way in your area, the area of London etc
59 go all the way (with sb) to have sex with someone

→ HALFWAY, ONE-WAY, RIGHT OF WAY, TWO-WAY, → **that's the way the cookie crumbles** at COOKIE(3), → **cut both ways** at CUT[1](36), → **in the family way** at FAMILY(7), → **go the way of all flesh** at FLESH[1](9), → **go your separate ways** at SEPARATE[1](4), → **know your way around (sth)** at KNOW[1](10), → **be laughing all the way to the bank** at LAUGH[1](8), → **lead the way** at LEAD[1](7), → **look the other way** at LOOK[1](9), → **out of harm's way** at HARM[1](6), → **parting of the ways** at PARTING[1](3), → **pay your way** at PAY[1](13), → **to put it another way** at PUT(4), → **rub sb up the wrong way** at RUB[1](7), → **see which way the wind is blowing** at WIND[1](6), → **see your way (clear) to doing sth** at SEE[1](38), → **any way you slice it** at SLICE[2], → **stand in sb's way** at STAND[1](30), → **where there's a will there's a way** at WILL[2](5), → **work your way to/through etc sth** at WORK[1](12)

THESAURUS
A WAY OF DOING SOMETHING

way something you can do in order to achieve what you want or deal with a problem: *Visiting a country is a great way to learn a language.* | *a good way to lose weight*
method a way of doing something, especially one that a lot of people know about and use: *They still use traditional methods of farming.* | *modern teaching methods*
approach a general way of dealing with a particular problem or situation, especially a way that has been carefully thought about: *We need a whole new approach to environmental issues.* | *There will be considerable advantages to adopting this approach.*
technique a way of doing something for which you need a skill that must be learned and practised: *I went to a class to learn relaxation techniques.* | *new surgical techniques* | *techniques for improving staff performance*
strategy a carefully planned way to achieve something difficult or complicated that may take a long time: *They met to discuss the company's business strategy.* | *the government's long-term strategy for reducing crime*

way² ●●○ S3 *adv*
1 very far: **[+ahead/behind/out etc]** *The other cyclists were way behind.* | *She lives way out of town.*
2 by a large amount: **[+above/below/past etc]** *Her IQ is way above average.* | **[+out]** *Your guess was way out* (=completely incorrect), *he's actually thirty-eight.* | **[+back]** *We first met way back* (=a long time ago) *in the seventies.* | **way heavier/smarter/bigger etc** (=much heavier etc) *The tickets were way more expensive than I thought.*
3 *AmE informal* very: *I think she's way cool, man.*

way·bill /ˈweɪbɪl/ *n* [C] a document sent with goods that says where the goods are to be delivered, how much they are worth, and how much they weigh

way·far·er /ˈweɪˌfeərə $ -ˌferər/ *n* [C] *literary* someone who travels from one place to another on foot

way·lay /weɪˈleɪ/ *v* (*past tense and past participle* **way-laid**) [T] **1** if someone waylays you, they stop you when you are going somewhere, for example to attack you or talk to you: *They used to waylay him as he came out of the factory.* **2** if you are waylaid, you are delayed when you are doing something – often used humorously to say why you are late: *Sorry, we* ***got waylaid*** *at the bar.*

ˌway of ˈlife ●●○ *n* (*plural* **ways of life**) [C]
1 the behaviour, habits, customs etc that are typical of a particular society or person: *The tribe's* ***traditional way of life*** *is under threat.* | **the American/British etc way of life**
2 a job or interest that is so important that it affects everything you do: *For Mark, travelling has* ***become a way of life.***

ˌway ˈout *n* (*plural* **ways out**) [C] **1** *BrE* a door or passage through which you leave a building SYN **exit** **2** a way to escape a difficult or bad situation: *He was in a dilemma, and could see no way out.* **3 on the/your way out a)** if you do something on the way out, you do it as you leave a place: *Pick up your mail on the way out.* **b)** soon to be replaced by someone or something else: *The old type of passport is on its way out.* → **take the easy way out** at EASY[1](6), → **way out** at WAY[1](3)

ˌway-ˈout *adj informal* very modern, unusual, and strange

way·side /ˈweɪsaɪd/ *n* [C] *literary* the side of a road → **fall by the wayside** at FALL[1](16)

ˈway ˌstation *n* [C] *AmE* **1** *old-fashioned* a place to stop between the main stations of a railway **2** a place where you can stop before going on somewhere else: **[+to]** *The refugee camps, however dreadful, were a way station to their dream.*

way·ward /ˈweɪwəd $ -wərd/ *adj* behaving badly, in a way that is difficult to control: *a wayward teenager* —**waywardness** *n* [U]

wa·zoo /wəˈzuː/ *n AmE* **out/up the wazoo** *informal* in a large amount, or to a great degree

WC /ˌdʌbəljuː ˈsiː/ *n* [C] *BrE* (***water closet***) a toilet – used especially on signs in public places

we /wi; *strong* wiː/ ●●● S1 W1 *pron* [used as the subject of a verb]
1 used by the person speaking or writing to refer to himself or herself and one or more other people: *'Did you go into the supermarket?' 'No, we didn't.'* | *Shall we stop for a coffee?* | *So we all travelled down to Brighton together.* | *We declare our support for a government of national unity.* | *We Italians are proud of our history.*
2 used by a writer or speaker to include themselves and their readers or listeners: *As we saw in Chapter 4, slavery was not the only cause of the Civil War.*
3 people in general: *We live on a complex planet.*
4 *formal* used by a king or queen to refer to himself or herself
5 *spoken* sometimes used to mean 'you' when speaking to children or people who are ill: *How are we feeling today, Mr Robson?*

weak /wiːk/ ●●● S3 W2 *adj*
1 PHYSICAL not physically strong: *The illness left her* ***feeling weak.*** | *Poor light produces weak plants.* | **be too weak to do sth** *She's too weak to feed herself.* | **[+with/from]** *Nina was* ***weak with hunger.*** | *The animal was weak from loss of blood.* | **weak heart/lungs etc** *My grandfather had a weak heart.*
2 LIKELY TO BREAK unable to support much weight: *a weak bridge* | **too weak to do sth** *The branch was too weak to support his weight.*
3 CHARACTER easily influenced by other people – used to show disapproval: *a weak indecisive man*
4 WITHOUT POWER not having much power or influence: **weak leader/ruler/king etc** *a weak and ineffective president* | *The party was left weak and divided.* | *The country is in a* ***weak position*** *economically.*
5 WITHOUT INTEREST without the power to interest or amuse people: *The play is well acted but the plot is weak.* | *a* ***weak joke***
6 WITHOUT ENERGY done without energy or confidence: *He managed a* ***weak smile.***

W

7 NOT GOOD AT DOING STH not good at a particular skill or subject, or in a particular area of activity or knowledge: **[+in]** *New Zealand was weak in defence.* | **[+on]** *She speaks quite fluently but she's weak on grammar.* | *Be honest about your* ***weak points*** (=your faults or the things you do not do well).
8 MONEY not financially successful: **weak currency/economy etc** *The pound was weak against the dollar.*
9 ARGUMENT/IDEA not likely to make people believe that something is true or right: *She's washing her hair? That sounds like a* ***weak excuse****!* | *There are some* ***weak points*** *in her argument.* | *The defence lawyer clearly knew that his case was weak.*
10 DRINK weak tea, beer etc contains a lot of water and has little taste OPP **strong**
11 LIGHT/SOUND difficult to see or hear SYN **faint**: *a* ***weak*** *radio* ***signal*** | *He had only a* ***weak light*** *to see by.*
12 weak points/spots the parts of something that can easily be attacked or criticized: *Check your house for weak spots where a thief could enter.*
13 weak at the knees feeling strange because of strong emotions: *His smile* ***made*** *her* ***go weak at the knees****.*
14 weak moment a time when you can be persuaded more easily than usual: *Dave caught me at a weak moment and I lent him £10.*
15 the weak/weakest link the person or thing in a situation that is less strong, skilful etc than the others: *Goalkeeper Gouter proved to be the weakest link.*
16 weak verb *technical* a verb that forms regular past tenses OPP **strong verb**
17 weak consonant/syllable one that is not emphasized
—**weakly** *adv*: *'I'm sorry,' she said, smiling weakly.* | *He sank down weakly beside her.*

THESAURUS

NOT PHYSICALLY STRONG

weak not physically strong, sometimes because you are ill: *Tom's had flu and he's still feeling weak.* | *The doctors said she was too weak to have an operation.*
frail weak and thin, especially because you are old: *a frail 85-year-old lady* | *My grandfather's becoming quite frail now.*
shaky feeling weak in your legs and only able to walk slowly and unsteadily: *When I came out of hospital I was a bit shaky for a while.*
puny /ˈpjuːni/ *especially disapproving* small, thin, and looking very weak: *his puny white arms* | *He was a puny little boy who was often bullied at school.*
feeble *especially written* weak and unable to do much because you are very ill, very old or very young: *For a week she was too feeble to get out of bed.* | *a tiny, feeble baby*
delicate weak and often becoming ill easily: *a delicate child* | *She had rather a* ***delicate constitution*** (=her body easily became ill).
infirm *formal* weak or ill for a long time, especially because you are old: *a residential home for people who are elderly and infirm*

LIKELY TO BREAK

weak unable to support much weight, and likely to break: *The foundations of the building are rather weak.* | *an old chair with weak legs*
fragile made of a thin material that is easy to break or damage – used when something needs to be handled carefully: *a fragile china vase* | *Be careful of those glasses – they're very fragile.*
delicate easy to break or damage – used especially about soft materials, skin etc: *Wash delicate fabrics separately.* | *This soap is good for delicate skin.*
flimsy not well-made from strong materials and so easily damaged – used about furniture, houses etc: *a flimsy plastic table* | *This keyboard's very cheap but it's a bit flimsy.*
rickety /ˈrɪkəti/ in very bad condition and likely to break – used about a building, piece of furniture, vehicle etc: *a rickety old bicycle* | *He lived in a rickety hut on the beach for several years.*

weak·en /ˈwiːkən/ ●●○ *v* [I,T]
1 to make someone or something less powerful or less important, or to become less powerful OPP **strengthen**: *Over the last two years the president's position has weakened.* | *Changes in policy have weakened the power of the trade unions.* | *The absence of this witness has weakened the case against the accused.*
2 to make someone lose their physical strength, or to become physically weak: *Julia was weakened by her long illness.*
3 to make someone less determined, or to become less determined: *Such policies weaken the resolve of potential troublemakers.* | *When she begged him to let her stay, he weakened.*
4 to make a building, structure etc less strong, or to become less strong: *The earthquake in Cairo weakened a number of structures.*
5 if a particular country's money or a company's SHARE prices weaken, or if they are weakened, their value is reduced: **[+against]** *The pound has weakened against the dollar.*

ˌweaker ˈsex *n* **the weaker sex** *old-fashioned* used to refer to women as a group, in a way that is now considered offensive

ˌweak-ˈkneed *adj informal* lacking courage and unable to make your own decisions

weak·ling /ˈwiːk-lɪŋ/ *n* [C] someone who is not physically strong

ˌweak-ˈminded *adj* showing little intelligence, or easily persuaded OPP **strong-minded**: *a weak-minded man*

weak·ness /ˈwiːknəs/ ●●○ W3 *n*
1 FAULT [C] a fault in someone's character or in a system, organization, design etc: *The legislation has a fundamental weakness.* | *The plan has* ***strengths and weaknesses****.* THESAURUS ▸ FAULT
2 LACK OF POWER [U] lack of strength, power, or influence: **[+in]** *weakness in the economy* | **[+of]** *the growing weakness of local government*
3 BODY [U] the state of being physically weak: *muscular weakness* | **[+in]** *weakness in the right arm*
4 CHARACTER [U] lack of determination shown in someone's behaviour: *He couldn't explain his weakness in giving in to her demands.* | *I dared not cry or show any* ***sign of weakness****.* | **[+of]** *his weakness of character*
5 MONEY [U] the condition of not being worth a lot of money: **[+of]** *the weakness of the pound against the dollar*
6 a weakness for sth if you have a weakness for something, you like it very much even though it may not be good for you: *I* ***have a*** *real* ***weakness for*** *fashionable clothes.*

ˌweak-ˈwilled *adj* someone who is weak-willed does not do something difficult that they had intended to do OPP **strong-willed**

weal /wiːl/ *n* [C] a red swollen mark on the skin where someone has been hit

wealth /welθ/ ●●○ W3 *n*
1 [U] a large amount of money, property etc that a person or country owns: *The country's wealth comes from its oil.* | *the* ***distribution of wealth*** (=the way wealth is divided among the people of a country or society) | *The purpose of industry is to* ***create wealth****.*
2 a wealth of sth a lot of something useful or good: *There is a wealth of information available about pregnancy and birth.*

wealth·y /ˈwelθi/ ●●○ *adj* (*comparative* **wealthier**, *superlative* **wealthiest**)
1 having a lot of money, possessions etc SYN **rich**: **very/extremely/immensely/fabulously etc wealthy** *He left as a poor, working class boy and returned as a wealthy man.* | *the wealthy nations of the world* THESAURUS ▸ RICH
2 the wealthy [plural] people who have a lot of money, possessions etc

wean /wiːn/ *v* [T] to gradually stop feeding a baby or young animal on its mother's milk and start giving it ordinary food: **wean sb onto sth** *It's time to start weaning her onto solid foods.*
wean sb **off/from** sth *phr v* to make someone gradually

W

stop doing something you disapprove of: *advice on how to wean yourself off nicotine*
be weaned on sth *phr v* to be influenced by something from a very early age: *I was weaned on a diet of Hollywood fantasy.*

weap·on /ˈwepən/ ●●● W2 *n* [C]
1 something that you use to fight with or attack someone with, such as a knife, bomb, or gun: *They all had sticks which they planned to use as weapons.*
2 an action, piece of information, piece of equipment etc that you can use to win or be successful in doing something: *a new weapon in the fight against AIDS | Right now, she felt the need of every* **weapon in** *her* **armoury** (=weapon that she had)*, including surprise.*

COLLOCATIONS

ADJECTIVES/NOUN + weapon

nuclear/atomic weapons *The country is thought to be developing nuclear weapons.*
conventional weapons (=not nuclear) | **chemical/biological weapons** | **an offensive weapon** (=one that can be used to attack someone illegally) | **a lethal/deadly weapon** (=one that can kill) | **the murder weapon** (=the weapon used to kill someone)

VERBS

carry a weapon *The man is believed to be carrying a weapon.*
use a weapon *They claim the government used chemical weapons against them.*
fire a weapon (=shoot a gun or missile)

weap·on·ry /ˈwepənri/ *n* [U] weapons of a particular type or belonging to a particular country or group: *nuclear weaponry*

ˈweapons inˌspector *n* [C] a scientist who is sent to a country that has or that might have BIOLOGICAL or NUCLEAR weapons in order to check that UN RESOLUTIONS (=laws) on these types of weapon are being obeyed

ˌweapons of ˌmass deˈstruction *n* [plural] chemical, NUCLEAR, or BIOLOGICAL weapons that are very powerful and could kill a lot of people or destroy large areas. This expression is used especially by politicians and news reporters to talk about weapons that are held by countries which are considered to be a threat to world peace.

wear[1] /weə $ wer/ ●●● S1 W1 *v* (*past tense* **wore** /wɔː $ wɔːr/, *past participle* **worn** /wɔːn $ wɔːrn/)
1 ON YOUR BODY [T] to have something such as clothes, shoes, or jewellery on your body: *Susanna was wearing a black silk dress. | He wore glasses for reading.* | **wear a seat belt** (=have it around yourself) | **wear black/white/red etc** *Usually I wear black, grey, or brown.* | **wear sth to a party/a dance/an interview etc** *I'm wearing a scarlet dress to the party.* **THESAURUS** DRESS
2 HAIR [T] to have your hair or BEARD in a particular style or shape: *She wore her hair loose.*
3 DAMAGE [I,T] to become thinner or weaker after continuous use, or to make something do this: *The cushions are starting to wear a little. | His jeans have* **worn thin** *at the knees. | You've* **worn a hole** *in your sock.*
4 wear well a) to remain in good condition after a period of time: *The tyres on the car seem to be wearing well.* **b)** if someone is wearing well, they look younger than they really are: *He must have been around his mid-forties at least, but he'd worn well.*
5 EXPRESSION [T] to have a particular expression on your face: **wear a smile/frown/grin etc** *His face wore a welcoming smile.*
6 sth is wearing thin a) if something is wearing thin, you are bored with it because it is not interesting anymore, or has become annoying: *The film begins well but the* **joke wears thin** *after about ten minutes.* **b)** if your patience is wearing thin, you have very little left, because of a delay or problem
7 wear the trousers *BrE*, **wear the pants** *AmE informal* to be the person in a family who makes the decisions
8 wear your heart on your sleeve *informal* to show your true feelings openly —**wearable** *adj*

wear away *phr v* to gradually become thinner or smoother, or to make something become like this, because of rubbing or touching: *The leather is starting to wear away at the seams.* | **wear sth ↔ away** *Most of the grass had already been worn away by the spectators.*

wear down *phr v*
1 to gradually become flatter or smoother, or to make something become like this, because of rubbing or use: *My shoes have worn down at the heel.* | **wear sth ↔ down** *Its teeth were worn down.*
2 wear sb ↔ down to gradually make someone physically weaker or less determined: *It was clear he was being worn down by the rumours over his future.*

wear off *phr v*
1 if pain or the effect of something wears off, it gradually stops: *The effects of the anaesthetic were starting to wear off.*
2 the novelty wears off used to say that you stop feeling interested or excited about something because it is no longer new: *It was funny for a while but the novelty soon wore off.*

wear on *phr v* if time wears on, it passes very slowly, especially when you are waiting for something to happen: *I was feeling more tired* **as the** *night* **wore on**.

wear out *phr v*
1 to become damaged and useless, or to make something like this, by using it a lot or for a long time: *My boots are beginning to wear out.* | **wear sth ↔ out** *He travels so much he actually wears out suitcases.*
2 wear sb out to make someone feel extremely tired SYN **exhaust**: *All this shopping has worn us out.* | **wear yourself out** *Illness and death came suddenly; over the years she had simply worn herself out.*
3 wear out your welcome to stay with someone longer than they want you to → WORN OUT

wear[2] ●○○ *n* [U]
1 the clothes worn for a particular occasion or activity, or by a particular group of people: **evening/casual/leisure etc wear** *a new range of casual wear | bridal wear | the children's wear department* → FOOTWEAR, MENSWEAR **THESAURUS** CLOTHES
2 damage caused by continuous use over a long period: *Replace your trainers when they start to show* **signs of wear**. *| Check the equipment for* **wear and tear**.
3 the amount of use an object, piece of clothing etc has had, or the use you can expect to get from it: *The dress stood up to the wear small children give their clothes. | You'll* **get years of wear out of** *that coat.* → **the worse for wear** at WORSE[1](7)

wear·a·ble /ˈweərəbəl $ ˈwer-/ (*also* **ˌwearable comˈputer**) *n* [C] a computer that is designed to be worn as an item of clothing

wear·er /ˈweərə $ ˈwerər/ *n* [C] someone who wears a particular type of clothing, jewellery etc: *Bicycle helmets offer wearers protection against head injury. | hearing aid wearers*

wear·ing /ˈweərɪŋ $ ˈwer-/ *adj* making you feel tired or annoyed: *Taking care of children can be wearing.* **THESAURUS** TIRING

wear·i·some /ˈwɪərisəm $ ˈwɪr-/ *adj formal* making you feel bored, tired, or annoyed: *a wearisome task*

wear·y[1] /ˈwɪəri $ ˈwɪr-/ ●○○ *adj*
1 very tired or bored, especially because you have been doing something for a long time: *She found Rachel in the kitchen, looking old and weary. | She sat down with a weary sigh.* | **weary of (doing) sth** *He was weary of the constant battle between them.* **THESAURUS** TIRED

REGISTER
In everyday English, people usually say **tired** rather than **weary**: *They were* **tired** *after their journey.*

2 *especially literary* very tiring: *a long and weary march* —**wearily** *adv* —**weariness** *n* [U]

W

weary² *v* (**wearied**, **wearying**, **wearies**) [I,T] *formal* to become very tired, or make someone very tired: *Amanda wouldn't admit how much the children wearied her.* | **weary of (doing) sth** *As the day wore on, we wearied of the journey.* —**wearying** *adj*

wea·sel¹ /ˈwiːzəl/ *n* [C] a small thin furry animal that kills and eats rats and birds

weasel² *v* (**weaselled**, **weaselling** *BrE*, **weaseled**, **weaseling** *AmE*)

weasel out *phr v informal* to avoid doing something you should do by using clever or dishonest excuses: **[+of]** *He's now in court trying to weasel out of $25 million in debts.*

ˈweasel ˌword *n* [C] *informal* a word used instead of another word when someone wants to be less direct, honest, or clear

weath·er¹ /ˈweðə $ -ər/ ●●● S1 W2 *n*

1 [singular, U] the temperature and other conditions such as sun, rain, and wind: *What's the weather like today?* | *The weather turned bitterly cold.*

GRAMMAR

- You often say **the weather**: *The weather seems to be getting worse.*
- You also often use **weather** with an adjective such as **good** or **bad**: *We had good weather all week.*| *Games are sometimes cancelled because of bad weather.*
- Don't use **weather** with 'a'. ✗ Don't say: *We had a good weather.*

GRAMMAR GUIDE ▸ NOUNS

2 the weather *informal* a description on radio or television, in newspapers etc of what the weather will be like in the near future SYN **the weather forecast**: *I always watch the weather after the news.*

3 in all weathers in all types of weather, even when it is very hot or cold: *There are homeless people sleeping on the streets in all weathers.*

4 under the weather *informal* slightly ill: *You look a bit under the weather.*

5 keep a weather eye on sth to watch a situation carefully so that you notice anything unusual or unpleasant: *Keep a weather eye on your finances.* → **make heavy weather of sth** at HEAVY¹(10)

COLLOCATIONS

ADJECTIVES

good/nice/lovely (=not wet) *We'll go out if the weather is good.*
bad (=wet or stormy) *Several flights were cancelled owing to bad weather.*
hot *Drink lots of water in hot weather.*
cold *The weather was cold and grey.*
fine/sunny/fair/dry | **wet/rainy** | **windy/stormy**

VERBS

have good/bad etc weather *We have had lovely weather all week.*

weather + NOUN

the weather forecast (=a description of what the weather is expected to be like in the near future) *What's the weather forecast like for the weekend?*
the weather map (=a map showing the current or expected future weather) | **weather conditions** | **weather patterns** (=the usual weather that comes at a particular time each year) | **a weather station** (=a place used for studying and recording weather conditions)

PHRASES

weather permitting (=if the weather is good enough) *Breakfast is served on the terrace, weather permitting.*

weather² *v* **1** [T] to come through a very difficult situation safely: *The company* ***weathered the storm*** *of objections to the scheme.* | *Northern Ireland weathered the recession better than any other region in the UK.* **2** [I,T] if rock, wood, or someone's face is weathered by the wind, sun, rain etc, or if it weathers, it changes colour or shape over a period of time: *The brick has weathered to a lovely pinky-brown.* | *Her face was weathered by the sun.*

ˈweather-ˌbeaten *adj* weather-beaten buildings, skin, clothing etc look old and damaged because they have been out in bad weather: *his weather-beaten face*

weath·er·board /ˈweðəbɔːd $ -ərbɔːrd/ *n* **1** [U] *BrE* boards covering the outer walls of a house SYN **clapboard** *AmE* **2** [C] a board fixed across the bottom of a door, to prevent water from getting inside

weath·er·cast·er /ˈweðəˌkɑːstə $ -ərˌkæstər/ *n* [C] a WEATHER GIRL or WEATHERMAN

weath·er·cock /ˈweðəkɒk $ -ərkɑːk/ *n* [C] a WEATHER VANE in the shape of a male chicken

ˈweather ˌgirl *n* [C] a woman on television or radio who tells you what the weather will be like

weath·er·man /ˈweðəmæn $ -ər-/ *n* (*plural* **weathermen** /-men/) [C] a man on television or radio who tells you what the weather will be like

weath·er·proof /ˈweðəpruːf $ -ər-/ *adj* weatherproof clothing or material can keep out wind and rain —**weatherproof** *v* [T]

ˈweather vane *n* [C] a metal object fixed to the top of a building that blows around to show the direction the wind is coming from

weave¹ /wiːv/ ●○○ *v* (*past tense* **wove** /wəʊv $ woʊv/, *past participle* **woven** /ˈwəʊvən $ ˈwoʊ-/)

1 CLOTH ETC [I,T] to make cloth, a carpet, a basket etc by crossing threads or thin pieces under and over each other by hand or on a LOOM: *hand-woven scarves* | *Only a few of the women still weave.* | *traditional basket weaving*

2 STORY [T] to put many different ideas, subjects, stories etc together and connect them smoothly: *She weaves a complicated plot of romance and intrigue.* | **weave sth together** *the complex patterns which evolve when individuals' lives are woven together*

3 weave your magic/weave a spell to attract or interest someone very much

4 MOVE (*past tense and past participle* **weaved**) [I always + adv/prep, T] to move somewhere by turning and changing direction a lot: *cyclists* ***weaving in and out of*** *the traffic* | **weave your way through/to etc sth** *Lori spotted them as they weaved their way through the tables.*

weave² *n* [C] the way in which a material is woven, and the pattern formed by this: *a fine weave*

weav·er /ˈwiːvə $ -ər/ *n* [C] someone whose job is to weave cloth

web /web/ ●●● S2 W2 *n*

1 [singular] **the Web** the system on the Internet that allows you to find and use information that is held on computers all over the world SYN **the World Wide Web**: **on the Web** *a guide to the best education-related sites on the Web* GRAMMAR ✗ Don't say: *in the Web/on Web*

2 [C] a net of thin threads made by a SPIDER to catch insects: *He watched a spider* ***spinning*** *its* ***web***. → COBWEB

3 [C usually singular] a closely related set of things that can be very complicated: **a web of intrigue/deceit/deception/lies etc** | *a* ***tangled web*** *of relationships*

4 [C] a piece of skin that connects the toes of ducks and some other birds, and helps them to swim well

ˈweb adˌdress *n* [C] a WEBSITE ADDRESS

webbed /webd/ *adj* webbed feet or toes have skin between the toes

web·bing /ˈwebɪŋ/ *n* [U] strong woven material in narrow bands, used for supporting seats, holding things etc

ˈweb ˌbrowser *n* [C] a computer program that finds information on the Internet and shows it on your computer screen

web·cam /ˈwebkæm/ *n* [C] a video camera that broadcasts what it is filming on a website

web·cast¹ /ˈwebkɑːst $ -kæst/ *n* [C] an event such as a musical performance which you can listen to or watch on the Internet THESAURUS PROGRAMME

webcast² *v* (*past tense and past participle* **webcast**) [I,T] to broadcast an event on the Internet, at the time the event happens: *Various local news sites plan to webcast each of the mayoral debates.*

web·cast·ing /ˈwebˌkɑːstɪŋ $ -ˌkæs-/ *n* [U] the use of the Internet to send information, especially news or entertainment, to many people at the same time

web·chat /ˈwebtʃæt/ *n* [C] a conversation that takes place on a website

ˈweb ˌcrawler *n* [C] a computer program that finds information on the Internet, especially so that this information can be used by a SEARCH ENGINE

ˈweb deˌsigner *n* [C] someone who designs websites, especially websites for businesses or organizations

ˌweb-ˈfooted *adj* having toes that are joined by pieces of skin

web·head /ˈwebhed/ *n* [C] *informal* someone who uses the Internet a lot, especially in a skilful way

web·i·nar /ˈwebɪnɑː $ -ɑːr/ *n* [C] a talk or meeting that people take part in using the Internet and often telephones as well

web·li·og·ra·phy /ˌwebliˈɒgrəfi $ -ˈɑːg-/ *n* (*plural* **webliographies**) [C] a list of the websites you used to get information when writing something

web·log, **ˈweb log** /ˈweblɒg $ -lɒːg, -lɑːg/ *n* [C] a website that is owned by a particular person or group of people rather than by an organization or company, and that has information about one or more subjects → **blog**

web·mas·ter /ˈwebˌmɑːstə $ -ˌmæstər/ *n* [C] someone who is in charge of a website

web·ol·o·gy /weˈbɒlədʒi $ -ˈbɑː-/ *n* [U] the study of the structure and content of the World Wide Web, and how the different websites are linked together

web·page, **ˈweb page** /ˈwebpeɪdʒ/ ●●● S2 *n* [C] all the information that you can see in one part of a website

ˈweb ring, **web·ring** /ˈwebrɪŋ/ *n* [C] a group of similar websites which are connected to each other by LINKS, so that it is easy for people to find a lot of information on a particular subject on the Internet: *a classical music web ring*

web·site /ˈwebsaɪt/ ●●● S2 W1 *n* [C] a place on the Internet where you can find information about something, especially a particular organization: *For more information on weight loss and healthy eating,* ***visit*** *our* ***website****.* | **on a website** *Responses will be* ***posted*** *(=put)* ***on*** *the* ***website****.*

ˈwebsite adˌdress *n* [C] the series of letters and other symbols that is the name of a website SYN **web address**

ˈweb ˌtraffic *n* [U] the number of people who visit a particular website

Web 2.0 /ˌweb tuː pɔɪnt ˈəʊ $ -ˈoʊ/ *n* [U] *technical* advanced ways of using the Internet, for example ways of sharing information using BLOGS and WIKIS

web·zine /ˈwebziːn/ *n* [C] a website that is like a magazine SYN **e-zine**

wed /wed/ *v* (*past tense and past participle* **wedded** *or* **wed**) [I,T not in progressive] to marry – used especially in literature or newspapers

we'd /wid; *strong* wiːd/ **1** the short form of 'we had': *We'd already eaten.* **2** the short form of 'we would': *We'd rather stay.*

Wed. (*also* **Weds** *BrE*) a written abbreviation of ***Wednesday***

wed·ded /ˈwedɪd/ *adj* [only before noun] **1** *formal* married: *a newly-wedded couple* | *my lawfully wedded wife* **2 wedded bliss** the happiness that comes when you are married – used humorously **3 be wedded to sth** to believe strongly in a particular idea or way of doing things: *On the whole the working class is still wedded to the Labour Party.*

wed·ding /ˈwedɪŋ/ ●●● S2 W3 *n* [C]
1 a marriage ceremony, especially one with a religious service: *She's busy planning her daughter's wedding.* | *When is the wedding?*
2 (hear the sound of) wedding bells *spoken* used to say that you think it is likely that two people will get married

COLLOCATIONS

VERBS

go to a wedding (*also* **attend a wedding** *formal*) *I'm going to a wedding on Saturday.*
come to the wedding *She wrote to say she couldn't come to the wedding.*
conduct a wedding *formal* (=say the official words and perform the actions at a wedding) *Their wedding was conducted by the local priest.*

ADJECTIVES/NOUN + wedding

a church wedding *I wanted a church wedding.*
a big wedding (=with a lot of guests) *They couldn't afford a big wedding.*
a white wedding (=a traditional wedding where the bride wears a white dress) | **a registry office wedding** *BrE* (=at a local government office, not in a church) | **a civil wedding** *AmE* (=a wedding that is not performed by a religious leader)

wedding + NOUN

sb's wedding day *She looked beautiful on her wedding day.*
sb's wedding night *They spent their wedding night in a hotel.*
sb's wedding anniversary *They celebrated their tenth wedding anniversary in May.*
the wedding ceremony | **the wedding service** (=the ceremony in a church) | **the wedding reception** (=the large formal meal or party after a wedding) | **the wedding breakfast** *BrE* (=the meal after a wedding, usually in the afternoon) | **the wedding cake** | **a wedding present/gift** | **a wedding guest** | **a wedding invitation** | **a wedding photograph/picture**

ˈwedding ˌchapel *n* [C] a building used in the US for wedding ceremonies

ˈwedding dress (*also* **ˈwedding gown**) *n* [C] a long dress, especially a white dress, worn at a traditional wedding

ˈwedding list *n* [C] a list of presents that two people who are getting married suggest that guests might buy for them: *These days, when a couple announce their wedding day and send out an invitation, they also add a wedding list.*

ˈwedding ring (*also* **ˈwedding band**) *n* [C] a ring that you wear to show that you are married

ˈwedding vows *n* [plural] the promises you make during your wedding ceremony

wedge¹ /wedʒ/ ●○○ *n* [C]
1 a piece of wood, metal etc that has one thick edge and one pointed edge and is used especially for keeping a door open or for splitting wood
2 a piece of food shaped like a wedge: *Garnish with lemon wedges.* | **[+of]** *a wedge of cheese*
3 wedges [plural] WEDGE HEELS → **drive a wedge between sb** at DRIVE¹(13), **the thin end of the wedge** at THIN¹(11)

wedge² *v* [T always + adv/prep] **1** to force something firmly into a narrow space: *The phone was wedged under his chin.* | *Victoria wedged herself into the passenger seat.* **2 wedge sth open/shut** to put something under a door, window etc to make it stay open or shut

ˌwedge ˈheels (*also* **wedg·es**) /ˈwedʒɪz/ *n* [plural] shoes worn by women, with high heels that are a solid block from the front of the shoe to the back —**ˈwedge-heel** *adj* [only before noun] → see picture at SHOE¹

wedg·ie /ˈwedʒi/ *n* [C] *informal* the situation of having your underwear pulled too tightly between your BUTTOCKS, or the action of pulling someone's underwear into this position as a joke: *He* ***gave*** *me a* ***wedgie****.*

wed·lock /ˈwedlɒk $ -lɑːk/ *n* [U] *old use* **1 born out of wedlock** if a child is born out of wedlock, its parents are not married when it is born **2** the state of being married

W

Wednes·day /ˈwenzdi, -deɪ/ ●●● S2 W2 (*written abbreviation* **Wed.** *or* **Weds**) *n* [C,U] the day between Tuesday and Thursday: **on Wednesday** *The sale starts on Wednesday.* | *We can go Wednesday. AmE* | **Wednesday morning/afternoon etc** *I saw Vicky on Wednesday evening.* | **last Wednesday** *They left last Wednesday.* | **this Wednesday** *Come down this Wednesday.* | **next Wednesday** (=Wednesday of next week) *I can let you know next Wednesday.* | **a Wednesday** (=one of the Wednesdays in the year) *'Are you free on the 19th?' 'Is that a Wednesday?'*

wee[1] /wiː/ *adj* [usually before noun] **1** *informal* very small – used especially in Scottish English: *My wee boy is three.* **2 a wee bit** *informal* to a small degree: *She looked a wee bit confused.* **3 the wee (small) hours** *AmE* the early hours of the morning, just after 12 o'clock at night SYN **the small hours** *BrE*: *The party continued into the wee small hours.*

wee[2] *v* [I] *BrE spoken* to pass water from your body – used by or to children SYN **urinate** —**wee** *n* [singular]: *Do you want a wee?*

weed[1] /wiːd/ ●○○ *n*

1 [C] a wild plant growing where it is not wanted that prevents crops or garden flowers from growing properly: *the constant battle against weeds*

2 [U] a plant without flowers that grows on water in a large green floating mass → **seaweed**

3 [C] *BrE informal* someone who is weak: *Nigel's such a weed, isn't he?*

4 like weeds in large numbers: *Cars clogged the roads like weeds.*

5 the weed *informal* cigarettes or tobacco

6 [U] CANNABIS

7 (widow's) weeds *old use* black clothes worn by a woman whose husband has died

weed[2] *v* [I,T] to remove unwanted plants from a garden or other place —**weeding** *n* [U]

weed sb/sth ↔ **out** *phr v* to get rid of people or things that are not very good: *The research will help governments to weed out ineffective aid schemes.*

weed·kil·ler /ˈwiːdˌkɪlə $ -ər/ *n* [C,U] poison used to kill unwanted plants

weed·y /ˈwiːdi/ *adj informal* **1** full of unwanted wild plants **2** *BrE* physically weak or having a weak character

week /wiːk/ ●●● S1 W1 *n* [C]

1 a period of seven days and nights, usually measured in Britain from Monday to Sunday and in the US from Sunday to Saturday: **once/twice/three times etc a week** *Letters were delivered twice a week only.* | *I can't see you **this week**.* | **last/next week** (=the week before or after this one) *See you next week.*

2 any period of seven days and nights: **for a week/two weeks etc** *I've been living here for six weeks.* | **in a week/two weeks etc** (=one, two etc weeks from now) *If he hasn't phoned in a week, I'll phone him.* | *It will cost you an estimated £10 **per week** to feed one dog.* | *The training program lasts three weeks.*

3 the part of the week when you go to work, usually from Monday to Friday SYN **working week**: *a 35-hour week* | **during the week** *I don't see her during the week.*

4 Monday week/Tuesday week etc *BrE* a week after the day that is mentioned: *We're off to Spain Sunday week.*

5 a week on Monday etc *BrE*, **a week from Monday etc** *AmE* a week after the day that is mentioned: *The Reids are coming for dinner a week from Sunday.* | *Keith's coming home two weeks on Saturday* (=two weeks after next Saturday).

6 week after week (*also* **week in week out**) continuously for many weeks: *We do the same things week in week out.*

GRAMMAR: Patterns with week

last week/this week etc

Don't use **in** with these words:

• You say **last week**: *I saw her last week.* ✗ Don't say: *I saw her in last week.*

• You say **this week**: *I'm going to be busy at work this week.* ✗ Don't say: *I'm going to be busy at work in this week.*

• You say **next week**: *Shall we meet for lunch next week?* ✗ Don't say: *Shall we meet for lunch in next week?*

• You say **that week**: *He was sick that week.* ✗ Don't say: *He was sick in that week.*

a week

• You use **a week** when saying how many times in a week something happens: *We have four English lessons a week.* ✗ Don't say: *We have four English lessons in a week.*

all week

• You use **all week** when talking about something that happens during every part of a week: *We had good weather all week.* ✗ Don't say: *We had good weather all the week.*

week·day /ˈwiːkdeɪ/ *n* [C] any day of the week except Saturday and Sunday

week·end[1] /ˌwiːkˈend◂ ˈwiːkend $ ˈwiːkend/ ●●● S1 W2 *n* [C] Saturday and Sunday, especially considered as time when you do not work: *Are you doing anything nice **this weekend**?* | **last/next weekend** (=the weekend before or after this one) | **at the weekend** *BrE*, **on the weekend** *AmE*: *I never work at the weekend.* | *What are you doing on the weekend?* | **at weekends** *BrE*, **on weekends** *AmE*: *I only see him at weekends.* | *Tony has been unwell **over the weekend*** (=during the weekend). | *We're going to Paris for a **long weekend*** (=Saturday and Sunday, and also Friday or Monday, or both). | **weekend cottage/cabin etc** (=a place in the country where you spend your weekends) → **dirty weekend** at DIRTY[1](2)

GRAMMAR: Patterns with weekend

at the weekend

• You use **at the weekend** in British English, when saying that something happens on Saturday or Sunday: *I went shopping at the weekend.* ✗ Don't say: *I went shopping at weekend.* | *in weekend*

on the weekend

• You use **on the weekend** in American English, when saying that something happens on Saturday or Sunday: *I went shopping on the weekend.* ✗ Don't say: *I went shopping on weekend.* | *in weekend*

at weekends/on weekends

You use these expressions when saying that something usually or regularly happens on Saturday or Sunday: *She is only home at weekends (BrE).* | *She is only home on weekends (AmE).* ✗ Don't say: *She is only home on weekend.* | *She is only home in weekend(s).*

this/next/last weekend

• Don't use **at** or **in** with these words.

• You say **this weekend**: *The festival will be held this weekend.* ✗ Don't say: *The festival will be held at this weekend.*

• You say **next weekend**: *Will you come to my house next weekend?* ✗ Don't say: *Will you come to my house in next weekend?*

• You say **last weekend**: *I visited my grandparents last weekend.* ✗ Don't say: *I visited my grandparents at last weekend.*

weekend[2] *v* [I always + adv/prep] to spend the weekend somewhere: *We're weekending on the coast.*

week·end·er /ˌwiːkˈendə $ ˈwiːkendər/ *n* [C] someone who spends time in a place only at weekends

ˌweekend ˈwarrior *n* [C] **1** someone who plays a sport or does some other type of exercise at the WEEKEND, but does not usually exercise during the week **2** someone who spends their weekends and holidays training to be part of an extra military force that is used only if it is needed to help the regular military forces

week·long /ˈwiːklɒŋ $ -lɒːŋ/ *adj* [only before noun] continuing for a week: *a weeklong training course*

week·ly[1] /ˈwiːkli/ ●●● W3 *adj* [only before noun] happening or done every week: *a weekly current affairs* *programme | twice-weekly flights* —**weekly** *adv*: *The magazine is published weekly.*

weekly² *n* (*plural* **weeklies**) [C] a magazine that appears once a week → **monthly**: *a popular news weekly*

week·night /ˈwiːknaɪt/ *n* [C] any night except Saturday and Sunday

wee·nie /ˈwiːni/ *n* [C] *AmE informal* **1** a type of SAUSAGE SYN **wiener**, **hot dog**: *a weenie roast* **2** someone who is weak, afraid, or stupid – used especially by children SYN **wimp**

wee·ny /ˈwiːni/ *BrE*, **ween·sie** /ˈwiːnzi/ *AmE adj spoken* extremely small → TEENY WEENY

weep /wiːp/ ●●○ *v* (*past tense and past participle* **wept** /wept/)

1 [I,T] *formal or literary* to cry, especially because you feel very sad: *James broke down and wept.* | **[+for]** *She wept for the loss of her mother.* | *He* ***wept bitterly*** (=cried a lot) *when it was time for us to leave.* THESAURUS ▸ CRY

> **REGISTER**
> In everyday English, people usually say **cry** rather than **weep**: *She was* ***crying*** *all the way through the movie.*

2 I could have wept *spoken* used to say that you felt very disappointed about something: *I could have wept thinking what I'd missed.*

3 [I] if a wound weeps, liquid comes out of it —**weep** *n* [singular]

weep·ie /ˈwiːpi/ *n* [C] another spelling of WEEPY²

weep·ing /ˈwiːpɪŋ/ *adj* **weeping willow/birch etc** a tree with branches that hang down towards the ground

weep·y¹ /ˈwiːpi/ *adj informal* tending to cry a lot

weepy², **weepie** *n* (*plural* **weepies**) [C] *informal* a film or story that is intended to make people cry

wee·vil /ˈwiːvəl/ *n* [C] a small insect that feeds on grain, flour etc and spoils it

ˈwee-wee *v* [I] *spoken* to pass water from your body – used by or to children SYN **urinate** —**wee-wee** *n* [singular]

weft /weft/ *n* **the weft** *technical* the threads in a piece of cloth that are woven across the threads that go from top to bottom SYN **woof** → **warp**

weigh /weɪ/ ●●● S3 W3 *v*

1 BE A PARTICULAR WEIGHT [linking verb] to have a particular weight: *The young birds weigh only a few grams.* | *Do you know* ***how much*** *it* ***weighs***? | ***What*** (=how much) *do you* ***weigh***? | *The box was full of books and* ***weighed a ton*** (=was very heavy).

> **GRAMMAR: Linking verbs**
> **Weigh** is a linking verb in this meaning. It links the subject of the sentence with a noun, often an amount: *The package weighed several kilos.*

2 MEASURE WEIGHT [T] to use a machine to discover how much something or someone weighs: *He weighed some potatoes on the scales.* | **weigh yourself** *Have you weighed yourself lately?*

3 CONSIDER/COMPARE (*also* **weigh up**) [T] to consider something carefully so that you can make a decision about it: *It is my job to weigh the evidence.* | **weigh sth against sth** *We have to weigh the benefits of the scheme against the costs.*

4 INFLUENCE [I always + adv/prep] *formal* to influence someone's opinion and the decision that they make: **[+against]** *This unfortunate experience will* ***weigh heavily*** *against further investment in the area.* | **weigh in sb's/sth's favour** *These facts will weigh in your favour.* | **[+with]** *Her evidence* ***weighed strongly*** *with the judge.*

5 weigh your words to think very carefully about what you say because you do not want to say the wrong thing: *He was weighing his words carefully.*

6 weigh anchor to raise an ANCHOR and sail away

weigh sb **down** *phr v*

1 if something weighs you down, it is heavy and difficult to carry: **be weighed down with sth** *Sally was weighed down with shopping bags.*

2 if a problem weighs you down, it makes you feel worried and upset: **be weighed down by/with sth** *He felt weighed down by his responsibilities.* | *a family weighed down with grief*

weigh in *phr v*

1 to have your weight measured before taking part in a competition: **[+at]** *Higgins weighed in at just over 100 kilos.* → WEIGH-IN

2 *informal* to join in an argument or fight: **[+with]** *The chairman then weighed in with his views.*

weigh on sb/sth *phr v* to make someone feel worried and upset: *The desire for peace will* ***weigh heavily on*** *the negotiators.* | *I'm sure there's something* ***weighing on*** *his* ***mind***. | *The burden of responsibility* ***weighed*** *heavily* ***on*** *his* ***shoulders***.

weigh sth ↔ **out** *phr v* to measure an amount of something by weighing it: *She weighed out half a kilo of rice.*

weigh sb/sth ↔ **up** *phr v*

1 to consider something carefully so that you can make a decision about it: *We're still* ***weighing up the pros and cons*** (=the advantages and disadvantages) *of the two options.*

2 to watch someone and listen to them carefully so that you can form an opinion about what they are like: *I could see that he was weighing me up.*

weigh·bridge /ˈweɪˌbrɪdʒ/ *n* [C] a machine that vehicles drive onto so that they can be weighed

ˈweigh-in *n* [C usually singular] a check on the weight of a BOXER or JOCKEY before a competition → WEIGH IN

weight¹ /weɪt/ ●●● S1 W2 *n*

1 AMOUNT SB/STH WEIGHS [C,U] how heavy something is when you measure it: *The average weight of a baby at birth is just over seven pounds.* | **in weight** *fish that are over two kilos in weight* | **by weight** *Fruit and vegetables are sold by weight.*

2 HOW FAT [U] how heavy and fat someone is: *You shouldn't worry about your weight.* → OVERWEIGHT, UNDERWEIGHT

3 HEAVINESS [U] the fact that something is heavy: *The weight of her boots made it hard for Sue to run.* | *I didn't know if the bridge would* ***support*** *our* ***weight***. | **under the weight of sth** *Karen staggered along under the weight of her backpack.*

4 HEAVY THING [C] something that is heavy: *I can't lift heavy weights because of my bad back.*

5 WORRY [singular] something that causes you a lot of worry because you have to deal with it: **[+of]** *She felt a great weight of responsibility.* | *families who are crumbling under the weight of increasing debt* | *Selling the house is* ***a weight off my mind*** (=something that no longer causes a lot of worry).

6 IMPORTANCE [U] if something has weight, it is important and influences people: *She knew that her opinion* ***carried*** *very little* ***weight***. | **give/add weight to sth** *This scandal adds more weight to their arguments.*

7 AMOUNT **weight of sth** a large amount of something: *The weight of evidence is that unemployment leads to all sorts of health problems.* | *The weight of public opinion is behind the teachers.* | *They won the battle by sheer* ***weight of numbers*** (=very large numbers of people).

8 FOR MEASURING QUANTITIES [C] a piece of metal that weighs an exact amount and is balanced against something else to measure how much the other thing weighs

9 FOR SPORT [C] a piece of metal that weighs an exact amount and is lifted by people as a sport: *I've been* ***lifting weights*** *since I was 18.* → WEIGHTLIFTING, see picture at GYM

10 throw your weight about/around *informal* to use your position of authority to tell people what to do in an unpleasant and unreasonable way

11 throw your weight behind sb/sth to use all your power and influence to support someone or something: *The US has thrown its weight behind the new leader.*

12 pull your weight to do your full share of work: *He accused me of not pulling my weight.*

13 take the weight off your feet *informal* used to tell someone to sit down: *Come in, take the weight off your feet.* → DEADWEIGHT

COLLOCATIONS - MEANING 2

VERBS

put on weight (*also* **gain weight** *formal*) *He had put on weight since she last saw him.*
lose/shed weight *She lost a lot of weight when she was ill.*
watch your weight (=try not to get fatter, by eating the correct foods) *He has to watch his weight because he has a heart condition.*
get/keep your weight down (=become thinner or stay thin) *How can I keep my weight down?*
get/keep the weight off (=become or stay thinner)

weight + NOUN

a weight problem (=a tendency to be too fat) *I've always had a weight problem.*
weight gain | **weight loss**

ADJECTIVES

sb's ideal weight *She weighs about 10lbs more than her ideal weight.*
excess weight *You'll feel better if you lose the excess weight.*

COMMON ERRORS

⚠ Don't say 'lose your weight'. Say **lose weight**. Do not use 'weight' as a verb, for example by saying 'I weight 55 kilos'. Say **I weigh 55 kilos**.

weight² *v* [T] **1** (*also* **weight down**) to fix a heavy object to something in order to keep it in place: **weight sth (down) with sth** *The fishing nets are weighted down with lead.* **2** to change something slightly so that you give more importance to particular ideas or people: **weight sth in favour of sb/sth** *a temptation to weight the report in favour of the option you want*

weight·ed /ˈweɪtɪd/ *adj* giving an advantage or disadvantage to one particular group or activity → **biased**: **[+against]** *The voting system is weighted against the smaller parties.* | **weighted in favour of sb/sth** *This year's pay increase is* ***heavily weighted*** *in favour of the lower paid staff.* | **[+towards]** *The course is weighted towards language skills.*

weight·ing /ˈweɪtɪŋ/ *n* [singular, U] *BrE* additional money that you get paid because of the high cost of living in a particular area: *salary £24,000 plus £2,400 London weighting*

weight·less /ˈweɪtləs/ *adj* something that is weightless seems to have no weight, especially when it is floating in space or water —**weightlessness** *n* [U]

weight·lift·ing /ˈweɪtˌlɪftɪŋ/ *n* [U] the sport of lifting specially shaped pieces of metal that weigh an exact amount —**weightlifter** *n* [C]

ˈweight ˌtraining *n* [U] the activity of lifting specially shaped pieces of metal that weigh an exact amount, as a form of exercise: *He does weight training at the gym twice a week.*

weight·y /ˈweɪti/ *adj* **1** important and serious: *She didn't feel like discussing weighty matters.* **2** *literary* heavy: *a weighty tome* (=a big and heavy book)

weir /wɪə $ wɪr/ *n* [C] a low fence or wall that is built across a river or stream to control the flow of water, or to make a pool where people can catch fish

weird¹ /wɪəd $ wɪrd/ ●●● S2 *adj informal* very strange and unusual, and difficult to understand or explain: *A really weird thing happened last night.* | *He's a weird bloke.* | *They sell all sorts of* ***weird and wonderful*** (=very strange) *products.* THESAURUS STRANGE —**weirdly** *adv*: *a weirdly shaped rock* —**weirdness** *n* [U]

weird² *v*
weird sb **out** *phr v informal* if something weirds you out, it is so strange that it makes you feel uncomfortable or worried

weird·o /ˈwɪədəʊ $ ˈwɪrdoʊ/ *n* (*plural* **weirdos**) [C] *informal* someone who wears strange clothes or behaves strangely: *Jenny's going out with a real weirdo.*

welch /welʃ $ welʃ, weltʃ/ *v* [I] another spelling of WELSH²

welcome¹ /ˈwelkəm/ ●●● S1 *interjection* used to greet someone who has just arrived: **[+to]** *Welcome to London!* | ***Welcome back*** *– it's good to see you again.* | *Hello,* ***welcome home***.

welcome² ●●● S2 W3 *adj*
1 you're welcome *spoken* a polite way of replying to someone who has just thanked you for something: *'Thanks for the coffee.' 'You're welcome.'*
2 if someone is welcome in a place, other people are glad that they are there: *I had the feeling I wasn't really welcome.* | *I didn't* ***feel welcome*** *in the club.* | *Mary* ***made*** *us very* ***welcome***. | *We try to* ***make*** *the new students* ***feel welcome***.
3 if something is welcome, you enjoy it because you feel that you need it: *The weekend was a* ***welcome break*** *from the pressures of work.* | *Six months in Scotland would* ***make a welcome change*** *from London.* | *A cup of tea would be very welcome.*
4 if something is welcome, you are glad that it has happened: *The increase in interest rates is welcome news for investors.* | *This new funding will come as a welcome boost for the industry.*
5 be welcome to sth *spoken* used to say that someone can have something if they want it, because you certainly do not want it: *If you want to take the job you're welcome to it!*
6 be welcome to do sth *spoken* used to invite someone to do something if they would like to: *You're welcome to stay for lunch.*

wel·come³ ●●● S3 W2 *v* [T]
1 to say hello in a friendly way to someone who has just arrived SYN **greet**: *I must be there to welcome my guests.* | *They* ***welcomed*** *us* ***warmly***. | *His family* ***welcomed*** *me* ***with open arms*** (=in a very friendly way).
2 to be glad to accept something: *The college welcomes applications from people of all races.* | *We would* ***welcome*** *any advice or suggestions* ***with open arms***.
3 to be glad that something has happened because you think it is a good idea: *Economists have welcomed the decision to raise interest rates.*

welcome⁴ ●●○ W3 *n* [singular]
1 the way in which you greet someone when they arrive at a place: **warm/friendly welcome** *His colleagues* ***gave*** *him a very warm* ***welcome*** *when he returned to work.* | *You can be sure of a friendly welcome at all our hotels.* | *The president* ***got*** *a tremendous* ***welcome*** *at the airport.*
2 the way in which people react to an idea, and show that they like it or do not like it: *Politicians have* ***given*** *an enthusiastic* ***welcome to*** *the Queen's speech.* | *The proposals have so far* ***received*** *a cautious* ***welcome*** *from government ministers.*
3 outstay/overstay your welcome to stay at someone's house longer than they want you to

ˈwelcome ˌwagon *n* [C] *AmE* an event that is organized to welcome someone who has just arrived in a new place: *The company is bringing out the welcome wagon for the new sales recruits.*

wel·com·ing /ˈwelkəmɪŋ/ *adj* **1** someone who is welcoming is friendly when you arrive in a place: *Everyone was very welcoming.* | *Stephanie was standing at the door with a welcoming smile.* THESAURUS FRIENDLY
2 a welcoming place is pleasant and makes you feel relaxed: *a restaurant with a welcoming atmosphere*
3 [only before noun] done or organized in order to welcome someone to a place: **welcoming committee/party** *I was met by a welcoming committee.* | *a welcoming speech*

weld¹ /weld/ *v* **1** [T] to join metals by melting their edges and pressing them together when they are hot: *The new handle will have to be welded on.* **2** [T always + adv/prep] to join or unite people into a single strong group: *His job is now to weld the players into a single team.* → ARC WELDING

W

weld² *n* [C] a joint that is made by welding two pieces of metal together

weld·er /ˈweldə $ -ər/ *n* [C] someone whose job is to weld metal in a factory

wel·fare /ˈwelfeə $ -fer/ ●●○ W2 AWL *n* [U]
1 someone's welfare is their health and happiness: *Our only concern is the children's welfare.*
2 help that is provided for people who have personal or social problems: **welfare benefits/services/programmes etc** *the provision of education and welfare services* | *The company's welfare officer deals with employees' personal problems.*
3 *AmE* money that is paid by the government in the US to people who are very poor or unemployed SYN **benefit** *BrE*: **on welfare** *Most of the people in this neighborhood are on welfare.*

ˌwelfare ˈstate / $ ˈ.../ *n* **1 the welfare state** a system in which the government provides money, free medical care etc for people who are unemployed, ill, or too old to work → **social security 2** [C] a country with such a system

well¹ /wel/ ●●● S1 W1 *adv* (*comparative* **better** /ˈbetə $ -ər/, *superlative* **best** /best/)
1 SATISFACTORILY in a successful or satisfactory way: *Did you sleep well?* | *James reads quite well for his age.* | *All the team played very well today.* | *Simon doesn't work well under pressure.* | *The festival was very well organized.* | *The concert* ***went*** *very* ***well***.
2 THOROUGHLY in a thorough way: *Mix the flour and butter well.* | *I know Birmingham quite well.*
3 A LOT **a)** a lot, or to a great degree: **[+before/after/above/below etc]** *Stand well back from the bonfire.* | *It was well after 12 o'clock when they arrived.* | *The village is well below sea level.* | *The amphitheatre is* ***well worth*** *a visit.* | *I'm* ***well aware*** *of the problems involved.* | *I went out and got* ***well and truly*** (=completely) *drunk.* **b)** [+adj] *BrE informal* very: *That was well funny!*
4 do well a) to be successful, especially in work or business: *He's doing very well at college.* | *Elizabeth's* ***done well for*** *herself since she moved to London.* **b)** if someone who has been ill is doing well, they are becoming healthy again: *He had the operation yesterday, and he's doing very well.*
5 as well in addition to something or someone else: *Why don't you come along as well?*

> **REGISTER**
> **As well** is used mostly in spoken English. In written English, people usually prefer to use **also**: *Parents are* ***also*** *welcome.*

6 as well as sth/sb in addition to something or someone else: *They own a house in France as well as a villa in Spain.* | **as well as doing sth** *The organization gives help and support to people in need, as well as raising money for local charities.*
7 may/might/could well used to say that something is likely to happen or is likely to be true: *What you say may well be true.* | *You could try the drugstore, but it might well be closed by now.*
8 may/might/could (just) as well a) *informal* used when you do not particularly want to do something but you decide you should do it: *I suppose we may as well get started.* **b)** used to mean that another course of action would have an equally good result: *The taxi was so slow we might just as well have gone on the bus.*
9 can't very well (do sth) used to say that you cannot do something because it would be unacceptable: *I can't very well tell him we don't want him at the party!*
10 know full/perfectly well used to say that someone does know something even though they are behaving as if they do not: *You know full well what I mean.*
11 speak/think well of sb to talk about someone in an approving way or to have a favourable opinion of them: *Sue has always spoken well of you.*
12 well done!/well played! *spoken* used to praise someone when you think they have done something very well
13 well said! *spoken* used to say that you agree with what someone has just said, or that you admire them for saying it
14 be well away *BrE informal* **a)** to be making good progress: *If we can get that grant from the local authority, we'll be well away.* **b)** to be very drunk
15 be well in with sb *informal* to have a friendly relationship with someone, especially someone important: *She's very well in with members of the management committee.*
16 be well out of sth *BrE spoken* to be lucky to no longer be involved in a particular situation
17 be well up in/on sth *informal especially BrE* to know a lot about a particular subject: *Geoff's always been well up on the internet.*
18 as well sb might/may *formal* used to say that there is a good reason for someone's feelings or reactions: *Marilyn looked guilty, as well she might.*
19 do well by sb *informal* to treat someone generously

well² ●●● S1 W1 *interjection*
1 EMPHASIZING STH used to emphasize something you are saying: *Well, I think it's a good idea anyway.* | *Well, I've had enough and I'm going home!* | *'James doesn't want to come to the cinema with us.' '****Well then****, let's go on our own.'*
2 PAUSING used to pause or give yourself time to think before saying something: *Well, let's see now, I could meet you on Thursday.*
3 ACCEPTING A SITUATION (*also* **oh well**) used to show that you accept a situation even though you feel disappointed or annoyed about it: *Well, I did my best – I can't do any more than that.* | *Oh well, we'll just have to cancel the holiday, I suppose.*
4 SHOWING SURPRISE (*also* **well, well, (well)**) used to express surprise or amusement: *Well, so Steve got the job?* | *Well, well, well, I didn't think I'd see you here.*
5 SHOWING ANGER used to express anger or disapproval: *Well, she could at least have phoned to say she wasn't coming!*
6 FINAL REMARK used to show that you are about to finish speaking or doing something: *Well, that's all for today.* | *Well, that's the last one done.*
7 EXPRESSING DOUBT used to show that you are not sure about something: *'Will you be in on Friday evening?' 'Well, it depends.'*
8 CHANGING STH used to slightly change something that you have said: *He's rolling in money! Well, he's got a lot more than me, anyway.*
9 AGREEING **very well** *formal* used to show that you agree with an idea or accept a suggestion: *'Very well,' he said. 'I accept.'*
10 CONTINUING A STORY used to continue a story you are telling people, especially in order to make it seem more interesting: *You know that couple I was telling you about the other day? Well, last night I saw a police car in front of their house!*
11 ASKING A QUESTION **Well?** used to ask someone to answer a question you have asked them, when you are angry with them: *Well? What have you got to say for yourself?*

well³ ●●● S1 W2 *adj* (*comparative* **better**, *superlative* **best**)
1 healthy: *'How are you?' 'Very well, thanks.'* | *I don't* ***feel*** *very* ***well***. | *You're* ***looking*** *very* ***well***. | *I hope you* ***get well*** *again soon.* THESAURUS HEALTHY
2 it's just as well (that) *spoken* used to say that things have happened in a good or fortunate way: *It's just as well I kept some money aside for emergencies.*
3 it's/that's all very well, but ... *spoken* used to say that something seems to be a good idea, but is not really possible or helpful: *It's all very well the doctors telling me I've got to rest, but who's going to look after my children?*
4 that's/it's all well and good *spoken especially BrE* used to say that something is good or enjoyable, but it also has some disadvantages: *Going off on foreign holidays is all well and good, but you've got to get back to reality sometime.*
5 it might/would be as well *spoken* used to give someone advice or make a helpful suggestion: *It might be as well to make him rest for a few days.*
6 all is well/all is not well *formal* used to say that a situation

W

is satisfactory or not satisfactory: *All is not well with their marriage.*
7 all's well that ends well used to say that a difficult situation has ended with a good result. It is the title of a humorous play by William Shakespeare about the relationship between the two main characters, Helena and Bertram.

well[4] ●●○ *n* [C]
1 a deep hole in the ground from which people take water: *She lowered her bucket into the well.*
2 an OIL WELL
3 the space in a tall building where the stairs are

well[5] (*also* **well up**) *v* [I] *literary* **1** if a liquid wells or wells up, it comes to the surface of something and starts to flow out: *I felt* ***tears well up*** *in my eyes.* **2** if a feeling wells or wells up in you, you start to feel it strongly: *Anger welled up within him.*

we'll /wil; *strong* wiːl/ the short form of 'we will' or 'we shall'

ˌwell-adˈjusted *adj* emotionally healthy and able to deal well with the problems of life OPP **maladjusted**: *a happy, well-adjusted child*

ˌwell-adˈvised *adj* **you would be well-advised to do sth** used when you are strongly advising someone to do something that will help them avoid trouble: *You would be well-advised to accept his offer.*

ˌwell-apˈpointed *adj formal* a well-appointed room, house, or hotel has attractive furniture and all the equipment that you need: *He showed me to a large, well-appointed room.*

ˌwell-atˈtended *adj* if a meeting, event etc is well-attended, a lot of people go to it

ˌwell-ˈbalanced *adj* **1** a well-balanced meal or DIET contains all the different things you need to keep you healthy **2** a well-balanced person is sensible and does not allow strong emotions to control their behaviour

ˌwell-beˈhaved *adj* behaving in a calm polite way, and not being rude or violent: *a well-behaved child | a very well-behaved dog | The crowd was well-behaved.* THESAURUS ▸ POLITE

> **REGISTER**
> In everyday English, people often say that a child is **good** rather than **well-behaved**: *Have the children been good?*

ˌwell-ˈbeing ●○○ *n* [U]
1 a feeling of being comfortable, healthy, and happy: **[+of]** *We are responsible for the care and well-being of all our patients.* | **a sense/feeling of well-being** *A good meal promotes a feeling of well-being.* | **physical/psychological/material etc well-being** *the physical and emotional well-being of the children*
2 the well-being of a country is the state in which it is strong and doing well: *We are now concerned for the* ***economic well-being*** *of the country.*

ˌwell-ˈborn *adj formal* born into a very rich or important family

ˌwell-ˈbred *adj old-fashioned* someone who is well-bred is polite, and behaves as if they come from a family of high social class: *a well-bred, courteous man*

ˌwell-brought-ˈup *adj* a child who is well-brought-up has been taught to be polite and to behave well

ˌwell-ˈbuilt *adj* someone who is well-built has a big strong body THESAURUS ▸ STRONG

ˌwell-ˈchosen *adj* chosen carefully and so very suitable: *good food and well-chosen wines | He encouraged us with a few* ***well-chosen words.***

ˌwell-conˈnected *adj* someone who is well-connected knows a lot of powerful important people

ˌwell-deˈfined *adj* clear and easy to see or understand: *well-defined limits on spending*

ˌwell-deˈserved *adj* deserved because of very good or bad behaviour, work, skill etc: *a well-deserved victory*

ˌwell-deˈveloped *adj* fully developed or formed and able to function very well: *well-developed back muscles | well-developed reading skills*

ˌwell-disˈposed *adj* feeling friendly towards a person or positive about an idea or plan: **[+to/towards]** *I did not* ***feel*** *particularly* ***well-disposed*** *towards him.*

ˌwell-ˈdocumented *adj* if something is well-documented, people have written a lot about it and so the facts about it are clear: *His life is remarkably well-documented. | These are all well-documented facts.*

ˌwell-ˈdone *adj* meat that is well-done has been cooked thoroughly → **rare** → **well done!** at WELL[1](12)

ˌwell-ˈdrained *adj* well-drained soil allows water to pass through it easily

ˌwell-ˈdressed *adj* wearing attractive fashionable clothes: *an attractive, well-dressed young woman*

ˌwell-ˈearned *adj* something that is well-earned is something you deserve because you have worked hard: *a well-earned rest | a well-earned drink*

ˌwell-ˈeducated *adj* someone who is well-educated has had a lot of education and has a lot of knowledge about many different things

ˌwell-enˈdowed *adj informal* **1** a woman who is well-endowed has large breasts – often used humorously **2** a man who is well-endowed has a large PENIS – often used humorously

ˌwell-esˈtablished ●○○ *adj* something that is well-established has existed for a long time and is respected or trusted by people: *a well-established law firm | a well-established scientific theory*

ˌwell-ˈfed *adj* having plenty of good food to eat: *The animals all look happy and well-fed.*

ˌwell-ˈfounded *adj* a belief or feeling etc that is well-founded is based on facts or good judgment: *My suspicions proved to be well-founded.*

ˌwell-ˈgroomed *adj* someone who is well-groomed looks very neat and clean

ˌwell-ˈgrounded *adj* **1 well-grounded in sth** fully trained in an activity or skill: *The soldiers were well-grounded in survival skills.* **2** WELL-FOUNDED: *My fears were well-grounded.*

ˌwell-ˈheeled *adj informal* rich: *a well-heeled businessman*

ˌwell-ˈhung *adj informal* a man who is well-hung has a large PENIS – used humorously

wel·lie /ˈweli/ *n BrE* **1** [C] *informal* a WELLINGTON **2** [U] *spoken informal* physical effort or force that you use to move or hit something: *You need to* ***give it some wellie.***

ˌwell-inˈformed *adj* someone who is well-informed knows a lot about one particular subject or about many subjects: **[+about]** *Most people are not very well-informed about the disease. | We had a serious and well-informed debate.*

wel·ling·ton /ˈwelɪŋtən/ (*also* **ˌwellington ˈboot**) *n* [C] *BrE* a rubber boot that stops your foot getting wet

ˌwell-inˈtentioned *adj* trying to be helpful to people, but actually making things worse for them: *well-intentioned grandparents who interfere between parents and children*

ˌwell-ˈkept *adj* **1** a well-kept building or garden is very well cared for and looks neat and clean THESAURUS ▸ TIDY **2** a well-kept secret is known only to a few people

ˌwell-ˈknown ●●○ *adj* (*comparative* **better-known**, *superlative* **best-known**) known by a lot of people → **notorious**: **it is well-known (that)** *It's a well-known fact that smoking can cause lung cancer. | This is probably their best-known song. | a well-known TV presenter |* **[+for]** *He was well-known for his extreme political views.* THESAURUS ▸ FAMOUS

ˌwell-ˈmannered *adj* talking and behaving in a polite way: *a well-mannered child* THESAURUS ▸ POLITE

ˌwell-ˈmeaning *adj* intending to be helpful, but not succeeding: *A lot of problems can be caused by well-meaning friends. | He's very well-meaning, but he doesn't really understand what's going on.*

W

ˌwell-ˈmeant *adj* something you say or do that is well-meant is intended to be helpful, but does not have the result you intended: *His comments were well-meant but a little tactless.*

well·ness /ˈwelnəs/ *n* [U] *AmE* the state of being healthy: *The college has established a wellness program for its students.*

ˈwell-nigh *adv old-fashioned* almost: *It will be* ***well-nigh impossible*** *to raise that amount of money.*

ˌwell-ˈoff *adj* (*comparative* **better-off**, *superlative* **best-off**) **1** having a lot of money, or enough money to have a good standard of living OPP **badly-off**: *children from well-off families* | *Many pensioners are* ***less well-off*** (=have less money) *than they used to be.* THESAURUS RICH **2 be well-off for sth** having plenty of something, or as much of it as you need: *We're well-off for public transport here.* **3 you don't know when you're well-off** *BrE spoken* used to tell someone that they are more fortunate than they realize

ˌwell-ˈoiled *adj* **a well-oiled machine** an organization or system that works very well

ˌwell-ˈpaid *adj* providing or receiving good wages: *a well-paid job* | *well-paid executives* THESAURUS EARN

ˌwell-preˈserved *adj* **1** someone who is well-preserved is getting old, but does not look as old as they are **2** a well-preserved building or object is old but still in good condition: *the remarkably well-preserved ruins of the church*

well-read /ˌwel ˈred◂/ *adj* someone who is well-read has read many books and knows a lot about different subjects

ˌwell-ˈrounded *adj* **1** a well-rounded person has a range of interests and skills and a variety of experience: *well-rounded graduates* **2** well-rounded education or experience of life is complete and varied: *She has a well-rounded background in management.* **3** a woman who is well-rounded has a pleasantly curved figure SYN **shapely**

ˌwell-ˈrun *adj* a well-run organization or business is managed well: *a small, well-run hotel*

ˌwell-ˈspoken *adj* speaking in a clear and polite way, and in a way that is considered correct

well·spring /ˈwelˌsprɪŋ/ *n* [C] *literary* **1** a large amount of a personal quality: **[+of]** *There was a wellspring of courage within her.* **2** the situation or place where something begins: **[+of]** *Las Vegas became the wellspring of a new style of family values.*

ˌwell-ˈstocked *adj* having a large supply and variety of things, especially food or drink: *a well-stocked supermarket*

ˌwell ˈthought of *adj* liked and admired by other people: *Her work is well thought of in academic circles.*

ˌwell-thought-ˈout *adj* carefully and thoroughly planned: *a well-thought-out design* | *All the menus are well-thought-out.*

ˌwell-ˈthumbed *adj* a well-thumbed book, magazine etc has been used a lot → **dog-eared**

ˌwell-ˈtimed *adj* said or done at the most suitable moment SYN **timely**: *a well-timed remark* | *My arrival wasn't very well-timed.*

ˌwell-to-ˈdo *adj* **1** rich and with a high social position: *well-to-do families* THESAURUS RICH **2 the well-to-do** people who are rich

ˌwell-ˈtried *adj* [only before noun] a well-tried method or principle has been used many times before and has always been successful SYN **tried and tested**: *a well-tried formula for success*

ˌwell-ˈtrodden *adj* **1 well-trodden path/track/route etc** *BrE* a path that is used a lot by people: *Follow the very well-trodden path to the summit.* **2** used to describe an idea or a course of action that has been used many times in the past: **well-trodden path/road/ground etc** *Andrew was on his well-trodden path to conquering another willing lady.*

ˌwell-ˈturned *adj* a well-turned phrase or sentence is carefully expressed

ˌwell-turned-ˈout *adj* someone who is well-turned-out wears nice, good quality clothes SYN **well-dressed**: *Our customers want to be served by people who are well-turned-out.*

ˌwell-ˈversed *adj* knowing a lot about something: **[+in]** *countries not so well-versed in technological advances as our own*

ˈwell-ˌwisher *n* [C] someone who shows by their behaviour that they like someone and want them to succeed, be happy etc: *The prince waved at the crowd of 600 well-wishers.*

ˌwell-ˈwoman *adj* [only before noun] providing medical care and advice for women, to make sure that they stay healthy: *a* ***well-woman clinic***

ˌwell-ˈworn *adj* **1** worn or used for a long time: *a well-worn jacket* **2** a well-worn expression, phrase etc has been repeated so often that it is no longer interesting or effective: *well-worn excuses*

wel·ly /ˈweli/ *n* (*plural* **wellies**) [C] *BrE informal* a WELLINGTON (=kind of boot)

welsh, **welch** /welʃ $ welʃ, weltʃ/ *v* [I] *informal* to not do something that you have promised to do, such as paying someone money that you owe: *I never welch on my bets.*

Welsh[1] /welʃ/ *adj* relating to Wales, its people, or its original language

Welsh[2] *n* **1 the Welsh** [plural] people from Wales **2** [U] the original language used in Wales

ˌWelsh ˈdresser *n* [C] *BrE* a piece of wooden furniture consisting of drawers and cupboards in the lower part and shelves on top SYN **hutch** *AmE*

ˌWelsh ˈrarebit (*also* **ˌWelsh ˈrabbit**) *n* [C,U] a dish of cheese melted on bread

welt /welt/ *n* [C] a painful raised mark on someone's skin, for example where they have been hit

wel·ter /ˈweltə $ -ər/ *n* **a welter of sth** a large and confusing amount or number of something: *There is a welter of information on the subject.*

wel·ter·weight /ˈweltəweɪt $ -ər-/ *n* [C] a BOXER who weighs less than 66.68 kilograms, and who is heavier than a LIGHTWEIGHT but lighter than a MIDDLEWEIGHT

Wem·bley /ˈwembli/ a large football ground in north-west London, England

wench /wentʃ/ *n* [C] *old use* a girl or young woman, especially a servant

wend /wend/ *v* **wend your way** *literary* to move or travel slowly from one place to another: **[+through/towards/home etc]** *The procession wended its way through the streets.*

wen·dy house /ˈwendi ˌhaʊs/ *n* [C] *BrE* a toy house that children can play inside SYN **playhouse** *AmE*

went /went/ *v* the past tense of GO

wept /wept/ the past tense and past participle of WEEP

were /wə; *strong* wɜː $ wər *strong* wɜːr/ a past tense of BE

we're /wɪə $ wɪr/ the short form of 'we are'

were·wolf /ˈweəwʊlf, ˈwɪə- $ ˈwer-, ˈwɪr-/ *n* (*plural* **werewolves** /-wʊlvz/) [C] a person who, in stories, changes into a WOLF every month when the moon is full

wert /wɜːt $ wɜːrt/ *v* **thou wert** *old use* you were

west[1], **West** /west/ ●●● S1 W2 *n* [singular, U]
1 the direction towards which the sun goes down, and which is on the left if you are facing north: **from/towards the west** *A damp wind blew from the west.* | **to the west (of sth)** *a village to the west of Brussels*
2 the west the western part of a country or area: *There's a slight chance of some sunshine in the west.* | **[+of]** *the west of the island*

west[2], **West** ●●● S3 W3 *adj* [only before noun] (*written abbreviation* **W**)
1 in the west or facing the west: *the west door of the church* | *farmers in West Africa*
2 a west wind comes from the west

west[3] ●●● S3 W3 *adv* (*written abbreviation* **W**)
1 towards the west: *The route then heads west over Gerrick*

Moor. | **[+of]** *The walk starts at Alnham, six miles west of Bridge of Aln.* | *a west-facing window*
2 out west to or in the western part of a country or area, especially the US: *The family moved out west to Kansas.*
3 go west *BrE old-fashioned* **a)** to die - used humorously **b)** to be damaged or ruined - used humorously

West *n* **1 the West** the western part of the world and the people that live there, especially Western Europe and North America: *the industrial countries of the West* **2** the western part of the US → MIDWEST, WEST COAST

west·bound /ˈwestbaʊnd/ *adj* travelling or leading towards the west: *Westbound traffic is moving very slowly.* | *an accident on the westbound carriageway of the motorway*

ˈWest Coast *n* **the West Coast** the part of the US that is next to the Pacific Ocean

ˈWest ˌCountry *n* **the West Country** the parts of England that are furthest south and west, especially Devon and Cornwall

ˌWest ˈEnd *n* **the West End** the western part of central London, where there are large shops, theatres, expensive hotels etc

west·er·ly¹ /ˈwestəli $ -ərli/ *adj* **1** towards or in the west: *We set off* ***in a westerly direction.*** **2** a westerly wind comes from the west

westerly² *n* (*plural* **westerlies**) [C] a wind that comes from the west

west·ern¹, **Western** /ˈwestən $ -ərn/ ●●● S2 W2 *adj* (*written abbreviation* **W**)
1 in or from the west of a country or area: *the western end of the bay* | *Western Australia*
2 relating to ideas and ways of doing things that come from Europe and the Americas: *Western philosophies*
→ COUNTRY AND WESTERN

western² *n* [C] a film about life in the 19th century in the American West, especially the lives of COWBOYS
THESAURUS ▸ MOVIE

West·ern·er /ˈwestənə $ -tərnər/ *n* [C] **1** someone from the western part of the world **2** *AmE* someone from the western part of the US

west·ern·ize (*also* **-ise** *BrE*) /ˈwestənaɪz $ -ər-/ *v* [T] to bring customs, business methods etc that are typical of Europe and the US to other countries: *Tunisian culture has been westernized.* GRAMMAR **Westernize** is usually passive. —**westernization** /ˌwestənaɪˈzeɪʃən $ -tərnə-/ *n* [U]

west·ern·ized (*also* **-ised** *BrE*) /ˈwestənaɪzd $ -ər/ *adj* using the customs, behaviour etc typical of the US or Europe: *westernised economies*

ˌwestern ˈmedicine *n* [U] the type of medical treatment that is standard in Europe and North America → **alternative medicine**

west·ern·most /ˈwestənməʊst $ -tərnmoʊst/ *adj* furthest west: *the westernmost tip of the island*

West·min·ster /ˈwestmɪnstəʳ, westˈmɪnstəʳ◂/ the British Houses of Parliament: *Westminster was buzzing with anticipation today as MPs gathered for tonight's crucial vote.*

west·ward /ˈwestwəd $ -wərd/ (*also* **west·wards** /-wədz $ -wərdz/) *adv* towards the west: *The ship turned westward, away from the coast.* —**westward** *adj*: *westward flights*

wet¹ /wet/ ●●● S2 W3 *adj* (*comparative* **wetter**, *superlative* **wettest**)
1 WATER/LIQUID covered in or full of water or another liquid OPP **dry**: *I've washed your shirt but it's still wet.* | *wet grass* | **get (sth) wet** *Take an umbrella or you'll get wet.* | **[+with]** *His face was wet with sweat.* | *The man in the boat was* ***wet through*** (=completely wet). | **soaking/dripping/sopping wet** (=very wet) *The towel was soaking wet.*
2 WEATHER rainy: *There's more* ***wet weather*** *on the way.* | ***It's*** *very* ***wet*** *outside.* | *the wettest summer on record*
3 PAINT/INK ETC not yet dry: *The paint's still wet.*
4 PERSON *BrE informal* someone who is wet does not have a strong character, or is not willing to do something that you think they should do - used to show disapproval: *Don't be so wet! Just tell them you don't want to go.*
5 BABY if a child or its NAPPY is wet, the nappy is full of URINE
6 sb is all wet *AmE informal* someone is completely wrong
7 wet behind the ears *informal* very young and without much experience of life —**wetly** *adv* —**wetness** *n* [U]

wet² ●●○ *v* (*past tense and past participle* **wet** *or* **wetted**, *present participle* **wetting**) [T]
1 to make something wet: *Wet your hair and apply the shampoo.*
2 to make yourself, your clothes, or your bed wet because you pass water from your body by accident: **wet yourself** *I nearly wet myself I was so scared.* | *Sam's* **wet** *his* **bed** *again.*

wet³ *n* **1 the wet** the rain: **in the wet** *The path is steep and dangerous in the wet.* **2** [C] *BrE* a politician who belongs to the CONSERVATIVE party, and who supports very MODERATE ideas - used to show disapproval: *Tory wets* **3** [C] *BrE informal* someone who does not have a strong character, or is not willing to do something that you think they should do - used to show disapproval: *Go on! Don't be such a wet!*

wet·back /ˈwetbæk/ *n* [C] *AmE taboo* a very offensive word for someone from Mexico who has come to the US illegally. Do not use this word.

ˈwet bar *n* [C] *AmE* a small bar with equipment for making alcoholic drinks, in a house, hotel room etc

ˌwet ˈblanket / $ ˈ. ˌ../ *n* [C] *informal* someone who seems to want to spoil other people's fun, for example by

THESAURUS: wet

wet covered in water or another liquid: *I've just washed my hair and it's still wet.* | *You'd better change out of those wet clothes.*
damp slightly wet: *Wipe the surfaces with a damp cloth.* | *The sheets are still a little damp.*
moist slightly wet, especially in a pleasant way - used about soil, food, or about someone's skin or eyes: *It's important to keep the soil moist.* | *a delicious moist chocolate cake* | *Her eyes became moist* (=she was almost crying).
clammy feeling slightly wet, cold, and sticky - used about someone's skin, especially when they are nervous or ill: *He had clammy hands.* | *Ruby was feverish and clammy with sweat.*
soggy unpleasantly wet and soft - used especially about food or the ground: *a bowl of soggy rice* | *It had been raining hard and the ground was soggy underfoot.*
humid/muggy used when the weather is hot but the air feels wet in a way that makes you uncomfortable: *Summers in Tokyo are hot and humid.* | *a hot muggy day*

VERY WET

soaked [not before noun] very wet all the way through - used especially about people and their clothes: *It absolutely poured with rain and we got soaked.* | *His shirt was soaked with blood.*
drenched [not before noun] very wet - used about a person or area after a lot of rain or water has fallen on them: *Everyone got drenched when a huge wave hit the boat.* | *The garden was completely drenched after the rain.*
saturated extremely wet, and unable to take in any more water or liquid: *His bandage was saturated with blood.* | *The floods were the result of heavy rainfall on already saturated soil.*
waterlogged /ˈwɔːtəlɒgd $ ˈwɒːtərlɒːgd, ˈwɑː-, -lɑːgd/ used about ground that has water on its surface because it is so wet that it cannot take in any more: *The game was cancelled because the field was waterlogged.*
sodden *BrE* very wet with water - used about clothes and the ground. **Sodden** is less common than **soaked**: *The ground was still sodden.* | *He took off his sodden shirt.*

refusing to join them in something enjoyable that they are doing

ˌwet ˈdream *n* [C] a sexually exciting dream that a man has, resulting in an ORGASM

ˌwet ˈfish *n* [U] *BrE* fresh uncooked fish that is on sale in a shop

wet·land /ˈwetlənd/ *n* [C often plural, U] an area of land that is partly covered with water, or is wet most of the time

ˈwet-look *adj* [only before noun] wet-look clothes have a shiny surface so that they look as if they are wet

ˈwet nurse *n* [C] *old use* a woman paid to give her breast milk to another woman's baby

ˈwet-nurse *v* [T] to give someone too much care and attention, as if they were a child

ˈwet suit *n* [C] a tight piece of clothing, usually made of rubber, worn by people who are swimming, SURFING etc in the sea

ˈwetting ˌagent *n* [C] a chemical substance which, when spread on a solid surface, makes it hold liquid

ˈwetting soˌlution *n* [C,U] a liquid used for storing CONTACT LENSes in, or for making them more comfortable to wear

we've /wiv; *strong* wiːv/ the short form of 'we have'

whack¹ /wæk/ *v* [T] *informal* **1** to hit someone or something hard: **whack sb/sth with sth** *He kept whacking the dog with a stick.* **THESAURUS** HIT **2** *BrE spoken* to put something somewhere: **whack sth in/on/under etc sth** *Just whack the bacon under the grill for a couple of minutes.*

whack² *n* [C] *especially spoken* **1** the act of hitting something hard, or the noise this makes: *She* ***gave*** *the ball* ***a whack.*** | *Singleton* ***took a whack at*** (=tried to hit) *Miller's head.* **2** *BrE* an amount of something: **(the) full whack** *If you're unemployed, you don't have to* ***pay*** *the* ***full whack*** (=the full amount). | *There's still* ***a fair whack*** (=quite a large amount) *of work to be done.* | *These agencies charge* ***top whack*** *for tickets.* **3 do your whack (of sth)** *BrE* to do a fair or equal share of a job or activity: *I've done my whack of the driving – it's your turn.* **4 have a whack at sth** *BrE*, **take a whack at sth** *AmE* to try to do something: *'Are you any good at doing maths?' 'I'll have a whack at it.'* **5 in one whack** *AmE* all on one occasion: *Steve lost $500 in one whack.* **6 out of whack** *AmE* if a system, machine etc is out of whack, the parts are not working together correctly: *The printer's out of whack again.*

whacked /wækt/ *adj* [not before noun] *informal* **1** (*also* **whacked out**) very tired: *You look absolutely whacked.* **2 whacked out** *AmE* behaving strangely, especially because of having too much alcohol or drugs **3** (*also* **whack**) *AmE informal* a whacked situation is very strange, especially in an unacceptable way: *Everyone was running around naked. It was totally whacked.*

whack·ing /ˈwækɪŋ/ *adv* **whacking great** *BrE spoken* very big SYN **whopping**: *a whacking great gas bill*

whac·ko /ˈwækəʊ $ -oʊ/ *n, adj* another spelling of WACKO

whac·ky /ˈwæki/ *adj* another spelling of WACKY

whale¹ /weɪl/ ●●○ *n* [C]

1 a very large animal that lives in the sea and looks like a fish, but is actually a MAMMAL

2 have a whale of a time *informal* to enjoy yourself very much

whale² *v* [I] *AmE* **whale into/on sb/sth** to start hitting someone or something

whale·bone /ˈweɪlbəʊn $ -boʊn/ *n* [U] a hard substance taken from the upper jaw of whales, used in the past for making women's clothes stiff

whal·er /ˈweɪlə $ -ər/ *n* [C] **1** someone who hunts whales **2** a boat used to hunt whales

whal·ing /ˈweɪlɪŋ/ *n* [U] the activity of hunting WHALES

wham /wæm/ *interjection* **1** used to describe the sound of something suddenly hitting something else very hard: *Wham! The car hit the wall.* **2** used to express the idea that something very unexpected suddenly happens: *Life is going along nicely and then, wham, you lose your job.* —**wham** *n* [C]

wham·my /ˈwæmi/ *n* [singular] *informal* **1 double/triple whammy** two or three unpleasant things that happen at or around the same time and cause problems or difficulties for someone or for people in general: *The government's policy is higher tax and higher interest rates. It's a double whammy.* **2 put the whammy on sb** *AmE* to use magic to make someone have bad luck

wharf /wɔːf $ wɔːrf/ *n* (*plural* **wharves** /wɔːvz $ wɔːrvz/) [C] a structure that is built out into the water so that boats can stop next to it

whas·sup, **wassup** /ˈwɒsʌp $ ˈwɑː-/ *interjection informal* used to say 'hello' to people you know very well – used especially by young people

what /wɒt $ wɑːt, wʌt/ ●●● S1 W1 *pron, determiner, predeterminer*

1 used to ask for information or for someone's opinion: *What are you doing?* | *What subjects did you enjoy most?* | *What colour is the new carpet?* | *What's your new boss like?* | *What do you think of my painting?* | *What do you mean, you want to spend Christmas alone?* | **what on earth/in the world/in heaven's name etc** (=used for emphasis when you are surprised, angry etc) *What on earth's going on?*

USAGE: What, which

When there are only a small number of possible things or people, you use **which**, not **what**: *Which leg did he break?* | *Which brother do you mean?* ✗ Don't say: *What leg did he break?* | *What brother do you mean?*

2 used to introduce a CLAUSE about something that is or was not known or not certain: *No one knows exactly what happened.* | *It is not clear to what extent these views were shared.* | **what to do/say/expect etc** *They're discussing what to do next.*

3 the thing which: *Show me what you bought.* | *I believe what he told me.* | *I could get you a job here if that's what you want.* | *What he did was morally wrong.* | *She gave him what money she had* (=all the money she had, although she did not have much).

GRAMMAR

What is not a relative pronoun and should not be used to begin a clause after a noun or pronoun. Use **that** instead. You say: *There are so many things that can go wrong.* ✗ Don't say: *There are so many things what can go wrong.*

4 used at the beginning of a statement to emphasize what you are going to say: *What that kid needs is some love and affection.* | *What we'll do is leave a note for Mum to tell her we won't be back till late.* | *What matters is the British people and British jobs.*

SPOKEN PHRASES

5 what? a) used to ask someone to repeat something they have just said because you did not hear it properly: *'Could you turn the music down a bit?' 'What?'* **b)** used when you have heard someone calling to you and you are asking them what they want: *'Elaine!' 'What?' 'Come on!'* **c)** used to show that you are surprised or shocked by something that someone has just said: *'I think I've lost my passport.' 'What?'*

6 used at the beginning of a sentence to emphasize that you think something or someone is very good, very bad etc: *What a lovely day!* | *What a horrible thing to do!* | *What nice people they are!*

7 used to ask someone to complete a name when they have only given you the first part of it: *'Do you know his name?' 'It's David.' 'David what?'*

8 what about ...? a) used to make a suggestion: *What about dinner at my place next week?* | **what about doing sth**

What about going to a movie? **b)** (*also* **what of ...?** *formal*) used to introduce a new subject into a conversation, or to mention something or someone else that also needs to be considered: *What about Patrick? What's he doing nowadays? | What about me? Aren't I coming too? | So that's the food – now what about the wine? | And what of her other job? How is that progressing?*

9 what (...) for? a) used to ask why someone does something: *'She's decided to work part-time.' 'What for?' | What did you do that for?* **b)** used to ask what purpose or use something has: *What's this gadget for?*

10 used to give yourself time to think before guessing a number or amount: *You're looking at, what, about £4,000 for a decent second-hand car.*

11 what's his/her/its name (*also* **what d'you call him/her/it, what's his/her face**) used when talking about a person or thing whose name you cannot immediately remember: *The hospital have just got a, what d'you call it, er ... a scanner. | Is what's his name still working there?*

12 (and) what's more used when adding information that emphasizes what you are saying: *Gas is a very efficient fuel. And what's more, it's clean.*

13 what's what the real facts about a situation that are important to know: *She's been working here long enough to know what's what.*

14 what's it to you? used to tell someone angrily that something does not concern them: *That's right, I didn't pass. What's it to you, anyway? | 'How did he die?' Suddenly Emily was angry. 'What's it to you?'*

15 ... or what a) used at the end of a question to show that you are impatient with someone or something: *Are you afraid of him, or what? | Is that work going to be finished by Friday, or what?* **b)** used after mentioning one or more possibilities to show that you are not certain about something: *I don't know whether it was an accident or on purpose or what.* **c)** used after a description of someone or something to emphasize it: *Nearby are the remains of a deserted village. Spooky or what? | Is that madness or what?*

16 so what? (*also* **what of it?**) used to say that you do not care about something or think it is important: *'Your room looks a real mess, Tracey.' 'So what?' | 'But, Paul, she's so much older than you.' 'What of it?'*

17 you what? a) *BrE* used to ask someone to repeat something they have just said. It is more polite to say PARDON: *'I want to tell you something.' 'You what? I can't hear what you're saying.'* **b)** used to show that you are surprised: *'So I resigned.' 'You what?'*

18 what if ...? a) used to ask what you should do or what the result will be if something happens, especially something unpleasant: *What if this plan of yours fails, what then? | 'What if it rains tomorrow?' 'We'll just have to postpone it.'* **b)** used to make a suggestion: *What if we moved the sofa over here? Would that look better?*

19 ... and what have you used at the end of a list of things to mean other things of a similar kind: *The shelves were crammed with books, documents, and what have you.*

20 what with sth used to introduce a list of reasons that have made something happen or made someone feel in a particular way: *She couldn't get to sleep, what with all the shooting and shouting.*

21 what's with sb? *AmE* used to ask why a person or group of people is behaving strangely: *What's with you people?*

22 what's with sth? *AmE* used to ask the reason for something: *What's with all the sad faces?*

23 now what? used to ask what is going to happen next, what you should do etc

24 what's not to like/love? *especially AmE* used to say that something has no bad qualities or features: *What's not to like about this book?*

→ **what does it matter?** at MATTER²(3), → **what does sb care** at CARE²(6), → **have what it takes** at TAKE¹(4), → **I/I'll tell you what** at TELL(13), → **guess what** at GUESS¹(6)

what·cha·ma·call·it /ˈwɒtʃəməˌkɔːlɪt $ ˈwɑːtʃəməˌkɒːl-, ˈwʌtʃ-/ *n* [C] *spoken* a word you use when you cannot remember the name of something: *I've broken the whatchamacallit on my bag.*

what·ev·er¹ /wɒtˈevə $ wɑːˈtevər, wʌt-/ ●●● S1 W1 *determiner, pron*

1 any or all of the things that are wanted, needed, or possible: *Help yourself to whatever you want. | The children were allowed to do whatever they liked. | He'll be ready to accept whatever help he can get. | I am willing to pay whatever price you ask.*

2 used to say that it is not important what happens, what you do etc because it does not change the situation: *Whatever I suggest, he always disagrees. | The building must be saved, whatever the cost. | If you are unable to attend the interview, for whatever reason, you should inform us immediately.*

SPOKEN PHRASES

3 whatever you do used to tell someone that it is very important that they do a particular thing, or do not do it: *Don't miss the train, whatever you do. | Whatever you do, slow down and take your time.*

4 used to say that you do not know the exact meaning of something, or the exact name of someone or something: *The doctor says she's got fibrositis, whatever that is. | Why don't you invite Seb, or whatever he's called, to supper?*

5 ... or/and whatever (else) used after mentioning one or two things to mean other things of the same kind: *You could put an advert in some magazine, journal, newspaper, or whatever.*

6 used when asking a question to emphasize that you are surprised or slightly angry about something: *Whatever can he mean? | 'Did you know she's dyed her hair orange?'* **'Whatever next?'**

7 used as a reply to say that you do not care what is done or chosen, or that the exact details of something do not matter: *'What flavour do you want? Strawberry, vanilla ...?' 'Whatever.' | 'It was Monday, not Tuesday.' 'Whatever.'*

8 whatever you say/think/want used to tell someone that you agree with them or will do what they want, especially when you do not really agree or want to do it: *'How about camping, just for a change?' 'OK, whatever you want.' | 'I think we'd better discuss this with your parents.' 'Whatever you think best.'*

whatever² ●●● S2 *adv* used to emphasize a negative statement SYN **whatsoever**: *She has shown no interest whatever in anything scientific. | This is just a stupid argument that has nothing whatever to do with your job.*

ˈwhat-if *n* [C usually plural] *informal* something that could happen in the future or could have happened in the past: *If I thought about all of the what-ifs in my life, I would go crazy.*

what·not /ˈwɒtnɒt $ ˈwɑːtnɑːt, ˈwʌt-/ *n* **and whatnot** *spoken* an expression used at the end of a list of things when you do not want to give the names of everything: *Put your bags, cases, and whatnot in the back of the car.*

whats·it /ˈwɒtsɪt $ ˈwɑːts-, ˈwʌts-/ *n* [C] *spoken* a word you use when you cannot think of the word you want: *Try and undo the screw to get the whatsit off.*

what·so·ev·er /ˌwɒtsəʊˈevə $ ˌwɑːtsoʊˈevər, ˌwʌt-/ ●●○ *adv* used to emphasize a negative statement SYN **whatever**: *He's had no luck whatsoever.*

wheat /wiːt/ ●●○ *n* [U]

1 the grain that bread is made from, or the plant that it grows on: *a field of wheat*

2 separate the wheat from the chaff to choose the good and useful things or people and get rid of the others

wheat·germ /ˈwiːtdʒɜːm $ -dʒɜːrm/ *n* [U] the centre of a grain of wheat, which is good for your health and is added to other food

wheat·meal /ˈwiːtmiːl/ *n* [U] *BrE* a brown flour made from whole grains of wheat

whee /wiː/ *interjection* used to express happiness or excitement, especially by or to children

whee·dle /ˈwiːdl/ *v* [T] to persuade someone to do or give you something, for example by saying nice things to them that you do not mean – used to show disapproval: **wheedle sth from/out of sb** *She even managed to wheedle more money out of him.* | **wheedle sb into doing sth** *You have* *to be able to wheedle your client into buying.* | **wheedle your way in/into/out of etc** *Don't think you can just wheedle your way in here!*

wheel¹ /wiːl/ ●●● S2 W3 *n* [C]
1 ON A VEHICLE one of the round things under a car, bus, bicycle etc that turns when it moves: **front/rear/back wheels** *The car slid sideways, its rear* ***wheels spinning.*** → FOUR-WHEEL DRIVE, see picture at MOTORBIKE
2 FOR CONTROLLING A VEHICLE [usually singular] the round piece of equipment that you turn to make a car, ship etc move in a particular direction: **at/behind the wheel** (=driving a car) *The driver must have* ***fallen asleep at the wheel.*** | *Shall I* ***take the wheel*** (=drive instead of someone else)? → STEERING WHEEL
3 IN A MACHINE a flat round part in a machine that turns round when the machine operates: *a gear wheel*
4 the wheels of sth the way in which a complicated organization, system etc works: *We hope that the next government will do more to keep* ***the wheels of industry*** *turning* (=help it to work smoothly and easily). | **oil/grease the wheels (of sth)** (=help something to work more smoothly and easily) *The money people spend at Christmas oils the wheels of the economy.*
5 the wheel of fortune/life/time etc the way in which things change in life, or in which the same things seem to happen again after a period of time: *We are powerless to stop the wheel of history.*
6 (set of) wheels *spoken* a car: *Do you like my new wheels?*
7 wheels within wheels *spoken* used to say that a situation is complicated and difficult to understand because it involves processes and decisions that you know nothing about
8 set the wheels in motion/set the wheels turning to make a particular process start: *It only took one phone call to set the wheels in motion.*
9 the wheels come off sth used to say that something suddenly stops being successful: *Why did the wheels come off his campaign?*
10 a/the big wheel *informal* an important person: *He became a big wheel in the East India Company.* → **put your shoulder to the wheel** at SHOULDER¹(8), → **put a spoke in sb's wheel** at SPOKE²(2), → **reinvent the wheel** at REINVENT(3)

wheel² ●○○ *v*
1 [T always + adv/prep] **a)** to push something that has wheels somewhere: *Kate wheeled her bike into the garage.* **b)** to move someone or something that is in or on something that has wheels: *Two nurses were wheeling him into the operating theatre.* THESAURUS PUSH
2 [I] if birds or planes wheel, they fly around in circles
3 [I] to turn around suddenly: **[+around]** *She wheeled around and started yelling at us.*
4 wheel and deal to do a lot of complicated and sometimes dishonest deals, especially in politics or business

wheel sb/sth ↔ **in/out** *phr v informal* to publicly produce someone or something and use them to help you achieve something: *Then the prosecution wheeled in a surprise witness.* | *The government wheeled out the same old arguments to support its election campaign.*

wheel·bar·row /ˈwiːlˌbærəʊ $ -roʊ/ *n* [C] a small CART with one wheel and two handles that you use outdoors to carry things, especially in the garden

wheel·base /ˈwiːlbeɪs/ *n* [C] *technical* the distance between the front and back AXLEs of a vehicle

wheel·chair /ˈwiːltʃeə $ -tʃer/ ●●○ *n* [C] a chair with wheels, used by people who cannot walk: **in a wheelchair** *He'll be in a wheelchair for the rest of his life.* | *Lynn has been* ***confined to a wheelchair*** (=has had to use a wheelchair) *for the last year.* | *special parking for* ***wheelchair users*** → see picture at CHAIR¹

ˈwheel clamp (*also* **clamp**) *n* [C] a metal object that is fastened to the wheel of an illegally parked car so that it cannot be driven away SYN **denver boot** *AmE* —**wheel-clamp** *v* [T]

wheeled /wiːld/ *adj* having wheels: **two-wheeled/three-wheeled/four-wheeled etc** (=having two, three etc wheels) *a three-wheeled car*

ˌwheeler-ˈdealer *n* [C] someone who does a lot of complicated, often dishonest deals, especially in business or politics

wheel·house /ˈwiːlhaʊs/ *n* [C] the place on a ship where the CAPTAIN stands at the WHEEL

wheel·ie /ˈwiːli/ *n informal* **do a wheelie** (*also* **pop a wheelie** *AmE*) to lift the front wheel of a bicycle that you are riding off the ground, so that you are balancing on the back wheel

ˈwheelie bin *n* [C] *BrE* a large container with wheels, that you keep outside your house for putting waste into → see picture at BIN¹

ˌwheeling and ˈdealing *n* [U] activities that involve a lot of complicated and sometimes dishonest deals, especially in business or politics

wheel·wright /ˈwiːlraɪt/ *n* [C] someone whose job was to make and repair the wooden wheels of vehicles pulled by horses in the past

wheeze¹ /wiːz/ *v* [I] to breathe with difficulty, making a noise in your throat and chest THESAURUS BREATHE

wheeze² *n* [C] **1** the act or sound of wheezing **2** *BrE old-fashioned* a clever and amusing idea or plan **3** *AmE* an old joke that no one thinks is funny now

wheez·y /ˈwiːzi/ *adj* making a noisy sound in your throat or chest, because you cannot breathe easily: *You sound wheezy.* | *a wheezy cough* —**wheezily** *adv* —**wheeziness** *n* [U]

whelk /welk/ *n* [C] a small sea animal that has a shell and can be eaten

whelp¹ /welp/ *n* [C] a young animal, especially a dog or lion

whelp² *v* [I] *old-fashioned* if a dog or lion whelps, it gives birth

when /wen/ ●●● S1 W1 *adv, conjunction, pron*
1 at what time: *When are we leaving?* | *When did you first meet Dr Darnall?* | *When will the work be finished?* | *I don't know when I'll see her again.* | **when to do sth** *I'll tell you when to stop.*
2 at or during the time that something happens: *Leonard was nine when his father died.* | *When the family came here from Russia, they were penniless.* | *When he was in the air force he flew Tornado jets.*
3 after or as soon as something happens: *When the meal was finished, Rachel washed up and made coffee.* | *I'll phone you again when I get home.*
4 used to mention a type of event or situation when talking about what happens on occasions of that type: *When lead is added to petrol, it improves the car's performance.* | *When mixed with water the powder forms a smooth paste.* | *He always wears glasses except when playing football.*
5 used to show which particular time or occasion you are talking about: *The best moment was when he scored the winning goal.* | *There are times when I hate him.* | **the day/time/afternoon etc when** *She remembered the day when Paula had first arrived.*
6 by/since when before or since which time: *The baby is due in May, by when the new house should be finished.* | *That was written in 1946, since when the education system has undergone great changes.*
7 since when ...? *spoken* used to show that you are very surprised or angry: *Since when have you been interested in my feelings?*
8 even though something is true: *Why does she steal things when she could easily afford to buy them?*
9 used to introduce a fact or statement that makes something seem surprising: *When you consider that the airline handled 80 million passengers last year, the accident figures are really very small.*

GRAMMAR: Choosing the right tense

• You use the present tense with **when**: *What are you planning to do when you leave college?*
• Don't use 'will' in the clause after **when**. ✗ Don't say: *What are you planning to do when you will leave college?*

• You can also use the present perfect tense with **when**: *What are you planning to do when your course has finished?*
• When talking about the past, you can use the past perfect tense with **when**: *When the rain had stopped, they went outside.*
GRAMMAR GUIDE ▶ **VERBS**

whence /wens/ *adv, pron old use* from where: *I walked to Rainbagh, whence I could complete the journey by car.* → **WHITHER**

when·ev·er /wen'evə $ -'evər/ ●●● S2 W3 *adv, conjunction*
1 every time that a particular thing happens: *Larry always blames me whenever anything goes wrong.* | *Whenever I hear that tune, it makes me think of you.*
2 at any time: *Come and visit me whenever you want.* | *a policy of using recycled paper* ***whenever possible***
3 *spoken* used as a reply to say that it does not matter what time something happens: *'I'll call you tomorrow or the day after.' 'Okay. Whenever.'*

where /weə $ wer/ ●●● S1 W1 *adv, conjunction, pron*
1 in or to which place: *Where are you going?* | *Where do they live?* | *Do you know where my glasses are?* | *Where would you like to sit?* | **where (...) to/from** *Where have you come from?* | *'We're going on a long journey.' 'Where to?'* | **where to do sth** *They're easy to find, if you know where to look.* | **where on earth/in the world etc** (=used for emphasis when you are surprised, angry etc) *Where on earth have you been all this time?*
2 used to talk about a particular place: *She was standing exactly where you are standing now.* | *Stay where you are.* | *This is the place where I hid the key.* | *In 1963 we moved to Boston, where my grandparents lived.*
3 used to talk about a particular stage in a process, conversation, story etc: *The treatment will continue until the patient reaches the point where he can walk correctly and safely.* | *You are saying that everyone should be equal, and this is where I disagree.* | *Now, where were we? Oh yes, we were talking about John.*
4 used to ask or talk about the origin of something or someone: *Where does the word 'super' come from?* | *Where does this man get the money to keep two houses?* | *I wonder where he gets these strange ideas.*
5 used to say that one person, thing, opinion etc is different from another: *Where others might have been satisfied, Dawson had higher ambitions.*
6 in or to any place SYN **wherever**: *You can sit where you like.* | *You're free to go where you please.*

where·a·bouts[1] /ˌweərə'baʊts◂ $ 'werəbaʊts/ ●●○ *adv spoken* used to ask in what general area something or someone is: *Whereabouts do you live?*

where·a·bouts[2] /'weərəbaʊts $ 'wer-/ ●○○ *n* [plural] the place or area where someone or something is: *He showed great reluctance to reveal his whereabouts.* | **[+of]** *The police want to know the whereabouts of his brother.*
THESAURUS ▶ **PLACE**

where·as /weər'æz $ wer-/ ●●○ W2 AWL *conjunction*
1 *formal* used to say that although something is true of one thing, it is not true of another: *The old system was fairly complicated whereas the new system is really very simple.* | *Whereas the city spent over $1 billion on its museums and stadium, it failed to look after its schools.*
THESAURUS ▶ **BUT**
2 *law* used at the beginning of an official document to mean 'because of a particular fact'

where·by /weə'baɪ $ wer-/ ●●○ AWL *adv formal* by means of which or according to which: *a proposal whereby EU citizens would be allowed to reside anywhere in the EU*

where·fore /'weəfɔː $ 'werfɔːr/ *adv, conjunction old use* used to ask why: *Wherefore art thou Romeo?* → **whys and wherefores** at **WHY**[3]

where·in /weər'ɪn $ wer-/ *adv, conjunction formal* in which place or part: *Wherein lies the difference between conservatism and liberalism?*

where·of /weər'ɒv $ wer'ʌv, -'ɑːv/ *adv, conjunction old use* of what or of which

where·on /weər'ɒn $ wer'ɒːn, -'ɑːn/ *adv, conjunction old use* on which

where·so·ever /ˌweəsəʊ'evə $ 'wersoʊˌevər/ *adv, conjunction literary* another word for WHEREVER

where·to /weə'tuː $ wer-/ *adv, conjunction old use* to which place

where·u·pon /ˌweərə'pɒn $ 'werəpɑːn, -pɒːn/ *conjunction formal* used when something happens immediately after something else, or as a result of something happening: *She refused to hand over her money, whereupon there was a fight.*

wher·ev·er /weər'evə $ wer'evər/ ●●● S2 *adv*
1 to or at any place, position, or situation: *Children will play wherever they happen to be.* | *Sit wherever you like.* | **... or wherever** (=used to emphasize that you are talking about any place and not a specific place) *Dublin people dress more individually than people in London or wherever.*
2 in all places that: *She is shadowed by detectives wherever she goes.* | *I feel I ought to be nice to them* ***wherever possible*** (=at all times when it is possible).
3 used at the beginning of a question to show surprise: *'Wherever did she find that?' Daisy wondered.*
4 wherever that is/may be used to say that you do not know where a place or town is or have never heard of it: *She wants to move to Far Flatley, wherever that is.*

where·with·al /'weəwɪðɔːl $ 'werwɪðɒːl/ *n* **the wherewithal to do sth** the money, skill etc that you need in order to do something SYN **means**: *Does Cath* ***have the*** *creative* ***wherewithal*** *to make it as a solo act?*

whet /wet/ *v* (**whetted**, **whetting**) [T] **1 whet sb's appetite (for sth)** if an experience whets your appetite for something, it increases your desire for it: *The view from the Quai bridge had whetted my appetite for a trip on the lake.*
2 *literary* to make the edge of a blade sharp

wheth·er /'weðə $ -ər/ ●●● S1 W1 *conjunction*
1 used when talking about a choice you have to make or about something that is not certain: *Maurice asked me whether I needed any help.* | *There were times when I wondered* ***whether or not*** *we would get there.* | **whether to do sth** *She was uncertain* ***whether*** *to stay* ***or*** *leave.* | *I didn't know* ***whether*** *to believe him* ***or not***. | *The question arose* ***as to whether*** *this behaviour was unlawful.*
2 used to say that something definitely will or will not happen whatever the situation is: *It seemed to me that she was in trouble whether Mahoney lived or died.* | *Look, Kate, I'm calling the doctor,* ***whether*** *you like it* ***or not***. | *Poor farmers, whether owners or tenants, will be worst affected.*
⚠ Do not confuse with the noun **weather** (=conditions outside such as rain, snow, sun, wind etc).

whet·stone /'wetstəʊn $ -stoʊn/ *n* [C] a stone used to make the blade of cutting tools sharp

whew /hjuː/ *interjection* used when you are surprised, very hot, or feeling glad that something bad did not happen SYN **phew**: *Whew, it was hot.*

whey /weɪ/ *n* [U] the watery liquid that is left after the solid part has been removed from sour milk

which /wɪtʃ/ ●●● S1 W1 *determiner, pron*
1 used to ask or talk about one or more members of a group of people or things, when you are uncertain about it or about them: *Which book are you looking for?* | *Which are the most important crops?* | *Miranda was sure it was one of them, but was not sure which.* | **[+of]** *I don't know which of us was the more scared.*
2 used after a noun to show what thing or things you mean: *Did you see the letter which came today?* | *Now they were driving by the houses which Andy had described.*
3 used, after a COMMA in writing, to add more information about the thing, situation, or event you have just mentioned: *The house, which was completed in 1856, was famous for its huge marble staircase.* | *One of the boys kept laughing, which annoyed Jane intensely.* | *He was educated at the local grammar school, after which he went on to*

W

Cambridge. | *She may have missed the train,* ***in which case*** (=if this has happened) *she won't arrive for another hour.*
4 don't know/can't tell etc which is which if you do not know which is which, you cannot see the difference between two very similar people or things: *The twins are so alike I can never tell which is which.*

which·ev·er /wɪtʃˈevə $ -ˈevər/ ●●○ *determiner, pron*
1 used to say that it does not matter which thing or person is chosen because the result will be the same: *It will be a difficult operation, whichever method you choose.* | *Whichever way you look at it, things are pretty bad.*
2 used to refer to the member of a group of people or things that does something, is wanted, is possible etc: *Whichever player scores the highest number of points will be the winner.* | *You can either have the double room or the family room, whichever you want.* | *'Do you want tea or coffee?' 'I don't mind –* ***whichever one*** *you're making.'*

whiff /wɪf/ *n* [C] **1** a very slight smell of something: **[+of]** *a whiff of tobacco* | **get/catch a whiff of sth** *As she walked past, I caught a whiff of her perfume.* **THESAURUS** SMELL **2 a whiff of danger/adventure/freedom etc** a slight sign that something dangerous, exciting etc might happen: *The whiff of danger filled her with excitement.*

Whig /wɪg/ *n* [C] a member of a British political party of the 18th and early 19th centuries which wanted to limit royal power, and later became the Liberal Party

while¹ /waɪl/ ●●● S1 W1 *conjunction*
1 during the time that something is happening: *They arrived while we were having dinner.* | *While she was asleep, thieves broke in and stole her handbag.* | *She met Andy while working on a production of 'Carmen'.*
2 all the time that something is happening: *Would you look after the children while I do the shopping?*

GRAMMAR: Choosing the right tense

You use the present tense, not 'will', with **while** when you are talking about the future: *I hope to visit the British Museum while I am in London.* ✗ Don't say *I hope to visit the British Museum while I will be in London.*

GRAMMAR GUIDE VERBS

3 used to emphasize the difference between two situations, activities etc: *Schools in the north tend to be better equipped, while those in the south are relatively poor.* **THESAURUS** BUT
4 in spite of the fact that SYN **although**: *While never a big eater, he did snack a lot.* | *While there was no conclusive evidence, most people thought he was guilty.*
5 while I'm/you're etc at/about it *spoken* used to suggest that someone should do something at the same time that they do something else: *Print out what you've written, and while you're at it make a copy for me.*

THESAURUS

while during the time that you are doing something, or something is happening: *I bought a magazine while I was waiting for the train.* | *While we were on holiday, my bag was stolen.*
meanwhile at the same time as something else is happening: *They're still working on our bedroom. Meanwhile, we're sleeping downstairs.* | *The Russians, meanwhile, declared war on August 8.*
in the meantime during the period of time between now and a future event, or between two events in the past: *More aid is expected soon, but in the meantime these people are going hungry.* | *My new job hadn't started, so in the meantime I tried to write a book.*
whilst *BrE* while. **Whilst** sounds a little more formal than **while**: *One American plane was forced to land whilst flying over North Korea.* | *Whilst all this was going on, the performers were getting ready for the show.*

while² ●●● S1 W2 *n*
1 a while a period of time, especially a short one: *It* ***takes a while*** *to recover from the operation.* | **in a while** *Mr Thomas will be with you in a while.* | **for a while** *At last, he could relax for a while.* | **a little/short while** *Wait a little while before deciding.* | *We talked for* ***quite a while*** (=a fairly long time) *on the phone.*
2 all the while all the time that something is happening: *He examined her thoroughly, talking softly all the while.* | *She continued working, all the while keeping an eye on the clock.*
→ **(every) once in a while** at ONCE¹(8), → **be worth sb's while (to do/doing sth)** at WORTH¹(5), → **make it worth sb's while** at WORTH¹(6)

while³ *v* **while away the hours/evening/days etc** to spend time in a pleasant and lazy way: *The evenings were whiled away in endless games of cards.*

whilst /waɪlst/ ●●○ *conjunction BrE formal* WHILE **THESAURUS** WHILE

whim /wɪm/ *n* [C usually singular] a sudden feeling that you would like to do or have something, especially when there is no important or good reason: **on a whim** *I didn't leave just on a whim* (=for no good reason). | **at the whim of sb** *At work they are at the whim of the boss.* | **sb's every whim** *Their father had always indulged her every whim.* | **at whim** *He appeared and disappeared at whim.*

whim·per /ˈwɪmpə $ -ər/ *v* [I,T] to make low crying sounds, or to speak in this way: *He heard the dog whimper.* | *'It's not my fault,' she whimpered.* **THESAURUS** CRY —**whimper** *n* [C]

whim·si·cal /ˈwɪmzɪkəl/ *adj* unusual or strange and often amusing: *He has a wonderful whimsical sense of humour.* —**whimsically** /-kli/ *adv*

whim·sy /ˈwɪmzi/ *n* [U] a way of thinking, behaving, or doing something that is unusual, strange, and often amusing: *a sense of fancy and whimsy*

whine /waɪn/ *v* **1** [I,T] to complain in a sad annoying voice about something SYN **moan**: *Oh Charlotte, please stop whining.* | *'I don't understand,' whined Rose.* | **[+about]** *The sergeant was whining about how hard he had been forced to work recently.* **2** [I] to make a long high sound because you are in pain or unhappy: *He could hear the dog whining behind the door.* **3** [I] if a machine whines, it makes a continuous high sound —**whine** *n* [C]: *The baby's howl turned to a high-pitched whine.* | *the whine of a vacuum cleaner*

whinge /wɪndʒ/ *v* (*present participle* **whingeing** *or* **whinging**) [I] *BrE* to keep complaining in an annoying way: **[+about]** *Stop whingeing about the situation and accept it.* —**whinge** *n* [C]: *His tale is one long whinge about his own suffering.* —**whinger** *n* [C]

whin·ny /ˈwɪni/ *v* (**whinnied**, **whinnying**, **whinnies**) [I] if a horse whinnies, it makes a high sound → **neigh** —**whinny** *n* [C]

whip¹ /wɪp/ ●●○ *v* (**whipped**, **whipping**)
1 [T] to hit someone or something with a whip: *He whipped the horse into a canter.*
2 [I,T always + adv/prep] to move quickly and violently, or to make something do this: *The wind whipped her hair into her eyes.* | **[+across/around/past etc]** *Rain whipped across the window pane.* | **whip sth about/around** *The branches were being whipped about in the storm.* | **[+round/around]** *He whipped round to face them.*
3 [T always + adv/prep] to move or remove something with a quick sudden movement: **whip sth off/out/back etc** *Annie whipped off her apron and put it into the drawer.* | *He whipped back the sheets.*
4 [T] to mix cream or the clear part of an egg very hard until it becomes stiff → **beat**, **whisk**: *Whip the cream until thick.*
5 [T] *BrE informal* to steal something

whip through sth *phr v informal* to finish a job very quickly: *He whipped through his routine paperwork before going home.*

whip sb/sth ↔ **up** *phr v*
1 to try to make people feel strongly about something: **whip up interest/opposition/support etc** *They'll do anything to whip up a bit of interest in a book.* | *an attempt to whip up the masses*

W

2 to quickly make something to eat: *Mother was in the kitchen whipping up a batch of cakes.*

whip² *n* **1** [C] a long thin piece of rope or leather with a handle, that you hit animals with to make them move or that you hit someone with to punish them: *The coachman* ***cracked*** *his* ***whip*** *and the carriage lurched forward.* **2** [C] a member of the US Congress or the British Parliament who is responsible for making sure that the members of their party attend and vote **3** [C] a written order sent to members of the British Parliament telling them when and how to vote → THREE-LINE WHIP **4** [C,U] *BrE* a sweet dish made from the white part of eggs and chocolate or fruit, beaten together to make a smooth light mixture: *pineapple whip* **5 have the whip hand** to have power and control over someone → **crack the whip** at CRACK¹(15), → **give sb a fair crack of the whip** at FAIR¹(9)

whip·lash /ˈwɪp-læʃ/ *n* [U] a neck injury caused when your head moves forward and back again suddenly and violently, especially in a car accident: *One officer suffered whiplash injuries.*

ˌwhipped ˈcream *n* [U] cream that has been beaten until it is thick

whip·per·snap·per /ˈwɪpəˌsnæpə $ ˈwɪpərˌsnæpər/ *n* [C] *old-fashioned* a young person who is too confident and does not show enough respect to older people

whip·pet /ˈwɪpɪt/ *n* [C] a small thin racing dog like a GREYHOUND

whip·ping /ˈwɪpɪŋ/ *n* [C usually singular] a punishment given to someone by whipping them

ˈwhipping boy *n* [singular] someone or something that is blamed for someone else's mistakes SYN **scapegoat**

ˈwhipping ˌcream *n* [U] a type of cream that becomes thick when you beat it

whip·py /ˈwɪpi/ *adj* long, thin, and easy to bend: *new growths of whippy little sapling twigs*

ˈwhip-round *n* **have a whip-round** *BrE informal* if a group of people have a whip-round, they all give some money so that they can buy something together: *We had a whip-round to pay for a taxi to the railway station.*

whir /wɜː $ wɜːr/ *v* [I] another spelling of WHIRR

whirl¹ /wɜːl $ wɜːrl/ *v* **1** [I,T] to turn or spin around very quickly, or to make someone or something do this: *We watched the seagulls whirling and shrieking over the harbour.* | **[+about/around/towards etc]** *She whirled around and her look shook him.* | **whirl sb/sth about/around/away etc** *He whirled her round in his arms.* **2** [I] if your head is whirling, or if thoughts are whirling in your head, your mind is full of thoughts and ideas, and you feel very confused or excited: *His head was whirling with excitement.* | *The implications began to whirl around in her head.*

whirl² *n* **1 give sth a whirl** *informal* to try something that you are not sure you are going to like or be able to do: *Why don't you give golf a whirl?* **2** [singular] a lot of activity of a particular kind: *the* ***social whirl*** *of New York publishing* | **[+of]** *The next two days passed in a* ***whirl of activity***. **3 be in a whirl** to feel very excited or confused about something: *His mind was in a whirl and he was worried.* **4** [C usually singular] a spinning movement or the shape of something that is spinning: **[+of]** *A car rumbled over the bumpy dirt road, leaving behind a whirl of white dust.*

whir·li·gig /ˈwɜːlɪɡɪɡ $ ˈwɜːr-/ *n* [C] a toy that spins SYN **top**

whirl·pool /ˈwɜːlpuːl $ ˈwɜːrl-/ *n* [C] **1** a powerful current of water that spins around and can pull things down into it **2** (*also* **whirlpool bath**) a large BATHTUB that makes hot water move in strong currents around your body **3 a whirlpool of emotion/activity etc** a very busy situation or a strong emotion, from which it is difficult to escape: *people who are caught in a whirlpool of grief*

whirl·wind¹ /ˈwɜːlˌwɪnd $ ˈwɜːrl-/ *n* [C] **1** an extremely strong wind that moves quickly with a circular movement, causing a lot of damage SYN **tornado, twister** *AmE* **2 a whirlwind of emotions/activity etc** a situation in which you experience a lot of different emotions, or a lot of different things happen, one after another

whirlwind² *adj* [only before noun] a whirlwind situation or event happens very quickly: *a whirlwind romance*

whirr, **whir** /wɜː $ wɜːr/ *v* (**whirred, whirring**) [I] to make a fairly quiet regular sound, like the sound of a bird or insect moving its wings very fast: *Helicopters whirred overhead.* —**whirr** *n* [C usually singular]: *the whirr of an electric motor*

whisk¹ /wɪsk/ ●○○ *v* [T]

1 to mix liquid, eggs etc very quickly so that air is mixed in, using a fork or a whisk THESAURUS ▸ MIX

2 [always + adv/prep] to take someone or something quickly away from a place: **whisk sb/sth away/off** *The waitress whisked our coffee cups away before we'd had a chance to finish.*

whisk² *n* [C] a small kitchen tool made of curved pieces of wire, used for mixing air into eggs, cream etc

ˈwhisk broom *n* [C] *AmE* a small stiff BROOM used especially for brushing clothes

whis·ker /ˈwɪskə $ -ər/ ●○○ *n* [C]

1 [usually plural] one of the long stiff hairs that grow near the mouth of a cat, mouse etc → see picture at BIG CAT

2 [usually plural] one of the hairs that grow on a man's face

3 win/lose by a whisker *informal* to win or lose by a very small amount: *Schmidt finished second, losing by a whisker in the final event.*

4 come within a whisker of (doing) sth to almost succeed or fail at doing something: *Doctors say he came within a whisker of dying on the operating table.*

whis·ky *BrE*, **whiskey** *especially AmE* /ˈwɪski/ ●●○ S3 *n* (*plural* **whiskies** *or* **whiskeys**) [C,U] a strong alcoholic drink made from grain, or a glass of this

whis·per¹ /ˈwɪspə $ -ər/ ●●● W3 *v*

1 [I,T] to speak or say something very quietly, using your breath rather than your voice: *You don't have to whisper, no one can hear us.* | **[+about]** *What are you two whispering about over there?* | **whisper sth to sb** *James leaned over to whisper something to Michael.* | *'I've missed you,' he* ***whispered in*** *her* ***ear***. THESAURUS ▸ SAY

2 [T] to say or suggest something privately or secretly: **whisper that** *Staff were whispering that the company was about to go out of business.*

whisper² ●●● W3 *n* [C]

1 a very quiet voice you make using your breath and no sound: **in a whisper** *'Where are we going?' he asked in a whisper.*

2 a piece of news or information that has not been officially announced and may or may not be true SYN **rumour**: **[+of]** *The first whisper of the redundancies came from the newspapers.* | **[+that]** *There are whispers that the actor was seen checking into a hospital last week.*

3 a whisper of sth *literary* a low soft sound made by something such as the wind

ˈwhispering camˌpaign *n* [C] a situation in which someone privately spreads criticism about another person in order to make people have a bad opinion of them

whist /wɪst/ *n* [U] a card game for four players in two pairs, in which each pair tries to win the most TRICKS

whis·tle¹ /ˈwɪsəl/ ●●○ *v*

1 HIGH SOUND [I,T] to make a high or musical sound by blowing air out through your lips: *Adam whistled happily on his way to work.* | *I heard this song on the radio and I've been whistling it all day.* | *He* ***whistled*** *a* ***tune*** *as he strolled down the corridor.* | **whistle to sb** (=whistle to get someone's attention) *Dad whistled to us to come home for dinner.* | **whistle at sb** (=whistle to let someone know that you think they are attractive) *Men are always whistling at Heidi on the street.*

2 USE A WHISTLE [I] to make a high sound by blowing into a whistle: *The referee whistled and the game began.*

3 GO/MOVE FAST [I always + adv/prep] to move quickly, making a whistling sound: *Bullets and shells were whistling overhead.* | *They listened to the* ***wind whistling*** *through the trees.*

W

4 STEAM TRAIN/KETTLE [I] if a steam train or KETTLE whistles, it makes a high sound when air or steam is forced through a small hole
5 BIRD [I] if a bird whistles, it makes a high musical sound
6 be whistling in the dark *informal* to be trying to show that you are brave when you are afraid, or that you know about something when you do not: *Does he know what he's talking about or is he just whistling in the dark?*
7 sb can whistle for sth *BrE spoken* used to tell someone that there is no chance of them getting what they have asked for

whistle² ●●○ *n* [C]
1 a small object that produces a high whistling sound when you blow into it: *The lifeguard* ***blew*** *his* ***whistle****.*
2 a high sound made by blowing a whistle, by blowing air out through your lips, or when air or steam is forced through a small opening: *Larsson scored just minutes before the final whistle.* | **low/shrill/high-pitched etc whistle** *Sanders* ***gave a*** *low* ***whistle*** *when he saw the contents of the box.*
3 a piece of equipment on a train or boat that makes a high noise when air is forced through it
4 the sound of something moving quickly through the air: **[+of]** *We could hear the whistle of the jets as they passed overhead.* → **blow the whistle on sth** at BLOW¹(17), → **clean as a whistle** at CLEAN¹(1), **PENNY WHISTLE**, **WOLF WHISTLE**

ˈwhistle-ˌblower *n* [C] someone who tells people in authority or the public about dishonest or illegal practices at the place where they work —**whistle-blowing** *n* [U]

ˈwhistle-ˌstop *adj AmE* **whistle-stop tour/trip** a trip during which someone, especially a politician, visits many different places in a short period of time: *a whistle-stop tour of Texas*

whit /wɪt/ *n* **not a whit** *old-fashioned* not at all: *Sara had not changed a whit.*

Whit *n* [C,U] *BrE* WHITSUN

white¹ /waɪt/ ●●● S1 W1 *adj*
1 COLOUR having the colour of milk, salt, or snow: *a white dress* | **pure/snow white** (=completely white) *snow white hair*
2 PEOPLE a) belonging to the race of people with pale skin → **black**: *young white males* **b)** relating to white people: *a white neighborhood*
3 PALE looking pale, because of illness, strong emotion etc: *Are you OK? You're* ***white as a sheet*** (=extremely pale). | **white with anger/fear etc** *Her voice shook, and her face was white with anger.*
4 COFFEE [usually before noun] *BrE* white coffee has milk or cream in it
5 WINE white wine is a pale yellow colour → **red**
6 a white Christmas a Christmas when there is snow
7 whiter than white completely morally good: *He said that he had never claimed to be whiter than white.* —**whiteness** *n* [U]

white² ●●● S3 W2 *n*
1 COLOUR [U] the colour of milk, salt, and snow
2 PEOPLE (*also* **White**) [C] someone who belongs to the race of people with pale skin → **black**: *The mayor is very popular among whites.*
3 WINE [C,U] wine that is pale yellow in colour: *a nice bottle of white* | *California has some of the finest whites in the world.*
4 EYE [C + of] the white part of your eye
5 EGG [C,U] the part of an egg that surrounds the YOLK (=yellow part) and becomes white when cooked
6 whites [plural] **a)** white clothes, sheets etc, which are separated from dark colours when they are washed **b)** white clothes that are worn for some sports, such as TENNIS

white³ *v*
white sth ↔ **out** *phr v* to cover something written on paper, especially a mistake, with a special white liquid so that it cannot be seen anymore

white·bait /ˈwaɪtbeɪt/ *n* [U] very young fish of several types, used as food: *deep-fried whitebait*

ˌwhite ˈblood cell *n* [C] one of the cells in your blood which fights against infection → **red blood cell**

white·board /ˈwaɪtbɔːd $ -bɔːrd/ *n* [C] a large board with a white smooth surface that you can write on, used, for example, in rooms where classes are taught → **blackboard**

ˈwhite-bread *adj AmE informal* relating to white people who are considered traditional and boring in their opinions and way of life: *a white-bread family*

white·caps /ˈwaɪtkæps/ *n* [plural] *AmE* WHITE HORSES

ˌwhite ˌcliffs of ˈDover, the the white cliffs made of CHALK, which are the first part of England that you see when crossing the English Channel from France

ˌwhite-ˈcollar *adj* **1** [only before noun] white-collar workers have jobs in offices, banks etc rather than jobs working in factories, building things etc → **blue-collar**, **pink-collar**: *white-collar jobs* **2 white-collar crime** crimes involving white-collar workers, for example when someone secretly steals money from the organization they work for

ˌwhite ˈcorpuscle *n* [C] a WHITE BLOOD CELL

ˌwhite ˈdwarf *n* [C] *technical* a hot star, near the end of its life, that is more solid but less bright than the Sun → **red giant**

ˌwhite ˈelephant *n* [C] something that is completely useless, although it may have cost a lot of money: *When the theatre first opened it was widely regarded as a white elephant.*

ˌwhite ˈflag *n* [C] a sign that you accept that you have failed or been defeated → **surrender**: **wave/raise/show etc the white flag** *Despite the loss, the team refuses to wave the white flag and give up on the season.*

ˌwhite ˈflour *n* [U] wheat flour from which the BRAN (=outer layer) and WHEATGERM (=inside seed) have been removed

ˈwhite goods *n* [plural] *BrE* equipment used in the home, for example washing machines and REFRIGERATORS → **brown goods**

White·hall /ˈwaɪthɔːl, ˌwaɪtˈhɔːl $ -hɒːl/ *n* **1** the British government, especially the government departments rather than parliament or the prime minister **2** the street in London where many of the government departments are

ˌwhite ˈheat *n* [U] the very high temperature at which a metal turns white → **WHITE-HOT**

ˌwhite ˈhorses *n* [plural] *BrE* waves in the sea or on a lake that are white at the top SYN **whitecaps** *AmE*

ˌwhite-ˈhot *adj* **1** white-hot metal is so hot that it shines white → **red-hot** **2** involving a lot of activity or strong feelings → **red-hot**: *white-hot passion*

ˈWhite House *n* **1 the White House** the official home in Washington D.C. of the president of the US **2** the president of the US and the people who advise him: *claims that* ***the White House*** *had received warnings of a possible terrorist attack before September 11th* | *White House officials refused to comment on the story.*

ˌwhite ˈknight *n* [C] a person or company that puts money into a business in order to save it from being controlled by another company

ˌwhite-ˈknuckle *adj* [only before noun] a white-knuckle ride at a FAIRGROUND makes you feel excited and afraid at the same time

ˌwhite-ˈknuckled *adj* if you have white-knuckled hands, your hands are held tightly in a FIST because you are anxious or afraid

ˌwhite ˈlie *n* [C] *informal* a lie that you tell someone in order to protect them or avoid hurting their feelings

ˌwhite ˈlightning *n* [U] *AmE* MOONSHINE

ˌwhite ˈmagic *n* [U] magic used for good purposes → **black magic**

ˈwhite meat *n* [U] the pale-coloured meat from the breast, wings etc of a cooked chicken, TURKEY, or other bird → **redmeat**, **red meat**

whit·en /ˈwaɪtn/ *v* [I,T] to become more white, or to

make something do this: *This stuff is supposed to whiten your teeth.*

whit·en·er /ˈwaɪtnə $ -ər/ (*also* **whit·en·ing** /ˈwaɪtnɪŋ/) *n* [C,U] a substance used to make something more white

ˌwhite ˈnoise *n* [U] noise coming from a radio or television which is turned on but not TUNEd to any programme

white·out /ˈwaɪtaʊt/ *n* [C] weather conditions in which there is so much cloud or snow that you cannot see anything

ˌWhite ˈPages *n* **the White Pages** the white part of a telephone DIRECTORY in the US with the names, addresses, and telephone numbers of people with telephones → **Yellow Pages**

ˌWhite ˈPaper *n* [C] an official report from the British government, explaining their ideas and plans concerning a particular subject before a new law is introduced → **Green Paper**

ˌwhite ˈpepper *n* [U] a white powder made from the crushed inside of a PEPPERCORN, which gives a slightly spicy taste to food → **black pepper**

ˌwhite ˈsauce / $ ˈ../ *n* [C,U] a thick white liquid made of flour, milk, and butter, which can be eaten with meat and vegetables

ˌwhite ˈspirit *n* [U] *BrE* a clear liquid made from petrol, used for making paint thinner, removing marks on clothes etc SYN **turpentine**

ˌwhite suˈpremacist *n* [C] someone who believes that white people are better than people of other races —**white supremacy** *n* [U]

ˌwhite-ˈtie *adj* [only before noun] a white-tie social occasion is a very formal one at which the men wear white BOW TIES and TAILS → **black-tie**

ˌwhite ˈtrash *n* [U] *AmE informal* an insulting expression used to talk about white people who are poor and uneducated

ˌwhite ˈvan man *n* [C] *BrE informal* a man who drives a white VAN, especially when delivering goods in a city, in an AGGRESSIVE and dangerous way

white·wall /ˈwaɪtwɔːl $ -wɒːl/ *n* [C] *AmE* a car tyre that has a wide white band on its side

white·wash¹ /ˈwaɪtwɒʃ $ -wɒːʃ, -wɑːʃ/ *n* **1** [singular, U] a report or examination of events that hides the true facts about something so that the person who is responsible will not be punished SYN **cover-up**: *The official report into the cause of the fire was labeled a whitewash.* **2** [U] a white liquid mixture used especially for painting walls **3** [C] an occasion in sport when one player or team defeats an opponent easily, without the opponent getting any points, GOALS etc

whitewash² *v* [T] **1** to cover something with whitewash: *The walls were whitewashed and covered with bullfighting posters.* **2** to hide the true facts about a serious accident or illegal action: *Investigators are accused of whitewashing the governor's record.* **3** to defeat an opponent in sport easily, without the opponent getting any points, GOALS etc

white·wa·ter, **white water** /ˌwaɪtˈwɔːtə◂ $ -ˈwɒːtər◂, -ˈwɑː-/ *n* [U] a part of a river that looks white because the water is running very quickly over rocks: *whitewater canoeing*

ˌwhite ˈwedding *n* [C] a traditional wedding at which the BRIDE wears a long white dress

whit·ey /ˈwaɪti/ *n* [C,U] an offensive word for a white person or white people in general

whith·er /ˈwɪðə $ -ər/ *adv* **1** *old use* to which place SYN **where**: *the place whither he went* **2** *formal* used to ask what the future of something will be or how it will develop: *Whither socialism?* → WHENCE

whit·ing /ˈwaɪtɪŋ/ *n* (*plural* **whiting**) [C] a black and silver fish that lives in the sea and can be eaten

whit·ish /ˈwaɪtɪʃ/ *adj* almost white in colour

Whit·sun /ˈwɪtsən/ *n* [C,U] *BrE* **1** (*also* **ˌWhit ˈSunday**) the seventh Sunday after Easter, when Christians celebrate the HOLY SPIRIT coming down from heaven SYN **Pentecost 2** (*also* **Whit·sun·tide** /ˈwɪtsəntaɪd/) the period around Whitsun

whit·tle /ˈwɪtl/ *v* **1** (*also* **whittle down**) [T] to gradually make something smaller by taking parts away: *We need to whittle down the list of guests for the party.* **2** [I,T] to cut a piece of wood into a particular shape by cutting off small pieces with a knife → **carve**

whittle away *phr v* to gradually reduce the amount or effectiveness of something, especially something that you think should not be reduced: **whittle sth ↔ away** *The museum is worried that government funding will be whittled away.* | **[+at]** *Congress is whittling away at our freedom of speech.*

whizz¹ *BrE*, **whiz** *AmE* /wɪz/ *v* [I] **1** [always + adv/prep] *informal* **a)** to move very quickly, often making a sound like something rushing through the air: *An ambulance whizzed past.* | *I saw a big piece of metal whizzing through the air.* **b)** to do something very quickly: **[+through]** *Let's just whizz through it one more time.* **2** *AmE spoken* to URINATE

whizz² *BrE*, **whiz** *AmE* *n* **1** [C] *informal* someone who is very fast, intelligent, or skilled in a particular activity: *a math whiz* **2 take a whiz** *AmE spoken* to URINATE **3** [C,U] *informal* AMPHETAMINE → **GEE WHIZ**

whizz-kid *BrE*, **whiz kid** *AmE* /ˈwɪzkɪd/ *n* [C] *informal* a young person who is very skilled or successful at something: *financial whizzkids in the City*

who /huː/ ●●● S1 W1 *pron*

1 used to ask or talk about which person is involved, or what the name of a person is: *Who locked the door?* | *Who do you work for?* | *Who's that guy with your wife?* | *They never found out who the murderer was.* | *She wondered who had sent the flowers.* | **who to ask/contact/blame etc** *He doesn't know who to vote for.* | **who on earth/in the world etc** (=used for emphasis when you are surprised, angry etc) *Who on earth would live in such a lonely place?* | *Who the hell are you?*

2 used after a noun to show which person or which people you are talking about: *Do you know the people who live over the road?* | *the woman who was driving* | *She was the one who did most of the talking.*

3 used, after a COMMA in writing, to add more information about a particular person or group of people that you have just mentioned: *I discussed it with my brother, who is a lawyer.* | *Alison Jones and her husband David, who live in Hartlepool, are celebrating their golden wedding anniversary.*

4 *informal* used to introduce a question that shows you think something is true of everyone or of no one: *We have the occasional argument. Who doesn't* (=everyone does)? | *Who wants to come second* (=no one does)?

5 who is sb to do sth? *spoken* used to say that someone does not have the right or the authority to say or do something: *Who is she to order me around?*

6 who's who a) if you know who is who within a particular organization or group, you know what each person's name is and what job they do or what position they have: *I'm just getting to know who's who in the department.* **b) a who's who of sth** a list of the important people within a particular organization or group – often used to emphasize that many important people are involved in something: *The list of competitors reads like a who's who of international tennis players.*

whoa /wəʊ, həʊ $ woʊ, hoʊ/ *interjection* **1** used to tell someone to become calmer or to do something more slowly: *Whoa! You're driving too fast.* **2** said to show that you are surprised or that you think something is impressive: *Whoa. That's a lot of money.* **3** used to tell a horse to stop

who·dun·it, **whodunnit** /ˌhuːˈdʌnɪt/ *n* [C] *informal* a book, film etc about a murder case, in which you do not find out who killed the person until the end

who·ev·er /huːˈevə $ -ˈevər/ ●●○ S3 *pron*

1 used to say that it does not matter who does something, is in a particular place etc: *I'll take whoever wants to*

W

go. | *When you're done with the book, just give it to Kristin or Shelley or whoever.*
2 used to talk about a specific person or people, although you do not know who they are: *Whoever is responsible for this will be punished.*
3 whoever he/she is (*also* **whoever he/she may be**) used to say that you do not know who someone is: *You've got a message from Tony Gower, whoever he is.*
4 used to mean 'who' at the beginning of a question to show surprise or anger: *Whoever would do a thing like that to an old woman?*

whole¹ /həʊl $ hoʊl/ ●●● S1 W1 *adj*
1 [only before noun] all of something SYN **entire**: *You have your whole life ahead of you!* | *His whole attitude bugs me.* | *We ate the whole cake in about ten minutes.* | ***The whole thing*** (=everything about the situation) *just makes me sick.* | *We just sat around and watched TV* ***the whole time*** (=the only thing we did was watch television). | *I don't believe she's telling us* ***the whole story*** (=all the facts). | *It was months before* ***the whole truth*** *came out.* | **the whole school/country/village etc** (=all the people in a school, country etc) *The whole town came out for the parade.*
2 whole lot *informal* **a) a whole lot** very much: *I'm feeling a whole lot better.* | *I don't cook a whole lot anymore.* **b) a whole lot (of sth)** a large quantity or number: *We're going to have a whole lot of problems if we don't finish this by tomorrow.* | *You can find a nice house in this neighborhood, and you don't have to spend a whole lot.* **c) the whole lot** *especially BrE* all of something: *She gave me the whole lot for 20 pounds.*
3 a whole range/series/variety etc (of sth) used to emphasize that there are a lot of things of a similar type: *There are a whole range of sizes to choose from.*
4 complete and not divided or broken into parts: *Place a whole onion inside the chicken.* | *a snake* ***swallowing*** *a mouse* ***whole*** (=swallowing it without chewing)
5 the whole point (of sth) used to emphasize the purpose for doing something, especially when you believe this is unclear or has been forgotten: *I thought the whole point of the meeting was to decide which offer to accept.*
6 in the whole (wide) world *informal* an expression meaning 'anywhere' or 'at all' – used to emphasize a statement: *I have the best job in the whole wide world.*
7 go the whole hog (*also* **go whole hog** *AmE*) *informal* to do something as completely or as well as you can, without any limits: *I'm gonna go whole hog and have a live band at the barbecue.*
8 the whole nine yards *AmE spoken* including everything that is typical of or possible in an activity, situation, set of things etc: *Our new apartment complex has a tennis court, swimming pool, playground – the whole nine yards.* —**wholeness** *n* [U] → **a whole new ball game** at BALL GAME(3), → **the whole shebang** at SHEBANG, → **the whole shooting match** at SHOOTING MATCH, → **the whole enchilada** at ENCHILADA(3), → WHOLLY

whole² ●●● S2 W2 *n*
1 the whole of sth all of something, especially something that is not a physical object: *The whole of the morning was wasted trying to find the documents.*
2 on the whole used to say that something is generally true: *On the whole, I thought the film was pretty good.*
3 as a whole used to say that all the parts of something are being considered together: *This project will be of great benefit to the region as a whole.*
4 [C usually singular] something that consists of a number of parts, but is considered as a single unit: *Two halves make a whole.*

whole·food /ˈhəʊlfuːd $ ˈhoʊl-/ *n* [C,U] food that is considered healthy because it only contains natural things rather than anything artificial

whole·heart·ed /ˌhəʊl ˈhɑːtɪd◂ $ ˌhoʊlˈhɑːr-/ *adj* [usually before noun] involving all your feelings, interest etc: **whole-hearted support/acceptance/cooperation etc** *Montgomery's new style of leadership met with Leslie's whole-hearted approval.* —**whole-heartedly** *adv*: *I agree whole-heartedly with the mayor on this issue.*

whole·meal /ˈhəʊlmiːl $ ˈhoʊl-/ *adj BrE* wholemeal flour or bread uses all of the grain, including the outer layer SYN **whole wheat** *AmE*

ˈwhole note *n* [C] *AmE* a musical note which continues for as long as two HALF NOTES SYN **semibreve** *BrE*

ˌwhole ˈnumber *n* [C] a number such as 0, 1, 2 etc that is not a FRACTION SYN **integer**

whole·sale¹ /ˈhəʊlseɪl $ ˈhoʊl-/ ●○○ *n* [U] the business of selling goods in large quantities at low prices to other businesses, rather than to the general public → **retail**

wholesale² ●○○ *adj*
1 relating to the business of selling goods in large quantities at low prices to other businesses, rather than to the general public → **retail**: *wholesale prices*
2 [usually before noun] affecting almost everything or everyone, and often done without any concern for the results: *the capture and wholesale destruction of a city* | *This company will not be successful until there are wholesale changes.* —**wholesale** *adv*: *I can get it for you wholesale.*

whole·sal·er /ˈhəʊlˌseɪlə $ ˈhoʊlˌseɪlər/ *n* [C] a person or company who sells goods wholesale → **retailer**

whole·some /ˈhəʊlsəm $ ˈhoʊl-/ *adj* **1** likely to make you healthy: **wholesome food/fare/meal etc** *well-balanced wholesome meals* **2** considered to have a good moral effect: *good wholesome fun* —**wholesomeness** *n* [U]

ˈwhole wheat *adj AmE* whole wheat flour or bread uses all of the grain, including the outer layer SYN **wholemeal** *BrE*

who'll /huːl/ the short form of 'who will'

whol·ly /ˈhəʊl-li $ ˈhoʊl-/ ●○○ *adv formal* completely: *a wholly satisfactory solution* | *The report claimed that the disaster was wholly unavoidable.*

whom /huːm/ ●●● W1 *pron* the object form of 'who', used especially in formal speech or writing: *Desperate for money, she called her sister, whom she hadn't spoken to in 20 years.* | *She brought with her three friends, none of whom I had ever met before.*

REGISTER
In everyday spoken or written English, people usually use **who** rather than **whom**: ***Who*** *did you send it to?* **Whom** is usually used only in the phrases **one of whom**, **none of whom**, **some of whom** etc.

whoop /wuːp, huːp/ *v* [I] **1** to shout loudly and happily: *Hundreds of people ran past them, whooping joyously.* **2 whoop it up** *informal* to enjoy yourself very much, especially in a large group —**whoop** *n* [C]: *whoops of victory*

whoop-de-do /ˌwuːp diː ˈduː, ˌhuːp-/ *interjection AmE* used to show that you do not think something that someone has told you is as exciting or impressive as they think it is: *'He says he'll give me a $20 raise.' 'Well, whoop-de-do.'*

whoo·pee¹ /wʊˈpiː/ *interjection* a shout of happiness

whoop·ee² /ˈwʊpi/ *n old-fashioned* **make whoopee a)** *BrE* to go out and enjoy yourself **b)** *AmE* to have sex

ˈwhoopee ˌcushion *n* [C] a rubber bag filled with air that makes a noise like a FART when you sit on it

whoop·ing cough /ˈhuːpɪŋ kɒf $ -kɒːf/ *n* [U] an infectious disease that especially affects children, and makes them cough and have difficulty breathing

whoops /wʊps/ ●○○ *interjection*
1 said when someone has fallen, dropped something, or made a small mistake: *Whoops! I nearly dropped it.*
2 whoops-a-daisy said when someone, usually a child, falls down

whoosh /wʊʃ $ wuːʃ/ *v* [I always + adv/prep] *informal* to move very fast with a soft rushing sound —**whoosh** *n* [C usually singular]: *a sudden whoosh of flame and then a big bang*

whop /wɒp $ wɑːp/ *v* (**whopped**, **whopping**) [T] *spoken* WHUP

whop·per /ˈwɒpə $ ˈwɑːpər/ *n* [C] *informal* **1** a lie: *She*

tells *one* **whopper** *after another.* **2** something unusually big: *The fish Mike caught was a whopper.*

whop·ping /ˈwɒpɪŋ $ ˈwɑː-/ *adj* [only before noun] *informal* very large: *a whopping fee*

whore /hɔː $ hɔːr/ *n* [C] *informal* **1** *taboo* an offensive word for a woman who has many sexual partners. Do not use this word. **2** a female PROSTITUTE

who're /ˈhuːə $ ˈhuːər/ the short form of 'who are'

whore·house /ˈhɔːhaʊs $ ˈhɔːr-/ *n* [C] *informal not polite* a place where men can pay to have sex SYN **brothel**

whor·ing /ˈhɔːrɪŋ/ *n* [U] *old-fashioned* the activity of having sex with a PROSTITUTE: *drinking, gambling, and whoring*

whorl /wɜːl $ wɔːrl/ *n* [C] **1** a pattern made of a line that curls out in circles that get bigger and bigger **2** *technical* a circular pattern of leaves or flowers on a stem

who's /huːz/ the short form of 'who is' or 'who has'

whose /huːz/ ●●● S2 W1 *determiner, pron*
1 used to ask which person or people a particular thing belongs to: *Whose is this?* | *Whose keys are those?*
2 used to show the relationship between a person or thing and something that belongs to that person or thing: *That's the man whose house has burned down.* | *Solar energy is an idea whose time has come.*
3 used to give additional information about a person or thing: *Jurors, whose identities will be kept secret, will be paid $40 a day.*

who·so·ev·er /ˌhuːsəʊˈevə $ -soʊˈevər/ *pron old use* WHOEVER

ˌWho's ˈWho *trademark* a book produced every year in the UK that contains an ALPHABETICAL list of famous and important people, such as politicians, writers, and entertainers, and provides information about their achievements, their families etc. If a list of people 'reads like a Who's Who' of something, it means that it contains a lot of famous people: *The list of guests read like a Who's Who of the pop industry.*

who've /huːv/ the short form of 'who have'

whup /wʌp/ (*also* **whop**) *v* (*past tense and past participle* **whupped**, *present participle* **whupping**) [T] *informal especially AmE* **1** to defeat someone easily in a sport or fight: *I'm gonna* ***whup*** *your* ***ass*** (=defeat you very easily). **2** to hit someone and hurt them very badly, especially using something such as a belt

why¹ /waɪ/ ●●● S1 W1 *adv*
1 used to ask or talk about the reason for something: *Why are you crying?* | *Why do we have to take all these tests?* | *'She wants to meet you.' 'Why?'* | *'I won't be able to come into work tomorrow.' '****Why not****?'* | *I have no idea why the television isn't working.* | *Simon loves you – that's why he wants to be with you.* | *He's angry with me and I don't know why.* | *There's no* ***reason why*** *we shouldn't be friends.* | **why on earth/why ever etc** (=used for emphasis when you are surprised, angry etc) *Why on earth didn't you ask me to help?* | *'I don't want us to be seen together.' 'Why ever not?'*
2 used to introduce a question that shows you do not think it is necessary to do something: *Why worry? You can't do anything about it.* | *Why waste time going to the bank when you can do it all over the Internet?*

SPOKEN PHRASES
3 why not? used to say that you agree with a suggestion: *'We could invite John and Barbara.' 'Yes, why not?'*
4 why doesn't sb do sth? a) (*also* **why not do sth?**) used to make a suggestion: *Why don't you bring over a video for us to watch?* | *Why not relax and enjoy the atmosphere?* **b)** used to say angrily that someone should do something: *Why don't you mind your own business?*
5 why sb? used to ask why a particular person has been chosen or is suffering: *Why me? Why can't someone else drive you?*
6 why oh why ...? used to show that you are very sorry or angry about something: *Why oh why did I say those horrible things?*

why² *interjection old-fashioned* used when you are surprised or have suddenly realized something: *Why, look who's here!* | *And I thought to myself, why, I can do that.*

why³ *n* **the whys and (the) wherefores** the reasons or explanations for something: *The whys and the wherefores of these procedures need to be explained.*

WI /ˌdʌbəljuː ˈaɪ/ the abbreviation of WOMEN'S INSTITUTE

wick /wɪk/ *n* [C] **1** the piece of thread in a CANDLE, that burns when you light it **2** a long piece of material in an oil lamp, that sucks up oil so that the lamp can burn **3 get on sb's wick** *BrE spoken informal* to annoy someone

wick·ed /ˈwɪkɪd/ ●●○ S3 *adj*
1 behaving in a way that is morally wrong SYN **evil**: *the wicked stepmother in 'Hansel and Gretel'* THESAURUS UNKIND
2 *informal* behaving badly in a way that is amusing: *Carl had a wicked grin on his face as he crept up behind Ellen.* | *Tara hasn't lost her* ***wicked sense of humour****.*
3 *spoken informal* very good: *That's a wicked bike!*
—**wickedly** *adv* —**wickedness** *n* [U]

wick·er /ˈwɪkə $ -ər/ *n* [U] thin dry branches or REEDS that are woven together: *a wicker basket*

wick·er·work /ˈwɪkəwɜːk $ ˈwɪkərwɜːrk/ *n* [U] objects made from wicker

wick·et /ˈwɪkɪt/ *n* [C] one of two sets of three wooden sticks that are stuck in the ground in a game of CRICKET, which the BOWLER tries to hit with the ball → **stump**, **bail** → **be on a sticky wicket** at STICKY

ˈwicket ˌgate *n* [C] *old use* a small door or gate that is part of a larger one

ˈwicket ˌkeeper *n* [C] a player who stands behind the wicket in CRICKET

wide¹ /waɪd/ ●●● S1 W1 *adj*
1 DISTANCE **a)** measuring a large distance from one side to the other SYN **broad** OPP **narrow**: *a wide tree-lined road* | *a hat with a wide brim* | **wide smile/grin** *As he ran toward me, his face broke into a wide grin.* **b)** measuring a particular distance from one side to the other: *How wide is the door?* | *The boat was nearly as wide as the canal.* | **five metres/two miles etc wide** *The river is more than fifty yards wide.*
2 VARIETY [usually before noun] including or involving a large variety of different people, things, or situations: *a man with a wide experience of foreign affairs* | *Our aim is to bring classical music to a wider audience.* | **a wide range/variety/choice etc (of sth)** *This year's festival includes a wide range of entertainers.* | *holidays to a wide choice of destinations*
3 IN MANY PLACES [usually before noun] happening among many people or in many places: *The radio and newspapers gave the trial wide coverage.*
4 a wide variation/difference/gap etc a large and noticeable difference: *the ever-wider gap between the richest and poorest countries*
5 the wider context/issues/picture etc the more general features of a situation, rather than the specific details: *We hope that by the end of the course students will be able to see their subject in a wider context.*
6 EYES *literary* wide eyes are fully open, especially when someone is very surprised, excited, or frightened: *Her eyes grew wide in anticipation.*
7 give sb/sth a wide berth to avoid someone or something
8 NOT HIT STH not hitting something you were aiming at: **[+of]** *His shot was just wide of the goal.*
9 the (big) wide world *especially spoken* places outside the small familiar place where you live: *Soon you'll leave school and go out into the big wide world.*
10 nationwide/city-wide etc affecting all the people in a nation, city etc: *a country-wide revolt against the government*

wide² ●●● W3 S3 *adv*
1 wide open/awake/apart completely open, awake, or apart: *Someone left the back door wide open.* | *At 2 a.m. I was still wide awake.* | *Sandy stood with his back to the fire, legs wide apart.*

W

2 opening or spreading as much as possible: **open/spread (sth) wide** *Spiro spread his arms wide in a welcoming gesture.* | *Leonora's eyes opened wide in horror.* | *The windows had been opened wide and she could feel a slight breeze.*
3 wide open if a competition, election etc is wide open, it is possible for anyone to succeed: *Most experts agree that the election is wide open at this point.*
4 not hitting something you were aiming at, and missing it by a large distance: *His throw to first base **went wide**.*
5 wide of the mark a) not correct about something, by a large amount: *The opinion polls were hopelessly wide of the mark.* **b)** not hitting something you were aiming at, and missing it by a large distance: *One of the bombs fell wide of the mark.* → **far and wide** at FAR[1](11)

ˌwide-angle ˈlens *n* [C] a camera LENS that lets you take photographs with a wider view than normal

ˈwide boy *n* [C] *BrE informal* a man who makes money in dishonest ways and uses it to buy expensive clothes, cars etc – used to show disapproval

ˌwide-ˈeyed *adj, adv written* **1** with your eyes wide open, especially because you are surprised or frightened: *He stood there wide-eyed at the appalling scene.* **2** too willing to believe, accept, or admire things because you do not have much experience of life SYN **naive**

wide·ly /ˈwaɪdli/ ●●● W2 *adv*
1 in a lot of different places or by a lot of people: *Organic food is now widely available.* | *an author who had travelled widely in the Far East* | *a widely used method* | *These laws were widely regarded as too strict.* | *This view was not widely held.*
2 to a large degree – used when talking about differences: *The quality of the applicants **varies widely**.*
3 widely read a) read by a lot of people: *a widely read magazine* **b)** having read many different books

wid·en /ˈwaɪdn/ ●●○ *v*
1 [I,T] to become wider, or to make something wider OPP **narrow**: *They're widening the road.* | *The river widens and splits.*
2 [I,T] to become larger in degree or range, or to make something do this OPP **narrow**: *The gap between income and expenditure has widened to 11%.* | *They are trying to widen the discussion to include environmental issues.*
3 [I] if your eyes widen, they open more, especially because you are surprised or frightened OPP **narrow**

ˌwide-ˈranging ●○○ *adj written* including a wide variety of subjects, things, or people: *a wide-ranging discussion* | *wide-ranging proposals to improve the rail network*

wide·screen[1] /ˈwaɪdskriːn/ *adj* **1** a widescreen television is much wider than it is high **2** made in a form that is intended to be seen on a screen much wider than it is high: *Widescreen movies are often shown on TV with the sides cut short.*

widescreen[2] *n* **in widescreen** in a form that is intended to be seen on a wide screen: *The series was shot in widescreen.*

wide·spread /ˈwaɪdspred/ ●●○ W3 AWL *adj* existing or happening in many places or situations, or among many people: *the **widespread use** of chemicals in agriculture* | **widespread support/acceptance/criticism/condemnation etc** *There was widespread support for the war.* | *The storm caused widespread damage.* THESAURUS▸ COMMON

wid·get /ˈwɪdʒɪt/ *n* [C] **1** *spoken* a small piece of equipment that you do not know the name for **2** *informal* used to refer to an imaginary product that a company might produce: *Company A produces 6,000 widgets a month at a unit price of $0.33.* **3** *technical* a small piece of software used as part of a WEBPAGE, or on a MOBILE PHONE, that shows information or does other things in a way that is controlled by the user

wid·ow /ˈwɪdəʊ $ -doʊ/ ●●○ *n* [C]
1 a woman whose husband has died and who has not married again: *an elderly widow who was attacked and robbed last month* | *a wealthy widow* THESAURUS▸ MARRIED
2 football/golf etc widow a woman whose husband spends all his free time watching football, playing golf etc – used humorously

wid·owed /ˈwɪdəʊd $ -doʊd/ *v* **be widowed** if someone is widowed, their husband or wife dies: *She was widowed at the age of 25.* THESAURUS▸ MARRIED —**widowed** *adj*: *his widowed mother*

wid·ow·er /ˈwɪdəʊə $ -doʊər/ *n* [C] a man whose wife has died and who has not married again THESAURUS▸ MARRIED

wid·ow·hood /ˈwɪdəʊhʊd $ -doʊ-/ *n* [U] the state of being a widow or widower

width /wɪdθ/ ●●○ *n*
1 [C,U] the distance from one side of something to the other → **breadth**, **length**: **[+of]** *What's the width of the desk?* | **three feet/two metres etc in width** *It's about six metres in width.* → see picture at DIMENSION
2 run/extend the (full) width of sth to exist from one side of something to the other: *a covered terrace extending the full width of the house*
3 [C] the distance from one side of a swimming pool to the other: *I **swam** ten **widths**.*
4 [C] a piece of cloth that has been measured and cut: **[+of]** *four widths of curtain material*

width·ways /ˈwɪdθweɪz/ *adv* across, between the two long sides of something → **lengthways**: *Cut each rectangular cake in half widthways.*

wield /wiːld/ ●○○ *v* [T]
1 wield power/influence/authority etc to have a lot of power or influence, and to use it: *The Church wields immense power in Ireland.*
2 to hold a weapon or tool that you are going to use: *She had her car windows smashed by a gang wielding baseball bats.*

wie·ner /ˈwiːnə $ -ər/ (*also* **wie·nie, weenie** /ˈwiːni/) *n* [C] *AmE* **1** a type of SAUSAGE **2** *spoken* someone who is silly or stupid **3** *spoken* a PENIS – used by children

wife /waɪf/ ●●● S1 W1 *n* (*plural* **wives** /waɪvz/) [C] the woman that a man is married to → **husband**, **spouse**: *Have you met my wife?* | *a refuge for battered wives* | *his second wife* | **ex-wife/former wife** *He threatened to kill his ex-wife's boyfriend.* THESAURUS▸ MARRIED

ˈwife-ˌbeater *n* [C] a man who often hits his wife

wife·ly /ˈwaɪfli/ *adj old-fashioned* wifely qualities or actions are supposed to be typical of a good wife – sometimes used humorously

ˈwife-ˌswapping *n* [U] an activity in which married couples have sex with each other's partners, for example at a party

wi-fi /ˈwaɪ faɪ/ ●●○ (*also* **wireless networking**) *n* [U] *trademark* (***wireless fidelity***) a way of connecting computers or other electronic machines to a network by using radio signals rather than wires

wig[1] /wɪg/ ●●○ *n* [C] artificial hair that you wear on your head → **toupée**

wig[2] *v* (**wigged, wigging**)
wig (sb) out *phr v AmE informal* to become very anxious, upset, or afraid, or to make someone very anxious, upset, or afraid

wig·gle /ˈwɪgəl/ *v* [I,T] to move with small movements from side to side or up and down, or to make something move like this: *Henry wiggled his toes.* —**wiggle** *n* [C]

ˈwiggle room *n* [U] if someone leaves themselves some wiggle room, they do or say something in a way that allows them to change it later

wig·gly /ˈwɪgəli/ *adj informal* a wiggly line is one that has small curves in it → **wavy**

wig·wam /ˈwɪgwæm $ -wɑːm/ *n* [C] a structure with a round or pointed roof used as a home by some Native American tribes in the past → **tepee**

wik·i /ˈwɪki/ *n* [C,U] a website with information that users can change or add things to

W

wild¹ /waɪld/ ●●● S2 W2 *adj*
1 PLANTS/ANIMALS [usually before noun] living in a natural state, not changed or controlled by people OPP **tame**: ***wild animals*** | *a field full of* ***wild flowers*** | **wild horse/dog/pig etc** | *animals both wild and domesticated* | **wild mushroom/garlic/rose etc**
2 LAND not used by people for farming, building etc: *Nepal is stunning, with its wild, untamed landscape.* | *the wild and lonely Scottish hills*
3 EMOTIONS feeling or expressing strong uncontrolled emotions, especially anger, happiness, or excitement: *wild laughter* | **[+with]** *He was wild with rage.*
4 BEHAVIOUR behaving in an uncontrolled, sometimes violent way: *She was completely wild in high school.* | *Donny could be* ***wild and crazy***. | *There was a* ***wild look*** *about her* (=she seemed a little crazy).
5 go wild a) to behave in a very excited uncontrolled way: *The crowd went wild as soon as the singer stepped onto the stage.* **b)** to get very angry: *When Tony heard how much it was going to cost, he just went wild.*
6 ENJOYABLE *informal* very enjoyable and exciting: *'How was the party?' 'It was wild!'*
7 be wild about sth/sb *informal* to like something or someone very much: *My son's wild about football.* | *I'm not that wild about rap music, to be honest.*
8 WITHOUT CAREFUL THOUGHT done or said without much thought or care, or without knowing all the facts: *wild accusations* | *I'm just making a* ***wild guess*** *here, so correct me if I'm wrong.*
9 beyond sb's wildest dreams beyond anything that someone imagined or hoped for: *an invention that was to change our lives beyond our wildest dreams*
10 not/never in your wildest dreams used to say that you did not expect or imagine that something would happen, especially after it has happened: *Never in my wildest dreams did I expect to win first place.*
11 WEATHER/SEA violent and strong: *a wild and angry sea*
12 CARD GAMES a card that is wild can be used to represent any other card in a game
13 wild horses would/could not ... used to say that someone is determined not to go somewhere, do something etc: *Wild horses would not have dragged him into a vegetarian restaurant.* —**wildness** *n* [U] → WILD CARD, → **sow your wild oats** at SOW¹(3)

wild² *adv* **1 run wild a)** if children or animals run wild, they behave in an uncontrolled way because there is no one to control them **b)** if something runs wild, it is not controlled and operates in an extremely free way: *Be creative – allow your* ***imagination*** *to* ***run wild***. **c)** if plants run wild, they grow a lot in an uncontrolled way **2 grow wild** if plants grow wild somewhere, they have not been planted by people

wild³ *n* **1 in the wild** in natural and free conditions, not kept or controlled by people: *There are very few pandas living in the wild now.* **2 the wilds of Africa/Alaska etc** areas where there are no towns and not many people live

ˌwild ˈboar *n* [C] a large wild pig with long hair

ˈwild ˌcard *n* [C] **1** a playing card that can represent any other card **2** someone whose behaviour or effect on a situation is difficult to guess **3** a player who is a wild card or who is given a wild card is chosen for a competition although they have not previously done well enough to take part **4** *technical* a symbol that can represent any letter in some computer instructions

wild·cat¹ /ˈwaɪldkæt/ *n* [C] a type of cat that looks similar to a pet cat and lives in mountains, forests etc

wildcat² *v* (**wildcatted**, **wildcatting**) [I] *AmE* to look for oil in a place where nobody has found any yet —**wildcatter** *n* [C]

ˌwildcat ˈstrike *n* [C] an occasion when workers suddenly stop working in order to protest about something, usually without the support of a TRADE UNION

wil·de·beest /ˈwɪldəbiːst/ *n* [C] a large Southern African animal with a tail and curved horns SYN **gnu**

wil·der·ness /ˈwɪldənəs $ -dər-/ ●●○ *n* [C usually singular]
1 a large area of land that has never been developed or farmed: *the Alaskan wilderness* THESAURUS COUNTRY
2 a place that seems no longer used or cared for by anyone: *The garden was a wilderness.* | *The south side of the city had become a lawless wilderness.*
3 in/from/out of the wilderness someone who is in the wilderness does not have power or is not involved in something in an important way at a particular time: *the re-emergence of Richard Nixon from the* ***political wilderness*** *in 1968*

ˈwilderness ˌarea *n* [C] an area of public land in the US where no buildings or roads are allowed to be built

wild·fire /ˈwaɪldfaɪə $ -faɪr/ *n* [C,U] *especially AmE* a fire that moves quickly and cannot be controlled → **spread like wildfire** at SPREAD¹(2)

wild·fowl /ˈwaɪldfaʊl/ *n* [plural] birds, especially ones that live near water such as DUCKS

ˌwild ˈgoose ˌchase *n* [C] a situation where you are looking for something that does not exist or that you are very unlikely to find, so that you waste a lot of time: *It looks like they've sent us on a wild goose chase.*

wild·life /ˈwaɪldlaɪf/ ●●○ *n* [U] animals and plants growing in natural conditions: *measures to protect the area's wildlife* | *the destruction of* ***wildlife habitats***

wild·ly /ˈwaɪldli/ ●●○ *adv*
1 in a very uncontrolled or excited way: *The audience cheered wildly.*
2 extremely: *The band is wildly popular in Cuba.* | *wildly inaccurate statements*

ˌwild ˈrice *n* [U] the seed of a type of grass that grows in parts of North America and China

ˌWild ˈWest, the the western US, where many European SETTLERS moved during the 19th century to establish new farms and new cities. In films it is often shown as a place where COWBOYS and INDIANS (=Native Americans) fight each other, and where cowboys use guns rather than the law to settle arguments. A situation where there are no laws or controls is sometimes described as being 'like the Wild West'.

wiles /waɪlz/ *n* [plural] clever talk or tricks used to persuade someone to do what you want: *It was impossible to resist her* ***feminine wiles***.

wil·ful *BrE*, **willful** *AmE* /ˈwɪlfəl/ *adj* **1** continuing to do what you want, even after you have been told to stop – used to show disapproval: *a wilful child* **2 wilful damage/disobedience/exaggeration etc** deliberate damage etc, when you know that what you are doing is wrong —**wilfully** *adv* —**wilfulness** *n* [U]

will¹ /wɪl/ ●●● S1 W1 *modal verb* (*negative short form* **won't**)
1 FUTURE used to make future tenses: *A meeting will be held next Tuesday at 3 p.m.* | *What time will she arrive?* | *I hope they won't be late.* | *Maybe by then you will have changed your mind.*
2 WILLING TO DO STH used to show that someone is willing or ready to do something: *Dr Weir will see you now.* | *The baby won't eat anything.*
3 REQUESTING *spoken* used to ask someone to do something: *Will you phone me later?* | *Shut the door, will you?*
4 WHAT GENERALLY HAPPENS used to say what always happens in a particular situation or what is generally true: *Oil will float on water.* | *Accidents will happen.*
5 POSSIBILITY used like 'can' to show what is possible: *This car will hold five people comfortably.*
6 BELIEF used to say that you think something is true: *That will be Tim coming home now.* | *As you will have noticed, there are some gaps in the data.*
7 GIVING ORDERS *spoken* used to give an order or to state a rule: *Will you be quiet!* | *You will do as I say.* | *Every employee will carry an identity card at all times.*
8 OFFERING/INVITING *spoken* used to offer something to someone or to invite them to do something: *Will you have some more tea?* | *Won't you have a seat?*

9 ANNOYING HABIT *spoken* used to describe someone's habits, especially when you think they are annoying: *Trish will keep asking silly questions.*

GRAMMAR: Choosing the right tense

• You use **will** when talking about the future: *I'm sure the party will be a big success.*
• Usually **will** changes to **would** when reporting what someone said or thought: *She said she was sure that the party would be a big success.*
• If the event is still in the future, **will** is sometimes used, especially after the present perfect tense: *Lots of people have said they will come to the party.*
GRAMMAR GUIDE ▸ VERBS

will² ●●● S2 W2 *n*
1 DETERMINATION [C,U] determination to do something that you have decided to do, even if this is difficult: *Children sometimes have strong wills.* | **the will to do sth** *Even though she was in terrible pain, Mary never lost the will to live.* → STRONG-WILLED, WEAK-WILLED
2 LEGAL DOCUMENT [C] a legal document that says who you want your money and property to be given to after you die: *Have you **made** a **will** yet?* | **in sb's will** *My grandfather left me some money in his will.* | *the senator's **last will and testament***
3 WHAT SB WANTS [singular] what someone wants to happen in a particular situation: *He accused her of trying to **impose** her **will** on others.* | **against your will** *Collier claims the police forced him to sign a confession against his will.* | **[+of]** *the will of the people* | *obedience to God's will* → FREE WILL
4 with the best will in the world *BrE spoken* used to say that something is not possible, even if you very much want to do it: *With the best will in the world, I don't see what more I can do.*
5 where there's a will there's a way *spoken* used to say that if you really want to do something, you will find a way to succeed
6 at will whenever you want and in whatever way you want: *He can't just fire people at will, can he?*
7 with a will *written* in an eager and determined way → GOODWILL, ILL WILL

COLLOCATIONS

ADJECTIVES

a strong will *She had a very strong will and a clear sense of purpose.*
an iron will (*also* **a will of iron**) (=an extremely strong will) *Her unassuming manner concealed an iron will.*
political will (=determination on the part of governments and politicians) *There was a lack of political will to do anything about global warming.*

PHRASES

strength of will *She had achieved success by sheer strength of will.*
an effort of will (=a determined effort to do something you do not want to do) *With a great effort of will, she resisted the temptation to look at the letter.*
a battle/clash/test of wills (=when two determined people oppose each other) *Even the smallest decision could become an exhausting battle of wills.*

VERBS

have the will to do sth (=be determined enough to do it) *Do you have the will to win?*
lack the will to do sth *He lacked the will to resist.*
lose the will to do sth *The country's troops had lost the will to fight.*

will³ *v* **1** [T] to try to make something happen by thinking about it very hard: **will sb to do sth** *She was willing herself not to cry.* **2** [T + to] to officially give something that you own to someone else after you die **3** [I,T] *old use* to want something to happen: *The King wills it.*

will·ful /ˈwɪlfəl/ *adj* the American spelling of WILFUL

wil·lie /ˈwɪli/ *n informal* **1 the willies** a nervous or frightened feeling: *All this talk about ghosts is **giving** me **the willies**.* **2** another spelling of WILLY

will·ing /ˈwɪlɪŋ/ ●●● S2 W3 *adj*
1 [not before noun] prepared to do something, or having no reason to not want to do it: **willing to do sth** *How much are they willing to pay?* | **quite/perfectly willing** *I told them I was perfectly willing to help.*
2 willing helper/volunteer/partner etc someone who is eager to help etc and does not have to be persuaded: *I soon had an army of willing helpers.* —**willingly** *adv*: *Sixty percent of voters said they would willingly pay higher taxes for better health care.*

will·ing·ness /ˈwɪlɪŋnəs/ ●○○ *n* [U] the state of being prepared to do something: *He has **shown** no **willingness to** compromise.*

ˌwill o' the ˈwisp *n* [C usually singular] **1** someone that you can never completely depend on, or something that you can never achieve **2** a blue moving light caused by natural gases, that can be seen over wet ground at night

wil·low /ˈwɪləʊ $ -loʊ/ *n* [C,U] a type of tree that has long thin branches and grows near water, or the wood from this tree

wil·low·y /ˈwɪləʊi $ -loʊi/ *adj* tall, thin, and graceful: *She was pale and willowy, with violet eyes.*

will·pow·er /ˈwɪlˌpaʊə $ -ˌpaʊr/ *n* [U] the ability to control your mind and body in order to achieve something that you want to do: *It took all his willpower to remain calm.*

wil·ly /ˈwɪli/ *n* (*plural* **willies**) [C] *BrE informal* a PENIS

willy-nil·ly /ˌwɪli ˈnɪli/ *adv* **1** if something happens willy-nilly, it happens whether you want it to or not: *He found himself drawn, willy-nilly, into the argument.* **2** without planning, organization, or control: *Companies were accused of raising prices willy-nilly.*

WILT

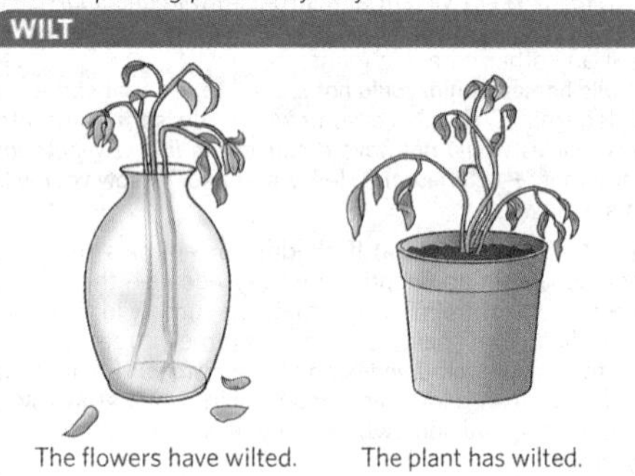

The flowers have wilted. The plant has wilted.

wilt¹ /wɪlt/ *v* [I] **1** if a plant wilts, it bends over because it is too dry or old → **droop 2** *informal* to feel weak or tired, especially because you are too hot

wilt² *v old use* **thou wilt** you will

wil·y /ˈwaɪli/ *adj* clever at getting what you want, especially by tricking people SYN **cunning**: *a wily politician* —**wiliness** *n* [U]

Wim·ble·don /ˈwɪmbəldən/ a tennis competition played every year in Wimbledon, south London. At Wimbledon, the games are played on grass and the players must wear all white. Wimbledon is also thought of as a typically English social occasion, and it is traditional to eat strawberries (STRAWBERRY) and cream there.

wimp¹ /wɪmp/ *n* [C] *informal* **1** someone who has a weak character and is afraid to do something difficult or unpleasant: *Don't be such a wimp!* **2** a man who is thin and physically weak —**wimpish, wimpy** *adj*

wimp² *v*
wimp out *phr v spoken* to not do something that you intended to do, because you do not feel brave enough, strong enough etc SYN **cop out**

wim·ple /ˈwɪmpəl/ *n* [C] a piece of cloth that a NUN wears over her head

win¹ /wɪn/ ●●● S1 W1 *v* (*past tense and past participle* **won** /wʌn/, *present participle* **winning**)
1 COMPETITION/RACE [I,T] to be the best or most successful in a competition, game, election etc OPP **lose**: **win a race/a game/an election etc** *Who do you think will win the next election?* | *He won the Tour de France last year.* | **win a war/battle** *the young pilots who won the Battle of Britain* | *Who's winning* (=who is most successful at this point in the game)? | **[+at]** *I never win at cards.* | **win by 10 points/70 metres etc** *We won by just one point.*
2 PRIZE [T] to get something as a prize for winning in a competition or game: *How does it feel to have* **won** *the gold* **medal**? | *She won £160 on the lottery.* | **win sth for sb** *the man who helped win the Cup for Arsenal*
3 GET/ACHIEVE [T] to get something that you want because of your efforts or abilities SYN **gain**: **win sb's approval/support/trust etc** *The proposal has won the approval of the city council.* | *Kramer has certainly won the respect of his peers.* | **win sb's heart** (=make them love you or feel sympathy for you) | *The company has* **won** *a* **contract** *to build a new power plant outside Houston.* | **win sth from sb** *Davis hopes to win financial backing from a London investment firm.*
4 MAKE SB WIN STH [T] if something, usually something that you do, wins you something, you win it or get it because of that thing: **win sb sth** *That performance won Hanks an Oscar.* | *That kind of behaviour won't win you any friends.*
5 you win *spoken* used to agree to what someone wants after you have tried to persuade them to do something else: *OK, you win – we'll go to the movies.*
6 you can't win *spoken* used to say that there is no satisfactory way of dealing with a particular situation: *You can't win, can you? You either work late and upset your family, or go home early and risk your job.*
7 you can't win them all (*also* **you win some, you lose some**) *spoken* used to show sympathy when someone has had a disappointing experience
8 win or lose *informal* no matter whether you win or lose: *Win or lose, I love competitive sports.*
9 win the day to finally be successful in a discussion or argument SYN **triumph**: *Common sense won the day, and the plans were dropped.* → **win the toss** at TOSS²(1), **WINNER**, **WINNING**

THESAURUS

win to be the best or most successful in a competition, game, election etc: *Italy won the World Cup in 2006.* | *He has a realistic chance of winning the Championship.*
come first/be first to win a race or competition: *Our team came first.* | *Jo was first in the race and I was second.*
finish in first place (*also* **come in first**) to win a race, competition, or election: *The Democratic candidate finished in first place.* | *I couldn't believe it when the horse I chose came in first.*
triumph *written* to win a great victory, especially after a long and difficult battle, game etc: *Britain triumphed over its enemies.* | *In the end, the Yankees triumphed.*
come out on top *informal* to win a game, competition, argument etc: *United came out on top after a thrilling game.* | *They did a survey and the Swedish car-maker came out on top.*
be leading/be in the lead to be winning a game, race, election etc at the moment: *The High School team are leading with sixty points.* | *With only two minutes left to play, we were still in the lead.*
be ahead to be doing better than someone else in a game, competition, or election: *He's still fifty seconds ahead of his nearest rival.* | *A week before the election, they were still ahead in the polls.*

win sb/sth ↔ **back** *phr v* to succeed in getting back something or someone that you had before SYN **regain**: *How can I win back her trust?*
win out *phr v* to finally succeed or defeat other people or things: **[+over]** *Often presentation wins out over content* (=is treated as more important than content).
win sb ↔ **over** (*also* **win sb ↔ round** *BrE*) *phr v* to get someone's support or friendship by persuading them or being nice to them: *We'll be working hard over the next ten days to win over the undecided voters.*
win through *phr v especially BrE* to finally succeed in spite of problems SYN **triumph**: *As in most of his films, it's the good guys who win through in the end.*

win² ●●● W3 *n* [C] a success or victory, especially in sport OPP **defeat**: *We've had two wins so far this season.* | **[+over]** *In the under-16 event England had their first win over Germany.* THESAURUS ▸ **VICTORY** → **NO-WIN**, **WIN-WIN**

wince /wɪns/ *v* [I] **1** to suddenly change the expression on your face as a reaction to something painful or upsetting: *Sandra winced as the dentist started to drill.* **2** to suddenly feel very uncomfortable or embarrassed because of something that happens, something you remember etc SYN **cringe**: **wince at the memory/thought/idea** *I still wince at the thought of that terrible evening.* —**wince** *n* [singular]

winch¹ /wɪntʃ/ *n* [C] a machine with a rope or chain for lifting heavy objects

winch² *v* [T always + adv/prep] to lift something or someone up using a winch: *The two men were winched out of the sinking boat by an RAF helicopter.*

wind¹ /wɪnd/ ●●● S2 W2 *n*
1 AIR (*also* **the wind**) [C,U] moving air, especially when it moves strongly or quickly in a current → **windy**: *The wind blew from the northeast.* | *Planes were unable to take off because of high winds.* → **CROSSWIND**, **DOWNWIND**, **HEADWIND**, **TAILWIND**, **TRADE WIND**, **UPWIND**
2 get/have wind of sth *informal* to hear or find out about something secret or private: *You'd better hope the press doesn't get wind of this.*
3 BREATH [U] your ability to breathe normally: **get your wind (back)** (=be able to breathe normally again, for example after running) | **knock the wind out of sb** (=hit someone in the stomach so that they cannot breathe for a moment) → **second wind** at SECOND¹(12), → **WINDPIPE**
4 IN YOUR STOMACH [U] *BrE* the condition of having air or gas in your stomach or INTESTINES, or the air or gas itself SYN **gas** *AmE*: *I can't drink beer – it gives me wind.* | *'What's wrong with the baby?' 'Just a little wind.'*
5 take the wind out of sb's sails *informal* to make someone lose their confidence, especially by saying or doing something unexpected
6 see which way the wind is blowing to find out what the situation is before you do something or make a decision
7 sth is in the wind used to say that something is happening or going to happen, but the details are not clear: *If there was a merger in the wind, I'm sure we'd hear about it.*
8 winds of change/freedom/public opinion etc used to refer to things that have important effects, and that cannot be stopped: *The* **winds** *of change are* **blowing** *through the entire organization.*
9 put the wind up sb/get the wind up *BrE informal* if you put the wind up someone, you make them feel anxious or frightened. If you get the wind up, you become anxious or frightened: *The threat of legal action will be enough to put the wind up them.*
10 MUSIC **the winds/the wind section** the people in an ORCHESTRA or band who play musical instruments that you blow through, such as a FLUTE
11 like the wind if someone or something moves or runs like the wind, they move or run very quickly: *She* **ran like the wind** *down the stairs to escape.*
12 TALK [U] *BrE informal* talk that does not mean anything → **break wind** at BREAK¹(31), → **it's an ill wind (that blows nobody any good)** at ILL¹(4), → **sail close to the wind** at SAIL¹(6), → **straw in the wind** at STRAW(5)

COLLOCATIONS

ADJECTIVES

strong *The wind was so strong he could hardly stand.*
light/gentle (=not strong) *Winds tomorrow will be light.*

W

high winds (=strong wind) *High winds are making driving conditions difficult.*
a cold/chill wind | an icy/biting/bitter wind (=very cold) | **a 20-/40-mile-an-hour wind | gale force/ hurricane force winds** (=very strong) | **the north/ south etc wind** (=coming from the north etc) | **a northerly/southerly etc wind** (=coming from the north etc) | **the prevailing wind** (=the most frequent wind in an area)

VERBS

the wind blows *A cold wind was blowing.*
the wind picks up (*also* **the wind gets up** *BrE*) (=becomes stronger) *The rain beat down and the wind was picking up.*
the wind drops/dies down (=becomes less strong) | **the wind changes** (=starts blowing from a different direction)

PHRASES

a gust of wind *A gust of wind rattled the window.*
be blowing/swaying/flapping etc in the wind *The trees were all swaying in the wind.*

wind + NOUN

wind speed *Wind speeds of up to 80 miles an hour were recorded.*

THESAURUS

wind air moving in a current, especially strongly or quickly: *A cold wind was blowing from the east. | Strong winds caused damage to many buildings.*
breeze a gentle pleasant wind: *The trees were moving gently in the breeze. | A slight breeze ruffled her hair.*
draught *BrE*, **draft** *AmE* /drɑːft $ dræft/ a current of cool air which blows into a room, especially one that makes you feel uncomfortable: *There's a bit of a draught in here - can you close the door?*

A STRONG WIND

gale a very strong wind: *The ship was blown off course in a severe gale.*
hurricane a storm that has very strong fast winds and that moves over water - used about storms in the North Atlantic Ocean: *The hurricane devastated Florida and killed at least 40 people.*
typhoon a violent tropical storm - used about storms in the Western Pacific Ocean: *A typhoon has hit the Philippines, lifting roofs off houses and uprooting trees.*
tornado (*also* **twister** *AmE informal*) a violent storm with strong winds that spin very quickly in a circle, often forming a cloud that is narrower at the bottom than the top: *The town was hit by a tornado that damaged several homes.*
cyclone a violent tropical storm with strong winds that spin in a circle: *A devastating cyclone struck Bangladesh in April that year.*

W

wind² /waɪnd/ ●●● S3 W3 *v* (*past tense and past participle* **wound** /waʊnd/)
1 [T always + adv/prep] to turn or twist something several times around something else: **wind sth around/round sth** *The hair is divided into sections and wound around heated rods.*
2 [T] (*also* **wind up**) to turn part of a machine around several times, in order to make it move or start working: *Did you remember to wind the clock?*
3 [I always + adv/prep] if a road, river etc winds somewhere, it has many smooth bends and is usually very long: **wind (its way) through/along etc sth** *Highway 99 winds its way along the coast. | a winding path*
4 [T] to make a tape move in a machine: **wind sth forward/back** *Can you wind the video back a little way - I want to see that bit again.* → REWIND —**wind** *n* [C]

wind down *phr v*
1 wind sth ↔ down to gradually reduce the work of a business or organization so that it can be closed down completely
2 to rest and relax after a lot of hard work or excitement: *I find it difficult to wind down after a day at work.*
3 wind sth ↔ down *BrE* to make something, especially a car window, move down by turning a handle or pressing a button

wind up *phr v*
1 to bring an activity, meeting etc to an end: *OK, just to wind up, could I summarize what we've decided?* | **wind sth ↔ up** *It's time to* **wind things up** *- I have a plane to catch.*
2 wind sth ↔ up to close down a company or organization: *Our operations in Jamaica are being wound up.*
3 [linking verb] *informal* to be in an unpleasant situation or place after a lot has happened SYN **end up**: **[+in/at/with etc]** *You know you're going to wind up in court over this.* | **wind up doing sth** *I wound up wishing I'd never come.*
4 wind sb ↔ up *BrE* to deliberately say or do something that will annoy or worry someone, as a joke → **tease**: *They're only winding you up.* → WOUND UP
5 wind sth ↔ up to turn part of a machine around several times, in order to make it move or start working
6 wind sth ↔ up *BrE* to make something, especially a car window, move up by turning a handle or pressing a button: *Could you wind the window up, please?*

wind³ /wɪnd/ *v* (*past tense and past participle* **winded**) [T] to make someone have difficulty breathing, as a result of falling on something or being hit: *The fall winded him and he lay still for a moment.*

wind·bag /ˈwɪndbæg/ *n* [C] *informal* someone who talks too much SYN **gasbag** *BrE*

wind·break /ˈwɪndbreɪk/ *n* [C] a fence, line of trees, or wall that is intended to protect a place from the wind

wind break·er /ˈwɪnd ˌbreɪkə $ -ər/ *AmE*, **windcheater** /ˈwɪndˌtʃiːtə $ -ər/ *BrE n* [C] a type of coat that protects you from the wind

wind chill /ˈwɪnd tʃɪl/ *n* [U] *technical* the cooling effect of the wind: *It must have been minus 5 with the* **wind chill factor**.

wind chimes /ˈwɪnd tʃaɪmz/ *n* [plural] long thin pieces of metal, wood etc hanging together in a group, that make musical sounds when the wind blows them against each other

wind·ed /ˈwɪndɪd/ *adj* unable to breathe easily, because you have been running or you have been hit in the stomach

wind·fall /ˈwɪndfɔːl $ -fɒːl/ *n* [C] **1** an amount of money that you get unexpectedly: *his £2 million windfall in the lottery* | **windfall gain/profit etc** (=high profit that you did not expect to make) **2** a piece of fruit that has fallen off a tree

ˈ**windfall ˌtax** *n* [C] an additional amount of tax that the British government sometimes takes from a company that has suddenly earned a large amount of money that it did not expect to earn

wind farm /ˈwɪnd fɑːm $ -fɑːrm/ *n* [C] a place where a lot of WINDMILLS have been built in order to produce electricity

winding sheet /ˈwaɪndɪŋ ʃiːt/ *n* [C] a cloth that is wrapped around a dead person's body before it is buried, used especially in the past SYN **shroud**

wind in·stru·ment /ˈwɪnd ˌɪnstrəmənt/ *n* [C] a musical instrument made of wood or metal that you play by blowing, such as a FLUTE, or one that air is passed through, such as an ORGAN → **brass**, **percussion**, **stringed instrument** → **the winds/the wind section** at WIND¹(10), → WOODWIND

wind·jam·mer /ˈwɪndˌdʒæmə $ -ər/ *n* [C] a large sailing ship of the type that was used for trade in the 19th century

wind·lass /ˈwɪndləs/ *n* [C] a machine for pulling or lifting heavy objects

wind·mill /ˈwɪndˌmɪl/ *n* [C] **1** a building or structure with parts that turn around in the wind, used for producing electrical power or crushing grain **2** *BrE* a toy consisting of a stick with curved pieces of plastic at the end that turn around when they are blown SYN **pinwheel** *AmE*

WINDOW

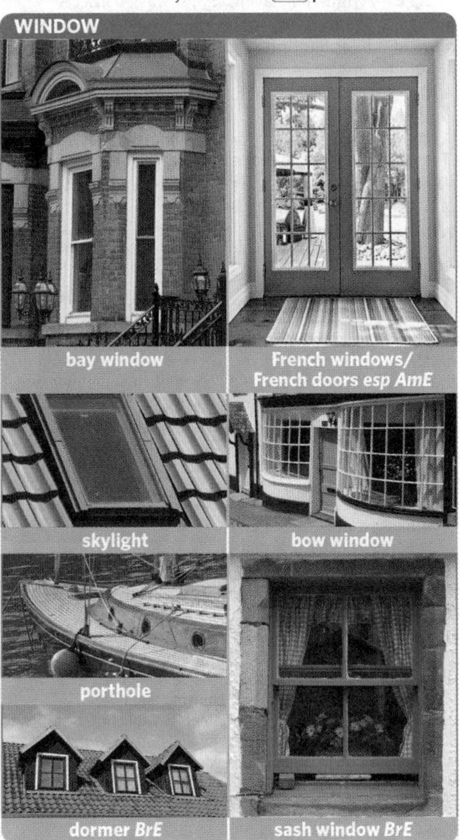

bay window

French windows/ French doors *esp AmE*

skylight

bow window

porthole

dormer *BrE*

sash window *BrE*

win·dow /ˈwɪndəʊ $ -doʊ/ ●●● S1 W1 *n* [C]
1 a space or an area of glass in the wall of a building or vehicle that lets in light: **open/close/shut a window** *Do you mind if I open the window?* | **out of/from/through the window** *She looked out of the window to see if it was raining.* | *The sun was shining through the windows.* | **in the window** (=just inside a window) *We were looking at the Christmas displays in the* ***shop windows***. | **bedroom/kitchen etc window** → BAY WINDOW, DORMER, FRENCH WINDOWS, PICTURE WINDOW, SASH WINDOW
2 one of the separate areas on a computer screen where different programs are operating
3 (*also* **window of opportunity**) a short period of time that is available for a particular activity: *Delay might open a window of opportunity for their rivals.*
4 an area on an envelope with clear plastic in it which lets you see the address written on the letter inside the envelope
5 a window on/to the world something that makes it possible to see and learn about what is happening in other parts of the world: *Television provides us with a useful window on the world.*
6 go out (of) the window *informal* to disappear completely or no longer have any effect: *One glass of wine, and all my good intentions went out the window.*

ˈwindow box *n* [C] a long narrow box in which you can grow plants outside your window

ˈwindow ˌcleaner *n* [C] someone whose job is to clean windows

ˈwindow ˌdresser *n* [C] someone whose job is to arrange goods attractively in shop windows

ˈwindow ˌdressing *n* [U] **1** something that is intended to make people like your plans or activities, and to stop them seeing the true situation – used to show disapproval: *All these glossy pamphlets are just window dressing – the fact is that the new mall will ruin the neighborhood.* **2** the art of arranging goods in a shop window so that they look attractive to customers

win·dow·less /ˈwɪndəʊləs $ -doʊ-/ *adj* without any windows: *a windowless basement room*

win·dow·pane /ˈwɪndəʊpeɪn $ -doʊ-/ *n* [C] a single whole piece of glass in a window

ˈwindow ˌseat *n* [C] **1** a seat next to the window on a bus, plane etc **2** a seat directly below a window

ˈwindow ˌshade *n* [C] *AmE* a BLIND³(1) → see picture at BLIND³

ˈwindow-ˌshopping *n* [U] the activity of looking at goods in shop windows without intending to buy them —**window-shopper** *n* [C]

win·dow·sill /ˈwɪndəʊˌsɪl $ -doʊ-/ (*also* **ˈwindow ˌledge**) *n* [C] a shelf fixed along the bottom of a window

wind·pipe /ˈwɪndpaɪp/ *n* [C] the tube through which air passes from your mouth to your lungs SYN **trachea**

wind·screen /ˈwɪndskriːn/ ●○○ *n* [C] *BrE* the large window at the front of a car, bus etc SYN **windshield** *AmE*

ˈwindscreen ˌwiper *n* [C] *BrE* a long thin piece of metal with a rubber edge that moves across a windscreen to remove rain SYN **windshield wiper** *AmE* → see picture at CAR

wind·shield /ˈwɪndʃiːld/ ●○○ *n* [C]
1 *AmE* a windscreen
2 a piece of glass or clear plastic fixed at the front of a MOTORCYCLE that protects the rider from wind

ˈwindshield ˌwiper *n* [C] *AmE* a windscreen wiper → see picture at CAR

wind·sock /ˈwɪndsɒk $ -sɑːk/ *n* [C] a tube of material fastened to a pole at airports to show the direction of the wind

Wind·sors, the /ˈwɪnzəz $ -zərz/ a name used especially by newspapers for the present British royal family, whose family name is Windsor

wind·storm /ˈwɪndstɔːm $ -stɔːrm/ *n* [C] a period of bad weather with strong winds but not much rain

wind-surf·ing /ˈwɪnd ˌsɜːfɪŋ $ -ˌsɜːr-/ *n* [U] the sport of sailing across water by standing on a SURFBOARD and holding on to a large sail attached to the surfboard —**wind-surfer** *n* [C] —**wind-surf** *v* [I]

wind·swept /ˈwɪndswept/ *adj* **1** a place that is windswept is often windy because there are not many trees or buildings to protect it: *windswept moors* **2** hair, clothes etc that are windswept have been blown around by the wind

wind tun·nel /ˈwɪnd ˌtʌnl/ *n* [C] a large enclosed passage where engineers test aircraft etc by forcing air past them

wind tur·bine /ˈwɪnd ˌtɜːbaɪn $ -ˌtɜːrbən, -baɪn/ *n* [C] a modern WINDMILL for providing electrical power

wind-up¹ *BrE*, **wind·up** *AmE* /ˈwaɪnd ʌp/ *n* **1** [C] *BrE informal* something that you say or do in order to make someone angry or worried, as a joke **2** [singular] a series of actions that are intended to complete a process, meeting etc: *The president made a statement at the windup of the summit in Helsinki.*

wind-up² /ˈwaɪnd ʌp/ *adj* [only before noun] relating to a machine or toy that you turn part of several times, in order to make it move or start working: *a wind-up gramophone*

wind·ward /ˈwɪndwəd $ -wərd/ *adj, adv* towards the direction from which the wind is blowing OPP **leeward**: *the windward side of the boat*

wind·y /ˈwɪndi/ ●●● S3 (*comparative* **windier**, *superlative* **windiest**) *adj*
1 if it is windy, there is a lot of wind: *It's too windy for a picnic.* | *a cold, windy day* | *a windy hillside*
2 windy talk is full of words that sound impressive but do not mean much: *politicians' windy generalizations*

W

ˌWindy ˈCity, the a NICKNAME for the US city of Chicago

wine¹ /waɪn/ ●●● S2 W2 *n* [C,U]
1 an alcoholic drink made from GRAPES, or a type of this drink: *a glass of wine* | **red/white wine** *a bottle of red wine* | **dry/sweet/sparkling wine** *a dry white wine*
2 an alcoholic drink made from another fruit or plant: *damson wine*

wine² *v* **wine and dine sb** to entertain someone well with a meal, wine etc: *Companies spend millions wining and dining clients.*

ˈwine bar *n* [C] a place that serves mainly wine and light meals

ˈwine ˌcellar *n* [C] an underground room where wine is stored to keep it at the right temperature

ˈwine ˌcooler *n* [C] *AmE* a drink made with wine, fruit juice, and water

ˈwine glass *n* [C] a tall glass with a thin stem, used for drinking wine → see picture at **GLASS¹**

win·e·ry /ˈwaɪnəri/ *n* (*plural* **wineries**) [C] a place where wine is made and stored → **vineyard**

ˈwine ˌtasting *n* [C,U] the activity or skill of tasting and comparing different wines to see if they are good, or an event where this happens

ˌwine ˈvinegar *n* [U] a type of VINEGAR made from sour wine, used in cooking

wing¹ /wɪŋ/ ●●● S2 W2 *n* [C]
1 BIRD/INSECT **a)** one of the parts of a bird's or insect's body that it uses for flying: *a butterfly with beautiful markings on its wings* | *The pheasant* ***flapped*** *its* ***wings*** *vigorously.* **b)** the meat on the wing bone of a chicken, duck etc, eaten as food: *spicy chicken wings*
2 PLANE one of the large flat parts that stick out from the side of a plane and help to keep it in the air → see picture at **PLANE¹**
3 BUILDING one of the parts of a large building, especially one that sticks out from the main part: **north/east etc wing** *the east wing of the palace* | *She works in the hospital's maternity wing.*
4 POLITICS a group of people within a political party or other organization who have a particular opinion or aim: *the moderate wing of the Republican Party* → **LEFT-WING, RIGHT-WING**
5 SPORT **a)** a WINGER **b)** the far left or right part of a sports field
6 CAR *BrE* the part of a car that is above a wheel SYN **fender** *AmE* → see picture at **CAR**
7 take sb under your wing to help and protect someone who is younger or less experienced than you are
8 (waiting/lurking) in the wings ready to do something or be used when the time is right: *Several junior managers are waiting in the wings for promotion.*
9 THEATRE **the wings** [plural] the parts at each side of a stage where actors are hidden from people who are watching the play
10 on a wing and a prayer if you do something on a wing and a prayer, you do not have much chance of succeeding
11 be on the wing *literary* if a bird is on the wing, it is flying
12 take wing *literary* to fly away
13 get your wings to pass the examinations you need to become a pilot → **clip sb's wings** at **CLIP²**(6), → **spread your wings** at **SPREAD¹**(10)

wing² *v* **1** [I always + adv/prep] *literary* to fly somewhere: *a flock of geese winging down the coast* | **wing its/their way to/across etc sth** *planes winging their way to exotic destinations* **2 wing its/their way** to go or be sent somewhere very quickly: **[+to]** *A bottle of champagne will soon be winging its way to 10 lucky winners.* **3 wing it** *spoken* to do something without planning or preparing it: *We'll just* ***have to wing it.***

ˈwing chair *n* [C] a comfortable chair with a high back and pieces pointing forward on each side where you can rest your head

ˌwing ˈcollar *n* [C] a type of shirt collar for men that is worn with very formal clothes

ˈwing comˌmander *n* [C] an officer of high rank in the British air force

winge /wɪndʒ/ *v* [I] another spelling of WHINGE

winged /wɪŋd/ *adj* having wings: *winged insects*

wing·er /ˈwɪŋə $ -ər/ (*also* **wing**) *n* [C] someone who plays in the far left or far right of the field in games such as football

ˈwing ˌmirror *n* [C] *BrE* a mirror on the side of a car → see picture at **CAR**

ˈwing nut *n* [C] a NUT for fastening things, which has sides that stick out to make it easier to turn

wing·span /ˈwɪŋspæn/ *n* [C] the distance from the end of one wing to the end of the other

wing·tip /ˈwɪŋtɪp/ *n* [C] **1** the point at the end of a bird's or a plane's wing **2** *AmE* a type of man's shoe with a pattern of small holes on the toe

wink¹ /wɪŋk/ ●●○ *v*
1 [I,T] to close and open one eye quickly to communicate something or show that something is a secret or joke: **[+at]** *He winked mischievously at Erica.* | *He winked an eye at his companion.*
2 [I] to shine with a light that flashes on and off SYN **blink**: *a Christmas tree with lights winking on and off*

WINK

wink at sth *phr v* to pretend not to notice something bad or illegal, in a way that suggests you approve of it

wink² ●●○ *n*
1 [C] a quick action of closing and opening one eye, usually as a signal to someone else: *He* ***gave*** *her* ***a wink.*** | *'You look tired,' he said with* ***a knowing wink.***
2 not get a wink of sleep/not sleep a wink not be able to sleep at all: *I didn't get a wink of sleep last night.* → **FORTY WINKS**, → **a nod's as good as a wink** at **NOD²**(4), → **tip sb the wink** at **TIP²**(11)

win·kle¹ /ˈwɪŋkəl/ *n* [C] *BrE* a small sea animal that lives in a shell and is eaten as food

winkle² *v*
winkle sb/sth ↔ **out** *phr v BrE* **1** to make someone leave a place: *Government critics were winkled out of their positions of influence.* **2** to get information from someone who does not want to give it to you: *Candy was very good at winkling out secrets.*

win·ner /ˈwɪnə $ -ər/ ●●● S3 W2 *n*
1 [C] a person or animal that has won something OPP **loser**: **[+of]** *the winner of the Ladies' Championship* | *Five* ***lucky winners*** *will each receive a signed copy of the album.* | *As a jockey he rode 10 winners.* | **prize/award/medal etc winner** *a Nobel prize winner*
2 [C] *informal* someone or something that is or is likely to be very popular and successful: *The book has proved to* ***be a winner with*** *young children.* | *The company seems to* ***be onto a winner*** (=doing something that is likely to be successful).
3 [singular] a GOAL or point that makes someone win a game such as football or tennis: *Moran* ***scored the winner*** *with only two minutes left.*
4 [C usually plural] the person who gets most of the advantages from a situation OPP **loser**: *In a capitalist society there will always be* ***winners and losers.*** | *The real winners this summer have been the sun cream manufacturers.*

win·ning /ˈwɪnɪŋ/ ●○○ *adj* [only before noun]
1 the winning person or thing is the one that wins or makes you win a competition or game: *the winning team* | *The winning design came from an architect in Glasgow.* | *Beckham scored the winning goal.*
2 making you very successful or likely to be successful: *a winning combination* | *As a business, they have found a winning formula.*

W

3 a winning quality or way of doing something is one that makes other people like you SYN **attractive**: *a* ***winning*** *smile*
4 a winning streak a period of time when you win every game or competition: *The team* ***are on a winning streak****.*
ˈwinning ˌpost *n* [singular] *BrE* the place where a race ends SYN **the finish line**
win·nings /ˈwɪnɪŋz/ *n* [plural] money that you have won: *lottery winnings*
win·now /ˈwɪnəʊ $ -noʊ/ (*also* **winnow down**) *v* [T] to make a list, group, or quantity smaller by getting rid of the things that you do not need or want SYN **whittle down**: *We need to winnow the list of candidates to three.*
winnow sb/sth ↔ **out** *phr v* to get rid of the things or people that you do not need or want from a group
wi·no /ˈwaɪnəʊ $ -noʊ/ *n* (*plural* **winos**) [C] *informal* someone who drinks a lot of alcohol and lives on the streets
win·some /ˈwɪnsəm/ *adj literary* behaving in a pleasant and attractive way: *a winsome smile*
win·ter¹ /ˈwɪntə $ -ər/ ●●● S2 W2 *n* [C,U] the season after autumn and before spring, when the weather is coldest → **summer**: *Soon it will be winter.* | **in (the) winter** *It usually snows here in the winter.* | **this/last/next winter** *Fuel supplies could be seriously disrupted this winter.*

GRAMMAR: Patterns with winter

in winter/in the winter
• You use **in winter** or **in the winter** when saying that something happens at that time: *It often snows here in winter.* | *We're going skiing in the winter.*

last winter/this winter etc
Don't use **in** with these words:
• You say **last winter**: *Last winter the temperature fell to minus 20 degrees.* ✗ Don't say: *In last winter the temperature fell to minus 20 degrees.*
• You say **this winter**: *We've had a lot of snow this winter.* ✗ Don't say: *We've had a lot of snow in this winter.*
• You say **next winter**: *Next winter she will turn 18.* ✗ Don't say: *In next winter she will turn 18.*
• You say **that winter**: *The lake froze over that winter.* ✗ Don't say: *The lake froze over in that winter.*

COLLOCATIONS

ADJECTIVES
cold *That winter was particularly cold.*
severe/hard/harsh (=very cold) *In a hard winter, many birds starve.*
mild *Winters here are generally mild.*

winter + NOUN
the winter months *During the winter months the town is often cut off.*
winter coat/shoes (=designed for winter)

PHRASES
in the depths of winter (=in the middle of the winter)

winter² *v* [I always + adv/prep] *formal* to spend the winter somewhere → **summer**: *Last year, over 11,000 Canadians wintered in Arizona.*
ˌwinter ˈsolstice *n* **the winter solstice** the shortest day of the year in the northern HEMISPHERE, usually around December 22nd → **summer solstice**
ˌwinter ˈsports *n* [plural] sports that are done on snow or ice, such as SKIing
win·ter·time /ˈwɪntətaɪm $ -ər-/ *n* [U] the time when it is winter → **summertime**: **in (the) wintertime** *The hills look very bleak in wintertime.*
win·try /ˈwɪntri/ (*also* **win·ter·y** /ˈwɪntəri/) *adj* **1** cold or typical of winter → **summery**: *a wintry day* | *wintry showers* **2** a wintry smile or expression is not very friendly
ˌwin-ˈwin *adj* [only before noun] a win-win situation, solution etc is one that will end well for everyone involved in it → **no-win situation**: *It's* ***a win-win situation*** *all around.* —**win-win** *n* [C]: *The agreement is a win-win for everyone.*
wipe¹ /waɪp/ ●●● S3 *v*
1 CLEAN/RUB [T] **a)** to rub a surface with something in order to remove dirt, liquid etc: **wipe sth with sth** *Wipe the table with a damp cloth.* | *Bill* ***wiped*** *his* ***eyes*** (=wiped the tears from his face) *and apologized.* | *He pulled a handkerchief from his pocket and* ***wiped*** *his* ***nose****.* **b)** to clean something by rubbing it against a surface: **wipe sth on sth** *He wiped his mouth on the back of his hand.* → see picture at **CLEAN** THESAURUS **CLEAN**
2 REMOVE DIRT [T always + adv/prep] to remove liquid, dirt, or marks by wiping: **wipe sth off/from etc sth** *Kim wiped the sweat from her face.* → see picture at **CLEAN²**
3 COMPUTER/TAPE [T] to remove all the information that is stored on a tape, video, or computer DISK
4 wipe sth from your mind/memory to try to forget an unpleasant experience
5 wipe the floor with sb *informal* to defeat someone completely in a competition or argument
6 wipe the slate clean to agree to forget about mistakes or arguments that happened in the past
7 wipe the smile/grin off sb's face *informal* to make someone feel less happy or confident, especially someone who is annoying because they think they are clever: *Tell him how much it'll cost – that should wipe the smile off his face!*
8 wipe sth off the face of the earth/wipe sth off the map to destroy something completely: *Another few years and this species could be wiped off the face of the earth.*
9 PLATES/CUPS ETC [I,T] to dry plates, cups etc that have been washed SYN **dry**: *You wash, I'll wipe.*
wipe sth ↔ **away** *phr v* to stop something existing: *A frown quickly wiped away her smile.*
wipe sth ↔ **down** *phr v* to completely clean a surface using a wet cloth
wipe sth **off** sth *phr v BrE* to reduce the value of SHARES or prices by a particular amount: *Nearly £7 billion has been wiped off share prices worldwide.*
wipe out *phr v*
1 wipe sth ↔ out to destroy, remove, or get rid of something completely: *Whole villages were wiped out by the floods.* | *Nothing could wipe out his bitter memories of the past.*
2 wipe sb ↔ out *informal* to make you feel extremely tired: *The heat had wiped us out.* → **WIPED OUT**
3 *AmE* to fall or hit an object when you are doing something: *Scott wiped out on his bike.*
wipe sth ↔ **up** *phr v* to remove liquid from a surface using a cloth: *I hastily wiped up the milk I had spilled.* → see picture at **CLEAN²**
wipe² *n* [C] **1** a wiping movement with a cloth: *An occasional wipe with a soft cloth will keep the surface shiny.* | ***Give*** *the baby's nose* ***a wipe,*** *would you?* **2** a special piece of wet material that you use to clean someone or something and then throw away: *a pack of baby wipes*
ˌwiped ˈout *adj* [not before noun] *informal* extremely tired SYN **exhausted**
wip·er /ˈwaɪpə $ -ər/ *n* [C] a piece of equipment on a car, that removes rain from the WINDSCREEN
wire¹ /waɪə $ waɪr/ ●●● S2 W3 *n*
1 [C,U] thin metal in the form of a thread, or a piece of this: *copper wire* | *a wire fence* → **BARBED WIRE, HIGH WIRE, TRIPWIRE**
2 [C] a piece of metal like this, used for carrying electrical currents or signals: *a telephone wire*
3 get your wires crossed to become confused about what someone is saying because you think they are talking about something else
4 go/come/be down to the wire *informal especially AmE* to be finished or achieved with very little time left: *The game was very close and went right down to the wire.*
5 [C] *AmE* a piece of electronic recording equipment, usually worn secretly on someone's clothes
6 [C] *AmE* a TELEGRAM
wire² ●○○ *v* [T]
1 (*also* **wire up**) **a)** to connect wires inside a building or

piece of equipment so that electricity can pass through: *Check that the plug has been wired up properly.* **b)** to connect electrical equipment to the electrical system using wires: **wire sth to sth** *The CD player had been wired up to the car's cigarette lighter.*
2 to send money electronically
3 to attach a piece of recording equipment to a person or room, especially secretly
4 be wired for sth to have all the necessary wires and connections for an electrical system to work: *All the rooms have been wired for cable TV.*
5 *AmE* to send a TELEGRAM to someone
6 to fasten two or more things together using wire: **wire sth together** *The poles had all been wired together.* → WIRING

ˈwire ˌcutters *n* [plural] a tool used for cutting wire

wired /waɪəd $ waɪrd/ *adj* **1** *AmE informal* feeling very active and excited, especially because you have drunk a lot of coffee or taken a drug → **high 2** *informal* connected to, and able to use, the Internet → **link, linkup 3** wired glass, cloth etc has wire in it to make it strong or stiff: *wired ribbon*

wire·less¹ /ˈwaɪələs $ ˈwaɪr-/ ●●○ *adj* relating to a system of communications that does not use electrical or telephone wires: *wireless Internet connections*

wireless² *n BrE old-fashioned* **1** [C] a radio **2** [U] a system of sending messages by radio

ˌwireless communiˈcations *n* [plural] a system of sending and receiving electronic signals that does not use electrical or telephone wires, for example the system used by MOBILE PHONES

ˌwireless ˈnetworking *n* [U] → **wi-fi**

ˌwire ˈnetting *BrE*, **ˌwire ˈmesh** *AmE n* [U] wires that have been woven together to form a net, used especially for fences

wire·tap·ping /ˈwaɪətæpɪŋ $ ˈwaɪr-/ *n* [U] the action of secretly listening to other people's telephone conversations, by connecting something to the wires of their telephone —**wiretap** *n* [C] —**wiretap** *v* [T]

ˌwire ˈwool *n* [U] *BrE* a mass of very thin pieces of wire, used for cleaning pans

wir·ing /ˈwaɪərɪŋ $ ˈwaɪr-/ *n* [U] the network of wires that form the electrical system in a building, vehicle, or piece of equipment: *The wiring needs to be replaced.*

wir·y /ˈwaɪəri $ ˈwaɪri/ *adj* **1** someone who is wiry is thin but has strong muscles **2** wiry hair or grass is stiff and strong

wis·dom /ˈwɪzdəm/ ●●○ *n* [U]
1 good sense and judgment, based especially on your experience of life: *a man of great wisdom* | **question/doubt the wisdom of (doing) sth** *Local people are questioning the wisdom of spending so much money on a new road.* | *You can always expect a few* **words of wisdom** *from Dave.* → **pearls of wisdom** at PEARL(3)
2 knowledge gained over a long period of time through learning or experience: *the collected wisdom of many centuries* THESAURUS KNOWLEDGE
3 (the) conventional/received/traditional etc wisdom a belief or opinion that most people have: *The conventional wisdom is that boys mature more slowly than girls.*
4 in sb's (infinite) wisdom *humorous* used to say that you do not understand why someone has decided to do something: *The boss, in her infinite wisdom, has decided to reorganize the whole office yet again.*

ˈwisdom tooth *n* [C] one of the four teeth at the back of your mouth that do not grow until you are an adult

wise¹ /waɪz/ ●●● S3 *adj*
1 DECISION/IDEA ETC wise decisions and actions are sensible and based on good judgment SYN **sensible**: **it is wise to do sth** *It's wise to check whether the flight times have changed before you leave for the airport.* | **be wise to do sth** *I think you were wise to leave when you did.* | *a wise precaution* | *I don't think that would be a very* **wise move** (=not be a sensible thing to do).
2 PERSON someone who is wise makes good decisions, gives good advice etc, especially because they have a lot of experience of life: *a wise old man* | *At the time I thought he was wonderful, but I'm* **older and wiser** *now.* | *As a manager, Sanford* **was wise in the ways of** (=knew a lot about) *company politics.* THESAURUS INTELLIGENT
3 be none the wiser/not be any the wiser a) to not understand something even after it has been explained to you: *Charlie explained how the system works, but I'm still none the wiser.* **b)** used for saying that no one will find out about something bad that someone has done: *He could easily have taken the money and no one would have been any the wiser.*
4 get/be wise to sb/sth *informal* to realize that someone is being dishonest: *Teachers quickly get wise to students who are cheating.* → **wise up** at WISE²
5 wise guy *informal especially AmE* an annoying person who thinks they know more than they really do: *OK, wise guy, shut up and listen!*
6 be wise after the event to realize what you should have done in a situation after it has happened: *It's easy to be wise after the event.* —**wisely** *adv*: *Invest the money wisely.* | *He nodded wisely.* → WISDOM, → **sadder but wiser** at SAD(6)

wise² *v*
wise up *phr v informal* to realize the truth about a bad situation: *Wise up, Vic – he's cheating you!* | **[+to]** *Consumers need to wise up to the effect that advertising has on them.*

wise³, **-wise** /waɪz/ *suffix* **1 price-wise/time-wise etc** *informal* used for saying which feature of a situation you are referring to: *Time-wise we're not doing too badly.* **2 crosswise/lengthwise etc** in a direction across something, along the length of something etc: *Cut the carrots lengthwise.* → CLOCKWISE, STREETWISE

wise·crack /ˈwaɪzkræk/ *n* [C] a clever and funny remark or reply SYN **joke** —**wisecrack** *v* [I]

wish¹ /wɪʃ/ ●●● S1 W1 *v*
1 [I,T] *formal* if you wish to do something or you wish to have it done for you, you want to do it or want to have it done SYN **like**: **wish to do sth** *I wish to make a complaint.* | *If you wish to discuss this matter further please do not hesitate to contact me.* | *You may leave now,* **if you wish**. | **(just) as you wish** (=used in formal situations to tell someone you will do what they want) *'I'd like it to be ready by six.' 'Just as you wish, sir.'* | *The cook will prepare whatever you wish.*

> **REGISTER**
> In everyday English, people usually say **want** rather than **wish**: *I* **want** *to see the manager.* | *You can go, if you* **want**.

2 [T] to want something to be true although you know it is either impossible or unlikely → **if only**: **wish (that)** *I wish I didn't have to go to work today.* | *I wish that I could afford a new car.* | *He wished Emily were with him.* | *Sometimes I wish I had never been born.*

> **GRAMMAR: Patterns with wish**
> • You **wish** that you **could** do something: *I wish I could speak Spanish.* ✗ Don't say: *I wish I can speak Spanish.*
> • You **wish** that something **would** happen: *I wish it would stop raining.* | *I wish you wouldn't do that.*
> • You **wish** that you **had done** something: *I wish I had paid more attention in class.*| *She wished she hadn't said that she was bored.*
> • You **wish** that you **could have done** something: *I wish I could have seen his face!*
> • In everyday spoken English, you say **I wish I was**: *I wish I was back home in Hong Kong.*
> • In more formal English, especially in American English, you use **I wish I were**: *I wish I were back home in Hong Kong.*
> • **I wish I were** is often used when talking about things that are impossible: *I wish I were you!* | *I wish I were younger.*
> GRAMMAR GUIDE VERBS

3 [T] to say that you hope someone will have good luck, a happy life etc: **wish sb sth** *We wish you a Merry Christmas and a Happy New Year!* | *We wish them every happiness in*

their new home. | *He shook my hand and* **wished** *me* **luck**. | **wish sb well** (=say that you hope that good things will happen to someone) *My friends wished me well in my new job.*
4 I couldn't wish for a nicer/better etc ... (*also* **the nicest/best etc ... I could have wished for**) used to emphasize that you are very happy with what you have and cannot imagine anyone or anything better: *I couldn't wish for a better husband.* | *It's the best birthday present I could have wished for.*
5 I wish (that) sb would do sth *spoken* used to say that you find someone's behaviour annoying and want them to change: *I wish you'd stop treating me like a child!*
6 [I] **a)** to want something to happen or to want to have something, especially when it seems unlikely or impossible → **long for**: **[+for]** *It was no use wishing for the impossible.* | *She was like the sister I never had but always wished for.* **b)** to silently ask for something you want and hope that it will happen by magic or good luck – used especially in children's stories: **[+for]** *One day she found a magic ring that brought her whatever she wished for.*
7 I wish! *spoken* used to say that something is not true, but you wish it was: *'I think he really likes you.' 'I wish!'*
8 you wish! *spoken* used to tell someone that what they want to happen or be true will definitely not happen or become true: *'I'm going to be famous one day.' 'You wish!'*
9 wouldn't wish sth on/upon sb *spoken* used to say that something is very unpleasant and that you would not like anyone to have to experience it: *Having your house broken into is terrible. I wouldn't wish it on anybody.*
10 I don't wish to interfere/be nosy etc *BrE spoken formal* used to show you are sorry if what you are going to say upsets or annoys someone: *I don't wish to seem ungrateful, but it's not quite what I expected.*
11 I (only) wish I knew *BrE spoken* used to emphasize that you do not know something, and you wish you did know: *'Where on earth have they gone?' 'I wish I knew!'*

wish sth ↔ **away** *phr v*
1 to make something unpleasant disappear by wanting it to disappear, without doing anything about it: *You can't just wish your problems away, you know!*
2 wish your life away to always be thinking about the future, so that you do not do or enjoy things now – used to show disapproval: *Don't wish your life away.*

wish² ●●● S3 *n* [C]

1 a desire to do something, to have something, or to have something happen: **[+of]** *It's important to listen to the wishes of the patient.* | **wish to do sth** *Despite her wish to continue working, she was forced to retire at the age of 62.* → DEATH WISH
2 a silent request for something to happen as if by magic: *Close your eyes and* **make a wish**.
3 against sb's wishes if you do something against someone's wishes, you do it even though you know they do not want you to: *She'd left school against her mother's wishes.* | **go against sb's wishes** (=do something against their wishes)
4 best/good/warmest etc wishes used, especially in cards and letters, to say that you hope someone will be happy, successful, or healthy: **[+for]** *Best wishes for a long and happy retirement!* | *She asked me to* **pass on** *her good* **wishes** *to all her friends and colleagues.* | **(With) best wishes** (=used at the end of a letter before you sign your name) *With best wishes, Celia.*
5 have no wish to do sth *formal* used to emphasize that you do not want or intend to do something: *I have no wish to speak to her ever again.*
6 your wish is my command used humorously to say that you will do whatever someone asks you to do

COLLOCATIONS

VERBS

make a wish (=silently ask for something that you want to happen) *He blew out the candles and made a wish.*
get/have your wish (=get what you want) *She wanted him to leave, and she got her wish.*
grant/fulfil sb's wish (=give someone what they want) *His parents would now be able to grant his wish.*
express a wish *He expressed a wish to go to the United States.*
respect sb's wishes (=do what someone wants) *We have to respect his wishes.*
ignore sb's wishes *It is important not to ignore the wishes of the patient.*

PHRASES

sb's wish comes true *His wish came true when he was called up to play for England.*

ADJECTIVES

sb's greatest/deepest wish (*also* **sb's dearest wish** *BrE*) (=what they want most of all) *Her greatest wish was to see her parents again.*
sb's last/final/dying wish

wish·bone /ˈwɪʃbəʊn $ -boʊn/ *n* [C] the V-shaped bone from a cooked chicken, duck etc, which two people pull apart to decide who will make a wish

ˌwishful ˈthinking *n* [U] when you believe that what you want to happen will happen, when in fact it is not possible: *I think she rather likes me. But maybe that's just wishful thinking.*

ˈwishing well *n* [C] a WELL or pool of water that people throw coins into while making a wish

ˈwish list *n* [C] *informal* all the things that you would like to have or would like to happen in a particular situation: **on sb's wish list** *Another player on Coach Beane's wish list is center fielder Jeffrey Hammonds.*

wish·y-wash·y /ˈwɪʃi ˌwɒʃi $ -ˌwɒːʃi, -ˌwɑːʃi/ *adj informal* **1** someone who is wishy-washy does not have firm or clear ideas and seems unable to decide what they want – used to show disapproval: *a bunch of wishy-washy liberals* **2** colours that are wishy-washy are pale and unexciting, not strong or dark – used to show disapproval

wisp /wɪsp/ *n* [C] **1** a wisp of hair, grass, HAY etc is a thin piece of it that is separate from the rest: **[+of]** *A wisp of hair had escaped from under her hat.* **2** a wisp of smoke, cloud, mist etc is a small thin line of it that rises upwards: **[+of]** *Wisps of smoke rose into the air.* → WILL O' THE WISP —**wispy** *adj*

wis·te·ri·a /wɪˈstɪəriə $ -ˈstɪr-/ *n* [C,U] a climbing plant with purple or white flowers

wist·ful /ˈwɪstfəl/ *adj* thinking sadly about something you would like to have but cannot have, especially something that you used to have in the past: *a wistful smile* —**wistfully** *adv*: *'That's the house where I was born,' she said wistfully.* —**wistfulness** *n* [U]

wit /wɪt/ ●○○ *n*

1 AMUSING [U] the ability to say things that are clever and amusing: *a woman of great wit and charm* | **quick/dry/sharp etc wit** *His sharp wit had them all smiling.*
2 AMUSING PERSON [C] someone who is able to say clever and amusing things
3 wits [plural] your ability to think quickly and make the right decisions: *Alone and penniless, I was forced to* **live on** *my* **wits**. | **keep/have your wits about you** (=be ready to think quickly and do what is necessary in a difficult situation)
4 frighten/scare/terrify sb out of their wits *informal* to frighten someone very much: *I was terrified out of my wits at the very idea.*
5 gather/collect/recover etc your wits to make yourself think about what you are going to do next after you have been surprised by something: *I felt helpless, but tried to gather my wits.*
6 pit your wits against sb to compete against someone in a test of knowledge or intelligence
7 be at your wits' end to be very upset and not know what to do, because you have tried everything possible to solve a problem
8 have the wit to do sth *formal* to be clever enough to know the right thing to do: *Thankfully, Reid had the wit to see what was wrong with the plan.*

W

9 not be beyond the wit of sb *formal* not be too difficult for someone to do: ***It's** surely **not beyond the wit** of man to come up with a solution.*
10 to wit *old use or formal* used to introduce additional information which makes it clear exactly who or what you are talking about SYN **namely**: *This does not stop me giving you a little treat. To wit, an invitation to dine at Brown's.*
→ **battle of wits** at BATTLE[1](5), → HALF-WIT, → **live by your wits** at LIVE[1](15), → OUTWIT, QUICK-WITTED, WITTY

witch /wɪtʃ/ ●●○ *n* [C]
1 a woman who is supposed to have magic powers, especially to do bad things → **wizard**
2 *informal* an insulting word for a woman who is old or unpleasant

witch·craft /ˈwɪtʃkrɑːft $ -kræft/ *n* [U] the use of magic powers, especially evil ones, to make things happen

ˈwitch-ˌdoctor *n* [C] a man who is believed to have magic powers and the ability to cure diseases, especially in parts of Africa → **medicine man**

ˈwitch-ˌhazel *n* [C,U] a substance used for treating small wounds on the skin, or the tree that produces it

ˈwitch-hunt *n* [C] an attempt to find and punish people in a society or organization whose opinions are regarded as wrong or dangerous - used to show disapproval: *anti-Communist witch-hunts*

ˈwitching ˌhour *n* **the witching hour** 12 o'clock at night

with /wɪð, wɪθ/ ●●● S1 W1 *prep*
1 used to say that two or more people or things are together in the same place: *I saw Bob in town with his girlfriend.* | *Put this bag with the others.* | *I always wear these shoes with this dress.* | *Mix the powder with boiling water.* | **have/bring/take sb/sth with you** *She had her husband with her.* | *You'd better bring your passport with you.*
2 having, possessing, or carrying something: *a tall gentleman with a beard* | *a book with a green cover* | *a man with a gun* | *We need someone with new ideas.* | *Only people with plenty of money can afford to shop here.* | *She came back with a letter in her hand.*
3 using something or by means of something: *Chop the onions with a sharp knife.* | *What will you buy with the money?* | *I amused myself with crossword puzzles.* | *a hat decorated with brightly coloured feathers*
4 because of a particular feeling or physical state: *They were trembling with fear.* | *Jack beamed with pleasure when he heard the news.* | *I was too weak with hunger to cry.* | *Mother became seriously ill with pneumonia.*
5 including: *Two nights' accommodation with breakfast and evening meal cost us just over £250.*
6 used to say what covers or fills something: *Her boots were covered with mud.* | *Fill the bowl with sugar.* | *In summer Venice is crammed with tourists.*
7 used to say what an action or situation is related to: *We have a problem with parking in this area.* | *Be careful with that glass.* | *Is there something wrong with your phone?* | *How are you getting on with your studies, David?* | *Compared with other children of the same age, Robert is very tall.*
8 used to say which person or thing someone has a particular feeling or attitude towards: *I hope you're not angry with me.* | *He thinks he's in love with Diana.* | *She's delighted with her new car.* | *Don't get too friendly with your students.*
9 supporting someone or sharing their opinion → **for**: *Some opposition MPs voted with the Government.* | *You're either with me or against me.* | *I'm with Harry all the way on this one.*
10 used when talking about an action or activity to say which other person, group, or country is involved: *Stop fighting with your brother!* | *I used to play chess with him.* | *It's a good idea to discuss the problem with a sympathetic teacher.* | *We're competing with foreign businesses.* | *Britain's trade with Japan* | *She left home after an argument with her parents.*
11 used to say how someone does something or how something happens: *He prepared everything with great care.* | *A rocket exploded with a blinding flash.* | *'Oh, I'm not in a hurry,' I said with a smile.* | *The day starts with a great American breakfast.*
12 used to say what position or state someone or something is in, or what is happening, when someone does something: *She stood with her back to me.* | *We lay in bed with the window open.* | *She was knitting, with the television on.* | **with sb/sth doing sth** *We jumped into the water with bullets whizzing past our ears.*
13 at the same rate as something else and because of it: *a skill which improves with practice* | *The risk of cancer increases with the number of cigarettes you smoke.*
14 because of a situation that exists: *With John away there's more room in the house.* | **with sth doing sth** *I can't do my homework with all this noise going on.*
15 employed by someone: *The manager is Stuart Walker, who has been with the company since 1970.*
16 used to say who is looking after something: *I left your keys with the janitor.*
17 used to say who or what someone becomes separated from: *Joan doesn't want to part with the money.* | *a complete break with tradition*
18 in the same direction as something: *We sailed with the wind.*
19 in spite of: *With all his faults, I still like him.*
20 used to show who or what a strong wish or order concerns: *Down with school!* | *Off to bed with you!*
21 be with you/me to understand what someone is telling you or explaining to you: *Sorry, I'm not with you - which room do you mean?* | *So that's how the system works. Are you with me?*
22 with it *informal* **a)** wearing fashionable clothes and knowing about new ideas SYN **trendy b)** able to understand clearly what is happening around you: *I'm sorry, I'm not feeling very with it today.* → WITH-IT
23 with that immediately after doing or saying something: *He gave a little wave and with that he was gone.*

with·draw /wɪðˈdrɔː, wɪθ- $ -ˈdrɒː/ ●●○ W2 *v* (*past tense* **withdrew** /-ˈdruː/, *past participle* **withdrawn** /-ˈdrɔːn $ -ˈdrɒːn/)
1 NOT TAKE PART [I,T] to stop taking part in an activity, belonging to an organization etc, or to make someone do this: **[+from]** *A knee injury forced her to withdraw from the competition.* | *calls for Britain to withdraw from the European Union* | **withdraw sth/sb from sth** *Parents have the right to withdraw their children from religious education lessons if they wish.*

> **REGISTER**
> In everyday English, people usually say that someone **pulls out** of something such as a competition or organization rather than **withdraws**: *She **pulled out** with a knee injury.*

2 STOP SUPPORTING [T] to stop giving support or money to someone or something, especially as the result of an official decision: *One of the minority parties had **withdrawn** its **support** for Chancellor Kohl.* | *Union members will vote on whether to **withdraw** their **labour** (=stop working).* | *a government decision to withdraw funding*
3 CHANGE YOUR MIND [T] if you withdraw a threat, offer, request etc, you say that you no longer will do what you said: *After much persuasion he agreed to withdraw his resignation.*
4 SAY STH IS NOT TRUE [T] *formal* if you withdraw a remark, criticism, statement etc, you say that what you said earlier was completely untrue SYN **retract**: *He refused to withdraw his remarks and was expelled from the Party.* | *The newspaper has agreed to withdraw its allegations.*
5 PRODUCT/SERVICE [T] if a product or service is withdrawn, it is no longer offered for sale or use: **withdraw sth from sale/from the market** *The drug has been withdrawn from the market for further tests.*
6 LEAVE A PLACE **a)** [I,T] if an army withdraws, or if it is withdrawn, it leaves a place SYN **pull out**: *the USA's decision to **withdraw** 40,000 **troops** from western Europe* **b)** [I] to leave a place, especially in order to be alone or go

somewhere quiet: **[+to]** *We withdrew to the garden for a private talk.*
7 MONEY [T] to take money out of a bank account SYN **take out**: **withdraw sth from sth** *I'd like to withdraw £500 from my current account.*

> **REGISTER**
> In everyday English, people often say that someone **takes** or **gets** money **out** rather than **withdraws** it: *Can we stop off at the bank? I need to* ***get*** *some money* ***out****.*

8 MOVE [T] if you withdraw your hand, arm, finger etc from somewhere, you move it from there to where it was before: *Claudia withdrew her hand from his.*
9 TAKE OUT [T] *literary* to take an object out from inside something: **withdraw sth from sth** *She withdrew a document from her briefcase.*
10 STOP COMMUNICATING [I] to become quieter, less friendly, and only concerned about your own thoughts → **withdrawn**: **[+into/from]** *Ralph has withdrawn from the other kids.* | *Many depressed people just withdraw into themselves.*

with·draw·al /wɪð'drɔːəl, wɪθ- $ -'drɒːəl/ ●○○ *n*
1 ARMY [C,U] the act of moving an army, weapons etc away from the area where they were fighting: **[+of]** *the withdrawal of UN forces* | **[+from]** *the Russian withdrawal from Afghanistan* | *large-scale* ***troop withdrawals***
2 REMOVAL/ENDING [U] the removal or stopping of something such as support, an offer, or a service: **[+of]** *withdrawal of government aid*
3 MONEY [C,U] the act of taking money from a bank account, or the amount you take out: *Customers can use the machine to* ***make withdrawals*** *of up to £250 a day.*
4 STOP TAKING PART [U] the act of no longer taking part in an activity or being a member of an organization: **[+from]** *Germany's withdrawal from the talks*
5 DRUGS [U] the period after someone has given up a drug that they were dependent on, and the unpleasant mental and physical effects that this causes
6 STATEMENT [U] the act of saying that something you previously said was in fact untrue SYN **retraction**: **[+of]** *the withdrawal of all allegations*

with'drawal ˌsymptoms *n* [plural] the painful or unpleasant feelings someone has after they have stopped taking a drug that they were dependent on

with·drawn /wɪð'drɔːn, wɪθ- $ -'drɒːn/ *adj* very shy and quiet, and concerned only about your own thoughts: *After his wife's death he* ***became*** *more and more* ***withdrawn****.* THESAURUS ▸ SHY

with·er /'wɪðə $ -ər/ (*also* **wither away**) *v* **1** [I,T] if plants wither, or if something withers them, they become drier and smaller and start to die **2** [I] to gradually become weaker or less successful and then end: *His career had withered.* | *The organization just withered away.* **3 wither on the vine** if something withers on the vine, it gradually ends because it is not given enough support: *The government has allowed the program to wither on the vine by reducing its funding.*

with·ered /'wɪðəd $ -ərd/ *adj* **1** a withered plant has become drier and smaller and is dead or dying **2** a withered person looks thin and weak and old **3** a withered arm or leg has not developed properly and is thin and weak

with·er·ing /'wɪðərɪŋ/ *adj* **a withering look/remark etc** a look, remark etc that makes someone feel stupid, embarrassed, or lose confidence —**witheringly** *adv*

with·ers /'wɪðəz $ -ərz/ *n* [plural] the highest part of a horse's back, above its shoulders

with·hold /wɪð'həʊld, wɪθ- $ -'hoʊld/ ●○○ *v* (*past tense and past participle* **withheld** /-'held/) [T] to refuse to give someone something: *I withheld payment until they had completed the work.* | *Ian was accused of withholding vital information from the police.*

with'holding ˌtax *n* [C,U] *AmE* money that is taken out of your wages as tax

with·in /wɪð'ɪn $ wɪð'ɪn, wɪθ'ɪn/ ●●● S1 W1 *prep, adv*
1 a) before a certain period of time has passed: *We should have the test results back within 24 hours.* | *He fell sick and died within a matter of weeks.* | *Within an hour of our arrival Caroline was starting to complain.* **b)** during a certain period of time: *the enormous success of televised sport within the last twenty years* | *Within the space of a year, three of the town's factories have closed down.* THESAURUS ▸ AFTER, DURING
2 less than a certain distance from a particular place: *The invading troops came within 50 miles of Paris.* | *Within a five mile radius of Ollerton there are several pubs and restaurants.* | *We live* ***within easy reach of*** (=close to) *the shops.* | *Adjust the driver's seat so that all the controls are* ***within reach*** (=close enough to touch). | **within sight/earshot (of sth)** (=close enough to see or hear) *As she came within sight of the house, she saw two men getting out of a car.*
3 inside a particular building or area OPP **outside**: *Prisoners who died were buried within the walls of the prison.* | *public footpaths within the national park* | *The rooms within were richly furnished.* | **apply/enquire within** (=used on notices on the outside of buildings) *Baby rabbits for sale. Enquire within.*
4 inside a society, organization, or group of people OPP **outside**: *There have been a lot of changes within the department since I joined.* | *an attempt to reform the system* ***from within***
5 if something stays within a particular limit or set of rules, it does not go beyond that limit: *We have to operate within a very tight budget.* | *Security firms have to work strictly within the law.* | *You can go anywhere you want* ***within reason*** (=within reasonable limits).
6 *literary or formal* inside a person's body or mind OPP **outside**: *Elaine felt a pain deep within her.* | *I'm feeling more relaxed within myself.*

'with-it *adj* fashionable and modern in the way that you dress, think etc SYN **trendy** → **with it** at WITH(22)

with·out /wɪð'aʊt $ wɪð'aut, wɪθ'aʊt/ ●●● S1 W1 *prep, adv*
1 not having something, especially something that is basic or necessary: *After the storm we were without electricity for five days.* | *a house without a garden* | *We passed two ruined abbeys, one with a tower and one without.* | *I'm getting used to managing without a car.* → **do without** at DO[2], → **go without** at GO[1]
2 used to say that a particular thing has not happened when someone does something: *Suddenly and without any warning, the army opened fire.* | *He had gone out without his parents' permission.* | *I accepted his offer without a moment's hesitation.* | *I got to my destination without too much difficulty.* | **without doing sth** *'What do you expect?' he said, without looking at her.* | ***Without so much as*** *a word of thanks, Ben turned and went back into the office* (=he did not even say thank you as he should have done).
3 not feeling or showing that you feel a particular emotion: *He told his story without anger or bitterness.*
4 not being with someone, or not having them to help you, especially someone you like or need: *I don't know what I'd do without you.* | *Won't you be lonely without her?* | *The rest of the group set off without him.*
5 without wanting/wishing to do sth used before a criticism, complaint, or other statement to make it less strong: *Without wanting to sound too boastful, I think we have the best television programmes in the world.*
6 *old use* outside → **reckon without** at RECKON

with·stand /wɪð'stænd, wɪθ-/ ●○○ *v* (*past tense and past participle* **withstood** /-'stʊd/) [T]
1 to be strong enough to remain unharmed by something such as great heat, cold, pressure etc SYN **resist**, **stand up to**: *This fabric can withstand steam and high temperatures.*
2 to defend yourself successfully against people who attack, criticize, or oppose you SYN **stand up to**: *The Chancellor has withstood the criticism and held firm.*

wit·less /ˈwɪtləs/ *adj* **1 be scared witless** feeling very frightened **2** not very intelligent or sensible SYN **stupid** —**witlessly** *adv* —**witlessness** *n* [U]

wit·ness¹ /ˈwɪtnəs/ ●●○ S3 W3 *n*
1 CRIME/ACCIDENT [C] someone who sees a crime or an accident and can describe what happened: *Police have appealed for witnesses to come forward.* | **[+to]** *One witness to the accident said the driver appeared to be drunk.* | *an* **eye witness** (=someone who sees an event) *to the robbery* → EYEWITNESS
2 IN A COURT OF LAW [C] someone who appears in a court of law to say what they know about a crime or other event → **testify**: **key/star/principal witness** *the key witness in the case against the brothers* | *The defence is expected to* **call** *them as* **witnesses**. | **witness for the prosecution/defence** (*also* **prosecution/defence witness**) (=someone the prosecution or defence lawyers choose as a witness in order to help prove their case) → EXPERT WITNESS
3 SIGNING A DOCUMENT [C] someone who is present when an official document is signed, and who signs it too, to say that they saw it being signed: **[+to]** *a witness to a will*
4 be witness to sth *formal* to be present when something happens, and watch it happening: *We were witness to the worst excesses of the military.*
5 CHRISTIAN BELIEF [C,U] *AmE* a public statement of strong Christian belief, or someone who makes such a statement → **bear witness** at BEAR¹(15)

witness² ●●○ *v*
1 CRIME/ACCIDENT [T] to see something happen, especially a crime or accident: *Several residents claim to have witnessed the attack.* THESAURUS NOTICE, SEE
2 EXPERIENCE STH [T] to experience important events or changes: *Priests have witnessed an increase in religious intolerance.*
3 TIME/PLACE [T] if a time or place witnesses an event, the event happens during that time or in that place: *Recent years have witnessed the collapse of the steel industry.*
4 OFFICIAL DOCUMENT [T] if you witness the signing of an official document, you are there when it is signed, and sign it yourself to prove this: *Will you* **witness** *my* **signature**?
5 witness sth (*also* **..., as witnessed by sth**) used to introduce an example that proves something you have just mentioned: *Bad economic times can result in political dictatorships. Witness Germany in the 1930s.*
6 RELIGION [I] to speak publicly about your Christian beliefs → **testify**

ˈwitness box *BrE*, **ˈwitness stand** *AmE* *n* [C] the place in a court of law where a witness stands to answer questions

wit·ter /ˈwɪtə $ -ər/ (*also* **witter on**) *v* [I] *BrE informal* to talk a lot in a boring way or about something unimportant SYN **ramble on**: **[+about]** *I'm sick of her wittering on about her boyfriend.*

wit·ti·cis·m /ˈwɪtɪsɪzəm/ *n* [C] a clever amusing remark

wit·ty /ˈwɪti/ ●○○ *adj* using words in a clever and amusing way: *witty remarks* | *Laura's very witty.* THESAURUS FUNNY —**wittily** *adv* —**wittiness** *n* [U]

wives /waɪvz/ the plural of WIFE

wiz·ard /ˈwɪzəd $ -ərd/ ●○○ *n* [C]
1 a man who is supposed to have magic powers → **witch**
2 someone who is very good at something: *a financial wizard* | **[+at]** *Ben's a real wizard at chess.*

wiz·ard·ry /ˈwɪzədri $ -ər-/ *n* [U] impressive ability at something or an impressive achievement: *high-speed Internet connections and other technical wizardry*

wiz·ened /ˈwɪzənd/ *adj* a wizened person, fruit etc is small and thin and has skin with a lot of lines and WRINKLES

wk. (*also* **wk** *BrE*) the written abbreviation of ***week***

WMD /ˌdʌbəljuː em ˈdiː/ *n* [plural] WEAPONS OF MASS DESTRUCTION

wob·ble /ˈwɒbəl $ ˈwɑː-/ *v* **1** [I,T] to move unsteadily from side to side, or make something do this: *The pile of bricks wobbled and fell.* | *Tom stopped, wobbling from the weight of his load.* THESAURUS MOVE **2** [I always + adv/prep] to go in a particular direction while moving unsteadily from side to side: **[+down/along/towards etc]** *Cindy wobbled along the street on her bike.* **3** [I] to be unsure whether to do something SYN **waver**: *The president appeared to wobble over sending the troops in.* —**wobble** *n* [C]

wob·bly¹ /ˈwɒbli $ ˈwɑː-/ *adj* **1** moving unsteadily from side to side: *a wobbly table* **2** *informal* if you or your legs feel wobbly, you feel weak and unable to keep your balance SYN **shaky** **3** a wobbly voice is weak and shakes, especially because you feel frightened or upset SYN **shaky** **4** not very good or not likely to be successful SYN **shaky**: *The meeting yesterday got off to a wobbly start.*

wobbly² *n* **throw a wobbly** *BrE informal* to suddenly become very angry or frightened

wodge /wɒdʒ $ wɑːdʒ/ *n* [C] *BrE informal* a thick solid piece or large amount of something: **[+of]** *a wodge of ten pound notes*

woe /wəʊ $ woʊ/ ●○○ *n*
1 woes [plural] *formal* the problems and troubles affecting someone: *the country's economic woes*
2 [U] *literary* great sadness
3 woe is me *spoken humorous* used to say that you are extremely unhappy or in a difficult situation
4 woe betide sb *BrE* used to warn someone that there will be trouble if they do something - especially used humorously: *Woe betide anyone who smokes in our house!*

woe·be·gone /ˈwəʊbɪɡɒn $ ˈwoʊbɪɡɒːn, -ɡɑːn/ *adj literary* looking very sad: *her woebegone expression*

woe·ful /ˈwəʊfəl $ ˈwoʊ-/ *adj* **1** very bad or serious SYN **deplorable**: *a woeful lack of information* **2** *literary* very sad SYN **pathetic**: *woeful eyes* —**woefully** *adv*: *woefully inadequate facilities*

wog /wɒɡ $ wɑːɡ/ *n* [C] *BrE taboo* a very offensive word for a black person. Do not use this word.

wok /wɒk $ wɑːk/ *n* [C] a wide pan shaped like a bowl, used in Chinese cooking → see picture at PAN¹

woke /wəʊk $ woʊk/ *v* the past tense of WAKE

wok·en /ˈwəʊkən $ ˈwoʊ-/ *v* the past participle of WAKE

wolds /wəʊldz $ woʊldz/ *n* [plural] *BrE* a word for an area of hilly countryside, especially used in the names of places: *the Lincolnshire Wolds*

wolf¹ /wʊlf/ ●●○ *n* (*plural* **wolves** /wʊlvz/) [C]
1 a wild animal that looks like a large dog and lives and hunts in groups: *a* **pack** *of wolves*
2 a wolf in sheep's clothing someone who seems to be friendly or harmless but is in fact dangerous, dishonest etc
3 keep the wolf from the door to earn just enough money to buy the basic things you need: *I work part-time in a coffee shop just to keep the wolf from the door.* —**wolfish** *adj*: *a wolfish grin* → **cry wolf** at CRY¹(7), → **lone wolf** at LONE(3)

wolf² (*also* **wolf down**) *v* [T] *informal* to eat something very quickly, swallowing it in big pieces SYN **gobble**

wolf·hound /ˈwʊlfhaʊnd/ *n* [C] a type of extremely large dog

ˈwolf ˌwhistle *n* [C] a way of whistling that men sometimes use to show that they think a woman is attractive —**wolf-whistle** *v* [I]

wolves /wʊlvz/ the plural of WOLF

W

wom·an /ˈwʊmən/ ●●● S1 W1 *n* (*plural* **women** /ˈwɪmɪn/)
1 FEMALE PERSON [C] an adult female person: *I was talking to a woman I met on the flight.* | *married women* | *a popular women's magazine* | *When a woman is pregnant, the levels of hormones in her body change.* | **woman priest/doctor etc** (=a priest etc who is a woman) *Ireland's first woman president* | *women artists*
2 ANY WOMAN [singular] *formal* women in general: *A woman's work is never done* (=used to say that women have a lot to do).
3 businesswoman/spokeswoman etc a woman who has a particular kind of job: *Congresswoman Ellen Tauscher*
4 another woman/the other woman *informal* a woman that a man is having a sexual relationship with, even though he is married to someone else: *I'm sure he's got another woman.*
5 be your own woman to make your own decisions and be in charge of your own life, without depending on anyone else
6 PARTNER [singular] *spoken* a word meaning a wife or girlfriend, which many women find offensive: *Did he bring his new woman with him?* → KEPT WOMAN
7 FORM OF ADDRESS [U] *old-fashioned not polite* a rude way of speaking to a woman when you are angry, annoyed etc
8 SERVANT [C] a female servant or person who does cleaning work for you in your house → **cleaner**, **daily help** → OLD WOMAN, → **make an honest woman (out) of sb** at HONEST(8), → **be a woman of the world** at WORLD[1](21)

THESAURUS

woman a female adult person: *a young woman with dark brown hair*
lady a polite word for a woman – used especially when you do not know the woman, or when the person you are talking to does not know the woman: *A glass of white wine please, for this lady here.* | *The young lady stood up and shook my hand.*
girl a young female person – usually used about someone younger than about twenty: *a very pretty girl* | *teenage girls*
female *formal* a woman – used especially when you are giving information about women, for example in formal surveys and reports: *Females account for 46% of Internet users.*

RELATING TO WOMEN

female relating to women or girls: *female voters* | *Advertisers try to sell things by using images of the female body.*
feminine used about qualities that are considered to be typical of women: *You must not cry or show any other feminine weakness.* | *the ideal of feminine beauty*
womanly behaving, dressing etc in a way that is thought to be typical of or suitable for a woman – used to show approval: *her womanly figure* | *the womanly virtues of compassion and patience*
girly/girlie *informal* behaving or dressing in a way that is thought to be typical of young girls, or suitable for a girl – often used disapprovingly: *Stop being so girly! It's only a mouse!* | *a very girlie pink dress*
effeminate *disapproving* a man who is effeminate looks or behaves like a woman: *His long blonde hair made him look rather effeminate.* | *a pale effeminate-looking young man*

wom·an·hood /ˈwʊmənhʊd/ *n* [U] **1** the state of being a woman, not a man or a girl **2** *formal* women in general → **manhood**

wom·an·ish /ˈwʊmənɪʃ/ *adj* a womanish man looks or behaves in a way that is thought to be typical of women → **mannish**

wom·an·izer (*also* **-iser** *BrE*) /ˈwʊmənaɪzə $ -ər/ *n* [C] a man who has sexual relationships with many different women – used to show disapproval → **man-eater** —**womanize** *v* [I] —**womanizing** *n* [U]

wom·an·kind /ˈwʊmənkaɪnd/ *n* [U] women considered together as a group → **mankind**

wom·an·ly /ˈwʊmənli/ *adj* behaving, dressing etc in a way that is thought to be typical of or suitable for a woman – used to show approval SYN **feminine** → **manly**: *her soft womanly figure* THESAURUS WOMAN —**womanliness** *n* [U]

womb /wuːm/ ●○○ *n* [C] the part of a woman's or female animal's body where her baby grows before it is born SYN **uterus**

wom·bat /ˈwɒmbæt $ ˈwɑːm-/ *n* [C] an Australian animal like a small bear whose babies live in a pocket of skin on its body

wom·en /ˈwɪmɪn/ the plural of WOMAN

wom·en·folk /ˈwɪmɪnfəʊk $ -foʊk/ *n* [plural] *old-fashioned* all the women in a particular family or society → **menfolk**

ˌwomen's ˈlib (*also* **ˌwomen's libeˈration**) *n* [U] *old-fashioned* all the ideas, actions, and politics relating to giving women the same rights and opportunities as men → **men's lib** —**women's libber** *n* [C]

ˈwomen's ˌmovement *n* **the women's movement** all the women who are involved in the aim of improving the social, economic, and political position of women and of ending sexual DISCRIMINATION

ˈwomen's room *n* [C] *AmE* a public TOILET for women SYN **ladies** *BrE* → **men's room**

ˈwomen's ˌstudies *n* [plural] the study of women in history, literature, and society

ˌWomen's ˈInstitute, the (*abbreviation* **WI**) a British organization for women, especially women in country areas, who meet for social and educational activities. Although the Women's Institute has members of all ages and all social classes, people generally imagine that a typical member is an older MIDDLE-CLASS woman who does not have a job and who enjoys activities such as cooking and sewing.

won[1] /wʌn/ the past tense and past participle of WIN[1]

won[2] /wɒn $ wɑːn/ *n* [C] the standard unit of money in South Korea and North Korea

won·der[1] /ˈwʌndə $ -ər/ ●●● S1 W2 *v* [I,T]
1 to think about something that you are not sure about and try to guess what is true, what will happen etc: **wonder who/what/how etc** *I wonder how James is getting on.* | *What are they going to do now,* **I wonder**? | **wonder if/whether** *I wonder if I'll recognize Philip after all these years.* | *He's been leaving work early a lot –* **it makes you wonder**, *doesn't it?*
2 I wonder if/whether *spoken* used to ask politely for something SYN **may I**: *I wonder if I might have a drink?*
3 I was wondering if/whether a) *spoken* used to ask someone politely to help you: *I was wondering if I could borrow your car?* **b)** used to ask someone politely if they would like to do something: *I was wondering if you'd like to come to dinner.*
4 to feel surprised and unable to believe something: **[+about/at]** *Sometimes I wonder about his behaviour.* | **wonder how** *I wonder how he dares to show his face!* | **I don't wonder** *BrE* (=I am not surprised) *I don't wonder you're tired.* | **I shouldn't wonder** *BrE* (=I would not be surprised about something) *He'll come back soon enough, I shouldn't wonder.*
5 to doubt or question whether something is true: *'Is she serious?' 'I wonder.'* | **wonder if/whether** *Sometimes I wonder if he's got any sense at all!*

GRAMMAR: Patterns with wonder

- You **wonder** what **will** happen: *I wonder what she'll say when she finds out.*
- You **wonder** what **would** happen if something else happened (when talking about imaginary situations): *I wonder what would happen if I said that I was leaving.*
- You **wonder** if you **should** do something: *I wonder if we should tell her.*

wonder² ●●○ *n*
1 ADMIRATION **a)** [U] a feeling of surprise and admiration for something very beautiful or new to you SYN **awe**: *The sight of the Taj Mahal filled us with wonder.* **b)** [C] something that makes you feel surprise and admiration: *technological wonders | the Seven Wonders of the World*
2 (it's) no/small/little wonder (that) *especially spoken* used to say that you are not surprised by something: *No wonder you've got a headache, the amount you drank last night.*
3 SURPRISING **it's a wonder (that)** *especially spoken* used to say that something is very surprising: *It's a wonder no one got hurt.*
4 do/work wonders to be very effective in solving a problem
5 wonders will never cease *spoken* used humorously to show you are surprised and pleased about something
6 CLEVER PERSON [singular] *BrE* someone who is good at doing difficult things → **a nine days' wonder** at NINE(3)

wonder³ *adj* [only before noun] very good and effective: *a new **wonder drug***

won·der·ful /ˈwʌndəfəl $ -dər-/ ●●● S1 W2 *adj*
1 making you feel very happy SYN **great**: *We had a wonderful time in Spain.* THESAURUS GOOD, NICE
2 making you admire someone or something very much SYN **amazing**: *It's wonderful what doctors can do nowadays.*

won·der·ful·ly /ˈwʌndəfəli $ -dər-/ ●○○ *adv* very well or to a very great degree, in a way that makes you feel happy: *All of the performers played wonderfully. | a wonderfully rich sauce*

won·der·ing·ly /ˈwʌndərɪŋli/ *adv* in a way that shows admiration, surprise, and pleasure

won·der·land /ˈwʌndəlænd $ -ər-/ *n* [U] an imaginary place in stories

won·der·ment /ˈwʌndəmənt $ -dər-/ *n* [U] *literary* a feeling of pleasant surprise or admiration

won·drous /ˈwʌndrəs/ *adj literary* good or impressive in a surprising way

wonk /wɒŋk $ wɑːŋk/ *n* [C] *informal* someone who works very hard and is very serious: *These are issues that would only interest **policy wonks*** (=people interested in details of government).

won·ky /ˈwɒŋki $ ˈwɑːŋki/ *adj BrE informal* unsteady or not straight or level: *a wonky table*

wont¹ /wəʊnt $ wɒːnt/ *n old-fashioned* **as is sb's wont** used to say that it is someone's habit to do something: *He spoke for too long, as is his wont.*

wont² *adj formal* **be wont to do sth** to be likely to do something

won't /wəʊnt $ woʊnt/ the short form of 'will not'

woo /wuː/ *v* [T] **1** to try to persuade someone to do something such as buy something from you, vote for you, or work for you – used in news reports: *the Party's efforts to woo working class voters* **2** *old-fashioned* to try to persuade a woman to love you and marry you SYN **court**

wood /wʊd/ ●●● S2 W2 *n*
1 [C,U] the material that trees are made of → **wooden**, **woody**: *Put some more wood on the fire. | a polished wood floor | Her house was **made of wood**.* → HARDWOOD, SOFTWOOD
2 [C] (*also* **the woods**) a small forest: *a walk in the woods*
3 touch wood *BrE*, **knock on wood** *AmE* said just after you have said that things are going well for you, when you want your good luck to continue
4 [C] one of a set of four GOLF CLUBS with wooden heads
5 not be out of the wood(s) yet *informal* used to say that there are likely to be more difficulties before things improve
6 not see the wood for the trees to not notice what is important about something because you give too much of your attention to small details → DEAD WOOD

COLLOCATIONS

ADJECTIVES

solid wood *You can install a solid wood door.*
bare wood (=not painted or covered) *The floors were of bare wood.*
a hard/soft wood *Oak is a hard wood.*

VERBS

chop wood *He was chopping wood for the fire.*
cut/saw wood *A local carpenter cut the wood to size.*

PHRASES

a piece of wood *He made a bench out of pieces of wood.*
a plank of wood (=a long thin flat piece) | **a block of wood** | **the grain of the wood** (=the natural lines in it)

wood + NOUN

wood chips (=small rough pieces) | **wood shavings** (=thin curly pieces) | **wood smoke**

wood·block /ˈwʊdblɒk $ -blɑːk/ *n* [C] **1** a piece of wood with a shape cut on it, used for printing **2** a block of wood used in making a floor

wood·carv·ing /ˈwʊdkɑːvɪŋ $ -kɑːr-/ *n* [C,U] the process of shaping wood with special tools, or a piece of art produced in this way

wood·chuck /ˈwʊdtʃʌk/ *n* [C] a GROUNDHOG

wood·craft /ˈwʊdkrɑːft $ -kræft/ *n* [U] the practical knowledge of woods and forests

wood·cut /ˈwʊdkʌt/ *n* [C] a picture made by pressing a shaped piece of wood and a colouring substance onto paper

wood·cut·ter /ˈwʊdˌkʌtə $ -ər/ *n* [C] *old-fashioned* someone whose job is to cut down trees in a forest

wood·ed /ˈwʊdɪd/ *adj* having woods or covered with trees: *the wooded hills of northern Virginia* | **thickly/heavily/densely etc wooded** *a thickly wooded area*

wood·en /ˈwʊdn/ ●●● S3 W3 *adj*
1 made of wood: *a wooden bench*
2 not showing enough expression, emotion, or movement, especially when performing in public —**woodenly** *adv* —**woodenness** *n* [U]

ˌwooden ˈspoon *n* [C] **1** a large spoon made of wood, used to mix things when cooking **2 win/collect/take etc the wooden spoon** *BrE* to come last in a competition

wood·land /ˈwʊdlənd, -lænd/ ●●○ *n* [U] (*also* **woodlands** [plural]) an area of land covered with trees → **wood**, **forest** THESAURUS FOREST

wood·louse /ˈwʊdlaʊs/ *n* (*plural* **woodlice** /-laɪs/) [C] a small grey creature like an insect that lives under wood, stones etc

wood·peck·er /ˈwʊdˌpekə $ -ər/ *n* [C] a bird with a long beak that it uses to make holes in trees

wood·pile /ˈwʊdpaɪl/ *n* [C] a pile of wood to be burned in a fire

ˈwood pulp *n* [U] wood crushed into a soft mass, used for making paper

wood·shed /ˈwʊdʃed/ *n* [C] a place for storing wood for burning

woods·man /ˈwʊdzmən/ *n* (*plural* **woodsmen** /-mən/) [C] someone who works in a forest taking care of, planting, and cutting down trees

wood·sy /ˈwʊdzi/ *adj AmE informal* relating to the woods: *a woodsy smell*

wood·wind /ˈwʊdˌwɪnd/ *n* **1** [U] musical instruments made of wood or metal that you play by blowing and that usually have finger holes or KEYS → **brass**, **percussion**, **stringed instrument**, **wind instrument**: ***woodwind instruments** such as the flute or saxophone* **2 woodwinds** [plural] (*also* **the woodwind (section)**) the people in an ORCHESTRA or band who play woodwind instruments

wood·work /ˈwʊdwɜːk $ -wɜːrk/ *n* [U] **1 woodwork** *BrE*, **woodwork·ing** *AmE* /ˈwʊdwɜːkɪŋ $ -ɜːr-/ the skill or activity of making wooden objects → **carpentry 2** the parts of a house or room that are made of wood **3 crawl/come out of the woodwork** if someone crawls out of the woodwork, they suddenly and unexpectedly appear in order to take advantage of a situation, express their opinion etc – used to show disapproval **4 fade/blend into the woodwork** to

W

WOODWIND INSTRUMENTS

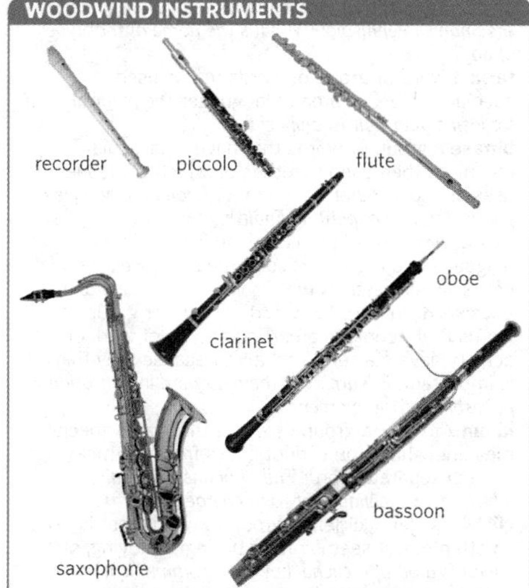

seem to disappear, or to behave in such a way that no one notices you —**woodworker** *n* [C]

wood·worm /ˈwʊdwɜːm $ -wɜːrm/ *n* **1** [C] a small insect that makes holes in wood **2** [U] the damage that is caused to wood by this creature

wood·y /ˈwʊdi/ *adj* **1** a woody plant has a stem like wood **2** a woody area of land has a lot of trees growing on it → **wooded**

woof¹ /wʊf/ *interjection* a word used for describing the sound a dog makes → **bark** —**woof** *n* [C] —**woof** *v* [I]

woof² /wuːf $ wʊf, wuːf/ *n* [C] the WEFT

wool /wʊl/ ●●● S3 *n* [U]
1 the soft thick hair that sheep and some goats have on their body → **LAMBSWOOL**
2 material made from wool: *a pure wool skirt | a mix of 80% wool and 20% man-made fibres*
3 thread made from wool that you use to KNIT clothes SYN **yarn** *AmE*: *a ball of wool*
4 pull the wool over sb's eyes to deceive someone by not telling the truth → **COTTON WOOL, DYED-IN-THE-WOOL, STEEL WOOL, WIRE WOOL**

wool·len *BrE*, **woolen** *AmE* /ˈwʊlən/ *adj* [only before noun] **1** made of wool SYN **wool**: *a woollen scarf* **2** relating to making cloth from wool: *the woollen industry | a woollen mill*

wool·lens *BrE*, **woolens** *AmE* /ˈwʊlənz/ *n* [plural] clothes made from wool, especially KNITTED clothes such as SWEATERS etc

wool·ly¹ *BrE*, **wooly** *AmE* /ˈwʊli/ *adj* **1** made of or feeling like wool: *a woolly hat* **2** not showing clear thinking SYN **vague**: *He gave a rather woolly argument.* —**woolliness** *n* [U]

wool·ly² *n* (*plural* **woollies**) [C] *BrE informal* a SWEATER or similar piece of KNITTED clothing: *You'll need your winter woollies!*

woo·zy /ˈwuːzi/ *adj informal* feeling weak and unsteady SYN **dizzy**: *Giving blood makes me feel really woozy.*

wop /wɒp $ wɑːp/ *n* [C] *taboo* a very offensive word for someone who is Italian. Do not use this word.

word¹ /wɜːd $ wɜːrd/ ●●● S1 W1 *n*
1 GROUP OF LETTERS [C] a single group of letters that are used together with a particular meaning: *Write an essay of about five hundred words. | What does that word mean? | 'Vater' is the German* **word for** (=that means) *'father'. | Perhaps 'lucky' is not exactly* **the right word**. → **BUZZWORD, FOUR-LETTER WORD, SWEAR WORD**
2 sb's words the things that someone says or writes: *Those are his words, not mine.* | **in sb's words** *Jones was, in the judge's words, 'an evil man'.* | **In your own words**, *explain the term 'personal service'.*
3 the words the words that are sung as part of a song: *I know the tune, but I've forgotten the words.* | **[+to]** *Many people don't know the words to the country's national anthem.*
4 have a word *especially spoken* to talk to someone quickly, especially because you need their advice about something or you want to tell them to do something: *Could I have a word?* | **[+with]** *I'll have a word with him and see if he'll help.* | **have a quick/brief word** *I was hoping to have a quick word with you.* | **have/exchange a few words** *Could I have a few words with you?*
5 want a word *spoken* to want to talk to someone, especially in order to criticize them: **[+with]** *Wait a minute! I want a word with you!*
6 not hear/understand/believe a word used to emphasize that you cannot hear, understand etc what someone says or writes: *No one could hear a word because someone had cut the amplifier cable.* | **[+of]** *I can't understand a word of Russian.*
7 without (saying) a word if you do something without a word, you do not say anything while you do it: *He left without a word.*
8 say a word/say a few words to make a short speech about something: *I'd like to say a few words about the plans.*
9 a word of warning/caution/advice/thanks etc something you say that warns someone, thanks them etc: *It's a beautiful city, but a word of warning: street robberies are very common. | He left without a word of apology.*
10 not say a word a) (*also* **not breathe a word**) to not say anything about something because it is a secret: *Promise you won't say a word to anyone?* **b)** to not say anything: *What's wrong? You haven't said a word since you got here.*
11 put your feelings/thoughts etc into words to express what you want to say clearly: *He found it difficult to put ideas into words.*
12 have/exchange words (with sb) to argue – use this when you do not want to make the argument seem serious: *I was in a bad mood and he kept pestering me, so we had words.*
13 a harsh/a cross/an angry etc word something you say that shows you are angry or want to criticize someone: *Mountain rescue teams have harsh words to say to people who climb without proper equipment. | They were married for 50 years and she says there was never an angry word between them.*
14 NEWS/INFORMATION [singular, U] a piece of news or a message: *Word came that our duties would be changed. | 'Have you heard from Ann?' 'No, not a word.' | There was still* **no word from** *John.* | **word gets out/around** (=people hear about something) *It's a very small town and if you do something bad, word gets around.* | **the word is (that)/word has it (that)** (=people are saying that) *The word is that the two companies are planning a merger.* | **spread/pass the word** (=tell other people some information or news) *Health officials are encouraging people to spread the word about the benefits of exercise.* | **send/bring word** *old-fashioned formal* (=send or bring a message) *The mayor sent word he'd be late.* | **Word of mouth** (=information you get by someone telling you) *is one of the best ways of getting business.* | **by word of mouth** *Much of this information is picked up by word of mouth from previous students.*
15 the last/final word a) the power to decide whether or how to do something: **[+on]** *The final word on policy determination belongs to the committee. | She* **has the final word** *on whether policies are put into action or not.* **b)** the last statement or speech in a discussion or argument: *The last word must go to Nick, who has organized the whole project. | Why must you always* **have the last word** *in any argument?* **c)** in sports, the last hit or kick in a game, especially when it is successful: *Adams* **had the final word** *with a last-minute goal.*
16 my/his/your etc word a sincere promise to do something, or a promise that what you say is true: *I trust him to* **keep** *his* **word**. | *I* **give** *you* **my word** (=I promise) *that it won't happen again. | They had* **given** *their* **word of honour** *that they*

W

would not attempt to escape. | We only **have** his **word** for it that he has already paid. | Delors claimed that Johnson had **gone back on** his **word** (=not done what he had promised to do). | The business is doing very well. You can **take my word for it** (=accept that what I say is true). | I never know whether to **take** him **at his word** (=believe what he says). | His **word is** his **bond** (=he always does what he promises to do). | **be true to your word/be as good as your word** (=do what you promise to do) | **a man of his word/a woman of her word** (=a man or woman who does what they have promised to do)

17 word for word a) in exactly the same words: *The newspaper printed his speech more or less word for word.* **b)** (*also* **word by word**) if you translate a piece of writing word for word, you translate the meaning of each single word rather than the meaning of a whole phrase or sentence

18 in a word used before giving a very simple answer or explanation: *We are, in a word, busy. Ridiculously busy.*

19 in words of one syllable saying something in a way that is very easy to understand, especially because the person you are talking to is stupid: *You have to put everything in words of one syllable for her.*

20 in so many words (*also* **in as many words**) [usually negative] in a direct way, or in a way that makes it very clear what you mean: *Aunt Fay wasn't happy and said so in as many words.*

21 take the words (right) out of sb's mouth *spoken* if someone takes the words out of your mouth, they have just said what you were going to say

22 put words into sb's mouth *spoken* to tell someone what you think they are trying to say, in a way that annoys them: *Will you stop putting words into my mouth – I never said I disliked the job.*

23 AN ORDER [singular] an order to do something: ***On the word*** *'go' everyone has to run to the end of the room and back.* | *When I* ***give the word,*** *grab him.*

24 (right) from the word go *spoken* from the beginning of something: *The marriage was a disaster from the word go.*

25 too silly/complicated/ridiculous etc for words *spoken* extremely silly, complicated etc: *His behaviour has been too pathetic for words.*

26 (have/drop) a word in sb's ear to say something to someone privately, especially to give them advice or a warning: *If I were you, I'd have a word in his ear before it's too late.*

27 get a word in (edgeways) to get a chance to say something: *Once George starts talking it's difficult to get a word in edgeways.*

28 put in a (good) word for sb to try to help someone get or achieve something by saying good things about them to someone else: *I got the job because Paul put in a good word for me.*

29 words fail me *spoken* used to say that you are so surprised, angry, or shocked that you do not know what to say: *I ... words fail me.*

30 word! *AmE informal* used to say that you understand or agree with what someone has just said

31 (Upon) my word! *spoken old-fashioned* used when you are very surprised: *My word! Hasn't she grown?*

32 surprised/angry/pleased etc isn't the word for it *spoken* used to say that you are extremely surprised, angry etc

33 a man/woman etc of few words someone who does not say very much: *My father was a man of few words.*

34 the Word (of God) the religious ideas and messages in the Bible → **eat your words** at EAT(3), → FOUR-LETTER WORD, → **a good word for sb/sth** at GOOD[1](31), → **in other words** at OTHER(11), → **be the last word in sth** at LAST[1](10), → **be lost for words** at LOST[2](10), → **mark my words** at MARK[1](12), → **not mince your words** at MINCE[1](3), → **play on words** at PLAY[2](6), → **say the word** at SAY[1](26), → **the spoken word** at SPOKEN[2](2), → **the written word** at WRITTEN[2](3)

THESAURUS

word a single group of letters that are used together with a particular meaning: *'Casa' is the Italian word for 'house'.* | *I looked up the word in a dictionary.*
name a word that you use for a particular thing, place, organization etc: *Iberia is the ancient name for the Spanish Peninsula.* | *What's the name of that type of dog?*
term a word or group of words that is used in a specific subject or area of language: *The medical term for losing your hair is 'alopecia'.*
phrase a group of words that have a particular meaning when used together, or which someone uses on a particular occasion: *We don't really have a phrase for 'bon appétit' in English.*
expression a fixed phrase which is used in a language and has a particular meaning: *He uses a lot of obscure expressions that I don't really understand.*
buzzword /ˈbʌzwɜːd $ -wɜːrd/ a word or group of words that people in a particular type of work or activity have started using a lot because they think it is important: *E-learning is the buzzword in educational publishing at the moment.*
idiom /ˈɪdiəm/ a group of words that has a special meaning which you cannot guess from the meanings of each separate word: *'Full of beans' is an idiom which means feeling lively and energetic.*
cliché /ˈkliːʃeɪ $ kliːˈʃeɪ/ a group of words that is used so often that it seems rather boring, annoying, or silly: *It's a bit of a cliché, but good communication skills are the key to success.*
slang very informal words used especially by a particular group of people such as young people, criminals, or soldiers: *Grass is slang for marijuana.* | *prison slang*
jargon words and phrases used in a particular profession or by a particular group of people, which are difficult for other people to understand – often used to show disapproval: *The instructions were full of technical jargon.* | *complicated legal jargon*

word² ●○○ *v* [T] to use words that are carefully chosen in order to express something SYN **phrase**: *How can we word the letter so as not to offend the parents?*

ˈword ˌblindness *n* [U] DYSLEXIA

ˈword cloud *n* [C] a drawing of the words used in a speech, on a website etc, with the more frequent words shown larger and the less frequent words shown smaller

word·ed /ˈwɜːdɪd $ ˈwɜːr-/ *adj* **carefully/clearly/strongly etc worded** using words that express an idea carefully or clearly: *a carefully worded question* | *a strongly worded letter*

word·ing /ˈwɜːdɪŋ $ ˈwɜːr-/ ●○○ *n* [U] the words and phrases used to express something SYN **phrasing**: **[+of]** *the exact wording of the contract*

word·less /ˈwɜːdləs $ ˈwɜːrd-/ *adj* without using words SYN **silent**: *a wordless prayer* | *She threw her arms around him in wordless grief.* —**wordlessly** *adv*: *She nodded wordlessly.*

ˌword-ˈperfect *adj BrE* able to remember and say every word of something correctly: *She rehearsed her speech until she was word-perfect.*

ˈword-play *n* [U] making jokes by using words in a clever way

ˈword ˌprocessor *n* [C] computer software or a small computer that you use for writing letters and other documents SYN **WP**: **on a word processor** *Most reports are produced on a word processor.* —**word processing** *n* [U]: *I mostly use my computer for word processing.* —**word processed** *adj*: *a word processed document*

word·search /ˈwɜːdsɜːtʃ $ ˈwɜːrdsɜːrtʃ/ *n* [C] a game in which you have to look at a square of letters and find words written in various directions

word·smith /ˈwɜːdsmɪθ $ ˈwɜːrd-/ *n* [C] someone who is clever at using language

word·y /ˈwɜːdi $ ˈwɜːrdi/ *adj* using too many words SYN **verbose**: *a wordy explanation* —**wordiness** *n* [U]

wore /wɔː $ wɔːr/ *v* the past tense of WEAR[1]

work¹ /wɜːk $ wɜːrk/ ●●● S1 W1 *v*

1 DO A JOB FOR MONEY [I] to do a job that you are paid for: *Where do you work?* | *Many young people in the area have* never worked. | *The injury means he'll probably never work again.* | **[+for]** *He works for a law firm.* | **[+at/in]** *I work at the university.* | **[+as]** *She works as a consultant for a design company.* | **work in industry/education/publishing etc** *The studies were undertaken by people working in education.* | **work part-time/full-time** *I work part-time in a library.*

GRAMMAR: Prepositions with work

- You **work in** a city or area: *He works in Manhattan.*
- You **work in** a type of place such as a bank, shop, or factory: *She works in a library.*
- You **work at** a particular place or organization: *She works at the Library of Congress.*
- You **work for** a person, company, or organization that employs you: *He works for his father.* | *We both work for the same company.*
- You **work in** an industry or a type of job, for example education, advertising, or IT: *He works in advertising.*
- You **work as** a waiter, cashier, accountant etc: *She works as a cook.* ✗ Don't say: *She works as cook.*
- You **work on** a project or task: *Several people worked on the report.*

2 DO YOUR JOB [I,T] to do the activities and duties that are part of your job: *Sally isn't working tomorrow.* | *Staff will have to get used to a new way of working.* | **[+with]** *One of the women I work with is getting married this weekend.* | **work under sb** (=have someone who is in charge of you) *Each site has a fully trained team who work under a site manager.* | **work days/nights/weekends etc** *I get paid more if I work nights.* | *We're sometimes expected to work twelve-hour days.* | *Are you **working late** (=working after the time you usually finish) again tonight?* | *Forty police officers are **working round the clock** (=working day and night without stopping) to find Murray's killer.* | *Nowadays, many people are able to **work from home**.*
3 HELP [I] if you work with someone or a group of people, your job involves trying to help them: **[+with/among]** *She's just retired after 38 years working with children.* | *He has worked among some of the world's poorest people.*
4 DO AN ACTIVITY [I] to spend time and effort doing something: *I've been working in the garden all afternoon.* | *I'm going to have to **work** really **hard** to pass these exams.* | *We're working together to develop a new system.*
5 TRY TO ACHIEVE STH [I] to try continuously to achieve a particular thing: **[+towards]** *They are working towards a solution to their problems.* | **[+for]** *We will work for the release of the hostages.* | **work to do sth** *The police are working to provide more help for victims of crime.* | *The company is **working hard** to improve its image.* | *He **worked tirelessly** (=worked very hard in a determined way) for the charity throughout his life.*
6 MACHINE/EQUIPMENT **a)** [I] if a machine or piece of equipment works, it does what it is supposed to do: *You should check that the smoke alarm is working properly.* | *The delete key doesn't work.* | **get sth to work** *I can't get the heater to work.* **b)** [T] to make a machine or piece of equipment do what it is supposed to do: *My parents can't even work the video.*
7 BE EFFECTIVE/SUCCESSFUL [I] to be effective or successful: *Making a marriage work can take a lot of effort.* | *I've never found a diet that works.* | *The recipe works just as well if you use margarine instead of butter.* | *The cream works immediately to relieve sore skin.* | **[+for]** *You need to find which method works best for you.* | **[+against]** *a drug that works against some types of cancer*
8 HAVE AN EFFECT [I always + adv/prep] if something such as a fact, situation, or system works in a particular way, it has a particular effect on someone or something: *The arrangement works well for everyone involved.* | *The French team are the heavier crew, which should **work in** their **favour*** (=help them). | *Sexism still **works against*** (=harms or causes problems for) *women in many professions.* | *Loyalty **works both ways*** (=involves two opposite or matching effects): *we are loyal to our employees and, in turn, they are loyal to us.*
9 ART/STYLE/LITERATURE [I] if a painting, design, piece of writing etc works, it is successful because it has the effect on you that the painter, writer etc intended: *I don't think the scene with the horses really works, do you?* | **[+for]** *The colour combination just doesn't work for me.*
10 SHAPE/CUT STH [T] if you work a material such as metal, leather, or clay, you cut, sew, or shape it in order to make something
11 USE A SUBSTANCE [I] to use a particular material or substance in order to make something such as a picture, design, jewellery etc: **[+in/with]** *a sculptor who works in steel* | *a jeweller who works with silver*
12 work your way to/through etc sth a) to move somewhere slowly and with difficulty: *From here, we worked our way carefully across the rock base.* **b)** to achieve something gradually by working: *He had worked his way up to head of department.*
13 work your way through school/college/university etc to do a job while you are a student because you need the money to pay for your courses, books etc
14 MOVE GRADUALLY [I,T always + adv/prep] to move into a particular state or position very gradually, either in a series of small movements or after a long time: *Slowly he worked the screwdriver into the crack.* | **work (its way) loose** *One of the screws must have worked loose.*
15 EXERCISE [T] to use and exercise a muscle or part of your body: *Swimming is a form of exercise that works every muscle in your body.*
16 MOVE [I,T] *formal* if a part of your body works or you work it, it moves: *She was trembling and her mouth was working.*
17 WORK IN AN AREA [T] *especially AmE* if you work a particular area or type of place, you travel around the area for your job, or work in that type of place: *Markowitz works the Tri-State area.*
18 work the door to take tickets from people as they enter a club, theatre etc: *Binns worked the door at various Manhattan clubs.*
19 ENTERTAIN A CROWD [T] if an entertainer or politician works a crowd of people, they entertain them and get their interest or support: *She really knew how to work a crowd.*
20 LAND/SOIL [T] if you work the land, soil etc, you do all the work necessary to grow crops on it: *He was left to work the farm alone.*
21 MINE [T] to remove a substance such as coal, gold, or oil from under the ground
22 work like magic/work like a charm (*also* **work a treat** *BrE*) to be very effective: *a polish that works a treat on windows*
23 MIND/BRAIN [I] if your mind or brain is working, you are thinking or trying to solve a problem
24 work on the principle/assumption/basis etc that to base ideas, plans etc on a particular fact that you think is true: *We're working on the assumption that the conference will take place in Canada, as planned.*
25 work yourself into a frenzy/panic/state etc to make yourself become very nervous, angry etc: *He seemed to be working himself into a rage.*
26 work it/things *spoken* to make arrangements for something to happen, especially by behaving in a clever or skilful way: *We should try and work it so that we can all go together.*
27 work the system to understand how a system works so that you can get advantages for yourself, often in a slightly dishonest way: *Lynn could show the rest of us how to work the system.*
28 work sb hard (*also* **work sb into the ground** *informal*) to make someone work very hard: *The coach has been working us really hard this week.* | *People have complained that they are being worked into the ground.* | **work yourself into the ground** *I've worked myself into the ground setting up this interview.*
29 work your fingers to the bone (*also* **work your socks off** *informal*) to work very hard
30 work your butt/ass/arse off *not polite* to work very hard
31 CALCULATE [T] *AmE formal* to calculate the answer to a mathematical problem
32 work to rule *BrE* to protest about a situation at work by

doing your job slowly, with the excuse that you must obey all the rules exactly
33 (it) works for me/you etc *spoken* used to say that something is very suitable for someone and does exactly what they wanted or expected: *I meditate and do Yoga every day. It works for me and I think it could work for you too.*
34 work a trend/look etc to wear something fashionable – used especially in magazines: *Gemma looks great as she works the nautical look.* → **work wonders** at WONDER[2](4), → **work miracles** at MIRACLE(4), → **work your magic** at MAGIC[1](5)
work around sb/sth (*also* **work round sb/sth** *BrE*) *phr v* to arrange or organize something so that you avoid problems that may stop you from doing something: *John won't be here on the 15th so we'll have to work round that.*
work around to sth (*also* **work round to sth** *BrE*) *phr v* to gradually mention a subject in a conversation or piece of writing, especially because it is embarrassing: *You'll have to work round to the subject gradually.*
work at sth *phr v* to try hard to improve something or achieve something: *Learning a language isn't easy. You have to work at it.* | **work at doing sth** *couples who want to work at improving their relationship*
work sb/sth **in** *phr v*
1 work sth ↔ in (*also* **work sth into sth**) to include something in a speech, piece of writing, activity etc: *He managed to work in a few references to his new book.* | *Here are a few goodies you can work into your daily diet.*
2 work sth ↔ in (*also* **work sth into sth**) to add one substance to another and mix them together in a very thorough way: *Work the butter into the flour.*
3 *AmE spoken* to arrange to meet someone, even though you are very busy SYN **fit sb in** *BrE*: *My schedule's pretty full, but I think I can work you in.*
work sth ↔ **off** *phr v*
1 to get rid of something, especially a feeling such as anger, nervousness etc, by doing something that uses a lot of your energy: *Walking is excellent for working off tension.* | *I need to go and work off a few of these calories.*
2 to do a job for someone else because you owe them money or because they have helped you in the past: *She hasn't worked off her debts to me yet.*
work on sb/sth *phr v*
1 to spend time working in order to produce or repair something: *He has spent the last two years working on a book about childcare.* | *Every weekend you see him working on his car.*
2 to try very hard to improve or achieve something: *A trainer has been brought in to work on her fitness.* | **work on doing sth** *We need to work on ensuring that the children feel safe and confident.*
3 to try continuously to influence someone or persuade them to do something: *You leave him to me. I'll work on him.*
work out *phr v*
1 PLAN **work sth ↔ out** to think carefully about how you are going to do something and plan a good way of doing it: *UN negotiators have worked out a set of compromise proposals.* | **work out what/where/how etc** *We need to work out how we're going to get there.* | ***I had it all worked out*** (=had made very careful plans).
2 CALCULATE **work sth ↔ out** to calculate an answer, amount, price etc: *See if you can work this bill out.* | **work out how much/how many etc** *We'll have to work out how much food we'll need for the party.*
3 UNDERSTAND **work sth ↔ out** *especially BrE* to think about something and manage to understand it: *The plot is very complicated – it'll take you a while to work it out.* | **work sth out for yourself** *I'm sure you can work it out for yourself.*
4 COST if a cost or amount works out at a particular figure, it is found to be that much when you calculate it: **work out at/to £10/$500 etc** *The bill works out at £15 each.* | **work out expensive/cheap etc** (=be expensive or cheap) *If we go by taxi, it's going to work out very expensive.*
5 GET BETTER if a problem or complicated situation works out, it gradually gets better or gets solved: *Things will work out, you'll see.* | *I hope it all works out for Gina and Andy.* | **work itself out** *I'm sure everything will work itself out.*
6 HAPPEN if a situation works out in a particular way, it happens in that way SYN **turn out**: **work out well/badly** *Financially, things have worked out well for us.*
7 EXERCISE to make your body fit and strong by doing exercises: *He works out with weights twice a week.* → WORKOUT
8 I can't work sb out *BrE spoken* used to say that you cannot understand what someone is really like or why they behave in the way they do: *I couldn't work her out at all.*
9 be worked out if a mine is worked out, all the coal, gold etc has been removed from it
work sb **over** *phr v informal* to attack someone by hitting them several times
work through *phr v*
1 work through sth to deal with problems or unpleasant feelings: *After someone dies, it can take a long time to work through your grief.*
2 if the result or effect of something works through, it becomes noticeable: *The positive effect on businesses may take up to three years to work through.*
work up *phr v*
1 work up enthusiasm/interest/courage etc to make yourself feel interested, brave etc: *I'm trying to work up enough courage to go to the dentist.*
2 work up an appetite/a thirst/a sweat to make yourself hungry or THIRSTY, or make yourself SWEAT, especially by doing physical exercise: *You can work up a really big thirst playing tennis.*
3 work sb up to make someone very angry, excited, or upset about something: **work yourself up** *You're working yourself up again.* | *She had* ***worked*** *herself* ***up into a state.*** → WORKED UP
4 work sth ↔ up to develop and improve something such as a project or a piece of writing: *Jack took notes which he would work up into a report later.*
work up to sth *phr v* to gradually prepare yourself to do something difficult: **work up to doing sth** *He'd been working up to asking her for a date all week.*

work[2] ●●● S1 W1 *n*

1 JOB [U] a job or activity that you do regularly, especially in order to earn money → **employment**: *There isn't a lot of work at this time of the year.* | *He's been* ***out of work*** (=without a job) *for two years.* | *More people are* ***in work*** (=have a job) *than ten years ago.* | **before/after work** (=before a day of work or at the end of a day of work) *Do you want to go for a drink after work?* THESAURUS JOB

GRAMMAR: Comparison

work
• In this meaning, **work** is always an uncountable noun.
• You say: *It may be hard for older people to find work.* ✗ Don't say: *find a work*
job
• **Job** is a countable noun.
• You say: *I applied for a job as a reporter.* ✗ Don't say: *I applied for a work.*
• You say: *Her first job was in London.* ✗ Don't say: *Her first work was in London.*

2 PLACE [U] a place where you do your job, which is not your home: *I had an accident on the way to work.* | *He left work at the usual time.* | *I went out with the girls from work last night.* | **at work** *Dad's at work right now.*
3 DUTIES [U] the duties and activities that are part of your job: *A large part of the work we do involves using computers.* | *He* ***starts work*** *at 4 am.* | *He's started a business doing gardening and roofing work.*
4 RESULT [U] something that you produce as a result of doing your job or doing an activity: *Send a résumé and examples of your work.* | *The building is the work of architect Rafael Moneo.* | *The teacher should make sure that each child has* ***a piece of work*** *displayed on the wall.* | *The* ***standard of work*** *has declined.*
5 PAPERS ETC [U] the papers and other materials you

W

need for doing work: *Can you move some of your work off the kitchen table? | I often have to take work home with me.*
6 BOOK/PAINTING/MUSIC [C] something such as a painting, play, piece of music etc that is produced by a painter, writer, or musician: *the Collected Works of Shakespeare | It is another accomplished work by the artist.* → WORK OF ART THESAURUS▸ MUSIC
7 ACTIVITY [U] when you use physical or mental effort in order to achieve something: **[+on]** *Work will start next month on a new swimming pool in the centre of the city. | Looking after children can be* ***hard work****.* | **carry out/do work** *You should not allow unqualified people to carry out work on your house.* | **set to work/get down to work** (=start work) *He set to work immediately.*
8 STUDY [U] study or RESEARCH, especially for a particular purpose: **carry out/do work** *The centre carries out work to monitor trends in housing management. | He did his postgraduate work in Sociology.*
9 at work a) doing your job or a particular activity: *He spent most of his time watching the fishermen at work.* **b)** having a particular influence or effect: *Volcanoes display some of nature's most powerful forces at work.*
10 the (whole) works *spoken* used after mentioning several things, to emphasize that someone or something has everything you can think of: *The hotel had everything – sauna, swimming pool, the works.*
11 nice work/quick work *spoken* used to praise someone for doing something well or quickly: *That was quick work!*
12 sth is in the works/pipeline *informal* used to say that something is being planned or developed: *Upgrades to the existing software are in the works.*
13 works a) [plural] activities involved in building or repairing things such as roads, bridges etc: **engineering works/irrigation works/roadworks** *the official in charge of the engineering works* → PUBLIC WORKS **b)** [C] (*plural* **works**) a building or group of buildings in which goods are produced in large quantities or an industrial process happens: **ironworks/gasworks/cement etc works** *The brick works closed last year.*
14 the works the moving parts of a machine SYN **mechanism**
15 OPERATION [U] an operation to make you look younger or more attractive SYN **cosmetic surgery**: *All these celebrities have had work done.*
16 have your work cut out (for you) *informal* used to say that it will be very difficult to do something: *The team will have their work cut out if they are to win the competition.*
17 make short/light work of sth to do something very quickly and easily: *A microwave oven can make light work of the cooking.*
18 make heavy/hard work of sth to do something with difficulty: *They made hard work of what should have been an easy game.*
19 be a work in progress to not be finished or perfect yet: *The garden is still very much a work in progress.*
20 all work and no play (makes Jack a dull boy) used to say that you should not spend all your time working, but should spend some of your time relaxing
21 FORCE [U] *technical* force multiplied by distance → **be all in a day's work** at DAY(21), → **do sb's dirty work** at DIRTY[1](8), → **a nasty piece of work** at NASTY(7), → **nice work if you can get it** at NICE(12)

COLLOCATIONS – MEANINGS 1 & 3

VERBS

start work *He started work as a trainee accountant.*
look for work (*also* **seek work** *formal*) *Young people come to town looking for work.*
find work (=get a job) *It was difficult for them to find work.*
return to work/go back to work *His doctor agreed he was fit enough to return to work.*

ADJECTIVES/NOUN + work

part-time work *In recent years part-time work has become more popular.*
full-time work *Are you available for full-time work?*
paid work *She hasn't done any paid work since she had children.*
secretarial/clerical/office work | **legal work** (=work done by lawyers) | **manual work** (=work done with your hands) | **voluntary work** *BrE*, **volunteer work** *AmE* (=a job you are not paid for) | **sb's daily work** (=the work someone does every day)

PHRASES

sb's line of work (=type of work) *I meet lots of interesting people in my line of work.*

work·a·ble /ˈwɜːkəbəl $ ˈwɜːr-/ *adj* **1** a workable system, plan etc will be practical and effective: *a workable solution to the problem | a workable timetable* THESAURUS▸ POSSIBLE **2** a substance that is workable can be shaped with your hands: *workable clay for making pots*
work·a·day /ˈwɜːkədeɪ $ ˈwɜːr-/ *adj* [only before noun] ordinary and not interesting SYN **everyday**: *He promised to tackle the workaday matters affecting people's daily lives.*
work·a·hol·ic /ˌwɜːkəˈhɒlɪk $ ˌwɜːrkəˈhɒː-/ *n* [C] *informal* someone who chooses to work a lot, so that they do not have time to do anything else
work·a·round /ˈwɜːkəraʊnd $ ˈwɜːrk-/ *n* [C] a method, especially a temporary one, that you use to achieve something when the normal method is not successful. In computing, workarounds are used to solve problems with HARDWARE or software.
work·bas·ket /ˈwɜːkˌbɑːskɪt $ ˈwɜːrkˌbæs-/ *n* [C] a container for sewing equipment
work·bench /ˈwɜːkbentʃ $ ˈwɜːrk-/ *n* [C] a strong table used for working on with tools → see picture at TABLE[1]
work·book /ˈwɜːkbʊk $ ˈwɜːrk-/ *n* [C] a school book containing questions and exercises
work·day /ˈwɜːkdeɪ $ ˈwɜːrk-/ *n* [C] *AmE* **1** the amount of time that you spend working in a day SYN **working day**: *a 10-hour workday* **2** a day of the week when most people work SYN **working day**: *He commutes three hours on workdays. | workday traffic*
ˌworked ˈup *adj* [not before noun] *informal* very upset or excited about something: **[+about/over]** *You shouldn't* ***get*** *so* ***worked up*** *about it.* → **work up** at WORK[1]
work·er /ˈwɜːkə $ ˈwɜːrkər/ ●●● S2 W1 *n* [C]
1 someone who does a job, especially a particular type of job: *workers in the tourist industry | reports from local aid workers* → GUEST WORKER, SOCIAL WORKER
2 [usually plural] someone who works in an organization and who is not a manager: *conflicts between workers and management | attacks on workers' rights*
3 a good/hard/quick etc worker someone who works very well or quickly
4 the workers [plural] the members of the WORKING CLASS: *the workers' revolution*

COLLOCATIONS

ADJECTIVES/NOUN + worker

a skilled worker (=one who has special skills) *There is a shortage of skilled workers.*
an unskilled worker *Some ex-miners now had jobs as unskilled workers in factories.*
a part-time worker *A high percentage of the female staff were part-time workers.*
a full-time worker | **a temporary/casual worker** (=working somewhere for a limited period of time) | **a manual/blue-collar worker** (=someone who does physical work) | **a white-collar worker** (=someone who works in an office, a bank etc) | **a low-paid worker** | **a factory/farm/office worker** | **a research/rescue/health etc worker** | **a construction worker** (=someone who builds buildings, bridges etc)

ˈwork ˌethic *n* [singular] a belief in the moral value and importance of work: *They instilled the work ethic into their children.*
ˈwork exˌperience *n* [U] **1** the experience you have had of working in a particular type of job: *She's well qualified but has no relevant work experience.* **2** *BrE* a period

W

of time that a young person spends working in a particular place, as a form of training: **on work experience** *The teenagers spend two weeks on work experience in local businesses.* | *Why do I have to* ***do work experience****?* | **work experience placement/programme/scheme etc**

work·fare /ˈwɜːkfeə $ ˈwɜːrkfer/ *n* [U] a system in which unemployed people have to work before they are given money for food, rent etc by the government

work·flow /ˈwɜːkfləʊ $ ˈwɜːrkfloʊ/ *n* [U] the way that a particular project is organized by a company, including which part of a project someone is going to do, and when they are supposed to do it

work·force /ˈwɜːkfɔːs $ ˈwɜːrkfɔːrs/ ●○○ *n* [singular] all the people who work in a particular industry or company, or are available to work in a particular country or area → **staff**: *Women now represent almost 50% of the workforce.* | *The company is cutting its workforce.* | **skilled/educated/flexible etc workforce**

work·horse /ˈwɜːkhɔːs $ ˈwɜːrkhɔːrs/ *n* [C] a person, machine, or vehicle that does a lot of work, especially when it is hard or boring: *The Hercules aircraft has been the workhorse of the air force for over 25 years.*

work·house /ˈwɜːkhaʊs $ ˈwɜːrk-/ *n* [C] a building in Britain in the past where very poor people lived if they had nowhere else to go SYN **poorhouse**

work·ing¹ /ˈwɜːkɪŋ $ ˈwɜːr-/ ●●○ W2 *adj* [only before noun]

1 a) having a job that you are paid for → **employed**: *a* ***working mother*** | *Many* ***working women*** *rely on relatives for childcare.* | *A smaller* ***working population*** *will have to support a growing number of retired people.* **b)** *old-fashioned* having a physical or practical job: **working man/people/folk** *the ordinary working man*

2 working hours/day/week the time that people spend doing their job: *In a normal working day, I see around 6 or 7 clients.* | **during/outside working hours** *Telephone at any time during normal working hours.* | *Many mothers prefer* ***flexible working hours****.* | *We do a 37-hour working week.*

3 working day a day of the week when most people work. In Britain and the US this is usually Monday to Friday SYN **workday**: *It will be returned within three working days* (=three days, not including weekends or public holidays).

4 working conditions/environment etc the situation in which you work, especially the physical things such as pay or safety: *improvements in working conditions*

5 working practices/methods the way in which you do your job: *training in up-to-date working practices*

6 working life the part of your adult life when you have a paid job: *He* ***spent*** *all his* ***working life*** *in a factory.*

7 (in) working order working properly and not broken: **be in good/perfect/full etc working order** *The car was old, but the engine was still in good working order.* | *the amount of exercise needed to* ***keep*** *your body* ***in working order***

8 working relationship the way that people work together: **[+with/between]** *They want to establish a better working relationship between medical and nursing staff.* | **good/close/effective etc working relationship** *We* ***have*** *a close* ***working relationship*** *with other voluntary groups.*

9 a working knowledge of sth enough knowledge of a system, subject, language etc to be able to use it or to do a particular job: *A* ***good working knowledge*** *of the building regulations is necessary for the job.*

10 working clothes (*also* **work clothes**) clothes which you wear for work or are designed for people to work in

11 working model a model that has parts that move

12 working parts the parts of a machine that move

13 working definition/theory/title a DEFINITION, idea etc that may not be exactly right but is good enough to use when you start working on something

14 working majority *BrE* enough support in parliament for a government to continue making laws and ruling a country

15 working breakfast/lunch/dinner a breakfast, lunch etc which is also a business meeting

16 working memory *technical* the part of a person's or computer's memory which stores information about the thing being worked on now

working² *n* **1 the workings** [plural] the way something such as a system, piece of equipment, or organization works: **[+of]** *his knowledge of the inner workings of the department* | *I shall never understand* ***the workings of*** *his* ***mind*** (=how he thinks). **2 flexible/short-time etc working** a particular way of working, especially relating to the hours which someone works **3** [C usually plural] a mine or part of a mine where soil has been dug out in order to remove metals or stone → **quarry**

ˌworking ˈcapital *n* [U] the money that is available to be used for the costs of a business → VENTURE CAPITAL

ˌworking ˈclass ●●○ *n* [singular] (*also* **working classes** [plural]) the group of people in society who traditionally do physical work and do not have much money or power: *Marx wrote about the political struggles of the working class.* —**working-class** *adj*: *working-class women* | *the traditional working-class occupations* | *He is proud of his working-class background.* → LOWER CLASS, MIDDLE CLASS, UPPER CLASS

GRAMMAR: Singular or plural verb?

- **The working class** is usually followed by a singular verb: *The working class* ***has*** *suffered a lot.*
- In British English, you can also use a plural verb: *The working class* ***have*** *suffered a lot.*

GRAMMAR GUIDE ▸ NOUNS

working families tax credit (*also* **working tax credit**) *n* [U] money given by the government in Britain to parents who do not earn much money

ˈworking girl *n* [C] *old-fashioned* a woman who has sex for money – used when you want to avoid saying this directly SYN **prostitute**

ˈworking group *n* [C] a group that is formed to examine a particular situation or problem and suggest ways of dealing with it SYN **working party**: **set up/establish a working group (to do sth)** *The commission has set up a special working group to look at the problem.* | **[+on]** *a working group on constitutional reform*

ˈworking ˌpapers *n* [plural] an official document that you need in the US in order to get a job if you are young or were born in a different country

ˈworking ˌparty *n* [C] *BrE* a WORKING GROUP

ˌwork-ˈlife ˌbalance *n* [U] the ability to give a sensible amount of time and effort to your work and to your life outside work, for example to your family or to other interests: *You can't have a proper work-life balance if you're in the office for 12 hours a day.*

work·load /ˈwɜːkləʊd $ ˈwɜːrkloʊd/ ●○○ *n* [C] the amount of work that a person or organization has to do: *She's struggling to cope with the* ***heavy workload****.* | **increase/reduce/add to etc sb's workload** *We've got to find ways of reducing Gail's workload next year.*

work·man /ˈwɜːkmən $ ˈwɜːrk-/ ●○○ *n* (*plural* **workmen** /-mən/) [C] someone who does physical work such as building, repairing things etc

work·man·like /ˈwɜːkmənlaɪk $ ˈwɜːrk-/ *adj* done in a way which shows skill and hard work, but may not be exciting: *The team put up a good workmanlike performance to win 1–0.*

work·man·ship /ˈwɜːkmənʃɪp $ ˈwɜːrk-/ *n* [U] skill in making things, especially in a way that makes them look good SYN **craftsmanship**

work·mate /ˈwɜːkmeɪt $ ˈwɜːrk-/ *n* [C] *BrE* someone you work with SYN **colleague**

ˌwork of ˈart ●●○ *n* (*plural* **works of art**) [C]

1 a painting, SCULPTURE etc of high quality

2 something that is very attractive and skilfully made – often used humorously: *That cake's a real work of art!*

work·out /ˈwɜːkaʊt $ ˈwɜːrk-/ *n* [C] a period of physical exercise, especially as training for a sport: *a daily workout in the gym* → **work out** at WORK¹

ˈwork ˌpermit *n* [C] an official document that you need if you want to work in a foreign country → **visa**

work·place /ˈwɜːkpleɪs $ ˈwɜːrk-/ ●●○ *n* [C] the room,

building etc where you work: **in the workplace** *a report into discrimination in the workplace*

ˈ**work reˌlease** *n* [U] *AmE* a system in which a prisoner is allowed to work outside a prison

work·room /ˈwɜːkrʊm, -ruːm $ ˈwɜːrk-/ *n* [C] a room that you work in, especially making things, often in your home

work·sheet /ˈwɜːkʃiːt $ ˈwɜːrk-/ *n* [C] a piece of paper with questions and exercises for students

work·shop /ˈwɜːkʃɒp $ ˈwɜːrkʃɑːp/ ●●○ S3 W3 *n* [C]
1 a room or building where tools and machines are used for making or repairing things
2 a meeting at which people try to improve their skills by discussing their experiences and doing practical exercises: **writers'/drama/music etc workshop** *They held a number of music workshops and seminars.*

ˈ**work-shy** *adj* someone who is work-shy tries to avoid working because they do not like it SYN **lazy**

work·sta·tion /ˈwɜːkˌsteɪʃən $ ˈwɜːrk-/ ●○○ *n* [C]
1 a computer that is part of an office computer system
2 the desk where an office worker works

ˈ**work-ˌsurface** (*also* **work·top**) /ˈwɜːktɒp $ ˈwɜːrktɑːp/ *n* [C] *especially BrE* a flat surface for working on, especially in a kitchen SYN **counter** *AmE*

ˌ**work-to-ˈrule** *n* [singular] a situation in which people in a particular job refuse to do any additional work as a protest → **strike** → **work to rule** at WORK[1](32)

work·week /ˈwɜːkwiːk $ ˈwɜːrk-/ *n* [C] *AmE* the total amount of time that you spend working during a week SYN **working week** *BrE*: *a 40-hour workweek*

world[1] /wɜːld $ wɜːrld/ ●●● S1 W1 *n*
1 OUR PLANET/EVERYONE ON IT **the world** the PLANET we live on, and all the people, cities, and countries on it → **earth**: *Tuberculosis is still common in some* ***parts of the world****.* | *At that time China was* ***the most*** *powerful country* ***in the world****.* | ***the world's tallest*** *building* | *The Taj Mahal attracts visitors from* ***around the world****.* | *Students from* ***all over the world*** *come to study at Oxford.* | *Children are the same* ***the world over****.* | *The book has been published* ***throughout the world****.* | *There is nothing quite like it* ***anywhere in the world****.* | *Europe's relationship with* ***the rest of the world*** | *I decided to take a year off to* ***travel the world****.* | *a crime that shocked the world*

> **GRAMMAR**
> You say **in the world**: *the fastest sports car in the world*
> ✗ Don't say: *the fastest sports car in world* | *the fastest sport car on the world*
> GRAMMAR GUIDE ▸ NOUNS

2 in the world used to emphasize what you are saying: **the happiest/most exciting etc ... in the world** *I'm the luckiest man in the world!* | *Bali is my favourite place* ***in the whole world****.* | *Off he went,* ***without a care in the world*** (=not worried about anything at all). | ***Nothing in the world*** (=nothing at all) *can save them now.* | *Don't worry, we've got* ***all the time in the world*** (=plenty of time so you do not need to hurry). | **what/who/where/how etc in the world ...?** (=used when you are very surprised or annoyed) *What in the world are you doing here at seven in the morning?*
3 THE SOCIETY WE LIVE IN [singular] the society that we live in, the way people behave, and the kind of life we have: *Parents want a better world for their children.* | **the world** *The world is being transformed by information technology.* | *You had to go into politics if you wanted to change the world.* | **in an ideal/perfect world** (=used to say how you would like things to be) *In an ideal world, we would be able to recycle everything.* | **the real world** (=the way life really is, not how people would like it to be or imagine it) *In the real world, things are never quite so simple.* | **what is the world coming to?** (=used to say that you do not like the way society is changing) *Five pounds just to park your car! I don't know what the world's coming to.*
4 GROUP OF COUNTRIES [singular] a particular group of countries: **the Western/Arab etc world** *the highest unemployment rate in the Western world* | *the English-speaking world* | *agricultural practices in* ***the developing world*** | *the economies of* ***the industrialized world***
5 TIME IN HISTORY [singular] a particular period in history: **the modern/ancient world** *the peoples of the ancient world* | **the world of ...** *the world of the ancient Greeks*
6 SB'S LIFE AND EXPERIENCES [C] the life and experiences of a particular person or group of people: **[+of]** *the world of children* | *The diary gives us an insight into Hemingway's world.*
7 AREA OF ACTIVITY/WORK [C usually singular] a particular area of activity or work, and the people who are involved in it: **the world of politics/business/work etc** *She knew little about the world of politics.* | **the art/business/academic etc world** *personalities from the sporting world*
8 NATURE/ANIMALS/PLANTS **the natural/animal/plant world** all of nature, or all animals or plants considered as a group: *the wonders of the natural world*
9 PLACE/SITUATION [C usually singular] a particular kind of place or situation, especially one that someone describes or which you imagine: **[+of]** *the nightmare world of Orwell's novel '1984'* | *a world of lies and secrecy*
10 ANOTHER PLANET [C] a place like the Earth in another part of the universe where other things may live: *strange creatures from* ***another world***
11 STH IS VERY DIFFERENT [C] used in the following phrases to emphasize that something is very different: *There's* ***a world of difference*** *between the US and Europe.* | *I realized we were still* ***worlds apart*** (=very different, especially concerning your ideas, opinions etc). | *It was* ***a world away from*** (=completely different from) *the grand hotels she was used to.*
12 the outside world the people who live outside a particular place or country – used when the people of that place or country do not often meet other people: *Prisoners have little contact with the outside world.* | **be cut off from/closed to/isolated from the outside world** *Parts of the country have been virtually closed to the outside world for 20 years.*
13 the material world real things, rather than ideas and beliefs: *Is the material world all that exists?*
14 for all the world as if/as though/like *literary* exactly as if or exactly like: *She sat reading her paper,* ***looking for all the world as if*** *nothing had happened.*
15 out of this world *informal* extremely good, enjoyable etc: *The graphics and sounds are out of this world.*
16 do sb a/the world of good to be very good for someone's health or mental state: *A bit of fresh air and exercise will do her a world of good.*
17 in a world of your own/in your own little world used to say that someone seems to spend a lot of time thinking or imagining things, and does not seem to notice what is happening around them: *She was a shy child who seemed to* ***live in a world of her own****.*
18 mean the world to sb/think the world of sb if someone or something means the world to you, or if you think the world of them, they are very important to you and you love or respect them very much: *Lee thinks the world of that dog.*
19 sb would give the world to do sth used to say that someone would like to do something very much: *He would give the world to see her again.*
20 be/feel on top of the world *informal* to feel extremely happy
21 be a man/woman of the world to be someone who has had many experiences and is not easily shocked
22 not for the world used to emphasize that you would not do something: *I wouldn't* ***hurt*** *her* ***for the world****.* | *I wouldn't have missed it for the world.*
23 the world is your oyster there is no limit to the opportunities that someone has: *If you've got a good education, the world is your oyster.*
24 have the world at your feet a) to be very famous, popular, or successful: *In those days the band had the world at their feet.* **b)** to be in a position where you have the chance to become very successful: *a bright young lad with the world at his feet*
25 go up/come down in the world to move to a higher or

lower position in society: *He's gone up in the world a bit since I knew him at college.*
26 set the world on fire/alight *spoken* to have a big effect or be very successful: *Her last film didn't exactly set the world on fire.*
27 set/put the world to rights to discuss or say how the world should be changed to make people's lives better: *We were having a few beers and generally putting the world to rights.*
28 the Michael Jacksons/Mother Teresas/Microsofts etc of this world *spoken* used to talk about a particular kind of person or group, by using one person or group as an example: *The US team is new to the soccer scene, and can't expect to beat the Brazils of this world.*
29 think the world owes you a living to think that you should not have to work and that other people will provide you with everything you need - used to show disapproval
30 think (that) the world revolves around you to think that you are the most important person and everyone else should only be interested in making sure that you have what you want - used to show disapproval
31 the world and his wife *BrE* everyone or anybody - used when you want to emphasize that a lot of people do something or anyone can do something: *It seemed that the world and his wife had come to Madrid.*
32 come into the world *literary* to be born
33 bring a child into the world *literary* to have a baby, or help a baby to be born
34 sb is not long for this world *literary* used to say that someone is likely to die soon
35 NORMAL LIFE **the world** normal life in society, as opposed to a religious way of life, especially in a MONASTERY etc: *She* ***renounced the world*** *and entered a convent.*
→ **best of both worlds** at BEST[3](7), → **be dead to the world** at DEAD[1](9), → **it's not the end of the world** at END[1](18), → NEW WORLD, THIRD WORLD

world² ●●○ *adj* [only before noun]
1 existing in, involving, or affecting all or most countries in the world: **the World Cup/Championships etc** (=a competition involving people from many countries) *He won the world title in 2001.* | *the reigning Formula One* ***world champion*** | **world trade/economy etc** *the impact of the crisis on the world economy* → WORLD WAR
2 a world figure is one of the most important people in the world: *a meeting of* ***world leaders*** | *a* ***world authority*** *on climate change* → WORLD POWER

ˈworld-ˌbeater *n* [C] someone or something that is the best at a particular activity —**world-beating** *adj*

ˌworld-ˈclass ●○○ *adj* among the best in the world: *a world-class tennis champion* | *world-class research facilities*

ˌWorld ˈCup, the **1** the most important international competition in football, which is held every four years in a different country. The winners receive a gold cup called the Jules Rimet Trophy. **2** a similar international competition in some other sports, such as CRICKET or RUGBY

ˌWorld ˈEnglish *n* **1** [singular, U] English words that are understood and used by speakers of English everywhere **2** [U] (*also* **World Englishes** [plural]) the types of English used in particular countries

ˌworld-ˈfamous *adj* known about by people all over the world: *a world-famous singer*

world·ly /ˈwɜːldli $ ˈwɜːrld-/ *adj* [only before noun]
1 worldly goods/possessions *literary* everything you own
2 relating to ordinary life rather than SPIRITUAL or religious ideas SYN **mundane**: *He seemed very calm and far removed from worldly concerns.* **3** having a lot of experience and knowledge about people and life OPP **unworldly** —**worldliness** *n* [U]

ˌworldly-ˈwise / $ ˈ.. ./ *adj* having a lot of experience and knowledge about life so that you are not easily shocked or deceived OPP **naïve, naive**

ˈworld ˌmusic *n* [U] a type of popular music which has influences from traditional music from different countries

ˌworld ˈpower *n* [C] a country that has a lot of power and influence in many parts of the world → **superpower**

ˌworld ˈrecord *n* [C] the fastest time, longest distance, highest level etc which anyone has ever achieved anywhere in the world, especially in a sport: **set/break/beat a world record** *He set a new world record for the marathon.* | *the 800 m* ***world record holder*** —**world-record** *adj*: *a world-record time*

ˌWorld ˈSeries, the a set of up to seven baseball games played every year in the US or Canada between two professional teams, the winner of the American League and the winner of the National League. The winner of the World Series is considered to be the best team in the Major Leagues.

ˌWorld ˈService, the part of the BBC which broadcasts radio programmes, especially news, to all parts of the world. Its official name is the BBC World Service.

ˌworld ˈview, **world-view** *n* [C usually singular] someone's opinions and attitudes relating to the world and things in general: *the limited nineteenth-century world view*

ˌworld ˈwar *n* [C] a war involving many of the countries of the world: *fears of another world war* | *Churchill was prime minister during the Second World War.* | *the years after World War I*

World War I /ˌwɜːld wɔː ˈwʌn $ ˌwɜːrld wɔːr-/ (*also* **the First World War**) (1914-1918) a war in Europe fought between France, the UK and its EMPIRE, Russia, and the US on one side (known together as 'the Allies'), and Germany, Austria-Hungary, and Turkey on the other side. The war started as a result of the murder in Sarajevo of the Archduke Franz Ferdinand, a member of the Austrian royal family.

World War II /ˌwɜːld wɔː ˈtuː $ ˌwɜːrld wɔːr-/ (*also* **the Second World War**) (1939-1945) a war involving almost every major country in the world. On one side were the Allies (including the UK, France, and Poland, and after 1941 the US and the Soviet Union) and on the other side the Axis (including Germany, Japan, and Italy). The war was started by Adolf Hitler, the Nazi leader of Germany, who aimed to increase German power by attacking other countries and taking control of them.

ˌworld-ˈweary *adj* not feeling excited about anything anymore —**world-weariness** *n* [U]

world·wide /ˌwɜːldˈwaɪd◂ $ ˌwɜːrld-/ ●●○ *adj, adv* everywhere in the world → **globally**: *We have offices in over 56 countries worldwide.* | *cars with a worldwide reputation for reliability*

worm¹ /wɜːm $ wɜːrm/ ●●○ *n* [C]
1 a long thin creature with no bones and no legs that lives in soil → EARTHWORM, LUGWORM
2 the young form of an insect, which looks like a short worm → GLOW-WORM, SILKWORM, WOODWORM
3 have worms if a person or animal has worms, they have legless PARASITES (=small creatures that eat their food or their blood) in their body → ROUNDWORM, TAPEWORM
4 someone who you do not like or respect
5 a type of computer VIRUS that can make copies of itself and destroy information on computers that are connected to each other
6 the worm turns *literary* used to say that someone who normally obeys someone without complaining suddenly refuses to do this → **can of worms** at CAN[2](4)

worm² *v* [T] **1 worm (your way) into/through etc sth** to move through a small place or a crowd slowly, carefully, or with difficulty: *He wormed his way under the fence.* **2 worm your way into sb's affections/heart/confidence etc** to gradually make someone love or trust you, especially by being dishonest **3 worm your way out of (doing) sth** to avoid doing something that you have been asked to do by making an excuse that is dishonest but clever: *Steve wormed his way out of going to the meeting.* **4** to give an animal medicine in order to remove PARASITES that live inside it

worm sth **out of** sb *phr v* to get information from someone who does not want to give it

WORM /wɜːm $ wɜːrm/ *n* [C] (***write once, read many***) a

CD on which information can be stored only once, but seen or used many times

ˈworm-ˌeaten *adj* worm-eaten wood or fruit has holes in it because it has been eaten by worms

worm·hole /ˈwɜːmhəʊl $ ˈwɜːrmhoʊl/ *n* [C] **1** a hole, which may exist, that connects one part of the universe with another part far away **2** a hole in a piece of wood etc made by a type of WORM

worm·wood /ˈwɜːmwʊd $ ˈwɜːrm-/ *n* [U] a plant with a bitter taste

worm·y /ˈwɜːmi $ ˈwɜːrmi/ *adj* full of worms

worn¹ /wɔːn $ wɔːrn/ *v* the past participle of WEAR¹

worn² ●○○ *adj*
1 a worn object is old and damaged, especially because it has been used a lot: *a worn patch on the carpet | well worn stone steps*
2 someone who looks worn seems tired

ˌworn ˈout *adj* **1** very tired because you have been working hard SYN **exhausted**: *You must be absolutely worn out.* **2** too old or damaged to be used: *a pair of old worn-out walking boots*

wor·ried /ˈwʌrid $ ˈwɜːrid/ ●●● S2 W3 *adj*
1 unhappy because you keep thinking about a problem, or about something bad that might happen: *She gave me a worried look.* | **[+about]** *I'm really worried about my brother.* | **[+by]** *Local people are worried by the rise in crime.* | **worried (that)** *I was worried we wouldn't have enough money.* | *His parents must be* ***worried sick*** (=extremely worried).
2 you had me worried *spoken* used to say that someone made you feel anxious because you did not properly understand what they said, or did not realize that it was a joke: *You had me worried there for a minute!*
3 the worried well healthy people who are worried that they might be ill or become ill: *Health tests for the worried well should be strictly regulated.* —**worriedly** *adv*

THESAURUS

worried not feeling happy or relaxed because you keep thinking about a problem or something bad that might happen: *I was worried that you had forgotten our date.*
anxious worried because you think something bad might happen or has happened. **Anxious** is more formal than **worried**, and is often used about a general feeling of worry, when you are not sure what has happened: *A lot of employees are anxious about their jobs. | Anxious relatives waited for news.*
nervous worried or frightened about something you are going to do or experience, and unable to relax: *Everyone feels nervous before an exam.*
uneasy a little worried because you feel there may be something wrong and you are not sure what is going to happen: *When she still wasn't home by midnight, I began to feel uneasy.*
concerned *formal* worried, usually about a problem affecting someone else or affecting the country or the world: *Many people are concerned about the current economic situation.*
bothered [not before noun] worried by something that happens – often used in negative sentences: *She didn't seem particularly bothered by the news.*
troubled very worried, so that you think about something a lot: *She fell into a troubled sleep. | a troubled expression*
apprehensive *especially written* a little worried about something you are going to do, or about the future, because you are not sure what it will be like: *I felt a bit apprehensive about seeing him again after so long.*
stressed (out) *informal* very worried and tired because of problems, too much work etc, and unable to relax or enjoy life: *He'd been working ten hours a day for ages and was stressed out.*

wor·ri·er /ˈwʌriə $ ˈwɜːriər/ *n* [C] someone who often worries about things: *Her mother was a born worrier.*

wor·ri·some /ˈwʌrisəm $ ˈwɜːri-/ *adj formal* making you anxious: *a worrisome problem*

wor·ry¹ /ˈwʌri $ ˈwɜːri/ ●●● S1 W2 *v* (**worried, worrying, worries**)
1 BE ANXIOUS [I] to be anxious or unhappy about someone or something, so that you think about them a lot: **[+about]** *I worry about my daughter. | You've really got no need to worry about your weight.* | **worry (that)** *She worried that she wasn't doing enough to help.* | **[+over]** *Dad worries over the slightest thing. | Don't tell Mum about this – she's* ***got enough to worry about*** (=she already has a lot of problems or is very busy).

GRAMMAR: Prepositions with worry

• You **worry about** someone or something: *Don't worry about me. | They worry about the cost.*
• If you **worry over** something, you spend a lot of time worrying about it: *She worries over how to help him.* ✗ Don't say: *worry for something*

2 don't worry *spoken* **a)** used when you are trying to make someone feel less anxious: *Don't worry, darling, Daddy's here.* | **[+if]** *Don't worry if you can't finish all the questions.* **b)** used to tell someone that they do not need to do something: **[+about]** *Don't worry about sorting them out – I'll do it later.* **c)** used to tell someone that you will definitely do something: *Don't you worry, I'll make sure he does his fair share.*
3 MAKE SB ANXIOUS [T] to make someone feel anxious about something: *The recent changes in the Earth's climate are beginning to worry scientists. | I didn't tell Mum and Dad – I didn't want to worry them.* | **what worries me is .../the (only) thing that worries me is ...** *The only thing that worries me is the food. I don't want to get food poisoning.* | **it worries sb that/how/when** *Doesn't it worry you that Sarah spends so much time away from home?* | **worry yourself** (=feel anxious, especially when there is no need to) *You're worrying yourself unnecessarily.*
4 not to worry *BrE spoken* used to say that something is not important: *Not to worry, we can always go another time.*
5 nothing to worry about *spoken* used to tell someone that something is not as serious or difficult as they think: *It's just a check-up – nothing to worry about.*
6 ANNOY [T] to annoy someone SYN **bother**: *The heat didn't seem to worry him.*
7 ANIMAL [T] if a dog worries sheep, it tries to bite or kill them

worry at sth *phr v*
1 if an animal worries at a bone or piece of meat, it bites and shakes it
2 if you worry at a problem, you think about it a lot in order to find a solution

worry² ●●● S2 *n* (*plural* **worries**)
1 [C] a problem that you are anxious about or are not sure how to deal with: **sb's main/biggest/real etc worry** *My main worry is finding somewhere to live. | I had a lot of* ***financial worries***. | **be a worry to/for sb** *Money was always a big worry for us.*

REGISTER
In written English, people often prefer to use **concern** rather than **worry**, because it sounds more formal: *One of voters' key* ***concerns*** *is crime.*

2 [C,U] the feeling of being anxious about something: **be frantic/sick/desperate etc with worry** (=feel extremely anxious) *His mother was desperate with worry. | He's been a constant* ***source of worry***. | **[+about]** *We had no worries about safety.*
3 no worries *BrE spoken* used to agree to what someone wants and to say that it will be no problem: *'Can you deliver on Thursday?' 'Yeah, no worries, mate.'*

ˈworry beads *n* [plural] a set of BEADS on a string that you move about in order to keep yourself calm

wor·ry·ing /ˈwʌri-ɪŋ $ ˈwɜː-/ ●●○ S3 *adj* something that is worrying makes you feel anxious or worried: *The* *situation is extremely worrying.* | *This is a worrying development for small businesses.* | *It's been a worrying few weeks for us all.* —**worryingly** *adv*: *Levels of some pollutants are worryingly high.*

wor·ry·wart /ˈwʌriwɔːt $ ˈwɜːriwɔːrt/ *n* [C] *AmE informal* someone who worries a lot about unimportant things

worse¹ /wɜːs $ wɜːrs/ ●●● S1 W2 *adj*
1 [the comparative of bad] more unpleasant, bad, or severe → **better**: **[+than]** *The violence was worse than we expected.* | *The traffic is* ***much worse*** *after five o'clock.* | *The weather was* ***a lot worse*** *this year.* | *Conditions will* ***get worse*** *as the winter continues.* | *High inflation will* ***make*** *unemployment* ***worse***. | *Don't say anything, you'll only* ***make matters worse***. | *The bullying got* ***worse and worse*** *until finally he had to leave the school.* | ***There's nothing worse than*** *being robbed while you're on holiday.* | *The school's not perfect, but I suppose it* ***could be worse***.
2 more ill than before: *If she's worse in the morning, I'll call the doctor.* | *I was worried because he seemed to be* ***getting worse*** *rather than better.* | *The tablets seemed to* ***make*** *him* ***worse***.
3 be none the worse for sth to not have been harmed by something: *She seemed none the worse for her night out in the cold.*
4 worse luck *spoken* used to say that you are disappointed or annoyed by something: *I've got one more year of college, worse luck!*
5 sb could do worse than do sth *spoken* used to say that you think that someone should do something: *He could do worse than marry Eleanor.*
6 go from bad to worse to continue getting worse: ***Things went from bad to worse***, *and in the end she lost her job.*
7 the worse for wear (*also* **the worse for drink** *BrE*) *informal* drunk

GRAMMAR: Comparatives
The comparative form of **bad** is **worse**: *The problem is getting worse.* ✗ Don't say: *The problem is getting more worse.* | *The problem is getting worser.*

worse² ●●● S3 W2 *adv* [the comparative of badly] in a more severe or serious way than before → **better**: **[+than]** *By lunch time it was raining worse than ever.* | [sentence adverb] *The business could become less profitable* ***or, even worse***, *could close down.* | *Suppose Rose,* ***or worse still***, *Peter had seen the photograph?*

worse³ *n* [U] **1** something worse → **better**: *We thought the situation was bad, but worse was to follow.* **2 take a turn for the worse** to change and become worse: *Last year his health took a turn for the worse.*

wors·en /ˈwɜːsən $ ˈwɜːr-/ ●○○ *v* [I,T] to become worse, or make something worse OPP **improve** → **deteriorate**: *A lot of teachers expect the situation to worsen over the next few years.* | *Interfering now could worsen the problem.* —**worsening** *adj*: *We are now faced with a worsening economic recession.*

ˌworse ˈoff *adj* [not before noun] **1** if you are worse off, you have less money OPP **better off**: *The rent increases will leave us worse off.* | **[+than]** *I don't think we're any worse off than a lot of other people.* **2** in a worse situation OPP **better off**: *People in rural areas are even worse off, as they have no regular bus service.* | **[+than]** *Other sports are much worse off than athletics.*

wor·ship¹ /ˈwɜːʃɪp $ ˈwɜːr-/ ●●○ *v* (*past tense and past participle* **worshipped**, *present participle* **worshipping** *also* **worshiped**, **worshiping** *AmE*)
1 [I,T] to show respect and love for a god, especially by praying in a religious building: *They all worship the same god.* | *a church where people have worshipped for hundreds of years*
2 [T] to admire and love someone very much: *He absolutely worships her.*
3 worship the ground sb walks on to admire or love someone so much that you cannot see their faults —**worshipper** *n* [C]: *She was a regular worshipper at the parish church.* → HERO WORSHIP

worship² ●○○ *n* [U]
1 the activity of praying or singing in a religious building in order to show respect and love for a god: **in worship** *They bowed their heads in worship.* | **[+of]** *Worship of the old gods still continues in remote areas of the country.* | *The ceremony must take place in a recognized* ***place of worship***. | *We were invited to join in their* ***act of worship*** (=religious ceremony).
2 Your/His Worship *BrE formal* used to talk to or about a public official such as a MAYOR or MAGISTRATE

worst¹ /wɜːst $ wɜːrst/ ●●● S2 W1 *adj* [the superlative of bad]
1 [only before noun] worse than anything or anyone else → **best**: *This is the worst recession for fifty years.* | *My worst fear was that we would run out of food.* | *What is the* ***worst possible*** *thing that can happen?*
2 be your own worst enemy to cause a lot of problems for yourself because of your own behaviour
3 come off worst to lose a fight or argument

GRAMMAR: Comparatives
The superlative form of **bad** is **worst**: *It was the worst film I have ever seen.* ✗ Don't say: *It was the most worst film I have ever seen.* | *It was the worstest film I have ever seen.*

worst² ●●● S2 W3 *n*
1 the worst the person or thing that is worse than all others → **the best**: **worst (that)** *This year's harvest is the worst that people can remember.* | *Last year was* ***by far the worst*** (=much worse than any other) *for road accidents.* | *I think* ***the worst is over*** *now.* | ***The worst of it is*** (=the worst part of the situation is), *I can't tell anyone what's happening.* | **at its/his etc worst** *You saw the garden at its worst, I'm afraid* (=when it is worse than at any other time).
2 the worst of sth most of something, or the most unpleasant or difficult part of it: *The worst of the storm seemed to be over.*
3 expect/fear the worst to expect or fear that something will not be successful or something bad will happen: *When it got so late and they still weren't home, I began to fear the worst.*
4 get/have the worst of it *spoken* to lose a fight or argument
5 at (the) worst if things are as bad as they can be: *Choosing the right software can be time-consuming* ***at best*** *and confusing or frustrating* ***at worst***.
6 do your/his/her/their worst used to say that someone can try to harm you but they will not be able to: *They can do their worst now, because I'm leaving in three weeks.*
7 if the worst comes to the worst *especially BrE*, **if worst comes to worst** *especially AmE* if the situation develops in the worst possible way: *If the worst comes to the worst, we'll sell the car.*

worst³ *adv* [the superlative of badly] **1** most badly → **best**: *Aid is being sent to areas that have been worst affected by the earthquake.* | *the worst-dressed man in the office* **2 worst of all** used to say what is the worst part of a situation: *She had no office of her own and, worst of all, she didn't even have her own computer.*

wor·sted /ˈwʊstɪd/ *n* [U] a type of woollen cloth

worth¹ /wɜːθ $ wɜːrθ/ ●●● S1 W2 *adj*
1 be worth sth a) to have a value in money: *The house must be worth quite a lot of money now.* | *One of the pictures is worth £50,000.* | *Do you know* ***how much*** *the ring* ***is worth***? | *This art collection is* ***worth a fortune*** (=worth a very large amount of money). | **be worth nothing/not be worth anything** *It's a very old machine so I shouldn't think it's worth anything.* **b)** to have money or possessions that have value: *I've heard that he's worth over $2 million.* | *The man who founded the company must be* ***worth a fortune***.
⚠ **Worth** is not a verb. Do not say that something 'worths' something.
2 be worth (doing) sth a) used to say that something is interesting, useful, or helpful: *A lot of the small towns in the area are definitely worth visiting.* | *The film is* ***well worth***

W

seeing. | **worth a trip/visit etc** *The local museum is worth a visit.* **b)** used to say that someone should do something because they will gain something from it: **be worth doing sth** *It's worth checking the details of the contract before you sign it.* | ***It's well worth*** *getting there early if you want a good seat.* | **be worth the time/effort/work** *It was a great evening, and definitely worth all the hard work.*
3 be worth it *informal* used to say that you gain something from an action: *It was a lot of hard work, but* ***it was worth it****.*
4 be not worth it *informal* used to say that you do not gain anything from an action: *I thought about trying to talk to him about it, but decided* ***it wasn't worth it****.*
5 be worth sb's while (to do/doing sth) *spoken* used to say that someone should spend time or money on something because they will gain something from it: ***It might be worth*** *your* ***while*** *to talk to the head of department.* | *Some people feel it's not worth their while working if they can get money from the state.*
6 make it worth sb's while *spoken* to offer something to someone so that they will do something for you: *He promised to make it worth our while.*
7 what's it worth (to you)? *spoken* used humorously to ask someone how they will reward you if you do something for them
8 for what it's worth *spoken* used when you are giving someone information, to say that you are not sure how useful it is: *Here's the list of names, for what it's worth.*
9 for all you are/he is etc worth with as much effort as possible: *He was pulling the rope for all he was worth.*
10 worth his/her salt doing their job well or deserving respect: *Any player worth his salt would love to play for his country.*
11 worth your/its etc weight in gold very useful: *In these mountains, an experienced guide is worth his weight in gold.*

worth² ●●● W3 *n* [U]
1 ten pounds' worth/$500 worth etc of sth an amount of something worth ten pounds, $500 etc: *a chance to win £2,000 worth of computing equipment* | *The fire caused thousands of pounds' worth of damage.*
2 ten minutes' worth/a week's worth etc of sth something that takes ten minutes, a week etc to happen, do, or use: *We had only three days' worth of food left.*
3 how good or useful something is or how important it is to people SYN **value**: *The new computer system has already proved its worth.*
4 how much money something is worth SYN **value**: *It is difficult to estimate the current worth of the company.*

worth·less /ˈwɜːθləs $ ˈwɜːrθ-/ ●○○ *adj*
1 something that is worthless has no value, importance, or use OPP **valuable**: *The house was full of worthless junk.* | *The information was worthless to me.*
2 a worthless person has no good qualities or useful skills SYN **useless**: *His parents had made him feel worthless.* —**worthlessness** *n* [U]: *She struggled to overcome her feelings of worthlessness.*

worth·while /ˌwɜːθˈwaɪl◂ $ ˌwɜːrθ-/ ●●○ *adj* if something is worthwhile, it is important or useful, or you gain something from it: *He wanted to do a worthwhile job.* | *We decided to give the money to a* ***worthwhile cause*** (=one that helps people). | **it is worthwhile to do sth** *I thought it was worthwhile to clarify the matter.* | **it is worthwhile doing sth** *It wasn't worthwhile continuing with the project.* THESAURUS USEFUL

wor·thy¹ /ˈwɜːði $ ˈwɜːrði/ ●●○ *adj*
1 [only before noun] deserving respect from people: *Leeds United were worthy winners of the competition.* | *a worthy opponent*
2 be worthy of sth to deserve to be thought about or treated in a particular way: *A couple of other books are worthy of mention.* | *a teacher who is worthy of respect*
3 be worthy of sb *informal* to be as good as something that a particular person would do: *a goal that was worthy of any of the great footballers of the world*
4 I'm/We're not worthy *spoken* used humorously to say that you consider it a great honour to be with someone because they are famous, or much more skilful at doing something than you are
5 *formal* trying to help other people: *The money will go to a worthy cause.* | *I'm sure his motives were worthy.*

worthy² *n* (*plural* **worthies**) [C] *informal* someone who is important and should be respected: *We were met by a group of local worthies.*

wot /wɒt $ wɑːt, wʌt/ *pron, determiner, predeterminer BrE* an informal spelling of WHAT

would /wʊd/ ●●● S1 W1 *modal verb* (*negative short form* **wouldn't**)
1 PAST INTENTIONS/EXPECTATIONS used to say what someone intended to do or expected to happen: *They said they would meet us at 10.30 at the station.* | *She said she wouldn't be coming to the library anymore.* | *Arnold knew he would be tired the next day.* | *It would soon be dark.*
2 IMAGINED SITUATIONS **a)** used when talking about the result of a possible or imagined situation or event, or describing one: *What would you do if you won a million pounds?* | *I would be amazed if I got the job.* | *It would be lovely to see you.* **b)** used when talking about something that did not happen, or a situation that cannot exist: *I would have phoned you, but there wasn't time.* | *Alex would never have found out if you hadn't told him.* | *What would have happened if I hadn't been here?* | *Everything would be very different if your father were still alive.* **c)** used to mention an unlikely situation or event that you want to happen: ***I wish*** *they* ***would*** *come and visit us.* | ***If only*** *he* ***would*** *listen to me.*

GRAMMAR: Choosing the right tense
You usually use **would** in the main clause, and a past tense in the 'if' clause: *I would be surprised if he* ***agreed****.* | *She would love it if you* ***came****.* ✗ Don't say: *I would be surprised if he would agree.*
GRAMMAR GUIDE VERBS

3 PAST HABITS used to say that something happened often or regularly in the past: *When we worked in the same office, we would often have coffee together.* | *On summer evenings they would sit out in the garden.*
4 REQUESTING *spoken* used to ask someone politely to do something: *Would you shut the window, please?* | *Would you mind waiting outside?* | *Would someone please tell me what is going on?*
5 OFFERING/INVITING *spoken* used to offer something to someone or invite them somewhere politely: *Would you like a coffee?* | *We're going to the theatre this evening. Would you be interested in coming?*
6 WHAT SB WANTS *spoken* used to say that someone wants something or wants to do something: **would like/love/prefer** *Yes, please, I'd love a coffee.* | *My parents would like to meet you.* | *Claudia would have liked to refuse* (=wanted to refuse), *but she didn't dare.* | ***I'd hate*** (=I do not want) *to disappoint you.* | **would rather/sooner** (=used to say what someone prefers) *I'd rather stay in this evening, if that's all right with you.*
7 PAST PURPOSE used after 'so that' to show that someone was trying to make something happen or prevent something: *We packed all the books in wooden boxes so that they wouldn't get damaged.*
8 would not a) used to say that someone refused to do something: *He wouldn't give us any money.* **b)** used to say that something did not happen, even though someone was trying to make it happen: *The door wouldn't open, no matter how hard she pushed.*
9 ADVICE *spoken* used when giving or asking for advice: *I'd try to get there early if you can.* | ***I would*** *talk to the doctor* ***if I were you****.* | *What would you do if you were in my position?*
10 I would think/imagine/say *spoken* used to give your opinion about something when you are not very sure about it: *I would think you'd be happier in a different school.* | *'Will it cost a lot?' 'I would imagine so.'*
11 TYPICAL BEHAVIOUR *spoken* used to say that an action

W

is typical or expected - usually used to show disapproval: *You would go and spoil it, wouldn't you!* | *She insists that she did nothing wrong, but then she would say that, wouldn't she?*
12 would that ... *literary* used to express a strong wish or desire SYN **if only**: *Would that we had seen her before she died.*

'would-be ●○○ *adj* **would-be actor/murderer etc** someone who hopes to have a particular job or intends to do a particular thing

would·n't /ˈwʊdnt/ the short form of 'would not'

would've /ˈwʊdəv/ the short form of 'would have'

wound¹ /wuːnd/ ●●○ *n* [C]
1 an injury to your body that is made by a weapon such as a knife or a bullet: *A nurse cleaned and bandaged the wound.* | *It took several months for his* ***wounds*** *to* ***heal***. | **suffer/receive a wound** *Several of the victims suffered severe stab wounds.* | **head/leg etc wound** *He was treated in hospital for head wounds.* | **stab/knife/gunshot wound** *He died of gunshot wounds.* | *The doctor said it was only a* ***flesh wound*** (=one that does not cut the skin very deeply). | *a* ***gaping wound*** (=one that is wide and open) *on his thigh* THESAURUS ▸ INJURY
2 a feeling of emotional or mental pain that you get when someone says or does something unpleasant to you: *It will take much longer for the mental* ***wounds*** *to* ***heal***.
3 open old wounds to remind someone of unpleasant things that happened in the past → **lick your wounds** at LICK¹(6), → **rub salt into the wound** at RUB¹(6)

wound² ●●○ W3 *v* [T]
1 to injure someone with a knife, gun etc: *Gunmen killed two people and wounded six others in an attack today.* | **be badly/seriously/critically etc wounded** *Five people were killed and many others were seriously wounded in the attack.* | **be mortally/fatally wounded** (=be wounded so badly that you die) THESAURUS ▸ HURT
2 to make someone feel unhappy or upset SYN **hurt**: *I was* ***deeply wounded*** *by his comments.* | *He made some very wounding remarks.*

wound³ /waʊnd/ the past tense and past participle of WIND²

wound·ed /ˈwuːndɪd/ ●●○ *adj*
1 injured by a weapon such as a gun or knife: *a wounded soldier*
2 very upset because of something that someone has said or done: *It was only* ***wounded pride*** *that stopped him from apologizing.*
3 the wounded [plural] people who have been injured, especially in a war: *providing medical care for the wounded* | **the walking wounded** (=people who have been injured but are well enough to walk)

wound up /ˌwaʊnd ˈʌp/ *adj* [not before noun] anxious, worried, or excited: *I was too wound up to sleep.*

wove /wəʊv $ woʊv/ a past tense of WEAVE¹

wov·en /ˈwəʊvən $ ˈwoʊ-/ a past participle of WEAVE¹

wow¹ /waʊ/ ●○○ *interjection informal* used when you think something is very impressive or surprising: *Wow! Look at that!*

wow² *v* [T] *informal* to make people admire you a lot SYN **impress**: *The show has wowed audiences all over the country.*

wow³ *n* [singular] *informal* **1** a great success **2 the wow factor** an interesting, exciting, or unusual feature of something, that people will notice and think is very impressive

WPC /ˌdʌbəljuː piː ˈsiː◂/ *n* [C] *BrE* (***Woman Police Constable***) a female police officer

wpm /ˌdʌbəljuː piː ˈem/ (***words per minute***) used to describe the speed at which someone can write using a KEYBOARD

wrack /ræk/ *v* [T] another spelling of RACK²

wraith /reɪθ/ *n* [C] *literary* a GHOST

wran·gle¹ /ˈræŋɡəl/ *n* [C] a long and complicated argument SYN **battle**: **[+over]** *a* ***bitter wrangle*** *over copyright* | **[+with]** *He was involved in a long* ***legal wrangle*** *with his employers.*

wrangle² *v* [I] to argue with someone angrily for a long time: **[+over/about]** *They are still wrangling over ownership of the house.* | **[+with]** *The various government departments are wrangling with each other.*

wran·gler /ˈræŋɡlə $ -ər/ *n* [C] *AmE informal* a COWBOY

wrap¹ /ræp/ ●●● S3 *v* (**wrapped, wrapping**) [T]
1 (*also* **wrap up**) to put paper or cloth over something to cover it: **wrap sth in sth** *The* ***present*** *was beautifully* ***wrapped*** *in gold paper.* | **wrap sth around sb/sth** *Ella wrapped a thick coat around her shoulders.* | *He wrapped a bandage around my injured wrist.* | *I've still got a few Christmas presents to wrap up.*
2 if you wrap your arms, legs, or fingers around something, you use them to hold it: **wrap sth around sb/sth** *He wrapped his arms around her waist.* → **wrap sb in cotton wool** at COTTON WOOL(2), → **wrap sb around your little finger** at FINGER¹(8)

wrap up *phr v*
1 to put on warm clothes: **wrap up warm/well** *Make sure you wrap up warm – it's freezing.* | **be wrapped up in sth** *She was wrapped up in a thick winter coat.*
2 wrap sth ↔ up *informal* to finish a job, meeting etc: *We're hoping to wrap up the negotiations this week.*
3 be wrapped up in sth to give so much of your attention to something that you do not have time for anything else

wrap² ●○○ *n*
1 [C] a piece of thick cloth that a woman wears around her shoulders → **shawl**
2 [U] a type of thin clear plastic that is used to cover food SYN **clingfilm**
3 keep sth under wraps to keep something secret: *The project has been kept under wraps for years.*
4 take the wraps off sth to show or tell people about something new or secret
5 [C] a type of sandwich made with thin bread which is rolled around meat, vegetables etc
6 [singular] the end of a day's filming: *OK everybody, it's a wrap!*

'wrap-aˌround, wraparound *adj* [only before noun]
1 a wrap-around skirt is one that you wind around your body and fasten in place **2** wrap-around SUNGLASSES curve around the sides of your face

ˌwrap-a·round 'care, ˌwraparound 'childcare /ˌræpəraʊndˈkeə/ *n* [U] an arrangement in which young children in Britain can go to school early in the morning and stay at school after the normal school day has finished, and take part in organized activities until their parents can collect them after finishing work

wrap-a·rounds /ˈræpəraʊndz/ *n* [plural] SUNGLASSES that are curved in such a way that they fit close to your face, from one ear to the other

wrap·per /ˈræpə $ -ər/ *n* [C] the piece of paper or plastic that covers something when it is sold: *old sweet wrappers*

wrap·ping /ˈræpɪŋ/ *n* [C,U] the cloth, paper, or plastic that is wrapped around something to protect it: *I finally managed to get the plastic wrapping off.*

'wrapping ˌpaper *n* [U] coloured paper that you use for wrapping presents SYN **gift wrap**

'wrap-up *n* [C] *AmE informal* a short report that repeats the main points, for example of a news broadcast SYN **round-up**

wrath /rɒθ $ ræθ/ *n* [U] *formal* extreme anger: *He was scared of* ***incurring*** *his father's* ***wrath***.

wreak /riːk/ *v* **1 wreak havoc/mayhem/destruction (on sth)** to cause a lot of damage or problems: *These policies have wreaked havoc on the British economy.*
2 wreak revenge/vengeance (on sb) *formal* to do something unpleasant to someone to punish them for something they have done to you: *He promised to wreak vengeance on those who had betrayed him.*

wreath /riːθ/ *n* [C] **1** a circle made from leaves or flowers that you put on the place where a person is buried: *The prime minister **laid** a **wreath** at the war memorial.* **2** a circle of leaves or flowers that people use to decorate their houses at Christmas **3** a circle made from leaves that a person wore on their head in the past as a sign of honour: *a laurel wreath*

wreathe /riːð/ *v literary* **1 be wreathed in sth** to be covered in something: *The mountains were wreathed in mist.* **2 be wreathed in smiles** to be smiling and look very happy: *His plump face was wreathed in smiles.*

wreck¹ /rek/ ●●○ *v* [T]
1 to completely spoil something so that it cannot continue in a successful way SYN **ruin**: *Injury threatened to wreck his sporting career.* | *It was drink that wrecked their marriage.*
2 to damage something such as a building or vehicle so badly that it cannot be repaired: *The car was completely wrecked in the accident.* THESAURUS ▸ DESTROY
3 if a ship is wrecked, it is badly damaged and sinks SYN **shipwreck**: *The ship was wrecked off the coast of Africa.*

wreck² ●●○ *n* [C]
1 CAR/PLANE a car, plane, or train that has been damaged very badly, especially in a crash: *He was still alive when they pulled him from the wreck.* THESAURUS ▸ ACCIDENT
2 SHIP a ship that has sunk SYN **shipwreck**: **[+of]** *Divers discovered the wreck of an old German warship.*
3 PERSON *informal* someone who is very nervous, tired, or unhealthy: *He looked a complete wreck.* | **nervous/emotional wreck** *The attack had left her an emotional wreck.*
4 ACCIDENT *AmE* an accident involving cars or other vehicles SYN **crash**: **car/train/plane wreck** *My father died in a car wreck.*
5 PLACE a place that is very untidy: *When you're here, this place is a wreck!*
6 OLD CAR *informal* an old car that is in a very bad condition

wreck·age /ˈrekɪdʒ/ ●○○ *n* [singular, U]
1 the parts of something such as a plane, ship, or building that are left after it has been destroyed in an accident: *Firemen managed to pull some survivors from the wreckage.* | **[+of]** *Accident investigators will examine the wreckage of the plane.*
2 the parts of someone's relationships, hopes, or plans that remain after they have been spoiled: **[+of]** *She still hoped to salvage something from the wreckage of her marriage.*

wrecked /rekt/ *adj* [not before noun] *informal* **1** *BrE* very drunk **2** extremely tired

wreck·er /ˈrekə $ -ər/ *n* [C] **1** someone who deliberately destroys something: *She accused him of being a marriage wrecker.* **2** *AmE* a vehicle that is used to take away damaged cars after an accident

ˈwrecking ˌball *n* [C] a heavy metal ball attached to a chain or CABLE which is used to knock down buildings

ˈwrecking ˌcrew *n* [C] a group of workers whose job is to knock down buildings

wren /ren/ *n* [C] a very small brown bird

wrench¹ /rentʃ/ *v* **1** [T always + adv/prep] to twist and pull something roughly from the place where it is being held: *I wrenched the packet from his grasp.* | *The door had been wrenched open.* **2 wrench yourself away/free** to use your strength to pull yourself away from someone who is holding you: *She managed to wrench herself free.* **3** [T] to hurt a joint in your body by twisting it SYN **sprain**: *I think I've wrenched my knee.*

wrench² *n* **1** [C] *especially AmE* a metal tool that you use for turning NUTS SYN **spanner** *BrE* **2 throw a (monkey) wrench in sth** *AmE informal* to do something that will cause problems or spoil someone's plans SYN **throw/put a spanner in the works** *BrE* **3** [singular] a strong feeling of sadness that you get when you leave a person or place that you love: *Leaving New York had been a terrible wrench.* **4** [C usually singular] a twisting movement that pulls something violently: *He grabbed the rope and gave it a wrench.*

wrest /rest/ *v* [T always + adv/prep] **1** *formal* to take power or influence away from someone, especially when this is difficult: *They are fighting to wrest control of the party from the old leaders.* **2** *literary* to pull something away from someone violently: *I managed to wrest the photograph from his grasp.*

wres·tle /ˈresəl/ ●○○ *v*
1 [I,T] to fight someone by holding them and pulling or pushing them: **[+with]** *The two men wrestled with each other.* | *Police officers **wrestled** him **to the ground**.*
2 [I,T] to move something or try to move it when it is large, heavy, or difficult to move: **[+with]** *Ray continued to wrestle with the wheel.*
3 wrestle with sth to try to understand or find a solution to a difficult problem: *I have been wrestling with this problem for quite some time.*

wres·tler /ˈreslə $ -ər/ *n* [C] someone who takes part in wrestling

wres·tling /ˈreslɪŋ/ *n* [U] a sport in which two people fight by holding each other and trying to make each other fall to the ground

wretch /retʃ/ *n* [C] **1** someone that you feel sorry for: *He was a lonely, miserable wretch.* **2** someone you are annoyed with: *Stop pulling my hair, you wretch!*

wretch·ed /ˈretʃɪd/ *adj* **1** someone who is wretched is very unhappy or ill, and you feel sorry for them: *the poor, wretched girl* **2** if you feel wretched, you feel guilty and unhappy because of something bad that you have done: *Guy felt wretched about it now.* **3** [only before noun] making you feel annoyed or angry: *Where is that wretched boy?* **4** *literary* extremely bad or unpleasant SYN **miserable**: *I was shocked to see their wretched living conditions.* —**wretchedly** *adv* —**wretchedness** *n* [U]

wrig·gle¹ /ˈrɪɡəl/ *v* **1** [I] to twist your body from side to side with small quick movements: *Stop wriggling and let me put your T-shirt on.* | **[+under/through/into]** *He wriggled through the window.* | *The dog **wriggled free** and ran off.* THESAURUS ▸ MOVE **2** [T] to move a part of your body backwards and forwards with small movements: *She took off her shoes and wriggled her toes.* —**wriggly** *adj*: *a wriggly worm*

wriggle out of sth *phr v* **1** to avoid doing something by using clever excuses SYN **get out of sth**: *Don't try to wriggle out of your responsibilities.* **2** to take off a tight piece of clothing by twisting your body from side to side: *She wriggled out of her dress.*

wriggle² *n* [C] **1** a movement in which you twist your body from side to side **2 get a wriggle on** *BrE informal* used to tell someone to hurry SYN **get a move on**

wring /rɪŋ/ *v* (*past tense and past participle* **wrung** /rʌŋ/) [T] **1** [always + adv/prep] to succeed in getting something from someone, but only after a lot of effort SYN **squeeze**: **wring sth from/out of sb** *They are always trying to wring additional funds from the government.* | *I managed to wring the information out of him.* **2** (*also* **wring out**) to tightly twist a wet cloth or wet clothes in order to remove

W

water **3 wring your hands** to rub and twist your hands together because you are worried and upset **4 wring sb's hand** to shake hands very firmly with someone **5 wring sth's neck** to kill a small animal by twisting its neck **6 I'll wring sb's neck** *spoken* used when you are very angry with someone: *I'll wring her neck when I get hold of her!* **7 wringing wet** extremely wet: *This jacket's wringing wet!*

wring·er /ˈrɪŋə $ -ər/ *n* [C] **1** a machine with two parts that roll over each other and press on wet clothes to remove water SYN **mangle 2 go through the wringer** *AmE informal* to have a lot of problems and upsetting experiences: *She's really been through the wringer since her husband died.*

wrin·kle[1] /ˈrɪŋkəl/ *n* [C] **1** wrinkles are lines on your face and skin that you get when you are old: *Her face was a mass of wrinkles.* **2** a small untidy fold in a piece of clothing or paper SYN **crease**: *She walked over to the bed and smoothed out the wrinkles.* **3 iron out the wrinkles** to solve the small problems in something —**wrinkly** *adj*: *her thin, wrinkly face*

wrinkle[2] *v* **1** [I,T] (*also* **wrinkle up**) if you wrinkle a part of your face, or if it wrinkles, small lines appear on it: *Alex **wrinkled** up her **nose** at the smell.* | *Carter **wrinkled** his **forehead** in concentration.* | *His **brow wrinkled** when he saw us.* **2** [I] if a piece of clothing wrinkles, it gets small untidy folds in it SYN **crease**: *The trouble with linen is that it wrinkles so easily.*

wrin·kled /ˈrɪŋkəld/ *adj* skin or cloth that is wrinkled has small lines or folds in it: *her wrinkled old face*

wrin·kly /ˈrɪŋkli/ *n* (*plural* **wrinklies**) [C] *BrE informal not polite* an offensive word for someone who is old

wrist /rɪst/ ●●● W3 *n* [C] the part of your body where your hand joins your arm: **on/around your wrist** *She had a gold watch on her wrist.* → BODY, see picture at TABLE[1]

wrist·band /ˈrɪstbænd/ *n* [C] **1** a band that some tennis players wear around their wrists **2** a band with your name on it that you wear around your wrist, for example in a hospital

wrist·watch /ˈrɪstwɒtʃ $ -wɑːtʃ, -wɒːtʃ/ *n* [C] a watch that you wear on your wrist

writ[1] /rɪt/ *n* [C] a document from a court that orders someone to do or not to do something: *He **issued** a **writ** against the newspaper.* | *The company has been **served with a writ** for damages.* → HOLY WRIT

writ[2] *adj* **writ large** *literary* **a)** very easy to notice: *I could see the curiosity writ large on Rose's face.* **b)** in a very clear strong form: *This is an example of bureaucracy writ large.*

write /raɪt/ ●●● S1 W1 *v* (*past tense* **wrote** /rəʊt $ roʊt/, *past participle* **written** /ˈrɪtn/)

1 BOOK/ARTICLE/POEM ETC **a)** [I,T] to produce a new book, article, poem etc: *He wrote some very famous books.* | *Who wrote 'Harry Potter'?* | *I can't come with you – I have an essay to write.* | **[+about]** *O'Brien often writes about her native Ireland.* | **well/badly/poorly etc written** *The article is very well written.* **b)** [I] someone who writes earns money by writing books, plays, articles etc: *Sean decided he wanted to write, and quit his job.* | **[+for]** *Maureen Dowd writes for 'The New York Times'.*

2 LETTER [I,T] to put words in a letter to someone: **[+to]** *I've written to my MP, and to the city council.* | **write sb** *AmE*: *Chris hasn't written me for a long time.* | *I **wrote** her several **letters**, but she didn't reply.*

GRAMMAR: Patterns with write

- You **write to** someone: *She writes to me every month.*
- In American English, you can also **write** someone: *She writes me every month.*
- You **write** someone a letter, note, story etc: *Please write me a letter soon.* ✗ Don't say: *Please write to me a letter soon.*
- You **write** to someone **about** a subject or an experience: *He wrote to me about his trip to France.* ✗ Don't say: *He wrote to me his trip to France.*
- **Write** is often used in the progressive: *I am writing to tell you something important.*

3 FORM WORDS [I,T] to form letters or numbers with a pen or pencil: *Kerry could **read and write** when she was five.*

4 STATE STH [T] to state something in a book, letter, advertisement etc, or on a label: **write (that)** *Isabella wrote that she was dying, and asked him to visit her for the last time.* | **be written on sth** *The price is written on the label.*

5 MUSIC/SONG [T] to write a piece of music or a song: *Mozart wrote the music.* | *The song was originally written by Leonard Cohen.*

6 COMPUTER PROGRAM [T] to make a program for a computer to use: *He writes software programs for financial institutions.*

7 A COMPUTER RECORDS STH [I,T] if a computer writes something, it records it on a disk or in its memory: **[+to/onto]** *data that had been written to disk*

8 CHEQUE/DOCUMENT ETC (*also* **write out**) [T] to write information on a cheque, form etc: *Wouldn't it be easier if I just wrote a cheque for the lot?* | *The doctor wrote me a prescription for sleeping pills.*

9 PEN [I] if a pen writes, it works properly: *Do any of these pens write?*

10 have sth/be written all over your face to show very clearly what you are feeling or thinking: *He had guilt written all over his face.* | *I know you're lying, Tyrell – it's written all over your face.*

11 have sth written all over it to show a particular quality or fact very clearly: *This awful film has 'career-killer' written all over it for the actors involved.*

12 nothing to write home about *informal* not particularly good or special: *The hotel was good, but the food was nothing to write home about.*

13 sb wrote the book on sth *spoken* used to say that someone knows a lot about a subject or is very good at an activity: *Motorola wrote the book on quality control.*

14 that's all she wrote *AmE spoken* used to mean that you cannot stop what happens next in a situation, especially when it is bad

THESAURUS

write to use a pen or pencil to make words, letters etc: *Have you written a shopping list?* | *The children are learning to read and write.*

write sth down to write something on paper, in order to remember it or make a record: *He wrote down everything she said.*

put to write something in a particular place, or to write particular words: *I've put the dates of the meetings in my diary.* | *At the end of the email she put 'PS I love you'.*

put sth in writing to write something that you have agreed or promised, so that there is an official record: *They said they would pay me 50%, but they haven't actually put it in writing.*

make a note of sth to write information that you might need later: *I'll just make a note of your address.*

take notes to write things while someone is speaking or while something is happening, so that you can use them later: *His lawyer was with him taking notes.*

scrawl /skrɔːl $ skrɒːl/ to write something carelessly and untidily, especially in big letters – often used to show disapproval: *Someone had scrawled graffiti on the school wall.* | *He'd scrawled a few unhelpful comments at the bottom of my work.*

fill sth in/out to write information on a form or other official document: *Please fill in the application form in black ink.* | *Would you mind filling out a questionnaire?*

sign to write your name at the end of a letter, document etc: *Read the contract carefully, and then sign it.* | *Don't forget to sign your name.*

TO WRITE SOMETHING QUICKLY

jot sth down to write something very quickly: *Start your essay by jotting down a few ideas.*

scribble to write something quickly and in an untidy way: *Andy scribbled a quick note and handed it to the chairman.*

TO WRITE SOMETHING ON A COMPUTER

enter to make words or numbers appear on a computer screen by pressing the keys: *You have to enter your password twice.*

key sth in/type sth in to write or record information on a computer, especially something you are copying: *I've keyed in my credit card details.*

write away for sth *phr v* to write a letter to a company or organization asking them to send you goods or information: *I've written away for their free catalog.*

write back *phr v* to reply to a letter that someone sent you, by writing a letter to them: *I sent them a card once, but they never wrote back.* | **[+to]** *I wrote back to them immediately, thanking them for their kind invitation.*

write sth ↔ **down** *phr v*

1 to write something on a piece of paper: *This is the address. Do you want to write it down?*

2 to officially say that a debt no longer has to be paid, or officially accept that you cannot get back money you have spent or lost SYN **write off**

write in *phr v*

1 to write a letter to an organization to give an opinion, ask for information etc: *If you would like a copy of our fact sheet, please write in, enclosing a stamped addressed envelope.* | **[+to]** *And so I wrote in to Radio Brighton.*

2 write sth ↔ in to write a piece of information in the space provided for it on a form or document: *Provide some space for students to write in their hobbies.*

3 write sb ↔ in *AmE* to add someone's name to the official list on your voting form, to show that you want to vote for them: *The campaign to write in Johnson for governor failed.* → WRITE-IN

write sth **into** sth *phr v* to add or include something in a contract, agreement etc: *It was written into his contract that he had to make two records a year.*

write off *phr v*

1 to write a letter to a company or organization asking them to send you goods or information SYN **send off**, **write away**: **[+for]** *Are you going to write off for that free poster?*

2 write sb/sth ↔ off to decide that someone or something is useless, unimportant, or a failure SYN **dismiss**: **[+as]** *After six months of work, we eventually wrote the project off as a non-starter.* → WRITE-OFF

3 write sth ↔ off to officially say that a debt no longer has to be paid, or officially accept that you cannot get back money you have spent or lost: *The United States agreed to write off debts worth billions of dollars.* | *The Inland Revenue wrote off £900 million in unpaid taxes.*

4 write sth ↔ off to make an official record of the amount of money that you have spent on things relating to your business, in order to reduce the amount of tax that you have to pay: **[+against]** *The costs of setting up a business can be written off against tax.*

5 write sth ↔ off *BrE* to damage a vehicle so badly that it can never be used again: *At thirteen he stole a car and wrote it off.* → WRITE-OFF

write sb/sth ↔ **out** *phr v*

1 to write something on paper, especially in a neat and clear way, including all the necessary details: *The children were asked to choose their favourite poem and write it out in their best handwriting.*

2 to write information on a cheque or a form: *She calmly wrote out a check for $500 and handed it to Will.*

3 to remove a character from a regular radio or television programme, by making him or her leave or die in the story: **[+of]** *It was revealed last week that Alma is being written out of the series.*

write sth ↔ **up** *phr v*

1 to write a report, article etc using notes that you made earlier: *I have to write up my report before the meeting.*

2 to write something on a wall, board etc where people can see it: *The teacher repeated the word, and then wrote it up on the blackboard.*

3 be written up if something is written up in a newspaper, magazine etc, someone describes what it is like and gives their opinion of it: *We're going to a Spanish restaurant that was written up in Time Out's good food guide.* → WRITE-UP

ˈwrite-in *n* [C] *AmE* a vote you give to someone by writing their name on your BALLOT PAPER

ˈwrite-off *n* [C] **1** *BrE* a vehicle that has been so badly damaged that it can never be used again: *The car was a complete write-off.* **2** a period of time when you fail to achieve anything: *This morning was a complete write-off.* **3** an official agreement that someone does not have to pay a debt

ˈwrite-ˌprotected *adj* if a computer document or DISK is write-protected, the information in it cannot be changed or removed: *write-protected files* —**write-protect** *v* [T]

writ·er /ˈraɪtə $ -ər/ ●●● S3 W2 *n* [C]

1 someone who writes books, stories etc, especially as a job → **author**, **playwright**: *She's one of my favourite writers.* | *a science-fiction writer* | **[+on]** *a well-known writer on American music* | **[+of]** *a writer of children's stories*

2 someone who has written something or who writes in a particular way: *He's always been a sloppy writer.* | **[+of]** *the writer of the previous message on this topic*

ˌwriter's ˈblock *n* [U] the problem that a writer sometimes has of not being able to think of new ideas

ˌwriter's ˈcramp *n* [U] a feeling of stiffness in your hand that you get after writing for a long time

ˈwrite-up *n* [C] a written opinion about a new book, play, or product in a newspaper, magazine etc SYN **review**: *The play got a really **good write-up** (=it was praised) in the press.*

writhe /raɪð/ *v* [I] to twist your body from side to side violently, especially because you are suffering pain: **writhe in pain/agony etc** *He lay writhing in pain.*

writ·ing /ˈraɪtɪŋ/ ●●● S2 W3 *n*

1 [U] words that have been written or printed: *What does the writing on the back say?* | *a T-shirt with Japanese writing on it*

2 [U] books, poems, articles etc, especially those by a particular writer or about a particular subject: *Some of his most powerful writing is based on his childhood experiences.* | **travel/feminist/scientific etc writing**

3 [U] the activity of writing books, stories etc: *In 1991 she retired from politics and took up writing as a career.* | *a short story that stands out as a brilliant **piece of writing*** | *a class in **creative writing*** (=a subject studied at school or college, where you write your own stories, poems etc)

4 [U] the particular way that someone writes with a pen or pencil SYN **handwriting**: *Your writing is very neat.*

5 [U] the skill of writing: *At this age we concentrate on the children's **reading and writing** skills.*

6 in writing if you get something in writing, it is official proof of an agreement, promise etc: *Could you **put** that **in writing**, please?*

7 writings [plural] the books, stories etc that an important writer has written: *Darwin's scientific writings*

8 the writing is on the wall (*also* **see/read the writing on the wall**) used to say that it seems very likely that something will not exist much longer or someone will fail: **[+for]** *The writing is on the wall for old manufacturing industries.*

ˈwriting desk *n* [C] a desk with special places for pens, paper etc

ˈwriting ˌpaper *n* [U] good quality paper that you use for writing letters SYN **notepaper**

writ·ten¹ /ˈrɪtn/ *v* the past participle of WRITE

written² ●●● W3 *adj* [only before noun]

1 recorded in writing: *the development of written language* | **written agreement/reply/statement/report etc** *Please send a cheque with written confirmation of your booking.*

2 written test/exam a test etc in which you have to write the answers → **oral**

3 the written word *formal* writing as a way of expressing ideas, emotions etc, as opposed to speaking

wrong¹ /rɒŋ $ rɔːŋ/ ●●● S1 W1 *adj*

1 NOT CORRECT not correct, and not based on true facts OPP **right**: *Your calculations must be wrong.* | *I think I **got***

W

question 3 **wrong**. | **it is wrong to do sth** *It is wrong to assume that technological advance brings a higher quality of life.* | *I wish you'd stop trying to* ***prove*** *me* ***wrong*** (=show that I am wrong) *all the time.*
2 be wrong (about sb/sth) to not be right in what you think or believe about someone or something SYN **mistaken** OPP **right**: *No, you're wrong. Brett wouldn't do a thing like that.* | *I was wrong about the new guy – he's not Belgian, he's French.* | ***That's where you're wrong!*** *We never slept together.*
3 PROBLEMS used to describe a situation where there are problems, or when someone is ill or unhappy: **there is something wrong/something is wrong** *When he didn't come back that night, I knew that something was wrong.* | **[+with]** ***What is wrong*** *with our society? People just don't seem to care anymore.* | ***Is anything wrong?*** *You haven't said more than two words since you got here.* | *Dave's* ***got something wrong with*** *his foot.* | *Don't worry, there's* ***nothing wrong***.
4 NOT THE RIGHT ONE not the one that you intended or the one that you really want OPP **right**: *The letter was delivered to the wrong address.* | *driving on the wrong side of the road* | *You've got the wrong man. I didn't kill her.* | *I think we went the* ***wrong way*** *at that last turning.* | *There's no one called Julia here. You must have the* ***wrong number*** (=wrong telephone number).
5 NOT MORALLY RIGHT not morally right or acceptable OPP **right**: **it is wrong that** *It's wrong that people should have to sleep on the streets.* | **it is wrong to do sth** *We all accept that it is wrong to torture people.* | *We weren't* ***doing anything wrong!*** | **[+with]** ***There's nothing wrong with*** *making a profit, provided you don't cheat anyone.*
6 NOT SUITABLE not suitable for a particular purpose, situation, or person OPP **right**: *It's the wrong time of year to be planning a holiday.* | **[+for]** *Anna and I were wrong for each other in dozens of ways* (=not suited for a romantic relationship with each other).
7 NOT WORKING if something is wrong with a vehicle or machine, it stops working properly: **[+with]** ***There's something wrong with*** *the car again.* → **go wrong** at WRONG²(2)
8 UNPLEASANT *informal* unpleasant and upsetting or offensive – often used humorously: *That joke's just wrong, man!*
9 be the wrong way round/around a) to be in the wrong order: *These two paragraphs are the wrong way round.* **b)** if something is the wrong way round, the back is where the front should be: *You've got your T-shirt on the wrong way around.*
10 the wrong way up if something is the wrong way up, the top is where the bottom should be SYN **upside down**: *The painting was hung the wrong way up.*
11 take sth the wrong way to be offended by a remark because you have understood it wrongly: *I like you. Don't take this the wrong way, now. I mean as a friend.*
12 be in the wrong place at the wrong time *spoken* to get involved in trouble without intending to
13 get on the wrong side of sb to do something that gives someone a bad opinion of you, so that they do not like or respect you in the future: *I wouldn't like to get on the wrong side of her.*
14 get on the wrong side of the law to get into trouble with the police
15 get off on the wrong foot to start a job, relationship etc badly by making a mistake that annoys people
16 get the wrong end of the stick *BrE informal* to understand a situation in completely the wrong way: *Geoff had got the wrong end of the stick, and thought I was angry with him.*
17 be on the wrong track/tack to have the wrong idea about a situation so that you are unlikely to get the result you want
18 be from the wrong side of the tracks *AmE* to be from a poor part of a town or a poor part of society
19 be the wrong side of thirty/forty etc *informal* to be older than 30 etc → **get out of bed on the wrong side** at BED¹(8)
20 correct me if I'm wrong used as a polite way of saying that you think what you are going to say is correct: ***Correct me if I'm wrong, but*** *didn't you say you were going to do it?*
21 you're not wrong *spoken* used to agree with someone: *'This government is ruining the country!' 'You're not wrong there!'*
22 fall/get into the wrong hands if something secret or dangerous falls into the wrong hands, it is discovered by someone who may use it to harm people

THESAURUS

wrong not correct or right – used about facts, answers etc, or people: *For every wrong answer, you lose five points.* | *The figure he gave me was wrong.* | *I think you're wrong about that.*
incorrect something that is incorrect is wrong because someone has made a mistake. **Incorrect** is more formal than **wrong**: *I'm afraid these prices are incorrect.* | *The doctor had made an incorrect diagnosis.*
inaccurate something that is inaccurate is not exactly right and contains mistakes: *inaccurate information* | *The old maps were often inaccurate.*
false not based on true facts: *Are the following statements true or false?* | *He was accused of giving false information to the police.*
untrue [not usually before noun] not based on true facts, especially because someone is lying or guessing: *I can't believe he said that about me. It's completely untrue!* | *The allegations were untrue.*
misleading a misleading statement or piece of information makes people believe something that is wrong, especially because it does not give all the facts: *The article was very misleading.*
misguided a misguided decision, belief, action etc is wrong because it is based on bad judgment or understanding: *That decision seems misguided now.* | *It was the consequence of a misguided economic policy.*
mistaken wrong – used about ideas and beliefs. Also used about a person being wrong. **You're mistaken** sounds more polite and less direct than saying **you're wrong**: *She's completely mistaken if she thinks that I don't care about her.* | *a mistaken belief*

wrong² ●●● S2 *adv*
1 not in the correct way OPP **right**: *You've spelt my name wrong.* | *What? Have I* ***done it wrong?*** | *I asked him to sort those files, but he's* ***done it all wrong*** (=in completely the wrong way).
2 go wrong a) to stop working properly: ***Something's gone wrong*** *with my watch.* **b)** to make a mistake during a process so that you do not get the right result: *Follow these instructions and* ***you can't go wrong*** (=you are sure to succeed). **c)** to do something that makes a plan, relationship etc fail: *Thinking back on the marriage, I just don't know where we went wrong.*
3 get sth wrong to make a mistake in the way you write, judge, or understand something: *This isn't it. We must have got the address wrong.* | **get/have it all wrong** (=understand a situation in completely the wrong way) *No, no – you've got it all wrong! We're just friends!*
4 don't get me wrong *spoken* used when you think someone may understand your remarks wrongly, or be offended by them: *Don't get me wrong – I like Jenny.*
5 you can't go wrong (with sth) *spoken* used to say that a particular object will always be suitable, satisfactory, or work well: *You can't go wrong with a little black dress, can you?* → **come out wrong** at COME OUT

wrong³ ●●○ *n*
1 [U] behaviour that is not morally right: *He's too young to know* ***right from wrong***. | *Those who* ***do wrong*** *should be punished.* | **sb can do no wrong** (=they are perfect) *Nathan adored her, and she could do no wrong in his eyes.*
2 [C] an action, judgment, or situation that is unfair: *The black population suffered countless wrongs at the hands of a racist regime.* | **right a wrong** (=bring justice to an unfair situation)
3 be in the wrong to make a mistake or deserve the blame for something: *Which driver was in the wrong?*
4 do sb wrong to treat someone badly and unfairly – used humorously
5 two wrongs don't make a right *spoken* used to say that if

someone does something bad to you, you should not do something bad to them

wrong[4] *v* [T] *formal* to treat or judge someone unfairly: *Both sides felt that they had been wronged.*

wrong·do·ing /ˈrɒŋˌduːɪŋ $ ˌrɒːŋˈduːɪŋ/ *n* [C,U] *formal* illegal or immoral behaviour —**wrongdoer** *n*

wrong·foot /ˌrɒŋˈfʊt $ ˌrɒːŋ-/ *v* [T] to surprise and embarrass someone, especially by asking a question they did not expect: *Woo's political skill and ability to wrongfoot the opposition*

wrong·ful /ˈrɒŋfəl $ ˈrɒːŋ-/ *adj* **wrongful arrest/conviction/imprisonment/dismissal etc** a wrongful arrest etc is unfair or illegal because the person affected by it has done nothing wrong: *She's threatening to sue her employers for wrongful dismissal.* —**wrongfully** *adv*

wrong·head·ed /ˌrɒŋˈhedɪd◂ $ ˌrɒːŋ-/ *adj* used to describe an idea, plan, or belief that someone has, that is based on wrong ideas that they are not willing to change —**wrongheadedly** *adv* —**wrongheadedness** *n* [U]

wrong·ly /ˈrɒŋli $ ˈrɒːŋ-/ ●●○ *adv*
1 not correctly or in a way that is not based on facts OPP **rightly**: *Matthew was wrongly diagnosed as having a brain tumour.* | *His name had been wrongly spelt.*
2 in a way that is unfair or immoral OPP **rightly**: *Human rights organizations maintain that the men have been wrongly convicted.* → **rightly or wrongly** at RIGHTLY

wrote /rəʊt $ roʊt/ *v* the past tense of WRITE

wrought /rɔːt $ rɒːt/ the old past tense and past participle of WORK

ˌwrought ˈiron *n* [U] long thin pieces of iron formed into shapes to make gates, fences etc

ˌwrought-ˈup *adj* very nervous and excited SYN **wound up**, **tense**

WRT the written abbreviation of ***with regard to***, used in email or by people communicating in CHAT ROOMS on the Internet

wrung /rʌŋ/ the past tense and past participle of WRING

wry /raɪ/ *adj* [only before noun] a wry expression or wry humour shows that you know a situation is bad, but you also think it is slightly amusing: *'Was it as bad as you expected?' Travis gave a wry smile.* —**wryly** *adv*

wt. (*also* **wt** *BrE*) the written abbreviation of ***weight***

wun·der·kind /ˈwʌndəkɪnd $ -ər-/ *n* [C] a young person who is very successful → **child prodigy**

wu·shu /ˈwuːʃuː/ *n* [U] a Chinese fighting art in which you fight using your hands and feet

wuss /wʊs/ *n* [C] *spoken* someone who you think is weak or lacks courage

WWI, **WW1** the written abbreviation of ***World War I***

WWII, **WW2** the written abbreviation of ***World War II***

WWW /ˌdʌbəljuː dʌbəljuː ˈdʌbəljuː/ the abbreviation of ***World Wide Web***

WYSIWYG /ˈwɪziwɪg/ *n* [U] (***what you see is what you get***) a word used to mean that what you see on the computer screen is exactly what will be printed

wy·vern /ˈwaɪvən $ -ərn/ *n* [C] an imaginary animal that has two legs and wings and looks like a DRAGON

X[1], **x** /eks/ (*plural* **X's**, **x's**) *n*
1 LETTER [C,U] the 24th letter of the English alphabet
2 NUMBER [C] the number 10 in the system of ROMAN NUMERALS
3 MATHEMATICS [U] *technical* a letter used in mathematics to represent an unknown quantity or value: *if 3x = 6, x = 2*
4 ON SCHOOL WORK [C] a mark used on school work to show that a written answer is not correct
5 WHEN VOTING [C] a mark used to show that you have chosen something on an official piece of paper, for example when voting
6 ON A LETTER [C] a mark used to show a kiss, especially at the end of a letter: *Love, Cindy XXX*
7 FILM [singular, U] used in the past to describe a film that was officially approved as only suitable for people over 18 SYN **18** → X-RATED
8 UNKNOWN/SECRET NAME [U] a letter used instead of someone's or something's real name because you want to keep it secret or you do not know it: *At the trial, Ms X said that she had known the defendant for three years.*
9 WHEN SIGNING YOUR NAME [C] a mark used instead of a signature by someone who cannot write
10 X number of people/things used to say that there are a number of people or things when the exact number is not important
11 X marks the spot used on maps in adventure stories to show that something is buried in a particular place

X[2] *v*
X sth ↔ **out** *phr v AmE* to mark or remove a mistake in a piece of writing using an X SYN **cross out**

x-ax·is /ˈeks ˌæksɪs/ *n* [singular] *technical* the line marked with numbers or times that goes from left to right on a GRAPH SYN **horizontal axis** → **y-axis**

X-cer·tif·i·cate /ˈeks səˌtɪfɪkət $ -sər-/ *adj, n* an X-certificate film is one that people under 18 are not allowed to see in Britain because it contains sex or violence → **PG**, **R**[2], **U**[1](2)

X chro·mo·some /ˈeks ˌkrəʊməsəʊm $ -ˌkrouməsoum/ *n* [C] a type of CHROMOSOME that exists in pairs in female cells, and together with a Y CHROMOSOME in male cells

xen·on /ˈzenɒn $ ˈziːnɑːn, ˈze-/ *n* [U] a colourless gas that is found in very small quantities in the air. It is a chemical ELEMENT: symbol Xe

xen·o·pho·bi·a /ˌzenəˈfəʊbiə $ -ˈfoʊ-/ *n* [U] strong fear or dislike of people from other countries THESAURUS PREJUDICE —**xenophobic** *adj*

xen·o·trans·plant /ˌzenəʊˈtrænsplɑːnt $ -noʊˈtrænsplænt/ *n* **1** [C,U] the operation of putting an organ from an animal into a person's body: *Doctors in Mississippi performed the world's first heart xenotransplant.* **2** [C] the organ that is moved in a xenotransplant operation —**xenotransplant** *v* [T] —**xenotransplantation** /ˌzenəʊtrænsplɑːnˈteɪʃən $ -noʊtrænsplæn-/ *n* [U]: *health risks related to xenotransplantation*

XL (*extra large*) used on clothes to show their size

X·mas /ˈkrɪsməs, ˈeksməs/ *n* [C,U] *informal* a word that means Christmas, often written on signs or cards

XML /ˌeks em ˈel/ *n* [U] *technical* (***extensible markup language***) a way of writing a document on a computer so that its structure is clear, and so that it can easily be read on a different computer system

X-rated /ˈeks ˌreɪtɪd/ *adj* an X-rated film is one that people under 18 are not allowed to see because it includes sex or violence

X-ray[1] /ˈeks reɪ/ ●●○ *n* [C]
1 a beam of RADIATION(1) that can go through solid objects and is used for photographing the inside of the body
2 a photograph of part of someone's body, taken using X-rays to see if anything is wrong: *The X-ray showed that her leg was not broken.*
3 a medical examination made using X-rays → **radiography**: *I had to go to hospital for an X-ray.* | *a chest X-ray*

X-ray[2] *v* [T] to photograph the inside of someone's body using X-rays: *The problem was only discovered when her lungs were X-rayed.*

xy·lo·phone /ˈzaɪləfəʊn $ -foʊn/ *n* [C] a musical instrument which consists of metal or wooden bars of different lengths that you hit with a special stick → **glockenspiel**

Y, **y** /waɪ/ (*plural* **Y's**, **y's**) *n* [C,U] the 25th letter of the English alphabet → **Y CHROMOSOME**, **Y-FRONTS**

-y[1] /i/ *suffix* [in adjectives] **1** full of something or covered with something: *sugary desserts* (=full of sugar) | *dirty hands* (=covered with dirt) | *a hairy chest* (=covered with hair) **2** having a quality or feeling, or tending to do something: *a messy room* | *curly hair* (=hair that curls) | *feeling sleepy* **3** like or typical of something: *a cold wintry day* (=typical of winter) | *his long, horsy face* (=he looks like a horse) **4** fond of or interested in something: *a horsy woman* (=who likes riding horses) —**-ily** *suffix* [in adverbs] —**-iness** *suffix* [in nouns]

-y[2] *suffix* [in nouns] **1** (*also* **-ie**) used to make a word or name less formal, and often to show that you care about them – used especially when talking to children: *Where's little Johnny?* | *my daddy* (=my father) | *What a nice doggy* (=dog)! **2** used to make nouns from some verbs to show an action: *the expiry date* (=the date when something EXPIRES) | *an inquiry* (=the act of INQUIRING about something)

ya /jə, jʌ/ *pron spoken informal* you: *See ya later!*

yacht /jɒt $ jɑːt/ ●●○ *n* [C] a large boat with a sail, used for pleasure or sport, especially one that has a place where you can sleep → **sailing boat**, **sailboat**

yacht·ing /ˈjɒtɪŋ $ ˈjɑːtɪŋ/ *n* [U] *especially BrE* sailing, travelling, or racing in a yacht → **sailing**

yachts·man /ˈjɒtsmən $ ˈjɑːts-/ *n* (*plural* **yachtsmen** /-mən/) [C] a man who sails a yacht

yachts·wom·an /ˈjɒtsˌwʊmən $ ˈjɑːts-/ *n* (*plural* **yachtswomen** /-ˌwɪmɪn/) [C] a woman who sails a yacht

ya·da ya·da ya·da, **yadda yadda yadda** /jædə jædə ˈjædə/ *interjection AmE spoken* said when you do not want to give a lot of detailed information, because it is boring or because the person you are talking to already knows it SYN **blah, blah, blah**: *I started talking to her and – yada yada yada – it turns out she's from New York too.*

ya·hoo[1] /jɑːˈhuː/ *interjection spoken informal* shouted when you are very happy or excited about something

yahoo[2] *n* (*plural* **yahoos**) [C] *old-fashioned* someone who is rough, noisy, or rude: *a bunch of time-wasting yahoos*

Yah·weh /ˈjɑːweɪ/ *n* [singular] a Hebrew name for God

yak[1] /jæk/ *n* [C] an animal of central Asia that looks like a cow with long hair

yak² *v* (**yakked**, **yakking**) [I] *informal* to talk continuously about things that are not very serious, in a way that is annoying

y'all /jɔːl $ jɒːl/ *pron AmE spoken* a word meaning 'all of you', used mainly in the southern US states when speaking to more than one person: *I'm going home now. See y'all later.*

yam /jæm/ *n* [C] **1** a tropical climbing plant grown for its root, which is eaten as a vegetable **2** *AmE* a type of SWEET POTATO

yam·mer /ˈjæmə $ -ər/ (*also* **yammer on**) *v* [I] *informal* to talk continuously in a way that is annoying: *a crowd of yammering aunts and cousins*

yang /jæŋ/ *n* [U] the male principle in Chinese PHILOSOPHY which is active, light, and positive, and which combines with YIN (=the female principle) to influence everything in the world

yank /jæŋk/ *v* [I,T] *informal* to suddenly pull something quickly and with force: **yank sth out/back/open etc** *One of the men grabbed Tom's hair and yanked his head back.* | *Nick yanked the door open.* | **[+on/at]** *With both hands she yanked at the necklace.* —**yank** *n* [C]: *He* ***gave*** *the rope* ***a yank****.*

Yank (*also* **Yankee**) *n* [C] *BrE informal* an American - often used to show disapproval

Yan·kee /ˈjæŋki/ *n* [C] *informal* **1** a soldier who fought on the side of the Union (=the northern states) during the American Civil War **2** *AmE* someone born in or living in the northern states of the US - sometimes used in an insulting way by people from the southern US **3** *BrE* an American - often used to show disapproval SYN **Yank** **4** *AmE* someone from New England

yap¹ /jæp/ *v* (**yapped**, **yapping**) [I] **1** if a small dog yaps, it BARKS (=makes short loud sounds) in an excited way **2** *informal* to talk in a noisy and annoying way: *Some guy was yapping on his cell phone.*

yap² *n* [C] the sound a small dog makes when it yaps

yard /jɑːd $ jɑːrd/ ●●● S2 W2 *n* [C]
1 MEASURE (*written abbreviation* **yd**) a unit for measuring length, equal to three feet or 0.91 metres: *a hundred yards away* | *an area of 9,000* ***square yards***
2 ENCLOSED AREA an enclosed area next to a building or group of buildings, used for a special purpose, activity, or business: *a builder's yard* | *a timber yard* | **prison/school yard** (=an area outside a prison or school where prisoners or students do activities outdoors)
3 GARDEN *AmE* the area around a house, usually covered with grass SYN **garden** *BrE*: **front/back yard** *The kids were playing in the back yard.*
4 BACK OF HOUSE *BrE* an enclosed area without grass at the back of a small house → BACKYARD

Yard, the an informal name for Scotland Yard

yard·age /ˈjɑːdɪdʒ $ ˈjɑːr-/ *n technical* **1** [U] the number of yards that a team or player moves forward in a game of American football **2** [C,U] the size of something measured in yards or square yards: *a large yardage of sail*

yard·arm /ˈjɑːd-ɑːm $ ˈjɑːrd-ɑːrm/ *n* [C] one of the ends of the pole that supports a square sail

yard·bird /ˈjɑːdbɜːd $ ˈjɑːrdbɜːrd/ *n* [C] *AmE informal old-fashioned* someone who is in prison, especially for a long time SYN **jailbird**

ˈyard sale *n* [C] *AmE* a sale of used clothes and things from someone's house which takes place in their YARD → **garage sale**

yard·stick /ˈjɑːdˌstɪk $ ˈjɑːrd-/ *n* [C] **1** something that you compare another thing with, in order to judge how good or successful it is: **[+of]** *Profit is the most important yardstick of success for any business.* | **as a yardstick** *These subjects are used as a* ***yardstick*** *against which to* ***measure*** *the children's progress.* **2** a special stick used for measuring things, which is exactly one YARD long

yar·mul·ke /ˈjɑːmʊlkə $ ˈjɑːr-/ *n* [C] a small circular cap worn by some Jewish men

yarn /jɑːn $ jɑːrn/ ●○○ *n*
1 [U] thick thread made of cotton or wool, which is used to KNIT things
2 [C] *informal* a story of adventures, travels etc, usually made more exciting and interesting by adding things that never really happened: *The old captain would often* ***spin*** (=tell) *us a* ***yarn*** *about life aboard ship.*
THESAURUS ▸ STORY

YARN

ˈyarn ˌbombing *n* [U] the activity of secretly decorating public places with things that have been knitted (KNIT)

yash·mak /ˈjæʃmæk/ *n* [C] a piece of cloth that Muslim women wear across their faces in public

yaw /jɔː $ jɒː/ *v* [I] *technical* if a ship, aircraft etc yaws, it turns away from the direction it should be travelling in —**yaw** *n* [C,U]

yawn¹ /jɔːn $ jɒːn/ ●●○ *v* [I]
1 to open your mouth wide and breathe in deeply because you are tired or bored: *Alan stretched and yawned.*
2 **yawning gap/gulf/chasm (between sth)** a very large difference between two groups, things, or people: *the yawning gap between the two parties* | *the yawning gulf between the rich and the poor*
3 *literary* to be or become wide open, especially in a frightening way: *The pit* ***yawned open*** *in front of them.* | **yawning gap/hole etc** *the yawning gap between the two cliffs*

yawn² ●●○ *n*
1 [C] an act of yawning: *Kay shook her head and* ***stifled a yawn*** (=tried to stop yawning).
2 **a yawn** *informal* someone or something that is boring: *The party was a big yawn.*

yaws /jɔːz $ jɒːz/ *n* [U] a tropical skin disease

y-ax·is /ˈwaɪ ˌæksɪs/ *n* [singular] *technical* the line marked with numbers that goes from top to bottom on a GRAPH SYN **vertical axis** → **x-axis**

yay /jeɪ/ *interjection informal* said when you are very happy about something SYN **hooray**

Y chro·mo·some /ˈwaɪ ˌkrəʊməsəʊm $ -ˌkroʊməsoʊm/ *n* [C] the part of a GENE that makes someone a male instead of a female → **X chromosome**

yd *BrE*, **yd.** *AmE* (*plural* **yd** *or* **yds**) the written abbreviation of ***yard*** or ***yards***

ye¹ /jiː/ *pron old use* you - used especially when speaking to more than one person: *Abandon hope all ye who enter here.*

ye² *determiner* the - used in the names of shops and PUBS to make them seem old: *Ye Olde Antique Shoppe*

yea¹ /jeɪ/ *adv old use* yes OPP **nay**

yea² *n* [C] a YES² OPP **nay**

yeah /jeə/ ●●● S1 *adv spoken informal* yes

year /jɪə, jɜː $ jɪr/ ●●● S1 W1 *n* [C]
1 12 MONTHS a period of about 365 days or 12 months, measured from any particular time: *I arrived here two years ago.* | *We've known each other for over a year.* | *It's almost a year since Sue died.* | *Jodi is 15 years old.* | *a three-year business plan* | *a four-year-old child* | **be 12/21 etc years of age** (=be 12/21 etc years old) → FINANCIAL YEAR, FISCAL YEAR, LIGHT YEAR, TAX YEAR
2 JANUARY TO DECEMBER (*also* **calendar year**) a period of 365 or 366 days divided into 12 months beginning on January 1st and ending on December 31st: *the year that Kennedy died* | *in the year 1785* | **this/last/next year** *They moved here at the beginning of this year.* | *last year's cup final* | *She goes there every year.* | *The museum attracts 100,000 visitors a year.* | *in the early years of the last century* → LEAP YEAR, NEW YEAR
3 **years a)** *informal* a very long period of time SYN **ages**: ***It's years*** *since I rode a bike.* | **in/for years** *I haven't been there for years.* | *It was* ***the first time in years*** *I'd seen her.*

b) age, especially old age: **a man/woman/person etc of his/her etc years** *Gordon is very active for a man of his years.* | **getting on in years** (=no longer young)
4 all (the) year round during the whole year: *It's warm enough to swim all year round.* → YEAR-ROUND
5 year by year as each year passes: *Business has steadily increased year by year.*
6 year after year/year in, year out every year for many years: *Many birds return to the same spot year after year.*
7 PERIOD OF LIFE/HISTORY **years** [plural] a particular period of time in someone's life or in history: *the difficult years following the war* | *Sheila enjoyed her years as a student in Oxford.*
8 the school/academic year the time within a period of 12 months when students are studying at a school or university
9 SCHOOL/UNIVERSITY LEVEL *especially BrE* a particular level that a student stays at for one year: *a group of year seven students* | **in a year** *He was in my year at school.*
10 first/second etc year *BrE* someone who is in their first etc year at school or university: *The department offers a study skills programme for all first years.*
11 musician/player/car etc of the year the musician etc who was voted the best in a particular year: **vote/name sth ... of the year** *The new Renault was voted car of the year.*
12 year on year compared with the previous year: *Sales rose by 39 per cent year on year.*
13 never/not in a million years *spoken* used to say that something is extremely unlikely: *Never in a million years did I think we'd lose.*
14 the year dot *BrE informal* a very long time ago: *Scientists have been involved in war* ***since the year dot.***
15 put years on sb/take years off sb to make someone look or feel older or younger: *Tina's divorce has put years on her.*
→ **donkey's years** at DONKEY(2)

GRAMMAR: Patterns with year

last year/this year etc
Don't use **in** with these words:
• You say **last year**: *They got married last year.* ✗ Don't say: *They got married in last year.*
• You say **this year**: *I will turn 16 this year.* ✗ Don't say: *I will turn 16 in this year.*
• You say **next year**: *She's going on a trip to England next year.* ✗ Don't say: *She's going on a trip to England in next year.*
• You say **that year**: *We had a lot of rain that year.* ✗ Don't say: *We had a lot of rain in that year.*

a year
• You use **a year** when saying how many times in a year something happens: *I only see my sister about twice a year.* ✗ Don't say: *I only see my sister about twice in a year.*

in the year ...
• You use **in the year** when saying the year when something happens: *In the year 2050 sea levels could be much higher.* | *The record was a hit in the year that I was born.*

all year
• You use **all year** when talking about something that happens during every part of a year: *There is enough snow here to ski all year.* ✗ Don't say: *There is enough snow here to ski all the year.*

COLLOCATIONS - MEANING 7

ADJECTIVES/NOUN + years
early years *Little is known about his early years.*
the last/latter/closing years of sth *He changed his opinion during the last years of his life.*
sb's childhood/teenage years *the home in which she spent her childhood years*
the war years *She worked for the BBC during the war years.*
the boom years (=when an economy or industry is very successful) | **the Bush/Blair etc years** (=when Bush, Blair etc was leader)

PHRASES
in recent years *The number of cases has risen dramatically in recent years.*
in later years *In later years he regretted their argument.*
in years gone by (=in the past)

COMMON ERRORS
⚠ Don't say 'in ancient years' or 'in the ancient years'. Say **in ancient times** or **long ago**.

year·book /ˈjɪəbʊk, ˈjɜː- $ ˈjɪr-/ *n* [C] **1** a book printed once a year, with information about a particular subject or activity: *Rothman's Football Yearbook* **2** *AmE* a book printed once a year by a school or college, with information and pictures about what happened there in the past year: *a high-school yearbook*

year·ling /ˈjɪəlɪŋ, ˈjɜː- $ ˈjɪr-/ *n* [C] an animal, especially a young horse, between one and two years old

ˈyear-long, year·long /ˈjɪəlɒŋ, ˈjɜː- $ ˈjɪrlɒːŋ/ *adj* [only before noun] continuing for a year or all through the year: *a year-long study of the problem*

year·ly /ˈjɪəli, ˈjɜː- $ ˈjɪrli/ ●○○ *adj* happening or appearing every year or once a year → **annual**: *Salary levels are reviewed on a yearly basis.* | *a total yearly income of $78,000* | *The magazine is issued twice yearly* (=two times a year). | **three-yearly/five-yearly etc** (=every three years etc) *a checkup at five-yearly intervals* —**yearly** *adv*: *We pay the fee yearly.*

yearn /jɜːn $ jɜːrn/ *v* [I] *literary* to have a strong desire for something, especially something that is difficult or impossible to get SYN **long**: **[+for]** *Hannah yearned for a child.* | **yearn to be/do sth** *Phil had yearned to be a pilot from an early age.*

REGISTER
In everyday English, people usually say **long for sth** or **long to do sth** rather than **yearn**: *She* ***longed for*** *another child.*

yearn·ing /ˈjɜːnɪŋ $ ˈjɜːr-/ *n* [C,U] *literary* a strong desire for something SYN **longing**: **[+for]** *a yearning for travel* | **yearning to do sth** *He* ***had a*** *deep* ***yearning*** *to return to his home town.*

ˈyear-round *adj* [usually before noun] happening or continuing through the whole year: *a year-round supply of fresh fruit*

yeast /jiːst/ *n* [U] a type of FUNGUS used for producing alcohol in beer and wine, and for making bread rise —**yeasty** *adj*: *a yeasty taste*

ˌyeast ˈextract *n* [U] a thick sticky brown substance made from yeast, used in cooking or for spreading on bread

ˈyeast inˌfection *n* [C] an infectious condition that affects the VAGINA in women SYN **thrush**

yecch /jʌk/ *interjection AmE spoken informal* used to say that you think something is very unpleasant SYN **yuck**

yell¹ /jel/ ●●○ *v*
1 [I,T] (*also* **yell out**) to shout or say something very loudly, especially because you are frightened, angry, or excited: *'Help me!' she yelled hysterically.* | *I yelled out, 'Here I am!'* | *The crowd are on their feet yelling.* | **[+at]** *Don't you yell at me like that!* | **yell at sb to do sth** *They yelled at him to stop.* | **yell (out) in surprise/pain etc** *Clare yelled in pain as she fell.* | *He could hear Pete yelling* ***at the top of*** *his* ***voice*** (=very loudly). THESAURUS ▸ SHOUT
2 [I] *spoken* to ask for help: *If you need me, just yell.*

yell² *n* [C] **1** a loud shout: **let out/give a yell** *She let out a yell when she saw me.* | **a yell of surprise/delight/triumph etc** *Dan gave a yell of delight when Larsson scored.* **2** *AmE* words or phrases that students and CHEERLEADERS shout together to show support for their school, college etc

yel·low¹ /ˈjeləʊ $ -loʊ/ ●●● S2 W3 *adj*
1 having the colour of butter or the middle part of an egg:

yellow flowers → CHROME YELLOW, → **lemon yellow** at LEMON²(2), → **primrose yellow** at PRIMROSE(2)
2 *not polite* an offensive way of describing the skin colour of people from parts of Asia
3 (*also* **yellow-bellied**) *informal* not brave SYN **cowardly**

yellow² ●●● S3 W3 *n* [C,U] the colour of butter or the middle part of an egg: *Yellow doesn't suit me at all.* | *The room was decorated in a variety of reds, blues, and yellows.*

yellow³ *v* [I,T] to become yellow, or to make something become yellow: *The paper had yellowed with age.*

ˌyellow ˈcard *n* [C] a yellow card held up by a football REFEREE to show that a player has done something wrong → **red card**

ˌyellow ˈfever *n* [U] a dangerous tropical disease which makes your skin turn slightly yellow

yel·low·ham·mer /ˈjeləʊˌhæmə $ -loʊˌhæmər/ *n* [C] a small European bird with a yellow head

yel·low·ish /ˈjeləʊɪʃ $ -loʊ-/ *adj* slightly yellow: *yellowish teeth*

ˌyellow ˈline *n* [C] a line of yellow paint along the edge of a street in Britain which means you can only park your car for a short time or at particular times: **double yellow lines** (=two lines of paint that mean you cannot park there at any time)

ˌYellow ˈPages (*also* **yellow pages** *AmE*) *n trademark* **(the) Yellow Pages** a book that contains the telephone numbers of businesses and organizations in an area, arranged according to the type of service or goods they provide → **White Pages**

yel·low·y /ˈjeləʊi $ -loʊi/ *adj* slightly yellow: *The cream was thick and yellowy.*

yelp /jelp/ *n* [C] a short sharp high cry which a person or an animal makes because they are excited, in pain, surprised etc: **give/let out a yelp of pain/dismay/surprise etc** *The water was hotter than she had expected, and she gave an involuntary yelp.* —**yelp** *v* [I]: *The dog ran up and down, yelping.*

yen /jen/ *n* **1** [C] (*plural* **yen**) the standard unit of money in Japan: symbol ¥ **2 the yen** the value of Japanese money in relation to the money of other countries: *The dollar **fell** by 24 percent **against the yen*** (=decreased in value in relation to the yen) *between 1970 and 1973.* **3** [singular] a strong desire: **[+for]** *a yen for foreign travel* | **yen to do sth** *She'd always **had a yen** to write a book.*

yeo·man /ˈjəʊmən $ ˈjoʊ-/ *n* (*plural* **yeomen** /-mən/) [C] **1** an officer in the US navy who often works in an office **2** a farmer in Britain in the past who owned and worked on his own land

yeo·man·ry /ˈjəʊmənri $ ˈjoʊ-/ *n* [plural] *literary* the people in Britain in the past who owned and farmed their own land

yep /jep/ *adv spoken informal* yes

yer /jə $ jər/ *determiner written informal* your or you: *Keep yer mouth shut!*

yes¹ /jes/ ●●● S1 W1 *adv spoken*
1 ANSWER TO QUESTION/STATEMENT **a)** used as an answer to say that something is true or that you agree OPP **no**: *'Is that real gold?' 'Yes.'* | *'It was a great show.' 'Yes, it was.'* **b)** used as an answer to a question or statement containing a negative, to say that the opposite is true: *'Sarah isn't very intelligent, is she?' 'Yes, she is* (=in fact, she is intelligent)*!'* | *'There isn't any cereal left.' 'Yes, there is – it's in the cupboard.'*
2 ANSWER TO OFFER/INVITATION used as an answer to say that you want something or want to do something OPP **no**: *'Would you like a sandwich?' '**Yes, please**.'* | *'Would you like to come with us?' 'Yes, I'd love to.'*
3 ANSWER TO REQUEST used as an answer to say that you will do something, or that someone may do or have something OPP **no**: *'Can I have a glass of water?' 'Yes, of course.'* | *He proposed to me and I **said yes**.*
4 yes, but ... used to show that you agree with what someone has said, but there is another fact to consider: *'There are still a lot of problems with Jeff's proposal.' 'Yes, but it's the best one we have.'*
5 READY TO LISTEN/TALK used to show that you have heard someone or are ready to speak to someone: *'Mike?' 'Yes?'* | *Yes sir, how can I help you?*
6 LISTENING used to show that you are listening to someone and want them to continue: *'And so I tried phoning him ...' 'Yes ...'*
7 EXCITED/HAPPY used to show that you are very excited or happy about something: *Yes! Rivaldo's scored again!*
8 oh yes a) used to show that you do not believe what someone is saying: *'There's nothing going on between me and Jane. We're just good friends.' 'Oh yes?'* **b)** used to show that you have remembered something: *Where's my umbrella? Oh yes – I left it in the car.*
9 EMPHASIS used to emphasize that you mean what you have just said, even though it is surprising: *It took ten years – yes, ten whole years – to complete.* | *Yes, you heard me correctly – I said 1921.*
10 yes, yes used to show annoyance when someone is talking to you and you do not want to listen: *'And don't forget to lock the door!' 'Yes, yes, OK.'*
11 yes and no used to show that there is not one clear answer to a question: *'Were you surprised?' 'Well, yes and no. I knew they were planning something, but I wasn't sure what.'* → YEAH

yes² *n* (*plural* **yeses** *or* **yesses**) [C] a vote, voter, or reply that agrees with an idea, plan, law etc OPP **no**: *According to the latest opinion poll, the noes have 60%, and the yeses have 40%.* —**yes** *adj*: *a yes vote*

ye·shi·va, **yeshivah** /jəˈʃiːvə/ *n* [C] a school for Jewish students, where they can train to become RABBIS (=religious leaders)

ˈyes-man *n* (*plural* **yes-men**) [C] someone who always agrees with and obeys their employer, leader etc in order to gain some advantage – used to show disapproval

yes·ter·day¹ /ˈjestədi, -deɪ $ -ər-/ ●●● S1 W1 *adv* on or during the day before today → **tomorrow**: *What did you do yesterday?* | **yesterday morning/afternoon/evening** *Anna left yesterday afternoon.* → **I wasn't born yesterday** at BORN¹(5)

yesterday² *n* [U] **1** the day before today → **tomorrow**: *yesterday's meeting* | *They arrived **the day before yesterday**.* **2** the recent past: *the great champions of yesterday* **3 yesterday's news** information that is old and no longer interesting

yes·ter·year /ˈjestəjɪə, -jɜː $ ˈjestərjɪr/ *n* **of yesteryear** *literary* existing in the past: *the steam trains of yesteryear*

yet¹ /jet/ ●●● S1 W1 *adv*
1 a) used in negative statements and questions to talk about whether something that was expected has happened: *I haven't asked him yet* (=but I will). | *Has Edmund arrived yet?* | *'Have you finished your homework?' '**Not yet**.'* **b)** used in negative statements and questions to talk about whether a situation has started to exist: *'How are you going to get there?' 'I don't know yet.'* | *Women didn't yet have the vote* (=at that time). | *'Is supper ready?' 'No, **not yet**.'*

GRAMMAR
Word order
- In spoken English, **yet** usually comes at the end of the sentence: *They haven't finished the job yet.*
- **Yet** can also come after 'do not', 'have not', 'is not' etc: *They haven't yet finished the job.*
- **Yet** can also come before 'why', 'whether' etc: *They haven't decided yet whether to take part.*

Choosing the right tense
- In British English, **yet** is used with perfect tenses when referring to a past event: *Has Joe come back yet?*
- In American English, the simple past can also be used: *Did Joe come back yet?*

USAGE: Yet, still, already

- **Yet** is used to say that something has not happened or a situation has not started to exist: *It isn't time to go yet.*
- **Yet** is also used to ask if something has happened: *Have you seen him yet?*
- **Still** is used to say that an earlier situation has not changed: *This system is still used today.* | *I still don't understand.* ✗ Don't say: *This system is yet used today.*
- **Already** is used to emphasize that something has happened or a situation has started to exist: *He has already published two novels.* | *They already knew one another.*
- **Already** is also used in questions to show surprise that something has happened sooner than expected: *Has it all gone already?*

2 used in negative sentences to say that someone should not or need not do something now, although they may have to do it later: *You can't give up yet!* | *Don't go yet. I like talking to you.*
3 used to emphasize that something is even more than it was before or is in addition to what existed before SYN **still**: **yet more/bigger/higher etc** *He got a call from the factory, telling of yet more problems.* | *Inflation had risen to a yet higher level.* | ***yet another** reason to be cautious* | *The meeting has been cancelled **yet again*** (=one more time after many others).
4 the biggest/worst etc (sth) yet used to say that something is the biggest, worst etc of its kind that has existed up to now: *This could turn out to be our biggest mistake yet.* | *Nordstrom's latest novel looks like his best yet.*
5 as (of) yet used when saying that something has not happened up to now: *We've had no luck as yet.* | *on an as yet undecided date*
6 months/weeks/ages yet used to emphasize how much time will pass before something happens, or how long a situation will continue: *'When's your holiday?' 'Oh, not for ages yet.'* | *It could be months yet before they know their fate.*
7 could/may/might yet do sth used to say that something is still possible in the future, in spite of the way that things seem now: *We may win yet.* | *The plan could yet succeed.*
8 sb/sth has yet to do sth *formal* used to say that someone has not done something, or that something has not happened when you think it should already have been done or have happened: *I have yet to hear Ray's version of what happened.* | *The bank has yet to respond to our letter.*

yet² ●●● W2 *conjunction* used to introduce a fact, situation, or quality that is surprising after what you have just said: *Kelly was a convicted criminal, yet many people admired him.* | *She does not speak our language **and yet** she seems to understand what we say.* | *a story that is strange yet true* | *an inexpensive yet effective solution to our problem*

yet·i /ˈjeti/ *n* [C] a large hairy creature like a human which some people believe lives in the Himalayan mountains SYN **Abominable Snowman**

yew /juː/ *n* [C,U] a tree with dark green leaves and red berries, or the wood of this tree

Y-fronts /ˈwaɪ frʌnts/ *n* [plural] *trademark BrE* men's underwear which has a part at the front shaped like an upside down Y

yid /jɪd/ *n* [C] *taboo* a very offensive word for a Jewish person. Do not use this word.

Yid·dish /ˈjɪdɪʃ/ *n* [U] a language based on German used by older Jewish people, especially those who are from Eastern Europe → **Hebrew**

yield¹ /jiːld/ ●●○ *v*
1 RESULT [T] to produce a result, answer, or piece of information: *Our research has only recently begun to **yield** important **results**.*
2 CROPS/PROFITS [T] to produce crops, profits etc: *Each of these oilfields could yield billions of barrels of oil.* | *The tourist industry yielded an estimated $2.25 billion for the state last year.* | *These investments should **yield** a reasonable **return**.* | **high-yielding/low-yielding** *high-yielding crops*

REGISTER
In everyday English, people usually say that something **produces** a result, a profit etc rather than **yields** it: *Each cow **produces** almost 20 litres of milk a day.*

3 AGREE UNWILLINGLY [I,T] to allow yourself to be forced or persuaded to do something or stop having something: *The military has promised to yield power.* | **[+to]** *The hijackers refuse to yield to demands to release the passengers.* | *Further action may be necessary if the leaders do not **yield to** diplomatic **pressure**.* | *Finally she **yielded to temptation** and helped herself to a large slice of cake.*

REGISTER
In everyday English, people usually say someone **gives in to** pressures, demands etc rather than **yields to** them: *I very much doubt the boss will **give in to** her demands.*

4 TRAFFIC [I] *AmE* to allow other traffic on a bigger road to go first SYN **give way** *BrE*: **[+to]** *Yield to traffic on the left.*
5 MOVE/BEND/BREAK [I] to move, bend, or break because of physical force or pressure SYN **give**: *Ideally, the surface should yield slightly under pressure.*
6 GIVE UP FIGHTING [I] *literary* to stop fighting and accept defeat SYN **surrender**
yield to sth *phr v formal* if one thing yields to another, it is replaced by that thing SYN **give way to sth**: *Laughter quickly yielded to amazement as the show went on.*
yield sth ↔ **up** *phr v formal*
1 to show or produce something that was hidden or difficult to find, or that people did not know about SYN **throw up**: *New research has yielded up some surprising discoveries.*
2 *BrE* to give something that belongs to you to someone else, because you are forced to SYN **surrender**: *He would never yield up the castle to the English.*

yield² ●○○ *n* [C] the amount of profits, crops etc that something produces: *The average milk yield per cow has doubled.* | **high/low yield** *Shareholders are expecting a higher yield this year.* | **[+of]** *a yield of over six percent* THESAURUS ▸ AMOUNT

yield·ing /ˈjiːldɪŋ/ *adj* **1** a surface that is yielding is soft and will move or bend when you press it: *the yielding softness of the bed* **2** willing to agree with other people's wishes SYN **accommodating**

yikes /jaɪks/ *interjection informal* said when something frightens or shocks you

yin /jɪn/ *n* [U] the female principle in Chinese PHILOSOPHY which is inactive, dark, and negative, and which combines with YANG (=the male principle) to influence everything in the world

ˌyin and ˈyang *n* [U] the ancient Chinese PHILOSOPHY which is based on the idea that everything in the universe is formed and influenced by the combination of two forces called YIN and YANG

yip·pee /jɪˈpiː $ ˈjɪpi/ *interjection* used when you are very pleased or excited about something SYN **hurray**

yng·ling /ˈjɪŋlɪŋ, ˈɪŋ-/ *n* [C] a small boat with sails, used for racing

yo /jəʊ $ joʊ/ *interjection especially AmE informal* used to greet someone, to get their attention, or as a reply when someone says your name: *Yo, dude! How's it going?* | *'Darren?' 'Yo!'*

yob /jɒb $ jɑːb/ (*also* **yob·bo** /ˈjɒbəʊ $ ˈjɑːboʊ/) *n* [C] *BrE* a rude noisy and sometimes violent young man SYN **lout**: *drunken yobbos*

yo·del¹ /ˈjəʊdl $ ˈjoʊdl/ *v* (**yodelled**, **yodelling** *BrE*, **yodeled**, **yodeling** *AmE*) [I,T] to sing while changing between your natural voice and a very high voice, traditionally done in the mountains of countries such as Switzerland and Austria —**yodeller** *n* [C]

yodel[2] *n* [C] a song or sound made by yodelling

yo·ga /ˈjəʊɡə $ ˈjoʊɡə/ *n* [U] **1** a system of exercises that help you control your mind and body in order to relax **2** a Hindu PHILOSOPHY in which you learn exercises to control your mind and body in order to try to become closer to God

yo·ga·la·tes /ˈjəʊɡəˌlɑːtiz $ ˈjoʊ-/ *n* [U] a type of exercise that is a combination of YOGA and PILATES

yo·gi /ˈjəʊɡi $ ˈjoʊɡi/ *n* [C] someone who has a lot of knowledge about yoga, and who often teaches it to other people

yog·urt, **yoghurt** /ˈjɒɡət $ ˈjoʊɡərt/ ●●● S3 *n* [C,U] a thick liquid food that tastes slightly sour and is made from milk, or an amount of this food: *a pot of strawberry yogurt*

yoke[1] /jəʊk $ joʊk/ *n* [C] **1** a wooden bar used for keeping two animals together, especially cattle, when they are pulling heavy loads **2** a frame that you put across your shoulders so that you can carry two equal loads which hang from either side of it **3** **the yoke of sth** *literary* something that restricts your freedom, making life difficult: *the yoke of tradition* **4** a part of a skirt or shirt just below the waist or collar, from which the main piece of material hangs in folds

yoke[2] *v* [T] **1** to put a yoke on two animals **2** to closely connect two ideas, people, or things: **yoke sth to sth** *Beauty is forever yoked to youth in our culture.*

yo·kel /ˈjəʊkəl $ ˈjoʊ-/ *n* [C] someone who comes from the countryside, seems stupid, and does not know much about modern life, ideas etc – used humorously

yolk /jəʊk $ joʊk, jelk/ *n* [C,U] the yellow part in the centre of an egg → **white**, **albumen**

YOLK

yolk

white

YOLO /ˈjəʊləʊ $ ˈjoʊloʊ/ (*you only live once*) used in SOCIAL MEDIA to give a reason for doing something that is unusual or that involves spending a lot of money

Yom Kip·pur /ˌjɒm ˈkɪpə, -kɪˈpʊə $ ˌjoʊm ˈkɪpər, -kɪˈpʊr/ *n* [U] a Jewish religious holiday on which people do not eat, but pray to be forgiven for the things they have done wrong

yon·der /ˈjɒndə $ ˈjɑːndər/ (*also* **yon** /jɒn $ jɑːn/) *adv, determiner old use* over there – used to show or explain where something or someone is: *the fresh blooms on yonder tree*

yonks /jɒŋks $ jɑːŋks/ *n* [U] *BrE spoken informal* a long time SYN **ages**: ***It's yonks since*** *we had a good night out.* | *We went to Blackpool once,* ***yonks ago.*** | **not do sth for yonks** *We haven't seen Tom and Jean for yonks.*

yoof[1] /juːf/ *adj* [only before noun] *BrE* relating to or intended for young people – used humorously: *a yoof magazine*

yoof[2] *n* [U] *BrE* young people, considered as a group – used humorously: *British white yoof*

yoo-hoo /juː ˈhuː/ *interjection informal* used to attract someone's attention when they are a long way from you

yore /jɔː $ jɔːr/ *n* **of yore** *literary* existing a long time ago: *in* ***days of yore***

York·shire pud·ding /ˌjɔːkʃə ˈpʊdɪŋ $ ˌjɔːrkʃɪr-/ *n* [C,U] a food made from flour, eggs, and milk, baked and eaten with meat in Britain

Yorkshire ter·ri·er /ˌjɔːkʃə ˈteriə $ ˌjɔːrkʃɪr ˈteriər/ *n* [C] a type of dog that is very small and has long brown hair

you /jə, jʊ; *strong* juː/ ●●● S1 W1 *pron* [used as subject or object]

1 used to refer to a person or group of people when speaking or writing to them: *Hi, Kelly. How are you?* | *You must all listen carefully.* | *I have some news for you.* | *The letter is addressed to both of you.* | *Did Robin give you the money?* | *Only you can make this decision.* | *You idiot!* | *You boys have got to learn to behave yourselves.* | *Hey, you over there! Get out of the way!*

2 people in general: *You have to be 21 or over to buy alcohol in Florida.* | *You can never be sure what Emily is thinking.*

you'd /juːd/ **1** the short form of 'you had': *If you'd been more careful, this wouldn't have happened.* **2** the short form of 'you would': *You'd be amazed at how much she spends on clothes.*

you'll /juːl/ the short form of 'you will' or 'you shall': *You'll feel better soon.*

young[1] /jʌŋ/ ●●● S1 W1 *adj* (*comparative* **younger**, *superlative* **youngest**)

1 a young person, plant, or animal has not lived for very long: *a young child* | *He's younger than me.* | *You're too young to get married.* | *young trees* | ***When I was young****, I wanted to be a model.* | *John was a great footballer* ***in his younger days*** (=when he was younger).

2 a young country, organization, or type of science has existed for only a short time: *At that time, America was still a young nation.* | *Psychology is a young science.*

3 **young lady/man** *spoken* used to speak to a girl or boy when you are angry with them: *Now, you listen to me, young man!*

4 seeming or looking younger than you are SYN **youthful**: *Val is incredibly* ***young for her age.***

5 **young at heart** thinking and behaving as if you were young, even though you are old

6 **65/82/97 etc years young** *spoken* used humorously to give the age of an old person who seems or feels much younger: *Next week, Bessie will be 84 years young.*

7 designed or intended for young people: *I'm looking for something in a younger style.*

8 **young gun/Turk** a young person who has just started doing a job or being involved in something, and is eager to achieve things or make changes

9 **sb is not getting any younger** used to say that someone is no longer young, especially when they may soon be too old to do something

GRAMMAR: Order of adjectives

If there is more than one adjective, the adjectives are usually used in a fixed order.
You say: *He's a nice young man.* ✗ Don't say: *He's a young nice man.*
You say: *We met a young German couple.* ✗ Don't say: *We met a German young couple.*
GRAMMAR GUIDE ▸ ADJECTIVES

THESAURUS

young not old: *a young man of about 22* | *My dad died when I was young.* | *Young people are often unable to get jobs.*
small/little a small child is very young. **Little** sounds more informal than **small**, and is used especially in spoken English: *They have two small children.* | *We used to go camping a lot when the kids were little.*
teenage [only before noun] between the ages of 13 and 19: *a group of teenage boys*
adolescent *especially written* at the age when you change from being a child into an adult – used especially when talking about the problems that young people have at this age: *Sudden mood changes are common in adolescent girls.* | *adolescent behaviour*
juvenile /ˈdʒuːvənaɪl $ -nəl, -naɪl/ [only before noun] *formal* connected with young people who commit crime: *juvenile crime* | *a special prison for juvenile offenders* | ***juvenile delinquents*** (=young people who commit crimes)
youthful *especially written* seeming young, or typical of someone who is young – often used about someone who is no longer young: *a youthful*

Y

55-year-old | youthful enthusiasm | Andrew still has a slim youthful look about him.

COLLOCATIONS CHECK

small/little child/girl/boy
teenage girl/boy/daughter/mother/pregnancy
juvenile crime/offence/court/offender/delinquent
youthful enthusiasm/energy/face/look/appearance

young[2] *n* [plural] **1 the young** young people: *The young are easily misled.* THESAURUS BABY **2** a group of young animals that belong to a particular mother or type of animal: *The lioness fought to protect her young.*

young·er /ˈjʌŋgə $ -ər/ *adj* **sb the Younger** *old use* someone famous who lived in the past and had the same name as their mother or father → **elder**: *William Pitt the Younger*

ˌyoung ofˈfender *n* [C] a criminal in Britain who is not an adult according to the law

young·ster /ˈjʌŋstə $ -ər/ ●○○ *n* [C] *old-fashioned* a child or young person

your /jə; *strong* jɔː $ jər *strong* jɔːr/ ●●● S1 W1 *determiner* [possessive form of 'you']
1 used when speaking or writing to one or more people to show that something belongs to them or is connected with them: *Could you move your car? | Is that your brother over there? | Don't worry. It's not your fault. | Be aware of* ***your own*** *feelings.*
2 of or belonging to any person: *If you are facing north, east is on your right.*
3 *informal* used when mentioning something that is a typical example of a particular type of thing: *It was just your basic, ordinary hotel room – nothing special. | Your typical 60s pop group had three guitarists and a drummer.*

you're /jə; *strong* jɔː $ jər *strong* jʊr, jɔːr/ the short form of 'you are': *You're late.*

yours /jɔːz $ jɔːrz/ ●●● S1 W3 *pron* [possessive form of 'you']
1 used when speaking or writing to one or more people to refer to something that belongs to them or is connected with them: *This is our room, and yours is just across the hall. | A lot of people have money problems, but yours are more serious than most people's. | A cash prize of £10,000 or a new car – the choice is yours.* | **sth of yours** *Is Maria a* ***friend of yours****? | That bag of yours weighs a ton. | I've read that book of yours.*
2 be yours for the taking/asking if something desirable is yours for the taking or asking, you can easily obtain it: *If you want the job, it's yours for the asking.*
3 Yours faithfully *BrE* used to end a formal letter that begins 'Dear Sir' or 'Dear Madam'
4 Yours truly/Yours (*also* **Yours sincerely** *BrE*, **Sincerely yours** *AmE*) used to end a letter that begins with the title and name of the person you are writing to, for example 'Dear Mr. Graves'
5 yours truly *informal* used humorously to mean 'I' or 'me': *They all went out, leaving yours truly to clear up the mess.* → **up yours** at UP[1](30)

your·self /jɔːˈself $ jɔːr-/ ●●● S1 W2 *pron* [reflexive form of 'you'] (*plural* **yourselves** /-ˈselvz/)
1 used when talking to someone to show that they are affected by their own action: *Look at yourself in the mirror. | Come and warm yourselves by the fire. | Have you hurt yourself? | Go and buy yourself an ice cream.*
2 a) used to emphasize 'you': *If you don't trust me, you'd better go yourself. | You yourselves are the guilty ones. | It must be true. You told me so yourself.* **b)** used after 'like', 'as', or 'except' instead of 'you', especially to make what you are saying seem more formal or important: *Most of our customers are people like yourself.*
3 (all) by yourself a) alone: *You can't go home by yourself in the dark.* **b)** without help from anyone: *Do you think you can move the sofa by yourself?*
4 not seem/be/feel yourself *informal* to not feel or behave as you usually do, for example because you are upset or ill: *Are you all right? You don't seem yourself this morning.*
5 have sth (all) to yourself if you have something to yourself, you do not have to share it with anyone else: *I'm going out, so you'll have the place to yourself.* → DO-IT-YOURSELF, → **keep sth to yourself** at KEEP TO, → **keep yourself to yourself** at KEEP TO

youth /juːθ/ ●●● S2 W2 *n* (*plural* **youths** /juːðz $ juːðz, juːθs/)
1 [U] the period of time when someone is young, especially the period when someone is a teenager → **old age**: **in sb's youth** *Many of these people had used drugs in their youth.*

REGISTER
In everyday English, people usually say **when I was young**, rather than saying **in my youth**: *They were friends* ***when they were young****.*

2 [C] a teenage boy – used especially in newspapers to show disapproval: *a* ***gang of youths*** THESAURUS CHILD, MAN
3 [U] young people in general: **the youth of sth** ***The youth of today*** *are the pensioners of tomorrow.*
4 [U] the quality or state of being young OPP **age**: *Despite his youth, he had travelled alone. | The cream will restore youth and vitality to your skin.*

COLLOCATIONS

VERBS

spend your youth *She spent her youth in India.*
relive/recapture your youth (=do things you did when young, to try and experience youth again)

PHRASES

a misspent youth (=spent doing things that were bad or not useful) | **your lost youth** (=the time long ago when you were young) | **the days/dreams/friends etc of sb's youth**

ˈyouth club *n* [C] a meeting place for young people where they can have drinks, play games etc

ˈyouth ˌculture *n* [U] the interests and activities of young people, especially the music, films etc they enjoy

youth·ful /ˈjuːθfəl/ ●○○ *adj*
1 typical of young people, or seeming young: **youthful enthusiasm/energy/vigour** | **youthful appearance/looks/complexion** *She has managed to maintain her youthful appearance.* THESAURUS YOUNG
2 young: *The photo shows a smiling, youthful Burgos.* —**youthfully** *adv* —**youthfulness** *n* [U]

ˈyouth ˌhostel *n* [C] a place where people, especially young people who are travelling, can stay very cheaply for a short time

ˈyouth ˌhostelling *n* [U] *BrE* the activity of staying in youth hostels and walking or cycling between them: *I* ***went youth hostelling*** *in the Peak District.*

You·Tube /ˈjuːtjuːb $ -tuːb/ *trademark* a WEBSITE, started in 2005, where users can UPLOAD, watch, and share VIDEO CLIPS

you've /juːv/ the short form of 'you have': *You've broken it.*

yowl /jaʊl/ *v* [I] if an animal or a person yowls, they make a long loud cry, especially because they are unhappy or in pain SYN **howl**: *A tomcat was yowling out on the lawn.* —**yowl** *n* [C]

Yo-Yo /ˈjəʊ jəʊ $ ˈjoʊ joʊ/ *n* (*plural* **Yo-Yos**) [C] *trademark* a toy made of two circular parts that goes up and down a string that you hold in your hand

ˈyo-yo ˌdieting *n* [U] a situation in which someone loses weight by DIETing and then gains weight again, many times: *Yo-yo dieting is really bad for you.* —**yo-yo dieter** *n* [C]

yr. (*also* **yr** *BrE*) (*plural* **yrs.**) the written abbreviation of *year*

yu·an /jʊˈɑːn/ *n* (*plural* **yuan**) [C] the standard unit of money in China

yuc·ca /ˈjʌkə/ *n* [C] a desert plant with long pointed leaves on a thick straight stem

yuck, **yuk** /jʌk/ *interjection informal* used to show that you think something is very unpleasant: *Oh yuck! I hate mayonnaise.*

yuck·y /ˈjʌki/ *adj informal* extremely unpleasant: *They painted the bathroom a yucky green colour.* | *The food was yucky.*

yuk /jʌk/ *interjection* another spelling of YUCK

Yule /juːl/ *n* [C,U] *old use* Christmas

ˈyule log *n* [C] **1** a LOG (=thick piece of wood) that some people burn as a tradition on the evening before Christmas **2** *BrE* a chocolate cake shaped like a LOG and eaten at Christmas

Yule·tide /ˈjuːltaɪd/ *n* [C,U] *literary* Christmas: *Yuletide festivities*

yum /jʌm/ *interjection informal* said when you think something tastes very good

yum·my /ˈjʌmi/ ●●○ *adj informal* tasting very good: *This cake is really yummy.* | *'Treacle tart! Yummy!' said Simon.*

ˌyummy ˈmummy *n* [C] *BrE informal* a young mother who looks attractive and fashionable

yup·pie, **yuppy** /ˈjʌpi/ *n* [C] a young person with a professional job who seems to be interested only in earning a lot of money and buying expensive things

yup·pi·fy /ˈjʌpɪfaɪ/ *v* (**yuppified**, **yuppifying**, **yuppifies**) [T] *informal* to improve the buildings in an area, or to open expensive restaurants, shops etc so that YUPPIES will want to live in the buildings or use the restaurants etc: *The restaurant's yuppified interior was done in colors like teal and mauve.*

YURT

yurt /jɜːt $ jɜːrt/ *n* [C] a round tent used by NOMADS (=people who travel rather than living in one place) in central Asia

Zz

Z, **z** /zed $ ziː/ (*plural* **Z's, z's**) *n* **1** [C,U] the 26th and last letter of the English alphabet → **from A to Z** at A¹(7) **2 catch/get some Z's** *AmE informal* to sleep

za·ny /ˈzeɪni/ *adj* (*comparative* **zanier**, *superlative* **zaniest**) crazy or unusual in a way that is amusing: ***zany comedian*** *Vic Reeves*

zap /zæp/ *v* (**zapped**, **zapping**) *informal* **1** [T] to quickly attack or destroy something, especially using a beam of electricity: *Doctors have tried zapping tumors with high-voltage radiation.* | *The laser weapons are designed to zap enemy missiles.* **2** [I,T] to change CHANNELS on a television by using a REMOTE CONTROL: *Dave just sat there, zapping through all the channels.* **3** [T] to cook something in a MICROWAVE¹(1) **4** [T] to send information quickly from one computer to another: *Computers identify threats and zap the results back to US pilots in the war zone.*

zap·per /ˈzæpə $ -ər/ *n* [C] *informal* **1** a thing you use for changing CHANNELS on a television from a distance SYN **remote control 2** a piece of electrical equipment that attracts and kills insects

zeal /ziːl/ *n* [U] eagerness to do something, especially to achieve a particular religious or political aim: **religious/revolutionary/missionary etc zeal** *He approached the job with missionary zeal.* | **in your zeal to do sth** *In their zeal to catch drug dealers, police have ignored citizens' basic civil rights.* | **[+for]** *their zeal for privatization*

zeal·ot /ˈzelət/ *n* [C] someone who has extremely strong beliefs, especially religious or political beliefs, and is too eager to make other people share them: *religious zealots* —**zealotry** *n* [U]

zeal·ous /ˈzeləs/ *adj* someone who is zealous does or supports something with great energy: *a zealous preacher* | *zealous political activists* | **be zealous in (doing) sth** *No one was more zealous than Neil in supporting the proposal.* —**zealously** *adv*

ze·bra /ˈziːbrə, ˈze- $ ˈziːbrə/ *n* [C] an animal that looks like a horse but has black and white lines all over its body

ˌzebra ˈcrossing ●●○ *n* [C] *BrE* a place marked with black and white lines where people who are walking can cross a road safely SYN **crosswalk** *AmE* → **pelican crossing**

zed /zed/ *BrE*, **zee** /ziː/ *AmE n* [C] a way of writing the letter 'z' that shows how you pronounce it

zeit·geist /ˈzaɪtgaɪst/ *n* [singular] the general spirit or feeling of a period in history, as shown by people's ideas and beliefs at the time

Zen /zen/ (*also* **ˌZen ˈBuddhism**) *n* [U] a kind of Buddhism from Japan that emphasizes MEDITATION

zen·ith /ˈzenəθ $ ˈziː-/ *n* [C usually singular] **1** the most successful point in the development of something SYN **peak** OPP **nadir**: **reach its zenith/be at its zenith** *The Roman Empire reached its zenith around the year 100.* **2** *technical* the highest point that is reached by the Sun or the Moon in the sky

> **REGISTER**
> **Zenith** sounds rather literary. In everyday English, people usually say **peak**: *Her career was at its* ***peak****.*

zeph·yr /ˈzefə $ -ər/ *n* [C] *literary* a soft gentle wind

zep·pe·lin /ˈzepəlɪn/ *n* [C] a German AIRSHIP used in World War I

ze·ro¹ /ˈzɪərəʊ $ ˈziːroʊ/ ●●● S3 *number* (*plural* **zeros** *or* **zeroes**)

1 the number 0 SYN **nought** *BrE*: *Make x greater than or equal to zero.*

2 the point between + and - on a scale for measuring something, or the lowest point on a scale that shows how much there is left of something: *The petrol gauge was already at zero.*

3 a temperature of 0° on the Celsius or Fahrenheit scale: **above/below zero** *It was five degrees below zero last night.* → **ABSOLUTE ZERO, SUB-ZERO**

4 none at all, or the lowest possible amount: **sb's chances are zero** (=they have no chance of success) *Mike's chances of winning are virtually zero.* | *From 1971 to 1976 West Vancouver experienced zero population growth.*

zero² *v*

zero in on sb/sth *phr v* **1** to direct all your attention towards a particular person or thing SYN **home in on**: *She immediately zeroed in on the weak point in his argument.* **2** to aim a gun or other weapon towards something or someone

ˌzero ˈcarbon *adj* made or acting in a way that produces only a small amount of CARBON DIOXIDE, which is OFFSET (=balanced) by doing things that remove carbon dioxide from the air: *a zero carbon house*

ˈzero hour *n* [singular] the time when a military operation or an important event is planned to begin

ˈzero-hours *adj BrE* a zero-hours contract is one in which a worker may or may not be given any work in a week but must be available for work, and is only paid for the hours they work

ˌzero-sum ˈgame *n* [singular] a situation in which you receive as much money or advantages as you give away: *Diplomatic negotiations often aim at a zero-sum game.*

ˌzero ˈtolerance *n* [U] a way of dealing with crime in which every person who breaks the law, even in a very small way, is punished as severely as possible: *a policy of zero tolerance in inner-city areas*

zest /zest/ *n* **1** [U] eager interest and enjoyment: **[+for]** *She had a great* ***zest for life.*** **2** [singular, U] the quality of being exciting and interesting: *The danger of being caught* ***added*** *a certain* ***zest*** *to the affair.* **3** [U] the outer skin of an orange or LEMON, used in cooking → **peel**, **rind**: *grated orange zest* —**zestful** *adj* —**zestfully** *adv*

zet·ta·byte /ˈzetəbaɪt/ *n* [C] a BILLION TERABYTES

zig·gu·rat /ˈzɪgəræt/ *n* [C] an ancient Middle Eastern structure which has smaller and smaller upper levels and a TEMPLE on top

zig·zag¹ /ˈzɪgzæg/ *n* [C] a pattern that looks like a line of z's joined together: *a zigzag path along the cliff* → see picture at **PATTERN¹**

zigzag² *v* (**zigzagged**, **zigzagging**) [I] to move forward in sharp angles, first to the left and then to the right etc: *The path zigzagged down the hillside.*

zilch /zɪltʃ/ *n* [U] *informal* nothing at all: *'How much money is left?' 'Zilch.'*

zil·lion /ˈzɪljən/ *number informal* a very large number of things: **a zillion** *I've seen that movie a zillion times.* | **zillions of sth** *zillions of mosquitoes*

Zim·mer frame /ˈzɪmə ˌfreɪm $ -mər-/ *trademark BrE* a type of metal frame that people use to help them walk if they are old or ill

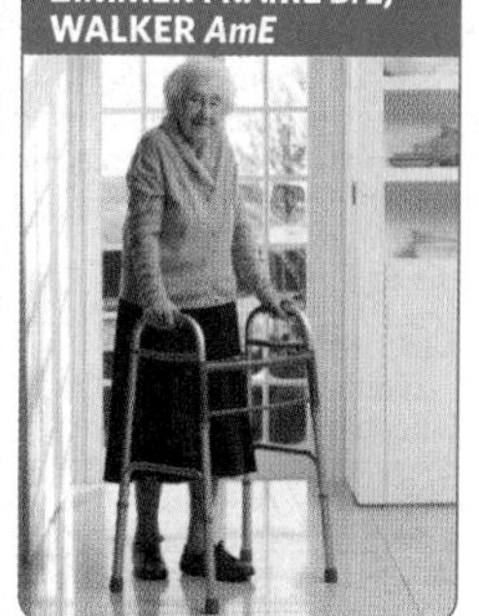

ZIMMER FRAME *BrE*/ WALKER *AmE*

zinc /zɪŋk/ *n* [U] a blue-white metal that is used to make BRASS and to cover and protect objects made of iron. It is a chemical ELEMENT: symbol Zn

zine /ziːn/ *n* [C] *informal* a small magazine, usually about popular culture, that is written by people who are not professional writers

zing¹ /zɪŋ/ *n* [U] *informal* the quality of being full of energy or taste: *Lemon juice adds zing to drinks.* —**zingy** *adj*

zing² *v* [I always + adv/prep] *informal* to move quickly, making a whistling noise SYN **whistle**: **[+past/off]** *He could hear the bullets zinging past his head.*

zing·er /ˈzɪŋə $ -ər/ *n* [C] *AmE informal* a clever humorous remark that might also be insulting

Zi·on·is·m /ˈzaɪənɪzəm/ *n* [U] support for the establishment and development of a state for the Jews in Israel —**Zionist** *n* [C], *adj*

zip¹ /zɪp/ ●●● S3 *n*

1 [C] *BrE* two lines of small metal or plastic pieces that slide together to fasten a piece of clothing SYN **zipper** *AmE*: *The zip on my skirt had broken.* | **do up/undo a zip** *Your zip's undone at the back.*

2 [U] *informal* speed, energy, or excitement: *This car goes with a bit more zip than my last one.* | *A spoonful of mustard will give the dish some zip.*

3 [singular] *AmE informal* nothing at all or zero: *We beat them 10 to zip.* | *'How much money do you have left?' 'Zip!'*

zip² *v* (**zipped**, **zipping**) **1** [T] to fasten something using a zip: *'I'll see you tomorrow,' said John, zipping his jacket.* | **zip sth shut/open** *Olsen zipped the bag shut.* | *He zipped open the case* (=unfastened it). | **zip sth together** *The two sleeping bags can be zipped together to make a double.* **2** [I always + adv/prep] *informal* to go somewhere or do something very quickly SYN **whizz**, **zoom**: **[+through/past/along etc]** *We zipped through customs in no time.* **3 zip it/zip your lip** *AmE spoken informal* used to tell someone not to say anything about something, or to tell them to be quiet: *You'd better zip your lip or you'll be in trouble!*

zip up *phr v* to fasten something using a zip, or to become fastened using a zip OPP **unzip**: *The dress zipped up at the front.* | **zip sth ↔ up** *He was zipping up a small brown suitcase.* | **zip sb up** *Could you zip me up* (=fasten my dress) *please? I can't reach.*

ˈzip code ●●○ *n* [C] *AmE* a number that you write at the end of an address on an envelope, package etc. The zip code shows the exact area where someone lives and helps the post office deliver the post more quickly. SYN **postcode** *BrE*

ˈzip file (*also* **ˈzipped file**) *n* [C] *technical* a computer FILE that has been made smaller so that it is easier to store and move

zip·per /ˈzɪpə $ -ər/ ●●● S3 *n* [C] *especially AmE* two lines of small metal or plastic pieces that slide together to fasten a piece of clothing SYN **zip** *BrE*

zip·po /ˈzɪpəʊ $ -poʊ/ *n* [singular] *AmE informal* nothing at all or zero

zip·py /ˈzɪpi/ *adj informal* **1** fast: *a zippy little sports car* **2** exciting: *a magazine with a zippy title*

ˈzip tie *n* [C] a thin piece of plastic that is used to fasten things together

zip-tie, **zip·tie** /ˈzɪptaɪ/ *v* [T] to fasten something together with a ZIP TIE

ˈzip wire (*also* **ˈzip line**) *n* [C] a strong wire going from a high place to a lower place, with a PULLEY hanging from it. People hold onto the pulley and travel along the wire, usually for fun.

zit /zɪt/ *n* [C] *informal* a PIMPLE

zith·er /ˈzɪðə $ -ər/ *n* [C] a musical instrument from Eastern Europe that consists of a flat box with strings stretched across it. You play it by pulling the strings with your fingers or a PLECTRUM (=small piece of plastic, metal etc).

Z-list /ˈzed ˌlɪst $ ˈziː-/ *adj informal* not very famous, or famous without having achieved anything - used to show disapproval: *pop stars' daughters and other Z-list celebrities*

Z-list·er /ˈzed ˌlɪstə $ ˈziː ˌlɪstər/ *n* [C] *informal* someone who appears on television, in magazines etc but is not very famous, or is famous without having achieved anything - used to show disapproval: *He can only get Z-listers to appear on his show nowadays.*

zo·di·ac /ˈzəʊdiæk $ ˈzoʊ-/ *n* **the zodiac** an imaginary area through which the Sun, Moon, and PLANETs appear to travel, which some people believe influences our lives → **astrology**: **sign of the zodiac** (=one of the 12 parts that this area is divided into) *'Which sign of the zodiac were you born under?' 'Leo.'* → **HOROSCOPE**

zom·bie /ˈzɒmbi $ ˈzɑːm-/ *n* [C] **1** *informal* someone who moves very slowly and does not seem to be thinking about what they are doing, especially because they are very tired: *I walked around like a zombie for most of the day.* **2** a dead person whose body is made to move by magic, according to some African and Caribbean religions **3** (*also* **zombie machine/computer**) a computer that someone has secretly gained control of and uses to do things such as send SPAM (=unwanted emails sent to a large number of people)

zon·al /ˈzəʊnl $ ˈzoʊnl/ *adj technical* relating to or arranged in zones

zone¹ /zəʊn $ zoʊn/ ●●○ W3 *n* [C]

1 a large area that is different from other areas around it in some way: *San Francisco and Tokyo are both located in earthquake zones.* | *The government has set up a special economic zone to promote private enterprise.* THESAURUS **AREA**

2 in the zone *informal* having all your attention on what you are doing, especially playing a sport, and doing it well: *When I'm in the zone, every shot seems easy.* → **buffer zone** at BUFFER[1](3), → NO-FLY ZONE, TIME ZONE

COLLOCATIONS

ADJECTIVES/NOUN + zone

a danger zone *Civilians were told to leave the danger zone.*
a war/battle/combat zone *Planes were diverted to avoid flying over the war zone.*
an earthquake zone (=where earthquakes are quite likely to happen) *It's not advisable to build nuclear reactors in an earthquake zone.*
a disaster zone *The damage is so serious that the government has declared the city a disaster zone.*
an economic zone | **an enterprise zone** (=where businesses are encouraged) | **a no-parking zone** | **a 20 mph/30 mph etc zone** (=where vehicles' speed is limited to 20 mph, 30 mph etc) | **a demilitarized zone** (=where soldiers and military activities are not allowed) | **a nuclear-free/smoke-free etc zone** (=where nuclear weapons, smoking etc is not allowed)

VERBS

set up/establish/create a zone *The government intends to set up an enterprise zone in the region.*
enter a zone *He didn't see the sign saying he'd entered a 20 mph zone.*

zone[2] *v* [T] *AmE* if an area of land is zoned, it is officially kept to be used for a particular purpose: **be zoned for sth** *The land is currently zoned for residential use.*

zone out *phr v informal* to stop paying attention, for example because you are bored or tired: *He tends to zone out when I talk to him about my job.*

zoned /zəʊnd $ zoʊnd/ (*also* ˌ**zoned ˈout**) *adj* [not before noun] *AmE informal* unable to think clearly and quickly, especially because you are tired or have taken drugs

zon·ing /ˈzəʊnɪŋ $ ˈzoʊ-/ *n* [U] a system of choosing areas to be developed for particular purposes, such as houses or shops, when planning a town

zonked /zɒŋkt $ zɑːŋkt/ (*also* ˌ**zonked ˈout**) *adj* [not before noun] *informal* very tired or suffering from the effects of drugs, so that you do not want to do anything: *I'm really zonked.*

zoo /zuː/ ●●● S3 *n* (*plural* **zoos**) [C] a place, usually in a city, where animals of many kinds are kept so that people can go to look at them → **wildlife park**

ˈ**zoo-ˌkeeper** *n* [C] someone who looks after animals in a zoo

ˌ**zoological ˈgarden** *n* [C] *formal* a zoo

zo·ol·o·gist /zuːˈɒlədʒəst, zəʊˈɒ- $ zoʊˈɑːl-/ *n* [C] a scientist who studies animals and their behaviour

zo·ol·o·gy /zuːˈɒlədʒi, zəʊˈɒ- $ zoʊˈɑːl-/ *n* [U] the scientific study of animals and their behaviour —**zoological** /ˌzuːəˈlɒdʒɪkəl◂, ˌzəʊ- $ ˌzoʊəˈlɑː-/ *adj* —**zoologically** /-kli/ *adv*

zoom[1] /zuːm/ *v* [I] *informal* **1** [always + adv/prep] to go somewhere or do something very quickly SYN **whizz, zip**: **zoom off/around/down etc** *Brenda jumped in the car and zoomed off.* | *The work was really easy and I was able to zoom through it in a couple of hours.* **2** (*also* **zoom up**) to increase suddenly and quickly SYN **escalate**: **[+to]** *Inflation zoomed to 123%.*

zoom in *phr v* if a camera zooms in, it makes the person or thing that you are taking a picture of seem bigger and closer: **[+on]** *The camera zoomed in on the child's face.*

zoom out *phr v* if a camera zooms out, it makes the person or thing that you are taking a picture of seem smaller and further away

zoom[2] *n* [singular] *informal* a sound made by a vehicle that is travelling fast

ˈ**zoom ˌlens** *n* [C] a camera LENS that can change from a distant to a close view

zoot suit /ˈzuːt suːt, -sjuːt $ -suːt/ *n* [C] a suit that consists of wide trousers and a JACKET with wide shoulders, worn especially in the 1940s and 1950s

zuc·chi·ni /zʊˈkiːni/ *n* [C] *AmE* a long vegetable with a dark green skin SYN **courgette** *BrE* → see picture at VEGETABLE[1]

Zu·lu /ˈzuːluː/ *n* **1** [C] someone who belongs to a race of black people who live in South Africa **2** [U] the language used by the Zulu people —**Zulu** *adj*

Zum·ba /ˈzʊmbə/ *n* [U] *trademark* a type of exercise that includes dance movements and is done to Latin American music

zwie·back /ˈzwiːbæk $ ˈzwaɪ-/ *n* [U] *AmE* a type of hard dry bread, often given to babies SYN **rusk** *BrE*

zy·de·co /ˈzaɪdəkəʊ $ -koʊ/ *n* [U] a type of Cajun music that is popular in southern Louisiana that combines the styles of French and Caribbean music with the BLUES

zy·gote /ˈzaɪgəʊt $ -goʊt/ *n* [C] *technical* a cell that is formed when an egg is FERTILIZEd

Zzz used in writing to represent sleep

Longman Communication 9000

Longman dictionaries have traditionally highlighted the 3000 most frequent words in English, so that learners know which words they need to learn first. These 3000 words enable you to understand 86% of the language. In order to understand a wide variety of authentic texts, however, research into vocabulary acquisition has shown that you may need to know as many as 8000 - 9000 word families. For this reason, we have now created a list of the 9000 most frequent words in English - the *Longman Communication 9000* - and we are highlighting it for the first time in this new edition of the *Longman Dictionary of Contemporary English.*

The *Longman Communication 9000* is divided into three bands (marked with circles):

●●● high frequency words - indicates the 3000 most frequent words

●●○ mid frequency words - indicates the next 3000 most frequent words (3000-6000)

●○○ lower frequency words - indicates the next 3000 most frequent words (6000-9000)

In addition to this new information, we have retained the spoken and written frequency information that is unique to Longman dictionaries. This information is marked with the following symbols:

W1 and S1 - indicate the 1000 most frequent words in written or spoken English

W2 and S2 - indicate the next 1000 most frequent words (1000-2000)

W3 and S3 - indicate the next 1000 most frequent words (2000-3000)

This frequency information is based on statistical analysis of the 390 million words contained in the Longman Corpus Network - a collection of corpuses, or databases, of authentic English language. The *Longman Communication 9000* represents the core of the English language and shows you which words are the most important to learn and study in order to communicate effectively in both speech and writing. The *Longman Communication 9000* is not, however, solely based on the raw frequency of words in speech and writing; it is also based on learner's needs, through an analysis of the *Longman Learner's Corpus*, and on an examination of coursebooks from elementary to advanced levels. This means that the *Communication 9000* takes account of, for example, words for food, or words that describe the language (*verb, adjective*) which are sometimes infrequent in written corpuses but commonly learned in classrooms.

Take for example the verb acquire. It is marked as ●●● W3 which means that it is in the top 3000-6000 words in English as a whole, and more specifically one of the top 3000 words in written English. Note that it has no marker for spoken English, because, according to corpus analysis, it is not part of the top 3000 most frequent words in spoken English. However, the entry also indicates that a synonym for *acquire* is *buy*, which is marked as ●●○ S1 W1. The conclusion to be drawn from this is that in speaking and writing, *buy* is the most frequent and often the most appropriate verb to use. In writing, however, you may want to use *acquire* in order to lift your writing to a more advanced level.

Learning a language can be exciting, but also sometimes difficult and frustrating because there are so many things to learn and it is difficult to know what to focus on. The frequency markers that identify the *Longman Communication 9000* help you see clearly how frequent words are, and which are frequent in written and spoken English. This enables you to focus more attention on mastering the meanings, grammatical patterns and collocations of these words.

The list printed here only shows the most frequent 3000 words in English and their spoken or written indicators. The full list of 9000 words is available in the *Longman Dictionary of Contemporary English* online at www.longmandictionaries.com.

●●● 3000 high frequency words | Full *Communication 9000* at www.longmandictionaries.com

The full list of 9000 words is available in the *Longman Dictionary of Contemporary English* online at www.longmandictionaries.com.

a *indefinite article, determiner* S1 W1
ability *n* S2 W1
able *adj* S1 W1
about *prep* S1 W1
about *adv* S1 W1
about *adj* S3 W2
above adv, *prep* S2 W1
abroad *adv* S2 W3
absence *n* S3 W2
absent *adj* W2
absolutely *adv* S1 W3
accept *v* S1 W1
access *n* S2 W1
accident *n* S2 W2
according to *prep* S2 W1
account *n* S1 W1
accurate *adj* S2 W3
achieve *v* S2 W1
achievement *n* S3 W2
across adv, *prep* S1 W1
act *n* S1 W1
act *v* S2 W1
action *n* S1 W1
active *adj* S2 W2
activity *n* S2 W1
actor *n* W3
actress *n* W3
actual *adj* S1 W2
actually *adv* S1 W1
ad *n* S3 W3
add *v* S1 W1
addition *n* S3 W1
address *n* S2 W2
adjective *n*
admire *v* S3
admit *v* S2 W1
adult *n* S2 W2
adult *adj* W3
advanced *adj* W3
advantage *n* S2 W1
adventure *n* W2
adverb *n*
advertisement *n* S3
advice *n* S2 W2
advise *v* S2 W2
affair *n* S2 W1
affect *v* S2 W1
afford *v* S1 W3
afraid *adj* S1 W2
after prep, *conjunction, adv* S1 W1
afternoon *n* S1 W2
afterwards *adv* S2 W3
again *adv* S1 W1
against *prep* S1 W1
age *n* S1 W1
ago *adv* S1 W1
agree *v* S1 W1
agreement *n* S2 W1
ahead *adv* S1 W2
aim *n* S2 W2
aim *v* S2 W2
air *n* S1 W1
aircraft *n* S2 W2
airport *n* S3 W3
alarm *n* S2
alcohol *n* S2 W2
alive *adj* S2 W3
all *determiner, predeterminer*, pron S1 W1
all *adv* S1 W1
allow *v* S1 W1
all right adj, adv, *interjection* S1 W2
almost *adv* S1 W1
alone adj, *adv* S2 W1
along *adv* S1 W1
along *prep* S1 W1
aloud *adv* S3 W2
alphabet *n* W3
alphabetical *adj* W3
already *adv* S1 W1
also *adv* S1 W1
alter *v* S3 W3
although *conjunction* S1 W1
altogether *adv* S2 W3
always *adv* S1 W1
a.m. W2
amazed *adj* S2
amazing *adj* S2
among *prep* S2 W1
amount *n* S1 W1
an *indefinite article, determiner* S1 W1
ancient *adj* W2
and *conjunction* S1 W1
angle *n* S3 W3
angry *adj* S2 W2
animal *n* S1 W1
announce *v* S2 W1
announcement *n* S3 W3
annoyed *adj* S2
annoying *adj* S2
another *determiner, pron* S1 W1
answer *n* S1 W1
answer *v* S1 W2
any *determiner, pron* S1 W1
any *adv* S2
anybody *pron* S1 W3
anymore *adv* S1 W3
anyone *pron* S1 W1
anything *pron* S1 W1
anytime *adv* S3
anyway *adv* S1 W2
anywhere *adv* S1 W3
apart adv, *adj* S2 W1
apartment *n* S2 W3
apologize *v* S2
apology *n* S3
apparently *adv* S1 W2
appeal *n* S2 W1
appeal *v* S3 W3
appear *v* S2 W1
appearance *n* W2
apple *n* S2 W3
application *n* S1 W1
apply *v* S1 W1
appointment *n* S2 W2
approach *n* S2 W1
approach *v* S3 W2
appropriate *adj* S2 W1
approve *v* S3 W2
April *n* S2 W2
area *n* S1 W1
argue *v* S2 W1
argument *n* S1 W1
arm *n* S1 W1
army *n* S1 W1
around adv, *prep* S1 W1
arrange *v* S2 W2
arrangement *n* S2 W2
arrest *v* S3 W2
arrest *n* S3 W2
arrival *n* W3
arrive *v* S2 W1
art *n* S1 W1
article *n* S2 W1
artificial *adj* S3
artist *n* S3 W2
as prep, *adv* S1 W1
as *conjunction* S1 W1
ask *v* S1 W1
asleep *adj* S2
aspect *n* S2 W1
assignment *n* S2
assume *v* S2 W1
at *prep* S1 W1
atmosphere *n* S3 W2
attach *v* S2 W2
attack *n* S2 W2
attack *v* S3 W2
attempt *n* S2 W1
attempt *v* S2 W2
attend *v* S2 W2
attention *n* S2 W1
attitude *n* S2 W1
attorney *n* S2 W3
attract *v* S2 W2
attractive *adj* S2 W2
audience *n* S2 W2
August *n* S2 W2
aunt *n* S3 W3
author *n* W2
authority *n* W1
autumn *n* W3
available *adj* S1 W1
average *adj* S2 W2
average *n* S2 W2
avoid *v* S2 W1
awake *adj* S2
award *n* S3 W2
aware *adj* S1 W1
away *adv* S1 W1
awful *adj* S1

baby *n* S1 W1
back *adv* S1 W1
back *n* S1 W1
back *v* S2 W3
back *adj* S2 W3
background *n* S2 W2
backwards *adv* S3
bad *adj* S1 W1
badly *adv* S3 W3
bag *n* S1 W2
bake *v* S3
balance *n* S2 W2
balance *v* S3
ball *n* S1 W2
banana *n* S2
band *n* S2 W2
bank *n* S1 W1
bar *n* S1 W1
barbecue *n* S3
base *v* S1 W1
base *n* S2 W2
baseball *n* S3 W2
basement *n* S2
basic *adj* S2 W1
basically *adv* S1
basis *n* S2 W1
basket *n* S3
basketball *n* S3
bat *n* S3
bath *n* S2 W3

S1 = one of the 1000 most frequent words in Spoken English W1 = one of the 1000 most frequent words in Written English
S2 = one of the 2000 most frequent words in Spoken English W2 = one of the 2000 most frequent words in Written English
S3 = one of the 3000 most frequent words in Spoken English W3 = one of the 3000 most frequent words in Written English

bathroom *n* S2 W3
battery *n* S2
battle *n* W2
be *auxiliary verb* S1 W1
be *v* S1 W1
beach *n* S2 W2
bean *n* S2
bear *v* S2 W2
beard *n* S3
beat *v* S2 W2
beautiful *adj* S1 W2
beauty *n* S3 W2
because *conjunction* S1 W1
because *prep* S1 W1
become *v* S1 W1
bed *n* S1 W1
bedroom *n* S1 W2
beef *n* S3
beer *n* S2 W3
before *conjunction* S1 W1
before *prep* S1 W1
before *adv* S1 W1
begin *v* S1 W1
beginner *n* W3
beginning *n* S1 W2
behave *v* S3 W3
behaviour *n* S2 W1
behind prep, *adv* S1 W1
belief *n* S3 W2
believe *v* S1 W1
bell *n* S2 W3
belong *v* S2 W2
below adv, *prep* S2 W2
belt *n* S2 W3
bench *n* S2 W3
bend *v* S3 W3
beneath adv, *prep* W2
benefit *n* S2 W1
beside *prep* S3 W2
best *adj* S1 W1
best *adv* S1 W2
best *n* S2 W2
bet *v* S1
bet *n* S3
better *adj* S1 W1
better *adv* S1 W1
between adv, *prep* S1 W1
beyond prep, *adv* S2 W1
bicycle *n* W3
big *adj* S1 W1
bike *n* S2
bill *n* S1 W1
billion number W2
bin *n* S2
biology *n* W3
bird *n* S2 W2
birth *n* S2 W2
birthday *n* S1 W3
biscuit *n* S2
bit adv, *pron* S1
bit *n* S1 W1
bite *v* S2
bite *n* S3
black *adj* S1 W1
black *n* S2 W2
blackboard *n* S3
blame *v* S2 W3
blame *n* S3 W2
blind *adj* S2 W3
block *n* S2 W2
block *v* S3
blond *adj* S3
blonde *adj* S3
blood *n* S2 W1
blouse *n* S3
blow *v* S2 W3
blue *adj* S1 W2
blue *n* S3 W3
board *n* S1 W1
boat *n* S1 W2
body *n* S1 W1
boil *v* S3
bomb *n* S3 W3
bomb *v* W3
bone *n* S2 W2
book *n* S1 W1
bookshelf *n* S3
bookshop *n* W3
boot *n* S2 W3
border *n* S3 W2
bored *adj* S3
boring *adj* S2
born *v* S1 W1
borrow *v* S2 W3
boss *n* S2 W3
both *determiner, predeterminer, pron* S1 W1
bother *v* S1 W3
bottle *n* S1 W2
bottom *n* S1 W3
bottom *adj* S1 W3
bounce *v* S3
bowl *n* S2 W3
bowling *n* S3
box *n* S1 W1
boy *n* S1 W1
boyfriend *n* S3
brain *n* S2 W2
brake *n* S3
branch *n* S2 W2
brave *adj* S3
bread *n* S2 W3
break *v* S1 W1
break *n* S2 W2
breakfast *n* S2 W2
breast *n* S3
breath *n* S3 W2
breathe *v* S3 W3
brick *n* S2 W3
bridge *n* S2 W2
brief *adj* S2 W2
bright *adj* S2 W2
brilliant *adj* S2 W3
bring *v* S1 W1
broad *adj* S2 W2
broken *adj* S3 W2
brother *n* S1 W1
brown *adj* S2 W2
brown *n* S2 W2
brush *n* S3
brush *v* S3
bucket *n* S2
build *v* S1 W1
building *n* S1 W1
bump *v* S3
bunch *n* S2
burger *n* S3
burn *v* S2 W3
bury *v* W3
bus *n* S1 W2
bush *n* S3
business *n* S1 W1
businessman *n* W3
busy *adj* S1 W2
but *conjunction* S1 W1
but *prep* S2 W3
butter *n* S2
button *n* S2
buy *v* S1 W1
by *prep* S1 W1
by *adv* S1 W1
bye *interjection* S1

---

cab *n* S3
cable *n* W3
café *n* S2
cafeteria *n* S3
cake *n* S2 W3
calculate *v* S2 W3
calculator *n* S3
calendar *n* S3
call *v* S1 W1
call *n* S1 W1
calm *adj* S3 W3
camera *n* S2 W3
camp *n* S3 W3
camping *n* S3
campus *n* S2 W3
can *modal verb* S1 W1
can *n* S2
cancel *v* S2
cancer *n* S2 W2
candidate *n* W2
candy *n* S3
cannot *modal verb* W1
can't S1
cap *n* S3
capital *n* S3 W1
captain *n* W3
car *n* S1 W1
card *n* S1 W2
cardigan *n* S3
care *n* S1 W1
care *v* S1 W2
career *n* S2 W2
careful *adj* S1 W2
carefully *adv* S2 W2
car park *n* S3
carpet *n* S2 W3
carrot *n* S3
carry *v* S1 W1
case *n* S1 W1
cash *n* S2 W2
castle *n* W3
cat *n* S1 W3
catch *v* S1 W1
category *n* S2 W2
cattle *n* W3
cause *v* S1 W1
cause *n* S2 W1
ceiling *n* S3 W3
celebrate *v* W3
cell *n* S3 W2
cellphone *n* S2 W3
cent *n* S1 W1
centimetre *n* S3 W3
central *adj* S1 W1
centre *n* S1 W1
century *n* S2 W1
cereal *n* S3
ceremony *n* S3 W2
certain *adj* S1 W1
certainly *adv* S1 W1
chain *n* S3 W2
chair *n* S1 W2
challenge *n* S2 W2
challenge *v* S3 W3
champion *n* W3
championship *n* W3
chance *n* S1 W1
change *v* S1 W1
change *n* S1 W1
channel *n* S3 W2
chapter *n* S3 W1
character *n* S1 W1
charge *n* S1 W1
charge *v* S1 W2
chart *n* S3 W3
chase *v* S3
cheap *adj* S1 W2
check *v* S1 W2
check *n* S1 W3
cheek *n* W3
cheese *n* S2 W3
chemical *n* S3 W3
chemical *adj* W3
chemistry *n* W3
cheque *n* S2
chest *n* S2 W3
chew *v* S2
chicken *n* S2
chief *adj* S2 W2

chief *n* W3
child *n* S1 W1
chin *n* W3
chip *n* S2 W3
chocolate *n* S2
choice *n* S1 W1
choose *v* S1 W1
chop *v* S3
Christmas *n* S2 W2
church *n* S1 W1
cigarette *n* S2 W3
cinema *n* S3
circle *n* S2 W2
circumstance *n* S2 W1
citizen *n* S2 W2
city *n* S1 W1
claim *v* S1 W1
claim *n* S2 W1
class *n* S1 W1
classroom *n* S3 W3
clean *adj* S2 W2
clean *v* S1 W3
clear *adj* S1 W1
clear *v* S1 W2
clearly *adv* S1 W1
clever *adj* S2
click *v* S3
client *n* S2 W1
climb *v* W2
clock *n* S2 W3
close *v* S1 W1
close *adj* S1 W1
close *adv* S2 W2
closed *adj* S3
closely *adv* S3 W2
closet *n* S3
clothes *n* S2 W2
clothing *n* S3 W3
cloud *n* S3 W3
cloudy *adj* S2 W3
club *n* S1 W1
clue *n* S2
coach *n* S3 W2
coal *n* S2 W2
coast *n* S3 W2
coat *n* S2 W3
code *n* S2 W2
coffee *n* S1 W2
coin *n* S3
cold *adj* S1 W1
cold *n* S2 W3
collar *n* S3
colleague *n* S2 W2
collect *v* S1 W2
collection *n* S2 W1
college *n* S1 W2
colour *n* S1 W1
comb *n* S3
comb *v* S3
combination *n* S3 W2
combine *v* S3 W2

come *v* S1 W1
comedy *n* W3
comfortable *adj* S2 W3
comment *n* S1 W2
commit *v* S2 W2
committee *n* S3 W1
common *adj* S1 W1
communicate *v* S3 W3
communication *n* S2 W1
community *n* S1 W1
company *n* S1 W1
compare *v* S1 W1
compete *v* S3 W3
competition *n* S2 W1
complain *v* S2 W3
complaint *n* S3 W3
complete *adj* S2 W1
complete *v* S2 W1
completely *adv* S1 W2
complicated *adj* S2 W3
computer *n* S1 W1
concentrate *v* S2 W2
concentration *n* S3 W2
concern *n* S3 W1
concerned *adj* S2 W2
concert *n* S3 W3
condition *n* S2 W1
conference *n* S2 W1
confidence *n* S2 W2
confident *adj* S3 W3
confirm *v* S2 W2
confused *adj* S3
confusing *adj* S3
congratulation *n* S3
connect *v* S2 W2
connected *adj* S3 W3
connection *n* S3 W2
consider *v* S1 W1
consist *v* W3
contact *n* S2 W2
contact *v* S2 W2
contain *v* S2 W1
content *n* S3 W2
continue *v* S1 W1
contract *n* S1 W1
control *n* S1 W1
control *v* S2 W1
conversation *n* S1 W2
cook *v* S1 W3
cook *n* S2
cookie *n* S3 W3
cool *adj* S2 W3
copy *n* S1 W2
copy *v* S2
corner *n* S1 W2
correct *adj* S1 W2
cost *n* S1 W1
cost *v* S1 W2
cotton *n* W3
couch *n* S3
cough *v* S3 W3

cough *n* S3 W3
could *modal verb* S1 W1
count *v* S2 W3
counter *n* S3
country *n* S1 W1
countryside *n* S3 W3
county *n* W2
couple *n* S1 W1
course *n* S1 W1
court *n* S1 W1
cousin *n* S2
cover *v* S1 W1
cover *n* S1 W2
cow *n* S2
crack *v* S2 W2
crack *n* S3
crash *v* S3 W2
crash *n* S3 W2
crazy *adj* S2
cream *n* S2
create *v* S2 W1
creature *n* W3
credit *n* S2 W2
credit card *n* S2
crew *n* S3 W3
crime *n* S2 W2
criminal *adj* S3 W2
criminal *n* W3
criticize *v* W3
crop *n* W3
cross *v* S2 W2
cross *n* S3 W3
cross *adj* S2
crowd *n* S3 W2
crowded *adj* S3
cruel *adj* S3
cry *v* S2 W2
cultural *adj* W2
culture *n* S2 W1
cup *n* S1 W1
cupboard *n* S2
curly *adj* S3
current *adj* S2 W2
currently *adv* S2 W2
curtain *n* S3 W3
cushion *n* S3
custom *n* W3
customer *n* S1 W1
cut *v* S1 W1
cut *n* S2 W2
cute *adj* S2

---

dad *n* S1 W3
daddy *n* S1
daily *adj* S3 W2
damage *n* S3 W2
damage *v* S3 W3
dance *n* S2 W3
dance *v* S2 W3
dancer *n* W3
danger *n* S2 W2

dangerous *adj* S2 W2
dark *adj* S2 W1
dark *n* S3 W3
darkness *n* W3
data *n* S1 W1
date *n* S1 W1
daughter *n* S1 W1
day *n* S1 W1
dead *adj* S1 W1
deal *n* S1 W1
deal *v* S1 W1
dear *interjection* S1
dear *adj* W1
death *n* S1 W1
debate *n* S2 W2
debt *n* S3 W2
decade *n* W1
December *n* S2 W2
decide *v* S1 W1
decision *n* S1 W1
deck *n* S3
deep *adj* S2 W1
deep *adv* W3
deeply *adv* W3
defeat *n* W3
defeat *v* W3
defence *n* S2 W1
defend *v* S3 W3
define *v* S2 W2
definitely *adv* S1
degree *n* S2 W1
delicious *adj* S2
deliver *v* S2 W2
delivery *n* S3 W3
demand *n* S2 W1
demand *v* W2
dentist *n* S3
deny *v* S3 W2
department *n* S2 W1
depend *v* S1 W2
depth *n* S3 W3
describe *v* S2 W1
description *n* S2 W2
deserve *v* S3 W3
design *n* S2 W1
design *v* S3 W1
desire *n* W2
desk *n* S2 W2
despite *prep* S3 W1
dessert *n* S2
destroy *v* S2 W2
detail *n* S2 W1
detailed *adj* W2
develop *v* S2 W1
development *n* S1 W1
dialogue *n* S3
dictionary *n* S3
die *v* S1 W1
diet *n* S3 W2
difference *n* S1 W1
different *adj* S1 W1

difficult *adj* S1 W1
difficulty *n* S2 W1
dig *v* S2
dining room *n* S3
dinner *n* S1 W2
direct *adj* S2 W1
direct *v* S3 W2
direction *n* S1 W1
directly *adv* S2 W2
director *n* S2 W1
dirt *n* S3
dirty *adj* S2 W3
disabled *adj* S3 W3
disadvantage *n* W2
disagree *v* S3
disappear *v* S2 W2
disappoint *v* W3
disappointed *adj* S3 W3
disaster *n* S3 W3
discover *v* S2 W1
discuss *v* S2 W1
discussion *n* S2 W1
disease *n* S3 W1
disgusting *adj* S2
dish *n* S2 W2
display *n* S3 W2
display *v* W2
distance *n* S2 W2
district *n* S3 W2
divide *v* S2 W2
division *n* S3 W1
divorce *n* S2 W2
divorce *v* S2 W3
divorced *adj* S2 W3
do *auxiliary verb* S1 W1
do *v* S1 W1
doctor *n* S1 W1
document *n* S2 W2
dog *n* S1 W1
doll *n* S3
dollar *n* S1 W2
door *n* S1 W1
dot *n* S2
double *adj* S1 W2
double *n* S3 W3
double *v* S3
doubt *n* S1 W1
doubt *v* S2
down *adv, prep, adj* S1 W1
download *v* S2 W2
downstairs *adv* S2
downtown *adv* S3 W3
dozen number S2 W3
Dr W2
drag *v* S3 W3
drama *n* W3
draw *v* S1 W1
drawer *n* S3
drawing *n* S3 W3
dream *n* S2 W2
dream *v* S3 W3
dress *n* S2 W2
dress *v* S2 W2
drink *v* S1 W2
drink *n* S1 W2
drive *v* S1 W1
drive *n* S2 W2
driver *n* S1 W2
drop *v* S1 W2
drop *n* S2 W3
drug *n* S2 W1
drugstore *n* S3
drum *n* S3
dry *adj* S2 W2
dry *v* S2 W3
duck *n* S3
due *adj* S1 W1
dump *v* S3
during *prep* S1 W1
dust *n* S3 W3
duty *n* S2 W1
DVD *n* S3 W3

---

each *determiner, pron, adv* S1 W1
each other *pron* S1 W1
ear *n* S2 W2
early *adj* S1 W1
early *adv* S1 W1
earn *v* S2 W2
earring *n* S3
earth *n* S2 W2
easily *adv* S2 W1
east *n* S2 W1
east *adj* S3 W3
east *adv* S2 W2
eastern *adj* S2 W2
easy *adj* S1 W1
easy *adv* S2
eat *v* S1 W1
economic *adj* S2 W1
economy *n* S2 W1
edge *n* S2 W2
education *n* S1 W1
effect *n* S1 W1
effective *adj* S2 W1
effectively *adv* S3 W2
efficient *adj* S3 W3
effort *n* S1 W1
egg *n* S1 W2
eight number, *n* S2 W2
eighteen number S3 W2
eighth *adj* S3 W3
eighty number W3
either *conjunction* S1 W1
either *determiner, pron* S1 W1
either *adv* S1 W2
elderly *adj* S3 W2
election *n* S2 W1
electric *adj* S2 W3
electricity *n* S2 W3
electronic *adj* S3 W3
element *n* S2 W1
elephant *n* W3
elevator *n* S3 W3
eleven number, *n* S3 W2
eleventh *adj* S3 W3
else *adv* S1 W1
elsewhere *adv* S3 W2
email *n* S1 W1
email *v* S1 W1
embarrassed *adj* S2
embarrassing *adj* S3
emergency *n* S3 W3
emotion *n* W3
emotional *adj* S3 W3
employ *v* S3 W2
employee *n* S2 W2
employer *n* S2 W2
employment *n* S2 W1
empty *adj* S2 W2
enable *v* S3 W1
encourage *v* S2 W1
end *n* S1 W1
end *v* S1 W1
enemy *n* W2
energy *n* S2 W1
engine *n* S2 W2
engineer *n* S3 W3
enjoy *v* S1 W1
enormous *adj* S2 W3
enough *adv* S1 W1
enough *determiner, pron* S1 W2
ensure *v* S2 W1
enter *v* S2 W1
entertainment *n* S3 W3
entire *adj* S3 W2
entirely *adv* S2 W2
entrance *n* S3 W3
entry *n* S3 W2
envelope *n* S3
environment *n* S1 W1
environmental *adj* S2 W2
equal *adj* S1 W2
equipment *n* S2 W2
eraser *n*
error *n* S3 W2
escape *v* S3 W2
especially *adv* S1 W1
essay *n* S3
essential *adj* S3 W2
establish *v* S2 W1
etc. *adv* W2
euro *n* S2 W2
even *adv* S1 W1
evening *n* S1 W1
event *n* S1 W1
eventually *adv* S1 W2
ever *adv* S1 W1
every *determiner* S1 W1
everybody *pron* S1 W3
everyone *pron* S1 W1
everything *pron* S1 W1
everywhere *adv* S2 W3
evidence *n* S2 W1
exact *adj* S2 W3
exactly *adv* S1 W2
exam *n* S1
examine *v* S3 W2
example *n* S1 W1
excellent *adj* S1 W2
except *conjunction, prep* S2 W2
exception *n* S3 W2
excited *adj* S2
exciting *adj* S2 W3
excuse *v* S1
excuse *n* S3
exercise *n* S2 W2
exhibition *n* W2
exist *v* S2 W1
exit *n* S3 W3
expect *v* S1 W1
expensive *adj* S1 W2
experience *n* S1 W1
experiment *n* S3 W2
expert *n* S3 W2
expert *adj* W3
explain *v* S1 W1
explanation *n* S3 W2
explode *v* W3
explore *v* S3 W2
explosion *n* W3
express *v* S2 W1
expression *n* S2 W2
extent *n* S2 W1
extra *adj* S1 W2
extremely *adv* S2 W2
eye *n* S1 W1

---

face *n* S1 W1
face *v* S1 W1
fact *n* S1 W1
factor *n* S3 W1
factory *n* S2 W2
fail *v* S2 W1
failure *n* S3 W2
fair *adj* S1 W2
fairly *adv* S1 W2
faith *n* S3 W2
fall *v* S1 W1
fall *n* S2 W2
false *adj* W3
family *n* S1 W1
famous *adj* S2 W2
fan *n* S3 W2
fantastic *adj* S3
far *adv* S1 W1
far *adj* S1 W1
farm *n* S2 W2
farmer *n* S2 W2
fashion *n* S3 W2

fashionable *adj* S3 W2
fast *adj* S2 W2
fast *adv* S2 W3
fat *adj* S1 W2
fat *n* S2 W2
father *n* S1 W1
fault *n* S2 W3
favour *n* S2 W3
favourite *adj* S2 W2
favourite *n* S2 W2
fear *n* S3 W1
feature *n* S2 W1
February *n* S2 W2
federal *adj* W1
fee *n* S3 W3
feed *v* S1 W2
feel *v* S1 W1
feeling *n* S1 W1
female *adj* S3 W2
female *n* W3
fence *n* S3
festival *n* S3 W3
fetch *v* S3
few *determiner*, pron, *adj* S1 W1
field *n* S1 W1
fifteen number, *n* S3 W3
fifth *adj* S3 W3
fifty number, *n* S3 W3
fight *v* S1 W1
fight *n* S2 W3
figure *n* S1 W1
figure *v* S1 W3
file *n* S1 W2
fill *v* S1 W1
film *n* S1 W1
final *adj* S1 W1
finally *adv* S2 W1
financial *adj* W1
find *v* S1 W1
fine *adj* S1 W1
fine *adv* S3
finger *n* S2 W2
finish *v* S1 W2
fire *n* S1 W1
firefighter *n* W3
firm *n* S1 W1
firm *adj* S3 W2
first *adj* S1 W1
first *adv* S1 W2
first *n* S2 W2
first *pron* S2 W2
first name *n* S2
fish *n* S1 W1
fishing *n* S3
fit *v* S1 W2
fit *adj* S2 W3
five number, *n* S2 W2
fix *v* S2 W2
flag *n* S2 W2
flat *adj* S2 W2
flat *n* S2 W3
flavour *n* S2 W2
flight *n* S3 W2
float *v* S3 W2
floor *n* S1 W1
flour *n* S3 W3
flow *n* S3 W2
flow *v* W3
flower *n* S2 W2
flu *n* S2
fly *v* S1 W1
fly *n* S3 W3
fog *n* S3 W3
foggy *adj* S3
folder *n* S2 W2
folk *n* S2 W3
follow *v* S1 W1
following *adj* S3 W1
food *n* S1 W1
foot *n* S1 W1
football *n* S1 W2
for *prep* S1 W1
force *n* S2 W1
force *v* S2 W1
foreign *adj* S3 W1
foreigner *n* W3
forest *n* S2 W2
forever *adv* S2 W3
forget *v* S1 W1
fork *n* S3
form *n* S1 W1
form *v* S2 W1
formal *adj* S2 W2
former *adj* S2 W1
forty number S3 W3
forward *adv* S1 W1
four number, *n* S2 W1
fourteen number S3 W3
fourth *adj* S3 W3
fourth *pron* S3 W3
frame *n* S3 W3
free *adj* S1 W1
free *v* W3
free *adv* S3
freedom *n* S3 W2
freeway *n* S2 W3
freeze *v* S3 W3
freezer *n* S3
freezing adj, *adv* S3
frequently *adv* S3 W2
fresh *adj* S2 W2
Friday *n* S2 W2
fridge *n* S2
friend *n* S1 W1
friendly *adj* S2 W3
frighten *v* S3 W3
frightened *adj* S3
frightening *adj* S3
from *prep* S1 W1
front *n* S1 W1
front *adj* S1 W2
frozen *adj* S2 W2
fruit *n* S2 W2
fry *v* S2 W3
fry *n* S2
fuel *n* S3 W2
full *adj* S1 W1
fully *adv* S2 W2
fun *n* S2 W3
fun *adj* S2 W3
function *n* S3 W1
funeral *n* S3 W3
funny *adj* S1 W3
furniture *n* S2 W3
further *adv* S1 W1
future *adj* S1 W1
future *n* S1 W1

---

gain *v* S3 W1
gallon *n* S3 W3
game *n* S1 W1
gang *n* S3
gap *n* S2 W2
garage *n* S2
garbage *n* S3
garden *n* S1 W1
gas *n* S1 W2
gate *n* S2 W2
gather *v* S3 W2
general *adj* S1 W1
generally *adv* S2 W1
generation *n* S3 W2
gentleman *n* S2 W2
geography *n* W3
get *v* S1 W1
ghost *n* S3
giant *adj* S3 W2
giant *n* W3
gift *n* S2 W2
girl *n* S1 W1
girlfriend *n* S3
give *v* S1 W1
glad *adj* S2 W3
glass *n* S1 W1
glove *n* S3 W3
go *v* S1 W1
go *n* S1
goal *n* S2 W1
god *n* S1 W1
gold *n* S2 W2
gold *adj* S3 W3
golden *adj* W3
golf *n* S2 W3
good *adj* S1 W1
good *n* S3 W2
good afternoon S3
goodbye S3
good evening S3
good-looking *adj* S2
good morning *interjection* S2
good night S3
government *n* S2 W1
governor *n* W3
grab *v* S1 W3
grade *n* S2 W3
gradually *adv* S3 W3
graduate *n* S2 W2
graduate *v* S2 W2
graduation *n* S3
gram *n* S3
grammar *n* S3 W3
grandad *n* S3
grandchild *n* S3 W3
granddaughter *n* S3 W3
grandfather *n* S2 W3
grandma *n* S2
grandmother *n* S2 W2
grandpa *n* S2
grandparent *n* W3
grandson *n* S3 W3
grape *n* S3
grapefruit *n* S3
graph *n* S3 W2
grass *n* S2 W2
gravy *n* S3
great *adj* S1 W1
green *adj* S1 W2
green *n* S2 W3
grey *adj* S2 W2
grey *n* S3 W3
grill *v* S3 W3
grill *n* S3 W3
grocery *n* S3
ground *n* S1 W1
group *n* S1 W1
grow *v* S1 W1
growth *n* S3 W1
guard *n* S2 W2
guard *v* W2
guess *v* S1 W3
guess *n* S3
guest *n* S3 W2
guide *n* S3 W2
guilty *adj* S2 W3
guitar *n* S3 W3
gum *n* S3
gun *n* S2 W2
guy *n* S1 W3
gym *n* S3

---

habit *n* S3 W3
hair *n* S1 W1
half *predeterminer*, *pron*, *adj* S1 W1
half *n* S1 W2
half *adv* S2
hall *n* S2 W2
Halloween *n* S3
ham *n* S3
hamburger *n* S3
hand *n* S1 W1
handle *v* S1 W2

handle *n* S1 W3
handsome *adj* W3
hang *v* S1 W2
happen *v* S1 W1
happiness *n* W3
happy *adj* S1 W1
hard *adj* S1 W1
hard *adv* S1 W2
hardly *adv* S2 W2
hat *n* S1 W3
hate *v* S1 W3
have *auxiliary verb* S1 W1
have *v* S1 W1
have *v* S1 W3
he *pron* S1 W1
head *n* S1 W1
head *v* S2 W2
headache *n* S2 W3
health *n* S1 W1
healthy *adj* S3 W3
hear *v* S1 W1
hearing *n* S3 W2
heart *n* S1 W1
heat *n* S2 W2
heat *v* S3 W3
heater *n* S3
heaven *n* S3 W3
heavy *adj* S1 W1
height *n* S2 W3
helicopter *n* S3
hello *interjection, n* S1
helmet *n* W3
help *v* S1 W1
help *n* S1 W1
helpful *adj* S2 W3
her *determiner* S1 W1
her *pron* S1 W1
here *adv* S1 W1
hero *n* W3
hers *pron* S3 W3
herself *pron* S2 W1
hi *interjection* S1
hide *v* S2 W2
high *adj* S1 W1
high *adv* S2 W3
highly *adv* S2 W2
high school *n* S2 W2
highway *n* S3 W2
hill *n* S2 W2
him *pron* S1 W1
himself *pron* S1 W1
hip *n* S3
hire *v* S2 W3
his *determiner, pron* S1 W1
history *n* S2 W1
hit *v* S1 W2
hit *n* S3 W3
hobby *n*
hold *v* S1 W1
hold *n* S2 W3
hole *n* S1 W2
holiday *n* S1 W2
holy *adj* W3
home *n* S1 W1
home *adv* S1 W1
home *adj* W3
homepage *n* S2 W1
homework *n* S2
honest *adj* S2 W3
honey *n* S2
hook *n* S3
hope *v* S1 W1
hope *n* S2 W2
hopefully *adv* S1
horrible *adj* S2
horse *n* S1 W1
hospital *n* S1 W1
hot *adj* S1 W2
hotel *n* S2 W1
hour *n* S1 W1
house *n* S1 W1
housewife *n* W3
how *adv* S1 W1
however *adv* S2 W1
however *conjunction* S2 W3
huge *adj* S1 W2
human *adj* S2 W1
human *n* W3
hundred number, *n* S2 W2
hungry *adj* S2
hunt *v* W3
hurry *v* S3 W3
hurry *n* S3
hurt *v* S1 W2
hurt *adj* S3
husband *n* S1 W1

I *pron* S1 W1
ice *n* S2 W3
ice cream *n* S2
idea *n* S1 W1
identify *v* W1
if *conjunction* S1 W1
ignore *v* S2 W2
ill *adj* S3 W2
illegal *adj* W3
illness *n* S3 W3
image *n* S2 W1
imagination *n* S3 W3
imagine *v* S1 W2
immediate *adj* S3 W2
immediately *adv* S2 W1
impact *n* S3 W2
importance *n* S3 W1
important *adj* S1 W1
impossible *adj* S2 W2
improve *v* S2 W1
improvement *n* S3 W2
in *prep* S1 W1
in *adv* S1 W1
inch *n* S2 W3
include *v* S1 W1
including *prep* S2 W1
income *n* S2 W1
increase *v* S2 W1
increase *n* S2 W1
indeed *adv* S1 W1
independence *n* W2
independent *adj* S2 W2
indicate *v* S3 W1
industrial *adj* S3 W1
industry *n* S2 W1
influence *n* S3 W1
influence *v* S3 W2
informal *adj* W3
information *n* S1 W1
injure *v* W3
injury *n* S3 W2
insect *n* W3
inside adv, *prep* S2 W2
inside *n* S3
inside *adj* S3
insist *v* S3 W2
instead *adv* S1 W1
instruction *n* S3 W2
instrument *n* W2
insurance *n* S2 W2
intelligence *n* S3 W3
intelligent *adj* S3 W3
intend *v* S2 W1
intention *n* S3 W2
interest *n* S2 W1
interest *v* W2
interested *adj* S1 W2
interesting *adj* S1 W2
intermediate *adj*
international *adj* S2 W1
Internet *n* S2 W2
interrupt *v* S3
intersection *n* S3
interview *n* S2 W1
into *prep* S1 W1
introduce *v* S2 W1
introduction *n* S3 W2
invent *v* S3 W3
invention *n* W3
investigate *v* W2
investigation *n* W2
invitation *n* S2
invite *v* S1 W2
involve *v* S2 W1
involved *adj* S2 W3
iron *n* S2 W3
iron *v* S3
island *n* S3 W2
issue *n* S1 W1
it *pron* S1 W1
item *n* S3 W2
its *determiner* S1 W1
itself *pron* S1 W1

---

jacket *n* S2 W3
jail *n* S3 W2
jam *n* S3
January *n* S2 W2
jar *n* S3
jealous *adj* S2
jeans *n* S2 W3
jelly *n* S3
job *n* S1 W1
join *v* S1 W1
joke *n* S2 W3
joke *v* S3
journalist *n* W3
journey *n* S3 W2
joy *n* W3
judge *n* S2 W2
judge *v* S3 W3
juice *n* S2
July *n* S2 W3
jump *v* S2 W3
jump *n* S3
June *n* S2 W3
junior *adj* W3
junk *n* S2
just *adv* S1 W1
justice *n* W2

---

keep *v* S1 W1
kettle *n* S3
key *n* S1 W2
keyboard *n* S3
kick *v* S2 W3
kid *n* S1 W2
kill *v* S1 W1
kilo *n* S3
kilogram *n* S3 W3
kilometre *n* S3 W3
kind *n* S1 W1
kind *adj* S3 W3
king *n* W1
kiss *v* S3 W3
kiss *n* S3
kitchen *n* S1 W2
kitten *n* S3
knee *n* S2 W2
knife *n* S3 W3
knock *v* S1 W3
know *v* S1 W1
knowledge *n* S2 W1

---

lab *n* S3
label *n* S3 W3
laboratory *n* W3
lack *n* S3 W2
ladder *n* S3
lady *n* S1 W2
lake *n* S3 W3
lamp *n* S3
land *n* S1 W1
land *v* S2 W3
landscape *n* W3

lane *n* S3 W3
language *n* S1 W1
laptop *n* S2 W2
large *adj* S1 W1
last *determiner, adj* S1 W1
last *adv* S1 W1
last n, *pron* S1 W1
last *v* S1 W2
last name *n* S2
late *adj* S1 W1
late *adv* S2 W3
lately *adv* S2
later *adv* S1 W1
latest *adj* S2 W2
laugh *v* S2 W2
laugh *n* S3
laughter *n* W3
laundry *n* S3
law *n* S1 W1
lawn *n* S2
lawyer *n* S3 W2
lay *v* S1 W2
layer *n* S3 W3
lazy *adj* S3
lead *v* S1 W1
leader *n* S2 W1
leaf *n* S2 W2
league *n* W2
learn *v* S1 W1
least *determiner, pron* S1 W1
leather *n* W3
leave *v* S1 W1
lecture *n* S2 W3
left *adj* S1 W1
left *adv* S3 W3
left *n* S3 W3
leg *n* S1 W1
legal *adj* S2 W1
lemon *n* S3
lend *v* S3 W3
length *n* S2 W2
less *adv* S1 W1
less *determiner, pron* S1 W1
lesson *n* S2 W3
let *v* S1 W1
let's S1
letter *n* S1 W1
lettuce *n* S3
level *n* S1 W1
library *n* S2 W1
licence *n* S3 W2
lick *v* S3
lid *n* S3
lie *v* S2 W1
lie *v* S3 W3
lie *n* S3
life *n* S1 W1
lift *v* S2 W2
lift *n* S3 W3
light *n* S1 W1
light *adj* S1 W1
light *v* S2 W3
like *prep* S1 W1
like *v* S1 W1
like *n* W3
like *conjunction* S1
likely *adj* S1 W1
limit *n* S2 W2
limit *v* S3 W2
limited *adj* W2
line *n* S1 W1
link *v* S3 W2
link *n* S3 W2
lion *n* S3 W3
lip *n* S3 W2
liquid *n* W3
list *n* S1 W1
list *v* S2 W3
listen *v* S1 W1
literature *n* S3 W2
litre *n* S3 W3
litter *n* S3 W3
little *adj* S1 W1
little *determiner, pron* S1 W1
little *adv* S1 W1
live *v* S1 W1
living room *n* S3
load *n* S1 W3
load *v* S2 W3
loaf *n* S3
loan *n* S2 W2
local *adj* S1 W1
location *n* S3 W2
lock *v* S2 W3
lock *n* S2
lonely *adj* S3
long *adj* S1 W1
long *adv* S1 W1
look *v* S1 W1
look *n* S1 W1
loose *adj* S3 W3
lorry *n* S3
lose *v* S1 W1
loss *n* S2 W1
lost *adj* S2 W3
lot pron, *adv* S1 W1
lot *n* S2
loud *adj* S2 W3
loud *adv* S3
love *v* S1 W1
love *n* S1 W1
lovely *adj* S1 W3
low *adj* S1 W1
low *adv* W1
lower *adj* W3
luck *n* S2 W3
lucky *adj* S2 W3
lunch *n* S1 W2

machine *n* S1 W1
mad *adj* S2 W3
magazine *n* S2 W2
magic *n* S3 W3
magic *adj* S3 W3
mail *n* S3 W3
mail *v* S3
main *adj* S1 W1
mainly *adv* S2 W2
maintain *v* S2 W1
major *adj* S1 W1
majority *n* S2 W1
make *v* S1 W1
male *adj* S3 W2
male *n* W3
mall *n* S3 W3
man *n* S1 W1
manage *v* S1 W1
management *n* S1 W1
manager *n* S1 W1
manner *n* S3 W2
many *determiner*, pron, *adj* S1 W1
map *n* S2 W2
March *n* S2 W2
mark *v* S2 W2
mark *n* S3 W2
market *n* S1 W1
marriage *n* S2 W2
married *adj* S2 W2
marry *v* S1 W2
massive *adj* S2 W3
match *n* S2 W2
match *v* S3 W2
material *n* S1 W1
math *n* S2
mathematics *n* W3
maths *n* S2
matter *n* S1 W1
matter *v* S1 W3
maximum *adj* S3 W2
maximum *n* S3 W3
may *modal verb* S1 W1
May *n* S2 W3
maybe *adv* S1 W1
mayor *n* W2
me *pron* S1 W1
meal *n* S2 W2
mean *v* S1 W1
mean *adj* S3
meaning *n* S2 W1
meanwhile *adv* W2
measure *v* S2 W2
measurement *n* W3
meat *n* S2 W3
medal *n* W3
media *n* S2 W2
medical *adj* S2 W2
medicine *n* S2 W3
medium *adj* S3
meet *v* S1 W1
meeting *n* S1 W1
member *n* S1 W1
membership *n* S3 W2
memory *n* S2 W1
mental *adj* S2 W2
mention *v* S1 W1
menu *n* S3
mess *n* S2
message *n* S1 W2
messy *adj* S3
metal *n* S2 W2
method *n* S1 W1
metre *n* S2 W3
microwave *n* S2
middle *n* S1 W2
middle *adj* S1 W2
midnight *n* S3
might *modal verb* S1 W1
mile *n* S1 W1
military *adj* S2 W1
milk *n* S2 W3
million number S3 W1
mind *n* S1 W1
mind *v* S1 W2
mine *pron* S1
minimum *adj* S3 W2
minimum *n* S3 W2
minor *adj* S2 W2
minority *n* S3 W2
minus *prep* S3
minute *n* S1 W1
mirror *n* S3 W3
miserable *adj* S3 W3
miss *v* S1 W2
miss *n* S2 W2
mistake *n* S2 W2
mix *v* S2 W3
mixture *n* S3 W3
mobile *n* S1 W2
mobile phone *n* S2 W2
model *n* S2 W1
modern *adj* S1 W1
mom *n* S1
moment *n* S1 W1
mommy *n* S3
Monday *n* S2 W2
money *n* S1 W1
monkey *n* S3
month *n* S1 W1
mood *n* S3 W3
moon *n* S3 W3
more *adv* S1 W1
more *determiner, pron* S1 W1
morning *n* S1 W1
morning *interjection* S2
most *adv* S1 W1
most *determiner, pron* S1 W1
mostly *adv* S2 W3
mother *n* S1 W1

motorway *n* S2
mountain *n* S3 W3
mouse *n* S2 W3
moustache *n* S3
mouth *n* S2 W1
move *v* S1 W1
move *n* S2 W1
movement *n* S1 W1
movie *n* S2 W2
movie theater *n* S3
Mr W2
Mrs W2
Ms W2
much *adv* S1 W1
much *determiner, pron* S1 W1
mum *n* S1 W2
mummy *n* S1
murder *n* S3 W2
murder *v* W3
muscle *n* S2 W3
museum *n* S3 W2
mushroom *n* S3
music *n* S1 W1
musical *adj* S3 W3
musician *n* W3
must *modal verb* S1 W1
my *determiner* S1 W1
myself *pron* S1 W1
mystery *n* W3
myth *n* S3 W3

---

nail *n* S3
naked *adj* S3
name *n* S1 W1
name *v* S2 W2
narrow *adj* S3 W2
nasty *adj* S2
nation *n* S3 W2
national *adj* S1 W1
natural *adj* S2 W1
nature *n* S1 W1
near adv, *prep* S1 W1
near *adj* S2 W3
nearby *adj* W3
nearly *adv* S1 W1
neat *adj* S2
necessarily *adv* S2 W2
necessary *adj* S2 W1
neck *n* S2 W2
necklace *n* S3
need *v* S1 W1
need *n* S1 W1
negative *adj* S2 W2
neighbour *n* S2 W2
neither *determiner, pron* S3 W2
neither *adv* S3
neither *conjunction* W2
nephew *n* S3
nervous *adj* S3 W3
net *n* S2 W2
network *n* S3 W2
never *adv* S1 W1
new *adj* S1 W1
news *n* S1 W1
newspaper *n* S2 W2
next *determiner, adj* S1 W1
next *adv* S1 W1
next *pron* S3 W3
next door *adv* S2
next to *prep* S3 W3
nice *adj* S1 W2
niece *n* S3
night *n* S1 W1
nine number S2 W2
nineteen number S3 W3
ninety number S3 W3
ninth *adj* S3 W3
no *adv* S1 W1
no *determiner* S1 W1
nobody *pron* S1 W2
noise *n* S2 W2
noisy *adj* S3
none *pron* S1 W2
noon *n* W3
no one *pron* S1 W2
nor *conjunction, adv* S2 W1
normal *adj* S1 W1
normally *adv* S1 W2
north *n* S2 W1
north *adj* S3 W3
north *adv* S3 W1
northern *adj* S2 W2
nose *n* S2 W2
not *adv* S1 W1
note *n* S1 W2
notebook *n* S3
nothing *pron* S1 W1
notice *v* S1 W2
notice *n* S2 W2
noun *n*
novel *n* W3
November *n* S2 W2
now *adv* S1 W1
now *conjunction* S1 W3
nowhere *adv* S2
number *n* S1 W1
nurse *n* S2 W3
nut *n* S3

---

obey *v* W3
object *n* S2 W2
obtain *v* S3 W2
obvious *adj* S2 W2
obviously *adv* S1 W2
occasion *n* S1 W2
occasionally *adv* S2 W3
occupation *n* S3 W3
occur *v* S3 W1
ocean *n* S3 W2
o'clock *adv* S1 W3
October *n* S2 W2
odd *adj* S1 W3
of *prep* S1 W1
of course *adv* S1 W1
off adv, prep, *adj* S1 W1
offence *n* S3 W2
offer *v* S1 W1
offer *n* S2 W1
office *n* S1 W1
officer *n* S1 W1
official *n* S3 W1
official *adj* S3 W2
often *adv* S1 W1
oil *n* S2 W1
OK *interjection* S1
OK adj, *adv* S1
old *adj* S1 W1
old-fashioned *adj* W2
on *prep* S1 W1
on adj, *adv* S1 W1
once *adv* S1 W1
once *conjunction* S1 W1
one number S1 W1
one *pron* S1 W1
one *determiner* S1 W1
one *adj* S3 W3
onion *n* S3
online *adj* S2 W2
only *adv* S1 W1
only *adj* S1 W1
onto *prep* S1 W2
open *adj* S1 W1
open *v* S1 W1
operate *v* S3 W2
operation *n* S1 W1
opinion *n* S1 W2
opponent *n* W3
opportunity *n* S1 W1
opposite *prep* S2 W2
opposite *adj* S3 W2
option *n* S1 W2
or *conjunction* S1 W1
orange *n* S1 W2
orange *adj* S2 W2
order *n* S1 W1
order *v* S2 W2
ordinary *adj* S1 W2
organization *n* S2 W1
organize *v* S1 W2
origin *n* W2
original *adj* S1 W1
originally *adv* S2 W2
other *determiner*, adj, *pron* S1 W1
otherwise *adv* S1 W2
ought to *modal verb* S1 W1
ounce *n* S3 W3
our *determiner* S1 W1
ours *pron* S1
ourselves *pron* S1 W3
out *adv* S1 W1
out *prep* S1 W2
outside adv, *prep* S1 W1
outside *adj* S2 W2
outside *n* S3
oven *n* S3
over *prep* S1 W1
over adv, *adj* S1 W1
owe *v* S2 W3
own adj, *pron* S1 W1
own *v* S2 W2
owner *n* S2 W2

---

pack *v* S2 W3
pack *n* S2 W3
package *n* S2 W2
packet *n* S2
page *n* S1 W1
pain *n* S2 W2
painful *adj* W2
paint *n* S2 W2
paint *v* S2 W3
painting *n* S3 W2
pair *n* S2 W2
pan *n* S3 W3
pancake *n* S3
pants *n* S3
paper *n* S1 W1
paper *adj* S3 W2
paragraph *n* S2
pardon *interjection* S2
parent *n* S1 W1
park *n* S1 W2
park *v* S2
parking *n* S3
parking lot *n* S3
parliament *n* W2
part *n* S1 W1
particular *adj* S1 W1
particularly *adv* S1 W1
partly *adv* S2 W2
partner *n* S2 W2
party *n* S1 W1
pass *v* S1 W1
pass *n* S2 W3
passenger *n* S3 W2
password *n* S2 W2
past *adj* S1 W1
past prep, *adv* S1 W2
past *n* S1 W2
pasta *n* S2
path *n* S2 W2
patient *n* S2 W1
patient *adj* W3
pattern *n* S2 W1
pause *v* W2
pause *n* W2
pay *v* S1 W1
pay *n* S1 W2
payment *n* S2 W1
pea *n* S3

peace *n* S2 W2
peach *n* S3
peanut *n* S3
pear *n* S3
pen *n* S2
pencil *n* S2
penny *n* S1
people *n* S1 W1
pepper *n* S3
per *prep* S3 W1
percent adj, *adv* W1
percent *n* S3 W2
perfect *adj* S2 W2
perfectly *adv* S2 W3
perform *v* S3 W2
performance *n* S2 W1
perhaps *adv* S1 W1
period *n* S1 W1
permanent *adj* S2 W2
permission *n* S2 W3
person *n* S1 W1
personal *adj* S1 W1
personality *n* S3 W3
personally *adv* S2
persuade *v* S3 W2
pet *n* S2
petrol *n* S3
pharmacy *n* S3
philosophy *n* W3
phone *n* S1 W2
phone *v* S1
photo *n* S3 W3
photograph *n* S2 W2
phrase *n* S3 W3
physical *adj* S2 W1
physics *n* S3
piano *n* S3
pick *v* S1 W1
picnic *n* S3
picture *n* S1 W1
pie *n* S2
piece *n* S1 W1
pig *n* S2
pile *n* S2
pill *n* S3
pillow *n* S3
pilot *n* W3
pin *n* S3
pink *adj* S2
pink *n* S2
pipe *n* S2 W3
pizza *n* S2
place *n* S1 W1
plain *adj* S2 W3
plan *n* S1 W1
plan *v* S1 W1
plane *n* S2 W2
planet *n* W3
plant *n* S2 W1
plastic *adj* S2 W2
plastic *n* S3 W2
plate *n* S2 W2
play *v* S1 W1
play *n* S1 W2
player *n* S2 W1
playground *n* S3
please *interjection* S1 W2
please *v* W3
pleased *adj* S2 W3
pleasure *n* S2 W2
plenty *pron* S1 W1
plug *n* S3
plug *v* S3
plural *n*
plural *adj*
plus *prep* S1 W2
p.m. W2
pocket *n* S2 W2
poem *n* S3 W3
poet *n* W3
poetry *n* W3
point *n* S1 W1
point *v* S2 W2
pole *n* W3
police *n* S1 W1
policeman *n* S2 W3
police officer *n* S3 W2
policy *n* S3 W1
polish *v* S3
polish *n* S3
polite *adj* S3
political *adj* S2 W1
politician *n* W2
politics *n* S2 W2
pool *n* S2 W2
poor *adj* S1 W1
popcorn *n* S3
popular *adj* S2 W1
population *n* S2 W1
porch *n* S3
pork *n* S3
port *n* W2
position *n* S1 W1
positive *adj* S2 W2
possibility *n* S2 W2
possible *adj* S1 W1
possibly *adv* S1 W2
post *n* S2 W2
post *v* S3
postcard *n* S3
poster *n* S3
post office *n* S3
pot *n* S2 W2
potato *n* S2
potential *adj* S3 W2
pound *n* S1 W2
pour *v* S2 W3
power *n* S1 W1
powerful *adj* S3 W2
practical *adj* S3 W2
practice *n* S2 W1
practise *v* S3 W3
praise *v* W2
praise *n* W3
prayer *n* S3 W3
predict *v* W3
prefer *v* S2 W2
prepare *v* S1 W1
preposition *n*
present *adj* S2 W2
present *v* S2 W2
present *n* S2 W3
President *n* S2 W2
press *n* S2 W1
press *v* S1 W2
pressure *n* S1 W1
pretend *v* S2 W3
pretty *adv* S1 W3
pretty *adj* S2 W3
prevent *v* S2 W1
previous *adj* S1 W1
previously *adv* S3 W2
price *n* S1 W1
pride *n* S3 W3
priest *n* W3
prince *n* W3
princess *n* W3
principle *n* S2 W1
print *v* S2 W3
printer *n* S3 W3
prison *n* S2 W2
prisoner *n* S3 W2
private *adj* S1 W1
prize *n* S2 W2
probably *adv* S1 W1
problem *n* S1 W1
process *n* S1 W1
produce *v* S1 W1
producer *n* W3
product *n* S1 W1
production *n* S1 W1
professional *adj* S2 W1
professor *n* S3 W3
profit *n* S1 W1
program *n* W1
programme *n* S1 W1
progress *n* S2 W2
project *n* S1 W1
promise *v* S2 W2
promise *n* S3 W2
pronoun *n*
pronounce *v* S3
pronunciation *n* S3
proper *adj* S1 W2
properly *adv* S1 W2
property *n* S2 W1
protect *v* S2 W2
protection *n* S2 W2
proud *adj* S2 W3
prove *v* S2 W1
provide *v* S1 W1
pub *n* S2 W3
public *adj* S1 W1
public *n* S2 W2
publish *v* S3 W1
pudding *n* S3
pull *v* S1 W1
punch *v* S3
punishment *n* W3
pupil *n* S2 W1
puppy *n* S3
pure *adj* S3 W3
purple *n* S3 W3
purple *adj* S3 W3
purpose *n* S2 W2
purse *n* S3
push *v* S1 W1
put *v* S1 W1
puzzle *n* S3

---

quality *n* S1 W1
quantity *n* S3 W2
quarter *n* S1 W2
queen *n* S2 W2
question *n* S1 W1
question *v* S2 W3
quick *adj* S1 W2
quick *interjection* S1
quickly *adv* S1 W1
quiet *adj* S2 W2
quietly *adv* S3 W3
quite *predeterminer, adv* S1 W1
quiz *n* S3

---

rabbit *n* S3
race *n* S2 W2
race *v* S3 W3
radio *n* S1 W2
rail *n* S2 W2
railway *n* S2 W2
railway station *n* S3
rain *n* S2 W2
rain *v* S3
rainy *adj* S3
raise *v* S1 W1
range *n* S1 W1
rank *n* W3
rank *v* W3
rare *adj* S3 W2
rarely *adv* W2
raspberry *n* S3
rate *n* S1 W1
rather *predeterminer, adv* S1 W1
raw *adj* W3
reach *v* S1 W1
react *v* S3 W3
reaction *n* S2 W2
read *v* S1 W1
reader *n* S3 W2
reading *n* W2
ready *adj* S1 W2
real *adj* S1 W1

●●● 3000 high frequency words | Full *Communication 9000* at www.longmandictionaries.com

real *adv* S2
reality *n* S2 W2
realize *v* S1 W1
really *adv* S1 W1
reason *n* S1 W1
reasonable *adj* S1 W2
receipt *n* S2
receive *v* S1 W1
recent *adj* S2 W1
recently *adv* S1 W1
recipe *n* S3
recognize *v* S1 W1
recommend *v* S2 W2
record *n* S1 W1
record *v* S3 W2
recover *v* W2
rectangle *n*
red *adj* S1 W1
red *n* S2 W2
reduce *v* S1 W1
reduction *n* S3 W2
refer *v* S1 W1
reference *n* S2 W1
reflect *v* S2 W1
refrigerator *n* S3
refuse *v* S2 W1
region *n* S1 W1
regional *adj* S1 W2
regular *adj* S2 W2
regularly *adv* S3 W3
relate *v* S2 W1
related *adj* S2 W3
relation *n* S2 W1
relationship *n* S1 W1
relative *n* S3 W3
relax *v* S3 W3
relaxed *adj* S2 W3
release *v* S3 W1
relevant *adj* S2 W2
religion *n* S2 W2
religious *adj* S2 W2
rely *v* S3 W2
remain *v* S1 W1
remark *n* W3
remember *v* S1 W1
remind *v* S1 W2
remove *v* S2 W1
rent *v* S2 W3
rent *n* S2 W3
repeat *v* S2 W2
replace *v* S2 W1
reply *v* W2
reply *n* S3 W3
report *n* S2 W1
report *v* S2 W1
reporter *n* S3
represent *v* S2 W1
republic *n* W2
request *n* S3 W2
require *v* S1 W1
requirement *n* S2 W2
research *n* S2 W1
reservation *n* S3 W3
reserve *v* W3
resource *n* S2 W1
respect *n* S3 W2
respect *v* S3 W2
respond *v* S2 W2
response *n* S1 W1
responsibility *n* S2 W1
responsible *adj* S2 W2
rest *n* S1 W1
rest *v* S3 W3
restaurant *n* S2 W2
result *n* S1 W1
return *v* S2 W1
return *n* S2 W2
reveal *v* W1
review *n* S2 W2
review *v* S3 W3
reward *n* W3
rice *n* S3
rich *adj* S2 W2
ride *v* S2 W2
ride *n* S3
right *adj* S1 W1
right *adv* S1 W1
right *n* S1 W1
right *interjection* S2
ring *n* S1 W2
ring *v* S1 W2
rise *v* S2 W1
rise *n* S3 W2
risk *n* S2 W1
river *n* S2 W2
road *n* S1 W1
rock *n* S2 W2
role *n* S2 W1
roll *v* S1 W2
roof *n* S2 W2
room *n* S1 W1
root *n* S2 W2
rope *n* S3 W3
rose *n* S3
rough *adj* S2 W3
roughly *adv* S2
round adv, *prep* S2 W2
round *adj* S1 W2
route *n* S3 W2
row *n* S2 W2
royal *adj* S3 W1
rub *v* S2
rubbish *n* S2
rude *adj* S3
rug *n* S3
rugby *n* S3
rule *n* S1 W1
rule *v* W2
ruler *n* W3
run *v* S1 W1
run *n* S1 W1
running *n* S3
rush *v* S2 W3

---

sad *adj* S2 W3
safe *adj* S2 W2
safety *n* S2 W2
sail *v* S3
salad *n* S2
salary *n* S2 W3
sale *n* S1 W1
salt *n* S2 W3
same *adj* S1 W1
same *pron* S1 W1
same *adv* S1 W1
sample *n* S3 W2
sand *n* S3 W3
sandwich *n* S2
satisfied *adj* S3
Saturday *n* S2 W2
sauce *n* S3
sausage *n* S3
save *v* S1 W1
say *v* S1 W1
scale *n* S2 W2
scare *v* S2
scared *adj* S3
scarf *n* S3
scary *adj* S1
scene *n* S2 W2
schedule *n* S2 W3
schedule *v* S3
scheme *n* S2 W1
school *n* S1 W1
science *n* S1 W1
scientific *adj* S3 W2
scientist *n* S3 W2
scissors *n* S3
score *n* S2 W2
score *v* S3 W2
scratch *v* S3
scream *v* S3
scream *n* S3
screen *n* S2 W2
screw *n* S3
sea *n* S2 W1
search *n* S3 W2
search *v* W3
season *n* S2 W1
seat *n* S2 W1
second number S1 W1
second *n* S1 W2
second *adv* S2 W2
secret *adj* S3 W2
secret *n* S3 W3
secretary *n* S2 W1
section *n* S1 W1
secure *v* W3
security *n* W1
see *v* S1 W1
seed *n* S3 W3
seek *v* S2 W1
seem *v* S1 W1
select *v* S2 W2
selection *n* S3 W2
self *n* S2 W3
sell *v* S1 W1
semester *n* S2
send *v* S1 W1
senior *adj* W2
sense *n* S1 W1
sentence *n* S1 W2
separate *adj* S2 W2
separate *v* S2 W2
September *n* S2 W2
series *n* S2 W1
serious *adj* S1 W1
seriously *adv* S2 W2
serve *v* S1 W1
service *n* S1 W1
set *v* S1 W1
set *n* S1 W1
settle *v* S2 W2
seven number S2 W2
seventeen number S3 W3
seventh *adj* S3 W3
seventy number W3
several *determiner, pron* S1 W1
severe *adj* S3 W3
sew *v* S3
sex *n* S1 W2
sexual *adj* S3 W2
shadow *n* S3 W2
shake *v* S3 W2
shall *modal verb* S1 W1
shallow *adj* S3
shame *n* S2
shampoo *n* S3
shape *n* S2 W2
share *v* S1 W1
share *n* S1 W1
sharp *adj* S3 W2
shave *v* S3
she *pron* S1 W1
sheep *n* S2 W3
sheet *n* S1 W2
shelf *n* S3 W3
shell *n* S3 W3
shine *v* S3
ship *n* S2 W2
shirt *n* S2 W3
shock *n* S2 W2
shock *v* S2
shocked *adj* S3
shocking *adj* S3
shoe *n* S1 W3
shoot *v* S2 W2
shop *n* S1 W1
shop *v* S2
shopping *n* S2 W3
shopping centre *n* S3
shore *n* W3
short *adj* S1 W1

shortly *adv* S3 W3
shot *n* S2 W2
should *modal verb* S1 W1
shoulder *n* S2 W2
shout *v* S2 W2
shout *n* W3
show *v* S1 W1
show *n* S1 W1
shower *n* S2
shut *v* S1 W2
shut *adj* S3
sick *adj* S1 W3
side *n* S1 W1
side *adj* S3
sidewalk *n* S3
sight *n* S2 W2
sign *n* S1 W1
sign *v* S1 W1
signal *n* S2 W2
significant *adj* S2 W1
silence *n* W2
silent *adj* W3
silly *adj* S2
silver *n* W3
silver *adj* W3
similar *adj* S1 W1
simple *adj* S1 W1
simply *adv* S1 W1
since prep, *conjunction, adv* S1 W1
sing *v* S1 W2
singer *n* S3
single *adj* S1 W1
singular *adj*
singular *n*
sink *v* W3
sink *n* S3
sir *n* S1 W3
sister *n* S1 W1
sit *v* S1 W1
site *n* S1 W2
situation *n* S1 W1
six number S2 W2
sixteen number S3 W3
sixth *adj* S3 W3
sixty number W3
size *n* S1 W1
skating *n* S3
skiing *n* S3
skilful *adj* W2
skill *n* S2 W1
skin *n* S2 W2
skirt *n* S3
sky *n* S2 W2
sleep *v* S1 W2
sleep *n* S2 W3
sleepy *adj* S3
slice *n* S3
slide *v* S3 W3
slight *adj* S2 W3
slightly *adv* S1 W2
slip *v* S3 W2
slot *n* S3
slow *adj* S2 W2
slow *v* S3 W2
slowly *adv* S3 W2
small *adj* S1 W1
smart *adj* S2 W2
smell *n* S2 W3
smell *v* S2 W3
smile *v* S3 W1
smile *n* S2 W2
smoke *n* S1 W2
smoke *v* S2 W2
smoking *n* S2
smooth *adj* W3
snack *n* S2
snake *n* W3
snap *v* W3
sneeze *v* S3
snow *n* S2 W3
snow *v* S2
snowy *adj* S3
so *adv* S1 W1
so *conjunction* S1 W3
soap *n* S3
soccer *n* S2
social *adj* S1 W1
society *n* S1 W1
sock *n* S3
soda *n* S3
sofa *n* S3
soft *adj* S2 W2
software *n* S3 W1
soil *n* W2
soldier *n* S3 W2
solid *adj* S3 W3
solution *n* S2 W1
solve *v* S2 W3
some *determiner* S1 W1
some *pron* S1 W1
some *adv* S1 W1
somebody *pron* S1 W3
somehow *adv* S2 W2
someone *pron* S1 W1
something *pron* S1 W1
sometime *adv* S2
sometimes *adv* S1 W1
somewhat *adv* S3 W2
somewhere *adv* S1 W2
son *n* S1 W1
song *n* S1 W2
soon *adv* S1 W1
sore *adj* S3
sorry *adj* S1 W2
sort *n* S1 W1
sort *v* S1 W3
sound *n* S1 W1
sound *v* S1 W2
soup *n* S3
sour *adj* S3
source *n* S2 W1
south *n* S1 W1
south *adj* S2 W2
south *adv* S3 W3
southern *adj* S2 W2
space *n* S1 W1
spaghetti *n* S3
speak *v* S1 W1
speaker *n* S2 W2
special *adj* S1 W1
specific *adj* S1 W1
speech *n* S2 W2
speed *n* S2 W1
spell *v* S2
spelling *n* S2
spend *v* S1 W1
spicy *adj* S3
spider *n* S3
spill *v* S3
spin *v* S3
spirit *n* S2 W2
splash *v* W3
split *v* S2 W3
spoil *v* S3
spoon *n* S3
sport *n* S2 W2
spot *n* S2 W2
spray *v* S3
spray *n* S3
spread *v* S2 W2
spring *n* S2 W2
square *adj* S2 W3
square *n* S2 W3
squeeze *v* S3
stadium *n* W3
staff *n* S2 W2
stage *n* S1 W1
stair *n* S2 W3
stamp *n* S2
stand *v* S1 W1
stand *n* S2 W2
standard *n* S2 W2
standard *adj* S2 W2
star *n* S2 W2
stare *v* S3 W2
start *v* S1 W1
start *n* S1 W2
state *n* S1 W2
statement *n* S2 W1
station *n* S1 W1
stay *v* S1 W1
steak *n* S3
steal *v* S3 W3
step *n* S2 W1
step *v* S3 W3
stick *v* S1 W3
stick *n* S3
sticker *n* S3
still *adv* S1 W1
still *adj* S3
stir *v* S3 W3
stock *n* S2 W2
stomach *n* S3 W3
stomachache *n* S3
stone *n* S2 W1
stool *n* S3
stop *v* S1 W1
stop *n* S2 W3
store *n* S1 W1
store *v* S3 W3
storm *n* W3
stormy *adj* S3
story *n* S1 W1
straight *adv* S1 W2
straight *adj* S2 W3
strange *adj* S2 W2
strawberry *n* S3
stream *n* W3
street *n* S1 W1
strength *n* S2 W2
stress *n* S3 W3
stress *v* S3 W3
stretch *v* S3 W3
strike *v* S3 W3
strike *n* S3 W2
string *n* S3 W2
strip *n* W3
strong *adj* S1 W1
structure *n* S3 W2
student *n* S1 W1
studio *n* S3 W2
study *n* S1 W1
study *v* S1 W1
stuff *n* S1 W3
stupid *adj* S1 W3
style *n* S2 W1
subject *n* S2 W1
substance *n* W3
succeed *v* S3 W2
success *n* S1 W1
successful *adj* S2 W1
such *determiner, predeterminer, pron* S1 W1
sudden *adj* S2 W3
suddenly *adv* S1 W1
suffer *v* S1 W1
sugar *n* S2 W3
suggest *v* S1 W1
suggestion *n* S1 W2
suit *n* S2 W3
suit *v* S3 W3
suitable *adj* S3 W2
suitcase *n* S3
summer *n* S1 W1
sun *n* S2 W1
Sunday *n* S2 W2
sunglasses *n* S3
sunny *adj* S3
super *adj* S2
supermarket *n* S3
supper *n* S3
supply *n* S2 W2

supply *v* S3 W2
support *v* S2 W1
support *n* S2 W1
supporter *n* S3 W2
suppose *v* S1 W1
sure *adj* S1 W1
sure *adv* S1
surely *adv* S1 W2
surface *n* S3 W1
surname *n* S3
surprise *n* S3 W2
surprise *v* S3 W2
surprised *adj* S2 W2
surprising *adj* S3 W3
surround *v* W2
survive *v* S2 W2
sweater *n* S2
sweatshirt *n* S3
sweep *v* W3
sweet *adj* S2 W3
sweet *n* S2
swim *v* S3
swimming *n* S2
swimming costume *n* S3
swimming pool *n* S3
swimming trunks *n* S3
swing *v* W3
switch *v* S2 W3
switch *n* S3
symbol *n* W3
system *n* S1 W1

table *n* S1 W1
tablet *n* S3
tag *n* S3
tail *n* S2 W3
take *v* S1 W1
tale *n* W3
talent *n* W3
talk *v* S1 W1
talk *n* S1 W1
tall *adj* S2 W2
tank *n* S2 W2
tape *n* S3 W3
target *n* S2 W2
task *n* S2 W1
taste *n* S2 W2
taste *v* S2
tax *n* S1 W1
taxi *n* S3
tea *n* S1 W2
teach *v* S1 W2
teacher *n* S1 W1
teaching *n* S2 W2
team *n* S1 W1
tear *n* S2 W3
tear *v* S2 W3
technical *adj* S2 W2
technique *n* S3 W1
technology *n* S2 W1
teenager *n* S3
telephone *n* S1 W2
television *n* S1 W1
tell *v* S1 W1
temperature *n* S2 W2
temporary *adj* S3 W3
ten number, *n* S1 W2
tend *v* S1 W1
tennis *n* S3 W3
tenth *adj* S3 W3
term *n* S1 W1
terrible *adj* S1 W3
test *n* S1 W1
test *v* S3 W2
text *n* S2 W1
text *v* S2
textbook *n*
than *conjunction, prep* S1 W1
thank *v* S1 W2
thanks *interjection* S1
Thanksgiving *n* S2
thank you *interjection* S1
that *determiner, pron* S1 W1
that *conjunction* S1 W1
that *adv* S1 W2
the definite article, *determiner* S1 W1
the *adv* S3
theatre *n* S2 W2
their *determiner* S1 W1
theirs *pron* S3
them *pron* S1 W1
theme *n* S2 W2
themselves *pron* S1 W1
then *adv* S1 W1
theory *n* S2 W1
there *pron* S1 W1
there *adv* S1 W1
therefore *adv* S3 W1
they *pron* S1 W1
thick *adj* S2 W2
thin *adj* S2 W2
thing *n* S1 W1
think *v* S1 W1
third *adj* S2 W2
third *n* W3
thirsty *adj* S3
thirteen number S3 W3
thirty number S3 W3
this *determiner, pron* S1 W1
this *adv* S1
though *conjunction* S1 W1
though *adv* S1
thought *n* S1 W1
thousand number W3
threat *n* S3 W2
threaten *v* S3 W2
three number S1 W2
throat *n* S3 W3
through prep, *adv* S1 W1
throughout prep, *adv* S2 W1
throw *v* S1 W1
thumb *n* S3
Thursday *n* S2 W2
ticket *n* S1 W2
tidy *adj* S3
tie *v* S2 W3
tie *n* S3 W3
tiger *n* W3
tight *adj* S2 W3
tight *adv* S2
till prep, *conjunction* S1
time *n* S1 W1
time *v* S1 W2
timetable *n* W3
tiny *adj* S2 W2
tip *n* S2 W3
tired *adj* S1 W2
tiring *adj* S3
tissue *n* S2
title *n* S3 W1
to S1 W1
to *prep* S1 W1
today *adv* S1 W1
toe *n* S3
together *adv* S1 W1
toilet *n* S2
tomato *n* S2
tomorrow *adv* S1 W2
tongue *n* S3 W3
tonight *adv* S1 W2
too *adv* S1 W1
tool *n* S2 W2
tooth *n* S2 W2
toothache *n* S3
toothbrush *n* S3
toothpaste *n* S3
top *n* S1 W1
top *adj* S1 W1
topic *n* S3 W2
total *adj* S1 W1
total *n* S2 W2
totally *adv* S1 W2
touch *v* S2 W2
touch *n* S2 W2
tough *adj* S2 W2
tour *n* S3 W2
tourist *n* W3
towards *prep* S1 W1
towel *n* S3
town *n* S1 W1
toy *n* S3
track *n* S2 W2
trade *n* S3 W1
tradition *n* S2 W2
traditional *adj* S3 W1
traffic *n* S1 W2
traffic lights *n* S3
train *n* S1 W2
train *v* S1 W2
training *n* S2 W1
translate *v* S3
translation *n* S3
transport *n* S2 W2
transportation *n* W3
trash *n* S3
travel *v* S2 W2
travel *n* S2 W2
treat *v* S2 W1
treat *n* S3
treatment *n* S2 W1
tree *n* S1 W1
trial *n* S3 W2
triangle *n*
trick *n* S3
trick *v* S3
trip *n* S2 W2
troop *n* W2
trouble *n* S1 W2
trousers *n* S2
truck *n* S2 W3
true *adj* S1 W1
trunk *n* S3
trust *n* S1 W2
trust *v* S2 W3
truth *n* S1 W2
try *v* S1 W1
try *n* S3
T-shirt *n* S2
tube *n* S3 W3
Tuesday *n* S2 W2
tune *n* S3
tunnel *n* W3
turkey *n* S3
turn *v* S1 W1
turn *n* S1 W1
TV *n* S2 W2
twelve number S3 W2
twenty number, *n* S2 W2
twice *adv, predeterminer* S2 W2
twin *n* S3
two number S2 W1
type *n* S1 W1
type *v* S2 W3
typical *adj* S2 W2
tyre *n* S3

ugly *adj* S3
umbrella *n* S3
unable *adj* W2
uncle *n* S2 W3
uncomfortable *adj* W3
under prep, *adv* S1 W1
underneath prep, *adv* S2
understand *v* S1 W1
underwear *n* S3
unemployed *adj* S2 W3
unemployment *n* S2 W2
unfair *adj* S3

unfortunately *adv* S1 W3
unhappy *adj* S3
uniform *n* S3
unique *adj* S3 W2
unit *n* S2 W2
university *n* S2 W1
unknown adj, *adv* W2
unless *conjunction* S1 W1
unlike *prep* W3
unlikely *adj* S3 W2
until prep, *conjunction* S1 W1
unusual *adj* S2 W3
up adv, prep, *adj* S1 W1
upon *prep* S3 W2
upper *adj* W2
upset *adj* S2
upset *v* S2
upstairs *adv* S2
us *pron* S1 W1
use *v* S1 W1
use *n* S1 W1
used *adj* S1 W2
used to *modal verb* S1 W2
useful *adj* S1 W1
user *n* S3 W1
usual *adj* S2 W2
usually *adv* S1 W1

vacation n S2 W3
valley *n* S3 W3
valuable *adj* W3
value *n* S2 W1
van *n* S2 W3
variety *n* S2 W1
various *adj* S1 W1
vary *v* S3 W2
vegetable *n* S3 W3
vehicle *n* S2 W2
verb *n*
version *n* S2 W2
very *adv* S1 W1
victim *n* S3 W2
victory *n* W2
video *n* S1 W2
view *n* S1 W1
village *n* S1 W1
violence *n* S2 W2
violent *adj* S3 W3
virtually *adv* S2 W2
visit *v* S2 W1
visit *n* S3 W2
visitor *n* S3 W2
vital *adj* W2
vocabulary *n* S3
voice *n* S2 W1
volume *n* S3 W2
vote *v* S2 W2
vote *n* S2 W2

wage n S2 W2
waist *n* W3
wait *v* S1 W1
waiter *n* S3
waitress *n* S3
wake *v* S2 W3
walk *v* S1 W1
walk *n* S2 W2
wall *n* S1 W1
wallet *n* S2
want *v* S1 W1
war *n* S2 W1
wardrobe *n* S3
warm *adj* S2 W2
warn *v* S3 W2
warning *n* S3 W2
wash *v* S1 W3
washing *n* S2
washing machine *n* S3
waste *n* S2 W3
waste *v* S2 W3
watch *v* S1 W1
watch *n* S2 W3
water *n* S1 W1
wave *n* S3 W2
wave *v* S3 W3
way *n* S1 W1
we *pron* S1 W1
weak *adj* S3 W2
weapon *n* W2
wear *v* S1 W1
weather *n* S1 W2
web *n* S2 W2
webpage *n* S2
website *n* S2 W1
wedding *n* S2 W3
Wednesday *n* S2 W2
week *n* S1 W1
weekend *n* S1 W2
weekly *adj* W3
weigh *v* S3 W3
weight *n* S1 W2
weird *adj* S2
welcome *interjection* S1
welcome *adj* S2 W3
welcome *v* S3 W2
well *adv* S1 W1
well *interjection* S1 W1
well *adj* S1 W2
west *n* S1 W2
west *adj* S3 W3
west *adv* S3 W3
western *adj* S2 W2
wet *adj* S2 W3
what pron, *determiner, predeterminer* S1 W1
whatever *determiner, pron* S1 W1
whatever *adv* S2
wheel *n* S2 W3
when adv, *conjunction, pron* S1 W1
whenever adv, *conjunction* S2 W3
where adv, *conjunction, pron* S1 W1
wherever *adv* S2
whether *conjunction* S1 W1
which *determiner, pron* S1 W1
while *conjunction* S1 W1
while *n* S1 W2
whisper *v* W3
whisper *n* W3
white *adj* S1 W1
white *n* S3 W2
who *pron* S1 W1
whole *adj* S1 W1
whole *n* S2 W2
whom *pron* W1
whose *determiner, pron* S2 W1
why *adv* S1 W1
wide *adj* S1 W1
wide *adv* S3 W3
widely *adv* W2
wife *n* S1 W1
wild *adj* S2 W2
will *modal verb* S1 W1
will *n* S2 W2
willing *adj* S2 W3
win *v* S1 W1
win *n* W3
wind *n* S2 W2
wind *v* S3 W3
window *n* S1 W1
windy *adj* S3
wine *n* S2 W2
wing *n* S2 W2
winner *n* S3 W2
winter *n* S2 W2
wipe *v* S3
wire *n* S2 W3
wise *adj* S3
wish *v* S1 W1
wish *n* S3
with *prep* S1 W1
within prep, *adv* S1 W1
without prep, *adv* S1 W1
woman *n* S1 W1
wonder *v* S1 W2
wonderful *adj* S1 W2
wood *n* S2 W2
wooden *adj* S3 W3
wool *n* S3
word *n* S1 W1
work *v* S1 W1
work *n* S1 W1
worker *n* S2 W1
world *n* S1 W1
worried *adj* S2 W3
worry *v* S1 W2
worry *n* S2
worse *adj* S1 W2
worse *adv* S3 W2
worst *adj* S2 W1
worst *n* S2 W3
worth *adj* S1 W2
worth *n* W3
would *modal verb* S1 W1
wrap *v* S3
wrist *n* W3
write *v* S1 W1
writer *n* S3 W2
writing *n* S2 W3
written *adj* W3
wrong *adj* S1 W1
wrong *adv* S2

yard *n* S2 W2
yeah *adv* S1
year *n* S1 W1
yellow *adj* S2 W3
yellow *n* S3 W3
yes *adv* S1 W1
yesterday *adv* S1 W1
yet *adv* S1 W1
yet *conjunction* W2
yogurt *n* S3
you *pron* S1 W1
young *adj* S1 W1
your *determiner* S1 W1
yours *pron* S1 W3
yourself *pron* S1 W2
youth *n* S2 W2

zero number S3
zip *n* S3
zipper *n* S3
zoo *n* S3

The full list of 9000 words is available in the *Longman Dictionary of Contemporary English* online at www.longmandictionaries.com.

Longman Defining Vocabulary

The Longman Defining Vocabulary of around 2000 common words has been used to write all the definitions in this dictionary. The words in the Defining Vocabulary have been carefully chosen to ensure that the definitions are clear and easy to understand, and that the words used in explanations are easier than the words being defined. Words in the Defining Vocabulary are constantly being researched and checked to make sure that they are frequent in the Longman Corpus Network, and that they are used correctly by learners in the Longman Learners' Corpus.

The words listed below are the main forms which are used in definitions. However, there are other limits on which word forms and meanings may be used.

Word meanings

The definitions use only the most common meanings of the words in the list.

Word classes

For some words in the list, a word class label such as *n* or *adj* is shown. This means that this particular word is used in definitions only in the word class shown. So **anger**, for example, is used only as a noun and not as a verb.

Phrasal verbs

Phrasal verbs are not used in definitions, except for the ones included in the list. Other phrasal verbs which are common in English and could be formed from words in the Defining Vocabulary list (such as **put up with**) are not used.

Prefixes and suffixes

Some words on the list may have prefixes (like **un-**) or suffixes (like **-ly**) added to them to make different word forms in the definition. The list of these affixes is included below. The forms which are common, or which change their meaning when a prefix or suffix is added (such as **acceptable** and **agreement**), are included in the full list.

Prefixes and suffixes that can be used with words in the Defining Vocabulary

-able	-ed	-ical	ir-	-less	re-
-al	-ence	im-	-ish	-ly	self-
-ance	-er	in-	-ity	-ment	-th
-ation	-ful	-ing	-ive	-ness	un-
dis-	-ic	-ion	-ize	non-	-y

Proper names

The Defining Vocabulary does not include the names of actual places, nationalities, religions, and so on, which are occasionally mentioned in definitions.

Words not in the Defining Vocabulary

It is sometimes necessary or helpful to use a word that is not in the Defining Vocabulary. These are shown in SMALL CAPITAL LETTERS, and sometimes followed by an explanation in brackets. For example:

> **kan·ga·roo** /ˌkæŋɡəˈruː◂/ *n* (*plural* **kangaroos**) [C] an Australian animal that moves by jumping and carries its babies in a POUCH (=a special pocket of skin) on its stomach → **marsupial**

Sometimes a definition includes a word which has its own entry and definition very close by. This word is written in ordinary type, even if it is not in the Defining Vocabulary. For example:

> **crick·et·er** /ˈkrɪkɪtə $ -ər/ *n* [C] *BrE* someone who plays cricket → **batsman**, **bowler**, **fielder**: *Her father was a very good cricketer.*

The word **cricket** is not in the special list of defining words, but its own definition is the entry above, so it can be found very easily.

Example sentences

The example sentences in this dictionary are allowed to use words outside the Defining Vocabulary. They are based on corpus evidence, and show the ways in which a word or phrase is used in a natural, typical context. However, care has been taken to make sure that these examples are helpful to the student. Where necessary, changes have been made to sentences found in the Corpus, or new examples have been written, to show the uses found in the Corpus in a simpler form.

a
abbreviation
ability
able
about
above
abroad
absence
absent *adj*
accept
acceptable
accident
accidental
according (to)
account *n*
achieve
achievement
acid
across
act
action
active
activity
actor, actress
actual
actually
add
addition
additional
address
adjective
admire
admit
adult
advanced
advantage
adventure *n*
adverb
advertise
advertisement
advice
advise
affair
affect
afford
afraid
after *prep, conj, adv*
afternoon
afterwards
again
against
age *n*
ago
agree
agreement
ahead
aim
air *n*
aircraft
air force
airport
alcohol
alive
all
allow
almost
alone
along
alphabet
already
also
although
always
among
amount *n*
amuse
amusement
amusing
an
ancient *adj*
and
anger *n*
angle *n*
angry
animal
announce
annoy
annoying
another
answer
anxiety
anxious
any
anymore
anyone
anything
anywhere
apart
apartment
appear
appearance
apple
approval
approve
area
argue
argument
arm *n*
army
around
arrange
arrangement
arrival
arrive
art
article
artificial
as
ashamed
ask
asleep
association
at
atom
attach
attack
attempt
attend
attention
attitude
attract
attractive
authority
autumn
available
average *adj, n*
avoid
awake *adj*
award *n*
away *adv*
awkward

baby
back *adj, adv, n*
background
backward(s) *adv*
bad
bag *n*
bake *v*
balance
ball *n*
band *n*
bank *n*
bar *n*
base *n, v*
baseball
basic
basket
bath *n*
battle *n*
be
beach *n*
beak
beam *n*
bean
bear
beat
beautiful
beauty
because
become
bed
beer
before
begin
beginning
behave
behaviour
behind *adv, prep*
belief
believe
bell
belong
below
belt *n*
bend
beneath
beside(s)
best
better *adj, adv*
between
beyond *prep*
bicycle *n*
big *adj*
bill
biology
bird
birth
bit
bite
bitter *adj*
black *adj, n*
blade
blame
blind *adj*
block
blood
blow
blue
board *n*
boat
body
boil
bomb
bone *n*
book *n*
boot *n*
border *n*
bored
boring
born
borrow
both
bottle *n*
bottom *n*
bowl *n*
box *n*
boy
boyfriend
brain *n*
branch *n*
brave *adj*
bread
break *v*
breakfast *n*
breast
breath
breathe
breed
brick
bridge *n*
bright
bring
broad *adj*
broadcast *v*
brother
brown *adj, n*
brush
bubble *n*
build *v*
building
bullet
burn
burst *v*
bury
bus
bush
business
busy
but *conj*
butter *n*
button *n*
buy *v*
by *prep*

cake *n*
calculate
call *v*
calm *adj*
camera
camp *n, v*
can
cannot
cap
capital
car
card
care
careful
careless
carriage
carry
case *n*
castle
cat
catch *v*
cattle
cause
ceiling
celebrate
cell
central
centre *n*
century
ceremony
certain *adj*
chain *n*
chair *n*
chance *n*
change
character
charge
chase *v*
cheap
cheat *v*
check
cheek *n*
cheese
chemical
chemistry
cheque
chest
chew *v*
chicken
child
chin
chocolate
choice *n*
choose
church
cigarette
cinema
circle *n*
circular *adj*
citizen
city
claim *v*
class *n*
clay
clean *adj, v*
clear *adj, v*
clever
click *n, v*
cliff
climb *v*
clock *n*
close *adj, adv, v*
cloth
clothes
clothing
cloud *n*
club *n*
coal
coast *n*
coat *n*
coffee
coin *n*
cold *adj, n*
collar *n*
collect
college
colour
comb
combination
combine *v*
come
comfort
comfortable
commit
committee
common *adj*
communicate
communication
company
compare *v*
comparison
compete
competition
competitor
complain
complaint
complete
completely
complicated
computer
concern *v*
concerning
concert
condition *n*
confidence
confident
confuse
confusing
connect
connection
conscious
consider
consist
contain
container
continue
continuous
contract *n*
control
conversation
cook
cool *adj*
copy
corn
corner *n*
correct
cost
cotton
cough
could
council
count *v*
country *n*
countryside
courage
course *n*
court *n*
cover
cow *n*
crack *n, v*
crash
crazy
cream *n*
creature
crime
criminal
criticism
criticize
crop *n*
cross *n, v*
crowd

cruel
cruelty
crush *v*
cry
cup *n*
cupboard
cure
curl
current *n*
curtain *n*
curve
custom
customer
cut
cycle *v*

daily *adj, adv*
damage
dance
danger
dangerous
dark
date *n*
daughter
day
dead *adj*
deal *n*
deal with
death
debt
decay
deceive
decide
decision
decorate
decoration
decrease
deep *adj*
defeat
defence
defend
definite
definitely
degree
delay
deliberate *adj*
deliberately
delicate
deliver
demand
department
depend
dependent
depth
describe
description
desert *n*
deserve
design
desirable
desire *n*
desk
destroy
destruction
detail *n*
determination
determined
develop
dictionary
die *v*
difference
different
difficult
difficulty
dig *v*
dinner
direct
direction
dirt
dirty *adj*
disappoint
disappointing
discover
discovery
discuss
discussion
disease
dish *n*
dismiss
distance
distant
divide
do *v*
doctor *n*
document *n*
dog *n*
dollar
door
double
doubt
down *adv, prep*
draw *v*
drawer
drawing *n*
dream
dress
drink
drive
drop
drug *n*
drum *n*
drunk *adj, past part*
dry
duck
dull *adj*
during
dust *n*
duty

each
eager
ear
early
earn
earth *n*
east
eastern
easy *adj*
eat
economic
economy
edge *n*
educate
educated
education
effect *n*
effective
effort
egg
eight
either
elbow
elect *v*
election
electric
electrical
electricity
electronic
eleven
else
email
embarrass
embarrassing
emotion
emphasize
employ *v*
employee
employer
employment
empty *adj, v*
enclose
encourage
end
enemy
energy
engine
engineer *n*
enjoy
enjoyable
enjoyment
enough
enter
entertain
entertainment
entrance *n*
envelope
environment
equal *adj, n*
equipment
escape
especially
establish
etc
even *adj, adv*
evening
event
ever
every
everyone
everything
everywhere
evil
exact *adj*
exactly
examination
examine
example
excellent
except *conj, prep*
exchange
excite
exciting
excuse
exercise
exist
existence
expect
expensive
experience
explain
explanation
explode
explosion
explosive
express *v*
expression
extra *adj*
extreme *adj*
extremely
eye

face
fact
factory
fail *v*
failure
fair *adj*
fairly
faith
faithful *adj*
fall
false
familiar
family
famous
far
farm
farmer
fashion *n*
fashionable
fast *adj, adv*
fasten
fat
father *n*
fault *n*
favourable
favourite *adj*
fear *n*
feather *n*
feature *n*
feed *v*
feel *v*
feeling(s)
female
fence *n*
fever
few
field *n*
fight
figure *n*
fill *v*
film
final *adj*
finally
financial
find *v*
find out
fine *adj*
finger *n*
finish *v*
fire
firm *adj*
first *adj, adv, pron*
fish
fit *adj, v*
five
fix *v*
flag *n*
flame *n*
flash *n, v*
flat *adj*
flesh
flight
float *v*
flood
floor *n*
flour *n*
flow
flower *n*
fly *n, v*
fog
fold
follow
food
foot *n*
football
for *prep*
force
foreign
foreigner
forest
forever
forget
forgive
fork *n*
form
formal
former
fortunate
forward(s) *adv*
four
frame *n*
free
freedom
freeze *v*
frequent *adj*
fresh
friend
friendly
friendship
frighten
frightening
from
front *adj, n*
fruit *n*
full *adj*
fun
funeral
funny
fur *n*
furniture
further *adj, adv*
future

gain *v*
game *n*
garage *n*
garden
gas *n*
gate
gather *v*
general *adj*
generally
generous
gentle
get
gift
girl
girlfriend
give *v*
glad
glass *adj, n*
glue
go *v*
goat
god
gold
golf
good
goodbye
goods
govern
government
graceful
gradual
grain
gram
grammar
grandfather
grandmother
grandparent
grass *n*
grateful
great *adj*
green
greet
greeting
grey *adj, n*
ground *n*
group *n*
grow
growth
guard *v*
guess *v*
guest *n*
guide
guilty
gun *n*

habit
hair
half
hall
hammer *n*
hand *n*
handle
hang *v*
happen
happy
hard
hardly
harm
harmful
hat
hate *v*
hatred
have
he
head *n*
health
healthy
hear
heart
heat
heaven
heavy *adj*
heel *n*
height
hello
help
helpful
her(s)
herb
here
herself
hide *v*
high *adj, adv*
hill
him
himself
his

historical
history
hit
hold *v*
hole
holiday *n*
hollow *adj*
holy
home *adv, n*
honest
honour *n*
hook *n*
hope
hopeful
horizontal *adj*
horn
horse *n*
hospital
hot *adj*
hotel
hour
house *n*
how *adv*
human
humorous
humour
hundred(th)
hungry
hunt *v*
hurry
hurt *v*
husband *n*

ice *n*
idea
if
ignore
ill *adj*
illegal
illness
image
imaginary
imagination
imagine
immediately
importance
important
impressive
improve
improvement
in *adv, prep*
include
including
income
increase
independent
indoor(s)
industrial
industry
infect
infection
infectious
influence *v*
informal
information
injure
injury
ink *n*
inner
insect
inside
in spite of
instead
institution
instruction
instrument
insult *v*
insulting
insurance
insure
intelligence
intelligent
intend
intention
interest
interesting
international *adj*
interrupt
into
introduce
introduction
invent
invitation
invite *v*
involve
inwards
iron *adj, n*
island
it
its

jacket
jaw
jewel
jewellery
job
join
joint
joke
journey *n*
judge
judgment
juice
jump
just *adv*
justice

keen *adj*
keep *v*
key *n*
kick
kill *v*
kilogram
kilometre
kind
king
kiss
kitchen
knee *n*
kneel
knife *n*
knock *v*
knot
know *v*
knowledge

lack
lake
lamb
lamp
land
language
large
last
late
laugh *v*
laughter
law
lawyer
lay *v*
layer *n*
lazy
lead *v*
leaf *n*
lean *v*
learn
least
leather
leave *v*
left
leg *n*
legal
lend
length
less *adv, pron, determiner*
lesson
let *v*
let go of
letter
level *adv, adj, n*
library
lid
lie
lie down
life
lift
light
like *prep, v*
likely
limit
line *n*
lion
lip
liquid
list *n*
listen *v*
literature
litre
little
live *v*
load
local *adj*
lock
lonely
long *adj, adv*
look
look after
look for
loose *adj*
lord *n*
lose
loss
lot
loud
love
low *adj*
lower
loyal
loyalty
luck *n*
lucky
lung

machine *n*
machinery
magazine
magic
main *adj*
make *v*
make up
male
man *n*
manage
manager
manner
many
map *n*
march *v*
mark
market *n*
marriage
married
marry
mass *n*
match
material *n*
mathematics
matter
may *v*
me
meal
mean *v*
meaning *n*
means
measure
measurement
meat
medical *adj*
medicine
meet *v*
meeting
melt
member
membership
memory
mental
mention *v*
message
metal *n*
method
metre
middle
might *v*
mile
military *adj*
milk *n*
million
mind
mine *n, pron*
mineral
minister *n*
minute *n*
mirror *n*
miss *v*
mist *n*
mistake *n*
mix *v*
mixture
model *n*
modern *adj*
moment
money
monkey *n*
month
moon *n*
moral *adj*
more
morning
most
mother *n*
motor *adj, n*
mountain
mouse
mouth *n*
move *v*
movement
much
mud
multiply
murder
muscle *n*
music
musician
must *v*
my
mysterious
mystery

nail
name
narrow *adj*
nasty
nation
national *adj*
natural *adj*
nature
navy
near *adj, adv, prep*
nearly
neat
necessary
neck
need
needle *n*
negative *adj*
neither
nerve *n*
nervous
net *n*
network *n*
never
new
news
newspaper
next
nice
night
nine
no *adv, determiner*
noise *n*
none *pron*
nonsense
no one
nor
normal
north
northern
nose *n*
not
note *n*
nothing
notice
noticeable
noun
now
nowhere
number *n*
nurse
nut

obey
object *n*
obtain
occasion *n*
ocean
o'clock
of
off *adv, prep*
offence
offend
offensive *adj*
offer
office
officer
official
often
oil *n*
old
old-fashioned
on *adv, prep*
once *adv*
one
onion
only
only just
onto
open *adj, v*
operate
operation
opinion
opponent
opportunity
oppose
as opposed to
opposite
opposition
or
orange
order
ordinary
organ
organize
organization
origin
original
other
ought
our(s)
out *adj, adv*
outdoor(s)
outer
outside
over *adv, prep*
owe
own
owner
oxygen

pack *v*
package
page *n*
pain *n*
painful
paint
painting
pair *n*
pale *adj*
pan *n*
paper *n*

parallel *adj, n*
parent
park
parliament
part *n*
participle
particular *adj*
partly
partner *n*
party *n*
pass *v*
passage
passenger
past
path
patient *adj*
pattern *n*
pause
pay
payment
peace
peaceful
pen *n*
pence
pencil *n*
people *n*
pepper *n*
percent
perfect *adj*
perform
performance
perhaps
period *n*
permanent
permission
person
personal
persuade
pet *n*
petrol
photograph
phrase *n*
physical *adj*
physics
piano *n*
pick *v*
pick up
picture *n*
piece *n*
pig *n*
pile *n*
pilot *n*
pin
pink
pipe *n*
pity
place
plain *adj, n*
plan
plane *n*
plant
plastic
plate *n*
play
pleasant
please
pleased
pleasure *n*
plenty *pron*
plural
pocket *n*
poem
poet
poetry
point
pointed
poison
poisonous
pole *n*
police *n*
polish *v*
polite
political
politician
politics
pool *n*
poor
popular
population
port *n*
position *n*
positive
possess
possession
possibility
possible *adj*
possibly
post
pot *n*
potato
pound *n*
pour
powder *n*
power *n*
powerful
practical
practice
practise
praise
pray
prayer
prefer
preparation
prepare
present *adj, n*
preserve *v*
president
press *v*
pressure *n*
pretend
pretty *adj*
prevent
previous
price *n*
priest
prince
principle
print
prison
prisoner
private *adj*
prize *n*
probably
problem
process *n*
produce *v*
product
production
profession
profit *n*
program *n*
programme
progress *n*
project *n*
promise
pronounce
pronunciation
proof *n*
proper
property
proposal
protect
protection
protective
protest
proud
prove
provide
public
pull
pump
punish
punishment
pure
purple
purpose *n*
push
put

quality
quantity
quarrel
quarter *n*
queen *n*
question
quick *adj*
quiet

rabbit *n*
race
radio *n*
railway
rain
raise *v*
range *n*
rank *n*
rare
rat *n*
rate *n*
rather
raw
reach *v*
react
reaction
read *v*
ready *adj*
real
realize
really
reason
reasonable
receive
recent
recently
recognize
record *n, v*
red
reduce
reduction
refer
refusal
refuse *v*
regard *v*
regular *adj*
related
relating to
relative *n*
relation
relationship
relax
relaxing
religion
religious
remain
remark *n*
remember
remind
remove *v*
rent
repair
repeat *v*
replace
reply
report
represent
representative *n*
request *n*
respect
responsible
rest
restaurant
restrict
result
return *n, v*
reward
rice
rich
rid *adj*
ride
right *adj, adv, n*
ring
rise
risk
river
road
rob
rock *n*
roll *v*
romantic *adj*
roof *n*
room *n*
root *n*
rope *n*
rose
rough *adj*
round *adj, adv, prep*
row
royal *adj*
rub *v*
rubber
rude
ruin *v*
rule
ruler
run
rush *v*

sad
safe *adj*
safety
sail
sailor
salary
sale
salt *n*
same
sand *n*
sandwich *n*
satisfaction
satisfactory
satisfy
sauce
save *v*
say *v*
scale *n*
scatter *v*
scene
school *n*
science
scientific
scientist
scissors
score
screen *n*
screw
sea
search
season *n*
seat
second *adv, n, number*
secret
secretary
see *v*
seed *n*
seem
sell *v*
send
sense *n*
sensible
sensitive
sentence *n*
separate
series
serious
servant
serve
service *n*
set *n, v*
settle *v*
seven
several
severe
sew
sex *n*
sexual
shade
shadow *n*
shake
shall
shame *n*
shape
share
sharp *adj*
she
sheep
sheet
shelf
shell *n*
shelter
shine *v*
shiny
ship *n*
shirt
shock *n, v*
shocking
shoe n
shoot *v*
shop
shore *n*
short *adj*
shot *n*
should
shoulder *n*
shout
show
shut
shy *adj*
sick *adj*
side *n*
sideways
sight *n*
sign
signal
silence *n*
silent
silk
silly
silver *n, adj*
similar
simple
since
sincere
sing
single *adj*
singular
sink *v*
sister
sit
situation
six
size *n*
skilful
skill
skin *n*
skirt *n*
sky
sleep
sleeve
slide *v*
slight *adj*
slippery
slope
slow
small
smell
smile
smoke
smooth *adj*
snake *n*
snow
so
soap *n*
social *adj*
society
sock *n*
soft
software
soil *n*
soldier *n*
solid
solution
solve
some
somehow
someone
something
sometimes
somewhere
son
song

soon
sore *adj*
sorry
sort *n*
soul
sound *n, v*
soup
sour *adj*
south
southern
space *n*
spacecraft
speak
special *adj*
specific
speech
speed *n*
spell *v*
spend
spice *n*
spicy
spin *v*
in spite of
split *v*
spoil *v*
spoon *n*
sport *n*
spot *n*
spread *v*
spring *n*
square *adj, n*
stage *n*
stair
stamp
stand *v*
standard
star *n*
start
state
statement
station *n*
stay
steady *adj*
steal *v*
steam *n*
steel *n*
steep *adj*
stem *n*
step
stick
sticky
stiff *adj*
still *adj, adv*
sting *v*
stitch
stomach *n*
stone *n*
stop
store
storm *n*
story
straight *adj, adv*
strange
stream *n*
street
strength
stretch *v*
strict
strike *v*
string *n*
strong
structure *n*
struggle
student
study
stupid
style *n*
subject *n*
substance
succeed
success
successful
such
suck *v*
sudden
suffer
sugar *n*
suggest
suit
suitable
sum *n*
summer
sun *n*
supply
support
suppose
sure *adj*
surface *n*
surprise
surprising
surround *v*
swallow *v*
swear
sweep *v*
sweet
swell *v*
swim
swing
switch
sword
symbol
sympathetic
sympathy
system

table *n*
tail *n*
take *v*
talk
tall
tape *n*
taste
tax
taxi *n*
tea
teach
team *n*
tear
technical
technology
teenage
telephone
television
tell
temper *n*
temperature
temporary
ten
tend
tendency
tennis
tense *n*
tent
terrible
test
than
thank
that
the
theatre
their(s)
them
themself
themselves
then *adv*
there
therefore
these
they
thick *adj*
thief
thin *adj*
thing
think *v*
third
thirsty
this
thorough
those
though
thought
thousand
thread *n*
threat
threaten
three
throat
through
throw
thumb *n*
ticket *n*
tidy *adj, v*
tie
tight *adj*
time *n*
tired
tiring
title
to
tobacco
today
toe *n*
together
toilet
tomato
tomorrow
tongue
tonight
too
tool *n*
tooth
top *adj, n*
total
touch
tourist
towards
tower *n*
town
toy *n*
track *n*
trade *n*
traditional
traffic *n*
train
training
translate
transparent
transport *n*
trap
travel
treat *v*
treatment
tree
tribe
trick *n, v*
trip *n*
tropical
trouble
trousers
truck *n*
true *adj*
trust
truth
try *v*
tube
tune *n*
turn
TV
twelve
twice
twist
two
type *n*
typical
tyre

ugly
under *prep*
understand
underwear
undo
unexpected
uniform *n*
union
unit
unite
universe
university
unless
until
unusual
up *adj, adv, prep*
upper
upright *adj, adv*
upset *v, adj*
upside down
upstairs
urgent
us
use
useful
useless
usual

valley
valuable *adj*
value *n*
variety
various
vegetable
vehicle
verb
vertical *adj*
very *adv*
victory
video *n*
view *n*
village
violence
violent
visit
visitor
voice *n*
vote
vowel

wage(s)
waist
wait *v*
wake *v*
walk
wall *n*
want
war *n*
warm *adj, v*
warmth
warn
warning
wash
waste
watch
water
wave
way
we
weak
wealth
weapon
wear *v*
weather *n*
weave *v*
website
wedding
week
weekly *adj, adv*
weigh
weight *n*
welcome
well *adj, adv, n*
west
western *adj*
wet *adj*
what
whatever
wheat
wheel *n*
when
whenever
where
whether
which
while *conj*
whip
whistle
white *adj, n*
who
whole
whose
why
wide
width
wife
wild *adj, adv*
will
willing
win *v*
wind
window
wine *n*
wing *n*
winter
wire *n*
wise *adj*
wish
with
within
without
woman
wood
wooden
wool
word *n*
work
world
worry
worse
worst
worth
would
wound
wrap *v*
wrist
write
wrong *adj, adv, n*

year
yellow
yes
yet
you
young *adj*
your(s)

zero

Irregular verbs

VERB	PAST TENSE	PAST PARTICIPLE
abide	abided, abode	abided
arise	arose	arisen
awake	awoke	awoken
babysit	babysat	babysat
bear	bore	borne
beat	beat	beaten
become	became	become
befall	befell	befallen
beget	begot (*also* begat *biblical*)	begotten
begin	began	begun
behold	beheld	beheld
bend	bent	bent
beseech	besought, beseeched	besought, beseeched
beset	beset	beset
bet	bet	bet
bid	bade, bid	bid, bidden
bind	bound	bound
bite	bit	bitten
bleed	bled	bled
bless	blessed	blessed
blow	blew	blown
break	broke	broken
breast-feed	breast-fed	breast-fed
breed	bred	bred
bring	brought	brought
broadcast	broadcast	broadcast
browbeat	browbeat	browbeaten
build	built	built
burn	burned, burnt	burned, burnt
burst	burst	burst
bust	bust (*BrE*), busted (*esp. AmE*)	bust (*BrE*), busted (*esp.. AmE*)
buy	bought	bought
cast	cast	cast
catch	caught	caught
choose	chose	chosen
cleave	cleaved, cleft, clove	cleaved, cleft, cloven
cling	clung	clung
come	came	come
cost	cost	cost
could	(see dictionary entry)	
creep	crept	crept
cut	cut	cut
deal	dealt	dealt
dig	dug	dug
dive	dived, dove (*AmE*)	dived
do	did	done
draw	drew	drawn
dream	dreamed, dreamt	dreamed, dreamt
drink	drank	drunk
drive	drove	driven
dwell	dwelt, dwelled	dwelt, dwelled
eat	ate	eaten
fall	fell	fallen
feed	fed	fed
feel	felt	felt
fight	fought	fought
find	found	found
flee	fled	fled
fling	flung	flung
fly	flew	flown
forbid	forbade	forbidden
forecast	forecast, forecasted	forecast
foresee	foresaw	foreseen
foretell	foretold	foretold
forget	forgot	forgotten
forgive	forgave	forgiven
forego	forewent	foregone
forgo	forwent	forgone
forsake	forsook	forsaken
forswear	forswore	forsworn
freeze	froze	frozen
gainsay	gainsaid	gainsaid
get	got	got (*BrE*), gotten (*AmE*)
give	gave	given
go	went	gone
grind	ground	ground
grow	grew	grown
hamstring	hamstrung	hamstrung
hang	hung, hanged	hung, hanged
have	had	had
hear	heard	heard
heave	heaved, hove	heaved, hove
hide	hid	hidden, hid
hit	hit	hit
hold	held	held
hurt	hurt	hurt
input	inputted, input	inputted, input
inset	inset	inset
interbreed	interbred	interbred
interweave	interwove	interwoven
keep	kept	kept
kneel	knelt, kneeled (*esp. AmE*)	knelt, kneeled (*esp. AmE*)
knit	knitted, knit	knitted, knit
know	knew	known
lay	laid	laid
lead	led	led
lean	leaned, leant (*esp. BrE*)	leaned, leant (*esp. BrE*)
leap	leapt (*esp. BrE*), leaped (*esp. AmE*)	leapt (*esp. BrE*), leaped (*esp. AmE*)
learn	learned, learnt (*esp. BrE*)	learned, learnt (*esp. BrE*)
leave	left	left
lend	lent	lent
let	let	let
lie	lay	lain
light	lit, lighted	lit, lighted
lose	lost	lost
make	made	made
mean	meant	meant
meet	met	met
miscast	miscast	miscast
mishear	misheard	misheard
mislay	mislaid	mislaid
mislead	misled	misled
misread	misread	misread
misspell	misspelled, misspelt (*BrE*)	misspelled, misspelt (*BrE*)
misspend	misspent	misspent
mistake	mistook	mistaken
misunderstand	misunderstood	misunderstood
mow	mowed	mown, mowed
offset	offset	offset
outbid	outbid	outbid
outdo	outdid	outdone
outgrow	outgrew	outgrown
outrun	outran	outrun
outsell	outsold	outsold
outshine	outshone	outshone
overcome	overcame	overcome
overdo	overdid	overdone
overeat	overate	overeaten
overhang	overhung	overhung
overhear	overheard	overheard
overlay	overlaid	overlaid
overpay	overpaid	overpaid
override	overrode	overridden

VERB	PAST TENSE	PAST PARTICIPLE
overrun	overran	overrun
oversee	oversaw	overseen
overshoot	overshot	overshot
oversleep	overslept	overslept
overtake	overtook	overtaken
overthrow	overthrew	overthrown
partake	partook	partaken
pay	paid	paid
plead	pleaded, pled (*esp. AmE*)	pleaded, pled (*esp. AmE*)
proofread	proofread	proofread
prove	proved	proved (*also* proven *AmE*)
put	put	put
quit	quit	quit
read	read /red/	read /red/
rebuild	rebuilt	rebuilt
recast	recast	recast
redo	redid	redone
relay	relaid	relaid
remake	remade	remade
rend	rent	rent
repay	repaid	repaid
rerun	reran	rerun
resell	resold	resold
reset	reset	reset
resit	resat	resat
retell	retold	retold
rethink	rethought	rethought
rewind	rewound	rewound
rewrite	rewrote	rewritten
rid	rid	rid
ride	rode	ridden
ring	rang	rung
rise	rose	risen
run	ran	run
saw	sawed	sawn, sawed (*AmE*)
say	said	said
see	saw	seen
seek	sought	sought
sell	sold	sold
send	sent	sent
set	set	set
sew	sewed	sewn, sewed
shake	shook	shaken
shall	(see dictionary entry)	
shear	sheared	shorn, sheared
shed	shed	shed
shine	shone, shined	shone, shined
shit	shit, shat	shit, shat
shoe	shod	shod
shoot	shot	shot
should	(see dictionary entry)	
show	showed	shown, showed
shrink	shrank, shrunk (*AmE*)	shrunk
shut	shut	shut
sing	sang	sung
sink	sank, sunk (*AmE*)	sunk
sit	sat	sat
slay	slew	slain
sleep	slept	slept
slide	slid	slid
sling	slung	slung
slink	slunk	slunk
slit	slit	slit
smell	smelled, smelt (*esp. BrE*)	smelled, smelt (*esp. BrE*)
smite	smote	smitten
sow	sowed	sown, sowed
speak	spoke	spoken
speed	sped, speeded	sped, speeded
spell	spelled, spelt (*esp. BrE*)	spelled, spelt (*esp. BrE*)
spend	spent	spent
spill	spilled, spilt (*esp. BrE*)	spilled, spilt (*esp. BrE*)

VERB	PAST TENSE	PAST PARTICIPLE
spin	spun	spun
spit	spat (*also* spit *AmE*)	spat (*also* spit *AmE*)
split	split	split
spoil	spoiled, spoilt (*BrE*)	spoiled, spoilt (*BrE*)
spoon-feed	spoon-fed	spoon-fed
spotlight	spotlighted, spotlit	spotlighted, spotlit
spread	spread	spread
spring	sprang (*also* sprung *AmE*)	sprung
stand	stood	stood
steal	stole	stolen
stick	stuck	stuck
sting	stung	stung
stink	stank, stunk	stunk
strew	strewed	strewn, strewed
stride	strode	stridden
strike	struck	struck
string	strung	strung
strive	strove, strived	striven, strived
sublet	sublet	sublet
swear	swore	sworn
sweep	swept	swept
swell	swelled	swollen, swelled
swim	swam	swum
swing	swung	swung
take	took	taken
teach	taught	taught
tear	tore	torn
tell	told	told
think	thought	thought
thrive	thrived, throve	thrived
throw	threw	thrown
thrust	thrust	thrust
tread	trod	trodden, trod
unbend	unbent	unbent
undergo	underwent	undergone
underlie	underlay	underlaid
underpay	underpaid	underpaid
undersell	undersold	undersold
understand	understood	understood
undertake	undertook	undertaken
underwrite	underwrote	underwritten
undo	undid	undone
unwind	unwound	unwound
uphold	upheld	upheld
upset	upset	upset
wake	woke	woken
wear	wore	worn
weave	wove	woven
wed	wedded, wed	wedded, wed
weep	wept	wept
wet	wetted, wet	wetted, wet
win	won	won
wind /waɪnd/	wound	wound
withdraw	withdrew	withdrawn
withhold	withheld	withheld
withstand	withstood	withstood
wring	wrung	wrung
write	wrote	written

ATLANTIC OCEAN
NORTH SEA
IRISH SEA
CELTIC SEA
English Channel
UNITED KINGDOM
SCOTLAND
ENGLAND
WALES
IRELAND
NORTHERN IRELAND
Shetland Is.
Mainland
Lerwick
Foula
Fair Isle
Orkney Is.
Westray
Sanday
Stronsay
Kirkwall
Hoy
South Ronaldsay
Pentland Firth
C. Wrath
Thurso
Wick
Helmsdale
Lairg
Golspie
Moray Firth
Outer Hebrides
Inner Hebrides
Lewis
Stornoway
Harris
St. Kilda
North Uist
Benbecula
South Uist
Barra
North Minch
North West Highlands
Ullapool
Tain
Invergordon
Dingwall
Skye
Portree
Inverness
L. Ness
Nairn
Elgin
Buckie
Banff
Fraserburgh
Peterhead
Huntly
Inverurie
Aberdeen
Stonehaven
Ballater
Aviemore
Grampian Mts.
Mallaig
Rhum
Eigg
Ben Nevis
Fort William
Coll
Tiree
Tobermory
Mull
Oban
Montrose
Arbroath
Forfar
Dundee
St. Andrews
Perth
Glenrothes
Kirkcaldy
L. Lomond
Stirling
Dunfermline
Dunbar
Colonsay
Jura
Islay
Greenock
Paisley
Glasgow
Edinburgh
Berwick-upon-Tweed
East Kilbride
Hamilton
Irvine
Kilmarnock
Arran
Campbeltown
Ayr
Southern Uplands
Galashiels
Jedburgh
Hawick
Cheviot Hills
Alnwick
Firth of Clyde
North Channel
Girvan
Dumfries
Stranraer
Kirkcudbright
Annan
Carlisle
Hexham
Newcastle-upon-Tyne
South Shields
Gateshead
Sunderland
Durham
Hartlepool
Redcar
Middlesbrough
Stockton-on-Tees
Darlington
Scarborough
Pennines
Workington
Whitehaven
Cumbrian Mts.
Barrow-in-Furness
Lancaster
Harrogate
York
Bridlington
Beverley
Kingston upon Hull
Leeds
Bradford
Keighley
Blackpool
Preston
Burnley
Blackburn
Bolton
Halifax
Huddersfield
Barnsley
Scunthorpe
Grimsby
Humber
Manchester
Oldham
Rotherham
Doncaster
Liverpool
Warrington
Stockport
Sheffield
Lincoln
Louth
Skegness
Chesterfield
Mansfield
Nottingham
Boston
The Wash
Cromer
Malin Hd.
Buncrana
Aran I.
Letterkenny
Coleraine
Londonderry
Lifford
Ballymena
Larne
Donegal
Ulster
Lough Neagh
Antrim
Bangor
Belfast
Omagh
Bundoran
Lower L. Erne
Portadown
Lisburn
Lurgan
Mull of Galloway
Enniskillen
Armagh
Newry
Sligo
Ballina
L. Conn
Castlebar
Leitrim
Cavan
Clones
Dundalk
Douglas
I. of Man
Westport
Lough Mask
Roscommon
Longford
Ceanannus Mor
Drogheda
Boyne
Connemara
Lough Corrib
Athlone
Lough Ree
Mullingar
Galway B.
Galway
Ballinasloe
Tullamore
Dublin
Dun Laoghaire
Bray
Anglesey
Holyhead
Bangor
Colwyn Bay
Chester
Wrexham
Crewe
Stoke-on-Trent
Derby
Snowdon
Pwllheli
Lough Derg
Ennis
Birr
Port Laoise
Athy
Kilrush
Limerick
Nenagh
Thurles
Carlow
Kilkenny
Wicklow Mts.
Arklow
Listowel
Tralee
Tipperary
Clonmel
Carrick-on-Suir
Wexford
Rosslare
Waterford
Mallow
Killarney
Macgillycuddy's Reeks
Blackwater
Dungarvan
Cork
Cobh
Youghal
Bantry
Bandon
Kinsale
Stafford
Shrewsbury
Telford
Welshpool
Wolverhampton
BIRMINGHAM
Nuneaton
Leicester
Coventry
Rugby
Grantham
Trent
Corby
Peterborough
King's Lynn
Norwich
Great Yarmouth
Lowestoft
Thetford
Ely
Bury St. Edmunds
Cambridge
Ipswich
Felixstowe
Harwich
Colchester
Cardigan Bay
Aberystwyth
Cambrian Mts.
Redditch
Worcester
Royal Leamington Spa
Northampton
Bedford
Milton Keynes
Stevenage
Hereford
Cotswold Hills
St. George's Channel
Fishguard
Carmarthen
Brecon
Haverfordwest
Milford Haven
Pembroke
Merthyr Tydfil
Neath
Llanelli
Swansea
Port Talbot
Rhondda
Cwmbran
Newport
Cardiff
Barry
Cheltenham
Gloucester
Oxford
Hemel Hempstead
Luton
Harlow
Chelmsford
High Wycombe
Watford
Basildon
Southend-on-Sea
Swindon
Slough
LONDON
Thames
Chatham
Margate
Canterbury
Maidstone
Dover
Bristol Channel
Bristol
Bath
Newbury
Reading
Reigate
Weston-super-Mare
Basingstoke
Guildford
Crawley
Ashford
Folkestone
Barnstaple
Exmoor
Salisbury
Winchester
Taunton
Southampton
Fareham
Havant
Hastings
Str. of Dover
Bude
Yeovil
Exeter
Bournemouth
Poole
Brighton
Worthing
Eastbourne
Dartmoor
Exmouth
Weymouth
Newport
Isle of Wight
Portsmouth
Torbay
Newquay
Truro
Plymouth
St. Austell
Falmouth
Land's End
Penzance
Isles of Scilly
C. de la
Fécamp
Dunkerque
Calais
C. Gris-Nez
Boulogne-sur-Mer
Le Touquet-Paris-Plage
Abbeville
Le Tréport
Dieppe
1224
316
789
1182
1342
1214
1311
973
840
816
893
978
1085
926
886
618
636
238
99
36
33
16

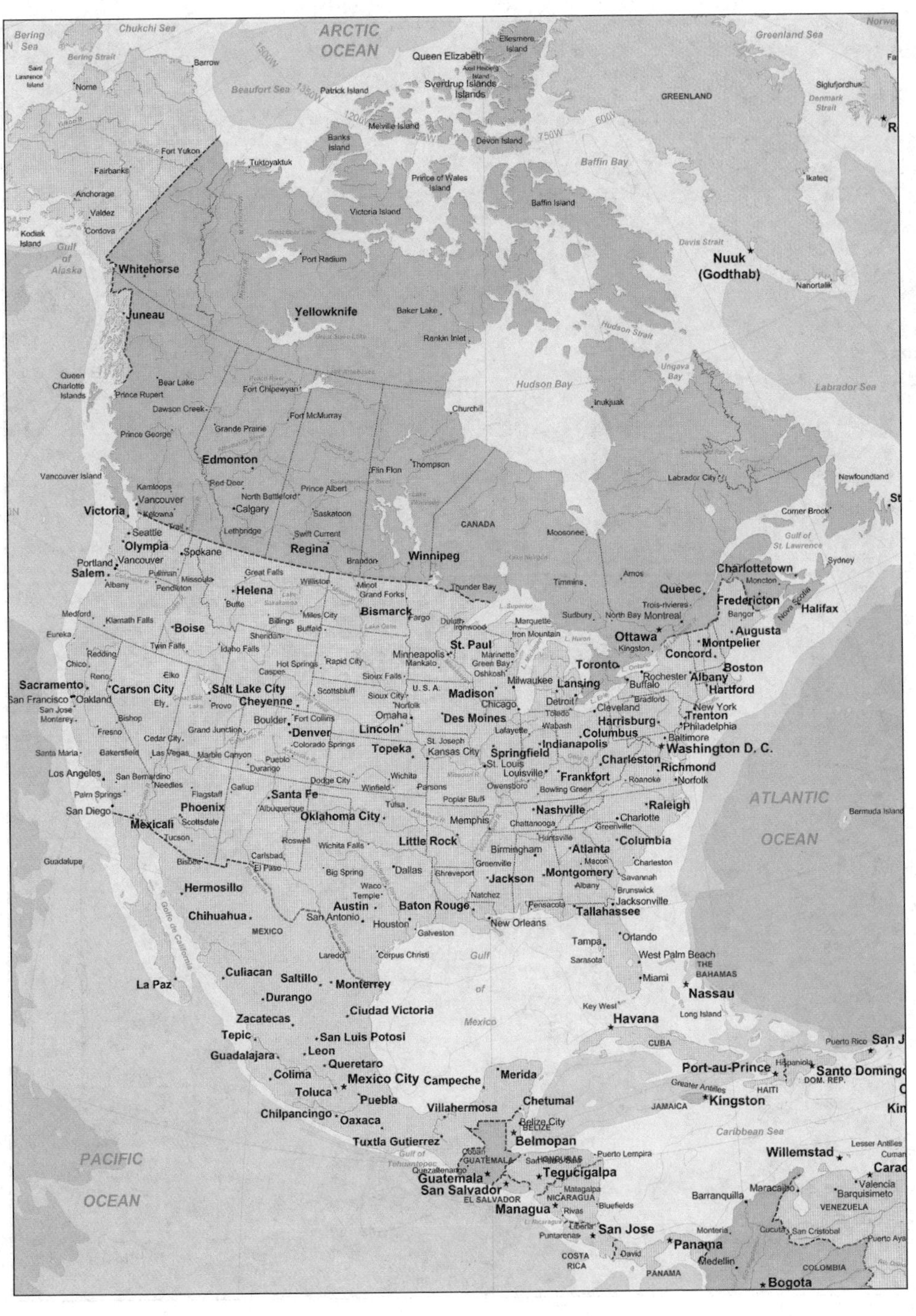
ARCTIC OCEAN
Chukchi Sea
Bering Sea
Bering Strait
Beaufort Sea
Greenland Sea
Baffin Bay
Davis Strait
Hudson Strait
Hudson Bay
Labrador Sea
Gulf of Alaska
Gulf of St. Lawrence
ATLANTIC OCEAN
PACIFIC OCEAN
Gulf of Mexico
Caribbean Sea
GREENLAND
CANADA
U. S. A.
MEXICO
CUBA
JAMAICA
HAITI
DOM. REP.
BELIZE
GUATEMALA
HONDURAS
EL SALVADOR
NICARAGUA
COSTA RICA
PANAMA
COLOMBIA
VENEZUELA
THE BAHAMAS
Queen Elizabeth
Ellesmere Island
Sverdrup Islands
Patrick Island
Melville Island
Banks Island
Devon Island
Prince of Wales Island
Victoria Island
Baffin Island
Queen Charlotte Islands
Vancouver Island
Newfoundland
Nome
Barrow
Fort Yukon
Fairbanks
Anchorage
Valdez
Cordova
Kodiak Island
Tuktoyaktuk
Port Radium
Whitehorse
Juneau
Yellowknife
Baker Lake
Rankin Inlet
Nuuk (Godthab)
Nanortalik
Ikateq
Siglufjordhur
Bear Lake
Prince Rupert
Fort Chipewyan
Dawson Creek
Fort McMurray
Churchill
Inukjuak
Grande Prairie
Prince George
Edmonton
Flin Flon
Thompson
Labrador City
Kamloops
Vancouver
Victoria
Kelowna
Red Deer
North Battleford
Prince Albert
Calgary
Saskatoon
Lethbridge
Swift Current
Regina
Winnipeg
Brandon
Moosonee
Corner Brook
Sydney
Charlottetown
Moncton
Fredericton
Halifax
Quebec
Trois-rivieres
Montreal
Ottawa
Kingston
Toronto
Timmins
Amos
Sudbury
North Bay
Thunder Bay
Seattle
Olympia
Spokane
Portland
Salem
Great Falls
Helena
Missoula
Williston
Minot
Grand Forks
Bismarck
Fargo
Duluth
Billings
Miles City
Boise
Twin Falls
Idaho Falls
Sheridan
Rapid City
Casper
Medford
Klamath Falls
Eureka
Redding
Chico
Reno
Sacramento
San Francisco
Oakland
San Jose
Monterey
Carson City
Salt Lake City
Cheyenne
Provo
Elko
Ely
Fresno
Bishop
Boulder
Fort Collins
Denver
Colorado Springs
Grand Junction
Pueblo
Durango
Las Vegas
Santa Maria
Bakersfield
Los Angeles
San Bernardino
Needles
Palm Springs
San Diego
Mexicali
Phoenix
Scottsdale
Tucson
Flagstaff
Gallup
Santa Fe
Albuquerque
Roswell
Carlsbad
El Paso
Sioux Falls
Sioux City
Norfolk
Omaha
Lincoln
Topeka
St. Joseph
Kansas City
Wichita
Dodge City
Winfield
Tulsa
Oklahoma City
Wichita Falls
Dallas
Big Spring
Waco
Temple
Austin
San Antonio
Houston
Galveston
Corpus Christi
Laredo
Minneapolis
Mankato
St. Paul
Madison
Milwaukee
Chicago
Des Moines
Springfield
St. Louis
Louisville
Frankfort
Indianapolis
Lansing
Detroit
Toledo
Cleveland
Columbus
Harrisburg
Buffalo
Rochester
Albany
Hartford
Boston
Concord
Montpelier
Augusta
Bangor
New York
Trenton
Philadelphia
Baltimore
Washington D. C.
Richmond
Norfolk
Charleston
Roanoke
Raleigh
Charlotte
Greenville
Columbia
Charleston
Nashville
Memphis
Little Rock
Chattanooga
Birmingham
Atlanta
Macon
Savannah
Montgomery
Jackson
Shreveport
Natchez
Baton Rouge
New Orleans
Pensacola
Tallahassee
Jacksonville
Brunswick
Orlando
Tampa
Sarasota
West Palm Beach
Miami
Key West
Nassau
Havana
Bermuda Island
Hermosillo
Chihuahua
Guadalupe
Golfo de California
La Paz
Culiacan
Saltillo
Monterrey
Durango
Ciudad Victoria
Zacatecas
Tepic
San Luis Potosi
Leon
Guadalajara
Queretaro
Colima
Mexico City
Campeche
Merida
Toluca
Puebla
Villahermosa
Chetumal
Chilpancingo
Oaxaca
Tuxtla Gutierrez
Belize City
Belmopan
Guatemala
San Salvador
Tegucigalpa
Puerto Lempira
Managua
Bluefields
San Jose
Panama
David
Port-au-Prince
Santo Domingo
Kingston
Puerto Rico
Willemstad
Barranquilla
Maracaibo
Barquisimeto
Cucuta
San Cristobal
Monteria
Medellin
Bogota

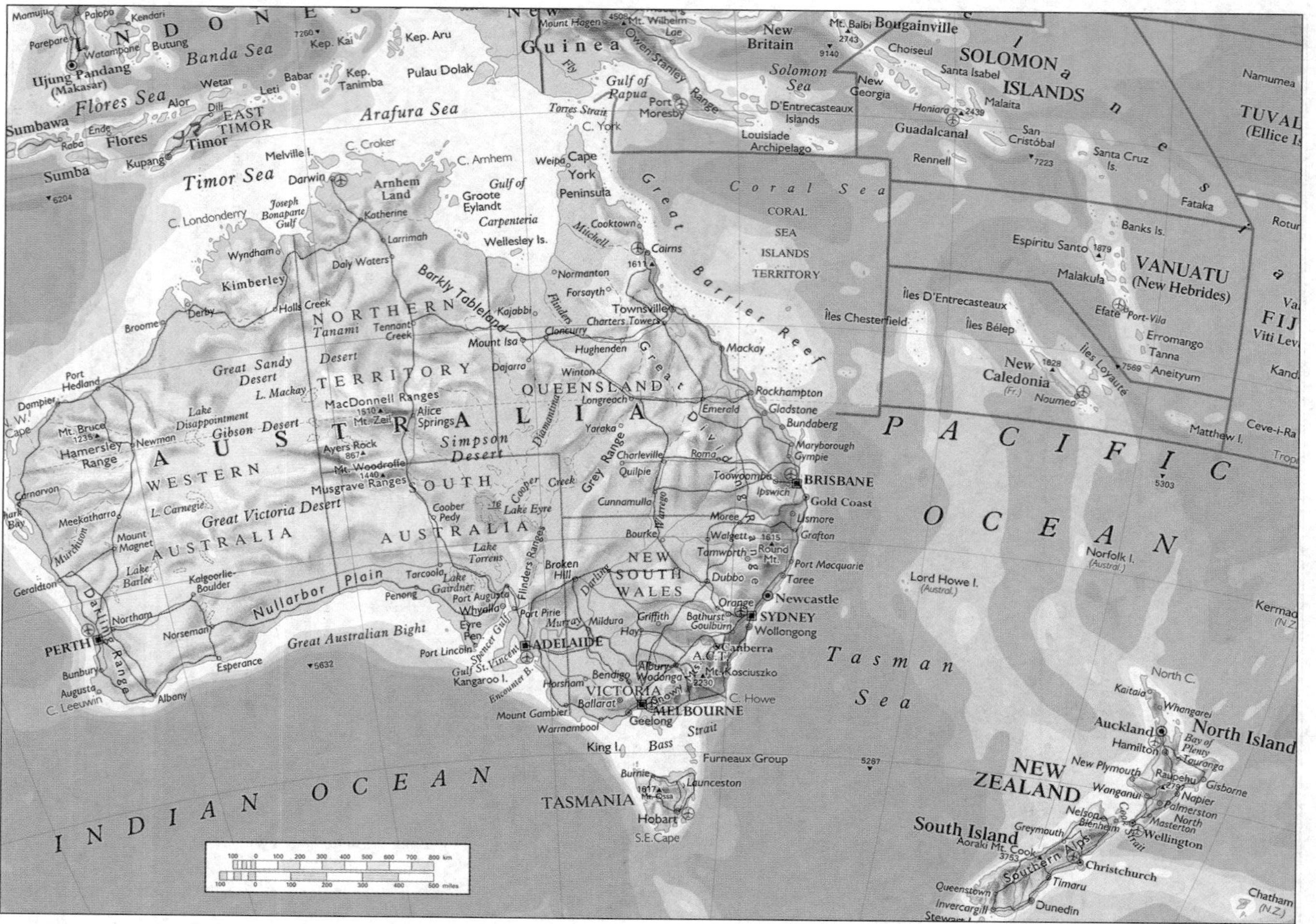
AUSTRALIA
NEW ZEALAND
North Island
South Island
TASMANIA
INDIAN OCEAN
PACIFIC OCEAN
Tasman Sea
Coral Sea
CORAL SEA ISLANDS TERRITORY
Great Barrier Reef
Arafura Sea
Timor Sea
Banda Sea
Flores Sea
Solomon Sea
Great Australian Bight
Bass Strait
Cook Strait
WESTERN AUSTRALIA
NORTHERN TERRITORY
SOUTH AUSTRALIA
QUEENSLAND
NEW SOUTH WALES
VICTORIA
A.C.T.
PERTH
ADELAIDE
MELBOURNE
SYDNEY
BRISBANE
Canberra
Darwin
Hobart
Alice Springs
Auckland
Wellington
Christchurch
Dunedin
SOLOMON ISLANDS
VANUATU (New Hebrides)
New Caledonia (Fr.)
FIJI
TUVALU (Ellice Is.)
Norfolk I. (Austral.)
Lord Howe I. (Austral.)
Great Sandy Desert
Gibson Desert
Great Victoria Desert
Simpson Desert
Tanami Desert
Nullarbor Plain
Barkly Tableland
Great Dividing Range
Darling Range
Hamersley Range
MacDonnell Ranges
Musgrave Ranges
Flinders Ranges
Kimberley
Arnhem Land
Cape York Peninsula
Gulf of Carpentaria
Lake Eyre
Lake Torrens
Ayers Rock
Mt. Kosciuszko
EAST TIMOR
New Guinea
New Britain
Bougainville
Guadalcanal

Geographical names

This list of geographical names is included to help advanced students in their reading of contemporary newspapers and magazines.

NAME	ADJECTIVE
Afghanistan /æf'gænɪstɑːn $ -stæn/	**Afghan** /'æfgæn/ *person:* **Afghanistani** /æf'gænɪ'stɑːni $ -æni/, **Afghan**
Africa /'æfrɪkə/	**African** /'æfrɪkən/
Alaska /ə'læskə/	**Alaskan** /ə'læskən/
Albania /æl'beɪniə/	**Albanian** /æl'beɪniən/
Algeria /æl'dʒɪəriə $ -'dʒɪr-/	**Algerian** /æl'dʒɪəriən $ -'dʒɪr-/
America /ə'merɪkə/	**American** /ə'merɪkən/
Andorra /æn'dɔːrə/	**Andorran** /æn'dɔːrən/
Angola /æŋ'gəʊlə $ -'goʊ-/	**Angolan** /æŋ'gəʊlən $ -'goʊ-/
Antarctic /æn'tɑːktɪk $ -ɑːr-/	**Antarctic**
Antigua & Barbuda /æn'tiːgə ən bɑː'bjuːdə/	**Antiguan** /æn'tiːgən/ **Barbudan** bɑː'bjuːdən/
Arctic /'ɑːktɪk $ 'ɑːrk-/	**Arctic**
Argentina /ˌɑːdʒən'tiːnə $ ˌɑːr-/	**Argentinian** *or* **-ean** /ˌɑːdʒən'tɪniən $ ˌɑːr-/
Armenia /ɑː'miːniə $ ɑːr-/	**Armenian** /ɑː'miːniən $ ɑːr-/
Asia /'eɪʃə, -ʒə $ -ʒə, -ʃə/	**Asian** /'eɪʃən, -ʒən $ -ʒən, -ʃən/
Atlantic /ət'læntɪk/	**Atlantic**
Australia /ɒ'streɪliə $ ɒː-, ɑː-/	**Australian** /ɒ'streɪliən $ ɒː-, ɑː-/
Austria /'ɒstriə $ 'ɒː-, 'ɑː-/	**Austrian** /'ɒstriən $ 'ɒː-, 'ɑː-/
Azerbaijan /ˌæzəbaɪ'dʒɑːn $ -zər-/	**Azerbaijani** /ˌæzəbaɪ'dʒɑːni $ -zər-/
Bahamas /bə'hɑːməz/	**Bahamian** /bə'heɪmiən/
Bahrain /bɑː'reɪn/	**Bahraini** /bɑː'reɪni/
Baltic /'bɔːltɪk $ 'bɒːl-/	**Baltic**
Bangladesh /ˌbæŋglə'deʃ/	**Bangladesh** *person:* **Bangladeshi** /ˌbæŋglə'deʃi/
Barbados /bɑː'beɪdɒs $ bɑːr'beɪdəs, -dɑːs/	**Barbadian** /bɑː'beɪdiən $ bɑːr-/
Belarus /ˌbelə'ruːs/ (Belorussia) /ˌbeləʊ'rʌʃə $ -loʊ-/	**Belorussian** /ˌbeləʊ'rʌʃən $ -loʊ-/
Belgium /'beldʒəm/	**Belgian** /'beldʒən/
Belize /bə'liːz/	**Belizean** /bə'liːziən/
Benin /be'niːn $ bə'nɪn/	**Beninese** /ˌbenɪ'niːz◂/
Bermuda /bə'mjuːdə $ bər-/	**Bermudan** /bə'mjuːdn $ bər-/
Bhutan /buː'tɑːn/	**Bhutanese** /buːtə'niːz◂ $ ˌbuːtn'iːz◂/
Bolivia /bə'lɪviə/	**Bolivian** /bə'lɪviən/

NAME	ADJECTIVE
Bosnia and Herzegovina /ˌbɒzniə ənd hɜːtsəgəʊ'viːnə $ ˌbɑːzniə ənd ˌhertsəgoʊ-/	**Bosnian** /'bɒzniən $ 'bɑːz-/
Botswana /bɒt'swɑːnə $ bɑːt-/	**Tswana** /'tswɑːnə, 'swɑː-/ *person: sing.* = **Motswana** /mɒt'swɑːnə $ mɑːt-/ *pl.* = **Batswana** /bæt'swɑːnə/
Brazil /brə'zɪl/	**Brazilian** /brə'zɪliən/
Brunei /'bruːnaɪ/	**Bruneian** /bruː'naɪən/
Bulgaria /bʌl'geəriə $ -'ger-/	**Bulgarian** /bʌl'geəriən $ -'ger-/
Burkina Faso /bɜːˌkiːnə 'fæsəʊ $ bʊrˌkiːnə 'fɑːsoʊ/	**Burkina** *person:* **Burkinabe** /ˌbɜːkiːnæ'beɪ $ ˌbʊr-/
Burma /'bɜːmə $ 'bɜːr-/ former name of Myanmar	
Burundi /bʊ'rʊndi $ -'ruː-/	**Burundian** /bʊ'rʊndiən $ -'ruː-/
Cambodia /kæm'bəʊdiə $ -'boʊ-/	**Cambodian** /kæm'bəʊdiən $ -'boʊ-/
Cameroon /ˌkæmə'ruːn/	**Cameroonian** /ˌkæmə'ruːniən◂/
Canada /'kænədə/	**Canadian** /kə'neɪdiən/
Cape Verde /keɪp 'vɜːd $ -'vɜːrd/	**Cape Verdean** /keɪp 'vɜːdiən $ -'vɜːr-/
Caribbean /ˌkærɪ'biːən $ kə'rɪbiən/	**Caribbean**
Cayman Islands /'keɪmən ˌaɪləndz/	**Cayman Island** /'keɪmən ˌaɪlənd◂/ *person:* **Cayman Islander** /'keɪmən ˌaɪləndə $ -dər/
Central African Republic /ˌsentrəl æfrɪkən rɪ'pʌblɪk/	**Central African** /ˌsentrəl æfrɪkən/
Chad /tʃæd/	**Chadian** /'tʃædiən/
Chile /'tʃɪli/	**Chilean** /'tʃɪliən/
China /'tʃaɪnə/	**Chinese** /ˌtʃaɪ'niːz◂/
Colombia /kə'lʌmbiə/	**Colombian** /kə'lʌmbiən/
Congo /'kɒŋgəʊ $ 'kɑːŋgoʊ/	**Congolese** /ˌkɒŋgə'liːz◂ $ ˌkɑːŋ-/
Costa Rica /ˌkɒstə 'riːkə $ ˌkoʊ-/	**Costa Rican** /ˌkɒstə 'riːkən◂ $ ˌkoʊ-/
Croatia /krəʊ'eɪʃə $ kroʊ-/	**Croatian** /krəʊ'eɪʃən $ kroʊ-/
Cuba /'kjuːbə/	**Cuban** /'kjuːbən/
Cyprus /'saɪprəs/	**Cypriot** /'sɪpriət/
Czech Republic /ˌtʃek rɪ'pʌblɪk/	**Czech** /tʃek/
Denmark /'denmɑːk $ -mɑːrk/	**Danish** /'deɪnɪʃ/ *person:* **Dane** /deɪn/
Djibouti /dʒɪ'buːti/	**Djiboutian** /dʒɪ'buːtiən/

NAME	ADJECTIVE
Dominica /ˌdɒmɪˈniːkə $ ˌdɑː-/	Dominican /ˌdɒmɪˈniːkən◂ $ ˌdɑː-/
Dominican Republic /dəˌmɪnɪkən rɪˈpʌblɪk/	Dominican /dəˈmɪnɪkən/
East Timor /ˌiːst ˈtiːmɔː $ -mɔːr/	Timorese /ˌtiːmɔːˈriːz◂/
Ecuador /ˈekwədɔː $ -ɔːr/	Ecuadorian /ˌekwəˈdɔːriən◂/
Egypt /ˈiːdʒɪpt/	Egyptian /ɪˈdʒɪpʃən/
El Salvador /el ˈsælvəˌdɔː $ -ɔːr/	Salvadorian /ˌsælvəˈdɔːriən◂/
Equatorial Guinea /ˌekwətɔːriəl ˈgɪni $ ˌiː-/	Equatorial Guinean /ˌekwətɔːriəl ˈgɪniən $ ˌiː-/
Eritrea /ˌerɪˈtreə/	Eritrean /ˌerɪˈtreɪən◂/
Estonia /eˈstəʊniə $ eˈstoʊ-/	Estonian /eˈstəʊniən $ eˈstoʊ-/
Ethiopia /ˌiːθiˈəʊpiə $ -ˈoʊ-/	Ethiopian /ˌiːθiˈəʊpiən◂ $ -ˈoʊ-/
Europe /ˈjʊərəp $ ˈjʊr-/	European /ˌjʊərəˈpiːən◂ $ ˈjʊr-/
Fiji /ˈfiːdʒiː/	Fijian /fiːˈdʒiːən $ ˈfiːdʒiən/
Finland /ˈfɪnlənd/	Finnish /ˈfɪnɪʃ/ *person:* Finn /fɪn/
France /frɑːns $ fræns/	French /frentʃ/ *person: sing.* = Frenchman /ˈfrentʃmən/ (*fem.*-woman) /-ˈwʊmən/: *pl.* = Frenchmen /ˈfrentʃmən/, *people:* French
Gabon /gæˈbɒn $ -ˈboʊn/	Gabonese /ˌgæbəˈniːz◂/
Gambia /ˈgæmbiə/	Gambian /ˈgæmbiən/
Georgia /ˈdʒɔːdʒə $ ˈdʒɔːr-/	Georgian /ˈdʒɔːdʒən $ ˈdʒɔːr-/
Germany /ˈdʒɜːməni $ -ɜːr-/	German /ˈdʒɜːmən◂ $ -ɜːr-/
Ghana /ˈgɑːnə/	Ghanaian /gɑːˈneɪən/
Gibraltar /dʒɪˈbrɔːltə $ -ˈbrɒːl-/	Gibraltarian /ˌdʒɪbrɒːlˈteəriən $ -brɒːlˈter-/
Greece /griːs/	Greek /griːk/
Greenland /ˈgriːnlənd, -lænd/	Greenlandic /griːnˈlændɪk/ *person:* Greenlander /ˈgriːnləndə $ -dər/
Grenada /grəˈneɪdə/	Grenadian /grəˈneɪdiən/
Guatemala /ˌgwɑːtəˈmɑːlə/	Guatemalan /ˌgwɑːtəˈmɑːlən◂/
Guiana /giˈɑːnə $ giˈænə, -ˈɑːnə/	Guianese /ˌgaɪəˈniːz◂/
Guinea /ˈgɪni/	Guinean /ˈgɪniən/
Guinea-Bissau /ˌgɪni bɪˈsaʊ/	Guinea-Bissauan /ˌgɪni bɪˈsaʊən/
Guyana /gaɪˈænə/	Guyanese /ˌgaɪəˈniːz◂/
Haiti /ˈheɪti/	Haitian /ˈheɪʃən/
Holland /ˈhɒlənd $ ˈhɑː-/ another name for The Netherlands	Dutch /dʌtʃ/
Honduras /hɒnˈdjʊərəs $ hɑːnˈdjʊrəs, -ˈdʊ-/	Honduran /hɒnˈdjʊərən $ hɑːnˈdjʊrən, -ˈdʊ-/
Hong Kong /ˌhɒŋ ˈkɒŋ $ ˈhɑːŋ ˌkɑːŋ/	Hong Konger /ˌhɒŋ ˈkɒŋə $ ˈhɑːŋ ˌkɑːŋər/

NAME	ADJECTIVE
Hungary /ˈhʌŋgəri/	Hungarian /hʌŋˈgeəriən $ -ˈger-/
Iceland /ˈaɪslənd/	Icelandic /aɪsˈlændɪk/ *person:* Icelander /ˈaɪsləndə $ -dər/
India /ˈɪndiə/	Indian /ˈɪndiən/
Indonesia /ˌɪndəˈniːʒə, -ziə $ -ʒə, -ʃə/	Indonesian /ˌɪndəˈniːʒən◂, -ziən◂ $ -ʒən, -ʃən◂/
Iran /ɪˈrɑːn,-æn/	Iranian /ɪˈreɪniən/
Iraq /ɪˈrɑːk, -æk/	Iraqi /ɪˈrɑːki, -æki/
Republic of Ireland /ripʌblɪk əv ˈaɪələnd $ - ˈaɪər-/	Irish /ˈaɪərɪʃ $ ˈaɪr-/ *person: sing.* = Irishman /ˈaɪərɪʃmən $ ˈaɪr-/ (*fem.* -woman) /-wʊmən/; *pl.* = Irishmen /ˈaɪərɪʃmən $ ˈaɪr-/ *people:* Irish
Israel /ˈɪzreɪl/	Israeli /ɪzˈreɪli/
Italy /ˈɪtəli/	Italian /ɪˈtæliən/
Ivory Coast /ˌaɪvəri ˈkəʊst $ -ˈkoʊst/	Ivorian /aɪˈvɔːriən/
Jamaica /dʒəˈmeɪkə/	Jamaican /dʒəˈmeɪkən/
Japan /dʒəˈpæn/	Japanese /ˈdʒæpəˌniːz◂/
Jordan /ˈdʒɔːdn $ ˈdʒɔːr-/	Jordanian /dʒɔːˈdeɪniən $ dʒɔːr-/
Kazakhstan /ˌkæzækˈstɑːn $ ˌkɑːzɑːk-/	Kazakh /kəˈzæk, -ˈzɑːk/
Kenya /ˈkenjə, ˈkiː-/	Kenyan /ˈkenjən, ˈkiː-/
Korea, North /ˌnɔːθ kəˈriːə $ ˌnɔːrθ-/	North Korean /ˌnɔːθ kəˈriːən $ ˌnɔːrθ-/
Korea, South /saʊθ kəˈriːə/	South Korean /saʊθ kəˈriːən/
Kosovo /ˈkɒsəvəʊ/ $ ˈkoʊsəvoʊ	Kosovan /ˈkɒsəvən/
Kuwait /kʊˈweɪt/	Kuwaiti /kʊˈweɪti/
Kyrgyzstan /ˌkɜːgɪˈstɑːn/	Kyrgz /ˌkɜːgɪz/
Laos /ˈlɑːɒs, laʊs $ laʊs, ˈleiɑːs/	Laotian /ˈlaʊʃən/
Latvia /ˈlætviə/	Latvian /ˈlætviən/
Lebanon /ˈlebənən/	Lebanese /ˌlebəˈniːz◂/
Lesotho /ləˈsuːtuː $ -ˈsoʊtoʊ/	Sotho /ˈsuːtuː $ ˈsoʊtoʊ/ *person: sing.* = Mosotho /məˈsuːtuː $ -ˈsoʊtoʊ/; *pl.* = Basotho /bəˈsuːtuː $ -ˈsoʊtoʊ/
Liberia /laɪˈbɪəriə $ -ˈbɪr-/	Liberian /laɪˈbɪəriən -ˈbɪr-/
Libya /ˈlɪbiə/	Libyan /ˈlɪbiən/
Liechtenstein /ˈlɪktənstaɪn/	Liechtenstein *person:* Liechtensteiner /ˈlɪktənstaɪnə $ -ər/
Lithuania /ˌlɪθjuˈeɪniə $ -θu-/	Lithuanian /ˌlɪθjuˈeɪniən◂ $ -θu-/
Luxemburg /ˈlʌksəmbɜːg $ -bɜːrg/	Luxemburg *person:* Luxemburger /ˈlʌksəmbɜːgə $ -bɜːrgər/
Macedonia /ˌmæsɪˈdəʊniə $ -ˈdoʊ-/	Macedonian /ˌmæsəˈdəʊniən◂ $ -ˈdoʊ-/
Madagascar /ˌmædəˈgæskə $ -kər/	Malagasy /ˌmæləˈgæsi◂/

NAME	ADJECTIVE
Malawi /məˈlɑːwi/	Malawian /məˈlɑːwiən/
Malaysia /məˈleɪziə $ -ʒə, -ʃə/	Malaysian /məˈleɪziən $ -ʒən, -ʃən/
Maldives /ˈmɔːldiːvz $ ˈmɒːl-/	Maldivian /mɔːlˈdɪviən $ mɒːl-/
Mali /ˈmɑːli/	Malian /ˈmɑːliən/
Malta /ˈmɔːltə $ ˈmɒːl-/	Maltese /ˌmɔːlˈtiːz $ ˌmɒːl-/
Marshall Islands /ˈmɑːʃəl ˌaɪləndz $ ˈmɑːr-/	Marshall Islander /ˌmɑːʃəl ˈaɪləndə $ ˌmɑːrʃəl ˈaɪləndər/
Mauritania /ˌmɒrɪˈteɪniə $ ˌmɔː-/	Mauritanian /ˌmɒrɪˈteɪniən◂ $ ˌmɔː-/
Mauritius /məˈrɪʃəs, mɔː-/	Mauritian /məˈrɪʃən, mɔː-/
Mediterranean /ˌmedɪtəˈreɪniən◂/	Mediterranean
Melanesia /ˌmeləˈniːziə $ -ʒə, -ʃə/	Melanesian /ˌmeləˈniːziən◂ $ -ʒən◂, -ʃən◂/
Mexico /ˈmeksɪkəʊ $ -koʊ/	Mexican /ˈmeksɪkən/
Micronesia /ˌmaɪkrəʊˈniːziə $ -kroʊˈniːʒə, -ʃə/	Micronesian /ˌmaɪkrəʊˈniːziən, -ʒən $ -kroʊˈniːʒən, -ʃən/
Moldova /mɒlˈdəʊvə $ mɑːlˈdoʊ-/	Moldovian /mɒlˈdəʊviən $ mɑːlˈdoʊ-/
Monaco /ˈmɒnəkəʊ $ ˈmɑːnəkoʊ/	Monegasque /ˌmɒnɪˈgæsk◂ $ ˌmɑː-/
Mongolia /mɒŋˈgəʊliə $ mɑːŋˈgoʊ-/	Mongolian /mɒŋˈgəʊliən $ mɑːŋˈgoʊ-/ *person:* Mongolian *or* Mongol /ˈmɒŋgɒl, -gəl $ ˈmɑːŋgəl/
Montenegro /ˌmɒntiˈniːgrəʊ/	Montenenegrin /ˌmɒntiˈniːgrɪn/
Montserrat /ˌmɒntseˈræt $ ˌmɑː-/	Montserratian /ˌmɒntseˈreɪʃən◂ $ ˌmɑː-/
Morocco /məˈrɒkəʊ $ -ˈrɑːkoʊ/	Moroccan /məˈrɒkən $ -ˈrɑː-/
Mozambique /ˌməʊzəmˈbiːk $ ˌmoʊ-/	Mozambican /ˌməʊzəmˈbiːkən◂ $ ˌmoʊ-/
Myanmar /ˈmjænmɑː $ ˈmjɑːnmɑːr/	Burmese /ˌbɜːˈmiːz◂ $ ˌbɜːr-/
Namibia /nəˈmɪbiə/	Namibian /nəˈmɪbiən/
Nauru /nɑːˈuːruː, nɑːˈruː/	Nauruan /nɑːˈuːruən, nɑːˈruːən/
Nepal /nɪˈpɔːl $ nəˈpɒːl, -ˈpɑːl/	Nepalese /ˌnepəˈliːz◂/
The Netherlands /ðə ˈneðələndz $ -ðər-/	Dutch /dʌtʃ/ *person: sing.* = Dutchman /ˈdʌtʃmən/ (*fem.* -woman) /-ˌwʊmən/; *pl.* = Dutchmen /ˈdʌtʃmən/; *people:* Dutch
New Zealand /njuː ˈziːlənd $ nuː-/	New Zealand, Maori /ˈmaʊri/ *person:* New Zealander /njuː ˈziːləndə $ nuː ˈziːləndər/
Nicaragua /ˌnɪkəˈrægjuə $ -ˈrɑːgwə/	Nicaraguan /ˌnɪkəˈrægjuən◂ $ -ˈrɑːgwən◂/
Niger /ˈnaɪdʒə, niːˈʒeə $ ər-/	Nigerien /niːˈʒeəriən -ˈʒer-/

NAME	ADJECTIVE
Nigeria /naɪˈdʒɪəriə $ -ˈdʒɪr-/	Nigerian /naɪˈdʒɪəriən -ˈdʒɪr-/
Norway /ˈnɔːweɪ $ ˈnɔːr-/	Norwegian /nɔːˈwiːdʒən $ nɔːr-/
Oman /əʊˈmɑːn $ oʊ-/	Omani /əʊˈmɑːni $ oʊ-/
Pacific /pəˈsɪfɪk/	Pacific
Pakistan /ˌpɑːkɪˈstɑːn, ˌpækɪˈstæn/	Pakistani /ˌpɑːkɪˈstɑːni◂, ˌpæk- $ -ˈstɑːni◂, -ˈstæni◂/
Palestine /ˈpæləstaɪn/	Palestinian /ˌpæləˈstɪniən/
Panama /ˌpænəˈmɑː◂ $ ˈpænəmɑː/	Panamanian /ˌpænəˈmeɪniən/
Papua New Guinea /ˌpæpuə njuː ˈgɪni $ ˌpæpjuə nuː-/	Papuan /ˈpæpuən $ ˈpæpjuən/
Paraguay /ˈpærəgwaɪ/	Paraguayan /ˌpærəˈgwaɪən◂/
Persia /ˈpɜːʃə, -ʒə $ ˈpɜːrʒə/ former name of Iran	
Peru /pəˈruː/	Peruvian /pəˈruːviən/
Philippines /ˈfɪləpiːnz $ ˌfɪləˈpiːnz/	Philippine /ˈfɪləpiːn $ ˌfɪləˈpiːn/ *person:* Filipino /ˌfɪləpiːnəʊ $ -noʊ/
Poland /ˈpəʊlənd $ ˈpoʊ-/	Polish /ˈpəʊlɪʃ $ ˈpoʊ-/ *person:* Pole /pəʊl $ poʊl/
Polynesia /ˌpɒlɪˈniːziə $ ˌpɑːləˈniːʒə/	Polynesian /ˌpɒlɪˈniːziən◂ $ ˌpɑːləˈniːʒən◂/
Portugal /ˈpɔːtʃʊgəl $ ˈpɔːr-/	Portuguese /ˌpɔːtʃʊˈgiːz◂ $ ˌpɔːr-/
Puerto Rico /ˌpwɜːtəʊ ˈriːkəʊ $ ˌpɔːrtoʊ ˈriːkoʊ/	Puerto Rican /ˌpwɜːtəʊ ˈriːkən $ ˌpɔːrtoʊ-/
Qatar /kʌˈtɑː $ ˈkɑːtər/	Qatari /kʌˈtɑːri/
Quebec /kwɪˈbek/	Quebecois /ˌkebeˈkwɑː/
Romania /ruːˈmeɪniə $ roʊ-/	Romanian /ruːˈmeɪniən $ roʊˈ-/
Russia /ˈrʌʃə/	Russian Federation, /ˌrʌʃən fedəˈreɪʃən/ *person:* Russian /ˈrʌʃən/
Rwanda /ruˈændə $ -ˈɑːn-/	Rwandan /ruˈændən $ -ˈɑːn-/
Saint Kitts & Nevis /sənt ˌkɪts ənd ˈniːvɪs $ seɪnt-/	Kittitian /kɪˈtɪʃən/ Nevisian /nɪˈvɪziən $ -ʒən/
Saint Lucia /sənt ˈluːʃə $ seɪnt-/	Saint Lucian /sənt ˈluːʃən $ seɪnt-/
Samoa /səˈməʊə $ -ˈmoʊə/	Samoan /səˈməʊən -ˈmoʊ-/
San Marino /sæn məˈriːnəʊ $ -noʊ/	Sanmarinese /ˌsænmærɪˈniːz/
São Tomé & Principe /ˌsaʊn təˌmeɪ ənd ˈprɪnsɪpeɪ $ -səpə/	São Toméan /ˌsaʊn təˈmeɪən/
Saudi Arabia /ˌsaʊdi əˈreɪbiə/	Saudi Arabian /ˌsaʊdi əˈreɪbiən/ *person:* Saudi *or* Saudi Arabian
Senegal /ˌsenɪˈgɔːl $ -ˈgɒːl/	Senegalese /ˌsenɪgəˈliːz◂/
Serbia /ˈsɜːbiə/	Serbian /ˈsɜːbiən/
Seychelles /seɪˈʃelz/	Seychellois /ˌseɪʃelˈwɑː◂/
Sierre Leone /siˈerə liˈəʊn $ -ˈoʊn/	Sierra Leonean /siˌerə liˈəʊniən $ -ˈoʊn-/
Singapore /ˌsɪŋəˈpɔː $ ˌsɪŋəpɔːr/	Singaporean /ˌsɪŋəˈpɔːriən◂/

NAME	ADJECTIVE
Slovak Republic /ˌsləʊvæk rɪˈpʌblɪk $ ˌsloʊvɑːk-/	Slovak /ˈsləʊvæk $ ˈsloʊvɑːk/
Slovenia /sləʊˈviːniə $ sloʊ-/	Slovene /ˈsləʊviːn $ ˈsloʊ-/ *person:* Slovenian /sləʊˈviːniən $ sloʊ-/
Solomon Islands /ˈsɒləmən ˌaɪləndz $ ˈsɑː-/	Solomon Islander /ˌsɒləmən ˈaɪləndə $ ˌsɑːləmən ˈaɪləndər/
Somalia /səʊˈmɑːliə $ soʊ-/	Somali /səʊˈmɑːli $ soʊ-/
South Africa /saʊθ ˈæfrɪkə/	South African /saʊθ ˈæfrɪkən/
South Sudan /saʊθ sʊˈdɑːn $ -dæn/	South Sudanese /saʊθ sʊˈdəˈniːz/
Spain /speɪn/	Spanish /ˈspænɪʃ/ *person:* Spaniard /ˈspænjəd $ -jərd/
Sri Lanka /sriː ˈlæŋkə $ -ˈlɑːŋ-/	Sri Lankan /sriː ˈlæŋkən $ -ˈlɑːŋ-/
Sudan /sʊˈdæn, -ˈdɑːn/	Sudanese /ˌsuːdəˈnɪːz◂/
Surinam /ˌsʊərɪˈnæm $ ˌsʊrəˈnɑːm/	Surinamese /ˌsʊərɪnəˈmiːz◂ $ -sʊr-/ *person:* Surinamer /ˌsʊərɪˈnɑːmə $ ˌsʊrəˈnɑːmər/
Swaziland /ˈswɑːzilænd/	Swazi /ˈswɑːzi/
Sweden /ˈswiːdn/	Swedish /ˈswiːdɪʃ/ *person:* Swede /swiːd/
Switzerland /ˈswɪtsələnd $ -sər-/	Swiss /swɪs/
Syria /ˈsɪriə/	Syrian /ˈsɪriən/
Tahiti /təˈhiːti/	Tahitian /təˈhiːʃən/
Tajikistan /tɑːˌdʒiːkɪˈstɑːn/	Tajik /tɑːˈdʒiːk $ -ˈdʒɪk, -ˈdʒiːk/
Tanzania /ˌtænzəˈnɪə/	Tanzanian /ˌtænzəˈnɪən◂/
Thailand /ˈtaɪlænd, -lənd/	Thai /taɪ/
Togo /ˈtəʊgəʊ $ ˈtoʊgoʊ/	Togolese /ˌtəʊgəˈliːz◂ $ ˌtoʊ-/
Tonga /ˈtɒŋgə $ ˈtɑːŋ-/	Tongan /ˈtɒŋgən $ ˈtɑːŋ-/
Trinidad & Tobago /ˌtrɪnɪdæd ən təˈbeɪgəʊ $ -goʊ/	Trinidadian /ˌtrɪnɪˈdædiən◂/ Tobagonian /ˌtəʊbəˈgəʊniən $ ˌtoʊbəˈgoʊ-/
Tunisia /tjʊˈnɪziə $ tuːˈniːʒə/	Tunisian /tjuːˈnɪziən $ tuːˈniːʒən/
Turkey /ˈtɜːki $ ˈtɜːr-/	Turkish /ˈtɜːkɪʃ $ ˈtɜːr-/ *person:* Turk /tɜːk $ tɜːrk/
Turkmenistan /ˌtɜːkmenɪˈstɑːn $ ˌtɜːrkmenɪˈstæn/	Turkmen /ˈtɜːkmən $ ˈtɜːrk-/
Uganda /juːˈgændə/	Ugandan /juːˈgændən/
Ukraine /juːˈkreɪn/	Ukrainian /juːˈkreɪniən/
United Arab Emirates /juːˌnaɪtɪd ˌærəb ˈemɪrəts/	Emirati /eˈmɪərɑːti/
United Kingdom /juːˌnaɪtɪd ˈkɪŋdəm/ of Great Britain /əv greɪt ˈbrɪtən/ and Northern Ireland /ənd ˌnɔːðən ˈaɪələnd $ -ˌnɔːrðərn ˈaɪrlənd/	British /ˈbrɪtɪʃ/ *person:* Briton /ˈbrɪtən/, *AmE people:* British
England /ˈɪŋglənd/	English /ˈɪŋglɪʃ/ *person: sing.* = Englishman /ˈɪŋglɪʃmən (*fem.* -woman) /-wʊmən/; *pl.* = Englishmen /ˈɪŋglɪʃmən/; *people:* English
Northern Ireland /ˈnɔːðən ˈaɪələnd/	British, Northern Irish /ˈbrɪtɪʃ/, /ˈnɔːðən ˈaɪərɪʃ $ ˈaɪrɪʃ/
Scotland /ˈskɒtlənd $ ˈskɑːt-/	Scottish /ˈskɒtɪʃ $ ˈskɑː-/ *or* Scots /skɒts $ skɑːts/ *person: sing.* = Scot *or* Scotsman /ˈskɒtsmən $ ˈskɑː-/ (*fem.* -woman) /-ˌwʊmən/; *pl.* = Scotsmen /ˈskɒtsmən $ ˈskɑː-/; *people:* Scots
Wales /weɪlz/	Welsh /welʃ/ *person: sing.* = Welshman /ˈwelʃmən/ (*fem.* -woman) /ˈwʊmən/; *pl.* = Welshmen /ˈwelʃmən/; *people:* Welsh
United States /juːˌnaɪtɪd ˈsteɪts/	American /əˈmerɪkən/ US /juː ˈes/, *person:* American /əˈmerɪkən/
Upper Volta /ˌʌpə ˈvɒltə $ ˌʌpər ˈvɑːl-/ former name of Burkina Faso	
Uruguay /ˈjʊərəgwaɪ $ ˈjʊr-/	Uruguayan /ˌjʊərəˈgwaɪən◂ $ ˌjʊr-/
Uzbekistan /ˌʊzbekɪˈstɑːn $ ʊzˌbekɪˈstæn/	Uzbek /ˈʊzbek/
Vanuatu /ˌvænuˈɑːtuː $ ˌvænwɑːˈtuː/	Vanuatuan /ˌvænuˈɑːtuən $ ˌvænwɑːˈtuːən/
Venezuela /ˌvenəˈzweɪlə/	Venezuelan /ˌvenəˈzweɪlən◂/
Vietnam /ˌvjetˈnæm $ -ˈnɑːm/	Vietnamese /ˌvjetnəˈmiːz◂/
Yemen /ˈjemən/	Yemeni /ˈjeməni/
Zaïre /zaɪˈɪə $ zɑːˈɪr/ former name of the Democratic Republic of the Congo	
Zambia /ˈzæmbiə/	Zambian /ˈzæmbiən/
Zimbabwe /zɪmˈbɑːbweɪ/	Zimbabwean /zɪmˈbɑːbweɪən/

Numbers

HOW NUMBERS ARE SPOKEN

Numbers over 20

21	twenty-one
22	twenty-two
32	thirty-two
99	ninety-nine

Numbers over 100

101	a/one hundred (and) one
121	a/one hundred (and) twenty-one
200	two hundred
232	two hundred (and) thirty-two
999	nine hundred (and) ninety-nine

Note: In British English the 'and' is always used: *two hundred and thirty-two.* But in American English it is often left out: *two hundred thirty-two.*

Numbers over 1000

1001	a/one thousand (and) one
1121	one thousand one hundred (and) twenty-one
2000	two thousand
2232	two thousand two hundred (and) thirty-two
9999	nine thousand nine hundred (and) ninety-nine

Ordinal numbers

20th	twentieth
21st	twenty-first
25th	twenty-fifth
90th	ninetieth
99th	ninety-ninth
100th	hundredth
101st	hundred and first
225th	two hundred (and) twenty-fifth

Dates

1624	sixteen twenty-four
1903	nineteen-oh-three
1987	nineteen eighty-seven

WHAT NUMBERS REPRESENT

Numbers are often used on their own to show:

Price — *It cost eight seventy-five* (=8 pounds 75 pence or 8 dollars 75 cents: £8.75 or $8.75).

Time — *We left at two twenty-five* (=25 minutes after 2 o'clock).

Age — *She's forty-six* (=46 years old). | *He's in his sixties* (=between 60 and 69 years old).

Size — *This shirt is a thirty-eight* (=size 38).

Temperature — *The temperature fell to minus fourteen* (=-14°). | *The temperature was in the mid-thirties* (=about 34-36°).

The score in a game — *He won the first set six-three* (=by six games to three: 6-3).

Something marked with the stated number — *She played two nines and an eight* (=playing cards marked with these numbers).

A set or group of the stated number — *The teacher divided us into fours* (=groups of 4). | *You can buy cigarettes in tens or twenties* (=in packets containing 10 or 20).

NUMBERS AND GRAMMAR

Numbers can be used as:

Determiners — *Five people were hurt in the accident.* | *the three largest companies in the US* | *several hundred cars*

Pronouns — *We invited a lot of people but only twelve came/only twelve of them came.* | *Do exercise 5 on page 9.*

Nouns — *Six can be divided by two and three.* | *Three twos make six.*

IN TEXT MESSAGES

1 a way of writing 'one', for example SUM1 (=someone)

2 a way of writing 'to' or 'too': *Happy birthday 2 U!* (=to you) | *He's 2* (=too) *cool!*

4 a way of writing 'for': *a message 4 U* (=for you)

8 a way of writing parts of words that sound like '-ate', 'eat', or '-ait': *gr8* (=great) | *I h8* (=hate) *homework!* | *It's 2 l8* (=too late)

Weights and Measures

The words in **bold** are the most commonly used in everyday English.

METRIC

Units of length

	1 **millimetre**	= 0.03937 inch
10 mm	= 1 **centimetre**	= 0.3937 inch
10 cm	= 1 decimetre	= 3.937 inches
10 dm	= 1 **metre**	= 39.37 inches
10 m	= 1 decametre	= 10.94 yards
10 dam	= 1 hectometre	= 109.4 yards
10 hm	= 1 **kilometre**	= 0.6214 mile

Units of weight

	1 **milligram**	= 0.015 grain
10 mg	= 1 centigram	= 0.154 grain
10 cg	= 1 decigram	= 1.543 grains
10 dg	= 1 **gram**	= 15.43 grains = 0.035 ounce
10 g	= 1 decagram	= 0.353 ounce
10 dag	= 1 hectogram	= 3.527 ounces
10 hg	= 1 **kilogram**	= 2.205 pounds
1000 kg	= 1 **tonne** (metric ton)	= 0.984 (long) ton = 2204.62 pounds

Units of capacity

	1 millilitre	= 0.00176 pint
10 ml	= 1 centilitre	= 0.0176 pint
10 cl	= 1 decilitre	= 0.176 pint
10 dl	= 1 **litre**	= 1.76 pints = 0.22 UK gallon
10 l	= 1 decalitre	= 2.20 gallons
10 dal	= 1 hectolitre	= 22.0 gallons
10 hl	= 1 kilolitre	= 220.0 gallons

Square measure

1 square measure = 0.00155 square inch

100 mm^2	= 1 square centimetre	= 0.1550 square inch
100 cm^2	= 1 square metre	= 1.196 square yards
100 m^2	= 1 are	= 119.6 square yards
100 ares	= 1 **hectare**	= 2.471 acres
100 ha	= 1 square kilometre	= 247.1 acres

Cubic measure

1 cubic centimetre = 0.06102 cubic inch

1000 cm^3	= 1 cubic decimetre	= 0.03532 cubic foot
1000 dm^3	= 1 cubic metre	= 1.308 cubic yards

Circular measure

1 microradian	= 0.206 seconds	
1000 µrad	= 1 milliradian	= 3.438 minutes
1000 mrad	= 1 radian = 180/π degrees	= 57.296 degrees

Metric prefixes

	Abbreviation	*Factor*
tera-	T	10^{12}
giga-	G	10^{9}
mega-	M	10^{6}
kilo-	k	10^{3}
hecto-	h	10^{2}
deca-	da	10^{1}
deci-	d	10^{-1}
centi-	c	10^{-2}
milli-	m	10^{-3}
micro-	µ	10^{-6}
nano-	n	10^{-9}
pico-	p	10^{-12}
femto-	f	10^{-15}
atto-	a	10^{-18}

BRITISH AND AMERICAN

Units of length

	1 **inch**	= 2.54 cm
12 inches	= 1 **foot**	= 0.3048 m
3 feet	= 1 **yard**	= 0.9144 m
5½ yards	= 1 rod, pole, or perch	= 5.029 m
22 yards	= 1 chain	= 20.12 m
10 chains	= 1 furlong	= 0.2012 km
8 furlongs	= 1 **mile**	= 1.609 km
6076.12 feet	= 1 nautical mile	= 1852 m

Units of weight

1 grain	= 64.8 mg	
1 dram	= 1.772 g	
16 drams	= 1 **ounce**	= 28.35 g
16 ounces	= 1 **pound**	= 0.4536 kg
14 pounds	= 1 stone	= 6.350 kg
2 stones	= 1 quarter	= 12.70 kg
4 quarters	= 1 (long) **hundredweight**	= 50.80 kg
20 hundredweight	= 1 (long) **ton**	= 1.016 tonnes
100 pounds	= 1 (short) **hundredweight**	= 45.36 kg
2000 pounds	= 1 (short) **ton**	= 0.9072 tonnes

The short hundredweight and ton are more common in the US.

Units of capacity

1 fluid ounce	= 28.41 cm^3	
5 fluid ounces	= 1 gill	= 0.1421 dm^3
4 gills	= 1 **pint**	= 0.5683 dm^3
2 pints	= 1 **quart**	= 1.137 dm^3
4 quarts	= 1 (UK) **gallon**	= 4.546 dm^3
231 cubic inches	= 1 (US) **gallon**	= 3.785 dm^3
8 gallons	= 1 (UK) bushel	= 36.369 dm^3

Square measure

1 square inch	= 645.16 mm^2	
144 square inches	= 1 square foot	= 0.0929 m^2
9 square feet	= 1 square yard	= 0.8361 m^2
4840 square yards	= 1 acre	= 4047 m^2
640 acres	= 1 square mile	= 259 ha

Cubic measure

1 cubic inch	= 16.39 cm^3	
1728 cubic inches	= 1 cubic foot	= 0.02832 m^3 = 28.32 dm^3
27 cubic feet	= 1 cubic yard	= 0.7646 m^3 = 764.6 dm^3

Circular measure

1 second	= 4.868 µrad	
60 seconds	= 1 minute	= 0.2909 mrad
60 minutes	= 1 degree	= 17.45 mrad = π/180 rad
45 degrees	= 1 oxtant	= π/4 rad
60 degrees	= 1 sextant	= π/3 rad
90 degrees	= 1 quadrant or 1 right angle	= π/2 rad
360 degrees	= 1 circle or 1 circumference	= 2π rad
1 grade or gon	= 1/100th of a right angle	= π/200 rad

US dry measure

1 pint	= 0.9689 UK pint	= 0.5506 dm^3
1 bushel	= 0.9689 UK bushel	= 35.238 dm^3

US liquid measure

1 fluid ounce	= 1.0408 UK fluid ounces = 0.0296 dm^3
16 fluid ounces	= 1 pint = 0.8327 UK pint = 0.4732 dm^3
8 pints	= 1 gallon = 0.8327 UK gallon = 3.7853 dm^3

Temperature

° *Fahrenheit* = $(9/5 \times x\ °C) + 32$

° *Celsius* = $5/9 \times (x\ °F - 32)$

Word Formation

In English there are many word beginnings (prefixes) and word endings (suffixes) that can be added to a word to change its meaning or its word class. The most common ones are shown here, with examples of how they are used in the process of word formation. Many more are listed in the dictionary.

VERB FORMATION

The endings **-ize** and **-ify** can be added to many nouns and adjectives to form verbs, like this:

American	-ize	Americanize
legal		legalize
modern		modernize
popular		popularize

They want to make the factory more **modern**. *They want to* **modernize** *the factory.*

beauty	-ify	beautify
false		falsify
pure		purify
simple		simplify

These tablets make the water **pure**. *They* **purify** *the water.*

ADVERB FORMATION

The ending **-ly** can be added to most adjectives to form adverbs, like this:

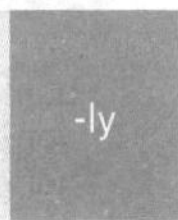

easy	-ly	easily
main		mainly
quick		quickly
stupid		stupidly

His behaviour was **stupid**. *He behaved* **stupidly**.

NOUN FORMATION

The endings **-er**, **-ment**, and **-ation** can be added to many verbs to form nouns, like this:

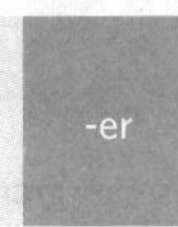

drive	-er	driver
fasten		fastener
open		opener
teach		teacher

John **drives** *a bus. He is a bus* **driver**.
A bottle **opener** *is a tool for* **opening** *bottles.*

amaze	-ment	amazement
develop		development
pay		payment
retire		retirement

Children **develop** *very quickly. Their* **development** *is very quick.*

admire	-ation	admiration
associate		association
examine		examination
organize		organization

The doctor **examined** *me carefully. He gave me a careful* **examination**.

The endings **-ity** and **-ness** can be added to many adjectives to form nouns, like this:

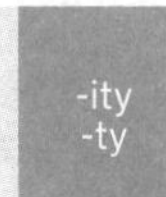

cruel	-ity -ty	cruelty
odd		oddity
pure		purity
stupid		stupidity

Don't be so **cruel**. *I hate* **cruelty**.

dark	-ness	darkness
deaf		deafness
happy		happiness
kind		kindness

It was very **dark**. *The* **darkness** *made it impossible to see.*

ADJECTIVE FORMATION

The endings **-y**, **-ic**, **-ical**, **-ful**, and **-less** can be added to many nouns to form adjectives, like this:

bush dirt hair smell	-y	bushy dirty hairy smelly

There was an awful **smell** *in the room. The room was very* **smelly**.

atom biology grammar poetry	-ic -ical	atomic biological grammatical poetic

This book contains exercises on **grammar**. *It contains* **grammatical** *exercises.*

pain hope care	-ful	painful hopeful careful

His broken leg caused him a lot of **pain**. *It was very* **painful**.

pain hope care	-less	painless hopeless careless

The operation didn't cause her any **pain**. *It was* **painless**.

The ending **-able** can be added to many verbs to form adjectives, like this:

wash love debate break	-able	washable lovable debatable breakable

You can **wash** *this coat. It's* **washable**.

OPPOSITES

The following prefixes can be used in front of many words to produce an opposite meaning. Note, however, that the words formed in this way are not always exact opposites and may have a slightly different meaning.

un-	happy fortunate wind block	unhappy unfortunate unwind unblock

I'm not very **happy**. *In fact, I'm very* **unhappy**.

in- im- il- ir-	efficient possible literate regular	inefficient impossible illiterate irregular

It's just not **possible** *to do that, it's* **impossible**.

dis-	agree approve honest	disagree disapprove dishonest

I don't **agree** *with everything you said. I* **disagree** *with the last part.*

de-	centralize increase ascend inflate	decentralize decrease descend deflate

Increase *means to make or become larger in amount or number.* **Decrease** *means to make or become smaller in amount or number.*

non-	sense payment resident conformist	nonsense non-payment non-resident nonconformist

The hotel serves meals to **residents** (=people who are staying in the hotel) *only.* **Non-residents** *are not allowed in.*

The publisher would like to thank the following for their kind permission to reproduce their photographs:

(Key: b-bottom; c-centre; l-left; r-right; t-top)

Alamy Images: 1864 (Workbench), Carlschneider.com / Ultimate Group, Llc 827, Chris Stock Photography 400, D.Hurst 1401, 1864 (Pool), Dex image 1287, Eileen Langsley 1984 (Judges), Haydn Hansell 1075 (Yale), Ian Nolan 691, ImageState 1993 (Camisole), Jason Wood 1984 (Umpire), Joe Fox 1984 (Referee), Kuttig - RF - Kids 992 (Leap), Marco Secchi 2089 (Sash), Martin Lee 383 (Bag crisps), Mike Booth 1864 (Dining), Mouse in the House 117 (Satchel), Neil McAllister 2089 (Bow), Graham Oliver 1490 (Magazine), Sigrid Dauth Stock photography 1224 (Hairnet), The Daniel Heighton Food Collection 383 (Tin beans), travelib europe 125br, V & A Images 1864 (Dressing table), WILDLIFE GmbH 685 (Swordfish); **Comstock Images:** 1784 (Coat stand); **Corbis:** Fancy / Lisa Pines 992 (Hop); **DK Images:** 117 (Laundry bag), 159 (Jaguar), 159 (Leopard), 159 (Lion), 159 (Panther), 159 (Tiger), 172 (Venetian blind), 181 (Snakes and ladders), 483 (Apple pie), 655 (Hook & eye), 655 (Toggle), 655 (Velcro), 685 (Eel), 685 (Mackerel), 685 (Shark), 788t, 842 (Beret), 880 (Hutch), 880 (Pigsty), 984 (Bangle), 984 (Brooch), 984 (Locket), 1008 (Palette), 1312 (Landscape), 1629 (Tack), Andy Crawford 198 (Lunchbox), 383 (Pot yoghurt), 1891b, Dave King 137 (Brown bear), 1769 (Cricket), 1769 (Hockey), David Murray / Jules Selmes 1773, Geoff Brightling 1229, Howard Shooter 1315 (Griddle), Jerry Young 137 (Polar bear), Steve Gorton 92 (Build), 141 (Futon), Susanna Price 383 (Pot honey), Tim Ridley 1379; **Dreamstime.com:** 194 (Carafe), 433 (Plastic cup), 781 (Boxing gloves), 991 (Carafe), 1020 (Chandelier), 1020 (Table lamp), 1020 (Torch), 1769 (Golf clubs), 1769 (Tennis ball), 1769 (Tennis racket), 1784 (Statue), 1858, 2023 (Squash); **Fotolia.com:** 11840812 740 (Star fruit), 2111, Accent 1624 (Mobility scooter), adw123 2089 (Dormer), Africa Studio 125tr, 433 (Coffee Cup), 701 (Lily), 723, 778 (Beer glass), 778 (Tumbler glass), 778 (Wine glass), 781 (Leather gloves), 789 (Swimming goggles), 842 (Baseball cap), 1106 (Eyeliner), 1106 (Foundation), 1792 (Ring binder), AGphotographer 720 (Fork lightning), Aleksandr Bryliaev 1792 (Pen), Aleksandr Volkov 980 (Denim), aleksangel 198 (TIn), Alekss 701 (Poppy), Alex_Mac 1677 (Football boots), Alexandra Karamyshev 1218 (Scoop neck), 1677 (Boots), alextan8 1805 (Precious stone), anandkrish16 1127 (Silver), Andi 678 (Footprint), Andres Rodriguez 825 (Layered), Antonio Gravante 773, Anyka 1004, apichai 740 (Slice Watermelon), apops 992 (Jump), 1123 (Surgical mask), 1400l, appujee 1333 (Paisley), arachi07 984 (Chain), arsdigital 1624 (Motor scooter), Art Allianz 1584 (Rope), 1769 (Snorkel), Artem Gorohov 781 (Mitten), ashumskiy 1289, auremar 825 (Bunches), 1994 (Loosen), AVD 1008 (Sheath knife), babimu 174 (Wooden blocks), 1251 (Peanuts), Andrey Bandurenko 117 (Handbag), 1677 (Pumps), 1677 (Slingbacks), 1864 (Bedside), below 778 (Shot glass), bergamont 740 (grapes), 1251 (Pistachio), 1351, Bernard GIRARDIN 834, bestfoto95 2089 (Skylight), blende40 1008 (Scalpel), bluebat 1769 (Badminton), Ionescu Bogdan 2023 (Brussels), Bombaert Patrick 842 (Bowler), borissos 1247, bornholm 684 (Scissors), Bozena Fulawka 740 (Watermelon), bramgino 1721, Brent Hofacker 1792 (Staple remover), bst2012 825 (Plait), by-studio 247 (Spray), 680, byggarn.se 984 (Medallion), bzyxx 880 (Stable), caimacanul 980 (Dinner), camellias 740 (Passion fruit), CandyBox Images 1490 (Luggage rack), charnsitr 148 (Bicycle bell), chayapol plairaharn 161 (Litter bin), chiyacat 1677 (Wedges), Christopher Dodge 1563, cocooo 984 (Pearls), 1677 (Mules), Comugnero Silvana 1251 (Pine nuts), cooperr 701 (Narcissus), 740 (Clementine), 1251 (Hazelnuts), Coprid 262 (Glasses case), 1629 (Nut bolt), CrackerClips 1769 (Baseball bat), Creative images 692 (flask), cretolamna 781 (Oven glove), Dani Simmonds 262 (Violin case), darak77 684 (Gauze), daseaford 880 (Hive), David Davis 1037, David Pruter 1020 (Lava lamp), davidyoung11111 1946 (Track), Deklofenak 825 (Bun), Denis Dryashkin 1629 (Nail), DenisNata 795 (Gosling), 1677 (Sandals), 1792 (Marker), design56 1075 (Bike lock), dianamower 842 (Bobble hat), 1400r, dimedrol68 842 (Peaked cap), Dimitar Bosakov 1008 (Flick Knife), Dimitri Surkov 210 (Viaduct), Direk Takmatcha 1792 (Notebooks), dja65 383 (Keg beer), Dmitry Naumov 197 (Garland), Dmitry Vereshchagin 15l, 1709 (Skate board), 1769 (Ice hockey), dmitrydesigner 1769 (Goggles), donyanedomam 976t, Egyptian Studio 1993 (Socks), ejkrouse 678 (Fingerprint), eldadcarin 174 (Breeze-block), Elemery 117 (Money bag), Elenathewise 141 (Twin bed), 425r, 701 (Daffodil), 713, 2089 (French windows), Elis Lasop 781 (Cycling gloves), Ella 1994 (Untie), Elnur 433 (Egg cup), 655 (Button), 1113, elzeva 984 (Ring), enzodebernardo 262 (Briefcase), epantha 701 (Sunflower), 795 (Canada goose), Eric Isselée 137 (Panda), 159 (Lynx), 159 (Puma), 163 (Eagle), 163 (Falcon), 665 (Ferret), 690, 880 (Kennel), 890, ESLINE 1361 (Upright piano), etiennevoss 571 (Fried egg), Eugen Wais 1315 (Cake tin), f9photos 1769 (Baseball glove), Fantini&Rossini 174 (Flats), 895 (Apartment), Faraways 740 (Peach), Fatih Kocyildir 1629 (Screw), Feng Yu 117 (Holdall), FirstBlood 684 (Antiseptic), flariv 1820 (Balalaika), flashon 820 (Treadmill), FomaA 701 (Violet), forevergreen 2023 (Kale), foto76 701 (Waterlily), fotomatrix 1388l, Fotoschlick 1792 (Paperclips), Frédéric Prochasson 210 (Suspension bridge), gavran333 692 (Hip flask), Gbuglok 740 (Melon), George Dolgikh 736l, Gert Vrey 1769 (Mask), Gino Santa Maria 701 (Clematis), Giuseppe Porzani 740 (Pineapple), Goran Bogicevic 865, Joe Gough 571 (Scrambled egg), 895 (Terraced), Graça Victoria 117 (Toilet bag), Gresei 740 (Papaya), Gudellaphoto 684 (Plaster), helenedevun 1251 (Chestnuts), Hellen Sergeyeva 210 (Footbridge), Himmelssturm 181 (Chessboard), HLPhoto 1016 (Care label), iava777 701 (Daisy), ibphoto 262 (Pencil case), 1075 (Combination), Ieva Geneviciene 161 (Recycling bin), Ignatius Wooster 799, Igor Negovelov 825 (Pigtails), iko 92 (Make), 1117 (Finger puppets), Illimity 1805 (Fossil), ILYA AKINSHIN 1411 (Flower pot), iMAGINE 706r, indigolotos 1784 (Tripod), infotrontof 2023 (Broad beans), injenerker 1584 (String), iofoto 210 (Flyover), IrisArt 1769 (Flippers), Ivonne Wierink 181 (Draughts), J.J.Brown 41l, JackF 141 (Double bed), 1677 (Slippers), Jakob Kamender 92 (Construct), James Steidl 665 (Barbed wire fence), jamiga • images 1075 (Mortise lock), Janina Dierks 198 (Cardboard box), Janis Smits 980 (Life), Jay Venkat 684 (Bandage), Jelena Ivanovic 820 (Push up), 1677 (Platforms), Jessmine 701 (Crocus), 2023 (Fennel), jianfei su 56, Jimi King 117 (Gift bag), Jiri Hera 299, Johanna Goodyear 1136 (Timer), JohanSwanepoel 163 (Vulture), Jouke van Keulen 1792 (Highlighter), jules 842 (Top hat), juliedeshaies 1522 (Fishing reel), Jürgen Fälchle 1946 (Railway track), Kamil Ćwiklewski 781 (Surgical glove), 1784 (Music stand), karandaev 778 (Champagne glass), Keith Wilson 740 (Satsuma), Kellis 789 (Safety goggles), Kesu 740 (Blackberries), Khvost 1218 (Crew neck), 1218 (v neck), 1993 (Vest), Kirsty Pargeter 161 (Wheelie bin), kittiyaporn1027 1009 (Door knob), Alexey Klementiev 781 (Rubber gloves), 1127 (Rubber), Kletr 842 (Cowboy hat), kmiragaya 1411 (Pot), koleg68 736r, kornienko 720 (Fork), 1106 (Mascara), kostrez 701 (Geranium), koya979 262 (Crate), 383 (Barrel), krsmanovic 125bl, Ruslan Kudrin 984 (Pendant), 1218 (Polo neck), 1993 (Boxer shorts), 1993 (Knickers), Kybele 1677 (Hiking boots), kyonnta 685 (Sardine), 701 (Azalea), La India Piaroa 825 (Curly), Laurin Rinder 1312 (Absract), Le Do 701 (Foxglove), 2023 (Watercress), Les Cunliffe 1152 (Microscope), 1792 (Elastic bands), lichtbildmaster 1132, lilithlita 685 (Flat fish), Liliya Sayfeeva 895 (Castle), Little_wine_fly 842 (Sun hat), Ljupco Smokovski 277 (Highchair), Marina Lohrbach 1864 (Patio), Luap Vision 1016 (Luggage), lucafranceschip 820 (Weights), Lucky Dragon 842 (Sombrero), Luis Santos 1677 (Kitten heels), luminastock 825 (Crew cut), Luminis 117 (Suitcase), 262 (Suitcase), 832 (Suitcase), Lusoimages 1709 (Roller skates), Maksym Dykha 1677 (Moccasins), mallivan 197 (Posy), Marek Kosmal 1020 (Uplighter), margo555 1251 (Almonds), Margrit Hirsch 1372b, marijicak 198 (Egg box), marilyn barbone 895 (Bungalow), Mariusz Blach 740 (Raspberry), Mark Aplet 433 (Paper cup), markus_marb 1677 (Trainers), marslander 740 (Mango), Mary Hommel 984 (Cameo), mashe 701 (Iris), mates 2023 (Spring onions), mbonaparte 895 (Chateau), mc81 984 (Solitaire), michaeljung 197 (Bunch roses), MIGUEL GARCIA SAAVED 1485 (Quiche), mihalec 125tl, milosluz 383 (Tube toothpaste), Monkey Business 2124, monstersparrow 1008 (Paper knife), 1117 (Glove puppet), MSPhotographic 1994 (Unbutton), mubus 895 (Cottage), narcis1 383 (Box matches), Natalia Merzlyakova 842 (Hard hat), Natika 740 (Half peach), 740 (Plum), nemans 318 (Clock radio), Nic Neish 1690, Nicholas Piccillo 820 (Arm curl), 1769 (Helmet), nick holdsworth 684 (Cotton wool), Nik 92 (Assemble), Nikolai Sorokin 1677 (Stilettos), nito 1677 (Flip flops), 1709 (Inline skates), 1792 (Sharpener), noomhh 1009 (Drawer knob), nrazumoff 740 (Lychee), nuttapongg 2023 (Beetroot), okinawakasawa 1624 (Scooter), oksun70 1023t, Olga Kovalenko 1805 (Pebbles), Olga Lyubkin 1251 (Coconut), olgades 984 (Casket), OMKAR A.V 1127 (Gold), onepony 665 (Picket fence), oriori 2023 (Cucumber), osorioartist 832 (Door handle), Pabkov 1792 (Fountain pen), pablocalvog 678, Paul Murphy 318 (Sundial), Paulista 740 (Coconut), Perytskyy 1000 (Keypad), Petr Malyshev 1000 (Keyboard), PhG 2123, picsfive 1564r, Picture Partners 2023 (Swede), Picture-Factory 820 (Sit up), pilipenkod 354l, pixelrobot 433 (Trophy cup), pixindy 1677 (Loafers), prosotphoto 1584 (Thread), prudkov 1342, R-O-M-A - 789 (Skiing goggles), Rafa Irusta 483 (Ice cream sundae), rangizzz 318 (Clock), redav 1816, reeel 1478, Restyler 181 (Chinese chequers), Richard Griffin 701 (Thistle), 1485 (Pie), Rido 706l, 825 (Frizzy), rimglow 2023 (Corn), goce risteski 1967 (Fork lift), 1967 (Pick up truck), Robert Lehmann 1792 (Drawing pin), Robert Mizerek 655 (Zip), robynmac 1564l, 1792 (Foldback clip), Roman Samokhin 383 (Can cola), ronstik 1333 (Floral), RTimages 778 (Long glass), 1769 (Baseball mitt), 1792 (Pencil), Ruslan Semichev 778 (Brandy glass), Sachs500 424, sarapulsar38 527 (Dominoes), 1792 (Felt tip), sbgoodwin 1252, schantalao 172 (Shutters), Schlierner 1677 (Court shoes), Christian Schwier 880 (Barn), scorpioart 1333 (Polka), senk 1411 (Paint pots), sepy 425l, Sergejs Rahunoks 825 (Flat top), Sergey Andrianov 197 (Bouquet), Sergey Skleznev 781 (Garden gloves), Sergey Yarochkin 354r, Sergey Zvyagintsev 1106 (Lipgloss), sergey02 1123 (Gas mask), Serghei Velusceac 1219 (Syringe), 1792 (Rubber), Gordana Sermek 1993 (Underpants), SerrNovik 825 (Wavy), Valery Shanin 976b, Shawn Hempel 1784 (Statue), simmittorok 1009 (Radio knob), 1677 (Mens shoes), skampixel 447, skouatroulio 113, Sly 1677 (Ballet shoes), Smileus 795 (White goose), sneekerp 1224 (Net), snowturtle 820 (Dumbbell), snyfer 820 (Stability ball), SokRom 832 (Draw Handle), sorapop 1175 (Model boat), soundsnaps 141 (Four-poster bed), 1075 (Latch), spaxiax 740 (Nectarine), 825 (Straight), spectr 194 (Thermos), 692 (Thermos flask), Sam Spiro 2089 (Bay window), starekase 1967 (Breakdown), starush 820 (Cross trainer), Stefano Neri 383 (Jar pickles), Stephen Coburn 383 (Carton milk), 1490 (Wine rack), Stian Iversen 1805 (Stones), stockcreations 991 (Decanter), SunnyS 2023 (Okra), sutsaiy 704r, talitha 842 (Motarboard), Taweesak Thiprod 161 (Wastepaper basket), terex 701 (carnation), 701 (Rose), thawats 1792 (Holepunch), Thomas Launois 1224 (mosquito net), Thomas Perkins 1792 (Folder), Jenny Thompson 1967 (Fire engine), Tiler84 121r, Oleh Tokarev 1136 (Kitchen scales), Tomas Sereda 701 (Tulip), Tsiumpa 1710, ucius 1946 (Tyre tracks), Tim UR 2023 (Aubergine), Valery Bareta 1946 (Running track), valery121283 740 (Avocado), 2023 (Carrots), Vasiliy Timofeev 1792 (Scissors & ruler), verdateo 148 (Bell), 684 (Syringe), Viacheslav Anyakin 655 (Buckle), Malyshchyts Viktar 2023 (Pumpkin), vlabo 117 (Briefcase), Vladimir Konjushenko 704l, Vladimir Melnikov 1784 (Easel), vnlit 1411 (Teapot), 1709 (ice skates), volff 740 (Apricot), WavebreakmediaMicro 1123 (Oxygen mask), Robert Wilson 1967 (Truck), windu 1522 (Cotton reel), Wisky 820 (Exercise bike), wolfelarry 1769 (Shuttlecock), wollertz 1771, womue 1251 (Walnut), WONG SZE FEI 825 (Ponytail), xrphoto 1136 (Thermometer), Yogesh More 148 (Door bell), zakaz 980 (Jacket), Zbyszek Nowak 740 (Cranberries), Zdenka Darula 820 (Stretch), Zee 590, zelenka68 1127 (Silk), Mara Zemgaliete 2023 (Cabbage), zotyaba 1820 (Viola); **Getty Images:** The Image Bank / Alistair Baker 992 (Vault); **Hemera Photo Objects:** 12, 78, 194 (Flask, Feeding, Hot water, Water, Hip flask, Olive oil, Carafe), 198 (Crate), 198 (First aid), 198 (Sewing), 203 (Bagel), 203 (Baguettes), 203 (Croissant), 203 (Dough), 203 (Loaf), 203 (Pitta), 203 (Rolls), 203 (Sliced), 203 (Toast), 210 (Hump), 218 (Broom), 218 (Dust brush), 218 (Hair), 218 (Nailbrush), 218 (Paintbrush), 218 (Scrub), 218 (Shaving), 218 (Shoe brush), 218 (Toothbrush), 247 (Oil), 247 (Tin), 247 (Watering can), 277 (Barber), 277 (Chair), 277 (Deck chair), 277 (Directors), 277 (Folding), 277 (Office), 277 (Rocking), 277 (Stool), 277 (Sun lounger), 277 (Swivel), 277 (Wheelchair), 292, 397, 426 (Squat), 433 (Mug), 649l, 649r, 655 (Safety pin), 685b (Fish), 686 (Bait), 686 (Float), 686 (Fly), 686 (Hook), 686 (Net), 686 (Rod), 686 (Tackle box), 722 (Garden fork), 740 (Figs), 740 (Orange), 757 (Fork), 757 (Gloves), 757 (Lawn mower), 757 (Pot), 757 (Rake), 757 (Shears), 757 (Spade), 757 (Sprinkler), 757 (Trowel), 757 (Watering can), 757 (Wheelbarrow), 788b, 818, 832 (Bag), 833, 842 (Bonnet), 857, 863, 870, 907 (Bucket), 929, 980 (Jack-O-Lantern), 1018 (Ladder), 1018 (Stepladder), 1054, 1108, 1127 (Cardboard), 1127 (Chrome), 1127 (Concrete), 1127 (Cotton), 1127 (Fur), 1127 (Glass), 1127 (Iron), 1127 (Leather), 1127 (Nylon), 1127 (Paper), 1127 (Plastic), 1127 (Steel), 1127 (Tin), 1127 (Wooden), 1127 (Wool), 1128 (Calculator), 1128 (Compass), 1128 (Dividers), 1128 (Protractor), 1128 (Ruler), 1128 (Set square), 1199, 1208 (Clippers), 1208 (File), 1208 (Kit), 1208 (Nailbrush), 1208 (Polish), 1283 (Binoculars), 1283 (Magnifying), 1283 (Microscope), 1283 (Opera), 1283 (Telescope), 1290, 1345, 1356, 1410l, 1410r, 1464, 1471 (Handbag),

471 (Purse), 1487, 1544 (Alligator), 1544 (Crocodile), 544 (Iguana), 1544 (Lizard), 1544 (Snake), 1544 Tortise), 1544 (Turtle), 1604 (Safety goggles), 1604 Safety harness), 1604 (Safety pin), 1624 (Scoop), 1645, 667, 1672 (Clam), 1672 (Lobster), 1672 (Mussel), 1672 (Oyster), 1672 (Prawn), 1780, 1895, 1936 (Chainsaw), 936 (Chisel), 1936 (Electric drill), 1936 (File), 1936 Hacksaw), 1936 (Hammer), 1936 (Handsaw), 1936 Jigsaw), 1936 (Pliers), 1936 (Screwdrivers), 1936 Spanner), 1936 (Toolbox), 1957 (Ashtray), 1957 Baking), 1957 (Breakfast), 1957 (Ice tray), 1957 (In ray), 1957 (Paint tray), 1964, 2056, 2117, 2121; **magemore Co., Ltd:** 1792 (Stapler); **iStockphoto:** 141 Hammock), 462, 665 (Railings), 720 (Tuning fork), 020 (Floor lamp), 1020 (Spot lamp), 1219 (Sewing), 1769 (Boxing gloves), 1769 (Paddle), 1792 (Push pins), 1792 (Tape), 2023 (Courgette), 2023 (Sweet potato); **Pearson Education Ltd:** 655 (Stud), Trevor Clifford 740 (Apple slice), 740 (Banana), 740 (Blackcurrant), 740 (Cherry), 740 (Grapefruit), 740 (Grapefruit slice), 740 (Kiwi), 740 (Kiwi slice), 740 (Lemon), 740 (Lime), 740 (Pears), 740 (Strawberry), 1993 (Tights), 2023 (Asparagus), 2023 (Broccoli), 2023 (Cauliflower), 2023 (Celery), 2023 (Garlic), 2023 (Green beans), 2023 (Leek), 2023 (Mushrooms), 2023 (Parsnip), 2023 (Peas), 2023 (Pepper), 2023 (Radish), Stuart Cox 825 (French plait), Cheuk-king Lo 202 (Tuba), Sozaijiten 832 (Umbrella); **PhotoDisc:** 1522 (Film), C Squared Studios 141 (Cot), C Squared Studios / Tony Gable 202 (Cornet), Karl Weatherly 1769 (Puck), www.photodisc.com / Musical Instruments 202 (French horn), 202 (Trombone), 202 (Trumpet), 1820 (Banjo), 1820 (Bass), 1820 (Guitar), 1820 (Harp), 1820 (Lute), 1820 (Mandolin), 1820 (Violin), 2099 (Bassoon), 2099 (Clarinet), 2099 (Flute), 2099 (Oboe), 2099 (Piccolo), 2099 (Recorder), 2099 (Saxophone); **Photolibrary.com:** Paul Massey 1864 (Trestle), Sven Olof Jonn 1677 (Clogs); **PunchStock:** Moodboard 820 (Rowing), PhotoDisc 850; **Shutterstock.com:** a454 1949l, Abramova Kseniya 665 (Show jumping), Alexey Lysenko 117 (Shopping bag), 383 (Grocery Bag), aquariagirl1970 699, arnet117 109, B Calkins 720 (Fork road), Blend Images 825 (Dreadlocks), Brian Maudsley 483 (Strawberry tart), Sandra Cunningham 1312 (Painting), Daniel Domanski 1949r, David Gilder 1036, Donald Joski 426 (Kneel), Elena Elisseeva 426 (Crouch), Eric Isselee 159 (Cheetah), 163 (Owl), Hugo Felix 1994 (Unzip), greatpapa 198 (Tool box), haveseen 462r, Igor Dutina 571 (Boiled eggs), Joe Gough 571 (Poached eggs), Johnny Lye 181 (Backgammon), Kasia Bialasiewicz 172 (Roman blinds), Kelvin Wong 483 (Chocolate cake), Kevin M. Kerfoot 665 (Electric fence), Kitch Bain 198 (Jewellery box), Luiz Rocha 198 (Trunk), Madlen 1011 (Loop), Mark William Richardson 895 (Semi-detatched), Michel Cecconi 913, mutation 728, Nikolai Pavlov 559, NKLRDVC 148 (Cowbell), Palto 383 (Oil drum), R. MACKAY PHOTOGRAPHY, LLC 383 (Sachet ketchup), Ragne Kabanova 172 (Roller blind), sagir 141 (Single), 1218 (Shirt), Sebastian Kaulitzki 531 (Double helix), SeDmi 117 (Sack), Sergey Toronto 701 (Chrysanthemum), Sharon Day 563, SteveWoods 684 (First aid box), StudioSmart 1033b, Repina Valeriya 2089 (Porthole), Piotr Wawrzyniuk 992 (Bounce), Yegor Korzh 760, Zsolt Biczo 698; **Thinkstock:** 1020 (Anglepoise), 1020 (Desk lamp), 1020 (Lamp post), 1020 (Oil lamp), 1033t, 1769 (Knee pad); **Veer / Corbis:** adsheyn 1190, Aleksandr Volkov 888 (Snail), Alexander Podshivalov 888 (Cow), alexraths 1016 (Parcel label), Andrey Kuzmin 984 (Tiara), anphotos 86, artush 1136 (Tape measure), aura 968, bds 2090, Blaj 1367, bmelofo 1333 (Tartan), boroda 1008 (craft knife), caimacanul 1016 (Bottle label), 1023b, 1106 (brush), cbrignell 15r, 318 (Grandfather clock), Norman Chan 2023 (Mangetout), christo 1123 (Face mask), cienpies 1864 (Coffee), Coprid 41r, 318 (Alarm clock), 1315 (Roasting pan), csjani 1820 (Cello), erierika 991 (Juggle), f9photos 1008 (Swiss Army knife), fajno 984 (Braclet), fckncg 895 (Motor home), fotoarek 983, Garsya 907 (Ice block), Givaga 991 (Pitcher), graja 125cl, Gregory Johnston 1700, happydancing 1008 (Carving Knife), Henryk Sadura 895 (Mansion), herreid 1891t, hoch2wo 161 (Dustbin), 1251 (Peacans), homestudio 1106 (Eyeshadow), iodrakon 1315 (Pancake), iofoto 825 (Bald), jgroupstudios 1361 (Grand piano), Karam Miri 1106 (Powder), Kitch 1315 (Wok), Konstantin Yuganov 1388r, Krasyuk Volodymyr 1152 (megaphone), Leobas 1106 (Blusher), Lightworks 1864 (Picnic), Ljupco 141 (Camp bed), lucadp 907 (Ice cube tray), lucielang 984 (Cuff links), 1123 (Mask), magraphics 161 (Pedal bin), Maksym Bondarchuk 141 (Bunk beds), 820 (Barbell), MaleWitch 1011 (Bow), maurotrb 1007, Mazzzur 1011 (Knot), mik122 1219 (Compass), MORNING LIGHT 1372t, mt kang 1016 (Address label), Nathan Till 126, nicemonkey 1333 (Zig zag), njnightsky 1136 (Stopwatch), nrey 701 (Orchid), 1152 (Microphone), Ohmega1982 121l, Pakhnyushchyy Vitaliy 885, 1219 (Pine), photobac 1864 (Desk), PicsFive 1075 (Padlock), Pitamaha 1075 (Bolt), pixelman 984 (Wedding ring), ribeiroantonio 1251 (Cashew), ronstik 2023 (Tomatoes), Kudrin Ruslan 1017, 1993 (Bra), Ruslan Grigolava 1076, sergej 1008 (Kitchen knife), 1315 (Frying pan), sheval 1136 (Thermometer(medical)), sirylok 125cr, Smit 2023 (Turnips), Stocksnapper 1066, studiofi 825 (Bob), Tanushka 907 (Ice cream), Tatyana Aleksieva-Sabeva 1117 (Marionette), Tom Gowanlock 1333 (Stripe), travismanley 1000 (Kettle), trekandscout 1136 (Bathroom scales), twixx 117 (Bin liner), Upsidedowncake 984 (Earrings), Vadim Zholobov 984 (Choker), Vasilius 1106 (Lipstick), ventdusud 1333 (Checked), Veronika Surovtseva 1312 (Still life), vnlit 1315 (Saucepan), Volodymyr Kaznovskyi 117 (Backpack), WorldsWildlifeWonders.com 1097, Yuriy Panyukov 1224 (Basket ball)

Picture Research by: Louise Edgeworth

Every effort has been made to trace the copyright holders and we apologize in advance for any unintentional omissions. We would be pleased to insert the appropriate acknowledgement in any subsequent edition of this publication.